GENERAL INFORMATION

CHRYSLER MOTORS

FORD MOTOR CO.

GENERAL MOTORS

JEEP

LATEST CHANGES & CORRECTIONS

Check these pages for updated info
in this and previous manuals.

CHRYSLER MOTORS
FORD MOTOR CO.
GENERAL MOTORS
JEEP

1991 MITCHELL® DOMESTIC LIGHT TRUCKS & VANS SERVICE & REPAIR

Mitchell®

The Leader in Professional Estimating and Repair Information.

Mitchell International

ACKNOWLEDGMENT

Mitchell International thanks the domestic manufacturers, distributors and dealers for their generous cooperation and assistance which make this manual possible.

Chrysler Motors
Ford Motor Company
General Motors Corporation

Published By

MITCHELL INTERNATIONAL
9889 Willow Creek Road
P.O. Box 26260
San Diego, California 92196-0260

ISBN 0-8470-0579-8

Customer Service Numbers:

Subscription/Billing Information:
1-800-648-8010 or 619-578-6550

Technical Information:
1-800-854-7030 or 619-578-6550

Or Write: P.O. Box 26260, San Diego, CA 92196-0260

1991 GENERAL INFORMATION CONTENTS

ALL MODELS **Page**

1991 GENERAL INFORMATION
How To Use The Engine Performance Section

We have redesigned Mitchell manuals to make them easier to use by organizing service and repair information by manufacturer. Also, major changes have taken place in the ENGINE PERFORMANCE section. Below is a brief description of what's been done and how it is organized.

INTRODUCTION

Here you will find out how to identify an engine by its Vehicle Identification Number (VIN). The manufacturer's MODEL COVERAGE chart lists each model and its engine option, fuel system, ignition system and engine code. Engine serial number locations are also shown here.

SERVICE & ADJUSTMENT SPECIFICATIONS

Here you will find easy-to-use tables covering *important* specifications. You can find valuable information like spark plug wire resistance, valve clearance, firing orders, etc.

EMISSION APPLICATIONS

Here you will find a chart listing emission control devices used on each model. These are helpful when performing government-required emissions inspections.

ON-VEHICLE ADJUSTMENTS

Here you will find adjustment procedures for checking/adjusting valves, base ignition timing and idle speed. Use this section when performing routine maintenance.

THEORY & OPERATION

Here you will find information on how various engine system and components work. Before diagnosing a vehicle or system with which you are not completely familiar, read this section.

BASIC DIAGNOSTIC PROCEDURES

This is the *first step* in diagnosing any driveability problem. These procedures can help you avoid skipping a simple step early, like checking base timing, which could be costly in both time and money later. Once all systems are "GO" here, proceed to SELF-DIAGNOSTICS or TROUBLE SHOOTING - NO CODES.

SELF-DIAGNOSTICS

Use this information to retrieve and interpret trouble codes accessed from the vehicle's self-diagnostic system. Once information is retrieved, diagnostic procedures are given to help pinpoint and repair computer system/component faults. Also included are steps for clearing trouble codes, once these faults are repaired. If there is a problem not indicated by trouble codes, proceed to TROUBLE SHOOTING - NO CODES.

TROUBLE SHOOTING – NO CODES

This is where to go when you have a problem that does not have a trouble code or when working on a non-computer controlled vehicle. It can help with symptoms and intermittent testing procedures. Procedures in this information should lead you to a specific component or system test.

SYSTEMS & COMPONENT TESTING

Here you will find various tests for engine performance systems and their components, such as air induction (turbochargers and superchargers), fuel control, ignition control and emission systems.

PIN VOLTAGE CHARTS

These are supplied (when available) to quicken the diagnostic process. By checking pin voltages at the electronic control unit, you can determine if the control unit is receiving and/or transmitting proper voltage signals.

SENSOR OPERATING RANGE CHARTS

These are supplied (when available) to determine if a sensor is out of calibration. An out-of-calibration sensor may not set a trouble code, but it will cause driveability problems.

WIRING DIAGRAMS

Here you can identify and trace component circuits or locate shorts and opens in circuits. They can also help you understand how individual circuits function within a system.

VACUUM DIAGRAMS

Here we give you underhood views of vacuum-hose routing which can help you find incorrectly routed hoses. Remember, a vacuum leak on computer-controlled vehicle can cause many driveability problems.

REMOVAL, OVERHAUL & INSTALLATION

After you've diagnosed the problem, this is where to go for the nuts-and-bolts of the job. Here you'll find procedures and specifications for removing, overhauling (if available) and installing components.

1991 GENERAL INFORMATION
Engine Performance Safety Precautions

- Always refer to Engine Tune-Up Decal in engine compartment before performing tune-up. If manual and decal differ, always use decal specifications.
- DO NOT allow or create a condition of misfire in more than one cylinder for an extended period of time. Damage to converter may occur if continually exposed to unburned fuel mixture.
- Always turn ignition off and disconnect negative battery cable BEFORE disconnecting or connecting computer or other electrical components.
- DO NOT drop or shock electrical components such as computer, airflow meter, etc.
- DO NOT use fuel system cleaning compounds that are not recommended by the manufacturer. Damage to gaskets, diaphragm materials and catalytic converter may result.
- Before performing a compression test or cranking engine using a remote starter switch, disconnect coil wire from distributor and secure it to a good engine ground, or disable ignition system.
- Before disconnecting any fuel system component, ensure fuel system pressure is released.
- Use a shop towel to absorb any spilled fuel to prevent fire.
- DO NOT create sparks or have an open flame near battery.
- If any Electronic Fuel Injection (EFI) components such as hoses or clamps are replaced, ensure they are replaced with components designed for EFI use.
- Always reassemble throttle body components using new gaskets, "O" rings and seals.
- If equipped with an inertia switch, DO NOT reset switch until after inspecting fuel system for leaks.
- Wear safety goggles when drilling or grinding.
- Wear proper clothing which protects against chemicals and other hazards.

1991 GENERAL INFORMATION
Diagnostic Routine Outline

WHERE TO BEGIN DIAGNOSING A DRIVEABILITY PROBLEM?

STEP 1 – PERFORM BASIC INSPECTION

a) Verify Customer Complaint
b) Perform Visual Inspection
(See BASIC DIAGNOSTIC PROCEDURES)
c) Test Engine Sub-Systems
(See BASIC DIAGNOSTIC PROCEDURES)
- Mechanical Condition (Compression)
- Ignition Output
- Fuel Delivery

d) Check Air Induction System For Leaks
e) Check & Adjust Basic Engine Settings
(See ON-VEHICLE ADJUSTMENTS)
- Ignition Timing
- Idle Speed

STEP 2 – CHECK FOR TROUBLE CODES

a) If equipped with self-diagnostics, check for trouble codes. *(See SELF-DIAGNOSTICS)*
b) Repair cause of trouble codes.
c) Clear control unit memory.

STEP 3 – DIAGNOSE SYMPTOM

a) If self-diagnostics and trouble codes are not available, identify complaint by symptom.
b) See trouble shooting procedure to identify problem.
(See TROUBLE SHOOTING – NO CODES)

STEP 4 – TEST & REPAIR SYSTEM

a) Perform required tests.
(See SYSTEMS & COMPONENT TESTING)
b) Verify complaint is repaired.

1991 GENERAL INFORMATION
1980-91 Maintenance Reminder Lights

AMERICAN MOTORS

1980-81 MODELS

Every 30,000 miles, an emission maintenance reminder light will illuminate on the instrument panel, indicating oxygen sensor requires servicing. If sensor is faulty, it must be replaced. After servicing sensor, reset light activating switch.

Locate switch in engine compartment, between upper and lower speedometer cables, next to firewall. Slide rubber boot up. With small screwdriver, turn reset screw clockwise 1/4 turn until detent resets in switch. *See Fig. 1*.

1982-84 MODELS (EXCEPT ALLIANCE & ENCORE)

The emission maintenance light illuminates after 1000 hours of engine operation, indicating service of the oxygen sensor is required. After servicing sensor, emission maintenance E-cell timer must be replaced.

Locate timer in passenger compartment within the wire harness leading to the microprocessor. Remove E-cell timer from its enclosure and insert a replacement timer.

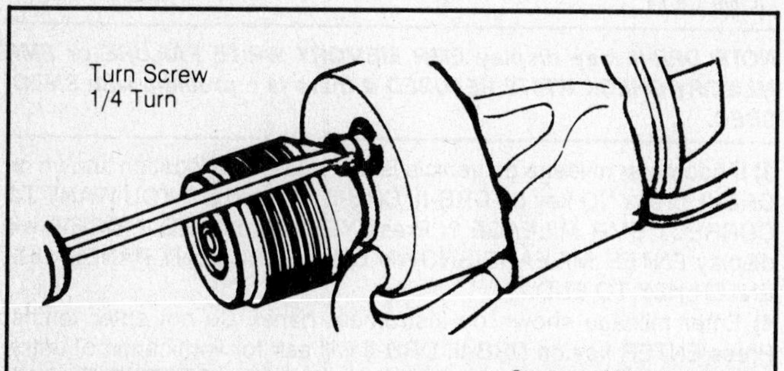
Turn Screw
1/4 Turn

Courtesy of Chrysler Motors.

Fig. 1: Resetting Maintenance Reminder Switch

1987 EAGLE WAGON

An emission light timer will start flashing the O_2 sensor service light at 82,500 miles. At this time, O_2 sensor and timer should both be replaced. Locate timer under the dash panel (to right of steering column). Remove mounting screws and disconnect wiring. To install, reverse procedure.

CHRYSLER MOTORS

1980 PASSENGER CARS, 1980-87 LIGHT DUTY TRUCKS & RWD VANS

A mileage counter activates the emission reminder light between 12,000 and 30,000 mile intervals, depending on model. Two types are used. If equipped with mechanical type, see AMERICAN MOTORS 1980-81 MODELS reset procedure. *See Fig. 1*. The electronic type uses a 9-volt battery which supplies power to the electronic counter, preventing memory loss when the vehicle battery is disconnected.

Electronic Type – On 1987 Dakota models, mileage counter in the odometer will illuminate reminder light at 52,500, 82,500 and 105,000 miles. On all other models reminder light will illuminate between 12,000 and 30,000 mile intervals.

NOTE: Vehicle battery MUST be connected during resetting procedure to prevent power loss to memory.

To reset electronic type, locate Green, Red, White or Tan plastic case behind instrument panel in lower left cluster area. Slide case from bracket and open cover. Remove 9-volt battery and insert a small rod or screwdriver into hole in switch, closing contacts. Replace battery with a new 9-volt alkaline type. Close case. Slide case back into bracket. *See Fig. 2*.

NOTE: Some models use a non-resettable mileage counter. Replace it with a resettable type.

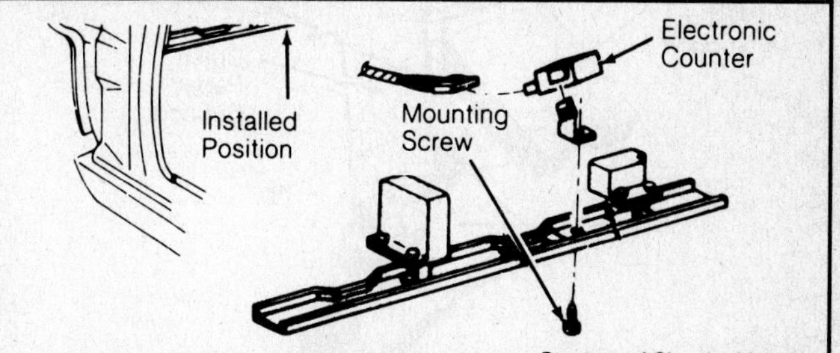
Electronic
Counter
Installed
Position
Mounting
Screw

Courtesy of Chrysler Motors.

Fig. 2: Chrysler Motors Electronic Type Switch

1987 FWD VANS & 1988 LIGHT DUTY TRUCKS & VANS

CAUTION: There is no test procedure for this system. Any attempt to test this system will damage system components.

The Emission Maintenance Reminder (EMR) module is designed to be a reminder to service the vehicle emissions control system. It is not an emissions warning system, only a reminder to perform emissions servicing. The components to be serviced include the EGR system, PCV valve, oxygen sensor, delay valves, and bi-level purge valve.

The EMR module will illuminate the MAINT REQD dash light after a predetermined time. Mileage will not cause the light to come on. The light will remain on until the EMR module is reset by inserting a small screwdriver into the hole in the module (RWD only) and depressing the reset switch (FWD and RWD).

The EMR module is located on the steering column, behind instrument panel on RWD vans and in the instrument cluster on FWD vans. *See Figs. 3 and 4*. On trucks, it is located behind the far right side of dash panel next to the glove box. *See Fig. 5*. On Dakota models, module is located on bracket below headlight switch, on rear of instrument panel. *See Fig. 6*.

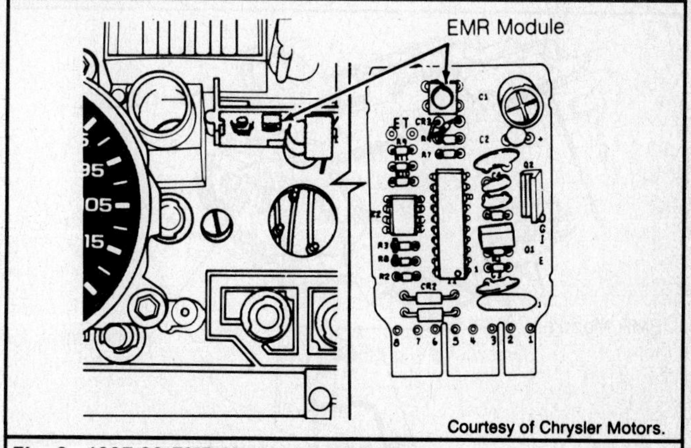
EMR Module

Courtesy of Chrysler Motors.

Fig. 3: 1987-88 EMR Module – FWD Van

1991 GENERAL INFORMATION
1980-91 Maintenance Reminder Lights (Cont.)

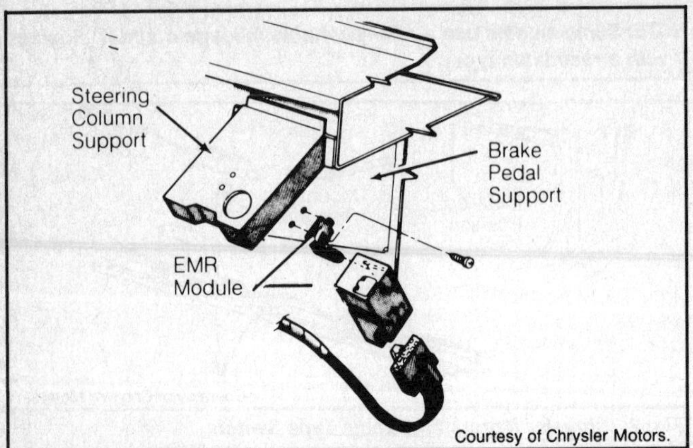
Steering
Column
Support
Brake
Pedal
Support
EMR
Module

Courtesy of Chrysler Motors.

Fig. 4: 1988 EMR Module – RWD Van

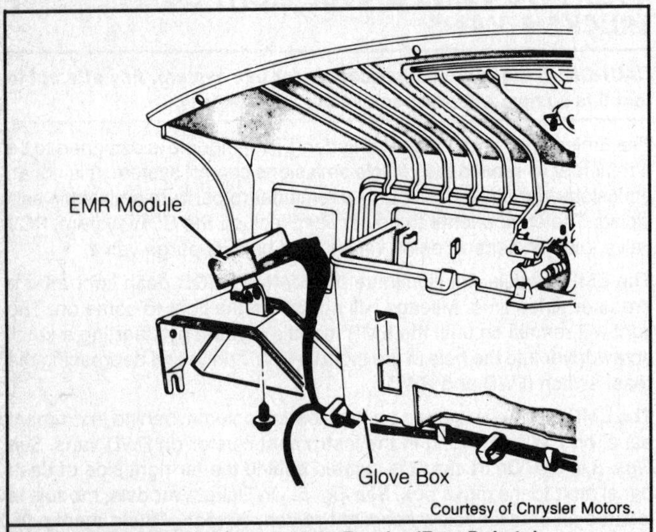
EMR Module
Glove Box

Courtesy of Chrysler Motors.

Fig. 5: 1988 EMR Module – Light Trucks (Exc. Dakota)

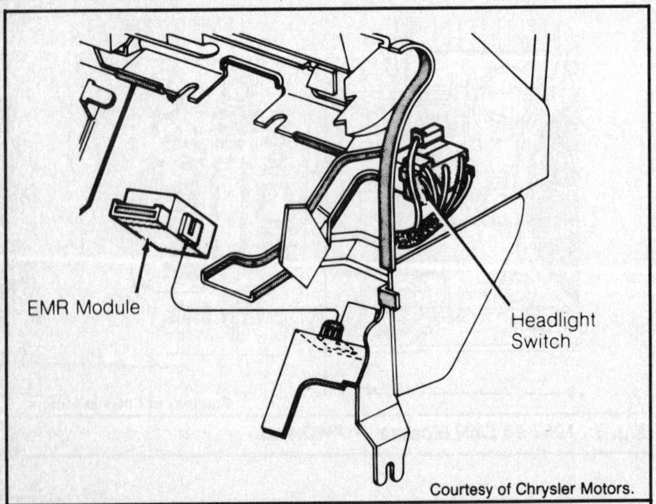
EMR Module
Headlight
Switch

Courtesy of Chrysler Motors.

Fig. 6: 1988 EMR Module – Dakota

1989-91 LIGHT DUTY TRUCKS & VANS

Emission Maintenance Reminder (EMR) Light Reset – The EMR light is designed to be a reminder to service the vehicle emissions control system. It is not an emissions warning system, only a reminder to perform emissions servicing.

The components to be serviced include the EGR system, PCV valve, oxygen sensor and some vacuum operated components. EMR light will illuminate after a predetermined mileage. To reset EMR light, Chrysler Diagnostic Readout Box (DRB-II) Tester (C-4805) is needed.

1) Using DRB-II tester, select EMISSIONS EMR TESTS. Select EMR MEMORY CHECK. Select RESET EMR LIGHT.

2) DRB-II display will read, RESET EMR LIGHT, ARE YOU SURE? YES, NO. Press YES key. When DRB-II is finished resetting light, DRB-II display will read EMR LIGHT IS RESET.

NOTE: If Single Module Engine Controller (SMEC) or Single Board Engine Controller (SBEC) is replaced, vehicle mileage must be programmed back into the SMEC/SBEC. If the following procedure is not performed, EMR light will not turn on at the proper mileage intervals to coincide with current vehicle mileage.

EMR Mileage Reset – **1)** Using DRB-II Tester, select EMISSIONS EMR TESTS. Select EMR MEMORY CHECK. DRB-II display will read, EMR MEMORY CHECK ARE YOU SURE? YES, NO. Press YES key.

2) Display will read, READING ENGINE DATA, WRITE TEST 1, WRITE TEST 2, WRITING ENGINE DATA, EMR: MILEAGE INVALID. DO YOU WANT TO CORRECT EMR MILEAGE?. Press YES or NO key. Display will read, IS INSTRUMENT PANEL MILEAGE BETWEEN XXXXXX AND XXXXXX ?. If odometer mileage on vehicle is within specification, press YES key. DRB-II will display EMR MEMORY CHECK TEST COMPLETE.

NOTE: DRB-II may display EMR MEMORY WRITE FAILURE or EMR MEMORY CHECK WRITE REFUSED if there is a problem with SMEC/SBEC.

3) If odometer mileage on vehicle is not within specification shown on DRB-II, press NO key on DRB-II. DRB-II will read DO YOU WANT TO CORRECT EMR MILEAGE ?. Press YES key on DRB-II. DRB-II will display ENTER MILEAGE SHOWN ON INSTRUMENT PANEL. USE ENTER KEY TO END.

4) Enter mileage shown on instrument panel. Do not enter tenths. Press ENTER key on DRB-II. DRB-II will ask for verification of entry. If mileage entry was correct, DRB-II will display SETTING ENGINE DATA and EMR MEMORY CHECK TEST COMPLETE. Vehicle must be driven for at least 8 miles for mileage reset to take place.

CHRYSLER MOTORS/EAGLE

1988-91 PREMIER & 1990-91 MONACO

Service Interval Reminder Light – Every 7500 miles, a Vehicle Maintenance Monitor (VMM) will illuminate a SERVICE interval reminder light. This indicates regular maintenance is due. After required service is performed, press RESET button on dash below VMM display. Hold button until a beep is heard. VMM display will now be clear.

FORD MOTOR CO.

1985-89 PASSENGER CARS

Service Interval Reminder Light – Every 5000 or 7500 miles, depending upon engine application, a SERVICE interval reminder light will illuminate (for approximately 30 seconds) on the dash, or begin flashing depending on model, indicating an oil change is due.

To reset reminder light, turn ignition on. Simultaneously depress and hold TRIP (ODO SEL on Taurus and Sable), (SYSTEM CHECK or CHECK OUT on Continental) and RESET or TRIP RESET buttons. On Probe models, depress and hold service reset button, located on speed alarm keyboard. On all models, 3 beeps will verify that reminder light has been reset.

1990-91 CONTINENTAL

Service Interval Reminder Light – During the system check sequence, the SERVICE symbol comes on and displays the number of miles to go before the next normal service. To reset the service interval reminder, press SYSTEM CHECK button. Press RESET button.

1991 GENERAL INFORMATION
1980-91 Maintenance Reminder Lights (Cont.)

Press SYSTEM CHECK and RESET buttons simultaneously. The display should now show 7200 miles. The service mileage will count down from here.

1989-91 COUGAR & THUNDERBIRD

Vehicle Maintenance Minder (VMM) - 1) Turn ignition off. Turn ignition switch to ON position. Within 16 seconds of turning ignition on, insert end of paper clip into reset switch hole and firmly push in switch. Reset switch hole is a small hole, located to left of word OK on VMM panel.
2) Keep switch depressed until left side of display stops flashing. If switch is not kept depressed until left side of display stops flashing, VMM will not be reset.

1990 PROBE (WITH STANDARD INSTRUMENT CLUSTER)

Vehicle Maintenance Minder (VMM) - 1) The SERVICE light will come on approximately every 7500 miles, indicating that it is time for next routine service. At 7500 miles, the light will remain on for 3 minutes every time vehicle is started.
2) To cancel the message and reset SERVICE light, depress and hold SERVICE RESET button until 3 beeps are sounded. This will verify that reminder light has been reset. SERVICE RESET button is located in VMM unit, in center of overhead console.

1990 PROBE (WITH ELECTRONIC INSTRUMENT CLUSTER)

Vehicle Maintenance Minder (VMM) - 1) SERVICE INTERVAL will be displayed on system scanner approximately every 7500 miles, indicating that it is time for next routine service. At 7500 miles, the message will remain on for 3 minutes every time vehicle is started.
2) To cancel message and reset service interval, press and hold SERVICE RESET button until 3 tones are heard. SERVICE RESET button is located on speed alarm keyboard.

1985-87 LIGHT DUTY TRUCKS, 1988 NON-EEC LIGHT DUTY TRUCKS & 1989-90 HEAVY DUTY TRUCKS

NOTE: 1980-84 trucks do not use an emission maintenance reminder light.

Maintenance Reminder Light - Ford Motor Co. 1985-87 light duty trucks (Aerostar vans, and Federal light and medium duty trucks), 1988 non-EEC equipped light duty trucks and 1989-90 heavy duty trucks use a maintenance reminder light to indicate emission system maintenance is required. Control unit (timer) for maintenance light is located under dash, near steering column or behind glove box. Control unit may be hidden behind bracket on some truck models. Maintenance light is triggered after 2000 key starts (about 60,000 miles). After servicing emission system, reset light on models with resettable timer.
1) Turn ignition off. Remove tape over reset hole in timer. Lightly push a small Phillips screwdriver into hole in timer unit marked RESET. With light pressure on screwdriver, turn ignition switch to RUN position.
2) Light should stay on while screwdriver is pressed down. Hold screwdriver down for approximately 5 seconds. Remove screwdriver. Light should go out within 2-5 seconds. If not, repeat steps **1)** and **2)**.
3) Cycle ignition from OFF to RUN position. Light should glow for 2 to 5 seconds. This verifies proper reset of maintenance reminder light.

NOTE: Some models use a non-resettable control unit. Replace it with a resettable type. Non-EEC vehicles for 1988 are the 2.0L Ranger, 6.1L and 7.0L gasoline trucks.

GENERAL MOTORS

NOTE: General Motors 1981-89 cars, trucks and vans do not use an emission maintenance warning light

1980 EXCEPT CADILLAC

Every 30,000 miles, a reminder flag appears in speedometer face, indicating service of oxygen sensor is necessary. *See Fig. 7*. To reset flag, remove instrument panel trim plate. Remove instrument cluster lens. Using pointed tool, apply light downward pressure on notches of flag until it is reset. An alignment mark will appear in left center of odometer window when flag is fully reset.

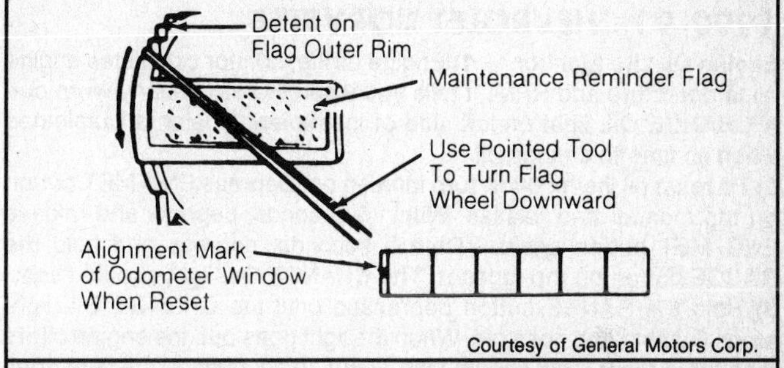
Detent on
Flag Outer Rim
Maintenance Reminder Flag
Use Pointed Tool
To Turn Flag
Wheel Downward
Alignment Mark
of Odometer Window
When Reset
Courtesy of General Motors Corp.

Fig. 7: Resetting Reminder Flag (1980 General Motors)

1980 CADILLAC

Every 15,000 miles, a reminder flag appears in speedometer face, indicating service of oxygen sensor is necessary. To reset flag, remove lower steering column cover. Sensor reset cable is located to the left of the speedometer cluster. Pull cable lightly (maximum 2 lbs. force). Reinstall lower steering column cover.

1989-91 CADILLAC ALLANTÉ

Engine Data Display - 1) An OIL LIFE INDEX is one of the displays on Driver Information Center (DIC). It will display remaining oil life as a percentage estimate of the useful life of oil.
2) It will show 100 percent when the system is reset. When the oil life is 0 percent, the display will show CHANGE ENGINE OIL. After performing necessary services, reset service reminder.
3) To reset service reminder on 1989 models, press RANGE button until OIL LIFE INDEX appears on display. Depress and hold in AVG ECON and RANGE buttons for more than 5 seconds or until 100 is displayed. This will reset remaining oil life to 100 percent.
4) On 1990-91 models, press RANGE button until OIL LIFE INDEX appears on display. Depress and hold in AVG SPEED and RANGE buttons for more than 5 seconds or until 100 is displayed. This will reset remaining oil life to 100 percent.

1989-91 CADILLAC ELDORADO & SEVILLE

Engine Data Display - 1) An OIL LIFE INDEX is one of 4 displays on Driver Information Center (DIC). It will display remaining oil life as a percentage estimate of the useful life of oil.
2) It will show 100 percent when the system is reset. When remaining oil life is 10 percent or less, the system will display CHANGE OIL SOON. When the oil life is 0 percent, the display will show CHANGE ENGINE OIL. After performing necessary services, reset service reminder.
3) To reset service reminder, press RANGE button until OIL LIFE INDEX appears on display. Depress and hold in ENG DATA and RANGE buttons until 100 is displayed. This will reset remaining oil life to 100 percent.

1991 GENERAL INFORMATION
1980-91 Maintenance Reminder Lights (Cont.)

1991 CADILLAC FLEETWOOD & DEVILLE

Engine Data Display – **1)** An OIL LIFE INDEX is one of the displays on Driver Information Center (DIC). It will display remaining oil life as a percentage estimate of the useful life of oil.
2) It will show 100 percent when the system is reset. When the oil life is 0 percent, the display will show CHANGE ENGINE OIL. After performing necessary services, reset service reminder.
3) To reset service reminder, depress and hold in RANGE and RESET buttons between 5 and 60 seconds. Once buttons are released, CHANGE OIL SOON light should flash 4 times. This will reset remaining oil life to 100 percent.
4) If CHANGE OIL SOON comes on and stays on for 5 seconds, display did not reset. Repeat step **3)**.

1990-91 CHEVROLET CORVETTE

Engine Oil Life Monitor – **1)** Engine oil life monitor calculates engine oil temperature and RPM. It tells you when the oil is nearly worn out. A CHANGE OIL light on left side of instrument cluster is illuminated when its time to change oil.
2) To reset oil life monitor, turn ignition on. Depress ENG MET button on trip monitor and release. Within 5 seconds, depress and release ENG MET button again. Within 5 seconds, depress and hold the RANGE button on trip monitor. The CHANGE OIL light should flash.
3) Hold the RANGE button depressed until the CHANGE OIL light stops flashing and goes out. When the light goes out, the engine oil life monitor is reset. This should take about 10 seconds. If the light does not reset, turn the ignition off and repeat the procedure.

1990-91 OLDSMOBILE CUTLASS CALAIS, CUTLASS SUPREME, CUTLASS CIERA, CUTLASS CRUISER, DELTA 88, NINETY-EIGHT & TOURING SEDAN

Engine Data Display – **1)** An OIL LIFE INDEX is one of 4 Engine Data Displays used on models with a Driver Information Center (DIC). It will display remaining oil life as a percentage estimate of the useful life of oil.
2) It will show 100 percent when the system is reset. When remaining oil life is 10 percent or less, the system will calculate distance to next oil change. When the car is started each day, a tone will sound and approximate distance to the next oil change will be displayed.
3) When the oil life is 0 percent, the display will show CHANGE OIL NOW. After performing necessary services, reset service reminder.
4) To reset the display, depress and hold in OIL button to select the oil life display. Then, depress and hold in RESET and OIL buttons for at least 5 seconds. This will reset remaining oil life to 100 percent.

1990-91 OLDSMOBILE TORONADO & TROFEO

Engine Data Display – **1)** An OIL LIFE INDEX is one of 4 Engine Data Displays used on models with a Driver Information Center (DIC). It will display remaining oil life as a percentage estimate of the useful life of oil. It will show 100 percent when the system is reset. When the oil life is 0, the display will show CHANGE OIL. After performing necessary services, reset service reminder.
2) To reset the display, depress and hold in ENG DATA button to select the oil life display. Then, depress and hold in RESET/ENTER and ENG DATA buttons for at least 5 seconds. This will reset remaining oil life to 100 percent.

1989 PONTIAC BONNEVILLE & 1987-89 6000 STE

Service Interval Reminder Light – A SERVICE light is used on models with a Driver Information Center (DIC). After performing necessary services, reset service reminder light.
1) Display the desired item on the DIC. Press and hold down the RESET button. While the button is depressed, the distance between service intervals will decrease at a rate of 500 miles for every 5 seconds.
2) When the button is released, the distance until the next service interval will be displayed on the DIC.
3) If the service interval light for each item is reset within 10 miles of coming on, the light will go out and stay out on reset.
4) If the service interval light is left on for longer than 10 miles of driving, the display will remain lit (after resetting) for an additional 10 miles before going out.

1990-91 PONTIAC BONNEVILLE

Service Interval Reminder Light – A SERVICE REMINDER light is used on models with a Driver Information Center (DIC). After performing necessary services, reset service reminder light.
1) To reset service reminder, push DIC button until you are about to get the correct service item. Press and hold down the DIC button. This will advance you to the desired service. While the button is depressed, the distance between service intervals will decrease at a rate of 500 miles for every 5 seconds.
2) When the button is released, the distance until the next service interval will be displayed on the DIC. If the service interval light for each item is reset within 10 miles of coming on, the light will go out and stay out on reset.
3) If the service interval light is left on for longer than 10 miles of driving, the display will remain lit (after resetting) for an additional 10 miles before going out.

JEEP

1988-90 CHEROKEE, COMANCHE, WAGONEER & WRANGLER

Emission Maintenance Indicator Light – Vehicles are equipped with an emission maintenance indicator light on instrument cluster. This light will come on one time at 82,500 miles to alert driver that emission service is required. At this time, oxygen sensor and PCV valve must be replaced and all other emission components should be inspected and serviced or replaced as necessary.

Indicator timer is located under dash, near accelerator pedal or to right of steering column. Timer cannot be reset. To turn off light, timer must be replaced or disconnected. Since timer and sensor are interdependent, if timer should fail prematurely, oxygen sensor should be replaced at same time to preserve correct replacement interval.

To replace timer on Cherokee, Comanche and Wagoneer models, remove cruise control module (if equipped). Remove timer mounting screws. Disconnect electrical connector. On Wrangler models, remove timer mounting screws. Disconnect electrical connector. To install, reverse removal procedure.

1991 CHEROKEE, COMANCHE & WRANGLER

Emission Maintenance Indicator Light – Vehicles are equipped with an emission maintenance indicator light on instrument cluster. This light will come on one time at 82,500 miles to alert driver that emission service is required. At this time, oxygen sensor must be replaced and all other emission components should be inspected and serviced or replaced as necessary. Chrysler's Diagnostic Readout Box (DRB-II) tester is required to reset the emission maintenance indicator light.

1991 GENERAL INFORMATION
Using Mitchell's Wiring Diagrams

INTRODUCTION

Mitchell obtains wiring diagrams and technical service bulletins, containing wiring diagram changes, from the domestic and import manufacturers. These are checked for accuracy and are all redrawn into a consistent format for easy use.

All diagrams are arranged with the front of the vehicle at the left side of the first page and the rear of the vehicle at the right side of the last page. Accessories are shown near the end of the diagram.
Components are shown in their approximate location on the vehicle. Due to the constantly increasing number of components on vehicles today, it is impossible to show exact locations.

In the past, when cars were simpler, diagrams were simpler. All components were connected by wires, and diagrams seldom exceeded 4 pages in length. Today, some wiring diagrams require more than 16 pages. It would be impractical to expect a service technician to trace a wire from page 1 across every page to page 16.
Removing some of the wiring maze reduces eyestrain and time wasted searching across several pages. Today, the majority of Mitchell diagrams now follow a much improved format, which permits space for internal switch details and connector shapes.

Any wires that don't connect directly to their components are identified on the diagram to indicate where they go. There is a legend on the first page of each diagram, detailing component location. It refers you to subsystems, using grid NUMBERS at the top and bottom of the page and grid LETTERS on each side. This grid system works in a manner similar to that of a road map.

HOW TO USE MITCHELL'S WIRING DIAGRAMS

1) On the first page of the diagram, you will find a listing of major electrical components or systems. Locate the specific component or system you wish to trace. A grid number and letter will follow the component's name.
2) Use the grid NUMBERS (arranged horizontally across the top and bottom of each page) to find the page of the wiring diagram that contains the component you're seeking. When you reach this page, use the grid LETTERS on the side of the page to determine the component's vertical location.
3) Locate the circuit you need to service. The internals are shown for switches and relays to assist you in understanding how the circuit operates.

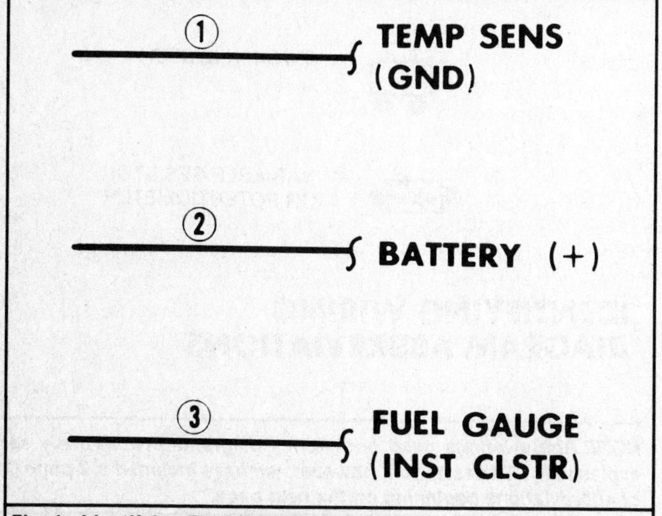
1
TEMP SENS
(GND)
2
BATTERY (+)
3
FUEL GAUGE
(INST CLSTR)

Fig. 1: Identifying Tie-Off Symbols

4) If the wires are not drawn all the way to another component (across several pages), a reference will tell you their final destination.
5) Again, use the legend on the first page of the wiring diagram to determine the grid number and letter of the referenced component. You can turn directly to it without tracing wires across several pages.

6) The symbols shown in *Fig. 1* are called tie-offs. The first tie-off shown indicates that the circuit goes to the temperature sensor, and is also a ground circuit.
7) The second symbol indicates that the circuit goes to a battery positive parallel circuit. The third symbol leads to a particular component and the location is also given.
8) The lines shown in *Fig. 2* are called options. Which path or option to take depends on what engine or systems the vehicle has.

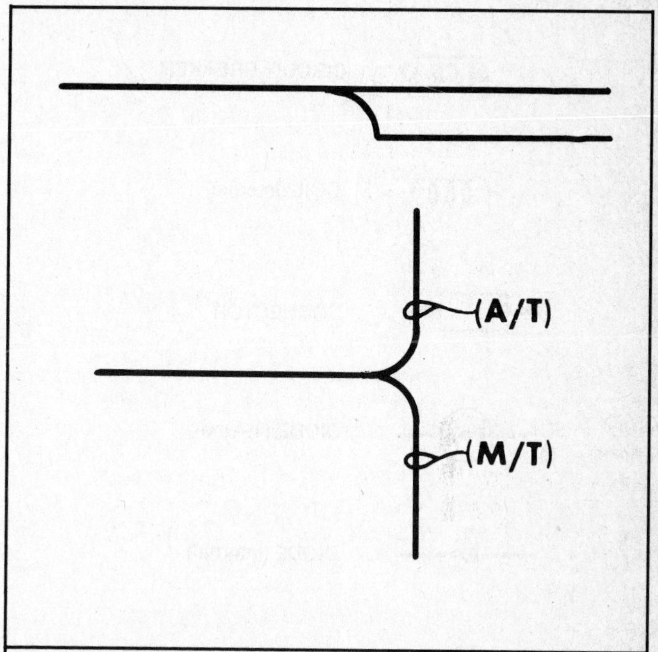
(A/T)
(M/T)

Fig. 2: Identifying Option Symbols

COLOR ABBREVIATIONS

Color	Abbreviation
Black	BLK
Blue	BLU
Brown	BRN
Clear	CLR
Dark Blue	DK BLU
Dark Green	DK GRN
Green	GRN
Gray	GRY
Light Blue	LT BLU
Light Green	LT GRN
Orange	ORG
Pink	PNK
Purple	PPL
Red	RED
Tan	TAN
Violet	VIO
White	WHT
Yellow	YEL

1991 GENERAL INFORMATION
Using Mitchell's Wiring Diagrams (Cont.)

IDENTIFYING WIRING DIAGRAM SYMBOLS

***NOTE:** Standard wiring symbols are used on Mitchell diagrams. The list below will help clarify any symbols that are not easily understood at a glance. Most components are labeled "Motor", "Switch" or "Relay" in addition to being drawn with the standard symbol.*

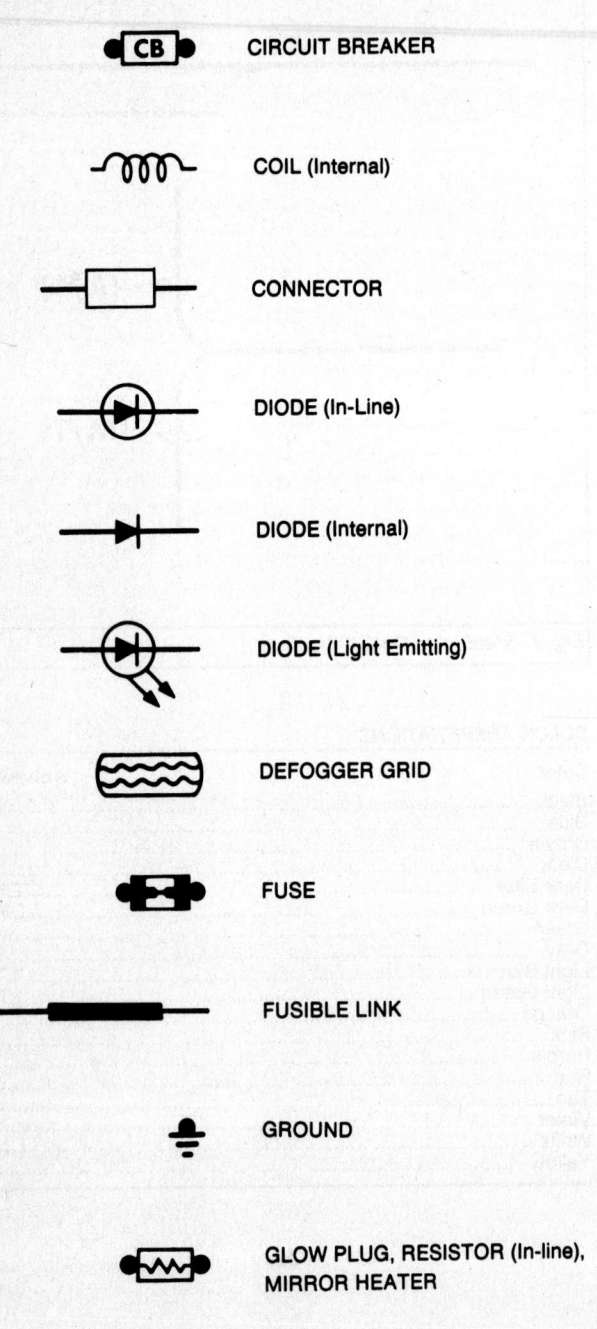

CIRCUIT BREAKER

COIL (Internal)

CONNECTOR

DIODE (In-Line)

DIODE (Internal)

DIODE (Light Emitting)

DEFOGGER GRID

FUSE

FUSIBLE LINK

GROUND

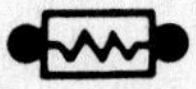
GLOW PLUG, RESISTOR (In-line), MIRROR HEATER

INJECTOR, PHOTOCELL

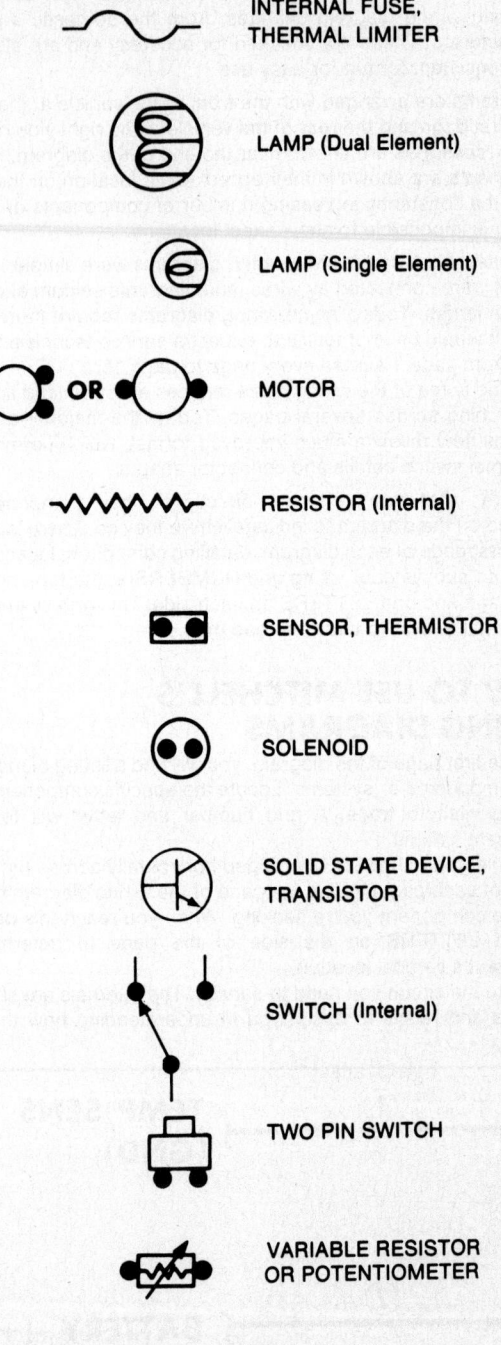

INTERNAL FUSE, THERMAL LIMITER

LAMP (Dual Element)

LAMP (Single Element)

OR

MOTOR

RESISTOR (Internal)

SENSOR, THERMISTOR

SOLENOID

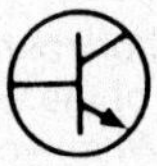
SOLID STATE DEVICE, TRANSISTOR

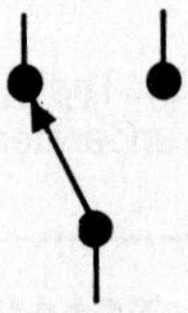
SWITCH (Internal)

TWO PIN SWITCH

VARIABLE RESISTOR OR POTENTIOMETER

IDENTIFYING WIRING DIAGRAM ABBREVIATIONS

***NOTE:** Abbreviations used on Mitchell diagrams are normally self-explanatory. To assist you, however, we have included a 2-page list of abbreviations beginning on the next page.*

1991 GENERAL INFORMATION
Commonly Used Abbreviations

"A"

A - Amperes
AAP - Auxiliary Accelerator Pump
AB - Air Bleed
ABDC - After Bottom Dead Center
ABS - Anti-Lock Brakes
ABRS - Air Bag Restraint System
Abs. - Absolute
AC - Alternating Current
A/C - Air Conditioning
ACCS - A/C Cycling Switch
ACCUM - Accumulator
ACCY - Accessory
ACT - Air Charge Temperature Sensor
ADJ - Adjust or Adjustable
ADV - Advance
AFS - Airflow Sensor
AI - Air Injection
AIR or A.I.R. - Air Injection Reactor
AIS - Air Injection System
ALCL - Assembly Line Communications Link
ALDL - Assembly Line Diagnostic Link
Alt. - Alternator or Altitude
Amp. - Ampere
ASCS - Air Suction Control Solenoid
ASD - Auto Shutdown
ASDM - Air Bag System Diagnostic Module
Assy. - Assembly
ASV - Air Suction Valve
A/T - Automatic Transmission/ Transaxle
ATC - Automatic Temperature Control
ATDC - After Top Dead Center
ATF - Automatic Transmission Fluid
ATS - Air Temperature Sensor
Aux. - Auxiliary
Avg. - Average
AXOD - Automatic Transaxle Overdrive

"B"

BAC - By-Pass Air Control
BAP - Barometric Absolute Pressure Sensor
BARO - Barometric
Batt. - Battery
BBDC - Before Bottom Dead Center
Bbl. - Barrel (Example: 4-Bbl.)
BCM - Body Control Module
BDC - Bottom Dead Center
BHP - Brake Horsepower
Blst. - Ballast
BMAP - Barometric and Manifold Absolute Pressure Sensor
BOO - Brake On-Off Switch
B/P - Backpressure
BPS - Barometric Pressure Sensor
BPT - Backpressure Transducer
BTDC - Before Top Dead Center
BTU - British Thermal Unit
BVSV - Bimetallic Vacuum Switching Valve

"C"

° C - Celsius (Degrees)
Calif. - California
CANP - Canister Purge
CARB - California Air Resources Board
CAT - Catalytic Converter
CB - Circuit Breaker
CBD - Closed Bowl Distributor
CBVV - Carburetor Bowl Vent Valve
cc - cubic centimeter
CCC - Computer Command Control
CCD - Computer Controlled Dwell
CCOT - Cycling Clutch Orifice Tube
CCW - Counterclockwise
CDI - Capacitor Discharge Ignition
CEC - Computerized Engine Control
CID - Cubic Inch Displacement
CIS - Continuous Injection System
CIS-E - Continuous Injection System-Electronic
cm - Centimeter
CO - Carbon Monoxide
CO_2 - Carbon Dioxide
Cont. - Continued
CONV - Convertible
CP - Canister Purge
CPS - Crank Position Sensor
CTS - Coolant Temperature Sensor
Cu. In. - Cubic Inch
CVC - Constant Vacuum Control
CV - Check Valve or Constant Velocity
CW - Clockwise
CYL or Cyl. - Cylinder
C^3 I - Computer Controlled Coil Ignition
C^4 - Computer Controlled Catalytic Converter

"D"

"D" - Drive
DBC - Dual Bed Catalyst
DC - Direct Current Or Discharge
DDD - Dual Diaphragm Distributor
Def. - Defrost
Defog. - Defogger
DERM - Diagnostic Energy Reserve Module
DFI - Digital Fuel Injection
Diag. - Diagnostic
DIC - Driver Information Center
DIS - Distributorless Ignition System
DIST - Distribution
DISTR - Distributor
DME - Digital Motor Electronics (Motronic System)
DOHC - Double Overhead Cam
DOT - Department of Transportation
DP - Dashpot
DRB-II - Diagnostic Readout Box
DVOM - Digital Volt-Ohmmeter

"E"

EAC - Electric Assist Choke
EACV - Electric Air Control Valve
EBCM - Electronic Brake Control Module
ECA - Electronic Control Assembly
ECM - Electronic Control Module
ECT - Engine Coolant Temperature Sensor
ECU - Electronic Control Unit
EDIS - Electronic Distributorless Ignition System
EEC - Electronic Engine Control
EECS - Evaporative Emission Control System
EEPROM - Electronically Erasable PROM
EFE - Early Fuel Evaporation
EGO - Exhaust Gas Oxygen Sensor
EGR - Exhaust Gas Recirculation
ESA - Electronic Spark Advance
ESC - Electronic Spark Control
EST - Electronic Spark Timing
EVAP - Fuel Evaporative System
EVIC - Electronic Vehicle Information Center
EVP - EGR Valve Position Sensor
Exc. - Except

"F"

° F - Fahrenheit (Degrees)
F/B - Fuse Block
FBC - Feedback Carburetor
Fed. - Federal
FI - Fuel Injection
FICD - Fast Idle Control Device
FIPL - Fuel Injector Pump Lever
FPR-VSV - Fuel Pressure Regulator Vacuum Switching Valve
Ft. Lbs. - Foot Pounds
FWD - Front Wheel Drive

"G"

g - grams
Gals. - gallons
GND or GRND - Ground
Gov. - Governor

"H"

HAC - High Altitude Compensation
HC - Hydrocarbons
H/D - Heavy Duty
HEGO - Heated Exhaust Gas Oxygen Sensor
HEI - High Energy Ignition
Hg - Mercury
Hgt. - Height
HLDT - Headlight
HO - High Output
HP - High Performance
HSC - High Swirl Combustion
HSO - High Specific Output
HTR - Heater
Hz - Hertz (Cycles Per Second)

1991 GENERAL INFORMATION
Commonly Used Abbreviations (Cont.)

"I"

IAC – Idle Air Control
IACV – Idle Air Control Valve
IC – Integrated Circuit
ID – Identification
I.D. – Inside Diameter
Ign. – Ignition
In. – Inches
INCH Lbs. – Inch Pounds
in. Hg – Inches of Mercury
Inj. – Injector
IP – Instrument Panel
IPC – Instrument Panel Cluster
ISC – Idle Speed Control
IVSV – Idle Vacuum Switching Valve

"J"

J/B – Junction Block

"K"

KAPWR – Keep Alive Power
k/ohms – 1000 ohms (kilo as in k/ohms)
kg – Kilograms (weight)
kg/cm² – Kilograms Per Square Centimeter
KM/H – Kilometers Per Hour
KOEO – Key On, Engine Off
KOER – Key On, Engine Running
KS – Knock Sensor

"L"

L – Liter
Lbs. – Pounds
LCD – Liquid Crystal Display
L/D – Light Duty
LED – Light Emitting Diode
LH – Left Hand

"M"

mA – Milliamps
MA or MAF – Mass Airflow
MAFS – Mass Airflow Sensor
MAP – Manifold Absolute Pressure
MAT – Manifold Air Temperature
MCU – Microprocessor Control Unit
MCV – Mixture Control Valve
Mem. – Memory
MEM-CAL – Memory Calibration Chip
mfd. – Microfarads
MFI – Multiport Fuel Injection
MIL – Malfunction Indicator Light
MPI – Multi-Point (Fuel) Injection
mm – Millimeters
MPH – Miles Per Hour
mV – Millivolts

"N"

NA – Not Available
N.m – Newton Meter
No. – Number
Nos. – Numbers
NOx – Oxides of Nitrogen

"O"

O – Oxygen
OC – Oxidation Catalyst
OD – Overdrive
O.D. – Outside Diameter
ODO – Odometer
OHC – Overhead Camshaft
O/S – Oversize
oz. – Ounce
ozs. – Ounces
O_2 – Oxygen

"P"

"P" – Park
PAV – Pulse Air Valve
P/C – Printed Circuit
PCM – Power Train Control Module
PCS – Purge Control Solenoid
PC-SOL – Purge Control Solenoid
PCV – Positive Crankcase Ventilation
PFI – Port Fuel Injection
PGM-CARB – Programmed Carburetor
PGM-FI – Programmed Fuel Injection
PIP – Profile Ignition Pick-up
P/N – Park/Neutral
PRNDL – Park Reverse Neutral Drive Low
PROM – Programmable Read-Only Memory
psi – Pounds Per Square Inch
P/S – Power Steering
PSPS – Power Steering Pressure Switch
PTC – Positive Temperature Coefficient
PTO – Power Take-Off
Pts. – Pints
Pwr. – Power

"Q"

Qts. – Quarts

R

RABS – Rear Anti-Lock Brake System
RECIRC – Recirculation
RH – Right Hand
RPM – Revolutions Per Minute
RWAL – Rear Wheel Anti-Lock Brake
RWD – Rear Wheel Drive

"S"

SBC – Single Bed Converter
SBEC – Single Board Engine Controller
SEN – Sensor
SES – Service Engine Soon
SFI – Sequential (Port) Fuel Injection
SIL – Shift Indicator Light
SIR – Supplemental Inflatable Restraint
SOHC – Single Overhead Cam
SOL or Sol. – Solenoid
SPFI – Sequential Port Fuel Injection
SPK – Spark Control
SPOUT – Spark Output
SRS – Supplemental Restraint System (Air Bag)
SSI – Solid State Ignition
STAR – Self-Test Automatic Readout
STO – Self-Test Output
SUB-O_2 – Sub Oxygen Sensor
Sw. – Switch
Sys. – System

"T"

TAB – Thermactor Air By-Pass
TAC – Thermostatic Air Cleaner
TAD – Thermactor Air Diverter
TBI – Throttle Body Injection
TCC – Torque Converter Clutch
TCCS – Toyota Computer Control System
TDC – Top Dead Center
Temp. – Temperature
TFI – Thick Film Ignition
THERMAC – Thermostatic Air Cleaner
TPS – Throttle Position Sensor/Switch
TS – Temperature Sensor
TV – Thermovalve
T.V. – Throttle Valve
TWC – Three-Way Catalyst

"V"

V – Valve
Vac. – Vacuum
VAF – Vane Airflow
VAPS – Variable Assist Power Steering
VCC – Viscous Converter Clutch
VIN – Vehicle Identification Number
VM – Vacuum Modulator
Volt. – Voltage
VOM – Volt-Ohmmeter (Analog)
VRV – Vacuum Regulator Valve
VSS – Vehicle Speed Sensor
VSV – Vacuum Switching Valve

"W"

W/ – With
W/O – Without
WAC – Wide Open Throttle A/C Switch
WOT – Wide Open Throttle

1991 GENERAL INFORMATION
Trouble Shooting

CHARGING SYSTEM

CHARGING SYSTEM TROUBLE SHOOTING

PROBLEM Possible Cause	Action
NO START CONDITION	
Dead Battery	Check/Replace Battery
Bad Cable Connections	Clean/Replace Cables
Ignition Switch/Circuit Fault	Check Switch/Circuit
CHARGING SYSTEM WARNING LIGHT STAYS ON	
Loose/Worn Alternator Belt	Tighten/Replace Belt
Loose Alternator Connections	Check/Repair Connections
Warning Light Wiring	Check/Repair Wiring
Faulty Stator/Diodes	Test/Repair Alternator
Faulty Voltage Regulator	Test/Repair Regulator
WARNING LIGHT OFF WITH IGNITION SWITCH ON	
Blown Fuse	Check/Replace Fuse
Faulty Alternator	Test Alternator
Bad Warning Light Bulb	Test/Replace Bulb
WARNING LIGHT ON WITH IGNITION SWITCH OFF	
Alternator Wiring Short	Check/Repair Wiring
Faulty Rectifier Bridge	Test/Repair Alternator
AMMETER INDICATES DISCHARGE	
Loose/Worn Alternator Belt	Tighten/Replace Belt
Loose Alternator Connections	Check/Repair Connections
Faulty Ammeter	Test/Replace Ammeter
NOISY ALTERNATOR	
Loose Drive Pulley	Check/Tighten Pulley Nut
Loose Mounting Bolts	Tighten Mounting Bolts
Worn/Dirty Alternator Bearings	Clean/Replace Alternator Bearings
Faulty Diodes/Stator	Replace Diodes/Stator
BATTERY WON'T STAY CHARGED	
Defective Battery	Test/Replace Battery
Accessories Left ON	Ensure Accessories OFF
Loose/Worn Alternator Belt	Tighten/Replace Belt
Loose Alternator Connections	Check/Repair Connections
Defective Alternator	Test/Repair Alternator
Short in System	Check/Repair Short
BATTERY OVERCHARGED	
Defective Battery	Replace Battery
Defective Alternator	Test/Repair Alternator
Defective Regulator	Test/Repair Regulator

STARTING SYSTEM

STARTING SYSTEM TROUBLE SHOOTING

PROBLEM Possible Cause	Action
STARTER FAILS TO OPERATE	
Dead Battery	Check/Replace Battery
Bad Connections/Wiring	Repair Connections/Wiring
Faulty Ignition Switch	Check Switch Circuit
Faulty Solenoid/Relay	Replace Solenoid/Relay
Faulty Ground	Check/Repair Ground
STARTER FAILS TO OPERATE – LIGHTS DIM	
Faulty Battery	Replace Battery
Bad Cable Connections	Check/Repair Connections
Grounded Starter Windings	Test/Repair Starter
Faulty Bearing/Bushing	Replace Bearing/Bushing
Faulty Ground	Check/Repair Ground
Corroded Terminals	Clean Terminals
STARTER TURNS – ENGINE DOES NOT	
Faulty Starter Drive	Replace Starter Drive
Broken Drive Housing	Replace Drive Housing
Faulty Pinion Shaft	Clean/Repair Shaft
Faulty Flywheel	Check Flywheel/Starter

STARTING SYSTEM TROUBLE SHOOTING (Cont.)

PROBLEM Possible Cause	Action
STARTER DOES NOT CRANK ENGINE	
Faulty Starter Drive	Replace Starter Drive
Broken Drive Housing	Replace Drive Housing
Missing Flywheel Teeth	Replace Flywheel
Faulty Ground	Check/Repair Ground
Frozen Engine	Check Engine
Liquid-Locked Engine	Test Cooling System
STARTER ROTATES ENGINE SLOWLY	
Faulty Battery	Replace Battery
Bad Connections/Wiring	Repair Connections/Wiring
Grounded Starter Windings	Test/Repair Starter
Faulty Starter Bearings	Replace Bearings
Faulty Ground	Check/Repair Ground
Engine Overheated	Check Cooling System
Timing Too Far Advanced	Reset Timing
Burned Solenoid Contacts	Replace Solenoid
High Current Draw	Test Starter Draw
STARTER ENGAGES ENGINE MOMENTARILY	
Timing Too Far Retarded	Reset Timing
Missing Flywheel Teeth	Replace Flywheel
Faulty Starter Drive	Replace Starter Drive
Broken Drive Housing	Replace Drive Housing
Weak Starter Solenoid	Replace Starter Solenoid
STARTER DRIVE DOES NOT ENGAGE	
Bad Solenoid Contacts	Replace Solenoid
Bad Solenoid Ground	Test Solenoid Ground
SOLENOID/RELAY DOES NOT CLOSE	
Faulty Battery	Replace Battery
Bad Connections/Wiring	Repair Connections/Wiring
Faulty Safety Switch	Replace Safety Switch
Faulty Solenoid/Relay	Replace Solenoid/Relay
STARTER DRIVE WILL NOT DISENGAGE	
Loose Starter Bolts	Tighten Starter Bolts
Worn Drive End Bushing	Replace Drive End Bushing
Missing Flywheel Teeth	Check Flywheel/Drive
Faulty Ignition Switch	Replace Ignition Switch
SOLENOID CLICKS	
Weak Battery	Charge/Replace Battery
Bad Solenoid Contacts	Replace Solenoid
Bad Connections/Wiring	Repair Connections/Wiring
Faulty Solenoid	Replace Solenoid
HIGH CURRENT DRAW	
Dragging Armature	Replace Starter Bushings
Shorted Armature Windings	Repair Starter
LOW CURRENT DRAW	
Worn Starter Brushes	Replace Brushes
Weak Brush Springs	Replace Brush Springs
Faulty Engine Ground	Check Ground Cable
High Resistance In Positive Battery Cable	Replace Cable
STARTER WHINES DURING CRANKING	
Starter Alignment	Check Starter Alignment
Too Much Distance Between Starter Drive & Flywheel	Ensure Flywheel is Okay Ensure Starter is Correct
STARTER WHINES AFTER STARTING	
Starter Alignment	Check Starter Alignment
Too Little Distance Between Starter Drive & Flywheel	Ensure Flywheel is Okay Ensure Starter is Correct

1991 GENERAL INFORMATION
Trouble Shooting (Cont.)

TUNE-UP

TUNE-UP TROUBLE SHOOTING

PROBLEM Possible Cause	Action
CARBON FOULED PLUGS	
Rich Air/Fuel Mixture	Adjust Air/Fuel Mixture
Faulty Choke	Replace Choke Assembly
Clogged Air Filter	Replace Air Filter
Incorrect Idle Speed	Reset Idle Speed
Faulty Ignition Wiring	Replace Ignition Wiring
Sticky Valves/Worn Valve Seal	Check Valve Train
Fuel Injection Operation	Check Fuel Injection
WET/OIL FOULED PLUGS	
Worn Rings/Pistons	Check Block Condition
Excessive Cylinder Wear	Rebore/Replace Block
PLUG GAP BRIDGED	
Combustion Chamber Carbon Deposits	Clean Combustion Chamber
BLISTERED ELECTRODE	
Engine Overheating	Check Cooling System
Loose Spark Plugs	Clean/Torque Plugs
Over-Advanced Timing	Reset Timing
Wrong Plug Heat Range	Install Correct Plug
MELTED ELECTRODES	
Incorrect Timing	Reset Timing
Burned Valves	Replace Valves
Engine Overheating	Check Cooling System
Wrong Plug Heat Range	Install Correct Plug
ENGINE WON'T START	
Loose Connections	Check Connections
No Power	Check Fuses/Battery
ENGINE RUNS ROUGH	
Leaky/Clogged Fuel Lines	Repair Fuel Lines
Incorrect Timing	Reset Timing/Check Advance
Faulty Plugs/Wires	Replace Plugs/Wires
COMPONENT FAILURE	
Spark Arcing	Replace Faulty Part
Defective Pick-Up Coil	Replace Pick-Up Coil
Defective Ignition Coil	Replace Ignition Coil
Defective Control Unit	Replace Control Unit
IGNITION DIAGNOSIS BY SCOPE PATTERN	
ALL FIRING LINES ABNORMALLY HIGH	
Retarded Ignition Timing	Reset Ignition Timing
Lean Air/Fuel Mixture	Adjust Fuel Mixture
High Secondary Resistance	Repair Secondary Ignition
ALL FIRING LINES ABNORMALLY LOW	
Rich Air/Fuel Mixture	Adjust Air/Fuel Mixture
Arcing Coil Wire	Replace Coil Wire
Cracked Coil Arcing	Replace Coil
Low Coil Output	Replace Coil
Low Compression	Check/Repair Engine
SEVERAL HIGH FIRING LINES	
Fuel Mixture Unbalanced	Adjust Fuel Mixture
EGR Valve Stuck Open	Clean/Replace EGR Valve
High Plug Wire Resistance	Replace Plug Wire
Cracked/Broken Plugs	Replace Plugs
Intake Vacuum Leak	Repair Leak
SEVERAL LOW FIRING LINES	
Fuel Mixture Unbalanced	Adjust Fuel Mixture
Plug Wires Arcing	Replace Plug Wires
Cracked Coil Arcing	Replace Coil
Low Compression	Check/Repair Engine
Faulty Spark Plugs	Replace Plugs

TUNE-UP TROUBLE SHOOTING (Cont.)

PROBLEM Possible Cause	Action
CYLINDERS NOT FIRING	
Cracked Distributor Cap	Replace Cap
Shorted Plug Wires	Replace Plug Wires
Mechanical Engine Fault	Check/Repair Engine
Spark Plugs Fouled	Replace Plugs
Carbon Track in Distributor Cap	Replace Cap
HARD STARTING	
Defective Ignition Coil(s)	Replace Coil(s)
Fouled Spark Plugs	Replace Plugs
Incorrect Timing	Reset Ignition Timing

CARBURETOR

CARBURETOR TROUBLE SHOOTING

PROBLEM Possible Cause	Action
ENGINE WON'T START	
Choke Not Closing	Check Choke/Linkage
Choke Linkage Bent	Check Linkage
Float Dry	Check/Reset Float Setting
ENGINE STARTS, THEN DIES	
Choke Breaker Setting Too Wide	Check Setting/Adjust
Fast Idle RPM Too Low	Reset Fast Idle
Fast Idle Cam Index Incorrect	Reset Fast Idle Cam Index
Vacuum Leak	Check For Vacuum Leaks
Low Fuel Pump Output	Repair/Replace Fuel Pump
Low Float Level	Check/Reset Float Setting
ENGINE QUITS UNDER LOAD	
Choke Breaker Setting Incorrect	Reset Choke Breaker
Fast Idle Cam Index Incorrect	Reset Fast Idle Cam Index
Hot Fast Idle Speed RPM Incorrect	Reset Fast Idle RPM
ENGINE IDLES SLOWLY WITH BLACK SMOKE	
Choke Breaker Setting Incorrect	Reset Choke Breaker
Fast Idle Cam Index Incorrect	Reset Fast Idle Cam Index
Hot Fast Idle RPM Too Low	Reset Fast Idle RPM
COLD ENGINE STALLS IN GEAR	
Choke Breaker Setting Incorrect	Reset Choke Breaker
Fast Idle RPM Incorrect	Reset Fast Idle RPM
Fast Idle Cam Index Incorrect	Reset Fast Idle Cam Index
ACCELERATION SAG OR STALL	
Defective Choke Heater	Replace Choke Heater
Choke Breaker Setting	Reset Choke Breaker
Float Level Too Low	Adjust Float Level
Accelerator Pump Defective	Repair Accelerator Pump
SAG OR STALL AFTER WARM-UP	
Defective Choke Heater	Replace Choke Heater
Faulty Accelerator Pump	Replace Accelerator Pump
Float Level Too Low	Adjust Float Level
WARM-UP BACKFIRING/BLACK SMOKE	
Choke Stuck Shut	Check/Replace Choke
TIP-IN HESITATION	
Vacuum Leak	Inspect Vacuum Lines
Accelerator Pump Weak	Replace Accelerator Pump
Float Level Setting Too Low	Reset Float Level
Metering Rods Sticking/Binding	Inspect/Replace Rods
Idle Passages Plugged	Clean/Rebuild Carburetor
WOT HESITATION	
Faulty Accelerator Pump	Replace Accelerator Pump
Large Vacuum Leak	Check For Vacuum Leaks
Float Level Too Low	Reset Float Level
Fuel Delivery Problem	Inspect Pump, Lines, Filter

1991 GENERAL INFORMATION
Trouble Shooting (Cont.)

FUEL INJECTION

FUEL INJECTION TROUBLE SHOOTING

PROBLEM Possible Cause	Action
ENGINE WON'T START	
Cold Start Valve Inoperative	Test Cold Start Valve
Poor Vacuum/Electrical Connection	Repair Connections
Contaminated Fuel	Test Fuel for Water/Alcohol
Bad Fuel Pump Relay/Circuit	Test Relay/Wiring
Battery Voltage Low	Charge/Test Battery
Low Fuel Pressure	Test Press. Regulator/Pump
No Distributor Reference Pulse	Repair Ignition System
Coolant Temp. Sensor Defective	Test Temp. Sensor/Circuit
Shorted WOT Switch	Check/Replace WOT Switch
Defective ECM	Replace ECM
HARD STARTING	
Defective Idle Air Control (IAC)	Test IAC and Circuit
EGR Valve Open	Test EGR Valve/Control Circuit
Stalls With A/C On	Check A/C "On" Signal to ECM
Restricted Fuel Lines	Inspect/Replace Fuel Lines
Poor MAP Sensor Signal	Test MAP Sensor/Circuit
Engine Stalls During Parking Maneuver	Check Power Steering Pressure
No Power To Injectors	Check Injector Fuse/Relay
ROUGH IDLE	
Poor MAP Sensor Signal	Test MAP Sensor/Circuit
Intermittent Fuel Injector Operation	Check Harness Connectors
Erratic Vehicle Speed Sensor Inputs	Harness Too Close to Plug Wires
Poor Temperature Sensor Signal	Test EGR Valve/Circuit
Poor O_2 Sensor Signal	Test O_2 Sensor/Circuit
Faulty PCV System	Check PCV Valve and Hoses
POOR HIGH SPEED OPERATION	
Low Fuel Pump Volume	Faulty Fuel Pump/Filter
Poor MAP Sensor Signal	Test Speed Sensor/Circuit
ACCELERATION PING/KNOCK	
Poor Knock Sensor Signal	Test Knock Sensor/Circuit
Poor Baro Sensor Signal	Test Baro Sensor/Circuit
Improper Ignition Timing	Adjust Timing
Engine Overheating	Check Cooling System

TURBOCHARGER

TURBOCHARGER TROUBLE SHOOTING

PROBLEM Possible Cause	Action
Faulty Spark Advance System	Check Distributor/Ignition
Defective EGR Operation	Check EGR System
Air Inlet Restriction	Clear Restriction
Excessive Boost	Check/Adjust Boost Pressure
Fuel System Fault	Check Fuel System
Internal Turbo Defect	Repair/Replace Turbo
LOW ENGINE POWER	
Faulty Spark Advance System	Check Distributor/Ignition
Defective EGR Operation	Check EGR System
Loose Turbo Bolts	Check/Tighten Bolts
BLUE EXHAUST SMOKE	
Oil Inlet Leak	Check/Repair Fittings
Oil Drain Leak/Plugged	Check/Repair Fittings
Turbo Seal Leak	Check/Replace Seal

GAS ENGINE

GAS ENGINE TROUBLE SHOOTING

PROBLEM Possible Cause	Action
ENGINE LOPES AT IDLE	
Leaky Intake Gasket	Replace Intake Gasket
Blown Head Gasket	Replace Head Gasket Test Cooling System
Worn Timing Chain/Gears	Replace Timing Chain/Gears
Worn Timing Belt	Inspect/Replace Belt
Worn Cam	Inspect Valve Train
Overheated Engine	Check Cooling System
Clogged PCV System	Check/Clear PCV System
Leaking EGR Valve	Check/Replace EGR Valve
Faulty Fuel Pump	Replace Fuel Pump
ENGINE LACKS POWER	
Low Fuel Pressure	Replace Fuel Pump
Leaky Fuel Pump	Replace Fuel Pump
Sticky Valves	Inspect Valve Train
Worn Timing Chain/Gears	Replace Timing Chain/Gears
Worn Piston Rings	Check Compression
Weak Valve Springs	Inspect Valve Train
Worn Cam	Inspect Cam (Lifters)
Blown Head Gasket	Replace Head Gasket Check Cooling System
Clutch Slipping	Adjust/Replace Clutch
Overheated Engine	Check Cooling System
A/T Slipping	Inspect/Repair A/T
Vacuum Leaks	Repair Vacuum Leaks
Restricted Exhaust	Clear Restriction
FAULTY HIGH SPEED OPERATION	
Low Fuel Pressure	Replace Fuel Pump
Leaky Fuel Pump	Replace Fuel Pump
Sticky Valves	Inspect Valve Train
Incorrect Valve Timing	Inspect Valve Train
Intake Manifold Restricted	Clear Restriction
Worn Distributor Shaft	Replace Distributor
POOR ACCELERATION	
Incorrect Ignition Timing	Reset Timing
Leaky Valves	Check Compression
Weak Fuel Pump	Test/Replace Fuel Pump
Clogged Injectors	Clean/Replace Injectors
Excessive Intake Valve Deposits	Clean Valve Deposits
BACKFIRE IN INTAKE MANIFOLD	
Improper Ignition Timing	Adjust Timing
Improper Valve Timing	Inspect Valve Train
Carbon Tracking/Crossfire	Inspect Cap/Rotor/Plug Wires
Faulty Plug Wires	Replace Plug Wires
Defective EGR Valve	Replace EGR Valve
Lean Fuel Mixture	Check/Adjust Mixture
Gas in Engine Oil	Check Fuel System
Sticky Intake Valve	Check Valve Train
Vacuum Leaks	Check for Vacuum Leaks
BACKFIRE IN EXHAUST	
Vacuum Leak	Repair Vacuum Leak
Faulty Diverter Valve	Replace Diverter Valve
Faulty Choke Operation	Adjust Choke
Exhaust System Leak	Repair Exhaust Leak
Carbon Tracking/Crossfire	Inspect Cap/Rotor/Plug Wires
ENGINE DETONATION/PRE-IGNITION	
Too Much Timing Advance	Reset Timing
Faulty Ignition System	Check Ignition System
Faulty Spark Plugs	Replace Spark Plugs
Lean Fuel Mixture	Check Fuel System
Carbon Deposit Build-Up	Remove Carbon
Low Octane Fuel	Try Different Fuel
Compression Too High	Check Compression

1991 GENERAL INFORMATION
Trouble Shooting (Cont.)

GAS ENGINE (Cont.)

GAS ENGINE TROUBLE SHOOTING (Cont.)

PROBLEM Possible Cause	Action
EXCESSIVE OIL CONSUMPTION	
Worn Valve Guides/Stems	Inspect Valve Train
Worn Piston Rings	Inspect Engine Block
Worn Cylinder Walls	Inspect Engine Block
Intake Manifold Leak	Replace Gasket
Excessive Bearing Clearance	Inspect Bearings/Crankshaft
NO OIL PRESSURE	
Low Oil Level	Add Oil/Check for Leaks
Faulty Oil Pump	Replace Oil Pump
Oil Pick-Up Screen Blocked	Clear Blockage
Loose Oil Pick-Up Tube	Check "O" Ring
Blocked Oil Passages	Inspect Engine Block
Faulty Pressure Relief Valve	Replace Relief Valve
Faulty Oil Light/Gauge	Check Light/Gauge
Worn Engine Bearings	Check/Replace Bearings
Faulty Cooling System	Check Cooling System
Excessive Backpressure	Check Exhaust System
LOW OIL PRESSURE	
Low Oil Level	Fill to Proper Level
Faulty Oil Pump	Replace Oil Pump
Oil Pick-Up Screen Blocked	Clear Blockage
Loose Oil Pick-Up Tube	Check "O" Ring
Blocked Oil Passages	Inspect Engine Block
Faulty Pressure Relief Valve	Replace Relief Valve
Faulty Oil Light/Gauge	Check Light/Gauge
Worn Engine Bearings	Check/Replace Bearings
HIGH OIL PRESSURE	
Faulty Pressure Relief Valve	Replace Relief Valve
Improper Grade of Oil	Change Oil/Grade
Faulty Oil Light/Gauge	Check Light/Gauge
NOISY MAIN BEARINGS	
Low Oil Level	Check Oil Level
Low Oil Pressure	Check Oil Pressure
Worn Main Bearings	Inspect Engine Block
Excessive Crankshaft End Play	Check Main Bearings Check Thrust Washer
Loose Flywheel/Torque Converter	Check Flywheel/Converter
Worn Vibration Damper	Replace Vibration Damper
Worn Crankshaft	Replace Crankshaft/Bearings
Excessive Belt Tension	Check/Loosen Belts
NOISY CONNECTING RODS	
Low Oil Level	Check/Fill Oil Level
Low Oil Pressure	Check Oil Pressure
Worn Rod Bearings	Inspect/Replace Bearings
Worn Crankshaft	Check/Replace Crankshaft/Bearings
Misaligned Rod/Cap	Check Rod/Cap
Excessive Belt Tension	Check/Loosen Belts
NOISY VALVE TRAIN	
Low Oil Pressure	Check Oil Level/Pressure
Improper Valve Lash	Check Valve Lash
Loose/Worn Timing Belt/Chain/Gears	Check Belt/Chain/Gears
Worn/Bent Push Rods	Check/Replace Push Rods
Worn Rocker Arms	Check/Replace Rocker Arms
Bent Valve	Check Valve Train/Head
Worn Camshaft	Check Camshaft/Bearings
Broken Valve Spring	Replace Valve Spring
Faulty Valve Lifters	Check Lifters/Camshaft
Worn Valve Guides	Check Valve Train
Missing Valve Keeper	Replace Valve Keeper
Loose Rocker Arm Studs	Replace Studs

DIESEL ENGINE

DIESEL ENGINE TROUBLE SHOOTING

PROBLEM Possible Cause	Action
ENGINE WON'T CRANK	
Bad Batteries	Test/Replace Batteries
Bad Cable Connections	Clean/Replace Cables
Bad Starter	Test/Repair/Replace Starter
Bad Neutral Safety Switch	Replace Neutral Safety Switch
ENGINE CRANKS SLOWLY	
Bad Batteries	Test/Replace Batteries
Bad Cable Connections	Clean/Replace Cables
Bad Starter	Test/Repair/Replace Starter
ENGINE CRANKS NORMALLY, WON'T START	
Faulty Glow Plugs	Test/Replace Glow Plugs
Faulty Glow Plug Controller	Test/Replace Controller
No Fuel To Cylinders	Test/Replace Injectors
No Fuel To Injector Pump	Check Fuel Delivery System
Plugged Air Filter	Replace Air Filter
Plugged Fuel Filter	Replace Fuel Filter
Plugged Fuel Tank Filter	Replace Tank Filter
Faulty Fuel Pump	Test/Replace Fuel Pump
Fuel Return System Blocked	Clear Restriction
No Voltage To Fuel Solenoid	Check Fuel Solenoid Wiring
Manual Shut-Off Lever Engaged	Disengage Shut-Off Lever
Incorrect/Contaminated Fuel	Flush/Refill Tank
Incorrect Inj. Pump Timing	Reset Inj. Pump Timing
Low Compression	Check Engine Condition
Faulty Injection Pump	Test/Replace Injection Pump
Fuel Solenoid Closed In RUN Position	Test/Replace Fuel Solenoid
ENGINE STARTS, WON'T IDLE	
Incorrect Slow Idle Setting	Adjust Slow Idle Setting
Plugged Air Filter	Replace Air Filter
Faulty Fast Idle Solenoid	Test/Replace Fast Idle Solenoid
Air In Fuel System	Bleed Air From System
Fuel Return System Blocked	Clear Restriction
Glow Plugs Off Too Soon	Test Glow Plugs
Incorrect Inj. Pump Timing	Reset Inj. Pump Timing
No Fuel To Injector Pump	Check Fuel Delivery System
Incorrect/Contaminated Fuel	Flush/Refill Tank
Low Compression	Check Engine Condition
Faulty Injection Pump	Test/Replace Injection Pump
ENGINE STARTS, IDLES ROUGH	
Incorrect Slow Idle Setting	Adjust Slow Idle Setting
Plugged Air Filter	Replace Air Filter
Fuel Leak at Injection Line	Repair Fuel Leak
Fuel Return System Blocked	Clear Restriction
Air In Fuel System	Bleed Air From System
Incorrect/Contaminated Fuel	Flush/Refill Tank
Faulty Injector Nozzle	Test/Replace Injector Nozzle
Low Compression	Check Engine Condition
ENGINE SMOKES, CLEARS AFTER WARM-UP	
Incorrect Inj. Pump Timing	Reset Inj. Pump Timing
Low Compression	Check Engine Condition
Faulty Injector Nozzle	Test/Replace Injector Nozzle
Air In Fuel System	Bleed Air From System
ENGINE MISFIRES ABOVE IDLE	
Plugged Fuel Filter	Replace Fuel Filter
Incorrect Inj. Pump Timing	Reset Inj. Pump Timing
Incorrect/Contaminated Fuel	Flush/Refill Tank
ENGINE WON'T RETURN TO IDLE	
Incorrect Fast Idle Setting	Adjust Fast Idle Setting
Faulty Injection Pump	Test/Replace Injection Pump
External Linkage Binding	Check/Repair Linkage
Air In Fuel System	Repair/Bleed Air From System

1991 GENERAL INFORMATION
Trouble Shooting (Cont.)

DIESEL ENGINE (Cont.)

DIESEL ENGINE TROUBLE SHOOTING (Cont.)

PROBLEM Possible Cause	Action
ENGINE LACKS POWER	
Restricted Air Intake	Clear Restriction
Faulty EGR Valve	Replace EGR Valve
Restricted Exhaust System	Repair Exhaust System
Blocked Fuel Cap Vent	Replace Fuel Cap
Restricted Fuel Supply From Tank to Injection Pump	Clear Restriction
Incorrect/Contaminated Fuel	Flush/Refill Tank
Faulty Injector Nozzle	Test/Replace Injector Nozzle
Low Compression	Check Engine Condition
Improper Throttle Linkage Adjustment	Adjust Throttle Linkage
CYLINDER KNOCKING NOISE	
Injector Nozzles Stuck Open	Test/Replace Injectors
Low Injector Nozzle Pressure	Test/Replace Injectors
Loose Wrist Pin	Disassemble Engine
Piston Slap	Disassemble Engine
ENGINE OVERHEATING	
Cooling System Leaks	Repair Cooling System
Loose/Damaged Belt	Tighten/Replace Belt
Plugged Radiator	Rod/Replace Radiator
Defective Fan	Replace Fan
Restricted Airflow Across Radiator	Clear Restriction
Thermostat Stuck Closed	Replace Thermostat
Leaking Head Gasket	Replace Head Gasket Test/Repair Cooling System
ENGINE WON'T SHUT OFF	
Injector Pump Fuel Solenoid Does Not Shut Off Fuel Valve	Test/Repair Fuel Solenoid

VACUUM PUMP TROUBLE SHOOTING

PROBLEM Possible Cause	Action
EXCESSIVE NOISE	
Loose Pump Mounting	Tighten Pump Mounting
Loose Pump Tube	Tighten Pump Tube
Faulty Pump Valves	Replace Pump Valves
OIL LEAKAGE	
Loose End Plug	Tighten End Plug
Bad Seal Crimp	Remove/Recrimp Seal

COOLING SYSTEM

COOLING SYSTEM TROUBLE SHOOTING

PROBLEM Possible Cause	Action
OVERHEATING	
Insufficient Coolant	Fill/Pressure Test System
Coolant Leak	Fill/Pressure Test System
Radiator Fins Clogged	Remove/Clean Radiator
Cooling Fan Malfunction	Test Cooling Fan/Circuit
Thermostat Stuck Closed	Replace Thermostat
Clogged Cooling System Passages	Clean/Flush Cooling System
Water Pump Malfunction	Replace Water Pump
Fan Clutch Malfunction	Replace Fan Clutch
Cooling Fan Motor Malfunction	Test Fan Motor
Cooling Fan Relay Malfunction	Test Fan Relay
Faulty Ignition Advance	Check/Replace Advance
Faulty Radiator Cap	Replace Radiator Cap
Broken/Slipping Fan Belt	Replace Fan Belt
Restricted Exhaust	Repair Exhaust System
CORROSION	
Impurities in Coolant	Clean/Flush System

COOLING SYSTEM (Cont.)

COOLING SYSTEM TROUBLE SHOOTING (Cont.)

PROBLEM Possible Cause	Action
COOLANT LEAKAGE	
Damaged Hose	Replace Hose
Leaky Water Pump Seal	Replace Water Pump
Damaged Radiator Seam	Replace/Repair Radiator
Leaky Thermostat Cover	Replace Thermostat Cover
Cylinder Head Problem	Check Head/Head Gasket
Cylinder Block Problem	Check Cylinder Block
Air in Cooling System	Bleed Cooling System
Leaky Freeze Plugs	Replace Freeze Plugs
RECOVERY SYSTEM INOPERATIVE	
Loose/Defective Radiator Cap	Replace Radiator Cap
Overflow Tube Clogged/Leaking	Repair Tube
Recovery Bottle Vent Restricted	Clean Vent
NO HEATER CORE FLOW	
Collapsed Heater Hose	Replace Heater Hose
Plugged Heater Core	Clean/Replace Heater Core
Faulty Heater Valve	Replace Heater Valve

CLUTCH

CLUTCH TROUBLE SHOOTING

PROBLEM Possible Cause	Action
CLUTCH CHATTERS/GRABS	
Incorrect Pedal Adjustment	Adjust Free Play
Worn Input Shaft Spline	Replace Input Shaft
Binding Pressure Plate	Replace Pressure Plate
Binding Throw-Out Lever	Check Throw-Out Lever Check Throw-Out Bearing Check Bearing Retainer
Uneven Pressure Plate Contact With Flywheel	Align/Replace Worn Parts
Transmission Misaligned	Align Transmission
Worn Pressure Plate	Replace Clutch Assembly
Oil-Saturated Disc	Replace Clutch Assembly Repair Oil Leak
Loose Engine Mounts	Replace Engine Mounts
CLUTCH PEDAL STICKS DOWN	
Clutch Cable Binding	Replace Clutch Cable
Weak Pressure Plate Springs	Replace Clutch Assembly
Binding Clutch Linkage	Lubricate Linkage
Broken Clutch Pedal Return Spring	Replace Return Spring
CLUTCH WILL NOT RELEASE	
Oil-Saturated Disc	Replace Clutch Assembly Repair Oil Leak
Defective Disc Face	Replace Clutch Assembly
Disc Sticking on Input Shaft Splines	Replace Disc/Input Shaft
Binding Pilot Bearing	Replace Pilot Bearing
Faulty Clutch Master Cylinder	Replace Master Cylinder
Faulty Clutch Slave Cylinder	Replace Slave Cylinder
Blown Clutch Flex Hose	Replace Flexhose
Sticky Throw-Out Bearing Sleeve	Clean/Lube Sleeve
Clutch Cable Binding	Replace Clutch Cable
Broken/Loose Bellhousing	Check Bellhousing
RATTLING/SQUEAKING	
Broken Throw-Out Lever Return Spring	Replace Return Spring
Faulty Throw-Out Bearing	Replace Throw-Out Bearing
Faulty Clutch Disc	Replace Clutch Disc
Faulty Pilot Bearing	Replace Pilot Bearing
Worn Throw-Out Bearing	Replace Throw-Out Bearing
Dry Bearing Retainer Slide For Throw-Out Bearing Sleeve	Lubricate Slide

1991 GENERAL INFORMATION
Trouble Shooting (Cont.)

CLUTCH (Cont.)

CLUTCH TROUBLE SHOOTING (Cont.)

PROBLEM / Possible Cause	Action
SLIPPING	
Faulty Pressure Plate	Replace Clutch Assembly
Worn Clutch Disc	Replace Clutch Assembly
Incorrect Alignment	Realign Clutch Assembly
Faulty Clutch Slave Cylinder	Replace Slave Cylinder
NO PEDAL PRESSURE	
Leaky Hydraulic System	Check Clutch Master Cylinder Check Clutch Slave Cylinder Check Clutch Flexhose
Broken Clutch Cable	Replace Clutch Cable
Faulty Throw-Out Lever	Replace Throw-Out Lever
Broken Clutch Linkage	Repair Clutch Linkage
NOISY CLUTCH PEDAL	
Faulty Safety Switch	Check/Replace Switch
Noisy Self-Adj. Ratchet	Replace Ratchet
Dry Throw-Out Bearing	Replace Throw-Out Bearing
Dry Pilot Bearing	Replace Pilot Bearing
Worn Input Shaft	Replace Input Shaft

DRIVE AXLE (RWD)

DRIVE AXLE (RWD) TROUBLE SHOOTING

PROBLEM / Possible Cause	Action
KNOCKING OR CLUNKING	
Differential Side Gear Clearance	Check Clearance
Worn Pinion Shaft	Replace Pinion Shaft
Axle Shaft End Play	Check End Play
Missing Gear Teeth	Check Diff./Replace Gear
Wrong Axle Backlash	Check Backlash
Misaligned Driveline	Realign Driveline
CLUNKING DURING ENGAGEMENT	
Side Gear Clearance	Check Side Gear Clearance
Ring and Pinion Backlash	Check Backlash
Worn/Loose Pinion Shaft	Replace Shaft/Bearing
Bad "U" Joint	Replace "U" Joint
Sticking Slip Yoke	Lube Slip Yoke
Broken Rear Axle Mount	Replace Mount
Loose Drive Shaft Flange	Check Flange
CLICK/CHATTER ON TURNS	
Differential Side Gear Clearance	Check Clearance
Worn Clutch Plates [1]	Replace Clutch Plates
Wrong Diff. Lubricant [1]	Change Lubricant
RHYTHMIC KNOCK OR CLICK	
Flat Spot on Rear Wheel Bearing	Replace Wheel Bearing
HUM/LOW VIBRATION AT ALL SPEEDS	
Faulty Wheel Bearings	Replace Bearings
Faulty "U" Joint	Replace "U" Joint
Faulty Drive Shaft	Balance Drive Shaft
Faulty Companion Flange	Replace Flange
Faulty Slip Yoke Flange	Replace Flange

[1] – Limited slip differential only.

DRIVE AXLE (FWD)

DRIVE AXLE (FWD) TROUBLE SHOOTING

PROBLEM / Possible Cause	Action
GREASE LEAKING	
Ripped CV Boot	Replace Boot
CLICKING NOISE WHILE CORNERING	
Dry/Worn CV Joints	Replace Outer CV Joints
CLUNK ON ACCELERATION	
Dry/Worn CV Joints	Replace Inner CV Joints
Worn Trans. Gears/Bearings	Inspect Trans.
VIBRATION/SHUDDER ON ACCELERATION	
Dry/Worn CV Joints	Replace CV Joints
Alignment Out	Check Alignment
Incorrect Spring Height	Check Spring Height
SQUEALING OR HUMMING	
Dry/Worn CV Joints	Lube/Replace CV Joints
Faulty Wheel Bearing	Replace Wheel Bearing

BRAKE

BRAKE TROUBLE SHOOTING

PROBLEM / Possible Cause	Action
CAR PULLS WHILE BRAKING	
Faulty Caliper	Rebuild/Replace Caliper
Restricted Brake Hose	Replace Hose
Faulty Rear Brakes	Inspect Rear Brakes
Worn Front Suspension	Check Suspension
Alignment Out	Check Alignment
Incorrect Tire Pressure	Check Pressure
Mismatched Tires	New Tires
HIGH-PITCHED SQUEAL (BRAKES OFF)	
Wear Indicators Rubbing	Replace Disc Pads
Faulty Wheel Bearing	Replace Bearing
HIGH-PITCHED SQUEAL (BRAKES ON)	
Worn Brake Pads	Replace Disc Pads
Glazed Rotors	Replace Pads/Resurface Rotor
CHATTERING/PULSATING	
Faulty Rotors/Drums	Check Runout/Parallelism
Loose Wheel Bearings	Check Bearings
Poorly Installed Pads	Correct Installation
EXCESSIVE PEDAL EFFORT	
Faulty Master Cylinder	Rebuild/Replace Cylinder
Faulty Power Booster	Repair/Replace Booster
Worn or Glazed Pads/Shoes	Replace Pads/Shoes
Frozen Caliper Piston	Replace Caliper
Poor Brake Adjustment	Adjust Brakes
Low Fluid Level	Fill Fluid/Inspect System
Air in Lines	Inspect/Bleed System
Heat Boiling Brake Fluid	Re-Route Brake Lines

BRAKE (Cont.)

BRAKE TROUBLE SHOOTING (Cont.)

PROBLEM Possible Cause	Action
EXCESSIVE PEDAL TRAVEL	
Brake Adjustment	Adjust Brakes
Low Fluid Level	Fill Fluid/Inspect System
Air in Lines	Inspect/Bleed System
Faulty Master Cylinder	Rebuild/Replace Cylinder
Faulty Brake Booster	Repair/Replace Booster
Worn or Glazed Pads/Shoes	Replace Pads/Shoes
Frozen Caliper Piston	Replace Caliper
Booster Actuator Rod Adjustment	Adjust Rod Clearance
Contaminated Fluid	Flush/Bleed System
BRAKES DRAG	
Faulty Master Cylinder	Rebuild/Replace Cylinder
Restricted Brake Lines	Clear Restrictions
Frozen Parking Brake Cables	Replace Cables
Gear Oil-Soaked Pads/Shoes	Repair Oil Leak Replace Pads/Shoes
Brake Fluid-Soaked Pads/Shoes	Repair Fluid Leak Replace Pads/Shoes
Oil Accidentally Mixed With Brake Fluid	Check/Replace All Cylinders/Calipers/Hoses Flush/Bleed System
BRAKES GRAB/UNEVEN ACTION	
Faulty Combination Valve	Replace Combination Valve
Faulty Power Booster	Repair/Replace Booster
Binding Brake Pedal	Check Pedal

WHEEL ALIGNMENT

WHEEL ALIGNMENT TROUBLE SHOOTING [1]

PROBLEM Possible Cause	Action
PREMATURE TIRE WEAR	
Incorrect Tire Pressure	Check Pressure
Alignment Out	Check Alignment
Worn Front Suspension	Check Suspension
Tires Out of Balance	Balance Tires
Worn Steering Linkage	Check/Replace Linkage
Improper Riding Height	Check/Adjust Riding Height
Uneven/Worn Springs	Replace Springs
Loose/Worn Wheel Bearings	Replace Bearings
Bent Wheel/Rim	Replace Wheel/Rim
Worn/Defective Shocks	Replace Shocks
PULLS TO ONE SIDE	
Incorrect Tire Pressure	Check Pressure
Brake Drag	Inspect Brakes
Mismatched Tires	New Tires
Radial Belt Separation [1]	Replace Tires
Alignment Out	Check Alignment
Frame Bent	Check Frame Damage
Worn Front Suspension	Check Suspension
Worn Steering Linkage	Check/Replace Linkage
Uneven/Worn Springs	Replace Springs
Loose/Worn Wheel Bearings	Replace Bearings
STEERING TOO HARD	
Tight Idler Arm Bushing	Retorque Idler Arm
Tight Ball Joint	Replace Ball Joint
Alignment Out	Check Alignment
Power Steering Fluid Low	Fill/Check Leaks
Power Steering Belt Loose	Tighten Belt
Power Steering Pump Faulty	Repair/Replace Pump
Faulty Steering Gear	Repair/Replace Gear
Faulty Steering Knuckle	Replace Steering Knuckle
Worn Front Suspension	Check Suspension
Incorrect Tire Pressure	Check Pressure

WHEEL ALIGNMENT (Cont.)

WHEEL ALIGNMENT TROUBLE SHOOTING [1] (Cont.)

PROBLEM Possible Cause	Action
VEHICLE WANDERS	
Incorrect Tire Pressure	Check Pressure
Loose/Worn Wheel Bearings	Replace Bearings
Alignment Out	Check Alignment
Loose Strut Rod (Bushings)	Repair Strut Rod
Faulty Stabilizer Bar	Repair Stabilizer Bar
Worn Spring/Shock	Replace Spring/Shock
Worn Front Suspension	Check Suspension
FRONT END SHIMMY	
Tires Out of Balance	Balance Tires
Radial Belt Separation	Replace Tires
Excessive Wheel Runout	Repair/Replace Wheel
Alignment Out	Check Alignment
Worn Rack Bushings	Replace Bushings
Worn Front Suspension	Check Suspension
Loose/Worn Wheel Bearings	Replace Bearings
Dry/Worn CV Joints	Lube/Replace CV Joints

SUSPENSION

SUSPENSION TROUBLE SHOOTING

PROBLEM Possible Cause	Action
FRONT END NOISE	
Loose/Worn Wheel Bearings	Replace Bearings
Worn Shocks/Struts	Replace Shocks/Struts
Worn Strut Mountings	Replace Mountings
Loose Steering Gear-to-Frame Mounting Bolts	Check Mounting
Worn Control Arm Bushings	Replace Bushings
Dry Ball Joints	Lubricate Ball Joints
FRONT END SHIMMY	
Tires Out of Balance	Balance Tires
Excessive Wheel Runout	Repair/Replace Wheel
Alignment Out	Check Alignment
Worn Rack Bushings	Replace Bushings
Worn Front Suspension	Check Suspension
Loose/Worn Wheel Bearings	Replace Bearings
Dry/Worn CV Joints	Lube/Replace CV Joints
PULLS TO ONE SIDE	
Incorrect Tire Pressure	Check Pressure
Brake Drag	Inspect Brakes
Mismatched Tires	New Tires
Alignment Out	Check Alignment
Frame Bent	Check Frame Damage
Worn Front Suspension	Check Suspension
Worn Steering Linkage	Check/Replace Linkage
Uneven/Worn Springs	Replace Springs
Loose/Worn Wheel Bearings	Replace Bearings
Power Steering Unbalance	Check Power Steering
SPRING NOISES	
Loose "U" Bolts	Check "U" Bolts
Loose/Worn Bushings	Replace Bushings
Worn/Missing Leaf Spacers	Replace Spacers
CAR LEANS/SWAYS ON CORNERS	
Loose Stabilizer Bar	Replace Bushings
Worn Shocks/Struts	Replace Shocks/Struts
Worn Spring/Shock	Replace Spring/Shock

1991 GENERAL INFORMATION
Trouble Shooting (Cont.)

STEERING COLUMN

STEERING COLUMN TROUBLE SHOOTING

PROBLEM Possible Cause	Action
NOISE IN COLUMN	
Coupling Pulled Apart	Check Coupling
Column Incorrectly Aligned	Align Column
Broken Lower Joint	Replace Joint
Dry Horn Contact Ring	Lube Contact Ring
Dry Column Bearings	Lube/Replace Bearings
Shaft Snap Ring Loose	Seat Snap Ring
Shroud Hits Wheel	Realign Shroud
Lock Plate Ring Loose	Seat Ring
Tight "U" Joint	Replace "U" Joint
STEERING SHAFT BINDS	
Column Misaligned	Align Column
Shroud Misaligned	Align Shroud
Faulty Column Bearings	Replace Bearings
Tight "U" Joint	Replace "U" Joint
SHIFT LEVER BINDS	
Column Misaligned	Align Column
Shroud Misaligned	Align Shroud
Faulty Column Bearings	Replace Bearings
Misadjusted Shifter	Adjust Shifter
Damaged Shift Tube	Replace Tube
EXCESS PLAY IN COLUMN	
Mounting Bracket Loose	Check Bolts
Broken Weld on Jacket	Repair/Replace Column
Broken Column Mount	Repair Column Mount
IGNITION SWITCH STICKY	
Poorly Installed Switch	Check Switch Installation
Worn Key Switch	Replace Key Switch

TILT STEERING COLUMN

TILT STEERING COLUMN TROUBLE SHOOTING

PROBLEM Possible Cause	Action
STEERING WHEEL LOOSE	
Housing/Pivot Pin Loose	Check Clearance
Faulty Anti-Lash Springs	Replace Springs
Upper Bearing Loose	Seat Upper Bearing
Misadjusted Tilt Lock	Adjust Tilt Lock
Loose Support Screws	Tighten Screws
Missing/Broken Bearing Preload Spring	Replace Spring
Housing Jacket Loose	Tighten Screws
PLAY IN COLUMN MOUNT	
Loose Support Screws	Tighten Screws/Bracket
Loose Housing Shoes	Check Housing Shoes
Loose Tilt Pivot Pins	Check Pivot Pins
Loose Shoe Lock Pin	Check Shoe Lock
HOUSING SCRAPES ON BOWL	
Damaged Bowl	Replace Bowl
WHEEL DOES NOT LOCK	
Shoe Seized on Pivot Pin	Check Shoe
Dirty/Damaged Shoe	Clean/Replace Shoe
Faulty Shoe Lock Spring	Replace Spring
WHEEL DOES NOT RETURN	
Bound Pivot Pins	Clean/Replace Pins
Damaged Tilt Spring	Replace Tilt Spring
Turn Signal Switch Wires Too Tight	Reset Wires
NOISE WHEN TILTING	
Worn Upper Tilt Bumpers	Replace Bumpers
Tilt Spring Rubs Housing	Adjust Springs

MANUAL STEERING GEAR

MANUAL STEERING GEAR TROUBLE SHOOTING

PROBLEM Possible Cause	Action
EXCESSIVE STEERING PLAY	
Wheel Bearing Misadjusted	Check Wheel Bearing
Worn/Loose Linkage	Check Linkage
Worn/Loose Ball Joints	Check Ball Joints
Loose Pitman Arm	Check Arm/Gear Splines
Loose Pitman Shaft	Check Gear
Loose Gear Mount	Check Gear Mount
Loose Rack Mount	Check Rack Mount
WHEEL CENTERS POORLY	
Steering Gear Adjusted Too Tightly	Check Gear Free Play
Dry Steering Linkage	Lubricate/Replace Linkage
Dry Ball Joints Bind	Lubricate/Replace Joints
Binding Rack Slide	Inspect Rack
Shaft Contacts Seals	Check Shaft/Replace Seal

POWER STEERING

POWER STEERING TROUBLE SHOOTING

PROBLEM Possible Cause	Action
POWER STEERING PUMP GROWLS/GROANS	
Air In System	Bleed/Check System
Low Fluid Level	Check Fluid/Leaks
High Pressure in Hoses	Clear Restriction
Scored Pump Plates	Check Pump Plates
Worn Cam Ring	Replace Cam Ring
POWER STEERING PUMP RATTLES	
Rotor Slot Vanes Sticking	Clean/Replace Vanes
POWER STEERING PUMP SWISHES	
Faulty Flow Control Valve	Replace Valve
POWER STEERING PUMP SQUAWKS DURING TURN	
Spool Valve "O" Ring Cut	Replace "O" Ring
POWER STEERING PUMP MOANS/WHINES	
Pump Shaft Bearing Scored	Inspect Bearing
Air In Fluid	Fill/Bleed System
Low Fluid Level	Fill/Bleed System
Poor Bracket Alignment	Correct Alignment
POWER STEERING PUMP HISSES DURING TURN	
Internal Leakage in Steering Gear	Check Steering Gear
POWER STEERING PUMP CHIRPS	
Loose Power Steering Belt	Tighten/Replace Belt
POWER STEERING PUMP BUZZES	
Bearing Loose on Shaft	Replace Bearing
POWER STEERING PUMP CLICKS	
Broken Vane Springs	Replace Springs
Worn/Nicked Rotors	Replace Rotors
FLUID FOAMY/MILKY	
Internal Pump Leakage	Reseal Pump
Power Steering Belt Slipping	Tighten/Replace Belt
Pump Output Low	Check Pressure
Faulty Steering Gear	Check Gear
WHEEL SURGES/JERKS	
Low Fluid Level	Check/Fill Fluid
Power Steering Belt Slipping	Tighten/Replace Belt
Pump Output Low	Check Pressure

1991 GENERAL INFORMATION
Engine Overhaul Procedures

DESCRIPTION

Examples used in this article are general in nature and do not necessarily relate to a specific engine or system. Illustrations and procedures have been chosen to guide mechanic through engine overhaul process. Descriptions of cleaning, inspection, and assembly processes are included.

ENGINE IDENTIFICATION

Engine may be identified from Vehicle Identification Number (VIN) stamped on a metal tab. Metal tab may be located in different locations depending on manufacturer. Engine identification number or serial number is located on cylinder block. Location varies with each manufacturer.

INSPECTION PROCEDURES

Engine components must be inspected to meet manufacturer's specifications and tolerances during overhaul. Proper dimensions and tolerances must be met to obtain proper performance and maximum engine life.

Micrometers, depth gauges and dial indicator are used for checking tolerances during engine overhaul. Magnaflux, Magnaglo, dye-check, ultrasonic and x-ray inspection procedures are used for parts inspection.

MAGNETIC PARTICLE INSPECTION

Magnaflux & Magnaglo – Magnaflux is an inspection technique used to locate material flaws and stress cracks. Component is subjected to a strong magnetic field. Entire component or a localized area can be magnetized. Component is coated with either a wet or dry material that contains fine magnetic particles.

Cracks which are outlined by the particles cause an interruption of magnetic field. Dry powder method of Magnaflux can be used in normal lighting and crack appears as a bright line.

Fluorescent liquid is used along with a Black light in the Magnaglo Magnaflux system. Darkened room is required for this procedure. The crack will appear as a glowing line. Complete demagnetizing of component upon completion is required on both procedures. Magnetic particle inspection applies to ferrous materials only.

PENETRANT INSPECTION

Zyglo – The Zyglo process coats material with a fluorescent dye penetrant. Component is often warmed to expand cracks that will be penetrated by the dye. Using darkened room and Black light, component is inspected for cracks. Crack will glow brightly.

Developing solution is often used to enhance results. Parts made of any material, such as aluminum cylinder heads or plastics, may be tested using this process.

Dye Check – Penetrating dye is sprayed on the previously cleaned component. Dye is left on component for 5-45 minutes, depending upon material density. Component is then wiped clean and sprayed with a developing solution. Surface cracks will show up as a bright line.

ULTRASONIC INSPECTION

If an expensive part is suspected of internal cracking, ultrasonic testing is used. Sound waves are used for component inspection.

X-RAY INSPECTION

This form of inspection is used on highly stressed components. X-ray inspection may be used to detect internal and external flaws in any material.

PRESSURE TESTING

Cylinder heads can be tested for cracks using a pressure tester. Pressure testing is performed by plugging all but one of the holes of cylinder head and injecting air or water into the open passage.

Leaks are indicated by the appearance of wet or damp areas when using water. When air is used, it is necessary to spray the head surface with a soap solution. Bubbles will indicate a leak. Cylinder head may also be submerged in water heated to specified temperature to check for cracks created during heat expansion.

CLEANING PROCEDURES

All components of an engine do not have the same cleaning requirements. Physical methods include bead blasting and manual removal. Chemical methods include solvent blast, solvent tank, hot tank, cold tank and steam cleaning of components.

BEAD BLASTING

Manual removal of deposits may be required prior to bead blasting, followed by some other cleaning method. Carbon, paint and rust may be removed using bead blasting method. Components must be free of oil and grease prior to bead blasting. Beads will stick to grease or oil soaked areas causing area not to be cleaned.

Use air pressure to remove all trapped residual beads from component after cleaning. After cleaning internal engine parts made of aluminum, wash thoroughly with hot soapy water. Component must be thoroughly cleaned as glass beads will enter engine oil resulting in bearing damage.

CHEMICAL CLEANING

Solvent tank is used for cleaning oily residue from components. Solvent blasting sprays solvent through a siphon gun using compressed air.

The hot tank, using heated caustic solvents, is used for cleaning ferrous materials only. DO NOT clean aluminum parts such as cylinder heads, bearings or other soft metals using the hot tank. After cleaning, flush parts with hot water.

A non-ferrous part will be ruined and caustic solution will be diluted if placed in the hot tank. Always use eye protection and gloves when using the hot tank.

Use of a cold tank is for cleaning aluminum cylinder heads, carburetors and other soft metals. A less caustic and unheated solution is used. Parts may be left in the tank for several hours without damage. After cleaning, flush parts with hot water.

Steam cleaning, with boiling hot water sprayed at high pressure, is recommended as the final cleaning process when using either hot or cold tank cleaning.

COMPONENT CLEANING

SHEET METAL PARTS

Examples of sheet metal parts are rocker covers, front and side covers, oil pan and bellhousing dust cover. Glass bead blasting or hot tank may be used for cleaning.

Ensure all mating surfaces are flat. Deformed surfaces should be straightened. Check all sheet metal parts for cracks and dents.

INTAKE & EXHAUST MANIFOLDS

Using solvent cleaning or bead blasting, clean manifolds for inspection. If intake manifold has an exhaust crossover, all carbon deposits must be removed. Inspect manifolds for cracks, burned or eroded areas, corrosion and damage to fasteners.

Exhaust heat and products of combustion cause threads of fasteners to corrode. Replace studs and bolts as necessary. On "V" type intake manifolds, sheet metal oil shield must be removed for proper cleaning and inspection. Ensure all manifold parting surfaces are flat and free of burrs.

1991 GENERAL INFORMATION
Engine Overhaul Procedures (Cont.)

CYLINDER HEAD REPLACEMENT

REMOVAL

Remove intake and exhaust manifolds and valve cover. Cylinder head and camshaft carrier bolts (if equipped) should be removed only when engine is cold. On many aluminum cylinder heads, removal while hot will cause cylinder head warpage. Mark rocker arm or overhead cam components for location.

Remove rocker arm components or overhead cam components. Components must be installed in original location. Individual design rocker arms may utilize shafts, ball-type pedestal mounts or no rocker arms. For all design types, wire components together and identify according to corresponding valve. Remove cylinder head bolts. Note length and location. Some applications require removing cylinder head bolts in proper sequence to prevent cylinder head damage. *See Fig. 1.* Remove cylinder head.

INSTALLATION

Ensure all surfaces and head bolts are clean. Check that head bolt holes of cylinder block are clean and dry to prevent block damage when bolts are tightened. Clean threads with tap to ensure accurate bolt torque.

Install head gasket on cylinder block. Some manufacturers may recommend sealant be applied to head gasket prior to installation. Note that all holes are aligned. Some gasket applications may be marked so that certain area faces upward. Install cylinder head using care not to damage head gasket. Ensure cylinder head is fully seated on cylinder block.

Some applications require coating head bolts with sealant prior to installation. This is done if head bolts are exposed to coolant passages. Some applications require coating head bolts with light coat of engine oil.

Install head bolts. Head bolts should be tightened in proper steps and sequence to specification. *See Fig. 1.* Install remaining components. Tighten all bolts to specification. Adjust valves if required. See VALVE ADJUSTMENT in this article.

NOTE: Some manufacturers require that head bolts be retightened after specified amount of operation. This must be done to prevent head gasket failure.

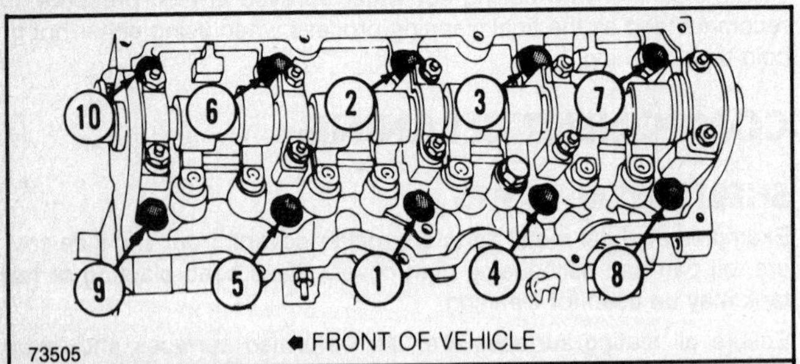
10
6
2
3
7
9
5
1
4
8
FRONT OF VEHICLE
73505

Fig. 1: Typical Cylinder Head Tightening or Loosening Sequence

VALVE ADJUSTMENT

Engine specifications will indicate valve train clearance and temperature at which adjustment is to be made on most models. In most cases, adjustment will be made with a cold engine. In some cases, both a cold and a hot clearance will be given for maintenance convenience.

On some models, adjustment is not required. Rocker arms are tightened to specification and valve lash is automatically set. On some models with push rod actuated valve train, adjustment is made at push rod end of rocker arm while other models do not require adjustment.

Clearance will be checked between tip of rocker arm and tip of valve stem in proper sequence using a feeler gauge. Adjustment is made by rotating adjusting screw until proper clearance is obtained. Lock nut is then tightened. Engine will be rotated to obtain all valve adjustments to manufacturer's specifications.

Some models require hydraulic lifter to be bled down and clearance measured. Push rods of different length can be used to obtain proper clearance. Clearance will be checked between tip of rocker arm and tip of valve stem in proper sequence using a feeler gauge.

Overhead cam engines designed without rocker arms actuate valves directly on a cam follower. A hardened, removable disc is installed between the cam lobe and lifter. Clearance will be checked between cam heel and adjusting disc in proper sequence using a feeler gauge. Engine will be rotated to obtain all valve adjustments.

On overhead cam engines designed with rocker arms, adjustment is made at valve end of rocker arm. Ensure valve to be adjusted is riding on heel of cam on all engines. Clearance will be checked between tip of rocker arm and tip of valve stem in proper sequence using a feeler gauge. Adjustment is made by rotating adjusting screw until proper clearance is obtained. Lock nut is then tightened. Engine will be rotated to obtain all valve adjustments to manufacturer's specifications.

CYLINDER HEAD OVERHAUL

CYLINDER HEAD DISASSEMBLY

Mark valves for location. Using valve spring compressor, compress valve springs. Remove valve locks. Carefully release spring compressor. Remove retainer or rotator, valve spring, spring seat and valve. *See Fig. 2.*

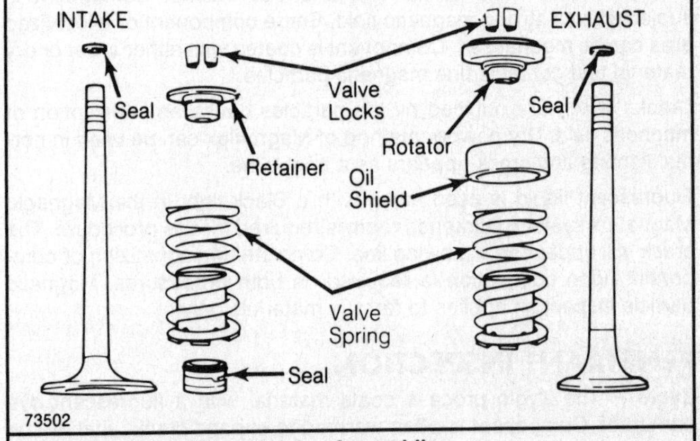
INTAKE
EXHAUST
Seal
Valve
Locks
Seal
Rotator
Retainer
Oil
Shield
Valve
Spring
Seal
73502

Fig. 2: Exploded View of Valve Assemblies

CYLINDER HEAD CLEANING & INSPECTION

Clean cylinder head and valve components using approved cleaning methods. Inspect cylinder head for cracks, damage or warped gasket surface. Place straightedge across gasket surface. Determine clearance at center of straightedge. Measure across both diagonals, longitudinal center line and across cylinder head at several points. *See Fig. 3.*

On cast iron cylinder heads, if warpage exceeds .003" (.08 mm) in a 6" span, or .006" (.15 mm) over total length, cylinder head must be resurfaced. On most aluminum cylinder heads, if warpage exceeds .002" (.05 mm) in any area, cylinder head must be resurfaced. Warpage specification may vary by manufacturer. If warpage exceeds specification on some cylinder heads, cylinder head must be replaced.

Cylinder head thickness should be measured to determine amount of material which can be removed before replacement is required. Cylinder head thickness must not be less than the manufacturer's specification.

If cylinder head required resurfacing, it may not align properly with intake manifold. On "V" type engines, misalignment is corrected by machining intake manifold surface that contacts cylinder head. Cylinder head may be machined on surface that contacts intake manifold. Using oil stone, remove burrs or scratches from all sealing surfaces.

1991 GENERAL INFORMATION
Engine Overhaul Procedures (Cont.)

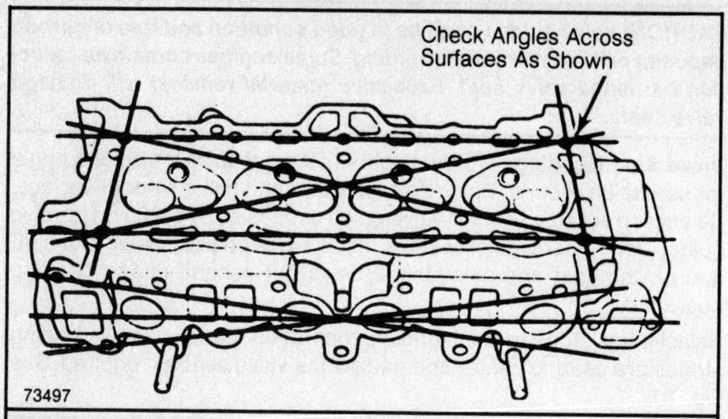
Check Angles Across
Surfaces As Shown
73497

Fig. 3: Checking Cylinder Head for Warpage

VALVE SPRINGS

Inspect valve springs for corroded or pitted valve spring surfaces which may lead to breakage. Polished spring ends caused by a rotating spring indicate that spring surge has occurred. Replace springs showing evidence of these conditions.

Inspect valve springs for squareness using a 90 degree straightedge. *See Fig. 4.* Replace valve spring if out-of-square exceeds manufacturer's specification.

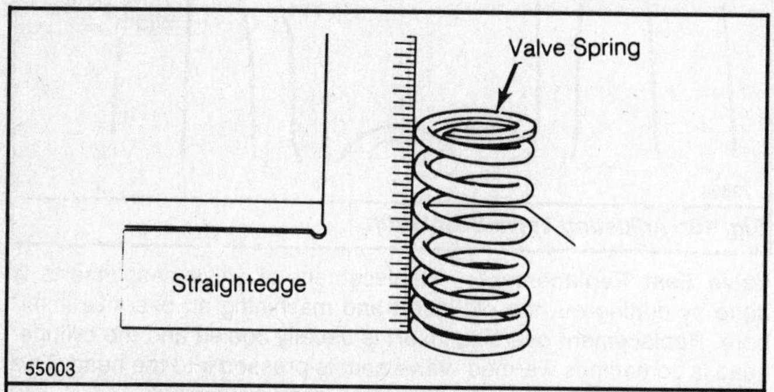
Valve Spring
Straightedge
55003

Fig. 4: Checking Valve Spring Squareness

Using vernier caliper, measure free length of all valve springs. Replace springs if not within specification. Using valve spring tester, test valve spring pressure at installed and compressed heights. *See Fig. 5.*

Usually compressed height is installed height minus valve lift. Replace valve spring if not within specification. It is recommended to replace all valve springs when overhauling cylinder head. Valve springs may need to be installed with color coded end or small coils at specified area according to manufacturer.

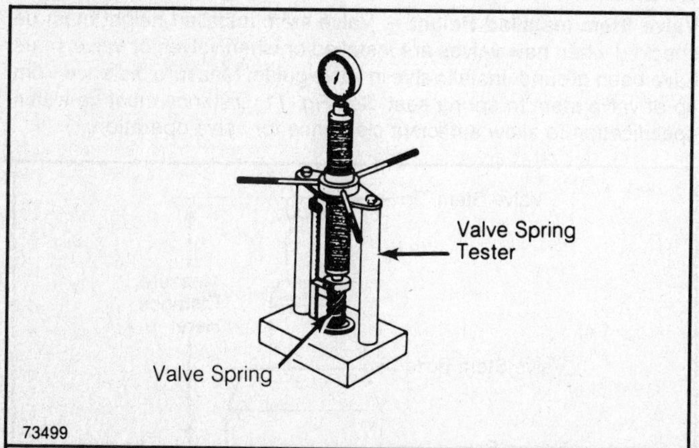
Valve Spring
Tester
Valve Spring
73499

Fig. 5: Checking Valve Spring Pressure

VALVE GUIDE

Measuring Valve Guide Clearance – Check valve stem-to-guide clearance. Ensure valve stem diameter is within specification. Install valve in valve guide. Install dial indicator assembly on cylinder head with tip resting against valve stem just above valve guide. *See Fig. 6.*

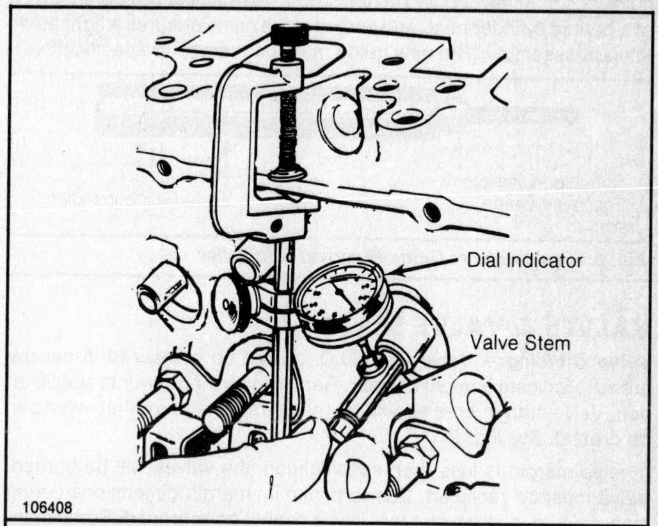
Dial Indicator
Valve Stem
106408

Fig. 6: Measuring Valve Stem-to-Guide Clearance

Lower valve approximately 1/16" below valve seat. Push valve stem against valve guide as far as possible. Adjust dial indicator to zero. Push valve stem in opposite direction and note reading. Clearance must be within specification.

If valve guide clearance exceeds specification, valves with oversize stems may be used and valve guides are reamed to larger size or valve guide must be replaced. On some applications, a false guide is installed, then reamed to proper specification. Valve guide reamer set is used to ream valve guide to obtain proper clearance for new valve.

Reaming Valve Guide – Select proper reamer for size of valve stem. Reamer must be of proper length to provide clean cut through entire length of valve guide. Install reamer in valve guide and rotate to cut valve guide. *See Fig. 7.*

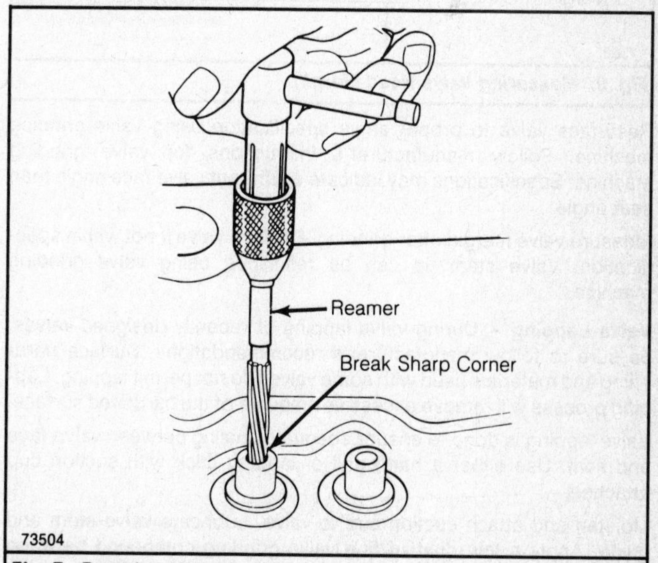
Reamer
Break Sharp Corner
73504

Fig. 7: Reaming Valve Guides

Replacing Valve Guide – Replace valve guide if clearance exceeds specification. Valve guides are either pressed, hammered or shrunk in place, depending upon cylinder head design and type of metal used.

1991 GENERAL INFORMATION
Engine Overhaul Procedures (Cont.)

Remove valve guide from cylinder head by pressing or tapping on a stepped drift. *See Fig. 8.* Once valve guide is installed, distance from cylinder head to top of valve guide must be checked. This distance must be within specification.

Aluminum heads are often heated before installing valve guide. Valve guide is sometimes cooled in dry ice prior to installation. Combination of a heated cylinder head and cooled valve guide ensures a tight guide fit upon assembly. The new guide must be reamed to specification.

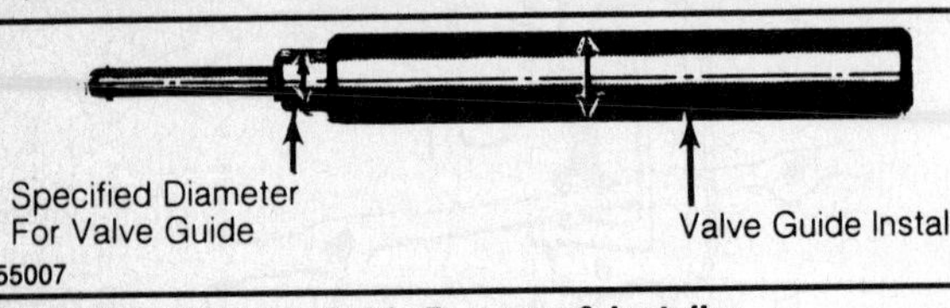
Specified Diameter
For Valve Guide
Valve Guide Installer
55007

Fig. 8: Typical Valve Guide Remover & Installer

VALVES & VALVE SEATS

Valve Grinding – Valve stem O.D. should be measured in several areas to indicate amount of wear. Replace valve if not within specification. Valve margin area should be measured to ensure that valve can be ground. *See Fig. 9.*

If valve margin is less than specification, the valves will be burned. Valve must be replaced. Due to minimum margin dimensions during manufacture, some new type valves cannot be reground. Some manufacturers use stellite coated valves that must NOT be machined. Valves can only be lapped into valve seat.

CAUTION: Some valves are sodium filled. Extreme care must be used when disposing of damaged or worn sodium-filled valves.

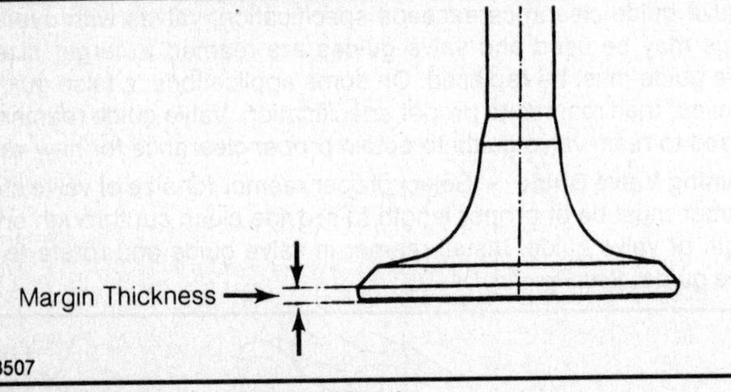
Margin Thickness
73507

Fig. 9: Measuring Valve Head Margin

Resurface valve to proper angle specification using valve grinding machine. Follow manufacturer's instructions for valve grinding machine. Specifications may indicate a different valve face angle than seat angle.

Measure valve margin after grinding. Replace valve if not within specification. Valve stem tip can be refinished using valve grinding machine.

Valve Lapping – During valve lapping of recently designed valves, be sure to follow manufacturer's recommendations. Surface hardening and materials used with some valves do not permit lapping. Lapping process will remove excessive amounts of the hardened surface.

Valve lapping is done to ensure adequate sealing between valve face and seat. Use either a hand drill or lapping stick with suction cup attached.

Moisten and attach suction cup to valve. Lubricate valve stem and guide. Apply a thin coat of fine valve grinding compound between valve and seat. Rotate lapping tool between the palms or with hand drill.

Lift valve upward off the seat and change position often. This is done to prevent grooving of valve seat. Lap valve until a smooth polished seat is obtained. Thoroughly clean grinding compound from components. Valve-to-valve seat concentricity should be checked. See VALVE SEAT CONCENTRICITY.

CAUTION: Valve guides must be in good condition and free of carbon deposits prior to valve seat grinding. Some engines contain an induction hardened valve seat. Excessive material removal will damage valve seats.

Valve Seat Grinding – Select coarse stone of correct size and angle for seat to be ground. Ensure stone is true and has a smooth surface. Select correct size pilot for valve guide dimension. Install pilot in valve guide. Lightly lubricate pilot shaft. Install stone on pilot. Move stone off and on the seat approximately 2 times per second during grinding operation.

Select a fine stone to finish grinding operation. Various angle grinding stones are used to center and narrow the valve seat as required. *See Fig. 10.*

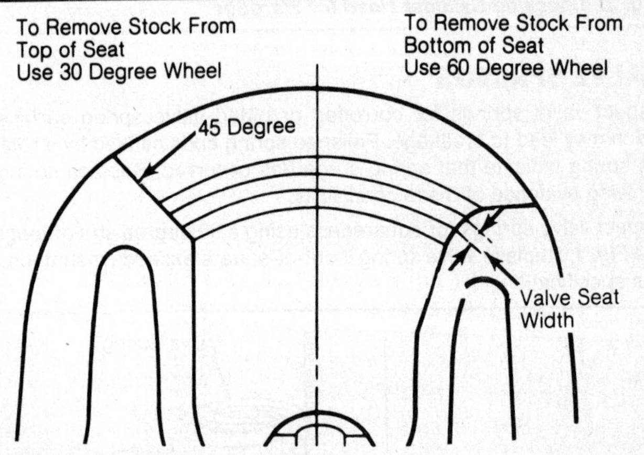
To Remove Stock From
Top of Seat
Use 30 Degree Wheel
To Remove Stock From
Bottom of Seat
Use 60 Degree Wheel
45 Degree
Valve Seat
Width
73508

Fig. 10: Adjusting Valve Seat Width

Valve Seat Replacement – Replacement of valve seat inserts is done by cutting out the old insert and machining an oversize insert bore. Replacement oversize insert is usually cooled and the cylinder head is sometimes warmed. Valve seat is pressed into the head. This operation requires specialized machine shop equipment.

Valve Seat Concentricity – Using dial gauge, install gauge pilot in valve guide. Position gauge arm on the valve seat. Adjust dial indicator to zero. Rotate arm 360 degrees and note reading. Runout should not exceed specification.

To check valve-to-valve seat concentricity, coat valve face lightly with Prussian Blue dye. Install valve and rotate it on valve seat. If pattern is even and entire seat is coated at valve contact point, valve is concentric with the valve seat.

CYLINDER HEAD REASSEMBLY

Valve Stem Installed Height – Valve stem installed height must be checked when new valves are installed or when valves or valve seats have been ground. Install valve in valve guide. Measure distance from tip of valve stem to spring seat. *See Fig. 11.* Distance must be within specification to allow sufficient clearance for valve operation.

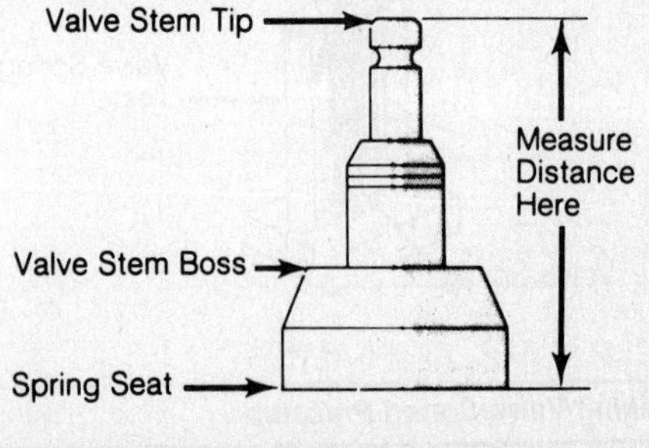
Valve Stem Tip
Measure
Distance
Here
Valve Stem Boss
Spring Seat
73500

Fig. 11: Measuring Valve Stem Installed Height

Remove valve and grind valve stem tip if height exceeds specification. Valve tips are surface hardened. DO NOT remove more than .010" (.25 mm) from tip. Chamfer sharp edge of reground valve tip. Recheck valve stem installed height.

VALVE STEM OIL SEALS

Valve stem oil seals must be installed on valve stem. *See Fig. 2.* Seals are needed due to pressure differential at the ends of valve guides. Atmospheric pressure above intake guide, combined with manifold vacuum below guide, causes oil to be drawn into the cylinder.

Exhaust guides also have pressure differential created by exhaust gas flowing past the guide, creating a low pressure area. This low pressure area draws oil into the exhaust system.

Some manufacturers require that special color code or specified height valve stem oil seal be installed in designated area.

Replacement (On-Vehicle) – Mark rocker arm or overhead cam components for location. Remove rocker arm components or overhead cam components. Components must be installed in original location. Remove spark plugs. Valve stem oil seals may be replaced by holding valves against seats using air pressure.

Air pressure must be installed in cylinder using an adapter for spark plug hole. An adapter can be constructed by welding air hose connection to spark plug body with porcelain removed.

Rotate engine until piston is at top of stroke. Install adapter in spark plug hole. Apply a minimum of 140 psi (9.8 kg/cm²) line pressure to adapter. Air pressure should hold valve closed. If air pressure does not hold valve closed, check for damaged or bent valve. Cylinder head must be removed for service.

Using valve spring compressor, compress valve springs. Remove valve locks. Carefully release spring compressor. Remove retainer or rotator and valve spring. Remove valve stem oil seal.

If oversize valves have been installed, oversize oil seals must be used. Coat valve stem with engine oil. Install protective sleeve over end of valve stem. Install new oil seal over valve stem and seat on valve guide. Remove protective sleeve. Install spring seat, valve spring and retainer or rotator. Compress spring and install valve locks. Remove spring compressor. Ensure valve locks are fully seated.

Install rocker arms or overhead cam components. Tighten all bolts to specification. Adjust valves if required. Remove adapter. Install spark plugs, valve cover and gasket.

VALVE SPRING INSTALLED HEIGHT

Valve spring installed height should be checked during reassembly. Measure height from lower edge of valve spring to the upper edge. DO NOT include valve spring seat or retainer. Distance must be within specification. If valves and/or seats have been ground, a valve spring shim may be required to correct spring height. *See Fig. 12.*

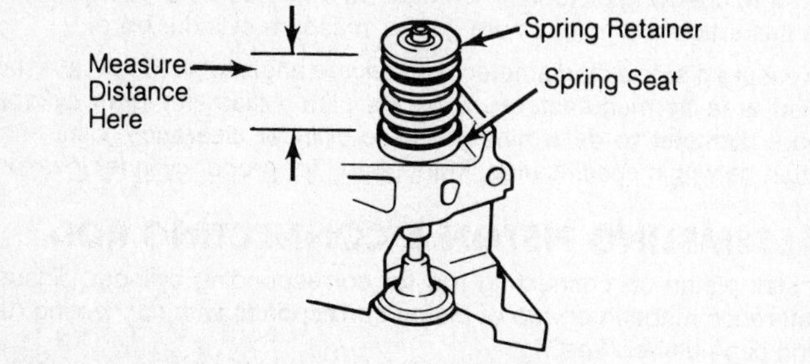

Spring Retainer
Measure Distance Here
Spring Seat
55011

Fig. 12: Measuring Valve Spring Installed Height

ROCKER ARMS & ASSEMBLIES

Rocker Studs – Rocker studs are either threaded or pressed in place. Threaded studs are removed by locking 2 nuts on the stud. Unscrew the stud by turning the jam nut. Coat new stud threads with Loctite and install. Tighten to specification.

Pressed-in stud can be removed using a stud puller. Ream stud bore to proper specification and press in a new oversize stud. Pressed-in studs are often replaced by cutting threads in the stud bore to accept a threaded stud.

Rocker Arms & Shafts – Mark rocker arms for location. Remove rocker arm retaining bolts. Remove rocker arms. Inspect rocker arms, shafts, bushings and pivot balls (if equipped) for excessive wear. Inspect rocker arms for wear in valve stem contact area. Measure rocker arm bushing I.D. Replace bushings if excessively worn.

The rocker arm valve stem contact point may be reground using special fixture for valve grinding machine. Remove minimum amount of material as possible. Ensure all oil passages are clear. Install rocker arm components in original location. Ensure rocker arm is properly seated in push rod. Tighten bolts to specification. Adjust valves if required. See VALVE ADJUSTMENT in this article.

PUSH RODS

Remove rocker arms. Mark push rods for location. Remove push rods. Push rods can be steel or aluminum, solid or hollow. Hollow push rods must be internally cleaned to ensure oil passage to rocker arms is cleaned. Check push rods for damage, such as loose ends on steel tipped aluminum types.

Check push rod for straightness. Roll push rod on a flat surface. Using feeler gauge, check clearance at center. Replace push rod if bent. The push rod can also be supported at each end and rotated. A dial indicator is used to detect a bent area in the push rod.

Lubricate ends of push rod and install push rod in original location. Ensure push rod is properly seated in lifter. Install rocker arm. Tighten bolts to specification. Adjust valves if required. See VALVE ADJUSTMENT in this article.

LIFTERS

Hydraulic Lifters – Before replacing a hydraulic lifter for noisy operation, ensure noise is not caused by worn rocker arms or valve tips. Also ensure sufficient oil pressure exists. Hydraulic lifters must be installed in original location. Remove rocker arm assembly and push rod. Mark components for location. Some applications require intake manifold, cylinder head or lifter cover removal. Remove lifter retainer plate (if used). To remove lifters, use a hydraulic lifter remover or magnet. Different type lifters are used. *See Fig. 13.*

On sticking lifters, disassemble and clean lifter. DO NOT mix lifter components or positions. Parts are select-fitted and are not interchangeable. Inspect all components for wear. Note amount of wear in lifter body-to-camshaft contact area. Surface must have smooth and convex contact face. If wear is apparent, carefully inspect cam lobe.

Inspect push rod contact area and lifter body for scoring or signs of wear. If body is scored, inspect lifter bore for damage and lack of lubrication. On roller type lifters, inspect roller for flaking, pitting, loss of needle bearings and roughness during rotation.

Measure lifter body O.D. in several areas. Measure lifter bore I.D. Ensure components or oil clearance is within specification. Some models offer oversize lifters. Replace lifter if damaged.

If lifter check valve is not operating, obstructions may be preventing it from closing or valve spring may be broken. Clean or replace components as necessary.

Check plunger operation. Plunger should drop to bottom of the body by its own weight when assembled dry. If plunger is not free, soak lifter in solvent to dissolve deposits.

Lifter leak-down test can be performed on lifter. Lifter must be filled with special test oil. New lifters contain special test oil. Using lifter leak-down tester, perform leak-down test following manufacturer's instructions. If leak-down time is not within specifications, replace lifter assembly.

Lifters should be soaked in clean engine oil several hours prior to installation. Coat lifter base, roller (if equipped) and lifter body with ample amount of Molykote or camshaft lubricant. *See Fig. 13.* Install lifter in original location. Install remaining components. Valve lash

1991 GENERAL INFORMATION
Engine Overhaul Procedures (Cont.)

adjustment is not required on most hydraulic lifters. Preload of hydraulic lifter is automatic. Some models may require adjustment.

NOTE: Some manufacturers require that a crankcase conditioner be added to engine oil and engine operated for specified amount of time to aid in lifter break-in procedure if new lifters or camshaft are installed.

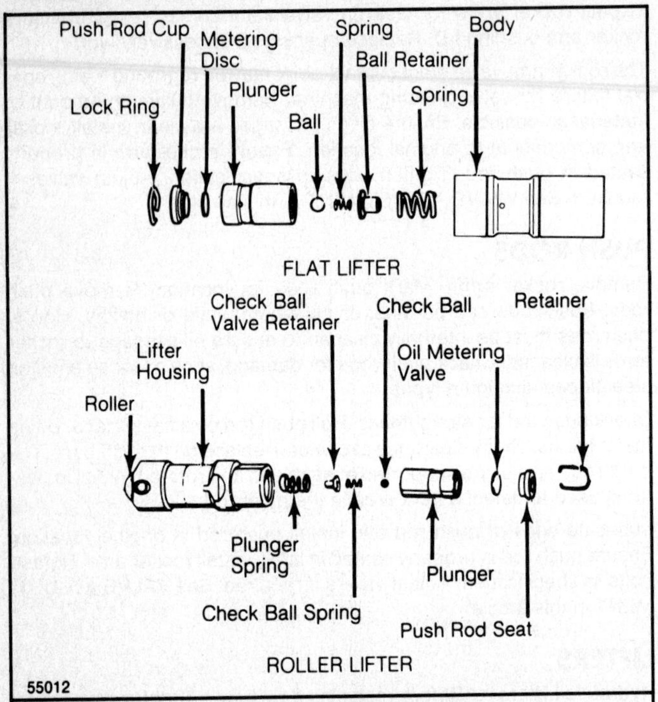
Push Rod Cup
Metering Disc
Spring
Body
Ball Retainer
Lock Ring
Plunger
Ball
Spring
FLAT LIFTER
Check Ball Valve Retainer
Check Ball
Retainer
Lifter Housing
Oil Metering Valve
Roller
Plunger Spring
Plunger
Check Ball Spring
Push Rod Seat
ROLLER LIFTER
55012

Fig. 13: Typical Hydraulic Valve Lifter Assemblies

Mechanical Lifters – Lifter assemblies must be installed in original locations. Remove rocker arm assembly and push rod. Mark components for location. Some applications require intake manifold or lifter cover removal. Remove lifter retainer plate (if used). To remove lifters, use lifter remover or magnet.

Inspect push rod contact area and lifter body for scoring or signs of wear. If body is scored, inspect lifter bore for damage and lack of lubrication. Note amount of wear in lifter body-to-camshaft contact area. Surface must have smooth and convex contact face. If wear is apparent, carefully inspect cam lobe.

Coat lifter base, roller (if equipped) and lifter body with ample amount of Molykote or camshaft lubricant. Install lifter in original location. Install remaining components. Tighten bolts to specification. Adjust valves. See VALVE ADJUSTMENT in this article.

PISTONS, CONNECTING RODS & BEARINGS

RIDGE REMOVAL

Ridge in cylinder wall must be removed prior to piston removal. Failure to remove ridge prior to removing pistons will cause piston damage in piston ring lands or grooves.

With piston at bottom dead center, place rag in bore to trap metal chips. Install ridge reamer in cylinder bore. Adjust ridge reamer using manufacturer's instructions. Remove ridge using ridge reamer. DO NOT remove an excessive amount of material. Ensure ridge is completely removed.

PISTON & CONNECTING ROD REMOVAL

Note top of piston. Some pistons may contain a notch, arrow or be marked FRONT. Piston must be installed in proper direction to prevent damage with valve operation.

Check that connecting rod and cap are numbered for cylinder location and which side of cylinder block the number faces. Proper cap and connecting rod must be installed together. Connecting rod cap must be installed on connecting rod in proper direction to ensure bearing lock procedure. Mark connecting rod and cap if necessary. Pistons must be installed in original location.

Remove cap retaining nuts or bolts. Remove bearing cap. Install tubing protectors on connecting rod bolts. This protects cylinder walls from scoring during removal. Ensure proper removal of ridge. Push piston and connecting rod from cylinder. Connecting rod boss can be tapped with a wooden dowel or hammer handle to aid in removal.

PISTON & CONNECTING ROD

Disassembly – Using ring expander, remove piston rings. Remove piston pin retaining rings (if equipped). Note direction of piston installation on connecting rod. On pressed type piston pins, special fixtures and procedures according to manufacturer must be used to remove piston pins. Follow manufacturer's recommendations to avoid piston distortion or breakage.

Cleaning – Remove all carbon and varnish from piston. Pistons and connecting rods may be cleaned in cold type chemical tank. Using ring groove cleaner, clean all deposits from ring grooves. Ensure all deposits are cleaned from ring grooves to prevent ring breakage or sticking. DO NOT attempt to clean pistons with wire brush.

Inspection – Inspect pistons for nicks, scoring, cracks or damage in ring areas. Connecting rod should be checked for cracks using Magnaflux procedure. Piston diameter must be measured in manufacturer's specified area.

Using telescopic gauge and micrometer, measure piston pin bore of piston in 2 areas, 90 degrees apart. This is done to check diameter and out-of-round.

Install proper bearing cap on connecting rod. Ensure bearing cap is installed in proper location. Tighten bolts or nuts to specification. Using inside micrometer, measure inside diameter in 2 areas, 90 degrees apart.

Connecting rod I.D. and out-of-round must be within specification. Measure piston pin bore I.D. and piston pin O.D. All components must be within specification. Subtract piston pin diameter from piston pin bore in piston and connecting rod to determine proper fit.

Connecting rod length must be measured from center of crankshaft journal inside diameter to center of piston pin bushing using proper caliper. Connecting rods must be the same length. Connecting rods should be checked on an alignment fixture for bent or twisted condition. Replace all components which are damaged or not within specification.

PISTON & CYLINDER BORE FIT

Ensure cylinder is checked for taper, out-of-round and properly honed prior to checking piston and cylinder bore fit. See CYLINDER BLOCK in this article. Using dial bore gauge, measure cylinder bore.

Measure piston skirt diameter at 90 degree angle to piston pin at specified area by manufacturer. Subtract piston diameter from cylinder bore diameter to determine piston-to-cylinder clearance. Clearance must be within specification. Mark piston for proper cylinder location.

ASSEMBLING PISTON & CONNECTING ROD

Install piston on connecting rod for corresponding cylinder. Ensure reference marking on top of piston corresponds with connecting rod and cap number. *See Fig. 14.*

Lubricate piston pin and install in connecting rod. Ensure piston pin retainers are fully seated (if equipped). On pressed type piston pins, follow manufacturer's recommended procedure to avoid distortion or breakage.

1991 GENERAL INFORMATION
Engine Overhaul Procedures (Cont.)

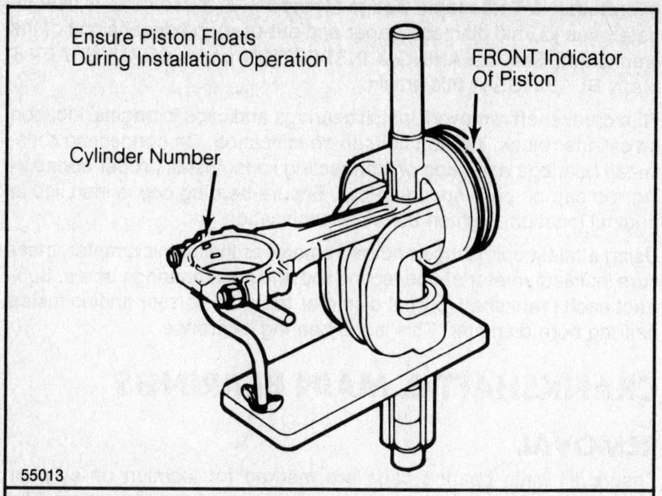
Ensure Piston Floats
During Installation Operation
FRONT Indicator
Of Piston
Cylinder Number
55013

Fig. 14: Installing Typical Piston Pin

CHECKING PISTON RING CLEARANCES

Piston rings must be checked for side clearance and end gap. To check end gap, install piston ring in cylinder in which it is to be installed. Using an inverted piston, push ring to bottom of cylinder in smallest cylinder diameter.

Using feeler gauge, check ring end gap. *See Fig. 15.* Piston ring end gap must be within specification. Ring breakage will occur if insufficient ring end gap exists.

Some manufacturers permit correcting insufficient ring end gap by using a fine file while other manufacturers recommend using another ring set. Mark rings for proper cylinder installation after checking end gap.

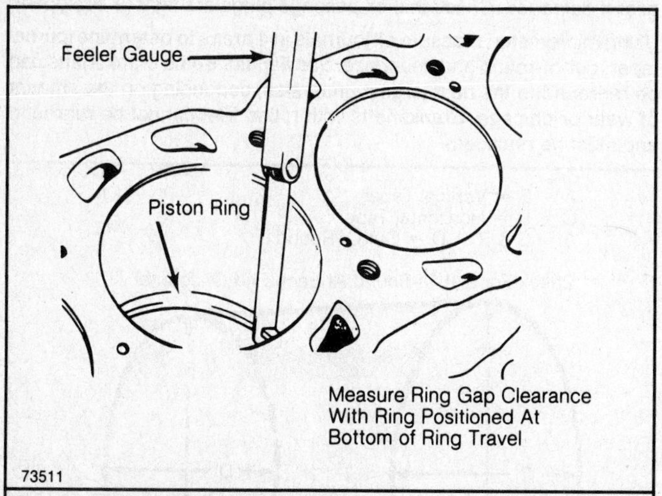
Feeler Gauge
Piston Ring
Measure Ring Gap Clearance
With Ring Positioned At
Bottom of Ring Travel
73511

Fig. 15: Checking Piston Ring End Gap

For checking side clearance, install rings on piston. Using feeler gauge, measure clearance between piston ring and piston ring land. Check side clearance in several areas around piston. Side clearance must be within specification.

If side clearance is excessive, piston ring grooves can be machined to accept oversize piston rings (if available). Normal practice is to replace piston.

PISTON & CONNECTING ROD INSTALLATION

Cylinders must be honed prior to piston installation. See CYLINDER HONING under CYLINDER BLOCK in this article.

Install upper connecting rod bearings. Lubricate upper bearings with engine oil. Install lower bearings in rod caps. Ensure bearing tabs are properly seated. Position piston ring gaps according to manufacturer's recommendations. *See Fig. 16.* Lubricate pistons, rings and cylinder walls.

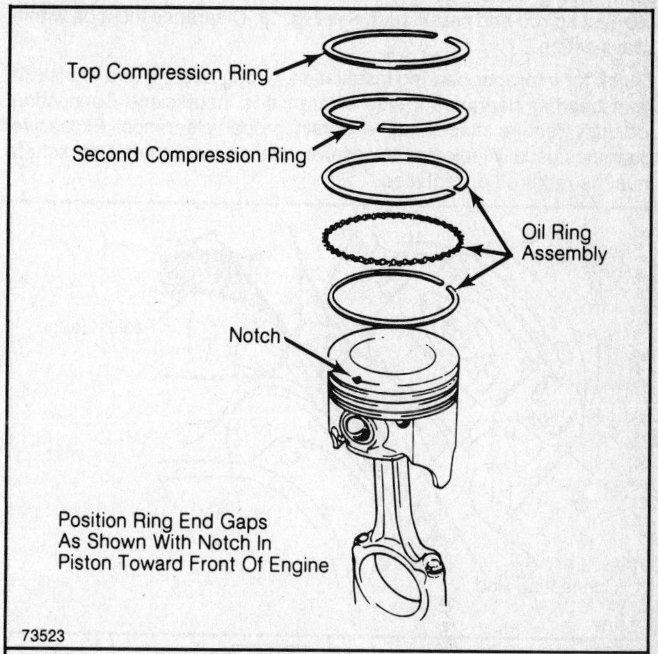
Top Compression Ring
Second Compression Ring
Oil Ring
Assembly
Notch
Position Ring End Gaps
As Shown With Notch In
Piston Toward Front Of Engine
73523

Fig. 16: Positioning Typical Piston Ring End Gap

Install ring compressor. Use care not to rotate piston rings. Compress rings with ring compressor. Install plastic tubing protectors over connecting rod bolts. Install piston and connecting rod assembly. Ensure piston notch, arrow or FRONT mark is toward front of engine. *See Fig. 17.*

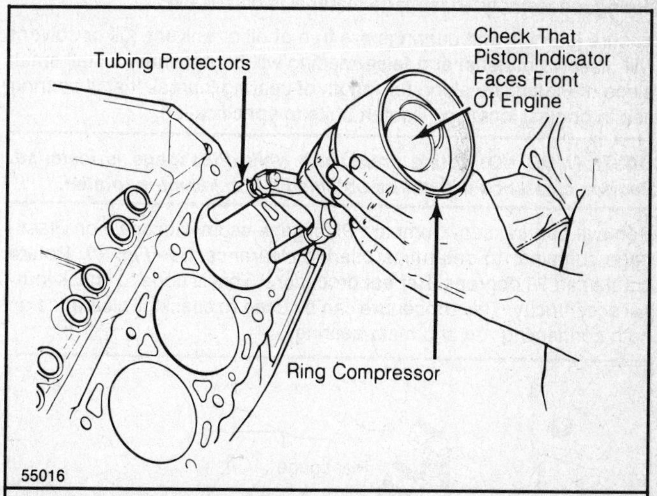
Tubing Protectors
Check That
Piston Indicator
Faces Front
Of Engine
Ring Compressor
55016

Fig. 17: Installing Piston & Connecting Rod Assembly

Carefully tap piston into cylinder until rod bearing is seated on crankshaft journal. Remove protectors. Install rod cap and bearing. Lightly tighten connecting rod bolts. Repeat procedure for remaining cylinders. Check bearing clearance. See MAIN & CONNECTING ROD BEARING CLEARANCE in this article.

Once clearance is checked, lubricate journals and bearings. Install bearing caps. Ensure marks are aligned on connecting rod and cap. Tighten rod nuts or bolts to specification. Ensure rod moves freely on crankshaft. Check connecting rod side clearance. See CONNECTING ROD SIDE CLEARANCE in this article.

1991 GENERAL INFORMATION
Engine Overhaul Procedures (Cont.)

CONNECTING ROD SIDE CLEARANCE

Position connecting rod toward one side of crankshaft as far as possible. Using feeler gauge, measure clearance between side of connecting rod and crankshaft. *See Fig. 18.* Clearance must be within specification.

Check for improper bearing installation, wrong bearing cap or insufficient bearing clearance if side clearance is insufficient. Connecting rod may require machining to obtain proper clearance. Excessive clearance usually indicates excessive wear at crankshaft. Crankshaft must be repaired or replaced.

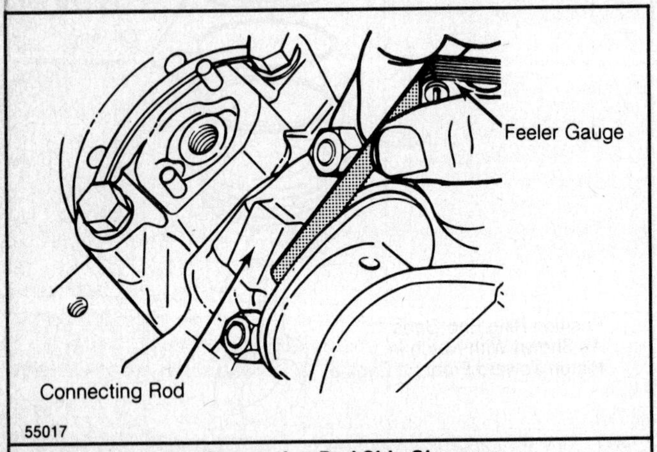
Feeler Gauge
Connecting Rod
55017

Fig. 18: Measuring Connecting Rod Side Clearance

MAIN & CONNECTING ROD BEARING CLEARANCE

Plastigage Method – Plastigage method may be used to determine bearing clearance. Plastigage can be used with an engine in service or during reassembly. Plastigage material is oil soluble.

Ensure journals and bearings are free of oil or solvent. Oil or solvent will dissolve material and false reading will be obtained. Install small piece of Plastigage along full length of bearing journal. Install bearing cap in original location. Tighten bolts to specification.

CAUTION: DO NOT rotate crankshaft while Plastigage is installed. Bearing clearance will not be obtained if crankshaft is rotated.

Remove bearing cap. Compare Plastigage width with scale on Plastigage container to determine bearing clearance. *See Fig. 19.* Rotate crankshaft 90 degrees. Repeat procedure. This is done to check journal eccentricity. This procedure can be used to check oil clearance on both connecting rod and main bearings.

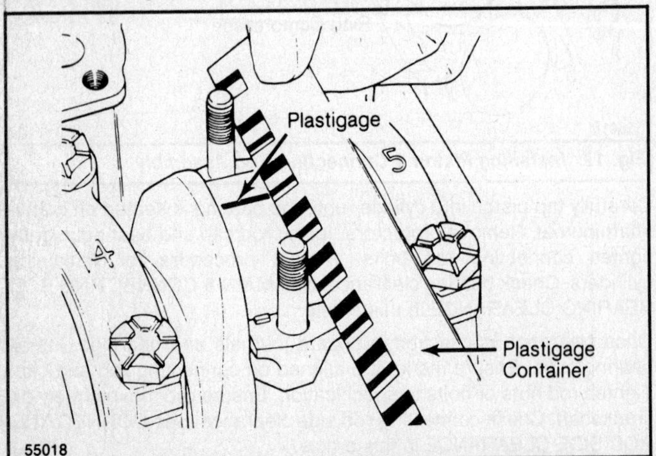
Plastigage
Plastigage Container
55018

Fig. 19: Measuring Bearing Clearance

Micrometer & Telescopic Gauge Method – A micrometer is used to determine journal diameter, taper and out-of-round dimensions of the crankshaft. See CLEANING & INSPECTION under CRANKSHAFT & MAIN BEARINGS in this article.

With crankshaft removed, install bearings and caps in original location on cylinder block. Tighten bolts to specification. On connecting rods, install bearings and caps on connecting rods. Install proper connecting rod cap on corresponding rod. Ensure bearing cap is installed in original location. Tighten bolts to specification.

Using a telescopic gauge and micrometer or inside micrometer, measure inside diameter of connecting rod and main bearings bores. Subtract each crankshaft journal diameter from the corresponding inside bearing bore diameter. This is the bearing clearance.

CRANKSHAFT & MAIN BEARINGS

REMOVAL

Ensure all main bearing caps are marked for location on cylinder block. Some main bearing caps have an arrow stamped on them. The arrow must face timing belt or timing chain end of engine. Remove main bearing cap bolts. Remove main bearing caps. Carefully remove crankshaft. Use care not to bind crankshaft in cylinder block during removal.

CLEANING & INSPECTION

Thoroughly clean crankshaft using solvent. Dry with compressed air. Ensure all oil passages are clear and free of sludge, rust, dirt and metal chips.

Inspect crankshaft for scoring and nicks. Inspect crankshaft for cracks using Magnaflux procedure. Inspect rear seal area for grooving or damage. Inspect bolt hole threads for damage. If pilot bearing or bushing is used, check pilot bearing or bushing fit in crankshaft. Inspect crankshaft gear for damaged or cracked teeth. Replace gear if damaged. Check that oil passage plugs are tight (if equipped).

Using micrometer, measure all journals in 4 areas to determine journal taper, out-of-round and undersize. *See Fig. 20.* Some crankshafts can be reground to the next largest undersize, depending on the amount of wear or damage. Crankshafts with rolled fillet cannot be reground and must be replaced.

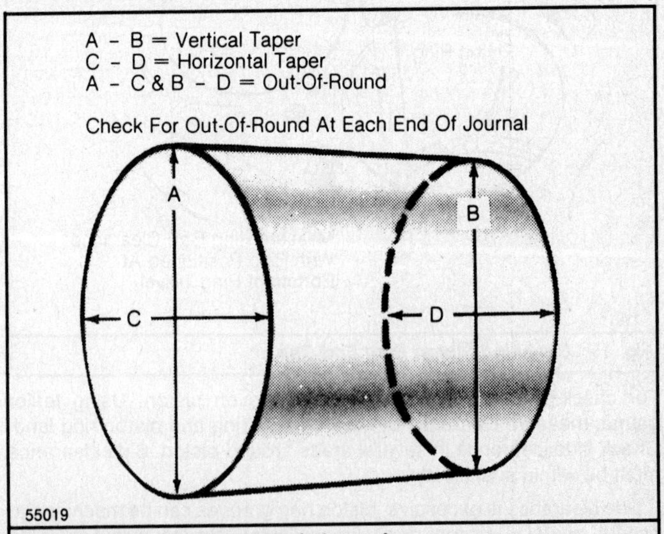
A - B = Vertical Taper
C - D = Horizontal Taper
A - C & B - D = Out-Of-Round
Check For Out-Of-Round At Each End Of Journal
A
B
C
D
55019

Fig. 20: Measuring Crankshaft Journals

Crankshaft journal runout should be checked. Install crankshaft in "V" blocks or bench center. Position dial indicator with tip resting on the main bearing journal area. *See Fig. 21.* Rotate crankshaft and note reading. Journal runout must not exceed specification. Repeat procedure on all main bearing journals. Crankshaft must be replaced if runout exceeds specification.

1991 GENERAL INFORMATION
Engine Overhaul Procedures (Cont.)

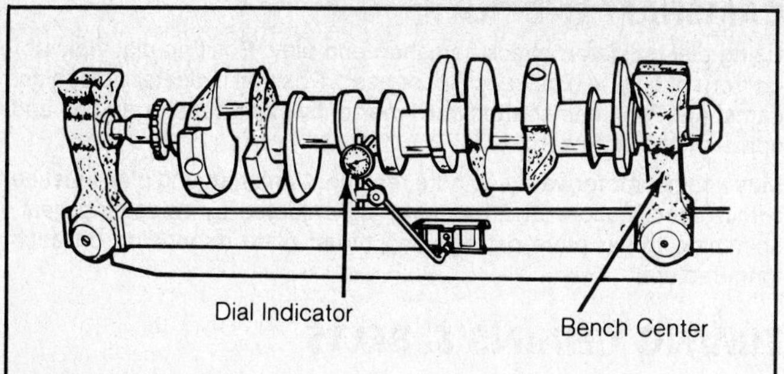
Dial Indicator
Bench Center
55020

Fig. 21: Measuring Crankshaft Main Bearing Journal Runout

INSTALLATION

Install upper main bearing in cylinder block. Ensure lock tab is properly located in cylinder block. Install bearings in main bearing caps. Ensure all oil passages are aligned. Install rear seal (if removed).

Ensure crankshaft journals are clean. Lubricate upper main bearings with clean engine oil. Carefully install crankshaft. Check each main bearing clearance using Plastigage method. See MAIN & CONNECTING ROD BEARING CLEARANCE in this article.

Once clearance is checked, lubricate lower main bearing and journals. Install main bearing caps in original location. Install rear seal in rear main bearing cap (if removed). Some rear main bearing caps require sealant to be applied in corners to prevent oil leakage.

Install and tighten all bolts except thrust bearing cap to specification. Tighten thrust bearing cap bolts finger tight only. Some models require that thrust bearing must be aligned. On most applications, crankshaft must be moved rearward then forward. Procedure may vary with manufacturer. Thrust bearing cap is then tightened to specification. Ensure crankshaft rotates freely. Crankshaft end play should be checked. See CRANKSHAFT END PLAY in this article.

CRANKSHAFT END PLAY

Dial Indicator Method – Crankshaft end play can be checked using dial indicator. Mount dial indicator on rear of cylinder block. Position dial indicator tip against rear of crankshaft. Ensure tip is resting against flat surface.

Pry crankshaft rearward. Adjust dial indicator to zero. Pry crankshaft forward and note reading. Crankshaft end play must be within specification. If end play is not within specification, check for faulty thrust bearing installation or worn crankshaft. Some applications offer oversize thrust bearings.

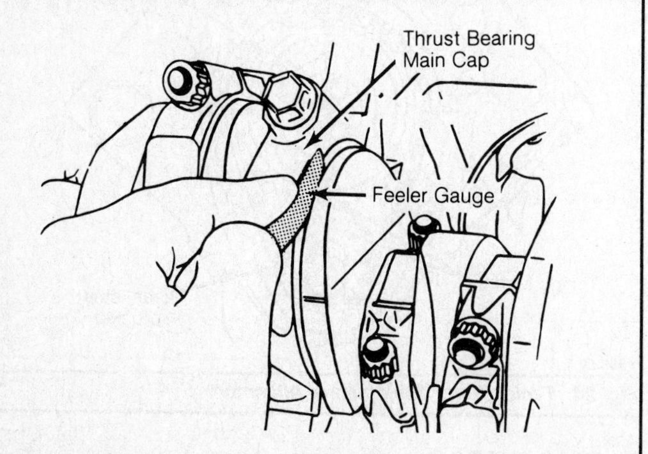
Thrust Bearing
Main Cap
Feeler Gauge
55021

Fig. 22: Checking Crankshaft End Play

Feeler Gauge Method – Crankshaft end play can be checked using feeler gauge. Pry crankshaft rearward. Pry crankshaft forward. Using feeler gauge, measure clearance between crankshaft and thrust bearing surface. *See Fig. 22.*

Crankshaft end play must be within specification. If end play is not within specification, check for faulty thrust bearing installation or worn crankshaft. Some applications offer oversize thrust bearings.

CYLINDER BLOCK

Block Cleaning – Only cast cylinder blocks should be hot tank cleaned. Aluminum cylinder blocks should be cleaned using cold tank method. Cylinder block is cleaned in order to remove carbon deposits, gasket residue and water jacket scale. Remove oil gallery plugs, freeze plugs and cam bearings prior to block cleaning.

Block Inspection – Visually inspect the block. Check suspected areas for cracks using the Dye Penetrant inspection method. Block may be checked for cracks using the Magnaflux method.

Cracks are most commonly found at the bottom of cylinders, main bearing saddles, near expansion plugs and between cylinders and water jackets. Inspect lifter bores for damage. Inspect all head bolt holes for damaged threads. Threads should be cleaned using tap to ensure proper head bolt torque. Consult machine shop concerning possible welding and machining (if required).

Cylinder Bore Inspection – Inspect bore for scoring or roughness. Cylinder bore is dimensionally checked for out-of-round and taper using dial bore gauge. For determining out-of-round, measure cylinder parallel and perpendicular to the block center line. Difference in the 2 readings is the bore out-of-round. Cylinder bore must be checked at top, middle and bottom of piston travel area.

Bore taper is obtained by measuring bore at the top and bottom. If wear has exceeded allowable limits, block must be honed or bored to next available oversize piston dimension.

Cylinder Honing – Cylinder must be properly honed to allow new piston rings to properly seat. Cross-hatching at correct angle and depth is critical to lubrication of cylinder walls and pistons.

A flexible drive hone and power drill are commonly used. Drive hone must be lubricated during operation. Mix equal parts of kerosene and SAE 20W engine oil for lubrication.

Apply lubrication to cylinder wall. Operate cylinder hone from top to bottom of cylinder using even strokes to produce 45 degree crosshatch pattern on the cylinder wall. DO NOT allow cylinder hone to extend below cylinder during operation.

Recheck bore dimension after final honing. Wash cylinder wall with hot soapy water to remove abrasive particles. Blow dry with compressed air. Coat cleaned cylinder walls with lubricating oil.

Deck Warpage – Check deck for damage or warped gasket surface. Place a straightedge across gasket surface of the deck. Using feeler gauge, measure clearance at center of straightedge. Measure across width and length of cylinder block at several points.

If warpage exceeds specifications, deck must be resurfaced. If warpage exceeds manufacturer's maximum tolerance for material removal, replace block.

Deck Height – Distance from crankshaft center line to block deck is called the deck height. Measure and record front and rear main journals of crankshaft. To compute this distance, install crankshaft and retain with center main bearing and cap only. Measure distance from crankshaft journal to block deck, parallel to cylinder center line.

Add one half of main bearing journal diameter to distance from crankshaft journal to block deck. This dimension should be checked at front and rear of cylinder block. Both readings should be the same.

If difference exceeds specification, cylinder block must be repaired or replaced. Deck height and warpage should be corrected at the same time.

1991 GENERAL INFORMATION
Engine Overhaul Procedures (Cont.)

Main Bearing Bore & Alignment – For checking main bearing bore, remove all bearings from cylinder block and main bearing caps. Install main bearing caps in original location. Tighten bolts to specification. Using inside micrometer, measure main bearing bore in 2 areas 90 degrees apart. Determine bore size and out-of-round. If diameter is not within specification, block must be align-bored.

For checking alignment, place a straightedge along center line of main bearing saddles. Check for clearance between straightedge and main bearing saddles. Block must be align-bored if clearance exists.

Expansion Plug Removal – Drill hole in center of expansion plug. Remove with screwdriver or punch. Use care not to damage sealing surface.

Expansion Plug Installation – Ensure sealing surface is free of burrs. Coat expansion plug with sealer. Using wooden dowel or pipe of slightly smaller diameter, install expansion plug. Ensure expansion plug is evenly located.

Oil Gallery Plug Removal – Remove threaded oil gallery plugs using appropriate wrench. Soft press-in plugs are removed by drilling into plug and installing a sheet metal screw. Remove plug with slide hammer or pliers.

Oil Gallery Plug Installation – Ensure threads or sealing surface is clean. Coat threaded oil gallery plugs with sealer and install. Replacement soft press-in plugs are installed with a hammer and drift.

CAMSHAFT

CLEANING & INSPECTION

Clean camshaft with solvent. Ensure all oil passages are clear. Inspect cam lobes and bearing journals for pitting, flaking or scoring. Using micrometer, measure bearing journal O.D.

Support camshaft at each end with "V" blocks. Position dial indicator with tip resting on center bearing journal. Rotate camshaft and note camshaft runout reading. If reading exceeds specification, replace camshaft.

Check cam lobe lift by measuring base circle of camshaft using micrometer. Measure again at 90 degree angle to tip of cam lobe. Cam lift can be determined by subtracting base circle diameter from tip of cam lobe measurement.

Different lift dimensions are given for intake and exhaust cam lobes. Reading must be within specification. Replace camshaft if cam lobes or bearing journals are not within specification.

Inspect camshaft gear for chipped, eroded or damaged teeth. Replace gear if damaged. On camshafts using thrust plate, measure distance between thrust plate and camshaft shoulder. Replace thrust plate if not within specification.

CAMSHAFT BEARINGS

Removal & Installation – Remove camshaft rear plug. Camshaft bearing remover is assembled with shoulder resting against bearing to be removed according to manufacturer's instructions. Tighten puller nut until bearing is removed. Remove remaining bearings, leaving front and rear bearings until last. These bearings act as a guide for camshaft bearing remover.

To install new bearings, puller is rearranged to pull bearings toward the center of block. Ensure all lubrication passages of bearing are aligned with cylinder block. Coat new camshaft rear plug with sealant. Install camshaft rear plug. Ensure plug is even in cylinder block.

CAMSHAFT INSTALLATION

Lubricate bearing surfaces and cam lobes with ample amount of Molykote or camshaft lubricant. Carefully install camshaft. Use care not to damage bearing journals during installation. Install thrust plate retaining bolts (if equipped). Tighten bolts to specification. On overhead camshafts, install bearing caps in original location. Tighten bolts to specification. On all applications, check camshaft end play.

CAMSHAFT END PLAY

Using dial indicator, check camshaft end play. Position dial indicator on front of engine block or cylinder head. Position indicator tip against camshaft. Push camshaft toward rear of cylinder head or engine and adjust indicator to zero.

Move camshaft forward and note reading. Camshaft end play must be within specification. End play may be adjusted by relocating gear, shimming thrust plate or replacing thrust plate depending on each manufacturer.

TIMING CHAINS & BELTS

TIMING CHAINS

Timing chains will stretch during operation. Limits are placed upon amount of stretch before replacement is required. Timing chain stretch will alter ignition timing and valve timing.

To check timing chain stretch, rotate crankshaft to eliminate slack from one side of timing chain. Mark reference point on cylinder block. Rotate crankshaft in opposite direction to eliminate slack from remaining side of timing chain. Force other side of chain outward and measure distance between reference point and timing chain. *See Fig. 23.* Replace timing chain and gears if not within specification.

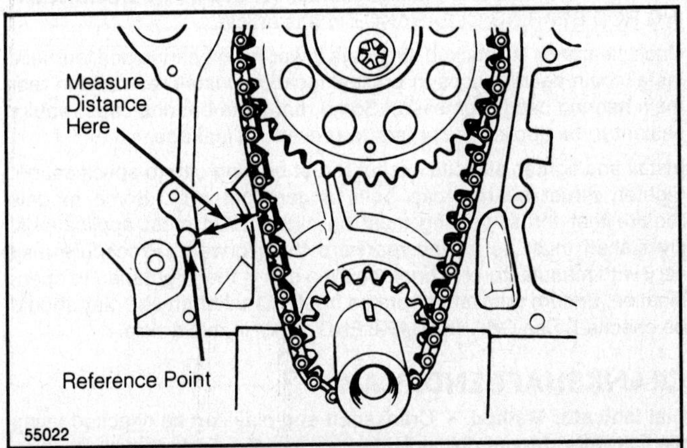
Measure
Distance
Here
Reference Point
55022

Fig. 23: Measuring Timing Chain Stretch

Timing chains must be installed so timing marks on camshaft gear and crankshaft gear are aligned according to manufacturer. *See Fig. 24.*

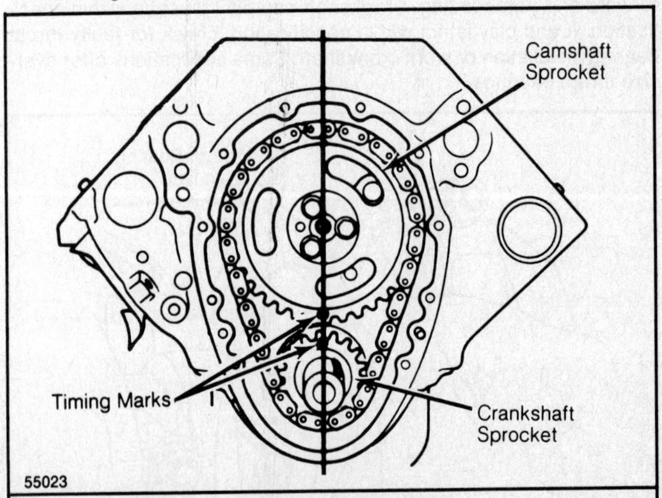
Camshaft
Sprocket
Timing Marks
Crankshaft
Sprocket
55023

Fig. 24: Typical Gear Timing Mark Alignment

TIMING BELTS

Cogged tooth belts are commonly used on overhead cam engines. Inspect belt teeth for rounded corners or cracking. Replace belt if it is cracked, damaged, missing teeth or oil soaked.

Used timing belt must be installed in original direction of rotation. Inspect all sprocket teeth for wear. Replace all worn sprockets. Sprockets are marked for timing purposes. Engine is positioned so that crankshaft sprocket mark will be upward. Camshaft sprocket is aligned with reference mark on cylinder head or timing belt cover and then timing belt can be installed. *See Fig. 25.*

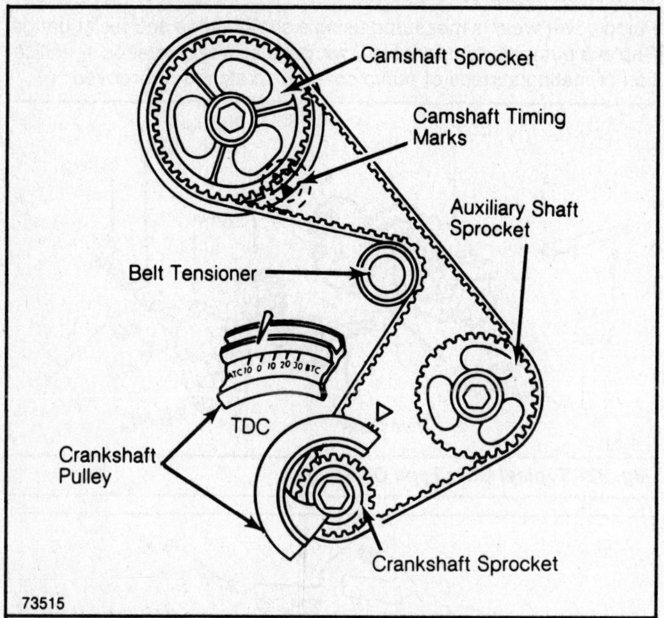
Camshaft Sprocket
Camshaft Timing
Marks
Auxiliary Shaft
Sprocket
Belt Tensioner
TDC
Crankshaft
Pulley
Crankshaft Sprocket
73515

Fig. 25: Typical Camshaft Belt Sprocket Alignment

TENSION ADJUSTMENT

If guide rails are used with spring loaded tensioners, ensure at least half of original rail thickness remains. Spring loaded tensioner should be inspected for damage.

Ensure all timing marks are aligned. Adjust belt tension using manufacturer's recommendations. Belt tension may require checking using tension gauge. *See Fig. 26.*

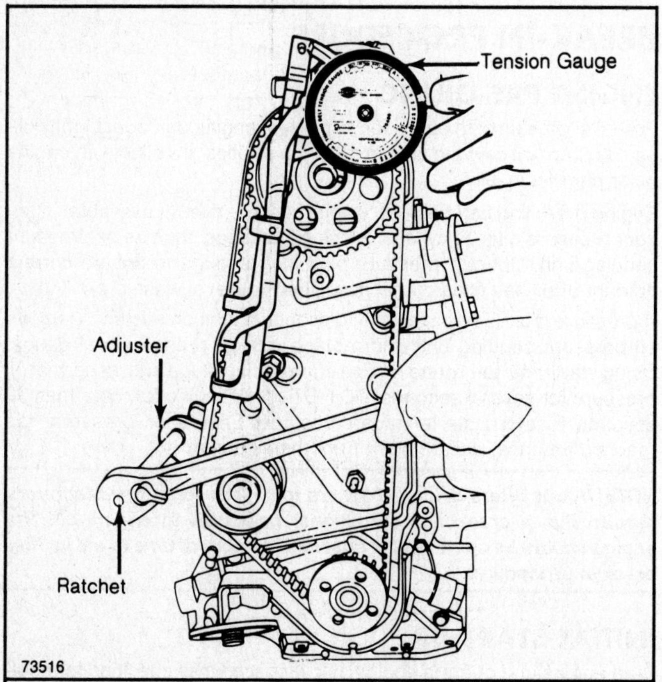
Tension Gauge
Adjuster
Ratchet
73516

Fig. 26: Typical Timing Belt Tension Adjustment

TIMING GEARS

TIMING GEAR BACKLASH & RUNOUT

On engines where camshaft gear operates directly on crankshaft gear, gear backlash and runout must be checked. To check backlash, install dial indicator with tip resting on tooth of camshaft gear. Rotate camshaft gear as far as possible. Adjust indicator to zero. Rotate camshaft gear in opposite direction as far as possible and note reading.

To determine timing gear runout, mount dial indicator with tip resting on face edge of camshaft gear. Adjust indicator to zero. Rotate camshaft gear 360 degrees and note reading. If backlash or runout exceeds specification, replace camshaft and/or crankshaft gear.

REAR MAIN OIL SEAL INSTALLATION

One-Piece Type Seal – For one-piece type oil seal installation, coat block contact surface of seal with sealer if seal is not factory coated. Ensure seal surface is free of burrs. Lubricate seal lip with engine oil and press seal into place using proper oil seal installer. *See Fig. 27.*

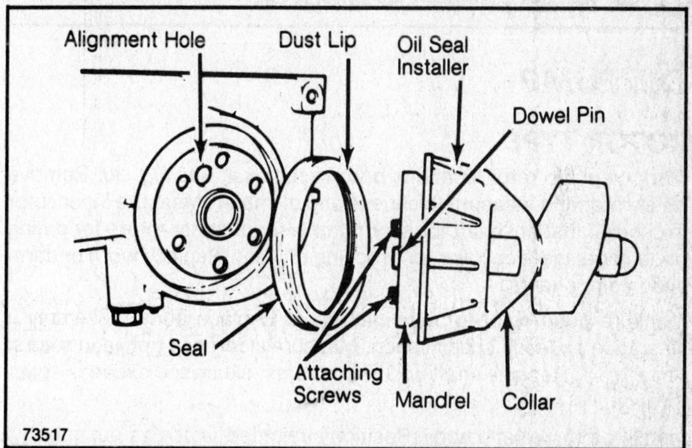
Alignment Hole
Dust Lip
Oil Seal
Installer
Dowel Pin
Seal
Attaching
Screws
Mandrel
Collar
73517

Fig. 27: Installing Typical One-Piece Oil Seal

Rope Type Seal – For rope type rear main oil seal installation, press seal lightly into seat area. Using seal installer, fully seat seal in bearing cap or cylinder block.

Trim seal ends even with cylinder block parting surface. Some applications require sealer to be applied on main bearing cap prior to installation. *See Fig. 28.*

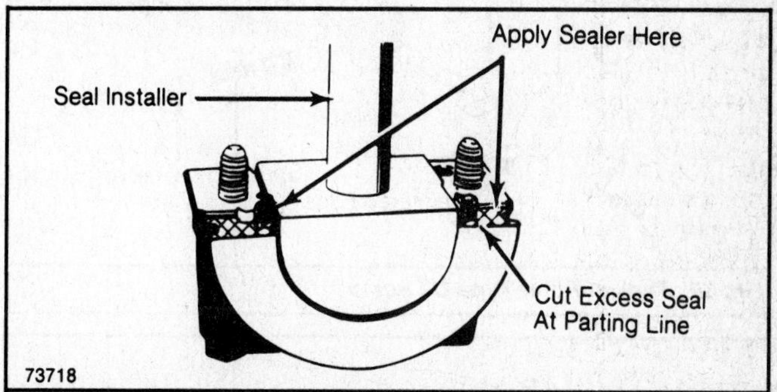
Apply Sealer Here
Seal Installer
Cut Excess Seal
At Parting Line
73718

Fig. 28: Installing Typical Rope Seal

Split-Rubber Type Seal – Follow manufacturer's procedures when installing split-rubber type rear main oil seals. Installation procedures vary with manufacturer and engine type. *See Fig. 29.*

1991 GENERAL INFORMATION
Engine Overhaul Procedures (Cont.)

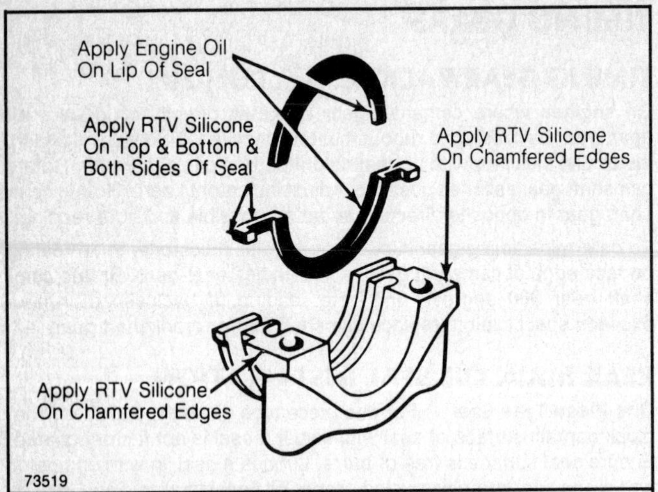
Apply Engine Oil
On Lip Of Seal
Apply RTV Silicone
On Top & Bottom &
Both Sides Of Seal
Apply RTV Silicone
On Chamfered Edges
Apply RTV Silicone
On Chamfered Edges
73519

Fig. 29: Installing Typical Split-Rubber Seal

OIL PUMP

ROTOR TYPE

Mark oil pump rotor locations prior to removal. *See Fig. 30.* Remove outer rotor and measure thickness and diameter. Measure inner rotor thickness. Inspect shaft for scoring or wear. Inspect rotors for pitting or damage. Inspect cover for grooving or wear. Replace worn or damaged components.

Measure outer rotor-to-body clearance. Replace pump assembly if clearance exceeds specification. Measure clearance between rotors. *See Fig. 31.* Replace shaft and both rotors if clearance exceeds specification.

Install rotors in pump body. Position straightedge across pump body. Using feeler gauge, measure clearance between rotors and straightedge. Pump cover wear is measured using a straightedge and feeler gauge. Replace pump if clearance exceeds specification.

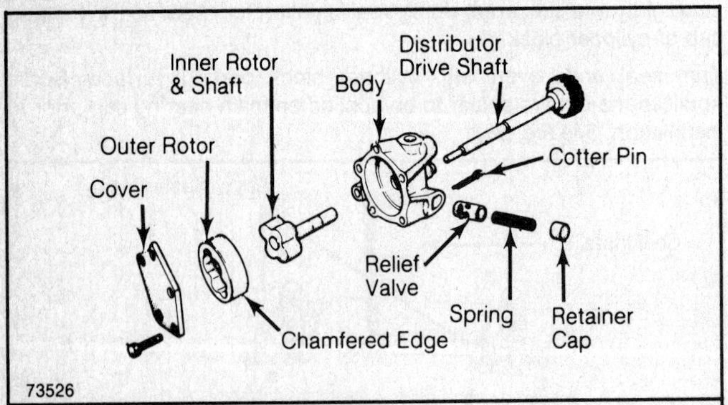
Inner Rotor
& Shaft
Body
Distributor
Drive Shaft
Outer Rotor
Cotter Pin
Cover
Relief
Valve
Spring
Retainer
Cap
Chamfered Edge
73526

Fig. 30: Typical Rotor Type Oil Pump

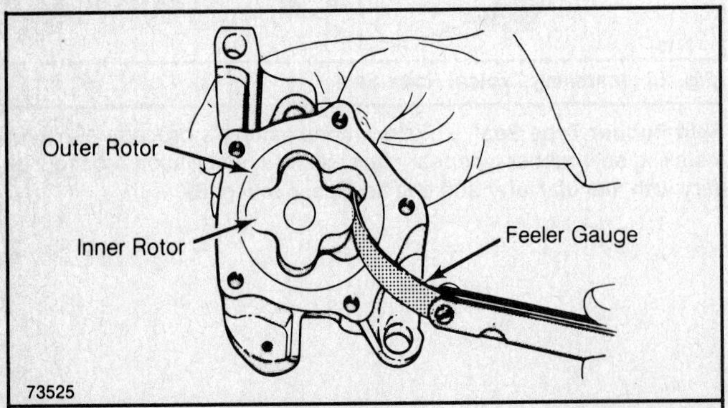
Outer Rotor
Inner Rotor
Feeler Gauge
73525

Fig. 31: Measuring Rotor Clearance

GEAR TYPE

Mark oil pump gear location prior to removal. *See Fig. 32.* Remove gears from pump body. Inspect gears for pitting or damage. Inspect cover for grooving or wear. Measure gear diameter and length. Measure gear housing cavity depth and diameter. *See Fig. 33.* Replace worn or damaged components.

Pump cover wear is measured using a straightedge and feeler gauge. Replace pump or components if warpage or wear exceeds specification or mating surface of pump cover is scratched or grooved.

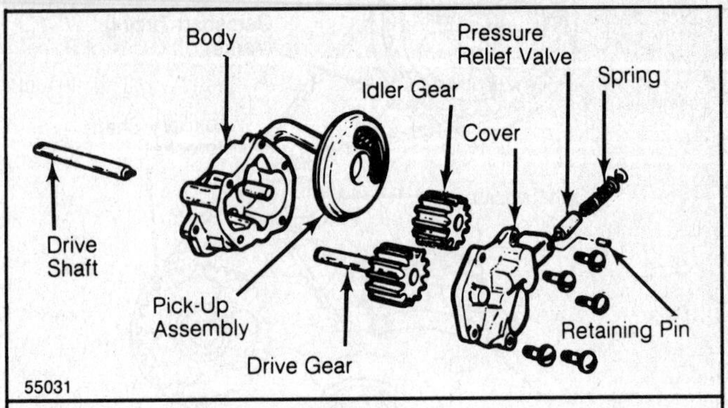
Body
Pressure
Relief Valve
Spring
Idler Gear
Cover
Drive
Shaft
Pick-Up
Assembly
Drive Gear
Retaining Pin
55031

Fig. 32: Typical Gear Type Oil Pump

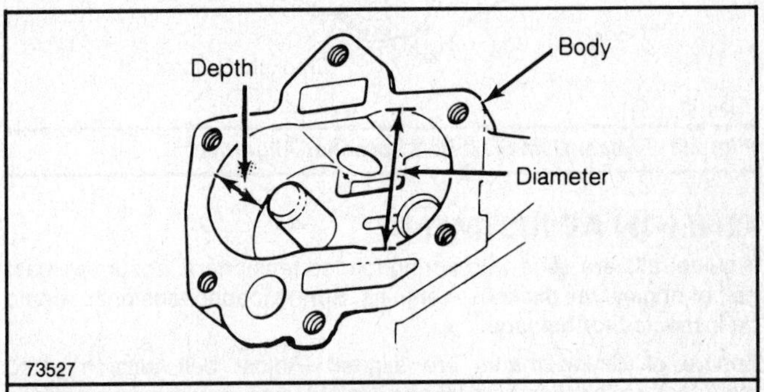
Depth
Body
Diameter
73527

Fig. 33: Measuring Oil Pump Gear Cavity

BREAK-IN PROCEDURE

ENGINE PRE-OILING

Pre-oil engine prior to operation to prevent engine damage. Lightly oiled oil pump will cavitate unless oil pump cavities are filled with engine oil or petroleum jelly.

Engine pre-oiling can be done using pressure oiler (if available). Connect pressure oiler to cylinder block oil passage such as oil pressure sending unit. Operate pressure oiler long enough to ensure correct amount of oil has filled crankcase. Check oil level while pre-oiling.

If pressure oiler is not available, disconnect ignition system. Remove oil pressure sending unit and replace with oil pressure test gauge. Using starter motor, rotate engine starter until gauge shows normal oil pressure for several seconds. DO NOT crank engine for more than 30 seconds to avoid starter motor damage. Ensure oil pressure has reached the most distant point from the oil pump.

NOTE: If new lifters or camshaft are installed, some manufacturers require that a crankcase conditioner be added to engine oil. The engine should be operated for specified amount of time to aid in lifter break-in procedure.

INITIAL START-UP

Start engine and operate engine at low speed while checking for coolant, fuel and oil leaks. Stop engine. Recheck coolant and oil level. Adjust if necessary.

1991 GENERAL INFORMATION
Engine Overhaul Procedures (Cont.)

CAMSHAFT

Break-in procedure is required when new or reground camshaft has been installed. Operate and maintain engine speed between 1500-2500 RPM for approximately 30 minutes. Procedure may vary due to manufacturer's recommendations.

PISTON RINGS

Piston rings require a break-in procedure to ensure seating of rings to cylinder walls. Serious damage may occur to rings if correct procedures are not followed.

Extremely high piston ring temperatures are obtained during break-in process. If rings are exposed to excessively high RPM or high cylinder pressures, ring damage can occur. Follow piston ring manufacturer's recommended break-in procedure.

FINAL ADJUSTMENTS

Check or adjust ignition timing and dwell (if applicable). Adjust valves (if necessary). Adjust idle speed and mixture. Retighten cylinder heads (if required). If cylinder head or block is aluminum, retighten bolts when engine is cold. Follow the engine manufacturer's recommended break-in procedure and maintenance schedule for new engines.

NOTE: Some manufacturers require that head bolts be retightened after specified amount of operation. This must be done to prevent head gasket failure.

1991 GENERAL INFORMATION
General Cooling System Servicing

All Models

DESCRIPTION

The basic liquid cooling system consists of a radiator, water pump, thermostat, electric or belt-driven cooling fan, pressure cap, heater, and various connecting hoses and cooling passages in the block and cylinder head.

MAINTENANCE

DRAINING

Remove radiator cap and open heater control valve to maximum heat position. Open drain cocks or remove plugs in bottom of radiator and engine block. In-line engines usually have one plug or drain cock, while "V" type engines will have 2, one in each bank of cylinders.

CLEANING

A good cleaning compound can remove most rust and scale. Follow manufacturer's instructions in the use of cleaner. If considerable rust and scale have to be removed, cooling system should be flushed. Clean radiator air passages with compressed air.

FLUSHING

CAUTION: Some manufacturers use an aluminum and plastic radiator. Flushing solution must be compatible with aluminum.

Back flushing is an effective means of removing cooling system rust and scale. The radiator, engine and heater core should be flushed separately.

Radiator - To flush radiator, connect flushing gun to water outlet of radiator and disconnect water inlet hose. To prevent flooding engine, use a hose connected to radiator inlet. Use air in short bursts to prevent damage to radiator. Continue flushing until water runs clear.

Engine - To flush engine, remove thermostat and replace housing. Connect flushing gun to water outlet of engine. Flush using short air bursts until water runs clean.

Heater Core - Flush heater core as described for radiator. Ensure heater control valve is set to maximum heat position before flushing heater.

REFILLING

To prevent air from being trapped in engine block, engine should be running when refilling cooling system. After system is full, continue running engine until thermostat is open, then recheck fill level. Do not overfill system.

TESTING

THERMOSTAT

1) Remove and visually inspect thermostat for corrosion and proper sealing of valve and seat. If okay, suspend thermostat and thermometer in a 50/50 mixture of coolant and water. *See Fig. 1.* DO NOT allow thermostat or thermometer to touch bottom of container. Heat water until thermostat begins to open.

2) Read temperature on thermometer. This is the initial opening temperature and should be within specification. Continue heating water until thermostat is fully open and note temperature. This is the fully open temperature. If either reading is not to specification, replace thermostat.

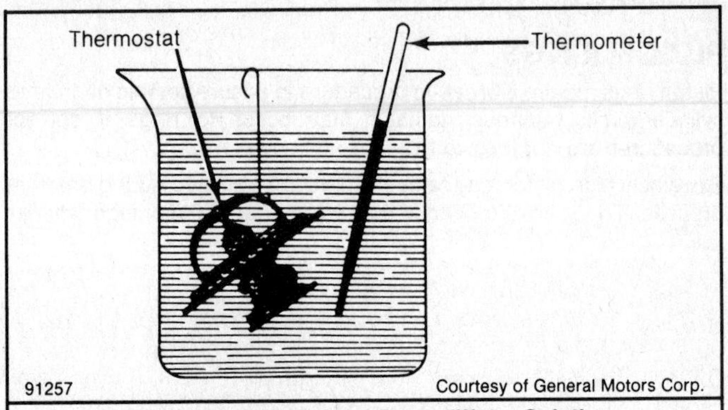
Thermostat
Thermometer
91257
Courtesy of General Motors Corp.

Fig. 1: Testing Thermostat in Anti-Freeze/Water Solution

PRESSURE TESTING

A pressure tester is used to check both radiator cap and complete cooling system. Follow pressure tester manufacturer's instructions and test components as follows:

Radiator Cap - Visually inspect radiator cap, then dip cap into water and connect to tester. Pump tester to bring pressure to upper limit of cap specification. *See Fig. 2.* If cap fails to hold pressure or releases at higher pressure than specification, replace cap.

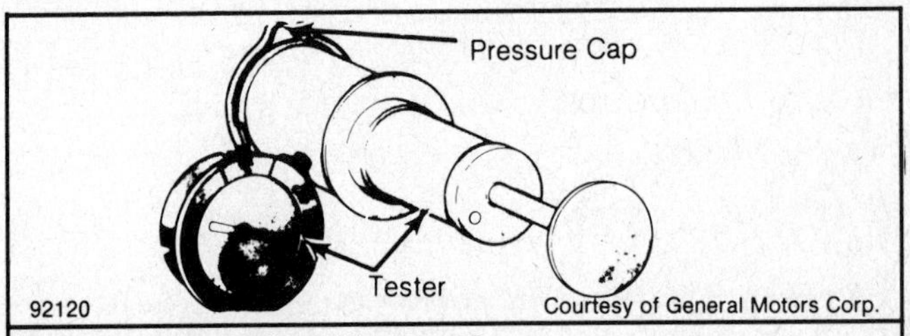
Pressure Cap
Tester
92120
Courtesy of General Motors Corp.

Fig. 2: Testing Radiator Pressure Cap

Cooling System - **1)** With engine off, clean radiator filler neck seat. Fill radiator to correct level. Attach tester to radiator and pump until pressure is at upper level of radiator rating.

2) If pressure drops, inspect for external leaks. If no leaks are apparent, detach tester and run engine until normal operating temperature is reached. Reattach tester and observe. If pressure builds up immediately, a possible leak exists from a faulty head gasket or crack in head or block.

NOTE: Pressure may build up quickly. Release excess pressure or cooling system damage may result.

3) If there is no immediate pressure build up, pump tester to within system pressure range (on radiator cap). Vibration of gauge pointer indicates compression or combustion leak into cooling system. Isolate leak by shorting each spark plug wire to cylinder block. Gauge pointer should stop or decrease vibration when leaking cylinder is shorted.

1991 GENERAL INFORMATION
Gear Tooth Contact Patterns

All Models

INSPECTION

Wipe lubricant from internal parts. Rotate gears and inspect for wear or damage. Mount dial indicator to housing and check backlash at several points around ring gear. Backlash must be within specification at all points. If no defects are found, check gear tooth pattern contact.

NOTE: Drive pattern should be well centered on ring gear teeth. Coast pattern should be centered, but may be slightly toward toe of ring gear teeth.

Gear Tooth Contact Pattern – 1) Paint ring gear teeth with marking compound. Wrap cloth or rope around drive pinion flange to act as brake. Rotate gear until clear contact pattern is obtained.

2) Contact pattern will indicate whether correct pinion bearing mounting shim has been installed and if drive gear backlash has been set properly. Backlash between drive gear pinion must be maintained within specified limits until correct tooth pattern is obtained.

ADJUSTMENTS

GEAR BACKLASH & PINION SHIM CHANGES

1) With no change in backlash, moving pinion further from ring gear moves drive pattern toward heel and top of tooth, and moves coast pattern toward toe and top of tooth.

2) With no change in backlash, moving pinion closer to ring gear moves drive pattern toward toe and bottom of tooth, and moves coast pattern toward heel and bottom of tooth.

3) With no change in pinion shim thickness, an increase in backlash moves ring gear further from pinion. Both drive and coast patterns move toward heel and top of tooth.

4) With no change in pinion shim thickness, a decrease in backlash moves ring gear closer to pinion gear. Both drive and coast patterns move toward toe and bottom of tooth.

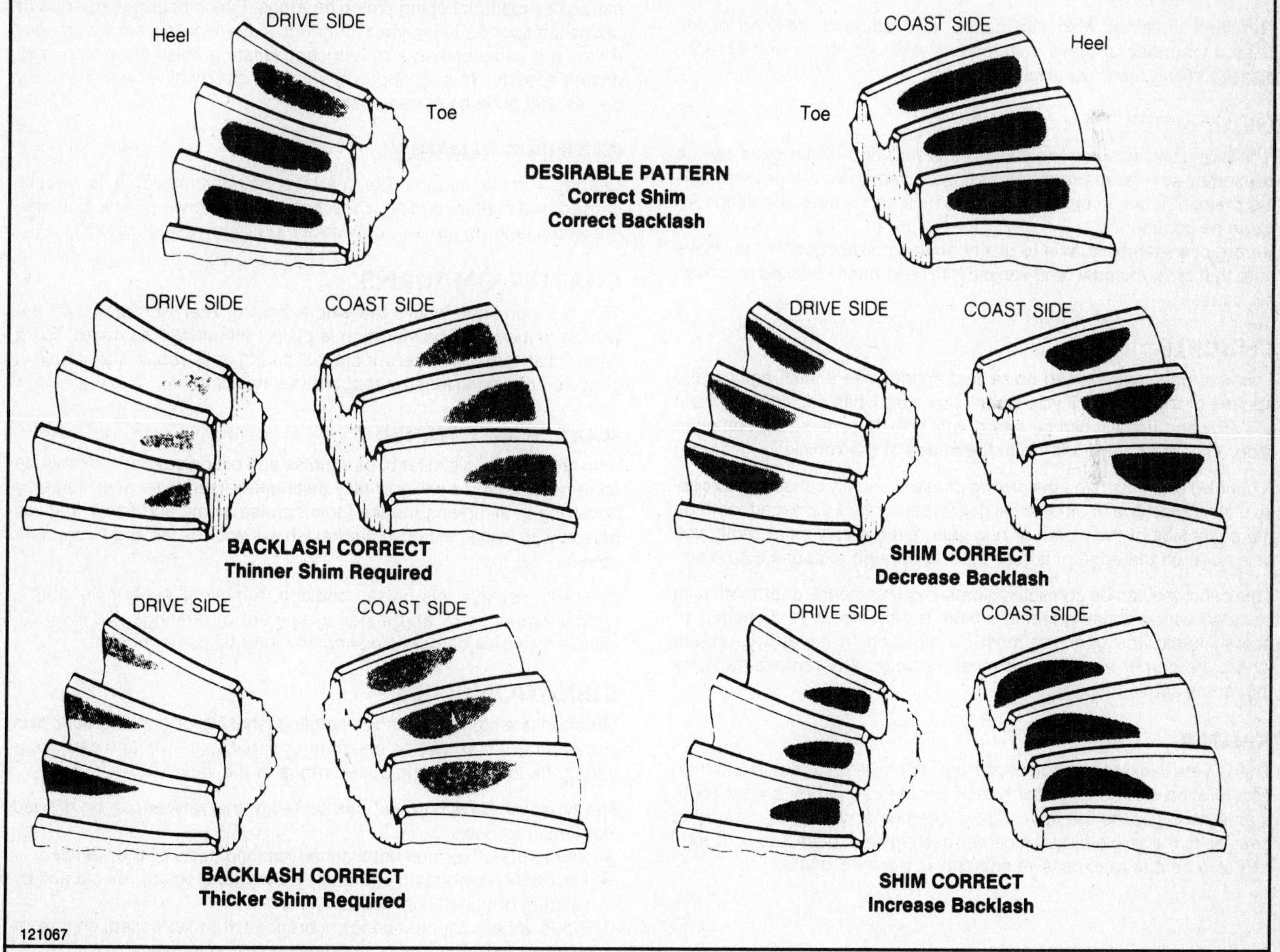
Heel
DRIVE SIDE
Toe
COAST SIDE
Heel
Toe
DESIRABLE PATTERN
Correct Shim
Correct Backlash
DRIVE SIDE
COAST SIDE
BACKLASH CORRECT
Thinner Shim Required
DRIVE SIDE
COAST SIDE
SHIM CORRECT
Decrease Backlash
DRIVE SIDE
COAST SIDE
BACKLASH CORRECT
Thicker Shim Required
DRIVE SIDE
COAST SIDE
SHIM CORRECT
Increase Backlash
121067

Fig. 1: Drive Axle Gear Tooth Patterns

1991 GENERAL INFORMATION
Drive Axle Noise Diagnosis

UNRELATED NOISES

Some driveline trouble symptoms are also common to the engine, transmission, wheel bearings, tires, and other parts of the vehicle. Make sure that cause of trouble actually is in the drive axle before adjusting, repairing, or replacing any of its parts.

NON-DRIVE AXLE NOISES

A few conditions can sound just like drive axle noise and have to be considered in pre-diagnosis. The 4 most common noises are exhaust, tires, CV/universal joints and trim moldings.

In certain conditions, the pitch of the exhaust gases may sound like gear whine. At other times, it may be mistaken for a wheel bearing rumble.

Tires, especially radial and snow tires, can have a high-pitched tread whine or roar, similar to gear noise. Also, some non-standard tires with an unusual tread construction may emit a roar or whine.

Defective CV/universal joints may cause clicking noises or excessive driveline play that can be improperly diagnosed as drive axle problems.

Trim and moldings also can cause a whistling or whining noise. Ensure that none of these components are causing the noise before disassembling the drive axle.

GEAR NOISE

A "howling" or "whining" noise from the ring and pinion gear can be caused by an improper gear pattern, gear damage, or improper bearing preload. It can occur at various speeds and driving conditions, or it can be continuous.

Before disassembling axle to diagnose and correct gear noise, make sure that tires, exhaust, and vehicle trim have been checked as possible causes.

CHUCKLE

This is a particular rattling noise that sounds like a stick against the spokes of a spinning bicycle wheel. It occurs while decelerating from 40 MPH and usually can be heard until vehicle comes to a complete stop. The frequency varies with the speed of the vehicle.

A chuckle that occurs on the driving phase is usually caused by excessive clearance due to differential gear wear, or by a damaged tooth on the coast side of the pinion or ring gear. Even a very small tooth nick or a ridge on the edge of a gear tooth is enough to cause the noise.

This condition can be corrected simply by cleaning the gear tooth nick or ridge with a small grinding wheel. If either gear is damaged or scored badly, the gear set must be replaced. If metal has broken loose, the carrier and housing must be cleaned to remove particles that could cause damage.

KNOCK

This is very similar to a chuckle, though it may be louder, and occur on acceleration or deceleration. Knock can be caused by a gear tooth that is damaged on the drive side of the ring and pinion gears. Ring gear bolts that are hitting the carrier casting can cause knock. Knock can also be due to excessive end play in the axle shafts.

CLUNK

Clunk is a metallic noise heard when an automatic transmission is engaged in Reverse or Drive, or when throttle is applied or released. It is caused by backlash somewhere in the driveline, but not necessarily in the axle. To determine whether driveline clunk is caused by the axle, check the total axle backlash as follows:

1) Raise vehicle on a frame or twinpost hoist so that drive wheels are free. Clamp a bar between axle companion flange and a part of the frame or body so that flange cannot move.

2) On conventional drive axles, lock the left wheel to keep it from turning. On all models, turn the right wheel slowly until it is felt to be in drive condition. Hold a chalk marker on side of tire about 12" from center of wheel. Turn wheel in the opposite direction until it is again felt to be in drive condition.

3) Measure the length of the chalk mark, which is the total axle backlash. If backlash is one inch or less, clunk will not be eliminated by overhauling drive axle.

BEARING WHINE

Bearing whine is a high-pitched sound similar to a whistle. It is usually caused by malfunctioning pinion bearings. Pinion bearings operate at driveshaft speed. Roller wheel bearings may whine in a similar manner if they run completely dry of lubricant. Bearing noise will occur at all driving speeds. This distinguishes it from gear whine, which usually comes and goes as speed changes.

BEARING RUMBLE

Bearing rumble sounds like marbles being tumbled. It is usually caused by a malfunctioning wheel bearing. The lower pitch is because the wheel bearing turns at only about 1/3 of driveshaft speed.

CHATTER ON TURNS

This is a condition where the whole front or rear vibrates when the vehicle is moving. The vibration is plainly felt as well as heard. Extra differential thrust washers installed during axle repair can cause a condition of partial lock-up that creates this chatter.

AXLE SHAFT NOISE

Axle shaft noise is similar to gear noise and pinion bearing whine. Axle shaft bearing noise will normally distinguish itself from gear noise by occurring in all driving modes (drive, cruise, coast and float), and will persist with transmission in neutral while vehicle is moving at problem speed.

If vehicle displays this noise condition, remove suspect axle shafts, replace wheel seals and install a new set of bearings. Re-evaluate vehicle for noise before removing any internal components.

VIBRATION

Vibration is a high-frequency trembling, shaking or grinding condition (felt or heard) that may be constant or variable in level and can occur during the total operating speed range of the vehicle.

The types of vibrations that can be felt in the vehicle can be divided into 3 main groups:

- Vibrations of various unbalanced rotating parts of the vehicle.
- Resonance vibrations of the body and frame structures caused by rotating of unbalanced parts.
- Tip-in moans of resonance vibrations from stressed engine or exhaust system mounts or driveline flexing modes.

1991 GENERAL INFORMATION
Anti-Lock Brake Safety Precautions

NOTE: Refer to appropriate Anti-Lock Brake System (ABS) article for description, operation, depressurizing, testing, system bleeding, trouble shooting and servicing of specific system. Failure to depressurize ABS could lead to physical injury.

- NEVER open a bleeder valve or loosen a hydraulic line while ABS is pressurized.
- NEVER disconnect or reconnect any electrical connectors while ignition is on. Damage to ABS control unit may result.
- DO NOT attempt to bleed hydraulic system without first referring to the appropriate article in your Mitchell service and repair manual.
- Only use specially designed brake hoses/lines on ABS-equipped vehicles.
- DO NOT tap on speed sensor components (sensor, sensor rings). Speed rings must be pressed, NOT hammered into hubs. Striking these components can cause demagnetization or a loss of polarization, affecting the accuracy of the speed signal returning to the ABS control unit.
- DO NOT mix tire sizes. Increasing the width, as long as tires remain close to the original diameter, is acceptable. Rolling diameter must be identical for all 4 tires. Some manufacturers recommend tires of the same brand, style and type. Failure to follow this precaution may cause inaccurate wheel speed readings.
- DO NOT contaminate speed sensor components with grease. Only use recommended anti-corrosion coating.
- When speed sensor components have been removed, ALWAYS check sensor-to-ring air gaps when applicable. These specifications can be found in each appropriate article.
- ONLY use recommended brake fluids. DO NOT use silicone brake fluids in an ABS-equipped vehicle.
- When installing transmitting devices (CB's, telephones, etc.) on ABS-equipped vehicles, DO NOT locate the antenna near the ABS control unit (or any control unit).
- Disconnect all on-board computers, when using electric welding equipment.
- DO NOT expose the ABS control unit to prolonged periods of high heat (185°F/85°C for 2 hours is generally considered a maximum limit).

1991 GENERAL INFORMATION
Wheel Alignment Theory & Operation

All Models

PRE-ALIGNMENT INSTRUCTIONS

Before adjusting wheel alignment, check the following:

- Ensure each axle uses tires of same construction and tread style, equal in tread wear and overall diameter. Using a dial indicator, verify that radial and axial runout of tires is not excessive. Inflation should be at manufacturer's specifications. *See Fig. 1.*
- Ensure steering linkage and suspension does not have excessive play. Check for wear in tie rod ends and ball joints. Springs must not be sagging. Check that control arm and strut rod bushings do not have excessive play.
- Vehicle must be on level floor with full fuel tank, no passenger load, spare tire in place and no load in trunk. Bounce front and rear end of vehicle several times. Confirm vehicle is at normal riding height.
- Ensure steering wheel is centered with wheels in straight ahead position. If required, shorten one tie rod adjusting sleeve and lengthen opposite sleeve (equal amount of turns). *See Fig. 2.*
- Ensure that wheel bearings have correct preload and that lug nuts are tightened to manufacturer's specifications. Adjust camber, caster and toe-in using this sequence. Follow instructions of the alignment equipment manufacturer.

CAUTION: DO NOT attempt to correct alignment by straightening parts. Damaged parts must be replaced.

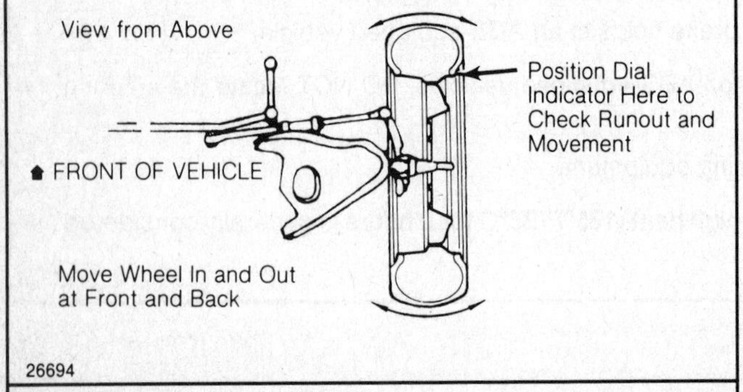
View from Above
Position Dial Indicator Here to Check Runout and Movement
FRONT OF VEHICLE
Move Wheel In and Out at Front and Back
26694

Fig. 1: Checking Steering Linkage

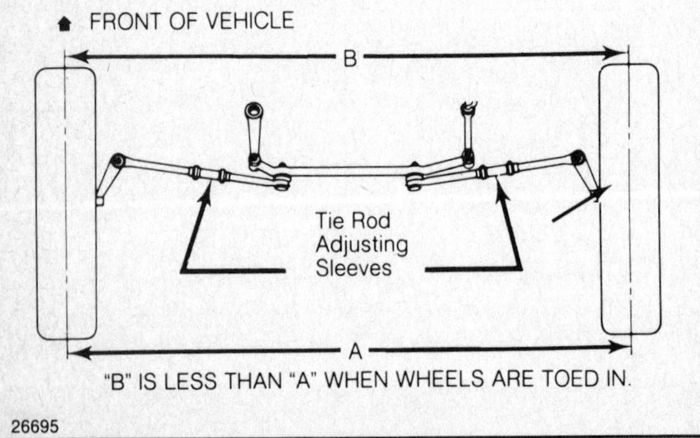
FRONT OF VEHICLE
B
Tie Rod Adjusting Sleeves
A
"B" IS LESS THAN "A" WHEN WHEELS ARE TOED IN.
26695

Fig. 2: Adjusting Tie Rod Sleeves (Top View)

CAMBER

1) Camber is the tilting of the wheel, outward at either top or bottom, as viewed from front of vehicle. *See Fig. 3.*

2) When wheels tilt outward at the top (from centerline of vehicle), camber is positive. When wheels tilt inward at top, camber is negative. Amount of tilt is measured in degrees from vertical.

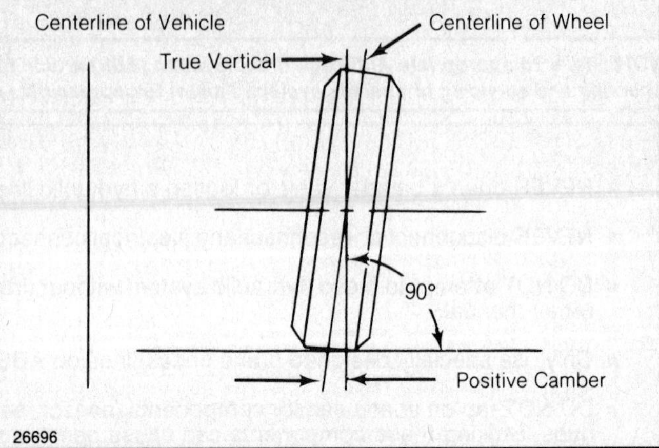
Centerline of Vehicle
Centerline of Wheel
True Vertical
90°
Positive Camber
26696

Fig. 3: Determining Camber Angle

CASTER

1) Caster is tilting of front steering axis either forward or backward from vertical, as viewed from side of vehicle. *See Fig. 4.*

2) When axis is tilted backward from vertical, caster is positive. This creates a trailing action on front wheels. When axis is tilted forward, caster is negative, causing a leading action on front wheels.

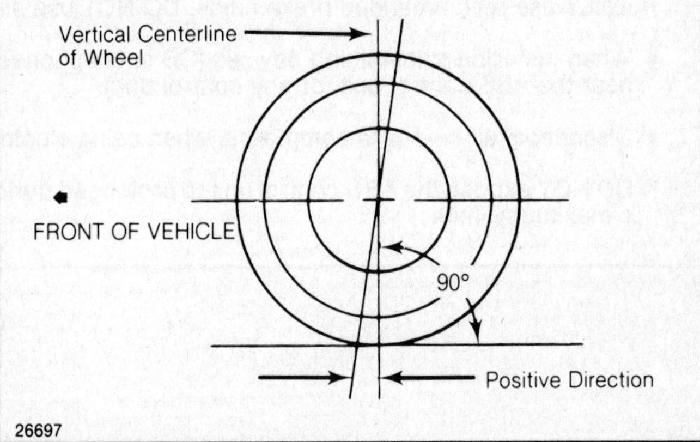
Vertical Centerline of Wheel
FRONT OF VEHICLE
90°
Positive Direction
26697

Fig. 4: Determining Caster Angle

TOE-IN ADJUSTMENT

Toe-in is the width measured at the rear of the tires subtracted by the width measured at the front of the tires at about spindle height. *See Fig. 5.* Toe-in specification is Dimension A less Dimension B. A positive figure would indicate toe-in and a negative figure would indicate toe-out. If the distance between the front and rear of the tires is the same, toe measurement would be zero. Use the following procedures to adjust toe-in:

1) Measure toe-in with front wheels in straight ahead position and steering wheel centered. To adjust toe-in, loosen clamps and turn adjusting sleeve or adjustable end on right and left tie rods. *See Figs. 2 and 5.*

2) Turn equally and in opposite directions to maintain steering wheel in centered position. Face of tie rod end must be parallel with machined surface of steering rod end to prevent binding.

3) When tightening clamps, make certain that clamp bolts are positioned so there will be no interference with other parts throughout the entire travel of the steering linkage.

1991 GENERAL INFORMATION
Wheel Alignment Theory & Operation (Cont.)

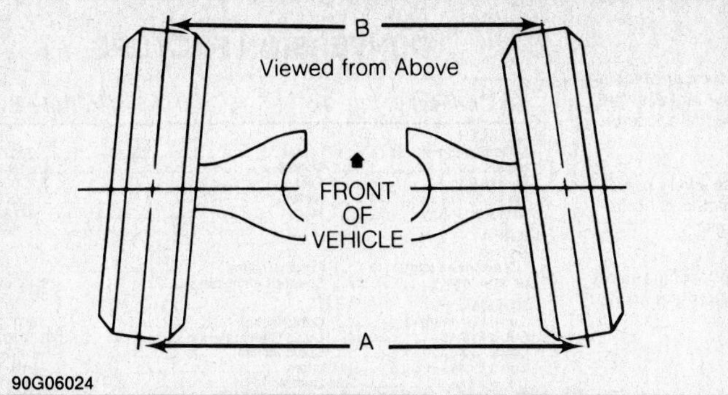
B
Viewed from Above
FRONT
OF
VEHICLE
A
90G06024

Fig. 5: Wheel Toe-In (Dimension A Less Dimension B)

TOE-OUT ON TURNS

1) Toe-out on turns (turning radius) is a check for bent or damaged parts, and not a service adjustment. With caster, camber, and toe-in properly adjusted, check toe-out with weight of vehicle on wheels.
2) Use a full floating turntable under each wheel, repeating test with each wheel positioned for right and left turns. Incorrect toe-out generally indicates a bent steering arm. Replace steering arm, if necessary, and recheck wheel alignment.

STEERING AXIS INCLINATION

1) Steering axis inclination is a check for bent or damaged parts, and not a service adjustment. Vehicle must be level and camber should be properly adjusted. *See Fig. 6.*

2) If camber cannot be brought within limits and steering axis inclination is correct, steering knuckle is bent. If camber and steering axis inclination are both incorrect by approximately the same amount, the upper and lower control arms are bent.

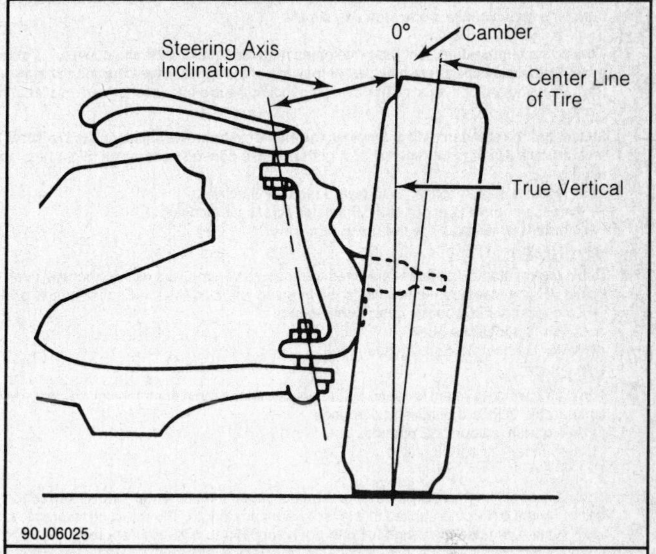
0°
Camber
Steering Axis
Inclination
Center Line
of Tire
True Vertical
90J06025

Fig. 6: Checking Steering Axis Inclination

1991 GENERAL INFORMATION
English-Metric Conversion Chart

METRIC CONVERSIONS

Metric conversions are making life more difficult for the mechanic. In addition to doubling the number of tools required, metric-dimensioned nuts and bolts are used alongside English components in many new vehicles. The mechanic has to decide which tool to use, slowing down the job. The tool problem can be solved by trial and error, but some metric conversions aren't so simple.

Converting temperature, lengths or volumes requires a calculator and conversion charts, or else a very nimble mind. Conversion charts are only part of the answer though, because they don't help you "think" metric, or "visualize" what you are converting. The following examples are intended to help you "see" metric sizes:

LENGTH

Meters are the standard unit of length in the metric system. The smaller units are 10ths (decimeter), 100ths (centimeter), and 1000ths (millimeter) of a meter. These common examples might help you to visualize the metric units:

- A meter is slightly longer than a yard (about 40 inches).
- An aspirin tablet is about one centimeter across (.4 inches).
- A millimeter is about the thickness of a dime.

VOLUME

Cubic meters and centimeters are used to measure volume, just as we normally think of cubic feet and inches. Liquid volume measurements include the liter and milliliter, like the English quarts or ounces.

- One teaspoon is about 4 cubic centimeters.
- A liter is about one quart.
- A liter is about 61 cubic inches.

WEIGHT

The metric weight system is based on the gram, with the most common unit being the kilogram (1000 grams). Our comparable units are ounces and pounds:

- A kilogram is about 2.2 pounds.
- An ounce is about 28 grams.

TORQUE

Torque is somewhat complicated. The term describes the amount of effort exerted to turn something. A chosen unit of weight or force is applied to a lever of standard length. The resulting leverage is called torque. In our standard system, we use the weight of one pound applied to a lever a foot long, resulting in the unit called a foot-pound. A smaller unit is the inch-pound (the lever is one inch long). Metric units include the meter kilogram (lever one meter long with a kilogram of weight applied) and the Newton-meter (lever one meter long with force of one Newton applied). Some conversions are:

- A meter kilogram is about 7.2 foot pounds.
- A foot pound is about 1.4 Newton-meters.
- A centimeter kilogram (cmkg) is equal to .9 inch pounds.

PRESSURE

Pressure is another complicated measurement. Pressure is described as a force or weight applied to a given area. Our common unit is pounds per square inch. Metric units can be expressed in several ways. One is the kilogram per square centimeter (kg/cm²). Another unit of pressure is the Pascal (force of one Newton on an area of one square meter), which equals about 4 ounces on a square yard. Since this is a very small amount of pressure, we usually see the kiloPascal, or kPa (1000 Pascals). Another common automotive term for pressure is the bar (used by German manufacturers), which equals 10 Pascals. Thoroughly confused? Try the examples below:

- Atmospheric pressure at sea level is about 14.7 psi.
- Atmospheric pressure at sea level is about 1 bar.
- Atomospheric pressure at sea level is about 1 kg/cm².
- One pound per square inch is about 7 kPa.

CONVERSION FACTORS

To Convert	To	Multiply By
LENGTH		
Millimeters (mm)	Inches	.03937
Inches	Millimeters	25.4
Meters (M)	Feet	3.28084
Feet	Meters	.3048
Kilometers (Km)	Miles	.62137
AREA		
Square Centimeters (cm²)	Square Inches	.155
Square Inches	Square Centimeters	6.45159
VOLUME		
Cubic Centimeters	Cubic Inches	.06103
Cubic Inches	Cubic Centimeters	16.38703
Liters	Cubic Inches	61.025
Cubic Inches	Liters	.01639
Liters	Quarts	1.05672
Quarts	Liters	.94633
Liters	Pints	2.11344
Pints	Liters	.47317
Liters	Ounces	33.81497
Ounces	Liters	.02957
WEIGHT		
Grams	Ounces	.03527
Ounces	Grams	28.34953
Kilograms	Pounds	2.20462
Pounds	Kilograms	.45359
WORK		
Centimeter Kilograms	Inch Pounds	.8676
Pounds/Sq. Inch	Kilograms/Sq. Centimeter	.07031
Bar	Pounds/Sq. Inch	14.504
Pounds/Sq. Inch	Bar	.06895
Atmosphere	Pounds/Sq. Inch	14.696
Pounds/Sq. Inch	Atmosphere	.06805
TEMPERATURE		
Centigrade Degrees	Fahrenheit Degrees	$(C° \times ^{9}/_{5}) + 32$
Fahrenheit Degrees	Centigrade Degrees	$(F° - 32) \times ^{5}/_{9}$

Inches	Decimals	mm
1/64	.016	.397
1/32	.031	.794
3/64	.047	1.191
1/16	.063	1.588
5/64	.078	1.984
3/32	.094	2.381
7/64	.109	2.778
1/8	.125	3.175
9/64	.141	3.572
5/32	.156	3.969
11/64	.172	4.366
3/16	.188	4.763
13/64	.203	5.159
7/32	.219	5.556
15/64	.234	5.953
1/4	.250	6.350
17/64	.266	6.747
9/32	.281	7.144
19/64	.297	7.541
5/16	.313	7.938
21/64	.328	8.334
11/32	.344	8.731
23/64	.359	9.128
3/8	.375	9.525
25/64	.391	9.992
13/32	.406	10.319
27/64	.422	10.716
7/16	.438	11.113
29/64	.453	11.509
15/32	.469	11.906
31/64	.484	12.303
1/2	.500	12.700
33/64	.516	13.097
17/32	.531	13.494
35/64	.547	13.891
9/16	.563	14.288
37/64	.578	14.684
19/32	.594	15.081
39/64	.609	15.478
5/8	.625	15.875
41/64	.641	16.272
21/32	.656	16.669
43/64	.672	17.066
11/16	.687	17.463
45/64	.703	17.859
23/32	.719	18.256
47/64	.734	18.653
3/4	.750	19.050
49/64	.766	19.447
25/32	.781	19.844
51/64	.797	20.241
13/16	.813	20.638
53/64	.828	21.034
27/32	.844	21.431
55/64	.859	21.828
7/8	.875	22.225
57/64	.891	22.622
29/32	.906	23.019
59/64	.922	23.416
15/16	.938	23.813
61/64	.953	24.209
31/32	.969	24.606
63/64	.984	25.003
1	1.000	25.400

MITCHELL INTERNATIONAL
9889 Willow Creek Road
P.O. Box 26260
San Diego, CA 92196-0260

CHRYSLER MOTORS

1991 CHRYSLER MOTORS CONTENTS

GENERAL INFORMATION [1]

[1] – For all GENERAL INFORMATION, see front of this manual.

ENGINE PERFORMANCE

ENGINE PERFORMANCE (Cont.)

ENGINE PERFORMANCE (Cont.)

ENGINE PERFORMANCE (Cont.)

1991 CHRYSLER MOTORS CONTENTS (Cont.)

ELECTRICAL

WIRING DIAGRAMS

SAFETY EQUIPMENT

SAFETY EQUIPMENT (Cont.)

ENGINES

ENGINES (Cont.)

3.0L V6

3.3L V6

3.9L V6, 5.2L & 5.9L V8

CUMMINS DIESEL "B" SERIES 5.9L 6-CYLINDER

ENGINE COOLING

SPECIFICATIONS & ELECTRIC COOLING FANS

CLUTCHES

SINGLE DISC

DRIVE AXLES

DANA FULL-FLOATING AXLES

1991 CHRYSLER MOTORS CONTENTS (Cont.)

DRIVE AXLES (Cont.)

DRIVE AXLES (Cont.)

BRAKES

ANTI-LOCK

DISC & DRUM

WHEEL ALIGNMENT

SPECIFICATIONS & PROCEDURES

SUSPENSION

FRONT - FWD

FRONT - 2WD COIL SPRING

FRONT - 4WD LEAF SPRING

FRONT - TORSION BAR

1991 CHRYSLER MOTORS CONTENTS (Cont.)

STEERING

TRANSMISSION SERVICING

1991 ENGINE PERFORMANCE
Chrysler Motors Introduction

1991 MODEL COVERAGE

MODEL	BODY CODE	ENGINE	ENGINE ID	FUEL SYSTEM	IGNITION SYSTEM
Caravan [1]	K, D [2]	2.5L	K	TBI	Magnetic [3]
		3.0L	3	PFI	Optical
		3.3L	R	PFI	DIS
Dakota	N	2.5L	K	TBI	Magnetic [3]
		3.9L	X	TBI	Magnetic [3]
		5.2L	Y	TBI	Magnetic [3]
Pickup (D150/350 & W150/350)	D	3.9L	X	TBI	Magnetic [3]
		5.2L	Y	TBI	Magnetic [3]
		5.9L	Z	TBI	Magnetic [3]
		5.9L [4]	5	TBI	Magnetic [3]
		5.9L Diesel	8	Turbo DFI	N/A
Ramcharger (AD150/350, & AW100/150)	D	5.2L	Y	TBI	Magnetic [3]
		5.9L	Z	TBI	Magnetic [3]
Town & Country	Y	3.3L	R	PFI	DIS
Van (B150/350) [5]	B	3.9L	X	TBI	Magnetic [3]
		5.2L	Y	TBI	Magnetic [3]
		5.9L	W or Z	TBI	Magnetic [3]
Voyager	H, P [2]	2.5L	K	TBI	Magnetic [3]
		3.0L	3	PFI	Optical
		3.3L	R	PFI	DIS

[1] – Includes Caravan C/V, Extended Caravan, Cargo Van and Extended Cargo Van.
[2] – All-Wheel Drive (AWD).
[3] – Uses a Single Board Electronic Controller (SBEC) with a Hall Effect distributor.
[4] – With heavy-duty emissions.
[5] – Includes Ram Wagon and Ram Van.

VIN DEFINITION

1B7FB35<u>X</u>9<u>M</u>S000001

① ② ③ ④ ⑤ ⑥ ⑦ ⑧ ⑨ ⑩ ⑪ ⑫ ⑬ ⑭ ⑮ ⑯ ⑰

① Indicates Nation of Origin.
② Indicates Manufacturer.
③ Indicates Vehicle Type.
④ Indicates Gross Vehicle Weight Rating.
⑤ Indicates Vehicle Line.
⑥ Indicates Vehicle Series.
⑦ Indicates Body Type.
⑧ Indicates Engine Code.
⑨ Indicates Check Digit.
⑩ Indicates Model Year.
⑪ Indicates Assembly Plant.
⑫-⑰ Indicate Plant Sequential Number.

MODEL YEAR VIN CODE APPLICATION

VIN Code	Model Year
K	1989
L	1990
M	1991

ENGINE CODE LOCATION

2.5L Engines – Engine serial number is located on rear face of engine block, below cylinder head.

3.0L & 3.3L Engines – Engine serial number is located on right front side of engine block, adjacent to exhaust manifold stud.

3.9L Engines – Engine serial number is on a pad located on right side of block.

5.2L & 5.9L Engines – Engine serial number is on left front corner of block, below cylinder head.

1991 ENGINE PERFORMANCE
Emission Applications

1991 CHRYSLER TRUCK EMISSION SYSTEMS

Model, Engine & Fuel System	Emission Control Systems & Devices	Remarks
2.5L (153") 4-Cyl. TBI	**PCV, TAC, EVAP, TWC, BP/EGR [1], SPK, O_2, CEC, EMR, CE,** EVAP-VC, EVAP-PRRV, EVAP-PS, BP/EGR-EET [2], BP/EGR-SOL [1], BP/EGR-BPT [1], SPK-CC	[1] - Except Federal with A/T. [2] - Calif. only with A/T. [3] - Some models.
3.0L (183") V6 PFI	**PCV, EVAP, TWC, SPK, O_2, CEC, EMR, CE,** EVAP-VC, EVAP-PRRV, EVAP-PS, SPK-CC	
3.3L (201") V6 PFI	**PCV, EVAP, TWC, SPK, O_2, CEC, EMR, CE,** EVAP-VC, EVAP-PRRV, EVAP-PS, SPK-CC	
3.9L (239") V6 TBI	**PCV, TAC, EVAP, TWC, BP/EGR, SPK, AP, O_2, CEC, EMR, CE,** EVAP-VC, EVAP-PRRV, EVAP-PS, BP/EGR-SOL, BP/EGR-BPT, SPK-CC, AP-DV [3], AP-ASS, AP-ASRV	
5.2L (318") V8 TBI	**PCV, TAC, EVAP, TWC, BP/EGR, SPK, AP, O_2, CEC, EMR, CE,** EVAP-VC, EVAP-PRRV, EVAP-PS, BP/EGR-SOL, BP/EGR-BPT, SPK-CC, AP-DV [3], AP-ASS, AP-ASRV	
5.9L (360") V8 TBI	**PCV, TAC, EVAP, TWC, BP/EGR, SPK, AP, O_2, CEC, EMR, CE,** EVAP-VC, EVAP-PRRV, EVAP-PS, BP/EGR-SOL, BP/EGR-BPT, SPK-CC, AP-DV [3], AP-ASS, AP-ASRV	
5.9L (360") V8 TBI (H/D)	**PCV, TAC, EVAP, TWC, BP/EGR [3], SPK, AP, O_2, CEC, EMR, CE,** EVAP-VC, EVAP-PRRV, EVAP-PS, BP/EGR-SOL, BP/EGR-BPT, SPK-CC, AP-DV [3], AP-ASS, AP-ASRV	

NOTE: Major emission control systems are listed in bold type; components are listed in light type.

AP - Air Pump
AP-ASS - AP Air Switching Solenoid
AP-DV - AP Diverter Valve
AP-ASRV - AP Air Switching Relief Valve
A/T - Automatic Transmission
BP/EGR - Backpressure EGR
BP/EET - BP/EGR Electric Transducer
BP/EGR-BPT - BP/EGR Backpressure Transducer
BP/EGR-SOL - BP/EGR Solenoid
CE - Check Engine Light
CEC - Computerized Engine Controls
EGR - Exhaust Gas Recirculation
EMR - Emission Maintenance Reminder Light
EVAP - Fuel Evaporation System
EVAP-PRRV - EVAP Pressure Relief Rollover Valve
EVAP-PS - EVAP Purge Solenoid
EVAP-VC - EVAP Vapor Canister
H/D - Heavy-Duty
O_2 - Oxygen Sensor
PCV - Positive Crankcase Ventilation
PFI - Port Fuel Injection
SPK - Spark Controls
SPK-CC - SPK Computer Controlled
TAC - Thermostatic Air Cleaner
TBI - Throttle Body Injection
TWC - Three-Way Catalyst

1991 ENGINE PERFORMANCE
Service & Adjustment Specifications – Gasoline

Caravan, Dakota, Pickup, Ramcharger RWD Van, Town & Country, Voyager

INTRODUCTION

Use this article to quickly find specifications related to servicing and on-vehicle adjustments. This article may be used for quick reference when you are familiar with proper adjustment procedures and only need a specification.

CAPACITIES

BATTERY SPECIFICATIONS

Load Test (Amps)	[1] CCA Rating @ 0°F (Amps)	[2] Reserve Capacity (Min.)
200	400	100
250	500	110
315	625	120
375	750	125

[1] – CCA rating is current a battery can deliver for 30 seconds and maintain a terminal voltage of 7.2 volts or greater at specified temperature.

[2] – Reserve capacity is length of time a battery can deliver 25 amps and maintain a minimum terminal voltage of 10.5 volts at 80°F (27°C).

FLUID CAPACITIES (AWD & FWD)

Application	Specification
Cooling System (Includes Heater)	
2.5L	[1] 9.5 qts. (9.0L)
3.0L & 3.3L	[1] 10.0 qts. (9.5L)
Crankcase (Includes Filter)	
All Models	4.5 qts. (4.3L)
Automatic Transaxle (Dexron-II)	
A-413 (Except Fleet)	8.9 qts. (8.4L)
A-413 (Fleet Only)	9.2 qts. (8.7L)
A-413/A-670 Lock-Up	8.5 qts. (8.0L)
A-604 Lock-Up	9.1 qts. (8.6L)
Power Steering (Dexron-II)	
All	1.7 pts. (0.8L)

[1] – Add 1 qt. (.95L) if equipped with rear heater.

FLUID CAPACITIES (RWD & 4WD)

Application	Specification
Cooling System (Includes Heater)	
Dakota	
2.5L	9.8 qts. (9.3L)
3.9L	14.0 qts. (13.2L)
5.2L (Dakota)	14.3 qts. (13.5L)
All Others	
2.5L & 3.9	15.1 qts. (14.3L)
5.2L (Except AW-150)	17.0 qts. (16.1L)
5.2L (AW-150)	16.5 qts. (15.6L)
5.9L (Except AW-150)	[1] 15.5 qts. (14.7L)
5.9L (AW-150)	15.0 qts. (14.2L)
Crankcase (Includes Filter)	
All	4.5 qts. (4.3L)
Transfer Case (Dexron-II)	
NP-205	4.5 pts. (2.1L)
NP-231	2.5 pts. (1.2L)
NP-241	6.0 pts. (2.8L)
Rear Axle (SAE 80W-90/API GL-4)	
Chrysler 7 1/4"	3.0 pts. (1.4L)
Chrysler 8 1/4"	4.4 pts. (2.1L)
Chrysler 9 1/4"	4.5 pts. (2.1L)
Dana 60	6.0 pts. (2.8L)
Dana 70	7.0 pts. (3.3L)
Front Axle (SAE 80W-90/API GL-4)	
Dakota	2.6 pts. (1.2L)
All Others	
Spicer 44FBJ	5.6 pts. (2.6L)
Spicer 60F	6.5 pts. (3.1L)

[1] – Add 1 qt. (.95L) if equipped with rear heater.

FLUID CAPACITIES (RWD & 4WD) (Cont.)

Application	Specification
Automatic Transmission (Dexron-II)	
A-500 (3.9L & 5.2L)	5.2 qts. (4.4L)
A-518 (5.2L & 5.9L)	10.2 qts. (9.6L)
A-727 (5.9L)	8.4 qts. (7.9L)
A-998 (3.9L)	8.6 qts. (8.1L)
A-999 (5.2L)	8.6 qts. (8.1L)
Manual Transmission (SAE 5W-30 SG/API GL-4)	
NP-435 (4-Speed)	3.5 qts. (3.3L)
NP-2500 (5-Speed)	2.0 qts. (1.9L)
Getrag 360 (5-speed)	3.5 qts. (3.3L)
Power Steering (DOT-3 Grade)	
Dakota RWD	1.7 pts. (0.8L)
Dakota 4WD	2.5 pts. (1.2L)
All Others	2.7 pts. (1.3L)

QUICK-SERVICE

SERVICE INTERVALS & SPECIFICATIONS

REPLACEMENT INTERVALS (AWD & FWD)

Component	Interval (Miles)
2.5L, 3.0L & 3.3L	
Air Filter	30,000
Coolant	[1] 52,500
Oil	7500
Oil Filter	[2] 15,000
Spark Plugs	30,000

[1] – Every 30,000 thereafter.

[2] – If mileage is less than 7500 miles (5000 miles on turbo) each 12 months, replace filter at each oil change.

REPLACEMENT INTERVALS (RWD & 4WD)

Component	Interval (Miles)
Light-Duty Service	
Air Filter	30,000
Coolant	30,000
Fuel Filter	As Necessary
Oil	7500
Oil Filter	[1] 15,000
Spark Plugs	30,000
Heavy-Duty Service	
Air Filter	24,000
Coolant	30,000
Fuel Filter	As Necessary
Oil	6000
Oil Filter	12,000
Spark Plugs	30,000

[1] – If mileage is less than 7500 miles each 12 months, replace filter at each oil change.

4-CYLINDER BELT ADJUSTMENT

Application	Tension Lbs. (kg)
2.5L	
A/C Compressor	
New Belt	125 (56.7)
Used Belt	80 (36.3)
Alternator/Water Pump Poly "V"	
New Belt	130 (59.0)
Used Belt	80 (36.3)
Power Steering Pump	
New Belt	105 (47.6)
Used Belt	80 (36.3)

1991 ENGINE PERFORMANCE
Service & Adjustment Specifications – Gasoline (Cont.)

V6 BELT ADJUSTMENT

Application	Tension Lbs. (kg)
3.0L	
A/C Compressor	
New Belt	125 (56.7)
Used Belt	80 (36.3)
Alternator/Water & Power Steering Pumps	
New or Used Belt	Dynamic Tensioner
3.3L	
New or Used Belt	Dynamic Tensioner
3.9L	
All Belts	
New Belt	100-140 (45.4-63.5)
Used Belt	60-90 (27.2-40.9)

V8 BELT ADJUSTMENT

Application	Tension Lbs. (kg)
5.2L & 5.9L	
All Belts	
New Belt	100-140 (45.4-63.5)
Used Belt	60-90 (27.2-40.9)

MECHANICAL CHECKS

ENGINE COMPRESSION

Check engine compression with engine at normal operating temperature at specified cranking speed, all spark plugs removed and throttle wide open.

COMPRESSION SPECIFICATIONS

Application	Specification
Compression Ratio	
2.5L	8.9:1
3.0L	8.85:1
3.3L	8.9:1
3.9L	9.0:1
5.2L	9.0:1
5.9L	8.1:1
Compression Pressure	
3.0L	[1] 178 psi (12.5 kg/cm²)
All Other Engines	[2] 100 psi (7.0 kg/cm²)

[1] – At 250 RPM.
[2] – Minimum compression pressure is given. Maximum difference between each cylinder should not exceed 25 percent.

VALVE CLEARANCE

All engines are equipped with hydraulic lifters and do not require valve adjustment. Valve clearance is zero lash with engine at operating temperature.

IGNITION SYSTEM

IGNITION COIL

IGNITION COIL RESISTANCE – Ohms @ 70-80°F (21-27°C)

Application	Primary	Secondary
2.5L & 3.0L		
Chrysler Prestolite	1.34-1.55	9400-11,700
Diamond	0.96-0.1.18	11,300-15,300
Toyodenso	0.95-1.20	11,300-13,300
3.3L		
Diamond	0.52-0.63	11,600-15,800
Toyodenso	0.51-0.61	11,500-13,500
3.9L, 5.2L & 5.9L		
Chrysler Essex	1.34-1.55	9000-12,200
Chrysler UTC	1.34-1.55	9000-12,200
Diamond	1.34-1.55	15,000-19,000

HIGH TENSION WIRE RESISTANCE

HIGH TENSION WIRE RESISTANCE

Application	Minimum Ohms	Maximum Ohms
All Wires	250 Per Inch	1000 Per Inch

SPARK PLUGS

SPARK PLUG TYPE

Application	Champion No.
2.5L	RN12YC
3.0L	
Standard	RN11YC4
Optional	BPR5ES-II
3.3L	RN16YC5
3.9L	RN12YC
5.2L & 5.9L	RN12YC

SPARK PLUG SPECIFICATIONS

Application	Gap In. (mm)	Torque Ft. Lbs. (N.m)
2.5L	.036 (.91)	20 (28)
3.0L	.041 (1.00)	20 (28)
3.3L	.050 (1.27)	20 (28)
3.9L, 5.2L & 5.9L	.035 (.89)	30 (41)

FIRING ORDER & TIMING MARKS

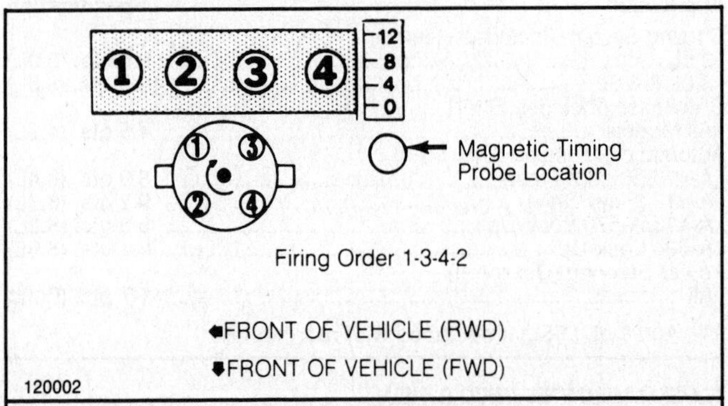
12
8
4
0
Magnetic Timing Probe Location
Firing Order 1-3-4-2
FRONT OF VEHICLE (RWD)
FRONT OF VEHICLE (FWD)
120002

Fig. 1: Firing Order & Distributor Rotation (2.5L)

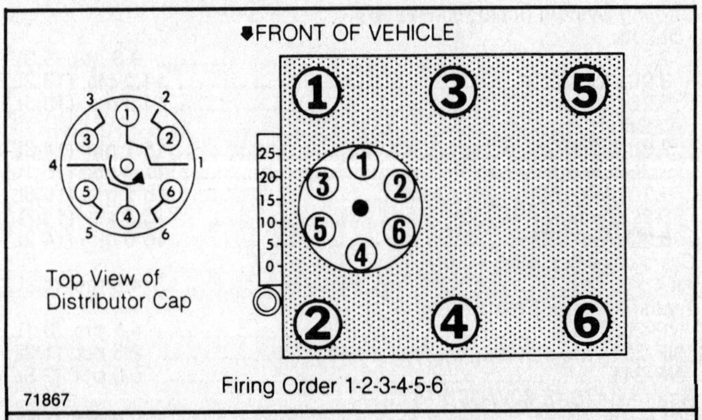
FRONT OF VEHICLE
Top View of Distributor Cap
Firing Order 1-2-3-4-5-6
71867

Fig. 2: Firing Order & Distributor Rotation (3.0L)

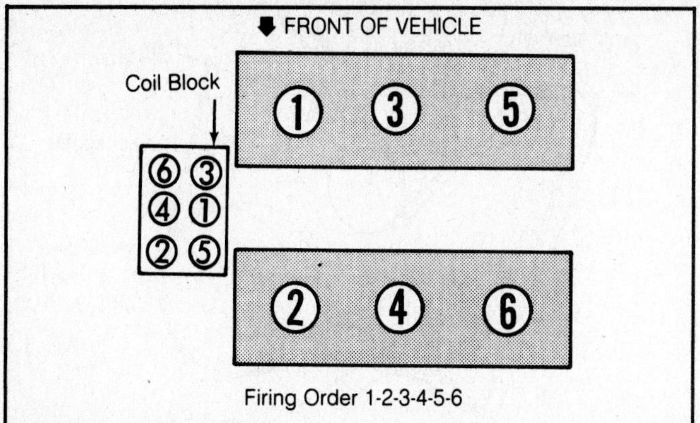

FRONT OF VEHICLE
Coil Block
Firing Order 1-2-3-4-5-6

91B13574

Fig. 3: Firing Order (3.3L)

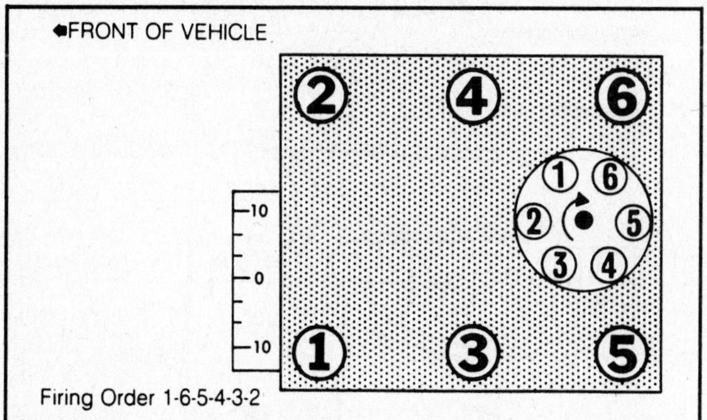

FRONT OF VEHICLE
Firing Order 1-6-5-4-3-2

71868

Fig. 4: Firing Order & Distributor Rotation (3.9L)

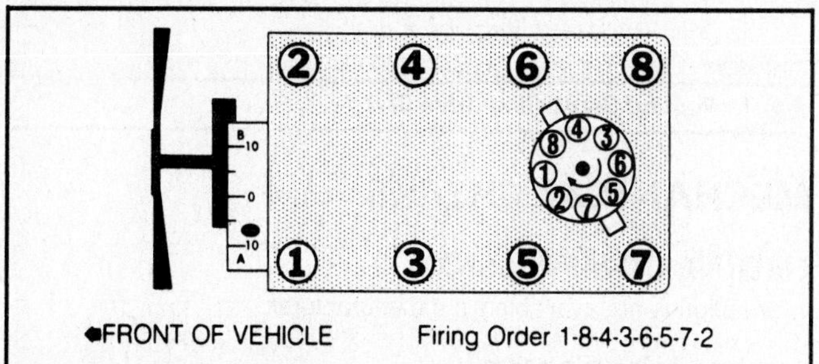

FRONT OF VEHICLE
Firing Order 1-8-4-3-6-5-7-2

9036

Fig. 5: Firing Order & Distributor Rotation (5.2L & 5.9L)

IGNITION TIMING

IGNITION TIMING (Degrees BTDC @ RPM)

Application	Man. Trans.	Auto. Trans.
2.5L	10-14 @ 850	10-14 @ 850
3.0L	.....	10-14 @ 700
3.3L	.....	[1] 14-18 @ 750
3.9L, 5.2L & 5.9L	[2] 8-12	[2] 8-12

[1] – Ignition timing is not adjustable.
[2] – At idle.

ELECTRONIC SPARK ADVANCE CHECK

***NOTE:* Always refer to Emissions Control Label in engine compartment before attempting service. If manual and label differ, always use emission label specifications.**

ELECTRONIC SPARK ADVANCE (Degrees BTDC @ RPM)

Application	Man. Trans.	Auto. Trans.
2.5L	17-25 @ 2000	17-25 @ 2000
3.0L	.....	34-42 @ 2000
3.3L [1]		
Federal	.....	24-32 @ 2000
California	.....	33-41 @ 2000
3.9L, 5.2L & 5.9L	N/A	N/A

[1] – Ignition timing is not adjustable.

FUEL SYSTEM

FUEL PUMP

***NOTE:* Fuel pump performance means fuel pressure and volume availability, not regulated fuel pressure.**

FUEL PUMP PERFORMANCE

Application	Pressure psi (kg/cm²)
2.5L	39 (2.7)
3.0L & 3.3L	48 (3.4)
3.9L, 5.2L & 5.9L	14.5 (1.0)

IDLE SPEED & MIXTURE

***NOTE:* Mixture is controlled by Single Board Engine Controller (SBEC). No adjustment is possible.**

CURB IDLE SPEED (RPM)

Application	Man. Trans.	Auto. Trans.
2.5L	850	850
3.0L	.....	700
3.3L	.....	750
3.9L, 5.2L & 5.9L	N/A	N/A

4-CYLINDER MINIMUM AIRFLOW RATE SPECIFICATIONS

Application	RPM
2.5L	1050-1250

V6 MINIMUM AIRFLOW RATE SPECIFICATIONS

Application	RPM
3.0L	750-950
3.3L & 3.9L	700-950

THROTTLE POSITION SENSOR

THROTTLE POSITION SENSOR VOLTAGE TEST

Terminals	Volts
All Models [1]	
At Idle	1.5
At Wide Open Throttle	3.4

[1] – Measure voltage at throttle position sensor center terminal.

1991 ENGINE PERFORMANCE
Service & Adjustment Specifications – Diesel

Pickup

INTRODUCTION

Use this article to quickly find specifications related to servicing and on-vehicle adjustments. This is a quick-reference article to use when you are familiar with an adjustment procedure and only need a specification.

CAPACITIES

BATTERY SPECIFICATIONS

Application	Cold Cranking Amperage
All Models	1025

FLUID CAPACITIES [1]

Application	Quantity
Cooling System (Includes Heater) [2]	
A/T	16.5 qts. (15.7L)
M/T	15.5 qts. (14.7L)
Crankcase (Includes Filter) [3]	12.0 qts. (11.4L)
Automatic Transmission (Dexron-II) [4]	
A518 & A727	11.0 qts. (10.4L)
Manual Transmission (SAE 5W-30 API SG or SG/CD)	
G360	3.5 qts. (3.3L)
Power Steering (Dexron-II)	2.7 pts. (1.3L)
Transfer Case [5]	
NP205	4.5 pts. (2.1L)
Front Axle [5]	6.5 pts. (3.1L)
Rear Axle [5]	7.0 pts. (3.3L)

1 – All capacities are approximate.
2 – Add 1 qt. (.95L) for coolant recovery tank.
3 – Engine oil must meet API rating of CC/CD-SF, CD/SF, CE/SF or CE/SG. Use 15W-40 weight oil for temperatures exceeding 10°F (-12°C) and 10W-30 for temperature less than 10°F (-12°C). Maximum sulfated ash content of 1.85% is recommended. DO NOT use single grade oil.
4 – Torque converters do not have drain plugs. DO NOT attempt to install drain plug. Add approximate amount of fluid and check fluid level several times while filling, and add fluid if necessary. Capacity is only approximate.
5 – Use gear oil with API rating of GL-5. Use SAE 140 for temperatures greater than 90°F (32°C). Use SAE 90 for temperatures between -10°F (-23°C) and 90°F (32°C). Use SAE 80 for temperatures less than -10°F (-23°C).

QUICK-SERVICE

SERVICE INTERVALS & SPECIFICATIONS

ADJUSTMENT OR REPLACEMENT INTERVALS

Component	Interval
Adjust Bands (A/T)	12 Months Or 12,000 Miles
Adjust Valve Clearance	24 Months Or 24,000 Miles
Air Filter	24 Months Or 24,000 Miles
Automatic Transmission	
Fluid & Filter	12 Months Or 12,000 Miles
Coolant	24 Months Or 24,000 Miles
Fuel Filter	12 Months Or 12,000 Miles
Oil & Filter	6 Months Or 6000 Miles

BELT ADJUSTMENT

A single serpentine drive belt is used. Proper belt tension is maintained by automatic belt tensioner. Ensure serpentine drive belt is properly routed. *See Fig. 1.*

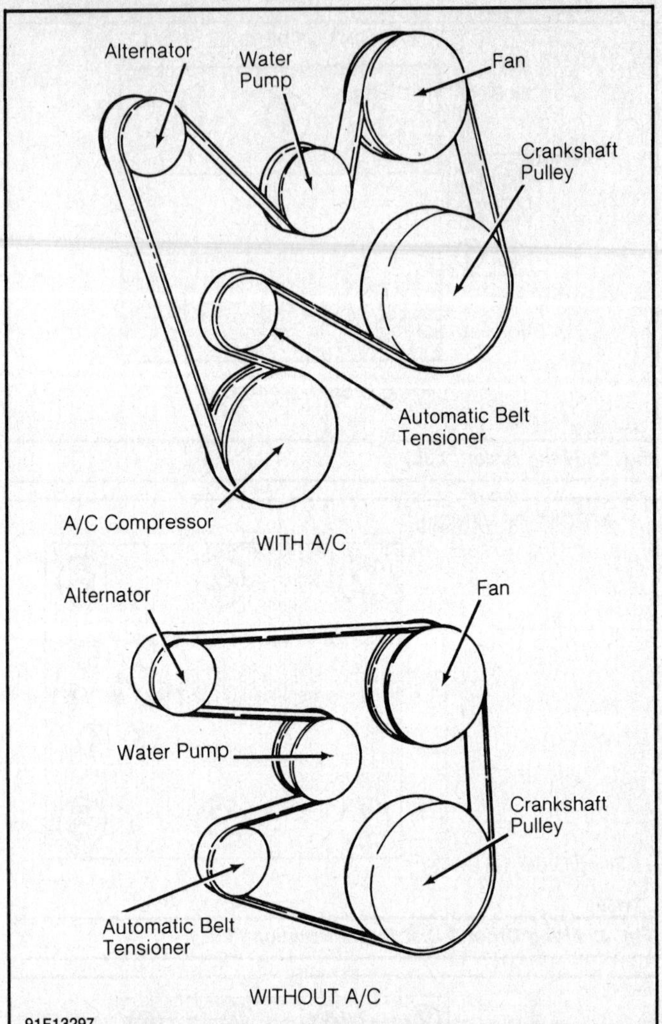
Alternator
Water Pump
Fan
Crankshaft Pulley
Automatic Belt Tensioner
A/C Compressor
WITH A/C
Alternator
Fan
Water Pump
Crankshaft Pulley
Automatic Belt Tensioner
WITHOUT A/C
91F13297
Fig. 1: Routing Serpentine Drive Belt

MECHANICAL CHECKS

ENGINE COMPRESSION

Information is not available from manufacturer.

VALVE CLEARANCE

Valve clearance must be adjusted with engine temperature less than 140°F (60°C). For valve clearance adjusting procedure, see ON-VEHICLE ADJUSTMENTS – DIESEL article in ENGINE PERFORMANCE.

VALVE ADJUSTING SEQUENCE [1]

Procedure	Cylinder Numbers
Step 1 [2]	
Exhaust Valves	1, 3 & 5
Intake Valves	1, 2 & 4
Step 2 [3]	
Exhaust Valves	2, 4 & 6
Intake Valves	3, 5 & 6

1 – Adjust valves with engine temperature less than 140°F (60°C).
2 – Adjust with timing pin engaged and No. 1 cylinder at TDC.
3 – Engine rotated 360 degrees from TDC of No. 1 cylinder and reference marks aligned.

1991 ENGINE PERFORMANCE
Service & Adjustment Specifications – Diesel (Cont.)

VALVE CLEARANCE SPECIFICATIONS [1]

Application	In. (mm)
Exhaust Valves	.020 (.51)
Intake Valves	.010 (.25)

[1] – Adjust valves with engine temperature less than 140°F (60°C).

FIRING ORDER

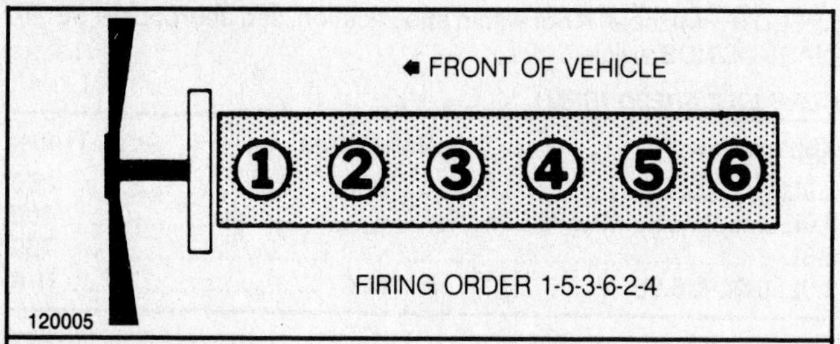

FRONT OF VEHICLE
1
2
3
4
5
6
FIRING ORDER 1-5-3-6-2-4
120005

Fig. 2: Firing Order

FUEL SYSTEM

FUEL INJECTOR

Fuel injector must have correct opening pressure. See FUEL INJECTOR OPENING PRESSURE table.

FUEL INJECTOR OPENING PRESSURE

Application	psi (kg/cm²)
Intercooled Models [1]	3625 (255)
Non-Intercooled Models	3550 (249)

[1] – In mid-year, an intercooler was installed in front of radiator.

FUEL INJECTION PUMP TIMING

See ON-VEHICLE ADJUSTMENTS – DIESEL article in ENGINE PERFORMANCE.

FUEL LIFT PUMP

For fuel lift pump testing procedure, see SYSTEM & COMPONENT TESTING – DIESEL article in ENGINE PERFORMANCE.

FUEL LIFT PUMP SPECIFICATIONS

Application	Output
Pump Pressure	3 psi Minimum (.2 kg/cm²)
Volume Within 30 Seconds	.7 qts. (.6L)

LOW IDLE SPEED

For low idle speed adjusting procedure, see ON-VEHICLE ADJUSTMENTS – DIESEL article in ENGINE PERFORMANCE.

LOW IDLE SPEED SPECIFICATIONS [1]

Application	RPM
A/T	700
M/T	750

[1] – Check low idle speed with A/C on.

FULL THROTTLE SPEED

Check full throttle speed with A/C on. If engine will not meet full throttle speed and low-pressure fuel system and fuel injectors are operating correctly, fuel injection pump must be removed for service. See FULL THROTTLE SPEED SPECIFICATIONS table.

FULL THROTTLE SPEED SPECIFICATIONS [1]

Application	RPM
All Models	2825-2925

[1] – Check with A/C on.

THROTTLE POSITION SENSOR (TPS)

NOTE: Throttle position sensor is only used on intercooled models with automatic transmissions.

For throttle position sensor adjusting procedure, see ON-VEHICLE ADJUSTMENTS – DIESEL article in ENGINE PERFORMANCE.

TURBOCHARGER

For turbocharger testing procedures, see SYSTEM & COMPONENT TESTING – DIESEL article in ENGINE PERFORMANCE.

TURBOCHARGER SPECIFICATIONS

Application	In. (mm)
Shaft Clearances	
End Play	[1]
Radial Clearance	.012-.018 (.30-.46)
Turbine Shaft Minimum O.D.	.432 (10.97)

[1] – On turbochargers with serial No. 840637 and earlier, end play should be .004-.006" (.10-.15 mm). On turbochargers with serial No. 840638 and later, end play should be .001-.003" (.03-.08 mm).

1991 ENGINE PERFORMANCE
On-Vehicle Adjustments – Gasoline

Caravan, Dakota, Pickup, Ramcharger, RWD Van, Town & Country, Voyager

ENGINE MECHANICAL

Before performing any on-vehicle adjustments to fuel or ignition systems, ensure engine mechanical condition is okay.

VALVE CLEARANCE

NOTE: All engines use hydraulic lifters. No adjustments are required.

IGNITION TIMING

NOTE: Always refer to Emission Control Information Label in engine compartment before service. If manual and emission label differ, always use emission label specifications. Basic timing is not adjustable on 3.3L.

ALL ENGINES EXCEPT 3.3L

CAUTION: Timing light secondary connection should be made with inductive pick-up. DO NOT puncture cables, boots or nipples with test probes.

1) Connect a suitable timing light to No. 1 cylinder. Refer to equipment manufacturer's instructions for proper connection. Turn selector switch to the appropriate cylinder position.
2) Start engine and warm to normal operating temperature. Connect tachometer and ensure idle RPM is within specification. See CURB IDLE SPEED (RPM) table under IDLE SPEED & MIXTURE. Disconnect engine coolant sensor lead wire. Radiator fan should come on and CHECK ENGINE light should illuminate.
3) Check timing through timing window in bellhousing on 4-cylinder models or crankshaft pulley for other engines. See IGNITION TIMING table. DO NOT adjust timing if it is within 2 degrees of specification. If timing is incorrect, loosen distributor hold-down bolt and turn housing until specified timing is obtained.
4) Recheck timing after tightening distributor hold-down bolt. Reconnect coolant lead wire. Erase any fault codes. Recheck curb idle and adjust (if necessary). Remove diagnostic equipment.

IGNITION TIMING (Degrees BTDC @ RPM)

Application	Man. Trans.	Auto. Trans.
2.5L	10-14 @ 850	10-14 @ 850
3.0L	......	10-14 @ 700
3.3L	......	14-18 @ 750
3.9L, 5.2L & 5.9L	[1] 8-12	[1] 8-12

[1] – At idle.

IDLE SPEED & MIXTURE

NOTE: Mixture is controlled by Single Board Engine Controller (SBEC). No adjustment is possible.

Electronically fuel injected vehicles use an Automatic Idle Speed (AIS) motor or Idle Speed Control (ISC) actuator to regulate idle RPM. AIS or ISC is controlled by SBEC, which uses information received from various sensors to determine, among other things, idle speed. Curb idle speed is not adjustable. See appropriate SELF-DIAGNOSTICS article for diagnosis of incorrect idle speed.

IDLE RPM TEST

NOTE: Engine idle set RPM should be tested and recorded when vehicle is first brought into shop for testing. This will assist in diagnosing complaints of engine stalling, creeping and hard shifting on vehicles equipped with automatic transmissions.

1) Connect tachometer Red lead to coil negative (–) terminal and tachometer Black lead to a chassis ground.
2) Turn selector switch to appropriate cylinder position of engine being tested. Start engine and warm to normal operating temperature.
3) Turn tachometer RPM switch to 1000 RPM position.
4) With engine at normal operating temperature, momentarily open throttle and release to ensure linkage is not binding and throttle lever is fully against its stop.
5) Note engine RPM, and compare with specification. See CURB IDLE SPEED (RPM) table. If not within specification, see appropriate SELF-DIAGNOSTICS article.

CURB IDLE SPEED (RPM)

Application	Man. Trans.	Auto. Trans.
2.5L	850	850
3.0L	.....	700
3.3L	.....	750
3.9L, 5.2L & 5.9L	N/A	N/A

MINIMUM AIRFLOW

NOTE: Minimum airflow testing procedures are provided for 2.5L, 3.0L, 3.3L & 3.9L engines equipped with Automatic Idle Speed (AIS) motor on throttle body.

1) Warm engine to normal operating temperature. Disconnect and plug heated air door vacuum hose. Connect timing light and tachometer. Disconnect engine coolant temperature sensor. Set basic timing to 10-14 degrees BTDC. Turn engine off. Reconnect coolant temperature sensor.
2) With engine off, disconnect hose from PCV valve, and plug PCV valve nipple. Disconnect idle purge hose from vacuum harness "T". *See Fig. 1.* Attach Air Metering Fitting (6457) to manifold-mounted idle purge hose. Orifice size is .125" (3 mm). Connect Diagnostic Readout Box II (DRB-II) to vehicle.
3) Start engine. Let engine idle for at least one minute. Using DRB-II, access MINIMUM AIRFLOW IDLE SPEED. When this mode is accessed, AIS motor will fully close, spark advance will fix, fuel delivery will not change and engine RPM will be displayed on DRB-II.
4) Check minimum airflow. See MINIMUM AIRFLOW IDLE SPEED table. If minimum airflow idle speed is not within specification, replace throttle body.

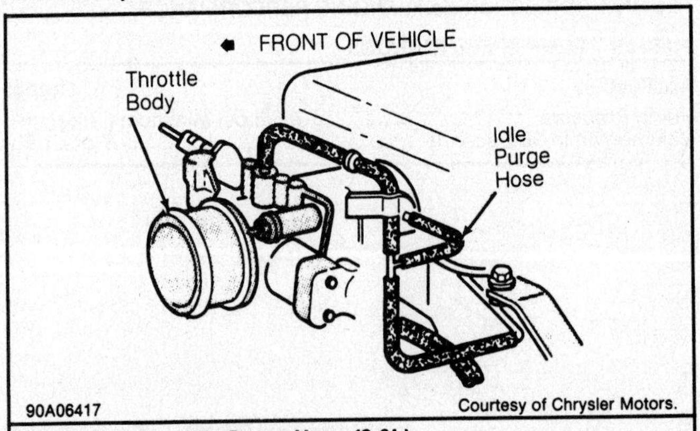
FRONT OF VEHICLE
Throttle Body
Idle Purge Hose
90A06417
Courtesy of Chrysler Motors.

Fig. 1: Locating Idle Purge Hose (3.0L)

MINIMUM AIRFLOW IDLE SPEED

Application	RPM
2.5L	1050-1250
3.0L	750-950
3.3L & 3.9L	700-950

THROTTLE POSITION SENSOR

NOTE: Throttle Position Sensor (TPS) is not adjustable. The following procedures may be used to check TPS calibration.

1) Turn ignition switch to "ON" position. DO NOT start engine. Measure voltage at center terminal of TPS, with throttle valve fully closed against stop. Voltage should be 1.5 volts or less. If voltage is not 1.5 volts or less, replace TPS.
2) Slowly open throttle valve to wide open throttle. TPS voltage should gradually increase to at least 3.4 volts. If voltage does not gradually increase to at least 3.4 volts, replace TPS.

1991 ENGINE PERFORMANCE
On-Vehicle Adjustments – Diesel

Pickup

***NOTE:** In mid-year, an intercooler was installed in front of the radiator. See Fig. 1. Note if vehicle contains an intercooler before servicing engine components. Service procedures may vary on models with intercooler.*

ENGINE COMPRESSION

Information not available from manufacturer.

VALVE CLEARANCE

***NOTE:** Valve clearance must be adjusted with engine temperature less than 140°F (60°C).*

1) Engine can be rotated by removing dust cover from transmission adapter plate and installing Engine Barring Tool (3377462) in adapter plate. *See Fig. 2.* Rotate engine clockwise until No. 1 cylinder is at TDC. Engage timing pin.

***CAUTION:** Use care when engaging timing pin to avoid breaking tip of pin. Ensure timing pin is disengaged before rotating engine.*

2) Remove rocker lever covers and ensure No. 1 cylinder push rods are loose and valves are closed. If not, disengage timing pin, and rotate engine 360 degrees in clockwise direction. With No. 1 cylinder at TDC, check clearance on proper valves. See VALVE ADJUSTING SEQUENCE table. Adjust clearance using rocker lever adjusting screw if not within specification. See VALVE CLEARANCE SPECIFICATIONS table.

3) Once correct valves are checked and adjusted, place reference marks on vibration damper and front timing gear cover. Disengage timing pin and rotate engine 360 degrees (clockwise) and realign reference marks. Clearance must be checked on proper valves. See VALVE ADJUSTING SEQUENCE table. Adjust clearance if not within specification. See VALVE CLEARANCE SPECIFICATIONS table.

VALVE ADJUSTING SEQUENCE [1]

Procedure	Cylinder Number
Step 1 [2]	
Exhaust Valves	1, 3 & 5
Intake Valves	1, 2 & 4
Step 2 [3]	
Exhaust Valves	2, 4 & 6
Intake Valves	3, 5 & 6

[1] – Adjust valves with engine temperature less than 140°F (60°C).
[2] – Adjust with engine cold, timing pin engaged and No. 1 cylinder at TDC.
[3] – Engine rotated 360 degrees from TDC of No. 1 cylinder and reference marks aligned.

VALVE CLEARANCE SPECIFICATIONS

Application	In. (mm)
Exhaust Valves	[1] .020 (.51)
Intake Valves	[1] .010 (.25)

[1] – Adjust valves with engine temperature less than 140°F (60°C).

FUEL INJECTION PUMP TIMING

***CAUTION:** Special washer must be installed under lock bolt before rotating engine to allow fuel injection pump to rotate. If special washer is not installed, loosen lock bolt and install special washer. Tighten lock bolt to 10 ft. lbs. (14 N.m). See Fig. 4.*

1) Ensure special washer is installed under lock bolt. *See Fig. 4.* Rotate engine clockwise until No. 1 cylinder is at TDC. Engage timing pin. *See Fig. 2.* Engine can be rotated by removing dust cover from transmission adapter plate and installing Engine Barring Tool (3377462) in adapter plate.

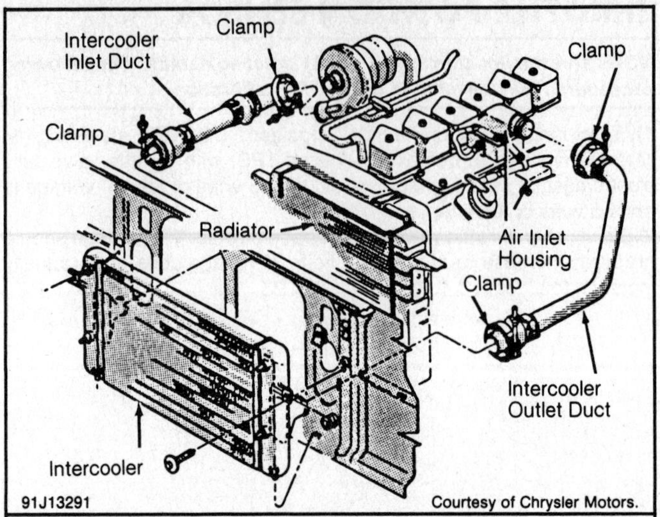
Clamp
Intercooler Inlet Duct
Clamp
Clamp
Radiator
Air Inlet Housing
Clamp
Intercooler Outlet Duct
Intercooler
91J13291
Courtesy of Chrysler Motors.

Fig. 1: Exploded View of Intercooler & Components

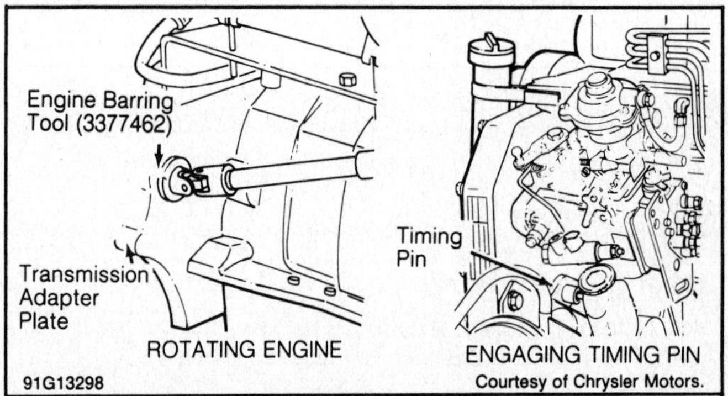
Engine Barring Tool (3377462)
Transmission Adapter Plate
ROTATING ENGINE
Timing Pin
ENGAGING TIMING PIN
91G13298
Courtesy of Chrysler Motors.

Fig. 2: Rotating Engine & Engaging Timing Pin

***CAUTION:** If it is necessary to remove some high-pressure fuel lines, ensure lines and fittings are thoroughly cleaned before removing. Cap all fuel lines and fittings when removed.*

2) Remove plug from end of fuel injection pump. Install timing indicator in end of fuel injection pump. *See Fig. 3.* If necessary, remove some high-pressure fuel lines to install timing indicator.

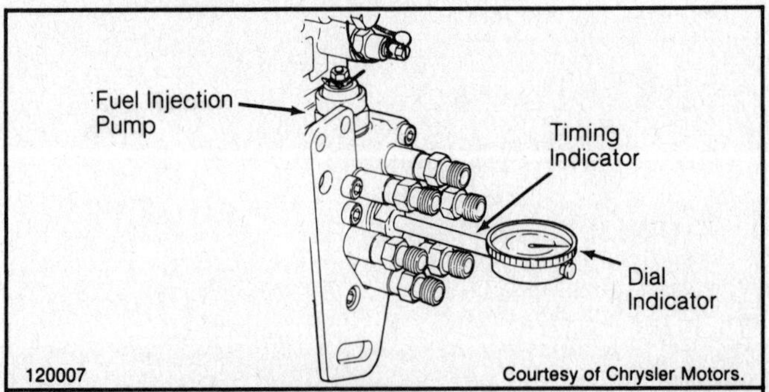
Fuel Injection Pump
Timing Indicator
Dial Indicator
120007
Courtesy of Chrysler Motors.

Fig. 3: Installing Timing Indicator

***CAUTION:** Note range of dial indicator and value of one revolution, as timing indicators may vary. Ensure timing indicator has at least .079" (2.00 mm) of travel.*

3) Disengage timing pin. DO NOT rotate engine until timing pin is disengaged. Rotate engine in opposite direction of rotation until needle on dial indicator stops moving. Adjust dial indicator to zero.

4) Rotate engine in direction of normal rotation to TDC of No. 1 cylinder, while counting number of revolutions of dial indicator. Ensure timing pin can be engaged. Current dial reading, plus previous rotations, is the plunger lift.

5) Plunger lift should be 1.25 mm for intercooled models or 1.4 mm for non-intercooler models. If lift is not within specification, loosen fuel injection pump mounting nuts, and rotate fuel injection pump on mounting studs to obtain correct plunger lift.

6) Tighten mounting nuts to 18 ft. lbs. (24 N.m). If installing new or replacement fuel injection pump is installed, place timing mark on fuel injection pump flange to align with timing mark on gear housing. *See Fig. 4.*

7) Remove timing indicator and install plug. Tighten plug to 84 INCH lbs. (10 N.m). Ensure timing pin is disengaged. Install and bleed high-pressure fuel lines. See FUEL LINE BLEEDING in REMOVAL, OVERHAUL & INSTALLATION - DIESEL article.

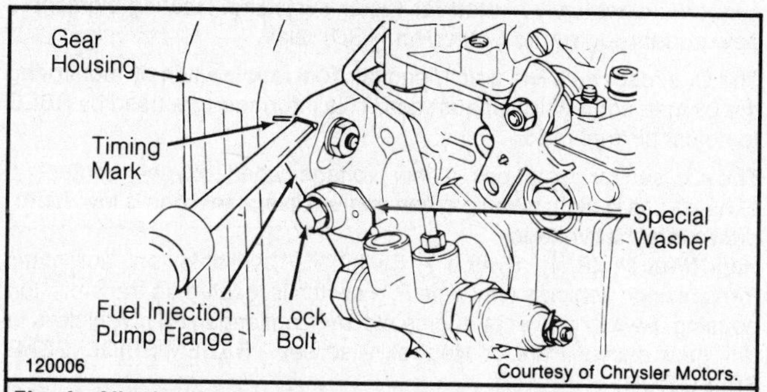
Gear
Housing
Timing
Mark
Special
Washer
Fuel Injection
Pump Flange
Lock
Bolt
120006
Courtesy of Chrysler Motors.

Fig. 4: Aligning Fuel Injection Pump Timing Marks

IDLE SPEED

LOW IDLE SPEED

Using optical tachometer, ensure low idle speed is 700 RPM (A/T) or 750 RPM (M/T) with A/C on. Adjust if necessary using low idle speed screw. *See Fig. 5.*

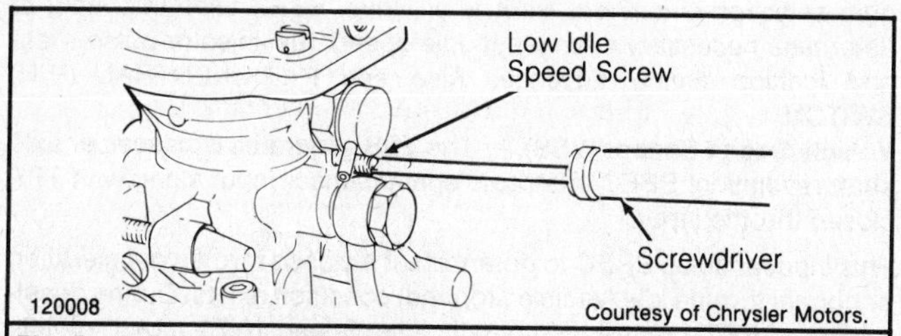
Low Idle
Speed Screw
Screwdriver
120008
Courtesy of Chrysler Motors.

Fig. 5: Adjusting Low Idle Speed

THROTTLE LINKAGE

1) Proper throttle linkage adjustment is required to obtain full travel of throttle lever. Check low idle speed before adjusting throttle linkage.

2) Using optical tachometer, ensure low idle speed is 700 RPM (A/T) or 750 RPM (M/T) with A/C on. Adjust if necessary using low idle speed screw. *See Fig. 5.* Once low idle speed is correct, disconnect throttle cable from ball on fuel injection pump.

3) Install a .020" (.51 mm) feeler gauge between throttle cam and cam stop. *See Fig. 6.* Ensure throttle lever contacts low idle speed screw and spring-loaded breakover lever has moved from stop area and is contacting breakover spring. *See Fig. 6.*

4) If low idle speed screw and breakover spring are not contacted, actuator rod must be adjusted. *See Fig. 6.* Hold rod while loosening lock nuts.

NOTE: One lock nut on actuator rod is left-hand thread. Flat area of actuator rod is marked "L" to indicate left-hand thread.

5) Adjust actuator rod to obtain correct adjustment. Tighten lock nuts. Remove feeler gauge. Reconnect throttle cable. Operate throttle and ensure breakover in both idle and full throttle positions. Ensure engine low idle speed is 700 RPM (A/T) or 750 RPM (M/T) with A/C on. Ensure full throttle speed is 2825-2925 RPM.

NOTE: If engine will does meet full throttle speed, and low pressure fuel system and fuel injectors are functioning correctly, fuel injection pump must be remove for service.

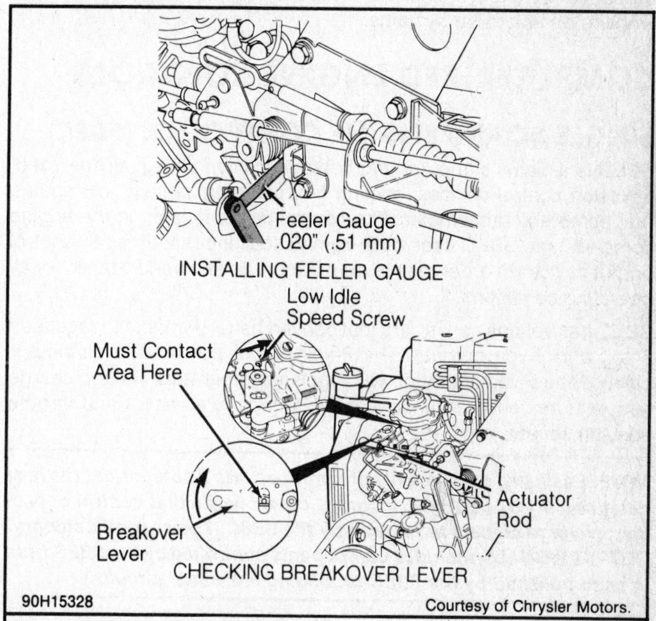
Feeler Gauge
.020" (.51 mm)
INSTALLING FEELER GAUGE
Low Idle
Speed Screw
Must Contact
Area Here
Actuator
Rod
Breakover
Lever
CHECKING BREAKOVER LEVER
90H15328
Courtesy of Chrysler Motors.

Fig. 6: Adjusting Throttle Linkage

THROTTLE POSITION SENSOR (TPS)

NOTE: Throttle Position Sensor (TPS) is used on intercooled models with A/T only.

CAUTION: Before adjusting TPS, ensure throttle linkage is properly adjusted. See THROTTLE LINKAGE.

1) Connect negative probe of voltmeter to ground. Turn ignition on. Backprobe center wire terminal at TPS electrical connector. With control lever contacting low-speed screw (idle position), voltage should be at least one volt. If voltage is not at least one volt, adjust TPS to obtain correct voltage using 10 mm wrench. *See Fig. 7.*

2) Open throttle to full throttle position. Backprobe center wire terminal at TPS electrical connector. Voltage should be at least 2.25 volts more than voltage obtained with throttle in idle position. If voltage is not at least 2.25 volts more than idle position voltage, adjust TPS to obtain correct voltage. *See Fig. 7.*

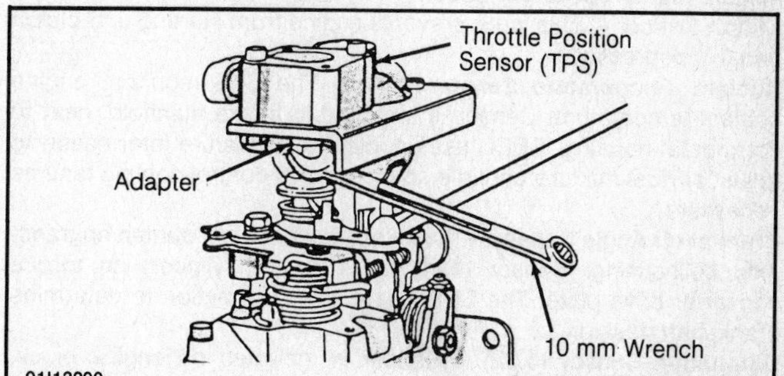
Throttle Position
Sensor (TPS)
Adapter
10 mm Wrench
91I13290
Courtesy of Chrysler Motors.

Fig. 7: Adjusting TPS

1991 ENGINE PERFORMANCE
Theory & Operation – Gasoline

Caravan, Dakota, Pickup, Ramcharger, RWD Van, Town & Country, Voyager

INTRODUCTION

This article covers the basic description and operation of engine performance related systems and components. Read this article before working on unfamiliar systems.

COMPUTERIZED ENGINE CONTROLS

SINGLE BOARD ENGINE CONTROLLER (SBEC)

SBEC is a digital computer that controls ignition timing, air/fuel ratio, emission control devices, cooling fan, charging system, idle speed, fuel pump and tachometer. The control unit is located in the engine compartment. SBEC uses data from various input sources to control output devices in order to achieve optimum engine performance for all operating conditions.

SBEC has voltage converters that convert battery voltage to regulated 5-volt and 8-volt outputs. The 8-volt output powers the distributor pickup. The 5-volt output powers coolant temperature sensor, charge temperature sensor, manifold absolute pressure sensor and throttle position sensor.

NOTE: Basically, components are grouped into 2 categories. The first category, INPUT DEVICES, includes components that control or produce voltage signals monitored by the SBEC. The second category, OUTPUT SIGNALS, includes components controlled by the SBEC (this is accomplished by the SBEC grounding individual circuits).

INPUT DEVICES

Vehicles are equipped with different combinations of input devices. Not all devices are used on all models. To determine the input usage on a specific model, see appropriate wiring diagram in WIRING DIAGRAMS article. Available input signals include the following:

A/C Switch – Switch signals SBEC that A/C has been selected. SBEC then activates A/C compressor clutch relay and maintains idle speed at a scheduled RPM. This is done through control of Idle Speed Control (ISC) actuator or Automatic Idle Speed (AIS) motor.

Battery Voltage – SBEC monitors battery voltage to determine fuel injector pulse width and alternator field control.

Brake Switch – SBEC uses this input to maintain idle speed at a scheduled RPM when brakes are applied.

Camshaft Angle Sensor – Camshaft angle sensor is mounted on top of timing chain cover. This sensor reads slots in cam timing sprocket. The SBEC uses this information along with information from crankshaft sensor to determine if fuel injectors and ignition coils are properly sequenced for correct cylinders.

Charge Temperature Sensor – Sensor measures temperature of incoming intake air. This information is used by SBEC to adjust air/fuel mixture and turbocharger boost.

Clutch Switch – This input prevents engine from starting until clutch pedal is depressed.

Coolant Temperature Sensor (CTS) – The CTS monitors engine coolant temperature. Sensor is mounted in intake manifold, next to thermostat housing. SBEC uses coolant temperature information to adjust air/fuel mixture and idle speed, and to control cooling fans as necessary.

Crankshaft Angle Sensor – Crankshaft sensor is mounted on transaxle bellhousing. Sensor reads slots (4 per cylinder) on torque converter drive plate. The SBEC uses this information to determine crankshaft position.

Detonation Sensor (3.3L) – Sensor is mounted on engine block. Positioning of detonation sensor enables it to detect detonation in any cylinder. Sensor generates an input signal to SBEC when detonation occurs. The SBEC uses this input to adjust spark advance and to eliminate detonation.

Hall Effect Switch – Hall Effect switch, sometimes called a Hall Effect pick-up, is located inside distributor. This switch supplies SBEC with engine RPM data and ignition timing information. SBEC uses this information to advance or retard ignition timing as necessary.

Idle Contact Switch – Idle contact switch provides an input signal that enables SBEC to increase or decrease throttle stop angle in response to engine operating conditions.

Manifold Absolute Pressure (MAP) Sensor – The MAP sensor monitors manifold vacuum. Sensor transmits information on manifold vacuum and barometric pressure to SBEC. MAP sensor information is used with information from other sensors to adjust air/fuel mixture.

Optical Distributor (3.0L) – Optical distributor provides engine speed and crankshaft position signals. SBEC uses this information to control fuel injection, ignition timing and idle speed.

Oxygen (O_2) Sensor – The O_2 sensor produces a small electrical voltage (.1-.9 volt) when exposed to oxygen in exhaust gas flow. O_2 sensor is electrically heated for faster switching. Heating element is powered through Auto Shutdown (ASD) relay.

The O_2 sensor acts like a rich/lean (air/fuel ratio) switch by monitoring the oxygen content in exhaust gas. This information is used by SBEC to adjust air/fuel ratio.

The O_2 sensor produces a low voltage when oxygen content in exhaust gas is high; when oxygen content in exhaust gas is low, it produces a higher voltage.

Park/Neutral (P/N) Switch – Switch is available on automatic transmission vehicles only. The P/N switch is located on transmission housing. Switch prevents engine starter from engaging if vehicle is in any gear except Park or Neutral. Also see TRANSMISSION GEAR SELECTION.

Throttle Body Temperature Sensor (5.2L & 5.9L) – Sensor is mounted in throttle body. Sensor monitors throttle body temperature so SBEC can adjust air/fuel mixture for a hot restart condition.

Throttle Position Sensor (TPS) – TPS is mounted on throttle body and monitors opening angle of throttle valve. Sensor varies its output voltage according to angle of throttle blade opening. SBEC uses this information and other sensor inputs to adjust air/fuel ratio.

Transmission Gear Selection – The P/N safety switch on the transmission housing provides an input to SBEC to indicate if transmission gear selection is in Park, Neutral or Drive. SBEC uses this input to determine necessary changes to idle speed, fuel injector pulse width and ignition timing advance. Also see PARK/NEUTRAL (P/N) SWITCH.

Vehicle Speed Sensor (VSS) – The VSS generates 8 pulses per axle shaft revolution. SBEC interprets speed sensor input along with TPS closed throttle input.

This input enables SBEC to determine if a closed throttle deceleration or normal throttle idle (vehicle stopped) condition exists. During deceleration, SBEC controls Automatic Idle Speed (AIS) motor or Idle Speed Control (ISC) actuator to maintain a desired manifold pressure. During idle (vehicle stopped), SBEC controls AIS motor or ISC actuator to maintain a desired idle speed.

OUTPUT SIGNALS

NOTE: Each vehicle may be equipped with different combinations of computer-controlled components. The following components may NOT be used on all models. For theory and operation on each output component, refer to the indicated system under appropriate heading.

A/C Clutch Relay – See MISCELLANEOUS CONTROLS.

Air Switching Solenoid – See AIR INJECTION SYSTEM under EMISSION SYSTEMS.

Alternator – See MISCELLANEOUS CONTROLS.

Automatic Idle Speed (AIS) Motor – See IDLE SPEED under FUEL SYSTEM.

Auto Shutdown (ASD) Relay – See MISCELLANEOUS CONTROLS.

Canister Purge Solenoid – See EVAPORATIVE EMISSION SYSTEM under EMISSION SYSTEMS.

CHECK ENGINE Light – See SELF-DIAGNOSTIC SYSTEM.

Electric EGR Transducer (EET) – See EXHAUST GAS RECIRCULATION (EGR) SYSTEM under EMISSION SYSTEMS.

Emission Maintenance Reminder (EMR) Light – See EMISSION MAINTENANCE REMINDER LIGHT under EMISSION SYSTEMS.
Exhaust Gas Recirculation (EGR) Solenoid – See EXHAUST GAS RECIRCULATION (EGR) SYSTEM under EMISSION SYSTEMS.
Fuel Injectors – See FUEL CONTROL under FUEL SYSTEM.
Idle Speed Control (ISC) Actuator – See IDLE SPEED under FUEL SYSTEM.
Direct Ignition System – See IGNITION SYSTEM.
Optical Ignition System – See IGNITION SYSTEM.
Magnetic Ignition System (Hall Effect) – See IGNITION SYSTEM.
In-Tank Fuel Pump – See FUEL DELIVERY under FUEL SYSTEM.
Limp-In Mode – See MISCELLANEOUS CONTROLS.
Lock-Up Torque Converter Solenoid – See MISCELLANEOUS CONTROLS.
Overdrive Solenoid – See MISCELLANEOUS CONTROLS.
Radiator Fan Relay – See MISCELLANEOUS CONTROLS.
Speed Control Servo – See MISCELLANEOUS CONTROLS.

FUEL SYSTEM

FUEL DELIVERY

Auto Shutdown (ASD) Relay – See AUTO SHUTDOWN (ASD) RELAY under MISCELLANEOUS CONTROLS.

Fuel Pressure Damper (3.3L) – Damper is located downstream of fuel pressure regulator. *See Fig. 1.* Damper dampens fuel pressure pulsations caused by injectors opening and closing to keep fuel pressure constant across injectors. Pressure pulses are absorbed by an internal rubber diaphragm with air pocket on one side.

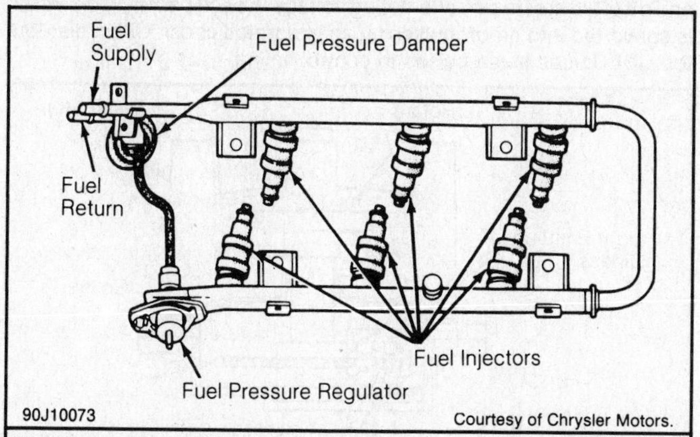
Fuel Supply
Fuel Pressure Damper
Fuel Return
Fuel Injectors
Fuel Pressure Regulator
90J10073
Courtesy of Chrysler Motors.

Fig. 1: Fuel Pressure Damper & Fuel Pressure Regulator (3.3L)

Fuel Pressure Regulator – Fuel pressure regulator is a mechanical device. Pressure regulator is located on top of throttle body on TBI engines. Pressure regulator is located on fuel injector rail on PFI engines. Regulator maintains constant fuel pressure across injectors. See FUEL PRESSURE table.

Inside pressure regulator is a spring-loaded diaphragm. *See Fig. 2.* When fuel pump is energized, fuel flows past fuel injectors into fuel pressure regulator. Pressure regulator restricts fuel from flowing any farther until proper pressure has been reached.

When proper fuel pressure is reached, fuel pressure pushes on a spring behind diaphragm. As fuel pressure moves spring and diaphragm, a return line to fuel tank is uncovered. This allows excess fuel to return to fuel tank, keeping fuel pressure constant across injectors.

In-Tank Fuel Pump (TBI) – Fuel pump is an immersible electric pump with permanent magnet motor. The pump incorporates a sock attached to pump pick-up. Fuel pump also contains a check valve which restricts fuel movement in either direction to maintain fuel line pressure when pump is not operating. Voltage to operate pump is supplied through ASD relay.

In-Tank Fuel Pump (PFI) – Fuel pump is a positive displacement, immersible gerotor pump with a permanent magnet motor. The pump incorporates a filter sock attached to pump pick-up. This fuel pump contains 2 check valves. One check valve is used to relieve internal pump pressure and regulate maximum fuel pump output. The other check valve, located near pump outlet, is used to restrict fuel movement in either direction when pump is not operational. Voltage to operate pump is supplied through ASD relay.

FUEL PRESSURE

Application	psi (kg/cm²)
2.5L	39 (2.7)
3.0L & 3.3L	48 (3.4)
3.9L, 5.2L & 5.9L	14.5 (1.0)

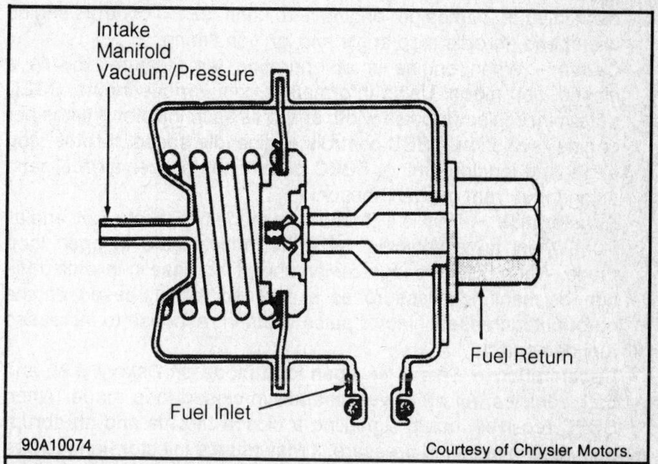
Intake Manifold Vacuum/Pressure
Fuel Return
Fuel Inlet
90A10074
Courtesy of Chrysler Motors.

Fig. 2: Cutaway View of Typical Fuel Pressure Regulator

FUEL CONTROL

Fuel Injectors – Fuel injectors are powered by electric solenoids and controlled by SBEC. SBEC determines when and time injectors should operate. Current is supplied to injectors through ASD relay, which is controlled by SBEC. When ground is supplied to injector by SBEC, armature and pintle inside injector move a short distance against spring and open a small orifice. Since fuel is under high pressure, a fine spray is developed.

Modes Of Operation – As input signals to SBEC change, SBEC adjusts its response to the output devices. Modes of operation come in 2 types, open loop and closed loop. In open loop mode, SBEC is not using input from oxygen sensor and is responding to preset programming to determine injector pulse width and ignition timing. In closed loop mode, SBEC is adjusting ignition timing and using the input from oxygen sensor to fine tune injector pulse width.

The following inputs are used to determine SBEC mode.

- Coolant Temperature Sensor (CTS)
- Idle Contact Switch
- MAP Sensor
- Engine Speed
- Throttle Position Sensor (TPS)
- Gear Position
- A/C Switch
- Battery Voltage
- Oxygen (O_2) Sensor
- A/C Control Positions

From these inputs, SBEC determines which mode vehicle is in and the appropriate response. Not all inputs are used in all modes. The 8 modes of operation are as follows:

- **Ignition Switch On** – This is an open loop mode. SBEC determines atmospheric pressure from MAP sensor and determines basic fuel strategy. SBEC modifies fuel strategy according to coolant temperature input.
- **Engine Start-Up** – This is an open loop mode. When starter is engaged, SBEC receives distributor signal and energizes Auto Shutdown (ASD) relay. See AUTO SHUTDOWN (ASD) RELAY under MISCELLANEOUS CONTROLS. Once ASD relay is

1991 ENGINE PERFORMANCE
Theory & Operation - Gasoline (Cont.)

energized, SBEC determines proper injector pulse width and ignition timing from input signals. During engine start-up, SBEC pulses each fuel injector 4 times per engine revolution instead of the normal 2 pulses per revolution.

- **Engine Warm-Up** - This is an open loop mode. SBEC determines injector pulse width using information from various inputs and fires each injector 2 times per engine revolution. SBEC controls engine idle speed, throttle stop angle and ignition timing.
- **Cruise** - When engine is at operating temperature, this is a closed loop mode. Using information from various inputs, SBEC determines injector pulse width and fires each injector 3 times per engine revolution. SBEC controls engine idle speed, throttle stop angle and ignition timing. SBEC determines proper air/fuel ratio using input from oxygen sensor.
- **Acceleration** - This is a closed loop mode on Dakota 2.5L and all front-wheel drive vehicles. All other vehicles are in open loop mode. When SBEC recognizes an abrupt increase in throttle position or manifold pressure as a demand for increased engine output, it increases injector pulse width in response to increased fuel demand.
- **Deceleration** - This is an open loop mode on Dakota 3.9L and 5.2L vehicles. All other vehicles are in closed loop mode. When SBEC receives inputs signalling a closed throttle and an abrupt decrease in manifold pressure, it may reduce injector firing to one pulse per engine revolution to lean air/fuel mixture. SBEC also prevents EGR and canister purge functions during deceleration by grounding EGR and evaporative purge solenoids. SBEC may cycle air switching solenoid for short periods of time in response to a high vacuum signal from MAP sensor.
- **Wide Open Throttle** - This is an open loop mode. When SBEC senses wide open throttle, it grounds EGR and evaporative purge solenoids to prevent EGR and canister purge functions. Oxygen sensor input is not utilized and SBEC adjusts injector pulse width to supply a predetermined amount of additional fuel.
- **Ignition Switch Off** - This is an open loop mode. All fuel injection is stopped. SBEC de-energizes auto shutdown relay and extends Idle Speed Control (ISC) actuator (if equipped) in anticipation of next start-up.

IDLE SPEED

Automatic Idle Speed Motor (2.5L, 3.0L & 3.3L) - Automatic Idle Speed (AIS) motor adjusts idle speed to compensate for engine load and ambient temperature. AIS motor does this by adjusting amount of air flowing through by-pass in throttle body. SBEC uses coolant temperature, distance (speed) sensor, throttle position and various switch input operations to adjust AIS to obtain optimum idle conditions. Deceleration stall is prevented by increasing airflow when throttle is closed suddenly.

Idle Speed Control (ISC) Actuator (3.9L, 5.2L & 5.9L) - The ISC actuator is a motor mounted to throttle body and controlled by SBEC. Using inputs from various engine control system sensors, SBEC extends or retracts actuator to control engine idle speed and to set throttle stop angle during deceleration.

NOTE: DO NOT attempt to correct a high idle speed condition by turning ISC adjustment screw. This will not change idle speed of warm engine, but may cause cold start problems due to restricted airflow.

IGNITION SYSTEM

DIRECT IGNITION SYSTEM (3.3L)

A Direct Ignition System (DIS) eliminates mechanical ignition components that can wear out. SBEC has complete ignition control and uses crankshaft and camshaft sensors to control ignition timing. Crankshaft position sensor senses slots (4 per cylinder, 20 degrees apart) around an extension of the drive plate. Basic timing is preset by crankshaft sensor position and is not adjustable. By using a crankshaft sensor, spark scatter has been eliminated.

A cam sensor is located on timing chain cover. Cam sensor senses slots on cam timing gear. Fuel injection synchronization and cylinder identification are provided through cam sensor. The unique combination of slots on cam gear are used to identify individual cylinders and initiate fuel and spark for start and run conditions.

This system uses 3 molded coils mounted on the intake manifold. Coil fires 2 spark plugs every power stroke. One cylinder is on compression stroke and the other cylinder is on exhaust stroke. A low primary resistance allows SBEC to fully charge ignition coil for each firing.

OPTICAL IGNITION SYSTEM (3.0L)

The timing member is a thin disk mounted on distributor shaft and driven at 1/2 crankshaft speed. Disk has 2 sets of slots on its surface. The outer, high data rate set of slots is positioned at intervals of 2 degrees of crankshaft rotation. Disk is used for ignition timing at engine speeds up to 1200 RPM to increase timing accuracy.

During cranking and idle, engine speed changes with firing pulse of each cylinder. High data rate signal is used to trigger ignition at correct crankshaft position regardless of these speed changes.

The inner, low data rate set contains 6 slots, which are correlated to piston TDC for each cylinder. This set is used to trigger fuel injection system operation at speeds greater than 1200 RPM, where speed changes because individual firing pulses are small. This set of slots is also used for ignition timing. Light Emitting Diodes (LED's) and photo diodes are mounted in facing positions on opposite sides of disk, in-line with slots. *See Fig. 3.*

Masks over LED's and photo diodes focus light beams onto photo diodes. As each slot passes between diodes, light beam is turned on and off. This creates an alternating voltage in each photo diode, which is converted into on-off pulses by an integrated circuit within distributor. SBEC uses these pulses to control timing.

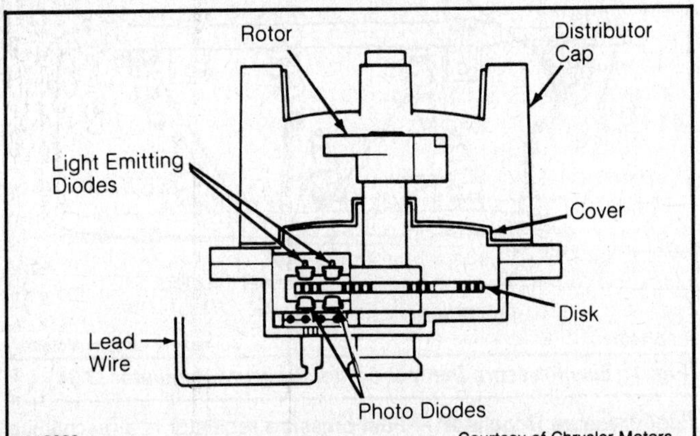
Rotor
Distributor Cap
Light Emitting Diodes
Cover
Disk
Lead Wire
Photo Diodes
113228
Courtesy of Chrysler Motors.

Fig. 3: Cutaway View of Optical Distributor (3.0L)

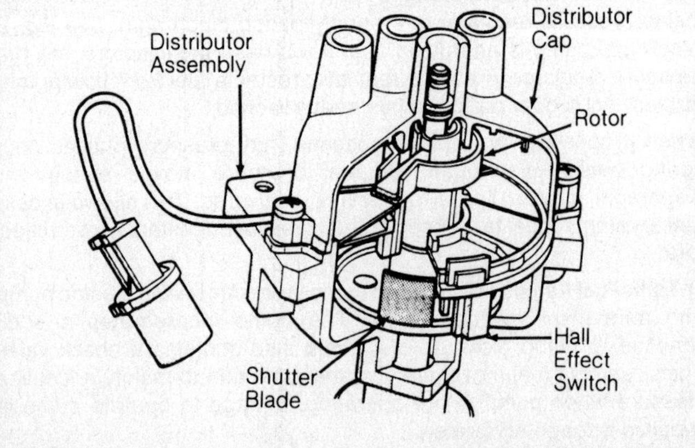
Distributor Assembly
Distributor Cap
Rotor
Hall Effect Switch
Shutter Blade
113226
Courtesy of Chrysler Motors.

Fig. 4: Cutaway View of Typical Hall Effect Distributor

MAGNETIC IGNITION SYSTEM (HALL EFFECT)

Ignition timing is controlled by Single Board Engine Controller (SBEC). SBEC uses engine RPM data from the Hall Effect switch to control ignition timing. Hall Effect switch is located inside distributor. Hall Effect distributor has a shutter attached to distributor shaft.

Shutter contains one blade per engine cylinder. *See Fig. 4.* A switch plate is mounted to distributor housing above shutter. Switch plate contains distributor pick-up (a Hall Effect device and magnet) through which shutter blades rotate. As shutter blades pass through pick-up, they interrupt the magnetic field. Hall Effect device in pick-up creates pulses by switching on and off when it senses change in magnetic field. These pulses generate the input signal to SBEC, which uses it to calculate engine speed.

IGNITION TIMING CONTROL SYSTEM

The Single Board Engine Controller (SBEC) completely controls ignition system. During a crank/start mode, SBEC will set a fixed amount of spark advance for an efficient engine start.

Ignition Timing Advance Control – The amount of spark advance or retard is determined by inputs that SBEC receives from coolant temperature, engine vacuum and engine RPM. During engine operation, SBEC can supply an infinite number of advance curves to ensure proper engine operation.

EMISSION SYSTEMS

AIR INJECTION SYSTEM

This system adds a controlled amount of air to exhaust gases to assist oxidation of hydrocarbons and carbon monoxide in exhaust stream. System does not interfere with ability of EGR system to control oxides of nitrogen emissions. Air is injected at either the exhaust manifold or the catalytic converter through air switching/relief valve. Air switching/relief valve is controlled by SBEC through air switching solenoid.

5.9L Heavy Duty Emissions engines are equipped with a dual air pump system, which does not include a air switching/relief valve.

Air Switching Solenoid – SBEC uses this solenoid to control discharge of air from air pump into exhaust system. This solenoid controls flow of vacuum to air switching/relief valve of air pump system. When solenoid is not energized, airflow is in downstream mode which means no vacuum is supplied to air switching/relief valve and air pump output is directed to catalytic converter. When solenoid is energized, airflow is in upstream mode, which means that vacuum is supplied to air switching/relief valve and air pump output is directed to exhaust manifolds.

EVAPORATIVE EMISSION SYSTEM

This system stores fuel vapors from fuel tank, preventing vapors from reaching the atmosphere. As fuel evaporates inside fuel tank, vapors are routed inside vent hoses to charcoal canister, located in wheelwell area, where they are stored until engine is started.

Canister Purge Solenoid – Charcoal canister purging is controlled by a canister purge solenoid. Canister purge solenoid is controlled by SBEC. During engine warm-up and for a short period after hot restarts, SBEC grounds canister purge solenoid winding causing solenoid to energize.

When canister purge solenoid is energized, engine vacuum signal to charcoal canister is interrupted. After engine reaches a predetermined operating temperature and SBEC internal timer has expired, SBEC will de-energize canister purge solenoid. This will allow engine vacuum to purge charcoal canister. Canister purge solenoid will also be de-energized during certain idle conditions so SBEC can update fuel delivery calibration.

HEATED AIR INLET SYSTEM

This device is an air preheater that controls air temperature entering throttle body when ambient temperatures are low. By maintaining temperature, throttle body can be calibrated much leaner to reduce hydrocarbon and carbon monoxide emissions, improve engine warm-up characteristics and minimize icing.

The heated air inlet system is a 2-circuit airflow system. When ambient temperature is above control temperature, airflow is through outside air inlet alone. When air temperature is below control temperature, airflow is through outside air inlet and through heated air inlet. The colder the ambient temperature, the greater the flow through heated air inlet. Airflow is controlled by a vacuum-operated, heat-controlled door located in snorkel.

POSITIVE CRANKCASE VENTILATION (PCV) SYSTEM

Crankcase blow-by gases are removed from crankcase with manifold vacuum. These gases are introduced into incoming air/fuel mixture and become part of the calibrated mixture. No fresh air enters crankcase with this PCV system.

EMISSION MAINTENANCE REMINDER LIGHT

SBEC activates the Emission Maintenance Reminder (EMR) light at scheduled mileage intervals to indicate need for servicing of certain emission system components. SBEC will also illuminate this light whenever a fault occurs in the emission systems.

To reset mileage interval, connect Diagnostic Readout Box II (DRB-II) to vehicles' diagnostic connector. Turn ignition switch to RUN position. Access EMISSIONS EMR TESTS on DRB-II. Select EMR MEMORY CHECK. Select RESET EMR LIGHT. Reset EMR light.

EXHAUST GAS RECIRCULATION (EGR) SYSTEM

EGR system allows a predetermined amount of exhaust gas to enter cylinder with the air/fuel mixture. This dilution of cylinder air/fuel volume reduces oxides of nitrogen (NOx) and helps prevent spark knock by reducing peak temperatures inside combustion chamber.

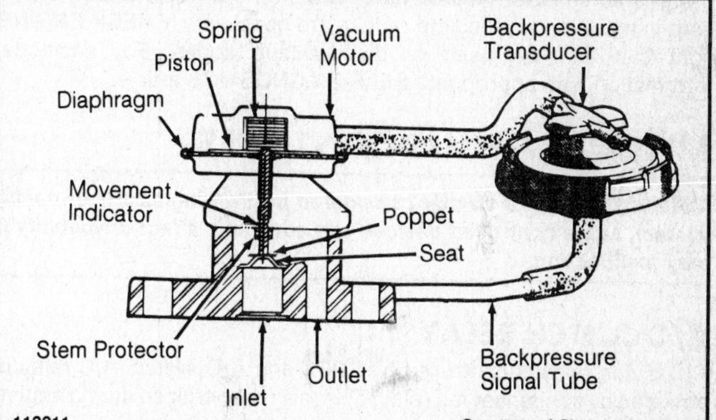
Spring
Vacuum Motor
Backpressure Transducer
Piston
Diaphragm
Movement Indicator
Poppet
Seat
Stem Protector
Outlet
Inlet
Backpressure Signal Tube
113211
Courtesy of Chrysler Motors.

Fig. 5: Typical Exhaust Gas Recirculation (EGR) System

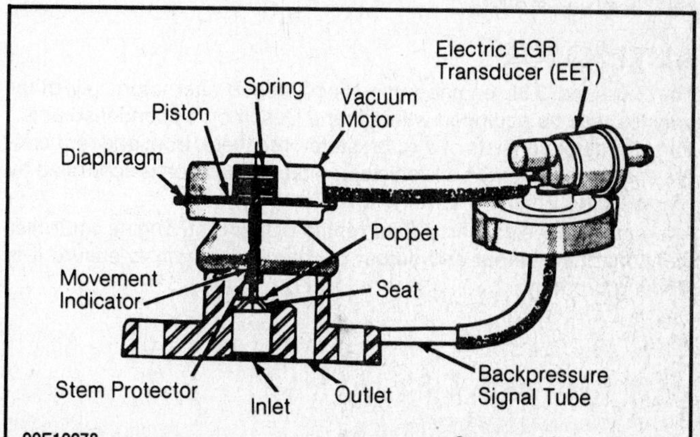
Electric EGR Transducer (EET)
Spring
Vacuum Motor
Piston
Diaphragm
Poppet
Movement Indicator
Seat
Stem Protector
Inlet
Outlet
Backpressure Signal Tube
90E10078
Courtesy of Chrysler Motors.

Fig. 6: Electric EGR Transducer (EET) System (3.3L)

1991 ENGINE PERFORMANCE
Theory & Operation – Gasoline (Cont.)

EGR system is a backpressure type. Backpressure transducer measures amount of exhaust gas backpressure on exhaust side of EGR valve and varies amount of vacuum applied to EGR valve. *See Fig. 5.*

This system allows backpressure transducer to provide proper vacuum signal to EGR valve for all engine operating conditions. EGR system is controlled by an EGR vacuum solenoid using a manifold vacuum signal from throttle body.

Exhaust Gas Recirculation (EGR) Solenoid – EGR solenoid does not allow EGR at idle. EGR system on 2.5L engines allows EGR at all temperatures. On all other EGR-equipped engines, EGR system does not function when ambient temperature is less than 40°F (4°C). EGR system is activated when coolant temperature reaches 170°F (77°C).

Electric EGR Transducer (EET) – On 2.5L, EGR system uses an Electric EGR Transducer (EET). This system incorporates backpressure transducer and EGR solenoid into one unit. *See Fig. 6.*

SELF-DIAGNOSTIC SYSTEM

The Single Board Engine Controller (SBEC) monitors several different circuits of engine control system. If a problem is sensed with a monitored circuit, SBEC will store a trouble code to aid technician in diagnosis of system. The CHECK ENGINE light or Diagnostic Readout Box-II (DRB-II) can be used to read trouble codes.

CHECK ENGINE LIGHT

CHECK ENGINE light comes on and remains on for 3 seconds as a bulb test each time ignition switch is turned to ON position. If SBEC receives an incorrect signal or receives no signal from battery voltage input, charging system, coolant temperature sensor, manifold absolute pressure sensor or throttle position sensor, CHECK ENGINE light will illuminate. On California vehicles only, light will also illuminate if there is an emission-related fault. This warns driver that SBEC is in limp-in mode and immediate repairs are necessary. CHECK ENGINE light can also be used to display fault codes. For additional information, see appropriate SELF-DIAGNOSTICS article.

MISCELLANEOUS CONTROLS

NOTE: Although not strictly considered part of engine performance system, some controlled devices can adversely affect driveability if they malfunction.

A/C CLUTCH RELAY

A/C clutch relay is controlled by SBEC and A/C switch. A/C relay is powered by condenser fan relay. This relay is energized during engine operation when A/C switch is closed and blower is on.

When SBEC senses low idle speed or wide open throttle through throttle position sensor, SBEC will de-energize A/C clutch relay, preventing A/C operation.

ALTERNATOR

The 3.0L and 3.3L engines use Nippondenso alternators. All other engines may be equipped with either a Bosch or Nippondenso unit. The alternator consists of a rotor, stator, rectifiers, front and rear covers and drive pulley. On all vehicles, voltage regulation is controlled by Single Board Engine Controller (SBEC).

Alternator diodes convert AC current to DC current. Engine controller monitors critical input and output of charging system to ensure it is working properly.

AUTO SHUTDOWN (ASD) RELAY

The ASD relay is a cut-off relay for the following components.

- Electric Fuel Pump
- Fuel Injectors
- Ignition Coil
- O_2 Sensor Heating Element

When ignition switch is turned to RUN position, SBEC energizes ASD relay which powers these components. If SBEC does not receive a distributor signal (cam or crankshaft signal on 3.3L) shortly thereafter, SBEC will de-energize ASD relay and power to these components is cut off.

LIMP-IN MODE

Limp-in mode is the attempt by SBEC to compensate for failure of certain components by substituting information from other sources. If SBEC senses incorrect data or no data at all from MAP sensor, throttle position sensor, coolant temperature sensor or battery voltage, system is placed into Limp-in mode and CHECK ENGINE light on instrument panel is illuminated.

LOCK-UP TORQUE CONVERTER SOLENOID

On vehicles equipped with A-999 or A-500 automatic transmission, SBEC controls torque converter lock-up through lock-up solenoid. SBEC controls lock-up according to various operating conditions.

OVERDRIVE SOLENOID

On vehicles equipped with overdrive transmissions, SBEC controls the 3-4 overdrive upshift and downshift through the overdrive solenoid. SBEC determines optimum overdrive shift scheduling for all operating conditions.

RADIATOR FAN RELAY

Single Board Engine Controller (SBEC) controls radiator fan relay. Radiator fan relay is energized during the following conditions:

- Fan relay is energized when A/C clutch is engaged.
- On non-A/C vehicles and A/C vehicles with A/C not engaged, fan relay energizes when vehicle speed is greater than 40 MPH and coolant temperature reaches 230°F (110°C). Fan relay turns off when coolant temperature drops to 220°F (104°C). When vehicle speed is less than 40 MPH, fan relay switches on at 210°F (99°C), and switches off at 200°F (93°C).
- Fan relay also prevents "steaming". "Steaming" occurs when moisture evaporates from outside of radiator and is not blown under the vehicle. Fan relay will energize when ambient temperature is less than 60°F (16°C), when coolant temperature is between 100-195°F (38-91°C), when engine is at idle and when vehicle is stopped. Fan relay will energize for 3 minutes only.

SPEED CONTROL SERVO

System is electrically actuated and vacuum operated. The controls are located on the steering wheel. Controls consist of 3 buttons: OFF/ON, RESUME/ACCEL. and SET/DECEL. Speed control servo is controlled by SBEC. System will operate at 35-85 MPH.

Pickup

NOTE: In mid-year, an intercooler was installed in front of the radiator. See Fig. 2. Note if vehicle contains an intercooler. Theory and operation are different on models without intercooler. For models without intercooler, see THEORY & OPERATION - DIESEL - NON-INTERCOOLED article.

INTRODUCTION

This article covers basic description and operation of engine performance-related systems and components. Read this article before diagnosing vehicles or systems with which you are not completely familiar.

AIR INDUCTION SYSTEM

TURBOCHARGERS

The Holset turbocharger is used to improve fuel efficiency and increase engine performance. Turbocharger consists of turbine section, bearing housing and compressor section. *See Fig. 1.* Turbocharger is mounted on exhaust manifold where exhaust gases drive the turbine wheel. Turbine wheel rotates compressor wheel, taking in outside air and compressing it for increased airflow through intercooler and then into the cylinders. The intercooler lowers intake manifold air temperature before reaching the cylinders.

Pressurized engine oil lubricates turbocharger. Excess oil is returned into cylinder block. Data plate, located on compressor housing, contains assembly number, serial number and type. This information is necessary for ordering replacement parts.

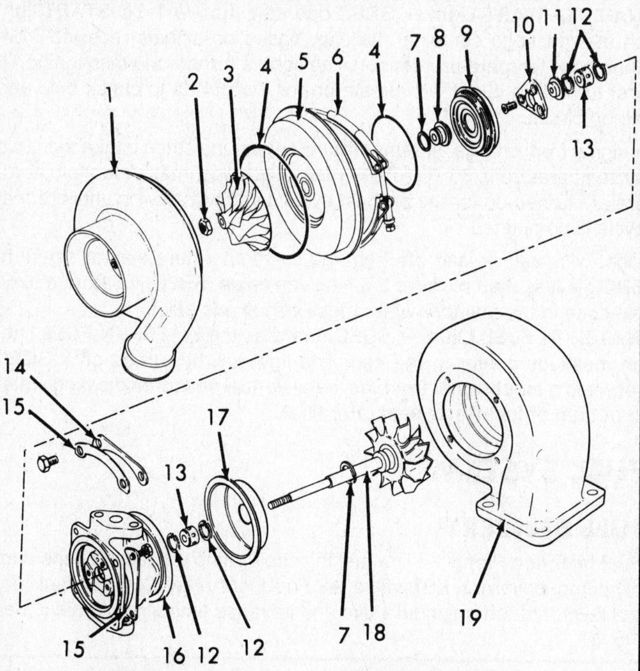
1
2
3
4
5
6
4
7
8
9
10
11
12
13
14
15
17
13
15
16
12
12
7
18
19

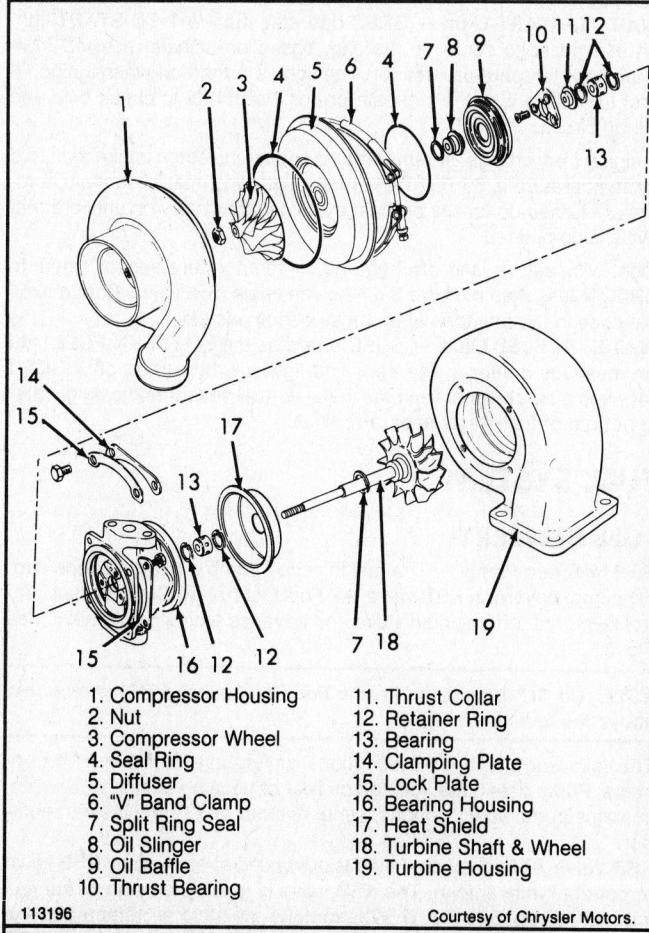

1. Compressor Housing
2. Nut
3. Compressor Wheel
4. Seal Ring
5. Diffuser
6. "V" Band Clamp
7. Split Ring Seal
8. Oil Slinger
9. Oil Baffle
10. Thrust Bearing
11. Thrust Collar
12. Retainer Ring
13. Bearing
14. Clamping Plate
15. Lock Plate
16. Bearing Housing
17. Heat Shield
18. Turbine Shaft & Wheel
19. Turbine Housing

113196 Courtesy of Chrysler Motors.

Fig. 1: Exploded View of Typical Turbocharger Assembly

INTERCOOLER

An intercooler is installed in front of the radiator. *See Fig. 2.* The intercooler is a heat exchanger, which is used to lower intake manifold air temperature before air reaches the cylinders.

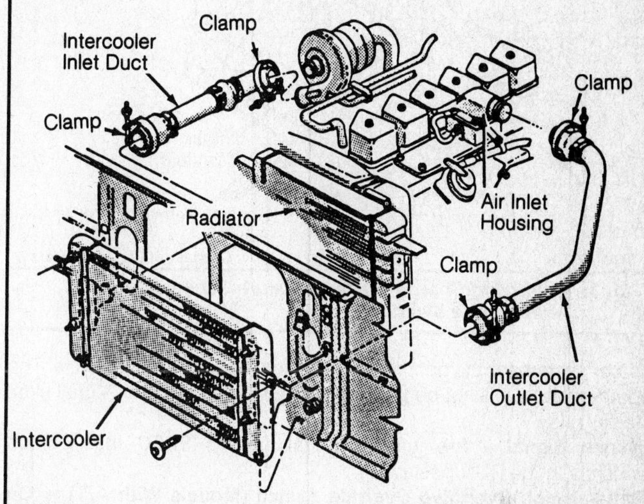
Clamp
Intercooler
Inlet Duct
Clamp
Clamp
Radiator
Air Inlet
Housing
Clamp
Intercooler
Outlet Duct
Intercooler

91J13291 Courtesy of Chrysler Motors.

Fig. 2: Exploded View of Intercooler Assembly

COMPUTERIZED ENGINE CONTROLS

SINGLE BOARD ENGINE CONTROLLER (SBEC)

SBEC is a microprocessor computer that controls the speed control system, intake manifold heater relays for intake manifold heater and transmission overdrive solenoid. SBEC also operates the WATER-IN-FUEL and WAIT-TO-START lights on the message center in the cab. SBEC is located on left front corner of engine compartment, near horns on left fender.

SBEC uses various input signals for controlling various systems. SBEC contains a memory to store trouble codes if a system failure exists. Trouble codes can be retrieved for system diagnosis. For system diagnosis, see SELF-DIAGNOSTICS - DIESEL - INTERCOOLED article in ENGINE PERFORMANCE.

NOTE: Components are grouped in 2 categories. The first category covers INPUT DEVICES, which control or produce voltage signals monitored by SBEC. The second category covers OUTPUT SIGNALS, which are components controlled by SBEC.

INPUT DEVICES

Battery Voltage - Battery voltage provides power to operate SBEC. The battery voltage also indicates to SBEC that the engine is running. SBEC checks battery voltage after a crank signal is received from the starter relay.

If battery voltage is more than 12.66 volts, SBEC assumes engine is running. If battery voltage is less than 12.66 volts, SBEC will abort the postheat (ignition on, engine running) cycle of the intake manifold heater system.

Brake Switch - If SBEC receives an input signal from brake switch when speed control system is on, SBEC will turn the speed control system off.

Charge Air Temperature Sensor - Charge air temperature sensor is located in intake manifold cover. *See Fig. 3.* Charge air temperature sensor monitors intake manifold air temperature and sends a signal to SBEC. SBEC uses this input signal to determine when and how long to operate intake manifold heaters.

Crank Signal - The crank signal is delivered from starter relay to SBEC when engine is cranking. SBEC will energize intake manifold

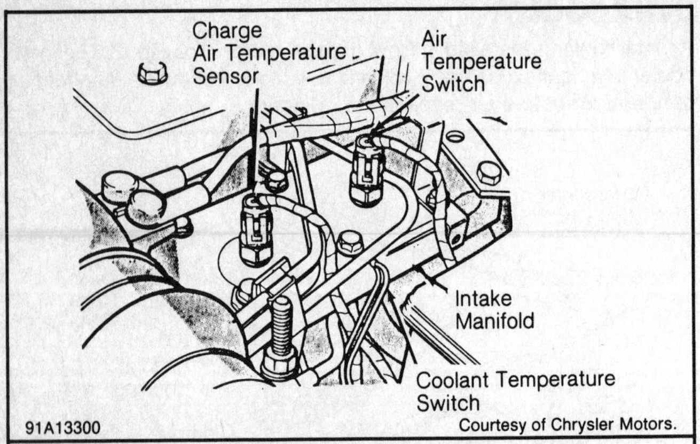
Charge
Air Temperature
Sensor
Air
Temperature
Switch
Intake
Manifold
Coolant Temperature
Switch
91A13300
Courtesy of Chrysler Motors.

Fig. 3: Identifying Charge Air Temperature Sensor & Air Temperature Switch

heater system for the postheat (ignition on, engine running) cycle. The postheat cycle will not begin unless SBEC receives crank signal from starter relay.

Ignition Signal – The ignition signal informs SBEC that ignition switch is in the RUN position.

Transmission Overdrive Override Switch (Models With A/T) – On models with overdrive, SBEC regulates overdrive upshift and downshift through the overdrive solenoid. The transmission overdrive override switch is mounted in the instrument panel.

The switch is normally closed. If switch is depressed and switch opens, transmission will not go into overdrive. Transmission will downshift if transmission is in overdrive and switch is depressed.

NOTE: Transmission overdrive circuit also contains a transmission thermoswitch and coolant temperature switch. If either switch is open, transmission will not shift into overdrive or will downshift if already in overdrive. For more information, see TRANSMISSION THERMOSWITCH and COOLANT TEMPERATURE SWITCH under MISCELLANEOUS CONTROLS.

Park/Neutral Switch (A/T) – The park/neutral switch is located on the side of transmission, near shift linkage. The park/neutral switch indicates to SBEC if transmission is in Drive, Neutral or Park. If transmission is in overdrive and driver shifts transmission in Neutral, and then back into gear, transmission will enter overdrive if SBEC determines all conditions are met.

SBEC uses input signal from park/neutral switch for speed control system operation. SBEC will disable speed control system if operator shifts transmission into Neutral. Speed control system will have to be reset if transmission is shifted into Neutral.

Throttle Position Sensor (A/T) – The Throttle Position Sensor (TPS) is mounted on top of the fuel injection pump. The TPS provides an input signal to SBEC ranging from one volt (idle position) to 5 volts (full throttle), depending on throttle position. SBEC uses input signal from TPS and vehicle speed sensor to determine transmission overdrive shift point.

Vehicle Speed Sensor – Vehicle speed sensor is mounted on rear of transmission. SBEC uses input signal from vehicle speed sensor and TPS to determine transmission overdrive shift point (A/T models) and speed control system operation.

Water-In-Fuel Sensor – Water-in-fuel sensor is located in bottom of fuel/water separator filter. *See Fig. 5.* The water-in-fuel sensor sends an input signal to SBEC when water exists in fuel/water separator filter. SBEC monitors input signal when ignition is on and intake manifold heater postheat cycle is complete. If water is detected, SBEC will turn on WATER-IN-FUEL light on message center in the cab.

OUTPUT SIGNALS

Intake Manifold Heater Relays – Intake manifold heater relays are mounted on the inner wheelwell. *See Fig. 4.* Intake manifold heater relays are energized by SBEC, depending on intake manifold air temperature, which is monitored by the charge air temperature sensor. intake manifold heater relays are not energized during engine cranking. A clicking sound will be heard when intake manifold relays are energized.

CAUTION: Intake manifold heater relays should not be cycled (ignition turned off and then on) more than once within 15 minutes. Wait 15 minutes before turning ignition on.

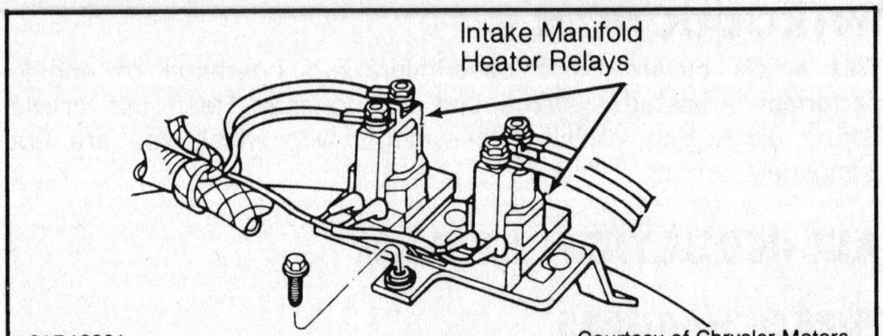
Intake Manifold
Heater Relays
91B13301
Courtesy of Chrysler Motors.

Fig. 4: Identifying Intake Manifold Heater Relays

Overdrive Solenoid (Models With A/T) – SBEC controls the overdrive solenoid for overdrive operation.

Serial Communications Interface (SCI) Receive & Transmit – The SCI receive and transmit outputs allow SBEC to communicate with DRB-II for system diagnosis.

Speed Control System – SBEC regulates vacuum and vent solenoid operation for speed control system operation. Vacuum solenoids maintain vacuum at a required pressure for speed control system operation. The vent solenoid allows vacuum to bleed off during deceleration, during brake application or when transmission is in gear or Neutral.

WAIT-TO-START Light – SBEC operates the WAIT-TO-START light on the message center in the cab, based on signals received from charge air temperature sensor. The light is turned on when ignition if first turned on. Light will remain on for 2 seconds to check bulb and wiring circuit.

If signal from charge air temperature sensor indicates intake manifold air temperature is 59°F (15°C) or less, light and intake manifold heaters are turned on for the preheat cycle. Light will stay on until preheat cycle is completed.

Light will flash on and off if charge air temperature sensor signal to SBEC is less than or more than a given value. SBEC will store a trouble code in the memory when these conditions exist.

WATER-IN-FUEL Light – SBEC operates the WATER-IN-FUEL light on message center in the cab. The light will be turned on if SBEC receives a input signal from the water-in-fuel sensor, indicating water in bottom of fuel/water separator filter.

FUEL SYSTEM

FUEL DELIVERY

Fuel Injection Pump – The fuel injection pump contains a vane supply pump, governor, KSB valve, Air Fuel Control (AFC) valve, fuel control lever, shutoff solenoid valve and advance timing mechanism. *See Fig. 5.*

NOTE: On A/T models, a Throttle Position Sensor (TPS) is mounted above the fuel control lever.

The following are brief descriptions of fuel injection pump components. Pump date plate, located on rear of housing behind KSB valve, contains pump specifications, serial number and Cummins part number.

KSB Valve – Fuel pump timing is advanced at start-up by KSB valve to control White smoke. The KSB valve is located on side of the fuel injection pump. *See Fig. 5.* When intake manifold air temperature is less than 54°F (12°C), air temperature switch provides voltage to KSB valve. Air temperature switch is located in the intake manifold cover. *See Fig. 3.*

When voltage is applied to KSB valve, valve closes and internal pressure in fuel injection pump increases. This causes fuel injection pump advance mechanism to advance fuel injection pump timing. Air temperature switch will open when intake manifold air temperature is more than 60°F (16°C°) and no voltage will be applied to KSB valve. The KSB valve will now open and fuel injection pump timing will return to normal operation.

CAUTION: DO NOT apply 12 volts to KSB valve. Wiring circuit contains a 3-ohm resistor to decrease voltage to KSB valve to 10 volts.

Air Fuel Control (AFC) Valve – The AFC valve is located on left side of engine, on top of fuel injection pump. *See Fig. 5.* The AFC valve controls Black smoke during engine acceleration by monitoring intake manifold air pressure and providing proper air/fuel ratio.

Shutoff Solenoid Valve – Shutoff solenoid valve is located on rear side of fuel injection pump. *See Fig. 5.* Shutoff solenoid valve controls fuel flow to high-pressure head of fuel injection pump. With ignition on, battery voltage is supplied to shutoff solenoid valve, pulling plunger away from fuel passage and allowing fuel into high-pressure head for engine operation. When ignition is off, plunger is closed to stop fuel flow.

Governor – Governor is located inside fuel injection pump. *See Fig. 6.* Balance between governor and fuel control lever position controls metering amount of fuel to be injected. Governor performance and setting can affect engine power.

Special tools and qualifications are required to adjust governor. If seals are broken on external adjustment screw, fuel rate may be out of adjustment. Warranty of pump governor and engine may be void if seals are tampered with or removed.

Fuel Control Lever – The amount of fuel injected and subsequently the speed and power from the engine is controlled by fuel control lever. *See Fig. 6.* Restricted travel of fuel control lever can cause loss of power.

Manual Shutdown Lever – Fuel injection pump is equipped with a manual shutdown lever. This lever is spring loaded in the RUN position. There is no cable or rod connected to the lever. *See Fig. 5.* Engine can be shut down by rotating manual shutdown.

Advance Timing Mechanism – Regulated pressure produced by vane supply pump in fuel injection pump is used to advance timing. Timing advances as engine speed increases. A return spring is used to retard timing as engine speed is reduced.

Fuel Lift Pump – Fuel lift pump is located on left side of engine block. *See Fig. 5.* The camshaft-driven fuel lift pump draws fuel from fuel tank to the fuel/water separator filter. Fuel lift pump contains a check valve to prevent fuel from bleeding back into fuel tank when engine is not operating. Fuel lift pump contains a hand lever for priming and bleeding air from fuel system. A defective fuel lift pump can create loss of engine power and long cranking periods.

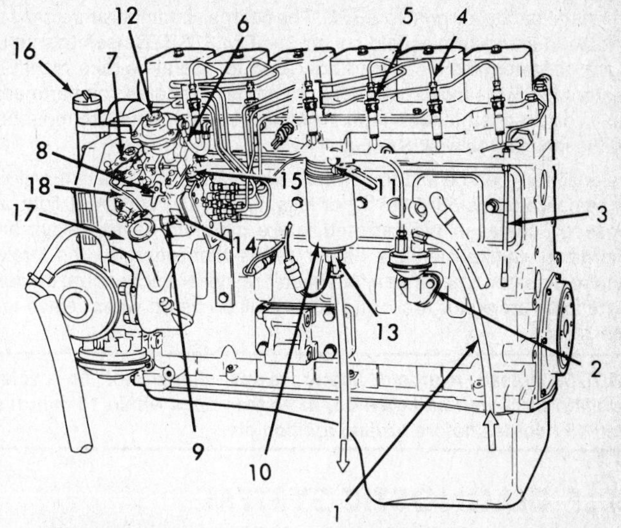

12
6
5
4
16
7
8
15
11
18
17
14
3
13
2
9
10
1

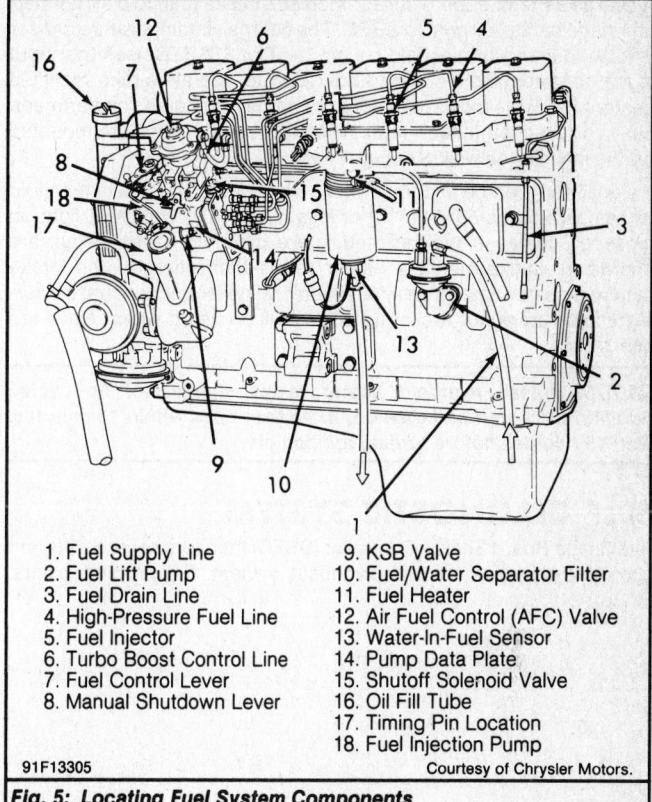

1. Fuel Supply Line
2. Fuel Lift Pump
3. Fuel Drain Line
4. High-Pressure Fuel Line
5. Fuel Injector
6. Turbo Boost Control Line
7. Fuel Control Lever
8. Manual Shutdown Lever
9. KSB Valve
10. Fuel/Water Separator Filter
11. Fuel Heater
12. Air Fuel Control (AFC) Valve
13. Water-In-Fuel Sensor
14. Pump Data Plate
15. Shutoff Solenoid Valve
16. Oil Fill Tube
17. Timing Pin Location
18. Fuel Injection Pump

91F13305 Courtesy of Chrysler Motors.

Fig. 5: Locating Fuel System Components

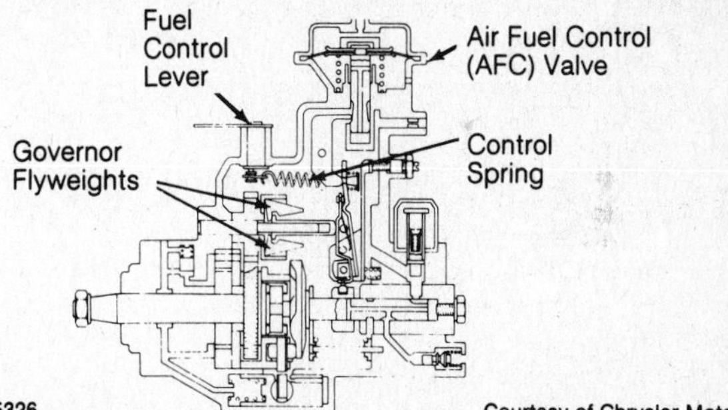

Fuel
Control
Lever
Air Fuel Control
(AFC) Valve
Governor
Flyweights
Control
Spring

90F15326 Courtesy of Chrysler Motors.

Fig. 6: Identifying Governor Assembly Components

FUEL CONTROL

Fuel Injectors – During the fuel injection cycle, fuel injection pressure increases to fuel injector opening pressure or POP pressure of 3625 psi (254 kg/cm²). The opening pressure is pressure required to lift injector needle valve from its seat.

With injector needle valve off its seat, fuel is injected into cylinders. A spring is used to force needle valve closed as injection pressure drops below opening pressure. Fuel injector opening pressure is adjusted with shims above needle valve return spring.

FUEL/WATER SEPARATOR FILTER

The fuel/water separator filter contains a water-in-fuel sensor and a water drain valve, located at bottom of fuel/water separator filter. *See Fig. 5.* The water-in-fuel sensor sends an input signal to SBEC when water exists in fuel/water separator filter.

SBEC will then turn on the WATER-IN-FUEL light on the message center in the cab. The WATER-IN-FUEL light informs operator to drain water from bottom of fuel/water separator filter or fuel system components may be damaged.

FUEL HEATER

Fuel flows from filter head and passes through the fuel heater, consisting of ceramic plates and a thermostat. Fuel heater is located between fuel/water separator filter and filter adapter on cylinder head. *See Fig. 5.* Voltage to operate fuel heater is provided from ignition switch.

A minimum of 7 volts is supplied from ignition switch to the ceramic plates. Thermostat senses fuel temperature and operates fuel heater to maintain a constant fuel viscosity to prevent fuel waxing. Fuel heater will turn on when temperature is approximately 43°F (6°C) and shut off at approximately 56°F (13°C).

EMISSIONS SYSTEMS

INTAKE MANIFOLD HEATER SYSTEM

Intake manifold heater is a grid heater installed between air inlet housing and intake manifold. The air inlet housing is attached to intercooler outlet duct which is connected to the intercooler. Intake manifold heater is used to warm intake manifold air before engine start-up.

1991 ENGINE PERFORMANCE
Theory & Operation - Diesel - Intercooled (Cont.)

A charge air temperature sensor monitors intake manifold air temperature and sends a signal to SBEC. The charge air temperature sensor is located in intake manifold cover. *See Fig. 3.* SBEC uses this input signal to determine when and how long to operate intake manifold heaters. SBEC is located on left front corner of engine compartment, near horns on left fender. Intake manifold heater relays are mounted on the inner wheelwell. *See Fig. 4.*

If signal from charge air temperature sensor indicates intake manifold air temperature is 59°F (15°C) or less, the WAIT-TO-START light on message center in the cab and intake manifold heater relays are energized. Intake manifold heater relays then energize the intake manifold heater. Intake manifold heater relays are not energized during engine cranking. A clicking sound will be heard when relays are energized.

CAUTION: Intake manifold heater relays should not be cycled (ignition turned off and then on) more than once within 15 minutes. Wait 15 minutes before turning ignition on.

SELF-DIAGNOSTIC SYSTEM

The Single Board Engine Controller (SBEC) monitors several different circuits and contains a self-diagnostic system. If a problem exists, SBEC will store a trouble code in the self-diagnostic system. Trouble code can be obtained using a DRB-II to determine circuit on which the problem exists. If problem is fixed, SBEC will cancel trouble code at 51 engine starts. For system diagnosis, see SELF-DIAGNOSTICS - DIESEL - INTERCOOLED article in ENGINE PERFORMANCE.

MISCELLANEOUS CONTROLS

TRANSMISSION

Coolant Temperature Switch (A/T) - Coolant temperature switch is located in the cylinder head, below intake manifold, near air temperature switch. *See Fig. 3.* Coolant temperature switch opens when coolant temperature is less than 60°F (16°C).

When coolant temperature switch opens, transmission will not shift into overdrive. Transmission will downshift if it is in overdrive when coolant temperature switch opens.

Transmission Thermoswitch (A/T) - Transmission thermoswitch is located in transmission-to-radiator oil cooler line. Transmission thermoswitch opens when transmission fluid temperature is more than 273°F (134°C) and closes at 240°F (116°C).

If transmission is in overdrive and thermoswitch opens, transmission will downshift. Once switch closes, SBEC will send a signal to transmission to shift into overdrive.

Pickup

NOTE: In mid-year, an intercooler was installed in front of the radiator and was connected to turbocharger and intake manifold. Note if vehicle contains an intercooler. Theory and operation are different on models with intercooler. For models with intercooler, see THEORY & OPERATION - DIESEL - INTERCOOLED article.

INTRODUCTION

This article covers basic description and operation of engine performance-related systems and components. Read this article before diagnosing vehicles or systems with which you are not completely familiar.

AIR INDUCTION SYSTEM

TURBOCHARGERS

The Holset turbocharger is used to improve fuel efficiency and increase engine performance. Turbocharger consists of turbine section, bearing housing and compressor section. *See Fig. 1.* Turbocharger is mounted on exhaust manifold where exhaust gases drive the turbine wheel. Turbine wheel rotates compressor wheel, taking in outside air and compressing it for increased airflow into cylinders.

Pressurized engine oil lubricates turbocharger. Excess oil is returned into cylinder block. Data plate, located on compressor housing, contains assembly number, serial number and type. This information is necessary for ordering replacement parts.

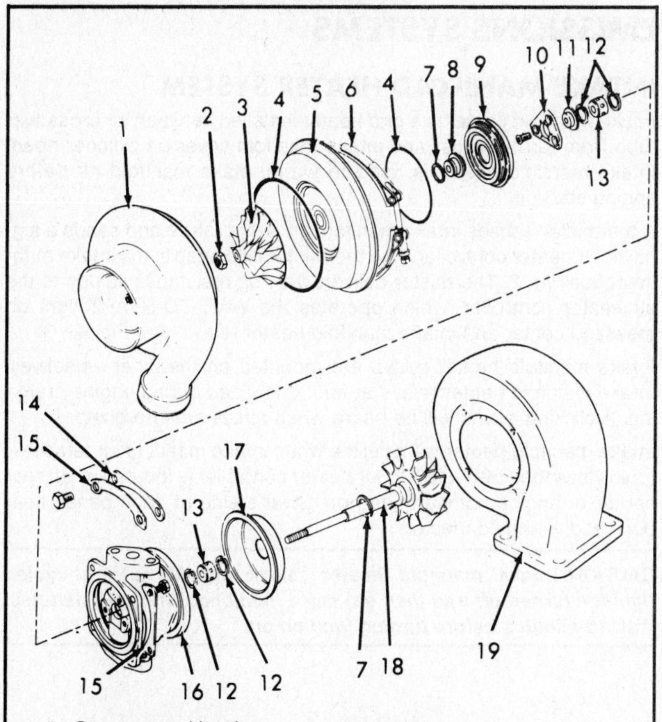
1
2
3
4
5
6
4
7 8
9
10 11 12
13
14
15
17
13
15
16 12
12
7 18
19

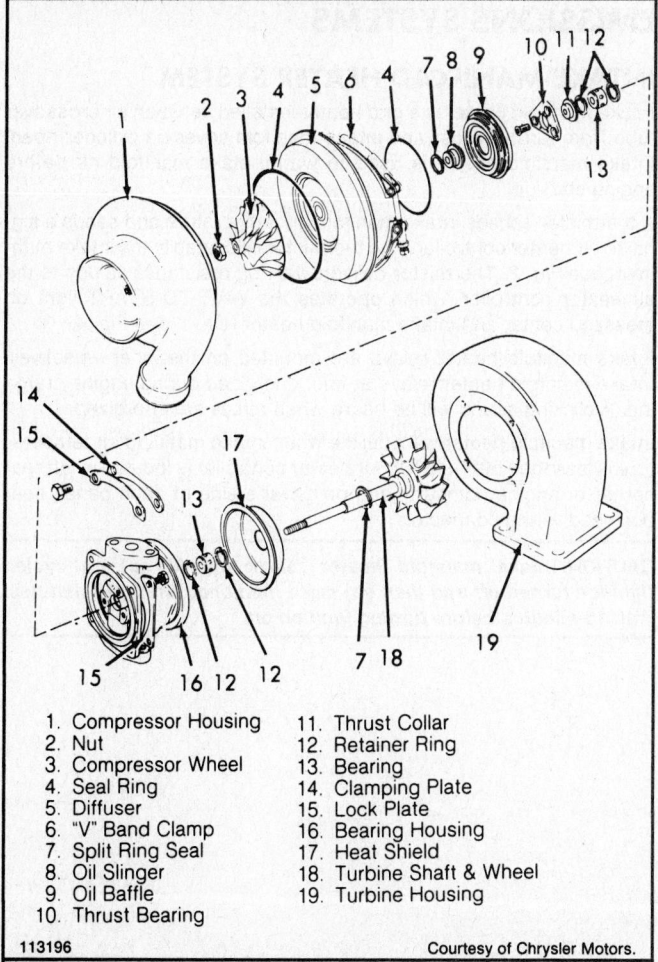

1. Compressor Housing
2. Nut
3. Compressor Wheel
4. Seal Ring
5. Diffuser
6. "V" Band Clamp
7. Split Ring Seal
8. Oil Slinger
9. Oil Baffle
10. Thrust Bearing
11. Thrust Collar
12. Retainer Ring
13. Bearing
14. Clamping Plate
15. Lock Plate
16. Bearing Housing
17. Heat Shield
18. Turbine Shaft & Wheel
19. Turbine Housing

113196 Courtesy of Chrysler Motors.

Fig. 1: Exploded View of Turbocharger Assembly

FUEL SYSTEM

FUEL DELIVERY

Fuel Injection Pump – The Bosch fuel injection pump contains a vane supply pump, governor, KSB valve, Air Fuel Control (AFC) valve, fuel control lever, shutoff solenoid valve and advance timing mechanism. *See Fig. 2.* Below is a brief description of fuel injection pump components. Pump date plate, located on rear of housing behind KSB valve, contains pump specifications, serial number and Cummins part number.

KSB Valve – Fuel pump timing is advanced at start-up by KSB valve to control White smoke. KSB valve is controlled by air heater controller. Air heater controller is located in left rear corner of engine compartment, on driver's side of dash panel, near bulkhead wiring connector.

A thermistor, located in intake manifold, senses intake manifold air temperature. *See Fig. 2.* When intake manifold air temperature is greater than 59°F (15°C), a specified resistance from thermistor is sensed by air heater controller.

The air heater controller then supplies battery voltage to heat the expansion element of KSB valve. As expansion element is heated, plunger of KSB valve is forced inward, opening secondary pressure regulator. This reduces internal pump pressure, allowing fuel injection pump timing to retard.

Air Fuel Control (AFC) Valve – The AFC valve is located on left side of engine, on top of fuel injection pump. *See Fig. 2.* The AFC valve controls Black smoke during engine acceleration by monitoring intake manifold air pressure and providing proper air/fuel ratio.

Shutoff Solenoid Valve – Shutoff solenoid valve is located on rear side of fuel injection pump. *See Fig. 2.* Shutoff solenoid valve controls fuel flow to high-pressure head of fuel injection pump. With ignition on, battery voltage is supplied to shutoff solenoid valve, pulling plunger away from fuel passage and allowing fuel into high-pressure head for engine operation. When ignition is off, plunger is closed to stop fuel flow.

Governor – Governor is located inside fuel injection pump. *See Fig. 3.* Balance between governor and fuel control lever position controls metering amount of fuel to be injected. Governor performance and setting can affect engine power.

Special tools and qualifications are required to adjust governor. If seals are broken on external adjustment screw, fuel rate may be out of adjustment. Warranty of pump governor and engine may be void if seals are tampered with or removed.

Fuel Control Lever – The amount of fuel injected and subsequently the speed and power from the engine is controlled by fuel control lever. *See Fig. 3.* Restricted travel of fuel control lever can cause loss of power.

Manual Shutdown Lever – Fuel injection pump is equipped with a manual shutdown lever. This lever is spring loaded in the RUN position. There is no cable or rod connected to the lever. *See Fig. 2.* Engine can be shut down by rotating manual shutdown lever counterclockwise.

Advance Timing Mechanism – Regulated pressure produced by vane supply pump in fuel injection pump is used to advance timing. Timing advances as engine speed increases. A return spring is used to retard timing as engine speed is reduced.

Fuel Lift Pump – Fuel lift pump is located on left side of engine block. *See Fig. 2.* The camshaft-driven fuel lift pump draws fuel from fuel tank to the fuel/water separator filter. Fuel lift pump contains a check valve to prevent fuel from bleeding back into fuel tank when engine is not operating. Fuel lift pump contains a hand lever for priming and bleeding air from fuel system. A defective fuel lift pump can create loss of engine power and long cranking periods.

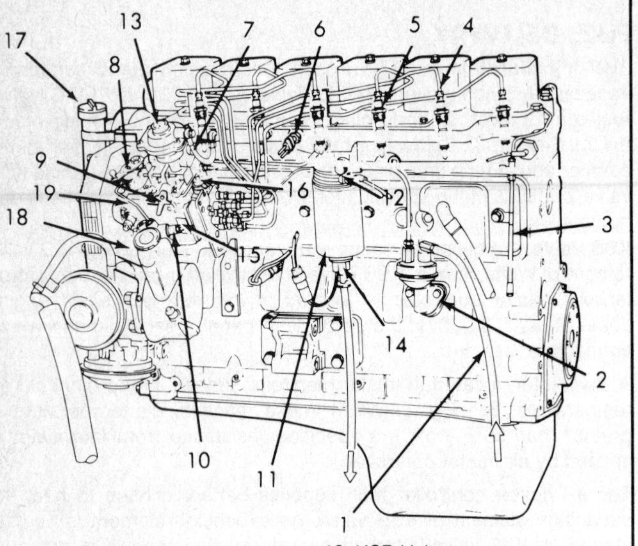
17
13
7
6
5
4
8
9
19
18
16
12
3
15
14
2
10
11
1

1. Fuel Supply Line
2. Fuel Lift Pump
3. Fuel Drain Line
4. High-Pressure Fuel Line
5. Fuel Injector
6. Thermistor
7. Turbo Boost Control Line
8. Fuel Control Lever
9. Manual Shutdown Lever
10. KSB Valve
11. Fuel/Water Separator Filter
12. Fuel Heater
13. Air Fuel Control (AFC) Valve
14. Water-In-Fuel Sensor
15. Pump Data Plate
16. Shutoff Solenoid Valve
17. Oil Fill Tube
18. Timing Pin Location
19. Fuel Injection Pump

90G15327 Courtesy of Chrysler Motors.

Fig. 2: Locating Fuel System Components

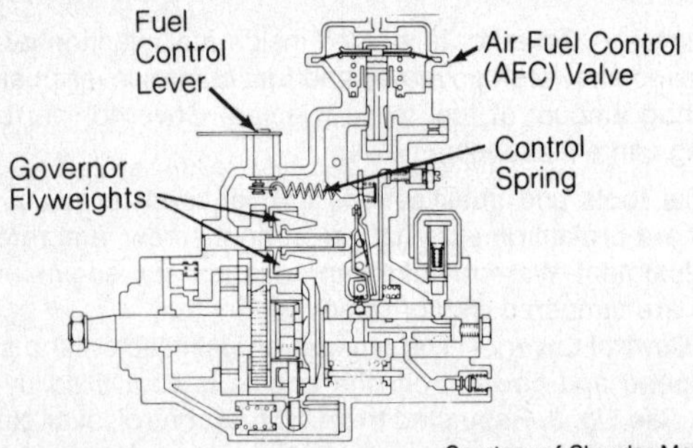
Fuel
Control
Lever
Air Fuel Control
(AFC) Valve
Governor
Flyweights
Control
Spring

90F15326 Courtesy of Chrysler Motors.

Fig. 3: Identifying Governor Assembly Components

FUEL CONTROL

Fuel Injectors - During the fuel injection cycle, fuel injection pressure increases to fuel injector opening pressure or POP pressure of 3550 psi (249 kg/cm²). The opening pressure is pressure required to lift injector needle valve from its seat.

With injector needle valve off its seat, fuel is injected into cylinders. A spring is used to force needle valve closed as injection pressure drops below opening pressure. Fuel injector opening pressure is adjusted with shims above needle valve return spring.

FUEL/WATER SEPARATOR FILTER

The fuel/water separator filter contains a water-in-fuel sensor and a water drain valve, located at bottom of fuel/water separator filter. *See Fig. 2.* The water-in-fuel sensor sends an input signal to air heater controller when water exists in fuel/water separator filter.

The air heater controller will then turn on the WATER-IN-FUEL light on the message center in the cab. The WATER-IN-FUEL light informs operator to drain water from bottom of fuel/water separator filter or fuel system components may be damaged.

FUEL HEATER

Fuel flows from filter head and passes through the fuel heater, consisting of ceramic plates and a thermostat. Fuel heater is located between fuel/water separator filter and filter adapter on cylinder head. *See Fig. 2.* Voltage to operate fuel heater is provided from ignition switch.

A minimum of 7 volts is supplied from ignition switch to the ceramic plates. Thermostat senses fuel temperature and operates fuel heater to maintain a constant fuel viscosity to prevent fuel waxing. Fuel heater will turn on when temperature is approximately 43°F (6°C) and shuts off at approximately 53°F (13°C).

EMISSIONS SYSTEMS

INTAKE MANIFOLD HEATER SYSTEM

Intake manifold heater is a grid heater installed between air crossover tube from turbocharger and intake manifold cover on cylinder head. Intake manifold heater is used to warm intake manifold air before engine start-up.

A thermistor senses intake manifold air temperature and sends a signal to air heater controller. The thermistor is located in the intake manifold. *See Fig. 2.* Thermistor delivers varying resistance values to the air heater controller, which operates the WAIT-TO-START light on message center and intake manifold heater relays. *See Fig. 4.*

Intake manifold heater relays are mounted on the inner wheelwell. Intake manifold heater relays are not energized during engine cranking. A clicking sound will be heard when relays are energized.

Intake manifold heater will operate when intake manifold air temperature is less than 59°F (15°C). Air heater controller is located in left rear corner of engine compartment, on driver's side of dash panel, near bulkhead wiring connector.

CAUTION: Intake manifold heater relays should not be cycled (ignition turned off and then on) more than once within 15 minutes. Wait 15 minutes before turning ignition on.

1991 ENGINE PERFORMANCE
Theory & Operation – Diesel – Non-Intercooled (Cont.)

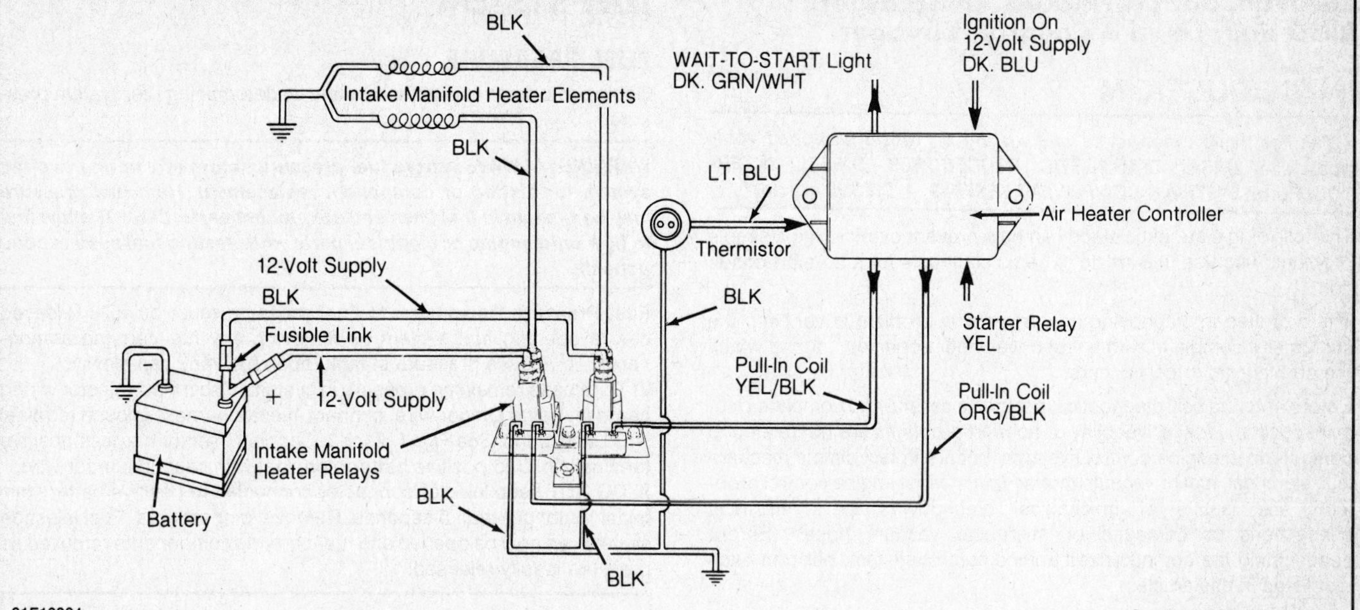
BLK
Intake Manifold Heater Elements
BLK
WAIT-TO-START Light
DK. GRN/WHT
Ignition On
12-Volt Supply
DK. BLU
LT. BLU
Air Heater Controller
Thermistor
12-Volt Supply
BLK
BLK
Fusible Link
+
12-Volt Supply
Starter Relay
YEL
Pull-In Coil
YEL/BLK
Pull-In Coil
ORG/BLK
Intake Manifold
Heater Relays
Battery
BLK
BLK
91E13304
Courtesy of Chrysler Motors.

Fig. 4: Identifying Intake Manifold Heater System Components

1991 ENGINE PERFORMANCE
Basic Diagnostic Procedures – Gasoline

Caravan, Dakota, Pickup, Ramcharger, RWD Van, Town & Country, Voyager

INTRODUCTION

NOTE: For basic diagnostics and testing on diesel equipped vehicles, see BASIC DIAGNOSTIC PROCEDURES – DIESEL – INTERCOOLED or SYSTEM & COMPONENT TESTING – DIESEL article.

The following diagnostic steps can help prevent overlooking a simple problem. Also use this article to begin diagnosis for a no-start condition.

The first step in diagnosing any driveability problem is verifying the customer's complaint with a test drive under conditions during which the problem reportedly occurs.

Before entering self-diagnostics, perform a careful and complete visual inspection. Most driveability or no-start problems are not related to computerized engine control systems, but are in fact simple mechanical, electrical, fuel or vacuum related faults. Most engine control problems are results of mechanical breakdowns, poor electrical connections or damaged or misrouted vacuum hoses. Before condemning the computerized engine control system, perform each test listed in this article.

NOTE: All voltage tests should be performed with a Digital Volt-Ohmmeter (DVOM) with a minimum 10-megohm input impedance, unless stated otherwise in testing procedures.

PRELIMINARY INSPECTION & ADJUSTMENTS

VISUAL INSPECTION

Perform a visual inspection of all electrical wirings. Look for chafed, stretched, cut or pinched wiring. Inspect electrical connectors and connections for tight fit and corrosion. Repair as necessary. Inspect all vacuum hoses for proper routing, cuts or pinches. If necessary, see VACUUM DIAGRAMS article to verify routing and connections. Repair as necessary. Inspect air induction system for possible vacuum leaks.

MECHANICAL INSPECTION

Compression – Check engine mechanical condition using a compression gauge, vacuum gauge, or an engine analyzer capable of performing a relative compression test. See engine analyzer instruction manual for availability and description of relative compression feature.

CAUTION: Use a remote starter to crank engine during compression test; DO NOT use ignition switch. Fuel injectors on many models are triggered by ignition switch during engine cranking. This could create a fire hazard or cause engine flooding, crankcase contamination, hydrostatic lock, or lubrication to be washed form cylinder walls.

ENGINE COMPRESSION

Application	psi (kg/cm²)
Minimum Compression Pressure	
All Models	100 (7.0)
Maximum Variation Between Cylinders	
All Models	25 (1.8)

Exhaust System Backpressure – Check exhaust system with a vacuum gauge or pressure gauge. Remove O_2 sensor or air injection check valve (if equipped). Connect a 1-5 psi pressure gauge, and run engine at 2500 RPM. If exhaust system backpressure is greater than 1 3/4 - 2 psi, exhaust system or catalytic converter is plugged.

If using a vacuum gauge, connect vacuum gauge hose to intake manifold vacuum port and start engine. Observe vacuum gauge. Open throttle part way and hold steady. If vacuum gauge reading slowly drops after stabilizing, check exhaust system for restriction.

FUEL SYSTEM

FUEL PRESSURE

Begin basic diagnosis of fuel system by determining fuel system pressure.

WARNING: ALWAYS relieve fuel pressure before attempting to open system for testing or component replacement. High fuel pressure may be present in fuel lines and component parts. DO NOT allow fuel to flow onto engine or electrical parts while testing fuel system components.

Fuel Pressure Release – **1)** Fuel pressure must be fully released before opening fuel system or removing any fuel-carrying components. To release pressure in tank, open fuel tank cap slowly.
2) To release remaining pressure in system, disconnect injector wiring harness. Using jumper wire, connect injector harness ground terminal No. 1 to ground. *See Fig. 1, 2 or 3*. Connect injector harness positive terminal No. 2 to positive battery terminal with second jumper wire.
3) DO NOT keep injector connector connected to positive battery terminal for longer than 5 seconds. Remove jumper wires. Fuel injection system can now be opened and fuel-carrying components removed as pressure is fully released.

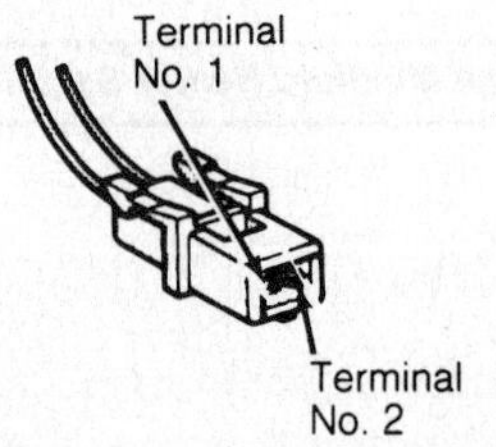
Terminal
No. 1
Terminal
No. 2

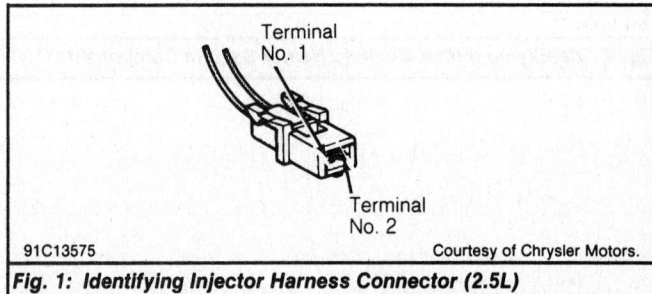

91C13575 Courtesy of Chrysler Motors.

Fig. 1: Identifying Injector Harness Connector (2.5L)

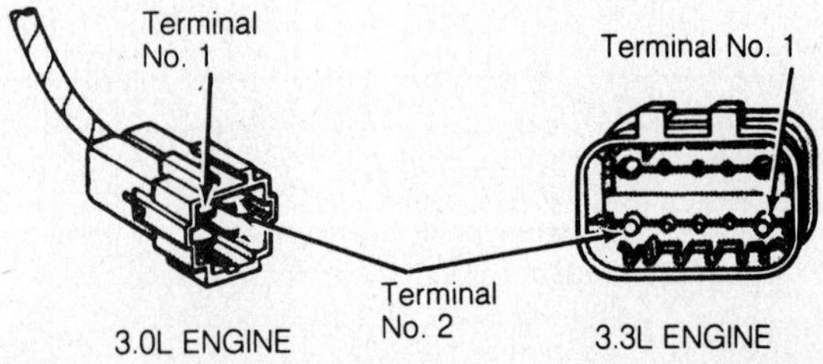
Terminal
No. 1
Terminal No. 1
Terminal
No. 2
3.0L ENGINE
3.3L ENGINE

90B13319 Courtesy of Chrysler Motors.

Fig. 2: Identifying Injector Harness Connectors (3.0L & 3.3L)

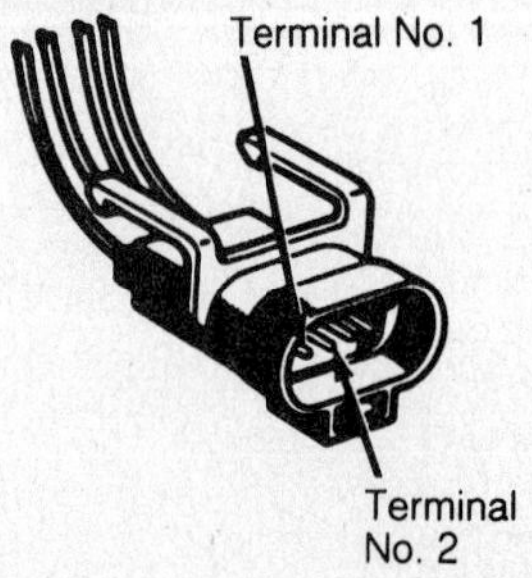
Terminal No. 1
Terminal
No. 2

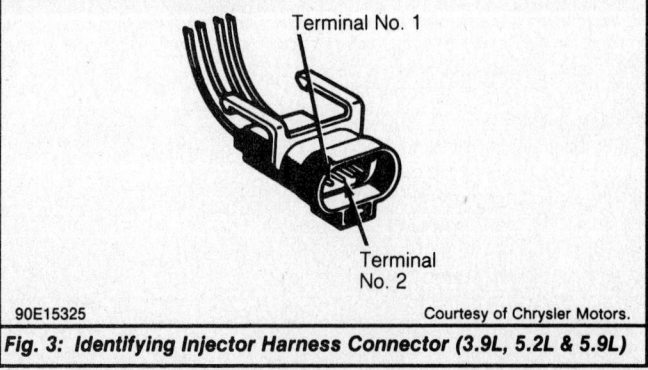

90E15325 Courtesy of Chrysler Motors.

Fig. 3: Identifying Injector Harness Connector (3.9L, 5.2L & 5.9L)

NOTE: Perform FUEL PUMP TEST with fuel tank at least half full. Before disconnecting a fuel line during testing, repeat FUEL PRESSURE RELEASE procedure.

Fuel Pump Test (2.5L, 3.9L, 5.2L & 5.9L) – 1) Release fuel pressure. See FUEL PRESSURE RELEASE. Disconnect 5/16" fuel supply hose. Connect fuel system pressure Gauge (C-4799) between fuel supply hose and engine fuel line.

2) Turn ignition on. Using Diagnostic Readout Box (DRB-II) (C-4805), activate fuel pump. If fuel pump pressure is at specification, fuel system is functioning properly. See FUEL PUMP PRESSURE SPECIFICATIONS table.

3) If fuel pressure is not to specification, record pressure. Install fuel pressure gauge in fuel supply line at rear of vehicle between fuel tank and fuel filter.

4) Using DRB-II, activate fuel pump. Record pressure reading. If fuel pressure is 5 psi (.4 kg/cm²) more than first pressure reading, replace fuel filter.

5) If no change in pressure reading is observed, gently squeeze fuel return hose. If fuel pressure increases, replace fuel pressure regulator. If no change in fuel pressure is observed, problem is plugged fuel pump filter sock or defective fuel pump.

6) If fuel pressure is more than specification, remove fuel return hose at rear of vehicle. Connect an extension hose to return hose. Place hose in an approved container with at least a 2 gallon capacity.

7) Using DRB-II, activate fuel pump. If fuel pressure is now within specification, check in-tank return fuel hose for kinking. Replace fuel pump assembly if in-tank reservoir check valve or aspirator jet is plugged.

8) If fuel pressure is still more than specification, remove fuel return hose from throttle body. Connect a substitute hose to throttle body return nipple. Place other end of hose in an approved container.

9) Using DRB-II, activate fuel pump. If fuel pressure is at specification, check for a restricted fuel return line between throttle body and fuel tank. If no change was observed, replace fuel pressure regulator.

FUEL PUMP PRESSURE SPECIFICATIONS

Application	psi (kg/cm²)
2.5L	39 (2.7)
3.0L & 3.3L	48 (3.4)
3.9L, 5.2L & 5.9L	14.5 (1.0)

NOTE: Perform FUEL PUMP TEST with fuel tank at least half full. Before disconnecting a fuel line during testing, repeat FUEL PRESSURE RELEASE procedure.

Fuel Pump Test (3.0L & 3.3L) – 1) Release fuel pressure. See FUEL PRESSURE RELEASE. Remove cap from service valve on fuel rail. Connect fuel system pressure Gauge (C-4799) to service valve.

2) Turn ignition on. Using Diagnostic Readout Box (DRB-II) (C-4805), activate fuel pump. If fuel pump pressure is at specification, fuel system is functioning properly. See FUEL PUMP PRESSURE SPECIFICATIONS table.

3) If fuel pressure is not to specification, record pressure and remove gauge. Using DRB-II, activate fuel pump. Ensure fuel is not leaking from service valve. Install cap on service valve.

4) If fuel pressure is not to specification, install pressure gauge in fuel supply line between fuel tank and fuel filter at rear of vehicle. See FUEL PUMP PRESSURE SPECIFICATIONS table. Using DRB-II, activate fuel pump.

5) Record pressure reading. If fuel pressure is 5 psi (.4 kg/cm²) higher than first pressure reading, replace fuel filter. If no change in pressure reading is observed, gently squeeze fuel return hose.

6) If fuel pressure increases, replace fuel pressure regulator. If no change in fuel pressure is observed, problem is plugged fuel pump filter sock or defective fuel pump.

7) If fuel pressure is more than specification, remove fuel return hose at rear of vehicle. See FUEL PUMP PRESSURE SPECIFICATIONS table. Connect an extension hose to return hose. Place hose in an approved container with at least 2 gallon capacity.

8) Using DRB-II, activate fuel pump. If fuel pressure is now within specification, check in-tank return fuel hose for kinking. Replace fuel pump assembly if in-tank reservoir check valve or aspirator jet is plugged.

9) If fuel pressure is still more than specification, remove fuel return hose from pressure regulator. Connect a substitute hose to fuel pressure regulator. Place other end of hose in an approved container.

10) Using DRB-II, activate fuel pump. If fuel pressure is at specification, check for a restricted fuel return line. If no change is observed, replace fuel pressure regulator.

AUTO SHUTDOWN (ASD) RELAY

NOTE: If ASD relay is suspected of causing a fuel or ignition system malfunction, it will be necessary to use Diagnostic Readout Box (DRB-II) to diagnose ASD relay. See appropriate SELF-DIAGNOSTICS article.

2.5L, 3.0L, 3.9L, 5.2L & 5.9L – When distributor signal is not present with ignition switch in RUN position, ASD relay turns off power to electric fuel pump, fuel injectors, ignition coil and O_2 sensor heating element.

3.3L – When there is no camshaft or crankshaft sensor signal with ignition switch in RUN position, ASD relay turns off power to electric fuel pump, fuel injectors, ignition coil and O_2 sensor heating element.

IGNITION CHECKS

TESTING SPARK AT COIL

2.5L, 3.0L, 3.9L, 5.2L & 5.9L – 1) Remove coil wire from distributor cap. Hold end of cable approximately 1/4" from ground. Crank engine and check for spark from coil wire. Spark should be present and constant.

2) If spark is present and constant, continue cranking engine. Slowly move coil wire away from ground. As coil wire is moved away from ground, check for arching at coil tower. If arching at coil tower is present, replace coil.

3) If spark is good and no arching is present, secondary ignition system is producing necessary voltage. Ensure spark reaches spark plugs by checking condition of rotor, cap, spark plug wires and spark plugs. Repair or replace as necessary. If ignition system components are in good condition, ignition system is okay.

3.3L – 1) This system has 3 independent coils. These coils must be tested separately. Remove spark plug wire from No. 2 spark plug. Insert a clean screwdriver into spark plug boot.

2) Hold screwdriver approximately 1/4" from ground. Crank engine and watch for spark between screwdriver and ground. Repeat this test for No. 4 and No. 6 spark plug wires.

3) If no spark is present on any cylinder tested, go to NO-START TEST. If one or more cylinders has weak or no spark, go to next step.

4) Remove spark plug wires individually. Using an ohmmeter, measure resistance of each spark plug wire. Resistance should be 3000-12,000 ohms per foot. Replace spark plug wire(s) if resistance is not within specification.

5) Measure resistance on primary side of each coil. Resistance should be .5-.7 ohm. Measure resistance between B+ terminal of ignition coil connector and corresponding cylinders. *See Fig. 4*. Replace coil if resistance is not within specification.

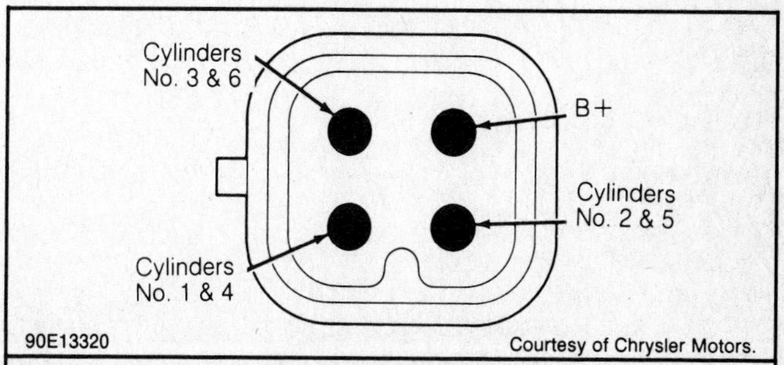
Cylinders
No. 3 & 6
B+
Cylinders
No. 2 & 5
Cylinders
No. 1 & 4
90E13320
Courtesy of Chrysler Motors.

Fig. 4: Identifying DIS Ignition Coil Terminals (3.3L)

6) Remove spark plug wires from coil one at a time. Measure secondary resistance of ignition coil between grouped cylinders and coil towers. Resistance should be 7000-15,800 ohms. Replace coil if resistance is not within specification.

NO-START TEST

NOTE: Perform TESTING SPARK AT COIL before proceeding with test.

2.5L, 3.0L, 3.9L, 5.2L & 5.9L - 1) Ensure sufficient battery voltage (12.4 volts) is available to crank engine and operate ignition systems. Crank engine for 5 seconds while monitoring voltage at coil positive terminal.

2) If voltage remains near zero during entire period of cranking, see appropriate SELF-DIAGNOSTICS article to check SBEC and ASD relay. If voltage is near battery voltage and drops to zero after 1-2 seconds of cranking, see appropriate SELF-DIAGNOSTICS article to check distributor pick-up circuit to SBEC.

3) If voltage remains near battery voltage during entire 5 seconds, turn ignition off. Disconnect SBEC 60-pin connector. Check 60-pin connector for loose terminals (push-outs).

4) Remove positive lead from coil. Connect a jumper wire between battery positive terminal and coil positive terminal. Using a specially constructed jumper wire, momentarily ground SBEC harness connector terminal No. 19. *See Figs. 5 and 6.* Spark should be generated when ground connection is disconnected.

5) If spark is generated, replace SBEC. If no spark is generated, use special jumper wire directly on coil negative terminal. If spark is produced, repair wiring harness for an open circuit. If no spark is produced, replace ignition coil.

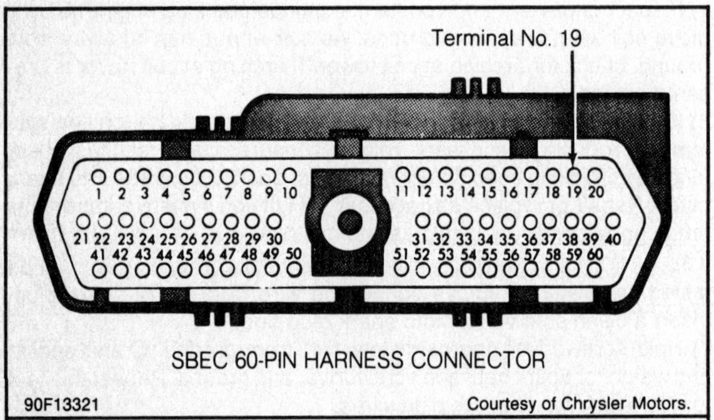
Terminal No. 19
1 2 3 4 5 6 7 8 9 10
11 12 13 14 15 16 17 18 19 20
21 22 23 24 25 26 27 28 29 30
31 32 33 34 35 36 37 38 39 40
41 42 43 44 45 46 47 48 49 50
51 52 53 54 55 56 57 58 59 60
SBEC 60-PIN HARNESS CONNECTOR
90F13321
Courtesy of Chrysler Motors.

Fig. 5: Identifying SBEC 60-Pin Harness Connector Terminals

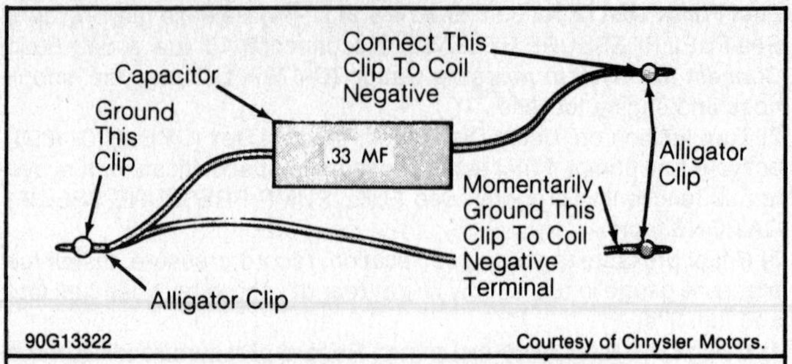
Connect This Clip To Coil Negative
Capacitor
Ground This Clip
.33 MF
Alligator Clip
Momentarily Ground This Clip To Coil Negative Terminal
Alligator Clip
90G13322
Courtesy of Chrysler Motors.

Fig. 6: Connecting Specially Constructed Jumper Wire

3.3L - 1) Ensure sufficient battery voltage (12.4 volts) is available to operate cranking and ignition systems. Connect voltmeter between B+ wiring harness coil connector and ground. *See Fig. 7.*

2) Crank engine for 5 seconds while monitoring voltage at B+ terminal. If voltage remains near zero during entire period of cranking, see appropriate SELF-DIAGNOSTICS article to check SBEC and ASD relay.

3) If voltage is near battery voltage and drops to zero after 1-2 seconds of cranking, see appropriate SELF-DIAGNOSTICS article to check cam and crank sensor circuits to SBEC.

4) If voltage remains near battery voltage during entire 5 seconds, turn ignition off. Disconnect SBEC 60-pin connector. Check 60-pin connector for loose terminals (push-outs).

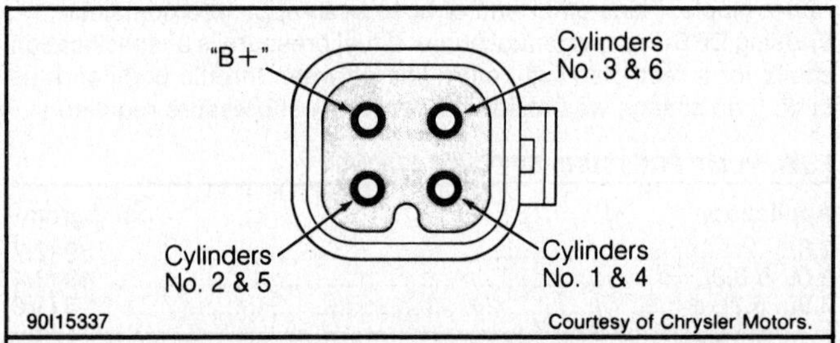
"B+"
Cylinders No. 3 & 6
Cylinders No. 2 & 5
Cylinders No. 1 & 4
90I15337
Courtesy of Chrysler Motors.

Fig. 7: Identifying Wiring Harness Coil Connector Terminals (3.3L)

IDLE SPEED & IGNITION TIMING

Ensure idle speed and ignition timing are set to specification. Always refer to Emissions Control Information label in engine compartment before servicing. If manual and emission label specifications differ, always use specifications on emission label. For adjustment procedures, see ON-VEHICLE ADJUSTMENTS - GASOLINE article.

SUMMARY

If no faults were found while performing BASIC DIAGNOSTIC PROCEDURES, proceed to appropriate SELF-DIAGNOSTICS article. If no hard codes are found in self-diagnostics, proceed to appropriate TROUBLE SHOOTING - NO CODES article for diagnosis by symptom (i.e., ROUGH IDLE, NO-START, etc.) or intermittent diagnostic procedures.

1991 ENGINE PERFORMANCE
Basic Diagnostic Procedures – Diesel – Intercooled

Pickup

INTRODUCTION

The following diagnostic steps will help prevent overlooking a simple problem. Also begin here to diagnose a no-start condition.

The first step in diagnosing any driveability problem is verifying the customer's complaint with a test drive under conditions during which the problem reportedly occurred.

Before entering self-diagnostics, perform a careful and complete visual inspection. Most engine control problems result from mechanical breakdowns or poor electrical connections. Before condemning the computerized system, perform each test listed in this article.

PRELIMINARY INSPECTION & ADJUSTMENTS

VISUAL INSPECTION

1) Ensure battery connections are tight and not corroded. Ensure 60-pin connector on Single Board Engine Controller (SBEC) is fully engaged and retaining screw is tight. The SBEC is located in left front corner of engine compartment, near horns on left fender.
2) Ensure electrical connections on intake manifold heater relays are tight and not corroded. Intake manifold heater relays are mounted on the inner wheelwell. *See Fig. 1.*
3) Check for loose or defective electrical connections on starter motor. Ensure electrical connections are installed on charge air temperature sensor and air temperature switch and wiring is okay. Charge air temperature sensor and air temperature switch are located in intake manifold cover. *See Fig. 2.*

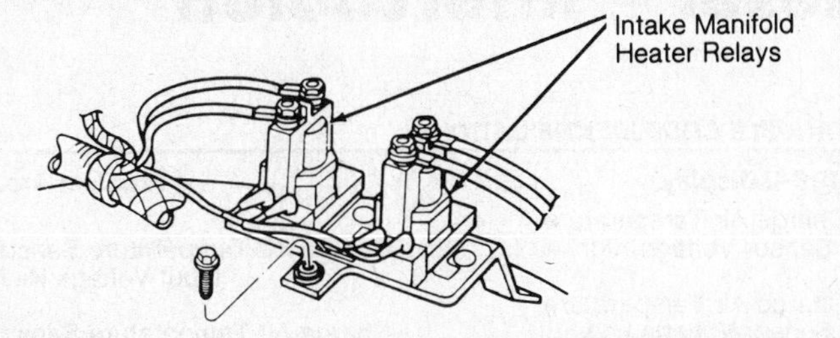
Intake Manifold
Heater Relays

91B13301 Courtesy of Chrysler Motors.

Fig. 1: Identifying Intake Manifold Heater Relays

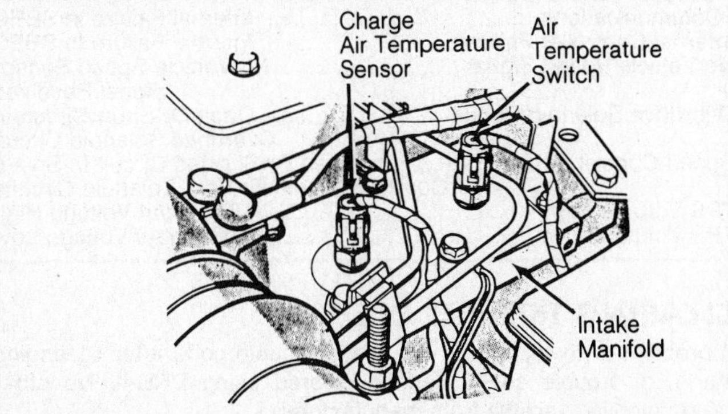
Charge
Air Temperature
Sensor
Air
Temperature
Switch
Intake
Manifold

91A13300 Courtesy of Chrysler Motors.

Fig. 2: Identifying Charge Air Temperature Sensor & Air Temperature Switch

4) Ensure electrical connector is installed on water-in-fuel sensor. The water-in-fuel sensor is located in bottom of fuel/water separator filter. *See Fig. 3.*
5) Ensure electrical connection is installed on shutoff solenoid valve and KSB valve on fuel injection pump. *See Fig. 3.*
6) Check for tightness and corrosion on electrical connections on intake manifold heater. Intake manifold heater is a grid heater installed between air inlet housing and intake manifold. The air inlet housing is attached to intercooler outlet duct, which is connected to the intercooler, located in front of the radiator.

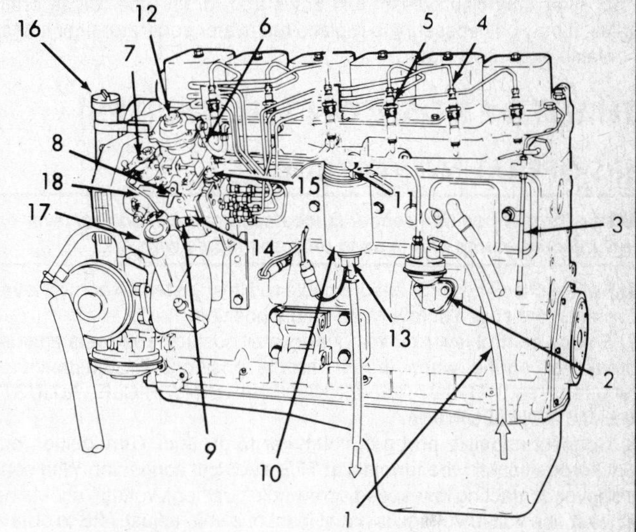
16
12
7
6
5
4
8
18
17
15
11
3
14
13
2
9
10
1

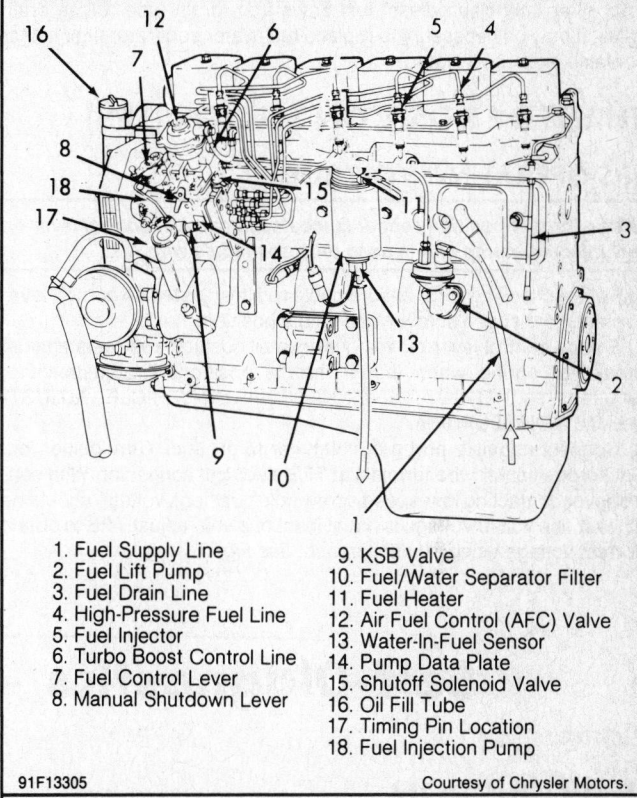

1. Fuel Supply Line
2. Fuel Lift Pump
3. Fuel Drain Line
4. High-Pressure Fuel Line
5. Fuel Injector
6. Turbo Boost Control Line
7. Fuel Control Lever
8. Manual Shutdown Lever
9. KSB Valve
10. Fuel/Water Separator Filter
11. Fuel Heater
12. Air Fuel Control (AFC) Valve
13. Water-In-Fuel Sensor
14. Pump Data Plate
15. Shutoff Solenoid Valve
16. Oil Fill Tube
17. Timing Pin Location
18. Fuel Injection Pump

91F13305 Courtesy of Chrysler Motors.

Fig. 3: Locating Fuel System Components

7) Check for binding throttle linkage or defective throttle return spring. Ensure ground cable, located near alternator, is tight. Check for leaking fuel lines.
8) Check air filter for restriction or damage. Ensure intercooler inlet and outlet ducts clamps are tight. *See Fig. 4.*

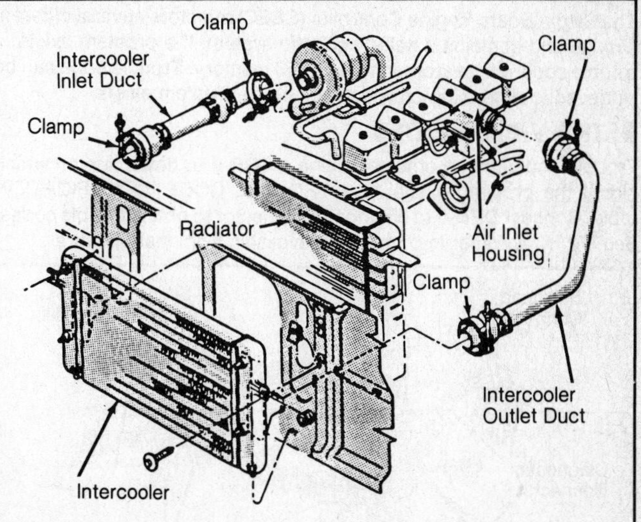
Clamp
Intercooler
Inlet Duct
Clamp
Clamp
Radiator
Air Inlet
Housing
Clamp
Intercooler
Outlet Duct
Intercooler

91J13291 Courtesy of Chrysler Motors.

Fig. 4: Exploded View of Intercooler Assembly

1991 ENGINE PERFORMANCE
Basic Diagnostic Procedures – Diesel – Intercooled (Cont.)

FUEL SYSTEM

FUEL/WATER SEPARATOR FILTER

Place drain pan under drain tube on fuel/water separator filter. *See Fig. 3.* With engine off, open drain valve on bottom of fuel/water separator filter until clean diesel fuel flows from drain tube. Close drain valve. It may be necessary to replace fuel/water separator filter if filter contains excessive water.

THROTTLE POSITION SENSOR (TPS)

TPS OPERATING VOLTAGE

NOTE: Throttle position sensor is located above fuel control lever on fuel injection pump and is used only on models with A/T.

1) Before checking TPS, ensure cable rod is adjusted so control lever contacts low-speed screw when in idle position.
2) Ensure control lever moves over center position and rests against breakover spring when in full throttle position. If adjustment is required, see THROTTLE LINKAGE in ON-VEHICLE ADJUSTMENTS - DIESEL article.
3) Connect negative probe of voltmeter to ground. Turn ignition on. Backprobe center wire terminal at TPS electrical connector. With control lever contacting low-speed screw (idle position), voltage should be at least one volt. If voltage is not at least one volt, adjust TPS to obtain correct voltage using 10 mm wrench. *See Fig. 5.*
4) Open throttle to full throttle position. Backprobe center wire terminal at TPS electrical connector. Voltage should be at least 2.25 volts more than voltage obtained with throttle in idle position. If voltage is not at least 2.25 volts more than idle position voltage, adjust TPS to obtain correct voltage. Replace TPS if it cannot be adjusted.

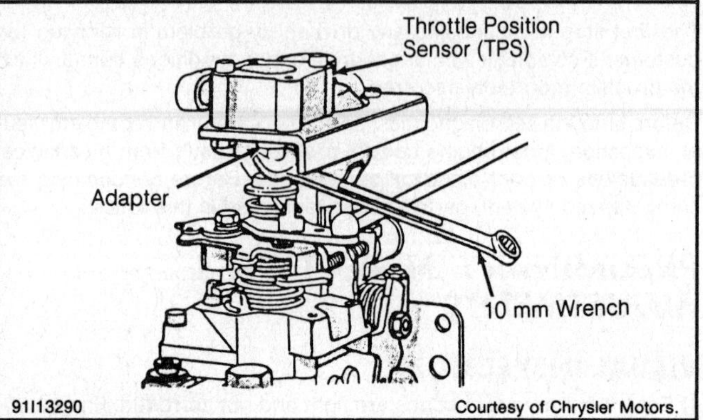
Throttle Position
Sensor (TPS)
Adapter
10 mm Wrench
91I13290
Courtesy of Chrysler Motors.

Fig. 5: Adjusting TPS

SUMMARY

If no faults were found while performing BASIC DIAGNOSTIC PROCEDURES, proceed to SELF-DIAGNOSTICS - DIESEL - INTERCOOLED article. If no trouble codes are found in self-diagnostics, proceed to TROUBLE SHOOTING - NO CODES - DIESEL article for diagnosis by symptom .

Self-Diagnostics – Diesel – Intercooled

Pickup

INTRODUCTION

If no faults were found while performing BASIC DIAGNOSTIC PROCEDURES - DIESEL - INTERCOOLED article, proceed with self-diagnostics. If no fault codes are present after entering self-diagnostics, proceed to TROUBLE SHOOTING - NO CODES - DIESEL article for diagnosis by symptom.

SELF-DIAGNOSTIC SYSTEM

The Single Board Engine Controller (SBEC) monitors several different circuits and contains a self-diagnostic system. If a problem exists, a trouble code will be stored in the SBEC memory. Trouble code can be retrieved to determine on which circuit the problem exists.

RETRIEVING CODES

Trouble code can be obtained using a DRB-II to determine on which circuit the problem exists. See TROUBLE CODE IDENTIFICATION table. Connect DRB-II to diagnostic connector to obtain trouble codes. *See Fig. 1.* No other information is available from manufacturer.

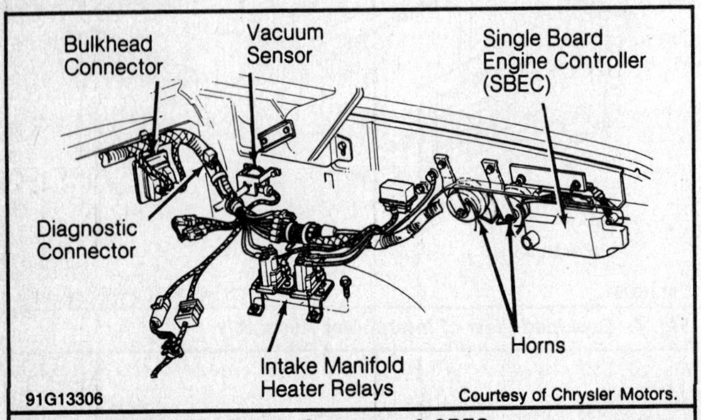
Bulkhead
Connector
Vacuum
Sensor
Single Board
Engine Controller
(SBEC)
Diagnostic
Connector
Intake Manifold
Heater Relays
Horns
91G13306
Courtesy of Chrysler Motors.

Fig. 1: Locating Diagnostic Connector & SBEC

TROUBLE CODE IDENTIFICATION

DRB-II Display	Problem Area
Charge Air Temperature Sensor Voltage High	Charge Air Temperature Sensor Input Voltage High
Charge Air Temperature Sensor Voltage Low	Charge Air Temperature Sensor Input Voltage Low
Controller Failure EEPROM Write Denied	EEPROM Failure In SBEC
Controller Failure - SPI Communications	Internal Failure In SBEC
Internal Controller Failure	Internal Failure In SBEC
No Vehicle Speed Signal	No Vehicle Speed Sensor Signal Received
Overdrive Solenoid Circuit	Open Or Short Circuit In Overdrive Solenoid Circuit
Speed Control Circuit	Open Or Shorted Circuit In Speed Control Vacuum Or Vent Solenoid Circuits
TPS Voltage High	TPS Input Voltage High
TPS Voltage Low	TPS Input Voltage Low

CLEARING TROUBLE CODES

If problem is fixed, SBEC will cancel trouble code after 51 engine starts, or trouble codes can be cleared using DRB-II. No other information is available from manufacturer.

SBEC LOCATION

The SBEC is located in left front corner of engine compartment, near horns on left fender. *See Fig. 1.*

SUMMARY

If no trouble codes are present and driveability symptoms exist, proceed to TROUBLE SHOOTING - NO CODES - DIESEL article for diagnosis by symptom.

1991 ENGINE PERFORMANCE
Self-Diagnostics – Gasoline

Caravan, Dakota, Pickup, Ramcharger, RWD Van, Town & Country, Voyager

INTRODUCTION

If no faults were found while performing BASIC DIAGNOSTIC PROCEDURES, proceed with self-diagnostics. If no fault codes or only pass codes are present after entering self-diagnostics, proceed to TROUBLE SHOOTING – NO CODES – GASOLINE article for diagnosis by symptom (i.e. ROUGH IDLE, NO START, etc.).

MODEL IDENTIFICATION

VEHICLE BODY IDENTIFICATION

Model Name	Body Type
Caravan, Town & Country, & Voyager	AS
Dakota	AN
Pickup & Ramcharger	AD
RWD Van	AB

NOTE: Fault code charts may contain references to body types not covered in this article.

SELF-DIAGNOSTIC SYSTEM

SELF-DIAGNOSTICS DIRECTORY

SYSTEM DIAGNOSIS

The self-diagnostic capabilities of this system, if properly utilized, can simplify testing. The Single-Board Engine Controller (SBEC) monitors several different engine control system circuits.

If a problem is sensed with a monitored circuit, a fault code is stored in the SBEC, the CHECK ENGINE light illuminates, and SBEC enters limp-in mode. In limp-in mode, SBEC compensates for component failure by substituting information from other sources. This allows vehicle operation until repairs can be made.

Once fault codes are known, refer to FAULT CODES table in this article to determine the questionable circuit. Test circuits and repair or replace components as required. If problem is repaired or ceases to exist, the SBEC cancels that fault code after approximately 50 ignition on-off cycles. To clear fault codes, see CLEARING FAULT CODES in this article.

A specific fault code is the result of a particular system failure, but it DOES NOT indicate that cause of failure is necessarily within system. The fault code DOES NOT condemn any specific component; it pinpoints a probable malfunctioning area.

Hard Failures – Hard failures cause CHECK ENGINE light to illuminate and remain on until the malfunction is repaired. If light comes on and remains on (light may flash) during vehicle operation, cause of malfunction must be determined using diagnostic (code) charts. If a sensor fails, SBEC will use a substitute value in its calculations, allowing engine operation in limp-in mode. In this condition, vehicle will run but driveability may be poor.

NOTE: A start counter (key counter) appears at bottom of fault message on DRB-II to show number of engine starts since fault code last occurred. This helps determine if fault is intermittent. As an example, if DRB-II displays 0 STARTS SINCE ERS, it indicates zero engine starts since fault occurred, and fault code is a hard failure. If start counter (key counter) shows more than zero engine starts since fault last occurred, then fault code is an intermittent failure.

Intermittent Failures – Intermittent failures may cause CHECK ENGINE light to flicker or illuminate and go out after the intermittent fault goes away. However, the corresponding fault code will be retained in SBEC memory.

If related fault does not reoccur within a certain time frame, fault code will be erased from SBEC memory. Intermittent failures can be caused by a defective sensor, connector, or wiring-related problems. See INTERMITTENTS in TROUBLE SHOOTING – NO CODES – GASOLINE article.

DIAGNOSTIC PROCEDURE

To obtain fault codes, see RETRIEVING FAULT CODES in this article. If fault codes are NOT present and/or Diagnostic Readout Box II (DRB-II) is used, proceed to one of the following tests.

- Go to NO START TEST 1A (NS-1A) chart if a no-start condition exists, or engine stalls after start-up. Perform indicated VERIFICATION PROCEDURE chart after repairs. Ensure charts apply to engine being tested.
- Go to DRIVEABILITY TEST 1A (DR-1A) chart if engine runs but has performance problems. Perform indicated VERIFICATION PROCEDURE chart after repairs. Ensure charts apply to engine being tested.

NOTE: When using trouble shooting charts for diagnosis, DO NOT skip any steps in chart, or incorrect diagnosis may result.

Before proceeding with diagnosis, the following precautions must be followed:

- Vehicle must have a fully charged battery, and functional charging system.
- Probe SBEC connector from pin side. DO NOT backprobe SBEC connector.
- DO NOT cause short circuits when performing electrical tests. This will set additional fault codes, making diagnosis of original problem more difficult.
- DO NOT use a test light in place of a voltmeter.
- When checking for spark, ensure coil wire is NO more than 1/4" from ground. If coil wire is more than 1/4" from ground, damage to vehicle electronics and/or SBEC may result.
- DO NOT prolong testing of fuel injectors, or engine may hydrostatically (liquid) lock.
- Always repair lowest fault code number (CHECK ENGINE light), or first fault displayed (DRB-II) first.
- Always perform VERIFICATION PROCEDURE test after repairs are made.
- Always disconnect DRB-II after use.
- Always disconnect DRB-II before charging battery.

RETRIEVING FAULT CODES

NOTE: Manufacturer recommends using DRB-II (Diagnostic Readout Box-II, C-4805) to diagnose the system. CHECK ENGINE light function can be used, but has limited diagnostic usage.

CHECK ENGINE Light Method – **1)** Start engine (if possible). Move transmission shift lever through all gear positions, ending in Park. Turn A/C switch on, then off (if equipped).

2) Turn engine off. Without starting engine again, turn ignition on, off, on, off, and on. Record 2-digit fault codes as displayed by the flashing CHECK ENGINE light.

3) For example, Code 23 is displayed as flash, flash, 4-second pause, flash, flash, flash. After a slightly longer pause, other codes stored are displayed in numerical order.

4) Once CHECK ENGINE light begins to flash fault codes, it cannot be stopped. If you lose count, it will be necessary to start over. Code 55 indicates end of fault code display.

5) Refer to FAULT CODES table to translate fault code number to a system fault description (display on DRB-II). Once fault code description is obtained, refer to appropriate NO START TEST 1A (NS-1A) or DRIVEABILITY TEST 1A (DR-1A) trouble shooting chart for additional testing procedures.

1991 ENGINE PERFORMANCE
Self-Diagnostics – Gasoline (Cont.)

6) As an example, a 3.0L engine starts and runs, but has a driveability problem, and CHECK ENGINE light indicates a Code 14. Refer to FAULT CODES table to translate fault code number to a system fault description (display on DRB-II).

7) When system fault description (display on DRB-II) is obtained, refer to appropriate DRIVEABILITY TEST 1A (DR-1A) trouble shooting chart, since vehicle has a driveability problem, for more testing procedures. Select fault message and corresponding test from table, and proceed to appropriate trouble shooting chart. Test procedure may vary depending whether fault code is a hard or intermittent failure.

NOTE: When using trouble shooting charts for diagnosis, DO NOT skip any steps in chart, or incorrect diagnosis may result.

NOTE: The DRB-II can also be used to perform the following: display the state or values of sensors, inputs/outputs and components, allow various outputs such as valves and hydraulics to be tested, and reset Emission Maintenance Reminder (EMR) functions. See OPERATING MODES and EMISSION MAINTENANCE REMINDER (EMR) in this article.

DRB-II Method – 1) Turn ignition off. Attach DRB-II Tester (C-4805) to diagnostic connector.

DIAGNOSTIC CONNECTOR LOCATIONS [1]

Application	Location
Caravan, Town & Country, & Voyager	In Engine Compartment, Near SBEC
Dakota	In Engine Compartment, On Right Corner Of Firewall
Pickup & Ramcharger	In Engine Compartment, Near Master Cylinder
RWD Van	On Center Of Firewall, Near SBEC

[1] – *See Figs. 1-5.*

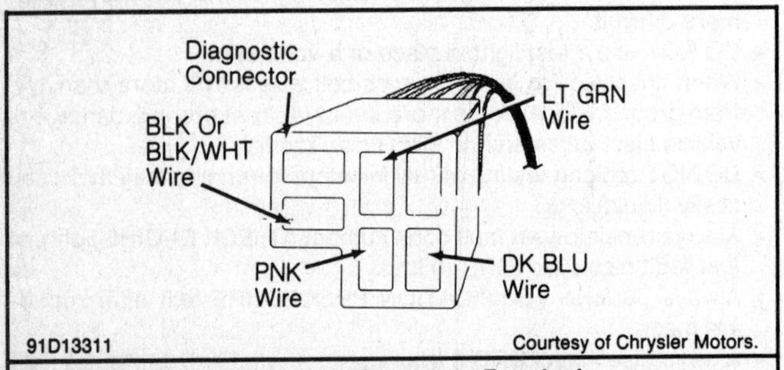
Diagnostic Connector
LT GRN Wire
BLK Or BLK/WHT Wire
PNK Wire
DK BLU Wire
91D13311
Courtesy of Chrysler Motors.

Fig. 1: Identifying Diagnostic Connector Terminals

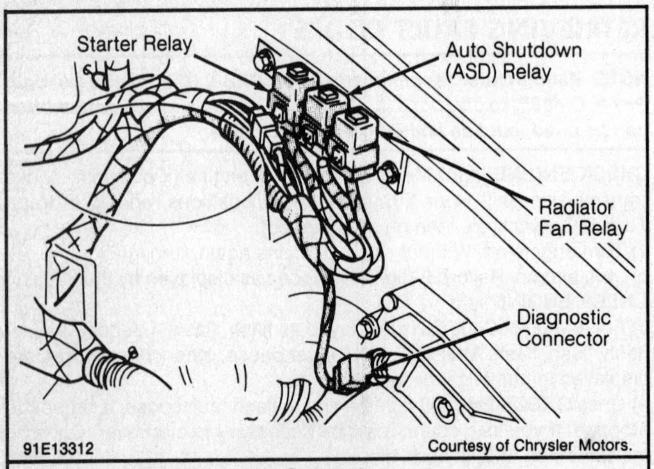
Starter Relay
Auto Shutdown (ASD) Relay
Radiator Fan Relay
Diagnostic Connector
91E13312
Courtesy of Chrysler Motors.

Fig. 2: Locating Diagnostic Connector (Caravan, Town & Country, & Voyager)

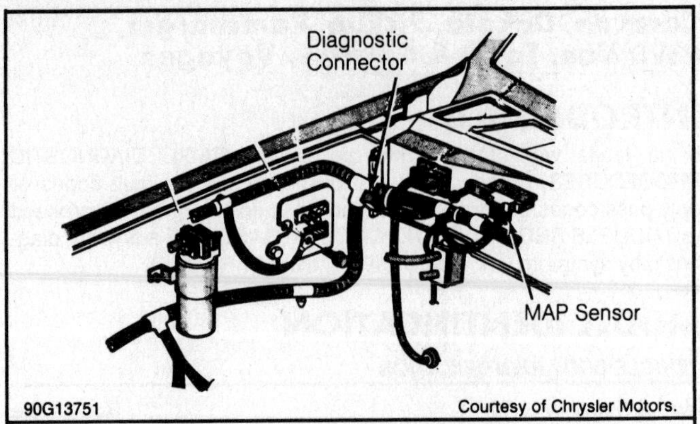
Diagnostic Connector
MAP Sensor
90G13751
Courtesy of Chrysler Motors.

Fig. 3: Locating Diagnostic Connector (Dakota)

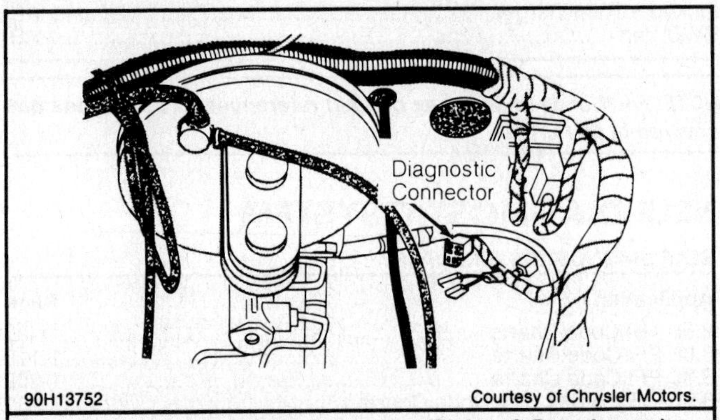
Diagnostic Connector
90H13752
Courtesy of Chrysler Motors.

Fig. 4: Locating Diagnostic Connector (Pickup & Ramcharger)

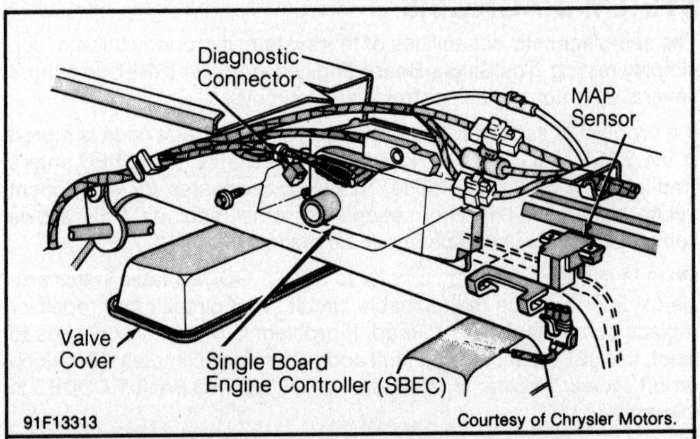
Diagnostic Connector
MAP Sensor
Valve Cover
Single Board Engine Controller (SBEC)
91F13313
Courtesy of Chrysler Motors.

Fig. 5: Locating Diagnostic Connector (RWD Van)

2) Start engine (if possible). Move transmission shift lever through all positions, ending in Park. Turn A/C switch on, then off (if equipped). Turn engine off. Without starting engine again, turn ignition on. DO NOT touch keypad on DRB-II during power-up sequence, or an error will result. The copyright date and diagnostic program will be displayed briefly.

3) If DRB-II screen is blank, or if an error message appears, proceed to DRB-II PROBLEMS & ERROR MESSAGES in this article. The following are possible error messages that may appear: BAD FRAMING, BAD OP CODE, CARTRIDGE ERROR, COMMAND REJECTED, HIGH BATTERY, KEYPAD TEST FAILURE, LOW BATTERY, NO RESPONSE or RAM TEST FAILURE.

4) After a few seconds, display will change to read as follows: DRB-II, 1) VEHICLES TESTED, or 2) HOW TO USE. Press ENTER button immediately. Press the down arrow twice. Display will now read as follows: DRB-II, 2) HOW TO USE, 3) CONFIGURE, and 4) SELECT SYSTEM.

FAULT CODES

FAULT CODES [1]

Code	Display On DRB-II	Fault Condition
11	NO REFERENCE SIGNAL DURING CRANKING	No distributor reference signal detected during cranking.
13 [2]	NO CHANGE IN MAP FROM START TO RUN OR	No difference is recognized between engine MAP reading and barometric pressure reading at start-up.
	SLOW CHANGE IN IDLE MAP SIGNAL	No difference in MAP sensor signal is detected.
14 [2]	MAP VOLTAGE TOO LOW	MAP sensor input less than minimum acceptable voltage.
	MAP VOLTAGE TOO HIGH	MAP sensor input greater than maximum acceptable voltage.
15 [3]	NO VEHICLE SPEED SIGNAL	No vehicle speed sensor signal detected.
17	ENGINE IS COLD TOO LONG	Coolant temperature less than normal operating temperature.
21 [3]	O_2 SIGNAL STAYS AT CENTER	No rich or lean signal is detected from O_2 sensor input.
	O_2 SIGNAL SHORTED TO VOLTAGE	Oxygen sensor input voltage greater than normal operating range.
22 [2]	COOLANT SENSOR VOLTAGE TOO LOW	Coolant temperature sensor input is low.
	COOLANT SENSOR VOLTAGE TOO HIGH	Coolant temperature sensor input is high.
23	[4] THROTTLE BODY TEMP VOLTAGE LOW	Throttle body temperature sensor input voltage is low.
	THROTTLE BODY TEMP VOLTAGE HIGH	Throttle body temperature sensor input voltage is high.
	[2] [5] CHARGE TEMPERATURE SENSOR VOLTAGE HIGH OR LOW	Charge temperature sensor input voltage is less than or greater than acceptable voltage.
24 [2]	TPS VOLTAGE LOW	TPS sensor output voltage is less than acceptable voltage.
	TPS VOLTAGE HIGH	TPS sensor output is greater than maximum acceptable voltage.
25 [3]	AUTOMATIC IDLE SPEED MOTOR CIRCUITS	Shorted condition detected in one or more AIS actuator circuits.
26 [2]	INJ 1 PEAK VOLTAGE NOT OBTAINED	High resistance in No. 1 injector circuit.
	INJ 2 PEAK VOLTAGE NOT OBTAINED	High resistance in No. 2 injector circuit.
	INJ 3 PEAK VOLTAGE NOT OBTAINED	High resistance in No. 3 injector circuit.
27	INJ 1 CONTROL CIRCUIT	Injector output driver does not respond correctly to control signal.
	INJ 2 CONTROL CIRCUIT	Injector output driver does not respond correctly to control signal.
	INJ 3 CONTROL CIRCUIT	Injector output driver does not respond correctly to control signal.
31 [3]	PURGE SOLENOID CIRCUIT	Open or shorted condition detected in purge solenoid circuit.
32 [3]	EGR SOLENOID CIRCUIT	Open or shorted condition detected in EGR solenoid circuit.
	EGR SYSTEM FAILURE	Controller did not detect required air/fuel mixture change. during diagnostic test (CA only).
33	A/C CLUTCH RELAY CIRCUIT	Open or shorted condition detected in A/C clutch relay circuit.
34	SPEED CONTROL SOLENOID CIRCUITS	Open or shorted condition detected in speed control vacuum or vent solenoid circuits.
35	[6] RADIATOR FAN RELAY CIRCUIT	Open or shorted circuit in radiator fan relay circuit.
	[7] IDLE SWITCH SHORTED	Idle contact switch input circuit shorted to ground.
	[7] IDLE SWITCH OPEN CIRCUIT	Idle contact switch input circuit open.
36	AIR SWITCHING SOLENOID CIRCUIT	Open or shorted condition detected in air switching solenoid circuit.
37	[8] TORQUE CONVERTER LOCK-UP SOLENOID CIRCUIT	Open or shorted condition detected in torque converter lockup solenoid circuit (A/T only).
41 [2]	ALTERNATOR FIELD NOT SWITCHING	Alternator field not switching properly.
42	ASD RELAY CONTROL CIRCUIT OR	Open or shorted condition detected in ASD relay circuit.
	NO ASD RELAY VOLTAGE SENSE AT SBEC	No ASD voltage sensed at controller.
43 [3]	IGNITION COIL NO. 1 PRIMARY CIRCUIT	Peak primary current not obtained with maximum dwell.
	IGNITION COIL NO. 2 PRIMARY CIRCUIT	Peak primary current not obtained with maximum dwell.
	IGNITION COIL NO. 3 PRIMARY CIRCUIT	Peak primary current not obtained with maximum dwell.
45	OVERDRIVE SOLENOID CIRCUIT	Open or shorted condition detected in overdrive solenoid circuit.
46 [2]	CHARGING SYSTEM VOLTAGE TOO HIGH	Charging system voltage is more than acceptable voltage.
47 [2]	CHARGING SYSTEM VOLTAGE TOO LOW	Charging system voltage is less than acceptable voltage.
51 [3]	O_2 SIGNAL STAYS BELOW CENTER (LEAN)	O_2 sensor signal stays lean.
	OR ADDITIVE ADAPTIVE MEMORY AT RICH LIMIT	Additive adaptive memory at rich limit.
52 [3]	O_2 SIGNAL STAYS ABOVE CENTER (RICH)	O_2 sensor signal stays rich.
	OR ADDITIVE ADAPTIVE MEMORY AT LEAN LIMIT	Additive adaptive memory at lean limit.
53	INTERNAL CONTROLLER FAILURE	Internal failure in controller.
54 [2]	NO SYNC PICK-UP SIGNAL	No fuel sync signal detected during engine rotation.
55	N/A	Completion of fault code display (CHECK ENGINE light).
62	CONTROLLER FAILURE EMR MILES NOT STORED	Controller failure, EMR miles not stored.
63	CONTROLLER FAILURE EEPROM WRITE DENIED	Controller failure, EEPROM write denied.

[1] – Fault code application will vary with model and engine application. Not all fault codes are used on all models.
[2] – CHECK ENGINE light will be on.
[3] – CHECK ENGINE light will be on (California models only).
[4] – Used on 2.5L (Dakota) and 5.2L and 5.9L.
[5] – Used on 3.3L only.
[6] – Used on 2.5L (Dakota), 3.0L and 3.3L.
[7] – Used on 3.9L, 5.2L and 5.9L.
[8] – On some models, this may be referred to as part throttle unlock solenoid.

5) Select No. 4 (SELECT SYSTEM) to enter the diagnostic system. Display will read as follows: SELECT SYSTEM, 1) ENGINE, and 2) TRANSMISSION. Select No. 1 (ENGINE) to enter the engine system part of the DRB-II program. Display will change to read as follows: 1991 XX, XXXX EMISSIONS, AUTOMATIC TRANS, SBEC XX,#XXXX-A.

NOTE: Display may vary slightly depending on engine package being diagnosed.

6) After a few seconds, display will change to read as follows: AIR COND, 1) WITH A/C, and 2) WITHOUT A/C. Press ENTER button to change display immediately. Select No. 1 or No. 2 as appropriate for vehicle being tested.

7) Display will now read as follows: ENGINE SYSTEM, 1) FUEL/IGNITION, and 2) CHARGING. Select No. 1 (FUEL/IGNITION) to bring up menu of test categories for the fuel/ignition system. Display will change to read as follows: FUEL/IGN MENU, 1) SYSTEM TEST, and 2) READ FAULTS.

8) Press the down arrow 3 times to view rest of menu. Display will read as follows: FUEL/IGN MENU, 3) STATE DISPLAY, 4) ACTUATOR TEST, and 5) ADJUSTMENTS. To read fault codes, select No. 2 (READ FAULTS).

9) If no fault code exists, display will read as follows: NO FAULTS DETECTED. If fault codes exist, display will show number of faults detected, such as 1 of 3 faults, and fault message. This is the fault counter. Below the fault message, the start counter (key counter) will list number of starts since fault code was set.

10) The start counter (key counter) helps to determine if fault is intermittent. As an example, if DRB-II displays 0 STARTS SINCE ERS, this indicates zero engine starts since fault occurred, and fault code is a hard failure. If start counter (key counter) on DRB-II shows more than zero engine starts since fault last occurred, fault code is an intermittent failure.

11) If more than one fault code exists, press the down arrow to display next fault code. All fault codes must be read before fault codes can be erased. Once fault codes are obtained, refer to appropriate NO START TEST 1A (NS-1A) or DRIVEABILITY TEST 1A (DR-1A) trouble shooting chart.

NOTE: When using trouble shooting charts for diagnosis, DO NOT skip any steps in chart, or incorrect diagnosis may result.

CLEARING FAULT CODES

NOTE: It will be necessary to place DRB-II in the FUEL/IGN MENU to erase fault codes. This menu is obtained when retrieving fault codes. See DRB-II METHOD under RETRIEVING FAULT CODES.

1) Once fault codes have been read and DRB-II is in FUEL/IGN MENU, press the down arrow. Display will read as follows: ERASE FAULTS, 1) DON'T ERASE, and 2) ERASE. Press the down arrow.

2) Display will ask you if you are sure you want to erase fault codes. Press ENTER button to erase fault codes. DRB-II will display FAULTS ERASED message.

OPERATING MODES

NOTE: Actuator, sensor, solenoid and switch tests available on DRB-II will vary depending on engine, transaxle and emission packages.

STATE DISPLAY MODE

The SBEC can only recognize high and low states on switch circuits. SBEC cannot tell the difference between switch position versus an open or short circuit, or a defective switch.

If a change is noted, it is assumed entire switch circuit to the SBEC is operating correctly. The following information can be selected from the state display mode: module, sensor, inputs/outputs, monitoring of system, and custom display.

Module Info – When module information is selected from STATE DISPLAY mode, information about the SBEC, such as, engine application, transmission application and identification number can be obtained. Information can be used to verify proper SBEC application.

Sensor – When sensor information is selected from STATE DISPLAY mode, information is provided about engine operation through various sensors and engine controls depending on engine and model application. The following information may be displayed.

- Added Adaptive Fuel
- Adaptive Fuel Factor
- Air Idle Speed (AIS) Motor Position
- Barometric Pressure
- Battery Temperature
- Battery Voltage
- Charging System Goal
- Charge Temperature
- Charge Temperature Sensor Reading
- Coolant Temperature
- Coolant Temperature Sensor Reading
- Distributorless Ignition System (DIS) Status
- Engine Speed
- Fault No. 1 Key-On Info
- Fault No. 2 Key-On Info
- Fault No. 3 Key-On Info
- Knock Sensor Signal
- Manifold Absolute Pressure Sensor Vacuum Reading
- Manifold Absolute Pressure Sensor Voltage Reading
- Minimum Idle Speed
- Minimum Throttle Position Sensor Voltage
- Module Spark Advance
- Overall Knock Retard
- Oxygen Sensor State
- Oxygen Sensor Voltage
- Theft Alarm Status
- Throttle Body Temperature
- Throttle Opening
- Throttle Position Sensor Voltage
- Total Spark Advance
- Speed Control Status
- Speed Control Target
- Vehicle Speed

Inputs/Outputs – When input/output information is selected from state display mode, information is provided about component operation through various lights, relays, solenoids and switches depending on engine and model application. The following information may be displayed.

- A/C Clutch Relay
- A/C Switch
- Air Switching Solenoid
- Auto Shutdown (ASD) Relay
- Brake Switch
- CHECK ENGINE Light
- Closed Throttle Switch
- EGR Solenoid
- Emission Maintenance Reminder (EMR) Light
- Idle Switch
- Lockup Solenoid
- Overdrive Override
- Overdrive Solenoid
- Park Neutral Switch (A/T Models)
- Part Throttle Unlock (PTU) A/T Only
- Purge Control Solenoid
- Radiator Fan Relay
- Shift Indicator Light
- Speed Control On/Off Switch
- Speed Control Resume
- Speed Control Setting
- Speed Control Vacuum Solenoid
- Speed Control Vent Solenoid

Monitors - When monitor information is selected from STATE DISPLAY mode, information is provided about various systems or components as they are monitored depending on engine and model application. The following possible information may be displayed.

- Adaptive Memory
- Engine RPM
- Fuel Control
- Fuel Mileage
- Interrogator
- Knock Retard
- No Start
- Secondary Indicators
- Spark Advance

Custom Display - When custom display is selected, information can be changed to what the technician wants to monitor.

ACTUATOR TEST MODE

Actuator test mode is used to check operation of output circuits of devices the SBEC cannot recognize. The following, depending on engine and model application, can be activated in actuator test mode to ensure component operation: relays, solenoids and various components. The following are information or components that may be accessed through actuator test mode.

- A/C Clutch Relay
- Air Idle Speed (AIS) Motor
- Air Switch Solenoid
- Alternator Field
- ASD (Auto Shutdown) Relay
- ASD (Auto Shutdown) System
- CHECK ENGINE Light
- EGR Solenoid
- Emission Maintenance Reminder (EMR) Light
- Fuel Injector
- Ignition Coil
- Overdrive Solenoid
- Part Throttle Unlock (PTU) A/T Only
- Purge Solenoid
- Radiator Fan Relay
- Shift Indicator Light (M/T Only)
- Solenoid/Relays
- Speed Control Servo Solenoids
- Stop All Tests
- Tachometer Output

ADJUSTMENTS MODE

In adjustments mode, fault codes can be erased and memory can be reset for the adaptive fuel, minimum TPS and all values. If SBEC is replaced, the Emission Maintenance Reminder (EMR) light can be reset, EMR light memory can be checked, and EMR mileage can be transferred.

DRB-II PROBLEMS & ERROR MESSAGES

BAD FRAMING

If message is displayed, replace cartridge with later version.

BAD OP CODE

If message is displayed, replace cartridge with later version.

BLANK MESSAGE

1) Connect DRB-II to a different vehicle. If message screen is still blank, DRB-II or adapter cable are faulty. Substitute to determine faulty component. If message screen is not blank, DRB-II and adapter cable are functioning properly.

2) Inspect diagnostic connector for proper wire placement, damaged terminals or pushed out pins. Repair as necessary. If connector is okay, check resistance between Black or Black/White wire of diagnostic connector and ground using an ohmmeter. *See Fig. 1.*

3) If resistance is less than 10 ohms, repair open circuit in Black or Black/White wire between diagnostic connector and 60-pin connector on the SBEC. See SBEC LOCATIONS table for component location.

SBEC LOCATIONS

Model	**Location**
Dakota	Right Front Fender, Above Tire
RWD Van	Center Of Firewall
All Others	Left Front Corner Of Engine Compartment

CARTRIDGE ERROR

If message is displayed, replace DRB-II cartridge and proceed with diagnostics.

COMMAND REJECTED

If message is displayed, replace cartridge with later version.

HIGH BATTERY

If message is displayed, connect DRB-II to a different vehicle. If message still exists, DRB-II or adapter cable are faulty. Substitute to determine faulty component. If message is not displayed, DRB-II and adapter cable are functioning properly. Repair charging system.

KEYPAD TEST FAILURE

Ensure ignition is off. DO NOT touch keypad on DRB-II. Turn ignition on. If DRB-II displays KEYPAD TEST FAILURE, replace DRB-II. If KEYPAD TEST FAILURE message is not displayed, proceed with diagnostics.

LOW BATTERY

If message is displayed, connect DRB-II to a different vehicle. If message still exists, DRB-II or adapter cable are faulty. Substitute to determine faulty component. If message is not displayed, DRB-II and adapter cable are functioning properly. Repair charging system.

NO RESPONSE

NOTE: No response may be caused by one of the following: DRB-II is connected to wrong diagnostic connector, ignition is off, defective adapter cable, cartridge or DRB-II, defective SBEC, connector or wiring.

1) Ensure DRB-II is connected to proper diagnostic connector. *See Figs. 2-5.* Ensure ignition is turned on and all wiring connections are secure.

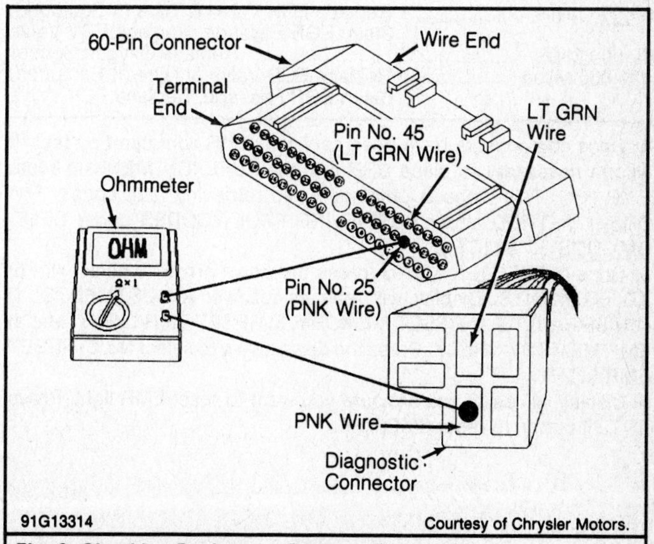
60-Pin Connector
Wire End
Terminal End
LT GRN Wire
Pin No. 45 (LT GRN Wire)
Ohmmeter
OHM
Ω×1
Pin No. 25 (PNK Wire)
PNK Wire
Diagnostic Connector
91G13314
Courtesy of Chrysler Motors.

Fig. 6: Checking Resistance Between Diagnostic Connector & 60-Pin Connector

1991 ENGINE PERFORMANCE
Self-Diagnostics – Gasoline (Cont.)

2) Turn ignition off. Disconnect DRB-II from diagnostic connector. Disconnect 60-pin connector from SBEC. See SBEC LOCATIONS table for component location. Using ohmmeter, check resistance between Pink wire terminal on diagnostic connector and pin No. 25 (Pink wire) on 60-pin connector. *See Figs. 1 and 6.*
3) If resistance is greater than 10 ohms, repair open circuit in Pink wire between diagnostic connector and 60-pin connector. If resistance is not greater than 10 ohms, check resistance between Light Green wire terminal on diagnostic connector and pin No. 45 (Light Green wire) on 60-pin connector.
4) If resistance is greater than 10 ohms, repair open circuit in Light Green wire between diagnostic connector and 60-pin connector. If resistance is not greater than 10 ohms, ensure DRB-II and adapter cable are okay.
5) If all above are okay and a no-start condition exists, proceed to appropriate no-start test. See TEST APPLICATION table.

TEST APPLICATION

Model	Test Number	Test Description
2.5L	NS-12A	Checking System Power, MAP Sensor & Engine Controller
3.0L	NS-8A	Checking System Power & Grounds, TPS, MAP Sensor & Engine Controller
3.3L	NS-10A	Checking System Power, MAP Sensor & Engine Controller
3.9L, 5.2L & 5.9L	NS-7A	Repairing NO RESPONSE

RAM TEST FAILURE

If message is displayed, replace DRB-II and proceed with diagnostics.

EMISSION MAINTENANCE REMINDER (EMR)

EMR LIGHT RESET PROCEDURE

1) The EMR light serves as the vehicle emissions control system service reminder. EMR light is not an emissions warning system; it is only a reminder to perform emissions servicing.
2) The EMR light will illuminate at 60,000, 82,500 and 120,000-mile intervals. Service specified components at designated interval. See EMR LIGHT COMPONENT SERVICE INTERVAL table.

EMR LIGHT COMPONENT SERVICE INTERVAL

Interval	Component To Be Serviced
60,000 Miles	Replace EGR Valve & Tube (If Equipped) Clean EGR Passage, Replace PCV Valve
82,500 Miles	Replace Oxygen Sensor
120,000 Miles	Replace EGR Valve & Tube (If Equipped) Clean EGR Passage, Replace PCV Valve

3) Once components have been serviced, EMR light can be reset. It will be necessary to place DRB-II in the FUEL/IGN MENU to reset EMR light. This menu is obtained when retrieving fault codes. See DRB-II METHOD under RETRIEVING FAULT CODES under SELF-DIAGNOSTIC SYSTEM.
4) Once in FUEL/IGN MENU, press the down arrow to select No. 5) ADJUSTMENTS. Display will read as follows: ADJUSTMENTS, 1) ERASE FAULTS, 2) RESET MEMORY, 3) RESET EMR LIGHT, and 4) EMR MEMORY CHECK. Press the down arrow to select No. 3) RESET EMR LIGHT.
5) Display will ask if you are sure you want to reset EMR light. Press ENTER button to reset EMR light.

EMR MILEAGE TRANSFER

1) When SBEC is replaced, vehicle mileage from odometer must be copied to the replacement SBEC memory. Transfer of vehicle mileage will enable replacement SBEC to operate EMR light properly.
2) It will be necessary to place DRB-II in the FUEL/IGN MENU to reset EMR light. This menu is obtained when retrieving fault codes. See DRB-II METHOD under RETRIEVING FAULT CODES under SELF-DIAGNOSTIC SYSTEM.
3) Once in FUEL/IGN MENU, press the down arrow to select No. 5) ADJUSTMENTS. Display will read as follows: ADJUSTMENTS, 1) ERASE FAULTS, 2) RESET MEMORY, 3) RESET EMR LIGHT, and 4) EMR MEMORY CHECK. Press the down arrow to select No. 4) EMR MEMORY CHECK.
4) Display will ask if you are sure you want to check EMR memory. Press ENTER button to continue. Display will read as follows: EMR MEMORY TEST, and WRITE TEST [------]. Display will now ask if instrument panel mileage is between a specified amount.
5) Press YES or NO button. If YES button is pressed, EMR memory check is completed. If NO button is pressed, enter mileage shown on the odometer. Press ENTER button to complete mileage transfer.

SBEC LOCATION

SBEC LOCATIONS

Model	Location
Dakota	Right Front Fender, Above Tire
RWD Van	Center Of Firewall
All Others	Left Front Corner Of Engine Compartment

SUMMARY

If no hard fault codes (or only pass codes) are present, driveability symptoms exist, or intermittent codes exist, proceed to TROUBLE SHOOTING – NO CODES – GASOLINE article for diagnosis by symptom (i.e. ROUGH IDLE, NO START, etc.), or intermittent diagnostic procedures.

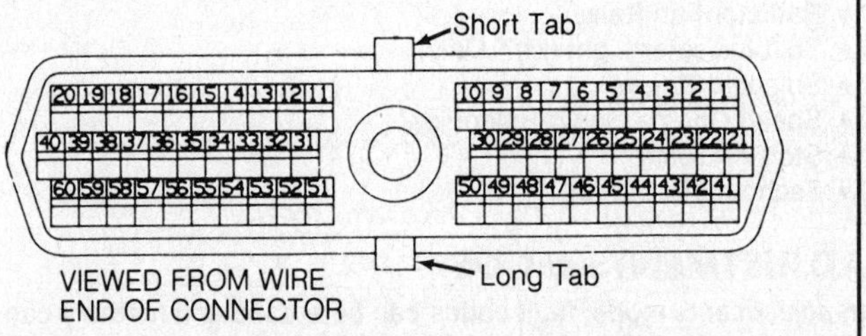
Short Tab
20 19 18 17 16 15 14 13 12 11
10 9 8 7 6 5 4 3 2 1
40 39 38 37 36 35 34 33 32 31
30 29 28 27 26 25 24 23 22 21
60 59 58 57 56 55 54 53 52 51
50 49 48 47 46 45 44 43 42 41
Long Tab
VIEWED FROM WIRE END OF CONNECTOR

91H13315 Courtesy of Chrysler Motors.

Fig. 7: Identifying SBEC 60-Pin Connector Terminals

FAULT CODE CHARTS

NOTE: Fault code charts may contain references to body types not covered in this article.

TROUBLE SHOOTING CHARTS

NOTE: The following trouble shooting charts and illustrations are courtesy of Chrysler Motors. To locate appropriate code chart for vehicle being worked on, see SELF-DIAGNOSTICS DIRECTORY table at beginning of article.

NS-1A: CHECKING FOR IGNITION SPARK & POWER FEED TO COIL (1 OF 3)

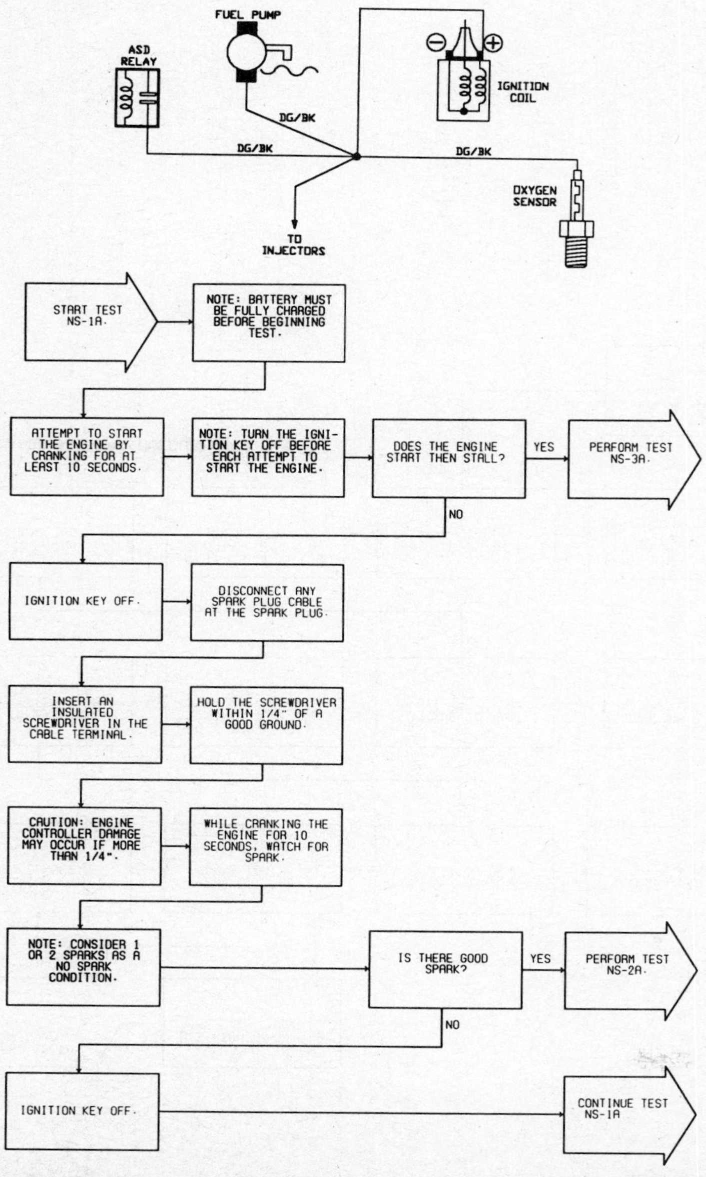
FUEL PUMP
ASD RELAY
IGNITION COIL
DG/BK
DG/BK
DG/BK
OXYGEN SENSOR
TO INJECTORS
START TEST NS-1A.
NOTE: BATTERY MUST BE FULLY CHARGED BEFORE BEGINNING TEST.
ATTEMPT TO START THE ENGINE BY CRANKING FOR AT LEAST 10 SECONDS.
NOTE: TURN THE IGNITION KEY OFF BEFORE EACH ATTEMPT TO START THE ENGINE.
DOES THE ENGINE START THEN STALL?
YES
PERFORM TEST NS-3A.
NO
IGNITION KEY OFF.
DISCONNECT ANY SPARK PLUG CABLE AT THE SPARK PLUG.
INSERT AN INSULATED SCREWDRIVER IN THE CABLE TERMINAL.
HOLD THE SCREWDRIVER WITHIN 1/4" OF A GOOD GROUND.
CAUTION: ENGINE CONTROLLER DAMAGE MAY OCCUR IF MORE THAN 1/4".
WHILE CRANKING THE ENGINE FOR 10 SECONDS, WATCH FOR SPARK.
NOTE: CONSIDER 1 OR 2 SPARKS AS A NO SPARK CONDITION.
IS THERE GOOD SPARK?
YES
PERFORM TEST NS-2A.
NO
IGNITION KEY OFF.
CONTINUE TEST NS-1A

91G08711 91I08731

Fig. 1: ***No Start Test 1A (2.2L & 2.5L) – Checking for Ignition Spark & Power Feed to Coil (1 of 3)***

NS-1A: CHECKING FOR IGNITION SPARK & POWER FEED TO COIL (2 OF 3)

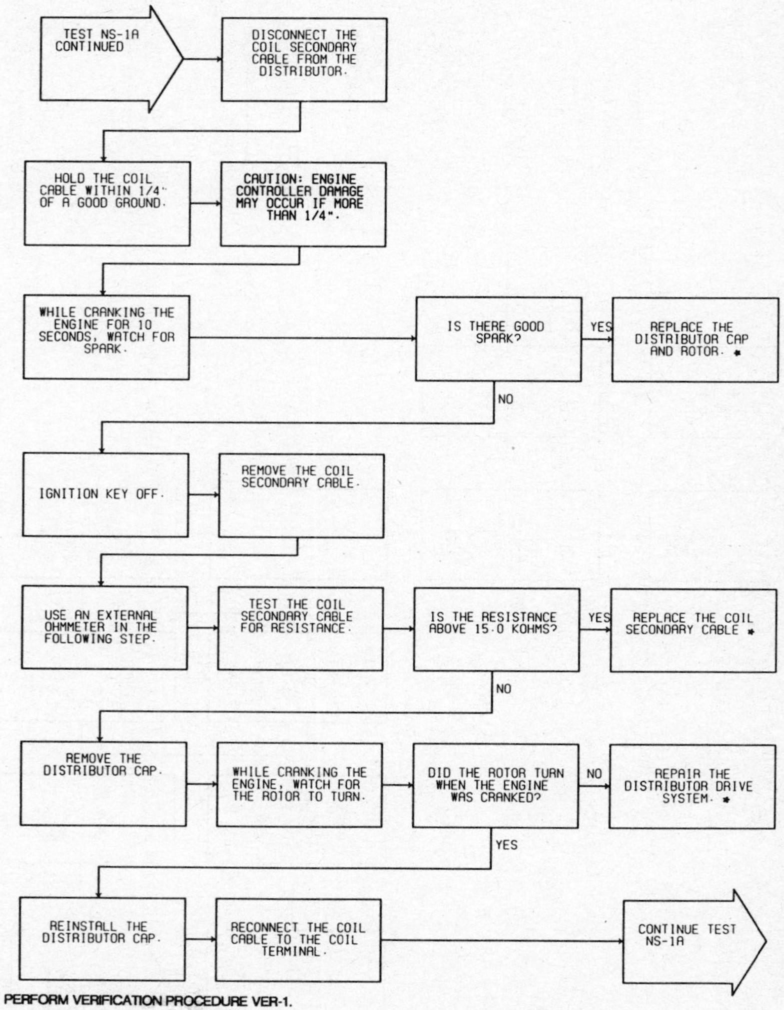
TEST NS-1A CONTINUED
DISCONNECT THE COIL SECONDARY CABLE FROM THE DISTRIBUTOR.
HOLD THE COIL CABLE WITHIN 1/4" OF A GOOD GROUND.
CAUTION: ENGINE CONTROLLER DAMAGE MAY OCCUR IF MORE THAN 1/4".
WHILE CRANKING THE ENGINE FOR 10 SECONDS, WATCH FOR SPARK.
IS THERE GOOD SPARK?
YES
REPLACE THE DISTRIBUTOR CAP AND ROTOR. *
NO
IGNITION KEY OFF.
REMOVE THE COIL SECONDARY CABLE.
USE AN EXTERNAL OHMMETER IN THE FOLLOWING STEP.
TEST THE COIL SECONDARY CABLE FOR RESISTANCE.
IS THE RESISTANCE ABOVE 15.0 KOHMS?
YES
REPLACE THE COIL SECONDARY CABLE *
NO
REMOVE THE DISTRIBUTOR CAP.
WHILE CRANKING THE ENGINE, WATCH FOR THE ROTOR TO TURN.
DID THE ROTOR TURN WHEN THE ENGINE WAS CRANKED?
NO
REPAIR THE DISTRIBUTOR DRIVE SYSTEM. *
YES
REINSTALL THE DISTRIBUTOR CAP.
RECONNECT THE COIL CABLE TO THE COIL TERMINAL.
CONTINUE TEST NS-1A

* PERFORM VERIFICATION PROCEDURE VER-1.

91A08732

Fig. 2: ***No Start Test 1A (2.2L & 2.5L) – Checking for Ignition Spark & Power Feed to Coil (2 of 3)***

1991 ENGINE PERFORMANCE
Self-Diagnostics – 2.5L TBI (Cont.)

NS-1A: CHECKING FOR IGNITION SPARK & POWER FEED TO COIL (3 OF 3)

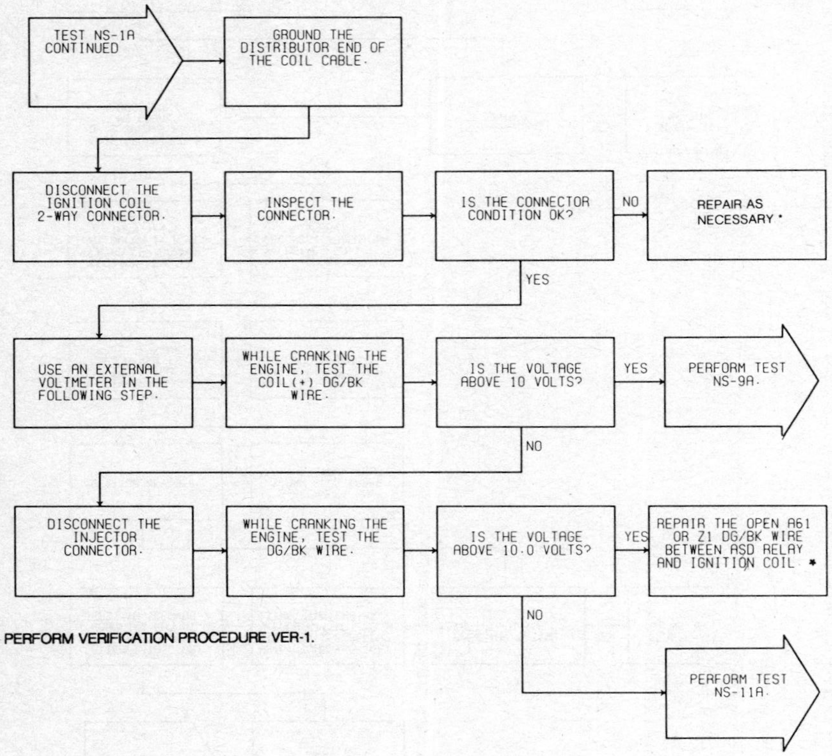
TEST NS-1A CONTINUED
GROUND THE DISTRIBUTOR END OF THE COIL CABLE.
DISCONNECT THE IGNITION COIL 2-WAY CONNECTOR.
INSPECT THE CONNECTOR.
IS THE CONNECTOR CONDITION OK?
NO
REPAIR AS NECESSARY *
YES
USE AN EXTERNAL VOLTMETER IN THE FOLLOWING STEP.
WHILE CRANKING THE ENGINE, TEST THE COIL(+) DG/BK WIRE.
IS THE VOLTAGE ABOVE 10 VOLTS?
YES
PERFORM TEST NS-9A.
NO
DISCONNECT THE INJECTOR CONNECTOR.
WHILE CRANKING THE ENGINE, TEST THE DG/BK WIRE.
IS THE VOLTAGE ABOVE 10.0 VOLTS?
YES
REPAIR THE OPEN A61 OR Z1 DG/BK WIRE BETWEEN ASD RELAY AND IGNITION COIL *
NO
PERFORM TEST NS-11A.

* PERFORM VERIFICATION PROCEDURE VER-1.

91C08733

Fig. 3: No Start Test 1A (2.2L & 2.5L) – Checking for Ignition Spark & Power Feed to Coil (3 of 3)

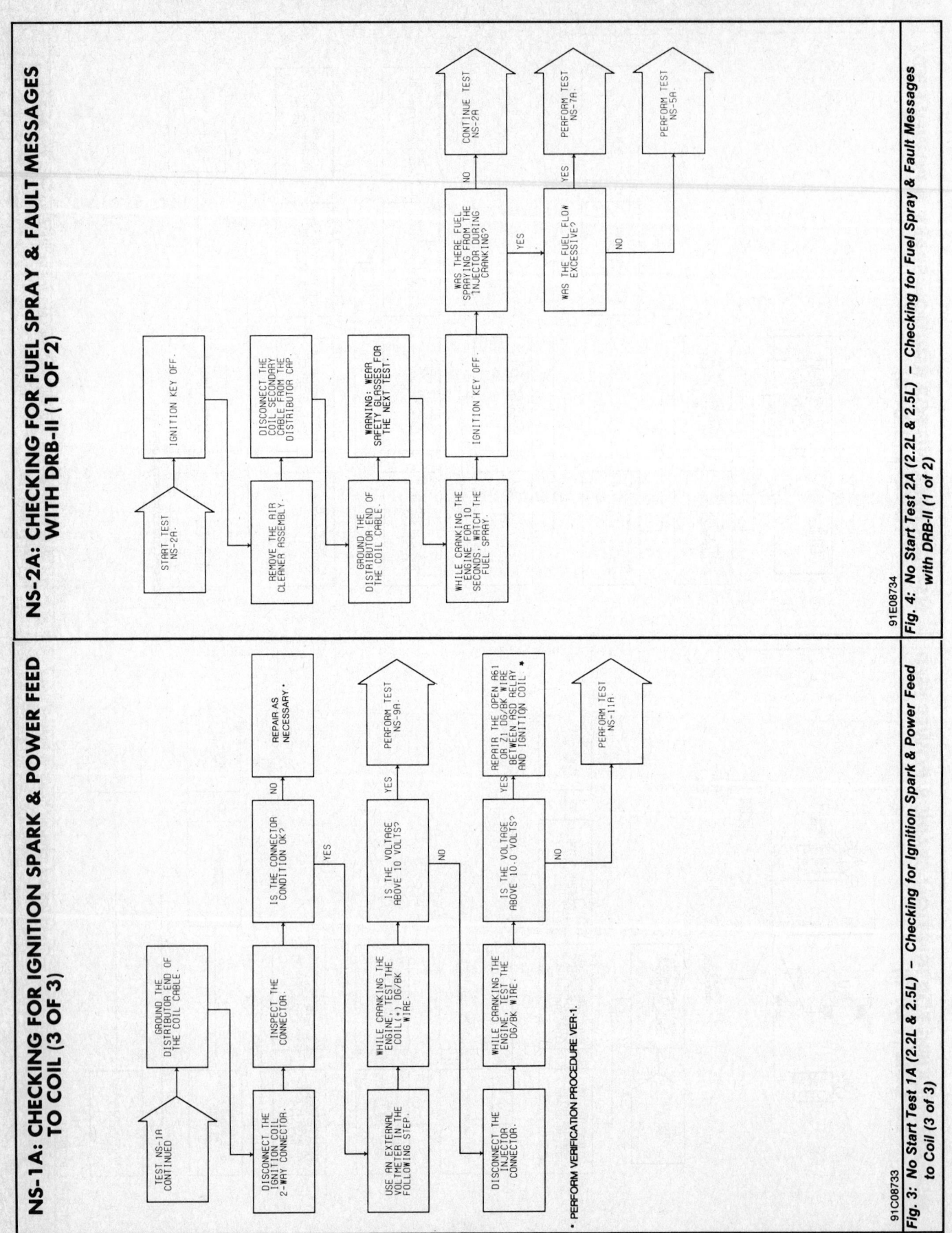

NS-2A: CHECKING FOR FUEL SPRAY & FAULT MESSAGES WITH DRB-II (1 OF 2)

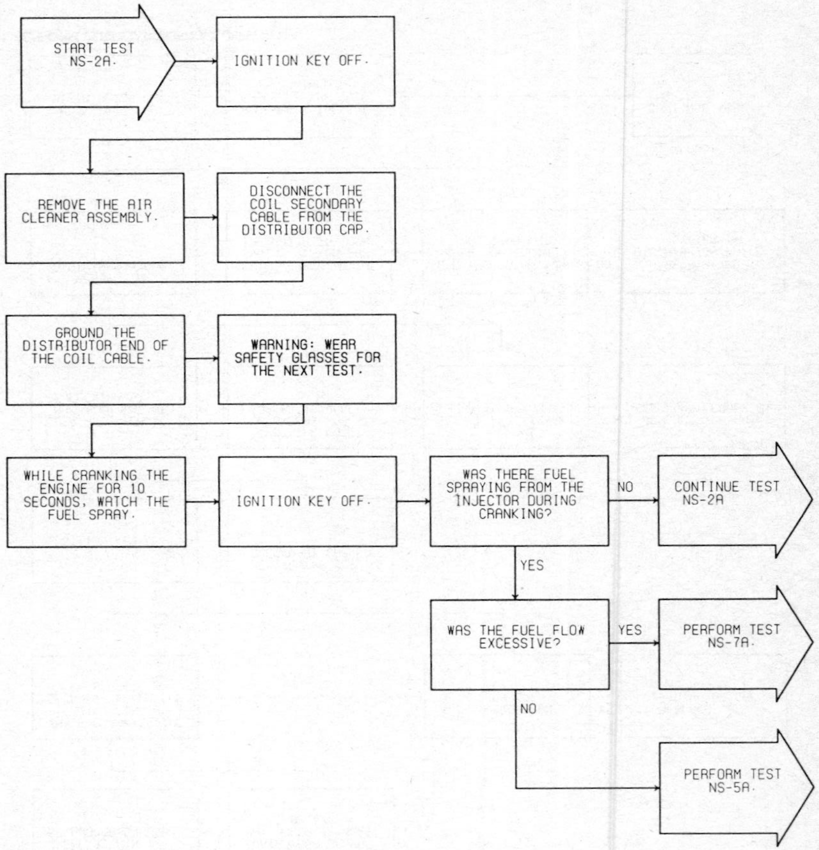
START TEST NS-2A.
IGNITION KEY OFF.
REMOVE THE AIR CLEANER ASSEMBLY.
DISCONNECT THE COIL SECONDARY CABLE FROM THE DISTRIBUTOR CAP.
GROUND THE DISTRIBUTOR END OF THE COIL CABLE.
WARNING: WEAR SAFETY GLASSES FOR THE NEXT TEST.
WHILE CRANKING THE ENGINE FOR 10 SECONDS, WATCH THE FUEL SPRAY.
IGNITION KEY OFF.
WAS THERE FUEL SPRAYING FROM THE INJECTOR DURING CRANKING?
NO
CONTINUE TEST NS-2A
YES
WAS THE FUEL FLOW EXCESSIVE?
YES
PERFORM TEST NS-7A.
NO
PERFORM TEST NS-5A.

91E08734

Fig. 4: No Start Test 2A (2.2L & 2.5L) – Checking for Fuel Spray & Fault Messages with DRB-II (1 of 2)

NS-2A: CHECKING FOR FUEL SPRAY & FAULT MESSAGES WITH DRB-II (2 OF 2)

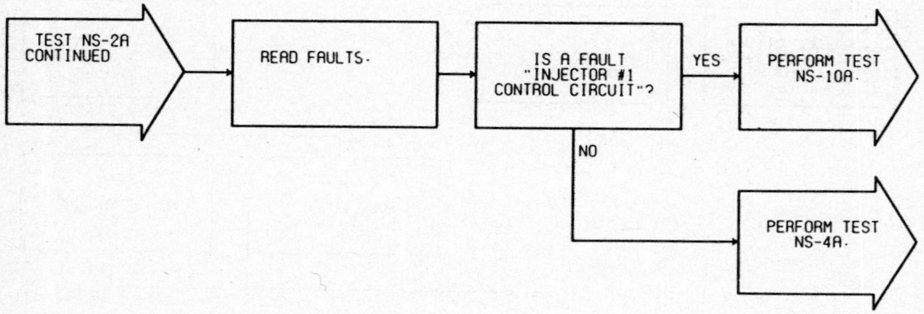
TEST NS-2A CONTINUED
READ FAULTS.
IS A FAULT "INJECTOR #1 CONTROL CIRCUIT"?
YES
PERFORM TEST NS-10A.
NO
PERFORM TEST NS-4A.

91H08735

Fig. 5: No Start Test 2A (2.2L & 2.5L) – Checking for Fuel Spray & Fault Messages with DRB-II (2 of 2)

NS-3A: CHECKING FOR INJECTOR FAULTS, POWER TO SBEC, MAP SENSOR & THEFT STATUS (1 OF 3)

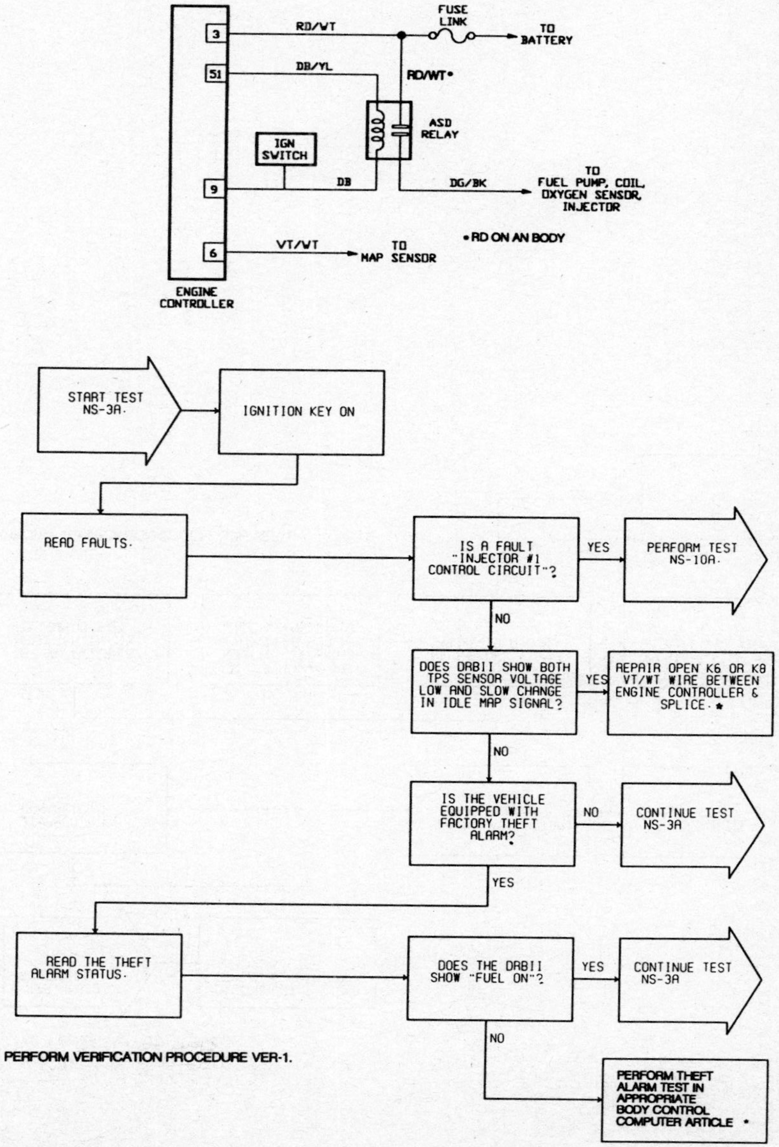
FUSE LINK
TO BATTERY
RD/WT
DB/YL
RD/WT•
ASD RELAY
IGN SWITCH
DB
DG/BK
TO FUEL PUMP, COIL, OXYGEN SENSOR, INJECTOR
•RD ON AN BODY
VT/WT
TO MAP SENSOR
3
51
9
6
ENGINE CONTROLLER
START TEST NS-3A.
IGNITION KEY ON
READ FAULTS.
IS A FAULT "INJECTOR #1 CONTROL CIRCUIT"?
YES
PERFORM TEST NS-10A.
NO
DOES DRBII SHOW BOTH TPS SENSOR VOLTAGE LOW AND SLOW CHANGE IN IDLE MAP SIGNAL?
YES
REPAIR OPEN K6 OR K8 VT/WT WIRE BETWEEN ENGINE CONTROLLER & SPLICE. *
NO
IS THE VEHICLE EQUIPPED WITH FACTORY THEFT ALARM?
NO
CONTINUE TEST NS-3A
YES
READ THE THEFT ALARM STATUS.
DOES THE DRBII SHOW "FUEL ON"?
YES
CONTINUE TEST NS-3A
NO
PERFORM THEFT ALARM TEST IN APPROPRIATE BODY CONTROL COMPUTER ARTICLE *
* PERFORM VERIFICATION PROCEDURE VER-1.

91I08712 91J08736

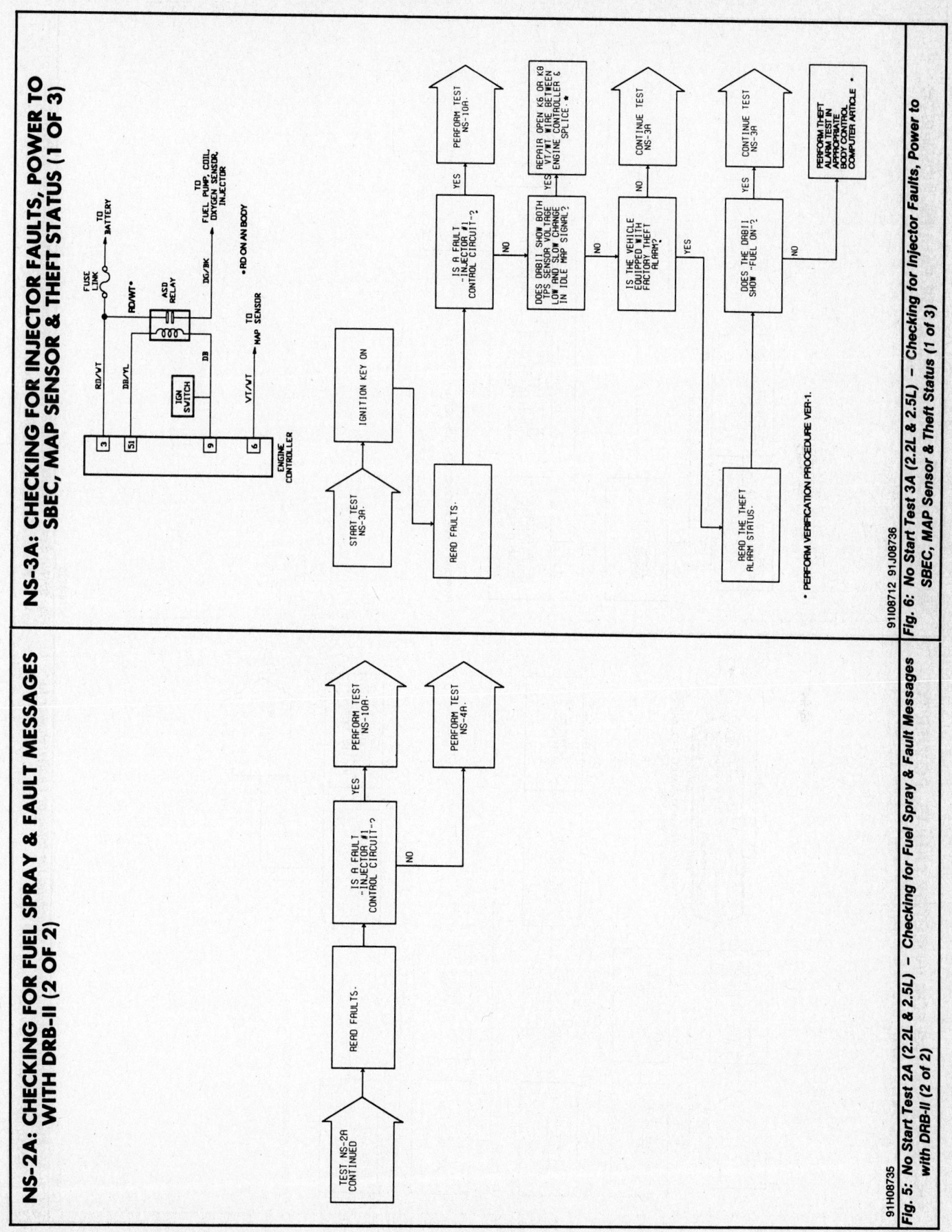

Fig. 6: No Start Test 3A (2.2L & 2.5L) – Checking for Injector Faults, Power to SBEC, MAP Sensor & Theft Status (1 of 3)

1991 ENGINE PERFORMANCE
Self-Diagnostics – 2.5L TBI (Cont.)

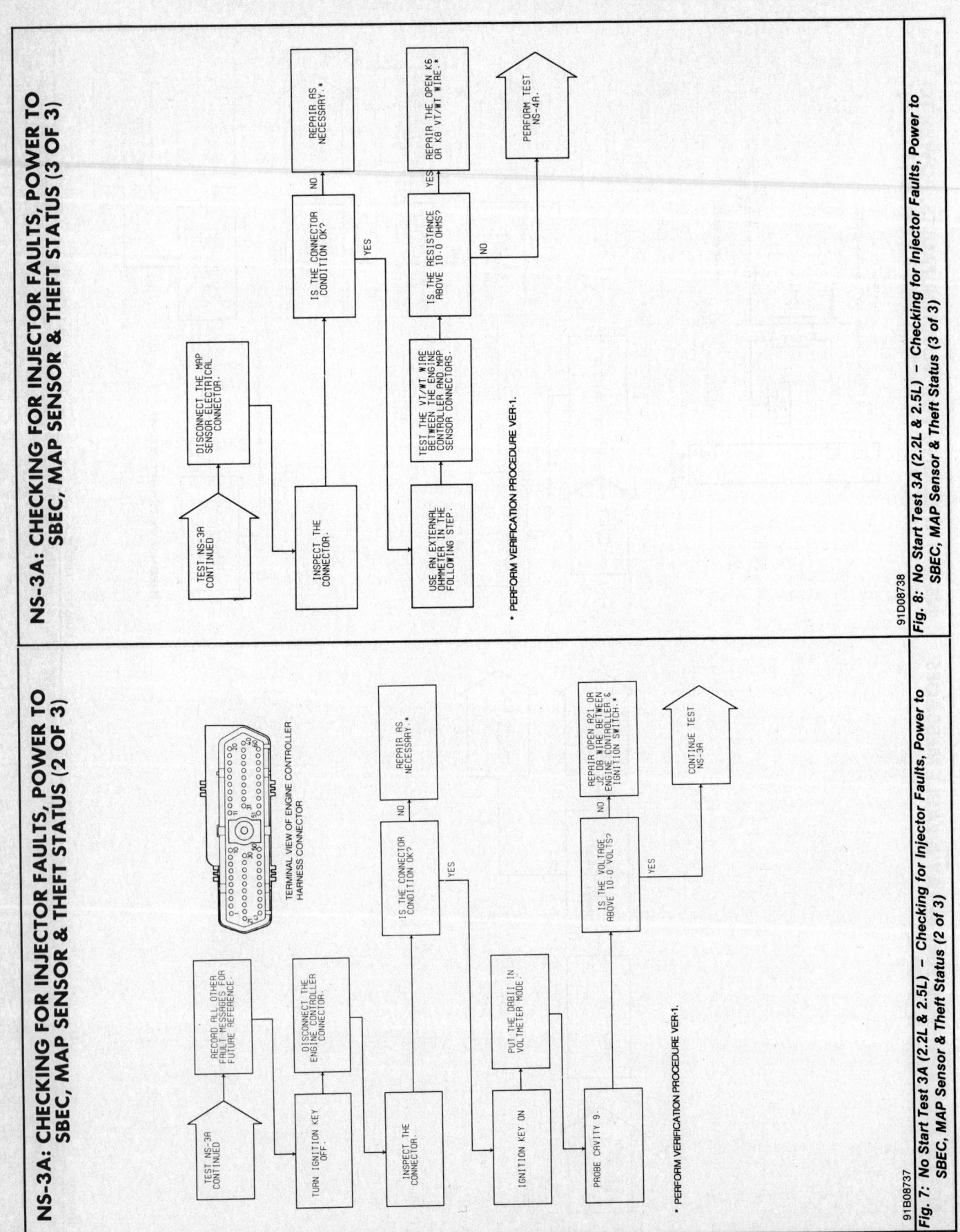

NS-3A: CHECKING FOR INJECTOR FAULTS, POWER TO SBEC, MAP SENSOR & THEFT STATUS (2 OF 3)

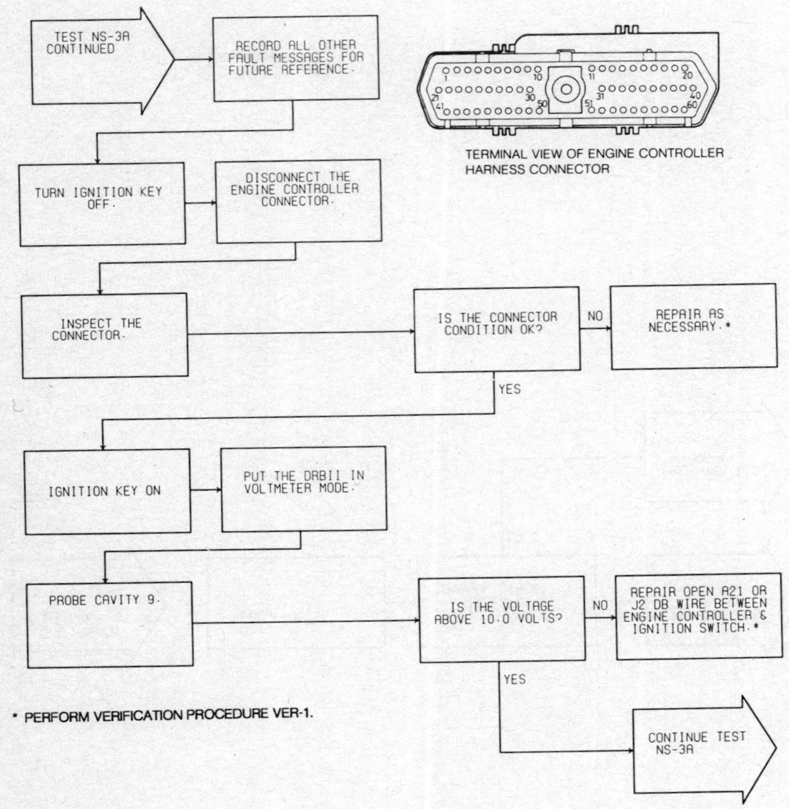
TEST NS-3A CONTINUED
RECORD ALL OTHER FAULT MESSAGES FOR FUTURE REFERENCE.
TERMINAL VIEW OF ENGINE CONTROLLER HARNESS CONNECTOR
TURN IGNITION KEY OFF.
DISCONNECT THE ENGINE CONTROLLER CONNECTOR.
INSPECT THE CONNECTOR.
IS THE CONNECTOR CONDITION OK?
NO
REPAIR AS NECESSARY.*
YES
IGNITION KEY ON
PUT THE DRBII IN VOLTMETER MODE.
PROBE CAVITY 9.
IS THE VOLTAGE ABOVE 10.0 VOLTS?
NO
REPAIR OPEN A21 OR J2 DB WIRE BETWEEN ENGINE CONTROLLER & IGNITION SWITCH.*
YES
CONTINUE TEST NS-3A

* PERFORM VERIFICATION PROCEDURE VER-1.

91B08737

Fig. 7: No Start Test 3A (2.2L & 2.5L) – Checking for Injector Faults, Power to SBEC, MAP Sensor & Theft Status (2 of 3)

NS-3A: CHECKING FOR INJECTOR FAULTS, POWER TO SBEC, MAP SENSOR & THEFT STATUS (3 OF 3)

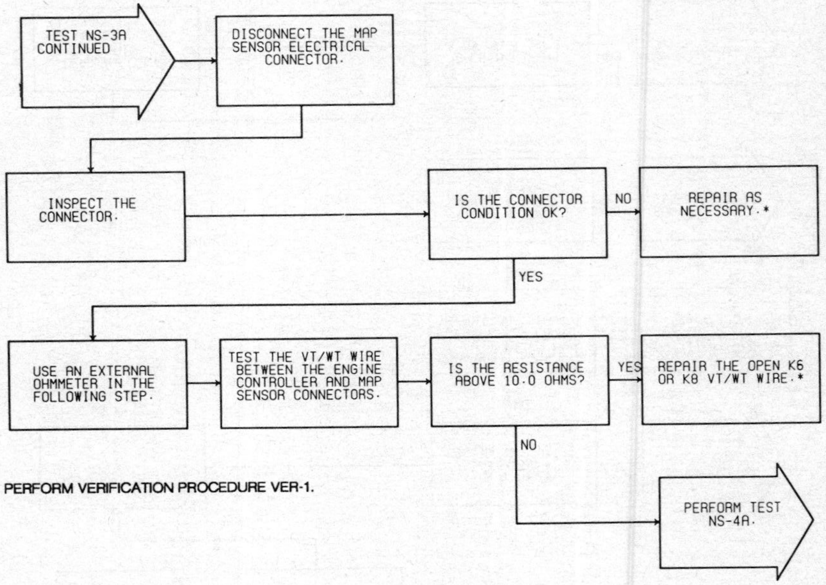
TEST NS-3A CONTINUED
DISCONNECT THE MAP SENSOR ELECTRICAL CONNECTOR.
INSPECT THE CONNECTOR.
IS THE CONNECTOR CONDITION OK?
NO
REPAIR AS NECESSARY.*
YES
USE AN EXTERNAL OHMMETER IN THE FOLLOWING STEP.
TEST THE VT/WT WIRE BETWEEN THE ENGINE CONTROLLER AND MAP SENSOR CONNECTORS.
IS THE RESISTANCE ABOVE 10.0 OHMS?
YES
REPAIR THE OPEN K6 OR K8 VT/WT WIRE.*
NO
PERFORM TEST NS-4A.

* PERFORM VERIFICATION PROCEDURE VER-1.

91D08738

Fig. 8: No Start Test 3A (2.2L & 2.5L) – Checking for Injector Faults, Power to SBEC, MAP Sensor & Theft Status (3 of 3)

NS-4A: CHECKING FOR FUEL PRESSURE, TPS & POWER FEED TO INJECTORS (1 OF 2)

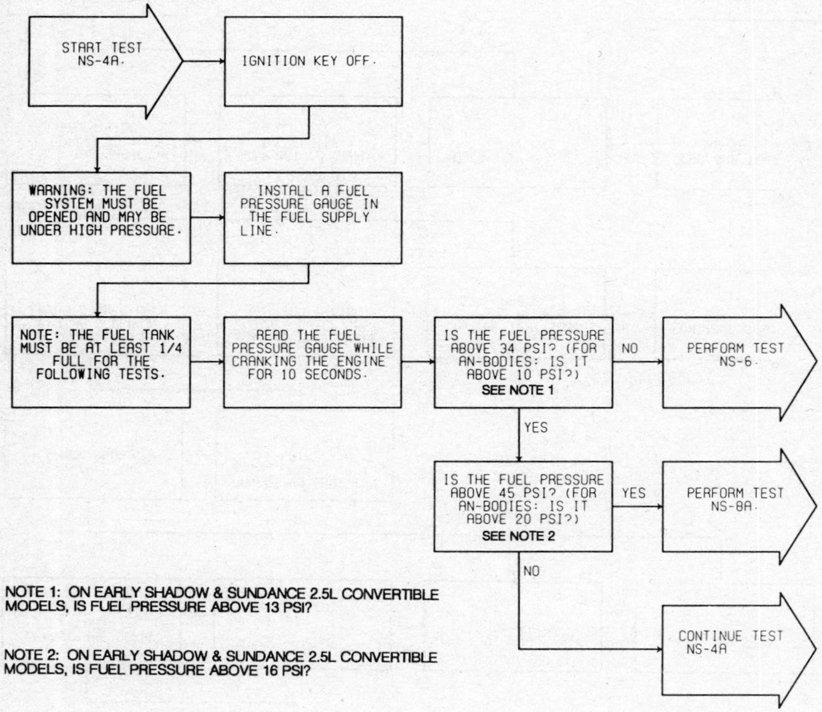
START TEST NS-4A.
IGNITION KEY OFF.
WARNING: THE FUEL SYSTEM MUST BE OPENED AND MAY BE UNDER HIGH PRESSURE.
INSTALL A FUEL PRESSURE GAUGE IN THE FUEL SUPPLY LINE.
NOTE: THE FUEL TANK MUST BE AT LEAST 1/4 FULL FOR THE FOLLOWING TESTS.
READ THE FUEL PRESSURE GAUGE WHILE CRANKING THE ENGINE FOR 10 SECONDS.
IS THE FUEL PRESSURE ABOVE 34 PSI? (FOR AN-BODIES: IS IT ABOVE 10 PSI?)
SEE NOTE 1
NO
PERFORM TEST NS-6.
YES
IS THE FUEL PRESSURE ABOVE 45 PSI? (FOR AN-BODIES: IS IT ABOVE 20 PSI?)
SEE NOTE 2
YES
PERFORM TEST NS-8A.
NO
CONTINUE TEST NS-4A

NOTE 1: ON EARLY SHADOW & SUNDANCE 2.5L CONVERTIBLE MODELS, IS FUEL PRESSURE ABOVE 13 PSI?

NOTE 2: ON EARLY SHADOW & SUNDANCE 2.5L CONVERTIBLE MODELS, IS FUEL PRESSURE ABOVE 16 PSI?

Shadow and Sundance Convertible models are manufactured with either early or late design fuel, ignition and emission systems. Late design vehicles use an epoxy ignition coil, mounted on thermostat housing, and a high pressure fuel system requiring quick-connect fuel fittings. Early design vehicles use an oil-filled ignition coil, mounted on right inner fender, and a low pressure fuel system using hoses and clamps.

91F08739

Fig. 9: No Start Test 4A (2.2L & 2.5L) – Checking for Fuel Pressure, TPS & Power Feed to Injectors (1 of 2)

NS-4A: CHECKING FOR FUEL PRESSURE, TPS & POWER FEED TO INJECTORS (2 OF 2)

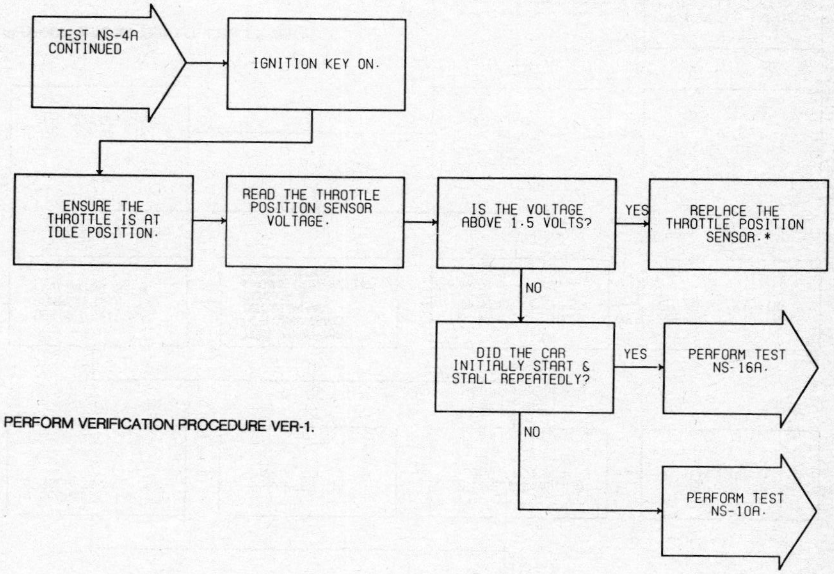
TEST NS-4A CONTINUED
IGNITION KEY ON.
ENSURE THE THROTTLE IS AT IDLE POSITION.
READ THE THROTTLE POSITION SENSOR VOLTAGE.
IS THE VOLTAGE ABOVE 1.5 VOLTS?
YES
REPLACE THE THROTTLE POSITION SENSOR.*
NO
DID THE CAR INITIALLY START & STALL REPEATEDLY?
YES
PERFORM TEST NS-16A.
NO
PERFORM TEST NS-10A.

* PERFORM VERIFICATION PROCEDURE VER-1.

91H08740

Fig. 10: No Start Test 4A (2.2L & 2.5L) – Checking for Fuel Pressure, TPS & Power Feed to Injectors (2 of 2)

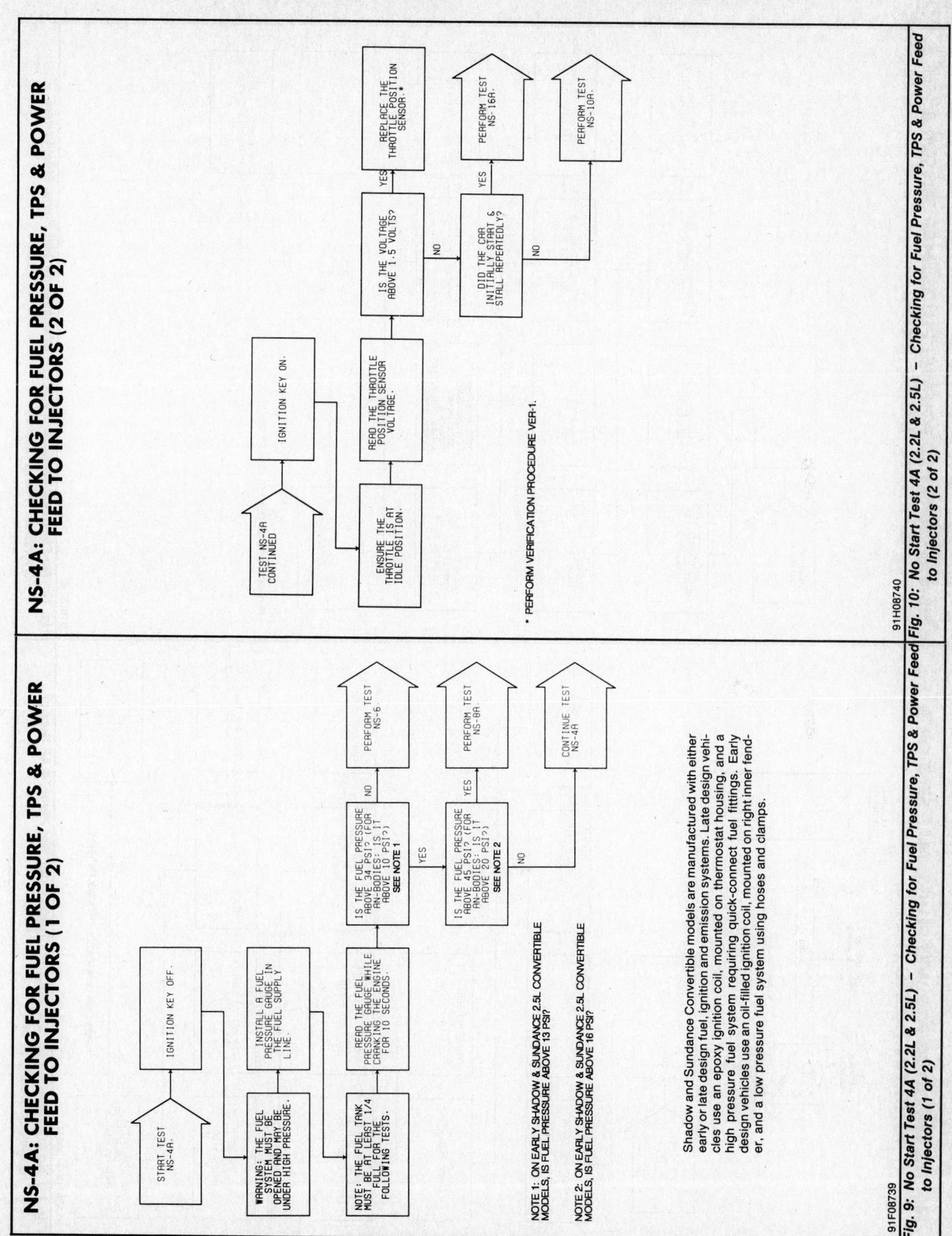

NS-5A: CHECKING FOR WET PLUGS, MAP SENSOR & IGNITION TIMING (1 OF 2)

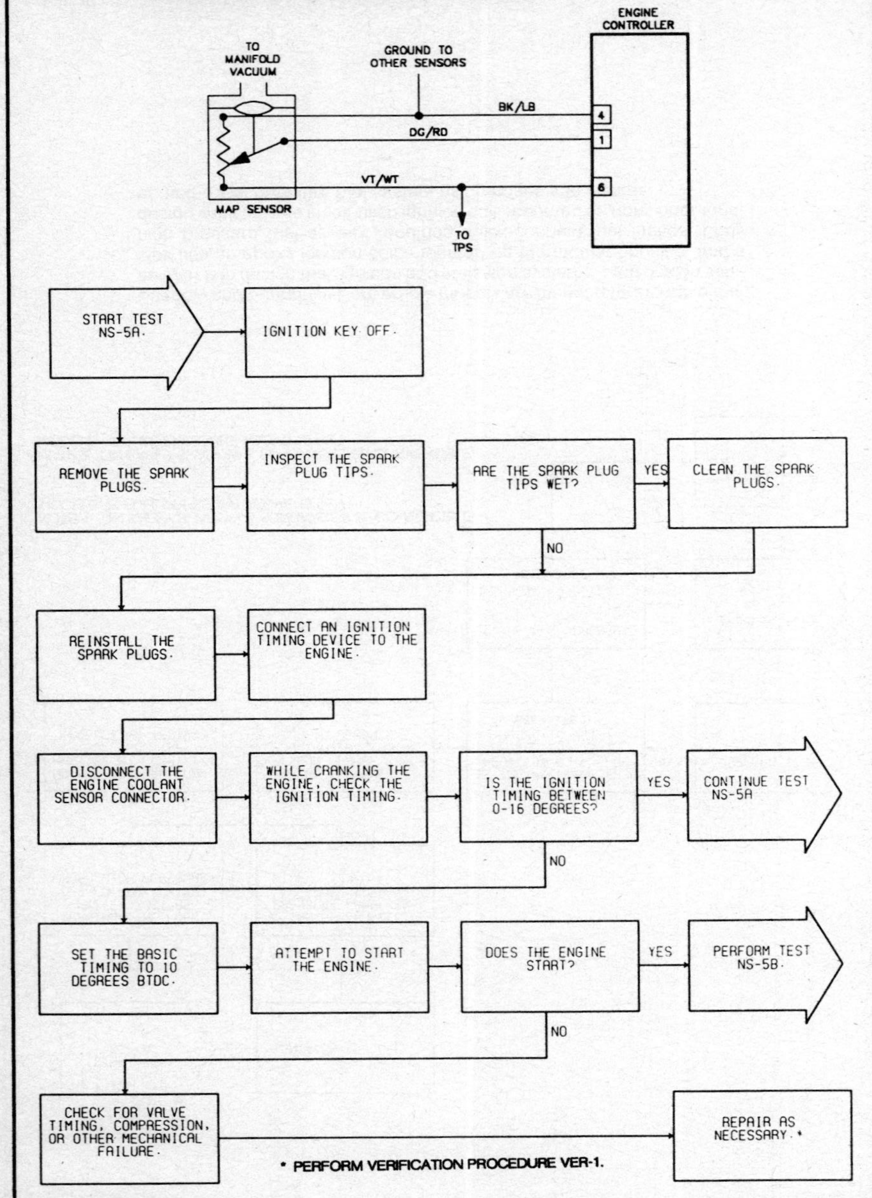
TO MANIFOLD VACUUM
GROUND TO OTHER SENSORS
ENGINE CONTROLLER
BK/LB
DG/RD
VT/WT
4
1
6
MAP SENSOR
TO TPS
START TEST NS-5A.
IGNITION KEY OFF.
REMOVE THE SPARK PLUGS.
INSPECT THE SPARK PLUG TIPS.
ARE THE SPARK PLUG TIPS WET?
YES
CLEAN THE SPARK PLUGS.
NO
REINSTALL THE SPARK PLUGS.
CONNECT AN IGNITION TIMING DEVICE TO THE ENGINE.
DISCONNECT THE ENGINE COOLANT SENSOR CONNECTOR.
WHILE CRANKING THE ENGINE, CHECK THE IGNITION TIMING.
IS THE IGNITION TIMING BETWEEN 0-16 DEGREES?
YES
CONTINUE TEST NS-5A
NO
SET THE BASIC TIMING TO 10 DEGREES BTDC.
ATTEMPT TO START THE ENGINE.
DOES THE ENGINE START?
YES
PERFORM TEST NS-5B.
NO
CHECK FOR VALVE TIMING, COMPRESSION, OR OTHER MECHANICAL FAILURE.
REPAIR AS NECESSARY.*
* PERFORM VERIFICATION PROCEDURE VER-1.

91A08713 91J08741

Fig. 11: No Start Test 5A (2.2L & 2.5L) – Checking for Wet Plugs, MAP Sensor & Ignition Timing (1 of 2)

NS-5A: CHECKING FOR WET PLUGS, MAP SENSOR & IGNITION TIMING (2 OF 2)

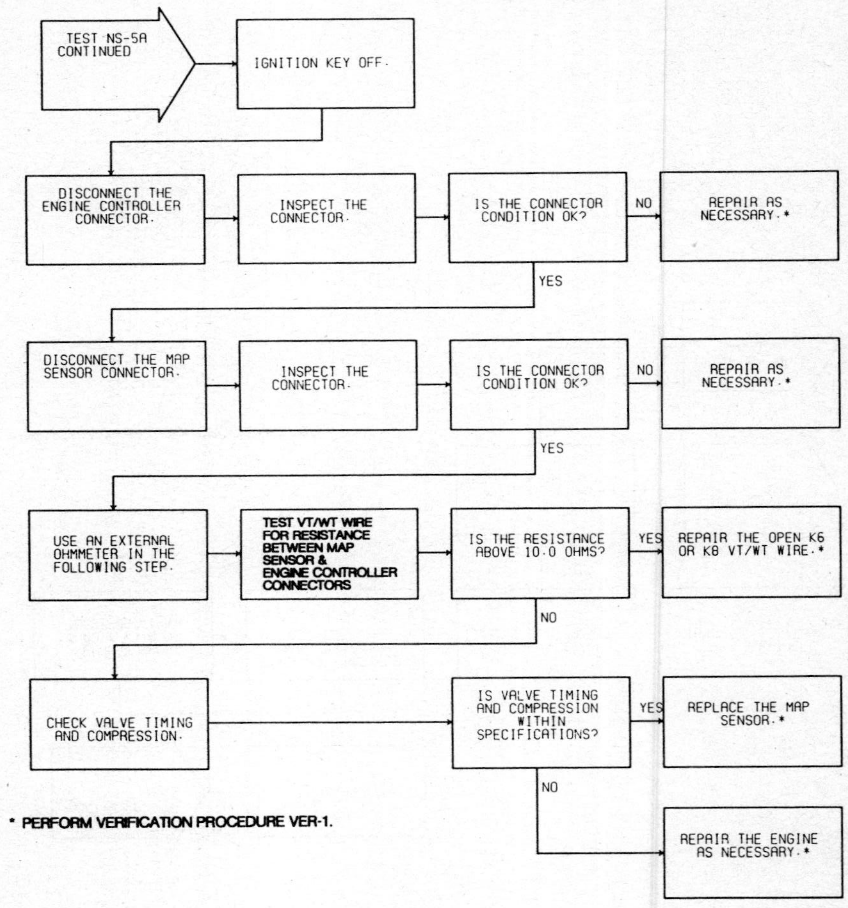
TEST NS-5A CONTINUED
IGNITION KEY OFF.
DISCONNECT THE ENGINE CONTROLLER CONNECTOR.
INSPECT THE CONNECTOR.
IS THE CONNECTOR CONDITION OK?
NO
REPAIR AS NECESSARY.*
YES
DISCONNECT THE MAP SENSOR CONNECTOR.
INSPECT THE CONNECTOR.
IS THE CONNECTOR CONDITION OK?
NO
REPAIR AS NECESSARY.*
YES
USE AN EXTERNAL OHMMETER IN THE FOLLOWING STEP.
TEST VT/WT WIRE FOR RESISTANCE BETWEEN MAP SENSOR & ENGINE CONTROLLER CONNECTORS
IS THE RESISTANCE ABOVE 10.0 OHMS?
YES
REPAIR THE OPEN K6 OR K8 VT/WT WIRE.*
NO
CHECK VALVE TIMING AND COMPRESSION.
IS VALVE TIMING AND COMPRESSION WITHIN SPECIFICATIONS?
YES
REPLACE THE MAP SENSOR.*
NO
REPAIR THE ENGINE AS NECESSARY.*
* PERFORM VERIFICATION PROCEDURE VER-1.

91B08742

Fig. 12: No Start Test 5A (2.2L & 2.5L) – Checking for Wet Plugs, MAP Sensor & Ignition Timing (2 of 2)

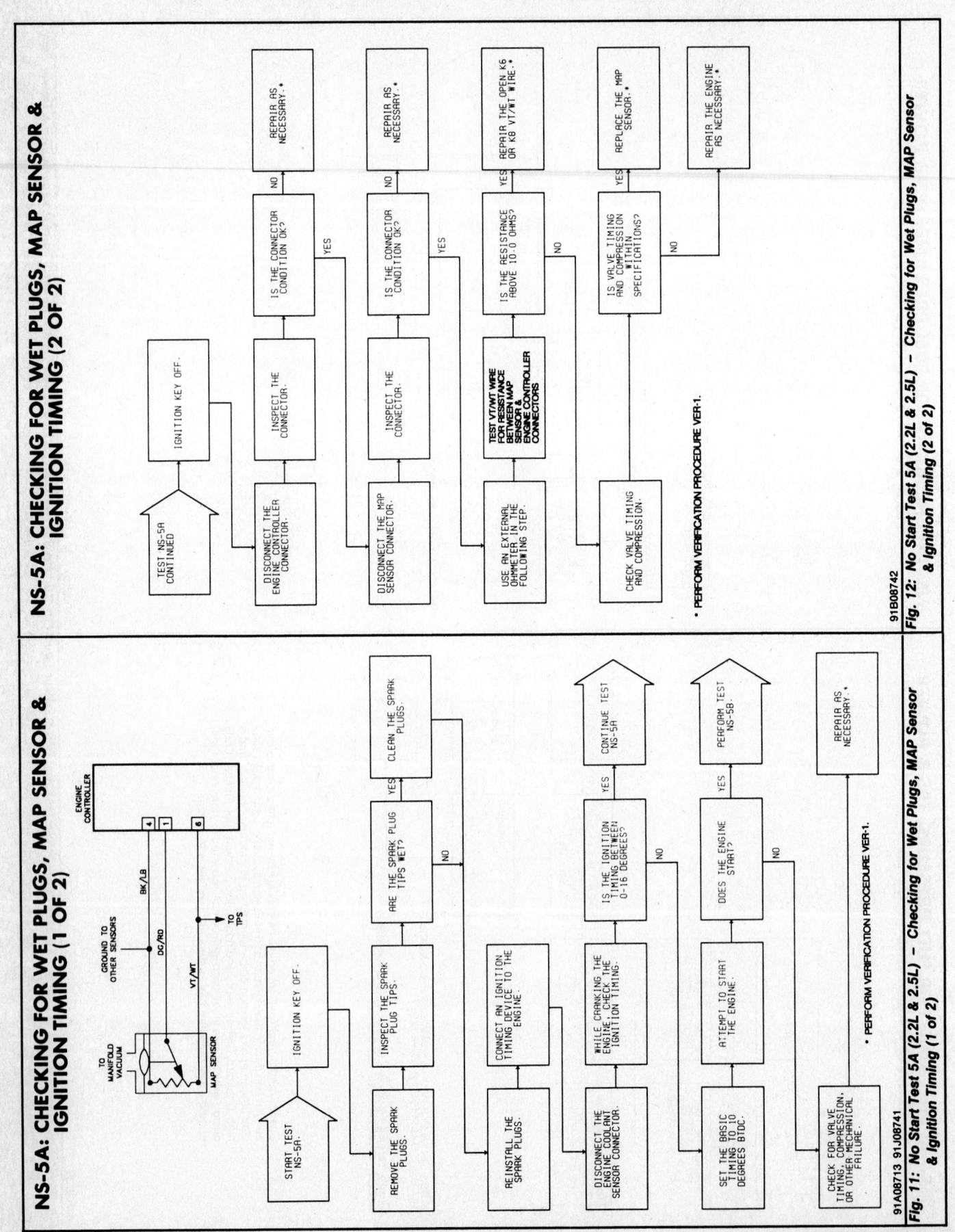

NS-5B: CHECKING VALVE GEAR

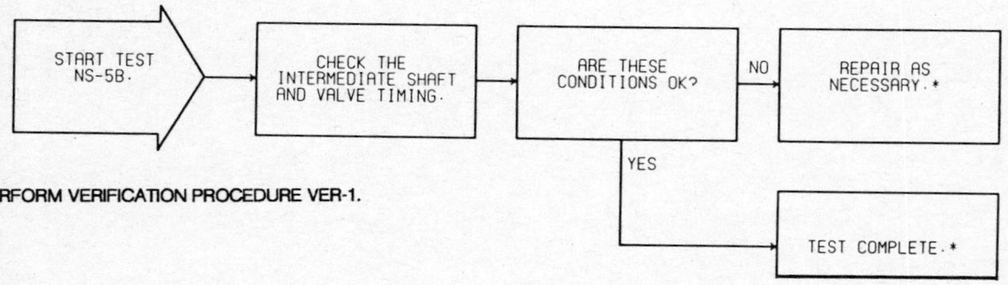
START TEST NS-5B.
CHECK THE INTERMEDIATE SHAFT AND VALVE TIMING.
ARE THESE CONDITIONS OK?
NO
REPAIR AS NECESSARY.*
YES
TEST COMPLETE.*

* PERFORM VERIFICATION PROCEDURE VER-1.

91D08743

Fig. 13: No Start Test 5B (2.2L & 2.5L) – Checking Valve Gear

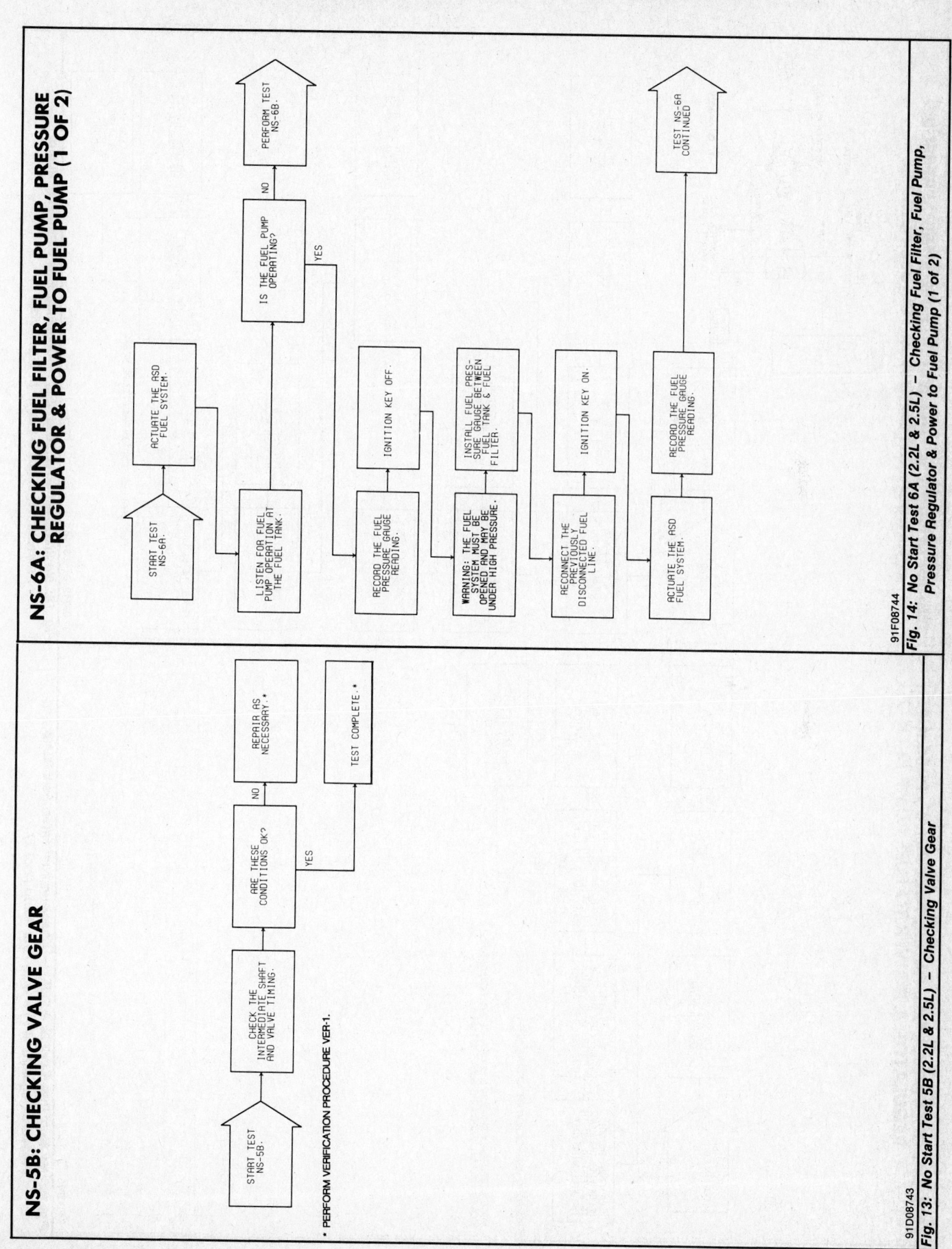

NS-6A: CHECKING FUEL FILTER, FUEL PUMP, PRESSURE REGULATOR & POWER TO FUEL PUMP (1 OF 2)

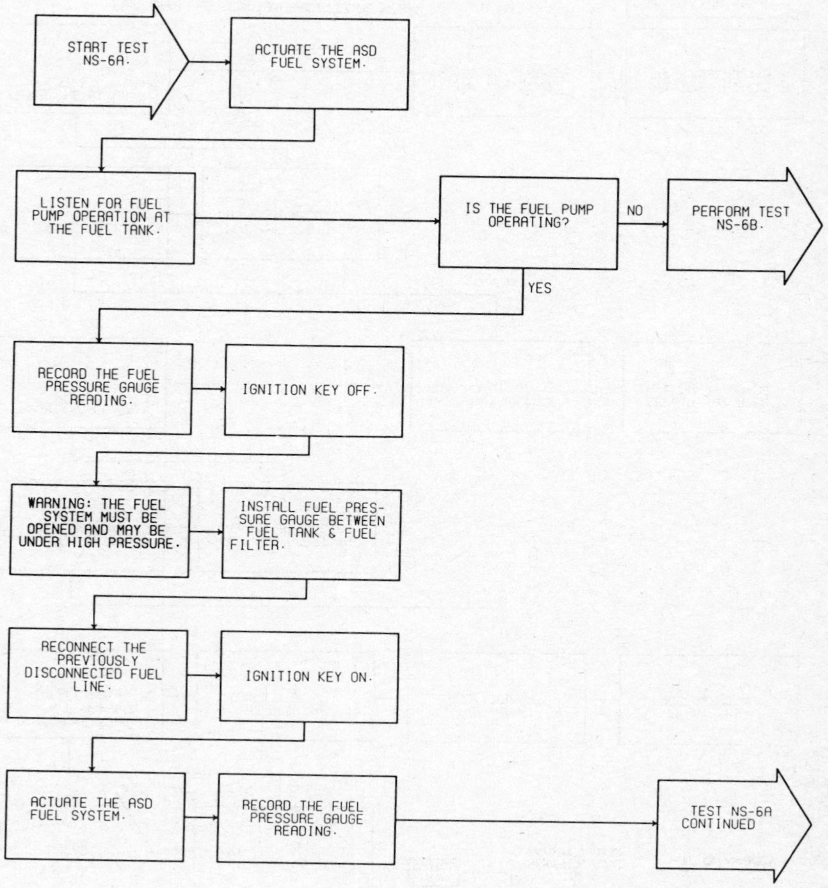
START TEST NS-6A.
ACTUATE THE ASD FUEL SYSTEM.
LISTEN FOR FUEL PUMP OPERATION AT THE FUEL TANK.
IS THE FUEL PUMP OPERATING?
NO
PERFORM TEST NS-6B.
YES
RECORD THE FUEL PRESSURE GAUGE READING.
IGNITION KEY OFF.
WARNING: THE FUEL SYSTEM MUST BE OPENED AND MAY BE UNDER HIGH PRESSURE.
INSTALL FUEL PRESSURE GAUGE BETWEEN FUEL TANK & FUEL FILTER.
RECONNECT THE PREVIOUSLY DISCONNECTED FUEL LINE.
IGNITION KEY ON.
ACTUATE THE ASD FUEL SYSTEM.
RECORD THE FUEL PRESSURE GAUGE READING.
TEST NS-6A CONTINUED

91F08744

Fig. 14: No Start Test 6A (2.2L & 2.5L) – Checking Fuel Filter, Fuel Pump, Pressure Regulator & Power to Fuel Pump (1 of 2)

1991 ENGINE PERFORMANCE
Self-Diagnostics – 2.5L TBI (Cont.)

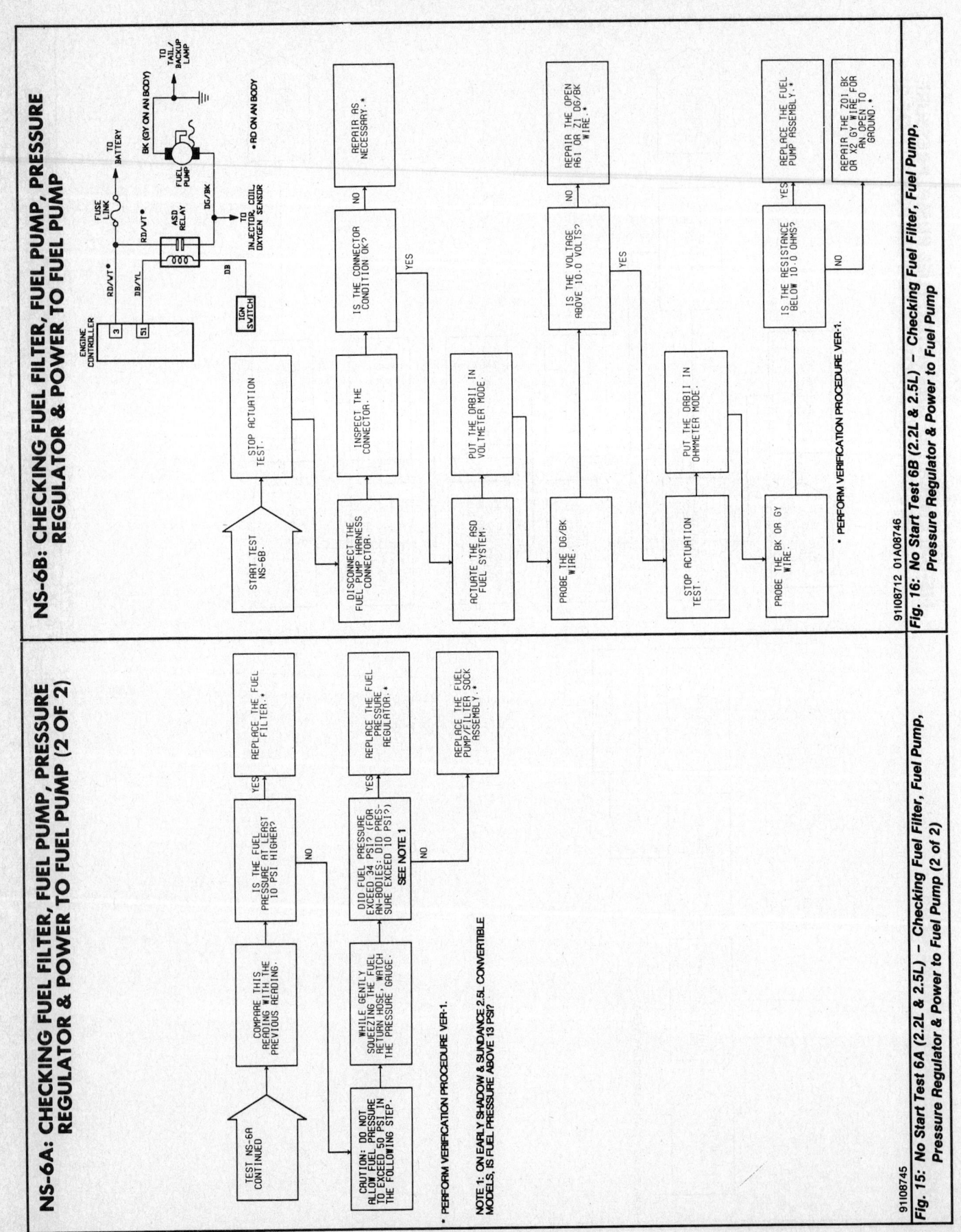

NS-6A: CHECKING FUEL FILTER, FUEL PUMP, PRESSURE REGULATOR & POWER TO FUEL PUMP (2 OF 2)

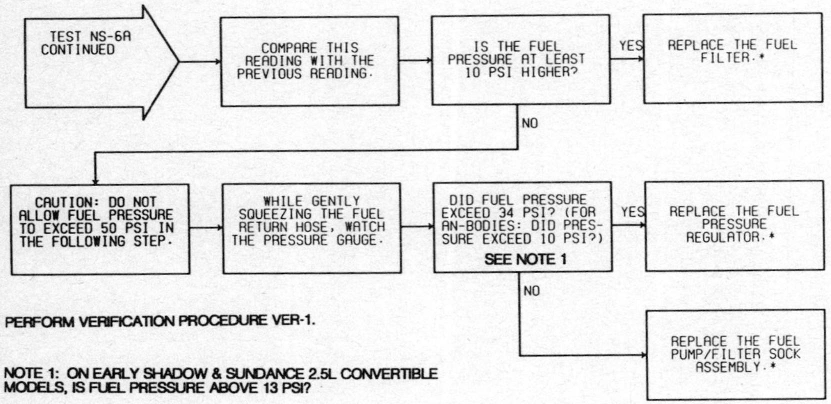
TEST NS-6A CONTINUED
COMPARE THIS READING WITH THE PREVIOUS READING.
IS THE FUEL PRESSURE AT LEAST 10 PSI HIGHER?
YES
REPLACE THE FUEL FILTER.*
NO
CAUTION: DO NOT ALLOW FUEL PRESSURE TO EXCEED 50 PSI IN THE FOLLOWING STEP.
WHILE GENTLY SQUEEZING THE FUEL RETURN HOSE, WATCH THE PRESSURE GAUGE.
DID FUEL PRESSURE EXCEED 34 PSI? (FOR AN-BODIES: DID PRESSURE EXCEED 10 PSI?)
SEE NOTE 1
YES
REPLACE THE FUEL PRESSURE REGULATOR.*
NO
REPLACE THE FUEL PUMP/FILTER SOCK ASSEMBLY.*

* PERFORM VERIFICATION PROCEDURE VER-1.

NOTE 1: ON EARLY SHADOW & SUNDANCE 2.5L CONVERTIBLE MODELS, IS FUEL PRESSURE ABOVE 13 PSI?

91I08745

Fig. 15: *No Start Test 6A (2.2L & 2.5L) – Checking Fuel Filter, Fuel Pump, Pressure Regulator & Power to Fuel Pump (2 of 2)*

NS-6B: CHECKING FUEL FILTER, FUEL PUMP, PRESSURE REGULATOR & POWER TO FUEL PUMP

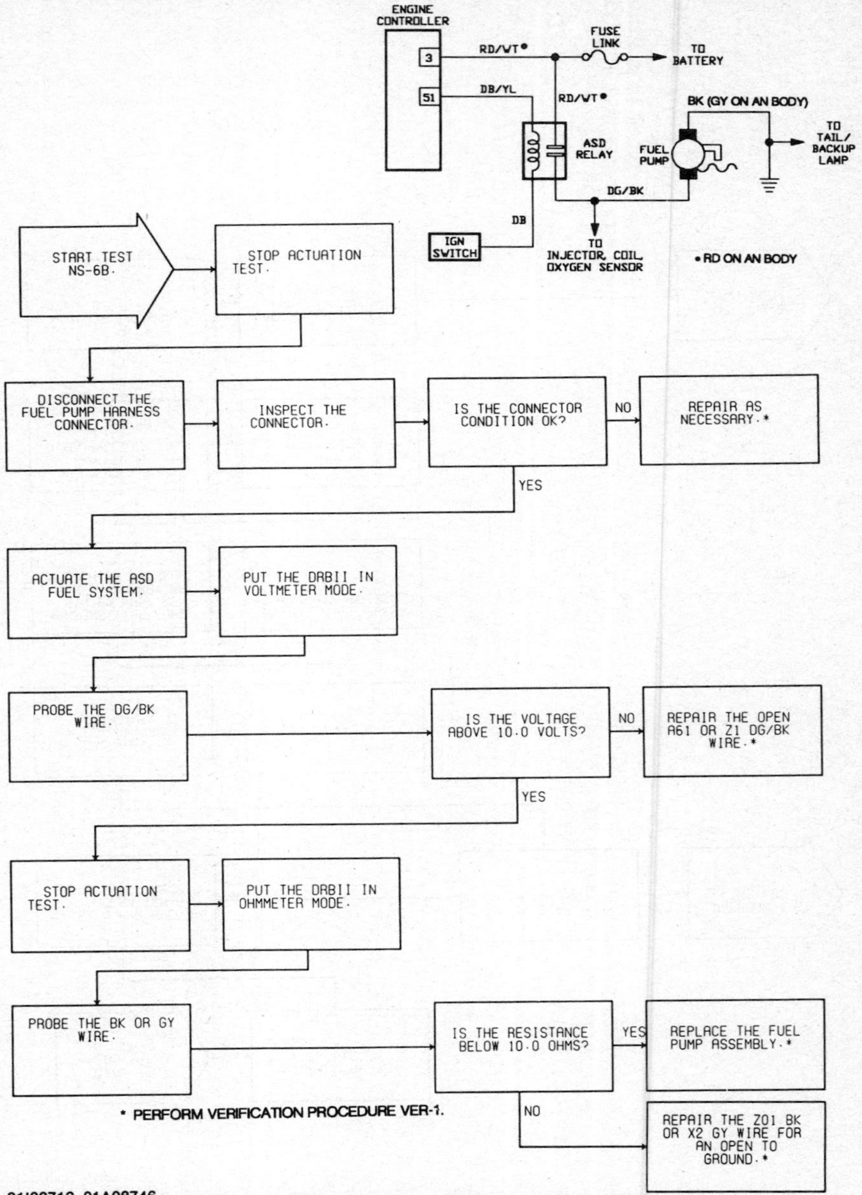
ENGINE CONTROLLER
3
51
RD/WT•
FUSE LINK
TO BATTERY
DB/YL
RD/WT•
BK (GY ON AN BODY)
ASD RELAY
FUEL PUMP
TO TAIL/ BACKUP LAMP
DG/BK
DB
IGN SWITCH
TO INJECTOR, COIL, OXYGEN SENSOR
• RD ON AN BODY
START TEST NS-6B.
STOP ACTUATION TEST.
DISCONNECT THE FUEL PUMP HARNESS CONNECTOR.
INSPECT THE CONNECTOR.
IS THE CONNECTOR CONDITION OK?
NO
REPAIR AS NECESSARY.*
YES
ACTUATE THE ASD FUEL SYSTEM.
PUT THE DRBII IN VOLTMETER MODE.
PROBE THE DG/BK WIRE.
IS THE VOLTAGE ABOVE 10.0 VOLTS?
NO
REPAIR THE OPEN A61 OR Z1 DG/BK WIRE.*
YES
STOP ACTUATION TEST.
PUT THE DRBII IN OHMMETER MODE.
PROBE THE BK OR GY WIRE.
IS THE RESISTANCE BELOW 10.0 OHMS?
YES
REPLACE THE FUEL PUMP ASSEMBLY.*
NO
REPAIR THE Z01 BK OR X2 GY WIRE FOR AN OPEN TO GROUND.*
* PERFORM VERIFICATION PROCEDURE VER-1.

91I08712 01A08746

Fig. 16: *No Start Test 6B (2.2L & 2.5L) – Checking Fuel Filter, Fuel Pump, Pressure Regulator & Power to Fuel Pump*

NS-7A: CHECKING FOR FLOODING FUEL INJECTOR (1 OF 3)

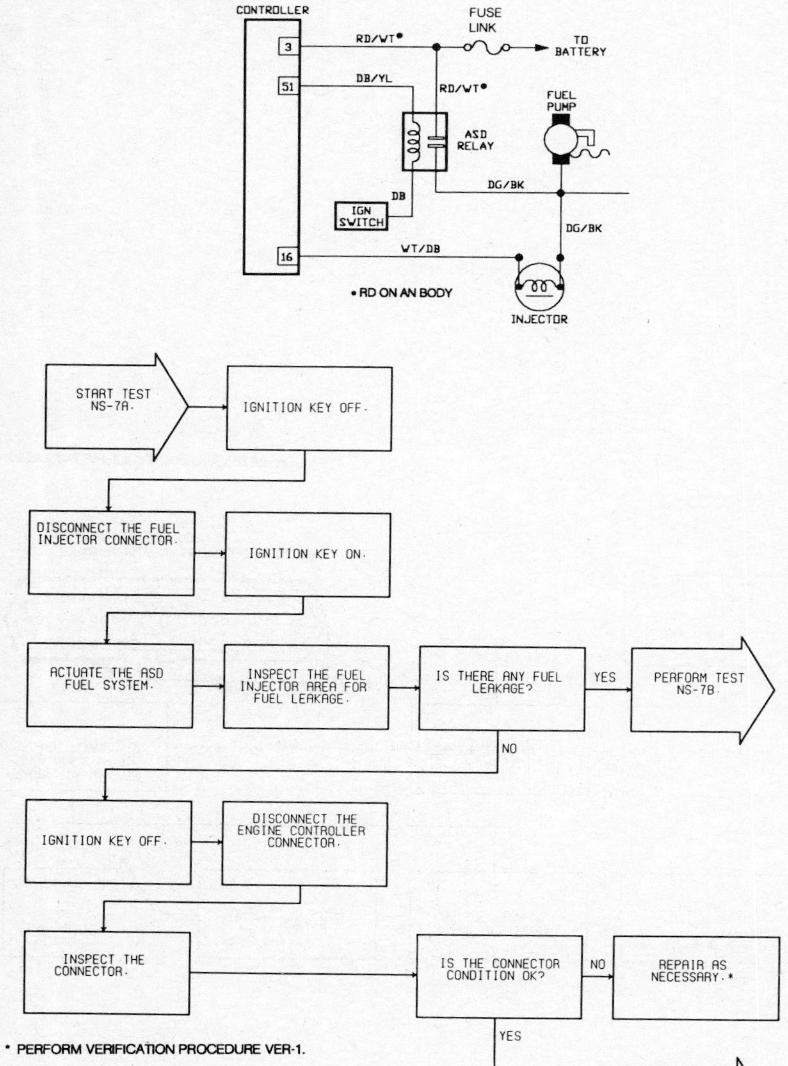
CONTROLLER
3
51
16
RD/WT•
DB/YL
FUSE LINK
TO BATTERY
RD/WT•
FUEL PUMP
ASD RELAY
DB
IGN SWITCH
DG/BK
DG/BK
WT/DB
• RD ON AN BODY
INJECTOR
START TEST NS-7A.
IGNITION KEY OFF.
DISCONNECT THE FUEL INJECTOR CONNECTOR.
IGNITION KEY ON.
ACTUATE THE ASD FUEL SYSTEM.
INSPECT THE FUEL INJECTOR AREA FOR FUEL LEAKAGE.
IS THERE ANY FUEL LEAKAGE?
YES
PERFORM TEST NS-7B.
NO
IGNITION KEY OFF.
DISCONNECT THE ENGINE CONTROLLER CONNECTOR.
INSPECT THE CONNECTOR.
IS THE CONNECTOR CONDITION OK?
NO
REPAIR AS NECESSARY.*
YES
CONTINUE TEST NS-7A
* PERFORM VERIFICATION PROCEDURE VER-1.

91C08714 91C08747

Fig. 17: No Start Test 7A (2.2L & 2.5L) – Checking for Flooding Fuel Injector (1 of 3)

NS-7A: CHECKING FOR FLOODING FUEL INJECTOR (2 OF 3)

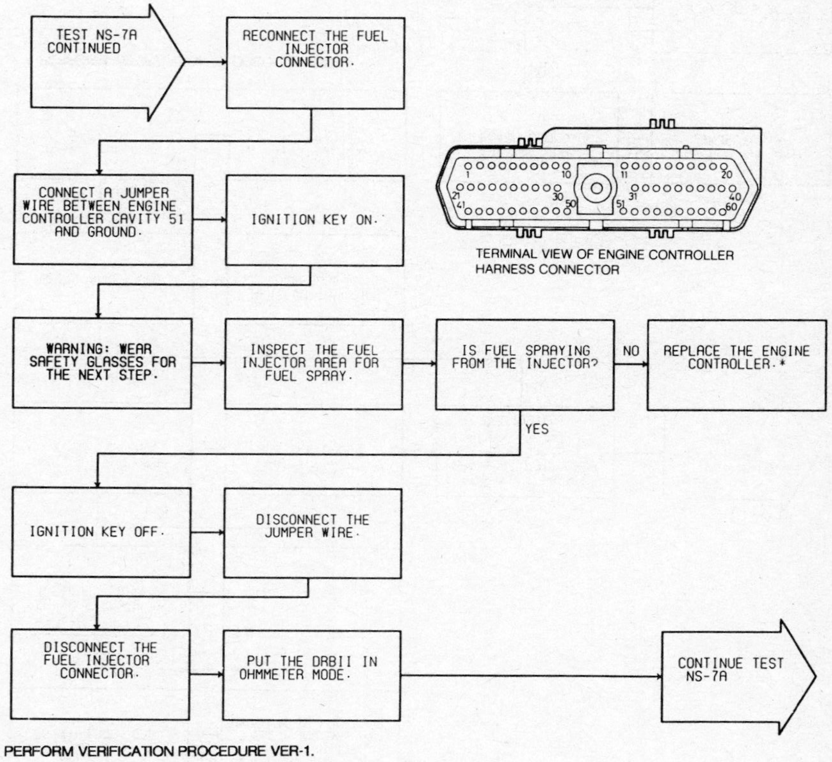
TEST NS-7A CONTINUED
RECONNECT THE FUEL INJECTOR CONNECTOR.
CONNECT A JUMPER WIRE BETWEEN ENGINE CONTROLLER CAVITY 51 AND GROUND.
IGNITION KEY ON.
TERMINAL VIEW OF ENGINE CONTROLLER HARNESS CONNECTOR
WARNING: WEAR SAFETY GLASSES FOR THE NEXT STEP.
INSPECT THE FUEL INJECTOR AREA FOR FUEL SPRAY.
IS FUEL SPRAYING FROM THE INJECTOR?
NO
REPLACE THE ENGINE CONTROLLER.*
YES
IGNITION KEY OFF.
DISCONNECT THE JUMPER WIRE.
DISCONNECT THE FUEL INJECTOR CONNECTOR.
PUT THE DRBII IN OHMMETER MODE.
CONTINUE TEST NS-7A
* PERFORM VERIFICATION PROCEDURE VER-1.

91E08748

Fig. 18: No Start Test 7A (2.2L & 2.5L) – Checking for Flooding Fuel Injector (2 of 3)

NS-7A: CHECKING FOR FLOODING FUEL INJECTOR (3 OF 3)

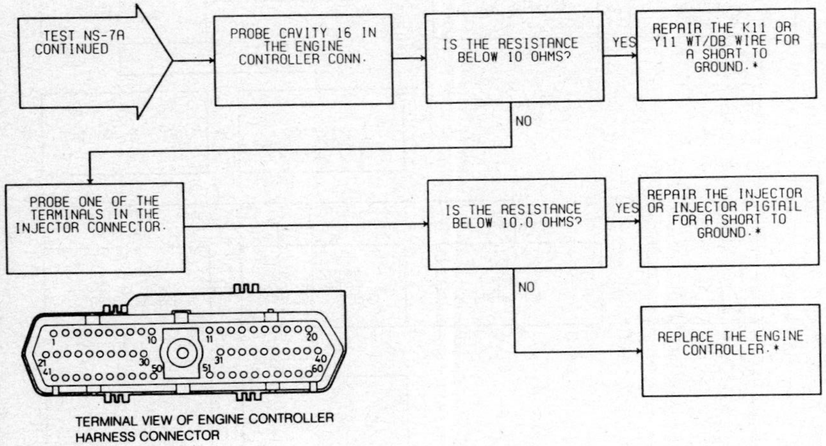
TEST NS-7A CONTINUED
PROBE CAVITY 16 IN THE ENGINE CONTROLLER CONN.
IS THE RESISTANCE BELOW 10 OHMS?
YES
REPAIR THE K11 OR Y11 WT/DB WIRE FOR A SHORT TO GROUND.*
NO
PROBE ONE OF THE TERMINALS IN THE INJECTOR CONNECTOR.
IS THE RESISTANCE BELOW 10.0 OHMS?
YES
REPAIR THE INJECTOR OR INJECTOR PIGTAIL FOR A SHORT TO GROUND.*
NO
REPLACE THE ENGINE CONTROLLER.*
1
10
11
20
21
30
31
40
41
50
51
60
TERMINAL VIEW OF ENGINE CONTROLLER HARNESS CONNECTOR

* PERFORM VERIFICATION PROCEDURE VER-1.

91G08749

Fig. 19: No Start Test 7A (2.2L & 2.5L) – Checking for Flooding Fuel Injector (3 of 3)

NS-7B: CHECKING FOR FLOODING FUEL INJ., KINKED FUEL LINES & PRESSURE REG. OPERATION (1 OF 2)

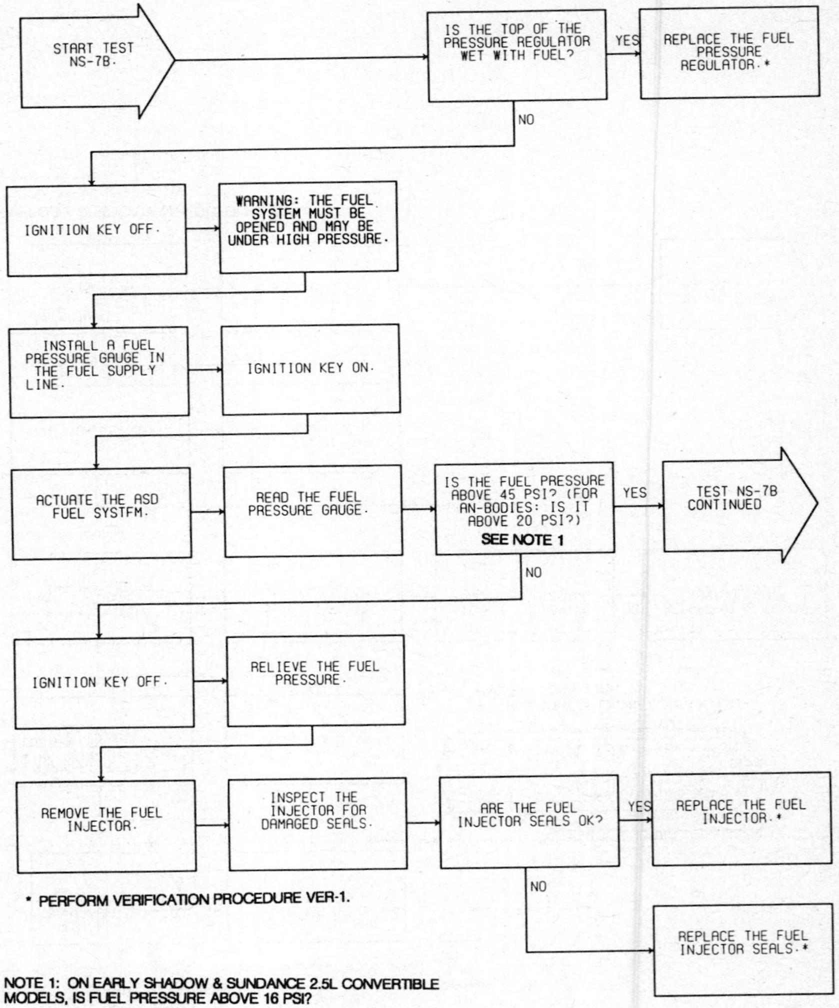
START TEST NS-7B.
IS THE TOP OF THE PRESSURE REGULATOR WET WITH FUEL?
YES
REPLACE THE FUEL PRESSURE REGULATOR.*
NO
IGNITION KEY OFF.
WARNING: THE FUEL SYSTEM MUST BE OPENED AND MAY BE UNDER HIGH PRESSURE.
INSTALL A FUEL PRESSURE GAUGE IN THE FUEL SUPPLY LINE.
IGNITION KEY ON.
ACTUATE THE ASD FUEL SYSTFM.
READ THE FUEL PRESSURE GAUGE.
IS THE FUEL PRESSURE ABOVE 45 PSI? (FOR AN-BODIES: IS IT ABOVE 20 PSI?)
SEE NOTE 1
YES
TEST NS-7B CONTINUED
NO
IGNITION KEY OFF.
RELIEVE THE FUEL PRESSURE.
REMOVE THE FUEL INJECTOR.
INSPECT THE INJECTOR FOR DAMAGED SEALS.
ARE THE FUEL INJECTOR SEALS OK?
YES
REPLACE THE FUEL INJECTOR.*
NO
REPLACE THE FUEL INJECTOR SEALS.*

* PERFORM VERIFICATION PROCEDURE VER-1.

NOTE 1: ON EARLY SHADOW & SUNDANCE 2.5L CONVERTIBLE MODELS, IS FUEL PRESSURE ABOVE 16 PSI?

91I08750

Fig. 20: No Start Test 7B (2.2L & 2.5L) – Checking for Flooding Fuel Injector, Kinked Fuel Lines & Pressure Regulator Operation (1 of 2)

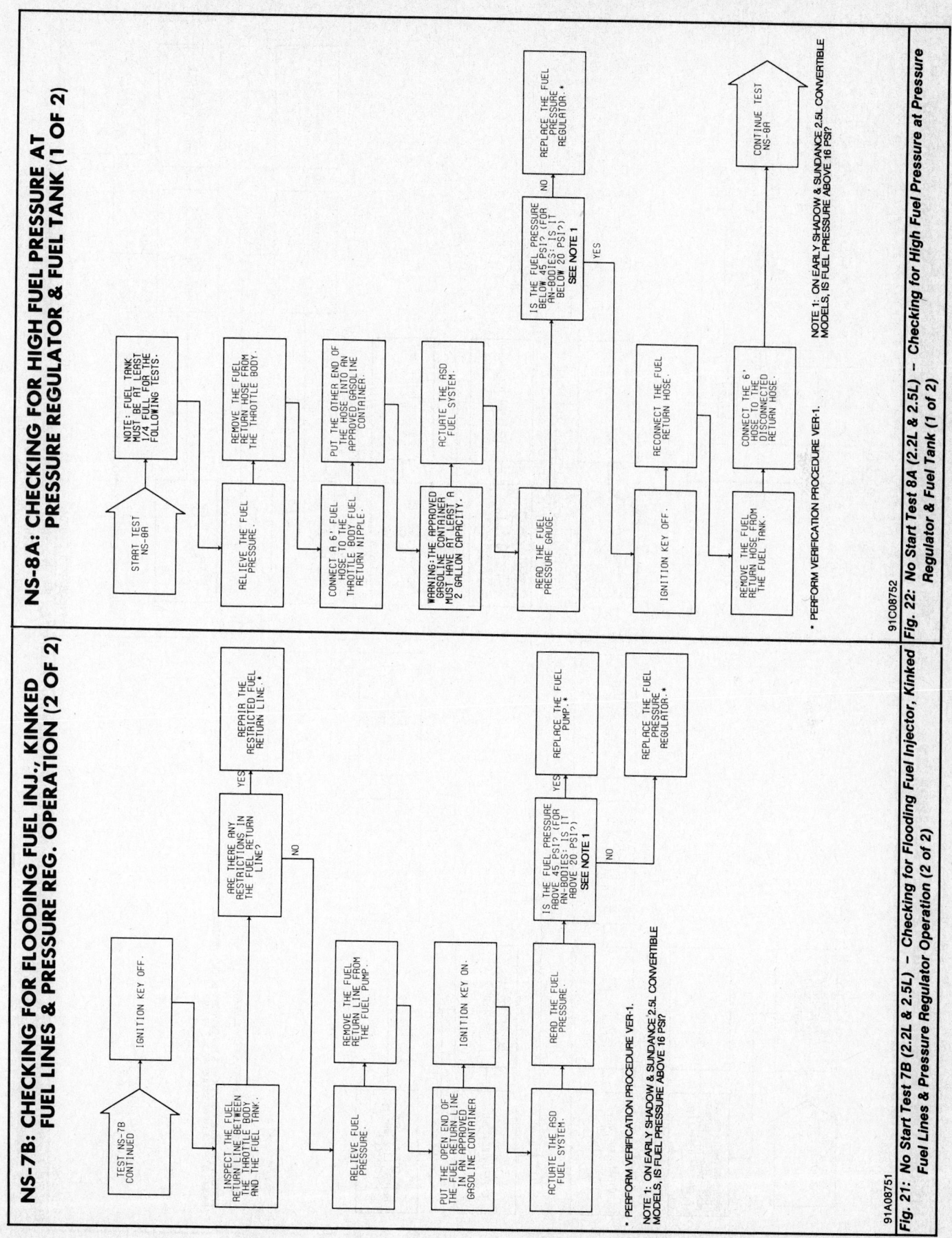

NS-7B: CHECKING FOR FLOODING FUEL INJ., KINKED FUEL LINES & PRESSURE REG. OPERATION (2 OF 2)

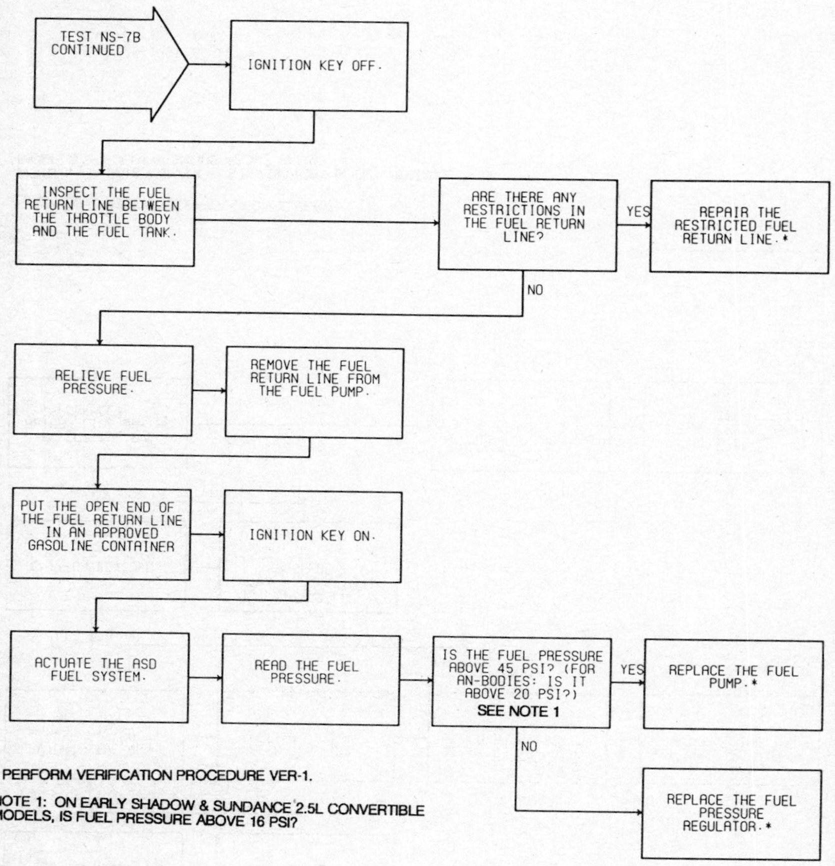

TEST NS-7B CONTINUED
IGNITION KEY OFF.
INSPECT THE FUEL RETURN LINE BETWEEN THE THROTTLE BODY AND THE FUEL TANK.
ARE THERE ANY RESTRICTIONS IN THE FUEL RETURN LINE?
YES
REPAIR THE RESTRICTED FUEL RETURN LINE.*
NO
RELIEVE FUEL PRESSURE.
REMOVE THE FUEL RETURN LINE FROM THE FUEL PUMP.
PUT THE OPEN END OF THE FUEL RETURN LINE IN AN APPROVED GASOLINE CONTAINER
IGNITION KEY ON.
ACTUATE THE ASD FUEL SYSTEM.
READ THE FUEL PRESSURE.
IS THE FUEL PRESSURE ABOVE 45 PSI? (FOR AN-BODIES: IS IT ABOVE 20 PSI?) SEE NOTE 1
YES
REPLACE THE FUEL PUMP.*
NO
REPLACE THE FUEL PRESSURE REGULATOR.*

* PERFORM VERIFICATION PROCEDURE VER-1.

NOTE 1: ON EARLY SHADOW & SUNDANCE 2.5L CONVERTIBLE MODELS, IS FUEL PRESSURE ABOVE 16 PSI?

91A08751

Fig. 21: No Start Test 7B (2.2L & 2.5L) – Checking for Flooding Fuel Injector, Kinked Fuel Lines & Pressure Regulator Operation (2 of 2)

NS-8A: CHECKING FOR HIGH FUEL PRESSURE AT PRESSURE REGULATOR & FUEL TANK (1 OF 2)

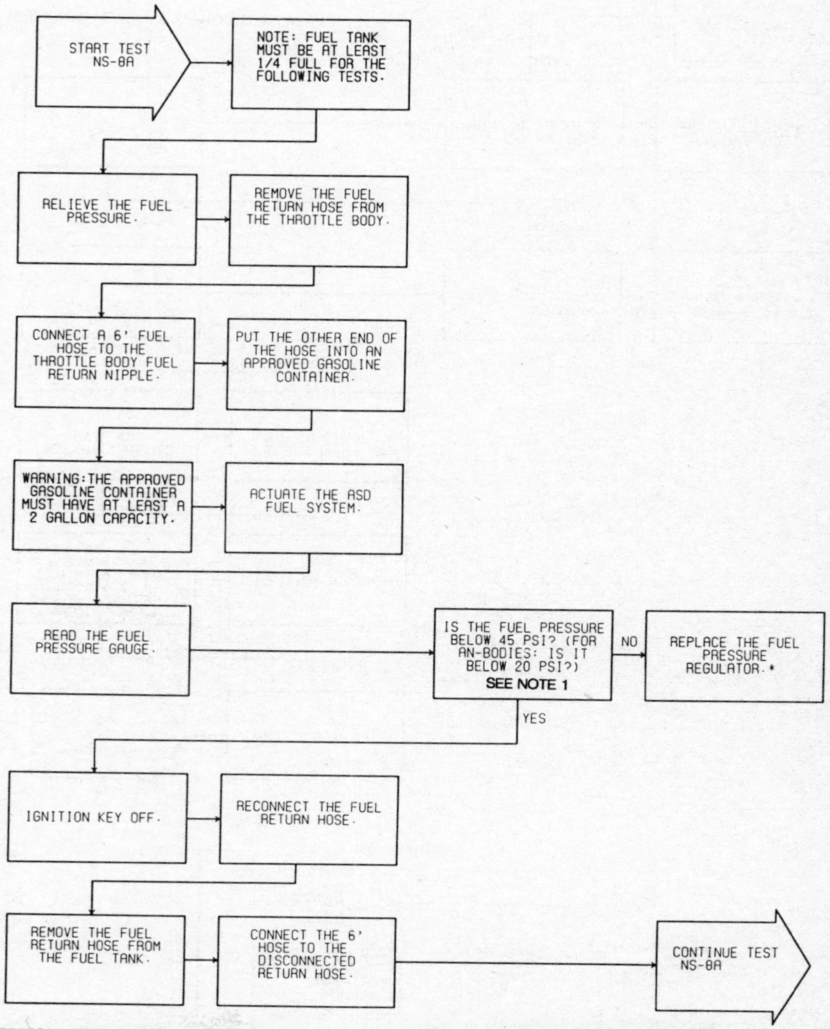

START TEST NS-8A
NOTE: FUEL TANK MUST BE AT LEAST 1/4 FULL FOR THE FOLLOWING TESTS.
RELIEVE THE FUEL PRESSURE.
REMOVE THE FUEL RETURN HOSE FROM THE THROTTLE BODY.
CONNECT A 6' FUEL HOSE TO THE THROTTLE BODY FUEL RETURN NIPPLE.
PUT THE OTHER END OF THE HOSE INTO AN APPROVED GASOLINE CONTAINER.
WARNING: THE APPROVED GASOLINE CONTAINER MUST HAVE AT LEAST A 2 GALLON CAPACITY.
ACTUATE THE ASD FUEL SYSTEM.
READ THE FUEL PRESSURE GAUGE.
IS THE FUEL PRESSURE BELOW 45 PSI? (FOR AN-BODIES: IS IT BELOW 20 PSI?) SEE NOTE 1
NO
REPLACE THE FUEL PRESSURE REGULATOR.*
YES
IGNITION KEY OFF.
RECONNECT THE FUEL RETURN HOSE.
REMOVE THE FUEL RETURN HOSE FROM THE FUEL TANK.
CONNECT THE 6' HOSE TO THE DISCONNECTED RETURN HOSE.
CONTINUE TEST NS-8A

* PERFORM VERIFICATION PROCEDURE VER-1.

NOTE 1: ON EARLY SHADOW & SUNDANCE 2.5L CONVERTIBLE MODELS, IS FUEL PRESSURE ABOVE 16 PSI?

91C08752

Fig. 22: No Start Test 8A (2.2L & 2.5L) – Checking for High Fuel Pressure at Pressure Regulator & Fuel Tank (1 of 2)

NS-8A: CHECKING FOR HIGH FUEL PRESSURE AT PRESSURE REGULATOR & FUEL TANK (2 OF 2)

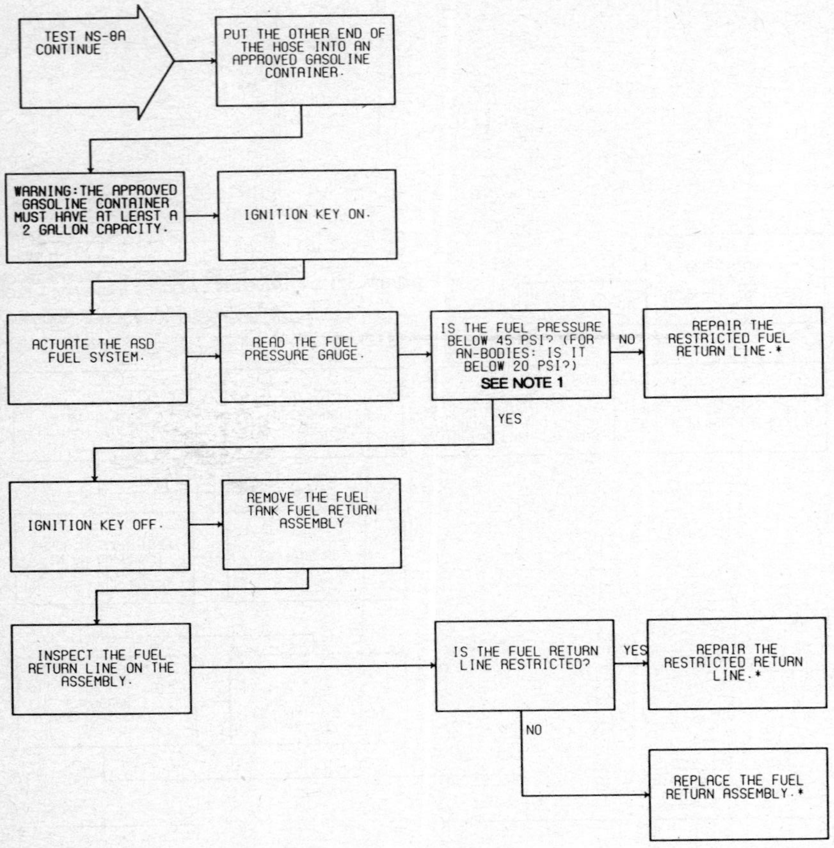
TEST NS-8A CONTINUE
PUT THE OTHER END OF THE HOSE INTO AN APPROVED GASOLINE CONTAINER.
WARNING: THE APPROVED GASOLINE CONTAINER MUST HAVE AT LEAST A 2 GALLON CAPACITY.
IGNITION KEY ON.
ACTUATE THE ASD FUEL SYSTEM.
READ THE FUEL PRESSURE GAUGE.
IS THE FUEL PRESSURE BELOW 45 PSI? (FOR AN-BODIES: IS IT BELOW 20 PSI?) SEE NOTE 1
NO
REPAIR THE RESTRICTED FUEL RETURN LINE.*
YES
IGNITION KEY OFF.
REMOVE THE FUEL TANK FUEL RETURN ASSEMBLY
INSPECT THE FUEL RETURN LINE ON THE ASSEMBLY.
IS THE FUEL RETURN LINE RESTRICTED?
YES
REPAIR THE RESTRICTED RETURN LINE.*
NO
REPLACE THE FUEL RETURN ASSEMBLY.*

* PERFORM VERIFICATION PROCEDURE VER-1.

NOTE 1: ON EARLY SHADOW & SUNDANCE 2.5L CONVERTIBLE MODELS, IS FUEL PRESSURE ABOVE 16 PSI?

91E08753

Fig. 23: No Start Test 8A (2.2L & 2.5L) – Checking for High Fuel Pressure at Pressure Regulator & Fuel Tank (2 of 2)

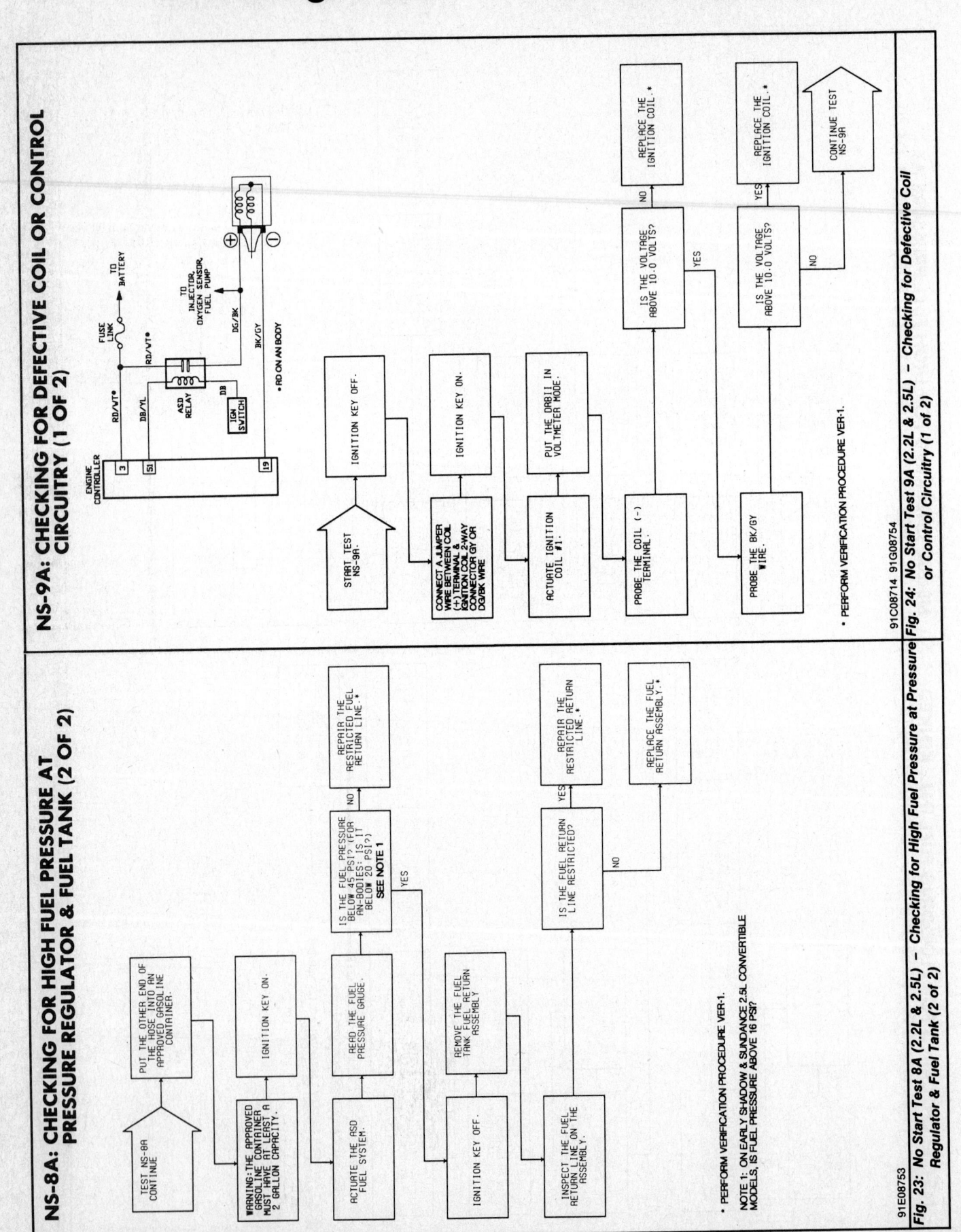

NS-9A: CHECKING FOR DEFECTIVE COIL OR CONTROL CIRCUITRY (1 OF 2)

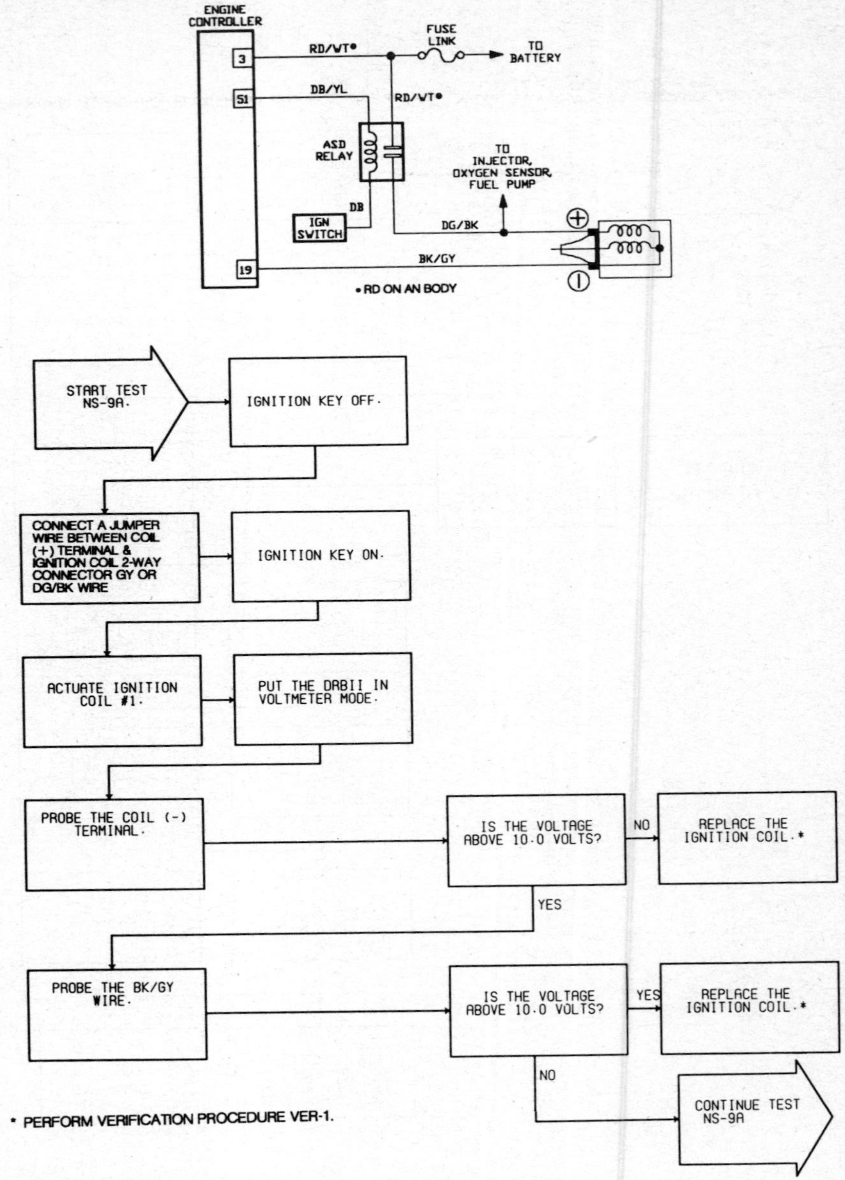
ENGINE CONTROLLER
3
51
19
RD/WT•
FUSE LINK
TO BATTERY
DB/YL
RD/WT•
ASD RELAY
TO INJECTOR, OXYGEN SENSOR, FUEL PUMP
DB
IGN SWITCH
DG/BK
BK/GY
• RD ON AN BODY
START TEST NS-9A.
IGNITION KEY OFF.
CONNECT A JUMPER WIRE BETWEEN COIL (+) TERMINAL & IGNITION COIL 2-WAY CONNECTOR GY OR DG/BK WIRE
IGNITION KEY ON.
ACTUATE IGNITION COIL #1.
PUT THE DRBII IN VOLTMETER MODE.
PROBE THE COIL (-) TERMINAL.
IS THE VOLTAGE ABOVE 10.0 VOLTS?
NO
REPLACE THE IGNITION COIL.*
YES
PROBE THE BK/GY WIRE.
IS THE VOLTAGE ABOVE 10.0 VOLTS?
YES
REPLACE THE IGNITION COIL.*
NO
CONTINUE TEST NS-9A

* PERFORM VERIFICATION PROCEDURE VER-1.

91C08714 91G08754

Fig. 24: No Start Test 9A (2.2L & 2.5L) – Checking for Defective Coil or Control Circuitry (1 of 2)

NS-9A: CHECKING FOR DEFECTIVE COIL OR CONTROL CIRCUITRY (2 OF 2)

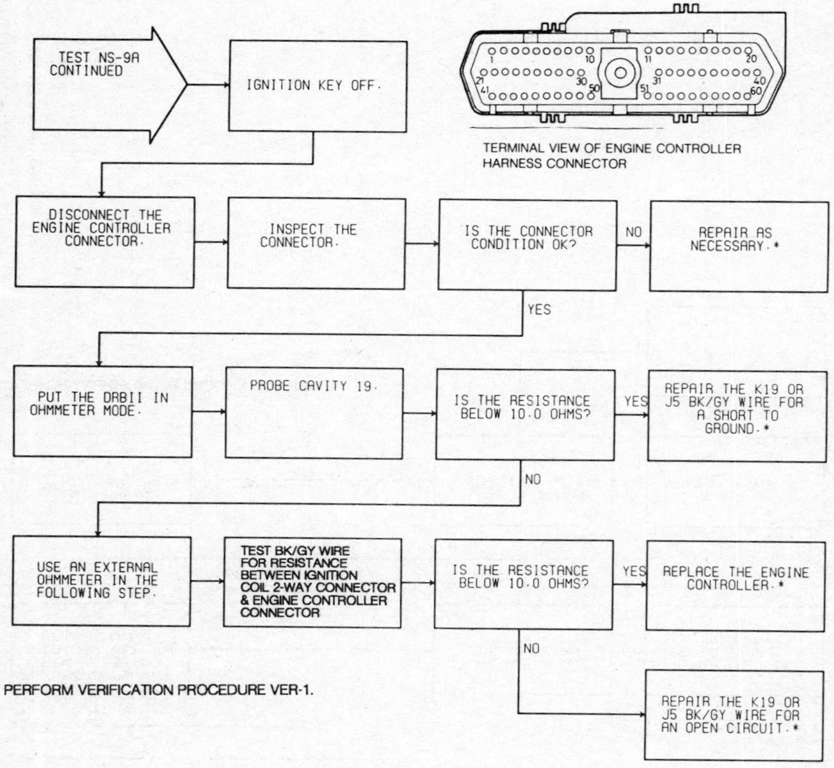
TEST NS-9A CONTINUED
IGNITION KEY OFF.
TERMINAL VIEW OF ENGINE CONTROLLER HARNESS CONNECTOR
DISCONNECT THE ENGINE CONTROLLER CONNECTOR.
INSPECT THE CONNECTOR.
IS THE CONNECTOR CONDITION OK?
NO
REPAIR AS NECESSARY.*
YES
PUT THE DRBII IN OHMMETER MODE.
PROBE CAVITY 19.
IS THE RESISTANCE BELOW 10.0 OHMS?
YES
REPAIR THE K19 OR J5 BK/GY WIRE FOR A SHORT TO GROUND.*
NO
USE AN EXTERNAL OHMMETER IN THE FOLLOWING STEP.
TEST BK/GY WIRE FOR RESISTANCE BETWEEN IGNITION COIL 2-WAY CONNECTOR & ENGINE CONTROLLER CONNECTOR
IS THE RESISTANCE BELOW 10.0 OHMS?
YES
REPLACE THE ENGINE CONTROLLER.*
NO
REPAIR THE K19 OR J5 BK/GY WIRE FOR AN OPEN CIRCUIT.*

* PERFORM VERIFICATION PROCEDURE VER-1.

91J08755

Fig. 25: No Start Test 9A (2.2L & 2.5L) – Checking for Defective Coil or Control Circuitry (2 of 2)

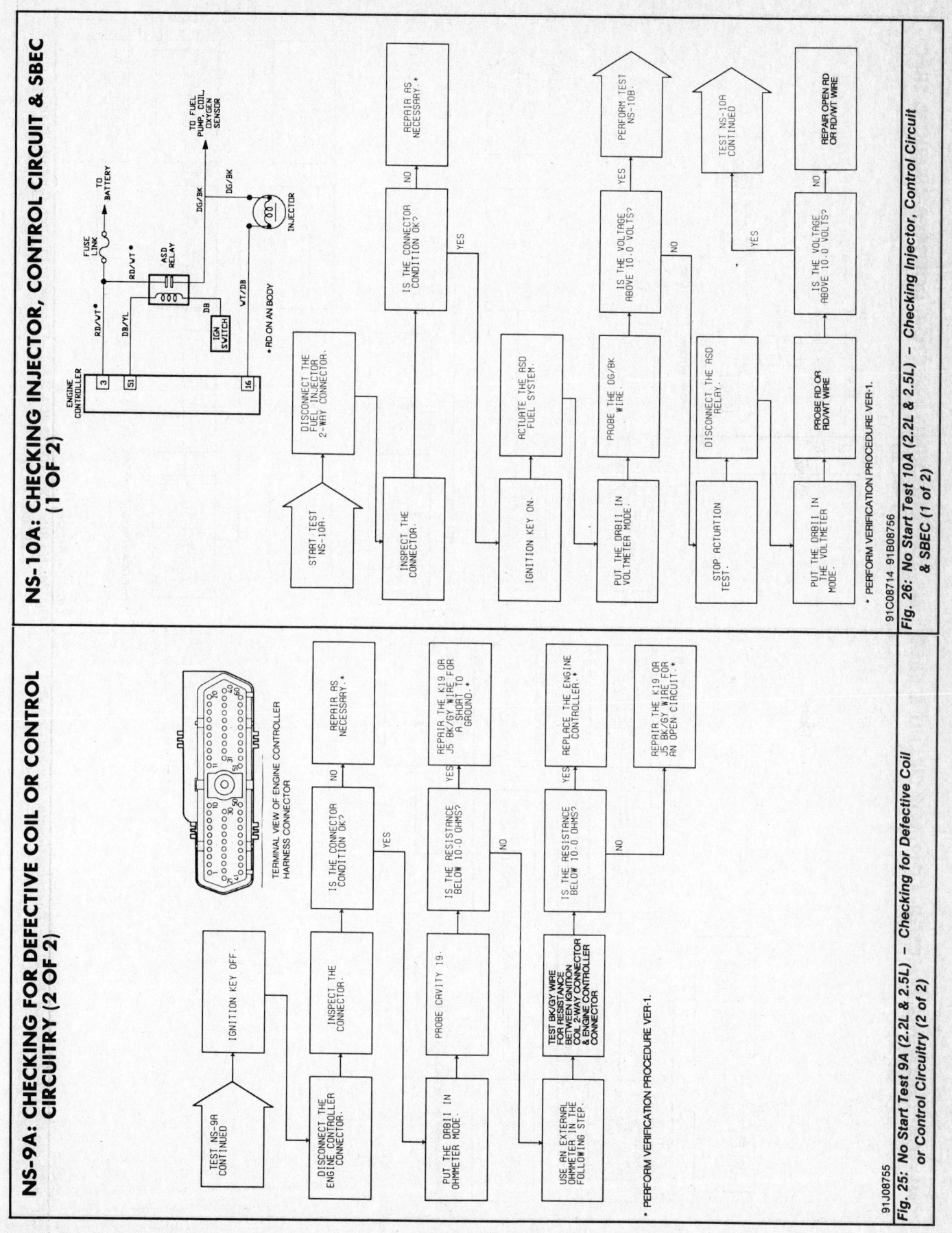

NS-10A: CHECKING INJECTOR, CONTROL CIRCUIT & SBEC (1 OF 2)

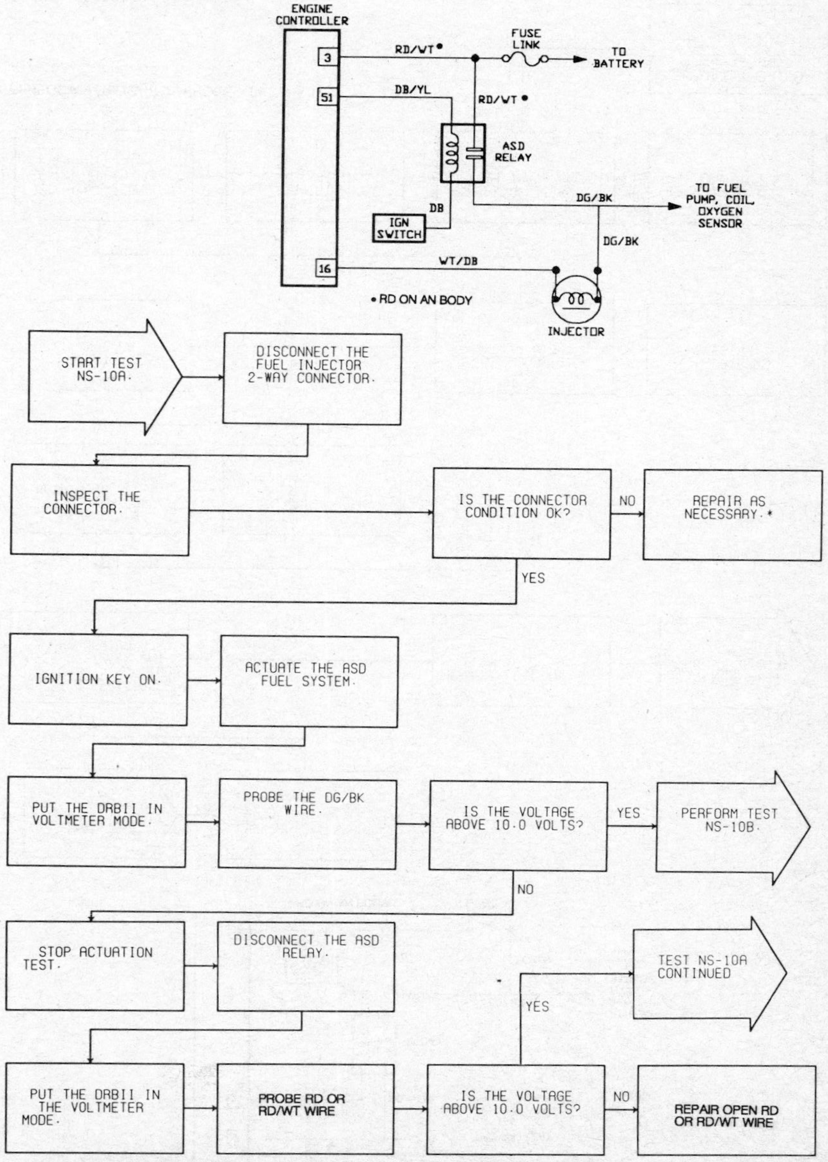
ENGINE CONTROLLER
RD/WT*
FUSE LINK
TO BATTERY
DB/YL
RD/WT*
ASD RELAY
DB
IGN SWITCH
DG/BK
TO FUEL PUMP, COIL, OXYGEN SENSOR
DG/BK
WT/DB
* RD ON AN BODY
INJECTOR
START TEST NS-10A.
DISCONNECT THE FUEL INJECTOR 2-WAY CONNECTOR.
INSPECT THE CONNECTOR.
IS THE CONNECTOR CONDITION OK?
NO
REPAIR AS NECESSARY.*
YES
IGNITION KEY ON.
ACTUATE THE ASD FUEL SYSTEM.
PUT THE DRBII IN VOLTMETER MODE.
PROBE THE DG/BK WIRE.
IS THE VOLTAGE ABOVE 10.0 VOLTS?
YES
PERFORM TEST NS-10B.
NO
STOP ACTUATION TEST.
DISCONNECT THE ASD RELAY.
TEST NS-10A CONTINUED
YES
PUT THE DRBII IN THE VOLTMETER MODE.
PROBE RD OR RD/WT WIRE
IS THE VOLTAGE ABOVE 10.0 VOLTS?
NO
REPAIR OPEN RD OR RD/WT WIRE

* PERFORM VERIFICATION PROCEDURE VER-1.

91C08714 91B08756

Fig. 26: No Start Test 10A (2.2L & 2.5L) – Checking Injector, Control Circuit & SBEC (1 of 2)

1991 ENGINE PERFORMANCE
Self-Diagnostics – 2.5L TBI (Cont.)

NS-10A: CHECKING INJECTOR, CONTROL CIRCUIT & SBEC (2 OF 2)

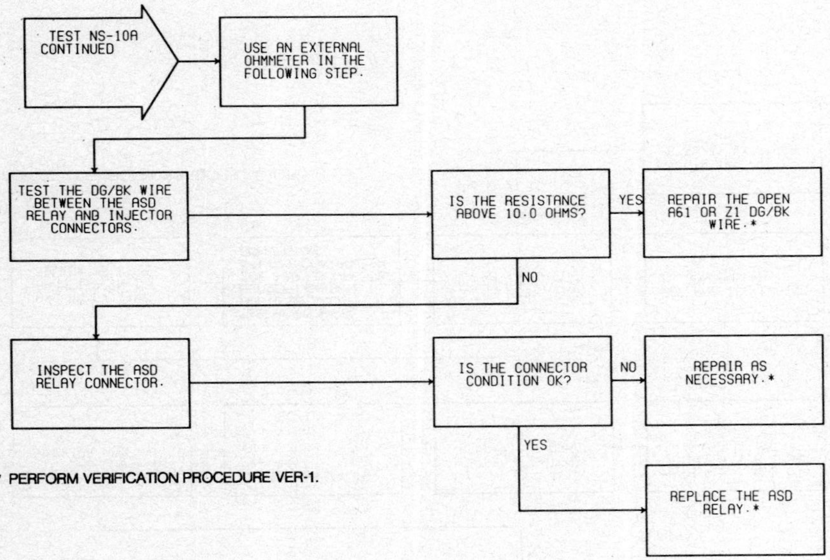
TEST NS-10A CONTINUED
USE AN EXTERNAL OHMMETER IN THE FOLLOWING STEP.
TEST THE DG/BK WIRE BETWEEN THE ASD RELAY AND INJECTOR CONNECTORS.
IS THE RESISTANCE ABOVE 10.0 OHMS?
YES
REPAIR THE OPEN A61 OR Z1 DG/BK WIRE.*
NO
INSPECT THE ASD RELAY CONNECTOR.
IS THE CONNECTOR CONDITION OK?
NO
REPAIR AS NECESSARY.*
YES
REPLACE THE ASD RELAY.*

* PERFORM VERIFICATION PROCEDURE VER-1.

91D08757

Fig. 27: No Start Test 10A (2.2L & 2.5L) – Checking Injector, Control Circuit & SBEC (2 of 2)

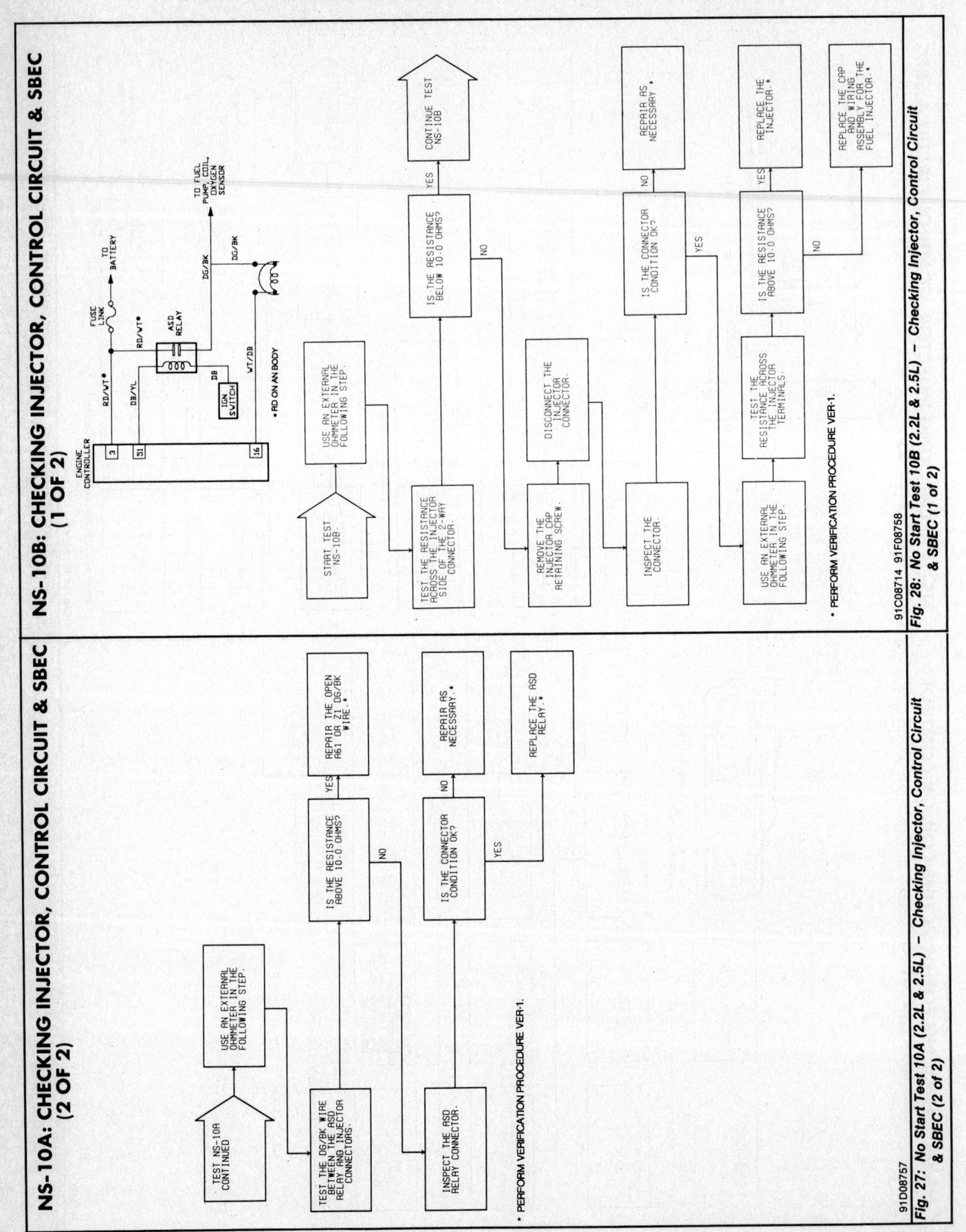

NS-10B: CHECKING INJECTOR, CONTROL CIRCUIT & SBEC (1 OF 2)

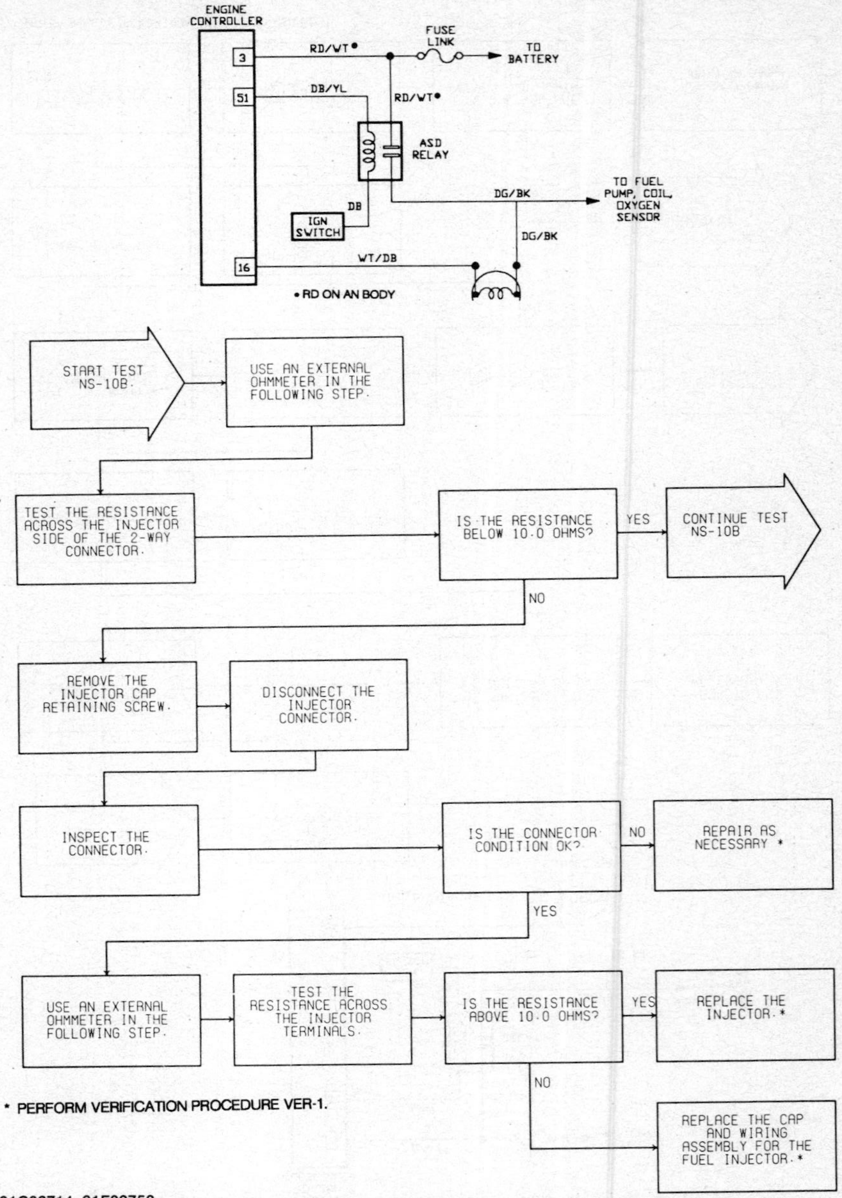
ENGINE CONTROLLER
3
51
16
RD/WT•
FUSE LINK
TO BATTERY
DB/YL
RD/WT•
ASD RELAY
DB
IGN SWITCH
DG/BK
TO FUEL PUMP, COIL, OXYGEN SENSOR
DG/BK
WT/DB
• RD ON AN BODY
START TEST NS-10B.
USE AN EXTERNAL OHMMETER IN THE FOLLOWING STEP.
TEST THE RESISTANCE ACROSS THE INJECTOR SIDE OF THE 2-WAY CONNECTOR.
IS THE RESISTANCE BELOW 10.0 OHMS?
YES
CONTINUE TEST NS-10B
NO
REMOVE THE INJECTOR CAP RETAINING SCREW.
DISCONNECT THE INJECTOR CONNECTOR.
INSPECT THE CONNECTOR.
IS THE CONNECTOR CONDITION OK?
NO
REPAIR AS NECESSARY.*
YES
USE AN EXTERNAL OHMMETER IN THE FOLLOWING STEP.
TEST THE RESISTANCE ACROSS THE INJECTOR TERMINALS.
IS THE RESISTANCE ABOVE 10.0 OHMS?
YES
REPLACE THE INJECTOR.*
NO
REPLACE THE CAP AND WIRING ASSEMBLY FOR THE FUEL INJECTOR.*

* PERFORM VERIFICATION PROCEDURE VER-1.

91C08714 91F08758

Fig. 28: No Start Test 10B (2.2L & 2.5L) – Checking Injector, Control Circuit & SBEC (1 of 2)

NS-10B: CHECKING INJECTOR, CONTROL CIRCUIT & SBEC (2 OF 2)

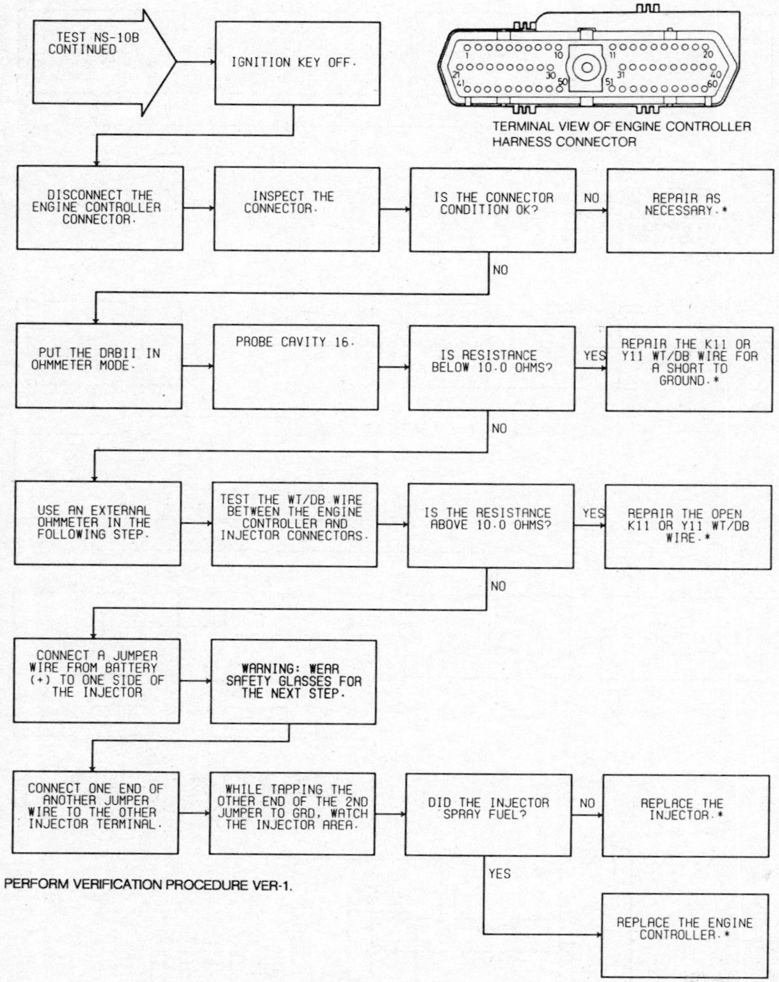

TEST NS-10B CONTINUED
IGNITION KEY OFF.
TERMINAL VIEW OF ENGINE CONTROLLER HARNESS CONNECTOR
DISCONNECT THE ENGINE CONTROLLER CONNECTOR.
INSPECT THE CONNECTOR.
IS THE CONNECTOR CONDITION OK?
NO
REPAIR AS NECESSARY.*
NO
PUT THE DRBII IN OHMMETER MODE.
PROBE CAVITY 16.
IS RESISTANCE BELOW 10.0 OHMS?
YES
REPAIR THE K11 OR Y11 WT/DB WIRE FOR A SHORT TO GROUND.*
NO
USE AN EXTERNAL OHMMETER IN THE FOLLOWING STEP.
TEST THE WT/DB WIRE BETWEEN THE ENGINE CONTROLLER AND INJECTOR CONNECTORS.
IS THE RESISTANCE ABOVE 10.0 OHMS?
YES
REPAIR THE OPEN K11 OR Y11 WT/DB WIRE.*
NO
CONNECT A JUMPER WIRE FROM BATTERY (+) TO ONE SIDE OF THE INJECTOR
WARNING: WEAR SAFETY GLASSES FOR THE NEXT STEP.
CONNECT ONE END OF ANOTHER JUMPER WIRE TO THE OTHER INJECTOR TERMINAL.
WHILE TAPPING THE OTHER END OF THE 2ND JUMPER TO GRD, WATCH THE INJECTOR AREA.
DID THE INJECTOR SPRAY FUEL?
NO
REPLACE THE INJECTOR.*
YES
REPLACE THE ENGINE CONTROLLER.*

* PERFORM VERIFICATION PROCEDURE VER-1.

91H08759

Fig. 29: No Start Test 10B (2.2L & 2.5L) – Checking Injector, Control Circuit & SBEC (2 of 2)

NS-11A: CHECKING DRB-II & SYSTEM FAULTS

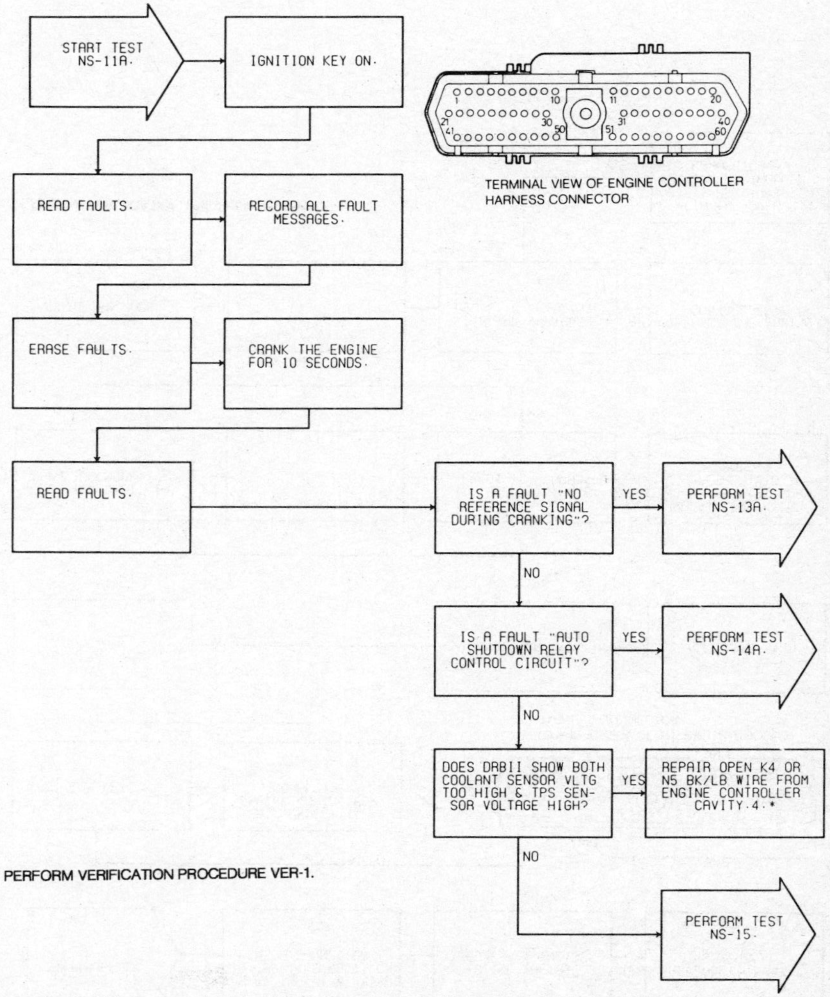

START TEST NS-11A.
IGNITION KEY ON.
TERMINAL VIEW OF ENGINE CONTROLLER HARNESS CONNECTOR
READ FAULTS.
RECORD ALL FAULT MESSAGES.
ERASE FAULTS.
CRANK THE ENGINE FOR 10 SECONDS.
READ FAULTS.
IS A FAULT "NO REFERENCE SIGNAL DURING CRANKING"?
YES
PERFORM TEST NS-13A.
NO
IS A FAULT "AUTO SHUTDOWN RELAY CONTROL CIRCUIT"?
YES
PERFORM TEST NS-14A.
NO
DOES DRBII SHOW BOTH COOLANT SENSOR VLTG TOO HIGH & TPS SENSOR VOLTAGE HIGH?
YES
REPAIR OPEN K4 OR N5 BK/LB WIRE FROM ENGINE CONTROLLER CAVITY 4.*
NO
PERFORM TEST NS-15.

* PERFORM VERIFICATION PROCEDURE VER-1.

91J08760

Fig. 30: No Start Test 11A (2.2L & 2.5L) – Checking DRB-II & System Faults

1991 ENGINE PERFORMANCE
Self-Diagnostics – 2.5L TBI (Cont.)

NS-12A: CHECKING FOR SYSTEM POWER, OPERATION OF MAP SENSOR & SBEC (1 OF 2)

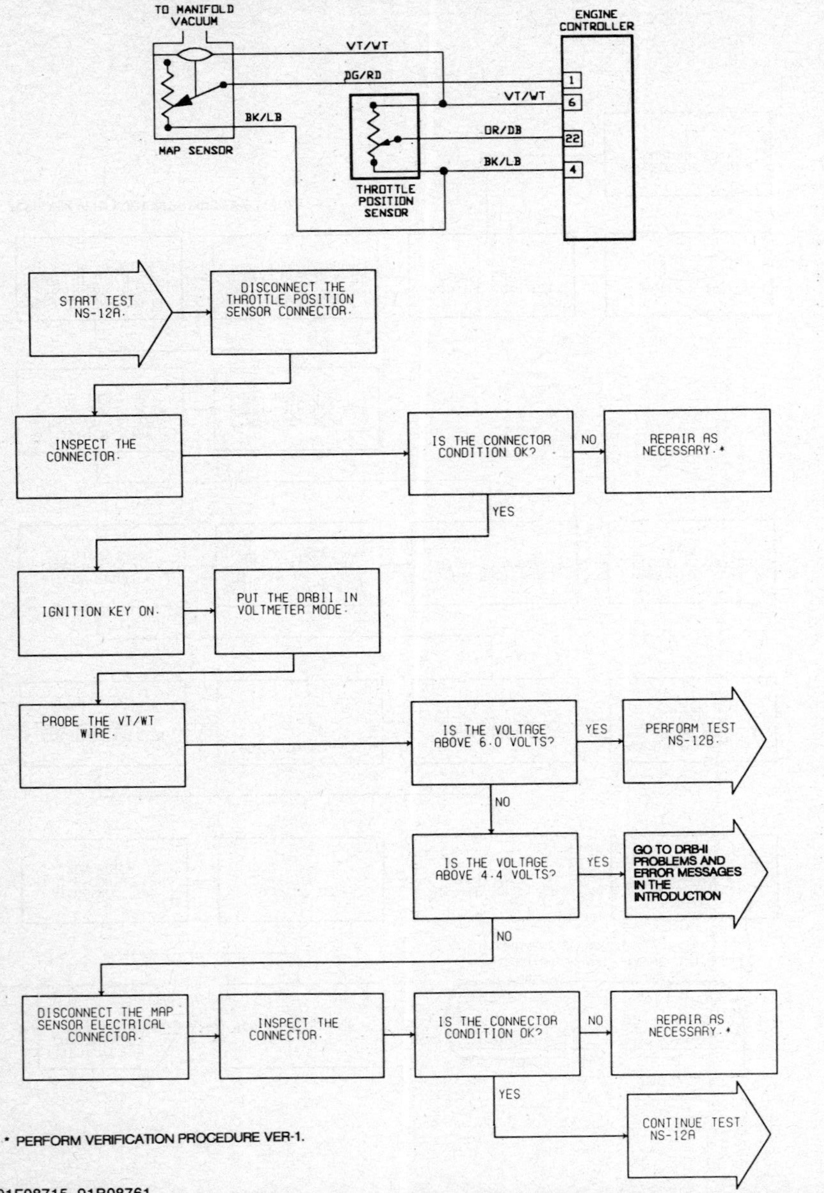
TO MANIFOLD VACUUM
MAP SENSOR
VT/WT
DG/RD
BK/LB
THROTTLE POSITION SENSOR
VT/WT
OR/DB
BK/LB
ENGINE CONTROLLER
1
6
22
4
START TEST NS-12A.
DISCONNECT THE THROTTLE POSITION SENSOR CONNECTOR.
INSPECT THE CONNECTOR.
IS THE CONNECTOR CONDITION OK?
NO
REPAIR AS NECESSARY.*
YES
IGNITION KEY ON.
PUT THE DRBII IN VOLTMETER MODE.
PROBE THE VT/WT WIRE.
IS THE VOLTAGE ABOVE 6.0 VOLTS?
YES
PERFORM TEST NS-12B.
NO
IS THE VOLTAGE ABOVE 4.4 VOLTS?
YES
GO TO DRB-II PROBLEMS AND ERROR MESSAGES IN THE INTRODUCTION
NO
DISCONNECT THE MAP SENSOR ELECTRICAL CONNECTOR.
INSPECT THE CONNECTOR.
IS THE CONNECTOR CONDITION OK?
NO
REPAIR AS NECESSARY.*
YES
CONTINUE TEST NS-12A

* PERFORM VERIFICATION PROCEDURE VER-1.

91F08715 91B08761

Fig. 31: No Start Test 12A (2.2L & 2.5L) – Checking for System Power, Operation of MAP Sensor & SBEC (1 of 2)

NS-12A: CHECKING FOR SYSTEM POWER, OPERATION OF MAP SENSOR & SBEC (2 OF 2)

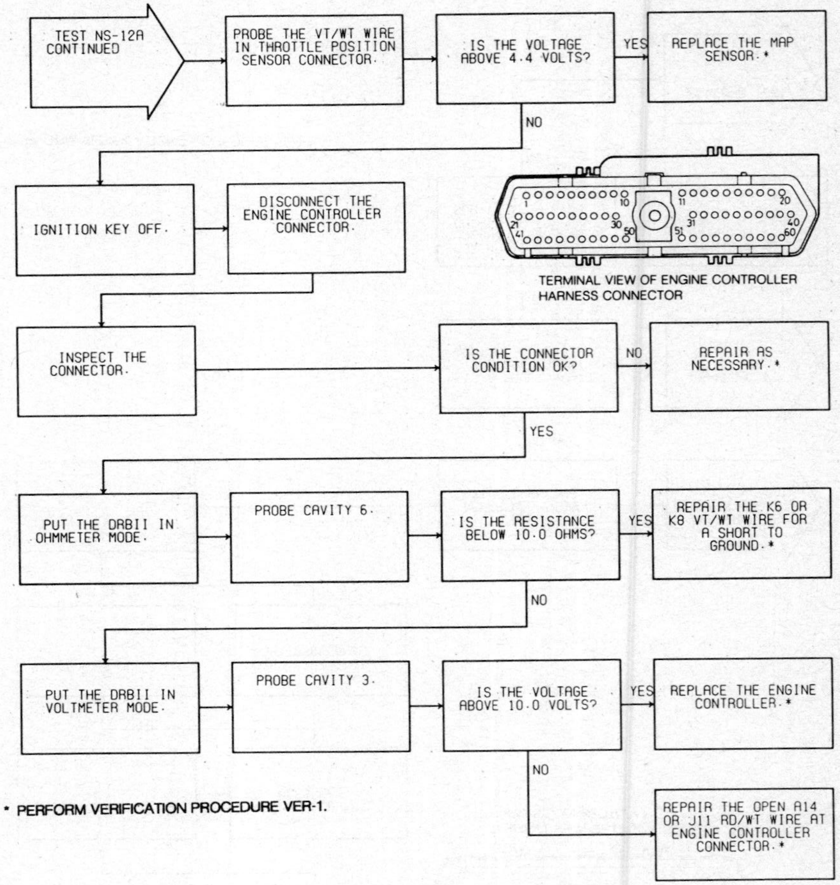
TEST NS-12A CONTINUED
PROBE THE VT/WT WIRE IN THROTTLE POSITION SENSOR CONNECTOR.
IS THE VOLTAGE ABOVE 4.4 VOLTS?
YES
REPLACE THE MAP SENSOR.*
NO
IGNITION KEY OFF.
DISCONNECT THE ENGINE CONTROLLER CONNECTOR.
TERMINAL VIEW OF ENGINE CONTROLLER HARNESS CONNECTOR
INSPECT THE CONNECTOR.
IS THE CONNECTOR CONDITION OK?
NO
REPAIR AS NECESSARY.*
YES
PUT THE DRBII IN OHMMETER MODE.
PROBE CAVITY 6.
IS THE RESISTANCE BELOW 10.0 OHMS?
YES
REPAIR THE K6 OR K8 VT/WT WIRE FOR A SHORT TO GROUND.*
NO
PUT THE DRBII IN VOLTMETER MODE.
PROBE CAVITY 3.
IS THE VOLTAGE ABOVE 10.0 VOLTS?
YES
REPLACE THE ENGINE CONTROLLER.*
NO
REPAIR THE OPEN A14 OR J11 RD/WT WIRE AT ENGINE CONTROLLER CONNECTOR.*

* PERFORM VERIFICATION PROCEDURE VER-1.

91D08762

Fig. 32: No Start Test 12A (2.2L & 2.5L) – Checking for System Power, Operation of MAP Sensor & SBEC (2 of 2)

NS-12B: CHECKING FOR SYSTEM POWER & OPERATION OF MAP SENSOR & SBEC (1 OF 2)

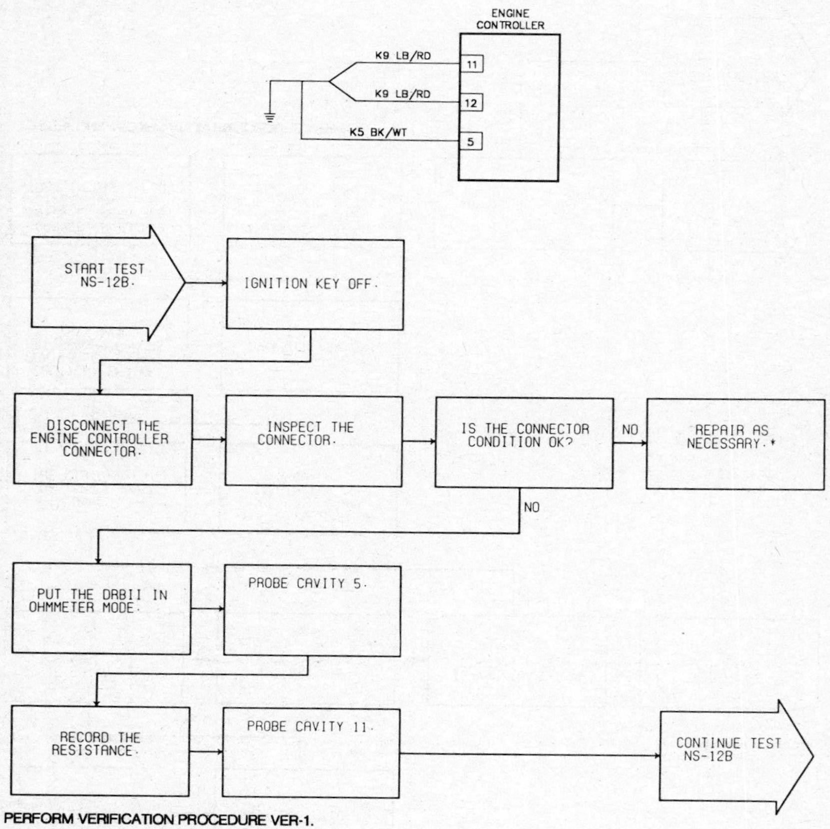
ENGINE CONTROLLER
K9 LB/RD
11
K9 LB/RD
12
K5 BK/WT
5
START TEST NS-12B.
IGNITION KEY OFF.
DISCONNECT THE ENGINE CONTROLLER CONNECTOR.
INSPECT THE CONNECTOR.
IS THE CONNECTOR CONDITION OK?
NO
REPAIR AS NECESSARY.*
NO
PUT THE DRBII IN OHMMETER MODE.
PROBE CAVITY 5.
RECORD THE RESISTANCE.
PROBE CAVITY 11.
CONTINUE TEST NS-12B

* PERFORM VERIFICATION PROCEDURE VER-1.

91H08716 91F08763

Fig. 33: No Start Test 12B (2.2L & 2.5L) – Checking for System Power & Operation of MAP Sensor & SBEC (1 of 2)

NS-12B: CHECKING FOR SYSTEM POWER & OPERATION OF MAP SENSOR & SBEC (2 OF 2)

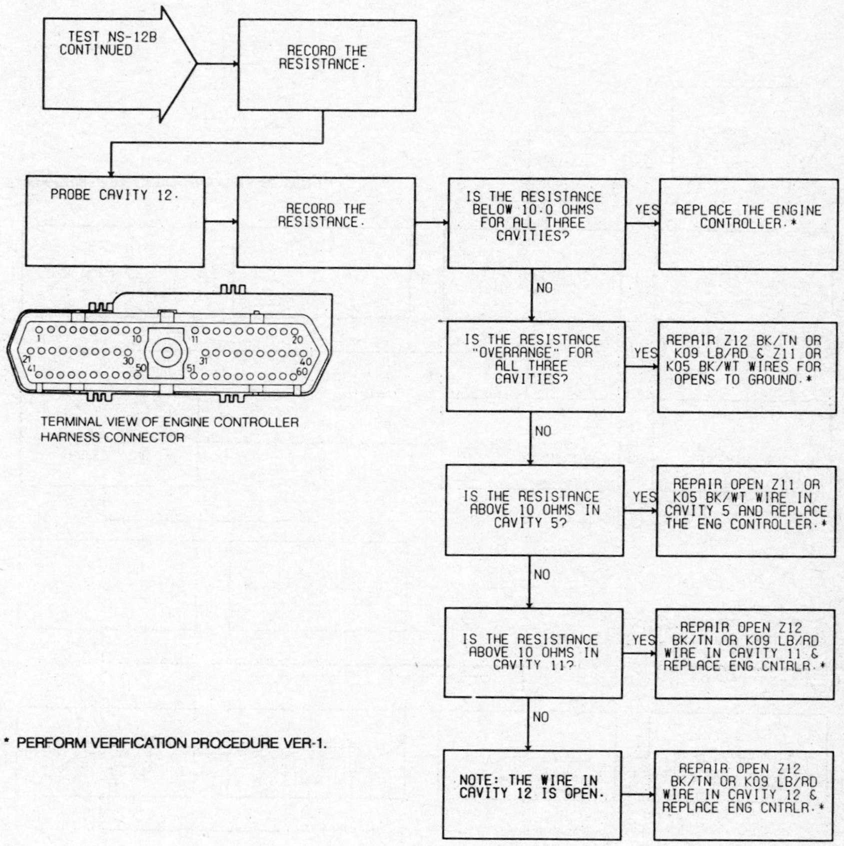
TEST NS-12B CONTINUED
RECORD THE RESISTANCE.
PROBE CAVITY 12.
RECORD THE RESISTANCE.
IS THE RESISTANCE BELOW 10.0 OHMS FOR ALL THREE CAVITIES?
YES
REPLACE THE ENGINE CONTROLLER.*
NO
IS THE RESISTANCE "OVERRANGE" FOR ALL THREE CAVITIES?
YES
REPAIR Z12 BK/TN OR K09 LB/RD & Z11 OR K05 BK/WT WIRES FOR OPENS TO GROUND.*
NO
IS THE RESISTANCE ABOVE 10 OHMS IN CAVITY 5?
YES
REPAIR OPEN Z11 OR K05 BK/WT WIRE IN CAVITY 5 AND REPLACE THE ENG CONTROLLER.*
NO
IS THE RESISTANCE ABOVE 10 OHMS IN CAVITY 11?
YES
REPAIR OPEN Z12 BK/TN OR K09 LB/RD WIRE IN CAVITY 11 & REPLACE ENG CNTRLR.*
NO
NOTE: THE WIRE IN CAVITY 12 IS OPEN.
REPAIR OPEN Z12 BK/TN OR K09 LB/RD WIRE IN CAVITY 12 & REPLACE ENG CNTRLR.*
1
10
11
20
21
30
31
40
41
50
51
60
TERMINAL VIEW OF ENGINE CONTROLLER HARNESS CONNECTOR

* PERFORM VERIFICATION PROCEDURE VER-1.

91H08764

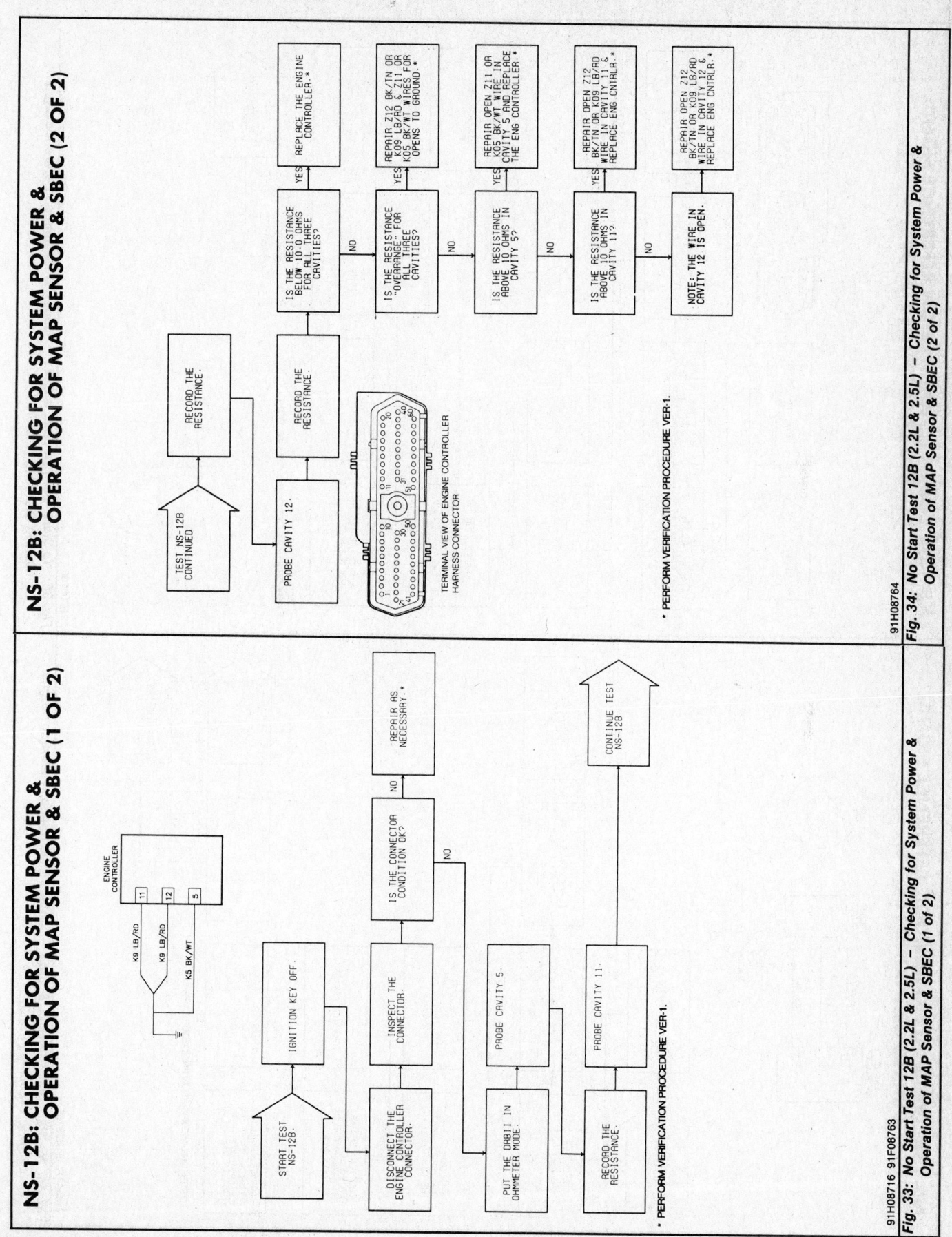

Fig. 34: No Start Test 12B (2.2L & 2.5L) – Checking for System Power & Operation of MAP Sensor & SBEC (2 of 2)

NS-13A: CODE 11, NO IGNITION REFERENCE SIGNAL DURING CRANKING (1 OF 3)

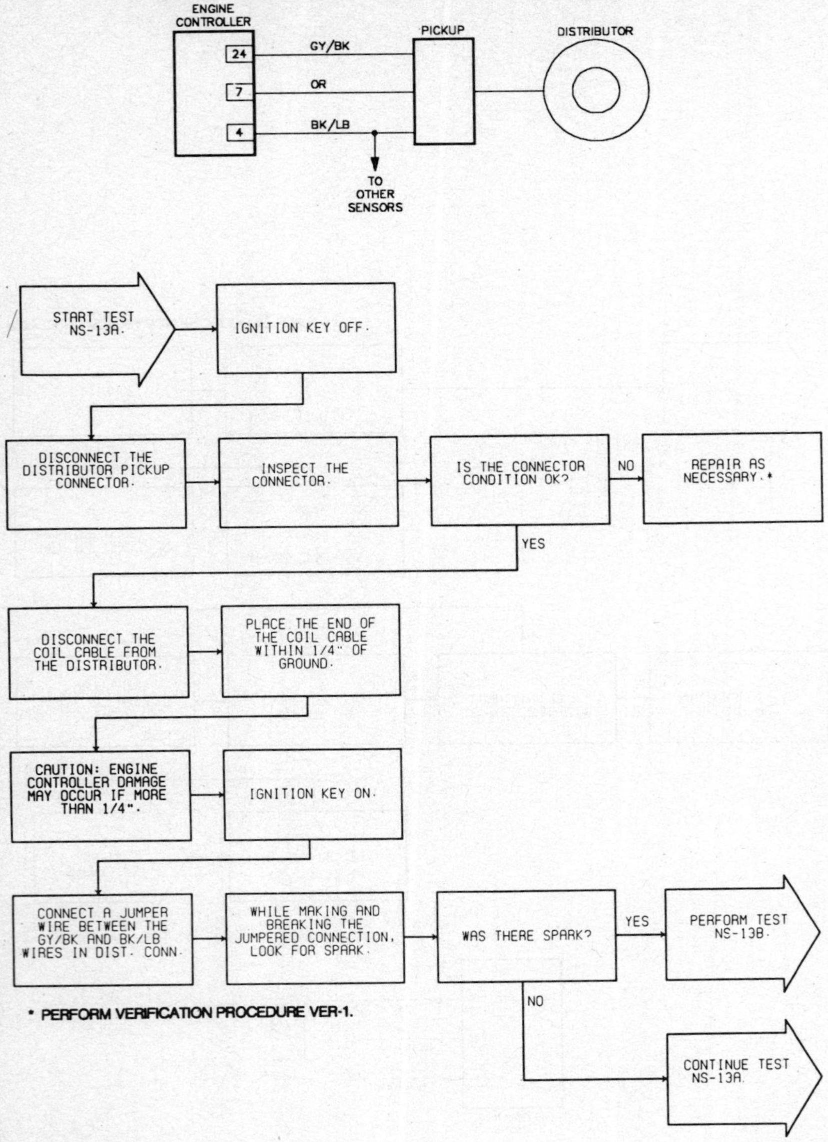
ENGINE CONTROLLER
24
7
4
GY/BK
OR
BK/LB
PICKUP
DISTRIBUTOR
TO OTHER SENSORS
START TEST NS-13A.
IGNITION KEY OFF.
DISCONNECT THE DISTRIBUTOR PICKUP CONNECTOR.
INSPECT THE CONNECTOR.
IS THE CONNECTOR CONDITION OK?
NO
REPAIR AS NECESSARY.*
YES
DISCONNECT THE COIL CABLE FROM THE DISTRIBUTOR.
PLACE THE END OF THE COIL CABLE WITHIN 1/4" OF GROUND.
CAUTION: ENGINE CONTROLLER DAMAGE MAY OCCUR IF MORE THAN 1/4".
IGNITION KEY ON.
CONNECT A JUMPER WIRE BETWEEN THE GY/BK AND BK/LB WIRES IN DIST. CONN.
WHILE MAKING AND BREAKING THE JUMPERED CONNECTION, LOOK FOR SPARK.
WAS THERE SPARK?
YES
PERFORM TEST NS-13B.
NO
CONTINUE TEST NS-13A.

* PERFORM VERIFICATION PROCEDURE VER-1.

91J08717 91A08765

Fig. 35: No Start Test 13A (2.2L & 2.5L) – Code 11, No Ignition Reference Signal During Cranking (1 of 3)

NS-13A: CODE 11, NO IGNITION REFERENCE SIGNAL DURING CRANKING (2 OF 3)

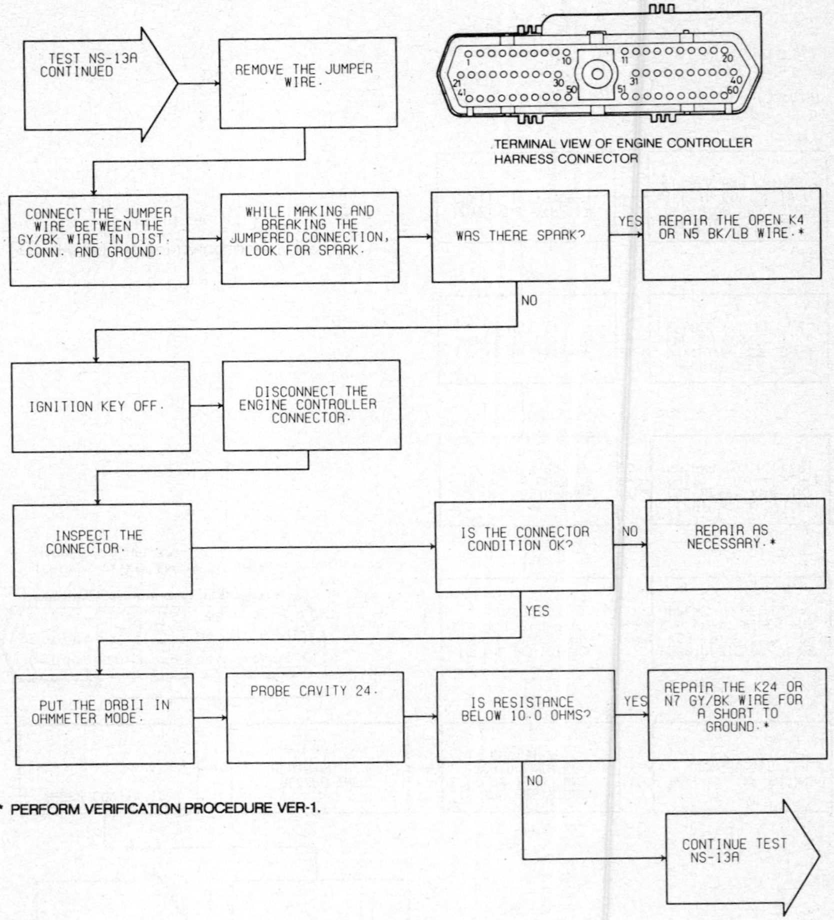
TEST NS-13A CONTINUED
REMOVE THE JUMPER WIRE.
TERMINAL VIEW OF ENGINE CONTROLLER HARNESS CONNECTOR
1
10
11
20
21
30
31
40
41
50
51
60
CONNECT THE JUMPER WIRE BETWEEN THE GY/BK WIRE IN DIST. CONN. AND GROUND.
WHILE MAKING AND BREAKING THE JUMPERED CONNECTION, LOOK FOR SPARK.
WAS THERE SPARK?
YES
REPAIR THE OPEN K4 OR N5 BK/LB WIRE.*
NO
IGNITION KEY OFF.
DISCONNECT THE ENGINE CONTROLLER CONNECTOR.
INSPECT THE CONNECTOR.
IS THE CONNECTOR CONDITION OK?
NO
REPAIR AS NECESSARY.*
YES
PUT THE DRBII IN OHMMETER MODE.
PROBE CAVITY 24.
IS RESISTANCE BELOW 10.0 OHMS?
YES
REPAIR THE K24 OR N7 GY/BK WIRE FOR A SHORT TO GROUND.*
NO
CONTINUE TEST NS-13A

* PERFORM VERIFICATION PROCEDURE VER-1.

91C08766

Fig. 36: No Start Test 13A (2.2L & 2.5L) – Code 11, No Ignition Reference Signal During Cranking (2 of 3)

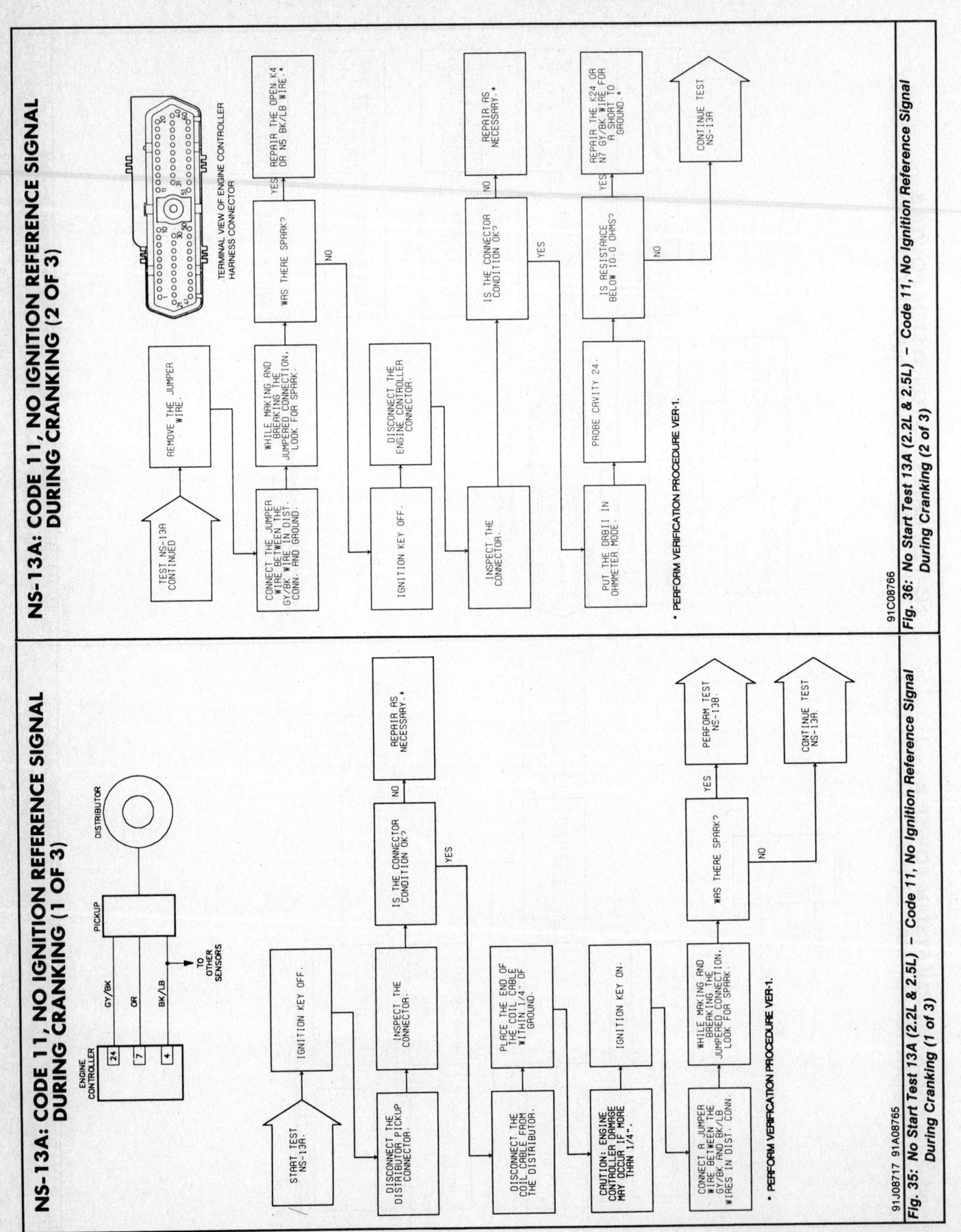

NS-13A: CODE 11, NO IGNITION REFERENCE SIGNAL DURING CRANKING (3 OF 3)

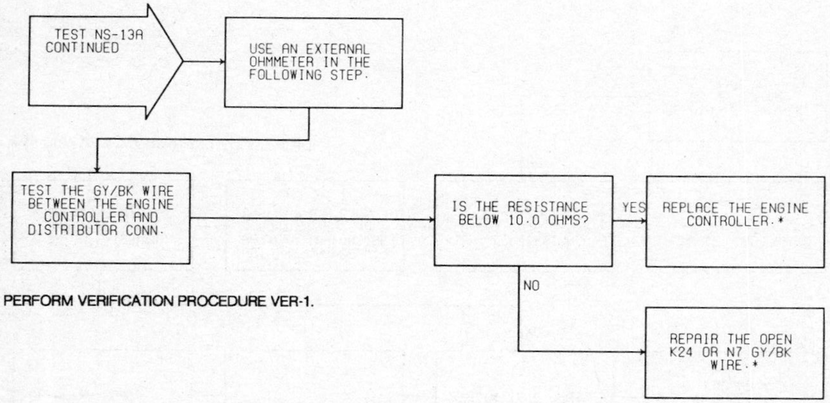
TEST NS-13A CONTINUED
USE AN EXTERNAL OHMMETER IN THE FOLLOWING STEP.
TEST THE GY/BK WIRE BETWEEN THE ENGINE CONTROLLER AND DISTRIBUTOR CONN.
IS THE RESISTANCE BELOW 10.0 OHMS?
YES
REPLACE THE ENGINE CONTROLLER.*
NO
REPAIR THE OPEN K24 OR N7 GY/BK WIRE.*

* PERFORM VERIFICATION PROCEDURE VER-1.

91E08767

Fig. 37: No Start Test 13A (2.2L & 2.5L) – Code 11, No Ignition Reference Signal During Cranking (3 of 3)

NS-13B: CODE 11, NO IGNITION REFERENCE SIGNAL DURING CRANKING (1 OF 2)

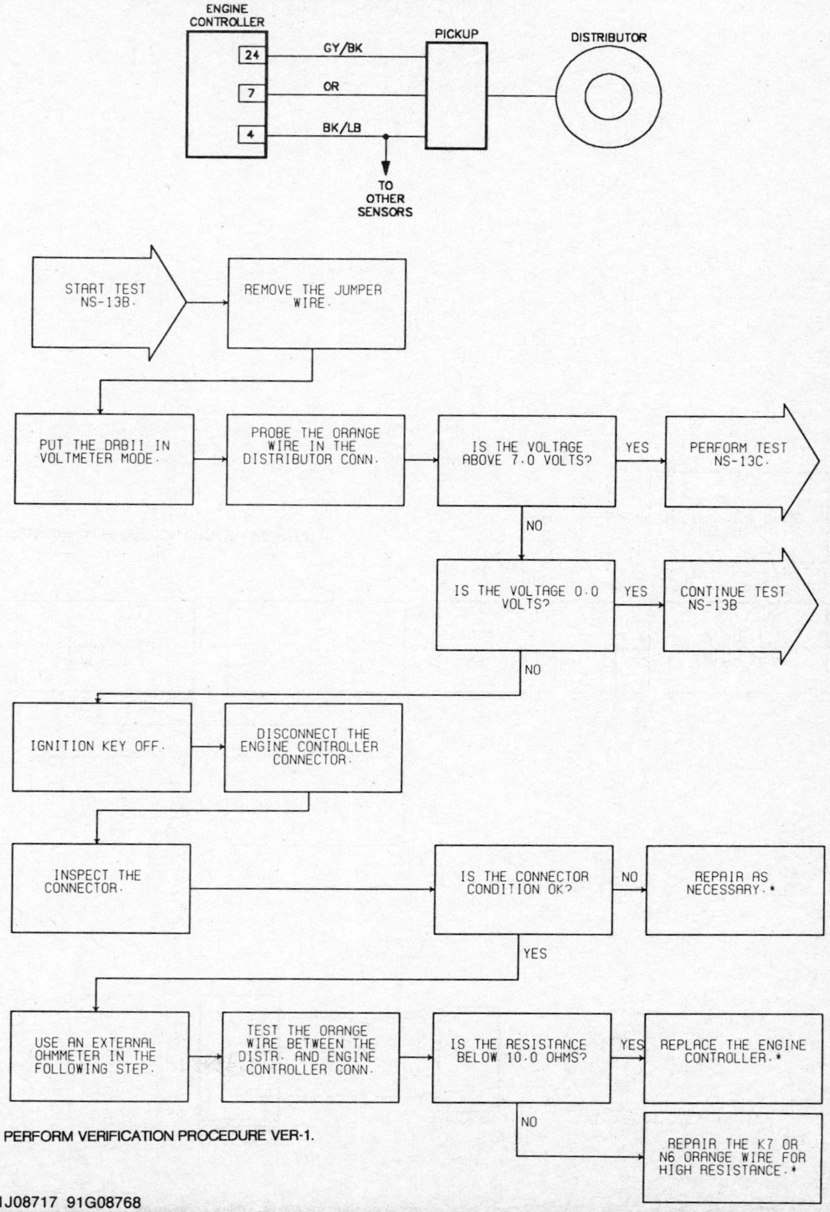
ENGINE CONTROLLER
24
7
4
GY/BK
OR
BK/LB
TO OTHER SENSORS
PICKUP
DISTRIBUTOR
START TEST NS-13B.
REMOVE THE JUMPER WIRE.
PUT THE DRBII IN VOLTMETER MODE.
PROBE THE ORANGE WIRE IN THE DISTRIBUTOR CONN.
IS THE VOLTAGE ABOVE 7.0 VOLTS?
YES
PERFORM TEST NS-13C.
NO
IS THE VOLTAGE 0.0 VOLTS?
YES
CONTINUE TEST NS-13B
NO
IGNITION KEY OFF.
DISCONNECT THE ENGINE CONTROLLER CONNECTOR.
INSPECT THE CONNECTOR.
IS THE CONNECTOR CONDITION OK?
NO
REPAIR AS NECESSARY.*
YES
USE AN EXTERNAL OHMMETER IN THE FOLLOWING STEP.
TEST THE ORANGE WIRE BETWEEN THE DISTR. AND ENGINE CONTROLLER CONN.
IS THE RESISTANCE BELOW 10.0 OHMS?
YES
REPLACE THE ENGINE CONTROLLER.*
NO
REPAIR THE K7 OR N6 ORANGE WIRE FOR HIGH RESISTANCE.*

* PERFORM VERIFICATION PROCEDURE VER-1.

91J08717 91G08768

Fig. 38: No Start Test 13B (2.2L & 2.5L) – Code 11, No Ignition Reference Signal During Cranking (1 of 2)

NS-13B: CODE 11, NO IGNITION REFERENCE SIGNAL DURING CRANKING (2 OF 2)

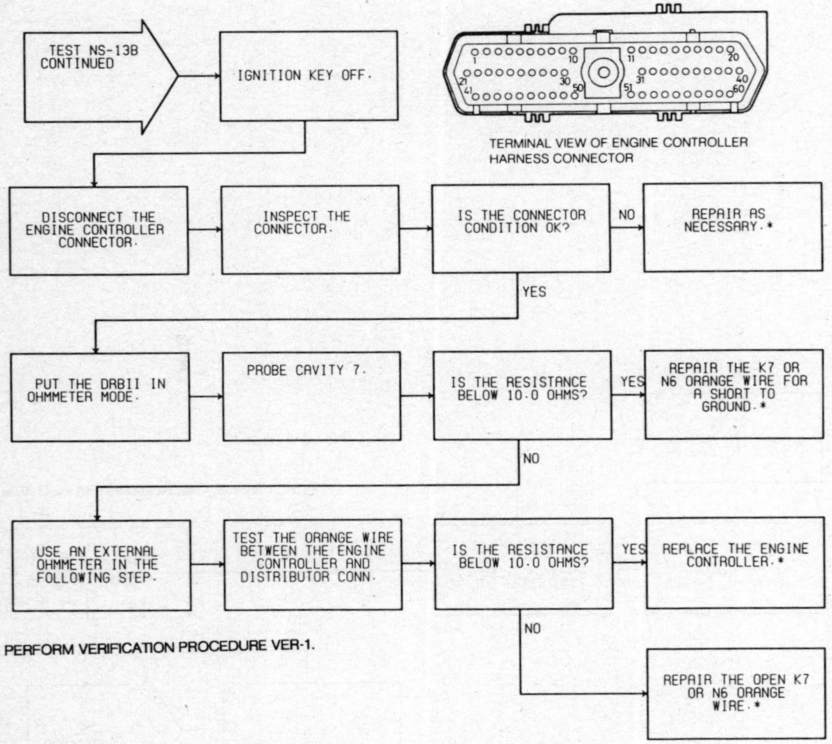
TEST NS-13B CONTINUED
IGNITION KEY OFF.
TERMINAL VIEW OF ENGINE CONTROLLER HARNESS CONNECTOR
DISCONNECT THE ENGINE CONTROLLER CONNECTOR.
INSPECT THE CONNECTOR.
IS THE CONNECTOR CONDITION OK?
NO
REPAIR AS NECESSARY.*
YES
PUT THE DRBII IN OHMMETER MODE.
PROBE CAVITY 7.
IS THE RESISTANCE BELOW 10.0 OHMS?
YES
REPAIR THE K7 OR N6 ORANGE WIRE FOR A SHORT TO GROUND.*
NO
USE AN EXTERNAL OHMMETER IN THE FOLLOWING STEP.
TEST THE ORANGE WIRE BETWEEN THE ENGINE CONTROLLER AND DISTRIBUTOR CONN.
IS THE RESISTANCE BELOW 10.0 OHMS?
YES
REPLACE THE ENGINE CONTROLLER.*
NO
REPAIR THE OPEN K7 OR N6 ORANGE WIRE.*

* PERFORM VERIFICATION PROCEDURE VER-1.

91I08769

Fig. 39: No Start Test 13B (2.2L & 2.5L) – Code 11, No Ignition Reference Signal During Cranking (2 of 2)

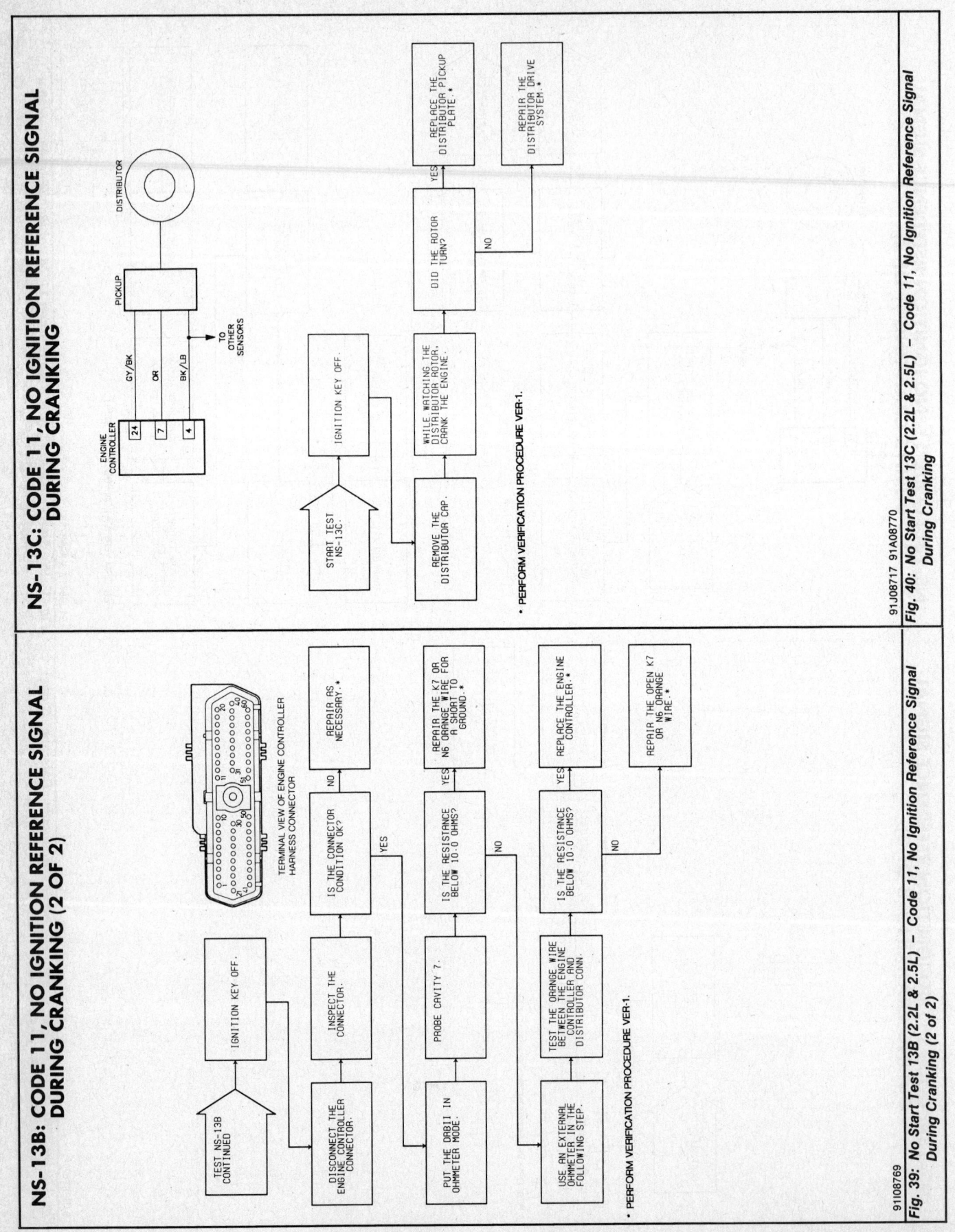

NS-13C: CODE 11, NO IGNITION REFERENCE SIGNAL DURING CRANKING

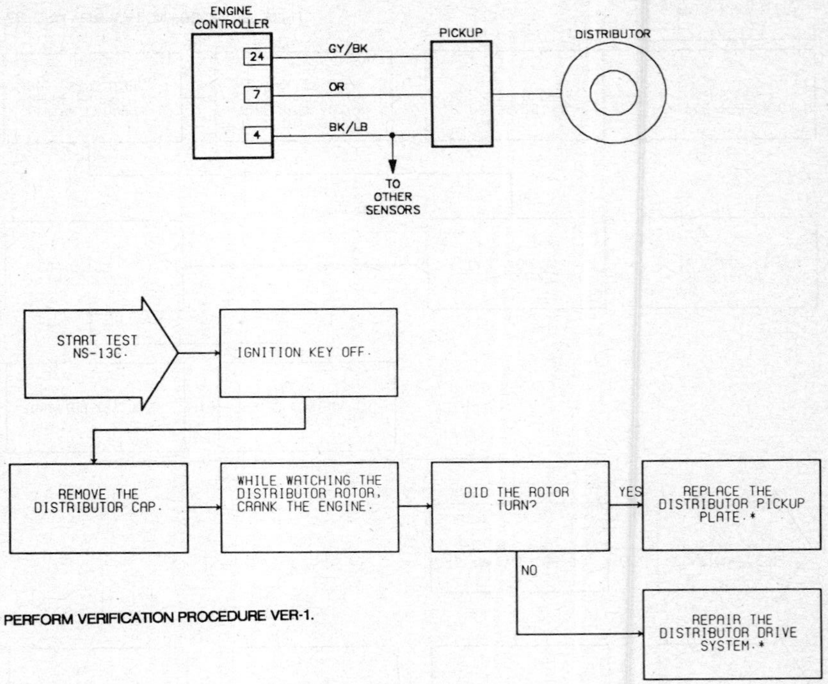
ENGINE CONTROLLER
24
7
4
GY/BK
OR
BK/LB
PICKUP
DISTRIBUTOR
TO OTHER SENSORS
START TEST NS-13C.
IGNITION KEY OFF.
REMOVE THE DISTRIBUTOR CAP.
WHILE WATCHING THE DISTRIBUTOR ROTOR, CRANK THE ENGINE.
DID THE ROTOR TURN?
YES
REPLACE THE DISTRIBUTOR PICKUP PLATE.*
NO
REPAIR THE DISTRIBUTOR DRIVE SYSTEM.*

* PERFORM VERIFICATION PROCEDURE VER-1.

91J08717 91A08770

Fig. 40: No Start Test 13C (2.2L & 2.5L) – Code 11, No Ignition Reference Signal During Cranking

NS-14A: CODE 42, ASD RELAY CIRCUIT (1 OF 2)

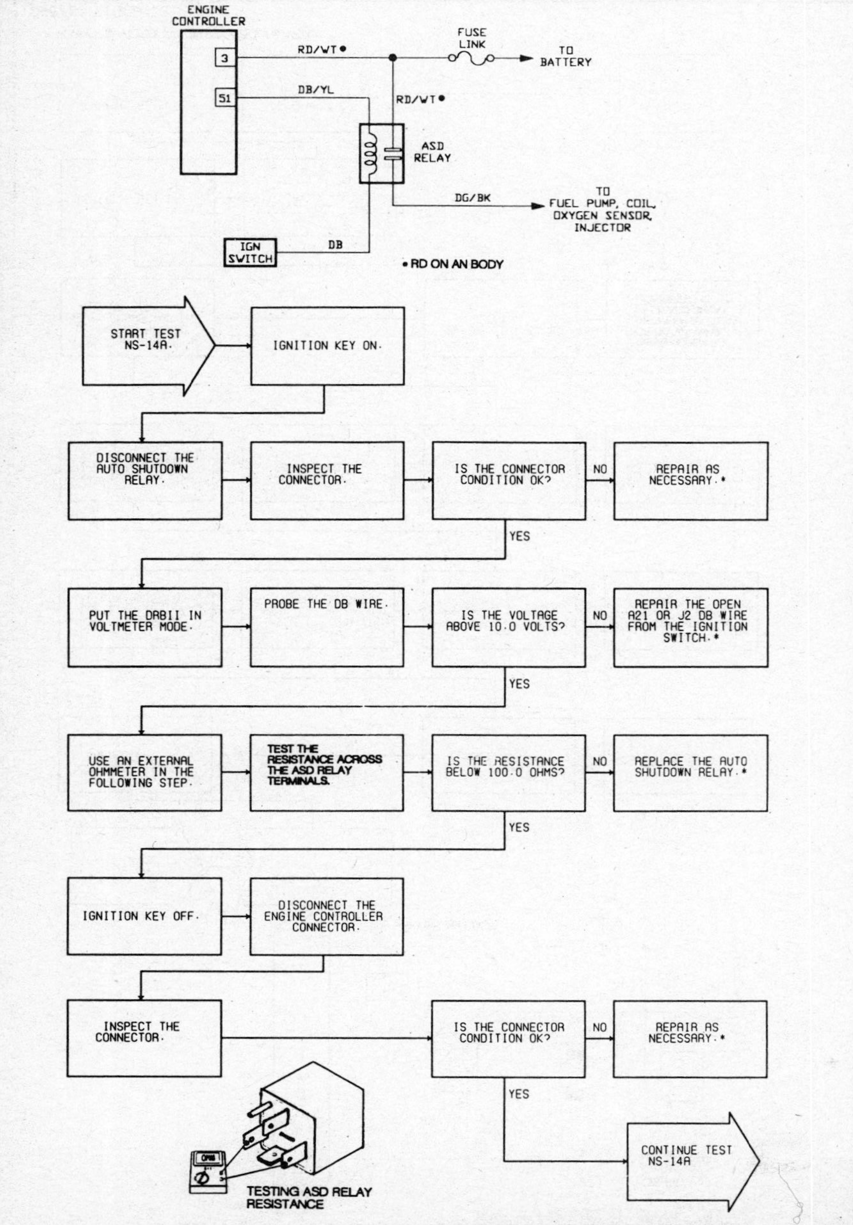

ENGINE CONTROLLER
3
51
RD/WT •
DB/YL
FUSE LINK
TO BATTERY
RD/WT •
ASD RELAY
DG/BK
TO FUEL PUMP, COIL, OXYGEN SENSOR, INJECTOR
IGN SWITCH
DB
• RD ON AN BODY
START TEST NS-14A.
IGNITION KEY ON.
DISCONNECT THE AUTO SHUTDOWN RELAY.
INSPECT THE CONNECTOR.
IS THE CONNECTOR CONDITION OK?
NO
REPAIR AS NECESSARY.*
YES
PUT THE DRBII IN VOLTMETER MODE.
PROBE THE DB WIRE.
IS THE VOLTAGE ABOVE 10.0 VOLTS?
NO
REPAIR THE OPEN A21 OR J2 DB WIRE FROM THE IGNITION SWITCH.*
YES
USE AN EXTERNAL OHMMETER IN THE FOLLOWING STEP.
TEST THE RESISTANCE ACROSS THE ASD RELAY TERMINALS.
IS THE RESISTANCE BELOW 100.0 OHMS?
NO
REPLACE THE AUTO SHUTDOWN RELAY.*
YES
IGNITION KEY OFF.
DISCONNECT THE ENGINE CONTROLLER CONNECTOR.
INSPECT THE CONNECTOR.
IS THE CONNECTOR CONDITION OK?
NO
REPAIR AS NECESSARY.*
YES
CONTINUE TEST NS-14A
TESTING ASD RELAY RESISTANCE

* PERFORM VERIFICATION PROCEDURE VER-1.

91C08714 91C08771

Fig. 41: No Start Test 14A (2.2L & 2.5L) – Code 42, ASD Relay Circuit (1 of 2)

NS-14A: CODE 42, ASD RELAY CIRCUIT (2 OF 2)

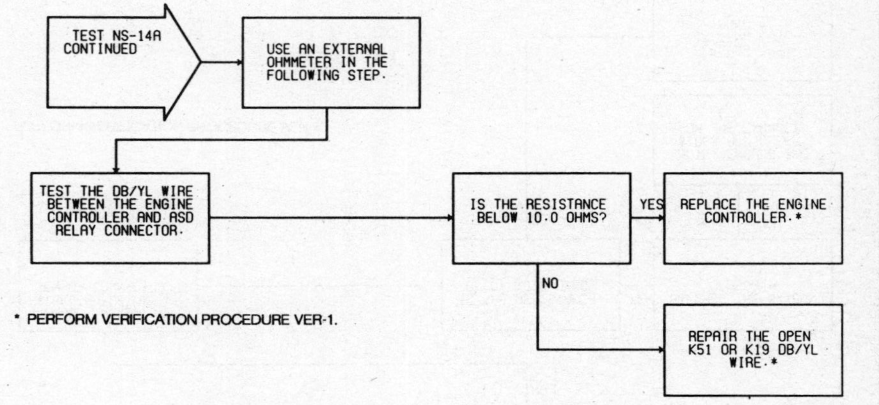

TEST NS-14A CONTINUED
USE AN EXTERNAL OHMMETER IN THE FOLLOWING STEP.
TEST THE DB/YL WIRE BETWEEN THE ENGINE CONTROLLER AND ASD RELAY CONNECTOR.
IS THE RESISTANCE BELOW 10.0 OHMS?
YES
REPLACE THE ENGINE CONTROLLER.*
NO
REPAIR THE OPEN K51 OR K19 DB/YL WIRE.*

* PERFORM VERIFICATION PROCEDURE VER-1.

91E08772

Fig. 42: No Start Test 14A (2.2L & 2.5L) – Code 42, ASD Relay Circuit (2 of 2)

NS-15A: CHECKING ASD RELAY, POWER FEED TO FUEL PUMP, OXYGEN SENSOR & INJECTORS (1 OF 3)

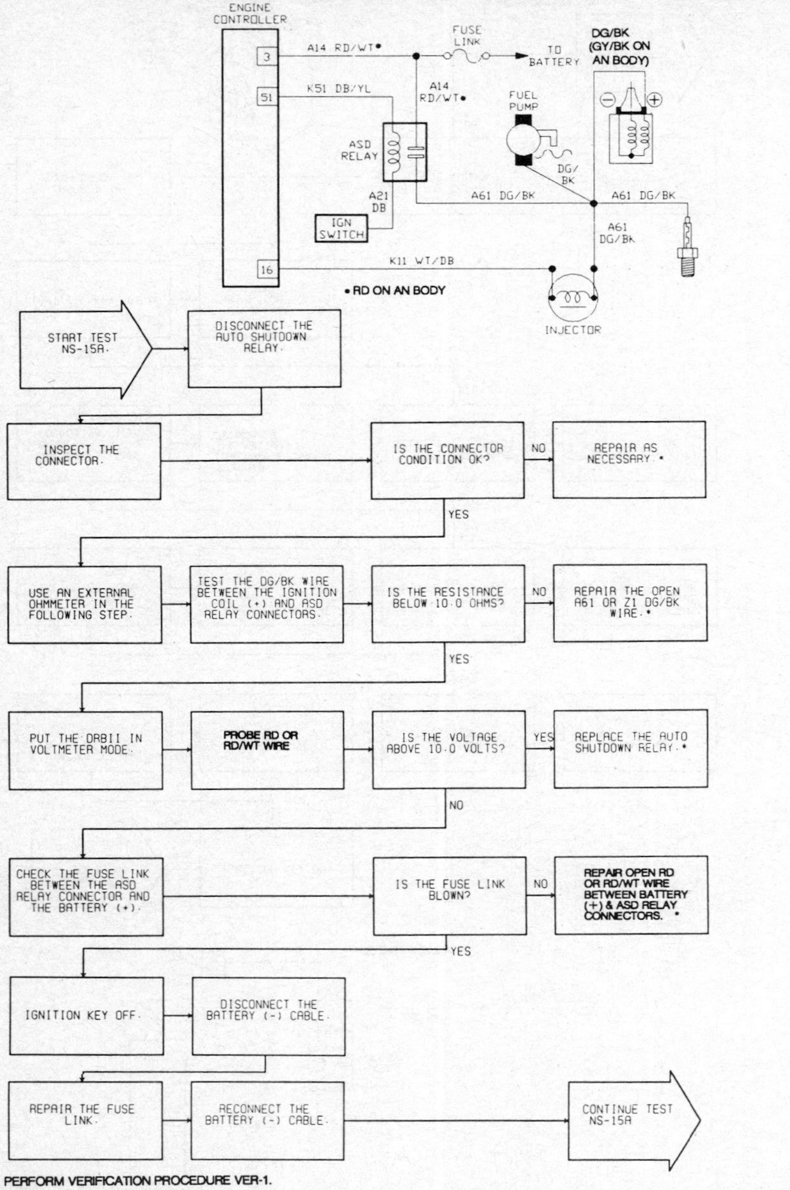
ENGINE CONTROLLER
3
51
16
A14 RD/WT•
K51 DB/YL
ASD RELAY
A21 DB
IGN SWITCH
K11 WT/DB
• RD ON AN BODY
FUSE LINK
TO BATTERY
A14 RD/WT•
FUEL PUMP
DG/BK
A61 DG/BK
DG/BK (GY/BK ON AN BODY)
A61 DG/BK
A61 DG/BK
INJECTOR
START TEST NS-15A.
DISCONNECT THE AUTO SHUTDOWN RELAY.
INSPECT THE CONNECTOR.
IS THE CONNECTOR CONDITION OK?
NO
REPAIR AS NECESSARY.*
YES
USE AN EXTERNAL OHMMETER IN THE FOLLOWING STEP.
TEST THE DG/BK WIRE BETWEEN THE IGNITION COIL (+) AND ASD RELAY CONNECTORS.
IS THE RESISTANCE BELOW 10.0 OHMS?
NO
REPAIR THE OPEN A61 OR Z1 DG/BK WIRE.*
YES
PUT THE DRBII IN VOLTMETER MODE.
PROBE RD OR RD/WT WIRE
IS THE VOLTAGE ABOVE 10.0 VOLTS?
YES
REPLACE THE AUTO SHUTDOWN RELAY.*
NO
CHECK THE FUSE LINK BETWEEN THE ASD RELAY CONNECTOR AND THE BATTERY (+).
IS THE FUSE LINK BLOWN?
NO
REPAIR OPEN RD OR RD/WT WIRE BETWEEN BATTERY (+) & ASD RELAY CONNECTORS.*
YES
IGNITION KEY OFF.
DISCONNECT THE BATTERY (-) CABLE.
REPAIR THE FUSE LINK.
RECONNECT THE BATTERY (-) CABLE.
CONTINUE TEST NS-15A

* PERFORM VERIFICATION PROCEDURE VER-1.

91C08714 91G08773

Fig. 43: No Start Test 15A (2.2L & 2.5L) – Checking ASD Relay, Power Feed to Fuel Pump, Oxygen Sensor & Injectors (1 of 3)

NS-15A: CHECKING ASD RELAY, POWER FEED TO FUEL PUMP, OXYGEN SENSOR & INJECTORS (2 OF 3)

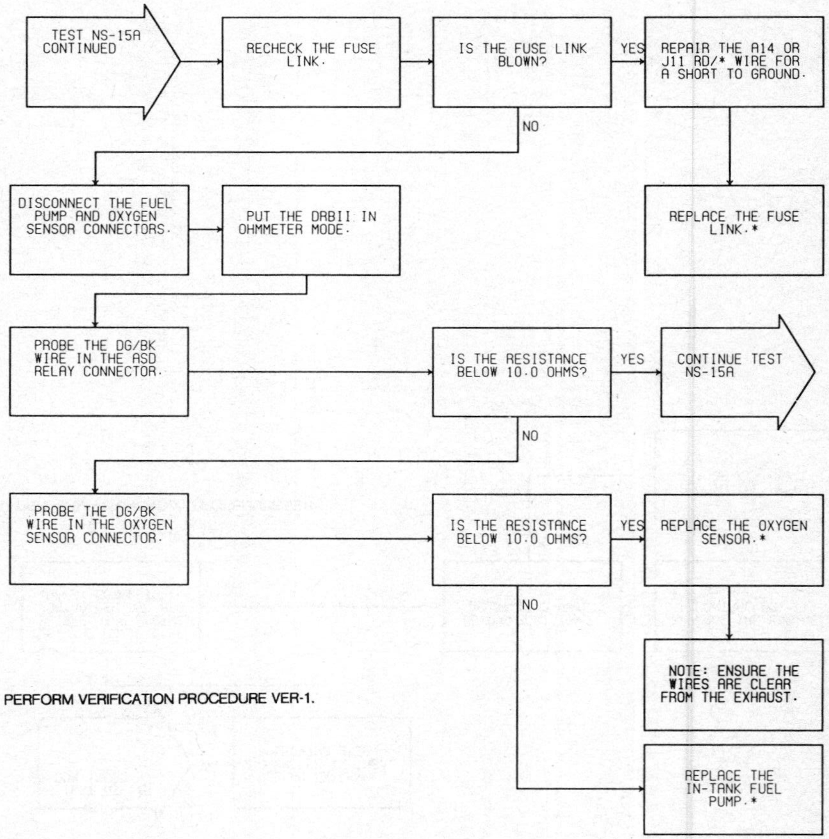
TEST NS-15A CONTINUED
RECHECK THE FUSE LINK.
IS THE FUSE LINK BLOWN?
YES
REPAIR THE A14 OR J11 RD/* WIRE FOR A SHORT TO GROUND.
REPLACE THE FUSE LINK.*
NO
DISCONNECT THE FUEL PUMP AND OXYGEN SENSOR CONNECTORS.
PUT THE DRBII IN OHMMETER MODE.
PROBE THE DG/BK WIRE IN THE ASD RELAY CONNECTOR.
IS THE RESISTANCE BELOW 10.0 OHMS?
YES
CONTINUE TEST NS-15A
NO
PROBE THE DG/BK WIRE IN THE OXYGEN SENSOR CONNECTOR.
IS THE RESISTANCE BELOW 10.0 OHMS?
YES
REPLACE THE OXYGEN SENSOR.*
NOTE: ENSURE THE WIRES ARE CLEAR FROM THE EXHAUST.
NO
REPLACE THE IN-TANK FUEL PUMP.*

* PERFORM VERIFICATION PROCEDURE VER-1.

91I08774

Fig. 44: No Start Test 15A (2.2L & 2.5L) – Checking ASD Relay, Power Feed to Fuel Pump, Oxygen Sensor & Injectors (2 of 3)

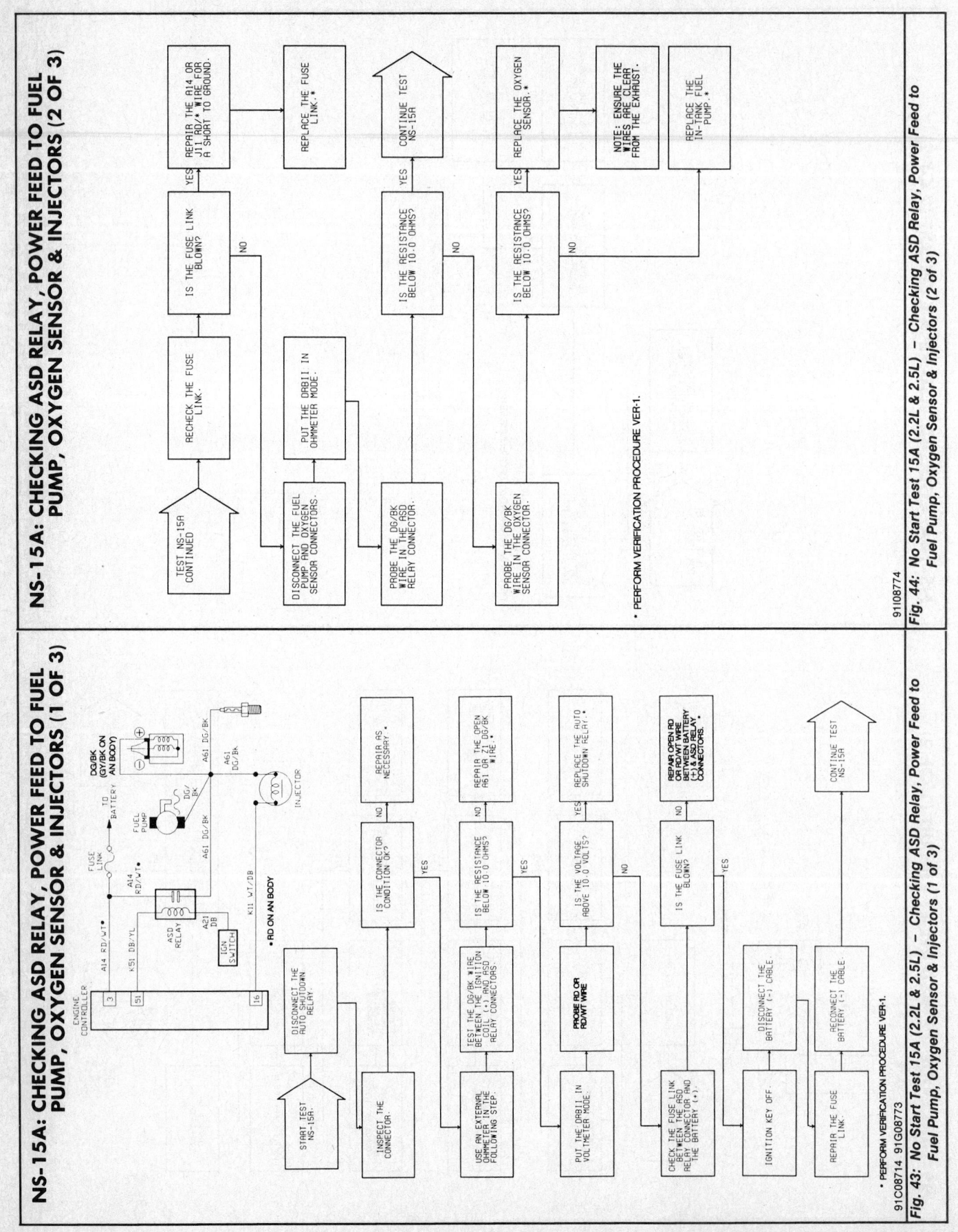

NS-15A: CHECKING ASD RELAY, POWER FEED TO FUEL PUMP, OXYGEN SENSOR & INJECTORS (3 OF 3)

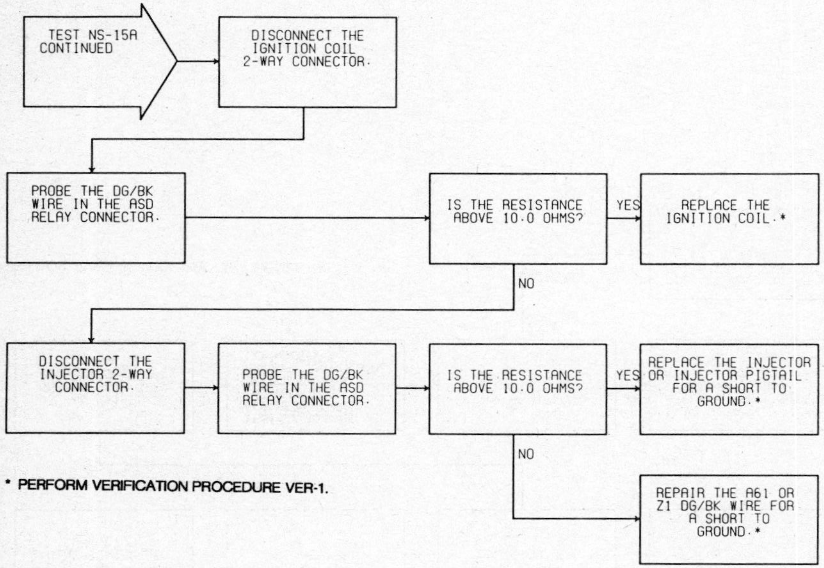
TEST NS-15A CONTINUED
DISCONNECT THE IGNITION COIL 2-WAY CONNECTOR.
PROBE THE DG/BK WIRE IN THE ASD RELAY CONNECTOR.
IS THE RESISTANCE ABOVE 10.0 OHMS?
YES
REPLACE THE IGNITION COIL.*
NO
DISCONNECT THE INJECTOR 2-WAY CONNECTOR.
PROBE THE DG/BK WIRE IN THE ASD RELAY CONNECTOR.
IS THE RESISTANCE ABOVE 10.0 OHMS?
YES
REPLACE THE INJECTOR OR INJECTOR PIGTAIL FOR A SHORT TO GROUND.*
NO
REPAIR THE A61 OR Z1 DG/BK WIRE FOR A SHORT TO GROUND.*

* PERFORM VERIFICATION PROCEDURE VER-1.

91B08775

Fig. 45: ***No Start Test 15A (2.2L & 2.5L) – Checking ASD Relay, Power Feed to Fuel Pump, Oxygen Sensor & Injectors (3 of 3)***

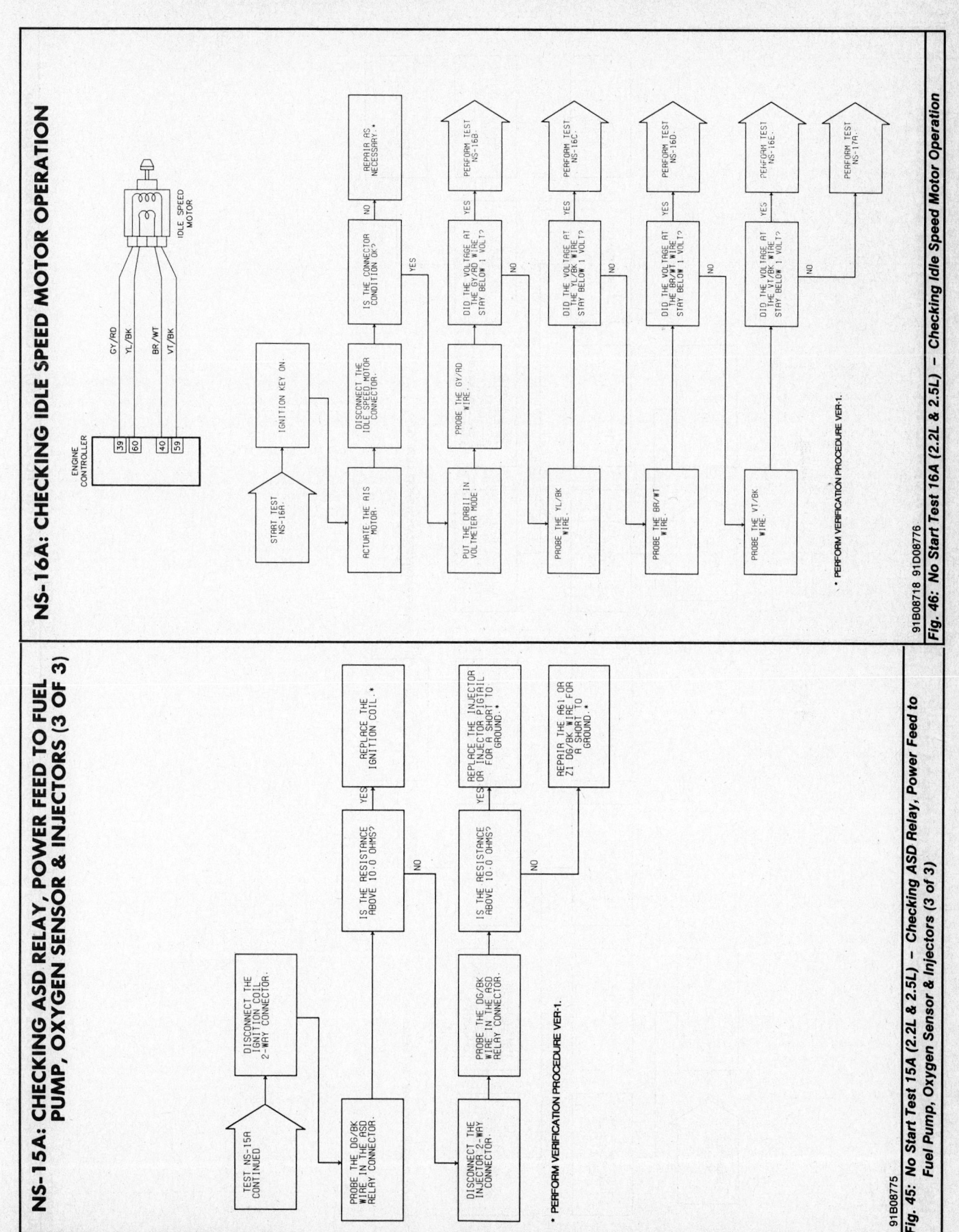

NS-16A: CHECKING IDLE SPEED MOTOR OPERATION

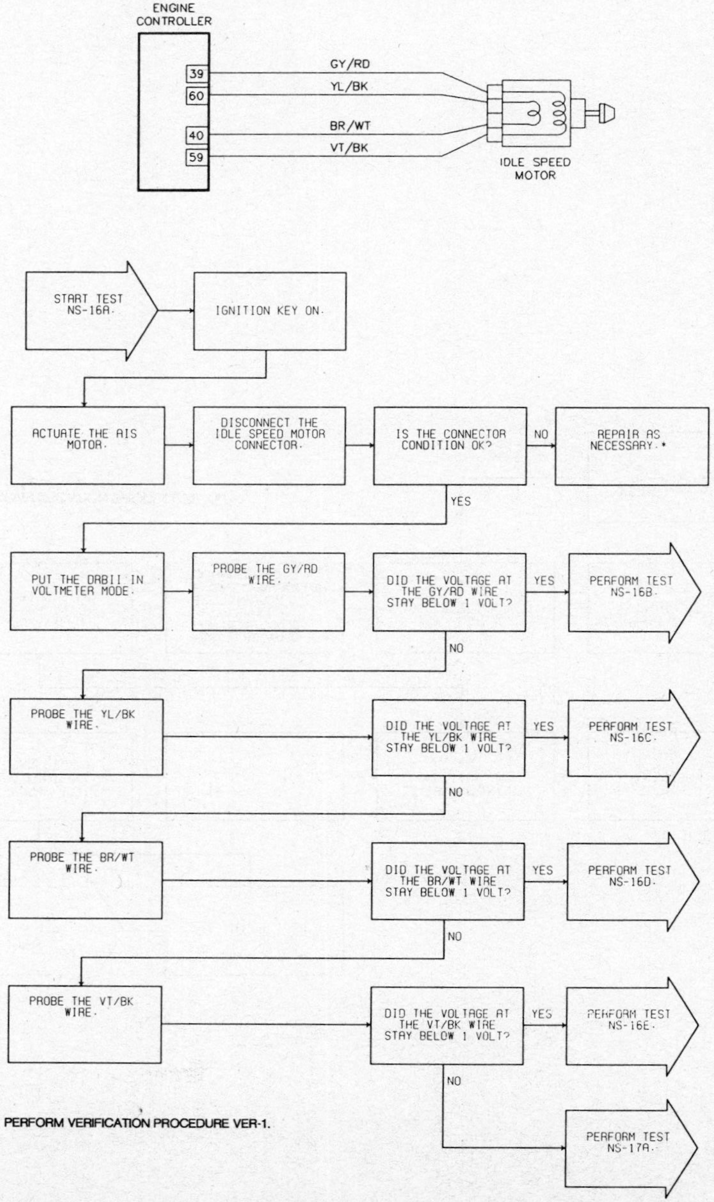
ENGINE CONTROLLER
39
60
40
59
GY/RD
YL/BK
BR/WT
VT/BK
IDLE SPEED MOTOR
START TEST NS-16A.
IGNITION KEY ON.
ACTUATE THE AIS MOTOR.
DISCONNECT THE IDLE SPEED MOTOR CONNECTOR.
IS THE CONNECTOR CONDITION OK?
NO
REPAIR AS NECESSARY.*
YES
PUT THE DRBII IN VOLTMETER MODE.
PROBE THE GY/RD WIRE.
DID THE VOLTAGE AT THE GY/RD WIRE STAY BELOW 1 VOLT?
YES
PERFORM TEST NS-16B.
NO
PROBE THE YL/BK WIRE.
DID THE VOLTAGE AT THE YL/BK WIRE STAY BELOW 1 VOLT?
YES
PERFORM TEST NS-16C.
NO
PROBE THE BR/WT WIRE.
DID THE VOLTAGE AT THE BR/WT WIRE STAY BELOW 1 VOLT?
YES
PERFORM TEST NS-16D.
NO
PROBE THE VT/BK WIRE.
DID THE VOLTAGE AT THE VT/BK WIRE STAY BELOW 1 VOLT?
YES
PERFORM TEST NS-16E.
NO
PERFORM TEST NS-17A.

* PERFORM VERIFICATION PROCEDURE VER-1.

91B08718 91D08776

Fig. 46: ***No Start Test 16A (2.2L & 2.5L) – Checking Idle Speed Motor Operation***

NS-16B: CHECKING IDLE SPEED MOTOR OPERATION

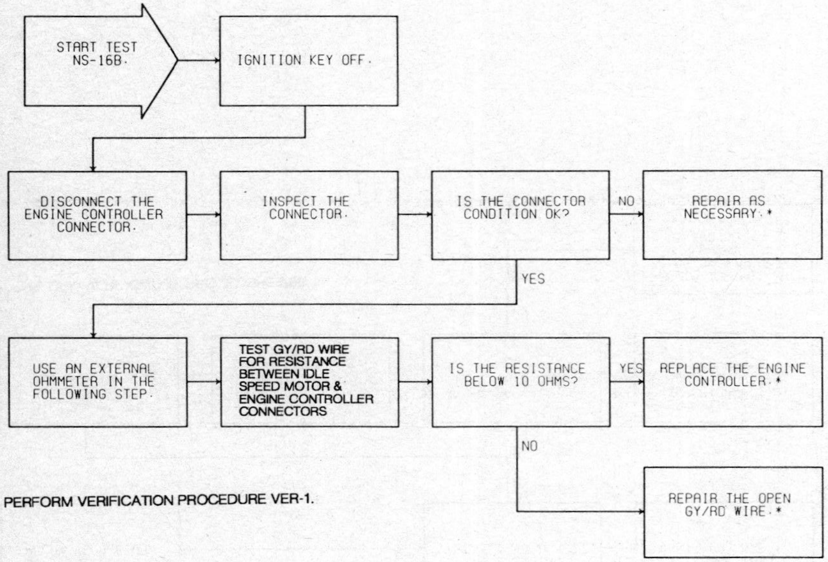
START TEST NS-16B.
IGNITION KEY OFF.
DISCONNECT THE ENGINE CONTROLLER CONNECTOR.
INSPECT THE CONNECTOR.
IS THE CONNECTOR CONDITION OK?
NO
REPAIR AS NECESSARY.*
YES
USE AN EXTERNAL OHMMETER IN THE FOLLOWING STEP.
TEST GY/RD WIRE FOR RESISTANCE BETWEEN IDLE SPEED MOTOR & ENGINE CONTROLLER CONNECTORS
IS THE RESISTANCE BELOW 10 OHMS?
YES
REPLACE THE ENGINE CONTROLLER.*
NO
REPAIR THE OPEN GY/RD WIRE.*

* PERFORM VERIFICATION PROCEDURE VER-1.

91F08777

Fig. 47: No Start Test 16B (2.2L & 2.5L) – Checking Idle Speed Motor Operation

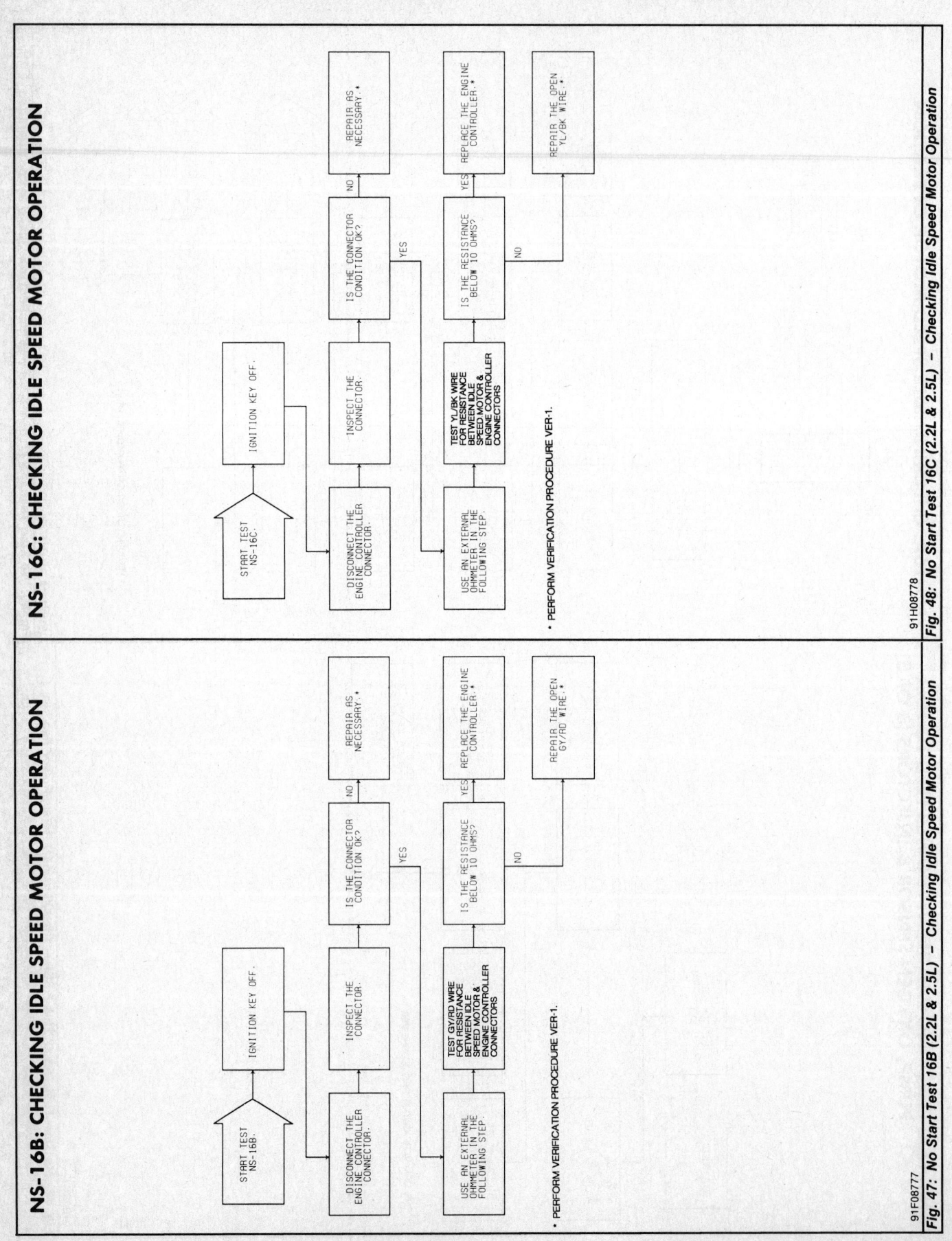

NS-16C: CHECKING IDLE SPEED MOTOR OPERATION

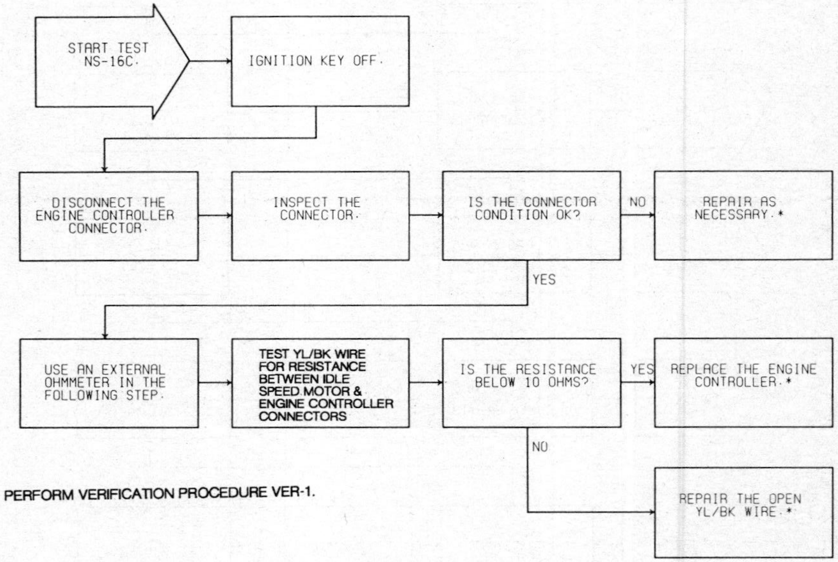
START TEST NS-16C.
IGNITION KEY OFF.
DISCONNECT THE ENGINE CONTROLLER CONNECTOR.
INSPECT THE CONNECTOR.
IS THE CONNECTOR CONDITION OK?
NO
REPAIR AS NECESSARY.*
YES
USE AN EXTERNAL OHMMETER IN THE FOLLOWING STEP.
TEST YL/BK WIRE FOR RESISTANCE BETWEEN IDLE SPEED MOTOR & ENGINE CONTROLLER CONNECTORS
IS THE RESISTANCE BELOW 10 OHMS?
YES
REPLACE THE ENGINE CONTROLLER.*
NO
REPAIR THE OPEN YL/BK WIRE.*

* PERFORM VERIFICATION PROCEDURE VER-1.

91H08778

Fig. 48: No Start Test 16C (2.2L & 2.5L) – Checking Idle Speed Motor Operation

NS-16D: CHECKING IDLE SPEED MOTOR OPERATION

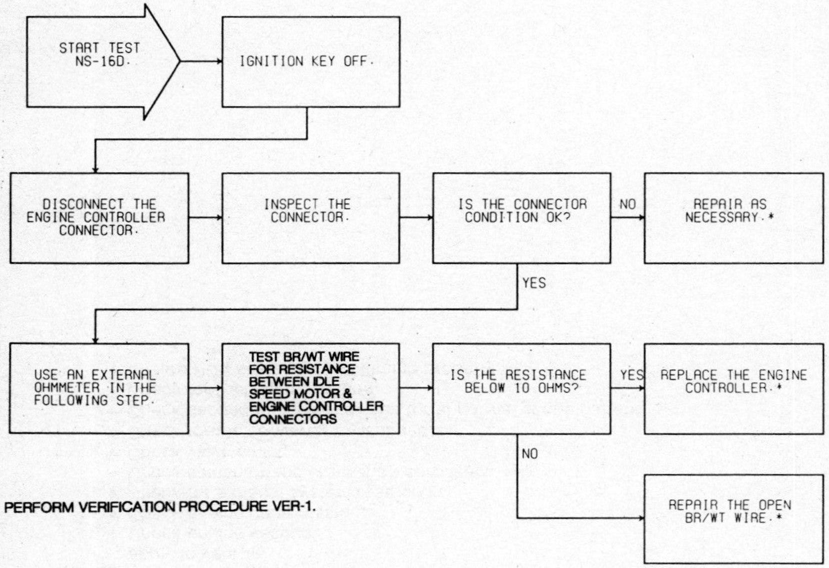
START TEST NS-16D.
IGNITION KEY OFF.
DISCONNECT THE ENGINE CONTROLLER CONNECTOR.
INSPECT THE CONNECTOR.
IS THE CONNECTOR CONDITION OK?
NO
REPAIR AS NECESSARY.*
YES
USE AN EXTERNAL OHMMETER IN THE FOLLOWING STEP.
TEST BR/WT WIRE FOR RESISTANCE BETWEEN IDLE SPEED MOTOR & ENGINE CONTROLLER CONNECTORS
IS THE RESISTANCE BELOW 10 OHMS?
YES
REPLACE THE ENGINE CONTROLLER.*
NO
REPAIR THE OPEN BR/WT WIRE.*

* PERFORM VERIFICATION PROCEDURE VER-1.

91J08779

Fig. 49: No Start Test 16D (2.2L & 2.5L) – Checking Idle Speed Motor Operation

NS-16E: CHECKING IDLE SPEED MOTOR OPERATION

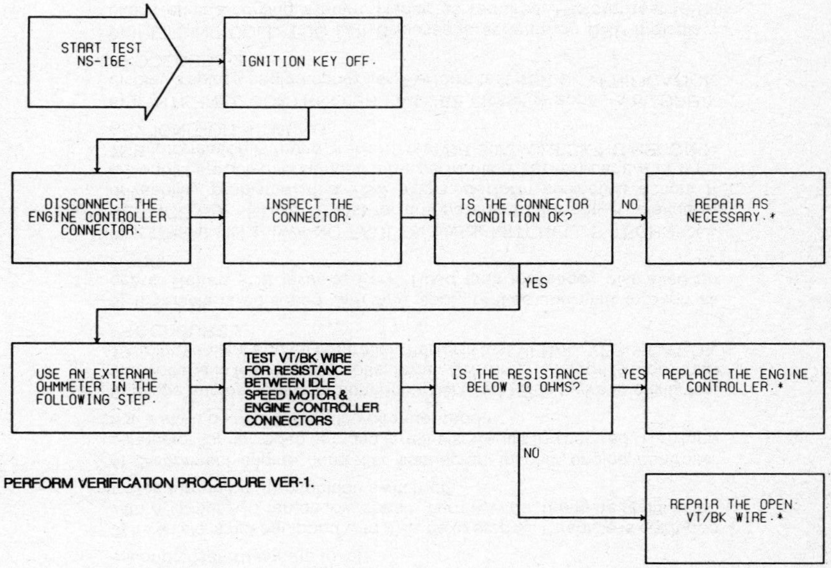
START TEST NS-16E.
IGNITION KEY OFF.
DISCONNECT THE ENGINE CONTROLLER CONNECTOR.
INSPECT THE CONNECTOR.
IS THE CONNECTOR CONDITION OK?
NO
REPAIR AS NECESSARY.*
YES
USE AN EXTERNAL OHMMETER IN THE FOLLOWING STEP.
TEST VT/BK WIRE FOR RESISTANCE BETWEEN IDLE SPEED MOTOR & ENGINE CONTROLLER CONNECTORS
IS THE RESISTANCE BELOW 10 OHMS?
YES
REPLACE THE ENGINE CONTROLLER.*
NO
REPAIR THE OPEN VT/BK WIRE.*

* PERFORM VERIFICATION PROCEDURE VER-1.

91B08780

Fig. 50: No Start Test 16E (2.2L & 2.5L) – Checking Idle Speed Motor Operation

NS-17A: PERFORMING NO FAULT CODE MECHANICAL TEST

At this point in the start-and-stall test procedure, if it is determined that all engine control systems are operating as designed and are not the cause of a no start-and-stall problem, the following additional items should be checked as possible causes:

- Check if any MITCHELL TECHNICAL SERVICE BULLETINS (TSBs) apply to vehicle.
- Check engine vacuum.
- Check engine compression.
- Check for exhaust system restriction.
- Check camshaft and crankshaft sprockets.
- Check valve timing.
- Check torque converter stall speed.
- Check secondary ignition circuit for abnormal scope pattern.
- Check for fuel contamination.
- Ensure PCV system is functioning properly.

Fig. 51: No Start Test 17A (2.2L & 2.5L) – Performing No Fault Code Mechanical Test

DR-1A: CHECKING SYSTEM FOR FAULTS

NOTE: Battery must be fully charged and at rated capacity before performing any driveability test procedure. If vehicle starts and stalls repeatedly, perform test NS-3A: CHECKING FOR INJECTOR FAULTS, POWER TO ENGINE CONTROLLER, MAP SENSOR & THEFT ALARM STATUS.

1) Connect DRB-II to engine diagnostic connector. Read fault messages. If DRB-II displays fault messages, go to DR-1B: DRB-II FAULT MESSAGES. Go to step **9)** if DRB-II displays ENGINE COLD TOO LONG. If DRB-II displays INTERNAL CONTROLLER FAILURE, go to step **8)**. If DRB-II displays NO FAULTS, go to next step.

2) If NO FAULTS message appears on DRB-II display, start engine. Allow engine to reach normal operating temperature. Set engine speed manually (DO NOT use DRB-II to set speed) to 2000 RPM for about 10 seconds. Return engine to idle.

3) If vehicle is not equipped with A/C, go to step **5)**. If vehicle is equipped with A/C, put A/C fan on low speed. Turn A/C on. If engine stalls when A/C is turned on, turn ignition switch off.

4) Disconnect engine controller connector. Inspect engine controller connector for corroded or loose terminals. Repair as required. Turn ignition switch on. Put DRB-II in voltmeter mode.

5) Probe engine controller connector DB (Dark/Blue) wire at cavity No. 9. If voltage is less than 10 volts, repair DB wire. If voltage is more than 10 volts, replace engine controller. Perform test VER-2: VERIFICATION PROCEDURE 2.

6) If vehicle is equipped with A/T, apply brakes and shift through all gears. Return shift lever to Park. Read fault messages displayed on DRB-II.

7) If DRB-II still shows NO FAULTS, check MITCHELL'S TECHNICAL SERVICE BULLETINS (TSBs) for any pertinent information relating to driveability problems. If a TSB exists, perform corrective action. If driveability problem continues after performing TSB procedure or if no TSB information is found, perform test DR-30A: CHECKING SECONDARY IGNITION & TIMING.

8) If INTERNAL CONTROLLER FAILURE message appears on DRB-II display, replace engine controller. Perform test VER-2: VERIFICATION PROCEDURE 2.

9) If ENGINE COLD TOO LONG message appears on DRB-II display, check engine cooling system. Repair as required. Perform test VER-3: VERIFICATION PROCEDURE 3.

Fig. 52: Driveability Test 1A (2.2L & 2.5L) – Checking System for Faults

DR-1B: DRB-II FAULT MESSAGES

Using the DRB-II FAULT MESSAGES table, select the fault message and corresponding test. Correct all hard fault messages before proceeding to intermittent fault message.

DRB-II FAULT MESSAGES

DRB-II Message	[1] Hard Fault	[2] Intermittent Fault
A/C Clutch Relay Circuit [3]	DR-19A	DR-42A
A/C Clutch Relay Circuit [4]	DR-20A	DR-42A
A/C Clutch Relay Circuit [5]	DR-21A	DR-42A
A/C Clutch Relay Circuit [6]	DR-22A	DR-42A
A/C Clutch Relay Circuit [7]	DR-23A	DR-42A
Automatic Idle Speed Motor Circuits	DR-15A	DR-44A
Controller Failure EEPROM Write Denied	DR-29A	DR-29A
Controller Failure EMR Mileage Not Stored	DR-29A	DR-29A
Coolant Sensor Voltage Too High	DR-9A	DR-43A
Coolant Sensor Voltage Too Low	DR-10A	DR-43A
EGR Solenoid Circuit	DR-17A	DR-42A
EGR System Failure	DR-18A	DR-42A
Injector No. 1 Control Circuit	DR-45A	DR-45A
Injector No. 1 Current Peak Not Reached	DR-45A	DR-45-A
MAP Voltage Too High	DR-5A	DR43-A
MAP Voltage Too Low	DR-4A	DR-43A
No Change In MAP From Start To Run	DR3A	DR-43B
No Vehicle Speed Signal	DR-6A	DR-6A
O_2 Signal Shorted To Voltage	DR-8A	DR-43A
O_2 Signal Stays At Center	DR-7A	DR-43A
Purge Solenoid Circuit	DR-16A	DR-42A
Radiator Fan Relay Circuit [8]	DR-24A	DR-42A
Radiator Fan Relay Circuit [4]	DR-25A	DR-42A
Radiator Fan Relay Circuit [5]	DR-26A	DR-42A
Radiator Fan Relay Circuit [6]	DR-27A	DR-42A
Slow Change In Idle MAP Signal	DR-2A	DR-43B
Throttle Body Temperature High	DR-11A	DR-43A
Throttle Body Temperature Low	DR-12A	DR-43A
Throttle Position Sensor Voltage High	DR-13A	DR-43A
Throttle Position Sensor Voltage Low	DR-14A	DR-43A
Torque Converter Lock-Up Solenoid	DR-28A	DR-42A

[1] – Key counter is "0".
[2] – Key counter is more than "0".
[3] – AA & AP bodies.
[4] – AC bodies.
[5] – AG & AJ bodies.
[6] – AN bodies.
[7] – AS bodies.
[8] – AP & AS bodies.

Fig. 53: Driveability Test 1B (2.2L & 2.5L) – DRB-II Fault Messages

DR-2A: CODE 13, SLOW CHANGE IN IDLE MAP SIGNAL (1 OF 2)

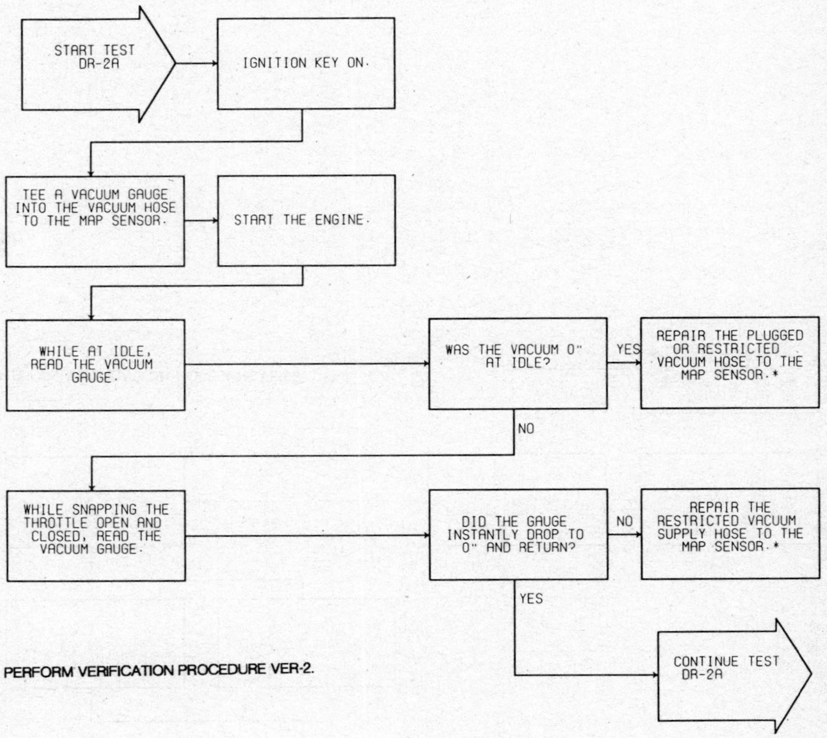
START TEST DR-2A
IGNITION KEY ON.
TEE A VACUUM GAUGE INTO THE VACUUM HOSE TO THE MAP SENSOR.
START THE ENGINE.
WHILE AT IDLE, READ THE VACUUM GAUGE.
WAS THE VACUUM 0" AT IDLE?
YES
REPAIR THE PLUGGED OR RESTRICTED VACUUM HOSE TO THE MAP SENSOR.*
NO
WHILE SNAPPING THE THROTTLE OPEN AND CLOSED, READ THE VACUUM GAUGE.
DID THE GAUGE INSTANTLY DROP TO 0" AND RETURN?
NO
REPAIR THE RESTRICTED VACUUM SUPPLY HOSE TO THE MAP SENSOR.*
YES
CONTINUE TEST DR-2A

* PERFORM VERIFICATION PROCEDURE VER-2.

91F08782

Fig. 54: Driveability Test 2A (2.2L & 2.5L) – Code 13, Slow Change in Idle MAP Signal (1 of 2)

DR-2A: CODE 13, SLOW CHANGE IN IDLE MAP SIGNAL (2 OF 2)

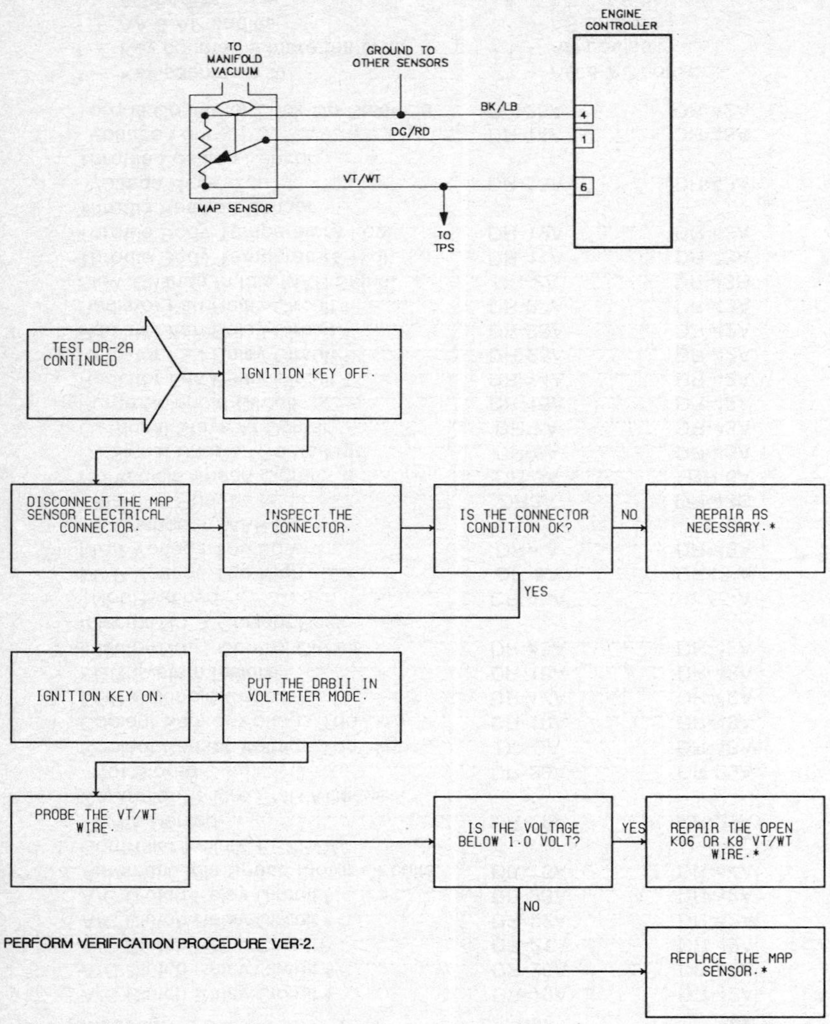
ENGINE CONTROLLER
TO MANIFOLD VACUUM
GROUND TO OTHER SENSORS
BK/LB
DG/RD
VT/WT
4
1
6
MAP SENSOR
TO TPS
TEST DR-2A CONTINUED
IGNITION KEY OFF.
DISCONNECT THE MAP SENSOR ELECTRICAL CONNECTOR.
INSPECT THE CONNECTOR.
IS THE CONNECTOR CONDITION OK?
NO
REPAIR AS NECESSARY.*
YES
IGNITION KEY ON.
PUT THE DRBII IN VOLTMETER MODE.
PROBE THE VT/WT WIRE.
IS THE VOLTAGE BELOW 1.0 VOLT?
YES
REPAIR THE OPEN K06 OR K8 VT/WT WIRE.*
NO
REPLACE THE MAP SENSOR.*
* PERFORM VERIFICATION PROCEDURE VER-2.

91F08715 91H08783

Fig. 55: Driveability Test 2A (2.2L & 2.5L) – Code 13, Slow Change in Idle MAP Signal (2 of 2)

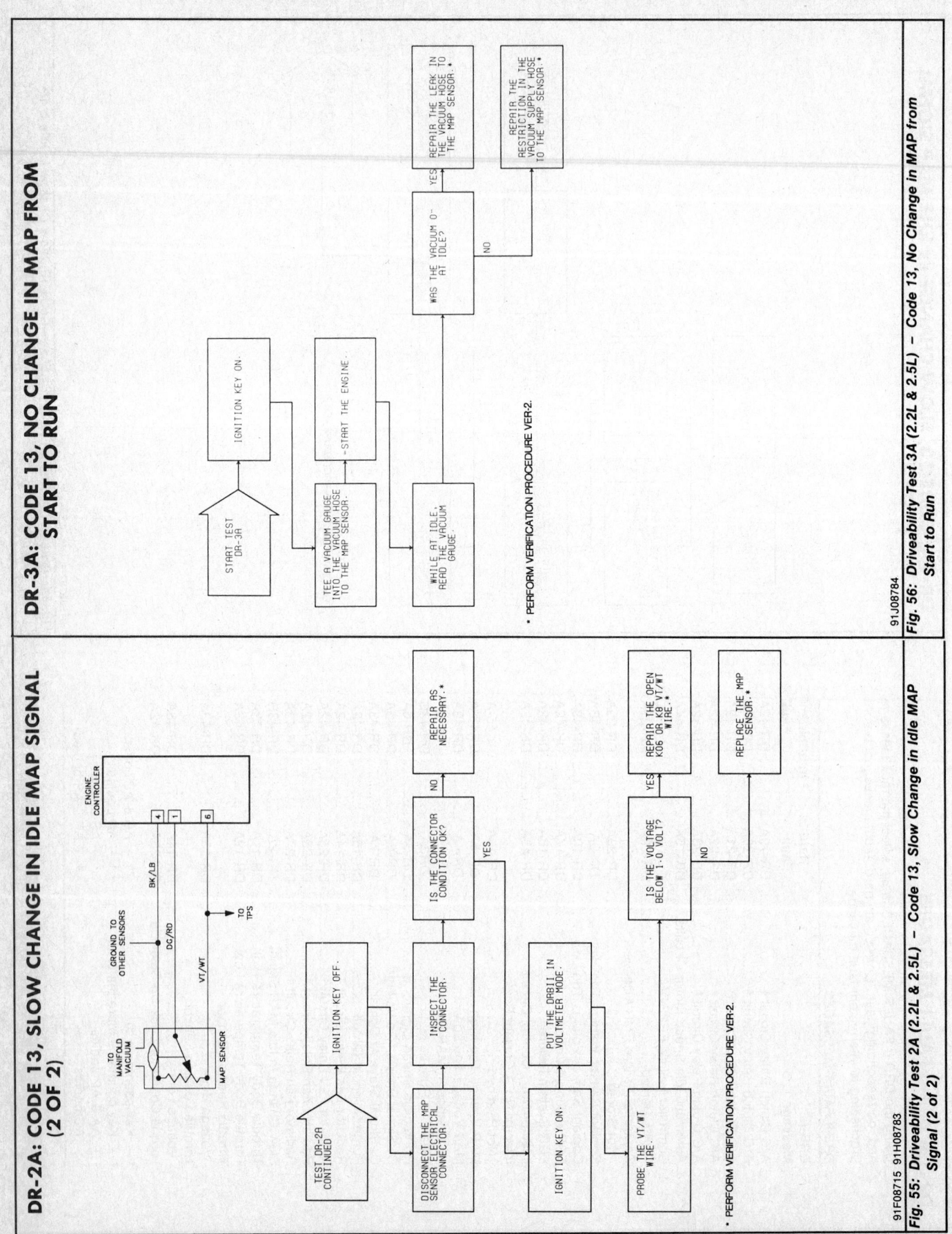

DR-3A: CODE 13, NO CHANGE IN MAP FROM START TO RUN

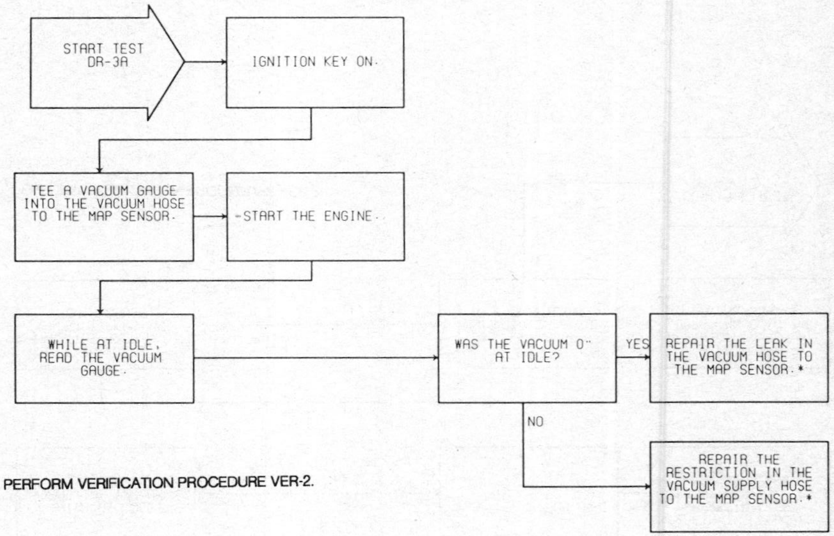
START TEST DR-3A
IGNITION KEY ON.
TEE A VACUUM GAUGE INTO THE VACUUM HOSE TO THE MAP SENSOR.
-START THE ENGINE.
WHILE AT IDLE, READ THE VACUUM GAUGE.
WAS THE VACUUM 0" AT IDLE?
YES
REPAIR THE LEAK IN THE VACUUM HOSE TO THE MAP SENSOR.*
NO
REPAIR THE RESTRICTION IN THE VACUUM SUPPLY HOSE TO THE MAP SENSOR.*

* PERFORM VERIFICATION PROCEDURE VER-2.

91J08784

Fig. 56: Driveability Test 3A (2.2L & 2.5L) – Code 13, No Change in MAP from Start to Run

DR-4A: CODE 14, MAP VOLTAGE TOO LOW

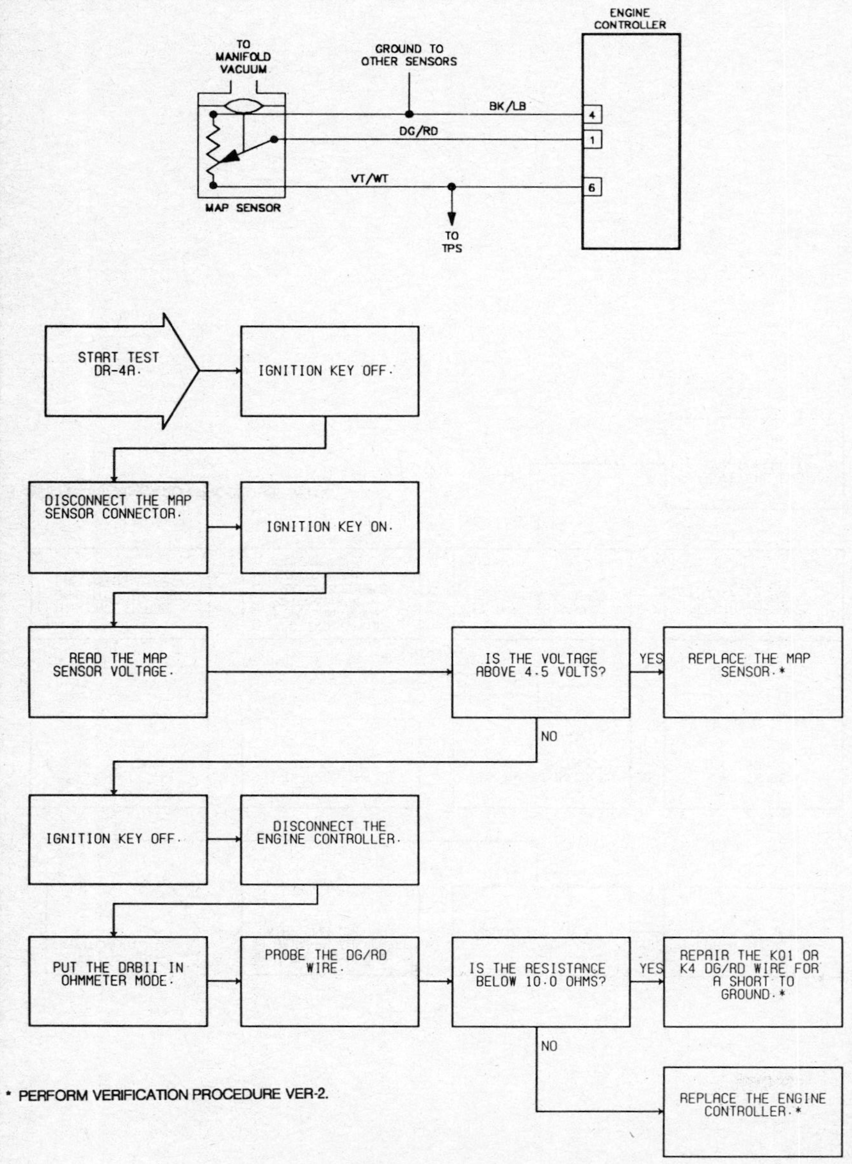
TO
MANIFOLD
VACUUM
GROUND TO
OTHER SENSORS
ENGINE
CONTROLLER
BK/LB
DG/RD
VT/WT
4
1
6
MAP SENSOR
TO
TPS
START TEST
DR-4A.
IGNITION KEY OFF.
DISCONNECT THE MAP
SENSOR CONNECTOR.
IGNITION KEY ON.
READ THE MAP
SENSOR VOLTAGE.
IS THE VOLTAGE
ABOVE 4.5 VOLTS?
YES
REPLACE THE MAP
SENSOR.*
NO
IGNITION KEY OFF.
DISCONNECT THE
ENGINE CONTROLLER.
PUT THE DRBII IN
OHMMETER MODE.
PROBE THE DG/RD
WIRE.
IS THE RESISTANCE
BELOW 10.0 OHMS?
YES
REPAIR THE K01 OR
K4 DG/RD WIRE FOR
A SHORT TO
GROUND.*
NO
REPLACE THE ENGINE
CONTROLLER.*

* PERFORM VERIFICATION PROCEDURE VER-2.

91F08715 91C08785

Fig. 57: Driveability Test 4A (2.2L & 2.5L) – Code 14, MAP Voltage Too Low

DR-5A: CODE 14, MAP VOLTAGE TOO HIGH (1 OF 2)

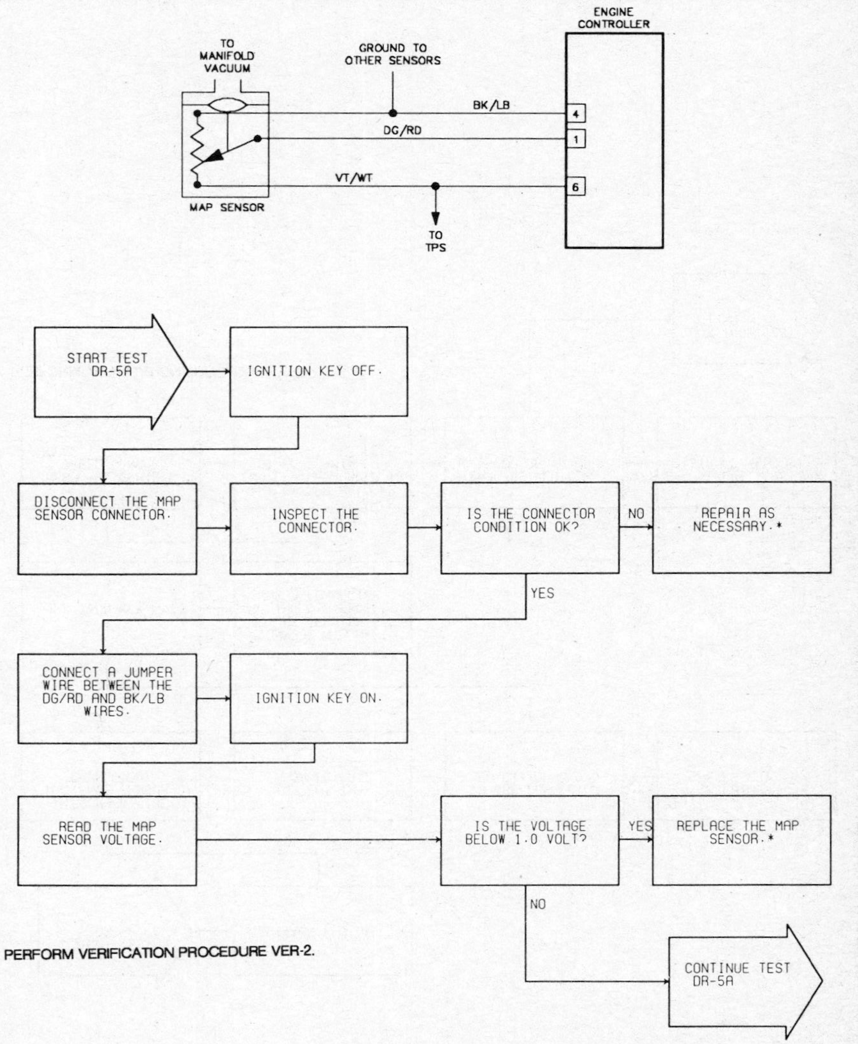
TO
MANIFOLD
VACUUM
GROUND TO
OTHER SENSORS
ENGINE
CONTROLLER
BK/LB
DG/RD
VT/WT
4
1
6
MAP SENSOR
TO
TPS
START TEST
DR-5A
IGNITION KEY OFF.
DISCONNECT THE MAP
SENSOR CONNECTOR.
INSPECT THE
CONNECTOR.
IS THE CONNECTOR
CONDITION OK?
NO
REPAIR AS
NECESSARY.*
YES
CONNECT A JUMPER
WIRE BETWEEN THE
DG/RD AND BK/LB
WIRES.
IGNITION KEY ON.
READ THE MAP
SENSOR VOLTAGE.
IS THE VOLTAGE
BELOW 1.0 VOLT?
YES
REPLACE THE MAP
SENSOR.*
NO
CONTINUE TEST
DR-5A

* PERFORM VERIFICATION PROCEDURE VER-2.

91F08715 91E08786

Fig. 58: Driveability Test 5A (2.2L & 2.5L) – Code 14, MAP Voltage Too High (1 of 2)

1991 ENGINE PERFORMANCE
Self-Diagnostics – 2.5L TBI (Cont.)

DR-5A: CODE 14, MAP VOLTAGE TOO HIGH (2 OF 2)

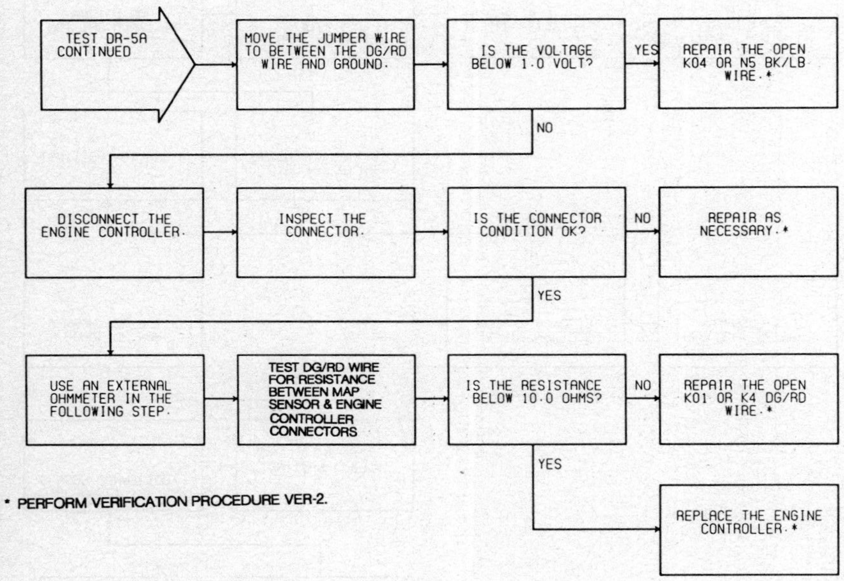
TEST DR-5A CONTINUED
MOVE THE JUMPER WIRE TO BETWEEN THE DG/RD WIRE AND GROUND.
IS THE VOLTAGE BELOW 1.0 VOLT?
YES
REPAIR THE OPEN K04 OR N5 BK/LB WIRE.*
NO
DISCONNECT THE ENGINE CONTROLLER.
INSPECT THE CONNECTOR.
IS THE CONNECTOR CONDITION OK?
NO
REPAIR AS NECESSARY.*
YES
USE AN EXTERNAL OHMMETER IN THE FOLLOWING STEP.
TEST DG/RD WIRE FOR RESISTANCE BETWEEN MAP SENSOR & ENGINE CONTROLLER CONNECTORS
IS THE RESISTANCE BELOW 10.0 OHMS?
NO
REPAIR THE OPEN K01 OR K4 DG/RD WIRE.*
YES
REPLACE THE ENGINE CONTROLLER.*
* PERFORM VERIFICATION PROCEDURE VER-2.

91G08787

Fig. 59: Driveability Test 5A (2.2L & 2.5L) – Code 14, MAP Voltage Too High (2 of 2)

DR-6A: CODE 15, NO VEHICLE SPEED SIGNAL (1 OF 3)

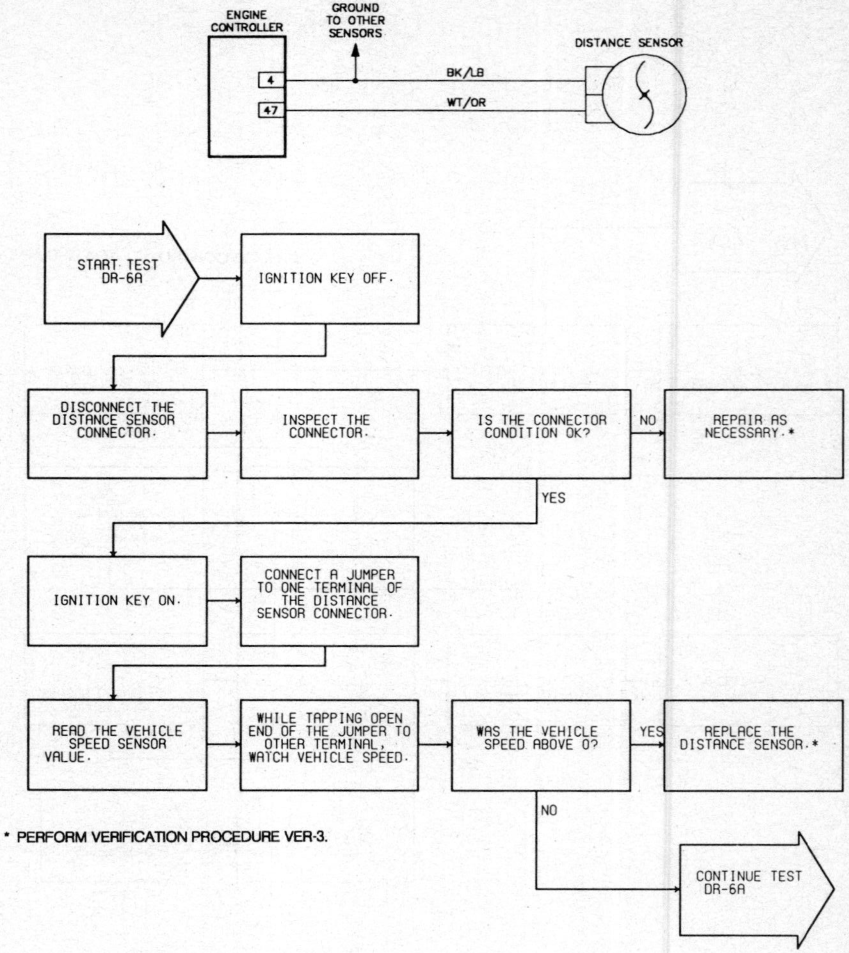
ENGINE CONTROLLER
GROUND TO OTHER SENSORS
DISTANCE SENSOR
4
47
BK/LB
WT/OR
START TEST DR-6A
IGNITION KEY OFF.
DISCONNECT THE DISTANCE SENSOR CONNECTOR.
INSPECT THE CONNECTOR.
IS THE CONNECTOR CONDITION OK?
NO
REPAIR AS NECESSARY.*
YES
IGNITION KEY ON.
CONNECT A JUMPER TO ONE TERMINAL OF THE DISTANCE SENSOR CONNECTOR.
READ THE VEHICLE SPEED SENSOR VALUE.
WHILE TAPPING OPEN END OF THE JUMPER TO OTHER TERMINAL, WATCH VEHICLE SPEED.
WAS THE VEHICLE SPEED ABOVE 0?
YES
REPLACE THE DISTANCE SENSOR.*
NO
CONTINUE TEST DR-6A
* PERFORM VERIFICATION PROCEDURE VER-3.

91D08719 91I08788

Fig. 60: Driveability Test 6A (2.2L & 2.5L) – Code 15, No Vehicle Speed Signal (1 of 3)

DR-6A: CODE 15, NO VEHICLE SPEED SIGNAL (2 OF 3)

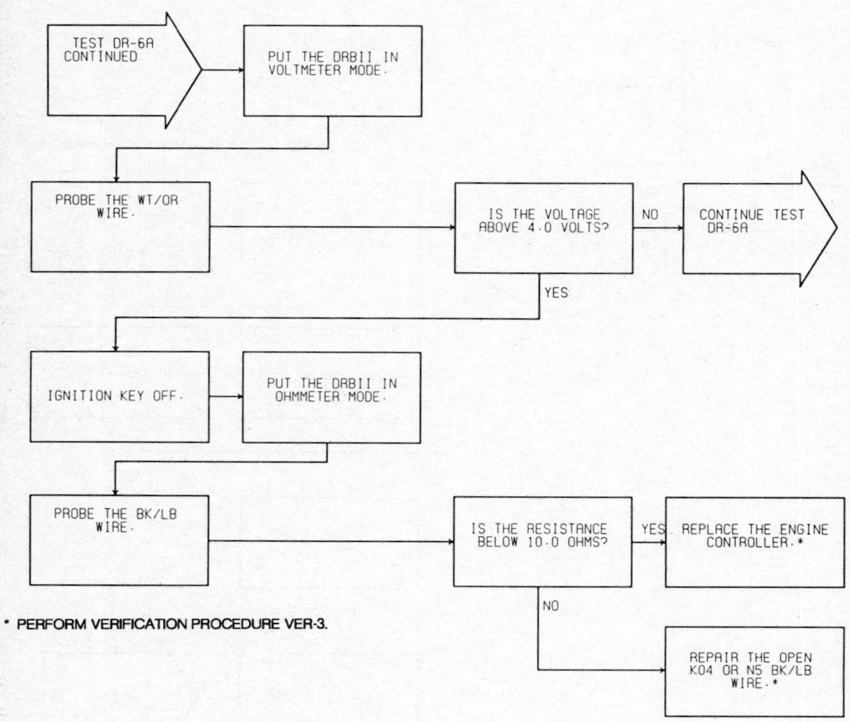
TEST DR-6A CONTINUED
PUT THE DRBII IN VOLTMETER MODE.
PROBE THE WT/OR WIRE.
IS THE VOLTAGE ABOVE 4.0 VOLTS?
NO
CONTINUE TEST DR-6A
YES
IGNITION KEY OFF.
PUT THE DRBII IN OHMMETER MODE.
PROBE THE BK/LB WIRE.
IS THE RESISTANCE BELOW 10.0 OHMS?
YES
REPLACE THE ENGINE CONTROLLER.*
NO
REPAIR THE OPEN K04 OR N5 BK/LB WIRE.*

* PERFORM VERIFICATION PROCEDURE VER-3.

91A08789

Fig. 61: Driveability Test 6A (2.2L & 2.5L) – Code 15, No Vehicle Speed Signal (2 of 3)

DR-6A: CODE 15, NO VEHICLE SPEED SIGNAL (3 OF 3)

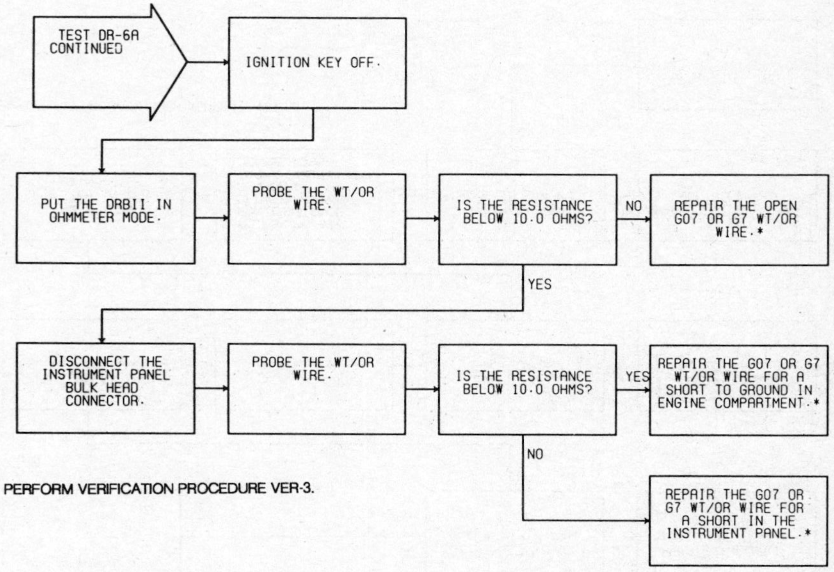
TEST DR-6A CONTINUED
IGNITION KEY OFF.
PUT THE DRBII IN OHMMETER MODE.
PROBE THE WT/OR WIRE.
IS THE RESISTANCE BELOW 10.0 OHMS?
NO
REPAIR THE OPEN G07 OR G7 WT/OR WIRE.*
YES
DISCONNECT THE INSTRUMENT PANEL BULK HEAD CONNECTOR.
PROBE THE WT/OR WIRE.
IS THE RESISTANCE BELOW 10.0 OHMS?
YES
REPAIR THE G07 OR G7 WT/OR WIRE FOR A SHORT TO GROUND IN ENGINE COMPARTMENT.*
NO
REPAIR THE G07 OR G7 WT/OR WIRE FOR A SHORT IN THE INSTRUMENT PANEL.*

* PERFORM VERIFICATION PROCEDURE VER-3.

91C08790

Fig. 62: Driveability Test 6A (2.2L & 2.5L) – Code 15, No Vehicle Speed Signal (3 of 3)

1991 ENGINE PERFORMANCE
Self-Diagnostics – 2.5L TBI (Cont.)

DR-7A: CODE 21, O_2 SIGNAL STAYS AT CENTER (1 OF 2)

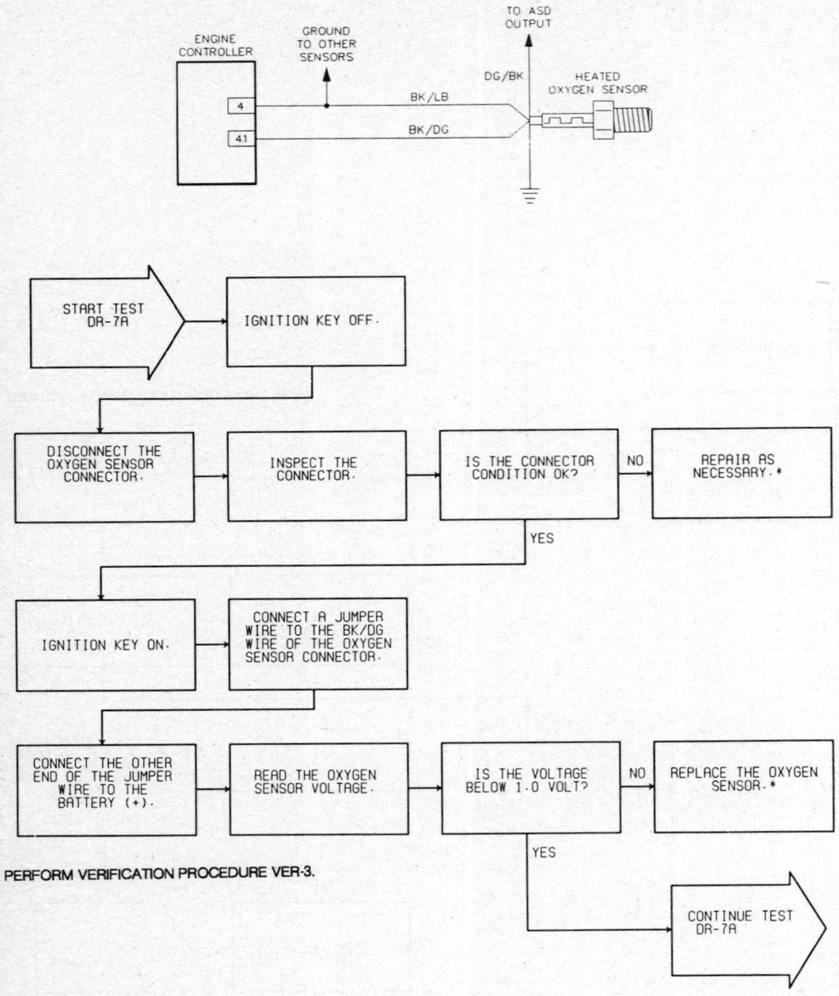
ENGINE CONTROLLER
GROUND TO OTHER SENSORS
TO ASD OUTPUT
DG/BK
HEATED OXYGEN SENSOR
4
41
BK/LB
BK/DG
START TEST DR-7A
IGNITION KEY OFF.
DISCONNECT THE OXYGEN SENSOR CONNECTOR.
INSPECT THE CONNECTOR.
IS THE CONNECTOR CONDITION OK?
NO
REPAIR AS NECESSARY.*
YES
IGNITION KEY ON.
CONNECT A JUMPER WIRE TO THE BK/DG WIRE OF THE OXYGEN SENSOR CONNECTOR.
CONNECT THE OTHER END OF THE JUMPER WIRE TO THE BATTERY (+).
READ THE OXYGEN SENSOR VOLTAGE.
IS THE VOLTAGE BELOW 1.0 VOLT?
NO
REPLACE THE OXYGEN SENSOR.*
YES
CONTINUE TEST DR-7A

* PERFORM VERIFICATION PROCEDURE VER-3.

91F08720 91E08791

Fig. 63: Driveability Test 7A (2.2L & 2.5L) – Code 21, O_2 Signal Stays at Center (1 of 2)

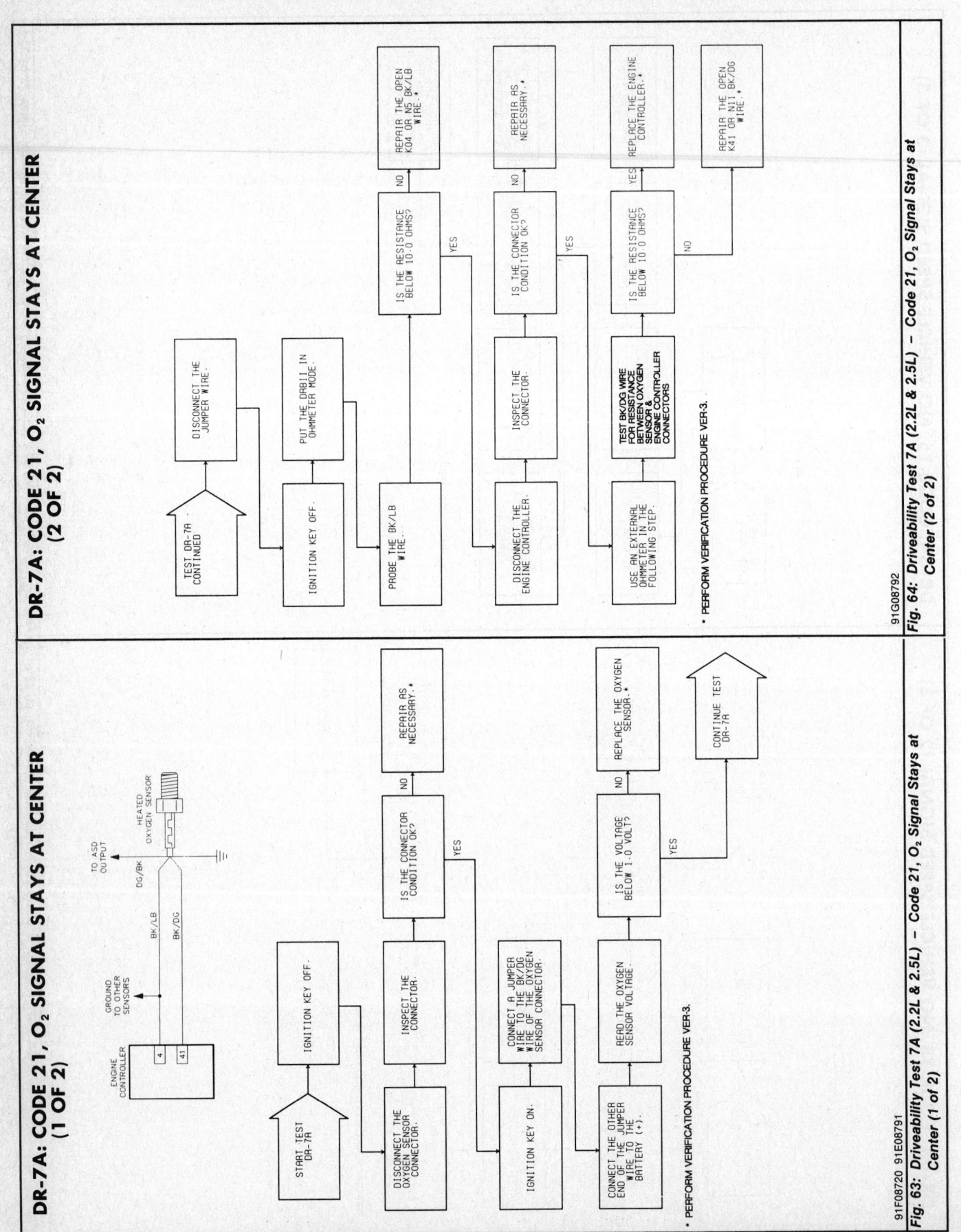

DR-7A: CODE 21, O_2 SIGNAL STAYS AT CENTER (2 OF 2)

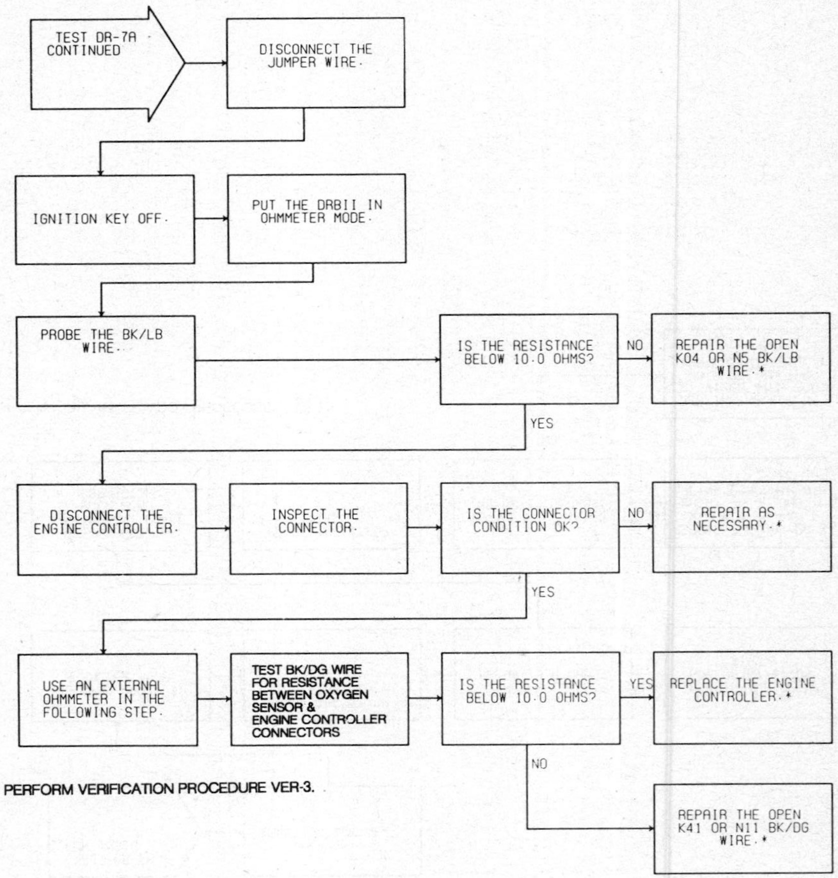
TEST DR-7A CONTINUED
DISCONNECT THE JUMPER WIRE.
IGNITION KEY OFF.
PUT THE DRBII IN OHMMETER MODE.
PROBE THE BK/LB WIRE.
IS THE RESISTANCE BELOW 10.0 OHMS?
NO
REPAIR THE OPEN K04 OR N5 BK/LB WIRE.*
YES
DISCONNECT THE ENGINE CONTROLLER.
INSPECT THE CONNECTOR.
IS THE CONNECTOR CONDITION OK?
NO
REPAIR AS NECESSARY.*
YES
USE AN EXTERNAL OHMMETER IN THE FOLLOWING STEP.
TEST BK/DG WIRE FOR RESISTANCE BETWEEN OXYGEN SENSOR & ENGINE CONTROLLER CONNECTORS
IS THE RESISTANCE BELOW 10.0 OHMS?
YES
REPLACE THE ENGINE CONTROLLER.*
NO
REPAIR THE OPEN K41 OR N11 BK/DG WIRE.*

* PERFORM VERIFICATION PROCEDURE VER-3.

91G08792

Fig. 64: Driveability Test 7A (2.2L & 2.5L) – Code 21, O_2 Signal Stays at Center (2 of 2)

DR-8A: CODE 21, O_2 SIGNAL SHORTED TO VOLTAGE (1 of 2)

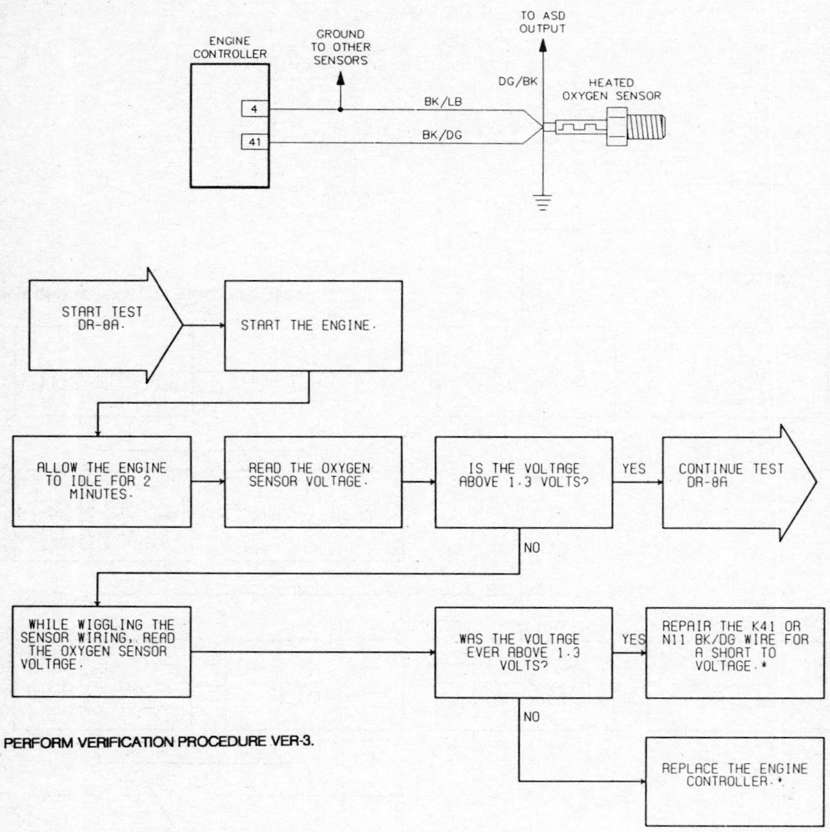
ENGINE CONTROLLER
4
41
GROUND TO OTHER SENSORS
BK/LB
BK/DG
TO ASD OUTPUT
DG/BK
HEATED OXYGEN SENSOR
START TEST DR-8A.
START THE ENGINE.
ALLOW THE ENGINE TO IDLE FOR 2 MINUTES.
READ THE OXYGEN SENSOR VOLTAGE.
IS THE VOLTAGE ABOVE 1.3 VOLTS?
YES
CONTINUE TEST DR-8A
NO
WHILE WIGGLING THE SENSOR WIRING, READ THE OXYGEN SENSOR VOLTAGE.
WAS THE VOLTAGE EVER ABOVE 1.3 VOLTS?
YES
REPAIR THE K41 OR N11 BK/DG WIRE FOR A SHORT TO VOLTAGE.*
NO
REPLACE THE ENGINE CONTROLLER.*

* PERFORM VERIFICATION PROCEDURE VER-3.

91F08720 91I08793

Fig. 65: Driveability Test 8A (2.2L & 2.5L) – Code 21, O_2 Signal Shorted to Voltage (1 of 2)

DR-8A: CODE 21, O_2 SIGNAL SHORTED TO VOLTAGE (2 of 2)

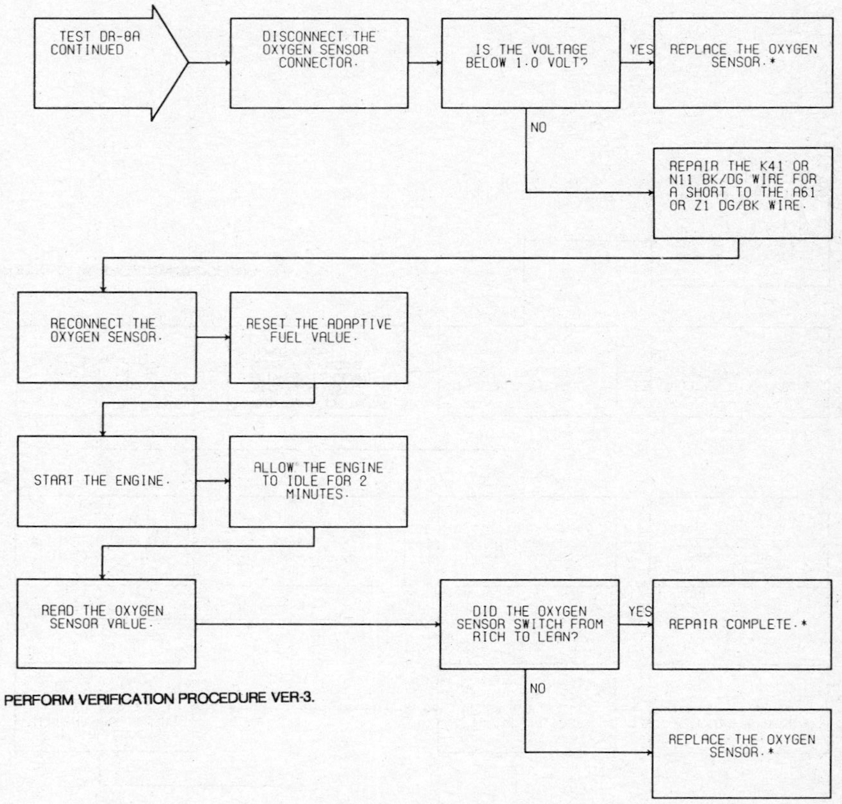
TEST DR-8A CONTINUED
DISCONNECT THE OXYGEN SENSOR CONNECTOR.
IS THE VOLTAGE BELOW 1.0 VOLT?
YES
REPLACE THE OXYGEN SENSOR.*
NO
REPAIR THE K41 OR N11 BK/DG WIRE FOR A SHORT TO THE A61 OR Z1 DG/BK WIRE.
RECONNECT THE OXYGEN SENSOR.
RESET THE ADAPTIVE FUEL VALUE.
START THE ENGINE.
ALLOW THE ENGINE TO IDLE FOR 2 MINUTES.
READ THE OXYGEN SENSOR VALUE.
DID THE OXYGEN SENSOR SWITCH FROM RICH TO LEAN?
YES
REPAIR COMPLETE.*
NO
REPLACE THE OXYGEN SENSOR.*

* PERFORM VERIFICATION PROCEDURE VER-3.

91A08794

Fig. 66: Driveability Test 8A (2.2L & 2.5L) – Code 21, O_2 Signal Shorted to Voltage (2 of 2)

1991 ENGINE PERFORMANCE
Self-Diagnostics – 2.5L TBI (Cont.)

DR-9A: CODE 22, COOLANT SENSOR VOLTAGE TOO HIGH (1 OF 2)

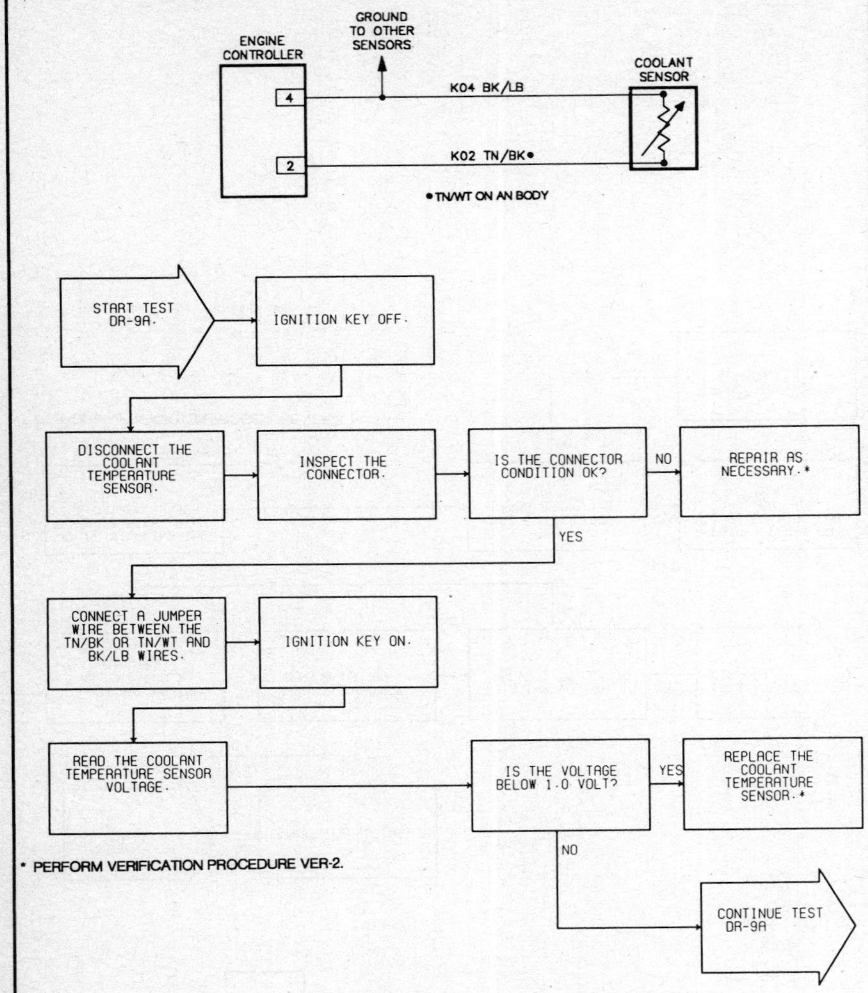
ENGINE CONTROLLER
GROUND TO OTHER SENSORS
COOLANT SENSOR
4
2
K04 BK/LB
K02 TN/BK•
•TN/WT ON AN BODY
START TEST DR-9A.
IGNITION KEY OFF.
DISCONNECT THE COOLANT TEMPERATURE SENSOR.
INSPECT THE CONNECTOR.
IS THE CONNECTOR CONDITION OK?
NO
REPAIR AS NECESSARY.*
YES
CONNECT A JUMPER WIRE BETWEEN THE TN/BK OR TN/WT AND BK/LB WIRES.
IGNITION KEY ON.
READ THE COOLANT TEMPERATURE SENSOR VOLTAGE.
IS THE VOLTAGE BELOW 1.0 VOLT?
YES
REPLACE THE COOLANT TEMPERATURE SENSOR.*
NO
CONTINUE TEST DR-9A
* PERFORM VERIFICATION PROCEDURE VER-2.

91H08721 91D08795

Fig. 67: *Driveability Test 9A (2.2L & 2.5L) – Code 22, Coolant Sensor Voltage Too High (1 of 2)*

DR-9A: CODE 22, COOLANT SENSOR VOLTAGE TOO HIGH (2 OF 2)

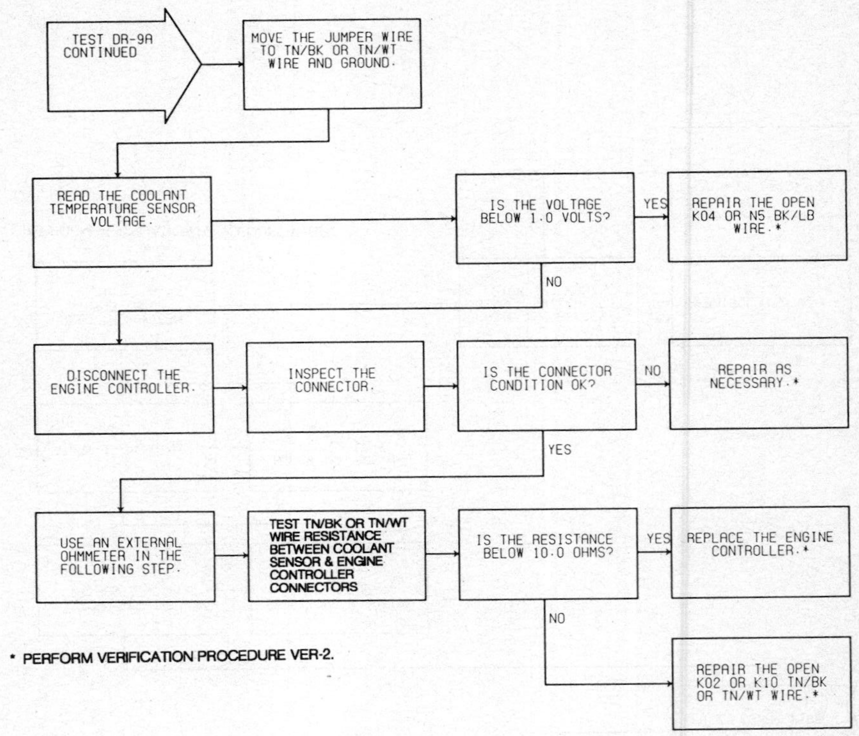
TEST DR-9A CONTINUED
MOVE THE JUMPER WIRE TO TN/BK OR TN/WT WIRE AND GROUND.
READ THE COOLANT TEMPERATURE SENSOR VOLTAGE.
IS THE VOLTAGE BELOW 1.0 VOLTS?
YES
REPAIR THE OPEN K04 OR N5 BK/LB WIRE.*
NO
DISCONNECT THE ENGINE CONTROLLER.
INSPECT THE CONNECTOR.
IS THE CONNECTOR CONDITION OK?
NO
REPAIR AS NECESSARY.*
YES
USE AN EXTERNAL OHMMETER IN THE FOLLOWING STEP.
TEST TN/BK OR TN/WT WIRE RESISTANCE BETWEEN COOLANT SENSOR & ENGINE CONTROLLER CONNECTORS
IS THE RESISTANCE BELOW 10.0 OHMS?
YES
REPLACE THE ENGINE CONTROLLER.*
NO
REPAIR THE OPEN K02 OR K10 TN/BK OR TN/WT WIRE.*
* PERFORM VERIFICATION PROCEDURE VER-2.

91F08796

Fig. 68: *Driveability Test 9A (2.2L & 2.5L) – Code 22, Coolant Sensor Voltage Too High (2 of 2)*

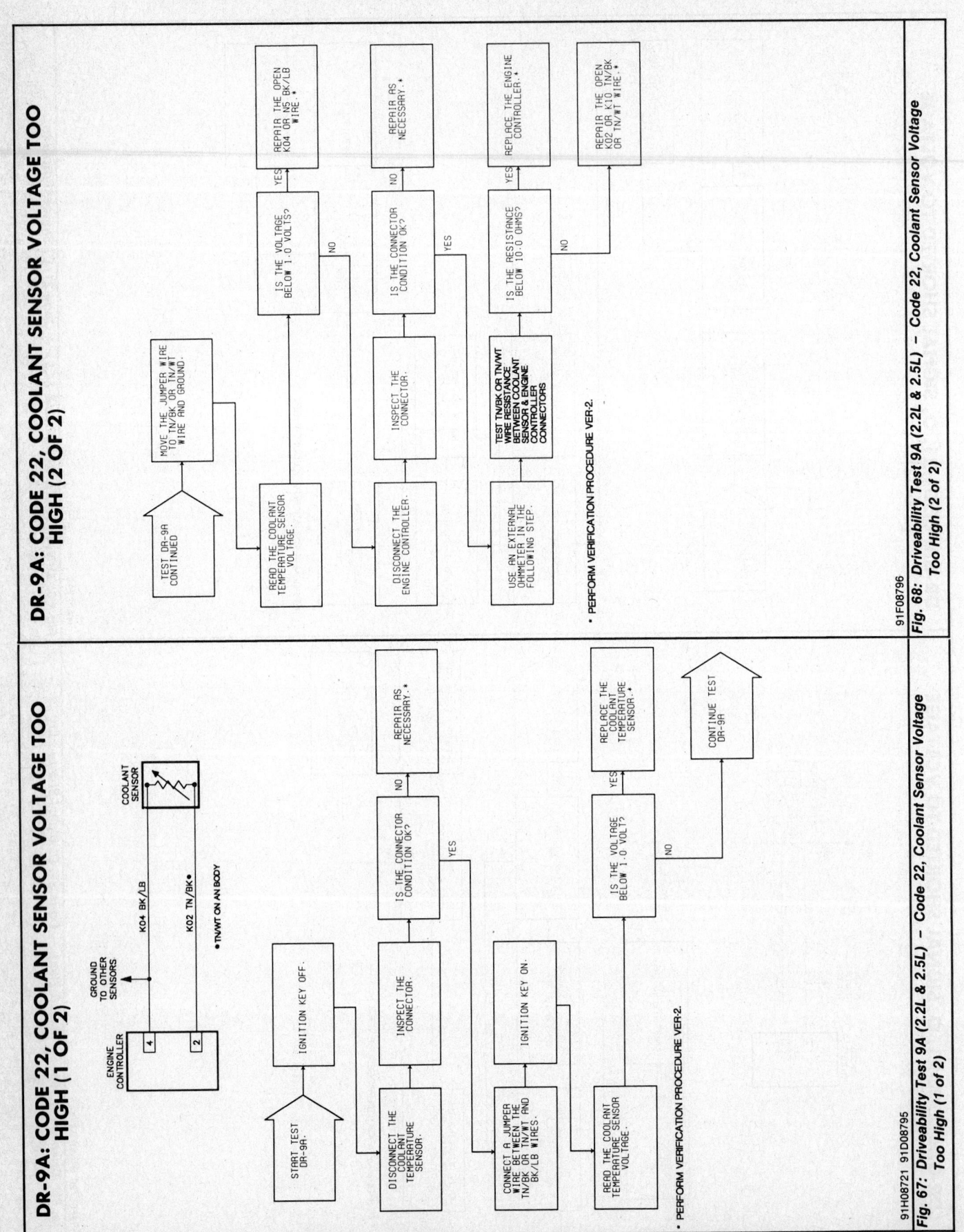

DR-10A: CODE 22, COOLANT SENSOR VOLTAGE TOO LOW

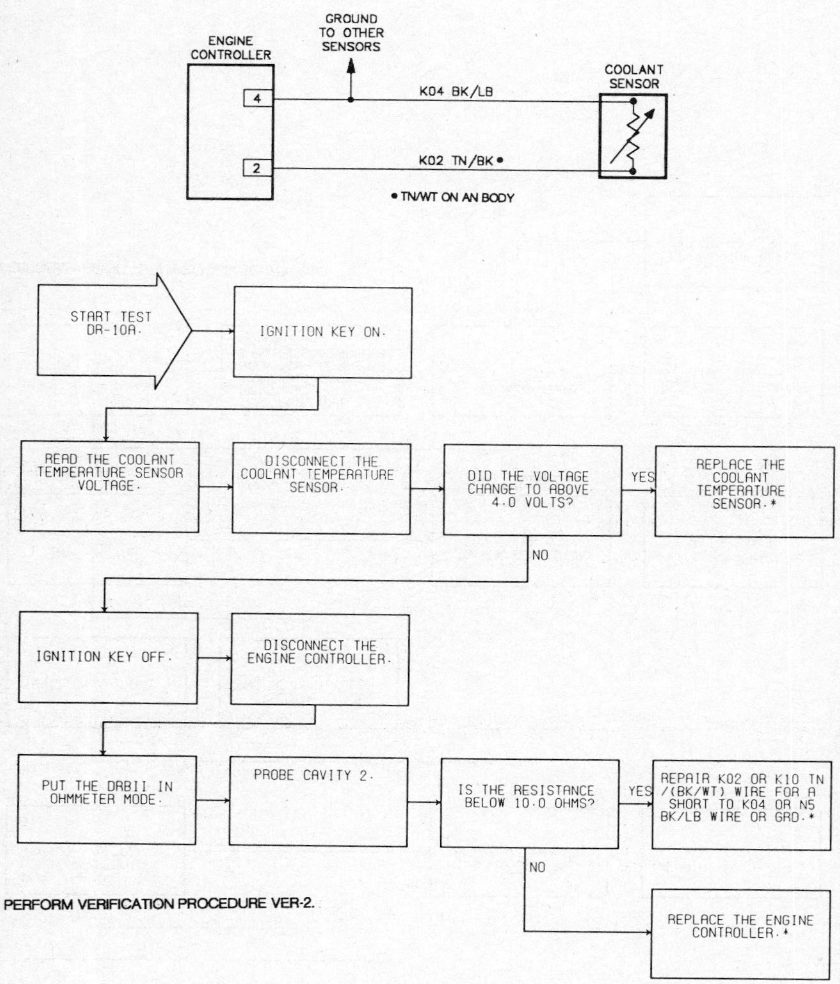
ENGINE CONTROLLER
GROUND TO OTHER SENSORS
4
2
K04 BK/LB
K02 TN/BK •
COOLANT SENSOR
• TN/WT ON AN BODY
START TEST DR-10A.
IGNITION KEY ON.
READ THE COOLANT TEMPERATURE SENSOR VOLTAGE.
DISCONNECT THE COOLANT TEMPERATURE SENSOR.
DID THE VOLTAGE CHANGE TO ABOVE 4.0 VOLTS?
YES
REPLACE THE COOLANT TEMPERATURE SENSOR.*
NO
IGNITION KEY OFF.
DISCONNECT THE ENGINE CONTROLLER.
PUT THE DRBII IN OHMMETER MODE.
PROBE CAVITY 2.
IS THE RESISTANCE BELOW 10.0 OHMS?
YES
REPAIR K02 OR K10 TN /(BK/WT) WIRE FOR A SHORT TO K04 OR N5 BK/LB WIRE OR GRD.*
NO
REPLACE THE ENGINE CONTROLLER.*
* PERFORM VERIFICATION PROCEDURE VER-2.

91H08721 91H08797

Fig. 69: *Driveability Test 10A (2.2L & 2.5L) – Code 22, Coolant Sensor Voltage Too Low*

DR-11A: CODE 23, THROTTLE BODY TEMPERATURE HIGH (1 OF 2)

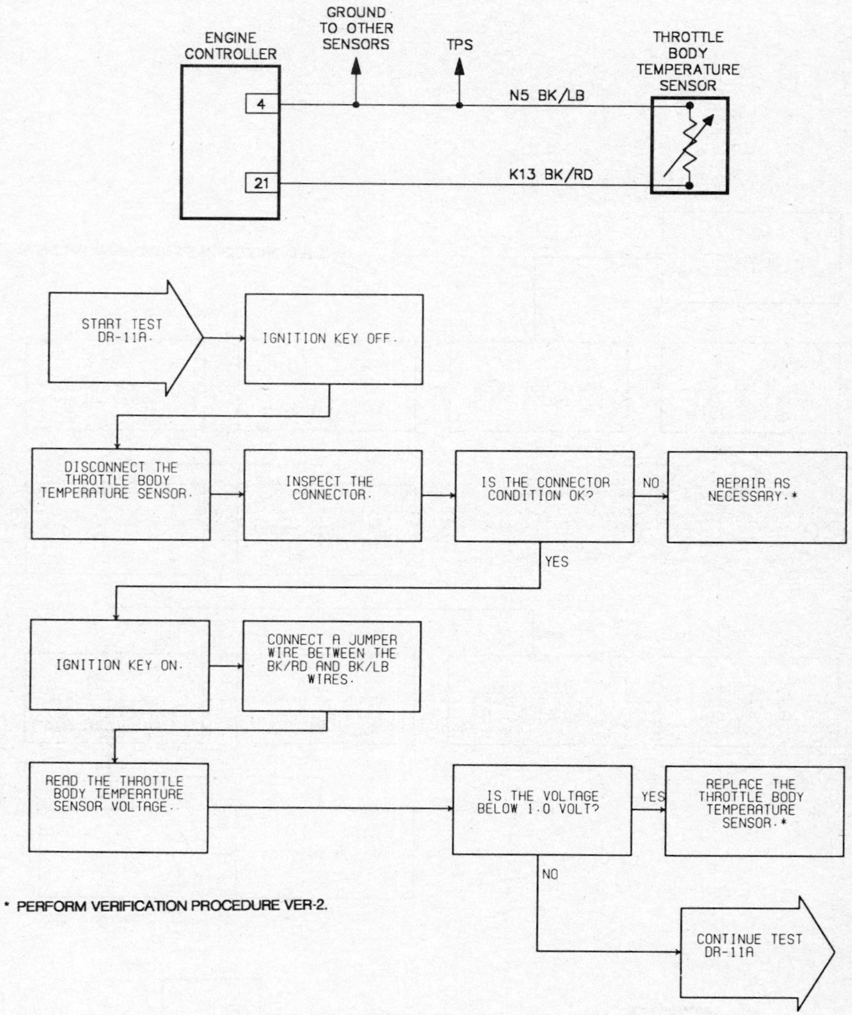
ENGINE CONTROLLER
GROUND TO OTHER SENSORS
TPS
THROTTLE BODY TEMPERATURE SENSOR
4
21
N5 BK/LB
K13 BK/RD
START TEST DR-11A.
IGNITION KEY OFF.
DISCONNECT THE THROTTLE BODY TEMPERATURE SENSOR.
INSPECT THE CONNECTOR.
IS THE CONNECTOR CONDITION OK?
NO
REPAIR AS NECESSARY.*
YES
IGNITION KEY ON.
CONNECT A JUMPER WIRE BETWEEN THE BK/RD AND BK/LB WIRES.
READ THE THROTTLE BODY TEMPERATURE SENSOR VOLTAGE.
IS THE VOLTAGE BELOW 1.0 VOLT?
YES
REPLACE THE THROTTLE BODY TEMPERATURE SENSOR.*
NO
CONTINUE TEST DR-11A
* PERFORM VERIFICATION PROCEDURE VER-2.

91J08722 91J08798

Fig. 70: *Driveability Test 11A (2.2L & 2.5L) – Code 23, Throttle Body Temperature High (1 of 2)*

1991 ENGINE PERFORMANCE
Self-Diagnostics – 2.5L TBI (Cont.)

DR-11A: CODE 23, THROTTLE BODY TEMPERATURE HIGH (2 OF 2)

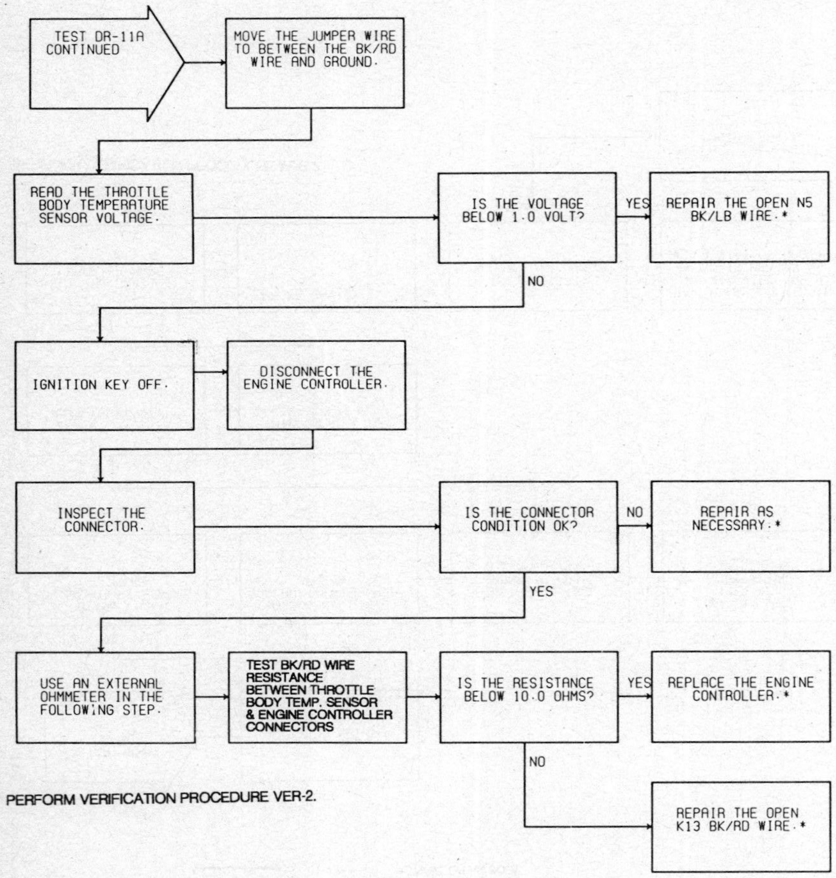
TEST DR-11A CONTINUED
MOVE THE JUMPER WIRE TO BETWEEN THE BK/RD WIRE AND GROUND.
READ THE THROTTLE BODY TEMPERATURE SENSOR VOLTAGE.
IS THE VOLTAGE BELOW 1.0 VOLT?
YES
REPAIR THE OPEN N5 BK/LB WIRE.*
NO
IGNITION KEY OFF.
DISCONNECT THE ENGINE CONTROLLER.
INSPECT THE CONNECTOR.
IS THE CONNECTOR CONDITION OK?
NO
REPAIR AS NECESSARY.*
YES
USE AN EXTERNAL OHMMETER IN THE FOLLOWING STEP.
TEST BK/RD WIRE RESISTANCE BETWEEN THROTTLE BODY TEMP. SENSOR & ENGINE CONTROLLER CONNECTORS
IS THE RESISTANCE BELOW 10.0 OHMS?
YES
REPLACE THE ENGINE CONTROLLER.*
NO
REPAIR THE OPEN K13 BK/RD WIRE.*

* PERFORM VERIFICATION PROCEDURE VER-2.

91B08799

Fig. 71: Driveability Test 11A (2.2L & 2.5L) – Code 23, Throttle Body Temperature High (2 of 2)

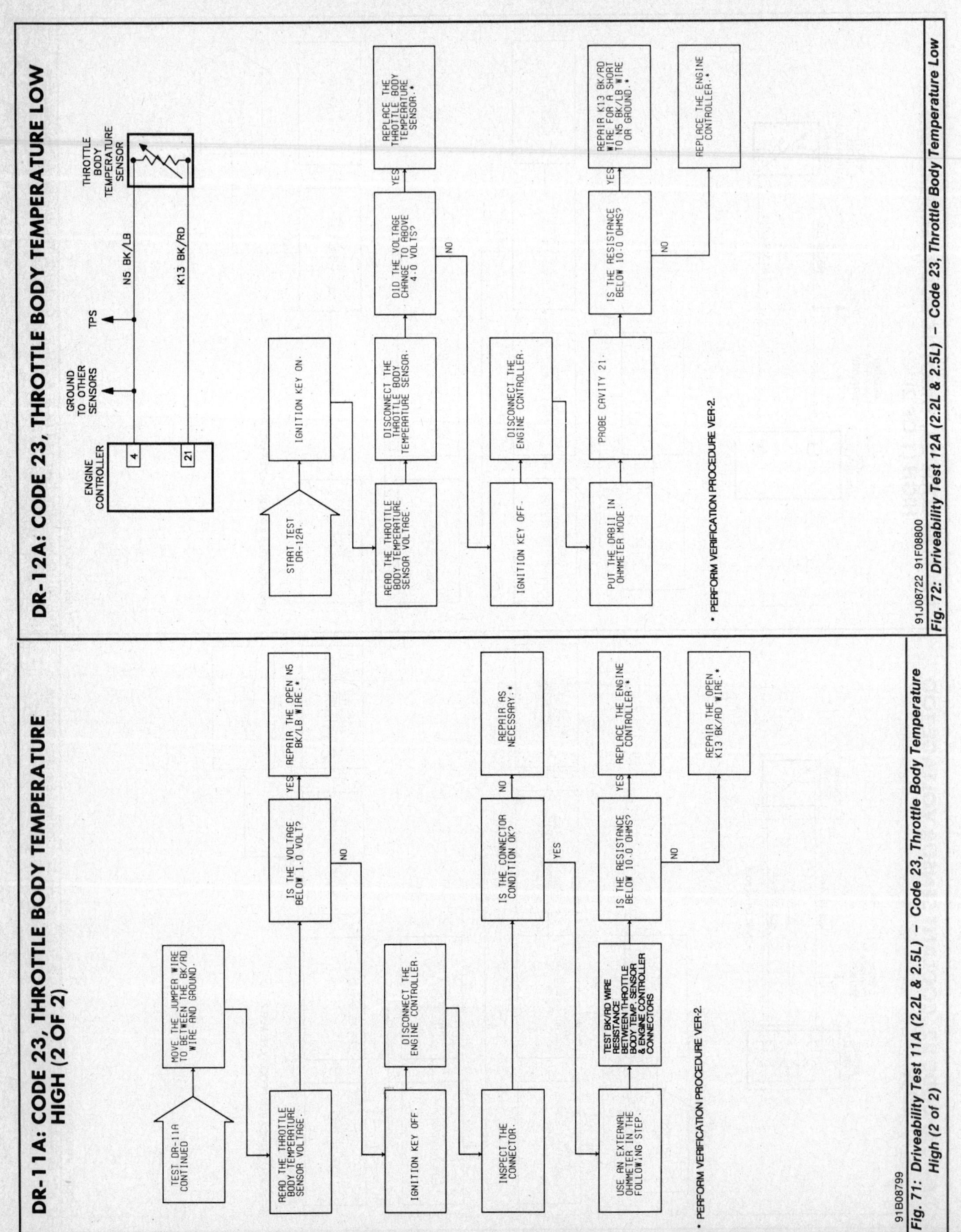

DR-12A: CODE 23, THROTTLE BODY TEMPERATURE LOW

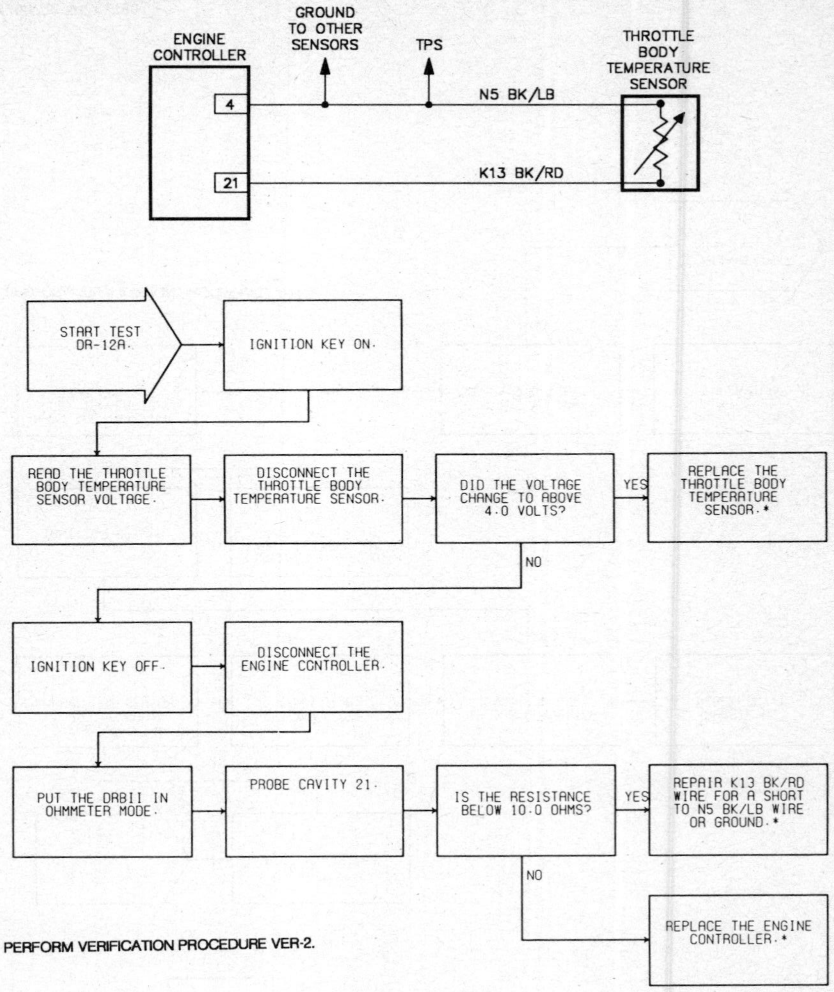
ENGINE CONTROLLER
4
21
GROUND TO OTHER SENSORS
TPS
N5 BK/LB
K13 BK/RD
THROTTLE BODY TEMPERATURE SENSOR
START TEST DR-12A.
IGNITION KEY ON.
READ THE THROTTLE BODY TEMPERATURE SENSOR VOLTAGE.
DISCONNECT THE THROTTLE BODY TEMPERATURE SENSOR.
DID THE VOLTAGE CHANGE TO ABOVE 4.0 VOLTS?
YES
REPLACE THE THROTTLE BODY TEMPERATURE SENSOR.*
NO
IGNITION KEY OFF.
DISCONNECT THE ENGINE CONTROLLER.
PUT THE DRBII IN OHMMETER MODE.
PROBE CAVITY 21.
IS THE RESISTANCE BELOW 10.0 OHMS?
YES
REPAIR K13 BK/RD WIRE FOR A SHORT TO N5 BK/LB WIRE OR GROUND.*
NO
REPLACE THE ENGINE CONTROLLER.*

* PERFORM VERIFICATION PROCEDURE VER-2.

91J08722 91F08800

Fig. 72: Driveability Test 12A (2.2L & 2.5L) – Code 23, Throttle Body Temperature Low

DR-13A: CODE 24, THROTTLE POSITION SENSOR VOLTAGE HIGH (1 OF 2)

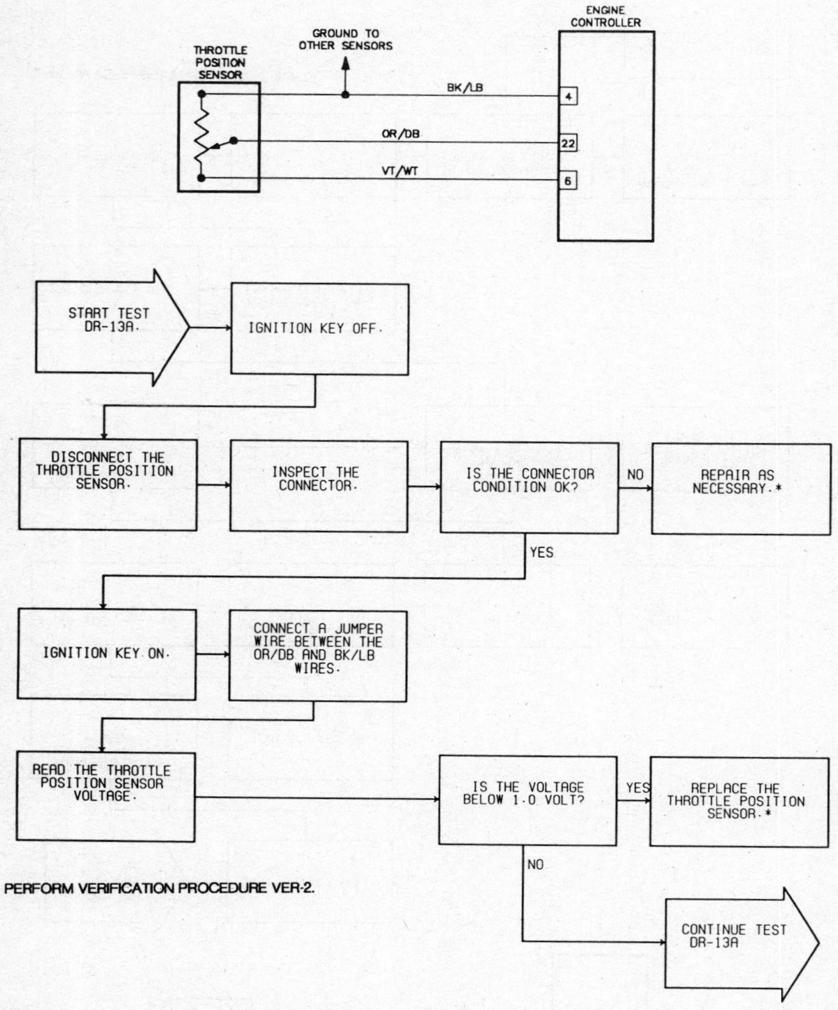
THROTTLE POSITION SENSOR
GROUND TO OTHER SENSORS
ENGINE CONTROLLER
BK/LB
OR/DB
VT/WT
4
22
6
START TEST DR-13A.
IGNITION KEY OFF.
DISCONNECT THE THROTTLE POSITION SENSOR.
INSPECT THE CONNECTOR.
IS THE CONNECTOR CONDITION OK?
NO
REPAIR AS NECESSARY.*
YES
IGNITION KEY ON.
CONNECT A JUMPER WIRE BETWEEN THE OR/DB AND BK/LB WIRES.
READ THE THROTTLE POSITION SENSOR VOLTAGE.
IS THE VOLTAGE BELOW 1.0 VOLT?
YES
REPLACE THE THROTTLE POSITION SENSOR.*
NO
CONTINUE TEST DR-13A

* PERFORM VERIFICATION PROCEDURE VER-2.

91B08723 91H08801

Fig. 73: Driveability Test 13A (2.2L & 2.5L) – Code 24, Throttle Position Sensor Voltage High (1 of 2)

DR-13A: CODE 24, THROTTLE POSITION SENSOR VOLTAGE HIGH (2 OF 2)

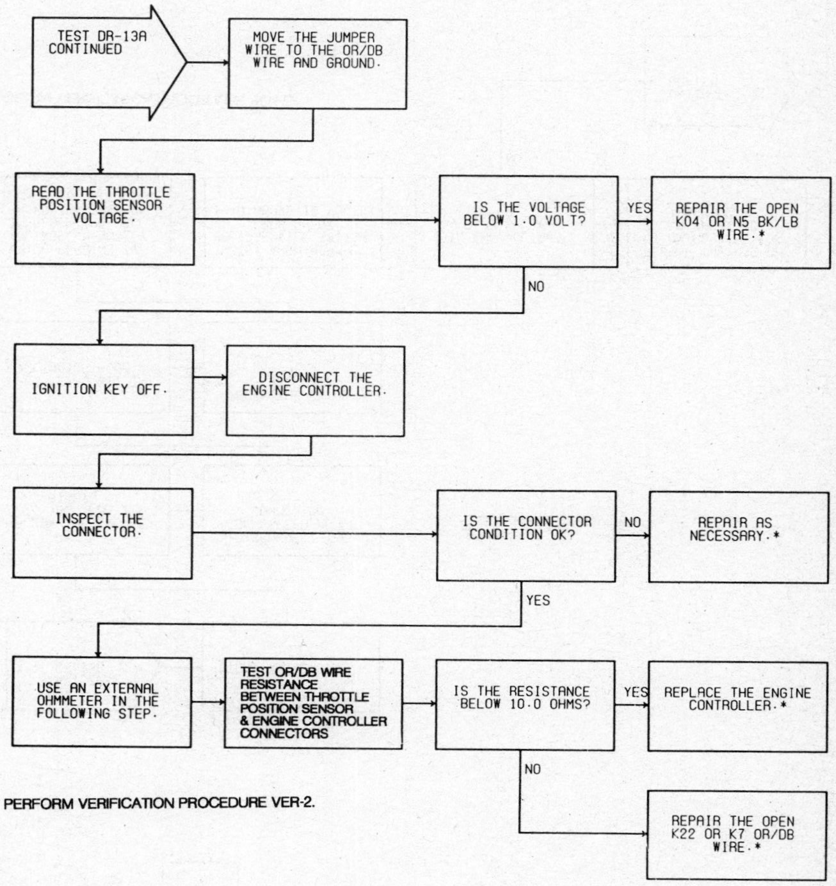
TEST DR-13A CONTINUED
MOVE THE JUMPER WIRE TO THE OR/DB WIRE AND GROUND.
READ THE THROTTLE POSITION SENSOR VOLTAGE.
IS THE VOLTAGE BELOW 1.0 VOLT?
YES
REPAIR THE OPEN K04 OR N5 BK/LB WIRE.*
NO
IGNITION KEY OFF.
DISCONNECT THE ENGINE CONTROLLER.
INSPECT THE CONNECTOR.
IS THE CONNECTOR CONDITION OK?
NO
REPAIR AS NECESSARY.*
YES
USE AN EXTERNAL OHMMETER IN THE FOLLOWING STEP.
TEST OR/DB WIRE RESISTANCE BETWEEN THROTTLE POSITION SENSOR & ENGINE CONTROLLER CONNECTORS
IS THE RESISTANCE BELOW 10.0 OHMS?
YES
REPLACE THE ENGINE CONTROLLER.*
NO
REPAIR THE OPEN K22 OR K7 OR/DB WIRE.*

* PERFORM VERIFICATION PROCEDURE VER-2.

91J08802

Fig. 74: Driveability Test 13A (2.2L & 2.5L) – Code 24, Throttle Position Sensor Voltage High (2 of 2)

1991 ENGINE PERFORMANCE
Self-Diagnostics – 2.5L TBI (Cont.)

DR-14A: CODE 24, THROTTLE POSITION SENSOR VOLTAGE LOW

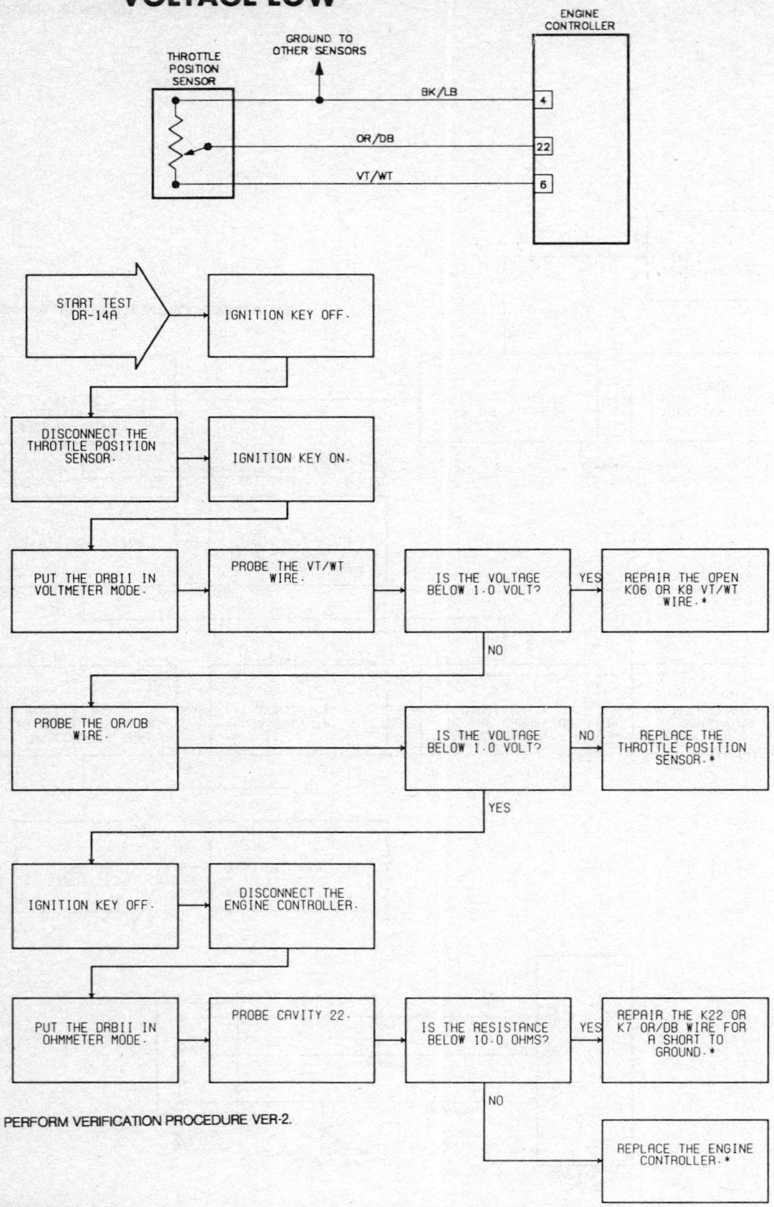
THROTTLE POSITION SENSOR
GROUND TO OTHER SENSORS
ENGINE CONTROLLER
BK/LB
OR/DB
VT/WT
4
22
6
START TEST DR-14A
IGNITION KEY OFF.
DISCONNECT THE THROTTLE POSITION SENSOR.
IGNITION KEY ON.
PUT THE DRBII IN VOLTMETER MODE.
PROBE THE VT/WT WIRE.
IS THE VOLTAGE BELOW 1.0 VOLT?
YES
REPAIR THE OPEN K06 OR K8 VT/WT WIRE.*
NO
PROBE THE OR/DB WIRE.
IS THE VOLTAGE BELOW 1.0 VOLT?
NO
REPLACE THE THROTTLE POSITION SENSOR.*
YES
IGNITION KEY OFF.
DISCONNECT THE ENGINE CONTROLLER.
PUT THE DRBII IN OHMMETER MODE.
PROBE CAVITY 22.
IS THE RESISTANCE BELOW 10.0 OHMS?
YES
REPAIR THE K22 OR K7 OR/DB WIRE FOR A SHORT TO GROUND.*
NO
REPLACE THE ENGINE CONTROLLER.*

* PERFORM VERIFICATION PROCEDURE VER-2.

91B08723 91B08803

Fig. 75: Driveability Test 14A (2.2L & 2.5L) – Code 24, Throttle Position Sensor Voltage Low

DR-15A: CODE 25, AUTOMATIC IDLE SPEED MOTOR CIRCUITS (1 OF 4)

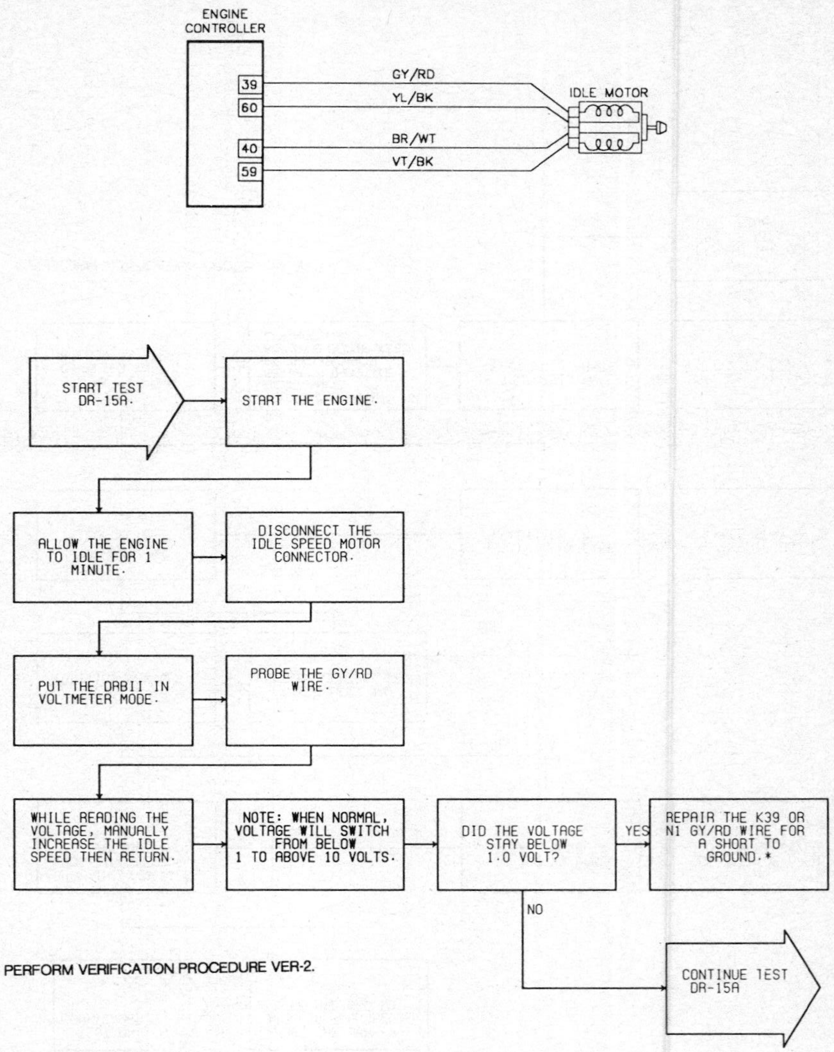
ENGINE CONTROLLER
39
60
40
59
GY/RD
YL/BK
BR/WT
VT/BK
IDLE MOTOR
START TEST DR-15A.
START THE ENGINE.
ALLOW THE ENGINE TO IDLE FOR 1 MINUTE.
DISCONNECT THE IDLE SPEED MOTOR CONNECTOR.
PUT THE DRBII IN VOLTMETER MODE.
PROBE THE GY/RD WIRE.
WHILE READING THE VOLTAGE, MANUALLY INCREASE THE IDLE SPEED THEN RETURN.
NOTE: WHEN NORMAL, VOLTAGE WILL SWITCH FROM BELOW 1 TO ABOVE 10 VOLTS.
DID THE VOLTAGE STAY BELOW 1.0 VOLT?
YES
REPAIR THE K39 OR N1 GY/RD WIRE FOR A SHORT TO GROUND.*
NO
CONTINUE TEST DR-15A

* PERFORM VERIFICATION PROCEDURE VER-2.

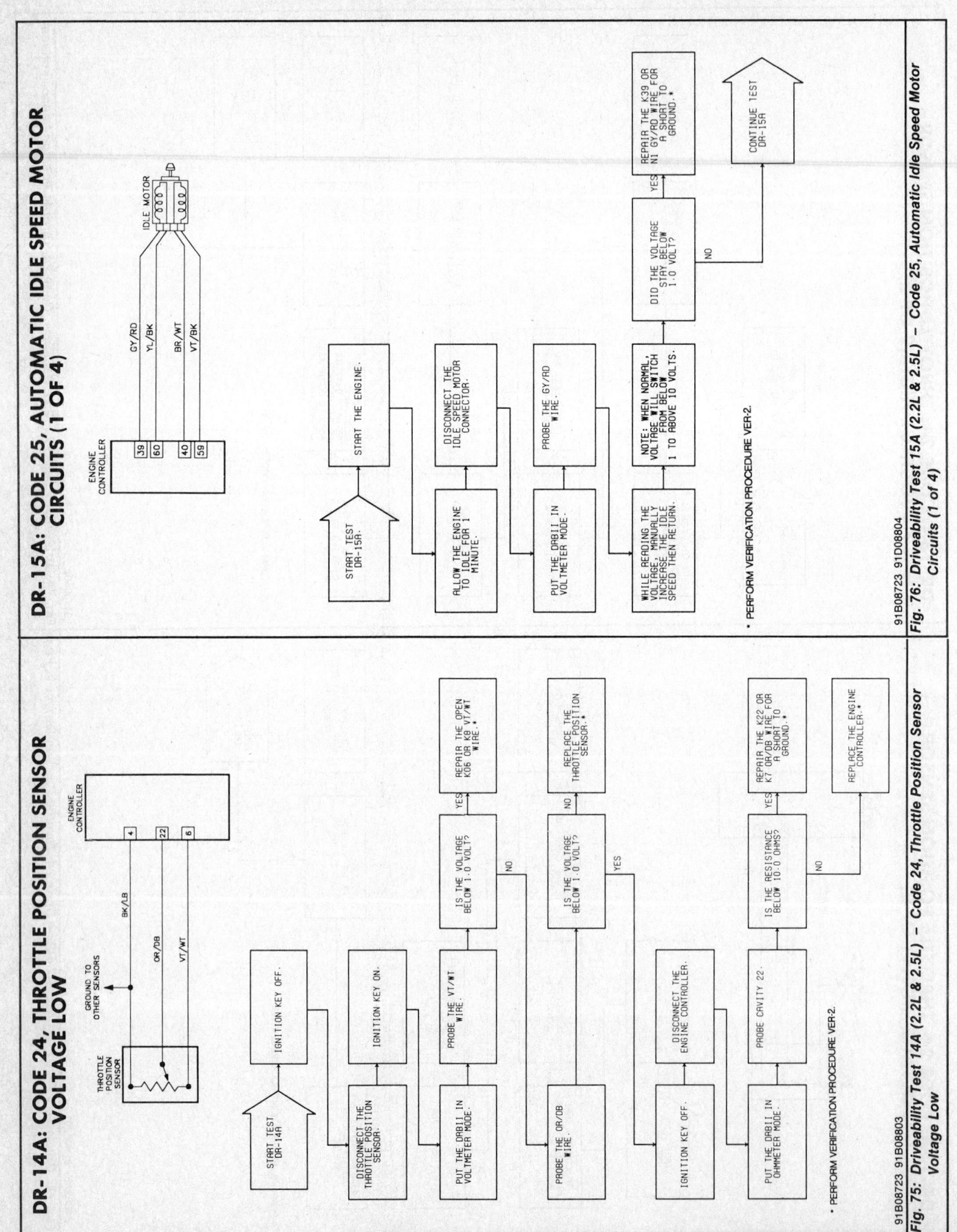

91B08723 91D08804

Fig. 76: Driveability Test 15A (2.2L & 2.5L) – Code 25, Automatic Idle Speed Motor Circuits (1 of 4)

DR-15A: CODE 25, AUTOMATIC IDLE SPEED MOTOR CIRCUITS (2 OF 4)

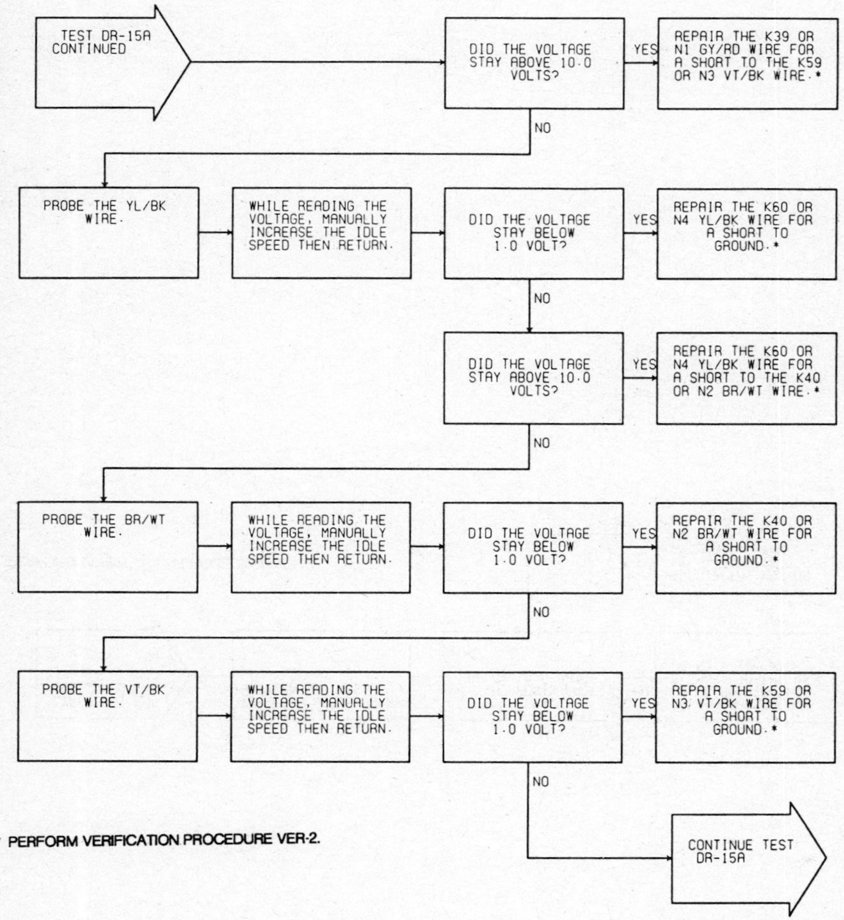
TEST DR-15A CONTINUED
DID THE VOLTAGE STAY ABOVE 10.0 VOLTS?
YES
REPAIR THE K39 OR N1 GY/RD WIRE FOR A SHORT TO THE K59 OR N3 VT/BK WIRE.*
NO
PROBE THE YL/BK WIRE.
WHILE READING THE VOLTAGE, MANUALLY INCREASE THE IDLE SPEED THEN RETURN.
DID THE VOLTAGE STAY BELOW 1.0 VOLT?
YES
REPAIR THE K60 OR N4 YL/BK WIRE FOR A SHORT TO GROUND.*
NO
DID THE VOLTAGE STAY ABOVE 10.0 VOLTS?
YES
REPAIR THE K60 OR N4 YL/BK WIRE FOR A SHORT TO THE K40 OR N2 BR/WT WIRE.*
NO
PROBE THE BR/WT WIRE.
WHILE READING THE VOLTAGE, MANUALLY INCREASE THE IDLE SPEED THEN RETURN.
DID THE VOLTAGE STAY BELOW 1.0 VOLT?
YES
REPAIR THE K40 OR N2 BR/WT WIRE FOR A SHORT TO GROUND.*
NO
PROBE THE VT/BK WIRE.
WHILE READING THE VOLTAGE, MANUALLY INCREASE THE IDLE SPEED THEN RETURN.
DID THE VOLTAGE STAY BELOW 1.0 VOLT?
YES
REPAIR THE K59 OR N3 VT/BK WIRE FOR A SHORT TO GROUND.*
NO
CONTINUE TEST DR-15A

* PERFORM VERIFICATION PROCEDURE VER-2.

91G08805

Fig. 77: Driveability Test 15A (2.2L & 2.5L) – Code 25, Automatic Idle Speed Motor Circuits (2 of 4)

DR-15A: CODE 25, AUTOMATIC IDLE SPEED MOTOR CIRCUITS (3 OF 4)

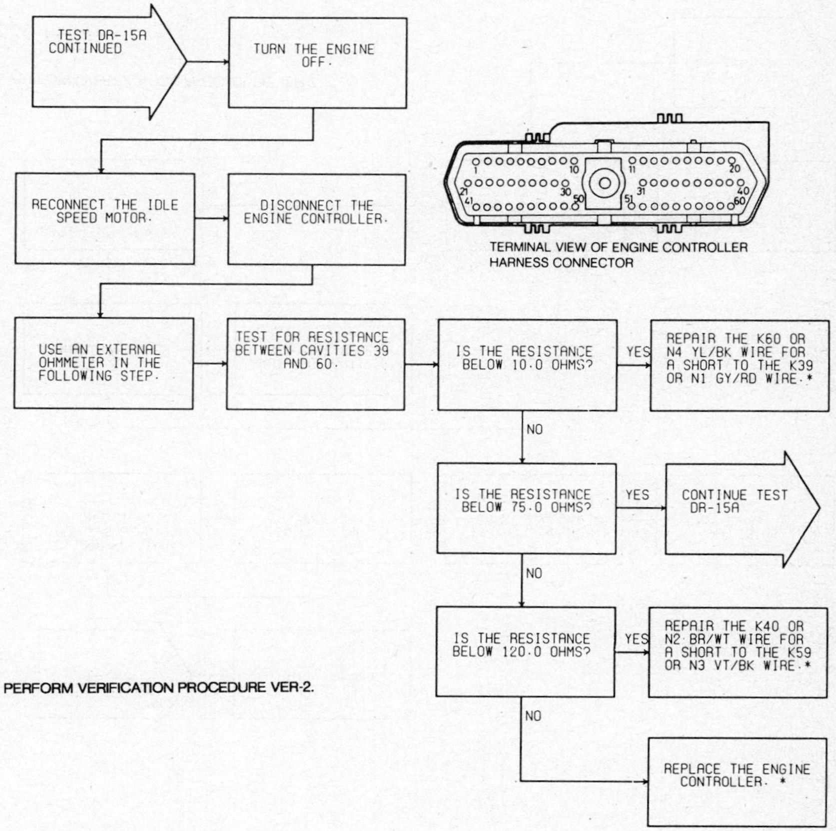
TEST DR-15A CONTINUED
TURN THE ENGINE OFF.
RECONNECT THE IDLE SPEED MOTOR.
DISCONNECT THE ENGINE CONTROLLER.
TERMINAL VIEW OF ENGINE CONTROLLER HARNESS CONNECTOR
1
10
11
20
21
30
31
40
41
50
51
60
USE AN EXTERNAL OHMMETER IN THE FOLLOWING STEP.
TEST FOR RESISTANCE BETWEEN CAVITIES 39 AND 60.
IS THE RESISTANCE BELOW 10.0 OHMS?
YES
REPAIR THE K60 OR N4 YL/BK WIRE FOR A SHORT TO THE K39 OR N1 GY/RD WIRE.*
NO
IS THE RESISTANCE BELOW 75.0 OHMS?
YES
CONTINUE TEST DR-15A
NO
IS THE RESISTANCE BELOW 120.0 OHMS?
YES
REPAIR THE K40 OR N2 BR/WT WIRE FOR A SHORT TO THE K59 OR N3 VT/BK WIRE.*
NO
REPLACE THE ENGINE CONTROLLER. *

* PERFORM VERIFICATION PROCEDURE VER-2.

91I08806

Fig. 78: Driveability Test 15A (2.2L & 2.5L) – Code 25, Automatic Idle Speed Motor Circuits (3 of 4)

DR-15A: CODE 25, AUTOMATIC IDLE SPEED MOTOR CIRCUITS (4 OF 4)

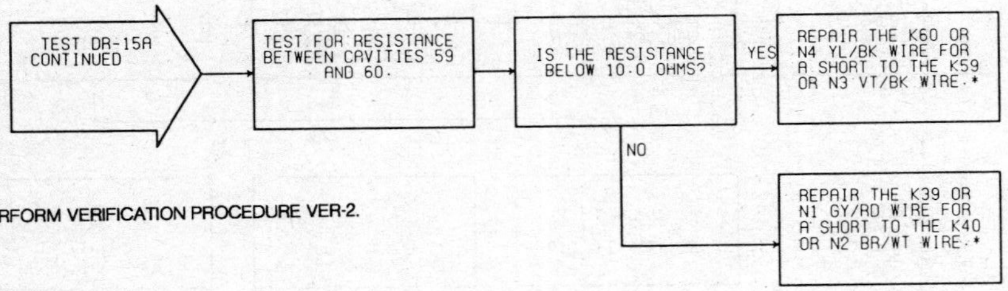
TEST DR-15A CONTINUED
TEST FOR RESISTANCE BETWEEN CAVITIES 59 AND 60.
IS THE RESISTANCE BELOW 10.0 OHMS?
YES
REPAIR THE K60 OR N4 YL/BK WIRE FOR A SHORT TO THE K59 OR N3 VT/BK WIRE.*
NO
REPAIR THE K39 OR N1 GY/RD WIRE FOR A SHORT TO THE K40 OR N2 BR/WT WIRE.*

* PERFORM VERIFICATION PROCEDURE VER-2.

91A08807

Fig. 79: Driveability Test 15A (2.2L & 2.5L) – Code 25, Automatic Idle Speed Motor Circuits (4 of 4)

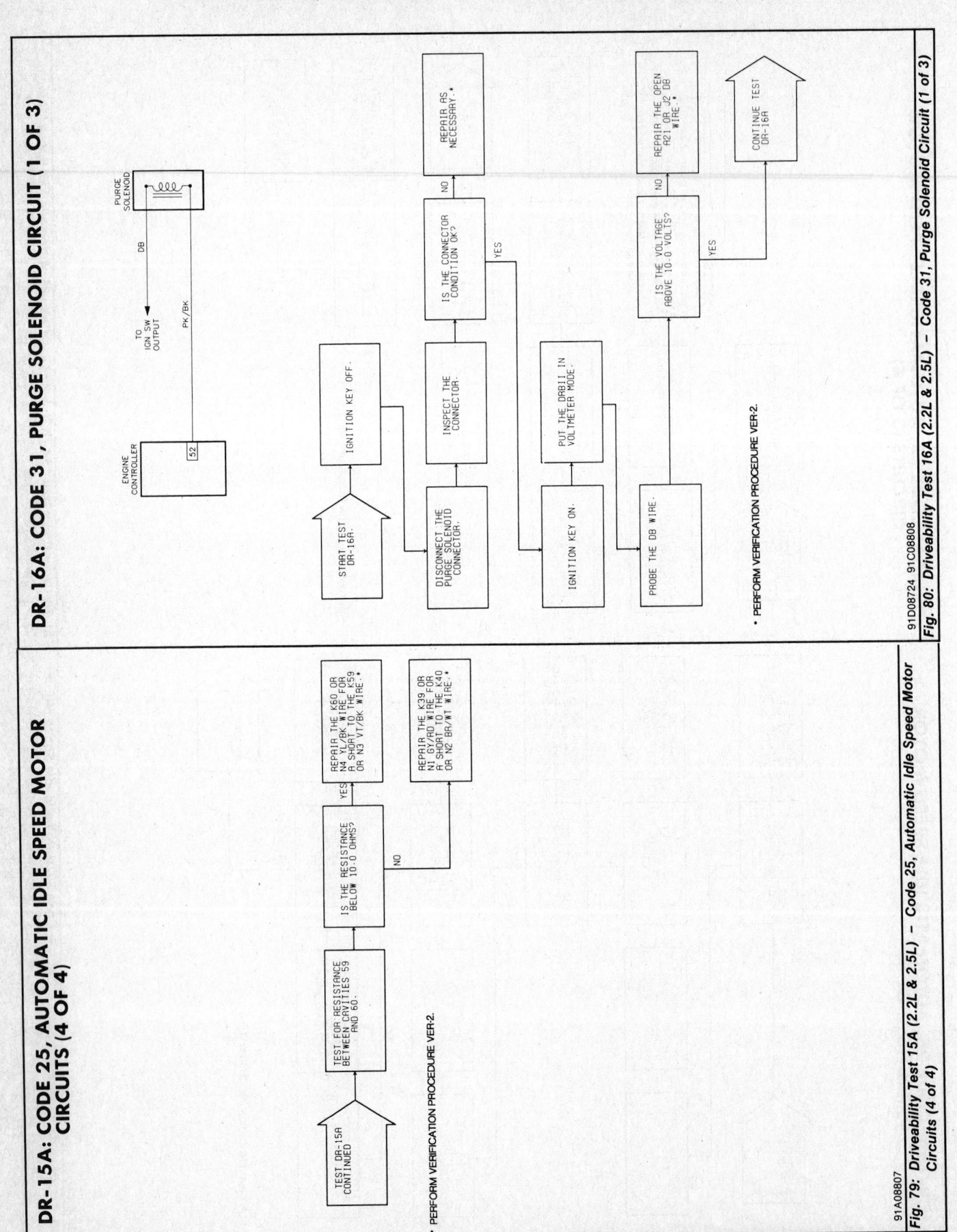

DR-16A: CODE 31, PURGE SOLENOID CIRCUIT (1 OF 3)

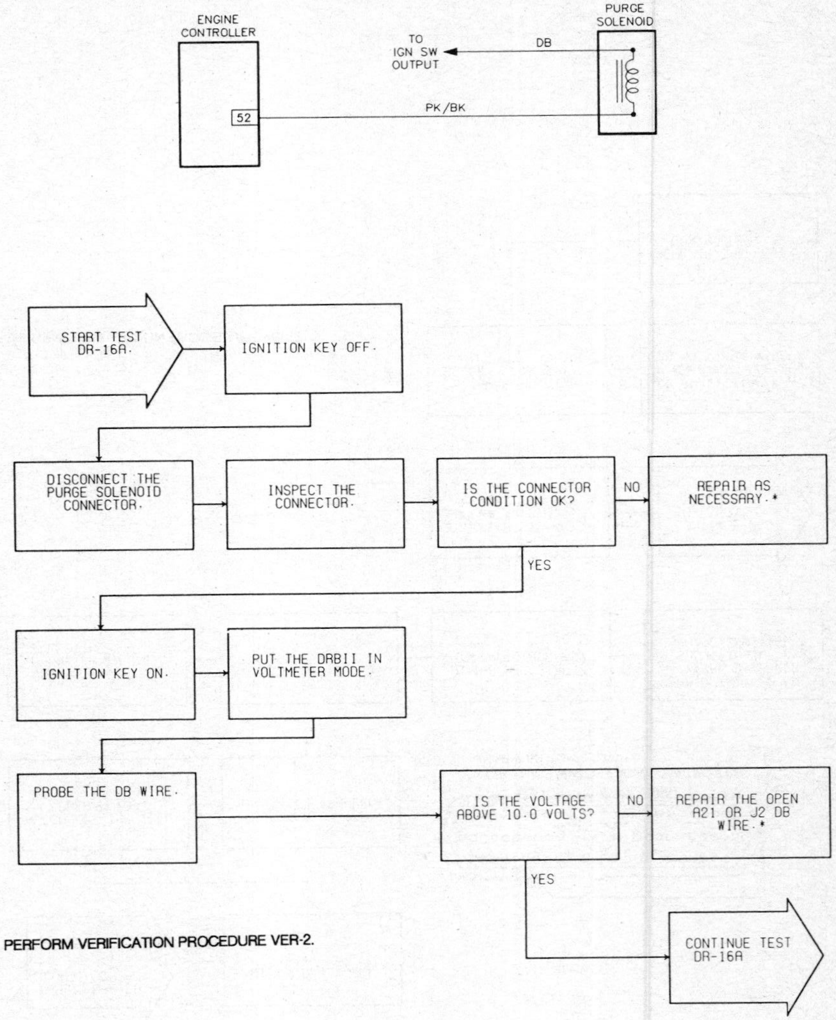
ENGINE CONTROLLER
52
TO IGN SW OUTPUT
DB
PK/BK
PURGE SOLENOID
START TEST DR-16A.
IGNITION KEY OFF.
DISCONNECT THE PURGE SOLENOID CONNECTOR.
INSPECT THE CONNECTOR.
IS THE CONNECTOR CONDITION OK?
NO
REPAIR AS NECESSARY.*
YES
IGNITION KEY ON.
PUT THE DRBII IN VOLTMETER MODE.
PROBE THE DB WIRE.
IS THE VOLTAGE ABOVE 10.0 VOLTS?
NO
REPAIR THE OPEN A21 OR J2 DB WIRE.*
YES
CONTINUE TEST DR-16A

* PERFORM VERIFICATION PROCEDURE VER-2.

91D08724 91C08808

Fig. 80: Driveability Test 16A (2.2L & 2.5L) – Code 31, Purge Solenoid Circuit (1 of 3)

DR-16A: CODE 31, PURGE SOLENOID CIRCUIT (2 OF 3)

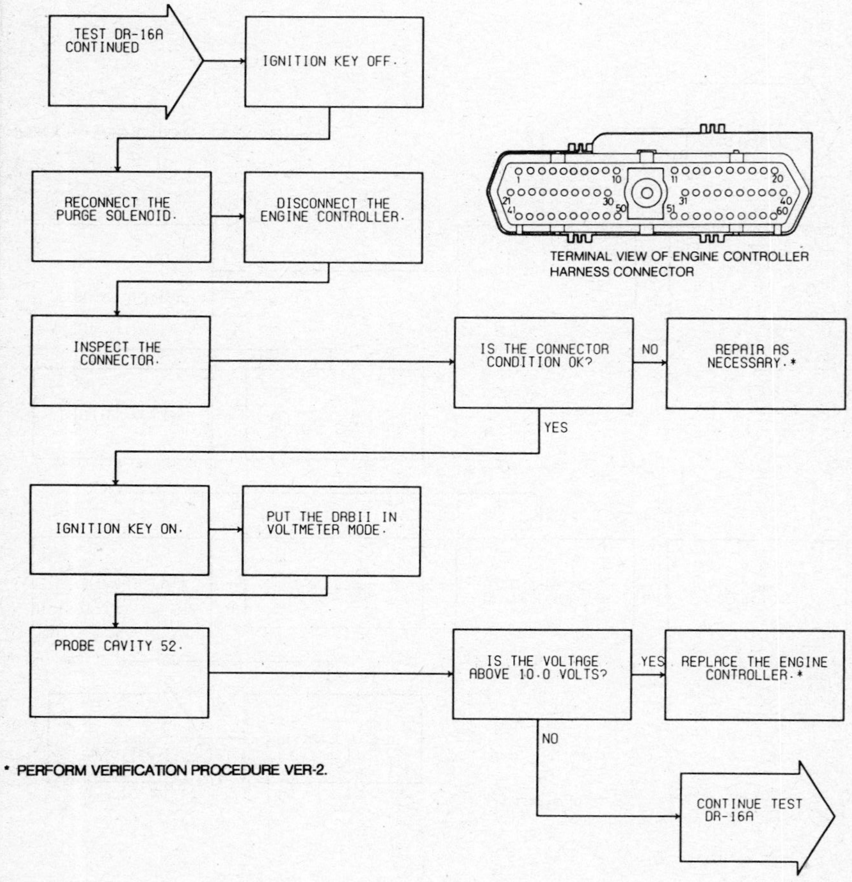
TEST DR-16A CONTINUED
IGNITION KEY OFF.
RECONNECT THE PURGE SOLENOID.
DISCONNECT THE ENGINE CONTROLLER.
INSPECT THE CONNECTOR.
IS THE CONNECTOR CONDITION OK?
NO
REPAIR AS NECESSARY.*
YES
IGNITION KEY ON.
PUT THE DRBII IN VOLTMETER MODE.
PROBE CAVITY 52.
IS THE VOLTAGE ABOVE 10.0 VOLTS?
YES
REPLACE THE ENGINE CONTROLLER.*
NO
CONTINUE TEST DR-16A
TERMINAL VIEW OF ENGINE CONTROLLER HARNESS CONNECTOR

* PERFORM VERIFICATION PROCEDURE VER-2.

91E08809

Fig. 81: Driveability Test 16A (2.2L & 2.5L) – Code 31, Purge Solenoid Circuit (2 of 3)

DR-16A: CODE 31, PURGE SOLENOID CIRCUIT (3 OF 3)

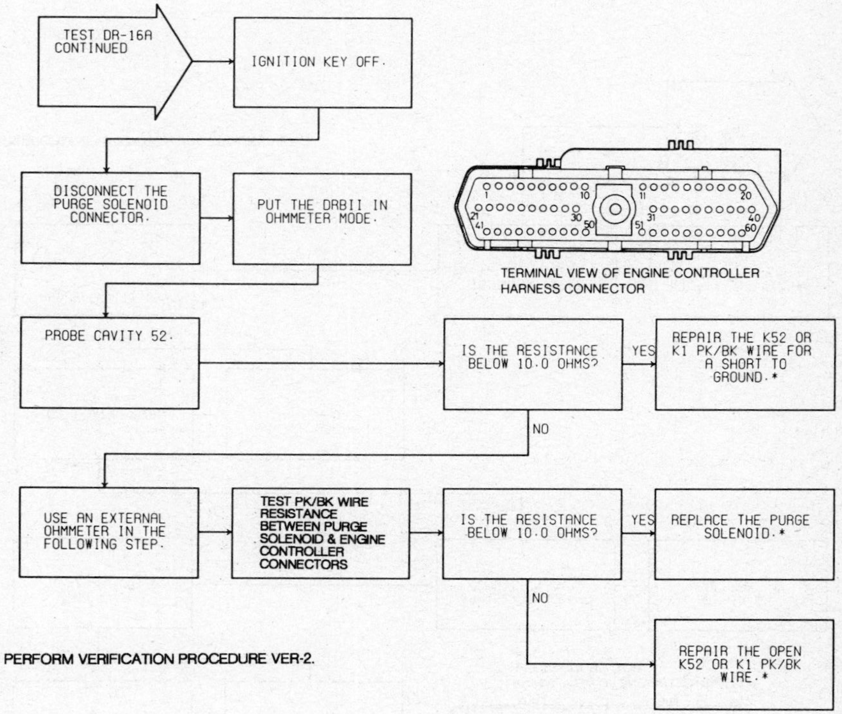
TEST DR-16A CONTINUED
IGNITION KEY OFF.
DISCONNECT THE PURGE SOLENOID CONNECTOR.
PUT THE DRBII IN OHMMETER MODE.
PROBE CAVITY 52.
IS THE RESISTANCE BELOW 10.0 OHMS?
YES
REPAIR THE K52 OR K1 PK/BK WIRE FOR A SHORT TO GROUND.*
NO
USE AN EXTERNAL OHMMETER IN THE FOLLOWING STEP.
TEST PK/BK WIRE RESISTANCE BETWEEN PURGE SOLENOID & ENGINE CONTROLLER CONNECTORS
IS THE RESISTANCE BELOW 10.0 OHMS?
YES
REPLACE THE PURGE SOLENOID.*
NO
REPAIR THE OPEN K52 OR K1 PK/BK WIRE.*
TERMINAL VIEW OF ENGINE CONTROLLER HARNESS CONNECTOR

* PERFORM VERIFICATION PROCEDURE VER-2.

91G08810

Fig. 82: Driveability Test 16A (2.2L & 2.5L) – Code 31, Purge Solenoid Circuit (3 of 3)

1991 ENGINE PERFORMANCE
Self-Diagnostics – 2.5L TBI (Cont.)

DR-17A: CODE 32, EGR SOLENOID CIRCUIT (1 OF 3)

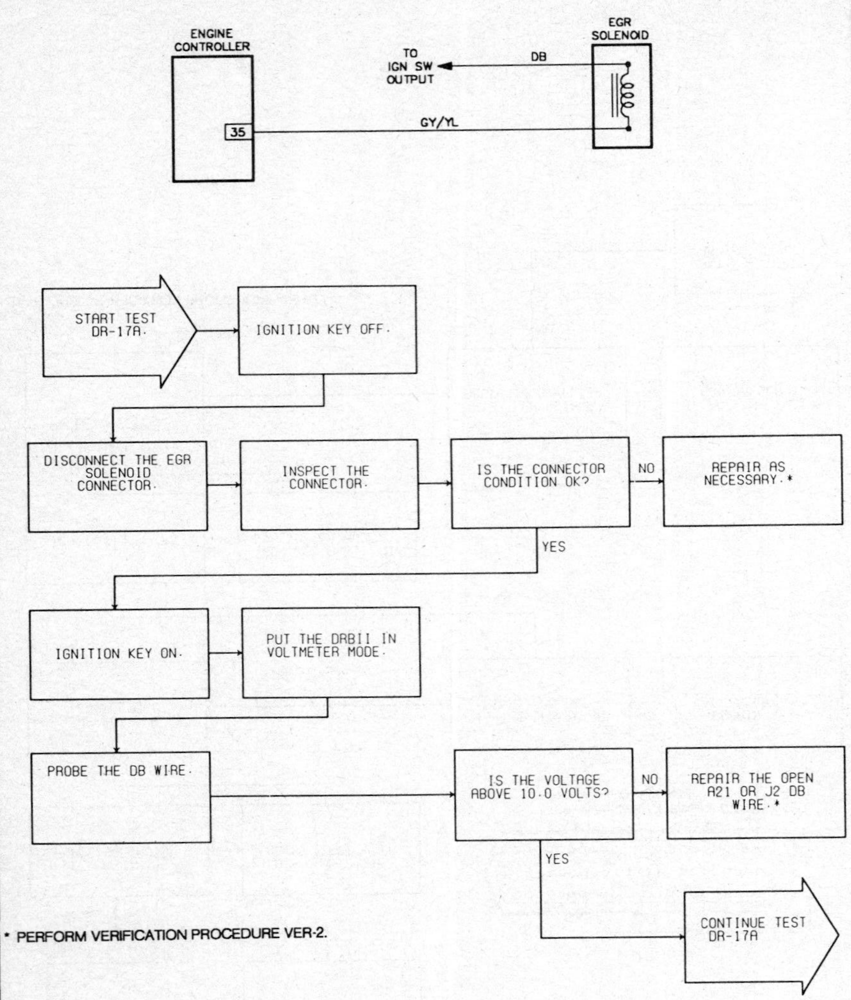
ENGINE CONTROLLER
35
TO IGN SW OUTPUT
DB
GY/YL
EGR SOLENOID
START TEST DR-17A.
IGNITION KEY OFF.
DISCONNECT THE EGR SOLENOID CONNECTOR.
INSPECT THE CONNECTOR.
IS THE CONNECTOR CONDITION OK?
NO
REPAIR AS NECESSARY.*
YES
IGNITION KEY ON.
PUT THE DRBII IN VOLTMETER MODE.
PROBE THE DB WIRE.
IS THE VOLTAGE ABOVE 10.0 VOLTS?
NO
REPAIR THE OPEN A21 OR J2 DB WIRE.*
YES
CONTINUE TEST DR-17A

* PERFORM VERIFICATION PROCEDURE VER-2.

91G08725 91I08811

Fig. 83: Driveability Test 17A (2.2L & 2.5L) – Code 32, EGR Solenoid Circuit (1 of 3)

DR-17A: CODE 32, EGR SOLENOID CIRCUIT (2 OF 3)

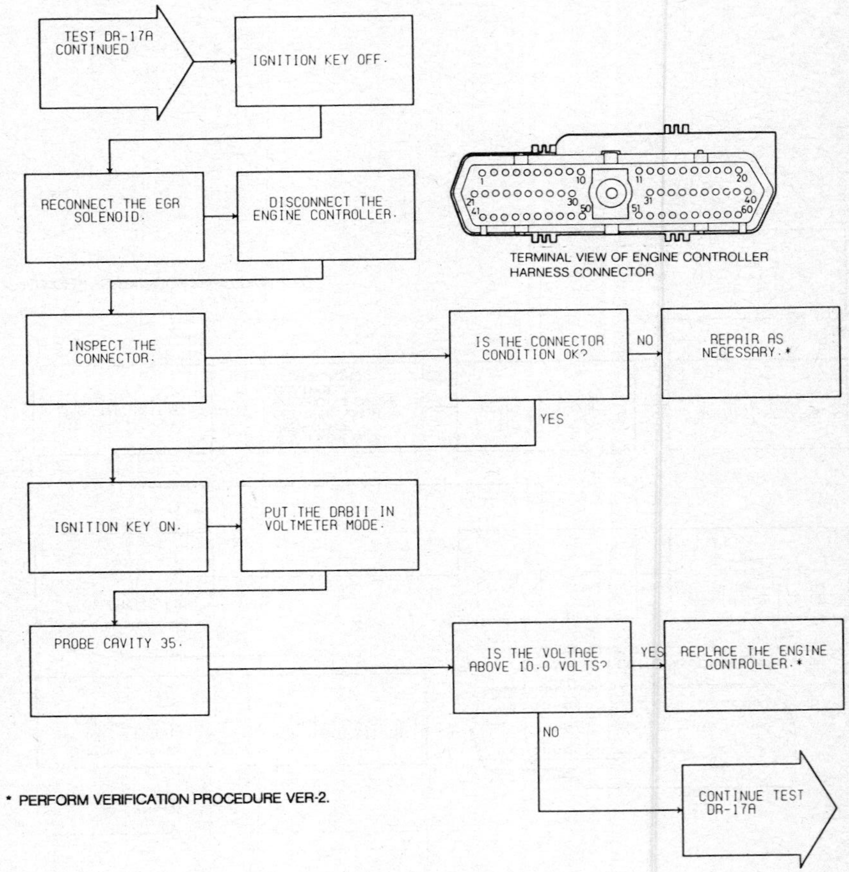
TEST DR-17A CONTINUED
IGNITION KEY OFF.
RECONNECT THE EGR SOLENOID.
DISCONNECT THE ENGINE CONTROLLER.
TERMINAL VIEW OF ENGINE CONTROLLER HARNESS CONNECTOR
INSPECT THE CONNECTOR.
IS THE CONNECTOR CONDITION OK?
NO
REPAIR AS NECESSARY.*
YES
IGNITION KEY ON.
PUT THE DRBII IN VOLTMETER MODE.
PROBE CAVITY 35.
IS THE VOLTAGE ABOVE 10.0 VOLTS?
YES
REPLACE THE ENGINE CONTROLLER.*
NO
CONTINUE TEST DR-17A

* PERFORM VERIFICATION PROCEDURE VER-2.

91A08812

Fig. 84: Driveability Test 17A (2.2L & 2.5L) – Code 32, EGR Solenoid Circuit (2 of 3)

DR-17A: CODE 32, EGR SOLENOID CIRCUIT (3 OF 3)

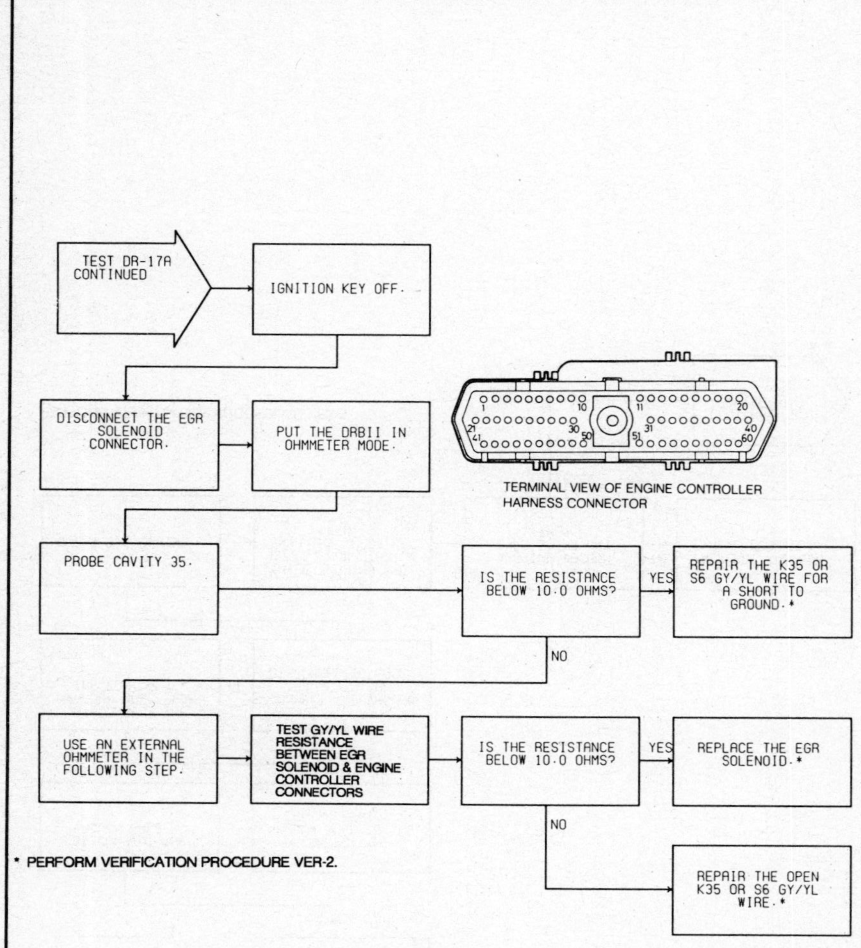
TEST DR-17A CONTINUED
IGNITION KEY OFF.
DISCONNECT THE EGR SOLENOID CONNECTOR.
PUT THE DRBII IN OHMMETER MODE.
TERMINAL VIEW OF ENGINE CONTROLLER HARNESS CONNECTOR
PROBE CAVITY 35.
IS THE RESISTANCE BELOW 10.0 OHMS?
YES
REPAIR THE K35 OR S6 GY/YL WIRE FOR A SHORT TO GROUND.*
NO
USE AN EXTERNAL OHMMETER IN THE FOLLOWING STEP.
TEST GY/YL WIRE RESISTANCE BETWEEN EGR SOLENOID & ENGINE CONTROLLER CONNECTORS
IS THE RESISTANCE BELOW 10.0 OHMS?
YES
REPLACE THE EGR SOLENOID.*
NO
REPAIR THE OPEN K35 OR S6 GY/YL WIRE.*
* PERFORM VERIFICATION PROCEDURE VER-2.

91C08813

Fig. 85: Driveability Test 17A (2.2L & 2.5L) – Code 32, EGR Solenoid Circuit (3 of 3)

DR-18A: CODE 32, EGR SYSTEM FAILURE (1 OF 5)

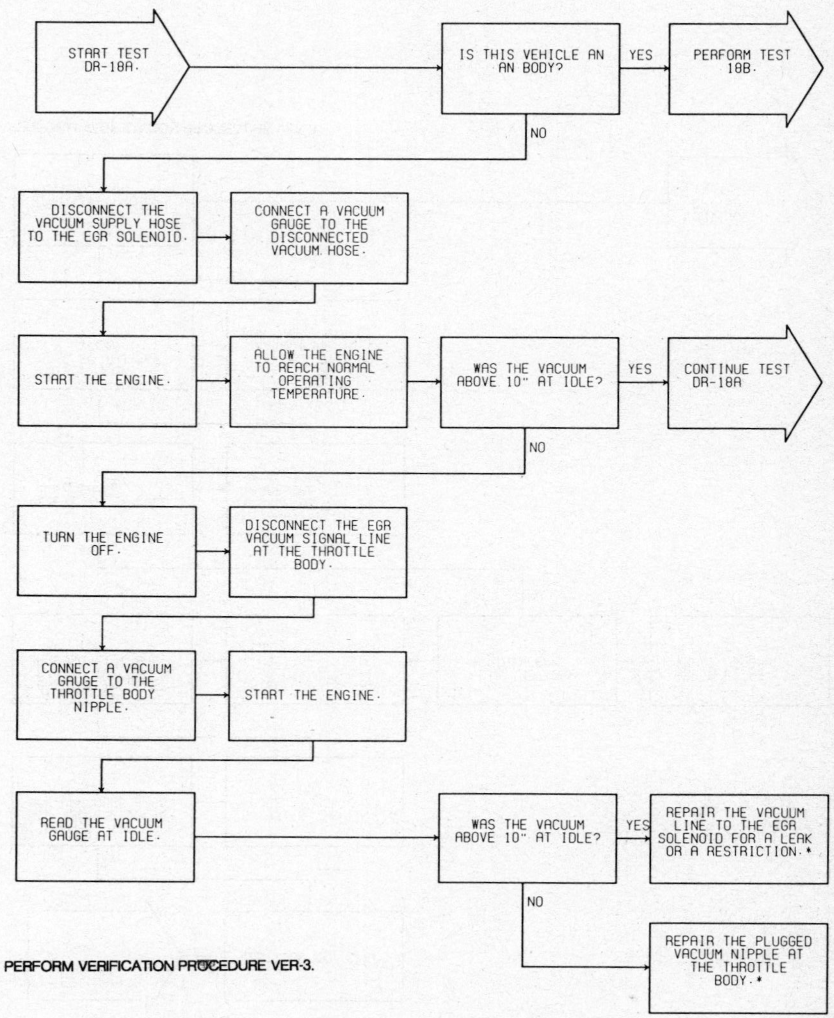
START TEST DR-18A.
IS THIS VEHICLE AN AN BODY?
YES
PERFORM TEST 18B.
NO
DISCONNECT THE VACUUM SUPPLY HOSE TO THE EGR SOLENOID.
CONNECT A VACUUM GAUGE TO THE DISCONNECTED VACUUM HOSE.
START THE ENGINE.
ALLOW THE ENGINE TO REACH NORMAL OPERATING TEMPERATURE.
WAS THE VACUUM ABOVE 10" AT IDLE?
YES
CONTINUE TEST DR-18A
NO
TURN THE ENGINE OFF.
DISCONNECT THE EGR VACUUM SIGNAL LINE AT THE THROTTLE BODY.
CONNECT A VACUUM GAUGE TO THE THROTTLE BODY NIPPLE.
START THE ENGINE.
READ THE VACUUM GAUGE AT IDLE.
WAS THE VACUUM ABOVE 10" AT IDLE?
YES
REPAIR THE VACUUM LINE TO THE EGR SOLENOID FOR A LEAK OR A RESTRICTION.*
NO
REPAIR THE PLUGGED VACUUM NIPPLE AT THE THROTTLE BODY.*
* PERFORM VERIFICATION PROCEDURE VER-3.

91E08814

Fig. 86: Driveability Test 18A (2.2L & 2.5L) – Code 32, EGR System Failure (1 of 5)

1991 ENGINE PERFORMANCE
Self-Diagnostics – 2.5L TBI (Cont.)

DR-18A: CODE 32, EGR SYSTEM FAILURE (2 OF 5)

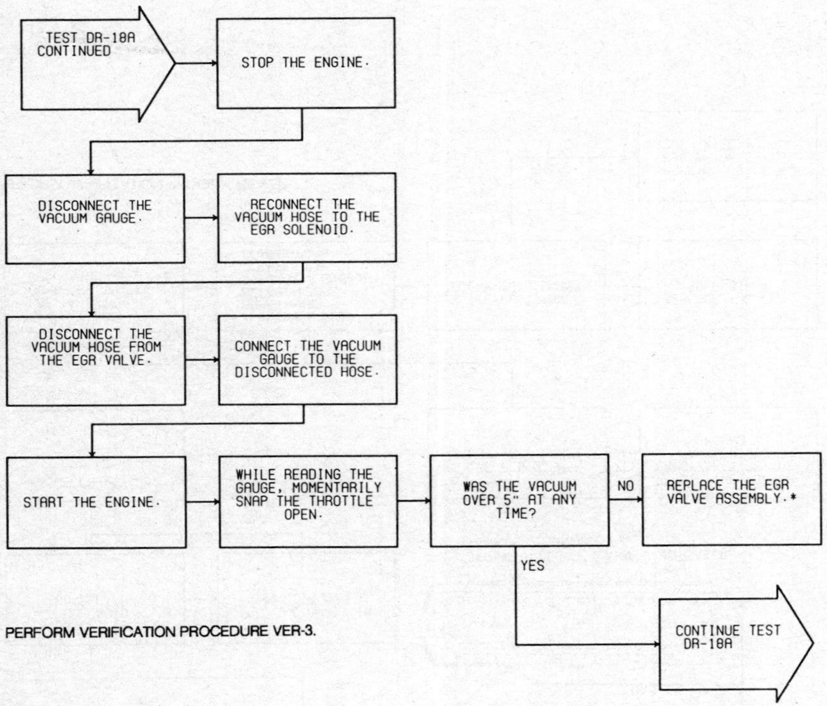
TEST DR-18A CONTINUED
STOP THE ENGINE.
DISCONNECT THE VACUUM GAUGE.
RECONNECT THE VACUUM HOSE TO THE EGR SOLENOID.
DISCONNECT THE VACUUM HOSE FROM THE EGR VALVE.
CONNECT THE VACUUM GAUGE TO THE DISCONNECTED HOSE.
START THE ENGINE.
WHILE READING THE GAUGE, MOMENTARILY SNAP THE THROTTLE OPEN.
WAS THE VACUUM OVER 5" AT ANY TIME?
NO
REPLACE THE EGR VALVE ASSEMBLY.*
YES
CONTINUE TEST DR-18A

* PERFORM VERIFICATION PROCEDURE VER-3.

91H08815

Fig. 87: Driveability Test 18A (2.2L & 2.5L) – Code 32, EGR System Failure (2 of 5)

DR-18A: CODE 32, EGR SYSTEM FAILURE (3 OF 5)

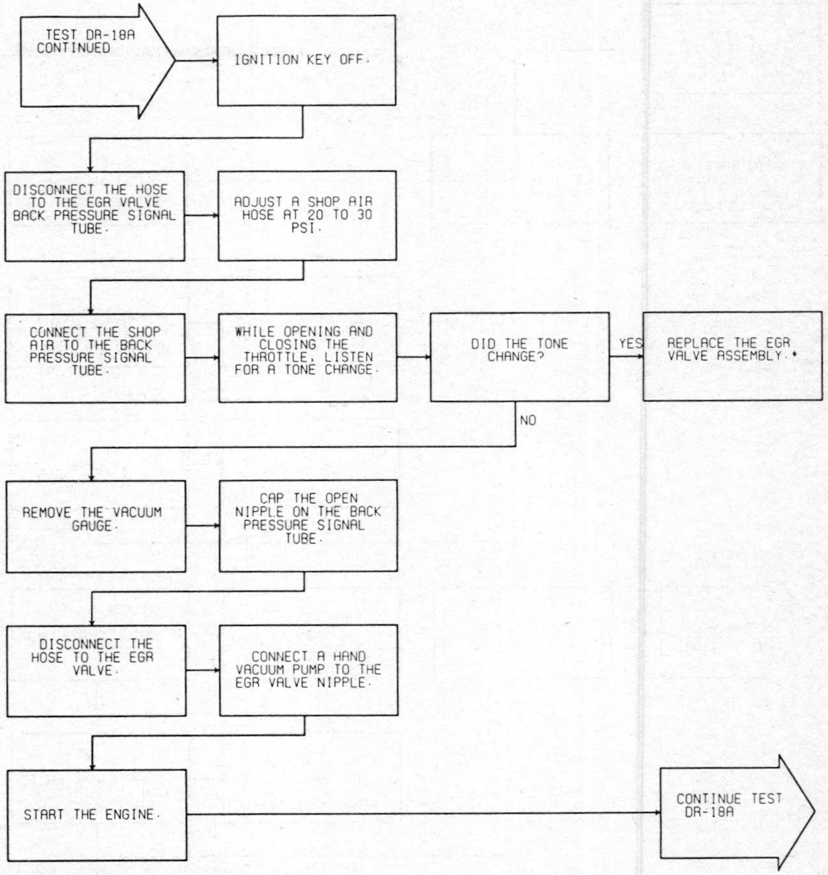
TEST DR-18A CONTINUED
IGNITION KEY OFF.
DISCONNECT THE HOSE TO THE EGR VALVE BACK PRESSURE SIGNAL TUBE.
ADJUST A SHOP AIR HOSE AT 20 TO 30 PSI.
CONNECT THE SHOP AIR TO THE BACK PRESSURE SIGNAL TUBE.
WHILE OPENING AND CLOSING THE THROTTLE, LISTEN FOR A TONE CHANGE.
DID THE TONE CHANGE?
YES
REPLACE THE EGR VALVE ASSEMBLY.*
NO
REMOVE THE VACUUM GAUGE.
CAP THE OPEN NIPPLE ON THE BACK PRESSURE SIGNAL TUBE.
DISCONNECT THE HOSE TO THE EGR VALVE.
CONNECT A HAND VACUUM PUMP TO THE EGR VALVE NIPPLE.
START THE ENGINE.
CONTINUE TEST DR-18A

* PERFORM VERIFICATION PROCEDURE VER-3.

91J08816

Fig. 88: Driveability Test 18A (2.2L & 2.5L) – Code 32, EGR System Failure (3 of 5)

DR-18A: CODE 32, EGR SYSTEM FAILURE (4 OF 5)

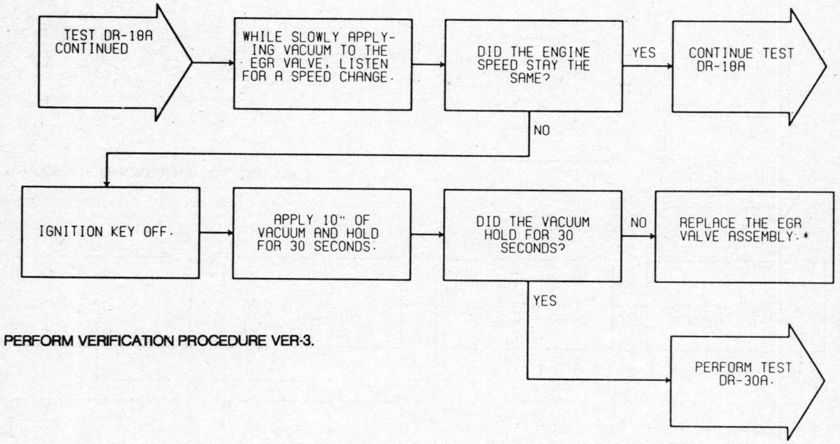
TEST DR-18A CONTINUED
WHILE SLOWLY APPLYING VACUUM TO THE EGR VALVE, LISTEN FOR A SPEED CHANGE.
DID THE ENGINE SPEED STAY THE SAME?
YES
CONTINUE TEST DR-18A
NO
IGNITION KEY OFF.
APPLY 10" OF VACUUM AND HOLD FOR 30 SECONDS.
DID THE VACUUM HOLD FOR 30 SECONDS?
NO
REPLACE THE EGR VALVE ASSEMBLY.*
YES
PERFORM TEST DR-30A.

* PERFORM VERIFICATION PROCEDURE VER-3.

91B08817

Fig. 89: Driveability Test 18A (2.2L & 2.5L) – Code 32, EGR System Failure (4 of 5)

DR-18A: CODE 32, EGR SYSTEM FAILURE (5 OF 5)

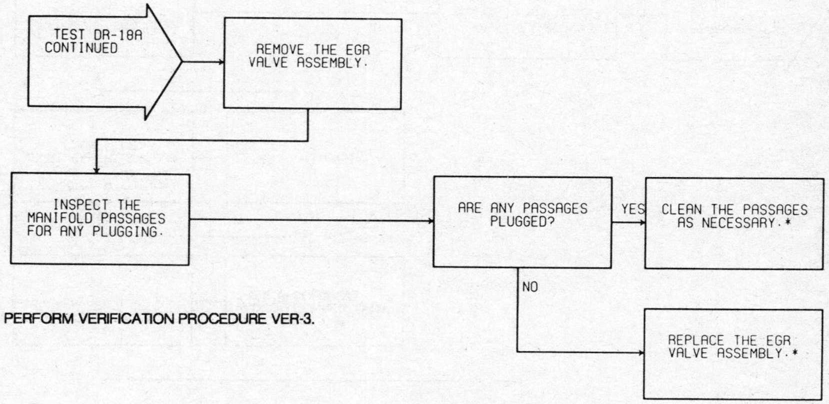
TEST DR-18A CONTINUED
REMOVE THE EGR VALVE ASSEMBLY.
INSPECT THE MANIFOLD PASSAGES FOR ANY PLUGGING.
ARE ANY PASSAGES PLUGGED?
YES
CLEAN THE PASSAGES AS NECESSARY.*
NO
REPLACE THE EGR VALVE ASSEMBLY.*

* PERFORM VERIFICATION PROCEDURE VER-3.

91D08818

Fig. 90: Driveability Test 18A (2.2L & 2.5L) – Code 32, EGR System Failure (5 of 5)

1991 ENGINE PERFORMANCE
Self-Diagnostics – 2.5L TBI (Cont.)

DR-18B: CODE 32, EGR SYSTEM FAILURE (1 OF 5)

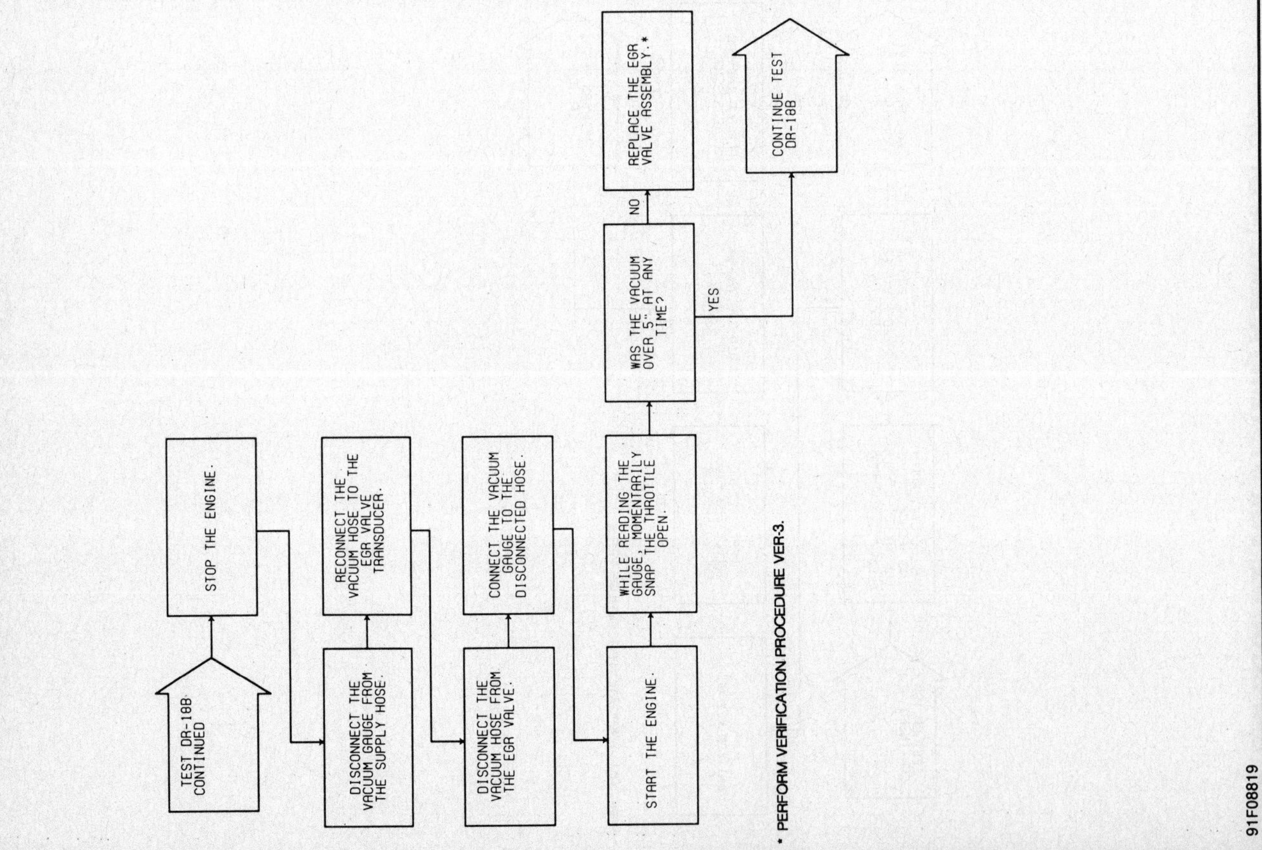
TEST DR-18B CONTINUED
STOP THE ENGINE.
DISCONNECT THE VACUUM GAUGE FROM THE SUPPLY HOSE.
RECONNECT THE VACUUM HOSE TO THE EGR VALVE TRANSDUCER.
DISCONNECT THE VACUUM HOSE FROM THE EGR VALVE.
CONNECT THE VACUUM GAUGE TO THE DISCONNECTED HOSE.
START THE ENGINE.
WHILE READING THE GAUGE, MOMENTARILY SNAP THE THROTTLE OPEN.
WAS THE VACUUM OVER 5" AT ANY TIME?
NO
REPLACE THE EGR VALVE ASSEMBLY.*
YES
CONTINUE TEST DR-18B
* PERFORM VERIFICATION PROCEDURE VER-3.
91F08819

Fig. 91: Driveability Test 18B (2.2L & 2.5L) – Code 32, EGR System Failure (1 of 5)

DR-18B: CODE 32, EGR SYSTEM FAILURE (2 OF 5)

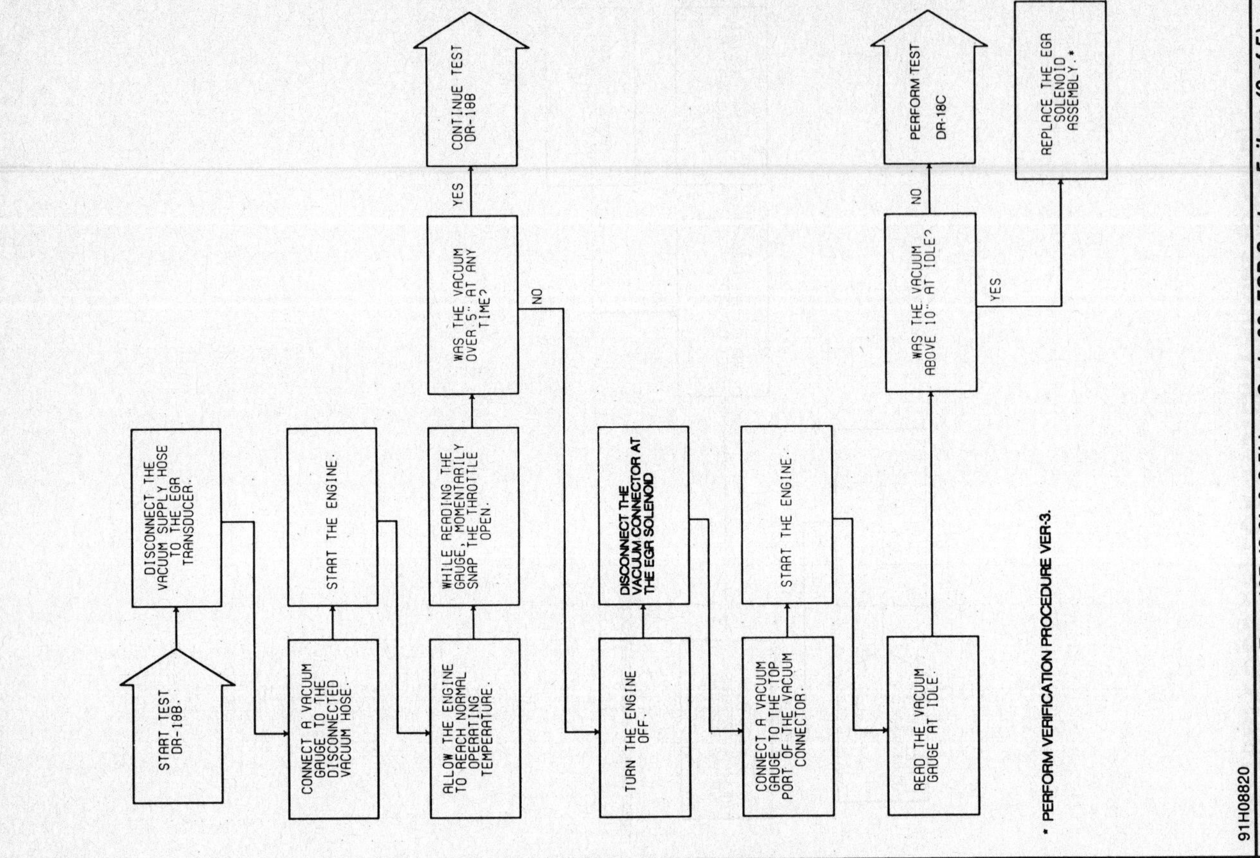
START TEST DR-18B.
DISCONNECT THE VACUUM SUPPLY HOSE TO THE EGR TRANSDUCER.
CONNECT A VACUUM GAUGE TO THE DISCONNECTED VACUUM HOSE.
START THE ENGINE.
ALLOW THE ENGINE TO REACH NORMAL OPERATING TEMPERATURE.
WHILE READING THE GAUGE, MOMENTARILY SNAP THE THROTTLE OPEN.
WAS THE VACUUM OVER 5" AT ANY TIME?
YES
CONTINUE TEST DR-18B
NO
TURN THE ENGINE OFF.
DISCONNECT THE VACUUM CONNECTOR AT THE EGR SOLENOID
CONNECT A VACUUM GAUGE TO THE TOP PORT OF THE VACUUM CONNECTOR.
START THE ENGINE.
READ THE VACUUM GAUGE AT IDLE.
WAS THE VACUUM ABOVE 10" AT IDLE?
NO
PERFORM TEST DR-18C
YES
REPLACE THE EGR SOLENOID ASSEMBLY.*
* PERFORM VERIFICATION PROCEDURE VER-3.
91H08820

Fig. 92: Driveability Test 18B (2.2L & 2.5L) – Code 32, EGR System Failure (2 of 5)

DR-18B: CODE 32, EGR SYSTEM FAILURE (3 OF 5)

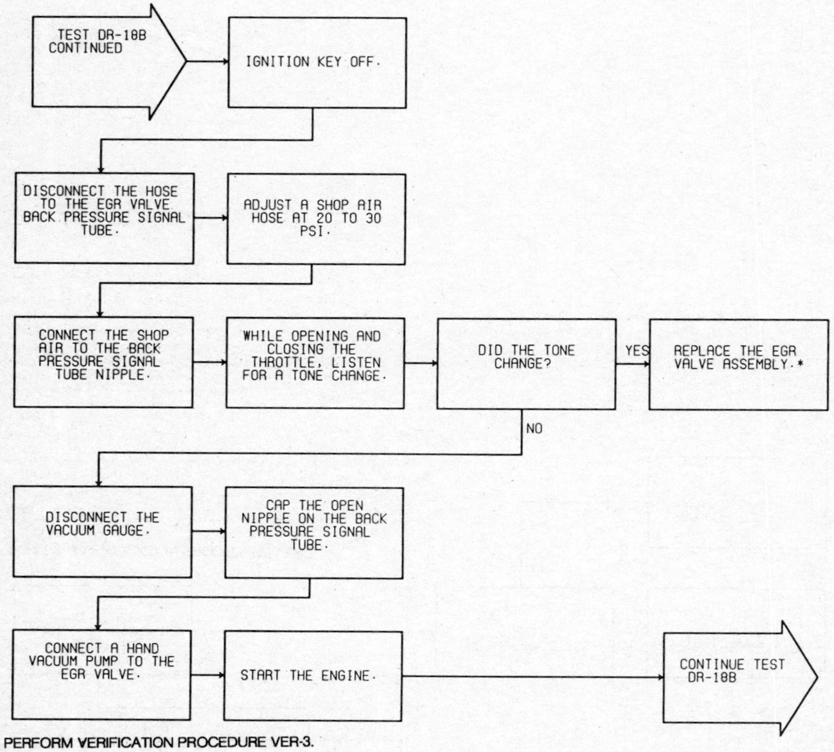
TEST DR-18B CONTINUED
IGNITION KEY OFF.
DISCONNECT THE HOSE TO THE EGR VALVE BACK PRESSURE SIGNAL TUBE.
ADJUST A SHOP AIR HOSE AT 20 TO 30 PSI.
CONNECT THE SHOP AIR TO THE BACK PRESSURE SIGNAL TUBE NIPPLE.
WHILE OPENING AND CLOSING THE THROTTLE, LISTEN FOR A TONE CHANGE.
DID THE TONE CHANGE?
YES
REPLACE THE EGR VALVE ASSEMBLY.*
NO
DISCONNECT THE VACUUM GAUGE.
CAP THE OPEN NIPPLE ON THE BACK PRESSURE SIGNAL TUBE.
CONNECT A HAND VACUUM PUMP TO THE EGR VALVE.
START THE ENGINE.
CONTINUE TEST DR-18B

* PERFORM VERIFICATION PROCEDURE VER-3.

91J08821

Fig. 93: Driveability Test 18B (2.2L & 2.5L) – Code 32, EGR System Failure (3 of 5)

DR-18B: CODE 32, EGR SYSTEM FAILURE (4 OF 5)

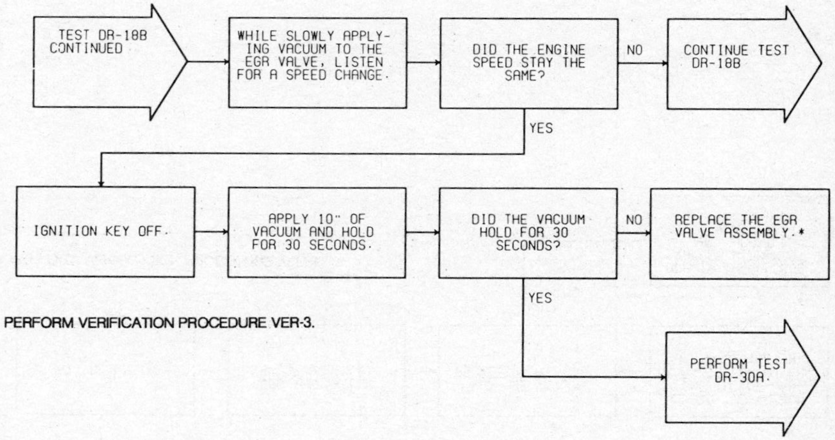
TEST DR-18B CONTINUED
WHILE SLOWLY APPLYING VACUUM TO THE EGR VALVE, LISTEN FOR A SPEED CHANGE.
DID THE ENGINE SPEED STAY THE SAME?
NO
CONTINUE TEST DR-18B
YES
IGNITION KEY OFF.
APPLY 10" OF VACUUM AND HOLD FOR 30 SECONDS.
DID THE VACUUM HOLD FOR 30 SECONDS?
NO
REPLACE THE EGR VALVE ASSEMBLY.*
YES
PERFORM TEST DR-30A.

* PERFORM VERIFICATION PROCEDURE VER-3.

91B08822

Fig. 94: Driveability Test 18B (2.2L & 2.5L) – Code 32, EGR System Failure (4 of 5)

1991 ENGINE PERFORMANCE
Self-Diagnostics – 2.5L TBI (Cont.)

DR-18B: CODE 32, EGR SYSTEM FAILURE (5 OF 5)

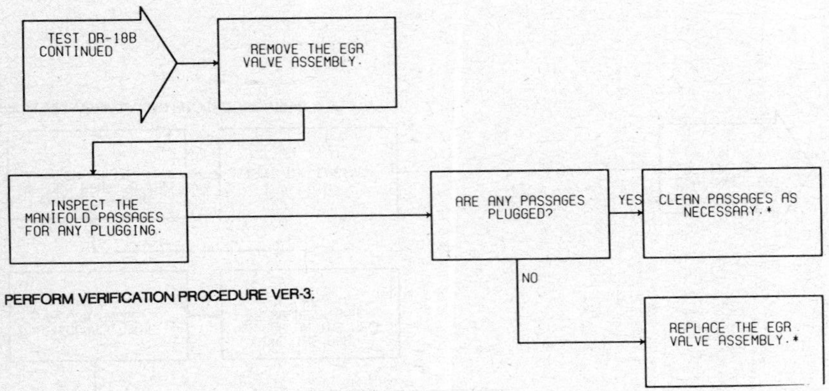
TEST DR-18B CONTINUED
REMOVE THE EGR VALVE ASSEMBLY.
INSPECT THE MANIFOLD PASSAGES FOR ANY PLUGGING.
ARE ANY PASSAGES PLUGGED?
YES
CLEAN PASSAGES AS NECESSARY.*
NO
REPLACE THE EGR VALVE ASSEMBLY.*

* PERFORM VERIFICATION PROCEDURE VER-3.

91D08823

Fig. 95: Driveability Test 18B (2.2L & 2.5L) – Code 32, EGR System Failure (5 of 5)

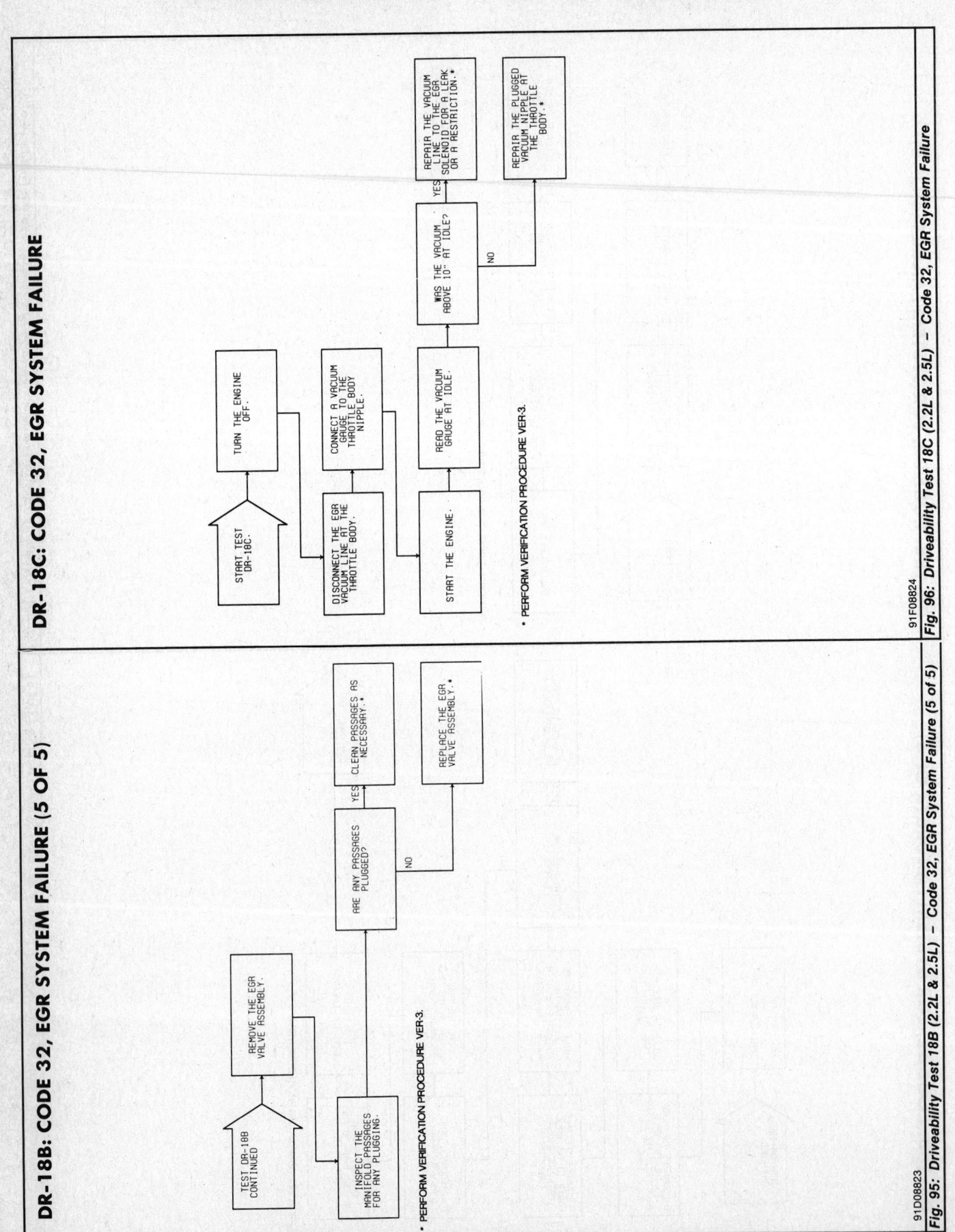

DR-18C: CODE 32, EGR SYSTEM FAILURE

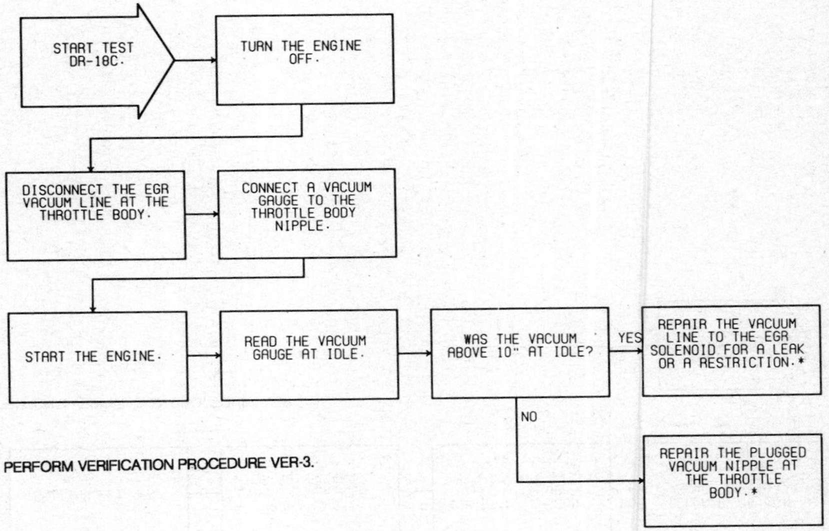
START TEST DR-18C.
TURN THE ENGINE OFF.
DISCONNECT THE EGR VACUUM LINE AT THE THROTTLE BODY.
CONNECT A VACUUM GAUGE TO THE THROTTLE BODY NIPPLE.
START THE ENGINE.
READ THE VACUUM GAUGE AT IDLE.
WAS THE VACUUM ABOVE 10" AT IDLE?
YES
REPAIR THE VACUUM LINE TO THE EGR SOLENOID FOR A LEAK OR A RESTRICTION.*
NO
REPAIR THE PLUGGED VACUUM NIPPLE AT THE THROTTLE BODY.*

* PERFORM VERIFICATION PROCEDURE VER-3.

91F08824

Fig. 96: Driveability Test 18C (2.2L & 2.5L) – Code 32, EGR System Failure

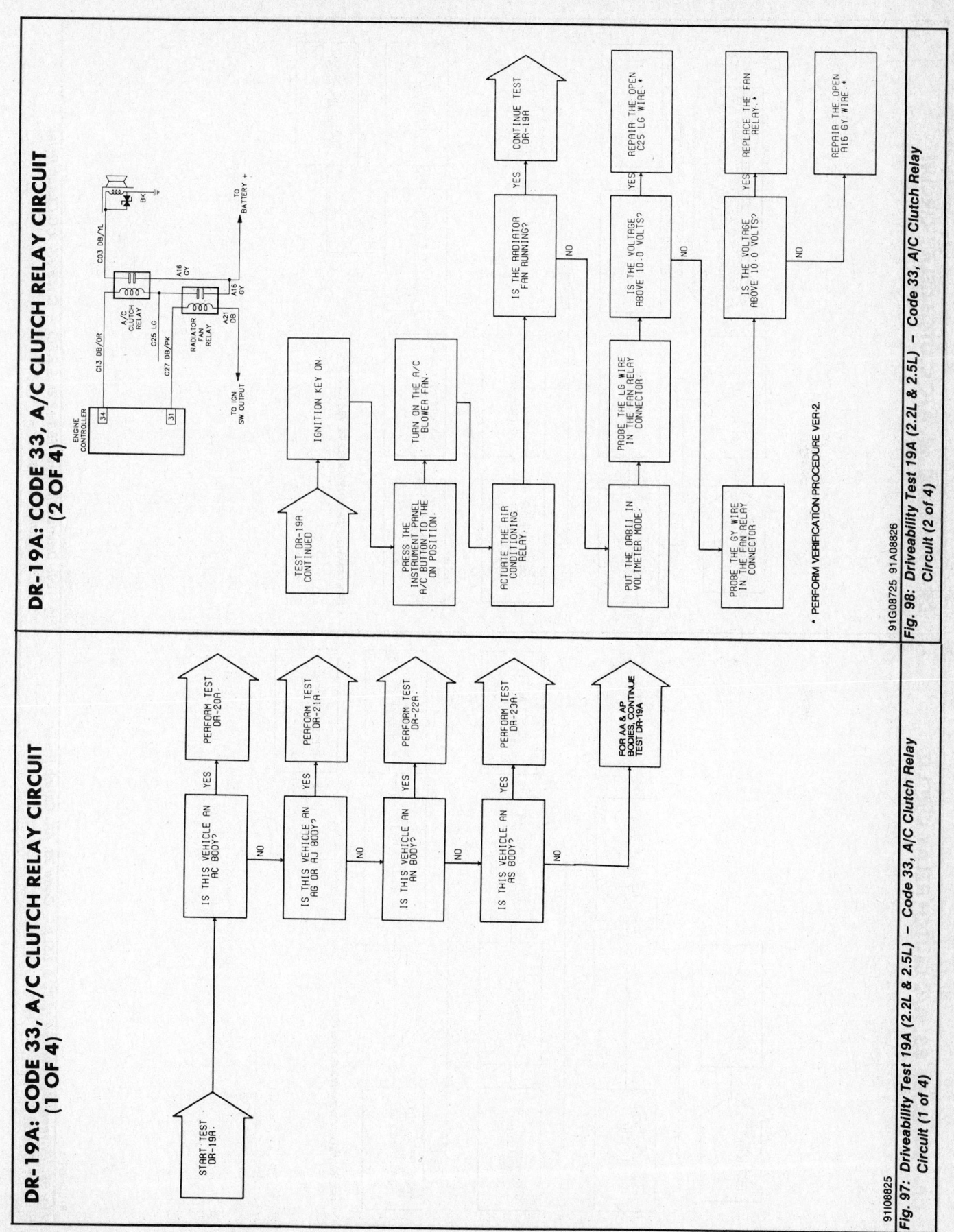

DR-19A: CODE 33, A/C CLUTCH RELAY CIRCUIT (1 OF 4)

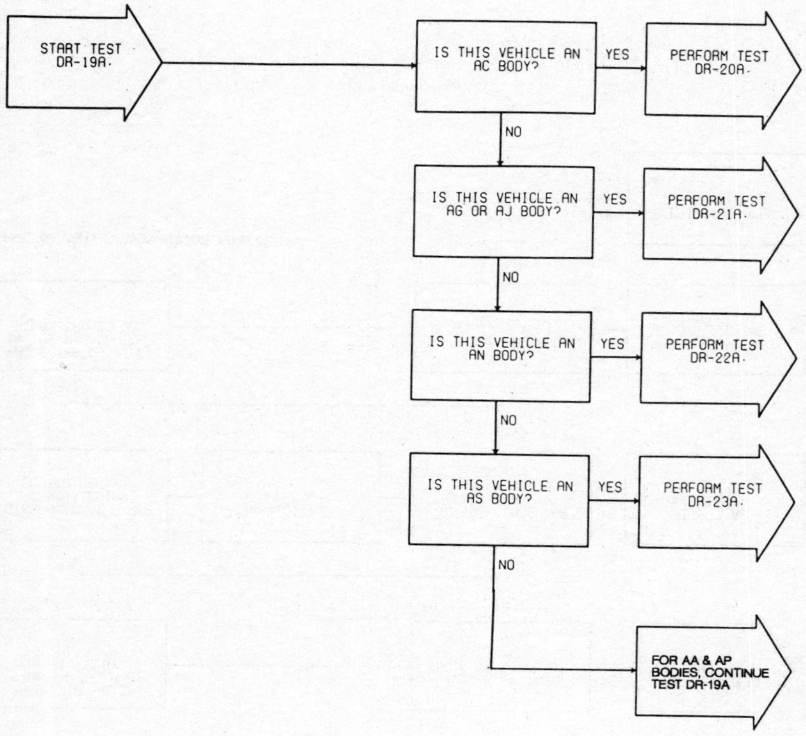
START TEST DR-19A.
IS THIS VEHICLE AN AC BODY?
YES
PERFORM TEST DR-20A.
NO
IS THIS VEHICLE AN AG OR AJ BODY?
YES
PERFORM TEST DR-21A.
NO
IS THIS VEHICLE AN AN BODY?
YES
PERFORM TEST DR-22A.
NO
IS THIS VEHICLE AN AS BODY?
YES
PERFORM TEST DR-23A.
NO
FOR AA & AP BODIES, CONTINUE TEST DR-19A

91I08825

Fig. 97: Driveability Test 19A (2.2L & 2.5L) – Code 33, A/C Clutch Relay Circuit (1 of 4)

DR-19A: CODE 33, A/C CLUTCH RELAY CIRCUIT (2 OF 4)

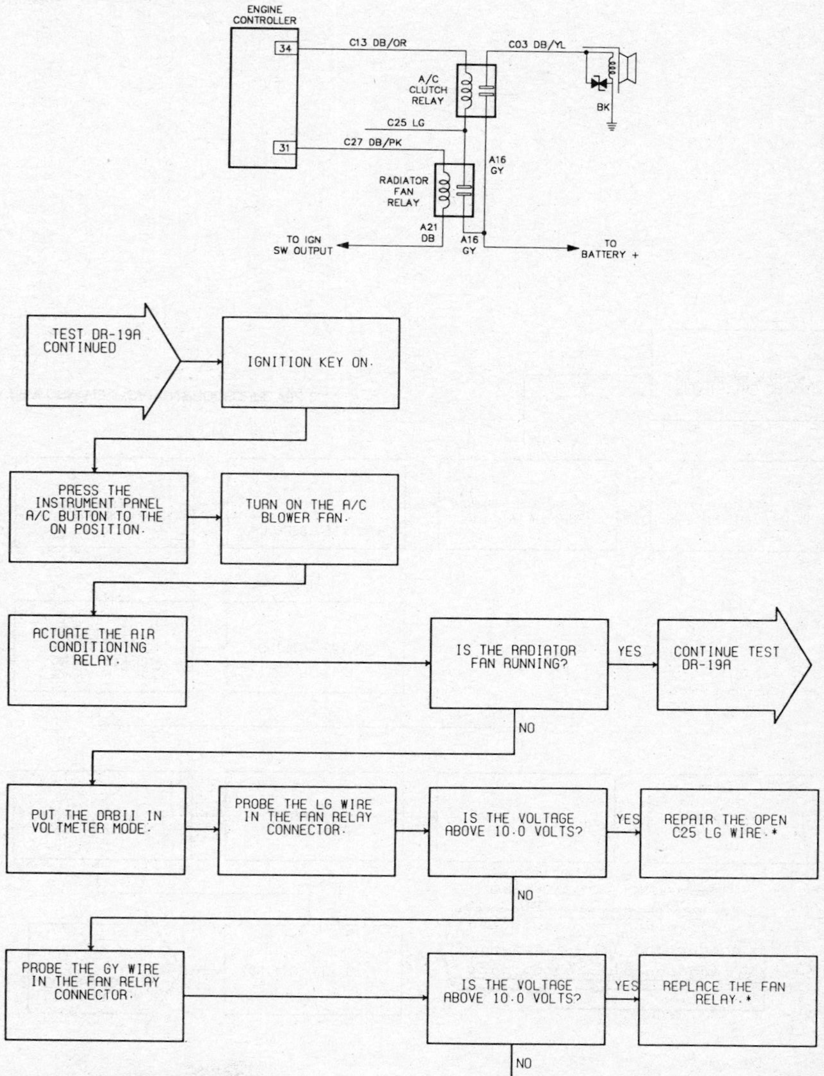
ENGINE CONTROLLER
34
31
C13 DB/OR
C03 DB/YL
A/C CLUTCH RELAY
BK
C25 LG
C27 DB/PK
A16 GY
RADIATOR FAN RELAY
A21 DB
A16 GY
TO IGN SW OUTPUT
TO BATTERY +
TEST DR-19A CONTINUED
IGNITION KEY ON.
PRESS THE INSTRUMENT PANEL A/C BUTTON TO THE ON POSITION.
TURN ON THE A/C BLOWER FAN.
ACTUATE THE AIR CONDITIONING RELAY.
IS THE RADIATOR FAN RUNNING?
YES
CONTINUE TEST DR-19A
NO
PUT THE DRBII IN VOLTMETER MODE.
PROBE THE LG WIRE IN THE FAN RELAY CONNECTOR.
IS THE VOLTAGE ABOVE 10.0 VOLTS?
YES
REPAIR THE OPEN C25 LG WIRE.*
NO
PROBE THE GY WIRE IN THE FAN RELAY CONNECTOR.
IS THE VOLTAGE ABOVE 10.0 VOLTS?
YES
REPLACE THE FAN RELAY.*
NO
REPAIR THE OPEN A16 GY WIRE.*

* PERFORM VERIFICATION PROCEDURE VER-2.

91G08725 91A08826

Fig. 98: Driveability Test 19A (2.2L & 2.5L) – Code 33, A/C Clutch Relay Circuit (2 of 4)

1991 ENGINE PERFORMANCE
Self-Diagnostics – 2.5L TBI (Cont.)

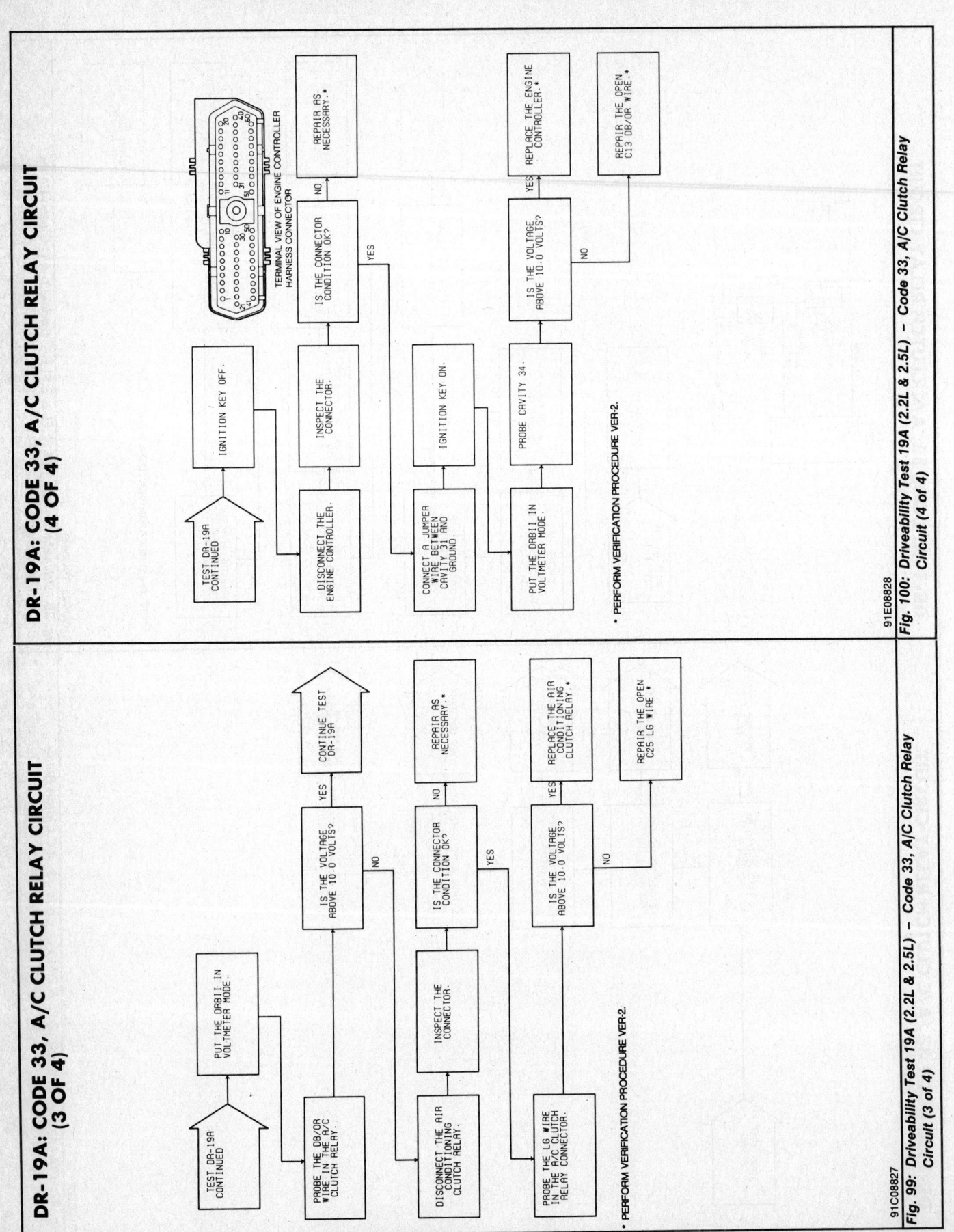

DR-19A: CODE 33, A/C CLUTCH RELAY CIRCUIT (3 OF 4)

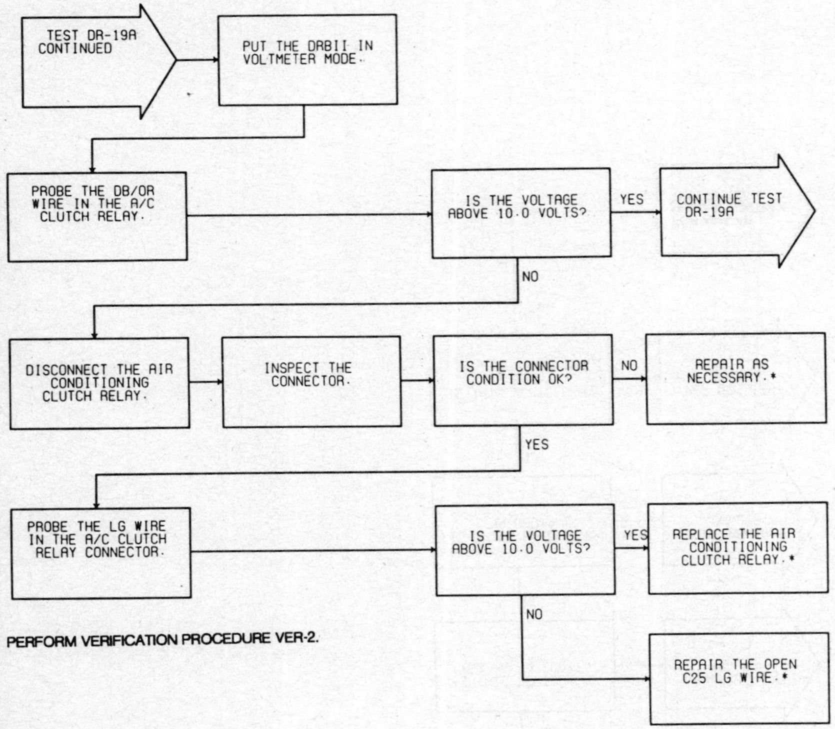
TEST DR-19A CONTINUED
PUT THE DRBII IN VOLTMETER MODE.
PROBE THE DB/OR WIRE IN THE A/C CLUTCH RELAY.
IS THE VOLTAGE ABOVE 10.0 VOLTS?
YES
CONTINUE TEST DR-19A
NO
DISCONNECT THE AIR CONDITIONING CLUTCH RELAY.
INSPECT THE CONNECTOR.
IS THE CONNECTOR CONDITION OK?
NO
REPAIR AS NECESSARY.*
YES
PROBE THE LG WIRE IN THE A/C CLUTCH RELAY CONNECTOR.
IS THE VOLTAGE ABOVE 10.0 VOLTS?
YES
REPLACE THE AIR CONDITIONING CLUTCH RELAY.*
NO
REPAIR THE OPEN C25 LG WIRE.*

* PERFORM VERIFICATION PROCEDURE VER-2.

91C08827

Fig. 99: Driveability Test 19A (2.2L & 2.5L) – Code 33, A/C Clutch Relay Circuit (3 of 4)

DR-19A: CODE 33, A/C CLUTCH RELAY CIRCUIT (4 OF 4)

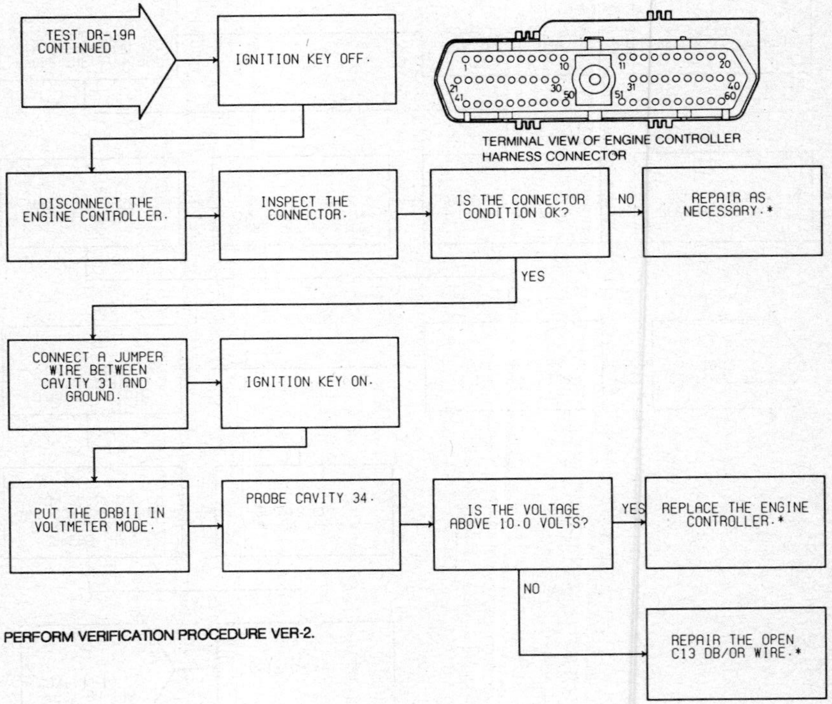
TEST DR-19A CONTINUED
IGNITION KEY OFF.
TERMINAL VIEW OF ENGINE CONTROLLER HARNESS CONNECTOR
1
10
11
20
21
30
31
40
41
50
51
60
DISCONNECT THE ENGINE CONTROLLER.
INSPECT THE CONNECTOR.
IS THE CONNECTOR CONDITION OK?
NO
REPAIR AS NECESSARY.*
YES
CONNECT A JUMPER WIRE BETWEEN CAVITY 31 AND GROUND.
IGNITION KEY ON.
PUT THE DRBII IN VOLTMETER MODE.
PROBE CAVITY 34.
IS THE VOLTAGE ABOVE 10.0 VOLTS?
YES
REPLACE THE ENGINE CONTROLLER.*
NO
REPAIR THE OPEN C13 DB/OR WIRE.*

* PERFORM VERIFICATION PROCEDURE VER-2.

91E08828

Fig. 100: Driveability Test 19A (2.2L & 2.5L) – Code 33, A/C Clutch Relay Circuit (4 of 4)

DR-20A: CODE 33, A/C CLUTCH RELAY CIRCUIT (1 OF 2)

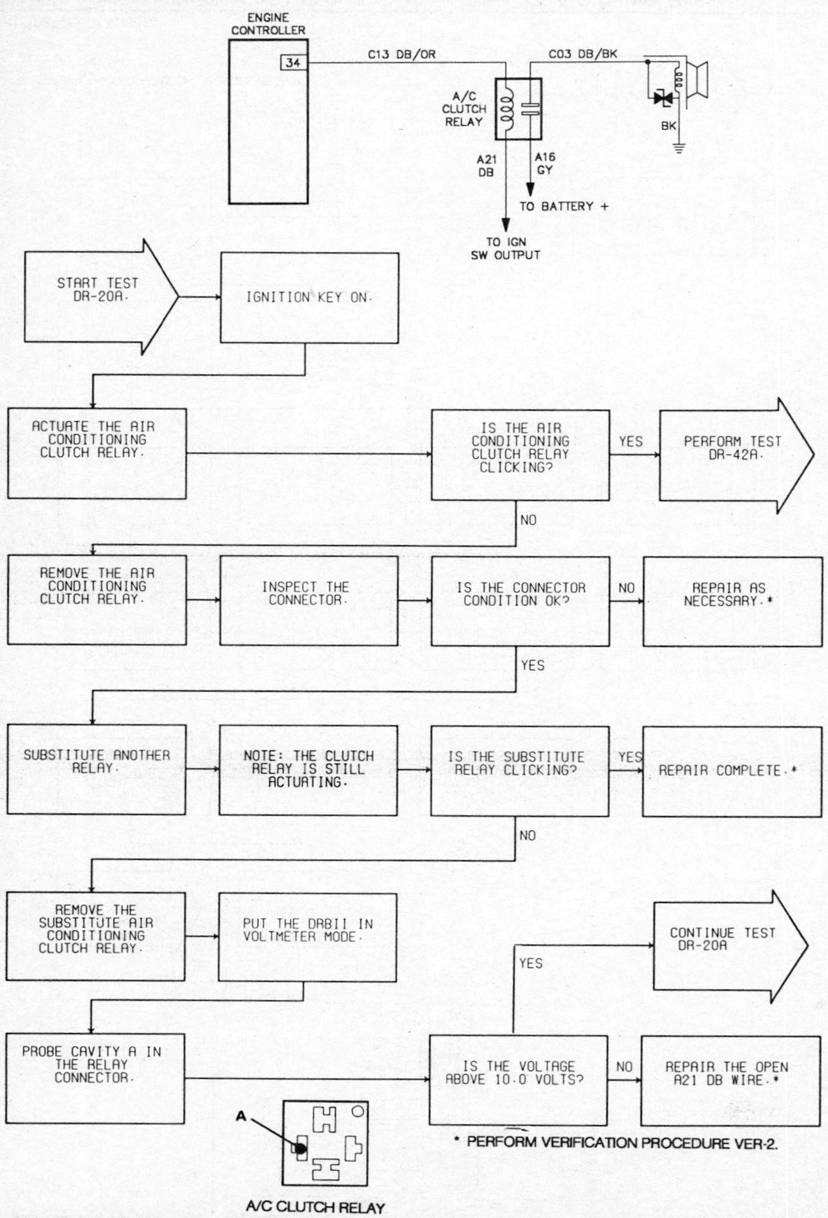
ENGINE CONTROLLER
34
C13 DB/OR
C03 DB/BK
A/C CLUTCH RELAY
A21 DB
A16 GY
BK
TO BATTERY +
TO IGN SW OUTPUT
START TEST DR-20A.
IGNITION KEY ON.
ACTUATE THE AIR CONDITIONING CLUTCH RELAY.
IS THE AIR CONDITIONING CLUTCH RELAY CLICKING?
YES
PERFORM TEST DR-42A.
NO
REMOVE THE AIR CONDITIONING CLUTCH RELAY.
INSPECT THE CONNECTOR.
IS THE CONNECTOR CONDITION OK?
NO
REPAIR AS NECESSARY.*
YES
SUBSTITUTE ANOTHER RELAY.
NOTE: THE CLUTCH RELAY IS STILL ACTUATING.
IS THE SUBSTITUTE RELAY CLICKING?
YES
REPAIR COMPLETE.*
NO
REMOVE THE SUBSTITUTE AIR CONDITIONING CLUTCH RELAY.
PUT THE DRBII IN VOLTMETER MODE.
CONTINUE TEST DR-20A
YES
PROBE CAVITY A IN THE RELAY CONNECTOR.
IS THE VOLTAGE ABOVE 10.0 VOLTS?
NO
REPAIR THE OPEN A21 DB WIRE.*
A
A/C CLUTCH RELAY

* PERFORM VERIFICATION PROCEDURE VER-2.

91G08725 91G08829

Fig. 101: Driveability Test 20A (2.2L & 2.5L) – Code 33, A/C Clutch Relay Circuit (1 of 2)

DR-20A: CODE 33, A/C CLUTCH RELAY CIRCUIT (2 OF 2)

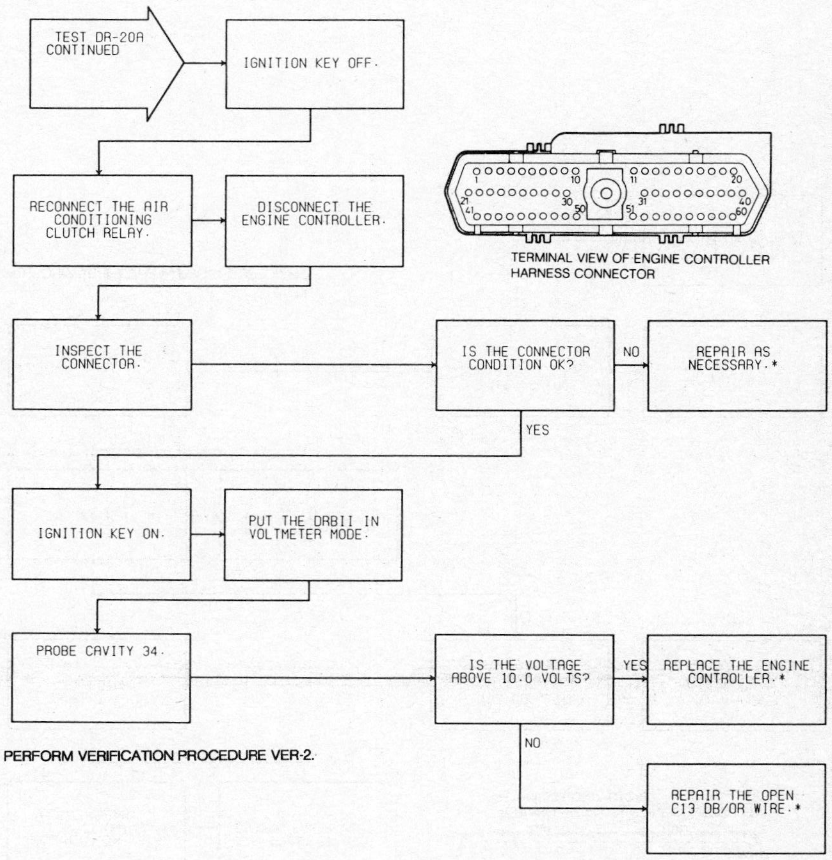
TEST DR-20A CONTINUED
IGNITION KEY OFF.
RECONNECT THE AIR CONDITIONING CLUTCH RELAY.
DISCONNECT THE ENGINE CONTROLLER.
TERMINAL VIEW OF ENGINE CONTROLLER HARNESS CONNECTOR
INSPECT THE CONNECTOR.
IS THE CONNECTOR CONDITION OK?
NO
REPAIR AS NECESSARY.*
YES
IGNITION KEY ON.
PUT THE DRBII IN VOLTMETER MODE.
PROBE CAVITY 34.
IS THE VOLTAGE ABOVE 10.0 VOLTS?
YES
REPLACE THE ENGINE CONTROLLER.*
NO
REPAIR THE OPEN C13 DB/OR WIRE.*

* PERFORM VERIFICATION PROCEDURE VER-2.

91I08830

Fig. 102: Driveability Test 20A (2.2L & 2.5L) – Code 33, A/C Clutch Relay Circuit (2 of 2)

1991 ENGINE PERFORMANCE
Self-Diagnostics – 2.5L TBI (Cont.)

DR-21A: CODE 33, A/C CLUTCH RELAY CIRCUIT (1 OF 2)

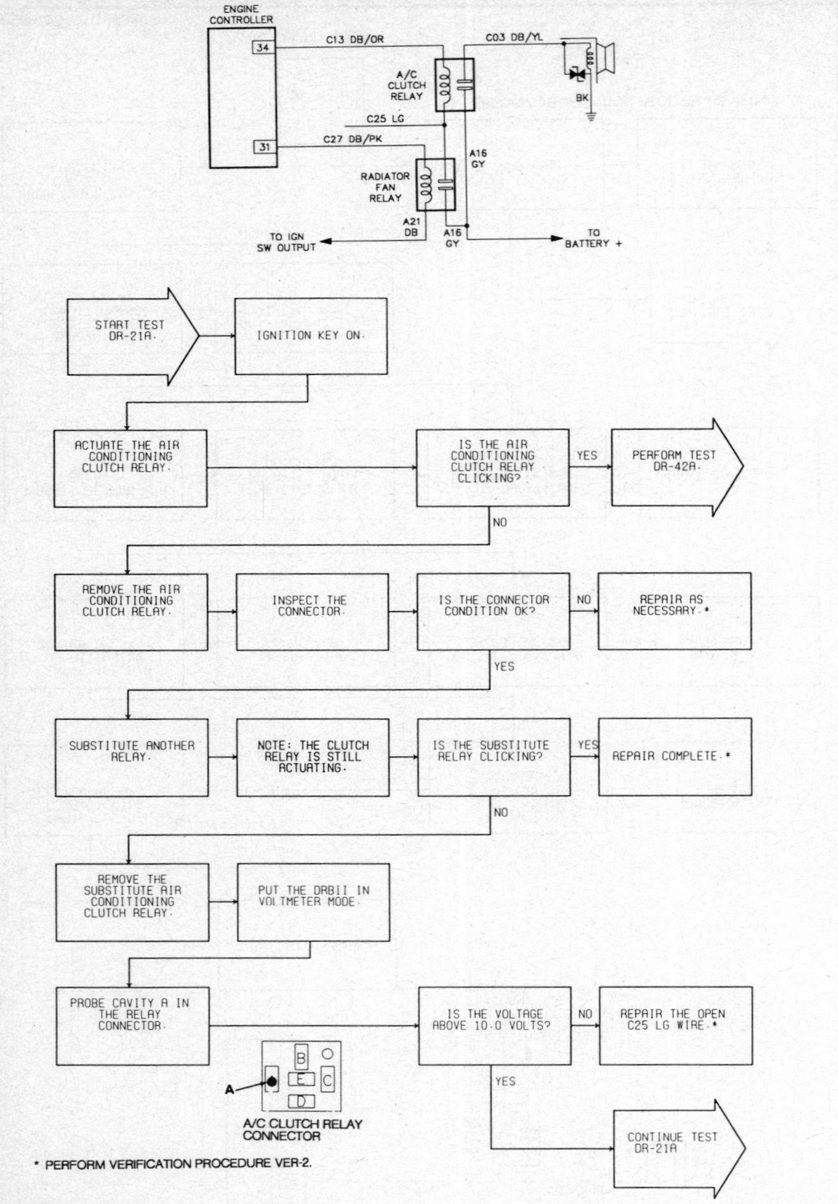
ENGINE CONTROLLER
34
31
C13 DB/OR
C03 DB/YL
A/C CLUTCH RELAY
BK
C25 LG
C27 DB/PK
A16 GY
RADIATOR FAN RELAY
A21 DB
A16 GY
TO IGN SW OUTPUT
TO BATTERY +
START TEST DR-21A.
IGNITION KEY ON.
ACTUATE THE AIR CONDITIONING CLUTCH RELAY.
IS THE AIR CONDITIONING CLUTCH RELAY CLICKING?
YES
PERFORM TEST DR-42A.
NO
REMOVE THE AIR CONDITIONING CLUTCH RELAY.
INSPECT THE CONNECTOR.
IS THE CONNECTOR CONDITION OK?
NO
REPAIR AS NECESSARY.*
YES
SUBSTITUTE ANOTHER RELAY.
NOTE: THE CLUTCH RELAY IS STILL ACTUATING.
IS THE SUBSTITUTE RELAY CLICKING?
YES
REPAIR COMPLETE.*
NO
REMOVE THE SUBSTITUTE AIR CONDITIONING CLUTCH RELAY.
PUT THE DRBII IN VOLTMETER MODE.
PROBE CAVITY A IN THE RELAY CONNECTOR.
IS THE VOLTAGE ABOVE 10.0 VOLTS?
NO
REPAIR THE OPEN C25 LG WIRE.*
YES
CONTINUE TEST DR-21A
B
E
C
D
A
A/C CLUTCH RELAY CONNECTOR
* PERFORM VERIFICATION PROCEDURE VER-2.
91G08725 91A08831

Fig. 103: Driveability Test 21A (2.2L & 2.5L) – Code 33, A/C Clutch Relay Circuit (1 of 2)

DR-21A: CODE 33, A/C CLUTCH RELAY CIRCUIT (2 OF 2)

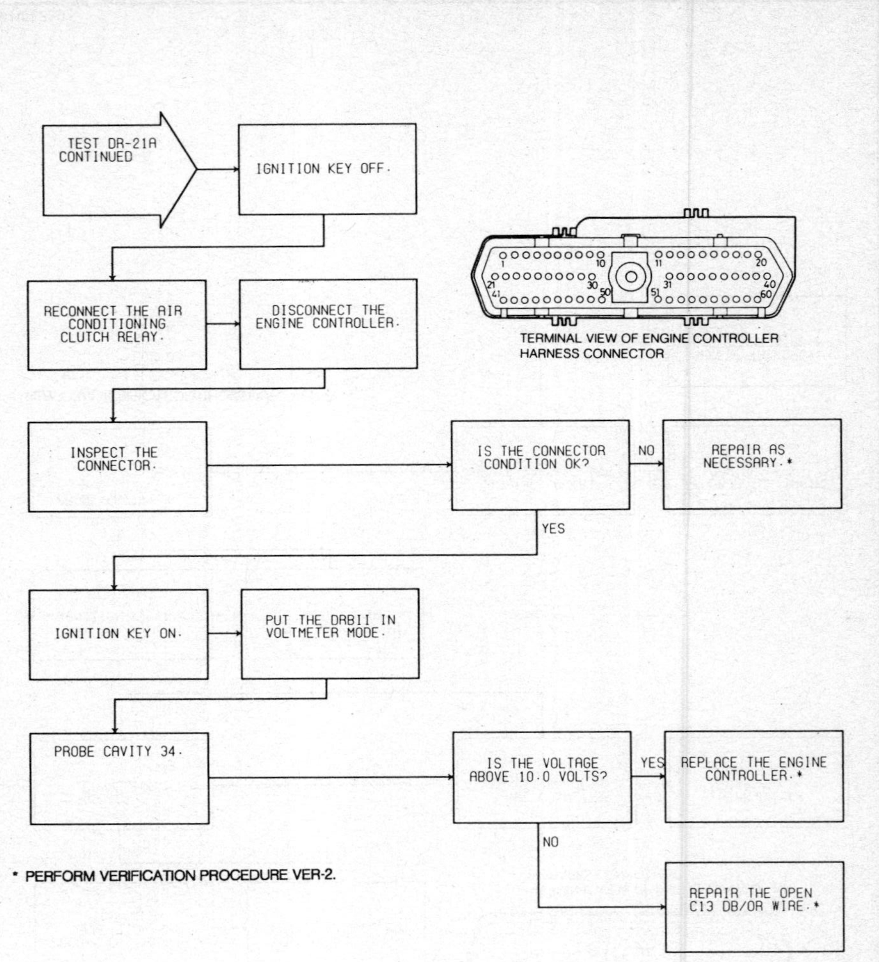
TEST DR-21A CONTINUED
IGNITION KEY OFF.
RECONNECT THE AIR CONDITIONING CLUTCH RELAY.
DISCONNECT THE ENGINE CONTROLLER.
TERMINAL VIEW OF ENGINE CONTROLLER HARNESS CONNECTOR
INSPECT THE CONNECTOR.
IS THE CONNECTOR CONDITION OK?
NO
REPAIR AS NECESSARY.*
YES
IGNITION KEY ON.
PUT THE DRBII IN VOLTMETER MODE.
PROBE CAVITY 34.
IS THE VOLTAGE ABOVE 10.0 VOLTS?
YES
REPLACE THE ENGINE CONTROLLER.*
NO
REPAIR THE OPEN C13 DB/OR WIRE.*
* PERFORM VERIFICATION PROCEDURE VER-2.
91C08832

Fig. 104: Driveability Test 21A (2.2L & 2.5L) – Code 33, A/C Clutch Relay Circuit (2 of 2)

DR-22A: CODE 33, A/C CLUTCH RELAY CIRCUIT (1 OF 2)

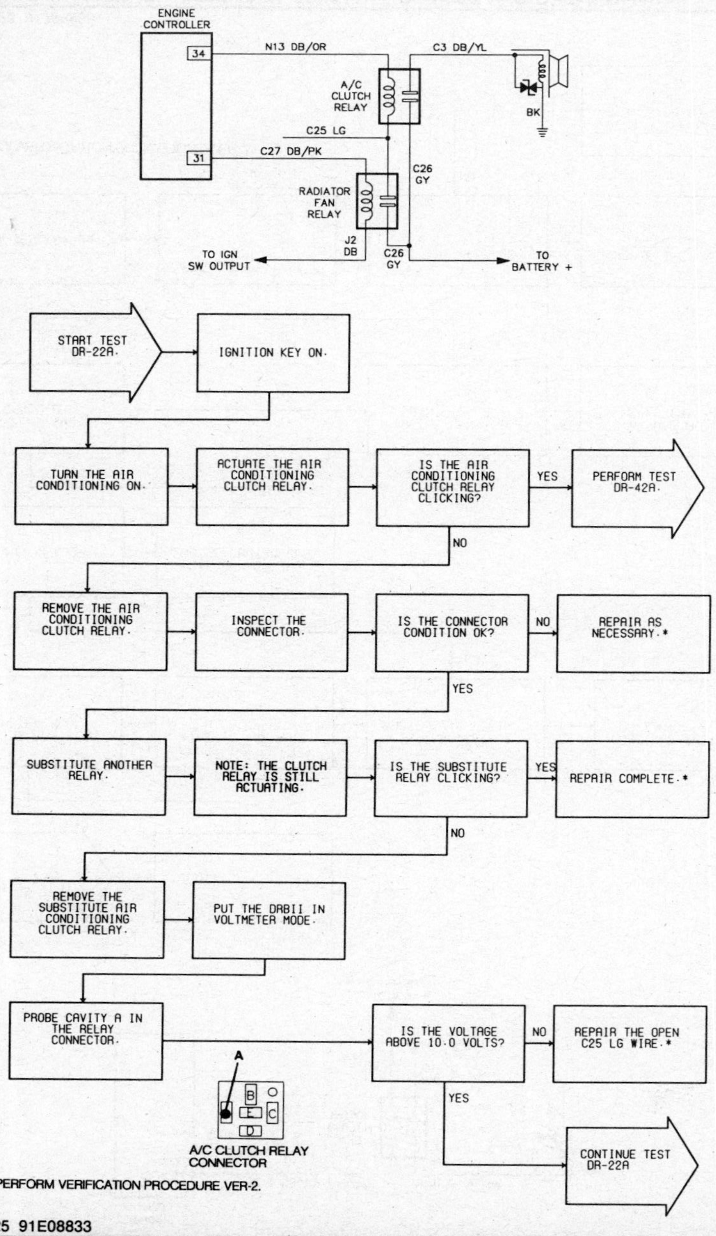
ENGINE CONTROLLER
34
31
N13 DB/OR
C3 DB/YL
A/C CLUTCH RELAY
BK
C25 LG
C27 DB/PK
C26 GY
RADIATOR FAN RELAY
J2 DB
C26 GY
TO IGN SW OUTPUT
TO BATTERY +
START TEST DR-22A.
IGNITION KEY ON.
TURN THE AIR CONDITIONING ON.
ACTUATE THE AIR CONDITIONING CLUTCH RELAY.
IS THE AIR CONDITIONING CLUTCH RELAY CLICKING?
YES
PERFORM TEST DR-42A.
NO
REMOVE THE AIR CONDITIONING CLUTCH RELAY.
INSPECT THE CONNECTOR.
IS THE CONNECTOR CONDITION OK?
NO
REPAIR AS NECESSARY.*
YES
SUBSTITUTE ANOTHER RELAY.
NOTE: THE CLUTCH RELAY IS STILL ACTUATING.
IS THE SUBSTITUTE RELAY CLICKING?
YES
REPAIR COMPLETE.*
NO
REMOVE THE SUBSTITUTE AIR CONDITIONING CLUTCH RELAY.
PUT THE DRBII IN VOLTMETER MODE.
PROBE CAVITY A IN THE RELAY CONNECTOR.
IS THE VOLTAGE ABOVE 10.0 VOLTS?
NO
REPAIR THE OPEN C25 LG WIRE.*
YES
CONTINUE TEST DR-22A
A
B
C
D
A/C CLUTCH RELAY CONNECTOR

* PERFORM VERIFICATION PROCEDURE VER-2.

91G08725 91E08833

Fig. 105: *Driveability Test 22A (2.2L & 2.5L) – Code 33, A/C Clutch Relay Circuit (1 of 2)*

DR-22A: CODE 33, A/C CLUTCH RELAY CIRCUIT (2 OF 2)

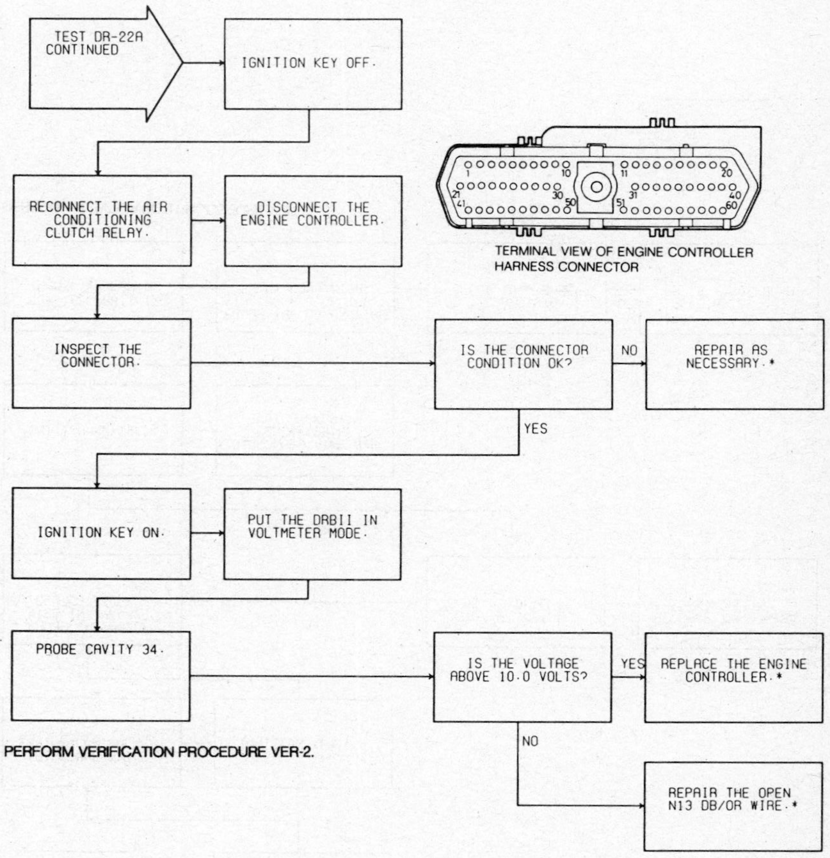
TEST DR-22A CONTINUED
IGNITION KEY OFF.
RECONNECT THE AIR CONDITIONING CLUTCH RELAY.
DISCONNECT THE ENGINE CONTROLLER.
TERMINAL VIEW OF ENGINE CONTROLLER HARNESS CONNECTOR
1
10
11
20
21
30
31
40
41
50
51
60
INSPECT THE CONNECTOR.
IS THE CONNECTOR CONDITION OK?
NO
REPAIR AS NECESSARY.*
YES
IGNITION KEY ON.
PUT THE DRBII IN VOLTMETER MODE.
PROBE CAVITY 34.
IS THE VOLTAGE ABOVE 10.0 VOLTS?
YES
REPLACE THE ENGINE CONTROLLER.*
NO
REPAIR THE OPEN N13 DB/OR WIRE.*

* PERFORM VERIFICATION PROCEDURE VER-2.

91G08834

Fig. 106: *Driveability Test 22A (2.2L & 2.5L) – Code 33, A/C Clutch Relay Circuit (2 of 2)*

DR-23A: CODE 33, A/C CLUTCH RELAY CIRCUIT (1 OF 3)

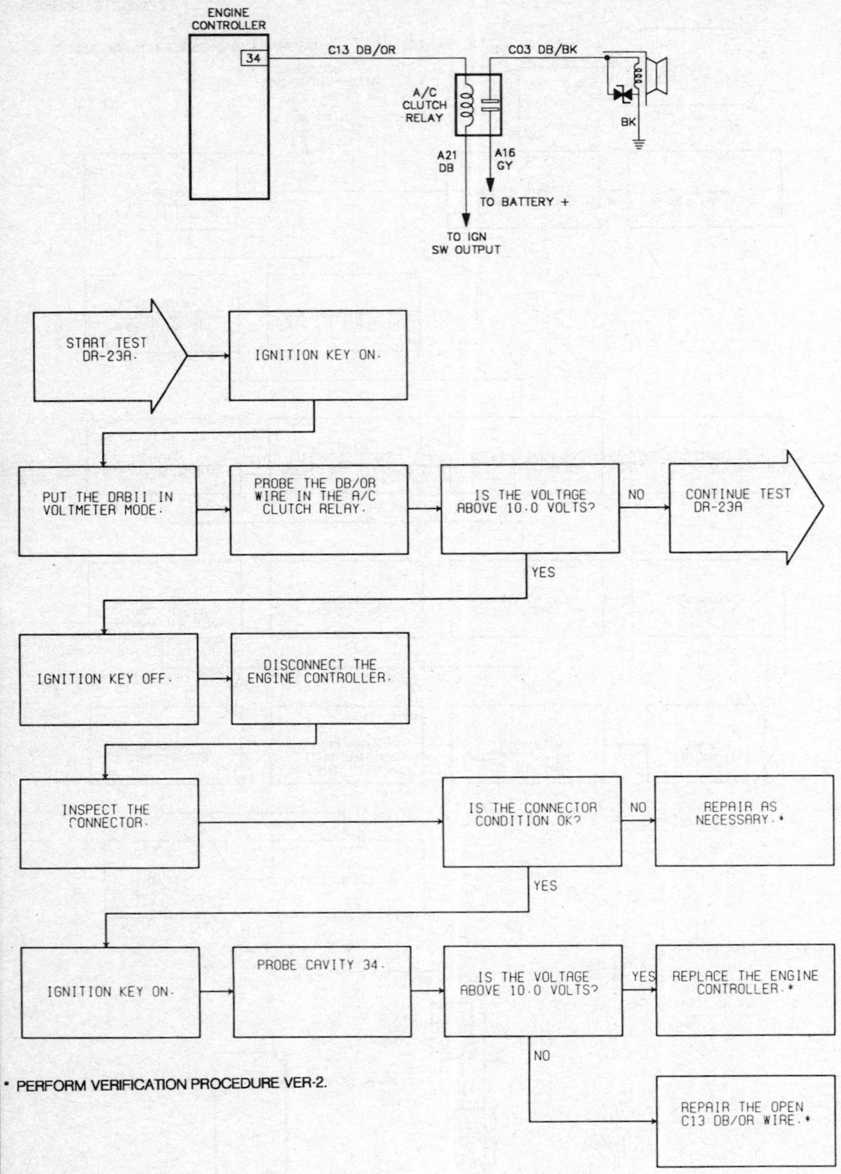
ENGINE CONTROLLER
34
C13 DB/OR
A/C CLUTCH RELAY
C03 DB/BK
BK
A21 DB
A16 GY
TO BATTERY +
TO IGN SW OUTPUT
START TEST DR-23A.
IGNITION KEY ON.
PUT THE DRBII IN VOLTMETER MODE.
PROBE THE DB/OR WIRE IN THE A/C CLUTCH RELAY.
IS THE VOLTAGE ABOVE 10.0 VOLTS?
NO
CONTINUE TEST DR-23A
YES
IGNITION KEY OFF.
DISCONNECT THE ENGINE CONTROLLER.
INSPECT THE CONNECTOR.
IS THE CONNECTOR CONDITION OK?
NO
REPAIR AS NECESSARY.*
YES
IGNITION KEY ON.
PROBE CAVITY 34.
IS THE VOLTAGE ABOVE 10.0 VOLTS?
YES
REPLACE THE ENGINE CONTROLLER.*
NO
REPAIR THE OPEN C13 DB/OR WIRE.*
* PERFORM VERIFICATION PROCEDURE VER-2.

91G08725 91J08835

Fig. 107: *Driveability Test 23A (2.2L & 2.5L) – Code 33, A/C Clutch Relay Circuit (1 of 3)*

DR-23A: CODE 33, A/C CLUTCH RELAY CIRCUIT (2 OF 3)

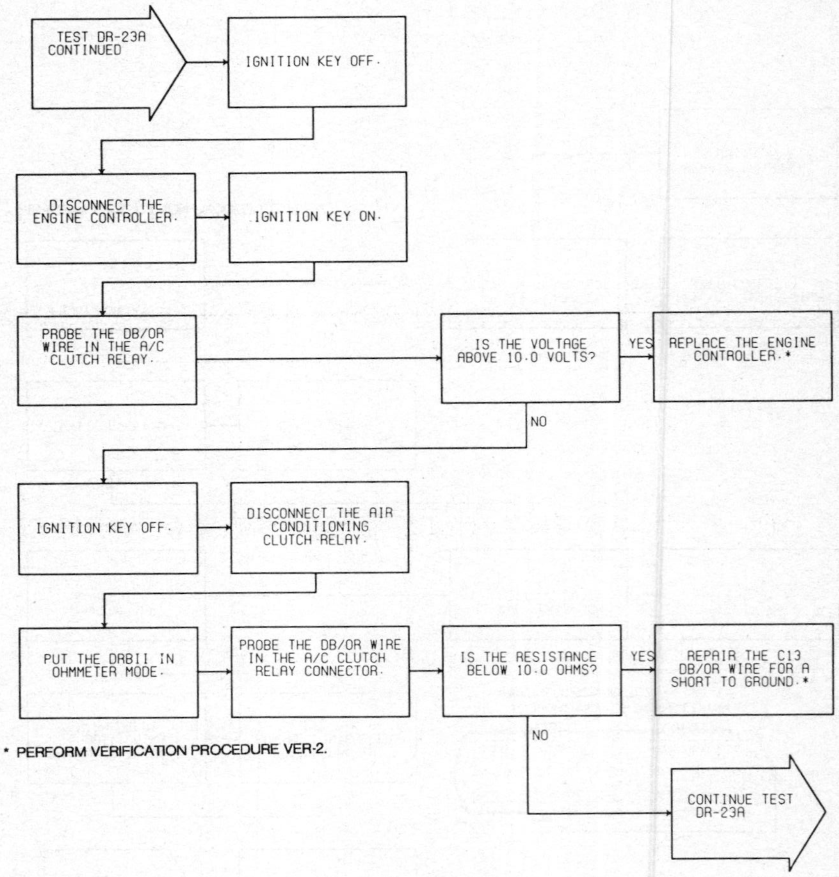
TEST DR-23A CONTINUED
IGNITION KEY OFF.
DISCONNECT THE ENGINE CONTROLLER.
IGNITION KEY ON.
PROBE THE DB/OR WIRE IN THE A/C CLUTCH RELAY.
IS THE VOLTAGE ABOVE 10.0 VOLTS?
YES
REPLACE THE ENGINE CONTROLLER.*
NO
IGNITION KEY OFF.
DISCONNECT THE AIR CONDITIONING CLUTCH RELAY.
PUT THE DRBII IN OHMMETER MODE.
PROBE THE DB/OR WIRE IN THE A/C CLUTCH RELAY CONNECTOR.
IS THE RESISTANCE BELOW 10.0 OHMS?
YES
REPAIR THE C13 DB/OR WIRE FOR A SHORT TO GROUND.*
NO
CONTINUE TEST DR-23A
* PERFORM VERIFICATION PROCEDURE VER-2.

91B08836

Fig. 108: *Driveability Test 23A (2.2L & 2.5L) – Code 33, A/C Clutch Relay Circuit (2 of 3)*

DR-23A: CODE 33, A/C CLUTCH RELAY CIRCUIT (3 OF 3)

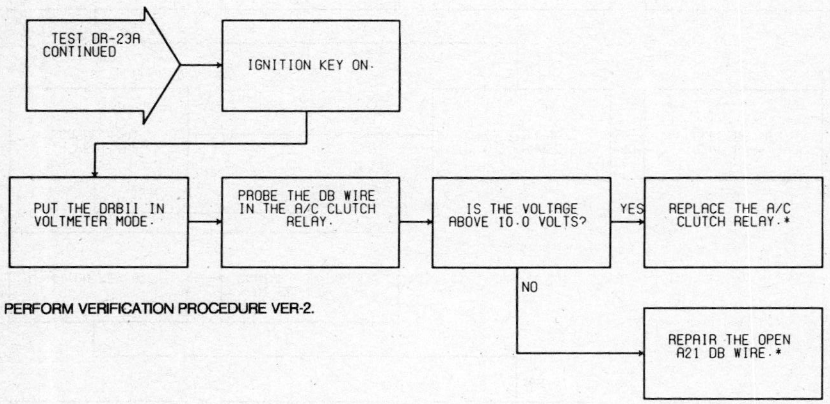
TEST DR-23A CONTINUED
IGNITION KEY ON.
PUT THE DRBII IN VOLTMETER MODE.
PROBE THE DB WIRE IN THE A/C CLUTCH RELAY.
IS THE VOLTAGE ABOVE 10.0 VOLTS?
YES
REPLACE THE A/C CLUTCH RELAY.*
NO
REPAIR THE OPEN A21 DB WIRE.*

* PERFORM VERIFICATION PROCEDURE VER-2.

91D08837

Fig. 109: Driveability Test 23A (2.2L & 2.5L) – Code 33, A/C Clutch Relay Circuit (3 of 3)

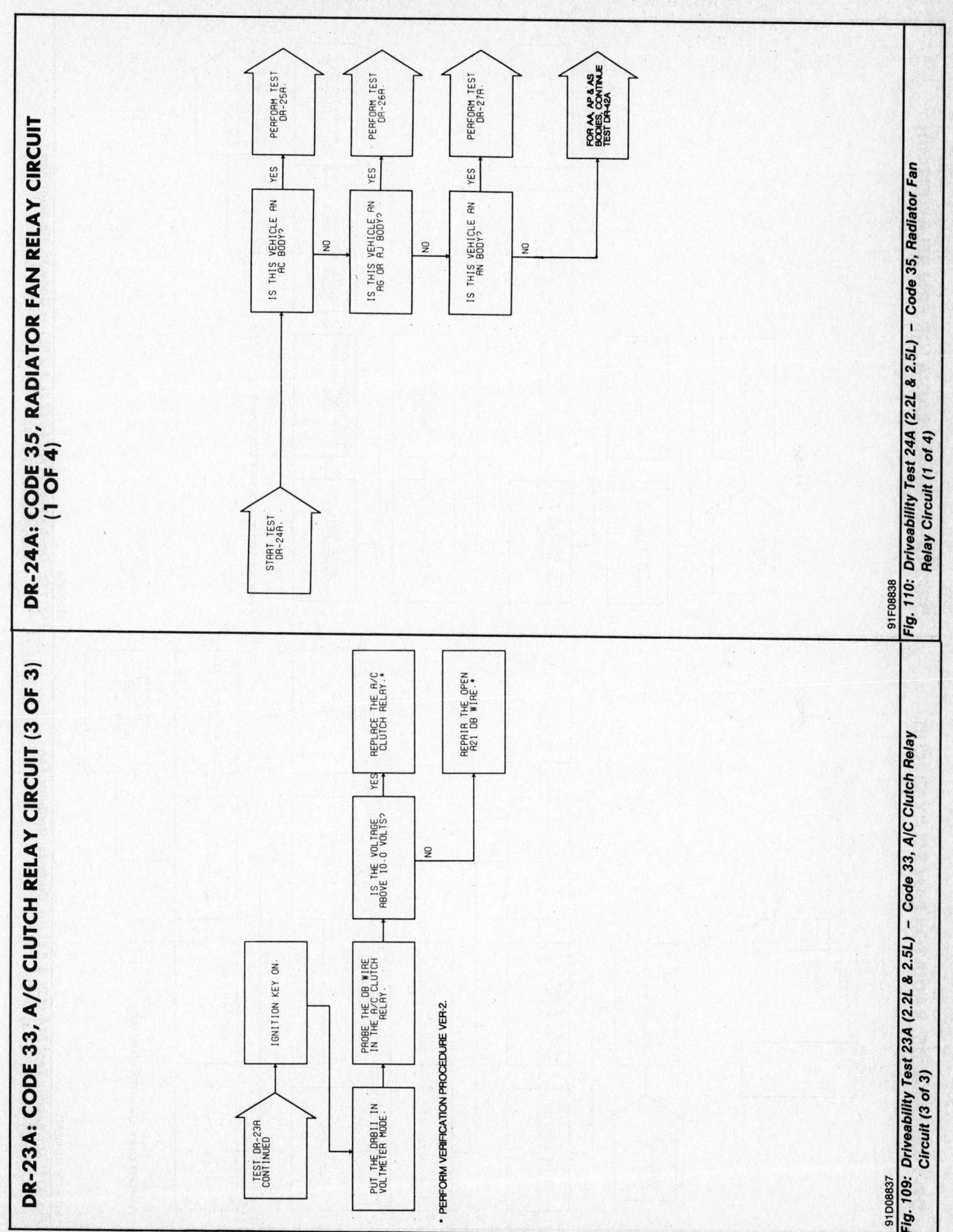

DR-24A: CODE 35, RADIATOR FAN RELAY CIRCUIT (1 OF 4)

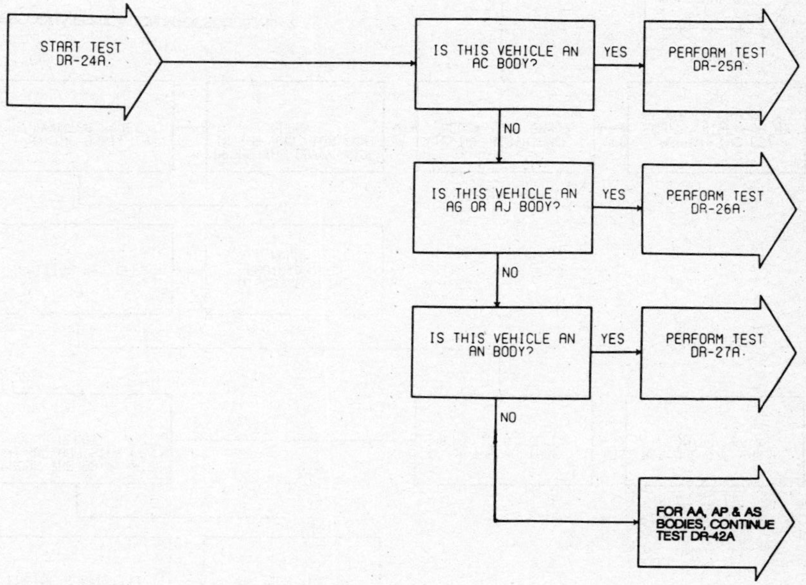
START TEST DR-24A.
IS THIS VEHICLE AN AC BODY?
YES
PERFORM TEST DR-25A.
NO
IS THIS VEHICLE AN AG OR AJ BODY?
YES
PERFORM TEST DR-26A.
NO
IS THIS VEHICLE AN AN BODY?
YES
PERFORM TEST DR-27A.
NO
FOR AA, AP & AS BODIES, CONTINUE TEST DR-42A

91F08838

Fig. 110: Driveability Test 24A (2.2L & 2.5L) – Code 35, Radiator Fan Relay Circuit (1 of 4)

DR-24A: CODE 35, RADIATOR FAN RELAY CIRCUIT (2 OF 4)

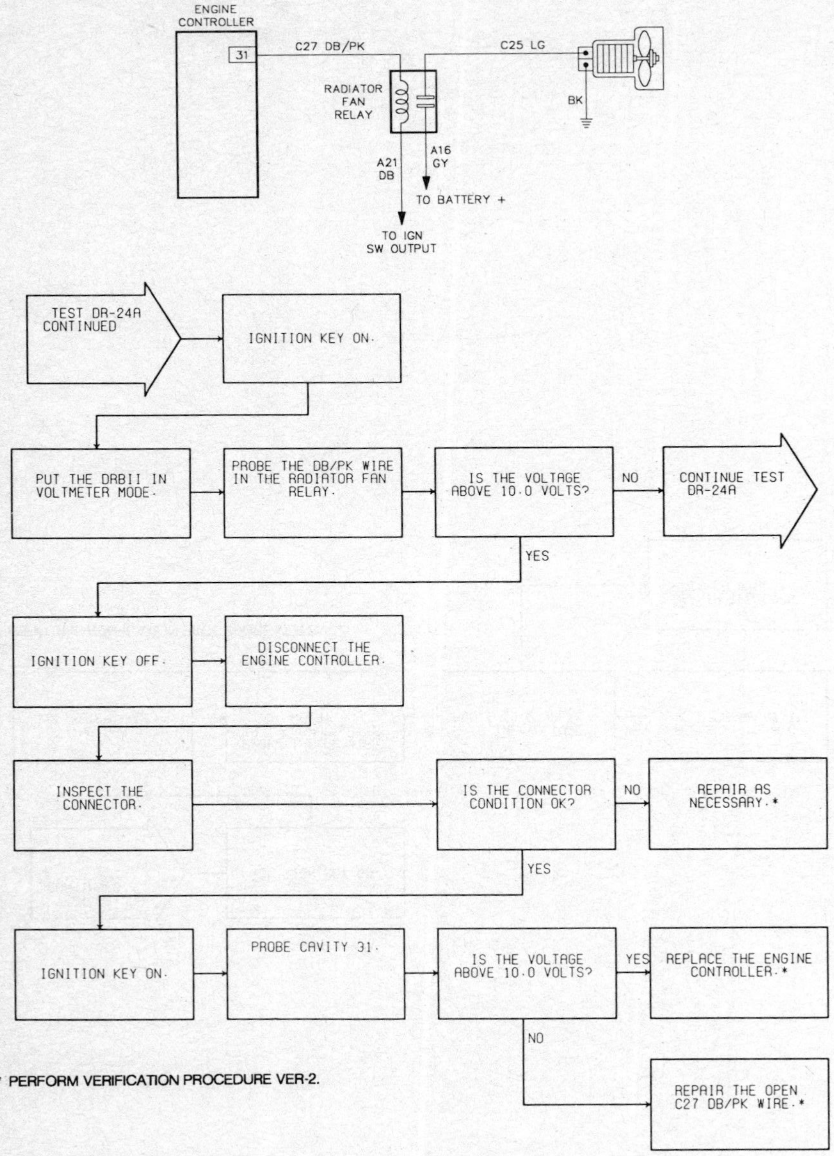
ENGINE CONTROLLER
31
C27 DB/PK
C25 LG
RADIATOR FAN RELAY
BK
A21 DB
A16 GY
TO BATTERY +
TO IGN SW OUTPUT
TEST DR-24A CONTINUED
IGNITION KEY ON.
PUT THE DRBII IN VOLTMETER MODE.
PROBE THE DB/PK WIRE IN THE RADIATOR FAN RELAY.
IS THE VOLTAGE ABOVE 10.0 VOLTS?
NO
CONTINUE TEST DR-24A
YES
IGNITION KEY OFF.
DISCONNECT THE ENGINE CONTROLLER.
INSPECT THE CONNECTOR.
IS THE CONNECTOR CONDITION OK?
NO
REPAIR AS NECESSARY.*
YES
IGNITION KEY ON.
PROBE CAVITY 31.
IS THE VOLTAGE ABOVE 10.0 VOLTS?
YES
REPLACE THE ENGINE CONTROLLER.*
NO
REPAIR THE OPEN C27 DB/PK WIRE.*

* PERFORM VERIFICATION PROCEDURE VER-2.

91I08726 91H08839

Fig. 111: Driveability Test 24A (2.2L & 2.5L) – Code 35, Radiator Fan Relay Circuit (2 of 4)

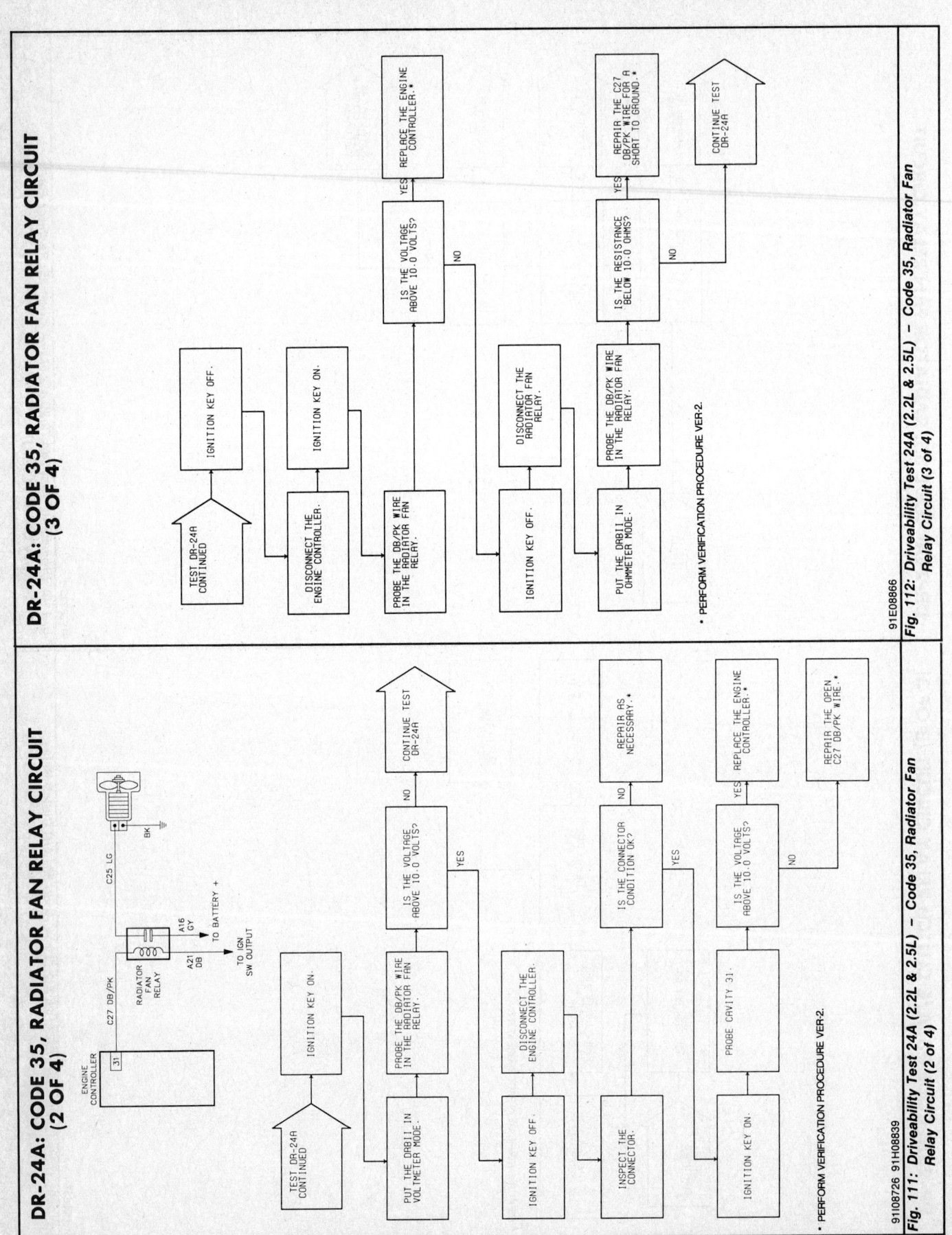

DR-24A: CODE 35, RADIATOR FAN RELAY CIRCUIT (3 OF 4)

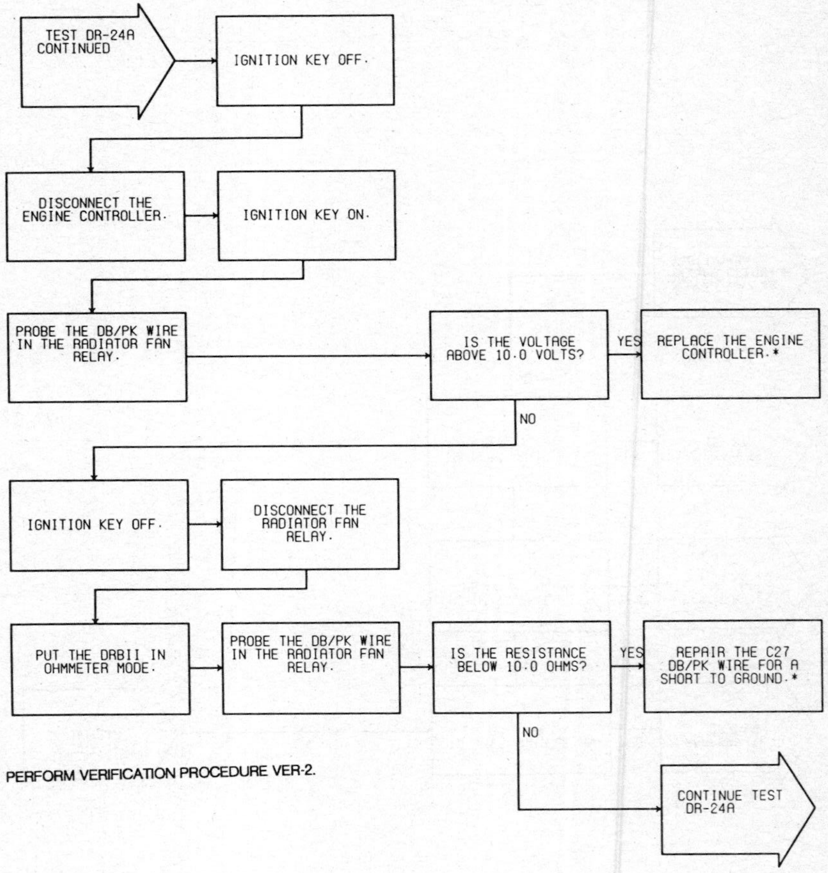
TEST DR-24A CONTINUED
IGNITION KEY OFF.
DISCONNECT THE ENGINE CONTROLLER.
IGNITION KEY ON.
PROBE THE DB/PK WIRE IN THE RADIATOR FAN RELAY.
IS THE VOLTAGE ABOVE 10.0 VOLTS?
YES
REPLACE THE ENGINE CONTROLLER.*
NO
IGNITION KEY OFF.
DISCONNECT THE RADIATOR FAN RELAY.
PUT THE DRBII IN OHMMETER MODE.
PROBE THE DB/PK WIRE IN THE RADIATOR FAN RELAY.
IS THE RESISTANCE BELOW 10.0 OHMS?
YES
REPAIR THE C27 DB/PK WIRE FOR A SHORT TO GROUND.*
NO
CONTINUE TEST DR-24A

* PERFORM VERIFICATION PROCEDURE VER-2.

91E08866

Fig. 112: Driveability Test 24A (2.2L & 2.5L) – Code 35, Radiator Fan Relay Circuit (3 of 4)

DR-24A: CODE 35, RADIATOR FAN RELAY CIRCUIT (4 OF 4)

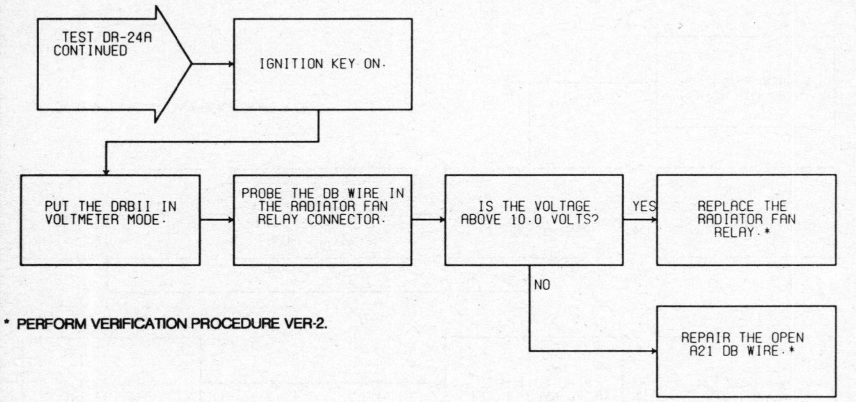
TEST DR-24A CONTINUED
IGNITION KEY ON.
PUT THE DRBII IN VOLTMETER MODE.
PROBE THE DB WIRE IN THE RADIATOR FAN RELAY CONNECTOR.
IS THE VOLTAGE ABOVE 10.0 VOLTS?
YES
REPLACE THE RADIATOR FAN RELAY.*
NO
REPAIR THE OPEN A21 DB WIRE.*

* PERFORM VERIFICATION PROCEDURE VER-2.

91G08867

Fig. 113: Driveability Test 24A (2.2L & 2.5L) – Code 35, Radiator Fan Relay Circuit (4 of 4)

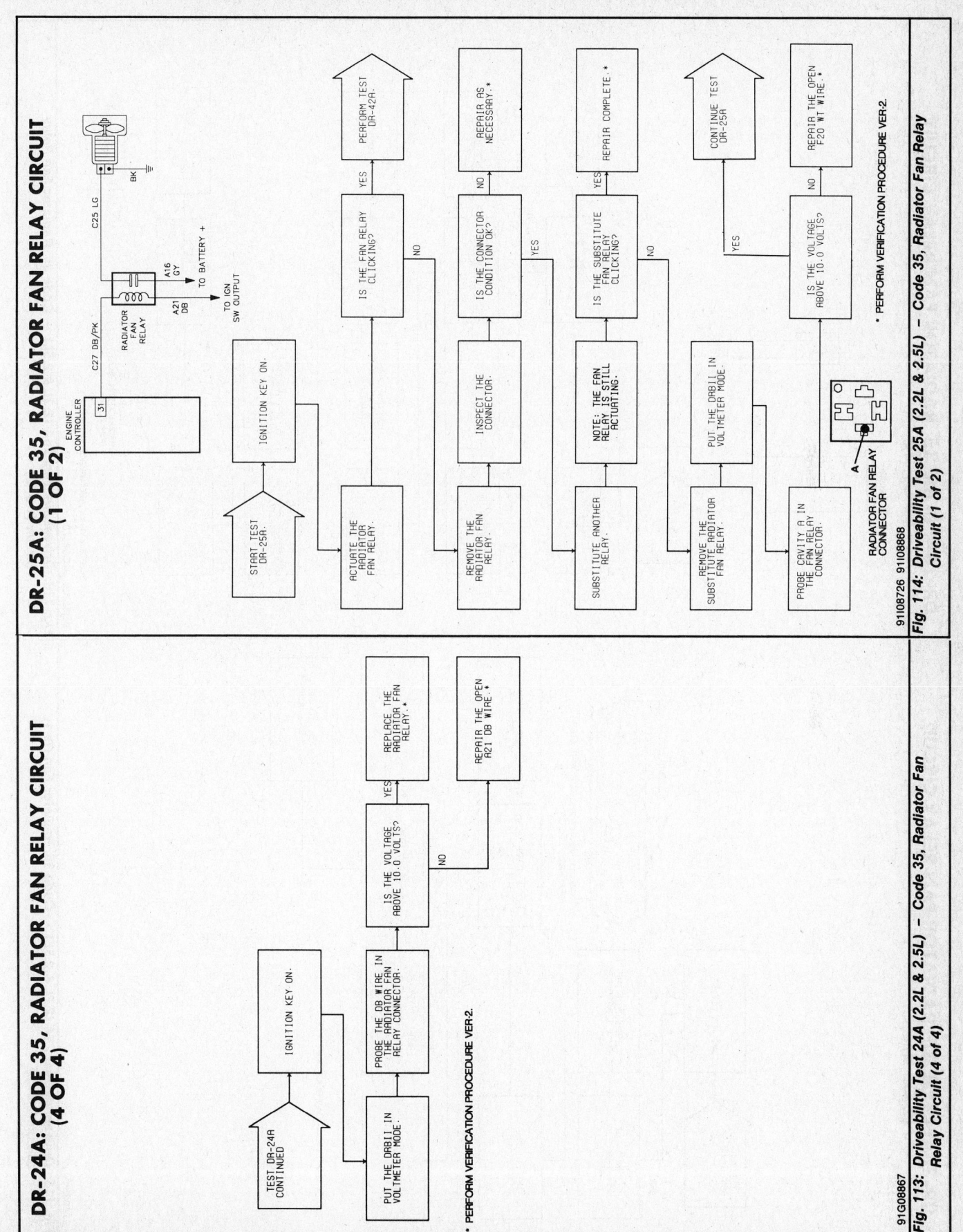

DR-25A: CODE 35, RADIATOR FAN RELAY CIRCUIT (1 OF 2)

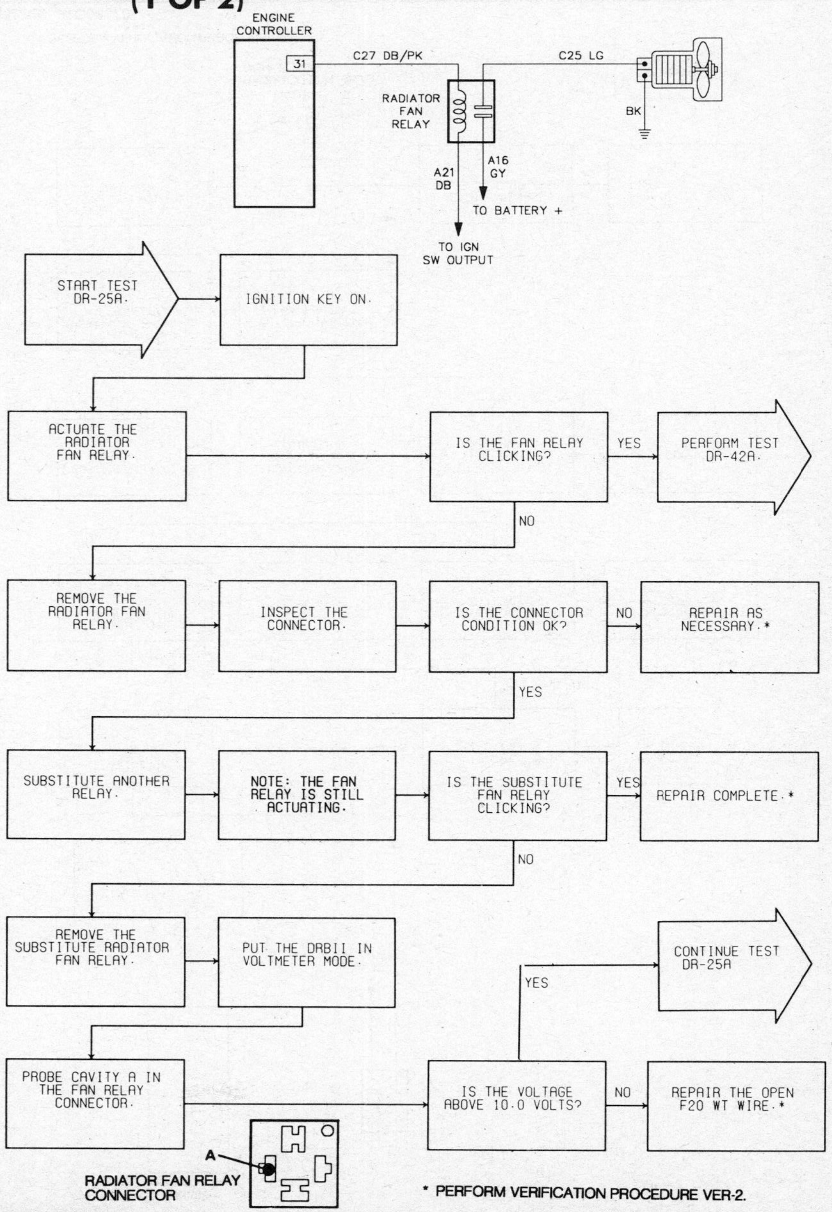
ENGINE CONTROLLER
31
C27 DB/PK
RADIATOR FAN RELAY
C25 LG
BK
A21 DB
A16 GY
TO BATTERY +
TO IGN SW OUTPUT
START TEST DR-25A.
IGNITION KEY ON.
ACTUATE THE RADIATOR FAN RELAY.
IS THE FAN RELAY CLICKING?
YES
PERFORM TEST DR-42A.
NO
REMOVE THE RADIATOR FAN RELAY.
INSPECT THE CONNECTOR.
IS THE CONNECTOR CONDITION OK?
NO
REPAIR AS NECESSARY.*
YES
SUBSTITUTE ANOTHER RELAY.
NOTE: THE FAN RELAY IS STILL ACTUATING.
IS THE SUBSTITUTE FAN RELAY CLICKING?
YES
REPAIR COMPLETE.*
NO
REMOVE THE SUBSTITUTE RADIATOR FAN RELAY.
PUT THE DRBII IN VOLTMETER MODE.
CONTINUE TEST DR-25A
YES
PROBE CAVITY A IN THE FAN RELAY CONNECTOR.
IS THE VOLTAGE ABOVE 10.0 VOLTS?
NO
REPAIR THE OPEN F20 WT WIRE.*
A
RADIATOR FAN RELAY CONNECTOR

* PERFORM VERIFICATION PROCEDURE VER-2.

91I08726 91I08868

Fig. 114: Driveability Test 25A (2.2L & 2.5L) – Code 35, Radiator Fan Relay Circuit (1 of 2)

DR-25A: CODE 35, RADIATOR FAN RELAY CIRCUIT (2 OF 2)

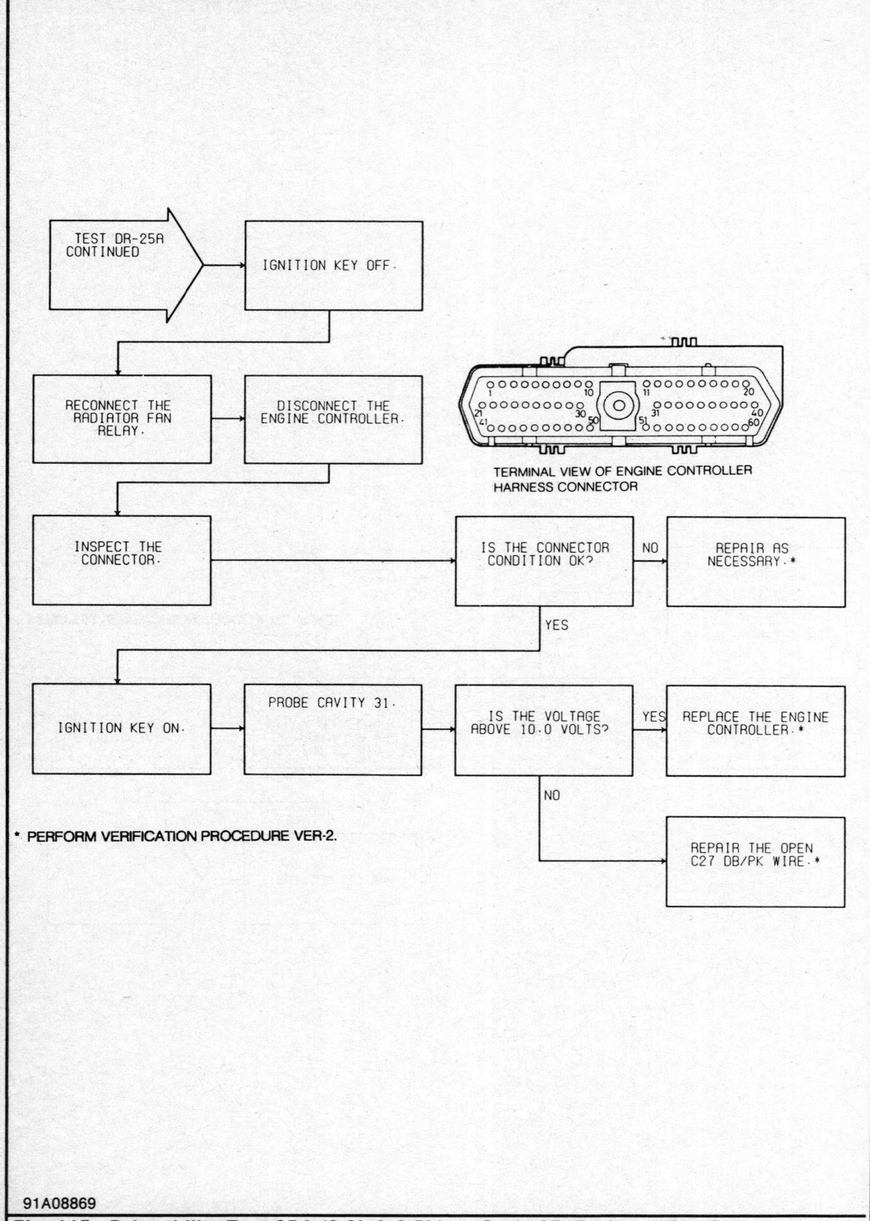
TEST DR-25A CONTINUED
IGNITION KEY OFF.
RECONNECT THE RADIATOR FAN RELAY.
DISCONNECT THE ENGINE CONTROLLER.
TERMINAL VIEW OF ENGINE CONTROLLER HARNESS CONNECTOR
INSPECT THE CONNECTOR.
IS THE CONNECTOR CONDITION OK?
NO
REPAIR AS NECESSARY.*
YES
IGNITION KEY ON.
PROBE CAVITY 31.
IS THE VOLTAGE ABOVE 10.0 VOLTS?
YES
REPLACE THE ENGINE CONTROLLER.*
NO
REPAIR THE OPEN C27 DB/PK WIRE.*
* PERFORM VERIFICATION PROCEDURE VER-2.
91A08869

Fig. 115: Driveability Test 25A (2.2L & 2.5L) – Code 35, Radiator Fan Relay Circuit (2 of 2)

DR-26A: CODE 35, RADIATOR FAN RELAY CIRCUIT (1 OF 2)

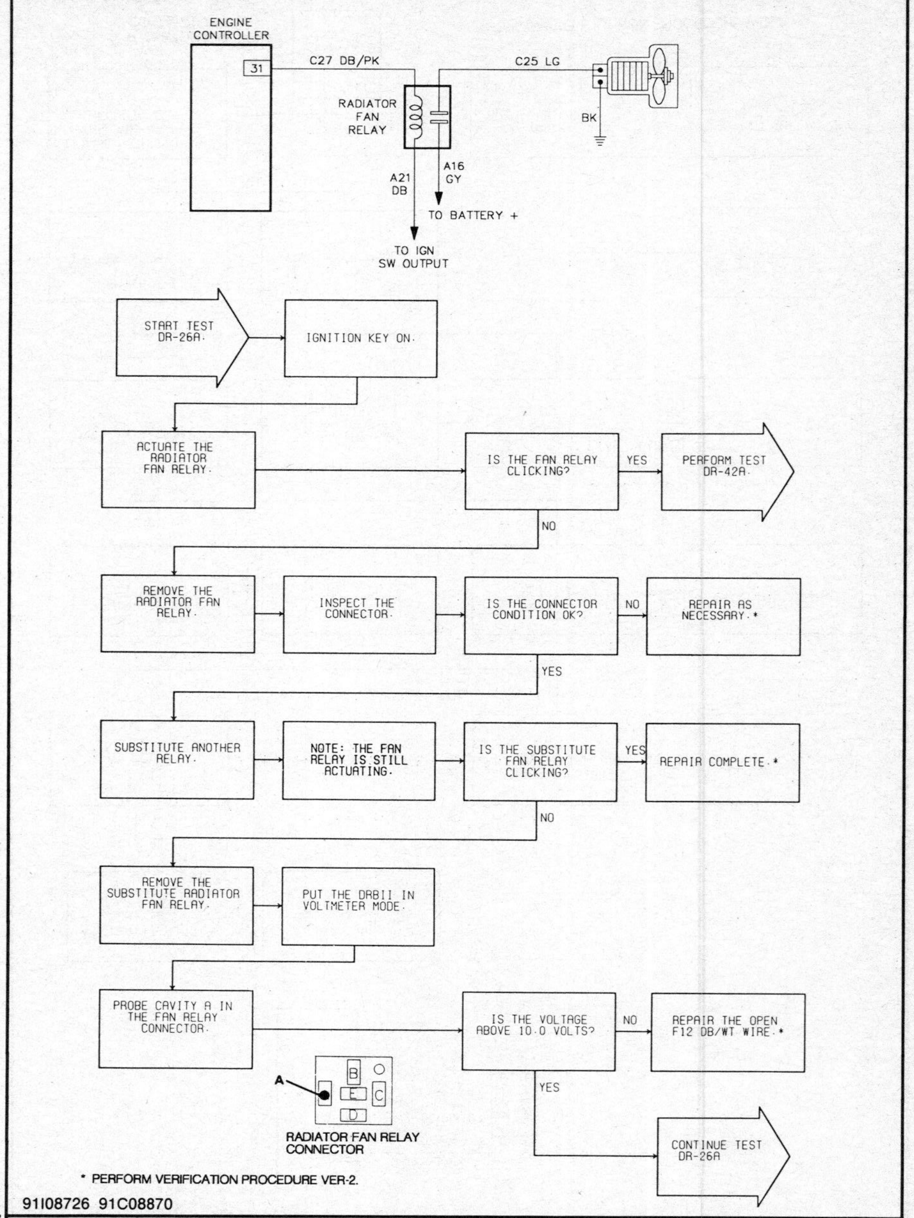
ENGINE CONTROLLER
31
C27 DB/PK
C25 LG
RADIATOR FAN RELAY
BK
A21 DB
A16 GY
TO BATTERY +
TO IGN SW OUTPUT
START TEST DR-26A.
IGNITION KEY ON.
ACTUATE THE RADIATOR FAN RELAY.
IS THE FAN RELAY CLICKING?
YES
PERFORM TEST DR-42A.
NO
REMOVE THE RADIATOR FAN RELAY.
INSPECT THE CONNECTOR.
IS THE CONNECTOR CONDITION OK?
NO
REPAIR AS NECESSARY.*
YES
SUBSTITUTE ANOTHER RELAY.
NOTE: THE FAN RELAY IS STILL ACTUATING.
IS THE SUBSTITUTE FAN RELAY CLICKING?
YES
REPAIR COMPLETE.*
NO
REMOVE THE SUBSTITUTE RADIATOR FAN RELAY.
PUT THE DRBII IN VOLTMETER MODE.
PROBE CAVITY A IN THE FAN RELAY CONNECTOR.
IS THE VOLTAGE ABOVE 10.0 VOLTS?
NO
REPAIR THE OPEN F12 DB/WT WIRE.*
YES
CONTINUE TEST DR-26A
A
B
C
D
E
RADIATOR FAN RELAY CONNECTOR
* PERFORM VERIFICATION PROCEDURE VER-2.
91I08726 91C08870

Fig. 116: Driveability Test 26A (2.2L & 2.5L) – Code 35, Radiator Fan Relay Circuit (1 of 2)

DR-26A: CODE 35, RADIATOR FAN RELAY CIRCUIT (2 OF 2)

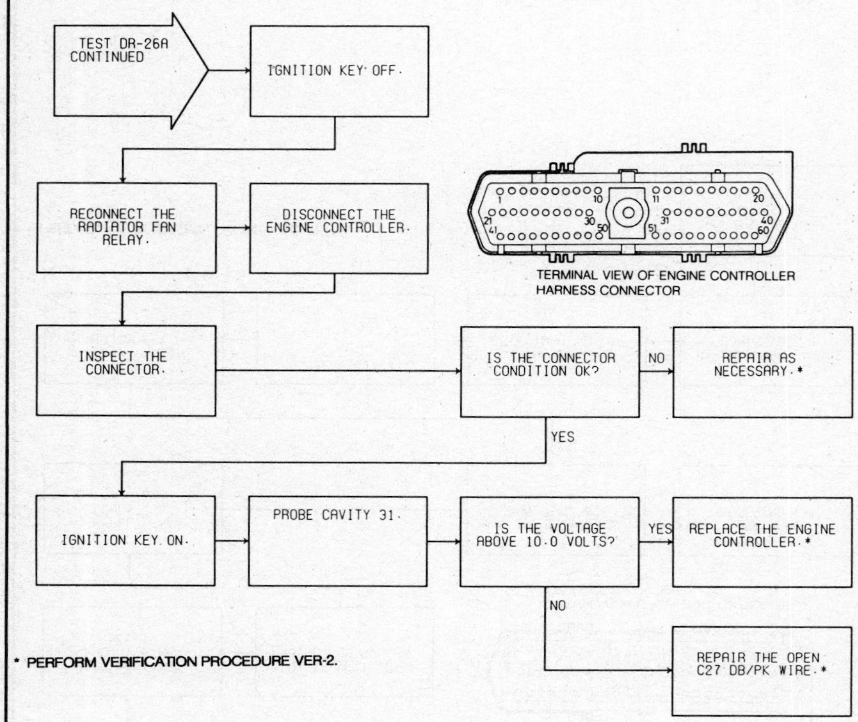
TEST DR-26A CONTINUED
IGNITION KEY OFF.
RECONNECT THE RADIATOR FAN RELAY.
DISCONNECT THE ENGINE CONTROLLER.
TERMINAL VIEW OF ENGINE CONTROLLER HARNESS CONNECTOR
INSPECT THE CONNECTOR.
IS THE CONNECTOR CONDITION OK?
NO
REPAIR AS NECESSARY.*
YES
IGNITION KEY ON.
PROBE CAVITY 31.
IS THE VOLTAGE ABOVE 10.0 VOLTS?
YES
REPLACE THE ENGINE CONTROLLER.*
NO
REPAIR THE OPEN C27 DB/PK WIRE.*

* PERFORM VERIFICATION PROCEDURE VER-2.

91E08871

Fig. 117: ***Driveability Test 26A (2.2L & 2.5L) – Code 35, Radiator Fan Relay Circuit (2 of 2)***

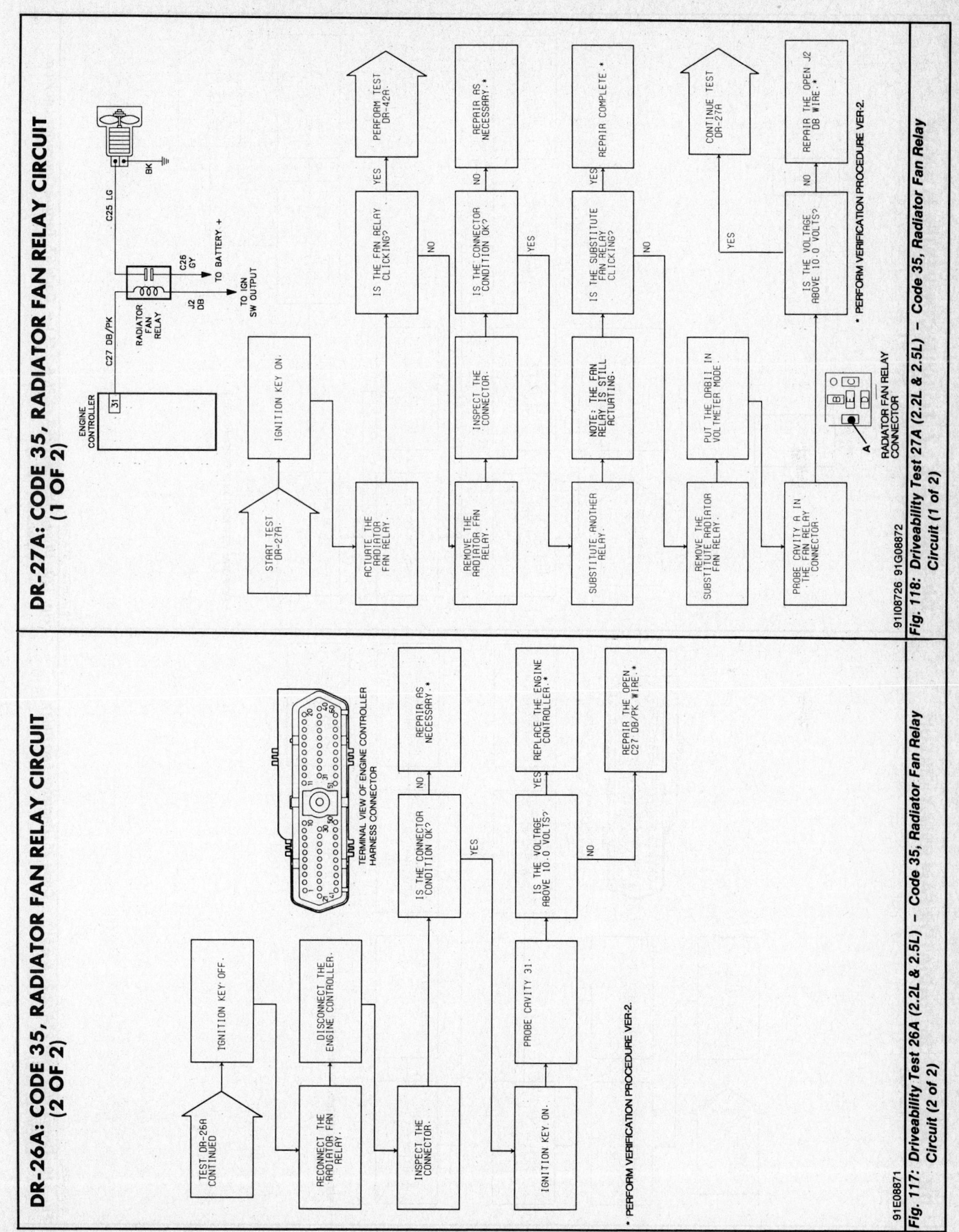

DR-27A: CODE 35, RADIATOR FAN RELAY CIRCUIT (1 OF 2)

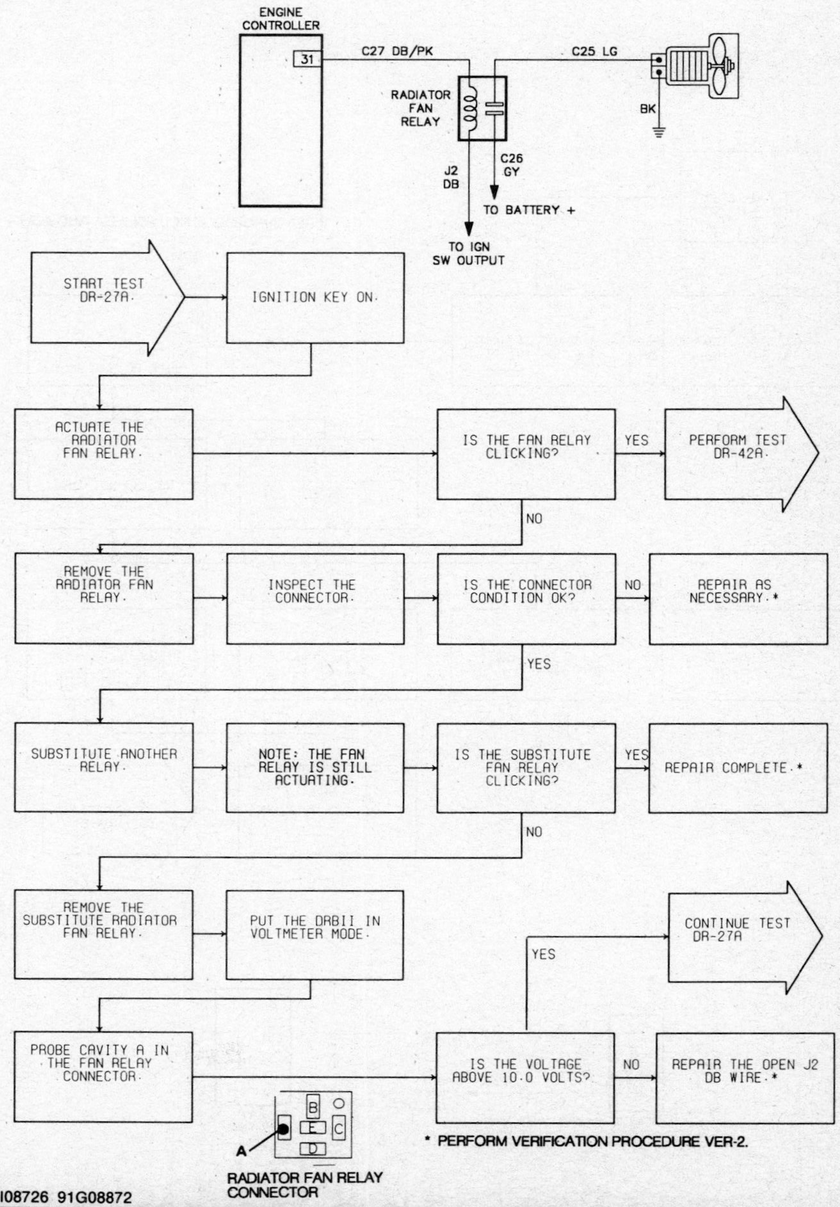
ENGINE CONTROLLER
31
C27 DB/PK
C25 LG
RADIATOR FAN RELAY
BK
J2 DB
C26 GY
TO BATTERY +
TO IGN SW OUTPUT
START TEST DR-27A.
IGNITION KEY ON.
ACTUATE THE RADIATOR FAN RELAY.
IS THE FAN RELAY CLICKING?
YES
PERFORM TEST DR-42A.
NO
REMOVE THE RADIATOR FAN RELAY.
INSPECT THE CONNECTOR.
IS THE CONNECTOR CONDITION OK?
NO
REPAIR AS NECESSARY.*
YES
SUBSTITUTE ANOTHER RELAY.
NOTE: THE FAN RELAY IS STILL ACTUATING.
IS THE SUBSTITUTE FAN RELAY CLICKING?
YES
REPAIR COMPLETE.*
NO
REMOVE THE SUBSTITUTE RADIATOR FAN RELAY.
PUT THE DRBII IN VOLTMETER MODE.
CONTINUE TEST DR-27A
YES
PROBE CAVITY A IN THE FAN RELAY CONNECTOR.
IS THE VOLTAGE ABOVE 10.0 VOLTS?
NO
REPAIR THE OPEN J2 DB WIRE.*
A
RADIATOR FAN RELAY CONNECTOR

* PERFORM VERIFICATION PROCEDURE VER-2.

91I08726 91G08872

Fig. 118: ***Driveability Test 27A (2.2L & 2.5L) – Code 35, Radiator Fan Relay Circuit (1 of 2)***

1991 ENGINE PERFORMANCE
Self-Diagnostics – 2.5L TBI (Cont.)

DR-27A: CODE 35, RADIATOR FAN RELAY CIRCUIT (2 OF 2)

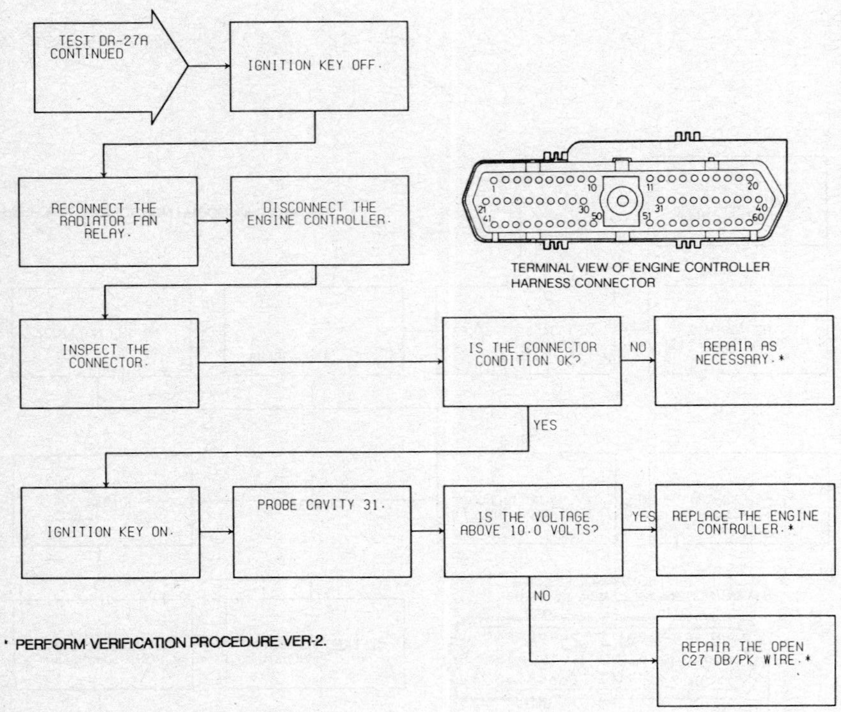
TEST DR-27A CONTINUED
IGNITION KEY OFF.
RECONNECT THE RADIATOR FAN RELAY.
DISCONNECT THE ENGINE CONTROLLER.
TERMINAL VIEW OF ENGINE CONTROLLER HARNESS CONNECTOR
INSPECT THE CONNECTOR.
IS THE CONNECTOR CONDITION OK?
NO
REPAIR AS NECESSARY.*
YES
IGNITION KEY ON.
PROBE CAVITY 31.
IS THE VOLTAGE ABOVE 10.0 VOLTS?
YES
REPLACE THE ENGINE CONTROLLER.*
NO
REPAIR THE OPEN C27 DB/PK WIRE.*

* PERFORM VERIFICATION PROCEDURE VER-2.

91I08873

Fig. 119: *Driveability Test 27A (2.2L & 2.5L) – Code 35, Radiator Fan Relay Circuit (2 of 2)*

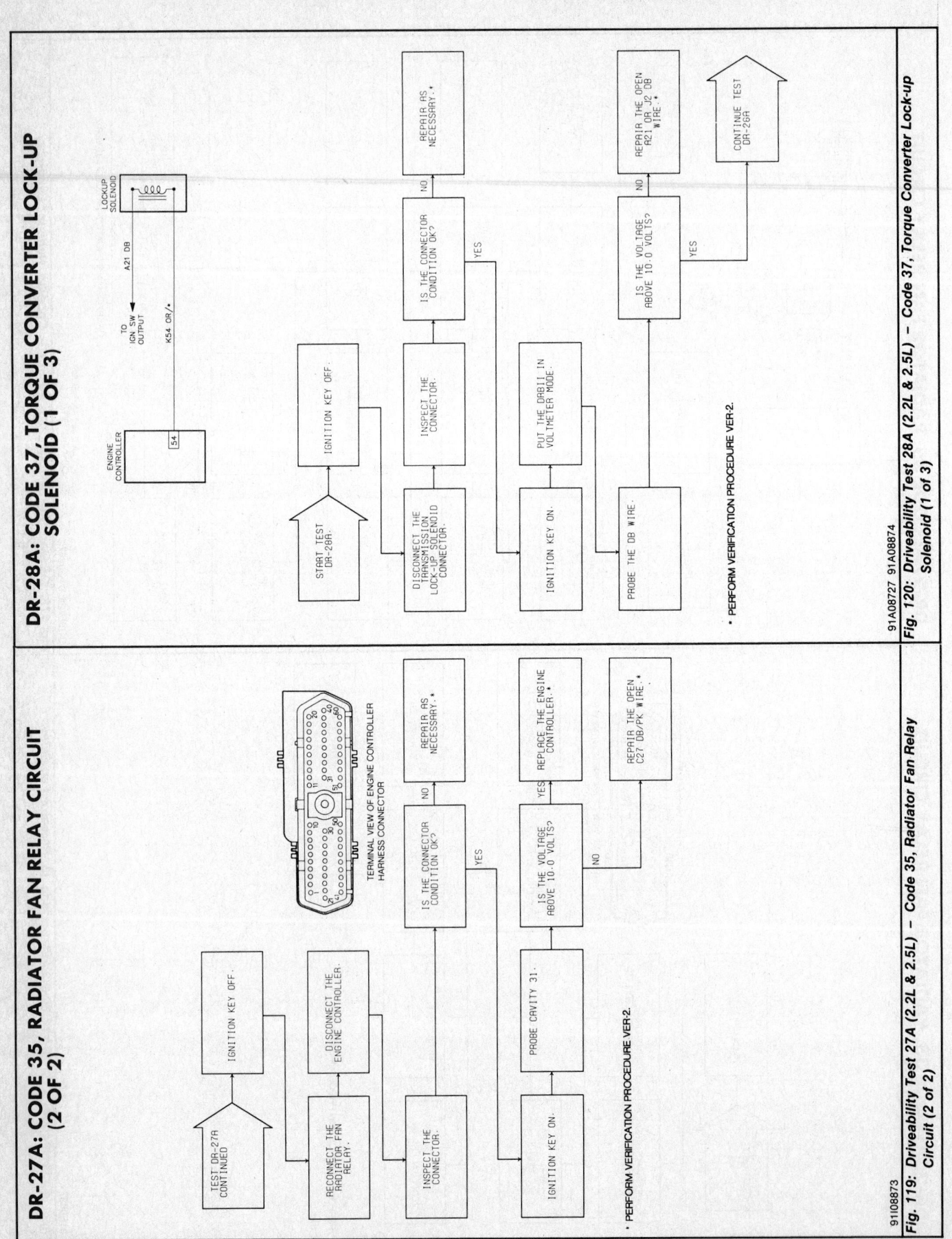

DR-28A: CODE 37, TORQUE CONVERTER LOCK-UP SOLENOID (1 OF 3)

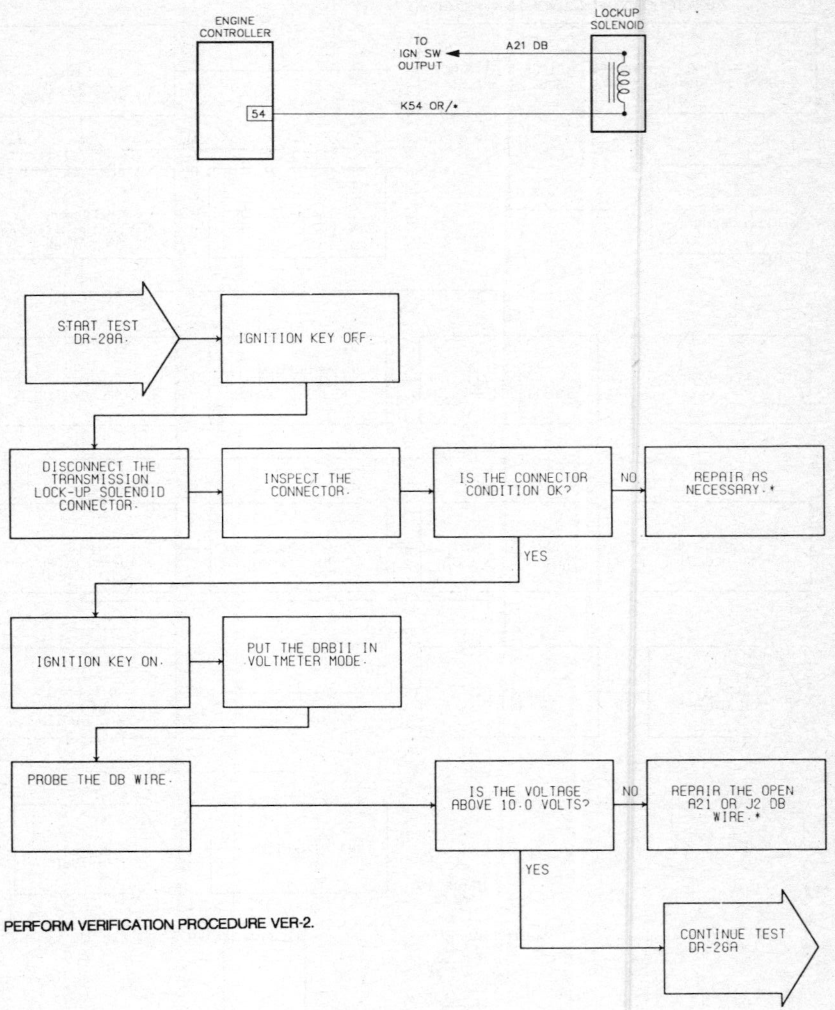
ENGINE CONTROLLER
54
TO IGN SW OUTPUT
A21 DB
K54 OR/*
LOCKUP SOLENOID
START TEST DR-28A.
IGNITION KEY OFF.
DISCONNECT THE TRANSMISSION LOCK-UP SOLENOID CONNECTOR.
INSPECT THE CONNECTOR.
IS THE CONNECTOR CONDITION OK?
NO
REPAIR AS NECESSARY.*
YES
IGNITION KEY ON.
PUT THE DRBII IN VOLTMETER MODE.
PROBE THE DB WIRE.
IS THE VOLTAGE ABOVE 10.0 VOLTS?
NO
REPAIR THE OPEN A21 OR J2 DB WIRE.*
YES
CONTINUE TEST DR-26A

* PERFORM VERIFICATION PROCEDURE VER-2.

91A08727 91A08874

Fig. 120: *Driveability Test 28A (2.2L & 2.5L) – Code 37, Torque Converter Lock-up Solenoid (1 of 3)*

DR-28A: CODE 37, TORQUE CONVERTER LOCK-UP SOLENOID (2 OF 3)

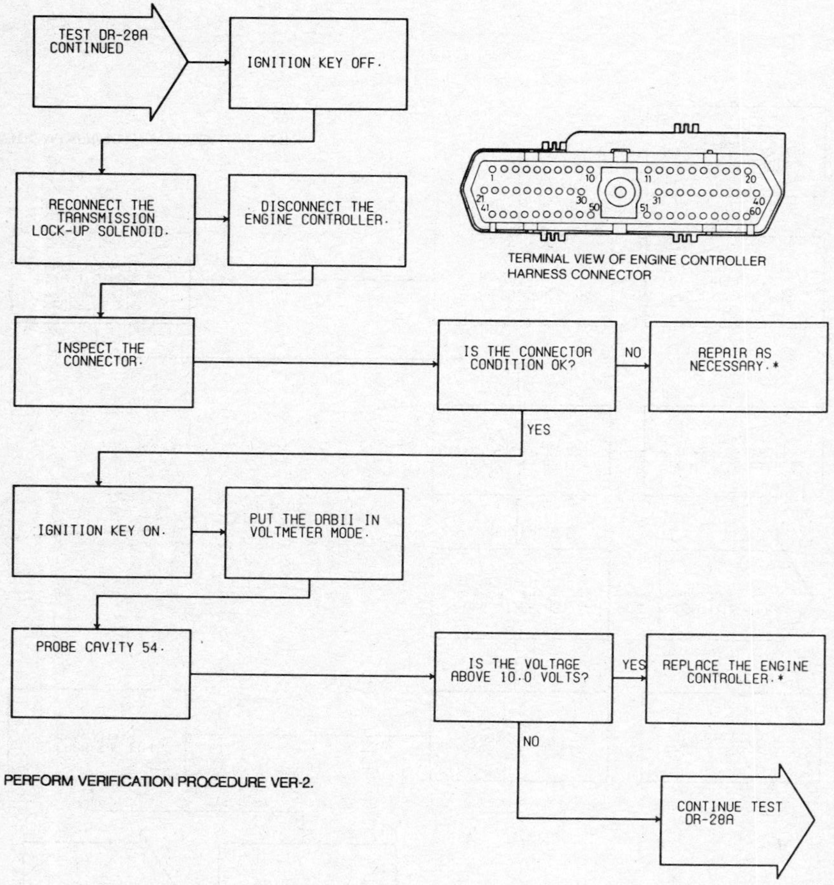
TEST DR-28A CONTINUED
IGNITION KEY OFF.
RECONNECT THE TRANSMISSION LOCK-UP SOLENOID.
DISCONNECT THE ENGINE CONTROLLER.
TERMINAL VIEW OF ENGINE CONTROLLER HARNESS CONNECTOR
INSPECT THE CONNECTOR.
IS THE CONNECTOR CONDITION OK?
NO
REPAIR AS NECESSARY.*
YES
IGNITION KEY ON.
PUT THE DRBII IN VOLTMETER MODE.
PROBE CAVITY 54.
IS THE VOLTAGE ABOVE 10.0 VOLTS?
YES
REPLACE THE ENGINE CONTROLLER.*
NO
CONTINUE TEST DR-28A

* PERFORM VERIFICATION PROCEDURE VER-2.

91D08875

Fig. 121: Driveability Test 28A (2.2L & 2.5L) – Code 37, Torque Converter Lock-up Solenoid (2 of 3)

DR-28A: CODE 37, TORQUE CONVERTER LOCK-UP SOLENOID (3 OF 3)

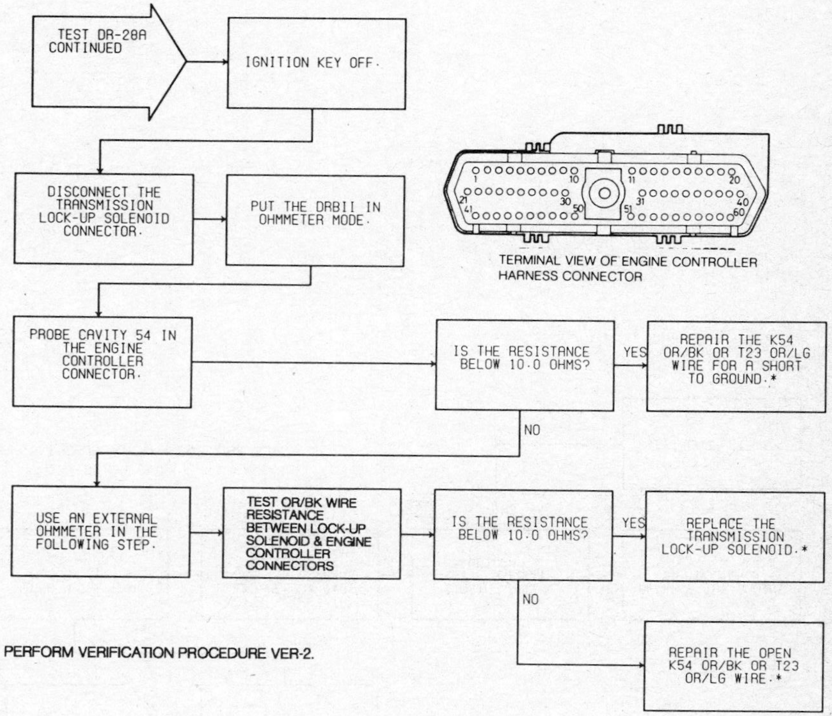
TEST DR-28A CONTINUED
IGNITION KEY OFF.
DISCONNECT THE TRANSMISSION LOCK-UP SOLENOID CONNECTOR.
PUT THE DRBII IN OHMMETER MODE.
TERMINAL VIEW OF ENGINE CONTROLLER HARNESS CONNECTOR
PROBE CAVITY 54 IN THE ENGINE CONTROLLER CONNECTOR.
IS THE RESISTANCE BELOW 10.0 OHMS?
YES
REPAIR THE K54 OR/BK OR T23 OR/LG WIRE FOR A SHORT TO GROUND.*
NO
USE AN EXTERNAL OHMMETER IN THE FOLLOWING STEP.
TEST OR/BK WIRE RESISTANCE BETWEEN LOCK-UP SOLENOID & ENGINE CONTROLLER CONNECTORS
IS THE RESISTANCE BELOW 10.0 OHMS?
YES
REPLACE THE TRANSMISSION LOCK-UP SOLENOID.*
NO
REPAIR THE OPEN K54 OR/BK OR T23 OR/LG WIRE.*

* PERFORM VERIFICATION PROCEDURE VER-2.

91F08876

Fig. 122: Driveability Test 28A (2.2L & 2.5L) – Code 37, Torque Converter Lock-up Solenoid (3 of 3)

DR-29A: CODE 63, SBEC FAILURE EMR MILEAGE NOT STORED & EEPROM WRITE DENIED (1 OF 2)

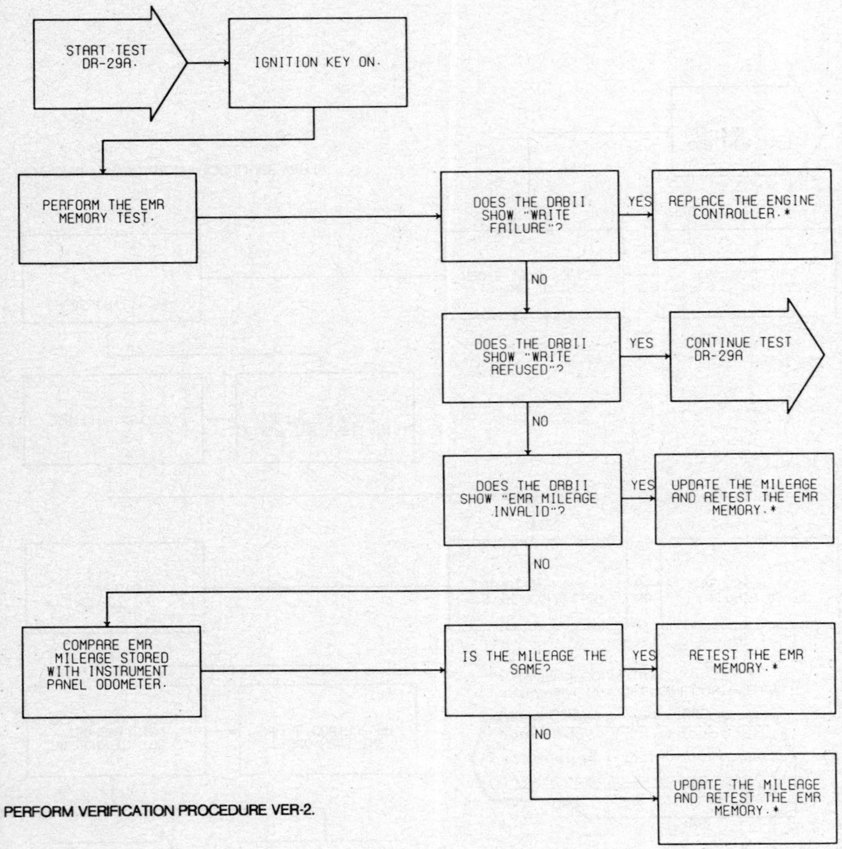
START TEST DR-29A.
IGNITION KEY ON.
PERFORM THE EMR MEMORY TEST.
DOES THE DRBII SHOW "WRITE FAILURE"?
YES
REPLACE THE ENGINE CONTROLLER.*
NO
DOES THE DRBII SHOW "WRITE REFUSED"?
YES
CONTINUE TEST DR-29A
NO
DOES THE DRBII SHOW "EMR MILEAGE INVALID"?
YES
UPDATE THE MILEAGE AND RETEST THE EMR MEMORY.*
NO
COMPARE EMR MILEAGE STORED WITH INSTRUMENT PANEL ODOMETER.
IS THE MILEAGE THE SAME?
YES
RETEST THE EMR MEMORY.*
NO
UPDATE THE MILEAGE AND RETEST THE EMR MEMORY.*

* PERFORM VERIFICATION PROCEDURE VER-2.

91H08877

Fig. 123: *Driveability Test 29A (2.2L & 2.5L) – Code 63, SBEC Failure EMR Mileage Not Stored & EEPROM Write Denied (1 of 2)*

DR-29A: CODE 63, SBEC FAILURE EMR MILEAGE NOT STORED & EEPROM WRITE DENIED (2 OF 2)

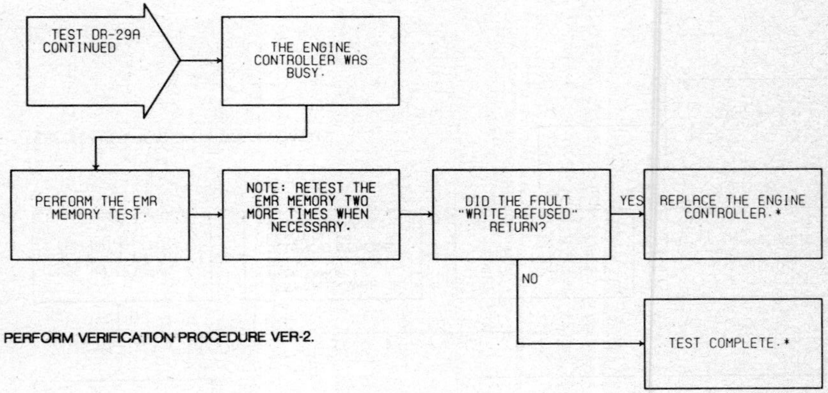
TEST DR-29A CONTINUED
THE ENGINE CONTROLLER WAS BUSY.
PERFORM THE EMR MEMORY TEST.
NOTE: RETEST THE EMR MEMORY TWO MORE TIMES WHEN NECESSARY.
DID THE FAULT "WRITE REFUSED" RETURN?
YES
REPLACE THE ENGINE CONTROLLER.*
NO
TEST COMPLETE.*

* PERFORM VERIFICATION PROCEDURE VER-2.

91J08878

Fig. 124: *Driveability Test 29A (2.2L & 2.5L) – Code 63, SBEC Failure EMR Mileage Not Stored & EEPROM Write Denied (2 of 2)*

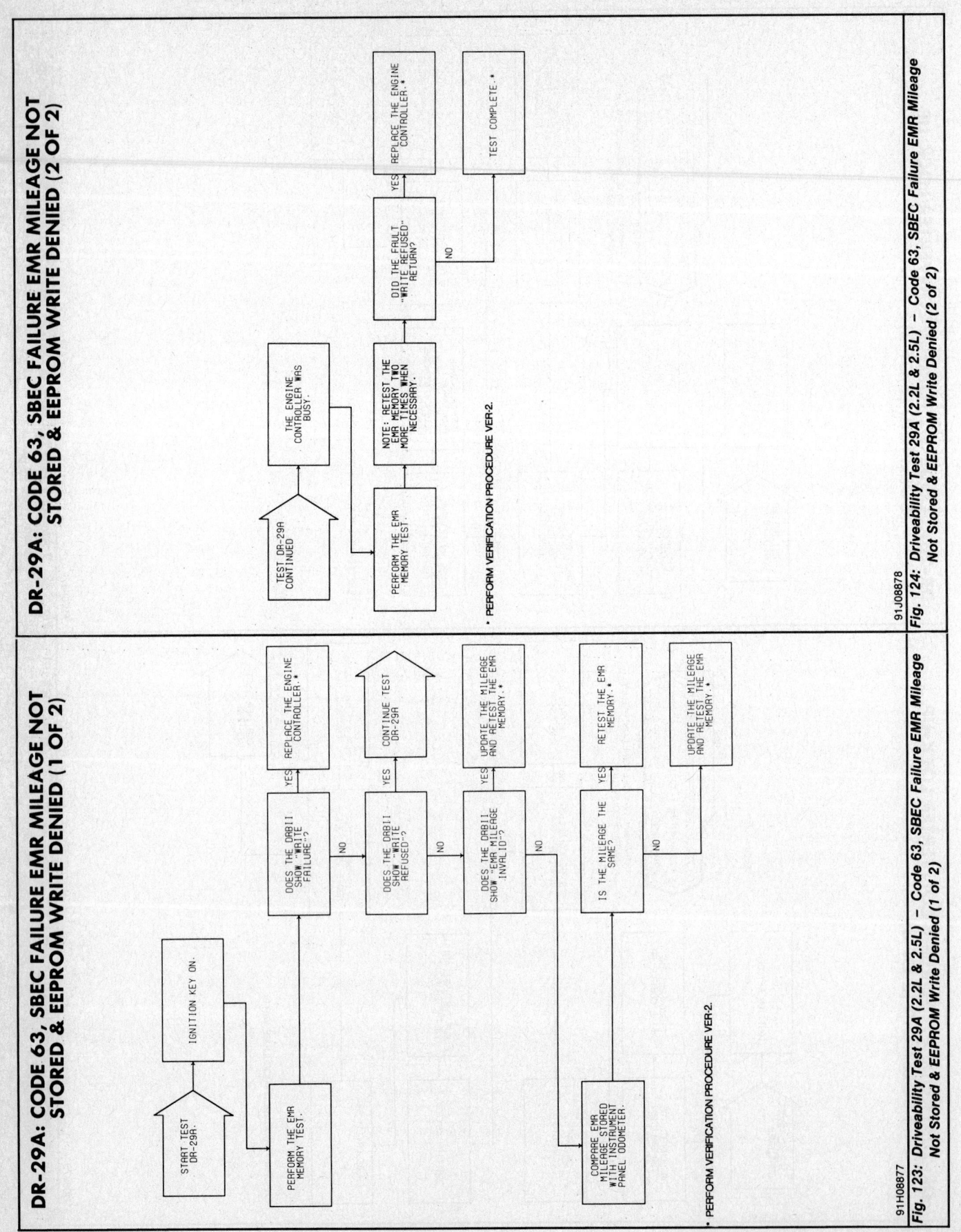

DR-30A: CHECKING SECONDARY IGNITION & TIMING (1 OF 2)

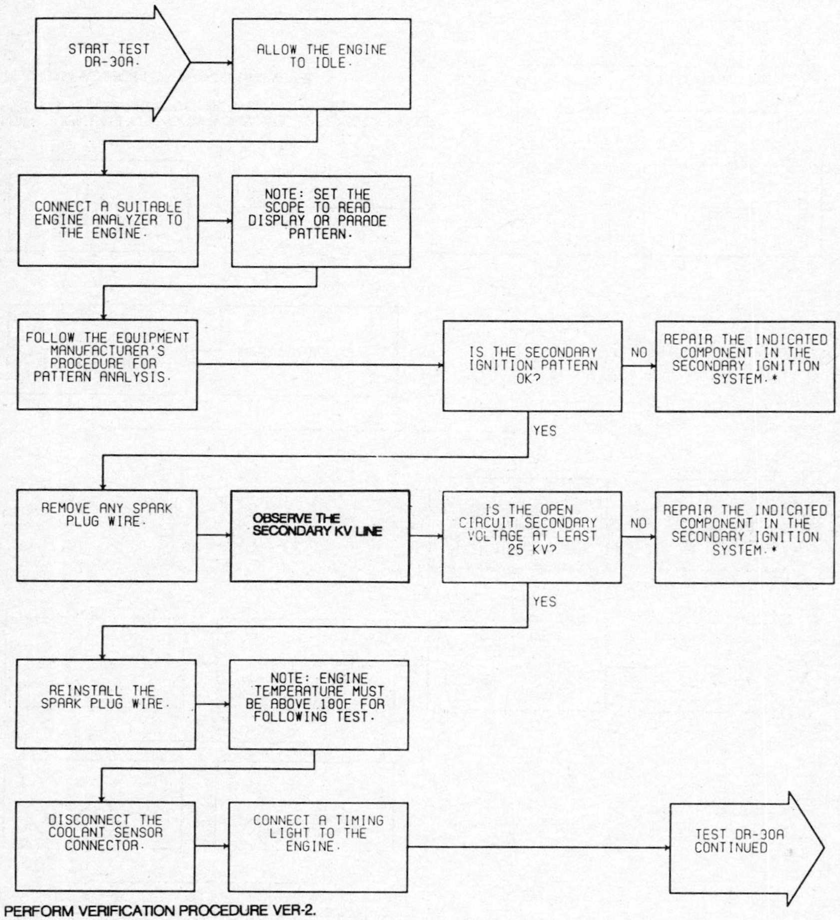
START TEST DR-30A.
ALLOW THE ENGINE TO IDLE.
CONNECT A SUITABLE ENGINE ANALYZER TO THE ENGINE.
NOTE: SET THE SCOPE TO READ DISPLAY OR PARADE PATTERN.
FOLLOW THE EQUIPMENT MANUFACTURER'S PROCEDURE FOR PATTERN ANALYSIS.
IS THE SECONDARY IGNITION PATTERN OK?
NO
REPAIR THE INDICATED COMPONENT IN THE SECONDARY IGNITION SYSTEM.*
YES
REMOVE ANY SPARK PLUG WIRE.
OBSERVE THE SECONDARY KV LINE
IS THE OPEN CIRCUIT SECONDARY VOLTAGE AT LEAST 25 KV?
NO
REPAIR THE INDICATED COMPONENT IN THE SECONDARY IGNITION SYSTEM.*
YES
REINSTALL THE SPARK PLUG WIRE.
NOTE: ENGINE TEMPERATURE MUST BE ABOVE 180F FOR FOLLOWING TEST.
DISCONNECT THE COOLANT SENSOR CONNECTOR.
CONNECT A TIMING LIGHT TO THE ENGINE.
TEST DR-30A CONTINUED

* PERFORM VERIFICATION PROCEDURE VER-2.

91B08879

Fig. 125: *Driveability Test 30A (2.2L & 2.5L) – Checking Secondary Ignition & Timing (1 of 2)*

DR-30A: CHECKING SECONDARY IGNITION & TIMING (2 OF 2)

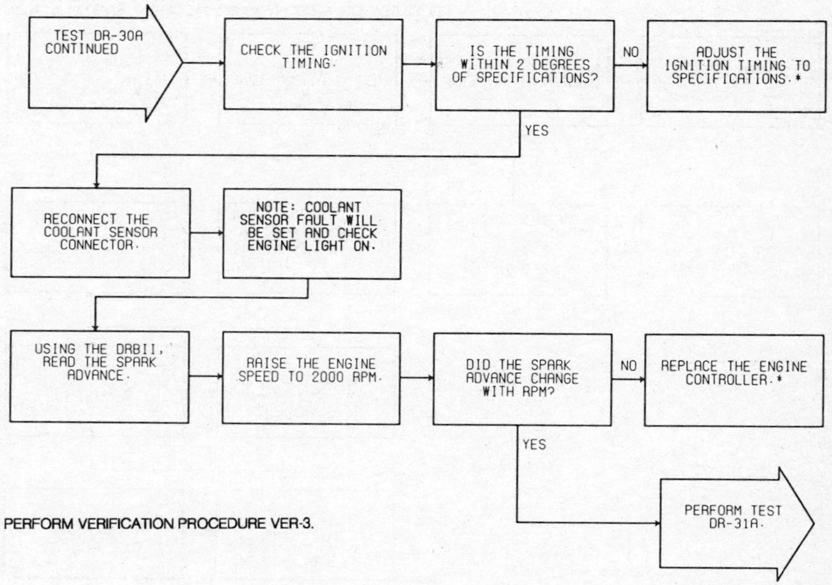
TEST DR-30A CONTINUED
CHECK THE IGNITION TIMING.
IS THE TIMING WITHIN 2 DEGREES OF SPECIFICATIONS?
NO
ADJUST THE IGNITION TIMING TO SPECIFICATIONS.*
YES
RECONNECT THE COOLANT SENSOR CONNECTOR.
NOTE: COOLANT SENSOR FAULT WILL BE SET AND CHECK ENGINE LIGHT ON.
USING THE DRBII, READ THE SPARK ADVANCE.
RAISE THE ENGINE SPEED TO 2000 RPM.
DID THE SPARK ADVANCE CHANGE WITH RPM?
NO
REPLACE THE ENGINE CONTROLLER.*
YES
PERFORM TEST DR-31A.

* PERFORM VERIFICATION PROCEDURE VER-3.

91D08880

Fig. 126: *Driveability Test 30A (2.2L & 2.5L) – Checking Secondary Ignition & Timing (2 of 2)*

DR-31A: CHECKING FUEL PRESSURE (1 OF 2)

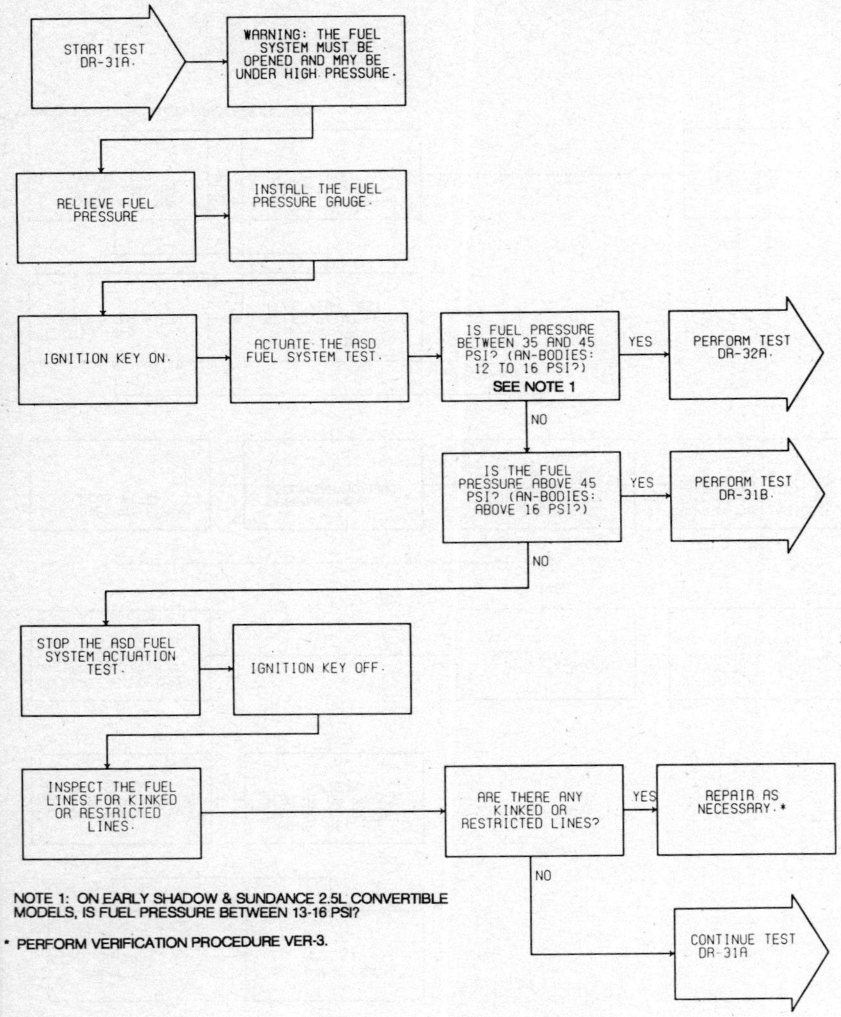
START TEST DR-31A.
WARNING: THE FUEL SYSTEM MUST BE OPENED AND MAY BE UNDER HIGH PRESSURE.
RELIEVE FUEL PRESSURE
INSTALL THE FUEL PRESSURE GAUGE.
IGNITION KEY ON.
ACTUATE THE ASD FUEL SYSTEM TEST.
IS FUEL PRESSURE BETWEEN 35 AND 45 PSI? (AN-BODIES: 12 TO 16 PSI?) SEE NOTE 1
YES
PERFORM TEST DR-32A.
NO
IS THE FUEL PRESSURE ABOVE 45 PSI? (AN-BODIES: ABOVE 16 PSI?)
YES
PERFORM TEST DR-31B.
NO
STOP THE ASD FUEL SYSTEM ACTUATION TEST.
IGNITION KEY OFF.
INSPECT THE FUEL LINES FOR KINKED OR RESTRICTED LINES.
ARE THERE ANY KINKED OR RESTRICTED LINES?
YES
REPAIR AS NECESSARY.*
NO
CONTINUE TEST DR-31A

NOTE 1: ON EARLY SHADOW & SUNDANCE 2.5L CONVERTIBLE MODELS, IS FUEL PRESSURE BETWEEN 13-16 PSI?

* PERFORM VERIFICATION PROCEDURE VER-3.

91F08881

Fig. 127: Driveability Test 31A (2.2L & 2.5L) – Checking Fuel Pressure (1 of 2)

DR-31A: CHECKING FUEL PRESSURE (2 OF 2)

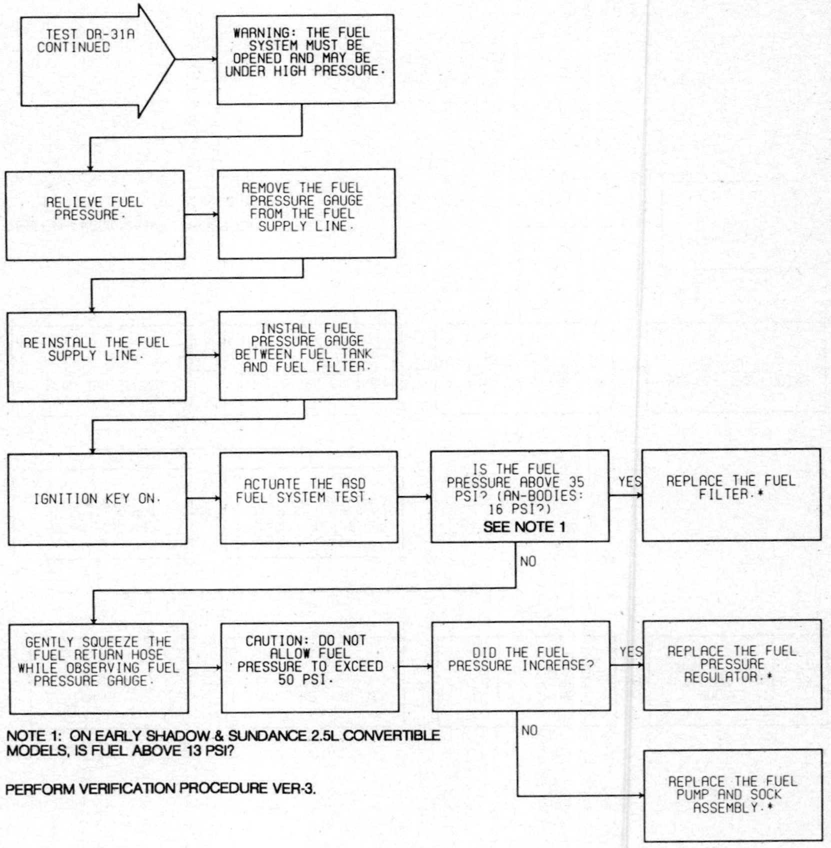
TEST DR-31A CONTINUED
WARNING: THE FUEL SYSTEM MUST BE OPENED AND MAY BE UNDER HIGH PRESSURE.
RELIEVE FUEL PRESSURE.
REMOVE THE FUEL PRESSURE GAUGE FROM THE FUEL SUPPLY LINE.
REINSTALL THE FUEL SUPPLY LINE.
INSTALL FUEL PRESSURE GAUGE BETWEEN FUEL TANK AND FUEL FILTER.
IGNITION KEY ON.
ACTUATE THE ASD FUEL SYSTEM TEST.
IS THE FUEL PRESSURE ABOVE 35 PSI? (AN-BODIES: 16 PSI?) SEE NOTE 1
YES
REPLACE THE FUEL FILTER.*
NO
GENTLY SQUEEZE THE FUEL RETURN HOSE WHILE OBSERVING FUEL PRESSURE GAUGE.
CAUTION: DO NOT ALLOW FUEL PRESSURE TO EXCEED 50 PSI.
DID THE FUEL PRESSURE INCREASE?
YES
REPLACE THE FUEL PRESSURE REGULATOR.*
NO
REPLACE THE FUEL PUMP AND SOCK ASSEMBLY.*

NOTE 1: ON EARLY SHADOW & SUNDANCE 2.5L CONVERTIBLE MODELS, IS FUEL ABOVE 13 PSI?

* PERFORM VERIFICATION PROCEDURE VER-3.

91H08882

Fig. 128: Driveability Test 31A (2.2L & 2.5L) – Checking Fuel Pressure (2 of 2)

DR-31B: CHECKING FUEL PRESSURE (1 OF 2)

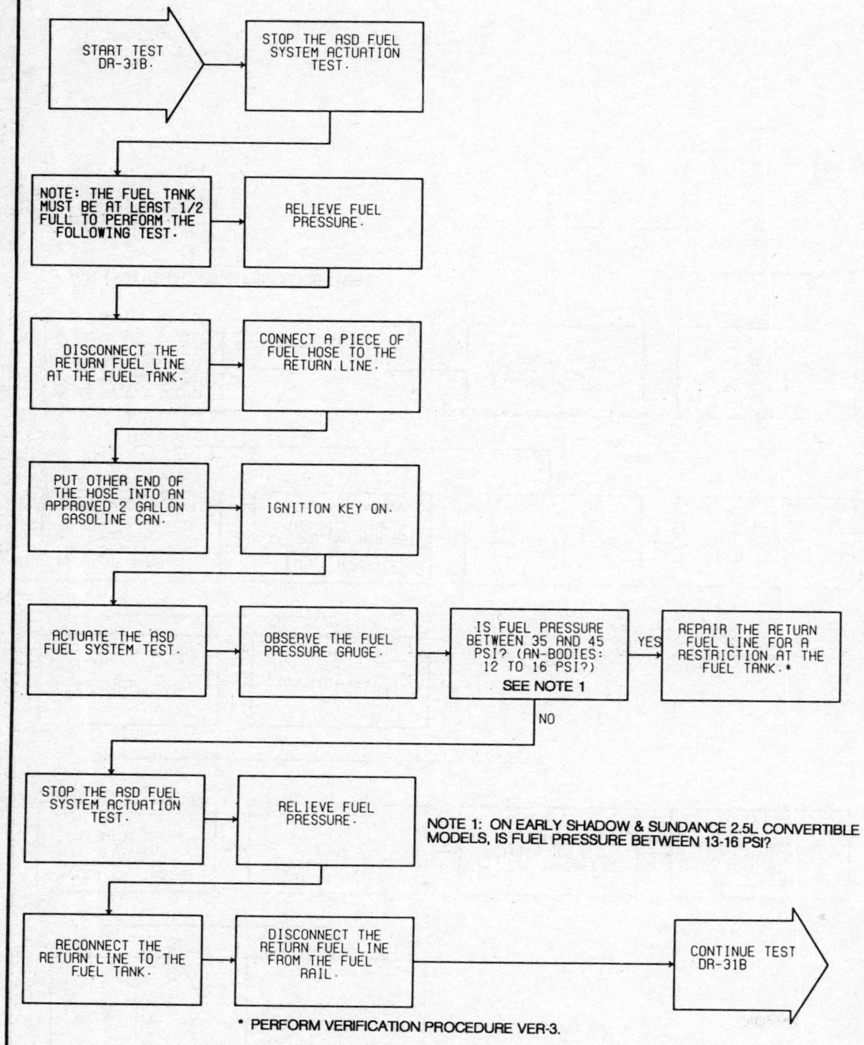
START TEST DR-31B.
STOP THE ASD FUEL SYSTEM ACTUATION TEST.
NOTE: THE FUEL TANK MUST BE AT LEAST 1/2 FULL TO PERFORM THE FOLLOWING TEST.
RELIEVE FUEL PRESSURE.
DISCONNECT THE RETURN FUEL LINE AT THE FUEL TANK.
CONNECT A PIECE OF FUEL HOSE TO THE RETURN LINE.
PUT OTHER END OF THE HOSE INTO AN APPROVED 2 GALLON GASOLINE CAN.
IGNITION KEY ON.
ACTUATE THE ASD FUEL SYSTEM TEST.
OBSERVE THE FUEL PRESSURE GAUGE.
IS FUEL PRESSURE BETWEEN 35 AND 45 PSI? (AN-BODIES: 12 TO 16 PSI?) SEE NOTE 1
YES
REPAIR THE RETURN FUEL LINE FOR A RESTRICTION AT THE FUEL TANK.*
NO
STOP THE ASD FUEL SYSTEM ACTUATION TEST.
RELIEVE FUEL PRESSURE.
NOTE 1: ON EARLY SHADOW & SUNDANCE 2.5L CONVERTIBLE MODELS, IS FUEL PRESSURE BETWEEN 13-16 PSI?
RECONNECT THE RETURN LINE TO THE FUEL TANK.
DISCONNECT THE RETURN FUEL LINE FROM THE FUEL RAIL.
CONTINUE TEST DR-31B
* PERFORM VERIFICATION PROCEDURE VER-3.

91J08883

Fig. 129: Driveability Test 31B (2.2L & 2.5L) – Checking Fuel Pressure (1 of 2)

DR-31B: CHECKING FUEL PRESSURE (2 OF 2)

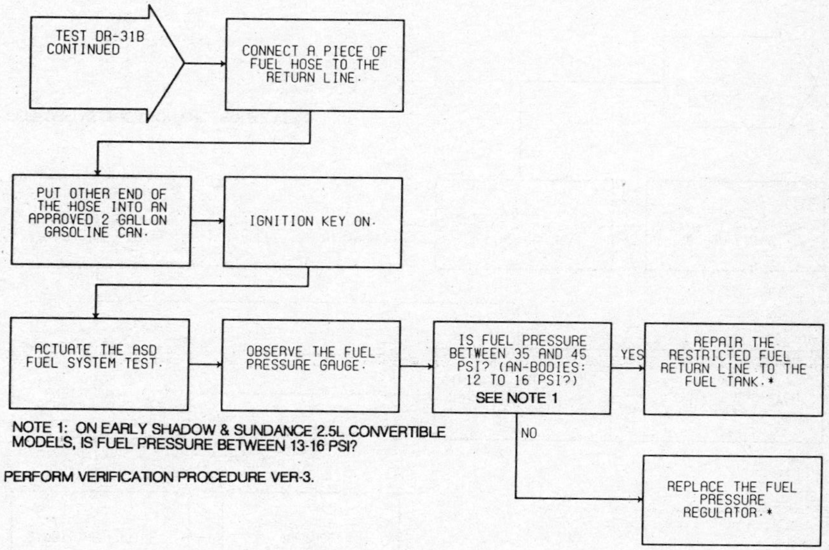
TEST DR-31B CONTINUED
CONNECT A PIECE OF FUEL HOSE TO THE RETURN LINE.
PUT OTHER END OF THE HOSE INTO AN APPROVED 2 GALLON GASOLINE CAN.
IGNITION KEY ON.
ACTUATE THE ASD FUEL SYSTEM TEST.
OBSERVE THE FUEL PRESSURE GAUGE.
IS FUEL PRESSURE BETWEEN 35 AND 45 PSI? (AN-BODIES: 12 TO 16 PSI?) SEE NOTE 1
YES
REPAIR THE RESTRICTED FUEL RETURN LINE TO THE FUEL TANK.*
NO
REPLACE THE FUEL PRESSURE REGULATOR.*
NOTE 1: ON EARLY SHADOW & SUNDANCE 2.5L CONVERTIBLE MODELS, IS FUEL PRESSURE BETWEEN 13-16 PSI?
* PERFORM VERIFICATION PROCEDURE VER-3.

91B08884

Fig. 130: Driveability Test 31B (2.2L & 2.5L) – Checking Fuel Pressure (2 of 2)

1991 ENGINE PERFORMANCE
Self-Diagnostics – 2.5L TBI (Cont.)

DR-32A: CHECKING COOLANT & TPS SENSOR CALIBRATION (1 OF 2)

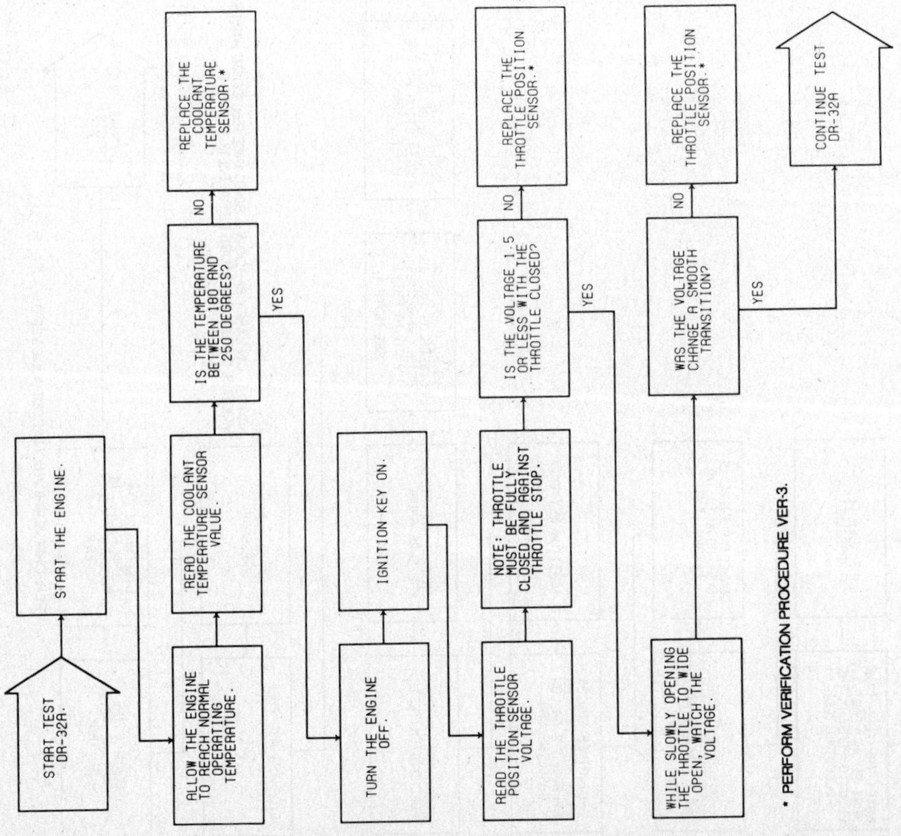
START TEST DR-32A.
START THE ENGINE.
ALLOW THE ENGINE TO REACH NORMAL OPERATING TEMPERATURE.
READ THE COOLANT TEMPERATURE SENSOR VALUE.
IS THE TEMPERATURE BETWEEN 180 AND 250 DEGREES?
NO
REPLACE THE COOLANT TEMPERATURE SENSOR.*
YES
TURN THE ENGINE OFF.
IGNITION KEY ON.
READ THE THROTTLE POSITION SENSOR VOLTAGE.
NOTE: THROTTLE MUST BE FULLY CLOSED AND AGAINST THROTTLE STOP.
IS THE VOLTAGE 1.5 OR LESS WITH THE THROTTLE CLOSED?
NO
REPLACE THE THROTTLE POSITION SENSOR.*
YES
WHILE SLOWLY OPENING THE THROTTLE TO WIDE OPEN, WATCH THE VOLTAGE.
WAS THE VOLTAGE CHANGE A SMOOTH TRANSITION?
NO
REPLACE THE THROTTLE POSITION SENSOR.*
YES
CONTINUE TEST DR-32A

* PERFORM VERIFICATION PROCEDURE VER-3.

91E08885

Fig. 131: Driveability Test 32A (2.2L & 2.5L) – Checking Coolant & TPS Calibration (1 of 2)

DR-32A: CHECKING COOLANT & TPS SENSOR CALIBRATION (2 OF 2)

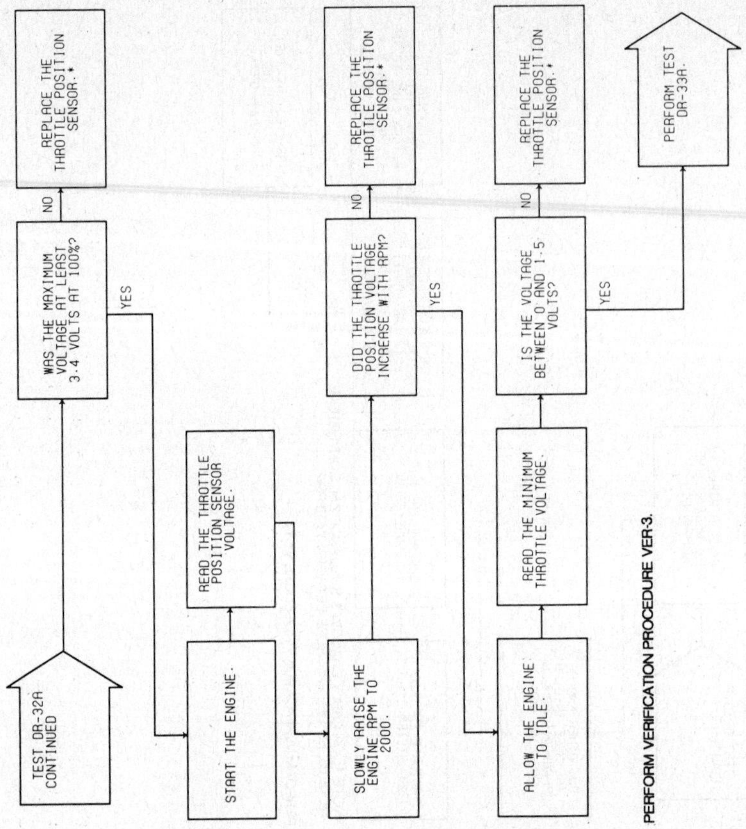
TEST DR-32A CONTINUED
WAS THE MAXIMUM VOLTAGE AT LEAST 3.4 VOLTS AT 100%?
NO
REPLACE THE THROTTLE POSITION SENSOR.*
YES
START THE ENGINE.
READ THE THROTTLE POSITION SENSOR VOLTAGE.
SLOWLY RAISE THE ENGINE RPM TO 2000.
DID THE THROTTLE POSITION VOLTAGE INCREASE WITH RPM?
NO
REPLACE THE THROTTLE POSITION SENSOR.*
YES
ALLOW THE ENGINE TO IDLE.
READ THE MINIMUM THROTTLE VOLTAGE.
IS THE VOLTAGE BETWEEN 0 AND 1.5 VOLTS?
NO
REPLACE THE THROTTLE POSITION SENSOR.*
YES
PERFORM TEST DR-33A.

* PERFORM VERIFICATION PROCEDURE VER-3.

91G08886

Fig. 132: Driveability Test 32A (2.2L & 2.5L) – Checking Coolant & TPS Calibration (2 of 2)

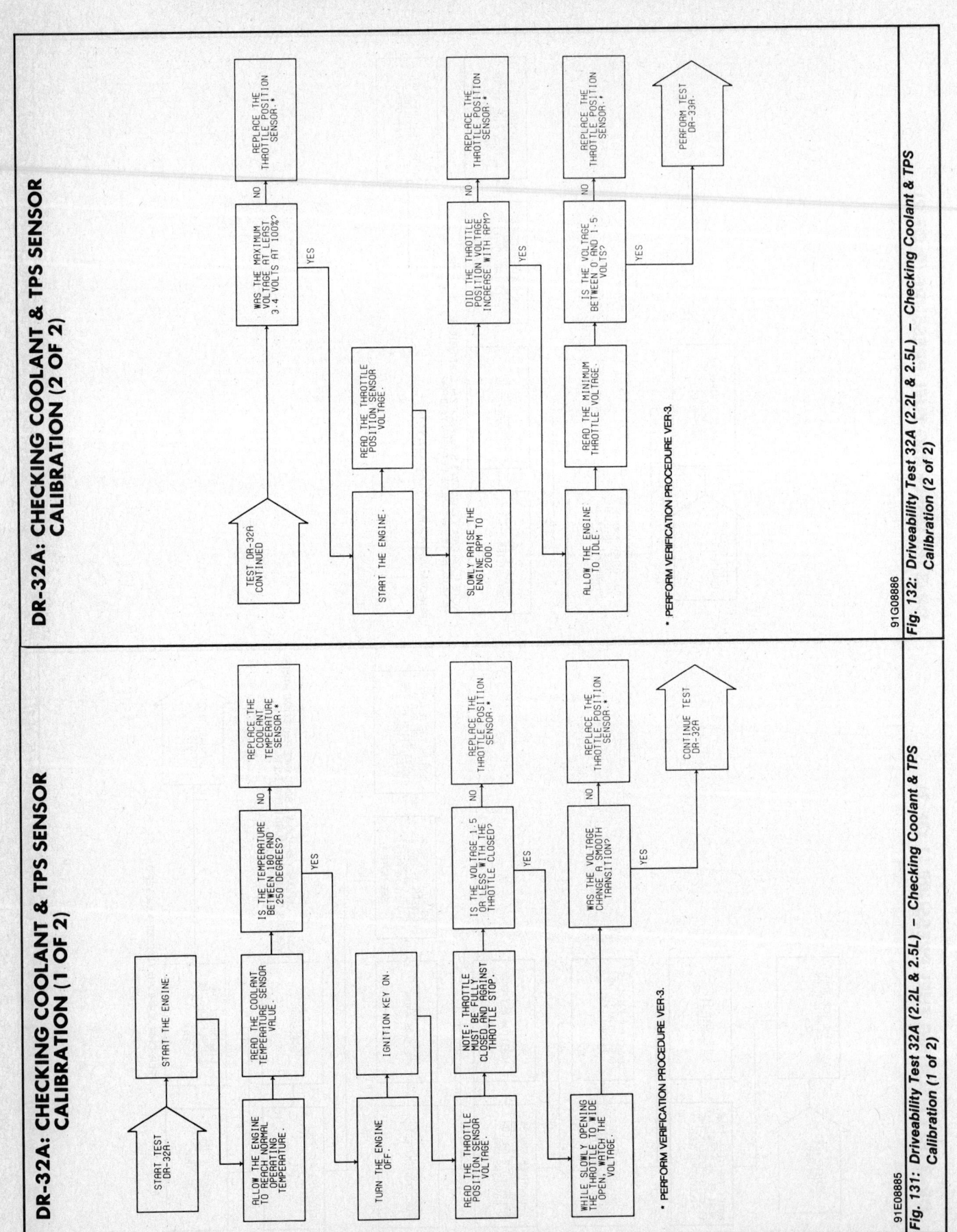

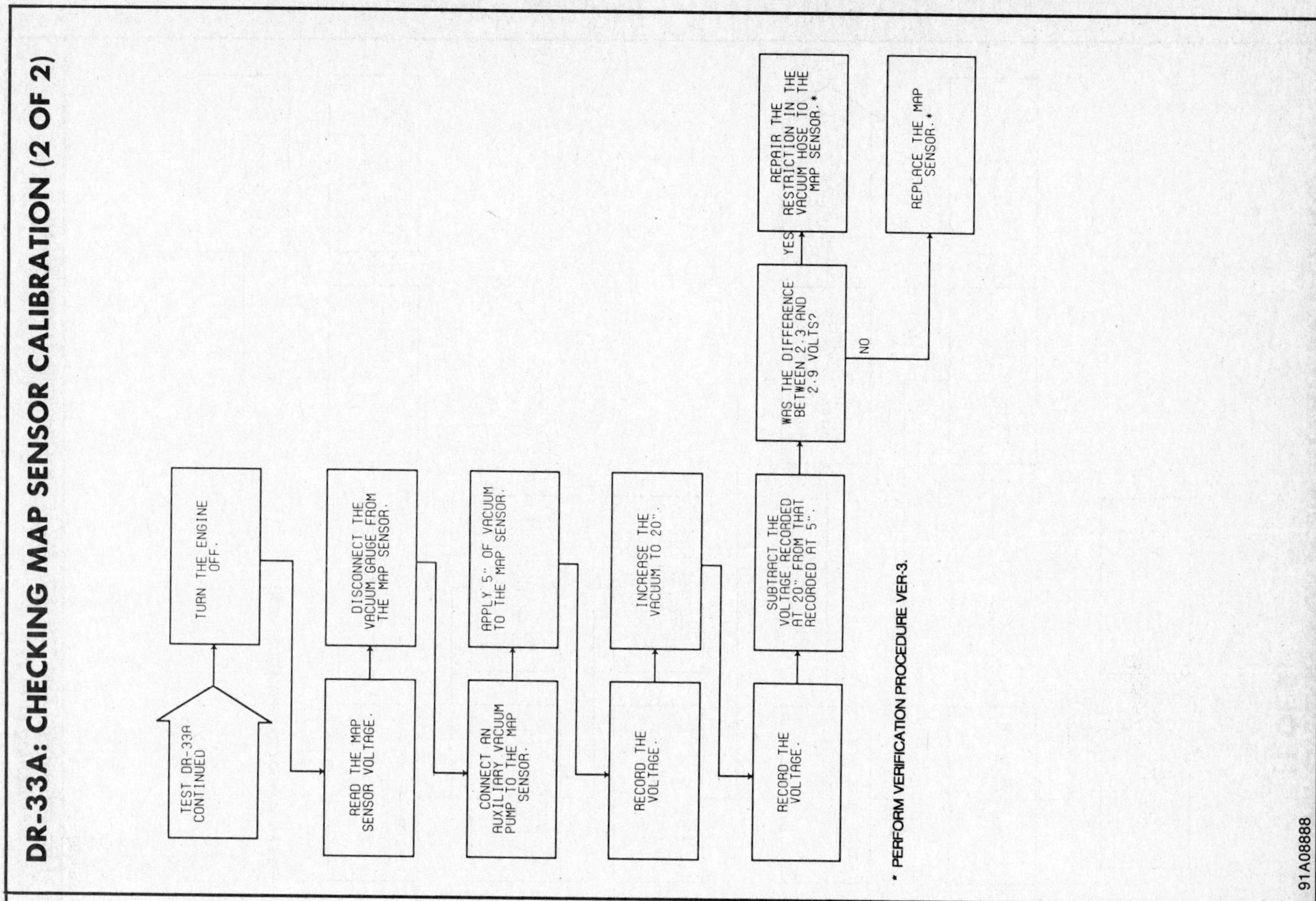

DR-33A: CHECKING MAP SENSOR CALIBRATION (2 OF 2)
TEST DR-33A CONTINUED
TURN THE ENGINE OFF.
READ THE MAP SENSOR VOLTAGE.
DISCONNECT THE VACUUM GAUGE FROM THE MAP SENSOR.
CONNECT AN AUXILIARY VACUUM PUMP TO THE MAP SENSOR.
APPLY 5" OF VACUUM TO THE MAP SENSOR.
RECORD THE VOLTAGE.
INCREASE THE VACUUM TO 20".
RECORD THE VOLTAGE.
SUBTRACT THE VOLTAGE RECORDED AT 20" FROM THAT RECORDED AT 5".
WAS THE DIFFERENCE BETWEEN 2.3 AND 2.9 VOLTS?
YES
REPAIR THE RESTRICTION IN THE VACUUM HOSE TO THE MAP SENSOR.*
NO
REPLACE THE MAP SENSOR.*
* PERFORM VERIFICATION PROCEDURE VER-3.
91A08888

Fig. 134: Driveability Test 33A (2.2L & 2.5L) – Checking MAP Sensor Calibration (2 of 2)

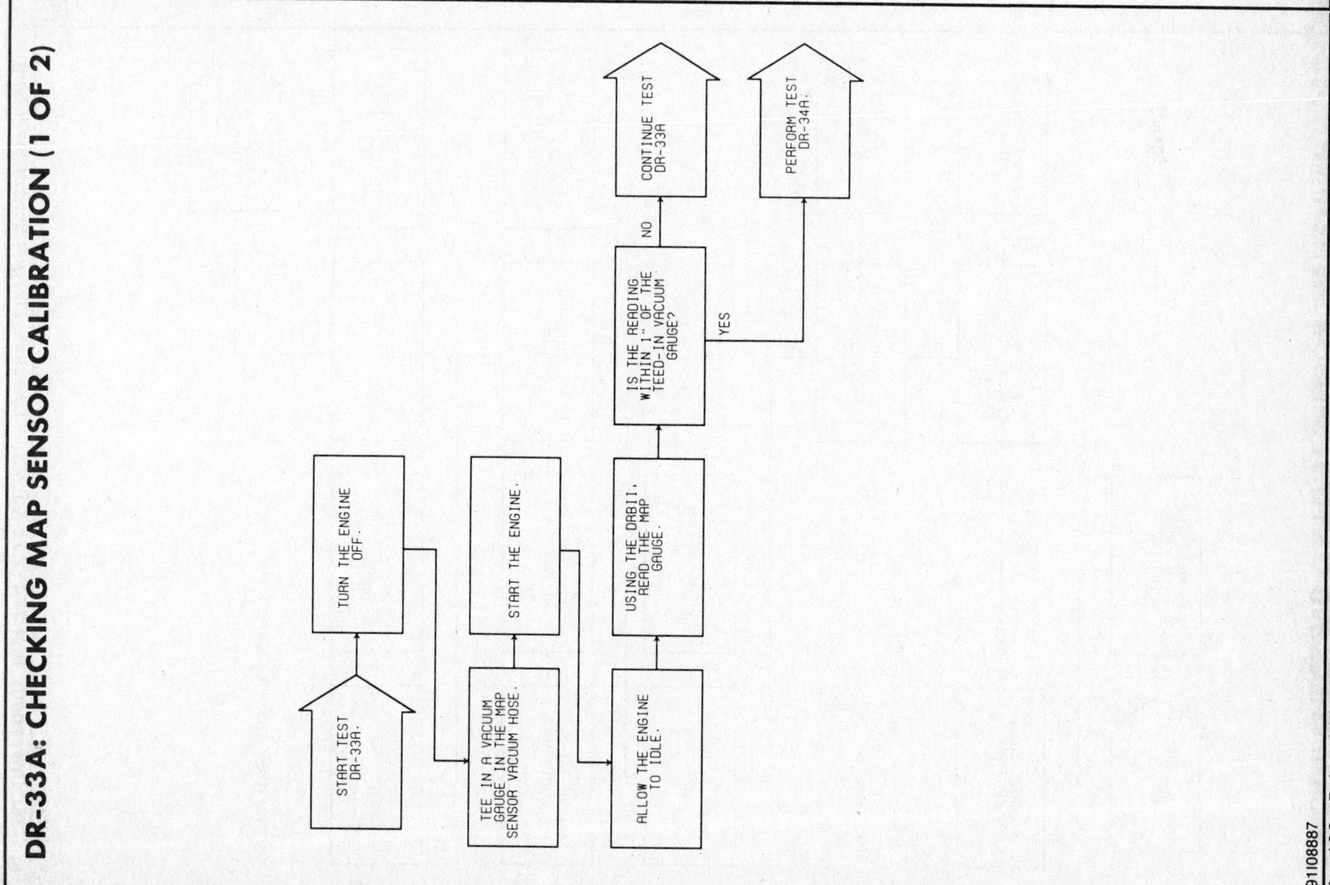

DR-33A: CHECKING MAP SENSOR CALIBRATION (1 OF 2)
START TEST DR-33A.
TURN THE ENGINE OFF.
TEE IN A VACUUM GAUGE IN THE MAP SENSOR VACUUM HOSE.
START THE ENGINE.
ALLOW THE ENGINE TO IDLE.
USING THE DRBII, READ THE MAP GAUGE.
IS THE READING WITHIN 1" OF THE TEED-IN VACUUM GAUGE?
NO
CONTINUE TEST DR-33A
YES
PERFORM TEST DR-34A.
91I08887

Fig. 133: Driveability Test 33A (2.2L & 2.5L) – Checking MAP Sensor Calibration (1 of 2)

DR-34A: CHECKING OXYGEN SENSOR SWITCHING

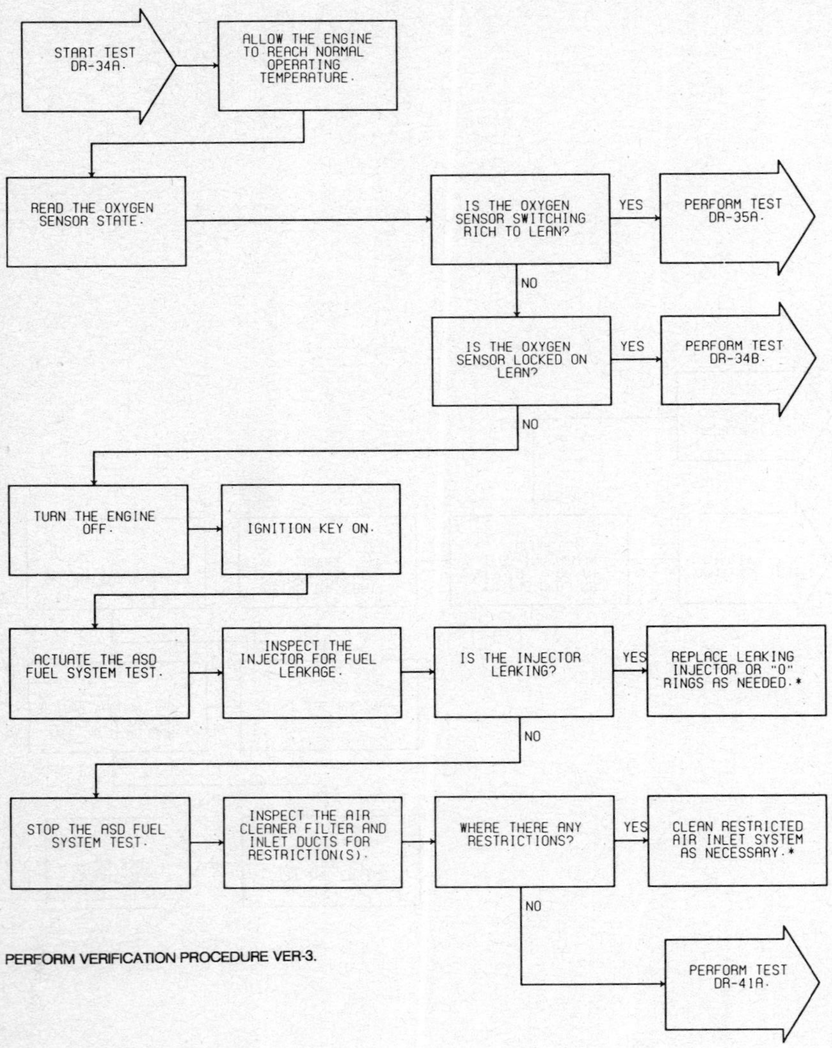
START TEST DR-34A.
ALLOW THE ENGINE TO REACH NORMAL OPERATING TEMPERATURE.
READ THE OXYGEN SENSOR STATE.
IS THE OXYGEN SENSOR SWITCHING RICH TO LEAN?
YES
PERFORM TEST DR-35A.
NO
IS THE OXYGEN SENSOR LOCKED ON LEAN?
YES
PERFORM TEST DR-34B.
NO
TURN THE ENGINE OFF.
IGNITION KEY ON.
ACTUATE THE ASD FUEL SYSTEM TEST.
INSPECT THE INJECTOR FOR FUEL LEAKAGE.
IS THE INJECTOR LEAKING?
YES
REPLACE LEAKING INJECTOR OR "O" RINGS AS NEEDED.*
NO
STOP THE ASD FUEL SYSTEM TEST.
INSPECT THE AIR CLEANER FILTER AND INLET DUCTS FOR RESTRICTION(S).
WHERE THERE ANY RESTRICTIONS?
YES
CLEAN RESTRICTED AIR INLET SYSTEM AS NECESSARY.*
NO
PERFORM TEST DR-41A.

* PERFORM VERIFICATION PROCEDURE VER-3.

91C08889

Fig. 135: Driveability Test 34A (2.2L & 2.5L) – Checking Oxygen Sensor Switching

DR-34B: CHECKING OXYGEN SENSOR SWITCHING (1 OF 2)

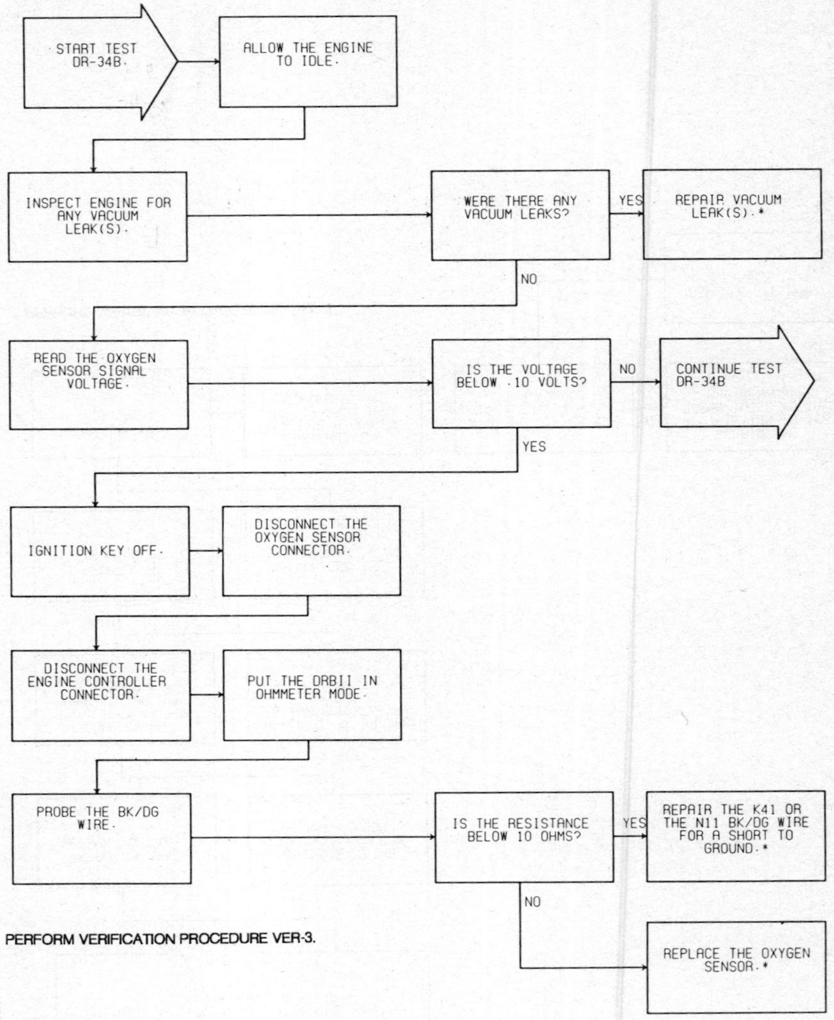
START TEST DR-34B.
ALLOW THE ENGINE TO IDLE.
INSPECT ENGINE FOR ANY VACUUM LEAK(S).
WERE THERE ANY VACUUM LEAKS?
YES
REPAIR VACUUM LEAK(S).*
NO
READ THE OXYGEN SENSOR SIGNAL VOLTAGE.
IS THE VOLTAGE BELOW .10 VOLTS?
NO
CONTINUE TEST DR-34B
YES
IGNITION KEY OFF.
DISCONNECT THE OXYGEN SENSOR CONNECTOR.
DISCONNECT THE ENGINE CONTROLLER CONNECTOR.
PUT THE DRBII IN OHMMETER MODE.
PROBE THE BK/DG WIRE.
IS THE RESISTANCE BELOW 10 OHMS?
YES
REPAIR THE K41 OR THE N11 BK/DG WIRE FOR A SHORT TO GROUND.*
NO
REPLACE THE OXYGEN SENSOR.*

* PERFORM VERIFICATION PROCEDURE VER-3.

91E08890

Fig. 136: Driveability Test 34B (2.2L & 2.5L) – Checking Oxygen Sensor Switching (1 of 2)

DR-34B: CHECKING OXYGEN SENSOR SWITCHING (2 OF 2)

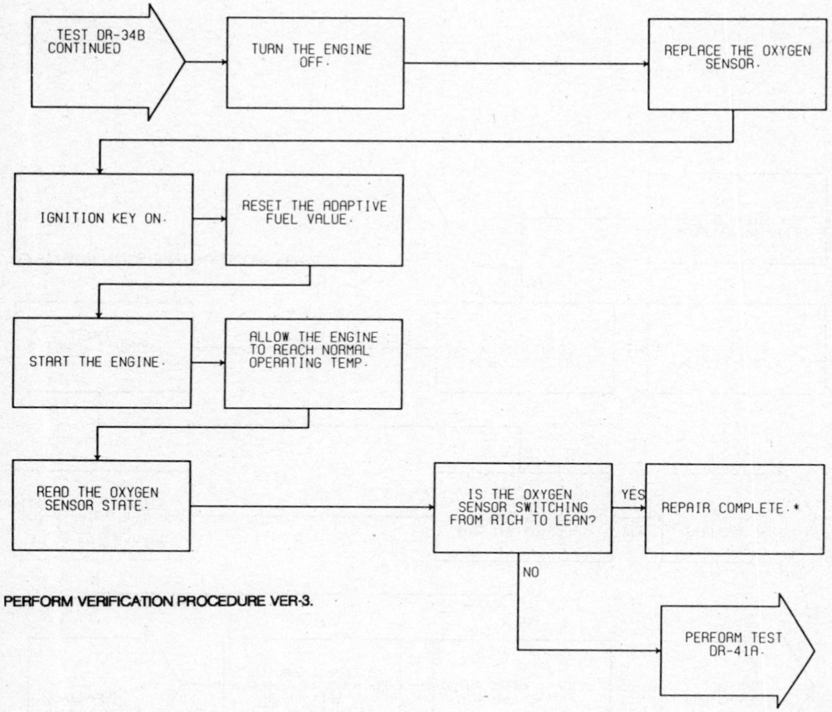
TEST DR-34B CONTINUED
TURN THE ENGINE OFF.
REPLACE THE OXYGEN SENSOR.
IGNITION KEY ON.
RESET THE ADAPTIVE FUEL VALUE.
START THE ENGINE.
ALLOW THE ENGINE TO REACH NORMAL OPERATING TEMP.
READ THE OXYGEN SENSOR STATE.
IS THE OXYGEN SENSOR SWITCHING FROM RICH TO LEAN?
YES
REPAIR COMPLETE.*
NO
PERFORM TEST DR-41A.

* PERFORM VERIFICATION PROCEDURE VER-3.

91G08891

Fig. 137: *Driveability Test 34B (2.2L & 2.5L) – Checking Oxygen Sensor Switching (2 of 2)*

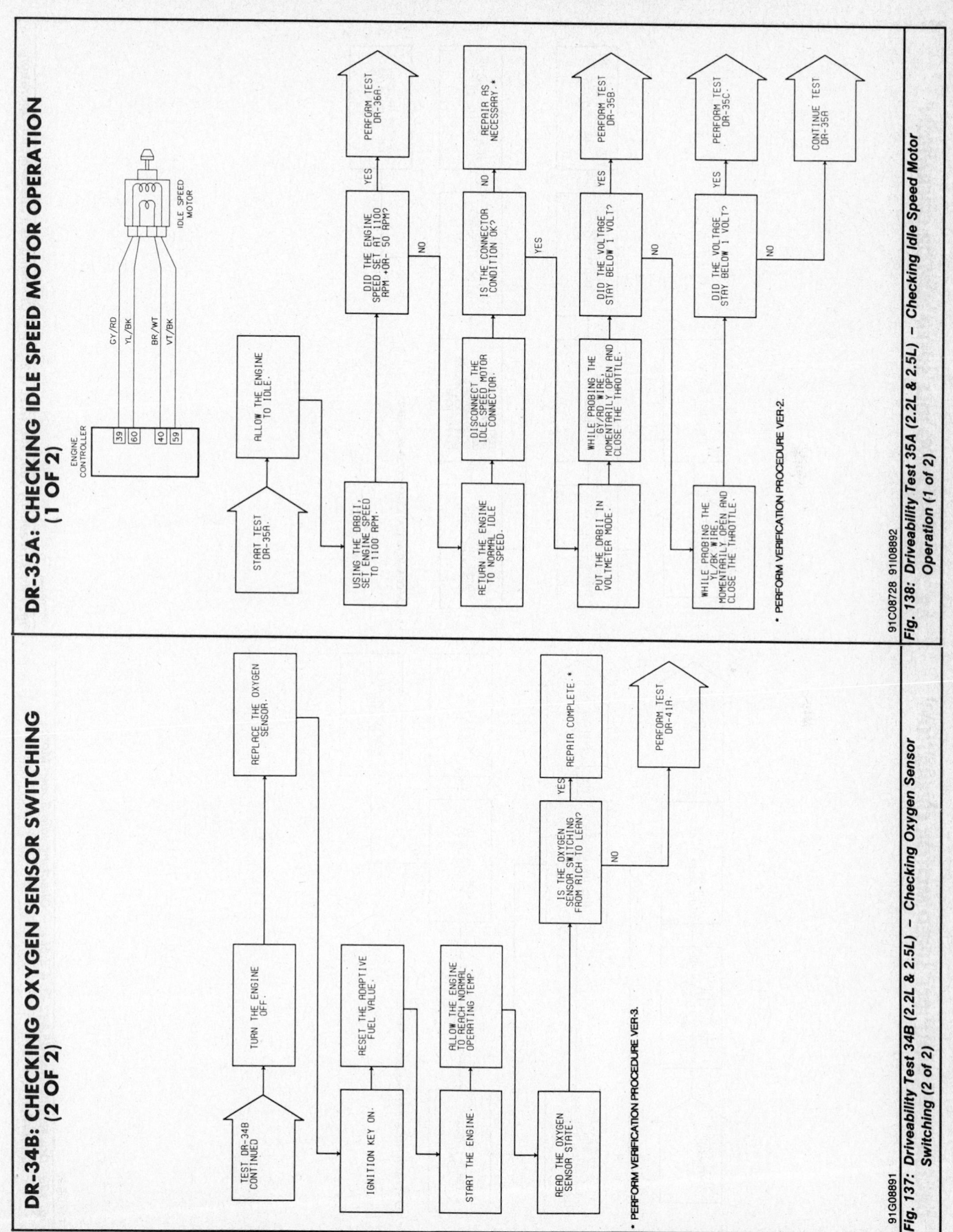

DR-35A: CHECKING IDLE SPEED MOTOR OPERATION (1 OF 2)

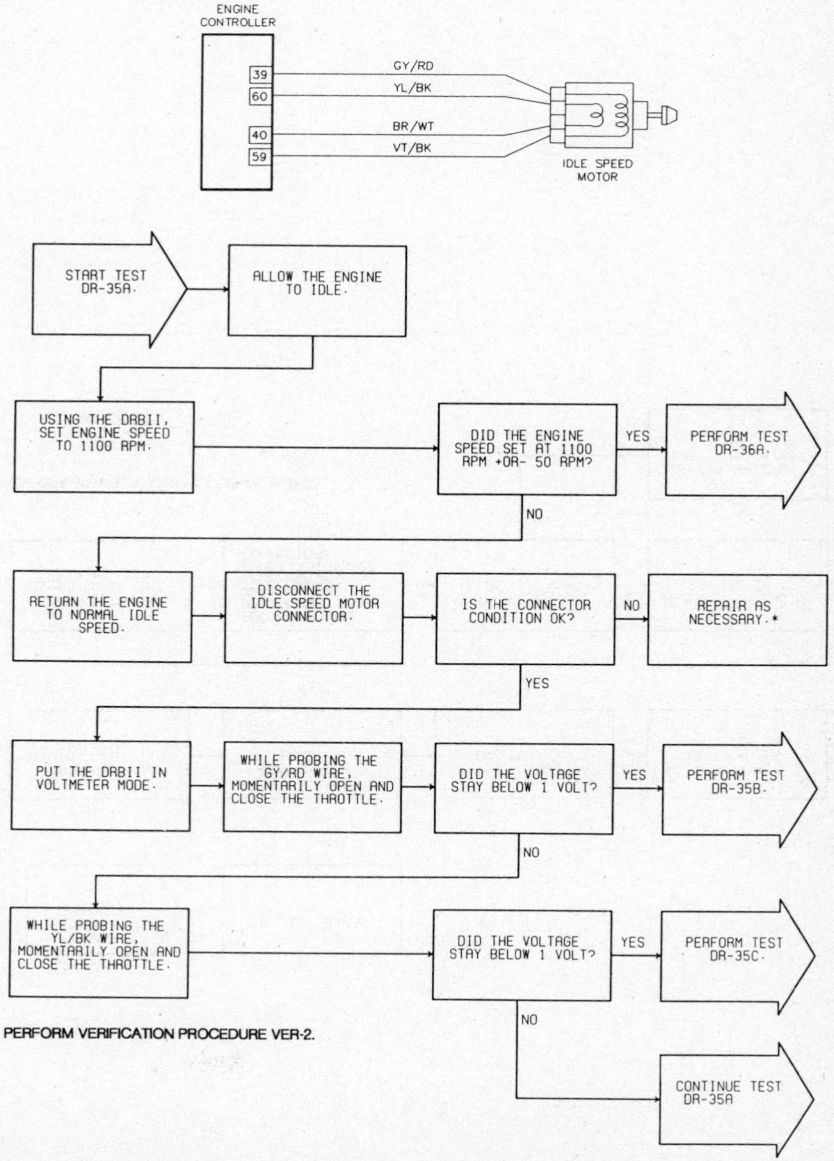
ENGINE CONTROLLER
39
60
40
59
GY/RD
YL/BK
BR/WT
VT/BK
IDLE SPEED MOTOR
START TEST DR-35A.
ALLOW THE ENGINE TO IDLE.
USING THE DRBII, SET ENGINE SPEED TO 1100 RPM.
DID THE ENGINE SPEED SET AT 1100 RPM +OR- 50 RPM?
YES
PERFORM TEST DR-36A.
NO
RETURN THE ENGINE TO NORMAL IDLE SPEED.
DISCONNECT THE IDLE SPEED MOTOR CONNECTOR.
IS THE CONNECTOR CONDITION OK?
NO
REPAIR AS NECESSARY.*
YES
PUT THE DRBII IN VOLTMETER MODE.
WHILE PROBING THE GY/RD WIRE, MOMENTARILY OPEN AND CLOSE THE THROTTLE.
DID THE VOLTAGE STAY BELOW 1 VOLT?
YES
PERFORM TEST DR-35B.
NO
WHILE PROBING THE YL/BK WIRE, MOMENTARILY OPEN AND CLOSE THE THROTTLE.
DID THE VOLTAGE STAY BELOW 1 VOLT?
YES
PERFORM TEST DR-35C.
NO
CONTINUE TEST DR-35A

* PERFORM VERIFICATION PROCEDURE VER-2.

91C08728 91I08892

Fig. 138: *Driveability Test 35A (2.2L & 2.5L) – Checking Idle Speed Motor Operation (1 of 2)*

1991 ENGINE PERFORMANCE
Self-Diagnostics – 2.5L TBI (Cont.)

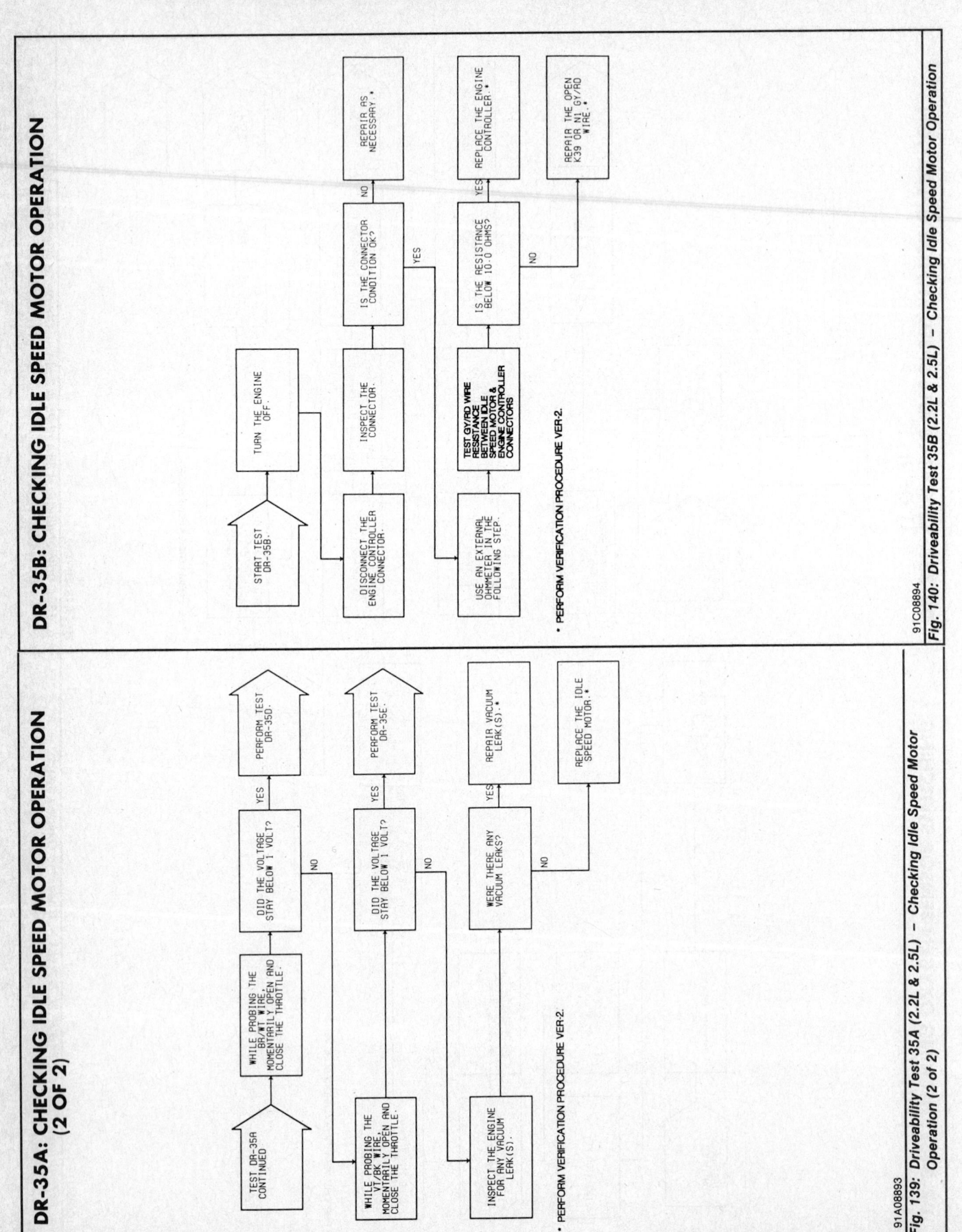

DR-35A: CHECKING IDLE SPEED MOTOR OPERATION (2 OF 2)

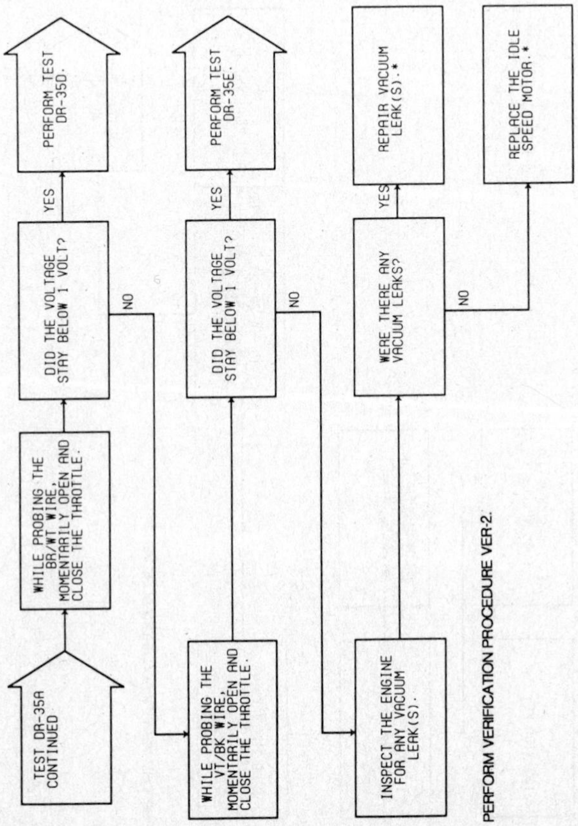
TEST DR-35A CONTINUED
WHILE PROBING THE BR/WT WIRE, MOMENTARILY OPEN AND CLOSE THE THROTTLE.
DID THE VOLTAGE STAY BELOW 1 VOLT?
YES
PERFORM TEST DR-35D.
NO
WHILE PROBING THE VT/BK WIRE, MOMENTARILY OPEN AND CLOSE THE THROTTLE.
DID THE VOLTAGE STAY BELOW 1 VOLT?
YES
PERFORM TEST DR-35E.
NO
INSPECT THE ENGINE FOR ANY VACUUM LEAK(S).
WERE THERE ANY VACUUM LEAKS?
YES
REPAIR VACUUM LEAK(S).*
NO
REPLACE THE IDLE SPEED MOTOR.*

* PERFORM VERIFICATION PROCEDURE VER-2.

91A08893

Fig. 139: Driveability Test 35A (2.2L & 2.5L) – Checking Idle Speed Motor Operation (2 of 2)

DR-35B: CHECKING IDLE SPEED MOTOR OPERATION

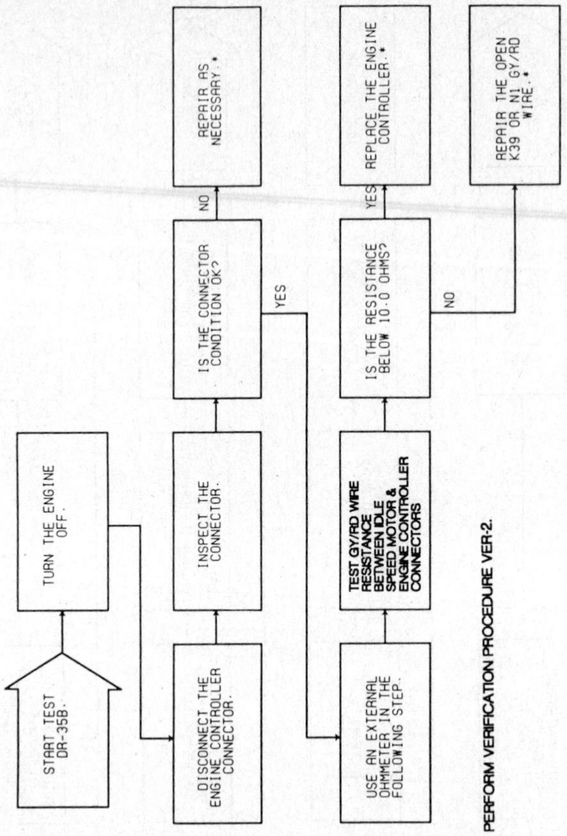
START TEST DR-35B.
TURN THE ENGINE OFF.
DISCONNECT THE ENGINE CONTROLLER CONNECTOR.
INSPECT THE CONNECTOR.
IS THE CONNECTOR CONDITION OK?
NO
REPAIR AS NECESSARY.*
YES
USE AN EXTERNAL OHMMETER IN THE FOLLOWING STEP.
TEST GY/RD WIRE RESISTANCE BETWEEN IDLE SPEED MOTOR & ENGINE CONTROLLER CONNECTORS
IS THE RESISTANCE BELOW 10.0 OHMS?
YES
REPLACE THE ENGINE CONTROLLER.*
NO
REPAIR THE OPEN K39 OR N1 GY/RD WIRE.*

* PERFORM VERIFICATION PROCEDURE VER-2.

91C08894

Fig. 140: Driveability Test 35B (2.2L & 2.5L) – Checking Idle Speed Motor Operation

DR-35C: CHECKING IDLE SPEED MOTOR OPERATION

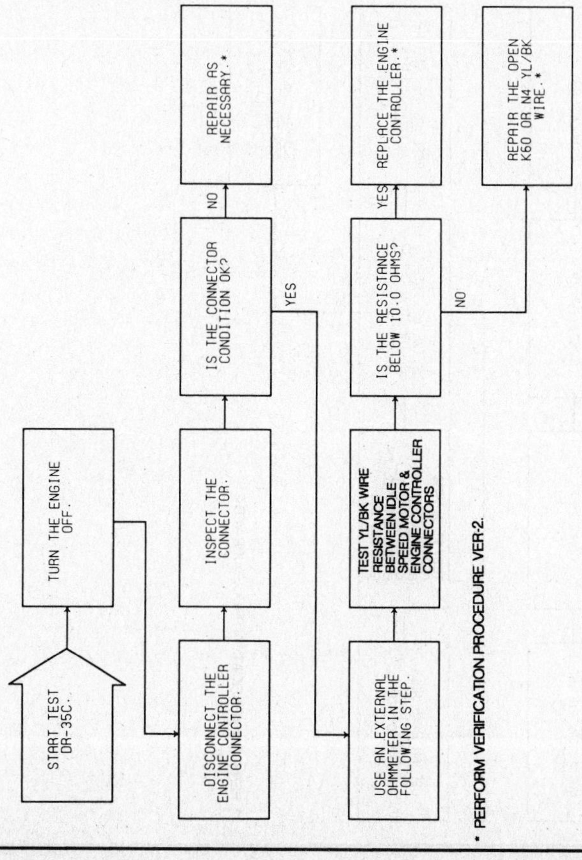
START TEST DR-35C.
TURN THE ENGINE OFF.
DISCONNECT THE ENGINE CONTROLLER CONNECTOR.
INSPECT THE CONNECTOR.
IS THE CONNECTOR CONDITION OK?
NO
REPAIR AS NECESSARY.*
YES
USE AN EXTERNAL OHMMETER IN THE FOLLOWING STEP.
TEST YL/BK WIRE RESISTANCE BETWEEN IDLE SPEED MOTOR & ENGINE CONTROLLER CONNECTORS
IS THE RESISTANCE BELOW 10.0 OHMS?
YES
REPLACE THE ENGINE CONTROLLER.*
NO
REPAIR THE OPEN K60 OR N4 YL/BK WIRE.*

* PERFORM VERIFICATION PROCEDURE VER-2.

91F08895

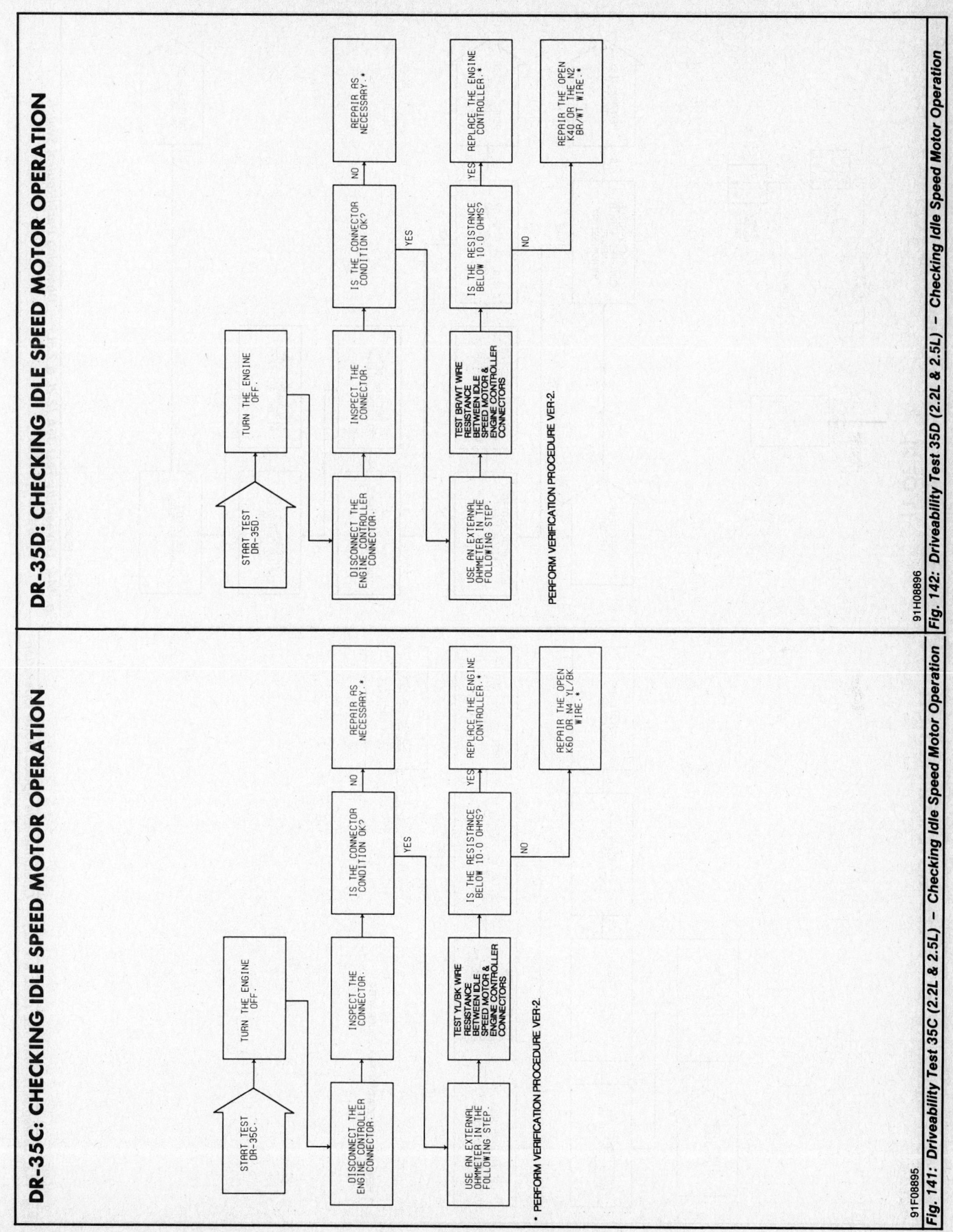

Fig. 141: Driveability Test 35C (2.2L & 2.5L) – Checking Idle Speed Motor Operation

DR-35D: CHECKING IDLE SPEED MOTOR OPERATION

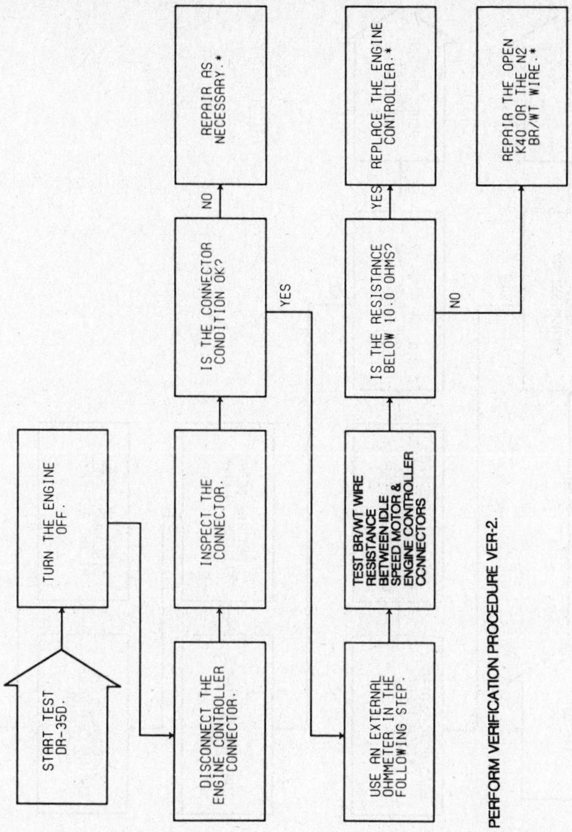
START TEST DR-35D.
TURN THE ENGINE OFF.
DISCONNECT THE ENGINE CONTROLLER CONNECTOR.
INSPECT THE CONNECTOR.
IS THE CONNECTOR CONDITION OK?
NO
REPAIR AS NECESSARY.*
YES
USE AN EXTERNAL OHMMETER IN THE FOLLOWING STEP.
TEST BR/WT WIRE RESISTANCE BETWEEN IDLE SPEED MOTOR & ENGINE CONTROLLER CCNNECTORS
IS THE RESISTANCE BELOW 10.0 OHMS?
YES
REPLACE THE ENGINE CONTROLLER.*
NO
REPAIR THE OPEN K40 OR THE N2 BR/WT WIRE.*

PERFORM VERIFICATION PROCEDURE VER-2.

91H08896

Fig. 142: Driveability Test 35D (2.2L & 2.5L) – Checking Idle Speed Motor Operation

1991 ENGINE PERFORMANCE
Self-Diagnostics – 2.5L TBI (Cont.)

DR-35E: CHECKING IDLE SPEED MOTOR OPERATION

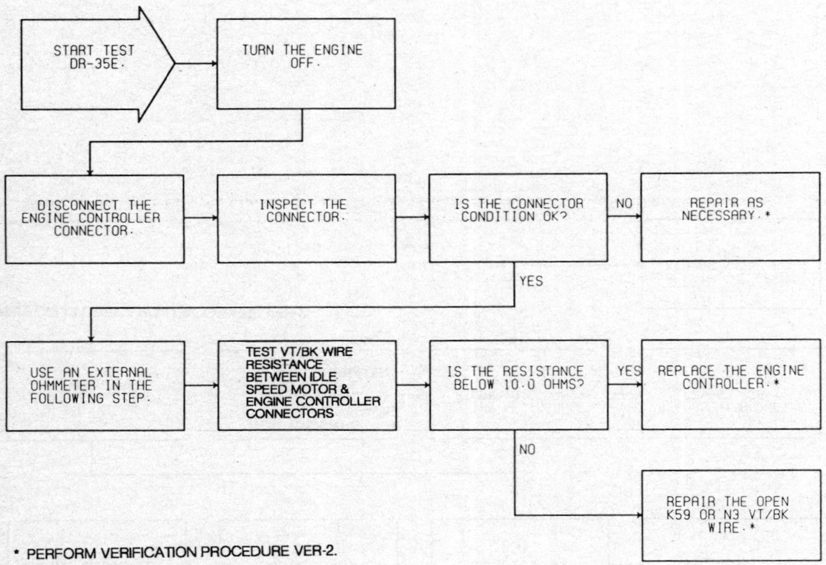
START TEST DR-35E.
TURN THE ENGINE OFF.
DISCONNECT THE ENGINE CONTROLLER CONNECTOR.
INSPECT THE CONNECTOR.
IS THE CONNECTOR CONDITION OK?
NO
REPAIR AS NECESSARY.*
YES
USE AN EXTERNAL OHMMETER IN THE FOLLOWING STEP.
TEST VT/BK WIRE RESISTANCE BETWEEN IDLE SPEED MOTOR & ENGINE CONTROLLER CONNECTORS
IS THE RESISTANCE BELOW 10.0 OHMS?
YES
REPLACE THE ENGINE CONTROLLER.*
NO
REPAIR THE OPEN K59 OR N3 VT/BK WIRE.*

* PERFORM VERIFICATION PROCEDURE VER-2.

91J08897

Fig. 143: Driveability Test 35E (2.2L & 2.5L) – Checking Idle Speed Motor Operation

DR-36A: CHECKING PARK/NEUTRAL SWITCH OPERATION (1 OF 2)

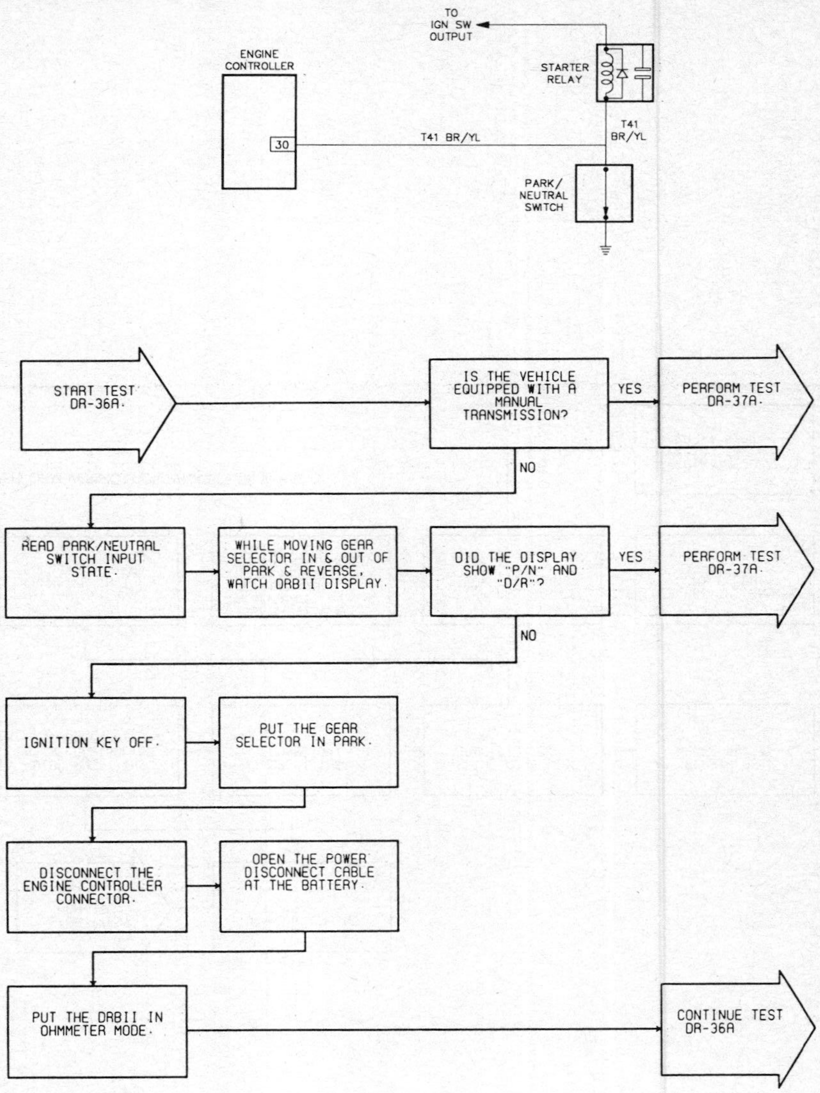
TO IGN SW OUTPUT
ENGINE CONTROLLER
30
T41 BR/YL
STARTER RELAY
T41 BR/YL
PARK/ NEUTRAL SWITCH
START TEST DR-36A.
IS THE VEHICLE EQUIPPED WITH A MANUAL TRANSMISSION?
YES
PERFORM TEST DR-37A.
NO
READ PARK/NEUTRAL SWITCH INPUT STATE.
WHILE MOVING GEAR SELECTOR IN & OUT OF PARK & REVERSE, WATCH DRBII DISPLAY.
DID THE DISPLAY SHOW "P/N" AND "D/R"?
YES
PERFORM TEST DR-37A.
NO
IGNITION KEY OFF.
PUT THE GEAR SELECTOR IN PARK.
DISCONNECT THE ENGINE CONTROLLER CONNECTOR.
OPEN THE POWER DISCONNECT CABLE AT THE BATTERY.
PUT THE DRBII IN OHMMETER MODE.
CONTINUE TEST DR-36A

91E08729 91B08898

Fig. 144: Driveability Test 36A (2.2L & 2.5L) – Checking Park/Neutral Switch Operation (1 of 2)

DR-36A: CHECKING PARK/NEUTRAL SWITCH OPERATION (2 OF 2)

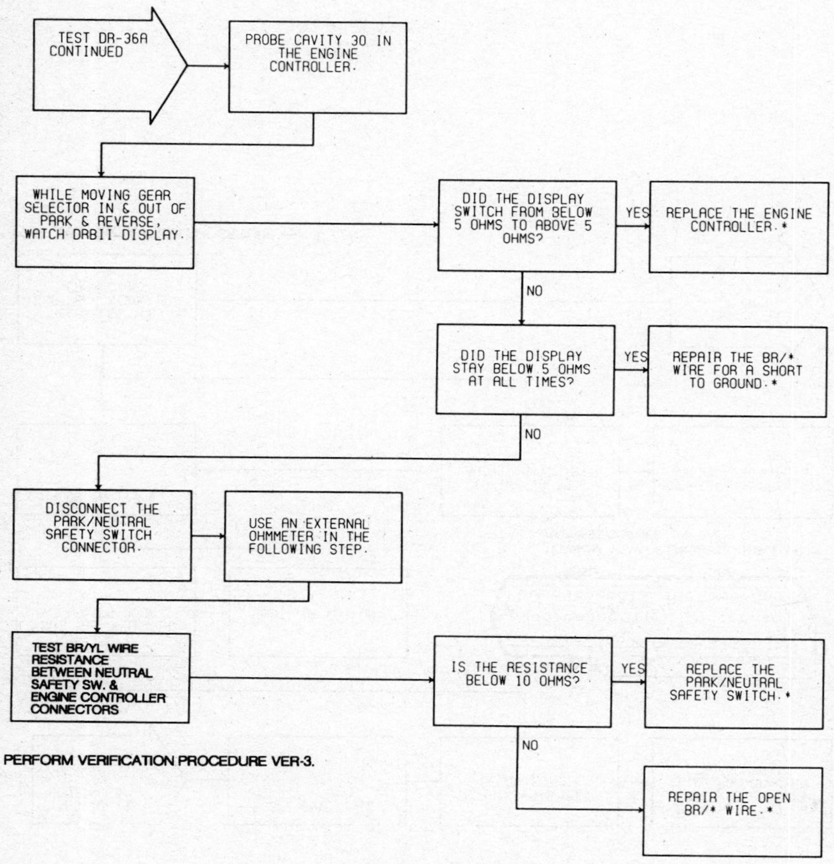
TEST DR-36A CONTINUED
PROBE CAVITY 30 IN THE ENGINE CONTROLLER.
WHILE MOVING GEAR SELECTOR IN & OUT OF PARK & REVERSE, WATCH DRBII DISPLAY.
DID THE DISPLAY SWITCH FROM BELOW 5 OHMS TO ABOVE 5 OHMS?
YES
REPLACE THE ENGINE CONTROLLER.*
NO
DID THE DISPLAY STAY BELOW 5 OHMS AT ALL TIMES?
YES
REPAIR THE BR/* WIRE FOR A SHORT TO GROUND.*
NO
DISCONNECT THE PARK/NEUTRAL SAFETY SWITCH CONNECTOR.
USE AN EXTERNAL OHMMETER IN THE FOLLOWING STEP.
TEST BR/YL WIRE RESISTANCE BETWEEN NEUTRAL SAFETY SW. & ENGINE CONTROLLER CONNECTORS
IS THE RESISTANCE BELOW 10 OHMS?
YES
REPLACE THE PARK/NEUTRAL SAFETY SWITCH.*
NO
REPAIR THE OPEN BR/* WIRE.*

* PERFORM VERIFICATION PROCEDURE VER-3.

91D08899

Fig. 145: ***Driveability Test 36A (2.2L & 2.5L) – Checking Park/Neutral Switch Operation (2 of 2)***

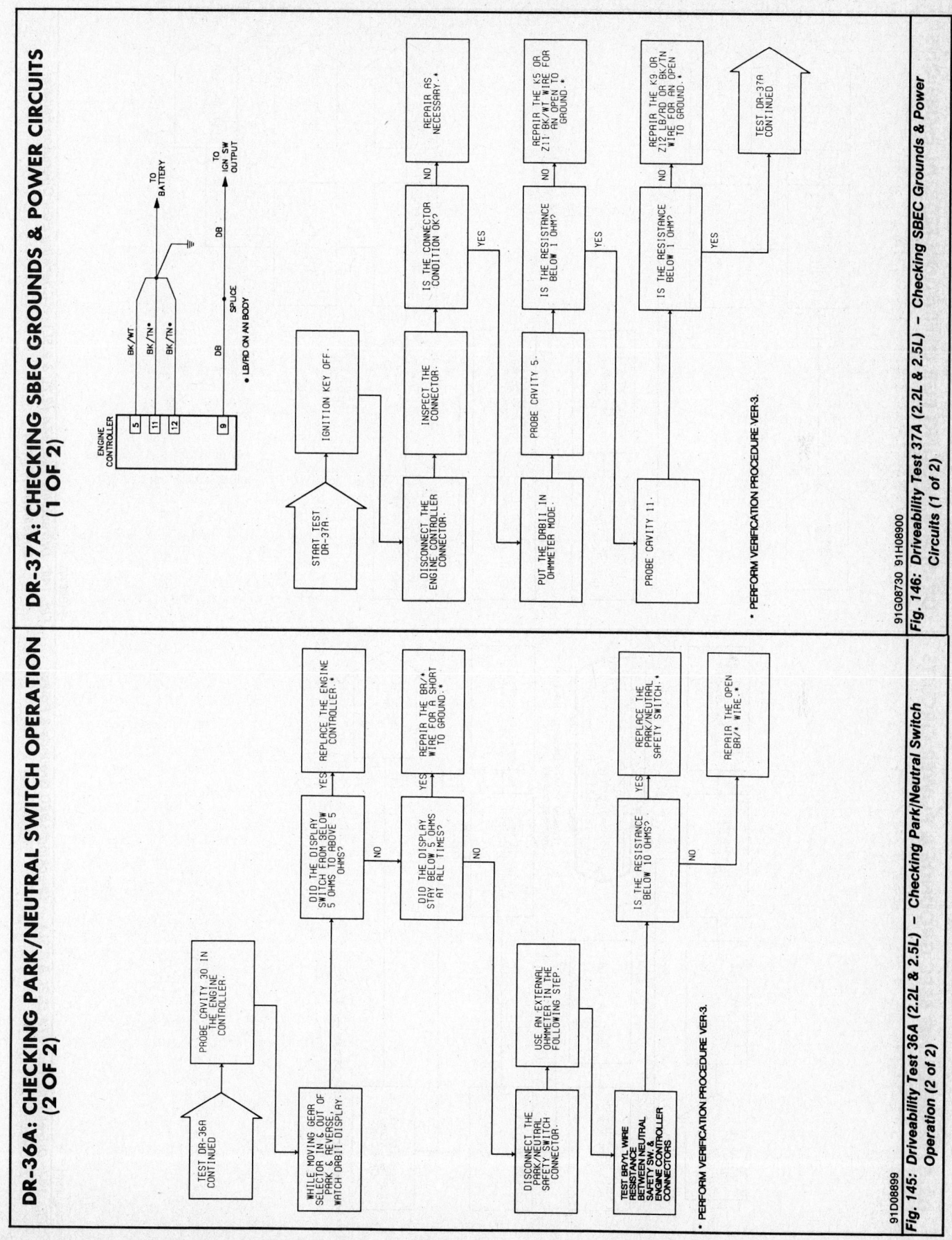

DR-37A: CHECKING SBEC GROUNDS & POWER CIRCUITS (1 OF 2)

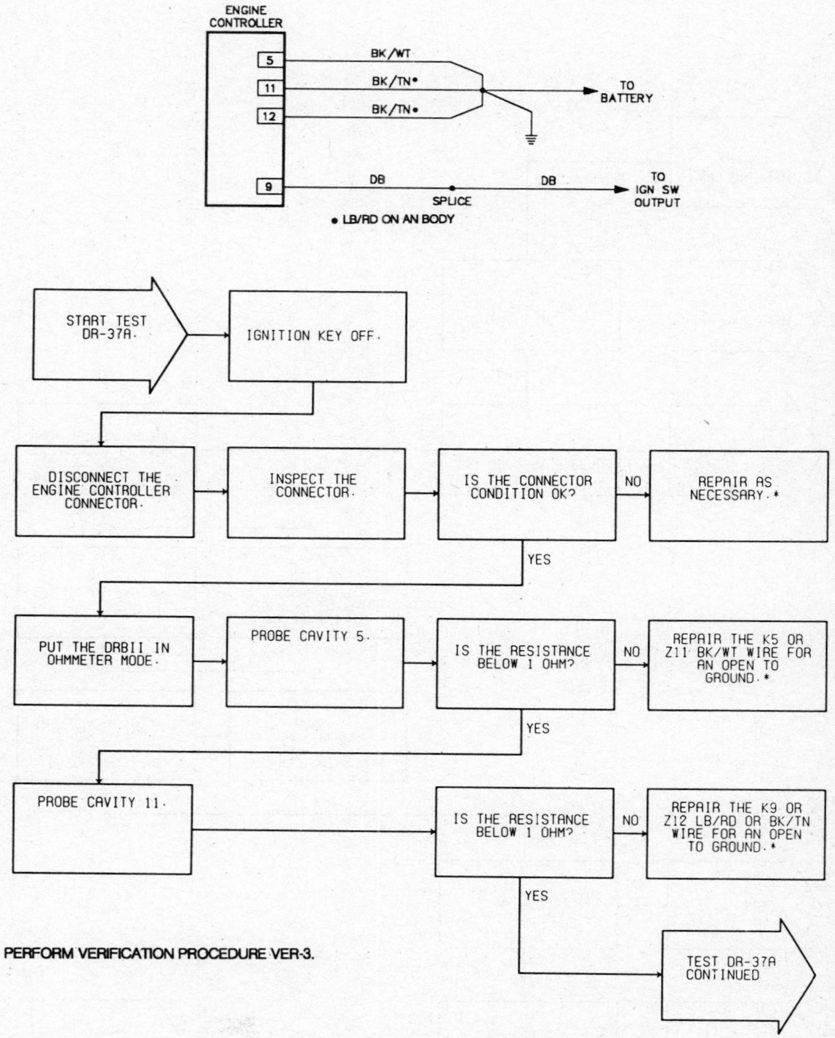
ENGINE CONTROLLER
5
11
12
9
BK/WT
BK/TN•
BK/TN•
TO BATTERY
DB
SPLICE
DB
TO IGN SW OUTPUT
• LB/RD ON AN BODY
START TEST DR-37A.
IGNITION KEY OFF.
DISCONNECT THE ENGINE CONTROLLER CONNECTOR.
INSPECT THE CONNECTOR.
IS THE CONNECTOR CONDITION OK?
NO
REPAIR AS NECESSARY.*
YES
PUT THE DRBII IN OHMMETER MODE.
PROBE CAVITY 5.
IS THE RESISTANCE BELOW 1 OHM?
NO
REPAIR THE K5 OR Z11 BK/WT WIRE FOR AN OPEN TO GROUND.*
YES
PROBE CAVITY 11.
IS THE RESISTANCE BELOW 1 OHM?
NO
REPAIR THE K9 OR Z12 LB/RD OR BK/TN WIRE FOR AN OPEN TO GROUND.*
YES
TEST DR-37A CONTINUED

* PERFORM VERIFICATION PROCEDURE VER-3.

91G08730 91H08900

Fig. 146: ***Driveability Test 37A (2.2L & 2.5L) – Checking SBEC Grounds & Power Circuits (1 of 2)***

1991 ENGINE PERFORMANCE
Self-Diagnostics – 2.5L TBI (Cont.)

DR-37A: CHECKING SBEC GROUNDS & POWER CIRCUITS (2 OF 2)

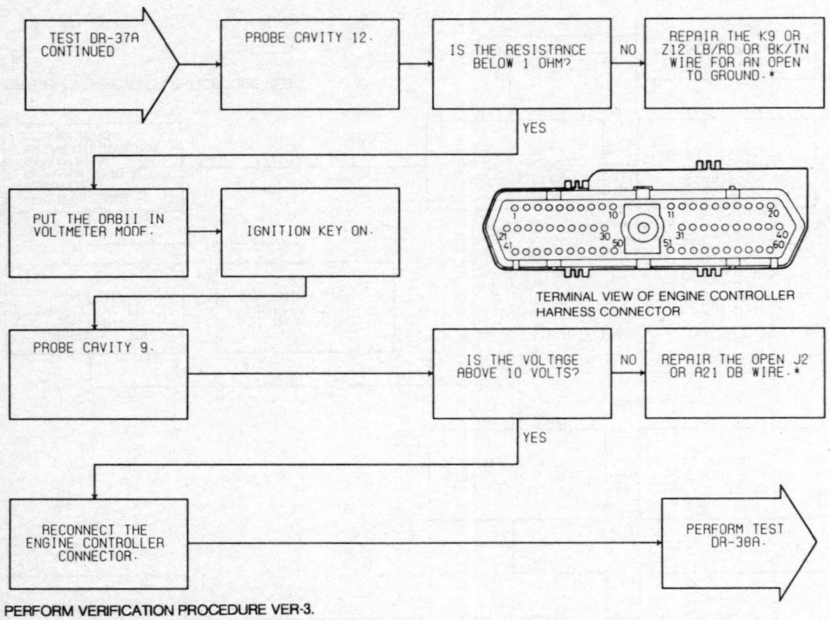
TEST DR-37A CONTINUED
PROBE CAVITY 12.
IS THE RESISTANCE BELOW 1 OHM?
NO
REPAIR THE K9 OR Z12 LB/RD OR BK/TN WIRE FOR AN OPEN TO GROUND.*
YES
PUT THE DRBII IN VOLTMETER MODE.
IGNITION KEY ON.
TERMINAL VIEW OF ENGINE CONTROLLER HARNESS CONNECTOR
PROBE CAVITY 9.
IS THE VOLTAGE ABOVE 10 VOLTS?
NO
REPAIR THE OPEN J2 OR A21 DB WIRE.*
YES
RECONNECT THE ENGINE CONTROLLER CONNECTOR.
PERFORM TEST DR-38A.

* PERFORM VERIFICATION PROCEDURE VER-3.

91J08901

Fig. 147: Driveability Test 37A (2.2L & 2.5L) – Checking SBEC Grounds & Power Circuits (2 of 2)

DR-38A: CHECKING EGR OPERATION FEDERAL EMISSIONS (1 OF 2)

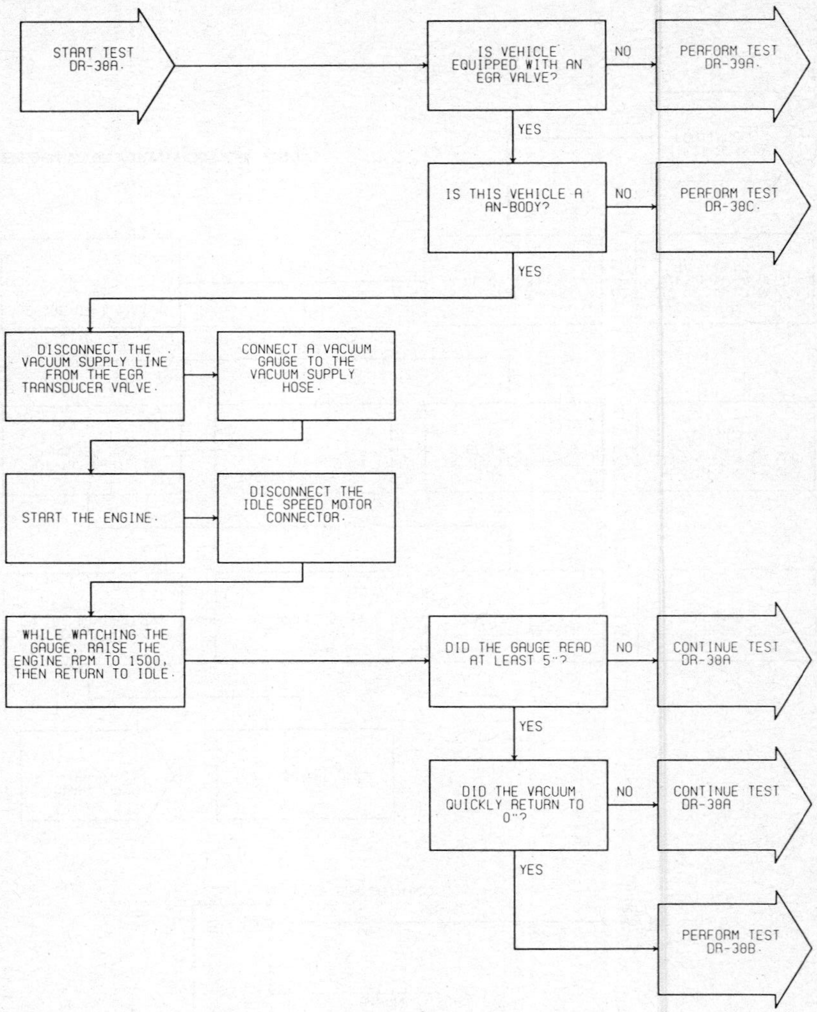
START TEST DR-38A.
IS VEHICLE EQUIPPED WITH AN EGR VALVE?
NO
PERFORM TEST DR-39A.
YES
IS THIS VEHICLE A AN-BODY?
NO
PERFORM TEST DR-38C.
YES
DISCONNECT THE VACUUM SUPPLY LINE FROM THE EGR TRANSDUCER VALVE.
CONNECT A VACUUM GAUGE TO THE VACUUM SUPPLY HOSE.
START THE ENGINE.
DISCONNECT THE IDLE SPEED MOTOR CONNECTOR.
WHILE WATCHING THE GAUGE, RAISE THE ENGINE RPM TO 1500, THEN RETURN TO IDLE.
DID THE GAUGE READ AT LEAST 5"?
NO
CONTINUE TEST DR-38A
YES
DID THE VACUUM QUICKLY RETURN TO 0"?
NO
CONTINUE TEST DR-38A
YES
PERFORM TEST DR-38B.

91B08902

Fig. 148: Driveability Test 38A (2.2L & 2.5L) – Checking EGR Operation Federal Emissions (1 of 2)

DR-38A: CHECKING EGR OPERATION FEDERAL EMISSIONS (2 OF 2)

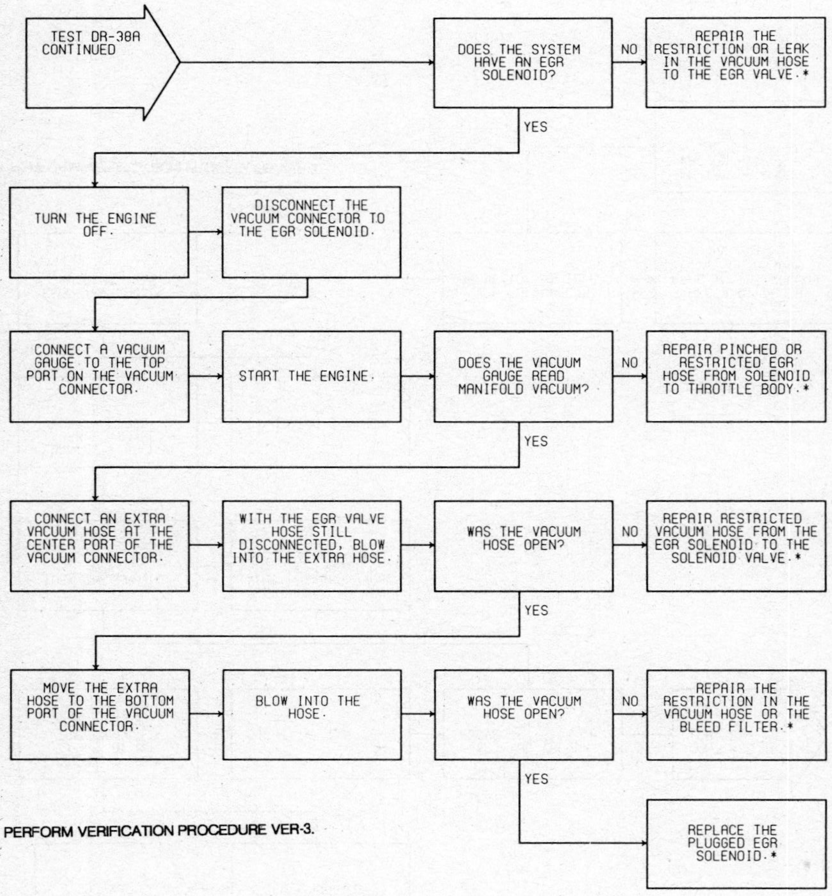
TEST DR-38A CONTINUED
DOES THE SYSTEM HAVE AN EGR SOLENOID?
NO
REPAIR THE RESTRICTION OR LEAK IN THE VACUUM HOSE TO THE EGR VALVE.*
YES
TURN THE ENGINE OFF.
DISCONNECT THE VACUUM CONNECTOR TO THE EGR SOLENOID.
CONNECT A VACUUM GAUGE TO THE TOP PORT ON THE VACUUM CONNECTOR.
START THE ENGINE.
DOES THE VACUUM GAUGE READ MANIFOLD VACUUM?
NO
REPAIR PINCHED OR RESTRICTED EGR HOSE FROM SOLENOID TO THROTTLE BODY.*
YES
CONNECT AN EXTRA VACUUM HOSE AT THE CENTER PORT OF THE VACUUM CONNECTOR.
WITH THE EGR VALVE HOSE STILL DISCONNECTED, BLOW INTO THE EXTRA HOSE.
WAS THE VACUUM HOSE OPEN?
NO
REPAIR RESTRICTED VACUUM HOSE FROM THE EGR SOLENOID TO THE SOLENOID VALVE.*
YES
MOVE THE EXTRA HOSE TO THE BOTTOM PORT OF THE VACUUM CONNECTOR.
BLOW INTO THE HOSE.
WAS THE VACUUM HOSE OPEN?
NO
REPAIR THE RESTRICTION IN THE VACUUM HOSE OR THE BLEED FILTER.*
YES
REPLACE THE PLUGGED EGR SOLENOID.*

* PERFORM VERIFICATION PROCEDURE VER-3.

91D08903

Fig. 149: Driveability Test 38A (2.2L & 2.5L) – Checking EGR Operation Federal Emissions (2 of 2)

DR-38B: CHECKING EGR OPERATION FEDERAL EMISSIONS

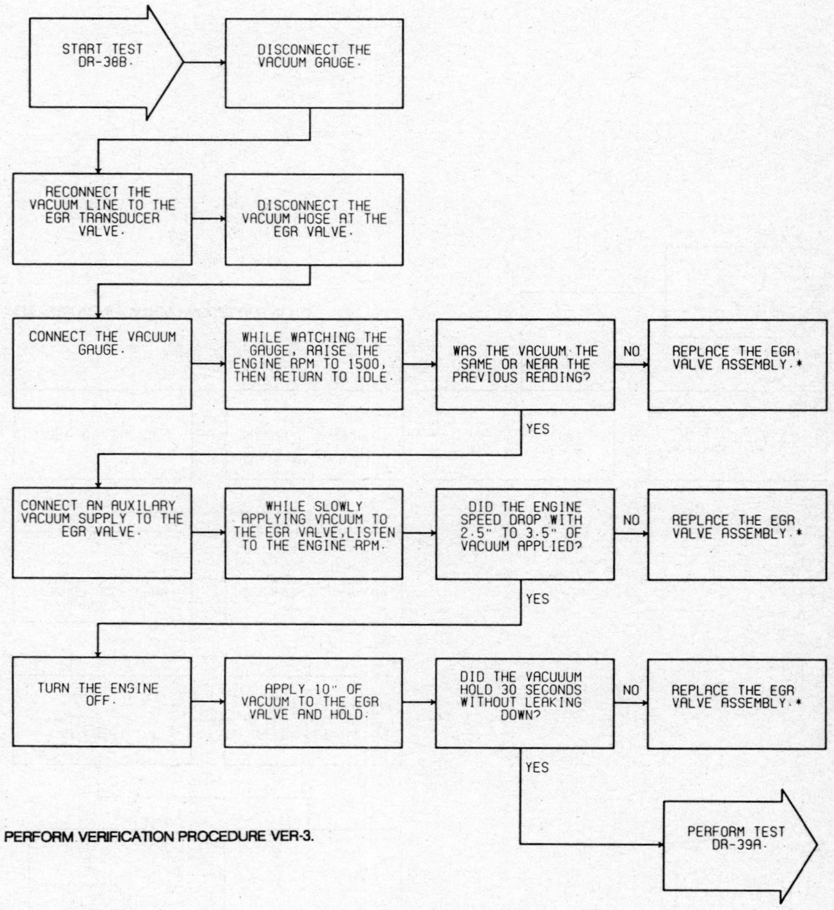
START TEST DR-38B.
DISCONNECT THE VACUUM GAUGE.
RECONNECT THE VACUUM LINE TO THE EGR TRANSDUCER VALVE.
DISCONNECT THE VACUUM HOSE AT THE EGR VALVE.
CONNECT THE VACUUM GAUGE.
WHILE WATCHING THE GAUGE, RAISE THE ENGINE RPM TO 1500, THEN RETURN TO IDLE.
WAS THE VACUUM THE SAME OR NEAR THE PREVIOUS READING?
NO
REPLACE THE EGR VALVE ASSEMBLY.*
YES
CONNECT AN AUXILARY VACUUM SUPPLY TO THE EGR VALVE.
WHILE SLOWLY APPLYING VACUUM TO THE EGR VALVE,LISTEN TO THE ENGINE RPM.
DID THE ENGINE SPEED DROP WITH 2.5" TO 3.5" OF VACUUM APPLIED?
NO
REPLACE THE EGR VALVE ASSEMBLY.*
YES
TURN THE ENGINE OFF.
APPLY 10" OF VACUUM TO THE EGR VALVE AND HOLD.
DID THE VACUUUM HOLD 30 SECONDS WITHOUT LEAKING DOWN?
NO
REPLACE THE EGR VALVE ASSEMBLY.*
YES
PERFORM TEST DR-39A.

* PERFORM VERIFICATION PROCEDURE VER-3.

91F08904

Fig. 150: Driveability Test 38B (2.2L & 2.5L) – Checking EGR Operation Federal Emissions

1991 ENGINE PERFORMANCE
Self-Diagnostics – 2.5L TBI (Cont.)

DR-38C: CHECKING EGR OPERATION FEDERAL EMISSIONS (1 OF 5)

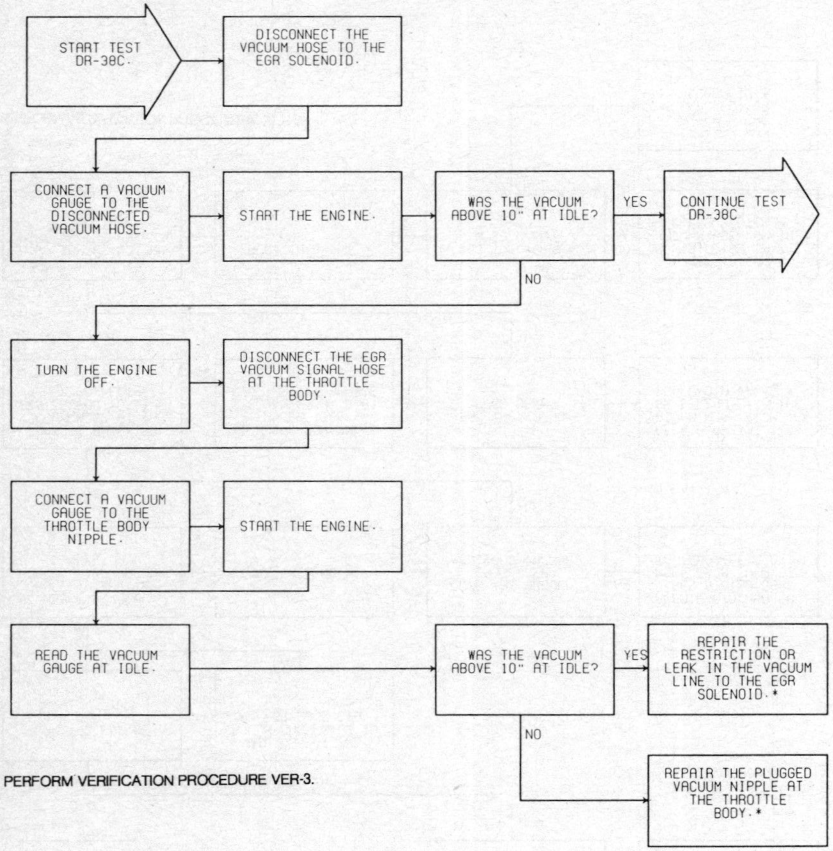
START TEST DR-38C.
DISCONNECT THE VACUUM HOSE TO THE EGR SOLENOID.
CONNECT A VACUUM GAUGE TO THE DISCONNECTED VACUUM HOSE.
START THE ENGINE.
WAS THE VACUUM ABOVE 10" AT IDLE?
YES
CONTINUE TEST DR-38C
NO
TURN THE ENGINE OFF.
DISCONNECT THE EGR VACUUM SIGNAL HOSE AT THE THROTTLE BODY.
CONNECT A VACUUM GAUGE TO THE THROTTLE BODY NIPPLE.
START THE ENGINE.
READ THE VACUUM GAUGE AT IDLE.
WAS THE VACUUM ABOVE 10" AT IDLE?
YES
REPAIR THE RESTRICTION OR LEAK IN THE VACUUM LINE TO THE EGR SOLENOID.*
NO
REPAIR THE PLUGGED VACUUM NIPPLE AT THE THROTTLE BODY.*

* PERFORM VERIFICATION PROCEDURE VER-3.

91I08905

Fig. 151: Driveability Test 38C (2.2L & 2.5L) – Checking EGR Operation Federal Emissions (1 of 5)

DR-38C: CHECKING EGR OPERATION FEDERAL EMISSIONS (2 OF 5)

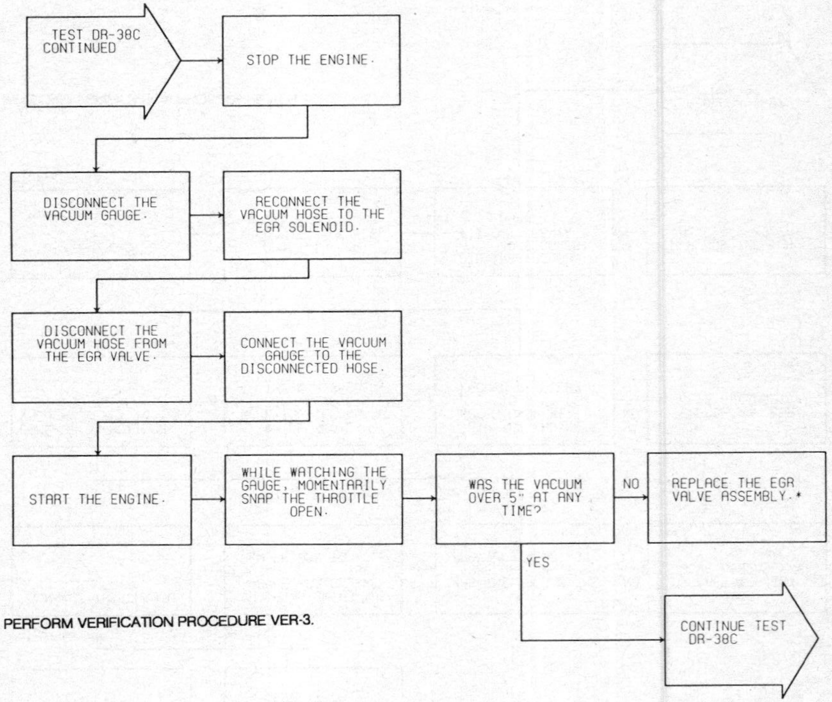
TEST DR-38C CONTINUED
STOP THE ENGINE.
DISCONNECT THE VACUUM GAUGE.
RECONNECT THE VACUUM HOSE TO THE EGR SOLENOID.
DISCONNECT THE VACUUM HOSE FROM THE EGR VALVE.
CONNECT THE VACUUM GAUGE TO THE DISCONNECTED HOSE.
START THE ENGINE.
WHILE WATCHING THE GAUGE, MOMENTARILY SNAP THE THROTTLE OPEN.
WAS THE VACUUM OVER 5" AT ANY TIME?
NO
REPLACE THE EGR VALVE ASSEMBLY.*
YES
CONTINUE TEST DR-38C

* PERFORM VERIFICATION PROCEDURE VER-3.

91A08906

Fig. 152: Driveability Test 38C (2.2L & 2.5L) – Checking EGR Operation Federal Emissions (2 of 5)

DR-38C: CHECKING EGR OPERATION FEDERAL EMISSIONS (3 OF 5)

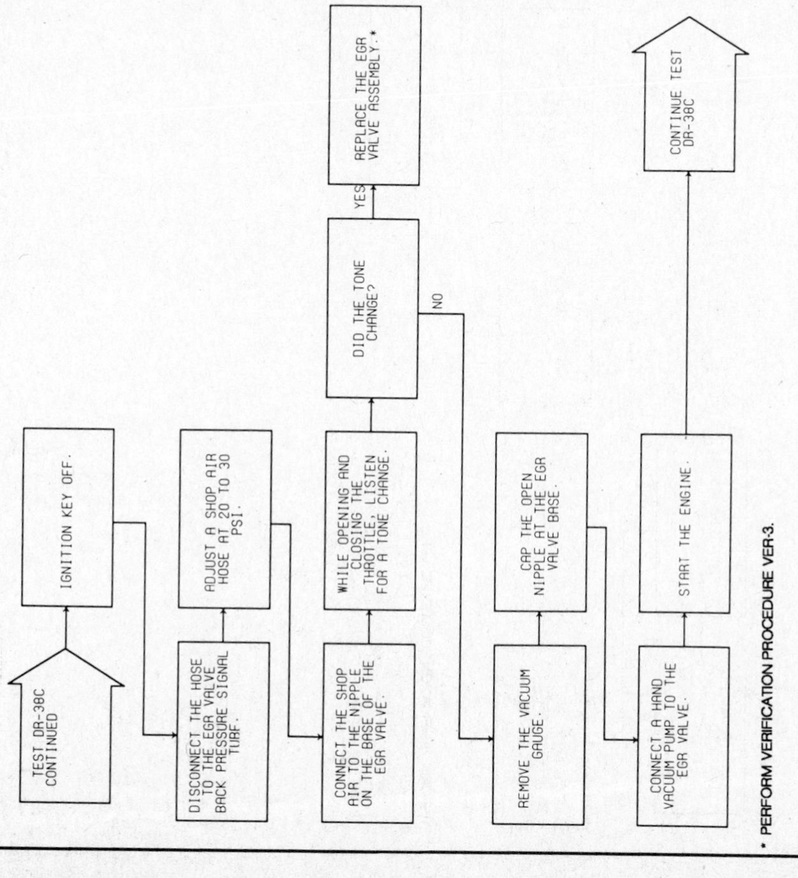

TEST DR-38C CONTINUED
IGNITION KEY OFF.
DISCONNECT THE HOSE TO THE EGR VALVE BACK PRESSURE SIGNAL TUBF.
ADJUST A SHOP AIR HOSE AT 20 TO 30 PSI.
CONNECT THE SHOP AIR TO THE NIPPLE ON THE BASE OF THE EGR VALVE.
WHILE OPENING AND CLOSING THE THROTTLE, LISTEN FOR A TONE CHANGE.
DID THE TONE CHANGE?
YES
REPLACE THE EGR VALVE ASSEMBLY.*
NO
REMOVE THE VACUUM GAUGE.
CAP THE OPEN NIPPLE AT THE EGR VALVE BASE.
CONNECT A HAND VACUUM PUMP TO THE EGR VALVE.
START THE ENGINE.
CONTINUE TEST DR-38C

* PERFORM VERIFICATION PROCEDURE VER-3.

91C08907

Fig. 153: Driveability Test 38C (2.2L & 2.5L) – Checking EGR Operation Federal Emissions (3 of 5)

DR-38C: CHECKING EGR OPERATION FEDERAL EMISSIONS (4 OF 5)

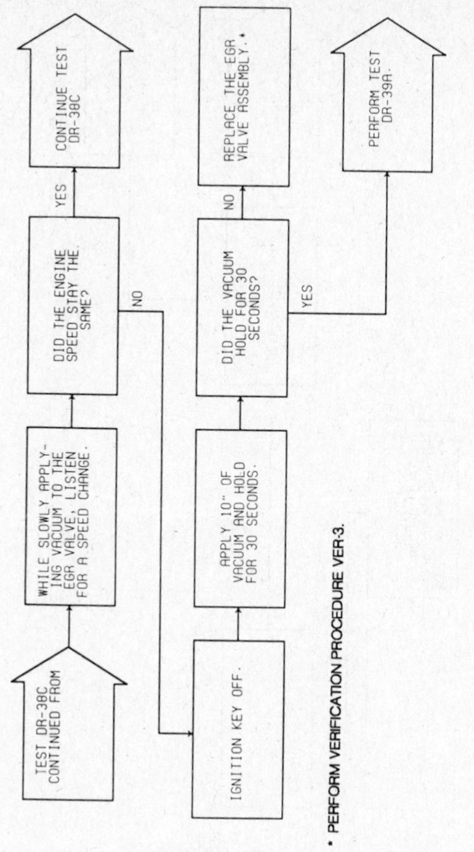

TEST DR-38C CONTINUED FROM
WHILE SLOWLY APPLYING VACUUM TO THE EGR VALVE, LISTEN FOR A SPEED CHANGE.
DID THE ENGINE SPEED STAY THE SAME?
YES
CONTINUE TEST DR-38C
NO
IGNITION KEY OFF.
APPLY 10" OF VACUUM AND HOLD FOR 30 SECONDS.
DID THE VACUUM HOLD FOR 30 SECONDS?
NO
REPLACE THE EGR VALVE ASSEMBLY.*
YES
PERFORM TEST DR-39A.

* PERFORM VERIFICATION PROCEDURE VER-3.

91H10683

Fig. 154: Driveability Test 38C (2.2L & 2.5L) – Checking EGR Operation Federal Emissions (4 of 5)

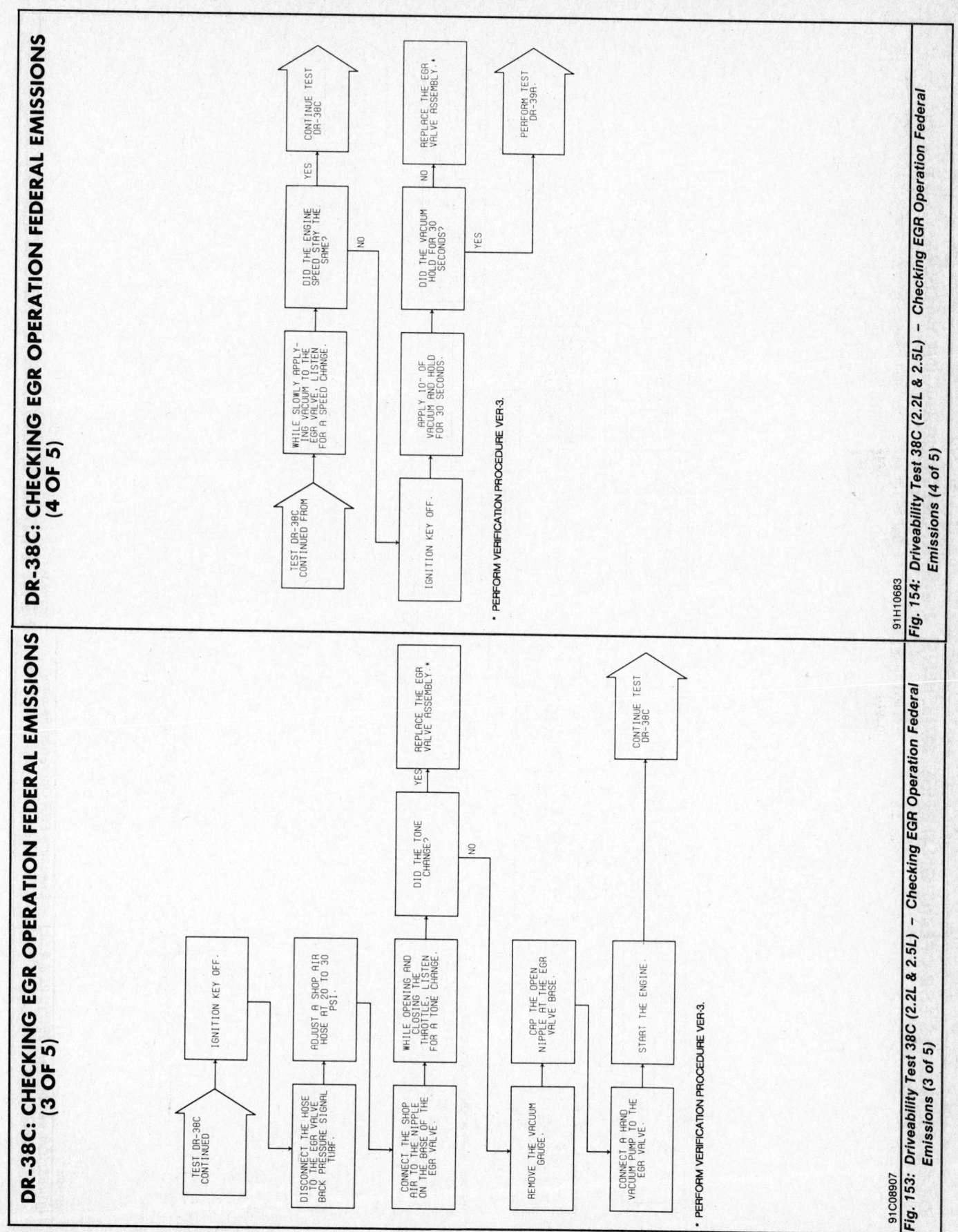

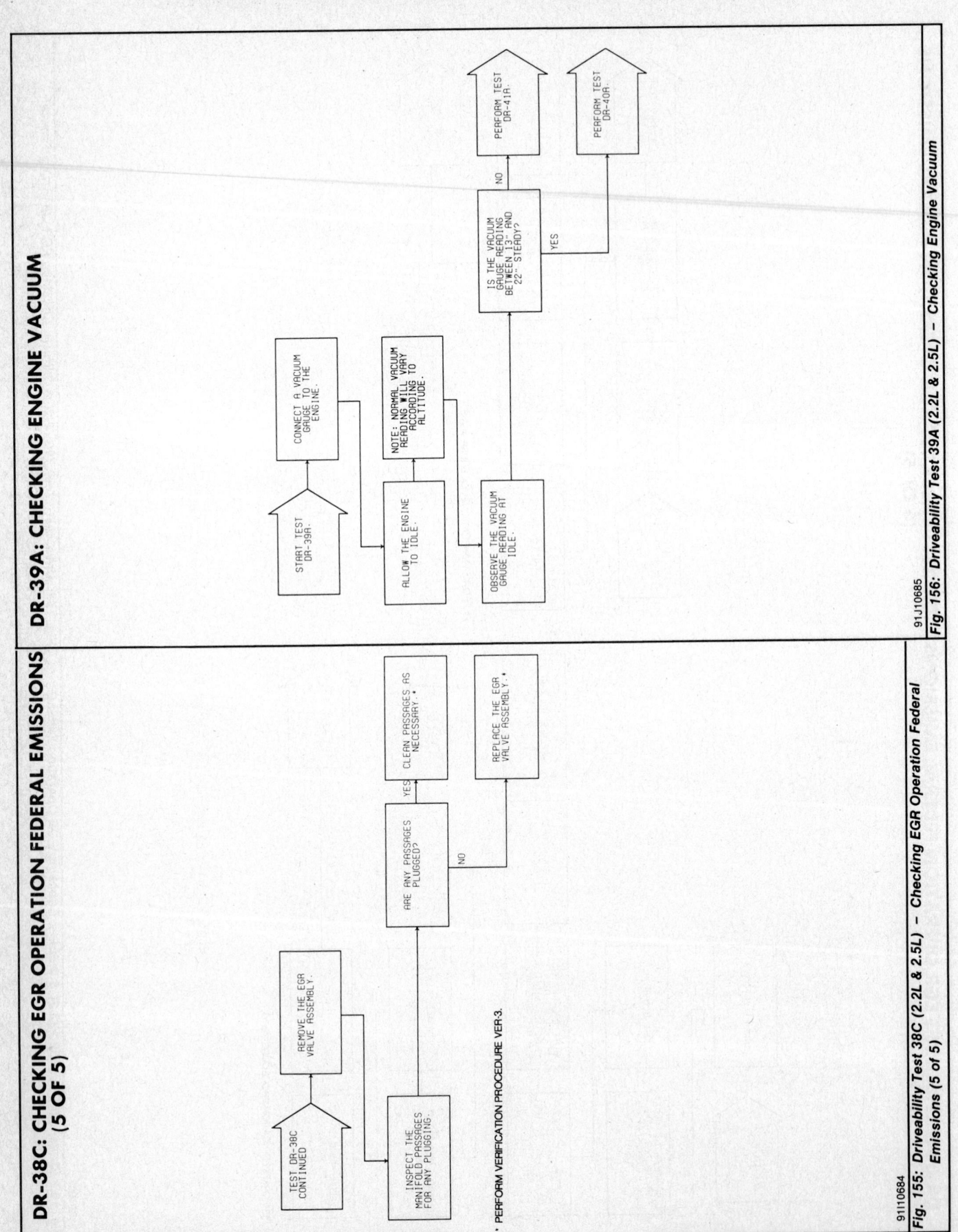

DR-38C: CHECKING EGR OPERATION FEDERAL EMISSIONS (5 OF 5)

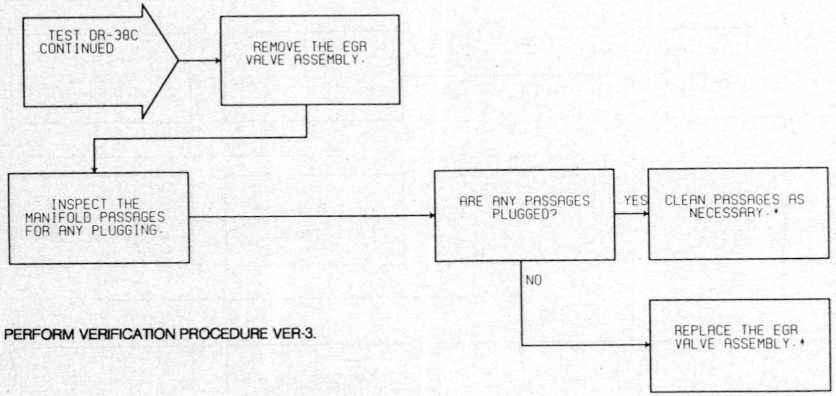
TEST DR-38C CONTINUED
REMOVE THE EGR VALVE ASSEMBLY.
INSPECT THE MANIFOLD PASSAGES FOR ANY PLUGGING.
ARE ANY PASSAGES PLUGGED?
YES
CLEAN PASSAGES AS NECESSARY.*
NO
REPLACE THE EGR VALVE ASSEMBLY.*

* PERFORM VERIFICATION PROCEDURE VER-3.

91I10684

Fig. 155: Driveability Test 38C (2.2L & 2.5L) – Checking EGR Operation Federal Emissions (5 of 5)

DR-39A: CHECKING ENGINE VACUUM

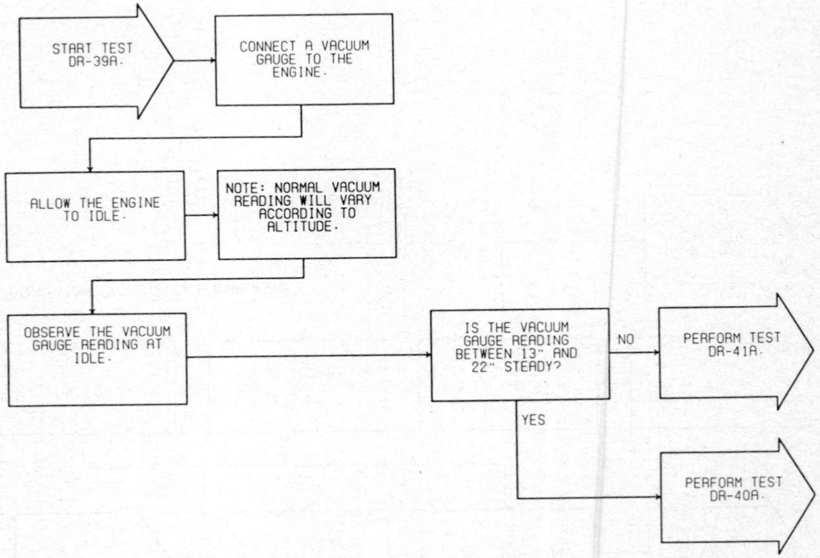
START TEST DR-39A.
CONNECT A VACUUM GAUGE TO THE ENGINE.
ALLOW THE ENGINE TO IDLE.
NOTE: NORMAL VACUUM READING WILL VARY ACCORDING TO ALTITUDE.
OBSERVE THE VACUUM GAUGE READING AT IDLE.
IS THE VACUUM GAUGE READING BETWEEN 13" AND 22" STEADY?
NO
PERFORM TEST DR-41A.
YES
PERFORM TEST DR-40A.

91J10685

Fig. 156: Driveability Test 39A (2.2L & 2.5L) – Checking Engine Vacuum

DR-40A: CHECKING MINIMUM IDLE AIR FLOW (1 OF 2)

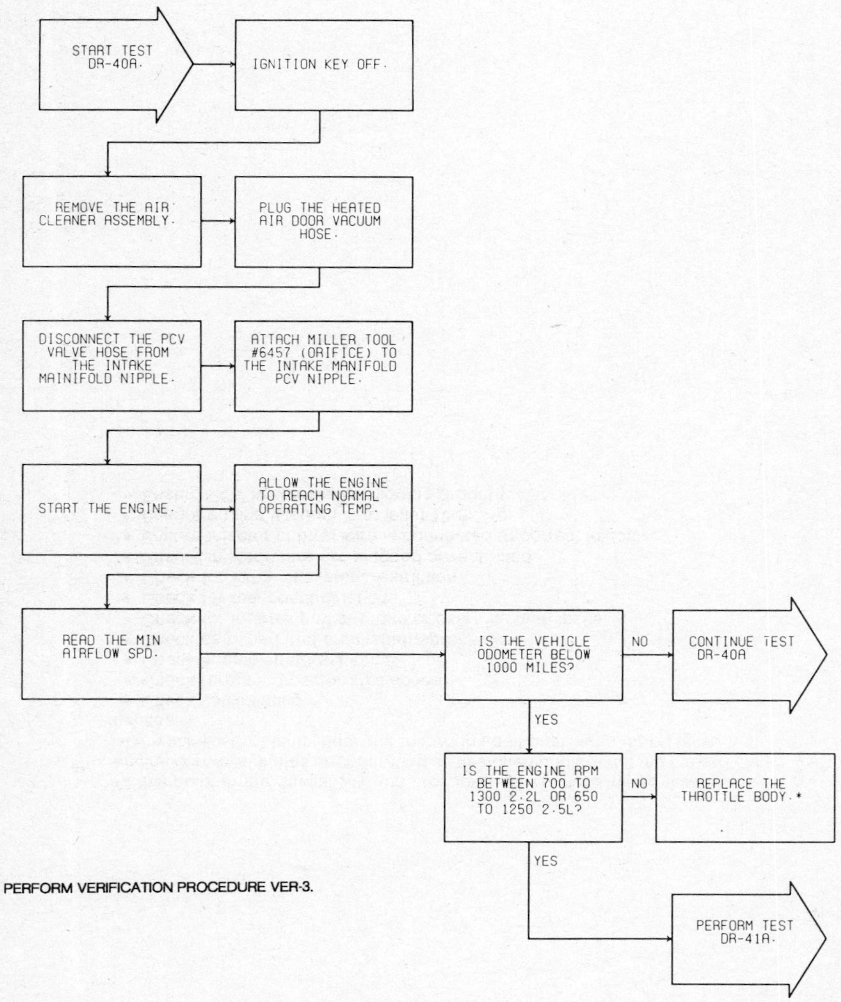
START TEST DR-40A.
IGNITION KEY OFF.
REMOVE THE AIR CLEANER ASSEMBLY.
PLUG THE HEATED AIR DOOR VACUUM HOSE.
DISCONNECT THE PCV VALVE HOSE FROM THE INTAKE MAINIFOLD NIPPLE.
ATTACH MILLER TOOL #6457 (ORIFICE) TO THE INTAKE MANIFOLD PCV NIPPLE.
START THE ENGINE.
ALLOW THE ENGINE TO REACH NORMAL OPERATING TEMP.
READ THE MIN AIRFLOW SPD.
IS THE VEHICLE ODOMETER BELOW 1000 MILES?
NO
CONTINUE TEST DR-40A
YES
IS THE ENGINE RPM BETWEEN 700 TO 1300 2.2L OR 650 TO 1250 2.5L?
NO
REPLACE THE THROTTLE BODY.*
YES
PERFORM TEST DR-41A.

* PERFORM VERIFICATION PROCEDURE VER-3.

91A10686

Fig. 157: Driveability Test 40A (2.2L & 2.5L) – Checking Minimum Idle Air Flow (1 of 2)

DR-40A: CHECKING MINIMUM IDLE AIR FLOW (2 OF 2)

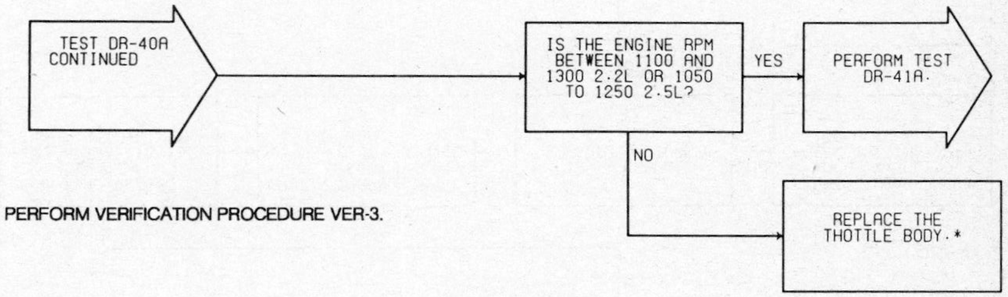
TEST DR-40A CONTINUED
IS THE ENGINE RPM BETWEEN 1100 AND 1300 2.2L OR 1050 TO 1250 2.5L?
YES
PERFORM TEST DR-41A.
NO
REPLACE THE THOTTLE BODY.*

* PERFORM VERIFICATION PROCEDURE VER-3.

91B10687

Fig. 158: Driveability Test 40A (2.2L & 2.5L) – Checking Minimum Idle Air Flow (2 of 2)

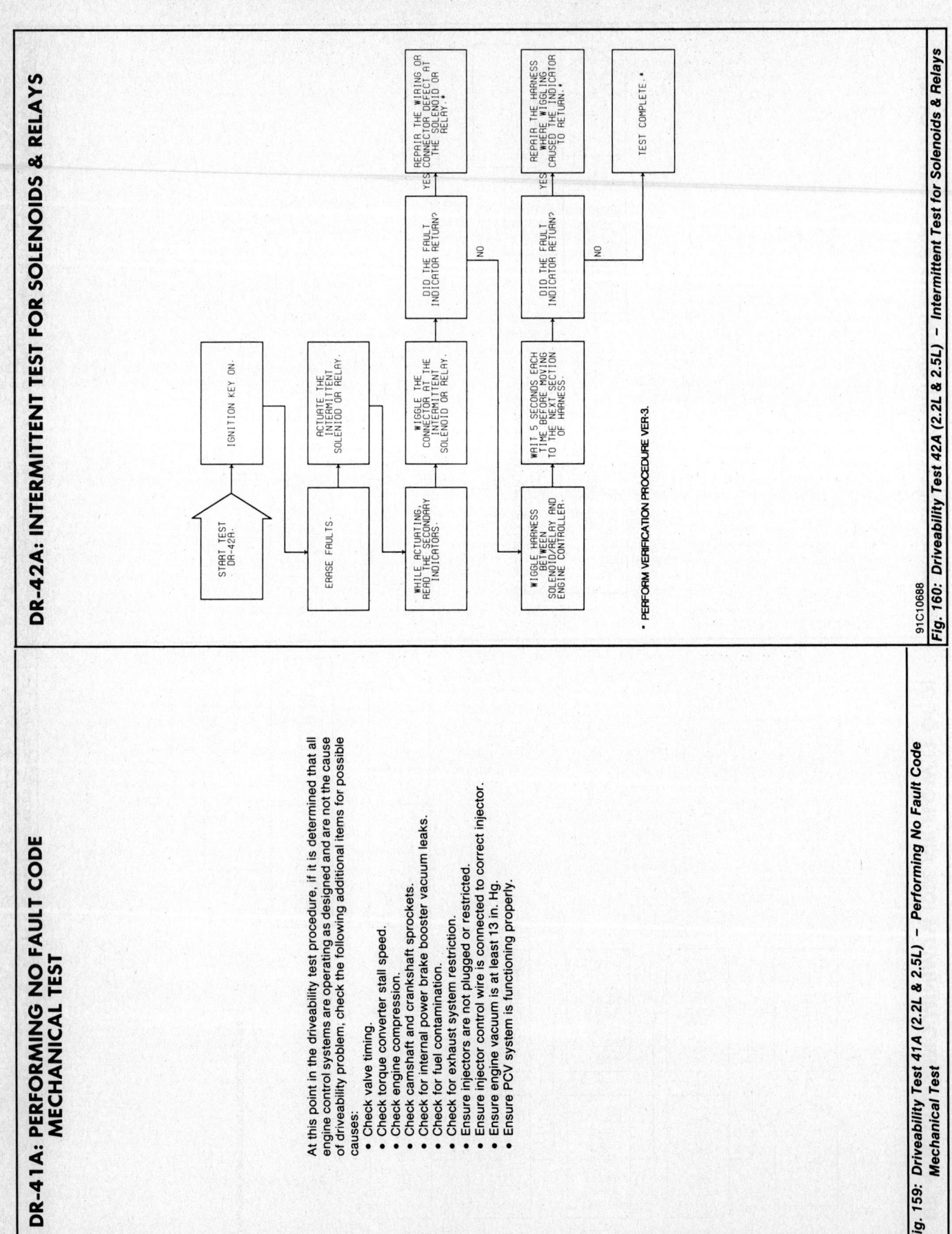

DR-41A: PERFORMING NO FAULT CODE MECHANICAL TEST

At this point in the driveability test procedure, if it is determined that all engine control systems are operating as designed and are not the cause of driveability problem, check the following additional items for possible causes:

- Check valve timing.
- Check torque converter stall speed.
- Check engine compression.
- Check camshaft and crankshaft sprockets.
- Check for internal power brake booster vacuum leaks.
- Check for fuel contamination.
- Check for exhaust system restriction.
- Ensure injectors are not plugged or restricted.
- Ensure injector control wire is connected to correct injector.
- Ensure engine vacuum is at least 13 in. Hg.
- Ensure PCV system is functioning properly.

Fig. 159: Driveability Test 41A (2.2L & 2.5L) – Performing No Fault Code Mechanical Test

DR-42A: INTERMITTENT TEST FOR SOLENOIDS & RELAYS

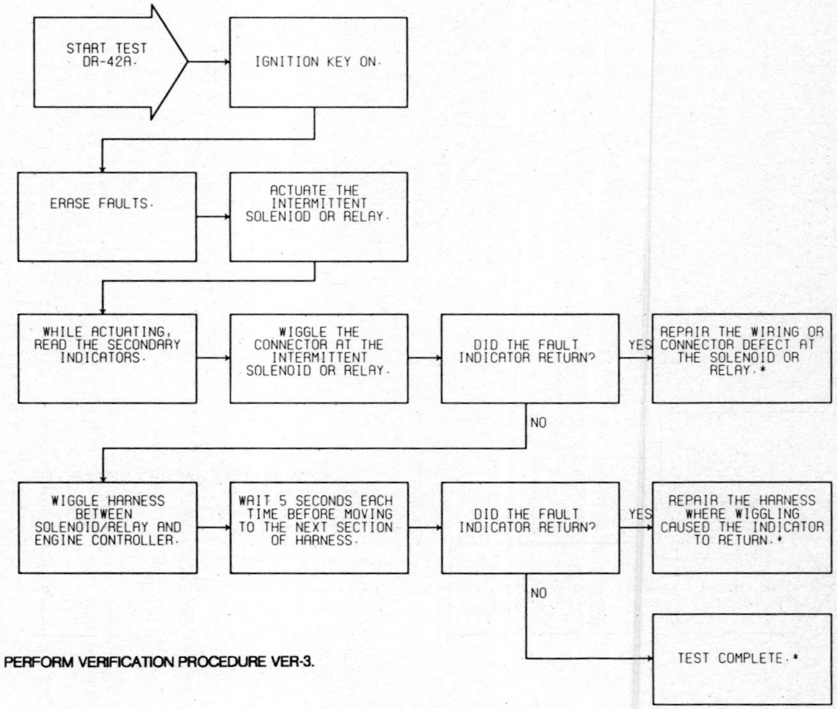
START TEST DR-42A.
IGNITION KEY ON.
ERASE FAULTS.
ACTUATE THE INTERMITTENT SOLENIOD OR RELAY.
WHILE ACTUATING, READ THE SECONDARY INDICATORS.
WIGGLE THE CONNECTOR AT THE INTERMITTENT SOLENOID OR RELAY.
DID THE FAULT INDICATOR RETURN?
YES
REPAIR THE WIRING OR CONNECTOR DEFECT AT THE SOLENOID OR RELAY.*
NO
WIGGLE HARNESS BETWEEN SOLENOID/RELAY AND ENGINE CONTROLLER.
WAIT 5 SECONDS EACH TIME BEFORE MOVING TO THE NEXT SECTION OF HARNESS.
DID THE FAULT INDICATOR RETURN?
YES
REPAIR THE HARNESS WHERE WIGGLING CAUSED THE INDICATOR TO RETURN.*
NO
TEST COMPLETE.*

* PERFORM VERIFICATION PROCEDURE VER-3.

91C10688

Fig. 160: Driveability Test 42A (2.2L & 2.5L) – Intermittent Test for Solenoids & Relays

DR-43A: INTERMITTENT TEST FOR VOLTAGE SENSOR

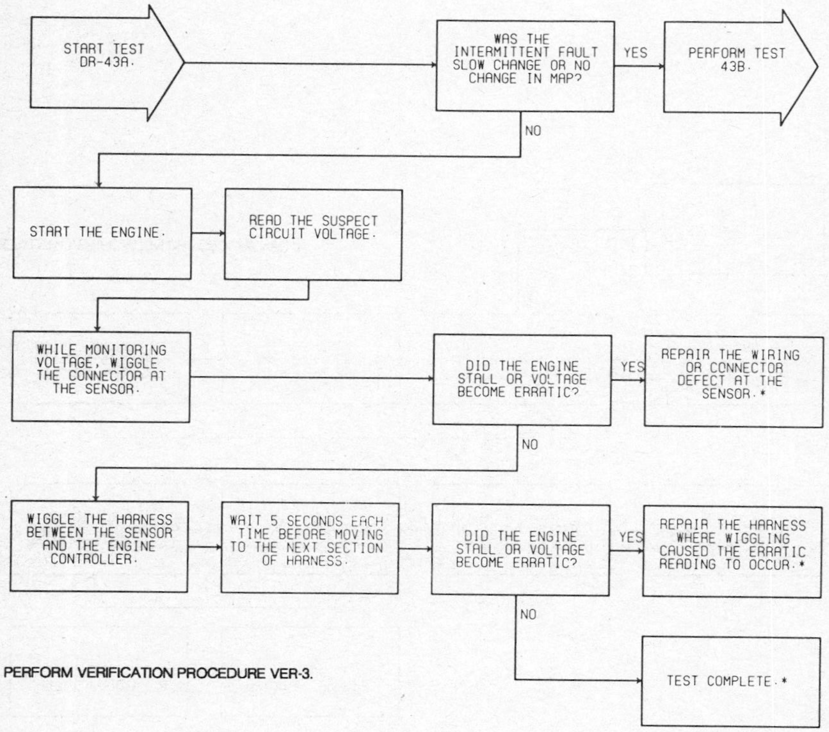
START TEST DR-43A.
WAS THE INTERMITTENT FAULT SLOW CHANGE OR NO CHANGE IN MAP?
YES
PERFORM TEST 43B.
NO
START THE ENGINE.
READ THE SUSPECT CIRCUIT VOLTAGE.
WHILE MONITORING VOLTAGE, WIGGLE THE CONNECTOR AT THE SENSOR.
DID THE ENGINE STALL OR VOLTAGE BECOME ERRATIC?
YES
REPAIR THE WIRING OR CONNECTOR DEFECT AT THE SENSOR.*
NO
WIGGLE THE HARNESS BETWEEN THE SENSOR AND THE ENGINE CONTROLLER.
WAIT 5 SECONDS EACH TIME BEFORE MOVING TO THE NEXT SECTION OF HARNESS.
DID THE ENGINE STALL OR VOLTAGE BECOME ERRATIC?
YES
REPAIR THE HARNESS WHERE WIGGLING CAUSED THE ERRATIC READING TO OCCUR.*
NO
TEST COMPLETE.*

* PERFORM VERIFICATION PROCEDURE VER-3.

91D10689

Fig. 161: Driveability Test 43A (2.2L & 2.5L) – Intermittent Test for Voltage Sensor

DR-43B: INTERMITTENT TEST FOR MAP SENSOR SIGNAL CHANGE

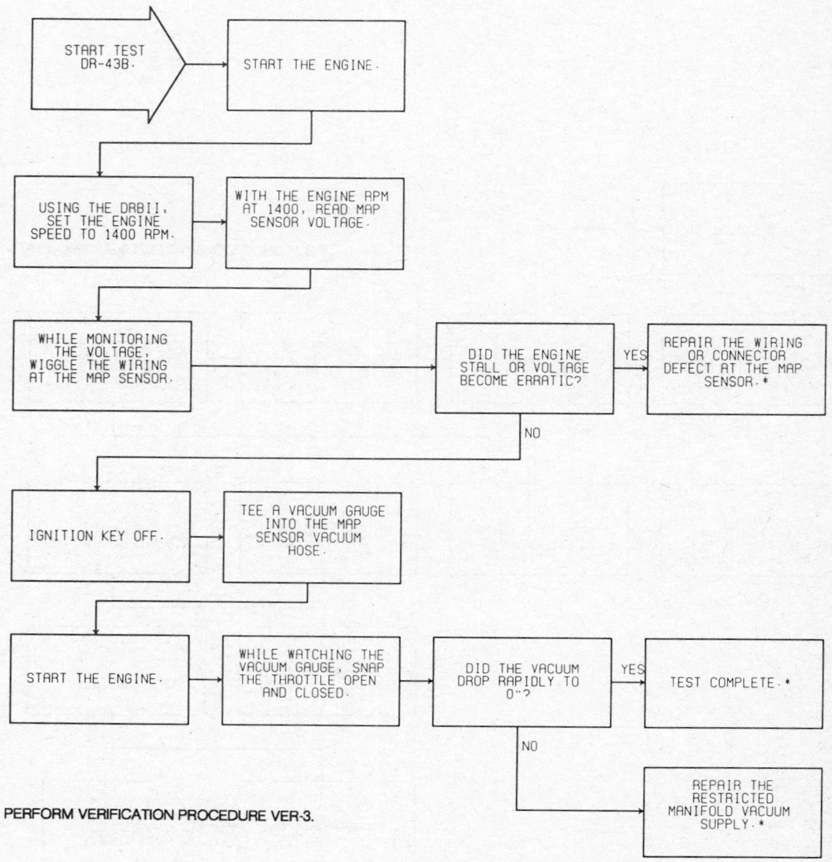
START TEST DR-43B.
START THE ENGINE.
USING THE DRBII, SET THE ENGINE SPEED TO 1400 RPM.
WITH THE ENGINE RPM AT 1400, READ MAP SENSOR VOLTAGE.
WHILE MONITORING THE VOLTAGE, WIGGLE THE WIRING AT THE MAP SENSOR.
DID THE ENGINE STALL OR VOLTAGE BECOME ERRATIC?
YES
REPAIR THE WIRING OR CONNECTOR DEFECT AT THE MAP SENSOR.*
NO
IGNITION KEY OFF.
TEE A VACUUM GAUGE INTO THE MAP SENSOR VACUUM HOSE.
START THE ENGINE.
WHILE WATCHING THE VACUUM GAUGE, SNAP THE THROTTLE OPEN AND CLOSED.
DID THE VACUUM DROP RAPIDLY TO 0"?
YES
TEST COMPLETE.*
NO
REPAIR THE RESTRICTED MANIFOLD VACUUM SUPPLY.*

* PERFORM VERIFICATION PROCEDURE VER-3.

91G10690

Fig. 162: Driveability Test 43B (2.2L & 2.5L) – Intermittent Test for MAP Sensor Signal Change

DR-44A: INTERMITTENT TEST FOR IDLE MOTOR CIRCUITS

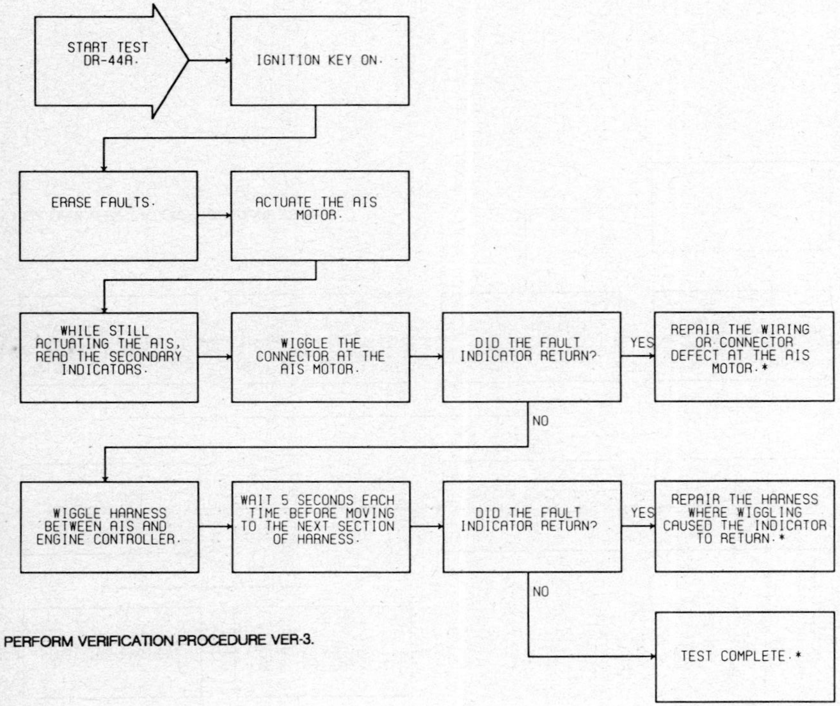
START TEST DR-44A.
IGNITION KEY ON.
ERASE FAULTS.
ACTUATE THE AIS MOTOR.
WHILE STILL ACTUATING THE AIS, READ THE SECONDARY INDICATORS.
WIGGLE THE CONNECTOR AT THE AIS MOTOR.
DID THE FAULT INDICATOR RETURN?
YES
REPAIR THE WIRING OR CONNECTOR DEFECT AT THE AIS MOTOR.*
NO
WIGGLE HARNESS BETWEEN AIS AND ENGINE CONTROLLER.
WAIT 5 SECONDS EACH TIME BEFORE MOVING TO THE NEXT SECTION OF HARNESS.
DID THE FAULT INDICATOR RETURN?
YES
REPAIR THE HARNESS WHERE WIGGLING CAUSED THE INDICATOR TO RETURN.*
NO
TEST COMPLETE.*

* PERFORM VERIFICATION PROCEDURE VER-3.

91H10691

Fig. 163: Driveability Test 44A (2.2L & 2.5L) – Intermittent Test for Idle Motor Circuits

DR-45A: INTERMITTENT TEST FOR INJECTOR CIRCUITS

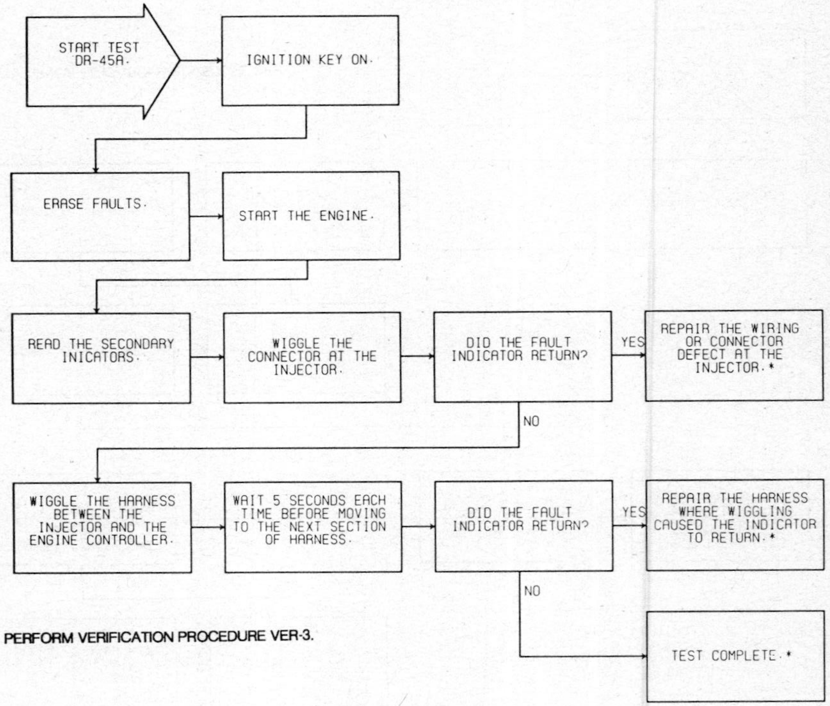
START TEST DR-45A.
IGNITION KEY ON.
ERASE FAULTS.
START THE ENGINE.
READ THE SECONDARY INICATORS.
WIGGLE THE CONNECTOR AT THE INJECTOR.
DID THE FAULT INDICATOR RETURN?
YES
REPAIR THE WIRING OR CONNECTOR DEFECT AT THE INJECTOR.*
NO
WIGGLE THE HARNESS BETWEEN THE INJECTOR AND THE ENGINE CONTROLLER.
WAIT 5 SECONDS EACH TIME BEFORE MOVING TO THE NEXT SECTION OF HARNESS.
DID THE FAULT INDICATOR RETURN?
YES
REPAIR THE HARNESS WHERE WIGGLING CAUSED THE INDICATOR TO RETURN.*
NO
TEST COMPLETE.*

* PERFORM VERIFICATION PROCEDURE VER-3.

91I10692

Fig. 164: Driveability Test 45A (2.2L & 2.5L) – Intermittent Test for Injector Circuits

VER-1: VERIFICATION PROCEDURE 1

1) Inspect vehicle to ensure all components are connected. Reassemble and reconnect components as necessary. Attempt to start engine. If engine does not start, return to test NS-1A: CHECKING FOR IGNITION SPARK & POWER FEED TO COIL.

2) If engine starts and engine controller has been changed, go to next step. If engine starts and engine controller has not been changed, connect DRB-II to engine diagnostic connector and erase faults. Repair is now complete.

3) If vehicle is equipped with factory theft alarm system, start engine about 20 times to activate theft alarm system. If vehicle is an AS or AN body, write EMR mileage into the new engine controller. Repair is now complete.

Fig. 165: Verification Procedure 1 (2.2L & 2.5L)

VER-2: VERIFICATION PROCEDURE 2

1) If test VER-3: VERIFICATION PROCEDURE 3 has been preformed previously, perform test VER-3 again. Inspect vehicle to ensure all engine components are connected. Reassemble and reconnect components as necessary.

2) If another fault exists that has not been corrected, return to DR-1B: DRB-II FAULT MESSAGES and follow path specified by other fault. If engine controller has been replaced and vehicle is equipped with factory theft alarm system, start engine about 20 times to activate theft alarm system. If vehicle is an AS or AN body, write EMR mileage into new engine controller.

3) Connect DRB-II to engine diagnostic connector and erase faults. Ensure no other faults are present. To ensure no other faults are present, start engine. Allow engine to reach normal operating temperature. Increase engine speed to 2000 RPM for about 10 seconds. Return engine to idle.

4) If vehicle is equipped with A/T, apply brakes and cycle through all transmission gear positions. Place gear selector in Park. If vehicle is equipped with A/C, turn A/C on. Set blower speed to LOW.

5) Turn engine off. Start engine. Allow engine to idle for about 2 minutes. Turn engine off. Using DRB-II, check for fault messages. If NO FAULT message appears on DRB-II display, test is complete.

6) If repaired fault resets or another fault sets, check MITCHELL'S TECHNICAL SERVICE BULLETINS (TSBs) for any pertinent information relating to driveability problem. If a TSB exists, perform corrective action. If another fault sets, return to DR-1B: DRB-II FAULT MESSAGES.

Fig. 166: Verification Procedure 2 (2.2L & 2.5L)

VER-3: VERIFICATION PROCEDURE 3

1) Inspect vehicle to ensure all engine components are connected. Reassemble and reconnect components as necessary. If another fault is present that has not been corrected, return to DR-1B: DRB-II FAULT MESSAGES and follow path specified by other fault.

2) If engine controller has been changed and vehicle is equipped with factory theft alarm system, start engine about 20 times to activate theft alarm system. If vehicle is an AS or AN body, write EMR mileage into new engine controller.

3) Connect DRB-II to engine diagnostic connector. Erase fault messages. Disconnect DRB-II. Ensure no other fault messages are present. To ensure no other fault messages are present, start engine. If vehicle is equipped with A/C, turn A/C on. Set blower speed to LOW.

4) Drive vehicle for about 5 minutes. During this time, attain a speed above 40 MPH or more. Ensure transmission shifts through all gears. Upon completion of road test, turn engine off.

5) Start engine. Allow engine to idle for about 2 minutes. Turn engine off. Connect DRB-II to engine diagnostic connector. Using DRB-II, check for fault messages. If no fault messages are present, test is complete.

6) If repaired fault message resets or another fault message sets, check MITCHELL'S TECHNICAL SERVICE BULLETINS (TSBs) for any pertinent information relating to driveability problems. If a TSB exists, perform corrective action. If another fault sets, return to DR-1B: DRB-II FAULT MESSAGES.

Fig. 167: Verification Procedure 3 (2.2L & 2.5L)

NS-1A: CHECKING FOR IGNITION SPARK & POWER FEED TO COIL (1 OF 3)

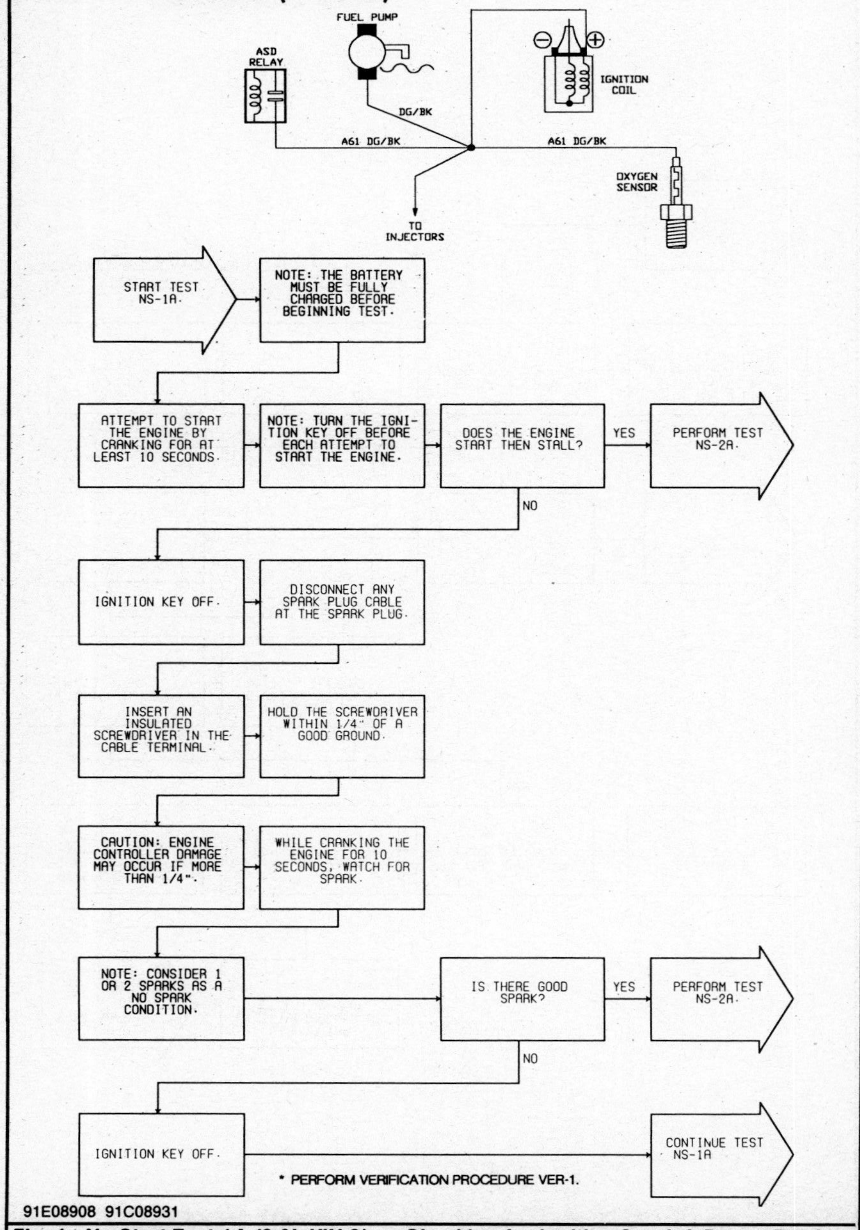
FUEL PUMP
ASD RELAY
DG/BK
A61 DG/BK
A61 DG/BK
IGNITION COIL
OXYGEN SENSOR
TO INJECTORS
START TEST NS-1A.
NOTE: THE BATTERY MUST BE FULLY CHARGED BEFORE BEGINNING TEST.
ATTEMPT TO START THE ENGINE BY CRANKING FOR AT LEAST 10 SECONDS.
NOTE: TURN THE IGNITION KEY OFF BEFORE EACH ATTEMPT TO START THE ENGINE.
DOES THE ENGINE START THEN STALL?
YES
PERFORM TEST NS-2A.
NO
IGNITION KEY OFF.
DISCONNECT ANY SPARK PLUG CABLE AT THE SPARK PLUG.
INSERT AN INSULATED SCREWDRIVER IN THE CABLE TERMINAL.
HOLD THE SCREWDRIVER WITHIN 1/4" OF A GOOD GROUND.
CAUTION: ENGINE CONTROLLER DAMAGE MAY OCCUR IF MORE THAN 1/4".
WHILE CRANKING THE ENGINE FOR 10 SECONDS, WATCH FOR SPARK.
NOTE: CONSIDER 1 OR 2 SPARKS AS A NO SPARK CONDITION.
IS THERE GOOD SPARK?
YES
PERFORM TEST NS-2A.
NO
IGNITION KEY OFF.
CONTINUE TEST NS-1A
* PERFORM VERIFICATION PROCEDURE VER-1.
91E08908 91C08931

Fig. 1: No Start Test 1A (3.0L VIN 3) – Checking for Ignition Spark & Power Feed to Coil (1 of 3)

NS-1A: CHECKING FOR IGNITION SPARK & POWER FEED TO COIL (2 OF 3)

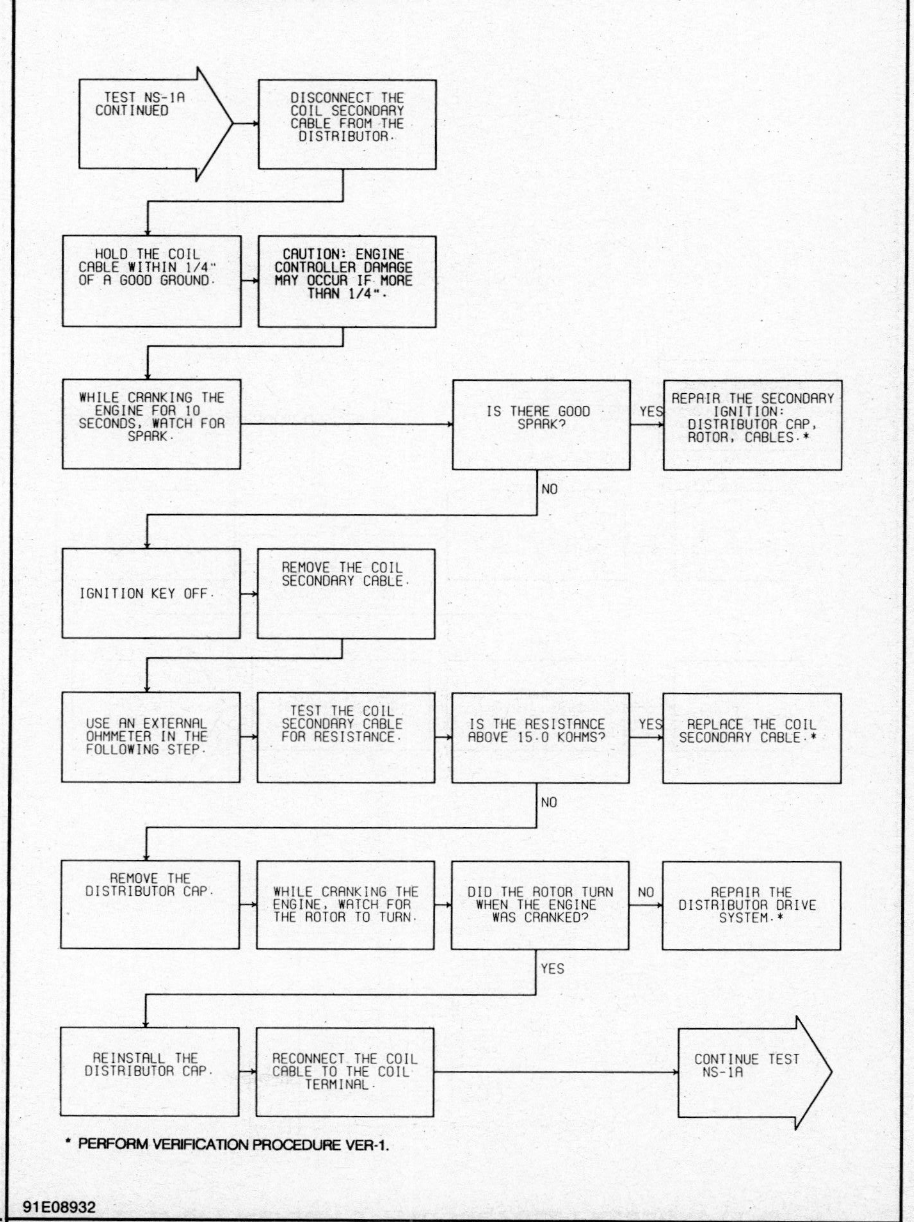
TEST NS-1A CONTINUED
DISCONNECT THE COIL SECONDARY CABLE FROM THE DISTRIBUTOR.
HOLD THE COIL CABLE WITHIN 1/4" OF A GOOD GROUND.
CAUTION: ENGINE CONTROLLER DAMAGE MAY OCCUR IF MORE THAN 1/4".
WHILE CRANKING THE ENGINE FOR 10 SECONDS, WATCH FOR SPARK.
IS THERE GOOD SPARK?
YES
REPAIR THE SECONDARY IGNITION: DISTRIBUTOR CAP, ROTOR, CABLES.*
NO
IGNITION KEY OFF.
REMOVE THE COIL SECONDARY CABLE.
USE AN EXTERNAL OHMMETER IN THE FOLLOWING STEP.
TEST THE COIL SECONDARY CABLE FOR RESISTANCE.
IS THE RESISTANCE ABOVE 15.0 KOHMS?
YES
REPLACE THE COIL SECONDARY CABLE.*
NO
REMOVE THE DISTRIBUTOR CAP.
WHILE CRANKING THE ENGINE, WATCH FOR THE ROTOR TO TURN.
DID THE ROTOR TURN WHEN THE ENGINE WAS CRANKED?
NO
REPAIR THE DISTRIBUTOR DRIVE SYSTEM.*
YES
REINSTALL THE DISTRIBUTOR CAP.
RECONNECT THE COIL CABLE TO THE COIL TERMINAL.
CONTINUE TEST NS-1A
* PERFORM VERIFICATION PROCEDURE VER-1.
91E08932

Fig. 2: No Start Test 1A (3.0L VIN 3) – Checking for Ignition Spark & Power Feed to Coil (2 of 3)

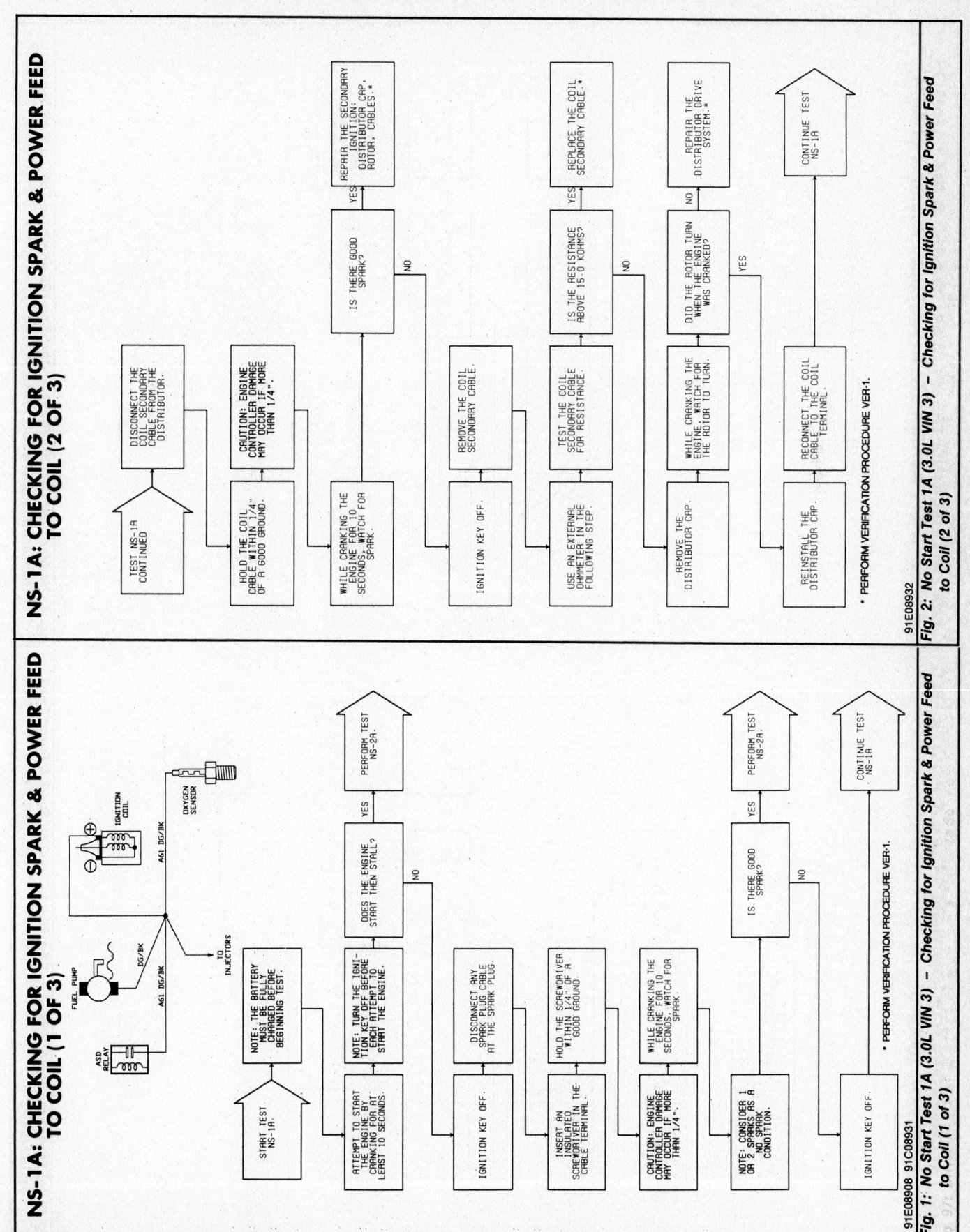

1991 ENGINE PERFORMANCE
Self-Diagnostics – 3.0L VIN 3 (Cont.)

NS-1A: CHECKING FOR IGNITION SPARK & POWER FEED TO COIL (3 OF 3)

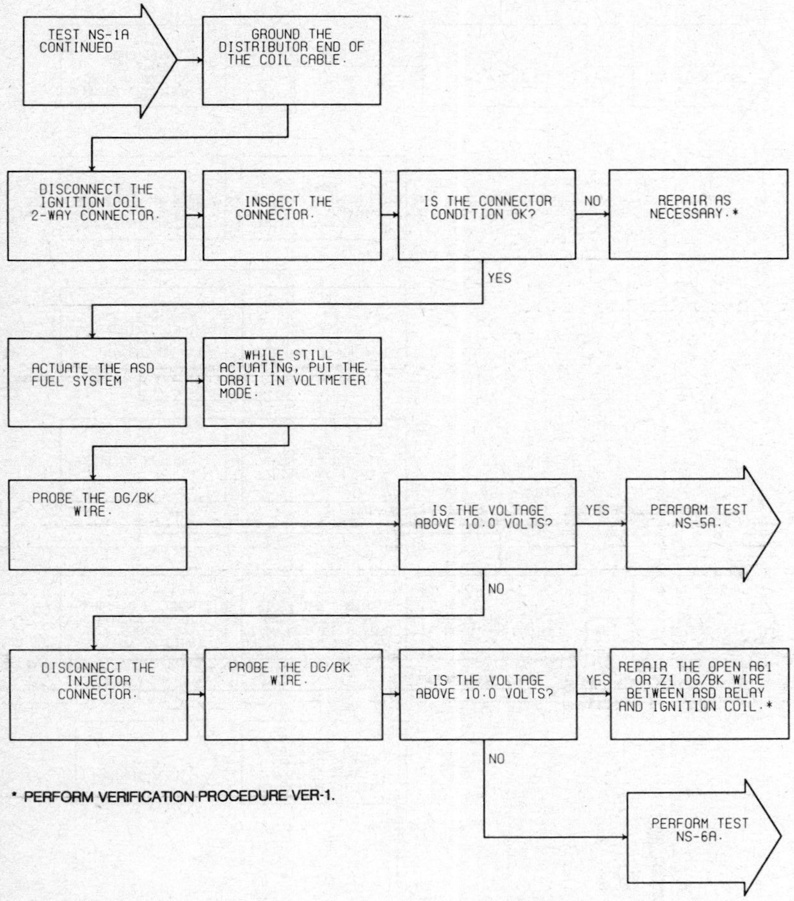
TEST NS-1A CONTINUED
GROUND THE DISTRIBUTOR END OF THE COIL CABLE.
DISCONNECT THE IGNITION COIL 2-WAY CONNECTOR.
INSPECT THE CONNECTOR.
IS THE CONNECTOR CONDITION OK?
NO
REPAIR AS NECESSARY.*
YES
ACTUATE THE ASD FUEL SYSTEM
WHILE STILL ACTUATING, PUT THE DRBII IN VOLTMETER MODE.
PROBE THE DG/BK WIRE.
IS THE VOLTAGE ABOVE 10.0 VOLTS?
YES
PERFORM TEST NS-5A.
NO
DISCONNECT THE INJECTOR CONNECTOR.
PROBE THE DG/BK WIRE.
IS THE VOLTAGE ABOVE 10.0 VOLTS?
YES
REPAIR THE OPEN A61 OR Z1 DG/BK WIRE BETWEEN ASD RELAY AND IGNITION COIL.*
NO
PERFORM TEST NS-6A.

* PERFORM VERIFICATION PROCEDURE VER-1.

91G08933

Fig. 3: No Start Test 1A (3.0L VIN 3) – Checking for Ignition Spark & Power Feed to Coil (3 of 3)

NS-2A: CHECKING TPS, POWER TO SBEC & MAP SENSOR, THEFT ALARM STATUS & FUEL PRESSURE (1 OF 4)

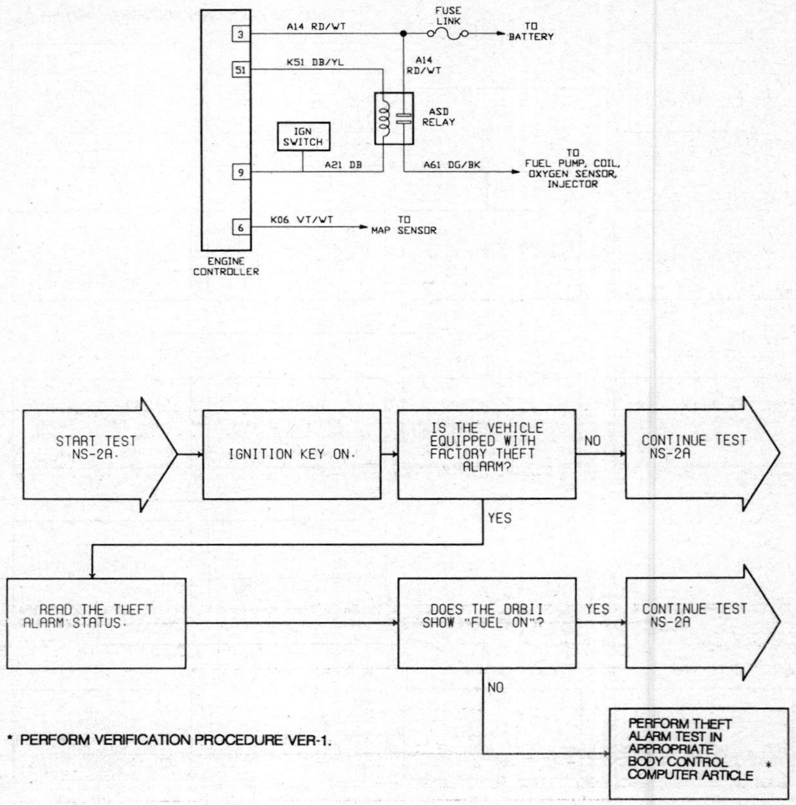
3
51
9
6
ENGINE CONTROLLER
A14 RD/WT
FUSE LINK
TO BATTERY
K51 DB/YL
A14 RD/WT
ASD RELAY
IGN SWITCH
A21 DB
A61 DG/BK
TO FUEL PUMP, COIL, OXYGEN SENSOR, INJECTOR
K06 VT/WT
TO MAP SENSOR
START TEST NS-2A.
IGNITION KEY ON.
IS THE VEHICLE EQUIPPED WITH FACTORY THEFT ALARM?
NO
CONTINUE TEST NS-2A
YES
READ THE THEFT ALARM STATUS.
DOES THE DRBII SHOW "FUEL ON"?
YES
CONTINUE TEST NS-2A
NO
PERFORM THEFT ALARM TEST IN APPROPRIATE BODY CONTROL COMPUTER ARTICLE *

* PERFORM VERIFICATION PROCEDURE VER-1.

91G08909 91I08934

Fig. 4: No Start Test 2A (3.0L VIN 3) – Checking TPS, Power to SBEC & MAP Sensor, Theft Alarm Status & Fuel Pressure (1 of 4)

NS-2A: CHECKING TPS, POWER TO SBEC & MAP SENSOR, THEFT ALARM STATUS & FUEL PRESSURE (2 OF 4)

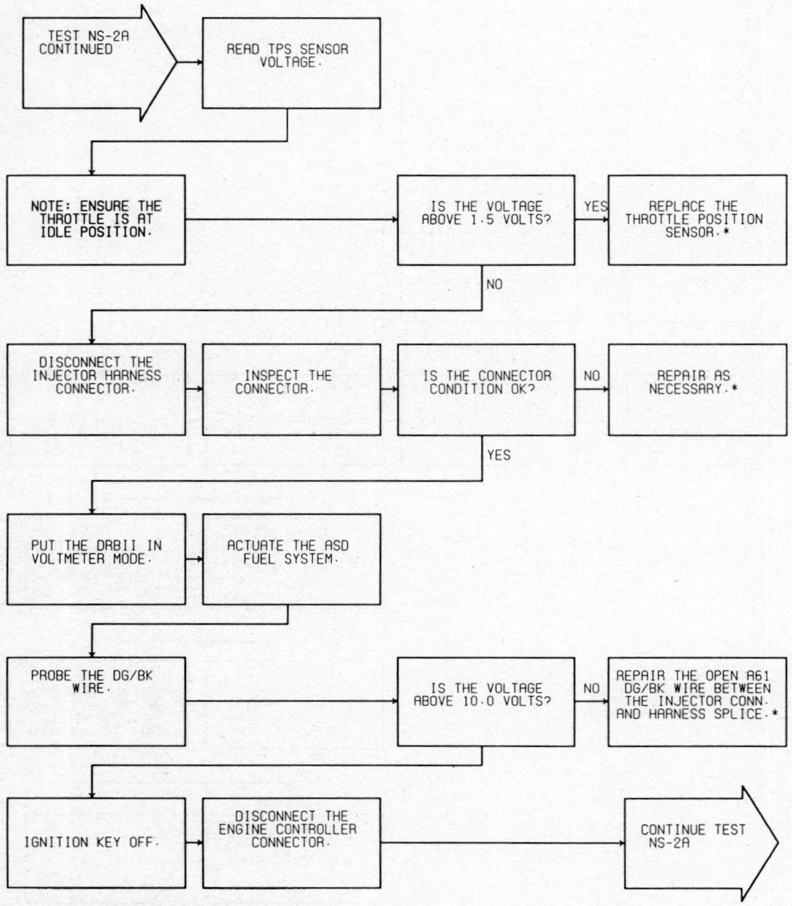
TEST NS-2A CONTINUED
READ TPS SENSOR VOLTAGE.
NOTE: ENSURE THE THROTTLE IS AT IDLE POSITION.
IS THE VOLTAGE ABOVE 1.5 VOLTS?
YES
REPLACE THE THROTTLE POSITION SENSOR.*
NO
DISCONNECT THE INJECTOR HARNESS CONNECTOR.
INSPECT THE CONNECTOR.
IS THE CONNECTOR CONDITION OK?
NO
REPAIR AS NECESSARY.*
YES
PUT THE DRBII IN VOLTMETER MODE.
ACTUATE THE ASD FUEL SYSTEM.
PROBE THE DG/BK WIRE.
IS THE VOLTAGE ABOVE 10.0 VOLTS?
NO
REPAIR THE OPEN A61 DG/BK WIRE BETWEEN THE INJECTOR CONN. AND HARNESS SPLICE.*
IGNITION KEY OFF.
DISCONNECT THE ENGINE CONTROLLER CONNECTOR.
CONTINUE TEST NS-2A

* PERFORM VERIFICATION PROCEDURE VER-1.

91B08935

Fig. 5: No Start Test 2A (3.0L VIN 3) – Checking TPS, Power to SBEC & MAP Sensor, Theft Alarm Status & Fuel Pressure (2 of 4)

NS-2A: CHECKING TPS, POWER TO SBEC & MAP SENSOR, THEFT ALARM STATUS & FUEL PRESSURE (3 OF 4)

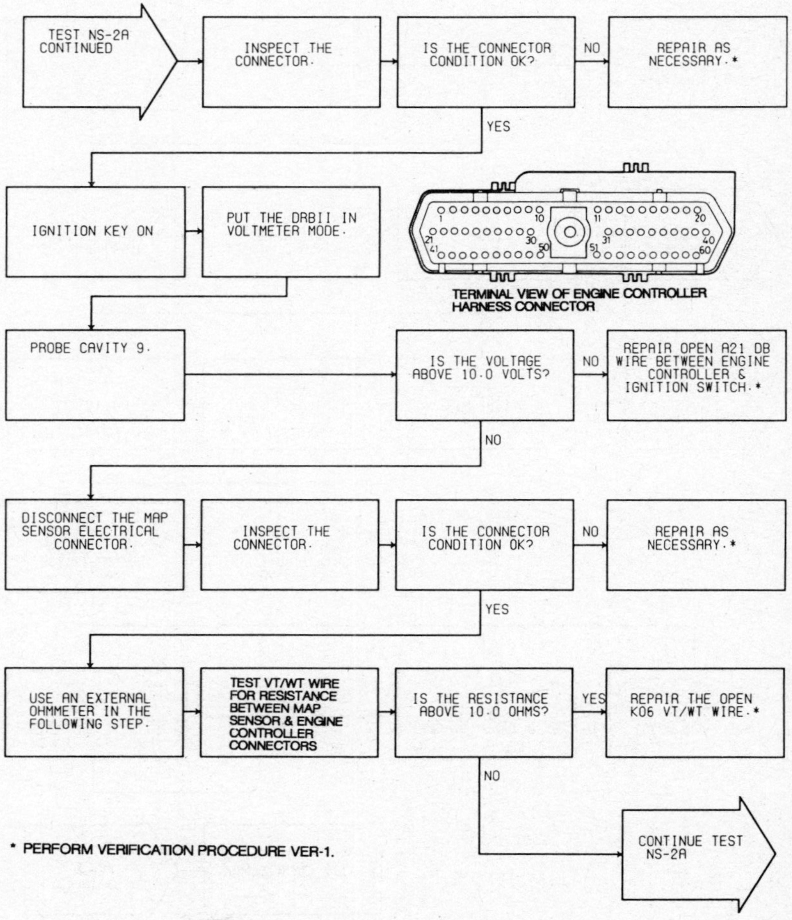
TEST NS-2A CONTINUED
INSPECT THE CONNECTOR.
IS THE CONNECTOR CONDITION OK?
NO
REPAIR AS NECESSARY.*
YES
IGNITION KEY ON
PUT THE DRBII IN VOLTMETER MODE.
1
10
11
20
21
30
31
40
41
50
51
60
TERMINAL VIEW OF ENGINE CONTROLLER HARNESS CONNECTOR
PROBE CAVITY 9.
IS THE VOLTAGE ABOVE 10.0 VOLTS?
NO
REPAIR OPEN A21 DB WIRE BETWEEN ENGINE CONTROLLER & IGNITION SWITCH.*
NO
DISCONNECT THE MAP SENSOR ELECTRICAL CONNECTOR.
INSPECT THE CONNECTOR.
IS THE CONNECTOR CONDITION OK?
NO
REPAIR AS NECESSARY.*
YES
USE AN EXTERNAL OHMMETER IN THE FOLLOWING STEP.
TEST VT/WT WIRE FOR RESISTANCE BETWEEN MAP SENSOR & ENGINE CONTROLLER CONNECTORS
IS THE RESISTANCE ABOVE 10.0 OHMS?
YES
REPAIR THE OPEN K06 VT/WT WIRE.*
NO
CONTINUE TEST NS-2A

* PERFORM VERIFICATION PROCEDURE VER-1.

91D08936

Fig. 6: No Start Test 2A (3.0L VIN 3) – Checking TPS, Power to SBEC & MAP Sensor, Theft Alarm Status & Fuel Pressure (3 of 4)

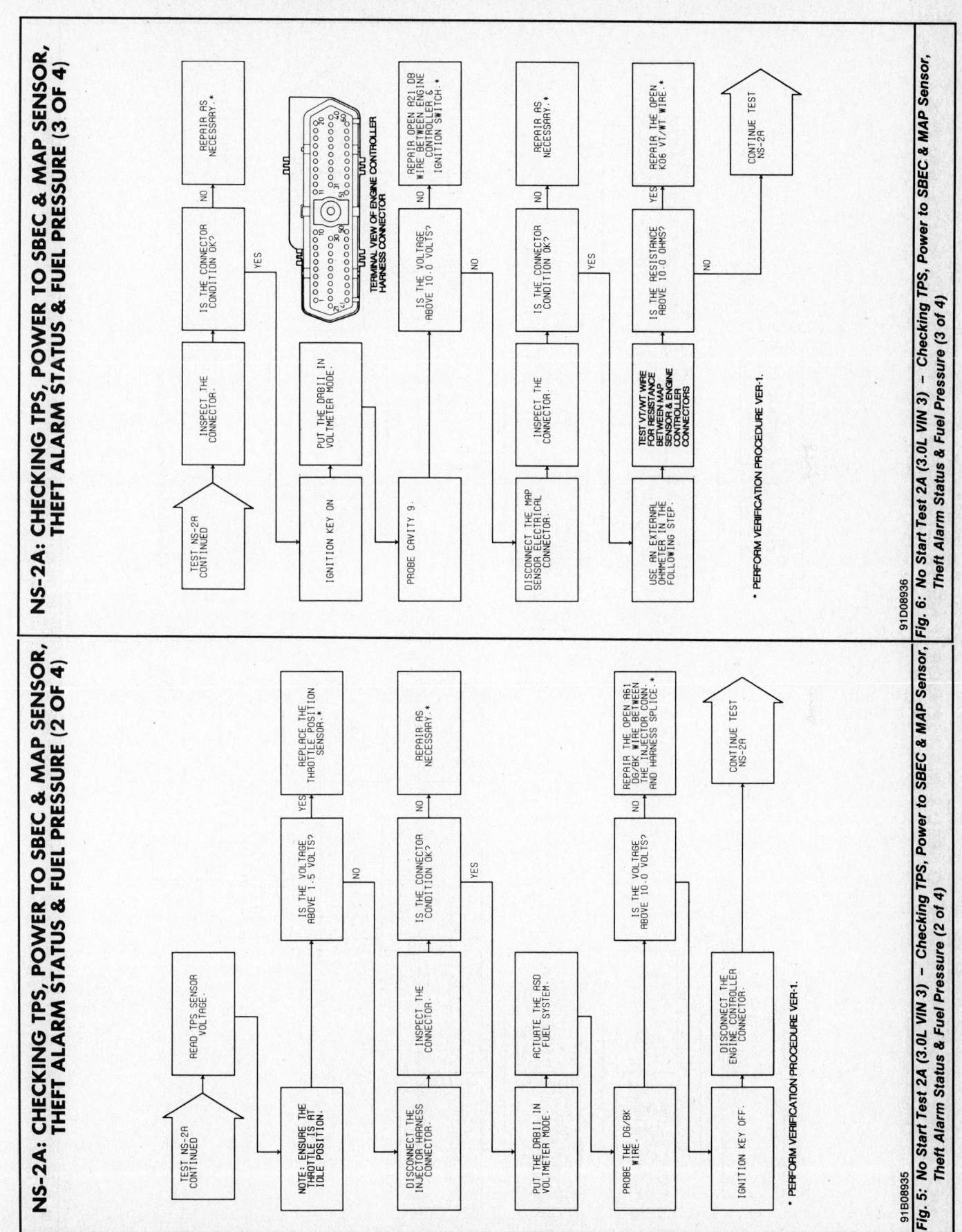

1991 ENGINE PERFORMANCE
Self-Diagnostics – 3.0L VIN 3 (Cont.)

NS-2A: CHECKING TPS, POWER TO SBEC & MAP SENSOR, THEFT ALARM STATUS & FUEL PRESSURE (4 OF 4)

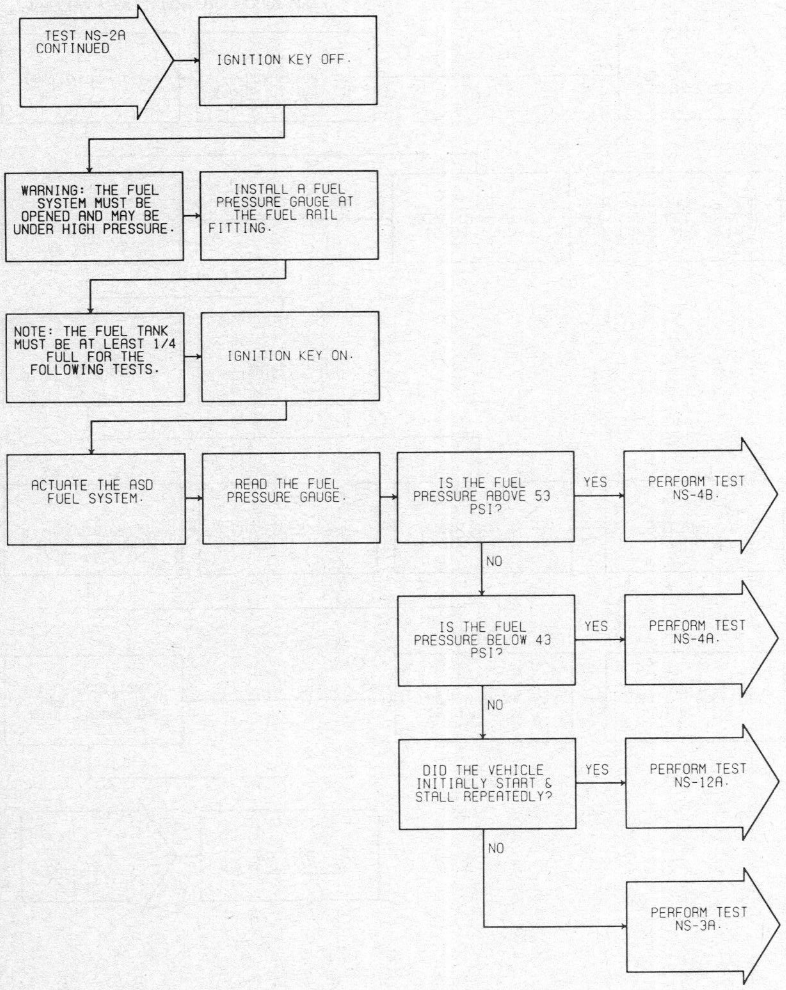
TEST NS-2A CONTINUED
IGNITION KEY OFF.
WARNING: THE FUEL SYSTEM MUST BE OPENED AND MAY BE UNDER HIGH PRESSURE.
INSTALL A FUEL PRESSURE GAUGE AT THE FUEL RAIL FITTING.
NOTE: THE FUEL TANK MUST BE AT LEAST 1/4 FULL FOR THE FOLLOWING TESTS.
IGNITION KEY ON.
ACTUATE THE ASD FUEL SYSTEM.
READ THE FUEL PRESSURE GAUGE.
IS THE FUEL PRESSURE ABOVE 53 PSI?
YES
PERFORM TEST NS-4B.
NO
IS THE FUEL PRESSURE BELOW 43 PSI?
YES
PERFORM TEST NS-4A.
NO
DID THE VEHICLE INITIALLY START & STALL REPEATEDLY?
YES
PERFORM TEST NS-12A.
NO
PERFORM TEST NS-3A.

91F08937

Fig. 7: No Start Test 2A (3.0L VIN 3) – Checking TPS, Power to SBEC & MAP Sensor, Theft Alarm Status & Fuel Pressure (4 of 4)

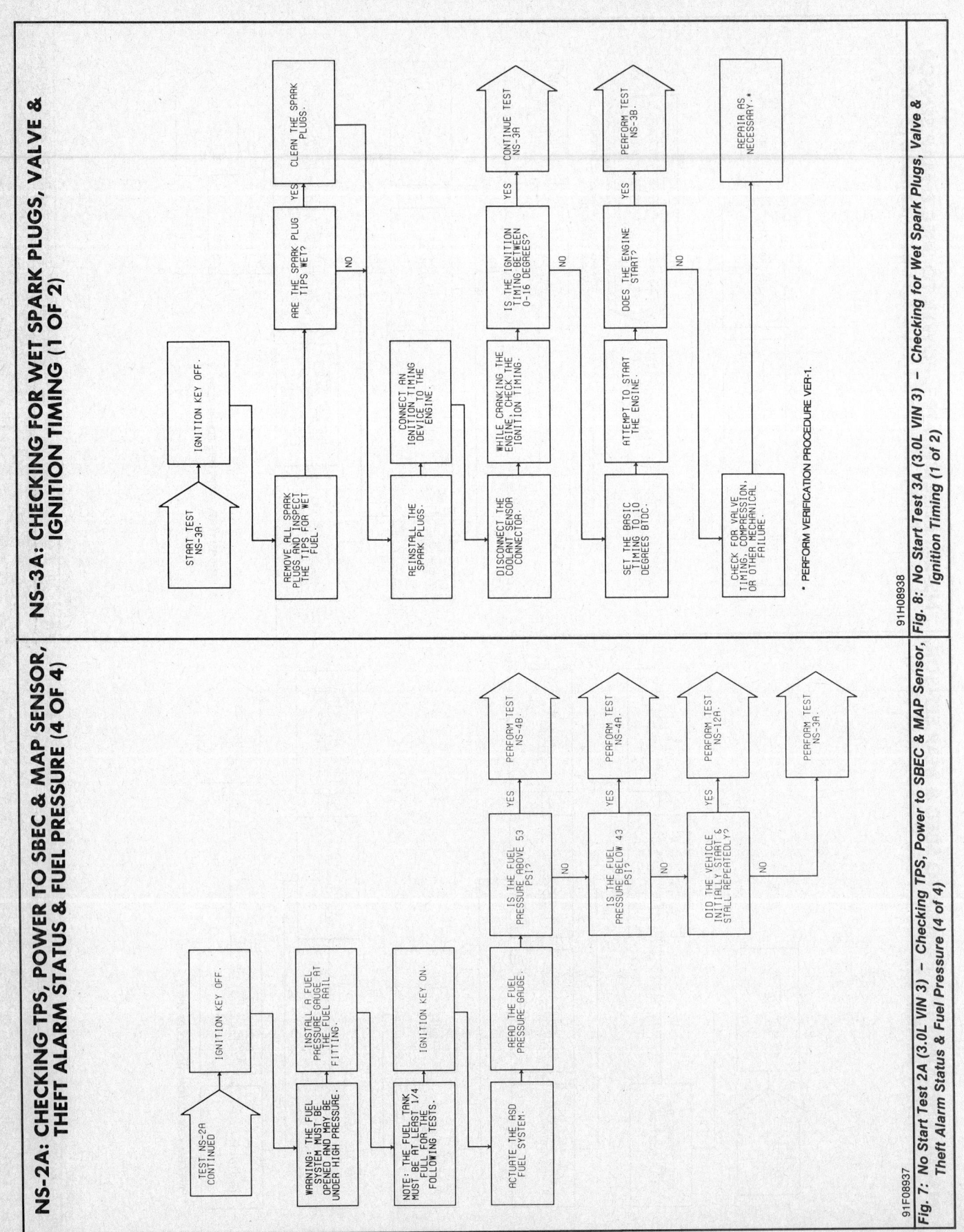

NS-3A: CHECKING FOR WET SPARK PLUGS, VALVE & IGNITION TIMING (1 OF 2)

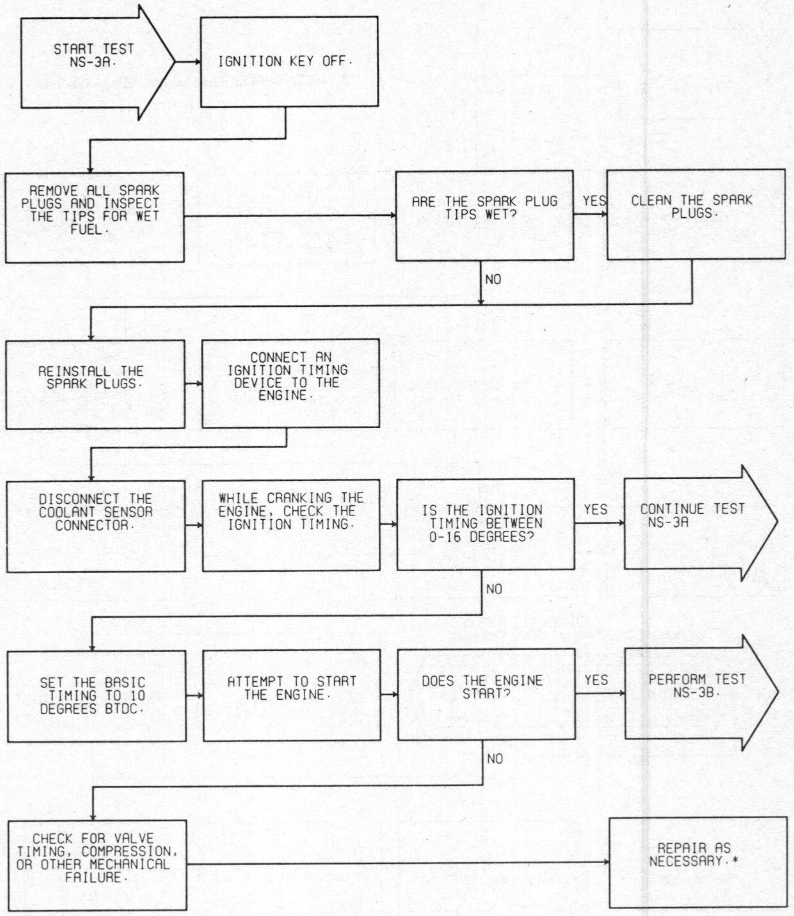
START TEST NS-3A.
IGNITION KEY OFF.
REMOVE ALL SPARK PLUGS AND INSPECT THE TIPS FOR WET FUEL.
ARE THE SPARK PLUG TIPS WET?
YES
CLEAN THE SPARK PLUGS.
NO
REINSTALL THE SPARK PLUGS.
CONNECT AN IGNITION TIMING DEVICE TO THE ENGINE.
DISCONNECT THE COOLANT SENSOR CONNECTOR.
WHILE CRANKING THE ENGINE, CHECK THE IGNITION TIMING.
IS THE IGNITION TIMING BETWEEN 0-16 DEGREES?
YES
CONTINUE TEST NS-3A
NO
SET THE BASIC TIMING TO 10 DEGREES BTDC.
ATTEMPT TO START THE ENGINE.
DOES THE ENGINE START?
YES
PERFORM TEST NS-3B.
NO
CHECK FOR VALVE TIMING, COMPRESSION, OR OTHER MECHANICAL FAILURE.
REPAIR AS NECESSARY.*

* PERFORM VERIFICATION PROCEDURE VER-1.

91H08938

Fig. 8: No Start Test 3A (3.0L VIN 3) – Checking for Wet Spark Plugs, Valve & Ignition Timing (1 of 2)

NS-3A: CHECKING FOR WET SPARK PLUGS, VALVE & IGNITION TIMING (2 OF 2)

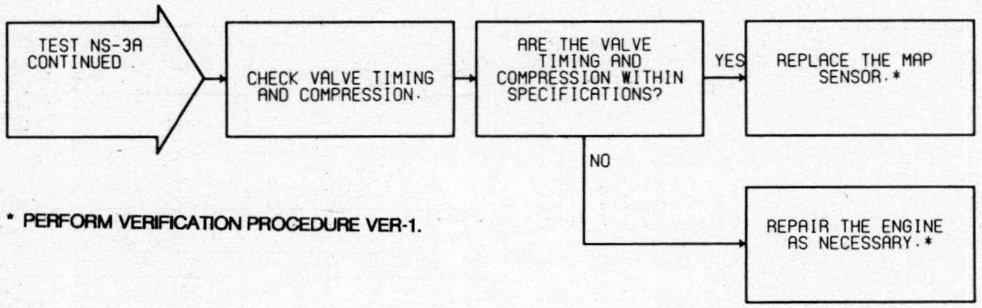
TEST NS-3A CONTINUED.
CHECK VALVE TIMING AND COMPRESSION.
ARE THE VALVE TIMING AND COMPRESSION WITHIN SPECIFICATIONS?
YES
REPLACE THE MAP SENSOR.*
NO
REPAIR THE ENGINE AS NECESSARY.*

* PERFORM VERIFICATION PROCEDURE VER-1.

91J08939

Fig. 9: No Start Test 3A (3.0L VIN 3) – Checking for Wet Spark Plugs, Valve & Ignition Timing (2 of 2)

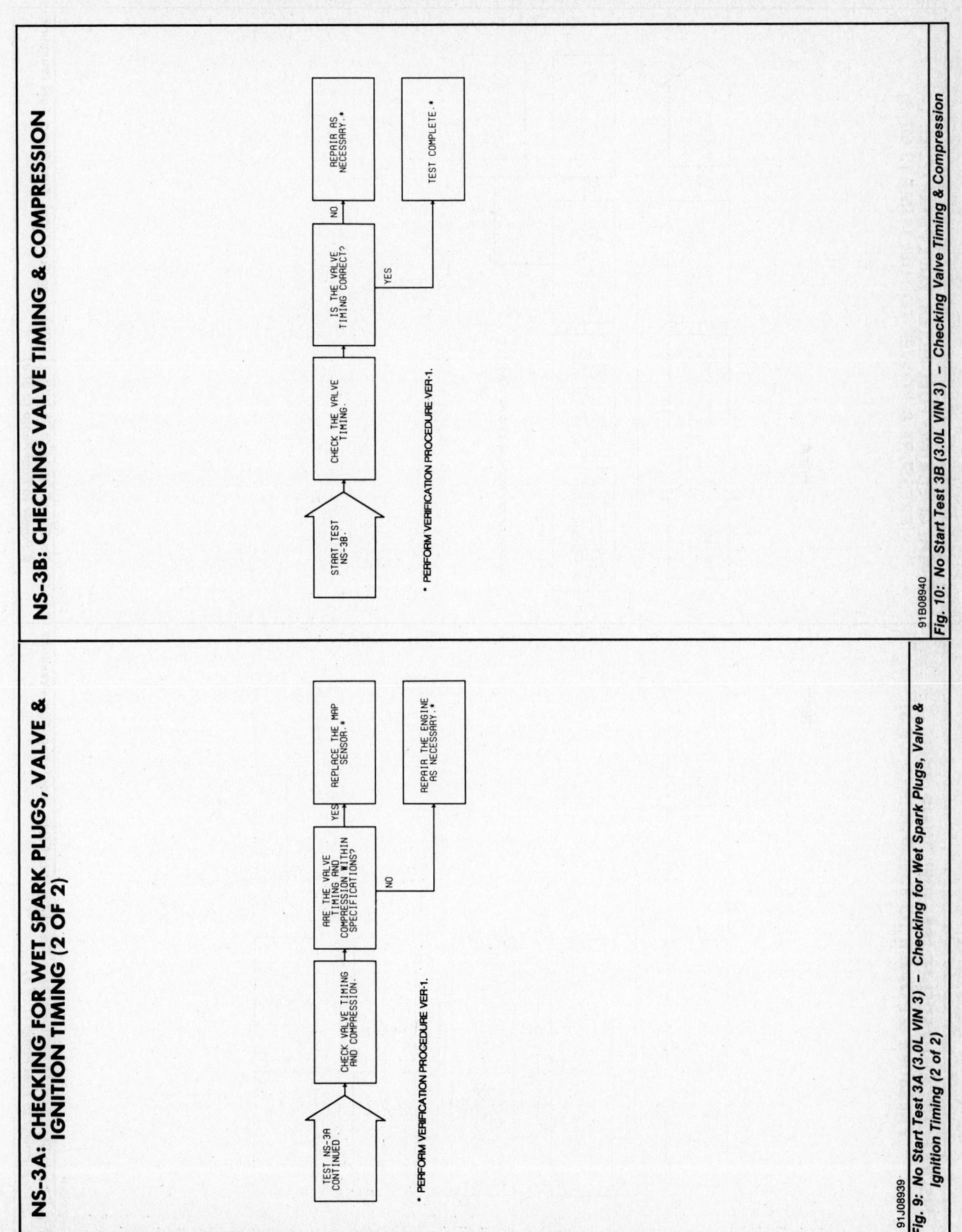

NS-3B: CHECKING VALVE TIMING & COMPRESSION

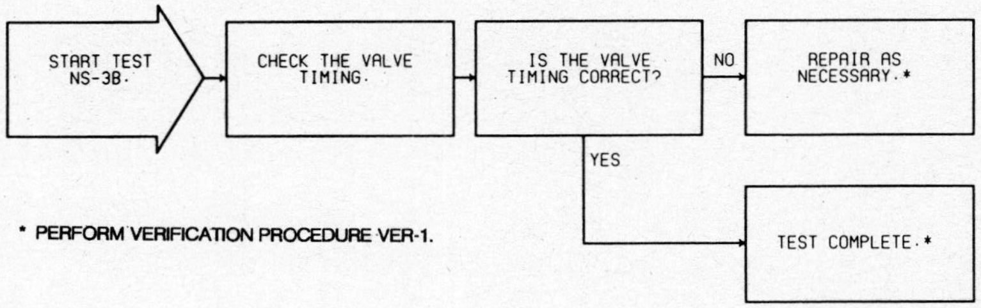
START TEST NS-3B.
CHECK THE VALVE TIMING.
IS THE VALVE TIMING CORRECT?
NO
REPAIR AS NECESSARY.*
YES
TEST COMPLETE.*

* PERFORM VERIFICATION PROCEDURE VER-1.

91B08940

Fig. 10: No Start Test 3B (3.0L VIN 3) – Checking Valve Timing & Compression

1991 ENGINE PERFORMANCE
Self-Diagnostics – 3.0L VIN 3 (Cont.)

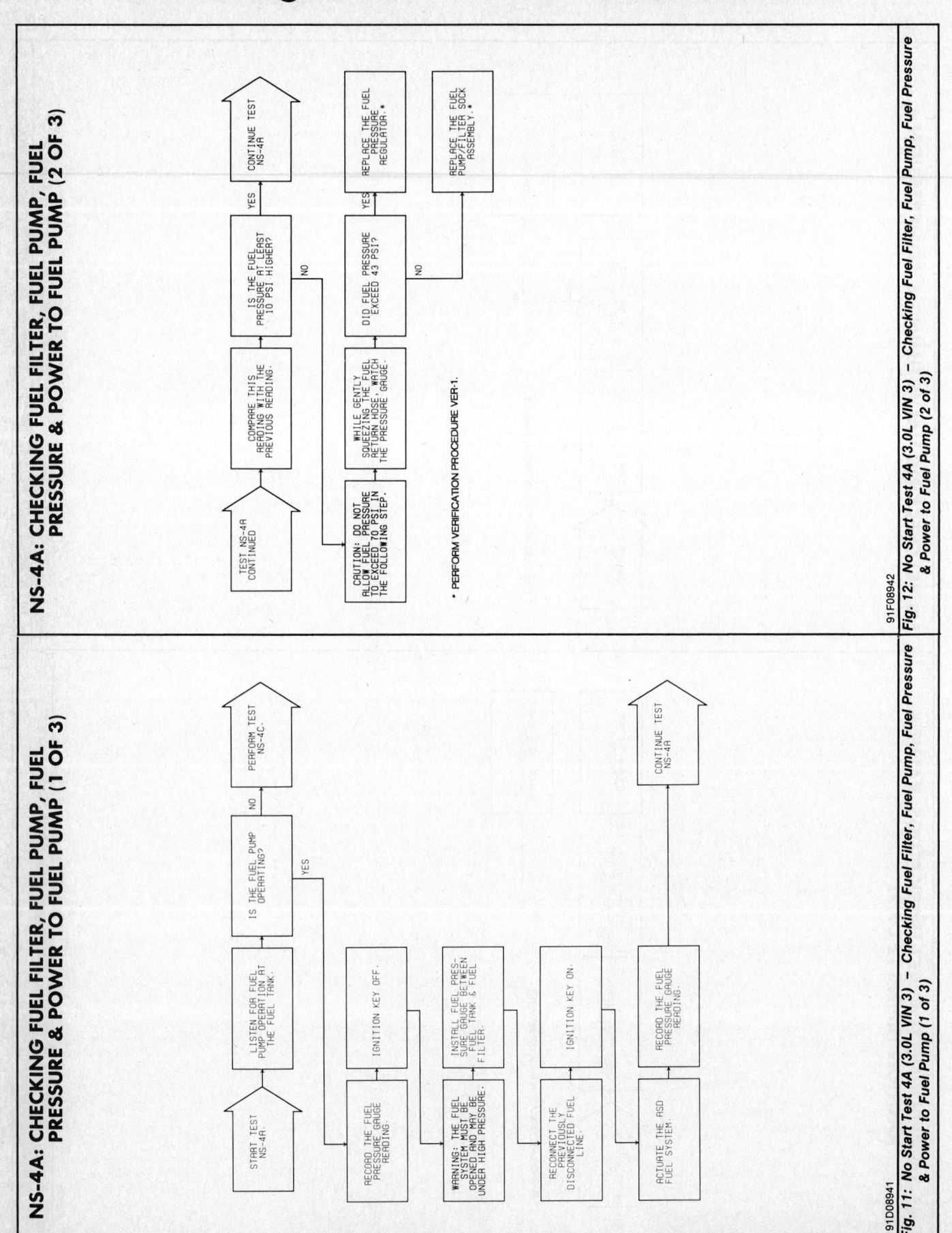

NS-4A: CHECKING FUEL FILTER, FUEL PUMP, FUEL PRESSURE & POWER TO FUEL PUMP (1 OF 3)

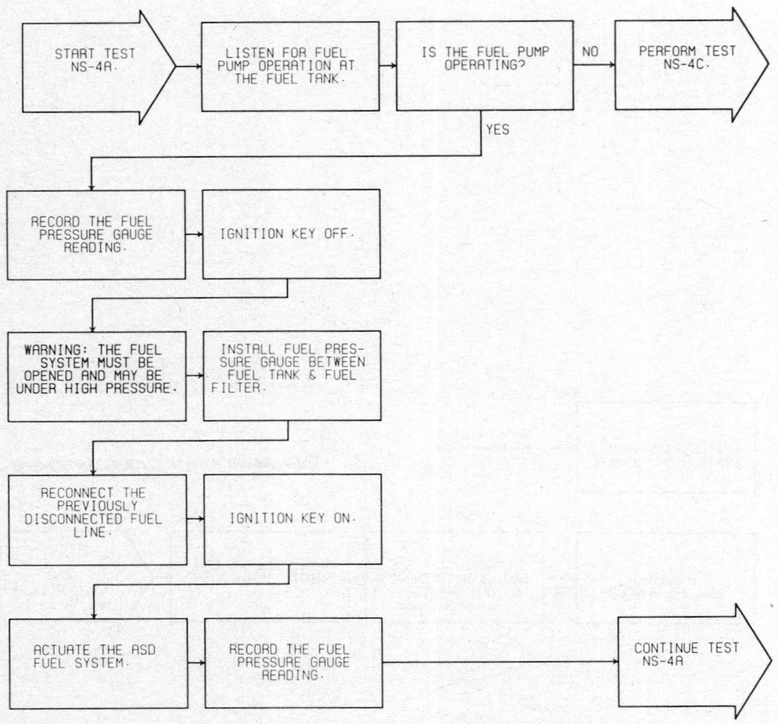
START TEST NS-4A.
LISTEN FOR FUEL PUMP OPERATION AT THE FUEL TANK.
IS THE FUEL PUMP OPERATING?
NO
PERFORM TEST NS-4C.
YES
RECORD THE FUEL PRESSURE GAUGE READING.
IGNITION KEY OFF.
WARNING: THE FUEL SYSTEM MUST BE OPENED AND MAY BE UNDER HIGH PRESSURE.
INSTALL FUEL PRESSURE GAUGE BETWEEN FUEL TANK & FUEL FILTER.
RECONNECT THE PREVIOUSLY DISCONNECTED FUEL LINE.
IGNITION KEY ON.
ACTUATE THE ASD FUEL SYSTEM.
RECORD THE FUEL PRESSURE GAUGE READING.
CONTINUE TEST NS-4A

91D08941

Fig. 11: No Start Test 4A (3.0L VIN 3) – Checking Fuel Filter, Fuel Pump, Fuel Pressure & Power to Fuel Pump (1 of 3)

NS-4A: CHECKING FUEL FILTER, FUEL PUMP, FUEL PRESSURE & POWER TO FUEL PUMP (2 OF 3)

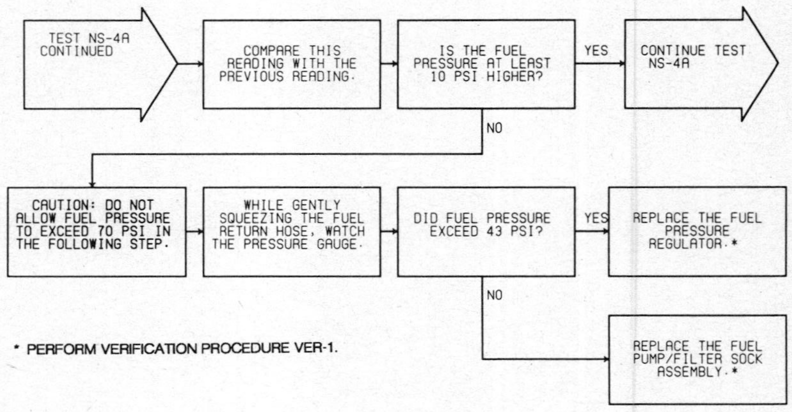
TEST NS-4A CONTINUED
COMPARE THIS READING WITH THE PREVIOUS READING.
IS THE FUEL PRESSURE AT LEAST 10 PSI HIGHER?
YES
CONTINUE TEST NS-4A
NO
CAUTION: DO NOT ALLOW FUEL PRESSURE TO EXCEED 70 PSI IN THE FOLLOWING STEP.
WHILE GENTLY SQUEEZING THE FUEL RETURN HOSE, WATCH THE PRESSURE GAUGE.
DID FUEL PRESSURE EXCEED 43 PSI?
YES
REPLACE THE FUEL PRESSURE REGULATOR.*
NO
REPLACE THE FUEL PUMP/FILTER SOCK ASSEMBLY.*

* PERFORM VERIFICATION PROCEDURE VER-1.

91F08942

Fig. 12: No Start Test 4A (3.0L VIN 3) – Checking Fuel Filter, Fuel Pump, Fuel Pressure & Power to Fuel Pump (2 of 3)

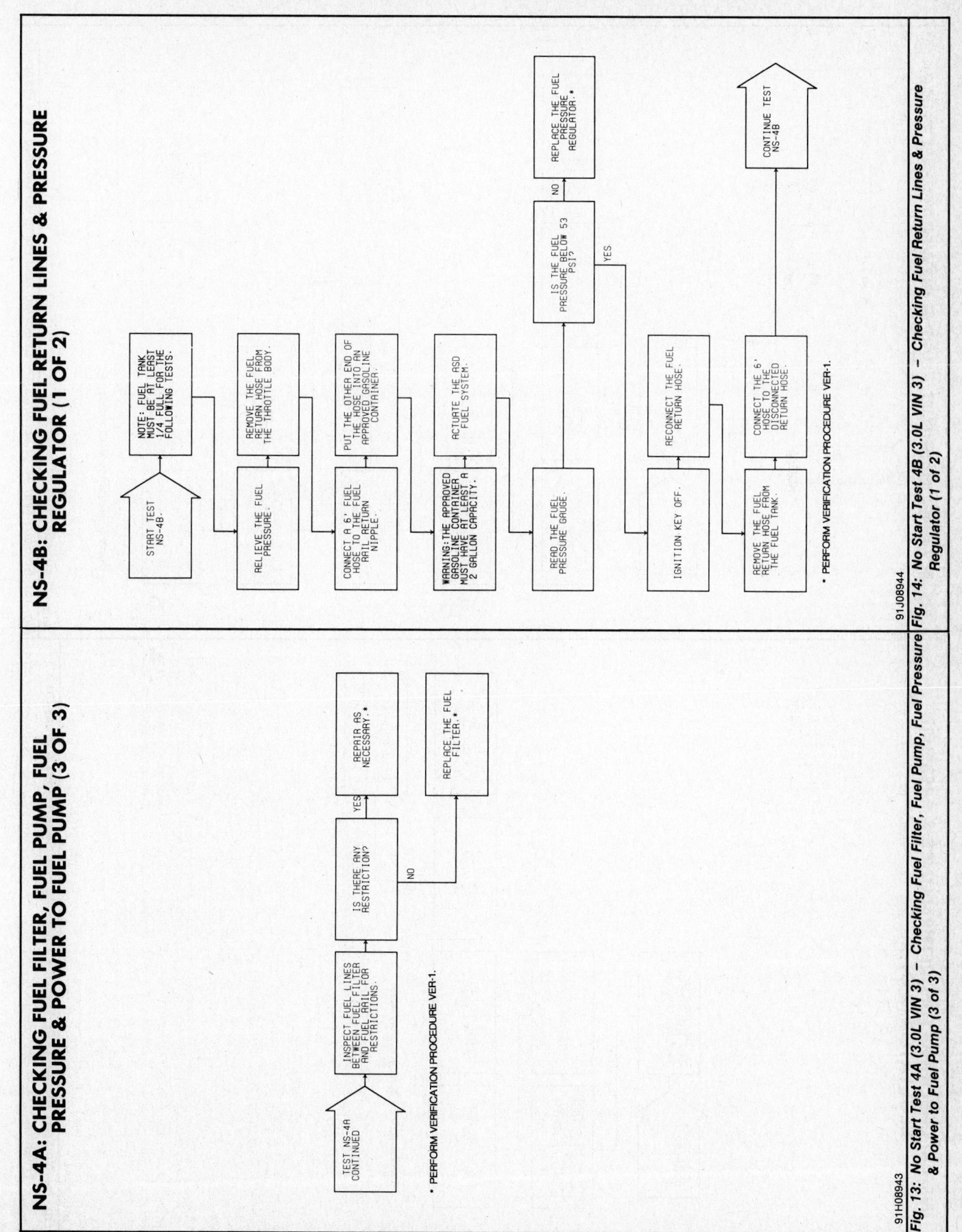

NS-4A: CHECKING FUEL FILTER, FUEL PUMP, FUEL PRESSURE & POWER TO FUEL PUMP (3 OF 3)

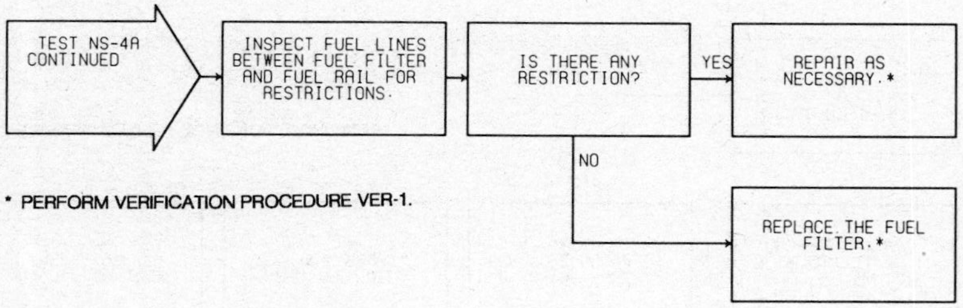
TEST NS-4A CONTINUED
INSPECT FUEL LINES BETWEEN FUEL FILTER AND FUEL RAIL FOR RESTRICTIONS.
IS THERE ANY RESTRICTION?
YES
REPAIR AS NECESSARY.*
NO
REPLACE THE FUEL FILTER.*

* PERFORM VERIFICATION PROCEDURE VER-1.

91H08943

Fig. 13: No Start Test 4A (3.0L VIN 3) – Checking Fuel Filter, Fuel Pump, Fuel Pressure & Power to Fuel Pump (3 of 3)

NS-4B: CHECKING FUEL RETURN LINES & PRESSURE REGULATOR (1 OF 2)

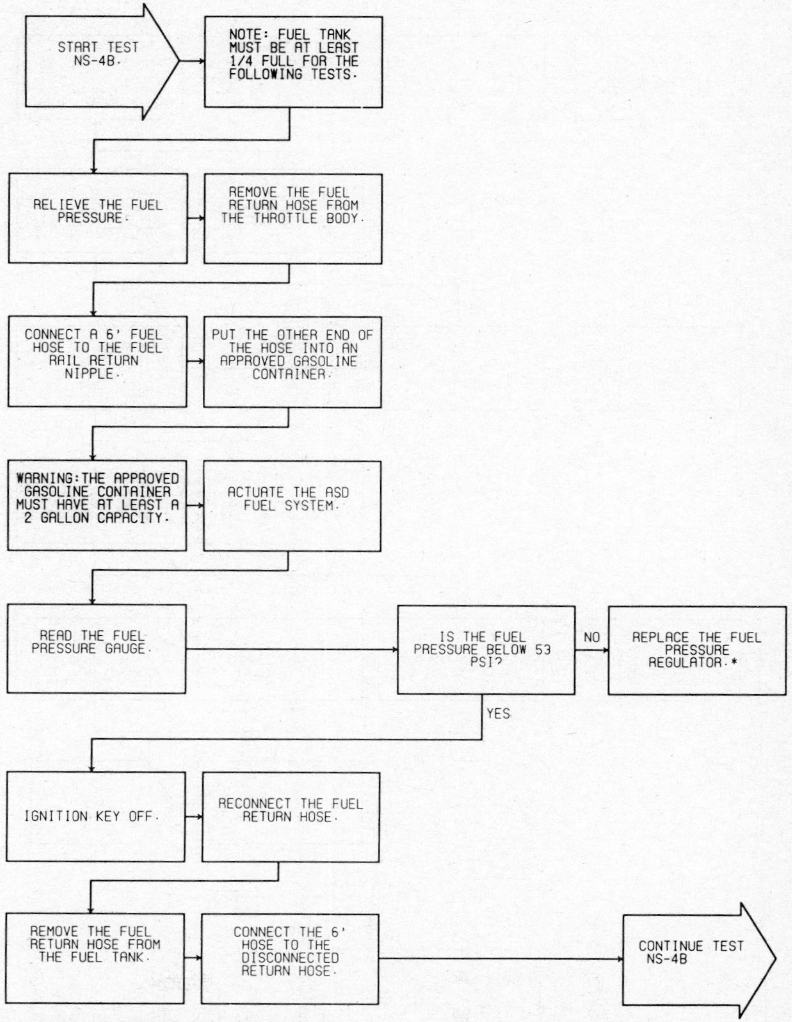
START TEST NS-4B.
NOTE: FUEL TANK MUST BE AT LEAST 1/4 FULL FOR THE FOLLOWING TESTS.
RELIEVE THE FUEL PRESSURE.
REMOVE THE FUEL RETURN HOSE FROM THE THROTTLE BODY.
CONNECT A 6' FUEL HOSE TO THE FUEL RAIL RETURN NIPPLE.
PUT THE OTHER END OF THE HOSE INTO AN APPROVED GASOLINE CONTAINER.
WARNING: THE APPROVED GASOLINE CONTAINER MUST HAVE AT LEAST A 2 GALLON CAPACITY.
ACTUATE THE ASD FUEL SYSTEM.
READ THE FUEL PRESSURE GAUGE.
IS THE FUEL PRESSURE BELOW 53 PSI?
NO
REPLACE THE FUEL PRESSURE REGULATOR.*
YES
IGNITION KEY OFF.
RECONNECT THE FUEL RETURN HOSE.
REMOVE THE FUEL RETURN HOSE FROM THE FUEL TANK.
CONNECT THE 6' HOSE TO THE DISCONNECTED RETURN HOSE.
CONTINUE TEST NS-4B

* PERFORM VERIFICATION PROCEDURE VER-1.

91J08944

Fig. 14: No Start Test 4B (3.0L VIN 3) – Checking Fuel Return Lines & Pressure Regulator (1 of 2)

1991 ENGINE PERFORMANCE
Self-Diagnostics – 3.0L VIN 3 (Cont.)

NS-4B: CHECKING FUEL RETURN LINES & PRESSURE REGULATOR (2 OF 2)

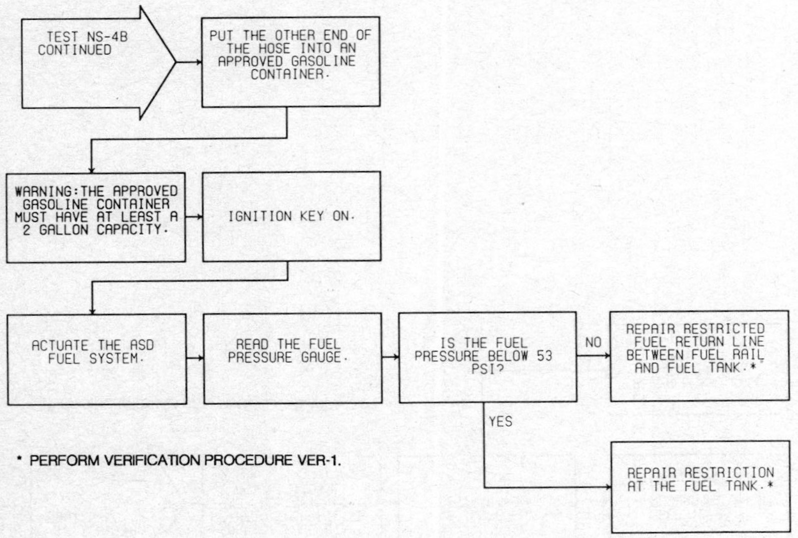
TEST NS-4B CONTINUED
PUT THE OTHER END OF THE HOSE INTO AN APPROVED GASOLINE CONTAINER.
WARNING: THE APPROVED GASOLINE CONTAINER MUST HAVE AT LEAST A 2 GALLON CAPACITY.
IGNITION KEY ON.
ACTUATE THE ASD FUEL SYSTEM.
READ THE FUEL PRESSURE GAUGE.
IS THE FUEL PRESSURE BELOW 53 PSI?
NO
REPAIR RESTRICTED FUEL RETURN LINE BETWEEN FUEL RAIL AND FUEL TANK.*
YES
REPAIR RESTRICTION AT THE FUEL TANK.*

* PERFORM VERIFICATION PROCEDURE VER-1.

91C08945

Fig. 15: No Start Test 4B (3.0L VIN 3) – Checking Fuel Return Lines & Pressure Regulator (2 of 2)

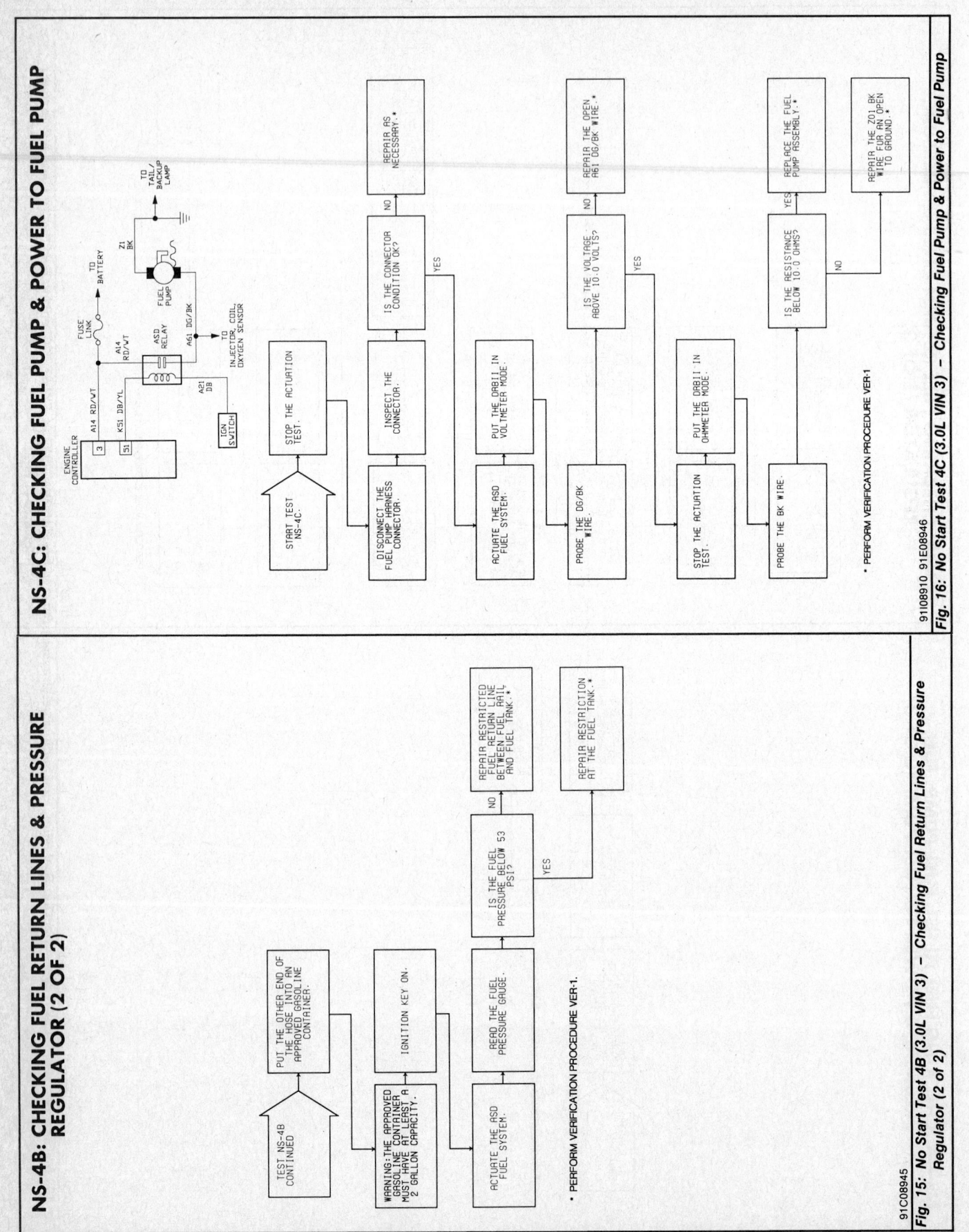

NS-4C: CHECKING FUEL PUMP & POWER TO FUEL PUMP

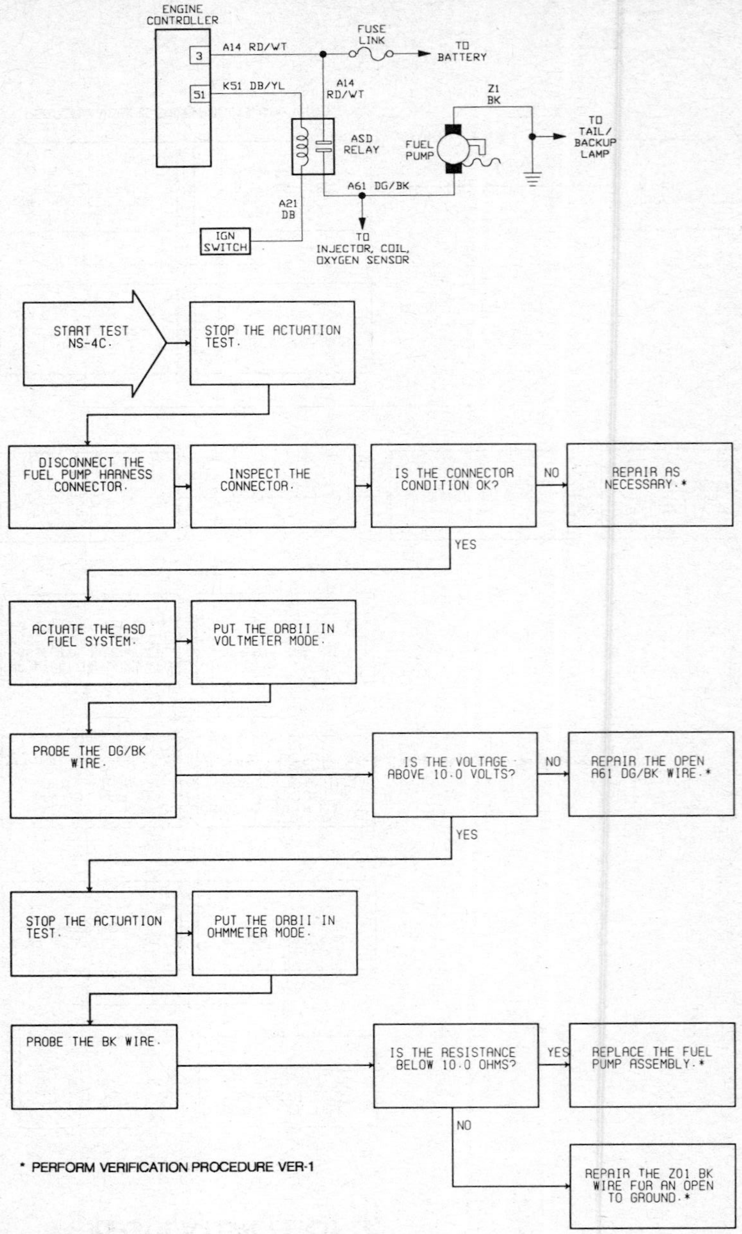
ENGINE CONTROLLER
3
51
A14 RD/WT
K51 DB/YL
FUSE LINK
TO BATTERY
A14 RD/WT
ASD RELAY
Z1 BK
FUEL PUMP
TO TAIL/ BACKUP LAMP
A61 DG/BK
A21 DB
IGN SWITCH
TO INJECTOR, COIL, OXYGEN SENSOR
START TEST NS-4C.
STOP THE ACTUATION TEST.
DISCONNECT THE FUEL PUMP HARNESS CONNECTOR.
INSPECT THE CONNECTOR.
IS THE CONNECTOR CONDITION OK?
NO
REPAIR AS NECESSARY.*
YES
ACTUATE THE ASD FUEL SYSTEM.
PUT THE DRBII IN VOLTMETER MODE.
PROBE THE DG/BK WIRE.
IS THE VOLTAGE ABOVE 10.0 VOLTS?
NO
REPAIR THE OPEN A61 DG/BK WIRE.*
YES
STOP THE ACTUATION TEST.
PUT THE DRBII IN OHMMETER MODE.
PROBE THE BK WIRE.
IS THE RESISTANCE BELOW 10.0 OHMS?
YES
REPLACE THE FUEL PUMP ASSEMBLY.*
NO
REPAIR THE Z01 BK WIRE FOR AN OPEN TO GROUND.*

* PERFORM VERIFICATION PROCEDURE VER-1

91I08910 91E08946

Fig. 16: No Start Test 4C (3.0L VIN 3) – Checking Fuel Pump & Power to Fuel Pump

NS-5A: CHECKING FOR DEFECTIVE COIL OR CONTROL CIRCUITRY (1 OF 2)

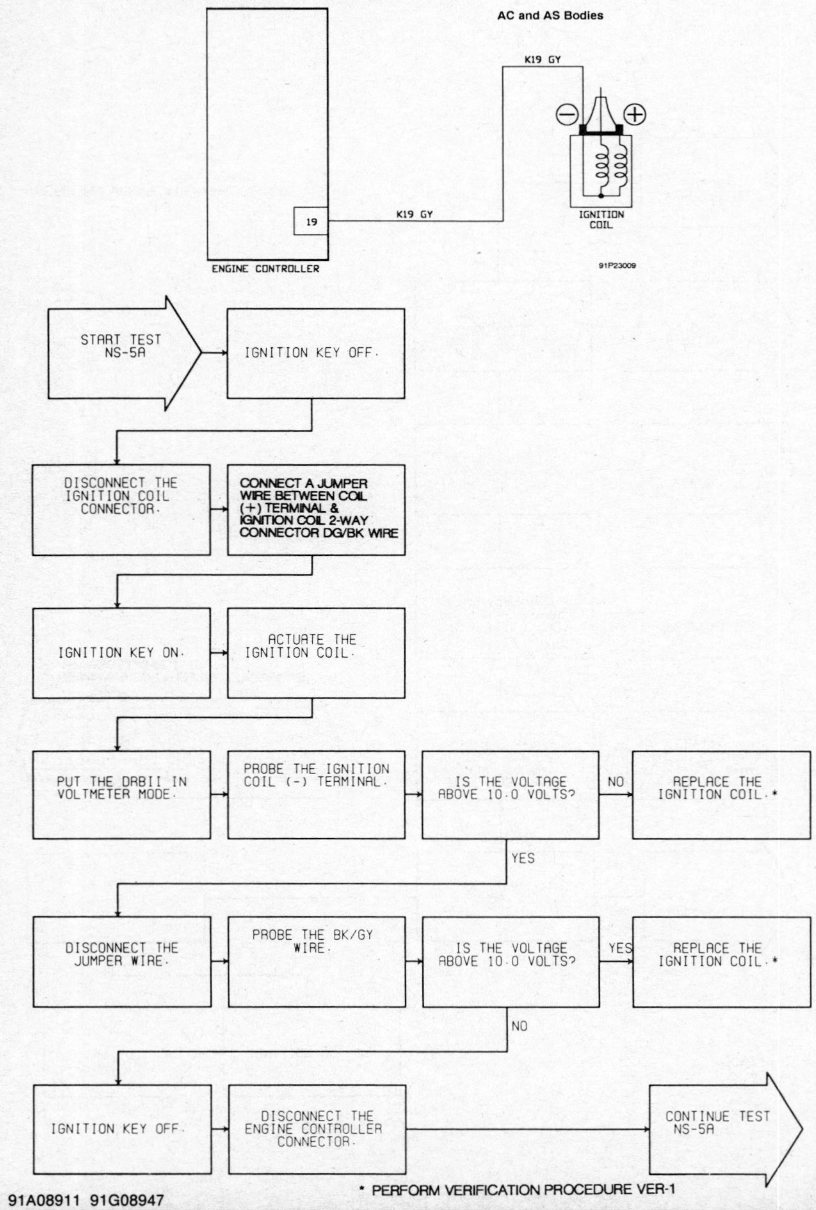
AC and AS Bodies
K19 GY
19
K19 GY
ENGINE CONTROLLER
IGNITION COIL
91P23009
START TEST NS-5A
IGNITION KEY OFF.
DISCONNECT THE IGNITION COIL CONNECTOR.
CONNECT A JUMPER WIRE BETWEEN COIL (+) TERMINAL & IGNITION COIL 2-WAY CONNECTOR DG/BK WIRE
IGNITION KEY ON.
ACTUATE THE IGNITION COIL.
PUT THE DRBII IN VOLTMETER MODE.
PROBE THE IGNITION COIL (-) TERMINAL.
IS THE VOLTAGE ABOVE 10.0 VOLTS?
NO
REPLACE THE IGNITION COIL.*
YES
DISCONNECT THE JUMPER WIRE.
PROBE THE BK/GY WIRE.
IS THE VOLTAGE ABOVE 10.0 VOLTS?
YES
REPLACE THE IGNITION COIL.*
NO
IGNITION KEY OFF.
DISCONNECT THE ENGINE CONTROLLER CONNECTOR.
CONTINUE TEST NS-5A
* PERFORM VERIFICATION PROCEDURE VER-1

91A08911 91G08947

Fig. 17: No Start Test 5A (3.0L VIN 3) – Checking for Defective Coil or Control Circuitry (1 of 2)

NS-5A: CHECKING FOR DEFECTIVE COIL OR CONTROL CIRCUITRY (2 OF 2)

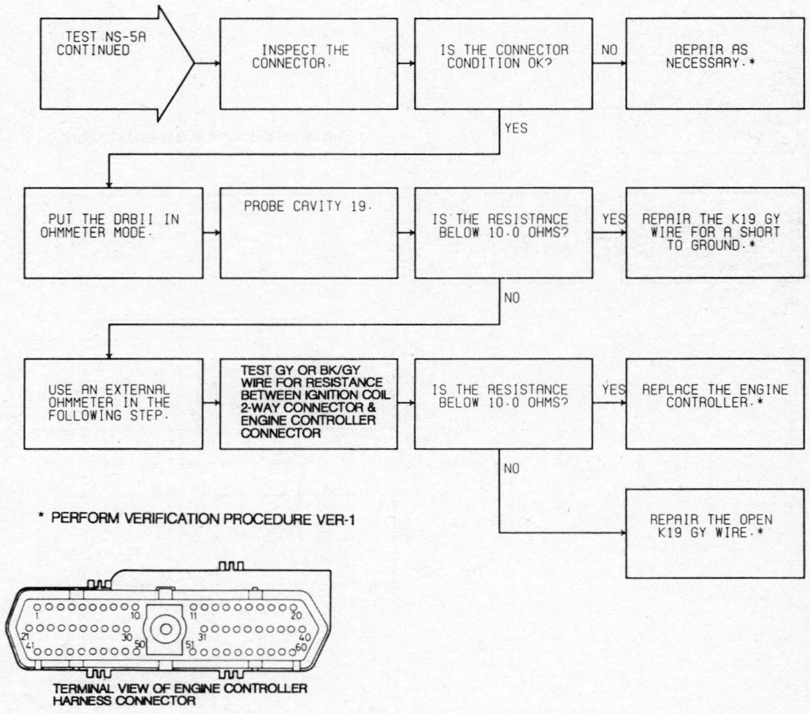
TEST NS-5A CONTINUED
INSPECT THE CONNECTOR.
IS THE CONNECTOR CONDITION OK?
NO
REPAIR AS NECESSARY.*
YES
PUT THE DRBII IN OHMMETER MODE.
PROBE CAVITY 19.
IS THE RESISTANCE BELOW 10.0 OHMS?
YES
REPAIR THE K19 GY WIRE FOR A SHORT TO GROUND.*
NO
USE AN EXTERNAL OHMMETER IN THE FOLLOWING STEP.
TEST GY OR BK/GY WIRE FOR RESISTANCE BETWEEN IGNITION COIL 2-WAY CONNECTOR & ENGINE CONTROLLER CONNECTOR
IS THE RESISTANCE BELOW 10.0 OHMS?
YES
REPLACE THE ENGINE CONTROLLER.*
NO
REPAIR THE OPEN K19 GY WIRE.*
* PERFORM VERIFICATION PROCEDURE VER-1
TERMINAL VIEW OF ENGINE CONTROLLER HARNESS CONNECTOR

91I08948

Fig. 18: No Start Test 5A (3.0L VIN 3) – Checking for Defective Coil or Control Circuitry (2 of 2)

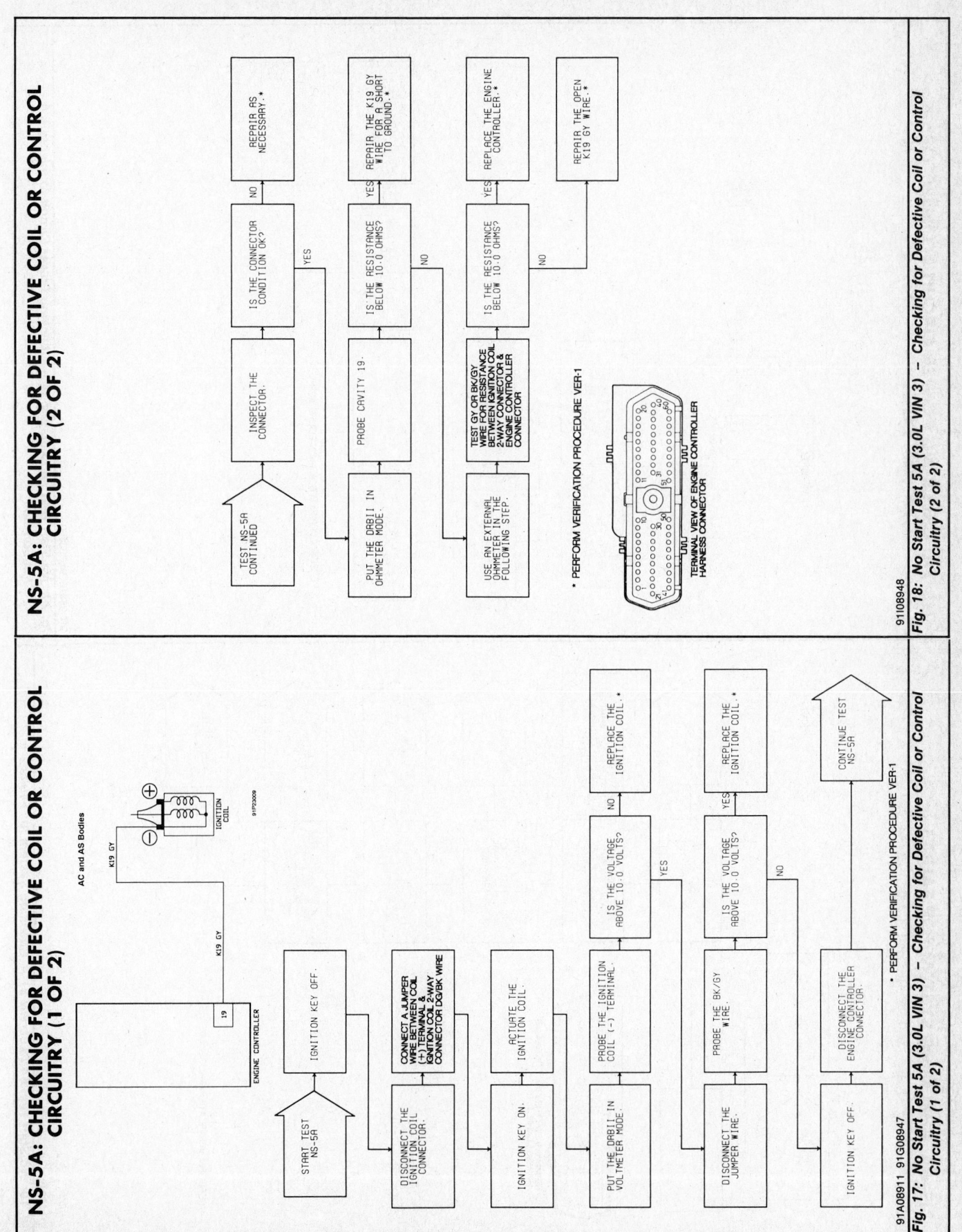

1991 ENGINE PERFORMANCE
Self-Diagnostics – 3.0L VIN 3 (Cont.)

NS-6A: CHECKING SYSTEM FOR FAULTS

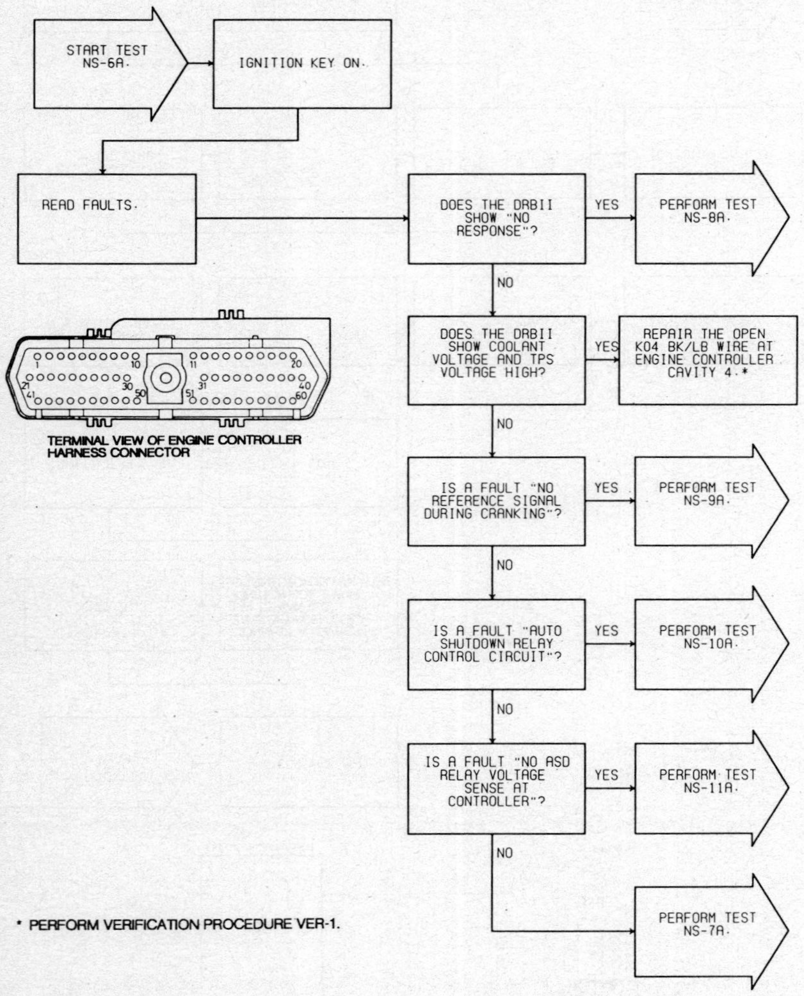
START TEST NS-6A.
IGNITION KEY ON.
READ FAULTS.
DOES THE DRBII SHOW "NO RESPONSE"?
YES
PERFORM TEST NS-8A.
NO
DOES THE DRBII SHOW COOLANT VOLTAGE AND TPS VOLTAGE HIGH?
YES
REPAIR THE OPEN K04 BK/LB WIRE AT ENGINE CONTROLLER CAVITY 4.*
NO
IS A FAULT "NO REFERENCE SIGNAL DURING CRANKING"?
YES
PERFORM TEST NS-9A.
NO
IS A FAULT "AUTO SHUTDOWN RELAY CONTROL CIRCUIT"?
YES
PERFORM TEST NS-10A.
NO
IS A FAULT "NO ASD RELAY VOLTAGE SENSE AT CONTROLLER"?
YES
PERFORM TEST NS-11A.
NO
PERFORM TEST NS-7A.
TERMINAL VIEW OF ENGINE CONTROLLER HARNESS CONNECTOR

* PERFORM VERIFICATION PROCEDURE VER-1.

91A08949

Fig. 19: No Start Test 6A (3.0L VIN 3) – Checking System for Faults

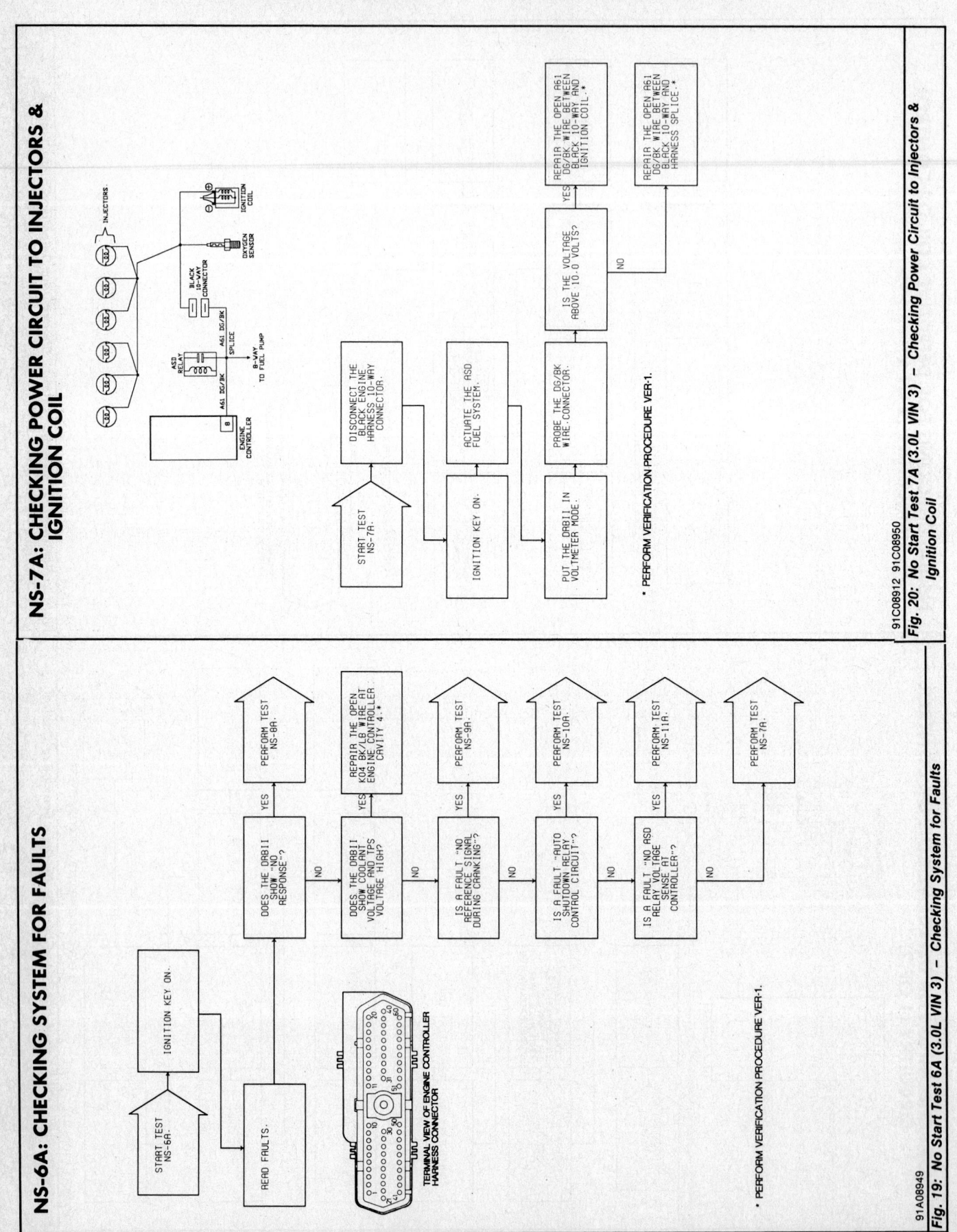

NS-7A: CHECKING POWER CIRCUIT TO INJECTORS & IGNITION COIL

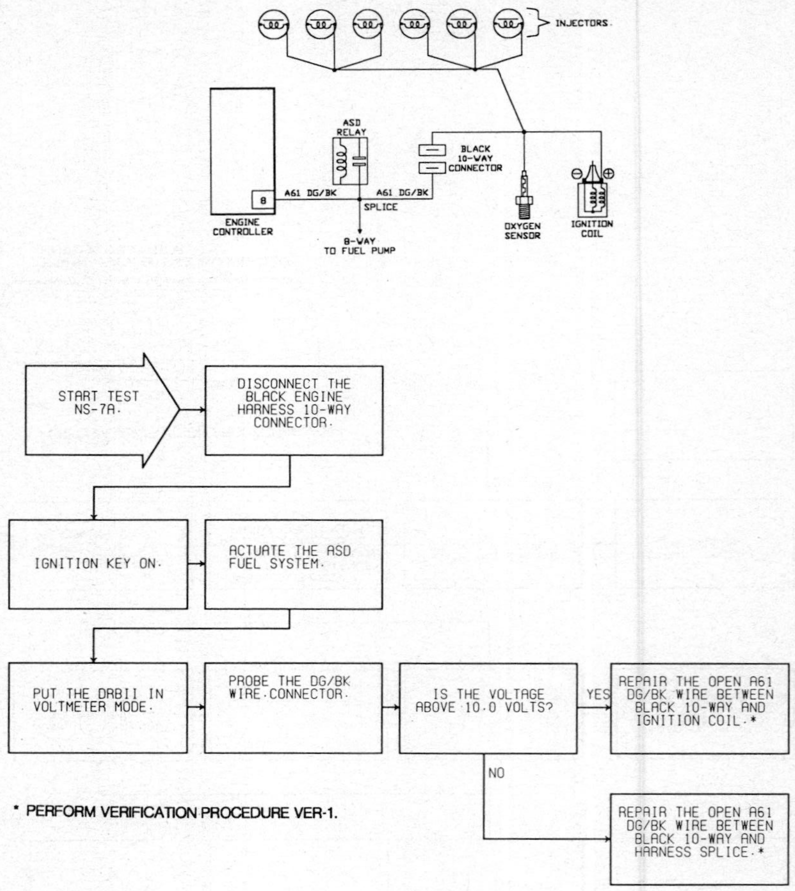
INJECTORS
ASD RELAY
BLACK 10-WAY CONNECTOR
A61 DG/BK
A61 DG/BK
SPLICE
8
ENGINE CONTROLLER
8-WAY TO FUEL PUMP
OXYGEN SENSOR
IGNITION COIL
START TEST NS-7A.
DISCONNECT THE BLACK ENGINE HARNESS 10-WAY CONNECTOR.
IGNITION KEY ON.
ACTUATE THE ASD FUEL SYSTEM.
PUT THE DRBII IN VOLTMETER MODE.
PROBE THE DG/BK WIRE CONNECTOR.
IS THE VOLTAGE ABOVE 10.0 VOLTS?
YES
REPAIR THE OPEN A61 DG/BK WIRE BETWEEN BLACK 10-WAY AND IGNITION COIL.*
NO
REPAIR THE OPEN A61 DG/BK WIRE BETWEEN BLACK 10-WAY AND HARNESS SPLICE.*

* PERFORM VERIFICATION PROCEDURE VER-1.

91C08912 91C08950

Fig. 20: No Start Test 7A (3.0L VIN 3) – Checking Power Circuit to Injectors & Ignition Coil

NS-8A: CHECKING SYSTEM PWR & GND & OPERATION OF TPS, MAP SENSOR & SBEC (1 OF 3)

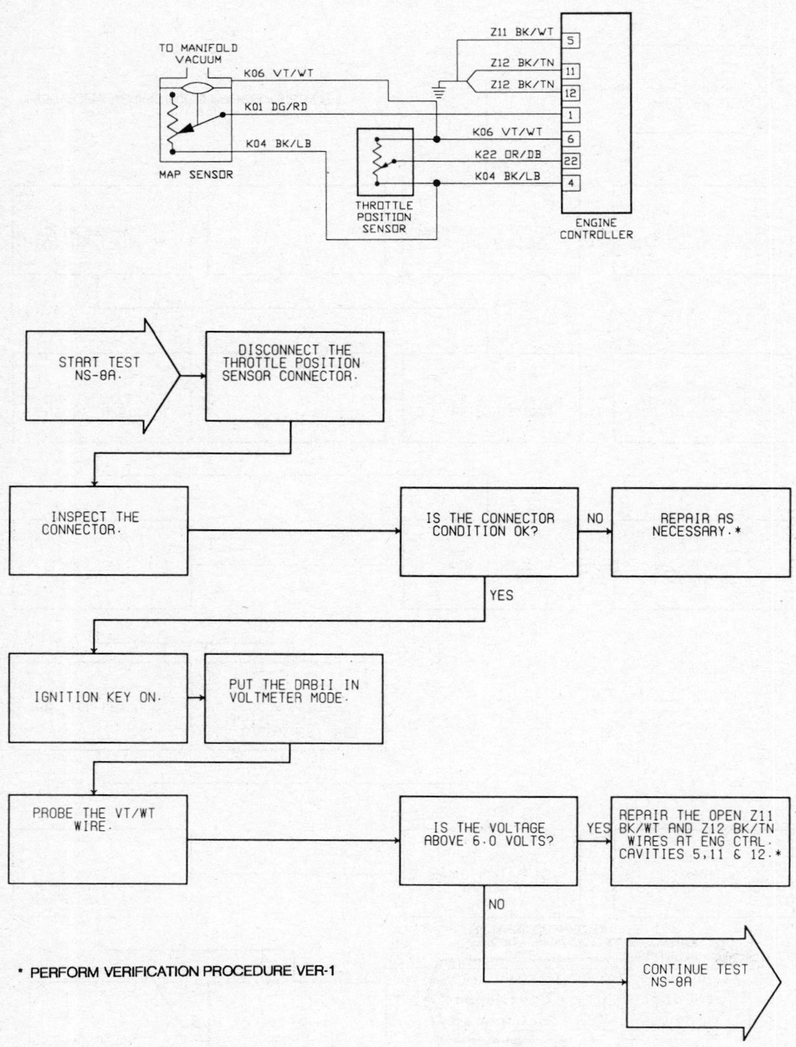
TO MANIFOLD VACUUM
MAP SENSOR
K06 VT/WT
K01 DG/RD
K04 BK/LB
Z11 BK/WT
Z12 BK/TN
Z12 BK/TN
K06 VT/WT
K22 OR/DB
K04 BK/LB
5
11
12
1
6
22
4
THROTTLE POSITION SENSOR
ENGINE CONTROLLER
START TEST NS-8A.
DISCONNECT THE THROTTLE POSITION SENSOR CONNECTOR.
INSPECT THE CONNECTOR.
IS THE CONNECTOR CONDITION OK?
NO
REPAIR AS NECESSARY.*
YES
IGNITION KEY ON.
PUT THE DRBII IN VOLTMETER MODE.
PROBE THE VT/WT WIRE.
IS THE VOLTAGE ABOVE 6.0 VOLTS?
YES
REPAIR THE OPEN Z11 BK/WT AND Z12 BK/TN WIRES AT ENG CTRL. CAVITIES 5,11 & 12.*
NO
CONTINUE TEST NS-8A
* PERFORM VERIFICATION PROCEDURE VER-1

91E08913 91E08951

Fig. 21: No Start Test 8A (3.0L VIN 3) – Checking System Pwr & Gnd & Operation of TPS, MAP Sensor & SBEC (1 of 3)

NS-8A: CHECKING SYSTEM PWR & GND & OPERATION OF TPS, MAP SENSOR & SBEC (2 OF 3)

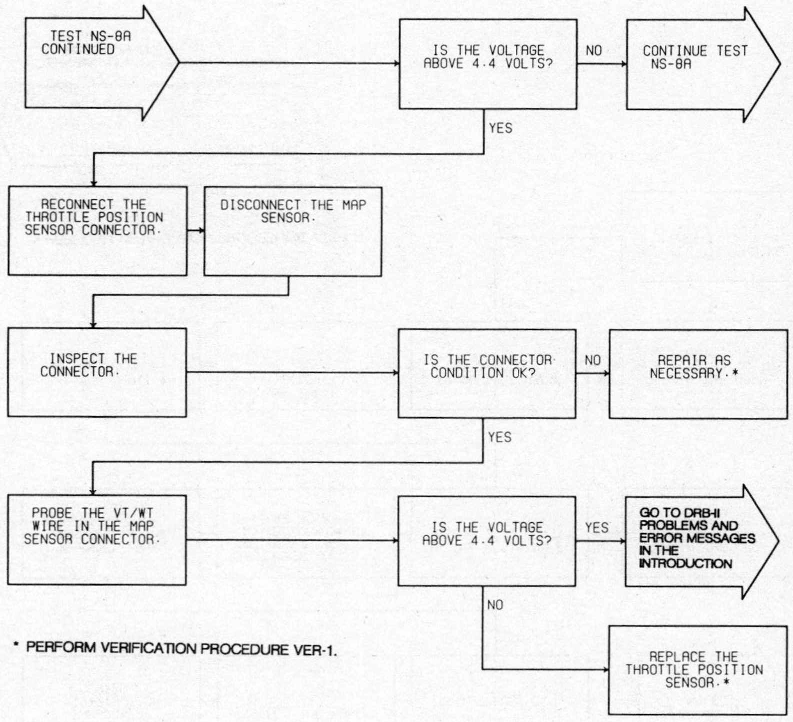
TEST NS-8A CONTINUED
IS THE VOLTAGE ABOVE 4.4 VOLTS?
NO
CONTINUE TEST NS-8A
YES
RECONNECT THE THROTTLE POSITION SENSOR CONNECTOR.
DISCONNECT THE MAP SENSOR.
INSPECT THE CONNECTOR.
IS THE CONNECTOR CONDITION OK?
NO
REPAIR AS NECESSARY.*
YES
PROBE THE VT/WT WIRE IN THE MAP SENSOR CONNECTOR.
IS THE VOLTAGE ABOVE 4.4 VOLTS?
YES
GO TO DRB-II PROBLEMS AND ERROR MESSAGES IN THE INTRODUCTION
NO
REPLACE THE THROTTLE POSITION SENSOR.*
* PERFORM VERIFICATION PROCEDURE VER-1.

91G08952

Fig. 22: No Start Test 8A (3.0L VIN 3) – Checking System Pwr & Gnd & Operation of TPS, MAP Sensor & SBEC (2 of 3)

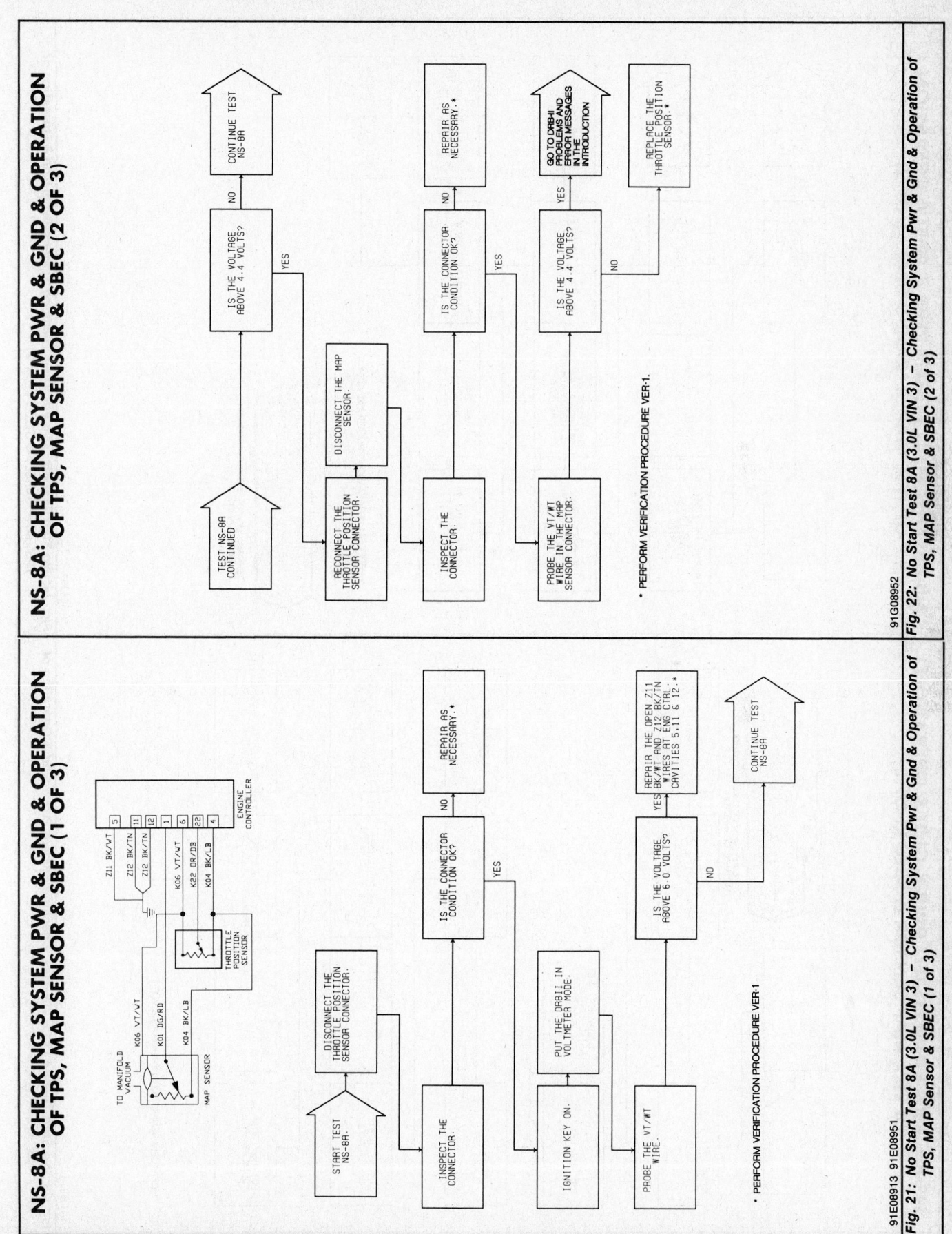

NS-8A: CHECKING SYSTEM PWR & GND & OPERATION OF TPS, MAP SENSOR & SBEC (3 OF 3)

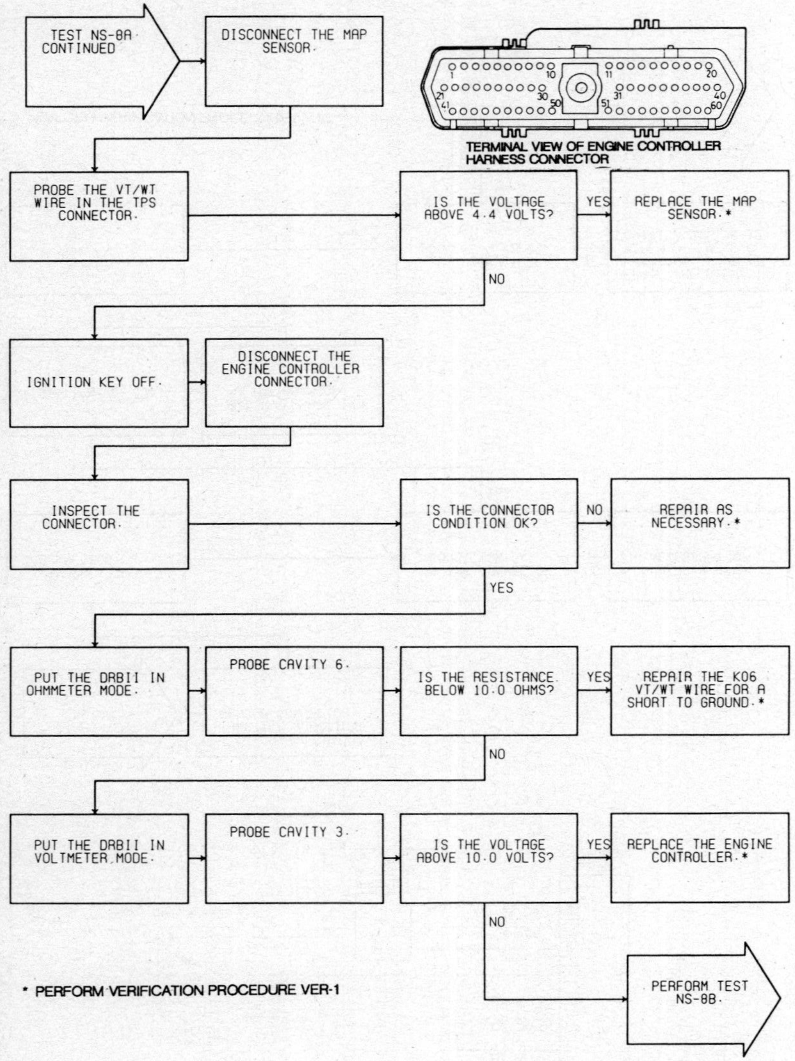
TEST NS-8A CONTINUED
DISCONNECT THE MAP SENSOR.
TERMINAL VIEW OF ENGINE CONTROLLER HARNESS CONNECTOR
PROBE THE VT/WT WIRE IN THE TPS CONNECTOR.
IS THE VOLTAGE ABOVE 4.4 VOLTS?
YES
REPLACE THE MAP SENSOR.*
NO
IGNITION KEY OFF.
DISCONNECT THE ENGINE CONTROLLER CONNECTOR.
INSPECT THE CONNECTOR.
IS THE CONNECTOR CONDITION OK?
NO
REPAIR AS NECESSARY.*
YES
PUT THE DRBII IN OHMMETER MODE.
PROBE CAVITY 6.
IS THE RESISTANCE BELOW 10.0 OHMS?
YES
REPAIR THE K06 VT/WT WIRE FOR A SHORT TO GROUND.*
NO
PUT THE DRBII IN VOLTMETER MODE.
PROBE CAVITY 3.
IS THE VOLTAGE ABOVE 10.0 VOLTS?
YES
REPLACE THE ENGINE CONTROLLER.*
NO
PERFORM TEST NS-8B.

* PERFORM VERIFICATION PROCEDURE VER-1

91I08953

Fig. 23: No Start Test 8A (3.0L VIN 3) – Checking System Pwr & Gnd & Operation of TPS, MAP Sensor & SBEC (3 of 3)

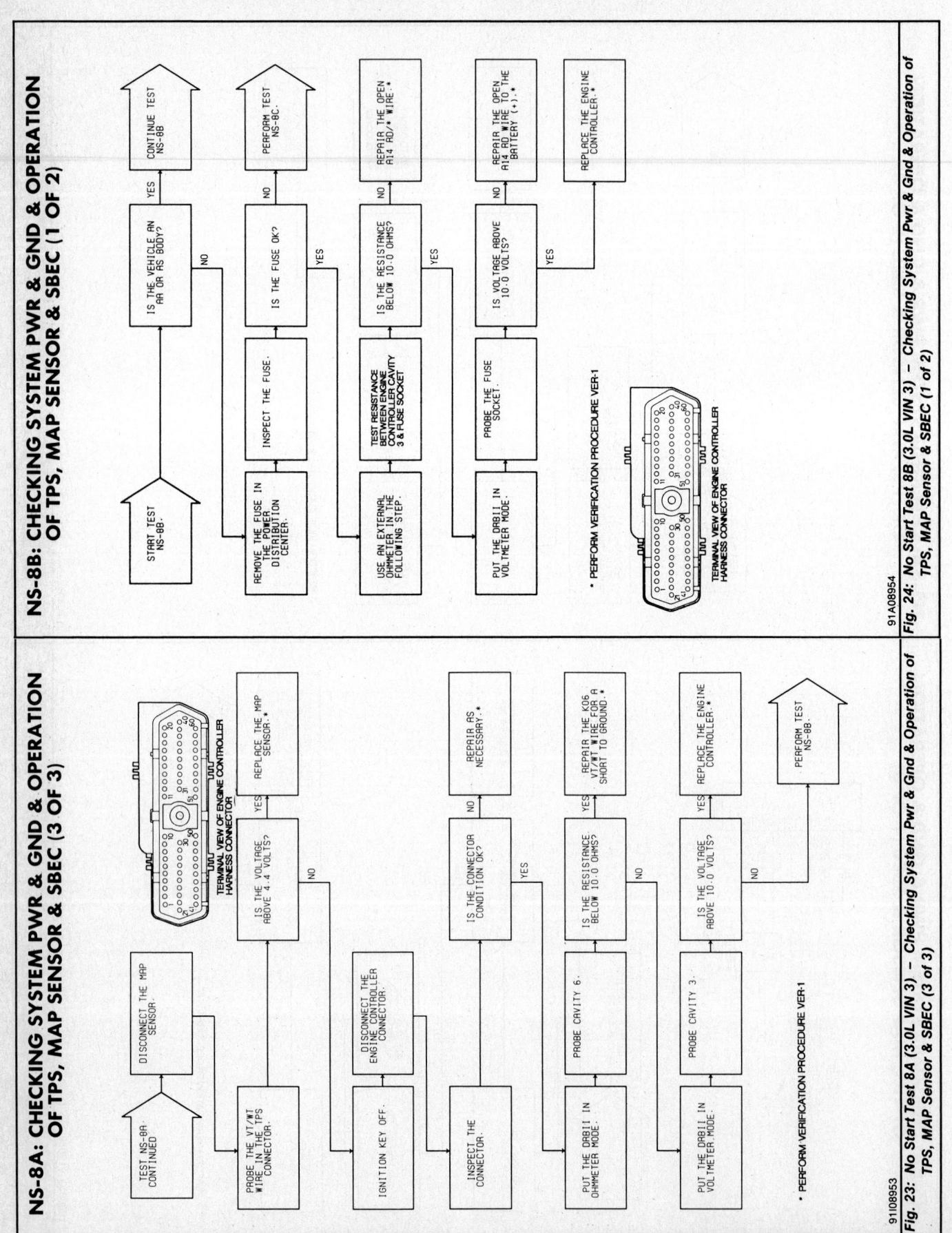

NS-8B: CHECKING SYSTEM PWR & GND & OPERATION OF TPS, MAP SENSOR & SBEC (1 OF 2)

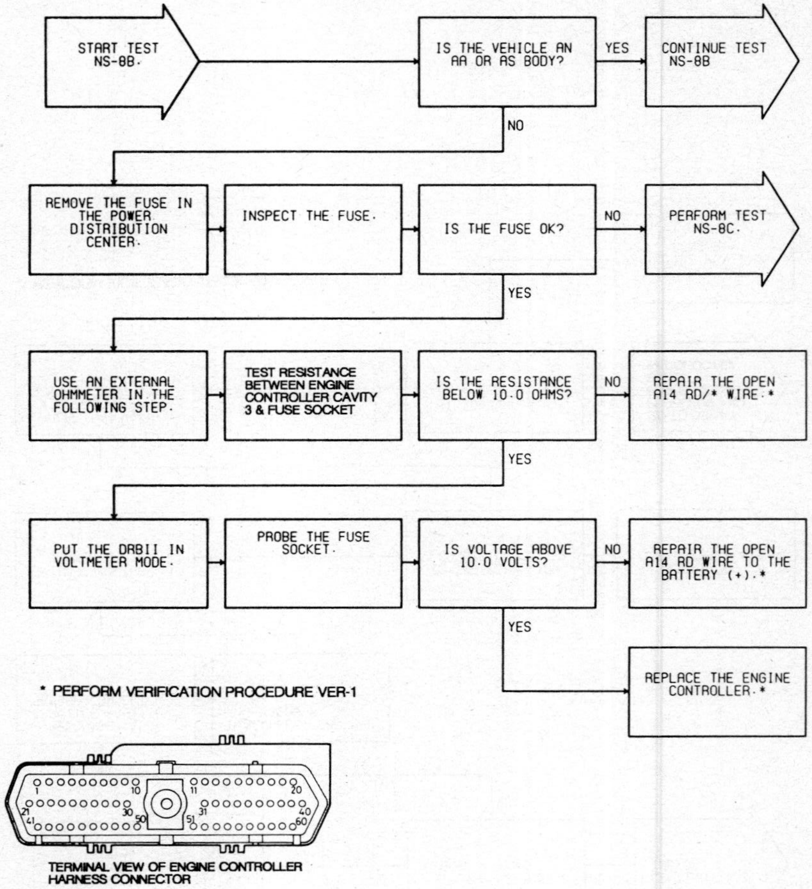
START TEST NS-8B.
IS THE VEHICLE AN AA OR AS BODY?
YES
CONTINUE TEST NS-8B
NO
REMOVE THE FUSE IN THE POWER DISTRIBUTION CENTER.
INSPECT THE FUSE.
IS THE FUSE OK?
NO
PERFORM TEST NS-8C.
YES
USE AN EXTERNAL OHMMETER IN THE FOLLOWING STEP.
TEST RESISTANCE BETWEEN ENGINE CONTROLLER CAVITY 3 & FUSE SOCKET
IS THE RESISTANCE BELOW 10.0 OHMS?
NO
REPAIR THE OPEN A14 RD/* WIRE.*
YES
PUT THE DRBII IN VOLTMETER MODE.
PROBE THE FUSE SOCKET.
IS VOLTAGE ABOVE 10.0 VOLTS?
NO
REPAIR THE OPEN A14 RD WIRE TO THE BATTERY (+).*
YES
REPLACE THE ENGINE CONTROLLER.*
TERMINAL VIEW OF ENGINE CONTROLLER HARNESS CONNECTOR

* PERFORM VERIFICATION PROCEDURE VER-1

91A08954

Fig. 24: No Start Test 8B (3.0L VIN 3) – Checking System Pwr & Gnd & Operation of TPS, MAP Sensor & SBEC (1 of 2)

NS-8B: CHECKING SYSTEM PWR & GND & OPERATION OF TPS, MAP SENSOR & SBEC (2 OF 2)

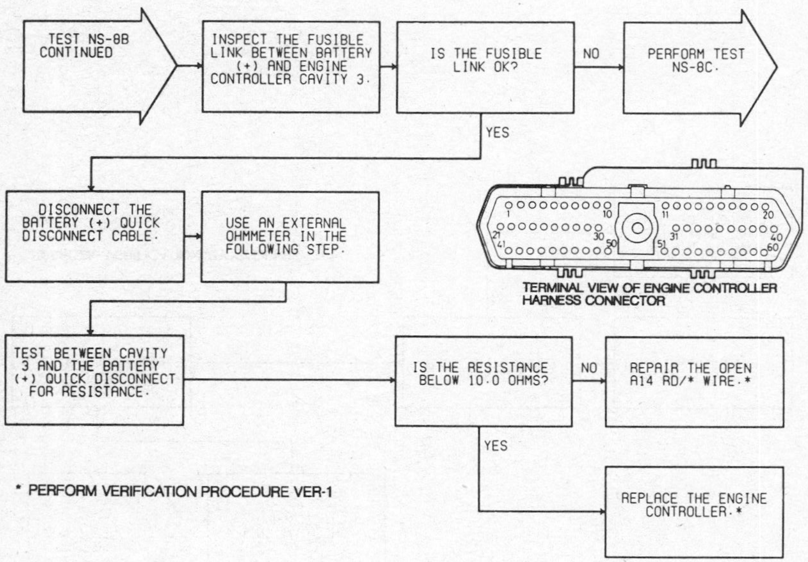
TEST NS-8B CONTINUED
INSPECT THE FUSIBLE LINK BETWEEN BATTERY (+) AND ENGINE CONTROLLER CAVITY 3.
IS THE FUSIBLE LINK OK?
NO
PERFORM TEST NS-8C.
YES
DISCONNECT THE BATTERY (+) QUICK DISCONNECT CABLE.
USE AN EXTERNAL OHMMETER IN THE FOLLOWING STEP.
TERMINAL VIEW OF ENGINE CONTROLLER HARNESS CONNECTOR
1
10
11
20
21
30
31
40
41
50
51
60
TEST BETWEEN CAVITY 3 AND THE BATTERY (+) QUICK DISCONNECT FOR RESISTANCE.
IS THE RESISTANCE BELOW 10.0 OHMS?
NO
REPAIR THE OPEN A14 RD/* WIRE.*
YES
REPLACE THE ENGINE CONTROLLER.*

* PERFORM VERIFICATION PROCEDURE VER-1

91D08955

Fig. 25: No Start Test 8B (3.0L VIN 3) – Checking System Pwr & Gnd & Operation of TPS, MAP Sensor & SBEC (2 of 2)

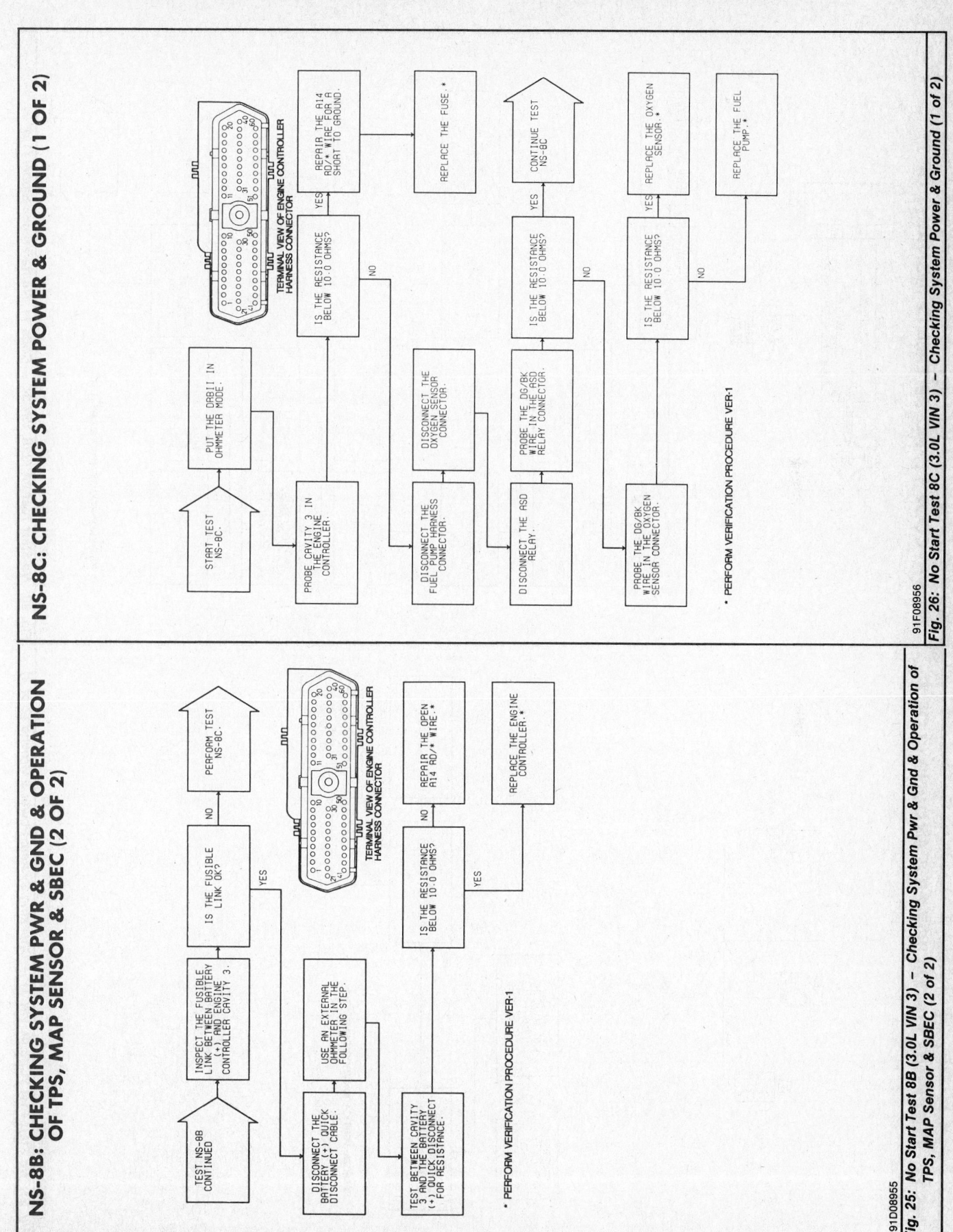

NS-8C: CHECKING SYSTEM POWER & GROUND (1 OF 2)

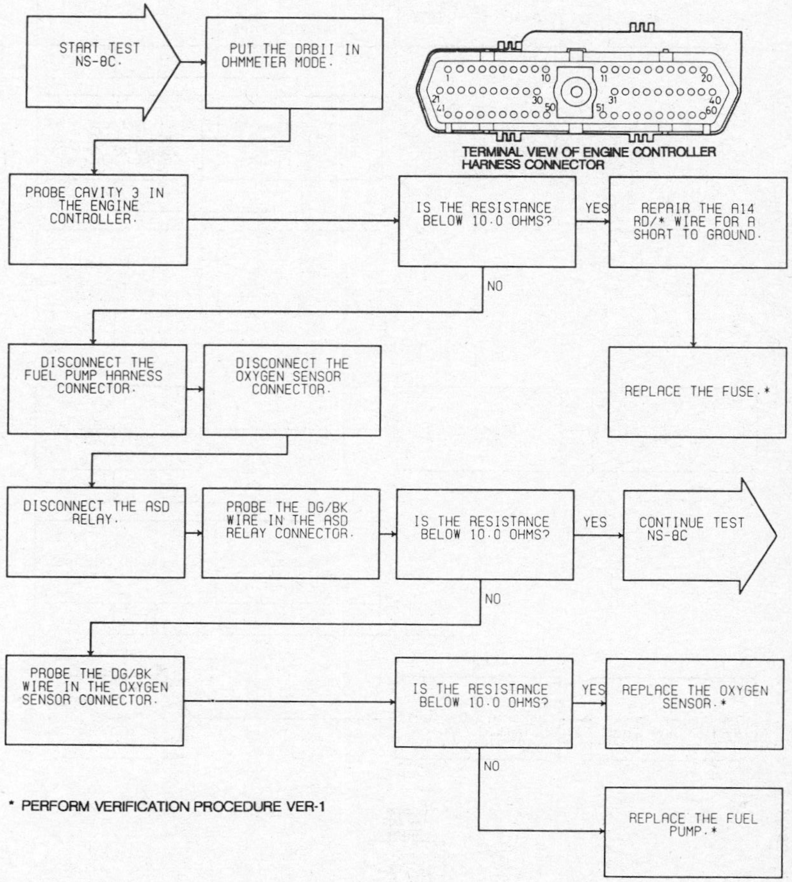
START TEST NS-8C.
PUT THE DRBII IN OHMMETER MODE.
TERMINAL VIEW OF ENGINE CONTROLLER HARNESS CONNECTOR
1
10
11
20
21
30
31
40
41
50
51
60
PROBE CAVITY 3 IN THE ENGINE CONTROLLER.
IS THE RESISTANCE BELOW 10.0 OHMS?
YES
REPAIR THE A14 RD/* WIRE FOR A SHORT TO GROUND.
REPLACE THE FUSE.*
NO
DISCONNECT THE FUEL PUMP HARNESS CONNECTOR.
DISCONNECT THE OXYGEN SENSOR CONNECTOR.
DISCONNECT THE ASD RELAY.
PROBE THE DG/BK WIRE IN THE ASD RELAY CONNECTOR.
IS THE RESISTANCE BELOW 10.0 OHMS?
YES
CONTINUE TEST NS-8C
NO
PROBE THE DG/BK WIRE IN THE OXYGEN SENSOR CONNECTOR.
IS THE RESISTANCE BELOW 10.0 OHMS?
YES
REPLACE THE OXYGEN SENSOR.*
NO
REPLACE THE FUEL PUMP.*

* PERFORM VERIFICATION PROCEDURE VER-1

91F08956

Fig. 26: No Start Test 8C (3.0L VIN 3) – Checking System Power & Ground (1 of 2)

NS-8C: CHECKING SYSTEM POWER & GROUND (2 OF 2)

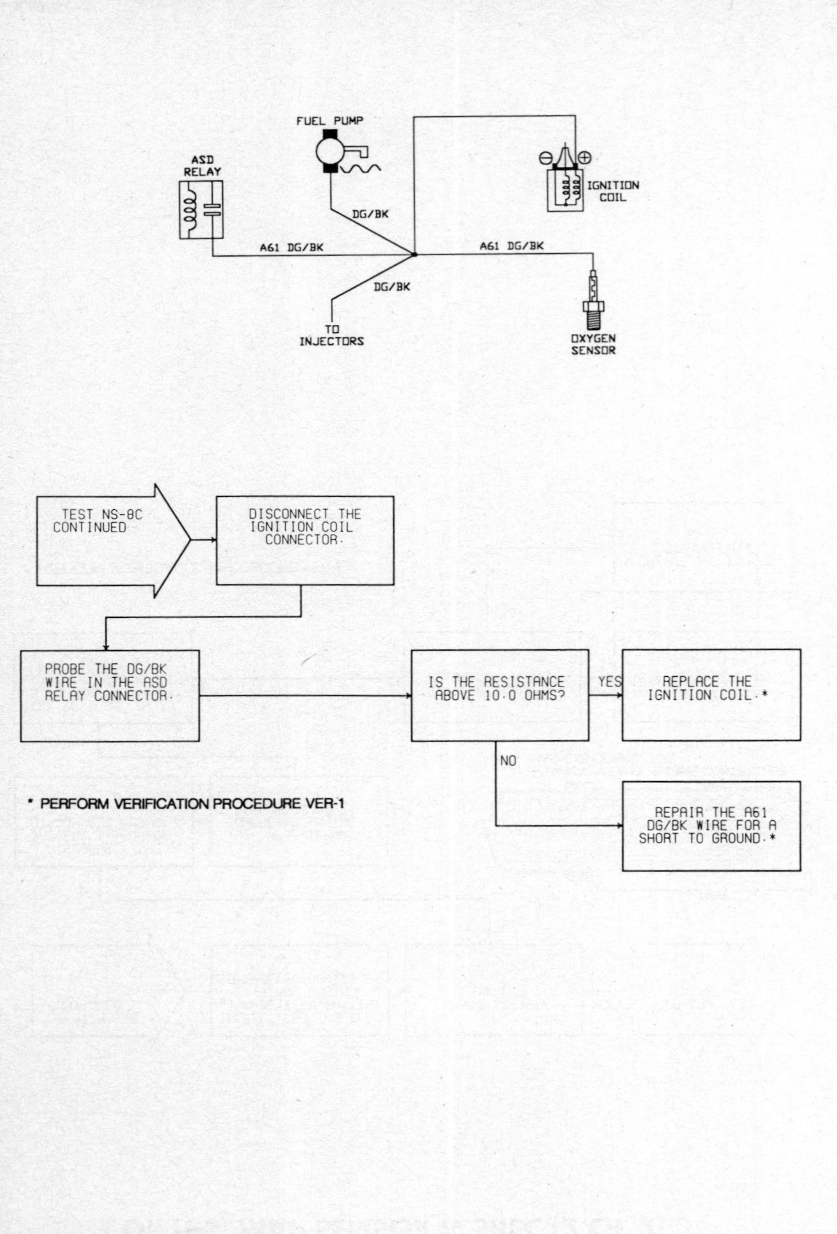
FUEL PUMP
ASD RELAY
IGNITION COIL
DG/BK
A61 DG/BK
A61 DG/BK
DG/BK
TO INJECTORS
OXYGEN SENSOR
TEST NS-8C CONTINUED
DISCONNECT THE IGNITION COIL CONNECTOR.
PROBE THE DG/BK WIRE IN THE ASD RELAY CONNECTOR.
IS THE RESISTANCE ABOVE 10.0 OHMS?
YES
REPLACE THE IGNITION COIL.*
NO
REPAIR THE A61 DG/BK WIRE FOR A SHORT TO GROUND.*
* PERFORM VERIFICATION PROCEDURE VER-1

91E08908 91H08957

Fig. 27: No Start Test 8C (3.0L VIN 3) – Checking System Power & Ground (2 of 2)

NS-9A: CODE 11, NO REFERENCE SIGNAL (1 OF 2)

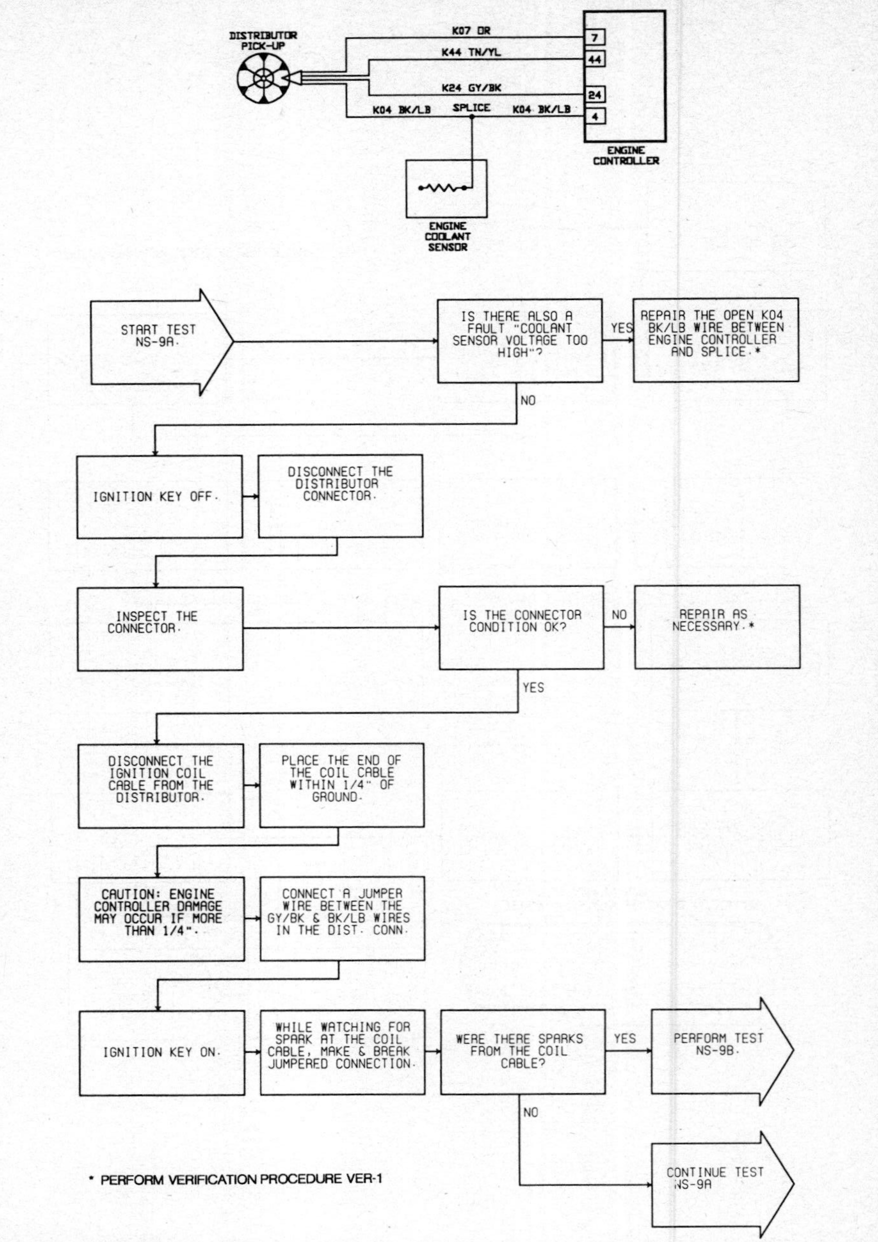
DISTRIBUTOR PICK-UP
K07 OR
K44 TN/YL
K24 GY/BK
K04 BK/LB
SPLICE
K04 BK/LB
7
44
24
4
ENGINE CONTROLLER
ENGINE COOLANT SENSOR
START TEST NS-9A.
IS THERE ALSO A FAULT "COOLANT SENSOR VOLTAGE TOO HIGH"?
YES
REPAIR THE OPEN K04 BK/LB WIRE BETWEEN ENGINE CONTROLLER AND SPLICE.*
NO
IGNITION KEY OFF.
DISCONNECT THE DISTRIBUTOR CONNECTOR.
INSPECT THE CONNECTOR.
IS THE CONNECTOR CONDITION OK?
NO
REPAIR AS NECESSARY.*
YES
DISCONNECT THE IGNITION COIL CABLE FROM THE DISTRIBUTOR.
PLACE THE END OF THE COIL CABLE WITHIN 1/4" OF GROUND.
CAUTION: ENGINE CONTROLLER DAMAGE MAY OCCUR IF MORE THAN 1/4".
CONNECT A JUMPER WIRE BETWEEN THE GY/BK & BK/LB WIRES IN THE DIST. CONN.
IGNITION KEY ON.
WHILE WATCHING FOR SPARK AT THE COIL CABLE, MAKE & BREAK JUMPERED CONNECTION.
WERE THERE SPARKS FROM THE COIL CABLE?
YES
PERFORM TEST NS-9B.
NO
CONTINUE TEST NS-9A
* PERFORM VERIFICATION PROCEDURE VER-1

91G08914 91J08958

Fig. 28: No Start Test 9A (3.0L VIN 3) – Code 11, No Reference Signal (1 of 2)

NS-9A: CODE 11, NO REFERENCE SIGNAL (2 OF 2)

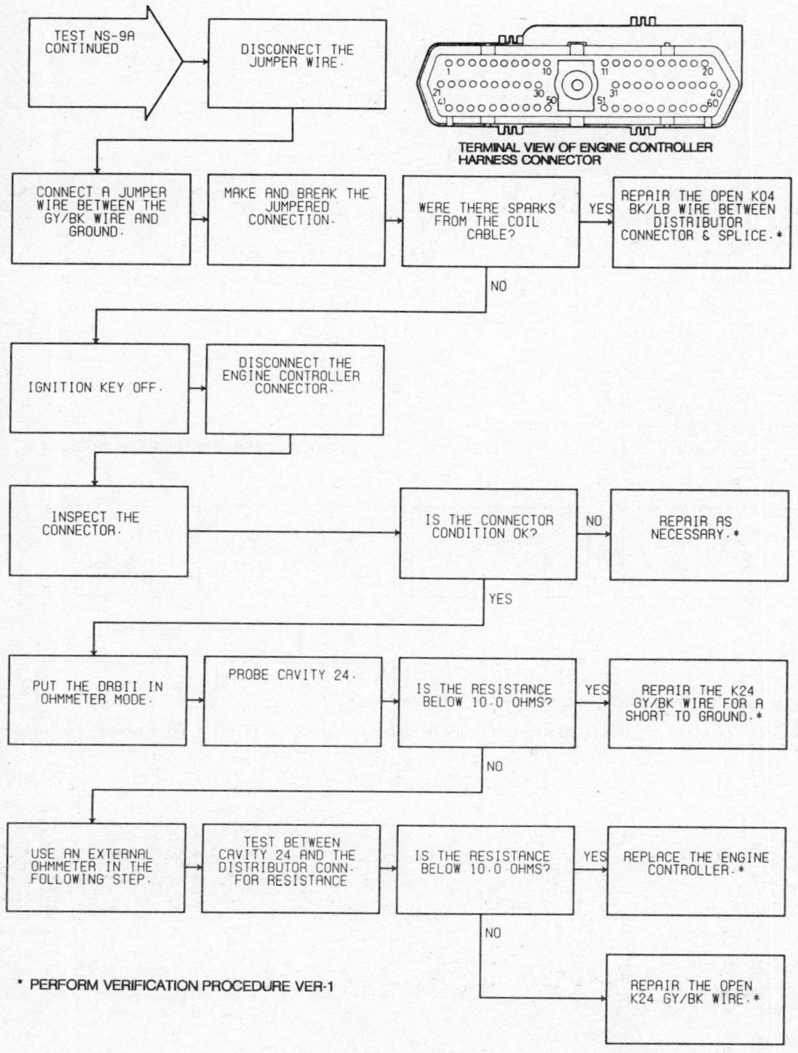
TEST NS-9A CONTINUED
DISCONNECT THE JUMPER WIRE.
TERMINAL VIEW OF ENGINE CONTROLLER HARNESS CONNECTOR
CONNECT A JUMPER WIRE BETWEEN THE GY/BK WIRE AND GROUND.
MAKE AND BREAK THE JUMPERED CONNECTION.
WERE THERE SPARKS FROM THE COIL CABLE?
YES
REPAIR THE OPEN K04 BK/LB WIRE BETWEEN DISTRIBUTOR CONNECTOR & SPLICE.*
NO
IGNITION KEY OFF.
DISCONNECT THE ENGINE CONTROLLER CONNECTOR.
INSPECT THE CONNECTOR.
IS THE CONNECTOR CONDITION OK?
NO
REPAIR AS NECESSARY.*
YES
PUT THE DRBII IN OHMMETER MODE.
PROBE CAVITY 24.
IS THE RESISTANCE BELOW 10.0 OHMS?
YES
REPAIR THE K24 GY/BK WIRE FOR A SHORT TO GROUND.*
NO
USE AN EXTERNAL OHMMETER IN THE FOLLOWING STEP.
TEST BETWEEN CAVITY 24 AND THE DISTRIBUTOR CONN. FOR RESISTANCE
IS THE RESISTANCE BELOW 10.0 OHMS?
YES
REPLACE THE ENGINE CONTROLLER.*
NO
REPAIR THE OPEN K24 GY/BK WIRE.*

* PERFORM VERIFICATION PROCEDURE VER-1

91B08959

Fig. 29: No Start Test 9A (3.0L VIN 3) – Code 11, No Reference Signal (2 of 2)

NS-9B: CODE 11, NO REFERENCE SIGNAL (1 OF 2)

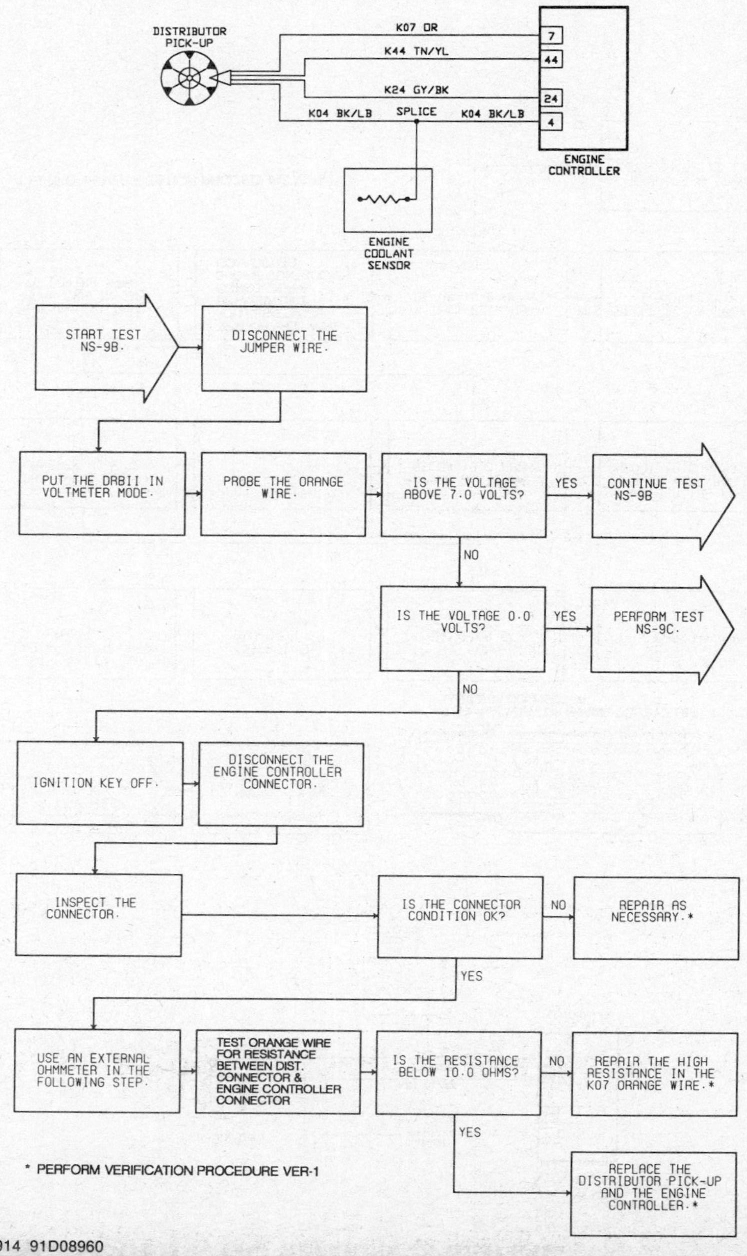
DISTRIBUTOR PICK-UP
K07 OR
K44 TN/YL
K24 GY/BK
K04 BK/LB
SPLICE
K04 BK/LB
7
44
24
4
ENGINE CONTROLLER
ENGINE COOLANT SENSOR
START TEST NS-9B.
DISCONNECT THE JUMPER WIRE.
PUT THE DRBII IN VOLTMETER MODE.
PROBE THE ORANGE WIRE.
IS THE VOLTAGE ABOVE 7.0 VOLTS?
YES
CONTINUE TEST NS-9B
NO
IS THE VOLTAGE 0.0 VOLTS?
YES
PERFORM TEST NS-9C.
NO
IGNITION KEY OFF.
DISCONNECT THE ENGINE CONTROLLER CONNECTOR.
INSPECT THE CONNECTOR.
IS THE CONNECTOR CONDITION OK?
NO
REPAIR AS NECESSARY.*
YES
USE AN EXTERNAL OHMMETER IN THE FOLLOWING STEP.
TEST ORANGE WIRE FOR RESISTANCE BETWEEN DIST. CONNECTOR & ENGINE CONTROLLER CONNECTOR
IS THE RESISTANCE BELOW 10.0 OHMS?
NO
REPAIR THE HIGH RESISTANCE IN THE K07 ORANGE WIRE.*
YES
REPLACE THE DISTRIBUTOR PICK-UP AND THE ENGINE CONTROLLER.*

* PERFORM VERIFICATION PROCEDURE VER-1

91G08914 91D08960

Fig. 30: No Start Test 9B (3.0L VIN 3) – Code 11, No Reference Signal (1 of 2)

1991 ENGINE PERFORMANCE
Self-Diagnostics – 3.0L VIN 3 (Cont.)

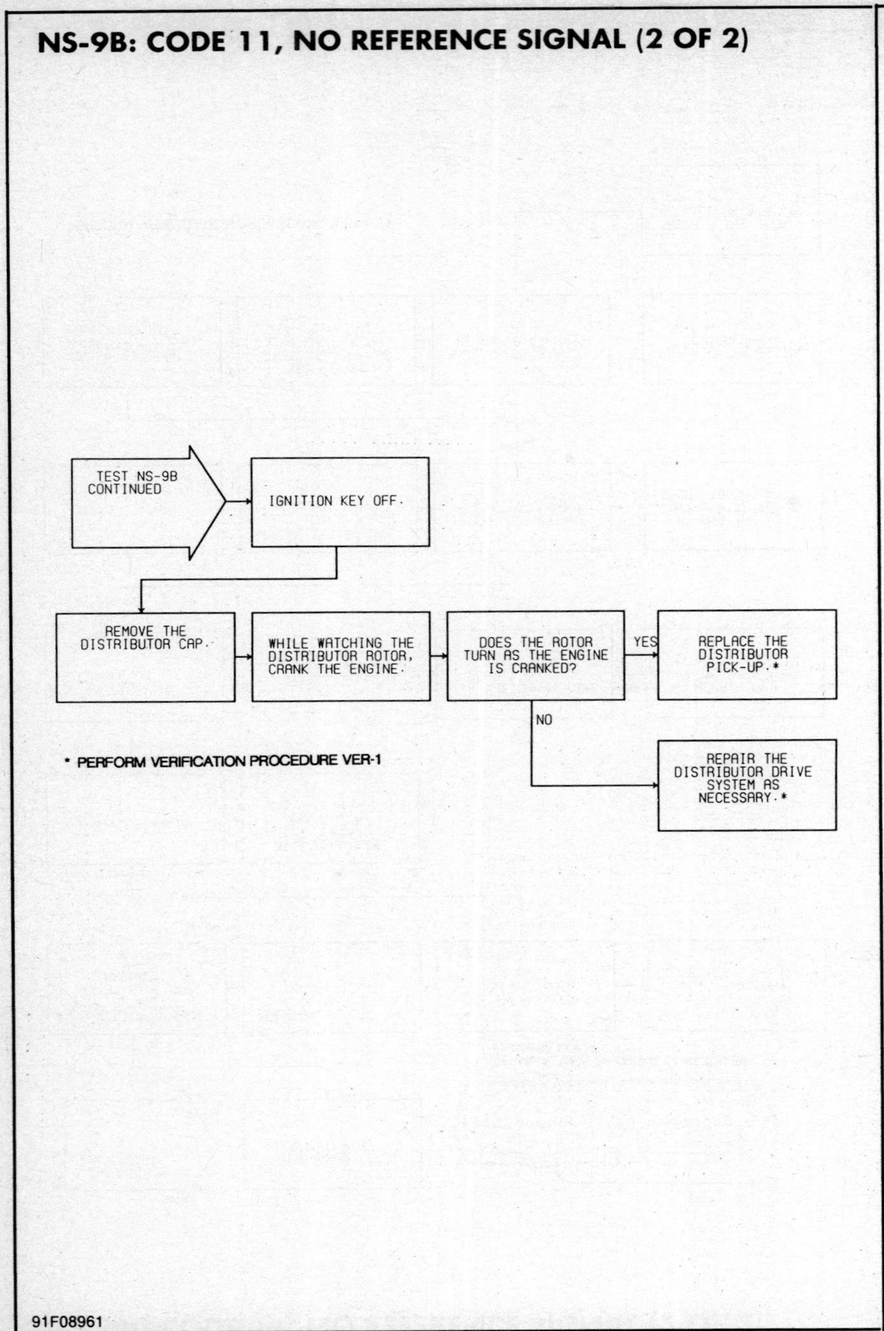
NS-9B: CODE 11, NO REFERENCE SIGNAL (2 OF 2)
TEST NS-9B CONTINUED
IGNITION KEY OFF.
REMOVE THE DISTRIBUTOR CAP.
WHILE WATCHING THE DISTRIBUTOR ROTOR, CRANK THE ENGINE.
DOES THE ROTOR TURN AS THE ENGINE IS CRANKED?
YES
REPLACE THE DISTRIBUTOR PICK-UP.*
NO
REPAIR THE DISTRIBUTOR DRIVE SYSTEM AS NECESSARY.*
* PERFORM VERIFICATION PROCEDURE VER-1
91F08961

Fig. 31: No Start Test 9B (3.0L VIN 3) – Code 11, No Reference Signal (2 of 2)

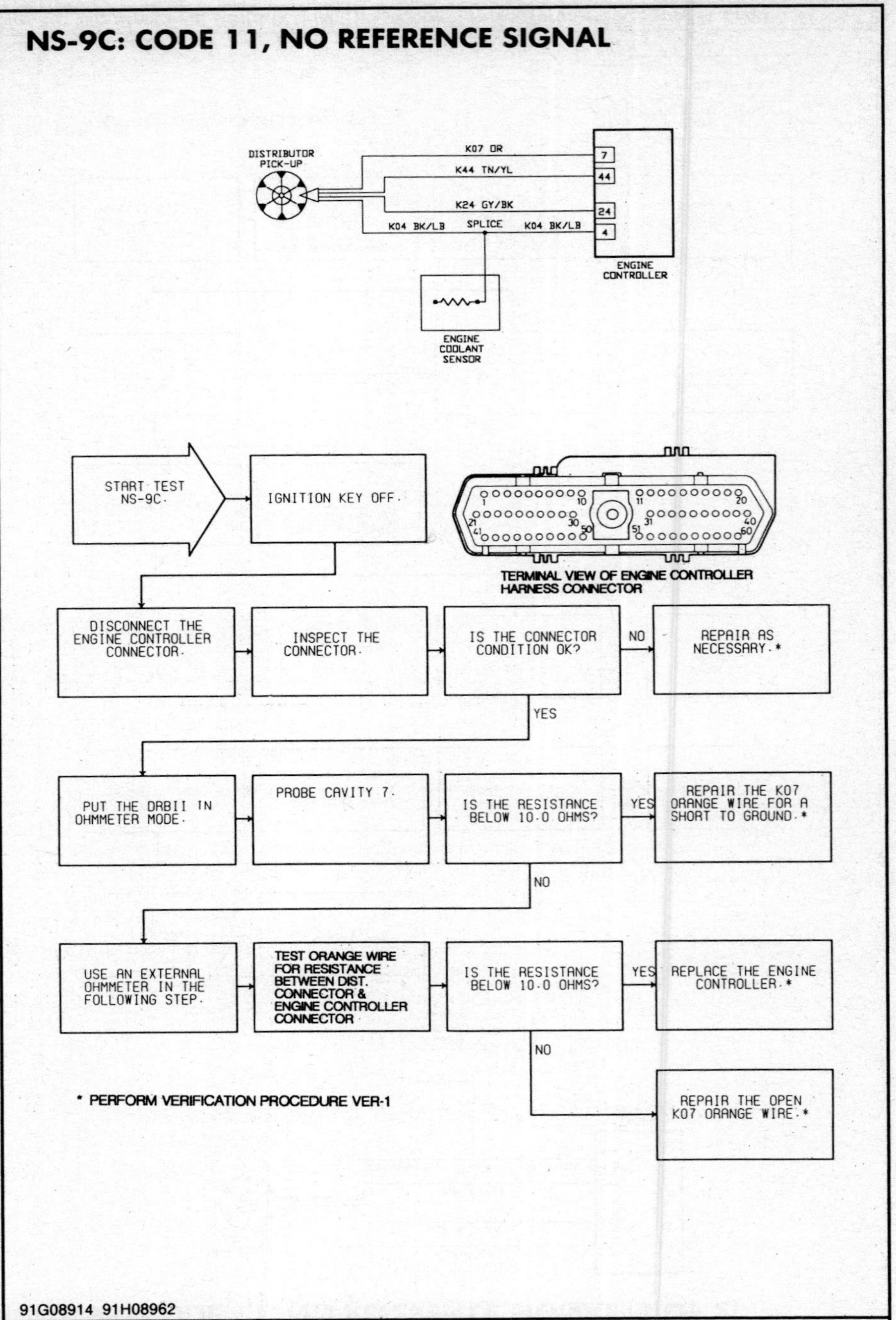
NS-9C: CODE 11, NO REFERENCE SIGNAL
DISTRIBUTOR PICK-UP
K07 OR
K44 TN/YL
K24 GY/BK
K04 BK/LB
SPLICE
K04 BK/LB
7
44
24
4
ENGINE CONTROLLER
ENGINE COOLANT SENSOR
START TEST NS-9C.
IGNITION KEY OFF.
TERMINAL VIEW OF ENGINE CONTROLLER HARNESS CONNECTOR
DISCONNECT THE ENGINE CONTROLLER CONNECTOR.
INSPECT THE CONNECTOR.
IS THE CONNECTOR CONDITION OK?
NO
REPAIR AS NECESSARY.*
YES
PUT THE DRBII IN OHMMETER MODE.
PROBE CAVITY 7.
IS THE RESISTANCE BELOW 10.0 OHMS?
YES
REPAIR THE K07 ORANGE WIRE FOR A SHORT TO GROUND.*
NO
USE AN EXTERNAL OHMMETER IN THE FOLLOWING STEP.
TEST ORANGE WIRE FOR RESISTANCE BETWEEN DIST. CONNECTOR & ENGINE CONTROLLER CONNECTOR
IS THE RESISTANCE BELOW 10.0 OHMS?
YES
REPLACE THE ENGINE CONTROLLER.*
NO
REPAIR THE OPEN K07 ORANGE WIRE.*
* PERFORM VERIFICATION PROCEDURE VER-1
91G08914 91H08962

Fig. 32: No Start Test 9C (3.0L VIN 3) – Code 11, No Reference Signal

NS-10A: CODE 42, AUTO SHUTDOWN (ASD) RELAY CIRCUIT (1 OF 2)

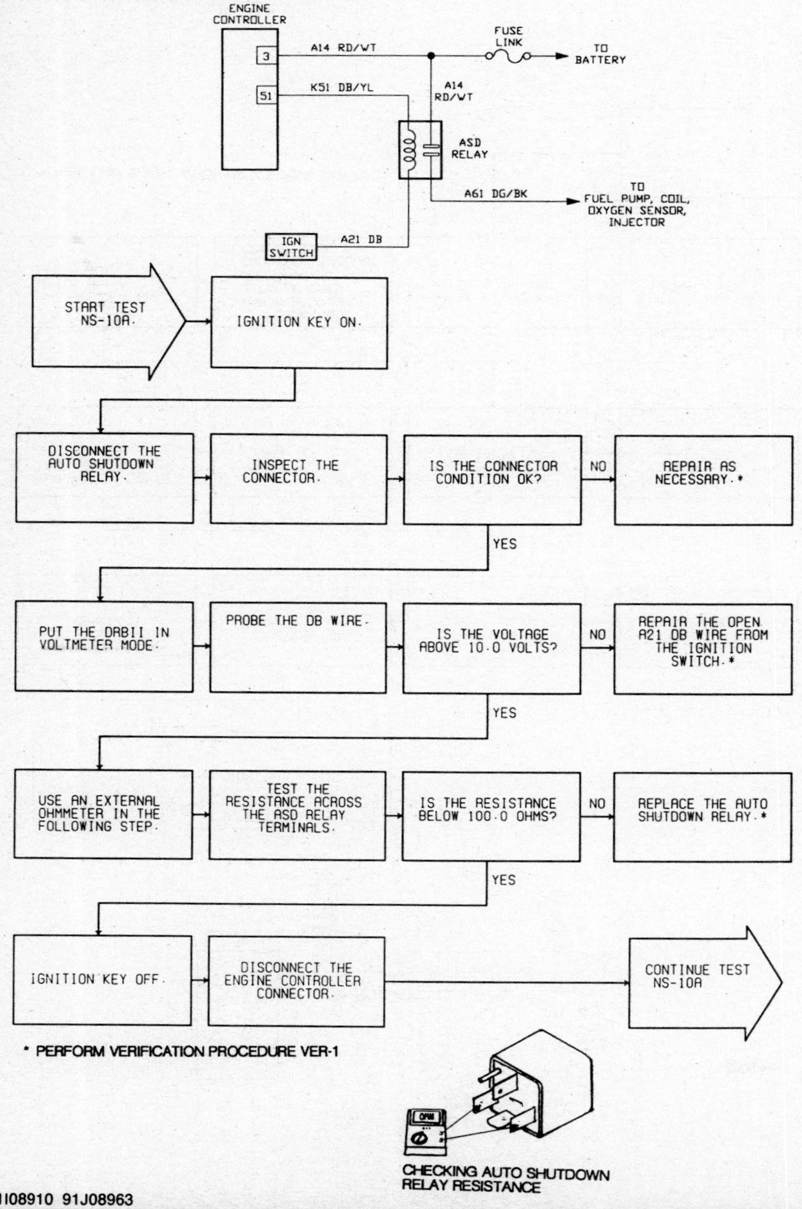
ENGINE CONTROLLER
3
51
A14 RD/WT
K51 DB/YL
FUSE LINK
TO BATTERY
A14 RD/WT
ASD RELAY
A61 DG/BK
TO FUEL PUMP, COIL, OXYGEN SENSOR, INJECTOR
IGN SWITCH
A21 DB
START TEST NS-10A.
IGNITION KEY ON.
DISCONNECT THE AUTO SHUTDOWN RELAY.
INSPECT THE CONNECTOR.
IS THE CONNECTOR CONDITION OK?
NO
REPAIR AS NECESSARY.*
YES
PUT THE DRBII IN VOLTMETER MODE.
PROBE THE DB WIRE.
IS THE VOLTAGE ABOVE 10.0 VOLTS?
NO
REPAIR THE OPEN A21 DB WIRE FROM THE IGNITION SWITCH.*
YES
USE AN EXTERNAL OHMMETER IN THE FOLLOWING STEP.
TEST THE RESISTANCE ACROSS THE ASD RELAY TERMINALS.
IS THE RESISTANCE BELOW 100.0 OHMS?
NO
REPLACE THE AUTO SHUTDOWN RELAY.*
YES
IGNITION KEY OFF.
DISCONNECT THE ENGINE CONTROLLER CONNECTOR.
CONTINUE TEST NS-10A
* PERFORM VERIFICATION PROCEDURE VER-1
CHECKING AUTO SHUTDOWN RELAY RESISTANCE

91I08910 91J08963

Fig. 33: No Start Test 10A (3.0L VIN 3) – Code 42, Auto Shutdown (ASD) Relay Circuit (1 of 2)

NS-10A: CODE 42, AUTO SHUTDOWN (ASD) RELAY CIRCUIT (2 OF 2)

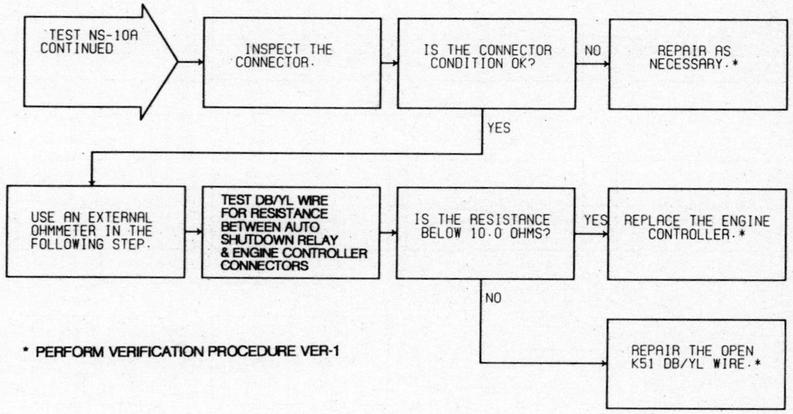
TEST NS-10A CONTINUED
INSPECT THE CONNECTOR.
IS THE CONNECTOR CONDITION OK?
NO
REPAIR AS NECESSARY.*
YES
USE AN EXTERNAL OHMMETER IN THE FOLLOWING STEP.
TEST DB/YL WIRE FOR RESISTANCE BETWEEN AUTO SHUTDOWN RELAY & ENGINE CONTROLLER CONNECTORS
IS THE RESISTANCE BELOW 10.0 OHMS?
YES
REPLACE THE ENGINE CONTROLLER.*
NO
REPAIR THE OPEN K51 DB/YL WIRE.*
* PERFORM VERIFICATION PROCEDURE VER-1

91B08964

Fig. 34: No Start Test 10A (3.0L VIN 3) – Code 42, Auto Shutdown (ASD) Relay Circuit (2 of 2)

NS-11A: CODE 42, NO AUTO SHUTDOWN (ASD) RELAY VOLTAGE SENSED AT SBEC

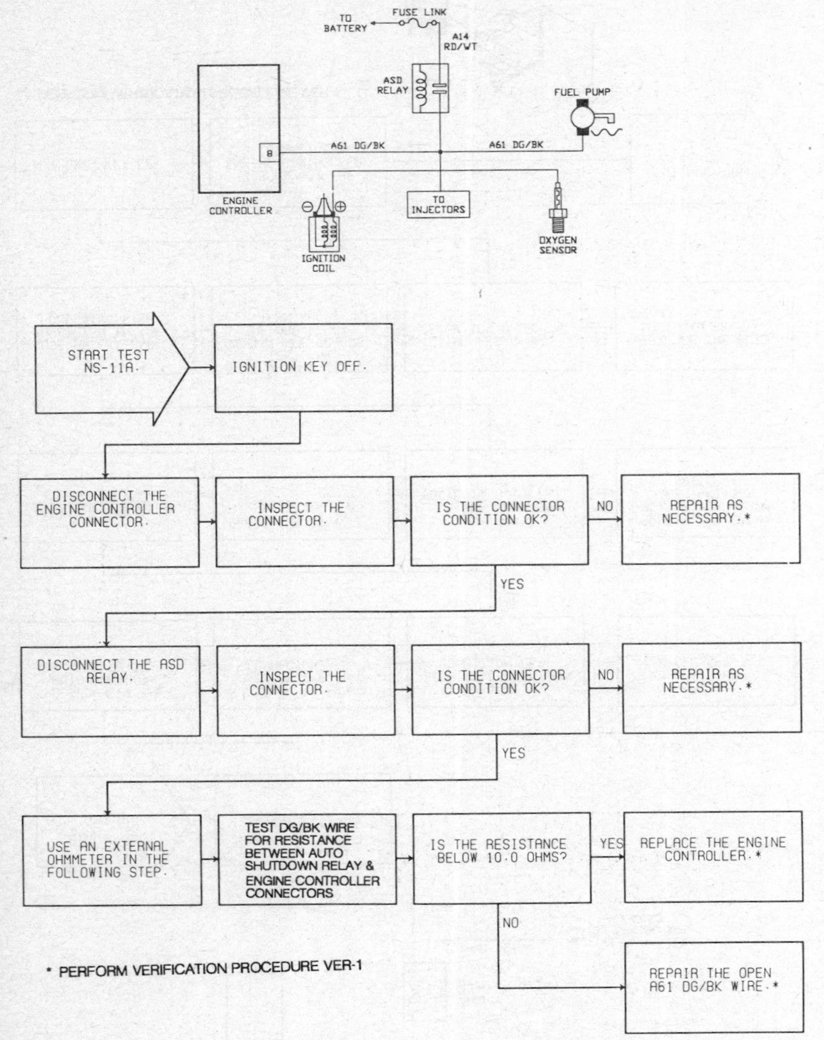
TO BATTERY
FUSE LINK
A14 RD/WT
ASD RELAY
FUEL PUMP
ENGINE CONTROLLER
8
A61 DG/BK
A61 DG/BK
TO INJECTORS
IGNITION COIL
OXYGEN SENSOR
START TEST NS-11A.
IGNITION KEY OFF.
DISCONNECT THE ENGINE CONTROLLER CONNECTOR.
INSPECT THE CONNECTOR.
IS THE CONNECTOR CONDITION OK?
NO
REPAIR AS NECESSARY.*
YES
DISCONNECT THE ASD RELAY.
INSPECT THE CONNECTOR.
IS THE CONNECTOR CONDITION OK?
NO
REPAIR AS NECESSARY.*
YES
USE AN EXTERNAL OHMMETER IN THE FOLLOWING STEP.
TEST DG/BK WIRE FOR RESISTANCE BETWEEN AUTO SHUTDOWN RELAY & ENGINE CONTROLLER CONNECTORS
IS THE RESISTANCE BELOW 10.0 OHMS?
YES
REPLACE THE ENGINE CONTROLLER.*
NO
REPAIR THE OPEN A61 DG/BK WIRE.*

* PERFORM VERIFICATION PROCEDURE VER-1

91J08915 91E08965

Fig. 35: *No Start Test 11A (3.0L VIN 3) – Code 42, No Auto Shutdown (ASD) Relay Voltage Sensed at SBEC*

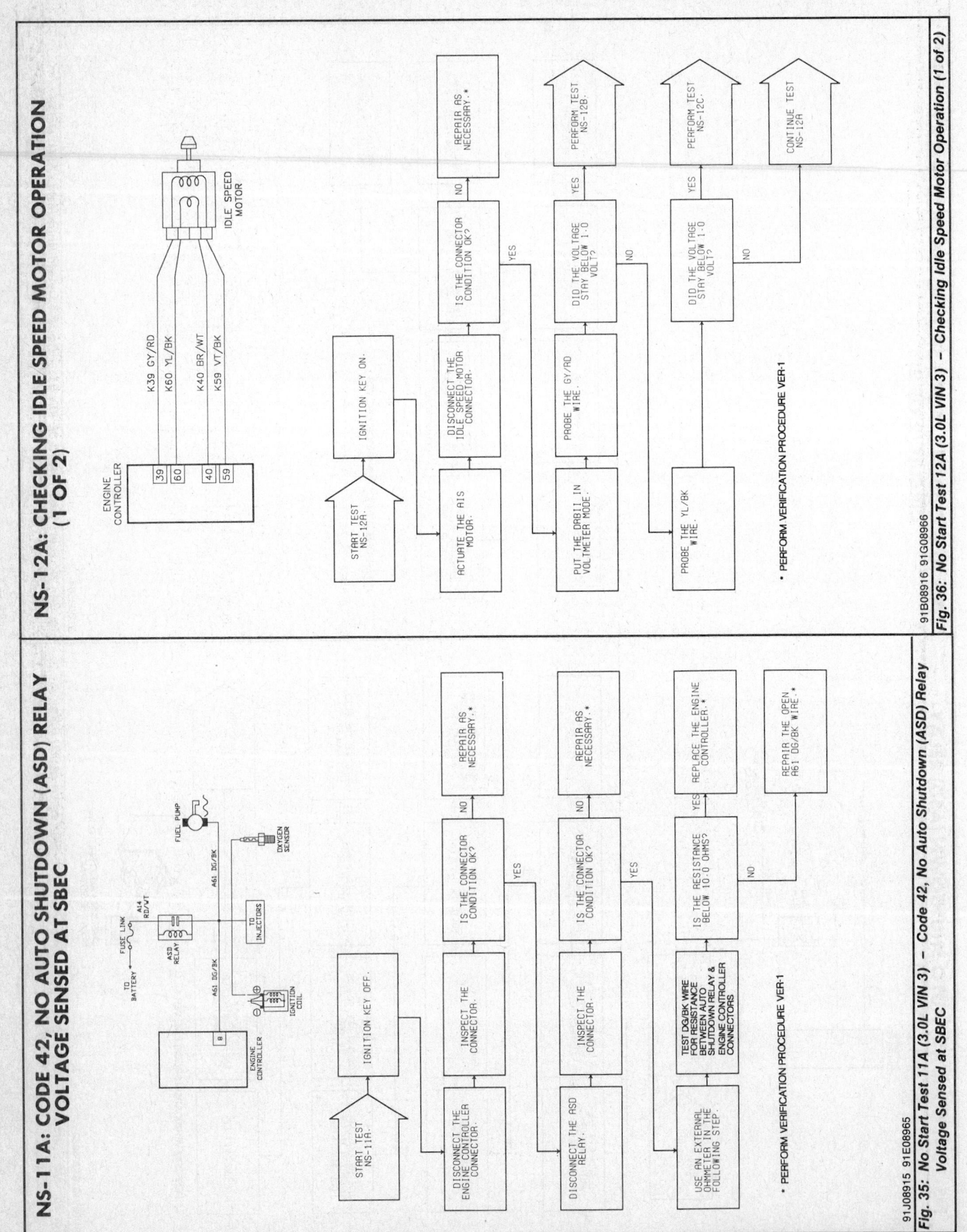

NS-12A: CHECKING IDLE SPEED MOTOR OPERATION (1 OF 2)

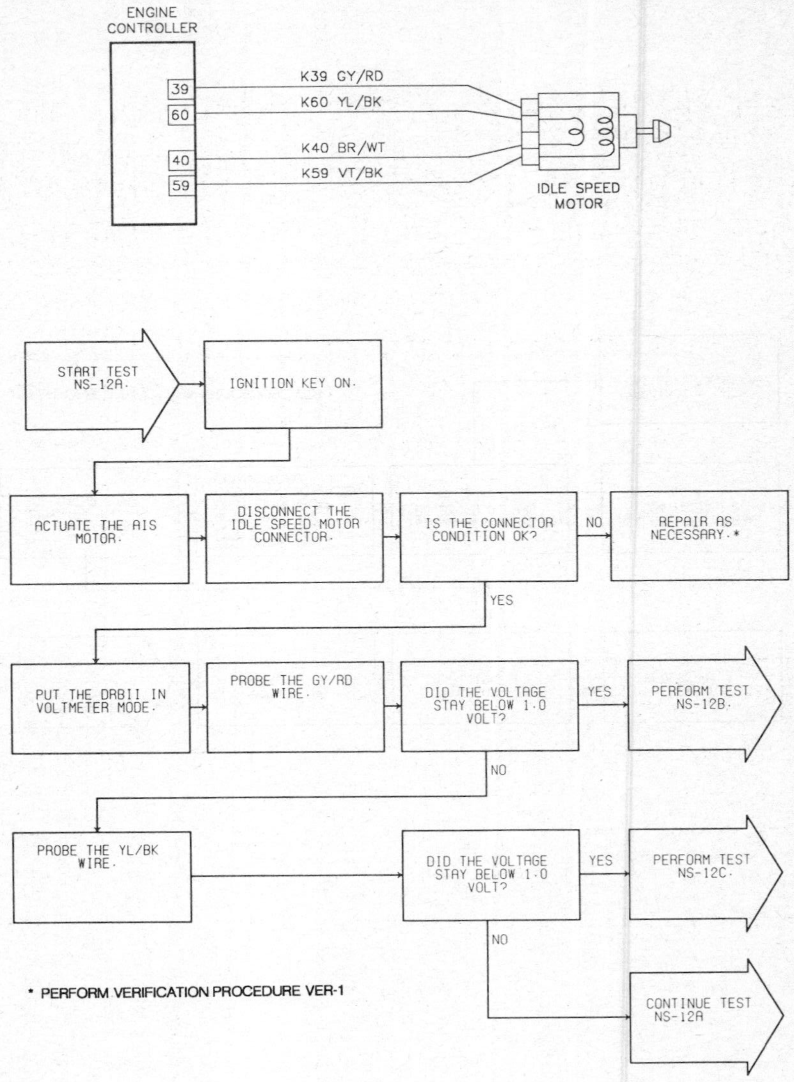
ENGINE CONTROLLER
39
60
40
59
K39 GY/RD
K60 YL/BK
K40 BR/WT
K59 VT/BK
IDLE SPEED MOTOR
START TEST NS-12A.
IGNITION KEY ON.
ACTUATE THE AIS MOTOR.
DISCONNECT THE IDLE SPEED MOTOR CONNECTOR.
IS THE CONNECTOR CONDITION OK?
NO
REPAIR AS NECESSARY.*
YES
PUT THE DRBII IN VOLTMETER MODE.
PROBE THE GY/RD WIRE.
DID THE VOLTAGE STAY BELOW 1.0 VOLT?
YES
PERFORM TEST NS-12B.
NO
PROBE THE YL/BK WIRE.
DID THE VOLTAGE STAY BELOW 1.0 VOLT?
YES
PERFORM TEST NS-12C.
NO
CONTINUE TEST NS-12A

* PERFORM VERIFICATION PROCEDURE VER-1

91B08916 91G08966

Fig. 36: *No Start Test 12A (3.0L VIN 3) – Checking Idle Speed Motor Operation (1 of 2)*

NS-12A: CHECKING IDLE SPEED MOTOR OPERATION (2 OF 2)

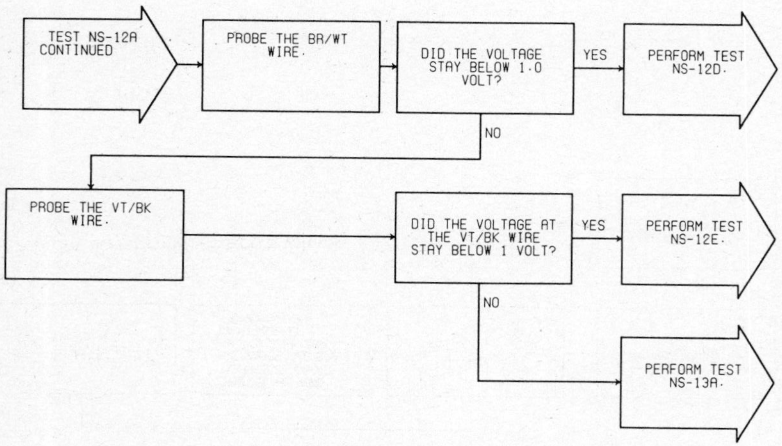
TEST NS-12A CONTINUED
PROBE THE BR/WT WIRE.
DID THE VOLTAGE STAY BELOW 1.0 VOLT?
YES
PERFORM TEST NS-12D.
NO
PROBE THE VT/BK WIRE.
DID THE VOLTAGE AT THE VT/BK WIRE STAY BELOW 1 VOLT?
YES
PERFORM TEST NS-12E.
NO
PERFORM TEST NS-13A.

91I08967

Fig. 37: No Start Test 12A (3.0L VIN 3) – Checking Idle Speed Motor Operation (2 of 2)

NS-12B: CHECKING IDLE SPEED MOTOR OPERATION

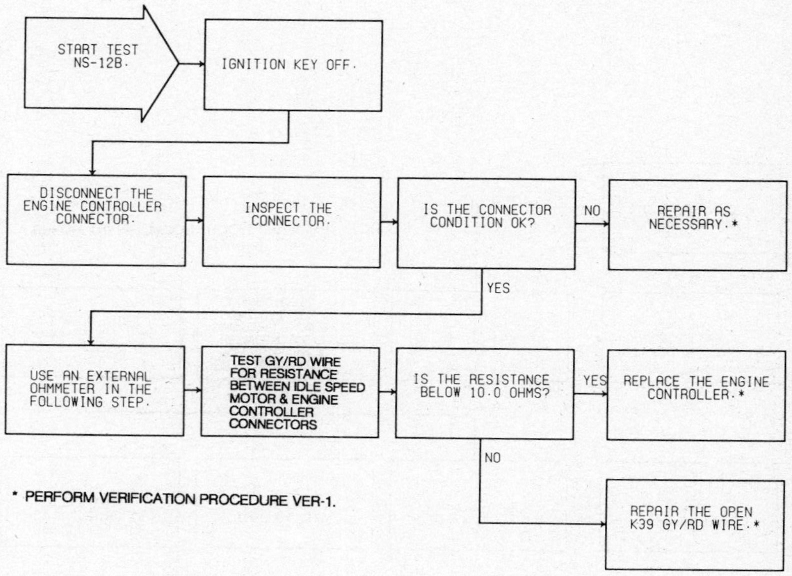
START TEST NS-12B.
IGNITION KEY OFF.
DISCONNECT THE ENGINE CONTROLLER CONNECTOR.
INSPECT THE CONNECTOR.
IS THE CONNECTOR CONDITION OK?
NO
REPAIR AS NECESSARY.*
YES
USE AN EXTERNAL OHMMETER IN THE FOLLOWING STEP.
TEST GY/RD WIRE FOR RESISTANCE BETWEEN IDLE SPEED MOTOR & ENGINE CONTROLLER CONNECTORS
IS THE RESISTANCE BELOW 10.0 OHMS?
YES
REPLACE THE ENGINE CONTROLLER.*
NO
REPAIR THE OPEN K39 GY/RD WIRE.*
* PERFORM VERIFICATION PROCEDURE VER-1.

91A08968

Fig. 38: No Start Test 12B (3.0L VIN 3) – Checking Idle Speed Motor Operation

NS-12C: CHECKING IDLE SPEED MOTOR OPERATION

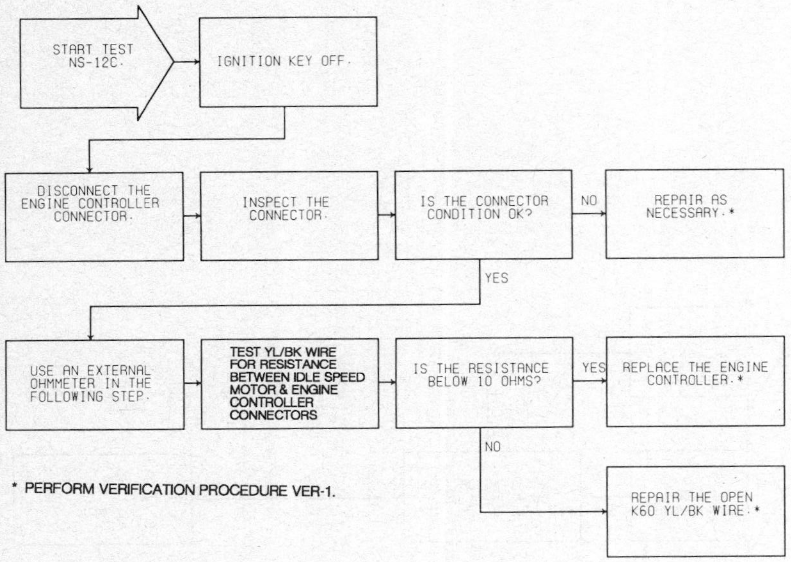
START TEST NS-12C.
IGNITION KEY OFF.
DISCONNECT THE ENGINE CONTROLLER CONNECTOR.
INSPECT THE CONNECTOR.
IS THE CONNECTOR CONDITION OK?
NO
REPAIR AS NECESSARY.*
YES
USE AN EXTERNAL OHMMETER IN THE FOLLOWING STEP.
TEST YL/BK WIRE FOR RESISTANCE BETWEEN IDLE SPEED MOTOR & ENGINE CONTROLLER CONNECTORS
IS THE RESISTANCE BELOW 10 OHMS?
YES
REPLACE THE ENGINE CONTROLLER.*
NO
REPAIR THE OPEN K60 YL/BK WIRE.*
* PERFORM VERIFICATION PROCEDURE VER-1.

91C08969

Fig. 39: No Start Test 12C (3.0L VIN 3) – Checking Idle Speed Motor Operation

NS-12D: CHECKING IDLE SPEED MOTOR OPERATION

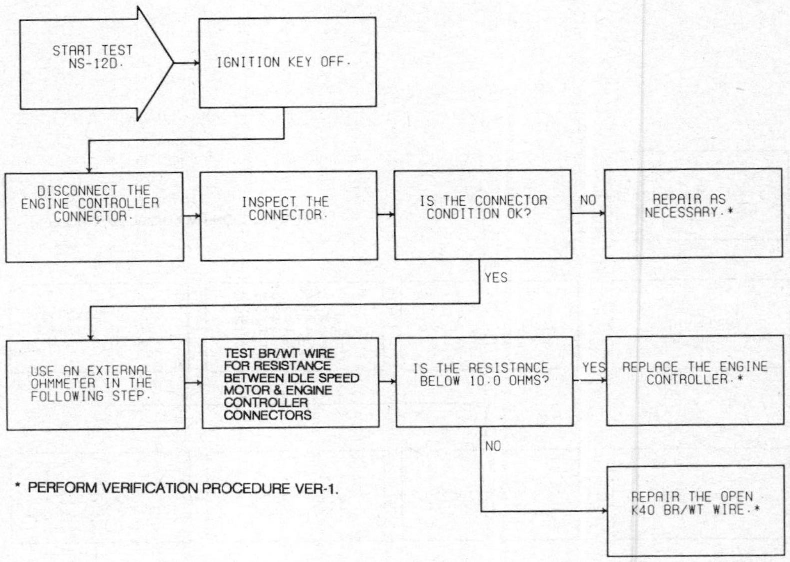
START TEST NS-12D.
IGNITION KEY OFF.
DISCONNECT THE ENGINE CONTROLLER CONNECTOR.
INSPECT THE CONNECTOR.
IS THE CONNECTOR CONDITION OK?
NO
REPAIR AS NECESSARY.*
YES
USE AN EXTERNAL OHMMETER IN THE FOLLOWING STEP.
TEST BR/WT WIRE FOR RESISTANCE BETWEEN IDLE SPEED MOTOR & ENGINE CONTROLLER CONNECTORS
IS THE RESISTANCE BELOW 10.0 OHMS?
YES
REPLACE THE ENGINE CONTROLLER.*
NO
REPAIR THE OPEN K40 BR/WT WIRE.*
* PERFORM VERIFICATION PROCEDURE VER-1.

91E08970

Fig. 40: No Start Test 12D (3.0L VIN 3) – Checking Idle Speed Motor Operation

NS-12E: CHECKING IDLE SPEED MOTOR OPERATION

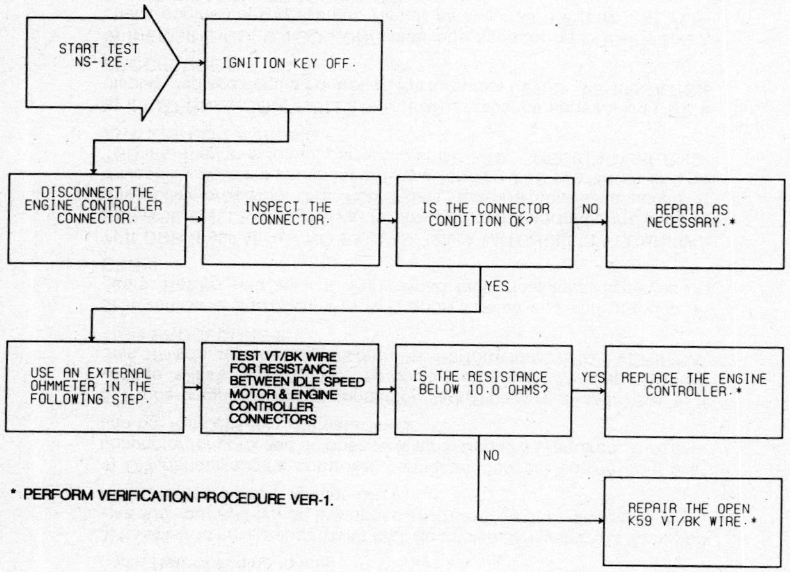
START TEST
NS-12E.
IGNITION KEY OFF.
DISCONNECT THE ENGINE CONTROLLER CONNECTOR.
INSPECT THE CONNECTOR.
IS THE CONNECTOR CONDITION OK?
NO
REPAIR AS NECESSARY.*
YES
USE AN EXTERNAL OHMMETER IN THE FOLLOWING STEP.
TEST VT/BK WIRE FOR RESISTANCE BETWEEN IDLE SPEED MOTOR & ENGINE CONTROLLER CONNECTORS
IS THE RESISTANCE BELOW 10.0 OHMS?
YES
REPLACE THE ENGINE CONTROLLER.*
NO
REPAIR THE OPEN K59 VT/BK WIRE.*
* PERFORM VERIFICATION PROCEDURE VER-1.

91G08971

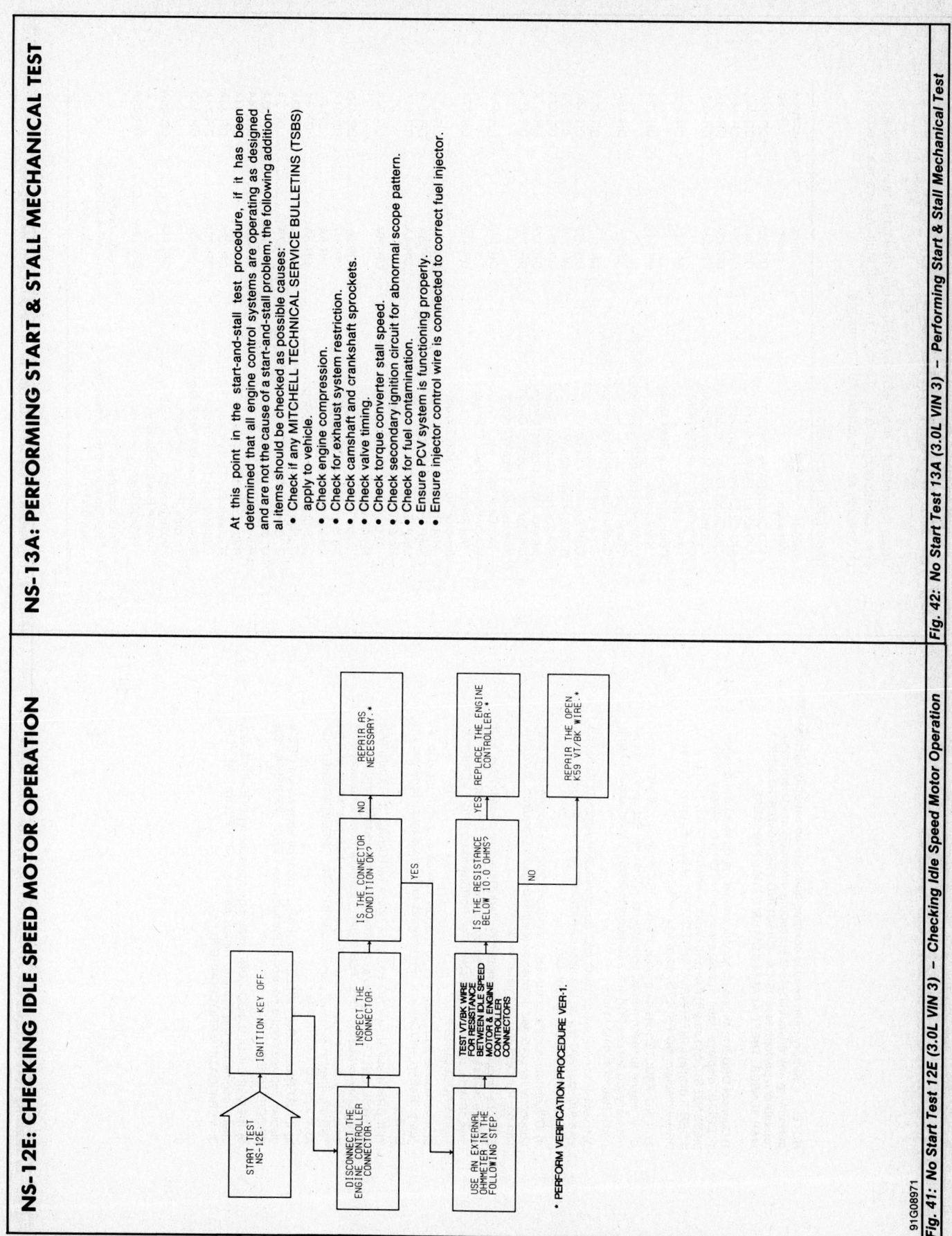

Fig. 41: No Start Test 12E (3.0L VIN 3) – Checking Idle Speed Motor Operation

NS-13A: PERFORMING START & STALL MECHANICAL TEST

At this point in the start-and-stall test procedure, if it has been determined that all engine control systems are operating as designed and are not the cause of a start-and-stall problem, the following additional items should be checked as possible causes:

- Check if any MITCHELL TECHNICAL SERVICE BULLETINS (TSBS) apply to vehicle.
- Check engine compression.
- Check for exhaust system restriction.
- Check camshaft and crankshaft sprockets.
- Check valve timing.
- Check torque converter stall speed.
- Check secondary ignition circuit for abnormal scope pattern.
- Check for fuel contamination.
- Ensure PCV system is functioning properly.
- Ensure injector control wire is connected to correct fuel injector.

Fig. 42: No Start Test 13A (3.0L VIN 3) – Performing Start & Stall Mechanical Test

1991 ENGINE PERFORMANCE
Self-Diagnostics – 3.0L VIN 3 (Cont.)

DR-1A: CHECKING SYSTEM FOR FAULTS

NOTE: Battery must be fully charged and at rated capacity before performing any driveability test procedure. If vehicle starts and stalls repeatedly, perform test NS-2A: CHECKING TPS, POWER TO SBEC & MAP SENSOR, THEFT ALARM STATUS & FUEL PRESSURE.

1) Connect DRB-II to engine diagnostic connector. Read fault messages. If DRB-II displays fault messages, go to DR-1B: DRB-II FAULT MESSAGES. Go to step **9)** if DRB-II displays ENGINE COLD TOO LONG. If DRB-II displays INTERNAL CONTROLLER FAILURE, go to step **8)**. If DRB-II displays NO FAULTS, go to next step.

2) If NO FAULTS message appears on DRB-II display, start engine. Allow engine to reach normal operating temperature. Set engine speed manually (do not use DRB-II to set speed) to 2000 RPM for about 10 seconds. Return engine to idle.

3) If vehicle is not equipped with A/C, go to step **5)**. If vehicle is equipped with A/C, put A/C fan on low speed. Turn A/C on. If engine stalls when A/C is turned on, turn ignition off.

4) Disconnect engine controller connector. Inspect engine controller connector for corroded or loose terminals. Repair as required. Turn ignition on. Put DRB-II in voltmeter mode.

5) Probe engine controller connector Dark/Blue wire at cavity No. 9. If voltage is less than 10 volts, repair Dark/Blue wire. If voltage is more than 10 volts, replace engine controller. Perform test VER-2: VERIFICATION PROCEDURE 2.

6) If vehicle is equipped with A/T, apply brakes and shift through all gears. Return shift lever to Park. Read fault messages displayed on DRB-II.

7) If DRB-II still shows NO FAULTS, check MITCHELL'S TECHNICAL SERVICE BULLETINS (TSB's) for any pertinent information relating to driveability problems. If a TSB exists, perform corrective action. If driveability problem continues after performing TSB procedure or if no TSB information is found, perform test DR-33A: CHECKING SECONDARY IGNITION & TIMING.

8) If INTERNAL CONTROLLER FAILURE message appears on DRB-II display, replace engine controller. Perform test VER-2: VERIFICATION PROCEDURE 2.

9) If ENGINE COLD TOO LONG message appears on DRB-II display, check engine cooling system. Repair as required. Perform test VER-3: VERIFICATION PROCEDURE 3.

Fig. 43: Driveability Test 1A (3.0L VIN 3) – Checking System for Faults

DR-1B: DRB-II FAULT MESSAGES

Using the DRB-II FAULT MESSAGES table, select the fault message and corresponding test. Correct all hard fault messages before proceeding to intermittent fault message.

DRB-II FAULT MESSAGES

DRB-II Message	[1] Hard Fault	[2] Intermittent Fault
A/C Clutch Relay Circuit [3]	DR-26A	DR-44A
A/C Clutch Relay Circuit [4]	DR-24A	DR-44A
A/C Clutch Relay Circuit [5]	DR-25A	DR-44A
A/C Clutch Relay Circuit [6]	DR-23A	DR-44A
Automatic Idle Motor Circuits	DR-13A	DR-46A
Controller Failure EEPROM Write Denied	DR-31A	DR-32A
Controller Failure EMR Miles Not Stored	DR-31A	DR-32A
Coolant Temperature Sensor Voltage Too High	DR-9A	DR-45A
Coolant Temperature Sensor Voltage Too Low	DR-10A	DR-45A
EGR Solenoid Circuit	DR-21A	DR-44A
EGR System Failure	DR-22A	DR-22A
Injector No. 1 Control Circuit	DR-15A	DR-47A
Injector No. 2 Control Circuit	DR-17A	DR-47A
Injector No. 3 Control Circuit	DR-19A	DR-47A
Injector No. 1 Peak Current Not Reached	DR-14A	DR-47A
Injector No. 2 Peak Current Not Reached	DR-16A	DR-47A
Injector No. 3 Peak Current Not Reached	DR-18A	DR-47A
MAP Voltage Too High	DR-5A	DR45-A
MAP Voltage Too Low	DR-4A	DR-45A
No ASD Relay Voltage Sense At Controller	DR-30A	DR-30A
No Change In MAP From Start To Run	DR3A	DR-45B
No Sync Pick-Up Signal	DR-31A	DR-31A
No Vehicle Speed Signal	DR-6A	DR-6A
O_2 Signal Shorted To Voltage	DR-8A	DR-8A
O_2 Signal Stays Above Center (Rich)	DR-33A	DR-33A
O_2 Signal Stays At Center	DR-7A	DR-7A
O_2 Signal Stays Below Center (Lean)	DR-33A	DR-33A
Purge Solenoid Circuit	DR-20A	DR-44A
Radiator Fan Relay Circuit [3,6]	DR-27A	DR-44A
Radiator Fan Relay Circuit [4]	DR-28A	DR-44A
Radiator Fan Relay Circuit [5]	DR-29A	DR-44A
Slow Change In Idle MAP Signal	DR-2A	DR-45B
Throttle Position Sensor Voltage High	DR-11A	DR-45A
Throttle Position Sensor Voltage Low	DR-12A	DR-45A

[1] – Key counter is "0".
[2] – Key counter is more than "0".
[3] – AA body.
[4] – AC body.
[5] – AG & AJ bodies.
[6] – AS body.

Fig. 44: Driveability Test 1B (3.0L VIN 3) – DRB-II Fault Messages

DR-2A: CODE 13, SLOW CHANGE IN MAP SIGNAL (1 OF 2)

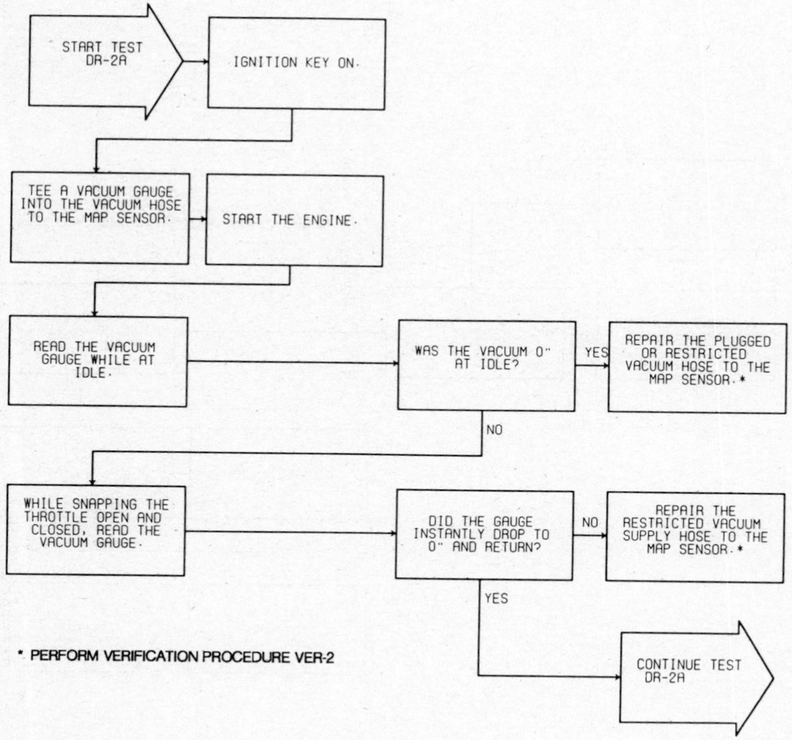
START TEST DR-2A
IGNITION KEY ON.
TEE A VACUUM GAUGE INTO THE VACUUM HOSE TO THE MAP SENSOR.
START THE ENGINE.
READ THE VACUUM GAUGE WHILE AT IDLE.
WAS THE VACUUM 0" AT IDLE?
YES
REPAIR THE PLUGGED OR RESTRICTED VACUUM HOSE TO THE MAP SENSOR.*
NO
WHILE SNAPPING THE THROTTLE OPEN AND CLOSED, READ THE VACUUM GAUGE.
DID THE GAUGE INSTANTLY DROP TO 0" AND RETURN?
NO
REPAIR THE RESTRICTED VACUUM SUPPLY HOSE TO THE MAP SENSOR.*
YES
CONTINUE TEST DR-2A

* PERFORM VERIFICATION PROCEDURE VER-2

91A08973

Fig. 45: Driveability Test 2A (3.0L VIN 3) – Code 13, Slow Change in MAP Signal (1 of 2)

DR-2A: CODE 13, SLOW CHANGE IN MAP SIGNAL (2 OF 2)

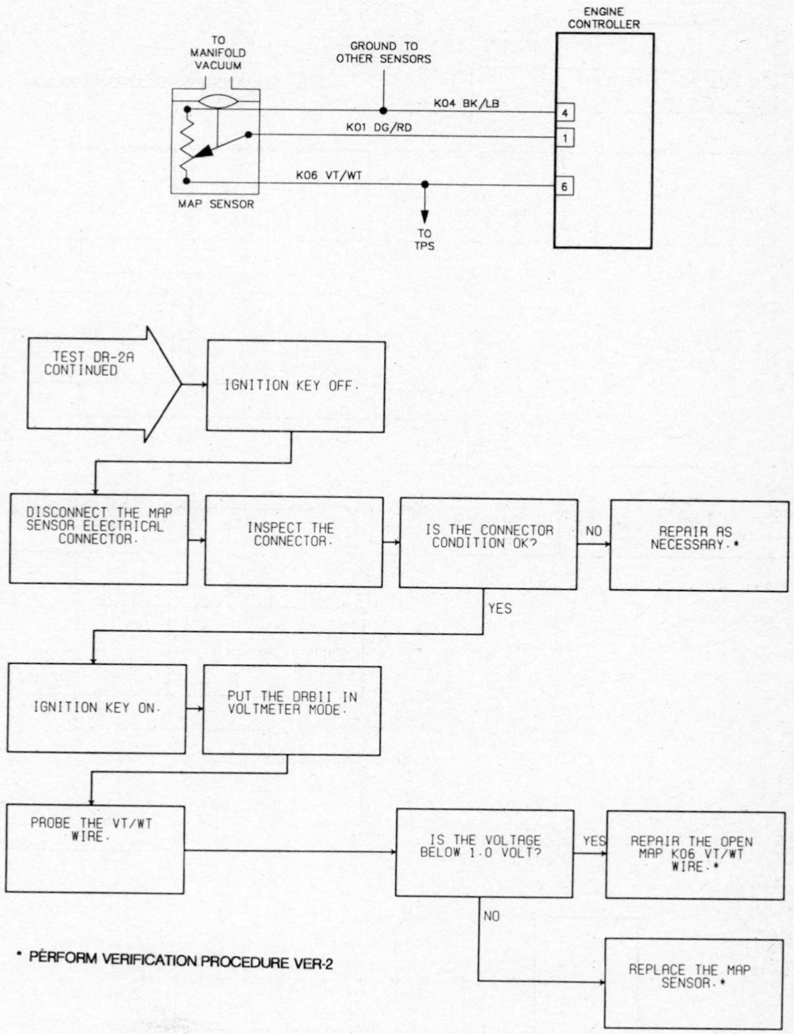
TO MANIFOLD VACUUM
GROUND TO OTHER SENSORS
ENGINE CONTROLLER
K04 BK/LB
K01 DG/RD
K06 VT/WT
4
1
6
MAP SENSOR
TO TPS
TEST DR-2A CONTINUED
IGNITION KEY OFF.
DISCONNECT THE MAP SENSOR ELECTRICAL CONNECTOR.
INSPECT THE CONNECTOR.
IS THE CONNECTOR CONDITION OK?
NO
REPAIR AS NECESSARY.*
YES
IGNITION KEY ON.
PUT THE DRBII IN VOLTMETER MODE.
PROBE THE VT/WT WIRE.
IS THE VOLTAGE BELOW 1.0 VOLT?
YES
REPAIR THE OPEN MAP K06 VT/WT WIRE.*
NO
REPLACE THE MAP SENSOR.*

* PERFORM VERIFICATION PROCEDURE VER-2

91E08913 91C08974

Fig. 46: Driveability Test 2A (3.0L VIN 3) – Code 13, Slow Change in MAP Signal (2 of 2)

DR-3A: CODE 13, NO CHANGE IN MAP FROM START TO RUN

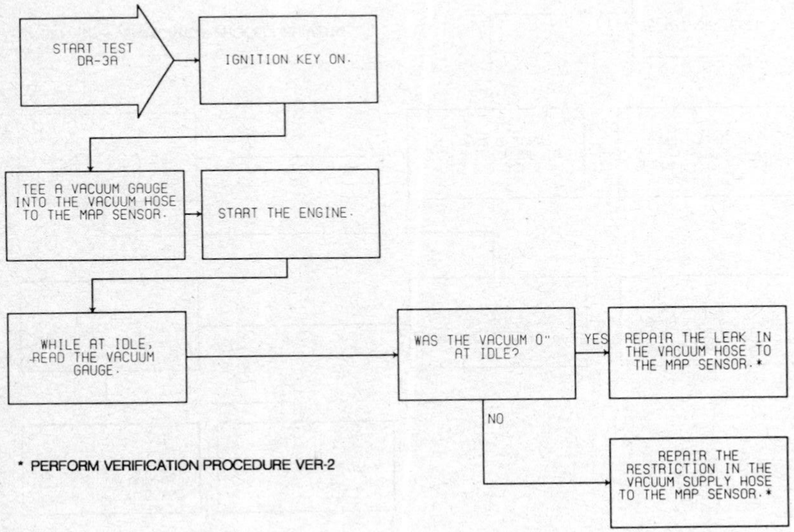
START TEST
DR-3A
IGNITION KEY ON.
TEE A VACUUM GAUGE INTO THE VACUUM HOSE TO THE MAP SENSOR.
START THE ENGINE.
WHILE AT IDLE, READ THE VACUUM GAUGE.
WAS THE VACUUM 0" AT IDLE?
YES
REPAIR THE LEAK IN THE VACUUM HOSE TO THE MAP SENSOR.*
NO
REPAIR THE RESTRICTION IN THE VACUUM SUPPLY HOSE TO THE MAP SENSOR.*

* PERFORM VERIFICATION PROCEDURE VER-2

91F08975

Fig. 47: Driveability Test 3A (3.0L VIN 3) – Code 13, No Change in MAP from Start to Run

DR-4A: CODE 14, MAP VOLTAGE TOO LOW

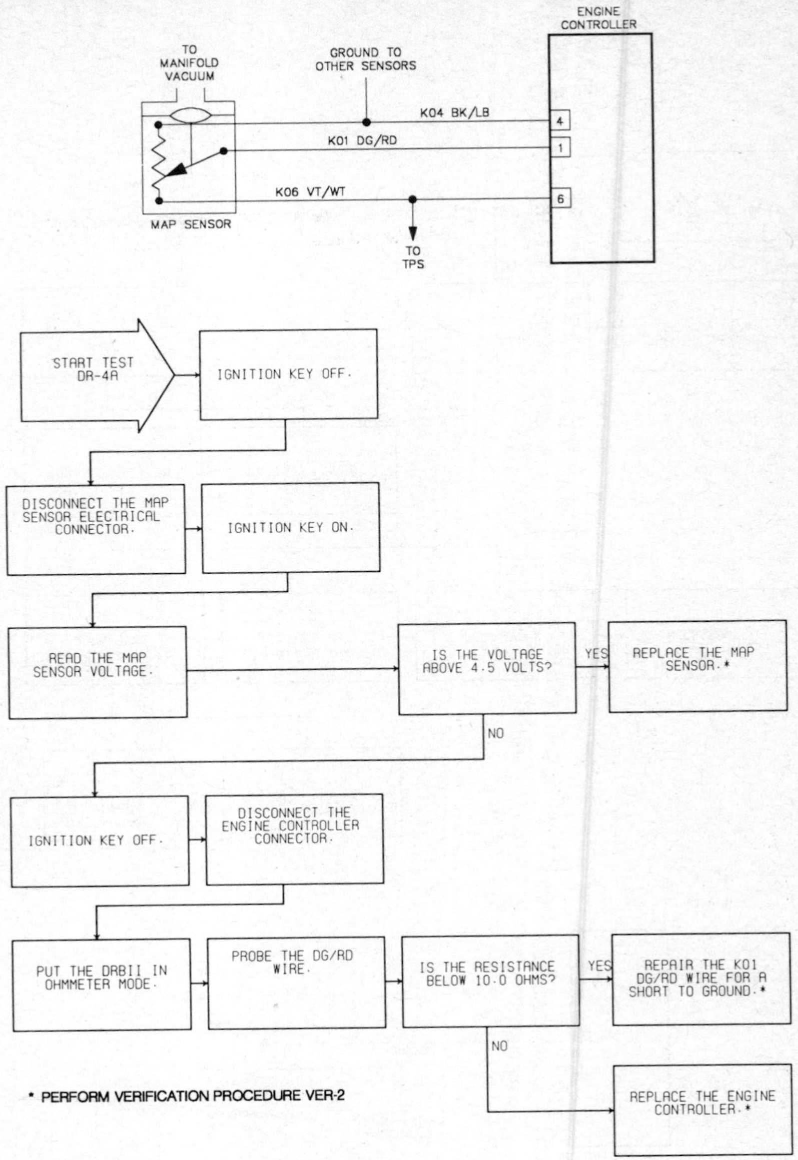
ENGINE CONTROLLER
TO MANIFOLD VACUUM
GROUND TO OTHER SENSORS
K04 BK/LB
K01 DG/RD
K06 VT/WT
4
1
6
MAP SENSOR
TO TPS
START TEST
DR-4A
IGNITION KEY OFF.
DISCONNECT THE MAP SENSOR ELECTRICAL CONNECTOR.
IGNITION KEY ON.
READ THE MAP SENSOR VOLTAGE.
IS THE VOLTAGE ABOVE 4.5 VOLTS?
YES
REPLACE THE MAP SENSOR.*
NO
IGNITION KEY OFF.
DISCONNECT THE ENGINE CONTROLLER CONNECTOR.
PUT THE DRBII IN OHMMETER MODE.
PROBE THE DG/RD WIRE.
IS THE RESISTANCE BELOW 10.0 OHMS?
YES
REPAIR THE K01 DG/RD WIRE FOR A SHORT TO GROUND.*
NO
REPLACE THE ENGINE CONTROLLER.*

* PERFORM VERIFICATION PROCEDURE VER-2

91E08913 91H08976

Fig. 48: Driveability Test 4A (3.0L VIN 3) – Code 14, MAP Voltage Too Low

DR-5A: CODE 14, MAP VOLTAGE TOO HIGH (1 OF 2)

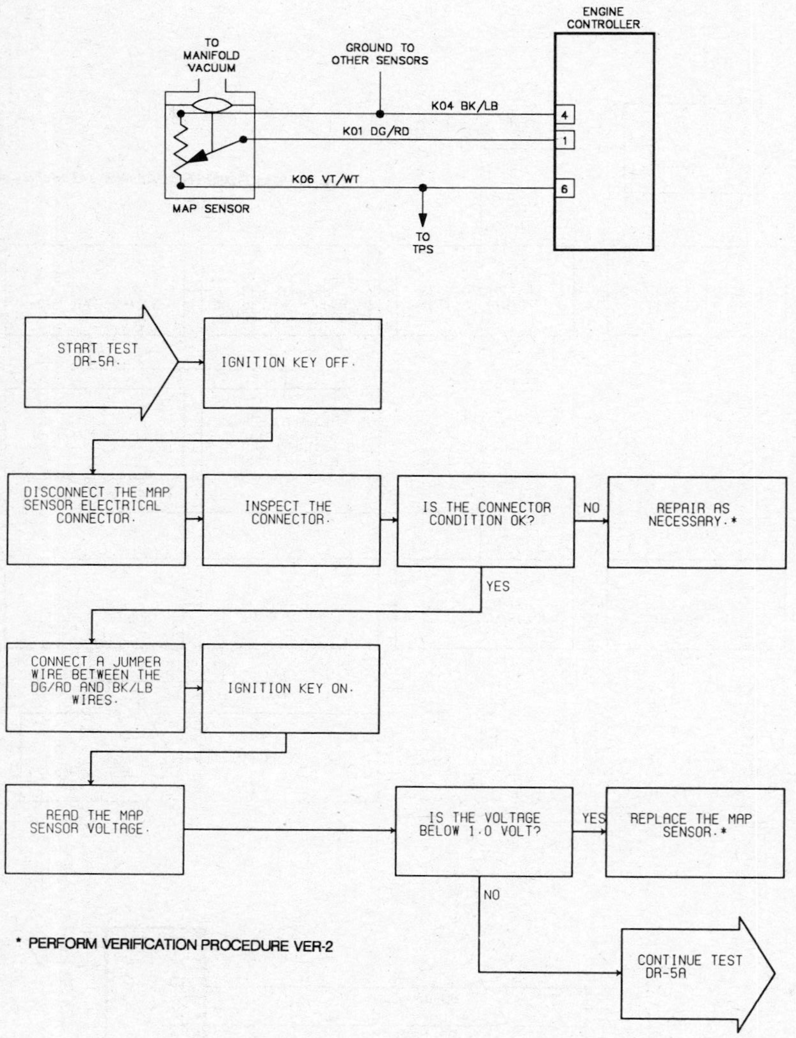
TO MANIFOLD VACUUM
GROUND TO OTHER SENSORS
ENGINE CONTROLLER
K04 BK/LB
K01 DG/RD
K06 VT/WT
4
1
6
MAP SENSOR
TO TPS
START TEST DR-5A.
IGNITION KEY OFF.
DISCONNECT THE MAP SENSOR ELECTRICAL CONNECTOR.
INSPECT THE CONNECTOR.
IS THE CONNECTOR CONDITION OK?
NO
REPAIR AS NECESSARY.*
YES
CONNECT A JUMPER WIRE BETWEEN THE DG/RD AND BK/LB WIRES.
IGNITION KEY ON.
READ THE MAP SENSOR VOLTAGE.
IS THE VOLTAGE BELOW 1.0 VOLT?
YES
REPLACE THE MAP SENSOR.*
NO
CONTINUE TEST DR-5A

* PERFORM VERIFICATION PROCEDURE VER-2

91E08913 91J08977

Fig. 49: Driveability Test 5A (3.0L VIN 3) – Code 14, MAP Voltage Too High (1 of 2)

DR-5A: CODE 14, MAP VOLTAGE TOO HIGH (2 OF 2)

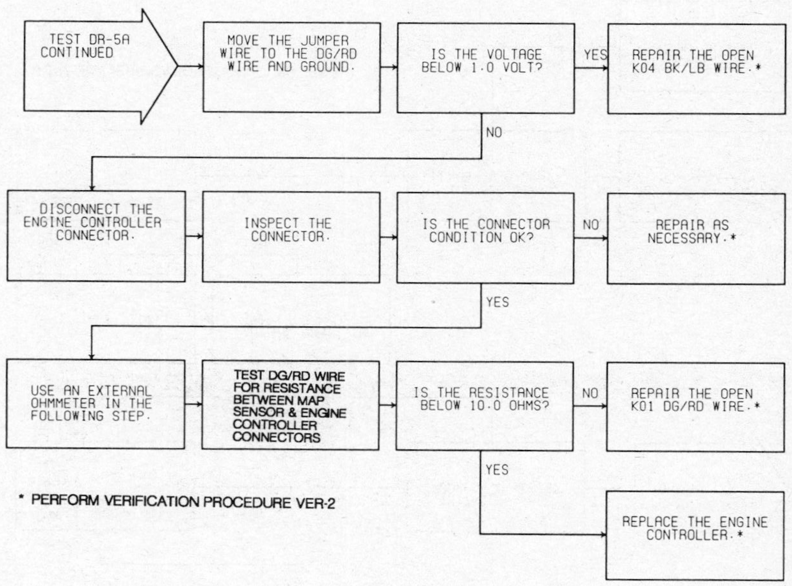
TEST DR-5A CONTINUED
MOVE THE JUMPER WIRE TO THE DG/RD WIRE AND GROUND.
IS THE VOLTAGE BELOW 1.0 VOLT?
YES
REPAIR THE OPEN K04 BK/LB WIRE.*
NO
DISCONNECT THE ENGINE CONTROLLER CONNECTOR.
INSPECT THE CONNECTOR.
IS THE CONNECTOR CONDITION OK?
NO
REPAIR AS NECESSARY.*
YES
USE AN EXTERNAL OHMMETER IN THE FOLLOWING STEP.
TEST DG/RD WIRE FOR RESISTANCE BETWEEN MAP SENSOR & ENGINE CONTROLLER CONNECTORS
IS THE RESISTANCE BELOW 10.0 OHMS?
NO
REPAIR THE OPEN K01 DG/RD WIRE.*
YES
REPLACE THE ENGINE CONTROLLER.*

* PERFORM VERIFICATION PROCEDURE VER-2

91B08978

Fig. 50: Driveability Test 5A (3.0L VIN 3) – Code 14, MAP Voltage Too High (2 of 2)

DR-6A: CODE 15, NO VEHICLE SPEED SIGNAL (1 OF 3)

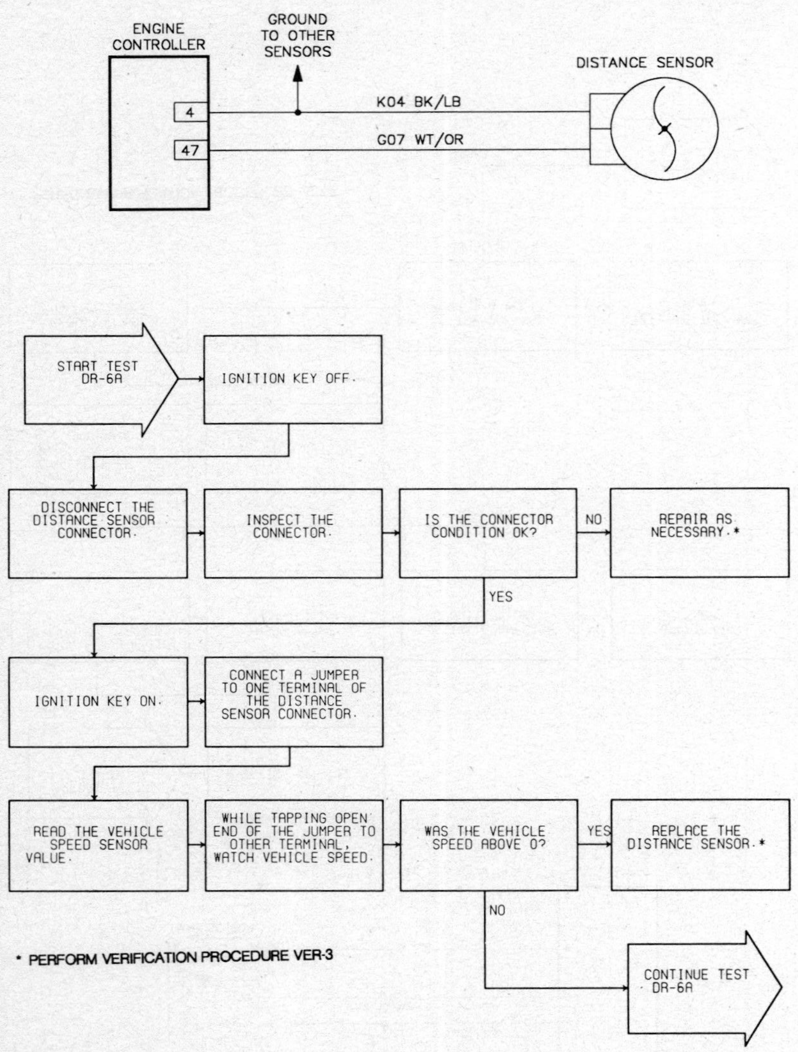
ENGINE CONTROLLER
GROUND TO OTHER SENSORS
DISTANCE SENSOR
4
47
K04 BK/LB
G07 WT/OR
START TEST DR-6A
IGNITION KEY OFF.
DISCONNECT THE DISTANCE SENSOR CONNECTOR.
INSPECT THE CONNECTOR.
IS THE CONNECTOR CONDITION OK?
NO
REPAIR AS NECESSARY.*
YES
IGNITION KEY ON.
CONNECT A JUMPER TO ONE TERMINAL OF THE DISTANCE SENSOR CONNECTOR.
READ THE VEHICLE SPEED SENSOR VALUE.
WHILE TAPPING OPEN END OF THE JUMPER TO OTHER TERMINAL, WATCH VEHICLE SPEED.
WAS THE VEHICLE SPEED ABOVE 0?
YES
REPLACE THE DISTANCE SENSOR.*
NO
CONTINUE TEST DR-6A

* PERFORM VERIFICATION PROCEDURE VER-3

91D08917 91D08979

Fig. 51: Driveability Test 6A (3.0L VIN 3) – Code 15, No Vehicle Speed Signal (1 of 3)

DR-6A: CODE 15, NO VEHICLE SPEED SIGNAL (2 OF 3)

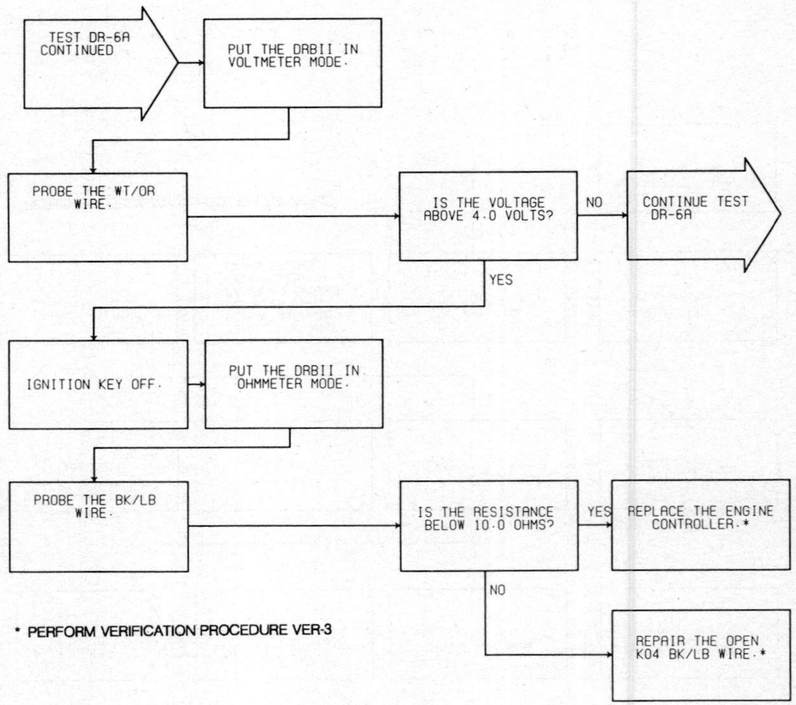
TEST DR-6A CONTINUED
PUT THE DRBII IN VOLTMETER MODE.
PROBE THE WT/OR WIRE.
IS THE VOLTAGE ABOVE 4.0 VOLTS?
NO
CONTINUE TEST DR-6A
YES
IGNITION KEY OFF.
PUT THE DRBII IN OHMMETER MODE.
PROBE THE BK/LB WIRE.
IS THE RESISTANCE BELOW 10.0 OHMS?
YES
REPLACE THE ENGINE CONTROLLER.*
NO
REPAIR THE OPEN K04 BK/LB WIRE.*

* PERFORM VERIFICATION PROCEDURE VER-3

91F08980

Fig. 52: Driveability Test 6A (3.0L VIN 3) – Code 15, No Vehicle Speed Signal (2 of 3)

DR-6A: CODE 15, NO VEHICLE SPEED SIGNAL (3 OF 3)

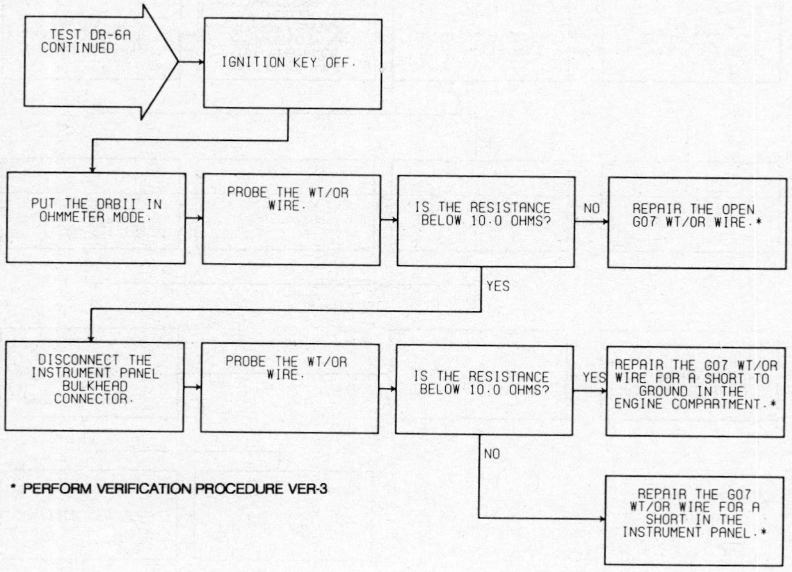
TEST DR-6A CONTINUED
IGNITION KEY OFF.
PUT THE DRBII IN OHMMETER MODE.
PROBE THE WT/OR WIRE.
IS THE RESISTANCE BELOW 10.0 OHMS?
NO
REPAIR THE OPEN G07 WT/OR WIRE.*
YES
DISCONNECT THE INSTRUMENT PANEL BULKHEAD CONNECTOR.
PROBE THE WT/OR WIRE.
IS THE RESISTANCE BELOW 10.0 OHMS?
YES
REPAIR THE G07 WT/OR WIRE FOR A SHORT TO GROUND IN THE ENGINE COMPARTMENT.*
NO
REPAIR THE G07 WT/OR WIRE FOR A SHORT IN THE INSTRUMENT PANEL.*
* PERFORM VERIFICATION PROCEDURE VER-3

91H08981

Fig. 53: Driveability Test 6A (3.0L VIN 3) – Code 15, No Vehicle Speed Signal (3 of 3)

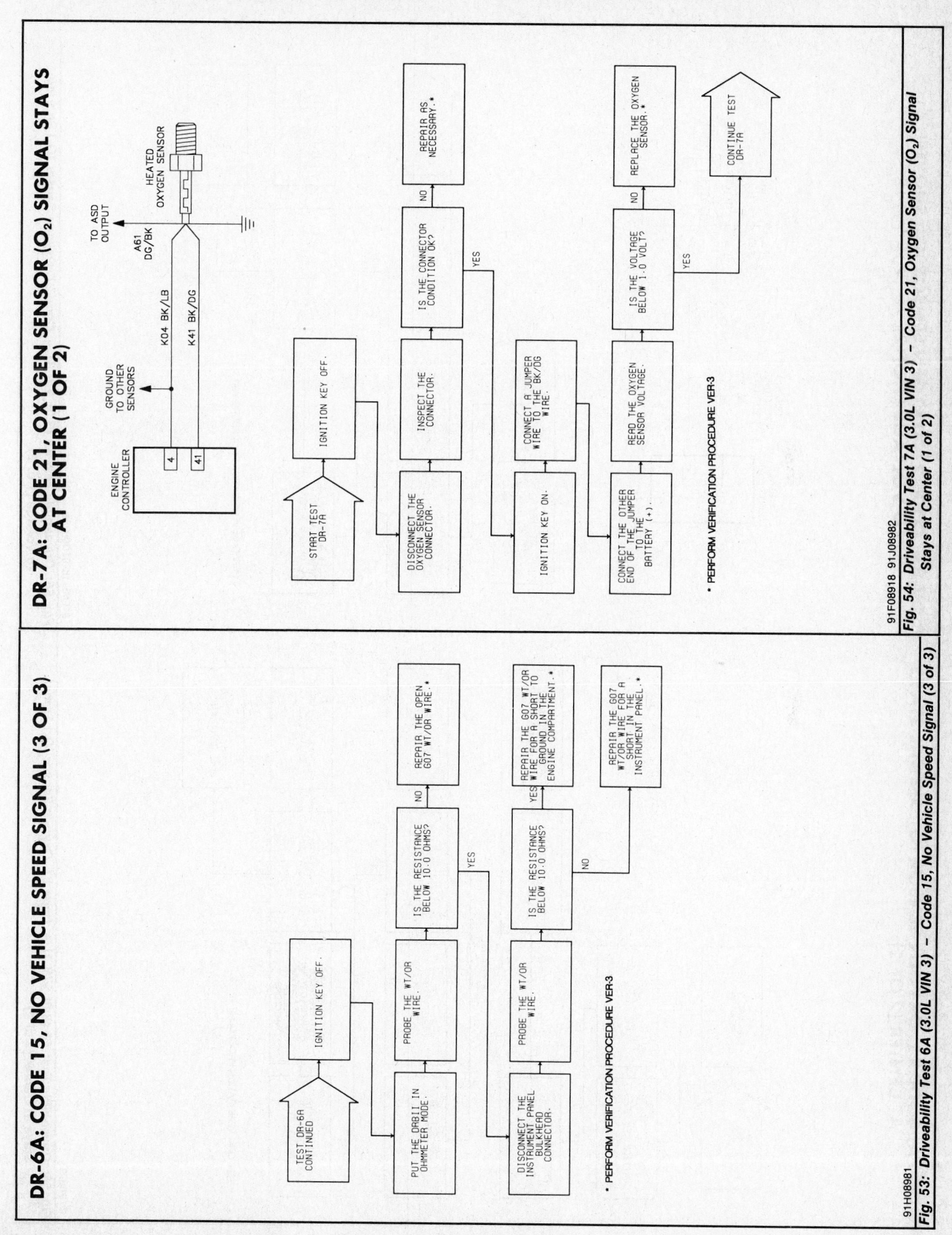

DR-7A: CODE 21, OXYGEN SENSOR (O_2) SIGNAL STAYS AT CENTER (1 OF 2)

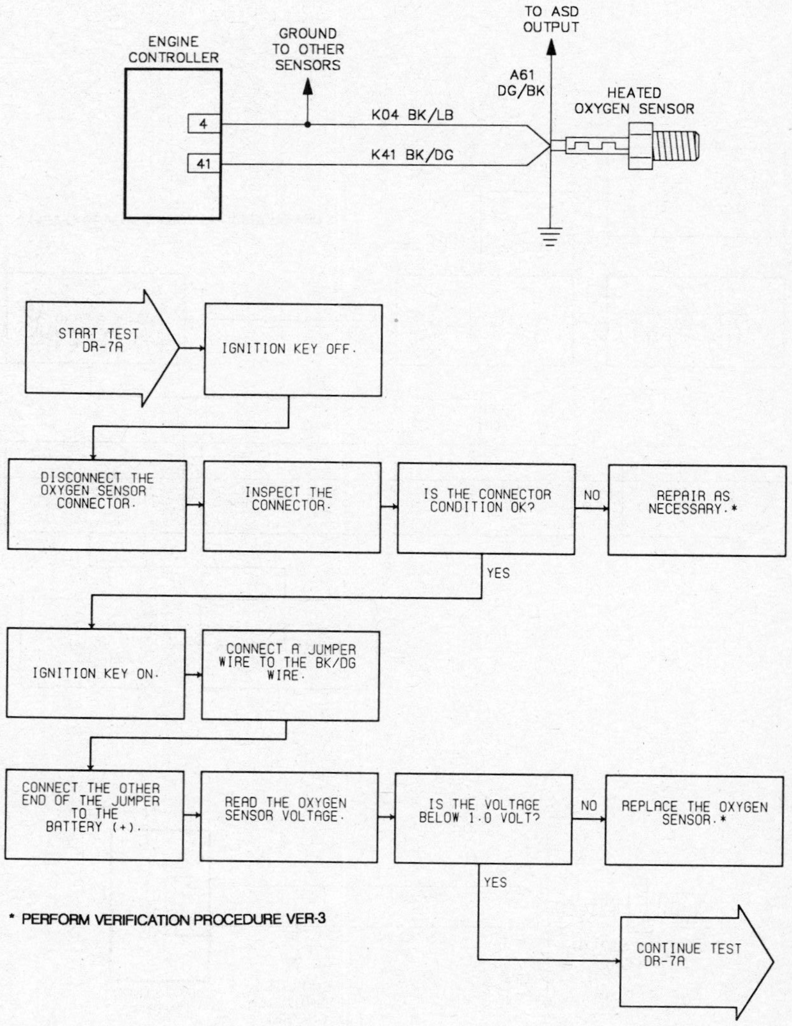
ENGINE CONTROLLER
4
41
GROUND TO OTHER SENSORS
K04 BK/LB
K41 BK/DG
TO ASD OUTPUT
A61 DG/BK
HEATED OXYGEN SENSOR
START TEST DR-7A
IGNITION KEY OFF.
DISCONNECT THE OXYGEN SENSOR CONNECTOR.
INSPECT THE CONNECTOR.
IS THE CONNECTOR CONDITION OK?
NO
REPAIR AS NECESSARY.*
YES
IGNITION KEY ON.
CONNECT A JUMPER WIRE TO THE BK/DG WIRE.
CONNECT THE OTHER END OF THE JUMPER TO THE BATTERY (+).
READ THE OXYGEN SENSOR VOLTAGE.
IS THE VOLTAGE BELOW 1.0 VOLT?
NO
REPLACE THE OXYGEN SENSOR.*
YES
CONTINUE TEST DR-7A
* PERFORM VERIFICATION PROCEDURE VER-3

91F08918 91J08982

Fig. 54: Driveability Test 7A (3.0L VIN 3) – Code 21, Oxygen Sensor (O_2) Signal Stays at Center (1 of 2)

DR-7A: CODE 21, OXYGEN SENSOR (O_2) SIGNAL STAYS AT CENTER (2 OF 2)

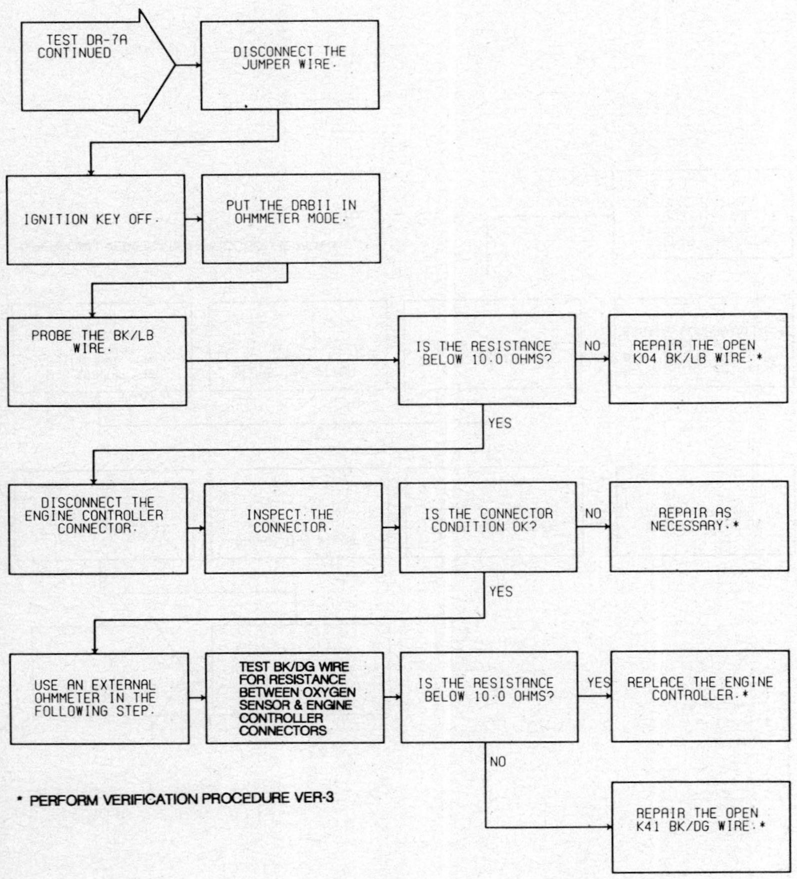
TEST DR-7A CONTINUED
DISCONNECT THE JUMPER WIRE.
IGNITION KEY OFF.
PUT THE DRBII IN OHMMETER MODE.
PROBE THE BK/LB WIRE.
IS THE RESISTANCE BELOW 10.0 OHMS?
NO
REPAIR THE OPEN K04 BK/LB WIRE.*
YES
DISCONNECT THE ENGINE CONTROLLER CONNECTOR.
INSPECT THE CONNECTOR.
IS THE CONNECTOR CONDITION OK?
NO
REPAIR AS NECESSARY.*
YES
USE AN EXTERNAL OHMMETER IN THE FOLLOWING STEP.
TEST BK/DG WIRE FOR RESISTANCE BETWEEN OXYGEN SENSOR & ENGINE CONTROLLER CONNECTORS
IS THE RESISTANCE BELOW 10.0 OHMS?
YES
REPLACE THE ENGINE CONTROLLER.*
NO
REPAIR THE OPEN K41 BK/DG WIRE.*

* PERFORM VERIFICATION PROCEDURE VER-3

91B08983

Fig. 55: Driveability Test 7A (3.0L VIN 3) – Code 21, Oxygen Sensor (O_2) Signal Stays at Center (2 of 2)

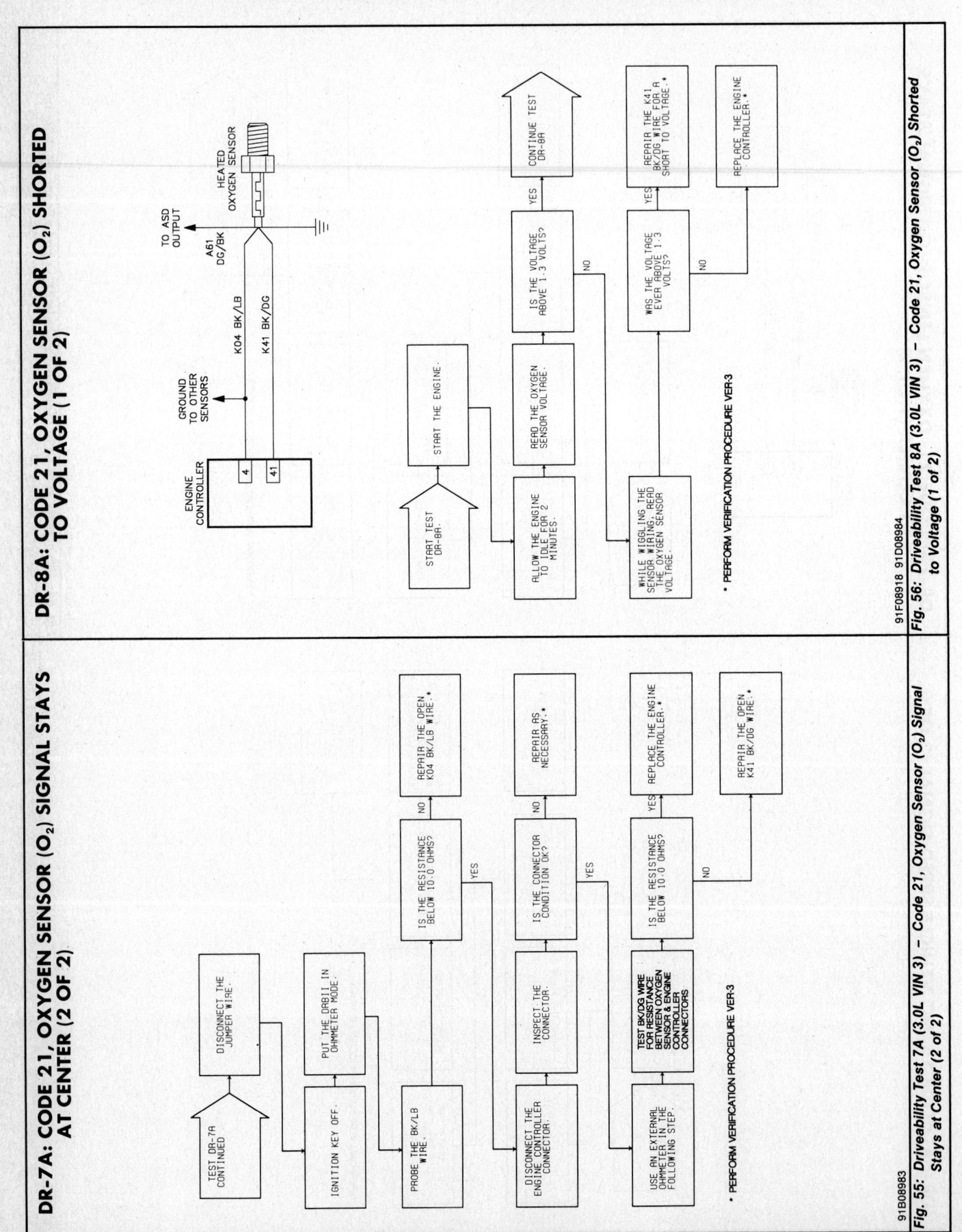

DR-8A: CODE 21, OXYGEN SENSOR (O_2) SHORTED TO VOLTAGE (1 OF 2)

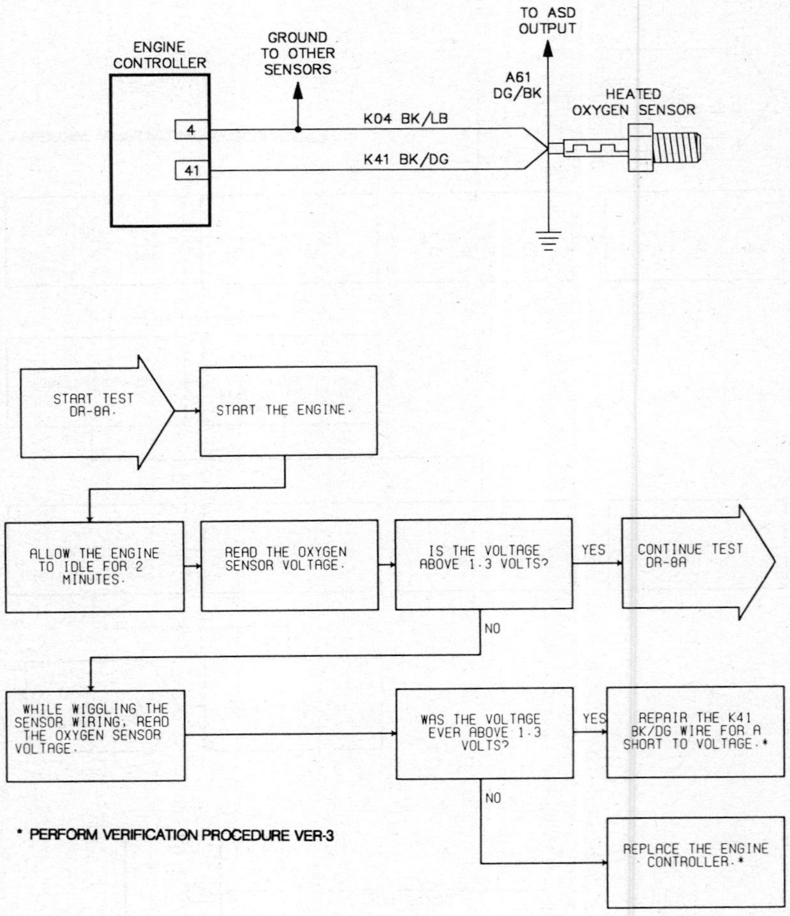
ENGINE CONTROLLER
4
41
GROUND TO OTHER SENSORS
K04 BK/LB
K41 BK/DG
TO ASD OUTPUT
A61 DG/BK
HEATED OXYGEN SENSOR
START TEST DR-8A.
START THE ENGINE.
ALLOW THE ENGINE TO IDLE FOR 2 MINUTES.
READ THE OXYGEN SENSOR VOLTAGE.
IS THE VOLTAGE ABOVE 1.3 VOLTS?
YES
CONTINUE TEST DR-8A
NO
WHILE WIGGLING THE SENSOR WIRING, READ THE OXYGEN SENSOR VOLTAGE.
WAS THE VOLTAGE EVER ABOVE 1.3 VOLTS?
YES
REPAIR THE K41 BK/DG WIRE FOR A SHORT TO VOLTAGE.*
NO
REPLACE THE ENGINE CONTROLLER.*

* PERFORM VERIFICATION PROCEDURE VER-3

91F08918 91D08984

Fig. 56: Driveability Test 8A (3.0L VIN 3) – Code 21, Oxygen Sensor (O_2) Shorted to Voltage (1 of 2)

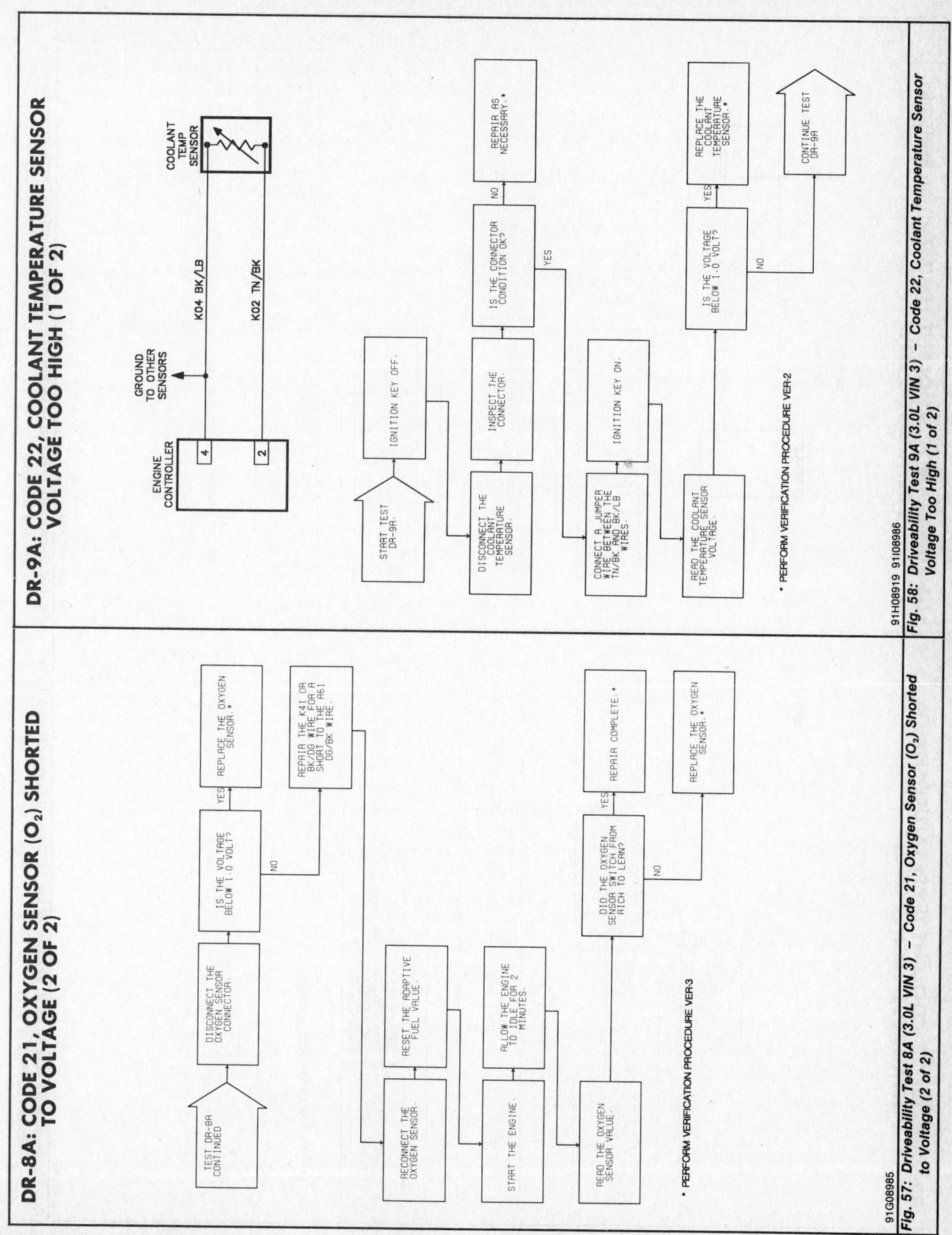

DR-8A: CODE 21, OXYGEN SENSOR (O_2) SHORTED TO VOLTAGE (2 OF 2)

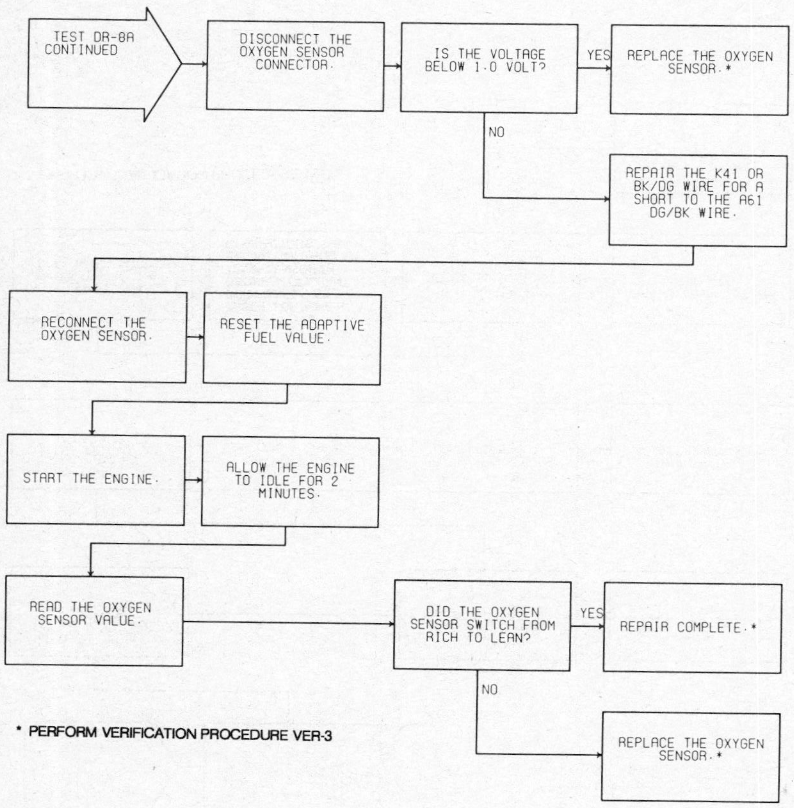
TEST DR-8A CONTINUED
DISCONNECT THE OXYGEN SENSOR CONNECTOR.
IS THE VOLTAGE BELOW 1.0 VOLT?
YES
REPLACE THE OXYGEN SENSOR.*
NO
REPAIR THE K41 OR BK/DG WIRE FOR A SHORT TO THE A61 DG/BK WIRE.
RECONNECT THE OXYGEN SENSOR.
RESET THE ADAPTIVE FUEL VALUE.
START THE ENGINE.
ALLOW THE ENGINE TO IDLE FOR 2 MINUTES.
READ THE OXYGEN SENSOR VALUE.
DID THE OXYGEN SENSOR SWITCH FROM RICH TO LEAN?
YES
REPAIR COMPLETE.*
NO
REPLACE THE OXYGEN SENSOR.*

* PERFORM VERIFICATION PROCEDURE VER-3

91G08985

Fig. 57: ***Driveability Test 8A (3.0L VIN 3) – Code 21, Oxygen Sensor (O_2) Shorted to Voltage (2 of 2)***

DR-9A: CODE 22, COOLANT TEMPERATURE SENSOR VOLTAGE TOO HIGH (1 OF 2)

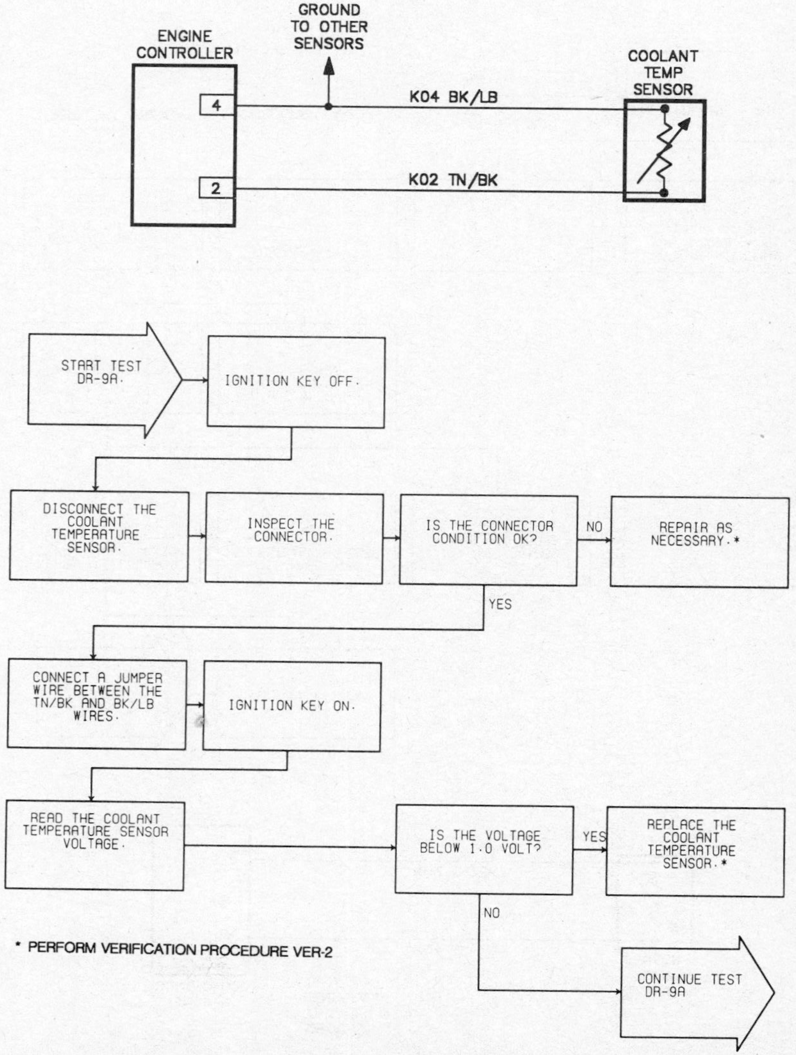
ENGINE CONTROLLER
GROUND TO OTHER SENSORS
COOLANT TEMP SENSOR
4
2
K04 BK/LB
K02 TN/BK
START TEST DR-9A.
IGNITION KEY OFF.
DISCONNECT THE COOLANT TEMPERATURE SENSOR.
INSPECT THE CONNECTOR.
IS THE CONNECTOR CONDITION OK?
NO
REPAIR AS NECESSARY.*
YES
CONNECT A JUMPER WIRE BETWEEN THE TN/BK AND BK/LB WIRES.
IGNITION KEY ON.
READ THE COOLANT TEMPERATURE SENSOR VOLTAGE.
IS THE VOLTAGE BELOW 1.0 VOLT?
YES
REPLACE THE COOLANT TEMPERATURE SENSOR.*
NO
CONTINUE TEST DR-9A

* PERFORM VERIFICATION PROCEDURE VER-2

91H08919 91I08986

Fig. 58: ***Driveability Test 9A (3.0L VIN 3) – Code 22, Coolant Temperature Sensor Voltage Too High (1 of 2)***

1991 ENGINE PERFORMANCE
Self-Diagnostics – 3.0L VIN 3 (Cont.)

DR-9A: CODE 22, COOLANT TEMPERATURE SENSOR VOLTAGE TOO HIGH (2 OF 2)

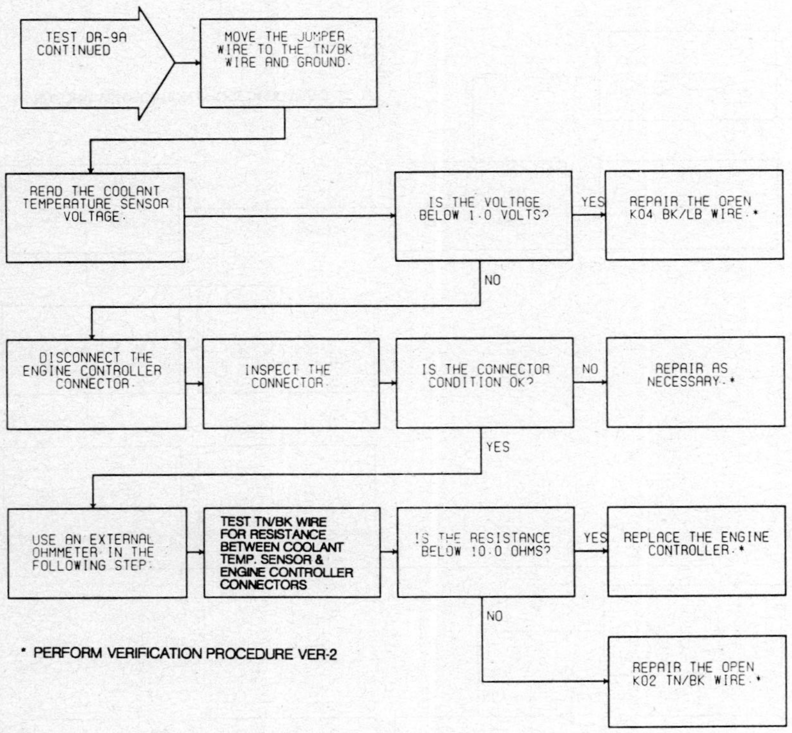
TEST DR-9A CONTINUED
MOVE THE JUMPER WIRE TO THE TN/BK WIRE AND GROUND.
READ THE COOLANT TEMPERATURE SENSOR VOLTAGE.
IS THE VOLTAGE BELOW 1.0 VOLTS?
YES
REPAIR THE OPEN K04 BK/LB WIRE.*
NO
DISCONNECT THE ENGINE CONTROLLER CONNECTOR.
INSPECT THE CONNECTOR.
IS THE CONNECTOR CONDITION OK?
NO
REPAIR AS NECESSARY.*
YES
USE AN EXTERNAL OHMMETER IN THE FOLLOWING STEP.
TEST TN/BK WIRE FOR RESISTANCE BETWEEN COOLANT TEMP. SENSOR & ENGINE CONTROLLER CONNECTORS
IS THE RESISTANCE BELOW 10.0 OHMS?
YES
REPLACE THE ENGINE CONTROLLER.*
NO
REPAIR THE OPEN K02 TN/BK WIRE.*

* PERFORM VERIFICATION PROCEDURE VER-2

91A08987

Fig. 59: Driveability Test 9A (3.0L VIN 3) – Code 22, Coolant Temperature Sensor Voltage Too High (2 of 2)

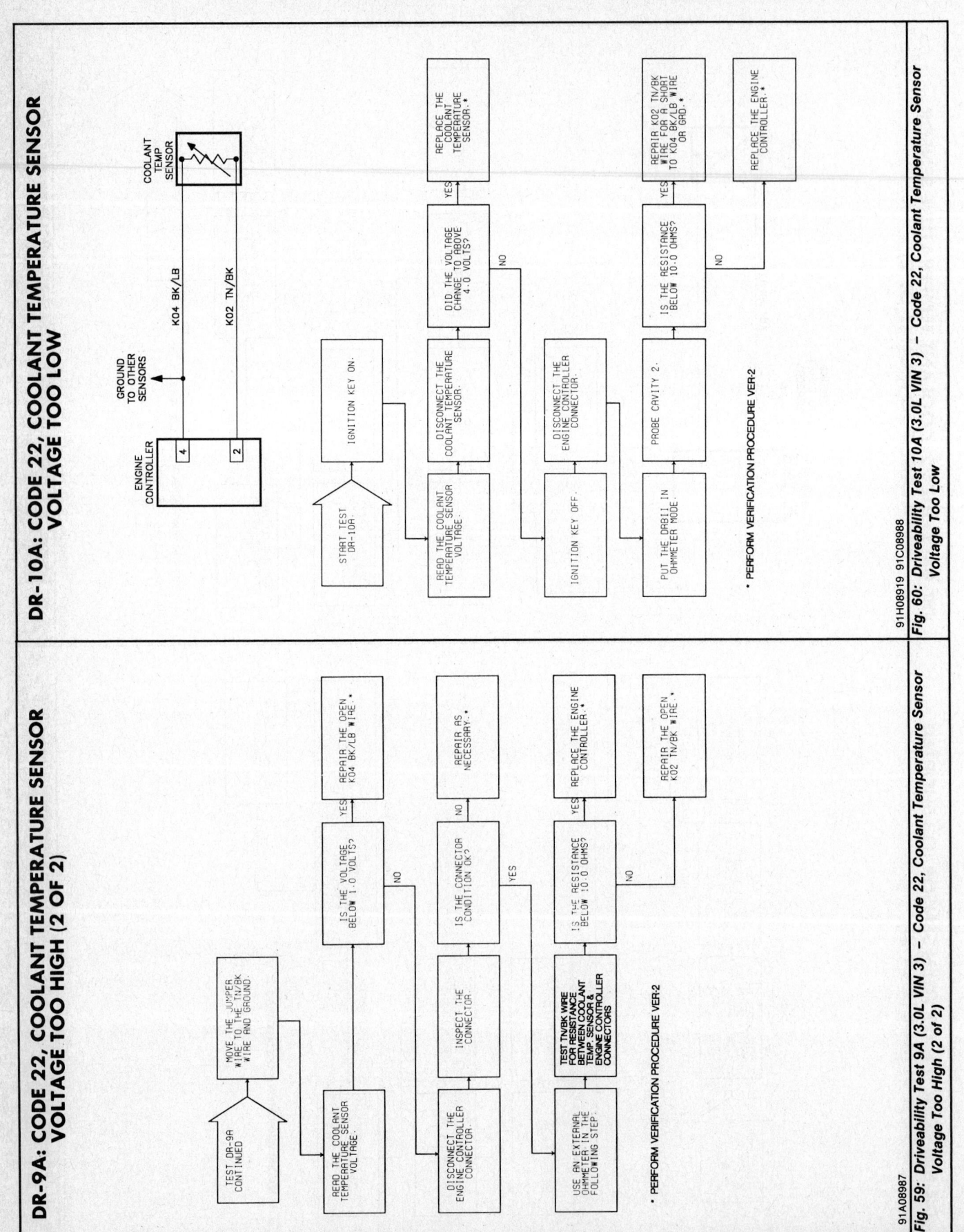

DR-10A: CODE 22, COOLANT TEMPERATURE SENSOR VOLTAGE TOO LOW

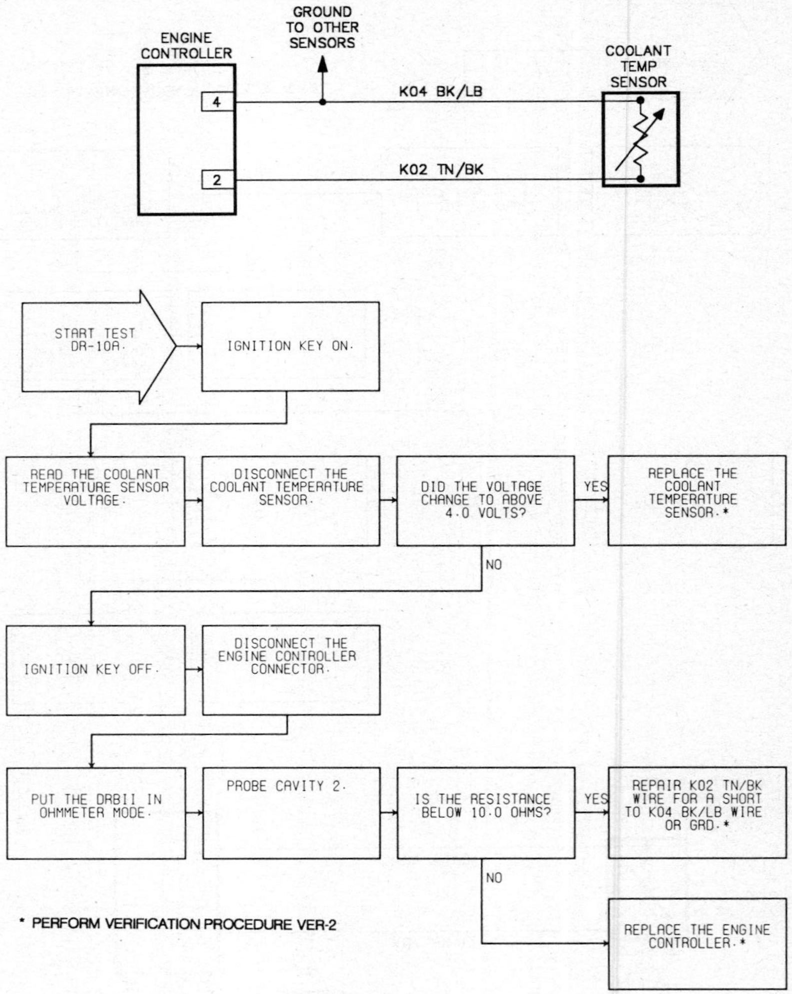
ENGINE CONTROLLER
4
2
GROUND TO OTHER SENSORS
K04 BK/LB
K02 TN/BK
COOLANT TEMP SENSOR
START TEST DR-10A.
IGNITION KEY ON.
READ THE COOLANT TEMPERATURE SENSOR VOLTAGE.
DISCONNECT THE COOLANT TEMPERATURE SENSOR.
DID THE VOLTAGE CHANGE TO ABOVE 4.0 VOLTS?
YES
REPLACE THE COOLANT TEMPERATURE SENSOR.*
NO
IGNITION KEY OFF.
DISCONNECT THE ENGINE CONTROLLER CONNECTOR.
PUT THE DRBII IN OHMMETER MODE.
PROBE CAVITY 2.
IS THE RESISTANCE BELOW 10.0 OHMS?
YES
REPAIR K02 TN/BK WIRE FOR A SHORT TO K04 BK/LB WIRE OR GRD.*
NO
REPLACE THE ENGINE CONTROLLER.*

* PERFORM VERIFICATION PROCEDURE VER-2

91H08919 91C08988

Fig. 60: Driveability Test 10A (3.0L VIN 3) – Code 22, Coolant Temperature Sensor Voltage Too Low

DR-11A: CODE 24, THROTTLE POSITION SENSOR (TPS) VOLTAGE HIGH (1 OF 2)

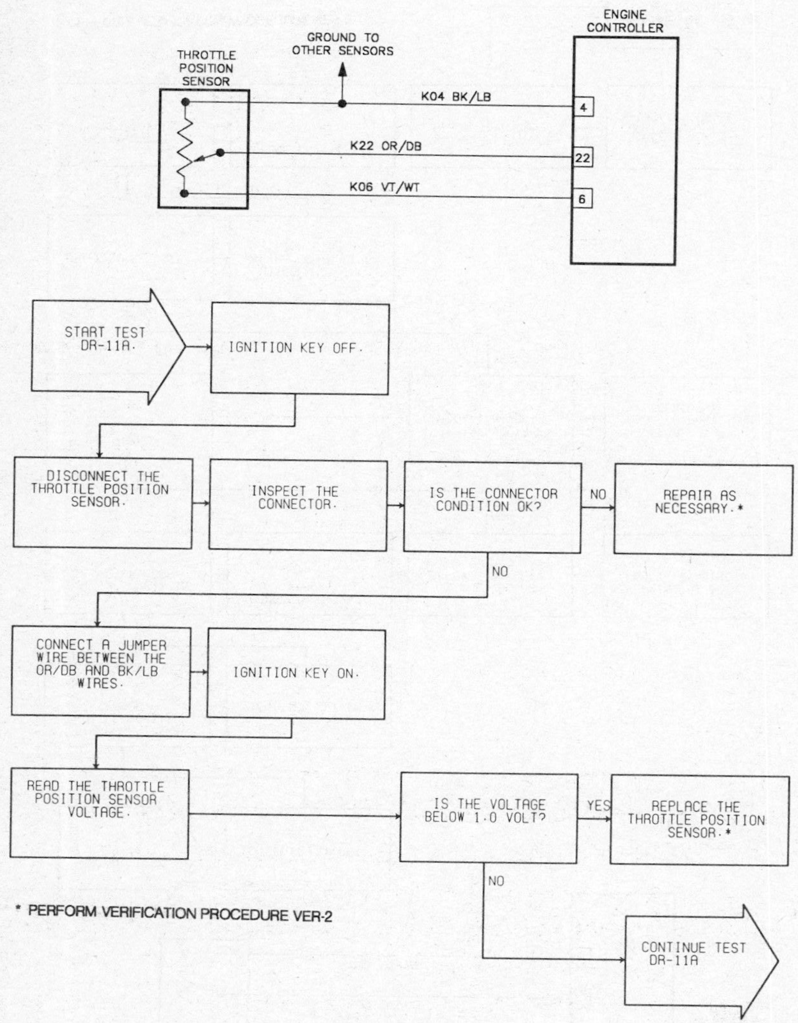

ENGINE CONTROLLER
THROTTLE POSITION SENSOR
GROUND TO OTHER SENSORS
K04 BK/LB
K22 OR/DB
K06 VT/WT
4
22
6
START TEST DR-11A.
IGNITION KEY OFF.
DISCONNECT THE THROTTLE POSITION SENSOR.
INSPECT THE CONNECTOR.
IS THE CONNECTOR CONDITION OK?
NO
REPAIR AS NECESSARY.*
NO
CONNECT A JUMPER WIRE BETWEEN THE OR/DB AND BK/LB WIRES.
IGNITION KEY ON.
READ THE THROTTLE POSITION SENSOR VOLTAGE.
IS THE VOLTAGE BELOW 1.0 VOLT?
YES
REPLACE THE THROTTLE POSITION SENSOR.*
NO
CONTINUE TEST DR-11A
* PERFORM VERIFICATION PROCEDURE VER-2

91J08920 91E08989

Fig. 61: Driveability Test 11A (3.0L VIN 3) – Code 24, Throttle Position Sensor (TPS) Voltage High (1 of 2)

DR-11A: CODE 24, THROTTLE POSITION SENSOR (TPS) VOLTAGE HIGH (2 OF 2)

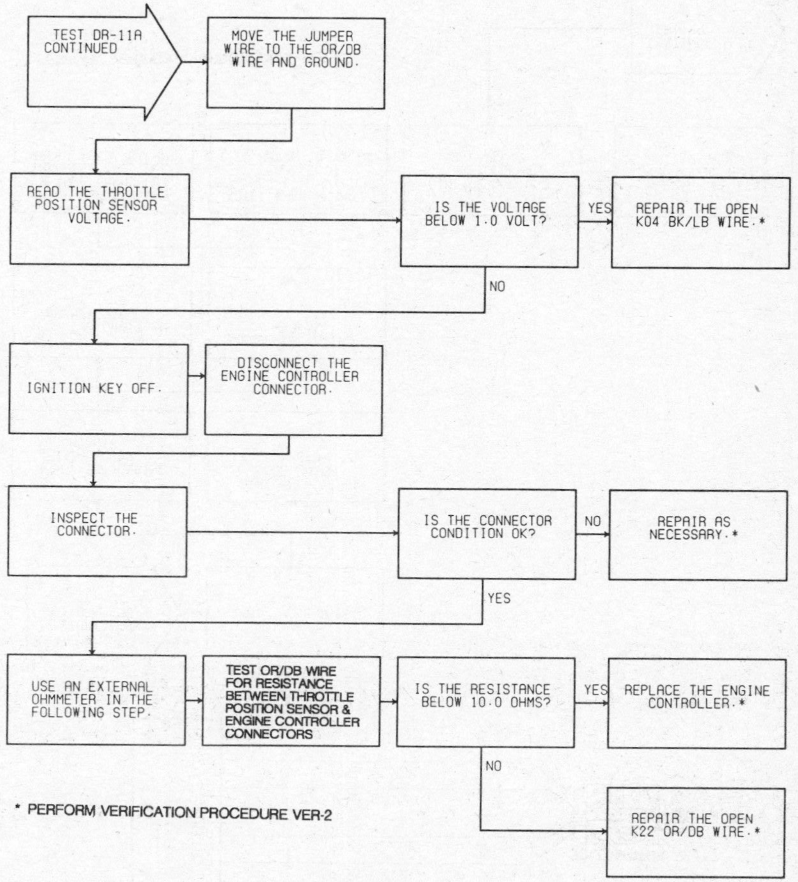

TEST DR-11A CONTINUED
MOVE THE JUMPER WIRE TO THE OR/DB WIRE AND GROUND.
READ THE THROTTLE POSITION SENSOR VOLTAGE.
IS THE VOLTAGE BELOW 1.0 VOLT?
YES
REPAIR THE OPEN K04 BK/LB WIRE.*
NO
IGNITION KEY OFF.
DISCONNECT THE ENGINE CONTROLLER CONNECTOR.
INSPECT THE CONNECTOR.
IS THE CONNECTOR CONDITION OK?
NO
REPAIR AS NECESSARY.*
YES
USE AN EXTERNAL OHMMETER IN THE FOLLOWING STEP.
TEST OR/DB WIRE FOR RESISTANCE BETWEEN THROTTLE POSITION SENSOR & ENGINE CONTROLLER CONNECTORS
IS THE RESISTANCE BELOW 10.0 OHMS?
YES
REPLACE THE ENGINE CONTROLLER.*
NO
REPAIR THE OPEN K22 OR/DB WIRE.*
* PERFORM VERIFICATION PROCEDURE VER-2

91G08990

Fig. 62: Driveability Test 11A (3.0L VIN 3) – Code 24, Throttle Position Sensor (TPS) Voltage High (2 of 2)

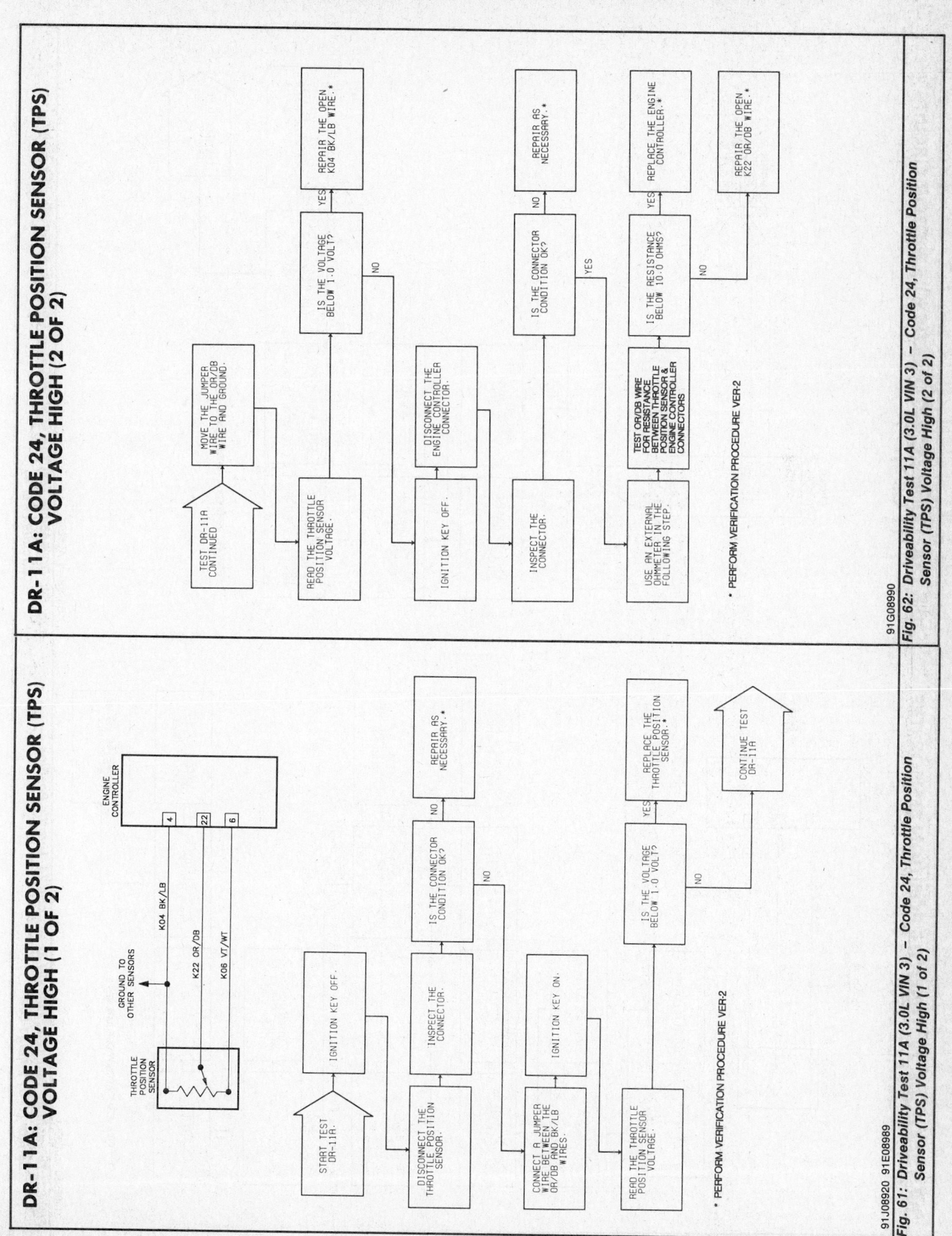

1991 ENGINE PERFORMANCE
Self-Diagnostics – 3.0L VIN 3 (Cont.)

DR-12A: CODE 24, THROTTLE POSITION SENSOR (TPS) VOLTAGE LOW

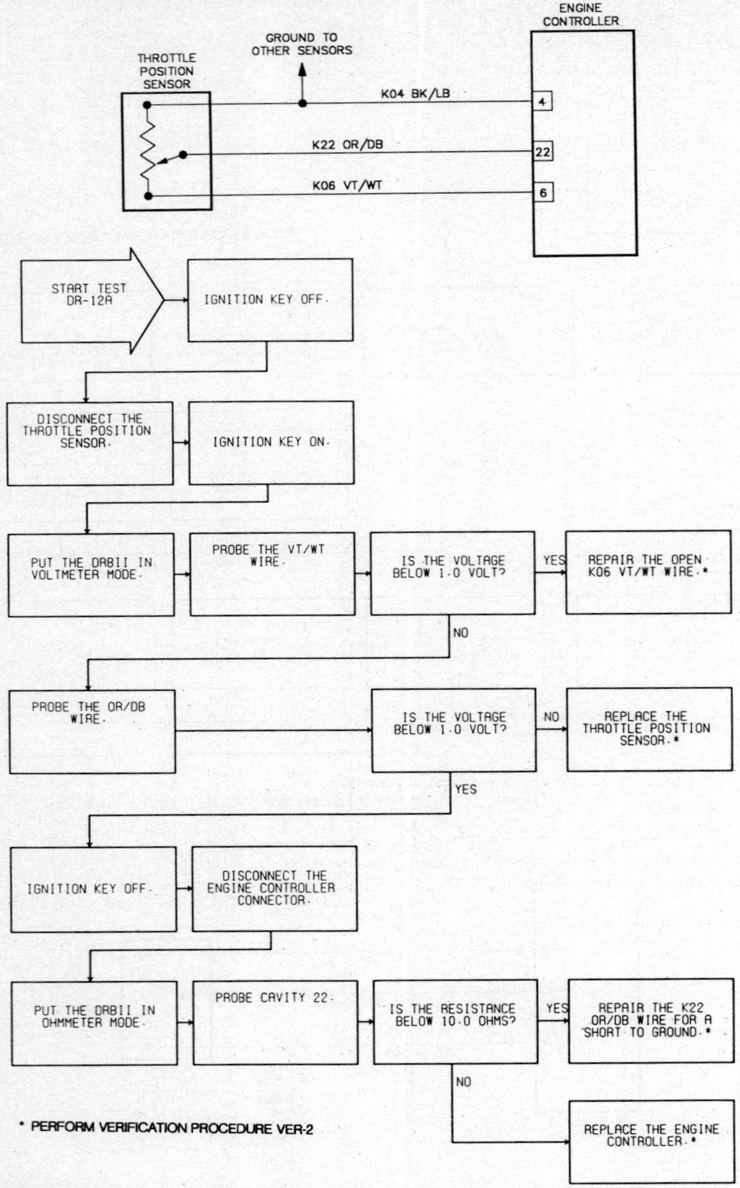
ENGINE CONTROLLER
THROTTLE POSITION SENSOR
GROUND TO OTHER SENSORS
K04 BK/LB
K22 OR/DB
K06 VT/WT
4
22
6
START TEST DR-12A
IGNITION KEY OFF.
DISCONNECT THE THROTTLE POSITION SENSOR.
IGNITION KEY ON.
PUT THE DRBII IN VOLTMETER MODE.
PROBE THE VT/WT WIRE.
IS THE VOLTAGE BELOW 1.0 VOLT?
YES
REPAIR THE OPEN K06 VT/WT WIRE.*
NO
PROBE THE OR/DB WIRE.
IS THE VOLTAGE BELOW 1.0 VOLT?
NO
REPLACE THE THROTTLE POSITION SENSOR.*
YES
IGNITION KEY OFF.
DISCONNECT THE ENGINE CONTROLLER CONNECTOR.
PUT THE DRBII IN OHMMETER MODE.
PROBE CAVITY 22.
IS THE RESISTANCE BELOW 10.0 OHMS?
YES
REPAIR THE K22 OR/DB WIRE FOR A SHORT TO GROUND.*
NO
REPLACE THE ENGINE CONTROLLER.*

* PERFORM VERIFICATION PROCEDURE VER-2

91J08920 91I08991

Fig. 63: ***Driveability Test 12A (3.0L VIN 3) – Code 24, Throttle Position Sensor (TPS) Voltage Low***

DR-13A: CODE 25, AUTOMATIC IDLE MOTOR CIRCUITS (1 OF 4)

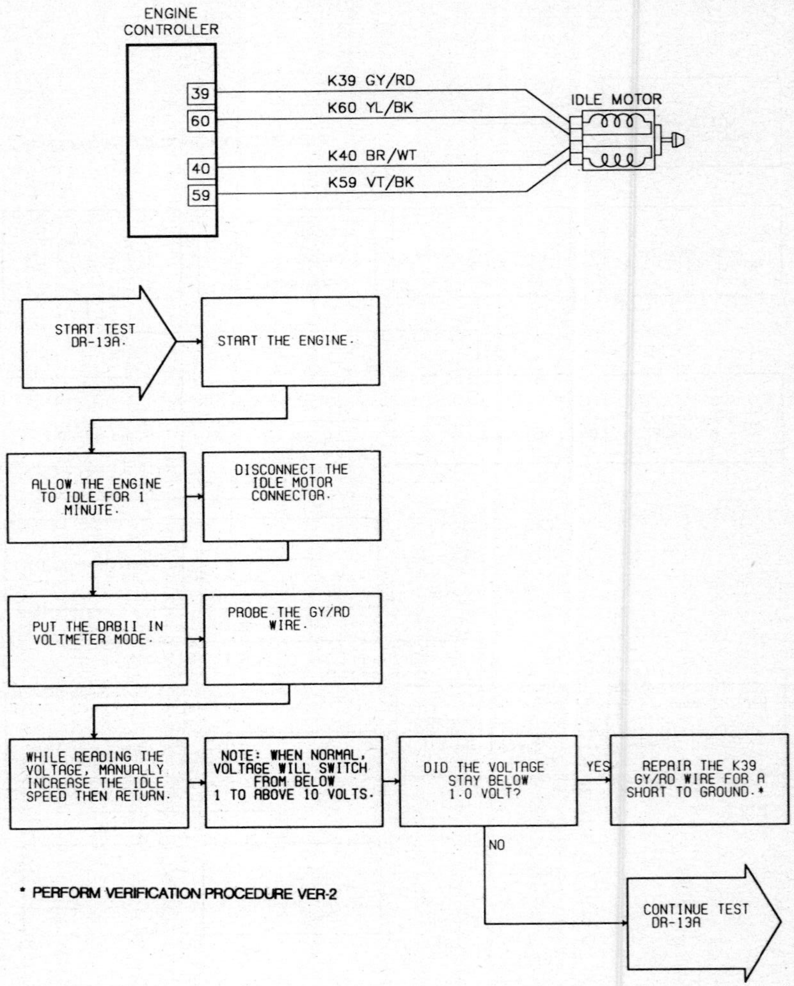
ENGINE CONTROLLER
39
60
40
59
K39 GY/RD
K60 YL/BK
K40 BR/WT
K59 VT/BK
IDLE MOTOR
START TEST DR-13A.
START THE ENGINE.
ALLOW THE ENGINE TO IDLE FOR 1 MINUTE.
DISCONNECT THE IDLE MOTOR CONNECTOR.
PUT THE DRBII IN VOLTMETER MODE.
PROBE THE GY/RD WIRE.
WHILE READING THE VOLTAGE, MANUALLY INCREASE THE IDLE SPEED THEN RETURN.
NOTE: WHEN NORMAL, VOLTAGE WILL SWITCH FROM BELOW 1 TO ABOVE 10 VOLTS.
DID THE VOLTAGE STAY BELOW 1.0 VOLT?
YES
REPAIR THE K39 GY/RD WIRE FOR A SHORT TO GROUND.*
NO
CONTINUE TEST DR-13A

* PERFORM VERIFICATION PROCEDURE VER-2

91B08921 91A08992

Fig. 64: ***Driveability Test 13A (3.0L VIN 3) – Code 25, Automatic Idle Motor Circuits (1 of 4)***

DR-13A: CODE 25, AUTOMATIC IDLE MOTOR CIRCUITS (2 OF 4)

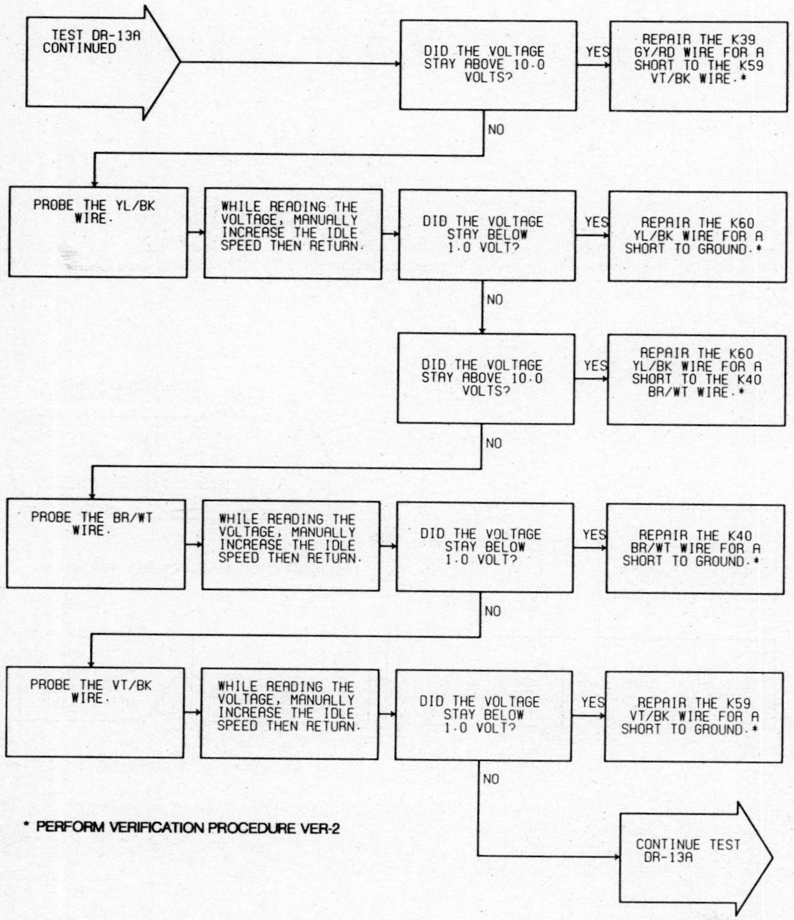
TEST DR-13A CONTINUED
DID THE VOLTAGE STAY ABOVE 10.0 VOLTS?
YES
REPAIR THE K39 GY/RD WIRE FOR A SHORT TO THE K59 VT/BK WIRE.*
NO
PROBE THE YL/BK WIRE.
WHILE READING THE VOLTAGE, MANUALLY INCREASE THE IDLE SPEED THEN RETURN.
DID THE VOLTAGE STAY BELOW 1.0 VOLT?
YES
REPAIR THE K60 YL/BK WIRE FOR A SHORT TO GROUND.*
NO
DID THE VOLTAGE STAY ABOVE 10.0 VOLTS?
YES
REPAIR THE K60 YL/BK WIRE FOR A SHORT TO THE K40 BR/WT WIRE.*
NO
PROBE THE BR/WT WIRE.
WHILE READING THE VOLTAGE, MANUALLY INCREASE THE IDLE SPEED THEN RETURN.
DID THE VOLTAGE STAY BELOW 1.0 VOLT?
YES
REPAIR THE K40 BR/WT WIRE FOR A SHORT TO GROUND.*
NO
PROBE THE VT/BK WIRE.
WHILE READING THE VOLTAGE, MANUALLY INCREASE THE IDLE SPEED THEN RETURN.
DID THE VOLTAGE STAY BELOW 1.0 VOLT?
YES
REPAIR THE K59 VT/BK WIRE FOR A SHORT TO GROUND.*
NO
CONTINUE TEST DR-13A

* PERFORM VERIFICATION PROCEDURE VER-2

91C08993

Fig. 65: Driveability Test 13A (3.0L VIN 3) – Code 25, Automatic Idle Motor Circuits (2 of 4)

DR-13A: CODE 25, AUTOMATIC IDLE MOTOR CIRCUITS (3 OF 4)

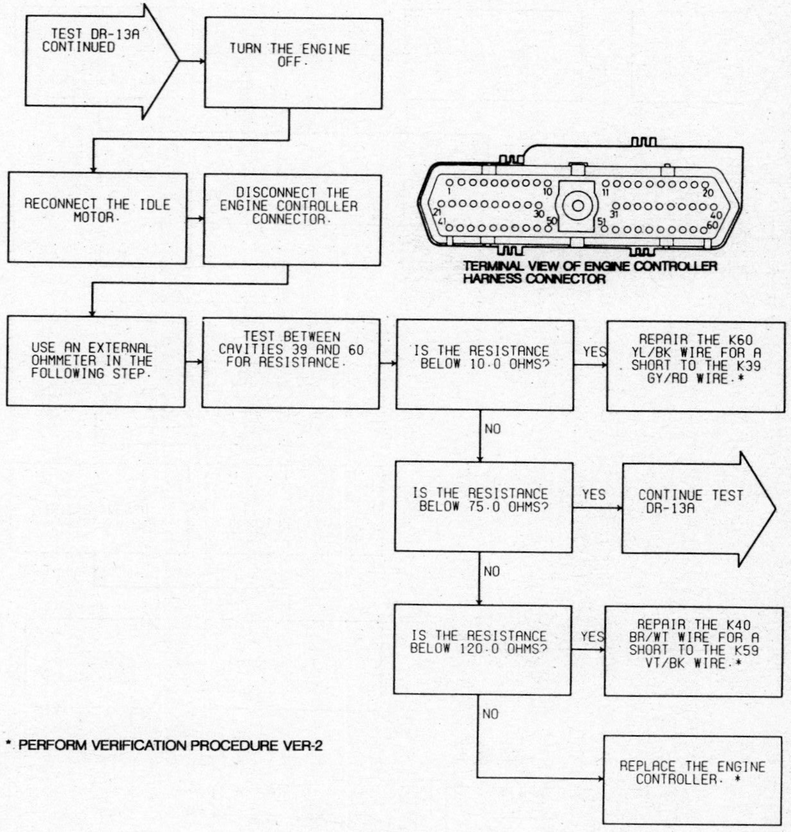
TEST DR-13A CONTINUED
TURN THE ENGINE OFF.
RECONNECT THE IDLE MOTOR.
DISCONNECT THE ENGINE CONTROLLER CONNECTOR.
TERMINAL VIEW OF ENGINE CONTROLLER HARNESS CONNECTOR
USE AN EXTERNAL OHMMETER IN THE FOLLOWING STEP.
TEST BETWEEN CAVITIES 39 AND 60 FOR RESISTANCE.
IS THE RESISTANCE BELOW 10.0 OHMS?
YES
REPAIR THE K60 YL/BK WIRE FOR A SHORT TO THE K39 GY/RD WIRE.*
NO
IS THE RESISTANCE BELOW 75.0 OHMS?
YES
CONTINUE TEST DR-13A
NO
IS THE RESISTANCE BELOW 120.0 OHMS?
YES
REPAIR THE K40 BR/WT WIRE FOR A SHORT TO THE K59 VT/BK WIRE.*
NO
REPLACE THE ENGINE CONTROLLER.*

* PERFORM VERIFICATION PROCEDURE VER-2

91E08994

Fig. 66: Driveability Test 13A (3.0L VIN 3) – Code 25, Automatic Idle Motor Circuits (3 of 4)

DR-13A: CODE 25, AUTOMATIC IDLE MOTOR CIRCUITS (4 OF 4)

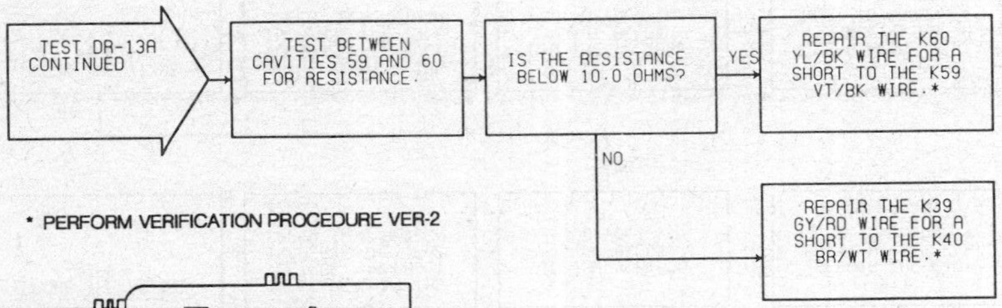
TEST DR-13A CONTINUED
TEST BETWEEN CAVITIES 59 AND 60 FOR RESISTANCE.
IS THE RESISTANCE BELOW 10.0 OHMS?
YES
REPAIR THE K60 YL/BK WIRE FOR A SHORT TO THE K59 VT/BK WIRE.*
NO
REPAIR THE K39 GY/RD WIRE FOR A SHORT TO THE K40 BR/WT WIRE.*

* PERFORM VERIFICATION PROCEDURE VER-2

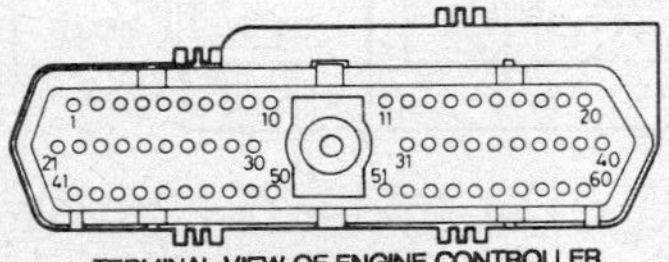
1
10
11
20
21
30
31
40
41
50
51
60

TERMINAL VIEW OF ENGINE CONTROLLER HARNESS CONNECTOR

91H08995

Fig. 67: Driveability Test 13A (3.0L VIN 3) – Code 25, Automatic Idle Motor Circuits (4 of 4)

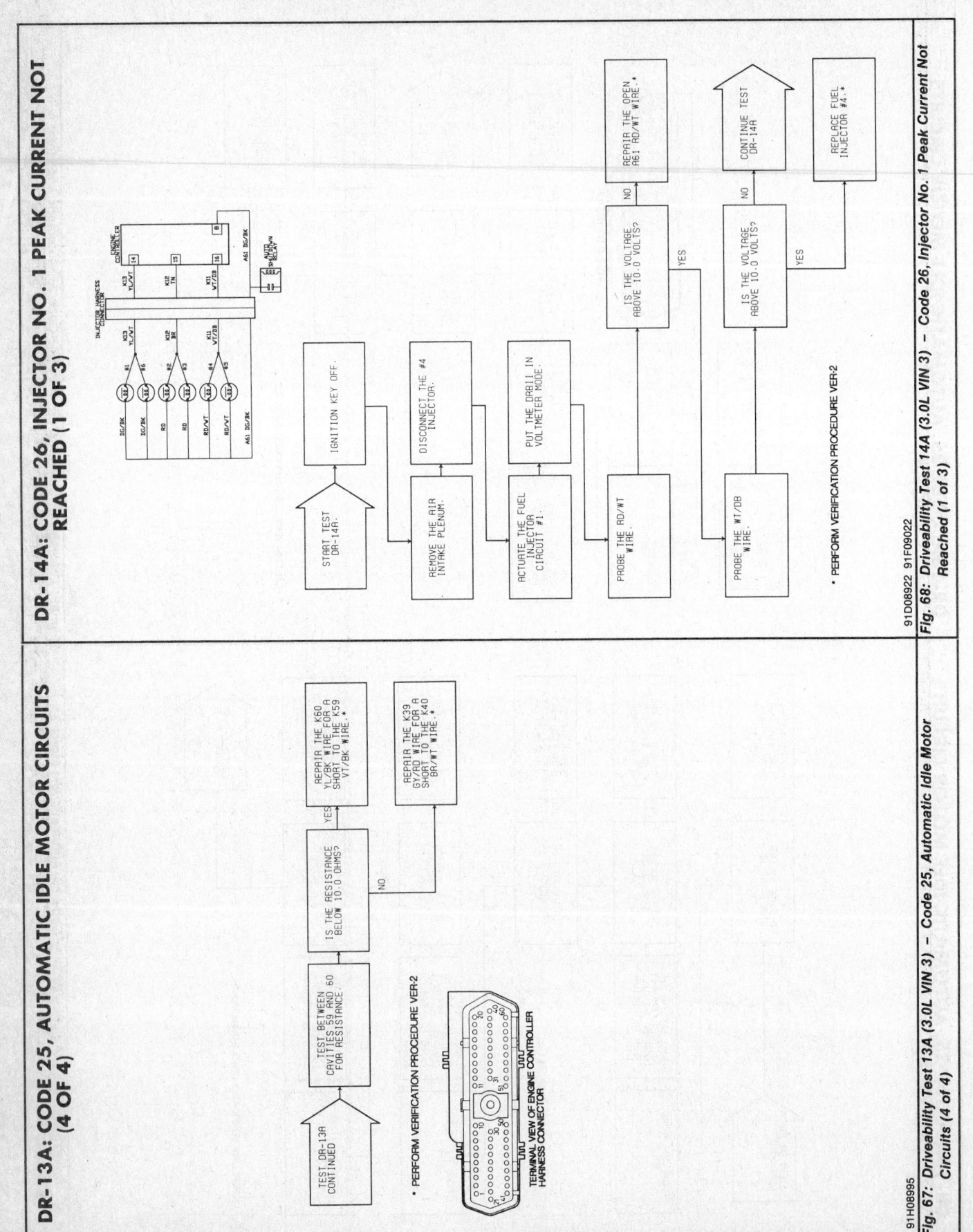

DR-14A: CODE 26, INJECTOR NO. 1 PEAK CURRENT NOT REACHED (1 OF 3)

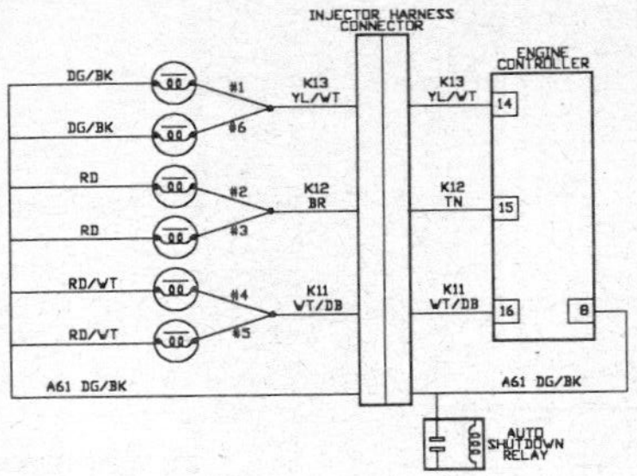
INJECTOR HARNESS CONNECTOR
ENGINE CONTROLLER
DG/BK
DG/BK
RD
RD
RD/WT
RD/WT
#1
#6
#2
#3
#4
#5
K13 YL/WT
K12 BR
K11 WT/DB
K13 YL/WT
K12 TN
K11 WT/DB
14
15
16
8
A61 DG/BK
A61 DG/BK
AUTO SHUTDOWN RELAY

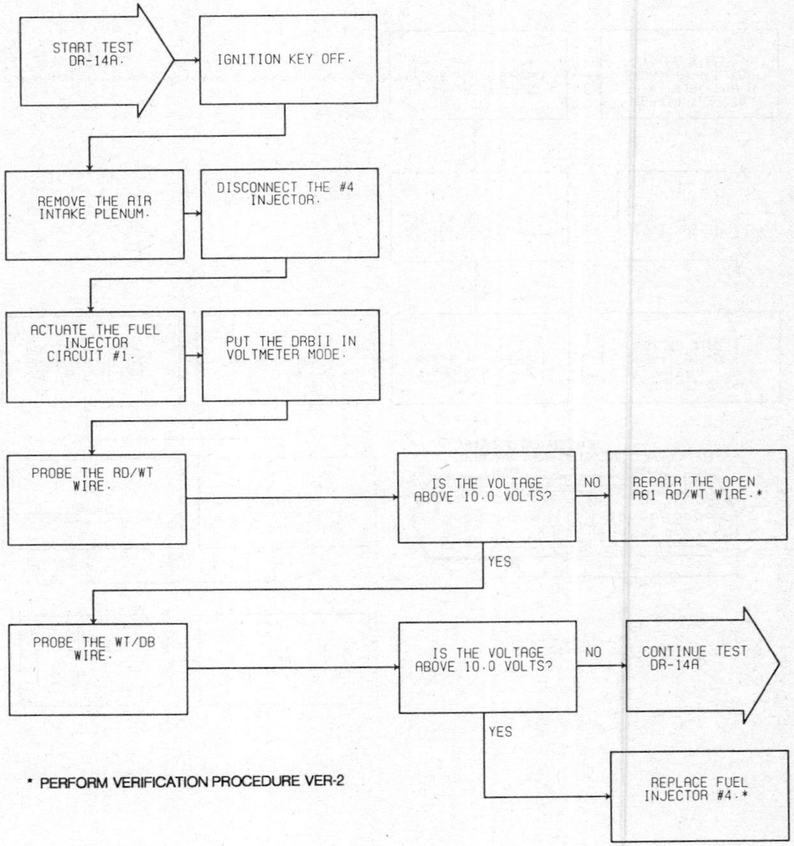
START TEST DR-14A.
IGNITION KEY OFF.
REMOVE THE AIR INTAKE PLENUM.
DISCONNECT THE #4 INJECTOR.
ACTUATE THE FUEL INJECTOR CIRCUIT #1.
PUT THE DRBII IN VOLTMETER MODE.
PROBE THE RD/WT WIRE.
IS THE VOLTAGE ABOVE 10.0 VOLTS?
NO
REPAIR THE OPEN A61 RD/WT WIRE.*
YES
PROBE THE WT/DB WIRE.
IS THE VOLTAGE ABOVE 10.0 VOLTS?
NO
CONTINUE TEST DR-14A
YES
REPLACE FUEL INJECTOR #4.*

* PERFORM VERIFICATION PROCEDURE VER-2

91D08922 91F09022

Fig. 68: Driveability Test 14A (3.0L VIN 3) – Code 26, Injector No. 1 Peak Current Not Reached (1 of 3)

DR-14A: CODE 26, INJECTOR NO. 1 PEAK CURRENT NOT REACHED (2 OF 3)

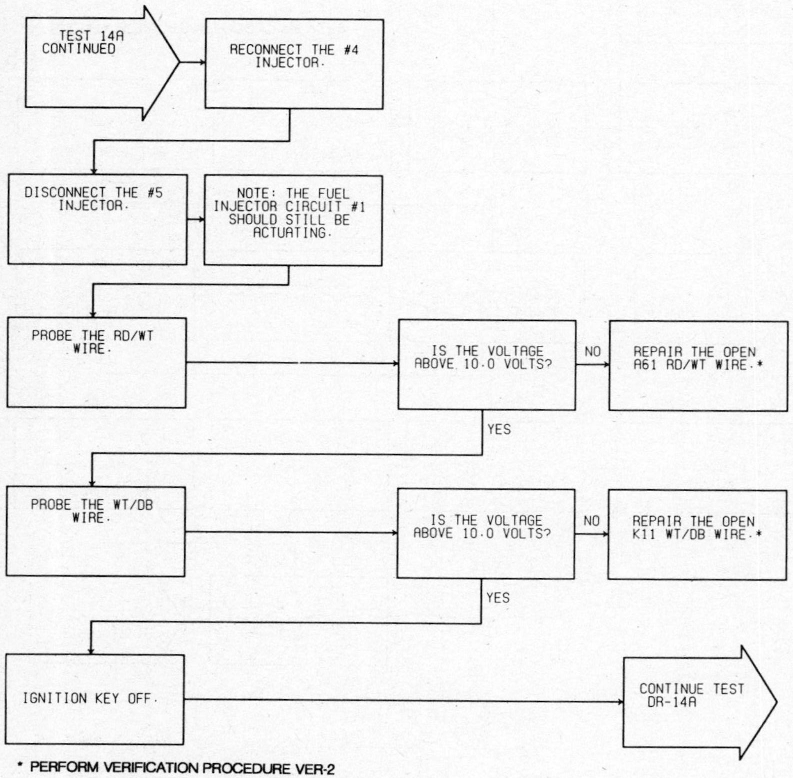
TEST 14A CONTINUED
RECONNECT THE #4 INJECTOR.
DISCONNECT THE #5 INJECTOR.
NOTE: THE FUEL INJECTOR CIRCUIT #1 SHOULD STILL BE ACTUATING.
PROBE THE RD/WT WIRE.
IS THE VOLTAGE ABOVE 10.0 VOLTS?
NO
REPAIR THE OPEN A61 RD/WT WIRE.*
YES
PROBE THE WT/DB WIRE.
IS THE VOLTAGE ABOVE 10.0 VOLTS?
NO
REPAIR THE OPEN K11 WT/DB WIRE.*
YES
IGNITION KEY OFF.
CONTINUE TEST DR-14A

* PERFORM VERIFICATION PROCEDURE VER-2

91H09023

Fig. 69: Driveability Test 14A (3.0L VIN 3) – Code 26, Injector No. 1 Peak Current Not Reached (2 of 3)

DR-14A: CODE 26, INJECTOR NO. 1 PEAK CURRENT NOT REACHED (3 OF 3)

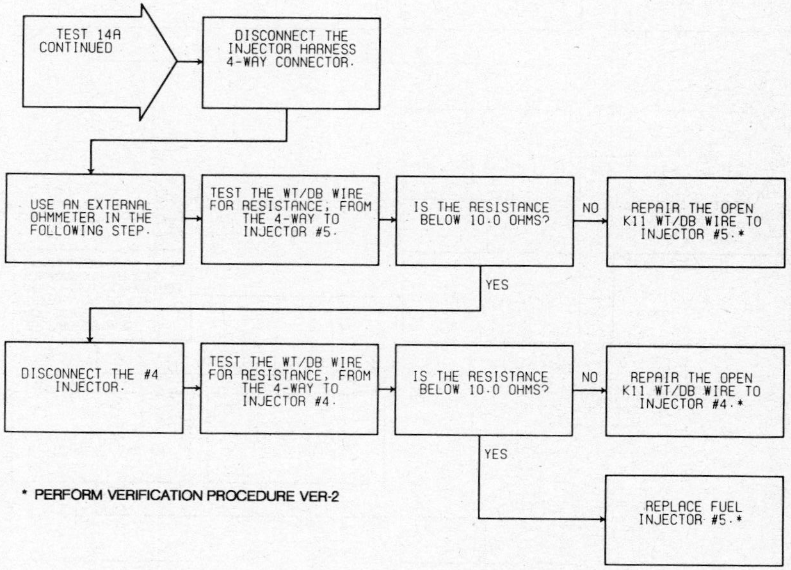
TEST 14A CONTINUED
DISCONNECT THE INJECTOR HARNESS 4-WAY CONNECTOR.
USE AN EXTERNAL OHMMETER IN THE FOLLOWING STEP.
TEST THE WT/DB WIRE FOR RESISTANCE, FROM THE 4-WAY TO INJECTOR #5.
IS THE RESISTANCE BELOW 10.0 OHMS?
NO
REPAIR THE OPEN K11 WT/DB WIRE TO INJECTOR #5.*
YES
DISCONNECT THE #4 INJECTOR.
TEST THE WT/DB WIRE FOR RESISTANCE, FROM THE 4-WAY TO INJECTOR #4.
IS THE RESISTANCE BELOW 10.0 OHMS?
NO
REPAIR THE OPEN K11 WT/DB WIRE TO INJECTOR #4.*
YES
REPLACE FUEL INJECTOR #5.*
* PERFORM VERIFICATION PROCEDURE VER-2

91J09024

Fig. 70: Driveability Test 14A (3.0L VIN 3) – Code 26, Injector No. 1 Peak Current Not Reached (3 of 3)

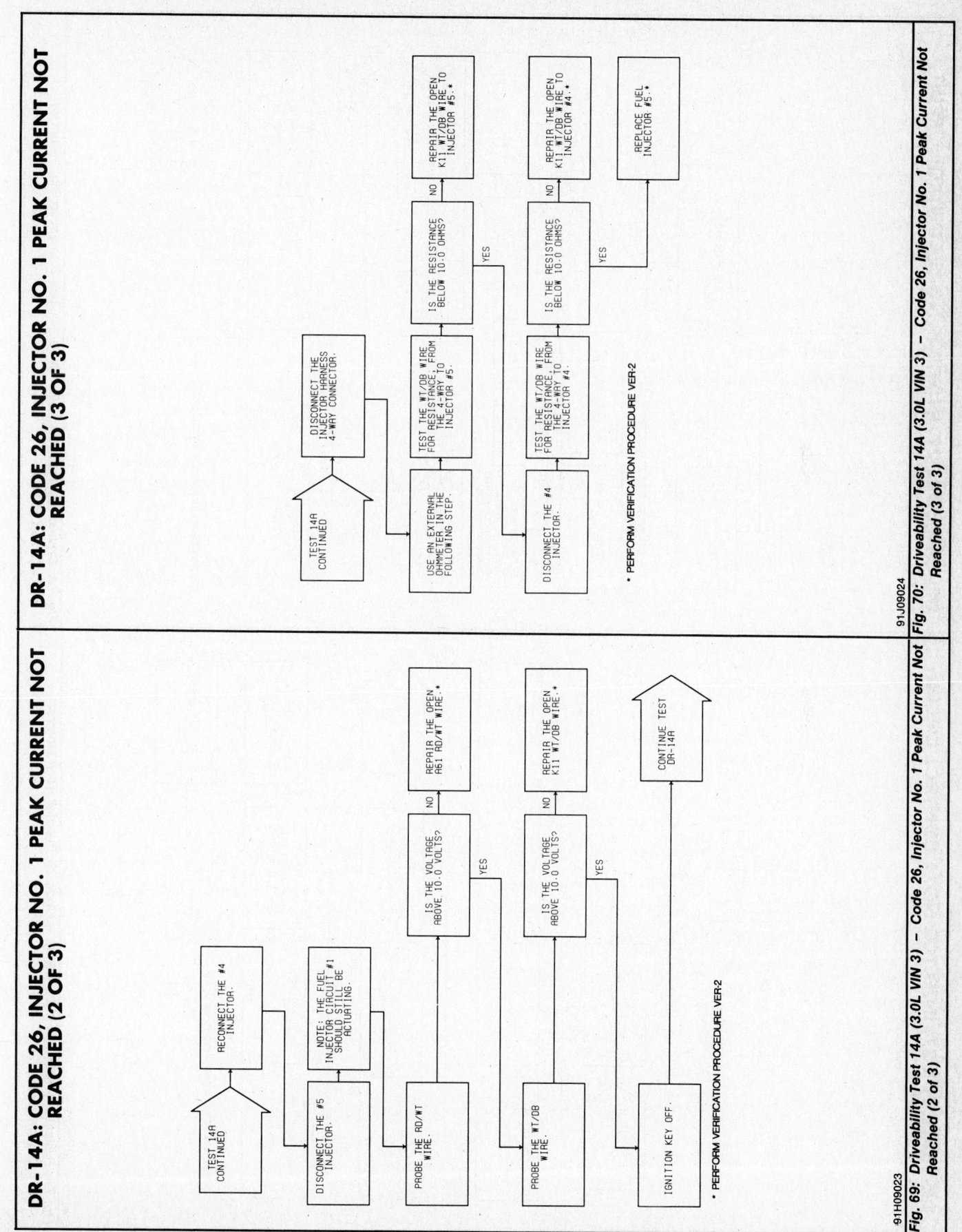

DR-15A: CODE 27, INJECTOR NO. 1 CONTROL CIRCUIT (1 OF 3)

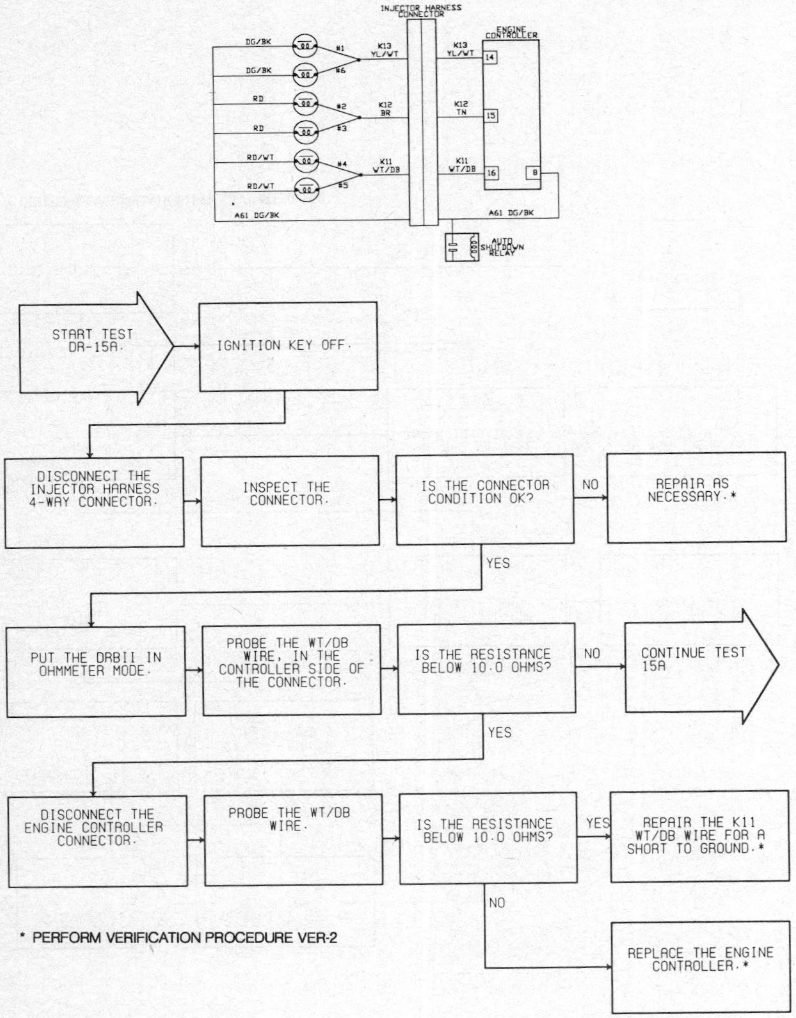
INJECTOR HARNESS CONNECTOR
ENGINE CONTROLLER
DG/BK
DG/BK
RD
RD
RD/WT
RD/WT
A61 DG/BK
#1
#6
#2
#3
#4
#5
K13 YL/WT
K12 BR
K11 WT/DB
K13 YL/WT
K12 TN
K11 WT/DB
14
15
16
8
A61 DG/BK
AUTO SHUTDOWN RELAY
START TEST DR-15A.
IGNITION KEY OFF.
DISCONNECT THE INJECTOR HARNESS 4-WAY CONNECTOR.
INSPECT THE CONNECTOR.
IS THE CONNECTOR CONDITION OK?
NO
REPAIR AS NECESSARY.*
YES
PUT THE DRBII IN OHMMETER MODE.
PROBE THE WT/DB WIRE, IN THE CONTROLLER SIDE OF THE CONNECTOR.
IS THE RESISTANCE BELOW 10.0 OHMS?
NO
CONTINUE TEST 15A
YES
DISCONNECT THE ENGINE CONTROLLER CONNECTOR.
PROBE THE WT/DB WIRE.
IS THE RESISTANCE BELOW 10.0 OHMS?
YES
REPAIR THE K11 WT/DB WIRE FOR A SHORT TO GROUND.*
NO
REPLACE THE ENGINE CONTROLLER.*
* PERFORM VERIFICATION PROCEDURE VER-2

91D08922 91C09025

Fig. 71: Driveability Test 15A (3.0L VIN 3) – Code 27, Injector No. 1 Control Circuit (1 of 3)

DR-15A: CODE 27, INJECTOR NO. 1 CONTROL CIRCUIT (2 OF 3)

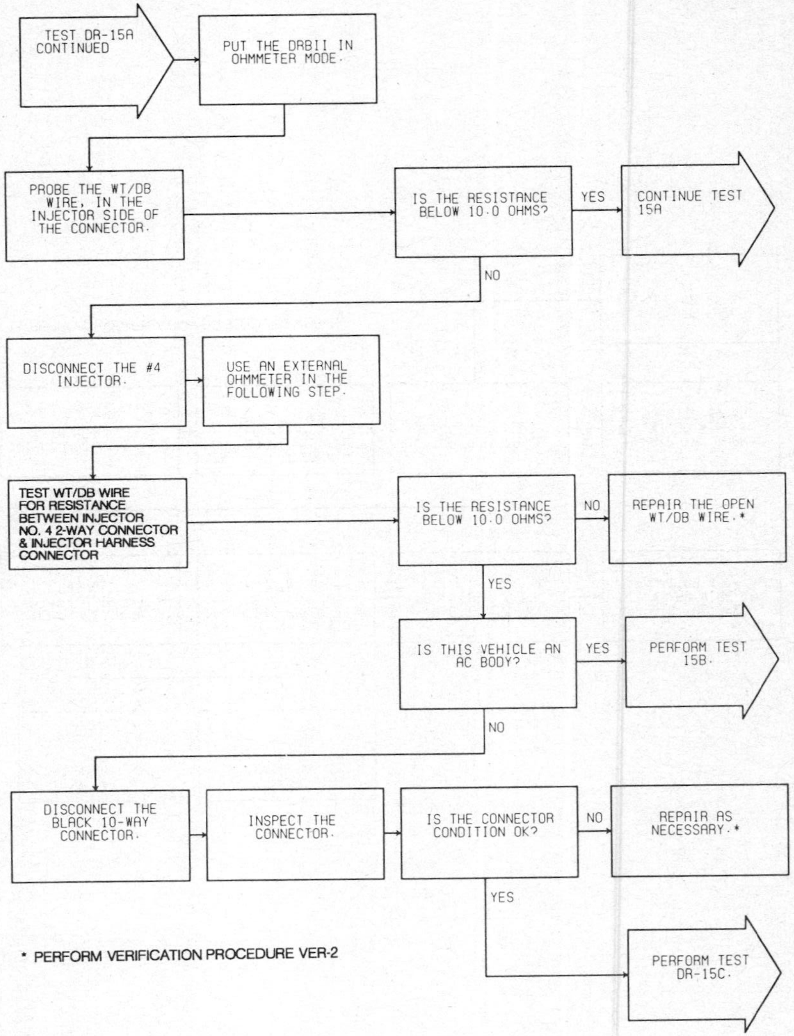
TEST DR-15A CONTINUED
PUT THE DRBII IN OHMMETER MODE.
PROBE THE WT/DB WIRE, IN THE INJECTOR SIDE OF THE CONNECTOR.
IS THE RESISTANCE BELOW 10.0 OHMS?
YES
CONTINUE TEST 15A
NO
DISCONNECT THE #4 INJECTOR.
USE AN EXTERNAL OHMMETER IN THE FOLLOWING STEP.
TEST WT/DB WIRE FOR RESISTANCE BETWEEN INJECTOR NO. 4 2-WAY CONNECTOR & INJECTOR HARNESS CONNECTOR
IS THE RESISTANCE BELOW 10.0 OHMS?
NO
REPAIR THE OPEN WT/DB WIRE.*
YES
IS THIS VEHICLE AN AC BODY?
YES
PERFORM TEST 15B.
NO
DISCONNECT THE BLACK 10-WAY CONNECTOR.
INSPECT THE CONNECTOR.
IS THE CONNECTOR CONDITION OK?
NO
REPAIR AS NECESSARY.*
YES
PERFORM TEST DR-15C.
* PERFORM VERIFICATION PROCEDURE VER-2

91E09026

Fig. 72: Driveability Test 15A (3.0L VIN 3) – Code 27, Injector No. 1 Control Circuit (2 of 3)

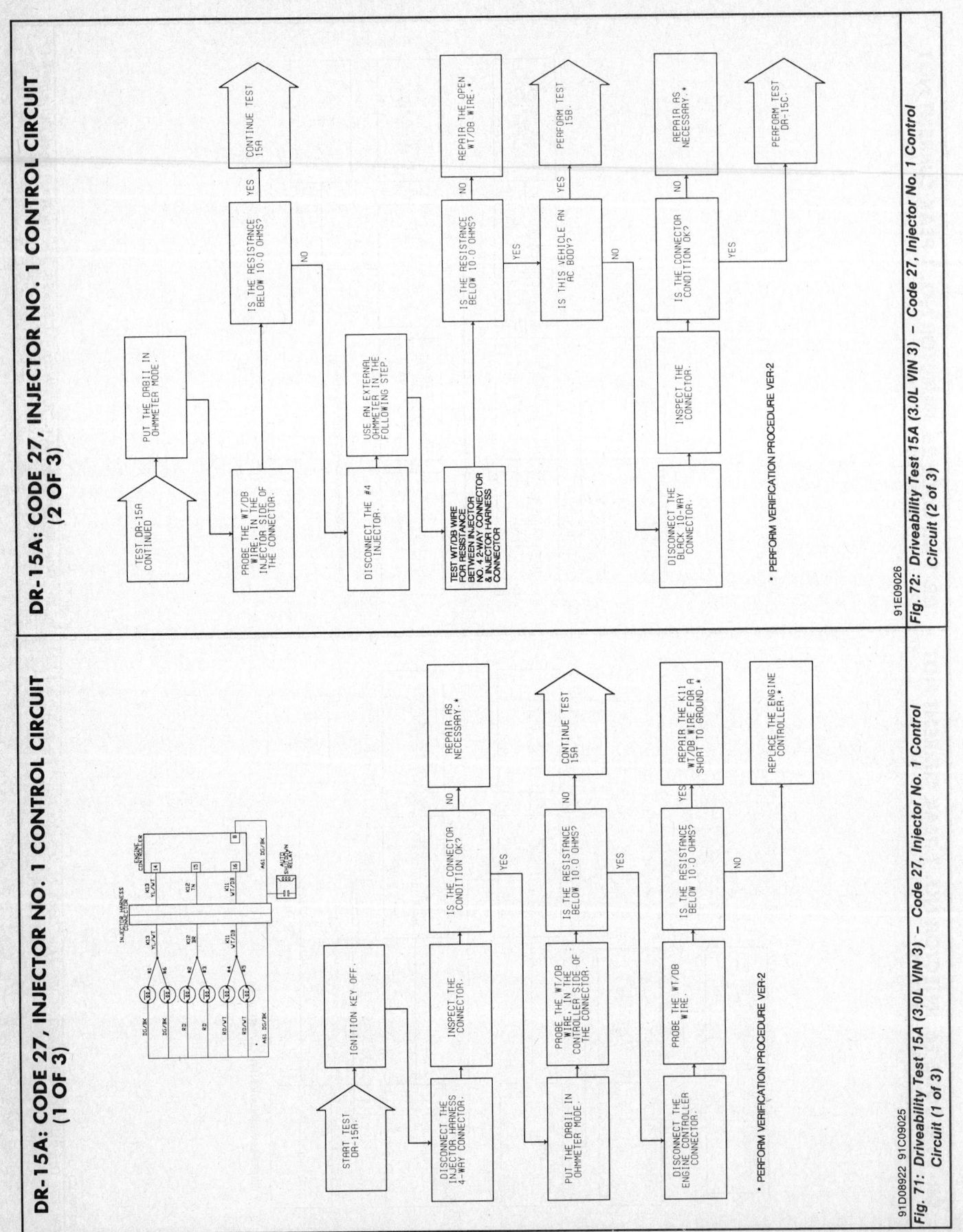

DR-15A: CODE 27, INJECTOR NO. 1 CONTROL CIRCUIT (3 OF 3)

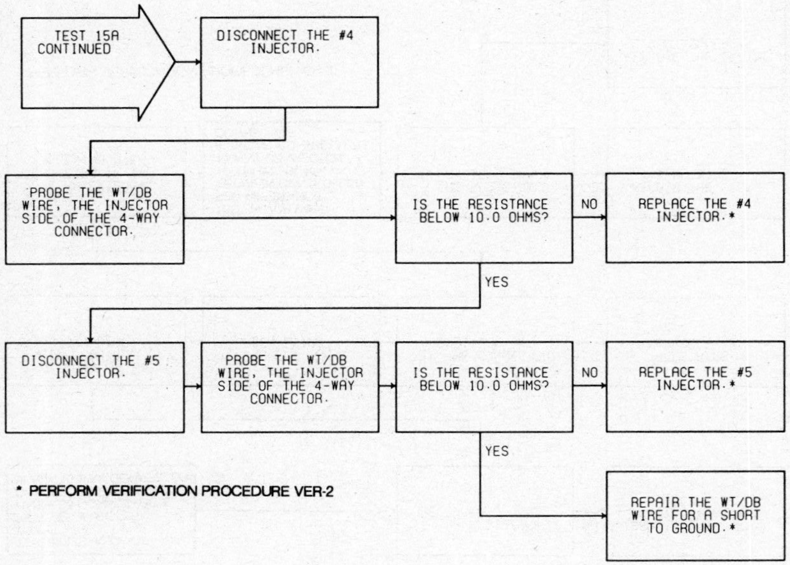
TEST 15A CONTINUED
DISCONNECT THE #4 INJECTOR.
PROBE THE WT/DB WIRE, THE INJECTOR SIDE OF THE 4-WAY CONNECTOR.
IS THE RESISTANCE BELOW 10.0 OHMS?
NO
REPLACE THE #4 INJECTOR.*
YES
DISCONNECT THE #5 INJECTOR.
PROBE THE WT/DB WIRE, THE INJECTOR SIDE OF THE 4-WAY CONNECTOR.
IS THE RESISTANCE BELOW 10.0 OHMS?
NO
REPLACE THE #5 INJECTOR.*
YES
REPAIR THE WT/DB WIRE FOR A SHORT TO GROUND.*
* PERFORM VERIFICATION PROCEDURE VER-2

91G09027

Fig. 73: Driveability Test 15A (3.0L VIN 3) – Code 27, Injector No. 1 Control Circuit (3 of 3)

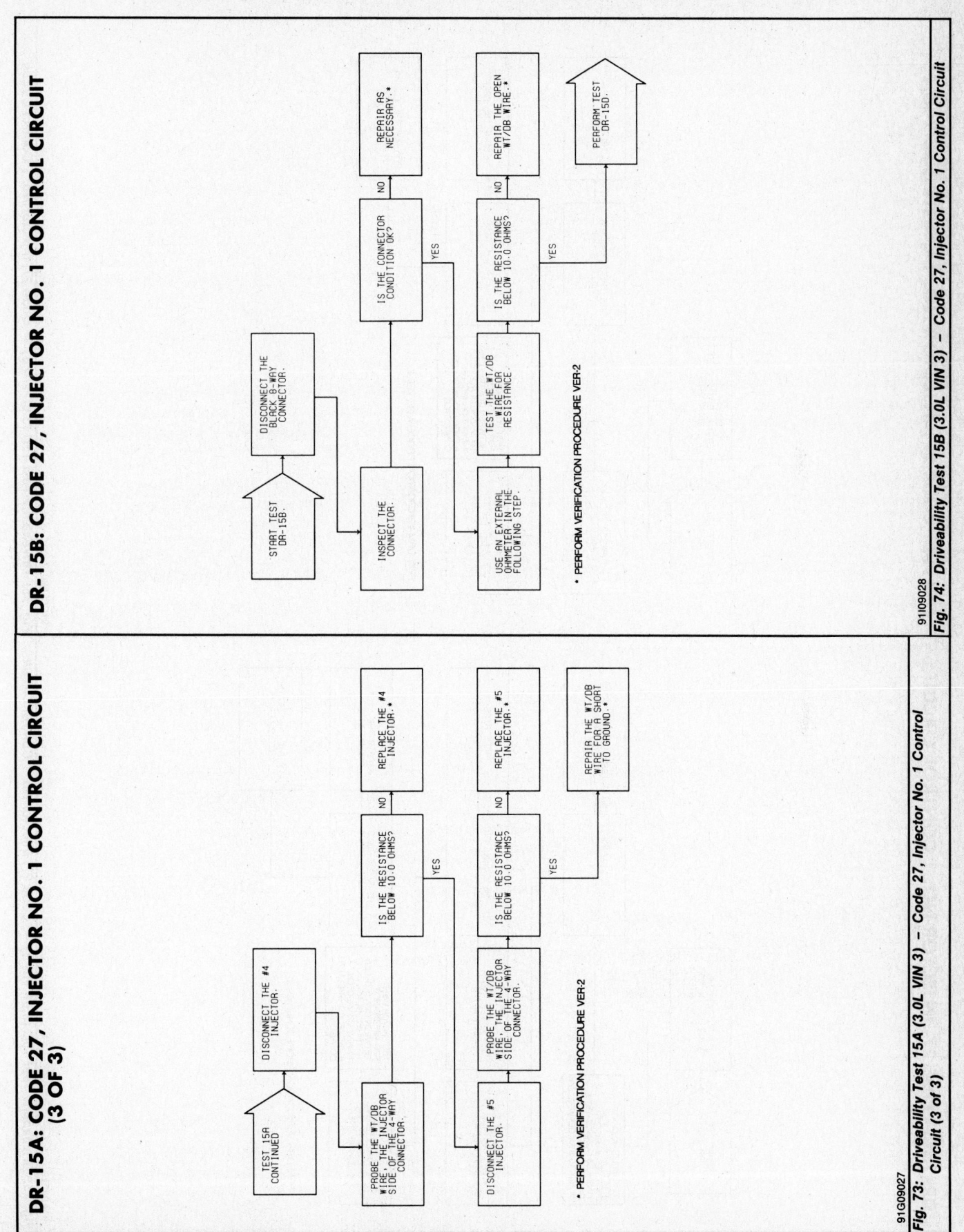

DR-15B: CODE 27, INJECTOR NO. 1 CONTROL CIRCUIT

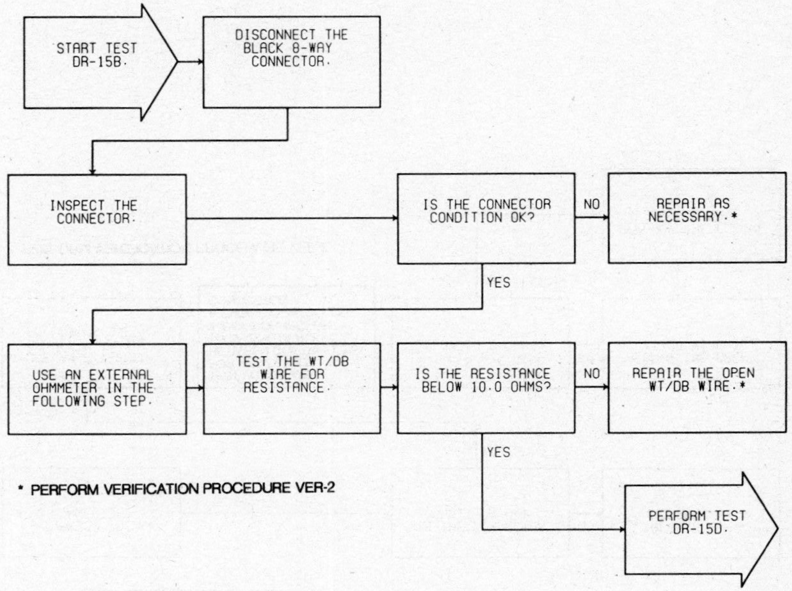
START TEST DR-15B.
DISCONNECT THE BLACK 8-WAY CONNECTOR.
INSPECT THE CONNECTOR.
IS THE CONNECTOR CONDITION OK?
NO
REPAIR AS NECESSARY.*
YES
USE AN EXTERNAL OHMMETER IN THE FOLLOWING STEP.
TEST THE WT/DB WIRE FOR RESISTANCE.
IS THE RESISTANCE BELOW 10.0 OHMS?
NO
REPAIR THE OPEN WT/DB WIRE.*
YES
PERFORM TEST DR-15D.
* PERFORM VERIFICATION PROCEDURE VER-2

91I09028

Fig. 74: Driveability Test 15B (3.0L VIN 3) – Code 27, Injector No. 1 Control Circuit

DR-15C: CODE 27, INJECTOR NO. 1 CONTROL CIRCUIT

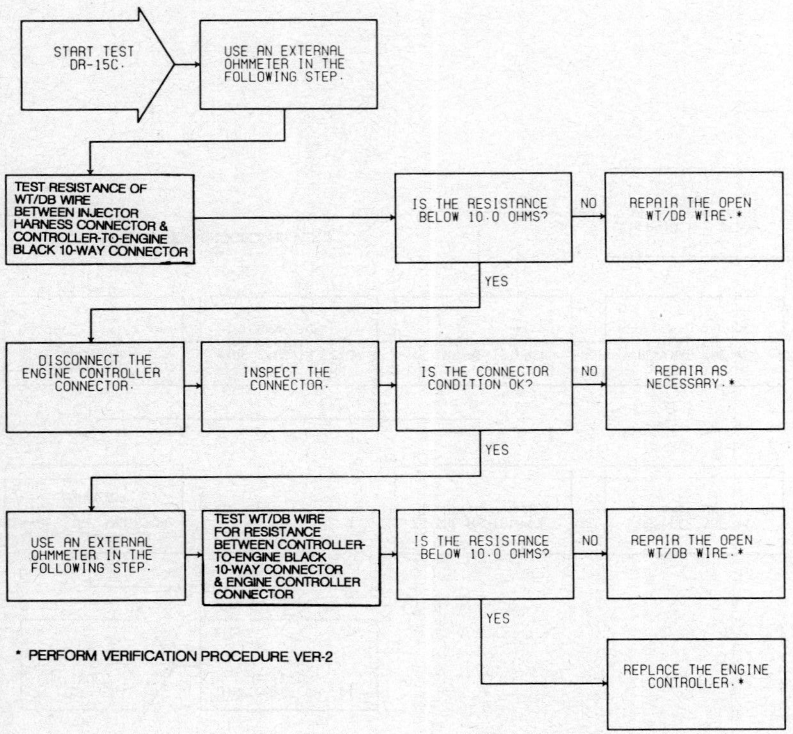
START TEST DR-15C.
USE AN EXTERNAL OHMMETER IN THE FOLLOWING STEP.
TEST RESISTANCE OF WT/DB WIRE BETWEEN INJECTOR HARNESS CONNECTOR & CONTROLLER-TO-ENGINE BLACK 10-WAY CONNECTOR
IS THE RESISTANCE BELOW 10.0 OHMS?
NO
REPAIR THE OPEN WT/DB WIRE.*
YES
DISCONNECT THE ENGINE CONTROLLER CONNECTOR.
INSPECT THE CONNECTOR.
IS THE CONNECTOR CONDITION OK?
NO
REPAIR AS NECESSARY.*
YES
USE AN EXTERNAL OHMMETER IN THE FOLLOWING STEP.
TEST WT/DB WIRE FOR RESISTANCE BETWEEN CONTROLLER-TO-ENGINE BLACK 10-WAY CONNECTOR & ENGINE CONTROLLER CONNECTOR
IS THE RESISTANCE BELOW 10.0 OHMS?
NO
REPAIR THE OPEN WT/DB WIRE.*
YES
REPLACE THE ENGINE CONTROLLER.*

* PERFORM VERIFICATION PROCEDURE VER-2

91A09029

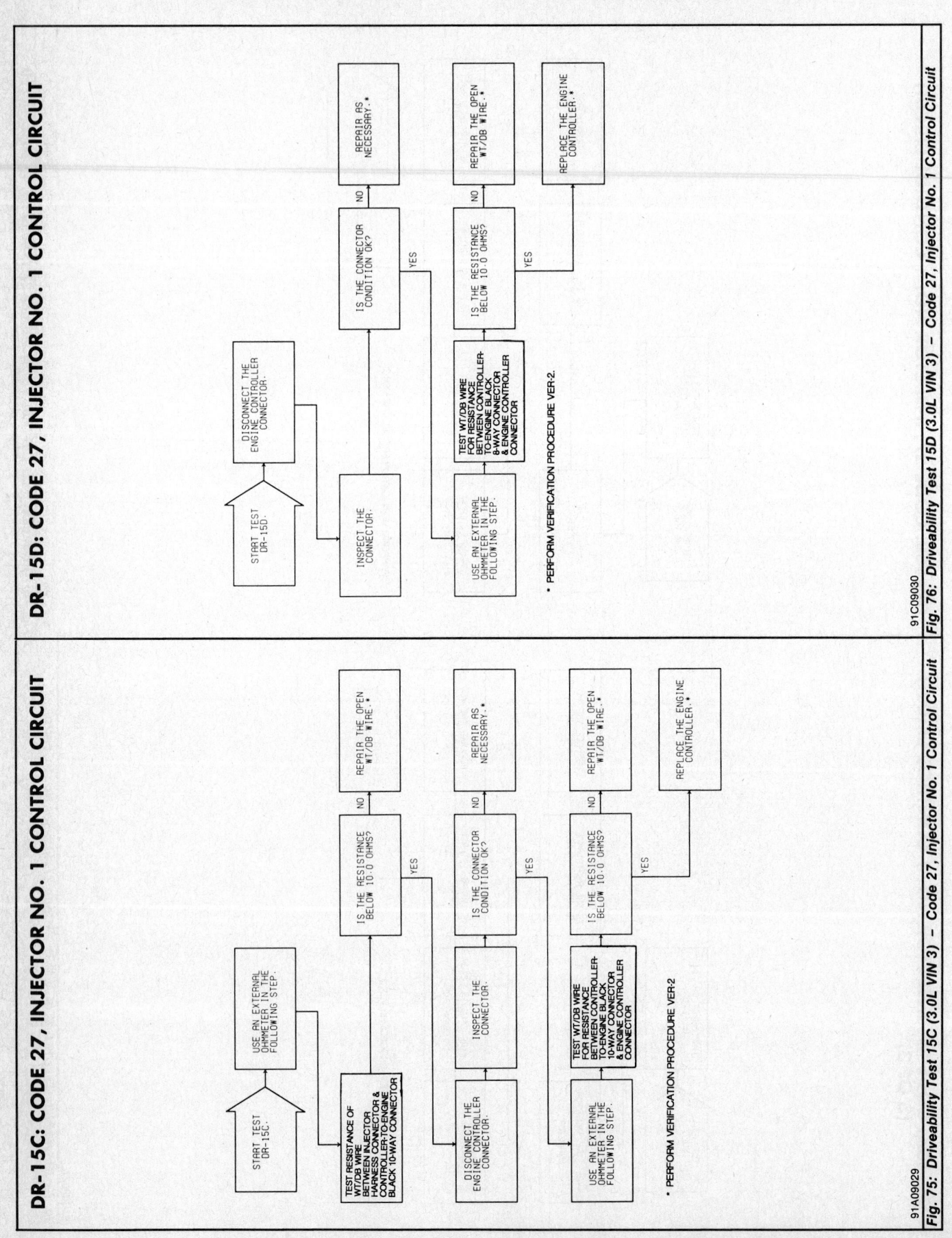

Fig. 75: Driveability Test 15C (3.0L VIN 3) – Code 27, Injector No. 1 Control Circuit

DR-15D: CODE 27, INJECTOR NO. 1 CONTROL CIRCUIT

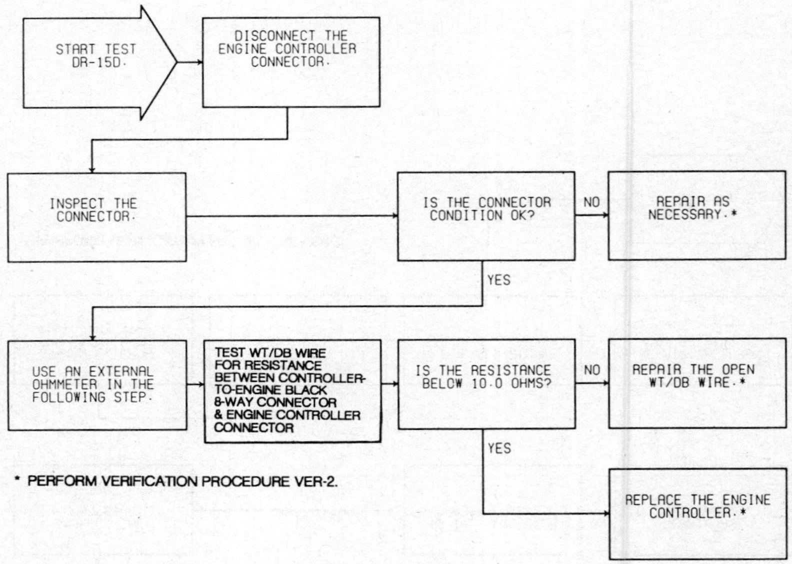
START TEST DR-15D.
DISCONNECT THE ENGINE CONTROLLER CONNECTOR.
INSPECT THE CONNECTOR.
IS THE CONNECTOR CONDITION OK?
NO
REPAIR AS NECESSARY.*
YES
USE AN EXTERNAL OHMMETER IN THE FOLLOWING STEP.
TEST WT/DB WIRE FOR RESISTANCE BETWEEN CONTROLLER-TO-ENGINE BLACK 8-WAY CONNECTOR & ENGINE CONTROLLER CONNECTOR
IS THE RESISTANCE BELOW 10.0 OHMS?
NO
REPAIR THE OPEN WT/DB WIRE.*
YES
REPLACE THE ENGINE CONTROLLER.*

* PERFORM VERIFICATION PROCEDURE VER-2.

91C09030

Fig. 76: Driveability Test 15D (3.0L VIN 3) – Code 27, Injector No. 1 Control Circuit

DR-16A: CODE 26, INJECTOR NO. 2 PEAK CURRENT NOT REACHED (1 OF 3)

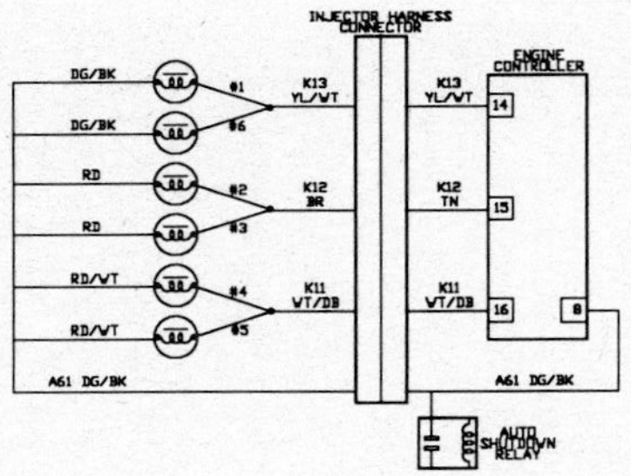
INJECTOR HARNESS CONNECTOR
ENGINE CONTROLLER
DG/BK
DG/BK
RD
RD
RD/VT
RD/VT
A61 DG/BK
#1
#6
#2
#3
#4
#5
K13 YL/WT
K12 BR
K11 WT/DB
K13 YL/WT
K12 TN
K11 WT/DB
14
15
16
8
A61 DG/BK
AUTO SHUTDOWN RELAY

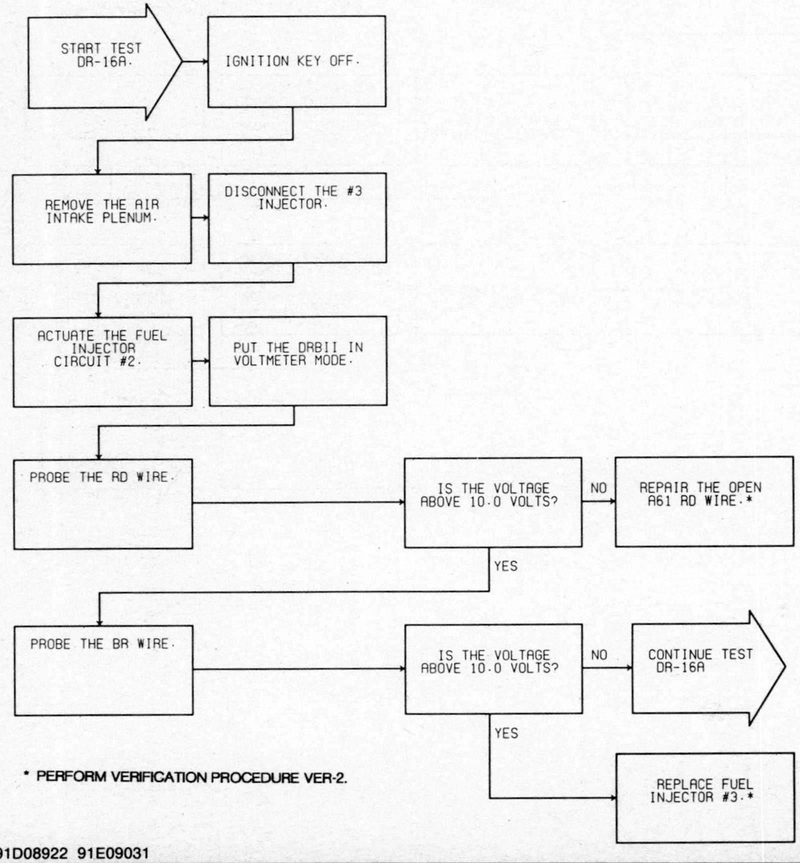
START TEST DR-16A.
IGNITION KEY OFF.
REMOVE THE AIR INTAKE PLENUM.
DISCONNECT THE #3 INJECTOR.
ACTUATE THE FUEL INJECTOR CIRCUIT #2.
PUT THE DRBII IN VOLTMETER MODE.
PROBE THE RD WIRE.
IS THE VOLTAGE ABOVE 10.0 VOLTS?
NO
REPAIR THE OPEN A61 RD WIRE.*
YES
PROBE THE BR WIRE.
IS THE VOLTAGE ABOVE 10.0 VOLTS?
NO
CONTINUE TEST DR-16A
YES
REPLACE FUEL INJECTOR #3.*

* PERFORM VERIFICATION PROCEDURE VER-2.

91D08922 91E09031

Fig. 77: Driveability Test 16A (3.0L VIN 3) – Code 26, Injector No. 2 Peak Current Not Reached (1 of 3)

DR-16A: CODE 26, INJECTOR NO. 2 PEAK CURRENT NOT REACHED (2 OF 3)

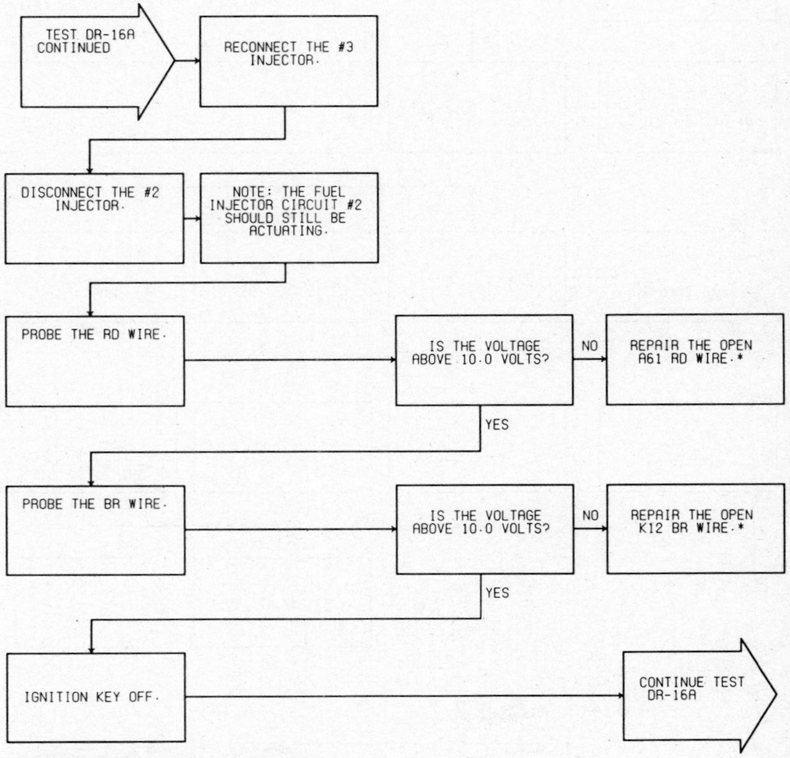
TEST DR-16A CONTINUED
RECONNECT THE #3 INJECTOR.
DISCONNECT THE #2 INJECTOR.
NOTE: THE FUEL INJECTOR CIRCUIT #2 SHOULD STILL BE ACTUATING.
PROBE THE RD WIRE.
IS THE VOLTAGE ABOVE 10.0 VOLTS?
NO
REPAIR THE OPEN A61 RD WIRE.*
YES
PROBE THE BR WIRE.
IS THE VOLTAGE ABOVE 10.0 VOLTS?
NO
REPAIR THE OPEN K12 BR WIRE.*
YES
IGNITION KEY OFF.
CONTINUE TEST DR-16A

* PERFORM VERIFICATION PROCEDURE VER-2.

91G09032

Fig. 78: Driveability Test 16A (3.0L VIN 3) – Code 26, Injector No. 2 Peak Current Not Reached (2 of 3)

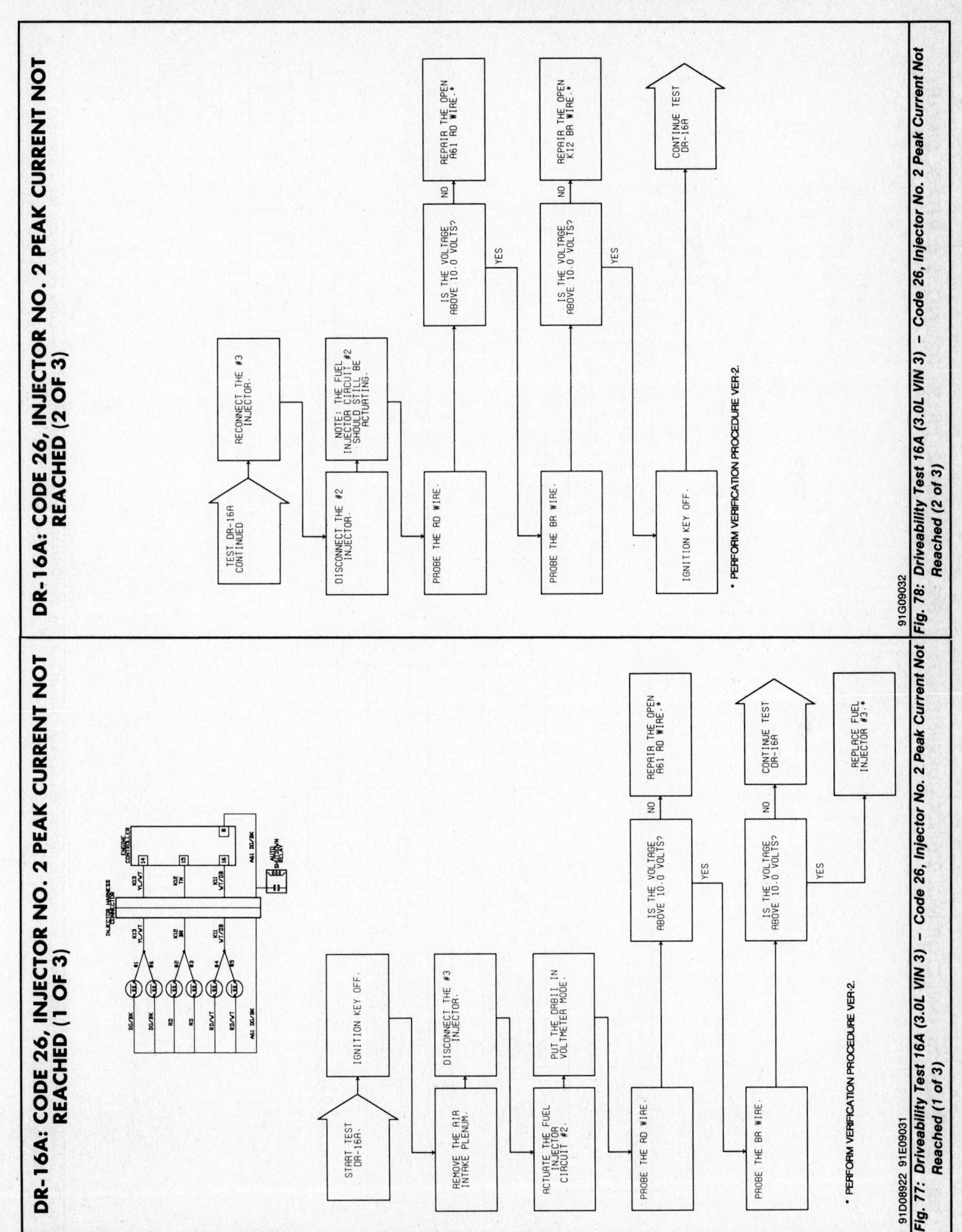

1991 ENGINE PERFORMANCE
Self-Diagnostics – 3.0L VIN 3 (Cont.)

DR-16A: CODE 26, INJECTOR NO. 2 PEAK CURRENT NOT REACHED (3 OF 3)

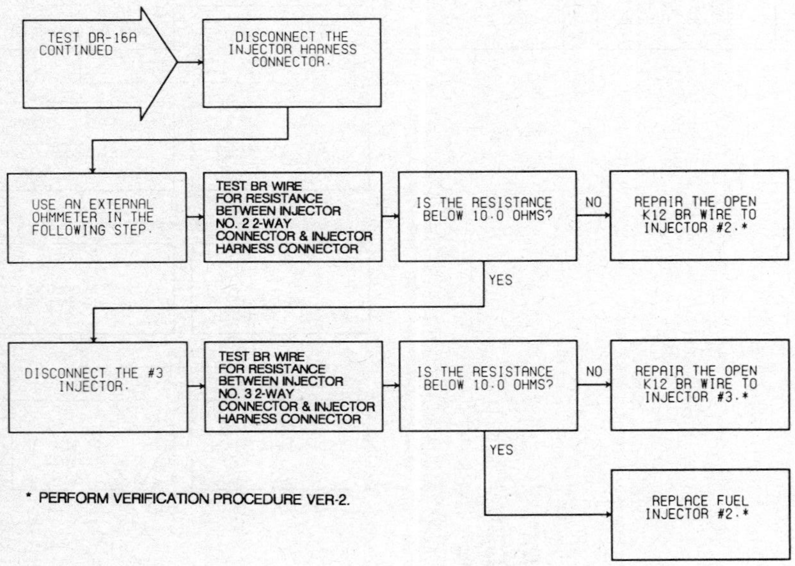
TEST DR-16A CONTINUED
DISCONNECT THE INJECTOR HARNESS CONNECTOR.
USE AN EXTERNAL OHMMETER IN THE FOLLOWING STEP.
TEST BR WIRE FOR RESISTANCE BETWEEN INJECTOR NO. 2 2-WAY CONNECTOR & INJECTOR HARNESS CONNECTOR
IS THE RESISTANCE BELOW 10.0 OHMS?
NO
REPAIR THE OPEN K12 BR WIRE TO INJECTOR #2.*
YES
DISCONNECT THE #3 INJECTOR.
TEST BR WIRE FOR RESISTANCE BETWEEN INJECTOR NO. 3 2-WAY CONNECTOR & INJECTOR HARNESS CONNECTOR
IS THE RESISTANCE BELOW 10.0 OHMS?
NO
REPAIR THE OPEN K12 BR WIRE TO INJECTOR #3.*
YES
REPLACE FUEL INJECTOR #2.*

* PERFORM VERIFICATION PROCEDURE VER-2.

91I09033

Fig. 79: Driveability Test 16A (3.0L VIN 3) – Code 26, Injector No. 2 Peak Current Not Reached (3 of 3)

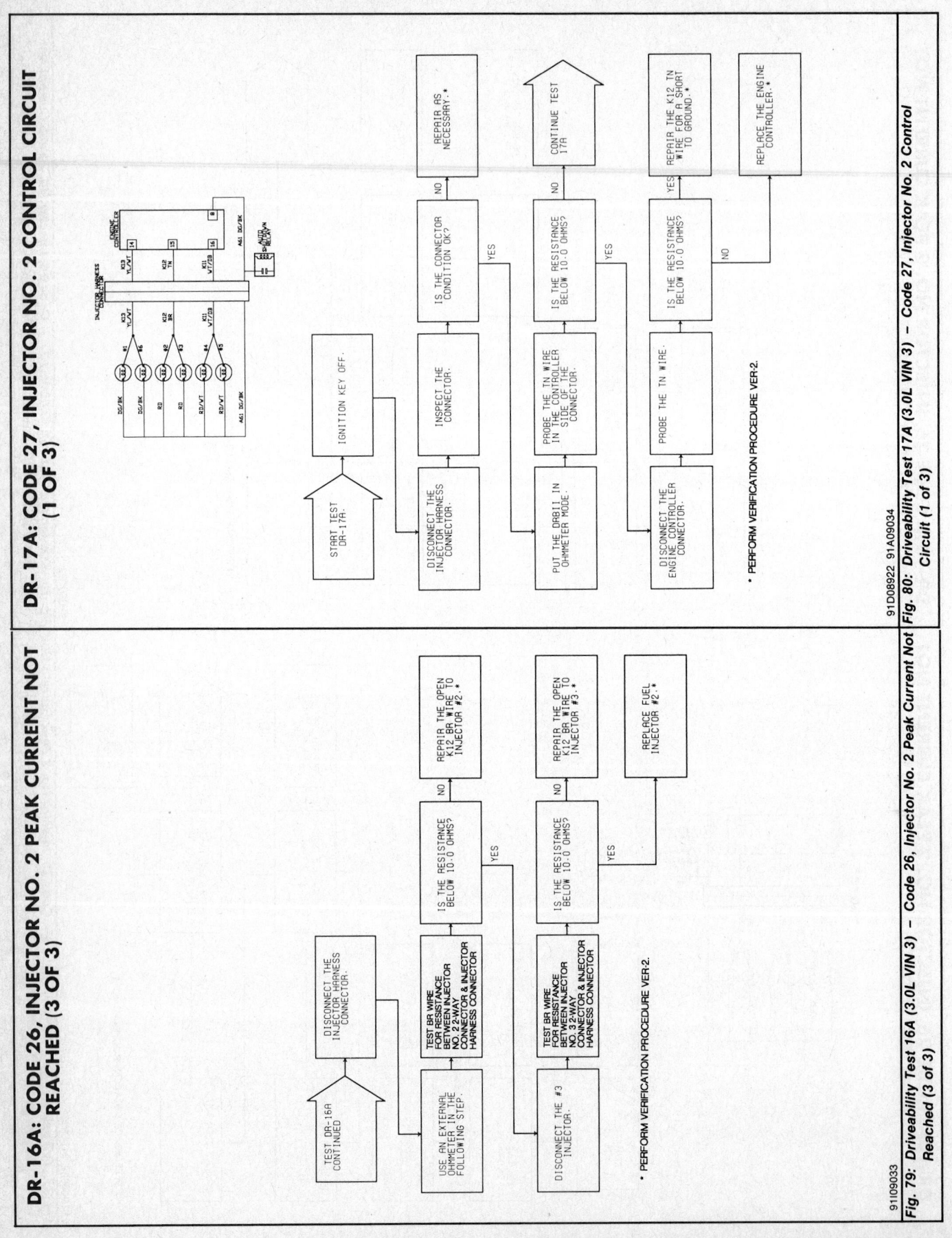

DR-17A: CODE 27, INJECTOR NO. 2 CONTROL CIRCUIT (1 OF 3)

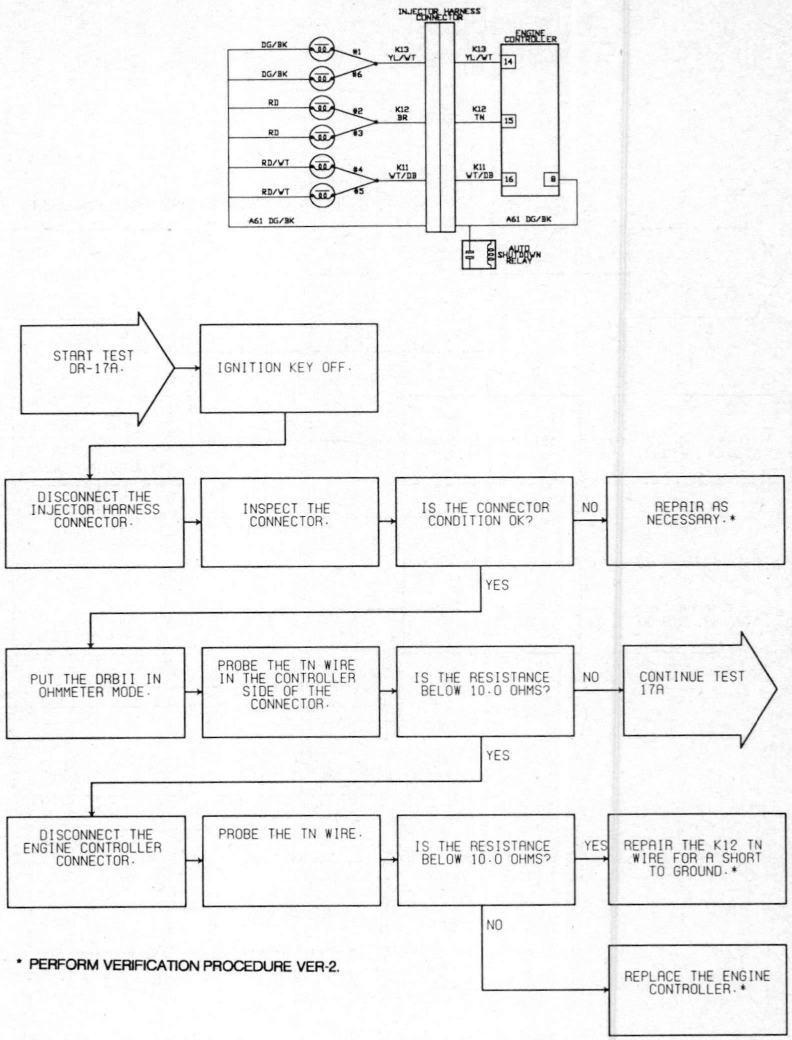
INJECTOR HARNESS CONNECTOR
ENGINE CONTROLLER
DG/BK
DG/BK
RD
RD
RD/WT
RD/WT
A61 DG/BK
#1
#6
#2
#3
#4
#5
K13 YL/WT
K12 BR
K11 WT/DB
K12 TN
14
15
16
8
A61 DG/BK
AUTO SHUTDOWN RELAY
START TEST DR-17A.
IGNITION KEY OFF.
DISCONNECT THE INJECTOR HARNESS CONNECTOR.
INSPECT THE CONNECTOR.
IS THE CONNECTOR CONDITION OK?
NO
REPAIR AS NECESSARY.*
YES
PUT THE DRBII IN OHMMETER MODE.
PROBE THE TN WIRE IN THE CONTROLLER SIDE OF THE CONNECTOR.
IS THE RESISTANCE BELOW 10.0 OHMS?
NO
CONTINUE TEST 17A
YES
DISCONNECT THE ENGINE CONTROLLER CONNECTOR.
PROBE THE TN WIRE.
IS THE RESISTANCE BELOW 10.0 OHMS?
YES
REPAIR THE K12 TN WIRE FOR A SHORT TO GROUND.*
NO
REPLACE THE ENGINE CONTROLLER.*

* PERFORM VERIFICATION PROCEDURE VER-2.

91D08922 91A09034

Fig. 80: Driveability Test 17A (3.0L VIN 3) – Code 27, Injector No. 2 Control Circuit (1 of 3)

DR-17A: CODE 27, INJECTOR NO. 2 CONTROL CIRCUIT (2 OF 3)

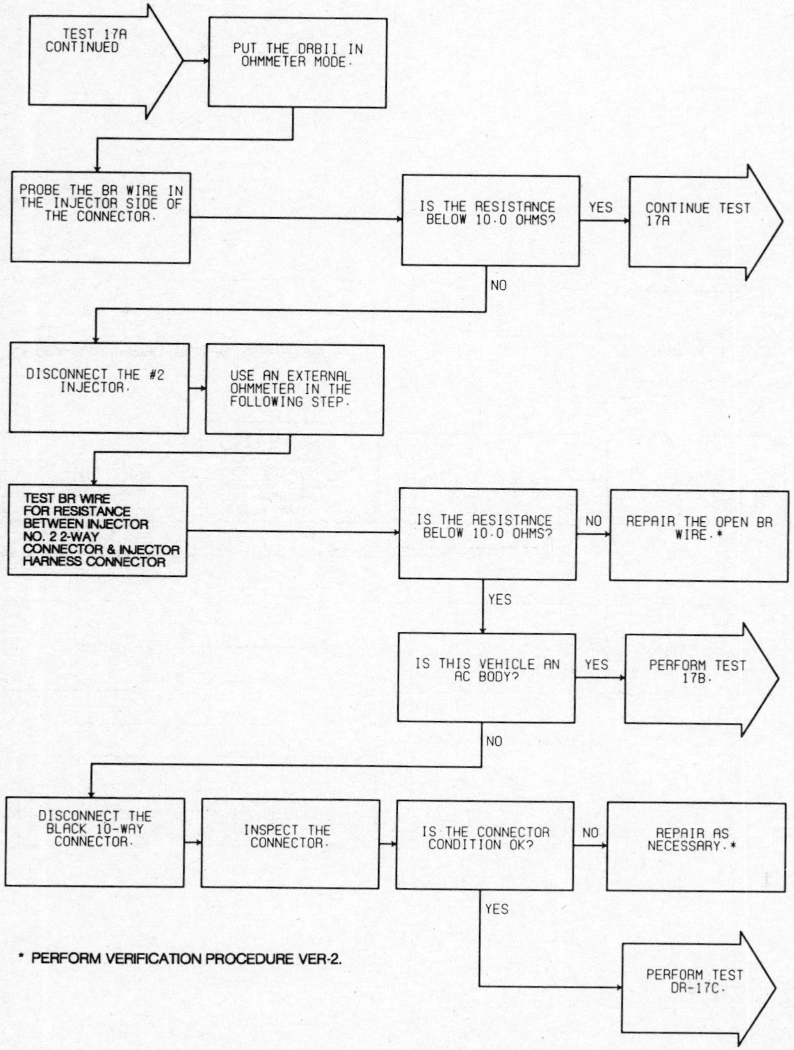
TEST 17A CONTINUED
PUT THE DRBII IN OHMMETER MODE.
PROBE THE BR WIRE IN THE INJECTOR SIDE OF THE CONNECTOR.
IS THE RESISTANCE BELOW 10.0 OHMS?
YES
CONTINUE TEST 17A
NO
DISCONNECT THE #2 INJECTOR.
USE AN EXTERNAL OHMMETER IN THE FOLLOWING STEP.
TEST BR WIRE FOR RESISTANCE BETWEEN INJECTOR NO. 2 2-WAY CONNECTOR & INJECTOR HARNESS CONNECTOR
IS THE RESISTANCE BELOW 10.0 OHMS?
NO
REPAIR THE OPEN BR WIRE.*
YES
IS THIS VEHICLE AN AC BODY?
YES
PERFORM TEST 17B.
NO
DISCONNECT THE BLACK 10-WAY CONNECTOR.
INSPECT THE CONNECTOR.
IS THE CONNECTOR CONDITION OK?
NO
REPAIR AS NECESSARY.*
YES
PERFORM TEST DR-17C.

* PERFORM VERIFICATION PROCEDURE VER-2.

91D09035

Fig. 81: Driveability Test 17A (3.0L VIN 3) – Code 27, Injector No. 2 Control Circuit (2 of 3)

DR-17A: CODE 27, INJECTOR NO. 2 CONTROL CIRCUIT (3 OF 3)

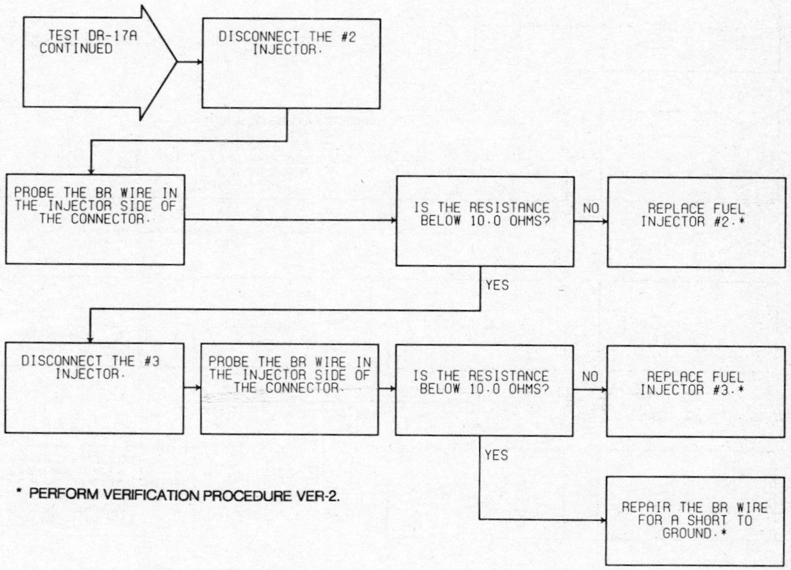
TEST DR-17A CONTINUED
DISCONNECT THE #2 INJECTOR.
PROBE THE BR WIRE IN THE INJECTOR SIDE OF THE CONNECTOR.
IS THE RESISTANCE BELOW 10.0 OHMS?
NO
REPLACE FUEL INJECTOR #2.*
YES
DISCONNECT THE #3 INJECTOR.
PROBE THE BR WIRE IN THE INJECTOR SIDE OF THE CONNECTOR.
IS THE RESISTANCE BELOW 10.0 OHMS?
NO
REPLACE FUEL INJECTOR #3.*
YES
REPAIR THE BR WIRE FOR A SHORT TO GROUND.*

* PERFORM VERIFICATION PROCEDURE VER-2.

91F09036

Fig. 82: Driveability Test 17A (3.0L VIN 3) – Code 27, Injector No. 2 Control Circuit (3 of 3)

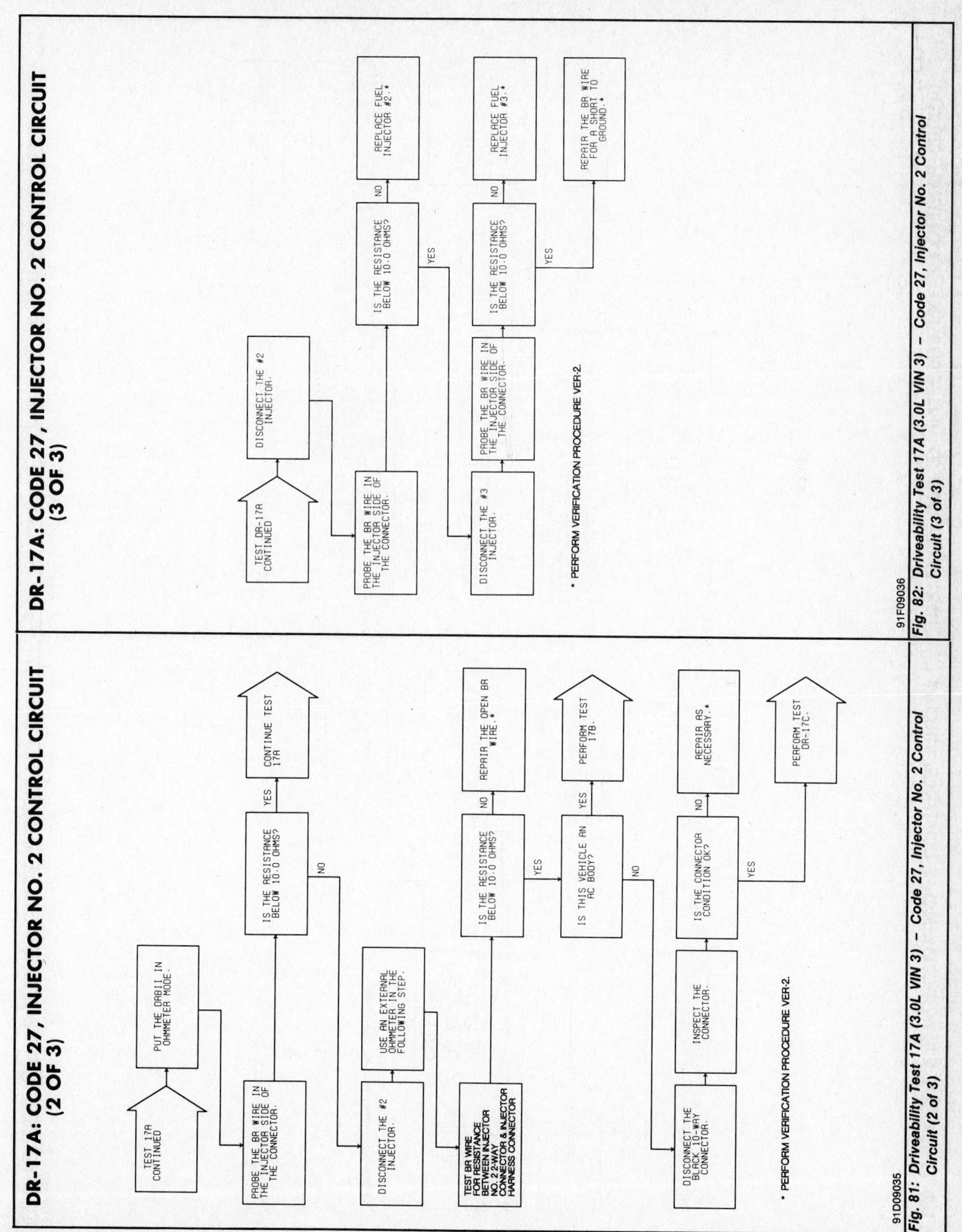

DR-17B: CODE 27, INJECTOR NO. 2 CONTROL CIRCUIT

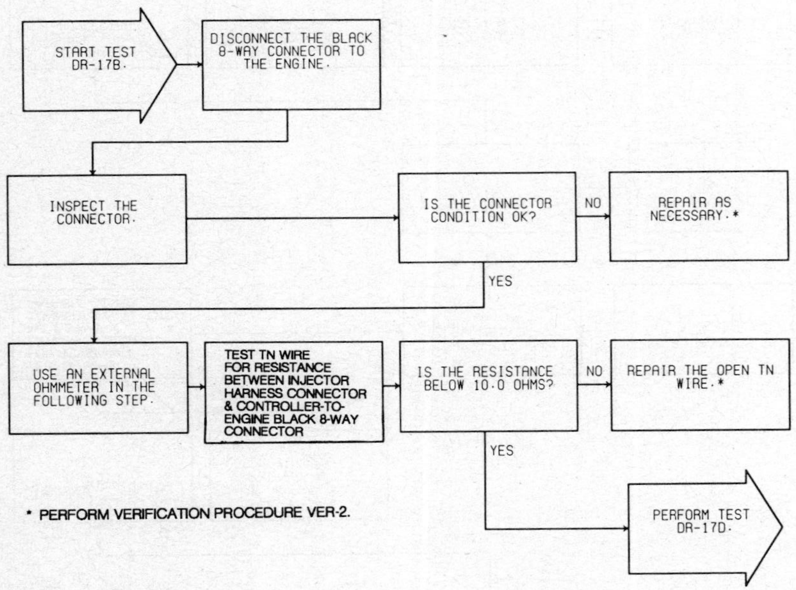
START TEST DR-17B.
DISCONNECT THE BLACK 8-WAY CONNECTOR TO THE ENGINE.
INSPECT THE CONNECTOR.
IS THE CONNECTOR CONDITION OK?
NO
REPAIR AS NECESSARY.*
YES
USE AN EXTERNAL OHMMETER IN THE FOLLOWING STEP.
TEST TN WIRE FOR RESISTANCE BETWEEN INJECTOR HARNESS CONNECTOR & CONTROLLER-TO-ENGINE BLACK 8-WAY CONNECTOR
IS THE RESISTANCE BELOW 10.0 OHMS?
NO
REPAIR THE OPEN TN WIRE.*
YES
PERFORM TEST DR-17D.
* PERFORM VERIFICATION PROCEDURE VER-2.

91H09037

Fig. 83: Driveability Test 17B (3.0L VIN 3) – Code 27, Injector No. 2 Control Circuit

DR-17C: CODE 27, INJECTOR NO. 2 CONTROL CIRCUIT

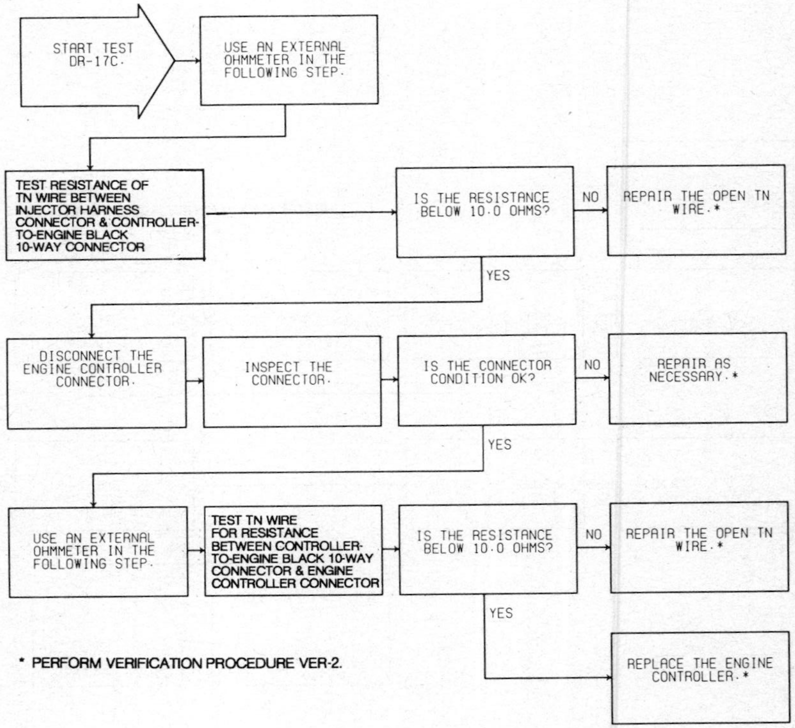
START TEST DR-17C.
USE AN EXTERNAL OHMMETER IN THE FOLLOWING STEP.
TEST RESISTANCE OF TN WIRE BETWEEN INJECTOR HARNESS CONNECTOR & CONTROLLER-TO-ENGINE BLACK 10-WAY CONNECTOR
IS THE RESISTANCE BELOW 10.0 OHMS?
NO
REPAIR THE OPEN TN WIRE.*
YES
DISCONNECT THE ENGINE CONTROLLER CONNECTOR.
INSPECT THE CONNECTOR.
IS THE CONNECTOR CONDITION OK?
NO
REPAIR AS NECESSARY.*
YES
USE AN EXTERNAL OHMMETER IN THE FOLLOWING STEP.
TEST TN WIRE FOR RESISTANCE BETWEEN CONTROLLER-TO-ENGINE BLACK 10-WAY CONNECTOR & ENGINE CONTROLLER CONNECTOR
IS THE RESISTANCE BELOW 10.0 OHMS?
NO
REPAIR THE OPEN TN WIRE.*
YES
REPLACE THE ENGINE CONTROLLER.*
* PERFORM VERIFICATION PROCEDURE VER-2.

91J09038

Fig. 84: Driveability Test 17C (3.0L VIN 3) – Code 27, Injector No. 2 Control Circuit

DR-17D: CODE 27, INJECTOR NO. 2 CONTROL CIRCUIT

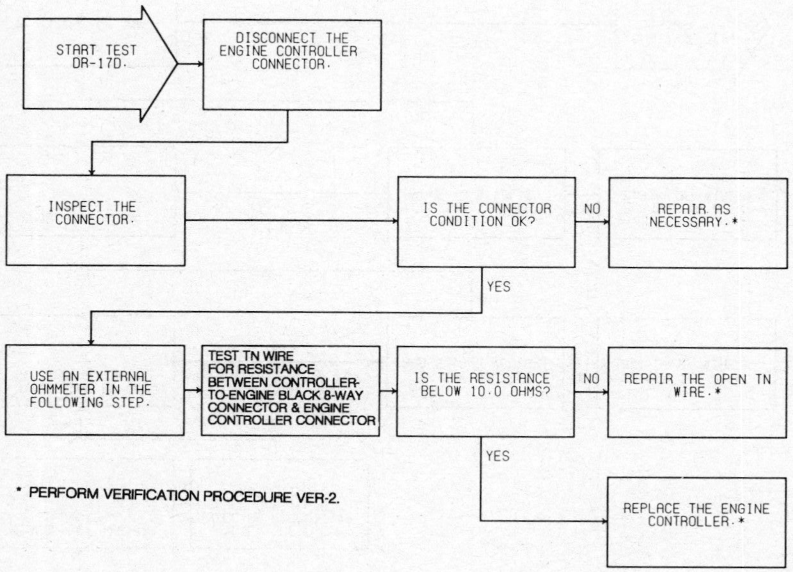
START TEST DR-17D.
DISCONNECT THE ENGINE CONTROLLER CONNECTOR.
INSPECT THE CONNECTOR.
IS THE CONNECTOR CONDITION OK?
NO
REPAIR AS NECESSARY.*
YES
USE AN EXTERNAL OHMMETER IN THE FOLLOWING STEP.
TEST TN WIRE FOR RESISTANCE BETWEEN CONTROLLER-TO-ENGINE BLACK 8-WAY CONNECTOR & ENGINE CONTROLLER CONNECTOR
IS THE RESISTANCE BELOW 10.0 OHMS?
NO
REPAIR THE OPEN TN WIRE.*
YES
REPLACE THE ENGINE CONTROLLER.*

* PERFORM VERIFICATION PROCEDURE VER-2.

91B09039

Fig. 85: Driveability Test 17D (3.0L VIN 3) – Code 27, Injector No. 2 Control Circuit

DR-18A: CODE 26, INJECTOR NO. 3 PEAK CURRENT NOT REACHED (1 OF 3)

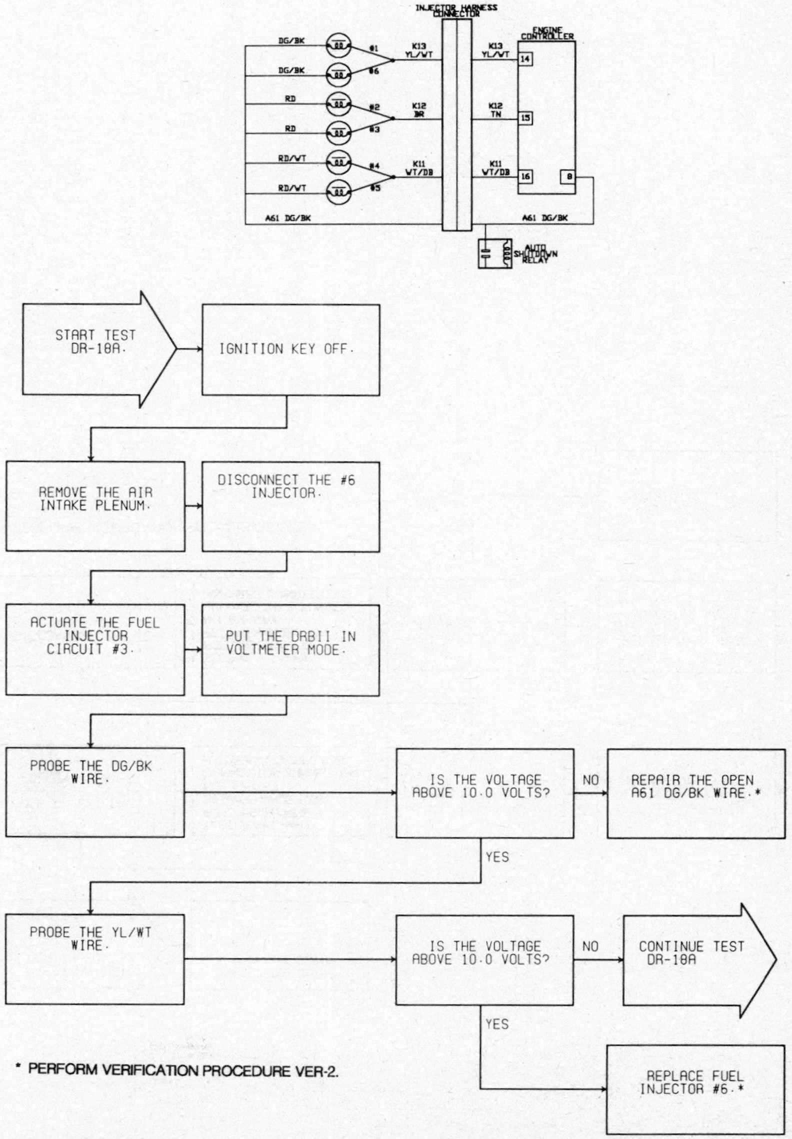
INJECTOR HARNESS CONNECTOR
ENGINE CONTROLLER
DG/BK
DG/BK
RD
RD
RD/WT
RD/WT
A61 DG/BK
#1
#6
#2
#3
#4
#5
K13 YL/WT
K12 BR
K11 WT/DB
K13 YL/WT
K12 TN
K11 WT/DB
14
15
16
8
A61 DG/BK
AUTO SHUTDOWN RELAY
START TEST DR-18A.
IGNITION KEY OFF.
REMOVE THE AIR INTAKE PLENUM.
DISCONNECT THE #6 INJECTOR.
ACTUATE THE FUEL INJECTOR CIRCUIT #3.
PUT THE DRBII IN VOLTMETER MODE.
PROBE THE DG/BK WIRE.
IS THE VOLTAGE ABOVE 10.0 VOLTS?
NO
REPAIR THE OPEN A61 DG/BK WIRE.*
YES
PROBE THE YL/WT WIRE.
IS THE VOLTAGE ABOVE 10.0 VOLTS?
NO
CONTINUE TEST DR-18A
YES
REPLACE FUEL INJECTOR #6.*

* PERFORM VERIFICATION PROCEDURE VER-2.

91D08922 91D09040

Fig. 86: Driveability Test 18A (3.0L VIN 3) – Code 26, Injector No. 3 Peak Current Not Reached (1 of 3)

DR-18A: CODE 26, INJECTOR NO. 3 PEAK CURRENT NOT REACHED (2 OF 3)

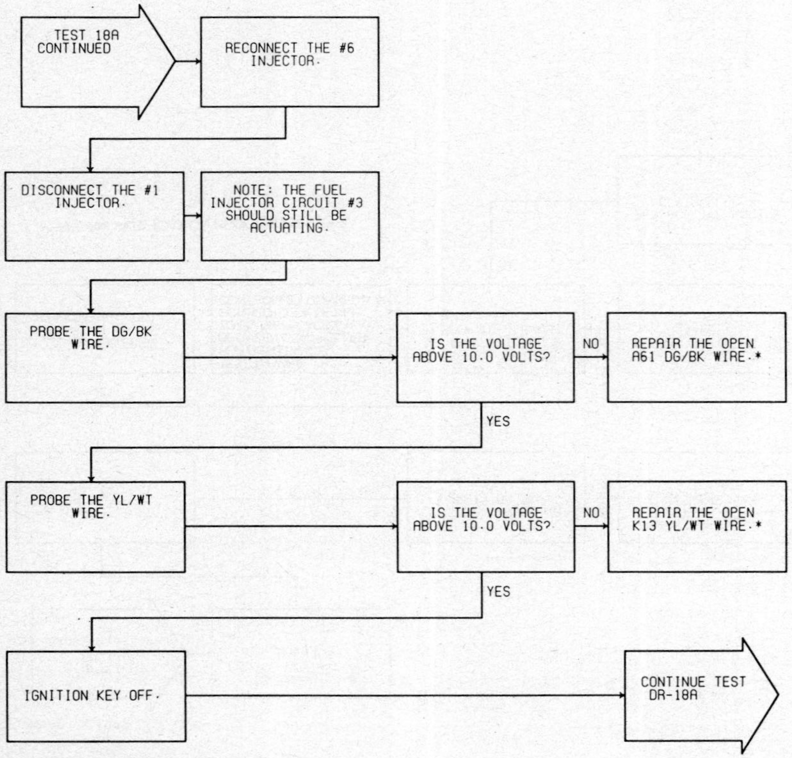
TEST 18A CONTINUED
RECONNECT THE #6 INJECTOR.
DISCONNECT THE #1 INJECTOR.
NOTE: THE FUEL INJECTOR CIRCUIT #3 SHOULD STILL BE ACTUATING.
PROBE THE DG/BK WIRE.
IS THE VOLTAGE ABOVE 10.0 VOLTS?
NO
REPAIR THE OPEN A61 DG/BK WIRE.*
YES
PROBE THE YL/WT WIRE.
IS THE VOLTAGE ABOVE 10.0 VOLTS?
NO
REPAIR THE OPEN K13 YL/WT WIRE.*
YES
IGNITION KEY OFF.
CONTINUE TEST DR-18A

* PERFORM VERIFICATION PROCEDURE VER-2.

91F09041

Fig. 87: Driveability Test 18A (3.0L VIN 3) – Code 26, Injector No. 3 Peak Current Not Reached (2 of 3)

DR-18A: CODE 26, INJECTOR NO. 3 PEAK CURRENT NOT REACHED (3 OF 3)

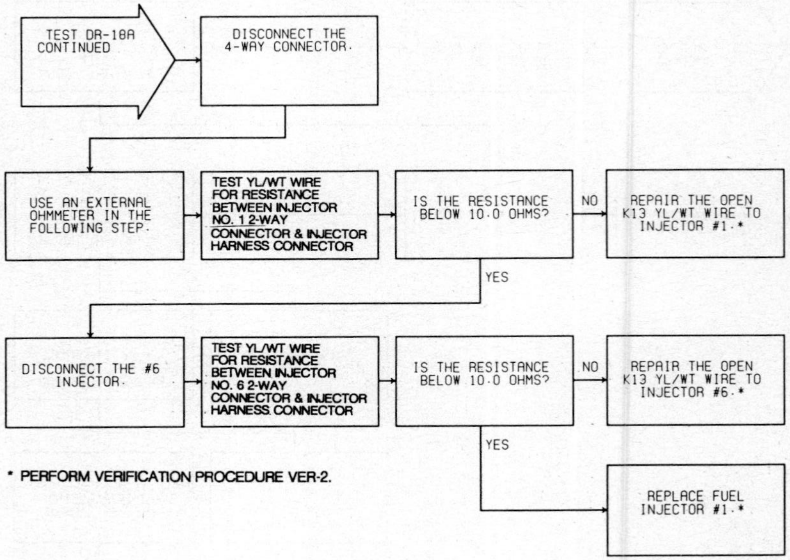
TEST DR-18A CONTINUED
DISCONNECT THE 4-WAY CONNECTOR.
USE AN EXTERNAL OHMMETER IN THE FOLLOWING STEP.
TEST YL/WT WIRE FOR RESISTANCE BETWEEN INJECTOR NO. 1 2-WAY CONNECTOR & INJECTOR HARNESS CONNECTOR
IS THE RESISTANCE BELOW 10.0 OHMS?
NO
REPAIR THE OPEN K13 YL/WT WIRE TO INJECTOR #1.*
YES
DISCONNECT THE #6 INJECTOR.
TEST YL/WT WIRE FOR RESISTANCE BETWEEN INJECTOR NO. 6 2-WAY CONNECTOR & INJECTOR HARNESS CONNECTOR
IS THE RESISTANCE BELOW 10.0 OHMS?
NO
REPAIR THE OPEN K13 YL/WT WIRE TO INJECTOR #6.*
YES
REPLACE FUEL INJECTOR #1.*

* PERFORM VERIFICATION PROCEDURE VER-2.

91H09042

Fig. 88: Driveability Test 18A (3.0L VIN 3) – Code 26, Injector No. 3 Peak Current Not Reached (3 of 3)

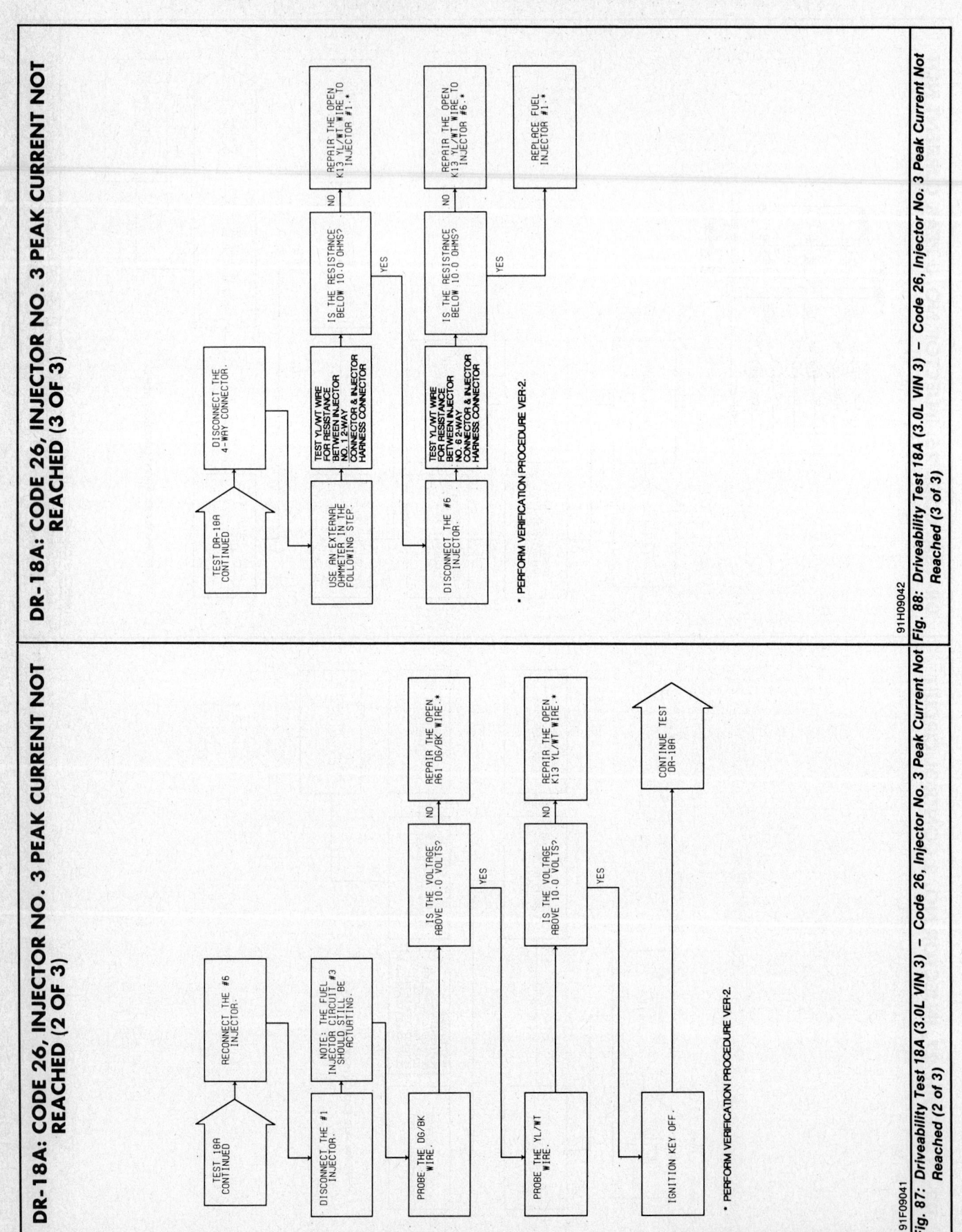

DR-19A: CODE 27, INJECTOR NO. 3 CONTROL CIRCUIT (1 OF 3)

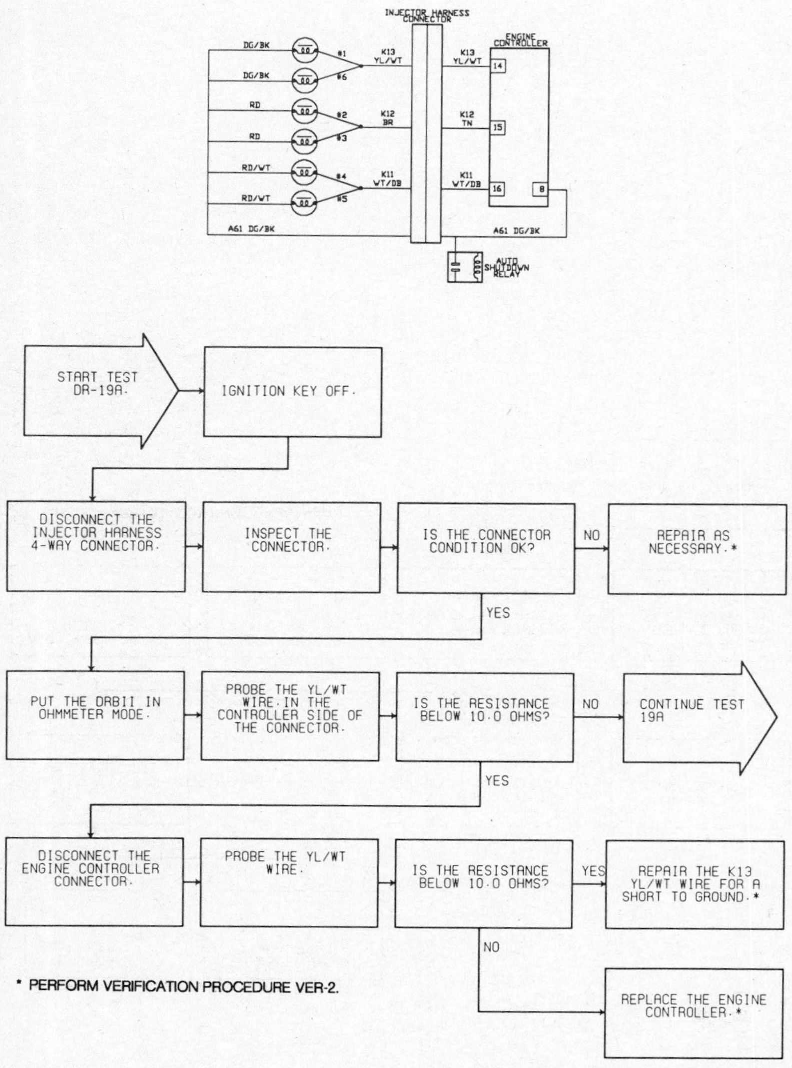
INJECTOR HARNESS CONNECTOR
ENGINE CONTROLLER
DG/BK
DG/BK
RD
RD
RD/WT
RD/WT
A61 DG/BK
#1
#6
#2
#3
#4
#5
K13 YL/WT
K12 BR
K11 WT/DB
K13 YL/WT
K12 TN
K11 WT/DB
14
15
16
8
A61 DG/BK
AUTO SHUTDOWN RELAY
START TEST DR-19A.
IGNITION KEY OFF.
DISCONNECT THE INJECTOR HARNESS 4-WAY CONNECTOR.
INSPECT THE CONNECTOR.
IS THE CONNECTOR CONDITION OK?
NO
REPAIR AS NECESSARY.*
YES
PUT THE DRBII IN OHMMETER MODE.
PROBE THE YL/WT WIRE IN THE CONTROLLER SIDE OF THE CONNECTOR.
IS THE RESISTANCE BELOW 10.0 OHMS?
NO
CONTINUE TEST 19A
YES
DISCONNECT THE ENGINE CONTROLLER CONNECTOR.
PROBE THE YL/WT WIRE.
IS THE RESISTANCE BELOW 10.0 OHMS?
YES
REPAIR THE K13 YL/WT WIRE FOR A SHORT TO GROUND.*
NO
REPLACE THE ENGINE CONTROLLER.*
* PERFORM VERIFICATION PROCEDURE VER-2.

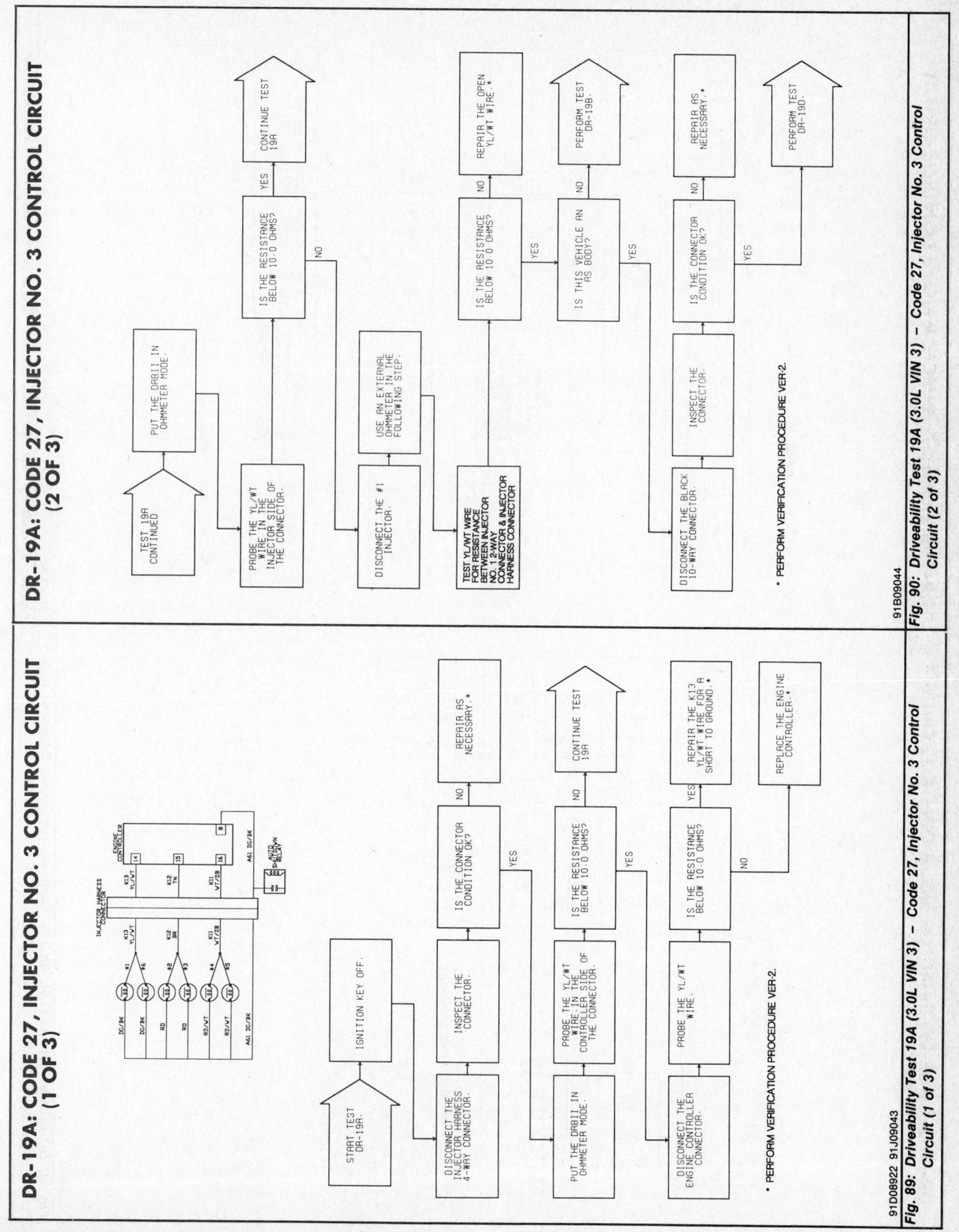

91D08922 91J09043

Fig. 89: Driveability Test 19A (3.0L VIN 3) – Code 27, Injector No. 3 Control Circuit (1 of 3)

DR-19A: CODE 27, INJECTOR NO. 3 CONTROL CIRCUIT (2 OF 3)

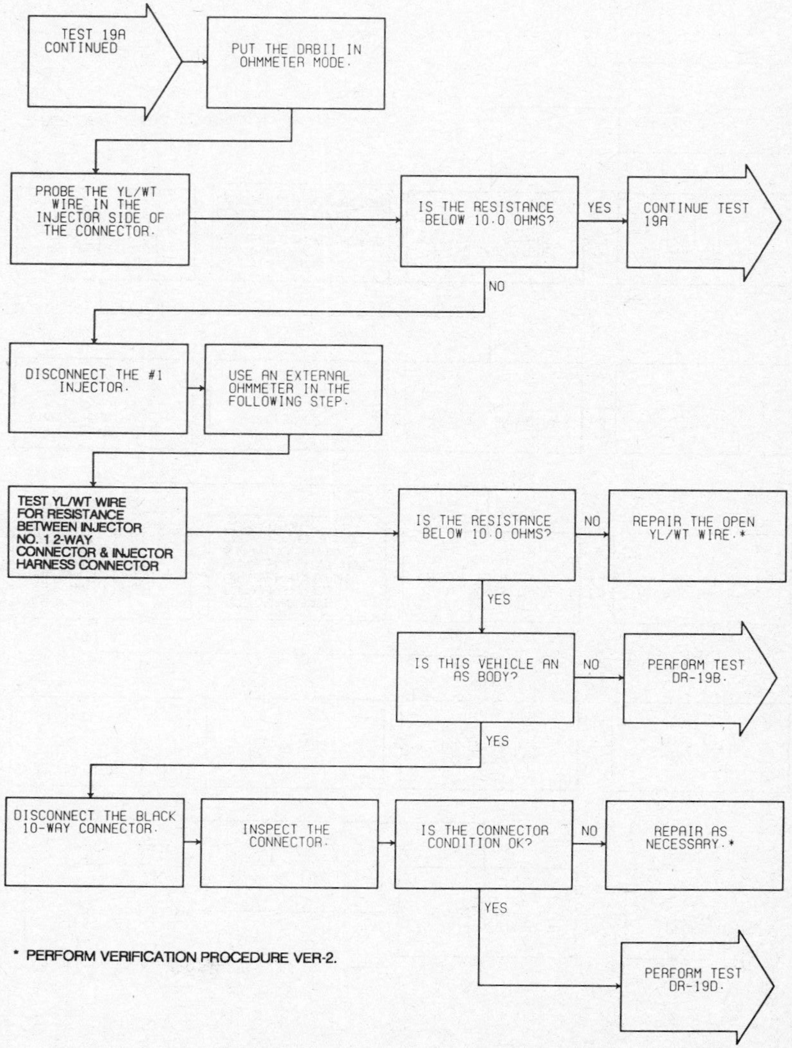
TEST 19A CONTINUED
PUT THE DRBII IN OHMMETER MODE.
PROBE THE YL/WT WIRE IN THE INJECTOR SIDE OF THE CONNECTOR.
IS THE RESISTANCE BELOW 10.0 OHMS?
YES
CONTINUE TEST 19A
NO
DISCONNECT THE #1 INJECTOR.
USE AN EXTERNAL OHMMETER IN THE FOLLOWING STEP.
TEST YL/WT WIRE FOR RESISTANCE BETWEEN INJECTOR NO. 1 2-WAY CONNECTOR & INJECTOR HARNESS CONNECTOR
IS THE RESISTANCE BELOW 10.0 OHMS?
NO
REPAIR THE OPEN YL/WT WIRE.*
YES
IS THIS VEHICLE AN AS BODY?
NO
PERFORM TEST DR-19B.
YES
DISCONNECT THE BLACK 10-WAY CONNECTOR.
INSPECT THE CONNECTOR.
IS THE CONNECTOR CONDITION OK?
NO
REPAIR AS NECESSARY.*
YES
PERFORM TEST DR-19D.
* PERFORM VERIFICATION PROCEDURE VER-2.

91B09044

Fig. 90: Driveability Test 19A (3.0L VIN 3) – Code 27, Injector No. 3 Control Circuit (2 of 3)

DR-19A: CODE 27, INJECTOR NO. 3 CONTROL CIRCUIT (3 OF 3)

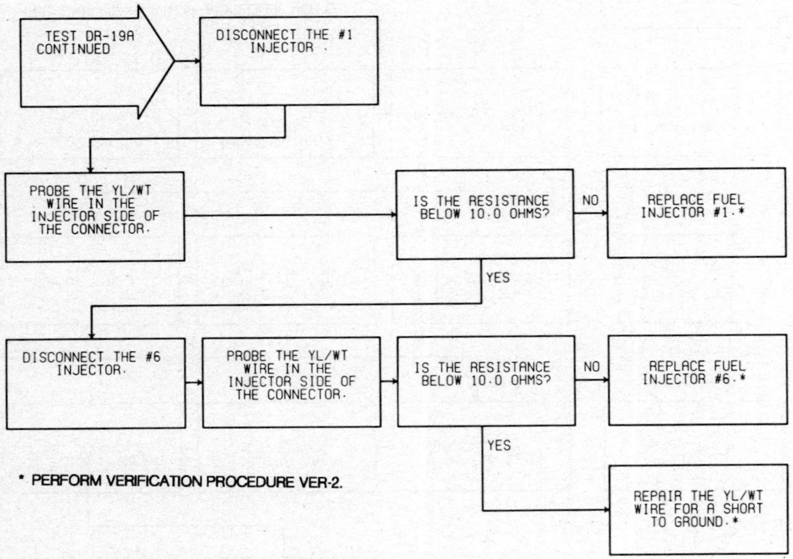
TEST DR-19A CONTINUED
DISCONNECT THE #1 INJECTOR.
PROBE THE YL/WT WIRE IN THE INJECTOR SIDE OF THE CONNECTOR.
IS THE RESISTANCE BELOW 10.0 OHMS?
NO
REPLACE FUEL INJECTOR #1.*
YES
DISCONNECT THE #6 INJECTOR.
PROBE THE YL/WT WIRE IN THE INJECTOR SIDE OF THE CONNECTOR.
IS THE RESISTANCE BELOW 10.0 OHMS?
NO
REPLACE FUEL INJECTOR #6.*
YES
REPAIR THE YL/WT WIRE FOR A SHORT TO GROUND.*
* PERFORM VERIFICATION PROCEDURE VER-2.

91E09045

Fig. 91: Driveability Test 19A (3.0L VIN 3) – Code 27, Injector No. 3 Control Circuit (3 of 3)

DR-19B: CODE 27, INJECTOR NO. 3 CONTROL CIRCUIT

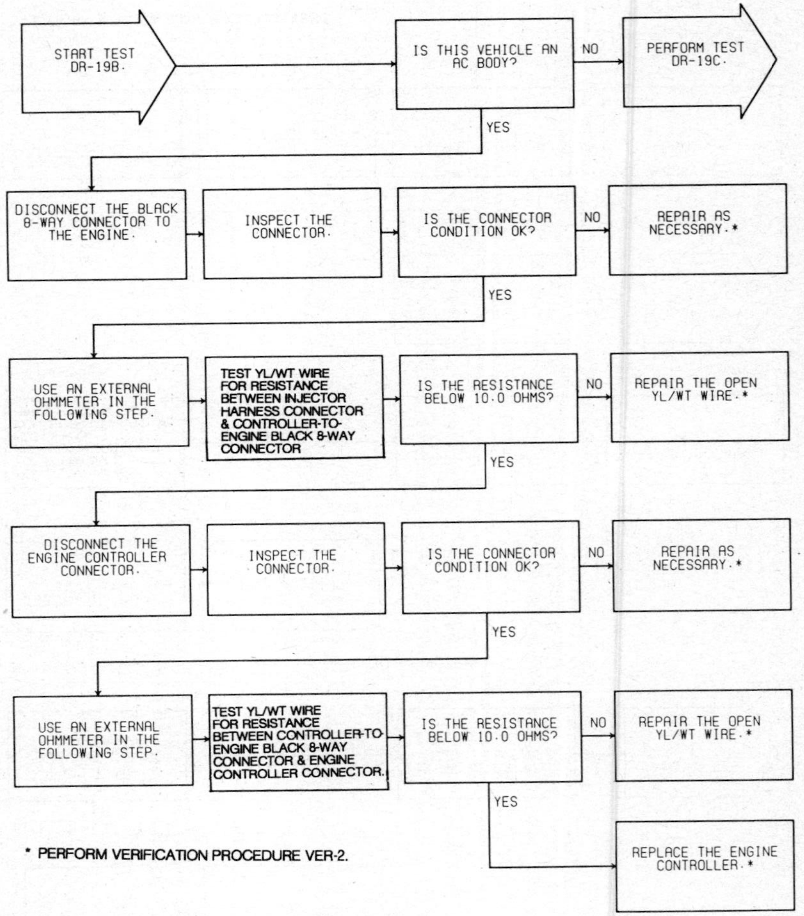
START TEST DR-19B.
IS THIS VEHICLE AN AC BODY?
NO
PERFORM TEST DR-19C.
YES
DISCONNECT THE BLACK 8-WAY CONNECTOR TO THE ENGINE.
INSPECT THE CONNECTOR.
IS THE CONNECTOR CONDITION OK?
NO
REPAIR AS NECESSARY.*
YES
USE AN EXTERNAL OHMMETER IN THE FOLLOWING STEP.
TEST YL/WT WIRE FOR RESISTANCE BETWEEN INJECTOR HARNESS CONNECTOR & CONTROLLER-TO-ENGINE BLACK 8-WAY CONNECTOR
IS THE RESISTANCE BELOW 10.0 OHMS?
NO
REPAIR THE OPEN YL/WT WIRE.*
YES
DISCONNECT THE ENGINE CONTROLLER CONNECTOR.
INSPECT THE CONNECTOR.
IS THE CONNECTOR CONDITION OK?
NO
REPAIR AS NECESSARY.*
YES
USE AN EXTERNAL OHMMETER IN THE FOLLOWING STEP.
TEST YL/WT WIRE FOR RESISTANCE BETWEEN CONTROLLER-TO-ENGINE BLACK 8-WAY CONNECTOR & ENGINE CONTROLLER CONNECTOR.
IS THE RESISTANCE BELOW 10.0 OHMS?
NO
REPAIR THE OPEN YL/WT WIRE.*
YES
REPLACE THE ENGINE CONTROLLER.*
* PERFORM VERIFICATION PROCEDURE VER-2.

91G09046

Fig. 92: Driveability Test 19B (3.0L VIN 3) – Code 27, Injector No. 3 Control Circuit

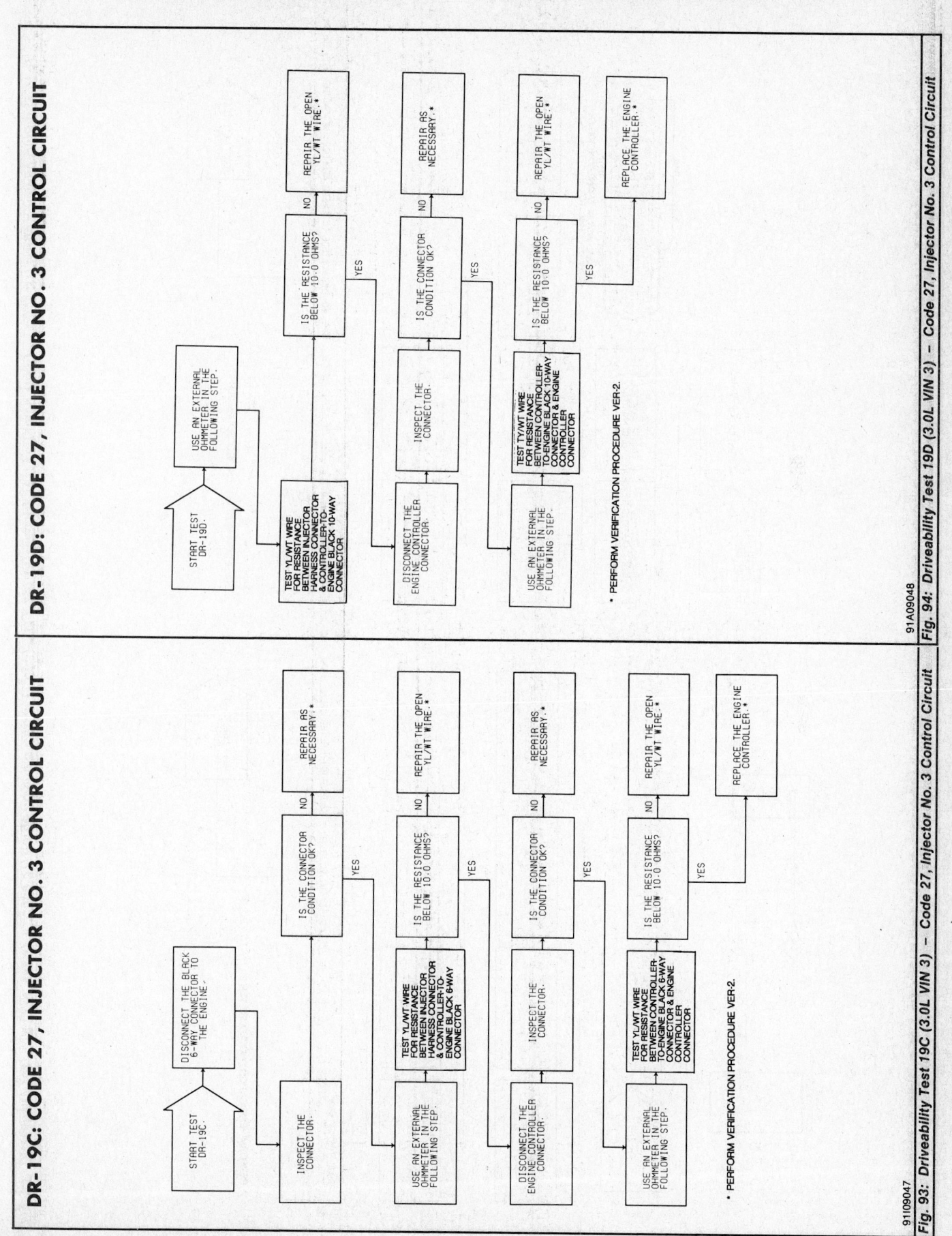

DR-19C: CODE 27, INJECTOR NO. 3 CONTROL CIRCUIT

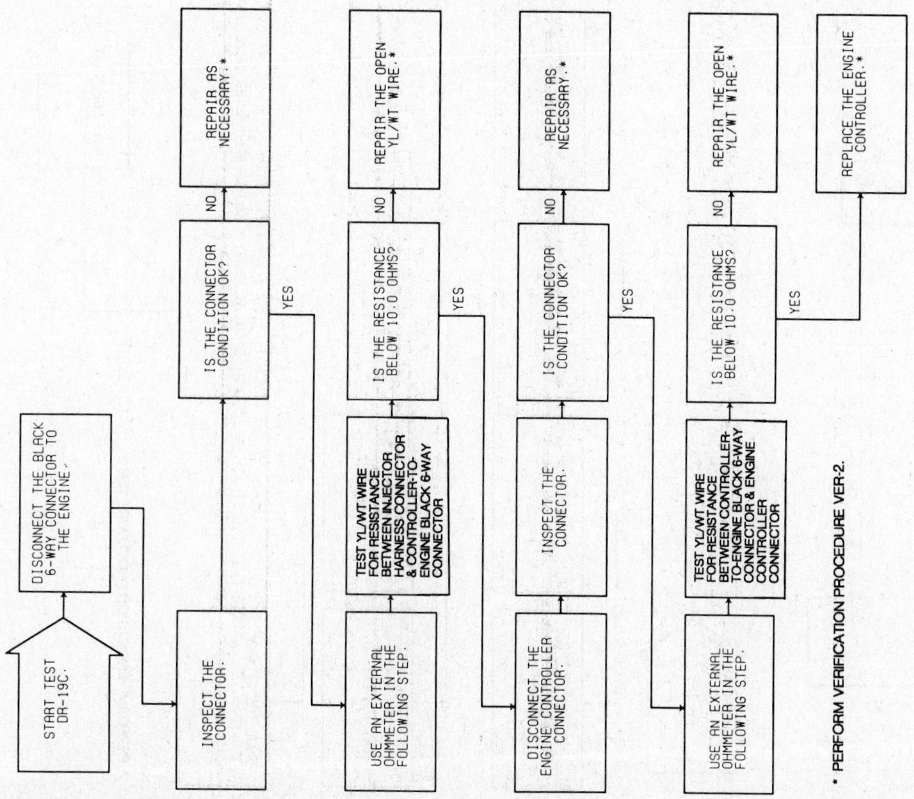

START TEST DR-19C.
DISCONNECT THE BLACK 6-WAY CONNECTOR TO THE ENGINE.
INSPECT THE CONNECTOR.
IS THE CONNECTOR CONDITION OK?
NO
REPAIR AS NECESSARY.*
YES
USE AN EXTERNAL OHMMETER IN THE FOLLOWING STEP.
TEST YL/WT WIRE FOR RESISTANCE BETWEEN INJECTOR HARNESS CONNECTOR & CONTROLLER-TO-ENGINE BLACK 6-WAY CONNECTOR
IS THE RESISTANCE BELOW 10.0 OHMS?
NO
REPAIR THE OPEN YL/WT WIRE.*
YES
DISCONNECT THE ENGINE CONTROLLER CONNECTOR.
INSPECT THE CONNECTOR.
IS THE CONNECTOR CONDITION OK?
NO
REPAIR AS NECESSARY.*
YES
USE AN EXTERNAL OHMMETER IN THE FOLLOWING STEP.
TEST YL/WT WIRE FOR RESISTANCE BETWEEN CONTROLLER-TO-ENGINE BLACK 6-WAY CONNECTOR & ENGINE CONTROLLER CONNECTOR
IS THE RESISTANCE BELOW 10.0 OHMS?
NO
REPAIR THE OPEN YL/WT WIRE.*
YES
REPLACE THE ENGINE CONTROLLER.*

* PERFORM VERIFICATION PROCEDURE VER-2.

91109047

Fig. 93: Driveability Test 19C (3.0L VIN 3) – Code 27, Injector No. 3 Control Circuit

DR-19D: CODE 27, INJECTOR NO. 3 CONTROL CIRCUIT

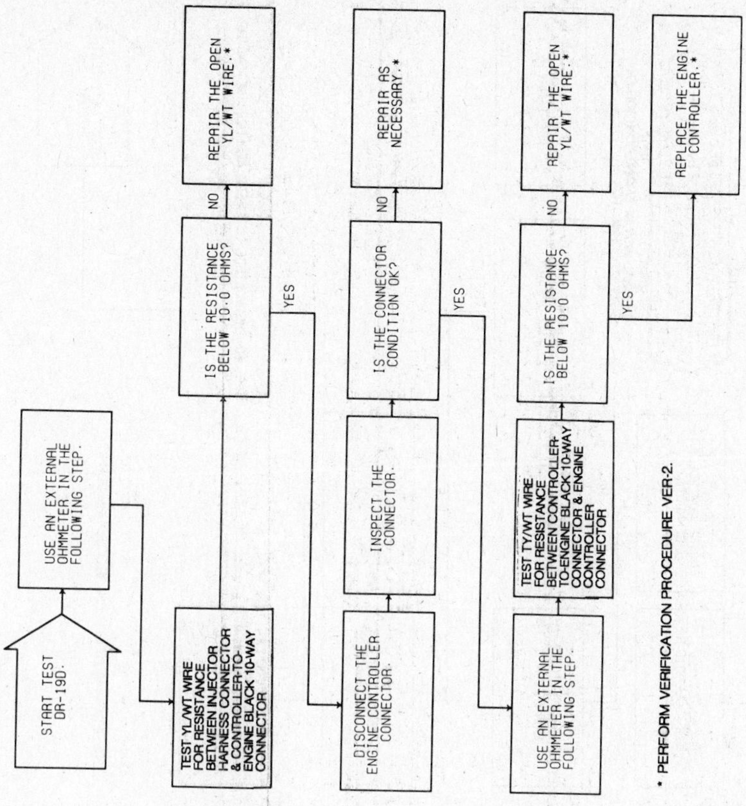

START TEST DR-19D.
USE AN EXTERNAL OHMMETER IN THE FOLLOWING STEP.
TEST YL/WT WIRE FOR RESISTANCE BETWEEN INJECTOR HARNESS CONNECTOR & CONTROLLER-TO-ENGINE BLACK 10-WAY CONNECTOR
IS THE RESISTANCE BELOW 10.0 OHMS?
NO
REPAIR THE OPEN YL/WT WIRE.*
YES
DISCONNECT THE ENGINE CONTROLLER CONNECTOR.
INSPECT THE CONNECTOR.
IS THE CONNECTOR CONDITION OK?
NO
REPAIR AS NECESSARY.*
YES
USE AN EXTERNAL OHMMETER IN THE FOLLOWING STEP.
TEST TY/WT WIRE FOR RESISTANCE BETWEEN CONTROLLER-TO-ENGINE BLACK 10-WAY CONNECTOR & ENGINE CONTROLLER CONNECTOR
IS THE RESISTANCE BELOW 10.0 OHMS?
NO
REPAIR THE OPEN YL/WT WIRE.*
YES
REPLACE THE ENGINE CONTROLLER.*

* PERFORM VERIFICATION PROCEDURE VER-2.

91A09048

Fig. 94: Driveability Test 19D (3.0L VIN 3) – Code 27, Injector No. 3 Control Circuit

DR-20A: CODE 31, PURGE SOLENOID CIRCUIT (1 OF 3)

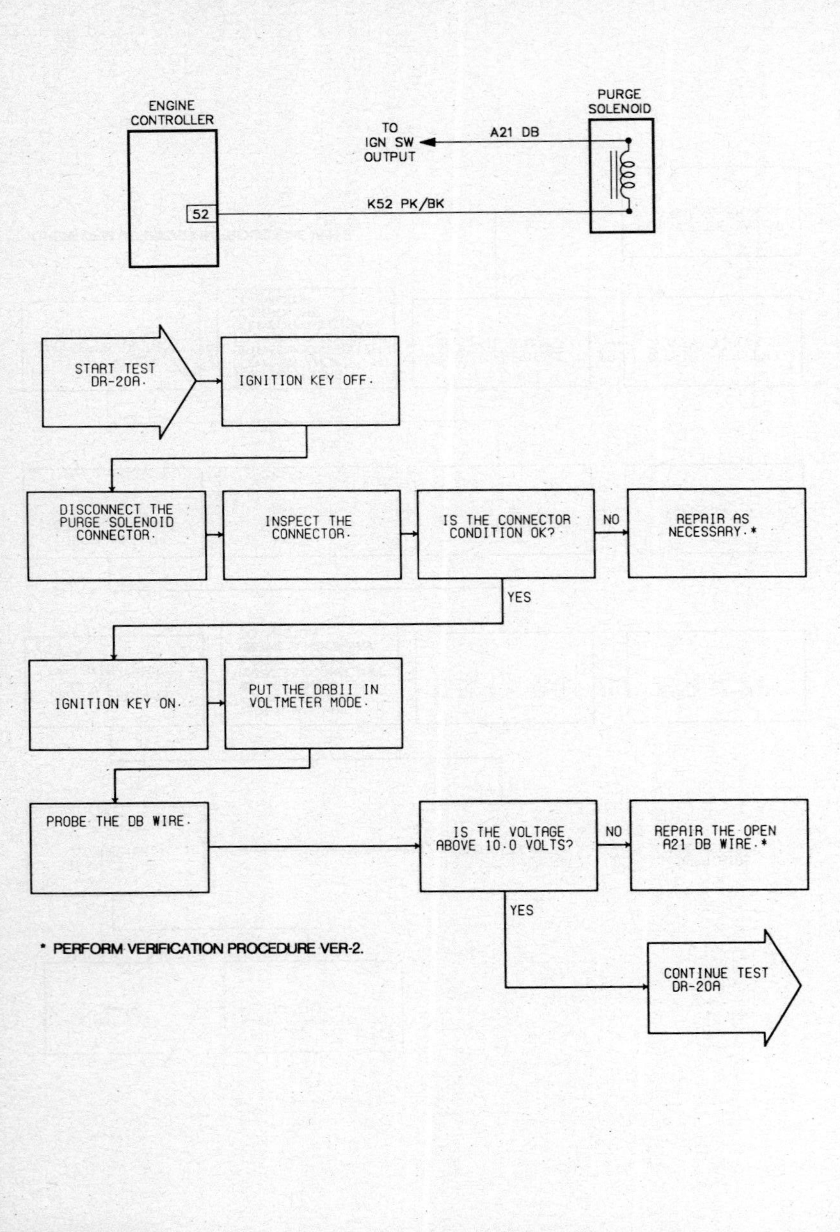
ENGINE CONTROLLER
52
TO IGN SW OUTPUT
A21 DB
K52 PK/BK
PURGE SOLENOID
START TEST DR-20A.
IGNITION KEY OFF.
DISCONNECT THE PURGE SOLENOID CONNECTOR.
INSPECT THE CONNECTOR.
IS THE CONNECTOR CONDITION OK?
NO
REPAIR AS NECESSARY.*
YES
IGNITION KEY ON.
PUT THE DRBII IN VOLTMETER MODE.
PROBE THE DB WIRE.
IS THE VOLTAGE ABOVE 10.0 VOLTS?
NO
REPAIR THE OPEN A21 DB WIRE.*
YES
CONTINUE TEST DR-20A
* PERFORM VERIFICATION PROCEDURE VER-2.

91F08923 91C09049

Fig. 95: Driveability Test 20A (3.0L VIN 3) – Code 31, Purge Solenoid Circuit (1 of 3)

DR-20A: CODE 31, PURGE SOLENOID CIRCUIT (2 OF 3)

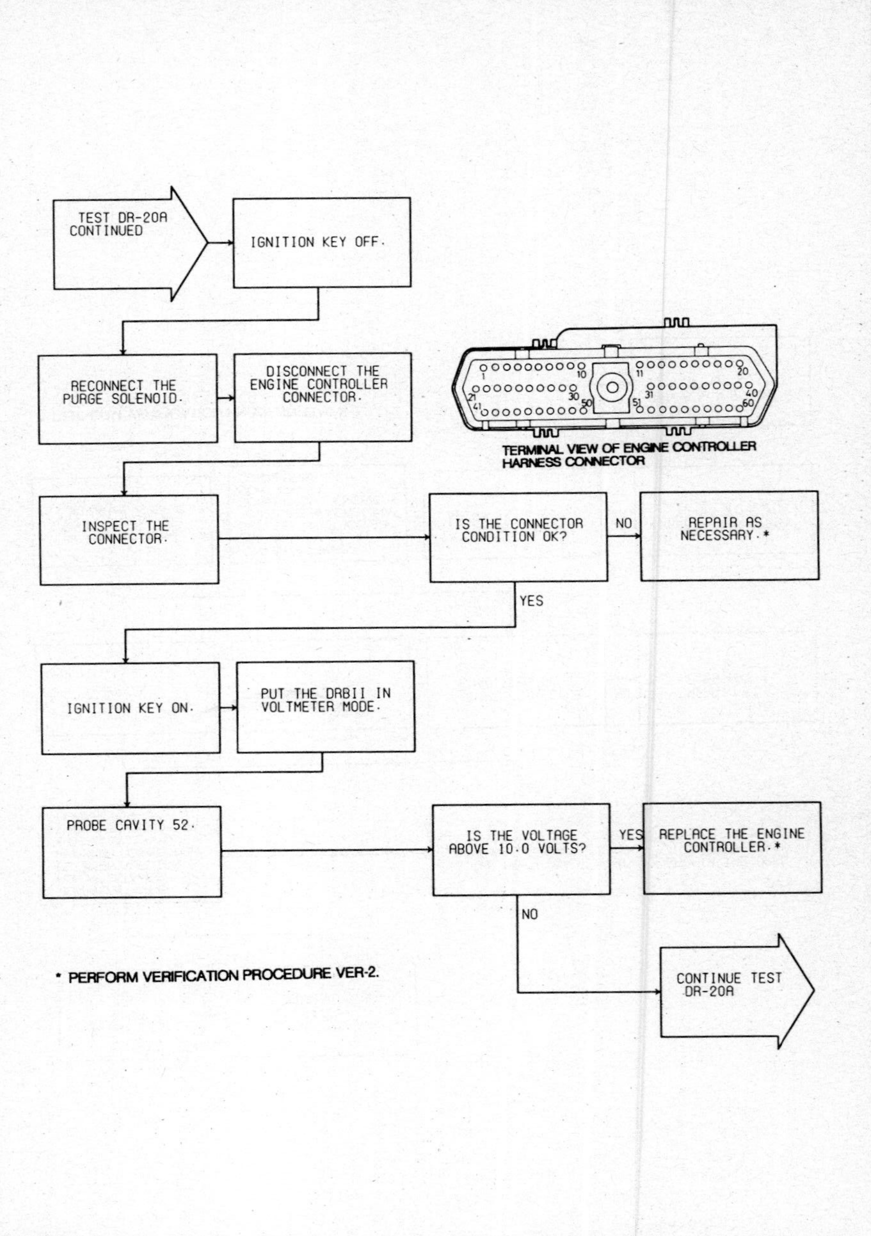
TEST DR-20A CONTINUED
IGNITION KEY OFF.
RECONNECT THE PURGE SOLENOID.
DISCONNECT THE ENGINE CONTROLLER CONNECTOR.
TERMINAL VIEW OF ENGINE CONTROLLER HARNESS CONNECTOR
INSPECT THE CONNECTOR.
IS THE CONNECTOR CONDITION OK?
NO
REPAIR AS NECESSARY.*
YES
IGNITION KEY ON.
PUT THE DRBII IN VOLTMETER MODE.
PROBE CAVITY 52.
IS THE VOLTAGE ABOVE 10.0 VOLTS?
YES
REPLACE THE ENGINE CONTROLLER.*
NO
CONTINUE TEST DR-20A
* PERFORM VERIFICATION PROCEDURE VER-2.

91E09050

Fig. 96: Driveability Test 20A (3.0L VIN 3) – Code 31, Purge Solenoid Circuit (2 of 3)

DR-20A: CODE 31, PURGE SOLENOID CIRCUIT (3 OF 3)

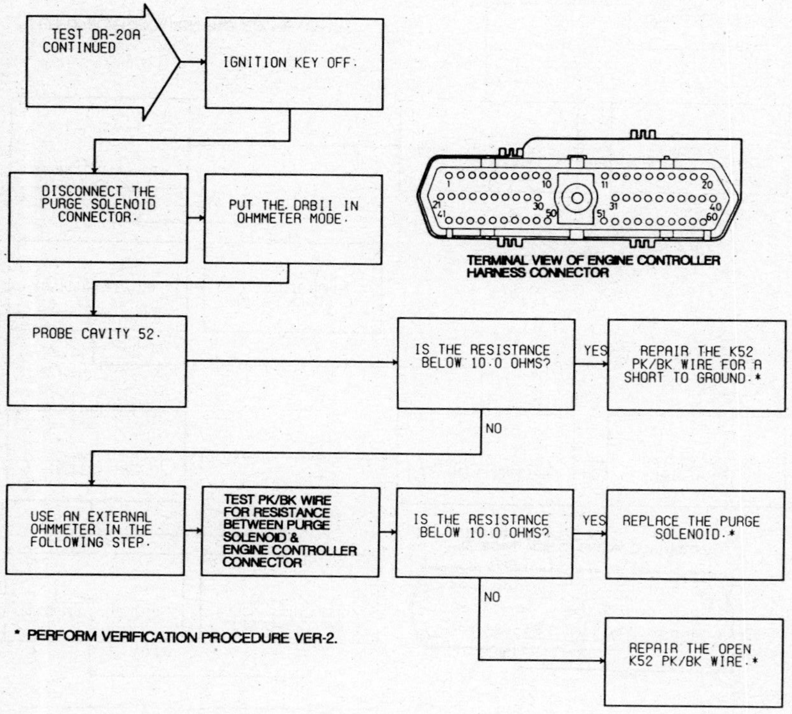
TEST DR-20A CONTINUED
IGNITION KEY OFF.
DISCONNECT THE PURGE SOLENOID CONNECTOR.
PUT THE DRBII IN OHMMETER MODE.
TERMINAL VIEW OF ENGINE CONTROLLER HARNESS CONNECTOR
PROBE CAVITY 52.
IS THE RESISTANCE BELOW 10.0 OHMS?
YES
REPAIR THE K52 PK/BK WIRE FOR A SHORT TO GROUND.*
NO
USE AN EXTERNAL OHMMETER IN THE FOLLOWING STEP.
TEST PK/BK WIRE FOR RESISTANCE BETWEEN PURGE SOLENOID & ENGINE CONTROLLER CONNECTOR
IS THE RESISTANCE BELOW 10.0 OHMS?
YES
REPLACE THE PURGE SOLENOID.*
NO
REPAIR THE OPEN K52 PK/BK WIRE.*

* PERFORM VERIFICATION PROCEDURE VER-2.

91G09051

Fig. 97: Driveability Test 20A (3.0L VIN 3) – Code 31, Purge Solenoid Circuit (3 of 3)

DR-21A: CODE 32, EGR SOLENOID CIRCUIT (1 OF 3)

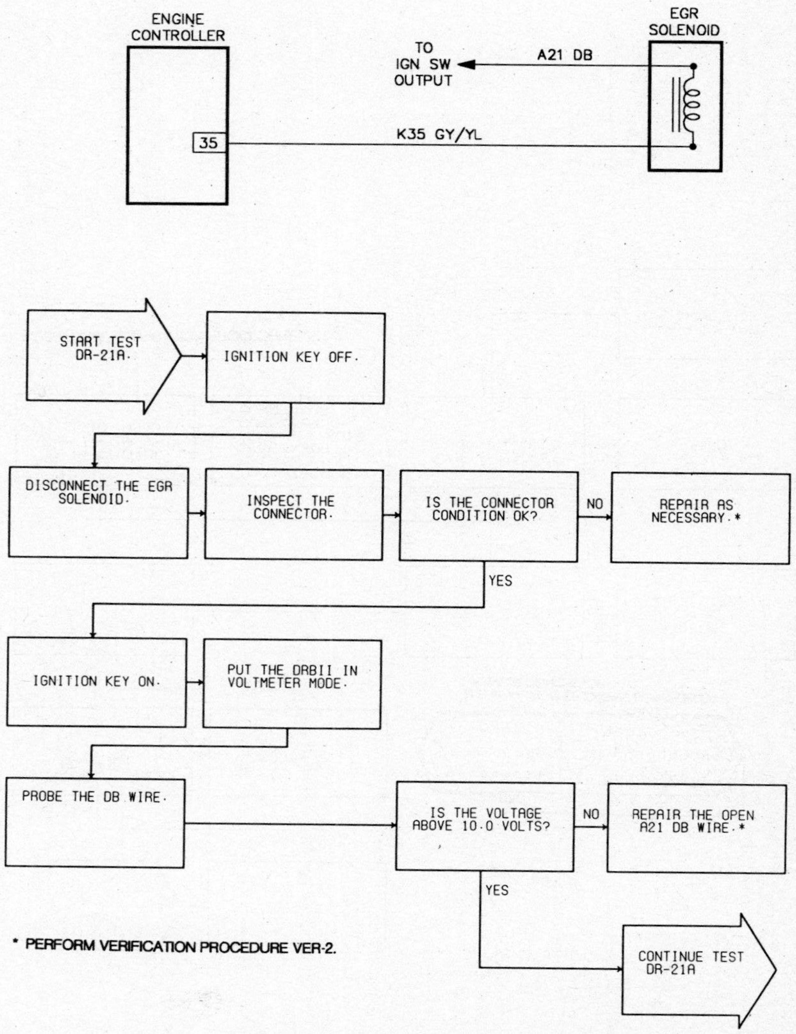
ENGINE CONTROLLER
35
EGR SOLENOID
TO IGN SW OUTPUT
A21 DB
K35 GY/YL
START TEST DR-21A.
IGNITION KEY OFF.
DISCONNECT THE EGR SOLENOID.
INSPECT THE CONNECTOR.
IS THE CONNECTOR CONDITION OK?
NO
REPAIR AS NECESSARY.*
YES
IGNITION KEY ON.
PUT THE DRBII IN VOLTMETER MODE.
PROBE THE DB WIRE.
IS THE VOLTAGE ABOVE 10.0 VOLTS?
NO
REPAIR THE OPEN A21 DB WIRE.*
YES
CONTINUE TEST DR-21A

* PERFORM VERIFICATION PROCEDURE VER-2.

91H08924 91I09052

Fig. 98: Driveability Test 21A (3.0L VIN 3) – Code 32, EGR Solenoid Circuit (1 of 3)

DR-21A: CODE 32, EGR SOLENOID CIRCUIT (2 OF 3)

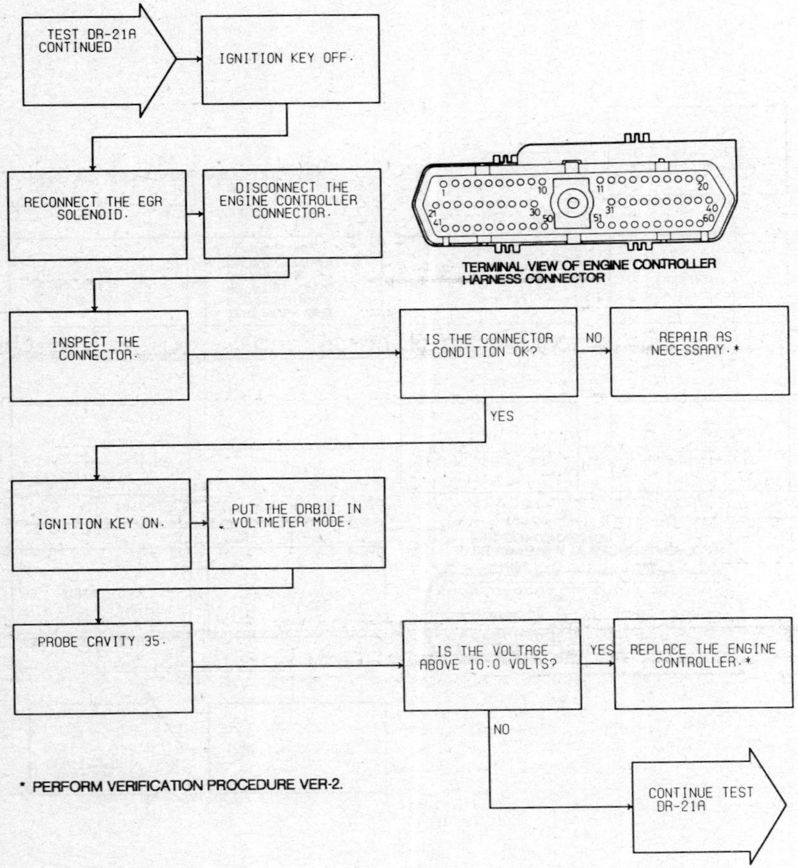
TEST DR-21A CONTINUED
IGNITION KEY OFF.
RECONNECT THE EGR SOLENOID.
DISCONNECT THE ENGINE CONTROLLER CONNECTOR.
TERMINAL VIEW OF ENGINE CONTROLLER HARNESS CONNECTOR
INSPECT THE CONNECTOR.
IS THE CONNECTOR CONDITION OK?
NO
REPAIR AS NECESSARY.*
YES
IGNITION KEY ON.
PUT THE DRBII IN VOLTMETER MODE.
PROBE CAVITY 35.
IS THE VOLTAGE ABOVE 10.0 VOLTS?
YES
REPLACE THE ENGINE CONTROLLER.*
NO
CONTINUE TEST DR-21A
* PERFORM VERIFICATION PROCEDURE VER-2.

91A09053

Fig. 99: Driveability Test 21A (3.0L VIN 3) – Code 32, EGR Solenoid Circuit (2 of 3)

DR-21A: CODE 32, EGR SOLENOID CIRCUIT (3 OF 3)

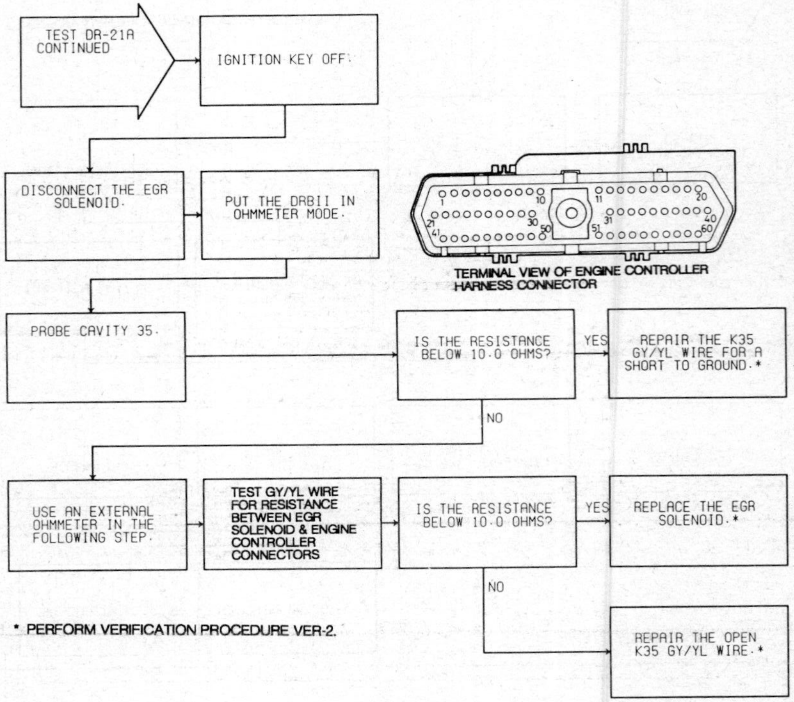
TEST DR-21A CONTINUED
IGNITION KEY OFF.
DISCONNECT THE EGR SOLENOID.
PUT THE DRBII IN OHMMETER MODE.
TERMINAL VIEW OF ENGINE CONTROLLER HARNESS CONNECTOR
PROBE CAVITY 35.
IS THE RESISTANCE BELOW 10.0 OHMS?
YES
REPAIR THE K35 GY/YL WIRE FOR A SHORT TO GROUND.*
NO
USE AN EXTERNAL OHMMETER IN THE FOLLOWING STEP.
TEST GY/YL WIRE FOR RESISTANCE BETWEEN EGR SOLENOID & ENGINE CONTROLLER CONNECTORS
IS THE RESISTANCE BELOW 10.0 OHMS?
YES
REPLACE THE EGR SOLENOID.*
NO
REPAIR THE OPEN K35 GY/YL WIRE.*
* PERFORM VERIFICATION PROCEDURE VER-2.

91C09054

Fig. 100: Driveability Test 21A (3.0L VIN 3) – Code 32, EGR Solenoid Circuit (3 of 3)

DR-22A: CODE 32, EGR SYSTEM FAILURE (1 OF 5)

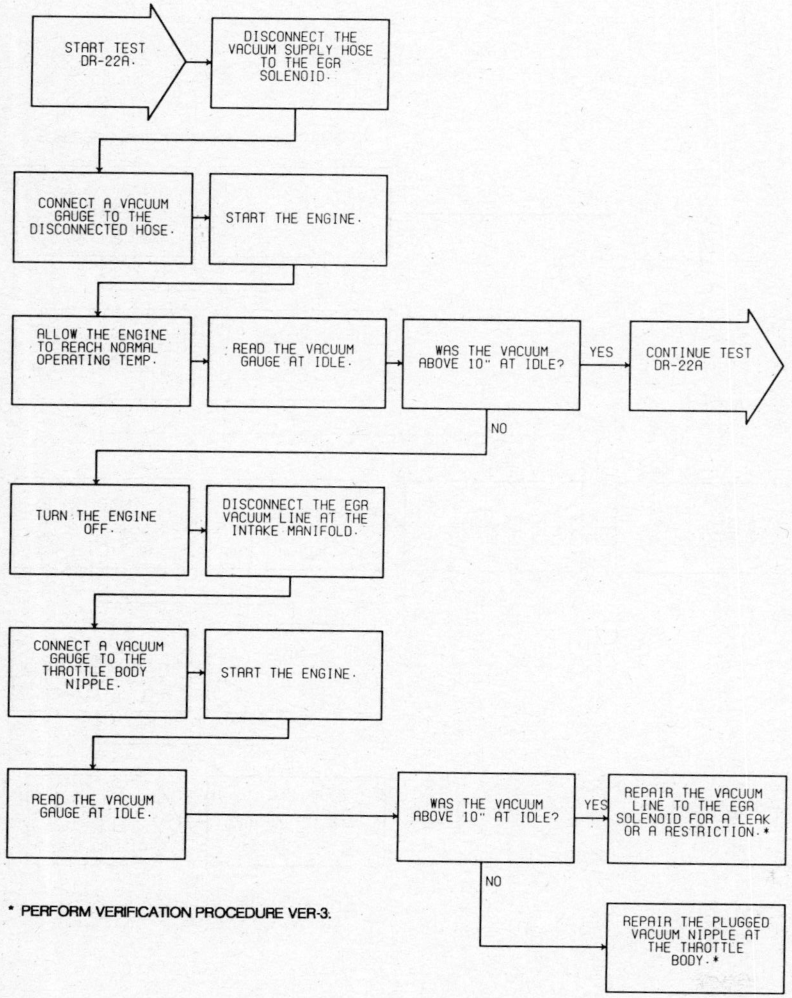

START TEST DR-22A.
DISCONNECT THE VACUUM SUPPLY HOSE TO THE EGR SOLENOID.
CONNECT A VACUUM GAUGE TO THE DISCONNECTED HOSE.
START THE ENGINE.
ALLOW THE ENGINE TO REACH NORMAL OPERATING TEMP.
READ THE VACUUM GAUGE AT IDLE.
WAS THE VACUUM ABOVE 10" AT IDLE?
YES
CONTINUE TEST DR-22A
NO
TURN THE ENGINE OFF.
DISCONNECT THE EGR VACUUM LINE AT THE INTAKE MANIFOLD.
CONNECT A VACUUM GAUGE TO THE THROTTLE BODY NIPPLE.
START THE ENGINE.
READ THE VACUUM GAUGE AT IDLE.
WAS THE VACUUM ABOVE 10" AT IDLE?
YES
REPAIR THE VACUUM LINE TO THE EGR SOLENOID FOR A LEAK OR A RESTRICTION.*
NO
REPAIR THE PLUGGED VACUUM NIPPLE AT THE THROTTLE BODY.*

* PERFORM VERIFICATION PROCEDURE VER-3.

91F09055

Fig. 101: Driveability Test 22A (3.0L VIN 3) – Code 32, EGR System Failure (1 of 5)

DR-22A: CODE 32, EGR SYSTEM FAILURE (2 OF 5)

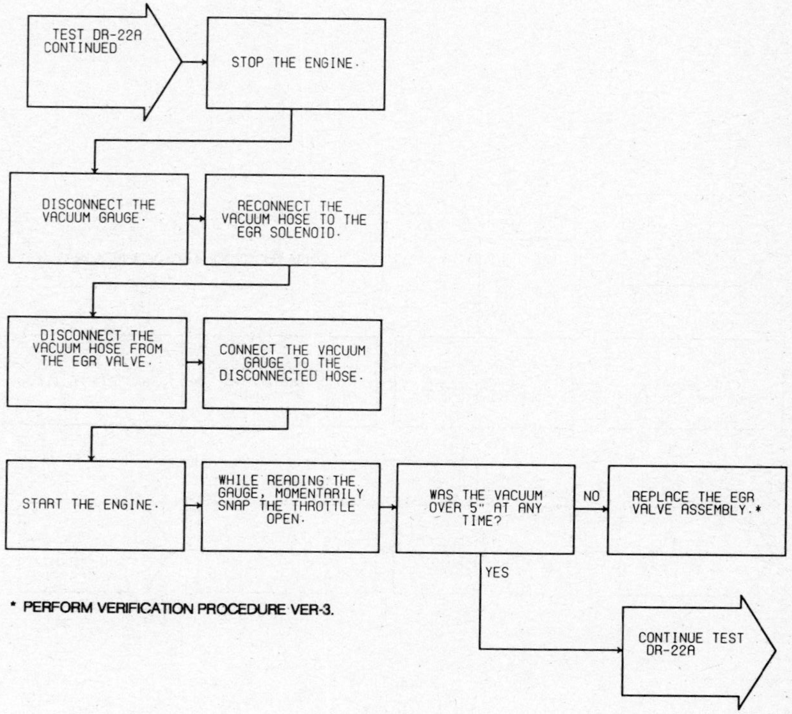

TEST DR-22A CONTINUED
STOP THE ENGINE.
DISCONNECT THE VACUUM GAUGE.
RECONNECT THE VACUUM HOSE TO THE EGR SOLENOID.
DISCONNECT THE VACUUM HOSE FROM THE EGR VALVE.
CONNECT THE VACUUM GAUGE TO THE DISCONNECTED HOSE.
START THE ENGINE.
WHILE READING THE GAUGE, MOMENTARILY SNAP THE THROTTLE OPEN.
WAS THE VACUUM OVER 5" AT ANY TIME?
NO
REPLACE THE EGR VALVE ASSEMBLY.*
YES
CONTINUE TEST DR-22A

* PERFORM VERIFICATION PROCEDURE VER-3.

91H09056

Fig. 102: Driveability Test 22A (3.0L VIN 3) – Code 32, EGR System Failure (2 of 5)

1991 ENGINE PERFORMANCE
Self-Diagnostics – 3.0L VIN 3 (Cont.)

DR-22A: CODE 32, EGR SYSTEM FAILURE (3 OF 5)

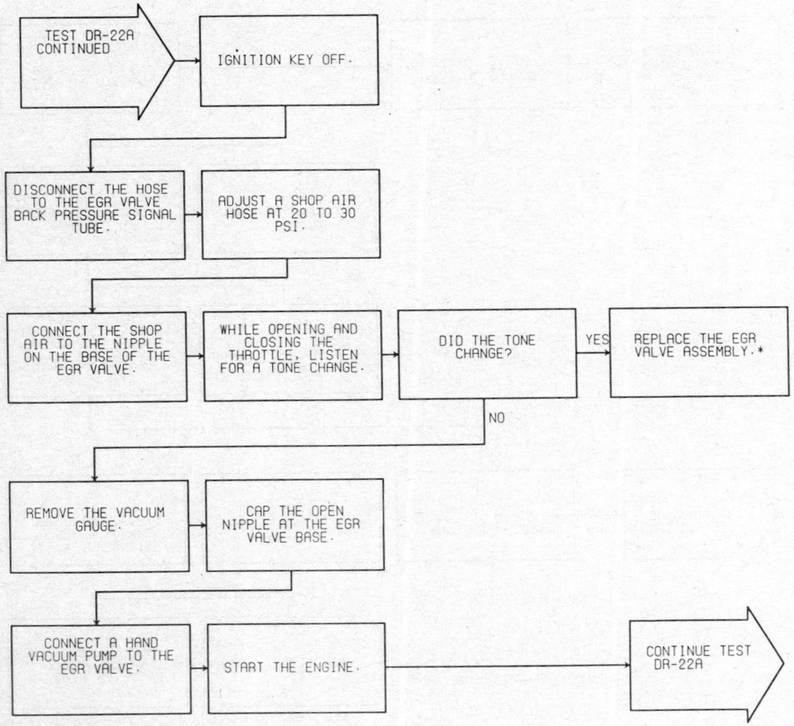
TEST DR-22A CONTINUED
IGNITION KEY OFF.
DISCONNECT THE HOSE TO THE EGR VALVE BACK PRESSURE SIGNAL TUBE.
ADJUST A SHOP AIR HOSE AT 20 TO 30 PSI.
CONNECT THE SHOP AIR TO THE NIPPLE ON THE BASE OF THE EGR VALVE.
WHILE OPENING AND CLOSING THE THROTTLE, LISTEN FOR A TONE CHANGE.
DID THE TONE CHANGE?
YES
REPLACE THE EGR VALVE ASSEMBLY.*
NO
REMOVE THE VACUUM GAUGE.
CAP THE OPEN NIPPLE AT THE EGR VALVE BASE.
CONNECT A HAND VACUUM PUMP TO THE EGR VALVE.
START THE ENGINE.
CONTINUE TEST DR-22A

* PERFORM VERIFICATION PROCEDURE VER-3.

91J09057

Fig. 103: Driveability Test 22A (3.0L VIN 3) – Code 32, EGR System Failure (3 of 5)

DR-22A: CODE 32, EGR SYSTEM FAILURE (4 OF 5)

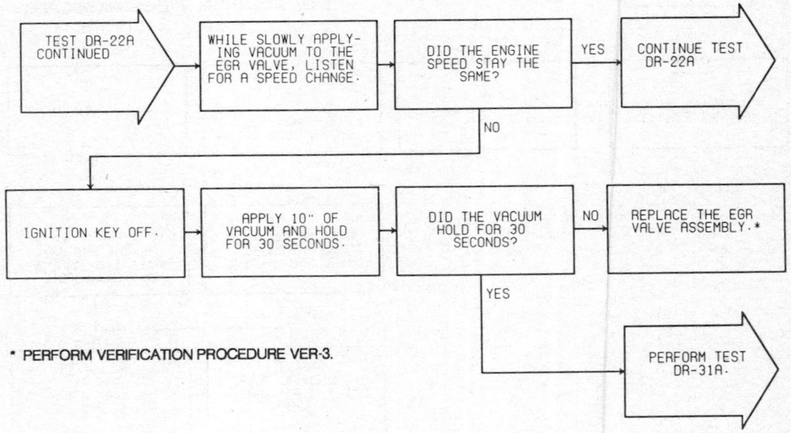
TEST DR-22A CONTINUED
WHILE SLOWLY APPLYING VACUUM TO THE EGR VALVE, LISTEN FOR A SPEED CHANGE.
DID THE ENGINE SPEED STAY THE SAME?
YES
CONTINUE TEST DR-22A
NO
IGNITION KEY OFF.
APPLY 10" OF VACUUM AND HOLD FOR 30 SECONDS.
DID THE VACUUM HOLD FOR 30 SECONDS?
NO
REPLACE THE EGR VALVE ASSEMBLY.*
YES
PERFORM TEST DR-31A.
* PERFORM VERIFICATION PROCEDURE VER-3.

91B09058

Fig. 104: Driveability Test 22A (3.0L VIN 3) – Code 32, EGR System Failure (4 of 5)

DR-22A: CODE 32, EGR SYSTEM FAILURE (5 OF 5)

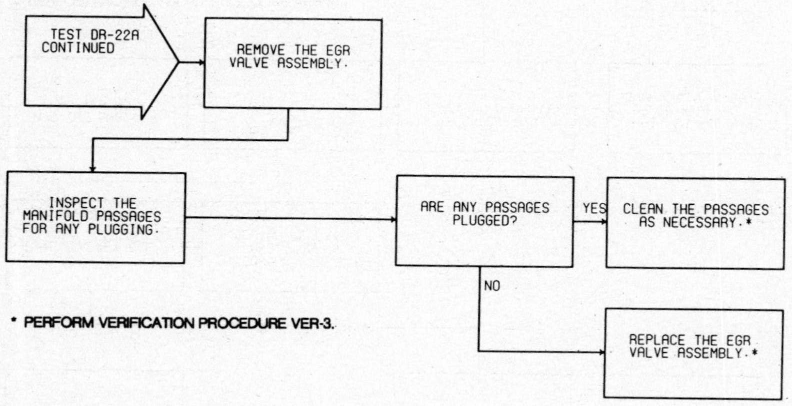
TEST DR-22A CONTINUED
REMOVE THE EGR VALVE ASSEMBLY.
INSPECT THE MANIFOLD PASSAGES FOR ANY PLUGGING.
ARE ANY PASSAGES PLUGGED?
YES
CLEAN THE PASSAGES AS NECESSARY.*
NO
REPLACE THE EGR VALVE ASSEMBLY.*

* PERFORM VERIFICATION PROCEDURE VER-3.

91D09059

Fig. 105: Driveability Test 22A (3.0L VIN 3) – Code 32, EGR System Failure (5 of 5)

DR-23A: CODE 33, A/C CLUTCH RELAY CIRCUIT (1 OF 3)

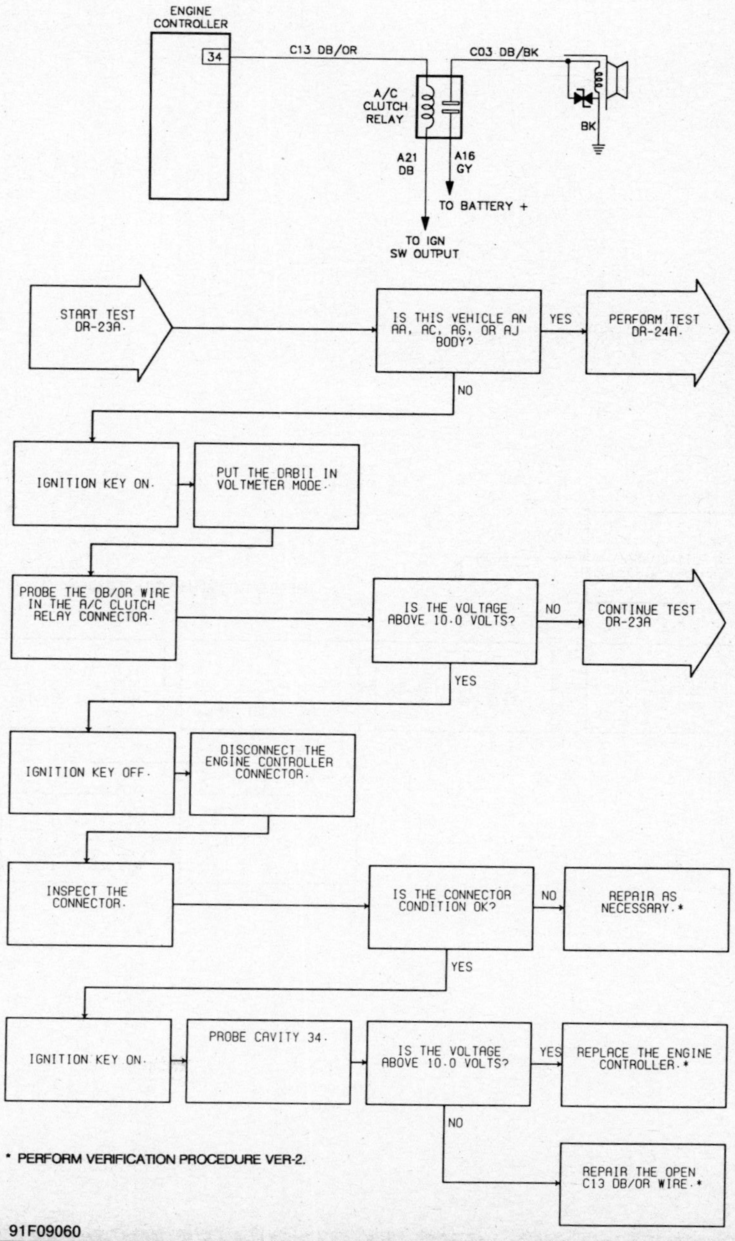
ENGINE CONTROLLER
34
C13 DB/OR
C03 DB/BK
A/C CLUTCH RELAY
BK
A21 DB
A16 GY
TO BATTERY +
TO IGN SW OUTPUT
START TEST DR-23A.
IS THIS VEHICLE AN AA, AC, AG, OR AJ BODY?
YES
PERFORM TEST DR-24A.
NO
IGNITION KEY ON.
PUT THE DRBII IN VOLTMETER MODE.
PROBE THE DB/OR WIRE IN THE A/C CLUTCH RELAY CONNECTOR.
IS THE VOLTAGE ABOVE 10.0 VOLTS?
NO
CONTINUE TEST DR-23A
YES
IGNITION KEY OFF.
DISCONNECT THE ENGINE CONTROLLER CONNECTOR.
INSPECT THE CONNECTOR.
IS THE CONNECTOR CONDITION OK?
NO
REPAIR AS NECESSARY.*
YES
IGNITION KEY ON.
PROBE CAVITY 34.
IS THE VOLTAGE ABOVE 10.0 VOLTS?
YES
REPLACE THE ENGINE CONTROLLER.*
NO
REPAIR THE OPEN C13 DB/OR WIRE.*

* PERFORM VERIFICATION PROCEDURE VER-2.

91A08925 91F09060

Fig. 106: Driveability Test 23A (3.0L VIN 3) – Code 33, A/C Clutch Relay Circuit (1 of 3)

DR-23A: CODE 33, A/C CLUTCH RELAY CIRCUIT (2 OF 3)

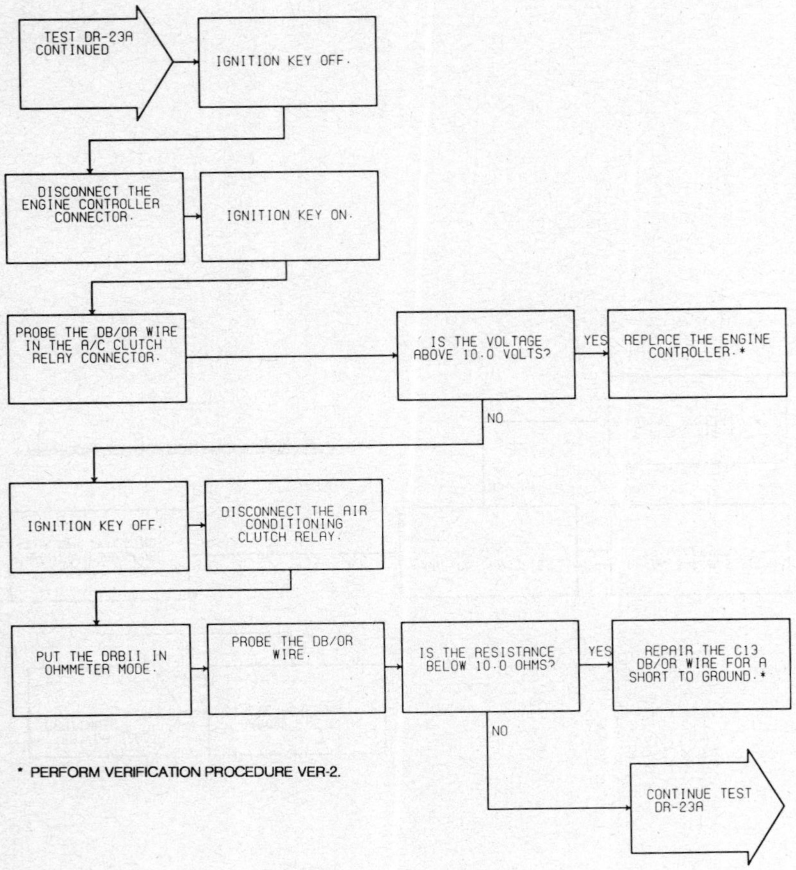
TEST DR-23A CONTINUED
IGNITION KEY OFF.
DISCONNECT THE ENGINE CONTROLLER CONNECTOR.
IGNITION KEY ON.
PROBE THE DB/OR WIRE IN THE A/C CLUTCH RELAY CONNECTOR.
IS THE VOLTAGE ABOVE 10.0 VOLTS?
YES
REPLACE THE ENGINE CONTROLLER.*
NO
IGNITION KEY OFF.
DISCONNECT THE AIR CONDITIONING CLUTCH RELAY.
PUT THE DRBII IN OHMMETER MODE.
PROBE THE DB/OR WIRE.
IS THE RESISTANCE BELOW 10.0 OHMS?
YES
REPAIR THE C13 DB/OR WIRE FOR A SHORT TO GROUND.*
NO
CONTINUE TEST DR-23A

* PERFORM VERIFICATION PROCEDURE VER-2.

91H09061

Fig. 107: Driveability Test 23A (3.0L VIN 3) – Code 33, A/C Clutch Relay Circuit (2 of 3)

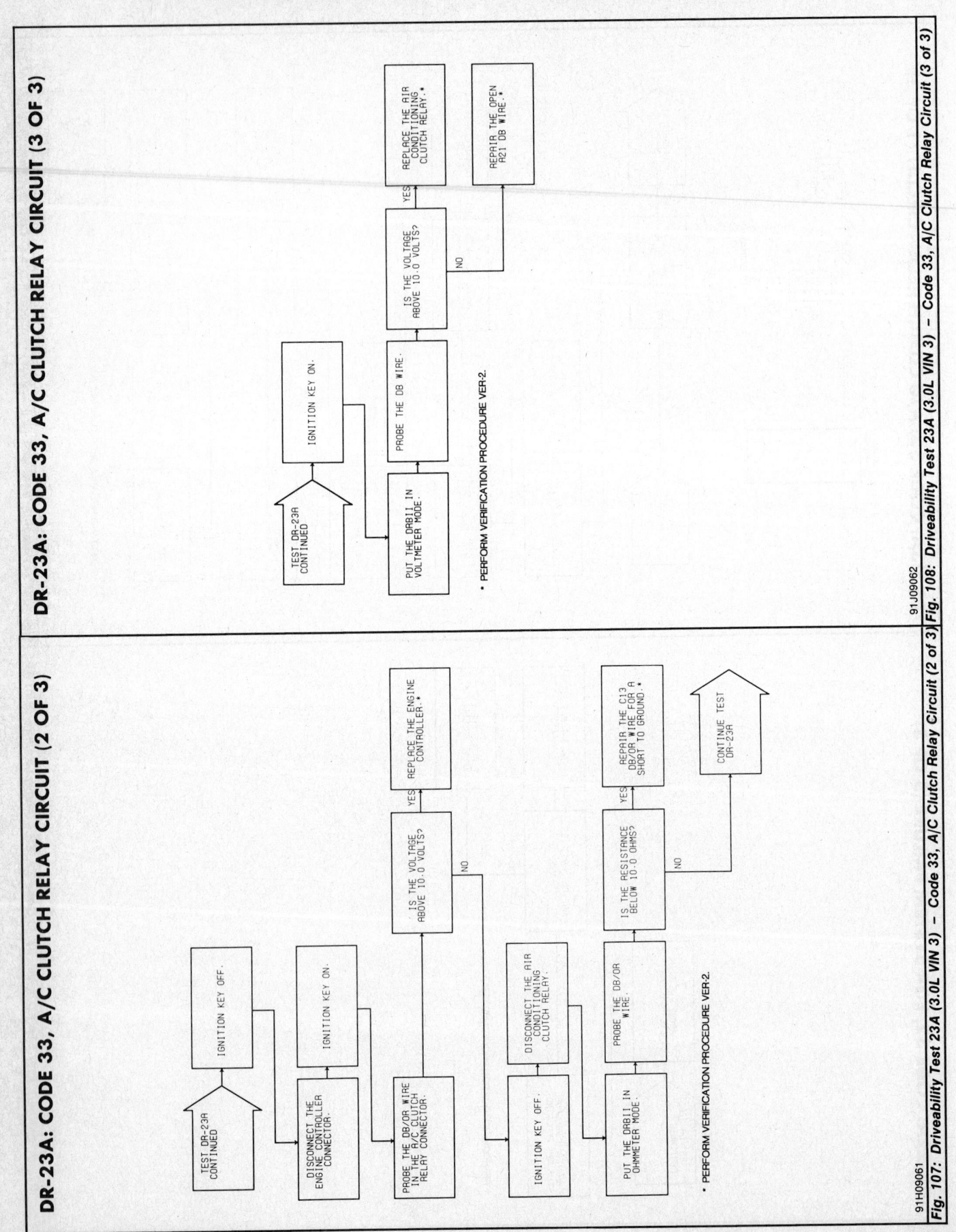

DR-23A: CODE 33, A/C CLUTCH RELAY CIRCUIT (3 OF 3)

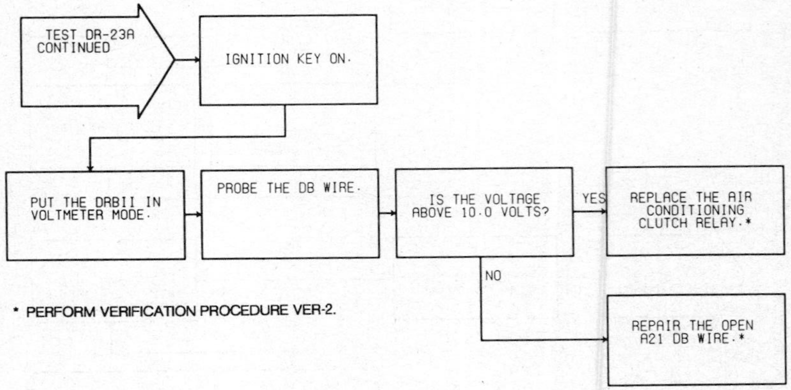
TEST DR-23A CONTINUED
IGNITION KEY ON.
PUT THE DRBII IN VOLTMETER MODE.
PROBE THE DB WIRE.
IS THE VOLTAGE ABOVE 10.0 VOLTS?
YES
REPLACE THE AIR CONDITIONING CLUTCH RELAY.*
NO
REPAIR THE OPEN A21 DB WIRE.*

* PERFORM VERIFICATION PROCEDURE VER-2.

91J09062

Fig. 108: Driveability Test 23A (3.0L VIN 3) – Code 33, A/C Clutch Relay Circuit (3 of 3)

DR-24A: CODE 33, A/C CLUTCH RELAY CIRCUIT (1 OF 2)

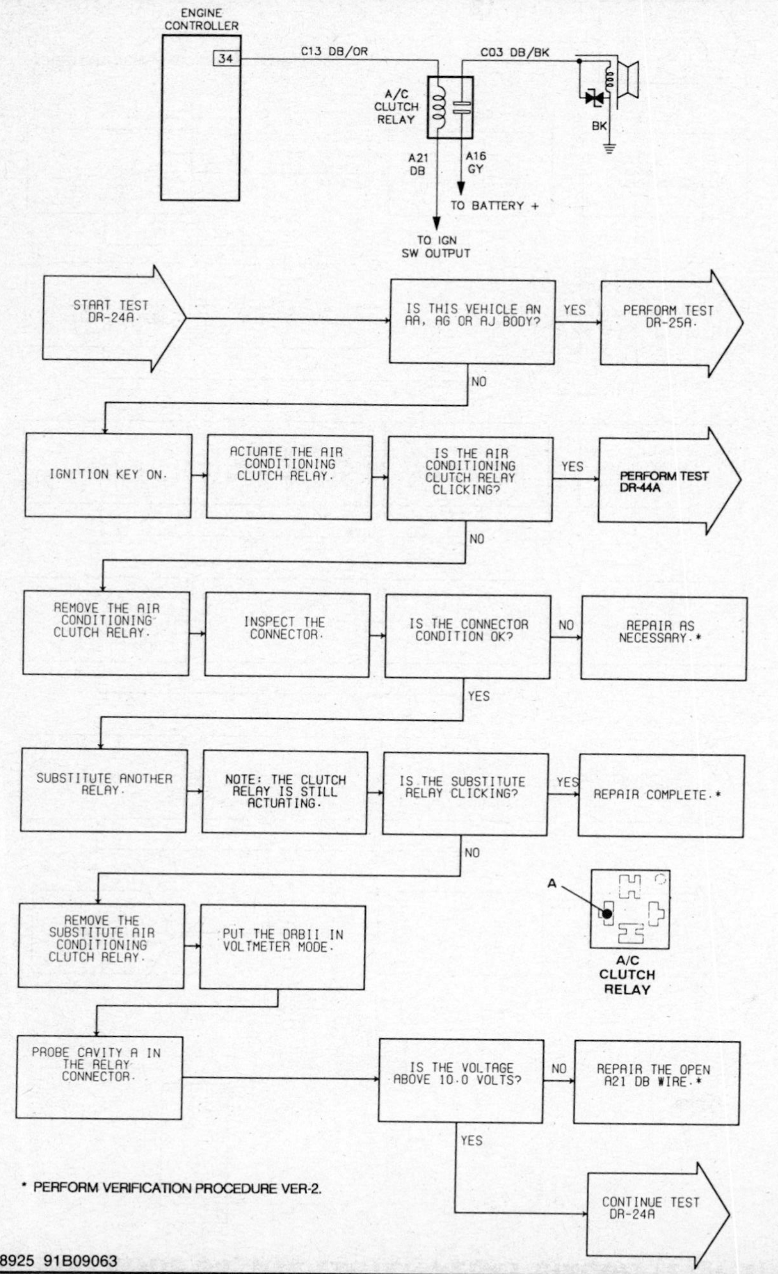
ENGINE CONTROLLER
34
C13 DB/OR
A/C CLUTCH RELAY
C03 DB/BK
BK
A21 DB
A16 GY
TO BATTERY +
TO IGN SW OUTPUT
START TEST DR-24A.
IS THIS VEHICLE AN AA, AG OR AJ BODY?
YES
PERFORM TEST DR-25A.
NO
IGNITION KEY ON.
ACTUATE THE AIR CONDITIONING CLUTCH RELAY.
IS THE AIR CONDITIONING CLUTCH RELAY CLICKING?
YES
PERFORM TEST DR-44A
NO
REMOVE THE AIR CONDITIONING CLUTCH RELAY.
INSPECT THE CONNECTOR.
IS THE CONNECTOR CONDITION OK?
NO
REPAIR AS NECESSARY.*
YES
SUBSTITUTE ANOTHER RELAY.
NOTE: THE CLUTCH RELAY IS STILL ACTUATING.
IS THE SUBSTITUTE RELAY CLICKING?
YES
REPAIR COMPLETE.*
NO
A
A/C CLUTCH RELAY
REMOVE THE SUBSTITUTE AIR CONDITIONING CLUTCH RELAY.
PUT THE DRBII IN VOLTMETER MODE.
PROBE CAVITY A IN THE RELAY CONNECTOR.
IS THE VOLTAGE ABOVE 10.0 VOLTS?
NO
REPAIR THE OPEN A21 DB WIRE.*
YES
CONTINUE TEST DR-24A
* PERFORM VERIFICATION PROCEDURE VER-2.

91A08925 91B09063

Fig. 109: Driveability Test 24A (3.0L VIN 3) – Code 33, A/C Clutch Relay Circuit (1 of 2)

DR-24A: CODE 33, A/C CLUTCH RELAY CIRCUIT (2 OF 2)

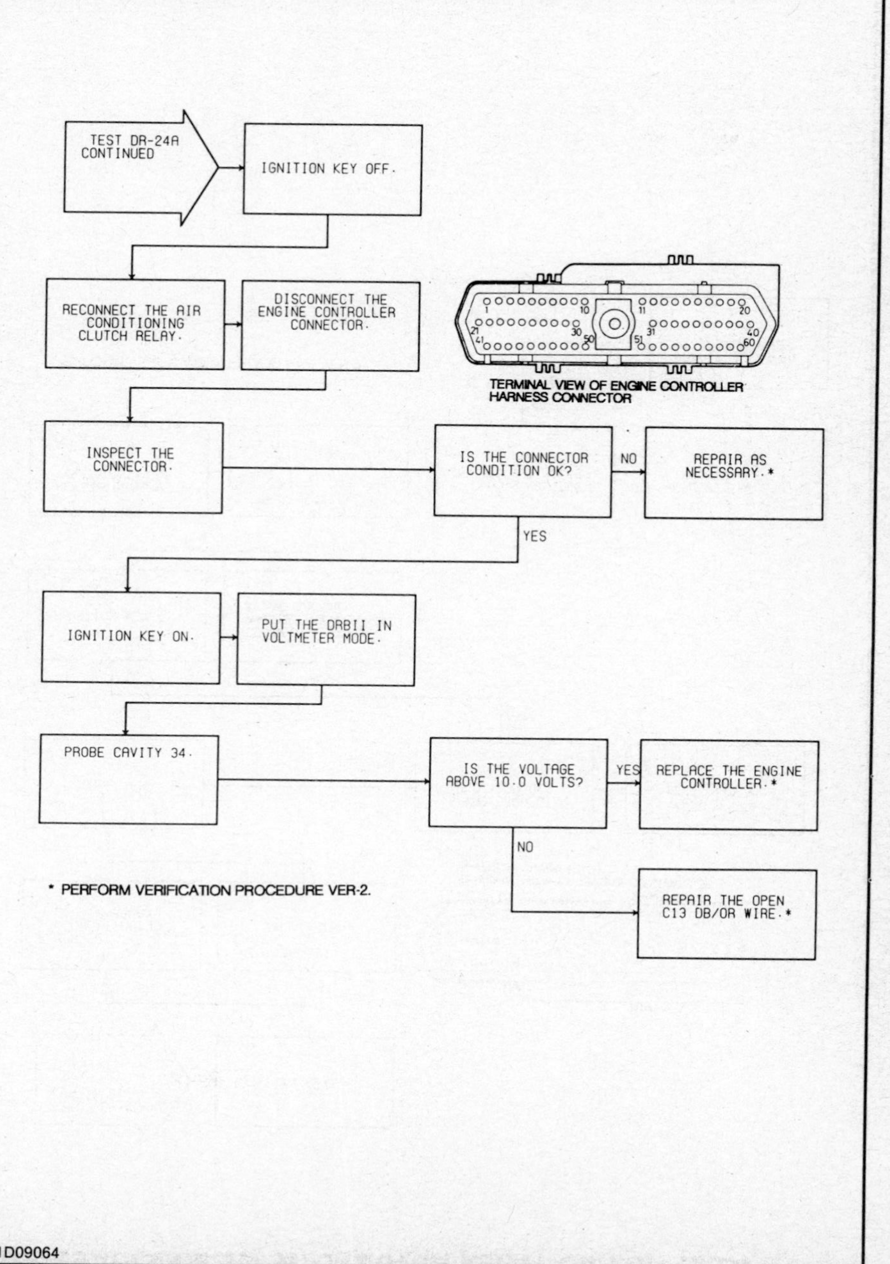
TEST DR-24A CONTINUED
IGNITION KEY OFF.
RECONNECT THE AIR CONDITIONING CLUTCH RELAY.
DISCONNECT THE ENGINE CONTROLLER CONNECTOR.
1
10
11
20
21
30
50
51
31
40
60
TERMINAL VIEW OF ENGINE CONTROLLER HARNESS CONNECTOR
INSPECT THE CONNECTOR.
IS THE CONNECTOR CONDITION OK?
NO
REPAIR AS NECESSARY.*
YES
IGNITION KEY ON.
PUT THE DRBII IN VOLTMETER MODE.
PROBE CAVITY 34.
IS THE VOLTAGE ABOVE 10.0 VOLTS?
YES
REPLACE THE ENGINE CONTROLLER.*
NO
REPAIR THE OPEN C13 DB/OR WIRE.*
* PERFORM VERIFICATION PROCEDURE VER-2.

91D09064

Fig. 110: Driveability Test 24A (3.0L VIN 3) – Code 33, A/C Clutch Relay Circuit (2 of 2)

1991 ENGINE PERFORMANCE
Self-Diagnostics – 3.0L VIN 3 (Cont.)

DR-25A: CODE 33, A/C CLUTCH RELAY CIRCUIT (1 OF 2)

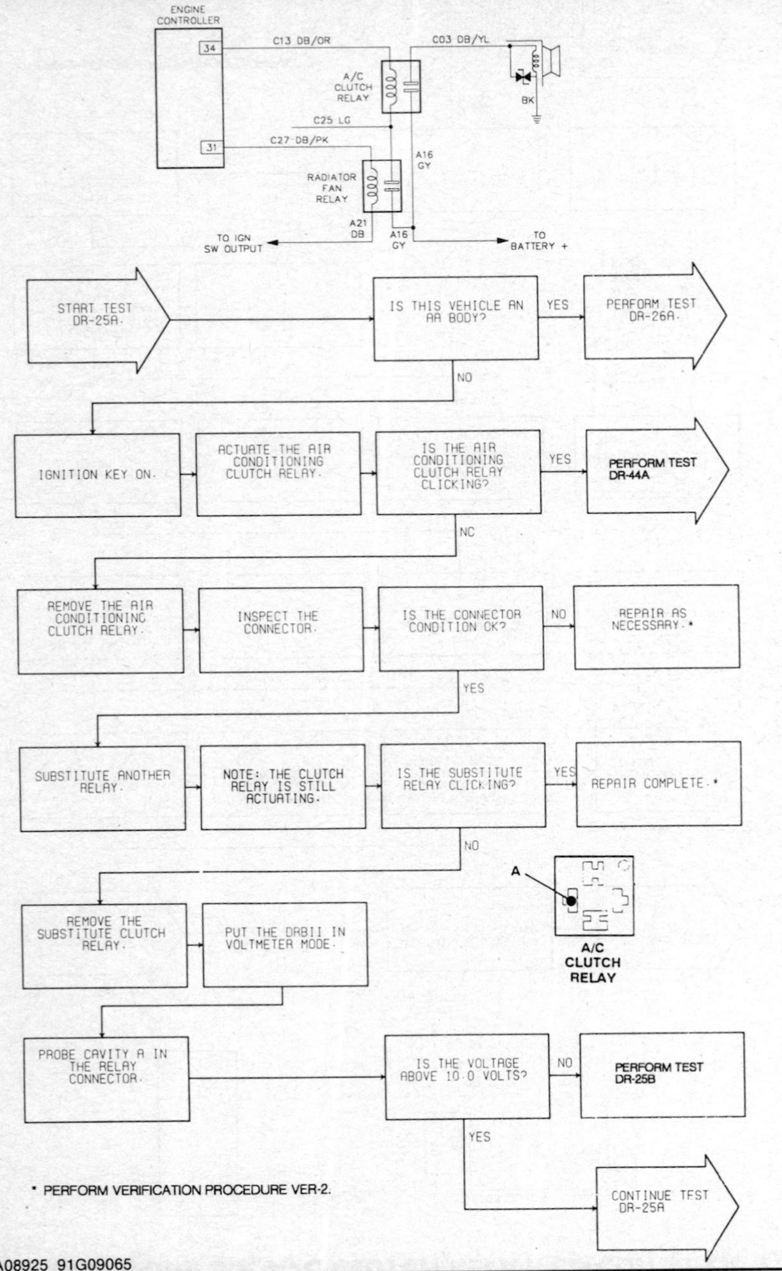
ENGINE CONTROLLER
34
31
C13 DB/OR
C03 DB/YL
A/C CLUTCH RELAY
BK
C25 LG
C27 DB/PK
A16 GY
RADIATOR FAN RELAY
A21 DB
TO IGN SW OUTPUT
TO BATTERY +
START TEST DR-25A.
IS THIS VEHICLE AN AA BODY?
YES
PERFORM TEST DR-26A.
NO
IGNITION KEY ON.
ACTUATE THE AIR CONDITIONING CLUTCH RELAY.
IS THE AIR CONDITIONING CLUTCH RELAY CLICKING?
YES
PERFORM TEST DR-44A
NC
REMOVE THE AIR CONDITIONING CLUTCH RELAY.
INSPECT THE CONNECTOR.
IS THE CONNECTOR CONDITION OK?
NO
REPAIR AS NECESSARY.*
YES
SUBSTITUTE ANOTHER RELAY.
NOTE: THE CLUTCH RELAY IS STILL ACTUATING.
IS THE SUBSTITUTE RELAY CLICKING?
YES
REPAIR COMPLETE.*
NO
A
A/C CLUTCH RELAY
REMOVE THE SUBSTITUTE CLUTCH RELAY.
PUT THE DRBII IN VOLTMETER MODE.
PROBE CAVITY A IN THE RELAY CONNECTOR.
IS THE VOLTAGE ABOVE 10.0 VOLTS?
NO
PERFORM TEST DR-25B
YES
CONTINUE TEST DR-25A
* PERFORM VERIFICATION PROCEDURE VER-2.
91A08925 91G09065

Fig. 111: Driveability Test 25A (3.0L VIN 3) – Code 33, A/C Clutch Relay Circuit (1 of 2)

DR-25A: CODE 33, A/C CLUTCH RELAY CIRCUIT (2 OF 2)

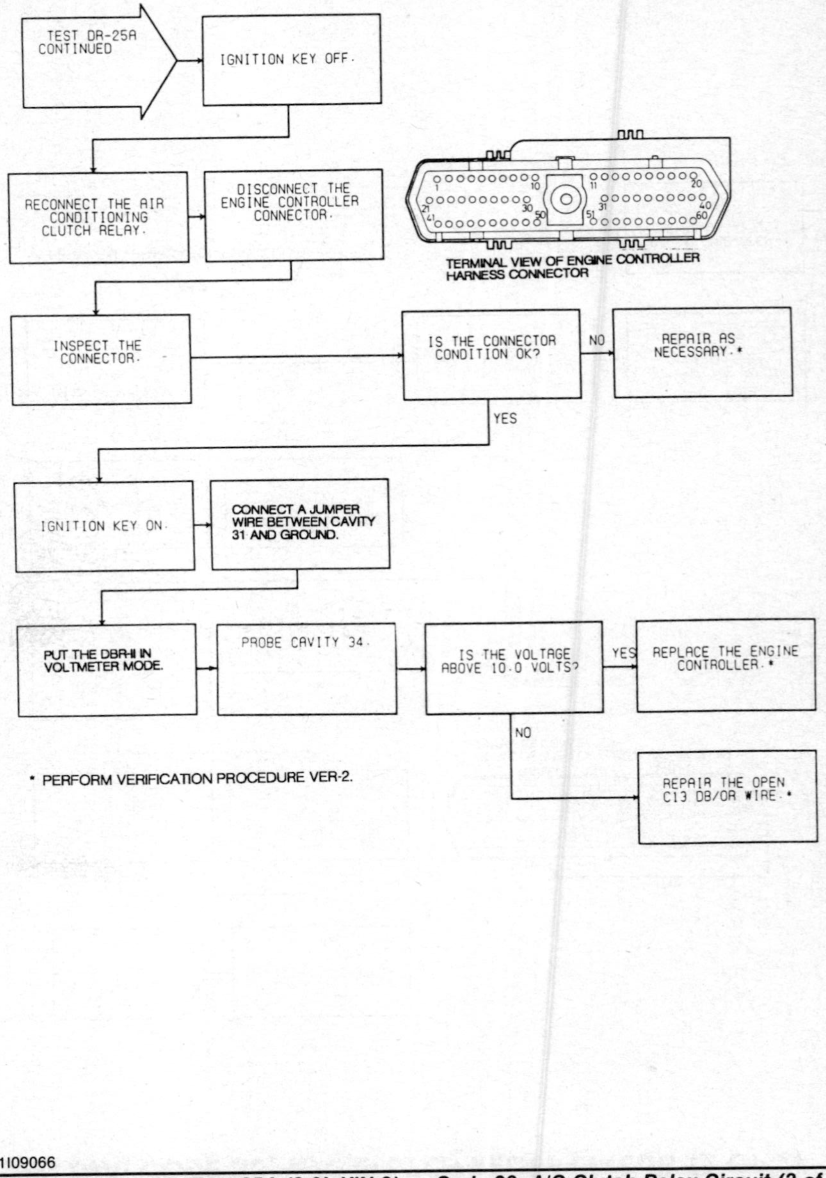
TEST DR-25A CONTINUED
IGNITION KEY OFF.
RECONNECT THE AIR CONDITIONING CLUTCH RELAY.
DISCONNECT THE ENGINE CONTROLLER CONNECTOR.
1
10
11
20
21
30
31
40
41
50
51
60
TERMINAL VIEW OF ENGINE CONTROLLER HARNESS CONNECTOR
INSPECT THE CONNECTOR.
IS THE CONNECTOR CONDITION OK?
NO
REPAIR AS NECESSARY.*
YES
IGNITION KEY ON.
CONNECT A JUMPER WIRE BETWEEN CAVITY 31 AND GROUND.
PUT THE DBR-II IN VOLTMETER MODE.
PROBE CAVITY 34.
IS THE VOLTAGE ABOVE 10.0 VOLTS?
YES
REPLACE THE ENGINE CONTROLLER.*
NO
REPAIR THE OPEN C13 DB/OR WIRE.*
* PERFORM VERIFICATION PROCEDURE VER-2.
91I09066

Fig. 112: Driveability Test 25A (3.0L VIN 3) – Code 33, A/C Clutch Relay Circuit (2 of 2)

DR-25B: CODE 33, A/C CLUTCH RELAY CIRCUIT

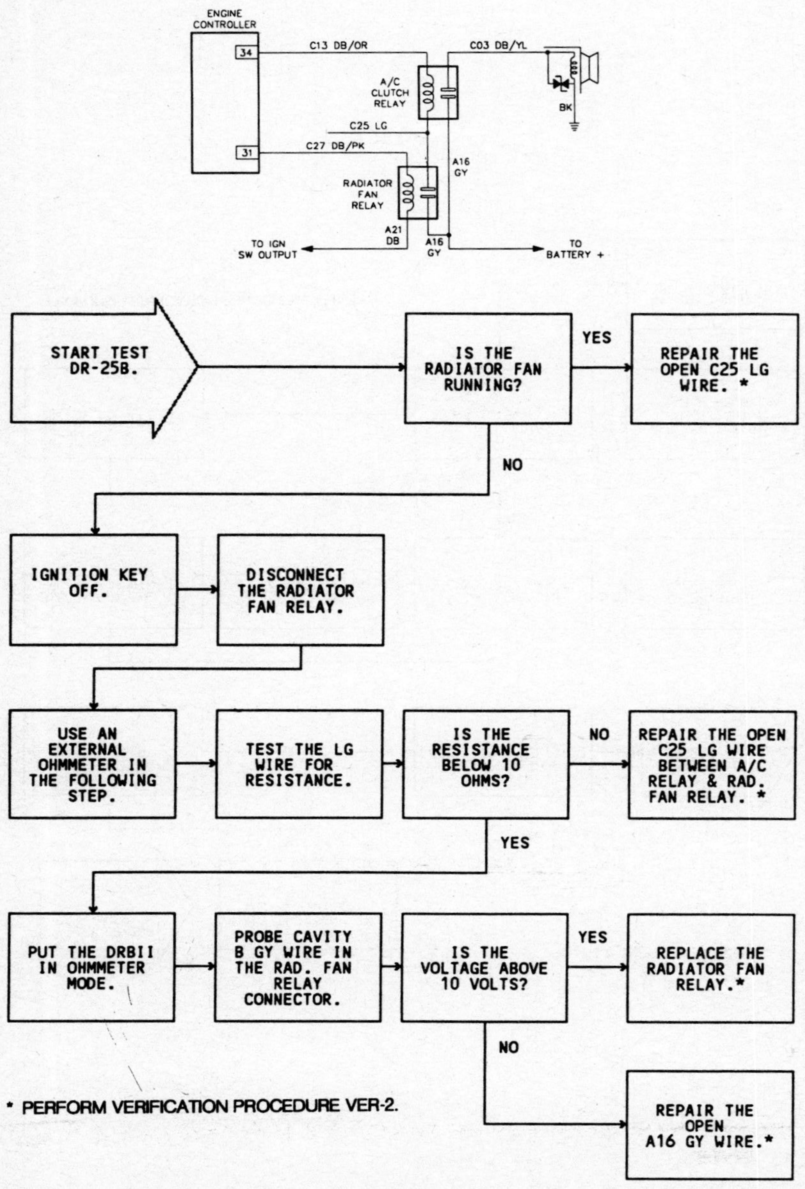
ENGINE CONTROLLER
34
31
C13 DB/OR
C03 DB/YL
A/C CLUTCH RELAY
BK
C25 LG
C27 DB/PK
A16 GY
RADIATOR FAN RELAY
A21 DB
A16 GY
TO IGN SW OUTPUT
TO BATTERY +
START TEST DR-25B.
IS THE RADIATOR FAN RUNNING?
YES
REPAIR THE OPEN C25 LG WIRE. *
NO
IGNITION KEY OFF.
DISCONNECT THE RADIATOR FAN RELAY.
USE AN EXTERNAL OHMMETER IN THE FOLLOWING STEP.
TEST THE LG WIRE FOR RESISTANCE.
IS THE RESISTANCE BELOW 10 OHMS?
NO
REPAIR THE OPEN C25 LG WIRE BETWEEN A/C RELAY & RAD. FAN RELAY. *
YES
PUT THE DRBII IN OHMMETER MODE.
PROBE CAVITY B GY WIRE IN THE RAD. FAN RELAY CONNECTOR.
IS THE VOLTAGE ABOVE 10 VOLTS?
YES
REPLACE THE RADIATOR FAN RELAY.*
NO
REPAIR THE OPEN A16 GY WIRE.*

* PERFORM VERIFICATION PROCEDURE VER-2.

91A08925 91A09067

Fig. 113: Driveability Test 25B (3.0L VIN 3) – Code 33, A/C Clutch Relay Circuit

DR-26A: CODE 33, A/C CLUTCH RELAY CIRCUIT (1 OF 3)

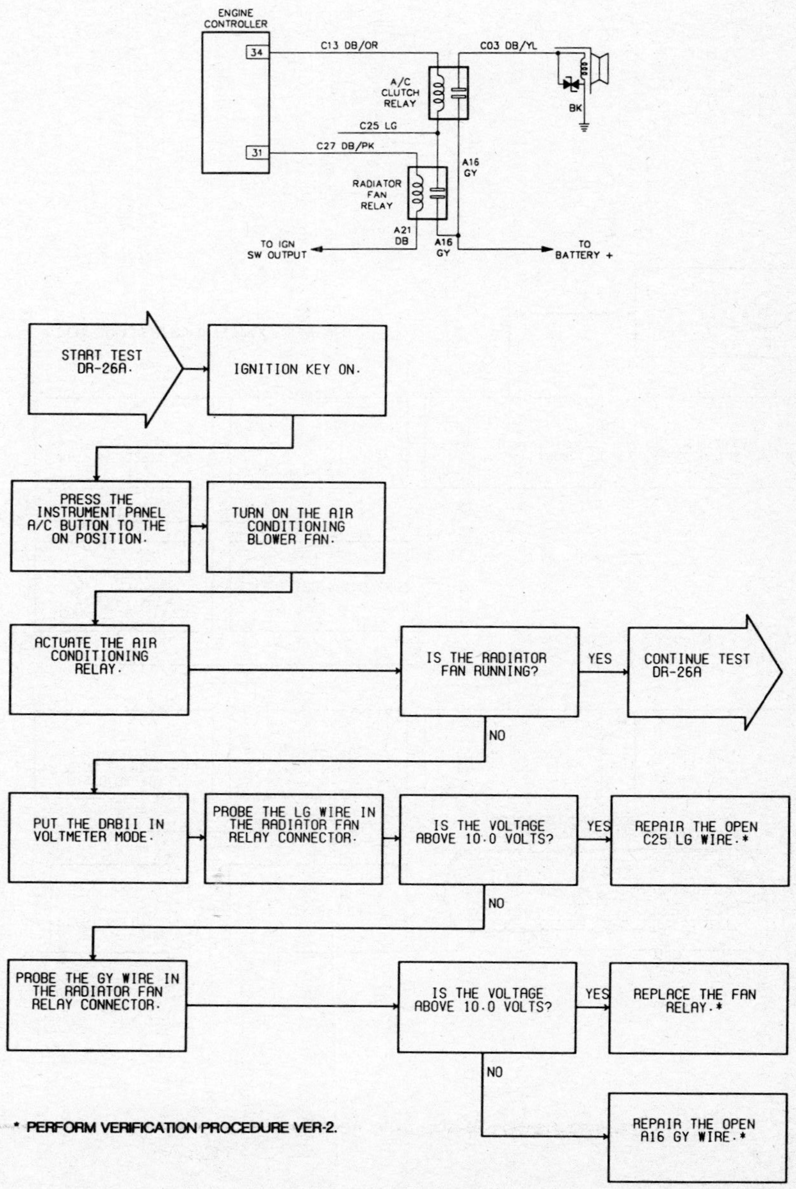
ENGINE CONTROLLER
34
31
C13 DB/OR
C03 DB/YL
A/C CLUTCH RELAY
BK
C25 LG
C27 DB/PK
A16 GY
RADIATOR FAN RELAY
A21 DB
A16 GY
TO IGN SW OUTPUT
TO BATTERY +
START TEST DR-26A.
IGNITION KEY ON.
PRESS THE INSTRUMENT PANEL A/C BUTTON TO THE ON POSITION.
TURN ON THE AIR CONDITIONING BLOWER FAN.
ACTUATE THE AIR CONDITIONING RELAY.
IS THE RADIATOR FAN RUNNING?
YES
CONTINUE TEST DR-26A
NO
PUT THE DRBII IN VOLTMETER MODE.
PROBE THE LG WIRE IN THE RADIATOR FAN RELAY CONNECTOR.
IS THE VOLTAGE ABOVE 10.0 VOLTS?
YES
REPAIR THE OPEN C25 LG WIRE.*
NO
PROBE THE GY WIRE IN THE RADIATOR FAN RELAY CONNECTOR.
IS THE VOLTAGE ABOVE 10.0 VOLTS?
YES
REPLACE THE FAN RELAY.*
NO
REPAIR THE OPEN A16 GY WIRE.*

* PERFORM VERIFICATION PROCEDURE VER-2.

91A08925 91C09068

Fig. 114: Driveability Test 26A (3.0L VIN 3) – Code 33, A/C Clutch Relay Circuit (1 of 3)

1991 ENGINE PERFORMANCE
Self-Diagnostics – 3.0L VIN 3 (Cont.)

DR-26A: CODE 33, A/C CLUTCH RELAY CIRCUIT (2 OF 3)

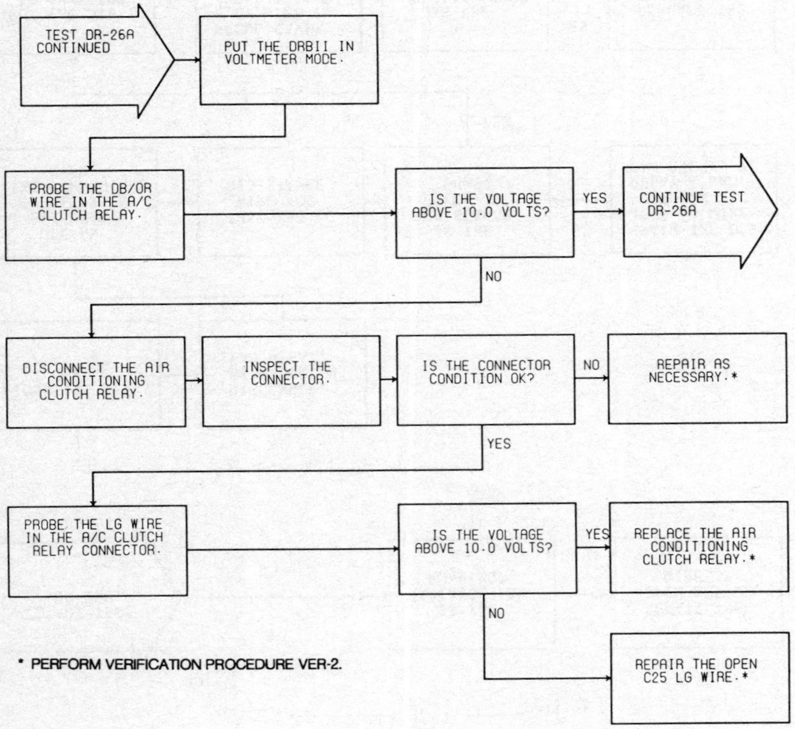
TEST DR-26A CONTINUED
PUT THE DRBII IN VOLTMETER MODE.
PROBE THE DB/OR WIRE IN THE A/C CLUTCH RELAY.
IS THE VOLTAGE ABOVE 10.0 VOLTS?
YES
CONTINUE TEST DR-26A
NO
DISCONNECT THE AIR CONDITIONING CLUTCH RELAY.
INSPECT THE CONNECTOR.
IS THE CONNECTOR CONDITION OK?
NO
REPAIR AS NECESSARY.*
YES
PROBE THE LG WIRE IN THE A/C CLUTCH RELAY CONNECTOR.
IS THE VOLTAGE ABOVE 10.0 VOLTS?
YES
REPLACE THE AIR CONDITIONING CLUTCH RELAY.*
NO
REPAIR THE OPEN C25 LG WIRE.*

* PERFORM VERIFICATION PROCEDURE VER-2.

91E09069

Fig. 115: Driveability Test 26A (3.0L VIN 3) – Code 33, A/C Clutch Relay Circuit (2 of 3)

DR-26A: CODE 33, A/C CLUTCH RELAY CIRCUIT (3 OF 3)

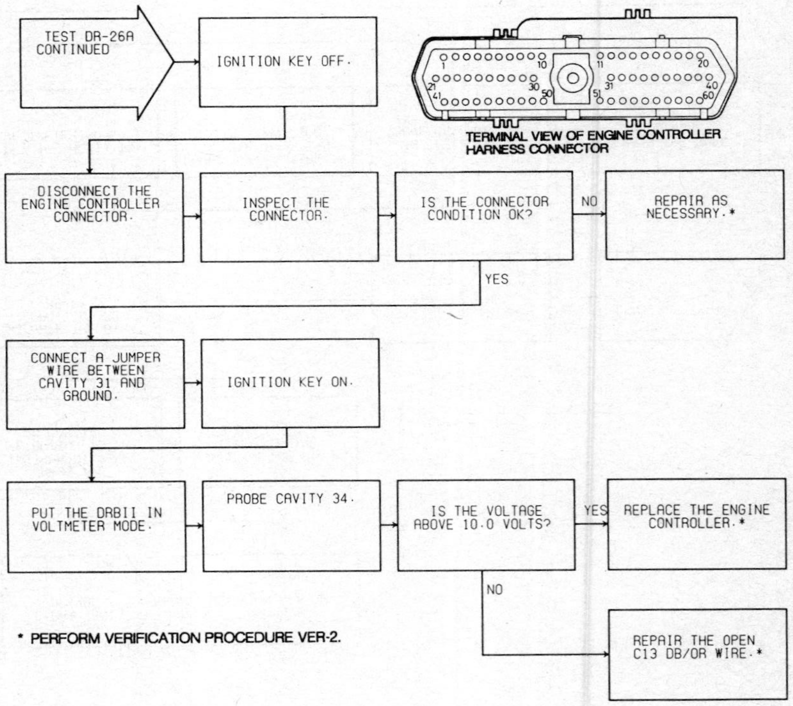
TEST DR-26A CONTINUED
IGNITION KEY OFF.
TERMINAL VIEW OF ENGINE CONTROLLER HARNESS CONNECTOR
DISCONNECT THE ENGINE CONTROLLER CONNECTOR.
INSPECT THE CONNECTOR.
IS THE CONNECTOR CONDITION OK?
NO
REPAIR AS NECESSARY.*
YES
CONNECT A JUMPER WIRE BETWEEN CAVITY 31 AND GROUND.
IGNITION KEY ON.
PUT THE DRBII IN VOLTMETER MODE.
PROBE CAVITY 34.
IS THE VOLTAGE ABOVE 10.0 VOLTS?
YES
REPLACE THE ENGINE CONTROLLER.*
NO
REPAIR THE OPEN C13 DB/OR WIRE.*

* PERFORM VERIFICATION PROCEDURE VER-2.

91G09070

Fig. 116: Driveability Test 26A (3.0L VIN 3) – Code 33, A/C Clutch Relay Circuit (3 of 3)

DR-27A: CODE 35, RADIATOR FAN RELAY CIRCUIT (1 OF 3)

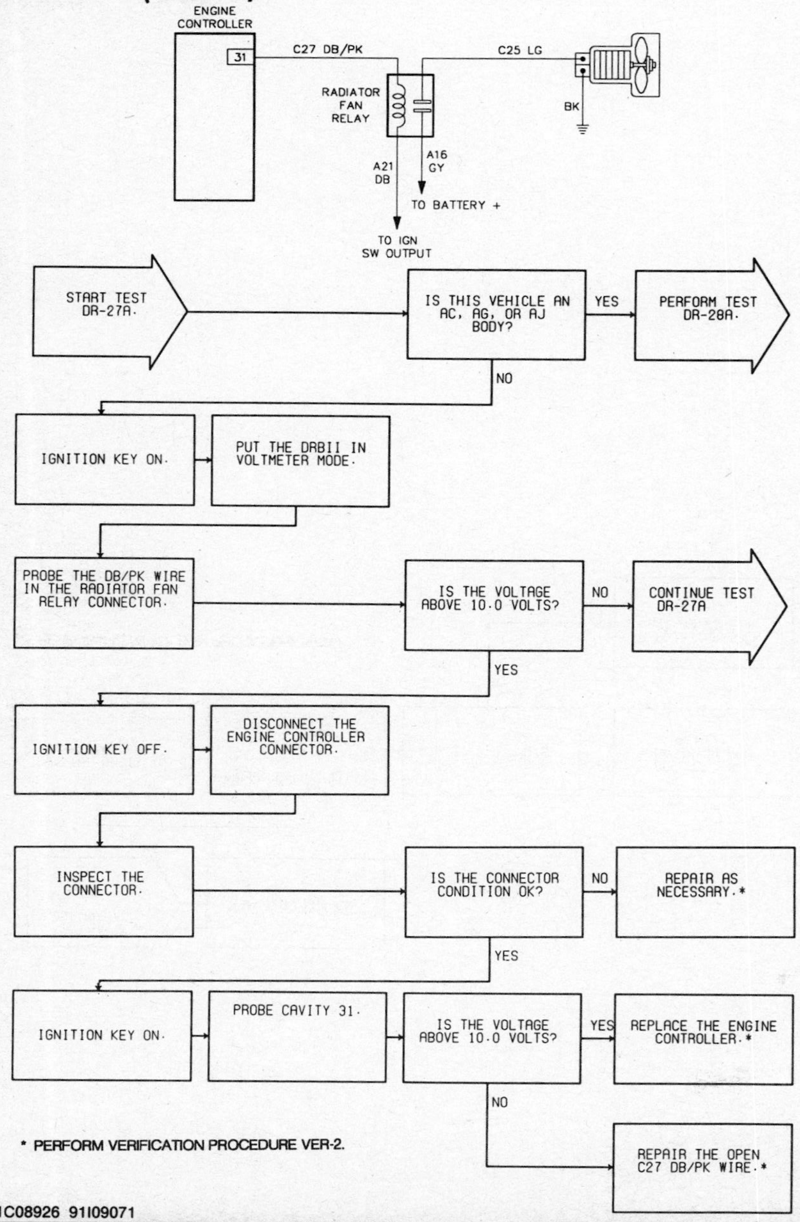
ENGINE CONTROLLER
31
C27 DB/PK
RADIATOR FAN RELAY
C25 LG
BK
A21 DB
A16 GY
TO BATTERY +
TO IGN SW OUTPUT
START TEST DR-27A.
IS THIS VEHICLE AN AC, AG, OR AJ BODY?
YES
PERFORM TEST DR-28A.
NO
IGNITION KEY ON.
PUT THE DRBII IN VOLTMETER MODE.
PROBE THE DB/PK WIRE IN THE RADIATOR FAN RELAY CONNECTOR.
IS THE VOLTAGE ABOVE 10.0 VOLTS?
NO
CONTINUE TEST DR-27A
YES
IGNITION KEY OFF.
DISCONNECT THE ENGINE CONTROLLER CONNECTOR.
INSPECT THE CONNECTOR.
IS THE CONNECTOR CONDITION OK?
NO
REPAIR AS NECESSARY.*
YES
IGNITION KEY ON.
PROBE CAVITY 31.
IS THE VOLTAGE ABOVE 10.0 VOLTS?
YES
REPLACE THE ENGINE CONTROLLER.*
NO
REPAIR THE OPEN C27 DB/PK WIRE.*

* PERFORM VERIFICATION PROCEDURE VER-2.

91C08926 91I09071

Fig. 117: Driveability Test 27A (3.0L VIN 3) – Code 35, Radiator Fan Relay Circuit (1 of 3)

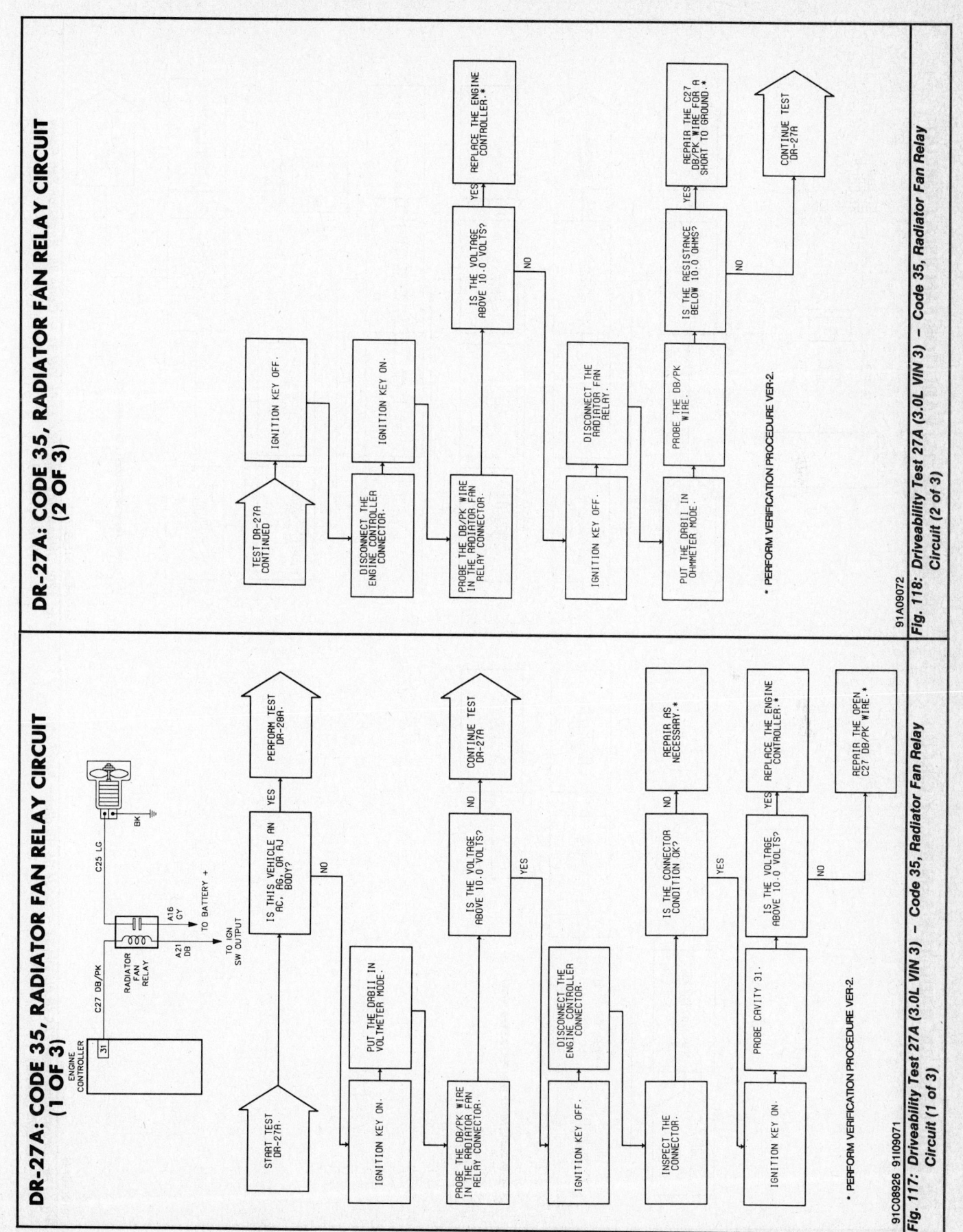

DR-27A: CODE 35, RADIATOR FAN RELAY CIRCUIT (2 OF 3)

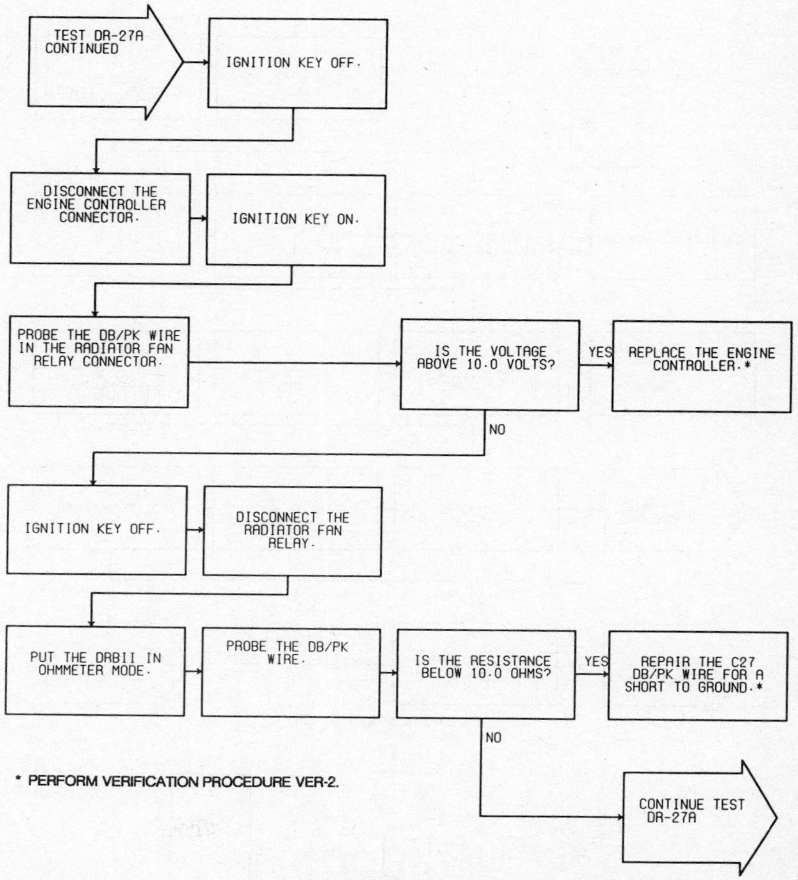
TEST DR-27A CONTINUED
IGNITION KEY OFF.
DISCONNECT THE ENGINE CONTROLLER CONNECTOR.
IGNITION KEY ON.
PROBE THE DB/PK WIRE IN THE RADIATOR FAN RELAY CONNECTOR.
IS THE VOLTAGE ABOVE 10.0 VOLTS?
YES
REPLACE THE ENGINE CONTROLLER.*
NO
IGNITION KEY OFF.
DISCONNECT THE RADIATOR FAN RELAY.
PUT THE DRBII IN OHMMETER MODE.
PROBE THE DB/PK WIRE.
IS THE RESISTANCE BELOW 10.0 OHMS?
YES
REPAIR THE C27 DB/PK WIRE FOR A SHORT TO GROUND.*
NO
CONTINUE TEST DR-27A

* PERFORM VERIFICATION PROCEDURE VER-2.

91A09072

Fig. 118: Driveability Test 27A (3.0L VIN 3) – Code 35, Radiator Fan Relay Circuit (2 of 3)

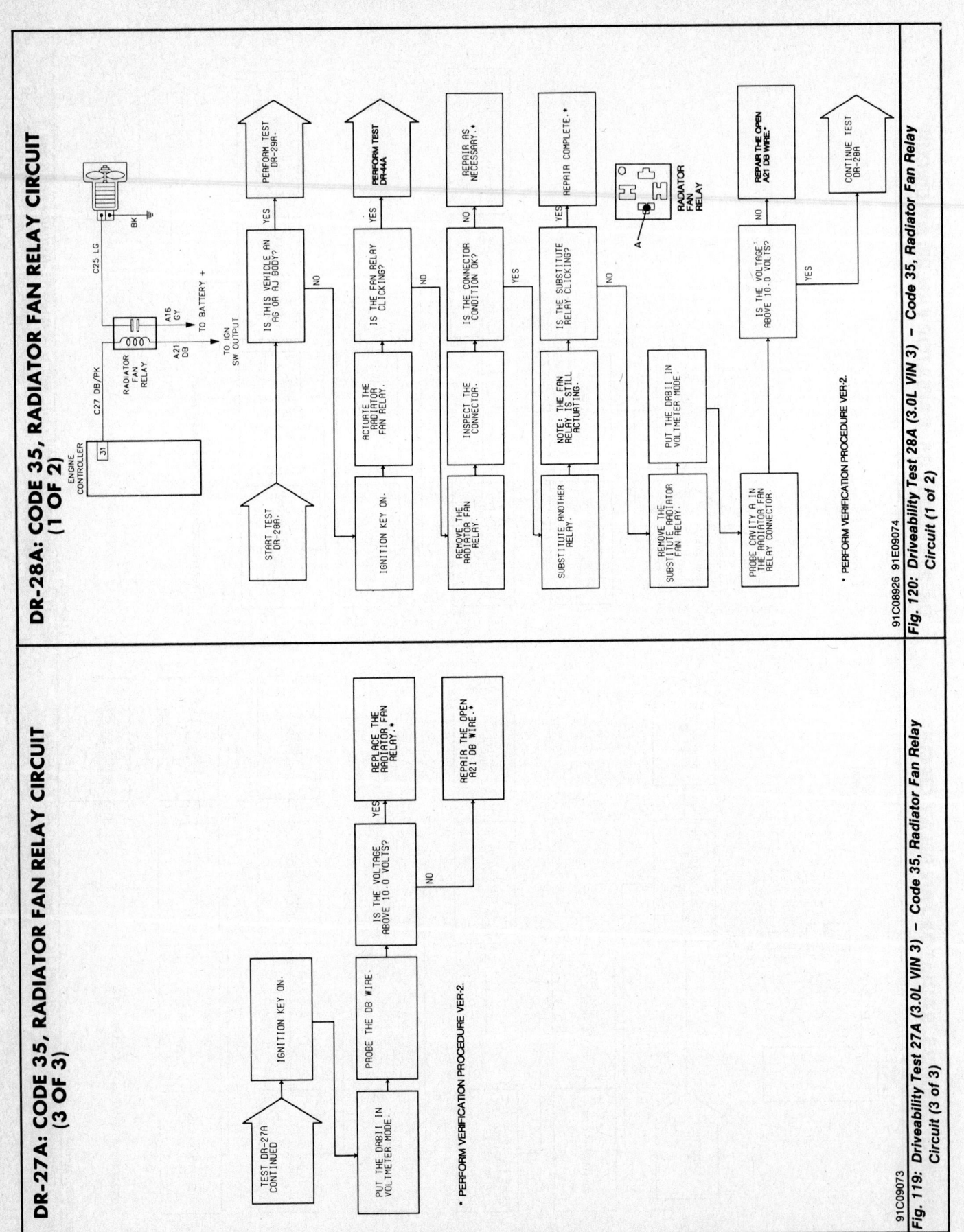

DR-27A: CODE 35, RADIATOR FAN RELAY CIRCUIT (3 OF 3)

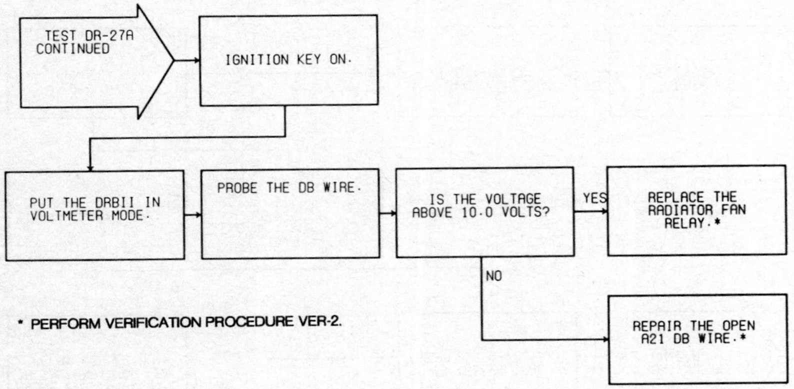
TEST DR-27A CONTINUED
IGNITION KEY ON.
PUT THE DRBII IN VOLTMETER MODE.
PROBE THE DB WIRE.
IS THE VOLTAGE ABOVE 10.0 VOLTS?
YES
REPLACE THE RADIATOR FAN RELAY.*
NO
REPAIR THE OPEN A21 DB WIRE.*

* PERFORM VERIFICATION PROCEDURE VER-2.

91C09073

Fig. 119: ***Driveability Test 27A (3.0L VIN 3) – Code 35, Radiator Fan Relay Circuit (3 of 3)***

DR-28A: CODE 35, RADIATOR FAN RELAY CIRCUIT (1 OF 2)

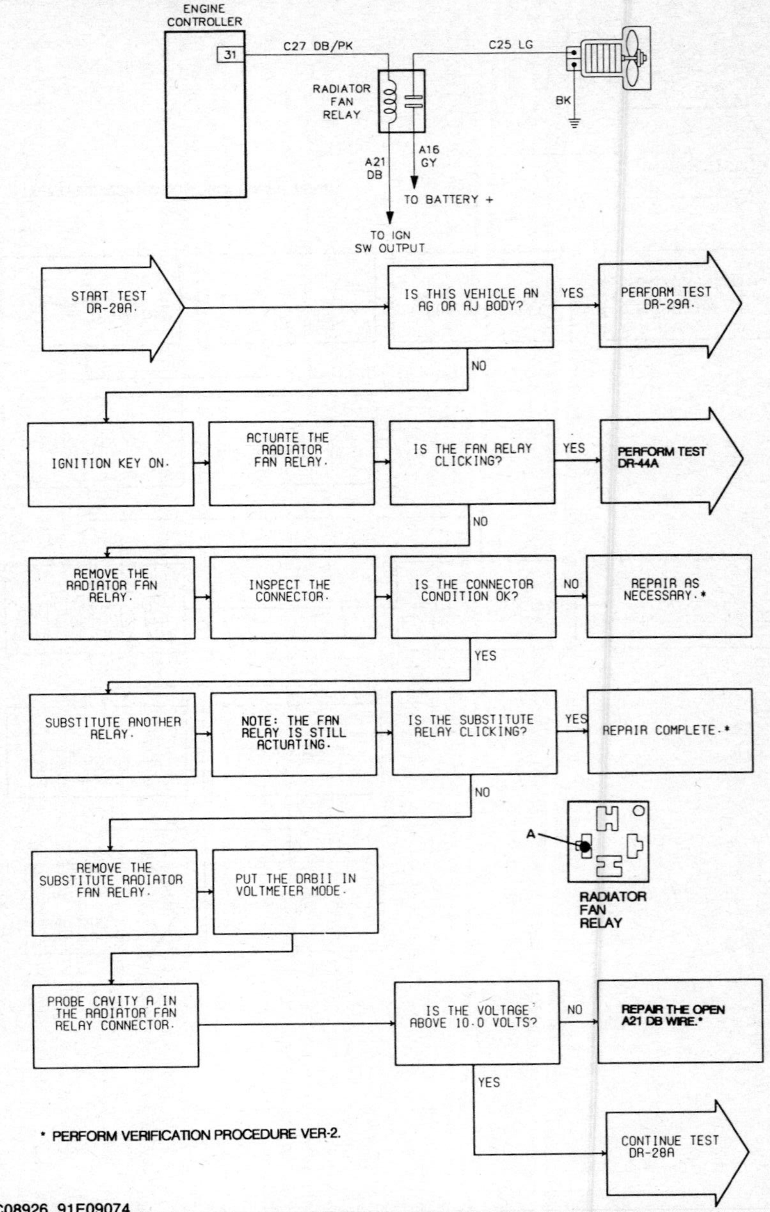
ENGINE CONTROLLER
31
C27 DB/PK
RADIATOR FAN RELAY
C25 LG
BK
A21 DB
A16 GY
TO BATTERY +
TO IGN SW OUTPUT
START TEST DR-28A.
IS THIS VEHICLE AN AG OR AJ BODY?
YES
PERFORM TEST DR-29A.
NO
IGNITION KEY ON.
ACTUATE THE RADIATOR FAN RELAY.
IS THE FAN RELAY CLICKING?
YES
PERFORM TEST DR-44A
NO
REMOVE THE RADIATOR FAN RELAY.
INSPECT THE CONNECTOR.
IS THE CONNECTOR CONDITION OK?
NO
REPAIR AS NECESSARY.*
YES
SUBSTITUTE ANOTHER RELAY.
NOTE: THE FAN RELAY IS STILL ACTUATING.
IS THE SUBSTITUTE RELAY CLICKING?
YES
REPAIR COMPLETE.*
NO
A
RADIATOR FAN RELAY
REMOVE THE SUBSTITUTE RADIATOR FAN RELAY.
PUT THE DRBII IN VOLTMETER MODE.
PROBE CAVITY A IN THE RADIATOR FAN RELAY CONNECTOR.
IS THE VOLTAGE ABOVE 10.0 VOLTS?
NO
REPAIR THE OPEN A21 DB WIRE.*
YES
CONTINUE TEST DR-28A

* PERFORM VERIFICATION PROCEDURE VER-2.

91C08926 91E09074

Fig. 120: ***Driveability Test 28A (3.0L VIN 3) – Code 35, Radiator Fan Relay Circuit (1 of 2)***

DR-28A: CODE 35, RADIATOR FAN RELAY CIRCUIT (2 OF 2)

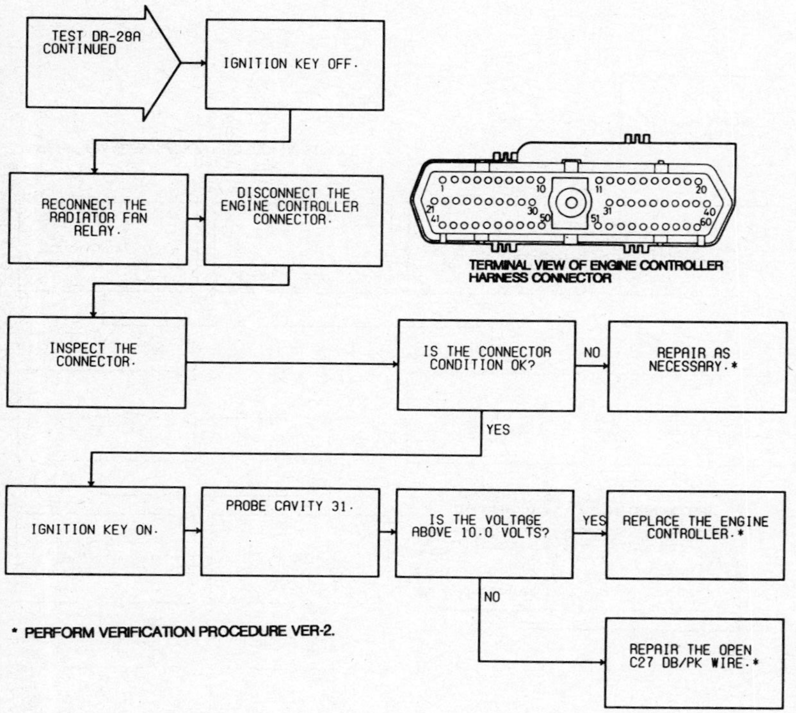
TEST DR-28A CONTINUED
IGNITION KEY OFF.
RECONNECT THE RADIATOR FAN RELAY.
DISCONNECT THE ENGINE CONTROLLER CONNECTOR.
TERMINAL VIEW OF ENGINE CONTROLLER HARNESS CONNECTOR
INSPECT THE CONNECTOR.
IS THE CONNECTOR CONDITION OK?
NO
REPAIR AS NECESSARY.*
YES
IGNITION KEY ON.
PROBE CAVITY 31.
IS THE VOLTAGE ABOVE 10.0 VOLTS?
YES
REPLACE THE ENGINE CONTROLLER.*
NO
REPAIR THE OPEN C27 DB/PK WIRE.*

* PERFORM VERIFICATION PROCEDURE VER-2.

91H09075

Fig. 121: Driveability Test 28A (3.0L VIN 3) – Code 35, Radiator Fan Relay Circuit (2 of 2)

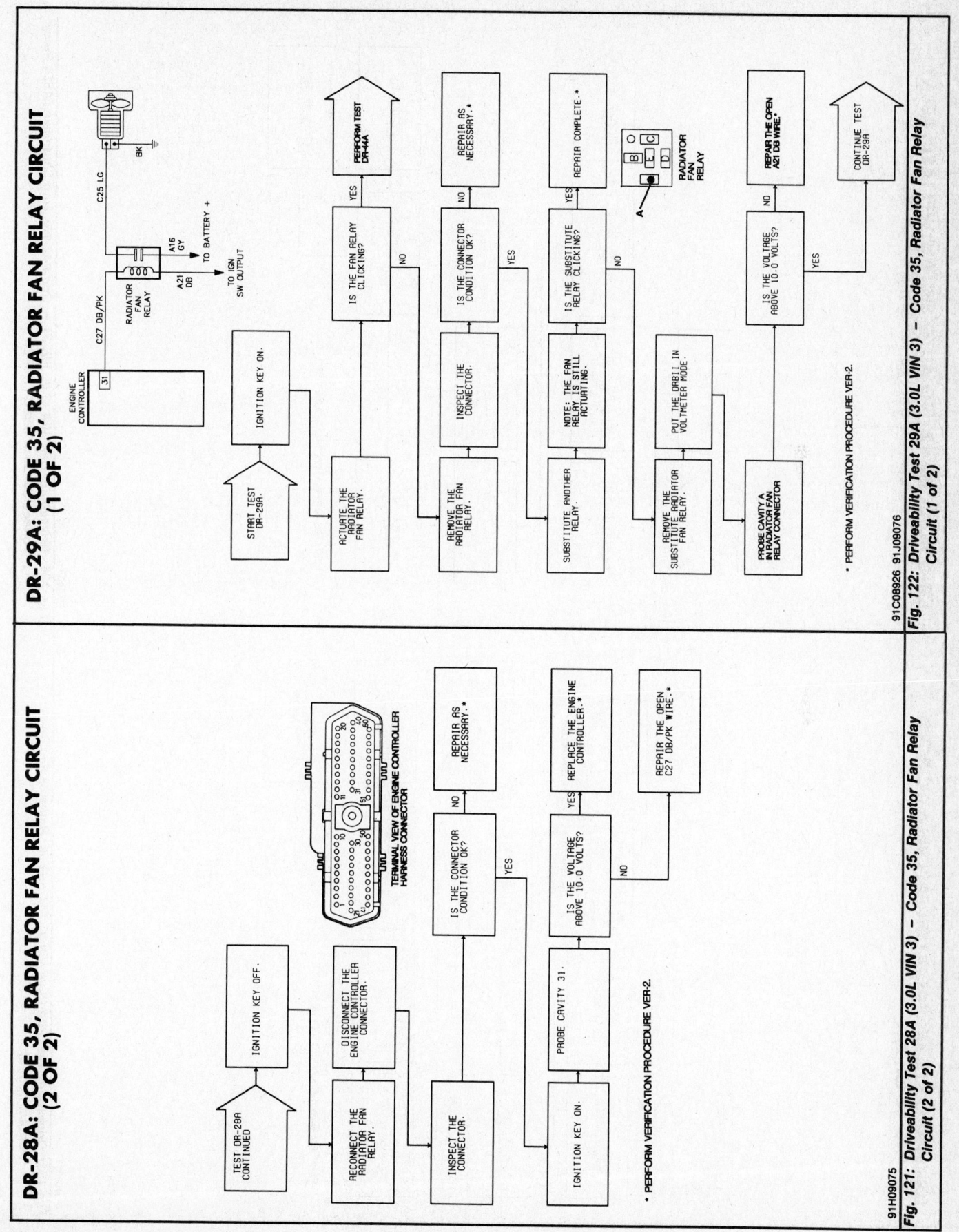

DR-29A: CODE 35, RADIATOR FAN RELAY CIRCUIT (1 OF 2)

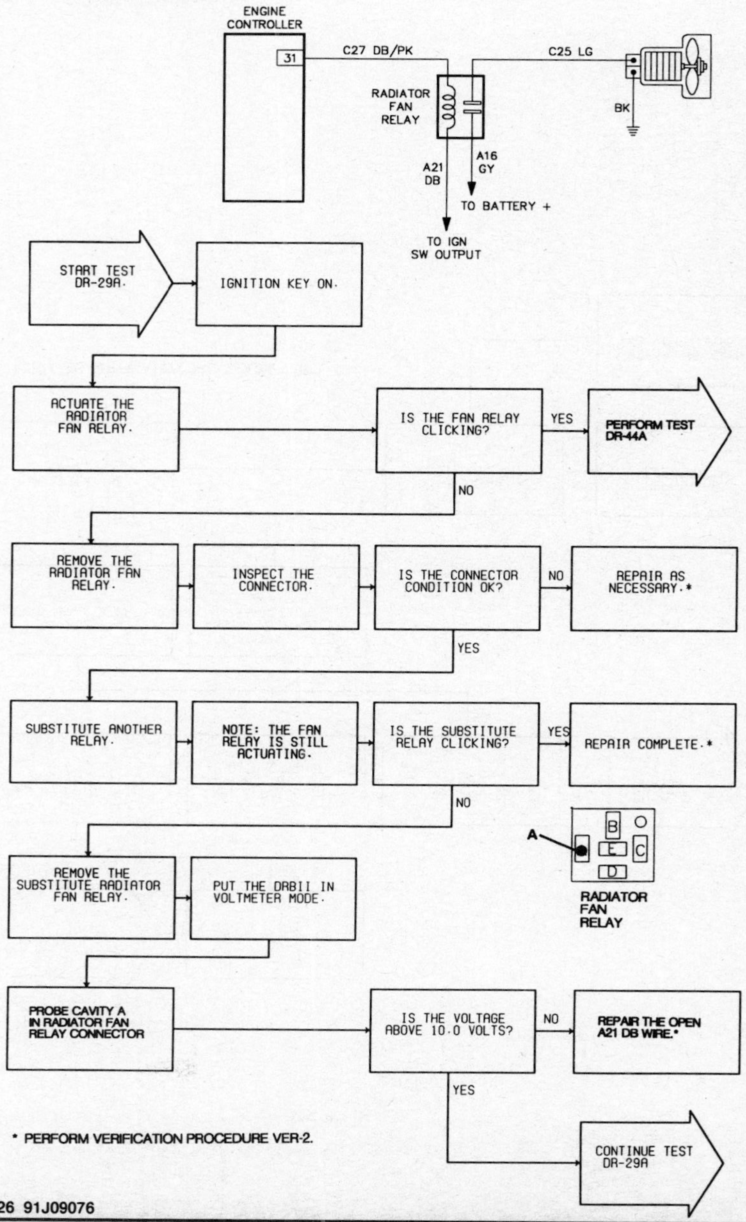
ENGINE CONTROLLER
31
C27 DB/PK
C25 LG
RADIATOR FAN RELAY
BK
A21 DB
A16 GY
TO BATTERY +
TO IGN SW OUTPUT
START TEST DR-29A.
IGNITION KEY ON.
ACTUATE THE RADIATOR FAN RELAY.
IS THE FAN RELAY CLICKING?
YES
PERFORM TEST DR-44A
NO
REMOVE THE RADIATOR FAN RELAY.
INSPECT THE CONNECTOR.
IS THE CONNECTOR CONDITION OK?
NO
REPAIR AS NECESSARY.*
YES
SUBSTITUTE ANOTHER RELAY.
NOTE: THE FAN RELAY IS STILL ACTUATING.
IS THE SUBSTITUTE RELAY CLICKING?
YES
REPAIR COMPLETE.*
NO
A
B
C
D
E
RADIATOR FAN RELAY
REMOVE THE SUBSTITUTE RADIATOR FAN RELAY.
PUT THE DRBII IN VOLTMETER MODE.
PROBE CAVITY A IN RADIATOR FAN RELAY CONNECTOR
IS THE VOLTAGE ABOVE 10.0 VOLTS?
NO
REPAIR THE OPEN A21 DB WIRE.*
YES
CONTINUE TEST DR-29A

* PERFORM VERIFICATION PROCEDURE VER-2.

91C08926 91J09076

Fig. 122: Driveability Test 29A (3.0L VIN 3) – Code 35, Radiator Fan Relay Circuit (1 of 2)

DR-29A: CODE 35, RADIATOR FAN RELAY CIRCUIT (2 OF 2)

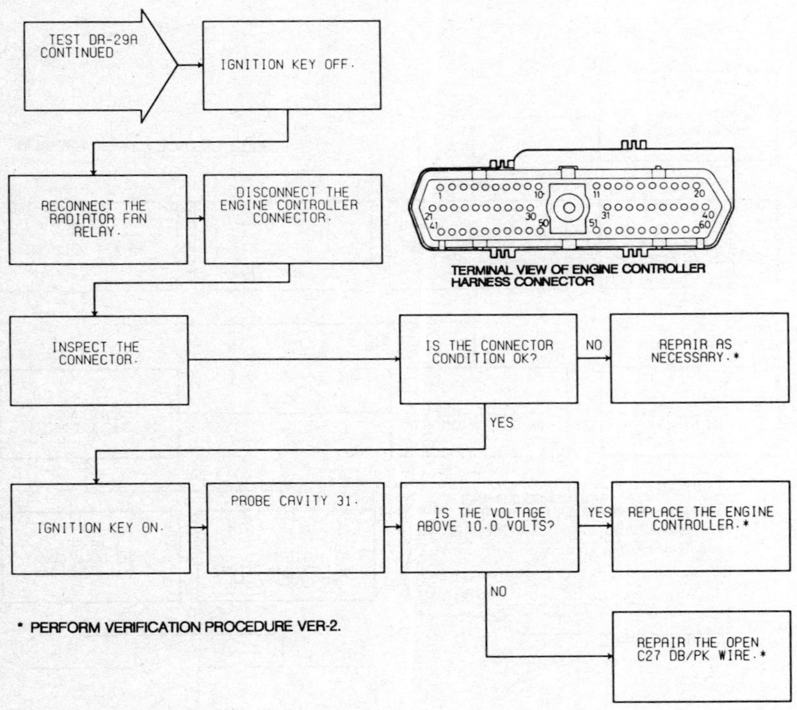
TEST DR-29A CONTINUED
IGNITION KEY OFF.
RECONNECT THE RADIATOR FAN RELAY.
DISCONNECT THE ENGINE CONTROLLER CONNECTOR.
TERMINAL VIEW OF ENGINE CONTROLLER HARNESS CONNECTOR
1
10
11
20
21
30
31
40
41
50
51
60
INSPECT THE CONNECTOR.
IS THE CONNECTOR CONDITION OK?
NO
REPAIR AS NECESSARY.*
YES
IGNITION KEY ON.
PROBE CAVITY 31.
IS THE VOLTAGE ABOVE 10.0 VOLTS?
YES
REPLACE THE ENGINE CONTROLLER.*
NO
REPAIR THE OPEN C27 DB/PK WIRE.*

* PERFORM VERIFICATION PROCEDURE VER-2.

91B09077

Fig. 123: Driveability Test 29A (3.0L VIN 3) – Code 35, Radiator Fan Relay Circuit (2 of 2)

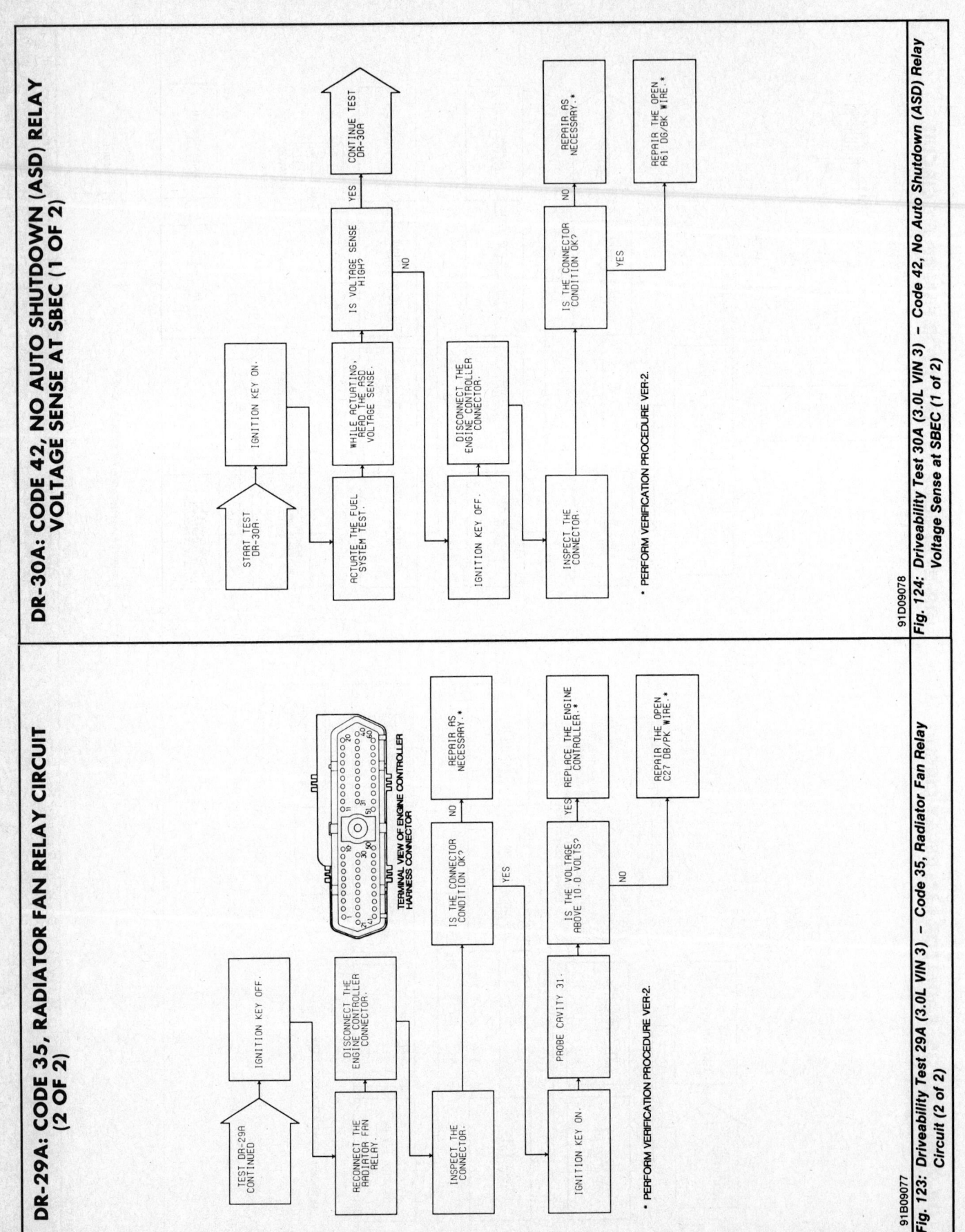

DR-30A: CODE 42, NO AUTO SHUTDOWN (ASD) RELAY VOLTAGE SENSE AT SBEC (1 OF 2)

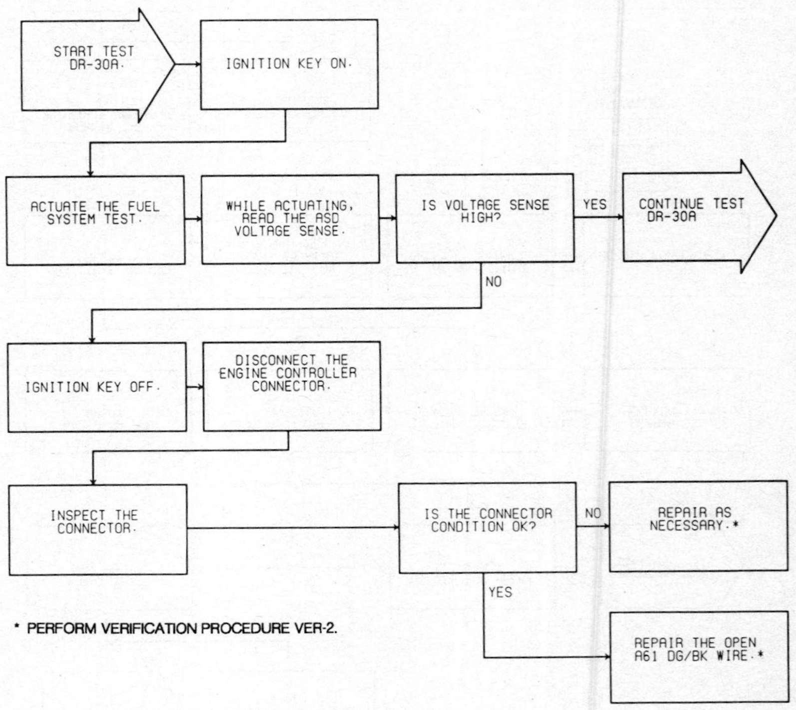
START TEST DR-30A.
IGNITION KEY ON.
ACTUATE THE FUEL SYSTEM TEST.
WHILE ACTUATING, READ THE ASD VOLTAGE SENSE.
IS VOLTAGE SENSE HIGH?
YES
CONTINUE TEST DR-30A
NO
IGNITION KEY OFF.
DISCONNECT THE ENGINE CONTROLLER CONNECTOR.
INSPECT THE CONNECTOR.
IS THE CONNECTOR CONDITION OK?
NO
REPAIR AS NECESSARY.*
YES
REPAIR THE OPEN A61 DG/BK WIRE.*

* PERFORM VERIFICATION PROCEDURE VER-2.

91D09078

Fig. 124: Driveability Test 30A (3.0L VIN 3) – Code 42, No Auto Shutdown (ASD) Relay Voltage Sense at SBEC (1 of 2)

DR-30A: CODE 42, NO AUTO SHUTDOWN (ASD) RELAY VOLTAGE SENSE AT SBEC (2 OF 2)

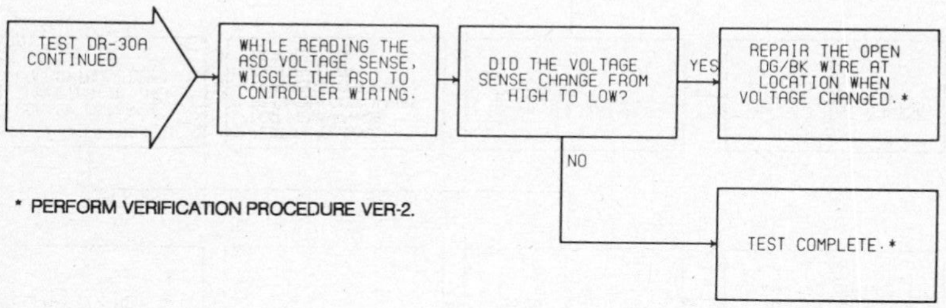
TEST DR-30A CONTINUED
WHILE READING THE ASD VOLTAGE SENSE, WIGGLE THE ASD TO CONTROLLER WIRING.
DID THE VOLTAGE SENSE CHANGE FROM HIGH TO LOW?
YES
REPAIR THE OPEN DG/BK WIRE AT LOCATION WHEN VOLTAGE CHANGED.*
NO
TEST COMPLETE.*

* PERFORM VERIFICATION PROCEDURE VER-2.

91F09079

Fig. 125: Driveability Test 30A (3.0L VIN 3) – Code 42, No Auto Shutdown (ASD) Relay Voltage Sense at SBEC (2 of 2)

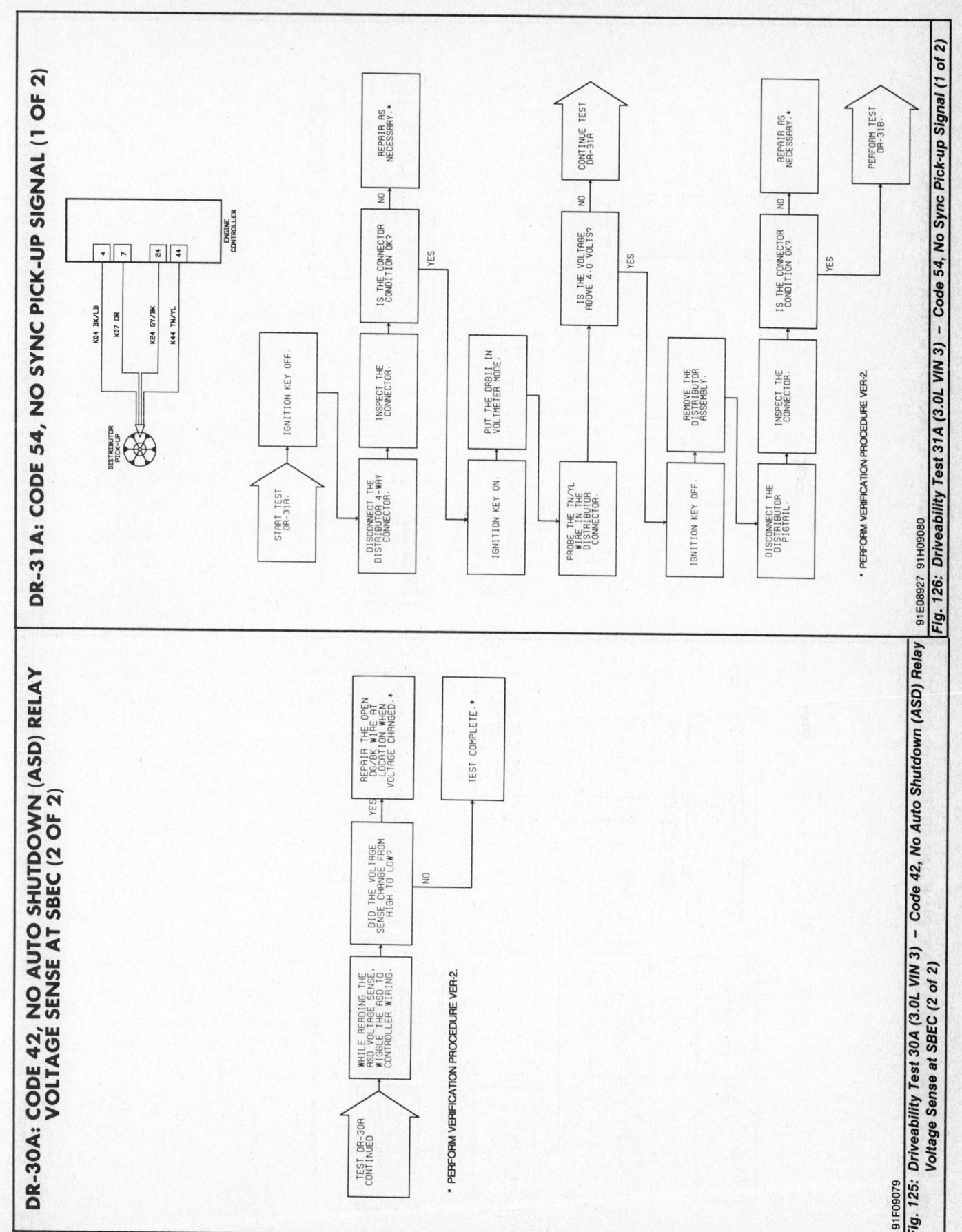

DR-31A: CODE 54, NO SYNC PICK-UP SIGNAL (1 OF 2)

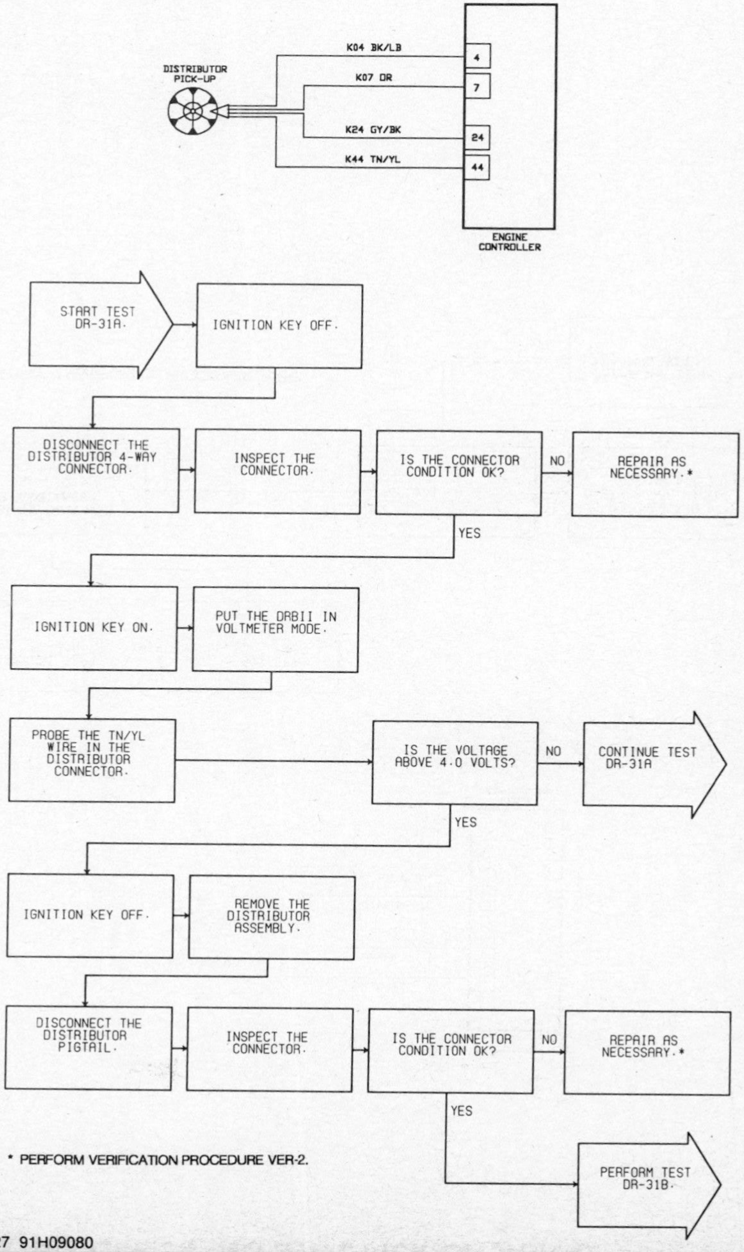
DISTRIBUTOR PICK-UP
K04 BK/LB
K07 OR
K24 GY/BK
K44 TN/YL
4
7
24
44
ENGINE CONTROLLER
START TEST DR-31A.
IGNITION KEY OFF.
DISCONNECT THE DISTRIBUTOR 4-WAY CONNECTOR.
INSPECT THE CONNECTOR.
IS THE CONNECTOR CONDITION OK?
NO
REPAIR AS NECESSARY.*
YES
IGNITION KEY ON.
PUT THE DRBII IN VOLTMETER MODE.
PROBE THE TN/YL WIRE IN THE DISTRIBUTOR CONNECTOR.
IS THE VOLTAGE ABOVE 4.0 VOLTS?
NO
CONTINUE TEST DR-31A
YES
IGNITION KEY OFF.
REMOVE THE DISTRIBUTOR ASSEMBLY.
DISCONNECT THE DISTRIBUTOR PIGTAIL.
INSPECT THE CONNECTOR.
IS THE CONNECTOR CONDITION OK?
NO
REPAIR AS NECESSARY.*
YES
PERFORM TEST DR-31B.

* PERFORM VERIFICATION PROCEDURE VER-2.

91E08927 91H09080

Fig. 126: Driveability Test 31A (3.0L VIN 3) – Code 54, No Sync Pick-up Signal (1 of 2)

1991 ENGINE PERFORMANCE
Self-Diagnostics – 3.0L VIN 3 (Cont.)

DR-31A: CODE 54, NO SYNC PICK-UP SIGNAL (2 OF 2)

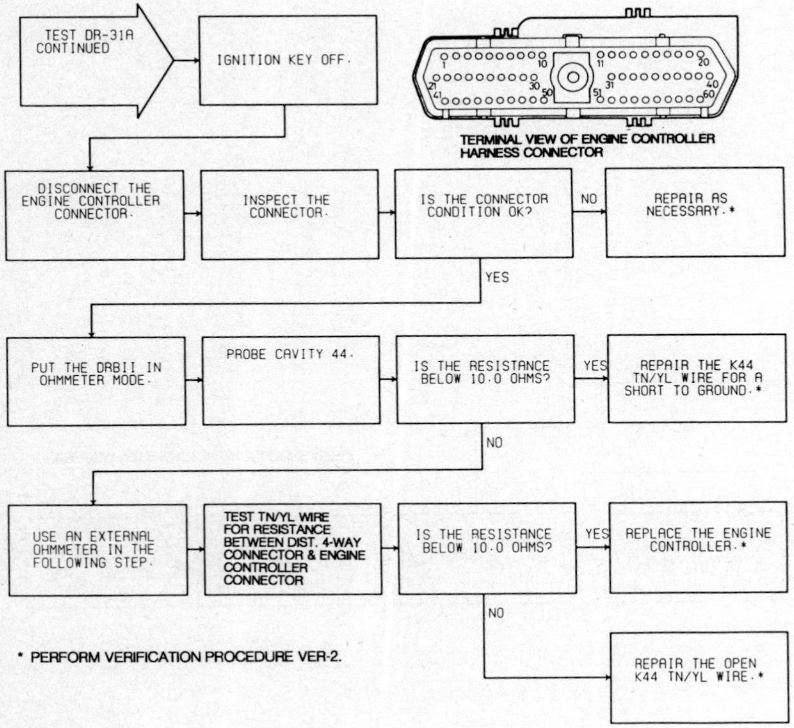
TEST DR-31A CONTINUED
IGNITION KEY OFF.
TERMINAL VIEW OF ENGINE CONTROLLER HARNESS CONNECTOR
DISCONNECT THE ENGINE CONTROLLER CONNECTOR.
INSPECT THE CONNECTOR.
IS THE CONNECTOR CONDITION OK?
NO
REPAIR AS NECESSARY.*
YES
PUT THE DRBII IN OHMMETER MODE.
PROBE CAVITY 44.
IS THE RESISTANCE BELOW 10.0 OHMS?
YES
REPAIR THE K44 TN/YL WIRE FOR A SHORT TO GROUND.*
NO
USE AN EXTERNAL OHMMETER IN THE FOLLOWING STEP.
TEST TN/YL WIRE FOR RESISTANCE BETWEEN DIST. 4-WAY CONNECTOR & ENGINE CONTROLLER CONNECTOR
IS THE RESISTANCE BELOW 10.0 OHMS?
YES
REPLACE THE ENGINE CONTROLLER.*
NO
REPAIR THE OPEN K44 TN/YL WIRE.*
* PERFORM VERIFICATION PROCEDURE VER-2.

91J09081

Fig. 127: Driveability Test 31A (3.0L VIN 3) – Code 54, No Sync Pick-up Signal (2 of 2)

DR-31B: CODE 54, NO SYNC PICK-UP SIGNAL

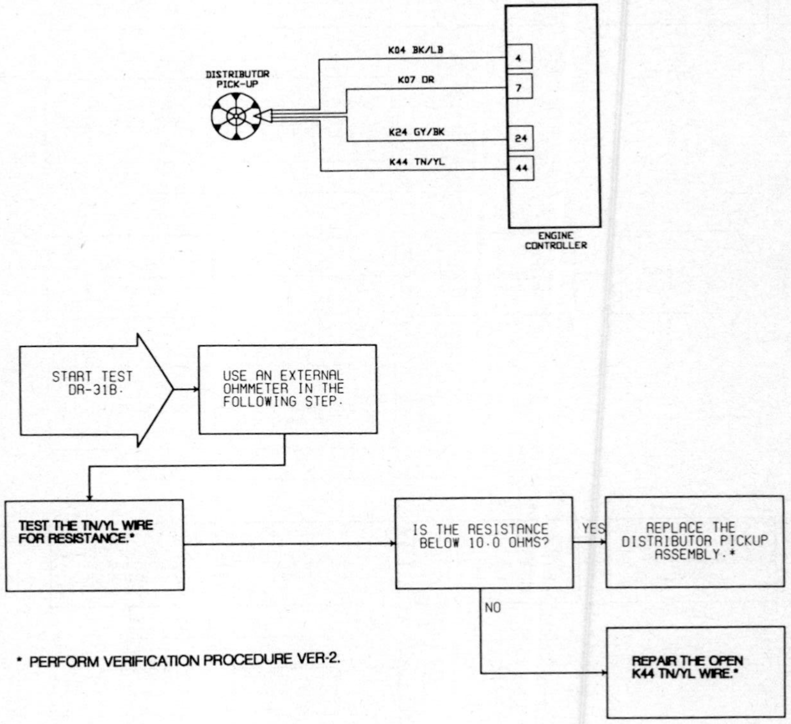
DISTRIBUTOR PICK-UP
K04 BK/LB
K07 OR
K24 GY/BK
K44 TN/YL
4
7
24
44
ENGINE CONTROLLER
START TEST DR-31B.
USE AN EXTERNAL OHMMETER IN THE FOLLOWING STEP.
TEST THE TN/YL WIRE FOR RESISTANCE.*
IS THE RESISTANCE BELOW 10.0 OHMS?
YES
REPLACE THE DISTRIBUTOR PICKUP ASSEMBLY.*
NO
REPAIR THE OPEN K44 TN/YL WIRE.*
* PERFORM VERIFICATION PROCEDURE VER-2.

91E08927 91B09082

Fig. 128: Driveability Test 31B (3.0L VIN 3) – Code 54, No Sync Pick-up Signal

DR-32A: CODE 63, SBEC FAILURE EMR MILES NOT STORED & EEPROM WRITE DENIED (1 OF 2)

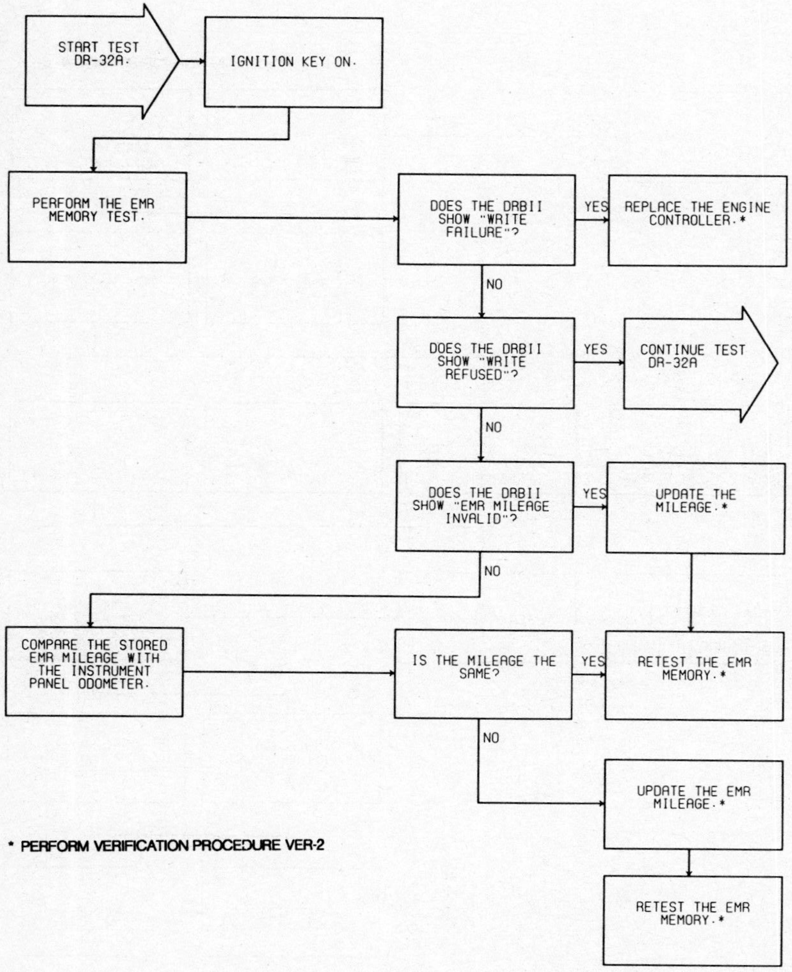
START TEST DR-32A.
IGNITION KEY ON.
PERFORM THE EMR MEMORY TEST.
DOES THE DRBII SHOW "WRITE FAILURE"?
YES
REPLACE THE ENGINE CONTROLLER.*
NO
DOES THE DRBII SHOW "WRITE REFUSED"?
YES
CONTINUE TEST DR-32A
NO
DOES THE DRBII SHOW "EMR MILEAGE INVALID"?
YES
UPDATE THE MILEAGE.*
NO
COMPARE THE STORED EMR MILEAGE WITH THE INSTRUMENT PANEL ODOMETER.
IS THE MILEAGE THE SAME?
YES
RETEST THE EMR MEMORY.*
NO
UPDATE THE EMR MILEAGE.*
RETEST THE EMR MEMORY.*

* PERFORM VERIFICATION PROCEDURE VER-2

91D09083

Fig. 129: Driveability Test 32A (3.0L VIN 3) – Code 63, SBEC Failure EMR Miles Not Stored & EEPROM Write Denied (1 of 2)

DR-32A: CODE 63, SBEC FAILURE EMR MILES NOT STORED & EEPROM WRITE DENIED (2 OF 2)

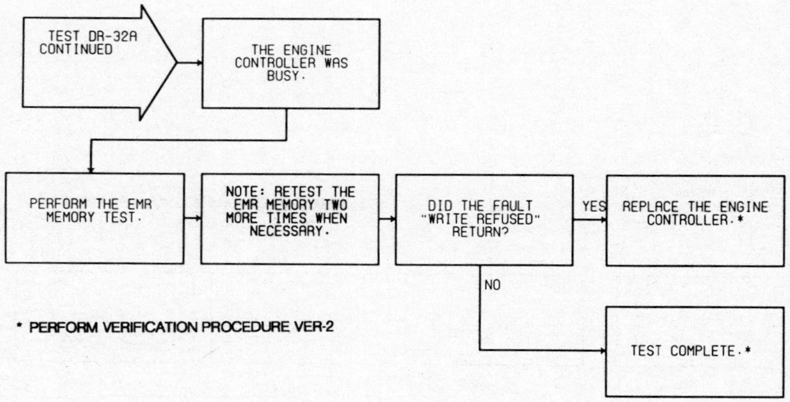
TEST DR-32A CONTINUED
THE ENGINE CONTROLLER WAS BUSY.
PERFORM THE EMR MEMORY TEST.
NOTE: RETEST THE EMR MEMORY TWO MORE TIMES WHEN NECESSARY.
DID THE FAULT "WRITE REFUSED" RETURN?
YES
REPLACE THE ENGINE CONTROLLER.*
NO
TEST COMPLETE.*

* PERFORM VERIFICATION PROCEDURE VER-2

91F09084

Fig. 130: Driveability Test 32A (3.0L VIN 3) – Code 63, SBEC Failure EMR Miles Not Stored & EEPROM Write Denied (2 of 2)

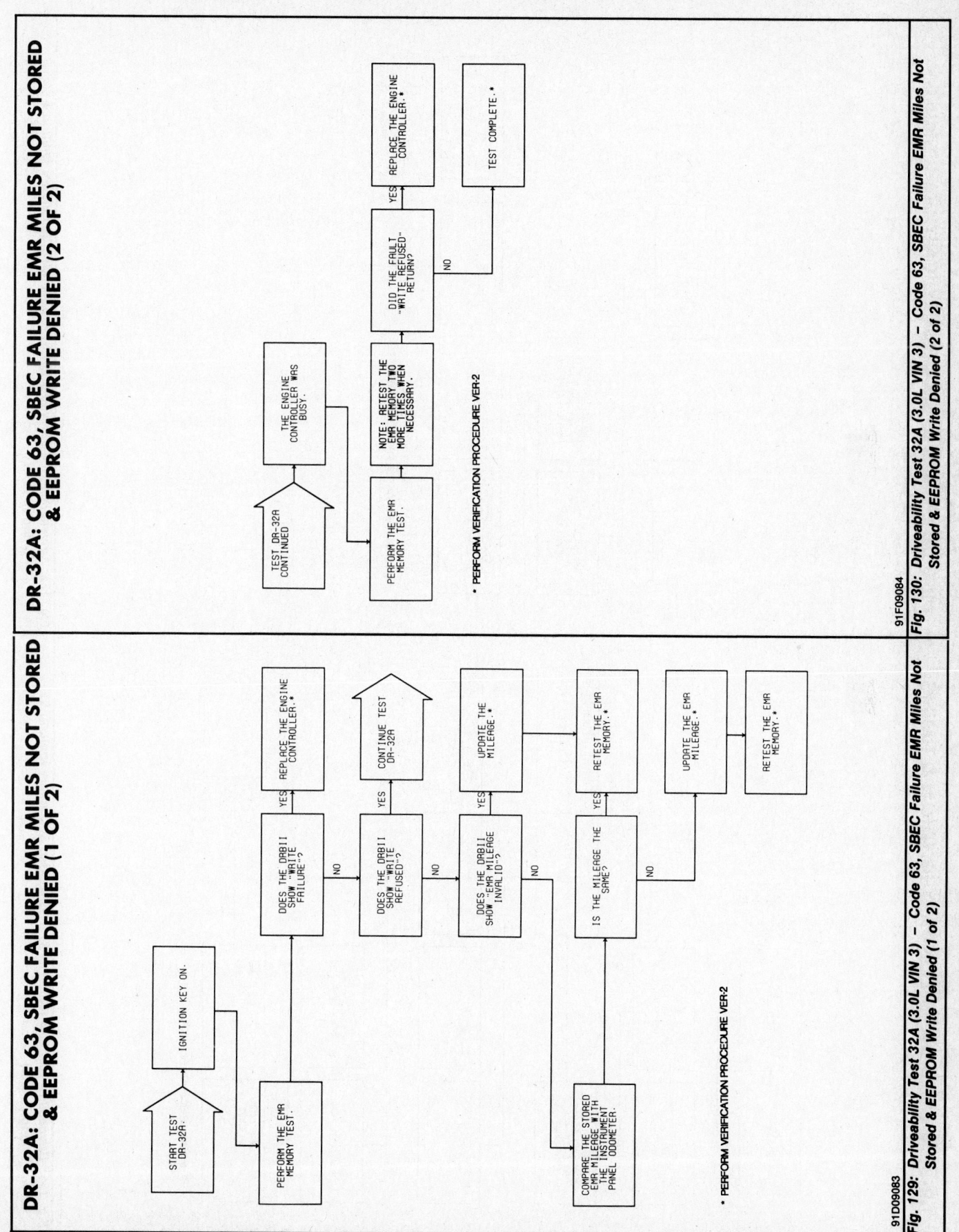

1991 ENGINE PERFORMANCE
Self-Diagnostics – 3.0L VIN 3 (Cont.)

DR-33A: CHECKING SECONDARY IGNITION & TIMING (1 OF 2)

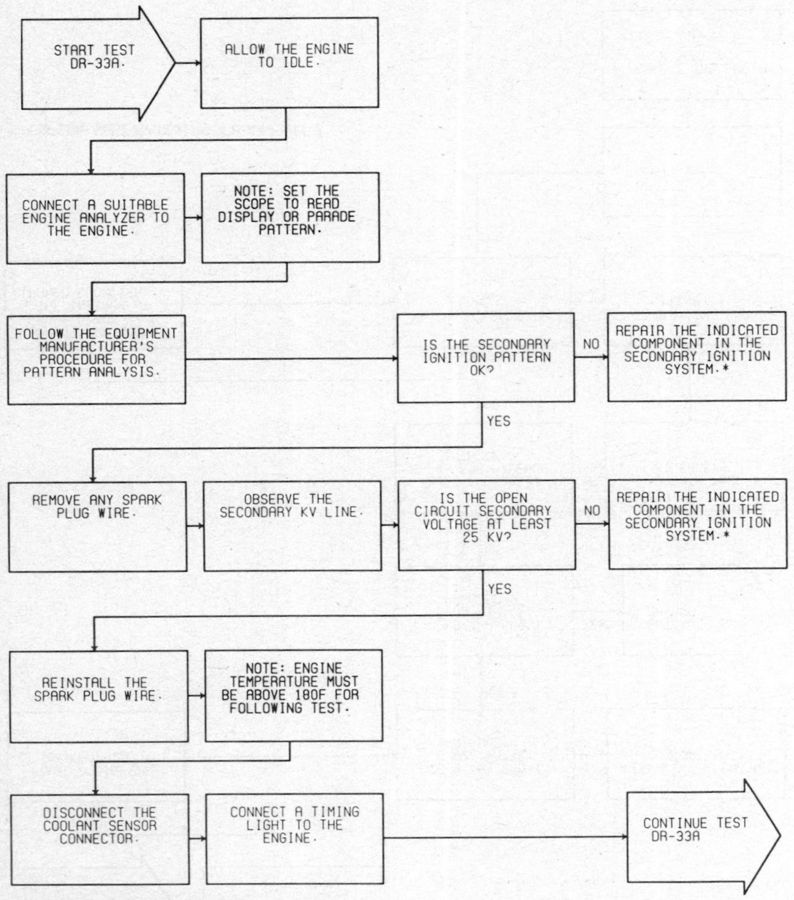
START TEST DR-33A.
ALLOW THE ENGINE TO IDLE.
CONNECT A SUITABLE ENGINE ANALYZER TO THE ENGINE.
NOTE: SET THE SCOPE TO READ DISPLAY OR PARADE PATTERN.
FOLLOW THE EQUIPMENT MANUFACTURER'S PROCEDURE FOR PATTERN ANALYSIS.
IS THE SECONDARY IGNITION PATTERN OK?
NO
REPAIR THE INDICATED COMPONENT IN THE SECONDARY IGNITION SYSTEM.*
YES
REMOVE ANY SPARK PLUG WIRE.
OBSERVE THE SECONDARY KV LINE.
IS THE OPEN CIRCUIT SECONDARY VOLTAGE AT LEAST 25 KV?
NO
REPAIR THE INDICATED COMPONENT IN THE SECONDARY IGNITION SYSTEM.*
YES
REINSTALL THE SPARK PLUG WIRE.
NOTE: ENGINE TEMPERATURE MUST BE ABOVE 180F FOR FOLLOWING TEST.
DISCONNECT THE COOLANT SENSOR CONNECTOR.
CONNECT A TIMING LIGHT TO THE ENGINE.
CONTINUE TEST DR-33A

* PERFORM VERIFICATION PROCEDURE VER-2

91I09085

Fig. 131: Driveability Test 33A (3.0L VIN 3) – Checking Secondary Ignition & Timing (1 of 2)

DR-33A: CHECKING SECONDARY IGNITION & TIMING (2 OF 2)

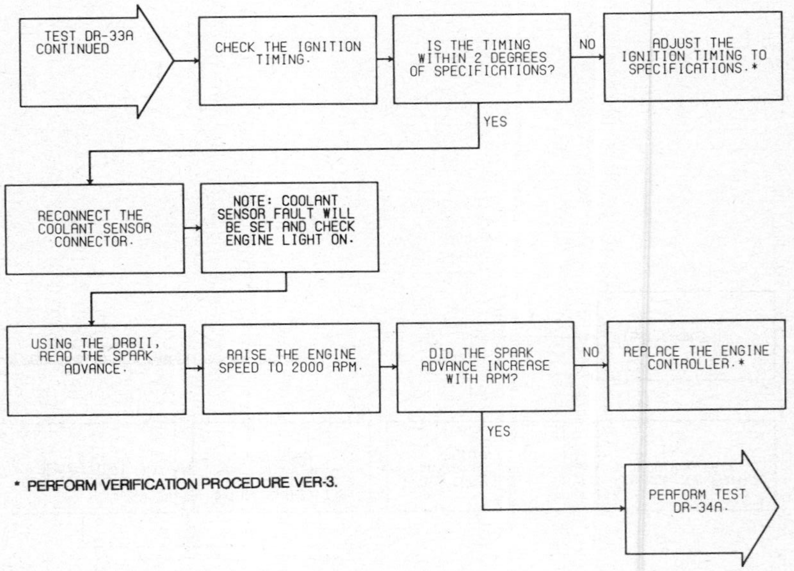
TEST DR-33A CONTINUED
CHECK THE IGNITION TIMING.
IS THE TIMING WITHIN 2 DEGREES OF SPECIFICATIONS?
NO
ADJUST THE IGNITION TIMING TO SPECIFICATIONS.*
YES
RECONNECT THE COOLANT SENSOR CONNECTOR.
NOTE: COOLANT SENSOR FAULT WILL BE SET AND CHECK ENGINE LIGHT ON.
USING THE DRBII, READ THE SPARK ADVANCE.
RAISE THE ENGINE SPEED TO 2000 RPM.
DID THE SPARK ADVANCE INCREASE WITH RPM?
NO
REPLACE THE ENGINE CONTROLLER.*
YES
PERFORM TEST DR-34A.

* PERFORM VERIFICATION PROCEDURE VER-3.

91A09086

Fig. 132: Driveability Test 33A (3.0L VIN 3) – Checking Secondary Ignition & Timing (2 of 2)

DR-34A: CHECKING FUEL PRESSURE (1 OF 2)

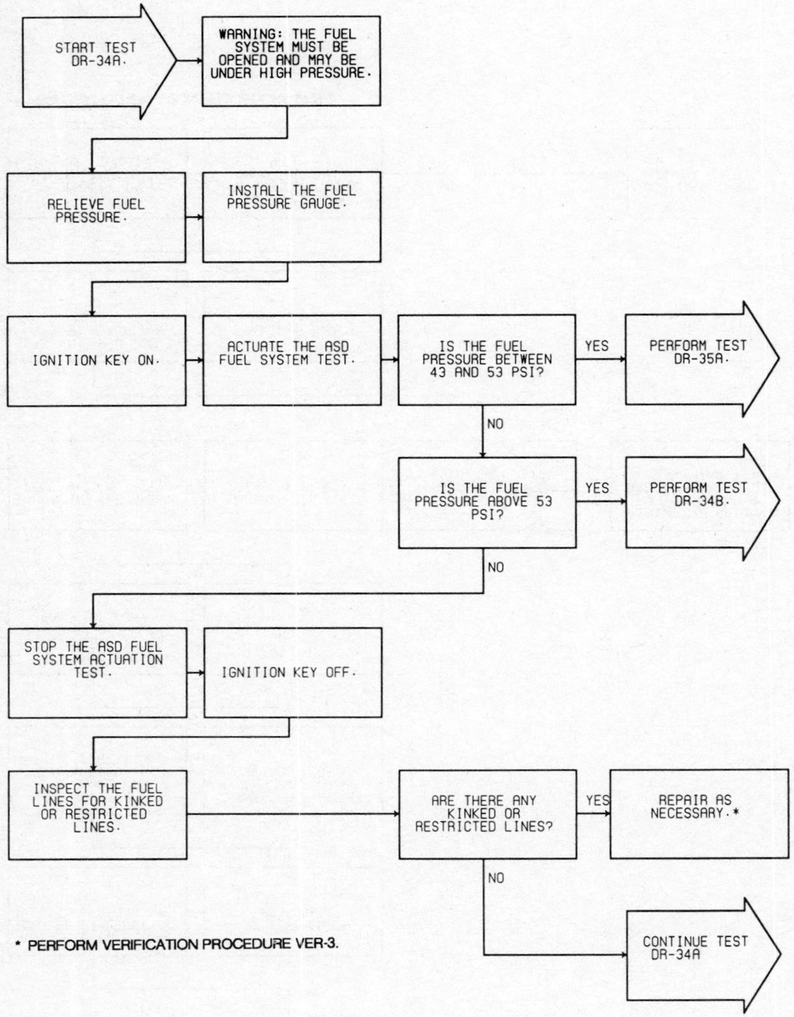
START TEST DR-34A.
WARNING: THE FUEL SYSTEM MUST BE OPENED AND MAY BE UNDER HIGH PRESSURE.
RELIEVE FUEL PRESSURE.
INSTALL THE FUEL PRESSURE GAUGE.
IGNITION KEY ON.
ACTUATE THE ASD FUEL SYSTEM TEST.
IS THE FUEL PRESSURE BETWEEN 43 AND 53 PSI?
YES
PERFORM TEST DR-35A.
NO
IS THE FUEL PRESSURE ABOVE 53 PSI?
YES
PERFORM TEST DR-34B.
NO
STOP THE ASD FUEL SYSTEM ACTUATION TEST.
IGNITION KEY OFF.
INSPECT THE FUEL LINES FOR KINKED OR RESTRICTED LINES.
ARE THERE ANY KINKED OR RESTRICTED LINES?
YES
REPAIR AS NECESSARY.*
NO
CONTINUE TEST DR-34A
* PERFORM VERIFICATION PROCEDURE VER-3.

91C09087

Fig. 133: Driveability Test 34A (3.0L VIN 3) – Checking Fuel Pressure (1 of 2)

DR-34A: CHECKING FUEL PRESSURE (2 OF 2)

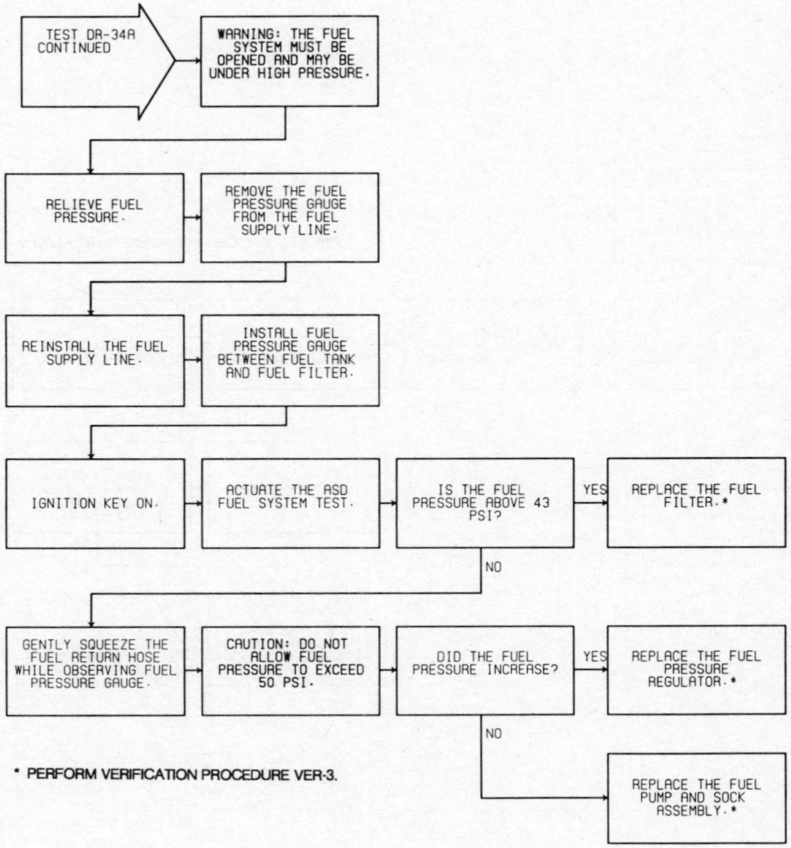
TEST DR-34A CONTINUED
WARNING: THE FUEL SYSTEM MUST BE OPENED AND MAY BE UNDER HIGH PRESSURE.
RELIEVE FUEL PRESSURE.
REMOVE THE FUEL PRESSURE GAUGE FROM THE FUEL SUPPLY LINE.
REINSTALL THE FUEL SUPPLY LINE.
INSTALL FUEL PRESSURE GAUGE BETWEEN FUEL TANK AND FUEL FILTER.
IGNITION KEY ON.
ACTUATE THE ASD FUEL SYSTEM TEST.
IS THE FUEL PRESSURE ABOVE 43 PSI?
YES
REPLACE THE FUEL FILTER.*
NO
GENTLY SQUEEZE THE FUEL RETURN HOSE WHILE OBSERVING FUEL PRESSURE GAUGE.
CAUTION: DO NOT ALLOW FUEL PRESSURE TO EXCEED 50 PSI.
DID THE FUEL PRESSURE INCREASE?
YES
REPLACE THE FUEL PRESSURE REGULATOR.*
NO
REPLACE THE FUEL PUMP AND SOCK ASSEMBLY.*
* PERFORM VERIFICATION PROCEDURE VER-3.

91E09088

Fig. 134: Driveability Test 34A (3.0L VIN 3) – Checking Fuel Pressure (2 of 2)

1991 ENGINE PERFORMANCE
Self-Diagnostics – 3.0L VIN 3 (Cont.)

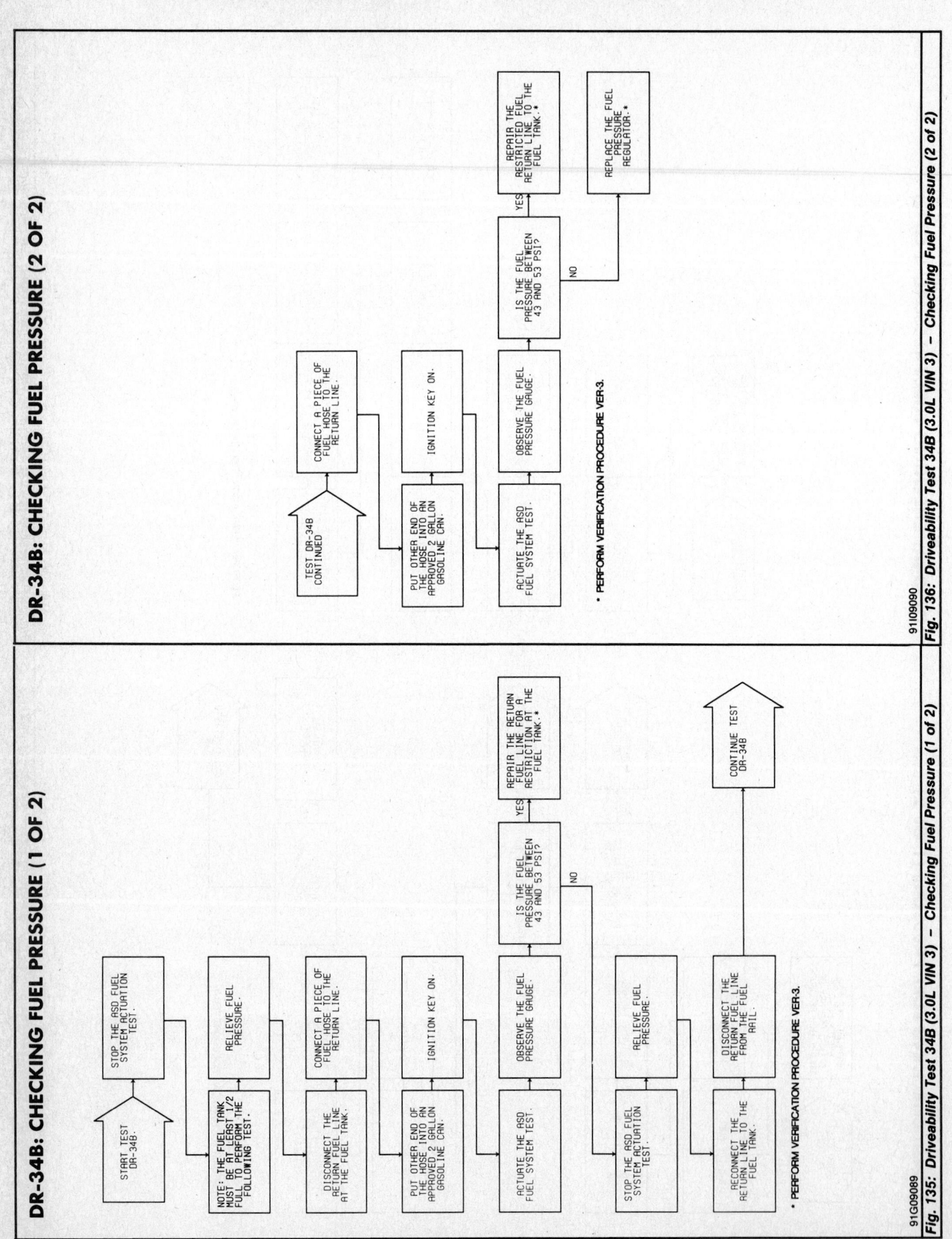

DR-34B: CHECKING FUEL PRESSURE (1 OF 2)

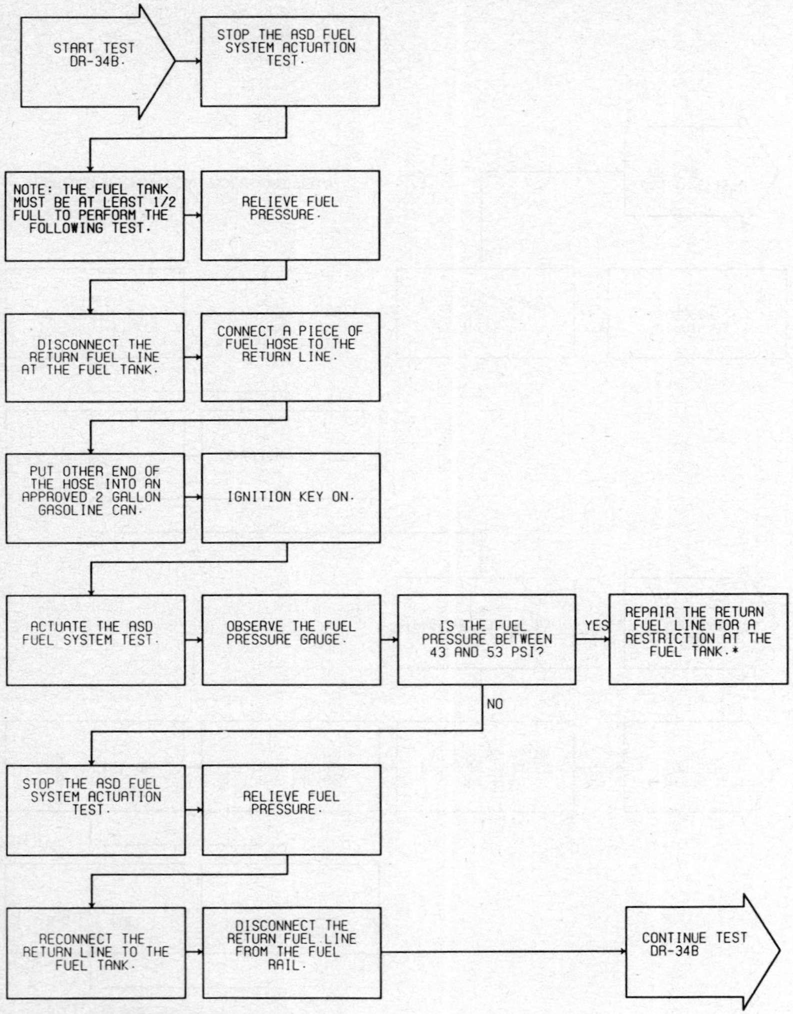
START TEST DR-34B.
STOP THE ASD FUEL SYSTEM ACTUATION TEST.
NOTE: THE FUEL TANK MUST BE AT LEAST 1/2 FULL TO PERFORM THE FOLLOWING TEST.
RELIEVE FUEL PRESSURE.
DISCONNECT THE RETURN FUEL LINE AT THE FUEL TANK.
CONNECT A PIECE OF FUEL HOSE TO THE RETURN LINE.
PUT OTHER END OF THE HOSE INTO AN APPROVED 2 GALLON GASOLINE CAN.
IGNITION KEY ON.
ACTUATE THE ASD FUEL SYSTEM TEST.
OBSERVE THE FUEL PRESSURE GAUGE.
IS THE FUEL PRESSURE BETWEEN 43 AND 53 PSI?
YES
REPAIR THE RETURN FUEL LINE FOR A RESTRICTION AT THE FUEL TANK.*
NO
STOP THE ASD FUEL SYSTEM ACTUATION TEST.
RELIEVE FUEL PRESSURE.
RECONNECT THE RETURN LINE TO THE FUEL TANK.
DISCONNECT THE RETURN FUEL LINE FROM THE FUEL RAIL.
CONTINUE TEST DR-34B

* PERFORM VERIFICATION PROCEDURE VER-3.

91G09089

Fig. 135: Driveability Test 34B (3.0L VIN 3) – Checking Fuel Pressure (1 of 2)

DR-34B: CHECKING FUEL PRESSURE (2 OF 2)

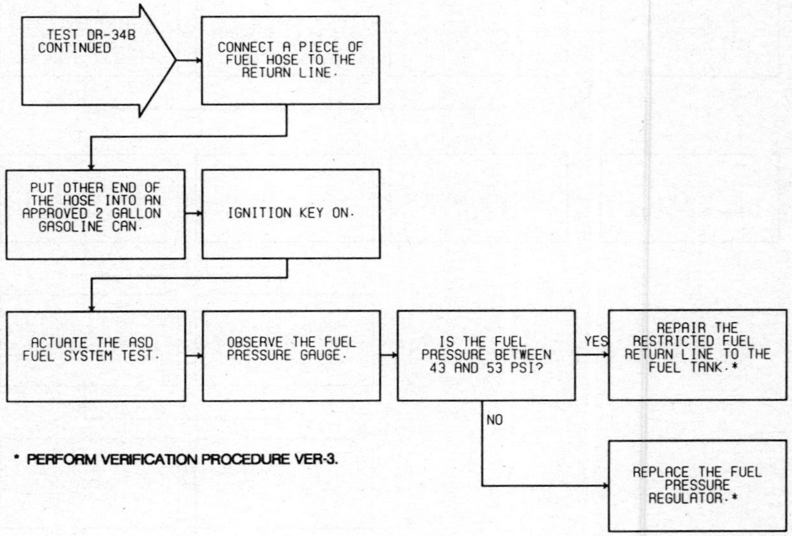
TEST DR-34B CONTINUED
CONNECT A PIECE OF FUEL HOSE TO THE RETURN LINE.
PUT OTHER END OF THE HOSE INTO AN APPROVED 2 GALLON GASOLINE CAN.
IGNITION KEY ON.
ACTUATE THE ASD FUEL SYSTEM TEST.
OBSERVE THE FUEL PRESSURE GAUGE.
IS THE FUEL PRESSURE BETWEEN 43 AND 53 PSI?
YES
REPAIR THE RESTRICTED FUEL RETURN LINE TO THE FUEL TANK.*
NO
REPLACE THE FUEL PRESSURE REGULATOR.*

* PERFORM VERIFICATION PROCEDURE VER-3.

91I09090

Fig. 136: Driveability Test 34B (3.0L VIN 3) – Checking Fuel Pressure (2 of 2)

DR-35A: CHECKING COOLANT & THROTTLE POSITION SENSOR (TPS) CALIBRATION (1 OF 2)

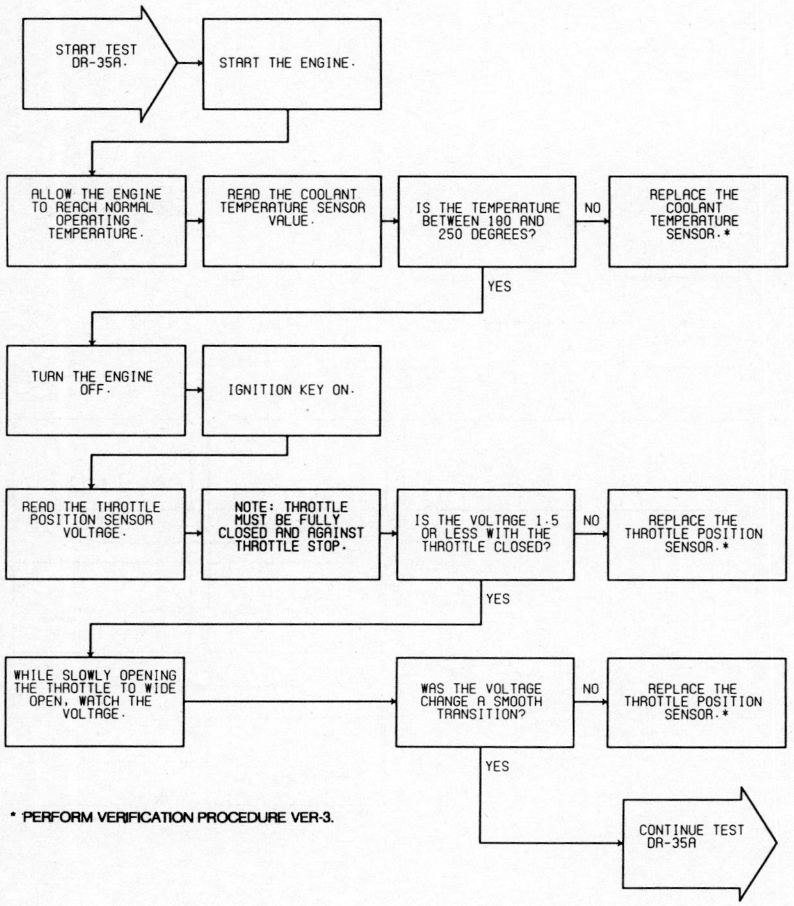
START TEST DR-35A.
START THE ENGINE.
ALLOW THE ENGINE TO REACH NORMAL OPERATING TEMPERATURE.
READ THE COOLANT TEMPERATURE SENSOR VALUE.
IS THE TEMPERATURE BETWEEN 180 AND 250 DEGREES?
NO
REPLACE THE COOLANT TEMPERATURE SENSOR.*
YES
TURN THE ENGINE OFF.
IGNITION KEY ON.
READ THE THROTTLE POSITION SENSOR VOLTAGE.
NOTE: THROTTLE MUST BE FULLY CLOSED AND AGAINST THROTTLE STOP.
IS THE VOLTAGE 1.5 OR LESS WITH THE THROTTLE CLOSED?
NO
REPLACE THE THROTTLE POSITION SENSOR.*
YES
WHILE SLOWLY OPENING THE THROTTLE TO WIDE OPEN, WATCH THE VOLTAGE.
WAS THE VOLTAGE CHANGE A SMOOTH TRANSITION?
NO
REPLACE THE THROTTLE POSITION SENSOR.*
YES
CONTINUE TEST DR-35A

* PERFORM VERIFICATION PROCEDURE VER-3.

91A09091

Fig. 137: Driveability Test 35A (3.0L VIN 3) – Checking Coolant & Throttle Position Sensor (TPS) Calibration (1 of 2)

DR-35A: CHECKING COOLANT & THROTTLE POSITION SENSOR (TPS) CALIBRATION (2 OF 2)

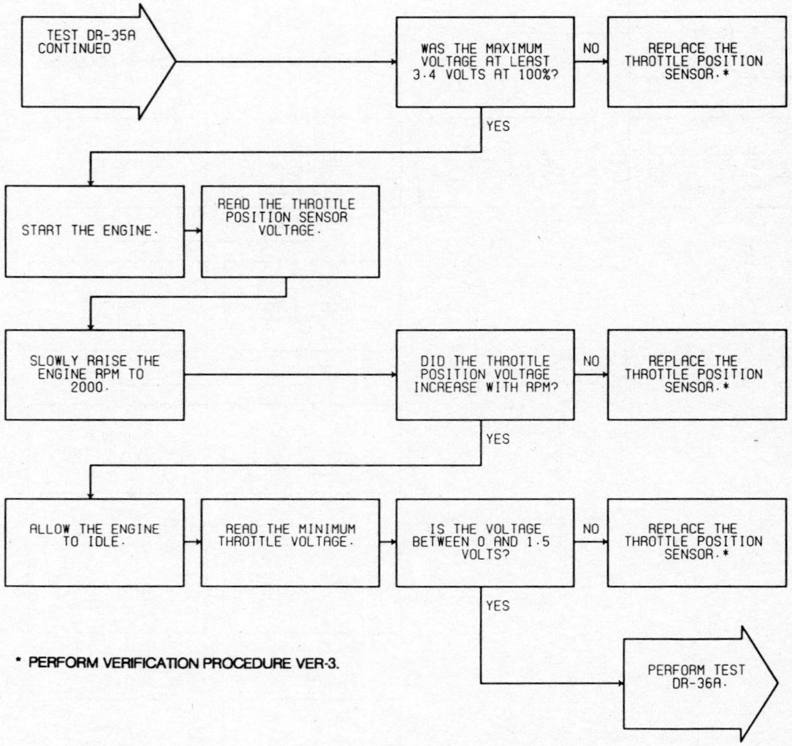
TEST DR-35A CONTINUED
WAS THE MAXIMUM VOLTAGE AT LEAST 3.4 VOLTS AT 100%?
NO
REPLACE THE THROTTLE POSITION SENSOR.*
YES
START THE ENGINE.
READ THE THROTTLE POSITION SENSOR VOLTAGE.
SLOWLY RAISE THE ENGINE RPM TO 2000.
DID THE THROTTLE POSITION VOLTAGE INCREASE WITH RPM?
NO
REPLACE THE THROTTLE POSITION SENSOR.*
YES
ALLOW THE ENGINE TO IDLE.
READ THE MINIMUM THROTTLE VOLTAGE.
IS THE VOLTAGE BETWEEN 0 AND 1.5 VOLTS?
NO
REPLACE THE THROTTLE POSITION SENSOR.*
YES
PERFORM TEST DR-36A.

* PERFORM VERIFICATION PROCEDURE VER-3.

91C09092

Fig. 138: Driveability Test 35A (3.0L VIN 3) – Checking Coolant & Throttle Position Sensor (TPS) Calibration (2 of 2)

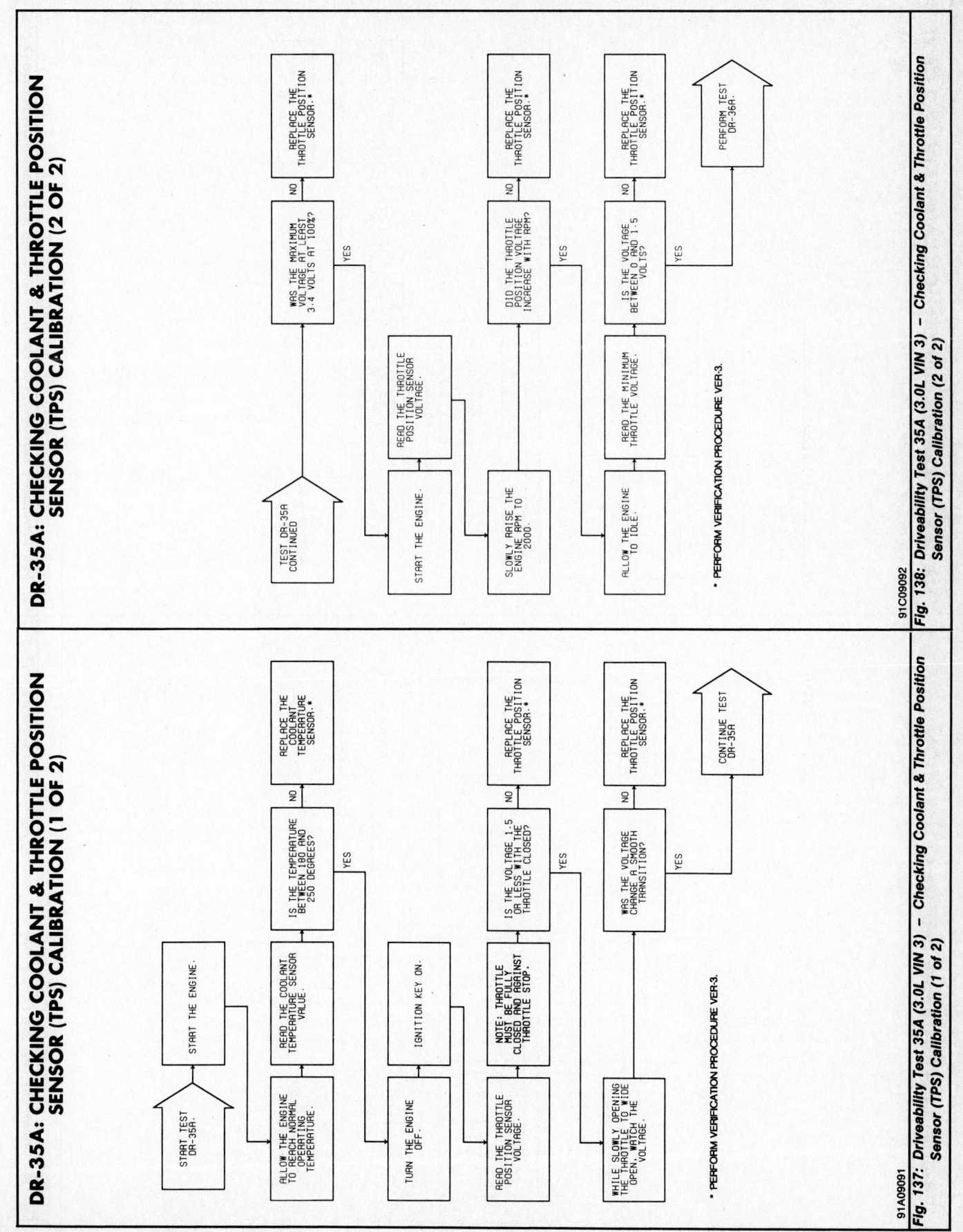

1991 ENGINE PERFORMANCE
Self-Diagnostics – 3.0L VIN 3 (Cont.)

DR-36A: CHECKING MAP SENSOR CALIBRATION (1 OF 2)

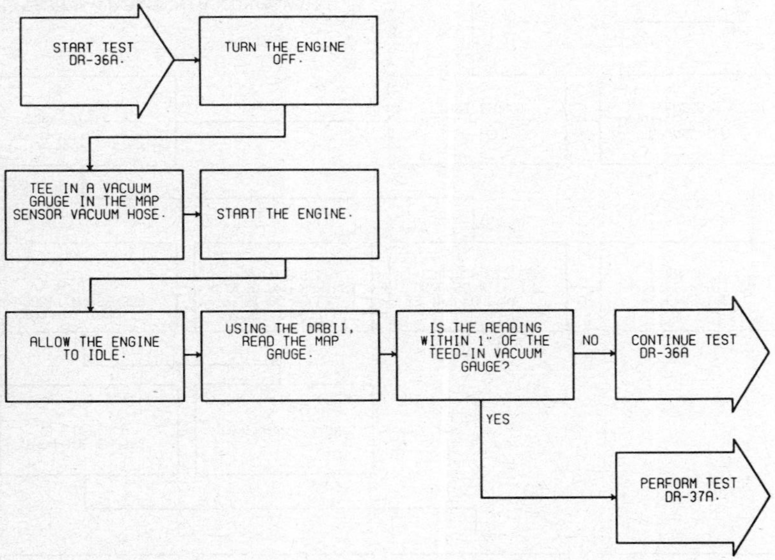
START TEST DR-36A.
TURN THE ENGINE OFF.
TEE IN A VACUUM GAUGE IN THE MAP SENSOR VACUUM HOSE.
START THE ENGINE.
ALLOW THE ENGINE TO IDLE.
USING THE DRBII, READ THE MAP GAUGE.
IS THE READING WITHIN 1" OF THE TEED-IN VACUUM GAUGE?
NO
CONTINUE TEST DR-36A
YES
PERFORM TEST DR-37A.

91E09093

Fig. 139: Driveability Test 36A (3.0L VIN 3) – Checking MAP Sensor Calibration (1 of 2)

DR-36A: CHECKING MAP SENSOR CALIBRATION (2 OF 2)

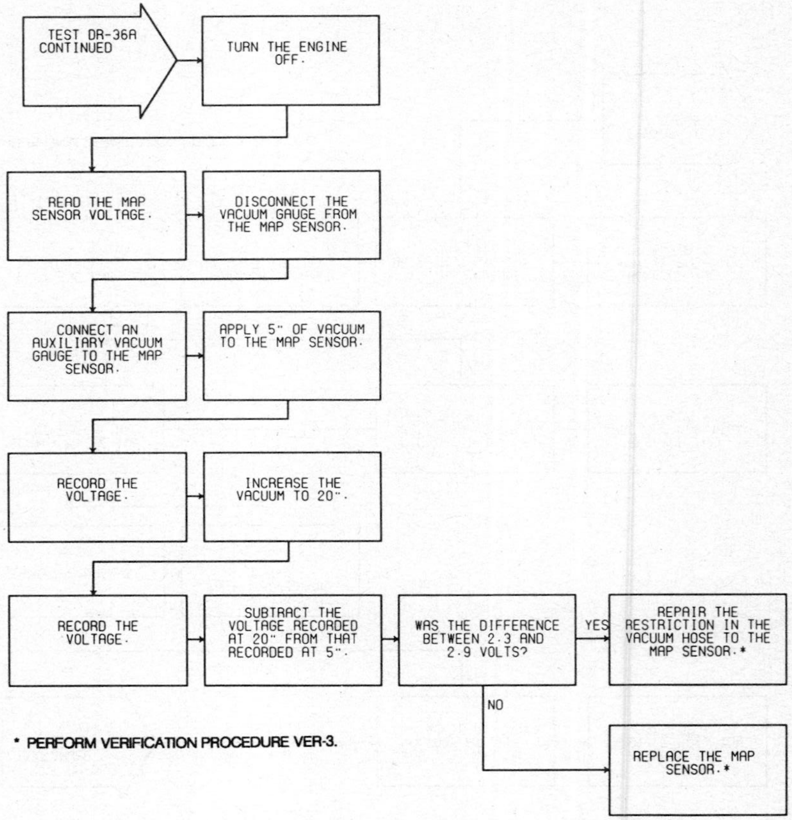
TEST DR-36A CONTINUED
TURN THE ENGINE OFF.
READ THE MAP SENSOR VOLTAGE.
DISCONNECT THE VACUUM GAUGE FROM THE MAP SENSOR.
CONNECT AN AUXILIARY VACUUM GAUGE TO THE MAP SENSOR.
APPLY 5" OF VACUUM TO THE MAP SENSOR.
RECORD THE VOLTAGE.
INCREASE THE VACUUM TO 20".
RECORD THE VOLTAGE.
SUBTRACT THE VOLTAGE RECORDED AT 20" FROM THAT RECORDED AT 5".
WAS THE DIFFERENCE BETWEEN 2.3 AND 2.9 VOLTS?
YES
REPAIR THE RESTRICTION IN THE VACUUM HOSE TO THE MAP SENSOR.*
NO
REPLACE THE MAP SENSOR.*

* PERFORM VERIFICATION PROCEDURE VER-3.

91G09094

Fig. 140: Driveability Test 36A (3.0L VIN 3) – Checking MAP Sensor Calibration (2 of 2)

DR-37A: CHECKING OXYGEN SENSOR SWITCHING

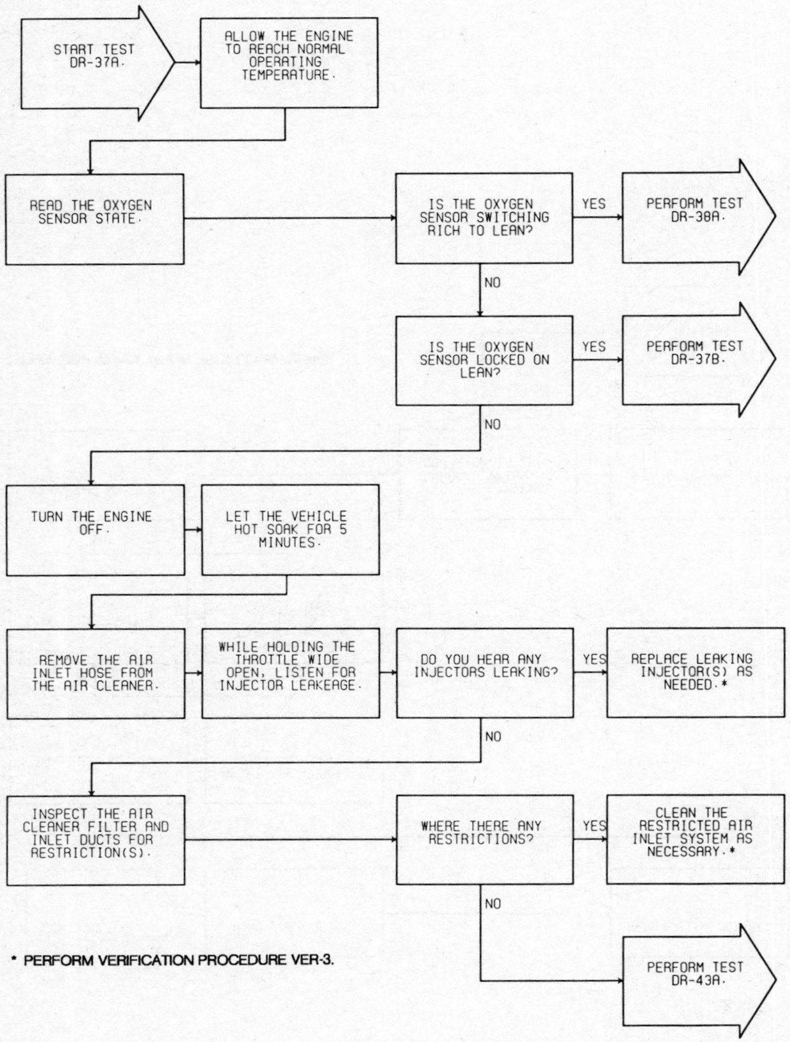
START TEST DR-37A.
ALLOW THE ENGINE TO REACH NORMAL OPERATING TEMPERATURE.
READ THE OXYGEN SENSOR STATE.
IS THE OXYGEN SENSOR SWITCHING RICH TO LEAN?
YES
PERFORM TEST DR-38A.
NO
IS THE OXYGEN SENSOR LOCKED ON LEAN?
YES
PERFORM TEST DR-37B.
NO
TURN THE ENGINE OFF.
LET THE VEHICLE HOT SOAK FOR 5 MINUTES.
REMOVE THE AIR INLET HOSE FROM THE AIR CLEANER.
WHILE HOLDING THE THROTTLE WIDE OPEN, LISTEN FOR INJECTOR LEAKEAGE.
DO YOU HEAR ANY INJECTORS LEAKING?
YES
REPLACE LEAKING INJECTOR(S) AS NEEDED.*
NO
INSPECT THE AIR CLEANER FILTER AND INLET DUCTS FOR RESTRICTION(S).
WHERE THERE ANY RESTRICTIONS?
YES
CLEAN THE RESTRICTED AIR INLET SYSTEM AS NECESSARY.*
NO
PERFORM TEST DR-43A.

* PERFORM VERIFICATION PROCEDURE VER-3.

91J09095

Fig. 141: Driveability Test 37A (3.0L VIN 3) – Checking Oxygen Sensor Switching

DR-37B: CHECKING OXYGEN SENSOR SWITCHING (1 OF 2)

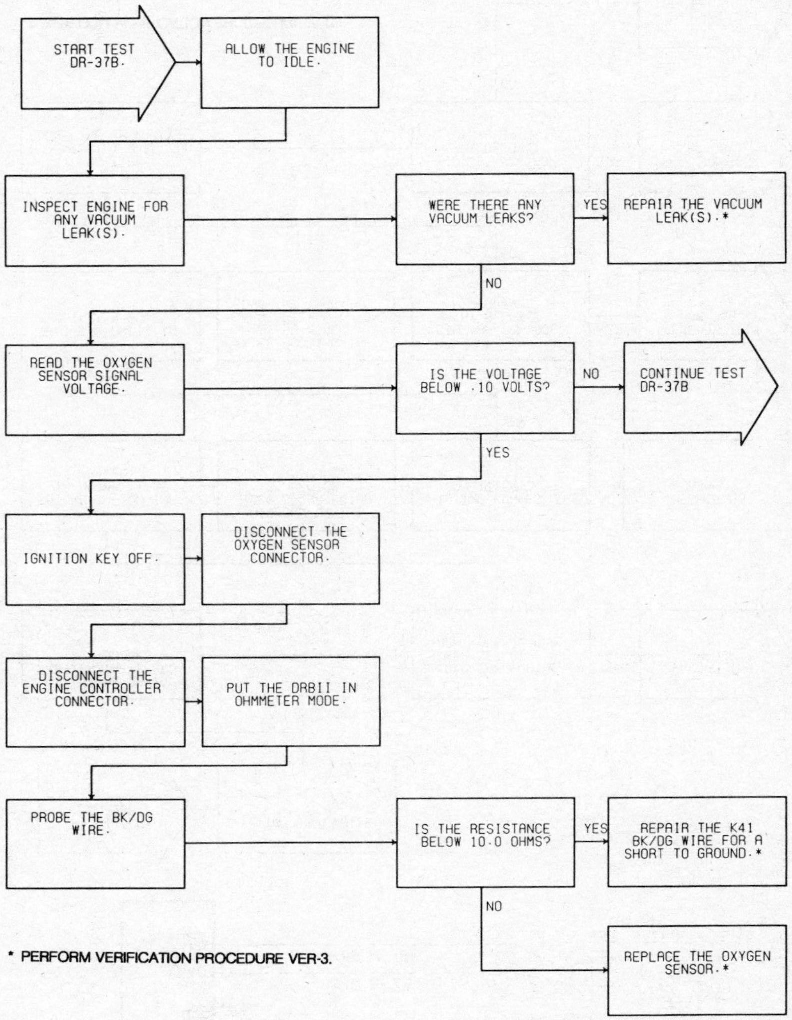
START TEST DR-37B.
ALLOW THE ENGINE TO IDLE.
INSPECT ENGINE FOR ANY VACUUM LEAK(S).
WERE THERE ANY VACUUM LEAKS?
YES
REPAIR THE VACUUM LEAK(S).*
NO
READ THE OXYGEN SENSOR SIGNAL VOLTAGE.
IS THE VOLTAGE BELOW .10 VOLTS?
NO
CONTINUE TEST DR-37B
YES
IGNITION KEY OFF.
DISCONNECT THE OXYGEN SENSOR CONNECTOR.
DISCONNECT THE ENGINE CONTROLLER CONNECTOR.
PUT THE DRBII IN OHMMETER MODE.
PROBE THE BK/DG WIRE.
IS THE RESISTANCE BELOW 10.0 OHMS?
YES
REPAIR THE K41 BK/DG WIRE FOR A SHORT TO GROUND.*
NO
REPLACE THE OXYGEN SENSOR.*

* PERFORM VERIFICATION PROCEDURE VER-3.

91B09096

Fig. 142: Driveability Test 37B (3.0L VIN 3) – Checking Oxygen Sensor Switching (1 of 2)

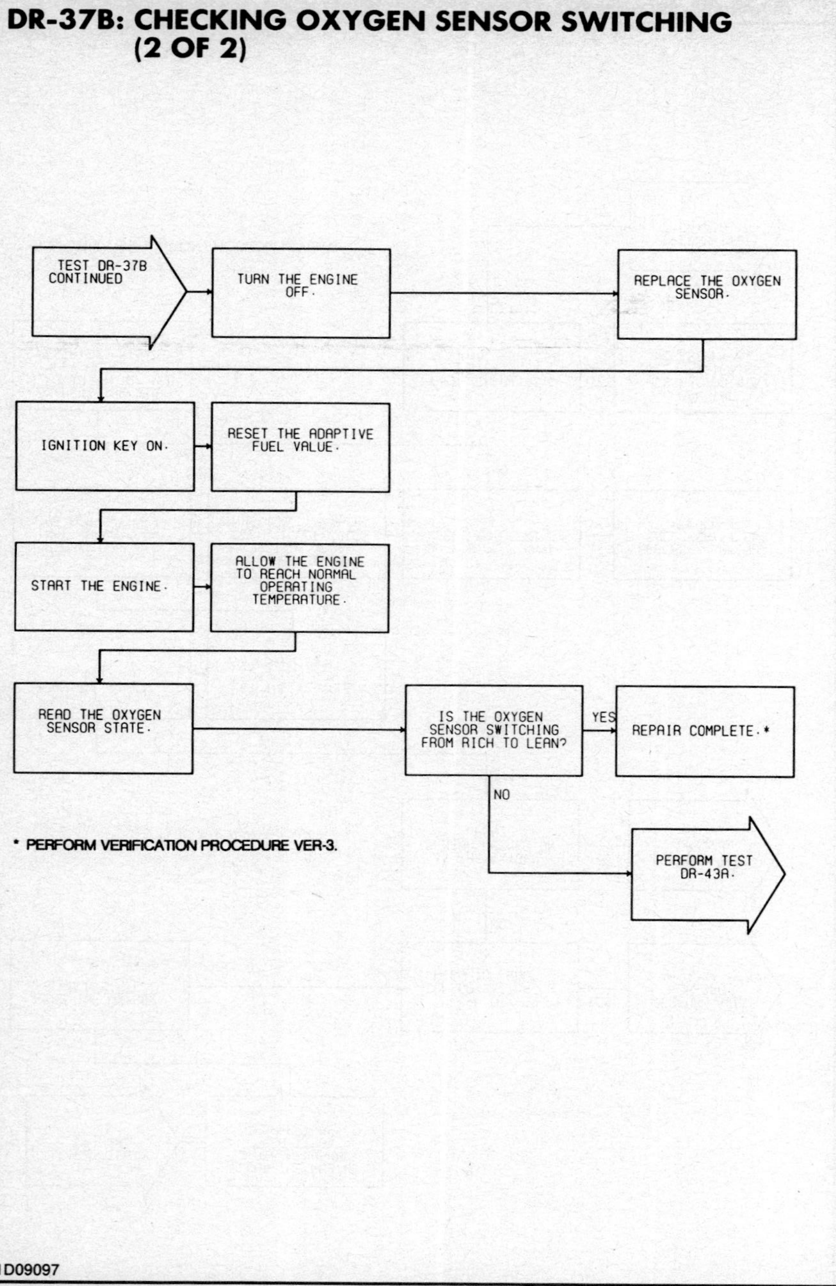
DR-37B: CHECKING OXYGEN SENSOR SWITCHING
(2 OF 2)
TEST DR-37B CONTINUED
TURN THE ENGINE OFF.
REPLACE THE OXYGEN SENSOR.
IGNITION KEY ON.
RESET THE ADAPTIVE FUEL VALUE.
START THE ENGINE.
ALLOW THE ENGINE TO REACH NORMAL OPERATING TEMPERATURE.
READ THE OXYGEN SENSOR STATE.
IS THE OXYGEN SENSOR SWITCHING FROM RICH TO LEAN?
YES
REPAIR COMPLETE.*
NO
PERFORM TEST DR-43A.
* PERFORM VERIFICATION PROCEDURE VER-3.
91D09097

Fig. 143: Driveability Test 37B (3.0L VIN 3) – Checking Oxygen Sensor Switching (2 of 2)

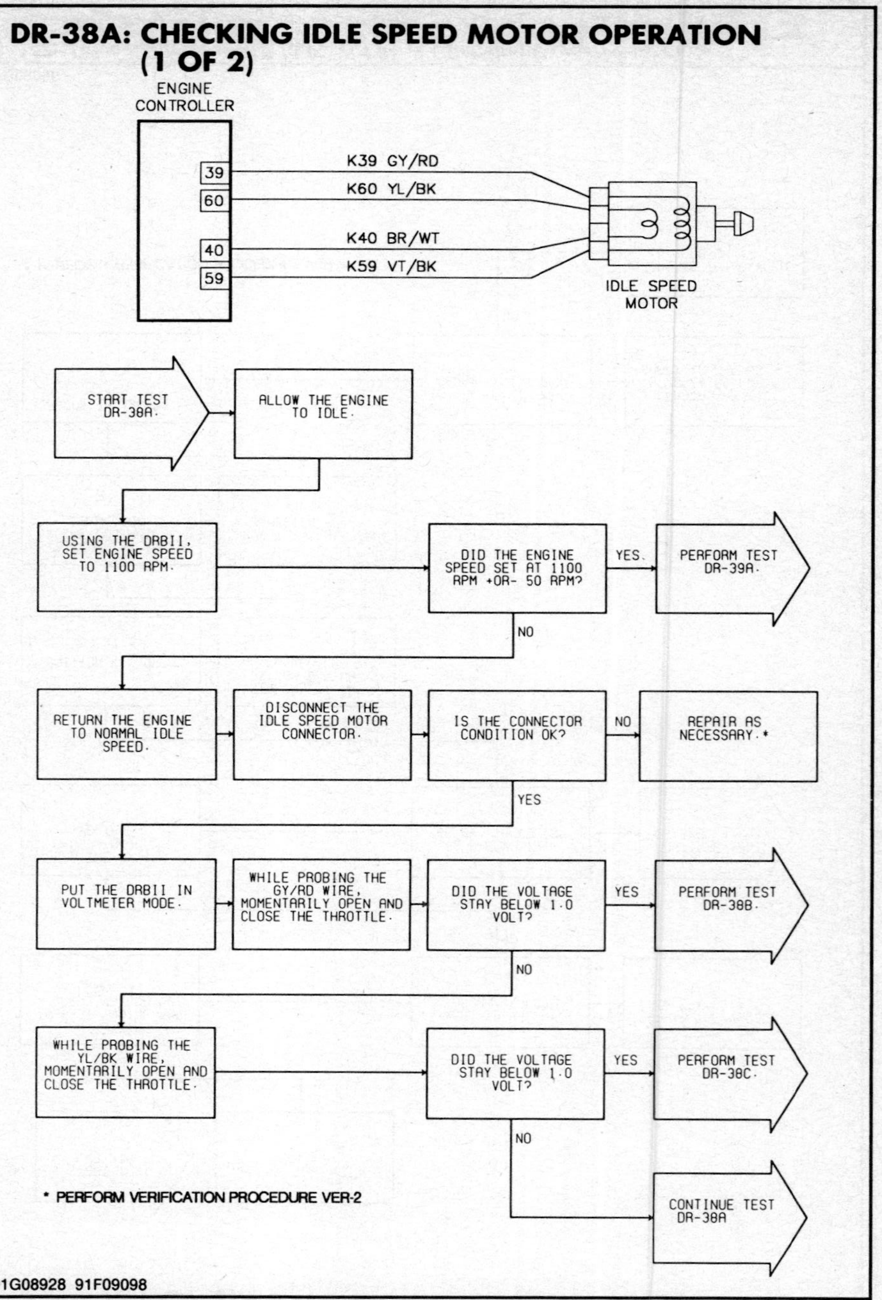
DR-38A: CHECKING IDLE SPEED MOTOR OPERATION
(1 OF 2)
ENGINE CONTROLLER
39
60
40
59
K39 GY/RD
K60 YL/BK
K40 BR/WT
K59 VT/BK
IDLE SPEED MOTOR
START TEST DR-38A.
ALLOW THE ENGINE TO IDLE.
USING THE DRBII, SET ENGINE SPEED TO 1100 RPM.
DID THE ENGINE SPEED SET AT 1100 RPM +OR- 50 RPM?
YES.
PERFORM TEST DR-39A.
NO
RETURN THE ENGINE TO NORMAL IDLE SPEED.
DISCONNECT THE IDLE SPEED MOTOR CONNECTOR.
IS THE CONNECTOR CONDITION OK?
NO
REPAIR AS NECESSARY.*
YES
PUT THE DRBII IN VOLTMETER MODE.
WHILE PROBING THE GY/RD WIRE, MOMENTARILY OPEN AND CLOSE THE THROTTLE.
DID THE VOLTAGE STAY BELOW 1.0 VOLT?
YES
PERFORM TEST DR-38B.
NO
WHILE PROBING THE YL/BK WIRE, MOMENTARILY OPEN AND CLOSE THE THROTTLE.
DID THE VOLTAGE STAY BELOW 1.0 VOLT?
YES
PERFORM TEST DR-38C.
NO
CONTINUE TEST DR-38A
* PERFORM VERIFICATION PROCEDURE VER-2
91G08928 91F09098

Fig. 144: Driveability Test 38A (3.0L VIN 3) – Checking Idle Speed Motor Operation (1 of 2)

DR-38A: CHECKING IDLE SPEED MOTOR OPERATION (2 OF 2)

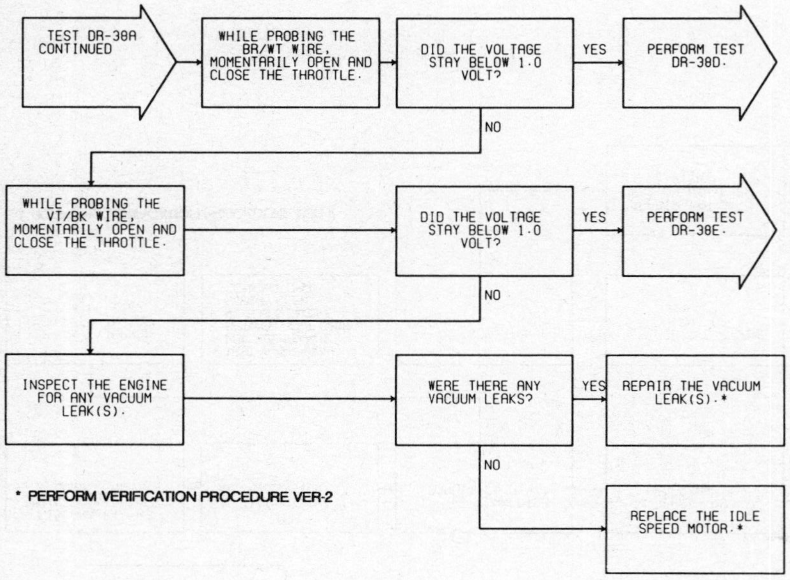
TEST DR-38A CONTINUED
WHILE PROBING THE BR/WT WIRE, MOMENTARILY OPEN AND CLOSE THE THROTTLE.
DID THE VOLTAGE STAY BELOW 1.0 VOLT?
YES
PERFORM TEST DR-38D.
NO
WHILE PROBING THE VT/BK WIRE, MOMENTARILY OPEN AND CLOSE THE THROTTLE.
DID THE VOLTAGE STAY BELOW 1.0 VOLT?
YES
PERFORM TEST DR-38E.
NO
INSPECT THE ENGINE FOR ANY VACUUM LEAK(S).
WERE THERE ANY VACUUM LEAKS?
YES
REPAIR THE VACUUM LEAK(S).*
NO
REPLACE THE IDLE SPEED MOTOR.*
* PERFORM VERIFICATION PROCEDURE VER-2

91H09099

Fig. 145: Driveability Test 38A (3.0L VIN 3) – Checking Idle Speed Motor Operation (2 of 2)

DR-38B: CHECKING IDLE SPEED MOTOR OPERATION

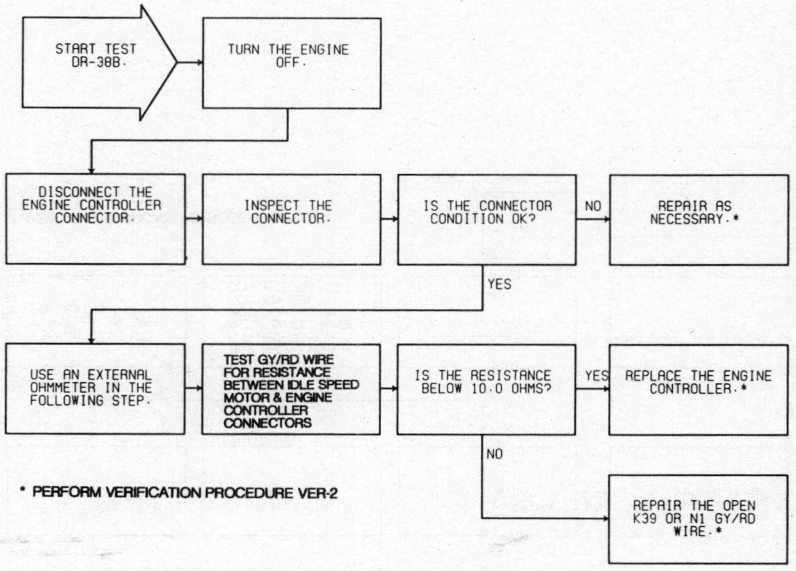
START TEST DR-38B.
TURN THE ENGINE OFF.
DISCONNECT THE ENGINE CONTROLLER CONNECTOR.
INSPECT THE CONNECTOR.
IS THE CONNECTOR CONDITION OK?
NO
REPAIR AS NECESSARY.*
YES
USE AN EXTERNAL OHMMETER IN THE FOLLOWING STEP.
TEST GY/RD WIRE FOR RESISTANCE BETWEEN IDLE SPEED MOTOR & ENGINE CONTROLLER CONNECTORS
IS THE RESISTANCE BELOW 10.0 OHMS?
YES
REPLACE THE ENGINE CONTROLLER.*
NO
REPAIR THE OPEN K39 OR N1 GY/RD WIRE.*
* PERFORM VERIFICATION PROCEDURE VER-2

91B09100

Fig. 146: Driveability Test 38B (3.0L VIN 3) – Checking Idle Speed Motor Operation

1991 ENGINE PERFORMANCE
Self-Diagnostics – 3.0L VIN 3 (Cont.)

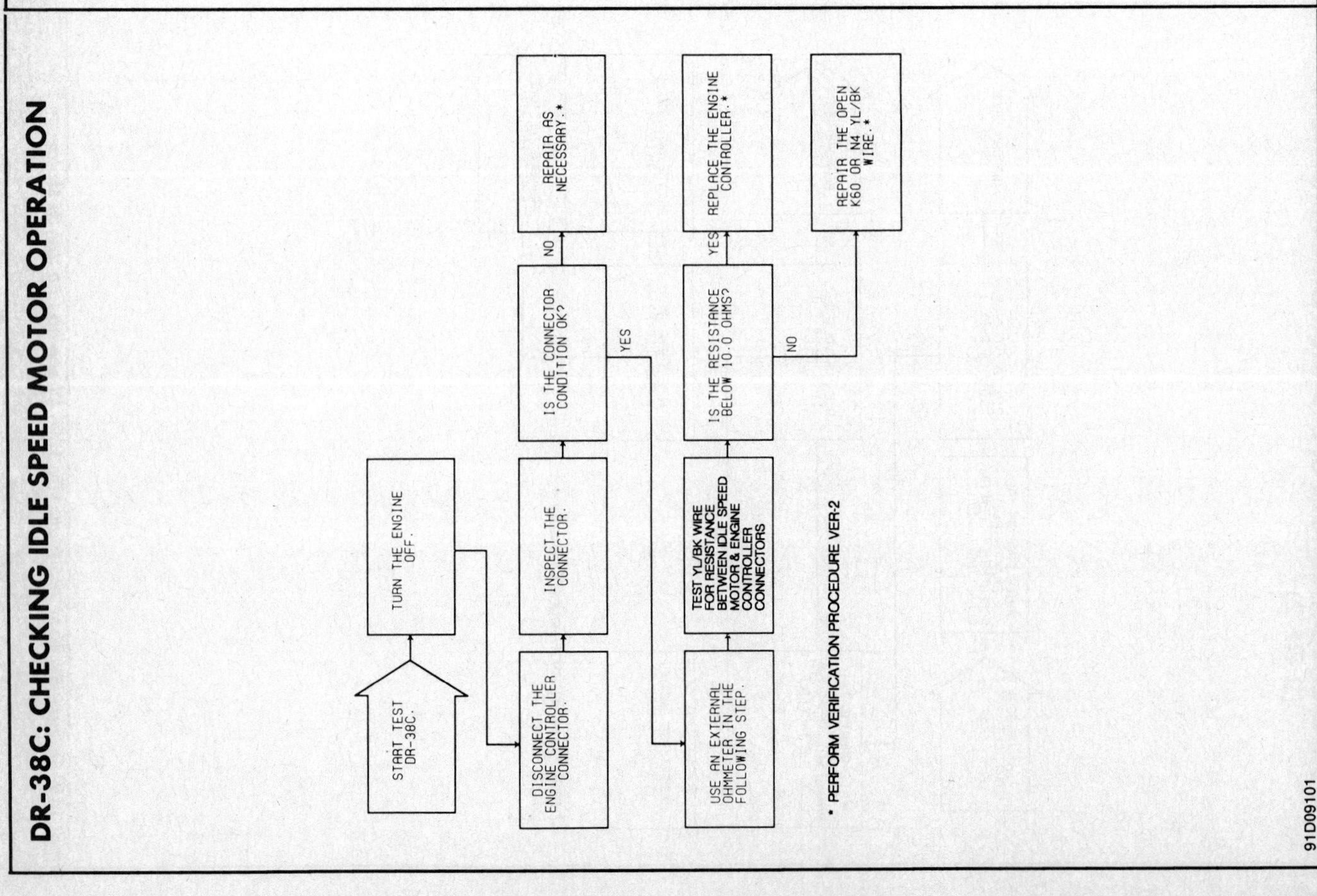
DR-38C: CHECKING IDLE SPEED MOTOR OPERATION
START TEST DR-38C.
TURN THE ENGINE OFF.
DISCONNECT THE ENGINE CONTROLLER CONNECTOR.
INSPECT THE CONNECTOR.
IS THE CONNECTOR CONDITION OK?
NO
REPAIR AS NECESSARY.*
YES
USE AN EXTERNAL OHMMETER IN THE FOLLOWING STEP.
TEST YL/BK WIRE FOR RESISTANCE BETWEEN IDLE SPEED MOTOR & ENGINE CONTROLLER CONNECTORS
IS THE RESISTANCE BELOW 10.0 OHMS?
YES
REPLACE THE ENGINE CONTROLLER.*
NO
REPAIR THE OPEN K60 OR N4 YL/BK WIRE.*
* PERFORM VERIFICATION PROCEDURE VER-2
91D09101

Fig. 147: Driveability Test 38C (3.0L VIN 3) – Checking Idle Speed Motor Operation

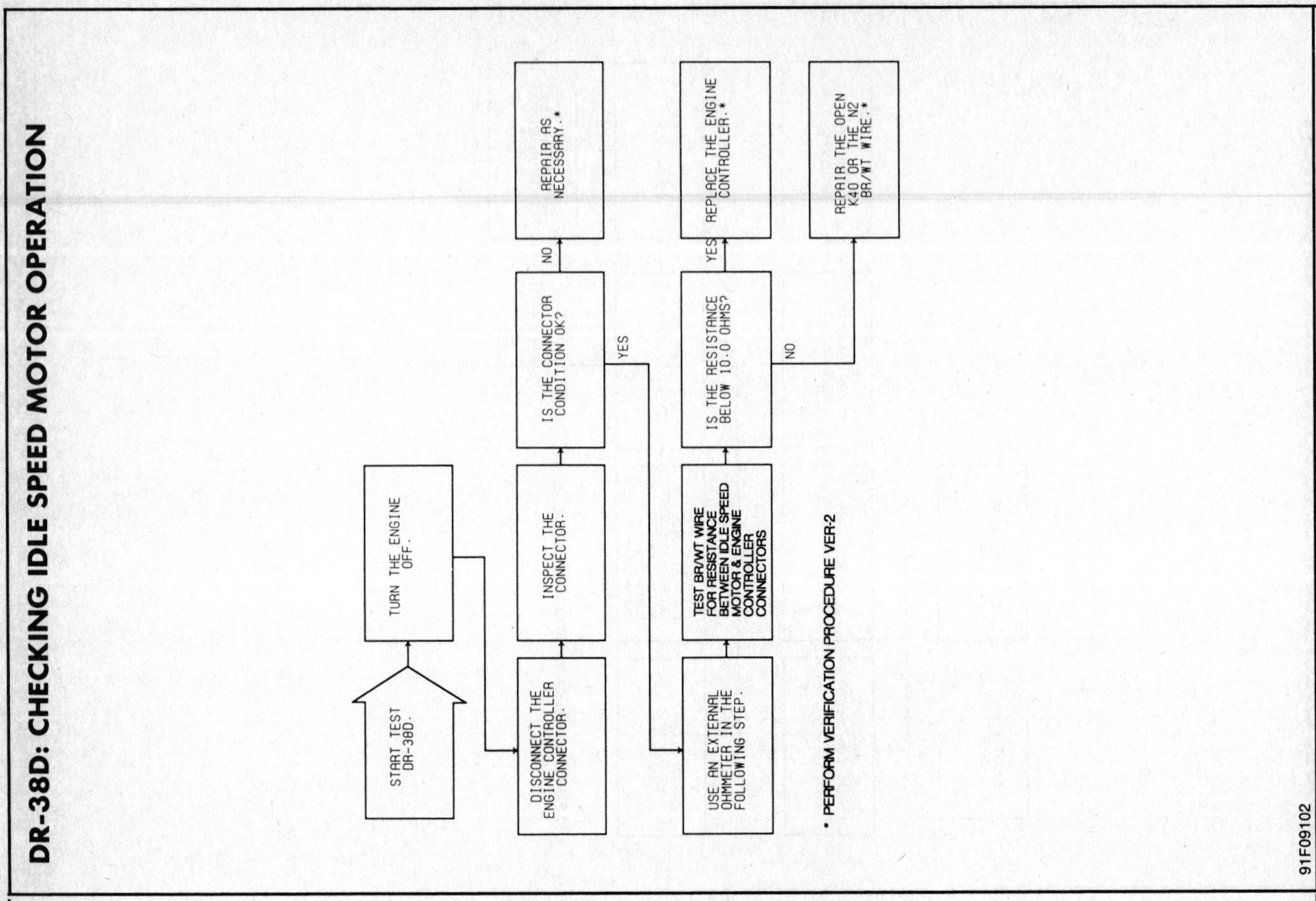
DR-38D: CHECKING IDLE SPEED MOTOR OPERATION
START TEST DR-38D.
TURN THE ENGINE OFF.
DISCONNECT THE ENGINE CONTROLLER CONNECTOR.
INSPECT THE CONNECTOR.
IS THE CONNECTOR CONDITION OK?
NO
REPAIR AS NECESSARY.*
YES
USE AN EXTERNAL OHMMETER IN THE FOLLOWING STEP.
TEST BR/WT WIRE FOR RESISTANCE BETWEEN IDLE SPEED MOTOR & ENGINE CONTROLLER CONNECTORS
IS THE RESISTANCE BELOW 10.0 OHMS?
YES
REPLACE THE ENGINE CONTROLLER.*
NO
REPAIR THE OPEN K40 OR THE N2 BR/WT WIRE.*
* PERFORM VERIFICATION PROCEDURE VER-2
91F09102

Fig. 148: Driveability Test 38D (3.0L VIN 3) – Checking Idle Speed Motor Operation

DR-38E: CHECKING IDLE SPEED MOTOR OPERATION

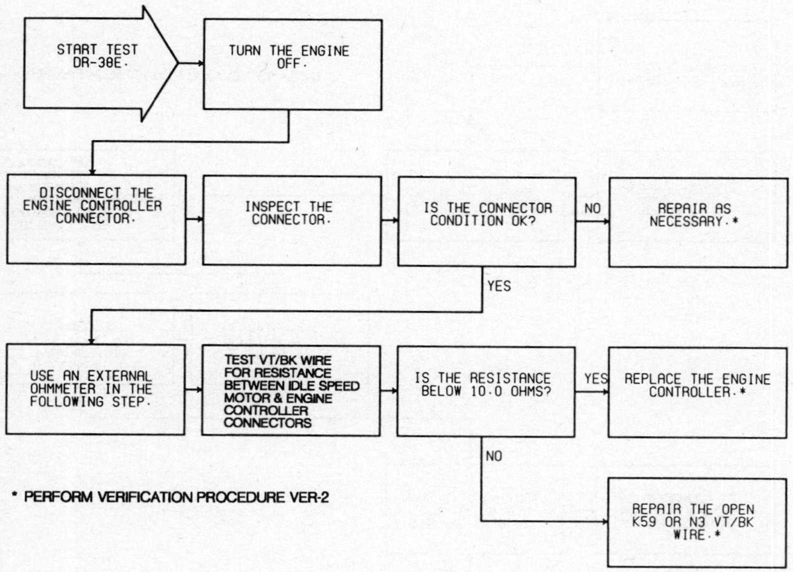
START TEST DR-38E.
TURN THE ENGINE OFF.
DISCONNECT THE ENGINE CONTROLLER CONNECTOR.
INSPECT THE CONNECTOR.
IS THE CONNECTOR CONDITION OK?
NO
REPAIR AS NECESSARY.*
YES
USE AN EXTERNAL OHMMETER IN THE FOLLOWING STEP.
TEST VT/BK WIRE FOR RESISTANCE BETWEEN IDLE SPEED MOTOR & ENGINE CONTROLLER CONNECTORS
IS THE RESISTANCE BELOW 10.0 OHMS?
YES
REPLACE THE ENGINE CONTROLLER.*
NO
REPAIR THE OPEN K59 OR N3 VT/BK WIRE.*
* PERFORM VERIFICATION PROCEDURE VER-2

91H09103

Fig. 149: Driveability Test 38E (3.0L VIN 3) – Checking Idle Speed Motor Operation

DR-39A: CHECKING PARK/NEUTRAL SWITCH INPUT (1 OF 2)

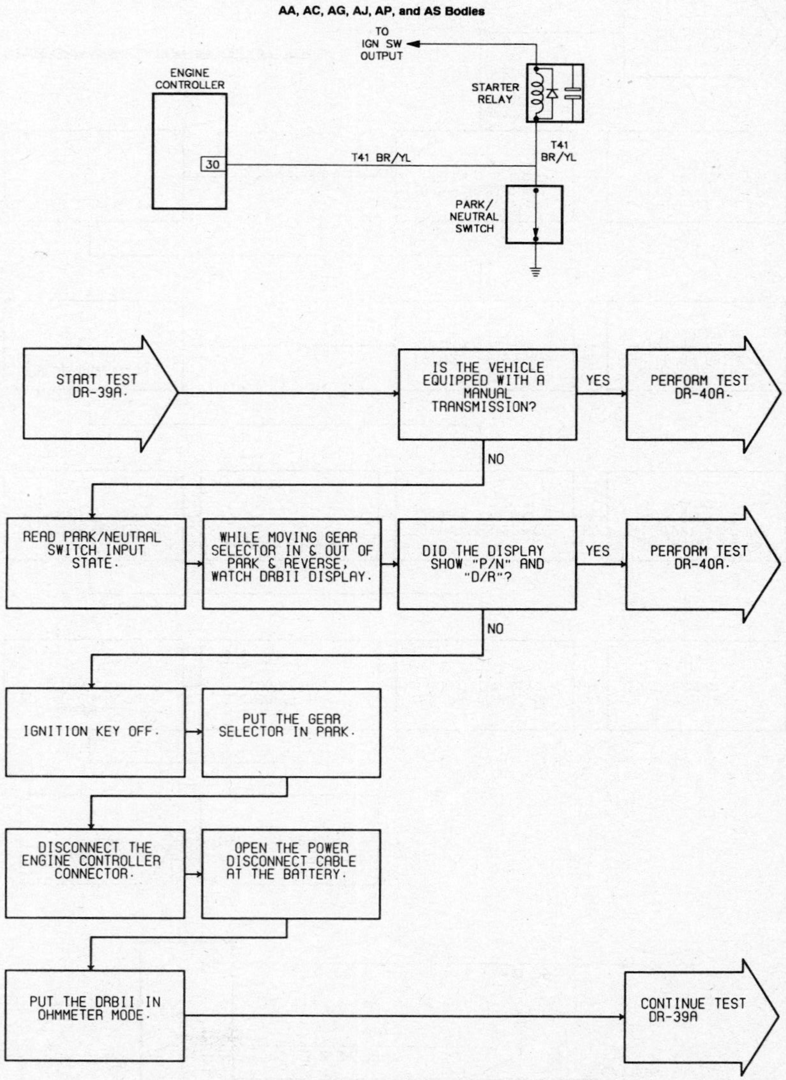
AA, AC, AG, AJ, AP, and AS Bodies
TO IGN SW OUTPUT
ENGINE CONTROLLER
30
STARTER RELAY
T41 BR/YL
T41 BR/YL
PARK/ NEUTRAL SWITCH
START TEST DR-39A.
IS THE VEHICLE EQUIPPED WITH A MANUAL TRANSMISSION?
YES
PERFORM TEST DR-40A.
NO
READ PARK/NEUTRAL SWITCH INPUT STATE.
WHILE MOVING GEAR SELECTOR IN & OUT OF PARK & REVERSE, WATCH DRBII DISPLAY.
DID THE DISPLAY SHOW "P/N" AND "D/R"?
YES
PERFORM TEST DR-40A.
NO
IGNITION KEY OFF.
PUT THE GEAR SELECTOR IN PARK.
DISCONNECT THE ENGINE CONTROLLER CONNECTOR.
OPEN THE POWER DISCONNECT CABLE AT THE BATTERY.
PUT THE DRBII IN OHMMETER MODE.
CONTINUE TEST DR-39A

91I08929 91J09104

Fig. 150: Driveability Test 39A (3.0L VIN 3) – Checking Park/Neutral Switch Input (1 of 2)

DR-39A: CHECKING PARK/NEUTRAL SWITCH INPUT (2 OF 2)

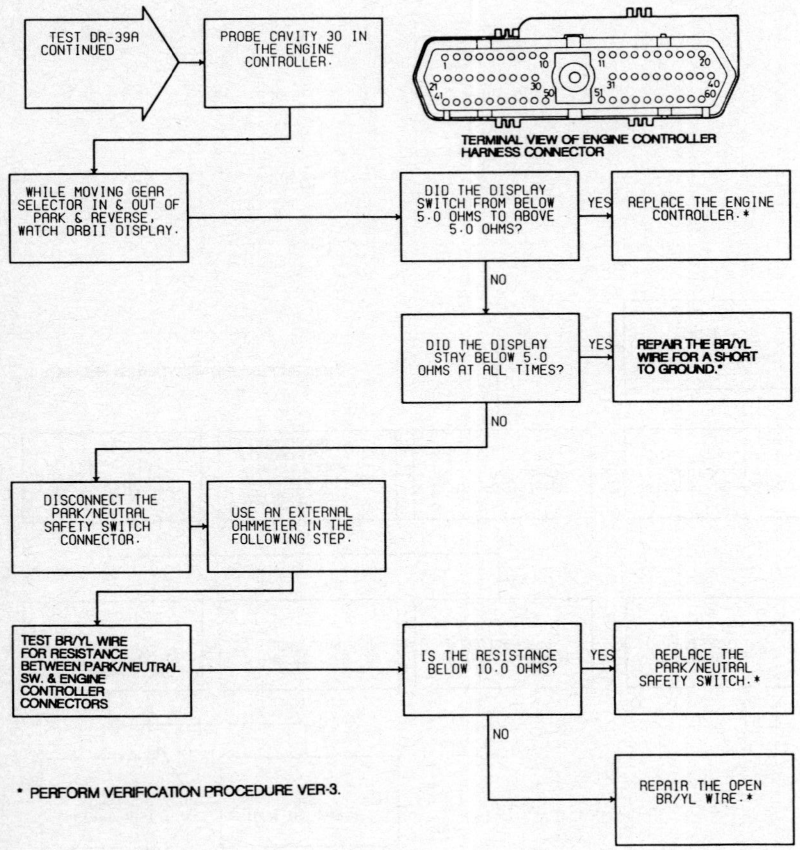
TEST DR-39A CONTINUED
PROBE CAVITY 30 IN THE ENGINE CONTROLLER.
TERMINAL VIEW OF ENGINE CONTROLLER HARNESS CONNECTOR
WHILE MOVING GEAR SELECTOR IN & OUT OF PARK & REVERSE, WATCH DRBII DISPLAY.
DID THE DISPLAY SWITCH FROM BELOW 5.0 OHMS TO ABOVE 5.0 OHMS?
YES
REPLACE THE ENGINE CONTROLLER.*
NO
DID THE DISPLAY STAY BELOW 5.0 OHMS AT ALL TIMES?
YES
REPAIR THE BR/YL WIRE FOR A SHORT TO GROUND.*
NO
DISCONNECT THE PARK/NEUTRAL SAFETY SWITCH CONNECTOR.
USE AN EXTERNAL OHMMETER IN THE FOLLOWING STEP.
TEST BR/YL WIRE FOR RESISTANCE BETWEEN PARK/NEUTRAL SW. & ENGINE CONTROLLER CONNECTORS
IS THE RESISTANCE BELOW 10.0 OHMS?
YES
REPLACE THE PARK/NEUTRAL SAFETY SWITCH.*
NO
REPAIR THE OPEN BR/YL WIRE.*

* PERFORM VERIFICATION PROCEDURE VER-3.

91C09105

Fig. 151: Driveability Test 39A (3.0L VIN 3) – Checking Park/Neutral Switch Input (2 of 2)

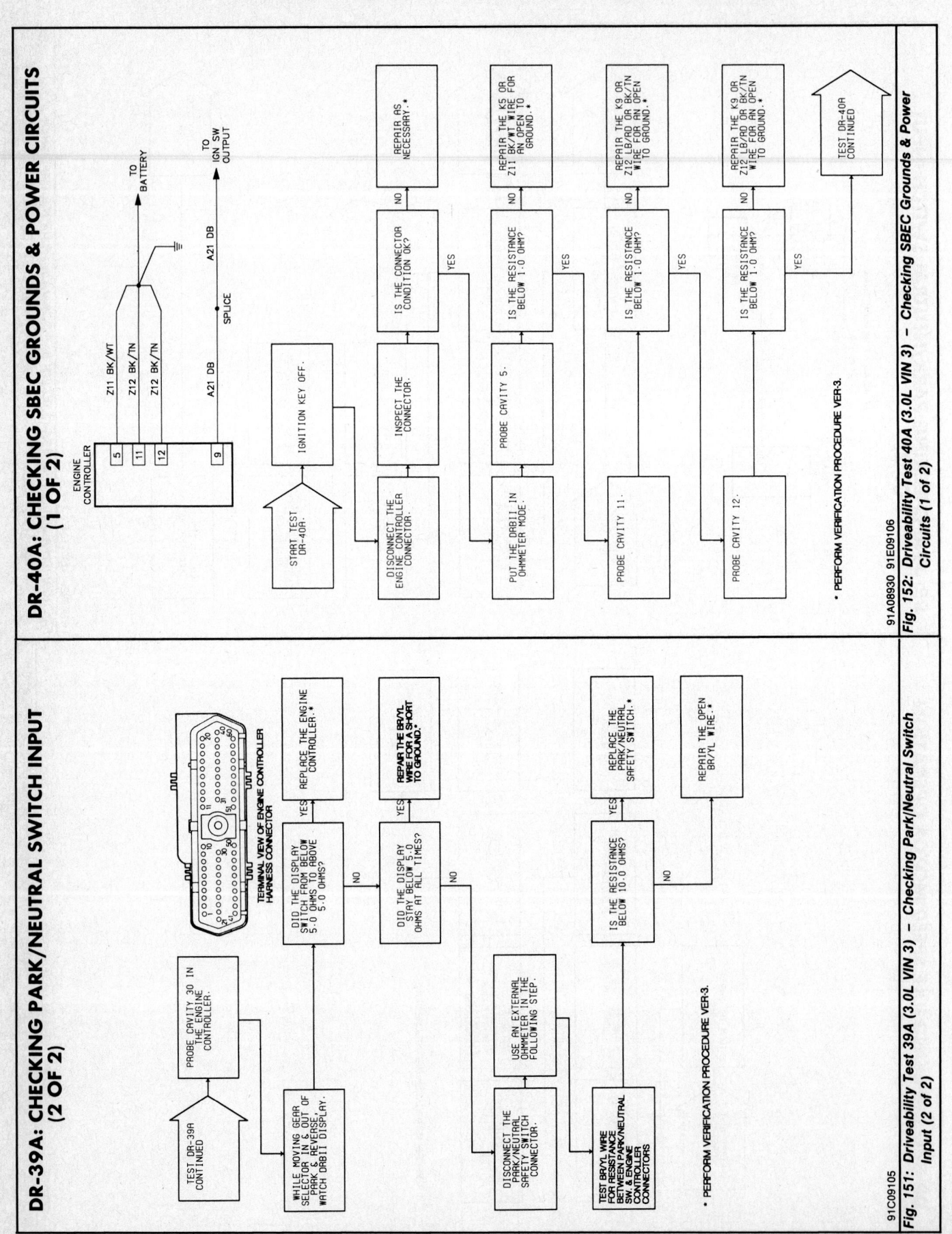

DR-40A: CHECKING SBEC GROUNDS & POWER CIRCUITS (1 OF 2)

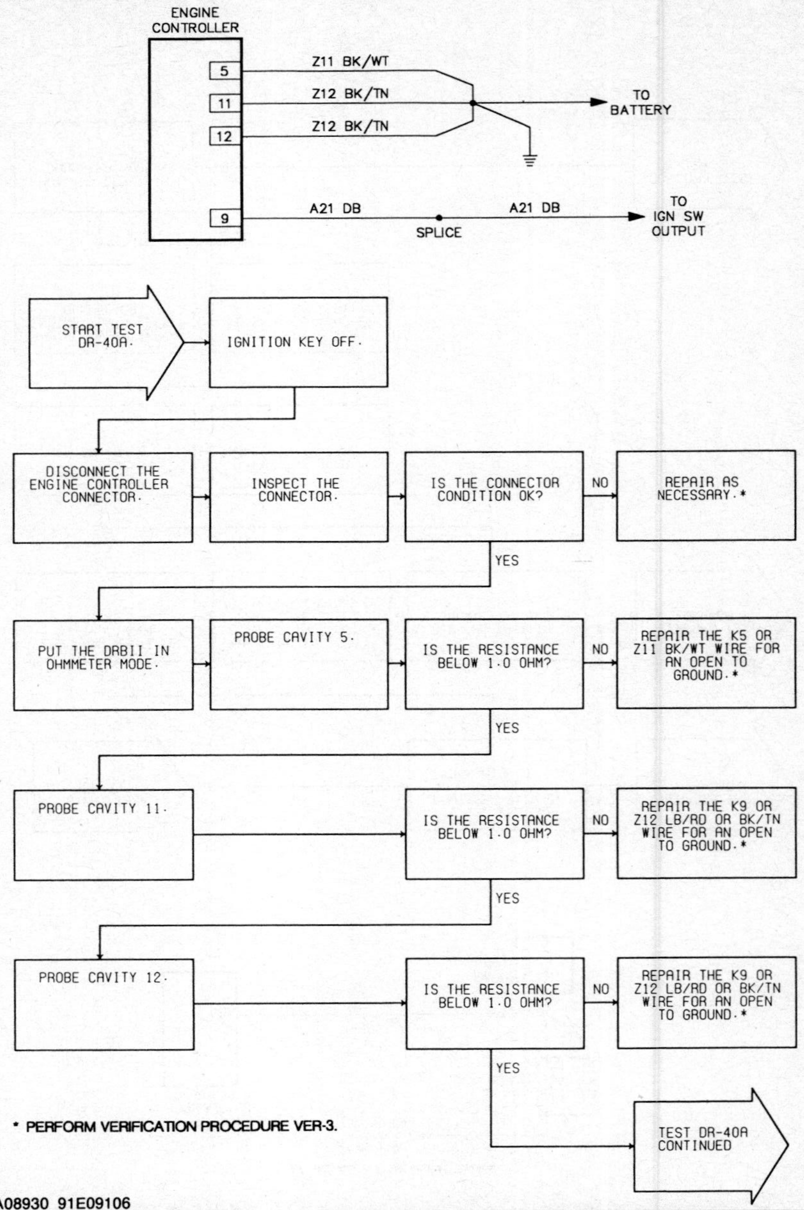
ENGINE CONTROLLER
5
11
12
9
Z11 BK/WT
Z12 BK/TN
Z12 BK/TN
TO BATTERY
A21 DB
SPLICE
A21 DB
TO IGN SW OUTPUT
START TEST DR-40A.
IGNITION KEY OFF.
DISCONNECT THE ENGINE CONTROLLER CONNECTOR.
INSPECT THE CONNECTOR.
IS THE CONNECTOR CONDITION OK?
NO
REPAIR AS NECESSARY.*
YES
PUT THE DRBII IN OHMMETER MODE.
PROBE CAVITY 5.
IS THE RESISTANCE BELOW 1.0 OHM?
NO
REPAIR THE K5 OR Z11 BK/WT WIRE FOR AN OPEN TO GROUND.*
YES
PROBE CAVITY 11.
IS THE RESISTANCE BELOW 1.0 OHM?
NO
REPAIR THE K9 OR Z12 LB/RD OR BK/TN WIRE FOR AN OPEN TO GROUND.*
YES
PROBE CAVITY 12.
IS THE RESISTANCE BELOW 1.0 OHM?
NO
REPAIR THE K9 OR Z12 LB/RD OR BK/TN WIRE FOR AN OPEN TO GROUND.*
YES
TEST DR-40A CONTINUED

* PERFORM VERIFICATION PROCEDURE VER-3.

91A08930 91E09106

Fig. 152: Driveability Test 40A (3.0L VIN 3) – Checking SBEC Grounds & Power Circuits (1 of 2)

DR-40A: CHECKING SBEC GROUNDS & POWER CIRCUITS (2 OF 2)

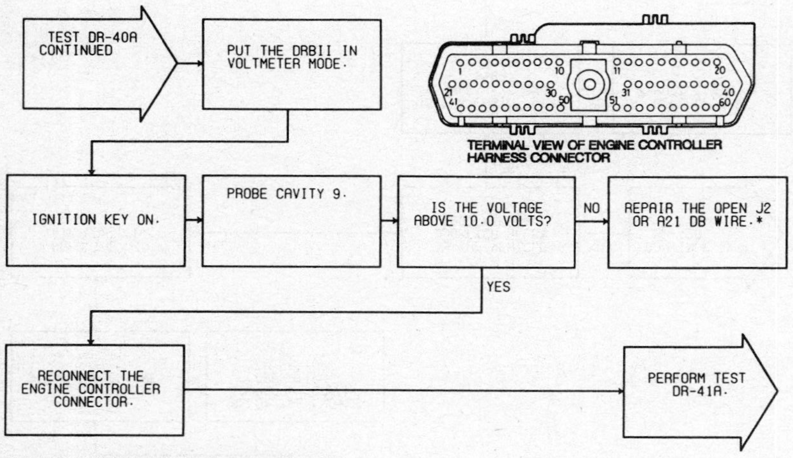
TEST DR-40A CONTINUED
PUT THE DRBII IN VOLTMETER MODE.
TERMINAL VIEW OF ENGINE CONTROLLER HARNESS CONNECTOR
IGNITION KEY ON.
PROBE CAVITY 9.
IS THE VOLTAGE ABOVE 10.0 VOLTS?
NO
REPAIR THE OPEN J2 OR A21 DB WIRE.*
YES
RECONNECT THE ENGINE CONTROLLER CONNECTOR.
PERFORM TEST DR-41A.

* PERFORM VERIFICATION PROCEDURE VER-3.

91G09107

Fig. 153: Driveability Test 40A (3.0L VIN 3) – Checking SBEC Grounds & Power Circuits (2 of 2)

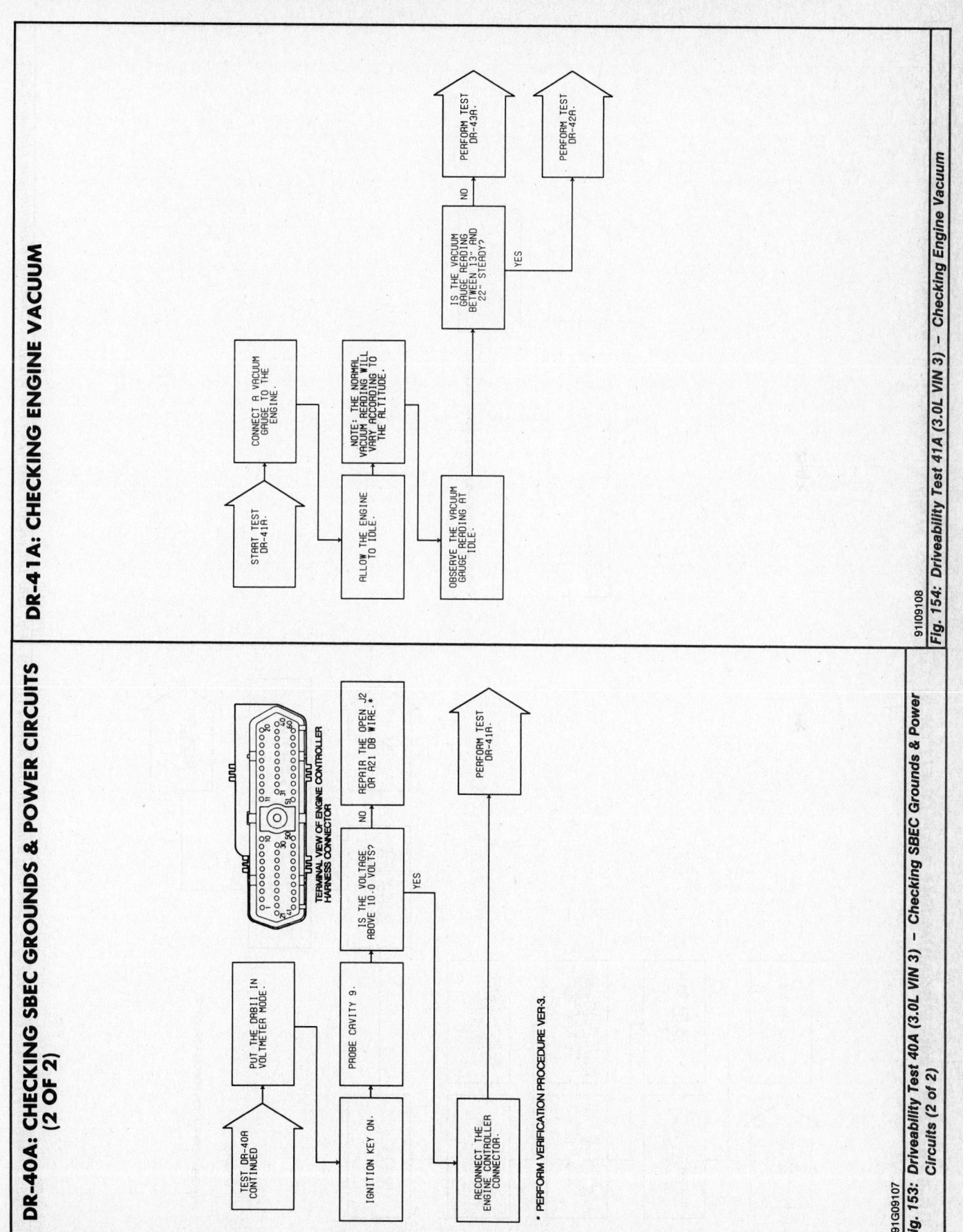

DR-41A: CHECKING ENGINE VACUUM

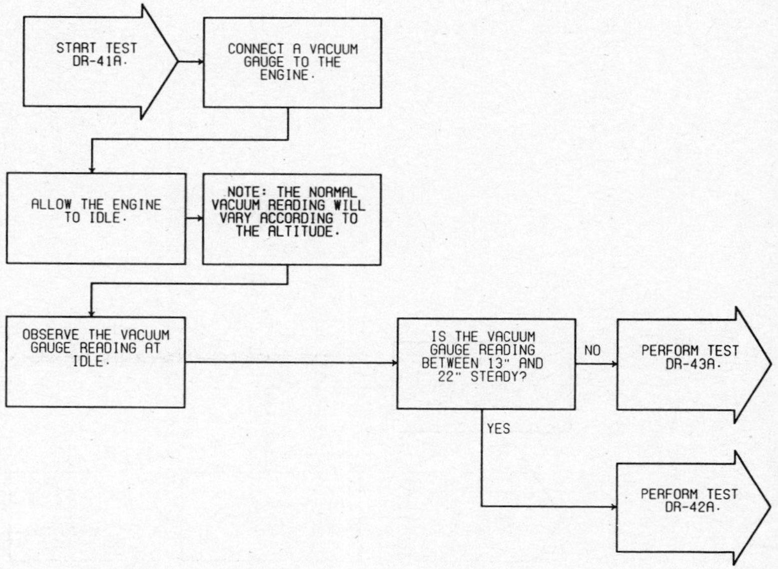
START TEST DR-41A.
CONNECT A VACUUM GAUGE TO THE ENGINE.
ALLOW THE ENGINE TO IDLE.
NOTE: THE NORMAL VACUUM READING WILL VARY ACCORDING TO THE ALTITUDE.
OBSERVE THE VACUUM GAUGE READING AT IDLE.
IS THE VACUUM GAUGE READING BETWEEN 13" AND 22" STEADY?
NO
PERFORM TEST DR-43A.
YES
PERFORM TEST DR-42A.

91I09108

Fig. 154: Driveability Test 41A (3.0L VIN 3) – Checking Engine Vacuum

DR-42A: CHECKING MINIMUM IDLE AIRFLOW (1 OF 2)

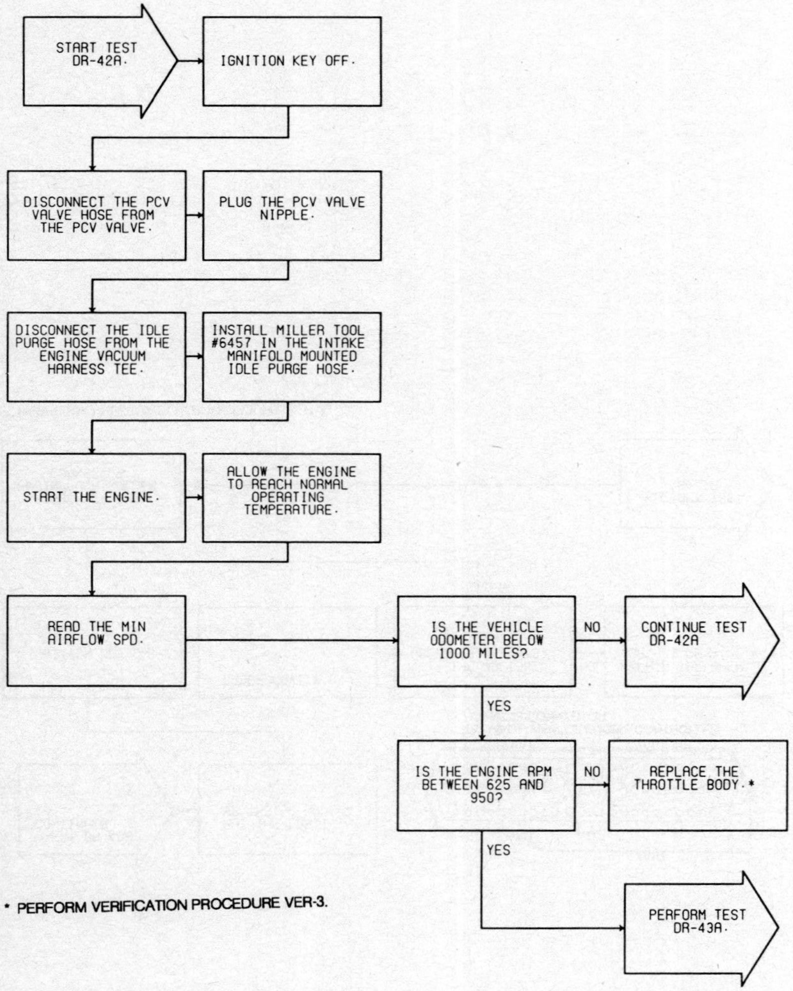
START TEST DR-42A.
IGNITION KEY OFF.
DISCONNECT THE PCV VALVE HOSE FROM THE PCV VALVE.
PLUG THE PCV VALVE NIPPLE.
DISCONNECT THE IDLE PURGE HOSE FROM THE ENGINE VACUUM HARNESS TEE.
INSTALL MILLER TOOL #6457 IN THE INTAKE MANIFOLD MOUNTED IDLE PURGE HOSE.
START THE ENGINE.
ALLOW THE ENGINE TO REACH NORMAL OPERATING TEMPERATURE.
READ THE MIN AIRFLOW SPD.
IS THE VEHICLE ODOMETER BELOW 1000 MILES?
NO
CONTINUE TEST DR-42A
YES
IS THE ENGINE RPM BETWEEN 625 AND 950?
NO
REPLACE THE THROTTLE BODY. *
YES
PERFORM TEST DR-43A.

* PERFORM VERIFICATION PROCEDURE VER-3.

91A09109

Fig. 155: Driveability Test 42A (3.0L VIN 3) – Checking Minimum Idle Airflow (1 of 2)

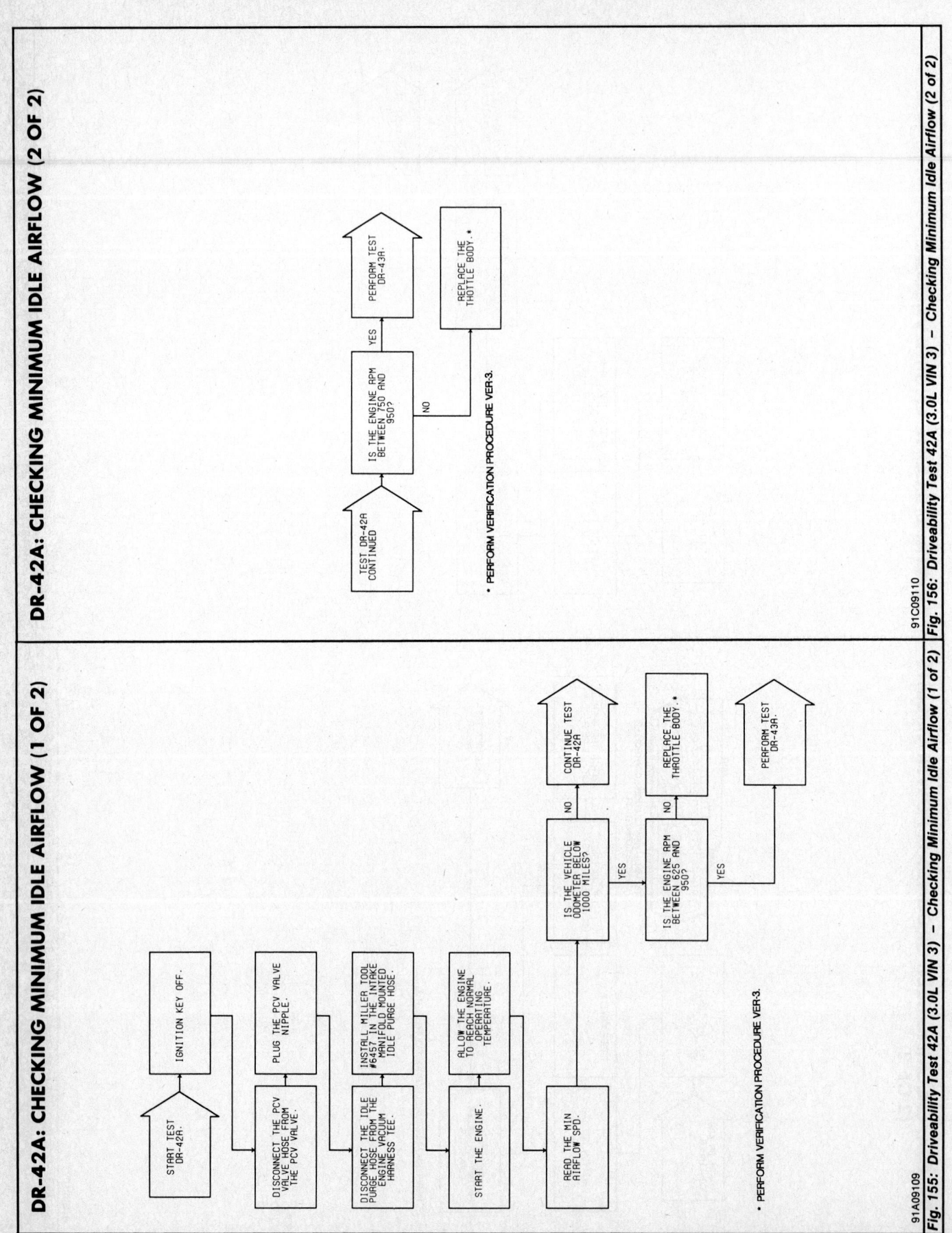

DR-42A: CHECKING MINIMUM IDLE AIRFLOW (2 OF 2)

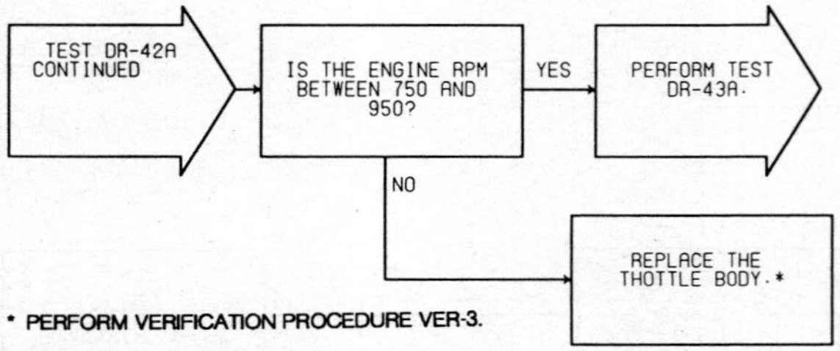
TEST DR-42A CONTINUED
IS THE ENGINE RPM BETWEEN 750 AND 950?
YES
PERFORM TEST DR-43A.
NO
REPLACE THE THOTTLE BODY. *

* PERFORM VERIFICATION PROCEDURE VER-3.

91C09110

Fig. 156: Driveability Test 42A (3.0L VIN 3) – Checking Minimum Idle Airflow (2 of 2)

DR-43A: PERFORMING NO FAULT CODE MECHANICAL TEST

At this point in the driveability test procedure, if it has been determined that all engine control systems are operating as designed and are not the cause of the driveability problem, check the following additional items for possible causes:

- Check valve timing.
- Check torque converter stall speed.
- Check engine compression.
- Check camshaft and crankshaft sprockets.
- Check for internal power brake booster vacuum leaks.
- Check for fuel contamination.
- Check for exhaust system restriction.
- Ensure injectors are not plugged or restricted.
- Ensure injector control wire is connected to correct injector.
- Ensure engine vacuum is at least 13 in. Hg.
- Ensure PCV system is functioning properly.

Fig. 157: Driveability Test 43A (3.0L VIN 3) – Performing No Fault Code Mechanical Test

DR-44A: INTERMITTENT TEST FOR SOLENOIDS & RELAYS

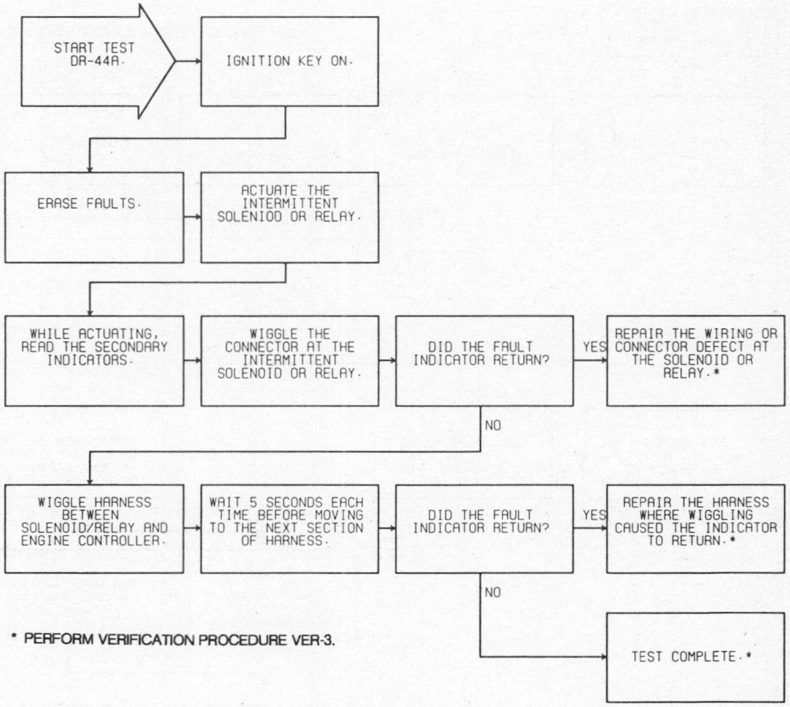
START TEST DR-44A.
IGNITION KEY ON.
ERASE FAULTS.
ACTUATE THE INTERMITTENT SOLENIOD OR RELAY.
WHILE ACTUATING, READ THE SECONDARY INDICATORS.
WIGGLE THE CONNECTOR AT THE INTERMITTENT SOLENOID OR RELAY.
DID THE FAULT INDICATOR RETURN?
YES
REPAIR THE WIRING OR CONNECTOR DEFECT AT THE SOLENOID OR RELAY.*
NO
WIGGLE HARNESS BETWEEN SOLENOID/RELAY AND ENGINE CONTROLLER.
WAIT 5 SECONDS EACH TIME BEFORE MOVING TO THE NEXT SECTION OF HARNESS.
DID THE FAULT INDICATOR RETURN?
YES
REPAIR THE HARNESS WHERE WIGGLING CAUSED THE INDICATOR TO RETURN.*
NO
TEST COMPLETE.*

* PERFORM VERIFICATION PROCEDURE VER-3.

91E09111

Fig. 158: Driveability Test 44A (3.0L VIN 3) – Intermittent Test for Solenoids & Relays

DR-45A: INTERMITTENT TEST FOR VOLTAGE SENSOR

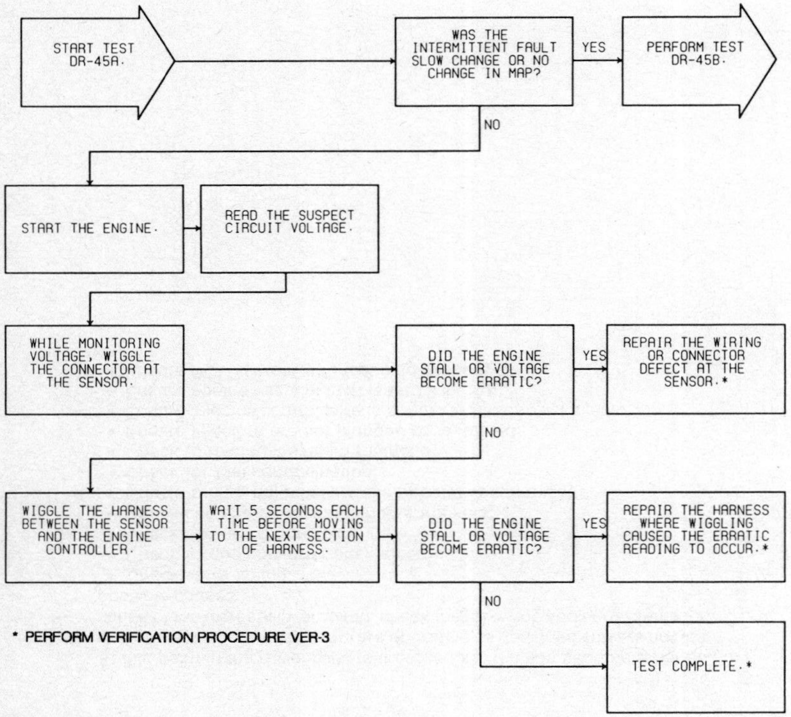
START TEST DR-45A.
WAS THE INTERMITTENT FAULT SLOW CHANGE OR NO CHANGE IN MAP?
YES
PERFORM TEST DR-45B.
NO
START THE ENGINE.
READ THE SUSPECT CIRCUIT VOLTAGE.
WHILE MONITORING VOLTAGE, WIGGLE THE CONNECTOR AT THE SENSOR.
DID THE ENGINE STALL OR VOLTAGE BECOME ERRATIC?
YES
REPAIR THE WIRING OR CONNECTOR DEFECT AT THE SENSOR.*
NO
WIGGLE THE HARNESS BETWEEN THE SENSOR AND THE ENGINE CONTROLLER.
WAIT 5 SECONDS EACH TIME BEFORE MOVING TO THE NEXT SECTION OF HARNESS.
DID THE ENGINE STALL OR VOLTAGE BECOME ERRATIC?
YES
REPAIR THE HARNESS WHERE WIGGLING CAUSED THE ERRATIC READING TO OCCUR.*
NO
TEST COMPLETE.*
* PERFORM VERIFICATION PROCEDURE VER-3

91G09112

Fig. 159: Driveability Test 45A (3.0L VIN 3) – Intermittent Test for Voltage Sensor

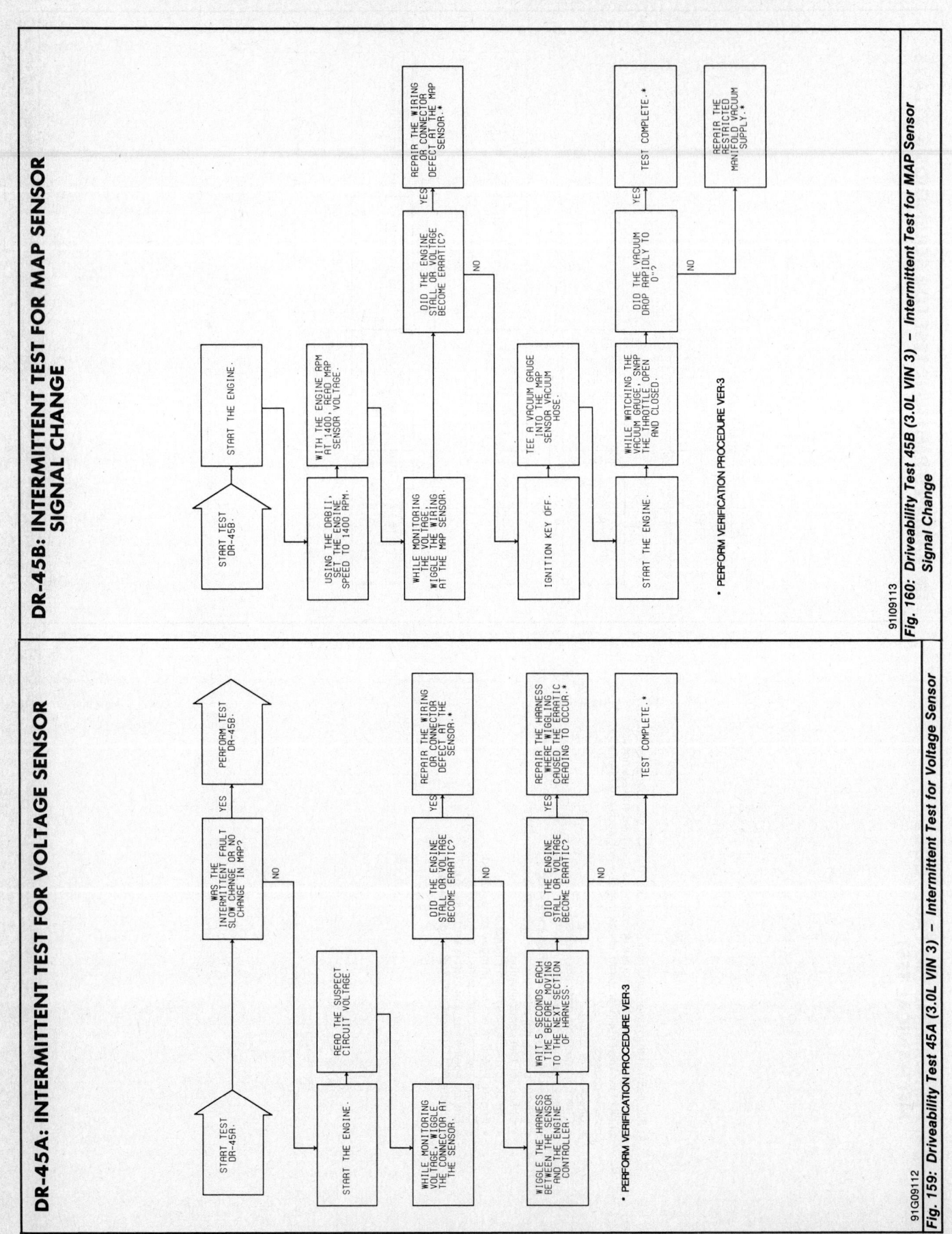

DR-45B: INTERMITTENT TEST FOR MAP SENSOR SIGNAL CHANGE

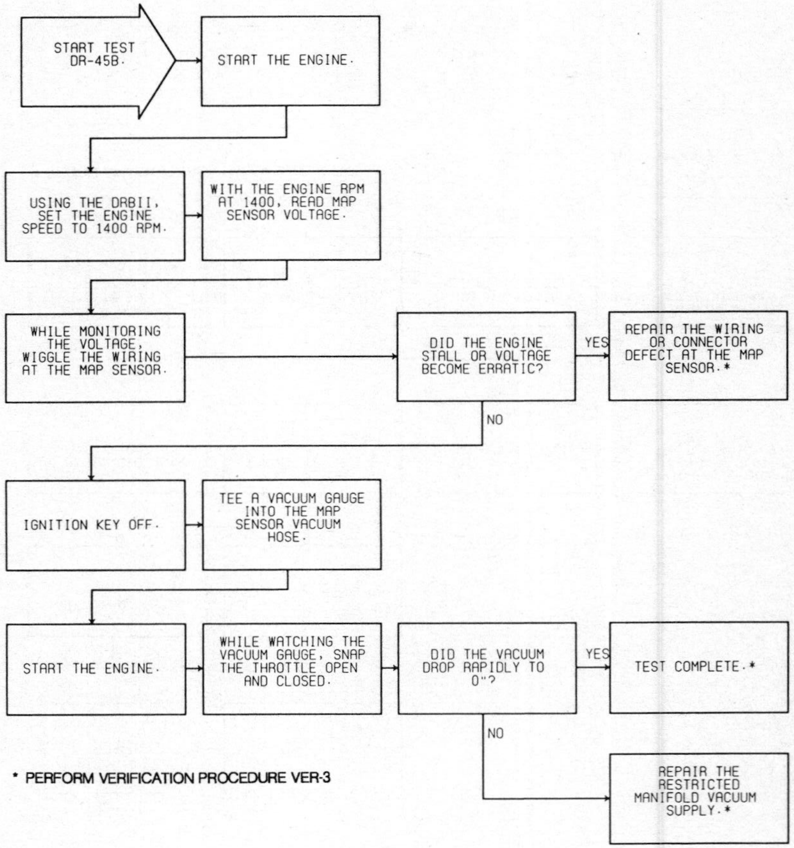
START TEST DR-45B.
START THE ENGINE.
USING THE DRBII, SET THE ENGINE SPEED TO 1400 RPM.
WITH THE ENGINE RPM AT 1400, READ MAP SENSOR VOLTAGE.
WHILE MONITORING THE VOLTAGE, WIGGLE THE WIRING AT THE MAP SENSOR.
DID THE ENGINE STALL OR VOLTAGE BECOME ERRATIC?
YES
REPAIR THE WIRING OR CONNECTOR DEFECT AT THE MAP SENSOR.*
NO
IGNITION KEY OFF.
TEE A VACUUM GAUGE INTO THE MAP SENSOR VACUUM HOSE.
START THE ENGINE.
WHILE WATCHING THE VACUUM GAUGE, SNAP THE THROTTLE OPEN AND CLOSED.
DID THE VACUUM DROP RAPIDLY TO 0"?
YES
TEST COMPLETE.*
NO
REPAIR THE RESTRICTED MANIFOLD VACUUM SUPPLY.*
* PERFORM VERIFICATION PROCEDURE VER-3

91I09113

Fig. 160: Driveability Test 45B (3.0L VIN 3) – Intermittent Test for MAP Sensor Signal Change

DR-46A: INTERMITTENT TEST FOR IDLE MOTOR CIRCUITS

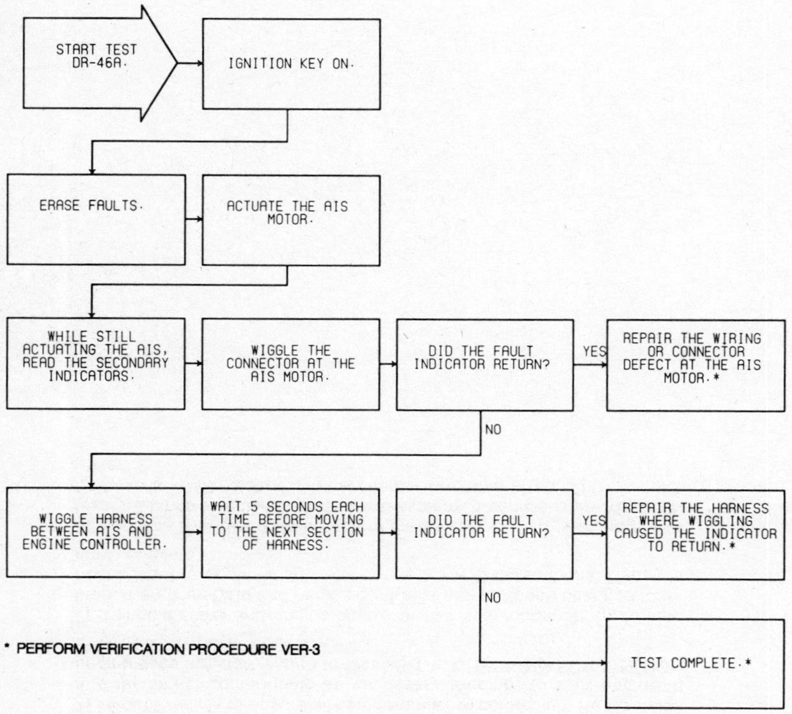
START TEST DR-46A.
IGNITION KEY ON.
ERASE FAULTS.
ACTUATE THE AIS MOTOR.
WHILE STILL ACTUATING THE AIS, READ THE SECONDARY INDICATORS.
WIGGLE THE CONNECTOR AT THE AIS MOTOR.
DID THE FAULT INDICATOR RETURN?
YES
REPAIR THE WIRING OR CONNECTOR DEFECT AT THE AIS MOTOR.*
NO
WIGGLE HARNESS BETWEEN AIS AND ENGINE CONTROLLER.
WAIT 5 SECONDS EACH TIME BEFORE MOVING TO THE NEXT SECTION OF HARNESS.
DID THE FAULT INDICATOR RETURN?
YES
REPAIR THE HARNESS WHERE WIGGLING CAUSED THE INDICATOR TO RETURN.*
NO
TEST COMPLETE.*

* PERFORM VERIFICATION PROCEDURE VER-3

91A09114

Fig. 161: Driveability Test 46A (3.0L VIN 3) – Intermittent Test for Idle Motor Circuits

DR-47A: INTERMITTENT TEST FOR IDLE MOTOR CIRCUITS

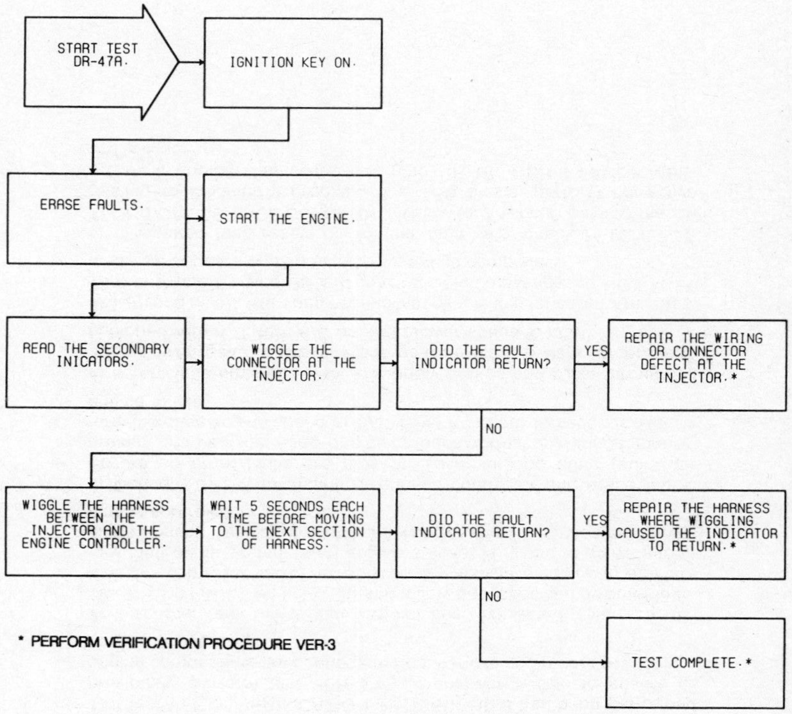
START TEST DR-47A.
IGNITION KEY ON.
ERASE FAULTS.
START THE ENGINE.
READ THE SECONDARY INICATORS.
WIGGLE THE CONNECTOR AT THE INJECTOR.
DID THE FAULT INDICATOR RETURN?
YES
REPAIR THE WIRING OR CONNECTOR DEFECT AT THE INJECTOR.*
NO
WIGGLE THE HARNESS BETWEEN THE INJECTOR AND THE ENGINE CONTROLLER.
WAIT 5 SECONDS EACH TIME BEFORE MOVING TO THE NEXT SECTION OF HARNESS.
DID THE FAULT INDICATOR RETURN?
YES
REPAIR THE HARNESS WHERE WIGGLING CAUSED THE INDICATOR TO RETURN.*
NO
TEST COMPLETE.*

* PERFORM VERIFICATION PROCEDURE VER-3

91D09115

Fig. 162: Driveability Test 47A (3.0L VIN 3) – Intermittent Test for Idle Motor Circuits

VER-1: VERIFICATION PROCEDURE 1

1) Inspect vehicle to ensure all components are connected. Reassemble and reconnect components as necessary. Attempt to start engine. If engine does not start, return to test NS-1A: CHECKING FOR IGNITION SPARK & POWER FEED TO COIL.

2) If engine starts and engine controller has been changed, go to next step. If engine starts and engine controller has not been changed, connect DRB-II to engine diagnostic connector and erase faults. Repair is now complete.

3) If vehicle is equipped with factory theft alarm system, start engine at least 20 times to activate theft alarm system. If vehicle is an AS or AN body, write EMR mileage into new engine controller. Repair is now complete.

Fig. 163: Verification Procedure 1 (3.0L VIN 3)

VER-2: VERIFICATION PROCEDURE 2

1) If test VER-3: VERIFICATION PROCEDURE 3 has been performed previously, perform test VER-3 again. Inspect vehicle to ensure all engine components are connected. Reassemble and reconnect components as necessary.

2) If another fault exists that has not been corrected, return to DR-1B: DRB-II FAULT MESSAGES and follow path specified by other fault. If engine controller has been replaced and vehicle is equipped with factory theft alarm system, start engine at least 20 times to activate theft alarm system. If vehicle is an AS or AN body, write EMR mileage into new engine controller.

3) Connect DRB-II to engine diagnostic connector and erase faults. Ensure no other faults are present. To ensure no other faults are present, start engine. Allow engine to reach normal operating temperature. Increase engine speed to 2000 RPM for about 10 seconds. Return engine to idle.

4) If vehicle is equipped with A/T, apply brakes and cycle through all transmission gear positions. Place gear selector in Park. If vehicle is equipped with A/C, turn A/C on. Set blower speed to LOW.

5) Turn engine off. Start engine. Allow engine to idle for about 2 minutes. Turn engine off. Using DRB-II, check for fault messages. If NO FAULT message appears on DRB-II display, test is complete.

6) If repaired fault resets or another fault sets, check MITCHELL'S TECHNICAL SERVICE BULLETINS (TSBs) for any pertinent information relating to driveability problem. If a TSB exists, perform corrective action. If another fault sets, return to DR-1B: DRB-II FAULT MESSAGES.

Fig. 164: Verification Procedure 2 (3.0L VIN 3)

VER-3: VERIFICATION PROCEDURE 3

1) Inspect vehicle to ensure all engine components are connected. Reassemble and reconnect components as necessary. If another fault is present that has not been corrected, return to DR-1B: DRB-II FAULT MESSAGES and follow path specified by other fault.

2) If engine controller has been changed and vehicle is equipped with factory theft alarm system, start engine at least 20 times to activate theft alarm system. If vehicle is an AS or AN body, write EMR mileage into new engine controller.

3) Connect DRB-II to engine diagnostic connector. Erase fault messages. Disconnect DRB-II. Ensure no other fault messages are present. To ensure no other fault messages are present, start engine. If vehicle is equipped with A/C, turn A/C on. Set blower speed to LOW.

4) Drive vehicle for about 5 minutes. During this time, attain a speed above 40 MPH or more. Ensure transmission shifts through all gears. Upon completion of road test, turn engine off.

5) Start engine. Allow engine to idle for about 2 minutes. Turn engine off. Connect DRB-II to engine diagnostic connector. Using DRB-II, check for fault messages. If no fault messages are present, test is complete.

6) If repaired fault message resets or another fault message sets, check MITCHELL'S TECHNICAL SERVICE BULLETINS (TSBs) for any pertinent information relating to driveability problems. If a TSB exists, perform corrective action. If another fault sets, return to DR-1B: DRB-II FAULT MESSAGES.

Fig. 165: Verification Procedure 3 (3.0L VIN 3)

NS-1A: CHECKING FOR IGNITION SPARK, FAULT MESSAGES & DIS SIGNAL STATUS (1 OF 4)

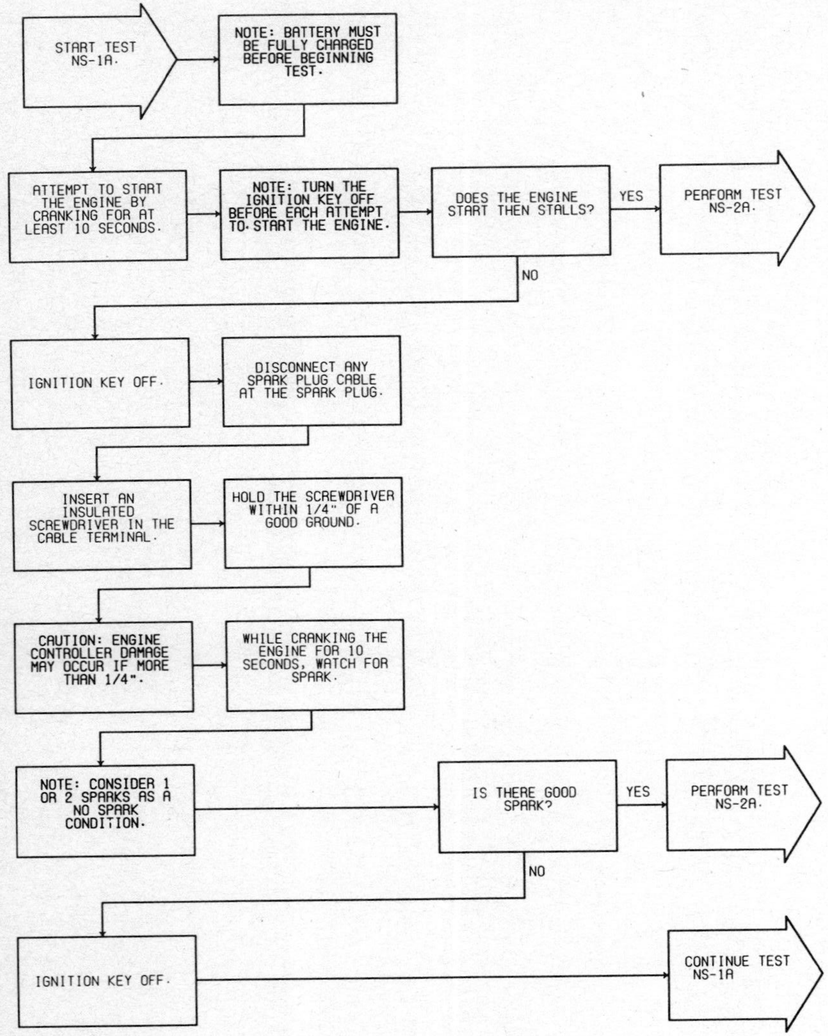
START TEST NS-1A.
NOTE: BATTERY MUST BE FULLY CHARGED BEFORE BEGINNING TEST.
ATTEMPT TO START THE ENGINE BY CRANKING FOR AT LEAST 10 SECONDS.
NOTE: TURN THE IGNITION KEY OFF BEFORE EACH ATTEMPT TO START THE ENGINE.
DOES THE ENGINE START THEN STALLS?
YES
PERFORM TEST NS-2A.
NO
IGNITION KEY OFF.
DISCONNECT ANY SPARK PLUG CABLE AT THE SPARK PLUG.
INSERT AN INSULATED SCREWDRIVER IN THE CABLE TERMINAL.
HOLD THE SCREWDRIVER WITHIN 1/4" OF A GOOD GROUND.
CAUTION: ENGINE CONTROLLER DAMAGE MAY OCCUR IF MORE THAN 1/4".
WHILE CRANKING THE ENGINE FOR 10 SECONDS, WATCH FOR SPARK.
NOTE: CONSIDER 1 OR 2 SPARKS AS A NO SPARK CONDITION.
IS THERE GOOD SPARK?
YES
PERFORM TEST NS-2A.
NO
IGNITION KEY OFF.
CONTINUE TEST NS-1A

91F09140

Fig. 1: No Start Test 1A (3.3L & 3.8L) – Checking for Ignition Spark, Fault Messages & DIS Signal Status (1 of 4)

NS-1A: CHECKING FOR IGNITION SPARK, FAULT MESSAGES & DIS SIGNAL STATUS (2 OF 4)

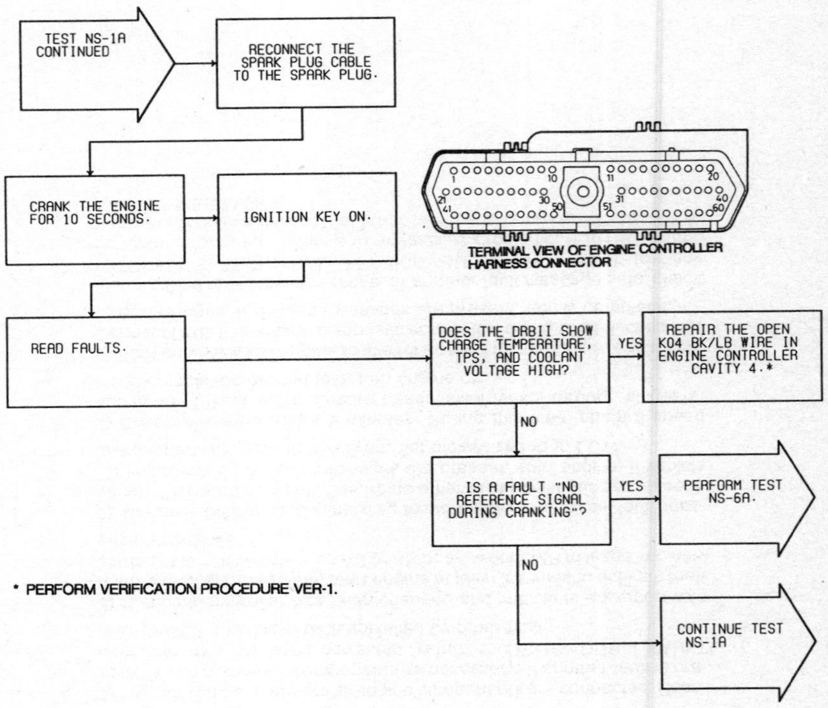
TEST NS-1A CONTINUED
RECONNECT THE SPARK PLUG CABLE TO THE SPARK PLUG.
CRANK THE ENGINE FOR 10 SECONDS.
IGNITION KEY ON.
TERMINAL VIEW OF ENGINE CONTROLLER HARNESS CONNECTOR
1
10
11
20
21
30
31
40
41
50
51
60
READ FAULTS.
DOES THE DRBII SHOW CHARGE TEMPERATURE, TPS, AND COOLANT VOLTAGE HIGH?
YES
REPAIR THE OPEN K04 BK/LB WIRE IN ENGINE CONTROLLER CAVITY 4.*
NO
IS A FAULT "NO REFERENCE SIGNAL DURING CRANKING"?
YES
PERFORM TEST NS-6A.
NO
CONTINUE TEST NS-1A

* PERFORM VERIFICATION PROCEDURE VER-1.

91H09141

Fig. 2: No Start Test 1A (3.3L & 3.8L) – Checking for Ignition Spark, Fault Messages & DIS Signal Status (2 of 4)

NS-1A: CHECKING FOR IGNITION SPARK, FAULT MESSAGES & DIS SIGNAL STATUS (3 OF 4)

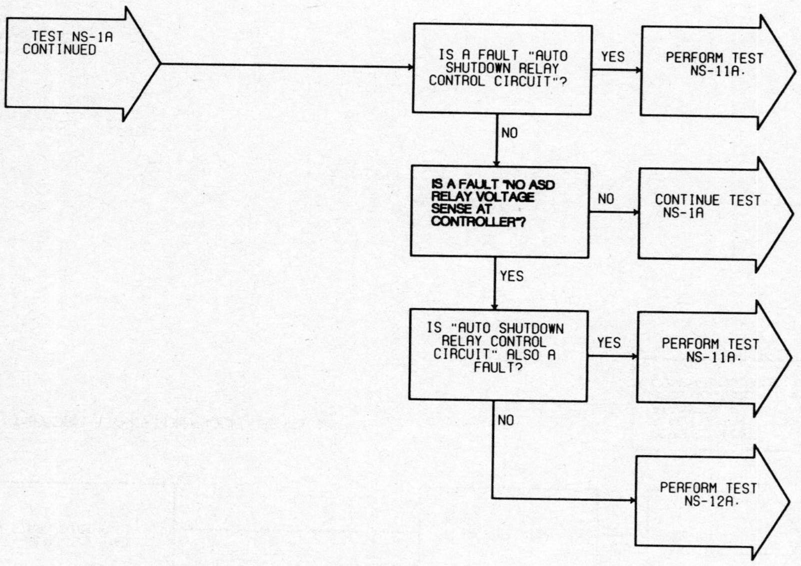
TEST NS-1A CONTINUED
IS A FAULT "AUTO SHUTDOWN RELAY CONTROL CIRCUIT"?
YES
PERFORM TEST NS-11A.
NO
IS A FAULT "NO ASD RELAY VOLTAGE SENSE AT CONTROLLER"?
NO
CONTINUE TEST NS-1A
YES
IS "AUTO SHUTDOWN RELAY CONTROL CIRCUIT" ALSO A FAULT?
YES
PERFORM TEST NS-11A.
NO
PERFORM TEST NS-12A.

91J09142

Fig. 3: ***No Start Test 1A (3.3L & 3.8L) – Checking for Ignition Spark, Fault Messages & DIS Signal Status (3 of 4)***

NS-1A: CHECKING FOR IGNITION SPARK, FAULT MESSAGES & DIS SIGNAL STATUS (4 OF 4)

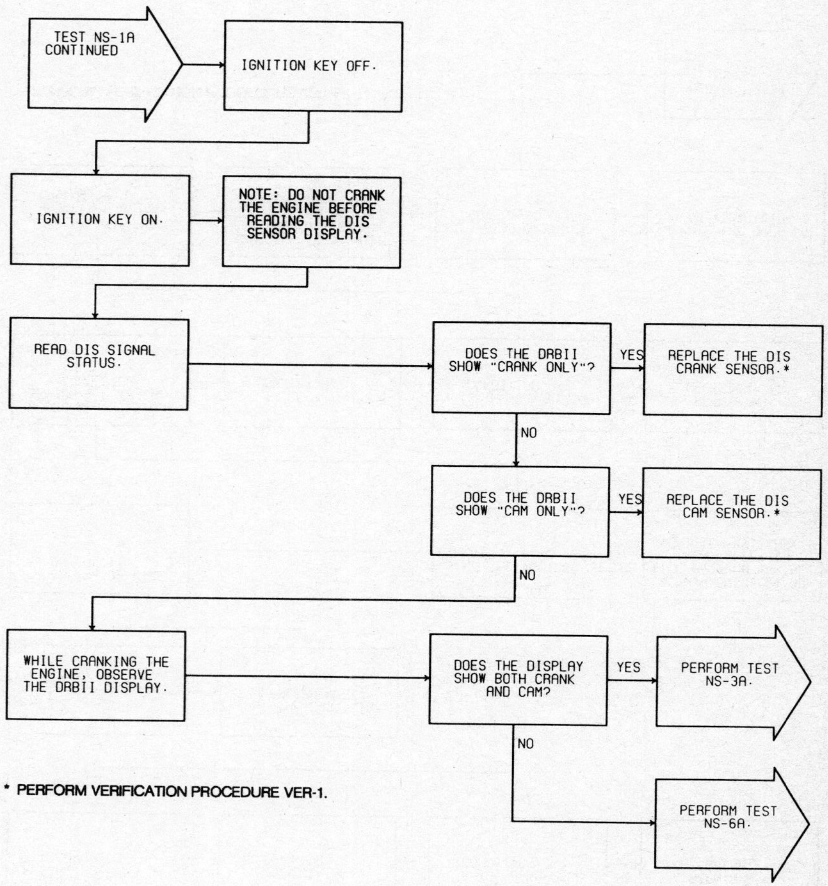
TEST NS-1A CONTINUED
IGNITION KEY OFF.
IGNITION KEY ON.
NOTE: DO NOT CRANK THE ENGINE BEFORE READING THE DIS SENSOR DISPLAY.
READ DIS SIGNAL STATUS.
DOES THE DRBII SHOW "CRANK ONLY"?
YES
REPLACE THE DIS CRANK SENSOR.*
NO
DOES THE DRBII SHOW "CAM ONLY"?
YES
REPLACE THE DIS CAM SENSOR.*
NO
WHILE CRANKING THE ENGINE, OBSERVE THE DRBII DISPLAY.
DOES THE DISPLAY SHOW BOTH CRANK AND CAM?
YES
PERFORM TEST NS-3A.
NO
PERFORM TEST NS-6A.

* PERFORM VERIFICATION PROCEDURE VER-1.

91B09143

Fig. 4: ***No Start Test 1A (3.3L & 3.8L) – Checking for Ignition Spark, Fault Messages & DIS Signal Status (4 of 4)***

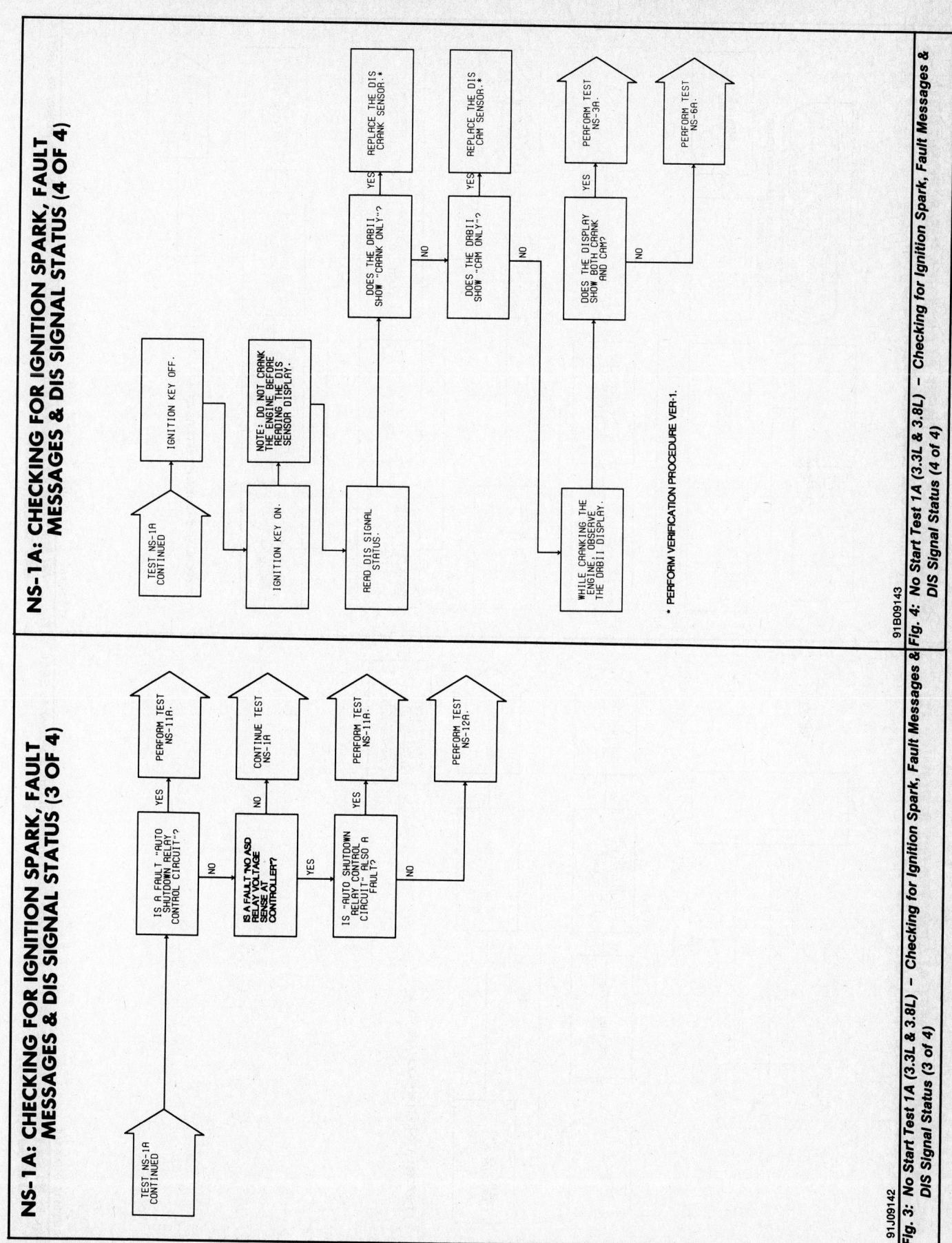

1991 ENGINE PERFORMANCE
Self-Diagnostics – 3.3L PFI (Cont.)

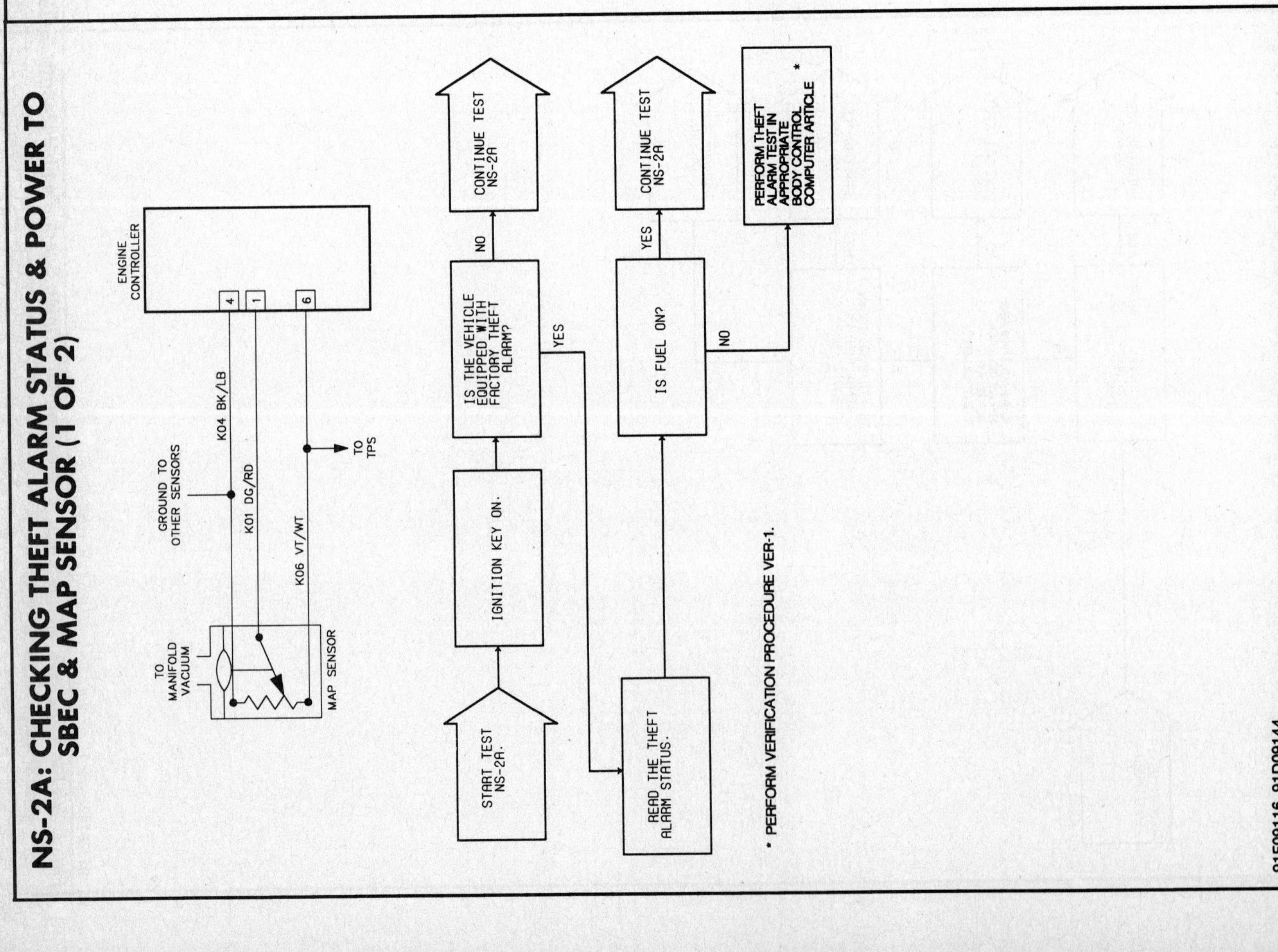
NS-2A: CHECKING THEFT ALARM STATUS & POWER TO SBEC & MAP SENSOR (1 OF 2)
TO MANIFOLD VACUUM
MAP SENSOR
GROUND TO OTHER SENSORS
K04 BK/LB
K01 DG/RD
K06 VT/WT
TO TPS
ENGINE CONTROLLER
4
1
6
START TEST NS-2A.
IGNITION KEY ON.
IS THE VEHICLE EQUIPPED WITH FACTORY THEFT ALARM?
NO
CONTINUE TEST NS-2A
YES
READ THE THEFT ALARM STATUS.
IS FUEL ON?
YES
CONTINUE TEST NS-2A
NO
PERFORM THEFT ALARM TEST IN APPROPRIATE BODY CONTROL COMPUTER ARTICLE *
* PERFORM VERIFICATION PROCEDURE VER-1.
91F09116 91D09144

Fig. 5: No Start Test 2A (3.3L & 3.8L) – Checking Theft Alarm Status & Power to SBEC & MAP Sensor (1 of 2)

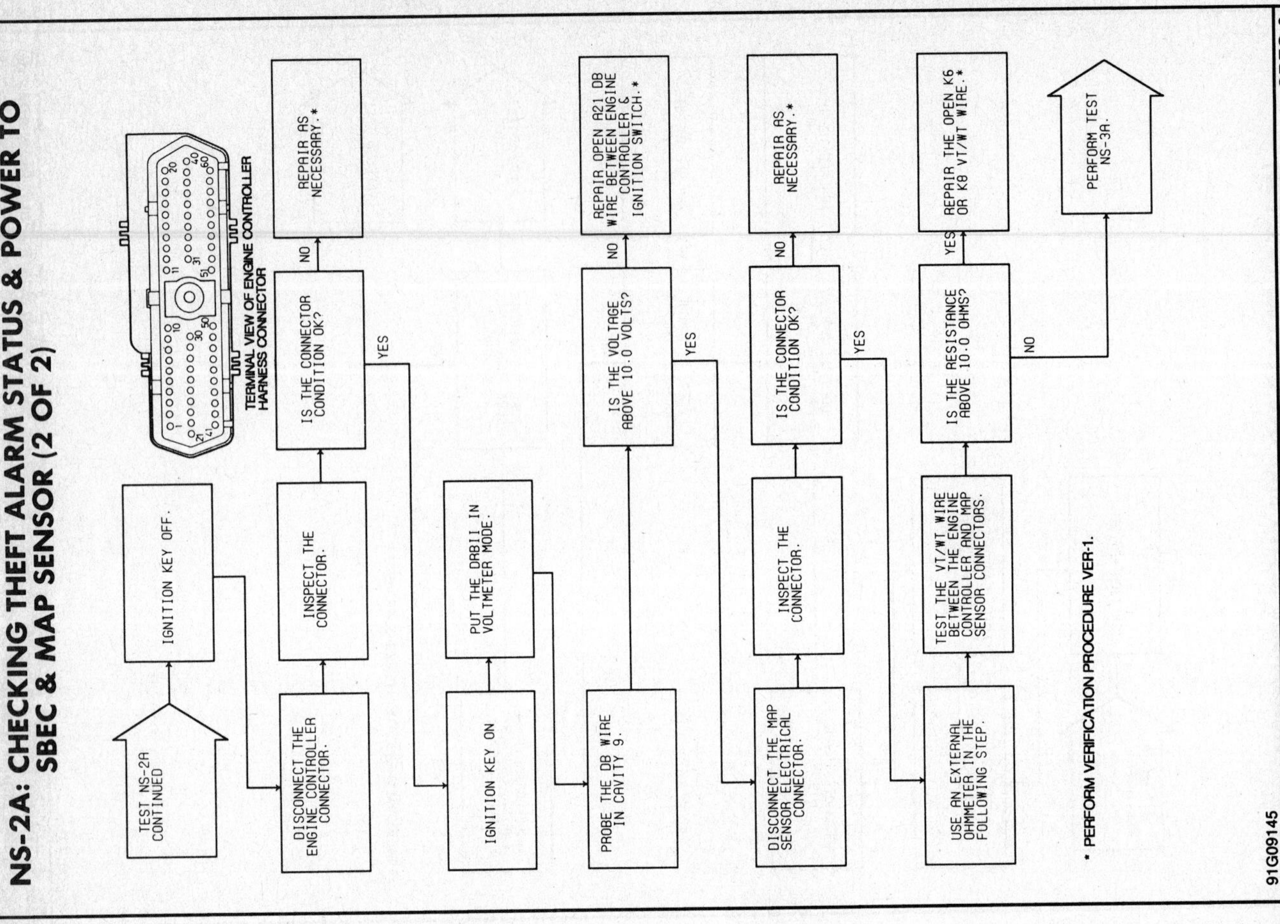
NS-2A: CHECKING THEFT ALARM STATUS & POWER TO SBEC & MAP SENSOR (2 OF 2)
TEST NS-2A CONTINUED
IGNITION KEY OFF.
DISCONNECT THE ENGINE CONTROLLER CONNECTOR.
INSPECT THE CONNECTOR.
IS THE CONNECTOR CONDITION OK?
NO
REPAIR AS NECESSARY.*
YES
TERMINAL VIEW OF ENGINE CONTROLLER HARNESS CONNECTOR
IGNITION KEY ON
PUT THE DRBII IN VOLTMETER MODE.
PROBE THE DB WIRE IN CAVITY 9.
IS THE VOLTAGE ABOVE 10.0 VOLTS?
NO
REPAIR OPEN A21 DB WIRE BETWEEN ENGINE CONTROLLER & IGNITION SWITCH.*
YES
DISCONNECT THE MAP SENSOR ELECTRICAL CONNECTOR.
INSPECT THE CONNECTOR.
IS THE CONNECTOR CONDITION OK?
NO
REPAIR AS NECESSARY.*
YES
USE AN EXTERNAL OHMMETER IN THE FOLLOWING STEP.
TEST THE VT/WT WIRE BETWEEN THE ENGINE CONTROLLER AND MAP SENSOR CONNECTORS.
IS THE RESISTANCE ABOVE 10.0 OHMS?
YES
REPAIR THE OPEN K6 OR K8 VT/WT WIRE.*
NO
PERFORM TEST NS-3A.
* PERFORM VERIFICATION PROCEDURE VER-1.
91G09145

Fig. 6: No Start Test 2A (3.3L & 3.8L) – Checking Theft Alarm Status & Power to SBEC & MAP Sensor (2 of 2)

NS-3A: CHECKING TPS, FUEL PRESSURE, POWER TO COIL, SPARK PLUGS & ENGINE TIMING (1 OF 3)

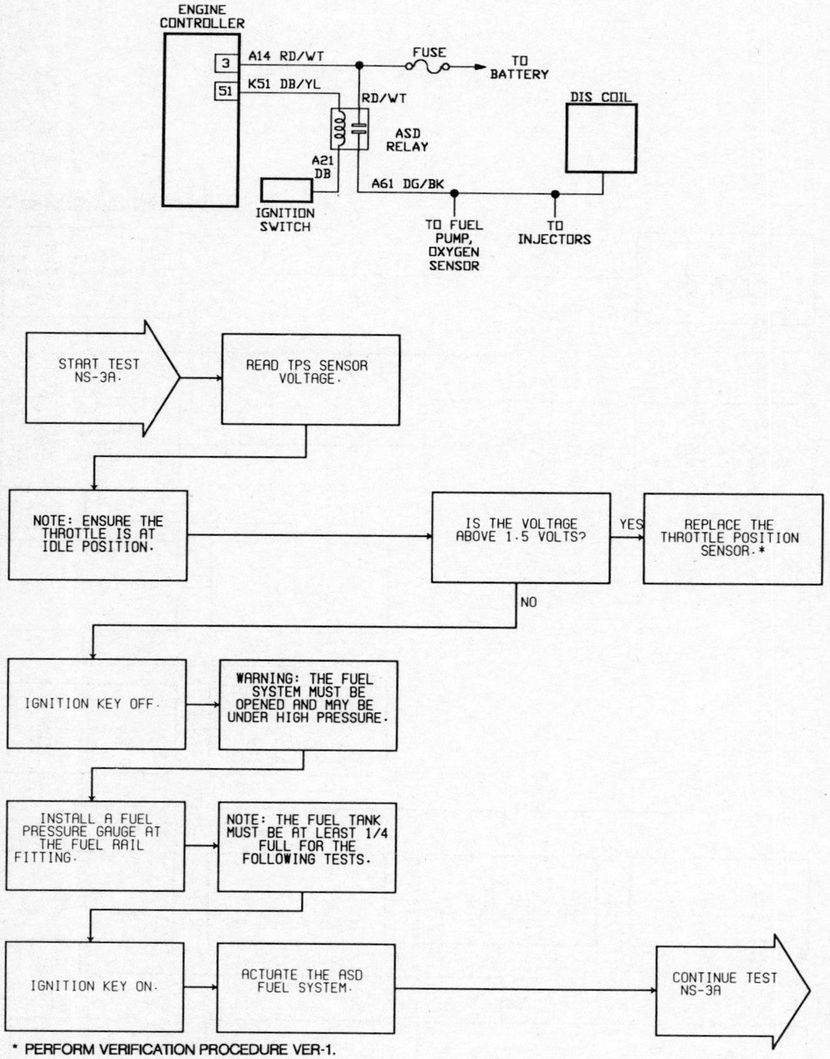
ENGINE CONTROLLER
3
51
A14 RD/WT
K51 DB/YL
FUSE
TO BATTERY
RD/WT
ASD RELAY
A21 DB
IGNITION SWITCH
A61 DG/BK
DIS COIL
TO FUEL PUMP, OXYGEN SENSOR
TO INJECTORS
START TEST NS-3A.
READ TPS SENSOR VOLTAGE.
NOTE: ENSURE THE THROTTLE IS AT IDLE POSITION.
IS THE VOLTAGE ABOVE 1.5 VOLTS?
YES
REPLACE THE THROTTLE POSITION SENSOR.*
NO
IGNITION KEY OFF.
WARNING: THE FUEL SYSTEM MUST BE OPENED AND MAY BE UNDER HIGH PRESSURE.
INSTALL A FUEL PRESSURE GAUGE AT THE FUEL RAIL FITTING.
NOTE: THE FUEL TANK MUST BE AT LEAST 1/4 FULL FOR THE FOLLOWING TESTS.
IGNITION KEY ON.
ACTUATE THE ASD FUEL SYSTEM.
CONTINUE TEST NS-3A

* PERFORM VERIFICATION PROCEDURE VER-1.

91H09117 91I09146

Fig. 7: No Start Test 3A (3.3L & 3.8L) – Checking TPS, Fuel Pressure, Power to Coil, Spark Plugs & Engine Timing (1 of 3)

NS-3A: CHECKING TPS, FUEL PRESSURE, POWER TO COIL, SPARK PLUGS & ENGINE TIMING (2 OF 3)

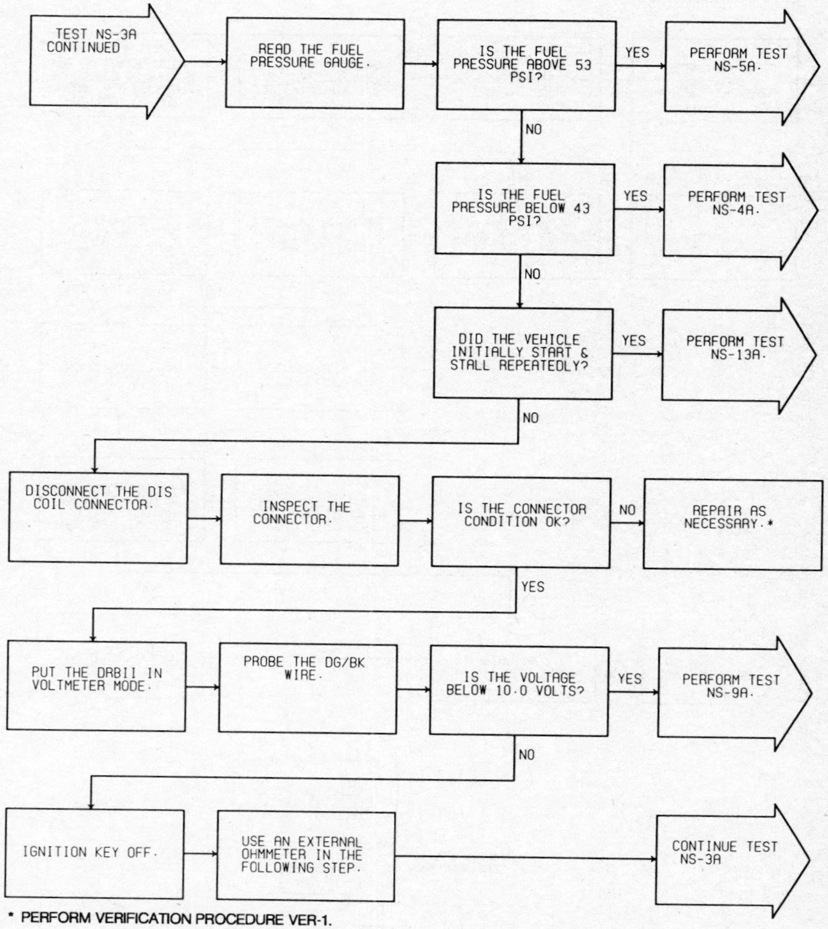
TEST NS-3A CONTINUED
READ THE FUEL PRESSURE GAUGE.
IS THE FUEL PRESSURE ABOVE 53 PSI?
YES
PERFORM TEST NS-5A.
NO
IS THE FUEL PRESSURE BELOW 43 PSI?
YES
PERFORM TEST NS-4A.
NO
DID THE VEHICLE INITIALLY START & STALL REPEATEDLY?
YES
PERFORM TEST NS-13A.
NO
DISCONNECT THE DIS COIL CONNECTOR.
INSPECT THE CONNECTOR.
IS THE CONNECTOR CONDITION OK?
NO
REPAIR AS NECESSARY.*
YES
PUT THE DRBII IN VOLTMETER MODE.
PROBE THE DG/BK WIRE.
IS THE VOLTAGE BELOW 10.0 VOLTS?
YES
PERFORM TEST NS-9A.
NO
IGNITION KEY OFF.
USE AN EXTERNAL OHMMETER IN THE FOLLOWING STEP.
CONTINUE TEST NS-3A

* PERFORM VERIFICATION PROCEDURE VER-1.

91A09147

Fig. 8: No Start Test 3A (3.3L & 3.8L) – Checking TPS, Fuel Pressure, Power to Coil, Spark Plugs & Engine Timing (2 of 3)

1991 ENGINE PERFORMANCE
Self-Diagnostics – 3.3L PFI (Cont.)

NS-3A: CHECKING TPS, FUEL PRESSURE, POWER TO COIL, SPARK PLUGS & ENGINE TIMING (3 OF 3)

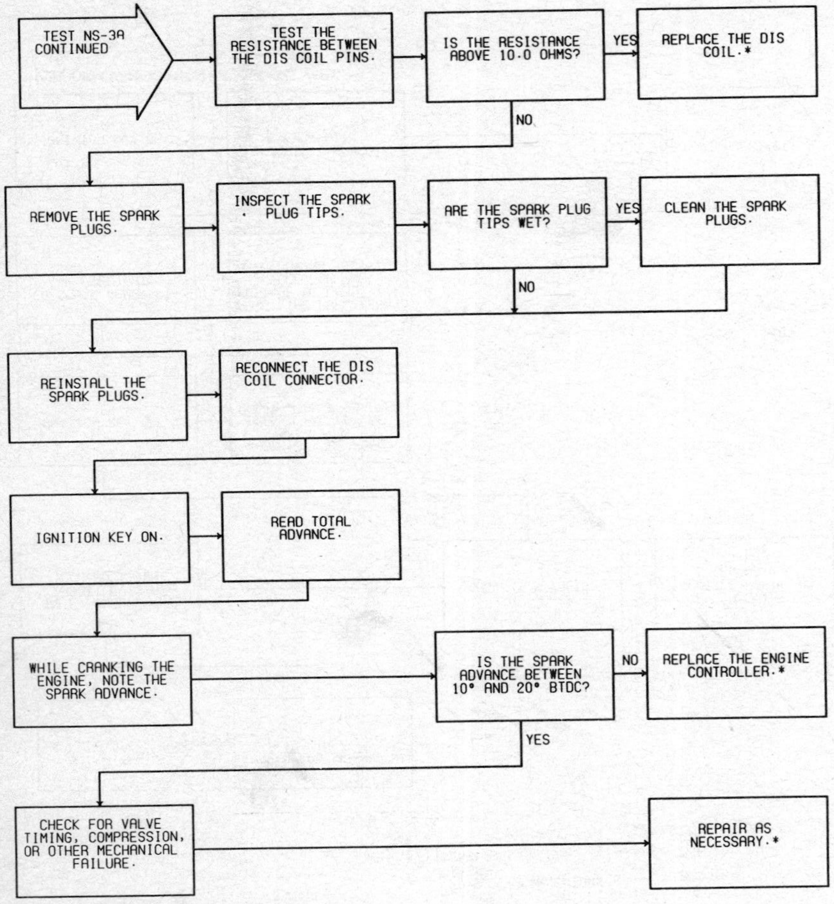
TEST NS-3A CONTINUED
TEST THE RESISTANCE BETWEEN THE DIS COIL PINS.
IS THE RESISTANCE ABOVE 10.0 OHMS?
YES
REPLACE THE DIS COIL.*
NO
REMOVE THE SPARK PLUGS.
INSPECT THE SPARK PLUG TIPS.
ARE THE SPARK PLUG TIPS WET?
YES
CLEAN THE SPARK PLUGS.
NO
REINSTALL THE SPARK PLUGS.
RECONNECT THE DIS COIL CONNECTOR.
IGNITION KEY ON.
READ TOTAL ADVANCE.
WHILE CRANKING THE ENGINE, NOTE THE SPARK ADVANCE.
IS THE SPARK ADVANCE BETWEEN 10° AND 20° BTDC?
NO
REPLACE THE ENGINE CONTROLLER.*
YES
CHECK FOR VALVE TIMING, COMPRESSION, OR OTHER MECHANICAL FAILURE.
REPAIR AS NECESSARY.*

* PERFORM VERIFICATION PROCEDURE VER-1.

91C09148

Fig. 9: No Start Test 3A (3.3L & 3.8L) – Checking TPS, Fuel Pressure, Power to Coil, Spark Plugs & Engine Timing (3 of 3)

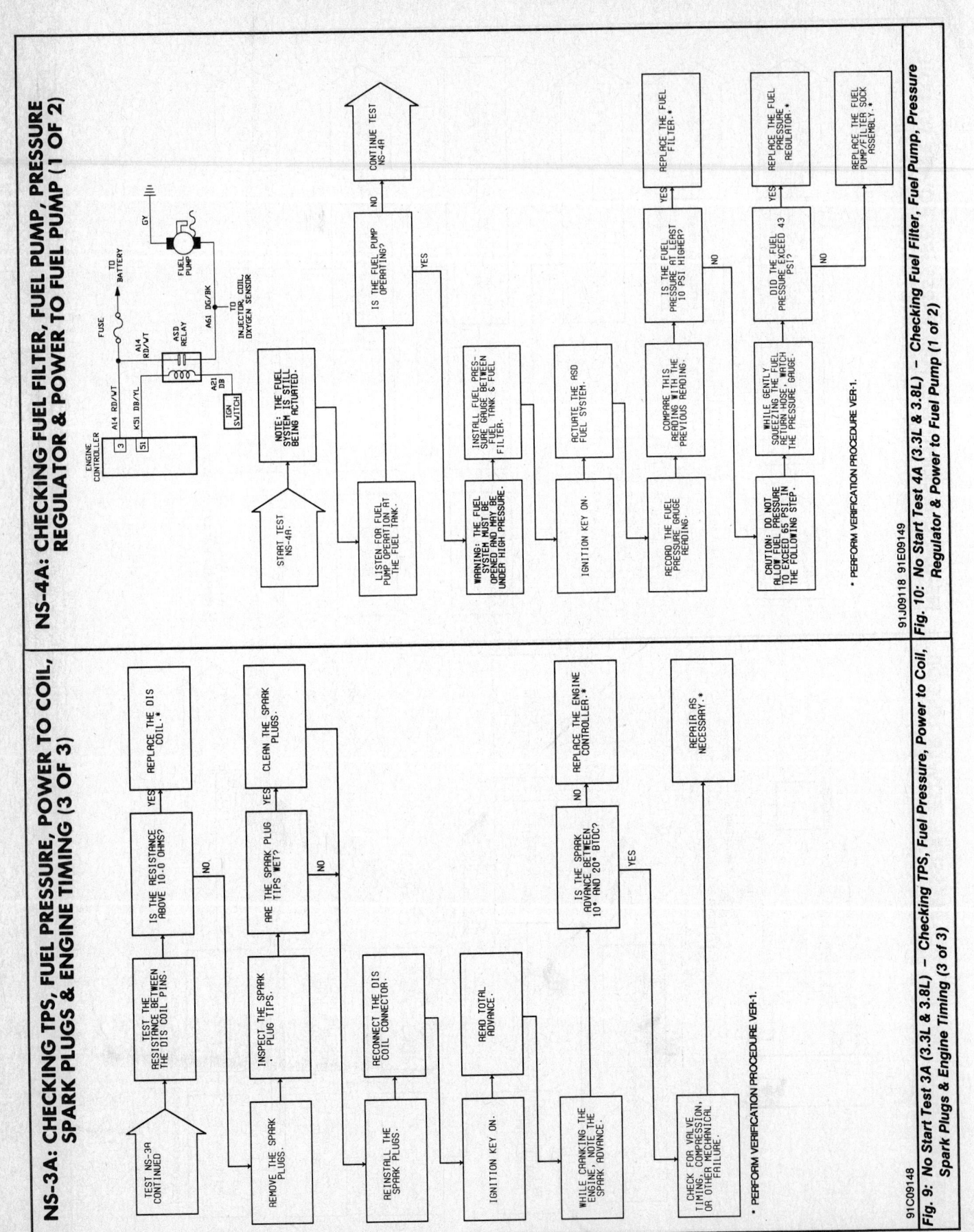

NS-4A: CHECKING FUEL FILTER, FUEL PUMP, PRESSURE REGULATOR & POWER TO FUEL PUMP (1 OF 2)

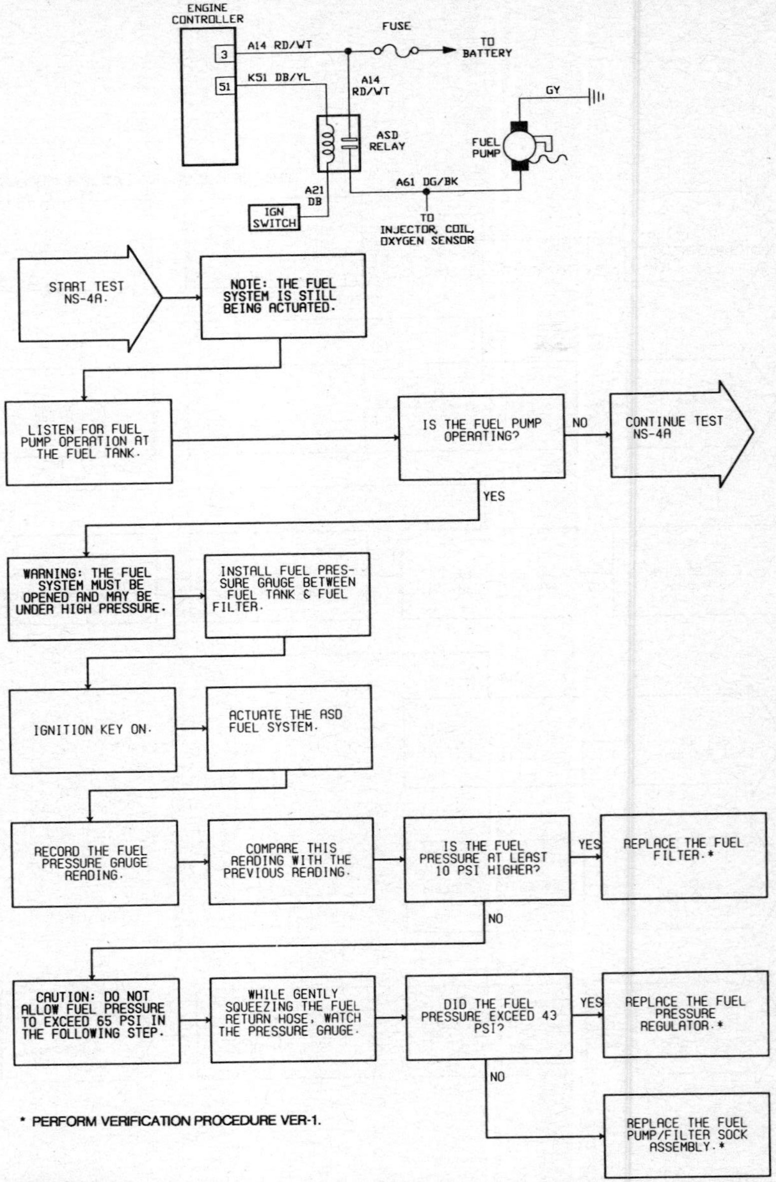
ENGINE CONTROLLER
3
51
A14 RD/WT
K51 DB/YL
FUSE
TO BATTERY
A14 RD/WT
ASD RELAY
GY
FUEL PUMP
A21 DB
IGN SWITCH
A61 DG/BK
TO INJECTOR, COIL, OXYGEN SENSOR
START TEST NS-4A.
NOTE: THE FUEL SYSTEM IS STILL BEING ACTUATED.
LISTEN FOR FUEL PUMP OPERATION AT THE FUEL TANK.
IS THE FUEL PUMP OPERATING?
NO
CONTINUE TEST NS-4A
YES
WARNING: THE FUEL SYSTEM MUST BE OPENED AND MAY BE UNDER HIGH PRESSURE.
INSTALL FUEL PRESSURE GAUGE BETWEEN FUEL TANK & FUEL FILTER.
IGNITION KEY ON.
ACTUATE THE ASD FUEL SYSTEM.
RECORD THE FUEL PRESSURE GAUGE READING.
COMPARE THIS READING WITH THE PREVIOUS READING.
IS THE FUEL PRESSURE AT LEAST 10 PSI HIGHER?
YES
REPLACE THE FUEL FILTER.*
NO
CAUTION: DO NOT ALLOW FUEL PRESSURE TO EXCEED 65 PSI IN THE FOLLOWING STEP.
WHILE GENTLY SQUEEZING THE FUEL RETURN HOSE, WATCH THE PRESSURE GAUGE.
DID THE FUEL PRESSURE EXCEED 43 PSI?
YES
REPLACE THE FUEL PRESSURE REGULATOR.*
NO
REPLACE THE FUEL PUMP/FILTER SOCK ASSEMBLY.*

* PERFORM VERIFICATION PROCEDURE VER-1.

91J09118 91E09149

Fig. 10: No Start Test 4A (3.3L & 3.8L) – Checking Fuel Filter, Fuel Pump, Pressure Regulator & Power to Fuel Pump (1 of 2)

NS-4A: CHECKING FUEL FILTER, FUEL PUMP, PRESSURE REGULATOR & POWER TO FUEL PUMP (2 OF 2)

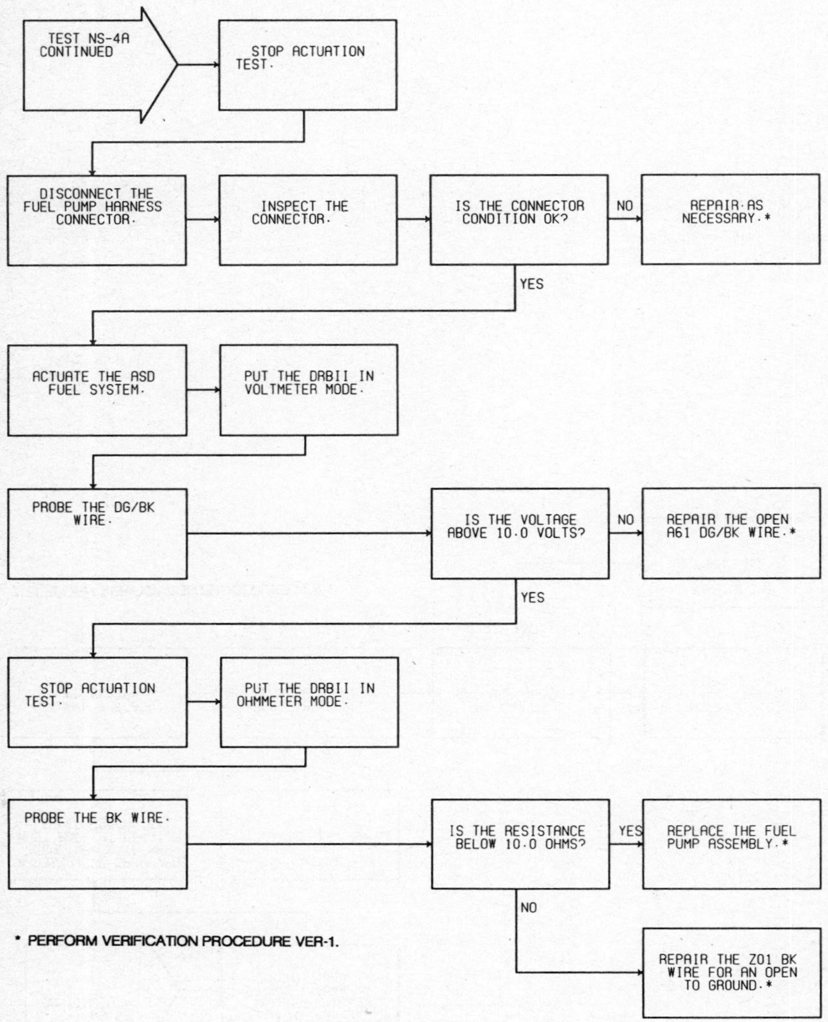
TEST NS-4A CONTINUED
STOP ACTUATION TEST.
DISCONNECT THE FUEL PUMP HARNESS CONNECTOR.
INSPECT THE CONNECTOR.
IS THE CONNECTOR CONDITION OK?
NO
REPAIR AS NECESSARY.*
YES
ACTUATE THE ASD FUEL SYSTEM.
PUT THE DRBII IN VOLTMETER MODE.
PROBE THE DG/BK WIRE.
IS THE VOLTAGE ABOVE 10.0 VOLTS?
NO
REPAIR THE OPEN A61 DG/BK WIRE.*
YES
STOP ACTUATION TEST.
PUT THE DRBII IN OHMMETER MODE.
PROBE THE BK WIRE.
IS THE RESISTANCE BELOW 10.0 OHMS?
YES
REPLACE THE FUEL PUMP ASSEMBLY.*
NO
REPAIR THE Z01 BK WIRE FOR AN OPEN TO GROUND.*

* PERFORM VERIFICATION PROCEDURE VER-1.

91G09150

Fig. 11: ***No Start Test 4A (3.3L & 3.8L) – Checking Fuel Filter, Fuel Pump, Pressure Regulator & Power to Fuel Pump (2 of 2)***

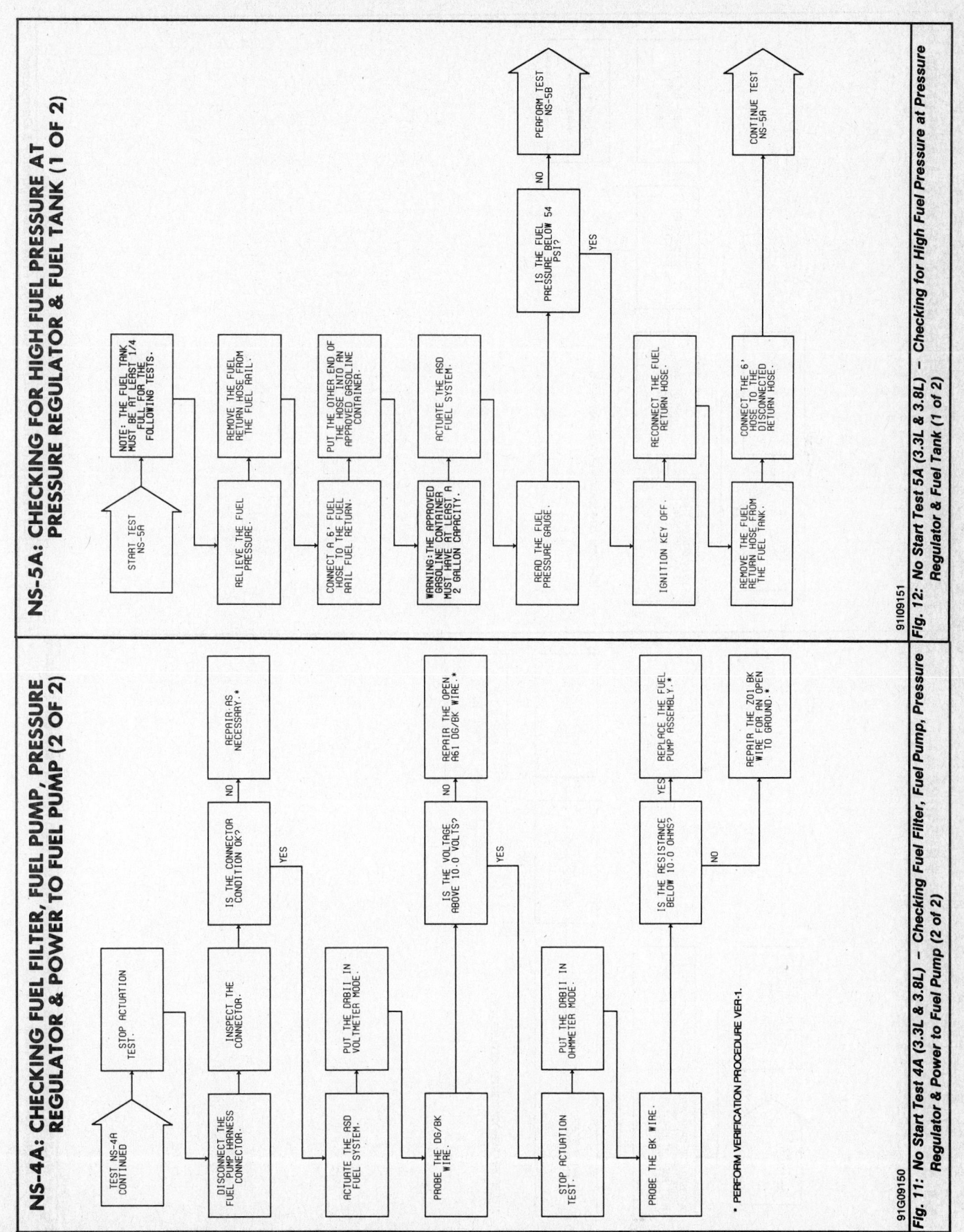

NS-5A: CHECKING FOR HIGH FUEL PRESSURE AT PRESSURE REGULATOR & FUEL TANK (1 OF 2)

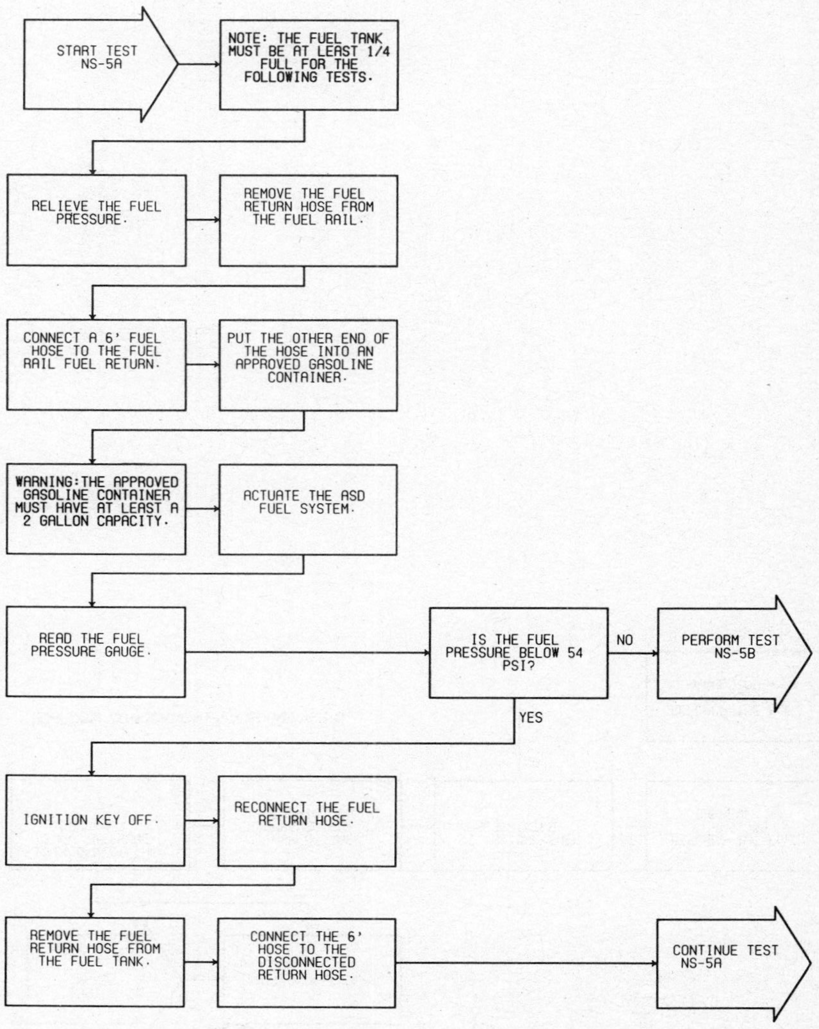
START TEST NS-5A
NOTE: THE FUEL TANK MUST BE AT LEAST 1/4 FULL FOR THE FOLLOWING TESTS.
RELIEVE THE FUEL PRESSURE.
REMOVE THE FUEL RETURN HOSE FROM THE FUEL RAIL.
CONNECT A 6' FUEL HOSE TO THE FUEL RAIL FUEL RETURN.
PUT THE OTHER END OF THE HOSE INTO AN APPROVED GASOLINE CONTAINER.
WARNING: THE APPROVED GASOLINE CONTAINER MUST HAVE AT LEAST A 2 GALLON CAPACITY.
ACTUATE THE ASD FUEL SYSTEM.
READ THE FUEL PRESSURE GAUGE.
IS THE FUEL PRESSURE BELOW 54 PSI?
NO
PERFORM TEST NS-5B
YES
IGNITION KEY OFF.
RECONNECT THE FUEL RETURN HOSE.
REMOVE THE FUEL RETURN HOSE FROM THE FUEL TANK.
CONNECT THE 6' HOSE TO THE DISCONNECTED RETURN HOSE.
CONTINUE TEST NS-5A

91I09151

Fig. 12: ***No Start Test 5A (3.3L & 3.8L) – Checking for High Fuel Pressure at Pressure Regulator & Fuel Tank (1 of 2)***

NS-5A: CHECKING FOR HIGH FUEL PRESSURE AT PRESSURE REGULATOR & FUEL TANK (2 OF 2)

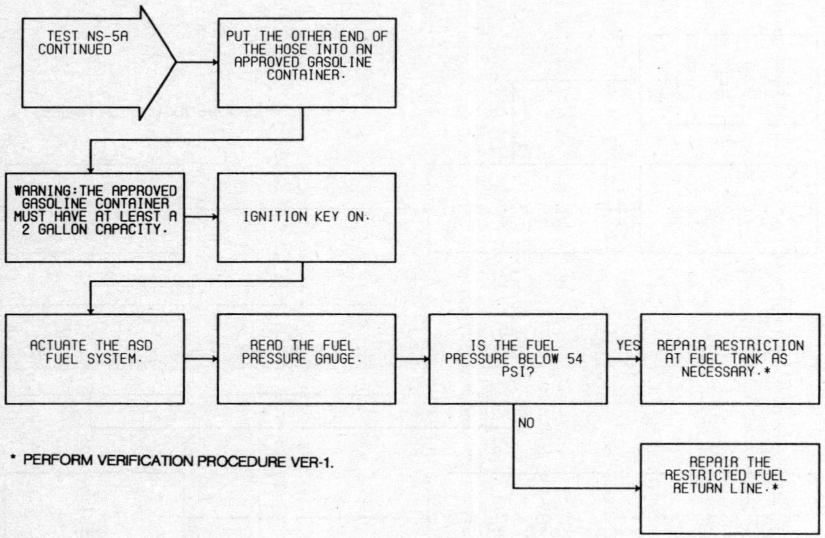
TEST NS-5A CONTINUED
PUT THE OTHER END OF THE HOSE INTO AN APPROVED GASOLINE CONTAINER.
WARNING: THE APPROVED GASOLINE CONTAINER MUST HAVE AT LEAST A 2 GALLON CAPACITY.
IGNITION KEY ON.
ACTUATE THE ASD FUEL SYSTEM.
READ THE FUEL PRESSURE GAUGE.
IS THE FUEL PRESSURE BELOW 54 PSI?
YES
REPAIR RESTRICTION AT FUEL TANK AS NECESSARY.*
NO
REPAIR THE RESTRICTED FUEL RETURN LINE.*

* PERFORM VERIFICATION PROCEDURE VER-1.

91F10400

Fig. 13: No Start Test 5A (3.3L & 3.8L) – Checking for High Fuel Pressure at Pressure Regulator & Fuel Tank (2 of 2)

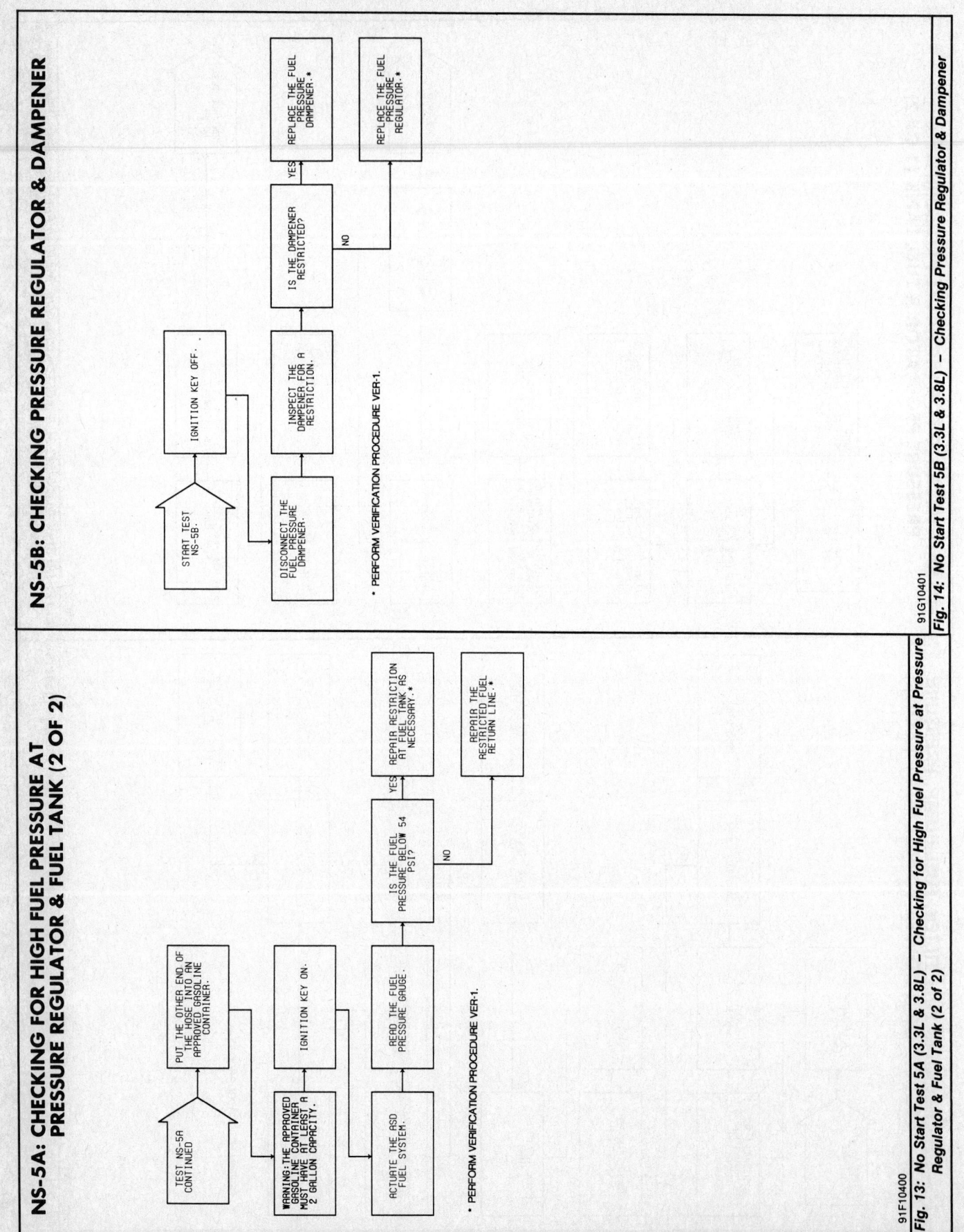

NS-5B: CHECKING PRESSURE REGULATOR & DAMPENER

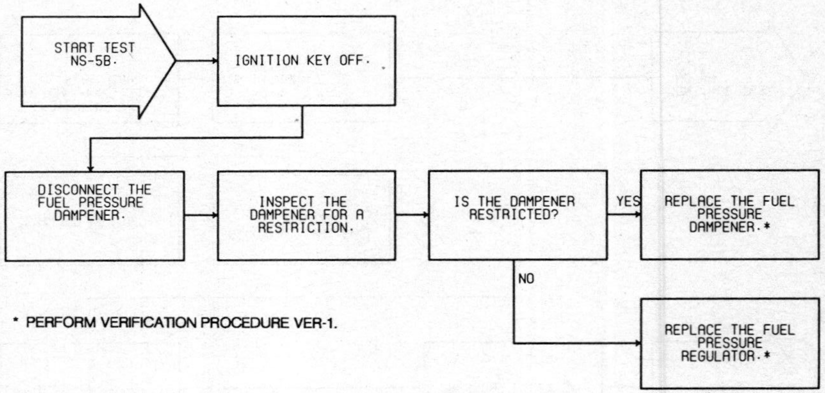
START TEST NS-5B.
IGNITION KEY OFF.
DISCONNECT THE FUEL PRESSURE DAMPENER.
INSPECT THE DAMPENER FOR A RESTRICTION.
IS THE DAMPENER RESTRICTED?
YES
REPLACE THE FUEL PRESSURE DAMPENER.*
NO
REPLACE THE FUEL PRESSURE REGULATOR.*

* PERFORM VERIFICATION PROCEDURE VER-1.

91G10401

Fig. 14: No Start Test 5B (3.3L & 3.8L) – Checking Pressure Regulator & Dampener

NS-6A: CHECKING DIS SIGNAL STATUS & DIS CRANKSHAFT SENSOR (1 OF 2)

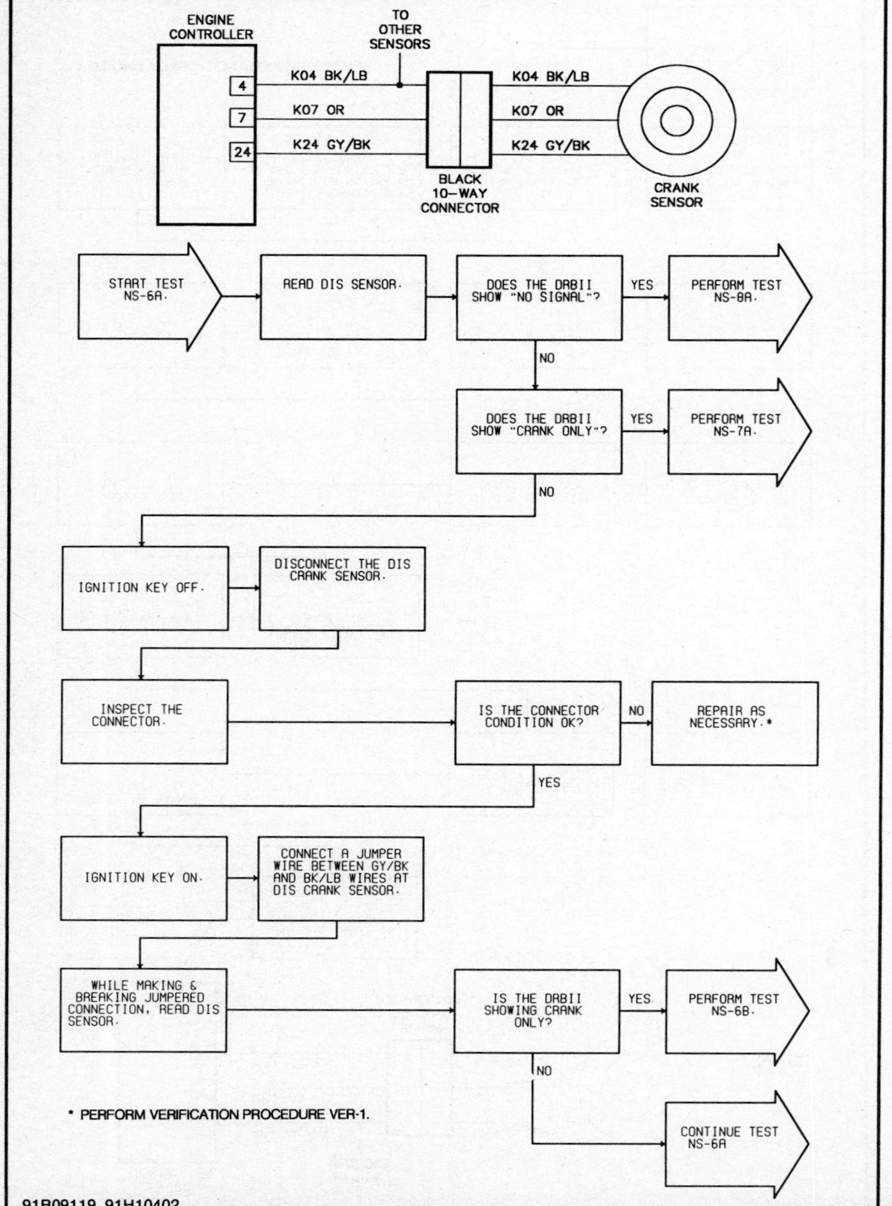
ENGINE CONTROLLER
4
7
24
K04 BK/LB
K07 OR
K24 GY/BK
TO OTHER SENSORS
BLACK 10-WAY CONNECTOR
K04 BK/LB
K07 OR
K24 GY/BK
CRANK SENSOR
START TEST NS-6A.
READ DIS SENSOR.
DOES THE DRBII SHOW "NO SIGNAL"?
YES
PERFORM TEST NS-8A.
NO
DOES THE DRBII SHOW "CRANK ONLY"?
YES
PERFORM TEST NS-7A.
NO
IGNITION KEY OFF.
DISCONNECT THE DIS CRANK SENSOR.
INSPECT THE CONNECTOR.
IS THE CONNECTOR CONDITION OK?
NO
REPAIR AS NECESSARY.*
YES
IGNITION KEY ON.
CONNECT A JUMPER WIRE BETWEEN GY/BK AND BK/LB WIRES AT DIS CRANK SENSOR.
WHILE MAKING & BREAKING JUMPERED CONNECTION, READ DIS SENSOR.
IS THE DRBII SHOWING CRANK ONLY?
YES
PERFORM TEST NS-6B.
NO
CONTINUE TEST NS-6A
* PERFORM VERIFICATION PROCEDURE VER-1.

91B09119 91H10402

Fig. 15: No Start Test 6A (3.3L & 3.8L) – Checking DIS Signal Status & DIS Crankshaft Sensor (1 of 2)

NS-6A: CHECKING DIS SIGNAL STATUS & DIS CRANKSHAFT SENSOR (2 OF 2)

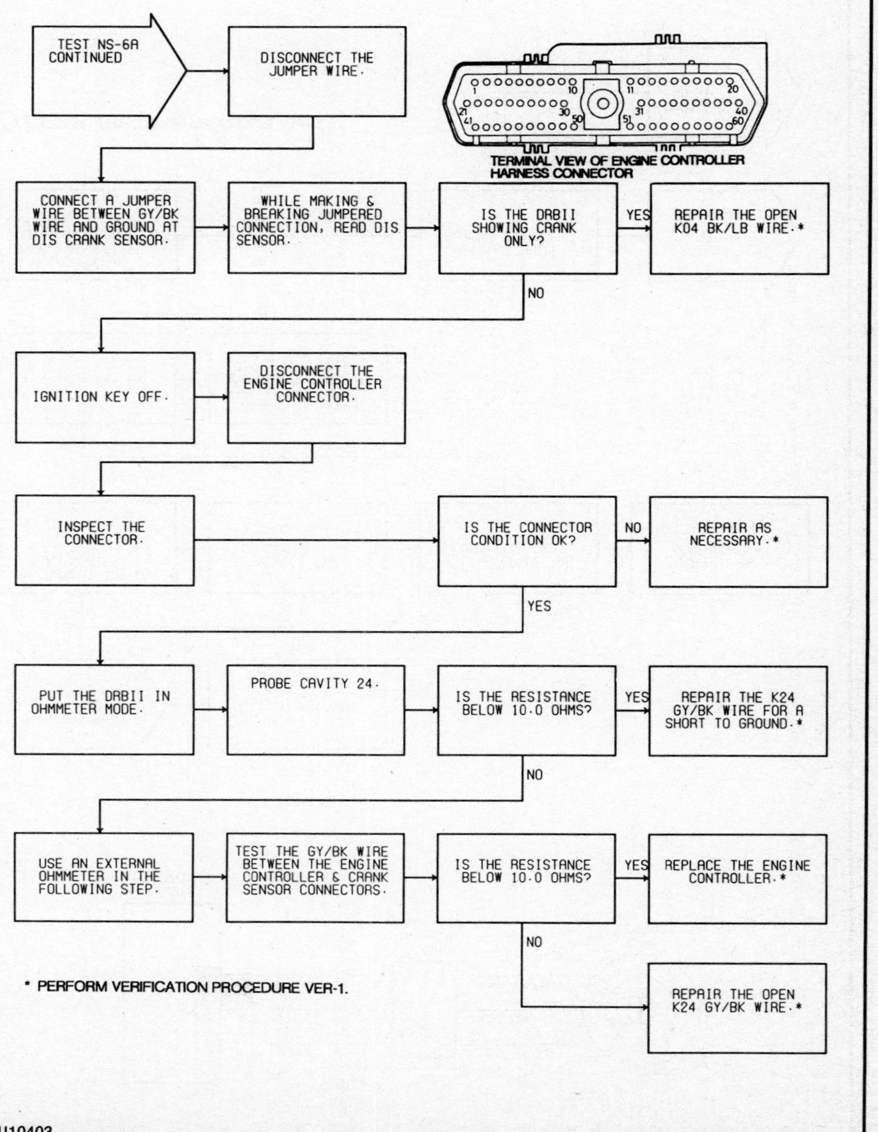
TEST NS-6A CONTINUED
DISCONNECT THE JUMPER WIRE.
TERMINAL VIEW OF ENGINE CONTROLLER HARNESS CONNECTOR
CONNECT A JUMPER WIRE BETWEEN GY/BK WIRE AND GROUND AT DIS CRANK SENSOR.
WHILE MAKING & BREAKING JUMPERED CONNECTION, READ DIS SENSOR.
IS THE DRBII SHOWING CRANK ONLY?
YES
REPAIR THE OPEN K04 BK/LB WIRE.*
NO
IGNITION KEY OFF.
DISCONNECT THE ENGINE CONTROLLER CONNECTOR.
INSPECT THE CONNECTOR.
IS THE CONNECTOR CONDITION OK?
NO
REPAIR AS NECESSARY.*
YES
PUT THE DRBII IN OHMMETER MODE.
PROBE CAVITY 24.
IS THE RESISTANCE BELOW 10.0 OHMS?
YES
REPAIR THE K24 GY/BK WIRE FOR A SHORT TO GROUND.*
NO
USE AN EXTERNAL OHMMETER IN THE FOLLOWING STEP.
TEST THE GY/BK WIRE BETWEEN THE ENGINE CONTROLLER & CRANK SENSOR CONNECTORS.
IS THE RESISTANCE BELOW 10.0 OHMS?
YES
REPLACE THE ENGINE CONTROLLER.*
NO
REPAIR THE OPEN K24 GY/BK WIRE.*
* PERFORM VERIFICATION PROCEDURE VER-1.

91I10403

Fig. 16: No Start Test 6A (3.3L & 3.8L) – Checking DIS Signal Status & DIS Crankshaft Sensor (2 of 2)

1991 ENGINE PERFORMANCE
Self-Diagnostics – 3.3L PFI (Cont.)

NS-6B: CHECKING DIS SIGNAL STATUS & DIS CRANKSHAFT SENSOR

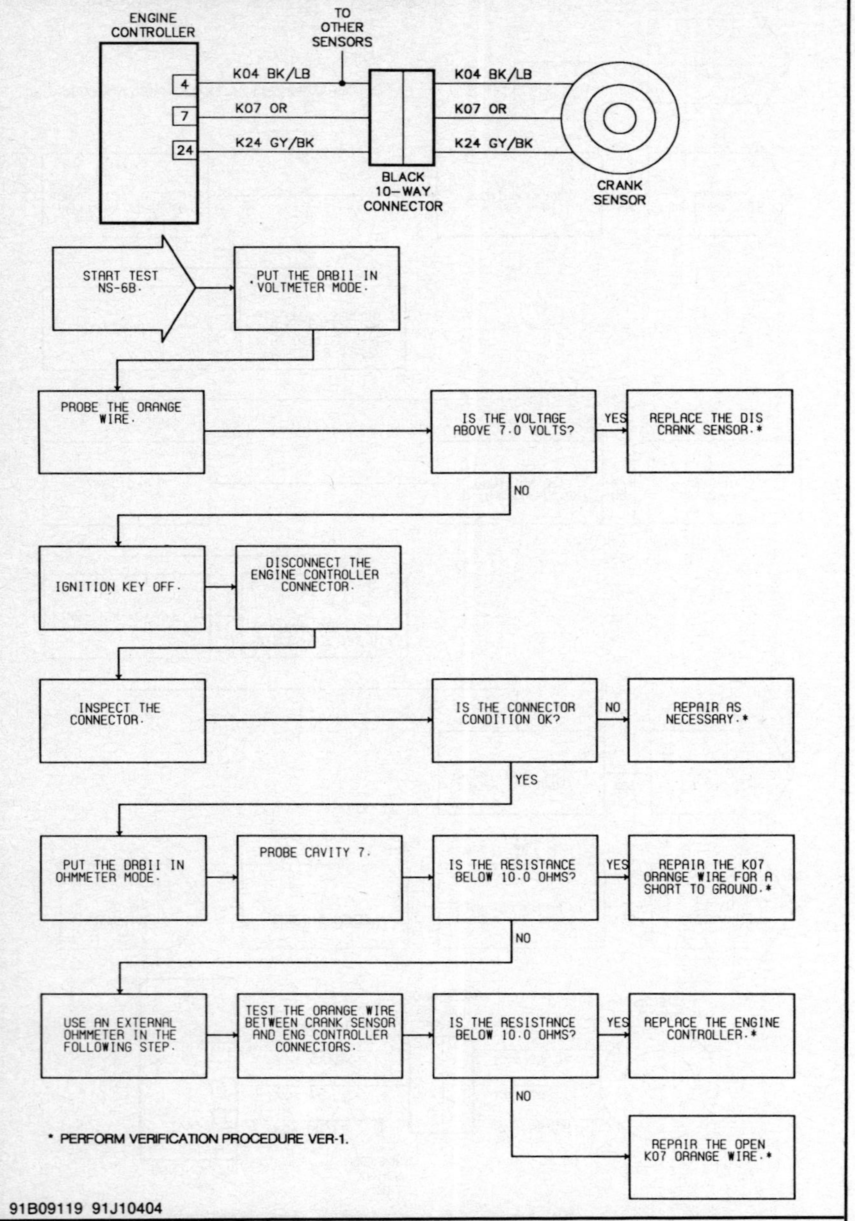
ENGINE CONTROLLER
TO OTHER SENSORS
4
7
24
K04 BK/LB
K07 OR
K24 GY/BK
BLACK 10–WAY CONNECTOR
CRANK SENSOR
START TEST NS-6B.
PUT THE DRBII IN VOLTMETER MODE.
PROBE THE ORANGE WIRE.
IS THE VOLTAGE ABOVE 7.0 VOLTS?
YES
REPLACE THE DIS CRANK SENSOR.*
NO
IGNITION KEY OFF.
DISCONNECT THE ENGINE CONTROLLER CONNECTOR.
INSPECT THE CONNECTOR.
IS THE CONNECTOR CONDITION OK?
NO
REPAIR AS NECESSARY.*
YES
PUT THE DRBII IN OHMMETER MODE.
PROBE CAVITY 7.
IS THE RESISTANCE BELOW 10.0 OHMS?
YES
REPAIR THE K07 ORANGE WIRE FOR A SHORT TO GROUND.*
NO
USE AN EXTERNAL OHMMETER IN THE FOLLOWING STEP.
TEST THE ORANGE WIRE BETWEEN CRANK SENSOR AND ENG CONTROLLER CONNECTORS.
IS THE RESISTANCE BELOW 10.0 OHMS?
YES
REPLACE THE ENGINE CONTROLLER.*
NO
REPAIR THE OPEN K07 ORANGE WIRE.*
* PERFORM VERIFICATION PROCEDURE VER-1.
91B09119 91J10404

Fig. 17: No Start Test 6B (3.3L & 3.8L) – Checking DIS Signal Status & DIS Crankshaft Sensor

NS-7A: CHECKING DIS CAMSHAFT SENSOR (1 OF 2)

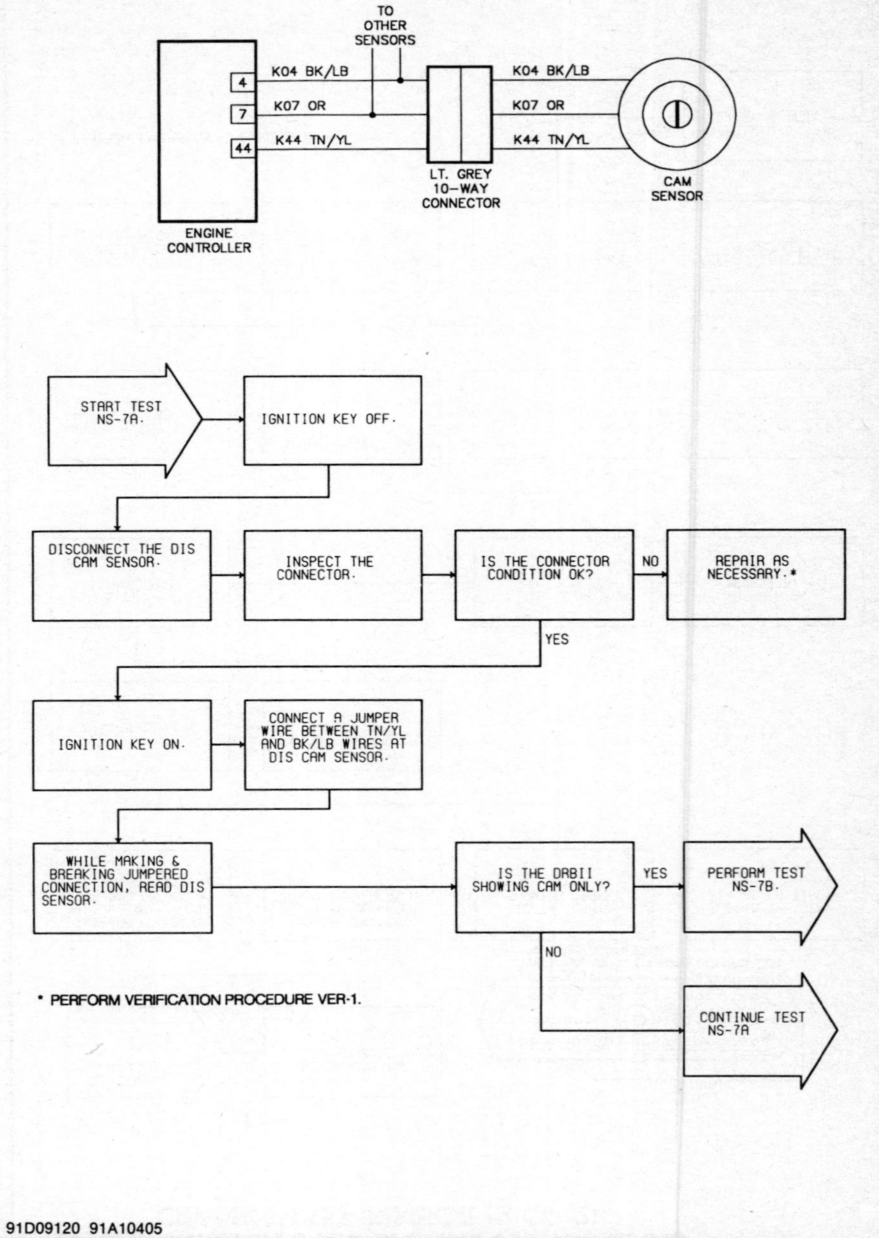
ENGINE CONTROLLER
TO OTHER SENSORS
4
7
44
K04 BK/LB
K07 OR
K44 TN/YL
LT. GREY 10–WAY CONNECTOR
CAM SENSOR
START TEST NS-7A.
IGNITION KEY OFF.
DISCONNECT THE DIS CAM SENSOR.
INSPECT THE CONNECTOR.
IS THE CONNECTOR CONDITION OK?
NO
REPAIR AS NECESSARY.*
YES
IGNITION KEY ON.
CONNECT A JUMPER WIRE BETWEEN TN/YL AND BK/LB WIRES AT DIS CAM SENSOR.
WHILE MAKING & BREAKING JUMPERED CONNECTION, READ DIS SENSOR.
IS THE DRBII SHOWING CAM ONLY?
YES
PERFORM TEST NS-7B.
NO
CONTINUE TEST NS-7A
* PERFORM VERIFICATION PROCEDURE VER-1.
91D09120 91A10405

Fig. 18: No Start Test 7A (3.3L & 3.8L) – Checking DIS Camshaft Sensor (1 of 2)

NS-7A: CHECKING DIS CAMSHAFT SENSOR (2 OF 2)

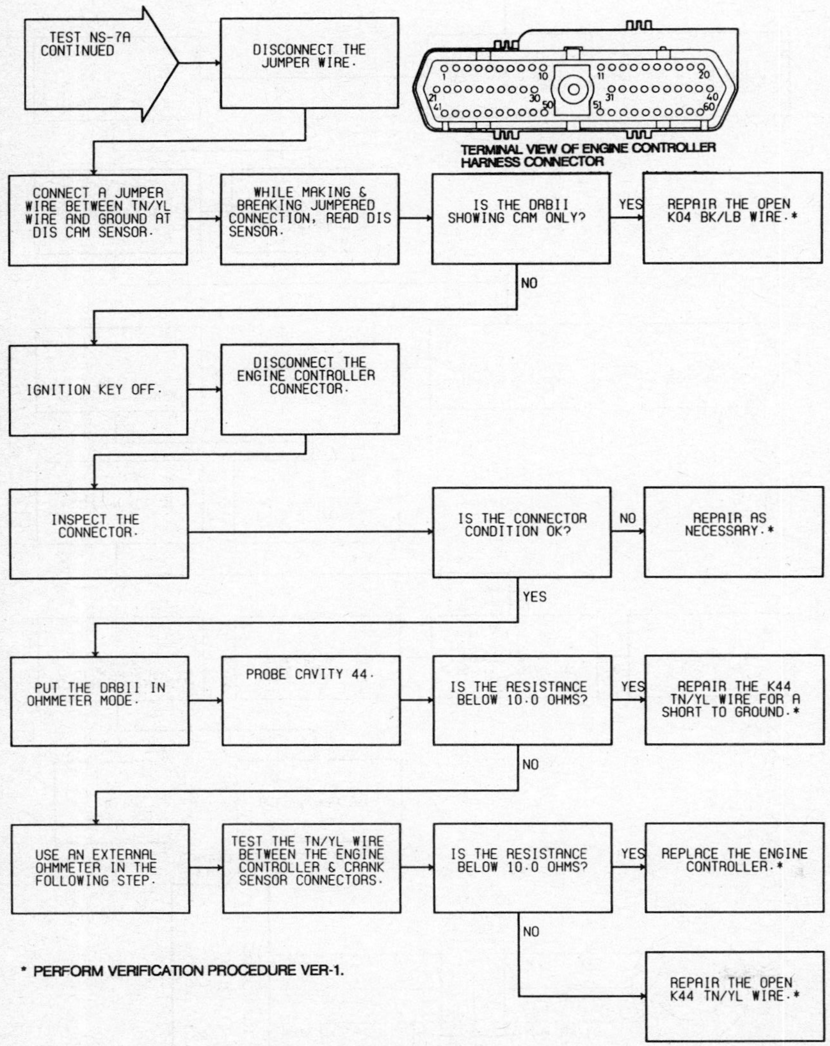
TEST NS-7A CONTINUED
DISCONNECT THE JUMPER WIRE.
TERMINAL VIEW OF ENGINE CONTROLLER HARNESS CONNECTOR
CONNECT A JUMPER WIRE BETWEEN TN/YL WIRE AND GROUND AT DIS CAM SENSOR.
WHILE MAKING & BREAKING JUMPERED CONNECTION, READ DIS SENSOR.
IS THE DRBII SHOWING CAM ONLY?
YES
REPAIR THE OPEN K04 BK/LB WIRE.*
NO
IGNITION KEY OFF.
DISCONNECT THE ENGINE CONTROLLER CONNECTOR.
INSPECT THE CONNECTOR.
IS THE CONNECTOR CONDITION OK?
NO
REPAIR AS NECESSARY.*
YES
PUT THE DRBII IN OHMMETER MODE.
PROBE CAVITY 44.
IS THE RESISTANCE BELOW 10.0 OHMS?
YES
REPAIR THE K44 TN/YL WIRE FOR A SHORT TO GROUND.*
NO
USE AN EXTERNAL OHMMETER IN THE FOLLOWING STEP.
TEST THE TN/YL WIRE BETWEEN THE ENGINE CONTROLLER & CRANK SENSOR CONNECTORS.
IS THE RESISTANCE BELOW 10.0 OHMS?
YES
REPLACE THE ENGINE CONTROLLER.*
NO
REPAIR THE OPEN K44 TN/YL WIRE.*
* PERFORM VERIFICATION PROCEDURE VER-1.

91B10406

Fig. 19: No Start Test 7A (3.3L & 3.8L) – Checking DIS Camshaft Sensor (2 of 2)

NS-7B: CHECKING DIS CAMSHAFT SENSOR

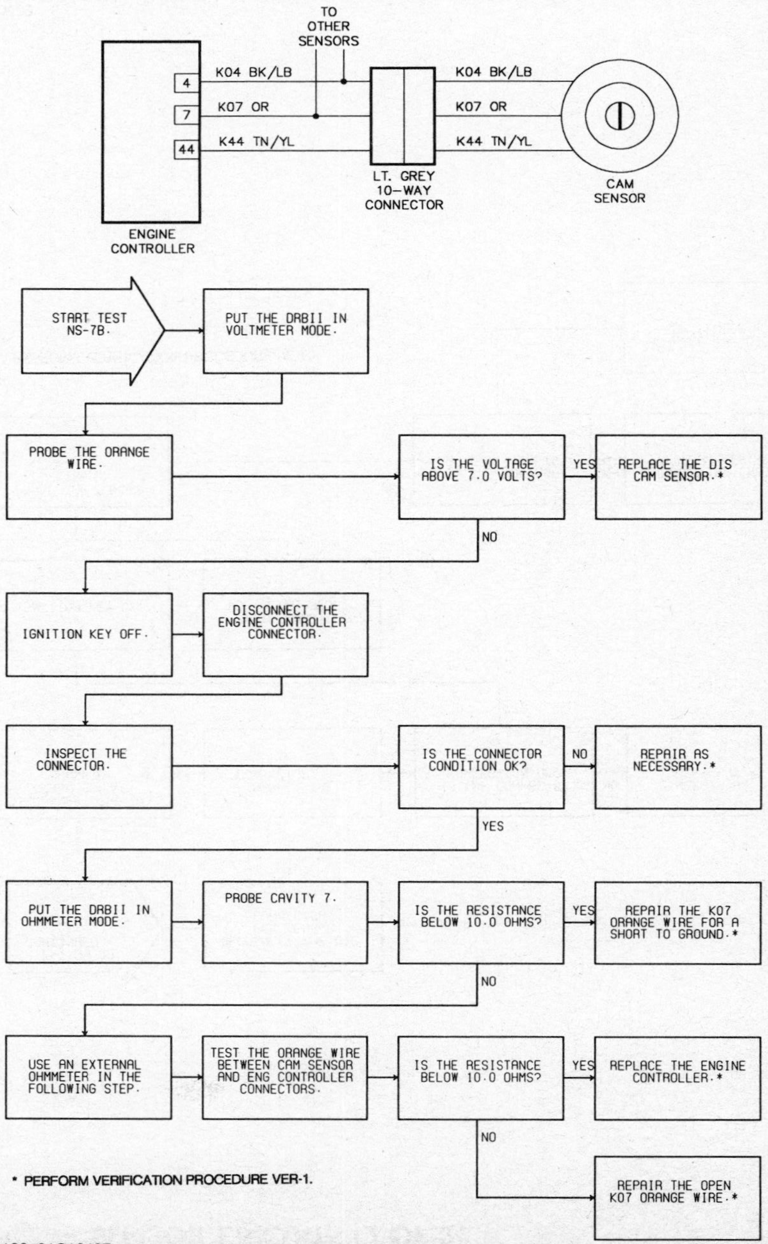
TO OTHER SENSORS
K04 BK/LB
K07 OR
K44 TN/YL
4
7
44
ENGINE CONTROLLER
LT. GREY 10-WAY CONNECTOR
CAM SENSOR
START TEST NS-7B.
PUT THE DRBII IN VOLTMETER MODE.
PROBE THE ORANGE WIRE.
IS THE VOLTAGE ABOVE 7.0 VOLTS?
YES
REPLACE THE DIS CAM SENSOR.*
NO
IGNITION KEY OFF.
DISCONNECT THE ENGINE CONTROLLER CONNECTOR.
INSPECT THE CONNECTOR.
IS THE CONNECTOR CONDITION OK?
NO
REPAIR AS NECESSARY.*
YES
PUT THE DRBII IN OHMMETER MODE.
PROBE CAVITY 7.
IS THE RESISTANCE BELOW 10.0 OHMS?
YES
REPAIR THE K07 ORANGE WIRE FOR A SHORT TO GROUND.*
NO
USE AN EXTERNAL OHMMETER IN THE FOLLOWING STEP.
TEST THE ORANGE WIRE BETWEEN CAM SENSOR AND ENG CONTROLLER CONNECTORS.
IS THE RESISTANCE BELOW 10.0 OHMS?
YES
REPLACE THE ENGINE CONTROLLER.*
NO
REPAIR THE OPEN K07 ORANGE WIRE.*
* PERFORM VERIFICATION PROCEDURE VER-1.

91D09120 91C10407

Fig. 20: No Start Test 7B (3.3L & 3.8L) – Checking DIS Camshaft Sensor

1991 ENGINE PERFORMANCE
Self-Diagnostics – 3.3L PFI (Cont.)

NS-8A: CHECKING DIS CAMSHAFT & CRANKSHAFT SENSOR CIRCUITS (1 OF 2)

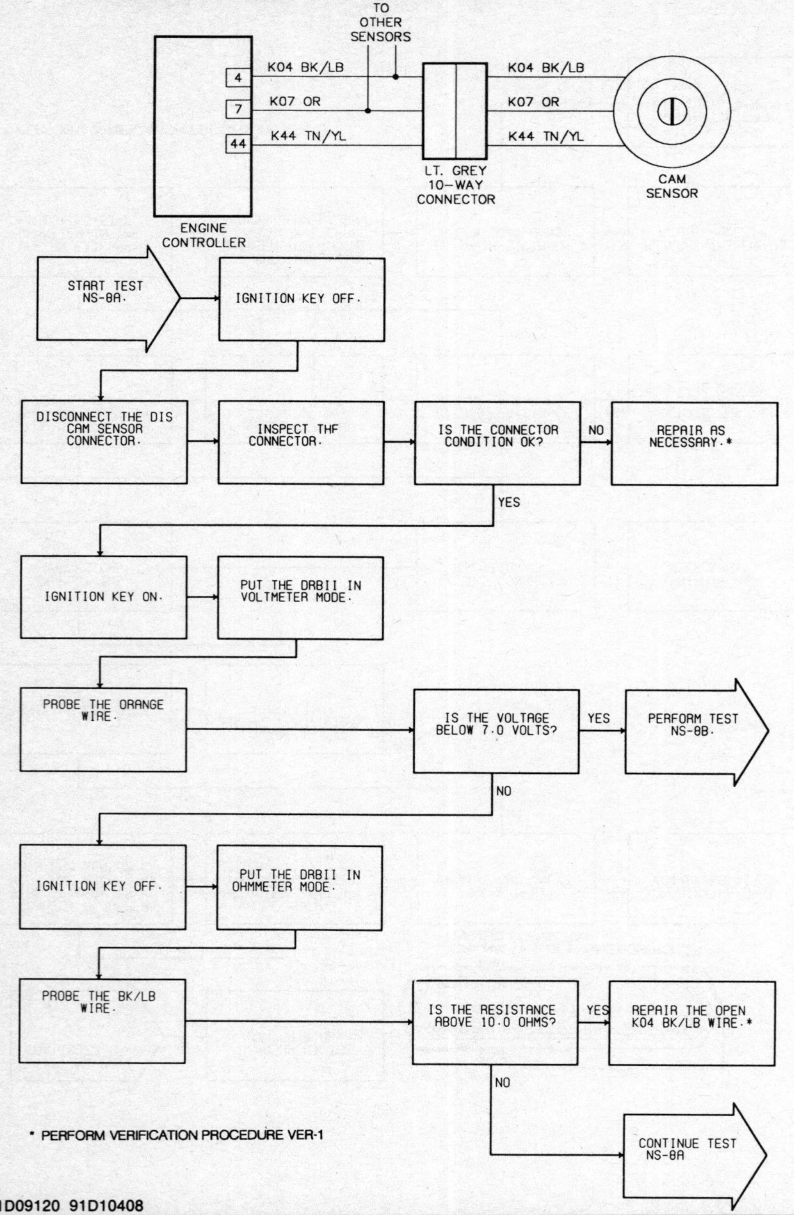
TO OTHER SENSORS
4
7
44
K04 BK/LB
K07 OR
K44 TN/YL
LT. GREY 10-WAY CONNECTOR
CAM SENSOR
ENGINE CONTROLLER
START TEST NS-8A.
IGNITION KEY OFF.
DISCONNECT THE DIS CAM SENSOR CONNECTOR.
INSPECT THF CONNECTOR.
IS THE CONNECTOR CONDITION OK?
NO
REPAIR AS NECESSARY.*
YES
IGNITION KEY ON.
PUT THE DRBII IN VOLTMETER MODE.
PROBE THE ORANGE WIRE.
IS THE VOLTAGE BELOW 7.0 VOLTS?
YES
PERFORM TEST NS-8B.
NO
IGNITION KEY OFF.
PUT THE DRBII IN OHMMETER MODE.
PROBE THE BK/LB WIRE.
IS THE RESISTANCE ABOVE 10.0 OHMS?
YES
REPAIR THE OPEN K04 BK/LB WIRE.*
NO
CONTINUE TEST NS-8A
* PERFORM VERIFICATION PROCEDURE VER-1

91D09120 91D10408

Fig. 21: No Start Test 8A (3.3L & 3.8L) – Checking DIS Camshaft & Crankshaft Sensor Circuits (1 of 2)

NS-8A: CHECKING DIS CAMSHAFT & CRANKSHAFT SENSOR CIRCUITS (2 OF 2)

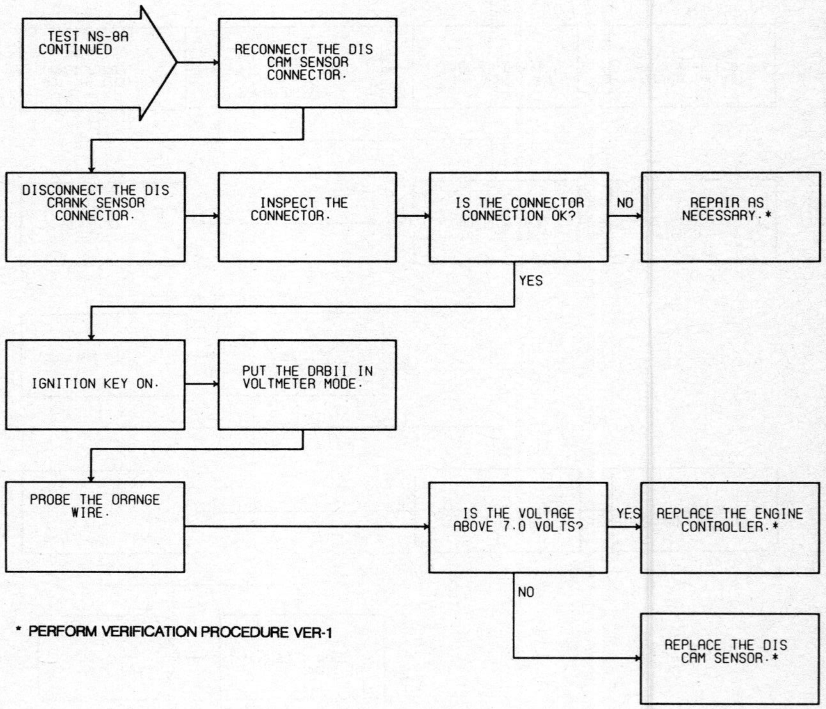
TEST NS-8A CONTINUED
RECONNECT THE DIS CAM SENSOR CONNECTOR.
DISCONNECT THE DIS CRANK SENSOR CONNECTOR.
INSPECT THE CONNECTOR.
IS THE CONNECTOR CONNECTION OK?
NO
REPAIR AS NECESSARY.*
YES
IGNITION KEY ON.
PUT THE DRBII IN VOLTMETER MODE.
PROBE THE ORANGE WIRE.
IS THE VOLTAGE ABOVE 7.0 VOLTS?
YES
REPLACE THE ENGINE CONTROLLER.*
NO
REPLACE THE DIS CAM SENSOR.*
* PERFORM VERIFICATION PROCEDURE VER-1

91E10409

Fig. 22: No Start Test 8A (3.3L & 3.8L) – Checking DIS Camshaft & Crankshaft Sensor Circuits (2 of 2)

NS-8B: CHECKING DIS CAMSHAFT & CRANKSHAFT SENSOR CIRCUITS

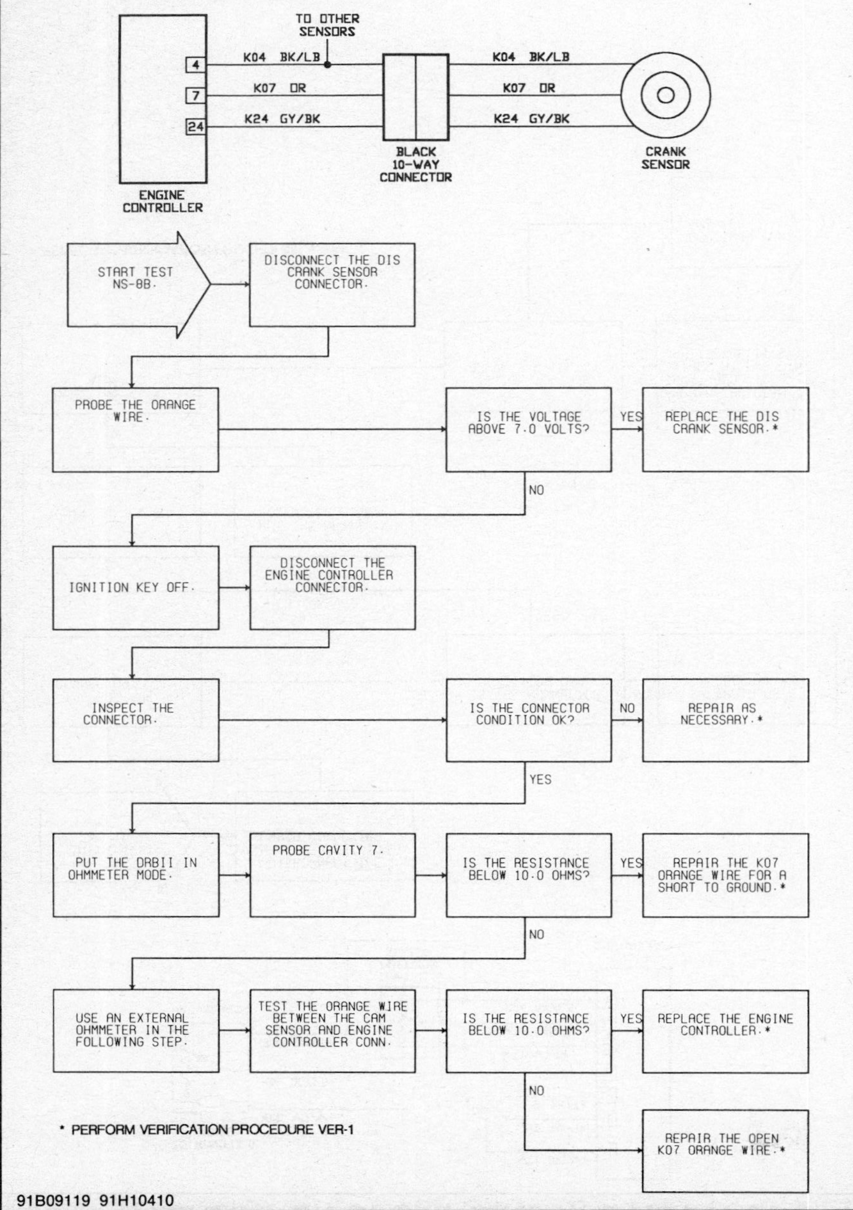

ENGINE CONTROLLER
TO OTHER SENSORS
4
7
24
K04 BK/LB
K07 OR
K24 GY/BK
BLACK 10-WAY CONNECTOR
CRANK SENSOR
START TEST NS-8B.
DISCONNECT THE DIS CRANK SENSOR CONNECTOR.
PROBE THE ORANGE WIRE.
IS THE VOLTAGE ABOVE 7.0 VOLTS?
YES
REPLACE THE DIS CRANK SENSOR.*
NO
IGNITION KEY OFF.
DISCONNECT THE ENGINE CONTROLLER CONNECTOR.
INSPECT THE CONNECTOR.
IS THE CONNECTOR CONDITION OK?
NO
REPAIR AS NECESSARY.*
YES
PUT THE DRBII IN OHMMETER MODE.
PROBE CAVITY 7.
IS THE RESISTANCE BELOW 10.0 OHMS?
YES
REPAIR THE K07 ORANGE WIRE FOR A SHORT TO GROUND.*
NO
USE AN EXTERNAL OHMMETER IN THE FOLLOWING STEP.
TEST THE ORANGE WIRE BETWEEN THE CAM SENSOR AND ENGINE CONTROLLER CONN.
IS THE RESISTANCE BELOW 10.0 OHMS?
YES
REPLACE THE ENGINE CONTROLLER.*
NO
REPAIR THE OPEN K07 ORANGE WIRE.*
* PERFORM VERIFICATION PROCEDURE VER-1
91B09119 91H10410

Fig. 23: No Start Test 8B (3.3L & 3.8L) – Checking DIS Camshaft & Crankshaft Sensor Circuits

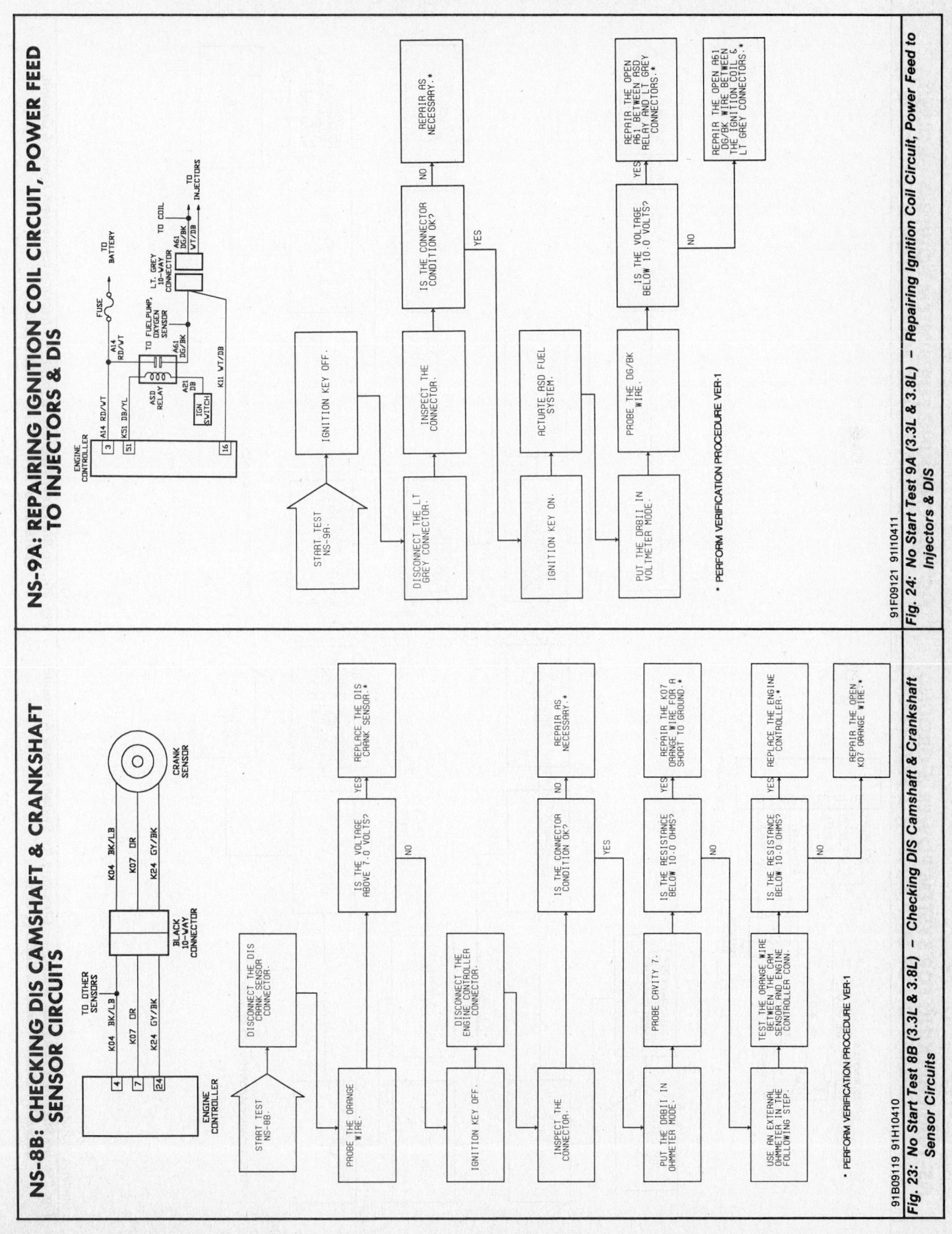

NS-9A: REPAIRING IGNITION COIL CIRCUIT, POWER FEED TO INJECTORS & DIS

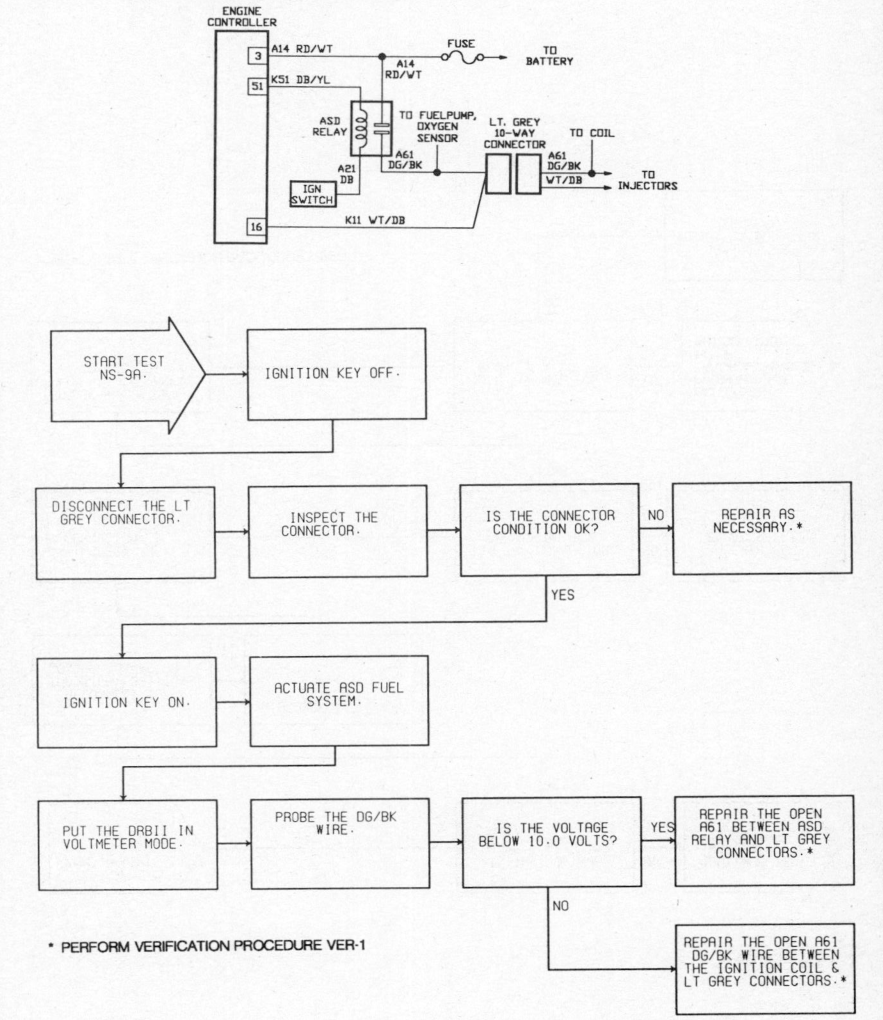

ENGINE CONTROLLER
3
51
16
A14 RD/WT
K51 DB/YL
FUSE
TO BATTERY
A14 RD/WT
ASD RELAY
TO FUELPUMP, OXYGEN SENSOR
A21 DB
IGN SWITCH
A61 DG/BK
LT. GREY 10-WAY CONNECTOR
TO COIL
A61 DG/BK
WT/DB
TO INJECTORS
K11 WT/DB
START TEST NS-9A.
IGNITION KEY OFF.
DISCONNECT THE LT GREY CONNECTOR.
INSPECT THE CONNECTOR.
IS THE CONNECTOR CONDITION OK?
NO
REPAIR AS NECESSARY.*
YES
IGNITION KEY ON.
ACTUATE ASD FUEL SYSTEM.
PUT THE DRBII IN VOLTMETER MODE.
PROBE THE DG/BK WIRE.
IS THE VOLTAGE BELOW 10.0 VOLTS?
YES
REPAIR THE OPEN A61 BETWEEN ASD RELAY AND LT GREY CONNECTORS.*
NO
REPAIR THE OPEN A61 DG/BK WIRE BETWEEN THE IGNITION COIL & LT GREY CONNECTORS.*
* PERFORM VERIFICATION PROCEDURE VER-1
91F09121 91I10411

Fig. 24: No Start Test 9A (3.3L & 3.8L) – Repairing Ignition Coil Circuit, Power Feed to Injectors & DIS

1991 ENGINE PERFORMANCE
Self-Diagnostics – 3.3L PFI (Cont.)

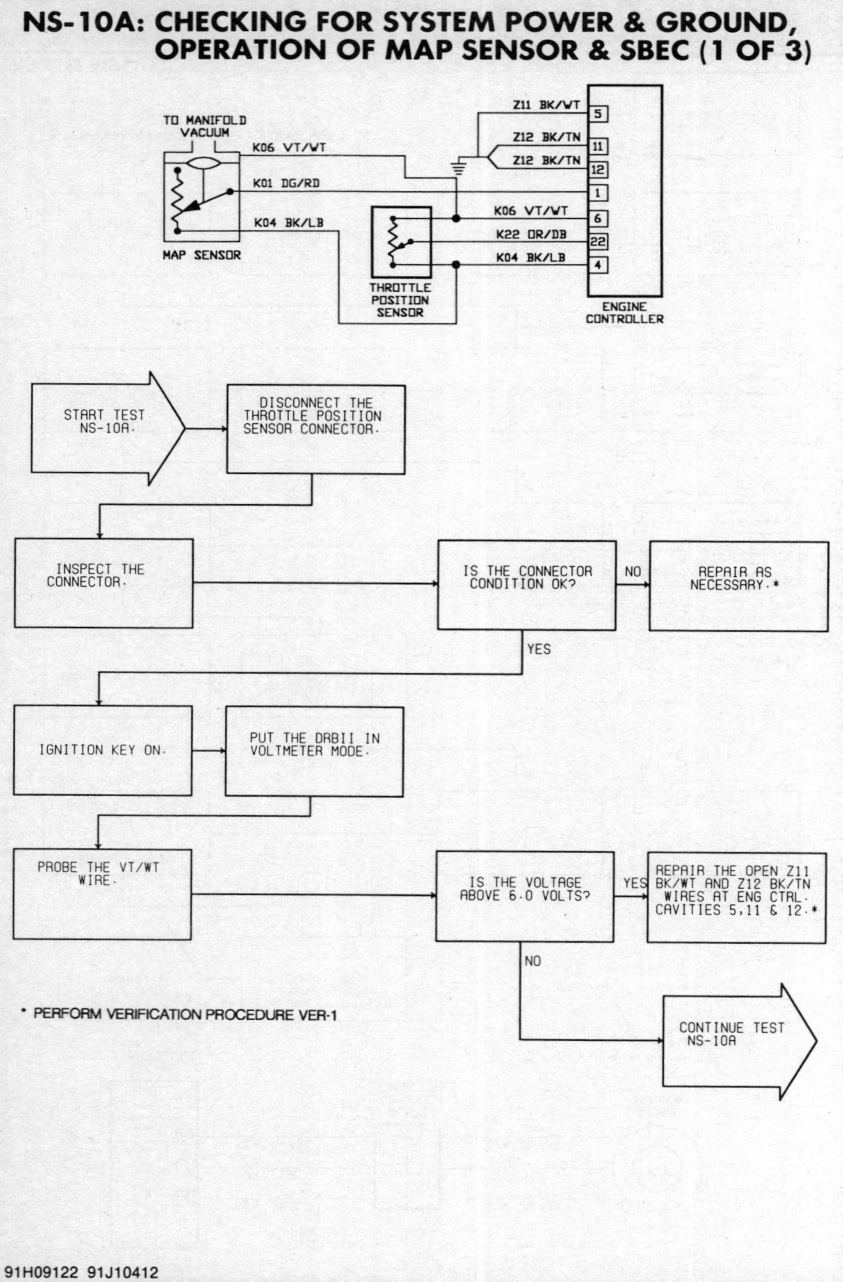
NS-10A: CHECKING FOR SYSTEM POWER & GROUND, OPERATION OF MAP SENSOR & SBEC (1 OF 3)
TO MANIFOLD VACUUM
K06 VT/WT
K01 DG/RD
K04 BK/LB
MAP SENSOR
THROTTLE POSITION SENSOR
Z11 BK/WT
Z12 BK/TN
Z12 BK/TN
K06 VT/WT
K22 OR/DB
K04 BK/LB
5
11
12
1
6
22
4
ENGINE CONTROLLER
START TEST NS-10A.
DISCONNECT THE THROTTLE POSITION SENSOR CONNECTOR.
INSPECT THE CONNECTOR.
IS THE CONNECTOR CONDITION OK?
NO
REPAIR AS NECESSARY.*
YES
IGNITION KEY ON.
PUT THE DRBII IN VOLTMETER MODE.
PROBE THE VT/WT WIRE.
IS THE VOLTAGE ABOVE 6.0 VOLTS?
YES
REPAIR THE OPEN Z11 BK/WT AND Z12 BK/TN WIRES AT ENG CTRL. CAVITIES 5,11 & 12.*
NO
CONTINUE TEST NS-10A
* PERFORM VERIFICATION PROCEDURE VER-1
91H09122 91J10412

Fig. 25: No Start Test 10A (3.3L & 3.8L) – Checking for System Power & Ground, Operation of MAP Sensor & SBEC (1 of 3)

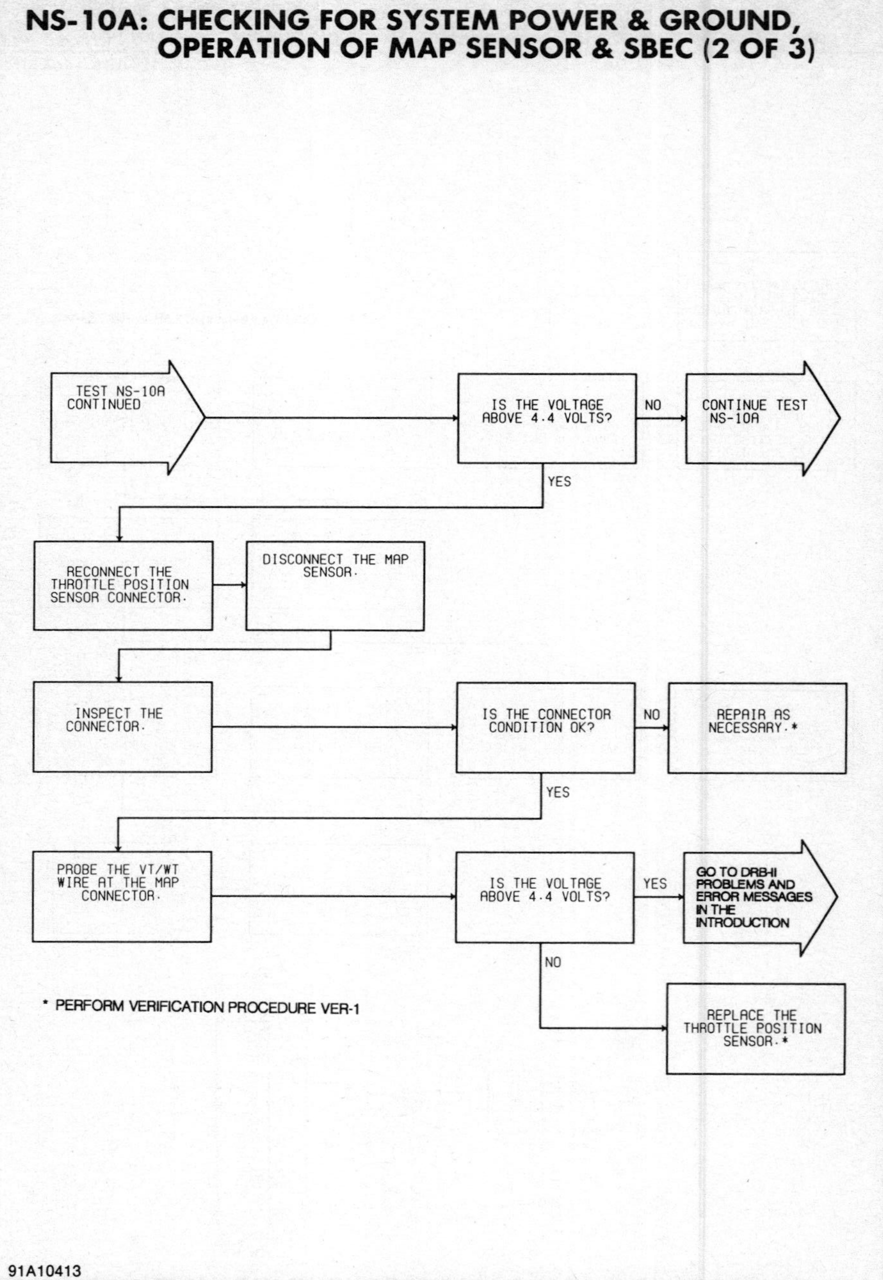
NS-10A: CHECKING FOR SYSTEM POWER & GROUND, OPERATION OF MAP SENSOR & SBEC (2 OF 3)
TEST NS-10A CONTINUED
IS THE VOLTAGE ABOVE 4.4 VOLTS?
NO
CONTINUE TEST NS-10A
YES
RECONNECT THE THROTTLE POSITION SENSOR CONNECTOR.
DISCONNECT THE MAP SENSOR.
INSPECT THE CONNECTOR.
IS THE CONNECTOR CONDITION OK?
NO
REPAIR AS NECESSARY.*
YES
PROBE THE VT/WT WIRE AT THE MAP CONNECTOR.
IS THE VOLTAGE ABOVE 4.4 VOLTS?
YES
GO TO DRB-II PROBLEMS AND ERROR MESSAGES IN THE INTRODUCTION
NO
REPLACE THE THROTTLE POSITION SENSOR.*
* PERFORM VERIFICATION PROCEDURE VER-1
91A10413

Fig. 26: No Start Test 10A (3.3L & 3.8L) – Checking for System Power & Ground, Operation of MAP Sensor & SBEC (2 of 3)

NS-10A: CHECKING FOR SYSTEM POWER & GROUND, OPERATION OF MAP SENSOR & SBEC (3 OF 3)

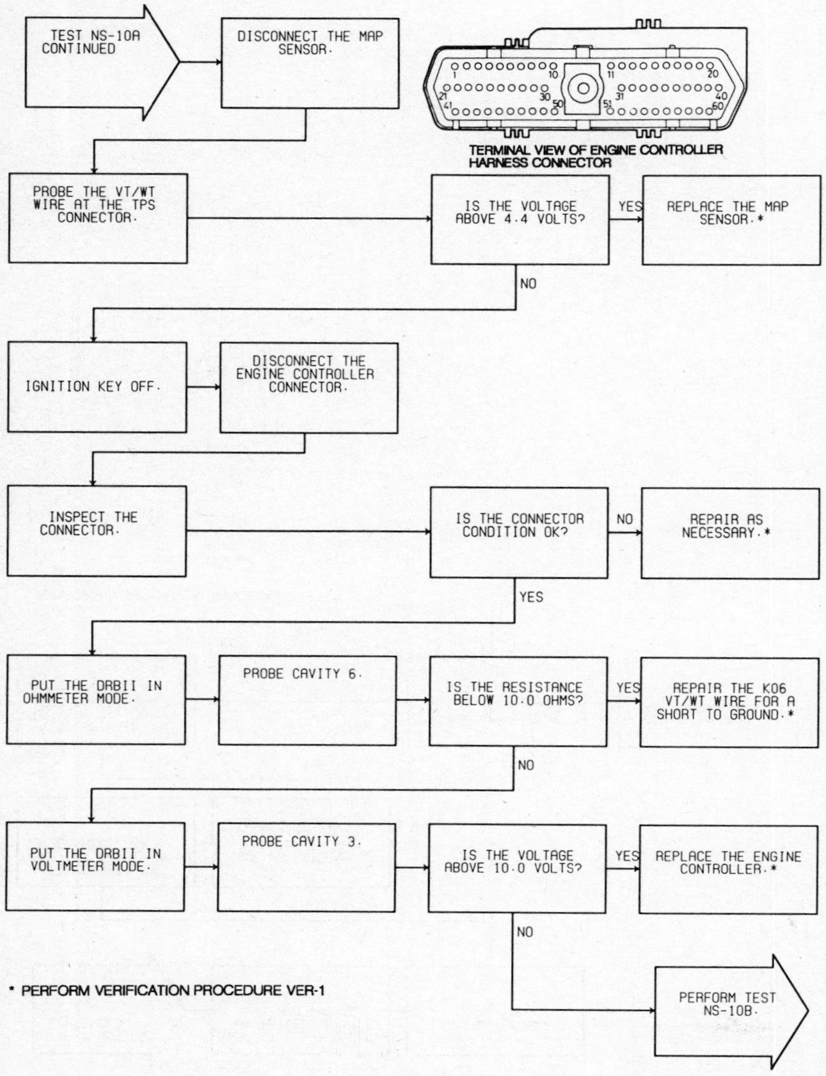
TEST NS-10A CONTINUED
DISCONNECT THE MAP SENSOR.
TERMINAL VIEW OF ENGINE CONTROLLER HARNESS CONNECTOR
PROBE THE VT/WT WIRE AT THE TPS CONNECTOR.
IS THE VOLTAGE ABOVE 4.4 VOLTS?
YES
REPLACE THE MAP SENSOR.*
NO
IGNITION KEY OFF.
DISCONNECT THE ENGINE CONTROLLER CONNECTOR.
INSPECT THE CONNECTOR.
IS THE CONNECTOR CONDITION OK?
NO
REPAIR AS NECESSARY.*
YES
PUT THE DRBII IN OHMMETER MODE.
PROBE CAVITY 6.
IS THE RESISTANCE BELOW 10.0 OHMS?
YES
REPAIR THE K06 VT/WT WIRE FOR A SHORT TO GROUND.*
NO
PUT THE DRBII IN VOLTMETER MODE.
PROBE CAVITY 3.
IS THE VOLTAGE ABOVE 10.0 VOLTS?
YES
REPLACE THE ENGINE CONTROLLER.*
NO
PERFORM TEST NS-10B.

* PERFORM VERIFICATION PROCEDURE VER-1

91B10414

Fig. 27: No Start Test 10A (3.3L & 3.8L) – Checking for System Power & Ground, Operation of MAP Sensor & SBEC (3 of 3)

NS-10B: CHECKING FOR SYSTEM POWER & GROUND, OPERATION OF MAP SENSOR & SBEC (1 OF 2)

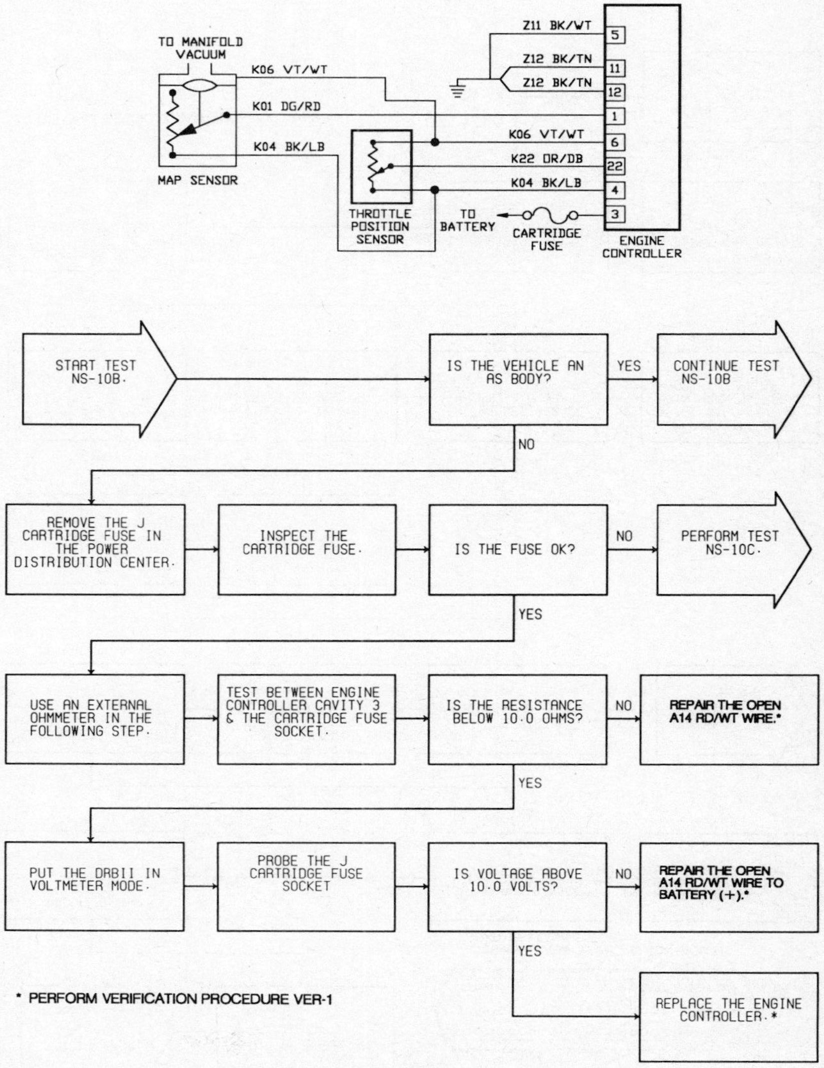
TO MANIFOLD VACUUM
K06 VT/WT
K01 DG/RD
K04 BK/LB
MAP SENSOR
THROTTLE POSITION SENSOR
Z11 BK/WT
Z12 BK/TN
Z12 BK/TN
K06 VT/WT
K22 OR/DB
K04 BK/LB
TO BATTERY
CARTRIDGE FUSE
ENGINE CONTROLLER
START TEST NS-10B.
IS THE VEHICLE AN AS BODY?
YES
CONTINUE TEST NS-10B
NO
REMOVE THE J CARTRIDGE FUSE IN THE POWER DISTRIBUTION CENTER.
INSPECT THE CARTRIDGE FUSE.
IS THE FUSE OK?
NO
PERFORM TEST NS-10C.
YES
USE AN EXTERNAL OHMMETER IN THE FOLLOWING STEP.
TEST BETWEEN ENGINE CONTROLLER CAVITY 3 & THE CARTRIDGE FUSE SOCKET.
IS THE RESISTANCE BELOW 10.0 OHMS?
NO
REPAIR THE OPEN A14 RD/WT WIRE.*
YES
PUT THE DRBII IN VOLTMETER MODE.
PROBE THE J CARTRIDGE FUSE SOCKET
IS VOLTAGE ABOVE 10.0 VOLTS?
NO
REPAIR THE OPEN A14 RD/WT WIRE TO BATTERY (+).*
YES
REPLACE THE ENGINE CONTROLLER.*

* PERFORM VERIFICATION PROCEDURE VER-1

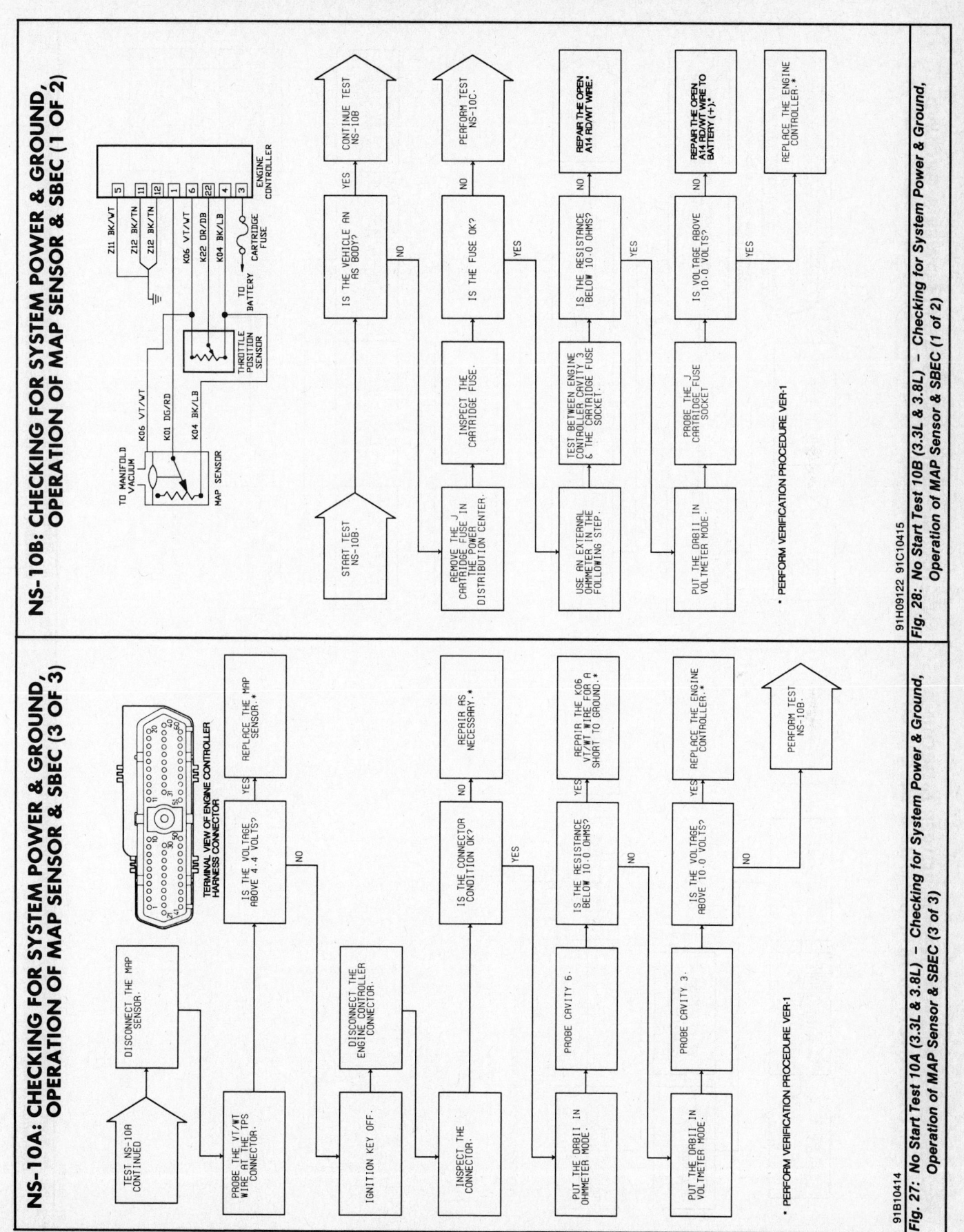

91H09122 91C10415

Fig. 28: No Start Test 10B (3.3L & 3.8L) – Checking for System Power & Ground, Operation of MAP Sensor & SBEC (1 of 2)

1991 ENGINE PERFORMANCE
Self-Diagnostics – 3.3L PFI (Cont.)

NS-10B: CHECKING FOR SYSTEM POWER & GROUND, OPERATION OF MAP SENSOR & SBEC (2 OF 2)

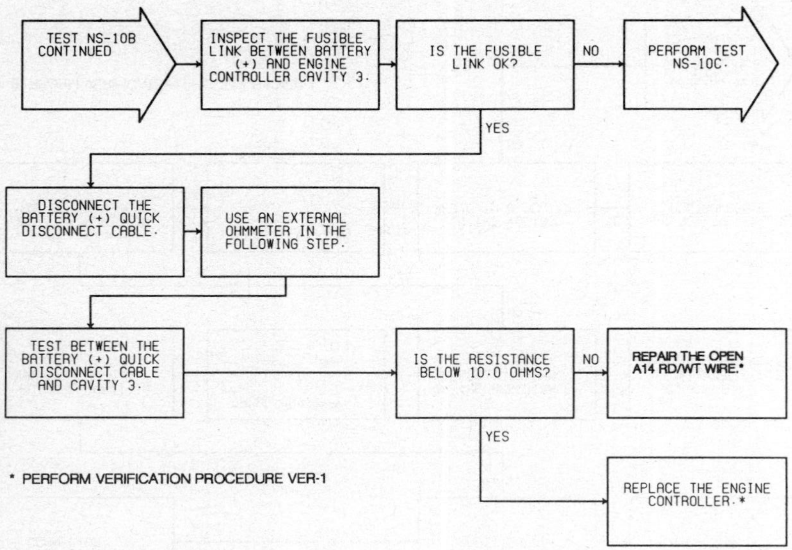
TEST NS-10B CONTINUED
INSPECT THE FUSIBLE LINK BETWEEN BATTERY (+) AND ENGINE CONTROLLER CAVITY 3.
IS THE FUSIBLE LINK OK?
NO
PERFORM TEST NS-10C.
YES
DISCONNECT THE BATTERY (+) QUICK DISCONNECT CABLE.
USE AN EXTERNAL OHMMETER IN THE FOLLOWING STEP.
TEST BETWEEN THE BATTERY (+) QUICK DISCONNECT CABLE AND CAVITY 3.
IS THE RESISTANCE BELOW 10.0 OHMS?
NO
REPAIR THE OPEN A14 RD/WT WIRE.*
YES
REPLACE THE ENGINE CONTROLLER.*

* PERFORM VERIFICATION PROCEDURE VER-1

91D10416

Fig. 29: No Start Test 10B (3.3L & 3.8L) – Checking for System Power & Ground, Operation of MAP Sensor & SBEC (2 of 2)

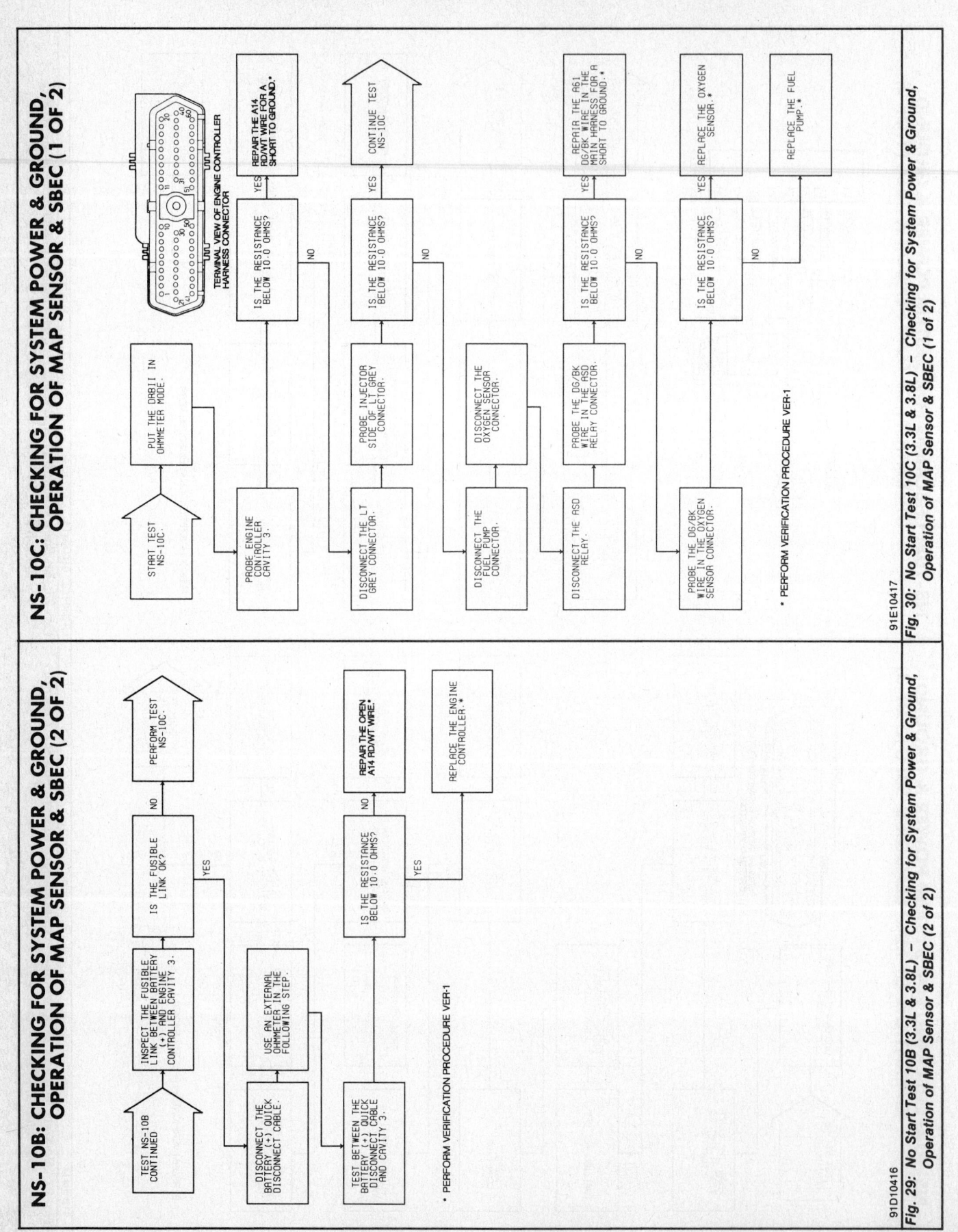

NS-10C: CHECKING FOR SYSTEM POWER & GROUND, OPERATION OF MAP SENSOR & SBEC (1 OF 2)

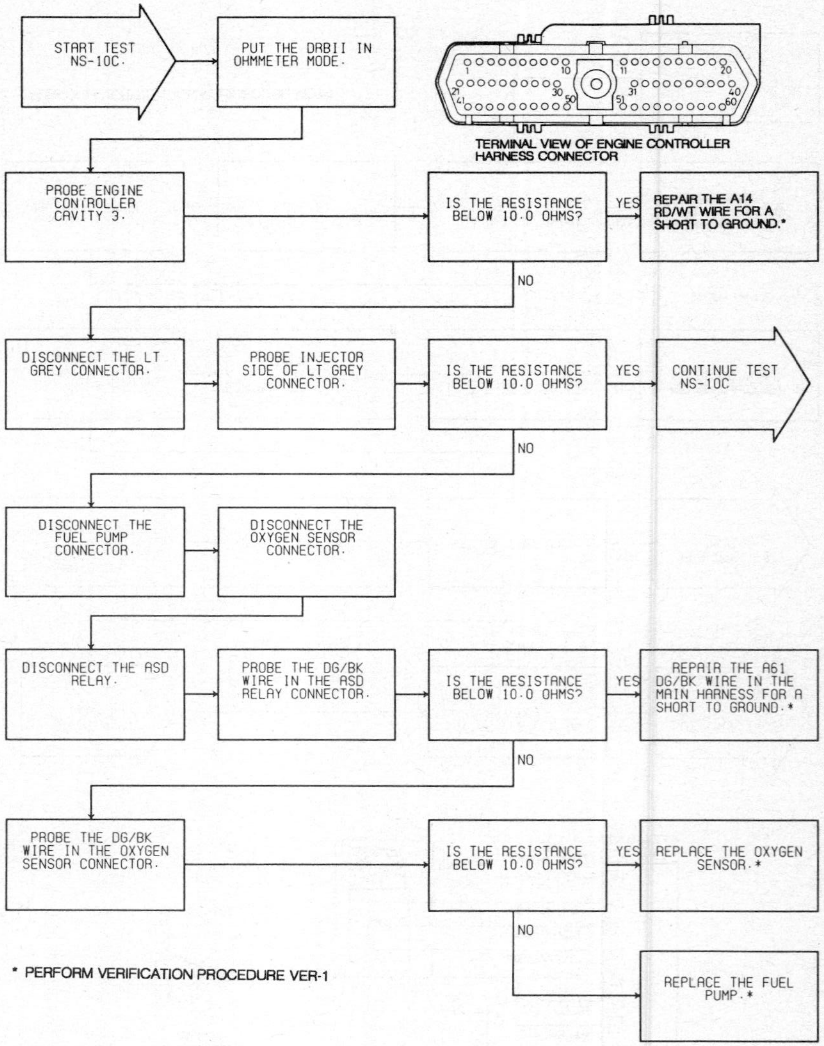
START TEST NS-10C.
PUT THE DRBII IN OHMMETER MODE.
1
10
11
20
21
30
31
40
41
50
51
60
TERMINAL VIEW OF ENGINE CONTROLLER HARNESS CONNECTOR
PROBE ENGINE CONTROLLER CAVITY 3.
IS THE RESISTANCE BELOW 10.0 OHMS?
YES
REPAIR THE A14 RD/WT WIRE FOR A SHORT TO GROUND.*
NO
DISCONNECT THE LT GREY CONNECTOR.
PROBE INJECTOR SIDE OF LT GREY CONNECTOR.
IS THE RESISTANCE BELOW 10.0 OHMS?
YES
CONTINUE TEST NS-10C
NO
DISCONNECT THE FUEL PUMP CONNECTOR.
DISCONNECT THE OXYGEN SENSOR CONNECTOR.
DISCONNECT THE ASD RELAY.
PROBE THE DG/BK WIRE IN THE ASD RELAY CONNECTOR.
IS THE RESISTANCE BELOW 10.0 OHMS?
YES
REPAIR THE A61 DG/BK WIRE IN THE MAIN HARNESS FOR A SHORT TO GROUND.*
NO
PROBE THE DG/BK WIRE IN THE OXYGEN SENSOR CONNECTOR.
IS THE RESISTANCE BELOW 10.0 OHMS?
YES
REPLACE THE OXYGEN SENSOR.*
NO
REPLACE THE FUEL PUMP.*

* PERFORM VERIFICATION PROCEDURE VER-1

91E10417

Fig. 30: No Start Test 10C (3.3L & 3.8L) – Checking for System Power & Ground, Operation of MAP Sensor & SBEC (1 of 2)

NS-10C: CHECKING FOR SYSTEM POWER & GROUND, OPERATION OF MAP SENSOR & SBEC (2 OF 2)

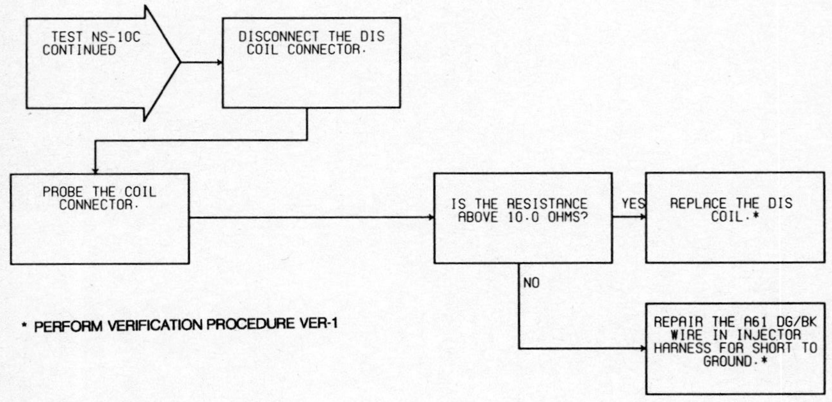
TEST NS-10C CONTINUED
DISCONNECT THE DIS COIL CONNECTOR.
PROBE THE COIL CONNECTOR.
IS THE RESISTANCE ABOVE 10.0 OHMS?
YES
REPLACE THE DIS COIL.*
NO
REPAIR THE A61 DG/BK WIRE IN INJECTOR HARNESS FOR SHORT TO GROUND.*
* PERFORM VERIFICATION PROCEDURE VER-1

91F10418

Fig. 31: No Start Test 10C (3.3L & 3.8L) – Checking for System Power & Ground, Operation of MAP Sensor & SBEC (2 of 2)

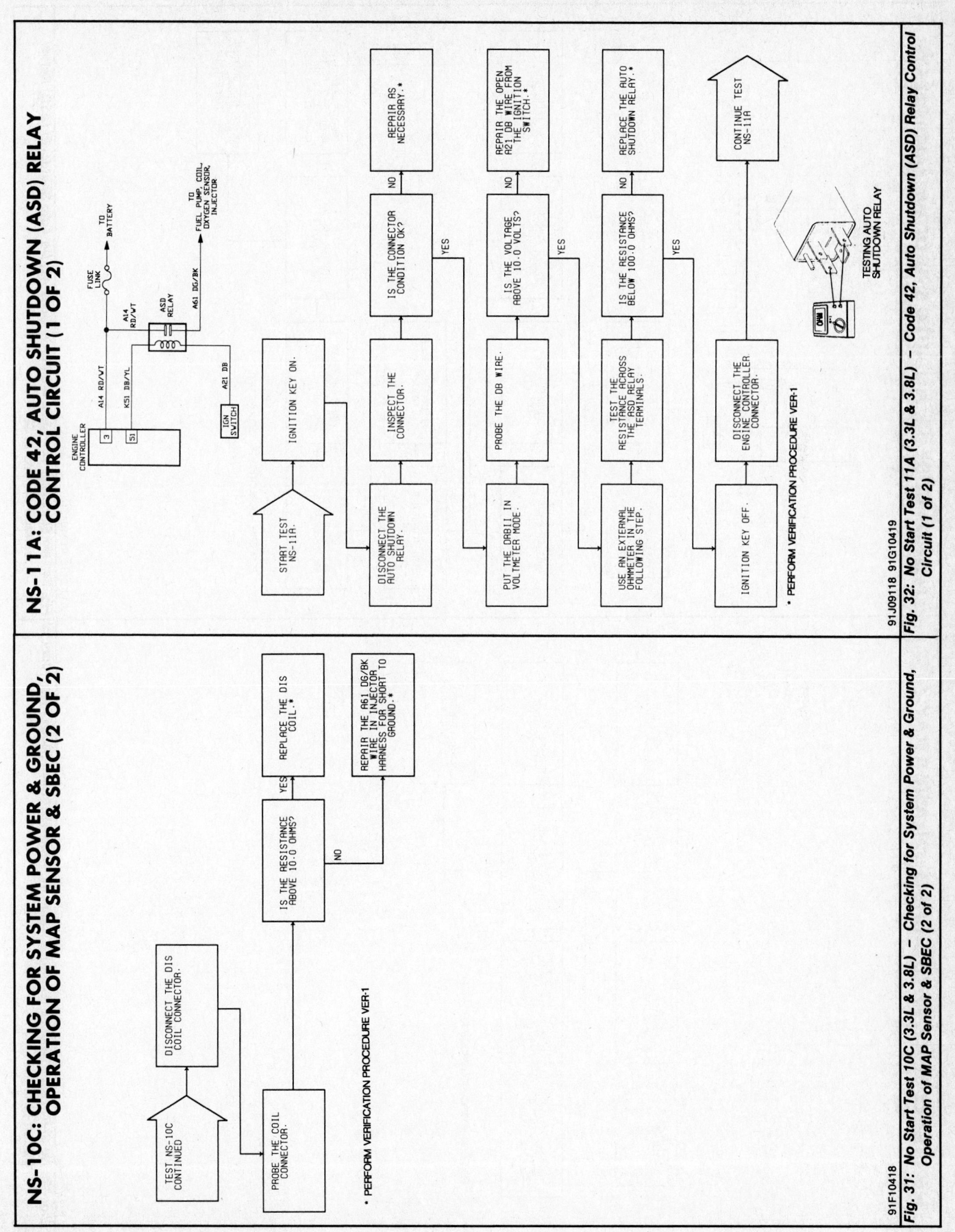

NS-11A: CODE 42, AUTO SHUTDOWN (ASD) RELAY CONTROL CIRCUIT (1 OF 2)

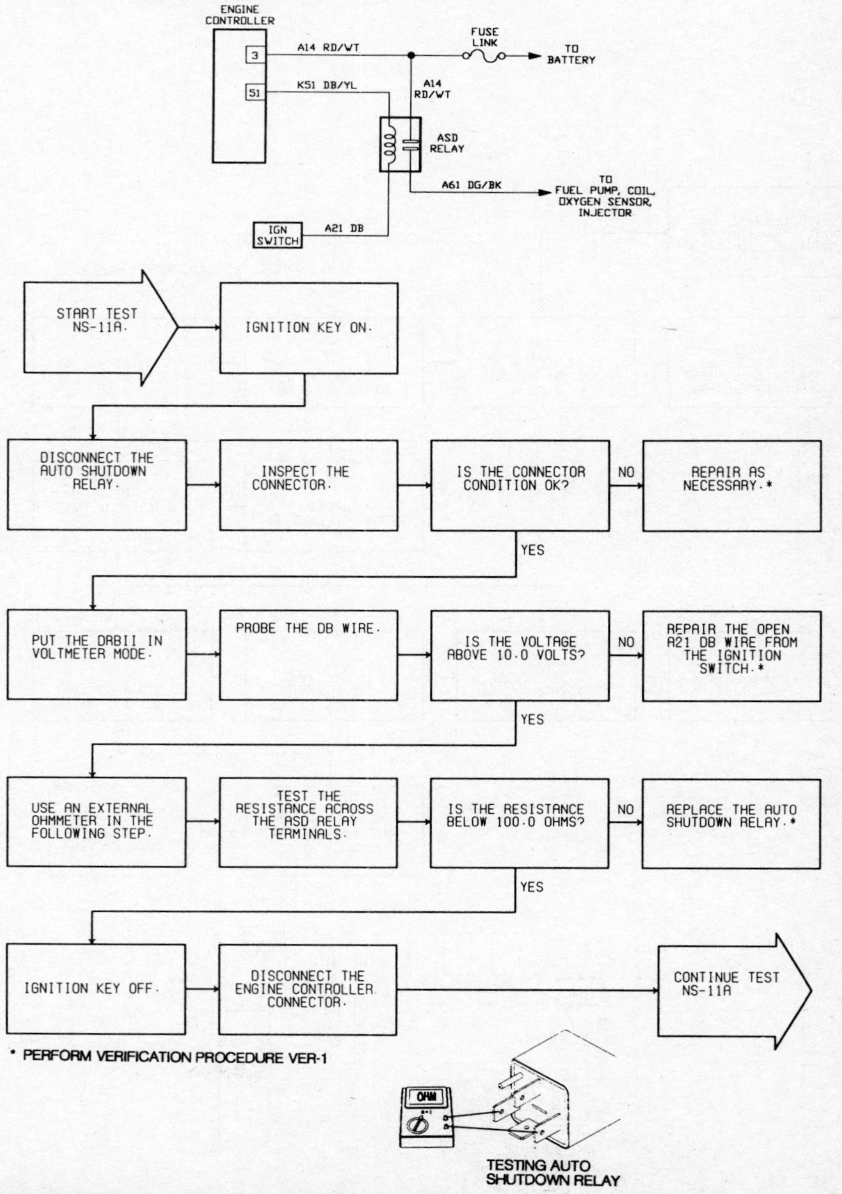
ENGINE CONTROLLER
3
51
A14 RD/WT
K51 DB/YL
FUSE LINK
TO BATTERY
A14 RD/WT
ASD RELAY
A61 DG/BK
TO FUEL PUMP, COIL, OXYGEN SENSOR, INJECTOR
IGN SWITCH
A21 DB
START TEST NS-11A.
IGNITION KEY ON.
DISCONNECT THE AUTO SHUTDOWN RELAY.
INSPECT THE CONNECTOR.
IS THE CONNECTOR CONDITION OK?
NO
REPAIR AS NECESSARY.*
YES
PUT THE DRBII IN VOLTMETER MODE.
PROBE THE DB WIRE.
IS THE VOLTAGE ABOVE 10.0 VOLTS?
NO
REPAIR THE OPEN A21 DB WIRE FROM THE IGNITION SWITCH.*
YES
USE AN EXTERNAL OHMMETER IN THE FOLLOWING STEP.
TEST THE RESISTANCE ACROSS THE ASD RELAY TERMINALS.
IS THE RESISTANCE BELOW 100.0 OHMS?
NO
REPLACE THE AUTO SHUTDOWN RELAY.*
YES
IGNITION KEY OFF.
DISCONNECT THE ENGINE CONTROLLER CONNECTOR.
CONTINUE TEST NS-11A
* PERFORM VERIFICATION PROCEDURE VER-1
OHM
TESTING AUTO SHUTDOWN RELAY

91J09118 91G10419

Fig. 32: No Start Test 11A (3.3L & 3.8L) – Code 42, Auto Shutdown (ASD) Relay Control Circuit (1 of 2)

1991 ENGINE PERFORMANCE
Self-Diagnostics – 3.3L PFI (Cont.)

NS-11A: CODE 42, AUTO SHUTDOWN (ASD) RELAY CONTROL CIRCUIT (2 OF 2)

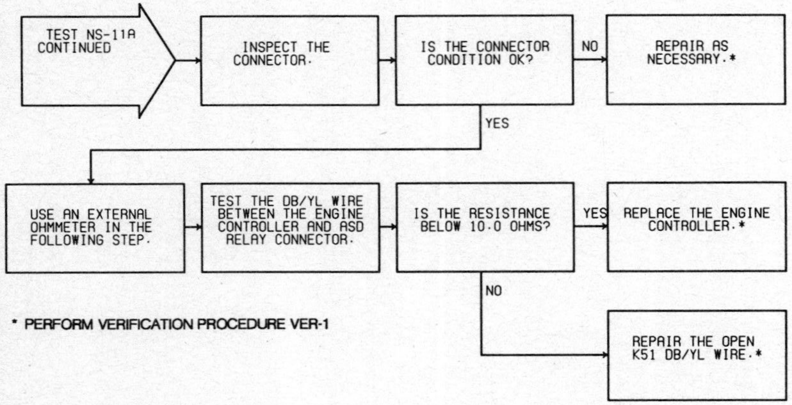
TEST NS-11A CONTINUED
INSPECT THE CONNECTOR.
IS THE CONNECTOR CONDITION OK?
NO
REPAIR AS NECESSARY.*
YES
USE AN EXTERNAL OHMMETER IN THE FOLLOWING STEP.
TEST THE DB/YL WIRE BETWEEN THE ENGINE CONTROLLER AND ASD RELAY CONNECTOR.
IS THE RESISTANCE BELOW 10.0 OHMS?
YES
REPLACE THE ENGINE CONTROLLER.*
NO
REPAIR THE OPEN K51 DB/YL WIRE.*
* PERFORM VERIFICATION PROCEDURE VER-1

91J10420

Fig. 33: No Start Test 11A (3.3L & 3.8L) – Code 42, Auto Shutdown (ASD) Relay Control Circuit (2 of 2)

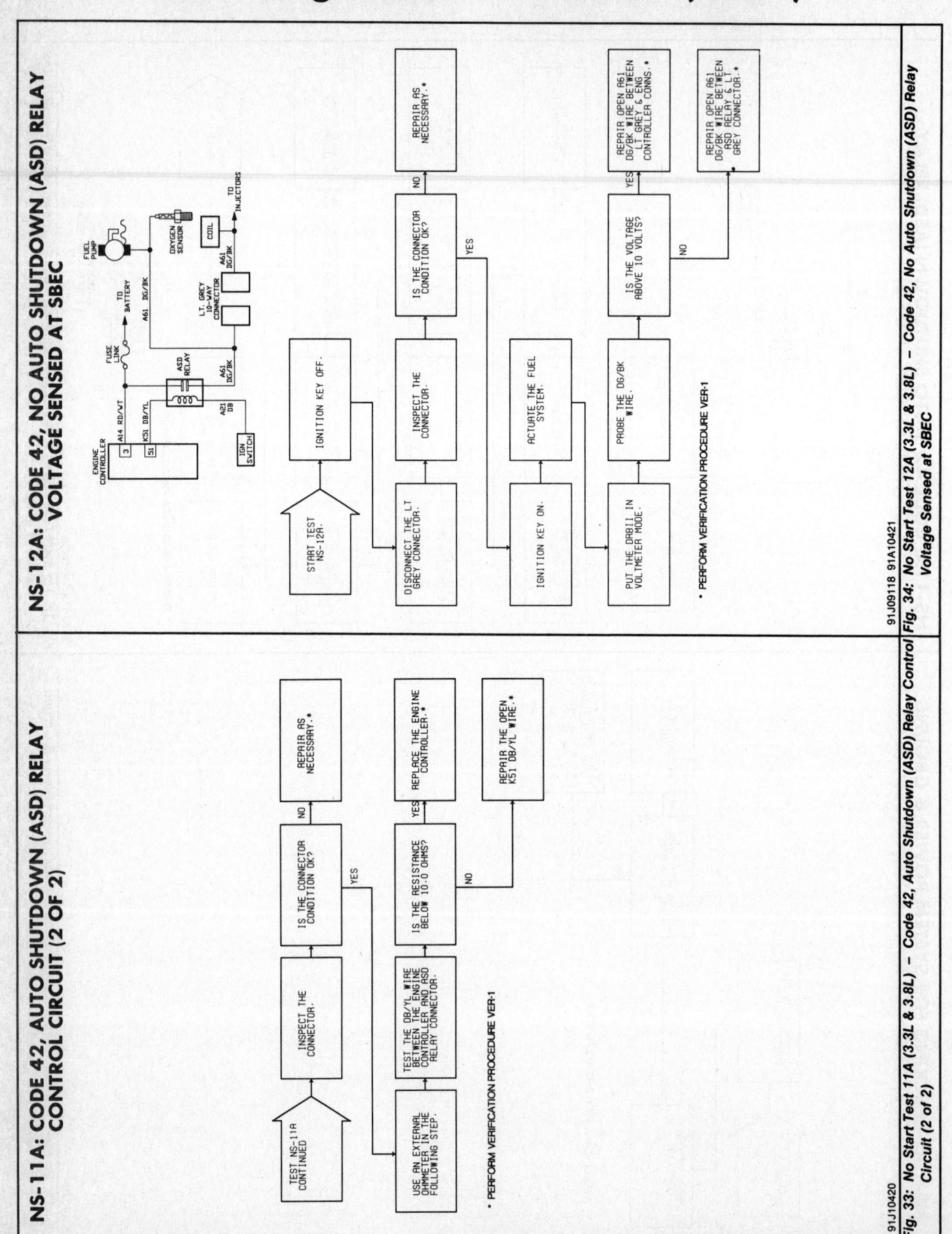

NS-12A: CODE 42, NO AUTO SHUTDOWN (ASD) RELAY VOLTAGE SENSED AT SBEC

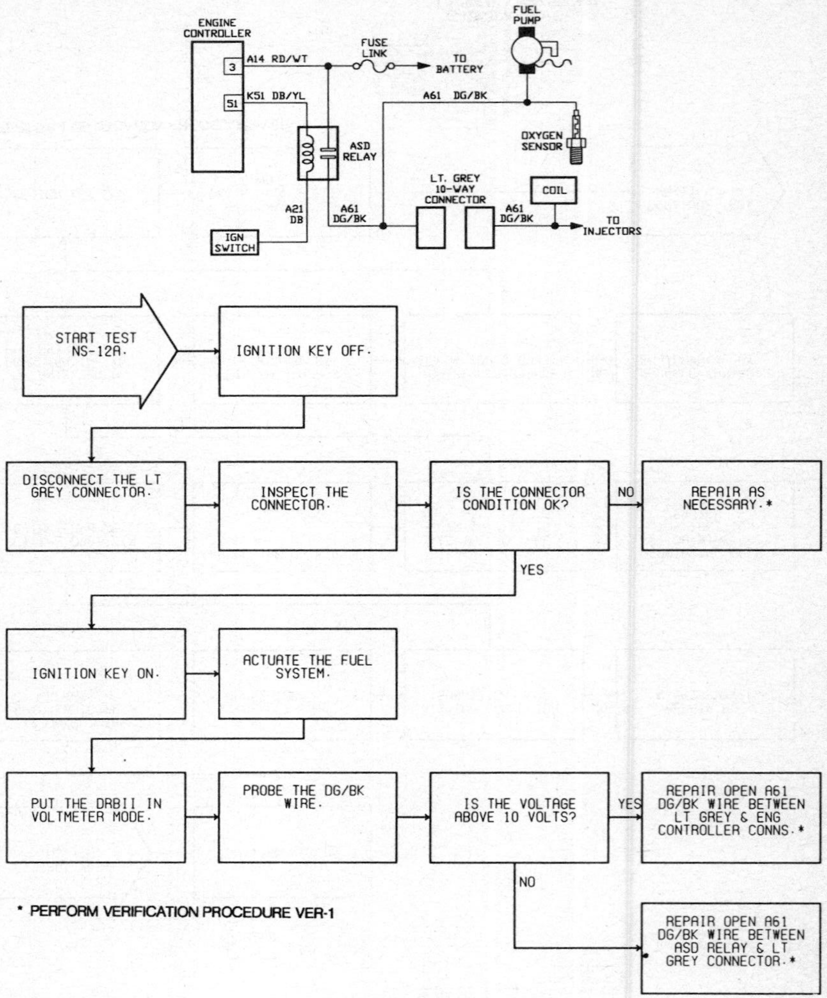
ENGINE CONTROLLER
3
51
A14 RD/WT
K51 DB/YL
FUSE LINK
TO BATTERY
FUEL PUMP
A61 DG/BK
OXYGEN SENSOR
ASD RELAY
A21 DB
IGN SWITCH
A61 DG/BK
LT. GREY 10-WAY CONNECTOR
COIL
A61 DG/BK
TO INJECTORS
START TEST NS-12A.
IGNITION KEY OFF.
DISCONNECT THE LT GREY CONNECTOR.
INSPECT THE CONNECTOR.
IS THE CONNECTOR CONDITION OK?
NO
REPAIR AS NECESSARY.*
YES
IGNITION KEY ON.
ACTUATE THE FUEL SYSTEM.
PUT THE DRBII IN VOLTMETER MODE.
PROBE THE DG/BK WIRE.
IS THE VOLTAGE ABOVE 10 VOLTS?
YES
REPAIR OPEN A61 DG/BK WIRE BETWEEN LT GREY & ENG CONTROLLER CONNS.*
NO
REPAIR OPEN A61 DG/BK WIRE BETWEEN ASD RELAY & LT GREY CONNECTOR.*
* PERFORM VERIFICATION PROCEDURE VER-1

91J09118 91A10421

Fig. 34: No Start Test 12A (3.3L & 3.8L) – Code 42, No Auto Shutdown (ASD) Relay Voltage Sensed at SBEC

NS-13A: CHECKING IDLE SPEED MOTOR OPERATION (1 OF 2)

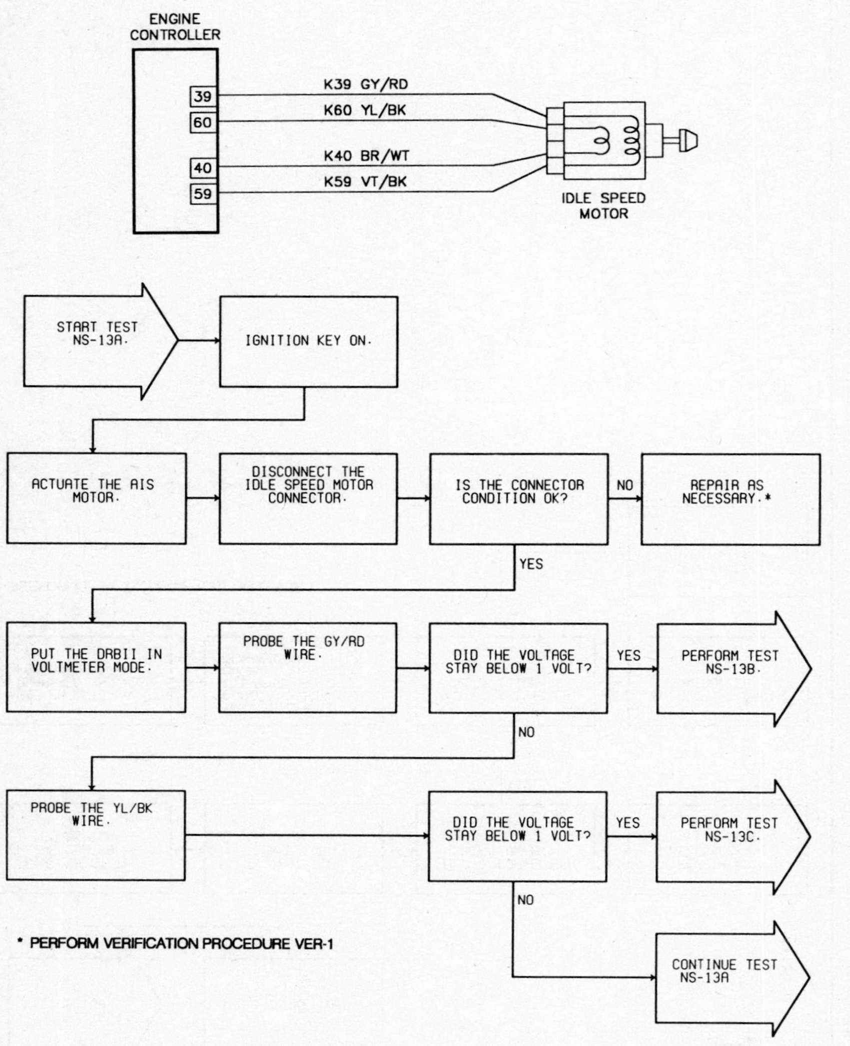
ENGINE CONTROLLER
39
60
40
59
K39 GY/RD
K60 YL/BK
K40 BR/WT
K59 VT/BK
IDLE SPEED MOTOR
START TEST NS-13A.
IGNITION KEY ON.
ACTUATE THE AIS MOTOR.
DISCONNECT THE IDLE SPEED MOTOR CONNECTOR.
IS THE CONNECTOR CONDITION OK?
NO
REPAIR AS NECESSARY.*
YES
PUT THE DRBII IN VOLTMETER MODE.
PROBE THE GY/RD WIRE.
DID THE VOLTAGE STAY BELOW 1 VOLT?
YES
PERFORM TEST NS-13B.
NO
PROBE THE YL/BK WIRE.
DID THE VOLTAGE STAY BELOW 1 VOLT?
YES
PERFORM TEST NS-13C.
NO
CONTINUE TEST NS-13A
* PERFORM VERIFICATION PROCEDURE VER-1

91J09123 91B10422

Fig. 35: No Start Test 13A (3.3L & 3.8L) – Checking Idle Speed Motor Operation (1 of 2)

NS-13A: CHECKING IDLE SPEED MOTOR OPERATION (2 OF 2)

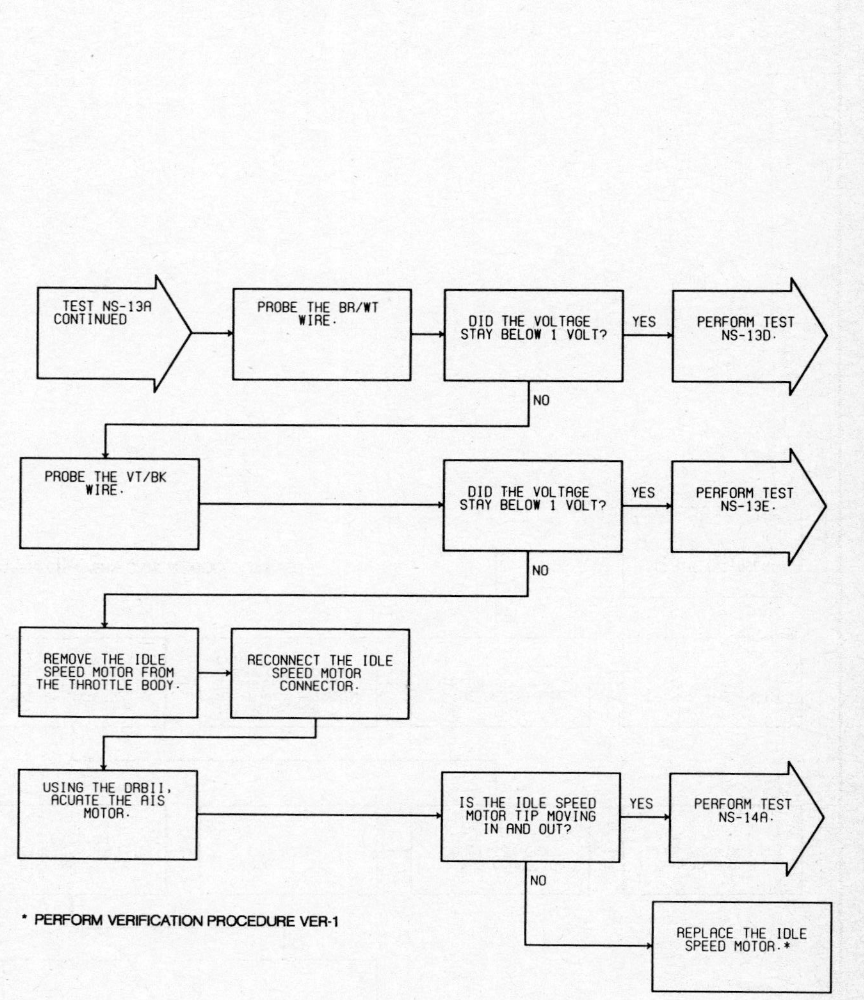
TEST NS-13A CONTINUED
PROBE THE BR/WT WIRE.
DID THE VOLTAGE STAY BELOW 1 VOLT?
YES
PERFORM TEST NS-13D.
NO
PROBE THE VT/BK WIRE.
DID THE VOLTAGE STAY BELOW 1 VOLT?
YES
PERFORM TEST NS-13E.
NO
REMOVE THE IDLE SPEED MOTOR FROM THE THROTTLE BODY.
RECONNECT THE IDLE SPEED MOTOR CONNECTOR.
USING THE DRBII, ACUATE THE AIS MOTOR.
IS THE IDLE SPEED MOTOR TIP MOVING IN AND OUT?
YES
PERFORM TEST NS-14A.
NO
REPLACE THE IDLE SPEED MOTOR.*
* PERFORM VERIFICATION PROCEDURE VER-1

91C10423

Fig. 36: No Start Test 13A (3.3L & 3.8L) – Checking Idle Speed Motor Operation (2 of 2)

NS-13B: CHECKING IDLE SPEED MOTOR OPERATION

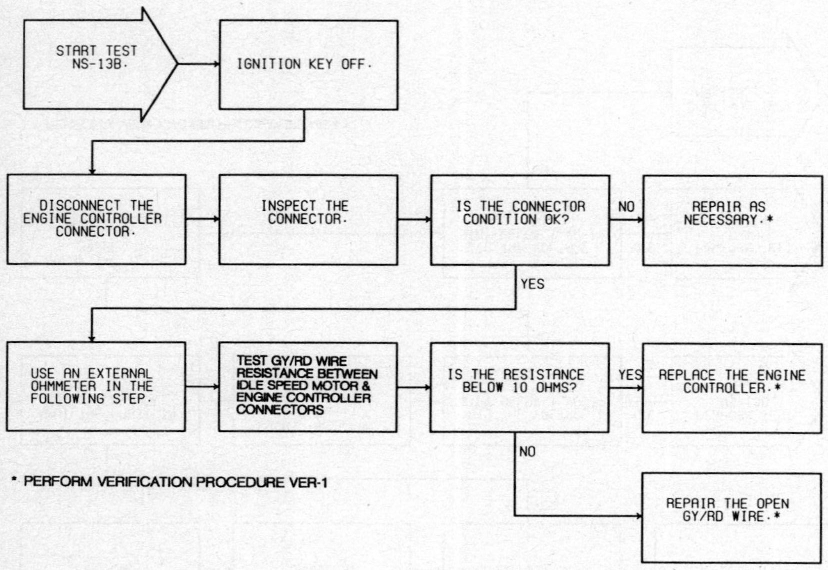
START TEST NS-13B.
IGNITION KEY OFF.
DISCONNECT THE ENGINE CONTROLLER CONNECTOR.
INSPECT THE CONNECTOR.
IS THE CONNECTOR CONDITION OK?
NO
REPAIR AS NECESSARY.*
YES
USE AN EXTERNAL OHMMETER IN THE FOLLOWING STEP.
TEST GY/RD WIRE RESISTANCE BETWEEN IDLE SPEED MOTOR & ENGINE CONTROLLER CONNECTORS
IS THE RESISTANCE BELOW 10 OHMS?
YES
REPLACE THE ENGINE CONTROLLER.*
NO
REPAIR THE OPEN GY/RD WIRE.*

* PERFORM VERIFICATION PROCEDURE VER-1

91D10424

Fig. 37: No Start Test 13B (3.3L & 3.8L) – Checking Idle Speed Motor Operation

NS-13C: CHECKING IDLE SPEED MOTOR OPERATION

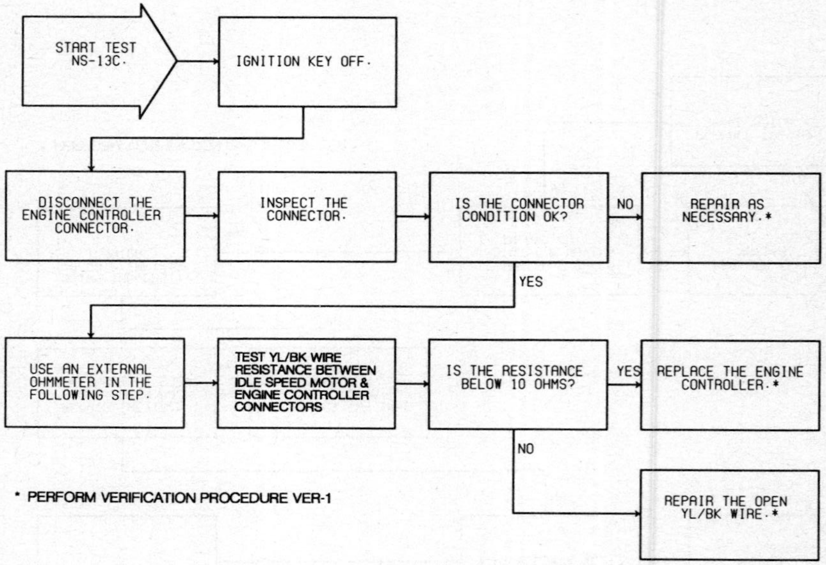
START TEST NS-13C.
IGNITION KEY OFF.
DISCONNECT THE ENGINE CONTROLLER CONNECTOR.
INSPECT THE CONNECTOR.
IS THE CONNECTOR CONDITION OK?
NO
REPAIR AS NECESSARY.*
YES
USE AN EXTERNAL OHMMETER IN THE FOLLOWING STEP.
TEST YL/BK WIRE RESISTANCE BETWEEN IDLE SPEED MOTOR & ENGINE CONTROLLER CONNECTORS
IS THE RESISTANCE BELOW 10 OHMS?
YES
REPLACE THE ENGINE CONTROLLER.*
NO
REPAIR THE OPEN YL/BK WIRE.*

* PERFORM VERIFICATION PROCEDURE VER-1

91E10425

Fig. 38: No Start Test 13C (3.3L & 3.8L) – Checking Idle Speed Motor Operation

NS-13D: CHECKING IDLE SPEED MOTOR OPERATION

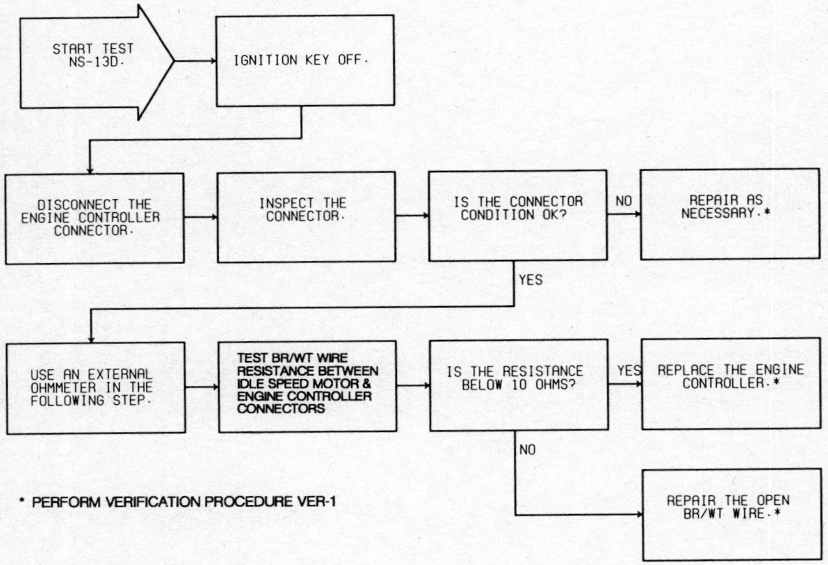
START TEST NS-13D.
IGNITION KEY OFF.
DISCONNECT THE ENGINE CONTROLLER CONNECTOR.
INSPECT THE CONNECTOR.
IS THE CONNECTOR CONDITION OK?
NO
REPAIR AS NECESSARY.*
YES
USE AN EXTERNAL OHMMETER IN THE FOLLOWING STEP.
TEST BR/WT WIRE RESISTANCE BETWEEN IDLE SPEED MOTOR & ENGINE CONTROLLER CONNECTORS
IS THE RESISTANCE BELOW 10 OHMS?
YES
REPLACE THE ENGINE CONTROLLER.*
NO
REPAIR THE OPEN BR/WT WIRE.*
* PERFORM VERIFICATION PROCEDURE VER-1

91F10426

Fig. 39: No Start Test 13D (3.3L & 3.8L) – Checking Idle Speed Motor Operation

NS-13E: CHECKING IDLE SPEED MOTOR OPERATION

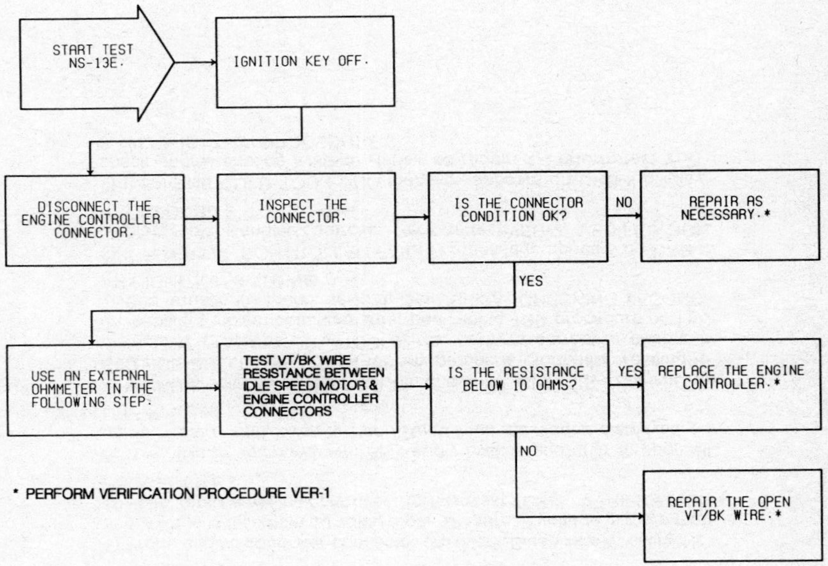
START TEST NS-13E.
IGNITION KEY OFF.
DISCONNECT THE ENGINE CONTROLLER CONNECTOR.
INSPECT THE CONNECTOR.
IS THE CONNECTOR CONDITION OK?
NO
REPAIR AS NECESSARY.*
YES
USE AN EXTERNAL OHMMETER IN THE FOLLOWING STEP.
TEST VT/BK WIRE RESISTANCE BETWEEN IDLE SPEED MOTOR & ENGINE CONTROLLER CONNECTORS
IS THE RESISTANCE BELOW 10 OHMS?
YES
REPLACE THE ENGINE CONTROLLER.*
NO
REPAIR THE OPEN VT/BK WIRE.*
* PERFORM VERIFICATION PROCEDURE VER-1

91G10427

Fig. 40: No Start Test 13E (3.3L & 3.8L) – Checking Idle Speed Motor Operation

NS-14A: PERFORMING NO FAULT CODE MECHANICAL TEST

At this point in the start-and-stall test procedure, if it is determined that all engine control systems are operating as designed and are not the cause of a no start-and-stall problem, the following additional items should be checked as possible causes:

- Check if any MITCHELL TECHNICAL SERVICE BULLETINS (TSB'S) apply to vehicle.
- Check engine compression.
- Check for exhaust system restriction.
- Check camshaft and crankshaft sprockets.
- Check valve timing.
- Check torque converter stall speed.
- Check secondary ignition circuit for abnormal scope pattern.
- Check for fuel contamination.
- Ensure engine vacuum is at least 13 in. Hg.
- Ensure PCV system is functioning properly.
- Ensure injector control wire is connected to correct fuel injector.

Fig. 41: No Start Test 14A (3.3L & 3.8L) – Performing No Fault Code Mechanical Test

DR-1A: CHECKING SYSTEM FOR FAULTS

NOTE: Battery must be fully charged and at rated capacity before performing any driveability test procedure. If vehicle starts and stalls repeatedly, perform test NS-2A: CHECKING THEFT ALARM STATUS & POWER TO ENGINE CONTROLLER & MAP SENSOR.

1) Connect DRB-II to engine diagnostic connector. Read fault messages. If DRB-II displays fault messages, go to DR-1B: DRB-II FAULT MESSAGES. Go to step **9)** if DRB-II displays ENGINE COLD TOO LONG. If DRB-II displays INTERNAL CONTROLLER FAILURE, go to step **8)**. If DRB-II displays NO FAULTS, go to next step.

2) If NO FAULTS message appears on DRB-II display, start engine. Allow engine to reach normal operating temperature. Set engine speed manually (DO NOT use DRB-II to set speed) to 2000 RPM for about 10 seconds. Return engine to idle.

3) If vehicle is not equipped with A/C, go to step **5)**. If vehicle is equipped with A/C, put A/C fan on low speed. Turn A/C on. If engine stalls when A/C is turned on, turn ignition switch off.

4) Disconnect engine controller connector. Inspect engine controller connector for corroded or loose terminals. Repair as required. Turn ignition switch on. Put DRB-II in voltmeter mode.

5) Probe engine controller connector DB (Dark/Blue) wire at cavity No. 9. If voltage is less than 10 volts, repair DB wire. If voltage is more than 10 volts, replace engine controller. Perform test VER-2: VERIFICATION PROCEDURE 2.

6) If vehicle is equipped with A/T, apply brakes and shift through all gears. Return shift lever to Park. Read fault messages displayed on DRB-II.

7) If DRB-II still shows NO FAULTS, check MITCHELL'S TECHNICAL SERVICE BULLETINS (TSBs) for any pertinent information relating to driveability problems. If a TSB exists, perform corrective action. If driveability problem continues after performing TSB procedure or if no TSB information is found, perform test DR-33A: CHECKING SECONDARY IGNITION & TIMING.

8) If INTERNAL CONTROLLER FAILURE message appears on DRB-II display, replace engine controller. Perform test VER-2: VERIFICATION PROCEDURE 2.

9) If ENGINE COLD TOO LONG message appears on DRB-II display, check engine cooling system. Repair as required. Perform test VER-3: VERIFICATION PROCEDURE 3.

Fig. 42: Driveability Test 1A (3.3L & 3.8L) – Checking System for Faults

DR-1B: DRB-II FAULT MESSAGES

Using the DRB-II FAULT MESSAGES table, select the fault message and corresponding test. Correct all hard fault messages before proceeding to intermittent fault message.

DRB-II FAULT MESSAGES

DRB-II Message	[1] Hard Fault	[2] Intermittent Fault
A/C Clutch Relay Circuit [3]	DR-25A	DR-46A
A/C Clutch Relay Circuit [4]	DR-24A	DR-46A
Automatic Idle Motor Circuits	DR-14A	DR-48A
Charge Temperature Sensor Voltage High	DR-10A	DR-47A
Charge Temperature Sensor Voltage Low	DR-11A	DR-47A
Controller Failure EMR Miles Not Stored	DR-32A	DR-32A
Coolant Sensor Voltage Too High	DR-8A	DR-47A
Coolant Sensor Voltage Too Low	DR-9A	DR-47A
EGR Solenoid Circuit	DR-22A	DR-46A
EGR System Failure	DR-23A	DR-23A
Injector Coil No. 1 Primary Circuit	DR-29A	DR-29A
Injector Coil No. 2 Primary Circuit	DR-30A	DR-30A
Injector Coil No. 3 Primary Circuit	DR-31A	DR-31A
Injector No. 1 Control Circuit	DR-16A	DR-49A
Injector No. 2 Control Circuit	DR-18A	DR-49A
Injector No. 3 Control Circuit	DR-20A	DR-49A
Injector No. 1 Peak Current Not Reached	DR-15A	DR-49A
Injector No. 2 Peak Current Not Reached	DR-17A	DR-49A
Injector No. 3 Peak Current Not Reached	DR-19A	DR-49A
MAP Voltage Too High	DR-4A	DR47-A
MAP Voltage Too Low	DR-3A	DR-47A
No ASD Relay Voltage Sense At Controller	DR-28A	DR-28A
No Change In MAP From Start To Run	DR2A	DR-47A
No Vehicle Speed Signal	DR-5A	DR-5A
O_2 Signal Shorted To Voltage	DR-7A	DR-7A
O_2 Signal Stays Above Center (Rich)	DR-33A	DR-33A
O_2 Signal Stays At Center	DR-6A	DR-6A
O_2 Signal Stays Below Center (Lean)	DR-33A	DR-33A
Purge Solenoid Circuit	DR-21A	DR-46A
Radiator Fan Relay Circuit [3]	DR-27A	DR-46A
Radiator Fan Relay Circuit [4]	DR-26A	DR-46A
Throttle Position Sensor Voltage High	DR-12A	DR-47A
Throttle Position Sensor Voltage Low	DR-13A	DR-47A

[1] – Key counter is "0".
[2] – Key counter is more than "0".
[3] – AC & AS bodies.
[4] – AS body.

Fig. 43: Driveability Test 1B (3.3L & 3.8L) – DRB-II Fault Messages

DR-2A: CODE 13, NO CHANGE IN MAP FROM START TO RUN

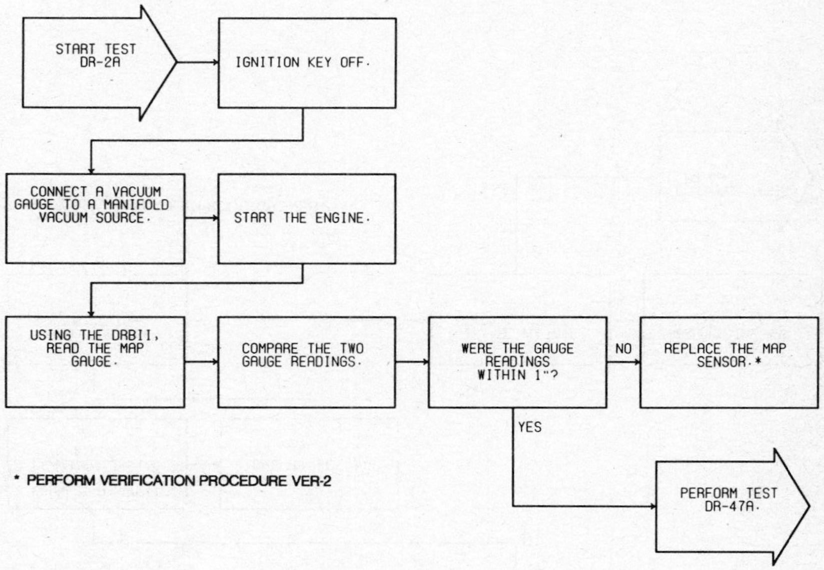
START TEST DR-2A
IGNITION KEY OFF.
CONNECT A VACUUM GAUGE TO A MANIFOLD VACUUM SOURCE.
START THE ENGINE.
USING THE DRBII, READ THE MAP GAUGE.
COMPARE THE TWO GAUGE READINGS.
WERE THE GAUGE READINGS WITHIN 1"?
NO
REPLACE THE MAP SENSOR.*
YES
PERFORM TEST DR-47A.
* PERFORM VERIFICATION PROCEDURE VER-2

91I10429

Fig. 44: Driveability Test 2A (3.3L & 3.8L) – Code 13, No Change in MAP from Start to Run

1991 ENGINE PERFORMANCE
Self-Diagnostics – 3.3L PFI (Cont.)

DR-3A: CODE 14, MAP VOLTAGE TOO LOW

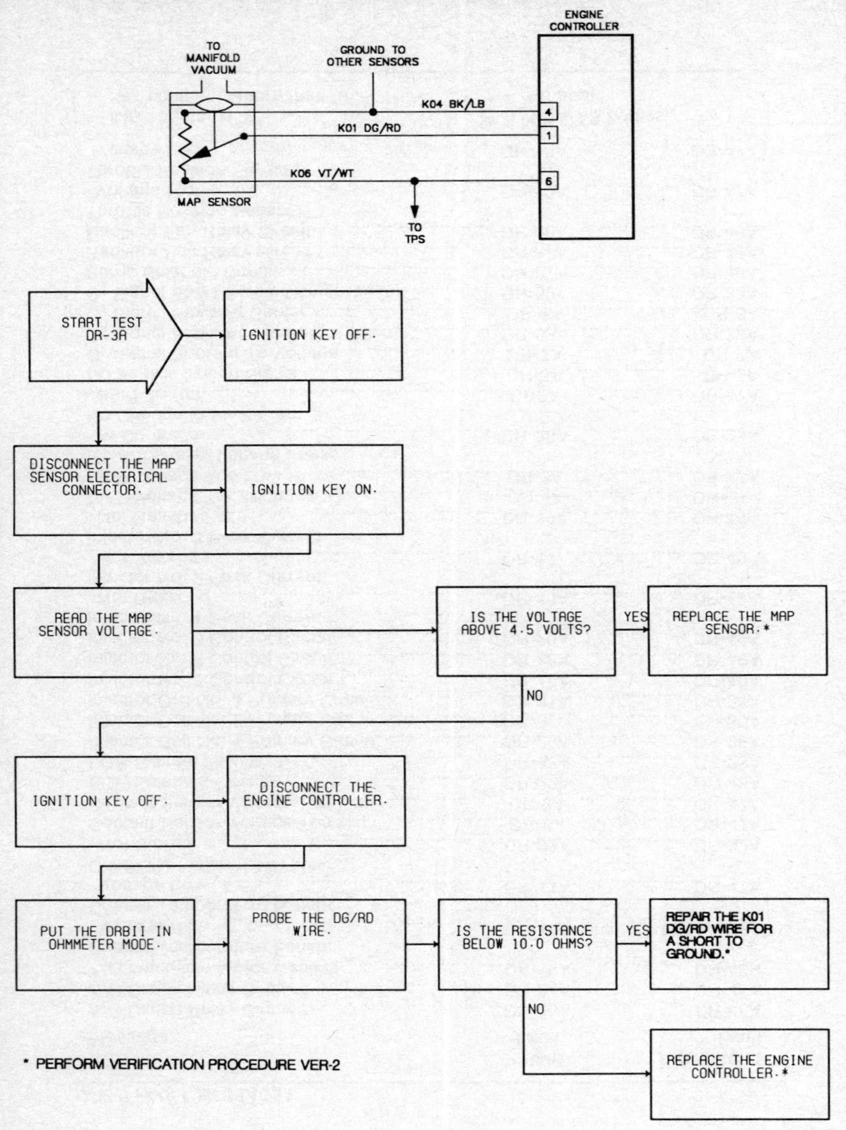
ENGINE CONTROLLER
TO MANIFOLD VACUUM
GROUND TO OTHER SENSORS
K04 BK/LB
K01 DG/RD
K06 VT/WT
4
1
6
MAP SENSOR
TO TPS
START TEST DR-3A
IGNITION KEY OFF.
DISCONNECT THE MAP SENSOR ELECTRICAL CONNECTOR.
IGNITION KEY ON.
READ THE MAP SENSOR VOLTAGE.
IS THE VOLTAGE ABOVE 4.5 VOLTS?
YES
REPLACE THE MAP SENSOR.*
NO
IGNITION KEY OFF.
DISCONNECT THE ENGINE CONTROLLER.
PUT THE DRBII IN OHMMETER MODE.
PROBE THE DG/RD WIRE.
IS THE RESISTANCE BELOW 10.0 OHMS?
YES
REPAIR THE K01 DG/RD WIRE FOR A SHORT TO GROUND.*
NO
REPLACE THE ENGINE CONTROLLER.*
* PERFORM VERIFICATION PROCEDURE VER-2

91H09122 91B10430

Fig. 45: Driveability Test 3A (3.3L & 3.8L) – Code 14, MAP Voltage Too Low

DR-4A: CODE 14, MAP VOLTAGE TOO HIGH (1 OF 2)

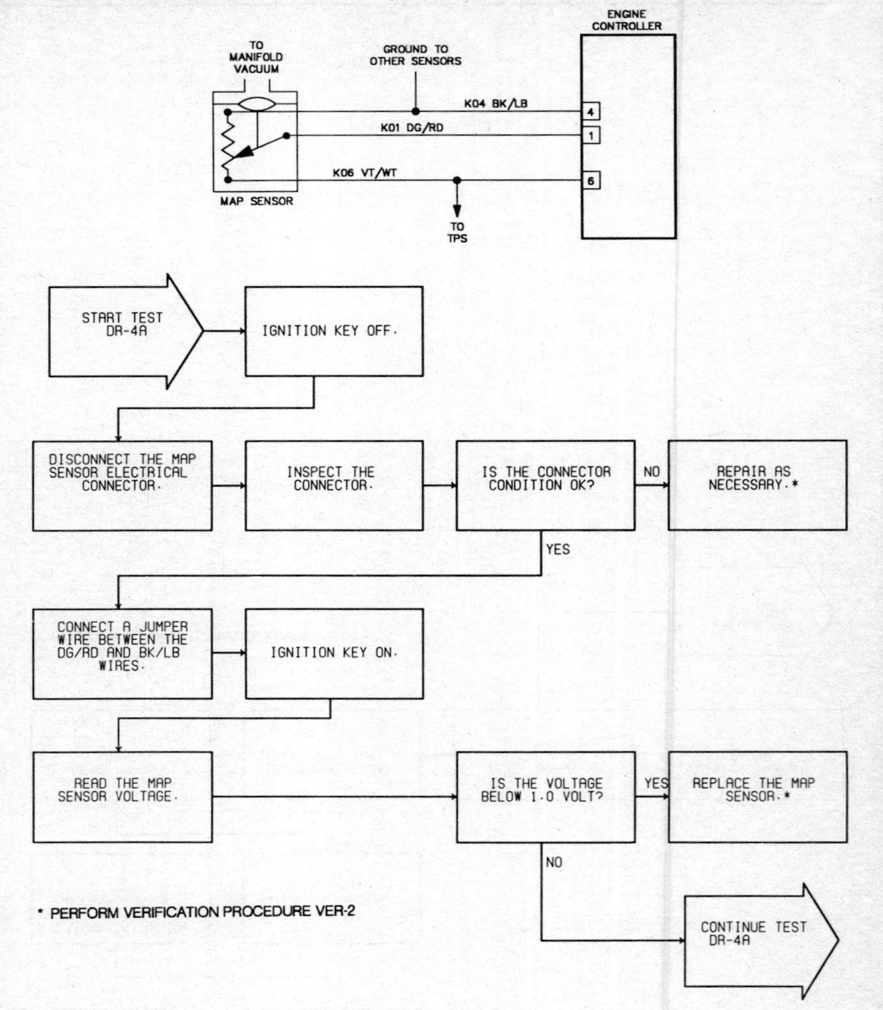
ENGINE CONTROLLER
TO MANIFOLD VACUUM
GROUND TO OTHER SENSORS
K04 BK/LB
K01 DG/RD
K06 VT/WT
4
1
6
MAP SENSOR
TO TPS
START TEST DR-4A
IGNITION KEY OFF.
DISCONNECT THE MAP SENSOR ELECTRICAL CONNECTOR.
INSPECT THE CONNECTOR.
IS THE CONNECTOR CONDITION OK?
NO
REPAIR AS NECESSARY.*
YES
CONNECT A JUMPER WIRE BETWEEN THE DG/RD AND BK/LB WIRES.
IGNITION KEY ON.
READ THE MAP SENSOR VOLTAGE.
IS THE VOLTAGE BELOW 1.0 VOLT?
YES
REPLACE THE MAP SENSOR.*
NO
CONTINUE TEST DR-4A
* PERFORM VERIFICATION PROCEDURE VER-2

91H09122 91C10431

Fig. 46: Driveability Test 4A (3.3L & 3.8L) – Code 14, MAP Voltage Too High (1 of 2)

DR-4A: CODE 14, MAP VOLTAGE TOO HIGH (2 OF 2)

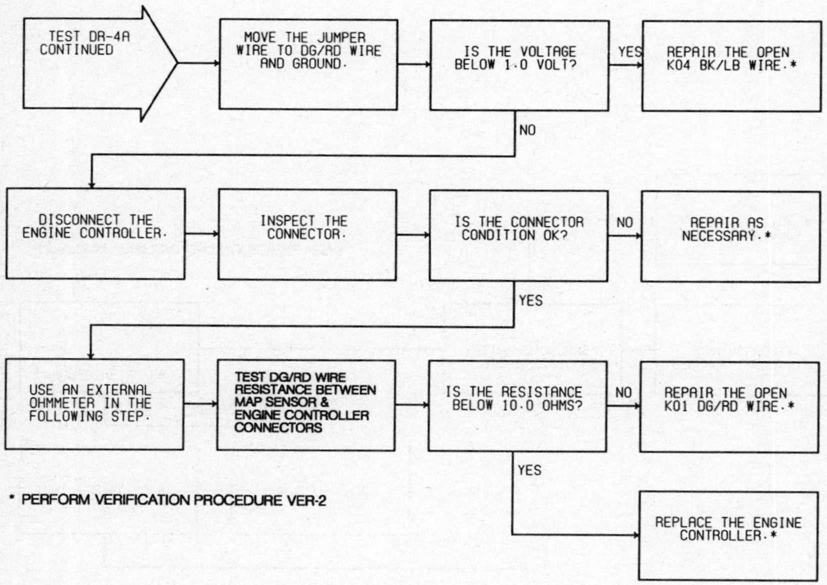
TEST DR-4A CONTINUED
MOVE THE JUMPER WIRE TO DG/RD WIRE AND GROUND.
IS THE VOLTAGE BELOW 1.0 VOLT?
YES
REPAIR THE OPEN K04 BK/LB WIRE.*
NO
DISCONNECT THE ENGINE CONTROLLER.
INSPECT THE CONNECTOR.
IS THE CONNECTOR CONDITION OK?
NO
REPAIR AS NECESSARY.*
YES
USE AN EXTERNAL OHMMETER IN THE FOLLOWING STEP.
TEST DG/RD WIRE RESISTANCE BETWEEN MAP SENSOR & ENGINE CONTROLLER CONNECTORS
IS THE RESISTANCE BELOW 10.0 OHMS?
NO
REPAIR THE OPEN K01 DG/RD WIRE.*
YES
REPLACE THE ENGINE CONTROLLER.*

* PERFORM VERIFICATION PROCEDURE VER-2

91D10432

Fig. 47: Driveability Test 4A (3.3L & 3.8L) – Code 14, MAP Voltage Too High (2 of 2)

DR-5A: CODE 15, NO VEHICLE SPEED SIGNAL (1 OF 3)

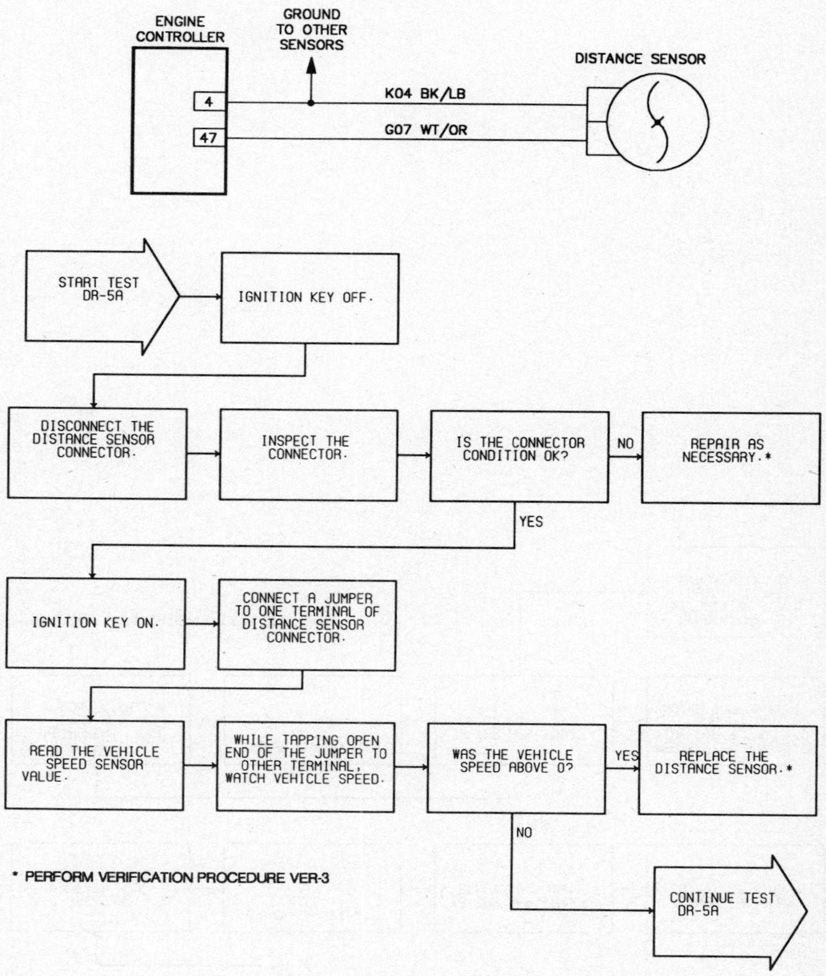
ENGINE CONTROLLER
GROUND TO OTHER SENSORS
DISTANCE SENSOR
4
47
K04 BK/LB
G07 WT/OR
START TEST DR-5A
IGNITION KEY OFF.
DISCONNECT THE DISTANCE SENSOR CONNECTOR.
INSPECT THE CONNECTOR.
IS THE CONNECTOR CONDITION OK?
NO
REPAIR AS NECESSARY.*
YES
IGNITION KEY ON.
CONNECT A JUMPER TO ONE TERMINAL OF DISTANCE SENSOR CONNECTOR.
READ THE VEHICLE SPEED SENSOR VALUE.
WHILE TAPPING OPEN END OF THE JUMPER TO OTHER TERMINAL, WATCH VEHICLE SPEED.
WAS THE VEHICLE SPEED ABOVE 0?
YES
REPLACE THE DISTANCE SENSOR.*
NO
CONTINUE TEST DR-5A

* PERFORM VERIFICATION PROCEDURE VER-3

91B09124 91E10433

Fig. 48: Driveability Test 5A (3.3L & 3.8L) – Code 15, No Vehicle Speed Signal (1 of 3)

DR-5A: CODE 15, NO VEHICLE SPEED SIGNAL (2 OF 3)

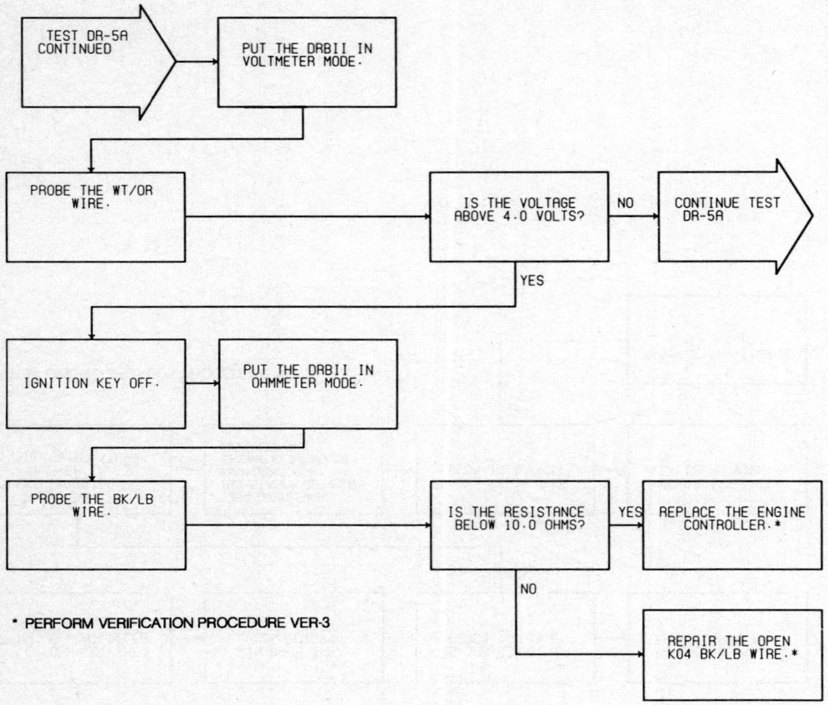
TEST DR-5A CONTINUED
PUT THE DRBII IN VOLTMETER MODE.
PROBE THE WT/OR WIRE.
IS THE VOLTAGE ABOVE 4.0 VOLTS?
NO
CONTINUE TEST DR-5A
YES
IGNITION KEY OFF.
PUT THE DRBII IN OHMMETER MODE.
PROBE THE BK/LB WIRE.
IS THE RESISTANCE BELOW 10.0 OHMS?
YES
REPLACE THE ENGINE CONTROLLER.*
NO
REPAIR THE OPEN K04 BK/LB WIRE.*
* PERFORM VERIFICATION PROCEDURE VER-3

91F10434

Fig. 49: Driveability Test 5A (3.3L & 3.8L) – Code 15, No Vehicle Speed Signal (2 of 3)

DR-5A: CODE 15, NO VEHICLE SPEED SIGNAL (3 OF 3)

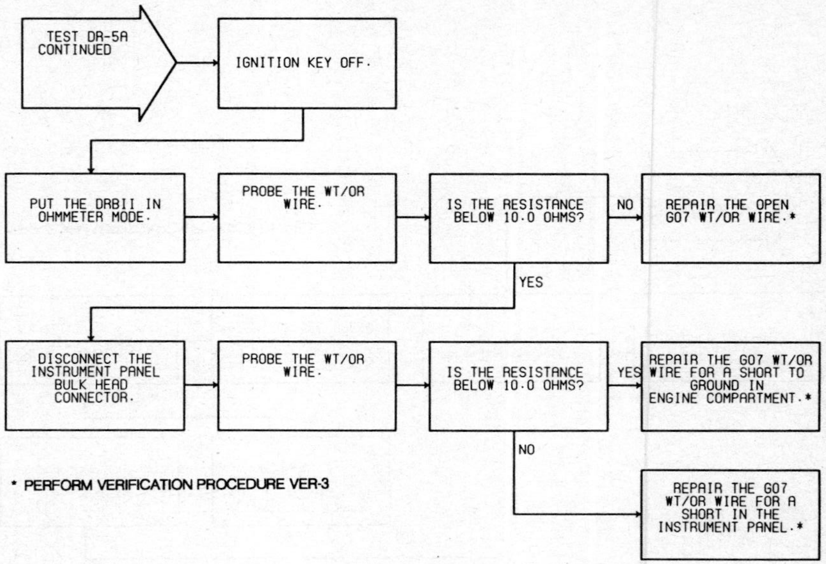
TEST DR-5A CONTINUED
IGNITION KEY OFF.
PUT THE DRBII IN OHMMETER MODE.
PROBE THE WT/OR WIRE.
IS THE RESISTANCE BELOW 10.0 OHMS?
NO
REPAIR THE OPEN G07 WT/OR WIRE.*
YES
DISCONNECT THE INSTRUMENT PANEL BULK HEAD CONNECTOR.
PROBE THE WT/OR WIRE.
IS THE RESISTANCE BELOW 10.0 OHMS?
YES
REPAIR THE G07 WT/OR WIRE FOR A SHORT TO GROUND IN ENGINE COMPARTMENT.*
NO
REPAIR THE G07 WT/OR WIRE FOR A SHORT IN THE INSTRUMENT PANEL.*
* PERFORM VERIFICATION PROCEDURE VER-3

91G10435

Fig. 50: Driveability Test 5A (3.3L & 3.8L) – Code 15, No Vehicle Speed Signal (3 of 3)

DR-6A: CODE 21, O_2 SIGNAL STAYS AT CENTER (1 OF 2)

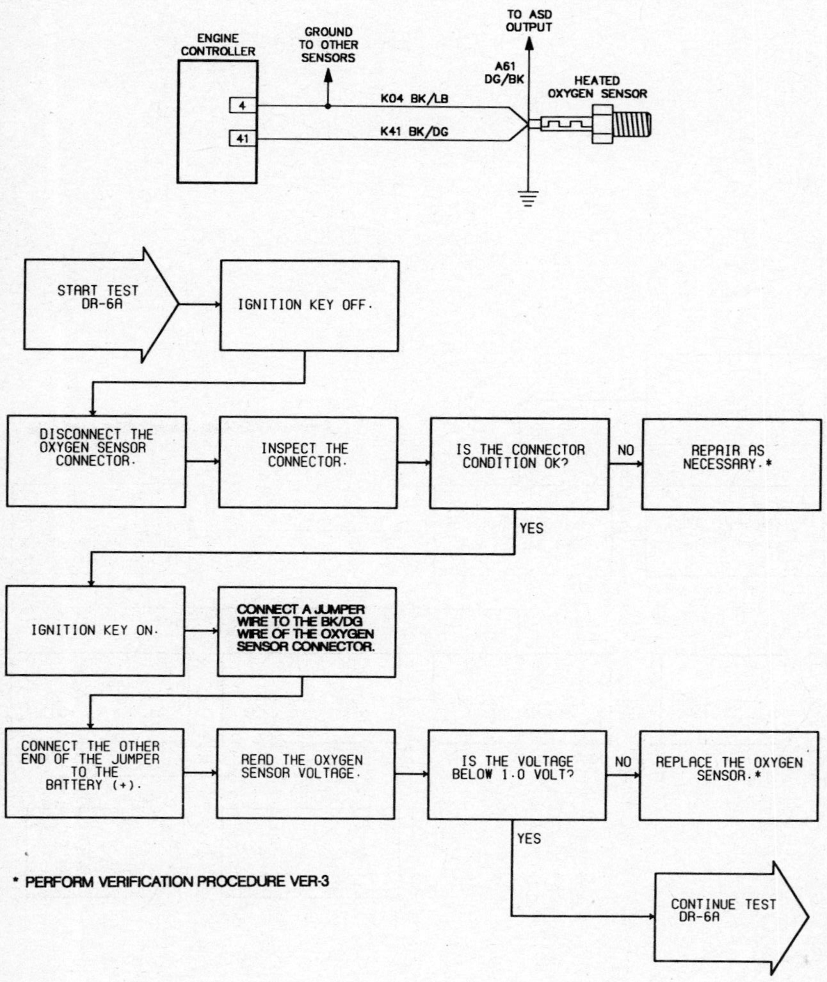

ENGINE CONTROLLER
4
41
GROUND TO OTHER SENSORS
K04 BK/LB
K41 BK/DG
A61 DG/BK
TO ASD OUTPUT
HEATED OXYGEN SENSOR
START TEST DR-6A
IGNITION KEY OFF.
DISCONNECT THE OXYGEN SENSOR CONNECTOR.
INSPECT THE CONNECTOR.
IS THE CONNECTOR CONDITION OK?
NO
REPAIR AS NECESSARY.*
YES
IGNITION KEY ON.
CONNECT A JUMPER WIRE TO THE BK/DG WIRE OF THE OXYGEN SENSOR CONNECTOR.
CONNECT THE OTHER END OF THE JUMPER TO THE BATTERY (+).
READ THE OXYGEN SENSOR VOLTAGE.
IS THE VOLTAGE BELOW 1.0 VOLT?
NO
REPLACE THE OXYGEN SENSOR.*
YES
CONTINUE TEST DR-6A

* PERFORM VERIFICATION PROCEDURE VER-3

91E09125 91H10436

Fig. 51: Driveability Test 6A (3.3L & 3.8L) – Code 21, O_2 Signal Stays at Center (1 of 2)

DR-6A: CODE 21, O_2 SIGNAL STAYS AT CENTER (2 OF 2)

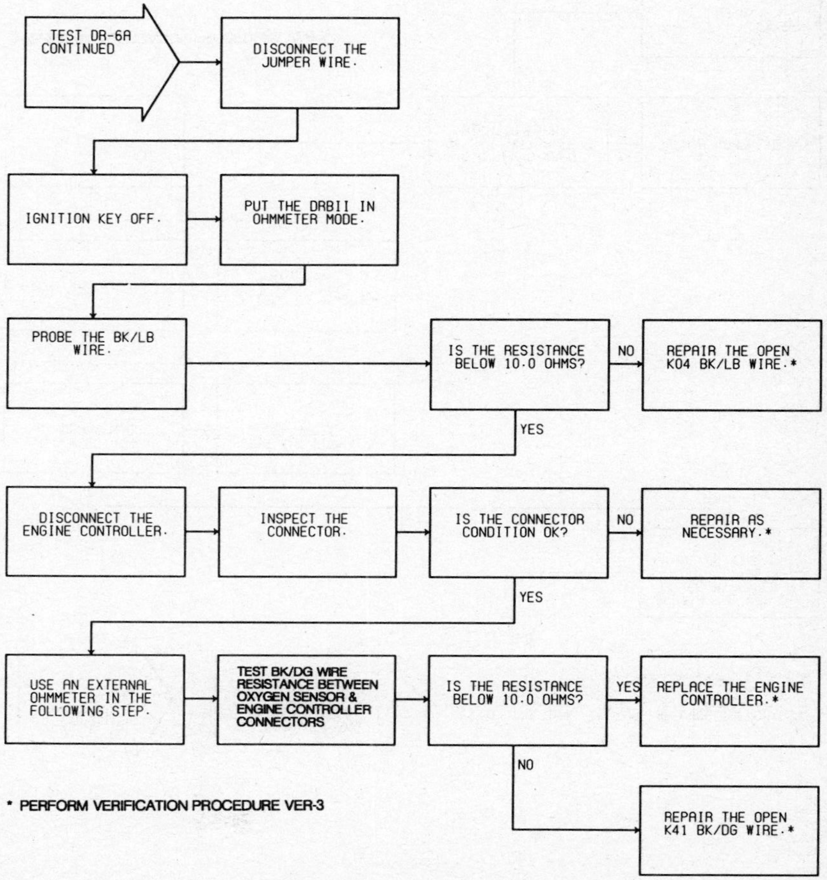

TEST DR-6A CONTINUED
DISCONNECT THE JUMPER WIRE.
IGNITION KEY OFF.
PUT THE DRBII IN OHMMETER MODE.
PROBE THE BK/LB WIRE.
IS THE RESISTANCE BELOW 10.0 OHMS?
NO
REPAIR THE OPEN K04 BK/LB WIRE.*
YES
DISCONNECT THE ENGINE CONTROLLER.
INSPECT THE CONNECTOR.
IS THE CONNECTOR CONDITION OK?
NO
REPAIR AS NECESSARY.*
YES
USE AN EXTERNAL OHMMETER IN THE FOLLOWING STEP.
TEST BK/DG WIRE RESISTANCE BETWEEN OXYGEN SENSOR & ENGINE CONTROLLER CONNECTORS
IS THE RESISTANCE BELOW 10.0 OHMS?
YES
REPLACE THE ENGINE CONTROLLER.*
NO
REPAIR THE OPEN K41 BK/DG WIRE.*

* PERFORM VERIFICATION PROCEDURE VER-3

91I10437

Fig. 52: Driveability Test 6A (3.3L & 3.8L) – Code 21, O_2 Sensor Signal Stays at Center (2 of 2)

DR-7A: CODE 21, O_2 SIGNAL SHORTED HIGH (1 OF 2)

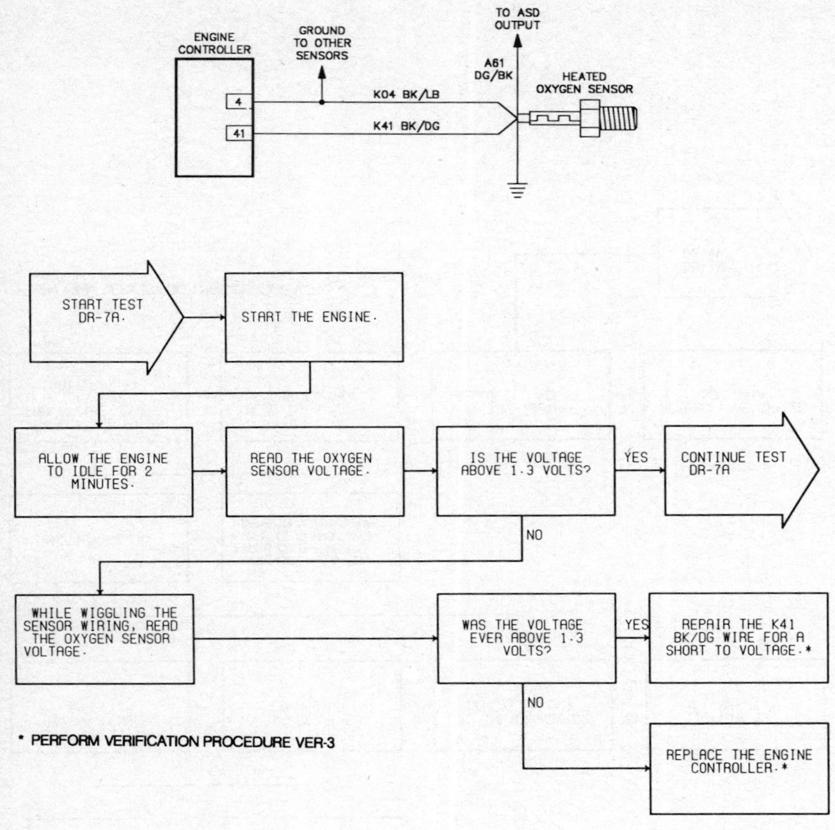
ENGINE CONTROLLER
GROUND TO OTHER SENSORS
TO ASD OUTPUT
A61 DG/BK
HEATED OXYGEN SENSOR
4
41
K04 BK/LB
K41 BK/DG
START TEST DR-7A.
START THE ENGINE.
ALLOW THE ENGINE TO IDLE FOR 2 MINUTES.
READ THE OXYGEN SENSOR VOLTAGE.
IS THE VOLTAGE ABOVE 1.3 VOLTS?
YES
CONTINUE TEST DR-7A
NO
WHILE WIGGLING THE SENSOR WIRING, READ THE OXYGEN SENSOR VOLTAGE.
WAS THE VOLTAGE EVER ABOVE 1.3 VOLTS?
YES
REPAIR THE K41 BK/DG WIRE FOR A SHORT TO VOLTAGE.*
NO
REPLACE THE ENGINE CONTROLLER.*
* PERFORM VERIFICATION PROCEDURE VER-3
91E09125 91J10438

Fig. 53: Driveability Test 7A (3.3L & 3.8L) – Code 21, O_2 Signal Shorted High (1 of 2)

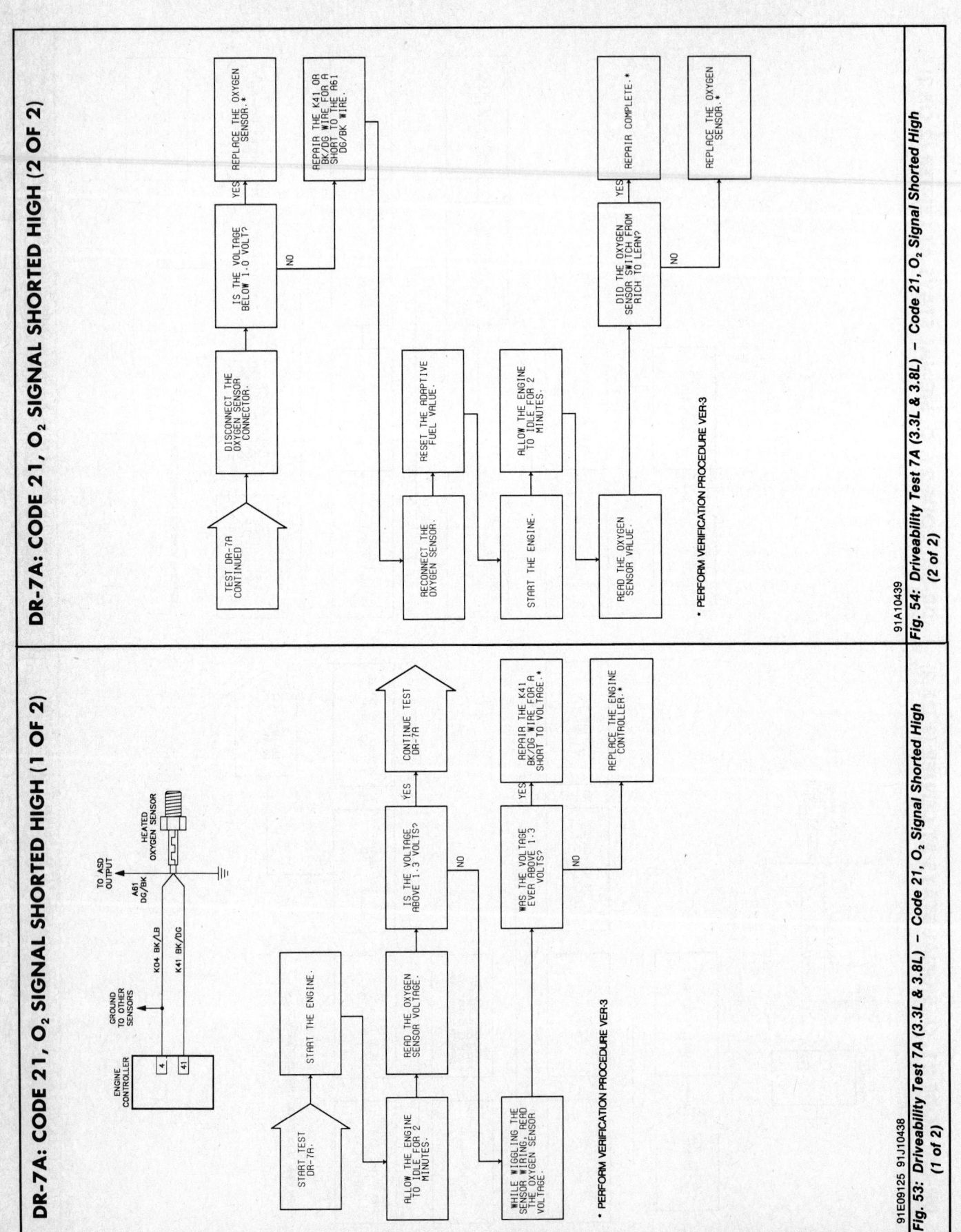

DR-7A: CODE 21, O_2 SIGNAL SHORTED HIGH (2 OF 2)

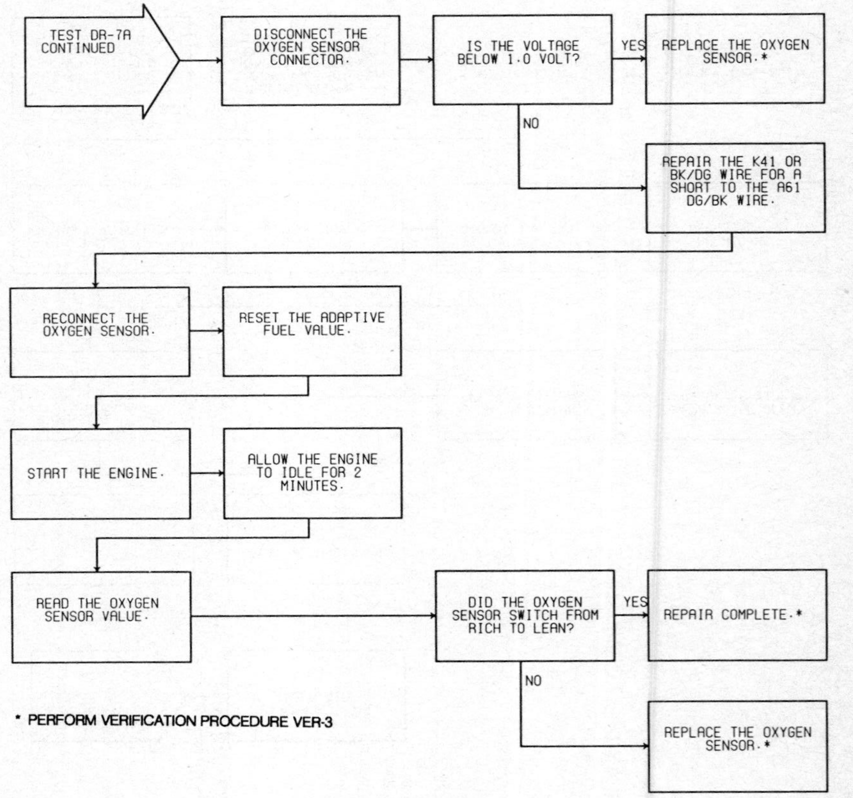
TEST DR-7A CONTINUED
DISCONNECT THE OXYGEN SENSOR CONNECTOR.
IS THE VOLTAGE BELOW 1.0 VOLT?
YES
REPLACE THE OXYGEN SENSOR.*
NO
REPAIR THE K41 OR BK/DG WIRE FOR A SHORT TO THE A61 DG/BK WIRE.
RECONNECT THE OXYGEN SENSOR.
RESET THE ADAPTIVE FUEL VALUE.
START THE ENGINE.
ALLOW THE ENGINE TO IDLE FOR 2 MINUTES.
READ THE OXYGEN SENSOR VALUE.
DID THE OXYGEN SENSOR SWITCH FROM RICH TO LEAN?
YES
REPAIR COMPLETE.*
NO
REPLACE THE OXYGEN SENSOR.*
* PERFORM VERIFICATION PROCEDURE VER-3
91A10439

Fig. 54: Driveability Test 7A (3.3L & 3.8L) – Code 21, O_2 Signal Shorted High (2 of 2)

DR-8A: CODE 22, COOLANT SENSOR VOLTAGE TOO HIGH (1 OF 2)

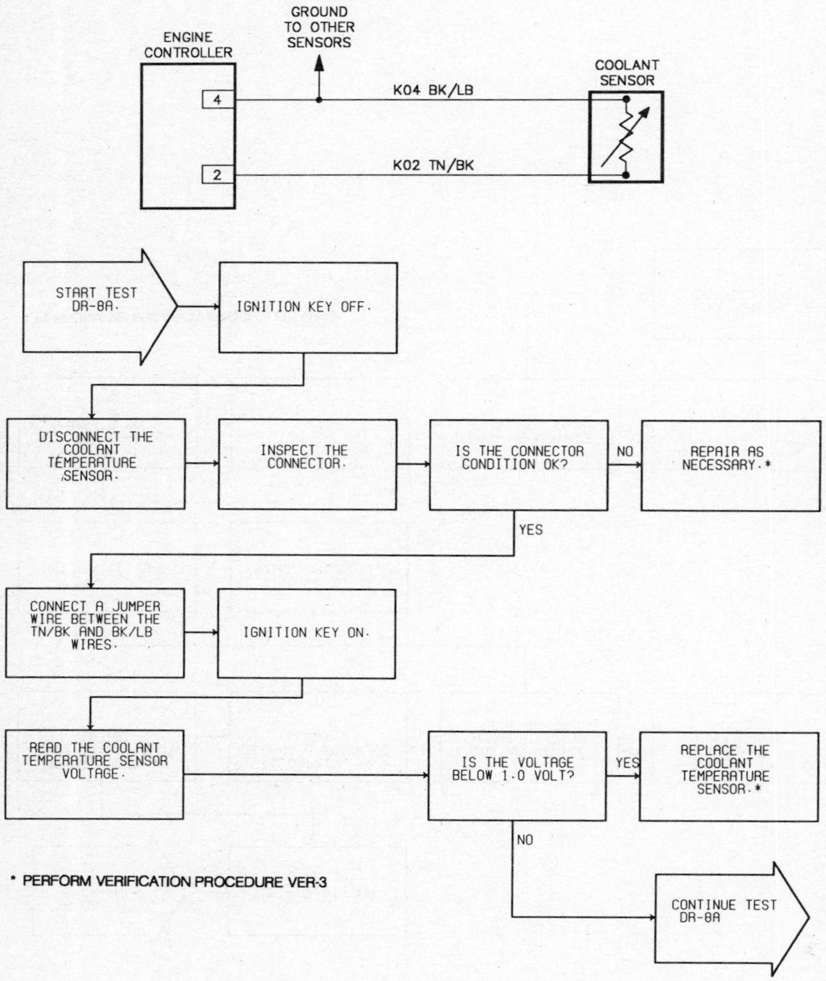
ENGINE CONTROLLER
4
2
GROUND TO OTHER SENSORS
K04 BK/LB
K02 TN/BK
COOLANT SENSOR
START TEST DR-8A.
IGNITION KEY OFF.
DISCONNECT THE COOLANT TEMPERATURE SENSOR.
INSPECT THE CONNECTOR.
IS THE CONNECTOR CONDITION OK?
NO
REPAIR AS NECESSARY.*
YES
CONNECT A JUMPER WIRE BETWEEN THE TN/BK AND BK/LB WIRES.
IGNITION KEY ON.
READ THE COOLANT TEMPERATURE SENSOR VOLTAGE.
IS THE VOLTAGE BELOW 1.0 VOLT?
YES
REPLACE THE COOLANT TEMPERATURE SENSOR.*
NO
CONTINUE TEST DR-8A

* PERFORM VERIFICATION PROCEDURE VER-3

91G09126 91D10440

Fig. 55: Driveability Test 8A (3.3L & 3.8L) – Code 22, Coolant Sensor Voltage Too High (1 of 2)

DR-8A: CODE 22, COOLANT SENSOR VOLTAGE TOO HIGH (2 OF 2)

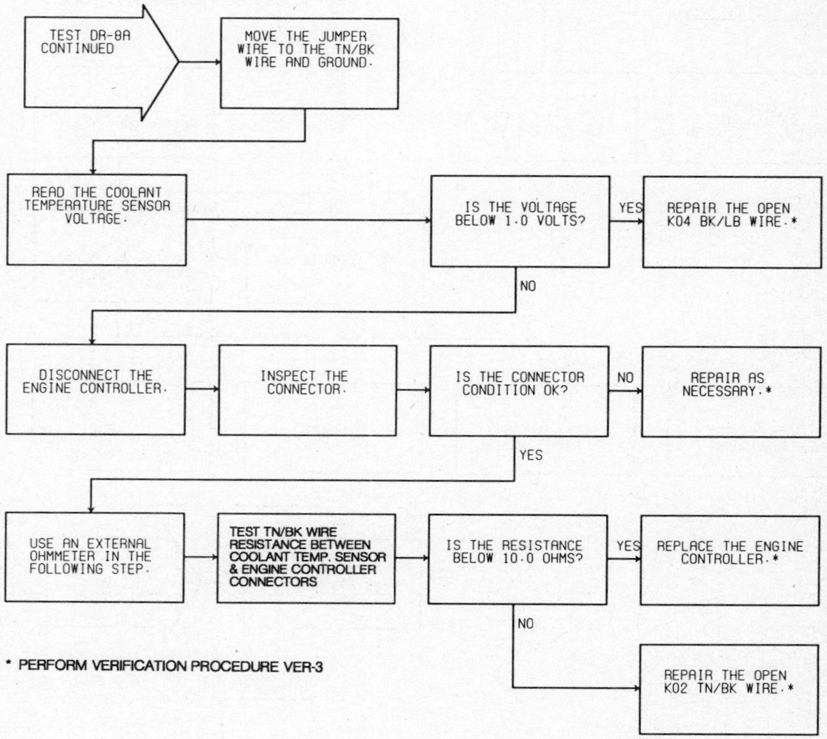
TEST DR-8A CONTINUED
MOVE THE JUMPER WIRE TO THE TN/BK WIRE AND GROUND.
READ THE COOLANT TEMPERATURE SENSOR VOLTAGE.
IS THE VOLTAGE BELOW 1.0 VOLTS?
YES
REPAIR THE OPEN K04 BK/LB WIRE.*
NO
DISCONNECT THE ENGINE CONTROLLER.
INSPECT THE CONNECTOR.
IS THE CONNECTOR CONDITION OK?
NO
REPAIR AS NECESSARY.*
YES
USE AN EXTERNAL OHMMETER IN THE FOLLOWING STEP.
TEST TN/BK WIRE RESISTANCE BETWEEN COOLANT TEMP. SENSOR & ENGINE CONTROLLER CONNECTORS
IS THE RESISTANCE BELOW 10.0 OHMS?
YES
REPLACE THE ENGINE CONTROLLER.*
NO
REPAIR THE OPEN K02 TN/BK WIRE.*

* PERFORM VERIFICATION PROCEDURE VER-3

91E10441

Fig. 56: Driveability Test 8A (3.3L & 3.8L) – Code 22, Coolant Sensor Voltage Too High (2 of 2)

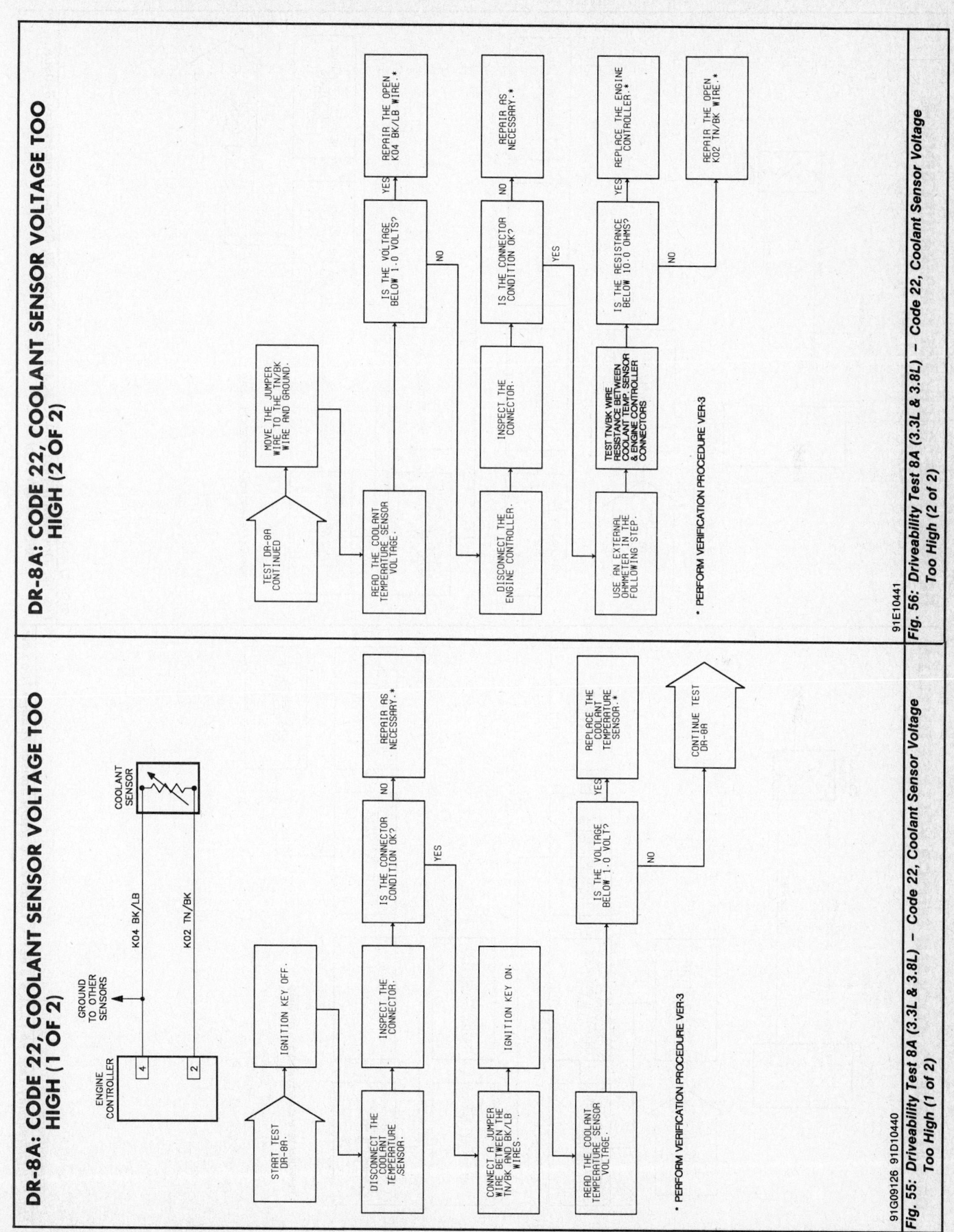

DR-9A: CODE 22, COOLANT SENSOR VOLTAGE TOO LOW

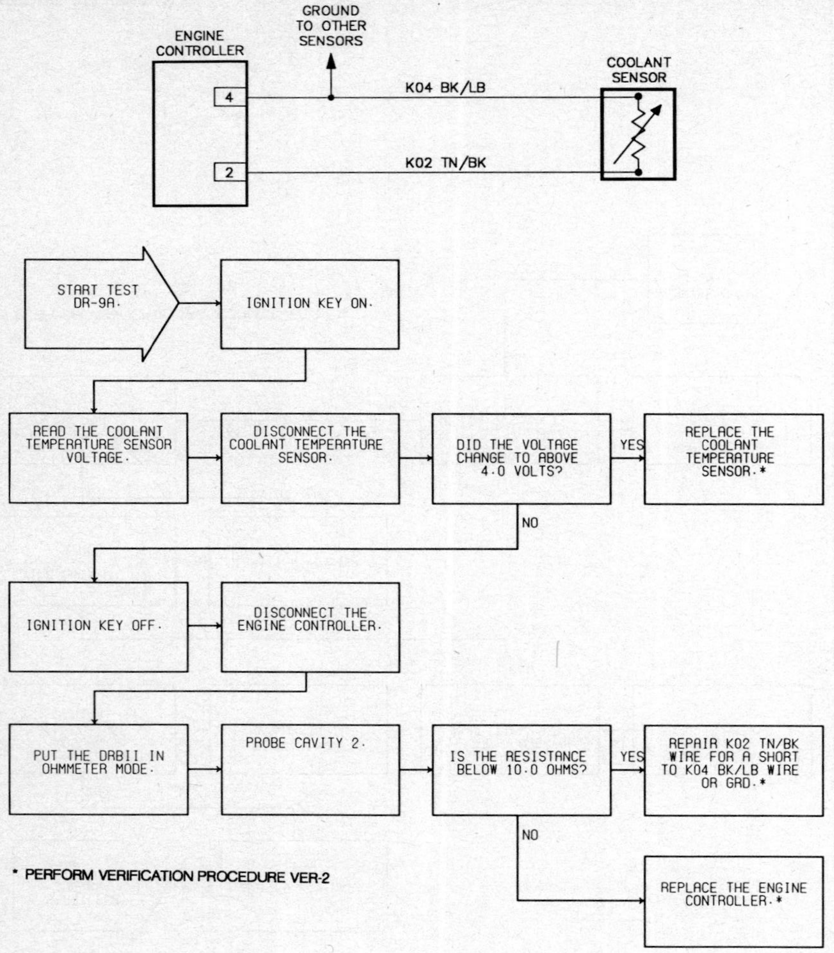
ENGINE CONTROLLER
GROUND TO OTHER SENSORS
COOLANT SENSOR
4
2
K04 BK/LB
K02 TN/BK
START TEST DR-9A.
IGNITION KEY ON.
READ THE COOLANT TEMPERATURE SENSOR VOLTAGE.
DISCONNECT THE COOLANT TEMPERATURE SENSOR.
DID THE VOLTAGE CHANGE TO ABOVE 4.0 VOLTS?
YES
REPLACE THE COOLANT TEMPERATURE SENSOR.*
NO
IGNITION KEY OFF.
DISCONNECT THE ENGINE CONTROLLER.
PUT THE DRBII IN OHMMETER MODE.
PROBE CAVITY 2.
IS THE RESISTANCE BELOW 10.0 OHMS?
YES
REPAIR K02 TN/BK WIRE FOR A SHORT TO K04 BK/LB WIRE OR GRD.*
NO
REPLACE THE ENGINE CONTROLLER.*
* PERFORM VERIFICATION PROCEDURE VER-2

91G09126 91F10442

Fig. 57: Driveability Test 9A (3.3L & 3.8L) – Code 22, Coolant Sensor Voltage Too Low

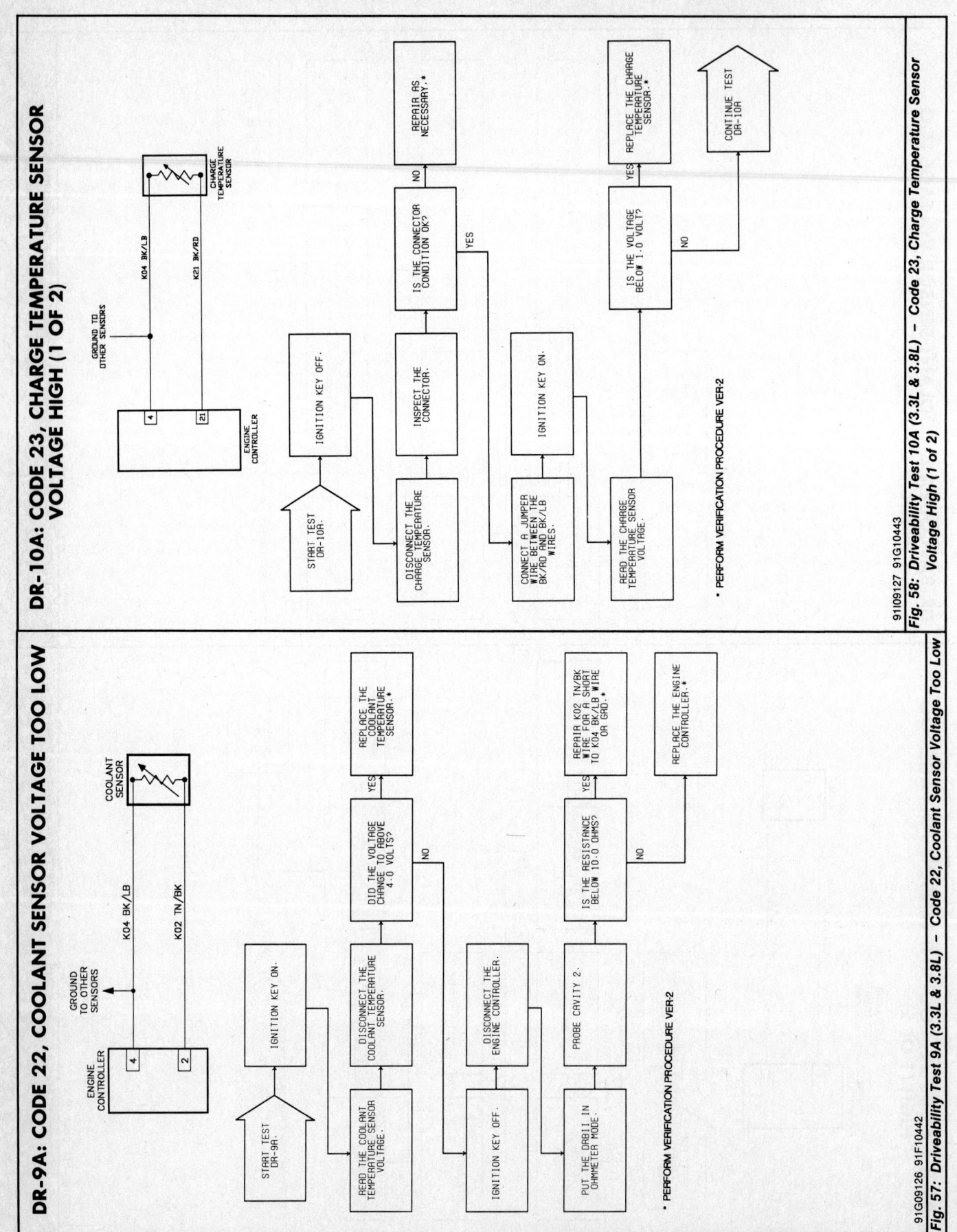

DR-10A: CODE 23, CHARGE TEMPERATURE SENSOR VOLTAGE HIGH (1 OF 2)

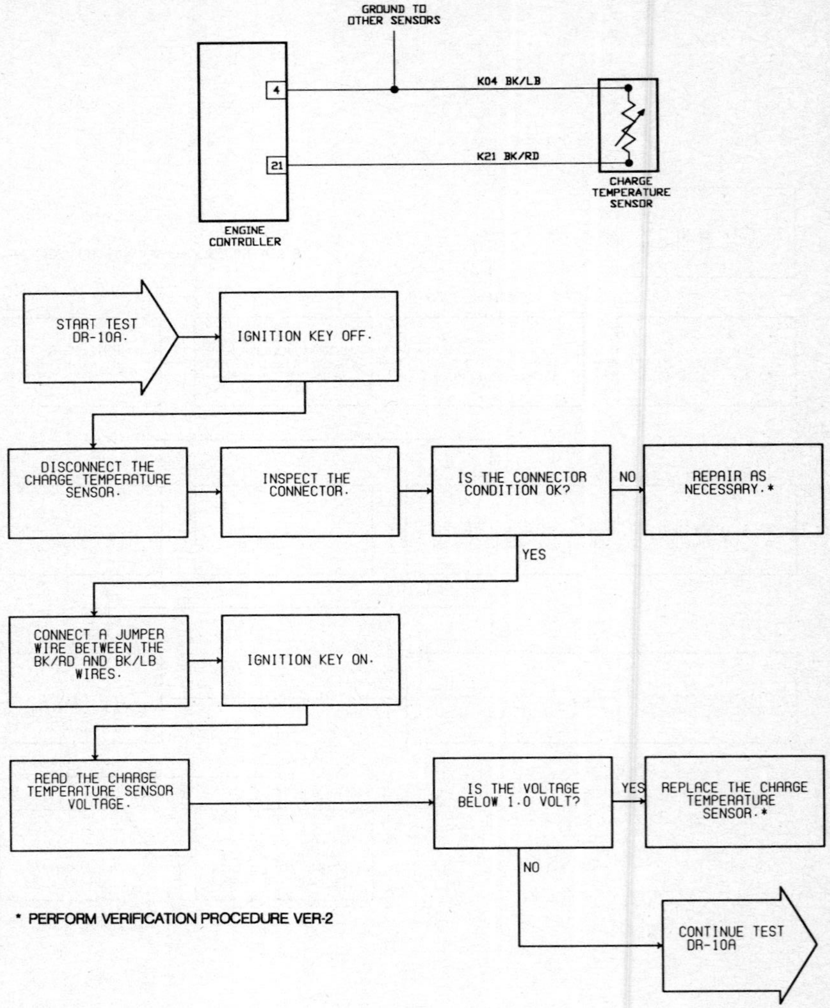
GROUND TO OTHER SENSORS
ENGINE CONTROLLER
CHARGE TEMPERATURE SENSOR
4
21
K04 BK/LB
K21 BK/RD
START TEST DR-10A.
IGNITION KEY OFF.
DISCONNECT THE CHARGE TEMPERATURE SENSOR.
INSPECT THE CONNECTOR.
IS THE CONNECTOR CONDITION OK?
NO
REPAIR AS NECESSARY.*
YES
CONNECT A JUMPER WIRE BETWEEN THE BK/RD AND BK/LB WIRES.
IGNITION KEY ON.
READ THE CHARGE TEMPERATURE SENSOR VOLTAGE.
IS THE VOLTAGE BELOW 1.0 VOLT?
YES
REPLACE THE CHARGE TEMPERATURE SENSOR.*
NO
CONTINUE TEST DR-10A
* PERFORM VERIFICATION PROCEDURE VER-2

91I09127 91G10443

Fig. 58: Driveability Test 10A (3.3L & 3.8L) – Code 23, Charge Temperature Sensor Voltage High (1 of 2)

DR-10A: CODE 23, CHARGE TEMPERATURE SENSOR VOLTAGE HIGH (2 OF 2)

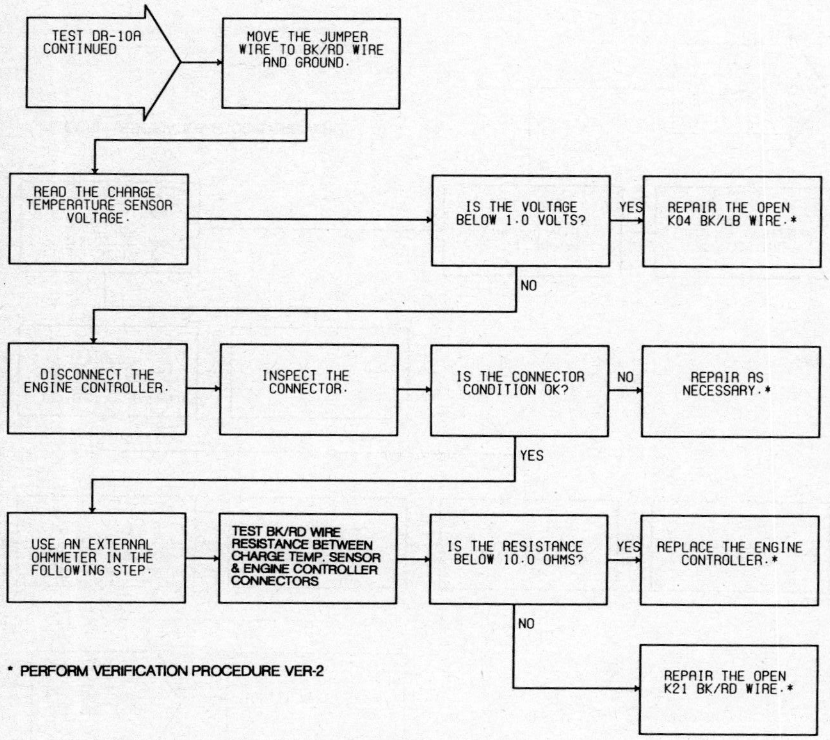
TEST DR-10A CONTINUED
MOVE THE JUMPER WIRE TO BK/RD WIRE AND GROUND.
READ THE CHARGE TEMPERATURE SENSOR VOLTAGE.
IS THE VOLTAGE BELOW 1.0 VOLTS?
YES
REPAIR THE OPEN K04 BK/LB WIRE.*
NO
DISCONNECT THE ENGINE CONTROLLER.
INSPECT THE CONNECTOR.
IS THE CONNECTOR CONDITION OK?
NO
REPAIR AS NECESSARY.*
YES
USE AN EXTERNAL OHMMETER IN THE FOLLOWING STEP.
TEST BK/RD WIRE RESISTANCE BETWEEN CHARGE TEMP. SENSOR & ENGINE CONTROLLER CONNECTORS
IS THE RESISTANCE BELOW 10.0 OHMS?
YES
REPLACE THE ENGINE CONTROLLER.*
NO
REPAIR THE OPEN K21 BK/RD WIRE.*

* PERFORM VERIFICATION PROCEDURE VER-2

91H10444

Fig. 59: Driveability Test 10A (3.3L & 3.8L) – Code 23, Charge Temperature Sensor Voltage High (2 of 2)

DR-11A: CODE 23, CHARGE TEMPERATURE VOLTAGE LOW

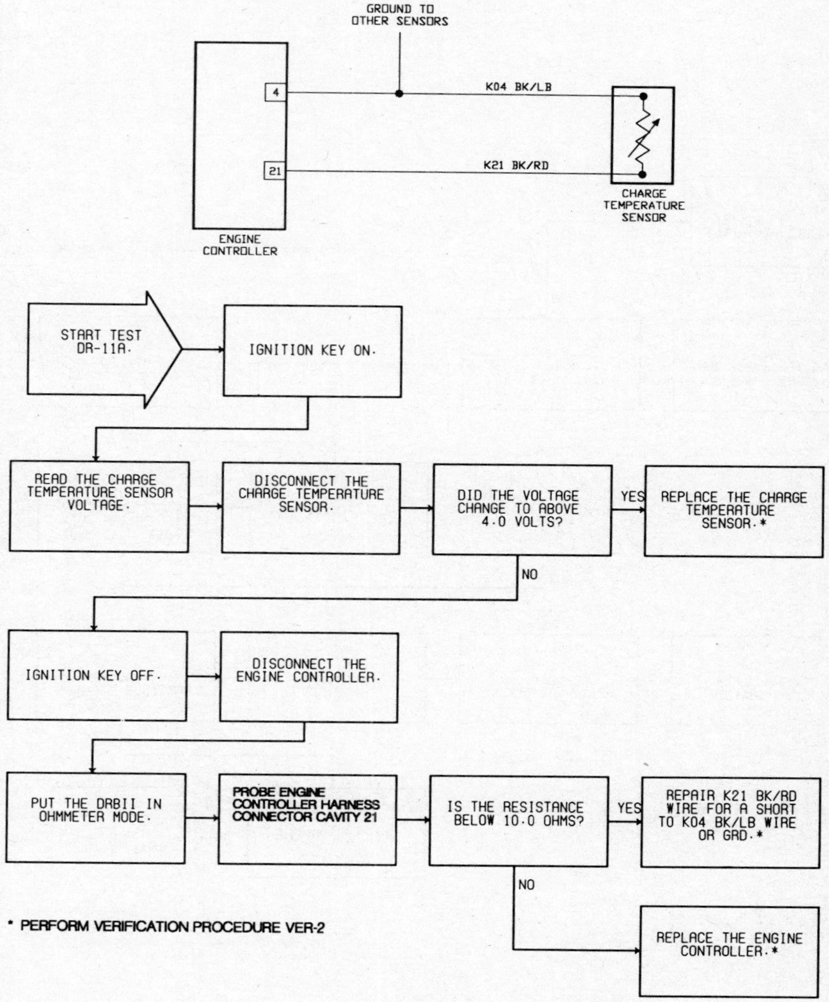
GROUND TO OTHER SENSORS
4
21
K04 BK/LB
K21 BK/RD
ENGINE CONTROLLER
CHARGE TEMPERATURE SENSOR
START TEST DR-11A.
IGNITION KEY ON.
READ THE CHARGE TEMPERATURE SENSOR VOLTAGE.
DISCONNECT THE CHARGE TEMPERATURE SENSOR.
DID THE VOLTAGE CHANGE TO ABOVE 4.0 VOLTS?
YES
REPLACE THE CHARGE TEMPERATURE SENSOR.*
NO
IGNITION KEY OFF.
DISCONNECT THE ENGINE CONTROLLER.
PUT THE DRBII IN OHMMETER MODE.
PROBE ENGINE CONTROLLER HARNESS CONNECTOR CAVITY 21
IS THE RESISTANCE BELOW 10.0 OHMS?
YES
REPAIR K21 BK/RD WIRE FOR A SHORT TO K04 BK/LB WIRE OR GRD.*
NO
REPLACE THE ENGINE CONTROLLER.*

* PERFORM VERIFICATION PROCEDURE VER-2

91I09127 91I10445

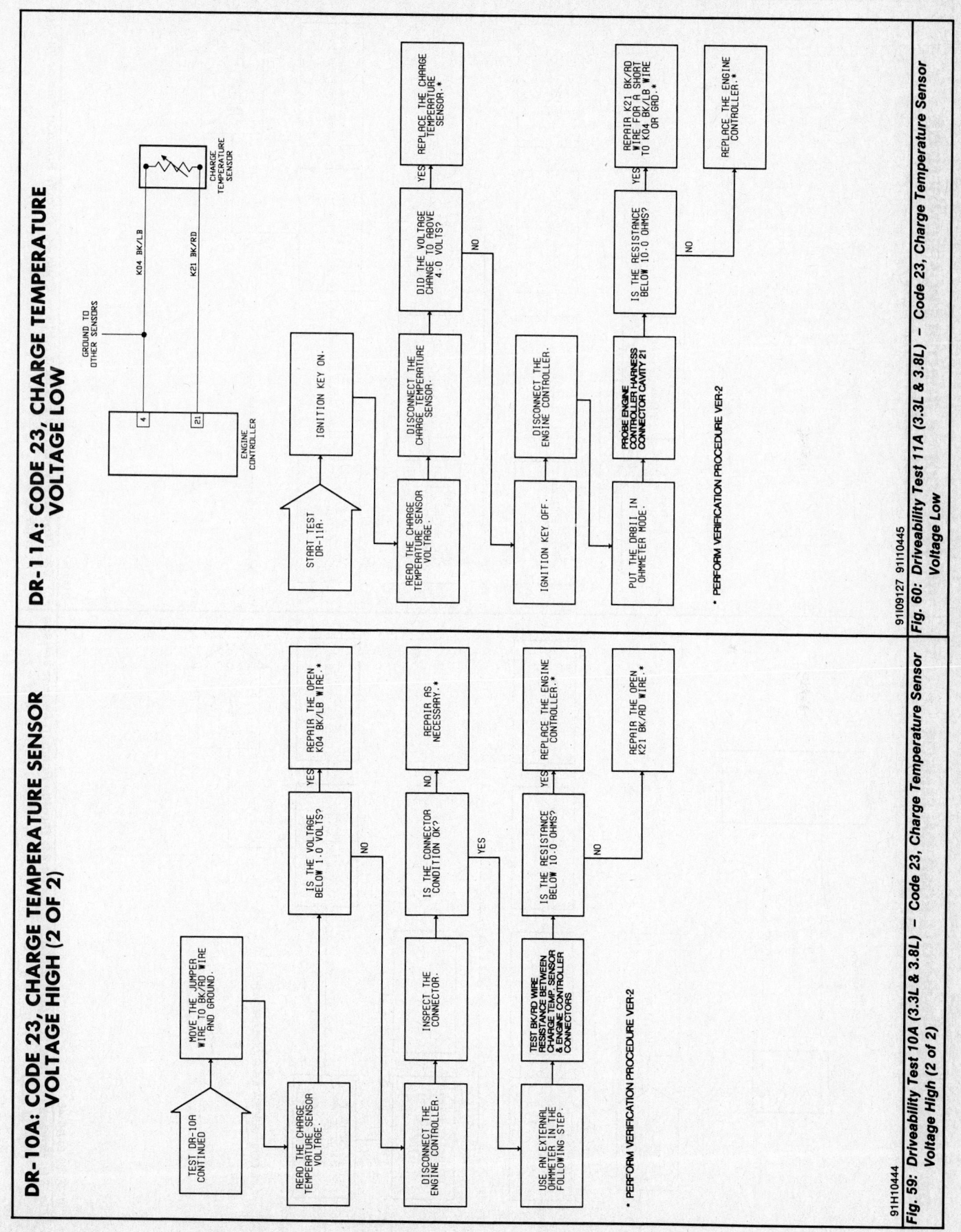

Fig. 60: Driveability Test 11A (3.3L & 3.8L) – Code 23, Charge Temperature Sensor Voltage Low

1991 ENGINE PERFORMANCE
Self-Diagnostics – 3.3L PFI (Cont.)

DR-12A: CODE 24, THROTTLE POSITION SENSOR VOLTAGE HIGH (1 OF 2)

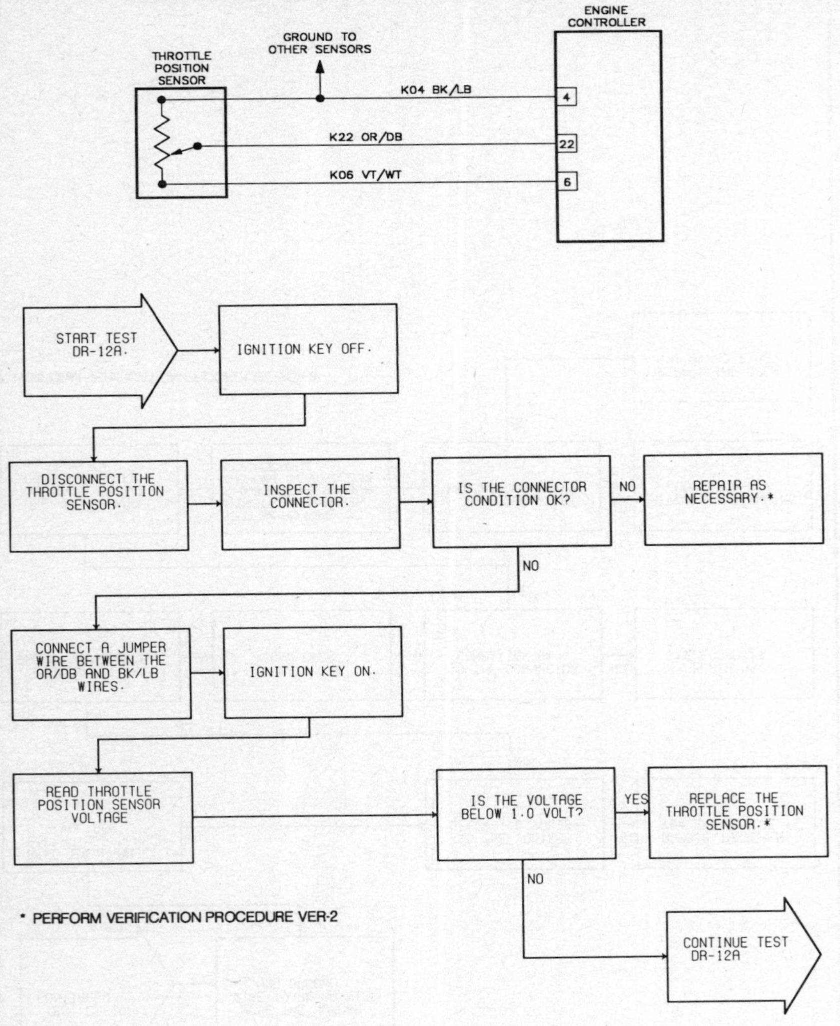
THROTTLE POSITION SENSOR
GROUND TO OTHER SENSORS
ENGINE CONTROLLER
K04 BK/LB
K22 OR/DB
K06 VT/WT
4
22
6
START TEST DR-12A.
IGNITION KEY OFF.
DISCONNECT THE THROTTLE POSITION SENSOR.
INSPECT THE CONNECTOR.
IS THE CONNECTOR CONDITION OK?
NO
REPAIR AS NECESSARY.*
NO
CONNECT A JUMPER WIRE BETWEEN THE OR/DB AND BK/LB WIRES.
IGNITION KEY ON.
READ THROTTLE POSITION SENSOR VOLTAGE
IS THE VOLTAGE BELOW 1.0 VOLT?
YES
REPLACE THE THROTTLE POSITION SENSOR.*
NO
CONTINUE TEST DR-12A

* PERFORM VERIFICATION PROCEDURE VER-2

91A09128 91J10446

Fig. 61: Driveability Test 12A (3.3L & 3.8L) – Code 24, Throttle Position Sensor Voltage High (1 of 2)

DR-12A: CODE 24, THROTTLE POSITION SENSOR VOLTAGE HIGH (2 OF 2)

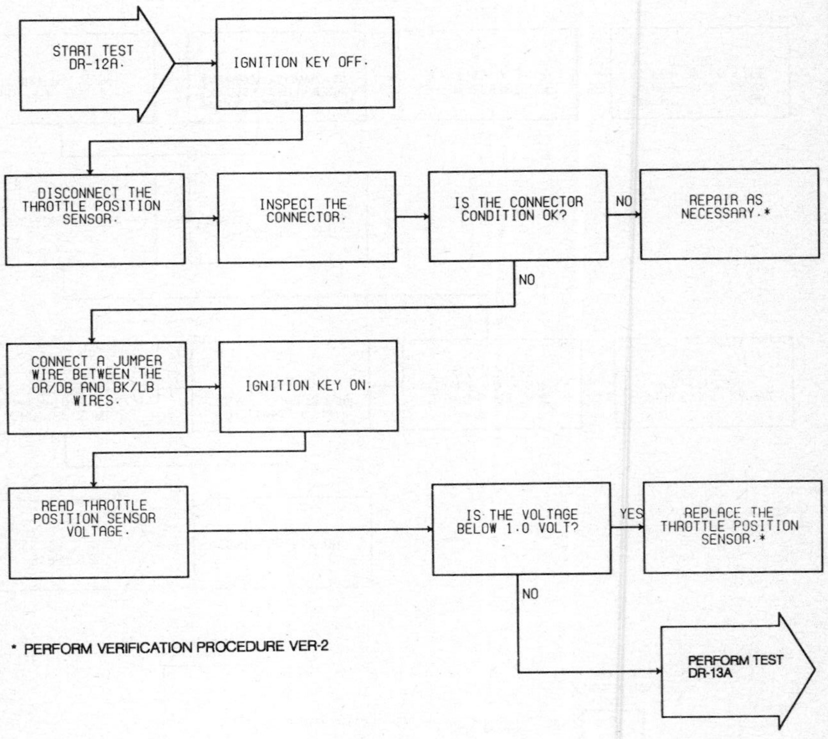
START TEST DR-12A.
IGNITION KEY OFF.
DISCONNECT THE THROTTLE POSITION SENSOR.
INSPECT THE CONNECTOR.
IS THE CONNECTOR CONDITION OK?
NO
REPAIR AS NECESSARY.*
NO
CONNECT A JUMPER WIRE BETWEEN THE OR/DB AND BK/LB WIRES.
IGNITION KEY ON.
READ THROTTLE POSITION SENSOR VOLTAGE.
IS THE VOLTAGE BELOW 1.0 VOLT?
YES
REPLACE THE THROTTLE POSITION SENSOR.*
NO
PERFORM TEST DR-13A

* PERFORM VERIFICATION PROCEDURE VER-2

91A10447

Fig. 62: Driveability Test 12A (3.3L & 3.8L) – Code 24, Throttle Position Sensor Voltage High (2 of 2)

DR-13A: CODE 24, THROTTLE POSITION SENSOR VOLTAGE LOW

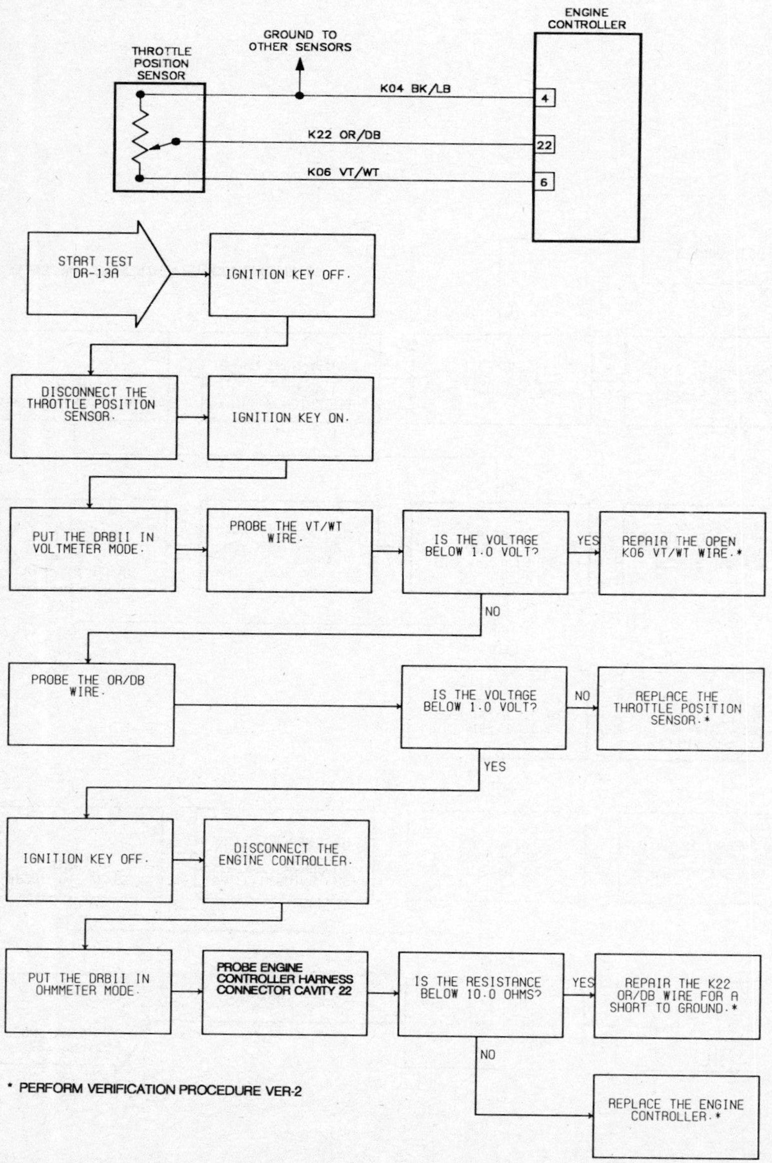
ENGINE CONTROLLER
THROTTLE POSITION SENSOR
GROUND TO OTHER SENSORS
K04 BK/LB
K22 OR/DB
K06 VT/WT
4
22
6
START TEST DR-13A
IGNITION KEY OFF.
DISCONNECT THE THROTTLE POSITION SENSOR.
IGNITION KEY ON.
PUT THE DRBII IN VOLTMETER MODE.
PROBE THE VT/WT WIRE.
IS THE VOLTAGE BELOW 1.0 VOLT?
YES
REPAIR THE OPEN K06 VT/WT WIRE.*
NO
PROBE THE OR/DB WIRE.
IS THE VOLTAGE BELOW 1.0 VOLT?
NO
REPLACE THE THROTTLE POSITION SENSOR.*
YES
IGNITION KEY OFF.
DISCONNECT THE ENGINE CONTROLLER.
PUT THE DRBII IN OHMMETER MODE.
PROBE ENGINE CONTROLLER HARNESS CONNECTOR CAVITY 22
IS THE RESISTANCE BELOW 10.0 OHMS?
YES
REPAIR THE K22 OR/DB WIRE FOR A SHORT TO GROUND.*
NO
REPLACE THE ENGINE CONTROLLER.*

* PERFORM VERIFICATION PROCEDURE VER-2

91A09128 91B10448

Fig. 63: Driveability Test 13A (3.3L & 3.8L) – Code 24, Throttle Position Sensor Voltage Low

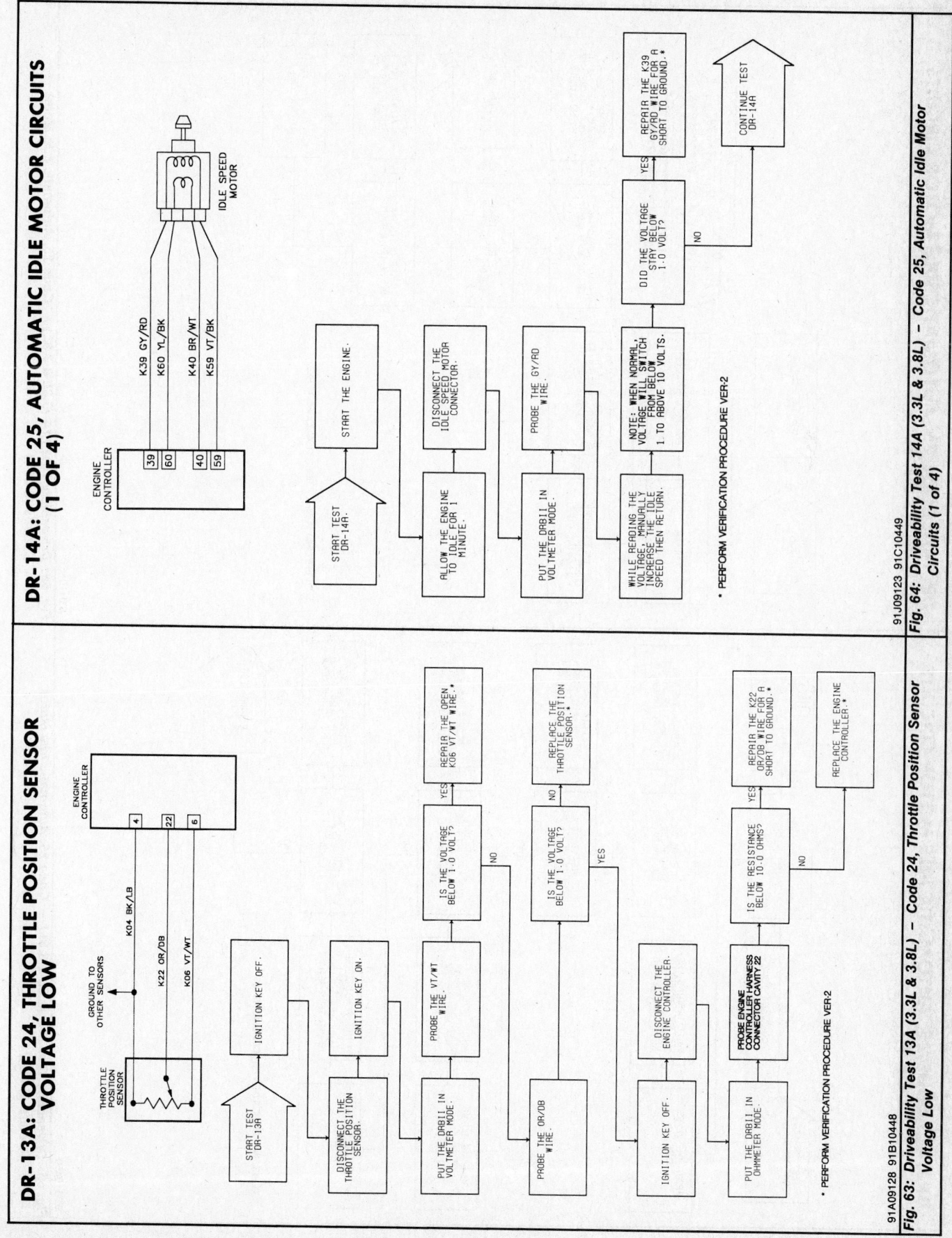

DR-14A: CODE 25, AUTOMATIC IDLE MOTOR CIRCUITS (1 OF 4)

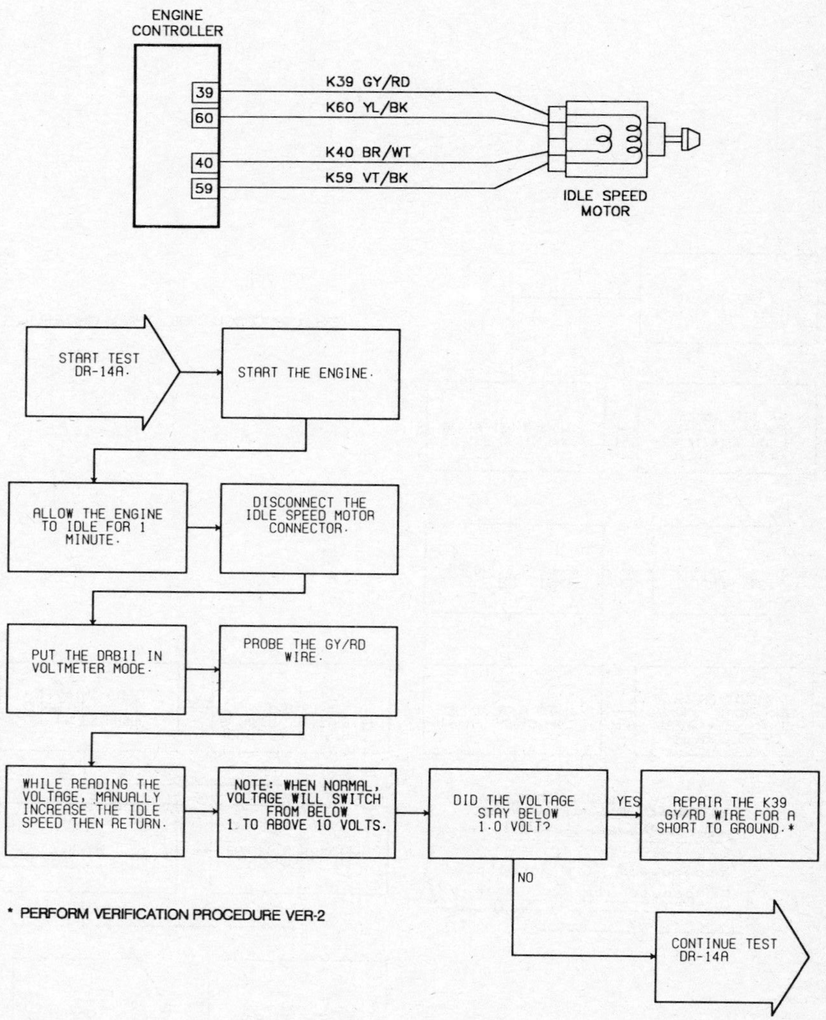
ENGINE CONTROLLER
39
60
40
59
K39 GY/RD
K60 YL/BK
K40 BR/WT
K59 VT/BK
IDLE SPEED MOTOR
START TEST DR-14A.
START THE ENGINE.
ALLOW THE ENGINE TO IDLE FOR 1 MINUTE.
DISCONNECT THE IDLE SPEED MOTOR CONNECTOR.
PUT THE DRBII IN VOLTMETER MODE.
PROBE THE GY/RD WIRE.
WHILE READING THE VOLTAGE, MANUALLY INCREASE THE IDLE SPEED THEN RETURN.
NOTE: WHEN NORMAL, VOLTAGE WILL SWITCH FROM BELOW 1 TO ABOVE 10 VOLTS.
DID THE VOLTAGE STAY BELOW 1.0 VOLT?
YES
REPAIR THE K39 GY/RD WIRE FOR A SHORT TO GROUND.*
NO
CONTINUE TEST DR-14A

* PERFORM VERIFICATION PROCEDURE VER-2

91J09123 91C10449

Fig. 64: Driveability Test 14A (3.3L & 3.8L) – Code 25, Automatic Idle Motor Circuits (1 of 4)

DR-14A: CODE 25, AUTOMATIC IDLE MOTOR CIRCUITS (2 OF 4)

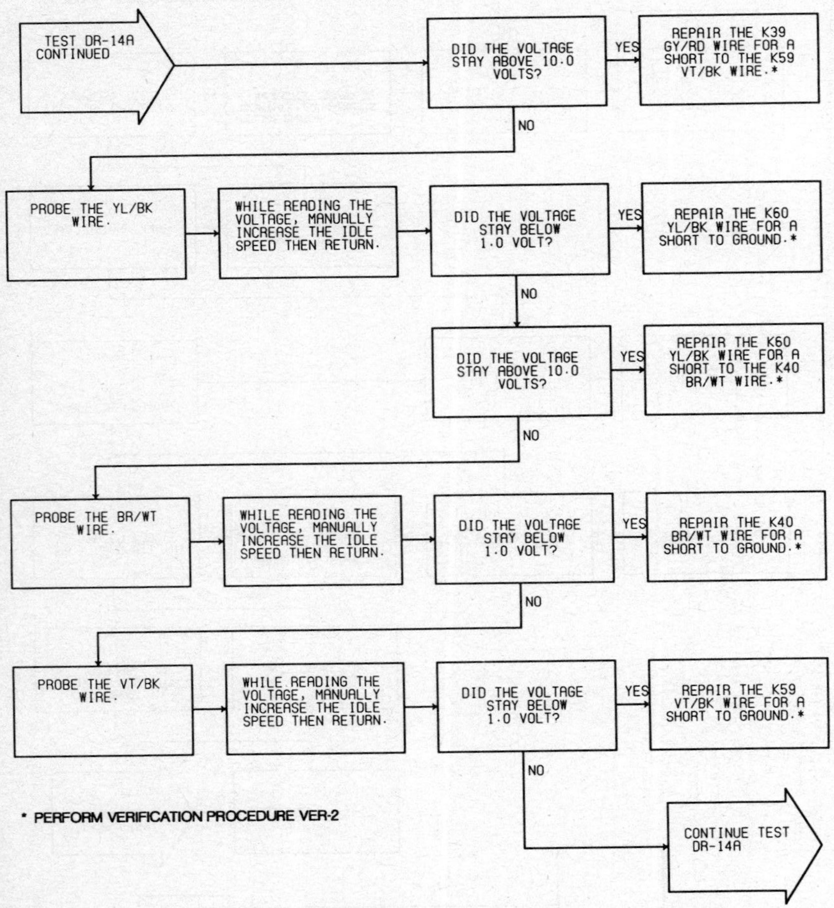
TEST DR-14A CONTINUED
DID THE VOLTAGE STAY ABOVE 10.0 VOLTS?
YES
REPAIR THE K39 GY/RD WIRE FOR A SHORT TO THE K59 VT/BK WIRE.*
NO
PROBE THE YL/BK WIRE.
WHILE READING THE VOLTAGE, MANUALLY INCREASE THE IDLE SPEED THEN RETURN.
DID THE VOLTAGE STAY BELOW 1.0 VOLT?
YES
REPAIR THE K60 YL/BK WIRE FOR A SHORT TO GROUND.*
NO
DID THE VOLTAGE STAY ABOVE 10.0 VOLTS?
YES
REPAIR THE K60 YL/BK WIRE FOR A SHORT TO THE K40 BR/WT WIRE.*
NO
PROBE THE BR/WT WIRE.
WHILE READING THE VOLTAGE, MANUALLY INCREASE THE IDLE SPEED THEN RETURN.
DID THE VOLTAGE STAY BELOW 1.0 VOLT?
YES
REPAIR THE K40 BR/WT WIRE FOR A SHORT TO GROUND.*
NO
PROBE THE VT/BK WIRE.
WHILE READING THE VOLTAGE, MANUALLY INCREASE THE IDLE SPEED THEN RETURN.
DID THE VOLTAGE STAY BELOW 1.0 VOLT?
YES
REPAIR THE K59 VT/BK WIRE FOR A SHORT TO GROUND.*
NO
CONTINUE TEST DR-14A

* PERFORM VERIFICATION PROCEDURE VER-2

91G10450

Fig. 65: Driveability Test 14A (3.3L & 3.8L) – Code 25, Automatic Idle Motor Circuits (2 of 4)

DR-14A: CODE 25, AUTOMATIC IDLE MOTOR CIRCUITS (3 OF 4)

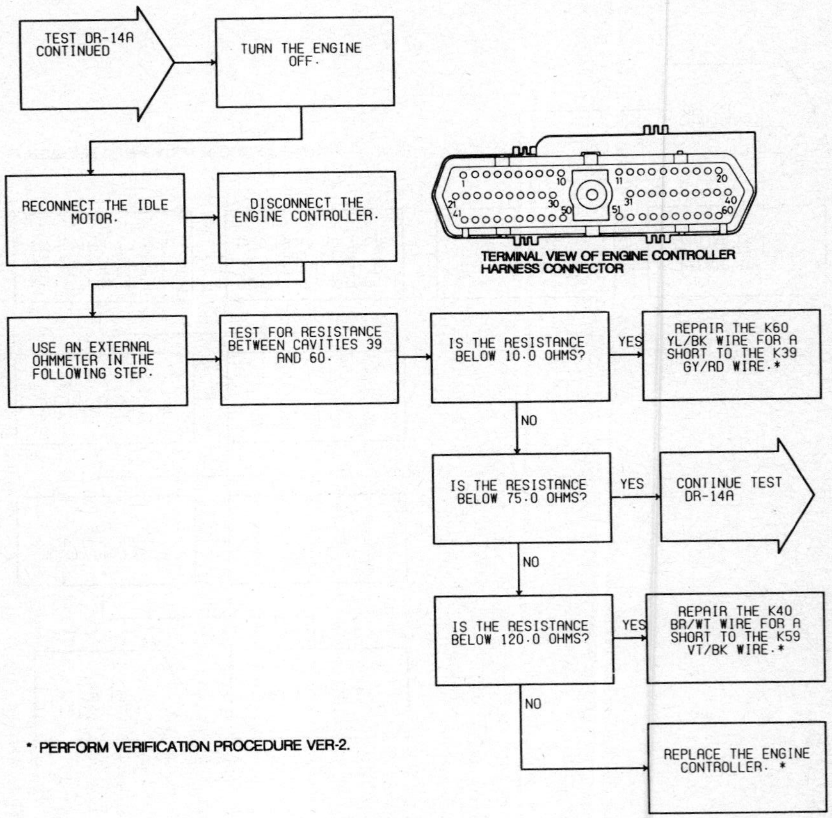
TEST DR-14A CONTINUED
TURN THE ENGINE OFF.
RECONNECT THE IDLE MOTOR.
DISCONNECT THE ENGINE CONTROLLER.
TERMINAL VIEW OF ENGINE CONTROLLER HARNESS CONNECTOR
1
10
11
20
21
30
31
40
41
50
51
60
USE AN EXTERNAL OHMMETER IN THE FOLLOWING STEP.
TEST FOR RESISTANCE BETWEEN CAVITIES 39 AND 60.
IS THE RESISTANCE BELOW 10.0 OHMS?
YES
REPAIR THE K60 YL/BK WIRE FOR A SHORT TO THE K39 GY/RD WIRE.*
NO
IS THE RESISTANCE BELOW 75.0 OHMS?
YES
CONTINUE TEST DR-14A
NO
IS THE RESISTANCE BELOW 120.0 OHMS?
YES
REPAIR THE K40 BR/WT WIRE FOR A SHORT TO THE K59 VT/BK WIRE.*
NO
REPLACE THE ENGINE CONTROLLER. *

* PERFORM VERIFICATION PROCEDURE VER-2.

91H10451

Fig. 66: Driveability Test 14A (3.3L & 3.8L) – Code 25, Automatic Idle Motor Circuits (3 of 4)

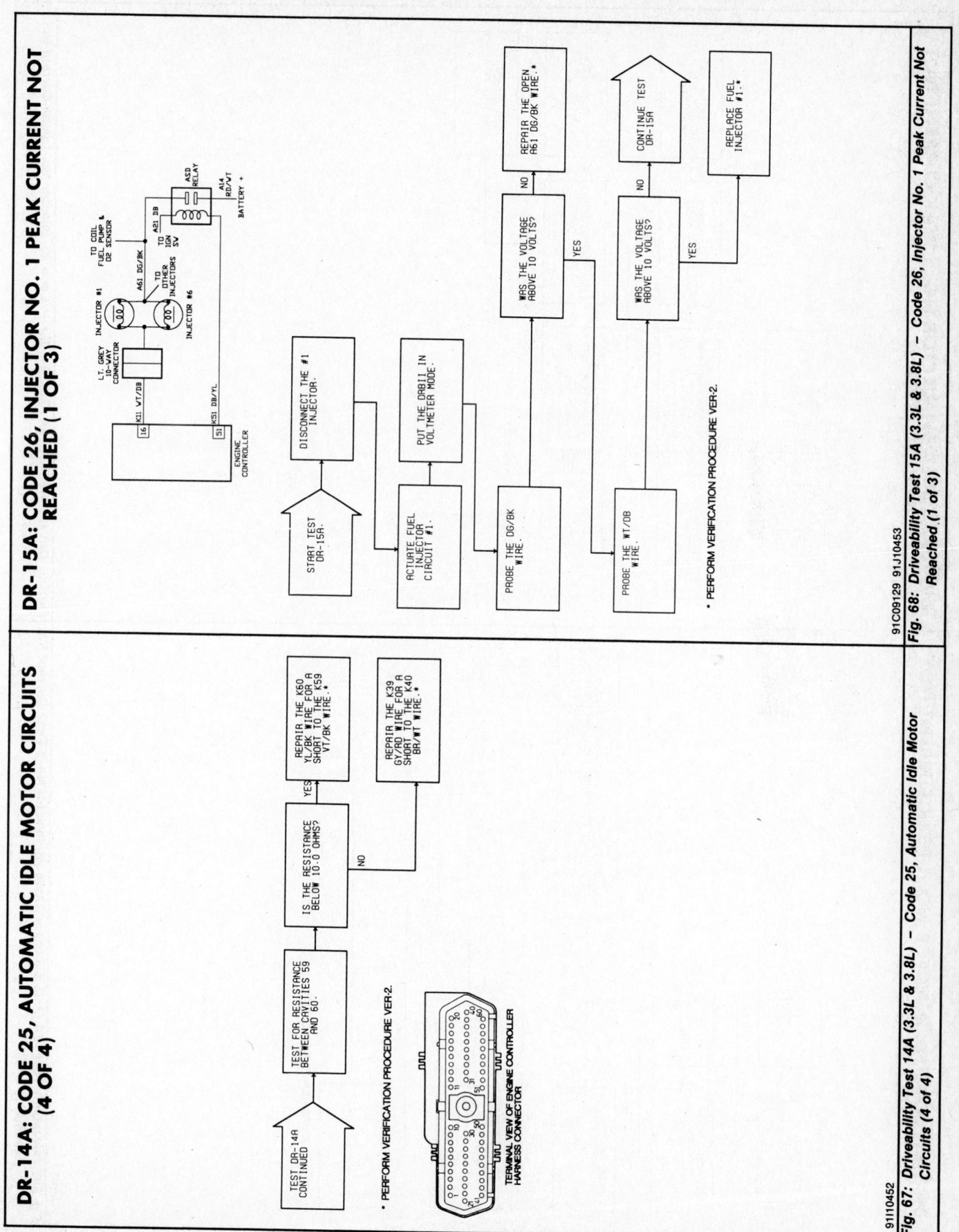

DR-14A: CODE 25, AUTOMATIC IDLE MOTOR CIRCUITS (4 OF 4)

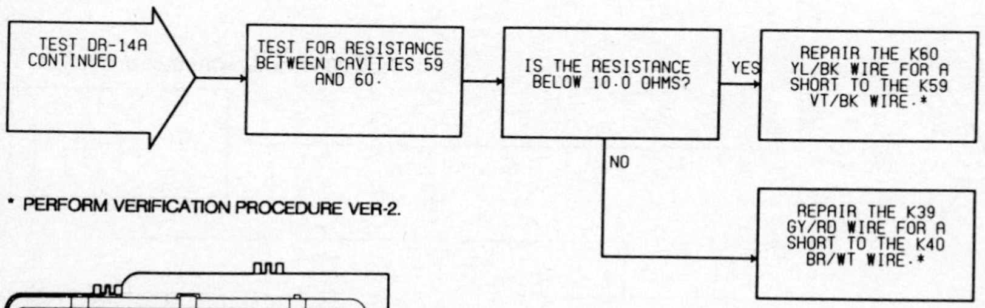
TEST DR-14A CONTINUED
TEST FOR RESISTANCE BETWEEN CAVITIES 59 AND 60.
IS THE RESISTANCE BELOW 10.0 OHMS?
YES
REPAIR THE K60 YL/BK WIRE FOR A SHORT TO THE K59 VT/BK WIRE.*
NO
REPAIR THE K39 GY/RD WIRE FOR A SHORT TO THE K40 BR/WT WIRE.*

* PERFORM VERIFICATION PROCEDURE VER-2.

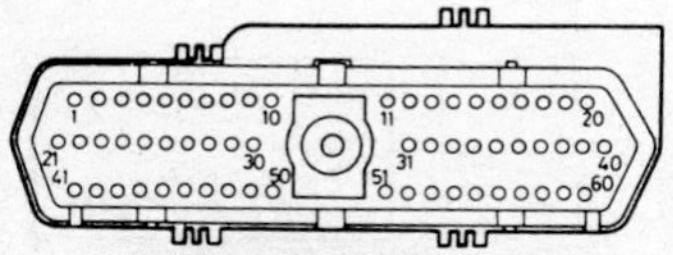
1
10
11
20
21
30
31
40
41
50
51
60

TERMINAL VIEW OF ENGINE CONTROLLER HARNESS CONNECTOR

91I10452

Fig. 67: Driveability Test 14A (3.3L & 3.8L) – Code 25, Automatic Idle Motor Circuits (4 of 4)

DR-15A: CODE 26, INJECTOR NO. 1 PEAK CURRENT NOT REACHED (1 OF 3)

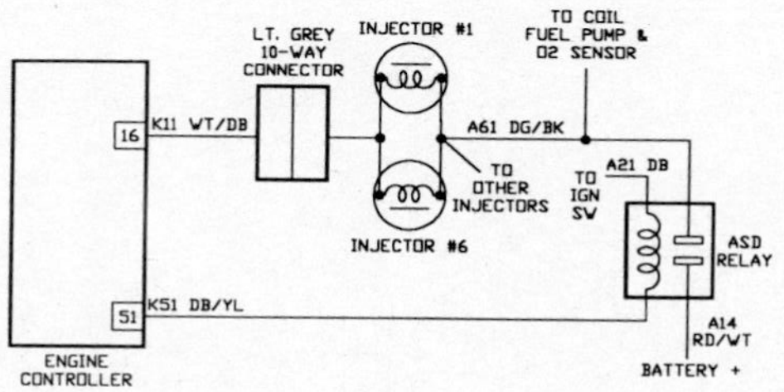
ENGINE CONTROLLER
16
K11 WT/DB
51
K51 DB/YL
LT. GREY 10-WAY CONNECTOR
INJECTOR #1
INJECTOR #6
TO OTHER INJECTORS
A61 DG/BK
TO COIL FUEL PUMP & O2 SENSOR
TO IGN SW
A21 DB
ASD RELAY
A14 RD/WT
BATTERY +

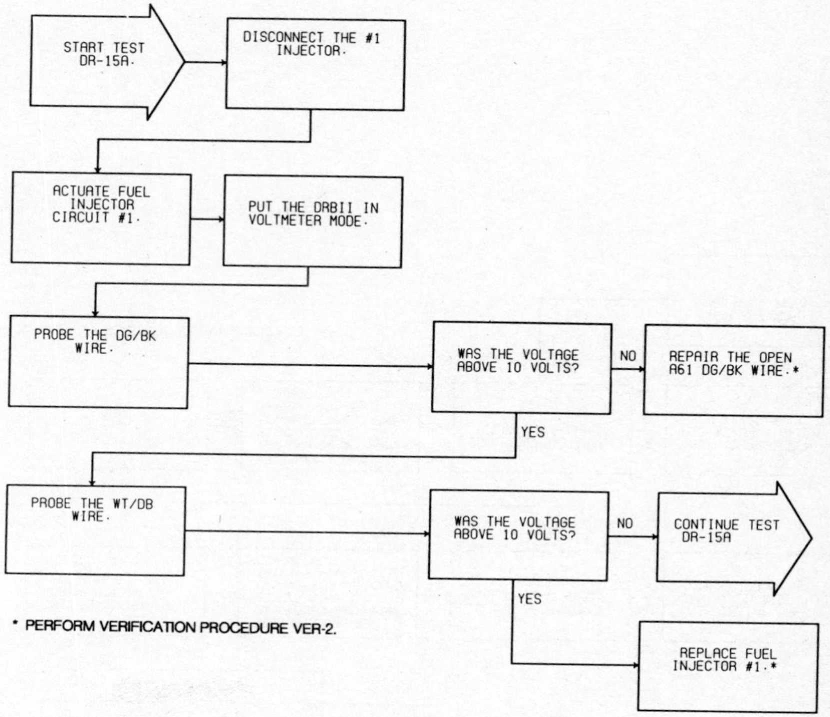
START TEST DR-15A.
DISCONNECT THE #1 INJECTOR.
ACTUATE FUEL INJECTOR CIRCUIT #1.
PUT THE DRBII IN VOLTMETER MODE.
PROBE THE DG/BK WIRE.
WAS THE VOLTAGE ABOVE 10 VOLTS?
NO
REPAIR THE OPEN A61 DG/BK WIRE.*
YES
PROBE THE WT/DB WIRE.
WAS THE VOLTAGE ABOVE 10 VOLTS?
NO
CONTINUE TEST DR-15A
YES
REPLACE FUEL INJECTOR #1.*

* PERFORM VERIFICATION PROCEDURE VER-2.

91C09129 91J10453

Fig. 68: Driveability Test 15A (3.3L & 3.8L) – Code 26, Injector No. 1 Peak Current Not Reached (1 of 3)

1991 ENGINE PERFORMANCE
Self-Diagnostics – 3.3L PFI (Cont.)

DR-15A: CODE 26, INJECTOR NO. 1 PEAK CURRENT NOT REACHED (2 OF 3)

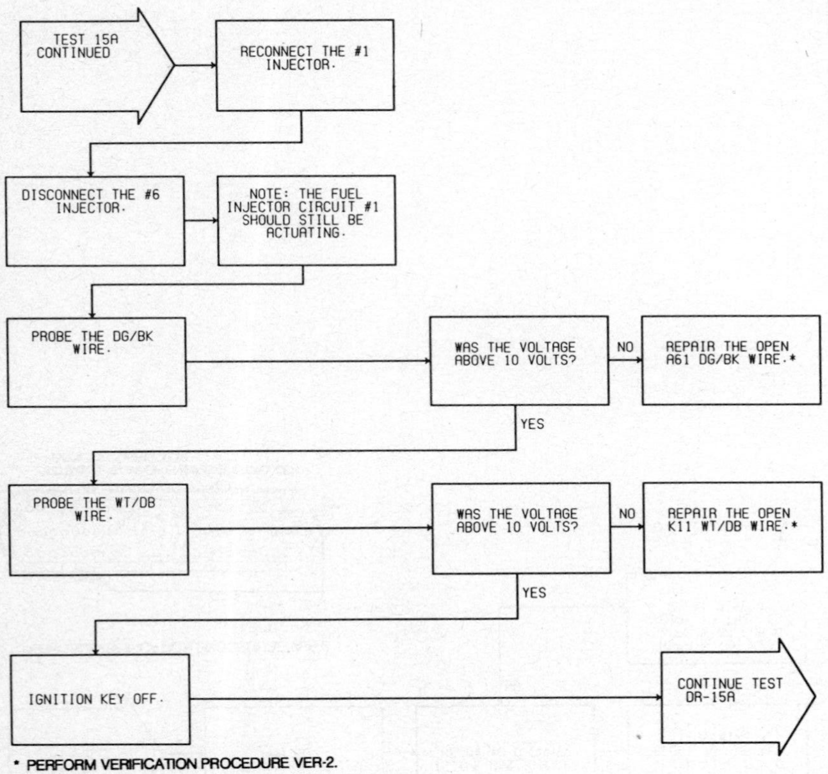
TEST 15A CONTINUED
RECONNECT THE #1 INJECTOR.
DISCONNECT THE #6 INJECTOR.
NOTE: THE FUEL INJECTOR CIRCUIT #1 SHOULD STILL BE ACTUATING.
PROBE THE DG/BK WIRE.
WAS THE VOLTAGE ABOVE 10 VOLTS?
NO
REPAIR THE OPEN A61 DG/BK WIRE.*
YES
PROBE THE WT/DB WIRE.
WAS THE VOLTAGE ABOVE 10 VOLTS?
NO
REPAIR THE OPEN K11 WT/DB WIRE.*
YES
IGNITION KEY OFF.
CONTINUE TEST DR-15A

* PERFORM VERIFICATION PROCEDURE VER-2.

91A10454

Fig. 69: *Driveability Test 15A (3.3L & 3.8L) – Code 26, Injector No. 1 Peak Current Not Reached (2 of 3)*

DR-15A: CODE 26, INJECTOR NO. 1 PEAK CURRENT NOT REACHED (3 OF 3)

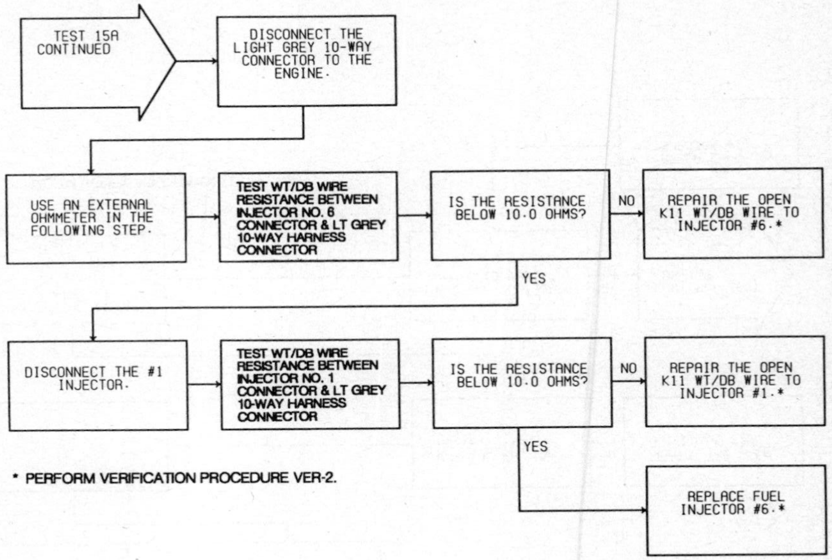
TEST 15A CONTINUED
DISCONNECT THE LIGHT GREY 10-WAY CONNECTOR TO THE ENGINE.
USE AN EXTERNAL OHMMETER IN THE FOLLOWING STEP.
TEST WT/DB WIRE RESISTANCE BETWEEN INJECTOR NO. 6 CONNECTOR & LT GREY 10-WAY HARNESS CONNECTOR
IS THE RESISTANCE BELOW 10.0 OHMS?
NO
REPAIR THE OPEN K11 WT/DB WIRE TO INJECTOR #6.*
YES
DISCONNECT THE #1 INJECTOR.
TEST WT/DB WIRE RESISTANCE BETWEEN INJECTOR NO. 1 CONNECTOR & LT GREY 10-WAY HARNESS CONNECTOR
IS THE RESISTANCE BELOW 10.0 OHMS?
NO
REPAIR THE OPEN K11 WT/DB WIRE TO INJECTOR #1.*
YES
REPLACE FUEL INJECTOR #6.*

* PERFORM VERIFICATION PROCEDURE VER-2.

91B10455

Fig. 70: *Driveability Test 15A (3.3L & 3.8L) – Code 26, Injector No. 1 Peak Current Not Reached (3 of 3)*

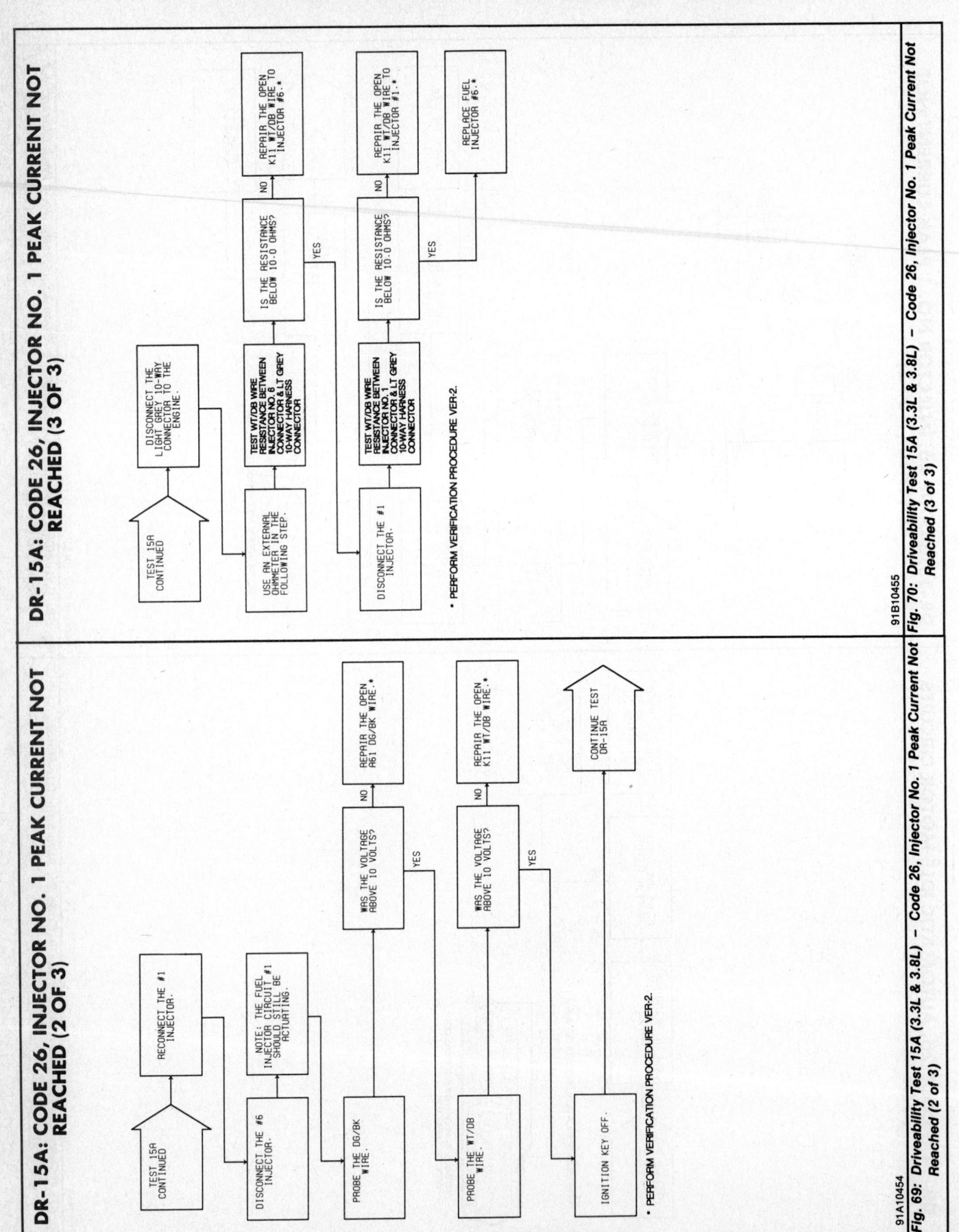

DR-16A: CODES 27 & 26, INJECTOR NO. 1 CONTROL CKT & PEAK CURRENT NOT REACHED (1 OF 3)

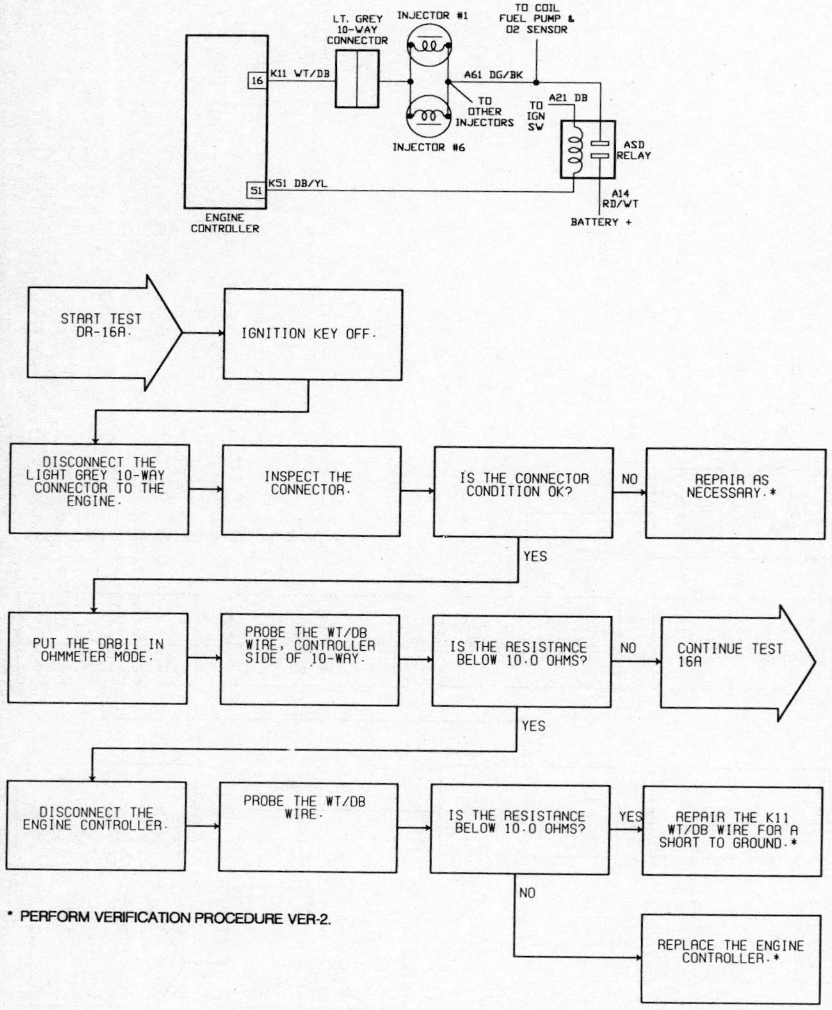
ENGINE CONTROLLER
16
K11 WT/DB
51
K51 DB/YL
LT. GREY 10-WAY CONNECTOR
INJECTOR #1
INJECTOR #6
TO OTHER INJECTORS
A61 DG/BK
TO COIL FUEL PUMP & O2 SENSOR
TO IGN SW
A21 DB
ASD RELAY
A14 RD/WT
BATTERY +
START TEST DR-16A.
IGNITION KEY OFF.
DISCONNECT THE LIGHT GREY 10-WAY CONNECTOR TO THE ENGINE.
INSPECT THE CONNECTOR.
IS THE CONNECTOR CONDITION OK?
NO
REPAIR AS NECESSARY.*
YES
PUT THE DRBII IN OHMMETER MODE.
PROBE THE WT/DB WIRE, CONTROLLER SIDE OF 10-WAY.
IS THE RESISTANCE BELOW 10.0 OHMS?
NO
CONTINUE TEST 16A
YES
DISCONNECT THE ENGINE CONTROLLER.
PROBE THE WT/DB WIRE.
IS THE RESISTANCE BELOW 10.0 OHMS?
YES
REPAIR THE K11 WT/DB WIRE FOR A SHORT TO GROUND.*
NO
REPLACE THE ENGINE CONTROLLER.*

* PERFORM VERIFICATION PROCEDURE VER-2.

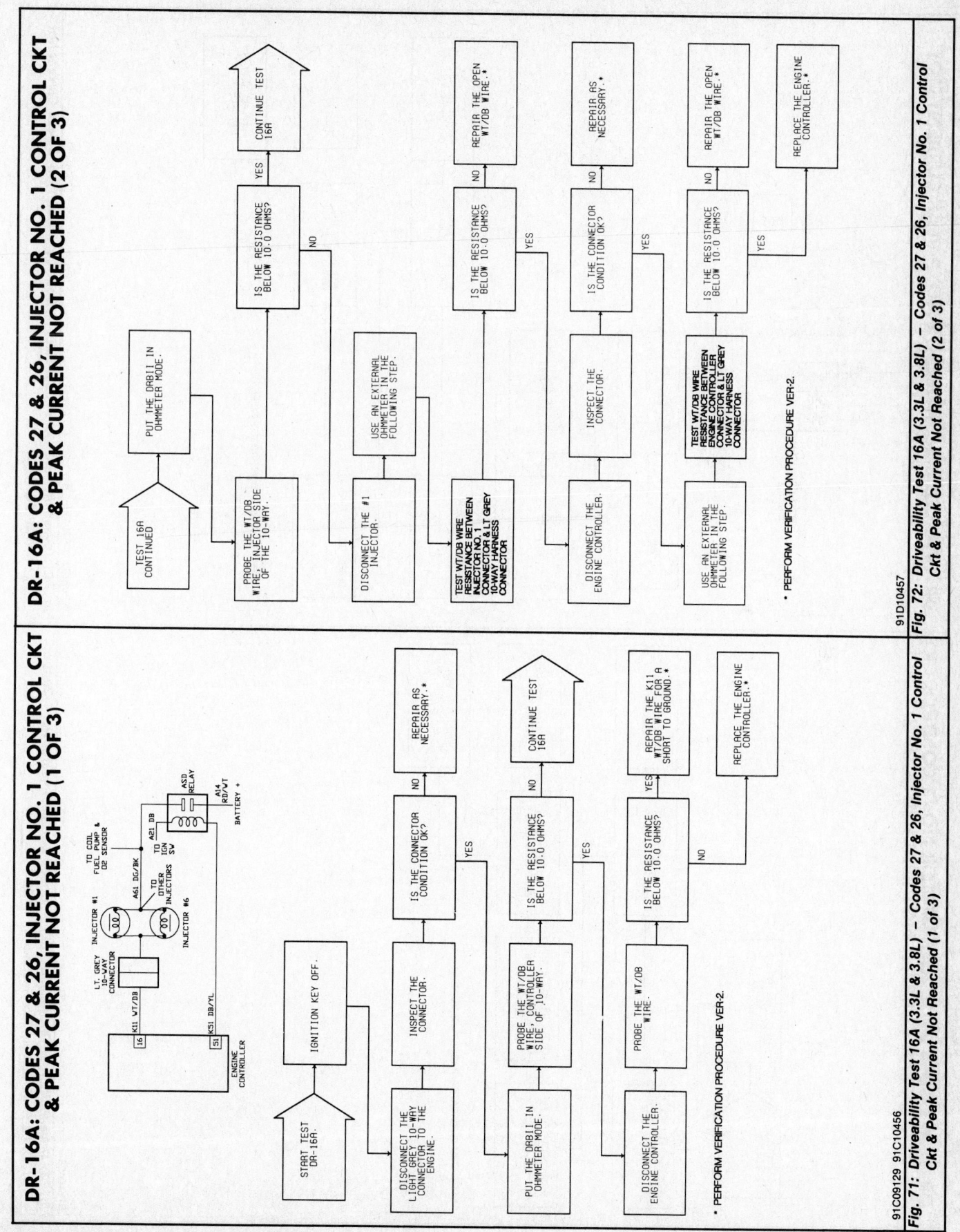

91C09129 91C10456

Fig. 71: ***Driveability Test 16A (3.3L & 3.8L) – Codes 27 & 26, Injector No. 1 Control Ckt & Peak Current Not Reached (1 of 3)***

DR-16A: CODES 27 & 26, INJECTOR NO. 1 CONTROL CKT & PEAK CURRENT NOT REACHED (2 OF 3)

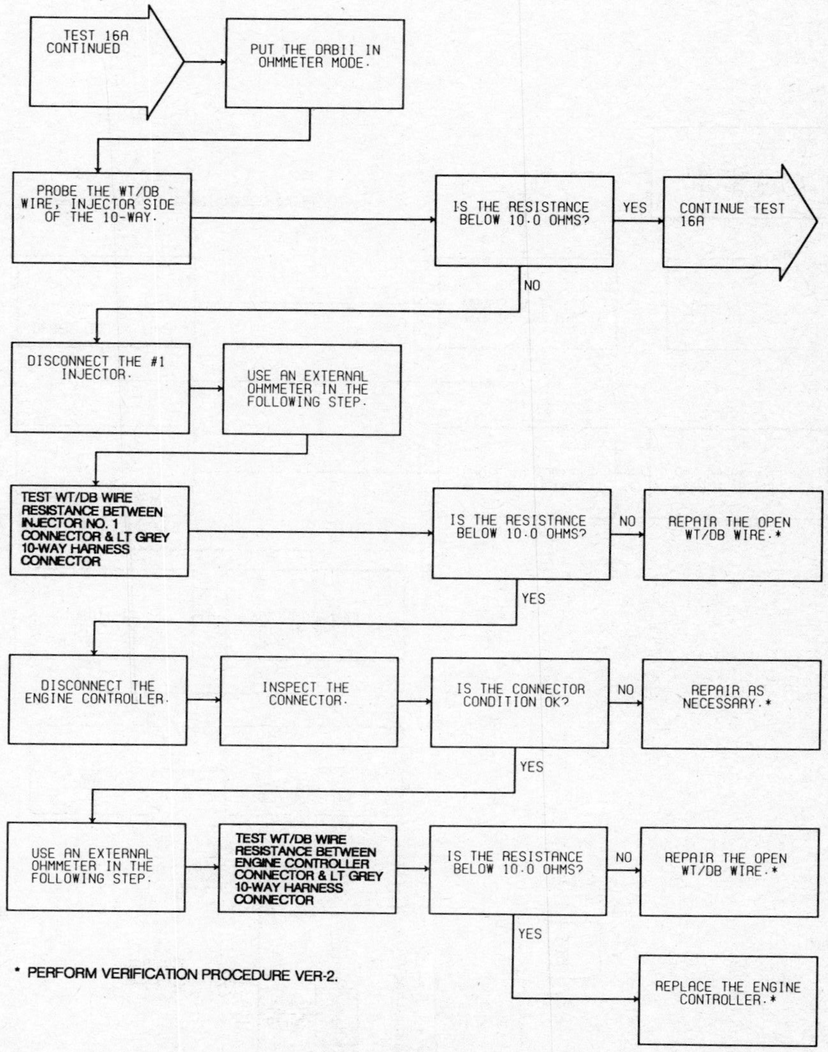
TEST 16A CONTINUED
PUT THE DRBII IN OHMMETER MODE.
PROBE THE WT/DB WIRE, INJECTOR SIDE OF THE 10-WAY.
IS THE RESISTANCE BELOW 10.0 OHMS?
YES
CONTINUE TEST 16A
NO
DISCONNECT THE #1 INJECTOR.
USE AN EXTERNAL OHMMETER IN THE FOLLOWING STEP.
TEST WT/DB WIRE RESISTANCE BETWEEN INJECTOR NO. 1 CONNECTOR & LT GREY 10-WAY HARNESS CONNECTOR
IS THE RESISTANCE BELOW 10.0 OHMS?
NO
REPAIR THE OPEN WT/DB WIRE.*
YES
DISCONNECT THE ENGINE CONTROLLER.
INSPECT THE CONNECTOR.
IS THE CONNECTOR CONDITION OK?
NO
REPAIR AS NECESSARY.*
YES
USE AN EXTERNAL OHMMETER IN THE FOLLOWING STEP.
TEST WT/DB WIRE RESISTANCE BETWEEN ENGINE CONTROLLER CONNECTOR & LT GREY 10-WAY HARNESS CONNECTOR
IS THE RESISTANCE BELOW 10.0 OHMS?
NO
REPAIR THE OPEN WT/DB WIRE.*
YES
REPLACE THE ENGINE CONTROLLER.*

* PERFORM VERIFICATION PROCEDURE VER-2.

91D10457

Fig. 72: ***Driveability Test 16A (3.3L & 3.8L) – Codes 27 & 26, Injector No. 1 Control Ckt & Peak Current Not Reached (2 of 3)***

DR-16A: CODES 27 & 26, INJECTOR NO. 1 CONTROL CKT & PEAK CURRENT NOT REACHED (3 OF 3)

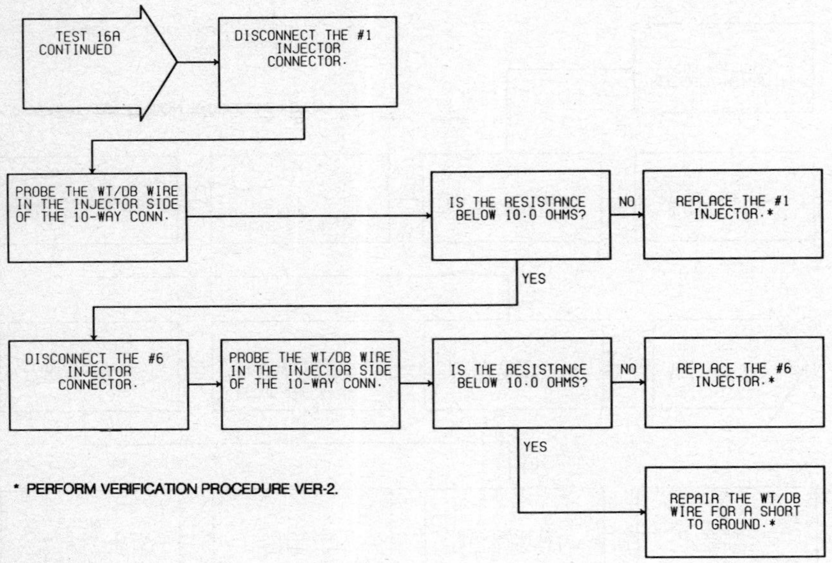
TEST 16A CONTINUED
DISCONNECT THE #1 INJECTOR CONNECTOR.
PROBE THE WT/DB WIRE IN THE INJECTOR SIDE OF THE 10-WAY CONN.
IS THE RESISTANCE BELOW 10.0 OHMS?
NO
REPLACE THE #1 INJECTOR.*
YES
DISCONNECT THE #6 INJECTOR CONNECTOR.
PROBE THE WT/DB WIRE IN THE INJECTOR SIDE OF THE 10-WAY CONN.
IS THE RESISTANCE BELOW 10.0 OHMS?
NO
REPLACE THE #6 INJECTOR.*
YES
REPAIR THE WT/DB WIRE FOR A SHORT TO GROUND.*

* PERFORM VERIFICATION PROCEDURE VER-2.

91E10458

Fig. 73: Driveability Test 16A (3.3L & 3.8L) – Codes 27 & 26, Injector No. 1 Control Ckt & Peak Current Not Reached (3 of 3)

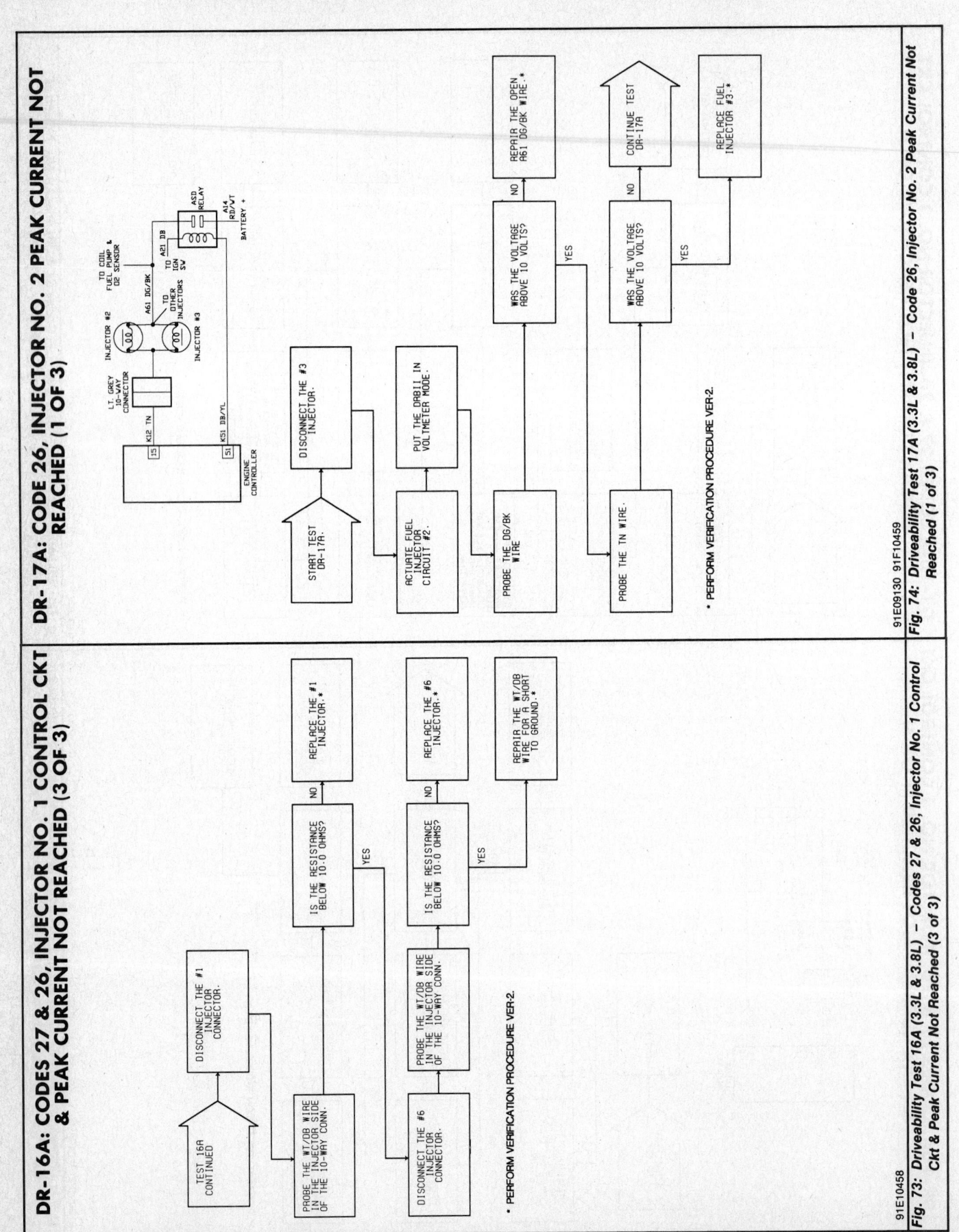

DR-17A: CODE 26, INJECTOR NO. 2 PEAK CURRENT NOT REACHED (1 OF 3)

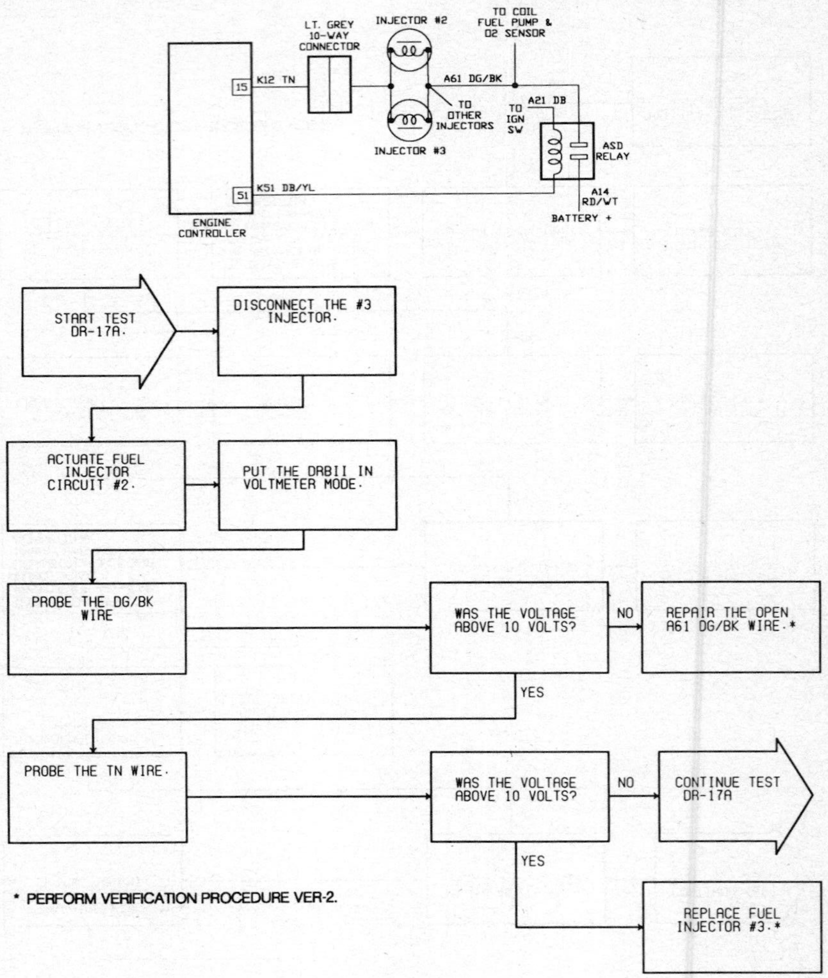
LT. GREY 10-WAY CONNECTOR
INJECTOR #2
TO COIL FUEL PUMP & O2 SENSOR
15
K12 TN
A61 DG/BK
TO OTHER INJECTORS
TO IGN SW
A21 DB
ASD RELAY
INJECTOR #3
51
K51 DB/YL
A14 RD/WT
BATTERY +
ENGINE CONTROLLER
START TEST DR-17A.
DISCONNECT THE #3 INJECTOR.
ACTUATE FUEL INJECTOR CIRCUIT #2.
PUT THE DRBII IN VOLTMETER MODE.
PROBE THE DG/BK WIRE
WAS THE VOLTAGE ABOVE 10 VOLTS?
NO
REPAIR THE OPEN A61 DG/BK WIRE.*
YES
PROBE THE TN WIRE.
WAS THE VOLTAGE ABOVE 10 VOLTS?
NO
CONTINUE TEST DR-17A
YES
REPLACE FUEL INJECTOR #3.*

* PERFORM VERIFICATION PROCEDURE VER-2.

91E09130 91F10459

Fig. 74: Driveability Test 17A (3.3L & 3.8L) – Code 26, Injector No. 2 Peak Current Not Reached (1 of 3)

DR-17A: CODE 26, INJECTOR NO. 2 PEAK CURRENT NOT REACHED (2 OF 3)

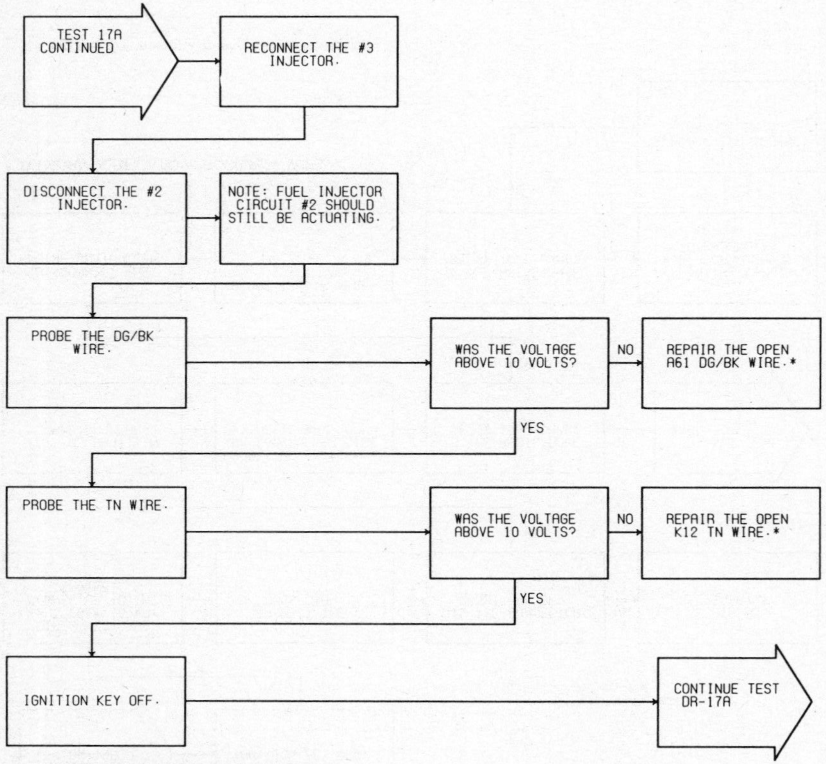
TEST 17A CONTINUED
RECONNECT THE #3 INJECTOR.
DISCONNECT THE #2 INJECTOR.
NOTE: FUEL INJECTOR CIRCUIT #2 SHOULD STILL BE ACTUATING.
PROBE THE DG/BK WIRE.
WAS THE VOLTAGE ABOVE 10 VOLTS?
NO
REPAIR THE OPEN A61 DG/BK WIRE.*
YES
PROBE THE TN WIRE.
WAS THE VOLTAGE ABOVE 10 VOLTS?
NO
REPAIR THE OPEN K12 TN WIRE.*
YES
IGNITION KEY OFF.
CONTINUE TEST DR-17A

* PERFORM VERIFICATION PROCEDURE VER-2.

91I10460

Fig. 75: Driveability Test 17A (3.3L & 3.8L) – Code 26, Injector No. 2 Peak Current Not Reached (2 of 3)

DR-17A: CODE 26, INJECTOR NO. 2 PEAK CURRENT NOT REACHED (3 OF 3)

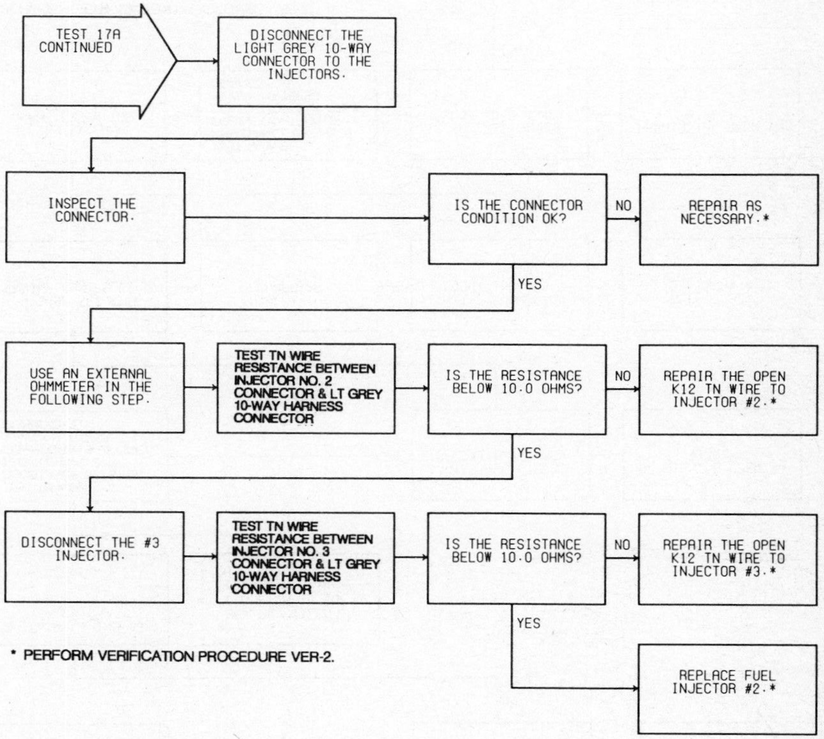
TEST 17A CONTINUED
DISCONNECT THE LIGHT GREY 10-WAY CONNECTOR TO THE INJECTORS.
INSPECT THE CONNECTOR.
IS THE CONNECTOR CONDITION OK?
NO
REPAIR AS NECESSARY.*
YES
USE AN EXTERNAL OHMMETER IN THE FOLLOWING STEP.
TEST TN WIRE RESISTANCE BETWEEN INJECTOR NO. 2 CONNECTOR & LT GREY 10-WAY HARNESS CONNECTOR
IS THE RESISTANCE BELOW 10.0 OHMS?
NO
REPAIR THE OPEN K12 TN WIRE TO INJECTOR #2.*
YES
DISCONNECT THE #3 INJECTOR.
TEST TN WIRE RESISTANCE BETWEEN INJECTOR NO. 3 CONNECTOR & LT GREY 10-WAY HARNESS CONNECTOR
IS THE RESISTANCE BELOW 10.0 OHMS?
NO
REPAIR THE OPEN K12 TN WIRE TO INJECTOR #3.*
YES
REPLACE FUEL INJECTOR #2.*

* PERFORM VERIFICATION PROCEDURE VER-2.

91J10461

Fig. 76: Driveability Test 17A (3.3L & 3.8L) – Code 26, Injector No. 2 Peak Current Not Reached (3 of 3)

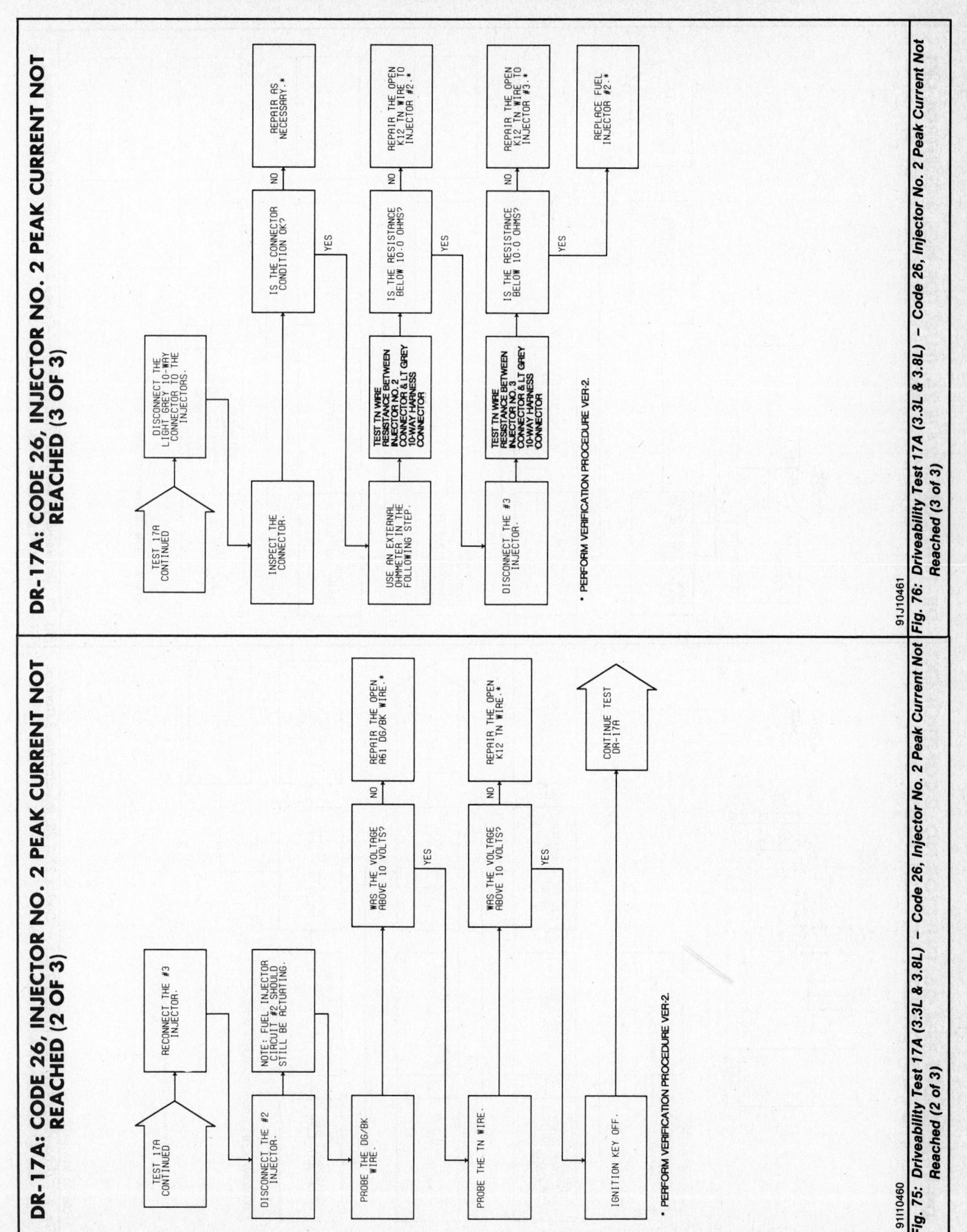

DR-18A: CODES 27 & 26, INJECTOR NO. 2 CONTROL CKT & PEAK CURRENT NOT REACHED (1 OF 3)

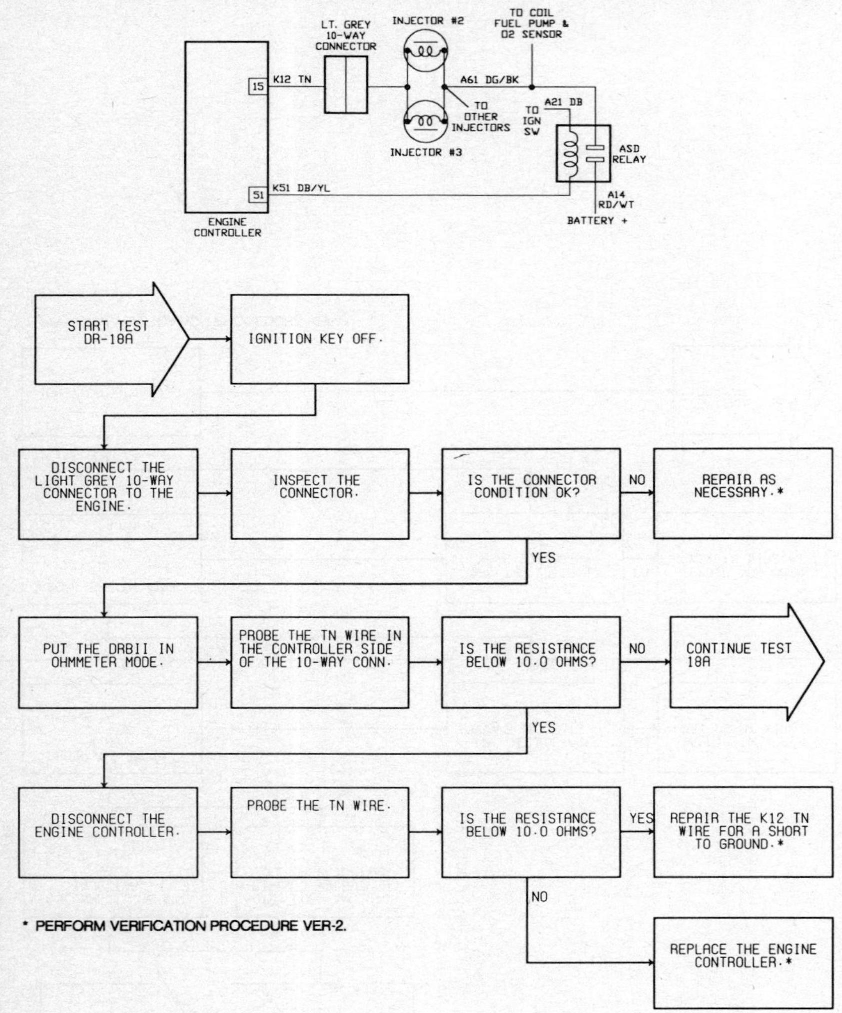
LT. GREY 10-WAY CONNECTOR
INJECTOR #2
TO COIL FUEL PUMP & O2 SENSOR
15
K12 TN
A61 DG/BK
TO OTHER INJECTORS
TO IGN SW
A21 DB
INJECTOR #3
ASD RELAY
51
K51 DB/YL
A14 RD/WT
BATTERY +
ENGINE CONTROLLER
START TEST DR-18A
IGNITION KEY OFF.
DISCONNECT THE LIGHT GREY 10-WAY CONNECTOR TO THE ENGINE.
INSPECT THE CONNECTOR.
IS THE CONNECTOR CONDITION OK?
NO
REPAIR AS NECESSARY.*
YES
PUT THE DRBII IN OHMMETER MODE.
PROBE THE TN WIRE IN THE CONTROLLER SIDE OF THE 10-WAY CONN.
IS THE RESISTANCE BELOW 10.0 OHMS?
NO
CONTINUE TEST 18A
YES
DISCONNECT THE ENGINE CONTROLLER.
PROBE THE TN WIRE.
IS THE RESISTANCE BELOW 10.0 OHMS?
YES
REPAIR THE K12 TN WIRE FOR A SHORT TO GROUND.*
NO
REPLACE THE ENGINE CONTROLLER.*

* PERFORM VERIFICATION PROCEDURE VER-2.

91E09130 91A10462

Fig. 77: *Driveability Test 18A (3.3L & 3.8L) – Codes 27 & 26, Injector No. 2 Control Ckt & Peak Current Not Reached (1 of 3)*

DR-18A: CODES 27 & 26, INJECTOR NO. 2 CONTROL CKT & PEAK CURRENT NOT REACHED (2 OF 3)

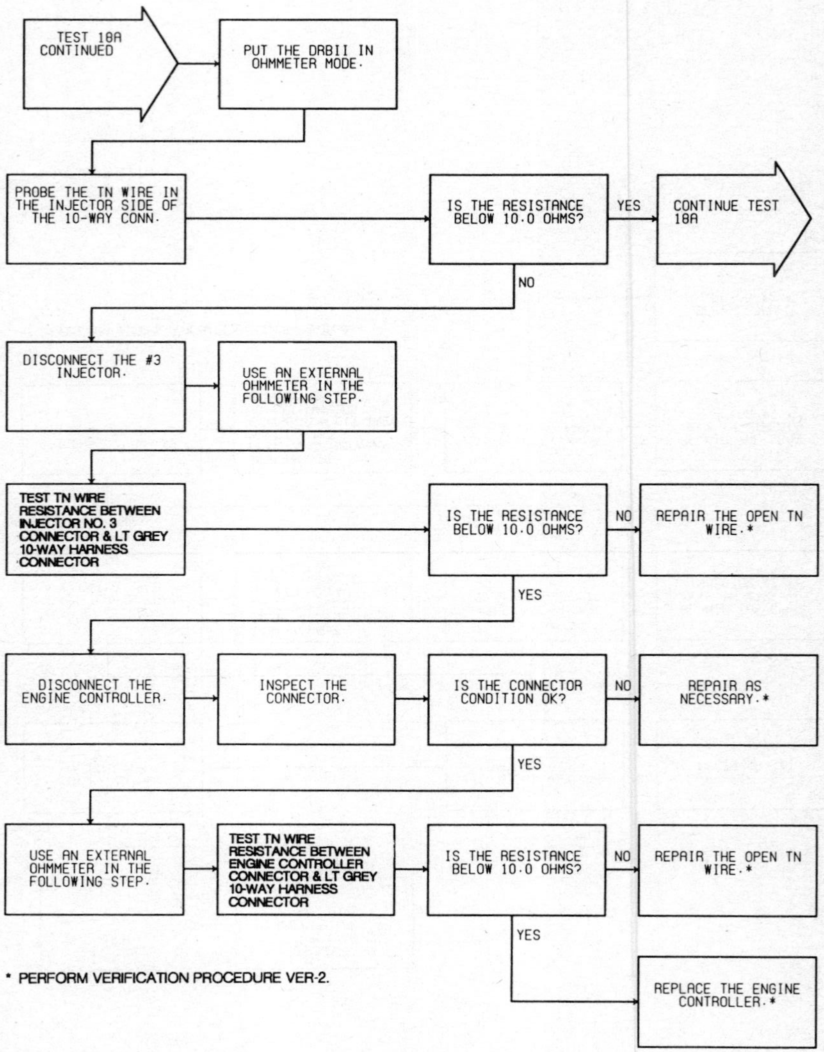
TEST 18A CONTINUED
PUT THE DRBII IN OHMMETER MODE.
PROBE THE TN WIRE IN THE INJECTOR SIDE OF THE 10-WAY CONN.
IS THE RESISTANCE BELOW 10.0 OHMS?
YES
CONTINUE TEST 18A
NO
DISCONNECT THE #3 INJECTOR.
USE AN EXTERNAL OHMMETER IN THE FOLLOWING STEP.
TEST TN WIRE RESISTANCE BETWEEN INJECTOR NO. 3 CONNECTOR & LT GREY 10-WAY HARNESS CONNECTOR
IS THE RESISTANCE BELOW 10.0 OHMS?
NO
REPAIR THE OPEN TN WIRE.*
YES
DISCONNECT THE ENGINE CONTROLLER.
INSPECT THE CONNECTOR.
IS THE CONNECTOR CONDITION OK?
NO
REPAIR AS NECESSARY.*
YES
USE AN EXTERNAL OHMMETER IN THE FOLLOWING STEP.
TEST TN WIRE RESISTANCE BETWEEN ENGINE CONTROLLER CONNECTOR & LT GREY 10-WAY HARNESS CONNECTOR
IS THE RESISTANCE BELOW 10.0 OHMS?
NO
REPAIR THE OPEN TN WIRE.*
YES
REPLACE THE ENGINE CONTROLLER.*

* PERFORM VERIFICATION PROCEDURE VER-2.

91B10463

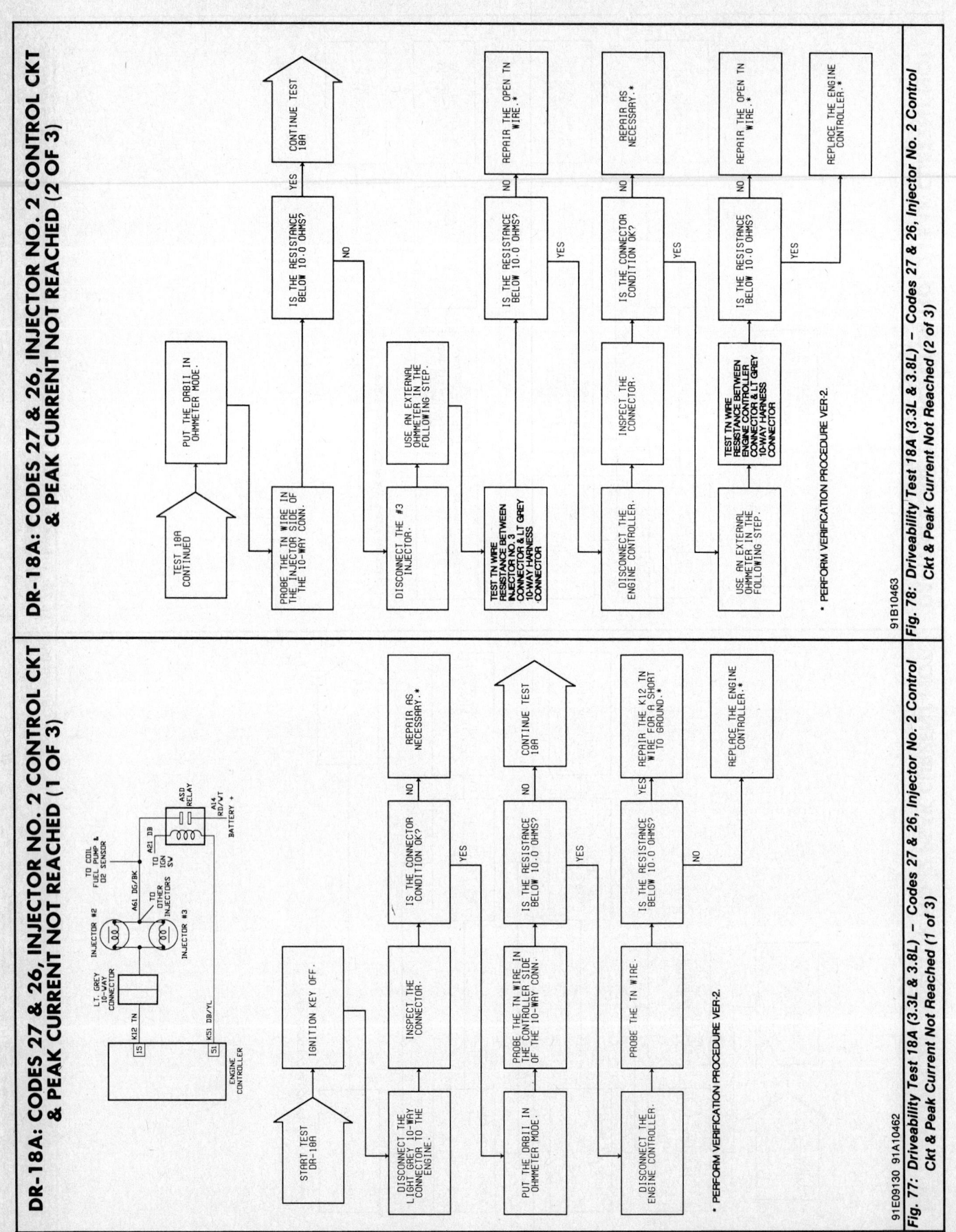

Fig. 78: *Driveability Test 18A (3.3L & 3.8L) – Codes 27 & 26, Injector No. 2 Control Ckt & Peak Current Not Reached (2 of 3)*

DR-18A: CODES 27 & 26, INJECTOR NO. 2 CONTROL CKT & PEAK CURRENT NOT REACHED (3 OF 3)

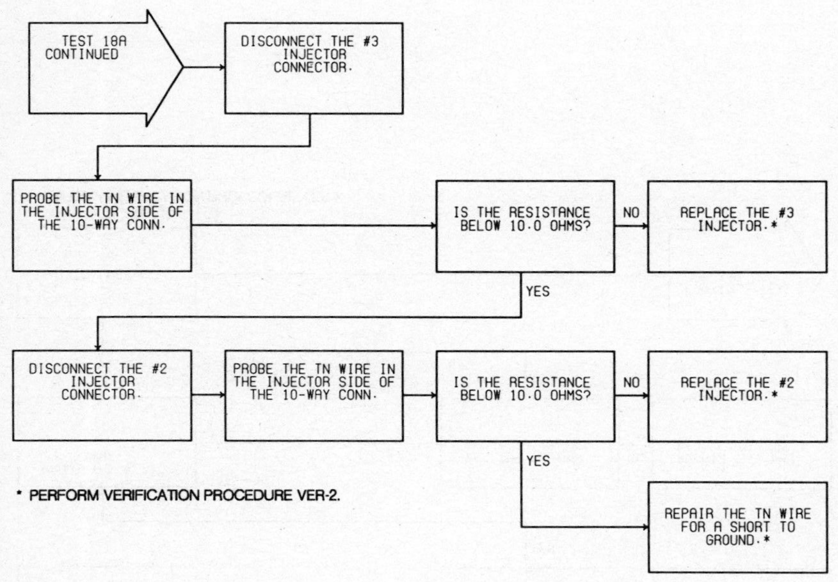
TEST 18A CONTINUED
DISCONNECT THE #3 INJECTOR CONNECTOR.
PROBE THE TN WIRE IN THE INJECTOR SIDE OF THE 10-WAY CONN.
IS THE RESISTANCE BELOW 10.0 OHMS?
NO
REPLACE THE #3 INJECTOR.*
YES
DISCONNECT THE #2 INJECTOR CONNECTOR.
PROBE THE TN WIRE IN THE INJECTOR SIDE OF THE 10-WAY CONN.
IS THE RESISTANCE BELOW 10.0 OHMS?
NO
REPLACE THE #2 INJECTOR.*
YES
REPAIR THE TN WIRE FOR A SHORT TO GROUND.*
* PERFORM VERIFICATION PROCEDURE VER-2.

91C10464

Fig. 79: Driveability Test 18A (3.3L & 3.8L) – Codes 27 & 26, Injector No. 2 Control Ckt & Peak Current Not Reached (3 of 3)

DR-19A: CODE 26, INJECTOR NO. 3 PEAK CURRENT NOT REACHED (1 OF 3)

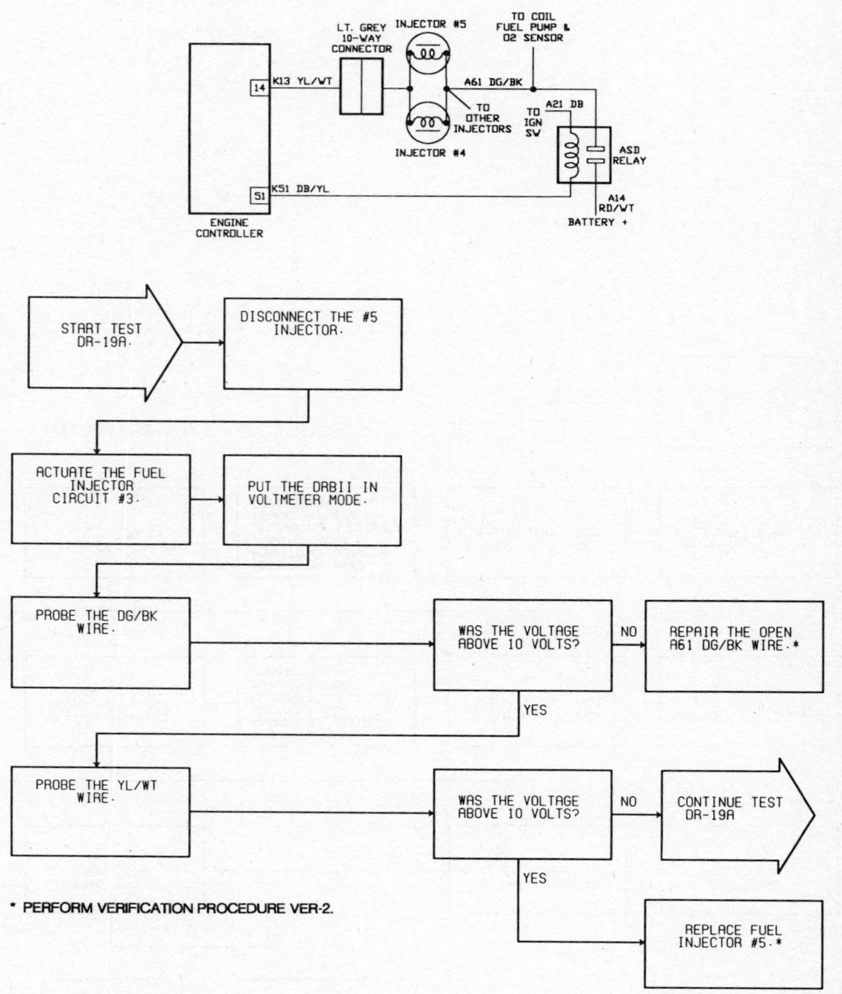
ENGINE CONTROLLER
14
K13 YL/WT
51
K51 DB/YL
LT. GREY 10-WAY CONNECTOR
INJECTOR #5
INJECTOR #4
TO OTHER INJECTORS
A61 DG/BK
TO COIL FUEL PUMP & O2 SENSOR
A21 DB
TO IGN SW
ASD RELAY
A14 RD/WT
BATTERY +
START TEST DR-19A.
DISCONNECT THE #5 INJECTOR.
ACTUATE THE FUEL INJECTOR CIRCUIT #3.
PUT THE DRBII IN VOLTMETER MODE.
PROBE THE DG/BK WIRE.
WAS THE VOLTAGE ABOVE 10 VOLTS?
NO
REPAIR THE OPEN A61 DG/BK WIRE.*
YES
PROBE THE YL/WT WIRE.
WAS THE VOLTAGE ABOVE 10 VOLTS?
NO
CONTINUE TEST DR-19A
YES
REPLACE FUEL INJECTOR #5.*
* PERFORM VERIFICATION PROCEDURE VER-2.

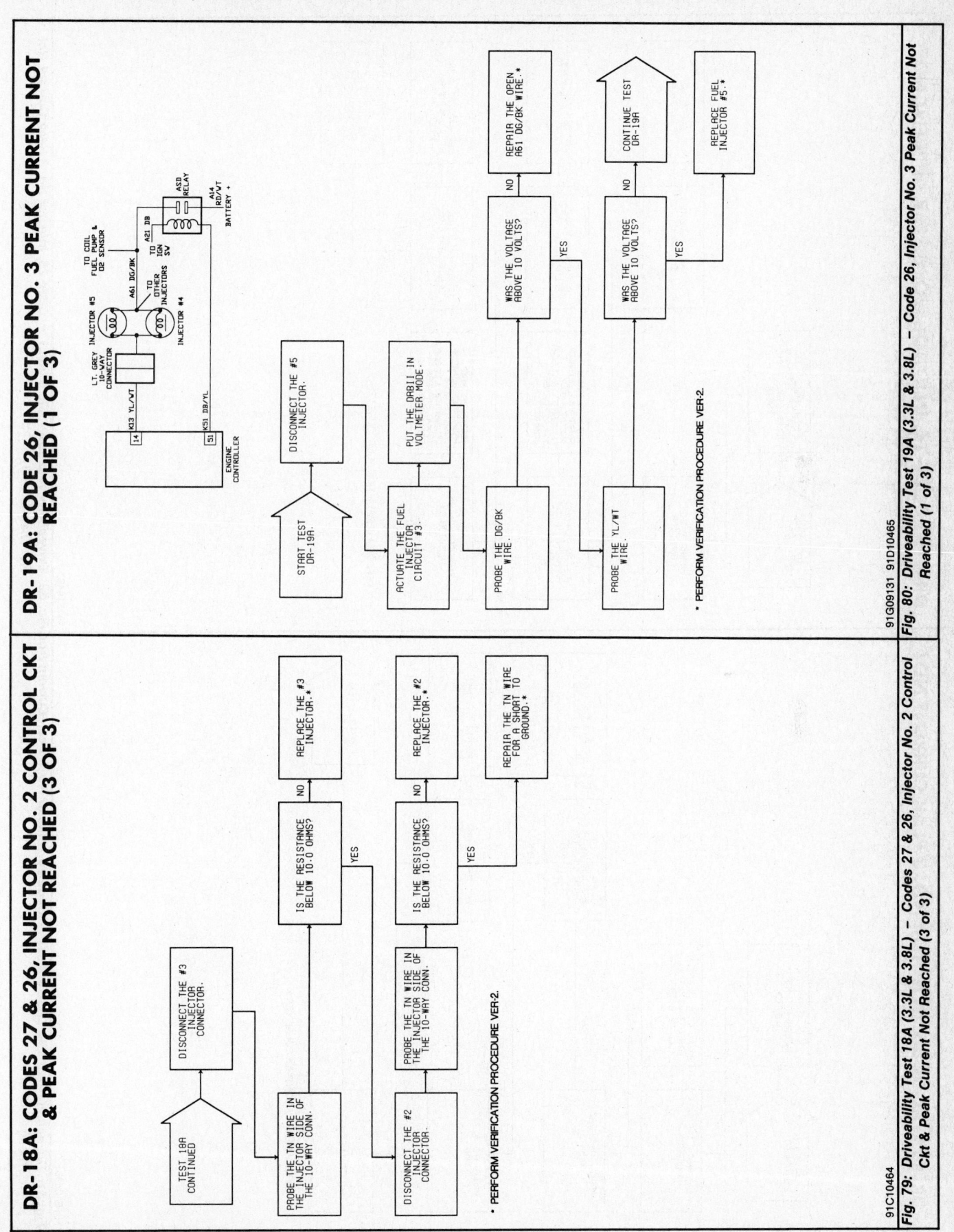

91G09131 91D10465

Fig. 80: Driveability Test 19A (3.3L & 3.8L) – Code 26, Injector No. 3 Peak Current Not Reached (1 of 3)

DR-19A: CODE 26, INJECTOR NO. 3 PEAK CURRENT NOT REACHED (2 OF 3)

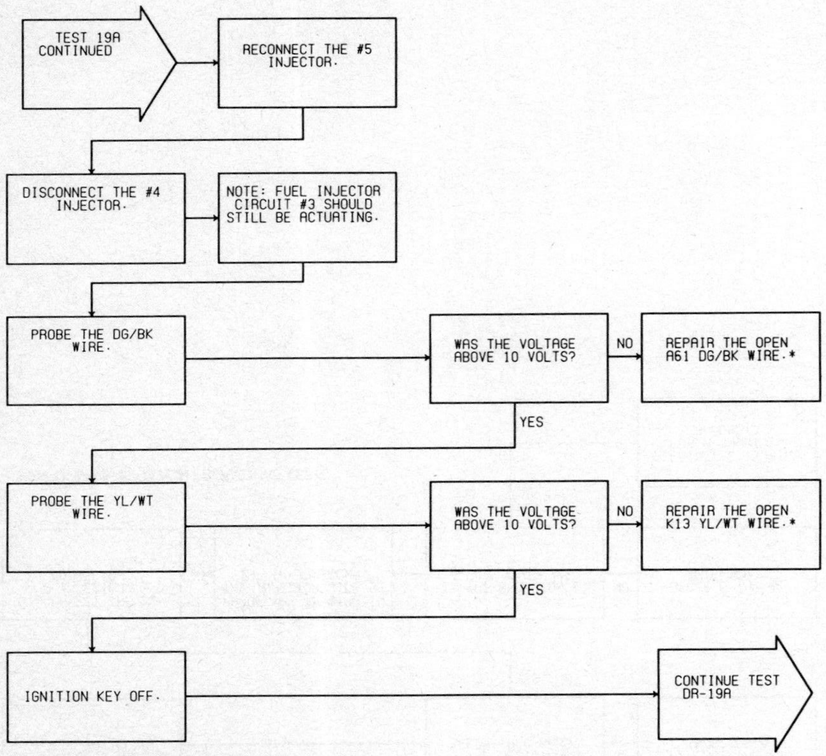
TEST 19A CONTINUED
RECONNECT THE #5 INJECTOR.
DISCONNECT THE #4 INJECTOR.
NOTE: FUEL INJECTOR CIRCUIT #3 SHOULD STILL BE ACTUATING.
PROBE THE DG/BK WIRE.
WAS THE VOLTAGE ABOVE 10 VOLTS?
NO
REPAIR THE OPEN A61 DG/BK WIRE.*
YES
PROBE THE YL/WT WIRE.
WAS THE VOLTAGE ABOVE 10 VOLTS?
NO
REPAIR THE OPEN K13 YL/WT WIRE.*
YES
IGNITION KEY OFF.
CONTINUE TEST DR-19A

* PERFORM VERIFICATION PROCEDURE VER-2.

91E10466

Fig. 81: Driveability Test 19A (3.3L & 3.8L) – Code 26, Injector No. 3 Peak Current Not Reached (2 of 3)

DR-19A: CODE 26, INJECTOR NO. 3 PEAK CURRENT NOT REACHED (3 OF 3)

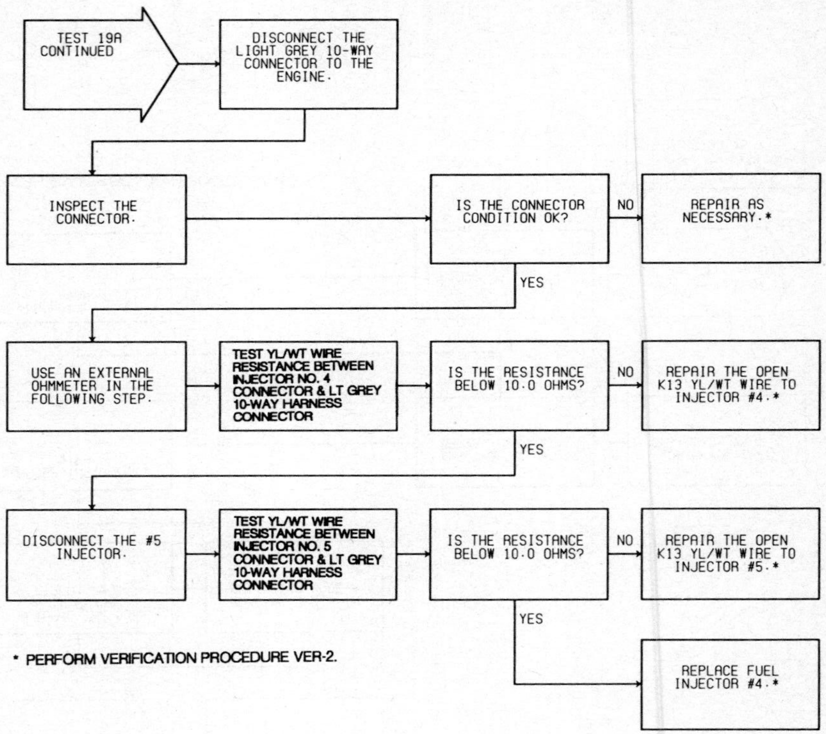
TEST 19A CONTINUED
DISCONNECT THE LIGHT GREY 10-WAY CONNECTOR TO THE ENGINE.
INSPECT THE CONNECTOR.
IS THE CONNECTOR CONDITION OK?
NO
REPAIR AS NECESSARY.*
YES
USE AN EXTERNAL OHMMETER IN THE FOLLOWING STEP.
TEST YL/WT WIRE RESISTANCE BETWEEN INJECTOR NO. 4 CONNECTOR & LT GREY 10-WAY HARNESS CONNECTOR
IS THE RESISTANCE BELOW 10.0 OHMS?
NO
REPAIR THE OPEN K13 YL/WT WIRE TO INJECTOR #4.*
YES
DISCONNECT THE #5 INJECTOR.
TEST YL/WT WIRE RESISTANCE BETWEEN INJECTOR NO. 5 CONNECTOR & LT GREY 10-WAY HARNESS CONNECTOR
IS THE RESISTANCE BELOW 10.0 OHMS?
NO
REPAIR THE OPEN K13 YL/WT WIRE TO INJECTOR #5.*
YES
REPLACE FUEL INJECTOR #4.*

* PERFORM VERIFICATION PROCEDURE VER-2.

91F10467

Fig. 82: Driveability Test 19A (3.3L & 3.8L) – Code 26, Injector No. 3 Peak Current Not Reached (3 of 3)

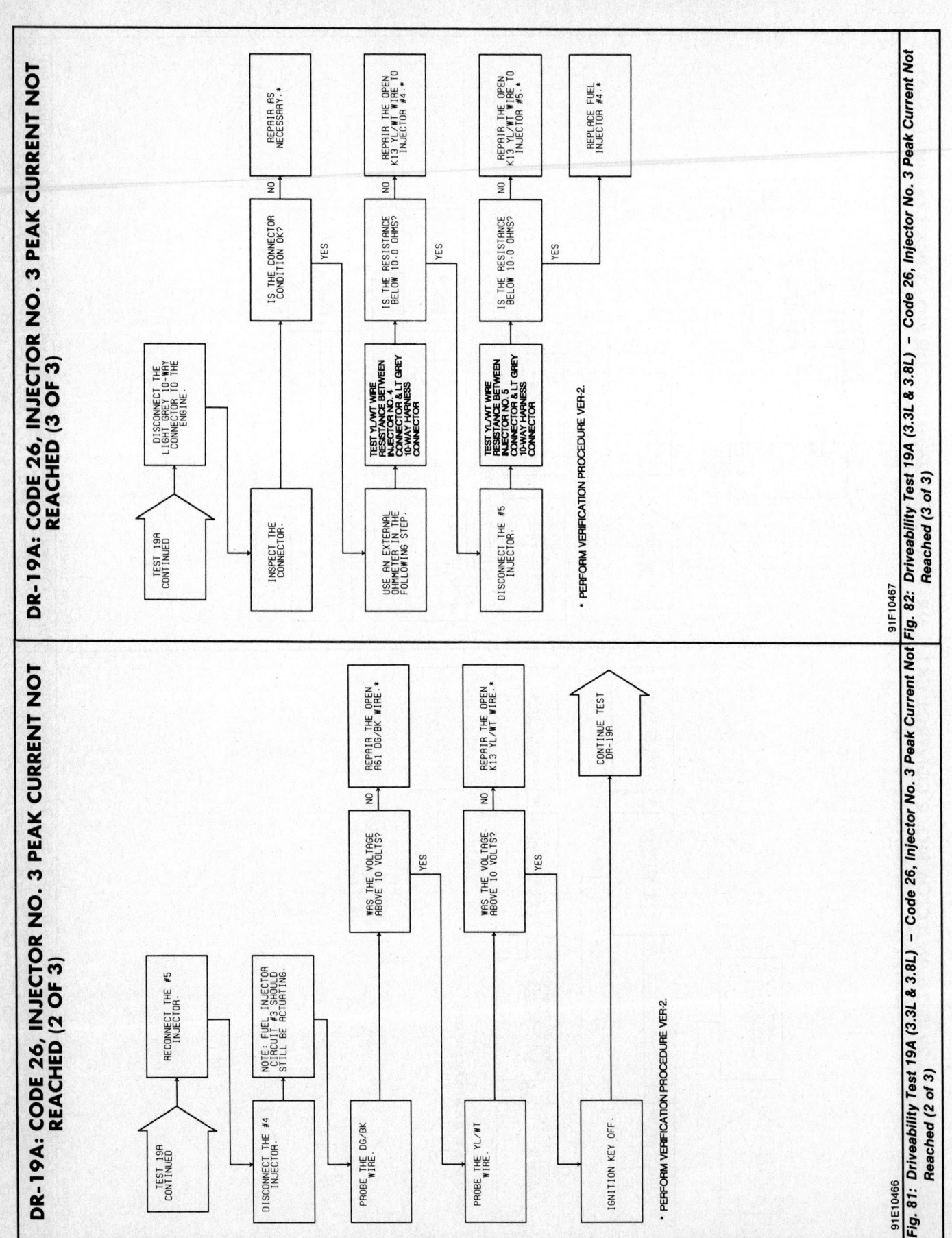

DR-20A: CODES 27 & 26, INJECTOR NO. 3 CONTROL CKT & PEAK CURRENT NOT REACHED (1 OF 3)

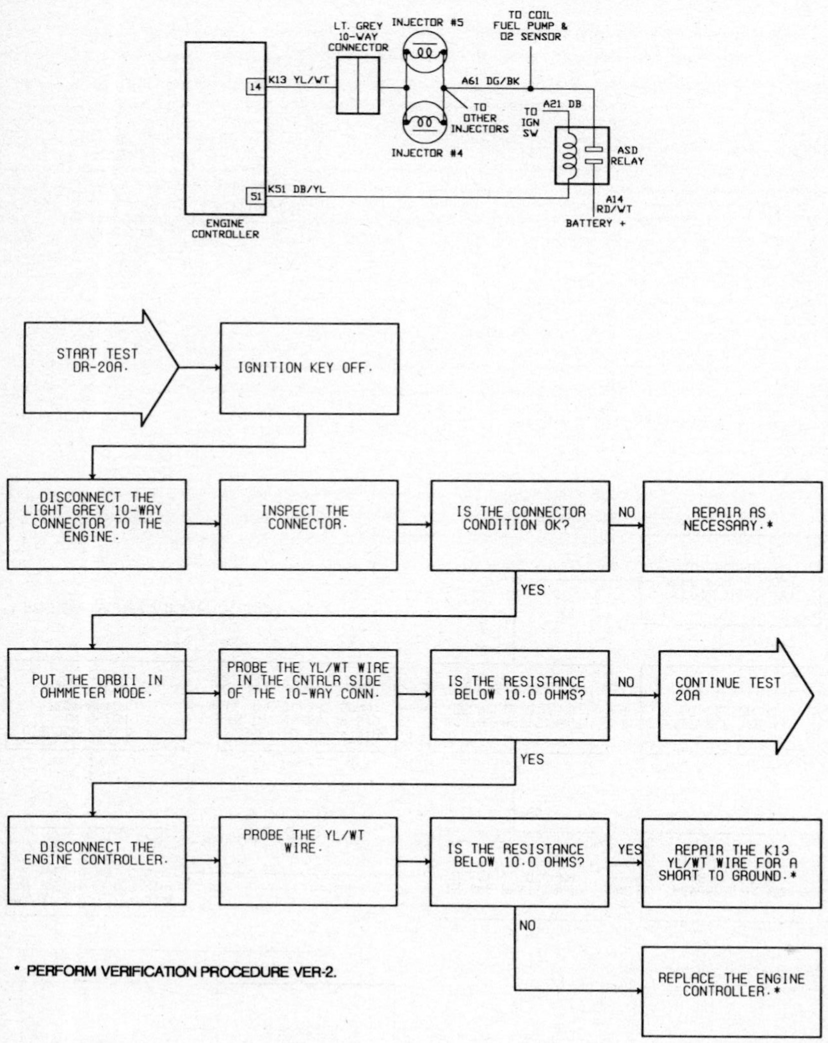
LT. GREY 10-WAY CONNECTOR
INJECTOR #5
TO COIL FUEL PUMP & O2 SENSOR
14
K13 YL/WT
A61 DG/BK
TO OTHER INJECTORS
TO IGN SW
A21 DB
ASD RELAY
INJECTOR #4
51
K51 DB/YL
A14 RD/WT
BATTERY +
ENGINE CONTROLLER
START TEST DR-20A.
IGNITION KEY OFF.
DISCONNECT THE LIGHT GREY 10-WAY CONNECTOR TO THE ENGINE.
INSPECT THE CONNECTOR.
IS THE CONNECTOR CONDITION OK?
NO
REPAIR AS NECESSARY.*
YES
PUT THE DRBII IN OHMMETER MODE.
PROBE THE YL/WT WIRE IN THE CNTRLR SIDE OF THE 10-WAY CONN.
IS THE RESISTANCE BELOW 10.0 OHMS?
NO
CONTINUE TEST 20A
YES
DISCONNECT THE ENGINE CONTROLLER.
PROBE THE YL/WT WIRE.
IS THE RESISTANCE BELOW 10.0 OHMS?
YES
REPAIR THE K13 YL/WT WIRE FOR A SHORT TO GROUND.*
NO
REPLACE THE ENGINE CONTROLLER.*

* PERFORM VERIFICATION PROCEDURE VER-2.

91G09131 91G10468

Fig. 83: Driveability Test 20A (3.3L & 3.8L) – Codes 27 & 26, Injector No. 3 Control Ckt & Peak Current Not Reached (1 of 3)

DR-20A: CODES 27 & 26, INJECTOR NO. 3 CONTROL CKT & PEAK CURRENT NOT REACHED (2 OF 3)

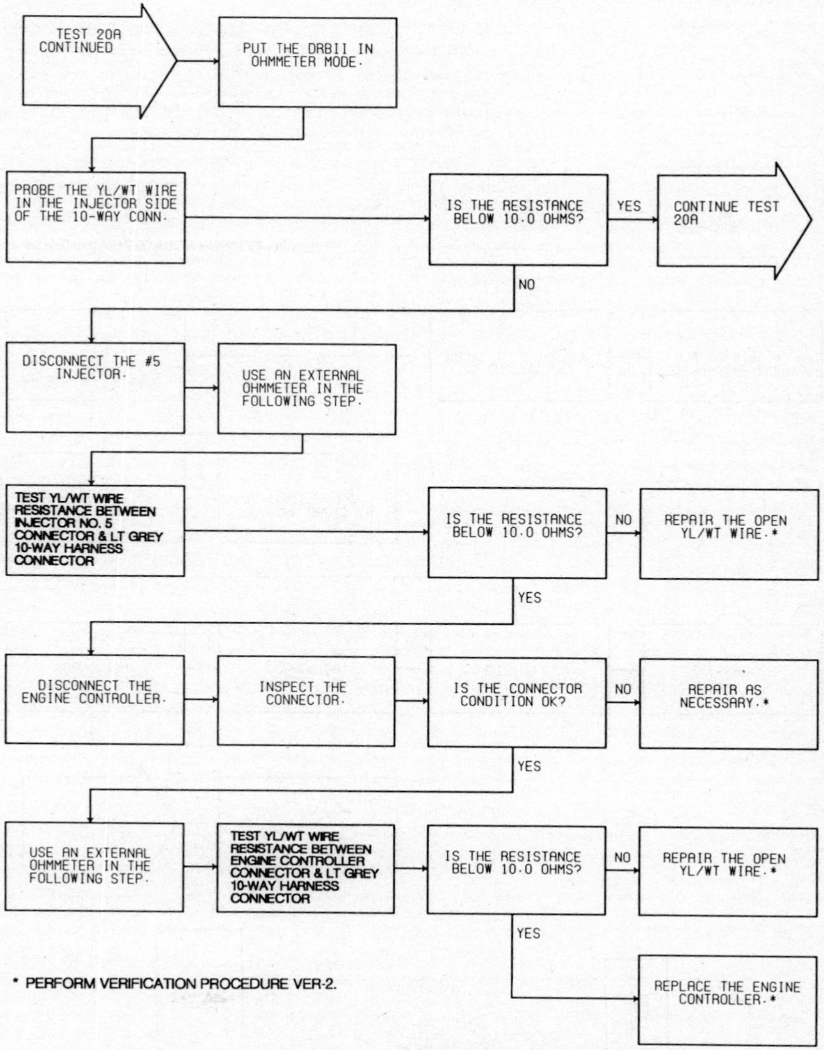
TEST 20A CONTINUED
PUT THE DRBII IN OHMMETER MODE.
PROBE THE YL/WT WIRE IN THE INJECTOR SIDE OF THE 10-WAY CONN.
IS THE RESISTANCE BELOW 10.0 OHMS?
YES
CONTINUE TEST 20A
NO
DISCONNECT THE #5 INJECTOR.
USE AN EXTERNAL OHMMETER IN THE FOLLOWING STEP.
TEST YL/WT WIRE RESISTANCE BETWEEN INJECTOR NO. 5 CONNECTOR & LT GREY 10-WAY HARNESS CONNECTOR
IS THE RESISTANCE BELOW 10.0 OHMS?
NO
REPAIR THE OPEN YL/WT WIRE.*
YES
DISCONNECT THE ENGINE CONTROLLER.
INSPECT THE CONNECTOR.
IS THE CONNECTOR CONDITION OK?
NO
REPAIR AS NECESSARY.*
YES
USE AN EXTERNAL OHMMETER IN THE FOLLOWING STEP.
TEST YL/WT WIRE RESISTANCE BETWEEN ENGINE CONTROLLER CONNECTOR & LT GREY 10-WAY HARNESS CONNECTOR
IS THE RESISTANCE BELOW 10.0 OHMS?
NO
REPAIR THE OPEN YL/WT WIRE.*
YES
REPLACE THE ENGINE CONTROLLER.*

* PERFORM VERIFICATION PROCEDURE VER-2.

91H10469

Fig. 84: Driveability Test 20A (3.3L & 3.8L) – Codes 27 & 26, Injector No. 3 Control Ckt & Peak Current Not Reached (2 of 3)

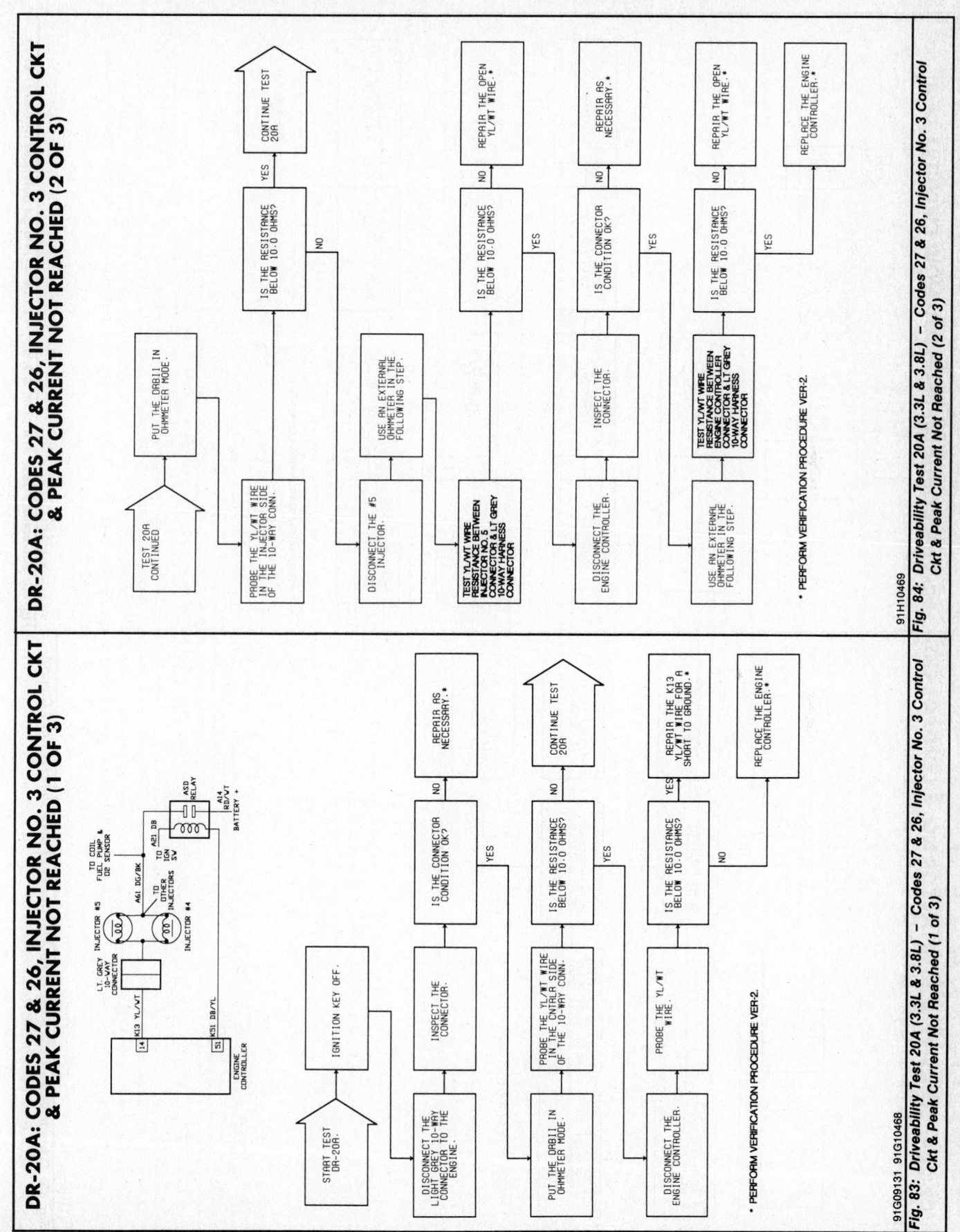

1991 ENGINE PERFORMANCE
Self-Diagnostics – 3.3L PFI (Cont.)

DR-20A: CODES 27 & 26, INJECTOR NO. 3 CONTROL CKT & PEAK CURRENT NOT REACHED (3 OF 3)

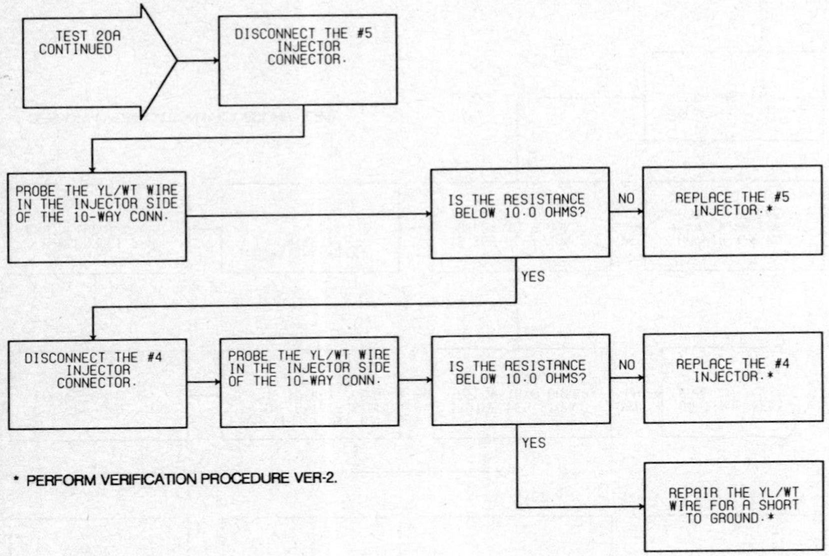
TEST 20A CONTINUED
DISCONNECT THE #5 INJECTOR CONNECTOR.
PROBE THE YL/WT WIRE IN THE INJECTOR SIDE OF THE 10-WAY CONN.
IS THE RESISTANCE BELOW 10.0 OHMS?
NO
REPLACE THE #5 INJECTOR.*
YES
DISCONNECT THE #4 INJECTOR CONNECTOR.
PROBE THE YL/WT WIRE IN THE INJECTOR SIDE OF THE 10-WAY CONN.
IS THE RESISTANCE BELOW 10.0 OHMS?
NO
REPLACE THE #4 INJECTOR.*
YES
REPAIR THE YL/WT WIRE FOR A SHORT TO GROUND.*

* PERFORM VERIFICATION PROCEDURE VER-2.

91A10470

Fig. 85: Driveability Test 20A (3.3L & 3.8L) – Codes 27 & 26, Injector No. 3 Control Ckt & Peak Current Not Reached (3 of 3)

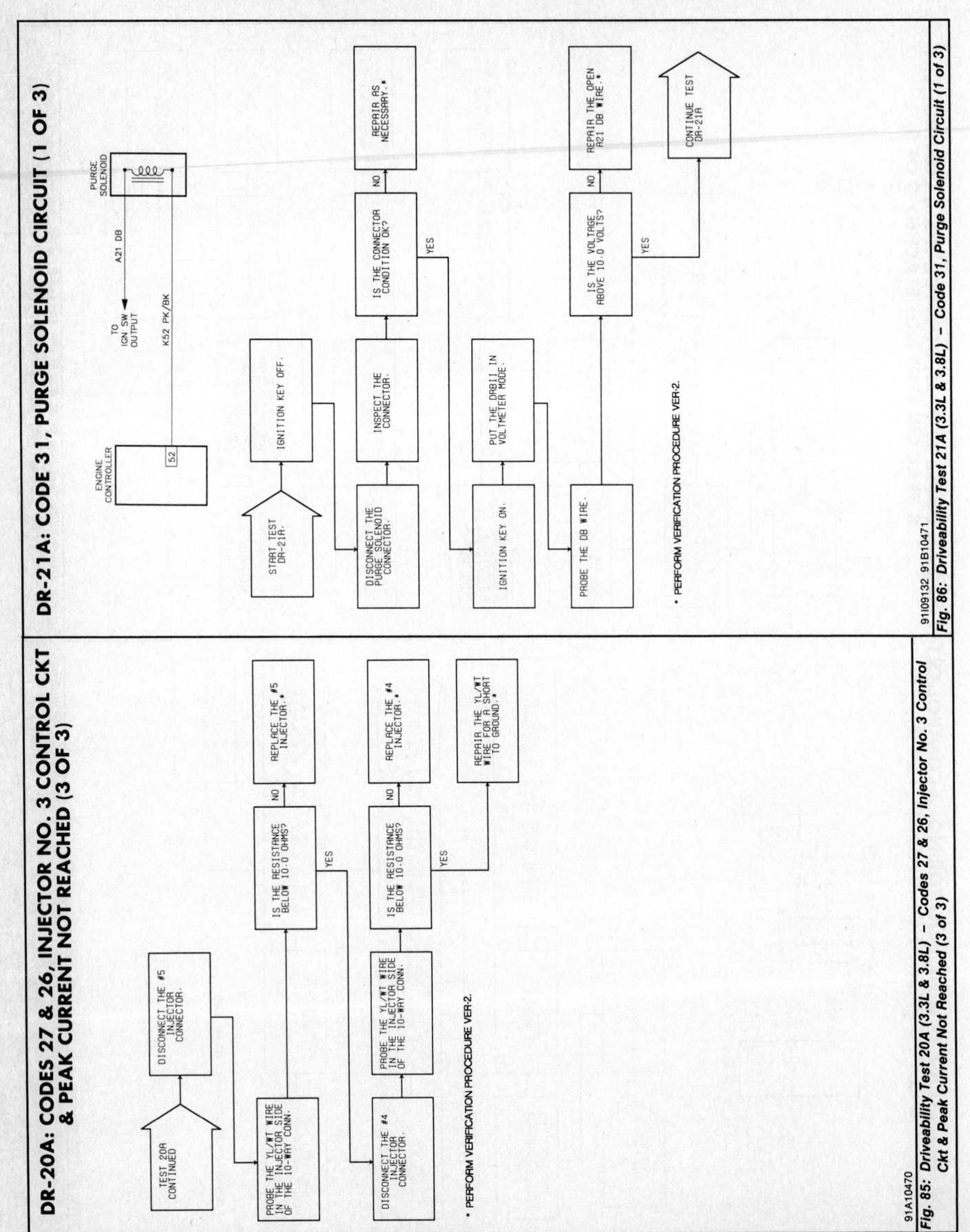

DR-21A: CODE 31, PURGE SOLENOID CIRCUIT (1 OF 3)

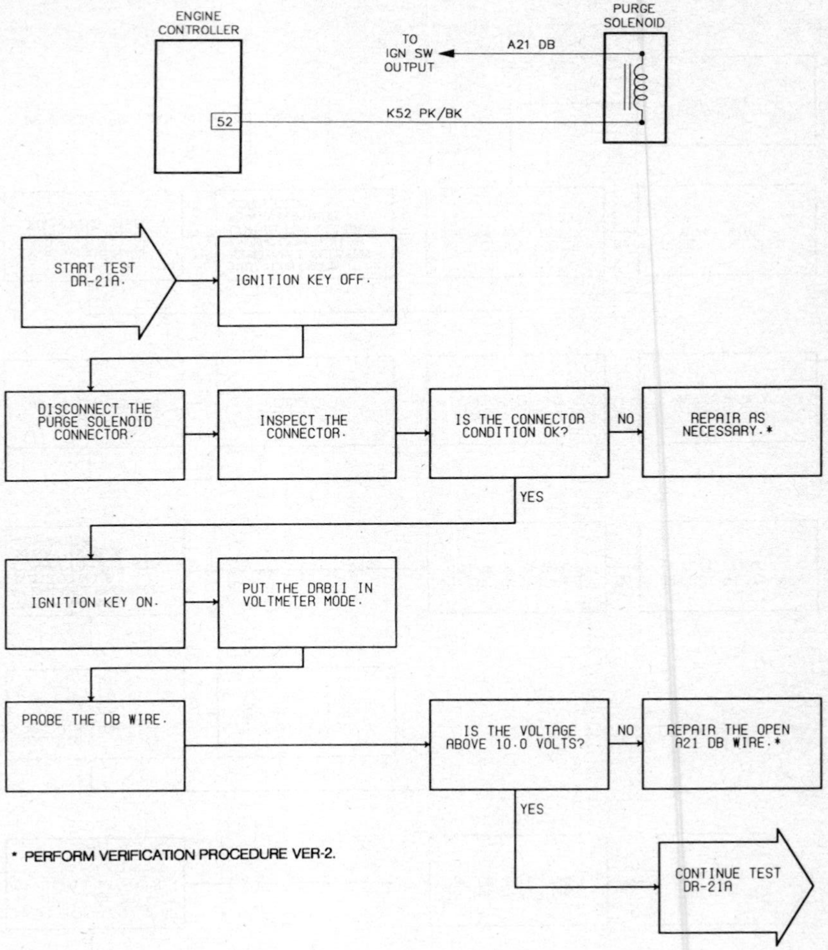
ENGINE CONTROLLER
52
TO IGN SW OUTPUT
A21 DB
K52 PK/BK
PURGE SOLENOID
START TEST DR-21A.
IGNITION KEY OFF.
DISCONNECT THE PURGE SOLENOID CONNECTOR.
INSPECT THE CONNECTOR.
IS THE CONNECTOR CONDITION OK?
NO
REPAIR AS NECESSARY.*
YES
IGNITION KEY ON.
PUT THE DRBII IN VOLTMETER MODE.
PROBE THE DB WIRE.
IS THE VOLTAGE ABOVE 10.0 VOLTS?
NO
REPAIR THE OPEN A21 DB WIRE.*
YES
CONTINUE TEST DR-21A

* PERFORM VERIFICATION PROCEDURE VER-2.

91I09132 91B10471

Fig. 86: Driveability Test 21A (3.3L & 3.8L) – Code 31, Purge Solenoid Circuit (1 of 3)

DR-21A: CODE 31, PURGE SOLENOID CIRCUIT (2 OF 3)

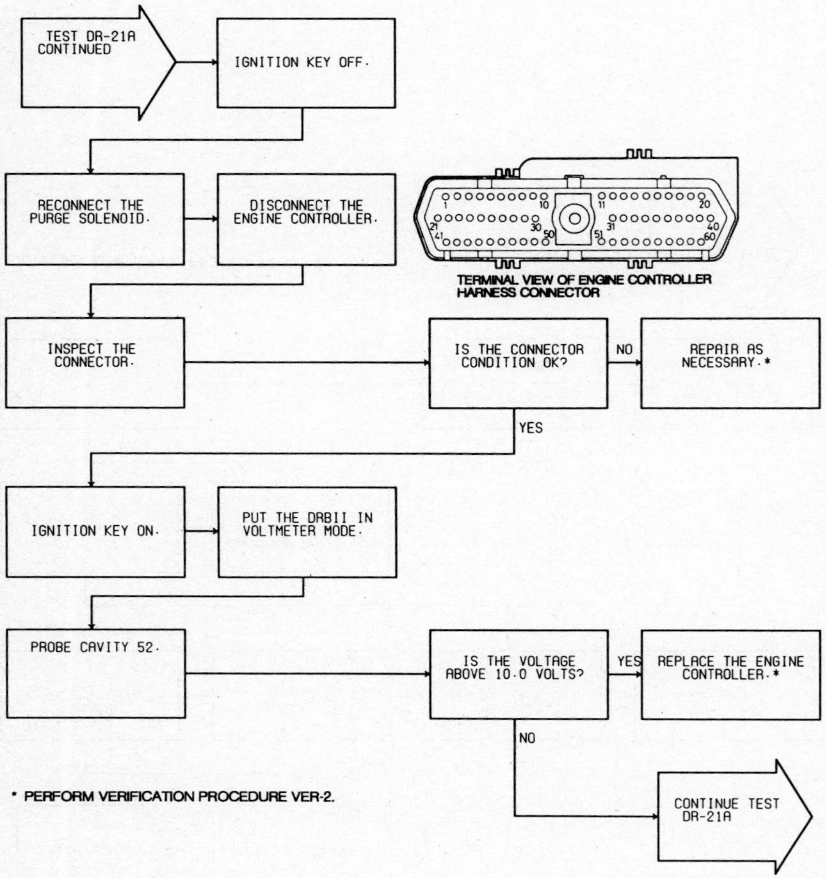
TEST DR-21A CONTINUED
IGNITION KEY OFF.
RECONNECT THE PURGE SOLENOID.
DISCONNECT THE ENGINE CONTROLLER.
TERMINAL VIEW OF ENGINE CONTROLLER HARNESS CONNECTOR
INSPECT THE CONNECTOR.
IS THE CONNECTOR CONDITION OK?
NO
REPAIR AS NECESSARY.*
YES
IGNITION KEY ON.
PUT THE DRBII IN VOLTMETER MODE.
PROBE CAVITY 52.
IS THE VOLTAGE ABOVE 10.0 VOLTS?
YES
REPLACE THE ENGINE CONTROLLER.*
NO
CONTINUE TEST DR-21A
* PERFORM VERIFICATION PROCEDURE VER-2.

91C10472

Fig. 87: Driveability Test 21A (3.3L & 3.8L) – Code 31, Purge Solenoid Circuit (2 of 3)

DR-21A: CODE 31, PURGE SOLENOID CIRCUIT (3 OF 3)

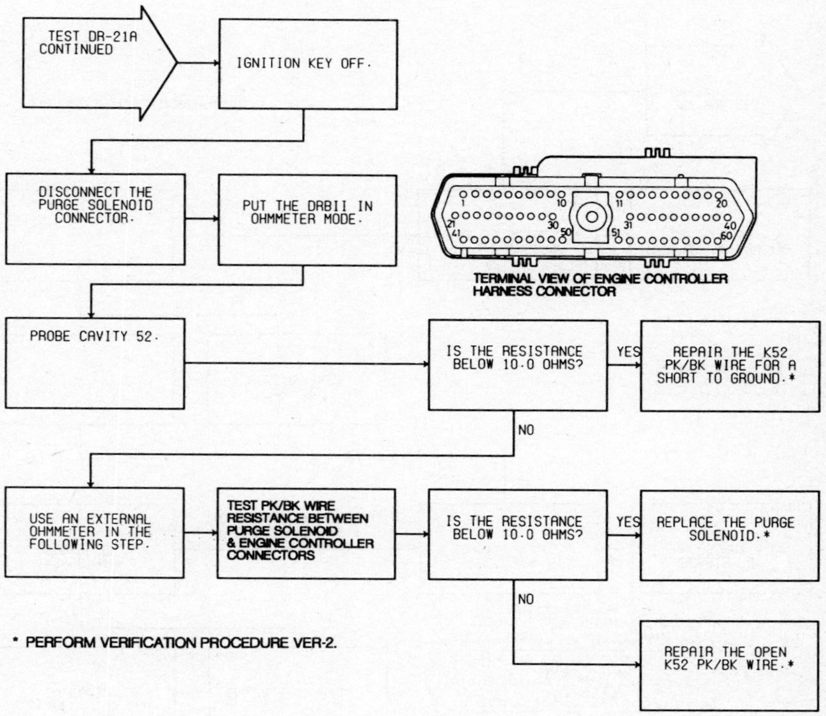
TEST DR-21A CONTINUED
IGNITION KEY OFF.
DISCONNECT THE PURGE SOLENOID CONNECTOR.
PUT THE DRBII IN OHMMETER MODE.
TERMINAL VIEW OF ENGINE CONTROLLER HARNESS CONNECTOR
PROBE CAVITY 52.
IS THE RESISTANCE BELOW 10.0 OHMS?
YES
REPAIR THE K52 PK/BK WIRE FOR A SHORT TO GROUND.*
NO
USE AN EXTERNAL OHMMETER IN THE FOLLOWING STEP.
TEST PK/BK WIRE RESISTANCE BETWEEN PURGE SOLENOID & ENGINE CONTROLLER CONNECTORS
IS THE RESISTANCE BELOW 10.0 OHMS?
YES
REPLACE THE PURGE SOLENOID.*
NO
REPAIR THE OPEN K52 PK/BK WIRE.*
* PERFORM VERIFICATION PROCEDURE VER-2.

91D10473

Fig. 88: Driveability Test 21A (3.3L & 3.8L) – Code 31, Purge Solenoid Circuit (3 of 3)

DR-22A: CODE 32, EGR SOLENOID CIRCUIT (1 OF 3)

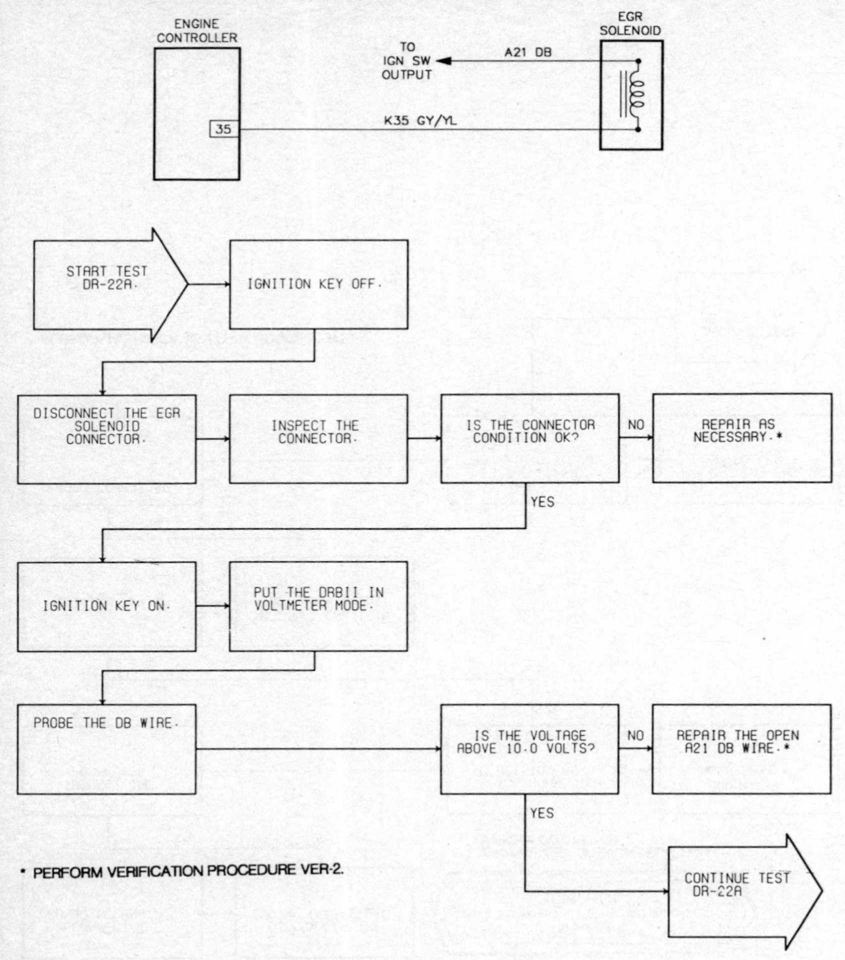
ENGINE CONTROLLER
35
TO IGN SW OUTPUT
A21 DB
K35 GY/YL
EGR SOLENOID
START TEST DR-22A.
IGNITION KEY OFF.
DISCONNECT THE EGR SOLENOID CONNECTOR.
INSPECT THE CONNECTOR.
IS THE CONNECTOR CONDITION OK?
NO
REPAIR AS NECESSARY.*
YES
IGNITION KEY ON.
PUT THE DRBII IN VOLTMETER MODE.
PROBE THE DB WIRE.
IS THE VOLTAGE ABOVE 10.0 VOLTS?
NO
REPAIR THE OPEN A21 DB WIRE.*
YES
CONTINUE TEST DR-22A
• PERFORM VERIFICATION PROCEDURE VER-2.

91A09133 91E10474

Fig. 89: Driveability Test 22A (3.3L & 3.8L) – Code 32, EGR Solenoid Circuit (1 of 3)

DR-22A: CODE 32, EGR SOLENOID CIRCUIT (2 OF 3)

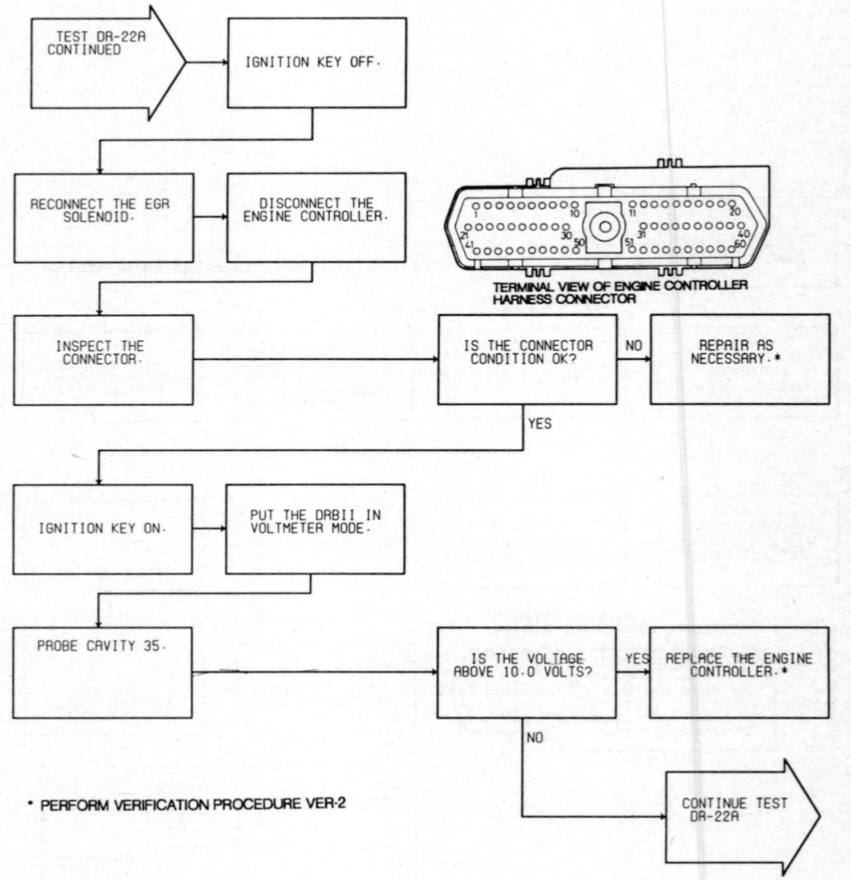
TEST DR-22A CONTINUED
IGNITION KEY OFF.
RECONNECT THE EGR SOLENOID.
DISCONNECT THE ENGINE CONTROLLER.
TERMINAL VIEW OF ENGINE CONTROLLER HARNESS CONNECTOR
INSPECT THE CONNECTOR.
IS THE CONNECTOR CONDITION OK?
NO
REPAIR AS NECESSARY.*
YES
IGNITION KEY ON.
PUT THE DRBII IN VOLTMETER MODE.
PROBE CAVITY 35.
IS THE VOLTAGE ABOVE 10.0 VOLTS?
YES
REPLACE THE ENGINE CONTROLLER.*
NO
CONTINUE TEST DR-22A
• PERFORM VERIFICATION PROCEDURE VER-2

91F10475

Fig. 90: Driveability Test 22A (3.3L & 3.8L) – Code 32, EGR Solenoid Circuit (2 of 3)

DR-22A: CODE 32, EGR SOLENOID CIRCUIT (3 OF 3)

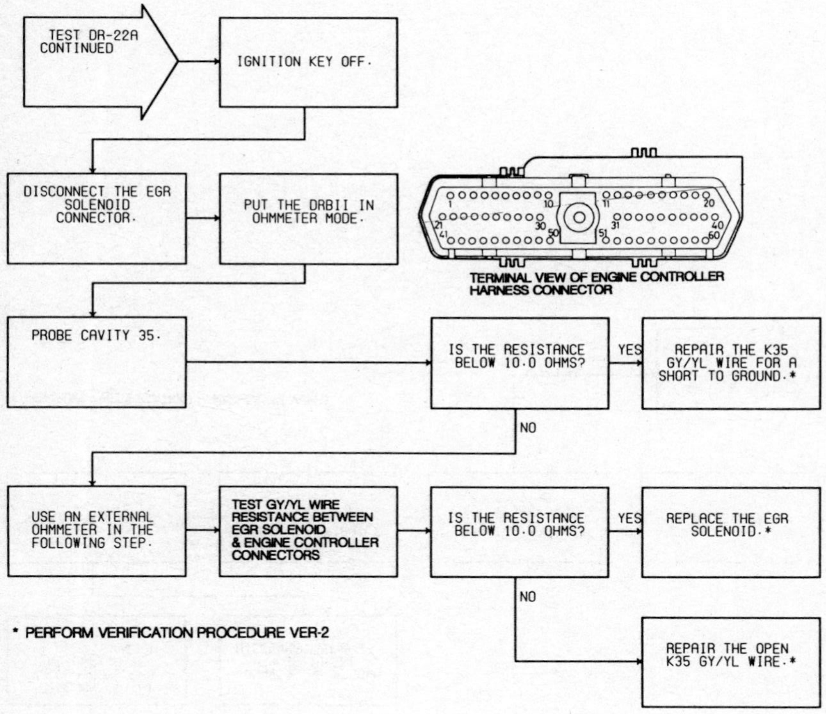
TEST DR-22A CONTINUED
IGNITION KEY OFF.
DISCONNECT THE EGR SOLENOID CONNECTOR.
PUT THE DRBII IN OHMMETER MODE.
TERMINAL VIEW OF ENGINE CONTROLLER HARNESS CONNECTOR
PROBE CAVITY 35.
IS THE RESISTANCE BELOW 10.0 OHMS?
YES
REPAIR THE K35 GY/YL WIRE FOR A SHORT TO GROUND.*
NO
USE AN EXTERNAL OHMMETER IN THE FOLLOWING STEP.
TEST GY/YL WIRE RESISTANCE BETWEEN EGR SOLENOID & ENGINE CONTROLLER CONNECTORS
IS THE RESISTANCE BELOW 10.0 OHMS?
YES
REPLACE THE EGR SOLENOID.*
NO
REPAIR THE OPEN K35 GY/YL WIRE.*

* PERFORM VERIFICATION PROCEDURE VER-2

91G10476

Fig. 91: Driveability Test 22A (3.3L & 3.8L) – Code 32, EGR Solenoid Circuit (3 of 3)

DR-23A: CODE 32, EGR SYSTEM FAILURE (1 OF 5)

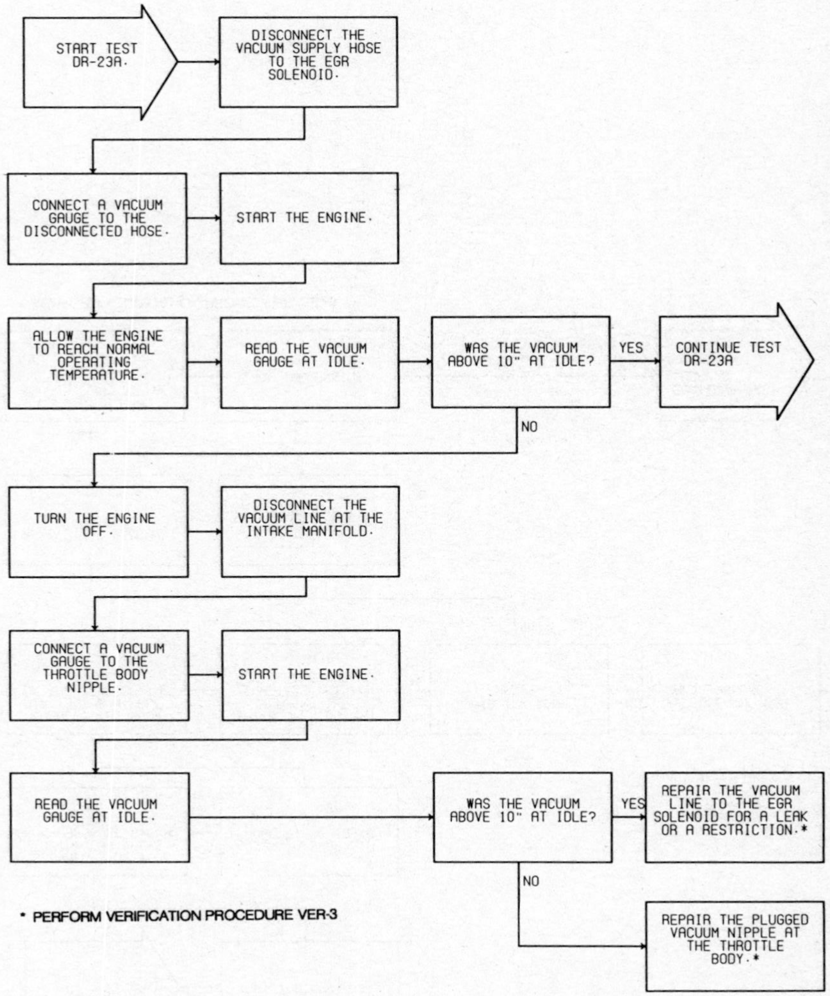
START TEST DR-23A.
DISCONNECT THE VACUUM SUPPLY HOSE TO THE EGR SOLENOID.
CONNECT A VACUUM GAUGE TO THE DISCONNECTED HOSE.
START THE ENGINE.
ALLOW THE ENGINE TO REACH NORMAL OPERATING TEMPERATURE.
READ THE VACUUM GAUGE AT IDLE.
WAS THE VACUUM ABOVE 10" AT IDLE?
YES
CONTINUE TEST DR-23A
NO
TURN THE ENGINE OFF.
DISCONNECT THE VACUUM LINE AT THE INTAKE MANIFOLD.
CONNECT A VACUUM GAUGE TO THE THROTTLE BODY NIPPLE.
START THE ENGINE.
READ THE VACUUM GAUGE AT IDLE.
WAS THE VACUUM ABOVE 10" AT IDLE?
YES
REPAIR THE VACUUM LINE TO THE EGR SOLENOID FOR A LEAK OR A RESTRICTION.*
NO
REPAIR THE PLUGGED VACUUM NIPPLE AT THE THROTTLE BODY.*

* PERFORM VERIFICATION PROCEDURE VER-3

91H10477

Fig. 92: Driveability Test 23A (3.3L & 3.8L) – Code 32, EGR System Failure (1 of 5)

1991 ENGINE PERFORMANCE
Self-Diagnostics – 3.3L PFI (Cont.)

DR-23A: CODE 32, EGR SYSTEM FAILURE (2 OF 5)

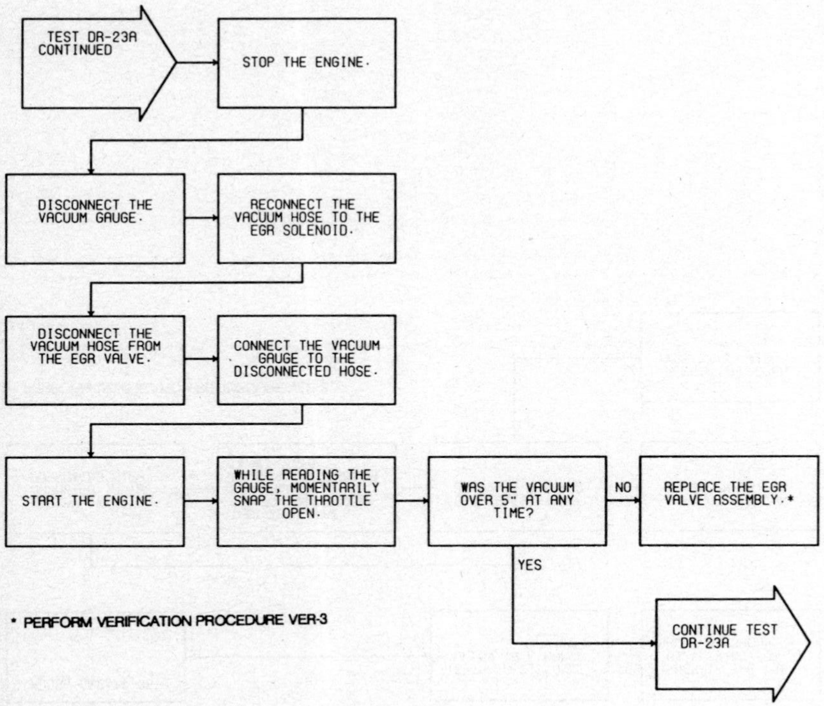
TEST DR-23A CONTINUED
STOP THE ENGINE.
DISCONNECT THE VACUUM GAUGE.
RECONNECT THE VACUUM HOSE TO THE EGR SOLENOID.
DISCONNECT THE VACUUM HOSE FROM THE EGR VALVE.
CONNECT THE VACUUM GAUGE TO THE DISCONNECTED HOSE.
START THE ENGINE.
WHILE READING THE GAUGE, MOMENTARILY SNAP THE THROTTLE OPEN.
WAS THE VACUUM OVER 5" AT ANY TIME?
NO
REPLACE THE EGR VALVE ASSEMBLY.*
YES
CONTINUE TEST DR-23A

* PERFORM VERIFICATION PROCEDURE VER-3

91I10478

Fig. 93: Driveability Test 23A (3.3L & 3.8L) – Code 32, EGR System Failure (2 of 5)

DR-23A: CODE 32, EGR SYSTEM FAILURE (3 OF 5)

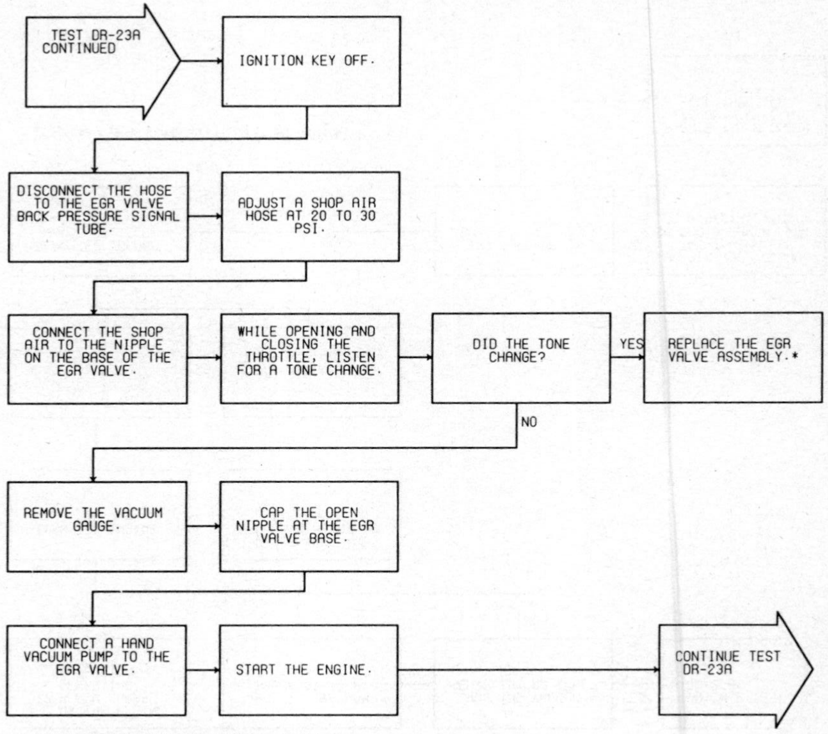
TEST DR-23A CONTINUED
IGNITION KEY OFF.
DISCONNECT THE HOSE TO THE EGR VALVE BACK PRESSURE SIGNAL TUBE.
ADJUST A SHOP AIR HOSE AT 20 TO 30 PSI.
CONNECT THE SHOP AIR TO THE NIPPLE ON THE BASE OF THE EGR VALVE.
WHILE OPENING AND CLOSING THE THROTTLE, LISTEN FOR A TONE CHANGE.
DID THE TONE CHANGE?
YES
REPLACE THE EGR VALVE ASSEMBLY.*
NO
REMOVE THE VACUUM GAUGE.
CAP THE OPEN NIPPLE AT THE EGR VALVE BASE.
CONNECT A HAND VACUUM PUMP TO THE EGR VALVE.
START THE ENGINE.
CONTINUE TEST DR-23A

* PERFORM VERIFICATION PROCEDURE VER-3

91J10479

Fig. 94: Driveability Test 23A (3.3L & 3.8L) – Code 32, EGR System Failure (3 of 5)

DR-23A: CODE 32, EGR SYSTEM FAILURE (4 OF 5)

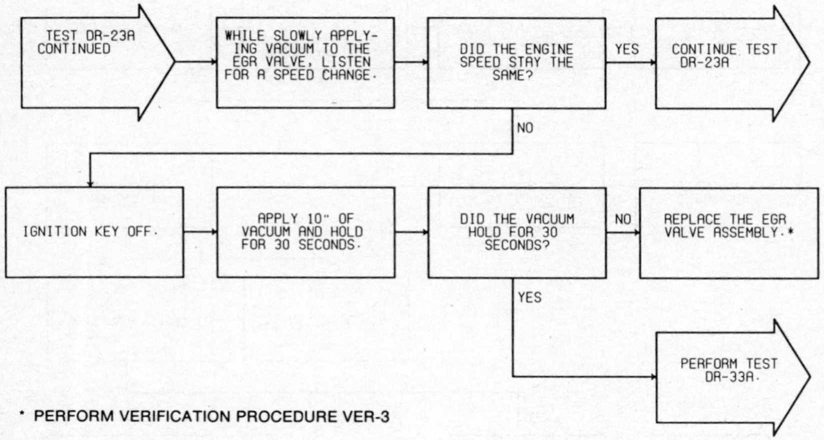
TEST DR-23A CONTINUED
WHILE SLOWLY APPLY-ING VACUUM TO THE EGR VALVE, LISTEN FOR A SPEED CHANGE.
DID THE ENGINE SPEED STAY THE SAME?
YES
CONTINUE TEST DR-23A
NO
IGNITION KEY OFF.
APPLY 10" OF VACUUM AND HOLD FOR 30 SECONDS.
DID THE VACUUM HOLD FOR 30 SECONDS?
NO
REPLACE THE EGR VALVE ASSEMBLY.*
YES
PERFORM TEST DR-33A.

* PERFORM VERIFICATION PROCEDURE VER-3

91C10480

Fig. 95: Driveability Test 23A (3.3L & 3.8L) – Code 32, EGR System Failure (4 of 5)

DR-23A: CODE 32, EGR SYSTEM FAILURE (5 OF 5)

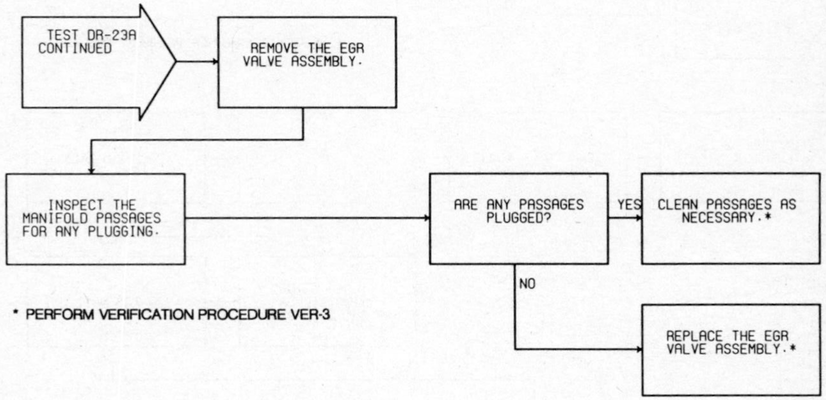
TEST DR-23A CONTINUED
REMOVE THE EGR VALVE ASSEMBLY.
INSPECT THE MANIFOLD PASSAGES FOR ANY PLUGGING.
ARE ANY PASSAGES PLUGGED?
YES
CLEAN PASSAGES AS NECESSARY.*
NO
REPLACE THE EGR VALVE ASSEMBLY.*

* PERFORM VERIFICATION PROCEDURE VER-3

91D10481

Fig. 96: Driveability Test 23A (3.3L & 3.8L) – Code 32, EGR System Failure (5 of 5)

DR-24A: CODE 33, A/C CLUTCH RELAY CIRCUIT (1 OF 3)

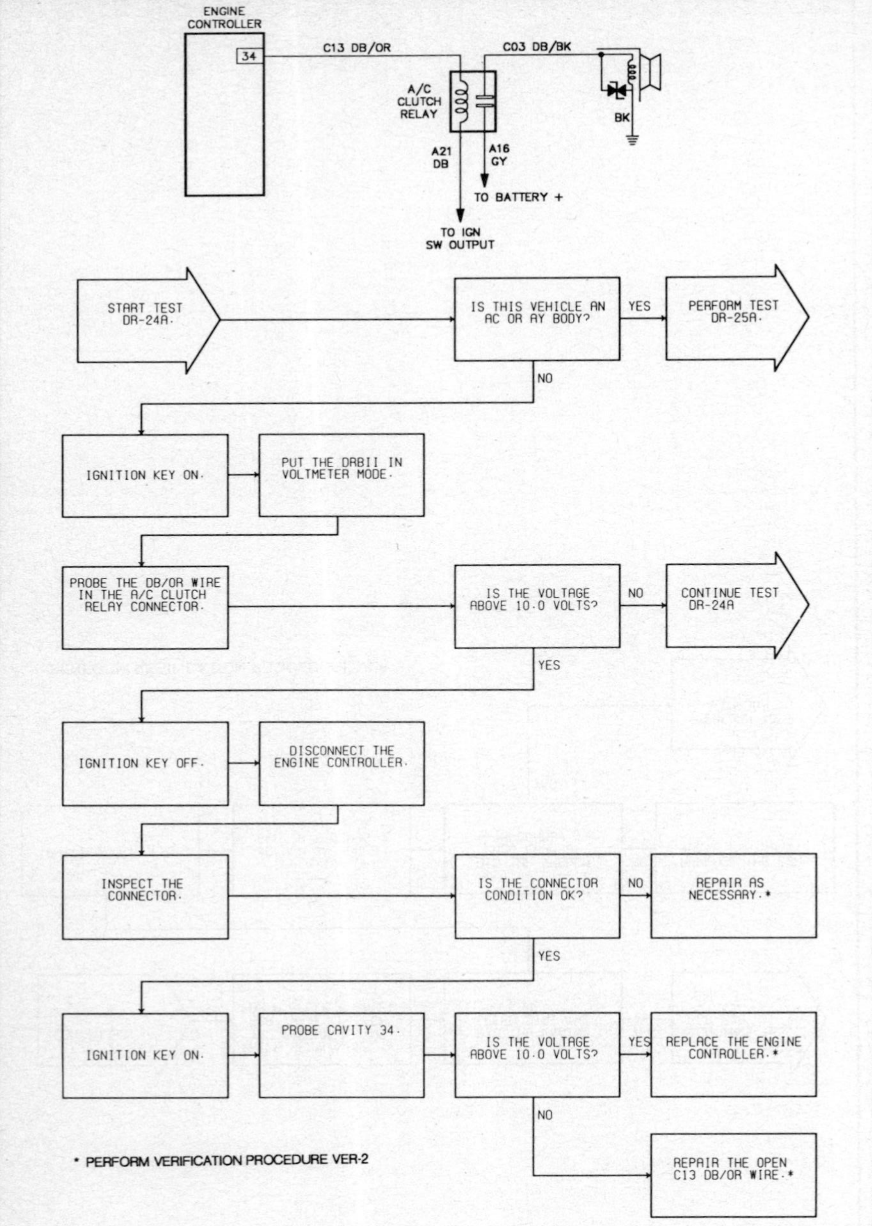
ENGINE CONTROLLER
34
C13 DB/OR
A/C CLUTCH RELAY
C03 DB/BK
BK
A21 DB
A16 GY
TO BATTERY +
TO IGN SW OUTPUT
START TEST DR-24A.
IS THIS VEHICLE AN AC OR AY BODY?
YES
PERFORM TEST DR-25A.
NO
IGNITION KEY ON.
PUT THE DRBII IN VOLTMETER MODE.
PROBE THE DB/OR WIRE IN THE A/C CLUTCH RELAY CONNECTOR.
IS THE VOLTAGE ABOVE 10.0 VOLTS?
NO
CONTINUE TEST DR-24A
YES
IGNITION KEY OFF.
DISCONNECT THE ENGINE CONTROLLER.
INSPECT THE CONNECTOR.
IS THE CONNECTOR CONDITION OK?
NO
REPAIR AS NECESSARY.*
YES
IGNITION KEY ON.
PROBE CAVITY 34.
IS THE VOLTAGE ABOVE 10.0 VOLTS?
YES
REPLACE THE ENGINE CONTROLLER.*
NO
REPAIR THE OPEN C13 DB/OR WIRE.*

* PERFORM VERIFICATION PROCEDURE VER-2

91C09134 91E10482

Fig. 97: Driveability Test 24A (3.3L & 3.8L) – Code 33, A/C Clutch Relay Circuit (1 of 3)

DR-24A: CODE 33, A/C CLUTCH RELAY CIRCUIT (2 OF 3)

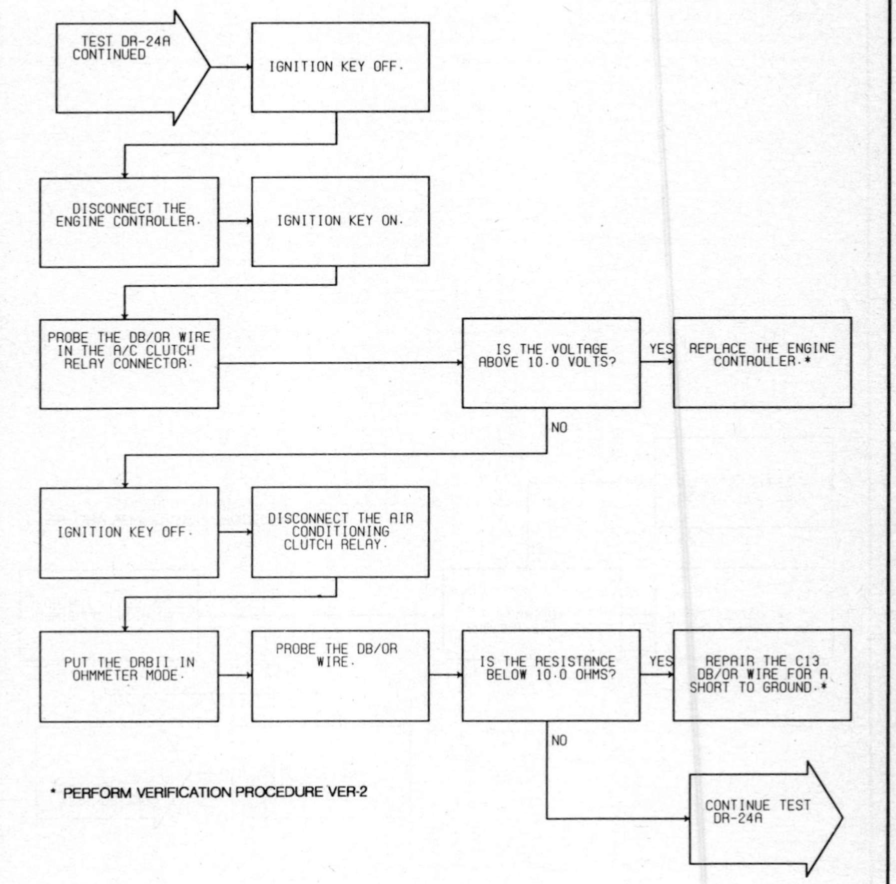
TEST DR-24A CONTINUED
IGNITION KEY OFF.
DISCONNECT THE ENGINE CONTROLLER.
IGNITION KEY ON.
PROBE THE DB/OR WIRE IN THE A/C CLUTCH RELAY CONNECTOR.
IS THE VOLTAGE ABOVE 10.0 VOLTS?
YES
REPLACE THE ENGINE CONTROLLER.*
NO
IGNITION KEY OFF.
DISCONNECT THE AIR CONDITIONING CLUTCH RELAY.
PUT THE DRBII IN OHMMETER MODE.
PROBE THE DB/OR WIRE.
IS THE RESISTANCE BELOW 10.0 OHMS?
YES
REPAIR THE C13 DB/OR WIRE FOR A SHORT TO GROUND.*
NO
CONTINUE TEST DR-24A

* PERFORM VERIFICATION PROCEDURE VER-2

91F10483

Fig. 98: Driveability Test 24A (3.3L & 3.8L) – Code 33, A/C Clutch Relay Circuit (2 of 3)

DR-24A: CODE 33, A/C CLUTCH RELAY CIRCUIT (3 OF 3)

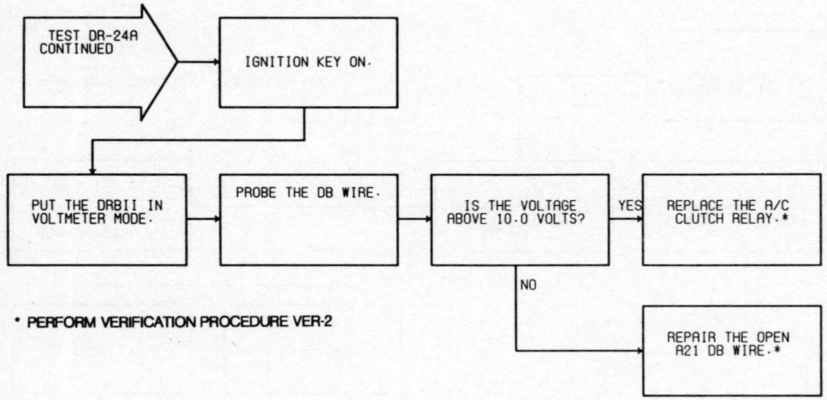
TEST DR-24A CONTINUED
IGNITION KEY ON.
PUT THE DRBII IN VOLTMETER MODE.
PROBE THE DB WIRE.
IS THE VOLTAGE ABOVE 10.0 VOLTS?
YES
REPLACE THE A/C CLUTCH RELAY.*
NO
REPAIR THE OPEN A21 DB WIRE.*

* PERFORM VERIFICATION PROCEDURE VER-2

91G10484

Fig. 99: Driveability Test 24A (3.3L & 3.8L) – Code 33, A/C Clutch Relay Circuit (3 of 3)

DR-25A: CODE 33, A/C CLUTCH RELAY CIRCUIT (1 OF 2)

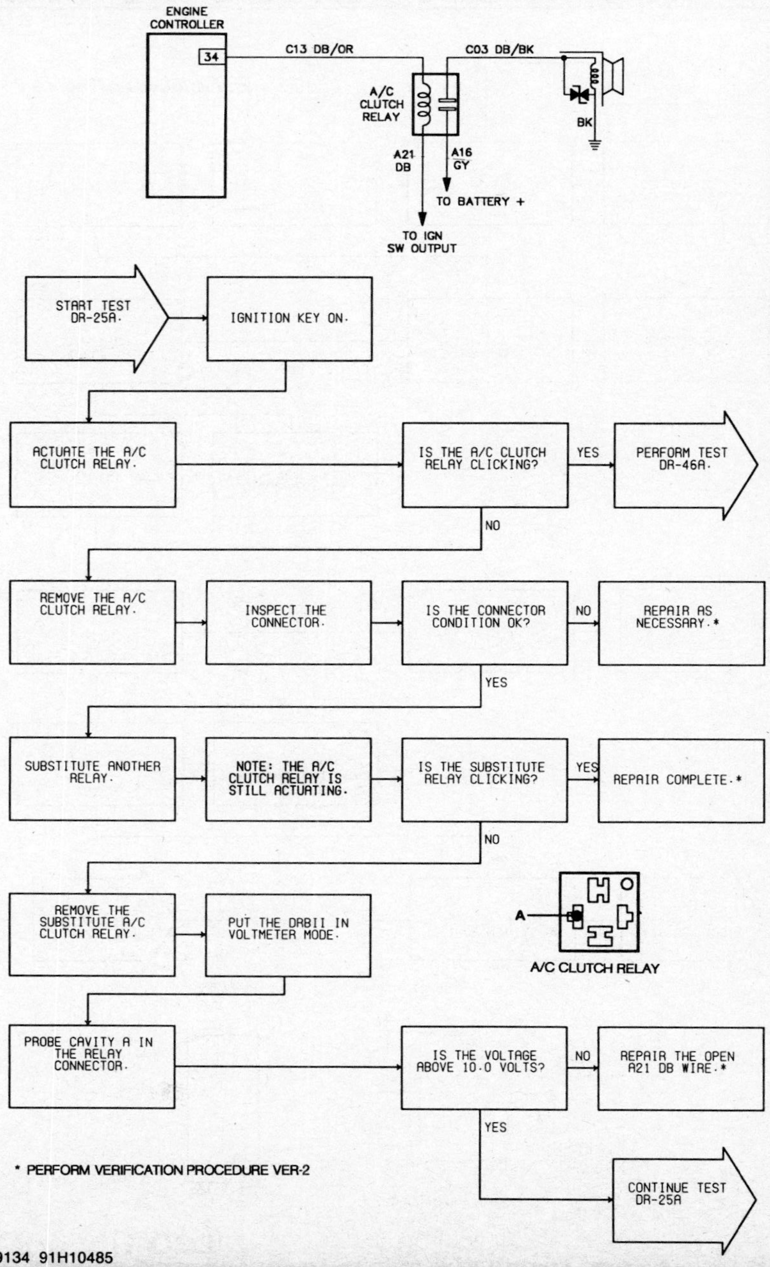
ENGINE CONTROLLER
34
C13 DB/OR
C03 DB/BK
A/C CLUTCH RELAY
BK
A21 DB
A16 GY
TO BATTERY +
TO IGN SW OUTPUT
START TEST DR-25A.
IGNITION KEY ON.
ACTUATE THE A/C CLUTCH RELAY.
IS THE A/C CLUTCH RELAY CLICKING?
YES
PERFORM TEST DR-46A.
NO
REMOVE THE A/C CLUTCH RELAY.
INSPECT THE CONNECTOR.
IS THE CONNECTOR CONDITION OK?
NO
REPAIR AS NECESSARY.*
YES
SUBSTITUTE ANOTHER RELAY.
NOTE: THE A/C CLUTCH RELAY IS STILL ACTUATING.
IS THE SUBSTITUTE RELAY CLICKING?
YES
REPAIR COMPLETE.*
NO
REMOVE THE SUBSTITUTE A/C CLUTCH RELAY.
PUT THE DRBII IN VOLTMETER MODE.
A
A/C CLUTCH RELAY
PROBE CAVITY A IN THE RELAY CONNECTOR.
IS THE VOLTAGE ABOVE 10.0 VOLTS?
NO
REPAIR THE OPEN A21 DB WIRE.*
YES
CONTINUE TEST DR-25A

* PERFORM VERIFICATION PROCEDURE VER-2

91C09134 91H10485

Fig. 100: Driveability Test 25A (3.3L & 3.8L) – Code 33, A/C Clutch Relay Circuit (1 of 2)

DR-25A: CODE 33, A/C CLUTCH RELAY CIRCUIT (2 OF 2)

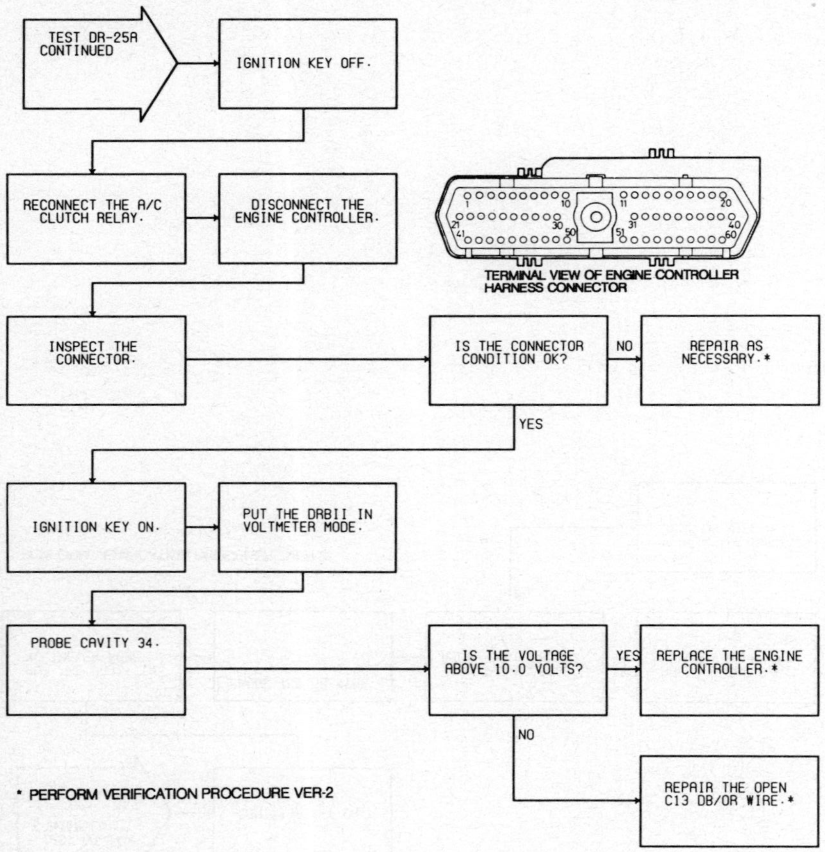
TEST DR-25A CONTINUED
IGNITION KEY OFF.
RECONNECT THE A/C CLUTCH RELAY.
DISCONNECT THE ENGINE CONTROLLER.
TERMINAL VIEW OF ENGINE CONTROLLER HARNESS CONNECTOR
INSPECT THE CONNECTOR.
IS THE CONNECTOR CONDITION OK?
NO
REPAIR AS NECESSARY.*
YES
IGNITION KEY ON.
PUT THE DRBII IN VOLTMETER MODE.
PROBE CAVITY 34.
IS THE VOLTAGE ABOVE 10.0 VOLTS?
YES
REPLACE THE ENGINE CONTROLLER.*
NO
REPAIR THE OPEN C13 DB/OR WIRE.*

* PERFORM VERIFICATION PROCEDURE VER-2

91I10486

Fig. 101: Driveability Test 25A (3.3L & 3.8L) – Code 33, A/C Clutch Relay Circuit (2 of 2)

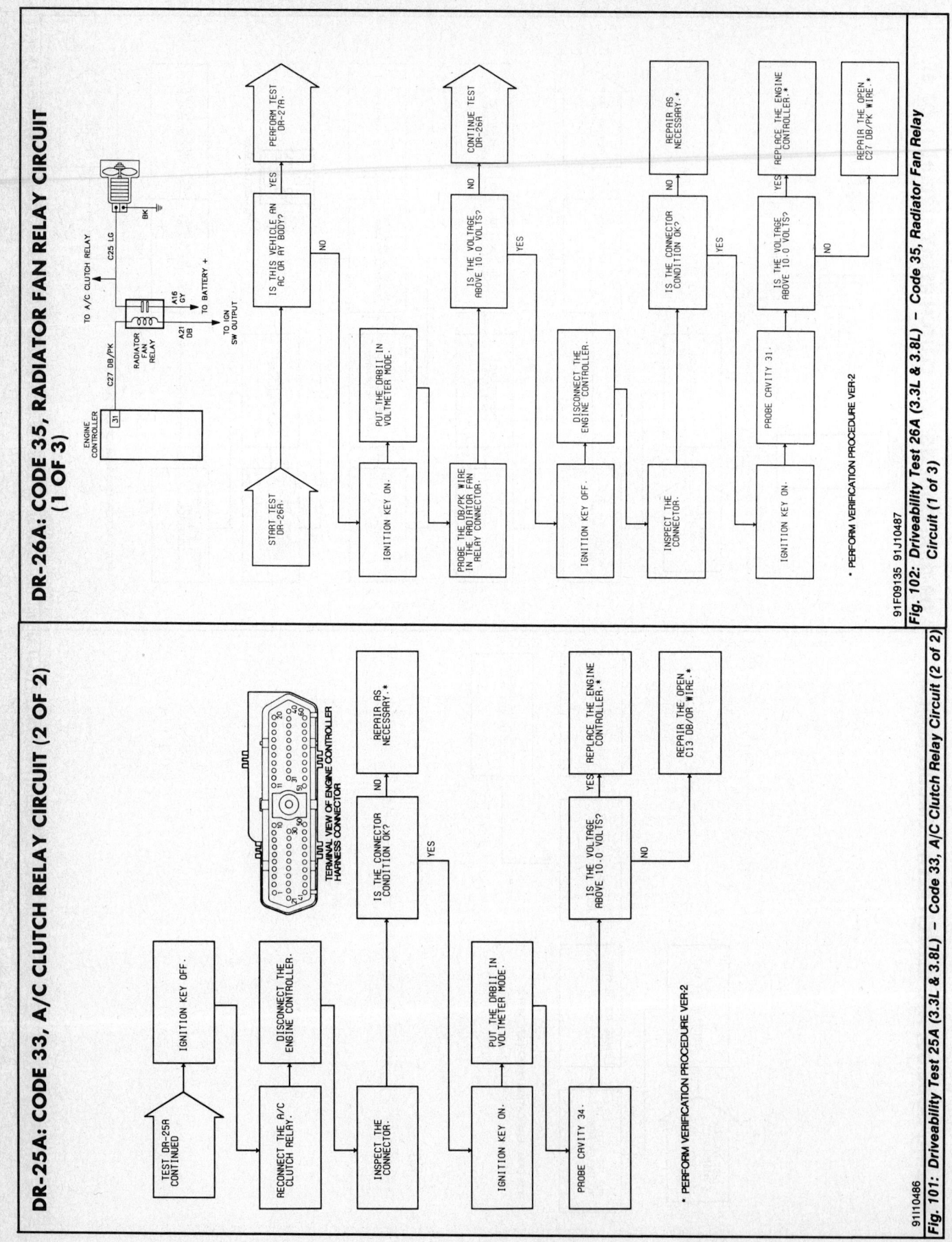

DR-26A: CODE 35, RADIATOR FAN RELAY CIRCUIT (1 OF 3)

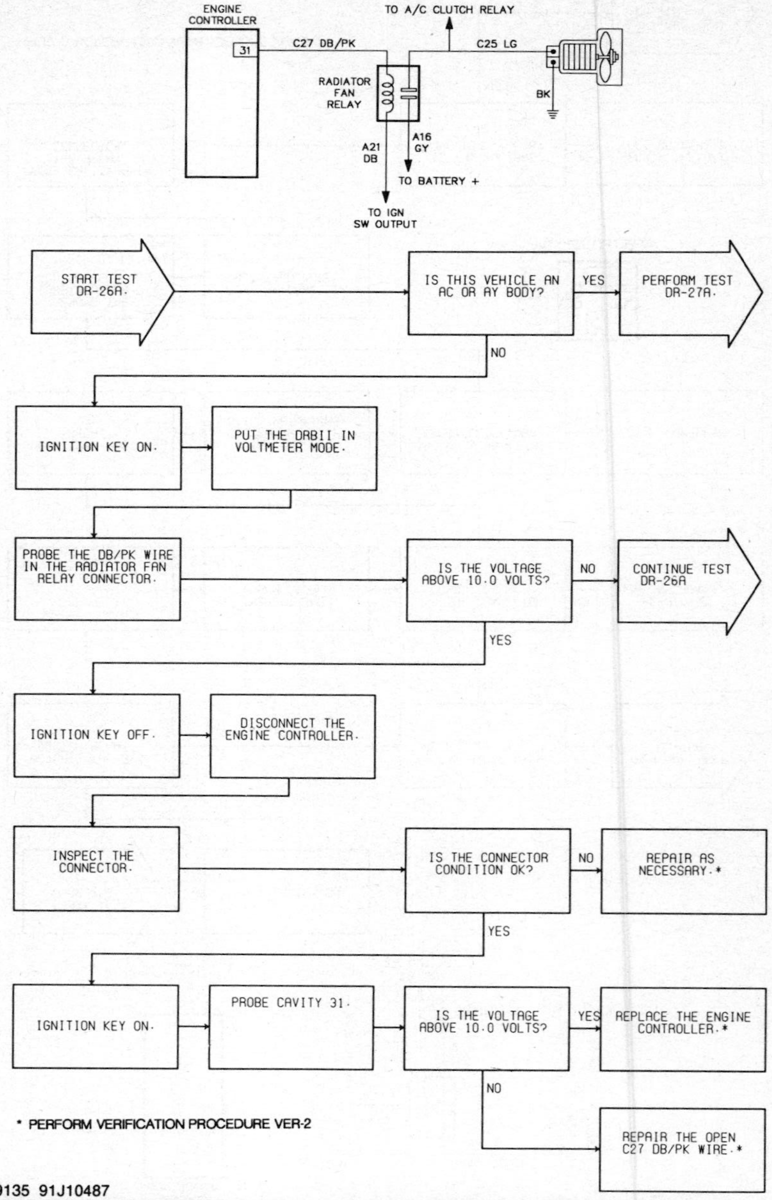
ENGINE CONTROLLER
31
C27 DB/PK
RADIATOR FAN RELAY
TO A/C CLUTCH RELAY
C25 LG
BK
A21 DB
A16 GY
TO BATTERY +
TO IGN SW OUTPUT
START TEST DR-26A.
IS THIS VEHICLE AN AC OR AY BODY?
YES
PERFORM TEST DR-27A.
NO
IGNITION KEY ON.
PUT THE DRBII IN VOLTMETER MODE.
PROBE THE DB/PK WIRE IN THE RADIATOR FAN RELAY CONNECTOR.
IS THE VOLTAGE ABOVE 10.0 VOLTS?
NO
CONTINUE TEST DR-26A
YES
IGNITION KEY OFF.
DISCONNECT THE ENGINE CONTROLLER.
INSPECT THE CONNECTOR.
IS THE CONNECTOR CONDITION OK?
NO
REPAIR AS NECESSARY.*
YES
IGNITION KEY ON.
PROBE CAVITY 31.
IS THE VOLTAGE ABOVE 10.0 VOLTS?
YES
REPLACE THE ENGINE CONTROLLER.*
NO
REPAIR THE OPEN C27 DB/PK WIRE.*

* PERFORM VERIFICATION PROCEDURE VER-2

91F09135 91J10487

Fig. 102: Driveability Test 26A (3.3L & 3.8L) – Code 35, Radiator Fan Relay Circuit (1 of 3)

DR-26A: CODE 35, RADIATOR FAN RELAY CIRCUIT (2 OF 3)

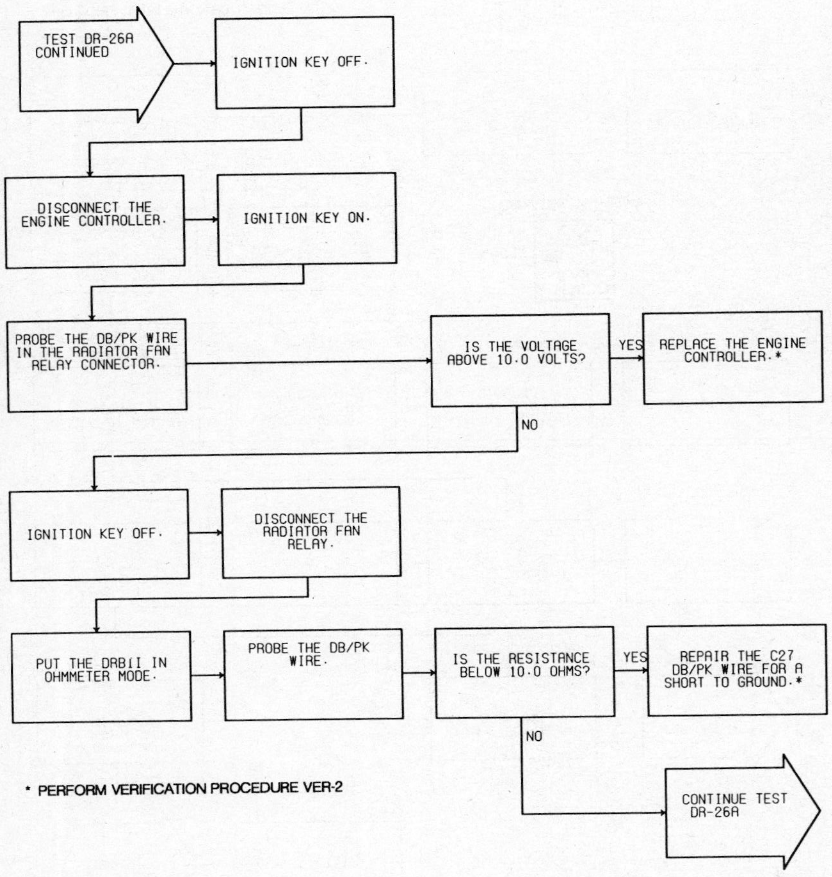
TEST DR-26A CONTINUED
IGNITION KEY OFF.
DISCONNECT THE ENGINE CONTROLLER.
IGNITION KEY ON.
PROBE THE DB/PK WIRE IN THE RADIATOR FAN RELAY CONNECTOR.
IS THE VOLTAGE ABOVE 10.0 VOLTS?
YES
REPLACE THE ENGINE CONTROLLER.*
NO
IGNITION KEY OFF.
DISCONNECT THE RADIATOR FAN RELAY.
PUT THE DRBII IN OHMMETER MODE.
PROBE THE DB/PK WIRE.
IS THE RESISTANCE BELOW 10.0 OHMS?
YES
REPAIR THE C27 DB/PK WIRE FOR A SHORT TO GROUND.*
NO
CONTINUE TEST DR-26A

* PERFORM VERIFICATION PROCEDURE VER-2

91A10488

Fig. 103: Driveability Test 26A (3.3L & 3.8L) – Code 35, Radiator Fan Relay Circuit (2 of 3)

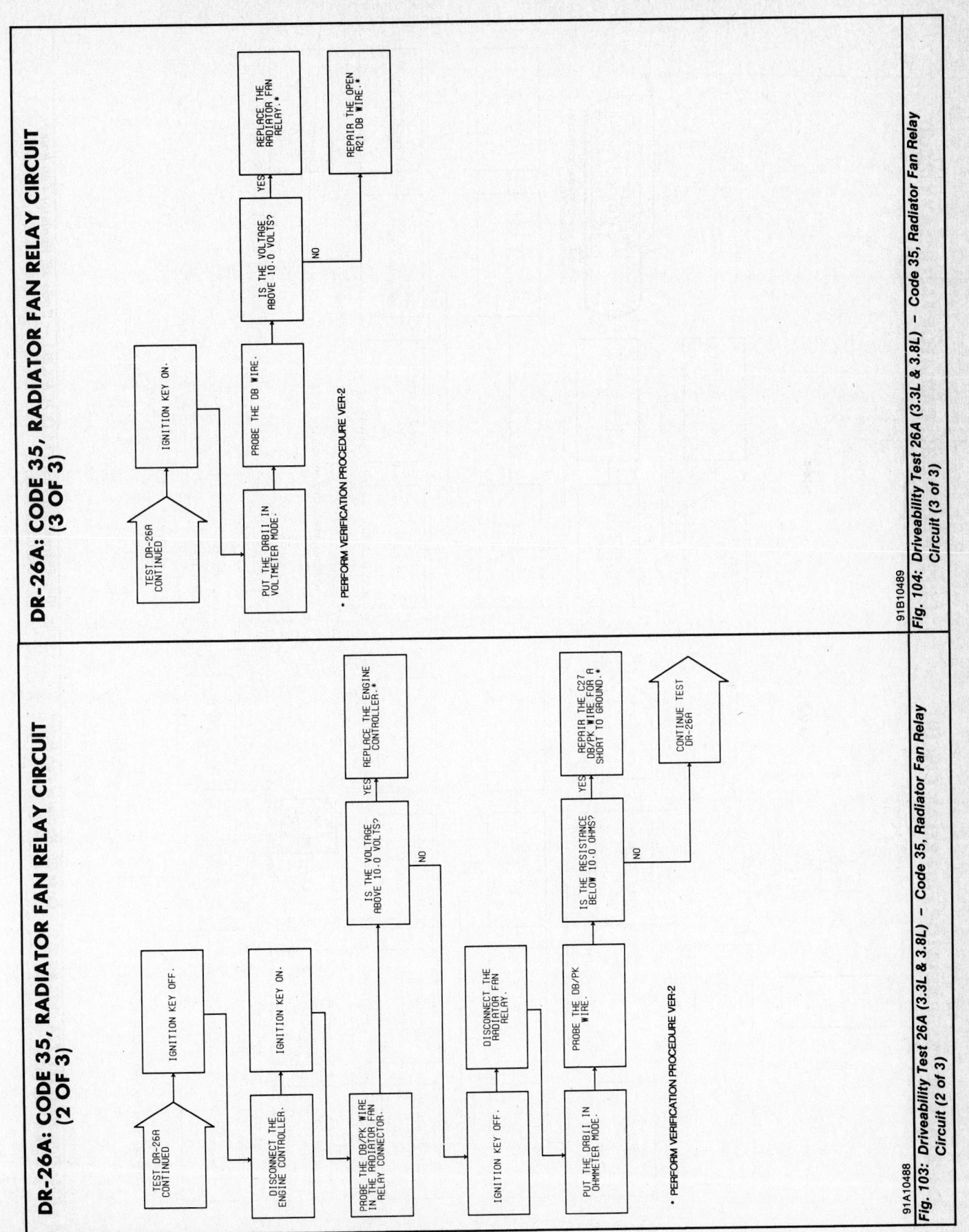

DR-26A: CODE 35, RADIATOR FAN RELAY CIRCUIT (3 OF 3)

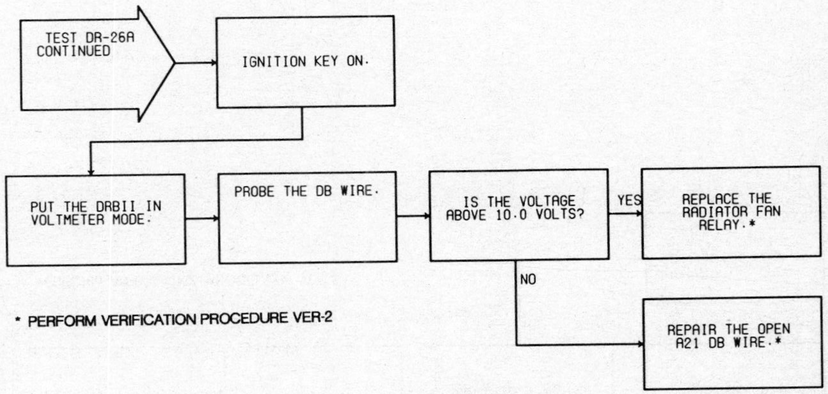
TEST DR-26A CONTINUED
IGNITION KEY ON.
PUT THE DRBII IN VOLTMETER MODE.
PROBE THE DB WIRE.
IS THE VOLTAGE ABOVE 10.0 VOLTS?
YES
REPLACE THE RADIATOR FAN RELAY.*
NO
REPAIR THE OPEN A21 DB WIRE.*

* PERFORM VERIFICATION PROCEDURE VER-2

91B10489

Fig. 104: Driveability Test 26A (3.3L & 3.8L) – Code 35, Radiator Fan Relay Circuit (3 of 3)

DR-27A: CODE 35, RADIATOR FAN RELAY CIRCUIT (1 OF 2)

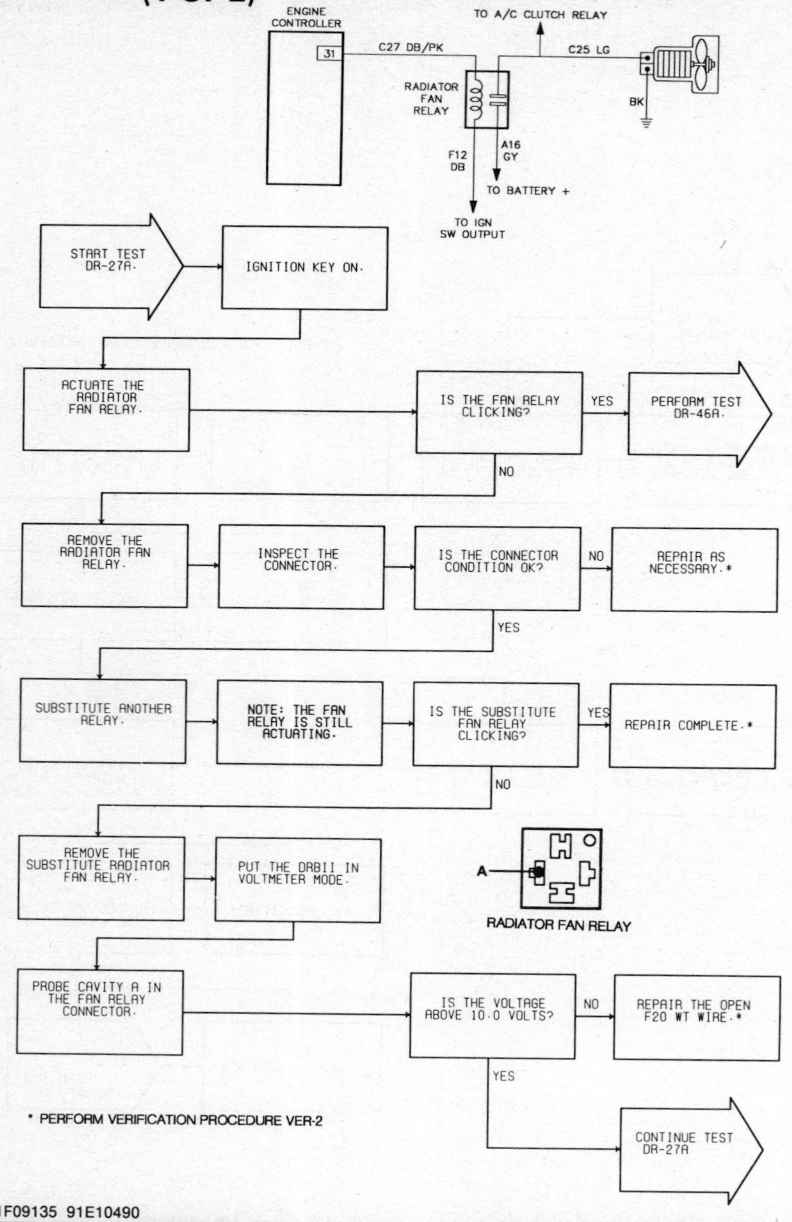
ENGINE CONTROLLER
31
C27 DB/PK
RADIATOR FAN RELAY
TO A/C CLUTCH RELAY
C25 LG
BK
F12 DB
A16 GY
TO BATTERY +
TO IGN SW OUTPUT
START TEST DR-27A.
IGNITION KEY ON.
ACTUATE THE RADIATOR FAN RELAY.
IS THE FAN RELAY CLICKING?
YES
PERFORM TEST DR-46A.
NO
REMOVE THE RADIATOR FAN RELAY.
INSPECT THE CONNECTOR.
IS THE CONNECTOR CONDITION OK?
NO
REPAIR AS NECESSARY.*
YES
SUBSTITUTE ANOTHER RELAY.
NOTE: THE FAN RELAY IS STILL ACTUATING.
IS THE SUBSTITUTE FAN RELAY CLICKING?
YES
REPAIR COMPLETE.*
NO
REMOVE THE SUBSTITUTE RADIATOR FAN RELAY.
PUT THE DRBII IN VOLTMETER MODE.
A
RADIATOR FAN RELAY
PROBE CAVITY A IN THE FAN RELAY CONNECTOR.
IS THE VOLTAGE ABOVE 10.0 VOLTS?
NO
REPAIR THE OPEN F20 WT WIRE.*
YES
CONTINUE TEST DR-27A

* PERFORM VERIFICATION PROCEDURE VER-2

91F09135 91E10490

Fig. 105: Driveability Test 27A (3.3L & 3.8L) – Code 35, Radiator Fan Relay Circuit (1 of 2)

DR-27A: CODE 35, RADIATOR FAN RELAY CIRCUIT (2 OF 2)

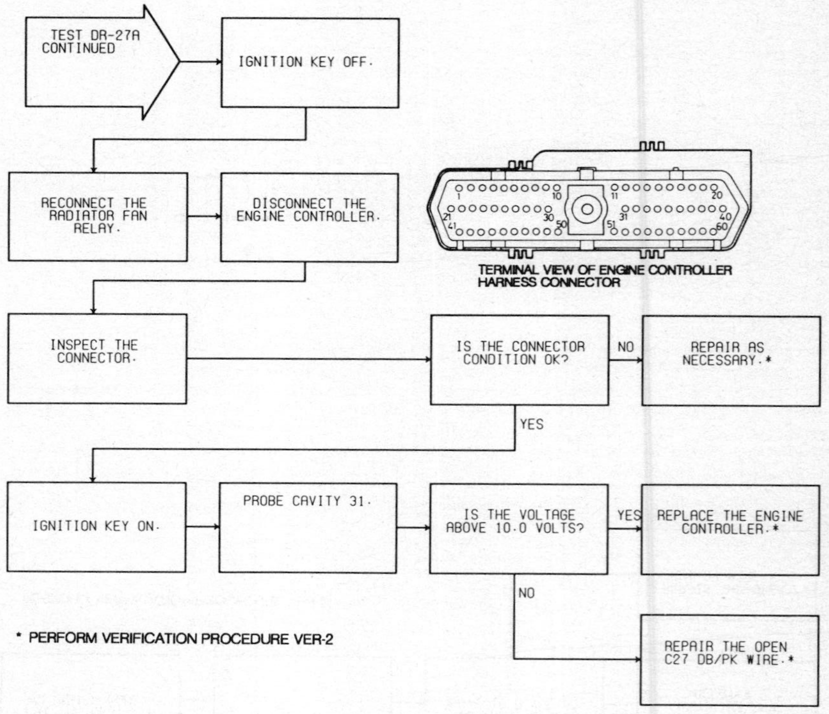
TEST DR-27A CONTINUED
IGNITION KEY OFF.
RECONNECT THE RADIATOR FAN RELAY.
DISCONNECT THE ENGINE CONTROLLER.
TERMINAL VIEW OF ENGINE CONTROLLER HARNESS CONNECTOR
INSPECT THE CONNECTOR.
IS THE CONNECTOR CONDITION OK?
NO
REPAIR AS NECESSARY.*
YES
IGNITION KEY ON.
PROBE CAVITY 31.
IS THE VOLTAGE ABOVE 10.0 VOLTS?
YES
REPLACE THE ENGINE CONTROLLER.*
NO
REPAIR THE OPEN C27 DB/PK WIRE.*

* PERFORM VERIFICATION PROCEDURE VER-2

91F10491

Fig. 106: Driveability Test 27A (3.3L & 3.8L) – Code 35, Radiator Fan Relay Circuit (2 of 2)

DR-28A: CODE 42, NO AUTO SHUTDOWN (ASD) RELAY VOLTAGE SENSED AT SBEC (1 OF 2)

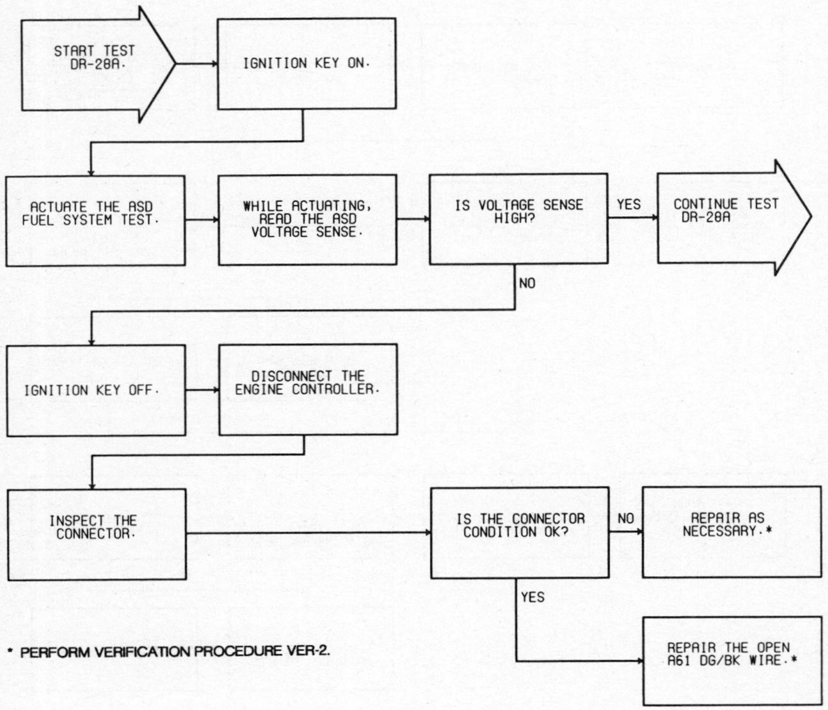
START TEST DR-28A.
IGNITION KEY ON.
ACTUATE THE ASD FUEL SYSTEM TEST.
WHILE ACTUATING, READ THE ASD VOLTAGE SENSE.
IS VOLTAGE SENSE HIGH?
YES
CONTINUE TEST DR-28A
NO
IGNITION KEY OFF.
DISCONNECT THE ENGINE CONTROLLER.
INSPECT THE CONNECTOR.
IS THE CONNECTOR CONDITION OK?
NO
REPAIR AS NECESSARY.*
YES
REPAIR THE OPEN A61 DG/BK WIRE.*

* PERFORM VERIFICATION PROCEDURE VER-2.

91G10492

Fig. 107: Driveability Test 28A (3.3L & 3.8L) – Code 42, No Auto Shutdown (ASD) Relay Voltage Sensed at SBEC (1 of 2)

DR-28A: CODE 42, NO AUTO SHUTDOWN (ASD) RELAY VOLTAGE SENSED AT SBEC (2 OF 2)

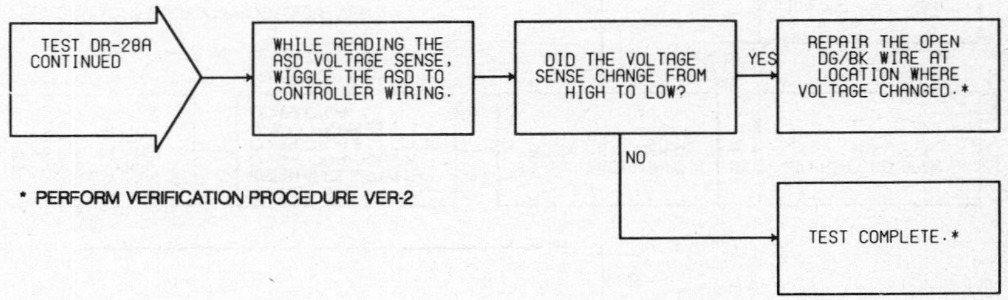
TEST DR-28A CONTINUED
WHILE READING THE ASD VOLTAGE SENSE, WIGGLE THE ASD TO CONTROLLER WIRING.
DID THE VOLTAGE SENSE CHANGE FROM HIGH TO LOW?
YES
REPAIR THE OPEN DG/BK WIRE AT LOCATION WHERE VOLTAGE CHANGED.*
NO
TEST COMPLETE.*

* PERFORM VERIFICATION PROCEDURE VER-2

91H10493

Fig. 108: Driveability Test 28A (3.3L & 3.8L) – Code 42, No Auto Shutdown (ASD) Relay Voltage Sensed at SBEC (2 of 2)

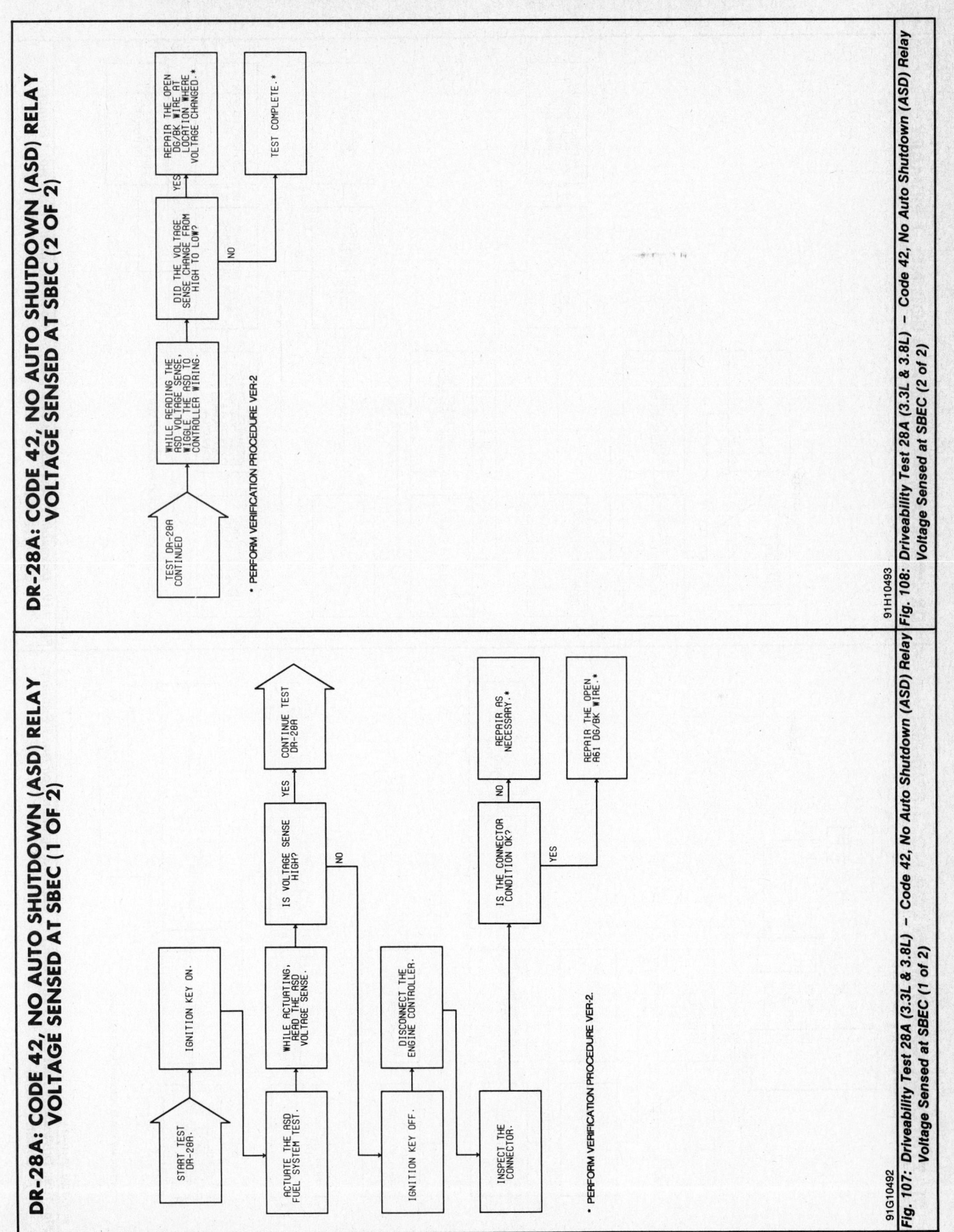

1991 ENGINE PERFORMANCE
Self-Diagnostics – 3.3L PFI (Cont.)

DR-29A: CODE 43, IGNITION COIL NO. 1 PRIMARY CIRCUIT (1 OF 2)

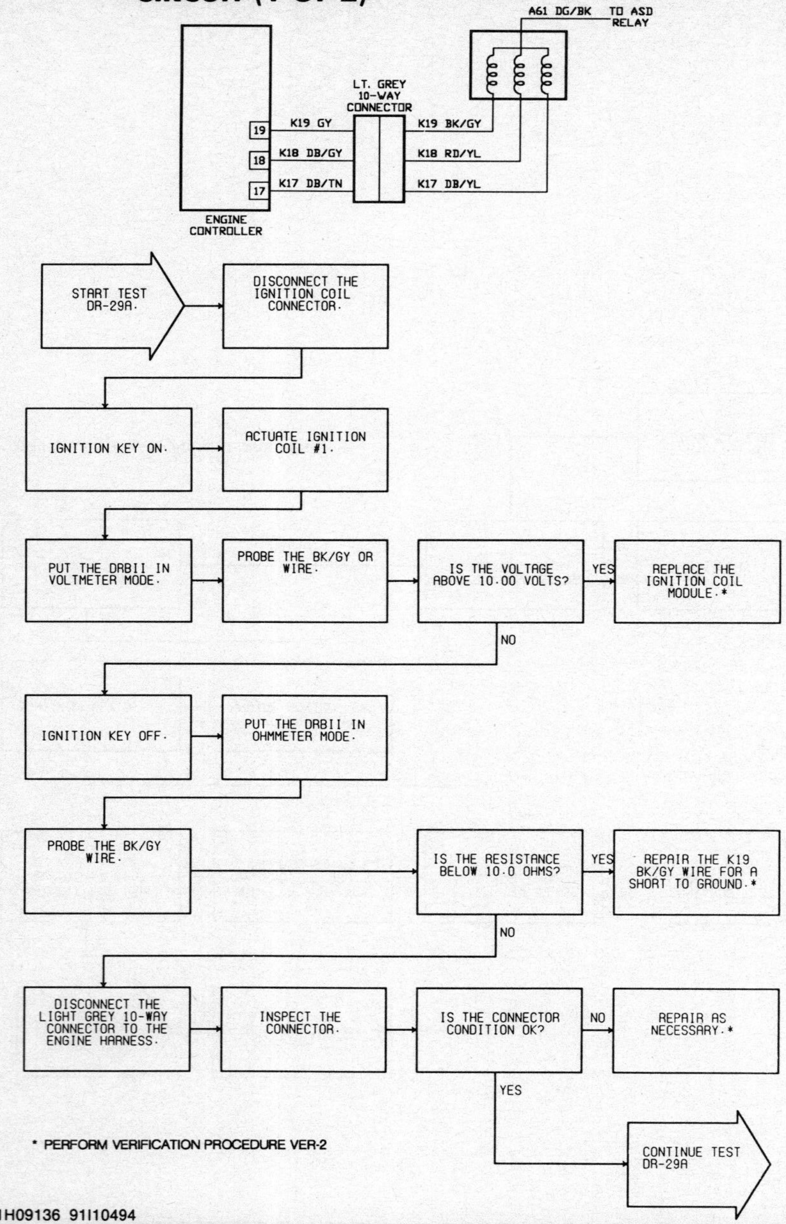
A61 DG/BK
TO ASD RELAY
LT. GREY 10-WAY CONNECTOR
19
18
17
K19 GY
K18 DB/GY
K17 DB/TN
K19 BK/GY
K18 RD/YL
K17 DB/YL
ENGINE CONTROLLER
START TEST DR-29A.
DISCONNECT THE IGNITION COIL CONNECTOR.
IGNITION KEY ON.
ACTUATE IGNITION COIL #1.
PUT THE DRBII IN VOLTMETER MODE.
PROBE THE BK/GY OR WIRE.
IS THE VOLTAGE ABOVE 10.00 VOLTS?
YES
REPLACE THE IGNITION COIL MODULE.*
NO
IGNITION KEY OFF.
PUT THE DRBII IN OHMMETER MODE.
PROBE THE BK/GY WIRE.
IS THE RESISTANCE BELOW 10.0 OHMS?
YES
REPAIR THE K19 BK/GY WIRE FOR A SHORT TO GROUND.*
NO
DISCONNECT THE LIGHT GREY 10-WAY CONNECTOR TO THE ENGINE HARNESS.
INSPECT THE CONNECTOR.
IS THE CONNECTOR CONDITION OK?
NO
REPAIR AS NECESSARY.*
YES
CONTINUE TEST DR-29A

* PERFORM VERIFICATION PROCEDURE VER-2

91H09136 91I10494

Fig. 109: *Driveability Test 29A (3.3L & 3.8L) – Code 43, Ignition Coil No. 1 Primary Circuit (1 of 2)*

DR-29A: CODE 43, IGNITION COIL NO. 1 PRIMARY CIRCUIT (2 OF 2)

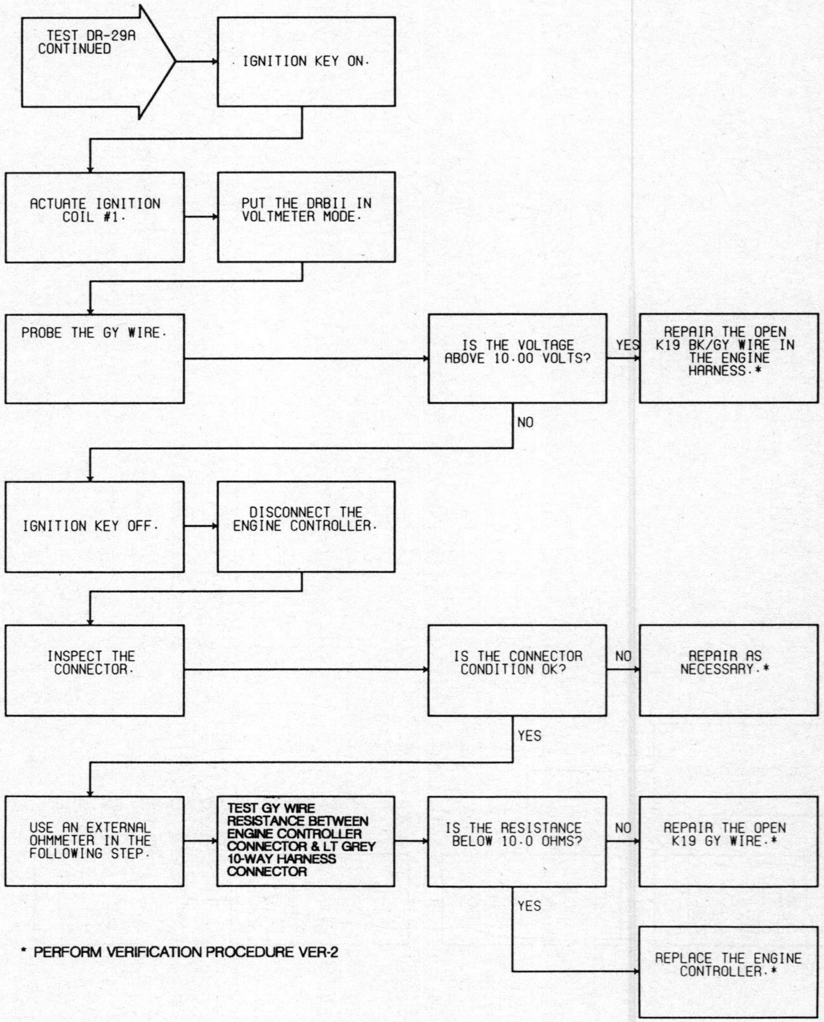
TEST DR-29A CONTINUED
IGNITION KEY ON.
ACTUATE IGNITION COIL #1.
PUT THE DRBII IN VOLTMETER MODE.
PROBE THE GY WIRE.
IS THE VOLTAGE ABOVE 10.00 VOLTS?
YES
REPAIR THE OPEN K19 BK/GY WIRE IN THE ENGINE HARNESS.*
NO
IGNITION KEY OFF.
DISCONNECT THE ENGINE CONTROLLER.
INSPECT THE CONNECTOR.
IS THE CONNECTOR CONDITION OK?
NO
REPAIR AS NECESSARY.*
YES
USE AN EXTERNAL OHMMETER IN THE FOLLOWING STEP.
TEST GY WIRE RESISTANCE BETWEEN ENGINE CONTROLLER CONNECTOR & LT GREY 10-WAY HARNESS CONNECTOR
IS THE RESISTANCE BELOW 10.0 OHMS?
NO
REPAIR THE OPEN K19 GY WIRE.*
YES
REPLACE THE ENGINE CONTROLLER.*

* PERFORM VERIFICATION PROCEDURE VER-2

91J10495

Fig. 110: *Driveability Test 29A (3.3L & 3.8L) – Code 43, Ignition Coil No. 1 Primary Circuit (2 of 2)*

DR-30A: CODE 43, IGNITION COIL NO. 2 PRIMARY CIRCUIT (1 OF 2)

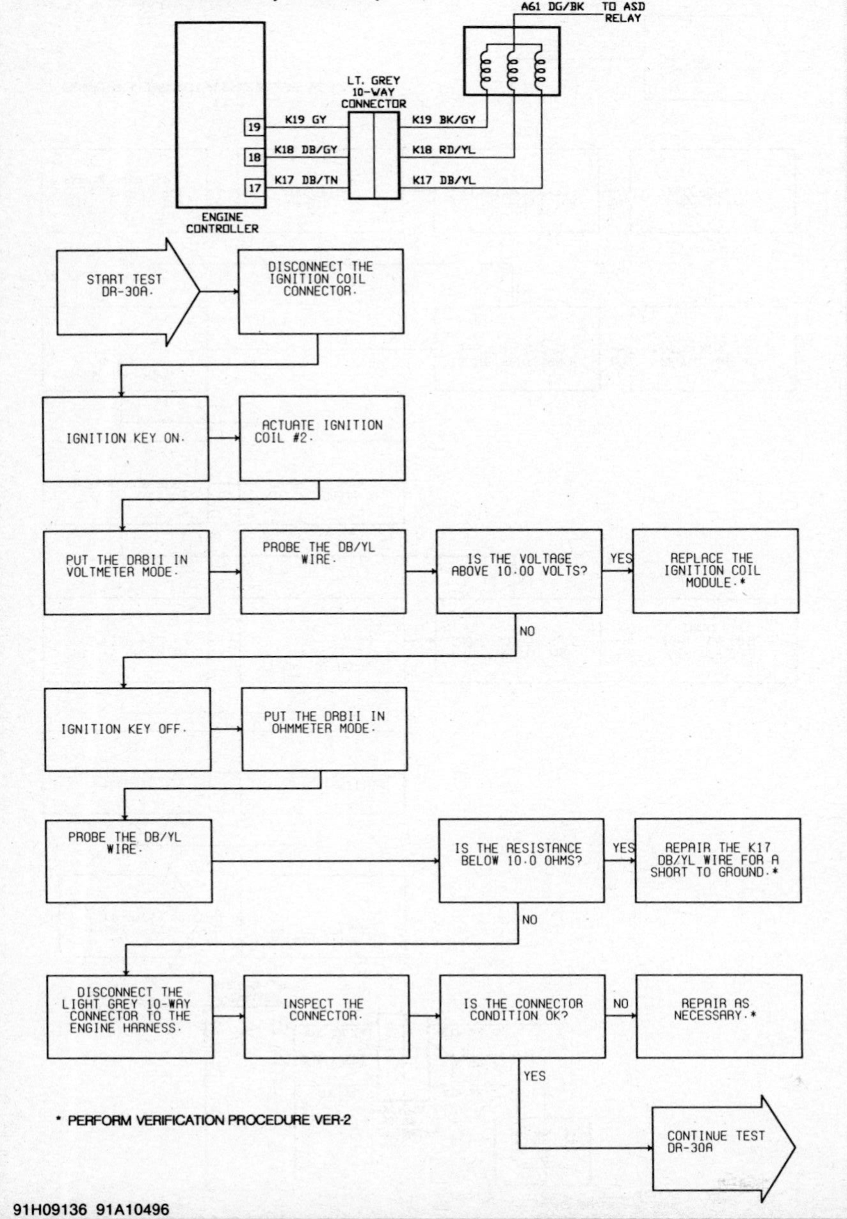
A61 DG/BK
TO ASD RELAY
LT. GREY 10-WAY CONNECTOR
K19 GY
K18 DB/GY
K17 DB/TN
K19 BK/GY
K18 RD/YL
K17 DB/YL
19
18
17
ENGINE CONTROLLER
START TEST DR-30A.
DISCONNECT THE IGNITION COIL CONNECTOR.
IGNITION KEY ON.
ACTUATE IGNITION COIL #2.
PUT THE DRBII IN VOLTMETER MODE.
PROBE THE DB/YL WIRE.
IS THE VOLTAGE ABOVE 10.00 VOLTS?
YES
REPLACE THE IGNITION COIL MODULE.*
NO
IGNITION KEY OFF.
PUT THE DRBII IN OHMMETER MODE.
PROBE THE DB/YL WIRE.
IS THE RESISTANCE BELOW 10.0 OHMS?
YES
REPAIR THE K17 DB/YL WIRE FOR A SHORT TO GROUND.*
NO
DISCONNECT THE LIGHT GREY 10-WAY CONNECTOR TO THE ENGINE HARNESS.
INSPECT THE CONNECTOR.
IS THE CONNECTOR CONDITION OK?
NO
REPAIR AS NECESSARY.*
YES
CONTINUE TEST DR-30A
* PERFORM VERIFICATION PROCEDURE VER-2
91H09136 91A10496

Fig. 111: Driveability Test 30A (3.3L & 3.8L) – Code 43, Ignition Coil No. 2 Primary Circuit (1 of 2)

DR-30A: CODE 43, IGNITION COIL NO. 2 PRIMARY CIRCUIT (2 OF 2)

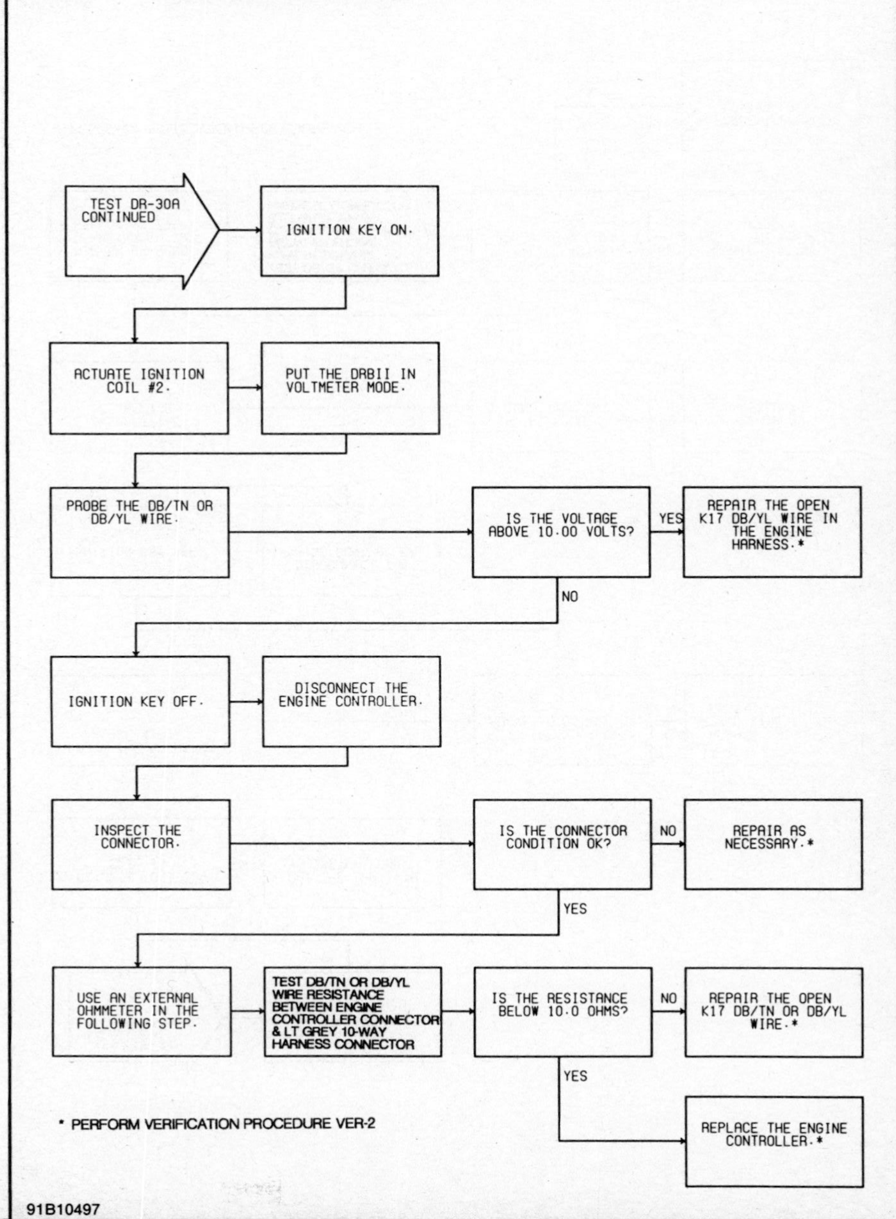
TEST DR-30A CONTINUED
IGNITION KEY ON.
ACTUATE IGNITION COIL #2.
PUT THE DRBII IN VOLTMETER MODE.
PROBE THE DB/TN OR DB/YL WIRE.
IS THE VOLTAGE ABOVE 10.00 VOLTS?
YES
REPAIR THE OPEN K17 DB/YL WIRE IN THE ENGINE HARNESS.*
NO
IGNITION KEY OFF.
DISCONNECT THE ENGINE CONTROLLER.
INSPECT THE CONNECTOR.
IS THE CONNECTOR CONDITION OK?
NO
REPAIR AS NECESSARY.*
YES
USE AN EXTERNAL OHMMETER IN THE FOLLOWING STEP.
TEST DB/TN OR DB/YL WIRE RESISTANCE BETWEEN ENGINE CONTROLLER CONNECTOR & LT GREY 10-WAY HARNESS CONNECTOR
IS THE RESISTANCE BELOW 10.0 OHMS?
NO
REPAIR THE OPEN K17 DB/TN OR DB/YL WIRE.*
YES
REPLACE THE ENGINE CONTROLLER.*
* PERFORM VERIFICATION PROCEDURE VER-2
91B10497

Fig. 112: Driveability Test 30A (3.3L & 3.8L) – Code 43, Ignition Coil No. 2 Primary Circuit (2 of 2)

1991 ENGINE PERFORMANCE
Self-Diagnostics – 3.3L PFI (Cont.)

DR-31A: CODE 43, IGNITION COIL NO. 3 PRIMARY CIRCUIT (1 OF 2)

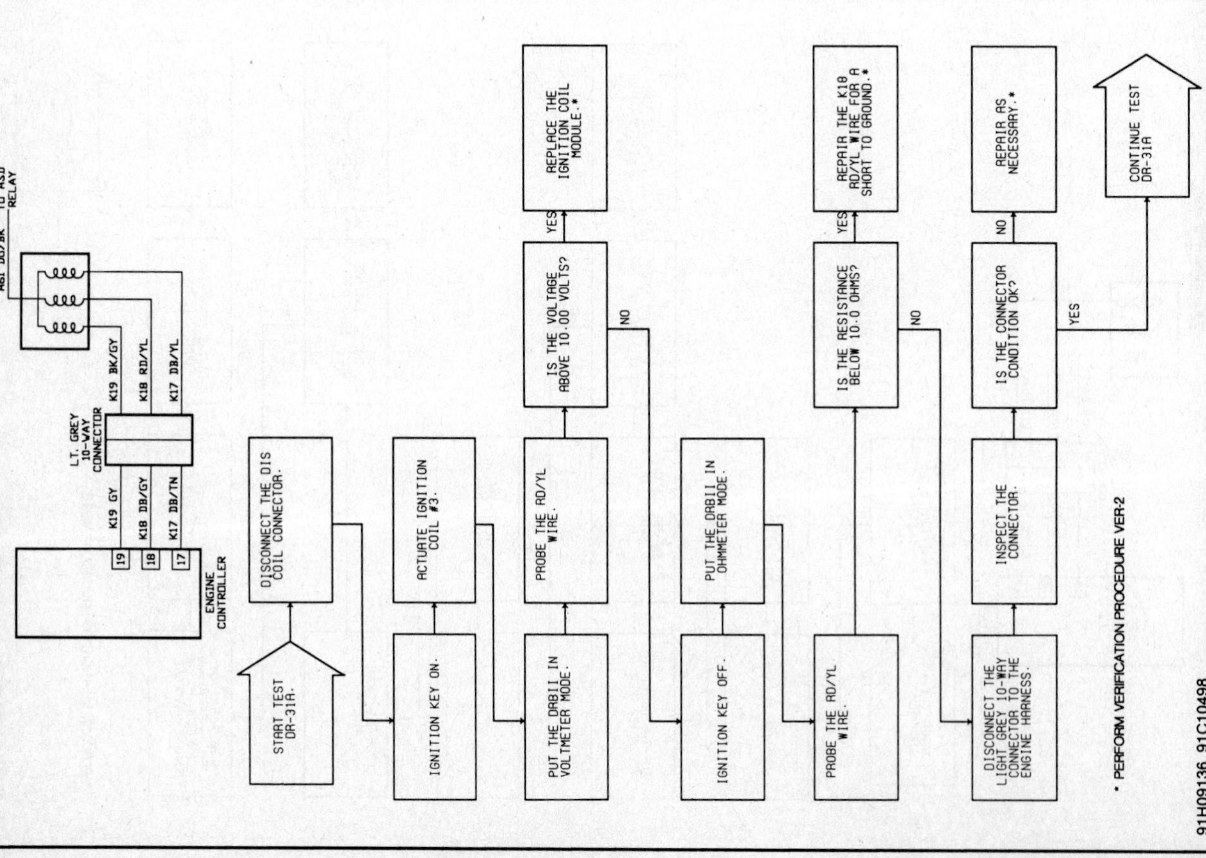
ENGINE CONTROLLER
19
18
17
K19 GY
K18 DB/GY
K17 DB/TN
LT. GREY 10-WAY CONNECTOR
K19 BK/GY
K18 RD/YL
K17 DB/YL
A61 DG/BK
TO ASD RELAY
START TEST DR-31A.
DISCONNECT THE DIS COIL CONNECTOR.
IGNITION KEY ON.
ACTUATE IGNITION COIL #3.
PUT THE DRBII IN VOLTMETER MODE.
PROBE THE RD/YL WIRE.
IS THE VOLTAGE ABOVE 10.00 VOLTS?
YES
REPLACE THE IGNITION COIL MODULE.*
NO
IGNITION KEY OFF.
PUT THE DRBII IN OHMMETER MODE.
PROBE THE RD/YL WIRE.
IS THE RESISTANCE BELOW 10.0 OHMS?
YES
REPAIR THE K18 RD/YL WIRE FOR A SHORT TO GROUND.*
NO
DISCONNECT THE LIGHT GREY 10-WAY CONNECTOR TO THE ENGINE HARNESS.
INSPECT THE CONNECTOR.
IS THE CONNECTOR CONDITION OK?
NO
REPAIR AS NECESSARY.*
YES
CONTINUE TEST DR-31A
* PERFORM VERIFICATION PROCEDURE VER-2

91H09136 91C10498

Fig. 113: Driveability Test 31A (3.3L & 3.8L) – Code 43, Ignition Coil No. 3 Primary Circuit (1 of 2)

DR-31A: CODE 43, IGNITION COIL NO. 3 PRIMARY CIRCUIT (2 OF 2)

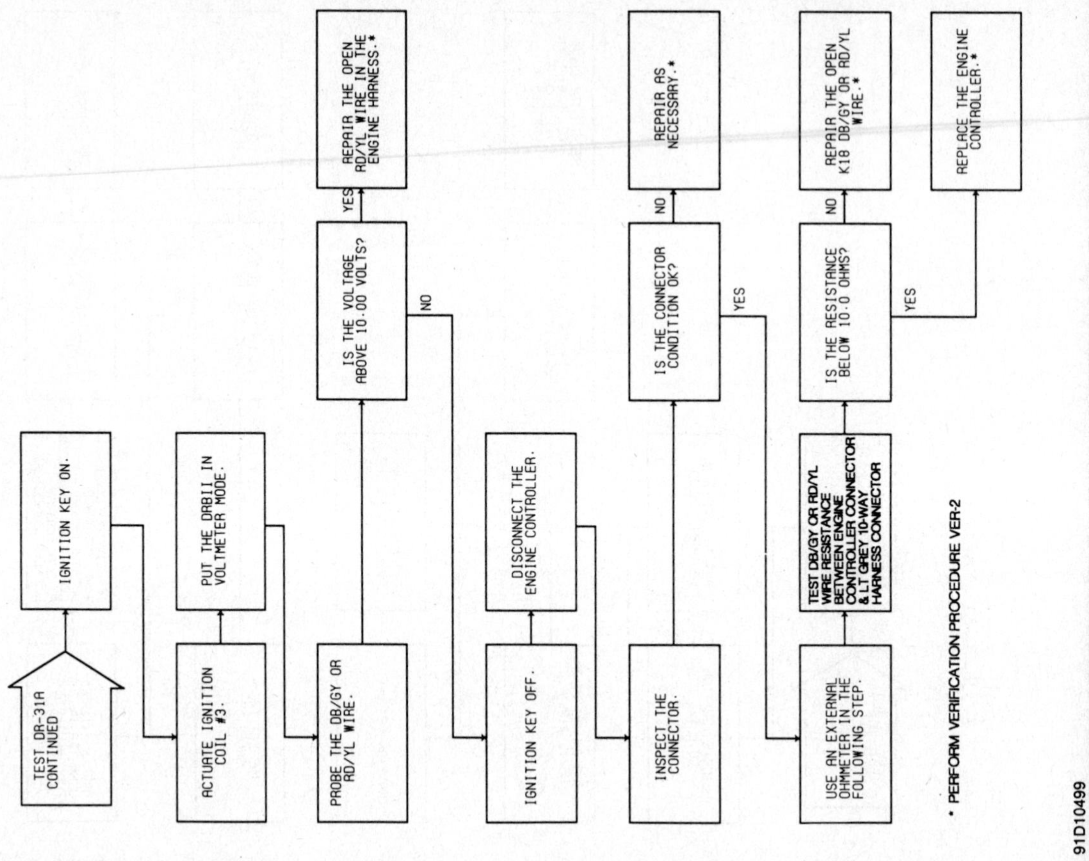
TEST DR-31A CONTINUED
IGNITION KEY ON.
ACTUATE IGNITION COIL #3.
PUT THE DRBII IN VOLTMETER MODE.
PROBE THE DB/GY OR RD/YL WIRE.
IS THE VOLTAGE ABOVE 10.00 VOLTS?
YES
REPAIR THE OPEN RD/YL WIRE IN THE ENGINE HARNESS.*
NO
IGNITION KEY OFF.
DISCONNECT THE ENGINE CONTROLLER.
INSPECT THE CONNECTOR.
IS THE CONNECTOR CONDITION OK?
NO
REPAIR AS NECESSARY.*
YES
USE AN EXTERNAL OHMMETER IN THE FOLLOWING STEP.
TEST DB/GY OR RD/YL WIRE RESISTANCE BETWEEN ENGINE CONTROLLER CONNECTOR & LT GREY 10-WAY HARNESS CONNECTOR
IS THE RESISTANCE BELOW 10.0 OHMS?
NO
REPAIR THE OPEN K18 DB/GY OR RD/YL WIRE.*
YES
REPLACE THE ENGINE CONTROLLER.*
* PERFORM VERIFICATION PROCEDURE VER-2

91D10499

Fig. 114: Driveability Test 31A (3.3L & 3.8L) – Code 43, Ignition Coil No. 3 Primary Circuit (2 of 2)

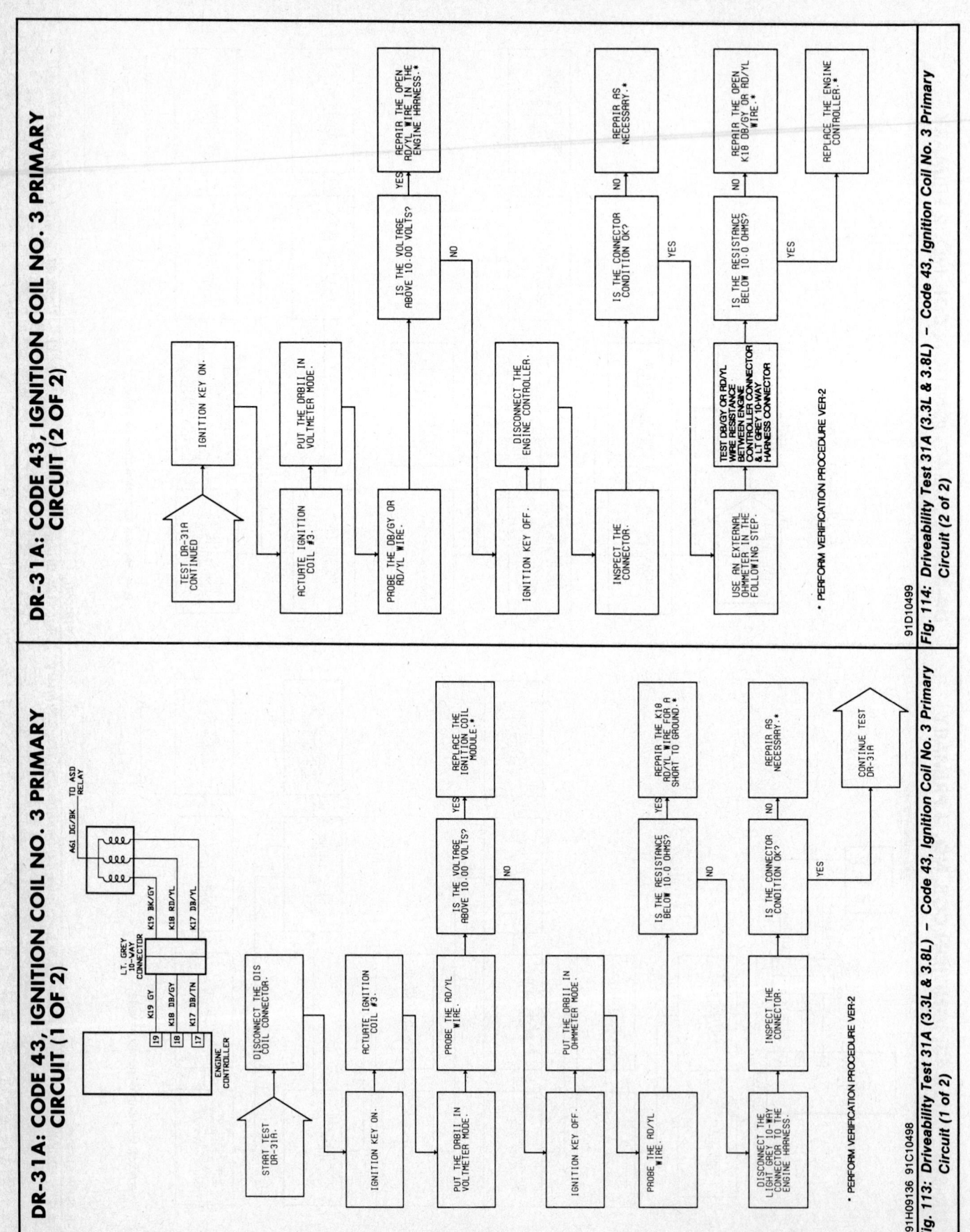

DR-32A: CODE 63, SBEC FAILURE EMR MILEAGE NOT STORED & EEPROM WRITE DENIED (1 OF 2)

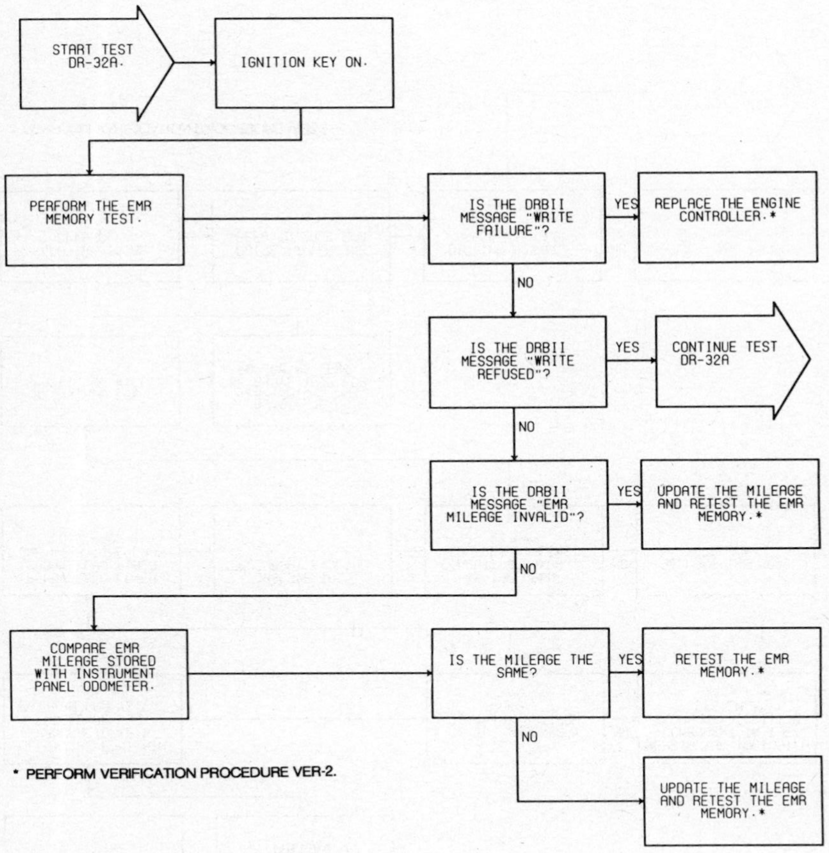
START TEST DR-32A.
IGNITION KEY ON.
PERFORM THE EMR MEMORY TEST.
IS THE DRBII MESSAGE "WRITE FAILURE"?
YES
REPLACE THE ENGINE CONTROLLER.*
NO
IS THE DRBII MESSAGE "WRITE REFUSED"?
YES
CONTINUE TEST DR-32A
NO
IS THE DRBII MESSAGE "EMR MILEAGE INVALID"?
YES
UPDATE THE MILEAGE AND RETEST THE EMR MEMORY.*
NO
COMPARE EMR MILEAGE STORED WITH INSTRUMENT PANEL ODOMETER.
IS THE MILEAGE THE SAME?
YES
RETEST THE EMR MEMORY.*
NO
UPDATE THE MILEAGE AND RETEST THE EMR MEMORY.*

* PERFORM VERIFICATION PROCEDURE VER-2.

91G10500

Fig. 115: Driveability Test 32A (3.3L & 3.8L) – Code 63, SBEC Failure EMR Mileage Not Stored & EEPROM Write Denied (1 of 2)

DR-32A: CODE 63, SBEC FAILURE EMR MILEAGE NOT STORED & EEPROM WRITE DENIED (2 OF 2)

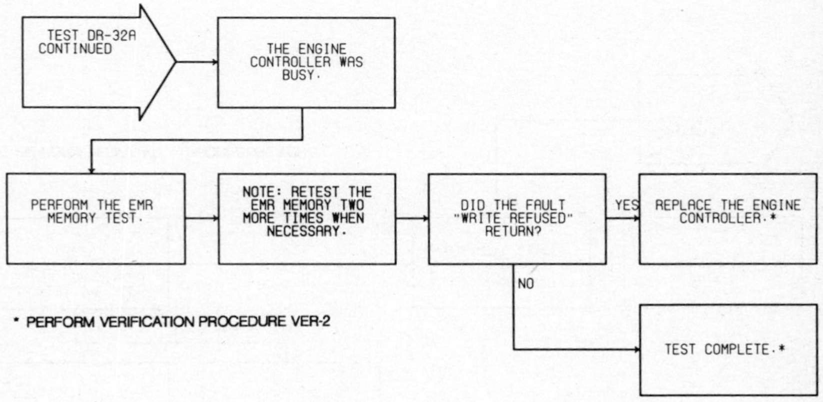
TEST DR-32A CONTINUED
THE ENGINE CONTROLLER WAS BUSY.
PERFORM THE EMR MEMORY TEST.
NOTE: RETEST THE EMR MEMORY TWO MORE TIMES WHEN NECESSARY.
DID THE FAULT "WRITE REFUSED" RETURN?
YES
REPLACE THE ENGINE CONTROLLER.*
NO
TEST COMPLETE.*

* PERFORM VERIFICATION PROCEDURE VER-2

91H10501

Fig. 116: Driveability Test 32A (3.3L & 3.8L) – Code 63, SBEC Failure EMR Mileage Not Stored & EEPROM Write Denied (2 of 2)

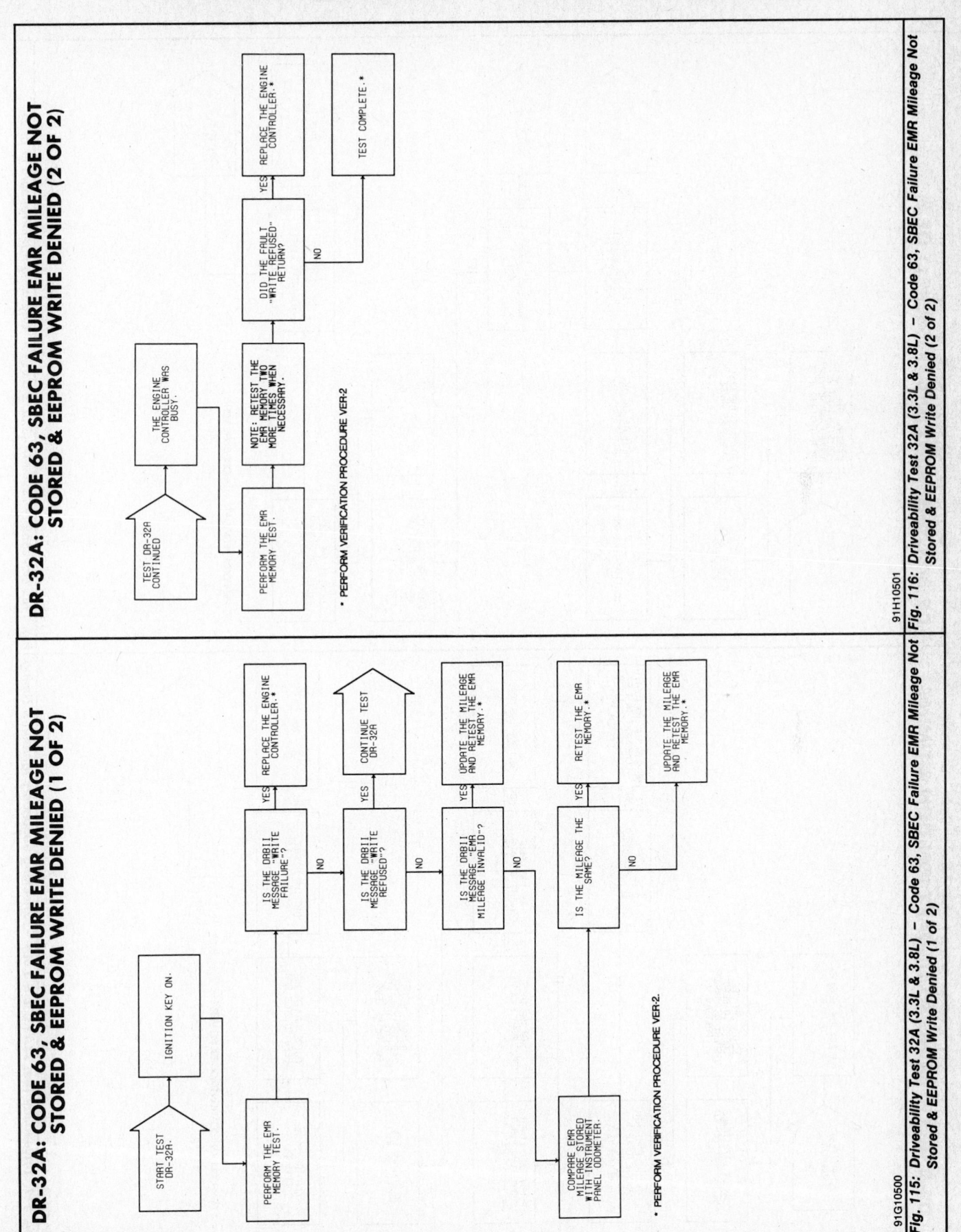

1991 ENGINE PERFORMANCE
Self-Diagnostics – 3.3L PFI (Cont.)

DR-33A: CHECKING SECONDARY IGNITION & TIMING

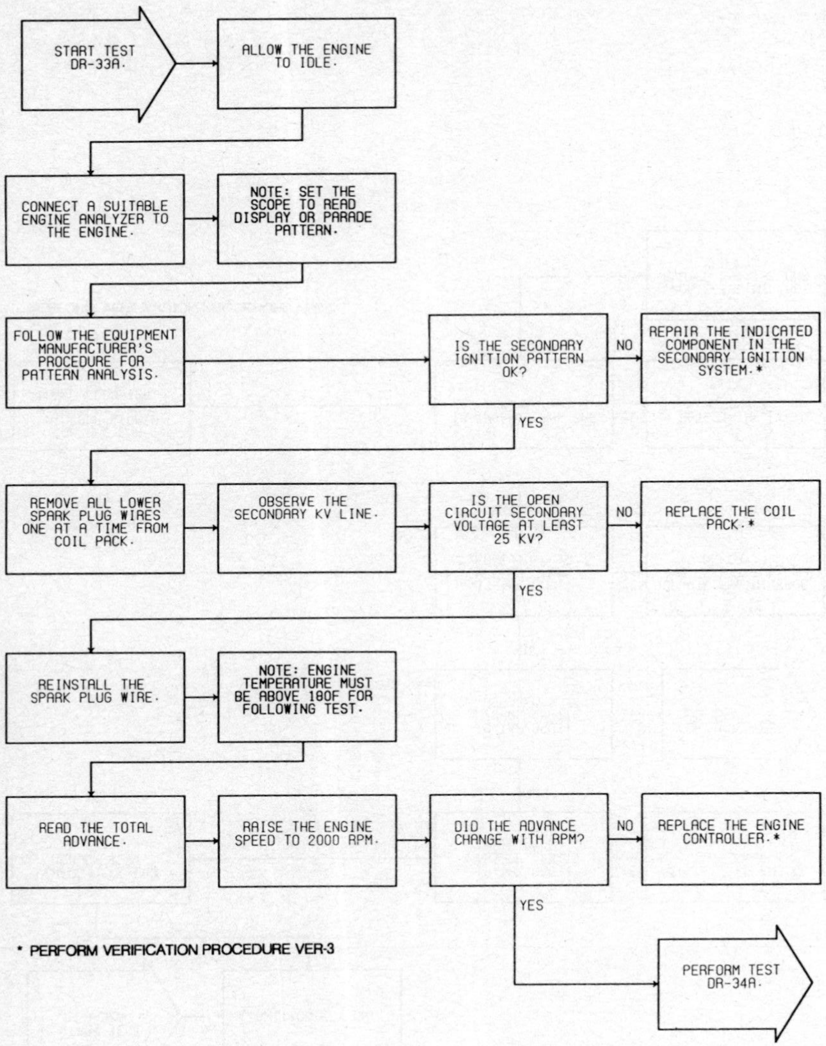
START TEST DR-33A.
ALLOW THE ENGINE TO IDLE.
CONNECT A SUITABLE ENGINE ANALYZER TO THE ENGINE.
NOTE: SET THE SCOPE TO READ DISPLAY OR PARADE PATTERN.
FOLLOW THE EQUIPMENT MANUFACTURER'S PROCEDURE FOR PATTERN ANALYSIS.
IS THE SECONDARY IGNITION PATTERN OK?
NO
REPAIR THE INDICATED COMPONENT IN THE SECONDARY IGNITION SYSTEM.*
YES
REMOVE ALL LOWER SPARK PLUG WIRES ONE AT A TIME FROM COIL PACK.
OBSERVE THE SECONDARY KV LINE.
IS THE OPEN CIRCUIT SECONDARY VOLTAGE AT LEAST 25 KV?
NO
REPLACE THE COIL PACK.*
YES
REINSTALL THE SPARK PLUG WIRE.
NOTE: ENGINE TEMPERATURE MUST BE ABOVE 180F FOR FOLLOWING TEST.
READ THE TOTAL ADVANCE.
RAISE THE ENGINE SPEED TO 2000 RPM.
DID THE ADVANCE CHANGE WITH RPM?
NO
REPLACE THE ENGINE CONTROLLER.*
YES
PERFORM TEST DR-34A.

* PERFORM VERIFICATION PROCEDURE VER-3

91I10502

Fig. 117: Driveability Test 33A (3.3L & 3.8L) – Checking Secondary Ignition & Timing

DR-34A: CHECKING FUEL PRESSURE (1 OF 2)

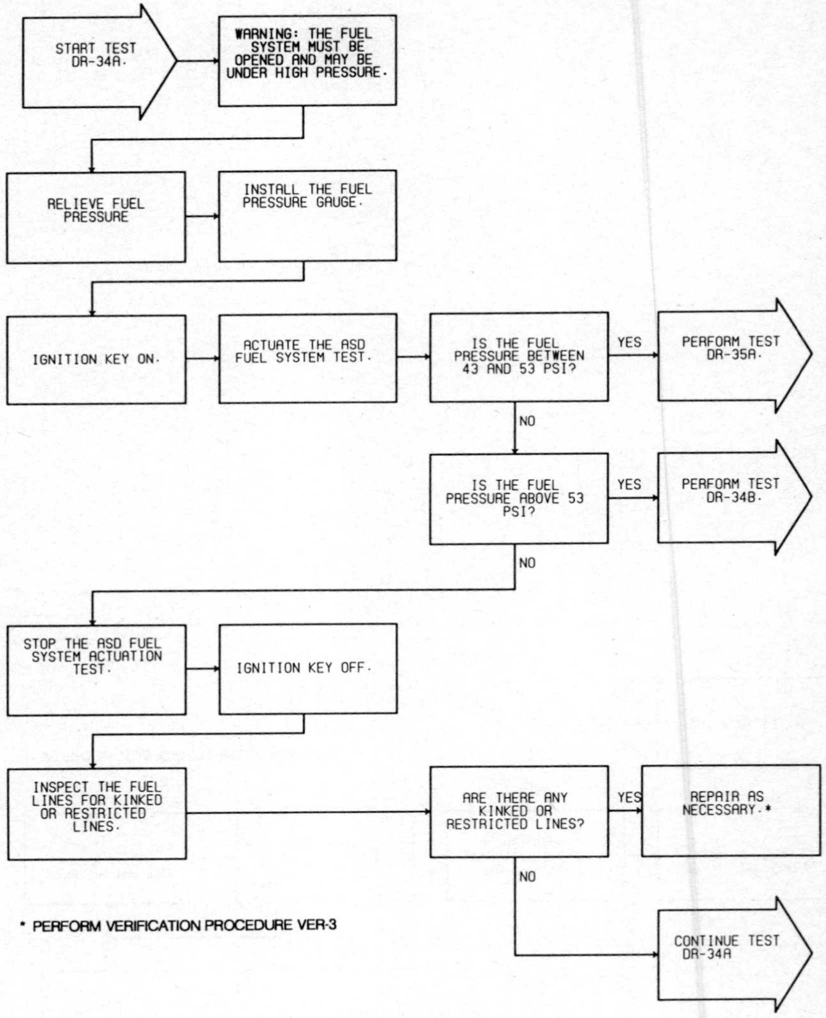
START TEST DR-34A.
WARNING: THE FUEL SYSTEM MUST BE OPENED AND MAY BE UNDER HIGH PRESSURE.
RELIEVE FUEL PRESSURE
INSTALL THE FUEL PRESSURE GAUGE.
IGNITION KEY ON.
ACTUATE THE ASD FUEL SYSTEM TEST.
IS THE FUEL PRESSURE BETWEEN 43 AND 53 PSI?
YES
PERFORM TEST DR-35A.
NO
IS THE FUEL PRESSURE ABOVE 53 PSI?
YES
PERFORM TEST DR-34B.
NO
STOP THE ASD FUEL SYSTEM ACTUATION TEST.
IGNITION KEY OFF.
INSPECT THE FUEL LINES FOR KINKED OR RESTRICTED LINES.
ARE THERE ANY KINKED OR RESTRICTED LINES?
YES
REPAIR AS NECESSARY.*
NO
CONTINUE TEST DR-34A

* PERFORM VERIFICATION PROCEDURE VER-3

91J10503

Fig. 118: Driveability Test 34A (3.3L & 3.8L) – Checking Fuel Pressure (1 of 2)

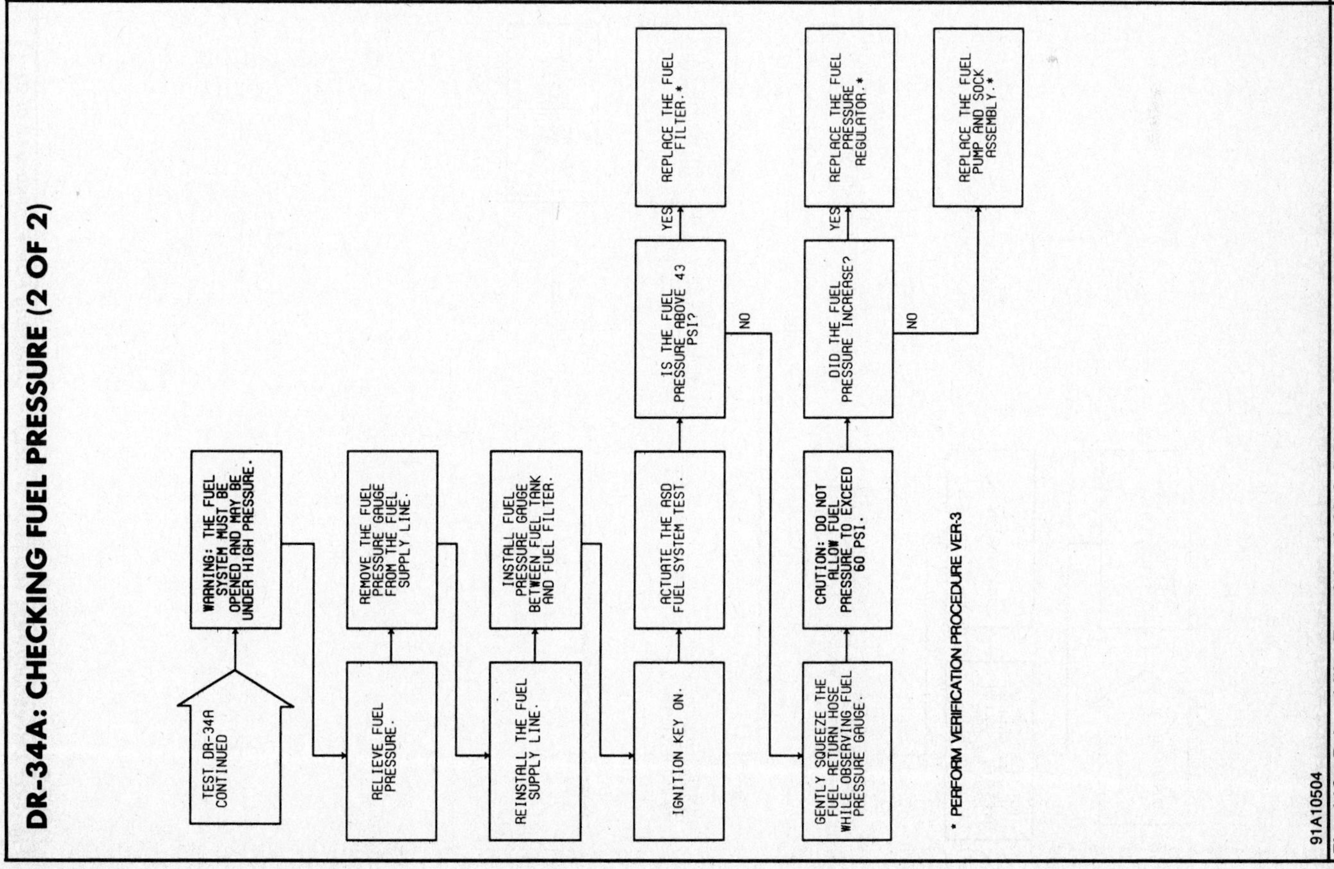

DR-34A: CHECKING FUEL PRESSURE (2 OF 2)
TEST DR-34A CONTINUED
WARNING: THE FUEL SYSTEM MUST BE OPENED AND MAY BE UNDER HIGH PRESSURE.
RELIEVE FUEL PRESSURE.
REMOVE THE FUEL PRESSURE GAUGE FROM THE FUEL SUPPLY LINE.
REINSTALL THE FUEL SUPPLY LINE.
INSTALL FUEL PRESSURE GAUGE BETWEEN FUEL TANK AND FUEL FILTER.
IGNITION KEY ON.
ACTUATE THE ASD FUEL SYSTEM TEST.
IS THE FUEL PRESSURE ABOVE 43 PSI?
YES
REPLACE THE FUEL FILTER.*
NO
GENTLY SQUEEZE THE FUEL RETURN HOSE WHILE OBSERVING FUEL PRESSURE GAUGE.
CAUTION: DO NOT ALLOW FUEL PRESSURE TO EXCEED 60 PSI.
DID THE FUEL PRESSURE INCREASE?
YES
REPLACE THE FUEL PRESSURE REGULATOR.*
NO
REPLACE THE FUEL PUMP AND SOCK ASSEMBLY.*
* PERFORM VERIFICATION PROCEDURE VER-3
91A10504

Fig. 119: Driveability Test 34A (3.3L & 3.8L) – Checking Fuel Pressure (2 of 2)

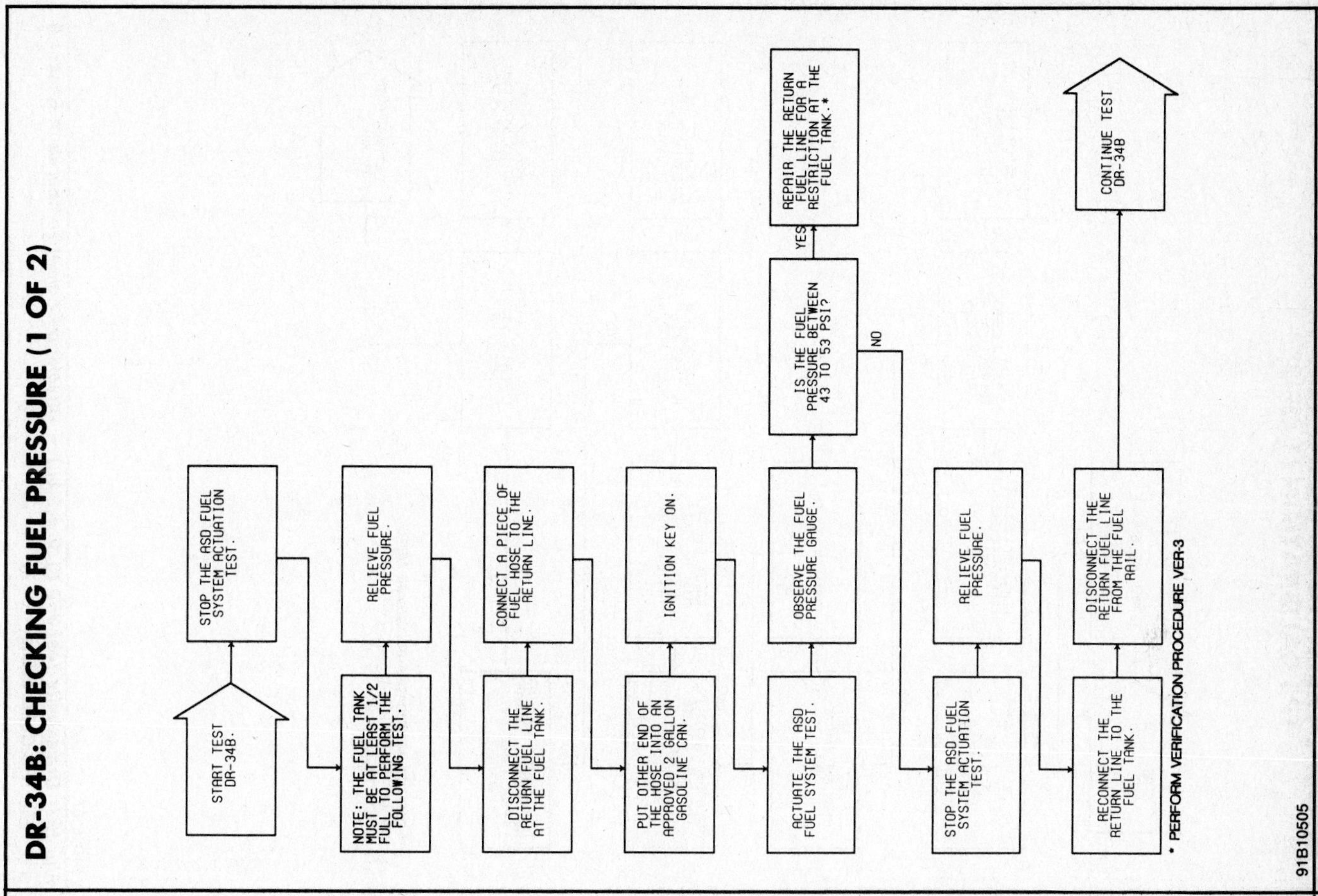

DR-34B: CHECKING FUEL PRESSURE (1 OF 2)
START TEST DR-34B.
STOP THE ASD FUEL SYSTEM ACTUATION TEST.
NOTE: THE FUEL TANK MUST BE AT LEAST 1/2 FULL TO PERFORM THE FOLLOWING TEST.
RELIEVE FUEL PRESSURE.
DISCONNECT THE RETURN FUEL LINE AT THE FUEL TANK.
CONNECT A PIECE OF FUEL HOSE TO THE RETURN LINE.
PUT OTHER END OF THE HOSE INTO AN APPROVED 2 GALLON GASOLINE CAN.
IGNITION KEY ON.
ACTUATE THE ASD FUEL SYSTEM TEST.
OBSERVE THE FUEL PRESSURE GAUGE.
IS THE FUEL PRESSURE BETWEEN 43 TO 53 PSI?
YES
REPAIR THE RETURN FUEL LINE FOR A RESTRICTION AT THE FUEL TANK.*
NO
STOP THE ASD FUEL SYSTEM ACTUATION TEST.
RELIEVE FUEL PRESSURE.
RECONNECT THE RETURN LINE TO THE FUEL TANK.
DISCONNECT THE RETURN FUEL LINE FROM THE FUEL RAIL.
CONTINUE TEST DR-34B
* PERFORM VERIFICATION PROCEDURE VER-3
91B10505

Fig. 120: Driveability Test 34B (3.3L & 3.8L) – Checking Fuel Pressure (1 of 2)

1991 ENGINE PERFORMANCE
Self-Diagnostics – 3.3L PFI (Cont.)

DR-34B: CHECKING FUEL PRESSURE (2 OF 2)

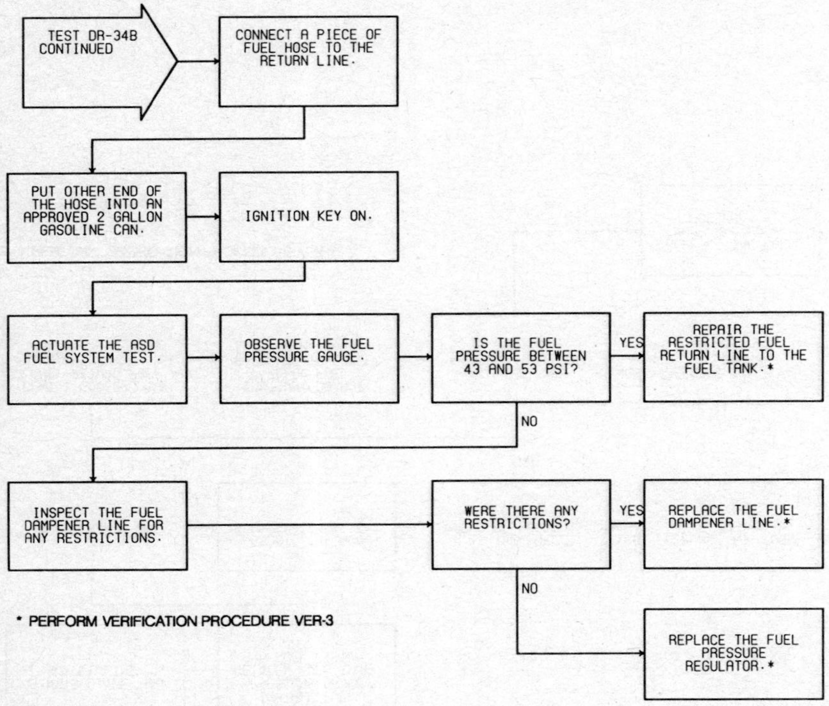
TEST DR-34B CONTINUED
CONNECT A PIECE OF FUEL HOSE TO THE RETURN LINE.
PUT OTHER END OF THE HOSE INTO AN APPROVED 2 GALLON GASOLINE CAN.
IGNITION KEY ON.
ACTUATE THE ASD FUEL SYSTEM TEST.
OBSERVE THE FUEL PRESSURE GAUGE.
IS THE FUEL PRESSURE BETWEEN 43 AND 53 PSI?
YES
REPAIR THE RESTRICTED FUEL RETURN LINE TO THE FUEL TANK.*
NO
INSPECT THE FUEL DAMPENER LINE FOR ANY RESTRICTIONS.
WERE THERE ANY RESTRICTIONS?
YES
REPLACE THE FUEL DAMPENER LINE.*
NO
REPLACE THE FUEL PRESSURE REGULATOR.*

* PERFORM VERIFICATION PROCEDURE VER-3

91C10506

Fig. 121: Driveability Test 34B (3.3L & 3.8L) – Checking Fuel Pressure (2 of 2)

DR-35A: CHECKING COOLANT TEMPERATURE SENSOR & TPS CALIBRATION (1 OF 2)

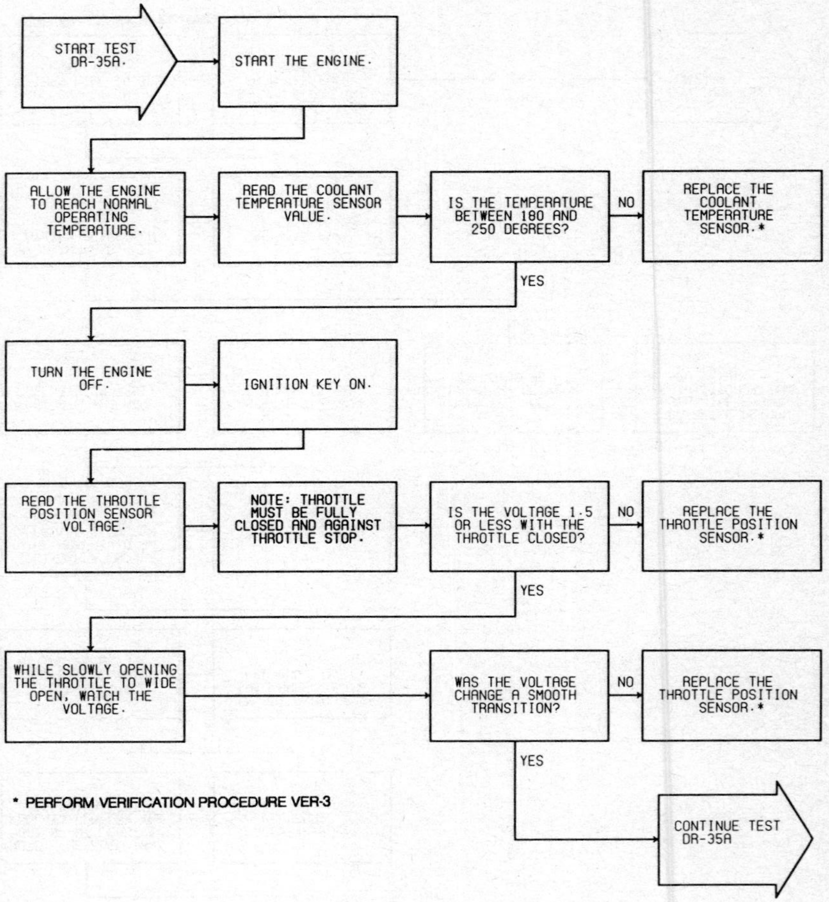
START TEST DR-35A.
START THE ENGINE.
ALLOW THE ENGINE TO REACH NORMAL OPERATING TEMPERATURE.
READ THE COOLANT TEMPERATURE SENSOR VALUE.
IS THE TEMPERATURE BETWEEN 180 AND 250 DEGREES?
NO
REPLACE THE COOLANT TEMPERATURE SENSOR.*
YES
TURN THE ENGINE OFF.
IGNITION KEY ON.
READ THE THROTTLE POSITION SENSOR VOLTAGE.
NOTE: THROTTLE MUST BE FULLY CLOSED AND AGAINST THROTTLE STOP.
IS THE VOLTAGE 1.5 OR LESS WITH THE THROTTLE CLOSED?
NO
REPLACE THE THROTTLE POSITION SENSOR.*
YES
WHILE SLOWLY OPENING THE THROTTLE TO WIDE OPEN, WATCH THE VOLTAGE.
WAS THE VOLTAGE CHANGE A SMOOTH TRANSITION?
NO
REPLACE THE THROTTLE POSITION SENSOR.*
YES
CONTINUE TEST DR-35A

* PERFORM VERIFICATION PROCEDURE VER-3

91D10507

Fig. 122: Driveability Test 35A (3.3L & 3.8L) – Checking Coolant Temperature Sensor & TPS Calibration (1 of 2)

DR-35A: CHECKING COOLANT TEMPERATURE SENSOR & TPS CALIBRATION (2 OF 2)

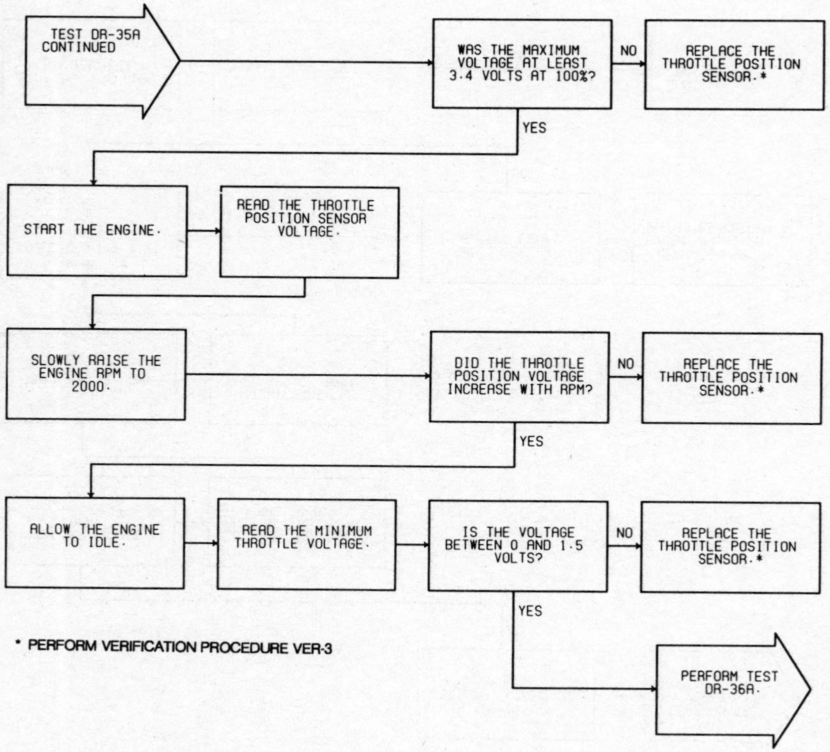
TEST DR-35A CONTINUED
WAS THE MAXIMUM VOLTAGE AT LEAST 3.4 VOLTS AT 100%?
NO
REPLACE THE THROTTLE POSITION SENSOR.*
YES
START THE ENGINE.
READ THE THROTTLE POSITION SENSOR VOLTAGE.
SLOWLY RAISE THE ENGINE RPM TO 2000.
DID THE THROTTLE POSITION VOLTAGE INCREASE WITH RPM?
NO
REPLACE THE THROTTLE POSITION SENSOR.*
YES
ALLOW THE ENGINE TO IDLE.
READ THE MINIMUM THROTTLE VOLTAGE.
IS THE VOLTAGE BETWEEN 0 AND 1.5 VOLTS?
NO
REPLACE THE THROTTLE POSITION SENSOR.*
YES
PERFORM TEST DR-36A.
* PERFORM VERIFICATION PROCEDURE VER-3

91E10508

Fig. 123: Driveability Test 35A (3.3L & 3.8L) – Checking Coolant Temperature Sensor & TPS Calibration (2 of 2)

DR-36A: CHECKING MAP SENSOR CALIBRATION

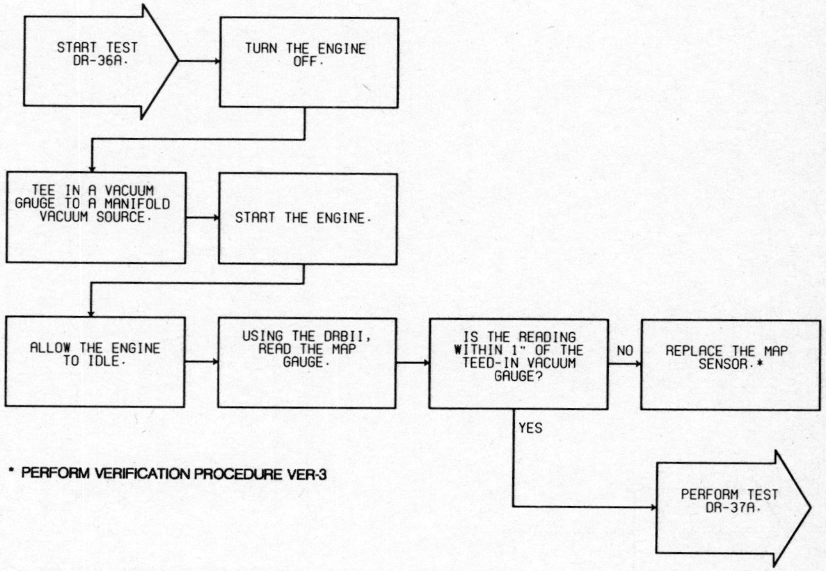
START TEST DR-36A.
TURN THE ENGINE OFF.
TEE IN A VACUUM GAUGE TO A MANIFOLD VACUUM SOURCE.
START THE ENGINE.
ALLOW THE ENGINE TO IDLE.
USING THE DRBII, READ THE MAP GAUGE.
IS THE READING WITHIN 1" OF THE TEED-IN VACUUM GAUGE?
NO
REPLACE THE MAP SENSOR.*
YES
PERFORM TEST DR-37A.
* PERFORM VERIFICATION PROCEDURE VER-3

91F10509

Fig. 124: Driveability Test 36A (3.3L & 3.8L) – Checking MAP Sensor Calibration

1991 ENGINE PERFORMANCE
Self-Diagnostics – 3.3L PFI (Cont.)

DR-37A: CHECKING OXYGEN SENSOR SWITCHING (1 OF 2)

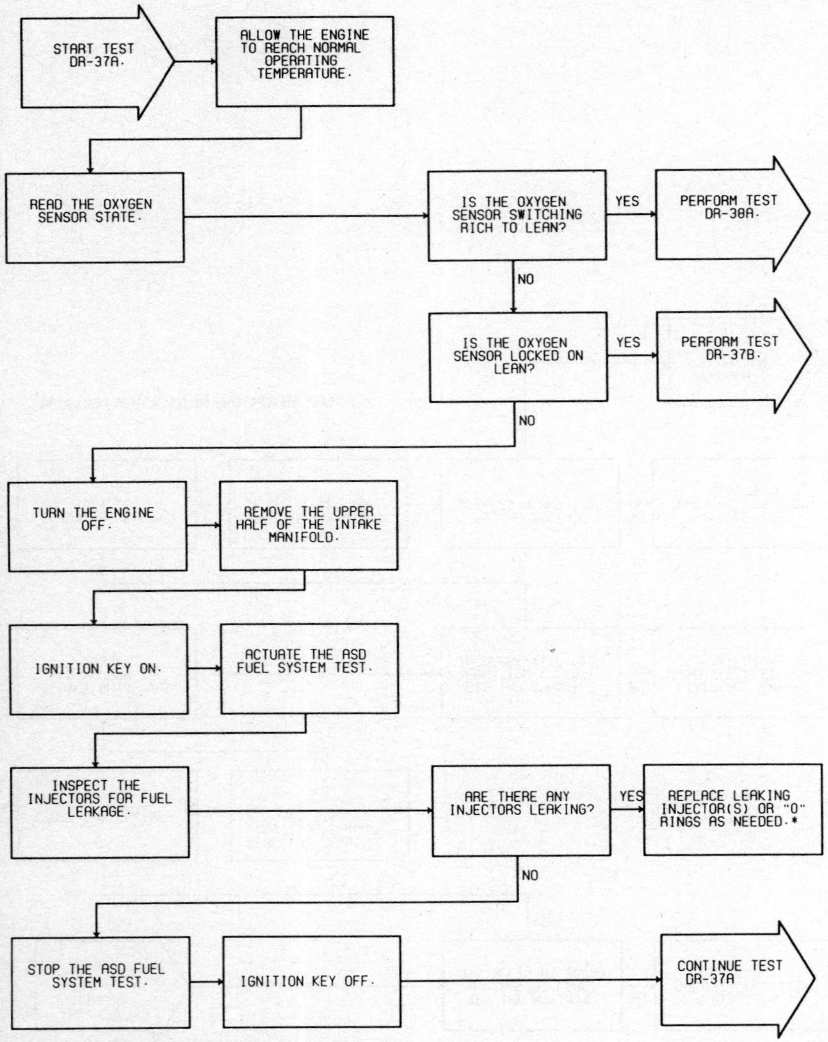
START TEST DR-37A.
ALLOW THE ENGINE TO REACH NORMAL OPERATING TEMPERATURE.
READ THE OXYGEN SENSOR STATE.
IS THE OXYGEN SENSOR SWITCHING RICH TO LEAN?
YES
PERFORM TEST DR-38A.
NO
IS THE OXYGEN SENSOR LOCKED ON LEAN?
YES
PERFORM TEST DR-37B.
NO
TURN THE ENGINE OFF.
REMOVE THE UPPER HALF OF THE INTAKE MANIFOLD.
IGNITION KEY ON.
ACTUATE THE ASD FUEL SYSTEM TEST.
INSPECT THE INJECTORS FOR FUEL LEAKAGE.
ARE THERE ANY INJECTORS LEAKING?
YES
REPLACE LEAKING INJECTOR(S) OR "O" RINGS AS NEEDED.*
NO
STOP THE ASD FUEL SYSTEM TEST.
IGNITION KEY OFF.
CONTINUE TEST DR-37A

* PERFORM VERIFICATION PROCEDURE VER-3

91I10510

Fig. 125: *Driveability Test 37A (3.3L & 3.8L) – Checking Oxygen Sensor Switching (1 of 2)*

DR-37A: CHECKING OXYGEN SENSOR SWITCHING (2 OF 2)

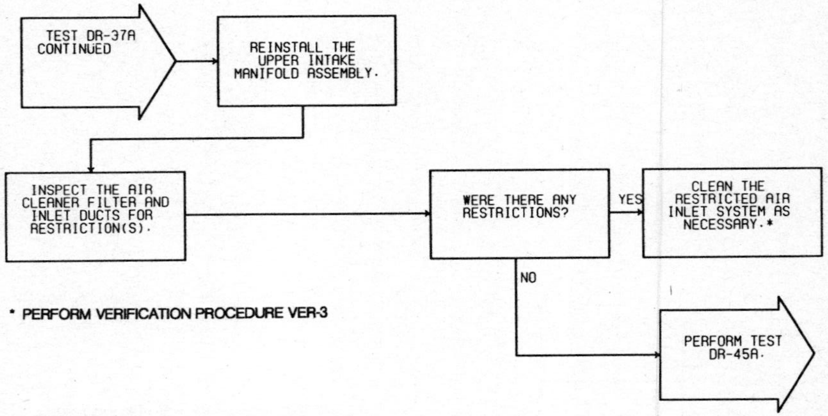
TEST DR-37A CONTINUED
REINSTALL THE UPPER INTAKE MANIFOLD ASSEMBLY.
INSPECT THE AIR CLEANER FILTER AND INLET DUCTS FOR RESTRICTION(S).
WERE THERE ANY RESTRICTIONS?
YES
CLEAN THE RESTRICTED AIR INLET SYSTEM AS NECESSARY.*
NO
PERFORM TEST DR-45A.

* PERFORM VERIFICATION PROCEDURE VER-3

91J10511

Fig. 126: *Driveability Test 37A (3.3L & 3.8L) – Checking Oxygen Sensor Switching (2 of 2)*

DR-37B: CHECKING OXYGEN SENSOR SWITCHING (1 OF 2)

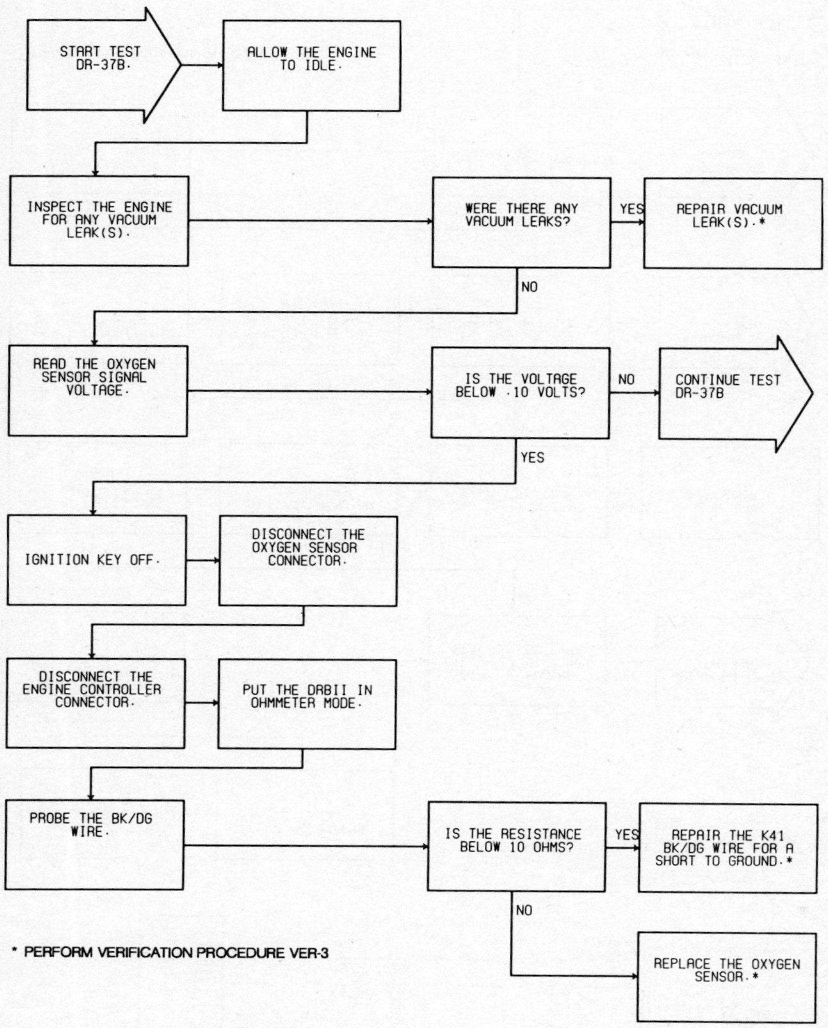
START TEST DR-37B.
ALLOW THE ENGINE TO IDLE.
INSPECT THE ENGINE FOR ANY VACUUM LEAK(S).
WERE THERE ANY VACUUM LEAKS?
YES
REPAIR VACUUM LEAK(S).*
NO
READ THE OXYGEN SENSOR SIGNAL VOLTAGE.
IS THE VOLTAGE BELOW .10 VOLTS?
NO
CONTINUE TEST DR-37B
YES
IGNITION KEY OFF.
DISCONNECT THE OXYGEN SENSOR CONNECTOR.
DISCONNECT THE ENGINE CONTROLLER CONNECTOR.
PUT THE DRBII IN OHMMETER MODE.
PROBE THE BK/DG WIRE.
IS THE RESISTANCE BELOW 10 OHMS?
YES
REPAIR THE K41 BK/DG WIRE FOR A SHORT TO GROUND.*
NO
REPLACE THE OXYGEN SENSOR.*
* PERFORM VERIFICATION PROCEDURE VER-3

91A10512

Fig. 127: Driveability Test 37B (3.3L & 3.8L) – Checking Oxygen Sensor Switching (1 of 2)

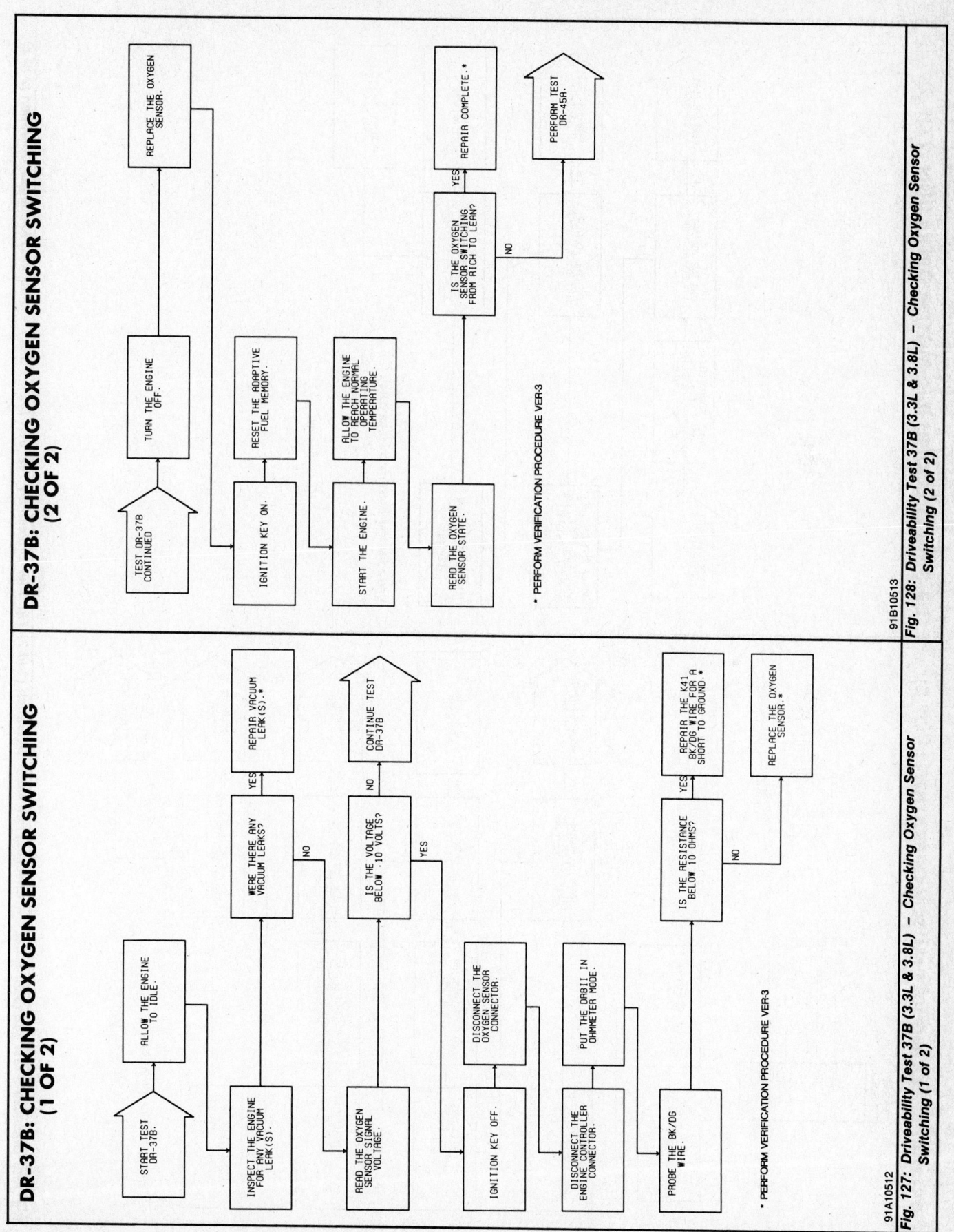

DR-37B: CHECKING OXYGEN SENSOR SWITCHING (2 OF 2)

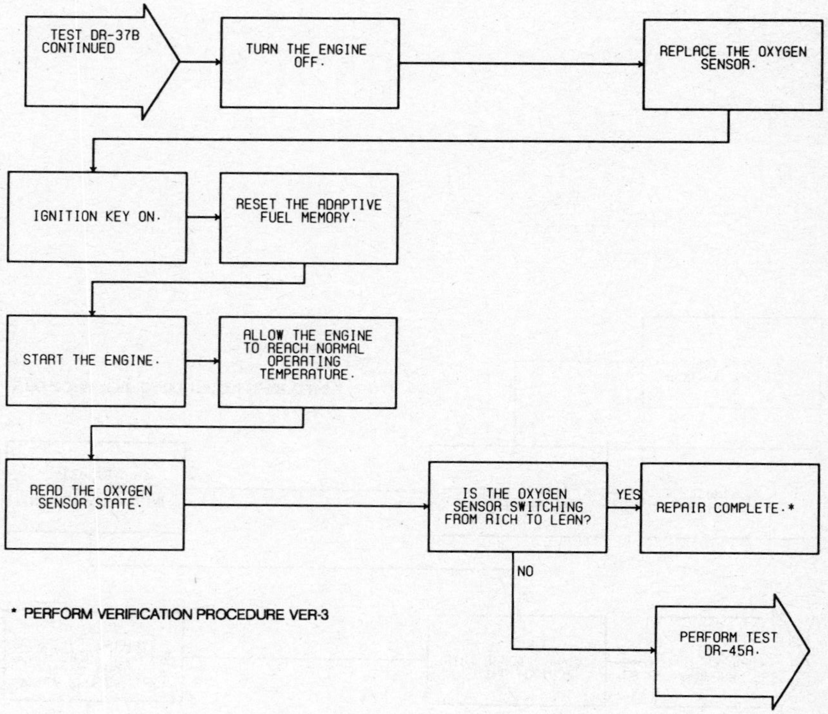
TEST DR-37B CONTINUED
TURN THE ENGINE OFF.
REPLACE THE OXYGEN SENSOR.
IGNITION KEY ON.
RESET THE ADAPTIVE FUEL MEMORY.
START THE ENGINE.
ALLOW THE ENGINE TO REACH NORMAL OPERATING TEMPERATURE.
READ THE OXYGEN SENSOR STATE.
IS THE OXYGEN SENSOR SWITCHING FROM RICH TO LEAN?
YES
REPAIR COMPLETE.*
NO
PERFORM TEST DR-45A.
* PERFORM VERIFICATION PROCEDURE VER-3

91B10513

Fig. 128: Driveability Test 37B (3.3L & 3.8L) – Checking Oxygen Sensor Switching (2 of 2)

DR-38A: CHECKING IDLE MOTOR OPERATION (1 OF 2)

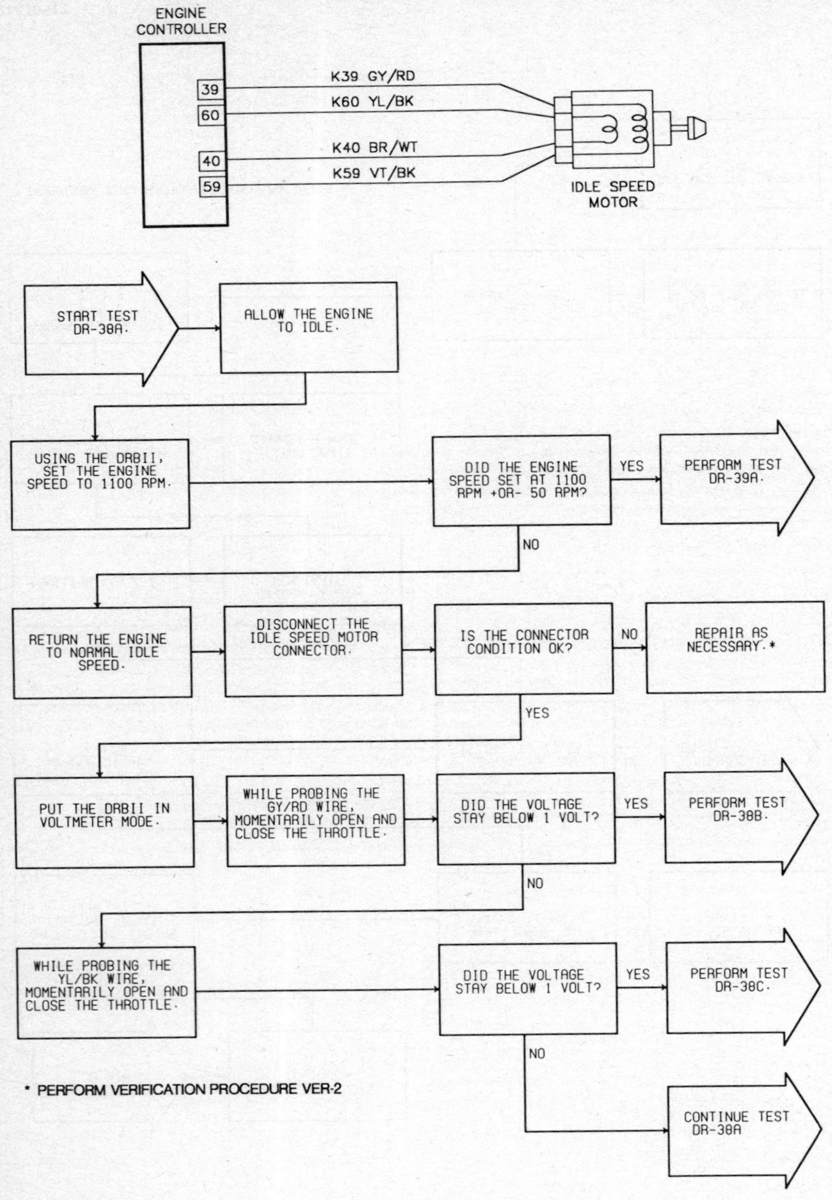
ENGINE CONTROLLER
39
60
40
59
K39 GY/RD
K60 YL/BK
K40 BR/WT
K59 VT/BK
IDLE SPEED MOTOR
START TEST DR-38A.
ALLOW THE ENGINE TO IDLE.
USING THE DRBII, SET THE ENGINE SPEED TO 1100 RPM.
DID THE ENGINE SPEED SET AT 1100 RPM +OR- 50 RPM?
YES
PERFORM TEST DR-39A.
NO
RETURN THE ENGINE TO NORMAL IDLE SPEED.
DISCONNECT THE IDLE SPEED MOTOR CONNECTOR.
IS THE CONNECTOR CONDITION OK?
NO
REPAIR AS NECESSARY.*
YES
PUT THE DRBII IN VOLTMETER MODE.
WHILE PROBING THE GY/RD WIRE, MOMENTARILY OPEN AND CLOSE THE THROTTLE.
DID THE VOLTAGE STAY BELOW 1 VOLT?
YES
PERFORM TEST DR-38B.
NO
WHILE PROBING THE YL/BK WIRE, MOMENTARILY OPEN AND CLOSE THE THROTTLE.
DID THE VOLTAGE STAY BELOW 1 VOLT?
YES
PERFORM TEST DR-38C.
NO
CONTINUE TEST DR-38A
* PERFORM VERIFICATION PROCEDURE VER-2

91J09123 91C10514

Fig. 129: Driveability Test 38A (3.3L & 3.8L) – Checking Idle Motor Operation (1 of 2)

DR-38A: CHECKING IDLE MOTOR OPERATION (2 OF 2)

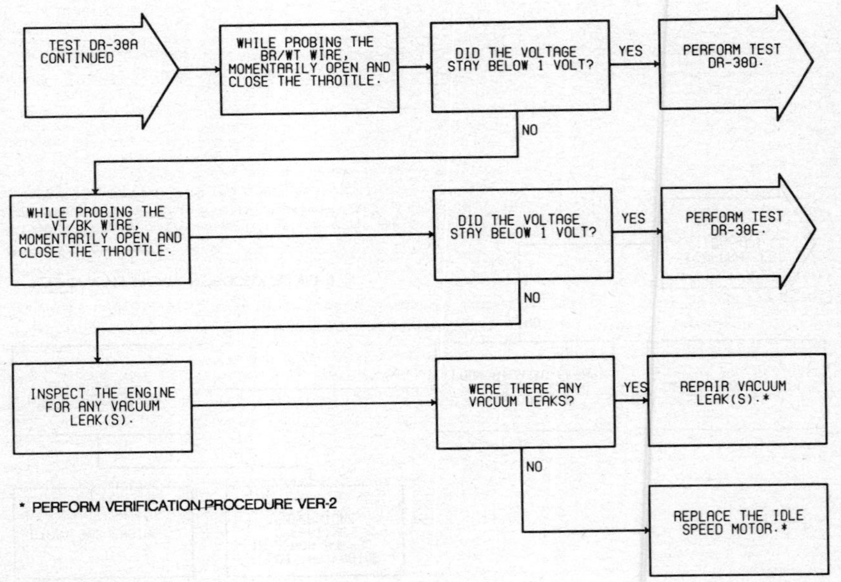
TEST DR-38A CONTINUED
WHILE PROBING THE BR/WT WIRE, MOMENTARILY OPEN AND CLOSE THE THROTTLE.
DID THE VOLTAGE STAY BELOW 1 VOLT?
YES
PERFORM TEST DR-38D.
NO
WHILE PROBING THE VT/BK WIRE, MOMENTARILY OPEN AND CLOSE THE THROTTLE.
DID THE VOLTAGE STAY BELOW 1 VOLT?
YES
PERFORM TEST DR-38E.
NO
INSPECT THE ENGINE FOR ANY VACUUM LEAK(S).
WERE THERE ANY VACUUM LEAKS?
YES
REPAIR VACUUM LEAK(S).*
NO
REPLACE THE IDLE SPEED MOTOR.*
* PERFORM VERIFICATION PROCEDURE VER-2

91D10515

Fig. 130: Driveability Test 38A (3.3L & 3.8L) – Checking Idle Motor Operation (2 of 2)

DR-38B: CHECKING IDLE MOTOR OPERATION

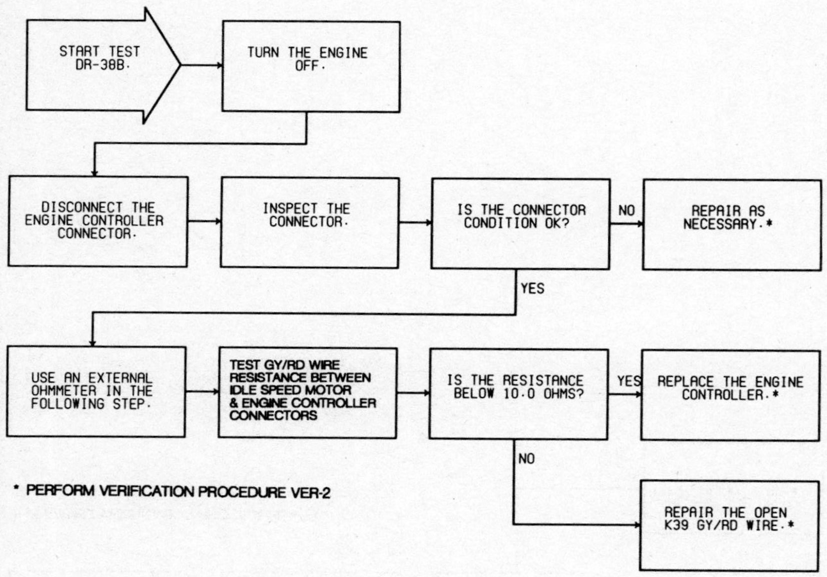
START TEST DR-38B.
TURN THE ENGINE OFF.
DISCONNECT THE ENGINE CONTROLLER CONNECTOR.
INSPECT THE CONNECTOR.
IS THE CONNECTOR CONDITION OK?
NO
REPAIR AS NECESSARY.*
YES
USE AN EXTERNAL OHMMETER IN THE FOLLOWING STEP.
TEST GY/RD WIRE RESISTANCE BETWEEN IDLE SPEED MOTOR & ENGINE CONTROLLER CONNECTORS
IS THE RESISTANCE BELOW 10.0 OHMS?
YES
REPLACE THE ENGINE CONTROLLER.*
NO
REPAIR THE OPEN K39 GY/RD WIRE.*

* PERFORM VERIFICATION PROCEDURE VER-2

91E10516

Fig. 131: Driveability Test 38B (3.3L & 3.8L) – Checking Idle Motor Operation

DR-38C: CHECKING IDLE MOTOR OPERATION

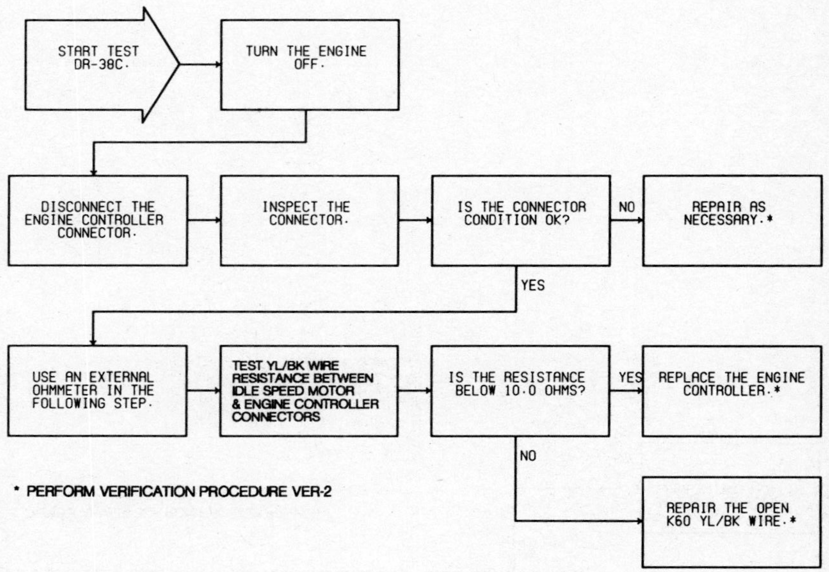
START TEST DR-38C.
TURN THE ENGINE OFF.
DISCONNECT THE ENGINE CONTROLLER CONNECTOR.
INSPECT THE CONNECTOR.
IS THE CONNECTOR CONDITION OK?
NO
REPAIR AS NECESSARY.*
YES
USE AN EXTERNAL OHMMETER IN THE FOLLOWING STEP.
TEST YL/BK WIRE RESISTANCE BETWEEN IDLE SPEED MOTOR & ENGINE CONTROLLER CONNECTORS
IS THE RESISTANCE BELOW 10.0 OHMS?
YES
REPLACE THE ENGINE CONTROLLER.*
NO
REPAIR THE OPEN K60 YL/BK WIRE.*

* PERFORM VERIFICATION PROCEDURE VER-2

91F10517

Fig. 132: Driveability Test 38C (3.3L & 3.8L) – Checking Idle Motor Operation

1991 ENGINE PERFORMANCE
Self-Diagnostics – 3.3L PFI (Cont.)

DR-38D: CHECKING IDLE MOTOR OPERATION

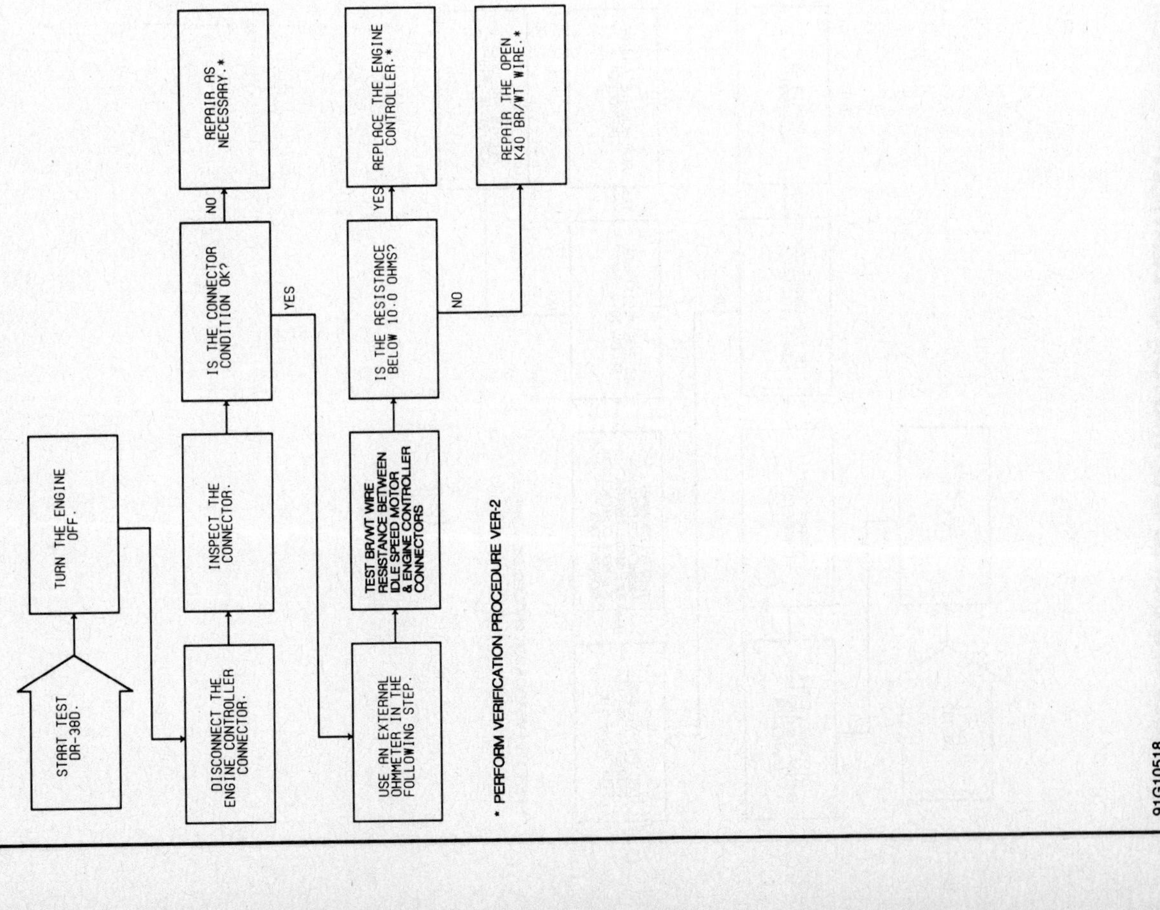
START TEST DR-38D.
TURN THE ENGINE OFF.
DISCONNECT THE ENGINE CONTROLLER CONNECTOR.
INSPECT THE CONNECTOR.
IS THE CONNECTOR CONDITION OK?
NO
REPAIR AS NECESSARY.*
YES
USE AN EXTERNAL OHMMETER IN THE FOLLOWING STEP.
TEST BR/WT WIRE RESISTANCE BETWEEN IDLE SPEED MOTOR & ENGINE CONTROLLER CONNECTORS
IS THE RESISTANCE BELOW 10.0 OHMS?
YES
REPLACE THE ENGINE CONTROLLER.*
NO
REPAIR THE OPEN K40 BR/WT WIRE.*
* PERFORM VERIFICATION PROCEDURE VER-2
91G10518

Fig. 133: Driveability Test 38D (3.3L & 3.8L) – Checking Idle Motor Operation

DR-38E: CHECKING IDLE MOTOR OPERATION

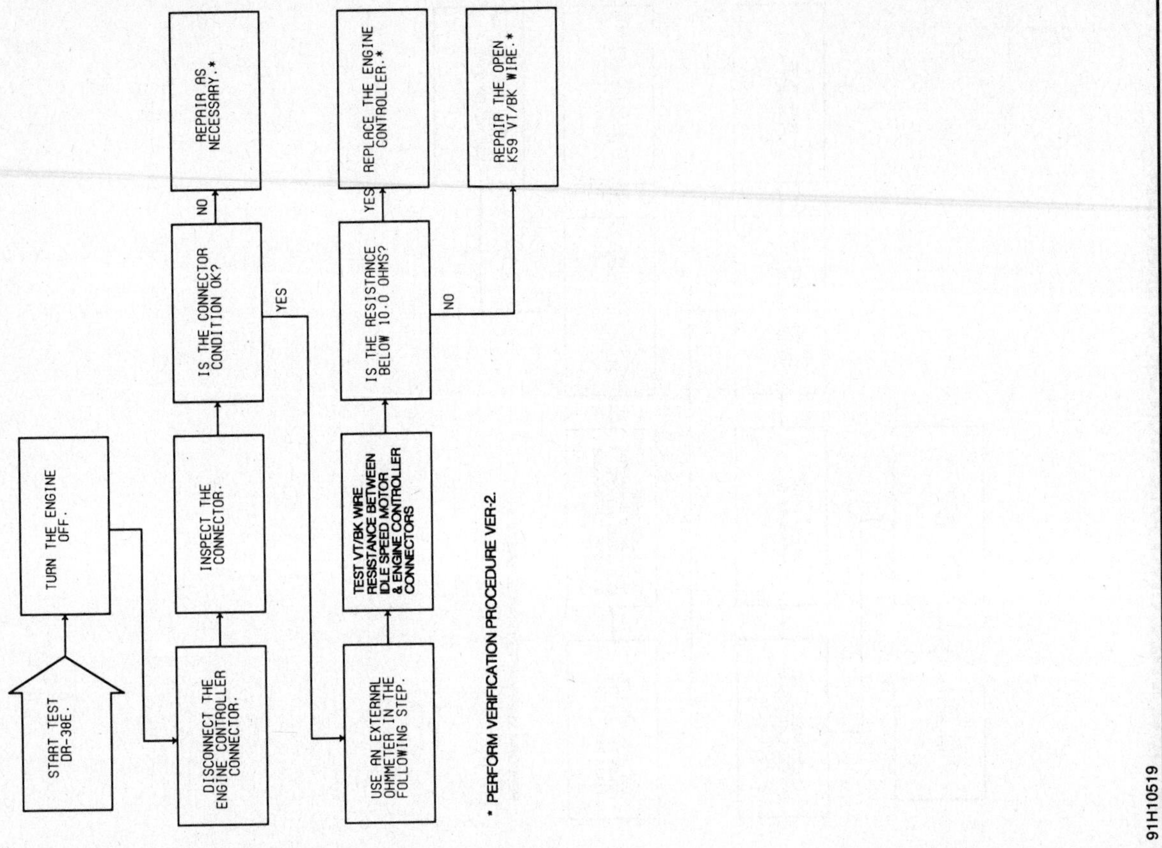
START TEST DR-38E.
TURN THE ENGINE OFF.
DISCONNECT THE ENGINE CONTROLLER CONNECTOR.
INSPECT THE CONNECTOR.
IS THE CONNECTOR CONDITION OK?
NO
REPAIR AS NECESSARY.*
YES
USE AN EXTERNAL OHMMETER IN THE FOLLOWING STEP.
TEST VT/BK WIRE RESISTANCE BETWEEN IDLE SPEED MOTOR & ENGINE CONTROLLER CONNECTORS
IS THE RESISTANCE BELOW 10.0 OHMS?
YES
REPLACE THE ENGINE CONTROLLER.*
NO
REPAIR THE OPEN K59 VT/BK WIRE.*
* PERFORM VERIFICATION PROCEDURE VER-2.
91H10519

Fig. 134: Driveability Test 38E (3.3L & 3.8L) – Checking Idle Motor Operation

DR-39A: CHECKING PARK/NEUTRAL SWITCH INPUT (1 OF 2)

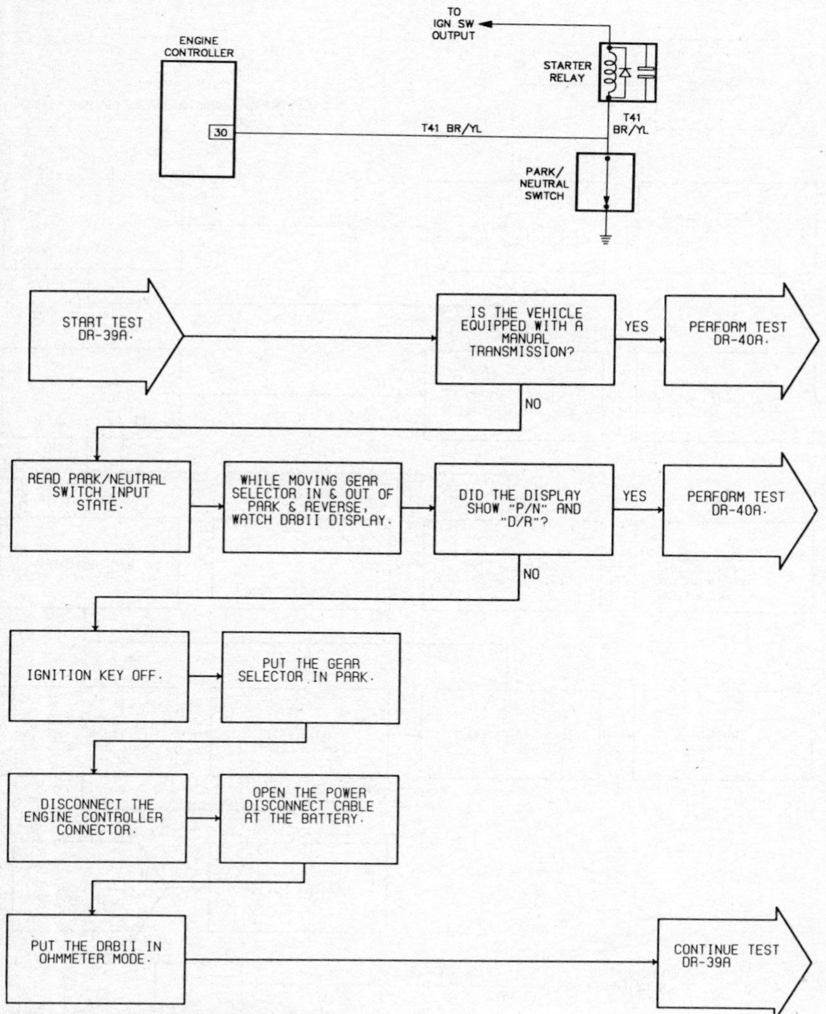
ENGINE CONTROLLER
30
T41 BR/YL
TO IGN SW OUTPUT
STARTER RELAY
T41 BR/YL
PARK/ NEUTRAL SWITCH
START TEST DR-39A.
IS THE VEHICLE EQUIPPED WITH A MANUAL TRANSMISSION?
YES
PERFORM TEST DR-40A.
NO
READ PARK/NEUTRAL SWITCH INPUT STATE.
WHILE MOVING GEAR SELECTOR IN & OUT OF PARK & REVERSE, WATCH DRBII DISPLAY.
DID THE DISPLAY SHOW "P/N" AND "D/R"?
YES
PERFORM TEST DR-40A.
NO
IGNITION KEY OFF.
PUT THE GEAR SELECTOR IN PARK.
DISCONNECT THE ENGINE CONTROLLER CONNECTOR.
OPEN THE POWER DISCONNECT CABLE AT THE BATTERY.
PUT THE DRBII IN OHMMETER MODE.
CONTINUE TEST DR-39A

* PERFORM VERIFICATION PROCEDURE VER-3

91J09137 91A10520

Fig. 135: Driveability Test 39A (3.3L & 3.8L) – Checking Park/Neutral Switch Input (1 of 2)

DR-39A: CHECKING PARK/NEUTRAL SWITCH INPUT (2 OF 2)

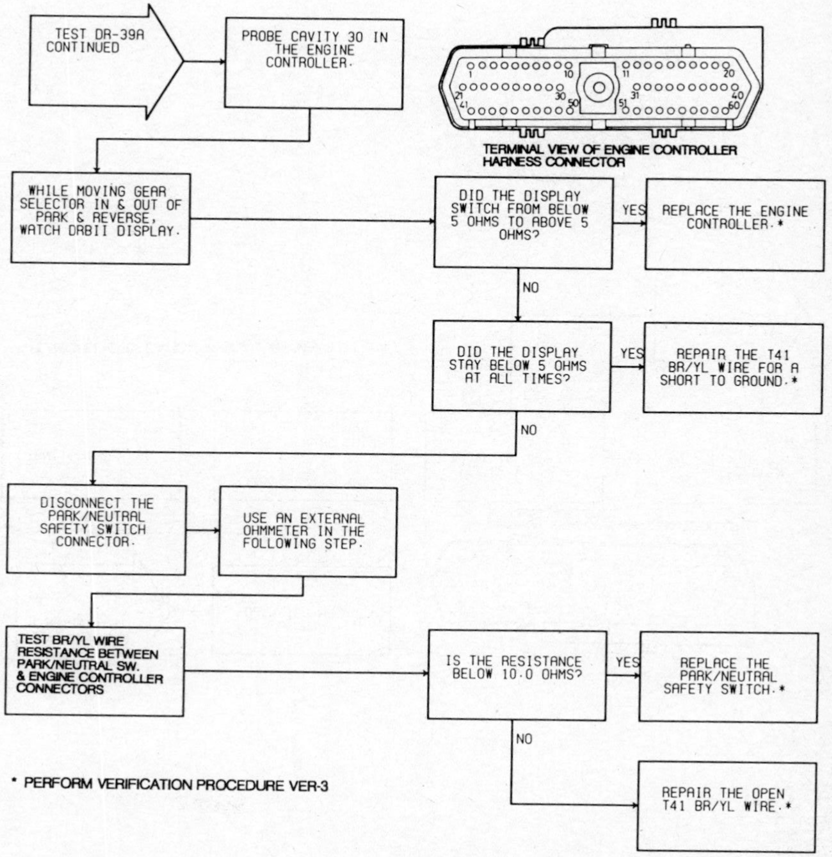
TEST DR-39A CONTINUED
PROBE CAVITY 30 IN THE ENGINE CONTROLLER.
TERMINAL VIEW OF ENGINE CONTROLLER HARNESS CONNECTOR
WHILE MOVING GEAR SELECTOR IN & OUT OF PARK & REVERSE, WATCH DRBII DISPLAY.
DID THE DISPLAY SWITCH FROM BELOW 5 OHMS TO ABOVE 5 OHMS?
YES
REPLACE THE ENGINE CONTROLLER.*
NO
DID THE DISPLAY STAY BELOW 5 OHMS AT ALL TIMES?
YES
REPAIR THE T41 BR/YL WIRE FOR A SHORT TO GROUND.*
NO
DISCONNECT THE PARK/NEUTRAL SAFETY SWITCH CONNECTOR.
USE AN EXTERNAL OHMMETER IN THE FOLLOWING STEP.
TEST BR/YL WIRE RESISTANCE BETWEEN PARK/NEUTRAL SW. & ENGINE CONTROLLER CONNECTORS
IS THE RESISTANCE BELOW 10.0 OHMS?
YES
REPLACE THE PARK/NEUTRAL SAFETY SWITCH.*
NO
REPAIR THE OPEN T41 BR/YL WIRE.*

* PERFORM VERIFICATION PROCEDURE VER-3

91B10521

Fig. 136: Driveability Test 39A (3.3L & 3.8L) – Checking Park/Neutral Switch Input (2 of 2)

1991 ENGINE PERFORMANCE
Self-Diagnostics – 3.3L PFI (Cont.)

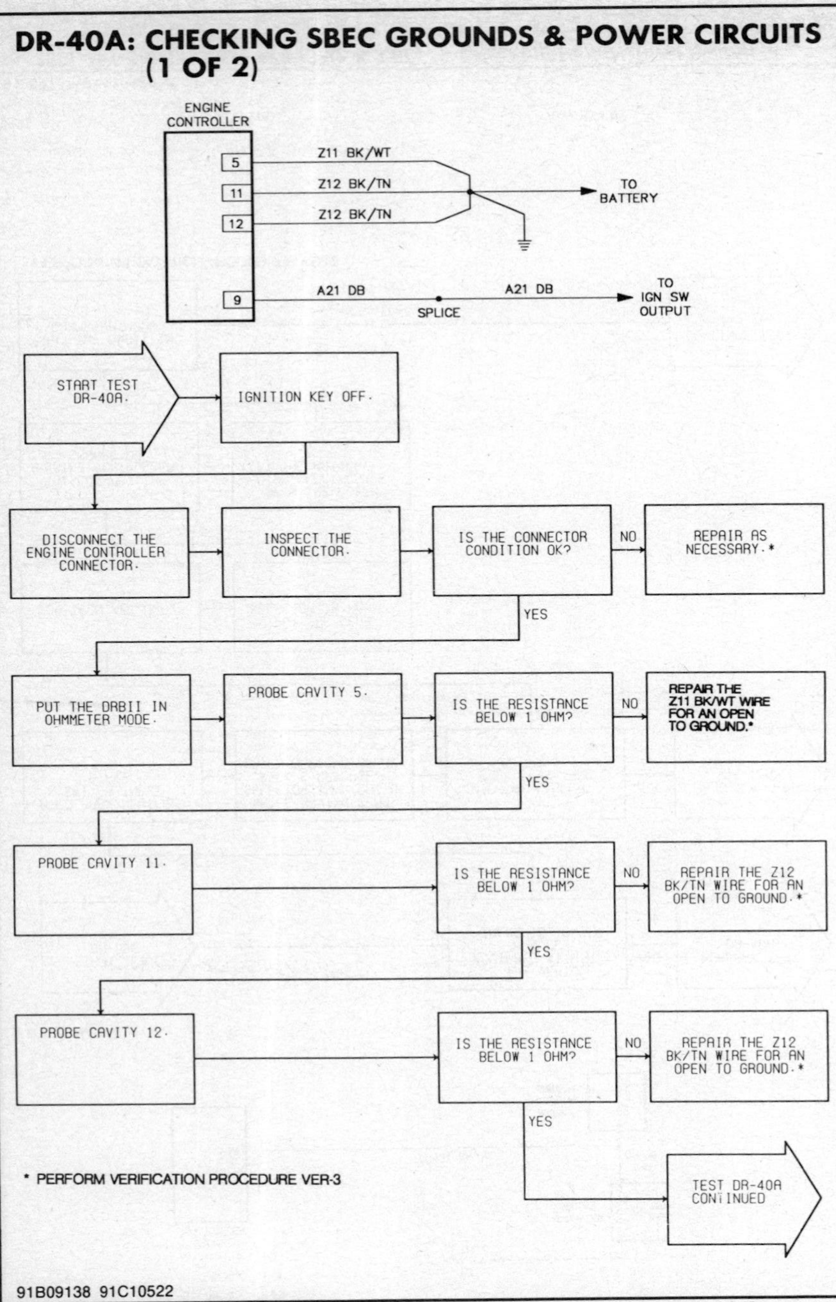
DR-40A: CHECKING SBEC GROUNDS & POWER CIRCUITS (1 OF 2)
ENGINE CONTROLLER
5
11
12
9
Z11 BK/WT
Z12 BK/TN
Z12 BK/TN
TO BATTERY
A21 DB
SPLICE
A21 DB
TO IGN SW OUTPUT
START TEST DR-40A.
IGNITION KEY OFF.
DISCONNECT THE ENGINE CONTROLLER CONNECTOR.
INSPECT THE CONNECTOR.
IS THE CONNECTOR CONDITION OK?
NO
REPAIR AS NECESSARY.*
YES
PUT THE DRBII IN OHMMETER MODE.
PROBE CAVITY 5.
IS THE RESISTANCE BELOW 1 OHM?
NO
REPAIR THE Z11 BK/WT WIRE FOR AN OPEN TO GROUND.*
YES
PROBE CAVITY 11.
IS THE RESISTANCE BELOW 1 OHM?
NO
REPAIR THE Z12 BK/TN WIRE FOR AN OPEN TO GROUND.*
YES
PROBE CAVITY 12.
IS THE RESISTANCE BELOW 1 OHM?
NO
REPAIR THE Z12 BK/TN WIRE FOR AN OPEN TO GROUND.*
YES
TEST DR-40A CONTINUED
* PERFORM VERIFICATION PROCEDURE VER-3
91B09138 91C10522

Fig. 137: Driveability Test 40A (3.3L & 3.8L) – Checking SBEC Grounds & Power Circuits (1 of 2)

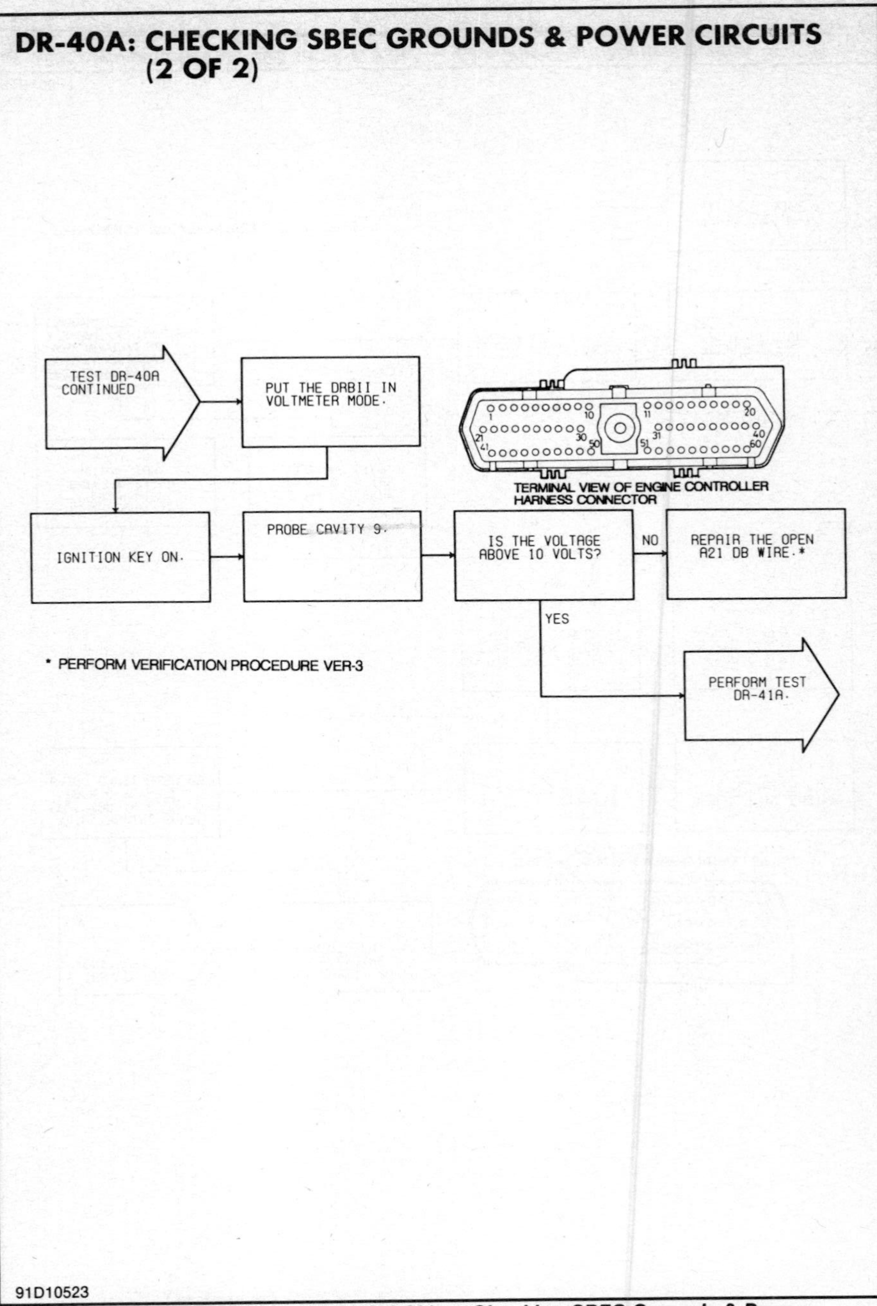
DR-40A: CHECKING SBEC GROUNDS & POWER CIRCUITS (2 OF 2)
TEST DR-40A CONTINUED
PUT THE DRBII IN VOLTMETER MODE.
TERMINAL VIEW OF ENGINE CONTROLLER HARNESS CONNECTOR
IGNITION KEY ON.
PROBE CAVITY 9.
IS THE VOLTAGE ABOVE 10 VOLTS?
NO
REPAIR THE OPEN A21 DB WIRE.*
YES
PERFORM TEST DR-41A.
* PERFORM VERIFICATION PROCEDURE VER-3
91D10523

Fig. 138: Driveability Test 40A (3.3L & 3.8L) – Checking SBEC Grounds & Power Circuits (2 of 2)

DR-41A: CHECKING EGR OPERATION, FEDERAL EMISSIONS (1 OF 6)

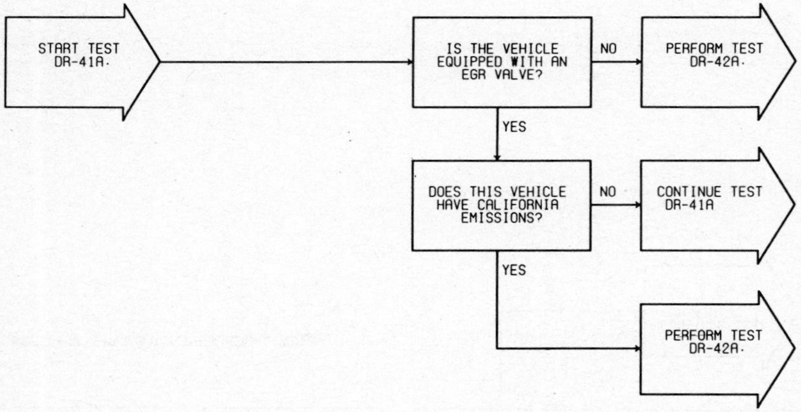
START TEST DR-41A.
IS THE VEHICLE EQUIPPED WITH AN EGR VALVE?
NO
PERFORM TEST DR-42A.
YES
DOES THIS VEHICLE HAVE CALIFORNIA EMISSIONS?
NO
CONTINUE TEST DR-41A
YES
PERFORM TEST DR-42A.

91E10524

Fig. 139: Driveability Test 41A (3.3L & 3.8L) – Checking EGR Operation, Federal Emissions (1 of 6)

DR-41A: CHECKING EGR OPERATION, FEDERAL EMISSIONS (2 OF 6)

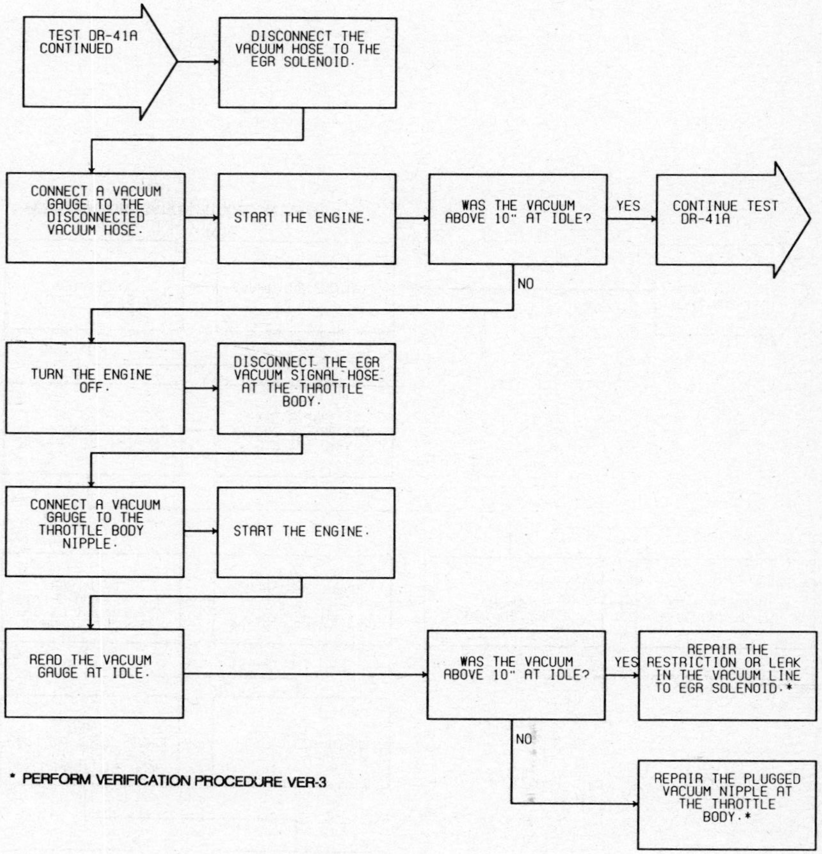
TEST DR-41A CONTINUED
DISCONNECT THE VACUUM HOSE TO THE EGR SOLENOID.
CONNECT A VACUUM GAUGE TO THE DISCONNECTED VACUUM HOSE.
START THE ENGINE.
WAS THE VACUUM ABOVE 10" AT IDLE?
YES
CONTINUE TEST DR-41A
NO
TURN THE ENGINE OFF.
DISCONNECT THE EGR VACUUM SIGNAL HOSE AT THE THROTTLE BODY.
CONNECT A VACUUM GAUGE TO THE THROTTLE BODY NIPPLE.
START THE ENGINE.
READ THE VACUUM GAUGE AT IDLE.
WAS THE VACUUM ABOVE 10" AT IDLE?
YES
REPAIR THE RESTRICTION OR LEAK IN THE VACUUM LINE TO EGR SOLENOID.*
NO
REPAIR THE PLUGGED VACUUM NIPPLE AT THE THROTTLE BODY.*
* PERFORM VERIFICATION PROCEDURE VER-3

91F10525

Fig. 140: Driveability Test 41A (3.3L & 3.8L) – Checking EGR Operation, Federal Emissions (2 of 6)

DR-41A: CHECKING EGR OPERATION, FEDERAL EMISSIONS (3 OF 6)

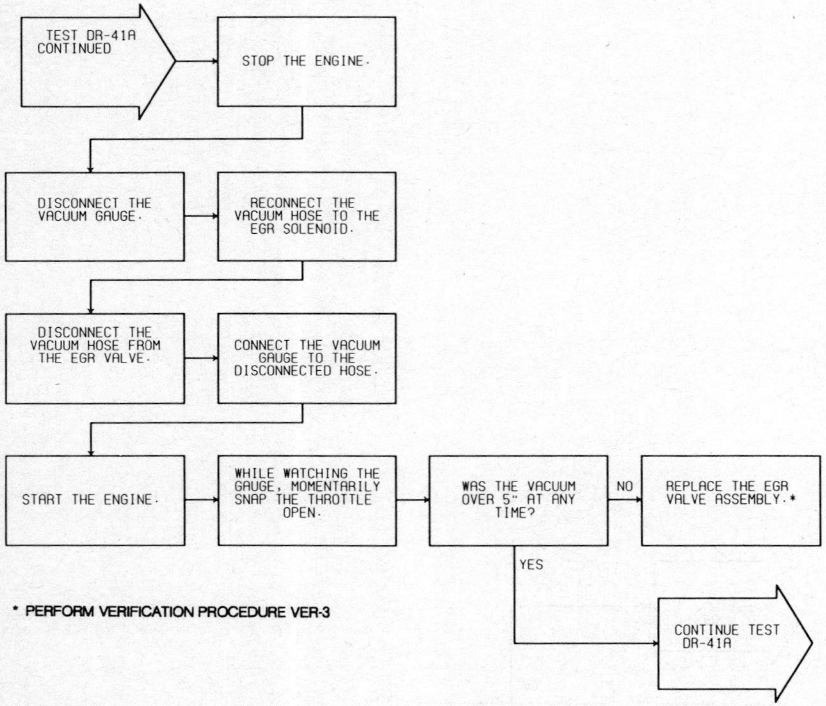
TEST DR-41A CONTINUED
STOP THE ENGINE.
DISCONNECT THE VACUUM GAUGE.
RECONNECT THE VACUUM HOSE TO THE EGR SOLENOID.
DISCONNECT THE VACUUM HOSE FROM THE EGR VALVE.
CONNECT THE VACUUM GAUGE TO THE DISCONNECTED HOSE.
START THE ENGINE.
WHILE WATCHING THE GAUGE, MOMENTARILY SNAP THE THROTTLE OPEN.
WAS THE VACUUM OVER 5" AT ANY TIME?
NO
REPLACE THE EGR VALVE ASSEMBLY.*
YES
CONTINUE TEST DR-41A

* PERFORM VERIFICATION PROCEDURE VER-3

91G10526

Fig. 141: Driveability Test 41A (3.3L & 3.8L) – Checking EGR Operation, Federal Emissions (3 of 6)

DR-41A: CHECKING EGR OPERATION, FEDERAL EMISSIONS (4 OF 6)

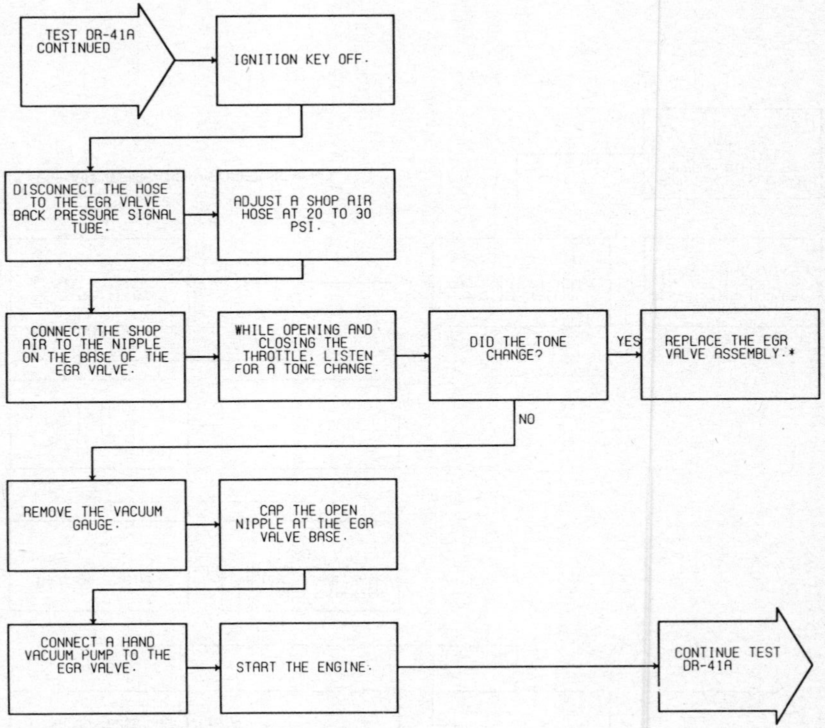
TEST DR-41A CONTINUED
IGNITION KEY OFF.
DISCONNECT THE HOSE TO THE EGR VALVE BACK PRESSURE SIGNAL TUBE.
ADJUST A SHOP AIR HOSE AT 20 TO 30 PSI.
CONNECT THE SHOP AIR TO THE NIPPLE ON THE BASE OF THE EGR VALVE.
WHILE OPENING AND CLOSING THE THROTTLE, LISTEN FOR A TONE CHANGE.
DID THE TONE CHANGE?
YES
REPLACE THE EGR VALVE ASSEMBLY.*
NO
REMOVE THE VACUUM GAUGE.
CAP THE OPEN NIPPLE AT THE EGR VALVE BASE.
CONNECT A HAND VACUUM PUMP TO THE EGR VALVE.
START THE ENGINE.
CONTINUE TEST DR-41A

* PERFORM VERIFICATION PROCEDURE VER-3

91H10527

Fig. 142: Driveability Test 41A (3.3L & 3.8L) – Checking EGR Operation, Federal Emissions (4 of 6)

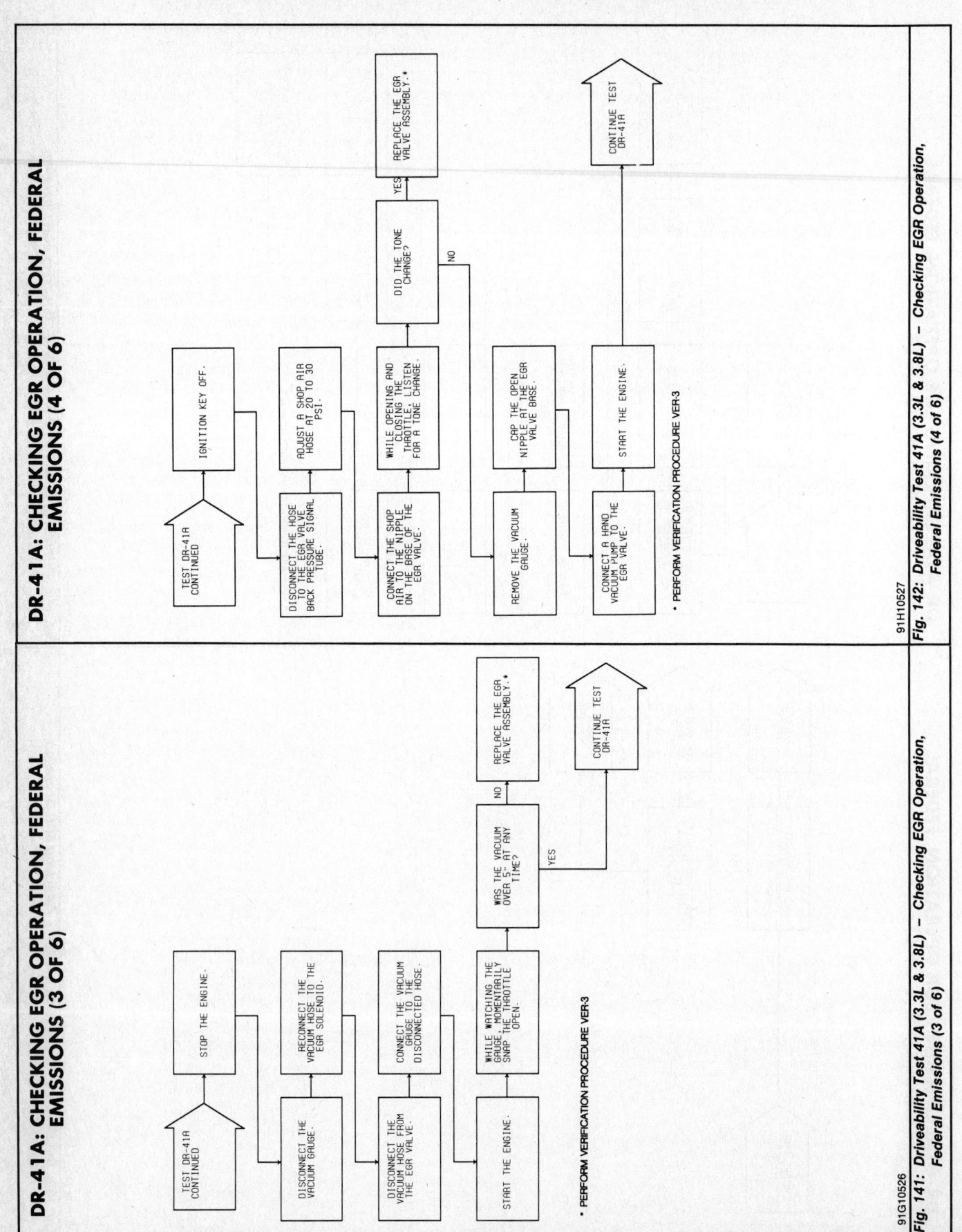

DR-41A: CHECKING EGR OPERATION, FEDERAL EMISSIONS (5 OF 6)

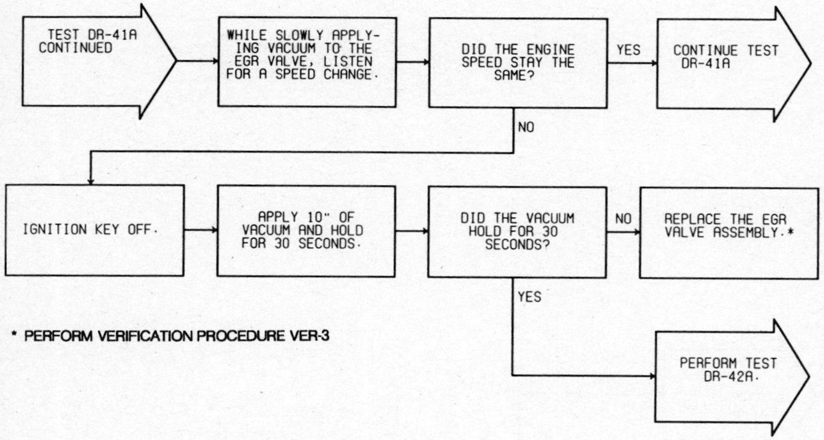
TEST DR-41A CONTINUED
WHILE SLOWLY APPLY-ING VACUUM TO THE EGR VALVE, LISTEN FOR A SPEED CHANGE.
DID THE ENGINE SPEED STAY THE SAME?
YES
CONTINUE TEST DR-41A
NO
IGNITION KEY OFF.
APPLY 10" OF VACUUM AND HOLD FOR 30 SECONDS.
DID THE VACUUM HOLD FOR 30 SECONDS?
NO
REPLACE THE EGR VALVE ASSEMBLY.*
YES
PERFORM TEST DR-42A.
* PERFORM VERIFICATION PROCEDURE VER-3

91I10528

Fig. 143: Driveability Test 41A (3.3L & 3.8L) – Checking EGR Operation, Federal Emissions (5 of 6)

DR-41A: CHECKING EGR OPERATION, FEDERAL EMISSIONS (6 OF 6)

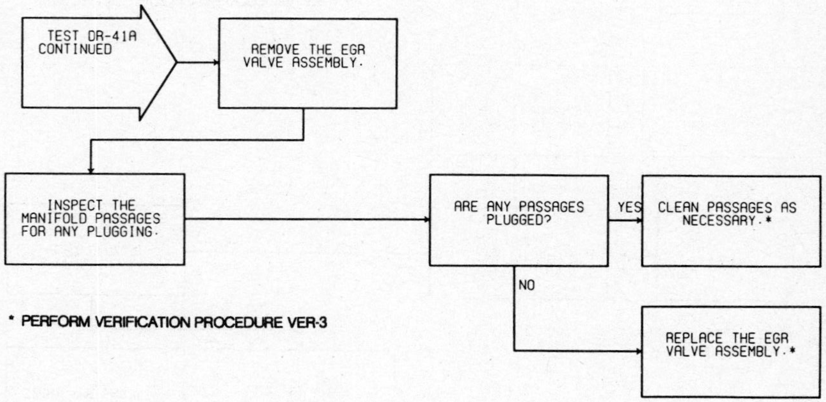
TEST DR-41A CONTINUED
REMOVE THE EGR VALVE ASSEMBLY.
INSPECT THE MANIFOLD PASSAGES FOR ANY PLUGGING.
ARE ANY PASSAGES PLUGGED?
YES
CLEAN PASSAGES AS NECESSARY.*
NO
REPLACE THE EGR VALVE ASSEMBLY.*
* PERFORM VERIFICATION PROCEDURE VER-3

91J10529

Fig. 144: Driveability Test 41A (3.3L & 3.8L) – Checking EGR Operation, Federal Emissions (6 of 6)

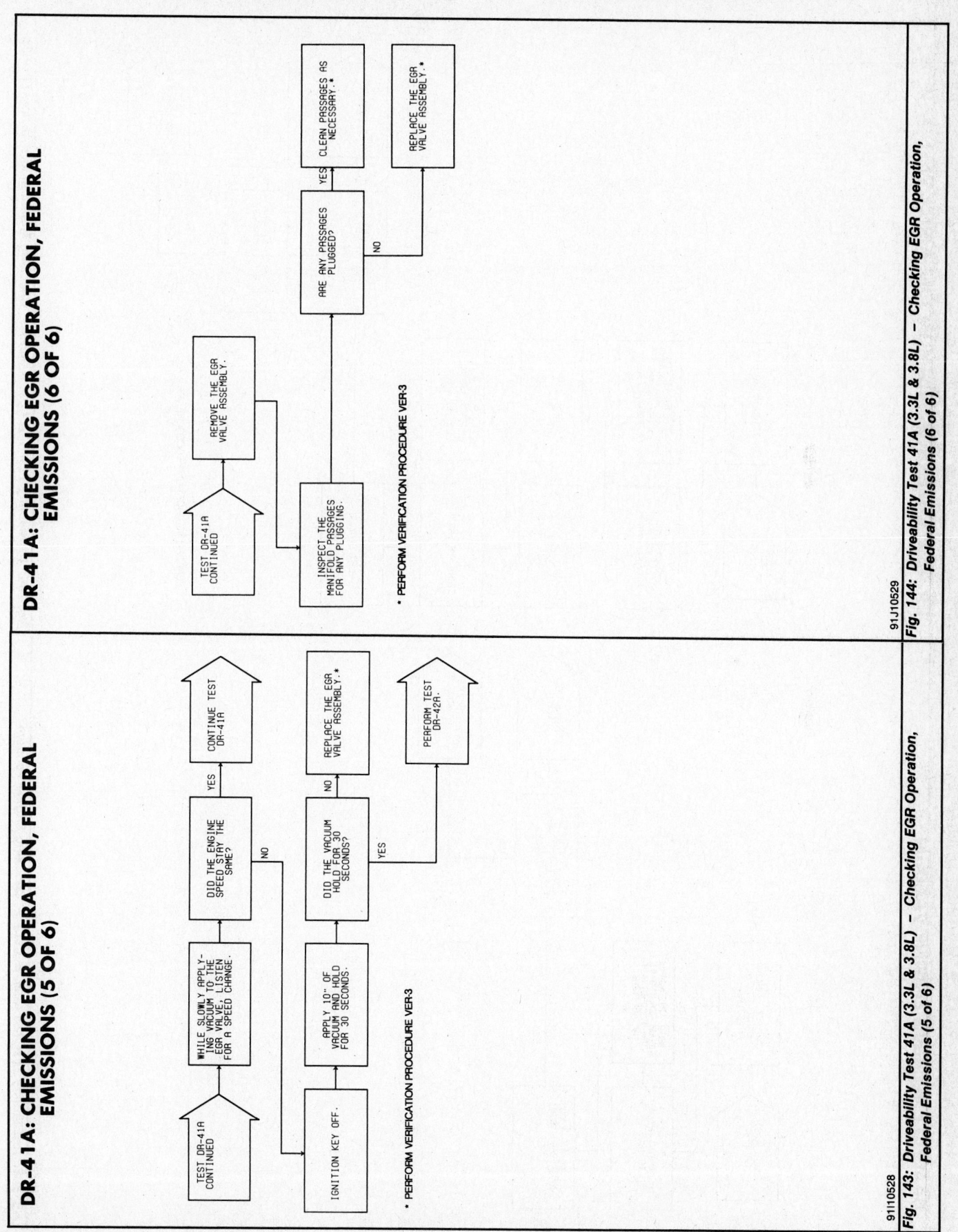

1991 ENGINE PERFORMANCE
Self-Diagnostics – 3.3L PFI (Cont.)

DR-42A: CHECKING ENGINE VACUUM

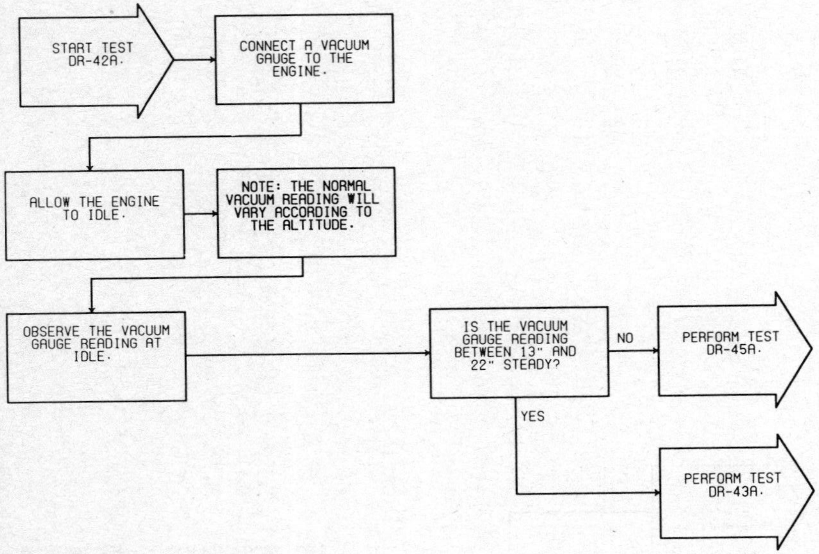
START TEST DR-42A.
CONNECT A VACUUM GAUGE TO THE ENGINE.
ALLOW THE ENGINE TO IDLE.
NOTE: THE NORMAL VACUUM READING WILL VARY ACCORDING TO THE ALTITUDE.
OBSERVE THE VACUUM GAUGE READING AT IDLE.
IS THE VACUUM GAUGE READING BETWEEN 13" AND 22" STEADY?
NO
PERFORM TEST DR-45A.
YES
PERFORM TEST DR-43A.

91C10530

Fig. 145: Driveability Test 42A (3.3L & 3.8L) – Checking Engine Vacuum

DR-43A: CHECKING MINIMUM IDLE AIRFLOW (1 OF 2)

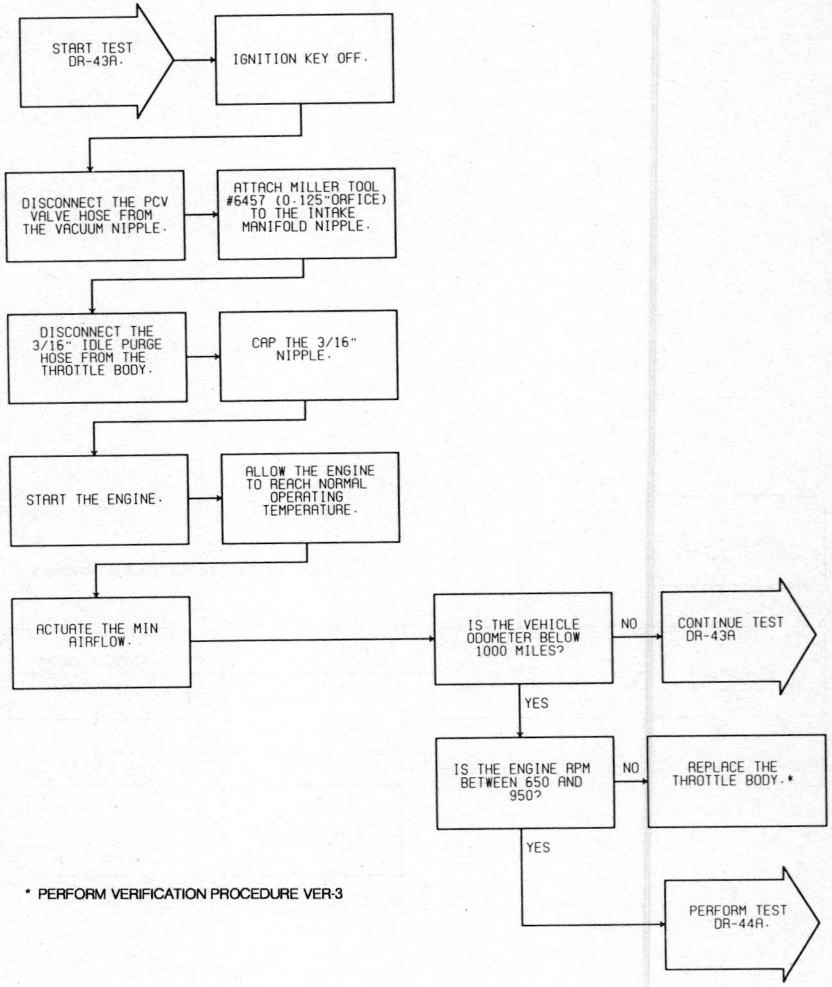
START TEST DR-43A.
IGNITION KEY OFF.
DISCONNECT THE PCV VALVE HOSE FROM THE VACUUM NIPPLE.
ATTACH MILLER TOOL #6457 (0.125" ORFICE) TO THE INTAKE MANIFOLD NIPPLE.
DISCONNECT THE 3/16" IDLE PURGE HOSE FROM THE THROTTLE BODY.
CAP THE 3/16" NIPPLE.
START THE ENGINE.
ALLOW THE ENGINE TO REACH NORMAL OPERATING TEMPERATURE.
ACTUATE THE MIN AIRFLOW.
IS THE VEHICLE ODOMETER BELOW 1000 MILES?
NO
CONTINUE TEST DR-43A
YES
IS THE ENGINE RPM BETWEEN 650 AND 950?
NO
REPLACE THE THROTTLE BODY.*
YES
PERFORM TEST DR-44A.

* PERFORM VERIFICATION PROCEDURE VER-3

91D10531

Fig. 146: Driveability Test 43A (3.3L & 3.8L) – Checking Minimum Idle Airflow (1 of 2)

DR-43A: CHECKING MINIMUM IDLE AIRFLOW (2 OF 2)

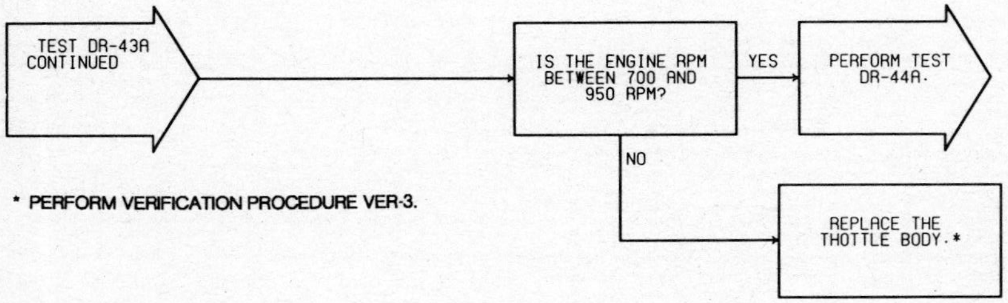
TEST DR-43A CONTINUED
IS THE ENGINE RPM BETWEEN 700 AND 950 RPM?
YES
PERFORM TEST DR-44A.
NO
REPLACE THE THOTTLE BODY.*

* PERFORM VERIFICATION PROCEDURE VER-3.

91E10532

Fig. 147: Driveability Test 43A (3.3L & 3.8L) – Checking Minimum Idle Airflow (2 of 2)

DR-44A: CHECKING KNOCK SENSOR CIRCUIT (1 OF 2)

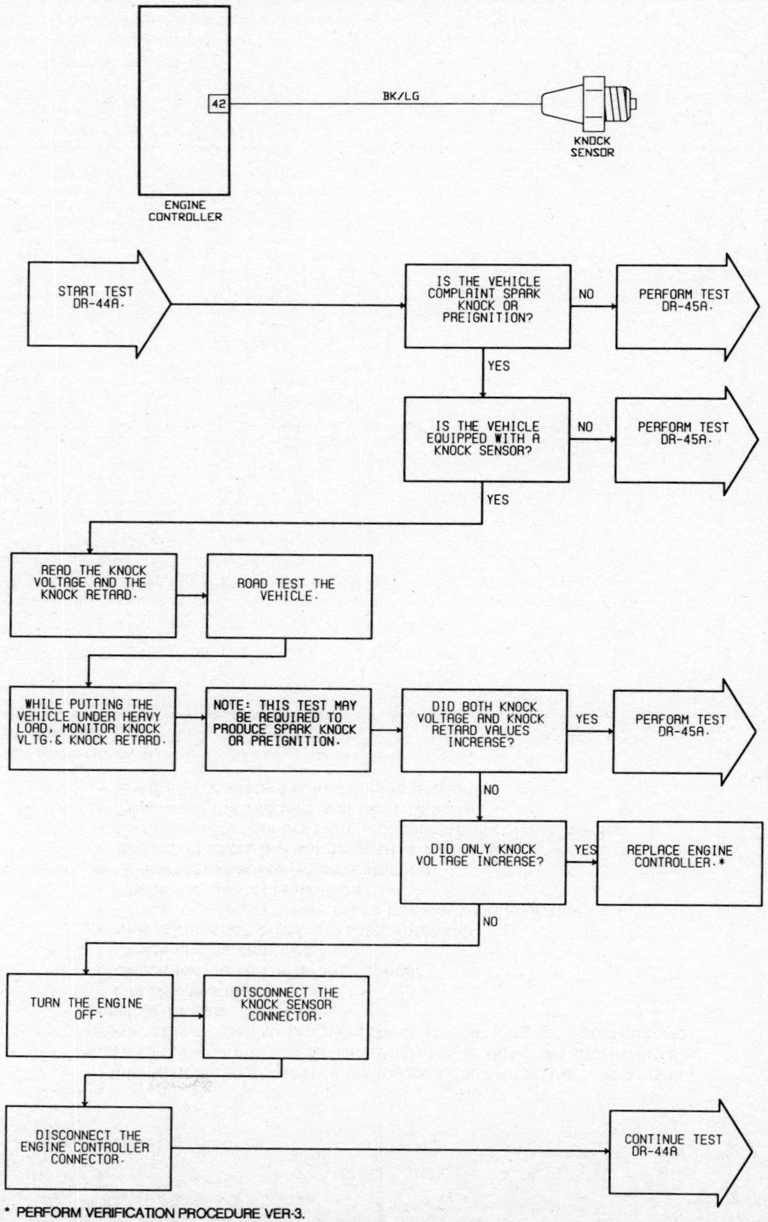
ENGINE CONTROLLER
42
BK/LG
KNOCK SENSOR
START TEST DR-44A.
IS THE VEHICLE COMPLAINT SPARK KNOCK OR PREIGNITION?
NO
PERFORM TEST DR-45A.
YES
IS THE VEHICLE EQUIPPED WITH A KNOCK SENSOR?
NO
PERFORM TEST DR-45A.
YES
READ THE KNOCK VOLTAGE AND THE KNOCK RETARD.
ROAD TEST THE VEHICLE.
WHILE PUTTING THE VEHICLE UNDER HEAVY LOAD, MONITOR KNOCK VLTG.& KNOCK RETARD.
NOTE: THIS TEST MAY BE REQUIRED TO PRODUCE SPARK KNOCK OR PREIGNITION.
DID BOTH KNOCK VOLTAGE AND KNOCK RETARD VALUES INCREASE?
YES
PERFORM TEST DR-45A.
NO
DID ONLY KNOCK VOLTAGE INCREASE?
YES
REPLACE ENGINE CONTROLLER.*
NO
TURN THE ENGINE OFF.
DISCONNECT THE KNOCK SENSOR CONNECTOR.
DISCONNECT THE ENGINE CONTROLLER CONNECTOR.
CONTINUE TEST DR-44A

* PERFORM VERIFICATION PROCEDURE VER-3.

91D09139 91F10533

Fig. 148: Driveability Test 44A (3.3L & 3.8L) – Checking Knock Sensor Circuit (1 of 2)

1991 ENGINE PERFORMANCE
Self-Diagnostics – 3.3L PFI (Cont.)

DR-44A: CHECKING KNOCK SENSOR CIRCUIT (2 OF 2)

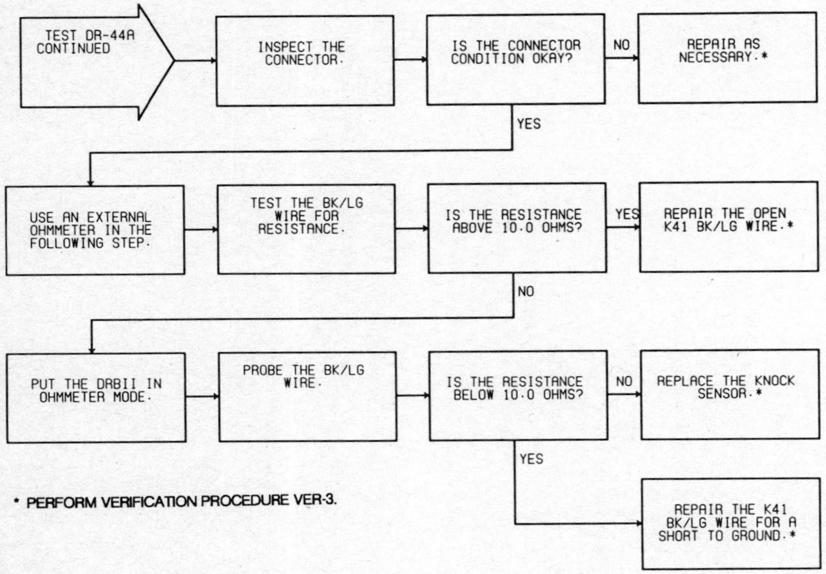
TEST DR-44A CONTINUED
INSPECT THE CONNECTOR.
IS THE CONNECTOR CONDITION OKAY?
NO
REPAIR AS NECESSARY.*
YES
USE AN EXTERNAL OHMMETER IN THE FOLLOWING STEP.
TEST THE BK/LG WIRE FOR RESISTANCE.
IS THE RESISTANCE ABOVE 10.0 OHMS?
YES
REPAIR THE OPEN K41 BK/LG WIRE.*
NO
PUT THE DRBII IN OHMMETER MODE.
PROBE THE BK/LG WIRE.
IS THE RESISTANCE BELOW 10.0 OHMS?
NO
REPLACE THE KNOCK SENSOR.*
YES
REPAIR THE K41 BK/LG WIRE FOR A SHORT TO GROUND.*

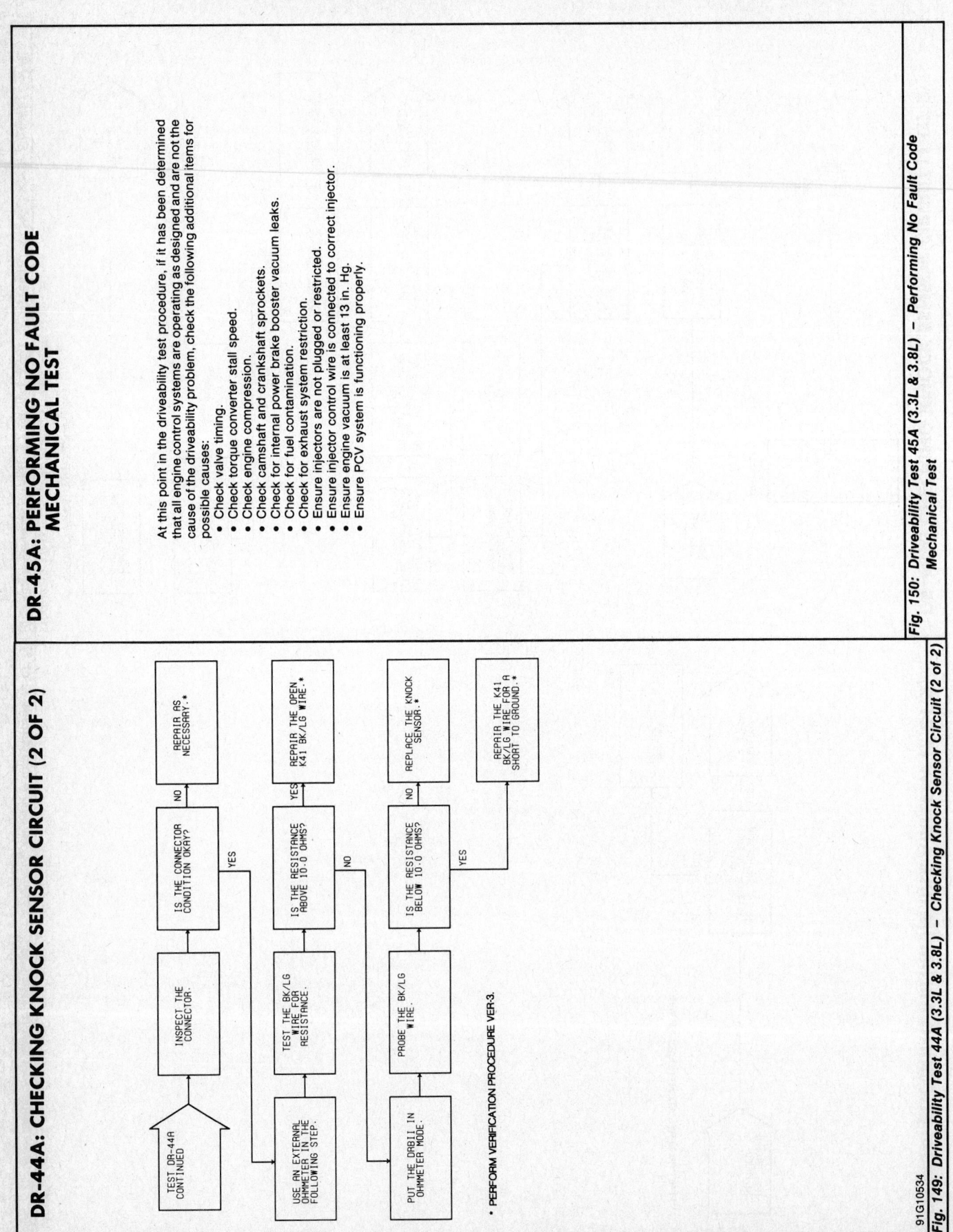

* PERFORM VERIFICATION PROCEDURE VER-3.

91G10534

Fig. 149: Driveability Test 44A (3.3L & 3.8L) – Checking Knock Sensor Circuit (2 of 2)

DR-45A: PERFORMING NO FAULT CODE MECHANICAL TEST

At this point in the driveability test procedure, if it has been determined that all engine control systems are operating as designed and are not the cause of the driveability problem, check the following additional items for possible causes:

- Check valve timing.
- Check torque converter stall speed.
- Check engine compression.
- Check camshaft and crankshaft sprockets.
- Check for internal power brake booster vacuum leaks.
- Check for fuel contamination.
- Check for exhaust system restriction.
- Ensure injectors are not plugged or restricted.
- Ensure injector control wire is connected to correct injector.
- Ensure engine vacuum is at least 13 in. Hg.
- Ensure PCV system is functioning properly.

Fig. 150: Driveability Test 45A (3.3L & 3.8L) – Performing No Fault Code Mechanical Test

DR-46A: INTERMITTENT TEST FOR SOLENOIDS & RELAYS

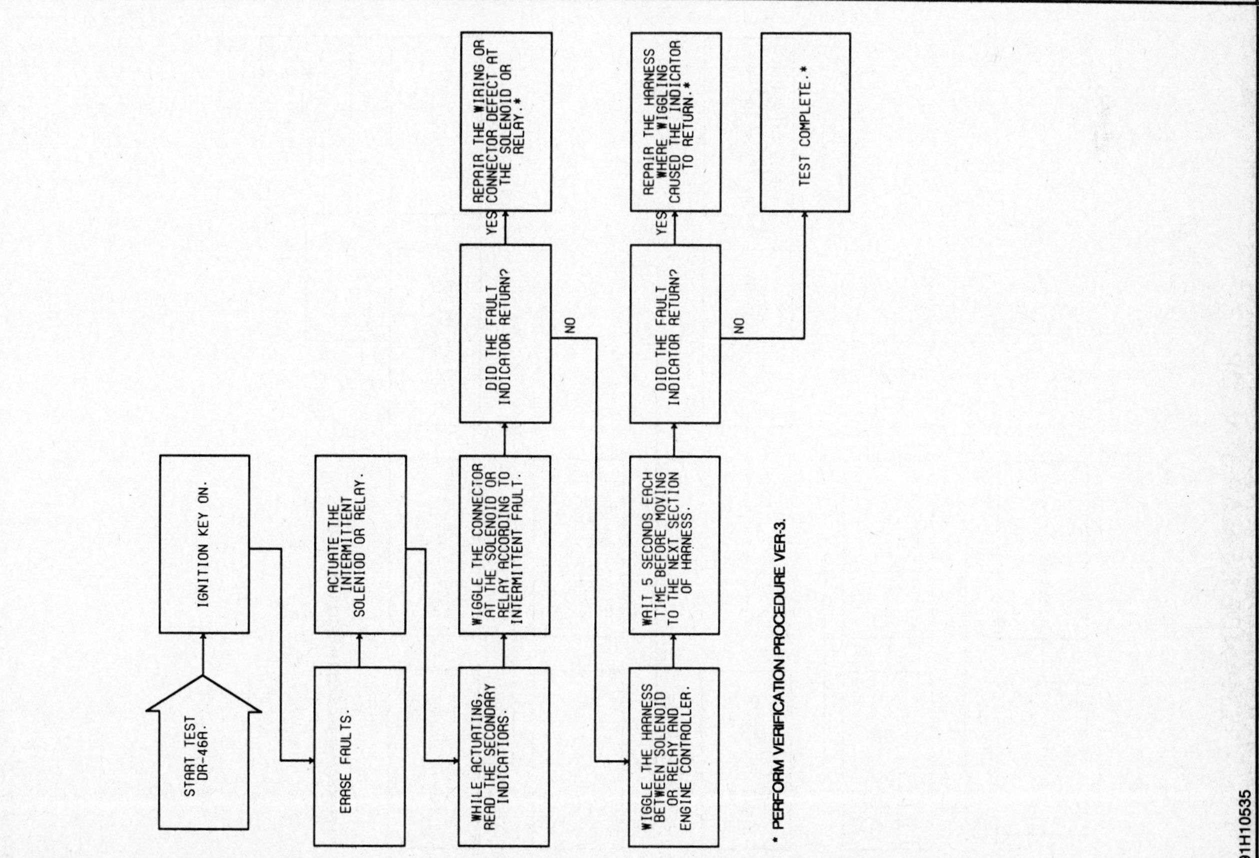

START TEST DR-46A.
IGNITION KEY ON.
ERASE FAULTS.
ACTUATE THE INTERMITTENT SOLENIOD OR RELAY.
WHILE ACTUATING, READ THE SECONDARY INDICATORS.
WIGGLE THE CONNECTOR AT THE SOLENOID OR RELAY ACCORDING TO INTERMITTENT FAULT.
DID THE FAULT INDICATOR RETURN?
YES
REPAIR THE WIRING OR CONNECTOR DEFECT AT THE SOLENOID OR RELAY.*
NO
WIGGLE THE HARNESS BETWEEN SOLENOID OR RELAY AND ENGINE CONTROLLER.
WAIT 5 SECONDS EACH TIME BEFORE MOVING TO THE NEXT SECTION OF HARNESS.
DID THE FAULT INDICATOR RETURN?
YES
REPAIR THE HARNESS WHERE WIGGLING CAUSED THE INDICATOR TO RETURN.*
NO
TEST COMPLETE.*
* PERFORM VERIFICATION PROCEDURE VER-3.
91H10535

Fig. 151: Driveability Test 46A (3.3L & 3.8L) – Intermittent Test for Solenoids & Relays

DR-47A: INTERMITTENT TEST FOR VOLTAGE SENSORS

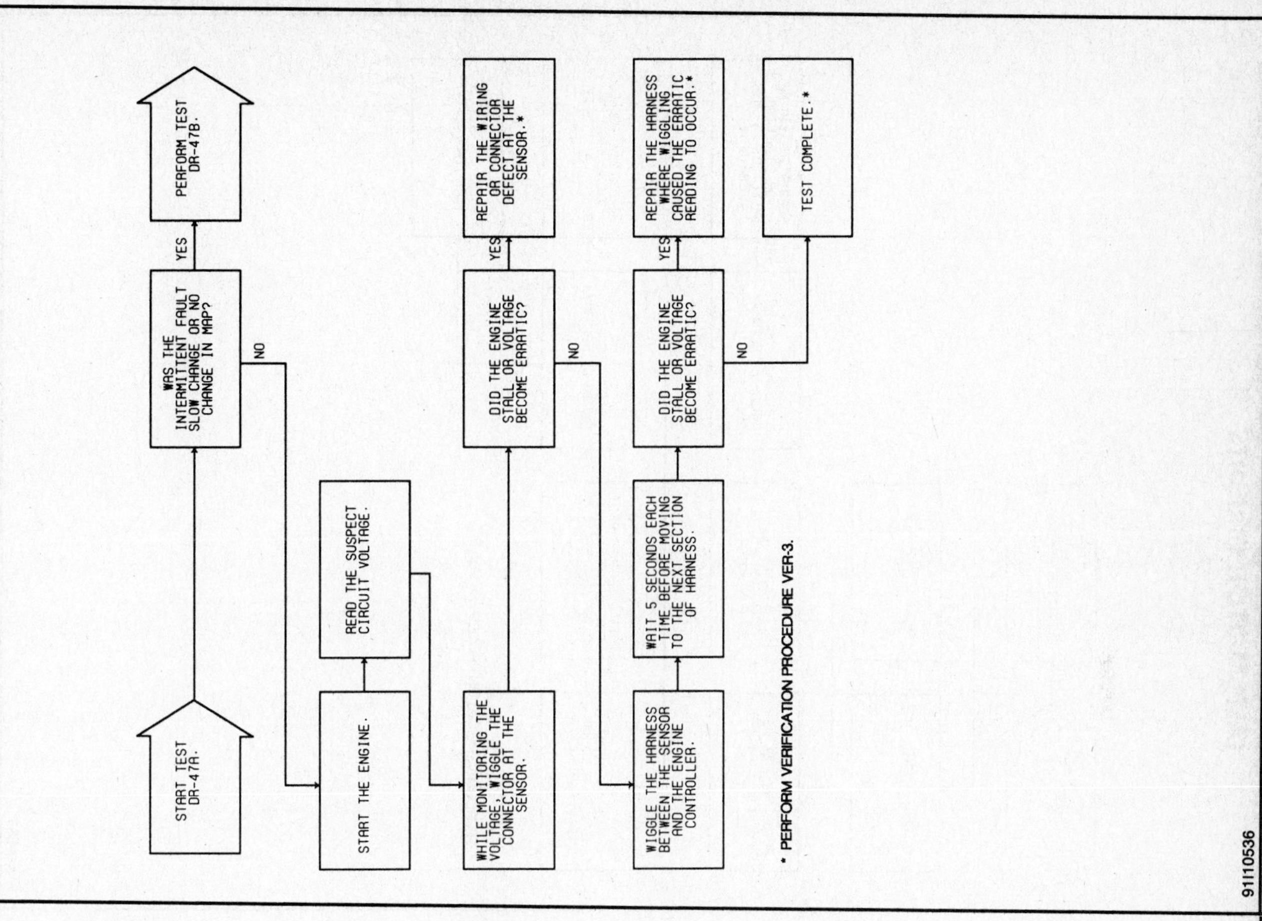

START TEST DR-47A.
WAS THE INTERMITTENT FAULT SLOW CHANGE OR NO CHANGE IN MAP?
YES
PERFORM TEST DR-47B.
NO
START THE ENGINE.
READ THE SUSPECT CIRCUIT VOLTAGE.
WHILE MONITORING THE VOLTAGE, WIGGLE THE CONNECTOR AT THE SENSOR.
DID THE ENGINE STALL OR VOLTAGE BECOME ERRATIC?
YES
REPAIR THE WIRING OR CONNECTOR DEFECT AT THE SENSOR.*
NO
WIGGLE THE HARNESS BETWEEN THE SENSOR AND THE ENGINE CONTROLLER.
WAIT 5 SECONDS EACH TIME BEFORE MOVING TO THE NEXT SECTION OF HARNESS.
DID THE ENGINE STALL OR VOLTAGE BECOME ERRATIC?
YES
REPAIR THE HARNESS WHERE WIGGLING CAUSED THE ERRATIC READING TO OCCUR.*
NO
TEST COMPLETE.*
* PERFORM VERIFICATION PROCEDURE VER-3.
91I10536

Fig. 152: Driveability Test 47A (3.3L & 3.8L) – Intermittent Test for Voltage Sensors

1991 ENGINE PERFORMANCE
Self-Diagnostics – 3.3L PFI (Cont.)

DR-47B: INTERMITTENT TEST FOR SLOW CHANGE OR NO CHANGE IN MAP SENSOR

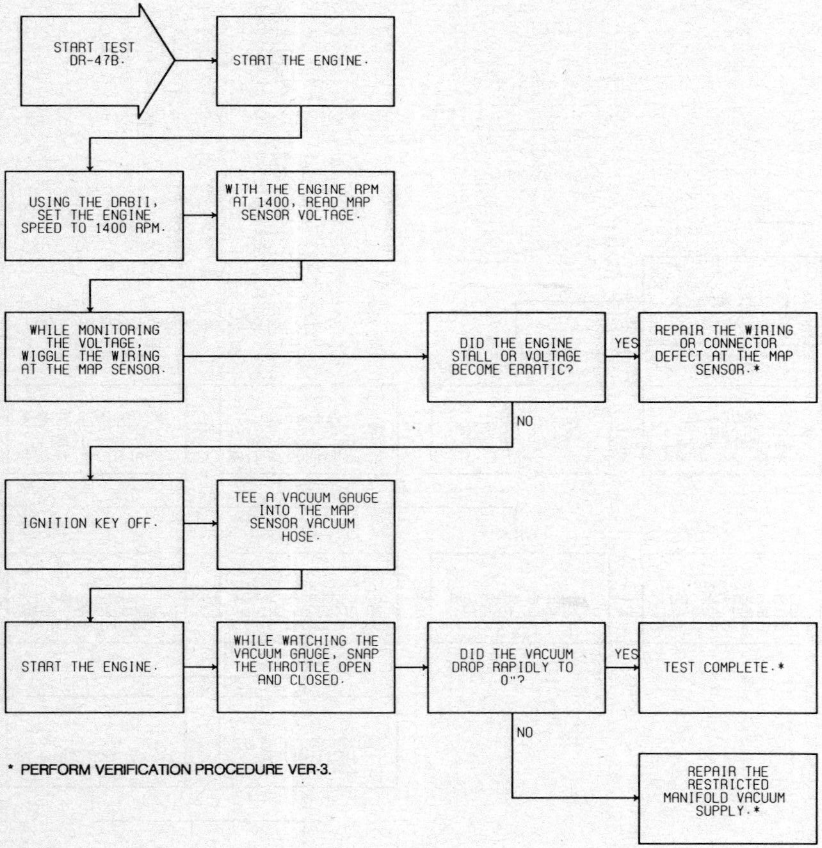
START TEST DR-47B.
START THE ENGINE.
USING THE DRBII, SET THE ENGINE SPEED TO 1400 RPM.
WITH THE ENGINE RPM AT 1400, READ MAP SENSOR VOLTAGE.
WHILE MONITORING THE VOLTAGE, WIGGLE THE WIRING AT THE MAP SENSOR.
DID THE ENGINE STALL OR VOLTAGE BECOME ERRATIC?
YES
REPAIR THE WIRING OR CONNECTOR DEFECT AT THE MAP SENSOR.*
NO
IGNITION KEY OFF.
TEE A VACUUM GAUGE INTO THE MAP SENSOR VACUUM HOSE.
START THE ENGINE.
WHILE WATCHING THE VACUUM GAUGE, SNAP THE THROTTLE OPEN AND CLOSED.
DID THE VACUUM DROP RAPIDLY TO 0"?
YES
TEST COMPLETE.*
NO
REPAIR THE RESTRICTED MANIFOLD VACUUM SUPPLY.*

* PERFORM VERIFICATION PROCEDURE VER-3.

91J10537

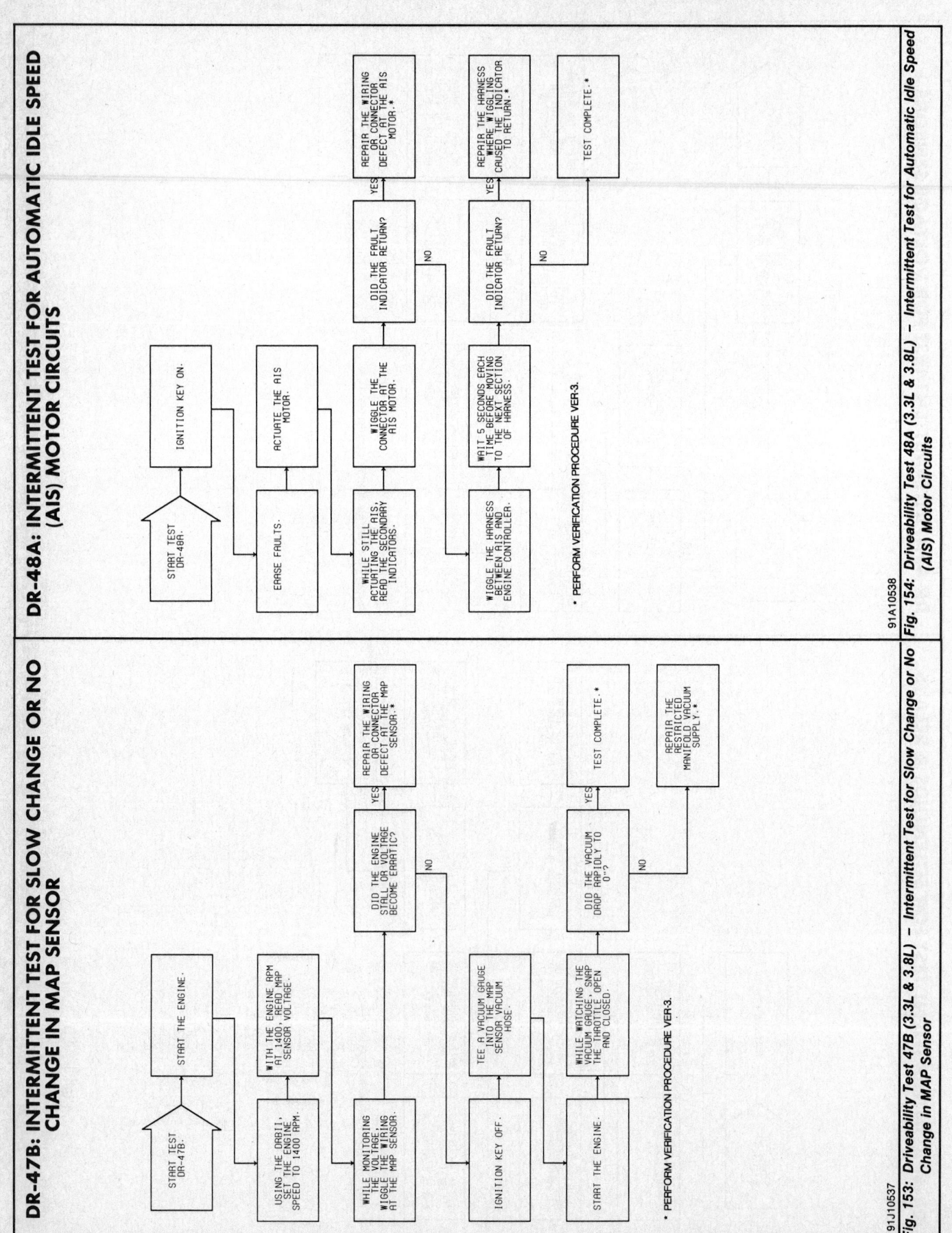

Fig. 153: Driveability Test 47B (3.3L & 3.8L) – Intermittent Test for Slow Change or No Change in MAP Sensor

DR-48A: INTERMITTENT TEST FOR AUTOMATIC IDLE SPEED (AIS) MOTOR CIRCUITS

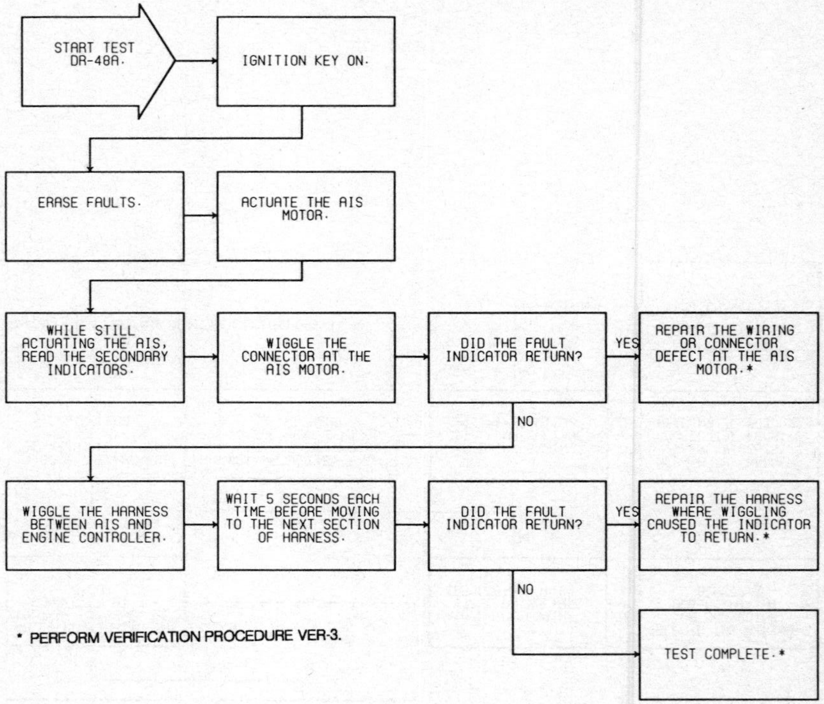
START TEST DR-48A.
IGNITION KEY ON.
ERASE FAULTS.
ACTUATE THE AIS MOTOR.
WHILE STILL ACTUATING THE AIS, READ THE SECONDARY INDICATORS.
WIGGLE THE CONNECTOR AT THE AIS MOTOR.
DID THE FAULT INDICATOR RETURN?
YES
REPAIR THE WIRING OR CONNECTOR DEFECT AT THE AIS MOTOR.*
NO
WIGGLE THE HARNESS BETWEEN AIS AND ENGINE CONTROLLER.
WAIT 5 SECONDS EACH TIME BEFORE MOVING TO THE NEXT SECTION OF HARNESS.
DID THE FAULT INDICATOR RETURN?
YES
REPAIR THE HARNESS WHERE WIGGLING CAUSED THE INDICATOR TO RETURN.*
NO
TEST COMPLETE.*

* PERFORM VERIFICATION PROCEDURE VER-3.

91A10538

Fig. 154: Driveability Test 48A (3.3L & 3.8L) – Intermittent Test for Automatic Idle Speed (AIS) Motor Circuits

DR-49A: INTERMITTENT TEST FOR FUEL INJECTORS

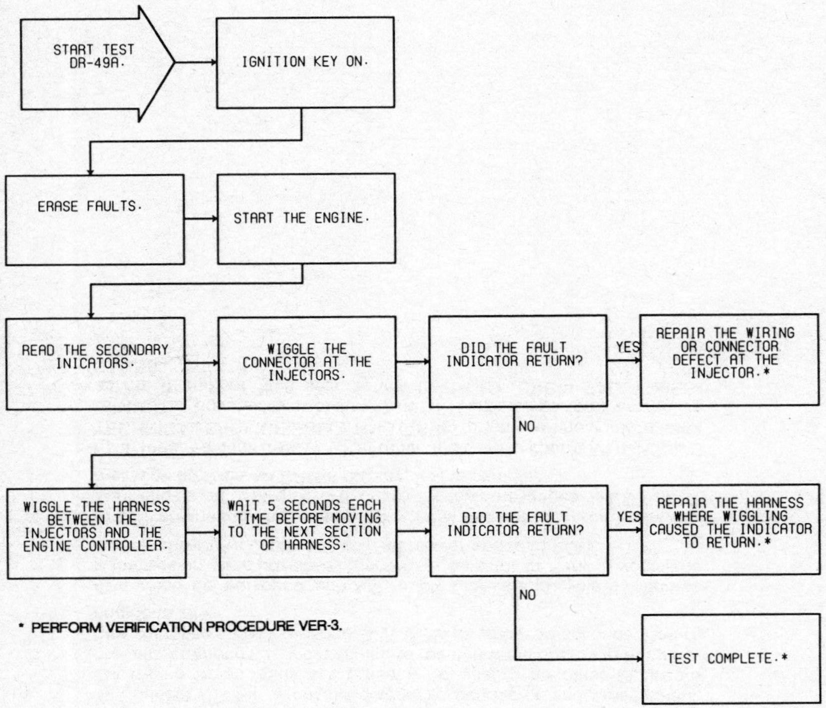
START TEST DR-49A.
IGNITION KEY ON.
ERASE FAULTS.
START THE ENGINE.
READ THE SECONDARY INICATORS.
WIGGLE THE CONNECTOR AT THE INJECTORS.
DID THE FAULT INDICATOR RETURN?
YES
REPAIR THE WIRING OR CONNECTOR DEFECT AT THE INJECTOR.*
NO
WIGGLE THE HARNESS BETWEEN THE INJECTORS AND THE ENGINE CONTROLLER.
WAIT 5 SECONDS EACH TIME BEFORE MOVING TO THE NEXT SECTION OF HARNESS.
DID THE FAULT INDICATOR RETURN?
YES
REPAIR THE HARNESS WHERE WIGGLING CAUSED THE INDICATOR TO RETURN.*
NO
TEST COMPLETE.*

* PERFORM VERIFICATION PROCEDURE VER-3.

91B10539

Fig. 155: Driveability Test 49A (3.3L & 3.8L) – Intermittent Test for Fuel Injectors

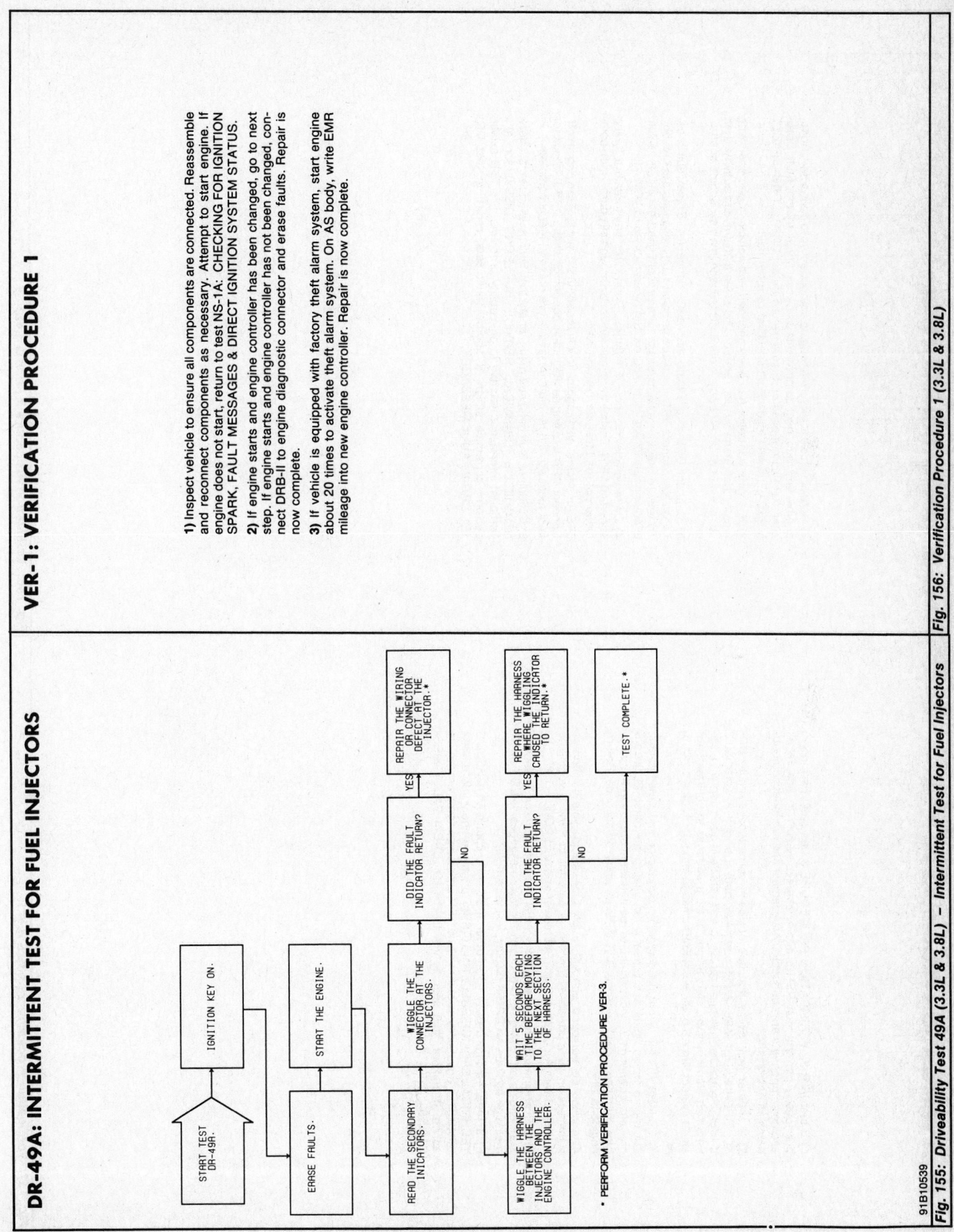

VER-1: VERIFICATION PROCEDURE 1

1) Inspect vehicle to ensure all components are connected. Reassemble and reconnect components as necessary. Attempt to start engine. If engine does not start, return to test NS-1A: CHECKING FOR IGNITION SPARK, FAULT MESSAGES & DIRECT IGNITION SYSTEM STATUS.

2) If engine starts and engine controller has been changed, go to next step. If engine starts and engine controller has not been changed, connect DRB-II to engine diagnostic connector and erase faults. Repair is now complete.

3) If vehicle is equipped with factory theft alarm system, start engine about 20 times to activate theft alarm system. On AS body, write EMR mileage into new engine controller. Repair is now complete.

Fig. 156: Verification Procedure 1 (3.3L & 3.8L)

VER-2: VERIFICATION PROCEDURE 2

1) If test VER-3: VERIFICATION PROCEDURE 3 has been performed previously, perform test VER-3 again. Inspect vehicle to ensure all engine components are connected. Reassemble and reconnect components as necessary.

2) If another fault exists that has not been corrected, return to DR-1B: DRB-II FAULT MESSAGES and follow path specified by other fault. If engine controller has been replaced and vehicle is equipped with factory theft alarm system, start engine at least 20 times to activate theft alarm system. On AS body, write EMR mileage into new engine controller.

3) Connect DRB-II to engine diagnostic connector and erase faults. Ensure no other faults are present. To ensure no other faults are present, start engine. Allow engine to reach normal operating temperature. Increase engine speed to 2000 RPM for about 10 seconds. Return engine to idle.

4) If vehicle is equipped with A/T, apply brakes and cycle through all transmission gear positions. Place gear selector in Park. If vehicle is equipped with A/C, turn A/C on. Set blower speed to LOW.

5) Turn engine off. Start engine. Allow engine to idle for about 2 minutes. Turn engine off. Using DRB-II, check for fault messages. If NO FAULT message appears on DRB-II display, test is complete.

6) If repaired fault resets or another fault sets, check MITCHELL'S TECHNICAL SERVICE BULLETINS (TSBs) for any pertinent information relating to driveability problem. If a TSB exists, perform corrective action. If another fault sets, return to DR-1B: DRB-II FAULT MESSAGES.

Fig. 157: Verification Procedure 2 (3.3L & 3.8L)

VER-3: VERIFICATION PROCEDURE 3

1) Inspect vehicle to ensure all engine components are connected. Reassemble and reconnect components as necessary. If another fault is present that has not been corrected, return to test DR-1B: DRB-II FAULT MESSAGES and follow path specified by other fault.

2) If engine controller has been changed and vehicle is equipped with factory theft alarm system, start engine at least 20 times to activate theft alarm system. On AS body, write EMR mileage into new engine controller.

3) Connect DRB-II to engine diagnostic connector. Erase fault messages. Disconnect DRB-II. Ensure no other fault messages are present. To ensure no other fault messages are present, start engine. If vehicle is equipped with A/C, turn A/C on. Set blower speed to LOW.

4) Drive vehicle for about 5 minutes. During this time, attain a speed above 40 MPH. Ensure transmission shifts through all gears. Upon completion of road test, turn engine off.

5) Start engine. Allow engine to idle for about 2 minutes. Turn engine off. Connect DRB-II to engine diagnostic connector. Using DRB-II, check for fault messages. If no fault messages are present, test is complete.

6) If repaired fault message resets or another fault message sets, check MITCHELL'S TECHNICAL SERVICE BULLETINS (TSBs) for any pertinent information relating to driveability problems. If a TSB exists, perform corrective action. If another fault sets, return to test DR-1B: DRB-II FAULT MESSAGES.

Fig. 158: Verification Procedure 3 (3.3L & 3.8L)

NS-1A – CHECKING FOR FAULTS & SPARK (1 OF 4)

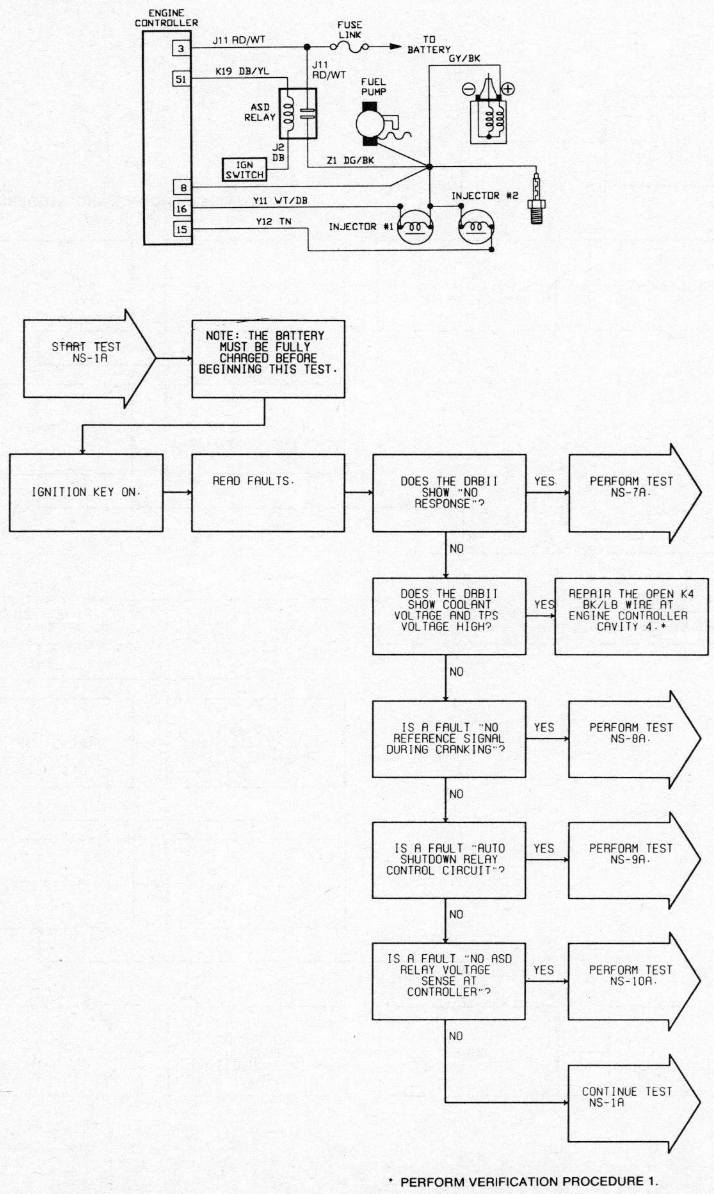
ENGINE CONTROLLER
3
51
8
16
15
J11 RD/WT
K19 DB/YL
FUSE LINK
TO BATTERY
GY/BK
J11 RD/WT
FUEL PUMP
ASD RELAY
J2 DB
IGN SWITCH
Z1 DG/BK
Y11 WT/DB
Y12 TN
INJECTOR #1
INJECTOR #2
START TEST NS-1A
NOTE: THE BATTERY MUST BE FULLY CHARGED BEFORE BEGINNING THIS TEST.
IGNITION KEY ON.
READ FAULTS.
DOES THE DRBII SHOW "NO RESPONSE"?
YES
PERFORM TEST NS-7A.
NO
DOES THE DRBII SHOW COOLANT VOLTAGE AND TPS VOLTAGE HIGH?
YES
REPAIR THE OPEN K4 BK/LB WIRE AT ENGINE CONTROLLER CAVITY 4.*
NO
IS A FAULT "NO REFERENCE SIGNAL DURING CRANKING"?
YES
PERFORM TEST NS-8A.
NO
IS A FAULT "AUTO SHUTDOWN RELAY CONTROL CIRCUIT"?
YES
PERFORM TEST NS-9A.
NO
IS A FAULT "NO ASD RELAY VOLTAGE SENSE AT CONTROLLER"?
YES
PERFORM TEST NS-10A.
NO
CONTINUE TEST NS-1A
* PERFORM VERIFICATION PROCEDURE 1.

91G14064 91H14065

Fig. 1: No Start Test 1A – Checking For Faults & Spark (1 of 4)

NS-1A – CHECKING FOR FAULTS & SPARK (2 OF 4)

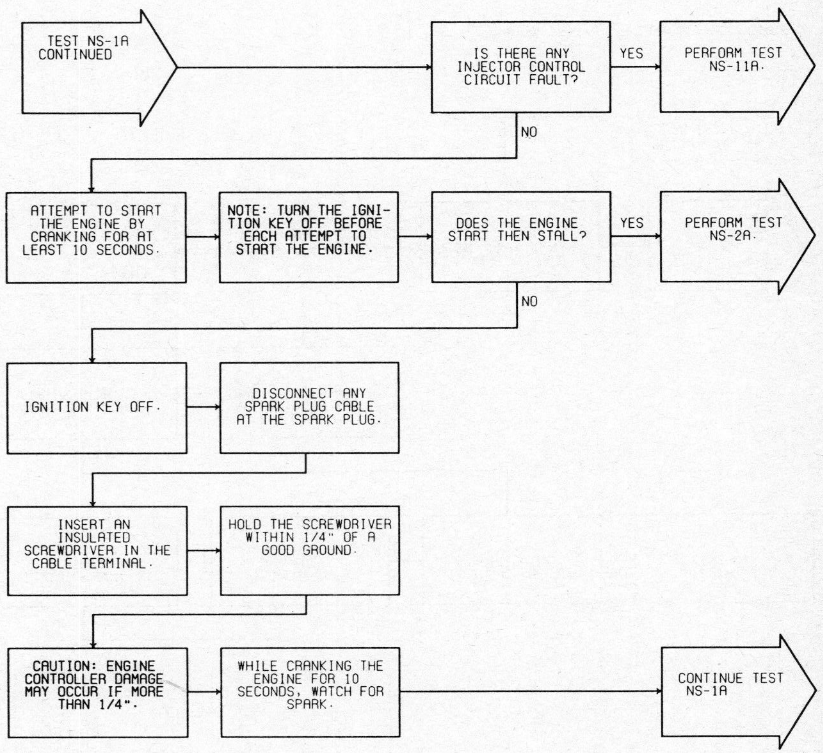
TEST NS-1A CONTINUED
IS THERE ANY INJECTOR CONTROL CIRCUIT FAULT?
YES
PERFORM TEST NS-11A.
NO
ATTEMPT TO START THE ENGINE BY CRANKING FOR AT LEAST 10 SECONDS.
NOTE: TURN THE IGNITION KEY OFF BEFORE EACH ATTEMPT TO START THE ENGINE.
DOES THE ENGINE START THEN STALL?
YES
PERFORM TEST NS-2A.
NO
IGNITION KEY OFF.
DISCONNECT ANY SPARK PLUG CABLE AT THE SPARK PLUG.
INSERT AN INSULATED SCREWDRIVER IN THE CABLE TERMINAL.
HOLD THE SCREWDRIVER WITHIN 1/4" OF A GOOD GROUND.
CAUTION: ENGINE CONTROLLER DAMAGE MAY OCCUR IF MORE THAN 1/4".
WHILE CRANKING THE ENGINE FOR 10 SECONDS, WATCH FOR SPARK.
CONTINUE TEST NS-1A

91I14066

Fig. 2: No Start Test 1A – Checking For Faults & Spark (2 of 4)

NS-1A – CHECKING FOR FAULTS & SPARK (3 OF 4)

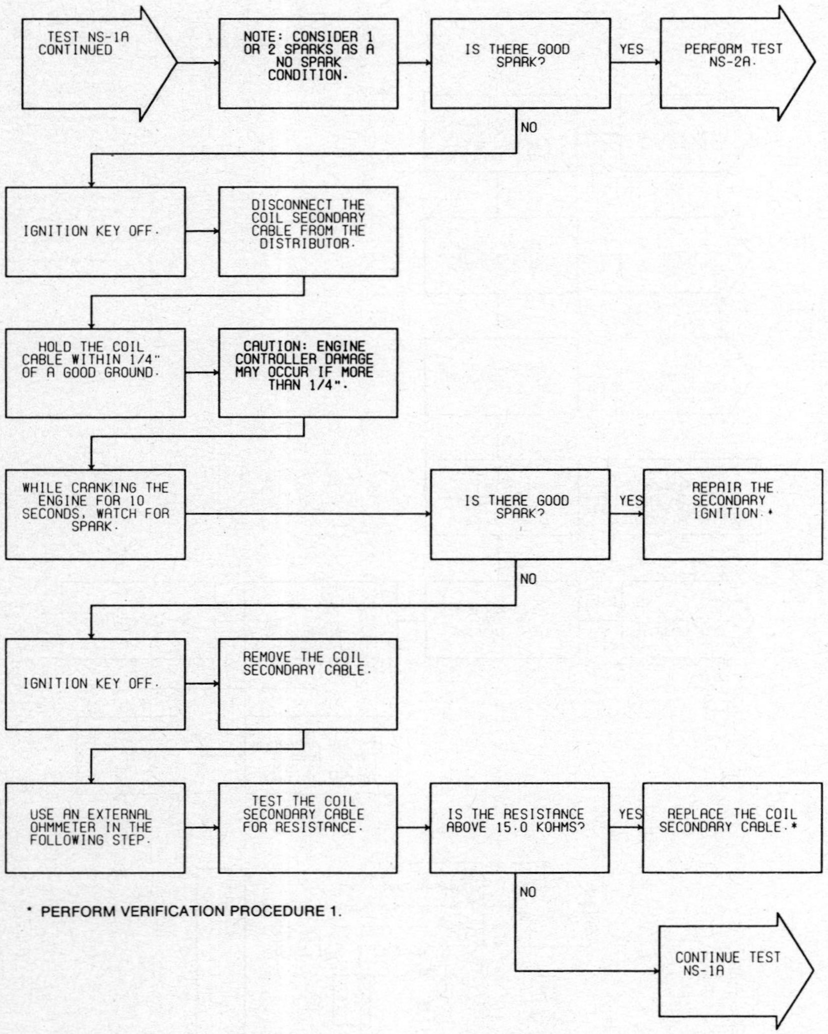
TEST NS-1A CONTINUED
NOTE: CONSIDER 1 OR 2 SPARKS AS A NO SPARK CONDITION.
IS THERE GOOD SPARK?
YES
PERFORM TEST NS-2A.
NO
IGNITION KEY OFF.
DISCONNECT THE COIL SECONDARY CABLE FROM THE DISTRIBUTOR.
HOLD THE COIL CABLE WITHIN 1/4" OF A GOOD GROUND.
CAUTION: ENGINE CONTROLLER DAMAGE MAY OCCUR IF MORE THAN 1/4".
WHILE CRANKING THE ENGINE FOR 10 SECONDS, WATCH FOR SPARK.
IS THERE GOOD SPARK?
YES
REPAIR THE SECONDARY IGNITION.*
NO
IGNITION KEY OFF.
REMOVE THE COIL SECONDARY CABLE.
USE AN EXTERNAL OHMMETER IN THE FOLLOWING STEP.
TEST THE COIL SECONDARY CABLE FOR RESISTANCE.
IS THE RESISTANCE ABOVE 15.0 KOHMS?
YES
REPLACE THE COIL SECONDARY CABLE.*
NO
CONTINUE TEST NS-1A
* PERFORM VERIFICATION PROCEDURE 1.

91J14067

Fig. 3: No Start Test 1A – Checking For Faults & Spark (3 of 4)

NS-1A – CHECKING FOR FAULTS & SPARK (4 OF 4)

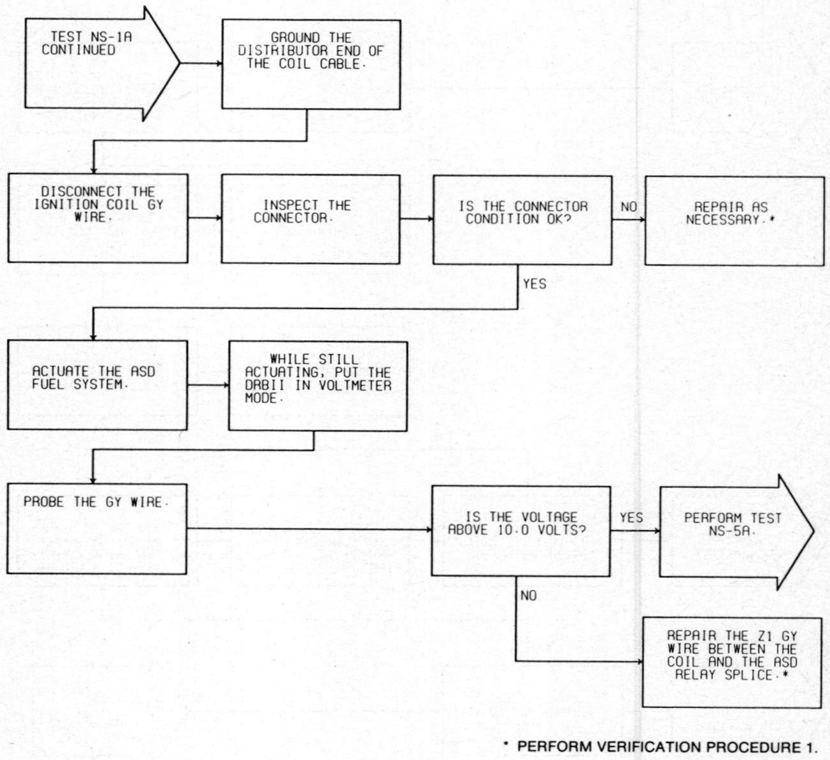
TEST NS-1A CONTINUED
GROUND THE DISTRIBUTOR END OF THE COIL CABLE.
DISCONNECT THE IGNITION COIL GY WIRE.
INSPECT THE CONNECTOR.
IS THE CONNECTOR CONDITION OK?
NO
REPAIR AS NECESSARY.*
YES
ACTUATE THE ASD FUEL SYSTEM.
WHILE STILL ACTUATING, PUT THE DRBII IN VOLTMETER MODE.
PROBE THE GY WIRE.
IS THE VOLTAGE ABOVE 10.0 VOLTS?
YES
PERFORM TEST NS-5A.
NO
REPAIR THE Z1 GY WIRE BETWEEN THE COIL AND THE ASD RELAY SPLICE.*
* PERFORM VERIFICATION PROCEDURE 1.

91A14068

Fig. 4: No Start Test 1A – Checking For Faults & Spark (4 of 4)

NS-2A – CHECKING FUEL SYSTEM (1 OF 2)

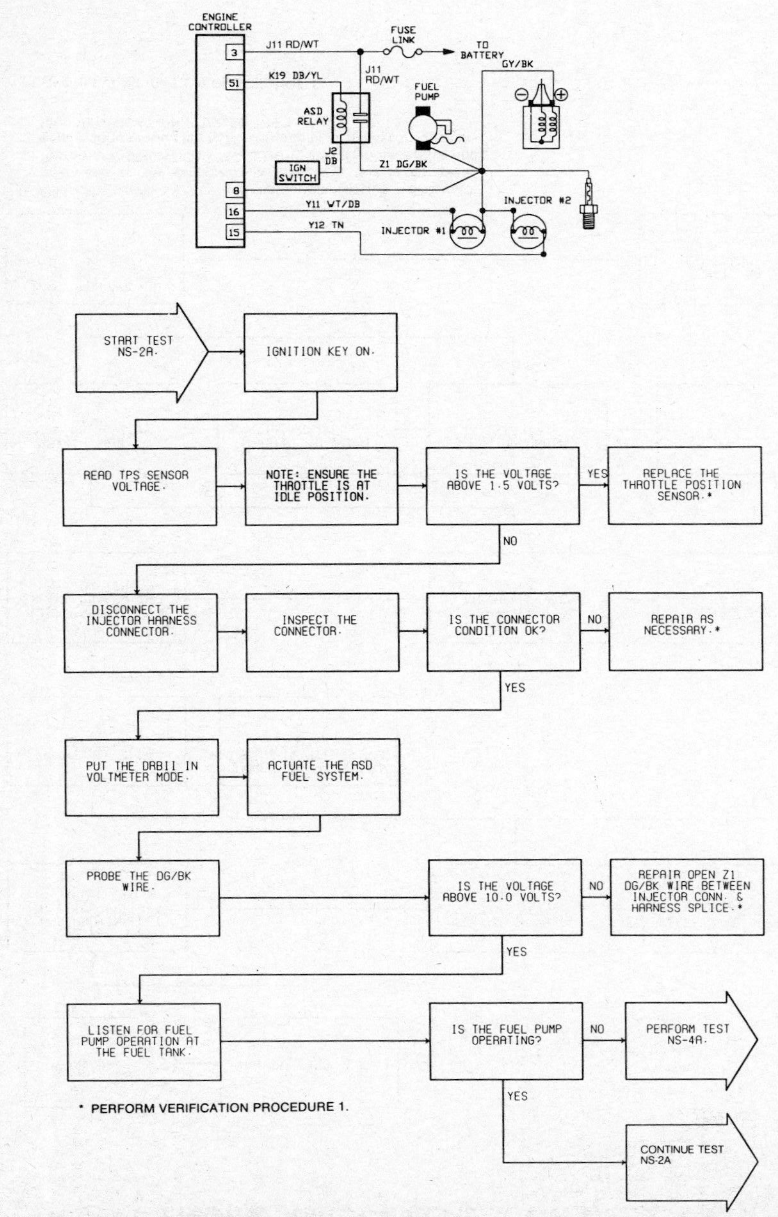
ENGINE CONTROLLER
3
51
8
16
15
J11 RD/WT
K19 DB/YL
FUSE LINK
TO BATTERY
J11 RD/WT
GY/BK
ASD RELAY
FUEL PUMP
J2 DB
IGN SWITCH
Z1 DG/BK
Y11 WT/DB
Y12 TN
INJECTOR #2
INJECTOR #1
START TEST NS-2A.
IGNITION KEY ON.
READ TPS SENSOR VOLTAGE.
NOTE: ENSURE THE THROTTLE IS AT IDLE POSITION.
IS THE VOLTAGE ABOVE 1.5 VOLTS?
YES
REPLACE THE THROTTLE POSITION SENSOR.*
NO
DISCONNECT THE INJECTOR HARNESS CONNECTOR.
INSPECT THE CONNECTOR.
IS THE CONNECTOR CONDITION OK?
NO
REPAIR AS NECESSARY.*
YES
PUT THE DRBII IN VOLTMETER MODE.
ACTUATE THE ASD FUEL SYSTEM.
PROBE THE DG/BK WIRE.
IS THE VOLTAGE ABOVE 10.0 VOLTS?
NO
REPAIR OPEN Z1 DG/BK WIRE BETWEEN INJECTOR CONN. & HARNESS SPLICE.*
YES
LISTEN FOR FUEL PUMP OPERATION AT THE FUEL TANK.
IS THE FUEL PUMP OPERATING?
NO
PERFORM TEST NS-4A.
YES
CONTINUE TEST NS-2A
* PERFORM VERIFICATION PROCEDURE 1.

91G14064 91B14069

Fig. 5: No Start Test 2A – Checking Fuel System (1 of 2)

NS-2A – CHECKING FUEL SYSTEM (2 OF 2)

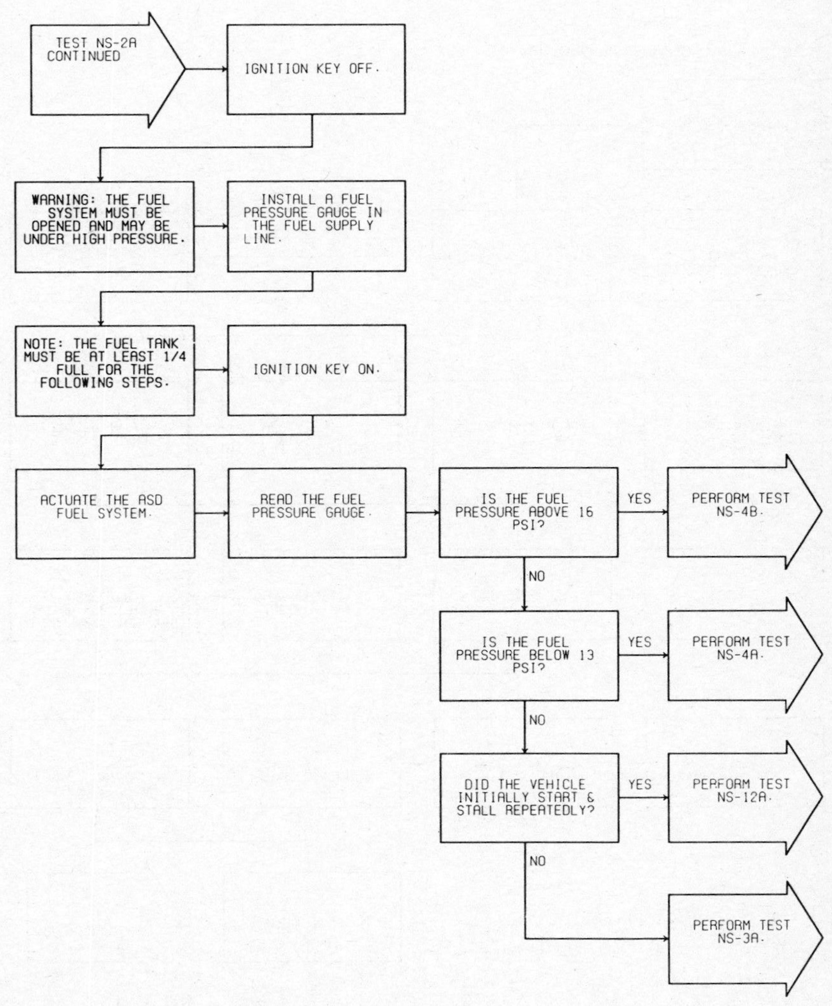
TEST NS-2A CONTINUED
IGNITION KEY OFF.
WARNING: THE FUEL SYSTEM MUST BE OPENED AND MAY BE UNDER HIGH PRESSURE.
INSTALL A FUEL PRESSURE GAUGE IN THE FUEL SUPPLY LINE.
NOTE: THE FUEL TANK MUST BE AT LEAST 1/4 FULL FOR THE FOLLOWING STEPS.
IGNITION KEY ON.
ACTUATE THE ASD FUEL SYSTEM.
READ THE FUEL PRESSURE GAUGE.
IS THE FUEL PRESSURE ABOVE 16 PSI?
YES
PERFORM TEST NS-4B.
NO
IS THE FUEL PRESSURE BELOW 13 PSI?
YES
PERFORM TEST NS-4A.
NO
DID THE VEHICLE INITIALLY START & STALL REPEATEDLY?
YES
PERFORM TEST NS-12A.
NO
PERFORM TEST NS-3A.

91E14070

Fig. 6: No Start Test 2A – Checking Fuel System (2 of 2)

NS-3A – CHECKING SPARK DELIVERY & ENGINE MECHANICAL (1 OF 2)

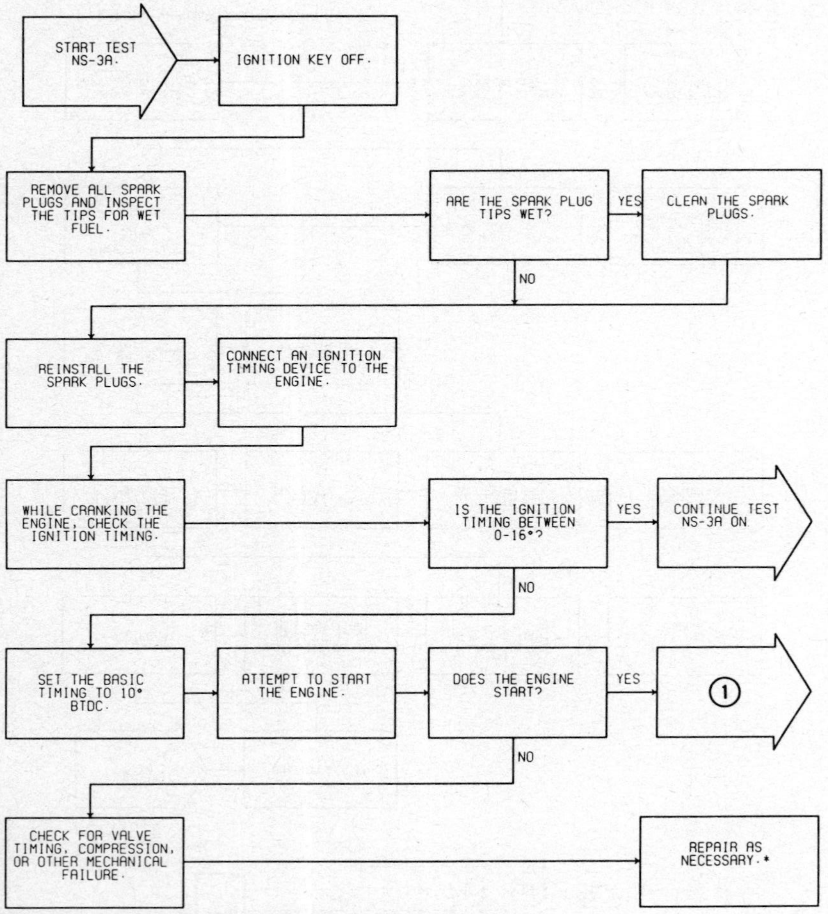
START TEST NS-3A.
IGNITION KEY OFF.
REMOVE ALL SPARK PLUGS AND INSPECT THE TIPS FOR WET FUEL.
ARE THE SPARK PLUG TIPS WET?
YES
CLEAN THE SPARK PLUGS.
NO
REINSTALL THE SPARK PLUGS.
CONNECT AN IGNITION TIMING DEVICE TO THE ENGINE.
WHILE CRANKING THE ENGINE, CHECK THE IGNITION TIMING.
IS THE IGNITION TIMING BETWEEN 0-16°?
YES
CONTINUE TEST NS-3A ON
NO
SET THE BASIC TIMING TO 10° BTDC.
ATTEMPT TO START THE ENGINE.
DOES THE ENGINE START?
YES
1
NO
CHECK FOR VALVE TIMING, COMPRESSION, OR OTHER MECHANICAL FAILURE.
REPAIR AS NECESSARY.*

① – Check the distributor drive and engine compression. If distributor drive and engine compression are okay, test is complete. Perform VERIFICATION PROCEDURE 1. If distributor drive and engine compression are NOT okay, repair as necessary and perform VERIFICATION PROCEDURE 1.

* PERFORM VERIFICATION PROCEDURE 1.

91F14071

Fig. 7: No Start Test 3A – Checking Spark Delivery & Engine Mechanical (1 of 2)

NS-3A – CHECKING SPARK DELIVERY & ENGINE MECHANICAL (2 OF 2)

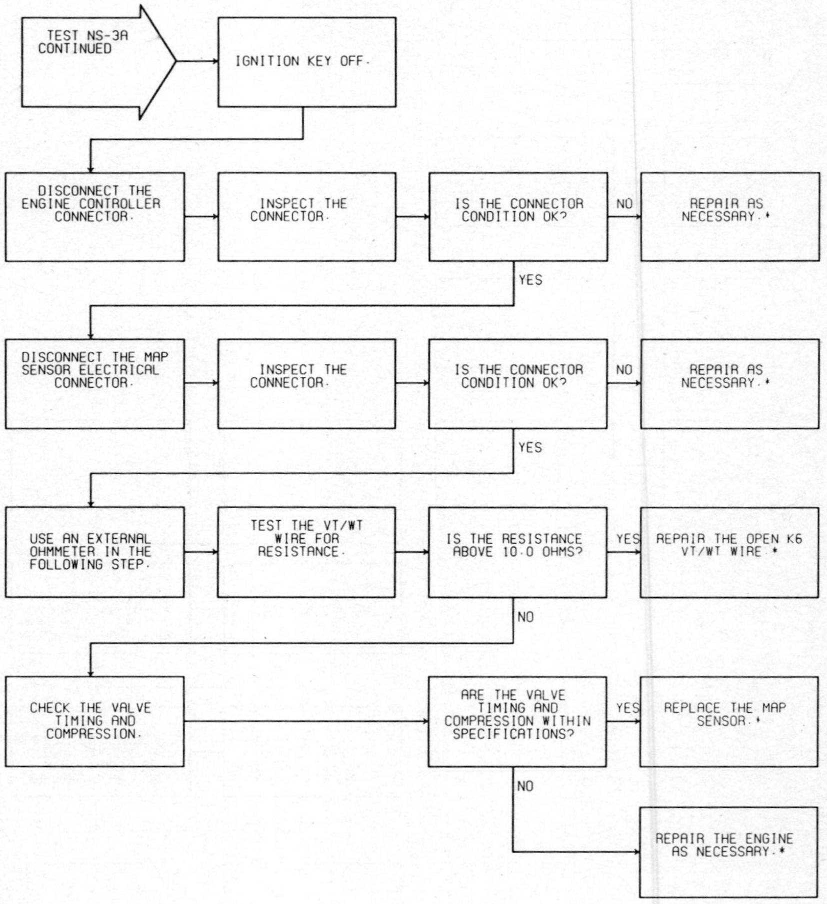
TEST NS-3A CONTINUED
IGNITION KEY OFF.
DISCONNECT THE ENGINE CONTROLLER CONNECTOR.
INSPECT THE CONNECTOR.
IS THE CONNECTOR CONDITION OK?
NO
REPAIR AS NECESSARY.*
YES
DISCONNECT THE MAP SENSOR ELECTRICAL CONNECTOR.
INSPECT THE CONNECTOR.
IS THE CONNECTOR CONDITION OK?
NO
REPAIR AS NECESSARY.*
YES
USE AN EXTERNAL OHMMETER IN THE FOLLOWING STEP.
TEST THE VT/WT WIRE FOR RESISTANCE.
IS THE RESISTANCE ABOVE 10.0 OHMS?
YES
REPAIR THE OPEN K6 VT/WT WIRE.*
NO
CHECK THE VALVE TIMING AND COMPRESSION.
ARE THE VALVE TIMING AND COMPRESSION WITHIN SPECIFICATIONS?
YES
REPLACE THE MAP SENSOR.*
NO
REPAIR THE ENGINE AS NECESSARY.*

* PERFORM VERIFICATION PROCEDURE 1.

91G14072

Fig. 8: No Start Test 3A – Checking Spark Delivery & Engine Mechanical (2 of 2)

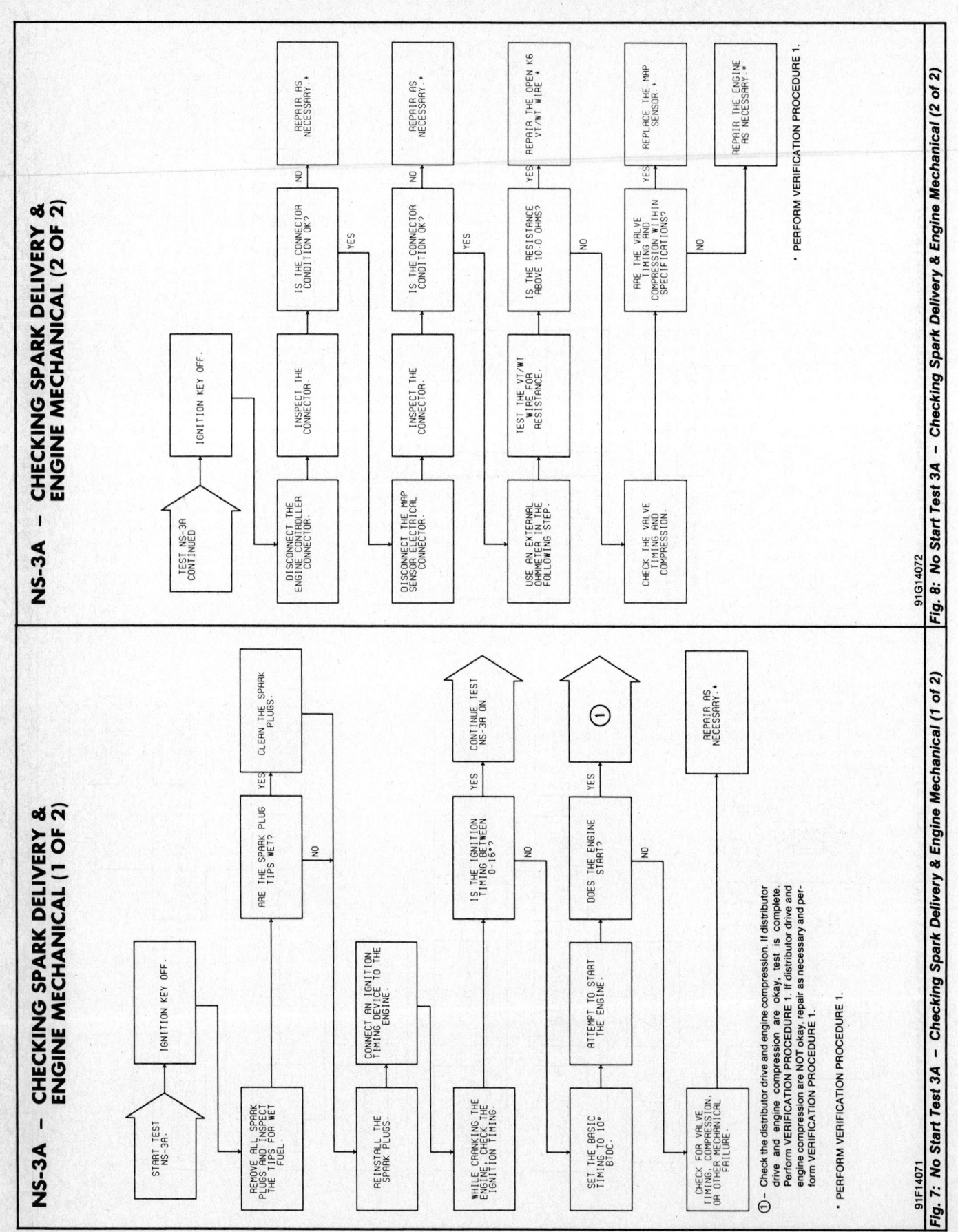

NS-4A – CHECKING LOW FUEL PRESSURE

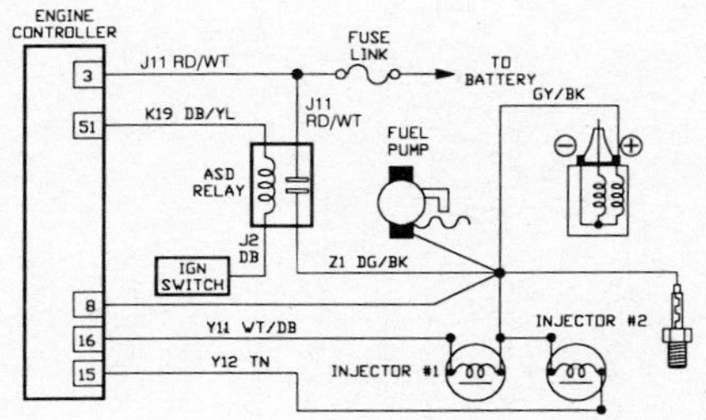
ENGINE CONTROLLER
3
51
8
16
15
J11 RD/WT
K19 DB/YL
FUSE LINK
TO BATTERY
GY/BK
J11 RD/WT
ASD RELAY
J2 DB
IGN SWITCH
FUEL PUMP
Z1 DG/BK
Y11 WT/DB
Y12 TN
INJECTOR #1
INJECTOR #2

START TEST NS-4A.

RECORD THE FUEL PRESSURE GAUGE READING.

IGNITION KEY OFF.

WARNING: THE FUEL SYSTEM MUST BE OPENED AND MAY BE UNDER HIGH PRESSURE.

INSTALL FUEL PRESSURE GAUGE BETWEEN FUEL TANK & FUEL FILTER.

RECONNECT THE PREVIOUSLY DISCONNECTED FUEL LINE.

IGNITION KEY ON.

ACTUATE THE ASD FUEL SYSTEM.

RECORD THE FUEL PRESSURE GAUGE READING.

COMPARE THIS READING WITH THE PREVIOUS READING.

IS THE FUEL PRESSURE AT LEAST 13 PSI?
- YES: ①
- NO: CAUTION: DO NOT ALLOW FUEL PRESSURE TO EXCEED 70 PSI IN THE FOLLOWING STEP.

WHILE GENTLY SQUEEZING THE FUEL RETURN HOSE, WATCH THE PRESSURE GAUGE.

DID FUEL PRESSURE EXCEED 13 PSI?
- YES: REPLACE THE FUEL PRESSURE REGULATOR.*
- NO: REPLACE THE FUEL PUMP/FILTER SOCK ASSEMBLY.*

① – Inspect fuel lines between fuel filter and throttle body for restrictions. If lines are restricted, repair as necessary and perform VERIFICATION PROCEDURE 1. If there is no restriction, replace fuel filter and perform VERIFICATION PROCEDURE 1.

* PERFORM VERIFICATION PROCEDURE 1.

91G14064 91I14074

Fig. 9: No Start Test 4A – Checking Low Fuel Pressure

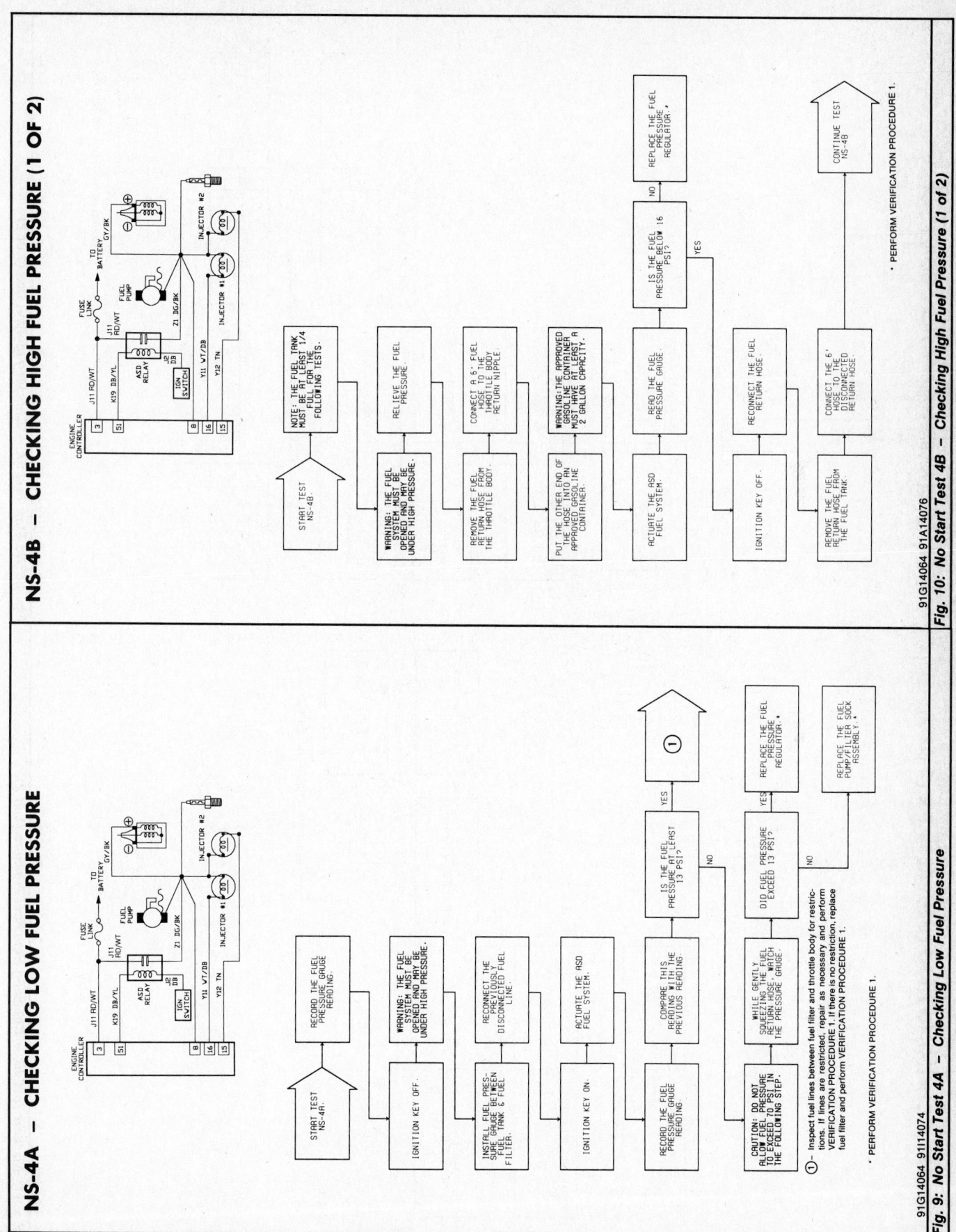

NS-4B – CHECKING HIGH FUEL PRESSURE (1 OF 2)

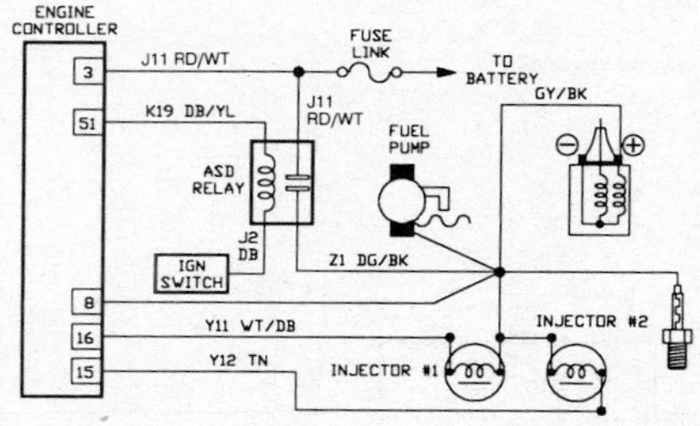
ENGINE CONTROLLER
3
51
8
16
15
J11 RD/WT
K19 DB/YL
FUSE LINK
TO BATTERY
GY/BK
J11 RD/WT
ASD RELAY
J2 DB
IGN SWITCH
FUEL PUMP
Z1 DG/BK
Y11 WT/DB
Y12 TN
INJECTOR #1
INJECTOR #2

START TEST NS-4B.

NOTE: THE FUEL TANK MUST BE AT LEAST 1/4 FULL FOR THE FOLLOWING TESTS.

WARNING: THE FUEL SYSTEM MUST BE OPENED AND MAY BE UNDER HIGH PRESSURE.

RELIEVE THE FUEL PRESSURE.

REMOVE THE FUEL RETURN HOSE FROM THE THROTTLE BODY.

CONNECT A 6' FUEL HOSE TO THE THROTTLE BODY RETURN NIPPLE.

PUT THE OTHER END OF THE HOSE INTO AN APPROVED GASOLINE CONTAINER.

WARNING: THE APPROVED GASOLINE CONTAINER MUST HAVE AT LEAST A 2 GALLON CAPACITY.

ACTUATE THE ASD FUEL SYSTEM.

READ THE FUEL PRESSURE GAUGE.

IS THE FUEL PRESSURE BELOW 16 PSI?
- NO: REPLACE THE FUEL PRESSURE REGULATOR.*
- YES: IGNITION KEY OFF.

RECONNECT THE FUEL RETURN HOSE.

REMOVE THE FUEL RETURN HOSE FROM THE FUEL TANK.

CONNECT THE 6' HOSE TO THE DISCONNECTED RETURN HOSE.

CONTINUE TEST NS-4B

* PERFORM VERIFICATION PROCEDURE 1.

91G14064 91A14076

Fig. 10: No Start Test 4B – Checking High Fuel Pressure (1 of 2)

1991 ENGINE PERFORMANCE
Self-Diagnostics – 3.9L, 5.2L & 5.9L TBI (Cont.)

NS-4B – CHECKING HIGH FUEL PRESSURE (2 OF 2)

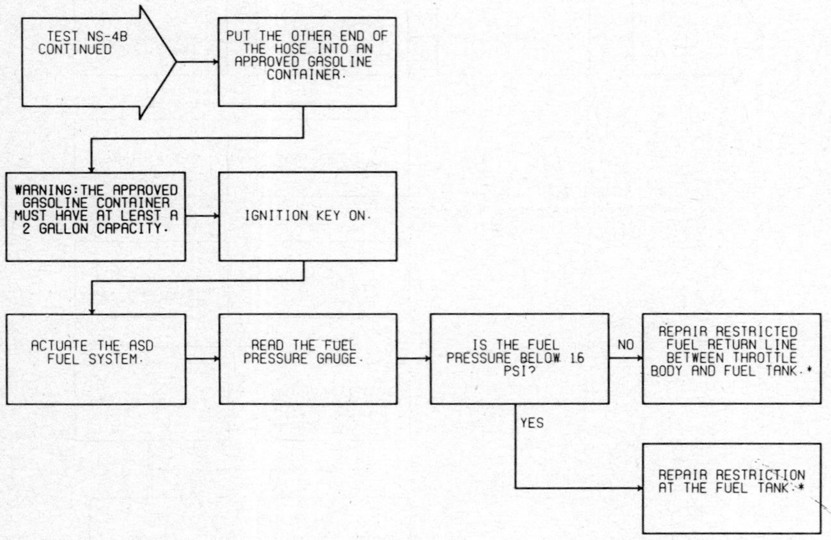
TEST NS-4B CONTINUED
PUT THE OTHER END OF THE HOSE INTO AN APPROVED GASOLINE CONTAINER.
WARNING: THE APPROVED GASOLINE CONTAINER MUST HAVE AT LEAST A 2 GALLON CAPACITY.
IGNITION KEY ON.
ACTUATE THE ASD FUEL SYSTEM.
READ THE FUEL PRESSURE GAUGE.
IS THE FUEL PRESSURE BELOW 16 PSI?
NO
REPAIR RESTRICTED FUEL RETURN LINE BETWEEN THROTTLE BODY AND FUEL TANK.*
YES
REPAIR RESTRICTION AT THE FUEL TANK.*

* PERFORM VERIFICATION PROCEDURE 1.

91B14077

Fig. 11: No Start Test 4B – Checking High Fuel Pressure (2 of 2)

NS-5A – CHECKING IGNITION COIL (1 OF 2)

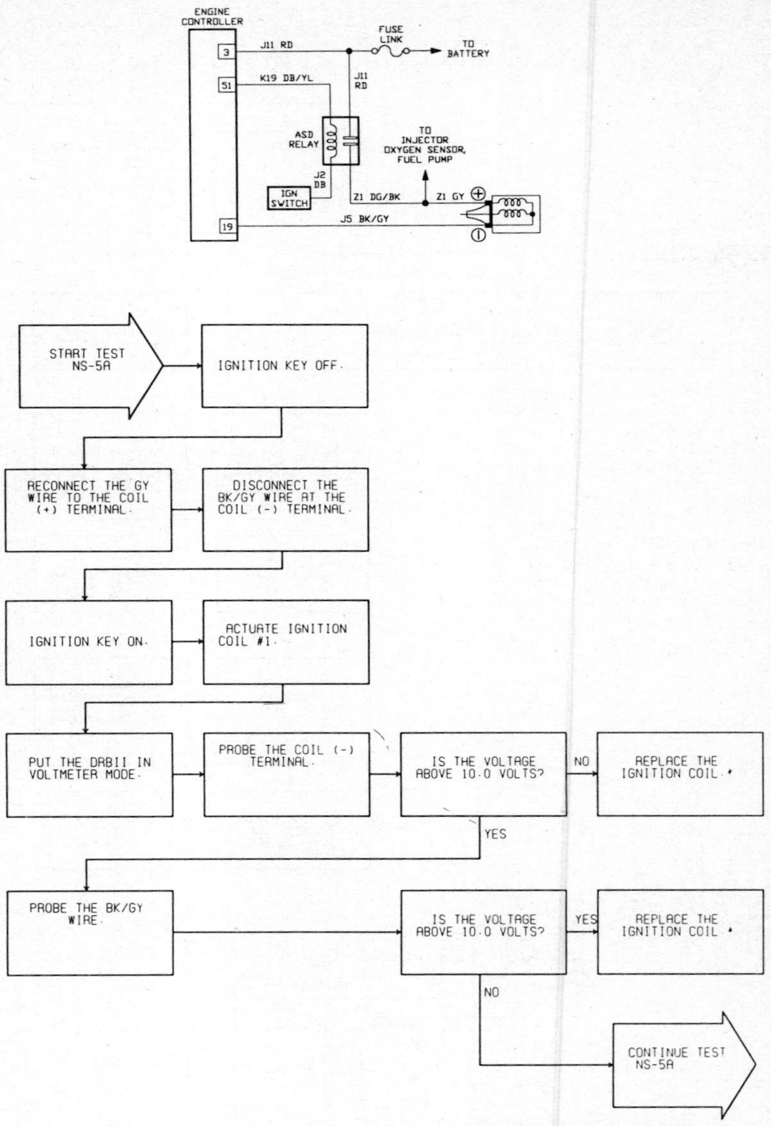
ENGINE CONTROLLER
3
51
19
J11 RD
FUSE LINK
TO BATTERY
K19 DB/YL
J11 RD
ASD RELAY
TO INJECTOR OXYGEN SENSOR, FUEL PUMP
J2 DB
IGN SWITCH
Z1 DG/BK
Z1 GY
J5 BK/GY
START TEST NS-5A
IGNITION KEY OFF.
RECONNECT THE GY WIRE TO THE COIL (+) TERMINAL.
DISCONNECT THE BK/GY WIRE AT THE COIL (-) TERMINAL.
IGNITION KEY ON.
ACTUATE IGNITION COIL #1.
PUT THE DRBII IN VOLTMETER MODE.
PROBE THE COIL (-) TERMINAL.
IS THE VOLTAGE ABOVE 10.0 VOLTS?
NO
REPLACE THE IGNITION COIL.*
YES
PROBE THE BK/GY WIRE.
IS THE VOLTAGE ABOVE 10.0 VOLTS?
YES
REPLACE THE IGNITION COIL.*
NO
CONTINUE TEST NS-5A

* PERFORM VERIFICATION PROCEDURE 1.

91C14078 91D14079

Fig. 12: No Start Test 5A – Checking Ignition Coil (1 of 2)

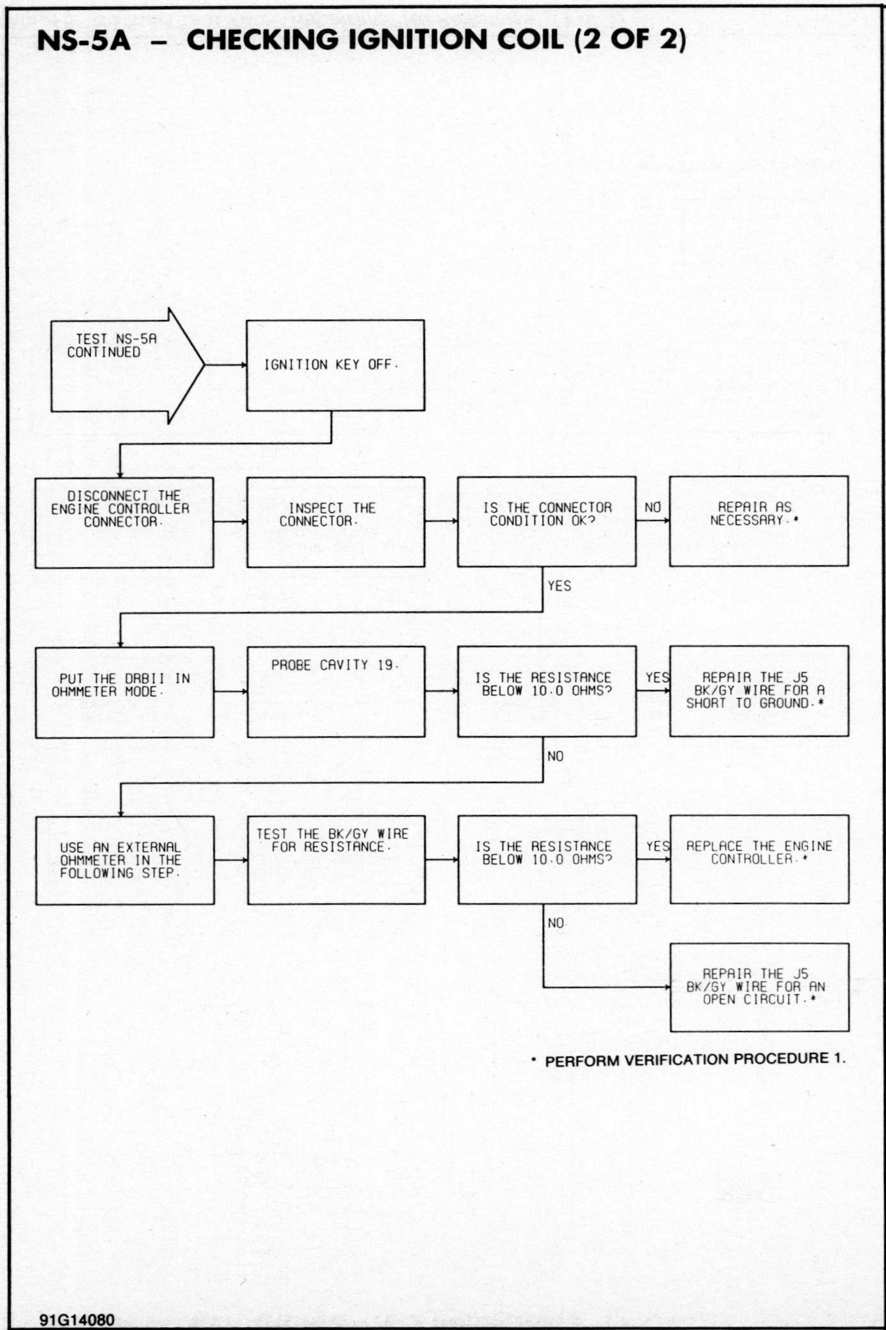
NS-5A – CHECKING IGNITION COIL (2 OF 2)
TEST NS-5A CONTINUED
IGNITION KEY OFF.
DISCONNECT THE ENGINE CONTROLLER CONNECTOR.
INSPECT THE CONNECTOR.
IS THE CONNECTOR CONDITION OK?
NO
REPAIR AS NECESSARY.*
YES
PUT THE DRBII IN OHMMETER MODE.
PROBE CAVITY 19.
IS THE RESISTANCE BELOW 10.0 OHMS?
YES
REPAIR THE J5 BK/GY WIRE FOR A SHORT TO GROUND.*
NO
USE AN EXTERNAL OHMMETER IN THE FOLLOWING STEP.
TEST THE BK/GY WIRE FOR RESISTANCE.
IS THE RESISTANCE BELOW 10.0 OHMS?
YES
REPLACE THE ENGINE CONTROLLER.*
NO
REPAIR THE J5 BK/GY WIRE FOR AN OPEN CIRCUIT.*
* PERFORM VERIFICATION PROCEDURE 1.
91G14080

Fig. 13: No Start Test 5A – Checking Ignition Coil (2 of 2)

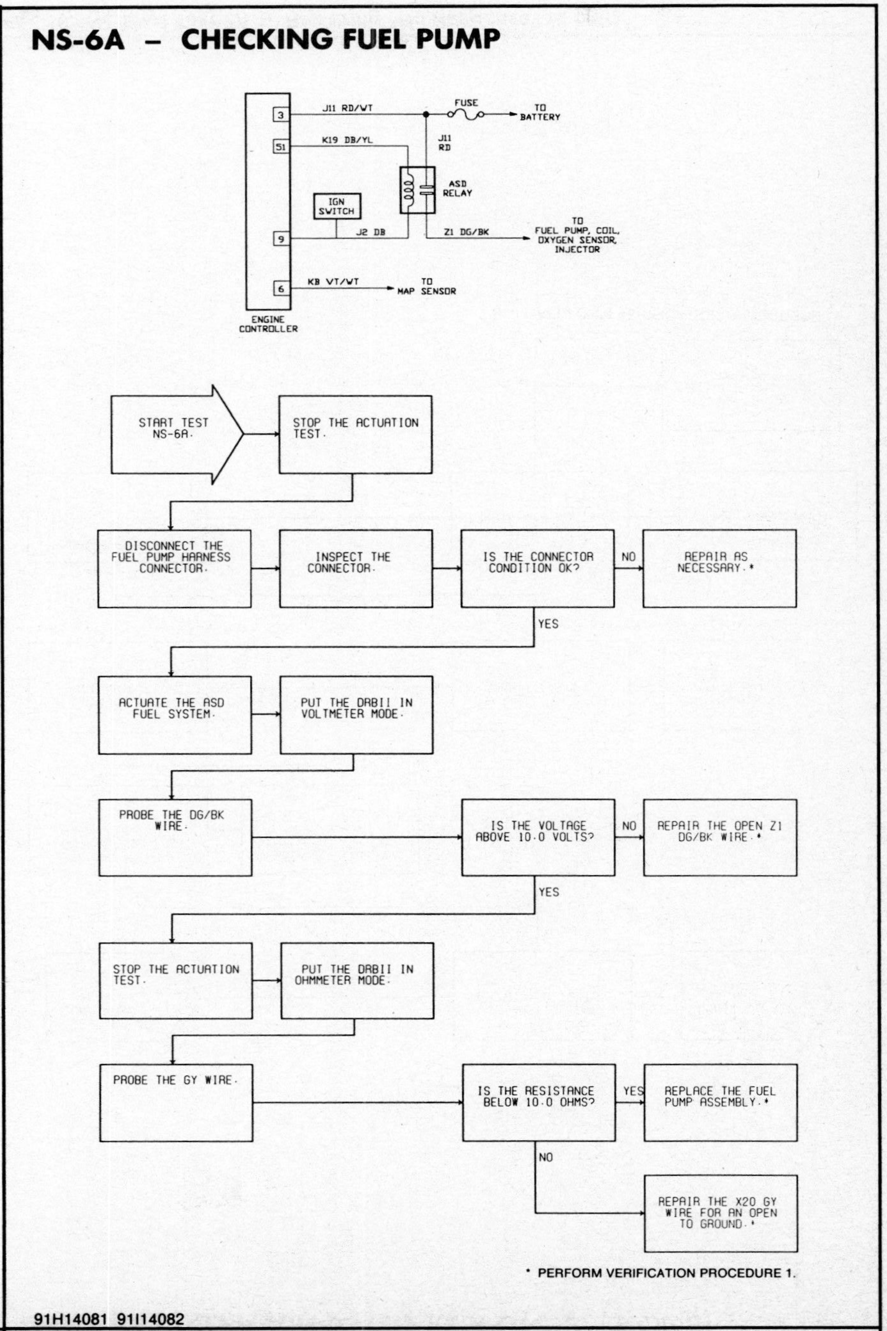
NS-6A – CHECKING FUEL PUMP
J11 RD/WT
FUSE
TO BATTERY
K19 DB/YL
J11 RD
ASD RELAY
IGN SWITCH
J2 DB
Z1 DG/BK
TO FUEL PUMP, COIL, OXYGEN SENSOR, INJECTOR
K8 VT/WT
TO MAP SENSOR
3
51
9
6
ENGINE CONTROLLER
START TEST NS-6A.
STOP THE ACTUATION TEST.
DISCONNECT THE FUEL PUMP HARNESS CONNECTOR.
INSPECT THE CONNECTOR.
IS THE CONNECTOR CONDITION OK?
NO
REPAIR AS NECESSARY.*
YES
ACTUATE THE ASD FUEL SYSTEM.
PUT THE DRBII IN VOLTMETER MODE.
PROBE THE DG/BK WIRE.
IS THE VOLTAGE ABOVE 10.0 VOLTS?
NO
REPAIR THE OPEN Z1 DG/BK WIRE.*
YES
STOP THE ACTUATION TEST.
PUT THE DRBII IN OHMMETER MODE.
PROBE THE GY WIRE.
IS THE RESISTANCE BELOW 10.0 OHMS?
YES
REPLACE THE FUEL PUMP ASSEMBLY.*
NO
REPAIR THE X20 GY WIRE FOR AN OPEN TO GROUND.*
* PERFORM VERIFICATION PROCEDURE 1.
91H14081 91I14082

Fig. 14: No Start Test 6A – Checking Fuel Pump

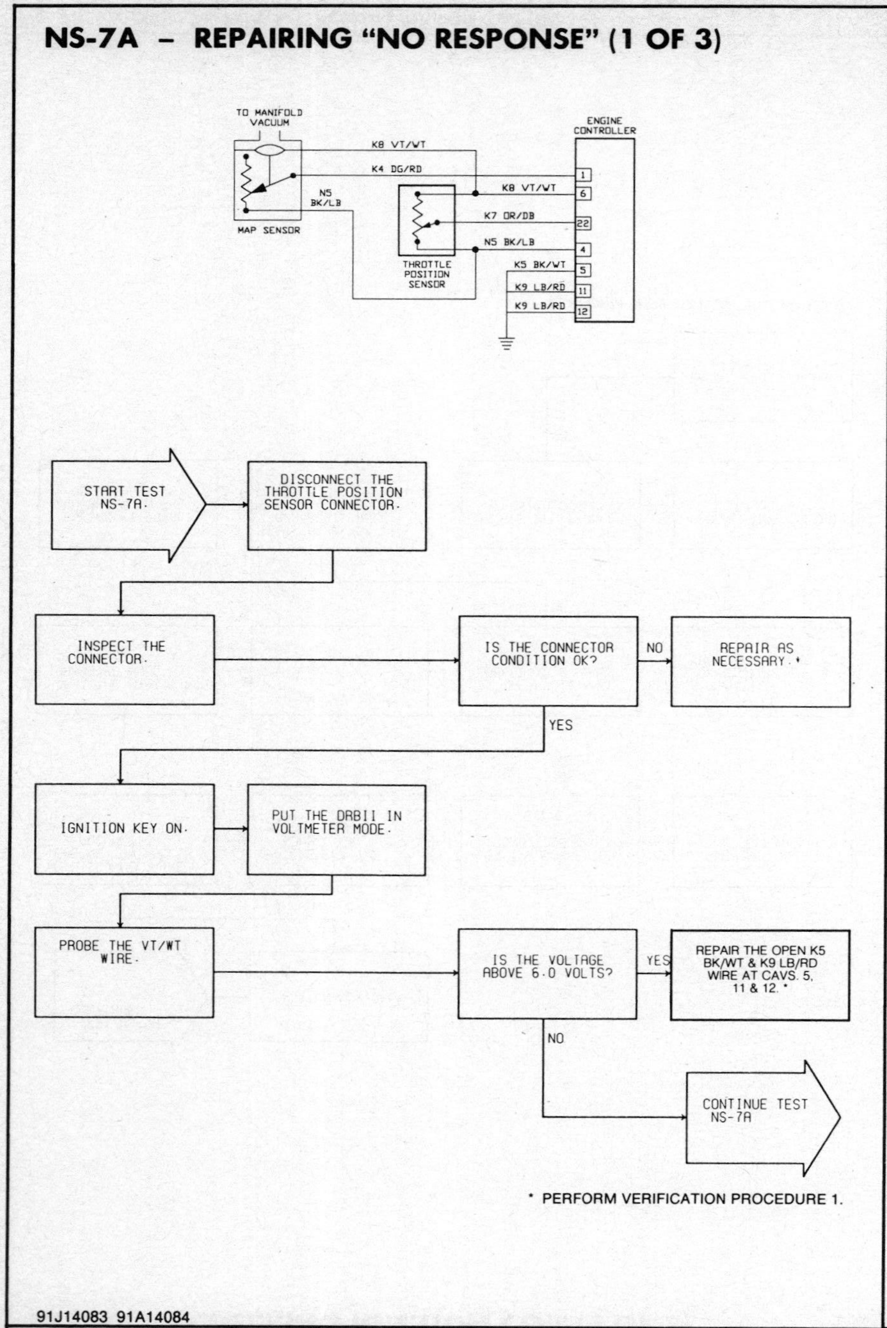
NS-7A – REPAIRING "NO RESPONSE" (1 OF 3)
TO MANIFOLD VACUUM
MAP SENSOR
K8 VT/WT
K4 DG/RD
N5 BK/LB
THROTTLE POSITION SENSOR
K8 VT/WT
K7 OR/DB
N5 BK/LB
K5 BK/WT
K9 LB/RD
K9 LB/RD
ENGINE CONTROLLER
1
6
22
4
5
11
12
START TEST NS-7A.
DISCONNECT THE THROTTLE POSITION SENSOR CONNECTOR.
INSPECT THE CONNECTOR.
IS THE CONNECTOR CONDITION OK?
NO
REPAIR AS NECESSARY.*
YES
IGNITION KEY ON.
PUT THE DRBII IN VOLTMETER MODE.
PROBE THE VT/WT WIRE.
IS THE VOLTAGE ABOVE 6.0 VOLTS?
YES
REPAIR THE OPEN K5 BK/WT & K9 LB/RD WIRE AT CAVS. 5, 11 & 12.*
NO
CONTINUE TEST NS-7A
* PERFORM VERIFICATION PROCEDURE 1.
91J14083 91A14084
Fig. 15: No Start Test 7A – Repairing "No Response" (1 of 3)

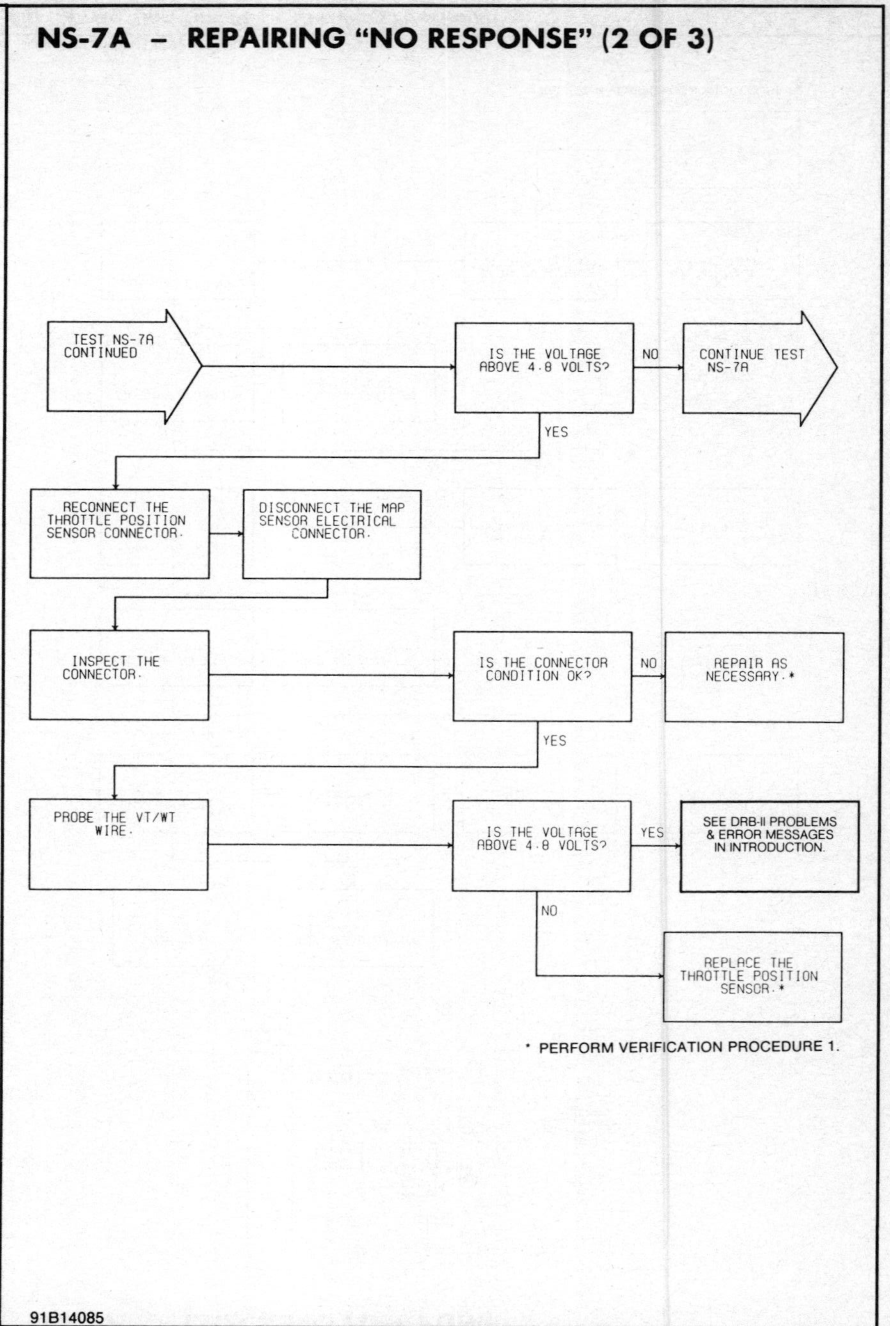
NS-7A – REPAIRING "NO RESPONSE" (2 OF 3)
TEST NS-7A CONTINUED
IS THE VOLTAGE ABOVE 4.8 VOLTS?
NO
CONTINUE TEST NS-7A
YES
RECONNECT THE THROTTLE POSITION SENSOR CONNECTOR.
DISCONNECT THE MAP SENSOR ELECTRICAL CONNECTOR.
INSPECT THE CONNECTOR.
IS THE CONNECTOR CONDITION OK?
NO
REPAIR AS NECESSARY.*
YES
PROBE THE VT/WT WIRE.
IS THE VOLTAGE ABOVE 4.8 VOLTS?
YES
SEE DRB-II PROBLEMS & ERROR MESSAGES IN INTRODUCTION.
NO
REPLACE THE THROTTLE POSITION SENSOR.*
* PERFORM VERIFICATION PROCEDURE 1.
91B14085
Fig. 16: No Start Test 7A – Repairing "No Response" (2 of 3)

NS-7A – REPAIRING "NO RESPONSE" (3 OF 3)

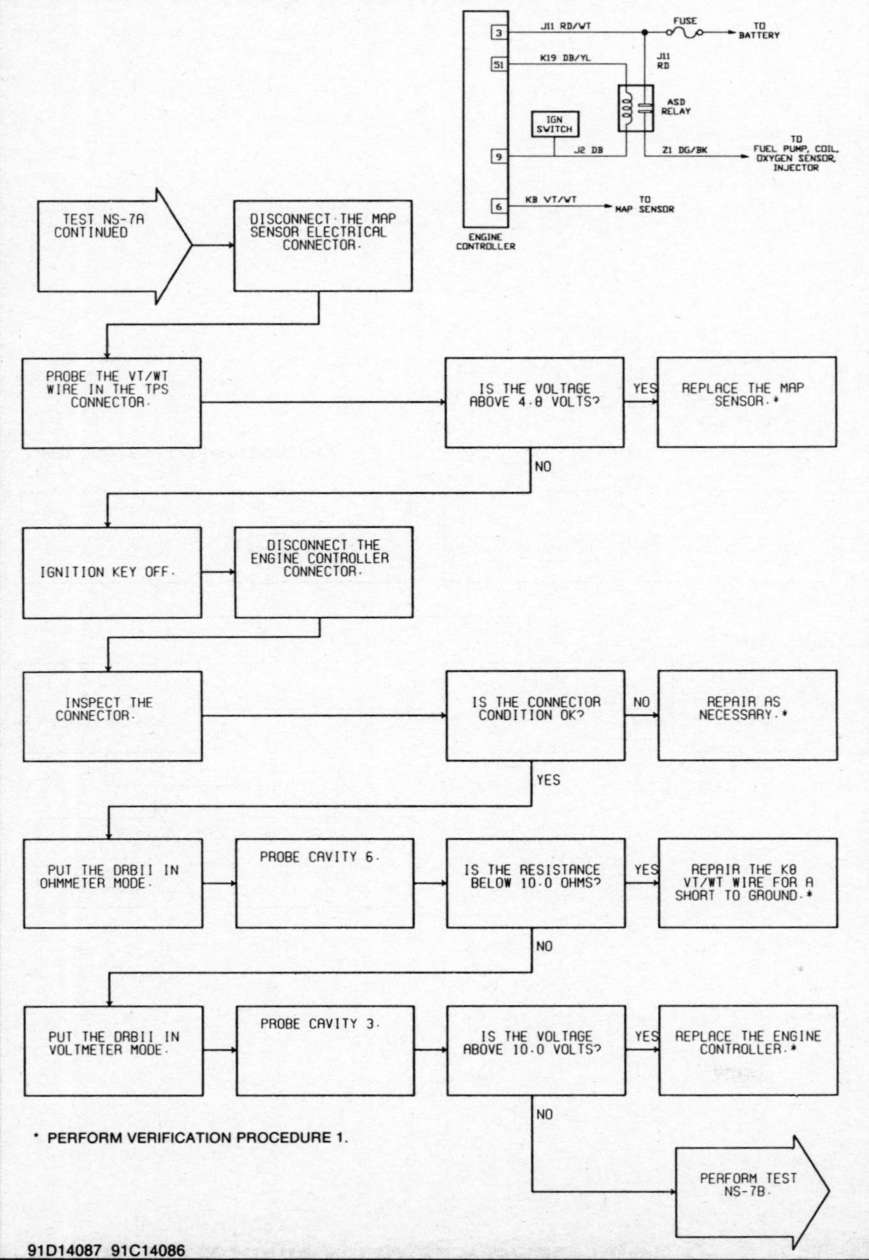
J11 RD/WT
FUSE
TO BATTERY
K19 DB/YL
J11 RD
ASD RELAY
IGN SWITCH
J2 DB
Z1 DG/BK
TO FUEL PUMP, COIL, OXYGEN SENSOR, INJECTOR
K8 VT/WT
TO MAP SENSOR
ENGINE CONTROLLER
3
51
9
6
TEST NS-7A CONTINUED
DISCONNECT THE MAP SENSOR ELECTRICAL CONNECTOR.
PROBE THE VT/WT WIRE IN THE TPS CONNECTOR.
IS THE VOLTAGE ABOVE 4.8 VOLTS?
YES
REPLACE THE MAP SENSOR.*
NO
IGNITION KEY OFF.
DISCONNECT THE ENGINE CONTROLLER CONNECTOR.
INSPECT THE CONNECTOR.
IS THE CONNECTOR CONDITION OK?
NO
REPAIR AS NECESSARY.*
YES
PUT THE DRBII IN OHMMETER MODE.
PROBE CAVITY 6.
IS THE RESISTANCE BELOW 10.0 OHMS?
YES
REPAIR THE K8 VT/WT WIRE FOR A SHORT TO GROUND.*
NO
PUT THE DRBII IN VOLTMETER MODE.
PROBE CAVITY 3.
IS THE VOLTAGE ABOVE 10.0 VOLTS?
YES
REPLACE THE ENGINE CONTROLLER.*
NO
PERFORM TEST NS-7B.
* PERFORM VERIFICATION PROCEDURE 1.
91D14087 91C14086

Fig. 17: No Start Test 7A – Repairing "No Response" (3 of 3)

NS-7B – REPAIRING "NO RESPONSE" (1 OF 2)

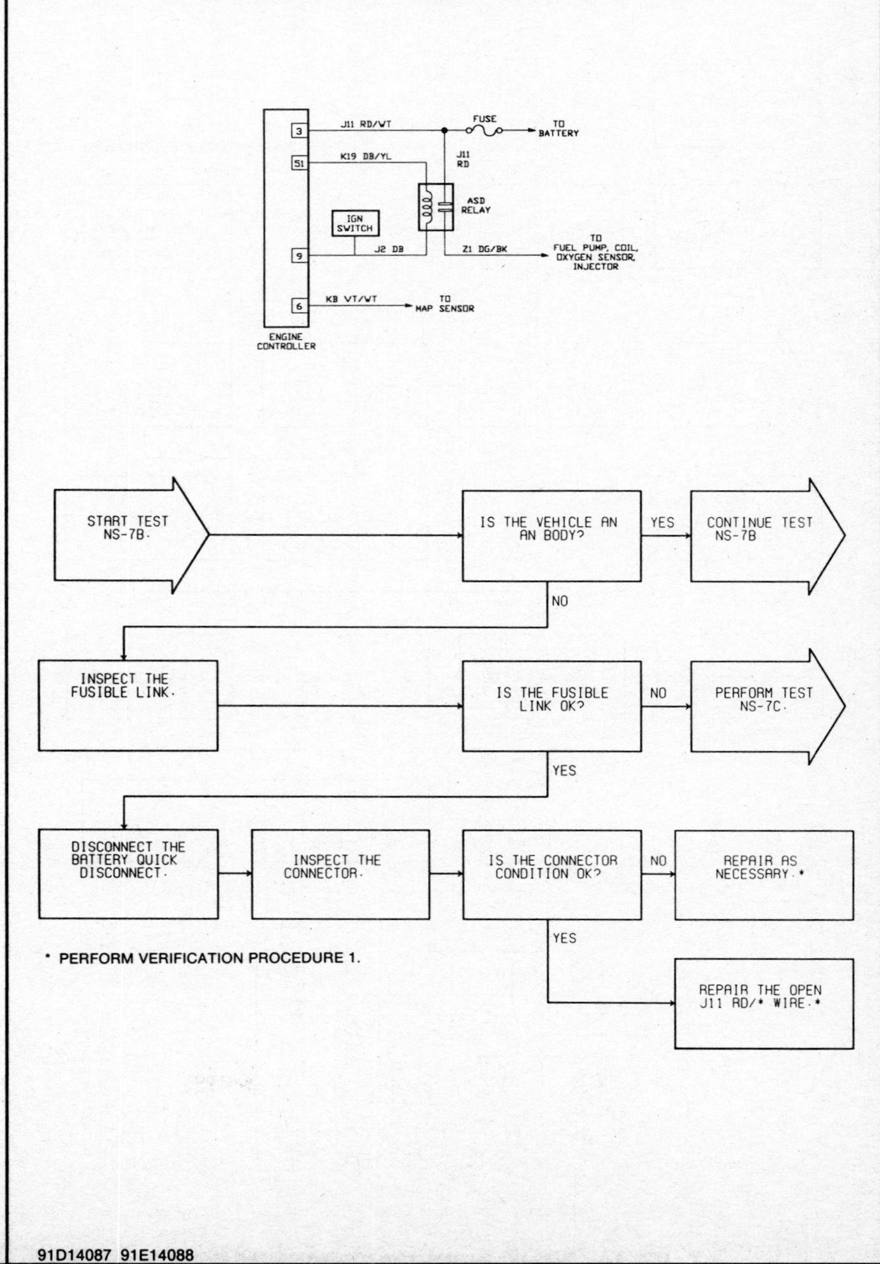
J11 RD/WT
FUSE
TO BATTERY
K19 DB/YL
J11 RD
ASD RELAY
IGN SWITCH
J2 DB
Z1 DG/BK
TO FUEL PUMP, COIL, OXYGEN SENSOR, INJECTOR
K8 VT/WT
TO MAP SENSOR
ENGINE CONTROLLER
3
51
9
6
START TEST NS-7B.
IS THE VEHICLE AN AN BODY?
YES
CONTINUE TEST NS-7B
NO
INSPECT THE FUSIBLE LINK.
IS THE FUSIBLE LINK OK?
NO
PERFORM TEST NS-7C.
YES
DISCONNECT THE BATTERY QUICK DISCONNECT.
INSPECT THE CONNECTOR.
IS THE CONNECTOR CONDITION OK?
NO
REPAIR AS NECESSARY.*
YES
REPAIR THE OPEN J11 RD/* WIRE.*
* PERFORM VERIFICATION PROCEDURE 1.
91D14087 91E14088

Fig. 18: No Start Test 7B – Repairing "No Response" (1 of 2)

1991 ENGINE PERFORMANCE
Self-Diagnostics – 3.9L, 5.2L & 5.9L TBI (Cont.)

NS-7B – REPAIRING "NO RESPONSE" (2 OF 2)

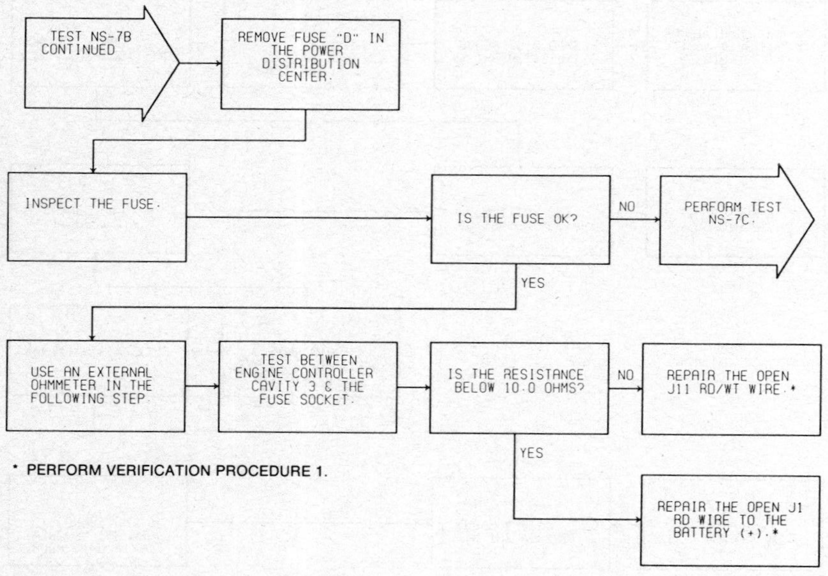
TEST NS-7B CONTINUED
REMOVE FUSE "D" IN THE POWER DISTRIBUTION CENTER.
INSPECT THE FUSE.
IS THE FUSE OK?
NO
PERFORM TEST NS-7C.
YES
USE AN EXTERNAL OHMMETER IN THE FOLLOWING STEP
TEST BETWEEN ENGINE CONTROLLER CAVITY 3 & THE FUSE SOCKET.
IS THE RESISTANCE BELOW 10.0 OHMS?
NO
REPAIR THE OPEN J11 RD/WT WIRE.*
YES
REPAIR THE OPEN J1 RD WIRE TO THE BATTERY (+).*
* PERFORM VERIFICATION PROCEDURE 1.

91F14089

Fig. 19: No Start Test 7B – Repairing "No Response" (2 of 2)

NS-7C – REPAIRING "NO RESPONSE" (1 OF 2)

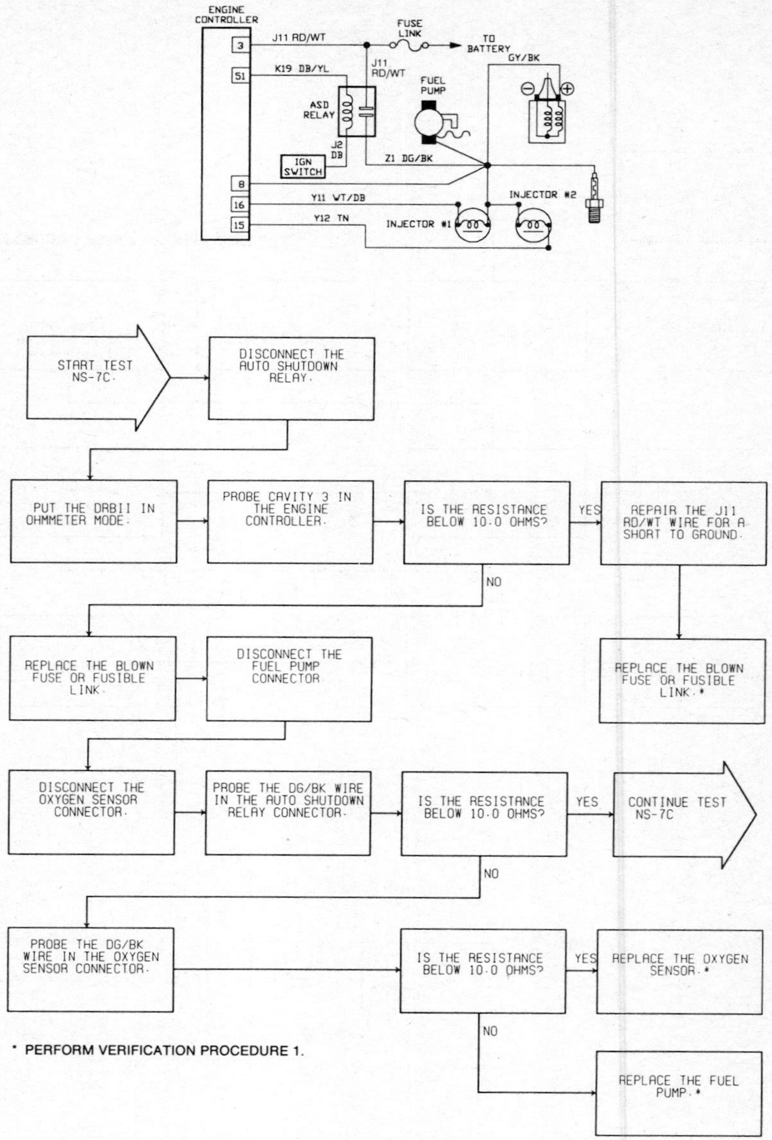
ENGINE CONTROLLER
3
51
8
16
15
J11 RD/WT
FUSE LINK
TO BATTERY
GY/BK
K19 DB/YL
J11 RD/WT
FUEL PUMP
ASD RELAY
J2 DB
IGN SWITCH
Z1 DG/BK
Y11 WT/DB
Y12 TN
INJECTOR #1
INJECTOR #2
START TEST NS-7C.
DISCONNECT THE AUTO SHUTDOWN RELAY.
PUT THE DRBII IN OHMMETER MODE.
PROBE CAVITY 3 IN THE ENGINE CONTROLLER.
IS THE RESISTANCE BELOW 10.0 OHMS?
YES
REPAIR THE J11 RD/WT WIRE FOR A SHORT TO GROUND.
REPLACE THE BLOWN FUSE OR FUSIBLE LINK.*
NO
REPLACE THE BLOWN FUSE OR FUSIBLE LINK.
DISCONNECT THE FUEL PUMP CONNECTOR
DISCONNECT THE OXYGEN SENSOR CONNECTOR.
PROBE THE DG/BK WIRE IN THE AUTO SHUTDOWN RELAY CONNECTOR.
IS THE RESISTANCE BELOW 10.0 OHMS?
YES
CONTINUE TEST NS-7C
NO
PROBE THE DG/BK WIRE IN THE OXYGEN SENSOR CONNECTOR.
IS THE RESISTANCE BELOW 10.0 OHMS?
YES
REPLACE THE OXYGEN SENSOR.*
NO
REPLACE THE FUEL PUMP.*
* PERFORM VERIFICATION PROCEDURE 1.

91G14064 91F14091

Fig. 20: No Start Test 7C – Repairing "No Response" (1 of 2)

NS-7C – REPAIRING "NO RESPONSE" (2 OF 2)

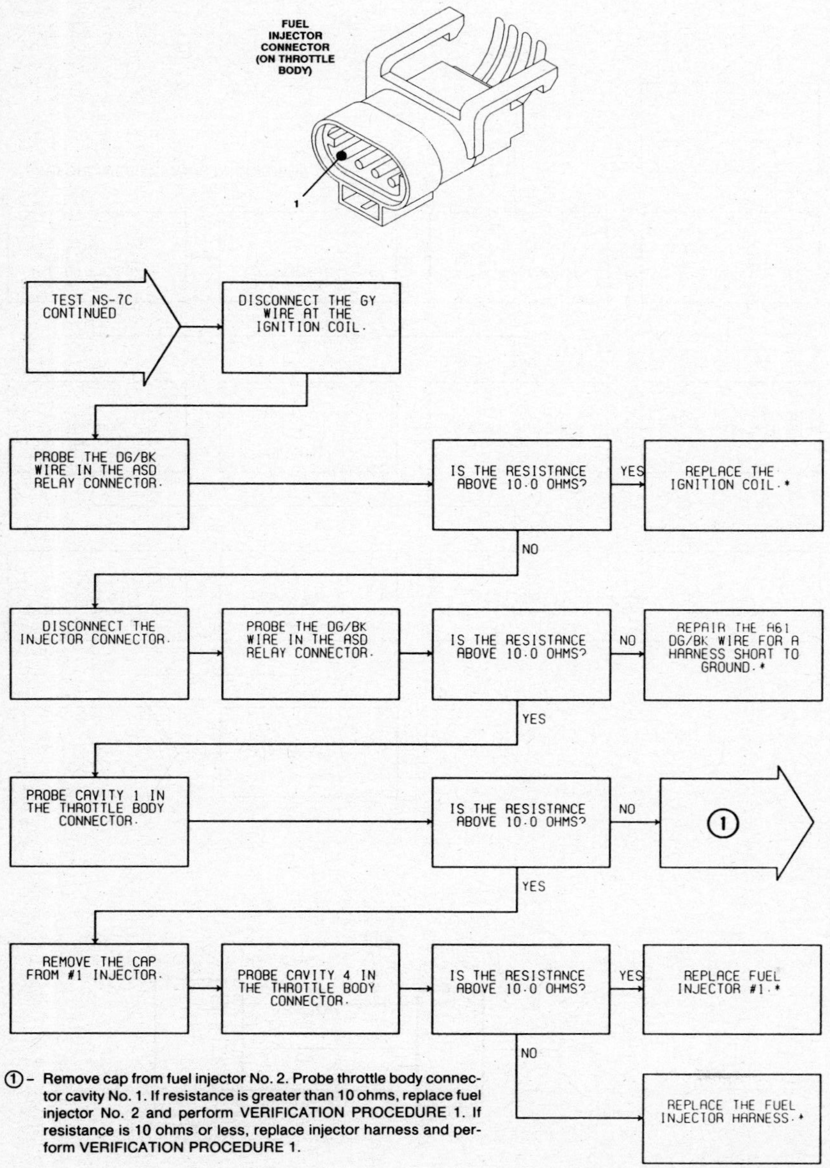

FUEL INJECTOR CONNECTOR (ON THROTTLE BODY)
1
TEST NS-7C CONTINUED
DISCONNECT THE GY WIRE AT THE IGNITION COIL.
PROBE THE DG/BK WIRE IN THE ASD RELAY CONNECTOR.
IS THE RESISTANCE ABOVE 10.0 OHMS?
YES
REPLACE THE IGNITION COIL.*
NO
DISCONNECT THE INJECTOR CONNECTOR.
PROBE THE DG/BK WIRE IN THE ASD RELAY CONNECTOR.
IS THE RESISTANCE ABOVE 10.0 OHMS?
NO
REPAIR THE A61 DG/BK WIRE FOR A HARNESS SHORT TO GROUND.*
YES
PROBE CAVITY 1 IN THE THROTTLE BODY CONNECTOR.
IS THE RESISTANCE ABOVE 10.0 OHMS?
NO
1
YES
REMOVE THE CAP FROM #1 INJECTOR.
PROBE CAVITY 4 IN THE THROTTLE BODY CONNECTOR.
IS THE RESISTANCE ABOVE 10.0 OHMS?
YES
REPLACE FUEL INJECTOR #1.*
NO
REPLACE THE FUEL INJECTOR HARNESS.*

① – Remove cap from fuel injector No. 2. Probe throttle body connector cavity No. 1. If resistance is greater than 10 ohms, replace fuel injector No. 2 and perform VERIFICATION PROCEDURE 1. If resistance is 10 ohms or less, replace injector harness and perform VERIFICATION PROCEDURE 1.

* PERFORM VERIFICATION PROCEDURE 1.

91A14092

Fig. 21: No Start Test 7C – Repairing "No Response" (2 of 2)

NS-8A – REPAIRING FAULT "NO REFERENCE SIGNAL DURING CRANKING"

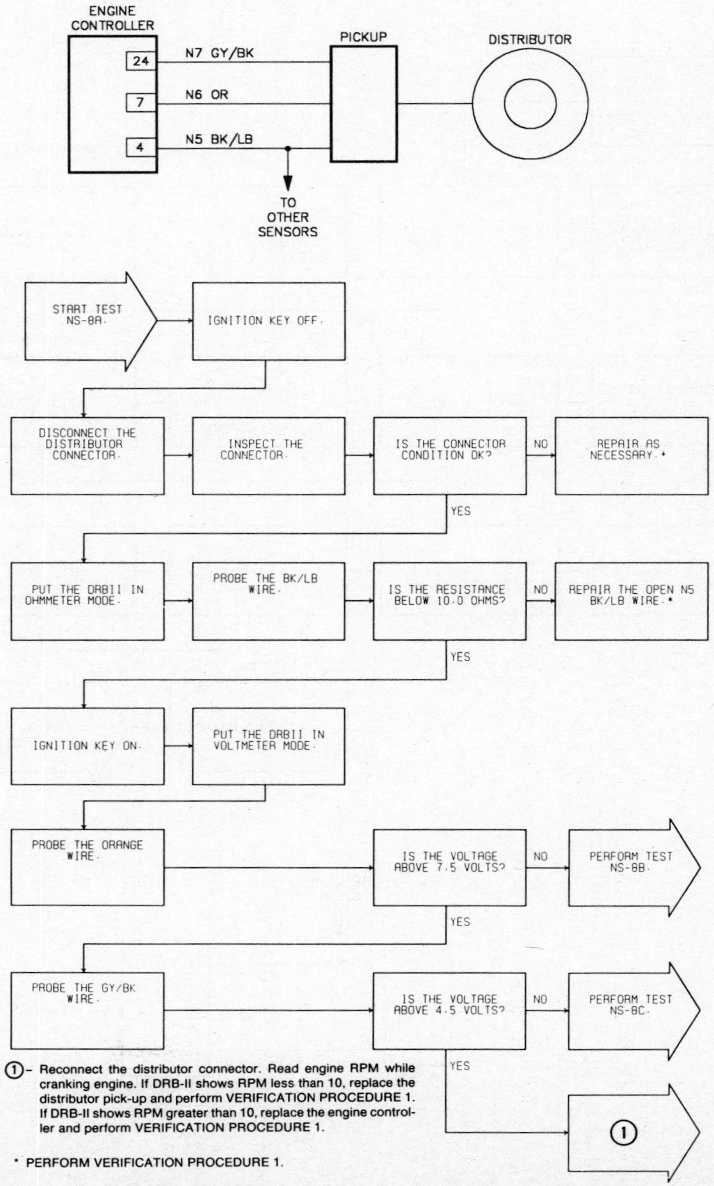

ENGINE CONTROLLER
24
7
4
N7 GY/BK
N6 OR
N5 BK/LB
PICKUP
DISTRIBUTOR
TO OTHER SENSORS
START TEST NS-8A.
IGNITION KEY OFF.
DISCONNECT THE DISTRIBUTOR CONNECTOR.
INSPECT THE CONNECTOR.
IS THE CONNECTOR CONDITION OK?
NO
REPAIR AS NECESSARY.*
YES
PUT THE DRBII IN OHMMETER MODE.
PROBE THE BK/LB WIRE.
IS THE RESISTANCE BELOW 10.0 OHMS?
NO
REPAIR THE OPEN N5 BK/LB WIRE.*
YES
IGNITION KEY ON.
PUT THE DRBII IN VOLTMETER MODE.
PROBE THE ORANGE WIRE.
IS THE VOLTAGE ABOVE 7.5 VOLTS?
NO
PERFORM TEST NS-8B.
YES
PROBE THE GY/BK WIRE.
IS THE VOLTAGE ABOVE 4.5 VOLTS?
NO
PERFORM TEST NS-8C.
YES
1

① – Reconnect the distributor connector. Read engine RPM while cranking engine. If DRB-II shows RPM less than 10, replace the distributor pick-up and perform VERIFICATION PROCEDURE 1. If DRB-II shows RPM greater than 10, replace the engine controller and perform VERIFICATION PROCEDURE 1.

* PERFORM VERIFICATION PROCEDURE 1.

91C14094 91D14095

Fig. 22: No Start Test 8A – Repairing Fault "No Reference Signal During Cranking"

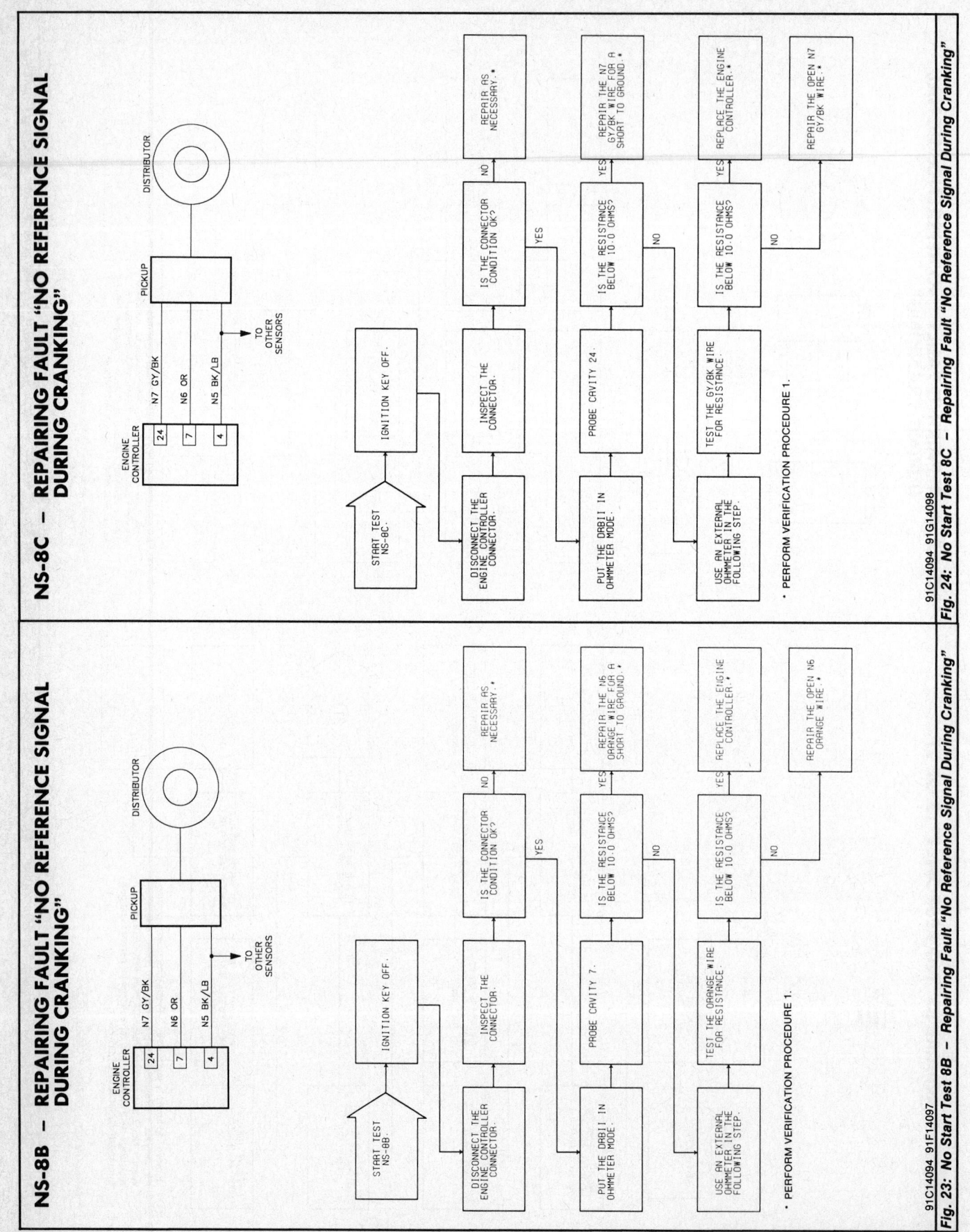

NS-8B – REPAIRING FAULT "NO REFERENCE SIGNAL DURING CRANKING"

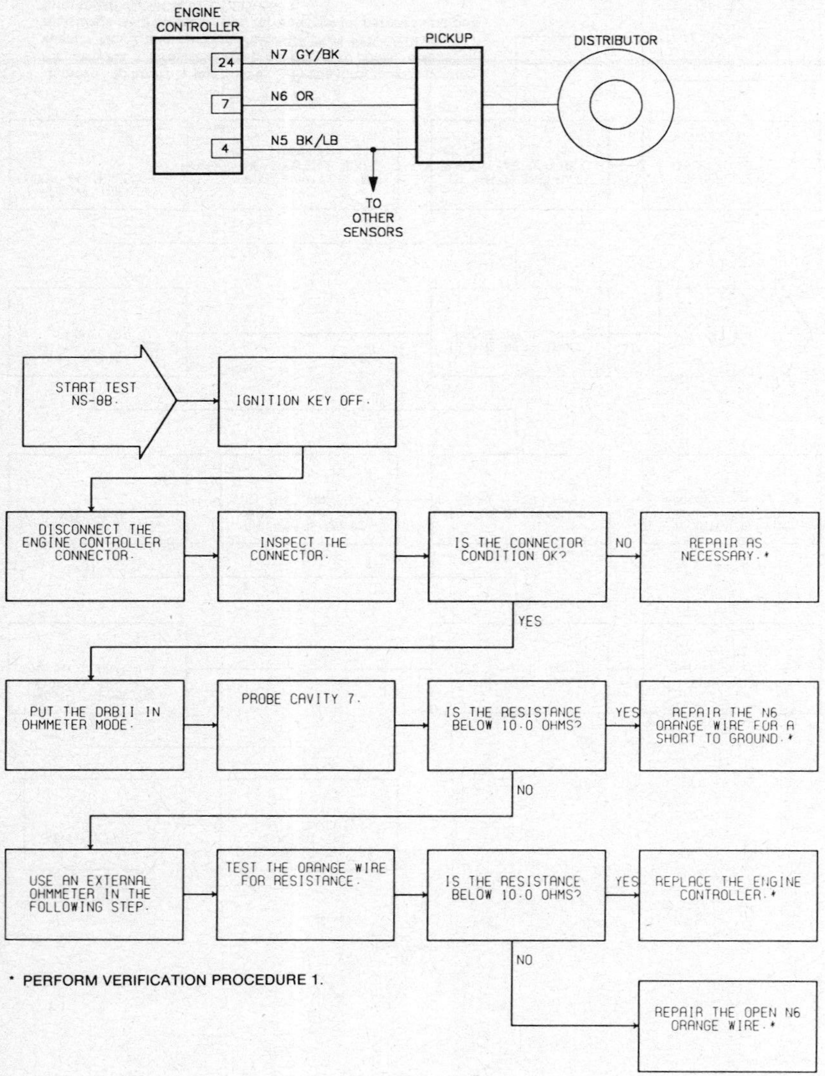
ENGINE CONTROLLER
24
7
4
N7 GY/BK
N6 OR
N5 BK/LB
PICKUP
DISTRIBUTOR
TO OTHER SENSORS
START TEST NS-8B.
IGNITION KEY OFF.
DISCONNECT THE ENGINE CONTROLLER CONNECTOR.
INSPECT THE CONNECTOR.
IS THE CONNECTOR CONDITION OK?
NO
REPAIR AS NECESSARY.*
YES
PUT THE DRBII IN OHMMETER MODE.
PROBE CAVITY 7.
IS THE RESISTANCE BELOW 10.0 OHMS?
YES
REPAIR THE N6 ORANGE WIRE FOR A SHORT TO GROUND.*
NO
USE AN EXTERNAL OHMMETER IN THE FOLLOWING STEP.
TEST THE ORANGE WIRE FOR RESISTANCE.
IS THE RESISTANCE BELOW 10.0 OHMS?
YES
REPLACE THE ENGINE CONTROLLER.*
NO
REPAIR THE OPEN N6 ORANGE WIRE.*

* PERFORM VERIFICATION PROCEDURE 1.

91C14094 91F14097

Fig. 23: No Start Test 8B – Repairing Fault "No Reference Signal During Cranking"

NS-8C – REPAIRING FAULT "NO REFERENCE SIGNAL DURING CRANKING"

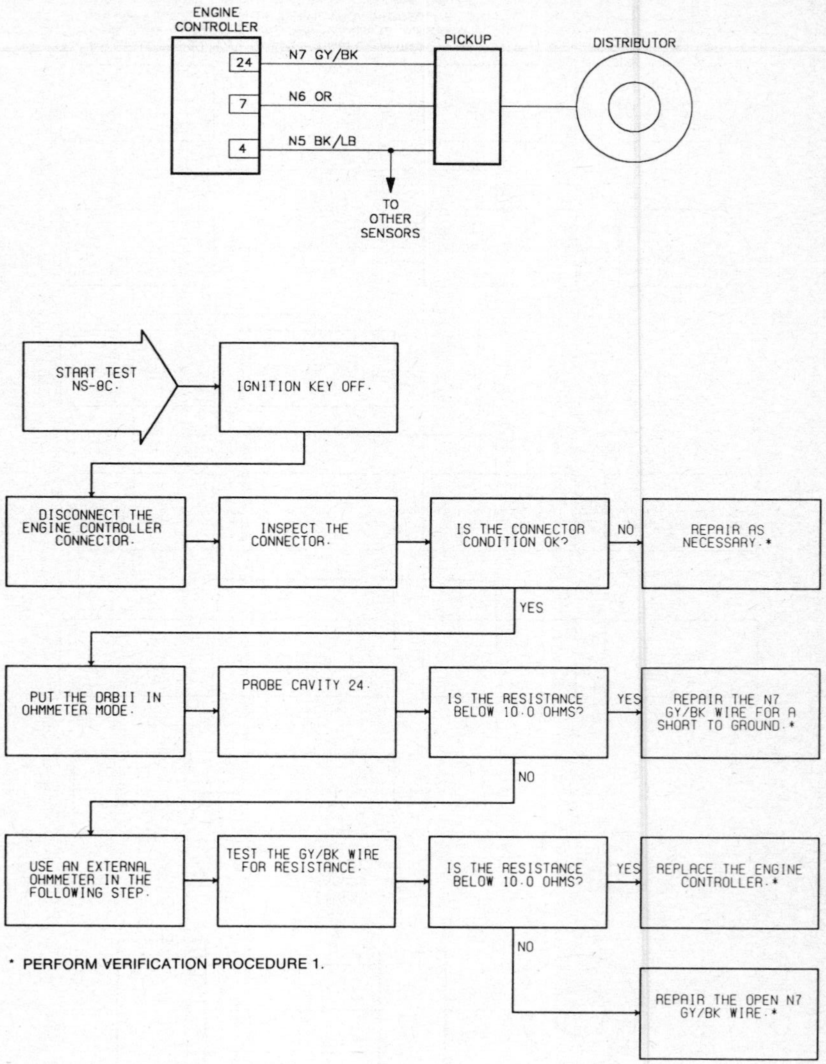
ENGINE CONTROLLER
24
7
4
N7 GY/BK
N6 OR
N5 BK/LB
PICKUP
DISTRIBUTOR
TO OTHER SENSORS
START TEST NS-8C.
IGNITION KEY OFF.
DISCONNECT THE ENGINE CONTROLLER CONNECTOR.
INSPECT THE CONNECTOR.
IS THE CONNECTOR CONDITION OK?
NO
REPAIR AS NECESSARY.*
YES
PUT THE DRBII IN OHMMETER MODE.
PROBE CAVITY 24.
IS THE RESISTANCE BELOW 10.0 OHMS?
YES
REPAIR THE N7 GY/BK WIRE FOR A SHORT TO GROUND.*
NO
USE AN EXTERNAL OHMMETER IN THE FOLLOWING STEP.
TEST THE GY/BK WIRE FOR RESISTANCE.
IS THE RESISTANCE BELOW 10.0 OHMS?
YES
REPLACE THE ENGINE CONTROLLER.*
NO
REPAIR THE OPEN N7 GY/BK WIRE.*

* PERFORM VERIFICATION PROCEDURE 1.

91C14094 91G14098

Fig. 24: No Start Test 8C – Repairing Fault "No Reference Signal During Cranking"

NS-9A – REPAIRING FAULT "AUTO SHUTDOWN RELAY CONTROL CIRCUIT" (1 OF 2)

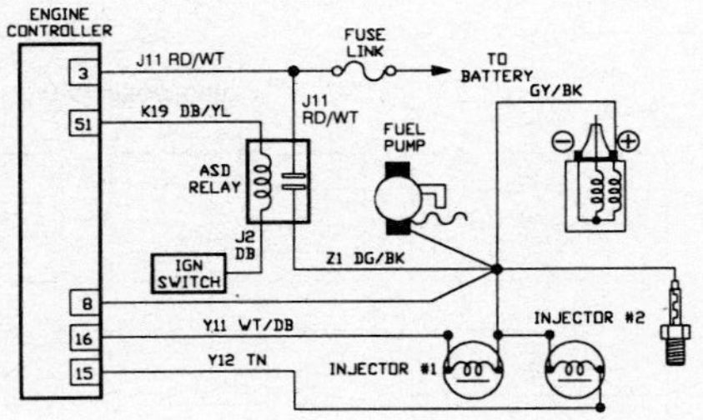
ENGINE CONTROLLER
3
51
8
16
15
J11 RD/WT
K19 DB/YL
FUSE LINK
TO BATTERY
GY/BK
J11 RD/WT
FUEL PUMP
ASD RELAY
J2 DB
IGN SWITCH
Z1 DG/BK
Y11 WT/DB
Y12 TN
INJECTOR #1
INJECTOR #2

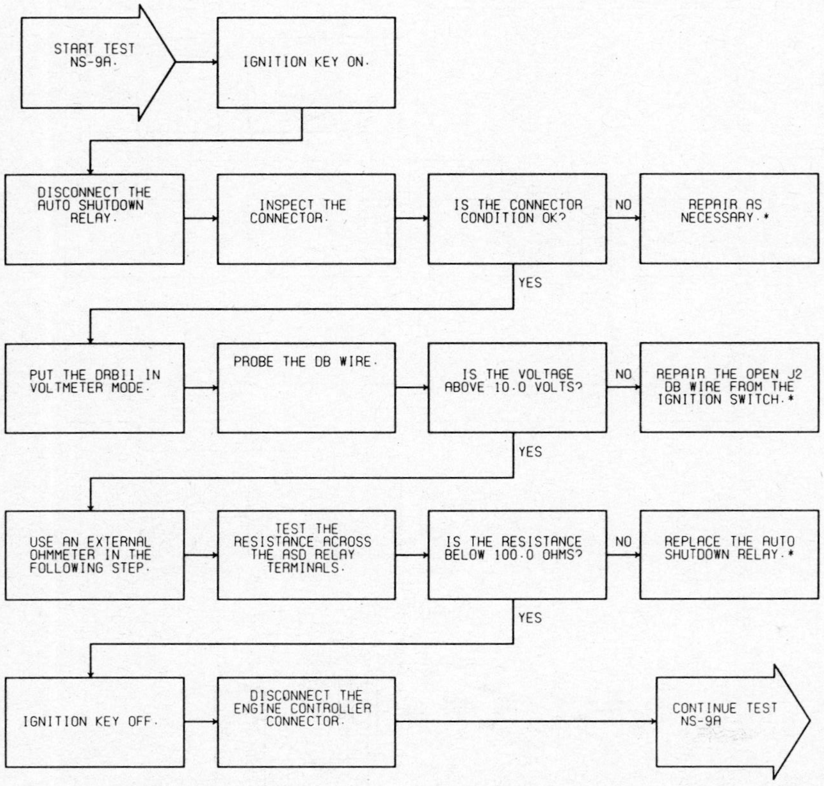
START TEST NS-9A.
IGNITION KEY ON.
DISCONNECT THE AUTO SHUTDOWN RELAY.
INSPECT THE CONNECTOR.
IS THE CONNECTOR CONDITION OK?
NO
REPAIR AS NECESSARY.*
YES
PUT THE DRBII IN VOLTMETER MODE.
PROBE THE DB WIRE.
IS THE VOLTAGE ABOVE 10.0 VOLTS?
NO
REPAIR THE OPEN J2 DB WIRE FROM THE IGNITION SWITCH.*
YES
USE AN EXTERNAL OHMMETER IN THE FOLLOWING STEP.
TEST THE RESISTANCE ACROSS THE ASD RELAY TERMINALS.
IS THE RESISTANCE BELOW 100.0 OHMS?
NO
REPLACE THE AUTO SHUTDOWN RELAY.*
YES
IGNITION KEY OFF.
DISCONNECT THE ENGINE CONTROLLER CONNECTOR.
CONTINUE TEST NS-9A

* PERFORM VERIFICATION PROCEDURE 1.

91G14064 91H14099

Fig. 25: No Start Test 9A – Repairing Fault "Auto Shutdown Relay Control Circuit" (1 of 2)

NS-9A – REPAIRING FAULT "AUTO SHUTDOWN RELAY CONTROL CIRCUIT" (2 OF 2)

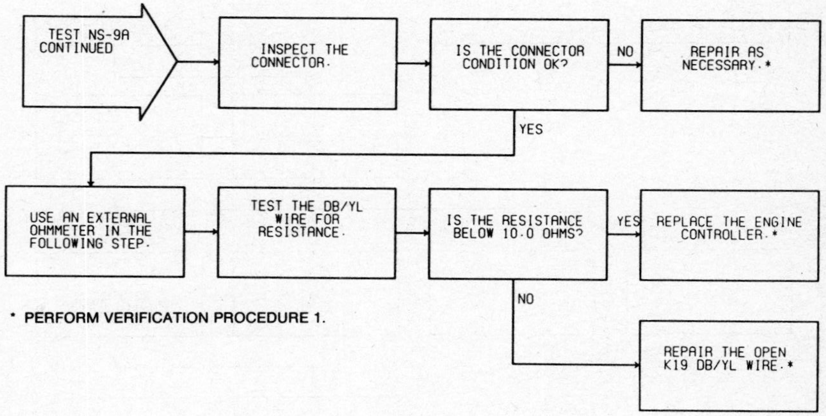
TEST NS-9A CONTINUED
INSPECT THE CONNECTOR.
IS THE CONNECTOR CONDITION OK?
NO
REPAIR AS NECESSARY.*
YES
USE AN EXTERNAL OHMMETER IN THE FOLLOWING STEP.
TEST THE DB/YL WIRE FOR RESISTANCE.
IS THE RESISTANCE BELOW 10.0 OHMS?
YES
REPLACE THE ENGINE CONTROLLER.*
NO
REPAIR THE OPEN K19 DB/YL WIRE.*

* PERFORM VERIFICATION PROCEDURE 1.

91A14100

Fig. 26: No Start Test 9A – Repairing Fault "Auto Shutdown Relay Control Circuit" (2 of 2)

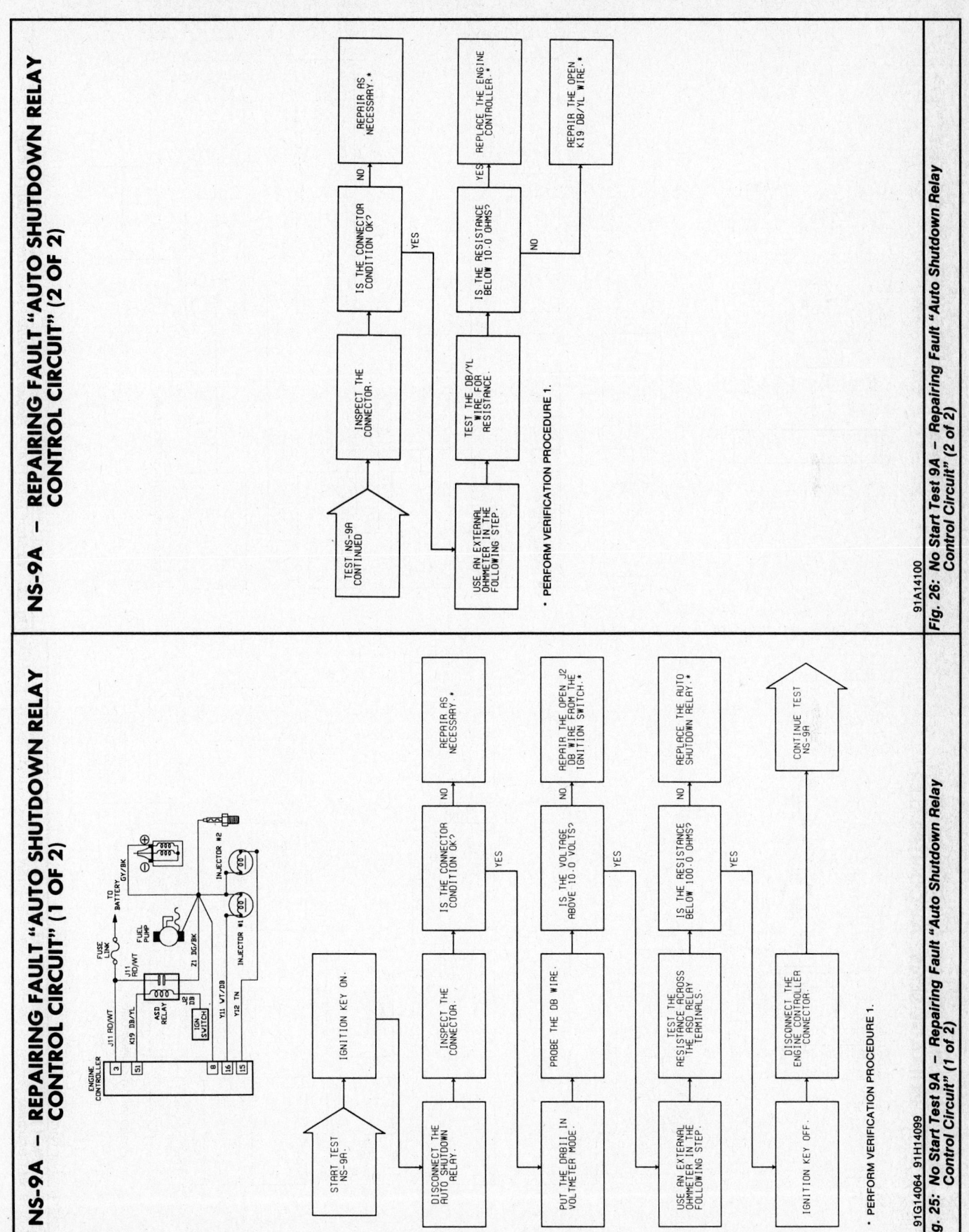

1991 ENGINE PERFORMANCE
Self-Diagnostics – 3.9L, 5.2L & 5.9L TBI (Cont.)

NS-10A – REPAIRING FAULT "NO ASD RELAY VOLTAGE SENSE AT CONTROLLER"

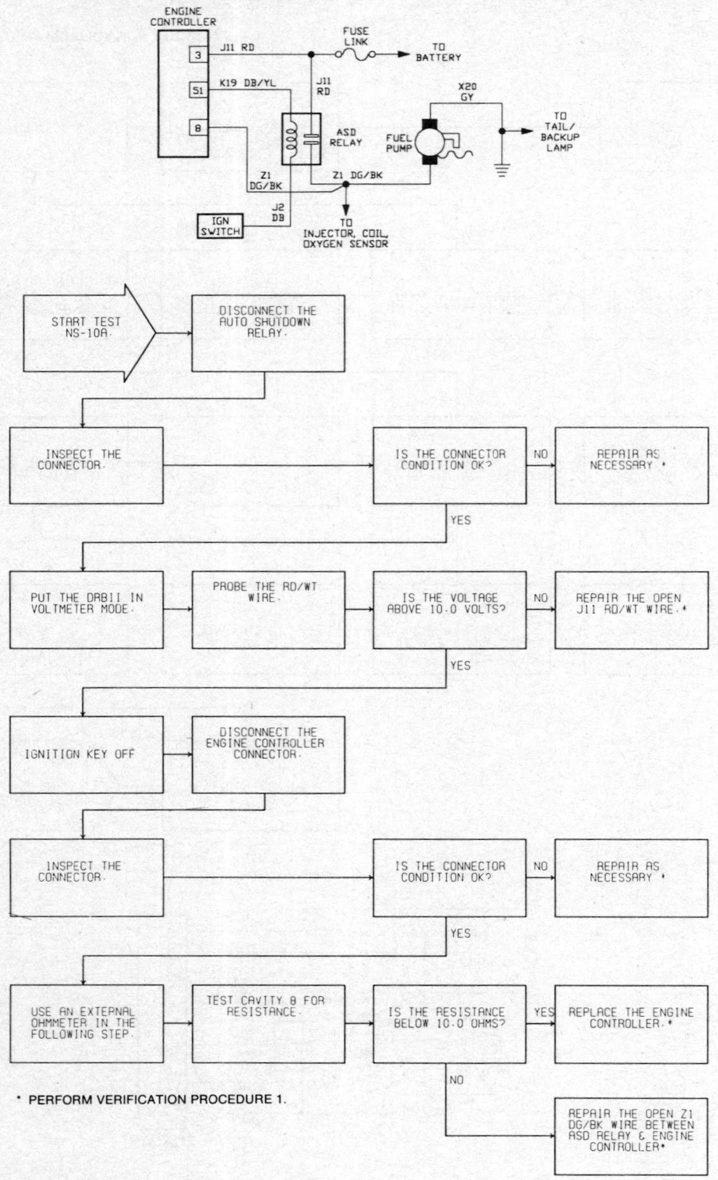
ENGINE CONTROLLER
3
51
8
J11 RD
K19 DB/YL
J11 RD
FUSE LINK
TO BATTERY
X20 GY
ASD RELAY
FUEL PUMP
TO TAIL/ BACKUP LAMP
Z1 DG/BK
Z1 DG/BK
J2 DB
IGN SWITCH
TO INJECTOR, COIL, OXYGEN SENSOR
START TEST NS-10A.
DISCONNECT THE AUTO SHUTDOWN RELAY.
INSPECT THE CONNECTOR.
IS THE CONNECTOR CONDITION OK?
NO
REPAIR AS NECESSARY.*
YES
PUT THE DRBII IN VOLTMETER MODE.
PROBE THE RD/WT WIRE.
IS THE VOLTAGE ABOVE 10.0 VOLTS?
NO
REPAIR THE OPEN J11 RD/WT WIRE.*
YES
IGNITION KEY OFF
DISCONNECT THE ENGINE CONTROLLER CONNECTOR.
INSPECT THE CONNECTOR.
IS THE CONNECTOR CONDITION OK?
NO
REPAIR AS NECESSARY.*
YES
USE AN EXTERNAL OHMMETER IN THE FOLLOWING STEP.
TEST CAVITY 8 FOR RESISTANCE.
IS THE RESISTANCE BELOW 10.0 OHMS?
YES
REPLACE THE ENGINE CONTROLLER.*
NO
REPAIR THE OPEN Z1 DG/BK WIRE BETWEEN ASD RELAY & ENGINE CONTROLLER*

* PERFORM VERIFICATION PROCEDURE 1.

91B14101 91C14102

Fig. 27: No Start Test 10A – Repairing Fault "No ASD Relay Voltage Sense At Controller"

NS-11A – REPAIRING FAULT IN INJECTOR CKT (1 OF 3)

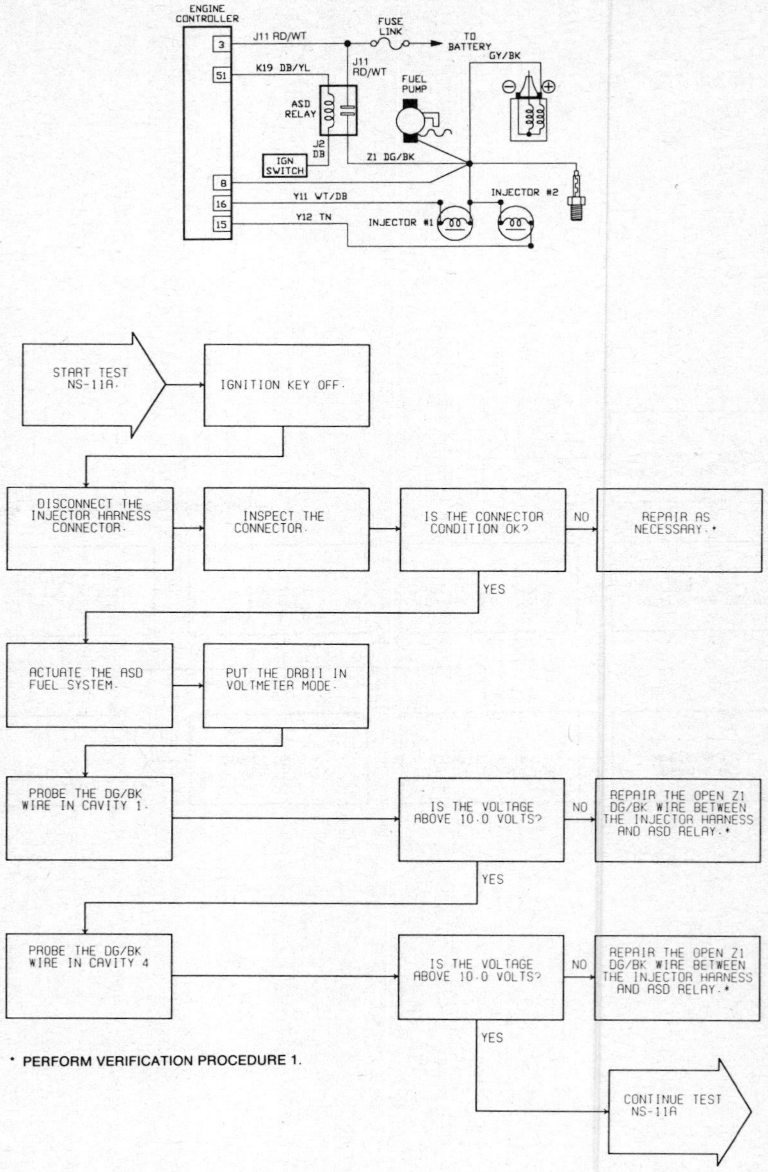
ENGINE CONTROLLER
3
51
8
16
15
J11 RD/WT
K19 DB/YL
FUSE LINK
TO BATTERY
J11 RD/WT
GY/BK
ASD RELAY
FUEL PUMP
J2 DB
IGN SWITCH
Z1 DG/BK
Y11 WT/DB
Y12 TN
INJECTOR #1
INJECTOR #2
START TEST NS-11A.
IGNITION KEY OFF.
DISCONNECT THE INJECTOR HARNESS CONNECTOR.
INSPECT THE CONNECTOR.
IS THE CONNECTOR CONDITION OK?
NO
REPAIR AS NECESSARY.*
YES
ACTUATE THE ASD FUEL SYSTEM.
PUT THE DRBII IN VOLTMETER MODE.
PROBE THE DG/BK WIRE IN CAVITY 1.
IS THE VOLTAGE ABOVE 10.0 VOLTS?
NO
REPAIR THE OPEN Z1 DG/BK WIRE BETWEEN THE INJECTOR HARNESS AND ASD RELAY.*
YES
PROBE THE DG/BK WIRE IN CAVITY 4
IS THE VOLTAGE ABOVE 10.0 VOLTS?
NO
REPAIR THE OPEN Z1 DG/BK WIRE BETWEEN THE INJECTOR HARNESS AND ASD RELAY.*
YES
CONTINUE TEST NS-11A

* PERFORM VERIFICATION PROCEDURE 1.

91G14064 91D14103

Fig. 28: No Start Test 11A – Repairing Fault in Injector Circuit (1 of 3)

NS-11A – REPAIRING FAULT IN INJECTOR CKT (2 OF 3)

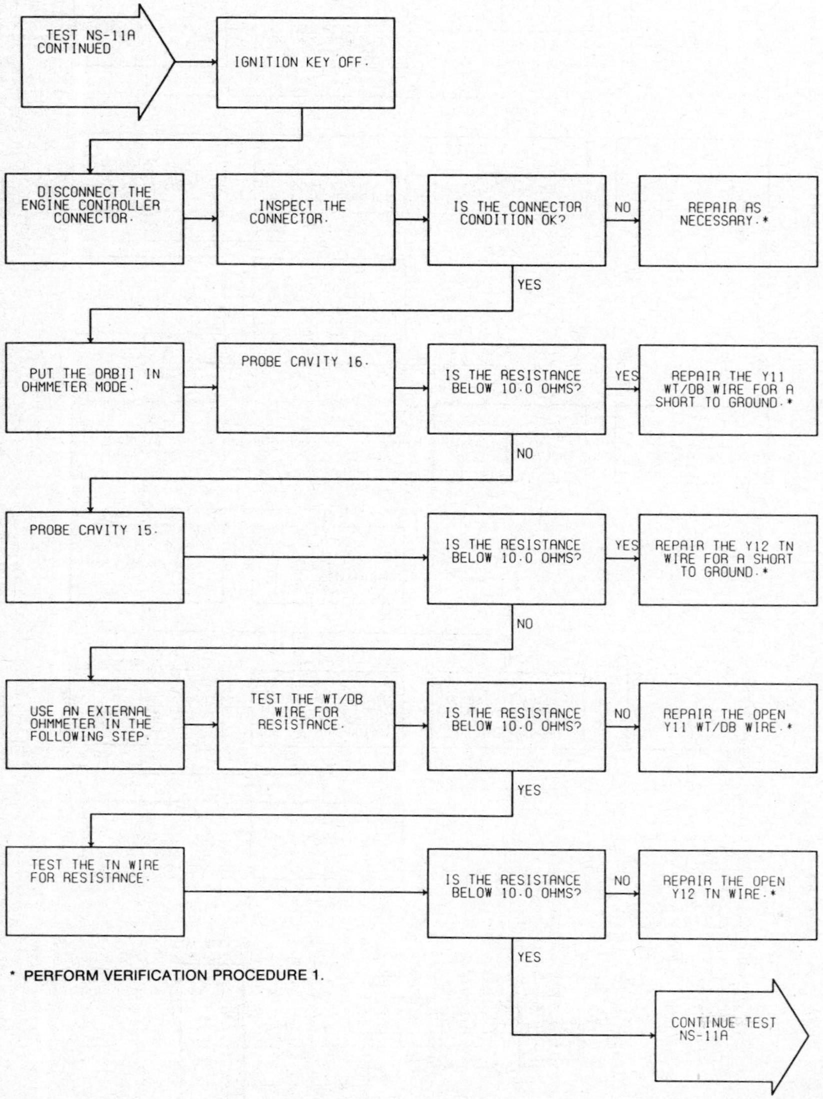
TEST NS-11A CONTINUED
IGNITION KEY OFF.
DISCONNECT THE ENGINE CONTROLLER CONNECTOR.
INSPECT THE CONNECTOR.
IS THE CONNECTOR CONDITION OK?
NO
REPAIR AS NECESSARY.*
YES
PUT THE DRBII IN OHMMETER MODE.
PROBE CAVITY 16.
IS THE RESISTANCE BELOW 10.0 OHMS?
YES
REPAIR THE Y11 WT/DB WIRE FOR A SHORT TO GROUND.*
NO
PROBE CAVITY 15.
IS THE RESISTANCE BELOW 10.0 OHMS?
YES
REPAIR THE Y12 TN WIRE FOR A SHORT TO GROUND.*
NO
USE AN EXTERNAL OHMMETER IN THE FOLLOWING STEP.
TEST THE WT/DB WIRE FOR RESISTANCE.
IS THE RESISTANCE BELOW 10.0 OHMS?
NO
REPAIR THE OPEN Y11 WT/DB WIRE.*
YES
TEST THE TN WIRE FOR RESISTANCE.
IS THE RESISTANCE BELOW 10.0 OHMS?
NO
REPAIR THE OPEN Y12 TN WIRE.*
YES
CONTINUE TEST NS-11A

* PERFORM VERIFICATION PROCEDURE 1.

91E14104

Fig. 29: No Start Test 11A – Repairing Fault in Injector Circuit (2 of 3)

NS-11A – REPAIRING FAULT IN INJECTOR CKT (3 OF 3)

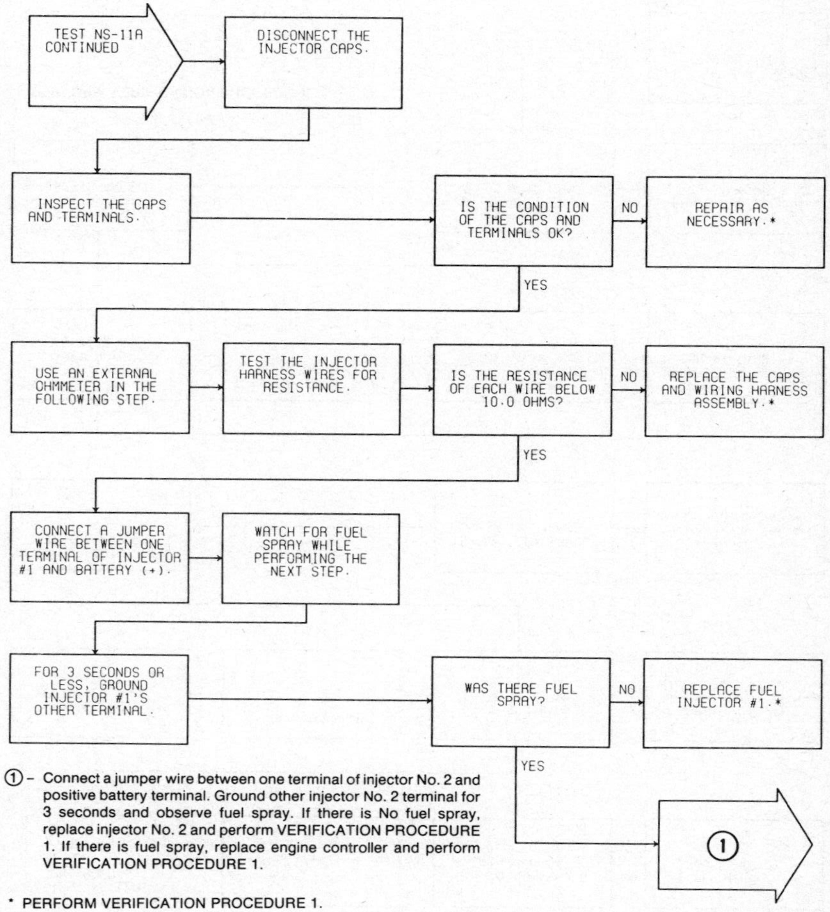
TEST NS-11A CONTINUED
DISCONNECT THE INJECTOR CAPS.
INSPECT THE CAPS AND TERMINALS.
IS THE CONDITION OF THE CAPS AND TERMINALS OK?
NO
REPAIR AS NECESSARY.*
YES
USE AN EXTERNAL OHMMETER IN THE FOLLOWING STEP.
TEST THE INJECTOR HARNESS WIRES FOR RESISTANCE.
IS THE RESISTANCE OF EACH WIRE BELOW 10.0 OHMS?
NO
REPLACE THE CAPS AND WIRING HARNESS ASSEMBLY.*
YES
CONNECT A JUMPER WIRE BETWEEN ONE TERMINAL OF INJECTOR #1 AND BATTERY (+).
WATCH FOR FUEL SPRAY WHILE PERFORMING THE NEXT STEP.
FOR 3 SECONDS OR LESS, GROUND INJECTOR #1'S OTHER TERMINAL.
WAS THERE FUEL SPRAY?
NO
REPLACE FUEL INJECTOR #1.*
YES
①

① – Connect a jumper wire between one terminal of injector No. 2 and positive battery terminal. Ground other injector No. 2 terminal for 3 seconds and observe fuel spray. If there is No fuel spray, replace injector No. 2 and perform VERIFICATION PROCEDURE 1. If there is fuel spray, replace engine controller and perform VERIFICATION PROCEDURE 1.

* PERFORM VERIFICATION PROCEDURE 1.

91F14105

Fig. 30: No Start Test 11A – Repairing Fault in Injector Circuit (3 of 3)

NS-12A – CHECKING IDLE SPEED MOTOR (1 OF 2)

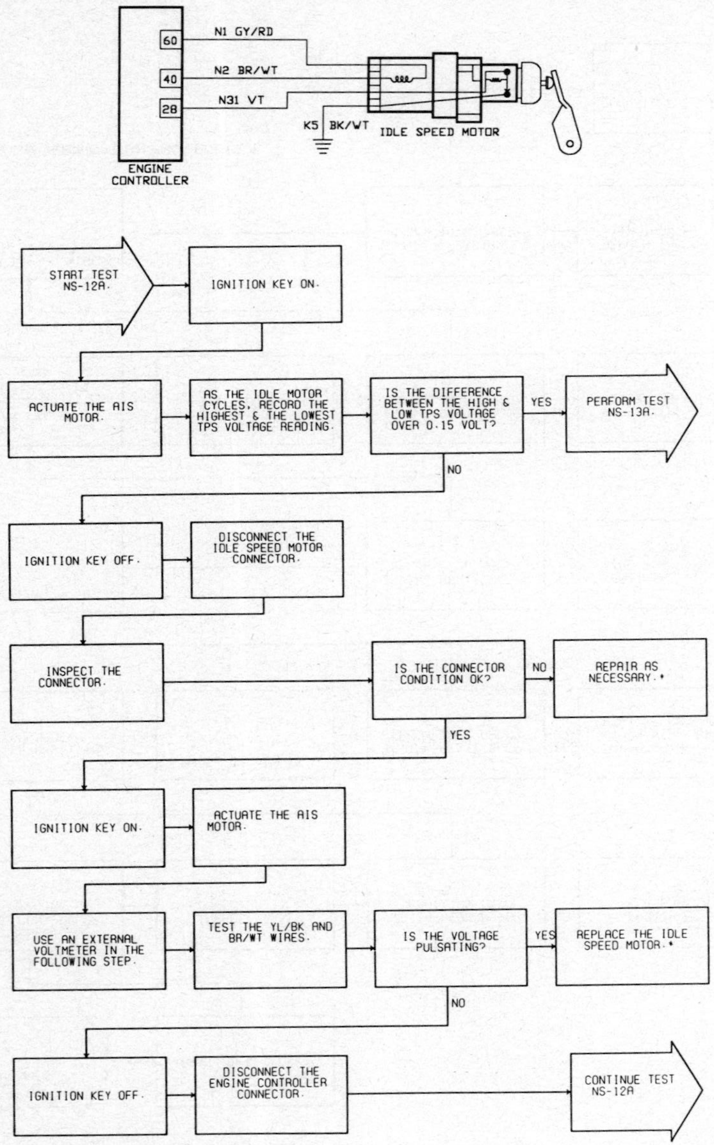
60
40
28
N1 GY/RD
N2 BR/WT
N31 VT
K5 BK/WT
IDLE SPEED MOTOR
ENGINE CONTROLLER
START TEST NS-12A.
IGNITION KEY ON.
ACTUATE THE AIS MOTOR.
AS THE IDLE MOTOR CYCLES, RECORD THE HIGHEST & THE LOWEST TPS VOLTAGE READING.
IS THE DIFFERENCE BETWEEN THE HIGH & LOW TPS VOLTAGE OVER 0.15 VOLT?
YES
PERFORM TEST NS-13A.
NO
IGNITION KEY OFF.
DISCONNECT THE IDLE SPEED MOTOR CONNECTOR.
INSPECT THE CONNECTOR.
IS THE CONNECTOR CONDITION OK?
NO
REPAIR AS NECESSARY.*
YES
IGNITION KEY ON.
ACTUATE THE AIS MOTOR.
USE AN EXTERNAL VOLTMETER IN THE FOLLOWING STEP.
TEST THE YL/BK AND BR/WT WIRES.
IS THE VOLTAGE PULSATING?
YES
REPLACE THE IDLE SPEED MOTOR.*
NO
IGNITION KEY OFF.
DISCONNECT THE ENGINE CONTROLLER CONNECTOR.
CONTINUE TEST NS-12A

* PERFORM VERIFICATION PROCEDURE 1.

91H14107 91I14108

Fig. 31: No Start Test 12A – Checking Idle Speed Motor (1 of 2)

NS-12A – CHECKING IDLE SPEED MOTOR (2 OF 2)

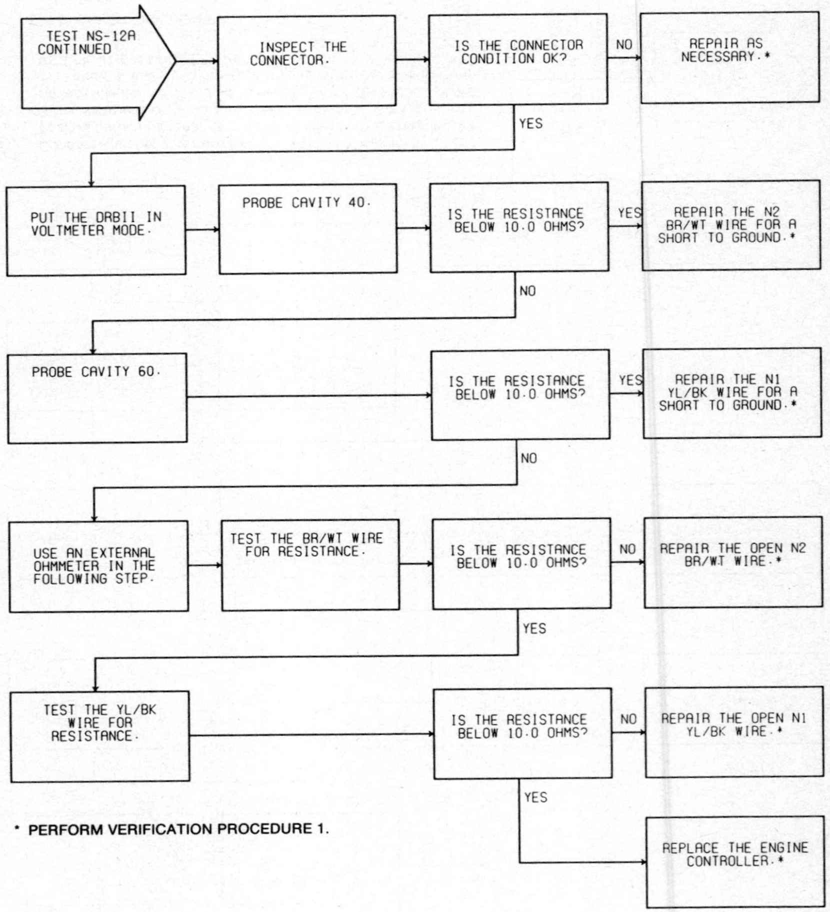
TEST NS-12A CONTINUED
INSPECT THE CONNECTOR.
IS THE CONNECTOR CONDITION OK?
NO
REPAIR AS NECESSARY.*
YES
PUT THE DRBII IN VOLTMETER MODE.
PROBE CAVITY 40.
IS THE RESISTANCE BELOW 10.0 OHMS?
YES
REPAIR THE N2 BR/WT WIRE FOR A SHORT TO GROUND.*
NO
PROBE CAVITY 60.
IS THE RESISTANCE BELOW 10.0 OHMS?
YES
REPAIR THE N1 YL/BK WIRE FOR A SHORT TO GROUND.*
NO
USE AN EXTERNAL OHMMETER IN THE FOLLOWING STEP.
TEST THE BR/WT WIRE FOR RESISTANCE.
IS THE RESISTANCE BELOW 10.0 OHMS?
NO
REPAIR THE OPEN N2 BR/WT WIRE.*
YES
TEST THE YL/BK WIRE FOR RESISTANCE.
IS THE RESISTANCE BELOW 10.0 OHMS?
NO
REPAIR THE OPEN N1 YL/BK WIRE.*
YES
REPLACE THE ENGINE CONTROLLER.*

* PERFORM VERIFICATION PROCEDURE 1.

91J14109

Fig. 32: No Start Test 12A – Checking Idle Speed Motor (2 of 2)

DR-1A – CHECKING SYSTEM FOR FAULTS (1 OF 2)

NOTE: Battery must be fully charged and at rated capacity before performing any driveability test procedure. If vehicle starts and stalls repeatedly, perform TEST NS-2A.

1) Connect DRB-II to underhood diagnostic connector and then read fault messages. If there are no faults, start engine and allow it to reach normal operating temperature. Set engine speed to 2000 RPM for at least 10 seconds manually, not using DRB-II.
2) Return engine to idle. If vehicle is equipped with A/C, set A/C fan on low speed. Turn A/C on. If vehicle stalls when A/C is turned on, perform steps **3)** and **4)**. If vehicle does not stall, go to step **5)**.
3) Disconnect and inspect engine controller connector for damaged terminals. Repair connector as necessary. Turn ignition on. Put DRB-II in voltmeter mode. Probe engine controller connector cavity No. 9 (Dark Blue wire).
4) If there is less than 10 volts at cavity No. 9, repair Dark Blue wire. If there are 10 volts or more at cavity No. 9, replace engine controller. Perform VERIFICATION PROCEDURE 2.
5) If vehicle is equipped with automatic transmission, depress brake pedal and shift transmission through all gears. Return shifter to Park. Read faults on DRB-II. If there are still no faults, check if any MITCHELL TECHNICAL SERVICE BULLETINS (TSBs) apply to vehicle relating to driveability problem.
6) If there are no TSBs, perform TEST DR-31A. If there is a TSB, perform corrective action. If driveability problems continue, perform TEST DR-31A.
7) If DRB-II message is "INTERNAL CONTROLLER FAILURE", replace engine controller and perform VERIFICATION PROCEDURE 2. If DRB-II message is "ENGINE IS COLD TOO LONG", repair cooling system as necessary and perform VERIFICATION PROCEDURE 3.
8) Using the DRB-II FAULT MESSAGES table, select the fault message and corresponding test. Correct all hard fault messages before proceeding to intermittent fault message.

Fig. 33: Driveability Test 1A – Checking System for Faults (1 of 2)

DR-1A – CHECKING SYSTEM FOR FAULTS (2 OF 2)

DRB-II FAULT MESSAGES

DRB-II Message	[1] Hard Fault	[2] Intermittent Fault
A/C Clutch Relay Circuit		
AB & AD Bodies	DR-22A	DR-46A
AN Body	DR-21A	DR-46A
Additive Adaptive Memory At Lean Limit	DR-31A	DR-31A
Additive Adaptive Memory At Rich Limit	DR-31A	DR-31A
Air Switching Solenoid Circuit	DR-25A	DR-46A
Automatic Idle Speed Motor Circuits	DR-15A	DR-48A
Controller Failure EEPROM Write Denied	DR-30A	DR-30A
Controller Failure EMR Mileage Not Stored	DR-30A	DR-30A
Coolant Sensor Voltage Too High	DR-9A	DR-47A
Coolant Sensor Voltage Too Low	DR-10A	DR-47A
EGR Solenoid Circuit	DR-19A	DR-46A
EGR System Failure	DR-20A	DR-20A
Idle Switch Shorted Low	DR-23A	DR-23A
Idle Switch Open Circuit	DR-24A	DR-24A
Injector No. 1 Control Circuit	DR-16A	DR-49A
Injector No. 2 Control Circuit	DR-17A	DR-49A
MAP Voltage Too High	DR-5A	DR-47B
MAP Voltage Too Low	DR-4A	DR-47B
No ASD Relay Voltage Sense At Controller	DR-27A	DR-27A
No Change In MAP From Start To Run	DR-3A	DR-47B
No Vehicle Speed Signal	DR-6A	DR-6A
Overdrive Solenoid Circuit		
With Lock-Up	DR-29A	DR-29A
Without Lock-Up	DR-28A	DR-28A
O_2 Signal Shorted To Voltage	DR-8A	DR-8A
O_2 Signal Stays At Center	DR-7A	DR-7A
O_2 Signal Stays Below Center (Lean)	DR-31A	DR-31A
O_2 Signal Stays Above Center (Rich)	DR-31A	DR-31A
Purge Solenoid Circuit	DR-18A	DR-46A
Slow Change In Idle MAP Signal	DR-2A	DR-47B
Throttle Body Temperature High	DR-11A	DR-47A
Throttle Body Temperature Low	DR-12A	DR-47A
Throttle Position Sensor Voltage High	DR-13A	DR-47A
Throttle Position Sensor Voltage Low	DR-14A	DR-47A
Torque Converter Lock-Up Solenoid	DR-26A	DR-46A

[1] – Key counter is "0".
[2] – Key counter is greater than "0".

Fig. 34: Driveability Test 1A – Checking System for Faults (2 of 2)

DR-2A – REPAIRING FAULT "SLOW CHANGE IN IDLE MAP SIGNAL" (1 OF 2)

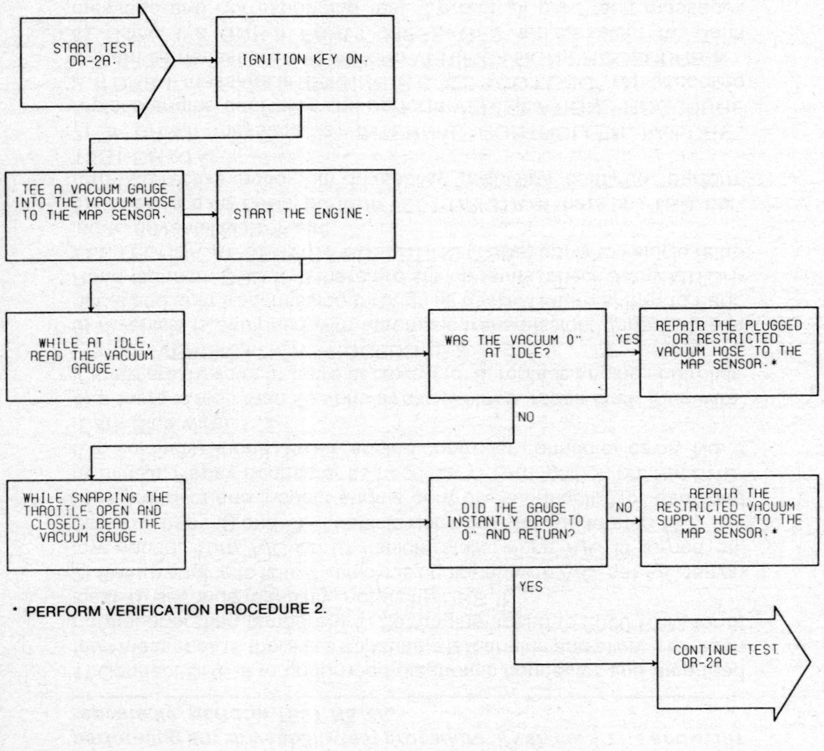
START TEST DR-2A.
IGNITION KEY ON.
TEE A VACUUM GAUGE INTO THE VACUUM HOSE TO THE MAP SENSOR.
START THE ENGINE.
WHILE AT IDLE, READ THE VACUUM GAUGE.
WAS THE VACUUM 0" AT IDLE?
YES
REPAIR THE PLUGGED OR RESTRICTED VACUUM HOSE TO THE MAP SENSOR.*
NO
WHILE SNAPPING THE THROTTLE OPEN AND CLOSED, READ THE VACUUM GAUGE.
DID THE GAUGE INSTANTLY DROP TO 0" AND RETURN?
NO
REPAIR THE RESTRICTED VACUUM SUPPLY HOSE TO THE MAP SENSOR.*
YES
CONTINUE TEST DR-2A

* PERFORM VERIFICATION PROCEDURE 2.

91C14110

Fig. 35: Driveability Test 2A – Repairing Fault "Slow Change In Idle MAP Signal" (1 of 2)

DR-2A – REPAIRING FAULT "SLOW CHANGE IN IDLE MAP SIGNAL" (2 OF 2)

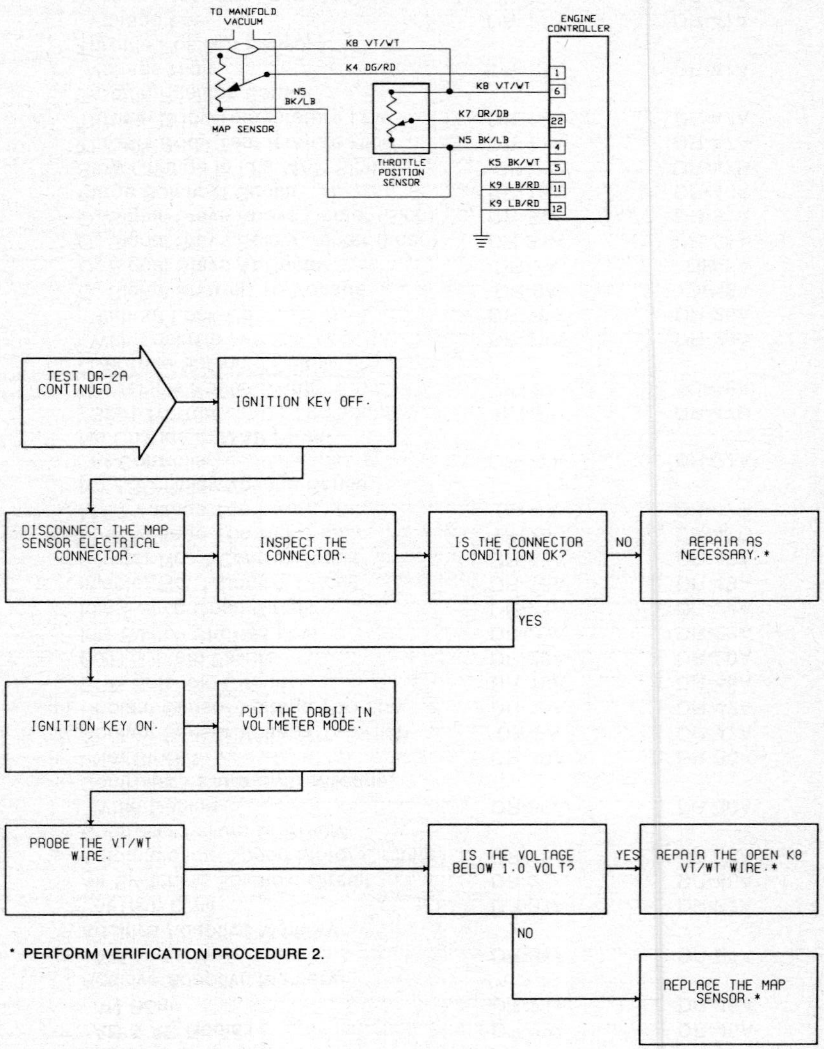
TO MANIFOLD VACUUM
MAP SENSOR
K8 VT/WT
K4 DG/RD
N5 BK/LB
THROTTLE POSITION SENSOR
ENGINE CONTROLLER
K8 VT/WT
K7 OR/DB
N5 BK/LB
K5 BK/WT
K9 LB/RD
K9 LB/RD
1
6
22
4
5
11
12
TEST DR-2A CONTINUED
IGNITION KEY OFF.
DISCONNECT THE MAP SENSOR ELECTRICAL CONNECTOR.
INSPECT THE CONNECTOR.
IS THE CONNECTOR CONDITION OK?
NO
REPAIR AS NECESSARY.*
YES
IGNITION KEY ON.
PUT THE DRBII IN VOLTMETER MODE.
PROBE THE VT/WT WIRE.
IS THE VOLTAGE BELOW 1.0 VOLT?
YES
REPAIR THE OPEN K8 VT/WT WIRE.*
NO
REPLACE THE MAP SENSOR.*

* PERFORM VERIFICATION PROCEDURE 2.

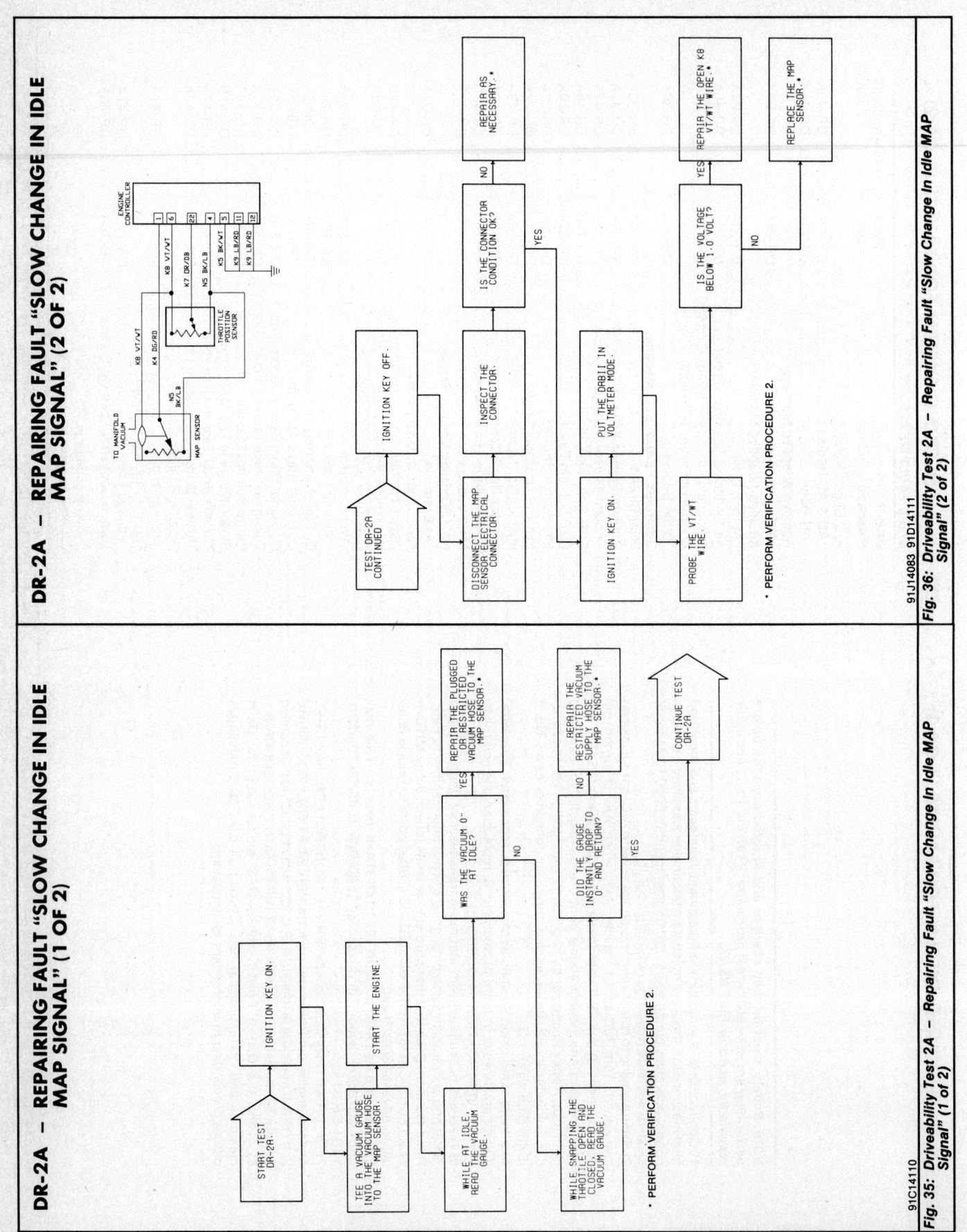

91J14083 91D14111

Fig. 36: Driveability Test 2A – Repairing Fault "Slow Change In Idle MAP Signal" (2 of 2)

DR-3A – REPAIRING FAULT "NO CHANGE IN MAP FROM START TO RUN"

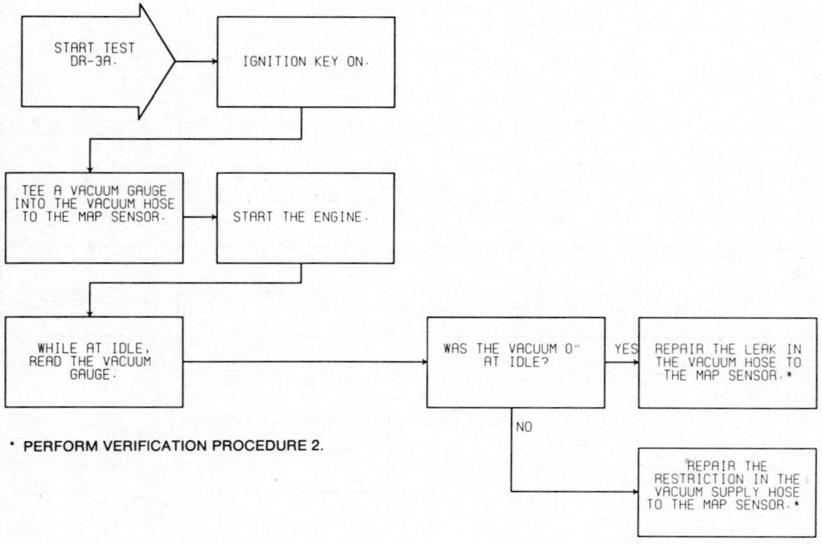
START TEST DR-3A.
IGNITION KEY ON.
TEE A VACUUM GAUGE INTO THE VACUUM HOSE TO THE MAP SENSOR.
START THE ENGINE.
WHILE AT IDLE, READ THE VACUUM GAUGE.
WAS THE VACUUM 0" AT IDLE?
YES
REPAIR THE LEAK IN THE VACUUM HOSE TO THE MAP SENSOR.*
NO
REPAIR THE RESTRICTION IN THE VACUUM SUPPLY HOSE TO THE MAP SENSOR.*

* PERFORM VERIFICATION PROCEDURE 2.

91E14112

Fig. 37: Driveability Test 3A – Repairing Fault "No Change In MAP From Start To Run"

DR-4A – REPAIRING FAULT "MAP VOLTAGE TOO LOW"

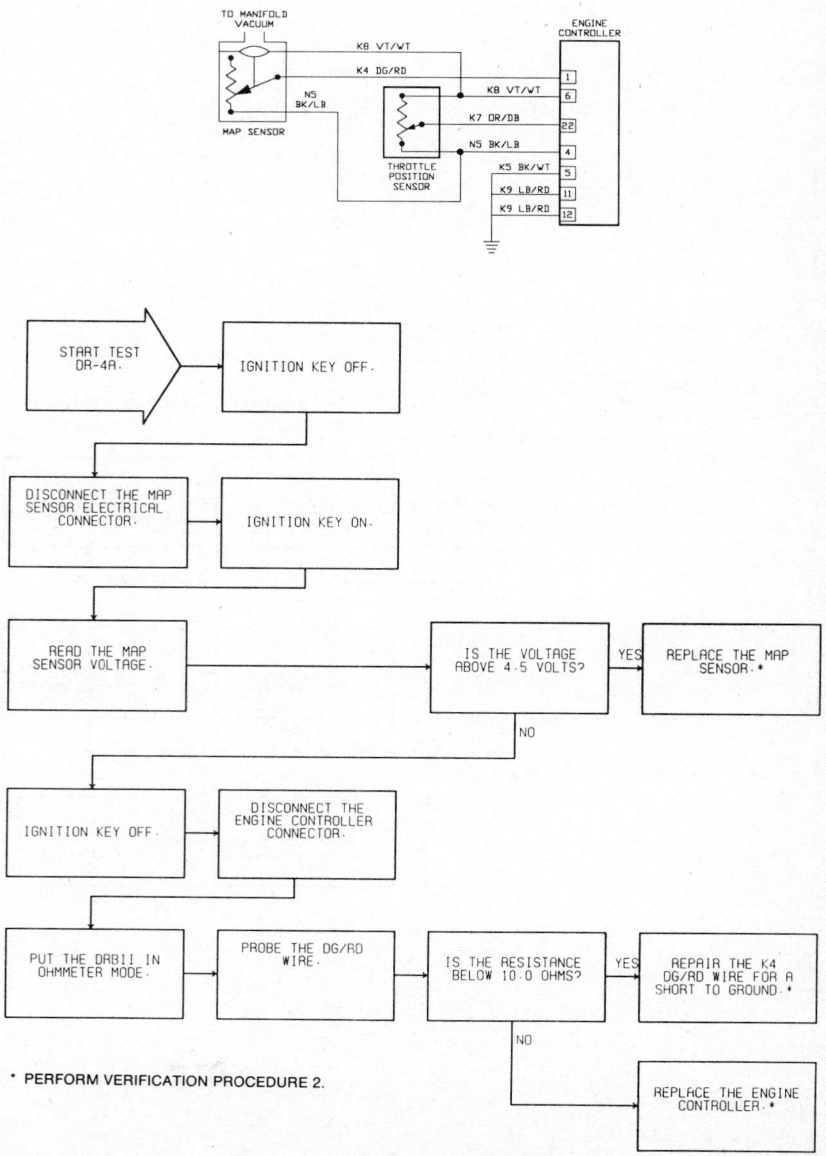
TO MANIFOLD VACUUM
MAP SENSOR
K8 VT/WT
K4 DG/RD
N5 BK/LB
THROTTLE POSITION SENSOR
K7 OR/DB
K5 BK/WT
K9 LB/RD
ENGINE CONTROLLER
1
6
22
4
5
11
12
START TEST DR-4A.
IGNITION KEY OFF.
DISCONNECT THE MAP SENSOR ELECTRICAL CONNECTOR.
IGNITION KEY ON.
READ THE MAP SENSOR VOLTAGE.
IS THE VOLTAGE ABOVE 4.5 VOLTS?
YES
REPLACE THE MAP SENSOR.*
NO
IGNITION KEY OFF.
DISCONNECT THE ENGINE CONTROLLER CONNECTOR.
PUT THE DRBII IN OHMMETER MODE.
PROBE THE DG/RD WIRE.
IS THE RESISTANCE BELOW 10.0 OHMS?
YES
REPAIR THE K4 DG/RD WIRE FOR A SHORT TO GROUND.*
NO
REPLACE THE ENGINE CONTROLLER.*

* PERFORM VERIFICATION PROCEDURE 2.

91J14083 91F14113

Fig. 38: Driveability Test 4A – Repairing Fault "MAP Voltage Too Low"

DR-5A – REPAIRING FAULT "MAP VOLTAGE TOO HIGH" (1 OF 2)

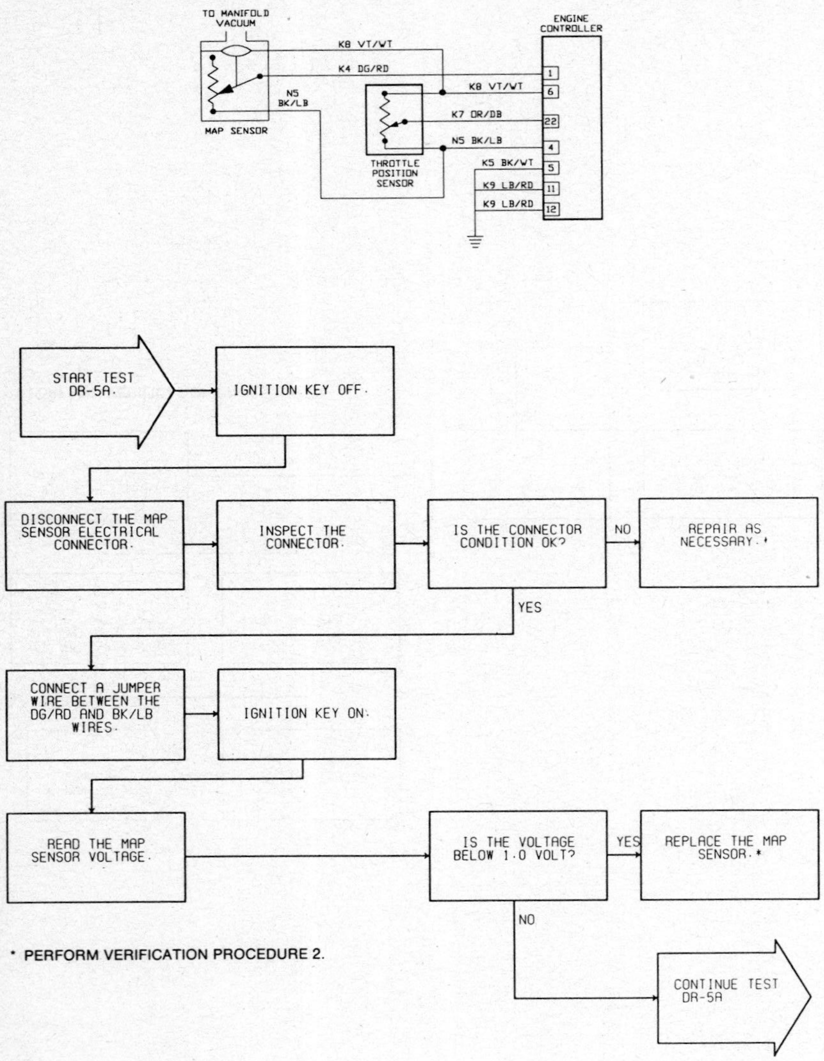
TO MANIFOLD VACUUM
MAP SENSOR
K8 VT/WT
K4 DG/RD
N5 BK/LB
THROTTLE POSITION SENSOR
K8 VT/WT
K7 OR/DB
N5 BK/LB
K5 BK/WT
K9 LB/RD
K9 LB/RD
ENGINE CONTROLLER
1
6
22
4
5
11
12
START TEST DR-5A.
IGNITION KEY OFF.
DISCONNECT THE MAP SENSOR ELECTRICAL CONNECTOR.
INSPECT THE CONNECTOR.
IS THE CONNECTOR CONDITION OK?
NO
REPAIR AS NECESSARY.*
YES
CONNECT A JUMPER WIRE BETWEEN THE DG/RD AND BK/LB WIRES.
IGNITION KEY ON.
READ THE MAP SENSOR VOLTAGE.
IS THE VOLTAGE BELOW 1.0 VOLT?
YES
REPLACE THE MAP SENSOR.*
NO
CONTINUE TEST DR-5A
* PERFORM VERIFICATION PROCEDURE 2.

91J14083 91G14114

Fig. 39: Driveability Test 5A – Repairing Fault "MAP Voltage Too High" (1 of 2)

DR-5A – REPAIRING FAULT "MAP VOLTAGE TOO HIGH" (2 OF 2)

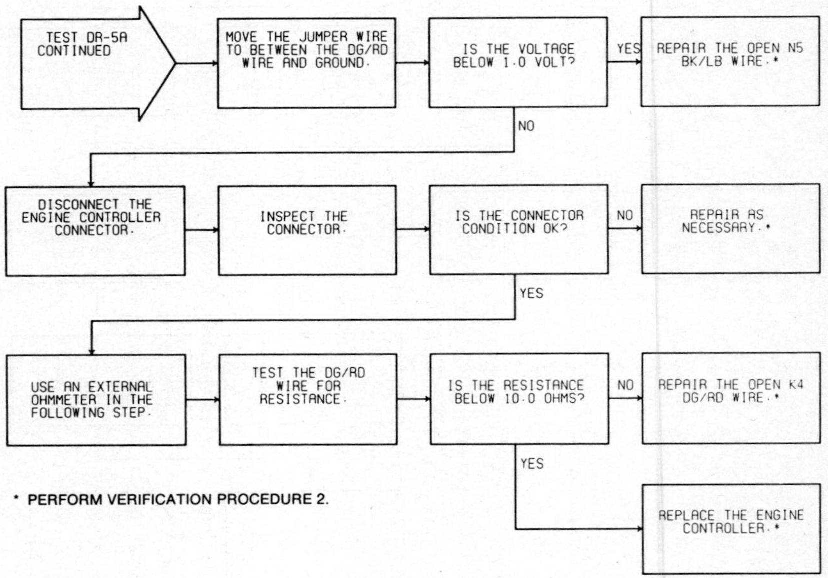
TEST DR-5A CONTINUED
MOVE THE JUMPER WIRE TO BETWEEN THE DG/RD WIRE AND GROUND.
IS THE VOLTAGE BELOW 1.0 VOLT?
YES
REPAIR THE OPEN N5 BK/LB WIRE.*
NO
DISCONNECT THE ENGINE CONTROLLER CONNECTOR.
INSPECT THE CONNECTOR.
IS THE CONNECTOR CONDITION OK?
NO
REPAIR AS NECESSARY.*
YES
USE AN EXTERNAL OHMMETER IN THE FOLLOWING STEP.
TEST THE DG/RD WIRE FOR RESISTANCE.
IS THE RESISTANCE BELOW 10.0 OHMS?
NO
REPAIR THE OPEN K4 DG/RD WIRE.*
YES
REPLACE THE ENGINE CONTROLLER.*
* PERFORM VERIFICATION PROCEDURE 2.

91H14115

Fig. 40: Driveability Test 5A – Repairing Fault "MAP Voltage Too High" (2 of 2)

DR-6A – REPAIRING FAULT "NO VEHICLE SPEED SIGNAL" (1 OF 3)

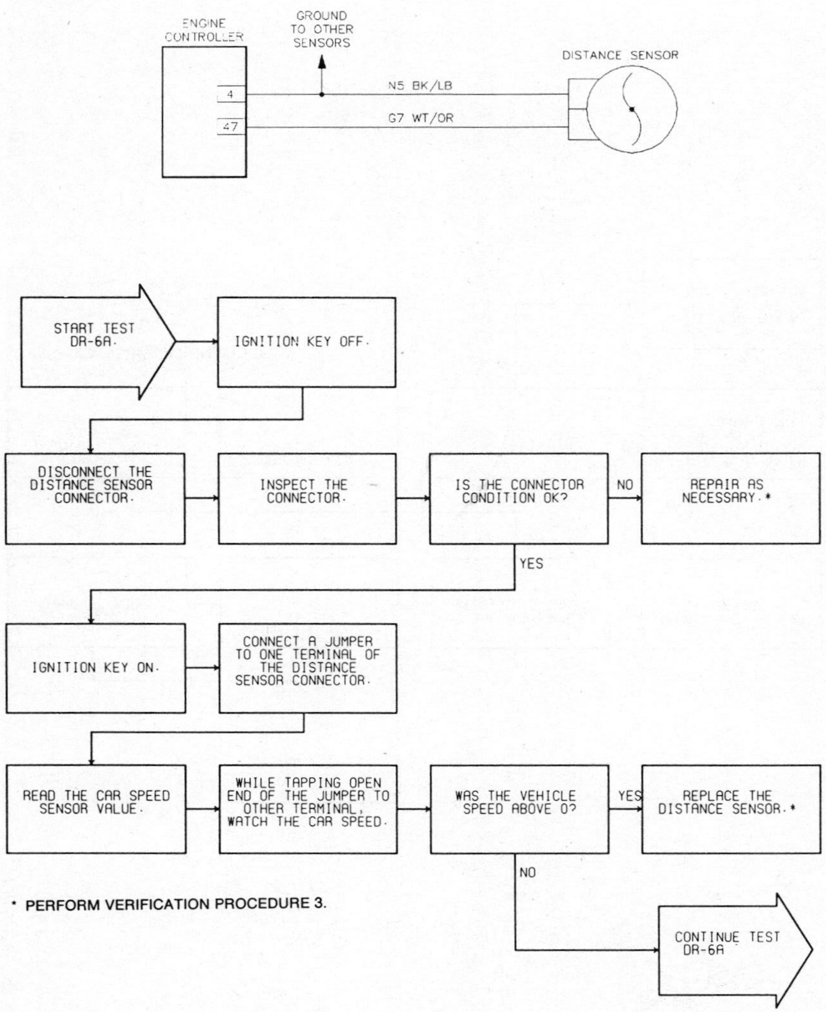
ENGINE CONTROLLER
GROUND TO OTHER SENSORS
DISTANCE SENSOR
4
47
N5 BK/LB
G7 WT/OR
START TEST DR-6A.
IGNITION KEY OFF.
DISCONNECT THE DISTANCE SENSOR CONNECTOR.
INSPECT THE CONNECTOR.
IS THE CONNECTOR CONDITION OK?
NO
REPAIR AS NECESSARY.*
YES
IGNITION KEY ON.
CONNECT A JUMPER TO ONE TERMINAL OF THE DISTANCE SENSOR CONNECTOR.
READ THE CAR SPEED SENSOR VALUE.
WHILE TAPPING OPEN END OF THE JUMPER TO OTHER TERMINAL, WATCH THE CAR SPEED.
WAS THE VEHICLE SPEED ABOVE 0?
YES
REPLACE THE DISTANCE SENSOR.*
NO
CONTINUE TEST DR-6A

* PERFORM VERIFICATION PROCEDURE 3.

91I14116 91J14117

Fig. 41: Driveability Test 6A – Repairing Fault "No Vehicle Speed Signal" (1 of 3)

DR-6A – REPAIRING FAULT "NO VEHICLE SPEED SIGNAL" (2 OF 3)

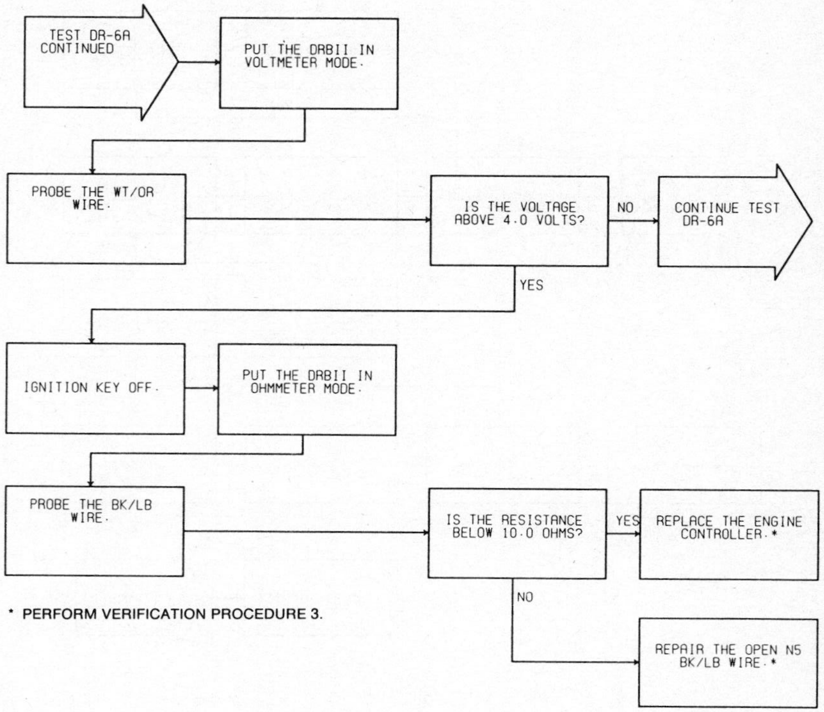
TEST DR-6A CONTINUED
PUT THE DRBII IN VOLTMETER MODE.
PROBE THE WT/OR WIRE.
IS THE VOLTAGE ABOVE 4.0 VOLTS?
NO
CONTINUE TEST DR-6A
YES
IGNITION KEY OFF.
PUT THE DRBII IN OHMMETER MODE.
PROBE THE BK/LB WIRE.
IS THE RESISTANCE BELOW 10.0 OHMS?
YES
REPLACE THE ENGINE CONTROLLER.*
NO
REPAIR THE OPEN N5 BK/LB WIRE.*

* PERFORM VERIFICATION PROCEDURE 3.

91A14118

Fig. 42: Driveability Test 6A – Repairing Fault "No Vehicle Speed Signal" (2 of 3)

DR-6A – REPAIRING FAULT "NO VEHICLE SPEED SIGNAL" (3 OF 3)

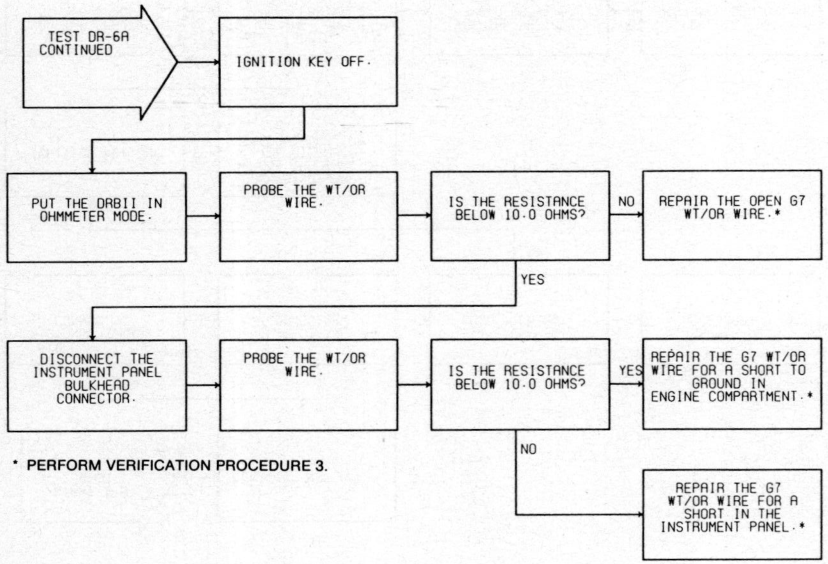
TEST DR-6A CONTINUED
IGNITION KEY OFF.
PUT THE DRBII IN OHMMETER MODE.
PROBE THE WT/OR WIRE.
IS THE RESISTANCE BELOW 10.0 OHMS?
NO
REPAIR THE OPEN G7 WT/OR WIRE.*
YES
DISCONNECT THE INSTRUMENT PANEL BULKHEAD CONNECTOR.
PROBE THE WT/OR WIRE.
IS THE RESISTANCE BELOW 10.0 OHMS?
YES
REPAIR THE G7 WT/OR WIRE FOR A SHORT TO GROUND IN ENGINE COMPARTMENT.*
NO
REPAIR THE G7 WT/OR WIRE FOR A SHORT IN THE INSTRUMENT PANEL.*

* PERFORM VERIFICATION PROCEDURE 3.

91B14119

Fig. 43: Driveability Test 6A – Repairing Fault "No Vehicle Speed Signal" (3 of 3)

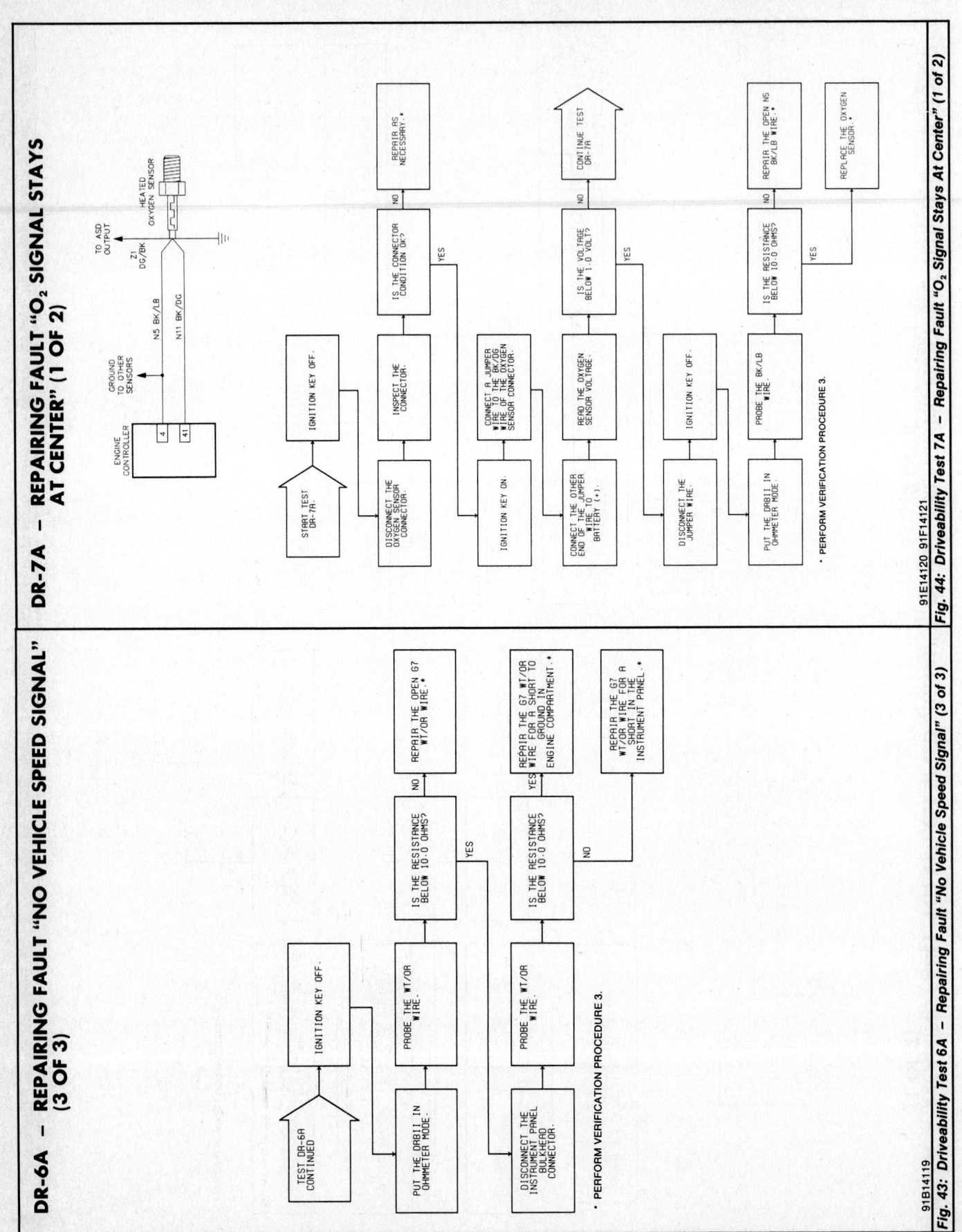

DR-7A – REPAIRING FAULT "O_2 SIGNAL STAYS AT CENTER" (1 OF 2)

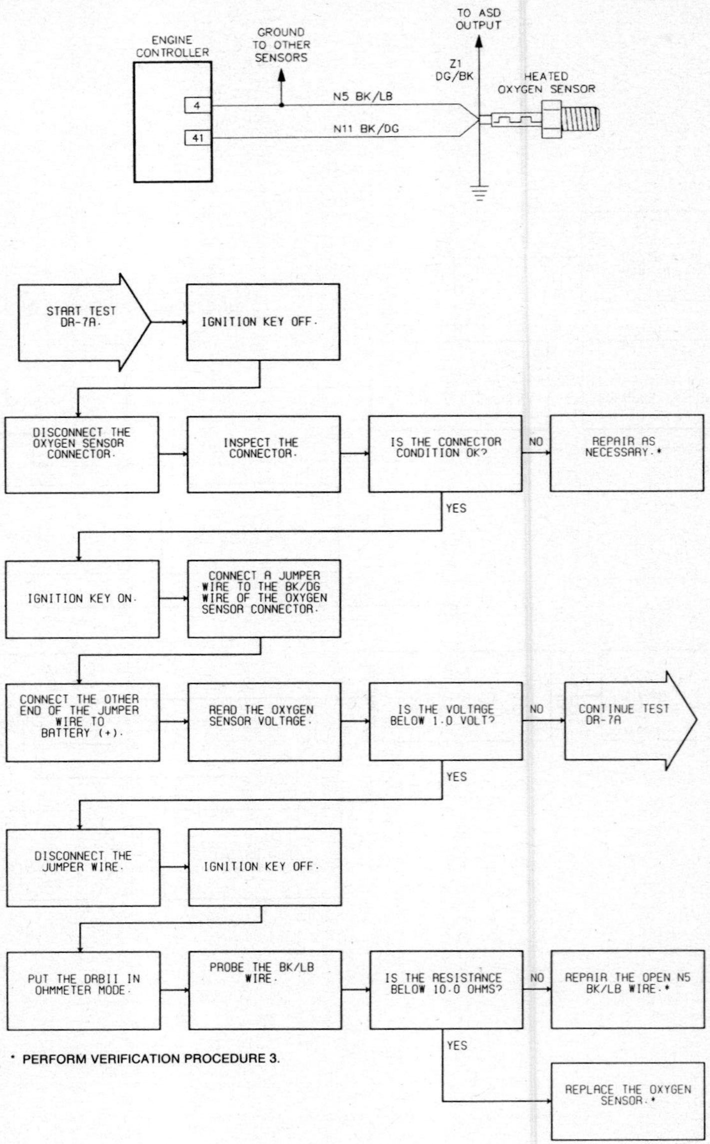
ENGINE CONTROLLER
4
41
GROUND TO OTHER SENSORS
N5 BK/LB
N11 BK/DG
Z1 DG/BK
TO ASD OUTPUT
HEATED OXYGEN SENSOR
START TEST DR-7A.
IGNITION KEY OFF.
DISCONNECT THE OXYGEN SENSOR CONNECTOR.
INSPECT THE CONNECTOR.
IS THE CONNECTOR CONDITION OK?
NO
REPAIR AS NECESSARY.*
YES
IGNITION KEY ON.
CONNECT A JUMPER WIRE TO THE BK/DG WIRE OF THE OXYGEN SENSOR CONNECTOR.
CONNECT THE OTHER END OF THE JUMPER WIRE TO BATTERY (+).
READ THE OXYGEN SENSOR VOLTAGE.
IS THE VOLTAGE BELOW 1.0 VOLT?
NO
CONTINUE TEST DR-7A
YES
DISCONNECT THE JUMPER WIRE.
IGNITION KEY OFF.
PUT THE DRBII IN OHMMETER MODE.
PROBE THE BK/LB WIRE.
IS THE RESISTANCE BELOW 10.0 OHMS?
NO
REPAIR THE OPEN N5 BK/LB WIRE.*
YES
REPLACE THE OXYGEN SENSOR.*

* PERFORM VERIFICATION PROCEDURE 3.

91E14120 91F14121

Fig. 44: Driveability Test 7A – Repairing Fault "O_2 Signal Stays At Center" (1 of 2)

DR-7A – REPAIRING FAULT "O_2 SIGNAL STAYS AT CENTER" (2 OF 2)

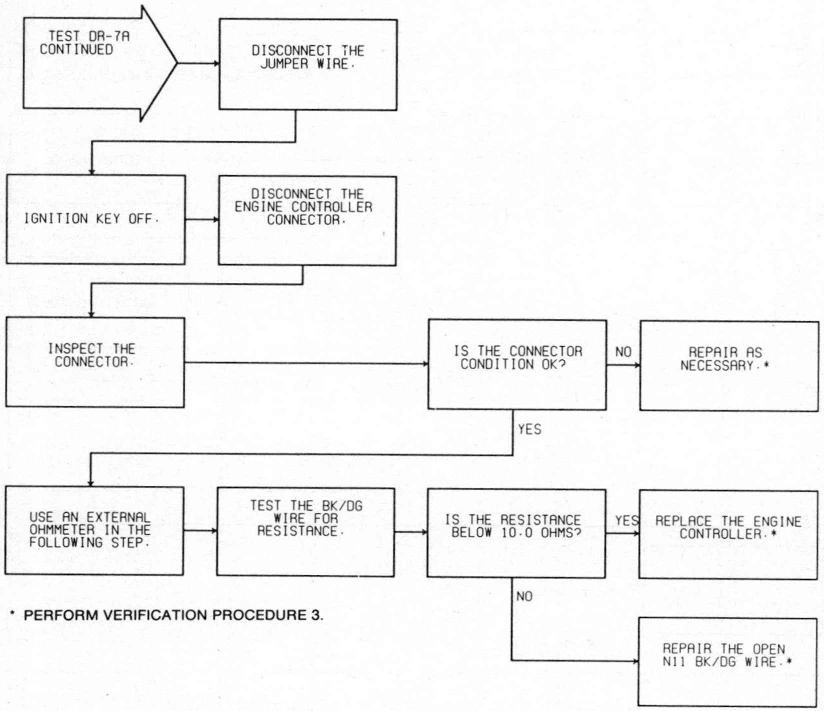
TEST DR-7A CONTINUED
DISCONNECT THE JUMPER WIRE.
IGNITION KEY OFF.
DISCONNECT THE ENGINE CONTROLLER CONNECTOR.
INSPECT THE CONNECTOR.
IS THE CONNECTOR CONDITION OK?
NO
REPAIR AS NECESSARY.*
YES
USE AN EXTERNAL OHMMETER IN THE FOLLOWING STEP.
TEST THE BK/DG WIRE FOR RESISTANCE.
IS THE RESISTANCE BELOW 10.0 OHMS?
YES
REPLACE THE ENGINE CONTROLLER.*
NO
REPAIR THE OPEN N11 BK/DG WIRE.*

* PERFORM VERIFICATION PROCEDURE 3.

91G14122

Fig. 45: Driveability Test 7A – Repairing Fault "O_2 Signal Stays At Center" (2 of 2)

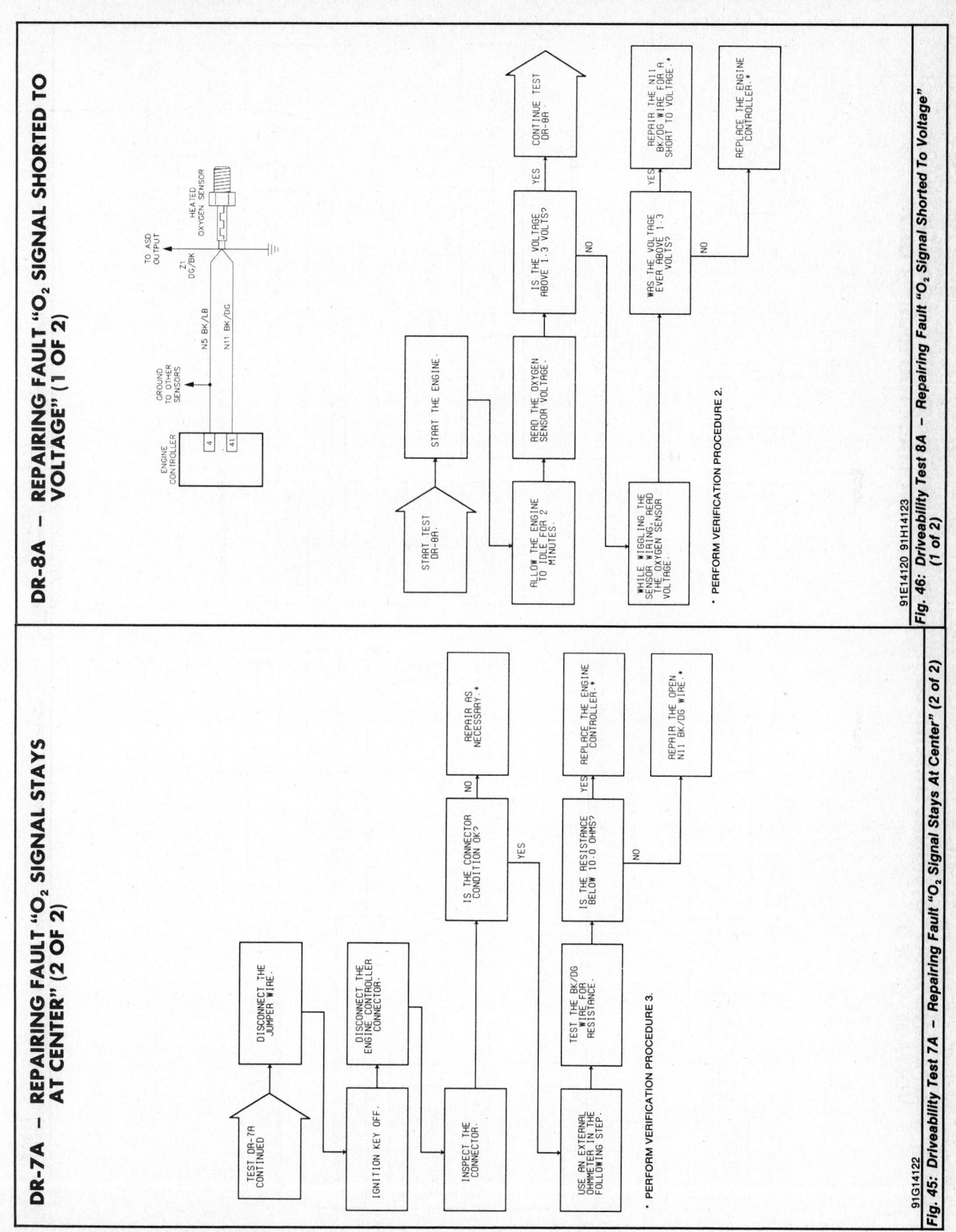

DR-8A – REPAIRING FAULT "O_2 SIGNAL SHORTED TO VOLTAGE" (1 OF 2)

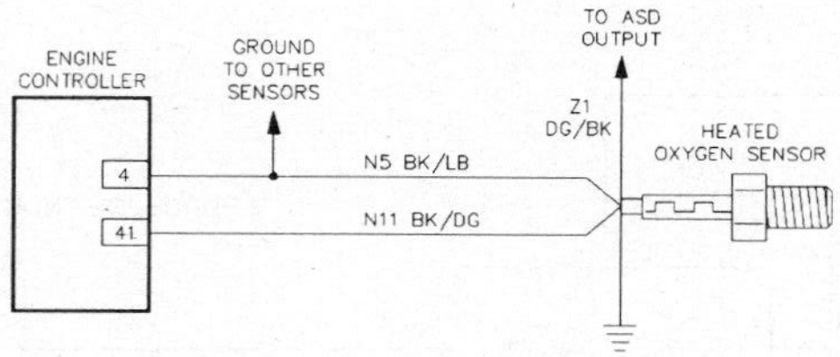
ENGINE CONTROLLER
4
41
GROUND TO OTHER SENSORS
N5 BK/LB
N11 BK/DG
TO ASD OUTPUT
Z1 DG/BK
HEATED OXYGEN SENSOR

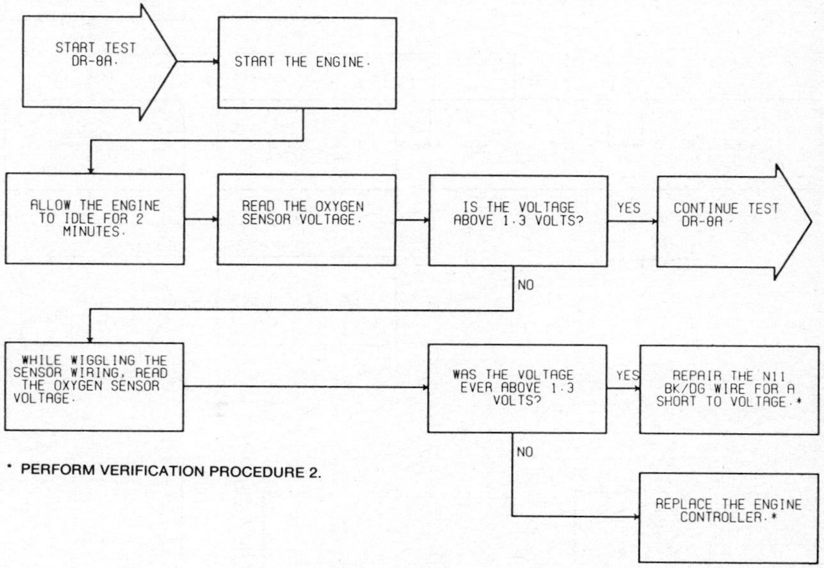
START TEST DR-8A.
START THE ENGINE.
ALLOW THE ENGINE TO IDLE FOR 2 MINUTES.
READ THE OXYGEN SENSOR VOLTAGE.
IS THE VOLTAGE ABOVE 1.3 VOLTS?
YES
CONTINUE TEST DR-8A.
NO
WHILE WIGGLING THE SENSOR WIRING, READ THE OXYGEN SENSOR VOLTAGE.
WAS THE VOLTAGE EVER ABOVE 1.3 VOLTS?
YES
REPAIR THE N11 BK/DG WIRE FOR A SHORT TO VOLTAGE.*
NO
REPLACE THE ENGINE CONTROLLER.*

* PERFORM VERIFICATION PROCEDURE 2.

91E14120 91H14123

Fig. 46: Driveability Test 8A – Repairing Fault "O_2 Signal Shorted To Voltage" (1 of 2)

1991 ENGINE PERFORMANCE
Self-Diagnostics – 3.9L, 5.2L & 5.9L TBI (Cont.)

DR-8A – REPAIRING FAULT "O_2 SIGNAL SHORTED TO VOLTAGE" (2 OF 2)

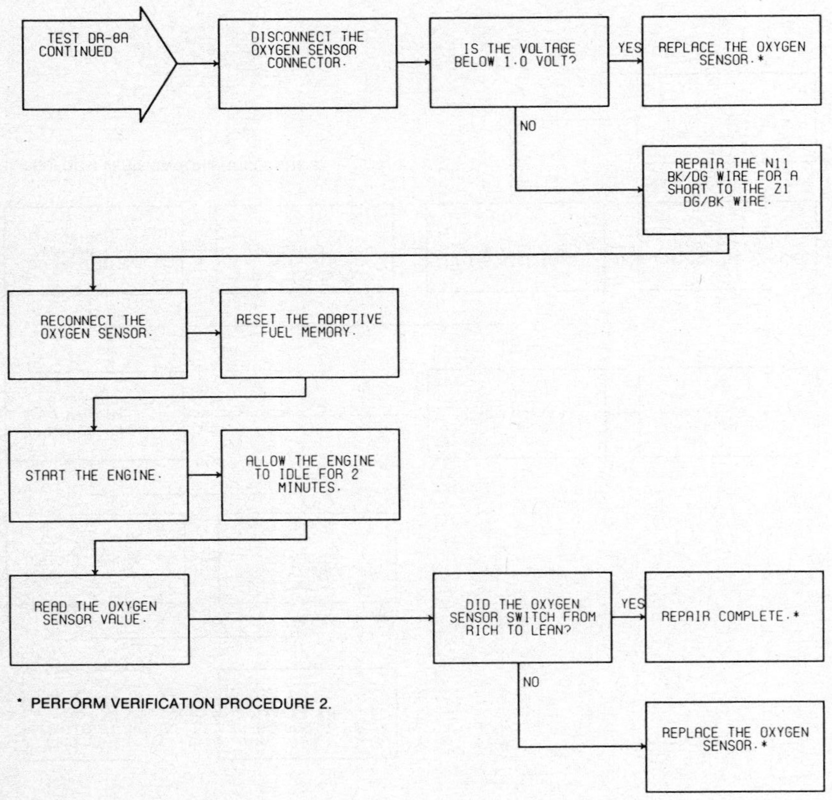
TEST DR-8A CONTINUED
DISCONNECT THE OXYGEN SENSOR CONNECTOR.
IS THE VOLTAGE BELOW 1.0 VOLT?
YES
REPLACE THE OXYGEN SENSOR.*
NO
REPAIR THE N11 BK/DG WIRE FOR A SHORT TO THE Z1 DG/BK WIRE.
RECONNECT THE OXYGEN SENSOR.
RESET THE ADAPTIVE FUEL MEMORY.
START THE ENGINE.
ALLOW THE ENGINE TO IDLE FOR 2 MINUTES.
READ THE OXYGEN SENSOR VALUE.
DID THE OXYGEN SENSOR SWITCH FROM RICH TO LEAN?
YES
REPAIR COMPLETE.*
NO
REPLACE THE OXYGEN SENSOR.*

* PERFORM VERIFICATION PROCEDURE 2.

91I14124

Fig. 47: Driveability Test 8A – Repairing Fault "O_2 Signal Shorted To Voltage" (2 of 2)

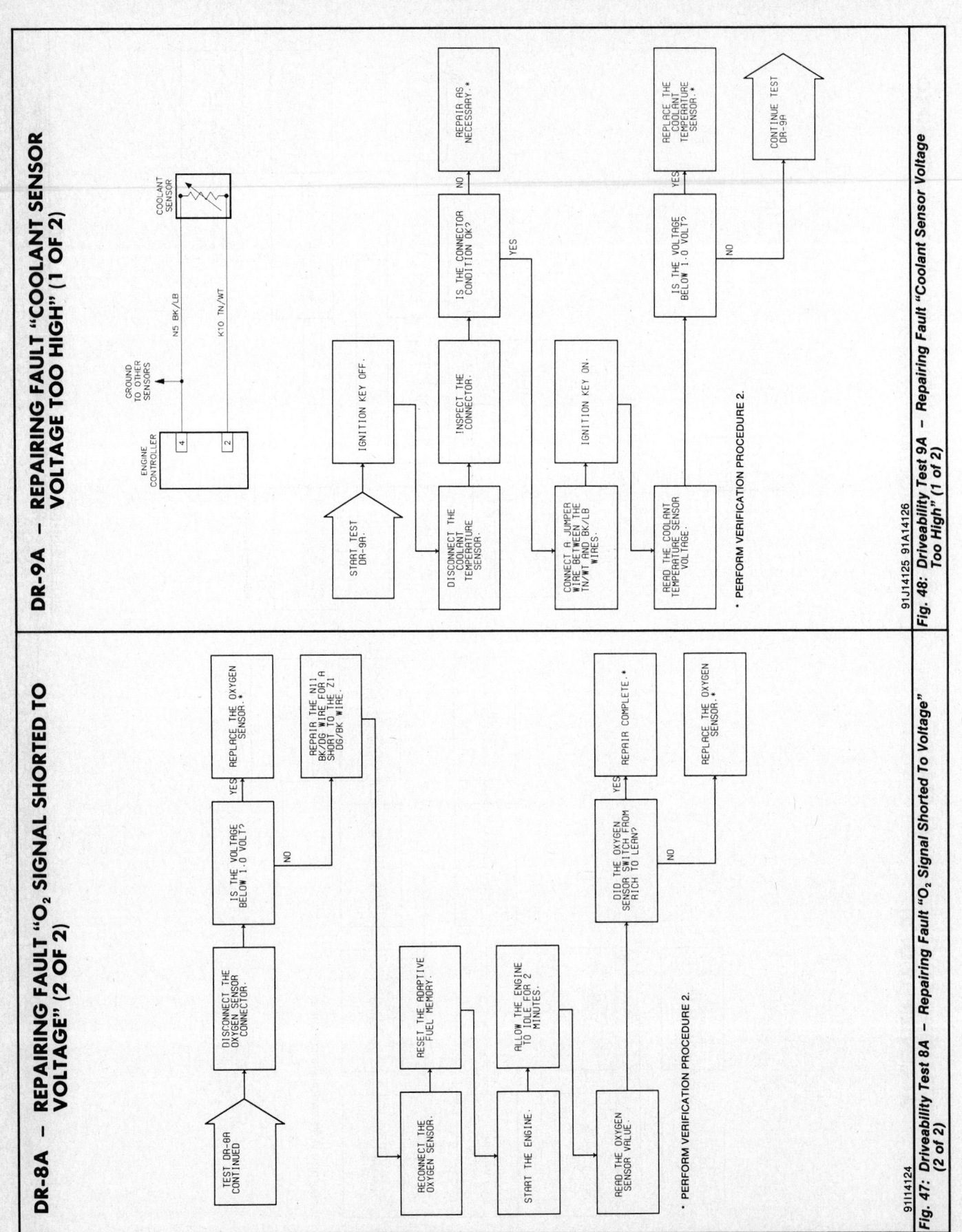

DR-9A – REPAIRING FAULT "COOLANT SENSOR VOLTAGE TOO HIGH" (1 OF 2)

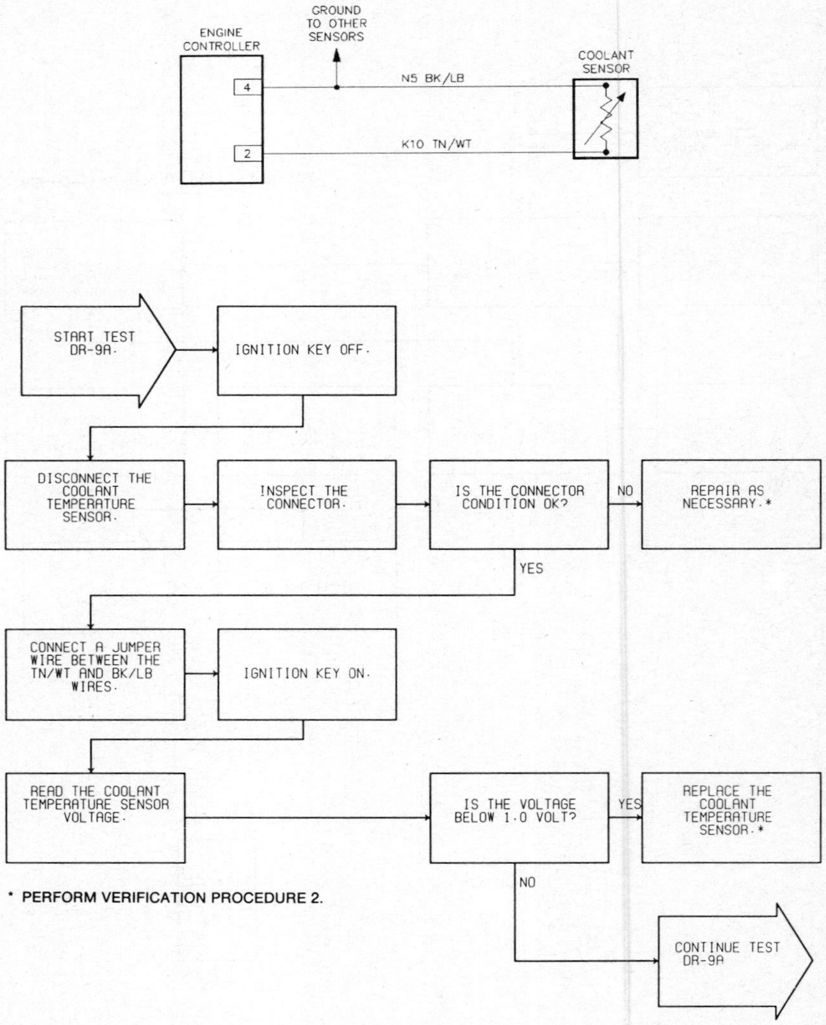
ENGINE CONTROLLER
GROUND TO OTHER SENSORS
COOLANT SENSOR
4
2
N5 BK/LB
K10 TN/WT
START TEST DR-9A.
IGNITION KEY OFF.
DISCONNECT THE COOLANT TEMPERATURE SENSOR.
INSPECT THE CONNECTOR.
IS THE CONNECTOR CONDITION OK?
NO
REPAIR AS NECESSARY.*
YES
CONNECT A JUMPER WIRE BETWEEN THE TN/WT AND BK/LB WIRES.
IGNITION KEY ON.
READ THE COOLANT TEMPERATURE SENSOR VOLTAGE.
IS THE VOLTAGE BELOW 1.0 VOLT?
YES
REPLACE THE COOLANT TEMPERATURE SENSOR.*
NO
CONTINUE TEST DR-9A

* PERFORM VERIFICATION PROCEDURE 2.

91J14125 91A14126

Fig. 48: Driveability Test 9A – Repairing Fault "Coolant Sensor Voltage Too High" (1 of 2)

DR-9A – REPAIRING FAULT "COOLANT SENSOR VOLTAGE TOO HIGH" (2 OF 2)

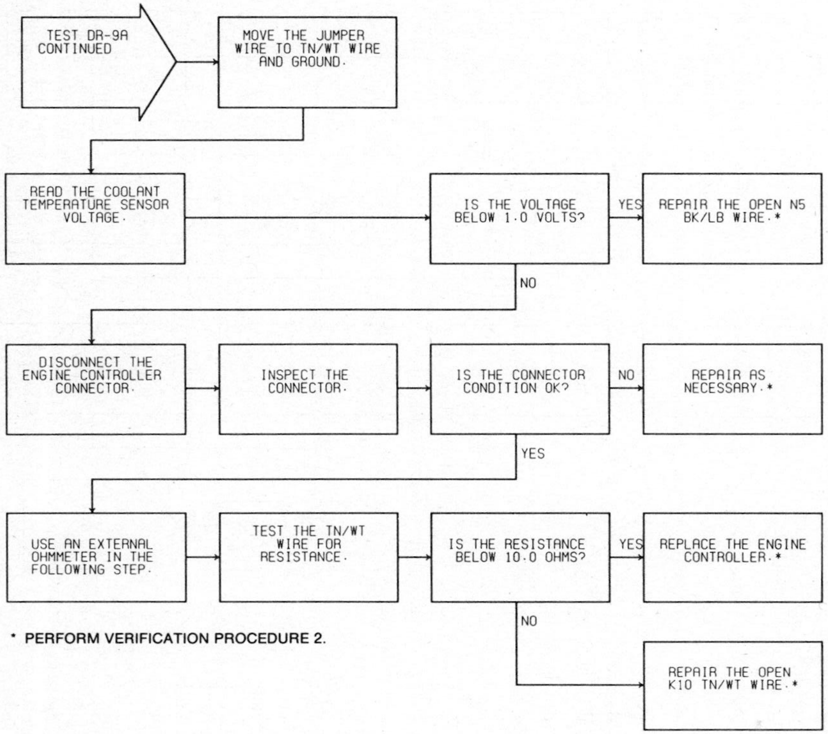
TEST DR-9A CONTINUED
MOVE THE JUMPER WIRE TO TN/WT WIRE AND GROUND.
READ THE COOLANT TEMPERATURE SENSOR VOLTAGE.
IS THE VOLTAGE BELOW 1.0 VOLTS?
YES
REPAIR THE OPEN N5 BK/LB WIRE.*
NO
DISCONNECT THE ENGINE CONTROLLER CONNECTOR.
INSPECT THE CONNECTOR.
IS THE CONNECTOR CONDITION OK?
NO
REPAIR AS NECESSARY.*
YES
USE AN EXTERNAL OHMMETER IN THE FOLLOWING STEP.
TEST THE TN/WT WIRE FOR RESISTANCE.
IS THE RESISTANCE BELOW 10.0 OHMS?
YES
REPLACE THE ENGINE CONTROLLER.*
NO
REPAIR THE OPEN K10 TN/WT WIRE.*

* PERFORM VERIFICATION PROCEDURE 2.

91B14127

Fig. 49: Driveability Test 9A – Repairing Fault "Coolant Sensor Voltage Too High" (2 of 2)

DR-10A – REPAIRING FAULT "COOLANT SENSOR VOLTAGE TOO LOW"

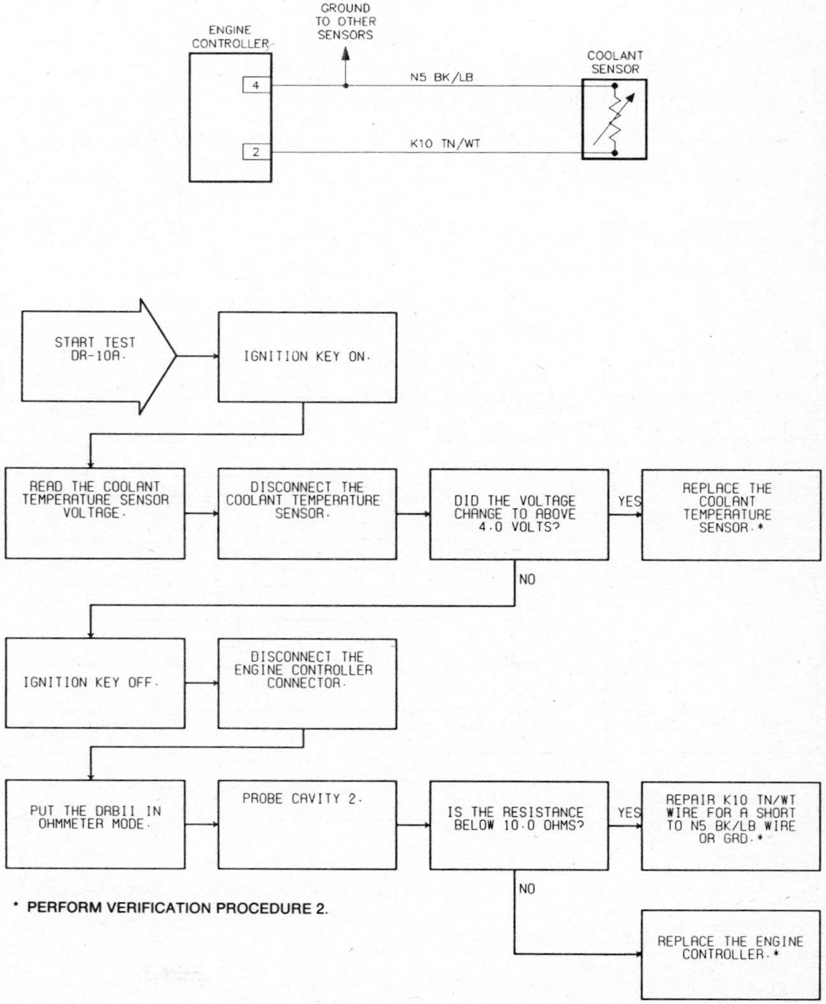
ENGINE CONTROLLER
GROUND TO OTHER SENSORS
4
2
N5 BK/LB
K10 TN/WT
COOLANT SENSOR
START TEST DR-10A.
IGNITION KEY ON.
READ THE COOLANT TEMPERATURE SENSOR VOLTAGE.
DISCONNECT THE COOLANT TEMPERATURE SENSOR.
DID THE VOLTAGE CHANGE TO ABOVE 4.0 VOLTS?
YES
REPLACE THE COOLANT TEMPERATURE SENSOR.*
NO
IGNITION KEY OFF.
DISCONNECT THE ENGINE CONTROLLER CONNECTOR.
PUT THE DRBII IN OHMMETER MODE.
PROBE CAVITY 2.
IS THE RESISTANCE BELOW 10.0 OHMS?
YES
REPAIR K10 TN/WT WIRE FOR A SHORT TO N5 BK/LB WIRE OR GRD.*
NO
REPLACE THE ENGINE CONTROLLER.*

* PERFORM VERIFICATION PROCEDURE 2.

91J14125 91C14128

Fig. 50: Driveability Test 10A – Repairing Fault "Coolant Sensor Voltage Too Low"

1991 ENGINE PERFORMANCE
Self-Diagnostics – 3.9L, 5.2L & 5.9L TBI (Cont.)

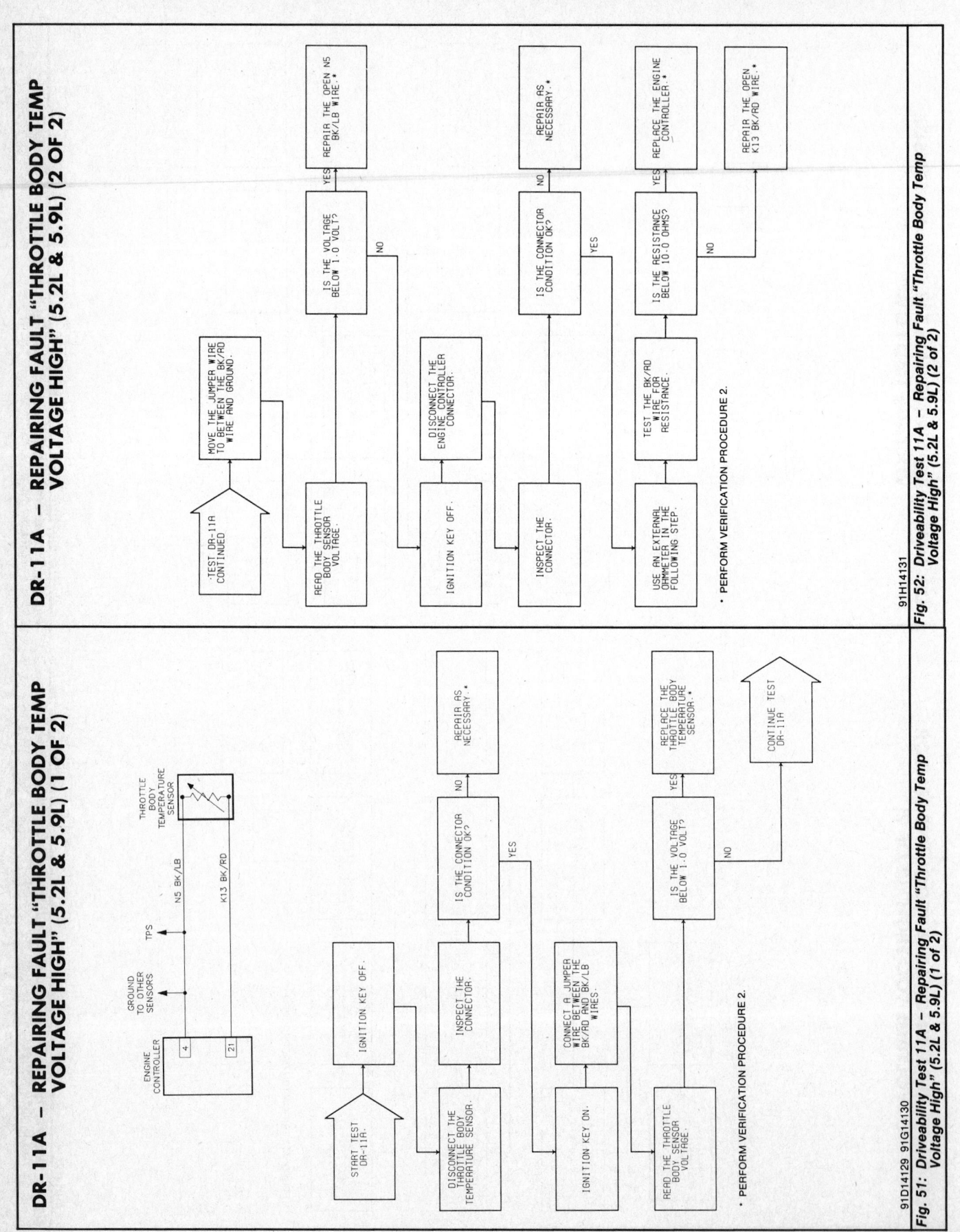

DR-11A – REPAIRING FAULT "THROTTLE BODY TEMP VOLTAGE HIGH" (5.2L & 5.9L) (1 OF 2)

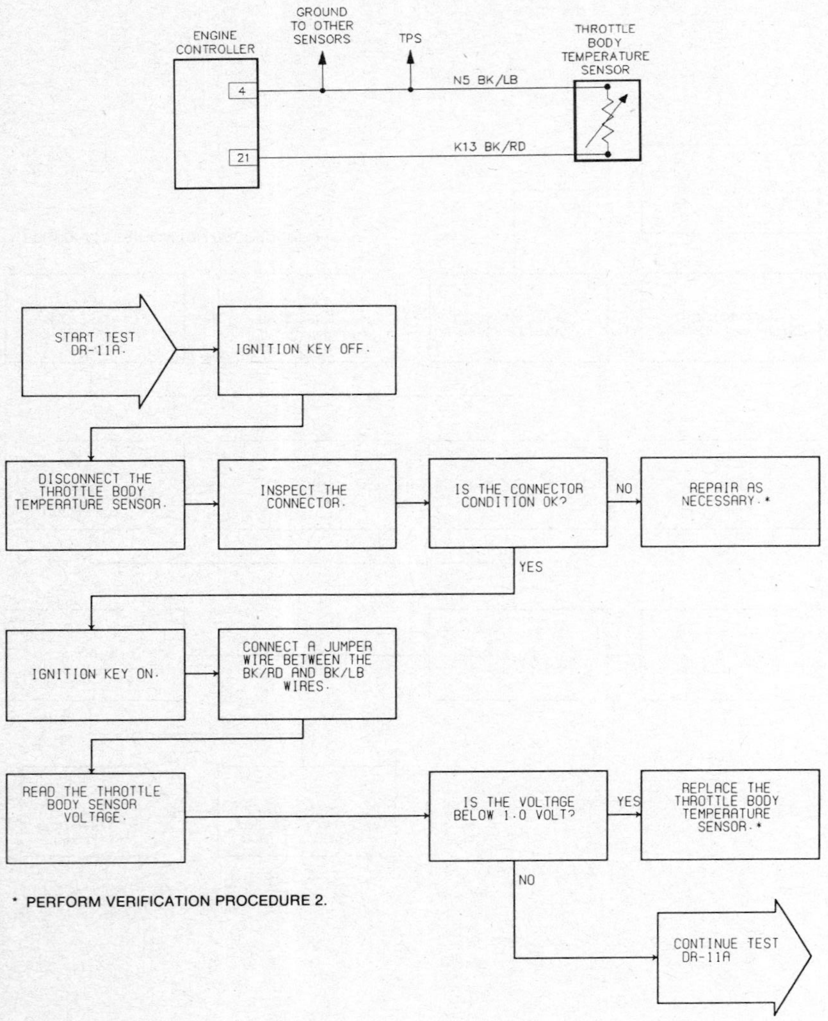
ENGINE CONTROLLER
GROUND TO OTHER SENSORS
TPS
THROTTLE BODY TEMPERATURE SENSOR
4
21
N5 BK/LB
K13 BK/RD
START TEST DR-11A.
IGNITION KEY OFF.
DISCONNECT THE THROTTLE BODY TEMPERATURE SENSOR.
INSPECT THE CONNECTOR.
IS THE CONNECTOR CONDITION OK?
NO
REPAIR AS NECESSARY.*
YES
IGNITION KEY ON.
CONNECT A JUMPER WIRE BETWEEN THE BK/RD AND BK/LB WIRES.
READ THE THROTTLE BODY SENSOR VOLTAGE.
IS THE VOLTAGE BELOW 1.0 VOLT?
YES
REPLACE THE THROTTLE BODY TEMPERATURE SENSOR.*
NO
CONTINUE TEST DR-11A

* PERFORM VERIFICATION PROCEDURE 2.

91D14129 91G14130

Fig. 51: Driveability Test 11A – Repairing Fault "Throttle Body Temp Voltage High" (5.2L & 5.9L) (1 of 2)

DR-11A – REPAIRING FAULT "THROTTLE BODY TEMP VOLTAGE HIGH" (5.2L & 5.9L) (2 OF 2)

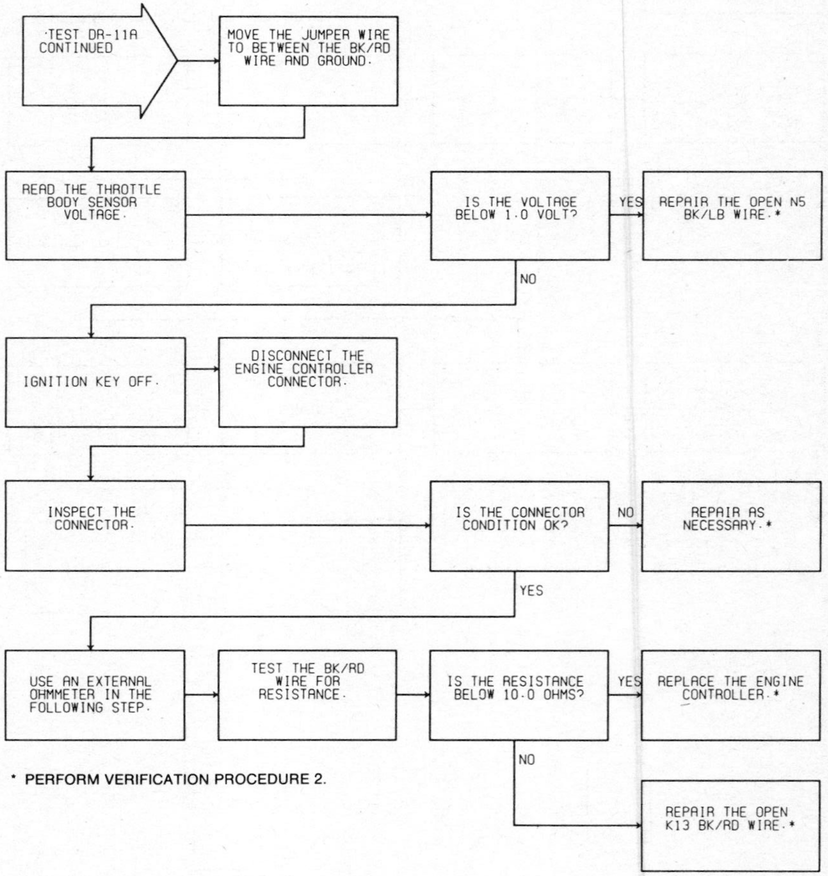
TEST DR-11A CONTINUED
MOVE THE JUMPER WIRE TO BETWEEN THE BK/RD WIRE AND GROUND.
READ THE THROTTLE BODY SENSOR VOLTAGE.
IS THE VOLTAGE BELOW 1.0 VOLT?
YES
REPAIR THE OPEN N5 BK/LB WIRE.*
NO
IGNITION KEY OFF.
DISCONNECT THE ENGINE CONTROLLER CONNECTOR.
INSPECT THE CONNECTOR.
IS THE CONNECTOR CONDITION OK?
NO
REPAIR AS NECESSARY.*
YES
USE AN EXTERNAL OHMMETER IN THE FOLLOWING STEP.
TEST THE BK/RD WIRE FOR RESISTANCE.
IS THE RESISTANCE BELOW 10.0 OHMS?
YES
REPLACE THE ENGINE CONTROLLER.*
NO
REPAIR THE OPEN K13 BK/RD WIRE.*

* PERFORM VERIFICATION PROCEDURE 2.

91H14131

Fig. 52: Driveability Test 11A – Repairing Fault "Throttle Body Temp Voltage High" (5.2L & 5.9L) (2 of 2)

DR-12A – REPAIRING FAULT "THROTTLE BODY TEMP VOLTAGE LOW" (5.2L & 5.9L)

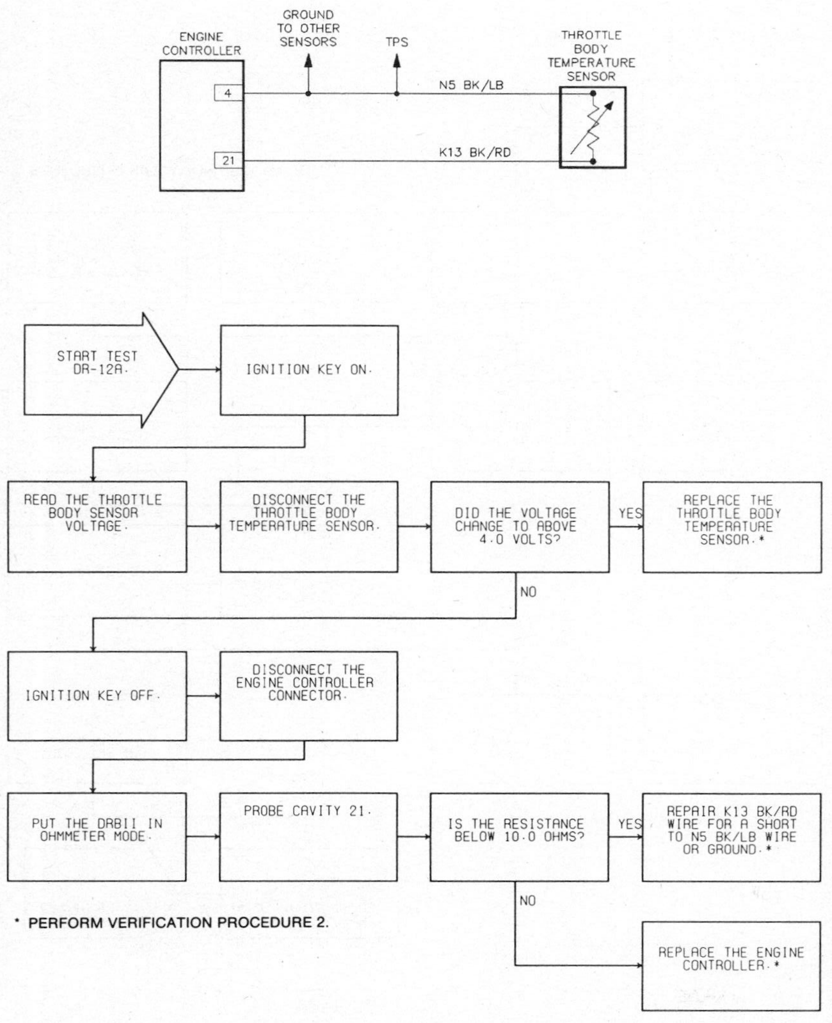
ENGINE CONTROLLER
4
21
GROUND TO OTHER SENSORS
TPS
N5 BK/LB
K13 BK/RD
THROTTLE BODY TEMPERATURE SENSOR
START TEST DR-12A.
IGNITION KEY ON.
READ THE THROTTLE BODY SENSOR VOLTAGE.
DISCONNECT THE THROTTLE BODY TEMPERATURE SENSOR.
DID THE VOLTAGE CHANGE TO ABOVE 4.0 VOLTS?
YES
REPLACE THE THROTTLE BODY TEMPERATURE SENSOR.*
NO
IGNITION KEY OFF.
DISCONNECT THE ENGINE CONTROLLER CONNECTOR.
PUT THE DRBII IN OHMMETER MODE.
PROBE CAVITY 21.
IS THE RESISTANCE BELOW 10.0 OHMS?
YES
REPAIR K13 BK/RD WIRE FOR A SHORT TO N5 BK/LB WIRE OR GROUND.*
NO
REPLACE THE ENGINE CONTROLLER.*

* PERFORM VERIFICATION PROCEDURE 2.

91D14129 91I14132

Fig. 53: Driveability Test 12A – Repairing Fault "Throttle Body Temp Voltage Low" (5.2L & 5.9L)

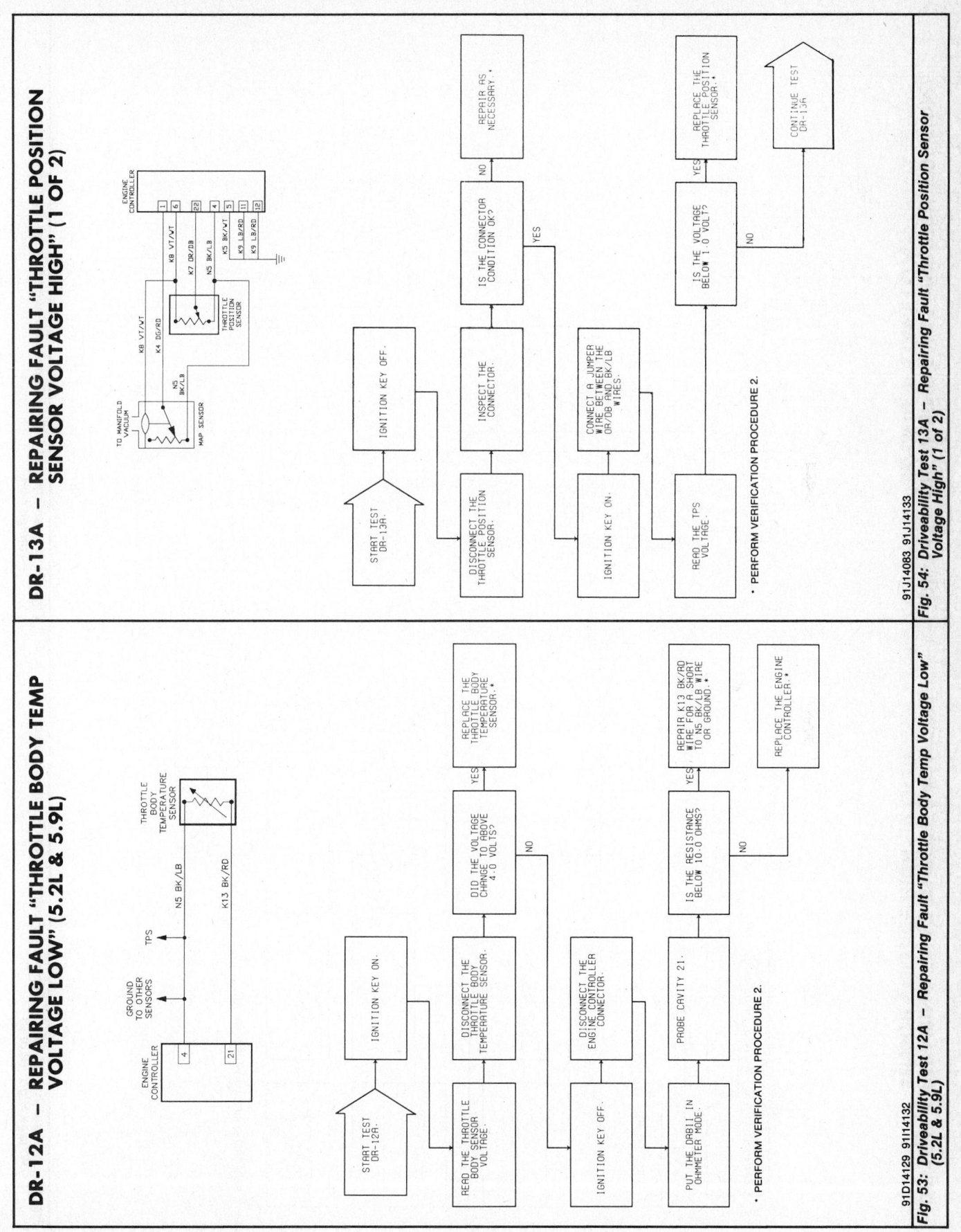

DR-13A – REPAIRING FAULT "THROTTLE POSITION SENSOR VOLTAGE HIGH" (1 OF 2)

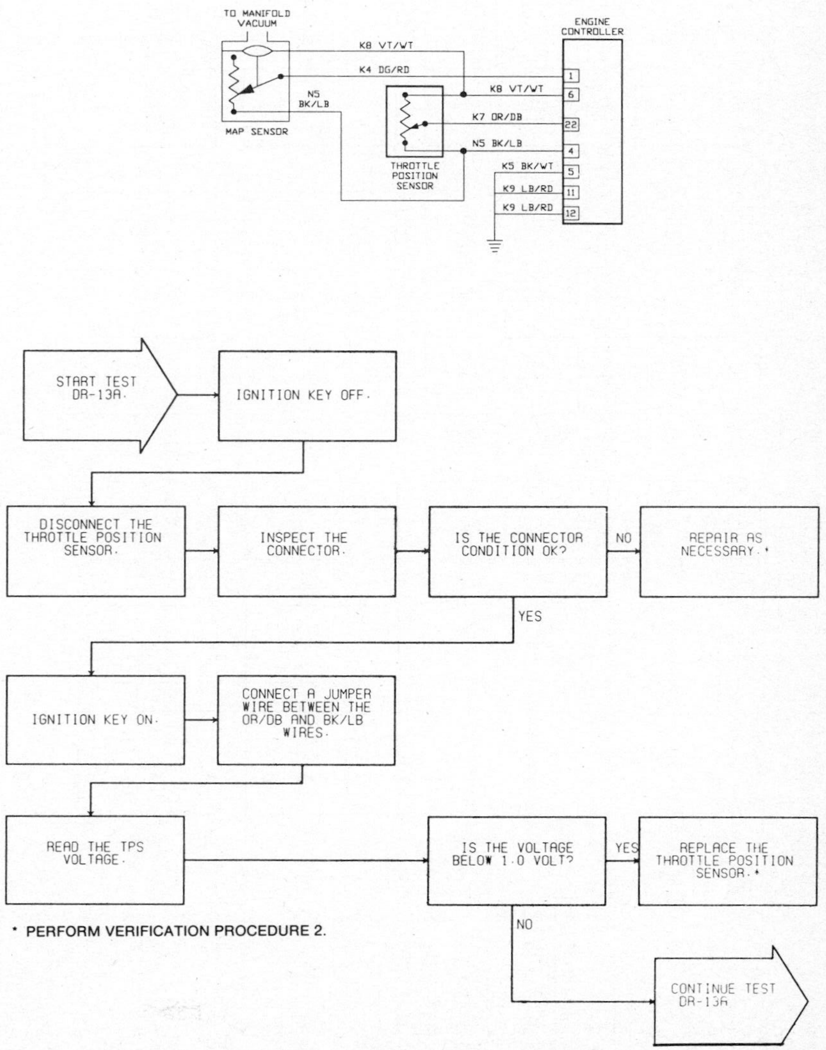
TO MANIFOLD VACUUM
MAP SENSOR
K8 VT/WT
K4 DG/RD
N5 BK/LB
THROTTLE POSITION SENSOR
ENGINE CONTROLLER
K8 VT/WT
K7 OR/DB
N5 BK/LB
K5 BK/WT
K9 LB/RD
K9 LB/RD
1
6
22
4
5
11
12
START TEST DR-13A.
IGNITION KEY OFF.
DISCONNECT THE THROTTLE POSITION SENSOR.
INSPECT THE CONNECTOR.
IS THE CONNECTOR CONDITION OK?
NO
REPAIR AS NECESSARY.*
YES
IGNITION KEY ON.
CONNECT A JUMPER WIRE BETWEEN THE OR/DB AND BK/LB WIRES.
READ THE TPS VOLTAGE.
IS THE VOLTAGE BELOW 1.0 VOLT?
YES
REPLACE THE THROTTLE POSITION SENSOR.*
NO
CONTINUE TEST DR-13A

* PERFORM VERIFICATION PROCEDURE 2.

91J14083 91J14133

Fig. 54: Driveability Test 13A – Repairing Fault "Throttle Position Sensor Voltage High" (1 of 2)

1991 ENGINE PERFORMANCE
Self-Diagnostics – 3.9L, 5.2L & 5.9L TBI (Cont.)

DR-13A – REPAIRING FAULT "THROTTLE POSITION SENSOR VOLTAGE HIGH" (2 OF 2)

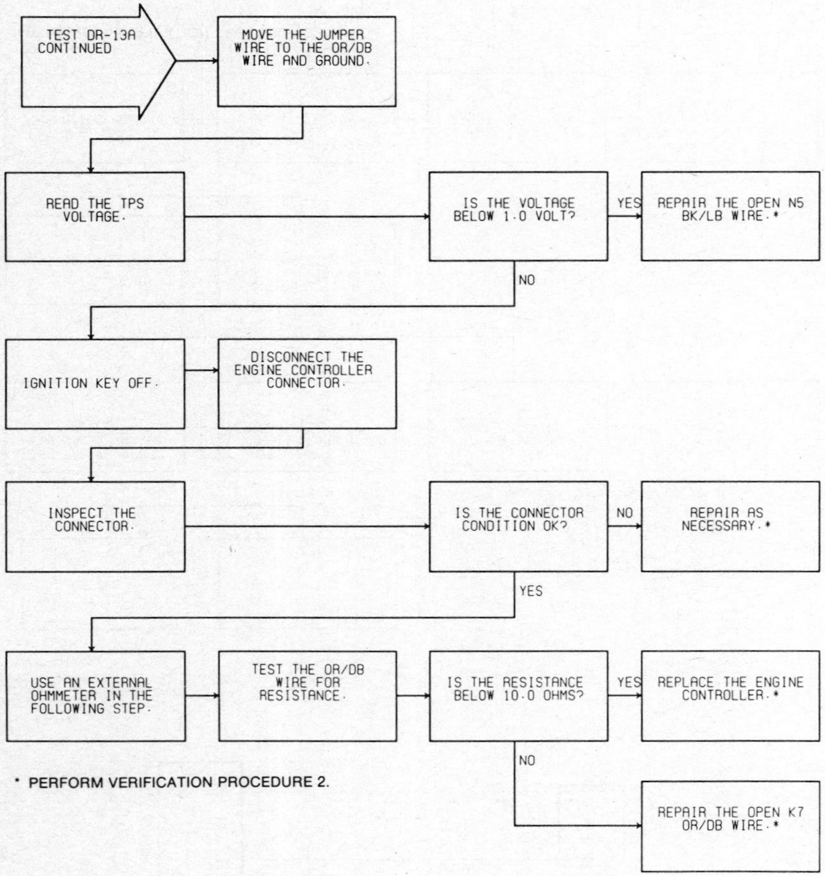
TEST DR-13A CONTINUED
MOVE THE JUMPER WIRE TO THE OR/DB WIRE AND GROUND.
READ THE TPS VOLTAGE.
IS THE VOLTAGE BELOW 1.0 VOLT?
YES
REPAIR THE OPEN N5 BK/LB WIRE.*
NO
IGNITION KEY OFF.
DISCONNECT THE ENGINE CONTROLLER CONNECTOR.
INSPECT THE CONNECTOR.
IS THE CONNECTOR CONDITION OK?
NO
REPAIR AS NECESSARY.*
YES
USE AN EXTERNAL OHMMETER IN THE FOLLOWING STEP.
TEST THE OR/DB WIRE FOR RESISTANCE.
IS THE RESISTANCE BELOW 10.0 OHMS?
YES
REPLACE THE ENGINE CONTROLLER.*
NO
REPAIR THE OPEN K7 OR/DB WIRE.*
* PERFORM VERIFICATION PROCEDURE 2.

91A14134

Fig. 55: Driveability Test 13A – Repairing Fault "Throttle Position Sensor Voltage High" (2 of 2)

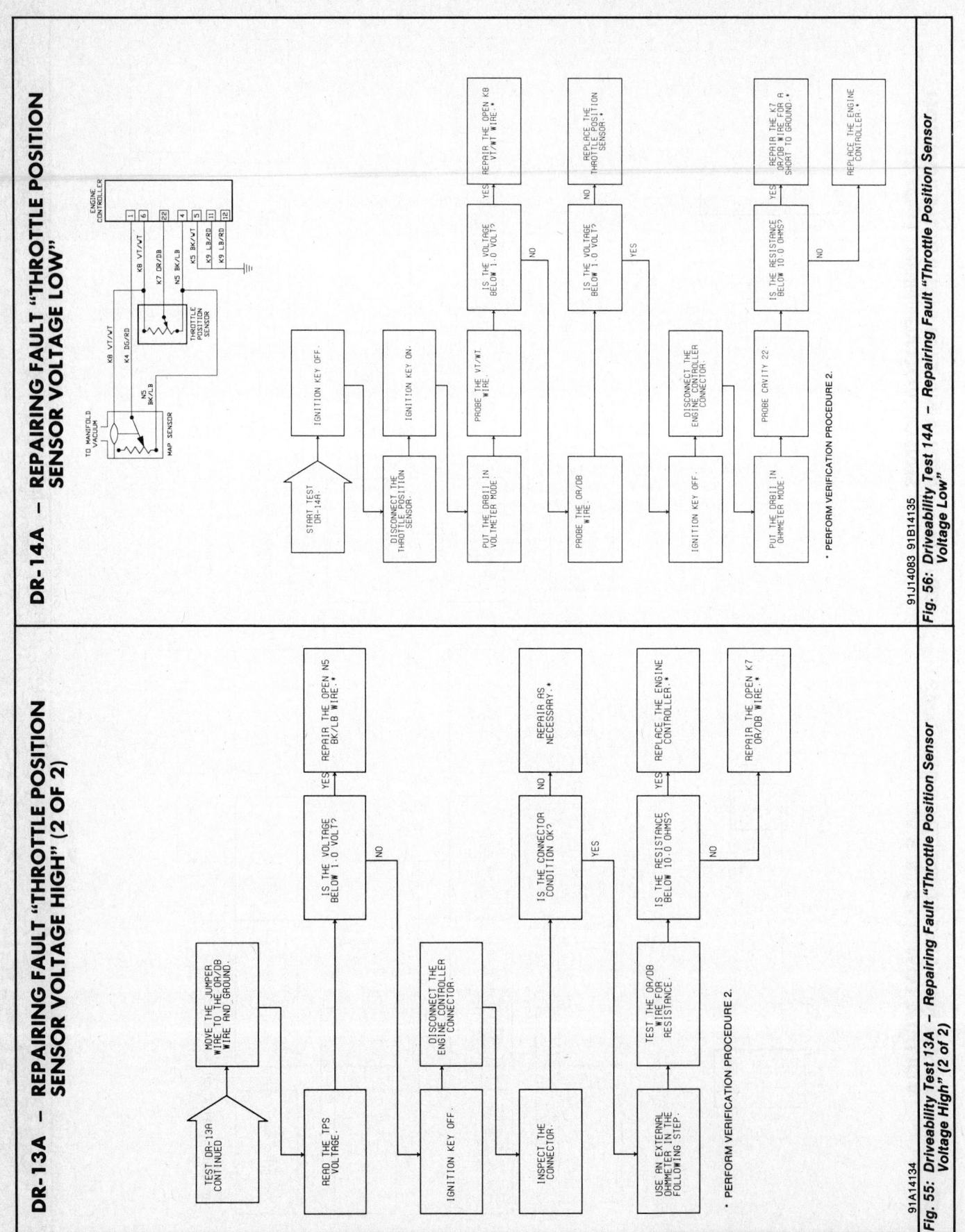

DR-14A – REPAIRING FAULT "THROTTLE POSITION SENSOR VOLTAGE LOW"

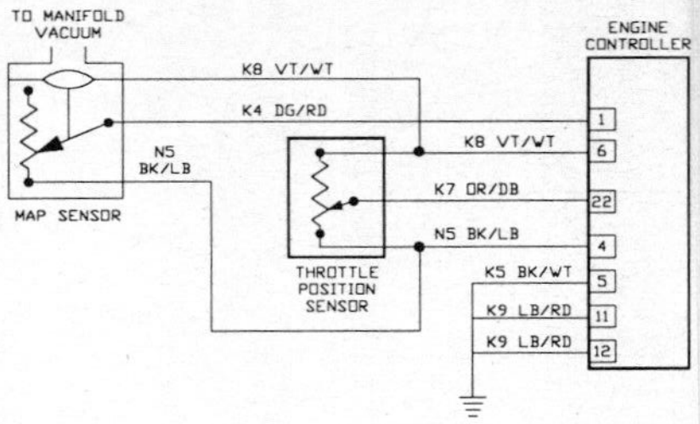
TO MANIFOLD VACUUM
MAP SENSOR
K8 VT/WT
K4 DG/RD
N5 BK/LB
THROTTLE POSITION SENSOR
K7 OR/DB
N5 BK/LB
K5 BK/WT
K9 LB/RD
K9 LB/RD
ENGINE CONTROLLER
1
6
22
4
5
11
12

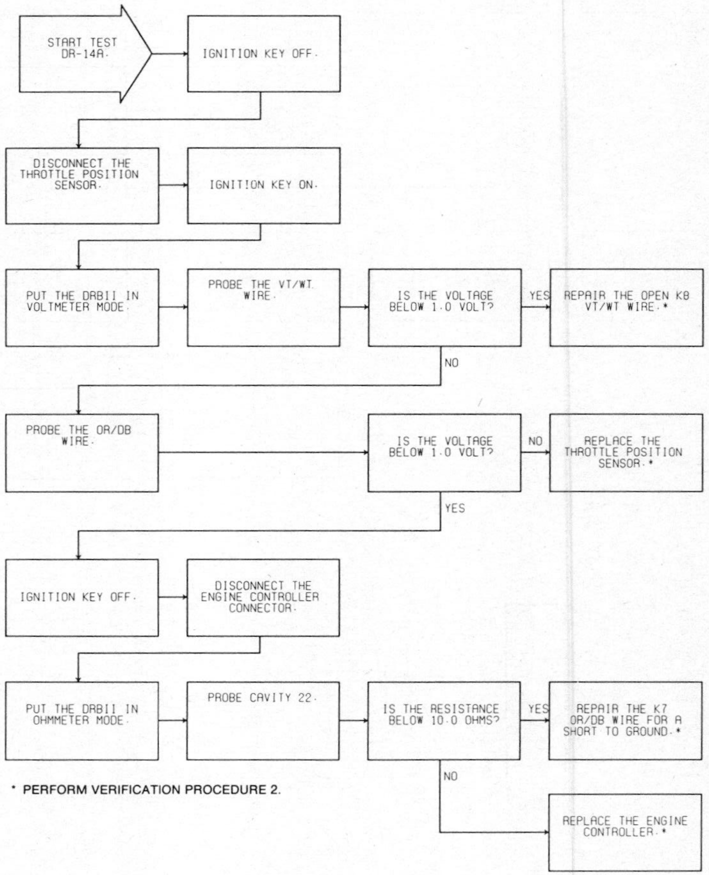
START TEST DR-14A.
IGNITION KEY OFF.
DISCONNECT THE THROTTLE POSITION SENSOR.
IGNITION KEY ON.
PUT THE DRBII IN VOLTMETER MODE.
PROBE THE VT/WT. WIRE.
IS THE VOLTAGE BELOW 1.0 VOLT?
YES
REPAIR THE OPEN K8 VT/WT WIRE.*
NO
PROBE THE OR/DB WIRE.
IS THE VOLTAGE BELOW 1.0 VOLT?
NO
REPLACE THE THROTTLE POSITION SENSOR.*
YES
IGNITION KEY OFF.
DISCONNECT THE ENGINE CONTROLLER CONNECTOR.
PUT THE DRBII IN OHMMETER MODE.
PROBE CAVITY 22.
IS THE RESISTANCE BELOW 10.0 OHMS?
YES
REPAIR THE K7 OR/DB WIRE FOR A SHORT TO GROUND.*
NO
REPLACE THE ENGINE CONTROLLER.*
* PERFORM VERIFICATION PROCEDURE 2.

91J14083 91B14135

Fig. 56: Driveability Test 14A – Repairing Fault "Throttle Position Sensor Voltage Low"

DR-15A – REPAIRING FAULT "AUTOMATIC IDLE SPEED MOTOR CIRCUITS" (1 OF 2)

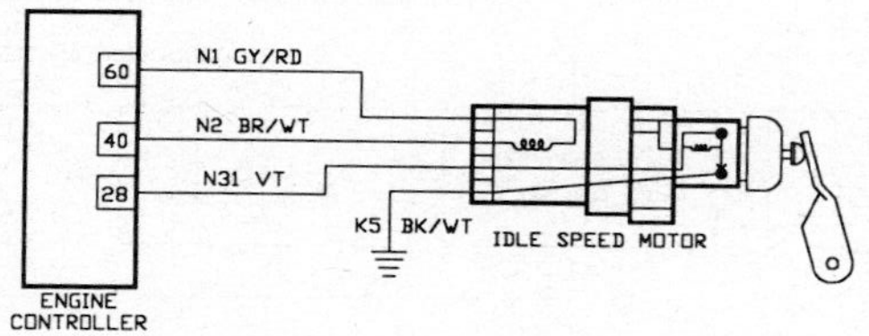
60
40
28
ENGINE CONTROLLER
N1 GY/RD
N2 BR/WT
N31 VT
K5 BK/WT
IDLE SPEED MOTOR

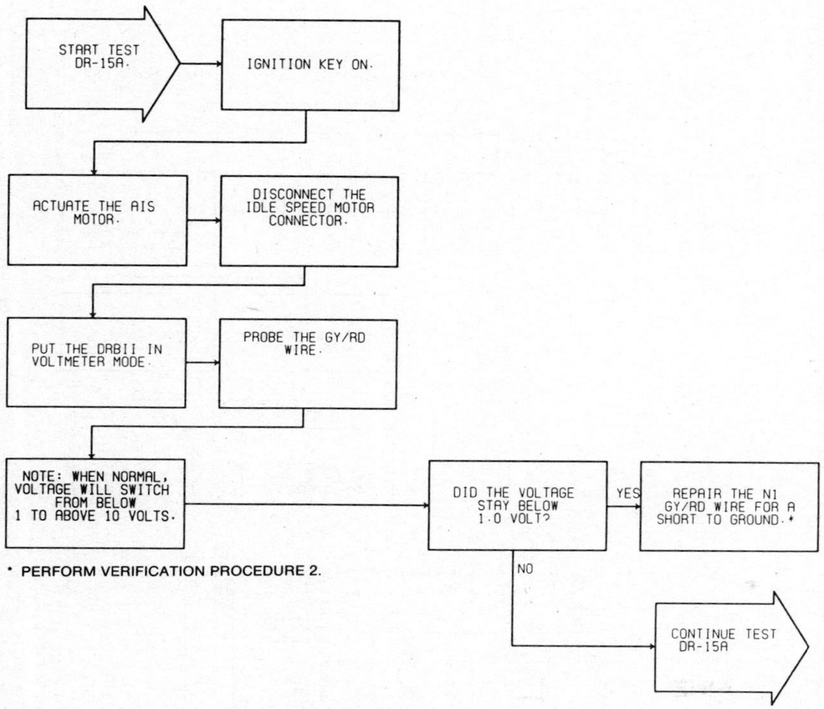
START TEST DR-15A.
IGNITION KEY ON.
ACTUATE THE AIS MOTOR.
DISCONNECT THE IDLE SPEED MOTOR CONNECTOR.
PUT THE DRBII IN VOLTMETER MODE.
PROBE THE GY/RD WIRE.
NOTE: WHEN NORMAL, VOLTAGE WILL SWITCH FROM BELOW 1 TO ABOVE 10 VOLTS.
DID THE VOLTAGE STAY BELOW 1.0 VOLT?
YES
REPAIR THE N1 GY/RD WIRE FOR A SHORT TO GROUND. *
NO
CONTINUE TEST DR-15A
* PERFORM VERIFICATION PROCEDURE 2.

91H14107 91C14136

Fig. 57: Driveability Test 15A – Repairing Fault "Automatic Idle Speed Motor Circuits" (1 of 2)

DR-15A – REPAIRING FAULT "AUTOMATIC IDLE SPEED MOTOR CIRCUITS" (2 OF 2)

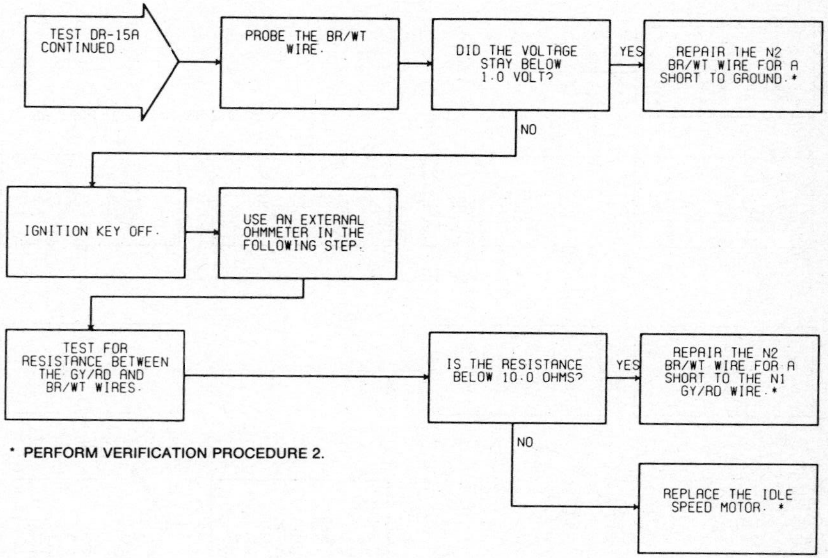
TEST DR-15A CONTINUED
PROBE THE BR/WT WIRE.
DID THE VOLTAGE STAY BELOW 1.0 VOLT?
YES
REPAIR THE N2 BR/WT WIRE FOR A SHORT TO GROUND. *
NO
IGNITION KEY OFF.
USE AN EXTERNAL OHMMETER IN THE FOLLOWING STEP.
TEST FOR RESISTANCE BETWEEN THE GY/RD AND BR/WT WIRES.
IS THE RESISTANCE BELOW 10.0 OHMS?
YES
REPAIR THE N2 BR/WT WIRE FOR A SHORT TO THE N1 GY/RD WIRE. *
NO
REPLACE THE IDLE SPEED MOTOR. *
* PERFORM VERIFICATION PROCEDURE 2.

91D14137

Fig. 58: Driveability Test 15A – Repairing Fault "Automatic Idle Speed Motor Circuits" (2 of 2)

DR-16A – REPAIRING FAULT "INJECTOR NO. 1 CONTROL CIRCUIT" (1 OF 2)

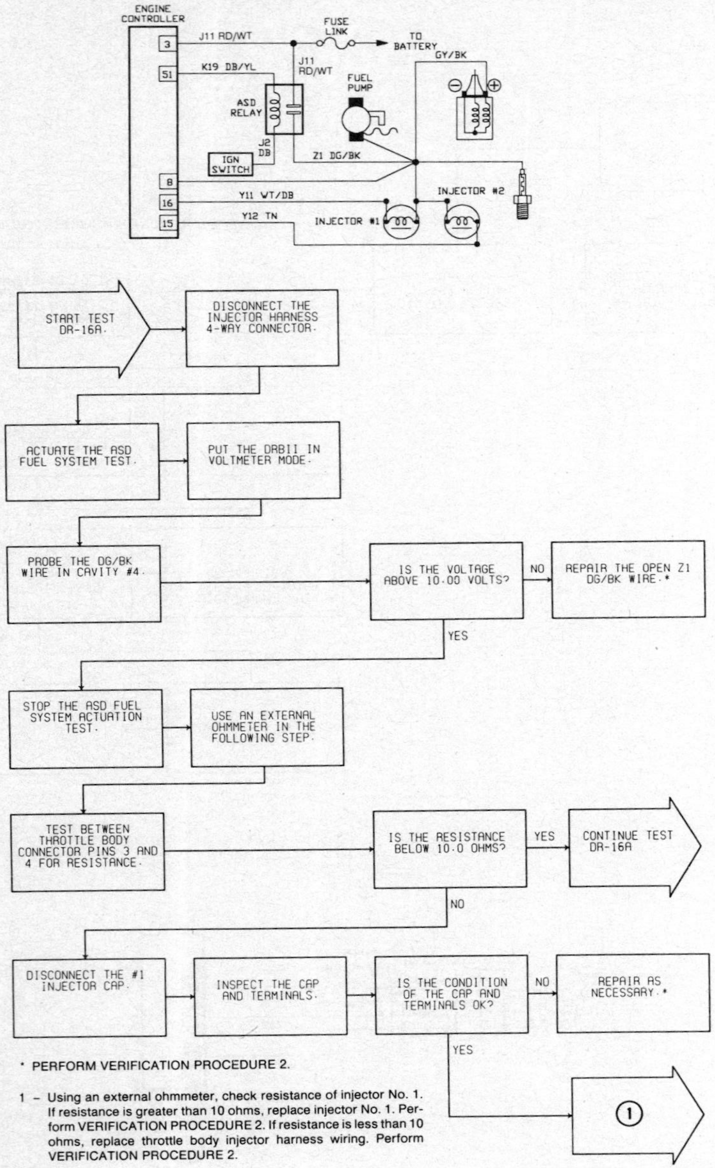
ENGINE CONTROLLER
3
51
8
16
15
J11 RD/WT
K19 DB/YL
FUSE LINK
TO BATTERY
GY/BK
J11 RD/WT
FUEL PUMP
ASD RELAY
J2 DB
IGN SWITCH
Z1 DG/BK
Y11 WT/DB
Y12 TN
INJECTOR #1
INJECTOR #2
START TEST DR-16A.
DISCONNECT THE INJECTOR HARNESS 4-WAY CONNECTOR.
ACTUATE THE ASD FUEL SYSTEM TEST.
PUT THE DRBII IN VOLTMETER MODE.
PROBE THE DG/BK WIRE IN CAVITY #4.
IS THE VOLTAGE ABOVE 10.00 VOLTS?
NO
REPAIR THE OPEN Z1 DG/BK WIRE.*
YES
STOP THE ASD FUEL SYSTEM ACTUATION TEST.
USE AN EXTERNAL OHMMETER IN THE FOLLOWING STEP.
TEST BETWEEN THROTTLE BODY CONNECTOR PINS 3 AND 4 FOR RESISTANCE.
IS THE RESISTANCE BELOW 10.0 OHMS?
YES
CONTINUE TEST DR-16A
NO
DISCONNECT THE #1 INJECTOR CAP.
INSPECT THE CAP AND TERMINALS.
IS THE CONDITION OF THE CAP AND TERMINALS OK?
NO
REPAIR AS NECESSARY.*
YES
1

* PERFORM VERIFICATION PROCEDURE 2.

1 – Using an external ohmmeter, check resistance of injector No. 1. If resistance is greater than 10 ohms, replace injector No. 1. Perform VERIFICATION PROCEDURE 2. If resistance is less than 10 ohms, replace throttle body injector harness wiring. Perform VERIFICATION PROCEDURE 2.

91G14064 91E14138

Fig. 59: Driveability Test 16A – Repairing Fault "Injector No. 1 Control Circuit" (1 of 2)

DR-16A – REPAIRING FAULT "INJECTOR NO. 1 CONTROL CIRCUIT" (2 OF 2)

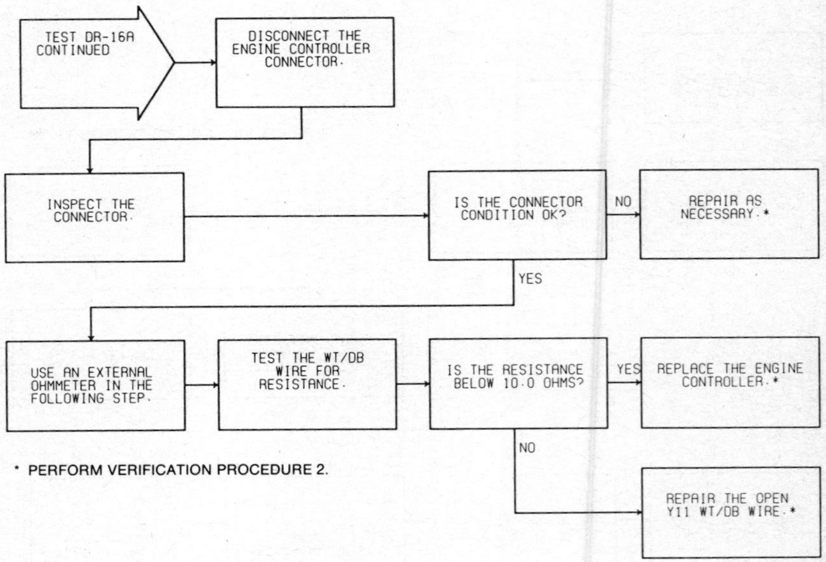
TEST DR-16A CONTINUED
DISCONNECT THE ENGINE CONTROLLER CONNECTOR.
INSPECT THE CONNECTOR.
IS THE CONNECTOR CONDITION OK?
NO
REPAIR AS NECESSARY.*
YES
USE AN EXTERNAL OHMMETER IN THE FOLLOWING STEP.
TEST THE WT/DB WIRE FOR RESISTANCE.
IS THE RESISTANCE BELOW 10.0 OHMS?
YES
REPLACE THE ENGINE CONTROLLER.*
NO
REPAIR THE OPEN Y11 WT/DB WIRE.*

* PERFORM VERIFICATION PROCEDURE 2.

91F14139

Fig. 60: Driveability Test 16A – Repairing Fault "Injector No. 1 Control Circuit" (2 of 2)

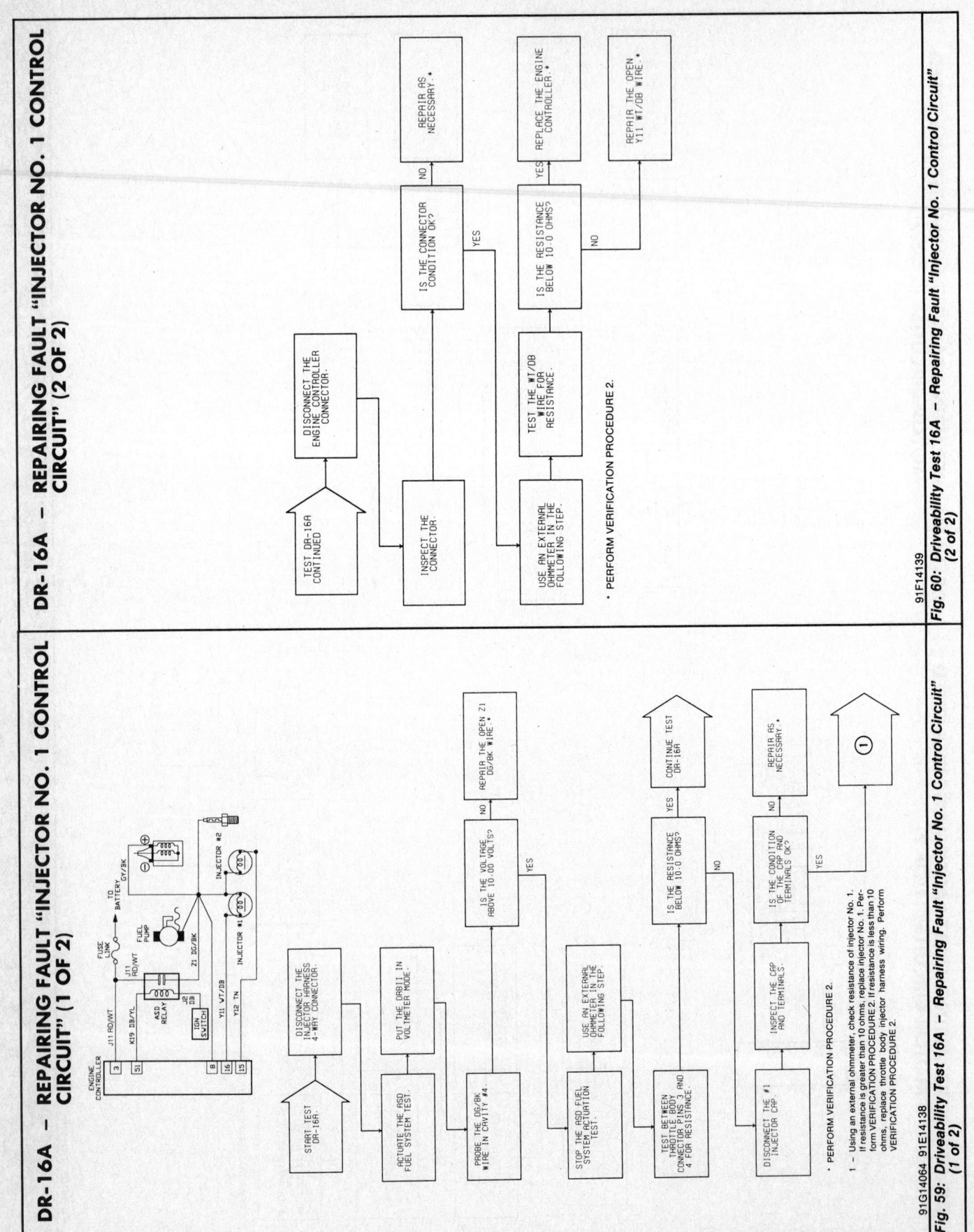

DR-17A – REPAIRING FAULT "INJECTOR NO. 2 CONTROL CIRCUIT" (1 OF 2)

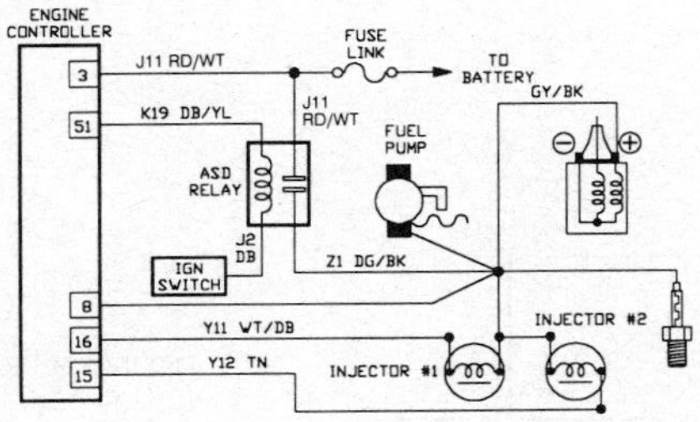
ENGINE CONTROLLER
3
51
8
16
15
J11 RD/WT
K19 DB/YL
FUSE LINK
TO BATTERY
GY/BK
J11 RD/WT
ASD RELAY
FUEL PUMP
J2 DB
IGN SWITCH
Z1 DG/BK
Y11 WT/DB
Y12 TN
INJECTOR #1
INJECTOR #2

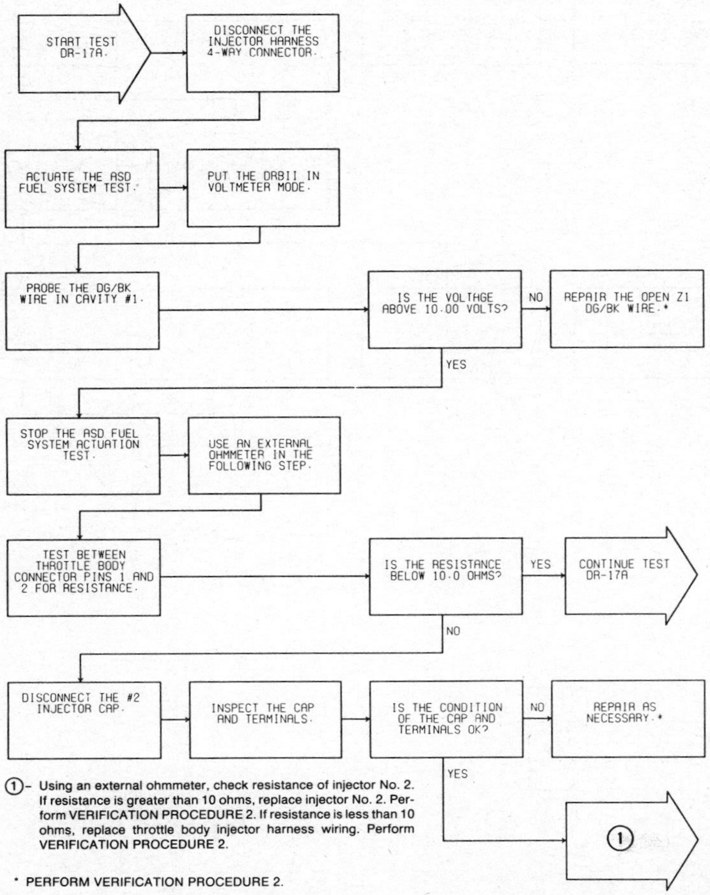
START TEST DR-17A.
DISCONNECT THE INJECTOR HARNESS 4-WAY CONNECTOR.
ACTUATE THE ASD FUEL SYSTEM TEST.
PUT THE DRBII IN VOLTMETER MODE.
PROBE THE DG/BK WIRE IN CAVITY #1.
IS THE VOLTAGE ABOVE 10.00 VOLTS?
NO
REPAIR THE OPEN Z1 DG/BK WIRE.*
YES
STOP THE ASD FUEL SYSTEM ACTUATION TEST.
USE AN EXTERNAL OHMMETER IN THE FOLLOWING STEP.
TEST BETWEEN THROTTLE BODY CONNECTOR PINS 1 AND 2 FOR RESISTANCE.
IS THE RESISTANCE BELOW 10.0 OHMS?
YES
CONTINUE TEST DR-17A
NO
DISCONNECT THE #2 INJECTOR CAP.
INSPECT THE CAP AND TERMINALS.
IS THE CONDITION OF THE CAP AND TERMINALS OK?
NO
REPAIR AS NECESSARY.*
YES
①

① – Using an external ohmmeter, check resistance of injector No. 2. If resistance is greater than 10 ohms, replace injector No. 2. Perform VERIFICATION PROCEDURE 2. If resistance is less than 10 ohms, replace throttle body injector harness wiring. Perform VERIFICATION PROCEDURE 2.

* PERFORM VERIFICATION PROCEDURE 2.

91G14064 91J14141

Fig. 61: Driveability Test 17A – Repairing Fault "Injector No. 2 Control Circuit" (1 of 2)

DR-17A – REPAIRING FAULT "INJECTOR NO. 2 CONTROL CIRCUIT" (2 OF 2)

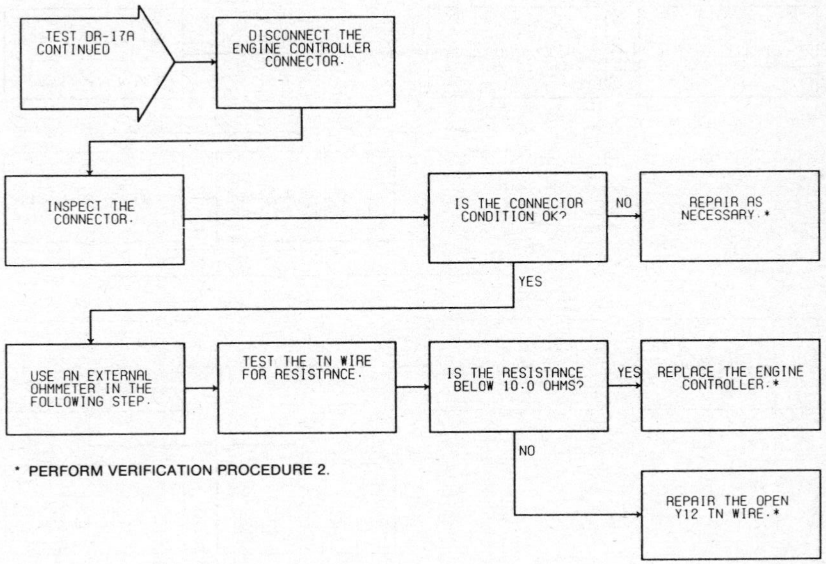
TEST DR-17A CONTINUED
DISCONNECT THE ENGINE CONTROLLER CONNECTOR.
INSPECT THE CONNECTOR.
IS THE CONNECTOR CONDITION OK?
NO
REPAIR AS NECESSARY.*
YES
USE AN EXTERNAL OHMMETER IN THE FOLLOWING STEP.
TEST THE TN WIRE FOR RESISTANCE.
IS THE RESISTANCE BELOW 10.0 OHMS?
YES
REPLACE THE ENGINE CONTROLLER.*
NO
REPAIR THE OPEN Y12 TN WIRE.*

* PERFORM VERIFICATION PROCEDURE 2.

91A14142

Fig. 62: Driveability Test 17A – Repairing Fault "Injector No. 2 Control Circuit" (2 of 2)

DR-18A – REPAIRING FAULT "PURGE SOLENOID CIRCUIT" (1 OF 3)

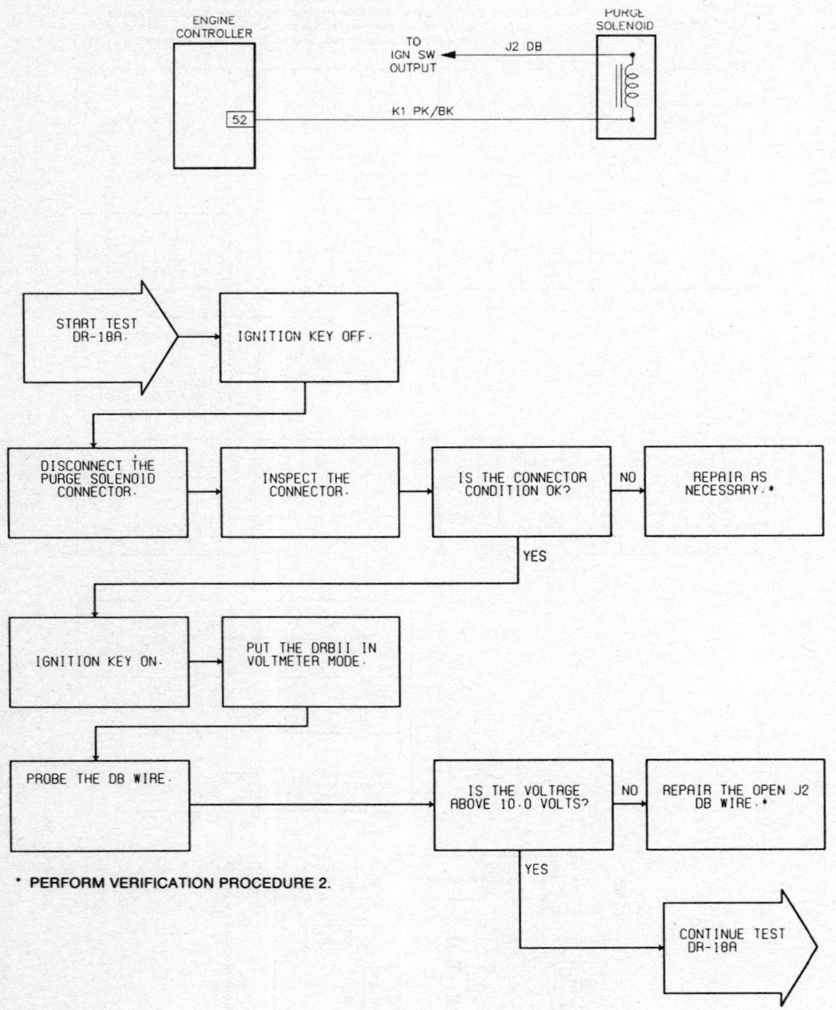
ENGINE CONTROLLER
52
TO IGN SW OUTPUT
J2 DB
K1 PK/BK
PURGE SOLENOID
START TEST DR-18A.
IGNITION KEY OFF.
DISCONNECT THE PURGE SOLENOID CONNECTOR.
INSPECT THE CONNECTOR.
IS THE CONNECTOR CONDITION OK?
NO
REPAIR AS NECESSARY.*
YES
IGNITION KEY ON.
PUT THE DRBII IN VOLTMETER MODE.
PROBE THE DB WIRE.
IS THE VOLTAGE ABOVE 10.0 VOLTS?
NO
REPAIR THE OPEN J2 DB WIRE.*
YES
CONTINUE TEST DR-18A

* PERFORM VERIFICATION PROCEDURE 2.

91C14144 91D14145

Fig. 63: Driveability Test 18A – Repairing Fault "Purge Solenoid Circuit" (1 of 3)

DR-18A – REPAIRING FAULT "PURGE SOLENOID CIRCUIT" (2 OF 3)

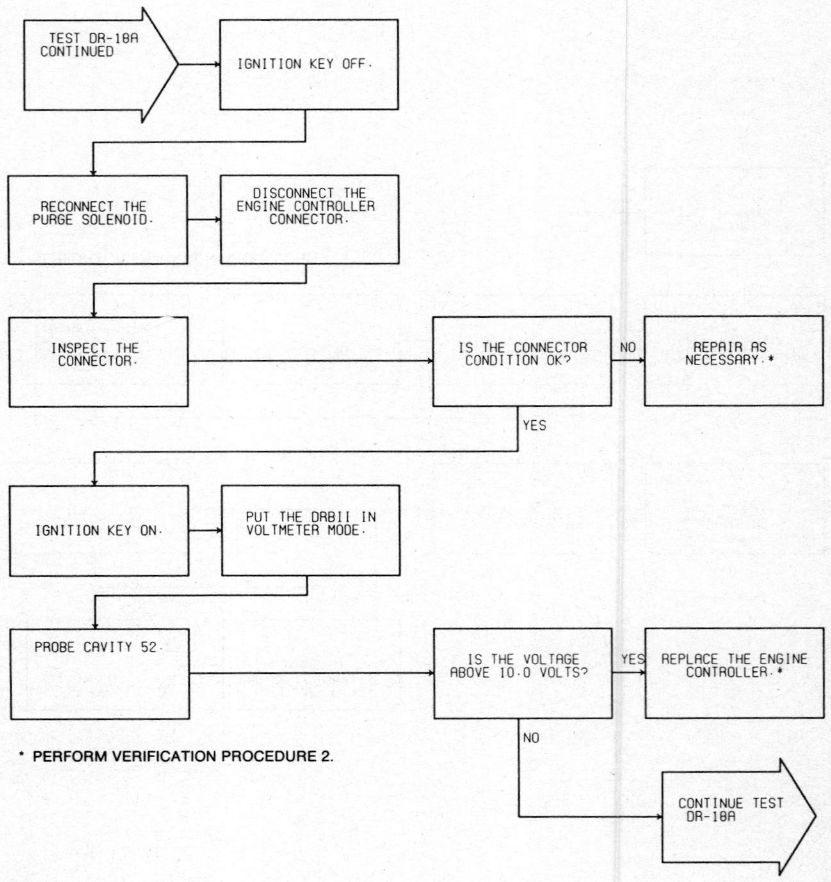
TEST DR-18A CONTINUED
IGNITION KEY OFF.
RECONNECT THE PURGE SOLENOID.
DISCONNECT THE ENGINE CONTROLLER CONNECTOR.
INSPECT THE CONNECTOR.
IS THE CONNECTOR CONDITION OK?
NO
REPAIR AS NECESSARY.*
YES
IGNITION KEY ON.
PUT THE DRBII IN VOLTMETER MODE.
PROBE CAVITY 52.
IS THE VOLTAGE ABOVE 10.0 VOLTS?
YES
REPLACE THE ENGINE CONTROLLER.*
NO
CONTINUE TEST DR-18A

* PERFORM VERIFICATION PROCEDURE 2.

91E14146

Fig. 64: Driveability Test 18A – Repairing Fault "Purge Solenoid Circuit" (2 of 3)

DR-18A – REPAIRING FAULT "PURGE SOLENOID CIRCUIT" (3 OF 3)

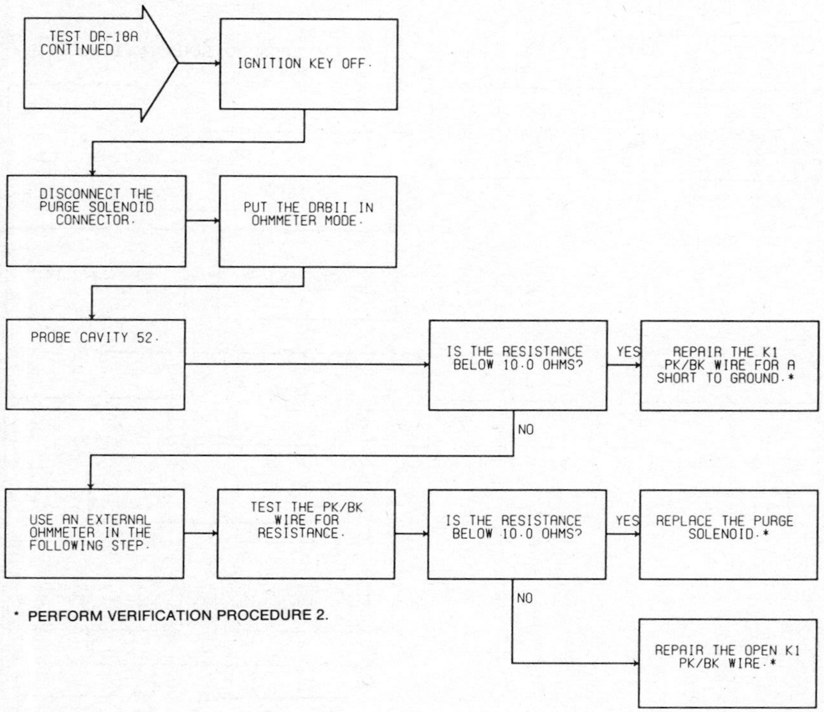
TEST DR-18A CONTINUED
IGNITION KEY OFF.
DISCONNECT THE PURGE SOLENOID CONNECTOR.
PUT THE DRBII IN OHMMETER MODE.
PROBE CAVITY 52.
IS THE RESISTANCE BELOW 10.0 OHMS?
YES
REPAIR THE K1 PK/BK WIRE FOR A SHORT TO GROUND.*
NO
USE AN EXTERNAL OHMMETER IN THE FOLLOWING STEP.
TEST THE PK/BK WIRE FOR RESISTANCE.
IS THE RESISTANCE BELOW 10.0 OHMS?
YES
REPLACE THE PURGE SOLENOID.*
NO
REPAIR THE OPEN K1 PK/BK WIRE.*

* PERFORM VERIFICATION PROCEDURE 2.

91F14147

Fig. 65: Driveability Test 18A – Repairing Fault "Purge Solenoid Circuit" (3 of 3)

DR-19A – REPAIRING FAULT "EGR SOLENOID CIRCUIT" (1 OF 3)

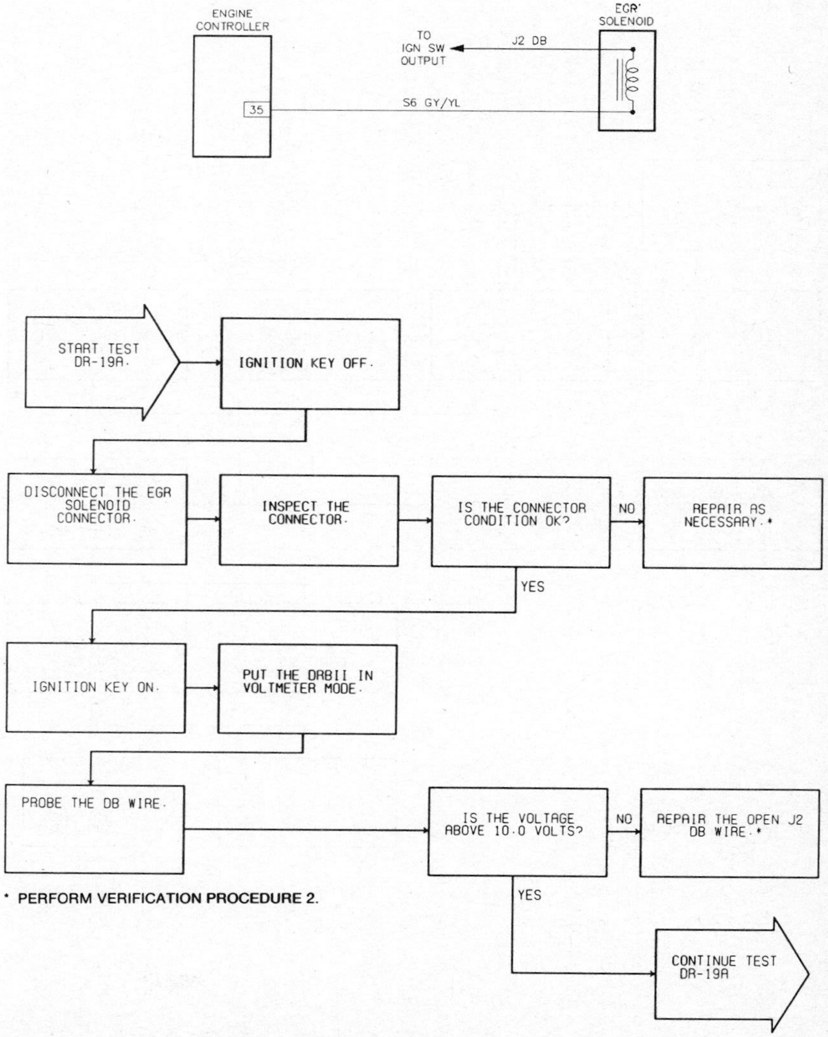
ENGINE CONTROLLER
35
EGR' SOLENOID
TO IGN SW OUTPUT
J2 DB
S6 GY/YL
START TEST DR-19A.
IGNITION KEY OFF.
DISCONNECT THE EGR SOLENOID CONNECTOR.
INSPECT THE CONNECTOR.
IS THE CONNECTOR CONDITION OK?
NO
REPAIR AS NECESSARY.*
YES
IGNITION KEY ON.
PUT THE DRBII IN VOLTMETER MODE.
PROBE THE DB WIRE.
IS THE VOLTAGE ABOVE 10.0 VOLTS?
NO
REPAIR THE OPEN J2 DB WIRE.*
YES
CONTINUE TEST DR-19A

* PERFORM VERIFICATION PROCEDURE 2.

91G14148 91H14149

Fig. 66: Driveability Test 19A – Repairing Fault "EGR Solenoid Circuit" (1 of 3)

1991 ENGINE PERFORMANCE
Self-Diagnostics – 3.9L, 5.2L & 5.9L TBI (Cont.)

DR-19A – REPAIRING FAULT "EGR SOLENOID CIRCUIT" (2 OF 3)

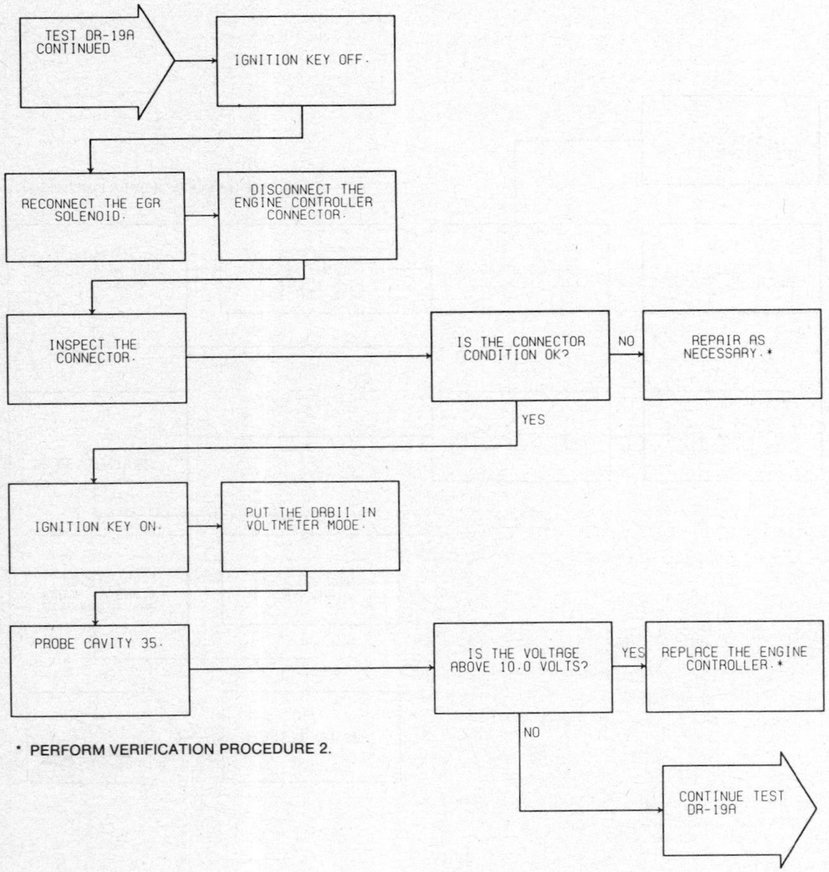
TEST DR-19A CONTINUED
IGNITION KEY OFF.
RECONNECT THE EGR SOLENOID.
DISCONNECT THE ENGINE CONTROLLER CONNECTOR.
INSPECT THE CONNECTOR.
IS THE CONNECTOR CONDITION OK?
NO
REPAIR AS NECESSARY.*
YES
IGNITION KEY ON.
PUT THE DRBII IN VOLTMETER MODE.
PROBE CAVITY 35.
IS THE VOLTAGE ABOVE 10.0 VOLTS?
YES
REPLACE THE ENGINE CONTROLLER.*
NO
CONTINUE TEST DR-19A

* PERFORM VERIFICATION PROCEDURE 2.

91B14150

Fig. 67: Driveability Test 19A – Repairing Fault "EGR Solenoid Circuit" (2 of 3)

DR-19A – REPAIRING FAULT "EGR SOLENOID CIRCUIT" (3 OF 3)

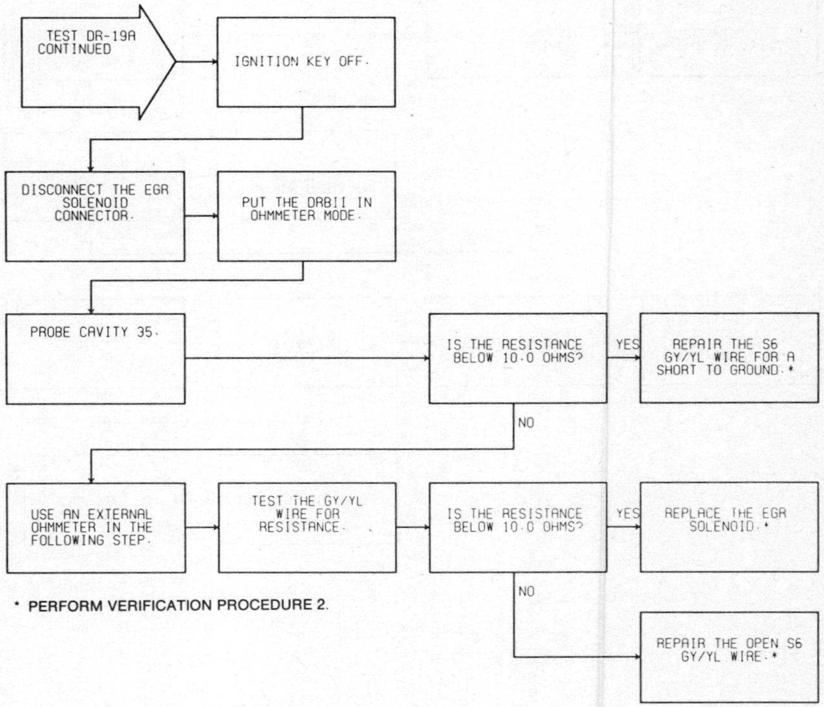
TEST DR-19A CONTINUED
IGNITION KEY OFF.
DISCONNECT THE EGR SOLENOID CONNECTOR.
PUT THE DRBII IN OHMMETER MODE.
PROBE CAVITY 35.
IS THE RESISTANCE BELOW 10.0 OHMS?
YES
REPAIR THE S6 GY/YL WIRE FOR A SHORT TO GROUND.*
NO
USE AN EXTERNAL OHMMETER IN THE FOLLOWING STEP.
TEST THE GY/YL WIRE FOR RESISTANCE.
IS THE RESISTANCE BELOW 10.0 OHMS?
YES
REPLACE THE EGR SOLENOID.*
NO
REPAIR THE OPEN S6 GY/YL WIRE.*

* PERFORM VERIFICATION PROCEDURE 2.

91C14151

Fig. 68: Driveability Test 19A – Repairing Fault "EGR Solenoid Circuit" (3 of 3)

DR-20A – REPAIRING FAULT "EGR SYSTEM FAILURE" (1 OF 4)

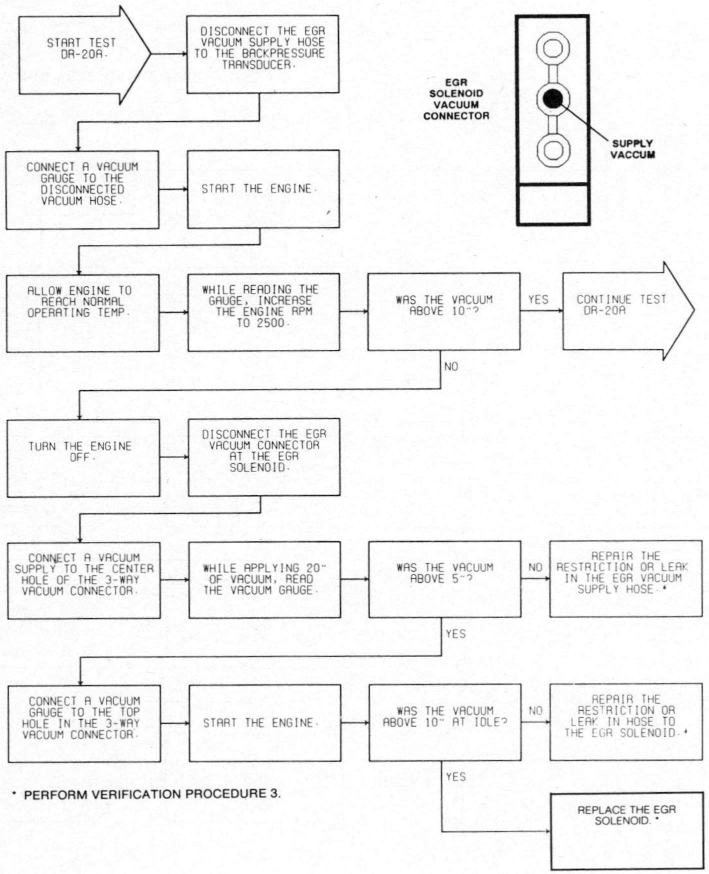
START TEST DR-20A.
DISCONNECT THE EGR VACUUM SUPPLY HOSE TO THE BACKPRESSURE TRANSDUCER.
EGR SOLENOID VACUUM CONNECTOR
SUPPLY VACCUM
CONNECT A VACUUM GAUGE TO THE DISCONNECTED VACUUM HOSE.
START THE ENGINE.
ALLOW ENGINE TO REACH NORMAL OPERATING TEMP.
WHILE READING THE GAUGE, INCREASE THE ENGINE RPM TO 2500.
WAS THE VACUUM ABOVE 10"?
YES
CONTINUE TEST DR-20A
NO
TURN THE ENGINE OFF.
DISCONNECT THE EGR VACUUM CONNECTOR AT THE EGR SOLENOID.
CONNECT A VACUUM SUPPLY TO THE CENTER HOLE OF THE 3-WAY VACUUM CONNECTOR.
WHILE APPLYING 20" OF VACUUM, READ THE VACUUM GAUGE.
WAS THE VACUUM ABOVE 5"?
NO
REPAIR THE RESTRICTION OR LEAK IN THE EGR VACUUM SUPPLY HOSE.*
YES
CONNECT A VACUUM GAUGE TO THE TOP HOLE IN THE 3-WAY VACUUM CONNECTOR.
START THE ENGINE.
WAS THE VACUUM ABOVE 10" AT IDLE?
NO
REPAIR THE RESTRICTION OR LEAK IN HOSE TO THE EGR SOLENOID.*
YES
REPLACE THE EGR SOLENOID.*

* PERFORM VERIFICATION PROCEDURE 3.

91D14152

Fig. 69: Driveability Test 20A – Repairing Fault "EGR System Failure" (1 of 4)

DR-20A – REPAIRING FAULT "EGR SYSTEM FAILURE" (2 OF 4)

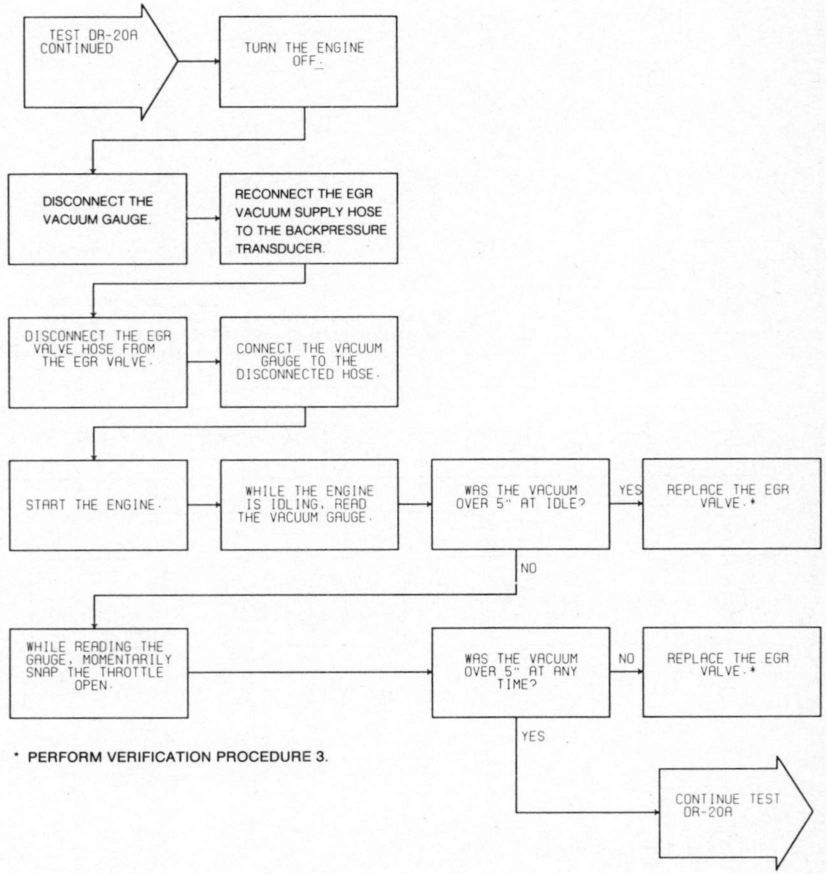
TEST DR-20A CONTINUED
TURN THE ENGINE OFF.
DISCONNECT THE VACUUM GAUGE.
RECONNECT THE EGR VACUUM SUPPLY HOSE TO THE BACKPRESSURE TRANSDUCER.
DISCONNECT THE EGR VALVE HOSE FROM THE EGR VALVE.
CONNECT THE VACUUM GAUGE TO THE DISCONNECTED HOSE.
START THE ENGINE.
WHILE THE ENGINE IS IDLING, READ THE VACUUM GAUGE.
WAS THE VACUUM OVER 5" AT IDLE?
YES
REPLACE THE EGR VALVE.*
NO
WHILE READING THE GAUGE, MOMENTARILY SNAP THE THROTTLE OPEN.
WAS THE VACUUM OVER 5" AT ANY TIME?
NO
REPLACE THE EGR VALVE.*
YES
CONTINUE TEST DR-20A

* PERFORM VERIFICATION PROCEDURE 3.

91E14153

Fig. 70: Driveability Test 20A – Repairing Fault "EGR System Failure" (2 of 4)

DR-20A – REPAIRING FAULT "EGR SYSTEM FAILURE" (3 OF 4)

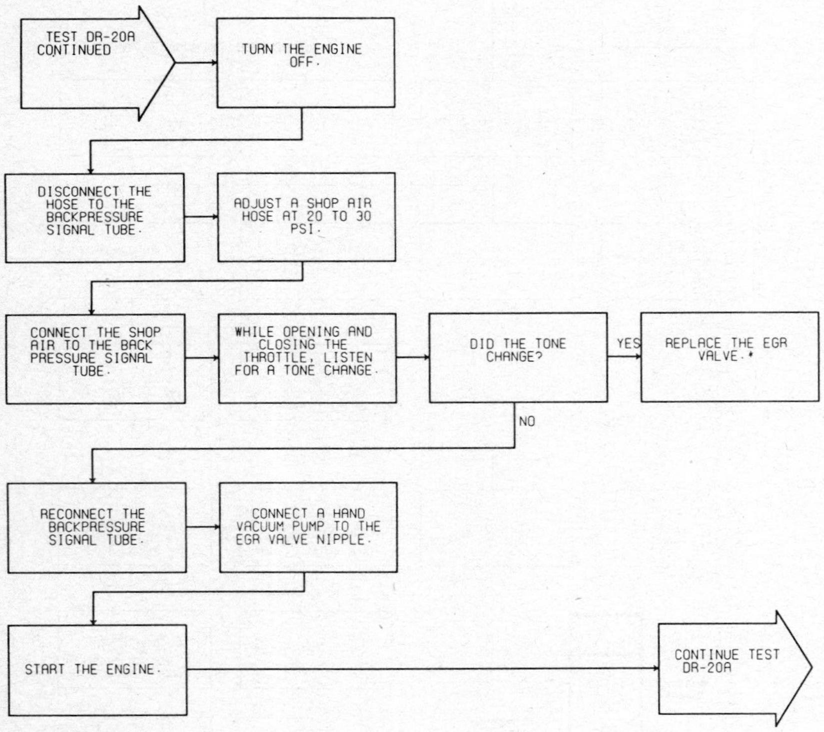
TEST DR-20A CONTINUED
TURN THE ENGINE OFF.
DISCONNECT THE HOSE TO THE BACKPRESSURE SIGNAL TUBE.
ADJUST A SHOP AIR HOSE AT 20 TO 30 PSI.
CONNECT THE SHOP AIR TO THE BACK PRESSURE SIGNAL TUBE.
WHILE OPENING AND CLOSING THE THROTTLE, LISTEN FOR A TONE CHANGE.
DID THE TONE CHANGE?
YES
REPLACE THE EGR VALVE.*
NO
RECONNECT THE BACKPRESSURE SIGNAL TUBE.
CONNECT A HAND VACUUM PUMP TO THE EGR VALVE NIPPLE.
START THE ENGINE.
CONTINUE TEST DR-20A

* PERFORM VERIFICATION PROCEDURE 3.

91F14154

Fig. 71: Driveability Test 20A – Repairing Fault "EGR System Failure" (3 of 4)

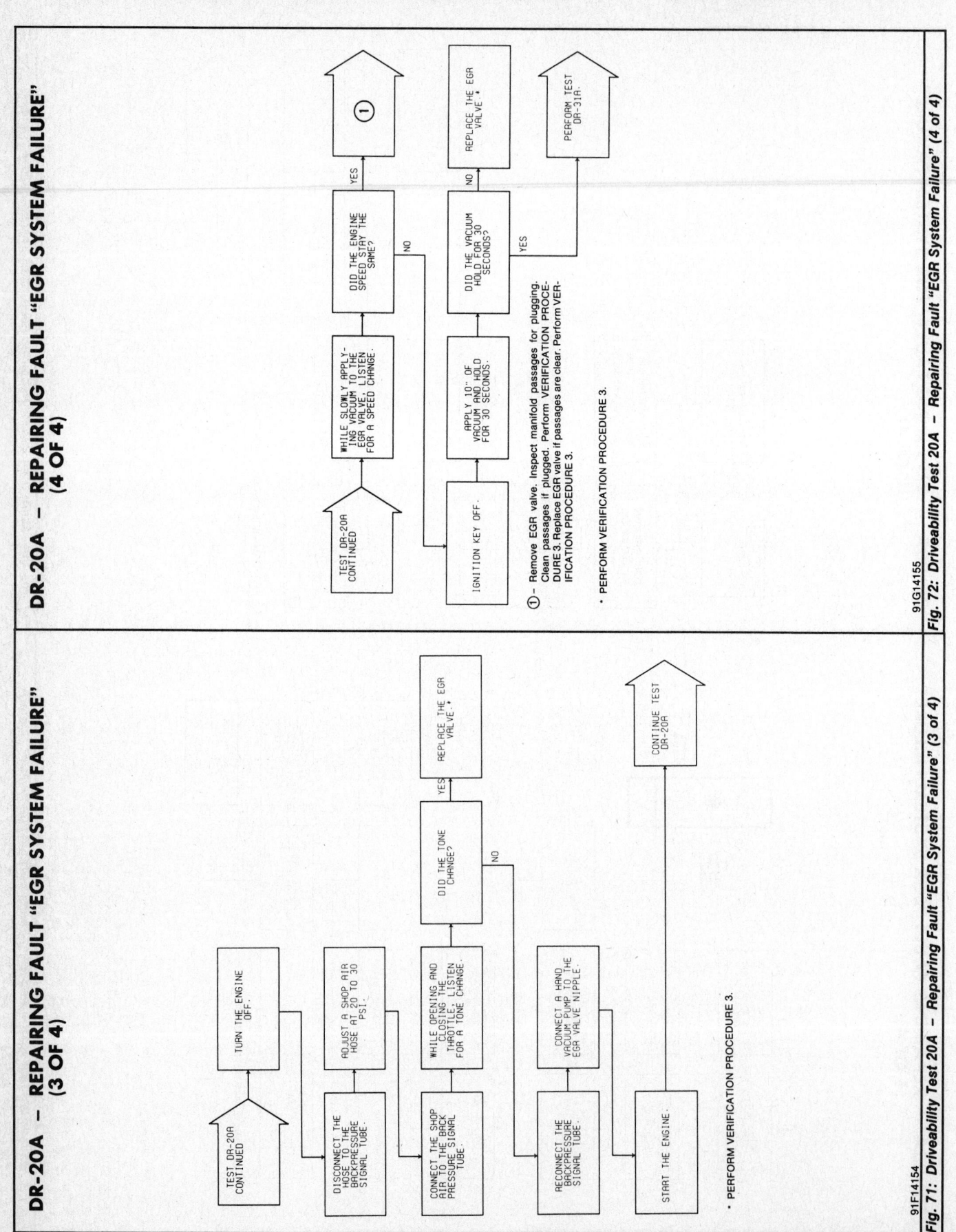

DR-20A – REPAIRING FAULT "EGR SYSTEM FAILURE" (4 OF 4)

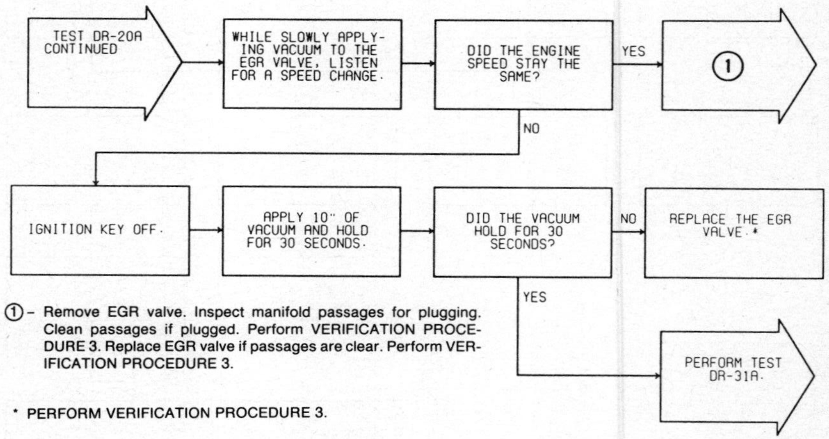
TEST DR-20A CONTINUED
WHILE SLOWLY APPLYING VACUUM TO THE EGR VALVE, LISTEN FOR A SPEED CHANGE.
DID THE ENGINE SPEED STAY THE SAME?
YES
1
NO
IGNITION KEY OFF.
APPLY 10" OF VACUUM AND HOLD FOR 30 SECONDS.
DID THE VACUUM HOLD FOR 30 SECONDS?
NO
REPLACE THE EGR VALVE.*
YES
PERFORM TEST DR-31A.

(1) – Remove EGR valve. Inspect manifold passages for plugging. Clean passages if plugged. Perform VERIFICATION PROCEDURE 3. Replace EGR valve if passages are clear. Perform VERIFICATION PROCEDURE 3.

* PERFORM VERIFICATION PROCEDURE 3.

91G14155

Fig. 72: Driveability Test 20A – Repairing Fault "EGR System Failure" (4 of 4)

DR-21A – REPAIRING FAULT "A/C CLUTCH RELAY CIRCUIT" (AN BODY) (1 OF 2)

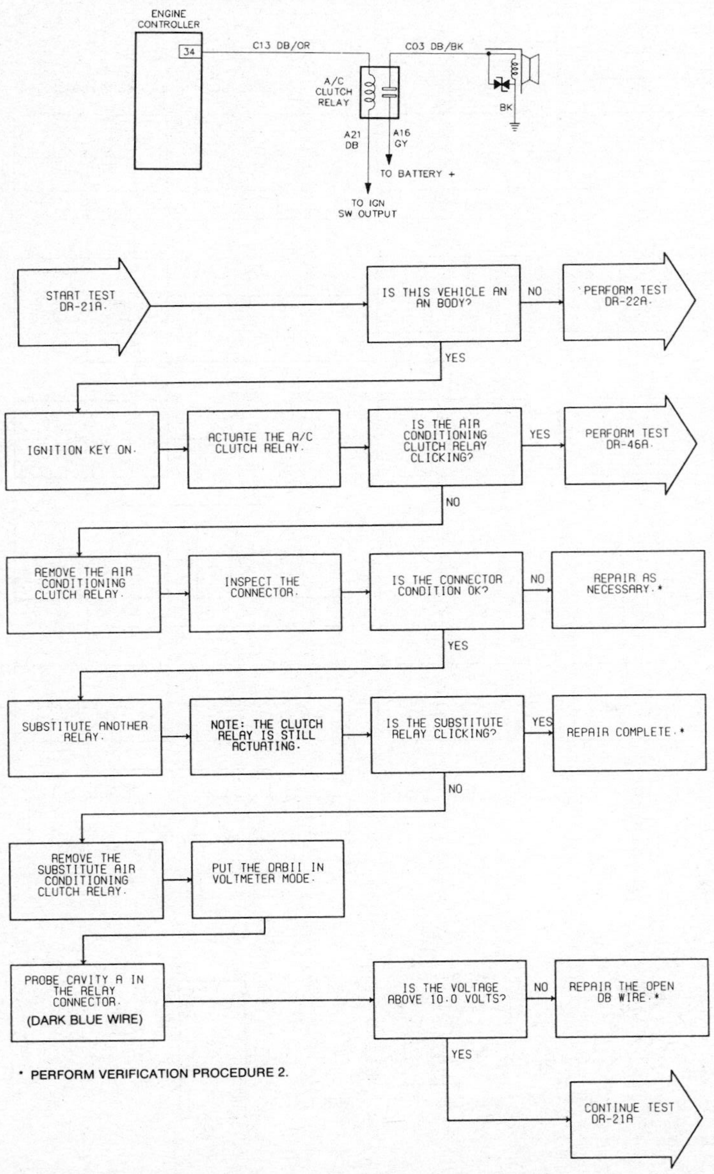
ENGINE CONTROLLER
34
C13 DB/OR
A/C CLUTCH RELAY
C03 DB/BK
BK
A21 DB
A16 GY
TO BATTERY +
TO IGN SW OUTPUT
START TEST DR-21A.
IS THIS VEHICLE AN AN BODY?
NO
PERFORM TEST DR-22A.
YES
IGNITION KEY ON.
ACTUATE THE A/C CLUTCH RELAY.
IS THE AIR CONDITIONING CLUTCH RELAY CLICKING?
YES
PERFORM TEST DR-46A.
NO
REMOVE THE AIR CONDITIONING CLUTCH RELAY.
INSPECT THE CONNECTOR.
IS THE CONNECTOR CONDITION OK?
NO
REPAIR AS NECESSARY.*
YES
SUBSTITUTE ANOTHER RELAY.
NOTE: THE CLUTCH RELAY IS STILL ACTUATING.
IS THE SUBSTITUTE RELAY CLICKING?
YES
REPAIR COMPLETE.*
NO
REMOVE THE SUBSTITUTE AIR CONDITIONING CLUTCH RELAY.
PUT THE DRBII IN VOLTMETER MODE.
PROBE CAVITY A IN THE RELAY CONNECTOR.
(DARK BLUE WIRE)
IS THE VOLTAGE ABOVE 10.0 VOLTS?
NO
REPAIR THE OPEN DB WIRE.*
YES
CONTINUE TEST DR-21A

* PERFORM VERIFICATION PROCEDURE 2.

91I14157 91J14158

Fig. 73: Driveability Test 21A – Repairing Fault "A/C Clutch Relay Circuit" (AN Body) (1 of 2)

DR-21A – REPAIRING FAULT "A/C CLUTCH RELAY CIRCUIT" (AN BODY) (2 OF 2)

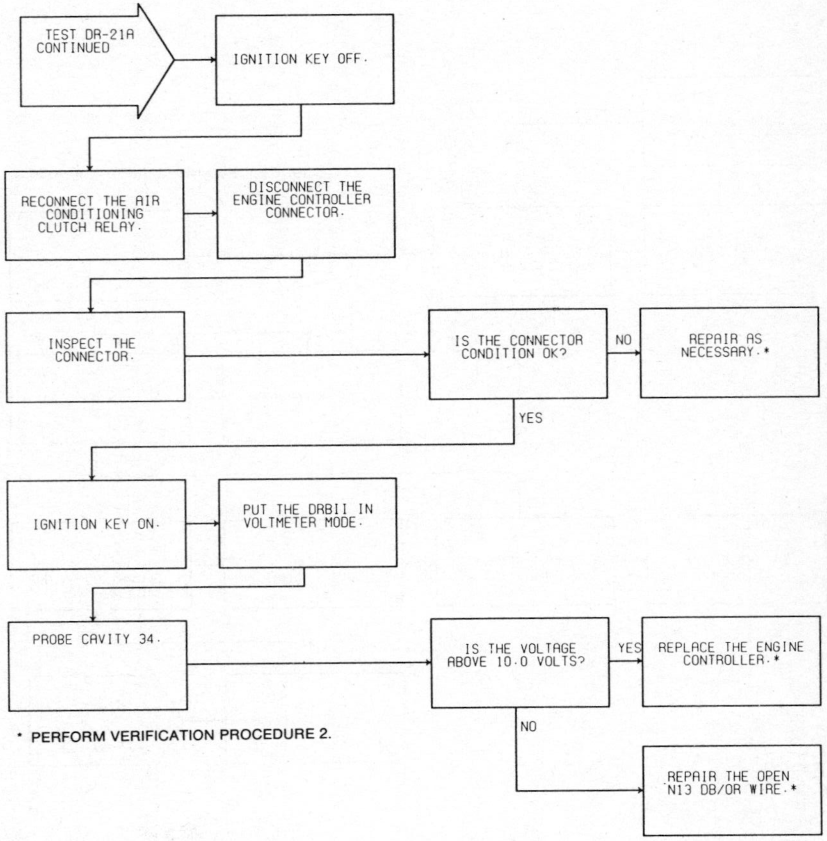
TEST DR-21A CONTINUED
IGNITION KEY OFF.
RECONNECT THE AIR CONDITIONING CLUTCH RELAY.
DISCONNECT THE ENGINE CONTROLLER CONNECTOR.
INSPECT THE CONNECTOR.
IS THE CONNECTOR CONDITION OK?
NO
REPAIR AS NECESSARY.*
YES
IGNITION KEY ON.
PUT THE DRBII IN VOLTMETER MODE.
PROBE CAVITY 34.
IS THE VOLTAGE ABOVE 10.0 VOLTS?
YES
REPLACE THE ENGINE CONTROLLER.*
NO
REPAIR THE OPEN N13 DB/OR WIRE.*

* PERFORM VERIFICATION PROCEDURE 2.

91A14159

Fig. 74: Driveability Test 21A – Repairing Fault "A/C Clutch Relay Circuit" (AN Body) (2 of 2)

1991 ENGINE PERFORMANCE
Self-Diagnostics – 3.9L, 5.2L & 5.9L TBI (Cont.)

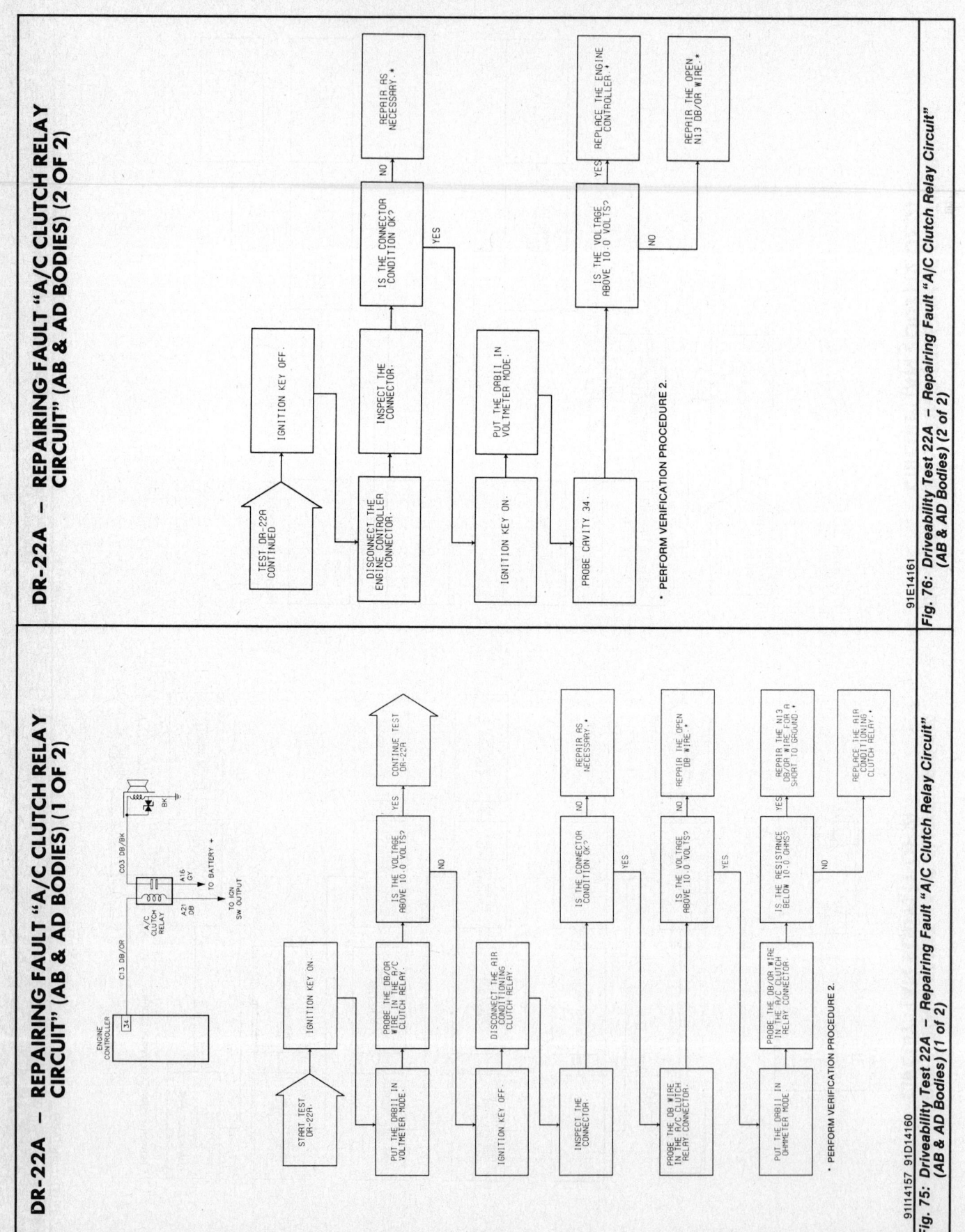

DR-22A – REPAIRING FAULT "A/C CLUTCH RELAY CIRCUIT" (AB & AD BODIES) (1 OF 2)

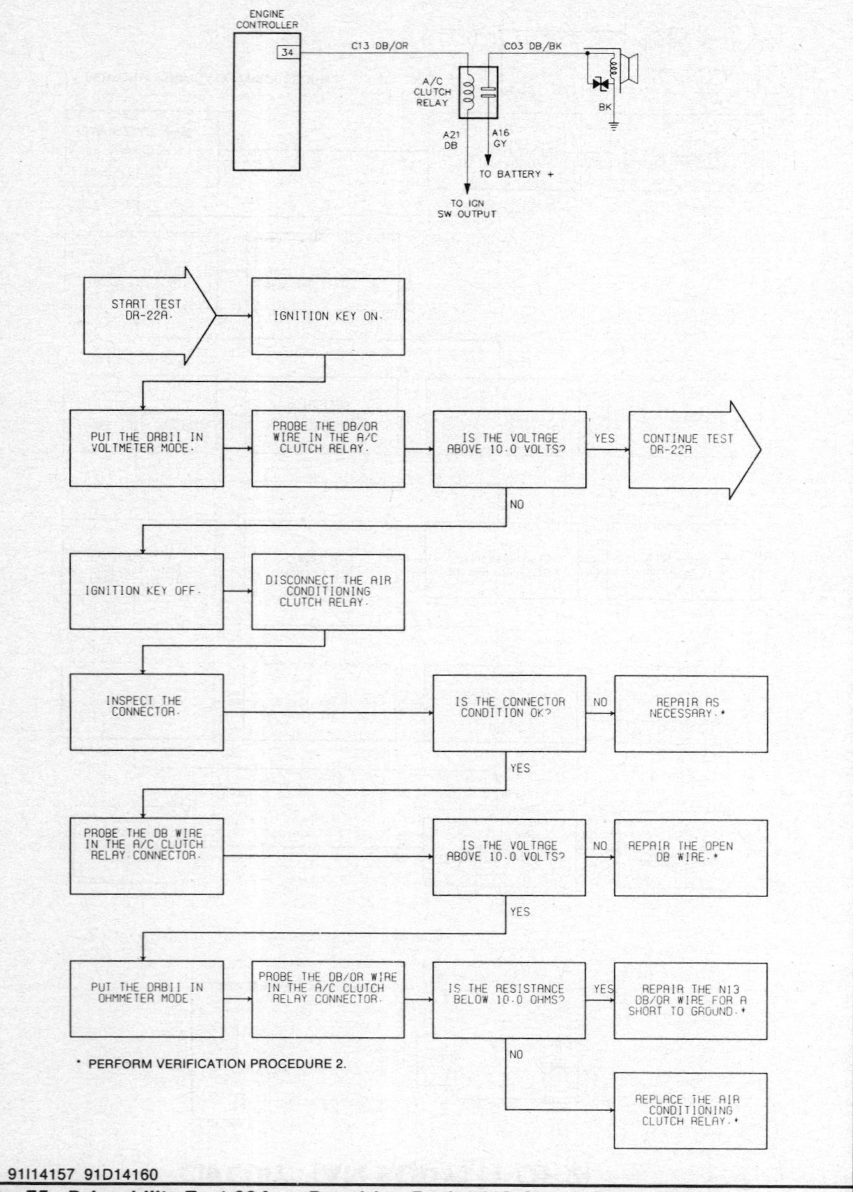
ENGINE CONTROLLER
34
C13 DB/OR
C03 DB/BK
A/C CLUTCH RELAY
BK
A21 DB
A16 GY
TO BATTERY +
TO IGN SW OUTPUT
START TEST DR-22A.
IGNITION KEY ON.
PUT THE DRBII IN VOLTMETER MODE.
PROBE THE DB/OR WIRE IN THE A/C CLUTCH RELAY.
IS THE VOLTAGE ABOVE 10.0 VOLTS?
YES
CONTINUE TEST DR-22A
NO
IGNITION KEY OFF.
DISCONNECT THE AIR CONDITIONING CLUTCH RELAY.
INSPECT THE CONNECTOR.
IS THE CONNECTOR CONDITION OK?
NO
REPAIR AS NECESSARY.*
YES
PROBE THE DB WIRE IN THE A/C CLUTCH RELAY CONNECTOR.
IS THE VOLTAGE ABOVE 10.0 VOLTS?
NO
REPAIR THE OPEN DB WIRE.*
YES
PUT THE DRBII IN OHMMETER MODE.
PROBE THE DB/OR WIRE IN THE A/C CLUTCH RELAY CONNECTOR.
IS THE RESISTANCE BELOW 10.0 OHMS?
YES
REPAIR THE N13 DB/OR WIRE FOR A SHORT TO GROUND.*
NO
REPLACE THE AIR CONDITIONING CLUTCH RELAY.*
* PERFORM VERIFICATION PROCEDURE 2.
91I14157 91D14160

Fig. 75: Driveability Test 22A – Repairing Fault "A/C Clutch Relay Circuit" (AB & AD Bodies) (1 of 2)

DR-22A – REPAIRING FAULT "A/C CLUTCH RELAY CIRCUIT" (AB & AD BODIES) (2 OF 2)

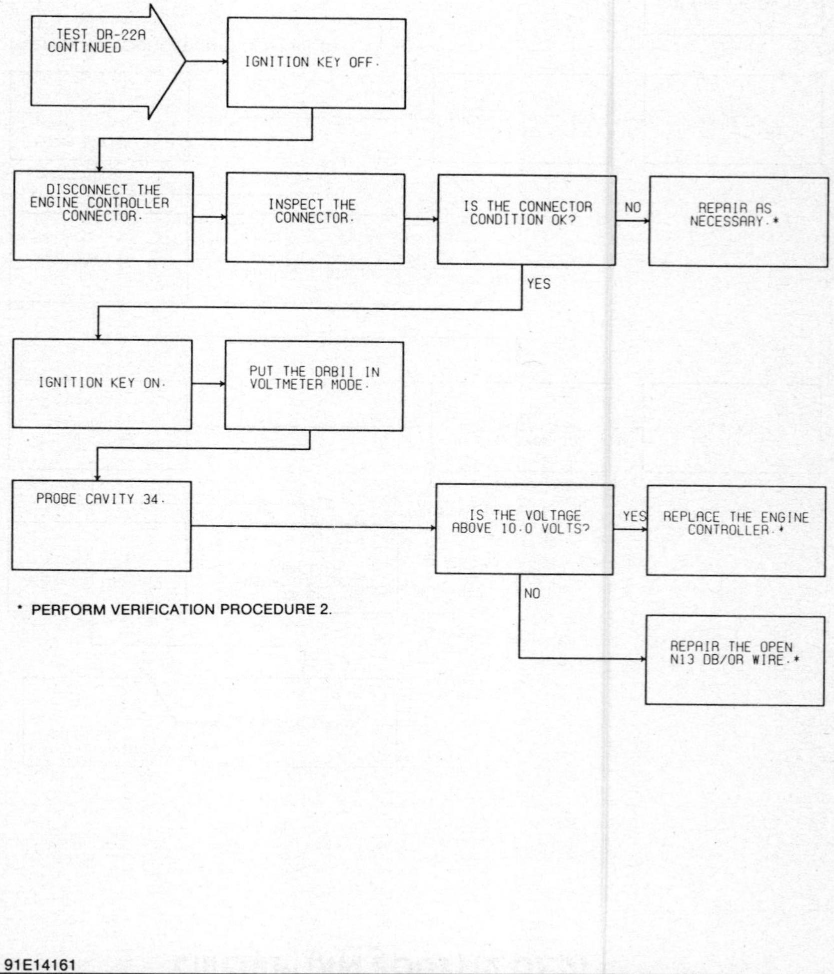
TEST DR-22A CONTINUED
IGNITION KEY OFF.
DISCONNECT THE ENGINE CONTROLLER CONNECTOR.
INSPECT THE CONNECTOR.
IS THE CONNECTOR CONDITION OK?
NO
REPAIR AS NECESSARY.*
YES
IGNITION KEY ON.
PUT THE DRBII IN VOLTMETER MODE.
PROBE CAVITY 34.
IS THE VOLTAGE ABOVE 10.0 VOLTS?
YES
REPLACE THE ENGINE CONTROLLER.*
NO
REPAIR THE OPEN N13 DB/OR WIRE.*
* PERFORM VERIFICATION PROCEDURE 2.
91E14161

Fig. 76: Driveability Test 22A – Repairing Fault "A/C Clutch Relay Circuit" (AB & AD Bodies) (2 of 2)

DR-23A – REPAIRING FAULT "IDLE SWITCH SHORTED LOW"

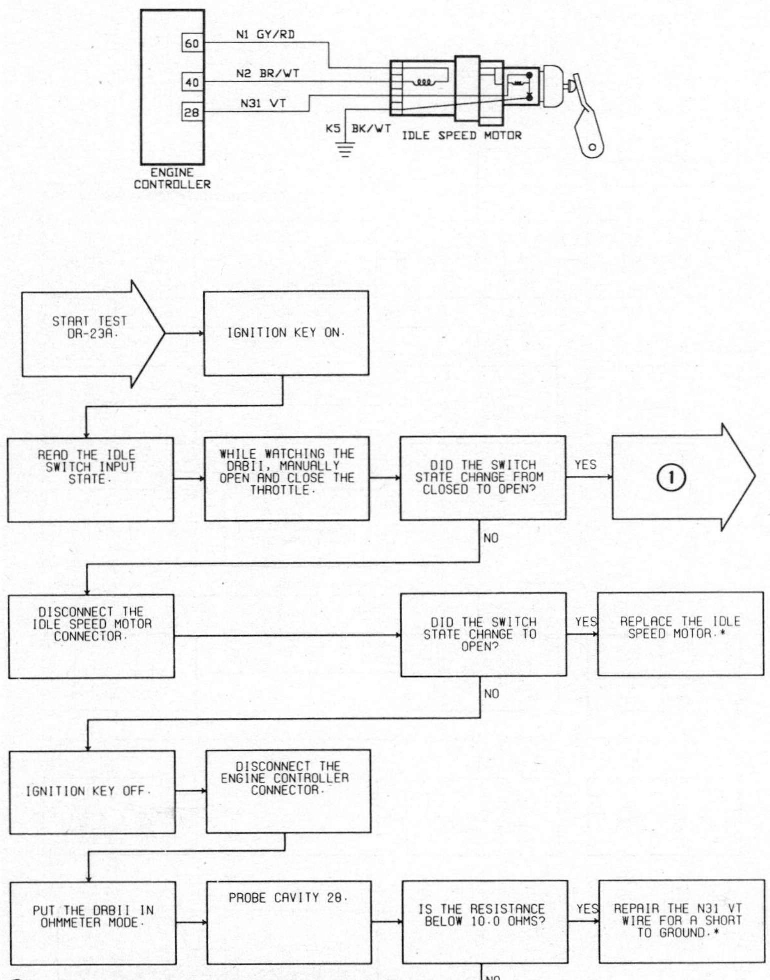
60
40
28
ENGINE CONTROLLER
N1 GY/RD
N2 BR/WT
N31 VT
K5 BK/WT
IDLE SPEED MOTOR
START TEST DR-23A.
IGNITION KEY ON.
READ THE IDLE SWITCH INPUT STATE.
WHILE WATCHING THE DRBII, MANUALLY OPEN AND CLOSE THE THROTTLE.
DID THE SWITCH STATE CHANGE FROM CLOSED TO OPEN?
YES
1
NO
DISCONNECT THE IDLE SPEED MOTOR CONNECTOR.
DID THE SWITCH STATE CHANGE TO OPEN?
YES
REPLACE THE IDLE SPEED MOTOR.*
NO
IGNITION KEY OFF.
DISCONNECT THE ENGINE CONTROLLER CONNECTOR.
PUT THE DRBII IN OHMMETER MODE.
PROBE CAVITY 28.
IS THE RESISTANCE BELOW 10.0 OHMS?
YES
REPAIR THE N31 VT WIRE FOR A SHORT TO GROUND.*
NO
REPLACE THE ENGINE CONTROLLER.*

① – While reading DRB-II, wiggle wiring harness to idle speed motor. If idle switch state changed from closed to open, repair Violet wire for a short to ground. Perform VERIFICATION PROCEDURE 2. If switch state did not change, test is complete. Perform VERIFICATION PROCEDURE 2.

* PERFORM VERIFICATION PROCEDURE 2.

91H14107 91F14162

Fig. 77: Driveability Test 23A – Repairing Fault "Idle Switch Shorted Low"

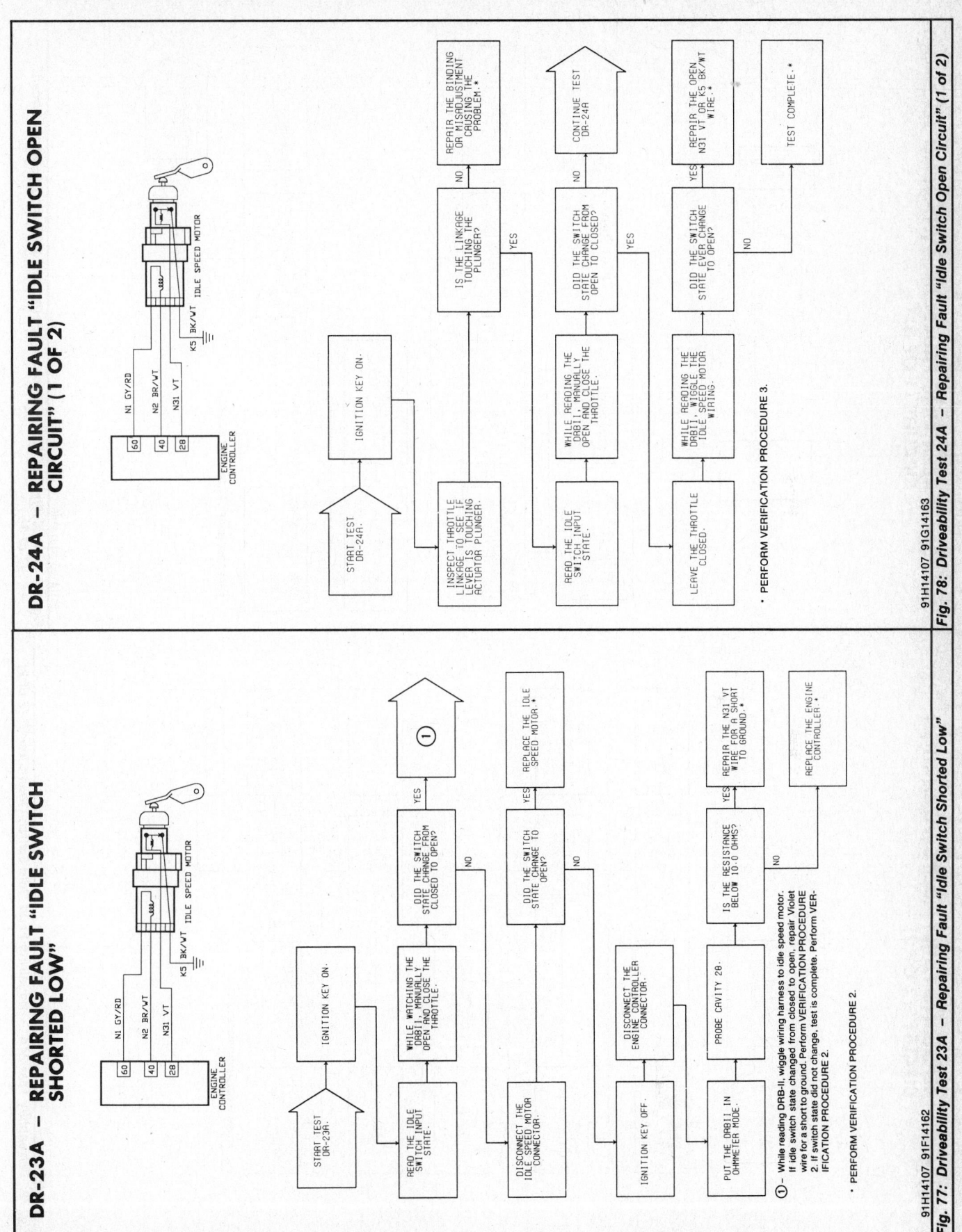

DR-24A – REPAIRING FAULT "IDLE SWITCH OPEN CIRCUIT" (1 OF 2)

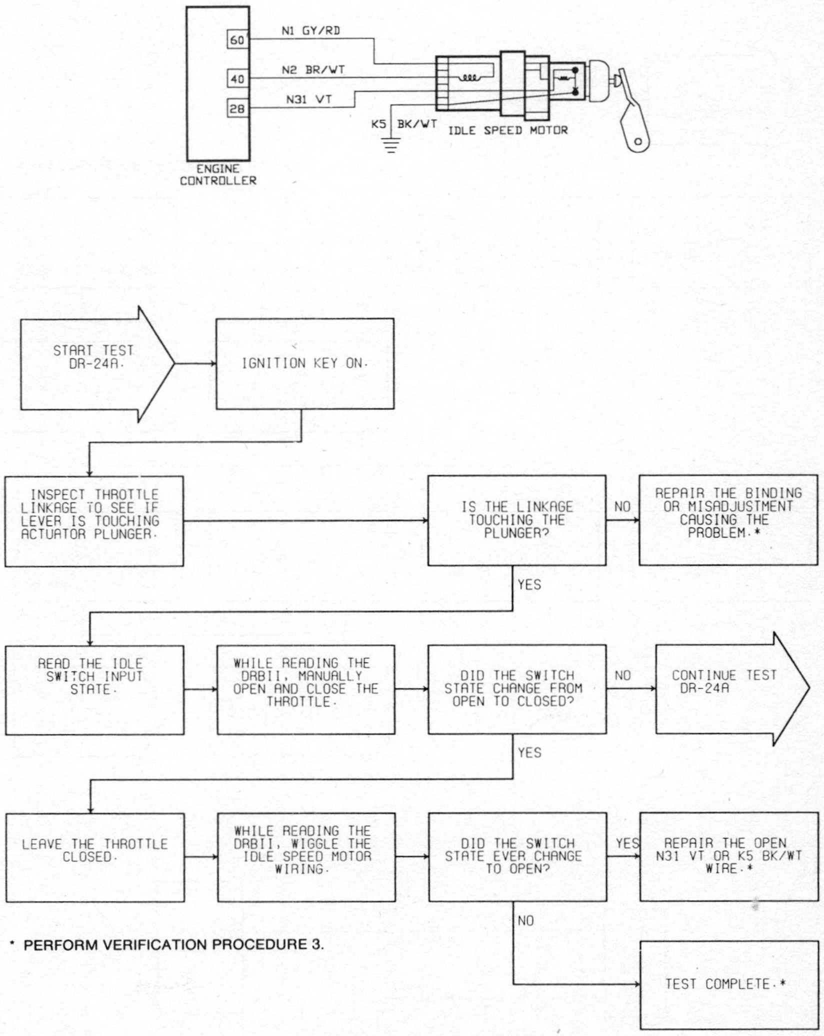
60
40
28
ENGINE CONTROLLER
N1 GY/RD
N2 BR/WT
N31 VT
K5 BK/WT
IDLE SPEED MOTOR
START TEST DR-24A.
IGNITION KEY ON.
INSPECT THROTTLE LINKAGE TO SEE IF LEVER IS TOUCHING ACTUATOR PLUNGER.
IS THE LINKAGE TOUCHING THE PLUNGER?
NO
REPAIR THE BINDING OR MISADJUSTMENT CAUSING THE PROBLEM.*
YES
READ THE IDLE SWITCH INPUT STATE.
WHILE READING THE DRBII, MANUALLY OPEN AND CLOSE THE THROTTLE.
DID THE SWITCH STATE CHANGE FROM OPEN TO CLOSED?
NO
CONTINUE TEST DR-24A
YES
LEAVE THE THROTTLE CLOSED.
WHILE READING THE DRBII, WIGGLE THE IDLE SPEED MOTOR WIRING.
DID THE SWITCH STATE EVER CHANGE TO OPEN?
YES
REPAIR THE OPEN N31 VT OR K5 BK/WT WIRE.*
NO
TEST COMPLETE.*

* PERFORM VERIFICATION PROCEDURE 3.

91H14107 91G14163

Fig. 78: Driveability Test 24A – Repairing Fault "Idle Switch Open Circuit" (1 of 2)

DR-24A – REPAIRING FAULT "IDLE SWITCH OPEN CIRCUIT" (2 OF 2)

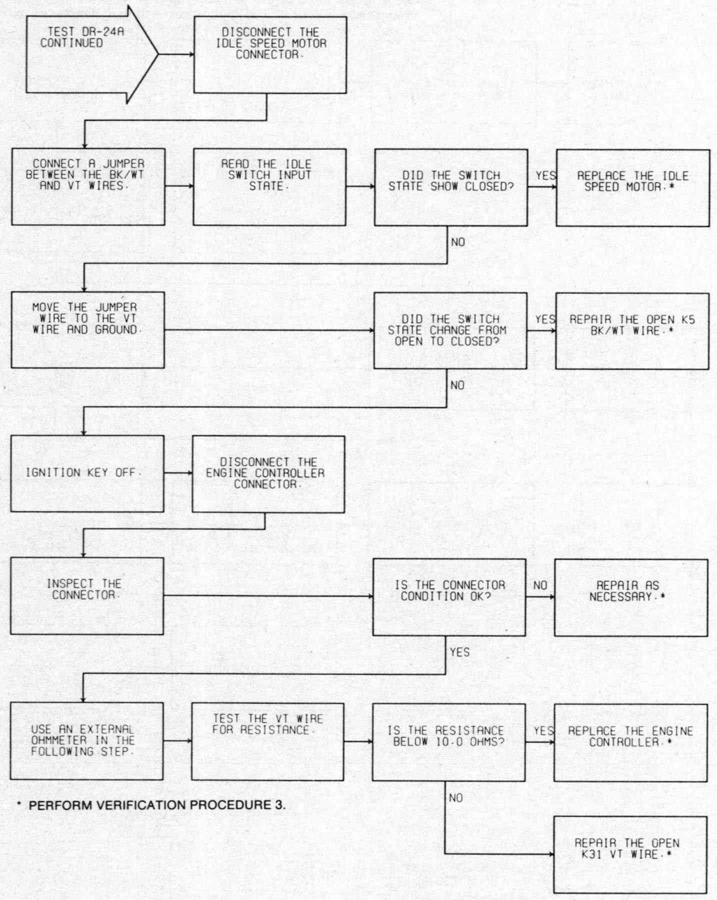
TEST DR-24A CONTINUED
DISCONNECT THE IDLE SPEED MOTOR CONNECTOR.
CONNECT A JUMPER BETWEEN THE BK/WT AND VT WIRES.
READ THE IDLE SWITCH INPUT STATE.
DID THE SWITCH STATE SHOW CLOSED?
YES
REPLACE THE IDLE SPEED MOTOR.*
NO
MOVE THE JUMPER WIRE TO THE VT WIRE AND GROUND.
DID THE SWITCH STATE CHANGE FROM OPEN TO CLOSED?
YES
REPAIR THE OPEN K5 BK/WT WIRE.*
NO
IGNITION KEY OFF.
DISCONNECT THE ENGINE CONTROLLER CONNECTOR.
INSPECT THE CONNECTOR.
IS THE CONNECTOR CONDITION OK?
NO
REPAIR AS NECESSARY.*
YES
USE AN EXTERNAL OHMMETER IN THE FOLLOWING STEP.
TEST THE VT WIRE FOR RESISTANCE.
IS THE RESISTANCE BELOW 10.0 OHMS?
YES
REPLACE THE ENGINE CONTROLLER.*
NO
REPAIR THE OPEN K31 VT WIRE.*
* PERFORM VERIFICATION PROCEDURE 3.

91H14164

Fig. 79: Driveability Test 24A – Repairing Fault "Idle Switch Open Circuit" (2 of 2)

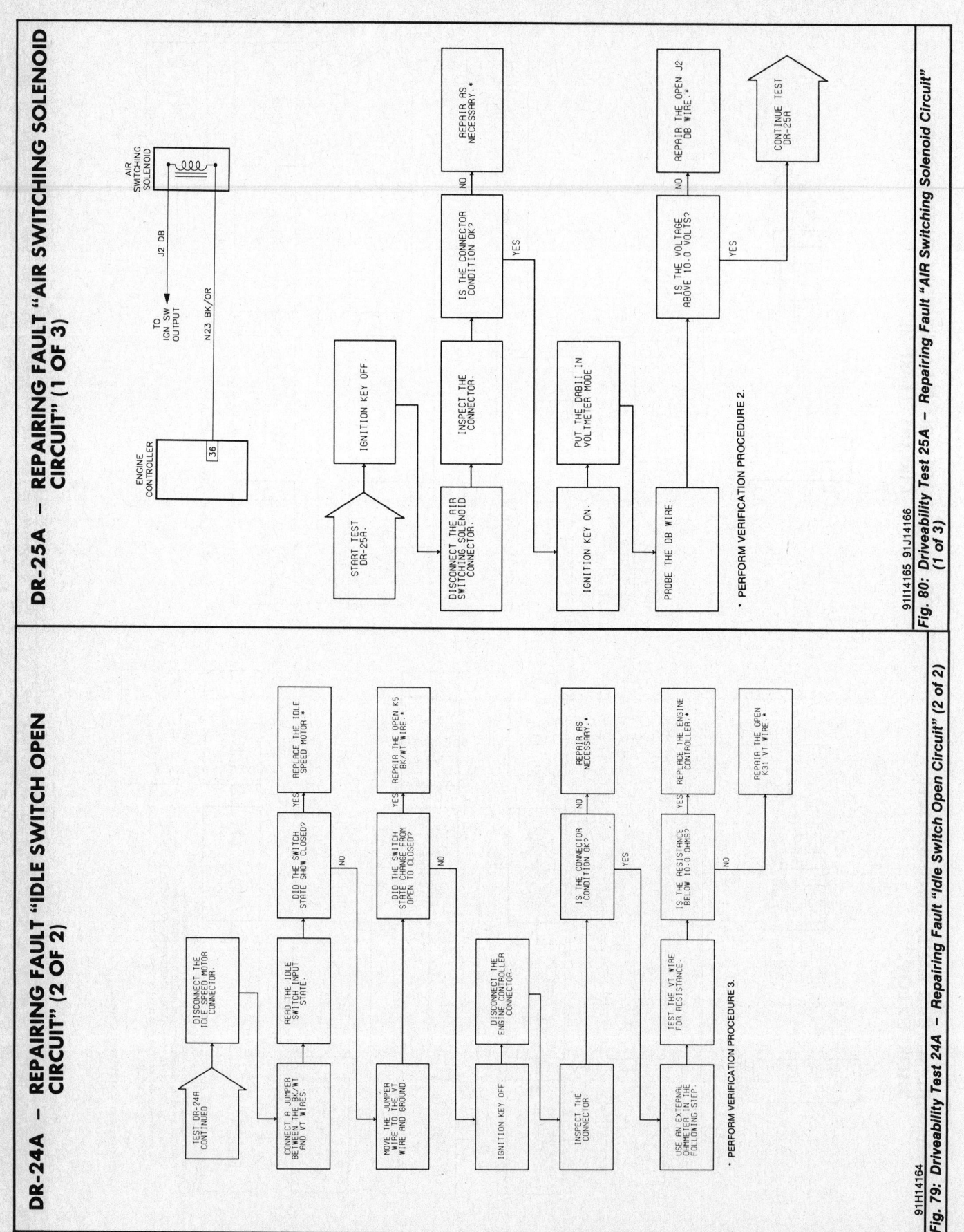

DR-25A – REPAIRING FAULT "AIR SWITCHING SOLENOID CIRCUIT" (1 OF 3)

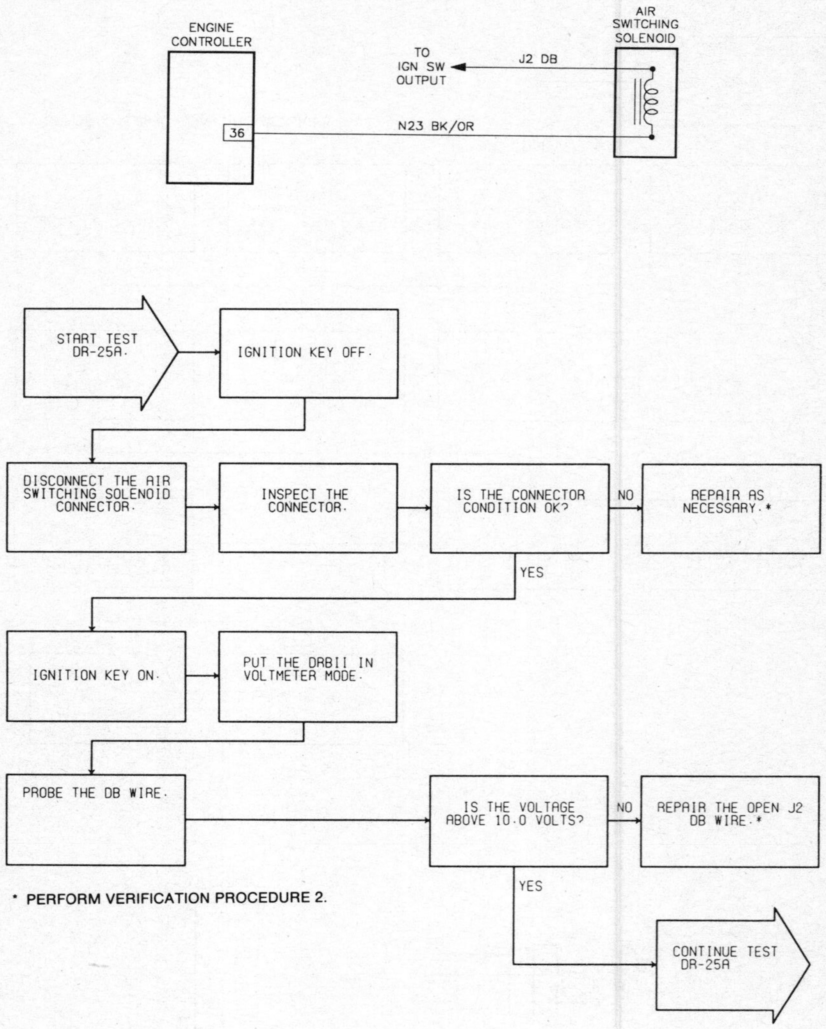
ENGINE CONTROLLER
36
TO IGN SW OUTPUT
J2 DB
N23 BK/OR
AIR SWITCHING SOLENOID
START TEST DR-25A.
IGNITION KEY OFF.
DISCONNECT THE AIR SWITCHING SOLENOID CONNECTOR.
INSPECT THE CONNECTOR.
IS THE CONNECTOR CONDITION OK?
NO
REPAIR AS NECESSARY.*
YES
IGNITION KEY ON.
PUT THE DRBII IN VOLTMETER MODE.
PROBE THE DB WIRE.
IS THE VOLTAGE ABOVE 10.0 VOLTS?
NO
REPAIR THE OPEN J2 DB WIRE.*
YES
CONTINUE TEST DR-25A
* PERFORM VERIFICATION PROCEDURE 2.

91I14165 91J14166

Fig. 80: Driveability Test 25A – Repairing Fault "AIR Switching Solenoid Circuit" (1 of 3)

DR-25A – REPAIRING FAULT "AIR SWITCHING SOLENOID CIRCUIT" (2 OF 3)

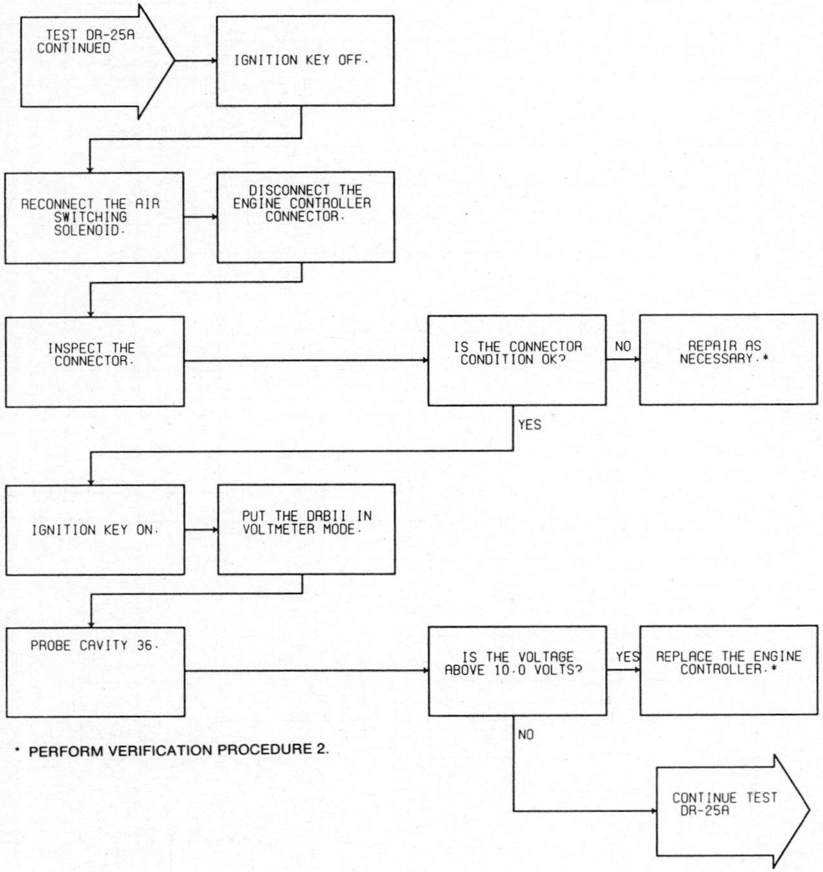
TEST DR-25A CONTINUED
IGNITION KEY OFF.
RECONNECT THE AIR SWITCHING SOLENOID.
DISCONNECT THE ENGINE CONTROLLER CONNECTOR.
INSPECT THE CONNECTOR.
IS THE CONNECTOR CONDITION OK?
NO
REPAIR AS NECESSARY.*
YES
IGNITION KEY ON.
PUT THE DRBII IN VOLTMETER MODE.
PROBE CAVITY 36.
IS THE VOLTAGE ABOVE 10.0 VOLTS?
YES
REPLACE THE ENGINE CONTROLLER.*
NO
CONTINUE TEST DR-25A

* PERFORM VERIFICATION PROCEDURE 2.

91A14167

Fig. 81: Driveability Test 25A – Repairing Fault "AIR Switching Solenoid Circuit" (2 of 3)

DR-25A – REPAIRING FAULT "AIR SWITCHING SOLENOID CIRCUIT" (3 OF 3)

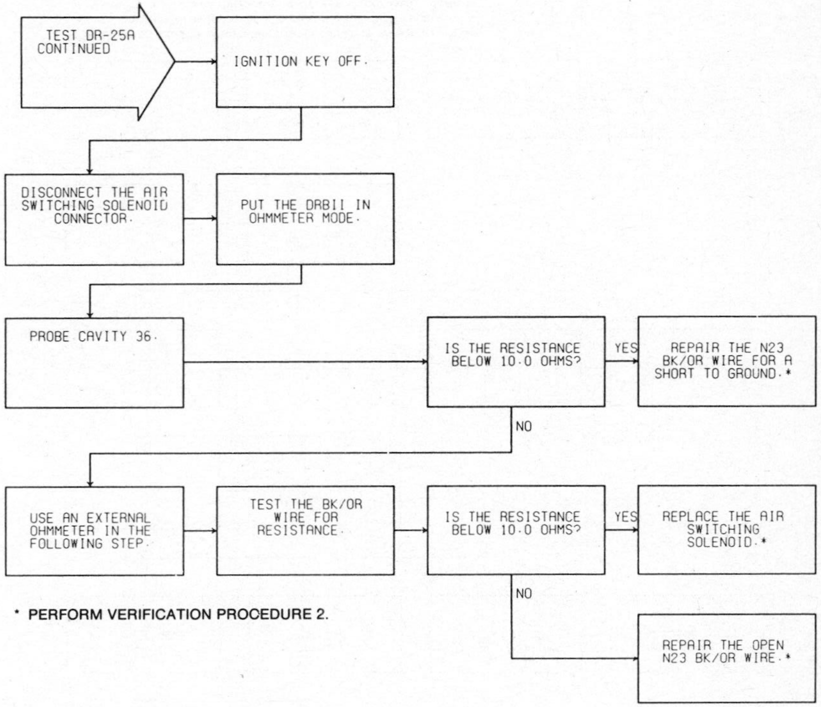
TEST DR-25A CONTINUED
IGNITION KEY OFF.
DISCONNECT THE AIR SWITCHING SOLENOID CONNECTOR.
PUT THE DRBII IN OHMMETER MODE.
PROBE CAVITY 36.
IS THE RESISTANCE BELOW 10.0 OHMS?
YES
REPAIR THE N23 BK/OR WIRE FOR A SHORT TO GROUND.*
NO
USE AN EXTERNAL OHMMETER IN THE FOLLOWING STEP.
TEST THE BK/OR WIRE FOR RESISTANCE.
IS THE RESISTANCE BELOW 10.0 OHMS?
YES
REPLACE THE AIR SWITCHING SOLENOID.*
NO
REPAIR THE OPEN N23 BK/OR WIRE.*

* PERFORM VERIFICATION PROCEDURE 2.

91B14168

Fig. 82: Driveability Test 25A – Repairing Fault "AIR Switching Solenoid Circuit" (3 of 3)

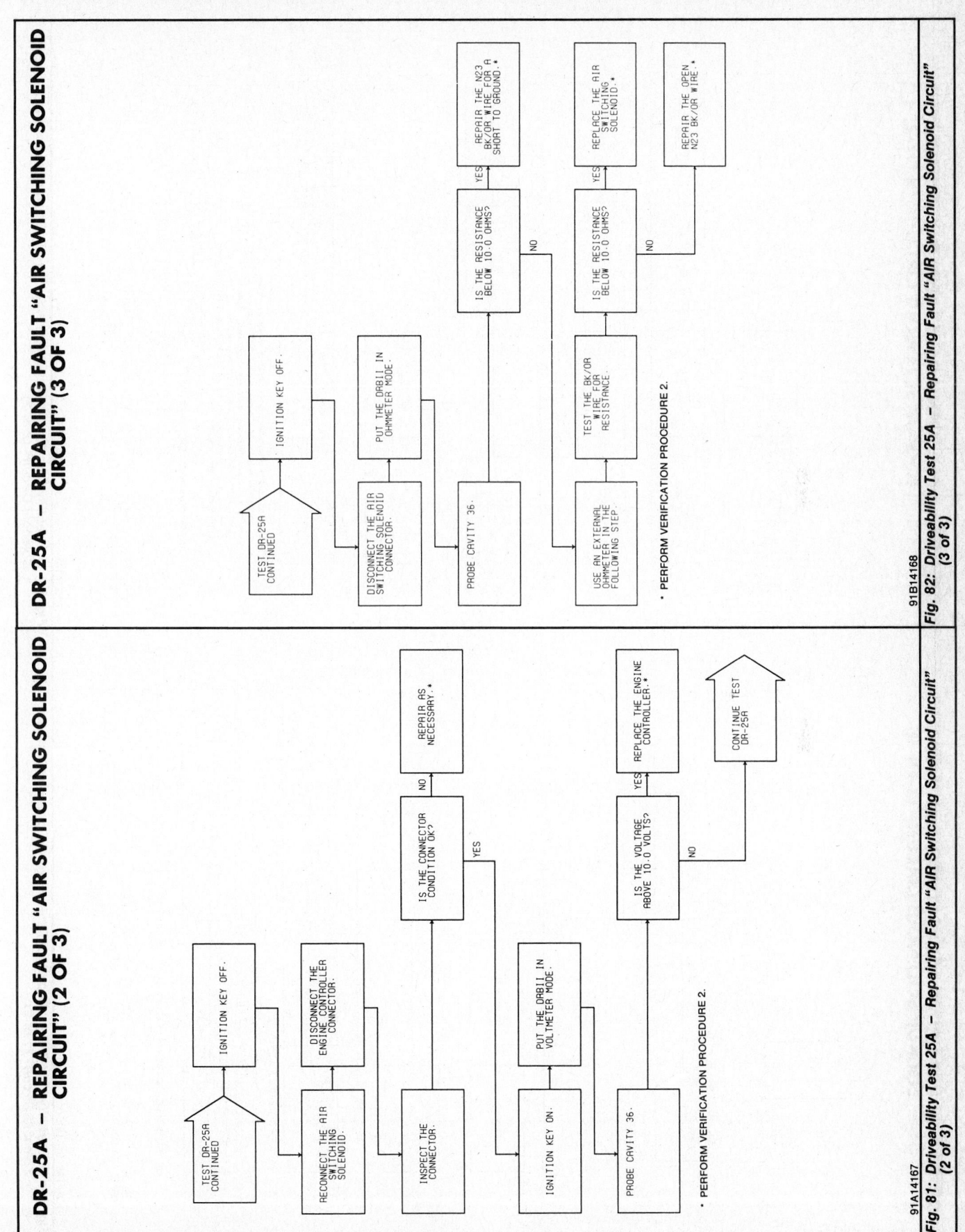

DR-26A – REPAIRING FAULT "TORQUE CONVERTER LOCKUP SOLENOID CIRCUIT" (1 OF 2)

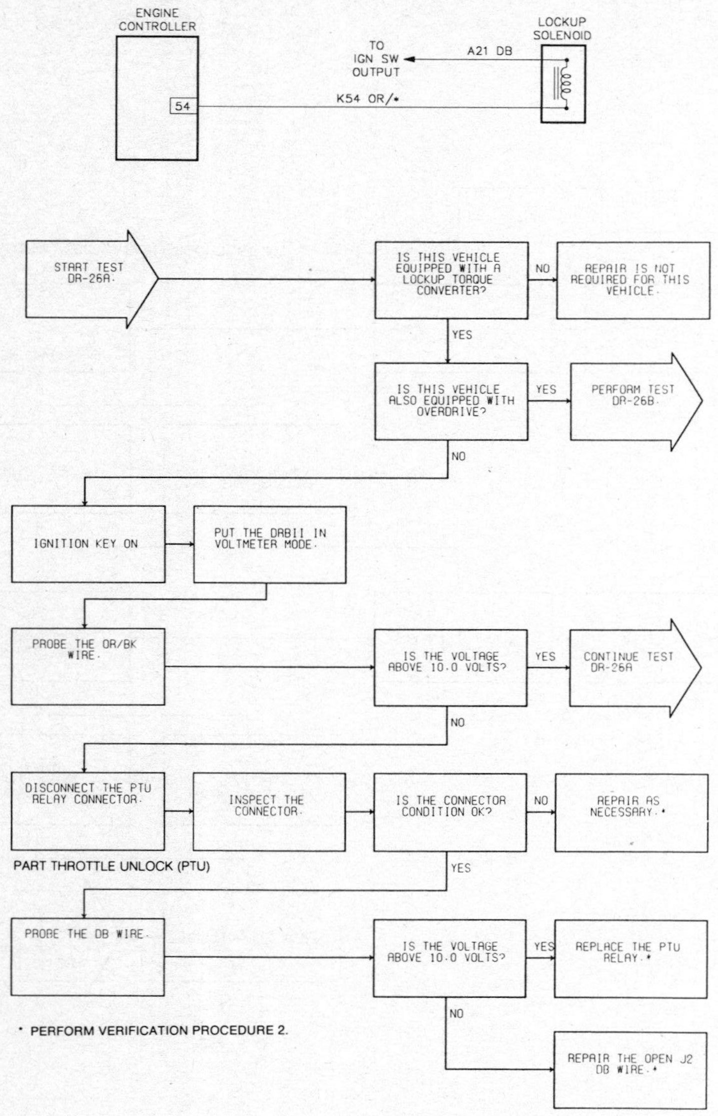
ENGINE CONTROLLER
54
K54 OR/*
TO IGN SW OUTPUT
A21 DB
LOCKUP SOLENOID
START TEST DR-26A.
IS THIS VEHICLE EQUIPPED WITH A LOCKUP TORQUE CONVERTER?
NO
REPAIR IS NOT REQUIRED FOR THIS VEHICLE.
YES
IS THIS VEHICLE ALSO EQUIPPED WITH OVERDRIVE?
YES
PERFORM TEST DR-26B.
NO
IGNITION KEY ON
PUT THE DRBII IN VOLTMETER MODE.
PROBE THE OR/BK WIRE.
IS THE VOLTAGE ABOVE 10.0 VOLTS?
YES
CONTINUE TEST DR-26A
NO
DISCONNECT THE PTU RELAY CONNECTOR.
INSPECT THE CONNECTOR.
IS THE CONNECTOR CONDITION OK?
NO
REPAIR AS NECESSARY.*
YES
PROBE THE DB WIRE.
IS THE VOLTAGE ABOVE 10.0 VOLTS?
YES
REPLACE THE PTU RELAY.*
NO
REPAIR THE OPEN J2 DB WIRE.*

PART THROTTLE UNLOCK (PTU)

* PERFORM VERIFICATION PROCEDURE 2.

91C14169 91F14170

Fig. 83: Driveability Test 26A – Repairing Fault "Torque Converter Lockup Solenoid Circuit" (1 of 2)

DR-26A – REPAIRING FAULT "TORQUE CONVERTER LOCKUP SOLENOID CIRCUIT" (2 OF 2)

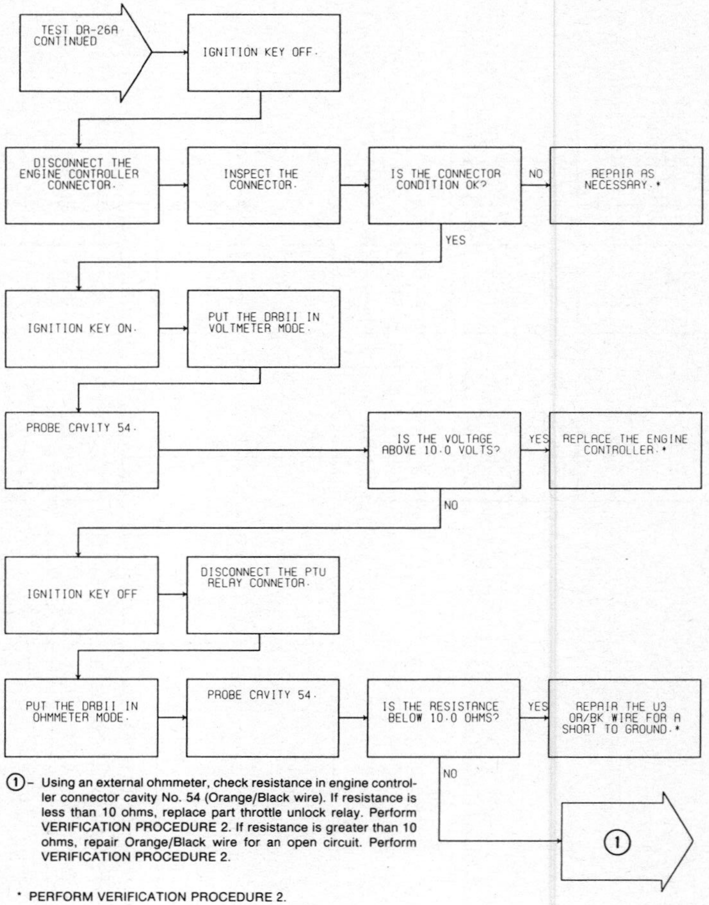
TEST DR-26A CONTINUED
IGNITION KEY OFF.
DISCONNECT THE ENGINE CONTROLLER CONNECTOR.
INSPECT THE CONNECTOR.
IS THE CONNECTOR CONDITION OK?
NO
REPAIR AS NECESSARY.*
YES
IGNITION KEY ON.
PUT THE DRBII IN VOLTMETER MODE.
PROBE CAVITY 54.
IS THE VOLTAGE ABOVE 10.0 VOLTS?
YES
REPLACE THE ENGINE CONTROLLER.*
NO
IGNITION KEY OFF
DISCONNECT THE PTU RELAY CONNETOR.
PUT THE DRBII IN OHMMETER MODE.
PROBE CAVITY 54.
IS THE RESISTANCE BELOW 10.0 OHMS?
YES
REPAIR THE U3 OR/BK WIRE FOR A SHORT TO GROUND.*
NO
1

① – Using an external ohmmeter, check resistance in engine controller connector cavity No. 54 (Orange/Black wire). If resistance is less than 10 ohms, replace part throttle unlock relay. Perform VERIFICATION PROCEDURE 2. If resistance is greater than 10 ohms, repair Orange/Black wire for an open circuit. Perform VERIFICATION PROCEDURE 2.

* PERFORM VERIFICATION PROCEDURE 2.

91G14171

Fig. 84: Driveability Test 26A – Repairing Fault "Torque Converter Lockup Solenoid Circuit" (2 of 2)

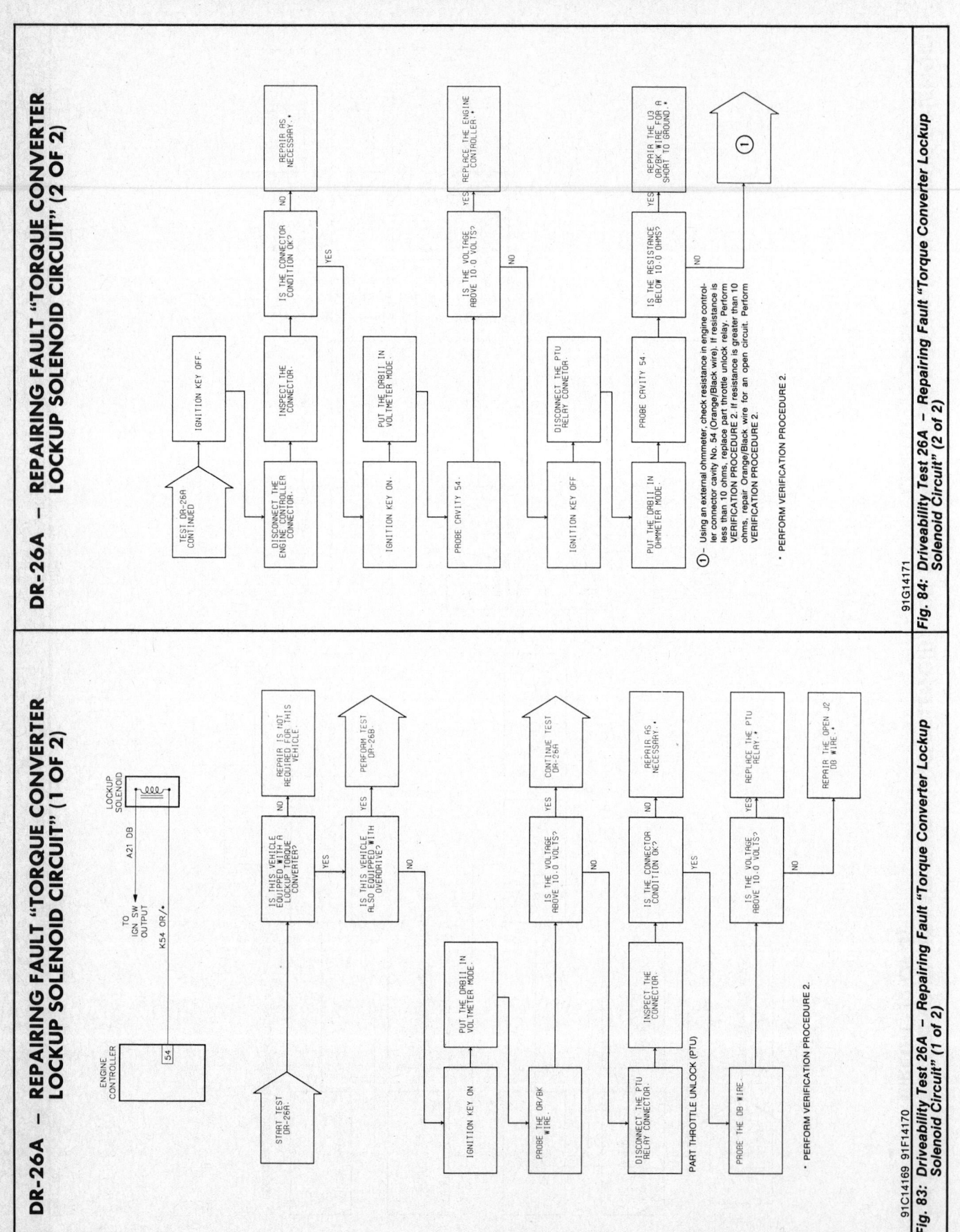

DR-26B – REPAIRING FAULT "TORQUE CONVERTER LOCKUP SOLENOID CIRCUIT" (W/OD) (1 OF 2)

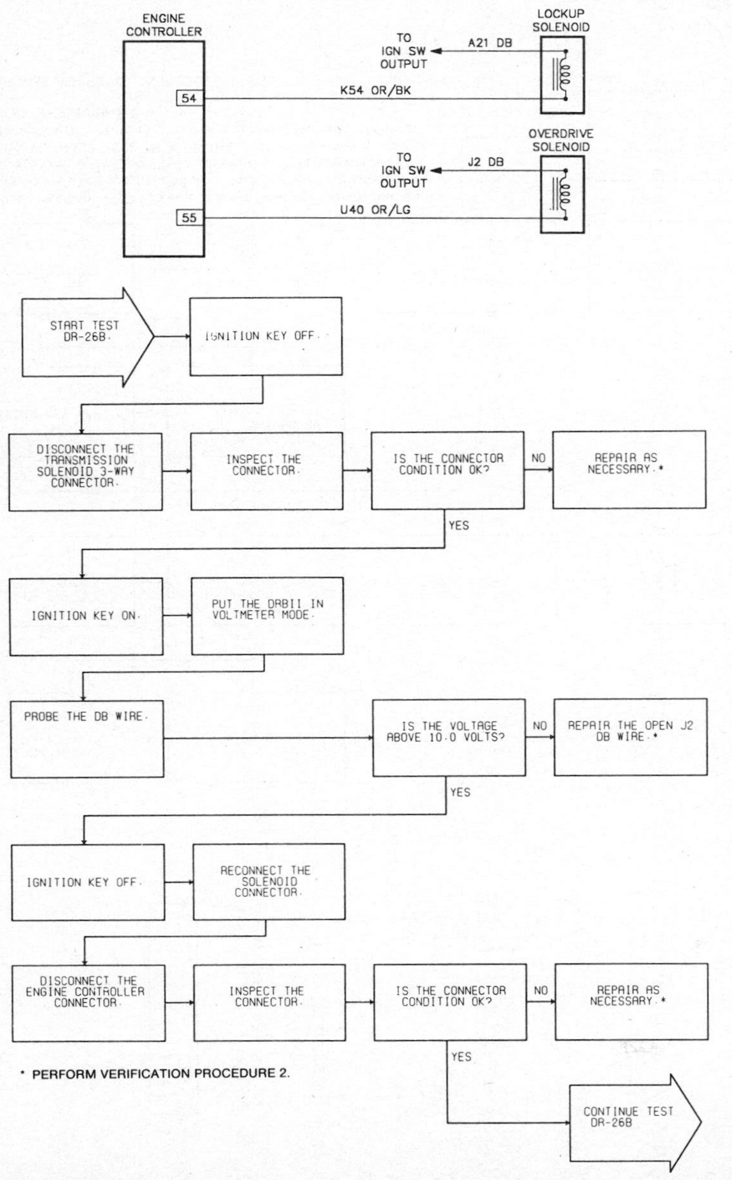
ENGINE CONTROLLER
LOCKUP SOLENOID
TO IGN SW OUTPUT
A21 DB
54
K54 OR/BK
OVERDRIVE SOLENOID
TO IGN SW OUTPUT
J2 DB
55
U40 OR/LG
START TEST DR-26B.
IGNITION KEY OFF.
DISCONNECT THE TRANSMISSION SOLENOID 3-WAY CONNECTOR.
INSPECT THE CONNECTOR.
IS THE CONNECTOR CONDITION OK?
NO
REPAIR AS NECESSARY.*
YES
IGNITION KEY ON.
PUT THE DRBII IN VOLTMETER MODE.
PROBE THE DB WIRE.
IS THE VOLTAGE ABOVE 10.0 VOLTS?
NO
REPAIR THE OPEN J2 DB WIRE.*
YES
IGNITION KEY OFF.
RECONNECT THE SOLENOID CONNECTOR.
DISCONNECT THE ENGINE CONTROLLER CONNECTOR.
INSPECT THE CONNECTOR.
IS THE CONNECTOR CONDITION OK?
NO
REPAIR AS NECESSARY.*
YES
CONTINUE TEST DR-26B
* PERFORM VERIFICATION PROCEDURE 2.

91H14172 91I14173

Fig. 85: Driveability Test 26B – Repairing Fault "Torque Converter Lockup Solenoid Circuit" (With Overdrive) (1 of 2)

DR-26B – REPAIRING FAULT "TORQUE CONVERTER LOCKUP SOLENOID CIRCUIT" (W/OD) (2 OF 2)

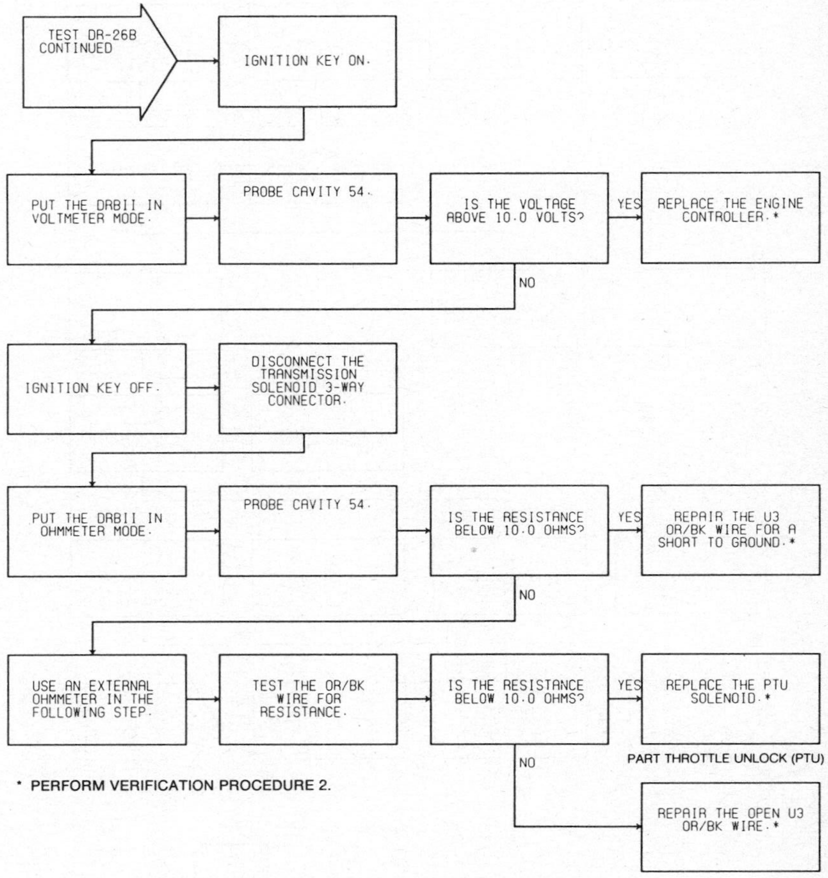
TEST DR-26B CONTINUED
IGNITION KEY ON.
PUT THE DRBII IN VOLTMETER MODE.
PROBE CAVITY 54.
IS THE VOLTAGE ABOVE 10.0 VOLTS?
YES
REPLACE THE ENGINE CONTROLLER.*
NO
IGNITION KEY OFF.
DISCONNECT THE TRANSMISSION SOLENOID 3-WAY CONNECTOR.
PUT THE DRBII IN OHMMETER MODE.
PROBE CAVITY 54.
IS THE RESISTANCE BELOW 10.0 OHMS?
YES
REPAIR THE U3 OR/BK WIRE FOR A SHORT TO GROUND.*
NO
USE AN EXTERNAL OHMMETER IN THE FOLLOWING STEP.
TEST THE OR/BK WIRE FOR RESISTANCE.
IS THE RESISTANCE BELOW 10.0 OHMS?
YES
REPLACE THE PTU SOLENOID.*
PART THROTTLE UNLOCK (PTU)
NO
REPAIR THE OPEN U3 OR/BK WIRE.*
* PERFORM VERIFICATION PROCEDURE 2.

91J14174

Fig. 86: Driveability Test 26B – Repairing Fault "Torque Converter Lockup Solenoid Circuit" (With Overdrive) (2 of 2)

1991 ENGINE PERFORMANCE
Self-Diagnostics – 3.9L, 5.2L & 5.9L TBI (Cont.)

DR-27A – REPAIRING FAULT "NO ASD RELAY VOLTAGE SENSE AT CONTROLLER"

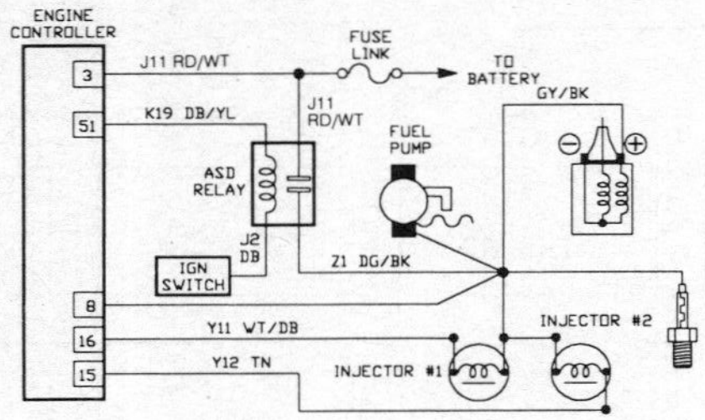
ENGINE CONTROLLER
3
51
8
16
15
J11 RD/WT
K19 DB/YL
FUSE LINK
TO BATTERY
GY/BK
J11 RD/WT
FUEL PUMP
ASD RELAY
J2 DB
IGN SWITCH
Z1 DG/BK
Y11 WT/DB
Y12 TN
INJECTOR #1
INJECTOR #2

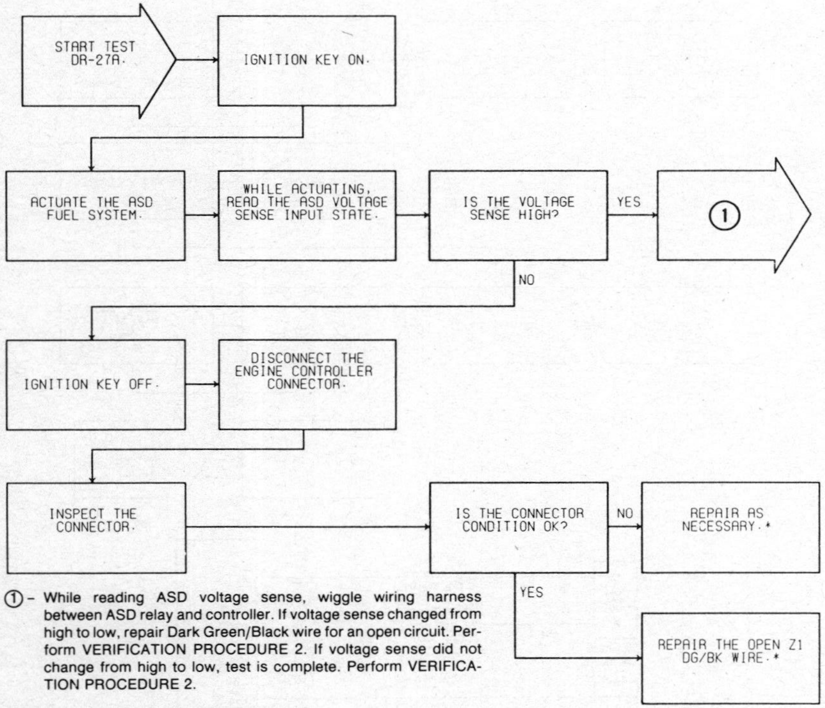
START TEST DR-27A.
IGNITION KEY ON.
ACTUATE THE ASD FUEL SYSTEM.
WHILE ACTUATING, READ THE ASD VOLTAGE SENSE INPUT STATE.
IS THE VOLTAGE SENSE HIGH?
YES
1
NO
IGNITION KEY OFF.
DISCONNECT THE ENGINE CONTROLLER CONNECTOR.
INSPECT THE CONNECTOR.
IS THE CONNECTOR CONDITION OK?
NO
REPAIR AS NECESSARY.*
YES
REPAIR THE OPEN Z1 DG/BK WIRE.*

① – While reading ASD voltage sense, wiggle wiring harness between ASD relay and controller. If voltage sense changed from high to low, repair Dark Green/Black wire for an open circuit. Perform VERIFICATION PROCEDURE 2. If voltage sense did not change from high to low, test is complete. Perform VERIFICATION PROCEDURE 2.

* PERFORM VERIFICATION PROCEDURE 2.

91G14064 91A14175

Fig. 87: Driveability Test 27A – Repairing Fault "No ASD Relay Voltage Sense At Controller"

DR-28A – REPAIRING FAULT "OVERDRIVE SOLENOID CIRCUIT" (WITHOUT LOCKUP) (1 OF 2)

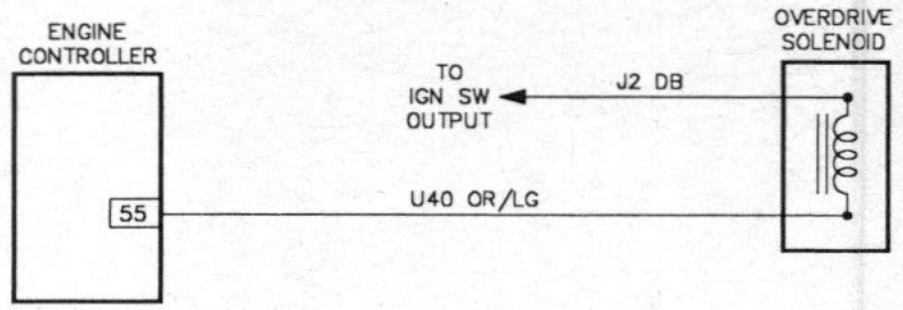
ENGINE CONTROLLER
55
OVERDRIVE SOLENOID
TO IGN SW OUTPUT
J2 DB
U40 OR/LG

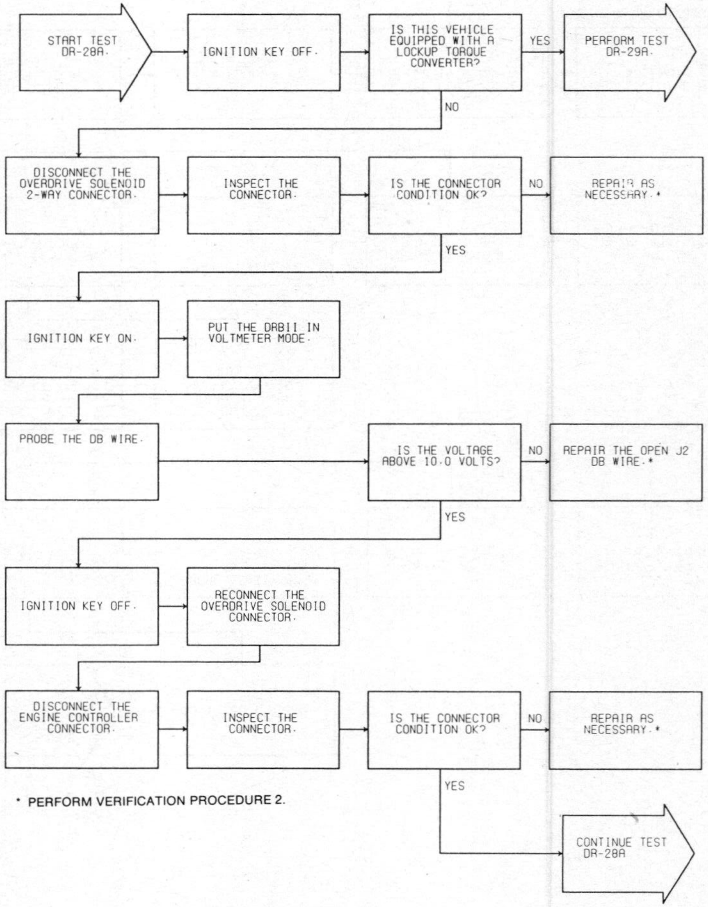
START TEST DR-28A.
IGNITION KEY OFF.
IS THIS VEHICLE EQUIPPED WITH A LOCKUP TORQUE CONVERTER?
YES
PERFORM TEST DR-29A.
NO
DISCONNECT THE OVERDRIVE SOLENOID 2-WAY CONNECTOR.
INSPECT THE CONNECTOR.
IS THE CONNECTOR CONDITION OK?
NO
REPAIR AS NECESSARY.*
YES
IGNITION KEY ON.
PUT THE DRBII IN VOLTMETER MODE.
PROBE THE DB WIRE.
IS THE VOLTAGE ABOVE 10.0 VOLTS?
NO
REPAIR THE OPEN J2 DB WIRE.*
YES
IGNITION KEY OFF.
RECONNECT THE OVERDRIVE SOLENOID CONNECTOR.
DISCONNECT THE ENGINE CONTROLLER CONNECTOR.
INSPECT THE CONNECTOR.
IS THE CONNECTOR CONDITION OK?
NO
REPAIR AS NECESSARY.*
YES
CONTINUE TEST DR-28A

* PERFORM VERIFICATION PROCEDURE 2.

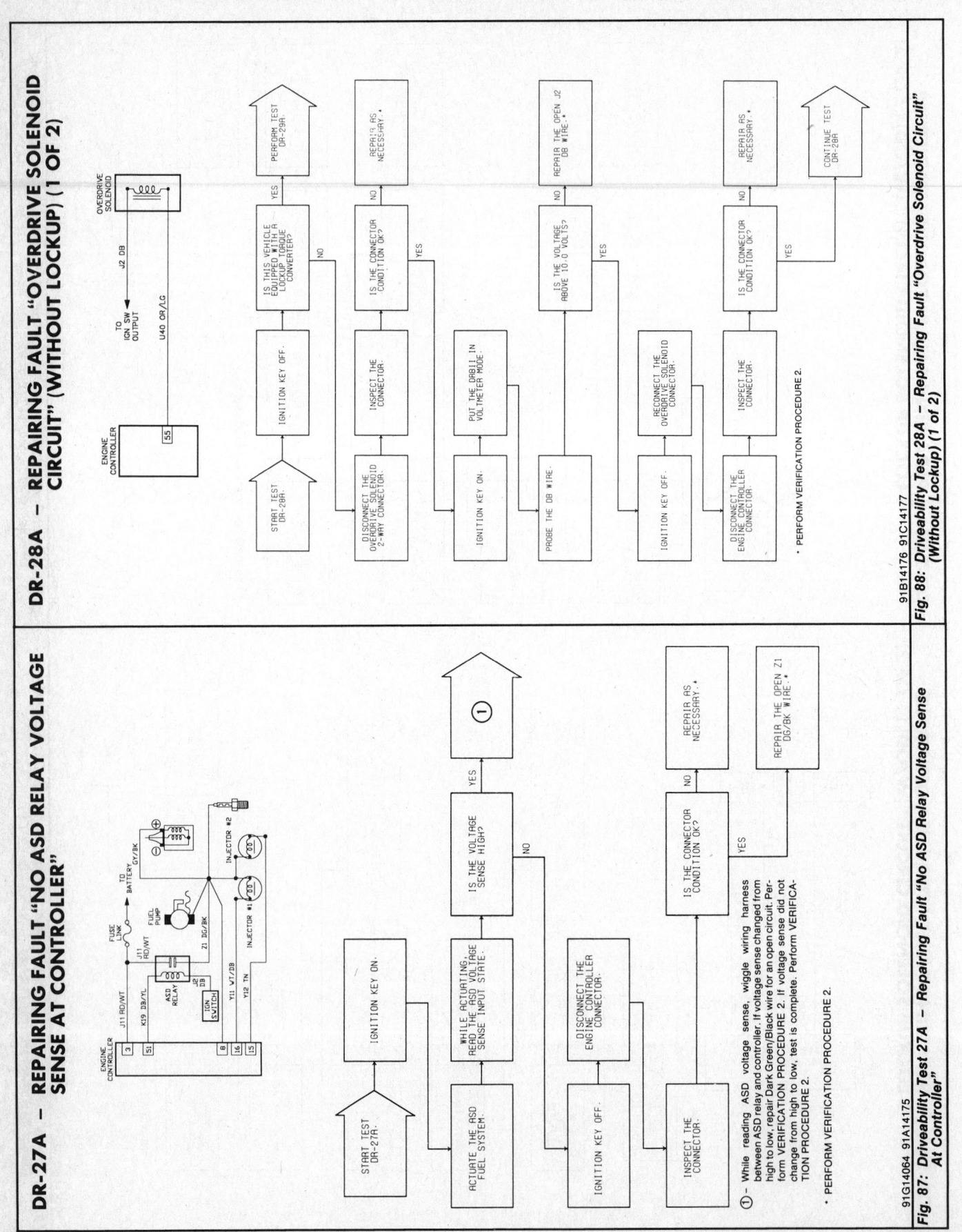

91B14176 91C14177

Fig. 88: Driveability Test 28A – Repairing Fault "Overdrive Solenoid Circuit" (Without Lockup) (1 of 2)

DR-28A – REPAIRING FAULT "OVERDRIVE SOLENOID CIRCUIT" (WITHOUT LOCKUP) (2 OF 2)

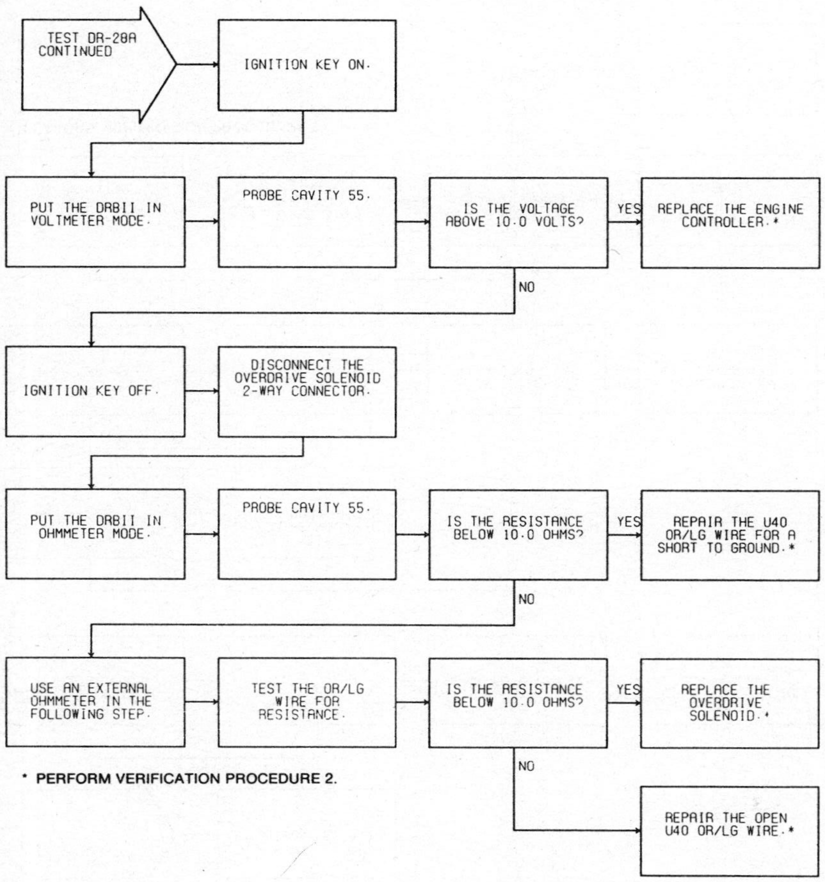
TEST DR-28A CONTINUED
IGNITION KEY ON.
PUT THE DRBII IN VOLTMETER MODE.
PROBE CAVITY 55.
IS THE VOLTAGE ABOVE 10.0 VOLTS?
YES
REPLACE THE ENGINE CONTROLLER.*
NO
IGNITION KEY OFF.
DISCONNECT THE OVERDRIVE SOLENOID 2-WAY CONNECTOR.
PUT THE DRBII IN OHMMETER MODE.
PROBE CAVITY 55.
IS THE RESISTANCE BELOW 10.0 OHMS?
YES
REPAIR THE U40 OR/LG WIRE FOR A SHORT TO GROUND.*
NO
USE AN EXTERNAL OHMMETER IN THE FOLLOWING STEP.
TEST THE OR/LG WIRE FOR RESISTANCE.
IS THE RESISTANCE BELOW 10.0 OHMS?
YES
REPLACE THE OVERDRIVE SOLENOID.*
NO
REPAIR THE OPEN U40 OR/LG WIRE.*

* PERFORM VERIFICATION PROCEDURE 2.

91D14178

Fig. 89: Driveability Test 28A – Repairing Fault "Overdrive Solenoid Circuit" (Without Lockup) (2 of 2)

DR-29A – REPAIRING FAULT "OVERDRIVE SOLENOID CIRCUIT" (WITH LOCKUP) (1 OF 2)

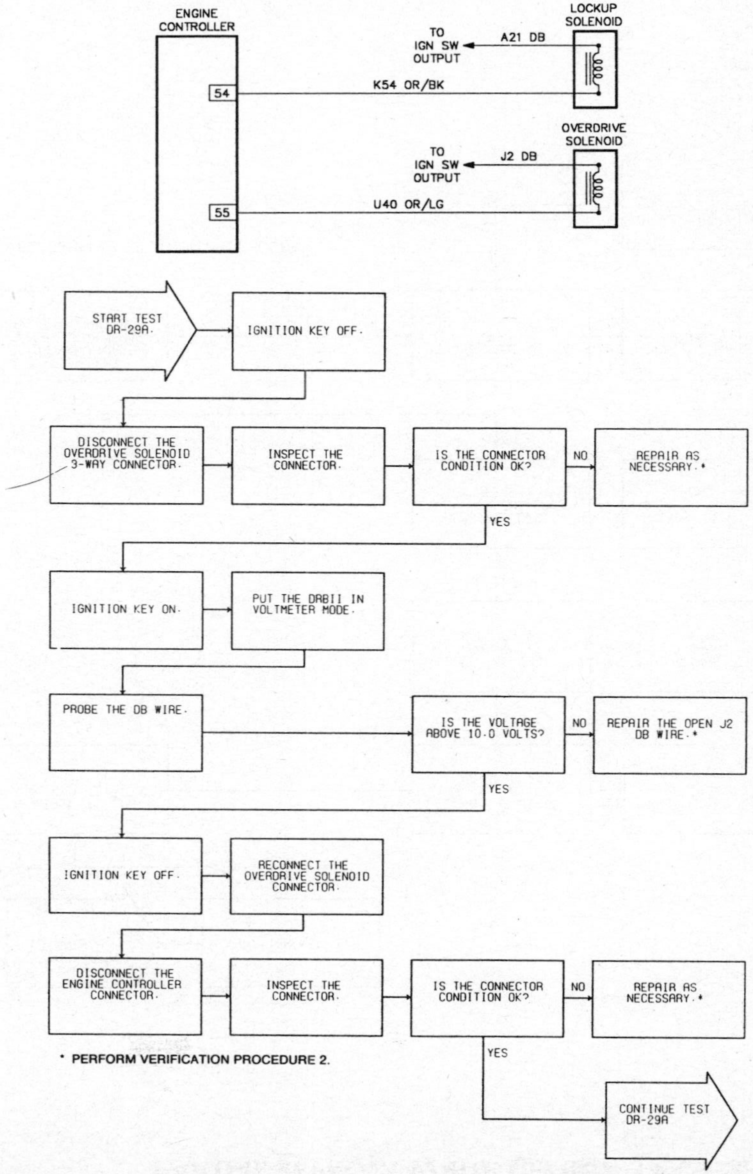
ENGINE CONTROLLER
54
55
TO IGN SW OUTPUT
A21 DB
LOCKUP SOLENOID
K54 OR/BK
TO IGN SW OUTPUT
J2 DB
OVERDRIVE SOLENOID
U40 OR/LG
START TEST DR-29A.
IGNITION KEY OFF.
DISCONNECT THE OVERDRIVE SOLENOID 3-WAY CONNECTOR.
INSPECT THE CONNECTOR.
IS THE CONNECTOR CONDITION OK?
NO
REPAIR AS NECESSARY.*
YES
IGNITION KEY ON.
PUT THE DRBII IN VOLTMETER MODE.
PROBE THE DB WIRE.
IS THE VOLTAGE ABOVE 10.0 VOLTS?
NO
REPAIR THE OPEN J2 DB WIRE.*
YES
IGNITION KEY OFF.
RECONNECT THE OVERDRIVE SOLENOID CONNECTOR.
DISCONNECT THE ENGINE CONTROLLER CONNECTOR.
INSPECT THE CONNECTOR.
IS THE CONNECTOR CONDITION OK?
NO
REPAIR AS NECESSARY.*
YES
CONTINUE TEST DR-29A

* PERFORM VERIFICATION PROCEDURE 2.

91H14172 91E14179

Fig. 90: Driveability Test 29A – Repairing Fault "Overdrive Solenoid Circuit" (With Lockup) (1 of 2)

DR-29A – REPAIRING FAULT "OVERDRIVE SOLENOID CIRCUIT" (WITH LOCKUP) (2 OF 2)

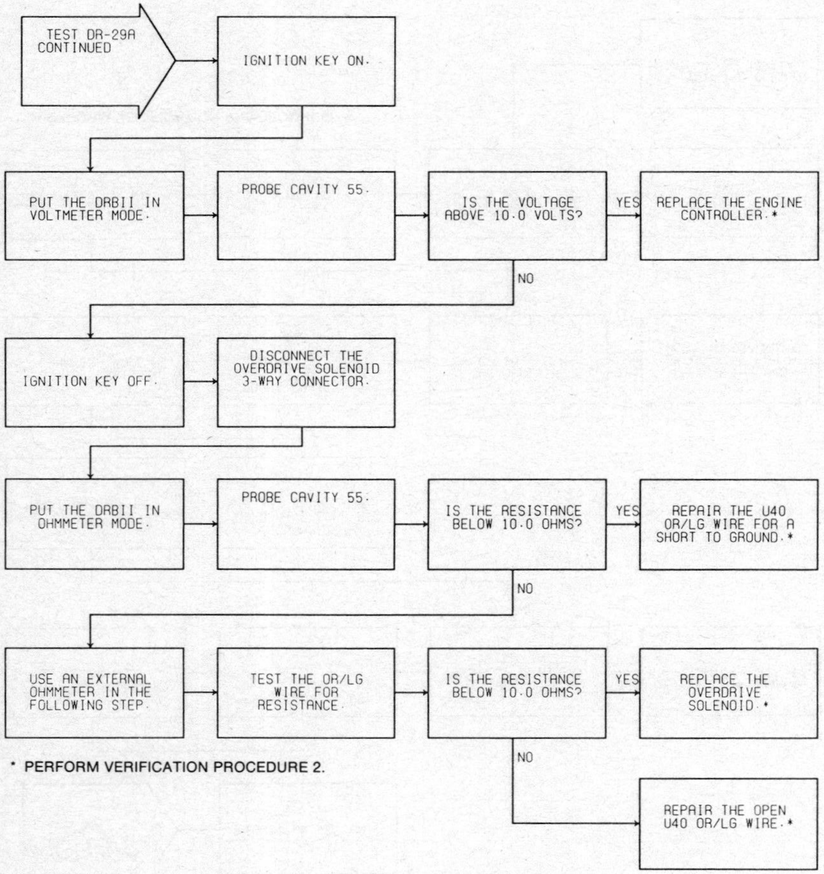
TEST DR-29A CONTINUED
IGNITION KEY ON.
PUT THE DRBII IN VOLTMETER MODE.
PROBE CAVITY 55.
IS THE VOLTAGE ABOVE 10.0 VOLTS?
YES
REPLACE THE ENGINE CONTROLLER.*
NO
IGNITION KEY OFF.
DISCONNECT THE OVERDRIVE SOLENOID 3-WAY CONNECTOR.
PUT THE DRBII IN OHMMETER MODE.
PROBE CAVITY 55.
IS THE RESISTANCE BELOW 10.0 OHMS?
YES
REPAIR THE U40 OR/LG WIRE FOR A SHORT TO GROUND.*
NO
USE AN EXTERNAL OHMMETER IN THE FOLLOWING STEP.
TEST THE OR/LG WIRE FOR RESISTANCE.
IS THE RESISTANCE BELOW 10.0 OHMS?
YES
REPLACE THE OVERDRIVE SOLENOID.*
NO
REPAIR THE OPEN U40 OR/LG WIRE.*

* PERFORM VERIFICATION PROCEDURE 2.

91H14180

Fig. 91: Driveability Test 29A – Repairing Fault "Overdrive Solenoid Circuit" (With Lockup) (2 of 2)

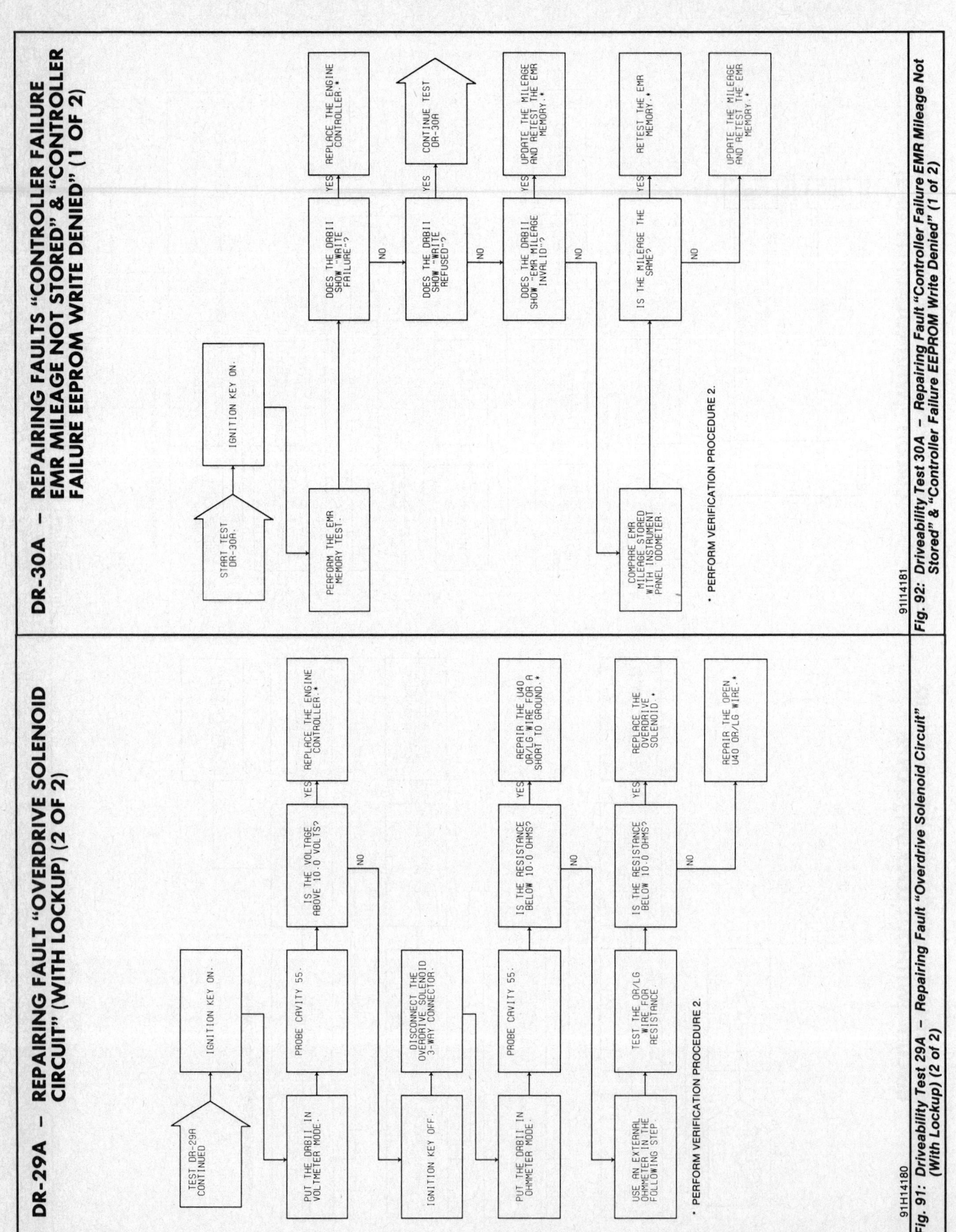

DR-30A – REPAIRING FAULTS "CONTROLLER FAILURE EMR MILEAGE NOT STORED" & "CONTROLLER FAILURE EEPROM WRITE DENIED" (1 OF 2)

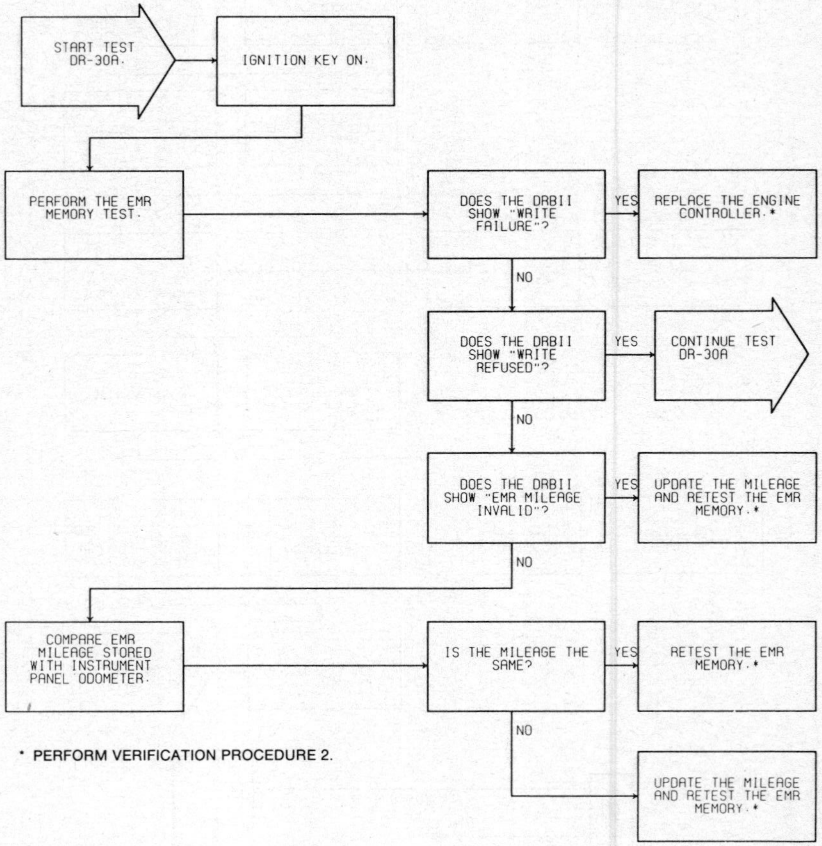
START TEST DR-30A.
IGNITION KEY ON.
PERFORM THE EMR MEMORY TEST.
DOES THE DRBII SHOW "WRITE FAILURE"?
YES
REPLACE THE ENGINE CONTROLLER.*
NO
DOES THE DRBII SHOW "WRITE REFUSED"?
YES
CONTINUE TEST DR-30A
NO
DOES THE DRBII SHOW "EMR MILEAGE INVALID"?
YES
UPDATE THE MILEAGE AND RETEST THE EMR MEMORY.*
NO
COMPARE EMR MILEAGE STORED WITH INSTRUMENT PANEL ODOMETER.
IS THE MILEAGE THE SAME?
YES
RETEST THE EMR MEMORY.*
NO
UPDATE THE MILEAGE AND RETEST THE EMR MEMORY.*

* PERFORM VERIFICATION PROCEDURE 2.

91I14181

Fig. 92: Driveability Test 30A – Repairing Fault "Controller Failure EMR Mileage Not Stored" & "Controller Failure EEPROM Write Denied" (1 of 2)

DR-30A – REPAIRING FAULTS "CONTROLLER FAILURE EMR MILEAGE NOT STORED" & "CONTROLLER FAILURE EEPROM WRITE DENIED" (2 OF 2)

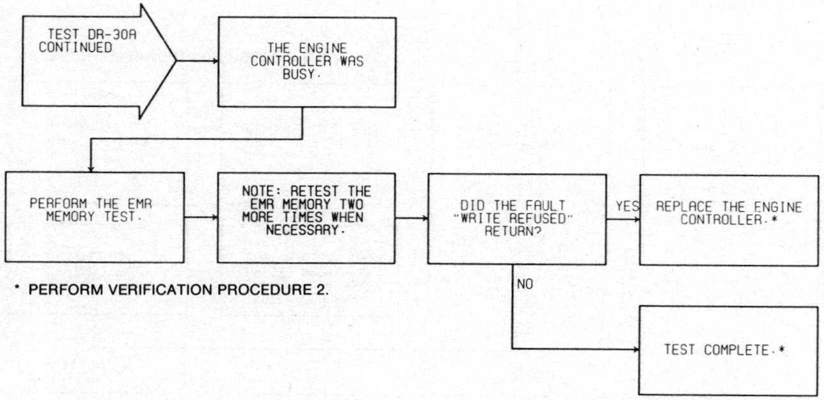
TEST DR-30A CONTINUED
THE ENGINE CONTROLLER WAS BUSY.
PERFORM THE EMR MEMORY TEST.
NOTE: RETEST THE EMR MEMORY TWO MORE TIMES WHEN NECESSARY.
DID THE FAULT "WRITE REFUSED" RETURN?
YES
REPLACE THE ENGINE CONTROLLER.*
NO
TEST COMPLETE.*

* PERFORM VERIFICATION PROCEDURE 2.

91J14182

Fig. 93: Driveability Test 30A – Repairing Fault "Controller Failure EMR Mileage Not Stored" & "Controller Failure EEPROM Write Denied" (2 of 2)

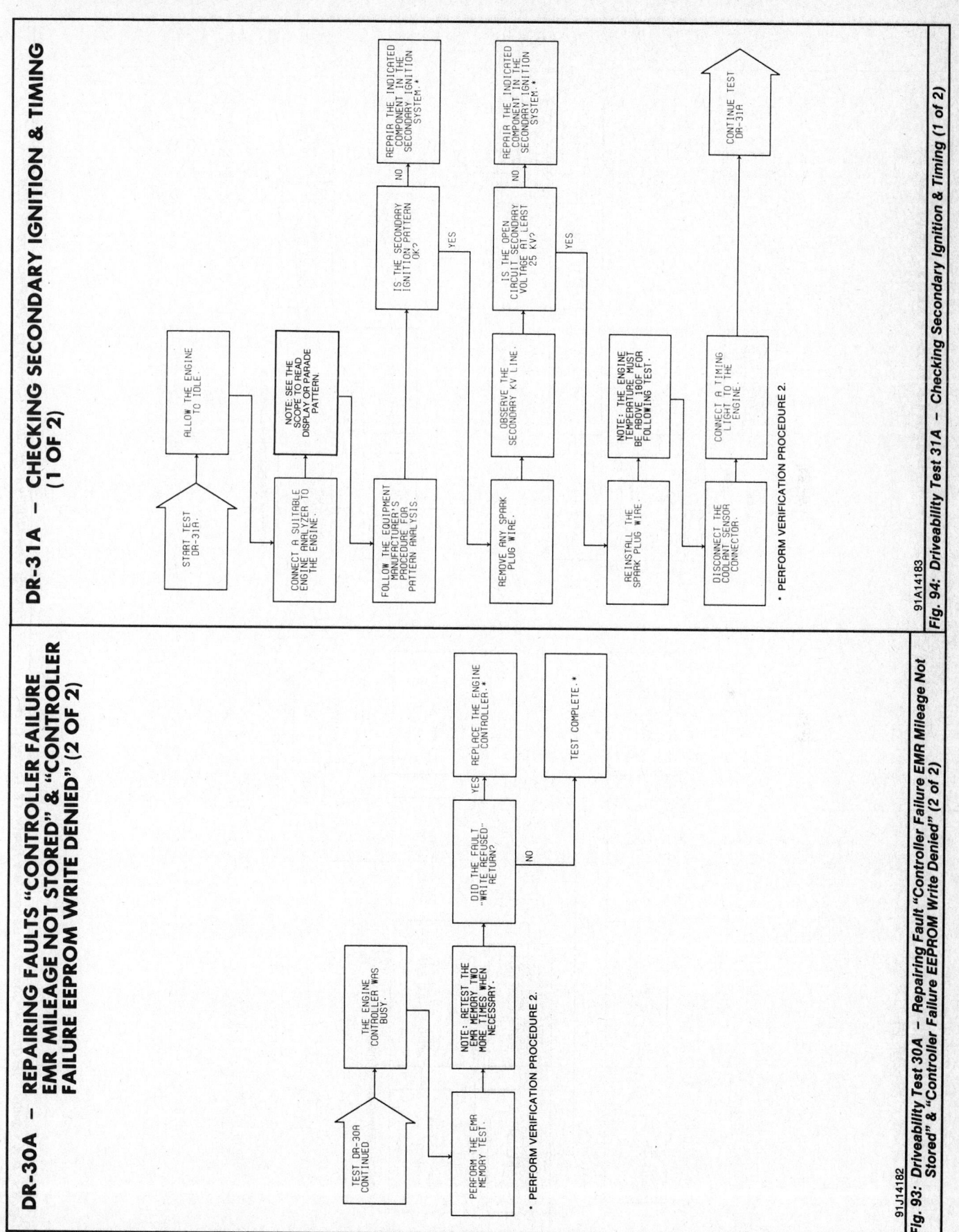

DR-31A – CHECKING SECONDARY IGNITION & TIMING (1 OF 2)

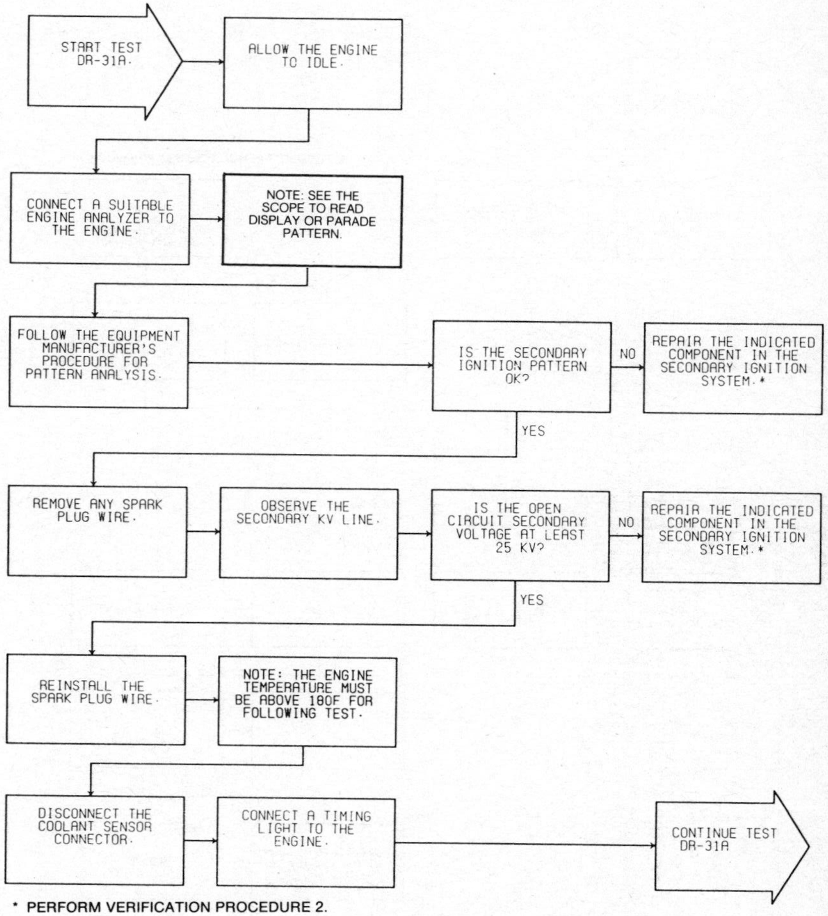
START TEST DR-31A.
ALLOW THE ENGINE TO IDLE.
CONNECT A SUITABLE ENGINE ANALYZER TO THE ENGINE.
NOTE: SEE THE SCOPE TO READ DISPLAY OR PARADE PATTERN.
FOLLOW THE EQUIPMENT MANUFACTURER'S PROCEDURE FOR PATTERN ANALYSIS.
IS THE SECONDARY IGNITION PATTERN OK?
NO
REPAIR THE INDICATED COMPONENT IN THE SECONDARY IGNITION SYSTEM.*
YES
REMOVE ANY SPARK PLUG WIRE.
OBSERVE THE SECONDARY KV LINE.
IS THE OPEN CIRCUIT SECONDARY VOLTAGE AT LEAST 25 KV?
NO
REPAIR THE INDICATED COMPONENT IN THE SECONDARY IGNITION SYSTEM.*
YES
REINSTALL THE SPARK PLUG WIRE.
NOTE: THE ENGINE TEMPERATURE MUST BE ABOVE 180F FOR FOLLOWING TEST.
DISCONNECT THE COOLANT SENSOR CONNECTOR.
CONNECT A TIMING LIGHT TO THE ENGINE.
CONTINUE TEST DR-31A

* PERFORM VERIFICATION PROCEDURE 2.

91A14183

Fig. 94: Driveability Test 31A – Checking Secondary Ignition & Timing (1 of 2)

1991 ENGINE PERFORMANCE
Self-Diagnostics – 3.9L, 5.2L & 5.9L TBI (Cont.)

DR-31A – CHECKING SECONDARY IGNITION & TIMING (2 OF 2)

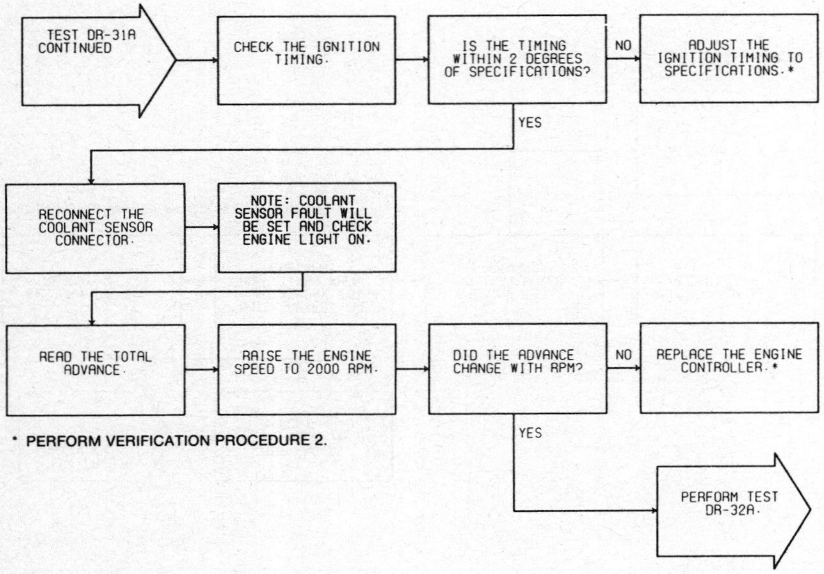
TEST DR-31A CONTINUED
CHECK THE IGNITION TIMING.
IS THE TIMING WITHIN 2 DEGREES OF SPECIFICATIONS?
NO
ADJUST THE IGNITION TIMING TO SPECIFICATIONS.*
YES
RECONNECT THE COOLANT SENSOR CONNECTOR.
NOTE: COOLANT SENSOR FAULT WILL BE SET AND CHECK ENGINE LIGHT ON.
READ THE TOTAL ADVANCE.
RAISE THE ENGINE SPEED TO 2000 RPM.
DID THE ADVANCE CHANGE WITH RPM?
NO
REPLACE THE ENGINE CONTROLLER.*
YES
PERFORM TEST DR-32A.

* PERFORM VERIFICATION PROCEDURE 2.

91B14184

Fig. 95: Driveability Test 31A – Checking Secondary Ignition & Timing (2 of 2)

DR-32A – CHECKING FUEL PRESSURE (1 OF 2)

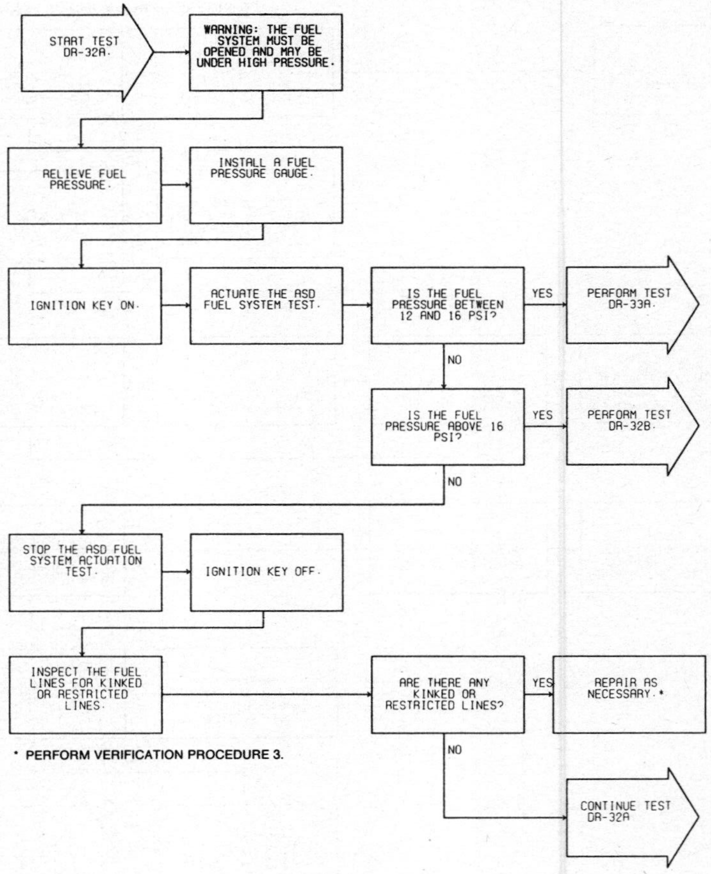
START TEST DR-32A.
WARNING: THE FUEL SYSTEM MUST BE OPENED AND MAY BE UNDER HIGH PRESSURE.
RELIEVE FUEL PRESSURE.
INSTALL A FUEL PRESSURE GAUGE.
IGNITION KEY ON.
ACTUATE THE ASD FUEL SYSTEM TEST.
IS THE FUEL PRESSURE BETWEEN 12 AND 16 PSI?
YES
PERFORM TEST DR-33A.
NO
IS THE FUEL PRESSURE ABOVE 16 PSI?
YES
PERFORM TEST DR-32B.
NO
STOP THE ASD FUEL SYSTEM ACTUATION TEST.
IGNITION KEY OFF.
INSPECT THE FUEL LINES FOR KINKED OR RESTRICTED LINES.
ARE THERE ANY KINKED OR RESTRICTED LINES?
YES
REPAIR AS NECESSARY.*
NO
CONTINUE TEST DR-32A

* PERFORM VERIFICATION PROCEDURE 3.

91C14185

Fig. 96: Driveability Test 32A – Checking Fuel Pressure (1 of 2)

DR-32A – CHECKING FUEL PRESSURE (2 OF 2)

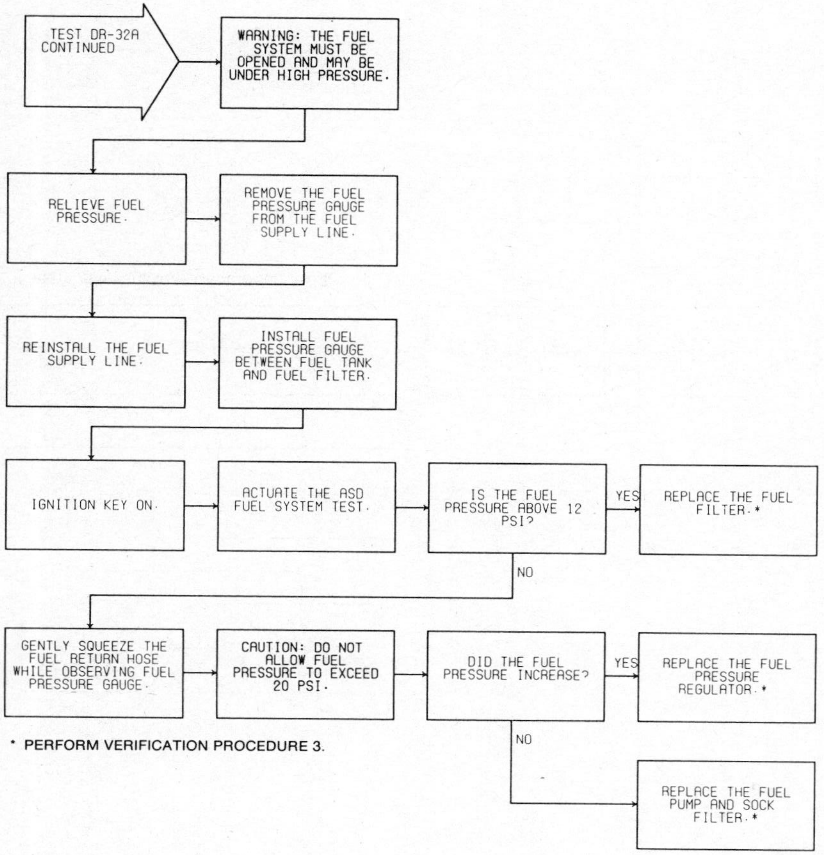
TEST DR-32A CONTINUED
WARNING: THE FUEL SYSTEM MUST BE OPENED AND MAY BE UNDER HIGH PRESSURE.
RELIEVE FUEL PRESSURE.
REMOVE THE FUEL PRESSURE GAUGE FROM THE FUEL SUPPLY LINE.
REINSTALL THE FUEL SUPPLY LINE.
INSTALL FUEL PRESSURE GAUGE BETWEEN FUEL TANK AND FUEL FILTER.
IGNITION KEY ON.
ACTUATE THE ASD FUEL SYSTEM TEST.
IS THE FUEL PRESSURE ABOVE 12 PSI?
YES
REPLACE THE FUEL FILTER.*
NO
GENTLY SQUEEZE THE FUEL RETURN HOSE WHILE OBSERVING FUEL PRESSURE GAUGE.
CAUTION: DO NOT ALLOW FUEL PRESSURE TO EXCEED 20 PSI.
DID THE FUEL PRESSURE INCREASE?
YES
REPLACE THE FUEL PRESSURE REGULATOR.*
NO
REPLACE THE FUEL PUMP AND SOCK FILTER.*

* PERFORM VERIFICATION PROCEDURE 3.

91D14186

Fig. 97: *Driveability Test 32A – Checking Fuel Pressure (2 of 2)*

DR-32B – CHECKING FUEL PRESSURE (1 OF 2)

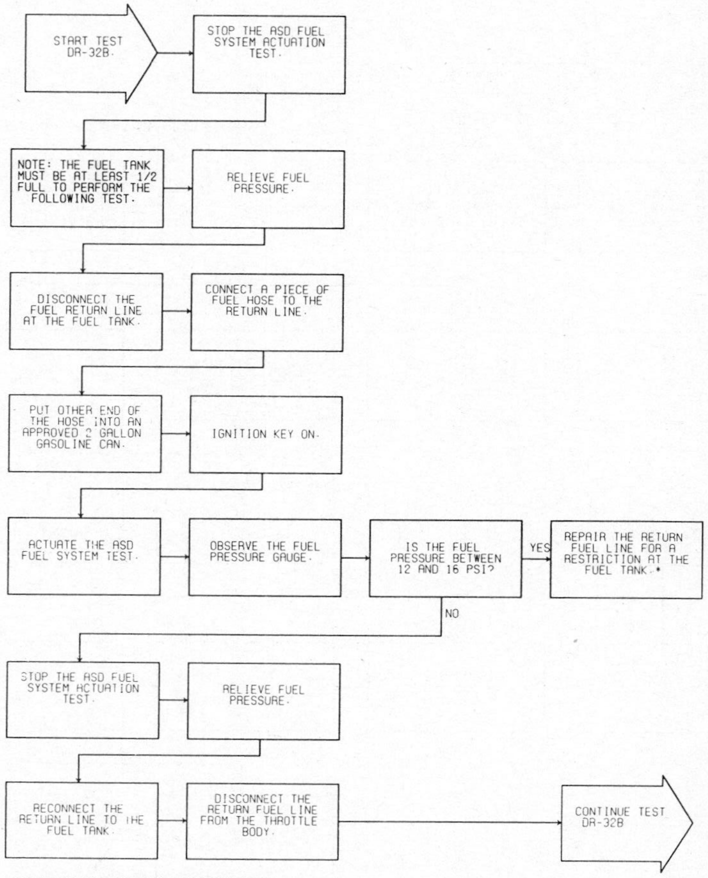
START TEST DR-32B.
STOP THE ASD FUEL SYSTEM ACTUATION TEST.
NOTE: THE FUEL TANK MUST BE AT LEAST 1/2 FULL TO PERFORM THE FOLLOWING TEST.
RELIEVE FUEL PRESSURE.
DISCONNECT THE FUEL RETURN LINE AT THE FUEL TANK.
CONNECT A PIECE OF FUEL HOSE TO THE RETURN LINE.
PUT OTHER END OF THE HOSE INTO AN APPROVED 2 GALLON GASOLINE CAN.
IGNITION KEY ON.
ACTUATE THE ASD FUEL SYSTEM TEST.
OBSERVE THE FUEL PRESSURE GAUGE.
IS THE FUEL PRESSURE BETWEEN 12 AND 16 PSI?
YES
REPAIR THE RETURN FUEL LINE FOR A RESTRICTION AT THE FUEL TANK.*
NO
STOP THE ASD FUEL SYSTEM ACTUATION TEST.
RELIEVE FUEL PRESSURE.
RECONNECT THE RETURN LINE TO THE FUEL TANK.
DISCONNECT THE RETURN FUEL LINE FROM THE THROTTLE BODY.
CONTINUE TEST DR-32B

* PERFORM VERIFICATION PROCEDURE 3.

91E14187

Fig. 98: *Driveability Test 32B – Checking Fuel Pressure (1 of 2)*

1991 ENGINE PERFORMANCE
Self-Diagnostics – 3.9L, 5.2L & 5.9L TBI (Cont.)

DR-32B – CHECKING FUEL PRESSURE (2 OF 2)

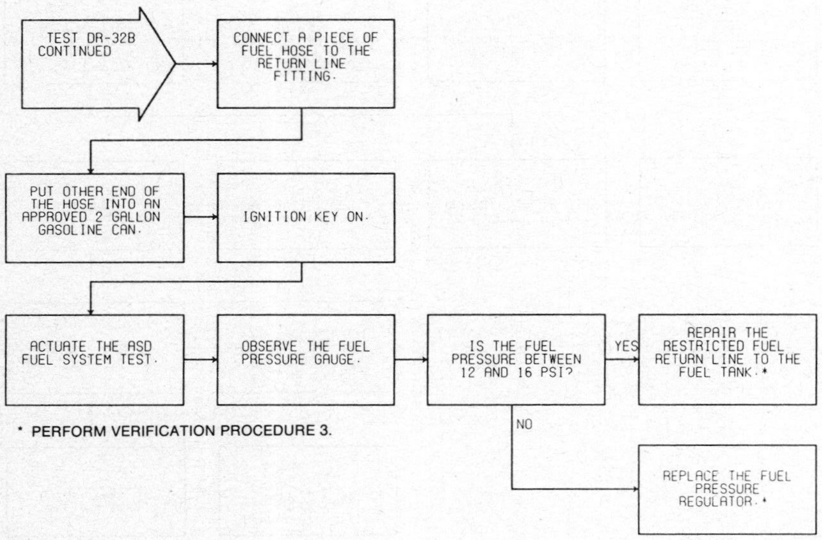
TEST DR-32B CONTINUED
CONNECT A PIECE OF FUEL HOSE TO THE RETURN LINE FITTING.
PUT OTHER END OF THE HOSE INTO AN APPROVED 2 GALLON GASOLINE CAN.
IGNITION KEY ON.
ACTUATE THE ASD FUEL SYSTEM TEST.
OBSERVE THE FUEL PRESSURE GAUGE.
IS THE FUEL PRESSURE BETWEEN 12 AND 16 PSI?
YES
REPAIR THE RESTRICTED FUEL RETURN LINE TO THE FUEL TANK.*
NO
REPLACE THE FUEL PRESSURE REGULATOR.*

* PERFORM VERIFICATION PROCEDURE 3.

91F14188

Fig. 99: Driveability Test 32B – Checking Fuel Pressure (2 of 2)

DR-33A – CHECKING COOLANT & TPS CALIBRATION (1 OF 2)

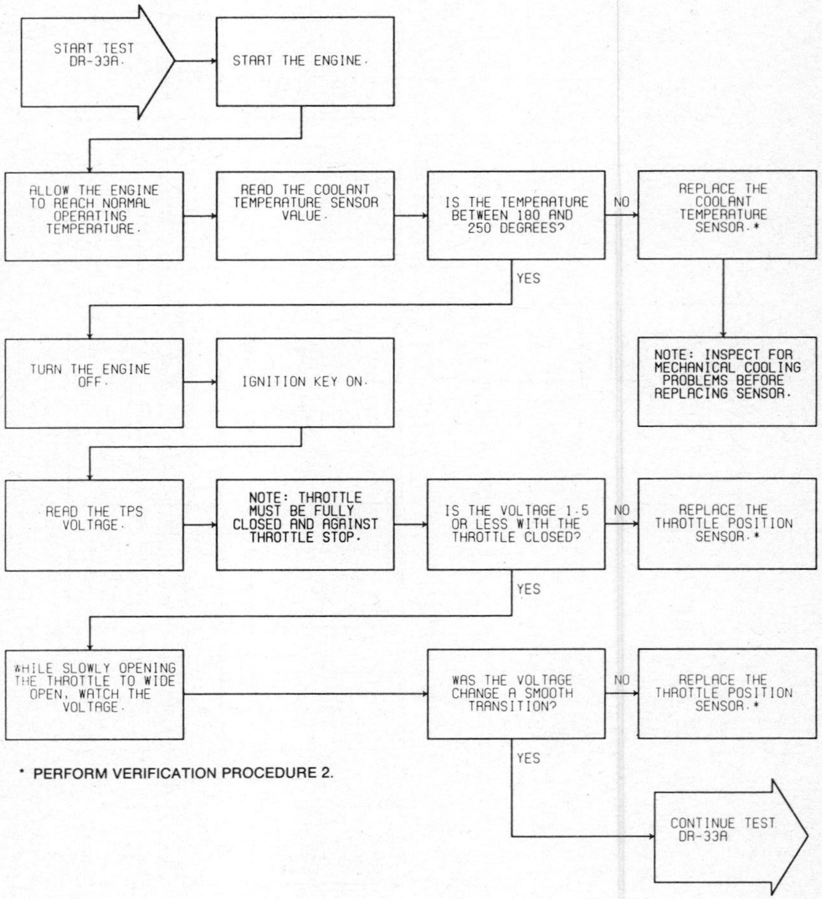
START TEST DR-33A.
START THE ENGINE.
ALLOW THE ENGINE TO REACH NORMAL OPERATING TEMPERATURE.
READ THE COOLANT TEMPERATURE SENSOR VALUE.
IS THE TEMPERATURE BETWEEN 180 AND 250 DEGREES?
NO
REPLACE THE COOLANT TEMPERATURE SENSOR.*
NOTE: INSPECT FOR MECHANICAL COOLING PROBLEMS BEFORE REPLACING SENSOR.
YES
TURN THE ENGINE OFF.
IGNITION KEY ON.
READ THE TPS VOLTAGE.
NOTE: THROTTLE MUST BE FULLY CLOSED AND AGAINST THROTTLE STOP.
IS THE VOLTAGE 1.5 OR LESS WITH THE THROTTLE CLOSED?
NO
REPLACE THE THROTTLE POSITION SENSOR.*
YES
WHILE SLOWLY OPENING THE THROTTLE TO WIDE OPEN, WATCH THE VOLTAGE.
WAS THE VOLTAGE CHANGE A SMOOTH TRANSITION?
NO
REPLACE THE THROTTLE POSITION SENSOR.*
YES
CONTINUE TEST DR-33A

* PERFORM VERIFICATION PROCEDURE 2.

91G14189

Fig. 100: Driveability Test 33A – Checking Coolant & TPS Calibration (1 of 2)

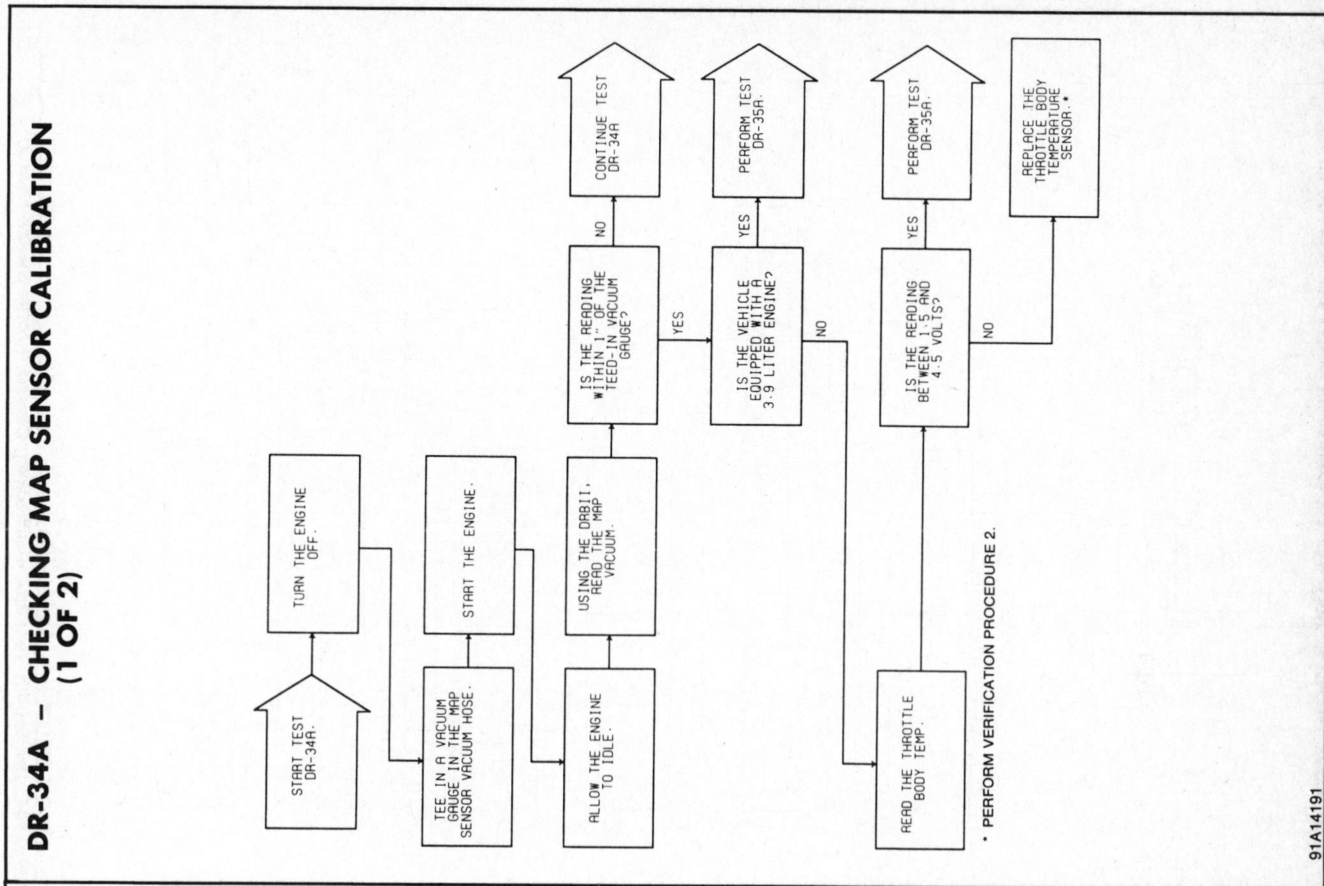

DR-34A – CHECKING MAP SENSOR CALIBRATION (1 OF 2)
START TEST DR-34A.
TURN THE ENGINE OFF.
TEE IN A VACUUM GAUGE IN THE MAP SENSOR VACUUM HOSE.
START THE ENGINE.
ALLOW THE ENGINE TO IDLE.
USING THE DRBII, READ THE MAP VACUUM.
IS THE READING WITHIN 1" OF THE TEED-IN VACUUM GAUGE?
NO
CONTINUE TEST DR-34A
YES
IS THE VEHICLE EQUIPPED WITH A 3.9 LITER ENGINE?
YES
PERFORM TEST DR-35A.
NO
READ THE THROTTLE BODY TEMP.
IS THE READING BETWEEN 1.5 AND 4.5 VOLTS?
YES
PERFORM TEST DR-35A.
NO
REPLACE THE THROTTLE BODY TEMPERATURE SENSOR.*
* PERFORM VERIFICATION PROCEDURE 2.
91A14191

Fig. 102: Driveability Test 34A – Checking MAP Sensor Calibration (1 of 2)

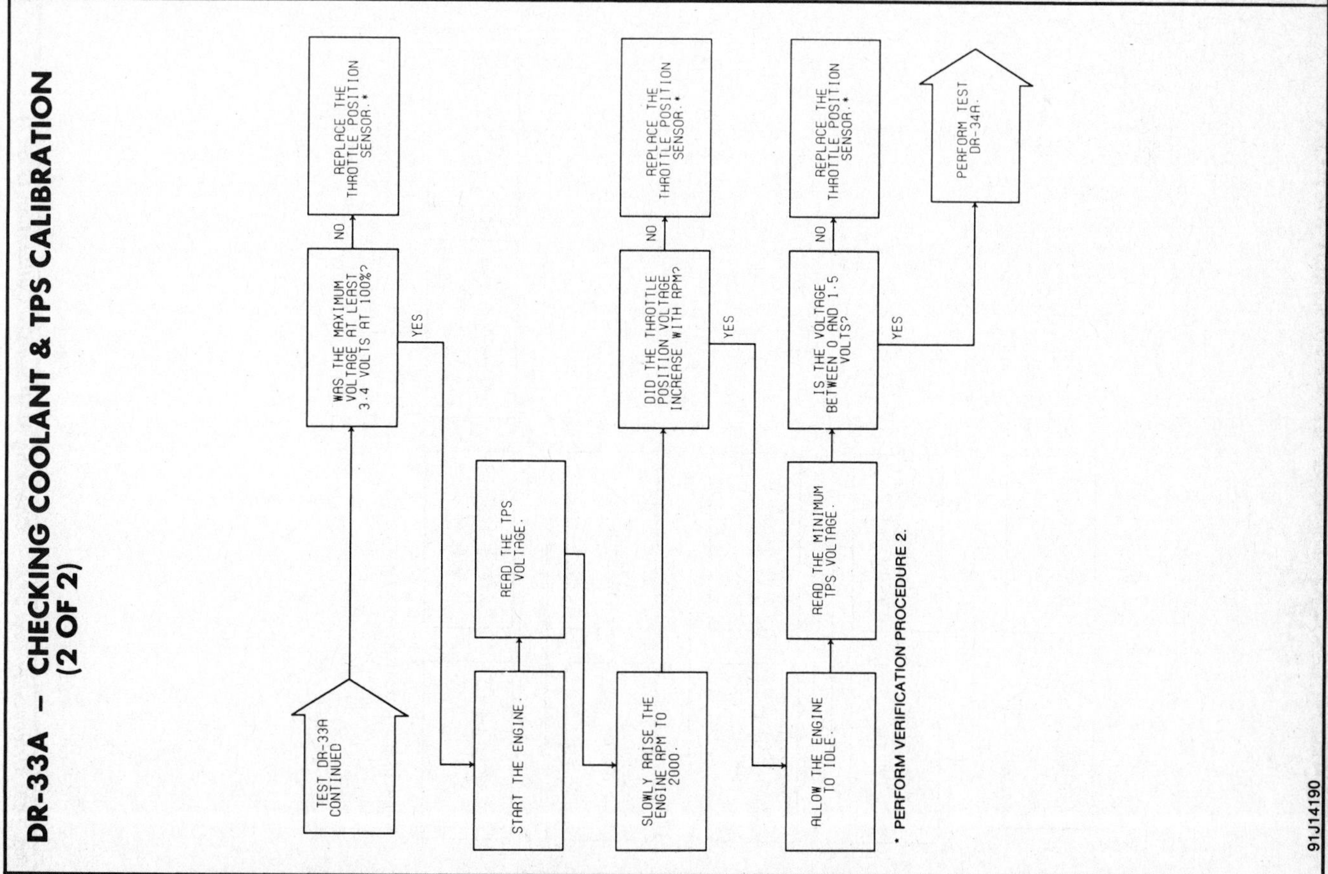

DR-33A – CHECKING COOLANT & TPS CALIBRATION (2 OF 2)
TEST DR-33A CONTINUED
START THE ENGINE.
READ THE TPS VOLTAGE.
SLOWLY RAISE THE ENGINE RPM TO 2000.
WAS THE MAXIMUM VOLTAGE AT LEAST 3.4 VOLTS AT 100%?
NO
REPLACE THE THROTTLE POSITION SENSOR.*
YES
DID THE THROTTLE POSITION VOLTAGE INCREASE WITH RPM?
NO
REPLACE THE THROTTLE POSITION SENSOR.*
YES
ALLOW THE ENGINE TO IDLE.
READ THE MINIMUM TPS VOLTAGE.
IS THE VOLTAGE BETWEEN 0 AND 1.5 VOLTS?
NO
REPLACE THE THROTTLE POSITION SENSOR.*
YES
PERFORM TEST DR-34A.
* PERFORM VERIFICATION PROCEDURE 2.
91J14190

Fig. 101: Driveability Test 33A – Checking Coolant & TPS Calibration (2 of 2)

DR-34A – CHECKING MAP SENSOR CALIBRATION (2 OF 2)

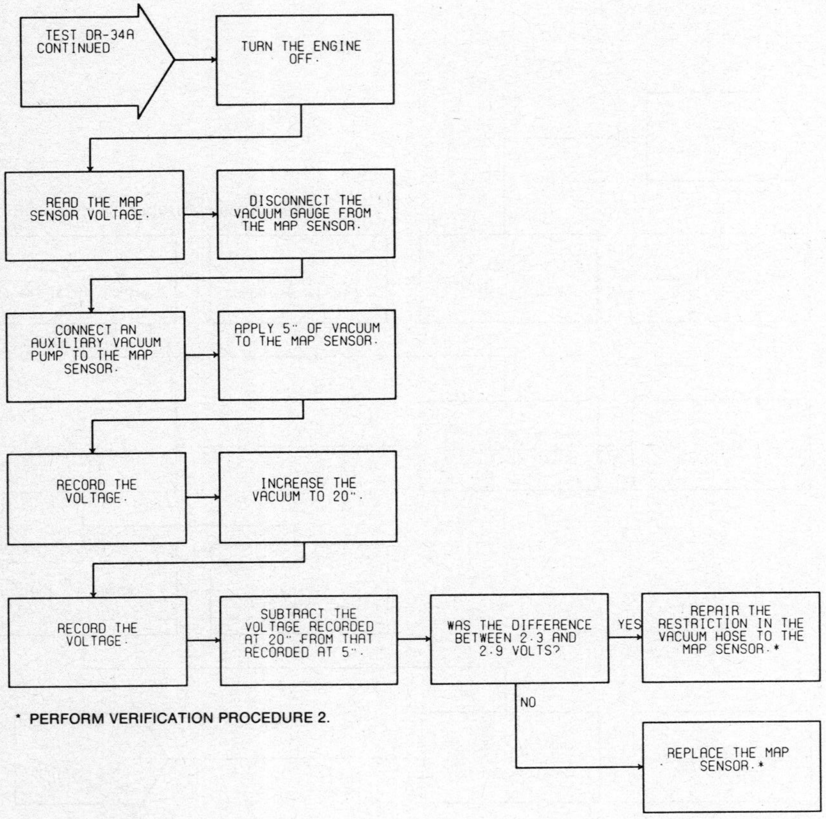
TEST DR-34A CONTINUED
TURN THE ENGINE OFF.
READ THE MAP SENSOR VOLTAGE.
DISCONNECT THE VACUUM GAUGE FROM THE MAP SENSOR.
CONNECT AN AUXILIARY VACUUM PUMP TO THE MAP SENSOR.
APPLY 5" OF VACUUM TO THE MAP SENSOR.
RECORD THE VOLTAGE.
INCREASE THE VACUUM TO 20".
RECORD THE VOLTAGE.
SUBTRACT THE VOLTAGE RECORDED AT 20" FROM THAT RECORDED AT 5".
WAS THE DIFFERENCE BETWEEN 2.3 AND 2.9 VOLTS?
YES
REPAIR THE RESTRICTION IN THE VACUUM HOSE TO THE MAP SENSOR.*
NO
REPLACE THE MAP SENSOR.*

* PERFORM VERIFICATION PROCEDURE 2.

91B14192

Fig. 103: Driveability Test 34A – Checking MAP Sensor Calibration (2 of 2)

DR-35A – CHECKING CLOSED THROTTLE SWITCH (1 OF 2)

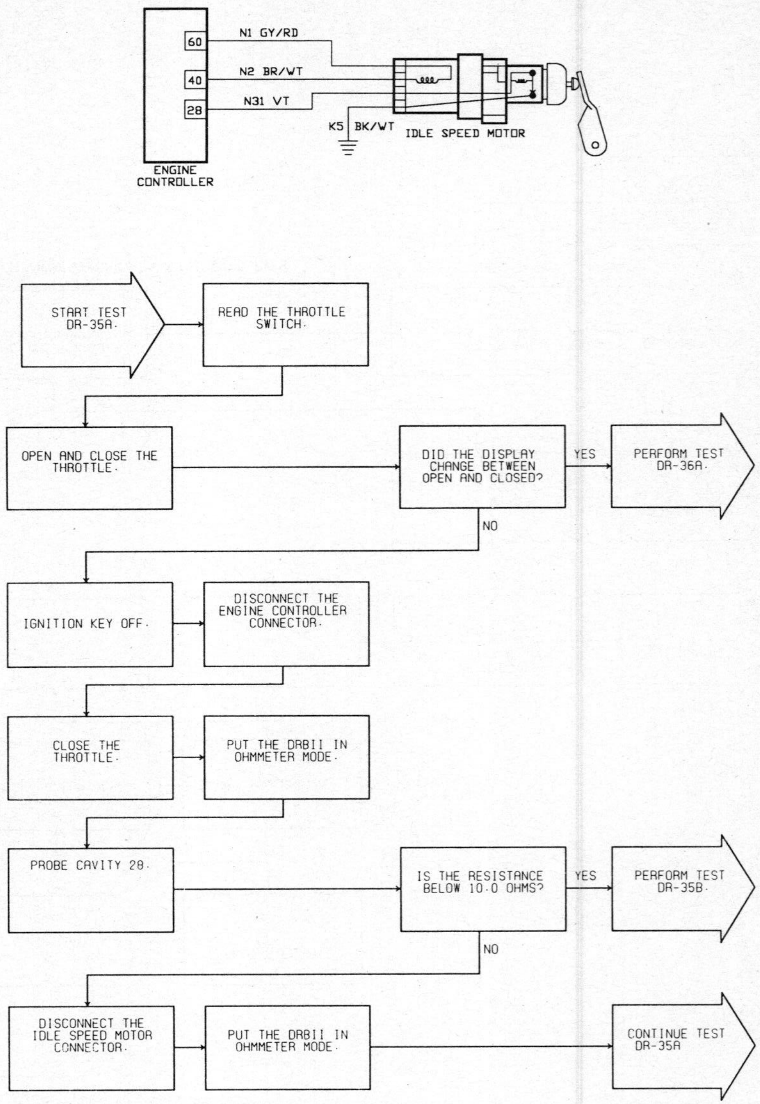
60
40
28
ENGINE CONTROLLER
N1 GY/RD
N2 BR/WT
N31 VT
K5 BK/WT
IDLE SPEED MOTOR
START TEST DR-35A.
READ THE THROTTLE SWITCH.
OPEN AND CLOSE THE THROTTLE.
DID THE DISPLAY CHANGE BETWEEN OPEN AND CLOSED?
YES
PERFORM TEST DR-36A.
NO
IGNITION KEY OFF.
DISCONNECT THE ENGINE CONTROLLER CONNECTOR.
CLOSE THE THROTTLE.
PUT THE DRBII IN OHMMETER MODE.
PROBE CAVITY 28.
IS THE RESISTANCE BELOW 10.0 OHMS?
YES
PERFORM TEST DR-35B.
NO
DISCONNECT THE IDLE SPEED MOTOR CONNECTOR.
PUT THE DRBII IN OHMMETER MODE.
CONTINUE TEST DR-35A

* PERFORM VERIFICATION PROCEDURE 2.

91H14107 91C14193

Fig. 104: Driveability Test 35A – Checking Closed Throttle Switch (1 of 2)

DR-35A – CHECKING CLOSED THROTTLE SWITCH (2 OF 2)

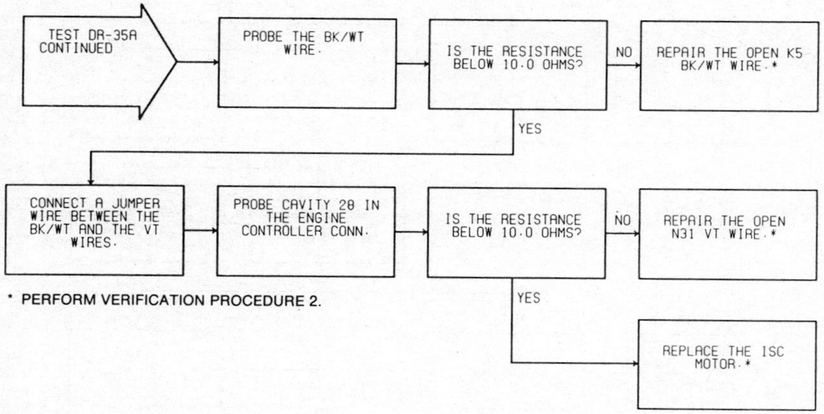
TEST DR-35A CONTINUED
PROBE THE BK/WT WIRE.
IS THE RESISTANCE BELOW 10.0 OHMS?
NO
REPAIR THE OPEN K5 BK/WT WIRE.*
YES
CONNECT A JUMPER WIRE BETWEEN THE BK/WT AND THE VT WIRES.
PROBE CAVITY 28 IN THE ENGINE CONTROLLER CONN.
IS THE RESISTANCE BELOW 10.0 OHMS?
NO
REPAIR THE OPEN N31 VT WIRE.*
YES
REPLACE THE ISC MOTOR.*

* PERFORM VERIFICATION PROCEDURE 2.

91D14194

Fig. 105: Driveability Test 35A – Checking Closed Throttle Switch (2 of 2)

DR-35B – CHECKING CLOSED THROTTLE SWITCH

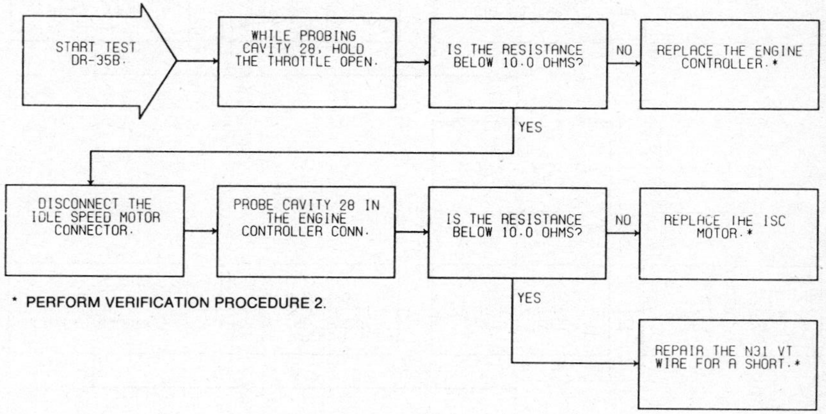
START TEST DR-35B.
WHILE PROBING CAVITY 28, HOLD THE THROTTLE OPEN.
IS THE RESISTANCE BELOW 10.0 OHMS?
NO
REPLACE THE ENGINE CONTROLLER.*
YES
DISCONNECT THE IDLE SPEED MOTOR CONNECTOR.
PROBE CAVITY 28 IN THE ENGINE CONTROLLER CONN.
IS THE RESISTANCE BELOW 10.0 OHMS?
NO
REPLACE THE ISC MOTOR.*
YES
REPAIR THE N31 VT WIRE FOR A SHORT.*

* PERFORM VERIFICATION PROCEDURE 2.

91E14195

Fig. 106: Driveability Test 35B – Checking Closed Throttle Switch

1991 ENGINE PERFORMANCE
Self-Diagnostics – 3.9L, 5.2L & 5.9L TBI (Cont.)

DR-36A – CHECKING IDLE SPEED ACTUATION OPERATION

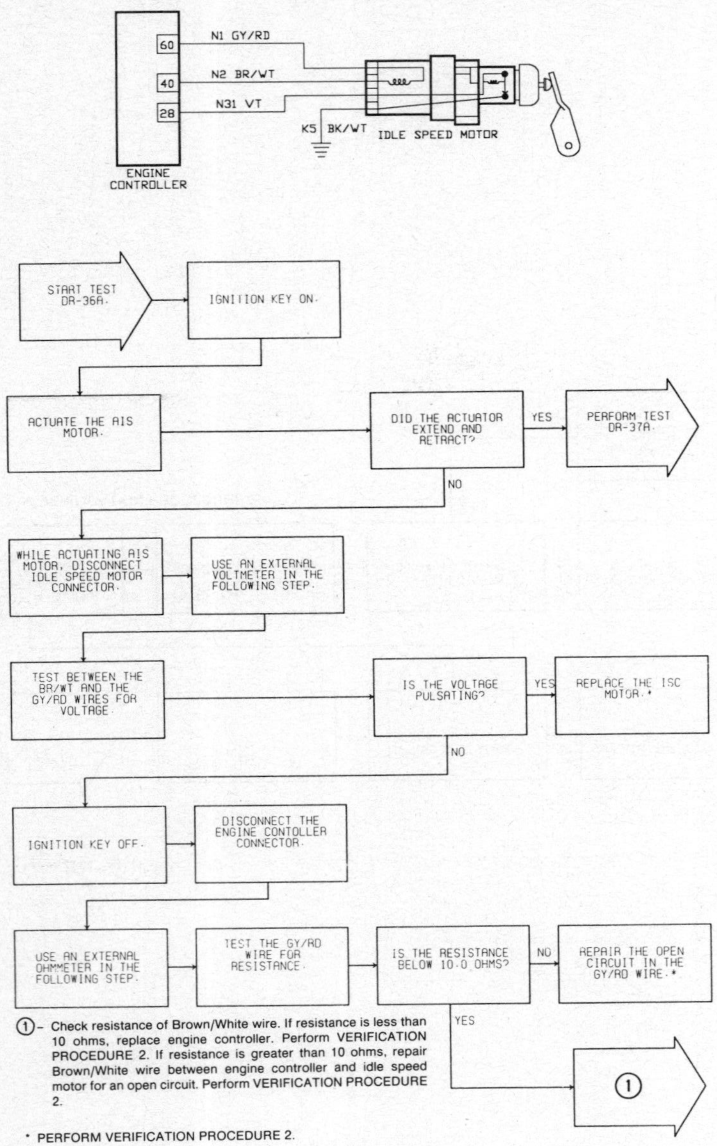
60
40
28
ENGINE CONTROLLER
N1 GY/RD
N2 BR/WT
N31 VT
K5 BK/WT
IDLE SPEED MOTOR
START TEST DR-36A.
IGNITION KEY ON.
ACTUATE THE AIS MOTOR.
DID THE ACTUATOR EXTEND AND RETRACT?
YES
PERFORM TEST DR-37A.
NO
WHILE ACTUATING AIS MOTOR, DISCONNECT IDLE SPEED MOTOR CONNECTOR.
USE AN EXTERNAL VOLTMETER IN THE FOLLOWING STEP.
TEST BETWEEN THE BR/WT AND THE GY/RD WIRES FOR VOLTAGE.
IS THE VOLTAGE PULSATING?
YES
REPLACE THE ISC MOTOR.*
NO
IGNITION KEY OFF.
DISCONNECT THE ENGINE CONTOLLER CONNECTOR.
USE AN EXTERNAL OHMMETER IN THE FOLLOWING STEP.
TEST THE GY/RD WIRE FOR RESISTANCE.
IS THE RESISTANCE BELOW 10.0 OHMS?
NO
REPAIR THE OPEN CIRCUIT IN THE GY/RD WIRE.*
YES
1

① – Check resistance of Brown/White wire. If resistance is less than 10 ohms, replace engine controller. Perform VERIFICATION PROCEDURE 2. If resistance is greater than 10 ohms, repair Brown/White wire between engine controller and idle speed motor for an open circuit. Perform VERIFICATION PROCEDURE 2.

* PERFORM VERIFICATION PROCEDURE 2.

91H14107 91F14196

Fig. 107: Driveability Test 36A – Checking Idle Speed Actuation Operation

DR-37A – CHECKING SOLENOID OPERATION

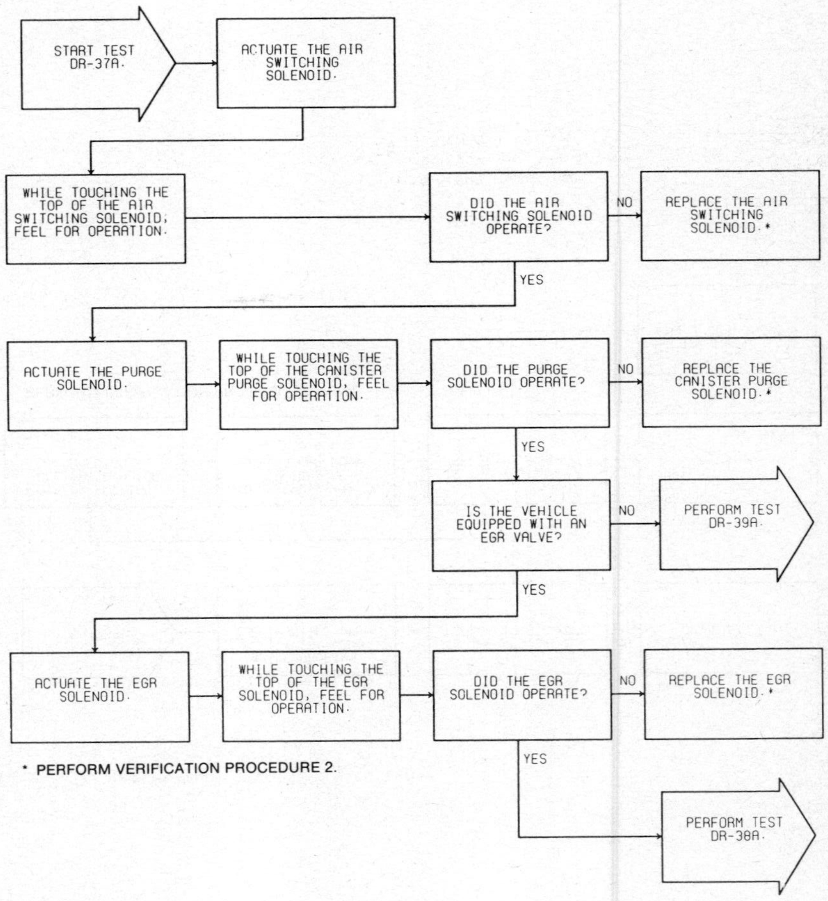
START TEST DR-37A.
ACTUATE THE AIR SWITCHING SOLENOID.
WHILE TOUCHING THE TOP OF THE AIR SWITCHING SOLENOID; FEEL FOR OPERATION.
DID THE AIR SWITCHING SOLENOID OPERATE?
NO
REPLACE THE AIR SWITCHING SOLENOID.*
YES
ACTUATE THE PURGE SOLENOID.
WHILE TOUCHING THE TOP OF THE CANISTER PURGE SOLENOID, FEEL FOR OPERATION.
DID THE PURGE SOLENOID OPERATE?
NO
REPLACE THE CANISTER PURGE SOLENOID.*
YES
IS THE VEHICLE EQUIPPED WITH AN EGR VALVE?
NO
PERFORM TEST DR-39A.
YES
ACTUATE THE EGR SOLENOID.
WHILE TOUCHING THE TOP OF THE EGR SOLENOID, FEEL FOR OPERATION.
DID THE EGR SOLENOID OPERATE?
NO
REPLACE THE EGR SOLENOID.*
YES
PERFORM TEST DR-38A.

* PERFORM VERIFICATION PROCEDURE 2.

91H14198

Fig. 108: Driveability Test 37A – Checking Solenoid Operation

DR-38A – CHECKING EGR VALVE OPERATION (1 OF 4)

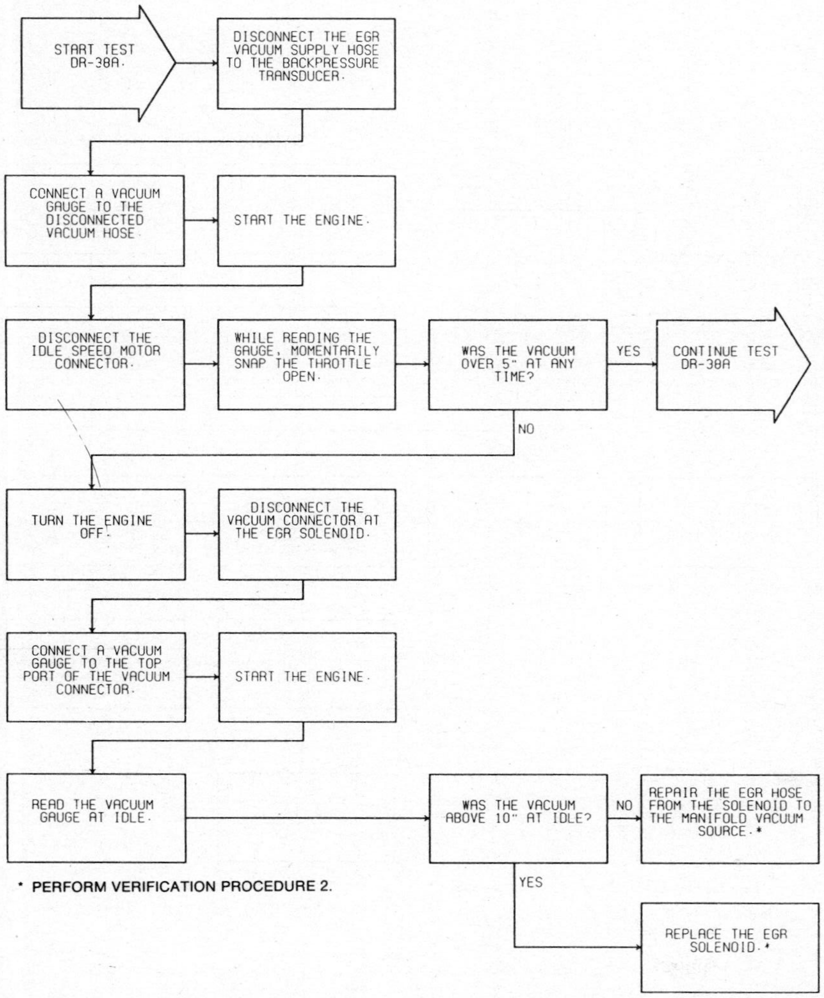
START TEST DR-38A.
DISCONNECT THE EGR VACUUM SUPPLY HOSE TO THE BACKPRESSURE TRANSDUCER.
CONNECT A VACUUM GAUGE TO THE DISCONNECTED VACUUM HOSE.
START THE ENGINE.
DISCONNECT THE IDLE SPEED MOTOR CONNECTOR.
WHILE READING THE GAUGE, MOMENTARILY SNAP THE THROTTLE OPEN.
WAS THE VACUUM OVER 5" AT ANY TIME?
YES
CONTINUE TEST DR-38A
NO
TURN THE ENGINE OFF.
DISCONNECT THE VACUUM CONNECTOR AT THE EGR SOLENOID.
CONNECT A VACUUM GAUGE TO THE TOP PORT OF THE VACUUM CONNECTOR.
START THE ENGINE.
READ THE VACUUM GAUGE AT IDLE.
WAS THE VACUUM ABOVE 10" AT IDLE?
NO
REPAIR THE EGR HOSE FROM THE SOLENOID TO THE MANIFOLD VACUUM SOURCE.*
YES
REPLACE THE EGR SOLENOID.*

* PERFORM VERIFICATION PROCEDURE 2.

91I14199

Fig. 109: Driveability Test 38A – Checking EGR Valve Operation (1 of 4)

DR-38A – CHECKING EGR VALVE OPERATION (2 OF 4)

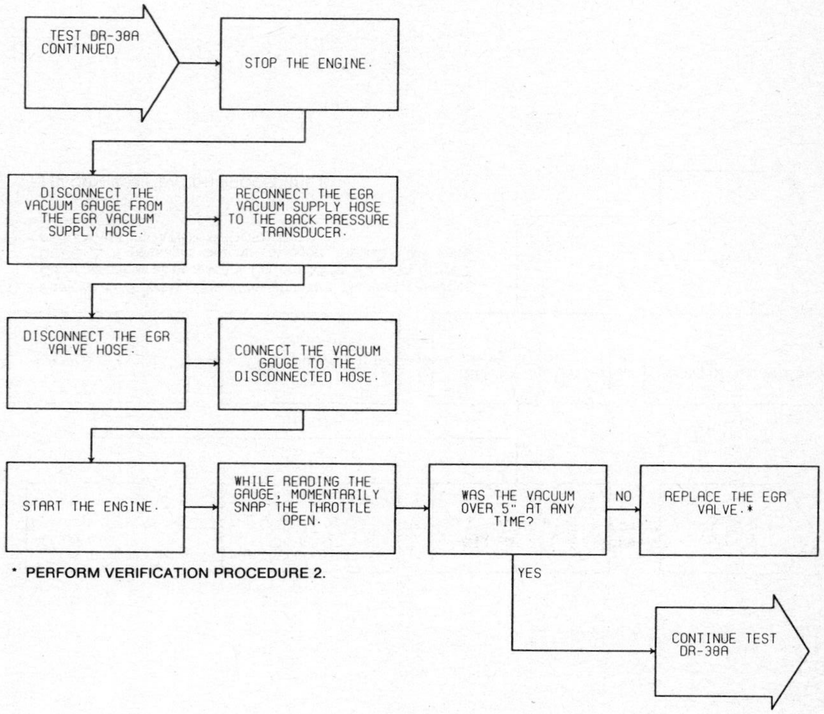
TEST DR-38A CONTINUED
STOP THE ENGINE.
DISCONNECT THE VACUUM GAUGE FROM THE EGR VACUUM SUPPLY HOSE.
RECONNECT THE EGR VACUUM SUPPLY HOSE TO THE BACK PRESSURE TRANSDUCER.
DISCONNECT THE EGR VALVE HOSE.
CONNECT THE VACUUM GAUGE TO THE DISCONNECTED HOSE.
START THE ENGINE.
WHILE READING THE GAUGE, MOMENTARILY SNAP THE THROTTLE OPEN.
WAS THE VACUUM OVER 5" AT ANY TIME?
NO
REPLACE THE EGR VALVE.*
YES
CONTINUE TEST DR-38A

* PERFORM VERIFICATION PROCEDURE 2.

91B14200

Fig. 110: Driveability Test 38A – Checking EGR Valve Operation (2 of 4)

DR-38A – CHECKING EGR VALVE OPERATION (3 OF 4)

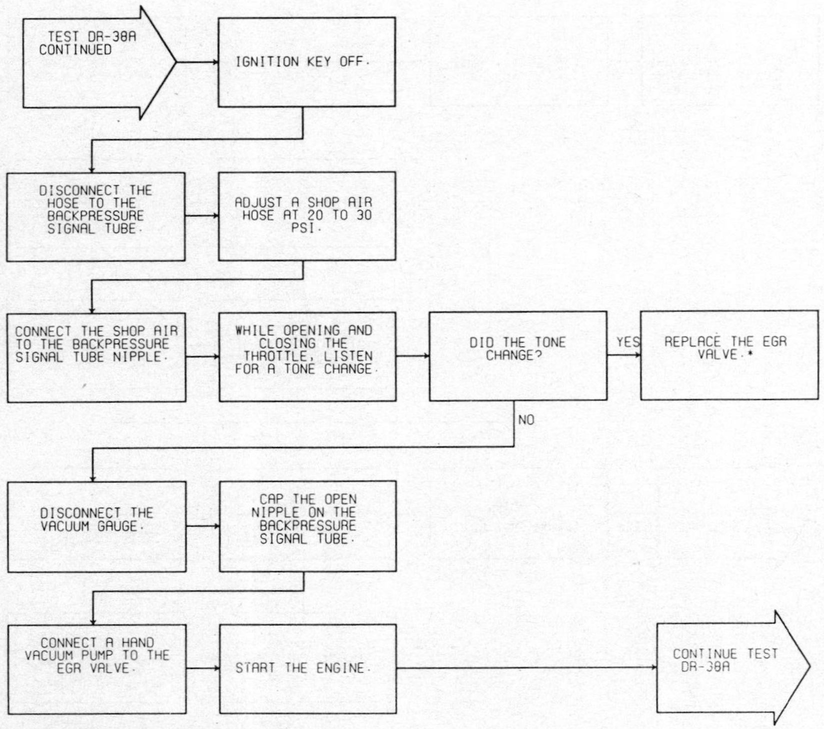
TEST DR-38A CONTINUED
IGNITION KEY OFF.
DISCONNECT THE HOSE TO THE BACKPRESSURE SIGNAL TUBE.
ADJUST A SHOP AIR HOSE AT 20 TO 30 PSI.
CONNECT THE SHOP AIR TO THE BACKPRESSURE SIGNAL TUBE NIPPLE.
WHILE OPENING AND CLOSING THE THROTTLE, LISTEN FOR A TONE CHANGE.
DID THE TONE CHANGE?
YES
REPLACE THE EGR VALVE.*
NO
DISCONNECT THE VACUUM GAUGE.
CAP THE OPEN NIPPLE ON THE BACKPRESSURE SIGNAL TUBE.
CONNECT A HAND VACUUM PUMP TO THE EGR VALVE.
START THE ENGINE.
CONTINUE TEST DR-38A

* PERFORM VERIFICATION PROCEDURE 2.

91C14201

Fig. 111: Driveability Test 38A – Checking EGR Valve Operation (3 of 4)

DR-38A – CHECKING EGR VALVE OPERATION (4 OF 4)

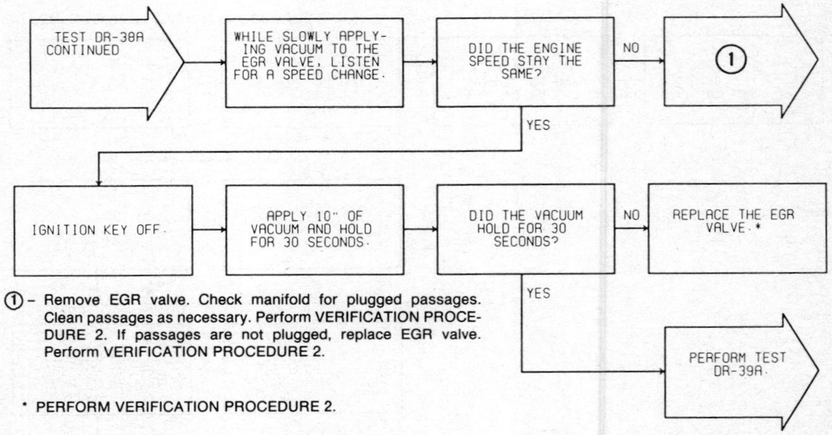
TEST DR-38A CONTINUED
WHILE SLOWLY APPLYING VACUUM TO THE EGR VALVE, LISTEN FOR A SPEED CHANGE.
DID THE ENGINE SPEED STAY THE SAME?
NO
①
YES
IGNITION KEY OFF.
APPLY 10" OF VACUUM AND HOLD FOR 30 SECONDS.
DID THE VACUUM HOLD FOR 30 SECONDS?
NO
REPLACE THE EGR VALVE.*
YES
PERFORM TEST DR-39A.

① – Remove EGR valve. Check manifold for plugged passages. Clean passages as necessary. Perform VERIFICATION PROCEDURE 2. If passages are not plugged, replace EGR valve. Perform VERIFICATION PROCEDURE 2.

* PERFORM VERIFICATION PROCEDURE 2.

91D14202

Fig. 112: Driveability Test 38A – Checking EGR Valve Operation (4 of 4)

DR-39A – CHECKING AIR SWITCHING SYSTEM (1 OF 2)

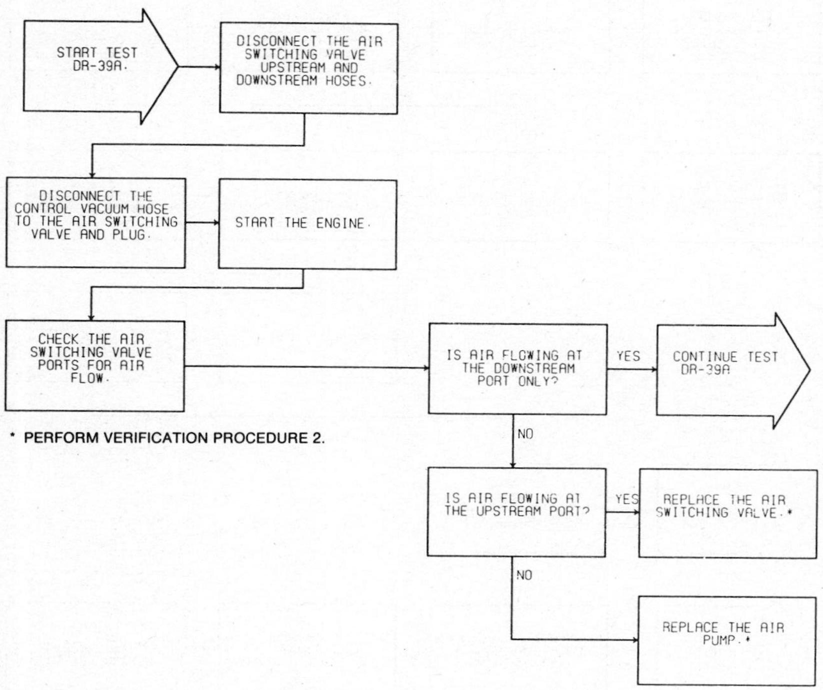
START TEST DR-39A.
DISCONNECT THE AIR SWITCHING VALVE UPSTREAM AND DOWNSTREAM HOSES.
DISCONNECT THE CONTROL VACUUM HOSE TO THE AIR SWITCHING VALVE AND PLUG.
START THE ENGINE.
CHECK THE AIR SWITCHING VALVE PORTS FOR AIR FLOW.
IS AIR FLOWING AT THE DOWNSTREAM PORT ONLY?
YES
CONTINUE TEST DR-39A
NO
IS AIR FLOWING AT THE UPSTREAM PORT?
YES
REPLACE THE AIR SWITCHING VALVE.*
NO
REPLACE THE AIR PUMP.*

* PERFORM VERIFICATION PROCEDURE 2.

91F14204

Fig. 113: Driveability Test 39A – Checking AIR Switching System (1 of 2)

DR-39A – CHECKING AIR SWITCHING SYSTEM (2 OF 2)

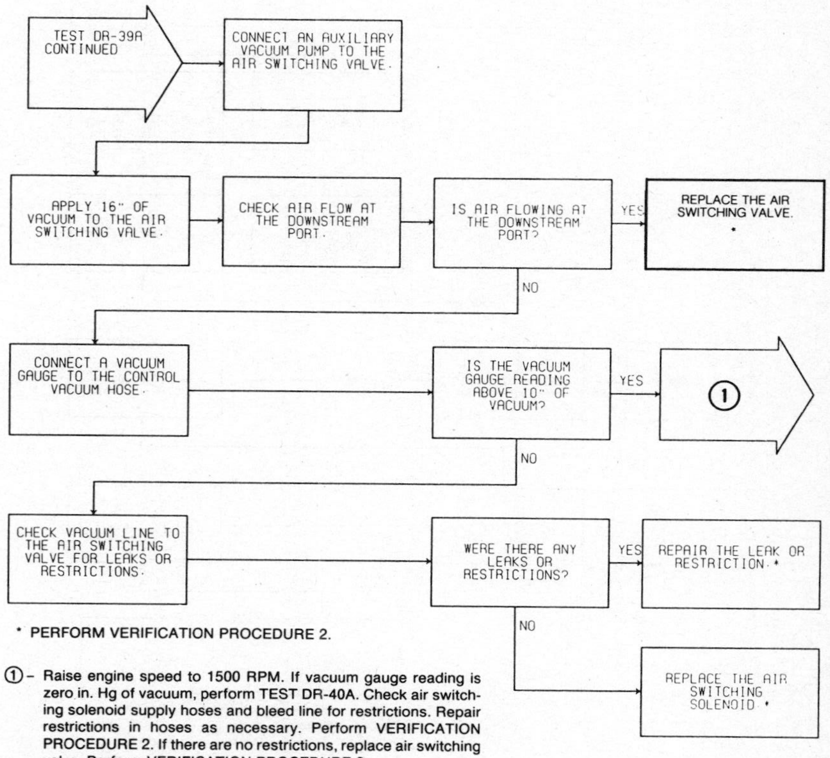
TEST DR-39A CONTINUED
CONNECT AN AUXILIARY VACUUM PUMP TO THE AIR SWITCHING VALVE.
APPLY 16" OF VACUUM TO THE AIR SWITCHING VALVE.
CHECK AIR FLOW AT THE DOWNSTREAM PORT.
IS AIR FLOWING AT THE DOWNSTREAM PORT?
YES
REPLACE THE AIR SWITCHING VALVE.
*
NO
CONNECT A VACUUM GAUGE TO THE CONTROL VACUUM HOSE.
IS THE VACUUM GAUGE READING ABOVE 10" OF VACUUM?
YES
1
NO
CHECK VACUUM LINE TO THE AIR SWITCHING VALVE FOR LEAKS OR RESTRICTIONS.
WERE THERE ANY LEAKS OR RESTRICTIONS?
YES
REPAIR THE LEAK OR RESTRICTION.*
NO
REPLACE THE AIR SWITCHING SOLENOID.*

* PERFORM VERIFICATION PROCEDURE 2.

① – Raise engine speed to 1500 RPM. If vacuum gauge reading is zero in. Hg of vacuum, perform TEST DR-40A. Check air switching solenoid supply hoses and bleed line for restrictions. Repair restrictions in hoses as necessary. Perform VERIFICATION PROCEDURE 2. If there are no restrictions, replace air switching valve. Perform VERIFICATION PROCEDURE 2.

91G14205

Fig. 114: Driveability Test 39A – Checking AIR Switching System (2 of 2)

1991 ENGINE PERFORMANCE
Self-Diagnostics – 3.9L, 5.2L & 5.9L TBI (Cont.)

DR-40A – CHECKING O_2 SENSOR SWITCHING

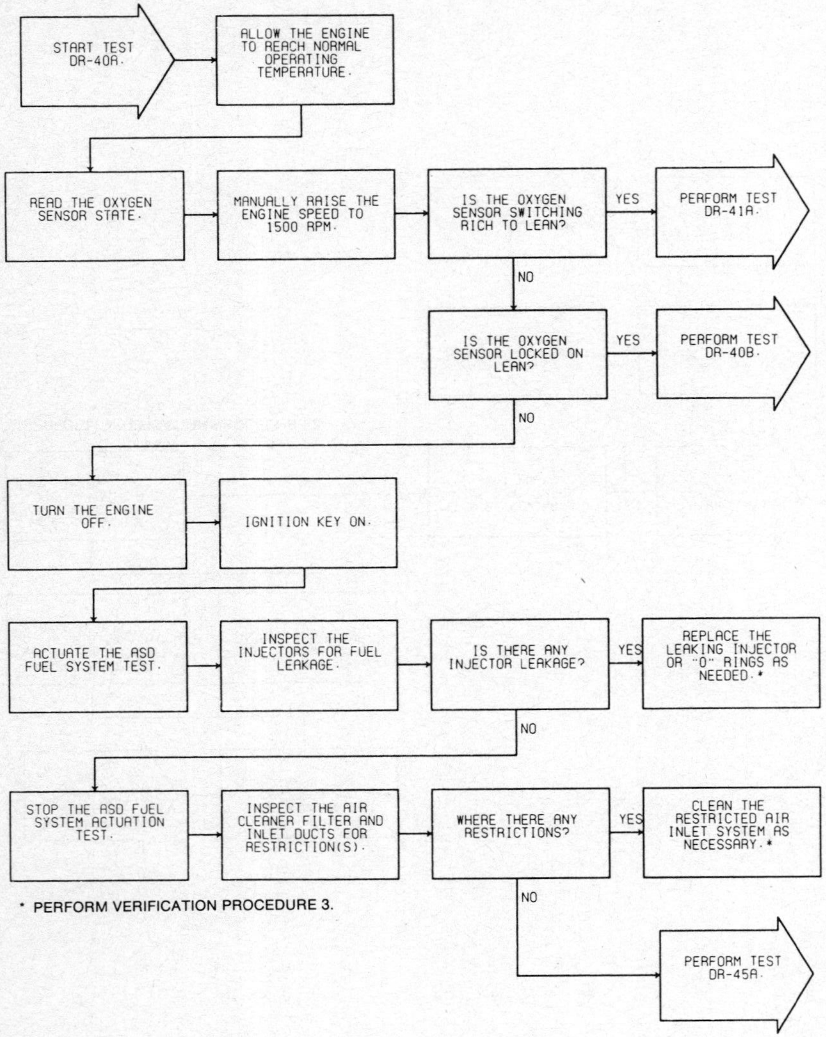
START TEST DR-40A.
ALLOW THE ENGINE TO REACH NORMAL OPERATING TEMPERATURE.
READ THE OXYGEN SENSOR STATE.
MANUALLY RAISE THE ENGINE SPEED TO 1500 RPM.
IS THE OXYGEN SENSOR SWITCHING RICH TO LEAN?
YES
PERFORM TEST DR-41A.
NO
IS THE OXYGEN SENSOR LOCKED ON LEAN?
YES
PERFORM TEST DR-40B.
NO
TURN THE ENGINE OFF.
IGNITION KEY ON.
ACTUATE THE ASD FUEL SYSTEM TEST.
INSPECT THE INJECTORS FOR FUEL LEAKAGE.
IS THERE ANY INJECTOR LEAKAGE?
YES
REPLACE THE LEAKING INJECTOR OR "O" RINGS AS NEEDED.*
NO
STOP THE ASD FUEL SYSTEM ACTUATION TEST.
INSPECT THE AIR CLEANER FILTER AND INLET DUCTS FOR RESTRICTION(S).
WHERE THERE ANY RESTRICTIONS?
YES
CLEAN THE RESTRICTED AIR INLET SYSTEM AS NECESSARY.*
NO
PERFORM TEST DR-45A.

* PERFORM VERIFICATION PROCEDURE 3.

91I14207

Fig. 115: Driveability Test 40A – Checking O_2 Sensor Switching

DR-40B – CHECKING O_2 SENSOR SWITCHING (LOCKED LEAN) (1 OF 2)

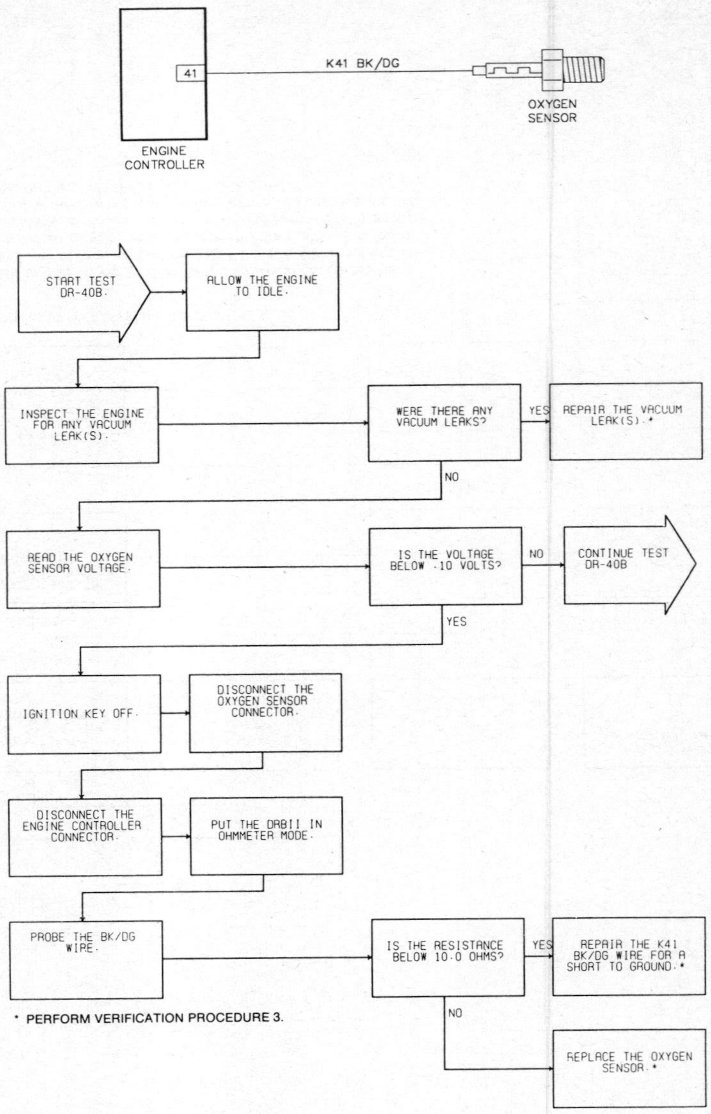
41
ENGINE CONTROLLER
K41 BK/DG
OXYGEN SENSOR
START TEST DR-40B.
ALLOW THE ENGINE TO IDLE.
INSPECT THE ENGINE FOR ANY VACUUM LEAK(S).
WERE THERE ANY VACUUM LEAKS?
YES
REPAIR THE VACUUM LEAK(S).*
NO
READ THE OXYGEN SENSOR VOLTAGE.
IS THE VOLTAGE BELOW .10 VOLTS?
NO
CONTINUE TEST DR-40B
YES
IGNITION KEY OFF.
DISCONNECT THE OXYGEN SENSOR CONNECTOR.
DISCONNECT THE ENGINE CONTROLLER CONNECTOR.
PUT THE DRBII IN OHMMETER MODE.
PROBE THE BK/DG WIRE.
IS THE RESISTANCE BELOW 10.0 OHMS?
YES
REPAIR THE K41 BK/DG WIRE FOR A SHORT TO GROUND.*
NO
REPLACE THE OXYGEN SENSOR.*

* PERFORM VERIFICATION PROCEDURE 3.

91J14208 91A14209

Fig. 116: Driveability Test 40B – Checking O_2 Sensor Switching (Locked Lean) (1 of 2)

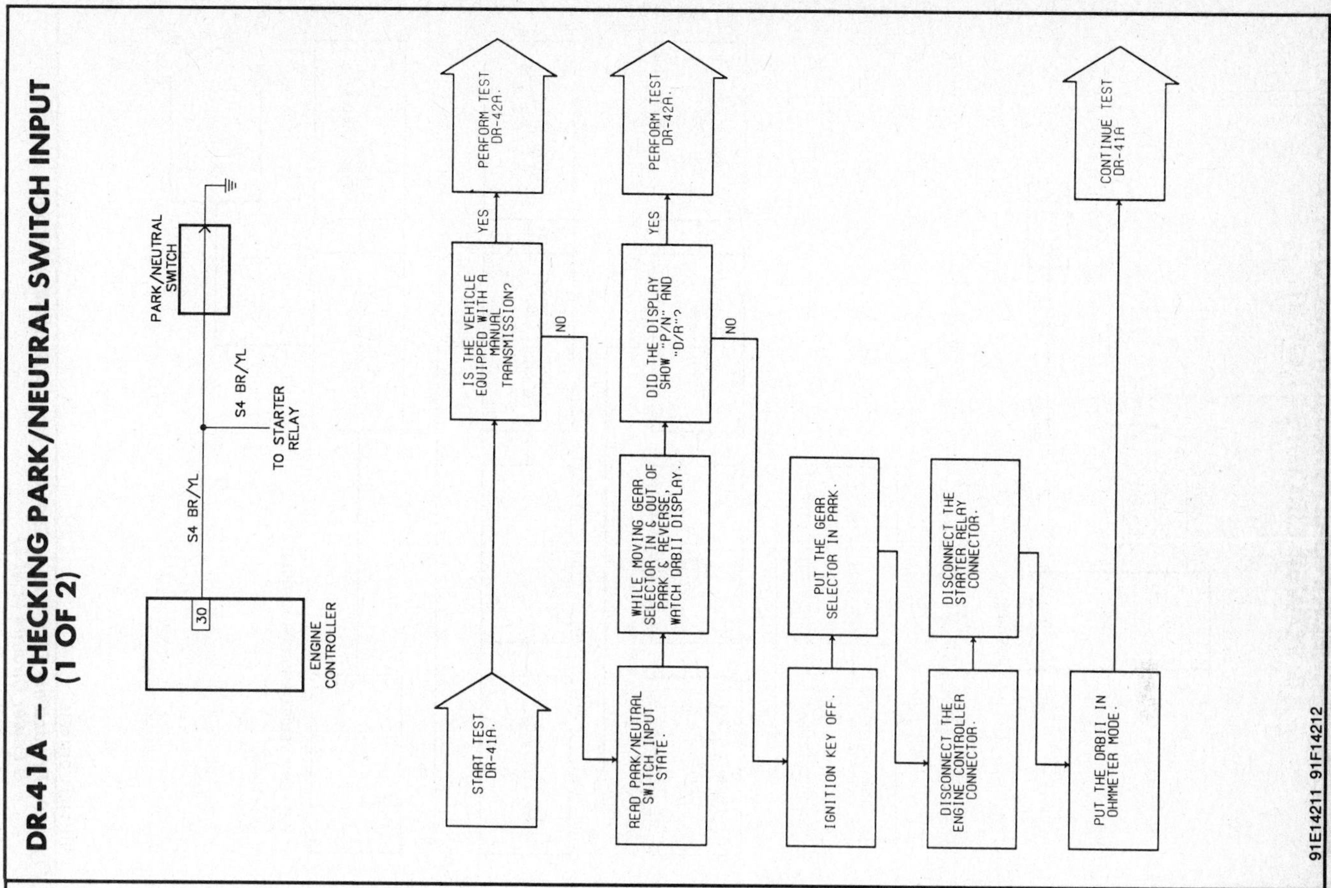

DR-41A – CHECKING PARK/NEUTRAL SWITCH INPUT (1 OF 2)
ENGINE CONTROLLER
30
S4 BR/YL
S4 BR/YL
TO STARTER RELAY
PARK/NEUTRAL SWITCH
START TEST DR-41A.
IS THE VEHICLE EQUIPPED WITH A MANUAL TRANSMISSION?
YES
NO
PERFORM TEST DR-42A.
READ PARK/NEUTRAL SWITCH INPUT STATE.
WHILE MOVING GEAR SELECTOR IN & OUT OF PARK & REVERSE, WATCH DRBII DISPLAY.
DID THE DISPLAY SHOW "P/N" AND "D/R"?
YES
NO
PERFORM TEST DR-42A.
IGNITION KEY OFF.
PUT THE GEAR SELECTOR IN PARK.
DISCONNECT THE ENGINE CONTROLLER CONNECTOR.
DISCONNECT THE STARTER RELAY CONNECTOR.
PUT THE DRBII IN OHMMETER MODE.
CONTINUE TEST DR-41A
91E14211 91F14212

Fig. 118: Driveability Test 41A – Checking Park/Neutral Switch Input (1 of 2)

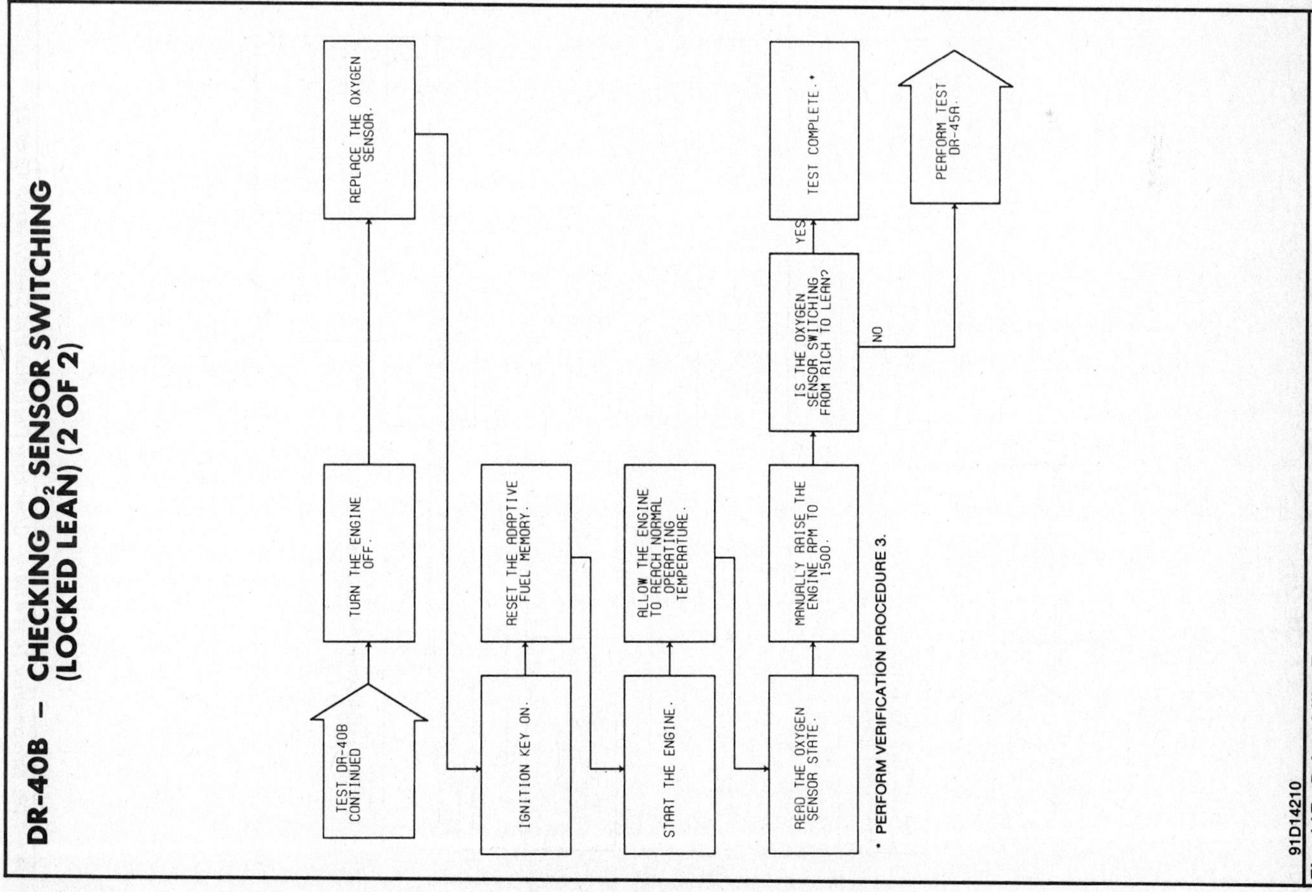

DR-40B – CHECKING O_2 SENSOR SWITCHING (LOCKED LEAN) (2 OF 2)
TEST DR-40B CONTINUED
TURN THE ENGINE OFF.
REPLACE THE OXYGEN SENSOR.
IGNITION KEY ON.
RESET THE ADAPTIVE FUEL MEMORY.
START THE ENGINE.
ALLOW THE ENGINE TO REACH NORMAL OPERATING TEMPERATURE.
READ THE OXYGEN SENSOR STATE.
MANUALLY RAISE THE ENGINE RPM TO 1500.
IS THE OXYGEN SENSOR SWITCHING FROM RICH TO LEAN?
YES
NO
TEST COMPLETE. *
PERFORM TEST DR-45A.
* PERFORM VERIFICATION PROCEDURE 3.
91D14210

Fig. 117: Driveability Test 40B – Checking O_2 Sensor Switching (Locked Lean) (2 of 2)

1991 ENGINE PERFORMANCE
Self-Diagnostics – 3.9L, 5.2L & 5.9L TBI (Cont.)

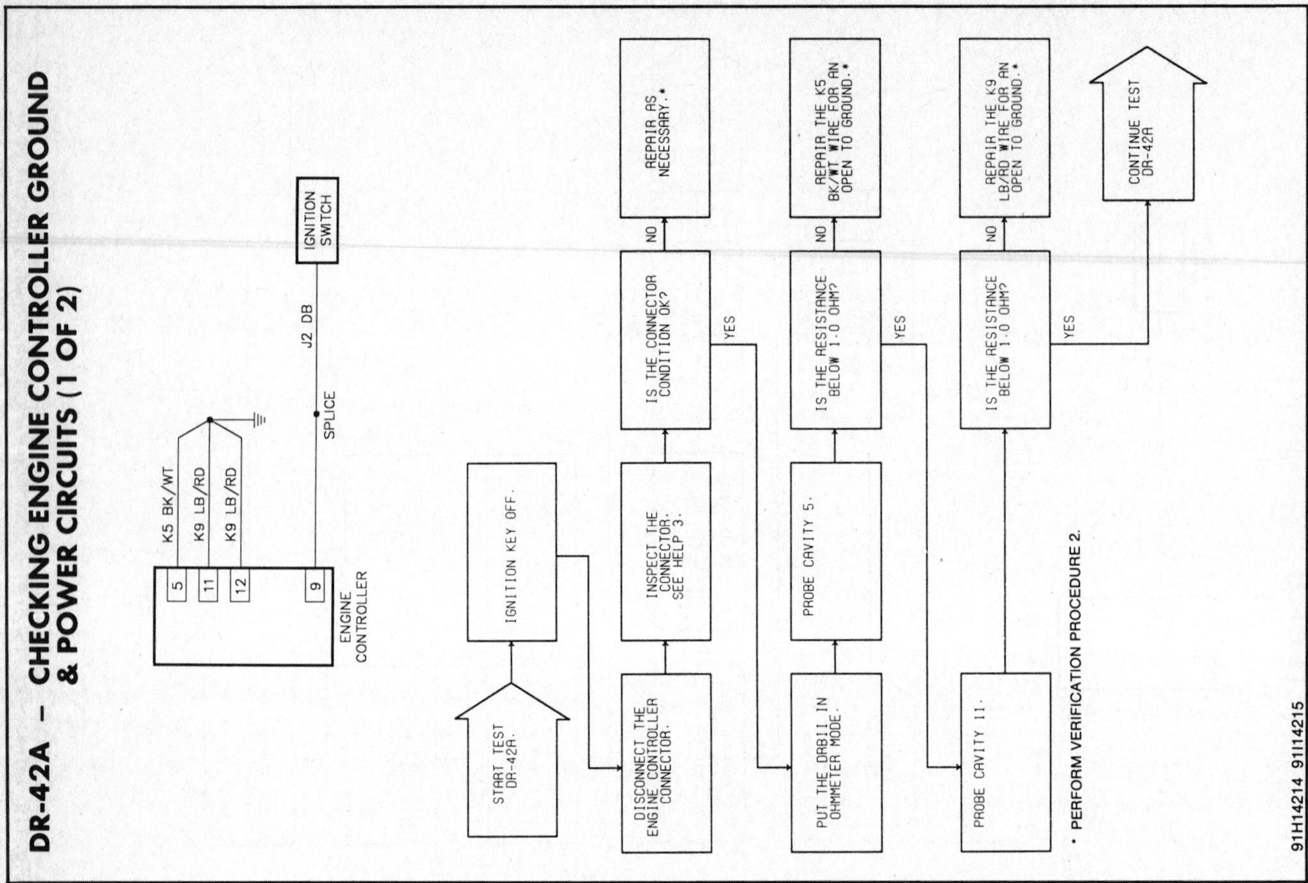
DR-42A – CHECKING ENGINE CONTROLLER GROUND & POWER CIRCUITS (1 OF 2)
ENGINE CONTROLLER
5
11
12
9
K5 BK/WT
K9 LB/RD
K9 LB/RD
SPLICE
J2 DB
IGNITION SWITCH
START TEST DR-42A.
IGNITION KEY OFF.
DISCONNECT THE ENGINE CONTROLLER CONNECTOR.
INSPECT THE CONNECTOR. SEE HELP 3.
IS THE CONNECTOR CONDITION OK?
NO
REPAIR AS NECESSARY.*
YES
PUT THE DRBII IN OHMMETER MODE.
PROBE CAVITY 5.
IS THE RESISTANCE BELOW 1.0 OHM?
NO
REPAIR THE K5 BK/WT WIRE FOR AN OPEN TO GROUND.*
YES
PROBE CAVITY 11.
IS THE RESISTANCE BELOW 1.0 OHM?
NO
REPAIR THE K9 LB/RD WIRE FOR AN OPEN TO GROUND.*
YES
CONTINUE TEST DR-42A
* PERFORM VERIFICATION PROCEDURE 2.
91H14214 91I14215

Fig. 120: Driveability Test 42A – Checking Engine Controller Ground & Power Circuits (1 of 2)

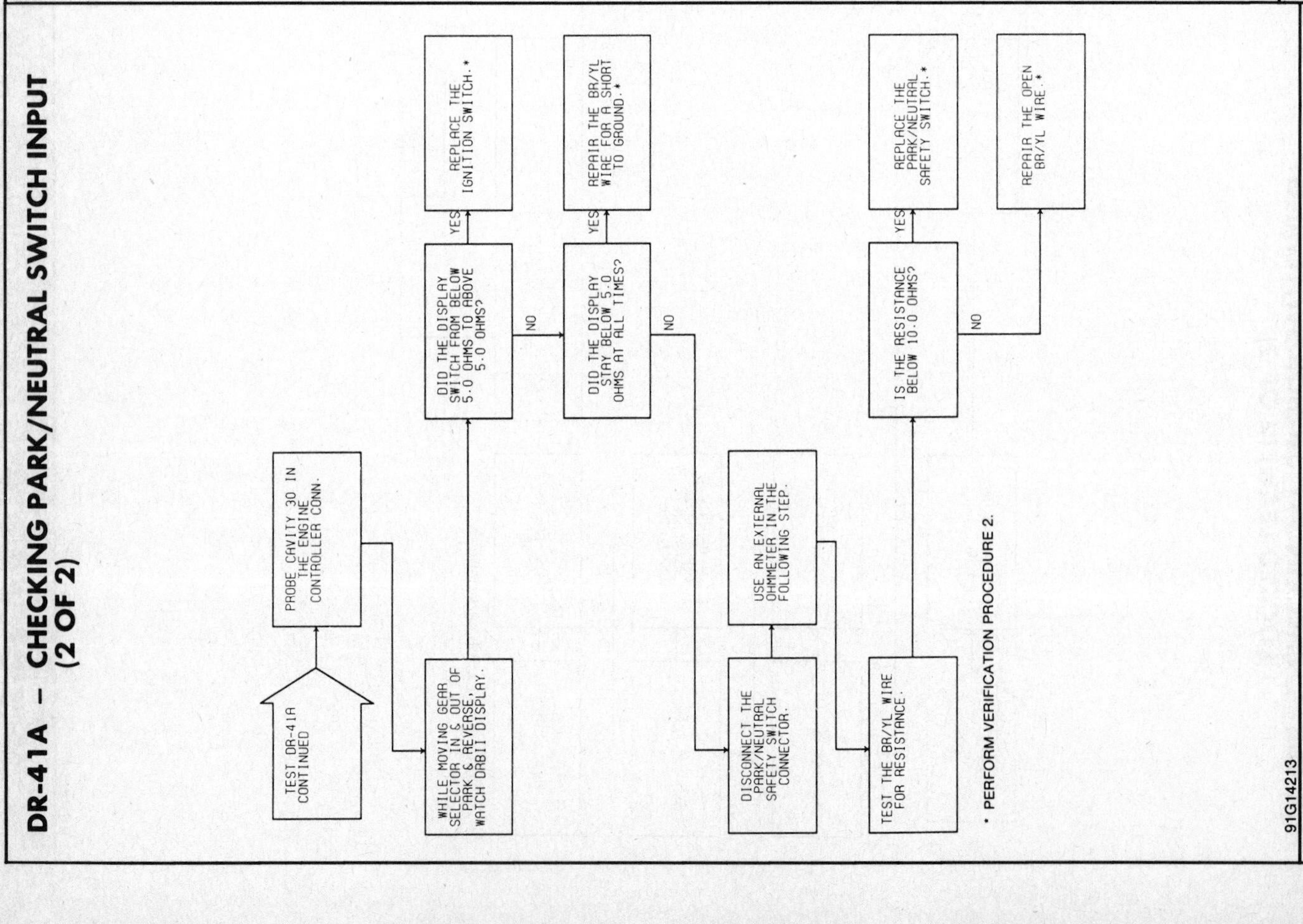
DR-41A – CHECKING PARK/NEUTRAL SWITCH INPUT (2 OF 2)
TEST DR-41A CONTINUED
PROBE CAVITY 30 IN THE ENGINE CONTROLLER CONN.
WHILE MOVING GEAR SELECTOR IN & OUT OF PARK & REVERSE, WATCH DRBII DISPLAY.
DID THE DISPLAY SWITCH FROM BELOW 5.0 OHMS TO ABOVE 5.0 OHMS?
YES
REPLACE THE IGNITION SWITCH.*
NO
DID THE DISPLAY STAY BELOW 5.0 OHMS AT ALL TIMES?
YES
REPAIR THE BR/YL WIRE FOR A SHORT TO GROUND.*
NO
DISCONNECT THE PARK/NEUTRAL SAFETY SWITCH CONNECTOR.
USE AN EXTERNAL OHMMETER IN THE FOLLOWING STEP.
TEST THE BR/YL WIRE FOR RESISTANCE.
IS THE RESISTANCE BELOW 10.0 OHMS?
YES
REPLACE THE PARK/NEUTRAL SAFETY SWITCH.*
NO
REPAIR THE OPEN BR/YL WIRE.*
* PERFORM VERIFICATION PROCEDURE 2.
91G14213

Fig. 119: Driveability Test 41A – Checking Park/Neutral Switch Input (2 of 2)

DR-42A – CHECKING ENGINE CONTROLLER GROUND & POWER CIRCUITS (2 OF 2)

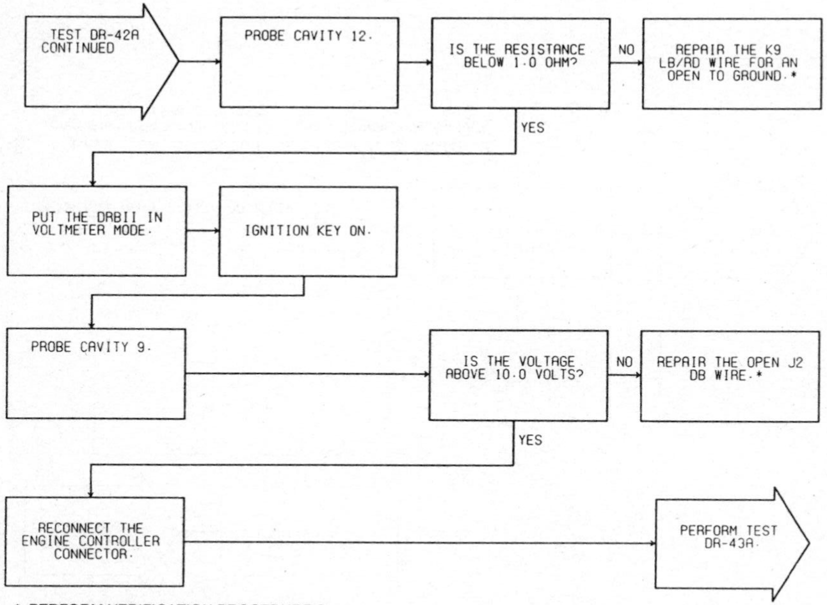
TEST DR-42A CONTINUED
PROBE CAVITY 12.
IS THE RESISTANCE BELOW 1.0 OHM?
NO
REPAIR THE K9 LB/RD WIRE FOR AN OPEN TO GROUND.*
YES
PUT THE DRBII IN VOLTMETER MODE.
IGNITION KEY ON.
PROBE CAVITY 9.
IS THE VOLTAGE ABOVE 10.0 VOLTS?
NO
REPAIR THE OPEN J2 DB WIRE.*
YES
RECONNECT THE ENGINE CONTROLLER CONNECTOR.
PERFORM TEST DR-43A.

* PERFORM VERIFICATION PROCEDURE 2.

91J14216

Fig. 121: Driveability Test 42A – Checking Engine Controller Ground & Power Circuits (2 of 2)

DR-43A – CHECKING ENGINE VACUUM

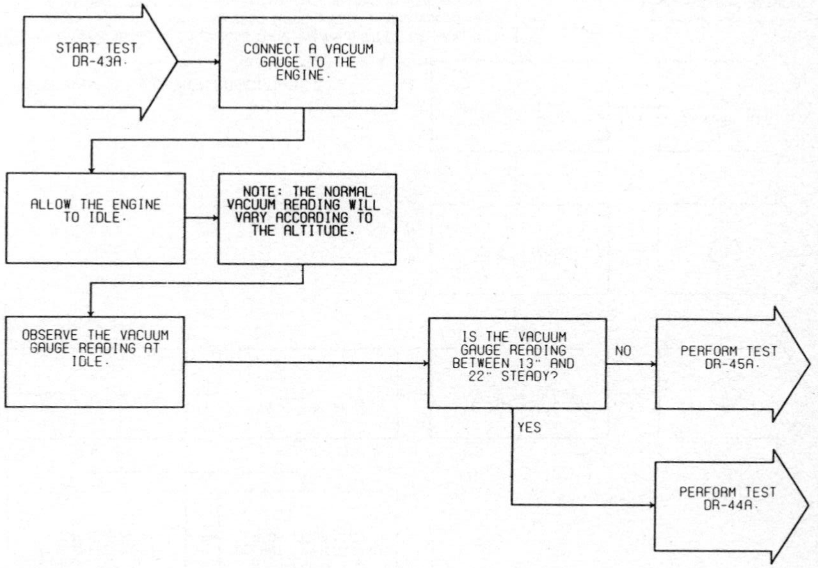
START TEST DR-43A.
CONNECT A VACUUM GAUGE TO THE ENGINE.
ALLOW THE ENGINE TO IDLE.
NOTE: THE NORMAL VACUUM READING WILL VARY ACCORDING TO THE ALTITUDE.
OBSERVE THE VACUUM GAUGE READING AT IDLE.
IS THE VACUUM GAUGE READING BETWEEN 13" AND 22" STEADY?
NO
PERFORM TEST DR-45A.
YES
PERFORM TEST DR-44A.

91A14217

Fig. 122: Driveability Test 43A – Checking Engine Vacuum

1991 ENGINE PERFORMANCE
Self-Diagnostics – 3.9L, 5.2L & 5.9L TBI (Cont.)

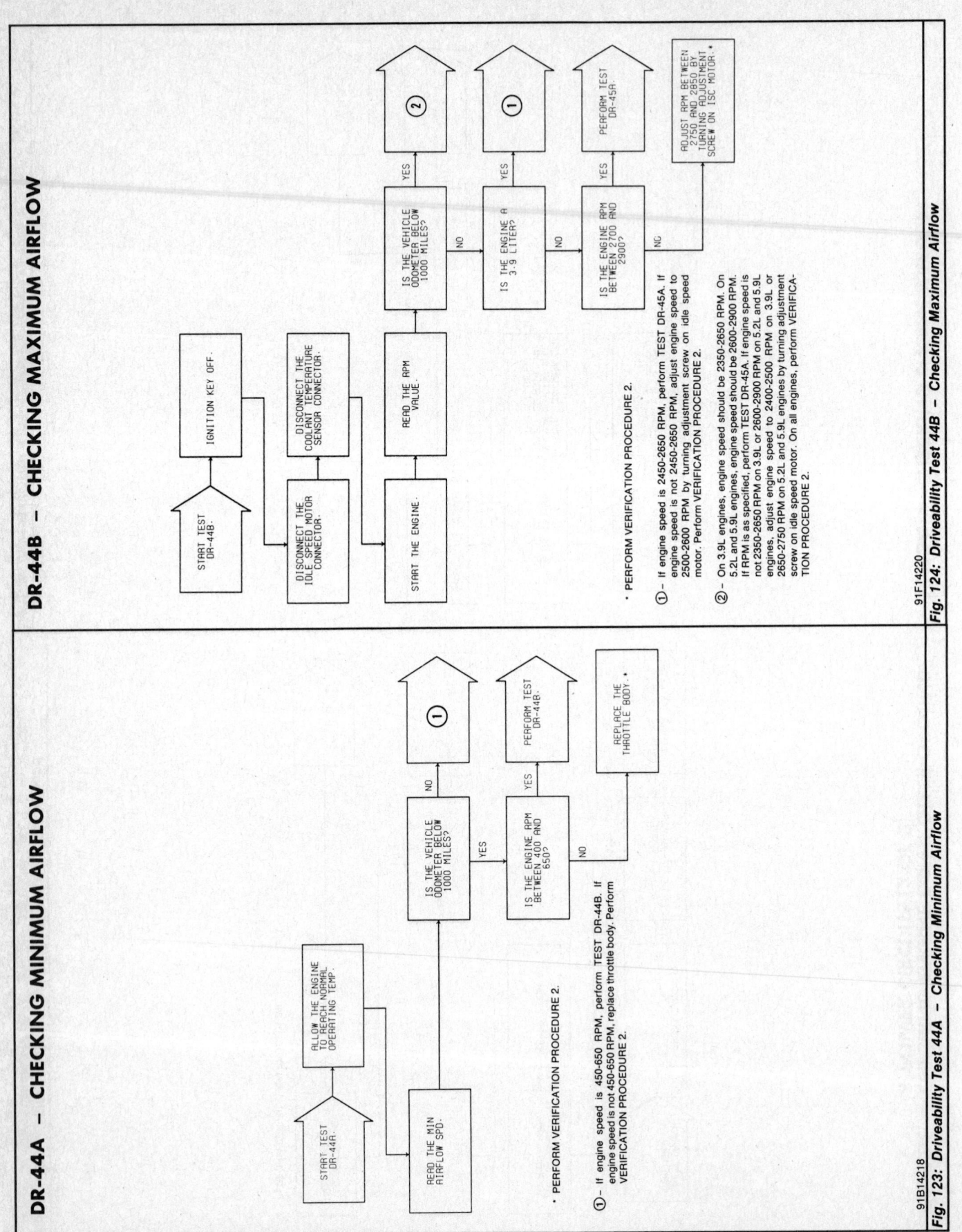

DR-44A – CHECKING MINIMUM AIRFLOW

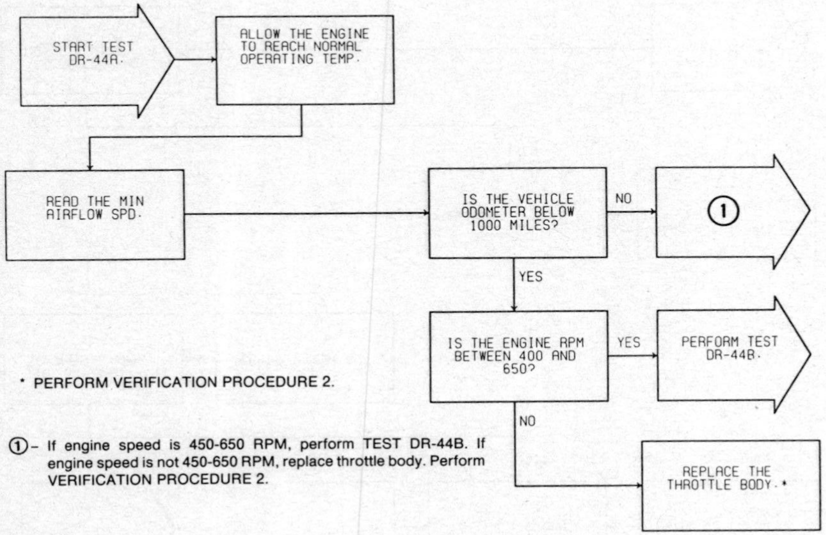
START TEST
DR-44A.
ALLOW THE ENGINE TO REACH NORMAL OPERATING TEMP.
READ THE MIN AIRFLOW SPD.
IS THE VEHICLE ODOMETER BELOW 1000 MILES?
NO
1
YES
IS THE ENGINE RPM BETWEEN 400 AND 650?
YES
PERFORM TEST DR-44B.
NO
REPLACE THE THROTTLE BODY.*

* PERFORM VERIFICATION PROCEDURE 2.

① – If engine speed is 450-650 RPM, perform TEST DR-44B. If engine speed is not 450-650 RPM, replace throttle body. Perform VERIFICATION PROCEDURE 2.

91B14218

Fig. 123: Driveability Test 44A – Checking Minimum Airflow

DR-44B – CHECKING MAXIMUM AIRFLOW

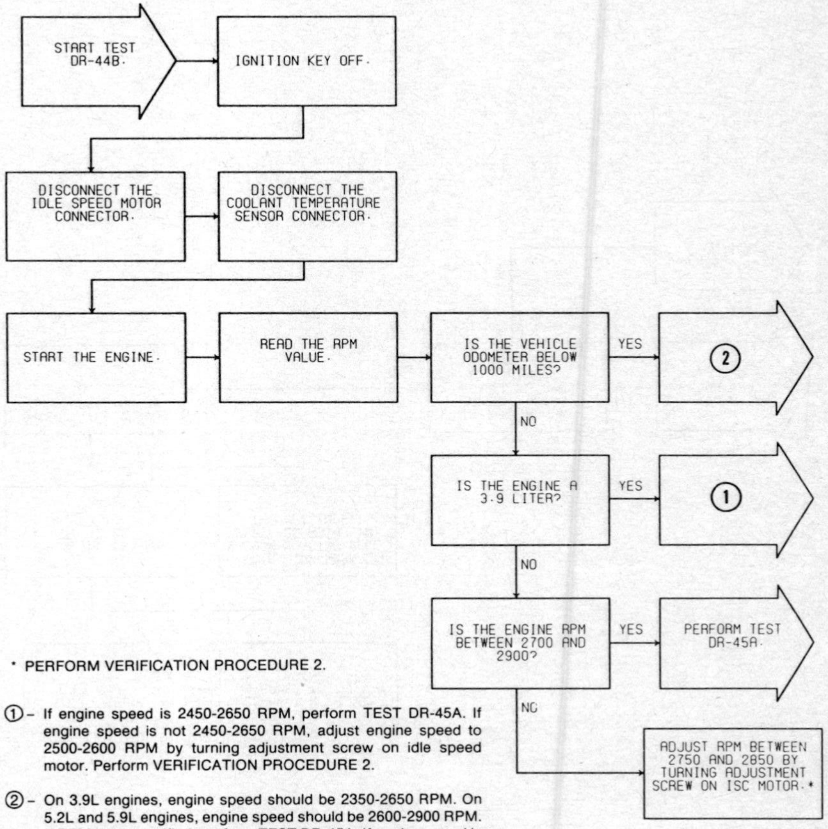
START TEST
DR-44B.
IGNITION KEY OFF.
DISCONNECT THE IDLE SPEED MOTOR CONNECTOR.
DISCONNECT THE COOLANT TEMPERATURE SENSOR CONNECTOR.
START THE ENGINE.
READ THE RPM VALUE.
IS THE VEHICLE ODOMETER BELOW 1000 MILES?
YES
2
NO
IS THE ENGINE A 3.9 LITER?
YES
1
NO
IS THE ENGINE RPM BETWEEN 2700 AND 2900?
YES
PERFORM TEST DR-45A.
NO
ADJUST RPM BETWEEN 2750 AND 2850 BY TURNING ADJUSTMENT SCREW ON ISC MOTOR.*

* PERFORM VERIFICATION PROCEDURE 2.

① – If engine speed is 2450-2650 RPM, perform TEST DR-45A. If engine speed is not 2450-2650 RPM, adjust engine speed to 2500-2600 RPM by turning adjustment screw on idle speed motor. Perform VERIFICATION PROCEDURE 2.

② – On 3.9L engines, engine speed should be 2350-2650 RPM. On 5.2L and 5.9L engines, engine speed should be 2600-2900 RPM. If RPM is as specified, perform TEST DR-45A. If engine speed is not 2350-2650 RPM on 3.9L or 2600-2900 RPM on 5.2L and 5.9L engines, adjust engine speed to 2400-2500 RPM on 3.9L or 2650-2750 RPM on 5.2L and 5.9L engines by turning adjustment screw on idle speed motor. On all engines, perform VERIFICATION PROCEDURE 2.

91F14220

Fig. 124: Driveability Test 44B – Checking Maximum Airflow

DR-45A – PERFORMING NO FAULT CODE MECHANICAL TEST

At this point in the driveability test procedure, it has been determined that all engine control systems are operating as designed and are not the cause of the driveability problem. Check the following additional items for possible causes:

- Check valve timing.
- Check torque converter stall speed.
- Check engine compression.
- Check camshaft and crankshaft sprockets.
- Check power brake booster for internal vacuum leaks.
- Check for fuel contamination.
- Check exhaust system for restriction.
- Ensure injectors are not plugged or restricted.
- Ensure engine vacuum is at least 13 in. Hg.
- Ensure PCV system is functioning properly.

NOTE: If you came to this test from the O_2 Sensor Test and the rich or lean condition is not caused by one of these mechanical systems, replace engine controller. Perform VERIFICATION PROCEDURE 2.

Fig. 125: Driveability Test 45A – Performing No Fault Code Mechanical Test

DR-46A – INTERMITTENT TEST FOR SOLENOIDS & RELAYS

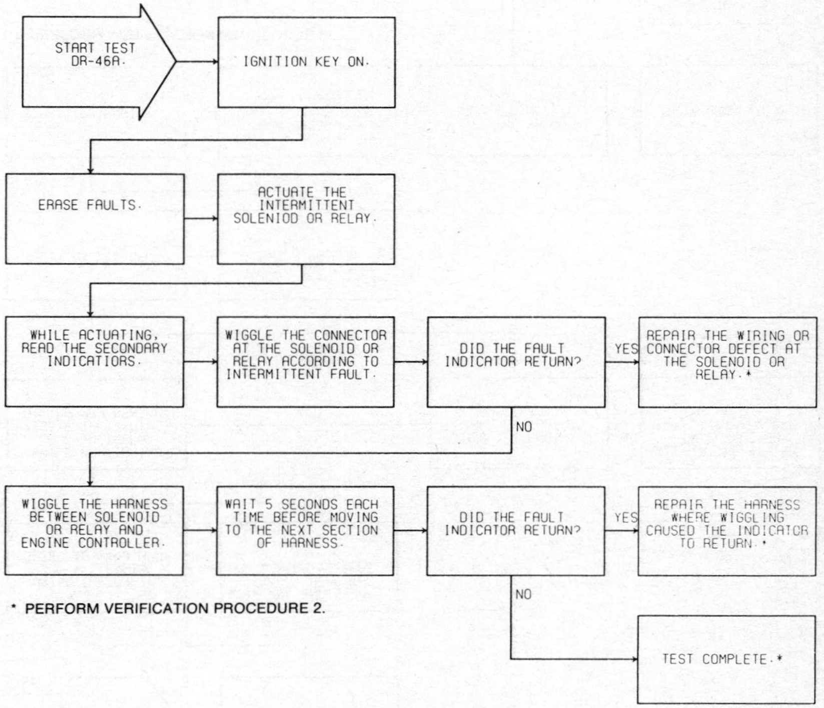
START TEST DR-46A.
IGNITION KEY ON.
ERASE FAULTS.
ACTUATE THE INTERMITTENT SOLENIOD OR RELAY.
WHILE ACTUATING, READ THE SECONDARY INDICATIORS.
WIGGLE THE CONNECTOR AT THE SOLENOID OR RELAY ACCORDING TO INTERMITTENT FAULT.
DID THE FAULT INDICATOR RETURN?
YES
REPAIR THE WIRING OR CONNECTOR DEFECT AT THE SOLENOID OR RELAY.*
NO
WIGGLE THE HARNESS BETWEEN SOLENOID OR RELAY AND ENGINE CONTROLLER.
WAIT 5 SECONDS EACH TIME BEFORE MOVING TO THE NEXT SECTION OF HARNESS.
DID THE FAULT INDICATOR RETURN?
YES
REPAIR THE HARNESS WHERE WIGGLING CAUSED THE INDICATOR TO RETURN.*
NO
TEST COMPLETE.*
* PERFORM VERIFICATION PROCEDURE 2.

91H14222

Fig. 126: Driveability Test 46A – Intermittent Test for Solenoids & Relays

1991 ENGINE PERFORMANCE
Self-Diagnostics – 3.9L, 5.2L & 5.9L TBI (Cont.)

DR-47A – INTERMITTENT TEST FOR VOLTAGE SENSORS

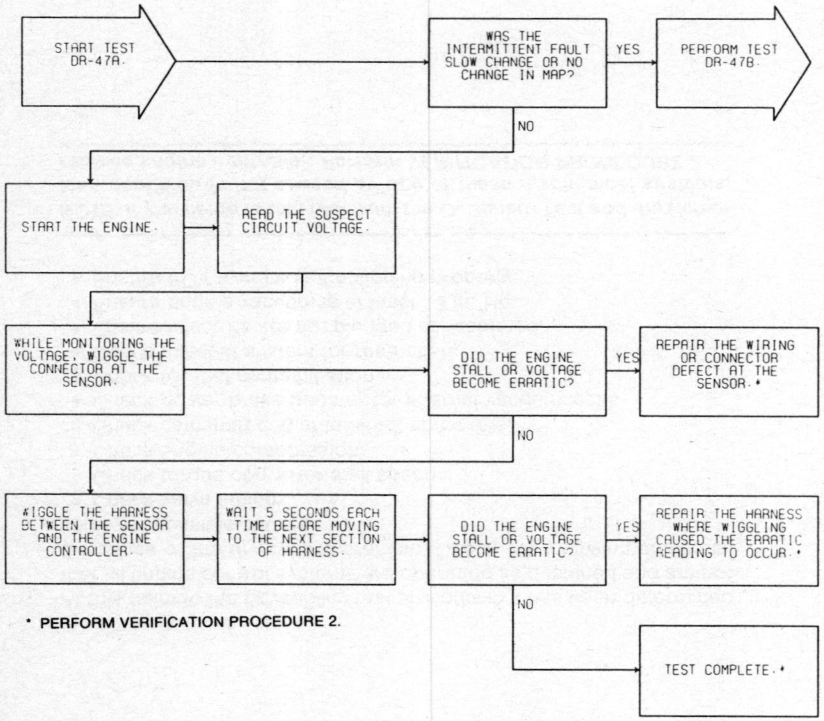
START TEST DR-47A.
WAS THE INTERMITTENT FAULT SLOW CHANGE OR NO CHANGE IN MAP?
YES
PERFORM TEST DR-47B.
NO
START THE ENGINE.
READ THE SUSPECT CIRCUIT VOLTAGE.
WHILE MONITORING THE VOLTAGE, WIGGLE THE CONNECTOR AT THE SENSOR.
DID THE ENGINE STALL OR VOLTAGE BECOME ERRATIC?
YES
REPAIR THE WIRING OR CONNECTOR DEFECT AT THE SENSOR.*
NO
WIGGLE THE HARNESS BETWEEN THE SENSOR AND THE ENGINE CONTROLLER.
WAIT 5 SECONDS EACH TIME BEFORE MOVING TO THE NEXT SECTION OF HARNESS.
DID THE ENGINE STALL OR VOLTAGE BECOME ERRATIC?
YES
REPAIR THE HARNESS WHERE WIGGLING CAUSED THE ERRATIC READING TO OCCUR.*
NO
TEST COMPLETE.*
* PERFORM VERIFICATION PROCEDURE 2.

91I14223

Fig. 127: Driveability Test 47A – Intermittent Test for Voltage Sensors

DR-47B – INTERMITTENT TEST FOR MAP SENSOR SIGNAL CHANGE

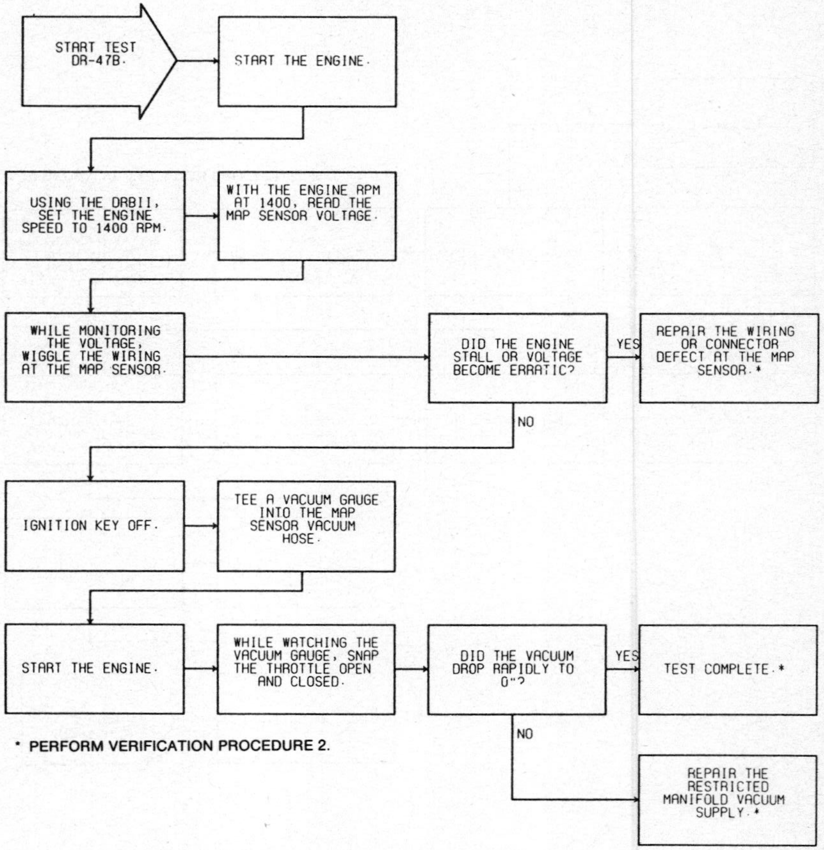
START TEST DR-47B.
START THE ENGINE.
USING THE DRBII, SET THE ENGINE SPEED TO 1400 RPM.
WITH THE ENGINE RPM AT 1400, READ THE MAP SENSOR VOLTAGE.
WHILE MONITORING THE VOLTAGE, WIGGLE THE WIRING AT THE MAP SENSOR.
DID THE ENGINE STALL OR VOLTAGE BECOME ERRATIC?
YES
REPAIR THE WIRING OR CONNECTOR DEFECT AT THE MAP SENSOR.*
NO
IGNITION KEY OFF.
TEE A VACUUM GAUGE INTO THE MAP SENSOR VACUUM HOSE.
START THE ENGINE.
WHILE WATCHING THE VACUUM GAUGE, SNAP THE THROTTLE OPEN AND CLOSED.
DID THE VACUUM DROP RAPIDLY TO 0"?
YES
TEST COMPLETE.*
NO
REPAIR THE RESTRICTED MANIFOLD VACUUM SUPPLY.*
* PERFORM VERIFICATION PROCEDURE 2.

91J14224

Fig. 128: Driveability Test 47B – Intermittent Test for MAP Sensor Signal Change

DR-48A – INTERMITTENT TEST FOR AIS MOTOR CIRCUITS

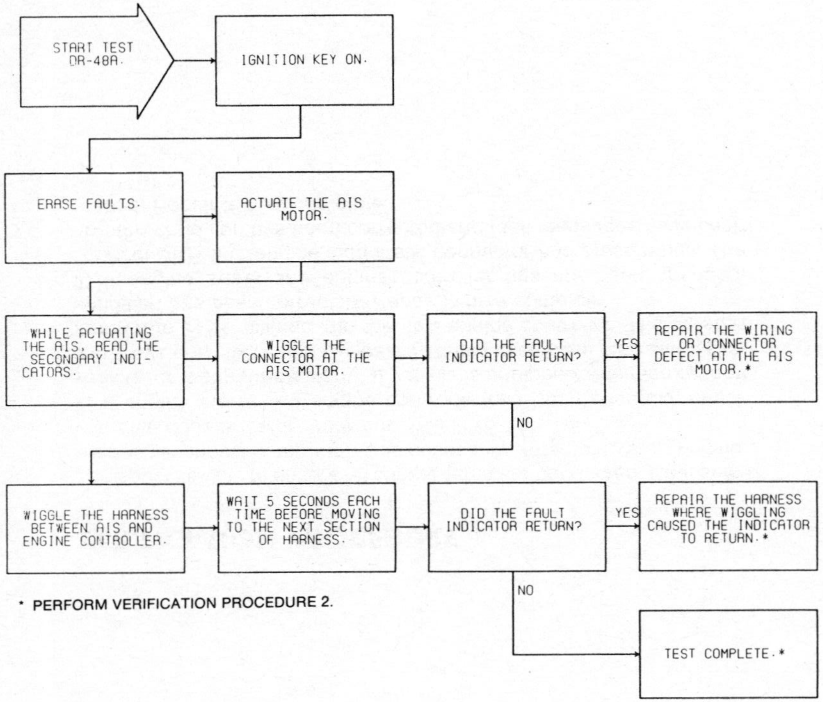
START TEST DR-48A.
IGNITION KEY ON.
ERASE FAULTS.
ACTUATE THE AIS MOTOR.
WHILE ACTUATING THE AIS, READ THE SECONDARY INDI- CATORS.
WIGGLE THE CONNECTOR AT THE AIS MOTOR.
DID THE FAULT INDICATOR RETURN?
YES
REPAIR THE WIRING OR CONNECTOR DEFECT AT THE AIS MOTOR.*
NO
WIGGLE THE HARNESS BETWEEN AIS AND ENGINE CONTROLLER.
WAIT 5 SECONDS EACH TIME BEFORE MOVING TO THE NEXT SECTION OF HARNESS.
DID THE FAULT INDICATOR RETURN?
YES
REPAIR THE HARNESS WHERE WIGGLING CAUSED THE INDICATOR TO RETURN.*
NO
TEST COMPLETE.*

* PERFORM VERIFICATION PROCEDURE 2.

91A14225

Fig. 129: Driveability Test 48A – Intermittent Test for AIS Motor Circuits

DR-49A – INTERMITTENT TEST FOR FUEL INJECTORS

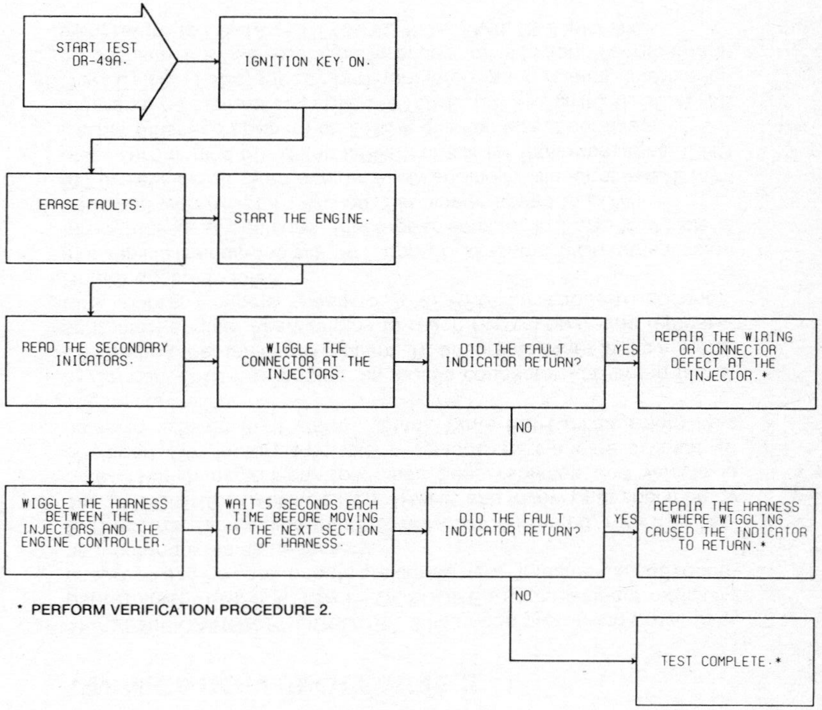
START TEST DR-49A.
IGNITION KEY ON.
ERASE FAULTS.
START THE ENGINE.
READ THE SECONDARY INICATORS.
WIGGLE THE CONNECTOR AT THE INJECTORS.
DID THE FAULT INDICATOR RETURN?
YES
REPAIR THE WIRING OR CONNECTOR DEFECT AT THE INJECTOR.*
NO
WIGGLE THE HARNESS BETWEEN THE INJECTORS AND THE ENGINE CONTROLLER.
WAIT 5 SECONDS EACH TIME BEFORE MOVING TO THE NEXT SECTION OF HARNESS.
DID THE FAULT INDICATOR RETURN?
YES
REPAIR THE HARNESS WHERE WIGGLING CAUSED THE INDICATOR TO RETURN.*
NO
TEST COMPLETE.*

* PERFORM VERIFICATION PROCEDURE 2.

91B14226

Fig. 130: Driveability Test 49A – Intermittent Test for Fuel Injectors

VER-1 – VERIFICATION PROCEDURE 1

VERIFICATION PROCEDURE 1

1) Inspect vehicle to ensure all components are connected. Reassemble and reconnect components as necessary. Attempt to start engine. If engine does not start, return to TEST NS-1A.
2) If engine starts and engine controller has been changed, check vehicle for factory theft alarm. If vehicle is equipped with factory theft alarm system, start engine at least 20 times to activate theft alarm system. Write EMR mileage into the new engine controller. The no-start condition has been corrected. Repair is now complete.
3) If engine starts and engine controller has not been changed, connect DRB-II to engine diagnostic connector and erase faults. The no-start condition has been corrected and fault messages have been erased. Repair is now complete.

Fig. 131: Verification Procedure 1

VER-2 – VERIFICATION PROCEDURE 2

VERIFICATION PROCEDURE 2

1) If VERIFICATION PROCEDURE 3 has been preformed previously, perform test VERIFICATION PROCEDURE 3 again. Inspect vehicle to ensure all engine components are connected. Reassemble and reconnect components as necessary.
2) If another fault exists that has not been corrected, return to DR-1A: CHECKING FOR FAULTS & SPARK and follow path specified by other fault. If engine controller has been replaced and vehicle is equipped with factory theft alarm system, start engine at least 20 times to activate theft alarm system. Write EMR mileage into new engine controller.
3) Connect DRB-II to engine diagnostic connector and erase faults. Ensure no other faults are present. To ensure no other faults are present, start engine. Allow engine to reach normal operating temperature. Increase engine speed to 2000 RPM for about 10 seconds. Return engine to idle.
4) If vehicle is equipped with A/T, apply brakes and cycle transmission through all gear positions. Place gear selector in Park. If vehicle is equipped with A/C, turn A/C on. Set blower speed to LOW.
5) Turn engine off. Start engine. Allow engine to idle for at least 2 minutes. Turn engine off. Using DRB-II, check for fault messages. If NO FAULT message appears on DRB-II display, test is complete.
6) If repaired fault resets, check MITCHELL'S TECHNICAL SERVICE BULLETINS (TSBs) for any pertinent information relating to driveability problem. If a TSB exists, perform corrective action. If another fault sets, return to DR-1A: CHECKING FOR FAULTS & SPARK.

Fig. 132: Verification Procedure 2

VER-3 – VERIFICATION PROCEDURE 3

VERIFICATION PROCEDURE 3

1) Inspect vehicle to ensure all engine components are connected. Reassemble and reconnect components as necessary. If another fault is present that has not been corrected, return to DR-1A: CHECKING FOR FAULTS & SPARK and follow path specified by other fault.
2) If engine controller has been changed and vehicle is equipped with factory theft alarm system, start engine at least 20 times to activate theft alarm system. Write EMR mileage into new engine controller.
3) Connect DRB-II to engine diagnostic connector. Erase fault messages. Disconnect DRB-II. Ensure no other fault messages are present. To ensure no other fault messages are present, start engine. If vehicle is equipped with A/C, turn A/C on. Set blower speed to LOW.
4) Drive vehicle for about 5 minutes. During this time, attain a speed of at least 40 MPH. Ensure transmission shifts through all gears. Upon completion of road test, turn engine off.
5) Start engine. Allow engine to idle for about 2 minutes. Turn engine off. Connect DRB-II to engine diagnostic connector. Using DRB-II, check for fault messages. If no fault messages are present, test is complete.
6) If repaired fault message resets, check MITCHELL'S TECHNICAL SERVICE BULLETINS (TSBs) for any pertinent information relating to driveability problems. If a TSB exists, perform corrective action. If another fault sets, return to DR-1A: CHECKING FOR FAULTS & SPARK.

Fig. 133: Verification Procedure 3

1991 ENGINE PERFORMANCE
Body Control Computer

Caravan, Town & Country, Voyager

DESCRIPTION

The body control computer system consists of a combination of modules that communicate over the Chrysler Collision Detection (CCD) bus system. Through the CCD bus, information related to the operation of vehicle components and circuits is relayed to the appropriate system module(s). Each module receives the same component information. This reduces the complexity of vehicle wiring and size of wiring harness.

The following body control computer systems are covered in this article: electronic instrument cluster, electro/mechanical instrument cluster and intermittent wipers. System failures within these systems can be diagnosed via the CCD bus diagnostic connector using Chrysler's Diagnostic Readout Box-II (DRB-II) tester.

OPERATION

Diagnostic test procedures are designed to detect system faults as quickly as possible. Body and chassis fault codes are accessed through CCD bus diagnostic connector. CCD bus diagnostic connector is located under left side of dash. *See Fig. 1.* DRB-II tester is used to access information from CCD bus.

BODY CONTROL COMPUTER

The body control computer is located behind center of dashboard. Body control computer stores odometer information for electronic instrument cluster and electro/mechanical instrument cluster display and provides power and ground for a variety of systems. Systems are monitored by body control computer through voltage drops.

CCD BUS

The CCD bus is a twisted pair of wires traveling from module to module receiving and delivering coded information. The code identifies the message and its importance. When multiple messages attempt to access CCD bus at once, code assigns priority ranking.

The 2 twisted wires used by the CCD bus system are called Bus "+" and Bus "–". Both wires carry approximately 2.5 volts.

SELF-DIAGNOSTIC SYSTEM

Use trouble shooting charts listed in BODY CONTROL COMPUTER DIRECTORY table when using DRB-II.

BODY CONTROL COMPUTER DIRECTORY

Application [1]	Page
Body Control Computer Trouble Shooting Charts	1-xxx
Vehicle Communications Trouble Shooting Charts [2]	1-xxx

[1] – Some trouble shooting charts may refer to body type with an "A" prefix.
[2] – Vehicle communications charts should only be used when instructed to do so by another chart.

PRETEST INSPECTION

Before proceeding with diagnosis, the following precautions must be followed:

- Vehicle must have a fully charged battery and functional charging system.
- Always start at TEST 1A: IDENTIFYING VEHICLE EQUIPMENT & SYSTEM PROBLEMS. Starting with any other test may result in incorrect results.
- Only perform test steps indicated. It is NOT necessary to perform all steps in a test.
- VEHICLE COMMUNICATIONS charts should only be used when instructed to do so by another chart. Always start at TEST 1A: GENERAL FAILURE MESSAGES.
- Always perform verification procedure test after repairs are made.
- At the end of each test step, reconnect all wires and install any components removed for testing.
- Use extreme care when connecting or disconnecting wiring during testing to prevent accidental grounding or shorting.
- DO NOT use a test light in place of a voltmeter.
- Always disconnect DRB-II after use.
- Always disconnect DRB-II before charging battery.

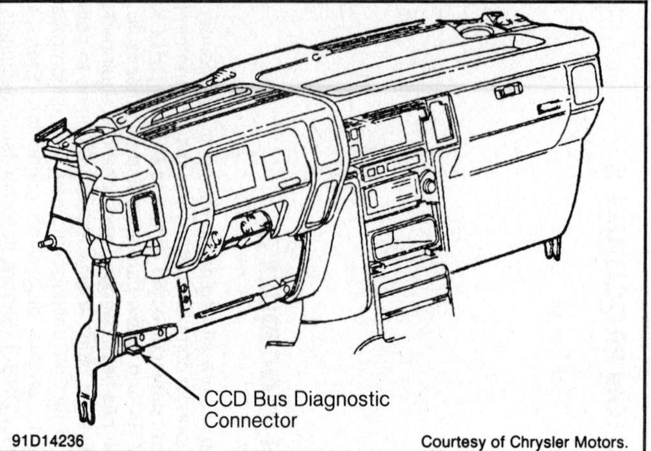
CCD Bus Diagnostic
Connector
91D14236
Courtesy of Chrysler Motors.

Fig. 1: Locating CCD Bus Diagnostic Connector

DIAGNOSTIC PROCEDURE

NOTE: Before proceeding with diagnosis, certain precautions must be followed. See PRETEST INSPECTION.

Diagnostic test procedures are designed to detect system faults as quickly as possible. Body fault codes are accessed through CCD bus diagnostic connector. *See Fig. 1.* DRB-II tester is used to access information from CCD bus diagnostic connector.

DRB-II tester, 1991 diagnostic program cartridge, body diagnostic cable, jumper wires, analog volt/ohmmeter and oil pressure gauge will be needed for testing. Proceed to TEST 1A: IDENTIFYING VEHICLE EQUIPMENT & SYSTEM PROBLEMS in TROUBLE SHOOTING CHARTS. When system problem is identified according to customer's complaint, perform the diagnostic test indicated.

DRB-II KEY FUNCTIONS

- **YES or Down Arrow & NO or Up Arrow** – Keys will move lines on screen up or down, allowing technician to choose an item or scroll through all selections available.
- **ATM Key** – Key will return technician to previous screen.
- **ENTER Key** – Allows technician to select a test or display. The flashing arrow must be on the display user wishes to select. Pressing the ENTER key in the sensor state will cause display to change from a 3-line display to a 1-line display.
- **F3 Key** – Key is used to display a help screen. This key may be used at any time.
- **READ/HOLD Key** – Key is used to freeze any sensor display.
- **MODE & ATM Keys** – Pressing MODE and ATM keys at the same time will cause DRB-II to reset to copyright screen.

ENTERING ON-BOARD DIAGNOSTICS

1) Before entering on-board diagnostics, refer to PRETEST INSPECTION. Turn ignition off. Attach appropriate cartridge to DRB-II. Connect DRB-II to CCD bus diagnostic connector. *See Fig. 1.*

2) Turn all accessories off. Turn ignition on. All character positions will illuminate and copyright information will appear on DRB-II screen for a few seconds. Display will then change to DRB-II menu.

3) If DRB-II displays an error message or screen is blank, refer to VEHICLE COMMUNICATIONS charts. See BODY CONTROL COMPUTER DIRECTORY table. Always start at TEST 1A: GENERAL MESSAGE FAILURES.

4) The following DRB-II modes can be accessed from DRB-II menu: VEHICLES TESTED, HOW TO USE, CONFIGURE and SELECT SYSTEM.

VEHICLES TESTED Mode - At DRB-II menu, press "1" (VEHICLES TESTED) key. Press ENTER key. At VEHICLES TESTED menu, DRB-II will display vehicles supported by cartridge used. This screen will display for 5 seconds and return to DRB-II menu. To return to DRB-II menu sooner, press ATM key.

HOW TO USE Mode - At DRB-II menu, press "2" (HOW TO USE) key. Press ENTER key. DRB-II will display instructions for use of DRB-II with cartridge being used.

CONFIGURE Mode - At DRB-II menu, press "3" (CONFIGURE) key. Press ENTER key. At CONFIGURE menu, technician can customize DRB-II display. For example, if metric system is more useful, simply select METRIC from the appropriate menu. All selections made under CONFIGURE option remain active until user changes selection.

SELECT SYSTEM Mode - 1) This mode enables the technician to select system to be diagnosed. At DRB-II menu, press "4" (SELECT SYSTEM) key. Press ENTER key. DRB-II will display SELECT SYSTEM menu.

2) At SELECT SYSTEM menu, press "3" (BODY) key. Press ENTER key. DRB-II should display BUS TEST IN PROGRESS and BUS OPERATIONAL. After a few seconds, display should change to BODY STYLE menu.

3) If a bus failure message appears during BUS TEST IN PROGRESS, proceed to VEHICLE COMMUNICATIONS charts. See BODY CONTROL COMPUTER DIRECTORY table. Always start at TEST 1A: GENERAL MESSAGE FAILURES. At BODY STYLE menu, select appropriate body style for vehicle being worked on. DRB-II will display SELECT MODULE MENU.

SELECT MODULE MENU - Menu will display body control systems available for the technician to diagnose. Select appropriate body system to be tested. DRB-II will then display a menu for specific system being tested. The following functions can be accessed from each system menu:

- **System Tests** - This function allows the technician to determine whether the Single Board Engine Controller (SBEC) is active over the CCD bus.
- **Read Faults** - This functions allows technician to read faults. If there are no faults, NO FAULTS DETECTED will be displayed. If there are faults, DRB-II will display number of faults, and fault code and message.
- **State Display** - This functions allows technician to read states or values of a variety of sensors, inputs/outputs and components.
- **Actuator Tests** - This function allows technician to activate various outputs, motors and relays to test their operation.
- **Adjustments** - This function allows the technician to change vehicle theft alarm system mode from disarmed to armed, or to put alarm system in self-diagnostics mode. Adjustments function is not available for testing of other body control modules.

DRB-II Volt-Ohmmeter Mode - 1) To access volt-ohmmeter mode of DRB-II, connect Red volt-ohmmeter test lead to Red port, located on right top side of DRB-II.

NOTE: Because DRB-II is grounded through engine diagnostic connector, only one volt-ohmmeter test lead is required when using volt-ohmmeter option. DRB-II volt-ohmmeter should only be used when trouble shooting charts require the use of this option.

2) To access voltmeter, press VOLT/OHM key once. DRB-II is now in voltmeter mode. Touch test probe to connector or wire to be measured. Read voltage on DRB-II display. When voltage testing is complete, press VOLT/OHM key 3 times to exit voltmeter mode.

3) To access ohmmeter, press VOLT/OHM key twice. DRB-II is now in ohmmeter mode. Touch test probe to connector or wire to be measured. Read resistance to circuit ground on DRB-II display. When resistance testing is complete, press VOLT/OHM key twice to exit ohmmeter mode.

DRB-II Continuity Meter Mode - Press VOLT/OHM key 3 times. Display will read NO CONTINUITY. Touch test probe to connector or wire to be measured. Read continuity on DRB-II display. When continuity testing is complete, press VOLT/OHM key once to exit continuity meter mode.

ELECTRONIC INSTRUMENT CLUSTER (EIC) ACTUATOR TESTS

After ACTUATOR TESTS is selected from ELEC CLUSTER menu, display will change to ACTUATOR TEST and the tests available for the technician to diagnose. Select appropriate test. DRB-II will then display a menu for specific test and ACTUATING/COMPLETED. To determine whether or not any of these tests pass or fail, observe EIC display as test is being actuated. The following tests can be accessed from menu:

- **INTERNAL CHECK** - This tests the internal functions of the EIC. This test also displays any fault codes present.
- **ALL SEGMENTS ON** - This test turns on all segments of EIC, and then turns them off. If all segments do not illuminate and then turn off, test fails.
- **SEQUENTIAL SEGMENTS TEST** - This test illuminates all vacuum fluorescent bars on all gauges in EIC, then turns them off. If any bar fails to illuminate, test fails.
- **SEQUENTIAL LEGENDS TEST** - This test illuminates all legends in EIC individually, and then turns them off. If any legend fails to illuminate or if 2 legends are illuminated together, test fails.
- **SEQUENTIAL LAMP CHECK** - This test illuminates all of the following lights in EIC display individually, and then turns them off: WASHER FLUID, DOOR/DECK, CHECK ENGINE, SEAT BELT, BRAKE and CHECK GAGES. If any light does not illuminate and then turn off, test fails.

DRB-II PROBLEMS & ERROR MESSAGES

If a problem exists with the operation of DRB-II, DRB-II displays a blank screen, CCD bus failure message or NO RESPONSE, RAM TEST FAILURE, CARTRIDGE ERROR, KEYPAD TEST FAILURE, HIGH BATTERY or LOW BATTERY error message appears, refer to VEHICLE COMMUNICATIONS charts. See BODY CONTROL COMPUTER DIRECTORY table. Always start at TEST 1A: GENERAL MESSAGE FAILURES.

BODY CONTROL SYSTEM CONNECTORS

NOTE: Use Figs. 2-4 to identify connector terminals referenced in TROUBLE SHOOTING CHARTS and VEHICLE COMMUNICATIONS.

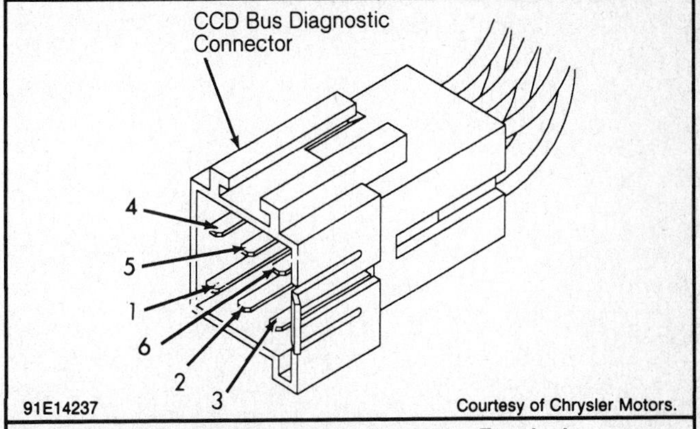

CCD Bus Diagnostic Connector
4
5
1
6
2
3
91E14237
Courtesy of Chrysler Motors.

Fig. 2: Identifying BUS Diagnostic Connector Terminals

1991 ENGINE PERFORMANCE
Body Control Computer (Cont.)

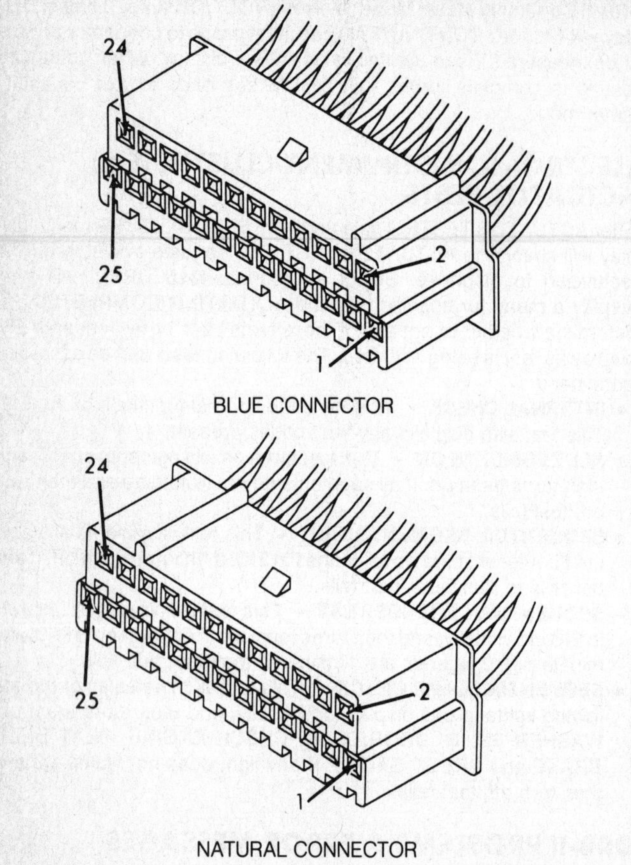
24
25
2
1
BLUE CONNECTOR
24
25
2
1
NATURAL CONNECTOR

91F14238 Courtesy of Chrysler Motors.

Fig. 3: Identifying Body Control Computer Terminals

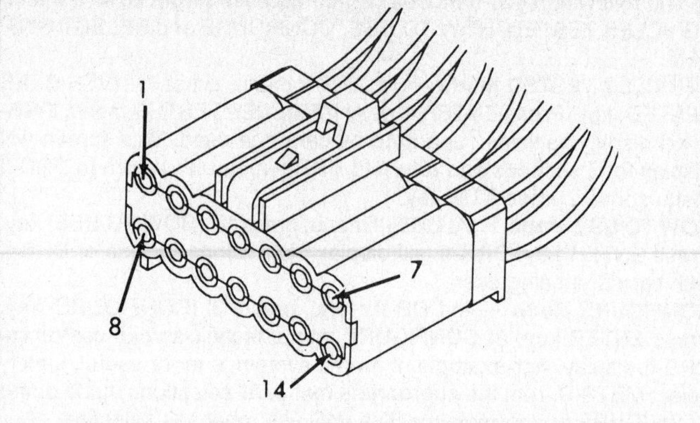
1
7
8
14

91G14239 Courtesy of Chrysler Motors.

Fig. 4: Identifying Instrument Cluster Connector Terminals

TROUBLE SHOOTING CHARTS

NOTE:* *The following trouble shooting charts and illustrations are courtesy of Chrysler Motors.

TEST 1A: IDENTIFYING VEHICLE EQUIPMENT & SYSTEM PROBLEMS (1 OF 2)

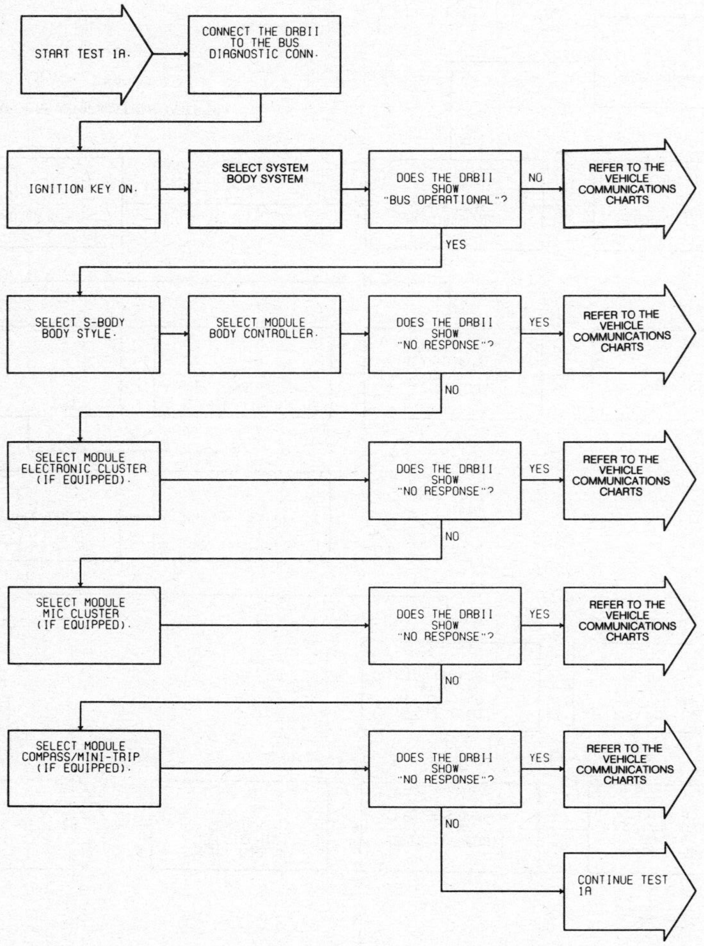
START TEST 1A.
CONNECT THE DRBII TO THE BUS DIAGNOSTIC CONN.
IGNITION KEY ON.
SELECT SYSTEM BODY SYSTEM
DOES THE DRBII SHOW "BUS OPERATIONAL"?
NO
REFER TO THE VEHICLE COMMUNICATIONS CHARTS
YES
SELECT S-BODY BODY STYLE.
SELECT MODULE BODY CONTROLLER.
DOES THE DRBII SHOW "NO RESPONSE"?
YES
REFER TO THE VEHICLE COMMUNICATIONS CHARTS
NO
SELECT MODULE ELECTRONIC CLUSTER (IF EQUIPPED).
DOES THE DRBII SHOW "NO RESPONSE"?
YES
REFER TO THE VEHICLE COMMUNICATIONS CHARTS
NO
SELECT MODULE MIC CLUSTER (IF EQUIPPED).
DOES THE DRBII SHOW "NO RESPONSE"?
YES
REFER TO THE VEHICLE COMMUNICATIONS CHARTS
NO
SELECT MODULE COMPASS/MINI-TRIP (IF EQUIPPED).
DOES THE DRBII SHOW "NO RESPONSE"?
YES
REFER TO THE VEHICLE COMMUNICATIONS CHARTS
NO
CONTINUE TEST 1A
91J14240

Fig. 5: Test 1A – Identifying Vehicle Equipment & System Problems (1 of 2)

TEST 1A: IDENTIFYING VEHICLE EQUIPMENT & SYSTEM PROBLEMS (2 OF 2)

The DIAGNOSTIC TEST OUTLINE table lists failures that can be diagnosed via the Chrysler Collision Detection (CCD) bus connector using the DRB-II. These failures may occur separately or in various combinations. When diagnosing a system with many apparent problems, choose a problem area in the DIAGNOSTIC TEST OUTLINE table and perform test indicated. Verify that the failure or group of failures has been corrected.

DIAGNOSTIC TEST OUTLINE

Problem	Test No.
Electronic Instrument Cluster	2A
Electro/Mechanical Instrument Cluster	9A
Headlight Time Delay Inoperative	37B
Headlights Will Not Turn Off	37A
Intermittent Wipers	22A

Fig. 6: Test 1A – Identifying Vehicle Equipment & System Problems (2 of 2)

1991 ENGINE PERFORMANCE
Body Control Computer (Cont.)

TEST 2A: ELECTRONIC CLUSTER DIAGNOSIS

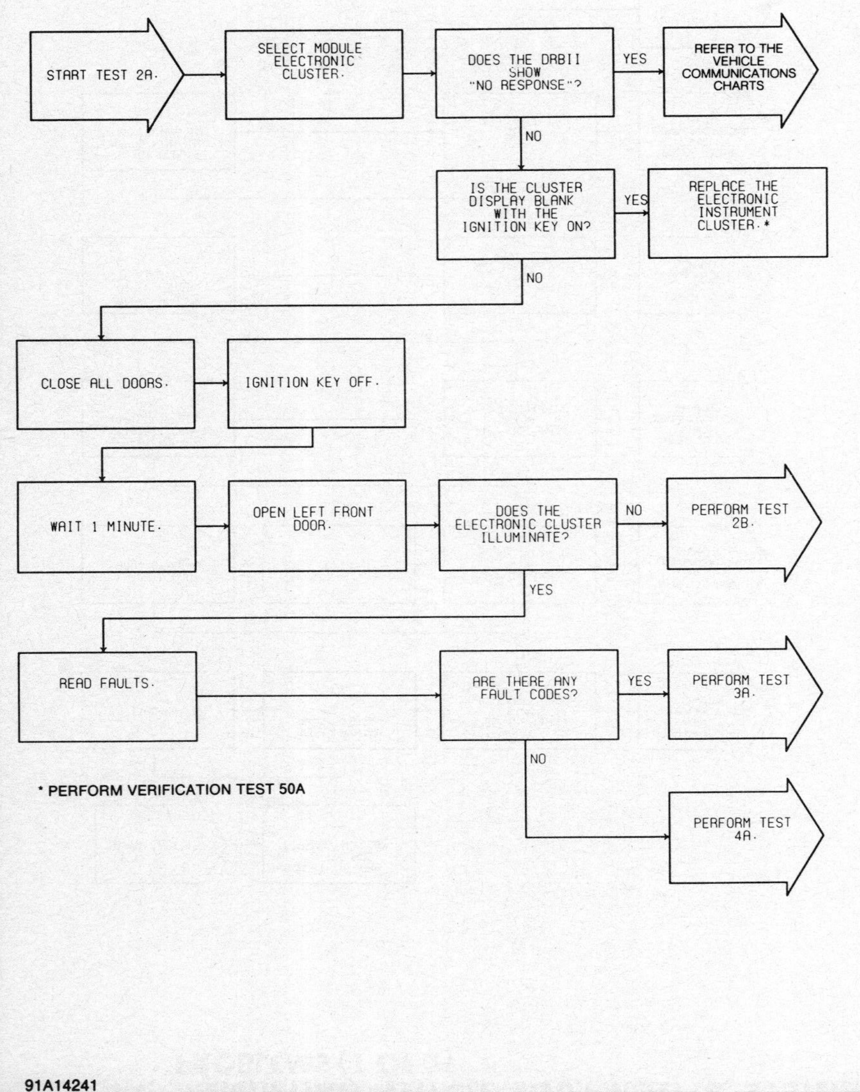
START TEST 2A.
SELECT MODULE ELECTRONIC CLUSTER.
DOES THE DRBII SHOW "NO RESPONSE"?
YES
REFER TO THE VEHICLE COMMUNICATIONS CHARTS
NO
IS THE CLUSTER DISPLAY BLANK WITH THE IGNITION KEY ON?
YES
REPLACE THE ELECTRONIC INSTRUMENT CLUSTER.*
NO
CLOSE ALL DOORS.
IGNITION KEY OFF.
WAIT 1 MINUTE.
OPEN LEFT FRONT DOOR.
DOES THE ELECTRONIC CLUSTER ILLUMINATE?
NO
PERFORM TEST 2B.
YES
READ FAULTS.
ARE THERE ANY FAULT CODES?
YES
PERFORM TEST 3A.
NO
PERFORM TEST 4A.
* PERFORM VERIFICATION TEST 50A
91A14241

Fig. 7: Test 2A – Electronic Cluster Diagnosis

TEST 2B: REPAIRING ELECTRONIC CLUSTER "POWER UP UPON ENTRY" (1 OF 2)

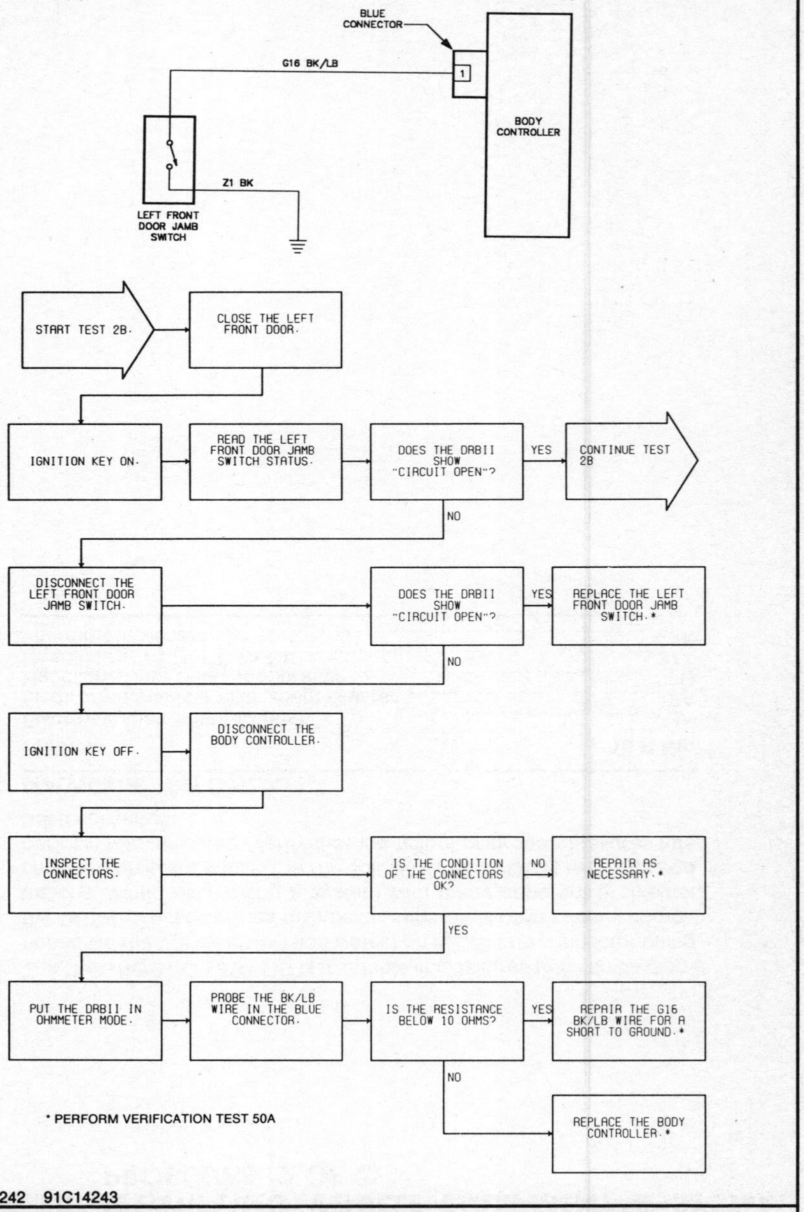
BLUE CONNECTOR
G16 BK/LB
1
BODY CONTROLLER
Z1 BK
LEFT FRONT DOOR JAMB SWITCH
START TEST 2B.
CLOSE THE LEFT FRONT DOOR.
IGNITION KEY ON.
READ THE LEFT FRONT DOOR JAMB SWITCH STATUS.
DOES THE DRBII SHOW "CIRCUIT OPEN"?
YES
CONTINUE TEST 2B
NO
DISCONNECT THE LEFT FRONT DOOR JAMB SWITCH.
DOES THE DRBII SHOW "CIRCUIT OPEN"?
YES
REPLACE THE LEFT FRONT DOOR JAMB SWITCH.*
NO
IGNITION KEY OFF.
DISCONNECT THE BODY CONTROLLER.
INSPECT THE CONNECTORS.
IS THE CONDITION OF THE CONNECTORS OK?
NO
REPAIR AS NECESSARY.*
YES
PUT THE DRBII IN OHMMETER MODE.
PROBE THE BK/LB WIRE IN THE BLUE CONNECTOR.
IS THE RESISTANCE BELOW 10 OHMS?
YES
REPAIR THE G16 BK/LB WIRE FOR A SHORT TO GROUND.*
NO
REPLACE THE BODY CONTROLLER.*
* PERFORM VERIFICATION TEST 50A
91B14242 91C14243

Fig. 8: Test 2B – Repairing Electronic Cluster "Power Up Upon Entry" (1 of 2)

TEST 2B: REPAIRING ELECTRONIC CLUSTER "POWER UP UPON ENTRY" (2 OF 2)

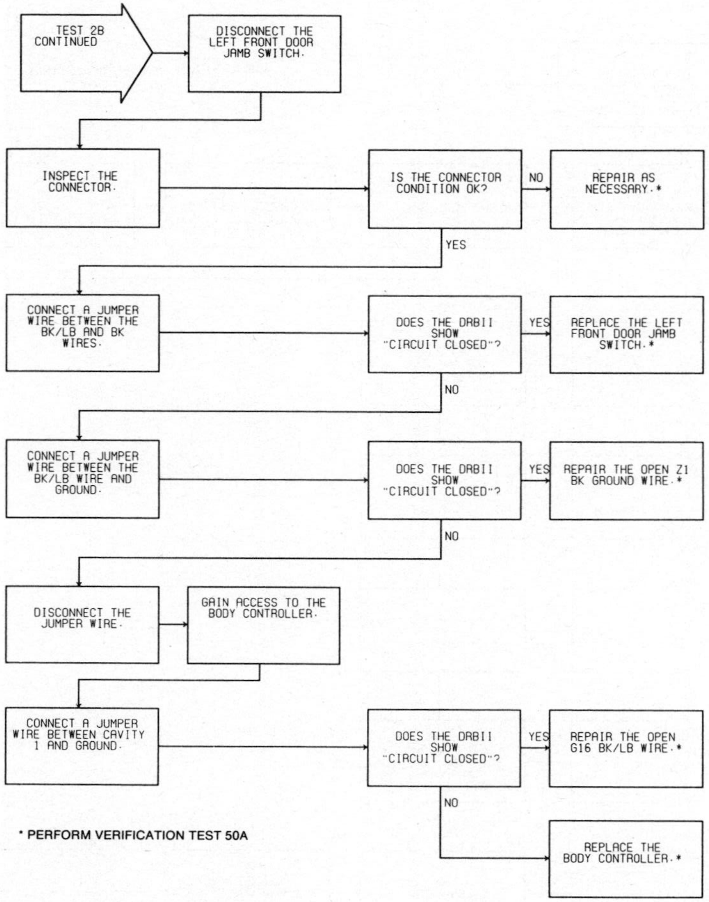

TEST 2B CONTINUED
DISCONNECT THE LEFT FRONT DOOR JAMB SWITCH.
INSPECT THE CONNECTOR.
IS THE CONNECTOR CONDITION OK?
NO
REPAIR AS NECESSARY.*
YES
CONNECT A JUMPER WIRE BETWEEN THE BK/LB AND BK WIRES.
DOES THE DRBII SHOW "CIRCUIT CLOSED"?
YES
REPLACE THE LEFT FRONT DOOR JAMB SWITCH.*
NO
CONNECT A JUMPER WIRE BETWEEN THE BK/LB WIRE AND GROUND.
DOES THE DRBII SHOW "CIRCUIT CLOSED"?
YES
REPAIR THE OPEN Z1 BK GROUND WIRE.*
NO
DISCONNECT THE JUMPER WIRE.
GAIN ACCESS TO THE BODY CONTROLLER.
CONNECT A JUMPER WIRE BETWEEN CAVITY 1 AND GROUND.
DOES THE DRBII SHOW "CIRCUIT CLOSED"?
YES
REPAIR THE OPEN G16 BK/LB WIRE.*
NO
REPLACE THE BODY CONTROLLER.*

* PERFORM VERIFICATION TEST 50A

91D14244

Fig. 9: Test 2B – Repairing Electronic Cluster "Power Up Upon Entry" (2 of 2)

TEST 3A: ELECTRONIC CLUSTER FAULT CODES

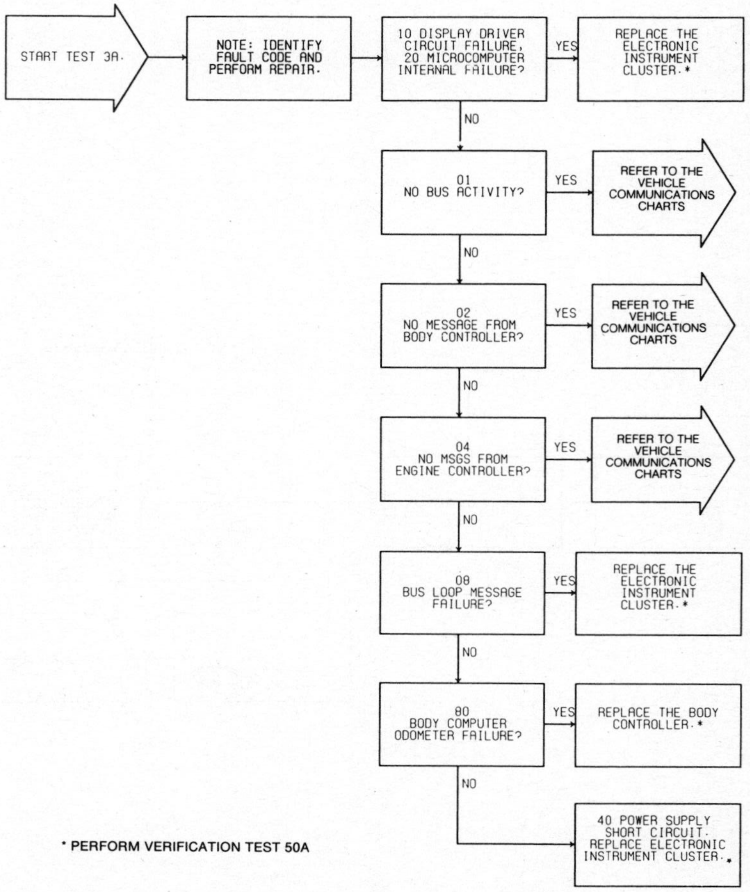

START TEST 3A.
NOTE: IDENTIFY FAULT CODE AND PERFORM REPAIR.
10 DISPLAY DRIVER CIRCUIT FAILURE, 20 MICROCOMPUTER INTERNAL FAILURE?
YES
REPLACE THE ELECTRONIC INSTRUMENT CLUSTER.*
NO
01 NO BUS ACTIVITY?
YES
REFER TO THE VEHICLE COMMUNICATIONS CHARTS
NO
02 NO MESSAGE FROM BODY CONTROLLER?
YES
REFER TO THE VEHICLE COMMUNICATIONS CHARTS
NO
04 NO MSGS FROM ENGINE CONTROLLER?
YES
REFER TO THE VEHICLE COMMUNICATIONS CHARTS
NO
08 BUS LOOP MESSAGE FAILURE?
YES
REPLACE THE ELECTRONIC INSTRUMENT CLUSTER.*
NO
80 BODY COMPUTER ODOMETER FAILURE?
YES
REPLACE THE BODY CONTROLLER.*
NO
40 POWER SUPPLY SHORT CIRCUIT. REPLACE ELECTRONIC INSTRUMENT CLUSTER.*

* PERFORM VERIFICATION TEST 50A

91E14245

Fig. 10: Test 3A – Electronic Cluster Fault Codes

1991 ENGINE PERFORMANCE
Body Control Computer (Cont.)

TEST 4A: ELECTRONIC CLUSTER PROBLEM NOT IDENTIFIED BY A FAULT CODE

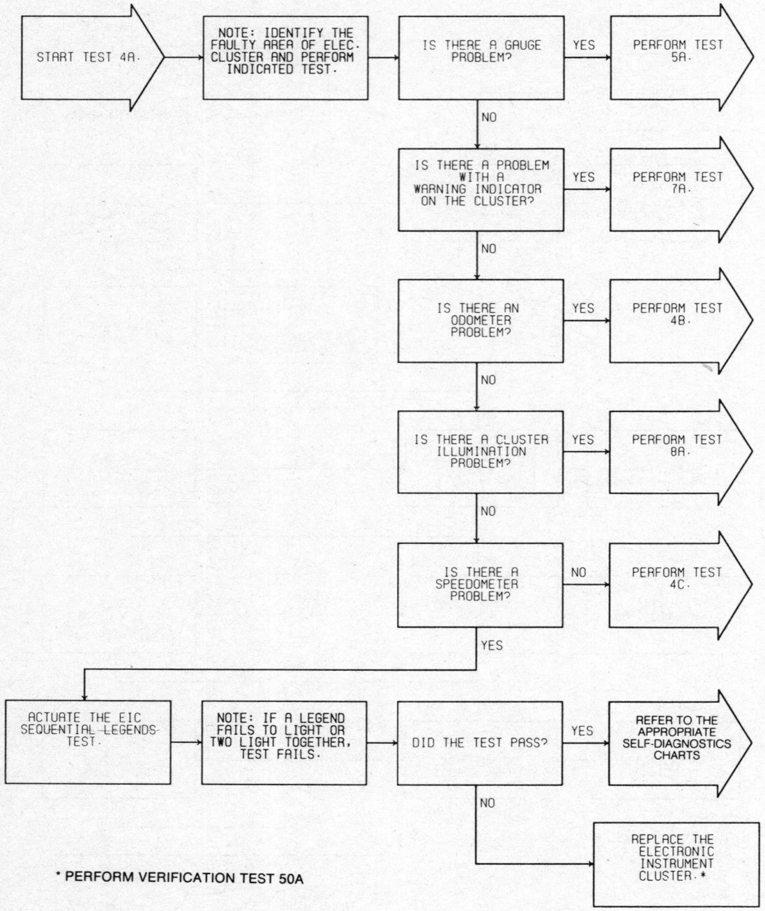
START TEST 4A.
NOTE: IDENTIFY THE FAULTY AREA OF ELEC. CLUSTER AND PERFORM INDICATED TEST.
IS THERE A GAUGE PROBLEM?
YES
PERFORM TEST 5A.
NO
IS THERE A PROBLEM WITH A WARNING INDICATOR ON THE CLUSTER?
YES
PERFORM TEST 7A.
NO
IS THERE AN ODOMETER PROBLEM?
YES
PERFORM TEST 4B.
NO
IS THERE A CLUSTER ILLUMINATION PROBLEM?
YES
PERFORM TEST 8A.
NO
IS THERE A SPEEDOMETER PROBLEM?
NO
PERFORM TEST 4C.
YES
ACTUATE THE EIC SEQUENTIAL LEGENDS TEST.
NOTE: IF A LEGEND FAILS TO LIGHT OR TWO LIGHT TOGETHER, TEST FAILS.
DID THE TEST PASS?
YES
REFER TO THE APPROPRIATE SELF-DIAGNOSTICS CHARTS
NO
REPLACE THE ELECTRONIC INSTRUMENT CLUSTER.*
* PERFORM VERIFICATION TEST 50A

91F14584

Fig. 11: Test 4A – Electronic Cluster Problem Not Identified By a Fault Code

TEST 4B: ELECTRONIC CLUSTER ODOMETER FAILURE

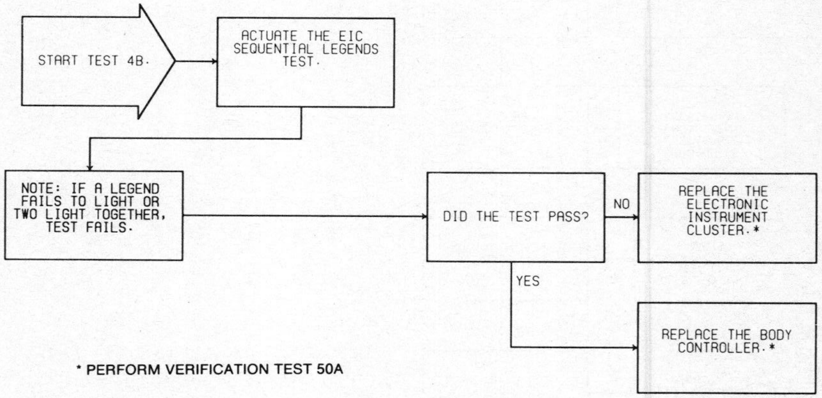
START TEST 4B.
ACTUATE THE EIC SEQUENTIAL LEGENDS TEST.
NOTE: IF A LEGEND FAILS TO LIGHT OR TWO LIGHT TOGETHER, TEST FAILS.
DID THE TEST PASS?
NO
REPLACE THE ELECTRONIC INSTRUMENT CLUSTER.*
YES
REPLACE THE BODY CONTROLLER.*
* PERFORM VERIFICATION TEST 50A

91G14585

Fig. 12: Test 4B – Electronic Cluster Odometer Failure

TEST 4C: ELECTRONIC CLUSTER SWITCH TEST

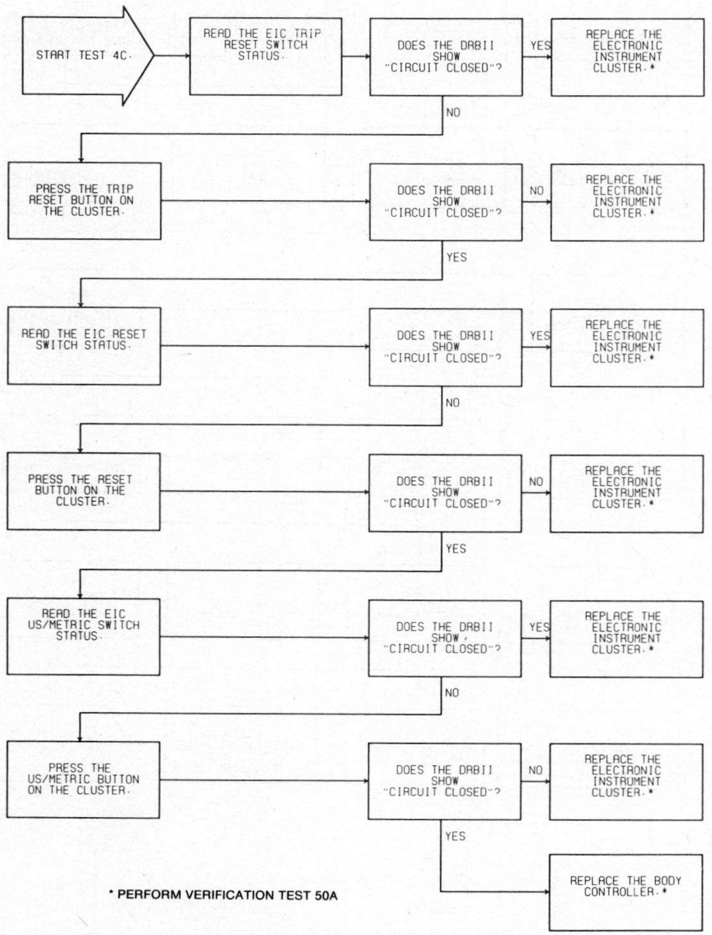
START TEST 4C.
READ THE EIC TRIP RESET SWITCH STATUS.
DOES THE DRBII SHOW "CIRCUIT CLOSED"?
YES
REPLACE THE ELECTRONIC INSTRUMENT CLUSTER.*
NO
PRESS THE TRIP RESET BUTTON ON THE CLUSTER.
DOES THE DRBII SHOW "CIRCUIT CLOSED"?
NO
REPLACE THE ELECTRONIC INSTRUMENT CLUSTER.*
YES
READ THE EIC RESET SWITCH STATUS.
DOES THE DRBII SHOW "CIRCUIT CLOSED"?
YES
REPLACE THE ELECTRONIC INSTRUMENT CLUSTER.*
NO
PRESS THE RESET BUTTON ON THE CLUSTER.
DOES THE DRBII SHOW "CIRCUIT CLOSED"?
NO
REPLACE THE ELECTRONIC INSTRUMENT CLUSTER.*
YES
READ THE EIC US/METRIC SWITCH STATUS.
DOES THE DRBII SHOW "CIRCUIT CLOSED"?
YES
REPLACE THE ELECTRONIC INSTRUMENT CLUSTER.*
NO
PRESS THE US/METRIC BUTTON ON THE CLUSTER.
DOES THE DRBII SHOW "CIRCUIT CLOSED"?
NO
REPLACE THE ELECTRONIC INSTRUMENT CLUSTER.*
YES
REPLACE THE BODY CONTROLLER.*

* PERFORM VERIFICATION TEST 50A

91H14586

Fig. 13: Test 4C – Electronic Cluster Odometer Failure

TEST 5A: IDENTIFYING FAULTY GAUGE

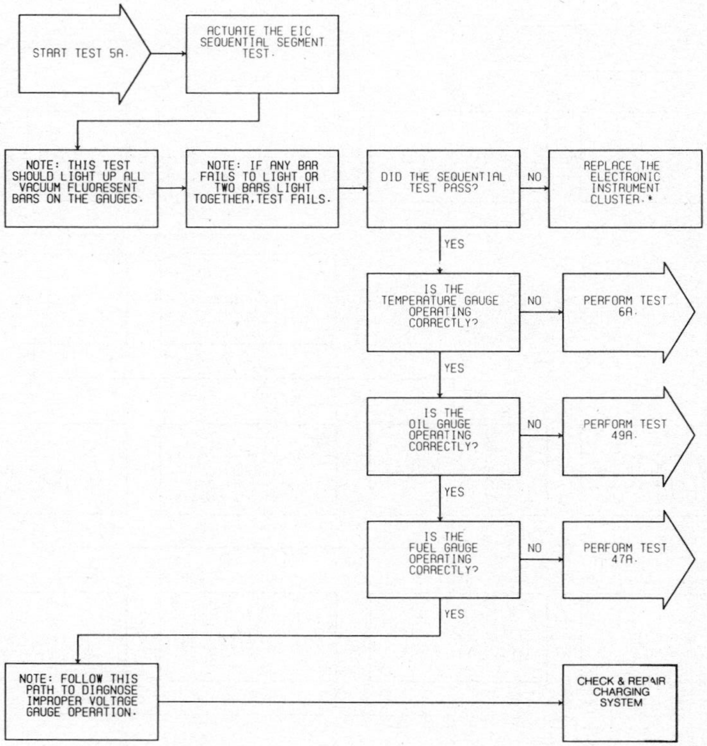
START TEST 5A.
ACTUATE THE EIC SEQUENTIAL SEGMENT TEST.
NOTE: THIS TEST SHOULD LIGHT UP ALL VACUUM FLUORESENT BARS ON THE GAUGES.
NOTE: IF ANY BAR FAILS TO LIGHT OR TWO BARS LIGHT TOGETHER, TEST FAILS.
DID THE SEQUENTIAL TEST PASS?
NO
REPLACE THE ELECTRONIC INSTRUMENT CLUSTER.*
YES
IS THE TEMPERATURE GAUGE OPERATING CORRECTLY?
NO
PERFORM TEST 6A.
YES
IS THE OIL GAUGE OPERATING CORRECTLY?
NO
PERFORM TEST 49A.
YES
IS THE FUEL GAUGE OPERATING CORRECTLY?
NO
PERFORM TEST 47A.
YES
NOTE: FOLLOW THIS PATH TO DIAGNOSE IMPROPER VOLTAGE GAUGE OPERATION.
CHECK & REPAIR CHARGING SYSTEM

* PERFORM VERIFICATION TEST 50A

91F14587

Fig. 14: Test 5A – Identifying Faulty Gauge

1991 ENGINE PERFORMANCE
Body Control Computer (Cont.)

TEST 6A: REPAIRING TEMPERATURE GAUGE PROBLEMS (1 OF 2)

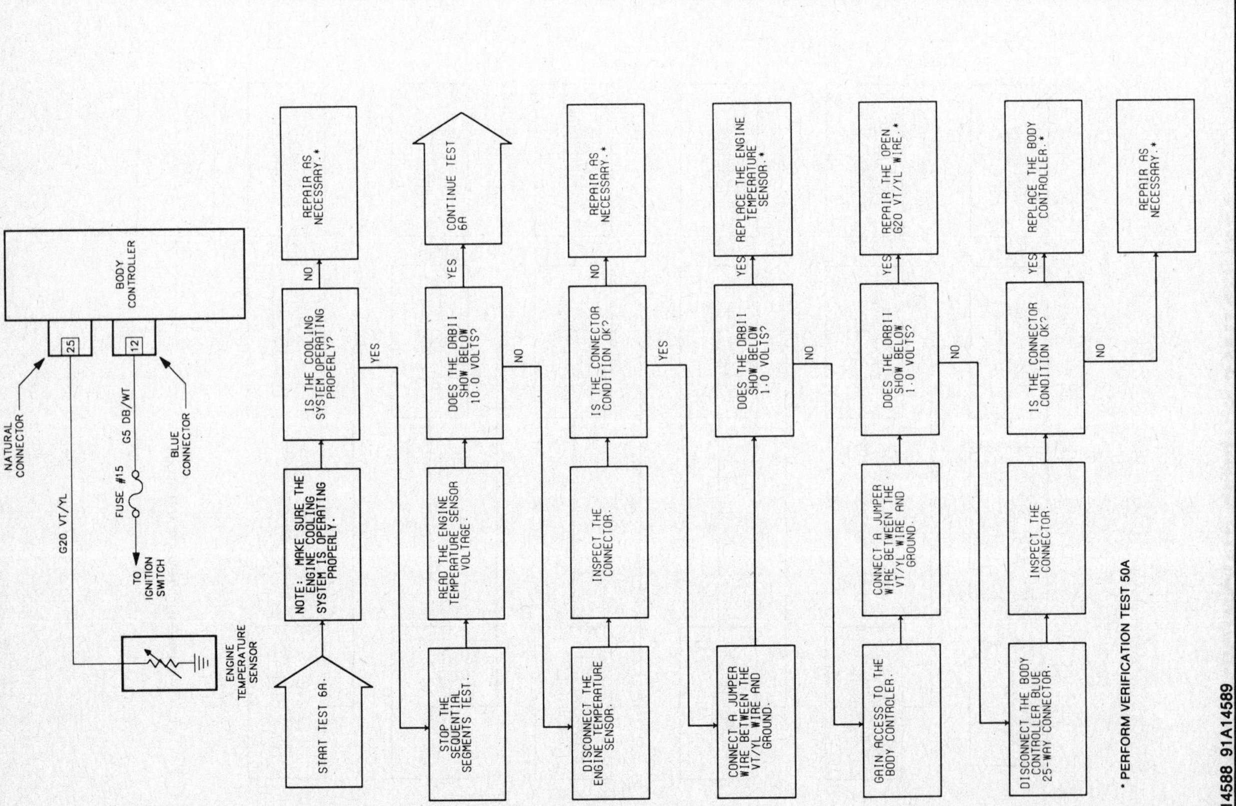
ENGINE TEMPERATURE SENSOR
G20 VT/YL
NATURAL CONNECTOR
25
BODY CONTROLLER
12
G5 DB/WT
BLUE CONNECTOR
FUSE #15
TO IGNITION SWITCH
START TEST 6A.
NOTE: MAKE SURE THE ENGINE COOLING SYSTEM IS OPERATING PROPERLY.
IS THE COOLING SYSTEM OPERATING PROPERLY?
NO
REPAIR AS NECESSARY.*
YES
STOP THE SEQUENTIAL SEGMENTS TEST.
READ THE ENGINE TEMPERATURE SENSOR VOLTAGE.
DOES THE DRBII SHOW BELOW 10.0 VOLTS?
YES
CONTINUE TEST 6A
NO
DISCONNECT THE ENGINE TEMPERATURE SENSOR.
INSPECT THE CONNECTOR.
IS THE CONNECTOR CONDITION OK?
NO
REPAIR AS NECESSARY.*
YES
CONNECT A JUMPER WIRE BETWEEN THE VT/YL WIRE AND GROUND.
DOES THE DRBII SHOW BELOW 1.0 VOLTS?
YES
REPLACE THE ENGINE TEMPERATURE SENSOR.*
NO
GAIN ACCESS TO THE BODY CONTROLER.
CONNECT A JUMPER WIRE BETWEEN THE VT/YL WIRE AND GROUND.
DOES THE DRBII SHOW BELOW 1.0 VOLTS?
YES
REPAIR THE OPEN G20 VT/YL WIRE.*
NO
DISCONNECT THE BODY CONTROLLER BLUE 25-WAY CONNECTOR.
INSPECT THE CONNECTOR.
IS THE CONNECTOR CONDITION OK?
YES
REPLACE THE BODY CONTROLLER.*
NO
REPAIR AS NECESSARY.*

* PERFORM VERIFICATION TEST 50A

91J14588 91A14589

Fig. 15: Test 6A – Repairing Temperature Gauge Problems (1 of 2)

TEST 6A: REPAIRING TEMPERATURE GAUGE PROBLEMS (2 OF 2)

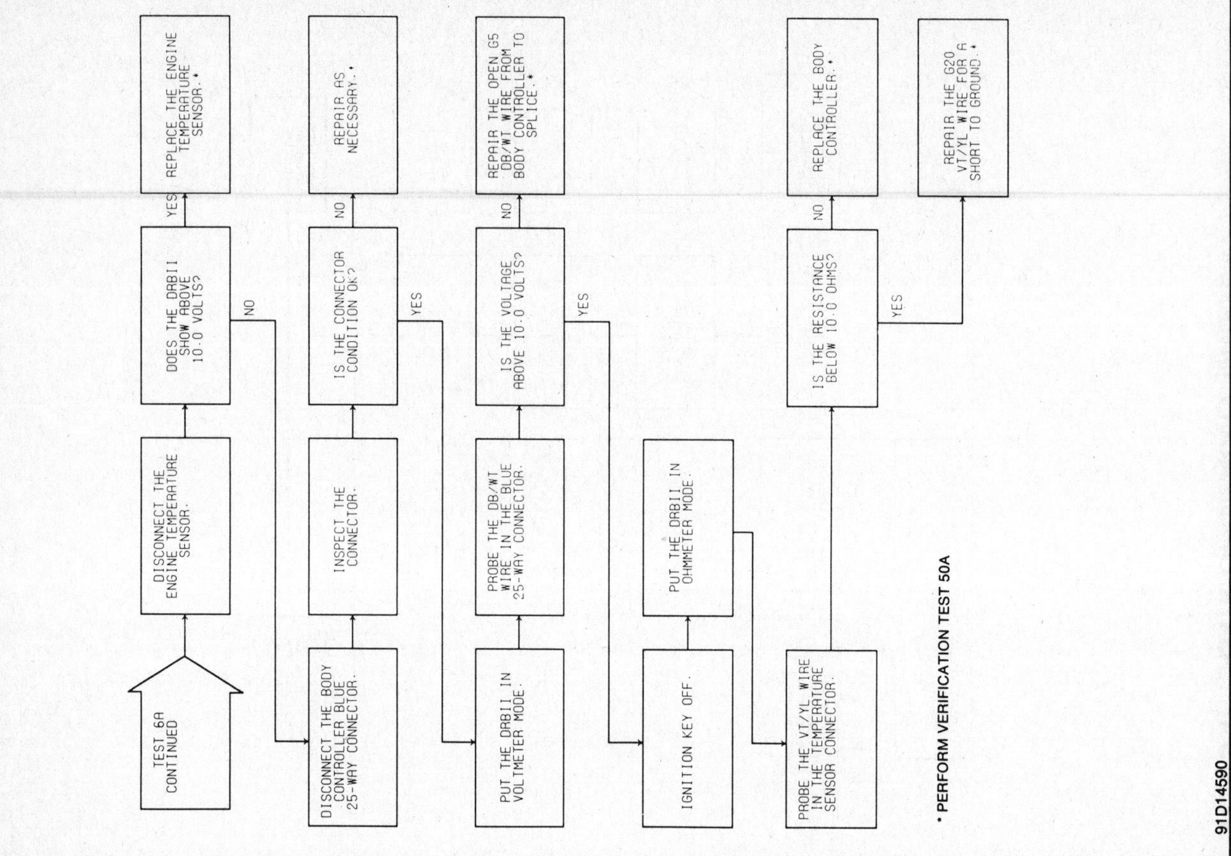
TEST 6A CONTINUED
DISCONNECT THE ENGINE TEMPERATURE SENSOR.
DOES THE DRBII SHOW ABOVE 10.0 VOLTS?
YES
REPLACE THE ENGINE TEMPERATURE SENSOR.*
NO
DISCONNECT THE BODY CONTROLLER BLUE 25-WAY CONNECTOR.
INSPECT THE CONNECTOR.
IS THE CONNECTOR CONDITION OK?
NO
REPAIR AS NECESSARY.*
YES
PUT THE DRBII IN VOLTMETER MODE.
PROBE THE DB/WT WIRE IN THE BLUE 25-WAY CONNECTOR.
IS THE VOLTAGE ABOVE 10.0 VOLTS?
NO
REPAIR THE OPEN G5 DB/WT WIRE FROM BODY CONTROLLER TO SPLICE.*
YES
IGNITION KEY OFF.
PUT THE DRBII IN OHMMETER MODE.
PROBE THE VT/YL WIRE IN THE TEMPERATURE SENSOR CONNECTOR.
IS THE RESISTANCE BELOW 10.0 OHMS?
NO
REPLACE THE BODY CONTROLLER.*
YES
REPAIR THE G20 VT/YL WIRE FOR A SHORT TO GROUND.*

* PERFORM VERIFICATION TEST 50A

91D14590

Fig. 16: Test 6A – Repairing Temperature Gauge Problems (2 of 2)

TEST 7A: IDENTIFYING FAULTY WARNING INDICATOR (1 OF 2)

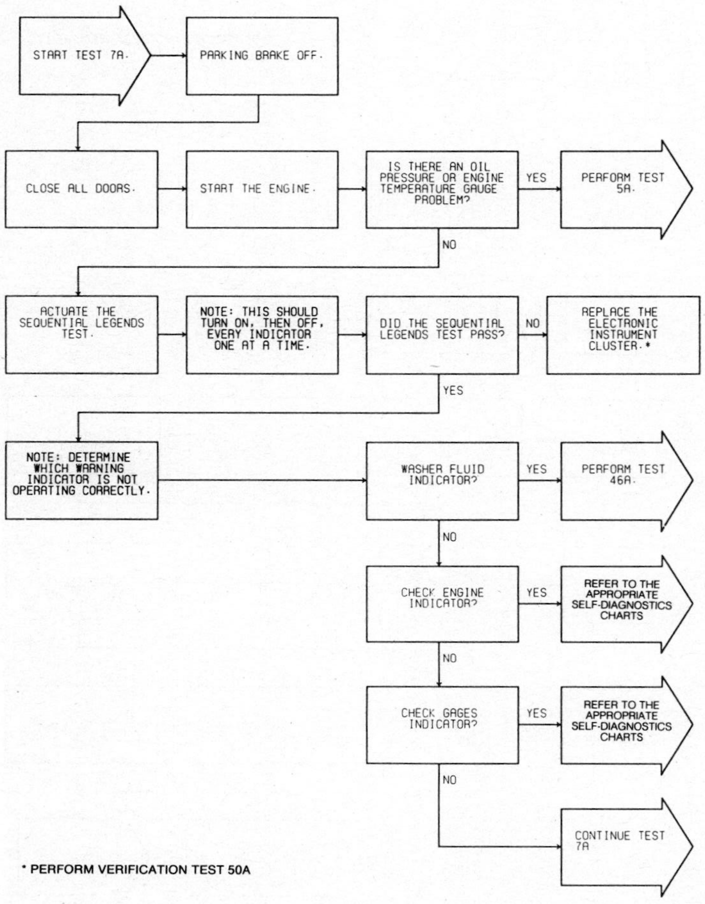
START TEST 7A.
PARKING BRAKE OFF.
CLOSE ALL DOORS.
START THE ENGINE.
IS THERE AN OIL PRESSURE OR ENGINE TEMPERATURE GAUGE PROBLEM?
YES
PERFORM TEST 5A.
NO
ACTUATE THE SEQUENTIAL LEGENDS TEST.
NOTE: THIS SHOULD TURN ON, THEN OFF, EVERY INDICATOR ONE AT A TIME.
DID THE SEQUENTIAL LEGENDS TEST PASS?
NO
REPLACE THE ELECTRONIC INSTRUMENT CLUSTER.*
YES
NOTE: DETERMINE WHICH WARNING INDICATOR IS NOT OPERATING CORRECTLY.
WASHER FLUID INDICATOR?
YES
PERFORM TEST 46A.
NO
CHECK ENGINE INDICATOR?
YES
REFER TO THE APPROPRIATE SELF-DIAGNOSTICS CHARTS
NO
CHECK GAGES INDICATOR?
YES
REFER TO THE APPROPRIATE SELF-DIAGNOSTICS CHARTS
NO
CONTINUE TEST 7A
* PERFORM VERIFICATION TEST 50A
91E14591

Fig. 17: Test 7A – Identifying Faulty Warning Indicator (1 of 2)

TEST 7A: IDENTIFYING FAULTY WARNING INDICATOR (2 OF 2)

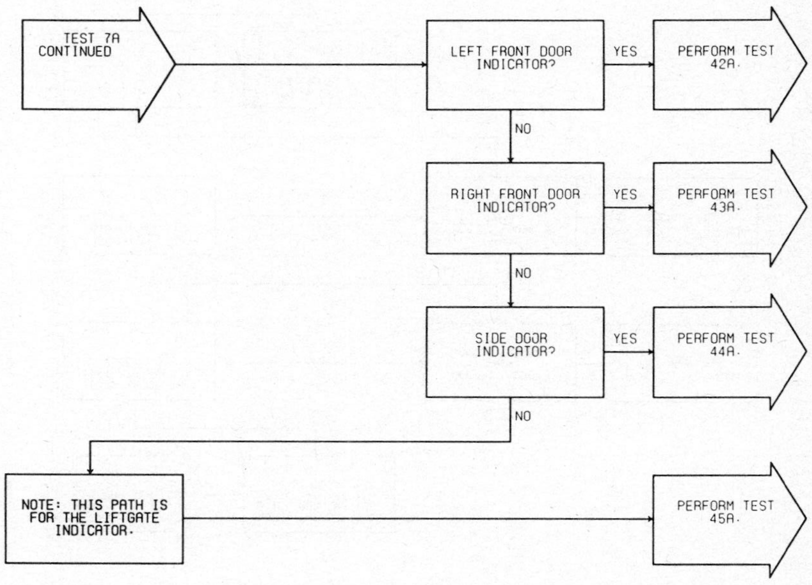
TEST 7A CONTINUED
LEFT FRONT DOOR INDICATOR?
YES
PERFORM TEST 42A.
NO
RIGHT FRONT DOOR INDICATOR?
YES
PERFORM TEST 43A.
NO
SIDE DOOR INDICATOR?
YES
PERFORM TEST 44A.
NO
NOTE: THIS PATH IS FOR THE LIFTGATE INDICATOR.
PERFORM TEST 45A.
91F14592

Fig. 18: Test 7A – Identifying Faulty Warning Indicator (2 of 2)

1991 ENGINE PERFORMANCE
Body Control Computer (Cont.)

TEST 8A: ELECTRONIC CLUSTER ILLUMINATION TEST

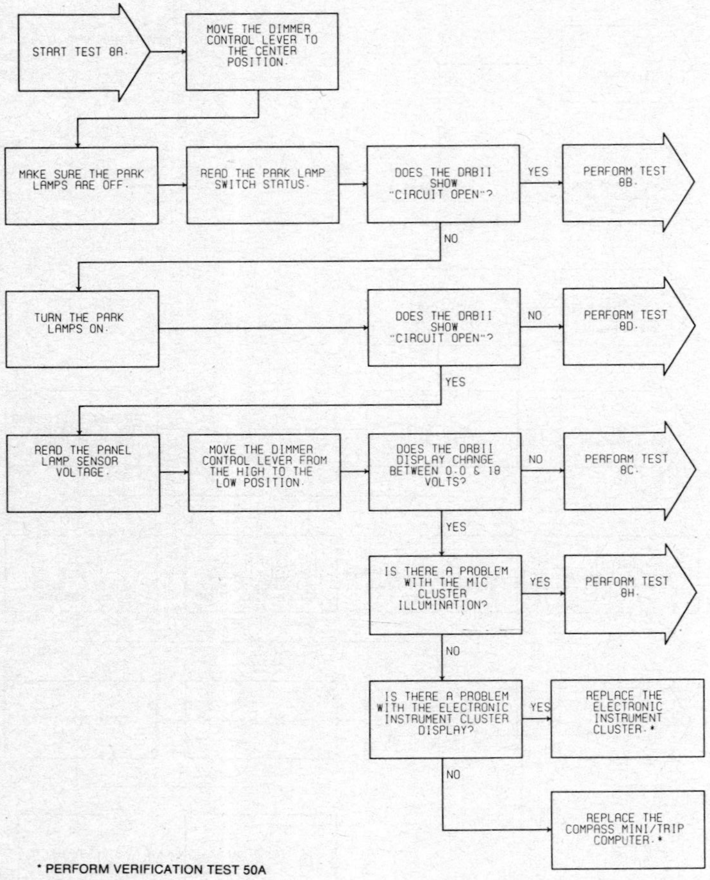
START TEST 8A.
MOVE THE DIMMER CONTROL LEVER TO THE CENTER POSITION.
MAKE SURE THE PARK LAMPS ARE OFF.
READ THE PARK LAMP SWITCH STATUS.
DOES THE DRBII SHOW "CIRCUIT OPEN"?
YES
PERFORM TEST 8B.
NO
TURN THE PARK LAMPS ON.
DOES THE DRBII SHOW "CIRCUIT OPEN"?
NO
PERFORM TEST 8D.
YES
READ THE PANEL LAMP SENSOR VOLTAGE.
MOVE THE DIMMER CONTROL LEVER FROM THE HIGH TO THE LOW POSITION.
DOES THE DRBII DISPLAY CHANGE BETWEEN 0.0 & 18 VOLTS?
NO
PERFORM TEST 8C.
YES
IS THERE A PROBLEM WITH THE MIC CLUSTER ILLUMINATION?
YES
PERFORM TEST 8H.
NO
IS THERE A PROBLEM WITH THE ELECTRONIC INSTRUMENT CLUSTER DISPLAY?
YES
REPLACE THE ELECTRONIC INSTRUMENT CLUSTER.*
NO
REPLACE THE COMPASS MINI/TRIP COMPUTER.*

* PERFORM VERIFICATION TEST 50A

91G14593

Fig. 19: Test 8A – Electronic Cluster Illumination Test

TEST 8B: ELECTRONIC CLUSTER ILLUMINATION TEST

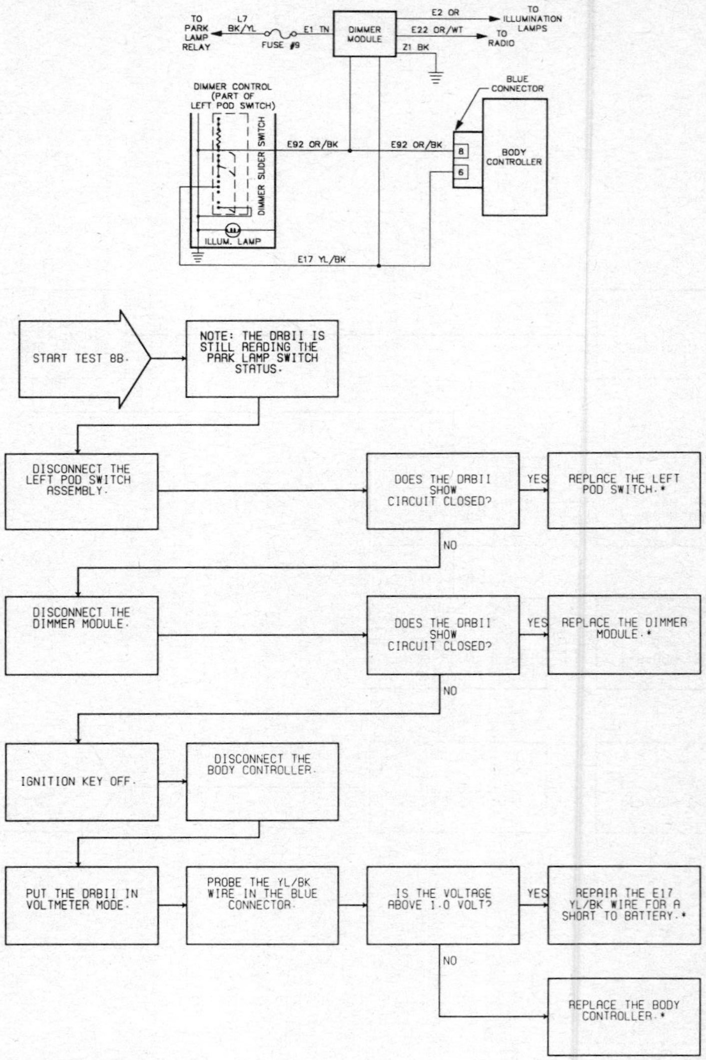
TO PARK LAMP RELAY
L7 BK/YL
FUSE #9
E1 TN
DIMMER MODULE
E2 OR
TO ILLUMINATION LAMPS
E22 OR/WT
TO RADIO
Z1 BK
DIMMER CONTROL (PART OF LEFT POD SWITCH)
DIMMER SLIDER SWITCH
ILLUM. LAMP
E92 OR/BK
E92 OR/BK
BLUE CONNECTOR
8
6
BODY CONTROLLER
E17 YL/BK
START TEST 8B.
NOTE: THE DRBII IS STILL READING THE PARK LAMP SWITCH STATUS.
DISCONNECT THE LEFT POD SWITCH ASSEMBLY.
DOES THE DRBII SHOW CIRCUIT CLOSED?
YES
REPLACE THE LEFT POD SWITCH.*
NO
DISCONNECT THE DIMMER MODULE.
DOES THE DRBII SHOW CIRCUIT CLOSED?
YES
REPLACE THE DIMMER MODULE.*
NO
IGNITION KEY OFF.
DISCONNECT THE BODY CONTROLLER.
PUT THE DRBII IN VOLTMETER MODE.
PROBE THE YL/BK WIRE IN THE BLUE CONNECTOR.
IS THE VOLTAGE ABOVE 1.0 VOLT?
YES
REPAIR THE E17 YL/BK WIRE FOR A SHORT TO BATTERY.*
NO
REPLACE THE BODY CONTROLLER.*

* PERFORM VERIFICATION TEST 50A

91H14594 91I14595

Fig. 20: Test 8B – Electronic Cluster Illumination Test

TEST 8C: ELECTRONIC CLUSTER ILLUMINATION TEST (1 OF 2)

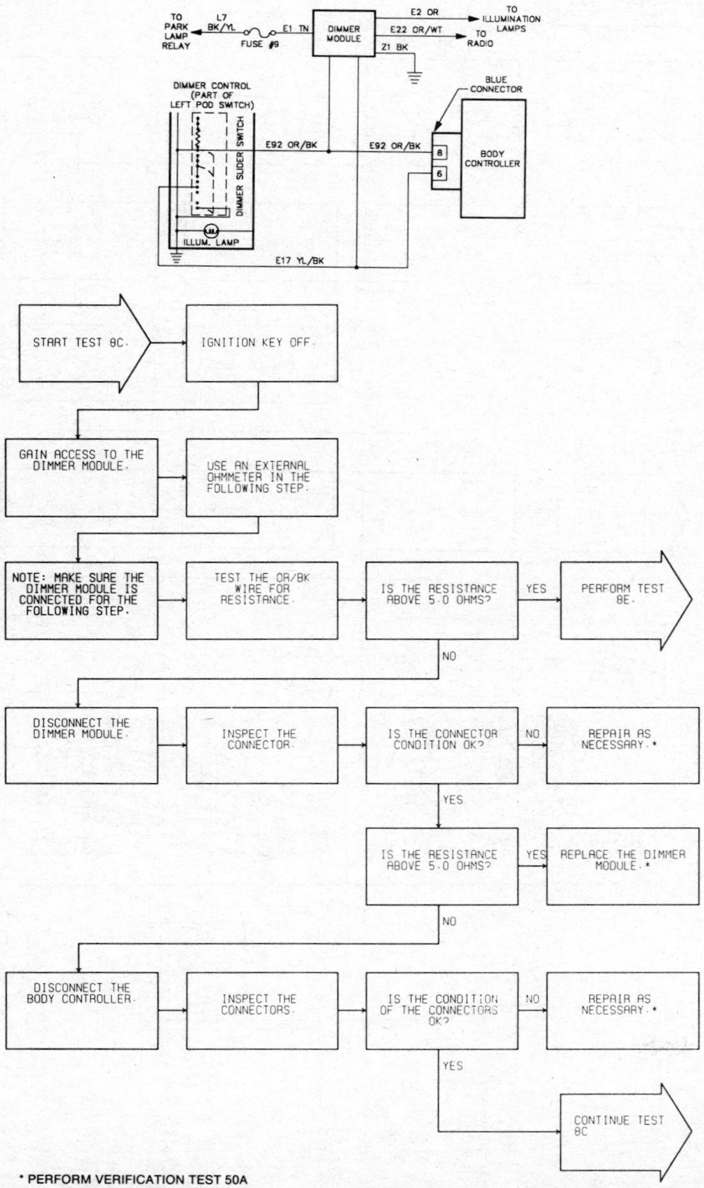
TO PARK LAMP RELAY
L7 BK/YL
FUSE #9
E1 TN
DIMMER MODULE
E2 OR
E22 OR/WT
Z1 BK
TO ILLUMINATION LAMPS
TO RADIO
DIMMER CONTROL (PART OF LEFT POD SWITCH)
DIMMER SLIDER SWITCH
ILLUM. LAMP
E92 OR/BK
BLUE CONNECTOR
BODY CONTROLLER
E17 YL/BK
START TEST 8C.
IGNITION KEY OFF.
GAIN ACCESS TO THE DIMMER MODULE.
USE AN EXTERNAL OHMMETER IN THE FOLLOWING STEP.
NOTE: MAKE SURE THE DIMMER MODULE IS CONNECTED FOR THE FOLLOWING STEP.
TEST THE OR/BK WIRE FOR RESISTANCE.
IS THE RESISTANCE ABOVE 5.0 OHMS?
YES
PERFORM TEST 8E.
NO
DISCONNECT THE DIMMER MODULE.
INSPECT THE CONNECTOR.
IS THE CONNECTOR CONDITION OK?
NO
REPAIR AS NECESSARY.*
YES
IS THE RESISTANCE ABOVE 5.0 OHMS?
YES
REPLACE THE DIMMER MODULE.*
NO
DISCONNECT THE BODY CONTROLLER.
INSPECT THE CONNECTORS.
IS THE CONDITION OF THE CONNECTORS OK?
NO
REPAIR AS NECESSARY.*
YES
CONTINUE TEST 8C

* PERFORM VERIFICATION TEST 50A

91H14594 91J14596

Fig. 21: Test 8C – Electronic Cluster Illumination Test (1 of 2)

TEST 8C: ELECTRONIC CLUSTER ILLUMINATION TEST (2 OF 2)

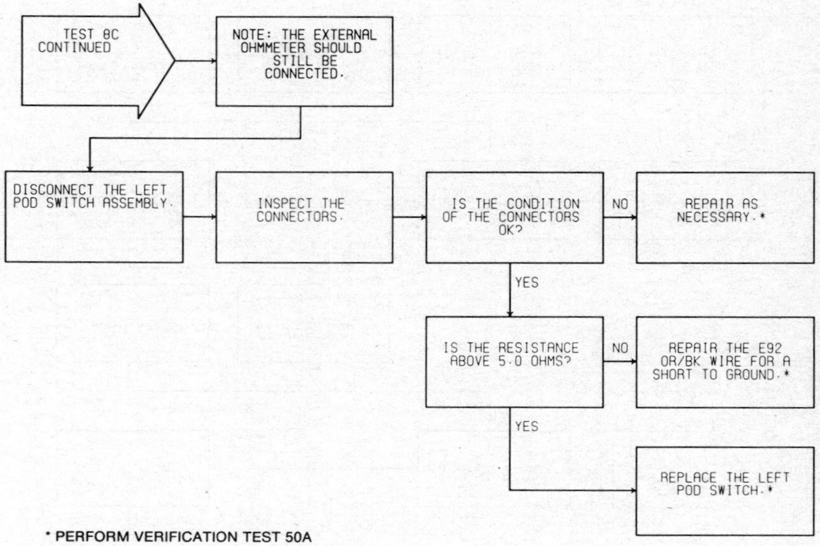
TEST 8C CONTINUED
NOTE: THE EXTERNAL OHMMETER SHOULD STILL BE CONNECTED.
DISCONNECT THE LEFT POD SWITCH ASSEMBLY.
INSPECT THE CONNECTORS.
IS THE CONDITION OF THE CONNECTORS OK?
NO
REPAIR AS NECESSARY.*
YES
IS THE RESISTANCE ABOVE 5.0 OHMS?
NO
REPAIR THE E92 OR/BK WIRE FOR A SHORT TO GROUND.*
YES
REPLACE THE LEFT POD SWITCH.*

* PERFORM VERIFICATION TEST 50A

91A14597

Fig. 22: Test 8C – Electronic Cluster Illumination Test (2 of 2)

TEST 8D: ELECTRONIC CLUSTER ILLUMINATION TEST (1 OF 2)

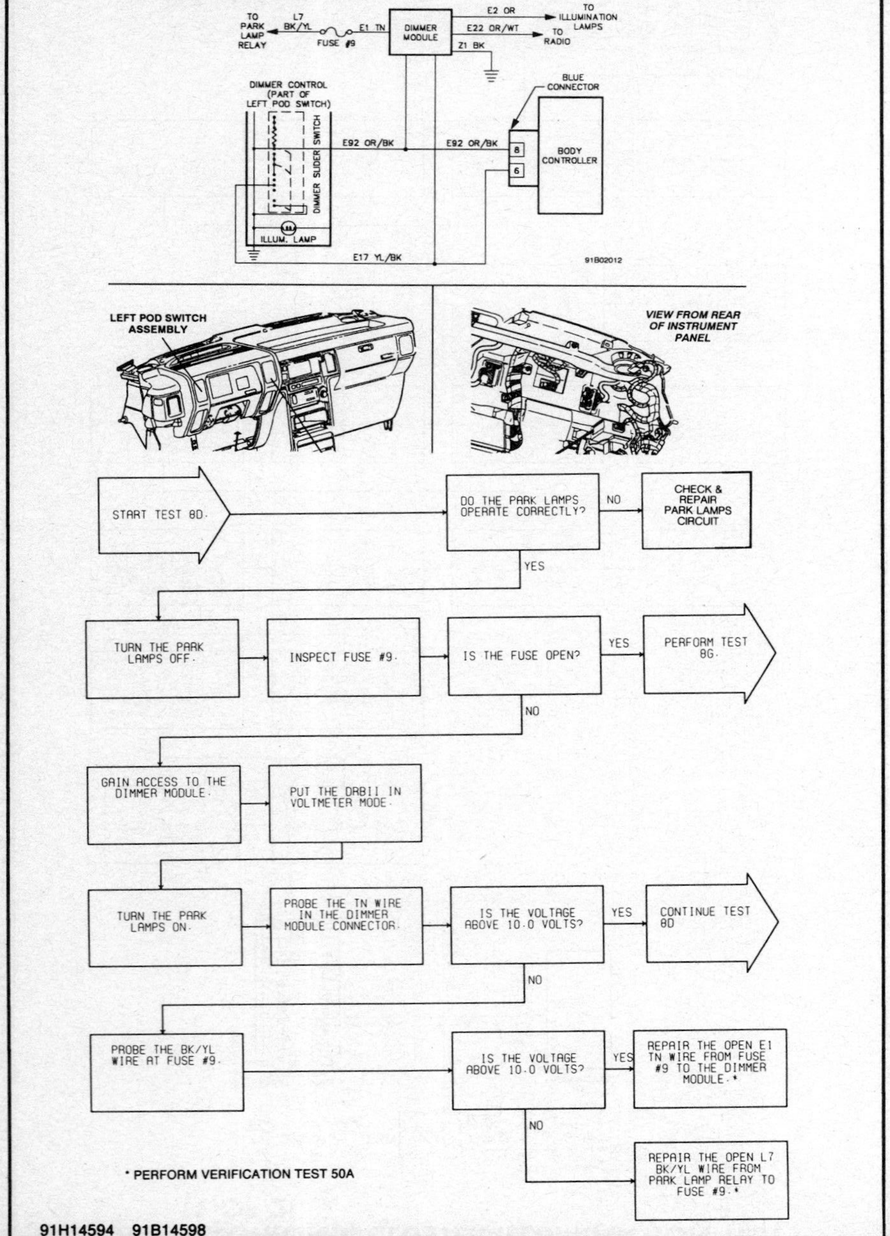
TO PARK LAMP RELAY
L7 BK/YL
FUSE #9
E1 TN
DIMMER MODULE
E2 OR
TO ILLUMINATION LAMPS
E22 OR/WT
TO RADIO
Z1 BK
DIMMER CONTROL (PART OF LEFT POD SWITCH)
DIMMER SLIDER SWITCH
ILLUM. LAMP
E92 OR/BK
E92 OR/BK
BLUE CONNECTOR
8
6
BODY CONTROLLER
E17 YL/BK
91B02012
LEFT POD SWITCH ASSEMBLY
VIEW FROM REAR OF INSTRUMENT PANEL
START TEST 8D.
DO THE PARK LAMPS OPERATE CORRECTLY?
NO
CHECK & REPAIR PARK LAMPS CIRCUIT
YES
TURN THE PARK LAMPS OFF.
INSPECT FUSE #9.
IS THE FUSE OPEN?
YES
PERFORM TEST 8G.
NO
GAIN ACCESS TO THE DIMMER MODULE.
PUT THE DRBII IN VOLTMETER MODE.
TURN THE PARK LAMPS ON.
PROBE THE TN WIRE IN THE DIMMER MODULE CONNECTOR.
IS THE VOLTAGE ABOVE 10.0 VOLTS?
YES
CONTINUE TEST 8D
NO
PROBE THE BK/YL WIRE AT FUSE #9.
IS THE VOLTAGE ABOVE 10.0 VOLTS?
YES
REPAIR THE OPEN E1 TN WIRE FROM FUSE #9 TO THE DIMMER MODULE.*
NO
REPAIR THE OPEN L7 BK/YL WIRE FROM PARK LAMP RELAY TO FUSE #9.*
* PERFORM VERIFICATION TEST 50A
91H14594 91B14598

Fig. 23: Test 8D – Electronic Cluster Illumination Test (1 of 2)

TEST 8D: ELECTRONIC CLUSTER ILLUMINATION TEST (2 OF 2)

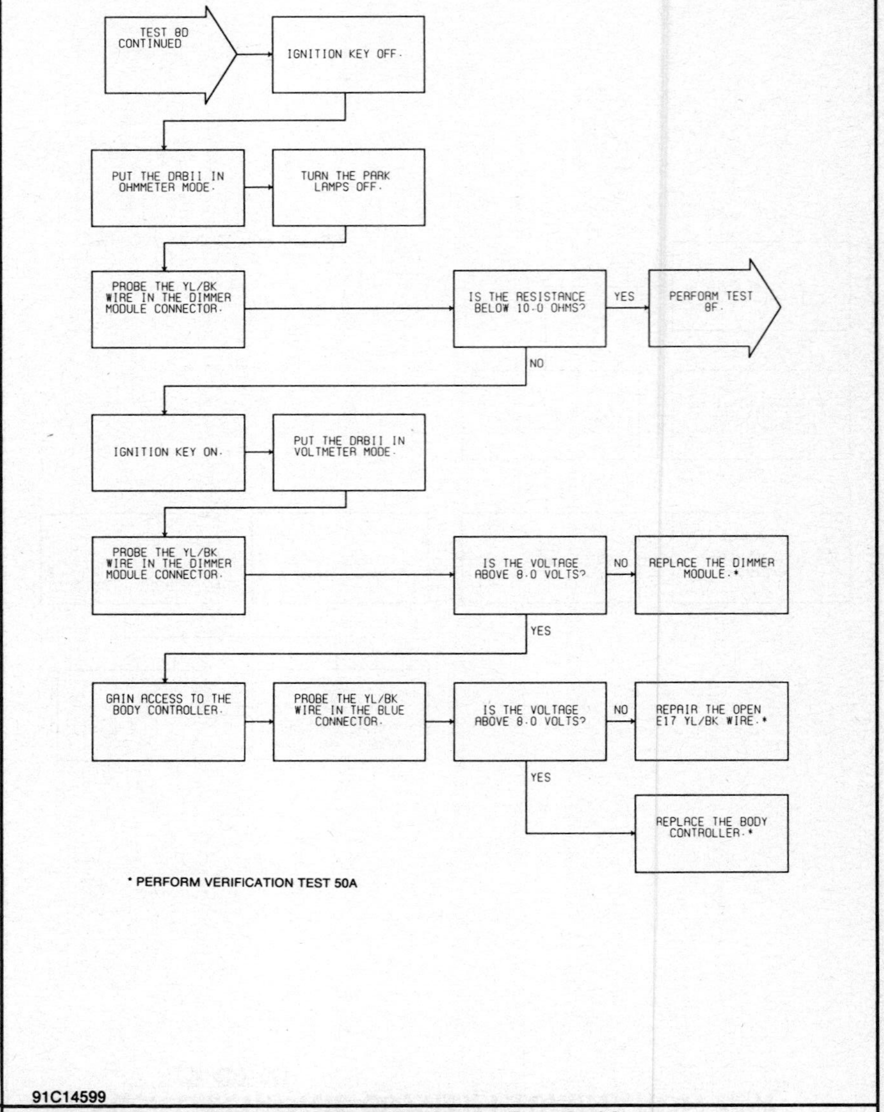
TEST 8D CONTINUED
IGNITION KEY OFF.
PUT THE DRBII IN OHMMETER MODE.
TURN THE PARK LAMPS OFF.
PROBE THE YL/BK WIRE IN THE DIMMER MODULE CONNECTOR.
IS THE RESISTANCE BELOW 10.0 OHMS?
YES
PERFORM TEST 8F.
NO
IGNITION KEY ON.
PUT THE DRBII IN VOLTMETER MODE.
PROBE THE YL/BK WIRE IN THE DIMMER MODULE CONNECTOR.
IS THE VOLTAGE ABOVE 8.0 VOLTS?
NO
REPLACE THE DIMMER MODULE.*
YES
GAIN ACCESS TO THE BODY CONTROLLER.
PROBE THE YL/BK WIRE IN THE BLUE CONNECTOR.
IS THE VOLTAGE ABOVE 8.0 VOLTS?
NO
REPAIR THE OPEN E17 YL/BK WIRE.*
YES
REPLACE THE BODY CONTROLLER.*
* PERFORM VERIFICATION TEST 50A
91C14599

Fig. 24: Test 8D – Electronic Cluster Illumination Test (2 of 2)

TEST 8E: ELECTRONIC CLUSTER ILLUMINATION TEST

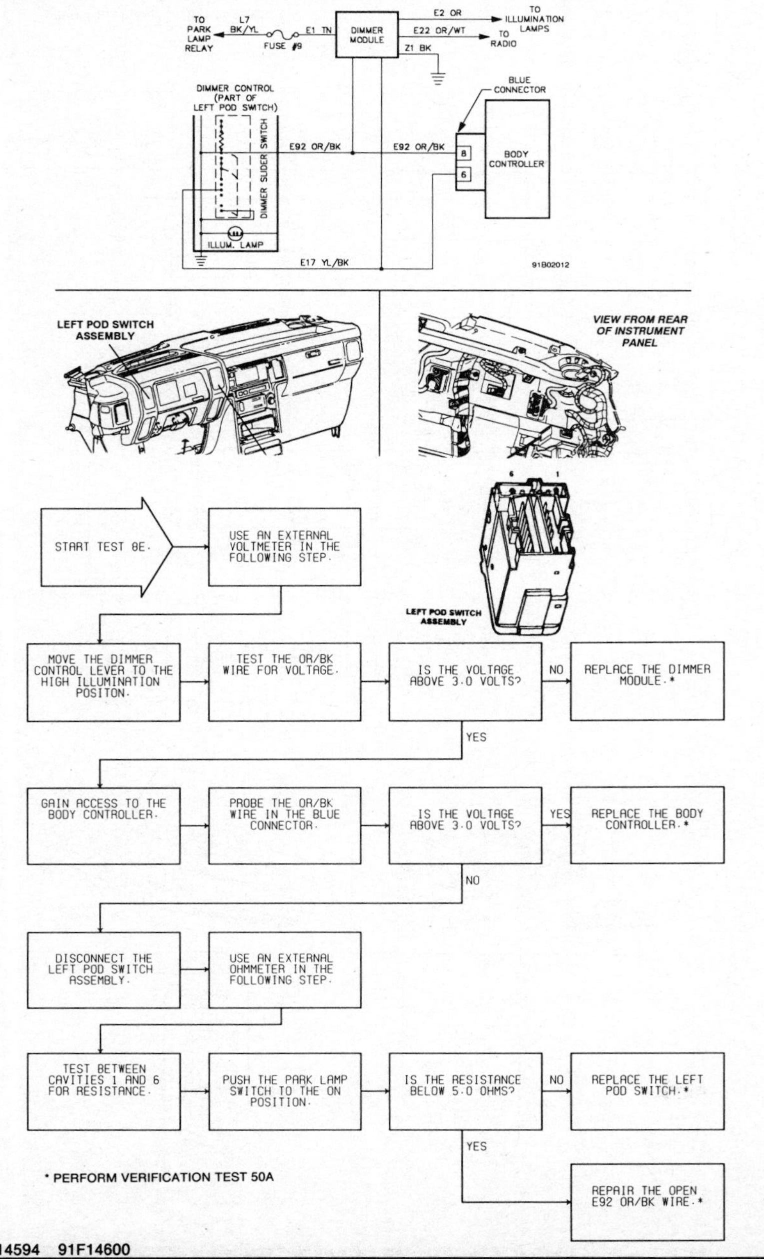
TO PARK LAMP RELAY
L7 BK/YL
FUSE #9
E1 TN
DIMMER MODULE
E2 OR
TO ILLUMINATION LAMPS
E22 OR/WT
TO RADIO
Z1 BK
DIMMER CONTROL (PART OF LEFT POD SWITCH)
DIMMER SLIDER SWITCH
ILLUM. LAMP
E92 OR/BK
E92 OR/BK
BLUE CONNECTOR
8
6
BODY CONTROLLER
E17 YL/BK
91B02012
LEFT POD SWITCH ASSEMBLY
VIEW FROM REAR OF INSTRUMENT PANEL
LEFT POD SWITCH ASSEMBLY
START TEST 8E.
USE AN EXTERNAL VOLTMETER IN THE FOLLOWING STEP.
MOVE THE DIMMER CONTROL LEVER TO THE HIGH ILLUMINATION POSITON.
TEST THE OR/BK WIRE FOR VOLTAGE.
IS THE VOLTAGE ABOVE 3.0 VOLTS?
NO
REPLACE THE DIMMER MODULE.*
YES
GAIN ACCESS TO THE BODY CONTROLLER.
PROBE THE OR/BK WIRE IN THE BLUE CONNECTOR.
IS THE VOLTAGE ABOVE 3.0 VOLTS?
YES
REPLACE THE BODY CONTROLLER.*
NO
DISCONNECT THE LEFT POD SWITCH ASSEMBLY.
USE AN EXTERNAL OHMMETER IN THE FOLLOWING STEP.
TEST BETWEEN CAVITIES 1 AND 6 FOR RESISTANCE.
PUSH THE PARK LAMP SWITCH TO THE ON POSITION.
IS THE RESISTANCE BELOW 5.0 OHMS?
NO
REPLACE THE LEFT POD SWITCH.*
YES
REPAIR THE OPEN E92 OR/BK WIRE.*

* PERFORM VERIFICATION TEST 50A

91H14594 91F14600

Fig. 25: Test 8E – Electronic Cluster Illumination Test

TEST 8F: ELECTRONIC CLUSTER ILLUMINATION TEST

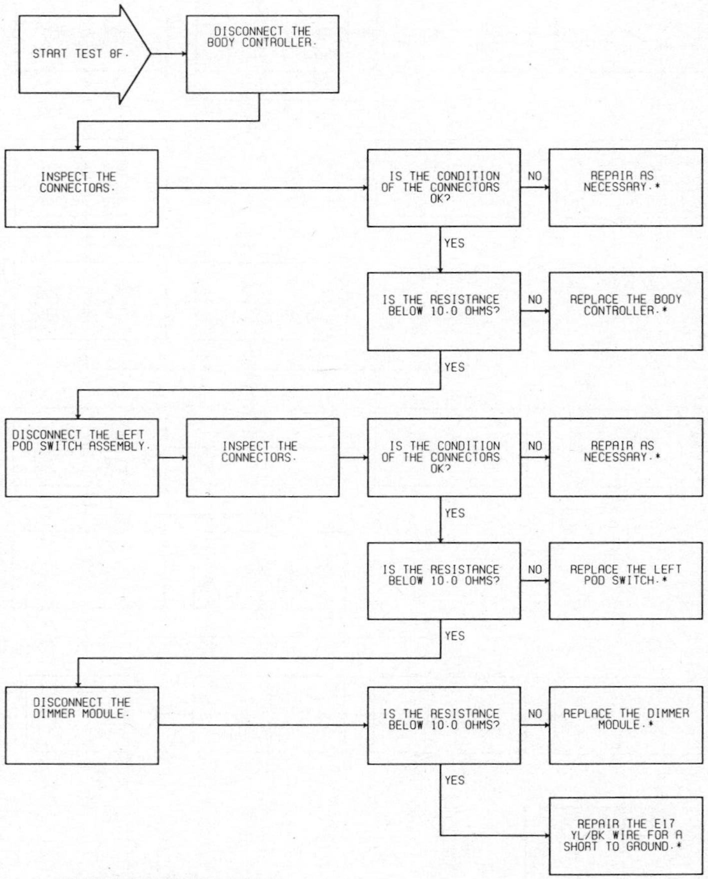
START TEST 8F.
DISCONNECT THE BODY CONTROLLER.
INSPECT THE CONNECTORS.
IS THE CONDITION OF THE CONNECTORS OK?
NO
REPAIR AS NECESSARY.*
YES
IS THE RESISTANCE BELOW 10.0 OHMS?
NO
REPLACE THE BODY CONTROLLER.*
YES
DISCONNECT THE LEFT POD SWITCH ASSEMBLY.
INSPECT THE CONNECTORS.
IS THE CONDITION OF THE CONNECTORS OK?
NO
REPAIR AS NECESSARY.*
YES
IS THE RESISTANCE BELOW 10.0 OHMS?
NO
REPLACE THE LEFT POD SWITCH.*
YES
DISCONNECT THE DIMMER MODULE.
IS THE RESISTANCE BELOW 10.0 OHMS?
NO
REPLACE THE DIMMER MODULE.*
YES
REPAIR THE E17 YL/BK WIRE FOR A SHORT TO GROUND.*

* PERFORM VERIFICATION TEST 50A

91G14601

Fig. 26: Test 8F – Electronic Cluster Illumination Test

1991 ENGINE PERFORMANCE
Body Control Computer (Cont.)

TEST 8G: ELECTRONIC CLUSTER ILLUMINATION TEST

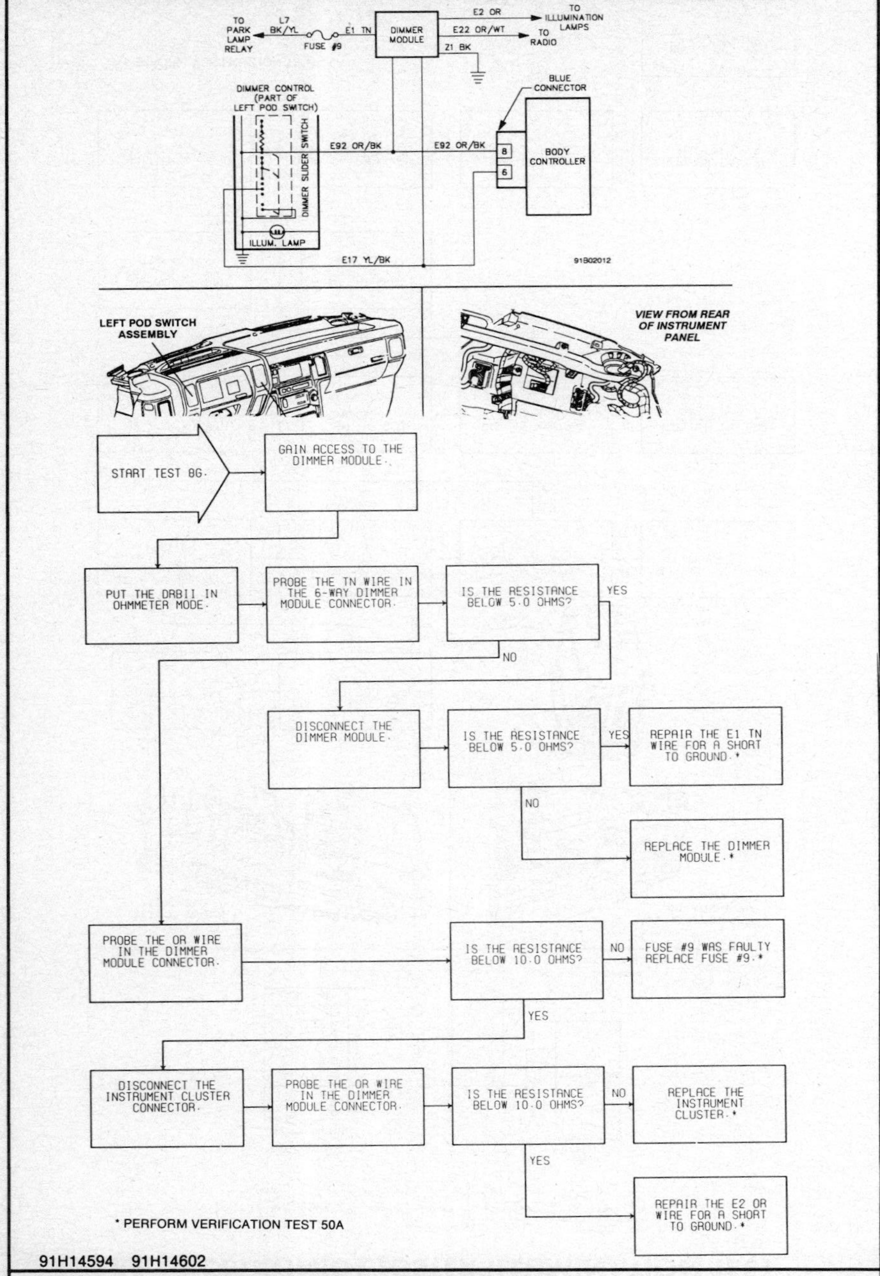
TO PARK LAMP RELAY
L7 BK/YL
FUSE #9
E1 TN
DIMMER MODULE
E2 OR
TO ILLUMINATION LAMPS
E22 OR/WT
TO RADIO
Z1 BK
BLUE CONNECTOR
DIMMER CONTROL (PART OF LEFT POD SWITCH)
DIMMER SLIDER SWITCH
ILLUM. LAMP
E92 OR/BK
E92 OR/BK
8
6
BODY CONTROLLER
E17 YL/BK
91B02012
LEFT POD SWITCH ASSEMBLY
VIEW FROM REAR OF INSTRUMENT PANEL
START TEST 8G.
GAIN ACCESS TO THE DIMMER MODULE.
PUT THE DRBII IN OHMMETER MODE.
PROBE THE TN WIRE IN THE 6-WAY DIMMER MODULE CONNECTOR.
IS THE RESISTANCE BELOW 5.0 OHMS?
YES
NO
DISCONNECT THE DIMMER MODULE.
IS THE RESISTANCE BELOW 5.0 OHMS?
YES
REPAIR THE E1 TN WIRE FOR A SHORT TO GROUND.*
NO
REPLACE THE DIMMER MODULE.*
PROBE THE OR WIRE IN THE DIMMER MODULE CONNECTOR.
IS THE RESISTANCE BELOW 10.0 OHMS?
NO
FUSE #9 WAS FAULTY REPLACE FUSE #9.*
YES
DISCONNECT THE INSTRUMENT CLUSTER CONNECTOR.
PROBE THE OR WIRE IN THE DIMMER MODULE CONNECTOR.
IS THE RESISTANCE BELOW 10.0 OHMS?
NO
REPLACE THE INSTRUMENT CLUSTER.*
YES
REPAIR THE E2 OR WIRE FOR A SHORT TO GROUND.*
* PERFORM VERIFICATION TEST 50A
91H14594 91H14602

Fig. 27: Test 8G – Electronic Cluster Illumination Test

TEST 8H: REPAIRING MIC CLUSTER ILLUMINATION (1 OF 2)

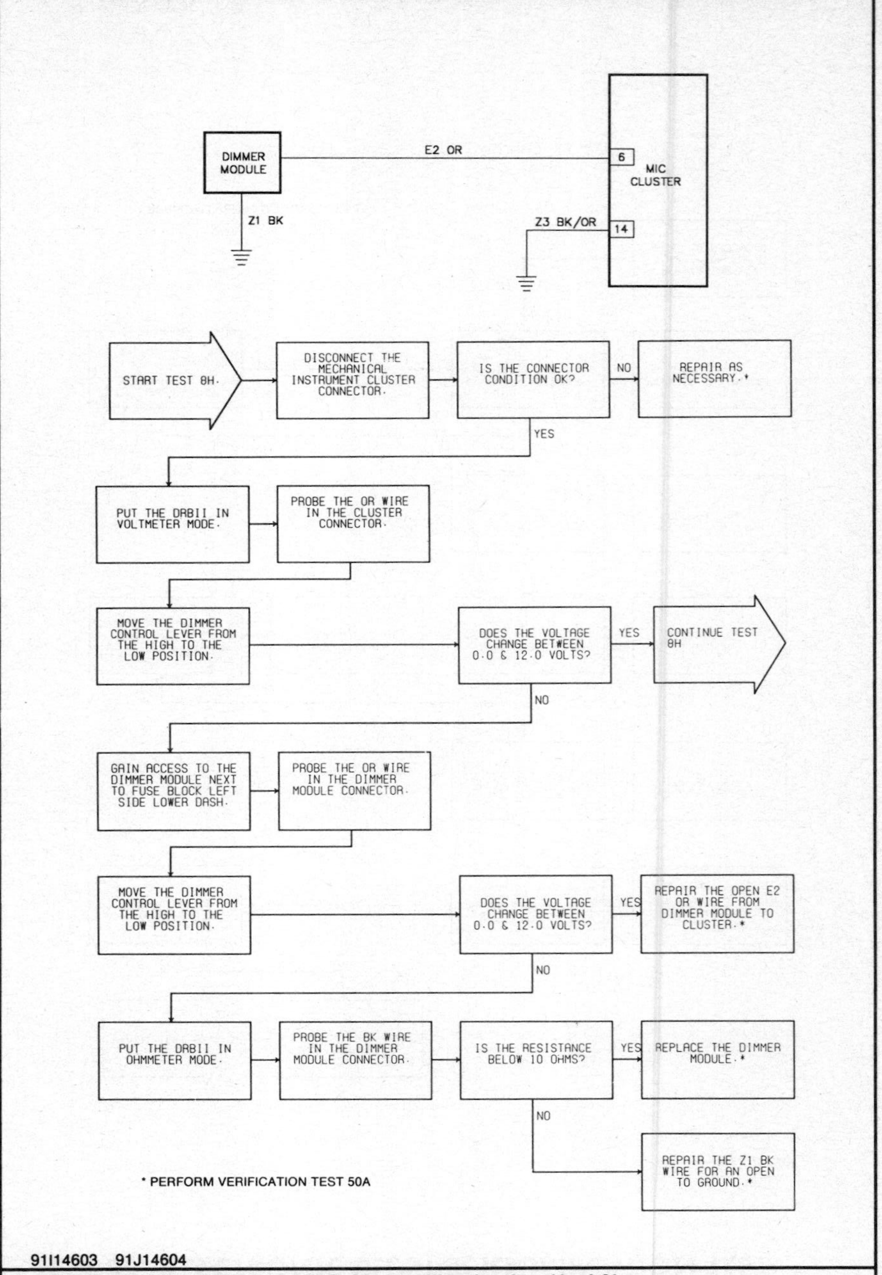
DIMMER MODULE
E2 OR
6
MIC CLUSTER
Z1 BK
Z3 BK/OR
14
START TEST 8H.
DISCONNECT THE MECHANICAL INSTRUMENT CLUSTER CONNECTOR.
IS THE CONNECTOR CONDITION OK?
NO
REPAIR AS NECESSARY.*
YES
PUT THE DRBII IN VOLTMETER MODE.
PROBE THE OR WIRE IN THE CLUSTER CONNECTOR.
MOVE THE DIMMER CONTROL LEVER FROM THE HIGH TO THE LOW POSITION.
DOES THE VOLTAGE CHANGE BETWEEN 0.0 & 12.0 VOLTS?
YES
CONTINUE TEST 8H
NO
GAIN ACCESS TO THE DIMMER MODULE NEXT TO FUSE BLOCK LEFT SIDE LOWER DASH.
PROBE THE OR WIRE IN THE DIMMER MODULE CONNECTOR.
MOVE THE DIMMER CONTROL LEVER FROM THE HIGH TO THE LOW POSITION.
DOES THE VOLTAGE CHANGE BETWEEN 0.0 & 12.0 VOLTS?
YES
REPAIR THE OPEN E2 OR WIRE FROM DIMMER MODULE TO CLUSTER.*
NO
PUT THE DRBII IN OHMMETER MODE.
PROBE THE BK WIRE IN THE DIMMER MODULE CONNECTOR.
IS THE RESISTANCE BELOW 10 OHMS?
YES
REPLACE THE DIMMER MODULE.*
NO
REPAIR THE Z1 BK WIRE FOR AN OPEN TO GROUND.*
* PERFORM VERIFICATION TEST 50A
91I14603 91J14604

Fig. 28: Test 8H – Repairing MIC Cluster Illumination (1 of 2)

TEST 8H: REPAIRING MIC CLUSTER ILLUMINATION (2 OF 2)

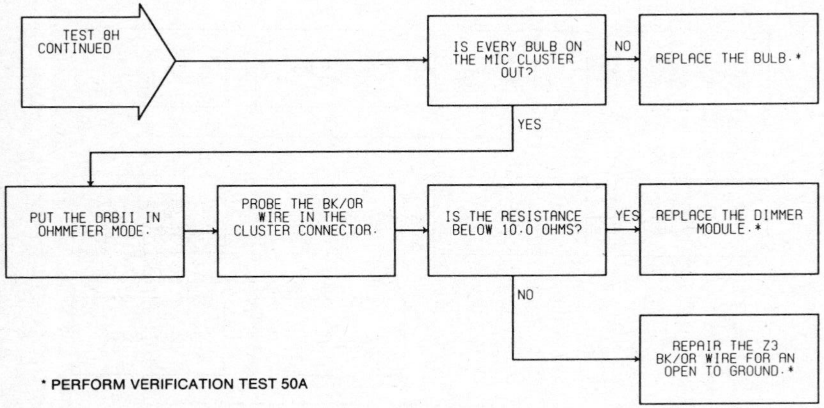
TEST 8H CONTINUED
IS EVERY BULB ON THE MIC CLUSTER OUT?
NO
REPLACE THE BULB.*
YES
PUT THE DRBII IN OHMMETER MODE.
PROBE THE BK/OR WIRE IN THE CLUSTER CONNECTOR.
IS THE RESISTANCE BELOW 10.0 OHMS?
YES
REPLACE THE DIMMER MODULE.*
NO
REPAIR THE Z3 BK/OR WIRE FOR AN OPEN TO GROUND.*

* PERFORM VERIFICATION TEST 50A

91A14605

Fig. 29: Test 8H – Repairing MIC Cluster Illumination (2 of 2)

TEST 9A: ELECTRO/MECHANICAL CLUSTER DIAGNOSIS (1 OF 2)

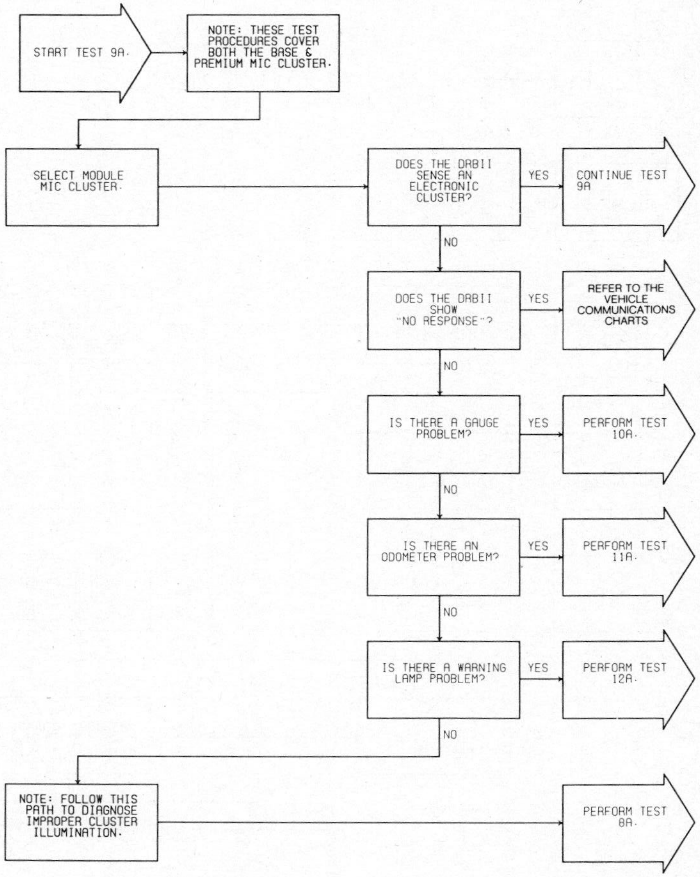
START TEST 9A.
NOTE: THESE TEST PROCEDURES COVER BOTH THE BASE & PREMIUM MIC CLUSTER.
SELECT MODULE MIC CLUSTER.
DOES THE DRBII SENSE AN ELECTRONIC CLUSTER?
YES
CONTINUE TEST 9A
NO
DOES THE DRBII SHOW "NO RESPONSE"?
YES
REFER TO THE VEHICLE COMMUNICATIONS CHARTS
NO
IS THERE A GAUGE PROBLEM?
YES
PERFORM TEST 10A.
NO
IS THERE AN ODOMETER PROBLEM?
YES
PERFORM TEST 11A.
NO
IS THERE A WARNING LAMP PROBLEM?
YES
PERFORM TEST 12A.
NO
NOTE: FOLLOW THIS PATH TO DIAGNOSE IMPROPER CLUSTER ILLUMINATION.
PERFORM TEST 8A.

91B14606

Fig. 30: Test 9A – Electro/Mechanical Cluster Diagnosis (1 of 2)

1991 ENGINE PERFORMANCE
Body Control Computer (Cont.)

TEST 9A: ELECTRO/MECHANICAL CLUSTER DIAGNOSIS (2 OF 2)

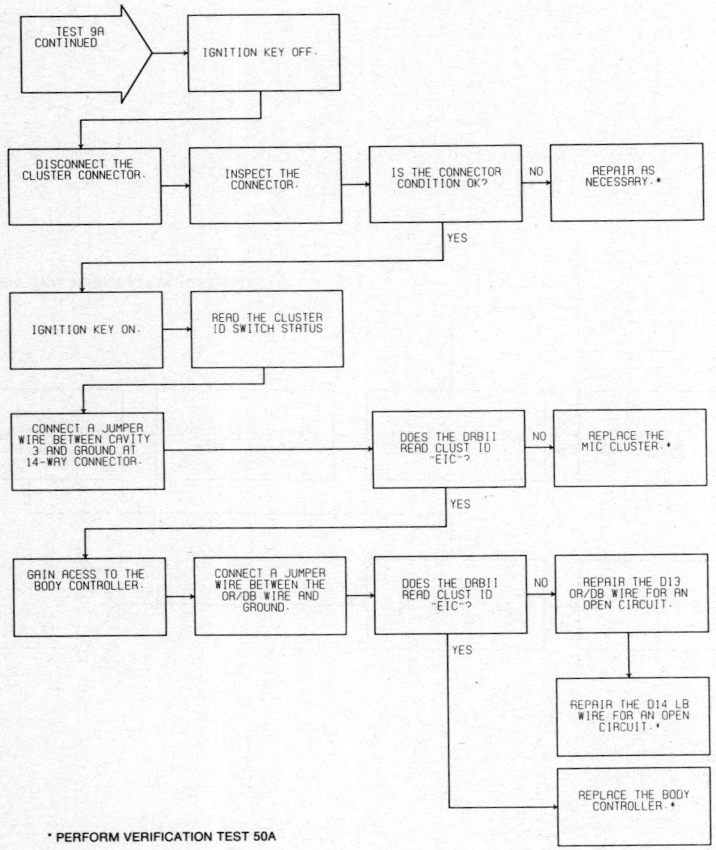
TEST 9A CONTINUED
IGNITION KEY OFF.
DISCONNECT THE CLUSTER CONNECTOR.
INSPECT THE CONNECTOR.
IS THE CONNECTOR CONDITION OK?
NO
REPAIR AS NECESSARY.*
YES
IGNITION KEY ON.
READ THE CLUSTER ID SWITCH STATUS
CONNECT A JUMPER WIRE BETWEEN CAVITY 3 AND GROUND AT 14-WAY CONNECTOR.
DOES THE DRBII READ CLUST ID "EIC"?
NO
REPLACE THE MIC CLUSTER.*
YES
GAIN ACESS TO THE BODY CONTROLLER.
CONNECT A JUMPER WIRE BETWEEN THE OR/DB WIRE AND GROUND.
DOES THE DRBII READ CLUST ID "EIC"?
NO
REPAIR THE D13 OR/DB WIRE FOR AN OPEN CIRCUIT.
REPAIR THE D14 LB WIRE FOR AN OPEN CIRCUIT.*
YES
REPLACE THE BODY CONTROLLER.*

* PERFORM VERIFICATION TEST 50A

91C14607

Fig. 31: Test 9A – Electro/Mechanical Cluster Diagnosis (2 of 2)

TEST 10A: IDENTIFYING FAULTY GAUGE ON ELECTRO/MECHANICAL CLUSTER (1 OF 2)

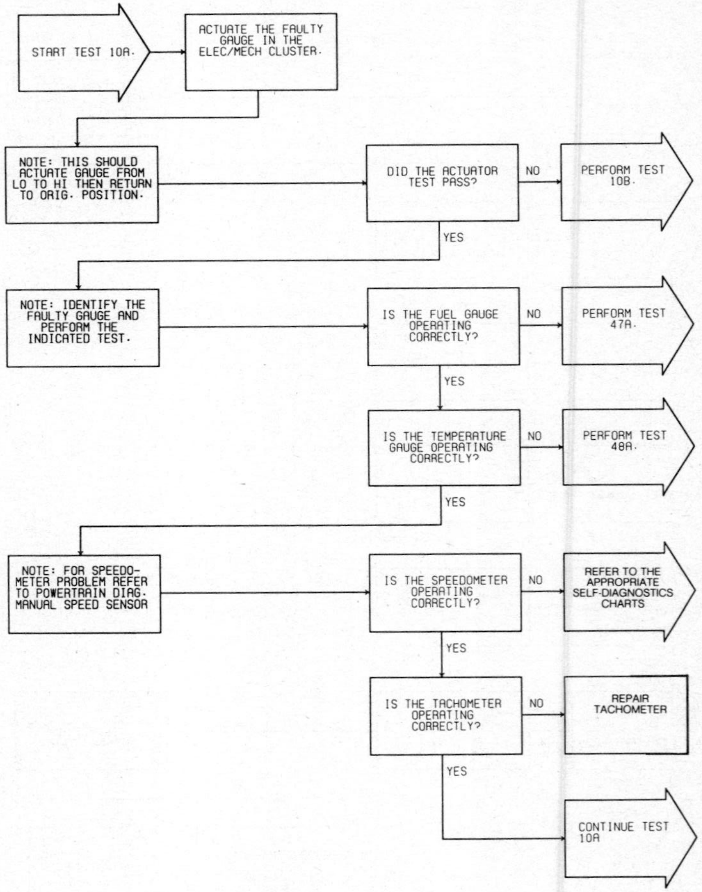
START TEST 10A.
ACTUATE THE FAULTY GAUGE IN THE ELEC/MECH CLUSTER.
NOTE: THIS SHOULD ACTUATE GAUGE FROM LO TO HI THEN RETURN TO ORIG. POSITION.
DID THE ACTUATOR TEST PASS?
NO
PERFORM TEST 10B.
YES
NOTE: IDENTIFY THE FAULTY GAUGE AND PERFORM THE INDICATED TEST.
IS THE FUEL GAUGE OPERATING CORRECTLY?
NO
PERFORM TEST 47A.
YES
IS THE TEMPERATURE GAUGE OPERATING CORRECTLY?
NO
PERFORM TEST 48A.
YES
NOTE: FOR SPEEDO-METER PROBLEM REFER TO POWERTRAIN DIAG. MANUAL SPEED SENSOR
IS THE SPEEDOMETER OPERATING CORRECTLY?
NO
REFER TO THE APPROPRIATE SELF-DIAGNOSTICS CHARTS
YES
IS THE TACHOMETER OPERATING CORRECTLY?
NO
REPAIR TACHOMETER
YES
CONTINUE TEST 10A

91D14608

Fig. 32: Test 10A – Identifying Faulty Gauge on Electro/Mechanical Cluster (1 of 2)

TEST 10A: IDENTIFYING FAULTY GAUGE ON ELECTRO/ MECHANICAL CLUSTER (2 OF 2)

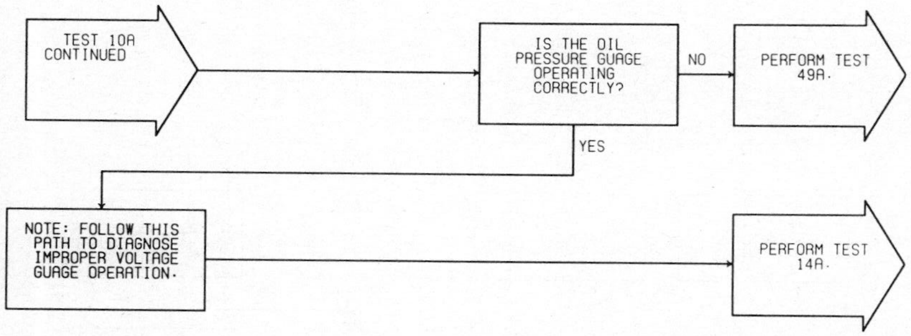
TEST 10A CONTINUED
IS THE OIL PRESSURE GUAGE OPERATING CORRECTLY?
NO
PERFORM TEST 49A.
YES
NOTE: FOLLOW THIS PATH TO DIAGNOSE IMPROPER VOLTAGE GUAGE OPERATION.
PERFORM TEST 14A.

91E14609

Fig. 33: Test 10A – Identifying Faulty Gauge on Electro/Mechanical Cluster (2 of 2)

TEST 10B: REPAIRING FAULTY GAUGE ON ELECTRO/ MECHANICAL CLUSTER

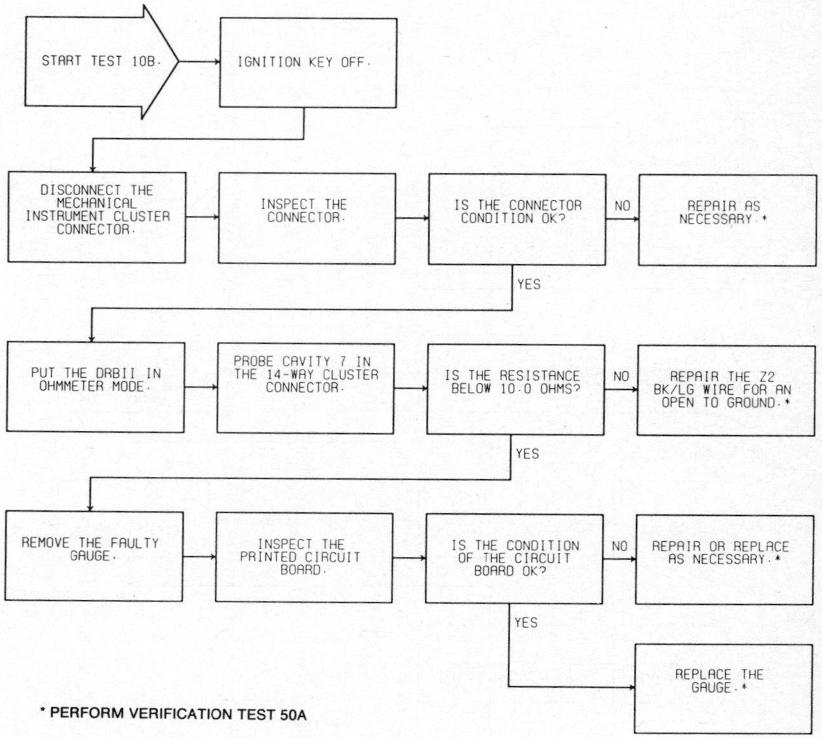
START TEST 10B.
IGNITION KEY OFF.
DISCONNECT THE MECHANICAL INSTRUMENT CLUSTER CONNECTOR.
INSPECT THE CONNECTOR.
IS THE CONNECTOR CONDITION OK?
NO
REPAIR AS NECESSARY.*
YES
PUT THE DRBII IN OHMMETER MODE.
PROBE CAVITY 7 IN THE 14-WAY CLUSTER CONNECTOR.
IS THE RESISTANCE BELOW 10.0 OHMS?
NO
REPAIR THE Z2 BK/LG WIRE FOR AN OPEN TO GROUND.*
YES
REMOVE THE FAULTY GAUGE.
INSPECT THE PRINTED CIRCUIT BOARD.
IS THE CONDITION OF THE CIRCUIT BOARD OK?
NO
REPAIR OR REPLACE AS NECESSARY.*
YES
REPLACE THE GAUGE.*

* PERFORM VERIFICATION TEST 50A

91H14610

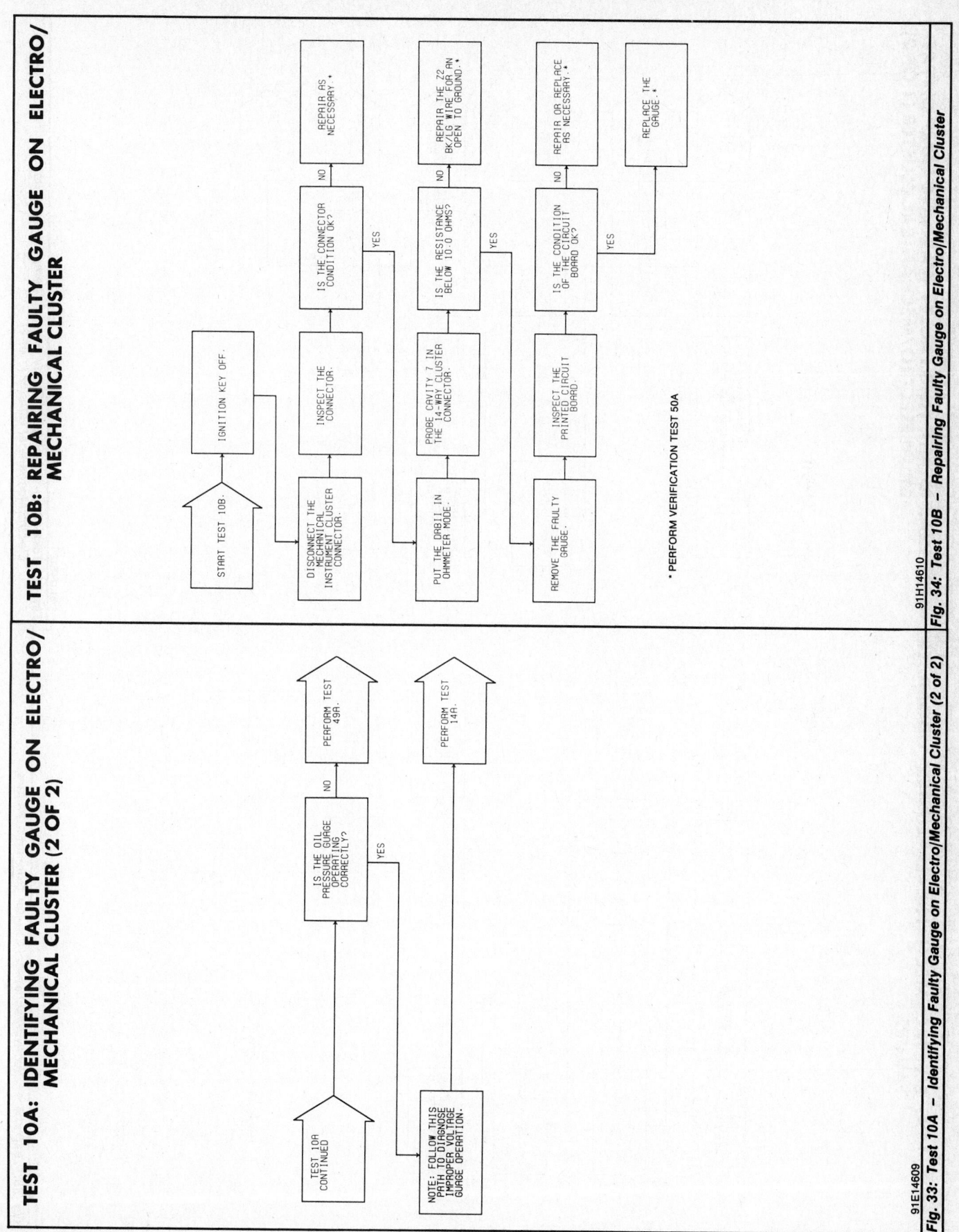

Fig. 34: Test 10B – Repairing Faulty Gauge on Electro/Mechanical Cluster

1991 ENGINE PERFORMANCE
Body Control Computer (Cont.)

TEST 11A: ELECTRO/MECHANICAL CLUSTER ODOMETER FAILURE

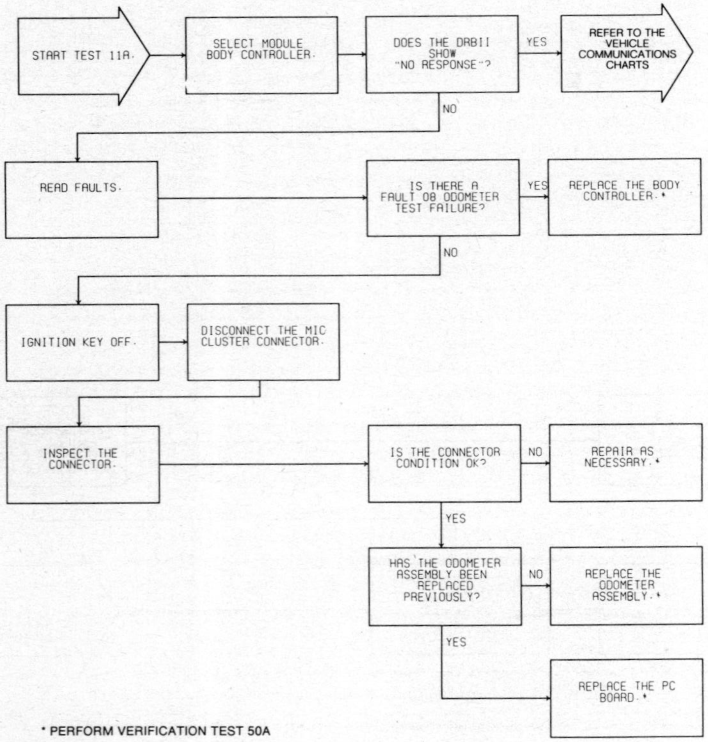
START TEST 11A.
SELECT MODULE BODY CONTROLLER.
DOES THE DRBII SHOW "NO RESPONSE"?
YES
REFER TO THE VEHICLE COMMUNICATIONS CHARTS
NO
READ FAULTS.
IS THERE A FAULT 08 ODOMETER TEST FAILURE?
YES
REPLACE THE BODY CONTROLLER.*
NO
IGNITION KEY OFF.
DISCONNECT THE MIC CLUSTER CONNECTOR.
INSPECT THE CONNECTOR.
IS THE CONNECTOR CONDITION OK?
NO
REPAIR AS NECESSARY.*
YES
HAS THE ODOMETER ASSEMBLY BEEN REPLACED PREVIOUSLY?
NO
REPLACE THE ODOMETER ASSEMBLY.*
YES
REPLACE THE PC BOARD.*

* PERFORM VERIFICATION TEST 50A

91I14611

Fig. 35: Test 11A – Electro/Mechanical Cluster Odometer Failure

TEST 12A: IDENTIFYING FAULTY WARNING LAMP ON PREMIUM ELECTRO/MECHANICAL CLUSTER (1 OF 2)

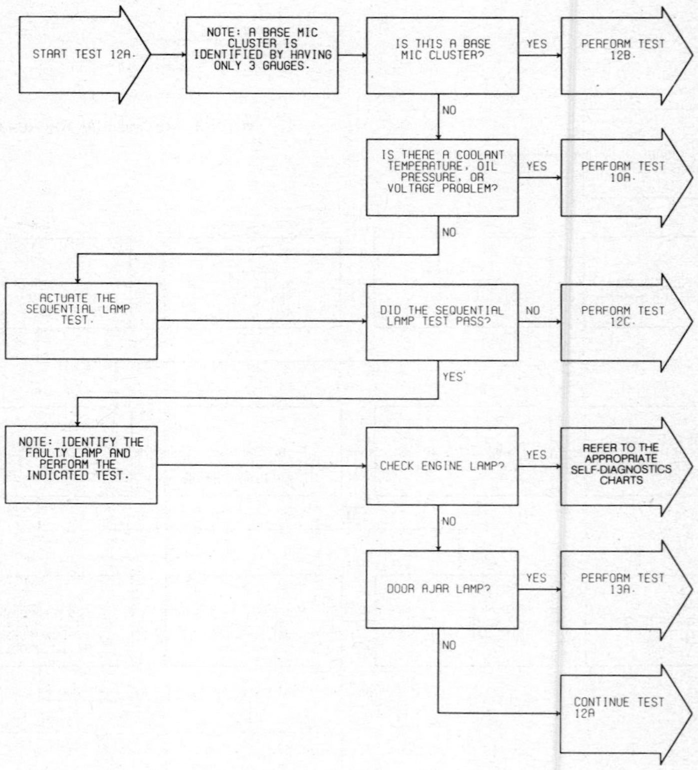
START TEST 12A.
NOTE: A BASE MIC CLUSTER IS IDENTIFIED BY HAVING ONLY 3 GAUGES.
IS THIS A BASE MIC CLUSTER?
YES
PERFORM TEST 12B.
NO
IS THERE A COOLANT TEMPERATURE, OIL PRESSURE, OR VOLTAGE PROBLEM?
YES
PERFORM TEST 10A.
NO
ACTUATE THE SEQUENTIAL LAMP TEST.
DID THE SEQUENTIAL LAMP TEST PASS?
NO
PERFORM TEST 12C.
YES
NOTE: IDENTIFY THE FAULTY LAMP AND PERFORM THE INDICATED TEST.
CHECK ENGINE LAMP?
YES
REFER TO THE APPROPRIATE SELF-DIAGNOSTICS CHARTS
NO
DOOR AJAR LAMP?
YES
PERFORM TEST 13A.
NO
CONTINUE TEST 12A

91J14612

Fig. 36: Test 12A – Identifying Faulty Warning Lamp on Premium Electro/Mechanical Cluster (1 of 2)

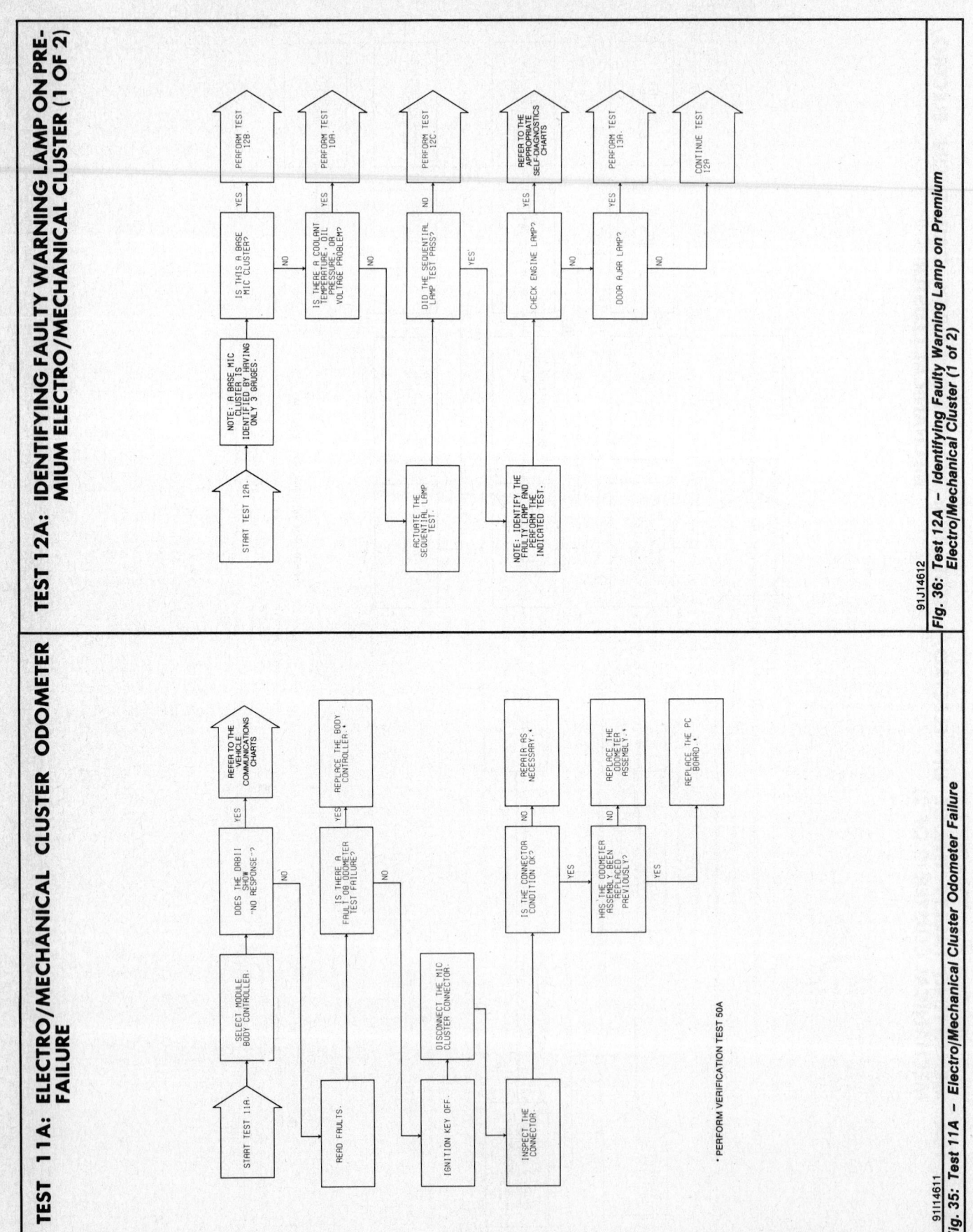

TEST 12A: IDENTIFYING FAULTY WARNING LAMP ON PREMIUM ELECTRO/MECHANICAL CLUSTER (2 OF 2)

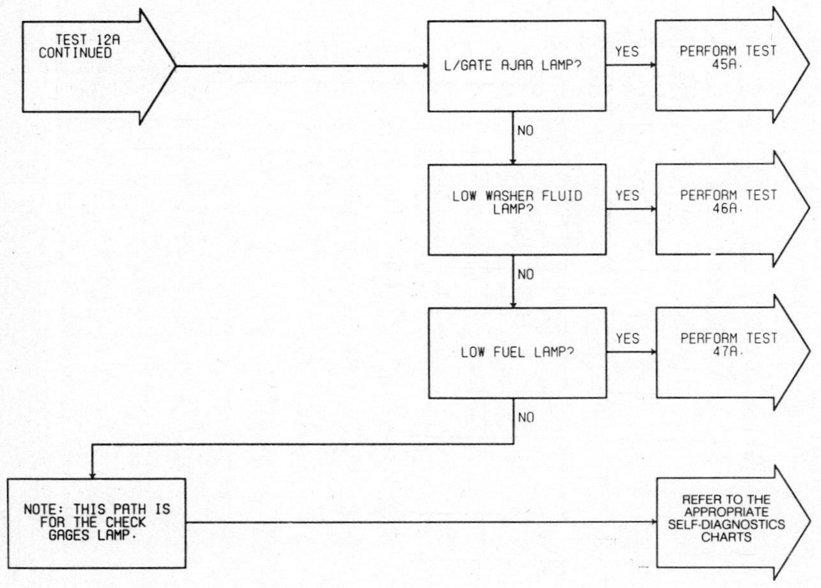
TEST 12A CONTINUED
L/GATE AJAR LAMP?
YES
PERFORM TEST 45A.
NO
LOW WASHER FLUID LAMP?
YES
PERFORM TEST 46A.
NO
LOW FUEL LAMP?
YES
PERFORM TEST 47A.
NO
NOTE: THIS PATH IS FOR THE CHECK GAGES LAMP.
REFER TO THE APPROPRIATE SELF-DIAGNOSTICS CHARTS

91A14613

Fig. 37: Test 12A – Identifying Faulty Warning Lamp on Premium Electro/Mechanical Cluster (2 of 2)

TEST 12B: IDENTIFYING FAULTY WARNING LAMP ON BASE ELECTRO/MECHANICAL CLUSTER (1 OF 2)

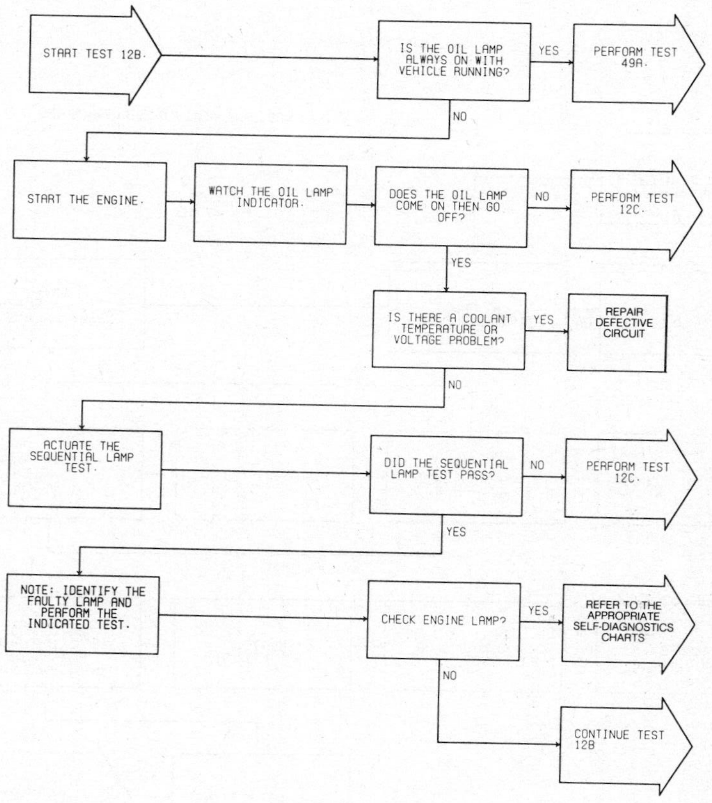
START TEST 12B.
IS THE OIL LAMP ALWAYS ON WITH VEHICLE RUNNING?
YES
PERFORM TEST 49A.
NO
START THE ENGINE.
WATCH THE OIL LAMP INDICATOR.
DOES THE OIL LAMP COME ON THEN GO OFF?
NO
PERFORM TEST 12C.
YES
IS THERE A COOLANT TEMPERATURE OR VOLTAGE PROBLEM?
YES
REPAIR DEFECTIVE CIRCUIT
NO
ACTUATE THE SEQUENTIAL LAMP TEST.
DID THE SEQUENTIAL LAMP TEST PASS?
NO
PERFORM TEST 12C.
YES
NOTE: IDENTIFY THE FAULTY LAMP AND PERFORM THE INDICATED TEST.
CHECK ENGINE LAMP?
YES
REFER TO THE APPROPRIATE SELF-DIAGNOSTICS CHARTS
NO
CONTINUE TEST 12B

91B14614

Fig. 38: Test 12B – Identifying Faulty Warning Lamp on Base Electro/Mechanical Cluster (1 of 2)

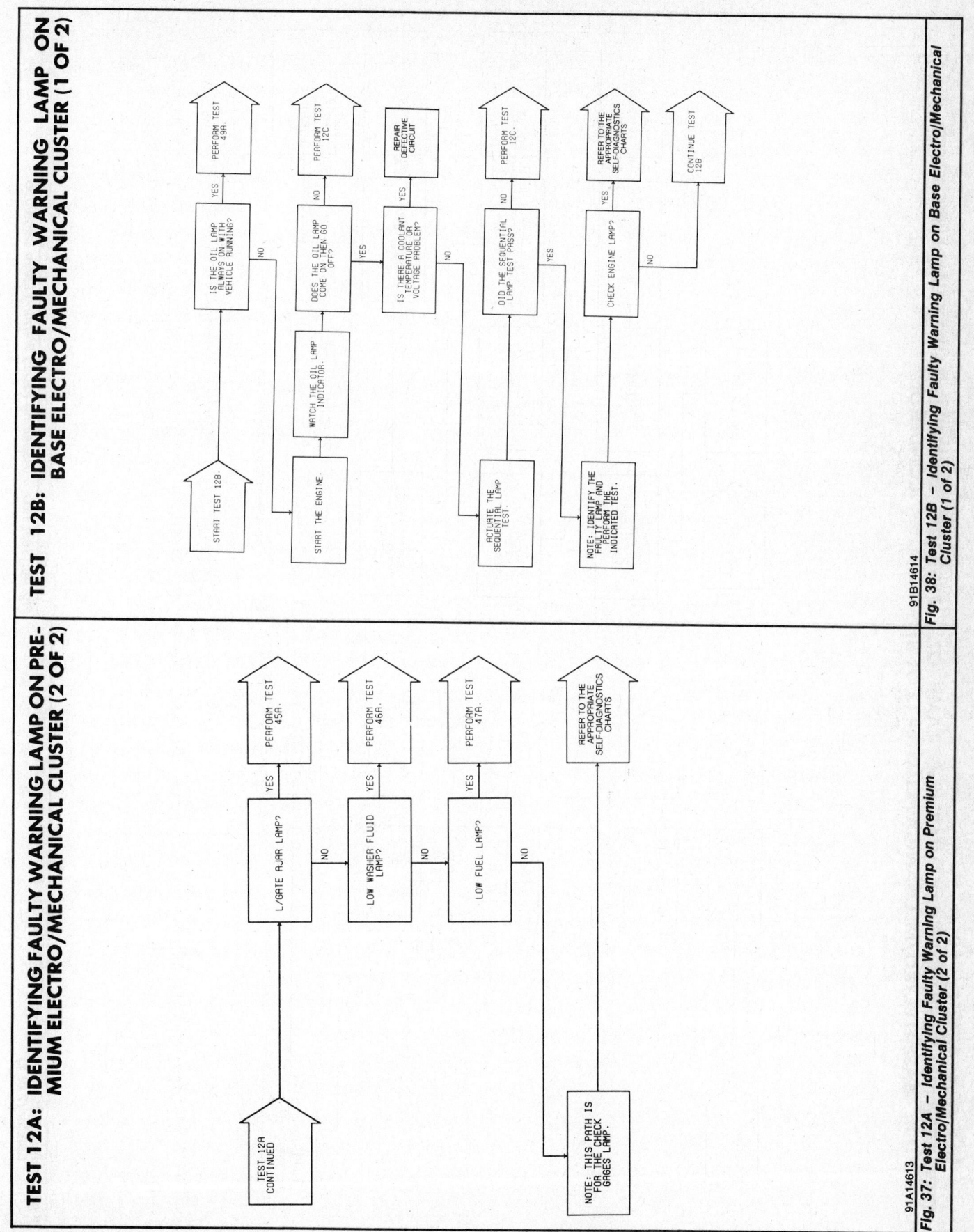

TEST 12B: IDENTIFYING FAULTY WARNING LAMP ON BASE ELECTRO/MECHANICAL CLUSTER (2 OF 2)

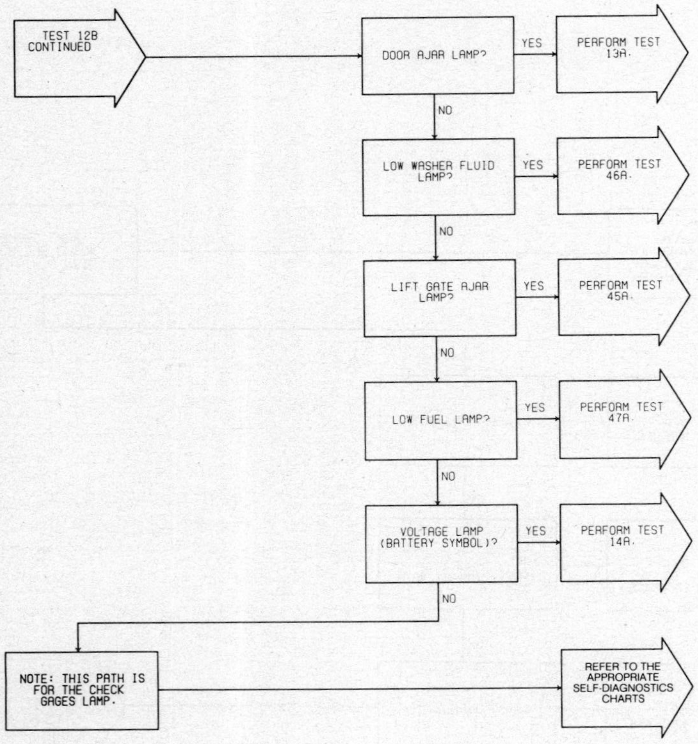
TEST 12B CONTINUED
DOOR AJAR LAMP?
YES
PERFORM TEST 13A.
NO
LOW WASHER FLUID LAMP?
YES
PERFORM TEST 46A.
NO
LIFT GATE AJAR LAMP?
YES
PERFORM TEST 45A.
NO
LOW FUEL LAMP?
YES
PERFORM TEST 47A.
NO
VOLTAGE LAMP (BATTERY SYMBOL)?
YES
PERFORM TEST 14A.
NO
NOTE: THIS PATH IS FOR THE CHECK GAGES LAMP.
REFER TO THE APPROPRIATE SELF-DIAGNOSTICS CHARTS

91C14615

Fig. 39: Test 12B – Identifying Faulty Warning Lamp on Base Electro/Mechanical Cluster (2 of 2)

TEST 12C: REPAIRING FAULTY WARNING LAMP CONDITION

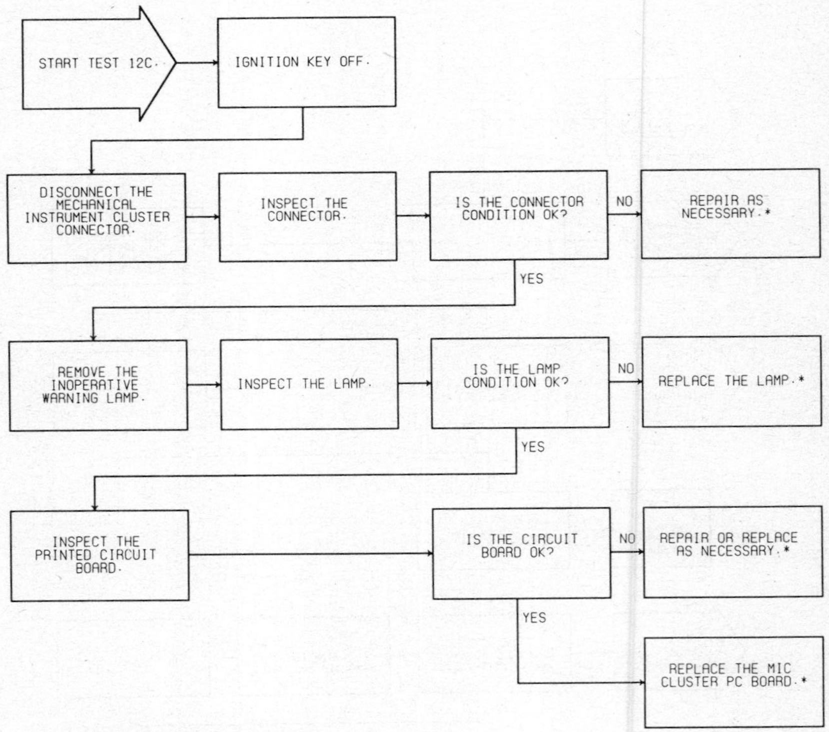
START TEST 12C.
IGNITION KEY OFF.
DISCONNECT THE MECHANICAL INSTRUMENT CLUSTER CONNECTOR.
INSPECT THE CONNECTOR.
IS THE CONNECTOR CONDITION OK?
NO
REPAIR AS NECESSARY.*
YES
REMOVE THE INOPERATIVE WARNING LAMP.
INSPECT THE LAMP.
IS THE LAMP CONDITION OK?
NO
REPLACE THE LAMP.*
YES
INSPECT THE PRINTED CIRCUIT BOARD.
IS THE CIRCUIT BOARD OK?
NO
REPAIR OR REPLACE AS NECESSARY.*
YES
REPLACE THE MIC CLUSTER PC BOARD.*

* PERFORM VERIFICATION TEST 50A

91D14616

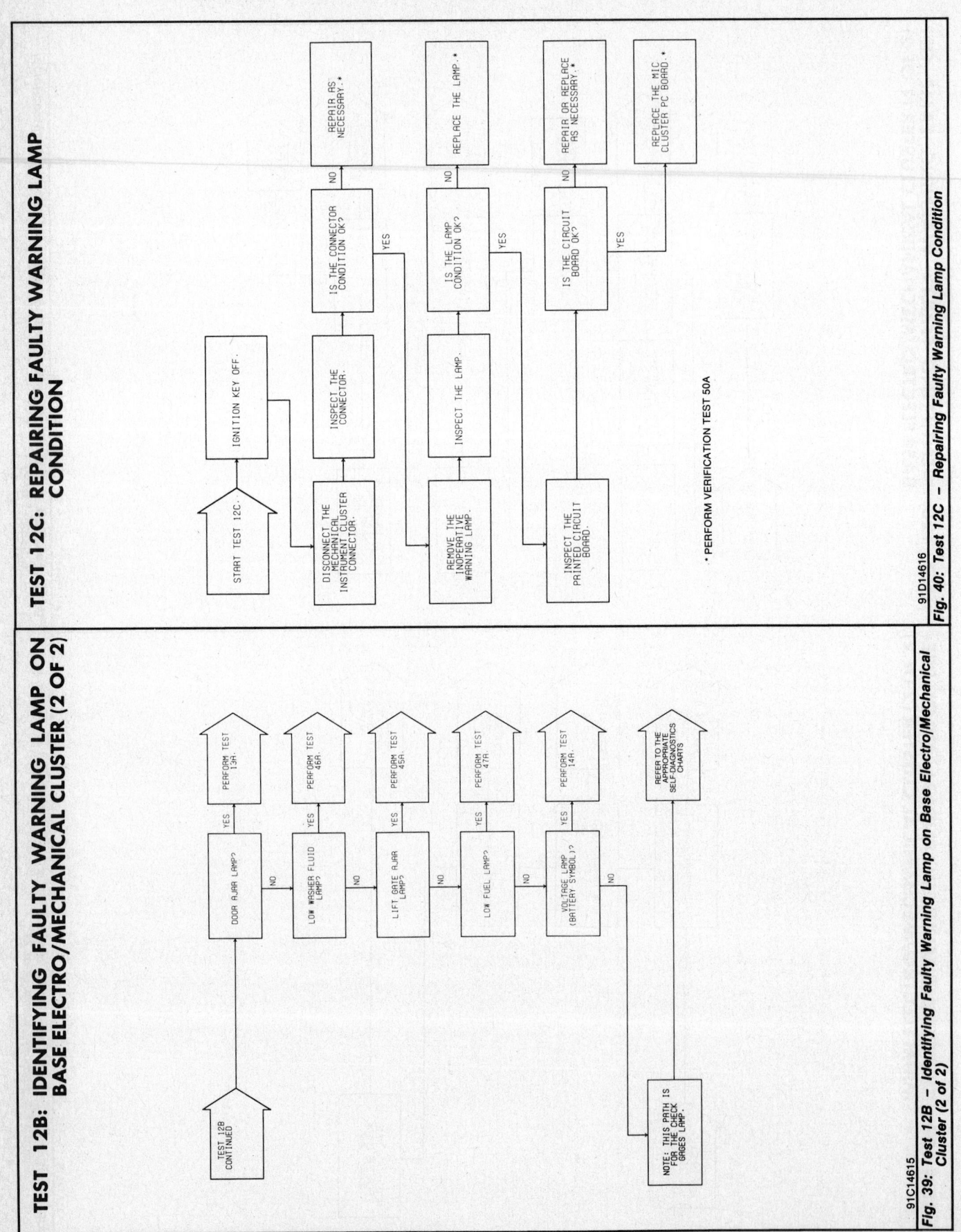

Fig. 40: Test 12C – Repairing Faulty Warning Lamp Condition

TEST 13A: REPAIRING DOOR AJAR WARNING LAMP

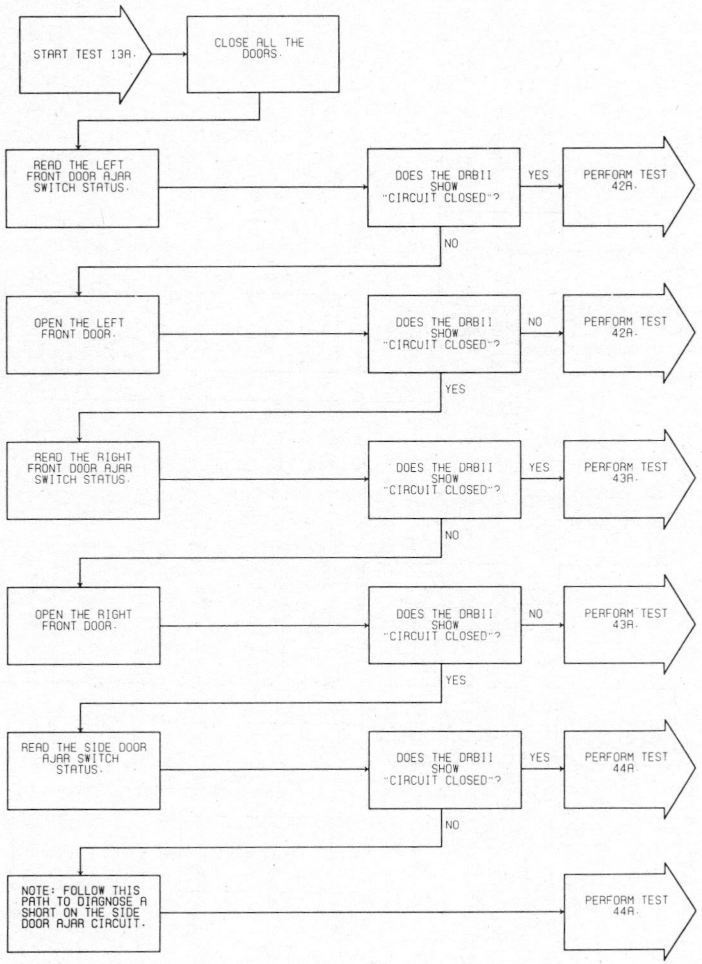
START TEST 13A.
CLOSE ALL THE DOORS.
READ THE LEFT FRONT DOOR AJAR SWITCH STATUS.
DOES THE DRBII SHOW "CIRCUIT CLOSED"?
YES
PERFORM TEST 42A.
NO
OPEN THE LEFT FRONT DOOR.
DOES THE DRBII SHOW "CIRCUIT CLOSED"?
NO
PERFORM TEST 42A.
YES
READ THE RIGHT FRONT DOOR AJAR SWITCH STATUS.
DOES THE DRBII SHOW "CIRCUIT CLOSED"?
YES
PERFORM TEST 43A.
NO
OPEN THE RIGHT FRONT DOOR.
DOES THE DRBII SHOW "CIRCUIT CLOSED"?
NO
PERFORM TEST 43A.
YES
READ THE SIDE DOOR AJAR SWITCH STATUS.
DOES THE DRBII SHOW "CIRCUIT CLOSED"?
YES
PERFORM TEST 44A
NO
NOTE: FOLLOW THIS PATH TO DIAGNOSE A SHORT ON THE SIDE DOOR AJAR CIRCUIT.
PERFORM TEST 44A.

91E14617

Fig. 41: Test 13A – Repairing Door Ajar Warning Lamp

TEST 14A: REPAIRING VOLTAGE GAUGE OR VOLTAGE LAMP PROBLEM

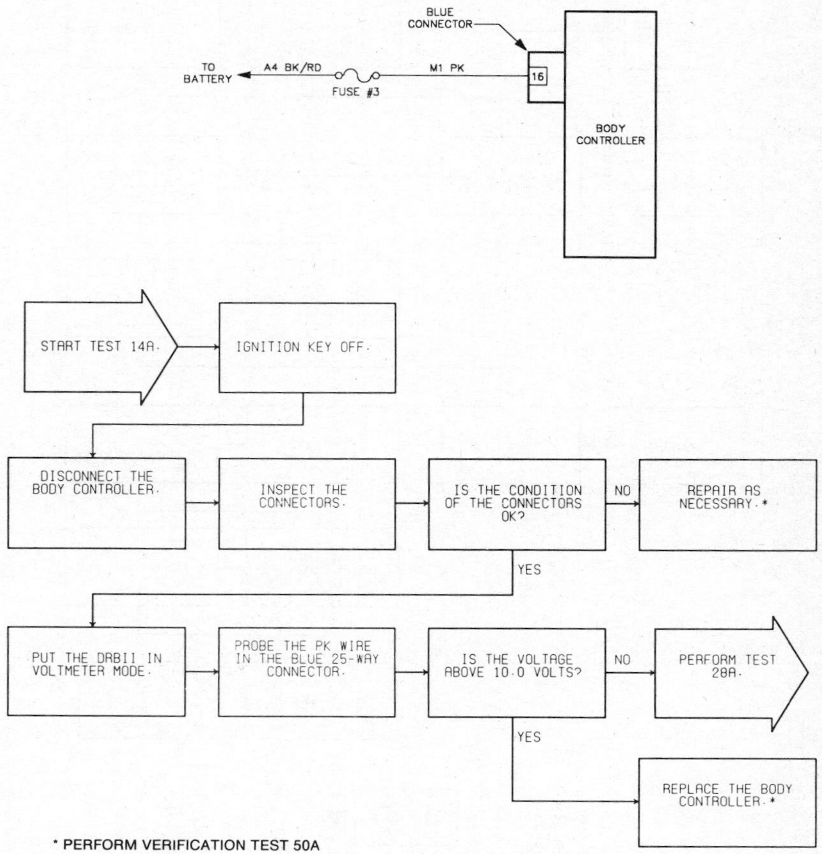
BLUE CONNECTOR
TO BATTERY
A4 BK/RD
FUSE #3
M1 PK
16
BODY CONTROLLER
START TEST 14A.
IGNITION KEY OFF.
DISCONNECT THE BODY CONTROLLER.
INSPECT THE CONNECTORS.
IS THE CONDITION OF THE CONNECTORS OK?
NO
REPAIR AS NECESSARY.*
YES
PUT THE DRBII IN VOLTMETER MODE.
PROBE THE PK WIRE IN THE BLUE 25-WAY CONNECTOR.
IS THE VOLTAGE ABOVE 10.0 VOLTS?
NO
PERFORM TEST 28A.
YES
REPLACE THE BODY CONTROLLER.*

* PERFORM VERIFICATION TEST 50A

91F14618 91G14619

Fig. 42: Test 13A – Repairing Door Ajar Warning Lamp

TEST 22A: IDENTIFYING INTERMITTENT WIPER PROBLEM (1 OF 3)

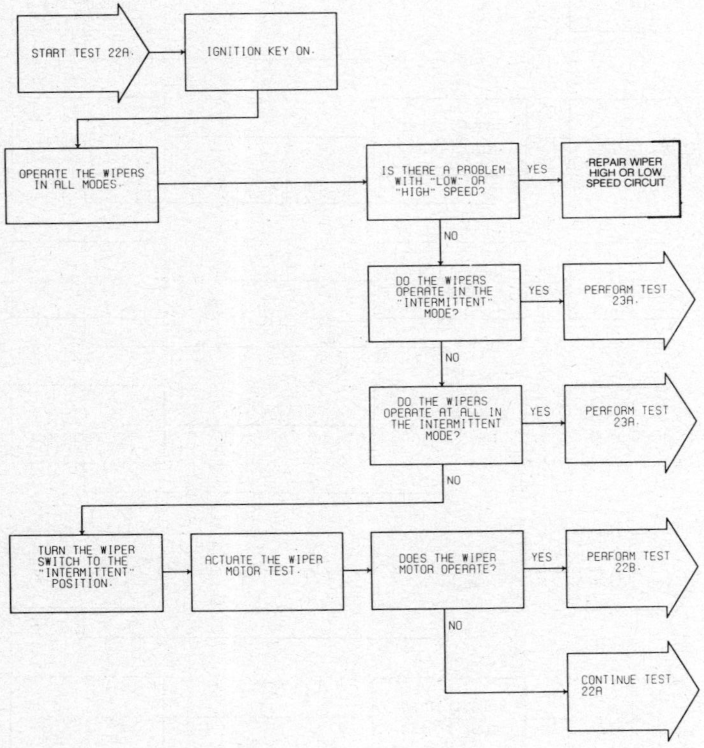
START TEST 22A.
IGNITION KEY ON.
OPERATE THE WIPERS IN ALL MODES.
IS THERE A PROBLEM WITH "LOW" OR "HIGH" SPEED?
YES
REPAIR WIPER HIGH OR LOW SPEED CIRCUIT
NO
DO THE WIPERS OPERATE IN THE "INTERMITTENT" MODE?
YES
PERFORM TEST 23A.
NO
DO THE WIPERS OPERATE AT ALL IN THE INTERMITTENT MODE?
YES
PERFORM TEST 23A.
NO
TURN THE WIPER SWITCH TO THE "INTERMITTENT" POSITION.
ACTUATE THE WIPER MOTOR TEST.
DOES THE WIPER MOTOR OPERATE?
YES
PERFORM TEST 22B.
NO
CONTINUE TEST 22A

91J14620

Fig. 43: Test 22A – Identifying Intermittent Wiper Problem (1 of 3)

TEST 22A: IDENTIFYING INTERMITTENT WIPER PROBLEM (2 OF 3)

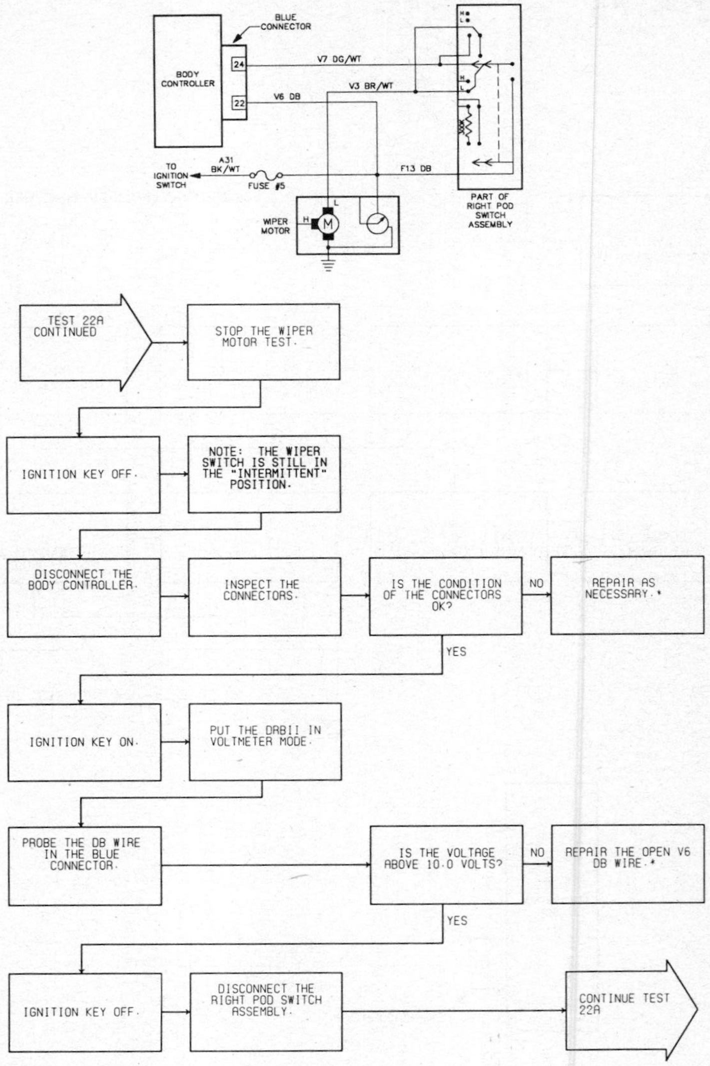
BLUE CONNECTOR
BODY CONTROLLER
24
22
V7 DG/WT
V3 BR/WT
V6 DB
TO IGNITION SWITCH
A31 BK/WT
FUSE #5
F13 DB
WIPER MOTOR
PART OF RIGHT POD SWITCH ASSEMBLY
TEST 22A CONTINUED
STOP THE WIPER MOTOR TEST.
IGNITION KEY OFF.
NOTE: THE WIPER SWITCH IS STILL IN THE "INTERMITTENT" POSITION.
DISCONNECT THE BODY CONTROLLER.
INSPECT THE CONNECTORS.
IS THE CONDITION OF THE CONNECTORS OK?
NO
REPAIR AS NECESSARY. *
YES
IGNITION KEY ON.
PUT THE DRBII IN VOLTMETER MODE.
PROBE THE DB WIRE IN THE BLUE CONNECTOR.
IS THE VOLTAGE ABOVE 10.0 VOLTS?
NO
REPAIR THE OPEN V6 DB WIRE. *
YES
IGNITION KEY OFF.
DISCONNECT THE RIGHT POD SWITCH ASSEMBLY.
CONTINUE TEST 22A

* PERFORM VERIFICATION TEST 50A

91A14621 91B14622

Fig. 44: Test 22A – Identifying Intermittent Wiper Problem (2 of 3)

TEST 22A: IDENTIFYING INTERMITTENT WIPER PROBLEM (3 OF 3)

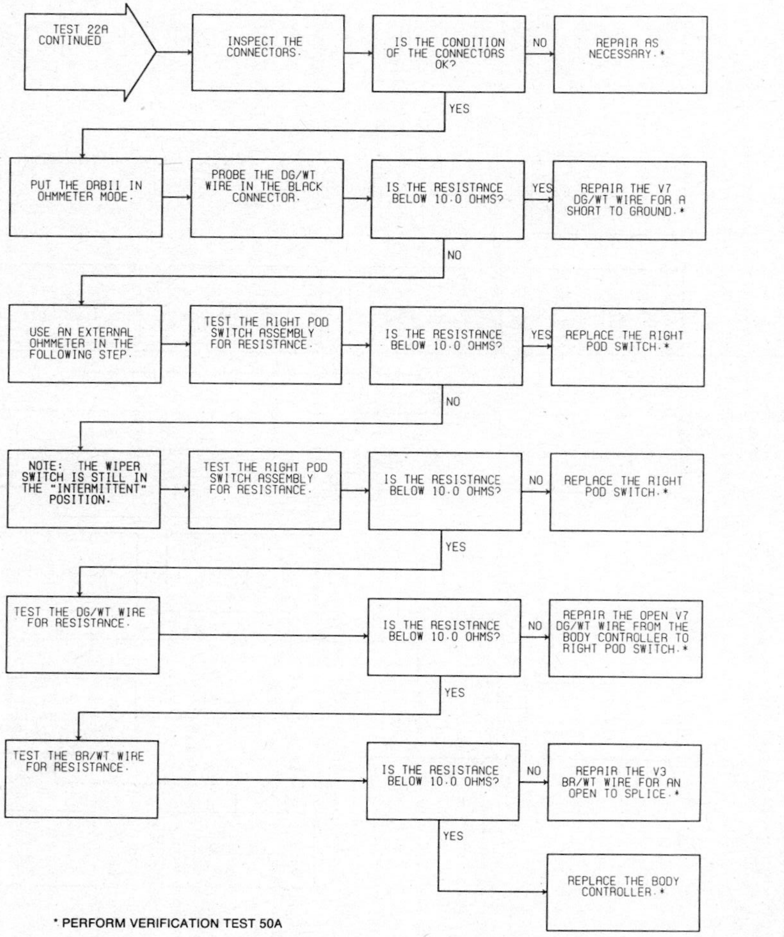
TEST 22A CONTINUED
INSPECT THE CONNECTORS.
IS THE CONDITION OF THE CONNECTORS OK?
NO
REPAIR AS NECESSARY.*
YES
PUT THE DRBII IN OHMMETER MODE.
PROBE THE DG/WT WIRE IN THE BLACK CONNECTOR.
IS THE RESISTANCE BELOW 10.0 OHMS?
YES
REPAIR THE V7 DG/WT WIRE FOR A SHORT TO GROUND.*
NO
USE AN EXTERNAL OHMMETER IN THE FOLLOWING STEP.
TEST THE RIGHT POD SWITCH ASSEMBLY FOR RESISTANCE.
IS THE RESISTANCE BELOW 10.0 OHMS?
YES
REPLACE THE RIGHT POD SWITCH.*
NO
NOTE: THE WIPER SWITCH IS STILL IN THE "INTERMITTENT" POSITION.
TEST THE RIGHT POD SWITCH ASSEMBLY FOR RESISTANCE.
IS THE RESISTANCE BELOW 10.0 OHMS?
NO
REPLACE THE RIGHT POD SWITCH.*
YES
TEST THE DG/WT WIRE FOR RESISTANCE.
IS THE RESISTANCE BELOW 10.0 OHMS?
NO
REPAIR THE OPEN V7 DG/WT WIRE FROM THE BODY CONTROLLER TO RIGHT POD SWITCH.*
YES
TEST THE BR/WT WIRE FOR RESISTANCE.
IS THE RESISTANCE BELOW 10.0 OHMS?
NO
REPAIR THE V3 BR/WT WIRE FOR AN OPEN TO SPLICE.*
YES
REPLACE THE BODY CONTROLLER.*

* PERFORM VERIFICATION TEST 50A

91C14623

Fig. 45: Test 22A – Identifying Intermittent Wiper Problem (3 of 3)

TEST 22B: CHECKING CONTROLLER & WIPER SWITCH (1 OF 2)

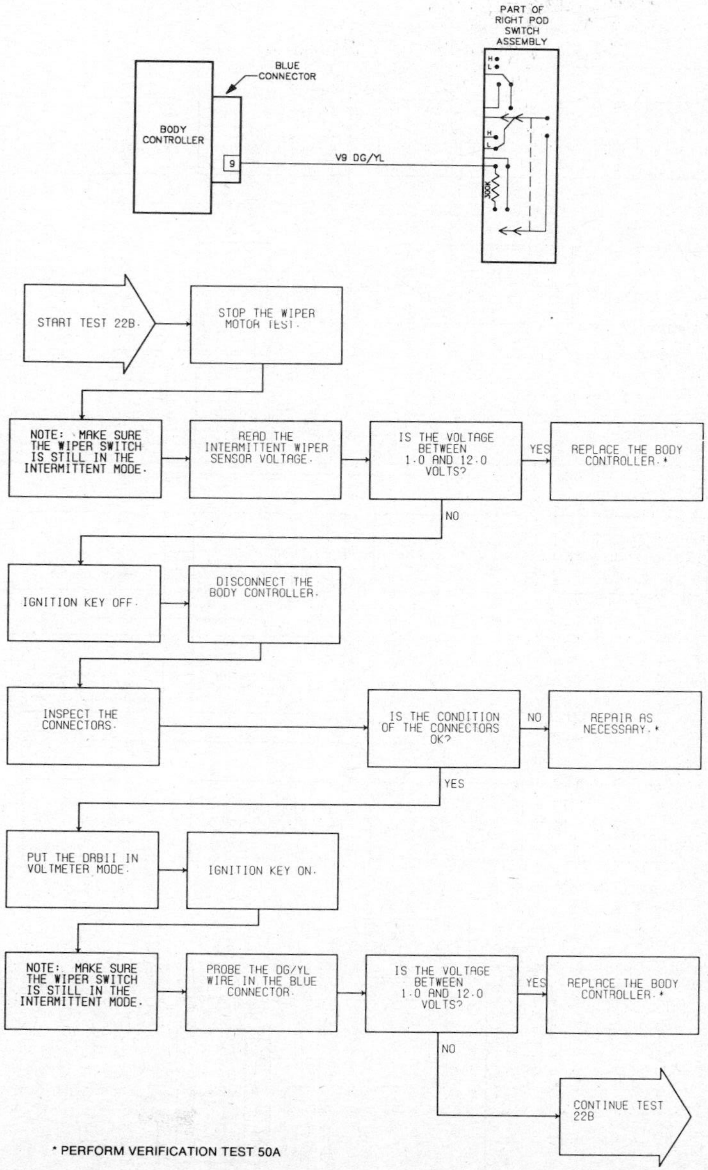
PART OF RIGHT POD SWITCH ASSEMBLY
BLUE CONNECTOR
BODY CONTROLLER
9
V9 DG/YL
H
L
300K
START TEST 22B.
STOP THE WIPER MOTOR TEST.
NOTE: MAKE SURE THE WIPER SWITCH IS STILL IN THE INTERMITTENT MODE.
READ THE INTERMITTENT WIPER SENSOR VOLTAGE.
IS THE VOLTAGE BETWEEN 1.0 AND 12.0 VOLTS?
YES
REPLACE THE BODY CONTROLLER.*
NO
IGNITION KEY OFF.
DISCONNECT THE BODY CONTROLLER.
INSPECT THE CONNECTORS.
IS THE CONDITION OF THE CONNECTORS OK?
NO
REPAIR AS NECESSARY.*
YES
PUT THE DRBII IN VOLTMETER MODE.
IGNITION KEY ON.
NOTE: MAKE SURE THE WIPER SWITCH IS STILL IN THE INTERMITTENT MODE.
PROBE THE DG/YL WIRE IN THE BLUE CONNECTOR.
IS THE VOLTAGE BETWEEN 1.0 AND 12.0 VOLTS?
YES
REPLACE THE BODY CONTROLLER.*
NO
CONTINUE TEST 22B

* PERFORM VERIFICATION TEST 50A

91D14624 91E14625

Fig. 46: Test 22B – Checking Controller & Wiper Switch (1 of 2)

1991 ENGINE PERFORMANCE
Body Control Computer (Cont.)

TEST 22B: CHECKING CONTROLLER & WIPER SWITCH (2 OF 2)

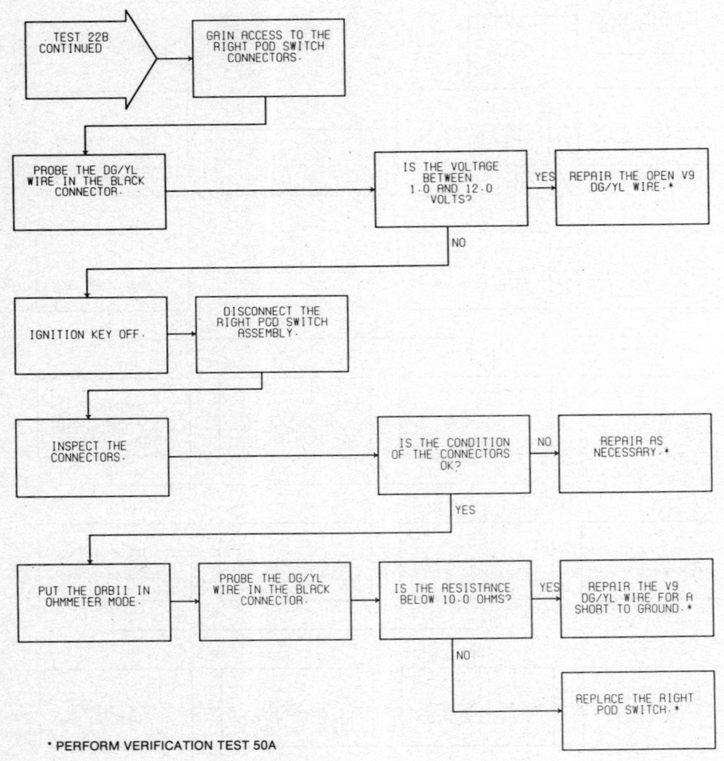
TEST 22B CONTINUED
GAIN ACCESS TO THE RIGHT POD SWITCH CONNECTORS.
PROBE THE DG/YL WIRE IN THE BLACK CONNECTOR.
IS THE VOLTAGE BETWEEN 1.0 AND 12.0 VOLTS?
YES
REPAIR THE OPEN V9 DG/YL WIRE.*
NO
IGNITION KEY OFF.
DISCONNECT THE RIGHT POD SWITCH ASSEMBLY.
INSPECT THE CONNECTORS.
IS THE CONDITION OF THE CONNECTORS OK?
NO
REPAIR AS NECESSARY.*
YES
PUT THE DRBII IN OHMMETER MODE.
PROBE THE DG/YL WIRE IN THE BLACK CONNECTOR.
IS THE RESISTANCE BELOW 10.0 OHMS?
YES
REPAIR THE V9 DG/YL WIRE FOR A SHORT TO GROUND.*
NO
REPLACE THE RIGHT POD SWITCH.*
* PERFORM VERIFICATION TEST 50A

91F14626

Fig. 47: Test 22B – Checking Controller & Wiper Switch (2 of 2)

TEST 23A: CHECKING POWER & GROUND SUPPLY (1 OF 3)

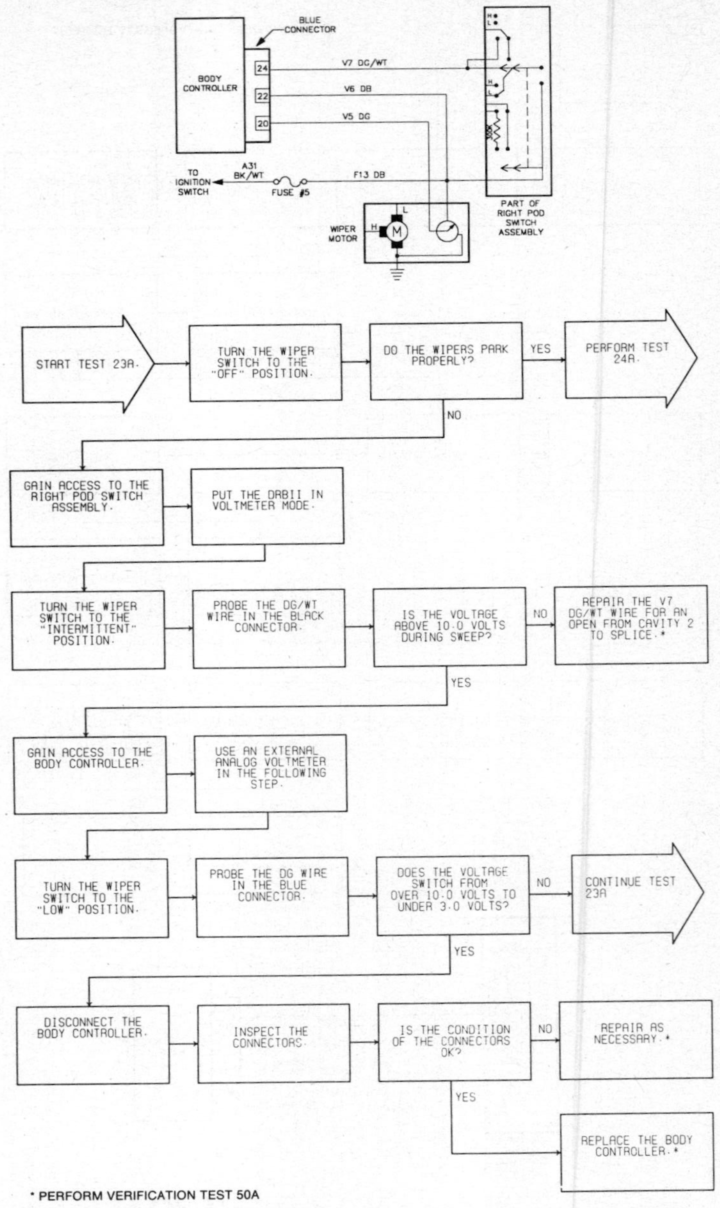
BODY CONTROLLER
BLUE CONNECTOR
24
22
20
V7 DG/WT
V6 DB
V5 DG
F13 DB
A31 BK/WT
TO IGNITION SWITCH
FUSE #5
WIPER MOTOR
PART OF RIGHT POD SWITCH ASSEMBLY
START TEST 23A.
TURN THE WIPER SWITCH TO THE "OFF" POSITION.
DO THE WIPERS PARK PROPERLY?
YES
PERFORM TEST 24A.
NO
GAIN ACCESS TO THE RIGHT POD SWITCH ASSEMBLY.
PUT THE DRBII IN VOLTMETER MODE.
TURN THE WIPER SWITCH TO THE "INTERMITTENT" POSITION.
PROBE THE DG/WT WIRE IN THE BLACK CONNECTOR.
IS THE VOLTAGE ABOVE 10.0 VOLTS DURING SWEEP?
NO
REPAIR THE V7 DG/WT WIRE FOR AN OPEN FROM CAVITY 2 TO SPLICE.*
YES
GAIN ACCESS TO THE BODY CONTROLLER.
USE AN EXTERNAL ANALOG VOLTMETER IN THE FOLLOWING STEP.
TURN THE WIPER SWITCH TO THE "LOW" POSITION.
PROBE THE DG WIRE IN THE BLUE CONNECTOR.
DOES THE VOLTAGE SWITCH FROM OVER 10.0 VOLTS TO UNDER 3.0 VOLTS?
NO
CONTINUE TEST 23A
YES
DISCONNECT THE BODY CONTROLLER.
INSPECT THE CONNECTORS.
IS THE CONDITION OF THE CONNECTORS OK?
NO
REPAIR AS NECESSARY.*
YES
REPLACE THE BODY CONTROLLER.*
* PERFORM VERIFICATION TEST 50A

91G14627 91H14628

Fig. 48: Test 23A – Checking Power & Ground Supply (1 of 3)

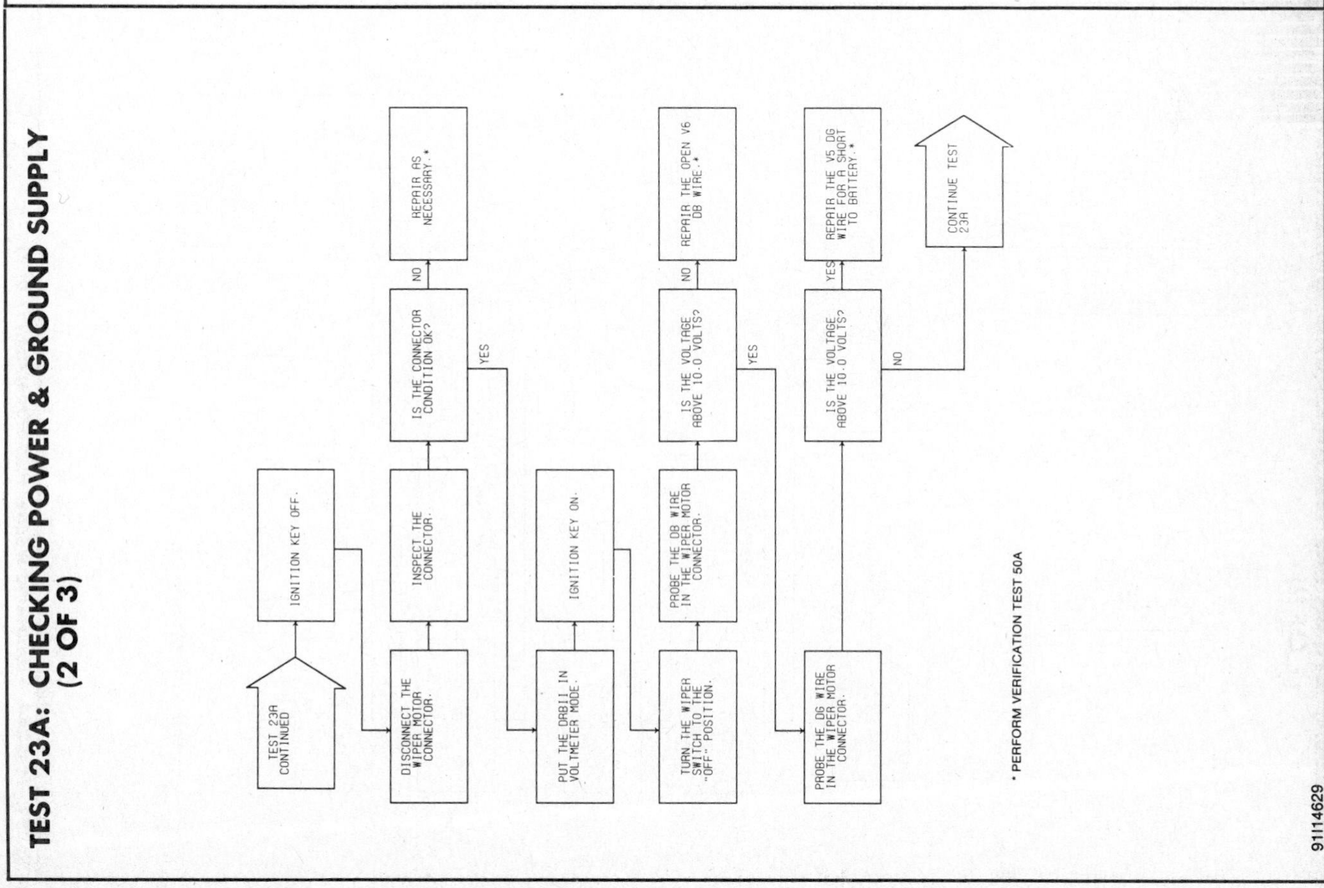

TEST 23A: CHECKING POWER & GROUND SUPPLY (2 OF 3)
TEST 23A CONTINUED
IGNITION KEY OFF.
DISCONNECT THE WIPER MOTOR CONNECTOR.
INSPECT THE CONNECTOR.
IS THE CONNECTOR CONDITION OK?
NO
REPAIR AS NECESSARY.*
YES
PUT THE DRBII IN VOLTMETER MODE.
IGNITION KEY ON.
TURN THE WIPER SWITCH TO THE "OFF" POSITION.
PROBE THE DB WIRE IN THE WIPER MOTOR CONNECTOR.
IS THE VOLTAGE ABOVE 10.0 VOLTS?
NO
REPAIR THE OPEN V6 DB WIRE.*
YES
PROBE THE DG WIRE IN THE WIPER MOTOR CONNECTOR.
IS THE VOLTAGE ABOVE 10.0 VOLTS?
YES
REPAIR THE V5 DG WIRE FOR A SHORT TO BATTERY.*
NO
CONTINUE TEST 23A
* PERFORM VERIFICATION TEST 50A
91I14629

Fig. 49: Test 23A – Checking Power & Ground Supply (2 of 3)

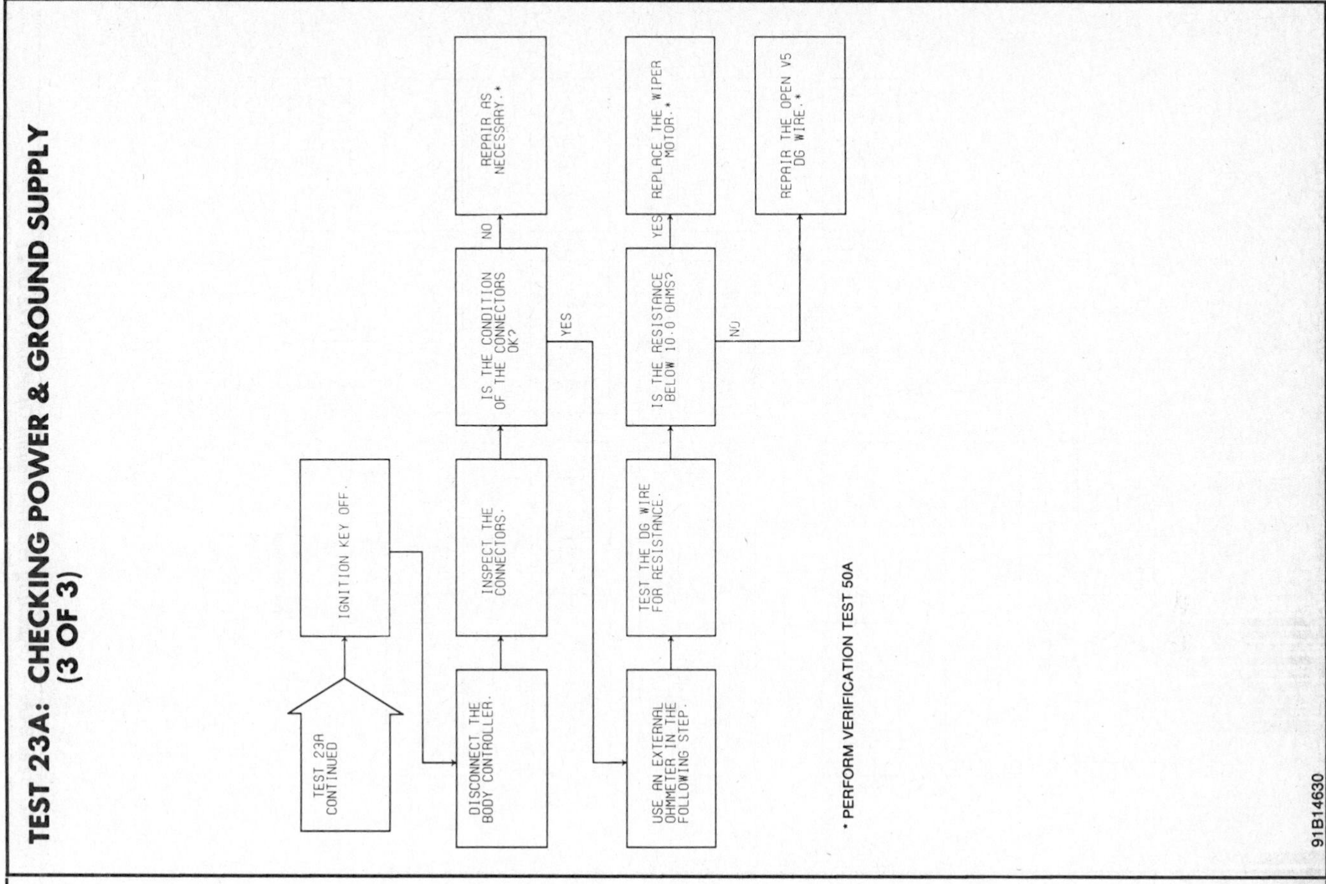

TEST 23A: CHECKING POWER & GROUND SUPPLY (3 OF 3)
TEST 23A CONTINUED
IGNITION KEY OFF.
DISCONNECT THE BODY CONTROLLER.
INSPECT THE CONNECTORS.
IS THE CONDITION OF THE CONNECTORS OK?
NO
REPAIR AS NECESSARY.*
YES
USE AN EXTERNAL OHMMETER IN THE FOLLOWING STEP.
TEST THE DG WIRE FOR RESISTANCE.
IS THE RESISTANCE BELOW 10.0 OHMS?
YES
REPLACE THE WIPER MOTOR.*
NO
REPAIR THE OPEN V5 DG WIRE.*
* PERFORM VERIFICATION TEST 50A
91B14630

Fig. 50: Test 23A – Checking Power & Ground Supply (3 of 3)

1991 ENGINE PERFORMANCE
Body Control Computer (Cont.)

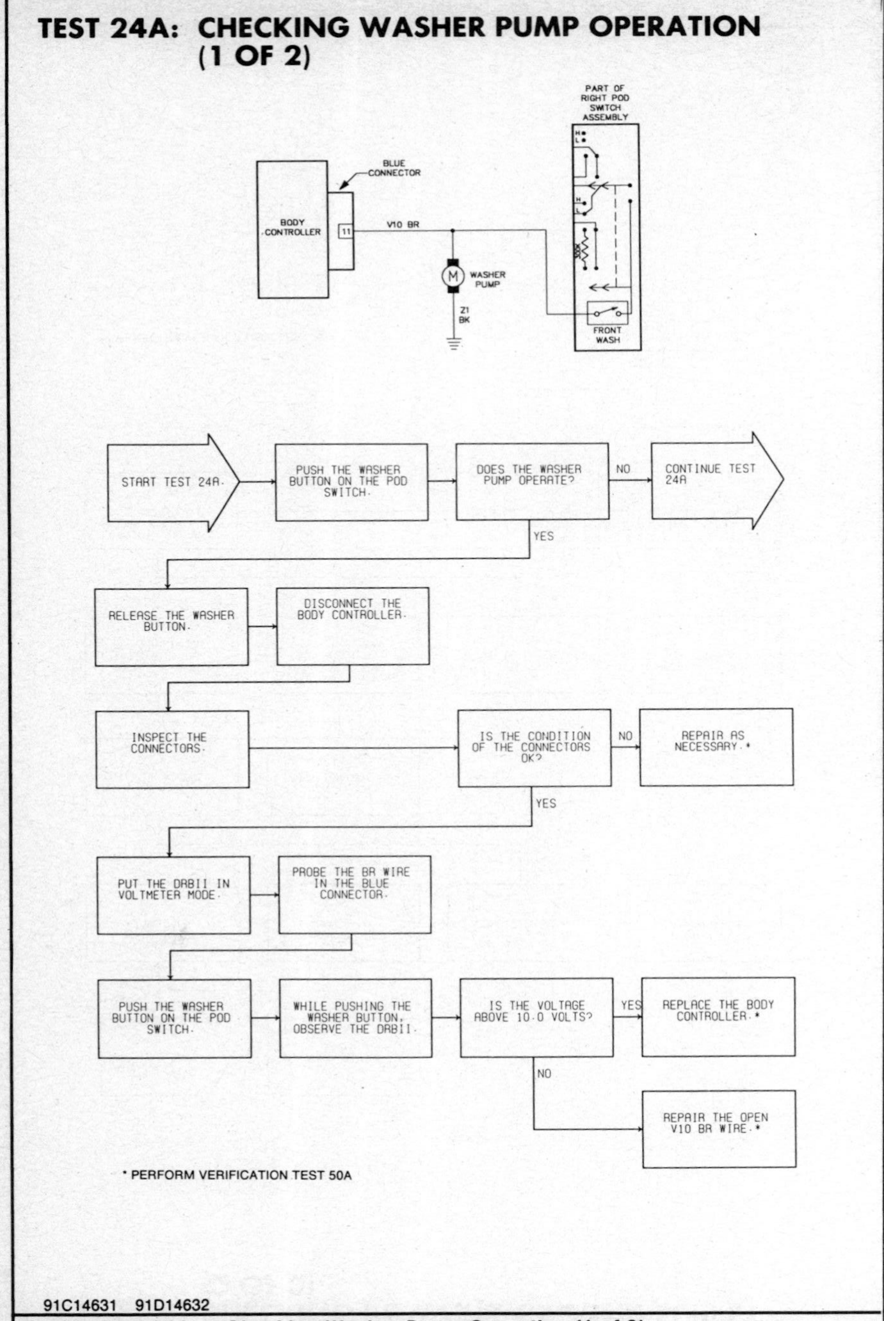
TEST 24A: CHECKING WASHER PUMP OPERATION (1 OF 2)
PART OF RIGHT POD SWITCH ASSEMBLY
BLUE CONNECTOR
BODY CONTROLLER
11
V10 BR
WASHER PUMP
Z1 BK
FRONT WASH
START TEST 24A.
PUSH THE WASHER BUTTON ON THE POD SWITCH.
DOES THE WASHER PUMP OPERATE?
NO
CONTINUE TEST 24A
YES
RELEASE THE WASHER BUTTON.
DISCONNECT THE BODY CONTROLLER.
INSPECT THE CONNECTORS.
IS THE CONDITION OF THE CONNECTORS OK?
NO
REPAIR AS NECESSARY.*
YES
PUT THE DRBII IN VOLTMETER MODE.
PROBE THE BR WIRE IN THE BLUE CONNECTOR.
PUSH THE WASHER BUTTON ON THE POD SWITCH.
WHILE PUSHING THE WASHER BUTTON, OBSERVE THE DRBII.
IS THE VOLTAGE ABOVE 10.0 VOLTS?
YES
REPLACE THE BODY CONTROLLER.*
NO
REPAIR THE OPEN V10 BR WIRE.*
* PERFORM VERIFICATION TEST 50A
91C14631 91D14632

Fig. 51: Test 24A – Checking Washer Pump Operation (1 of 2)

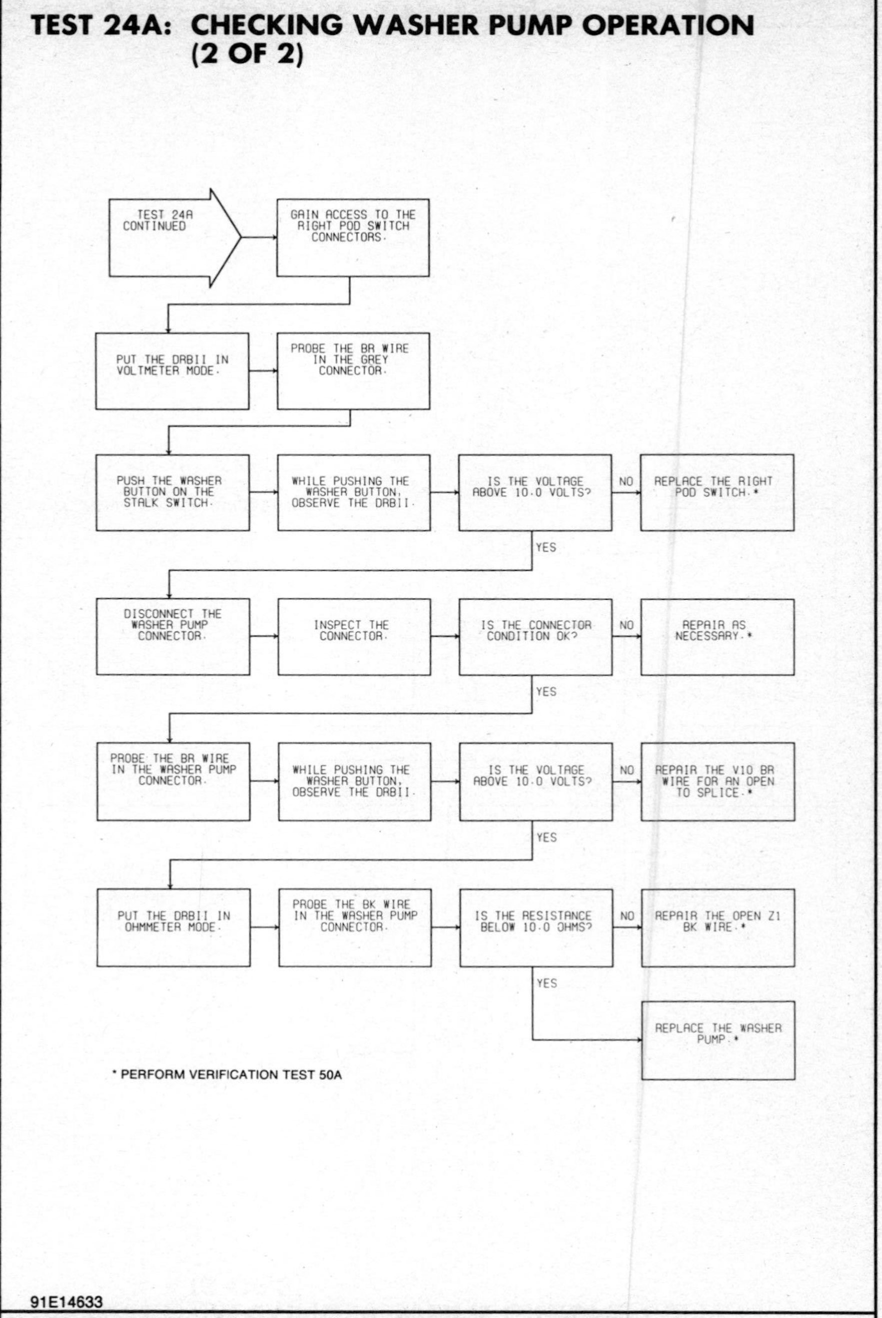
TEST 24A: CHECKING WASHER PUMP OPERATION (2 OF 2)
TEST 24A CONTINUED
GAIN ACCESS TO THE RIGHT POD SWITCH CONNECTORS.
PUT THE DRBII IN VOLTMETER MODE.
PROBE THE BR WIRE IN THE GREY CONNECTOR.
PUSH THE WASHER BUTTON ON THE STALK SWITCH.
WHILE PUSHING THE WASHER BUTTON, OBSERVE THE DRBII.
IS THE VOLTAGE ABOVE 10.0 VOLTS?
NO
REPLACE THE RIGHT POD SWITCH.*
YES
DISCONNECT THE WASHER PUMP CONNECTOR.
INSPECT THE CONNECTOR.
IS THE CONNECTOR CONDITION OK?
NO
REPAIR AS NECESSARY.*
YES
PROBE THE BR WIRE IN THE WASHER PUMP CONNECTOR.
WHILE PUSHING THE WASHER BUTTON, OBSERVE THE DRBII.
IS THE VOLTAGE ABOVE 10.0 VOLTS?
NO
REPAIR THE V10 BR WIRE FOR AN OPEN TO SPLICE.*
YES
PUT THE DRBII IN OHMMETER MODE.
PROBE THE BK WIRE IN THE WASHER PUMP CONNECTOR.
IS THE RESISTANCE BELOW 10.0 OHMS?
NO
REPAIR THE OPEN Z1 BK WIRE.*
YES
REPLACE THE WASHER PUMP.*
* PERFORM VERIFICATION TEST 50A
91E14633

Fig. 52: Test 24A – Checking Washer Pump Operation (2 of 2)

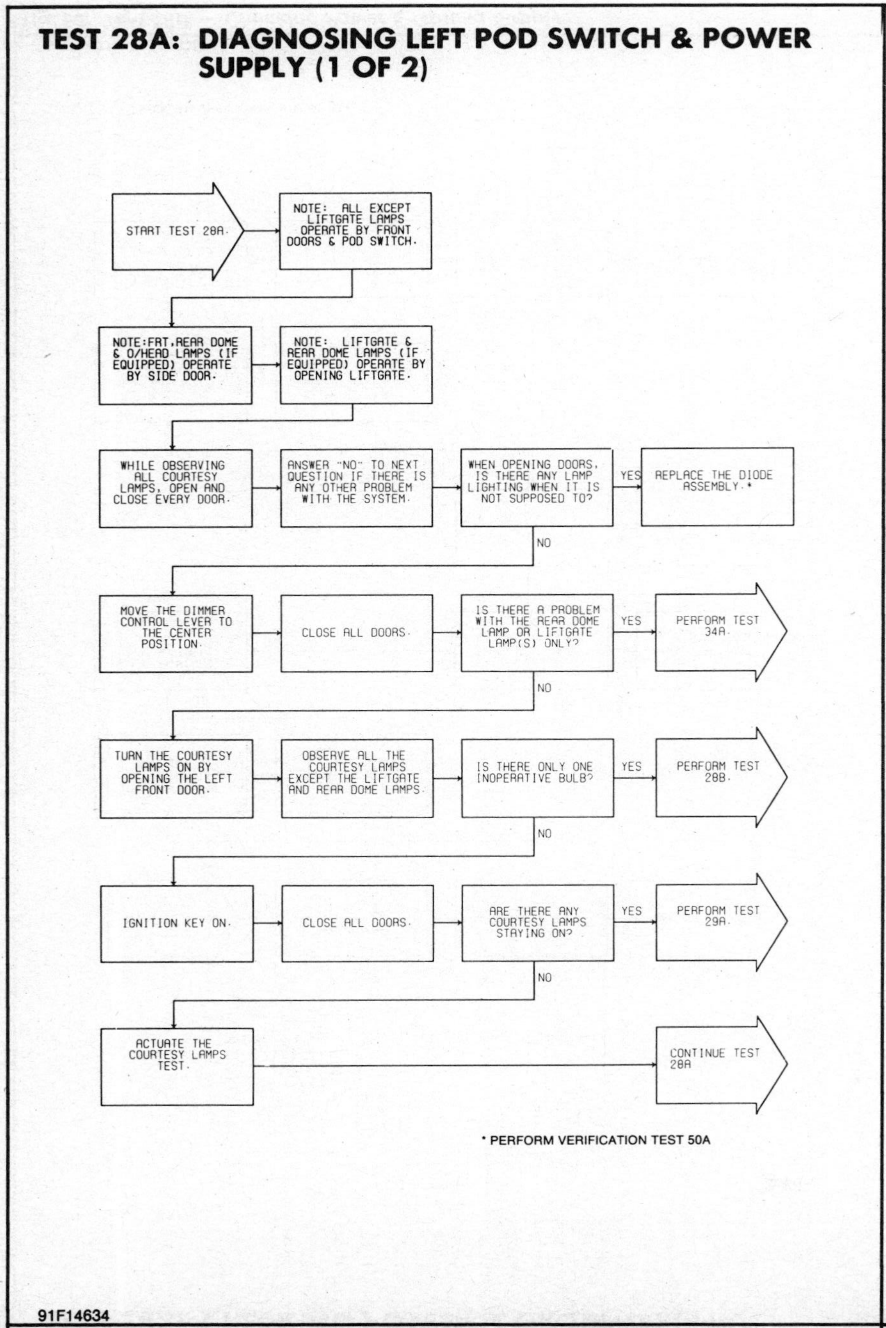
TEST 28A: DIAGNOSING LEFT POD SWITCH & POWER SUPPLY (1 OF 2)
START TEST 28A.
NOTE: ALL EXCEPT LIFTGATE LAMPS OPERATE BY FRONT DOORS & POD SWITCH.
NOTE: FRT, REAR DOME & O/HEAD LAMPS (IF EQUIPPED) OPERATE BY SIDE DOOR.
NOTE: LIFTGATE & REAR DOME LAMPS (IF EQUIPPED) OPERATE BY OPENING LIFTGATE.
WHILE OBSERVING ALL COURTESY LAMPS, OPEN AND CLOSE EVERY DOOR.
ANSWER "NO" TO NEXT QUESTION IF THERE IS ANY OTHER PROBLEM WITH THE SYSTEM.
WHEN OPENING DOORS, IS THERE ANY LAMP LIGHTING WHEN IT IS NOT SUPPOSED TO?
YES
REPLACE THE DIODE ASSEMBLY.*
NO
MOVE THE DIMMER CONTROL LEVER TO THE CENTER POSITION.
CLOSE ALL DOORS.
IS THERE A PROBLEM WITH THE REAR DOME LAMP OR LIFTGATE LAMP(S) ONLY?
YES
PERFORM TEST 34A.
NO
TURN THE COURTESY LAMPS ON BY OPENING THE LEFT FRONT DOOR.
OBSERVE ALL THE COURTESY LAMPS EXCEPT THE LIFTGATE AND REAR DOME LAMPS.
IS THERE ONLY ONE INOPERATIVE BULB?
YES
PERFORM TEST 28B.
NO
IGNITION KEY ON.
CLOSE ALL DOORS.
ARE THERE ANY COURTESY LAMPS STAYING ON?
YES
PERFORM TEST 29A.
NO
ACTUATE THE COURTESY LAMPS TEST.
CONTINUE TEST 28A
* PERFORM VERIFICATION TEST 50A
91F14634

Fig. 53: Test 28A – Diagnosing Left Pod Switch & Power Supply (1 of 2)

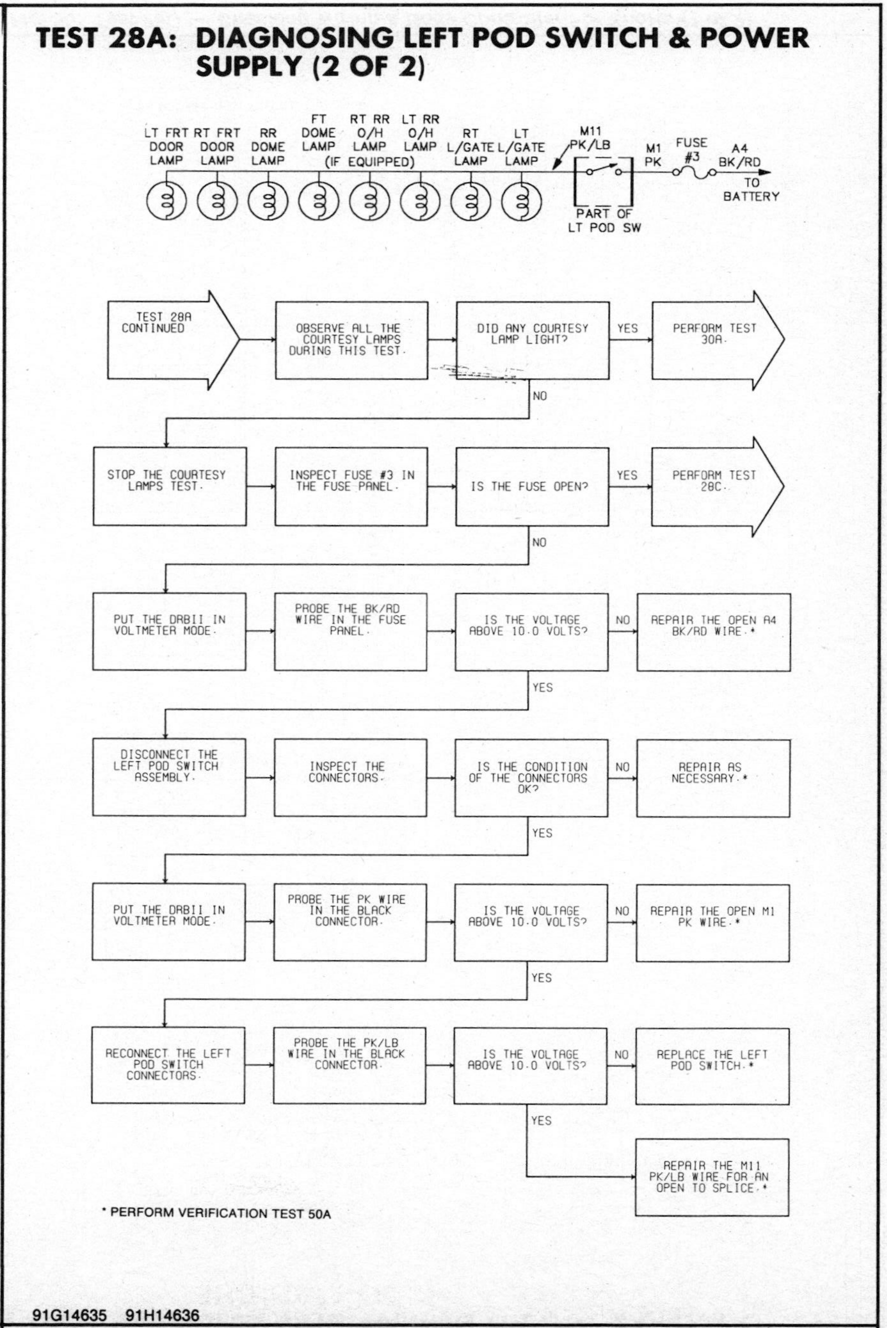
TEST 28A: DIAGNOSING LEFT POD SWITCH & POWER SUPPLY (2 OF 2)
LT FRT DOOR LAMP
RT FRT DOOR LAMP
RR DOME LAMP
FT DOME LAMP
RT RR O/H LAMP
LT RR O/H LAMP
(IF EQUIPPED)
RT L/GATE LAMP
LT L/GATE LAMP
M11 PK/LB
PART OF LT POD SW
M1 PK
FUSE #3
A4 BK/RD
TO BATTERY
TEST 28A CONTINUED
OBSERVE ALL THE COURTESY LAMPS DURING THIS TEST.
DID ANY COURTESY LAMP LIGHT?
YES
PERFORM TEST 30A.
NO
STOP THE COURTESY LAMPS TEST.
INSPECT FUSE #3 IN THE FUSE PANEL.
IS THE FUSE OPEN?
YES
PERFORM TEST 28C.
NO
PUT THE DRBII IN VOLTMETER MODE.
PROBE THE BK/RD WIRE IN THE FUSE PANEL.
IS THE VOLTAGE ABOVE 10.0 VOLTS?
NO
REPAIR THE OPEN A4 BK/RD WIRE.*
YES
DISCONNECT THE LEFT POD SWITCH ASSEMBLY.
INSPECT THE CONNECTORS.
IS THE CONDITION OF THE CONNECTORS OK?
NO
REPAIR AS NECESSARY.*
YES
PUT THE DRBII IN VOLTMETER MODE.
PROBE THE PK WIRE IN THE BLACK CONNECTOR.
IS THE VOLTAGE ABOVE 10.0 VOLTS?
NO
REPAIR THE OPEN M1 PK WIRE.*
YES
RECONNECT THE LEFT POD SWITCH CONNECTORS.
PROBE THE PK/LB WIRE IN THE BLACK CONNECTOR.
IS THE VOLTAGE ABOVE 10.0 VOLTS?
NO
REPLACE THE LEFT POD SWITCH.*
YES
REPAIR THE M11 PK/LB WIRE FOR AN OPEN TO SPLICE.*
* PERFORM VERIFICATION TEST 50A
91G14635 91H14636

Fig. 54: Test 28A – Diagnosing Left Pod Switch & Power Supply (2 of 2)

1991 ENGINE PERFORMANCE
Body Control Computer (Cont.)

TEST 28B: CHECKING POWER & GROUND SUPPLY

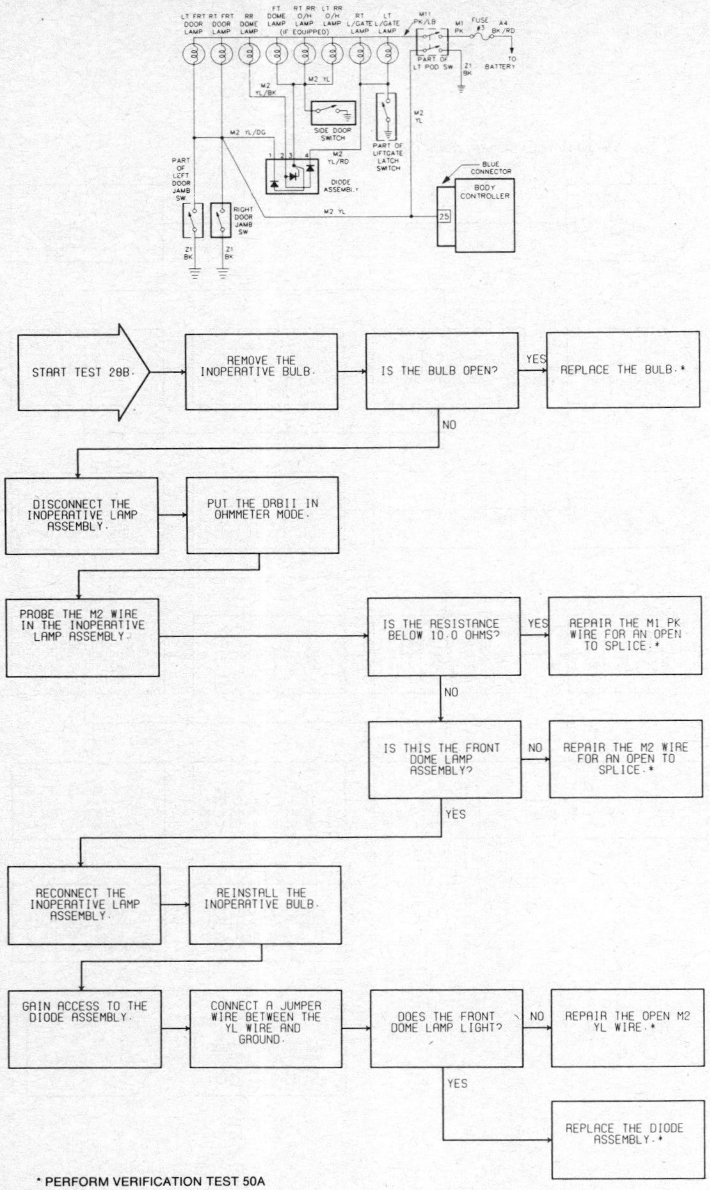
LT FRT DOOR LAMP
RT FRT DOOR LAMP
RR DOME LAMP
FT DOME LAMP
RT RR O/H LAMP
LT RR O/H LAMP
(IF EQUIPPED)
RT L/GATE LAMP
LT L/GATE LAMP
M11 PK/LB
M1 PK
FUSE #3
A4 BK/RD
TO BATTERY
PART OF LT POD SW
Z1 BK
M2 YL/BK
M2 YL
SIDE DOOR SWITCH
PART OF LIFTGATE LATCH SWITCH
M2 YL/DG
M2 YL/RD
DIODE ASSEMBLY
BLUE CONNECTOR
BODY CONTROLLER
25
PART OF LEFT DOOR JAMB SW
RIGHT DOOR JAMB SW
START TEST 28B.
REMOVE THE INOPERATIVE BULB.
IS THE BULB OPEN?
YES
REPLACE THE BULB.*
NO
DISCONNECT THE INOPERATIVE LAMP ASSEMBLY.
PUT THE DRBII IN OHMMETER MODE.
PROBE THE M2 WIRE IN THE INOPERATIVE LAMP ASSEMBLY.
IS THE RESISTANCE BELOW 10.0 OHMS?
YES
REPAIR THE M1 PK WIRE FOR AN OPEN TO SPLICE.*
NO
IS THIS THE FRONT DOME LAMP ASSEMBLY?
NO
REPAIR THE M2 WIRE FOR AN OPEN TO SPLICE.*
YES
RECONNECT THE INOPERATIVE LAMP ASSEMBLY.
REINSTALL THE INOPERATIVE BULB.
GAIN ACCESS TO THE DIODE ASSEMBLY.
CONNECT A JUMPER WIRE BETWEEN THE YL WIRE AND GROUND.
DOES THE FRONT DOME LAMP LIGHT?
NO
REPAIR THE OPEN M2 YL WIRE.*
YES
REPLACE THE DIODE ASSEMBLY.*

* PERFORM VERIFICATION TEST 50A

91I14637 91J14638

Fig. 55: Test 28B – Checking Power & Ground Supply

TEST 28C: CHECKING WIRING & BODY CONTROLLER FOR SHORTS (1 OF 2)

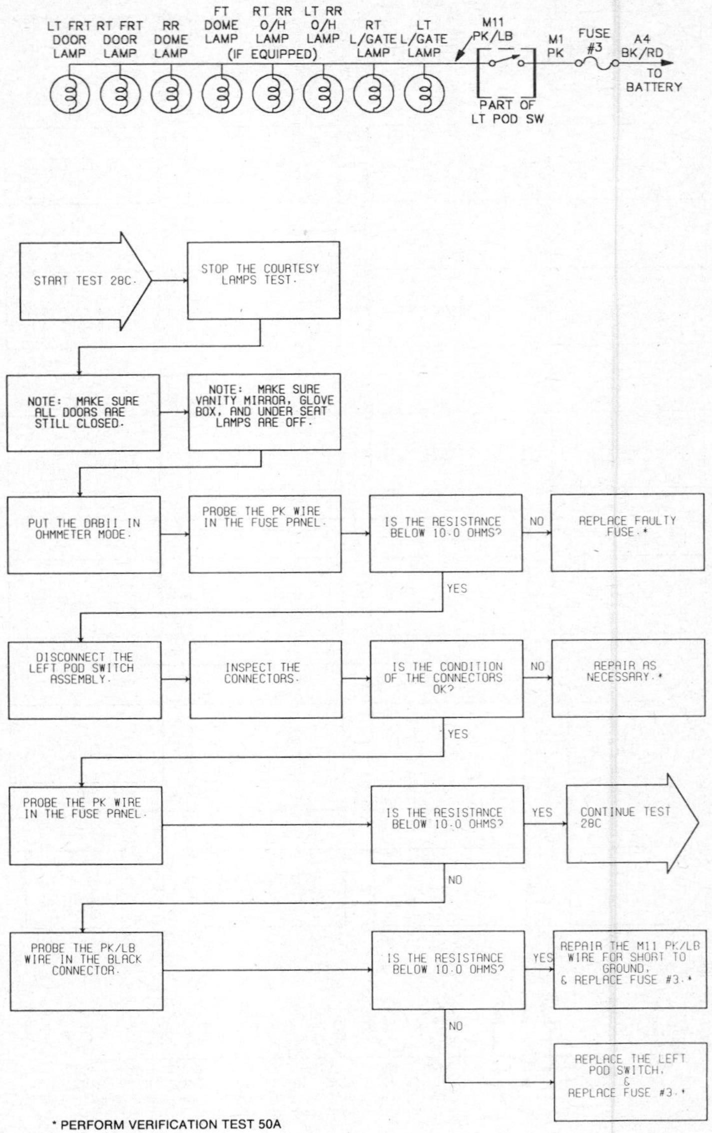
LT FRT DOOR LAMP
RT FRT DOOR LAMP
RR DOME LAMP
FT DOME LAMP
RT RR O/H LAMP
LT RR O/H LAMP
(IF EQUIPPED)
RT L/GATE LAMP
LT L/GATE LAMP
M11 PK/LB
PART OF LT POD SW
M1 PK
FUSE #3
A4 BK/RD
TO BATTERY
START TEST 28C.
STOP THE COURTESY LAMPS TEST.
NOTE: MAKE SURE ALL DOORS ARE STILL CLOSED.
NOTE: MAKE SURE VANITY MIRROR, GLOVE BOX, AND UNDER SEAT LAMPS ARE OFF.
PUT THE DRBII IN OHMMETER MODE.
PROBE THE PK WIRE IN THE FUSE PANEL.
IS THE RESISTANCE BELOW 10.0 OHMS?
NO
REPLACE FAULTY FUSE.*
YES
DISCONNECT THE LEFT POD SWITCH ASSEMBLY.
INSPECT THE CONNECTORS.
IS THE CONDITION OF THE CONNECTORS OK?
NO
REPAIR AS NECESSARY.*
YES
PROBE THE PK WIRE IN THE FUSE PANEL.
IS THE RESISTANCE BELOW 10.0 OHMS?
YES
CONTINUE TEST 28C
NO
PROBE THE PK/LB WIRE IN THE BLACK CONNECTOR.
IS THE RESISTANCE BELOW 10.0 OHMS?
YES
REPAIR THE M11 PK/LB WIRE FOR SHORT TO GROUND, & REPLACE FUSE #3.*
NO
REPLACE THE LEFT POD SWITCH, & REPLACE FUSE #3.*

* PERFORM VERIFICATION TEST 50A

91G14635 91A14639

Fig. 56: Test 28C – Checking Wiring & Body Controller For Shorts (1 of 2)

TEST 28C: CHECKING WIRING & BODY CONTROLLER FOR SHORTS (2 OF 2)

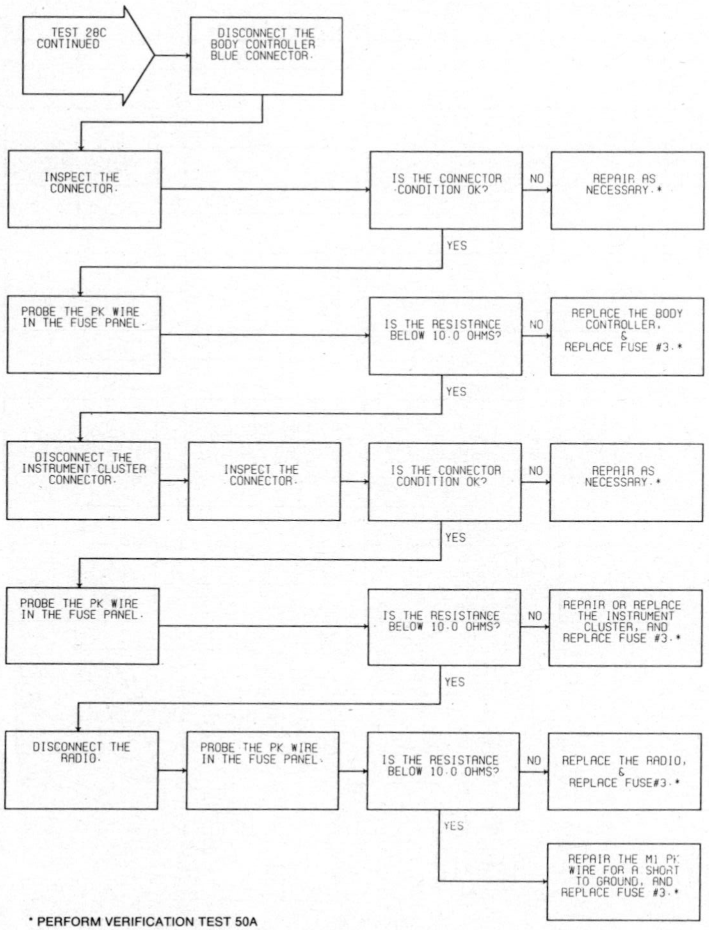
TEST 28C CONTINUED
DISCONNECT THE BODY CONTROLLER BLUE CONNECTOR.
INSPECT THE CONNECTOR.
IS THE CONNECTOR CONDITION OK?
NO
REPAIR AS NECESSARY.*
YES
PROBE THE PK WIRE IN THE FUSE PANEL.
IS THE RESISTANCE BELOW 10.0 OHMS?
NO
REPLACE THE BODY CONTROLLER, & REPLACE FUSE #3.*
YES
DISCONNECT THE INSTRUMENT CLUSTER CONNECTOR.
INSPECT THE CONNECTOR.
IS THE CONNECTOR CONDITION OK?
NO
REPAIR AS NECESSARY.*
YES
PROBE THE PK WIRE IN THE FUSE PANEL.
IS THE RESISTANCE BELOW 10.0 OHMS?
NO
REPAIR OR REPLACE THE INSTRUMENT CLUSTER, AND REPLACE FUSE #3.*
YES
DISCONNECT THE RADIO.
PROBE THE PK WIRE IN THE FUSE PANEL.
IS THE RESISTANCE BELOW 10.0 OHMS?
NO
REPLACE THE RADIO, & REPLACE FUSE#3.*
YES
REPAIR THE M1 PK WIRE FOR A SHORT TO GROUND, AND REPLACE FUSE #3.*

* PERFORM VERIFICATION TEST 50A

91D14640

Fig. 57: Test 28C – Checking Wiring & Body Controller For Shorts (2 of 2)

TEST 29A: CHECKING BODY CONTROLLER & WIRING FOR SHORTS TO GROUND

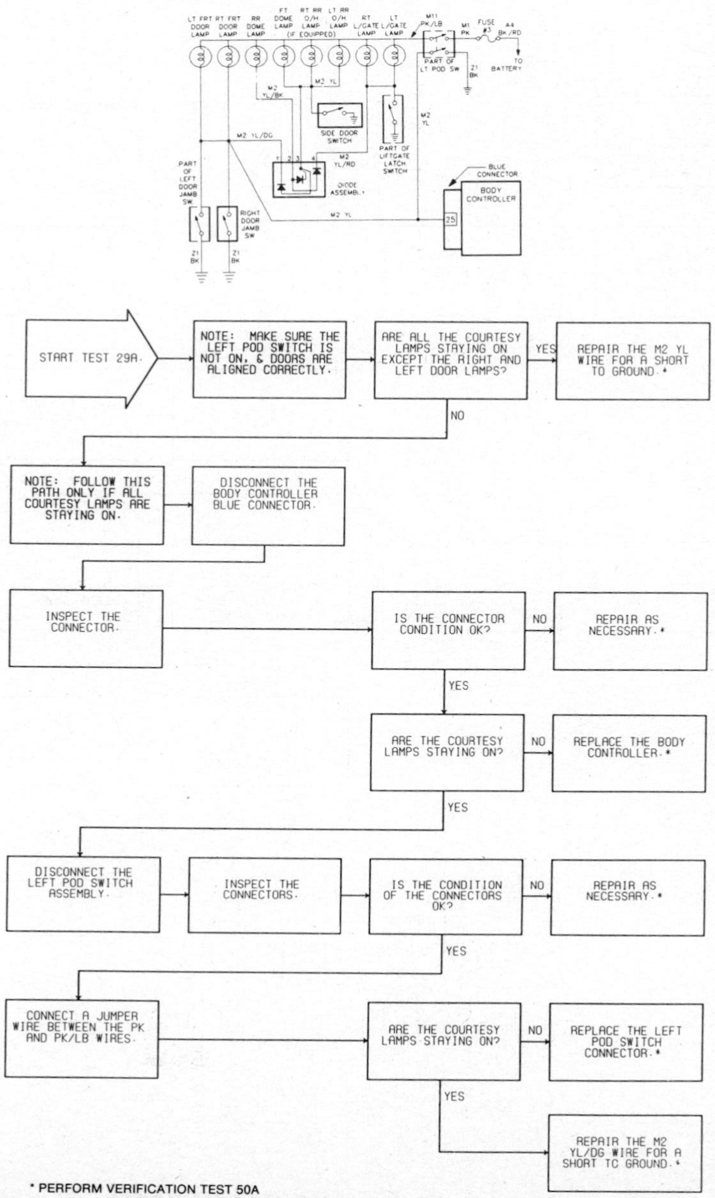
SIDE DOOR SWITCH
DIODE ASSEMBLY
BLUE CONNECTOR
BODY CONTROLLER
TO BATTERY
START TEST 29A.
NOTE: MAKE SURE THE LEFT POD SWITCH IS NOT ON, & DOORS ARE ALIGNED CORRECTLY.
ARE ALL THE COURTESY LAMPS STAYING ON EXCEPT THE RIGHT AND LEFT DOOR LAMPS?
YES
REPAIR THE M2 YL WIRE FOR A SHORT TO GROUND.*
NO
NOTE: FOLLOW THIS PATH ONLY IF ALL COURTESY LAMPS ARE STAYING ON.
DISCONNECT THE BODY CONTROLLER BLUE CONNECTOR.
INSPECT THE CONNECTOR.
IS THE CONNECTOR CONDITION OK?
NO
REPAIR AS NECESSARY.*
YES
ARE THE COURTESY LAMPS STAYING ON?
NO
REPLACE THE BODY CONTROLLER.*
YES
DISCONNECT THE LEFT POD SWITCH ASSEMBLY.
INSPECT THE CONNECTORS.
IS THE CONDITION OF THE CONNECTORS OK?
NO
REPAIR AS NECESSARY.*
YES
CONNECT A JUMPER WIRE BETWEEN THE PK AND PK/LB WIRES.
ARE THE COURTESY LAMPS STAYING ON?
NO
REPLACE THE LEFT POD SWITCH CONNECTOR.*
YES
REPAIR THE M2 YL/DG WIRE FOR A SHORT TO GROUND.*

* PERFORM VERIFICATION TEST 50A

91I14637 91E14641

Fig. 58: Test 29A – Checking Body Controller & Wiring For Shorts To Ground

1991 ENGINE PERFORMANCE
Body Control Computer (Cont.)

TEST 30A: CHECKING LEFT FRONT DOOR JAMB SWITCH & WIRING FOR OPEN

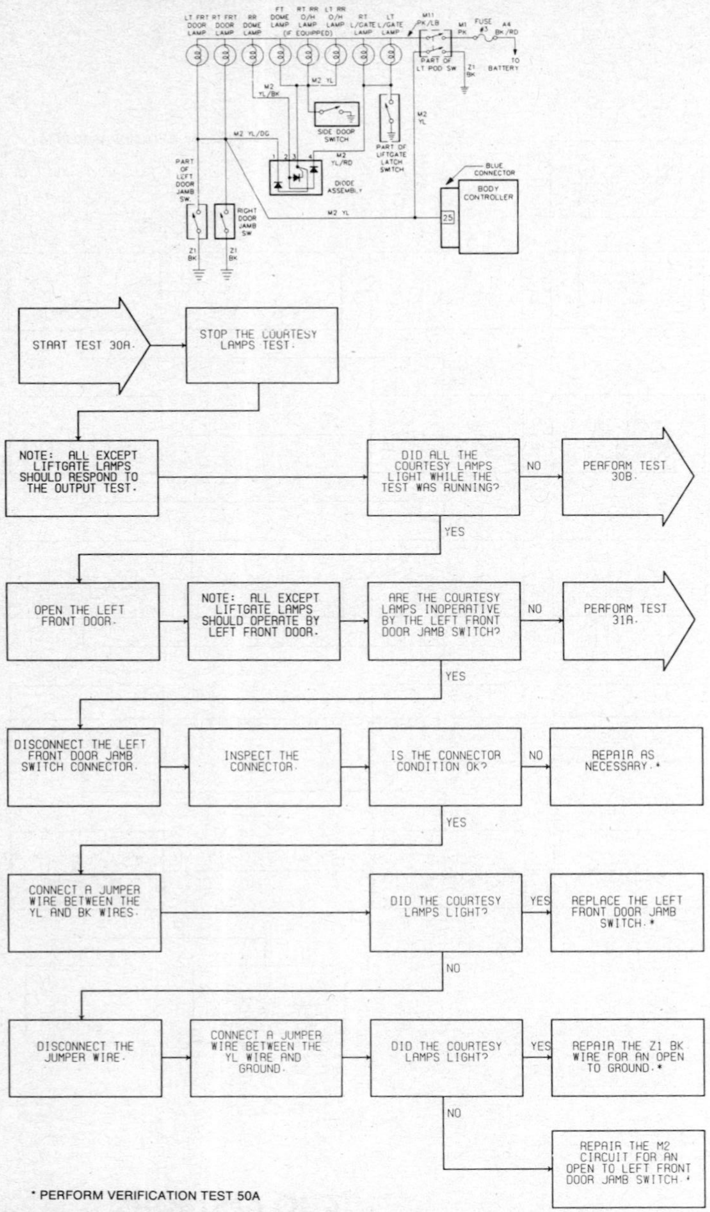
START TEST 30A.
STOP THE COURTESY LAMPS TEST.
NOTE: ALL EXCEPT LIFTGATE LAMPS SHOULD RESPOND TO THE OUTPUT TEST.
DID ALL THE COURTESY LAMPS LIGHT WHILE THE TEST WAS RUNNING?
NO
PERFORM TEST 30B.
YES
OPEN THE LEFT FRONT DOOR.
NOTE: ALL EXCEPT LIFTGATE LAMPS SHOULD OPERATE BY LEFT FRONT DOOR.
ARE THE COURTESY LAMPS INOPERATIVE BY THE LEFT FRONT DOOR JAMB SWITCH?
NO
PERFORM TEST 31A.
YES
DISCONNECT THE LEFT FRONT DOOR JAMB SWITCH CONNECTOR.
INSPECT THE CONNECTOR.
IS THE CONNECTOR CONDITION OK?
NO
REPAIR AS NECESSARY.*
YES
CONNECT A JUMPER WIRE BETWEEN THE YL AND BK WIRES.
DID THE COURTESY LAMPS LIGHT?
YES
REPLACE THE LEFT FRONT DOOR JAMB SWITCH.*
NO
DISCONNECT THE JUMPER WIRE.
CONNECT A JUMPER WIRE BETWEEN THE YL WIRE AND GROUND.
DID THE COURTESY LAMPS LIGHT?
YES
REPAIR THE Z1 BK WIRE FOR AN OPEN TO GROUND.*
NO
REPAIR THE M2 CIRCUIT FOR AN OPEN TO LEFT FRONT DOOR JAMB SWITCH.*

* PERFORM VERIFICATION TEST 50A

91I14637 91F14642

Fig. 59: Test 30A – Checking Left Front Door Jamb Switch & Wiring For Open

TEST 30B: CHECKING GROUND SUPPLY & DIODE ASSEMBLY FOR OPEN

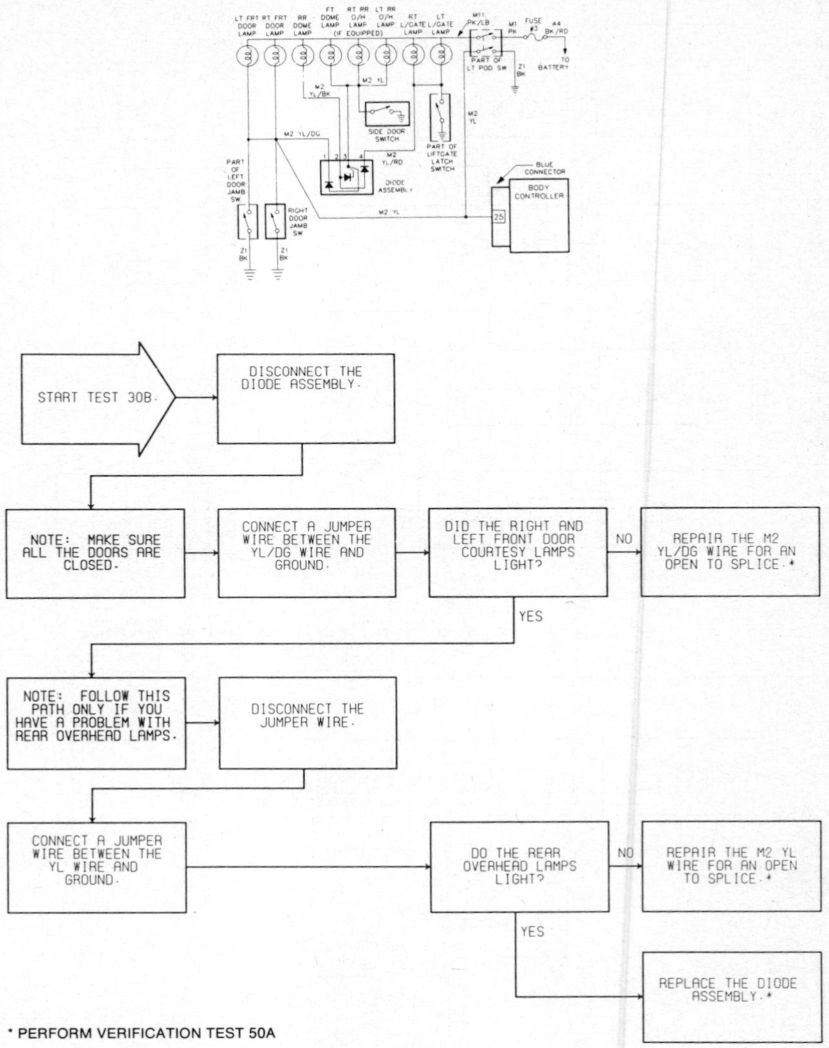
START TEST 30B.
DISCONNECT THE DIODE ASSEMBLY.
NOTE: MAKE SURE ALL THE DOORS ARE CLOSED.
CONNECT A JUMPER WIRE BETWEEN THE YL/DG WIRE AND GROUND.
DID THE RIGHT AND LEFT FRONT DOOR COURTESY LAMPS LIGHT?
NO
REPAIR THE M2 YL/DG WIRE FOR AN OPEN TO SPLICE.*
YES
NOTE: FOLLOW THIS PATH ONLY IF YOU HAVE A PROBLEM WITH REAR OVERHEAD LAMPS.
DISCONNECT THE JUMPER WIRE.
CONNECT A JUMPER WIRE BETWEEN THE YL WIRE AND GROUND.
DO THE REAR OVERHEAD LAMPS LIGHT?
NO
REPAIR THE M2 YL WIRE FOR AN OPEN TO SPLICE.*
YES
REPLACE THE DIODE ASSEMBLY.*

* PERFORM VERIFICATION TEST 50A

91I14637 91G14643

Fig. 60: Test 30B – Checking Ground Supply & Diode Assembly For Open

TEST 31A: CHECKING RIGHT FRONT DOOR JAMB SWITCH & WIRING FOR OPEN

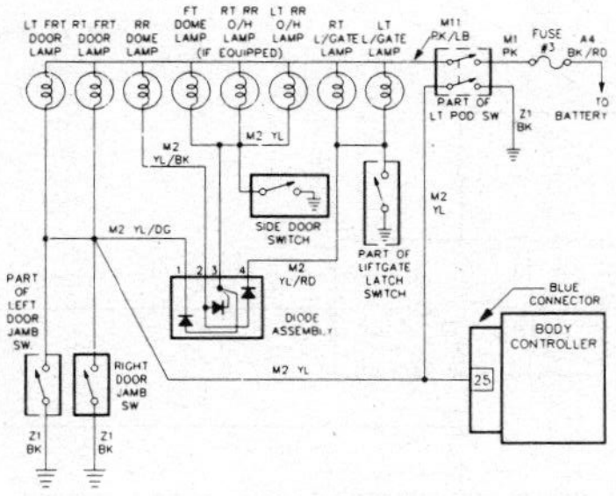
LT FRT DOOR LAMP
RT FRT DOOR LAMP
RR DOME LAMP
FT DOME LAMP
RT RR O/H LAMP
LT RR O/H LAMP
(IF EQUIPPED)
RT L/GATE LAMP
LT L/GATE LAMP
M11 PK/LB
M1 PK
FUSE #3
A4 BK/RD
TO BATTERY
PART OF LT POD SW
Z1 BK
M2 YL/BK
M2 YL
SIDE DOOR SWITCH
PART OF LIFTGATE LATCH SWITCH
M2 YL/DG
M2 YL/RD
DIODE ASSEMBLY
BLUE CONNECTOR
BODY CONTROLLER
25
PART OF LEFT DOOR JAMB SW
RIGHT DOOR JAMB SW

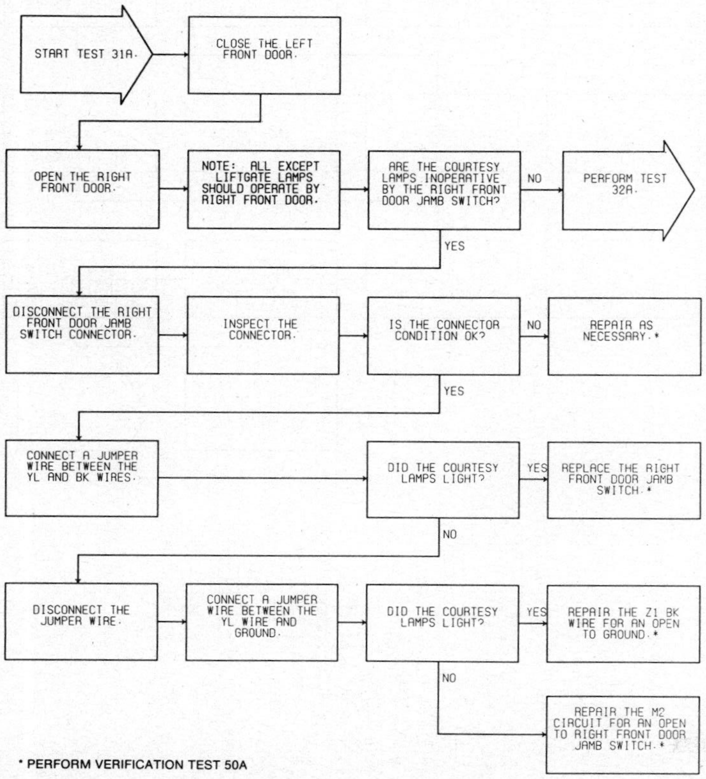
START TEST 31A.
CLOSE THE LEFT FRONT DOOR.
OPEN THE RIGHT FRONT DOOR.
NOTE: ALL EXCEPT LIFTGATE LAMPS SHOULD OPERATE BY RIGHT FRONT DOOR.
ARE THE COURTESY LAMPS INOPERATIVE BY THE RIGHT FRONT DOOR JAMB SWITCH?
NO
PERFORM TEST 32A.
YES
DISCONNECT THE RIGHT FRONT DOOR JAMB SWITCH CONNECTOR.
INSPECT THE CONNECTOR.
IS THE CONNECTOR CONDITION OK?
NO
REPAIR AS NECESSARY.*
YES
CONNECT A JUMPER WIRE BETWEEN THE YL AND BK WIRES.
DID THE COURTESY LAMPS LIGHT?
YES
REPLACE THE RIGHT FRONT DOOR JAMB SWITCH.*
NO
DISCONNECT THE JUMPER WIRE.
CONNECT A JUMPER WIRE BETWEEN THE YL WIRE AND GROUND.
DID THE COURTESY LAMPS LIGHT?
YES
REPAIR THE Z1 BK WIRE FOR AN OPEN TO GROUND.*
NO
REPAIR THE M2 CIRCUIT FOR AN OPEN TO RIGHT FRONT DOOR JAMB SWITCH.*

* PERFORM VERIFICATION TEST 50A

91I14637 91H14644

Fig. 61: Test 31A – Checking Left Front Door Jamb Switch & Wiring For Open

TEST 32A: CHECKING SIDE DOOR JAMB SWITCH & WIRING FOR OPEN

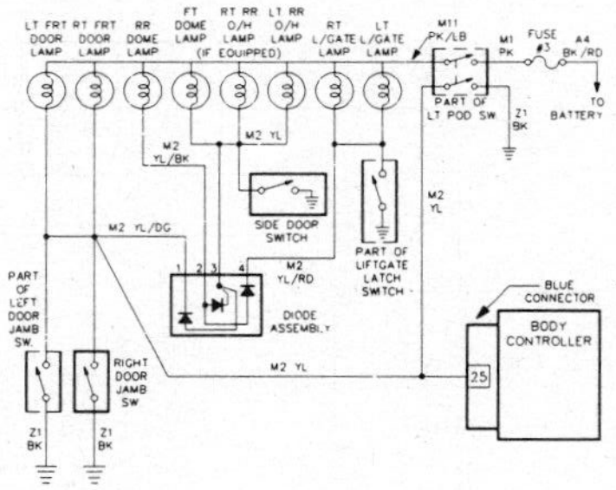
LT FRT DOOR LAMP
RT FRT DOOR LAMP
RR DOME LAMP
FT DOME LAMP
RT RR O/H LAMP
LT RR O/H LAMP
(IF EQUIPPED)
RT L/GATE LAMP
LT L/GATE LAMP
M11 PK/LB
M1 PK
FUSE #3
A4 BK/RD
TO BATTERY
PART OF LT POD SW
Z1 BK
M2 YL/BK
M2 YL
SIDE DOOR SWITCH
PART OF LIFTGATE LATCH SWITCH
M2 YL/DG
M2 YL/RD
DIODE ASSEMBLY
BLUE CONNECTOR
BODY CONTROLLER
25
PART OF LEFT DOOR JAMB SW
RIGHT DOOR JAMB SW

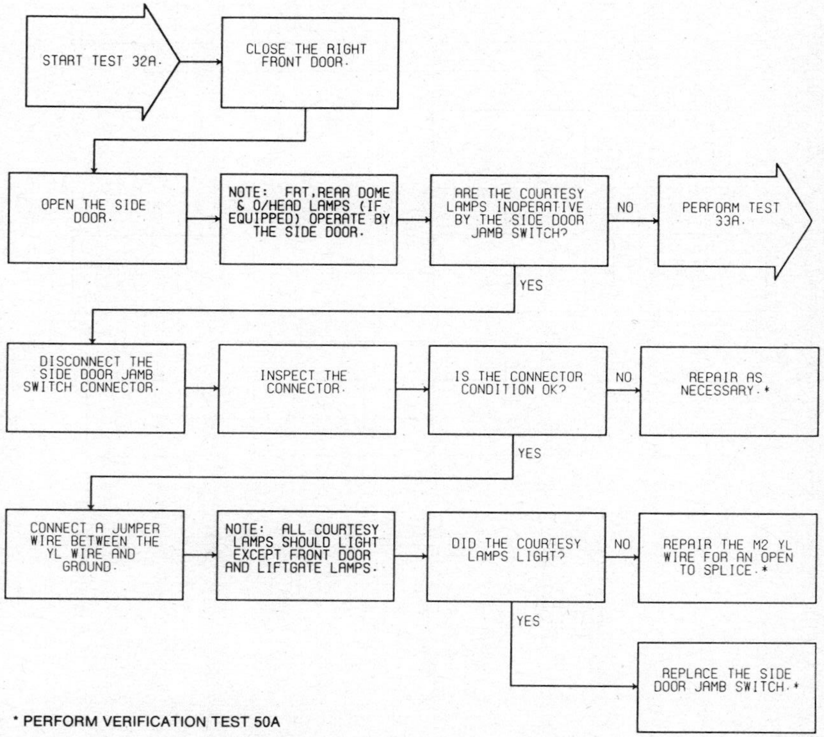
START TEST 32A.
CLOSE THE RIGHT FRONT DOOR.
OPEN THE SIDE DOOR.
NOTE: FRT,REAR DOME & O/HEAD LAMPS (IF EQUIPPED) OPERATE BY THE SIDE DOOR.
ARE THE COURTESY LAMPS INOPERATIVE BY THE SIDE DOOR JAMB SWITCH?
NO
PERFORM TEST 33A.
YES
DISCONNECT THE SIDE DOOR JAMB SWITCH CONNECTOR.
INSPECT THE CONNECTOR.
IS THE CONNECTOR CONDITION OK?
NO
REPAIR AS NECESSARY.*
YES
CONNECT A JUMPER WIRE BETWEEN THE YL WIRE AND GROUND.
NOTE: ALL COURTESY LAMPS SHOULD LIGHT EXCEPT FRONT DOOR AND LIFTGATE LAMPS.
DID THE COURTESY LAMPS LIGHT?
NO
REPAIR THE M2 YL WIRE FOR AN OPEN TO SPLICE.*
YES
REPLACE THE SIDE DOOR JAMB SWITCH.*

* PERFORM VERIFICATION TEST 50A

91I14637 91I14645

Fig. 62: Test 32A – Checking Side Door Jamb Switch & Wiring For Open

1991 ENGINE PERFORMANCE
Body Control Computer (Cont.)

TEST 33A: CHECKING LEFT POD SWITCH & FOR OPEN GROUND

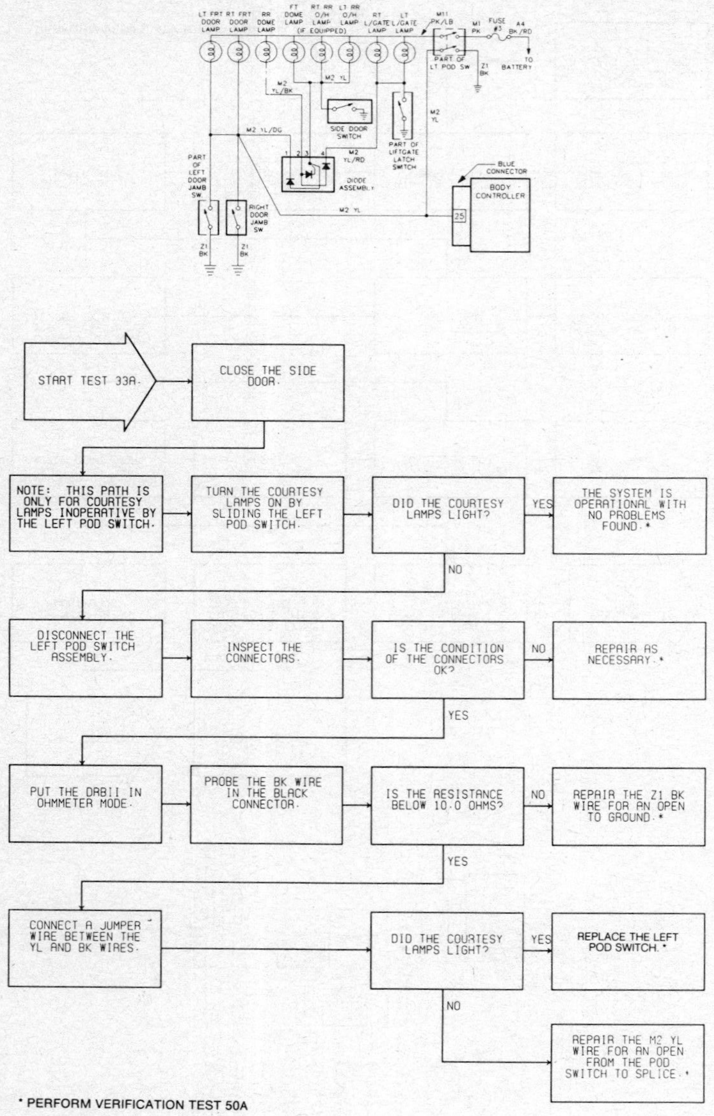
START TEST 33A.
CLOSE THE SIDE DOOR.
NOTE: THIS PATH IS ONLY FOR COURTESY LAMPS INOPERATIVE BY THE LEFT POD SWITCH.
TURN THE COURTESY LAMPS ON BY SLIDING THE LEFT POD SWITCH.
DID THE COURTESY LAMPS LIGHT?
YES
THE SYSTEM IS OPERATIONAL WITH NO PROBLEMS FOUND.*
NO
DISCONNECT THE LEFT POD SWITCH ASSEMBLY.
INSPECT THE CONNECTORS.
IS THE CONDITION OF THE CONNECTORS OK?
NO
REPAIR AS NECESSARY.*
YES
PUT THE DRBII IN OHMMETER MODE.
PROBE THE BK WIRE IN THE BLACK CONNECTOR.
IS THE RESISTANCE BELOW 10.0 OHMS?
NO
REPAIR THE Z1 BK WIRE FOR AN OPEN TO GROUND.*
YES
CONNECT A JUMPER WIRE BETWEEN THE YL AND BK WIRES.
DID THE COURTESY LAMPS LIGHT?
YES
REPLACE THE LEFT POD SWITCH.*
NO
REPAIR THE M2 YL WIRE FOR AN OPEN FROM THE POD SWITCH TO SPLICE.*
* PERFORM VERIFICATION TEST 50A

91I14637 91J14646

Fig. 63: Test 33A – Checking Left Pod Switch & For Open Ground

TEST 34A: REPAIRING FAULTY REAR DOME & LIFTGATE LAMPS (1 OF 2)

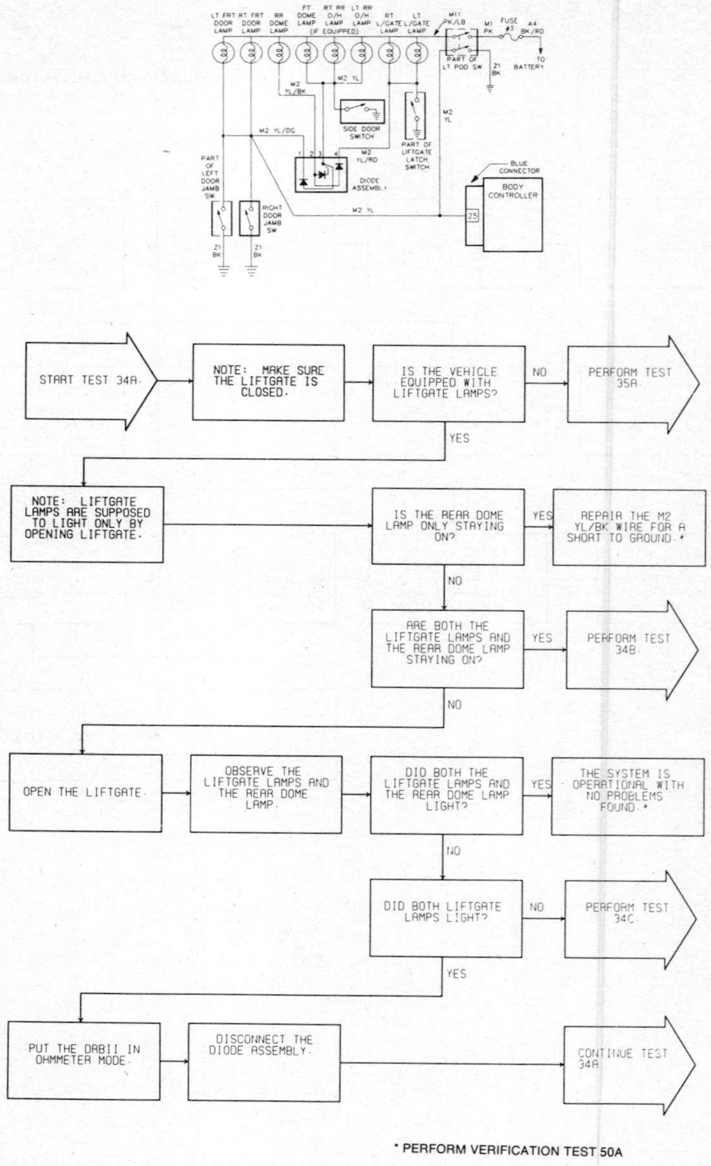
START TEST 34A.
NOTE: MAKE SURE THE LIFTGATE IS CLOSED.
IS THE VEHICLE EQUIPPED WITH LIFTGATE LAMPS?
NO
PERFORM TEST 35A.
YES
NOTE: LIFTGATE LAMPS ARE SUPPOSED TO LIGHT ONLY BY OPENING LIFTGATE.
IS THE REAR DOME LAMP ONLY STAYING ON?
YES
REPAIR THE M2 YL/BK WIRE FOR A SHORT TO GROUND.*
NO
ARE BOTH THE LIFTGATE LAMPS AND THE REAR DOME LAMP STAYING ON?
YES
PERFORM TEST 34B.
NO
OPEN THE LIFTGATE.
OBSERVE THE LIFTGATE LAMPS AND THE REAR DOME LAMP.
DID BOTH THE LIFTGATE LAMPS AND THE REAR DOME LAMP LIGHT?
YES
THE SYSTEM IS OPERATIONAL WITH NO PROBLEMS FOUND.*
NO
DID BOTH LIFTGATE LAMPS LIGHT?
NO
PERFORM TEST 34C.
YES
PUT THE DRBII IN OHMMETER MODE.
DISCONNECT THE DIODE ASSEMBLY.
CONTINUE TEST 34A
* PERFORM VERIFICATION TEST 50A

91I14637 91A14647

Fig. 64: Test 34A – Repairing Faulty Rear Dome & Liftgate Lamps (1 of 2)

TEST 34A: REPAIRING FAULTY REAR DOME & LIFTGATE LAMPS (2 OF 2)

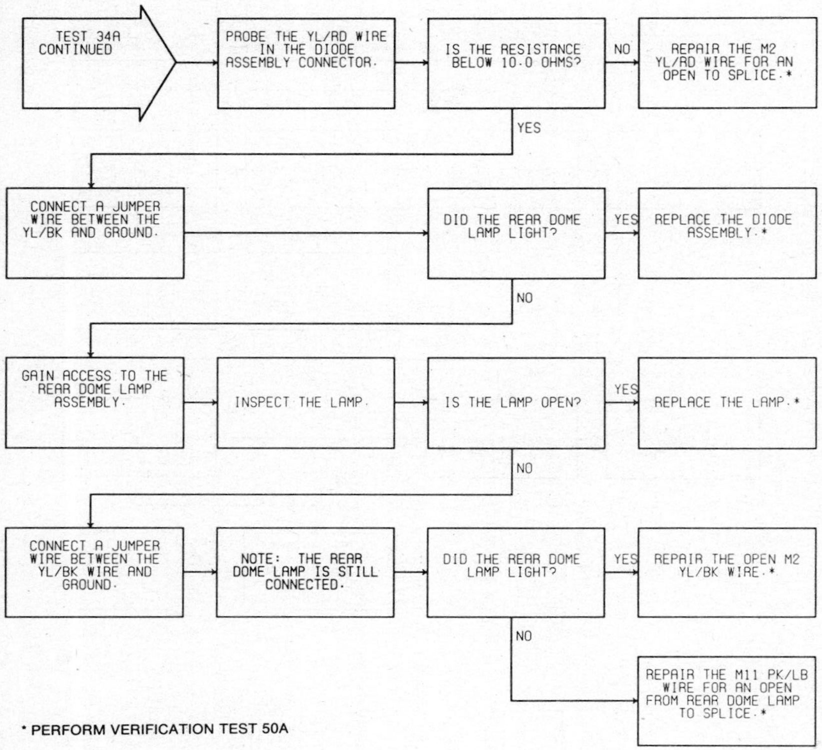
TEST 34A CONTINUED
PROBE THE YL/RD WIRE IN THE DIODE ASSEMBLY CONNECTOR.
IS THE RESISTANCE BELOW 10.0 OHMS?
NO
REPAIR THE M2 YL/RD WIRE FOR AN OPEN TO SPLICE.*
YES
CONNECT A JUMPER WIRE BETWEEN THE YL/BK AND GROUND.
DID THE REAR DOME LAMP LIGHT?
YES
REPLACE THE DIODE ASSEMBLY.*
NO
GAIN ACCESS TO THE REAR DOME LAMP ASSEMBLY.
INSPECT THE LAMP.
IS THE LAMP OPEN?
YES
REPLACE THE LAMP.*
NO
CONNECT A JUMPER WIRE BETWEEN THE YL/BK WIRE AND GROUND.
NOTE: THE REAR DOME LAMP IS STILL CONNECTED.
DID THE REAR DOME LAMP LIGHT?
YES
REPAIR THE OPEN M2 YL/BK WIRE.*
NO
REPAIR THE M11 PK/LB WIRE FOR AN OPEN FROM REAR DOME LAMP TO SPLICE.*

* PERFORM VERIFICATION TEST 50A

91B14648

Fig. 65: Test 34A – Repairing Faulty Rear Dome & Liftgate Lamps (2 of 2)

TEST 34B: CHECKING LIFTGATE LATCH SWITCH & WIRING FOR SHORTS

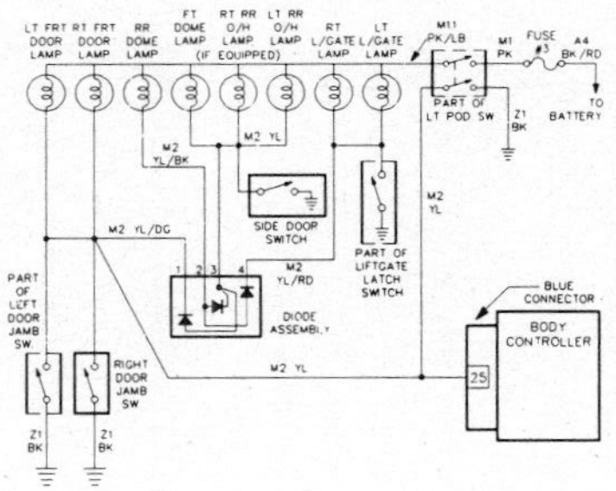

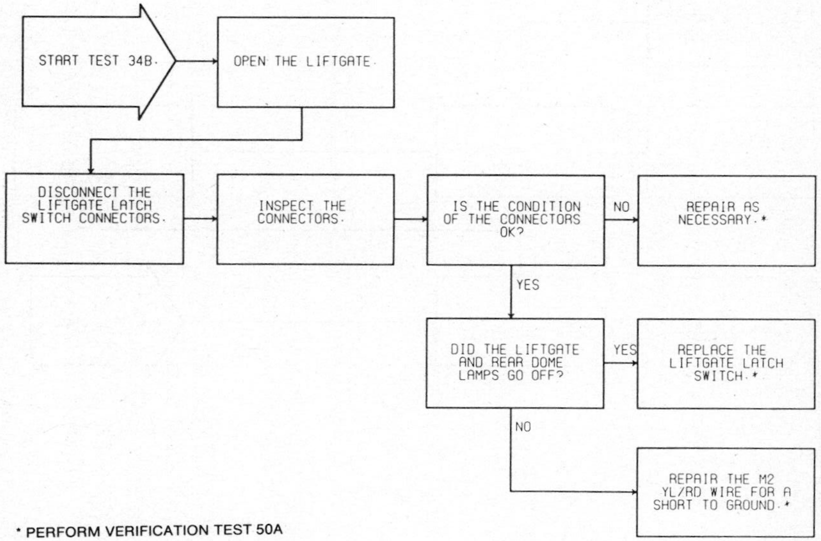
START TEST 34B.
OPEN THE LIFTGATE.
DISCONNECT THE LIFTGATE LATCH SWITCH CONNECTORS.
INSPECT THE CONNECTORS.
IS THE CONDITION OF THE CONNECTORS OK?
NO
REPAIR AS NECESSARY.*
YES
DID THE LIFTGATE AND REAR DOME LAMPS GO OFF?
YES
REPLACE THE LIFTGATE LATCH SWITCH.*
NO
REPAIR THE M2 YL/RD WIRE FOR A SHORT TO GROUND.*

* PERFORM VERIFICATION TEST 50A

91I14637 91C14649

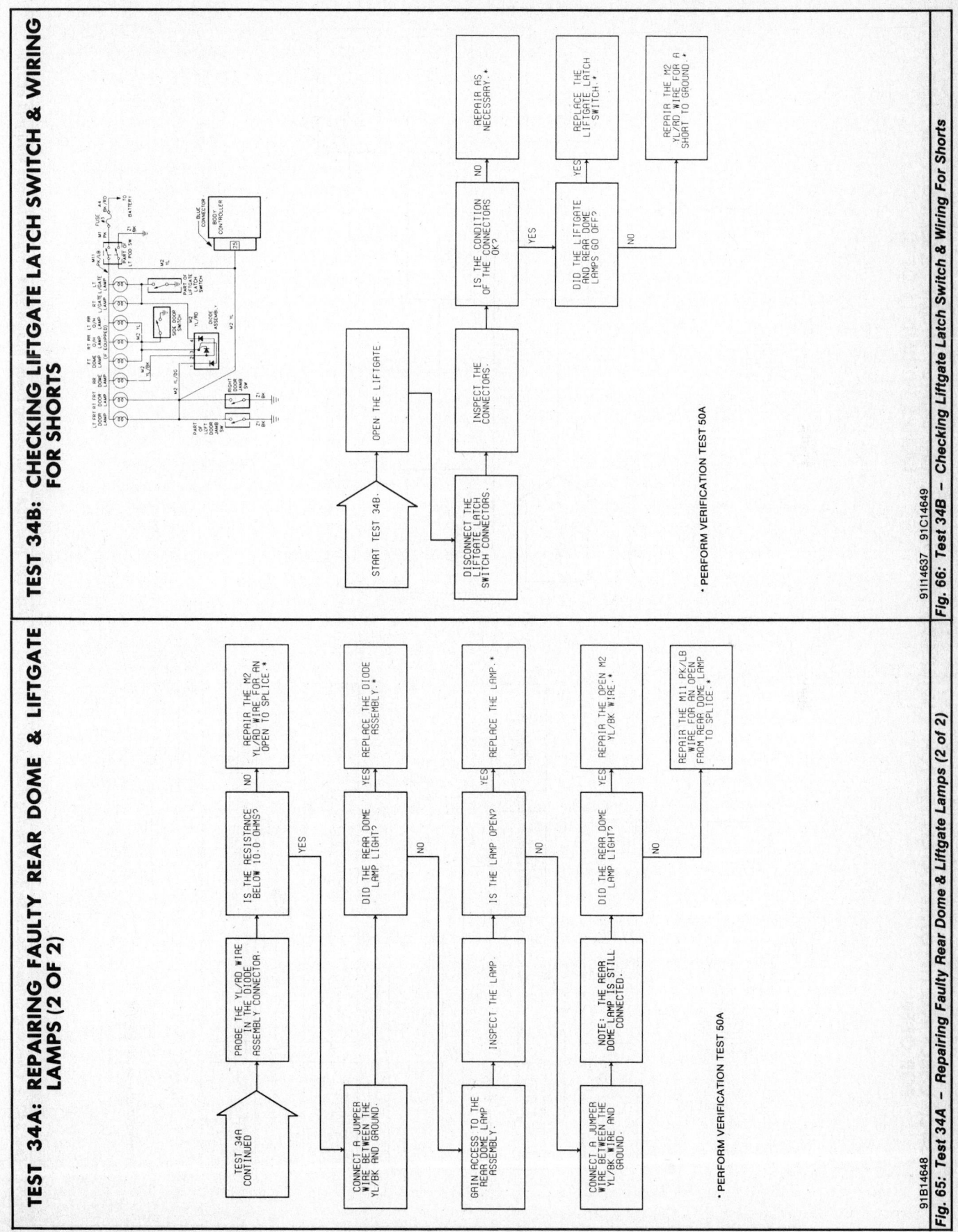

Fig. 66: Test 34B – Checking Liftgate Latch Switch & Wiring For Shorts

1991 ENGINE PERFORMANCE
Body Control Computer (Cont.)

TEST 34C: CHECKING LIFTGATE LATCH SWITCH & WIRING FOR OPEN

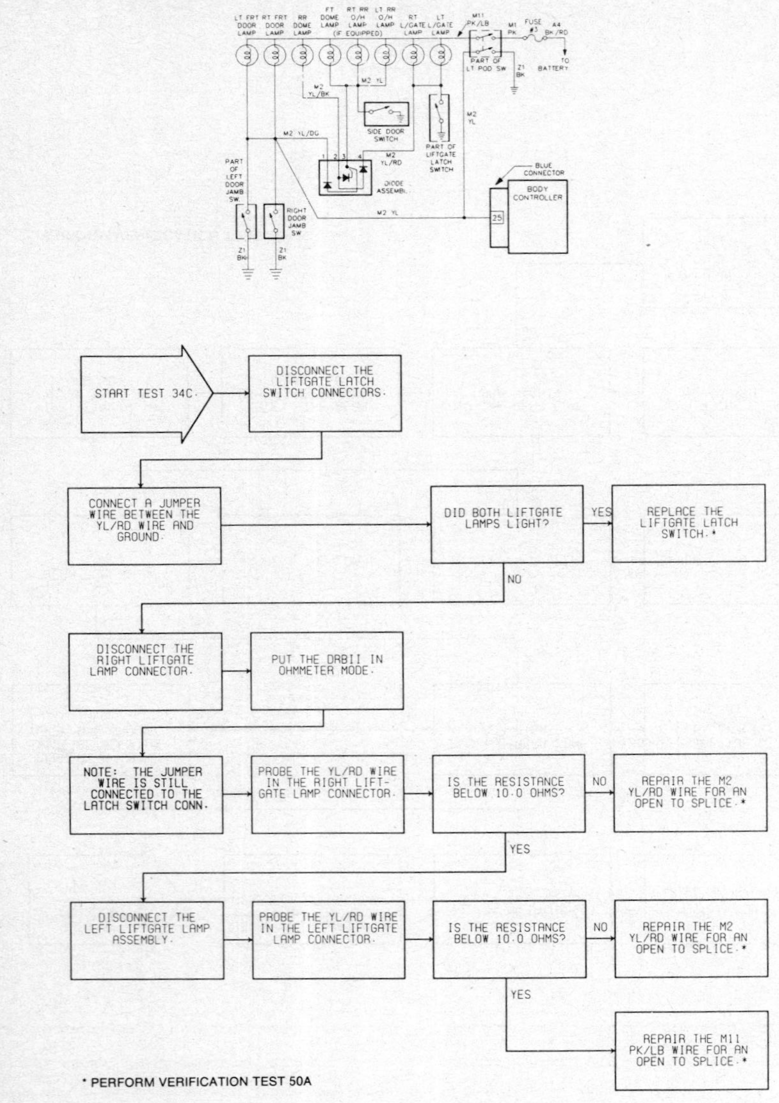
START TEST 34C.
DISCONNECT THE LIFTGATE LATCH SWITCH CONNECTORS.
CONNECT A JUMPER WIRE BETWEEN THE YL/RD WIRE AND GROUND.
DID BOTH LIFTGATE LAMPS LIGHT?
YES
REPLACE THE LIFTGATE LATCH SWITCH.*
NO
DISCONNECT THE RIGHT LIFTGATE LAMP CONNECTOR.
PUT THE DRBII IN OHMMETER MODE.
NOTE: THE JUMPER WIRE IS STILL CONNECTED TO THE LATCH SWITCH CONN.
PROBE THE YL/RD WIRE IN THE RIGHT LIFTGATE LAMP CONNECTOR.
IS THE RESISTANCE BELOW 10.0 OHMS?
NO
REPAIR THE M2 YL/RD WIRE FOR AN OPEN TO SPLICE.*
YES
DISCONNECT THE LEFT LIFTGATE LAMP ASSEMBLY.
PROBE THE YL/RD WIRE IN THE LEFT LIFTGATE LAMP CONNECTOR.
IS THE RESISTANCE BELOW 10.0 OHMS?
NO
REPAIR THE M2 YL/RD WIRE FOR AN OPEN TO SPLICE.*
YES
REPAIR THE M11 PK/LB WIRE FOR AN OPEN TO SPLICE.*

* PERFORM VERIFICATION TEST 50A

91I14637 91G14650

Fig. 67: Test 34C – Checking Liftgate Latch Switch & Wiring For Open

TEST 35A: CHECKING DIODE ASSEMBLY & LIFTGATE LAMPS WIRING (1 OF 3)

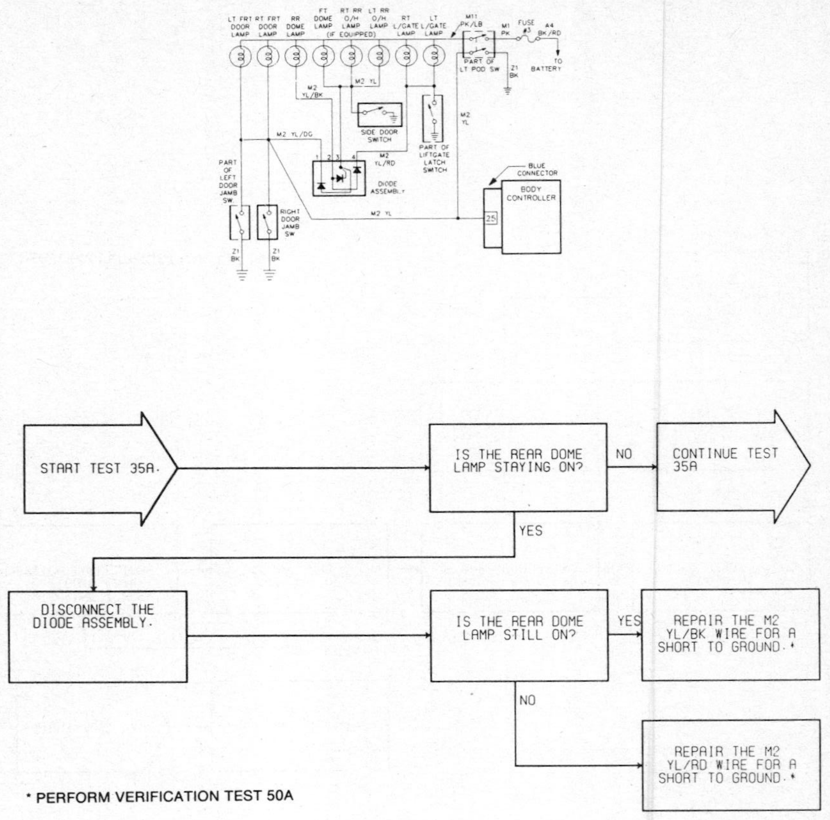
START TEST 35A.
IS THE REAR DOME LAMP STAYING ON?
NO
CONTINUE TEST 35A
YES
DISCONNECT THE DIODE ASSEMBLY.
IS THE REAR DOME LAMP STILL ON?
YES
REPAIR THE M2 YL/BK WIRE FOR A SHORT TO GROUND.*
NO
REPAIR THE M2 YL/RD WIRE FOR A SHORT TO GROUND.*

* PERFORM VERIFICATION TEST 50A

91I14637 91H14651

Fig. 68: Test 35A – Checking Diode Assembly & Liftgate Lamps Wiring (1 of 3)

TEST 35A: CHECKING DIODE ASSEMBLY & LIFTGATE LAMPS WIRING (2 OF 3)

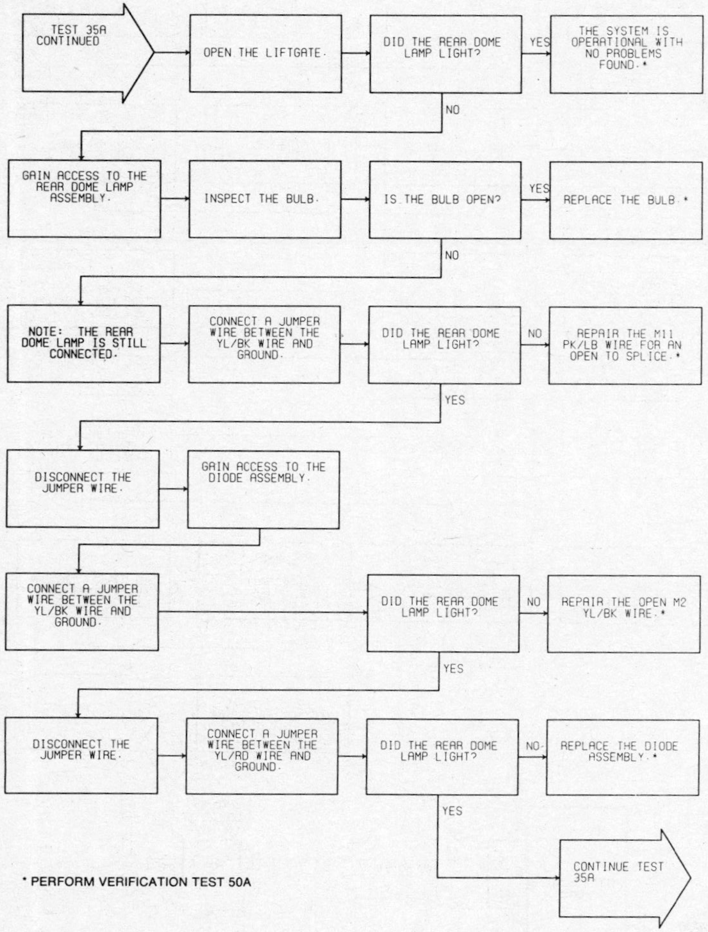
TEST 35A CONTINUED
OPEN THE LIFTGATE.
DID THE REAR DOME LAMP LIGHT?
YES
THE SYSTEM IS OPERATIONAL WITH NO PROBLEMS FOUND.*
NO
GAIN ACCESS TO THE REAR DOME LAMP ASSEMBLY.
INSPECT THE BULB.
IS THE BULB OPEN?
YES
REPLACE THE BULB.*
NO
NOTE: THE REAR DOME LAMP IS STILL CONNECTED.
CONNECT A JUMPER WIRE BETWEEN THE YL/BK WIRE AND GROUND.
DID THE REAR DOME LAMP LIGHT?
NO
REPAIR THE M11 PK/LB WIRE FOR AN OPEN TO SPLICE.*
YES
DISCONNECT THE JUMPER WIRE.
GAIN ACCESS TO THE DIODE ASSEMBLY.
CONNECT A JUMPER WIRE BETWEEN THE YL/BK WIRE AND GROUND.
DID THE REAR DOME LAMP LIGHT?
NO
REPAIR THE OPEN M2 YL/BK WIRE.*
YES
DISCONNECT THE JUMPER WIRE.
CONNECT A JUMPER WIRE BETWEEN THE YL/RD WIRE AND GROUND.
DID THE REAR DOME LAMP LIGHT?
NO
REPLACE THE DIODE ASSEMBLY.*
YES
CONTINUE TEST 35A

* PERFORM VERIFICATION TEST 50A

91I14652

Fig. 69: Test 35A – Checking Diode Assembly & Liftgate Lamps Wiring (2 of 3)

TEST 35A: CHECKING DIODE ASSEMBLY & LIFTGATE LAMPS WIRING (3 OF 3)

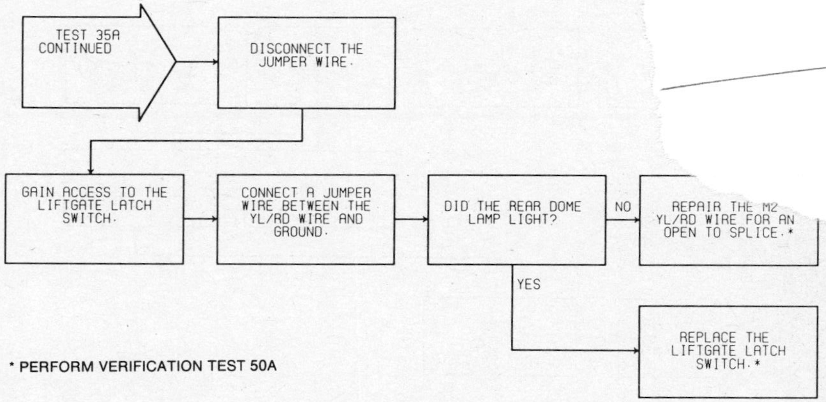
TEST 35A CONTINUED
DISCONNECT THE JUMPER WIRE.
GAIN ACCESS TO THE LIFTGATE LATCH SWITCH.
CONNECT A JUMPER WIRE BETWEEN THE YL/RD WIRE AND GROUND.
DID THE REAR DOME LAMP LIGHT?
NO
REPAIR THE M2 YL/RD WIRE FOR AN OPEN TO SPLICE.*
YES
REPLACE THE LIFTGATE LATCH SWITCH.*

* PERFORM VERIFICATION TEST 50A

91I14637 91H14653

Fig. 70: Test 35A – Checking Diode Assembly & Liftgate Lamps Wiring (3 of 3)

1991 ENGINE PERFORMANCE
Body Control Computer (Cont.)

TEST 37A: HEADLIGHTS WILL NOT TURN OFF

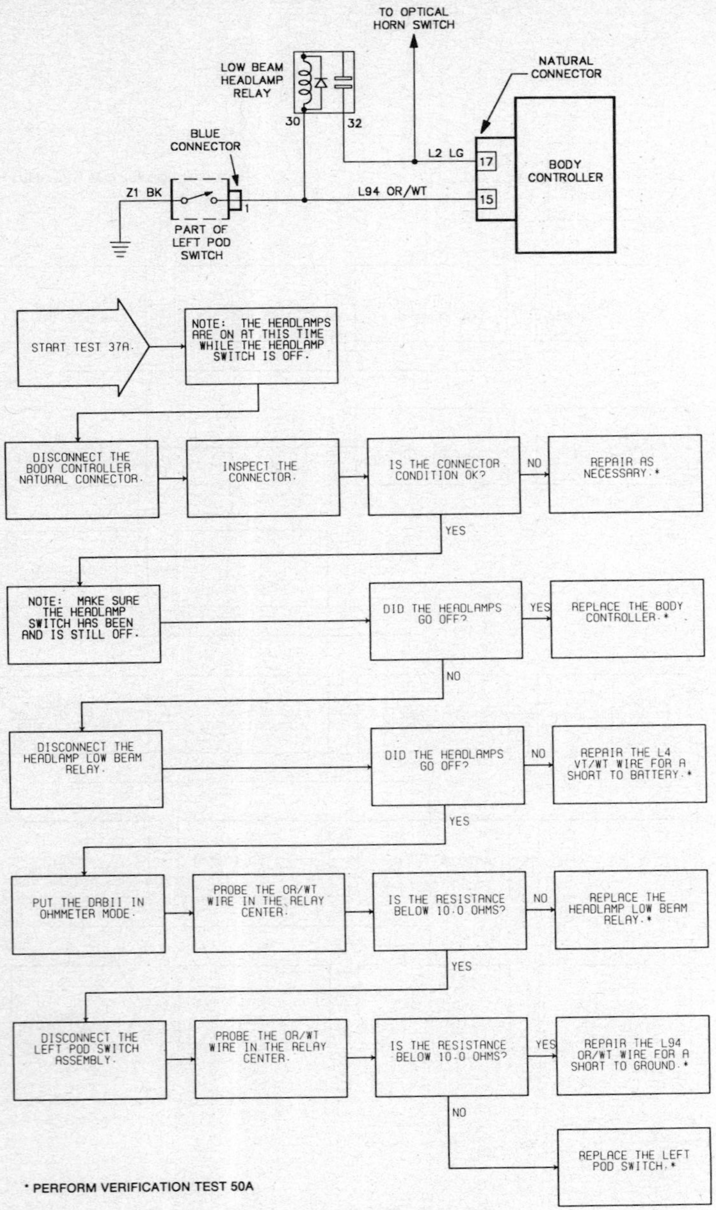
TO OPTICAL HORN SWITCH
LOW BEAM HEADLAMP RELAY
NATURAL CONNECTOR
30
32
BLUE CONNECTOR
L2 LG
17
BODY CONTROLLER
Z1 BK
L94 OR/WT
15
1
PART OF LEFT POD SWITCH
START TEST 37A.
NOTE: THE HEADLAMPS ARE ON AT THIS TIME WHILE THE HEADLAMP SWITCH IS OFF.
DISCONNECT THE BODY CONTROLLER NATURAL CONNECTOR.
INSPECT THE CONNECTOR.
IS THE CONNECTOR CONDITION OK?
NO
REPAIR AS NECESSARY.*
YES
NOTE: MAKE SURE THE HEADLAMP SWITCH HAS BEEN AND IS STILL OFF.
DID THE HEADLAMPS GO OFF?
YES
REPLACE THE BODY CONTROLLER.*
NO
DISCONNECT THE HEADLAMP LOW BEAM RELAY.
DID THE HEADLAMPS GO OFF?
NO
REPAIR THE L4 VT/WT WIRE FOR A SHORT TO BATTERY.*
YES
PUT THE DRBII IN OHMMETER MODE.
PROBE THE OR/WT WIRE IN THE RELAY CENTER.
IS THE RESISTANCE BELOW 10.0 OHMS?
NO
REPLACE THE HEADLAMP LOW BEAM RELAY.*
YES
DISCONNECT THE LEFT POD SWITCH ASSEMBLY.
PROBE THE OR/WT WIRE IN THE RELAY CENTER.
IS THE RESISTANCE BELOW 10.0 OHMS?
YES
REPAIR THE L94 OR/WT WIRE FOR A SHORT TO GROUND.*
NO
REPLACE THE LEFT POD SWITCH.*

* PERFORM VERIFICATION TEST 50A

91A14654 91B14655

Fig. 71: Test 37A – Headlights Will Not Turn Off

TEST 37B: HEADLIGHT TIME DELAY WILL NOT WORK

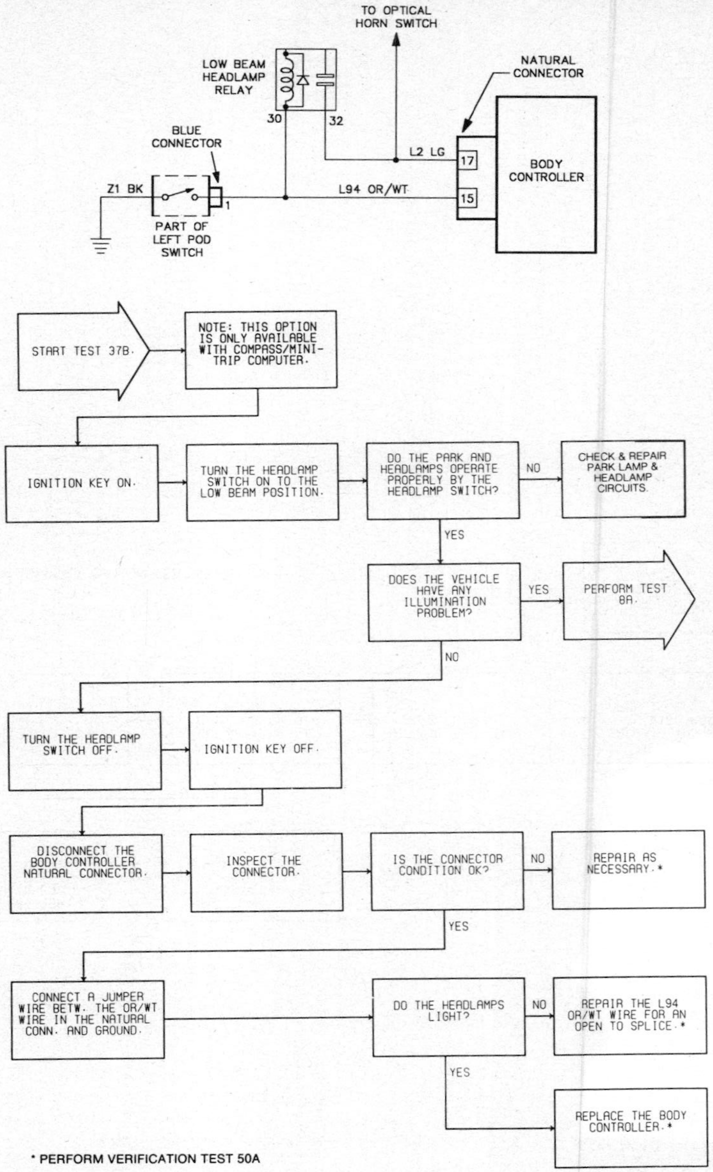
TO OPTICAL HORN SWITCH
LOW BEAM HEADLAMP RELAY
NATURAL CONNECTOR
30
32
BLUE CONNECTOR
L2 LG
17
BODY CONTROLLER
Z1 BK
L94 OR/WT
15
1
PART OF LEFT POD SWITCH
START TEST 37B.
NOTE: THIS OPTION IS ONLY AVAILABLE WITH COMPASS/MINI-TRIP COMPUTER.
IGNITION KEY ON.
TURN THE HEADLAMP SWITCH ON TO THE LOW BEAM POSITION.
DO THE PARK AND HEADLAMPS OPERATE PROPERLY BY THE HEADLAMP SWITCH?
NO
CHECK & REPAIR PARK LAMP & HEADLAMP CIRCUITS.
YES
DOES THE VEHICLE HAVE ANY ILLUMINATION PROBLEM?
YES
PERFORM TEST 8A.
NO
TURN THE HEADLAMP SWITCH OFF.
IGNITION KEY OFF.
DISCONNECT THE BODY CONTROLLER NATURAL CONNECTOR.
INSPECT THE CONNECTOR.
IS THE CONNECTOR CONDITION OK?
NO
REPAIR AS NECESSARY.*
YES
CONNECT A JUMPER WIRE BETW. THE OR/WT WIRE IN THE NATURAL CONN. AND GROUND.
DO THE HEADLAMPS LIGHT?
NO
REPAIR THE L94 OR/WT WIRE FOR AN OPEN TO SPLICE.*
YES
REPLACE THE BODY CONTROLLER.*

* PERFORM VERIFICATION TEST 50A

91A14654 91C14656

Fig. 72: Test 37B – Headlight Time Delay Will Not Work

TEST 42A: DIAGNOSING LEFT FRONT DOOR AJAR CIRCUIT (1 OF 2)

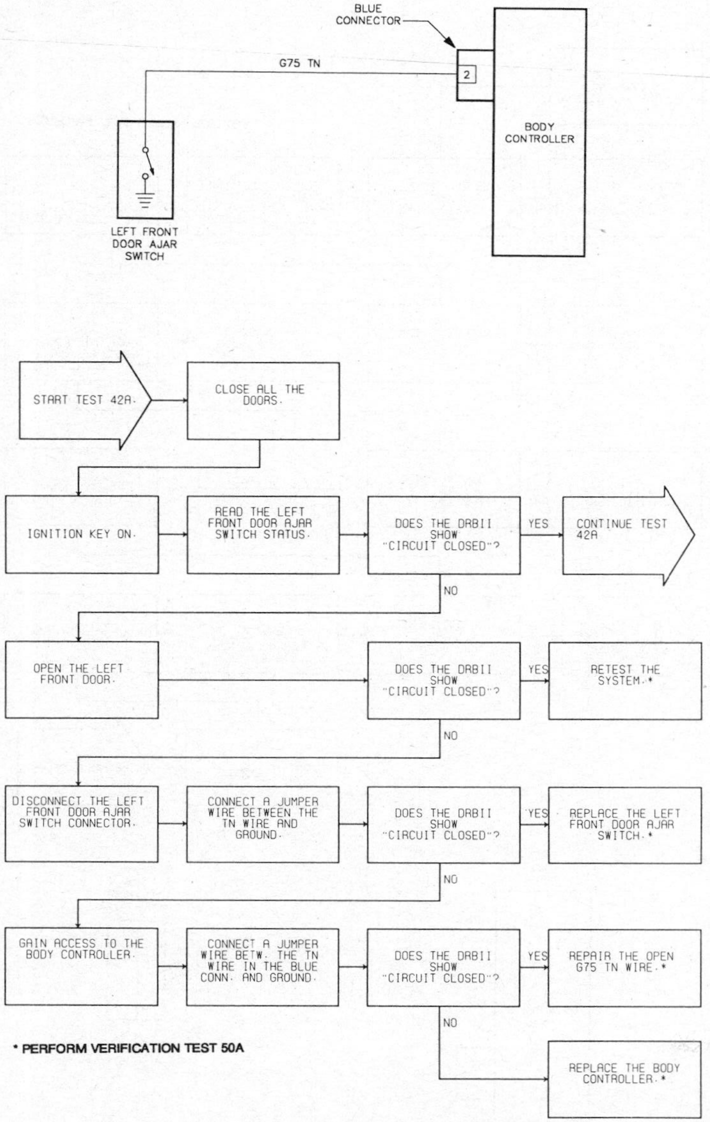
BLUE CONNECTOR
G75 TN
2
BODY CONTROLLER
LEFT FRONT DOOR AJAR SWITCH
START TEST 42A.
CLOSE ALL THE DOORS.
IGNITION KEY ON.
READ THE LEFT FRONT DOOR AJAR SWITCH STATUS.
DOES THE DRBII SHOW "CIRCUIT CLOSED"?
YES
CONTINUE TEST 42A
NO
OPEN THE LEFT FRONT DOOR.
DOES THE DRBII SHOW "CIRCUIT CLOSED"?
YES
RETEST THE SYSTEM.*
NO
DISCONNECT THE LEFT FRONT DOOR AJAR SWITCH CONNECTOR.
CONNECT A JUMPER WIRE BETWEEN THE TN WIRE AND GROUND.
DOES THE DRBII SHOW "CIRCUIT CLOSED"?
YES
REPLACE THE LEFT FRONT DOOR AJAR SWITCH.*
NO
GAIN ACCESS TO THE BODY CONTROLLER.
CONNECT A JUMPER WIRE BETW. THE TN WIRE IN THE BLUE CONN. AND GROUND.
DOES THE DRBII SHOW "CIRCUIT CLOSED"?
YES
REPAIR THE OPEN G75 TN WIRE.*
NO
REPLACE THE BODY CONTROLLER.*

* PERFORM VERIFICATION TEST 50A

91D14657 91E14658

Fig. 73: Test 42A – Diagnosing Left Front Door Ajar Circuit (1 of 2)

TEST 42A: DIAGNOSING LEFT FRONT DOOR AJAR CIRCUIT (2 OF 2)

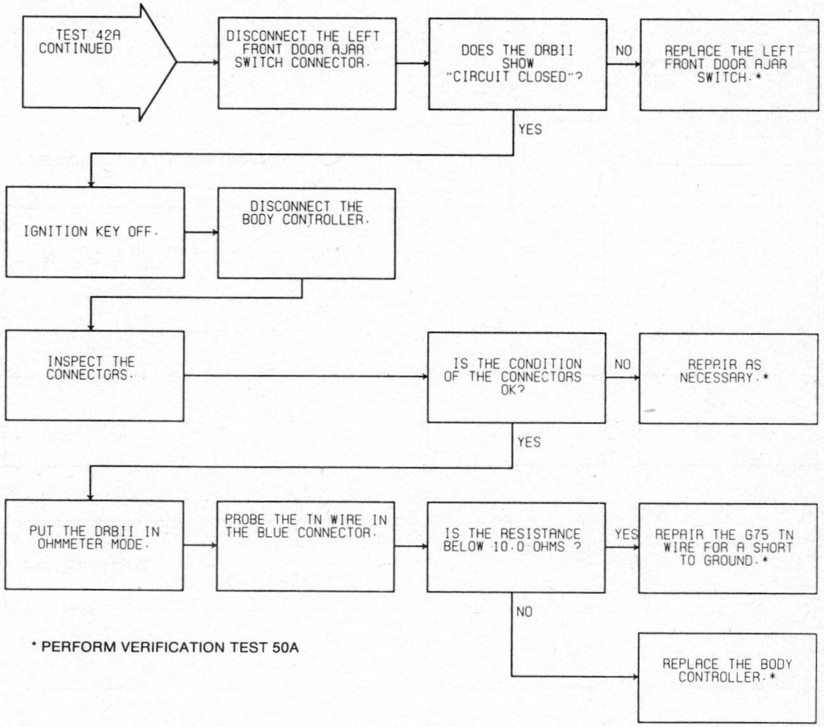
TEST 42A CONTINUED
DISCONNECT THE LEFT FRONT DOOR AJAR SWITCH CONNECTOR.
DOES THE DRBII SHOW "CIRCUIT CLOSED"?
NO
REPLACE THE LEFT FRONT DOOR AJAR SWITCH.*
YES
IGNITION KEY OFF.
DISCONNECT THE BODY CONTROLLER.
INSPECT THE CONNECTORS.
IS THE CONDITION OF THE CONNECTORS OK?
NO
REPAIR AS NECESSARY.*
YES
PUT THE DRBII IN OHMMETER MODE.
PROBE THE TN WIRE IN THE BLUE CONNECTOR.
IS THE RESISTANCE BELOW 10.0 OHMS ?
YES
REPAIR THE G75 TN WIRE FOR A SHORT TO GROUND.*
NO
REPLACE THE BODY CONTROLLER.*

* PERFORM VERIFICATION TEST 50A

91F14659

Fig. 74: Test 42A – Diagnosing Left Front Door Ajar Circuit (2 of 2)

1991 ENGINE PERFORMANCE
Body Control Computer (Cont.)

TEST 43A: DIAGNOSING RIGHT FRONT DOOR AJAR CIRCUIT (1 OF 2)

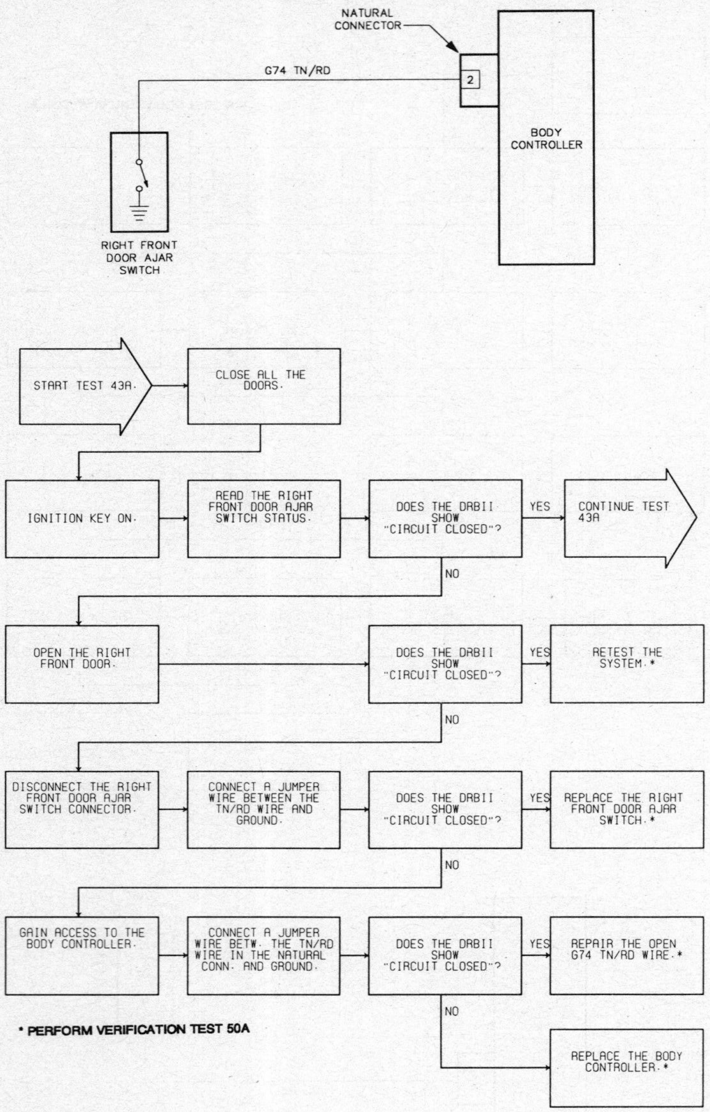
NATURAL CONNECTOR
G74 TN/RD
2
BODY CONTROLLER
RIGHT FRONT DOOR AJAR SWITCH
START TEST 43A.
CLOSE ALL THE DOORS.
IGNITION KEY ON.
READ THE RIGHT FRONT DOOR AJAR SWITCH STATUS.
DOES THE DRBII SHOW "CIRCUIT CLOSED"?
YES
CONTINUE TEST 43A
NO
OPEN THE RIGHT FRONT DOOR.
DOES THE DRBII SHOW "CIRCUIT CLOSED"?
YES
RETEST THE SYSTEM.*
NO
DISCONNECT THE RIGHT FRONT DOOR AJAR SWITCH CONNECTOR.
CONNECT A JUMPER WIRE BETWEEN THE TN/RD WIRE AND GROUND.
DOES THE DRBII SHOW "CIRCUIT CLOSED"?
YES
REPLACE THE RIGHT FRONT DOOR AJAR SWITCH.*
NO
GAIN ACCESS TO THE BODY CONTROLLER.
CONNECT A JUMPER WIRE BETW. THE TN/RD WIRE IN THE NATURAL CONN. AND GROUND.
DOES THE DRBII SHOW "CIRCUIT CLOSED"?
YES
REPAIR THE OPEN G74 TN/RD WIRE.*
NO
REPLACE THE BODY CONTROLLER.*

* PERFORM VERIFICATION TEST 50A

91I14660 91J14661

Fig. 75: Test 43A – Diagnosing Right Front Door Ajar Circuit (1 of 2)

TEST 43A: DIAGNOSING RIGHT FRONT DOOR AJAR CIRCUIT (2 OF 2)

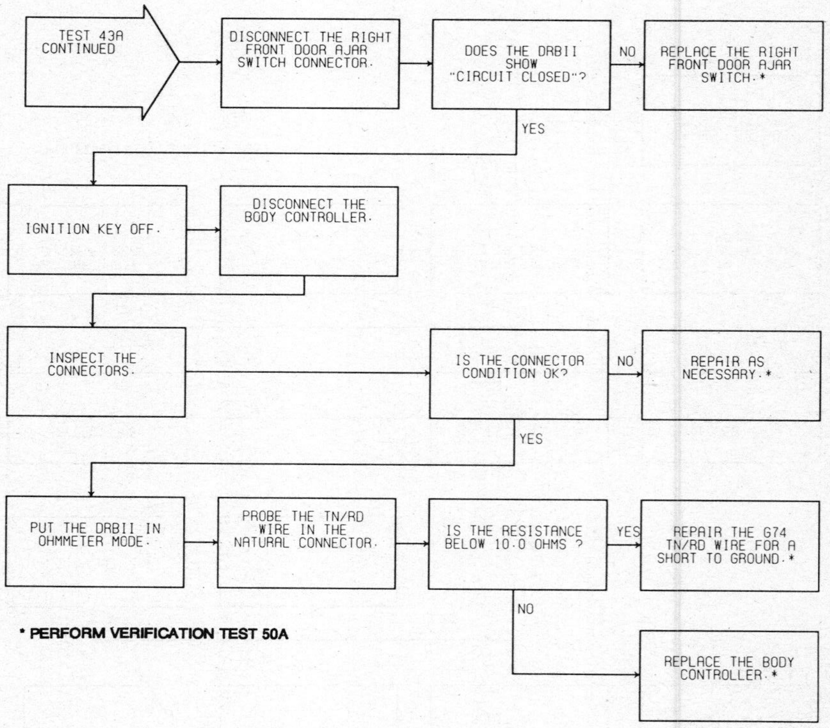
TEST 43A CONTINUED
DISCONNECT THE RIGHT FRONT DOOR AJAR SWITCH CONNECTOR.
DOES THE DRBII SHOW "CIRCUIT CLOSED"?
NO
REPLACE THE RIGHT FRONT DOOR AJAR SWITCH.*
YES
IGNITION KEY OFF.
DISCONNECT THE BODY CONTROLLER.
INSPECT THE CONNECTORS.
IS THE CONNECTOR CONDITION OK?
NO
REPAIR AS NECESSARY.*
YES
PUT THE DRBII IN OHMMETER MODE.
PROBE THE TN/RD WIRE IN THE NATURAL CONNECTOR.
IS THE RESISTANCE BELOW 10.0 OHMS ?
YES
REPAIR THE G74 TN/RD WIRE FOR A SHORT TO GROUND.*
NO
REPLACE THE BODY CONTROLLER.*

* PERFORM VERIFICATION TEST 50A

91A14662

Fig. 76: Test 43A – Diagnosing Right Front Door Ajar Circuit (2 of 2)

TEST 44A: DIAGNOSING SIDE DOOR AJAR CIRCUIT (1 OF 2)

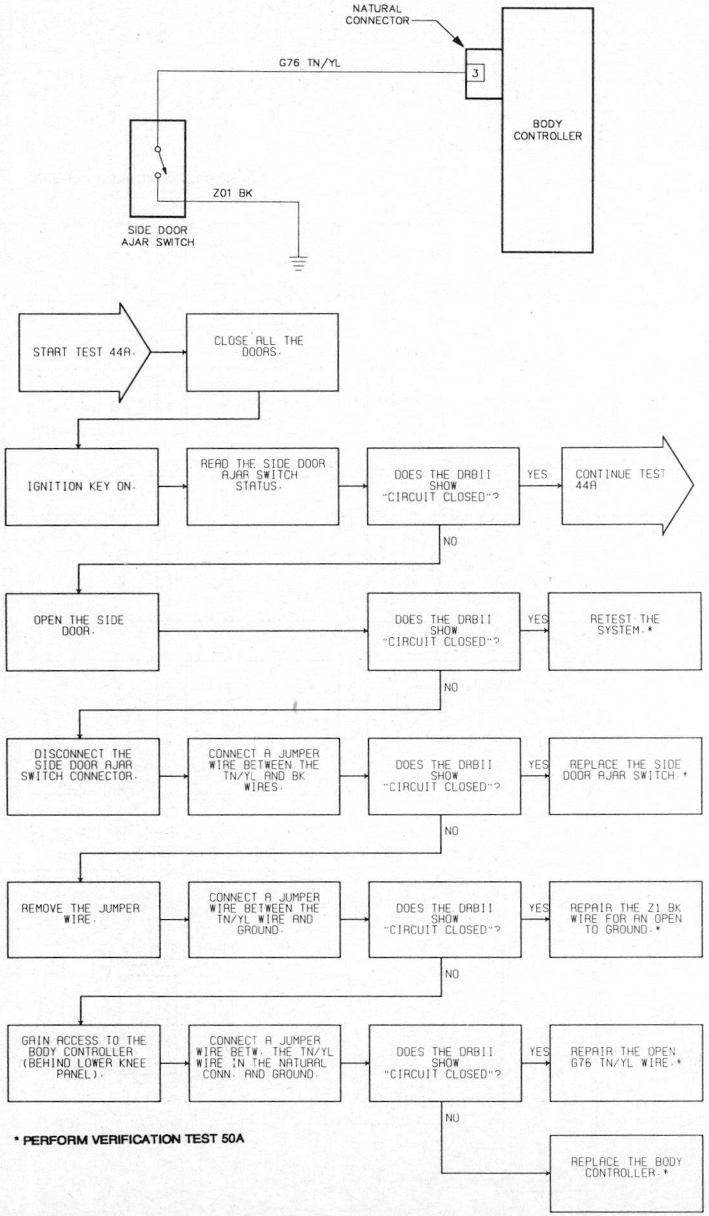
NATURAL CONNECTOR
G76 TN/YL
3
BODY CONTROLLER
Z01 BK
SIDE DOOR AJAR SWITCH
START TEST 44A.
CLOSE ALL THE DOORS.
IGNITION KEY ON.
READ THE SIDE DOOR AJAR SWITCH STATUS.
DOES THE DRBII SHOW "CIRCUIT CLOSED"?
YES
CONTINUE TEST 44A
NO
OPEN THE SIDE DOOR.
DOES THE DRBII SHOW "CIRCUIT CLOSED"?
YES
RETEST THE SYSTEM.*
NO
DISCONNECT THE SIDE DOOR AJAR SWITCH CONNECTOR.
CONNECT A JUMPER WIRE BETWEEN THE TN/YL AND BK WIRES.
DOES THE DRBII SHOW "CIRCUIT CLOSED"?
YES
REPLACE THE SIDE DOOR AJAR SWITCH.*
NO
REMOVE THE JUMPER WIRE.
CONNECT A JUMPER WIRE BETWEEN THE TN/YL WIRE AND GROUND.
DOES THE DRBII SHOW "CIRCUIT CLOSED"?
YES
REPAIR THE Z1 BK WIRE FOR AN OPEN TO GROUND.*
NO
GAIN ACCESS TO THE BODY CONTROLLER (BEHIND LOWER KNEE PANEL).
CONNECT A JUMPER WIRE BETW. THE TN/YL WIRE IN THE NATURAL CONN. AND GROUND.
DOES THE DRBII SHOW "CIRCUIT CLOSED"?
YES
REPAIR THE OPEN G76 TN/YL WIRE.*
NO
REPLACE THE BODY CONTROLLER.*

* PERFORM VERIFICATION TEST 50A

91B14663 91C14664

Fig. 77: Test 44A - Diagnosing Side Door Ajar Circuit (1 of 2)

TEST 44A: DIAGNOSING SIDE DOOR AJAR CIRCUIT (2 OF 2)

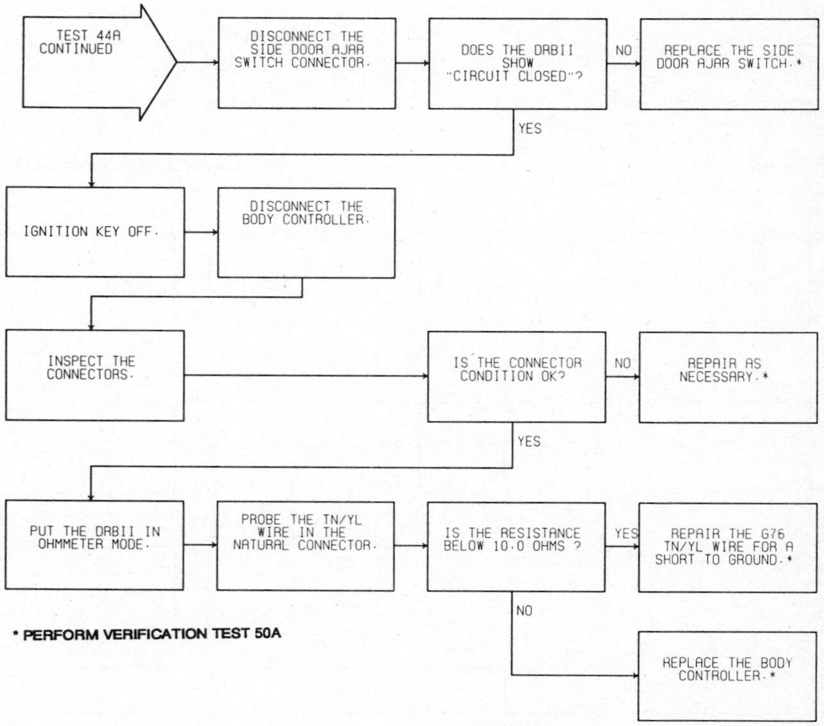
TEST 44A CONTINUED
DISCONNECT THE SIDE DOOR AJAR SWITCH CONNECTOR.
DOES THE DRBII SHOW "CIRCUIT CLOSED"?
NO
REPLACE THE SIDE DOOR AJAR SWITCH.*
YES
IGNITION KEY OFF.
DISCONNECT THE BODY CONTROLLER.
INSPECT THE CONNECTORS.
IS THE CONNECTOR CONDITION OK?
NO
REPAIR AS NECESSARY.*
YES
PUT THE DRBII IN OHMMETER MODE.
PROBE THE TN/YL WIRE IN THE NATURAL CONNECTOR.
IS THE RESISTANCE BELOW 10.0 OHMS ?
YES
REPAIR THE G76 TN/YL WIRE FOR A SHORT TO GROUND.*
NO
REPLACE THE BODY CONTROLLER.*

* PERFORM VERIFICATION TEST 50A

91D14665

Fig. 78: Test 44A - Diagnosing Side Door Ajar Circuit (2 of 2)

1991 ENGINE PERFORMANCE
Body Control Computer (Cont.)

TEST 45A: DIAGNOSING LIFTGATE AJAR CIRCUIT (1 OF 2)

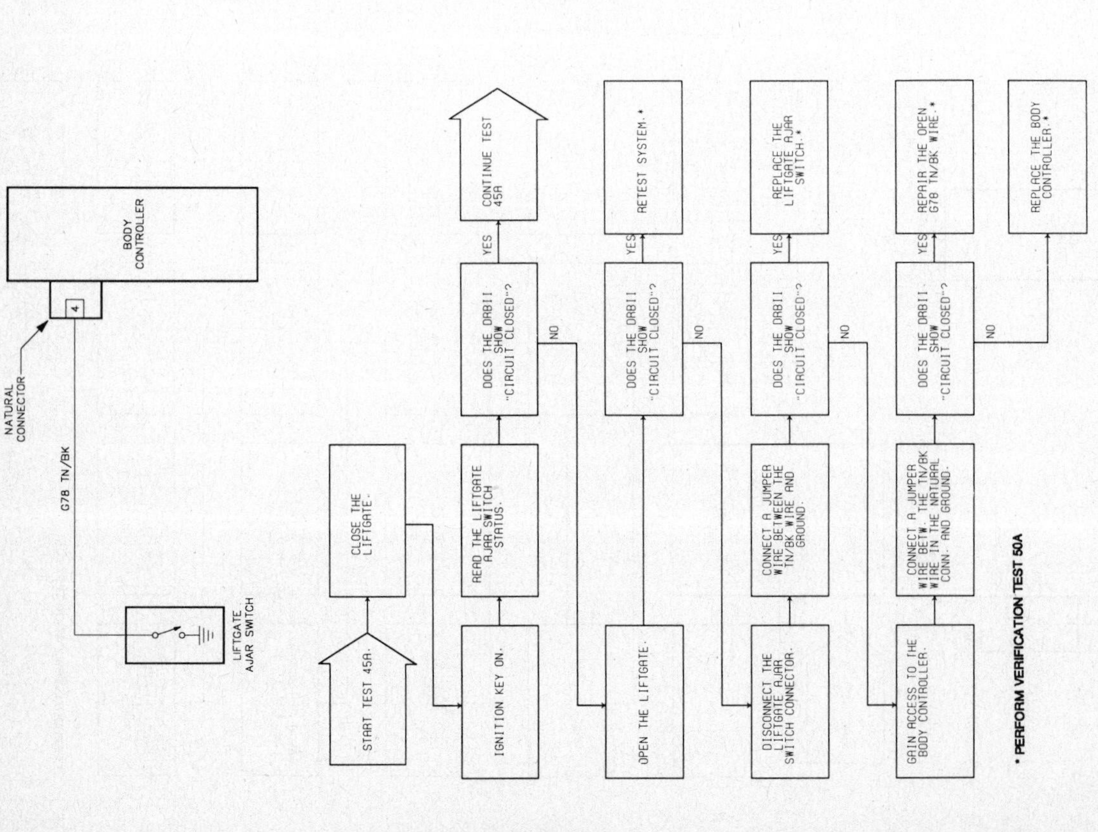
BODY CONTROLLER
NATURAL CONNECTOR
4
G78 TN/BK
LIFTGATE AJAR SWITCH
START TEST 45A.
CLOSE THE LIFTGATE.
IGNITION KEY ON.
READ THE LIFTGATE AJAR SWITCH STATUS.
DOES THE DRBII SHOW "CIRCUIT CLOSED"?
YES
CONTINUE TEST 45A
NO
OPEN THE LIFTGATE.
DOES THE DRBII SHOW "CIRCUIT CLOSED"?
YES
RETEST SYSTEM.*
NO
DISCONNECT THE LIFTGATE AJAR SWITCH CONNECTOR.
CONNECT A JUMPER WIRE BETWEEN THE TN/BK WIRE AND GROUND.
DOES THE DRBII SHOW "CIRCUIT CLOSED"?
YES
REPLACE THE LIFTGATE AJAR SWITCH.*
NO
GAIN ACCESS TO THE BODY CONTROLLER.
CONNECT A JUMPER WIRE BETW. THE TN/BK WIRE IN THE NATURAL CONN. AND GROUND.
DOES THE DRBII SHOW "CIRCUIT CLOSED"?
YES
REPAIR THE OPEN G78 TN/BK WIRE.*
NO
REPLACE THE BODY CONTROLLER.*
* PERFORM VERIFICATION TEST 50A

91E14666 91F14667

Fig. 79: Test 45A – Diagnosing Liftgate Ajar Circuit (1 of 2)

TEST 45A: DIAGNOSING LIFTGATE AJAR CIRCUIT (2 OF 2)

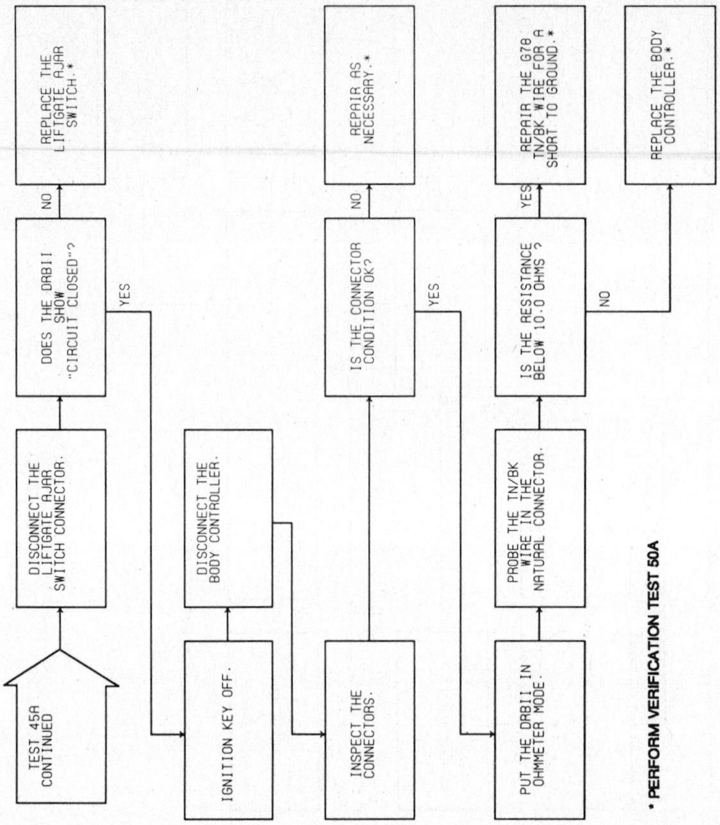
TEST 45A CONTINUED
DISCONNECT THE LIFTGATE AJAR SWITCH CONNECTOR.
DOES THE DRBII SHOW "CIRCUIT CLOSED"?
NO
REPLACE THE LIFTGATE AJAR SWITCH.*
YES
IGNITION KEY OFF.
DISCONNECT THE BODY CONTROLLER.
INSPECT THE CONNECTORS.
IS THE CONNECTOR CONDITION OK?
NO
REPAIR AS NECESSARY.*
YES
PUT THE DRBII IN OHMMETER MODE.
PROBE THE TN/BK WIRE IN THE NATURAL CONNECTOR.
IS THE RESISTANCE BELOW 10.0 OHMS?
YES
REPAIR THE G78 TN/BK WIRE FOR A SHORT TO GROUND.*
NO
REPLACE THE BODY CONTROLLER.*
* PERFORM VERIFICATION TEST 50A

91G14668

Fig. 80: Test 45A – Diagnosing Liftgate Ajar Circuit (2 of 2)

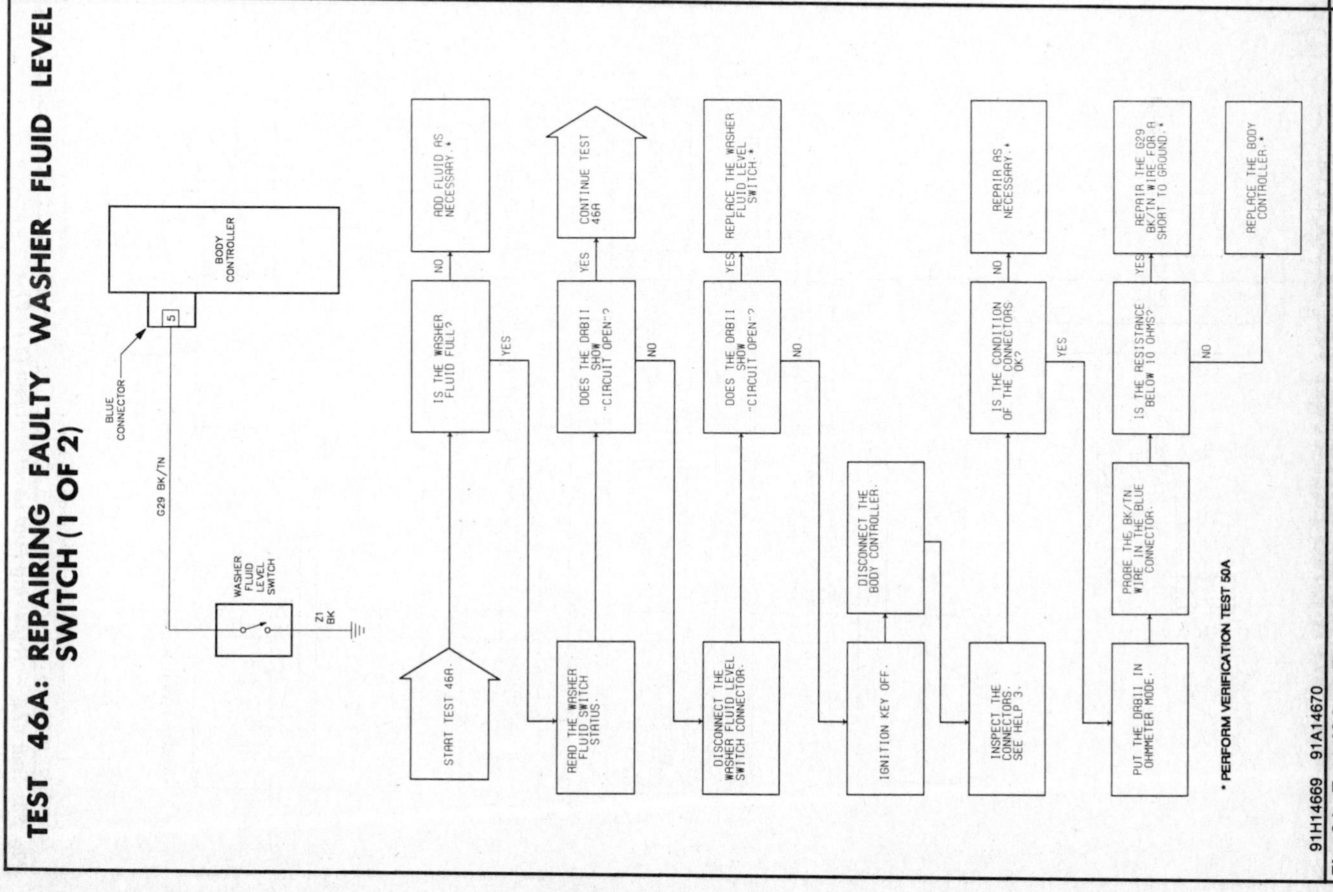

TEST 46A: REPAIRING FAULTY WASHER FLUID LEVEL SWITCH (1 OF 2)
BODY CONTROLLER
BLUE CONNECTOR
5
G29 BK/TN
WASHER FLUID LEVEL SWITCH
Z1 BK
START TEST 46A.
IS THE WASHER FLUID FULL?
NO
ADD FLUID AS NECESSARY.*
YES
READ THE WASHER FLUID SWITCH STATUS.
DOES THE DRBII SHOW "CIRCUIT OPEN"?
YES
CONTINUE TEST 46A
NO
DISCONNECT THE WASHER FLUID LEVEL SWITCH CONNECTOR.
DOES THE DRBII SHOW "CIRCUIT OPEN"?
YES
REPLACE THE WASHER FLUID LEVEL SWITCH.*
NO
IGNITION KEY OFF.
DISCONNECT THE BODY CONTROLLER.
INSPECT THE CONNECTORS. SEE HELP 3.
IS THE CONDITION OF THE CONNECTORS OK?
NO
REPAIR AS NECESSARY.*
YES
PUT THE DRBII IN OHMMETER MODE.
PROBE THE BK/TN WIRE IN THE BLUE CONNECTOR.
IS THE RESISTANCE BELOW 10 OHMS?
YES
REPAIR THE G29 BK/TN WIRE FOR A SHORT TO GROUND.*
NO
REPLACE THE BODY CONTROLLER.*
* PERFORM VERIFICATION TEST 50A
91H14669 91A14670

Fig. 81: Test 46A – Repairing Faulty Washer Fluid Level Switch (1 of 2)

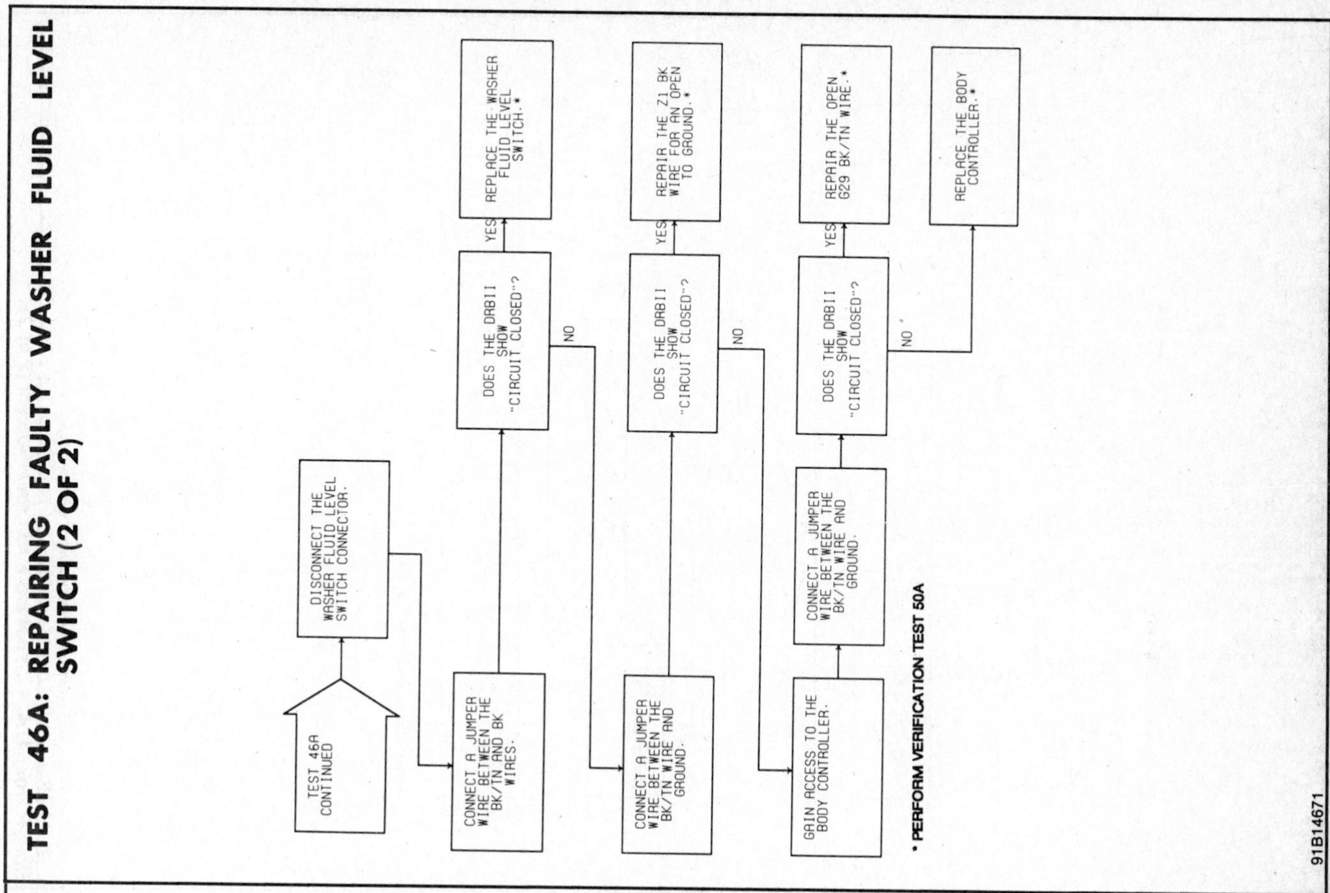

TEST 46A: REPAIRING FAULTY WASHER FLUID LEVEL SWITCH (2 OF 2)
TEST 46A CONTINUED
DISCONNECT THE WASHER FLUID LEVEL SWITCH CONNECTOR.
CONNECT A JUMPER WIRE BETWEEN THE BK/TN AND BK WIRES.
DOES THE DRBII SHOW "CIRCUIT CLOSED"?
YES
REPLACE THE WASHER FLUID LEVEL SWITCH.*
NO
CONNECT A JUMPER WIRE BETWEEN THE BK/TN WIRE AND GROUND.
DOES THE DRBII SHOW "CIRCUIT CLOSED"?
YES
REPAIR THE Z1 BK WIRE FOR AN OPEN TO GROUND.*
NO
GAIN ACCESS TO THE BODY CONTROLLER.
CONNECT A JUMPER WIRE BETWEEN THE BK/TN WIRE AND GROUND.
DOES THE DRBII SHOW "CIRCUIT CLOSED"?
YES
REPAIR THE OPEN G29 BK/TN WIRE.*
NO
REPLACE THE BODY CONTROLLER.*
* PERFORM VERIFICATION TEST 50A
91B14671

Fig. 82: Test 46A – Repairing Faulty Washer Fluid Level Switch (2 of 2)

1991 ENGINE PERFORMANCE
Body Control Computer (Cont.)

TEST 47A: REPAIRING FUEL LEVEL PROBLEM (1 OF 2)

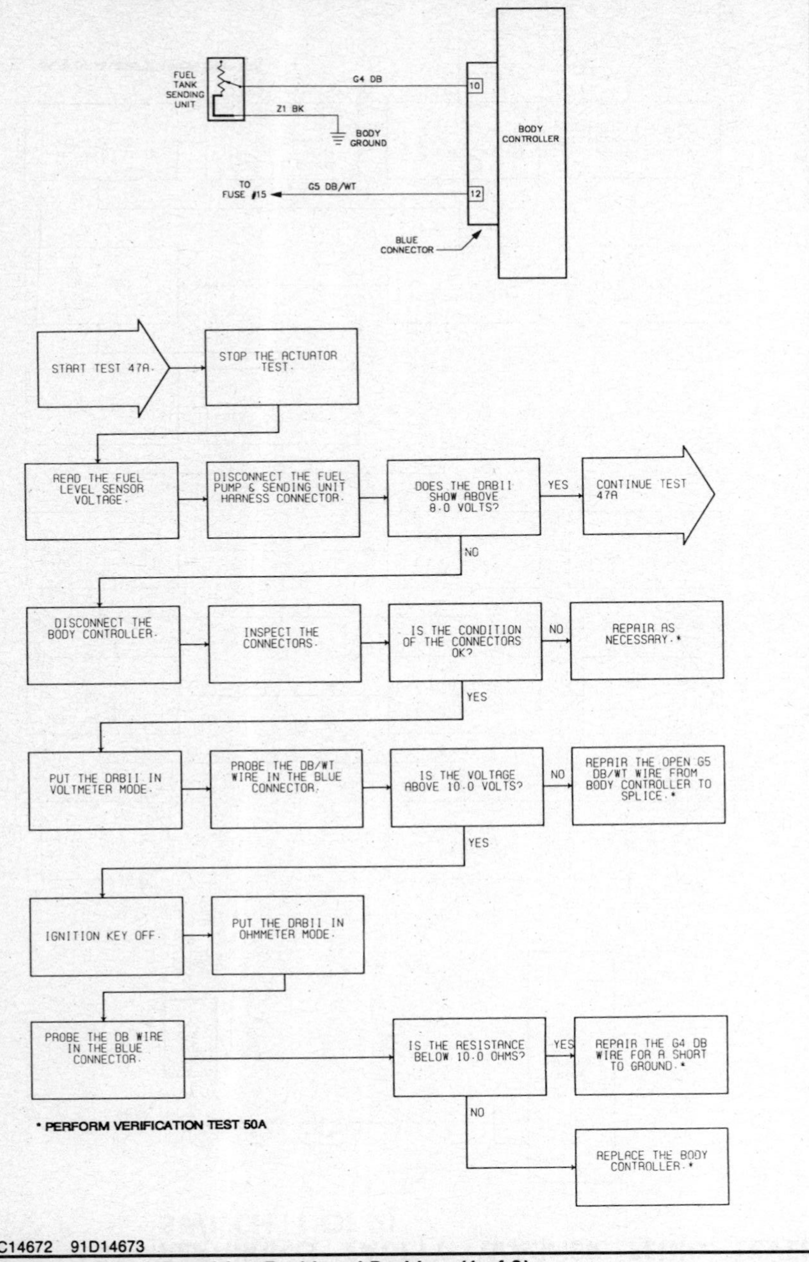
FUEL TANK SENDING UNIT
G4 DB
Z1 BK
BODY GROUND
BODY CONTROLLER
10
12
TO FUSE #15
G5 DB/WT
BLUE CONNECTOR
START TEST 47A.
STOP THE ACTUATOR TEST.
READ THE FUEL LEVEL SENSOR VOLTAGE.
DISCONNECT THE FUEL PUMP & SENDING UNIT HARNESS CONNECTOR.
DOES THE DRBII SHOW ABOVE 8.0 VOLTS?
YES
CONTINUE TEST 47A
NO
DISCONNECT THE BODY CONTROLLER.
INSPECT THE CONNECTORS.
IS THE CONDITION OF THE CONNECTORS OK?
NO
REPAIR AS NECESSARY.*
YES
PUT THE DRBII IN VOLTMETER MODE.
PROBE THE DB/WT WIRE IN THE BLUE CONNECTOR.
IS THE VOLTAGE ABOVE 10.0 VOLTS?
NO
REPAIR THE OPEN G5 DB/WT WIRE FROM BODY CONTROLLER TO SPLICE.*
YES
IGNITION KEY OFF.
PUT THE DRBII IN OHMMETER MODE.
PROBE THE DB WIRE IN THE BLUE CONNECTOR.
IS THE RESISTANCE BELOW 10.0 OHMS?
YES
REPAIR THE G4 DB WIRE FOR A SHORT TO GROUND.*
NO
REPLACE THE BODY CONTROLLER.*
* PERFORM VERIFICATION TEST 50A
91C14672 91D14673

Fig. 83: Test 47A – Repairing Fuel Level Problem (1 of 2)

TEST 47A: REPAIRING FUEL LEVEL PROBLEM (2 OF 2)

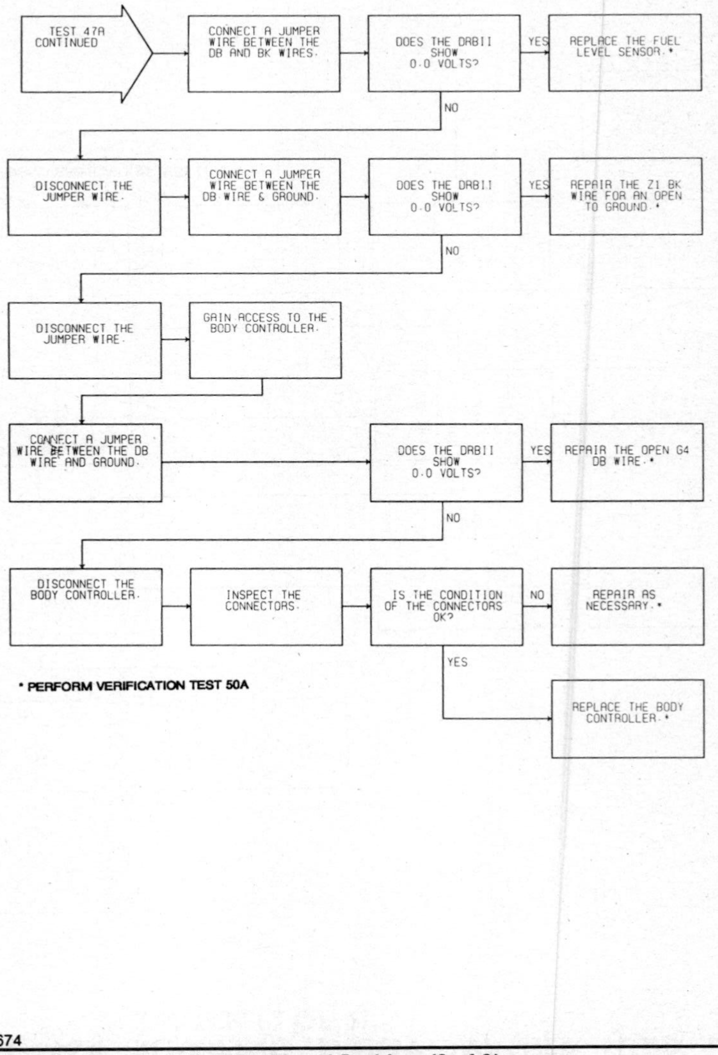
TEST 47A CONTINUED
CONNECT A JUMPER WIRE BETWEEN THE DB AND BK WIRES.
DOES THE DRBII SHOW 0.0 VOLTS?
YES
REPLACE THE FUEL LEVEL SENSOR.*
NO
DISCONNECT THE JUMPER WIRE.
CONNECT A JUMPER WIRE BETWEEN THE DB WIRE & GROUND.
DOES THE DRBII SHOW 0.0 VOLTS?
YES
REPAIR THE Z1 BK WIRE FOR AN OPEN TO GROUND.*
NO
DISCONNECT THE JUMPER WIRE.
GAIN ACCESS TO THE BODY CONTROLLER.
CONNECT A JUMPER WIRE BETWEEN THE DB WIRE AND GROUND.
DOES THE DRBII SHOW 0.0 VOLTS?
YES
REPAIR THE OPEN G4 DB WIRE.*
NO
DISCONNECT THE BODY CONTROLLER.
INSPECT THE CONNECTORS.
IS THE CONDITION OF THE CONNECTORS OK?
NO
REPAIR AS NECESSARY.*
YES
REPLACE THE BODY CONTROLLER.*
* PERFORM VERIFICATION TEST 50A
91E14674

Fig. 84: Test 47A – Repairing Fuel Level Problem (2 of 2)

TEST 48A: REPAIRING FUEL LEVEL PROBLEM (1 OF 2)

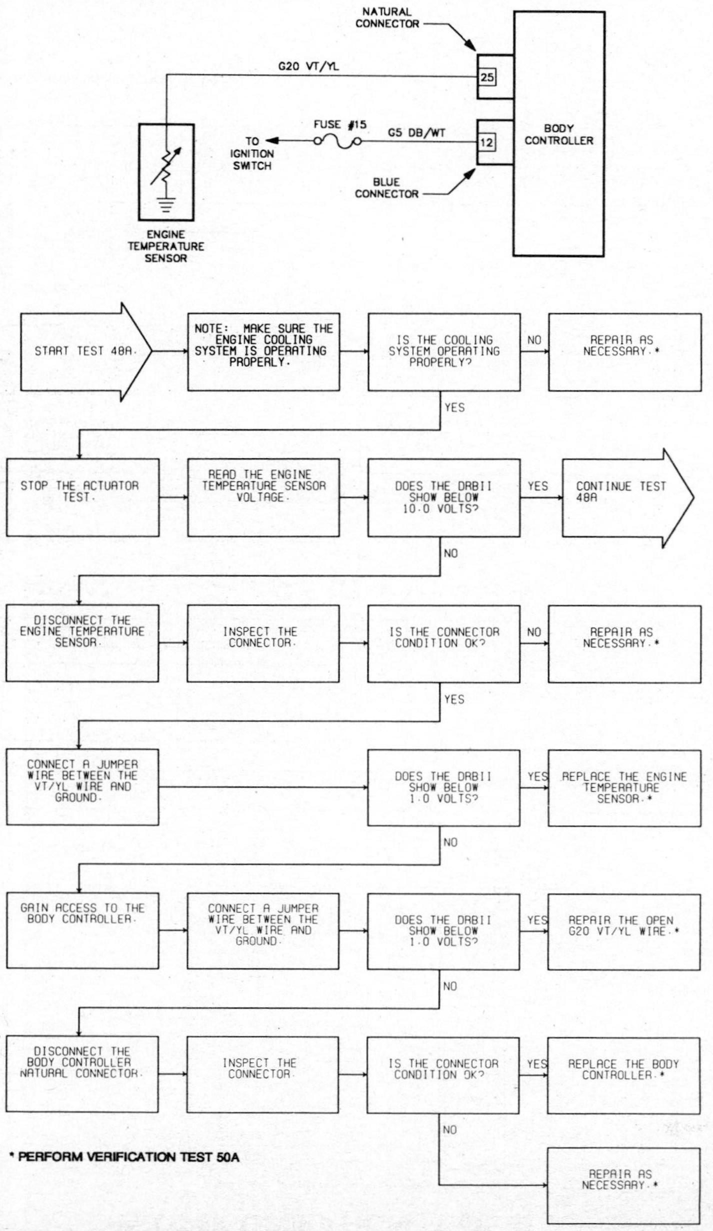
NATURAL CONNECTOR
G20 VT/YL
25
FUSE #15
G5 DB/WT
12
BODY CONTROLLER
TO IGNITION SWITCH
BLUE CONNECTOR
ENGINE TEMPERATURE SENSOR
START TEST 48A.
NOTE: MAKE SURE THE ENGINE COOLING SYSTEM IS OPERATING PROPERLY.
IS THE COOLING SYSTEM OPERATING PROPERLY?
NO
REPAIR AS NECESSARY.*
YES
STOP THE ACTUATOR TEST.
READ THE ENGINE TEMPERATURE SENSOR VOLTAGE.
DOES THE DRBII SHOW BELOW 10.0 VOLTS?
YES
CONTINUE TEST 48A
NO
DISCONNECT THE ENGINE TEMPERATURE SENSOR.
INSPECT THE CONNECTOR.
IS THE CONNECTOR CONDITION OK?
NO
REPAIR AS NECESSARY.*
YES
CONNECT A JUMPER WIRE BETWEEN THE VT/YL WIRE AND GROUND.
DOES THE DRBII SHOW BELOW 1.0 VOLTS?
YES
REPLACE THE ENGINE TEMPERATURE SENSOR.*
NO
GAIN ACCESS TO THE BODY CONTROLLER.
CONNECT A JUMPER WIRE BETWEEN THE VT/YL WIRE AND GROUND.
DOES THE DRBII SHOW BELOW 1.0 VOLTS?
YES
REPAIR THE OPEN G20 VT/YL WIRE.*
NO
DISCONNECT THE BODY CONTROLLER NATURAL CONNECTOR.
INSPECT THE CONNECTOR.
IS THE CONNECTOR CONDITION OK?
YES
REPLACE THE BODY CONTROLLER.*
NO
REPAIR AS NECESSARY.*

* PERFORM VERIFICATION TEST 50A

91F14675 91G14676

Fig. 85: Test 48A – Repairing Fuel Level Problem (1 of 2)

TEST 48A: REPAIRING FUEL LEVEL PROBLEM (2 OF 2)

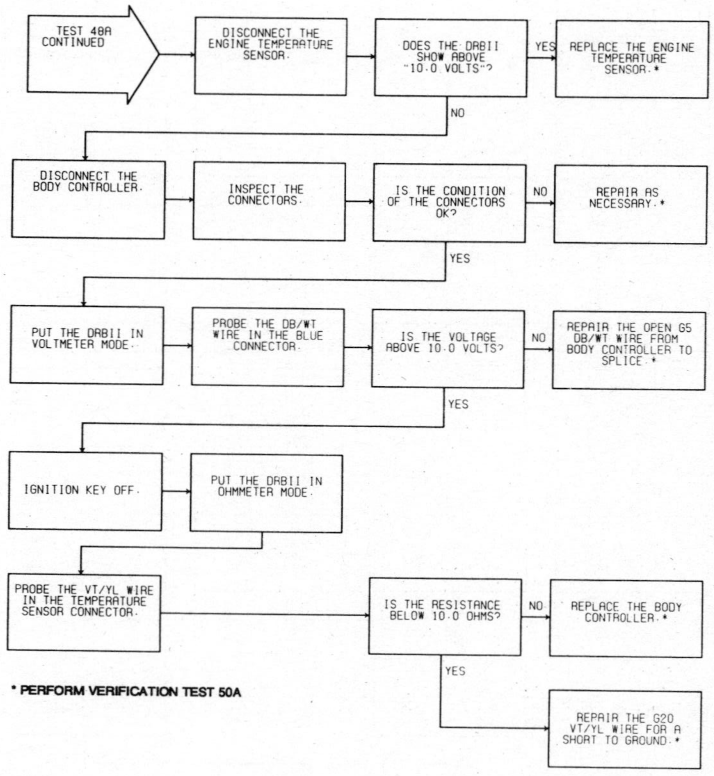
TEST 48A CONTINUED
DISCONNECT THE ENGINE TEMPERATURE SENSOR.
DOES THE DRBII SHOW ABOVE "10.0 VOLTS"?
YES
REPLACE THE ENGINE TEMPERATURE SENSOR.*
NO
DISCONNECT THE BODY CONTROLLER.
INSPECT THE CONNECTORS.
IS THE CONDITION OF THE CONNECTORS OK?
NO
REPAIR AS NECESSARY.*
YES
PUT THE DRBII IN VOLTMETER MODE.
PROBE THE DB/WT WIRE IN THE BLUE CONNECTOR.
IS THE VOLTAGE ABOVE 10.0 VOLTS?
NO
REPAIR THE OPEN G5 DB/WT WIRE FROM BODY CONTROLLER TO SPLICE.*
YES
IGNITION KEY OFF.
PUT THE DRBII IN OHMMETER MODE.
PROBE THE VT/YL WIRE IN THE TEMPERATURE SENSOR CONNECTOR.
IS THE RESISTANCE BELOW 10.0 OHMS?
NO
REPLACE THE BODY CONTROLLER.*
YES
REPAIR THE G20 VT/YL WIRE FOR A SHORT TO GROUND.*

* PERFORM VERIFICATION TEST 50A

91H14677

Fig. 86: Test 48A – Repairing Fuel Level Problem (2 of 2)

1991 ENGINE PERFORMANCE
Body Control Computer (Cont.)

TEST 49A: CHECKING WIRING & SENDING UNIT FOR PROPER OPERATION (1 OF 3)

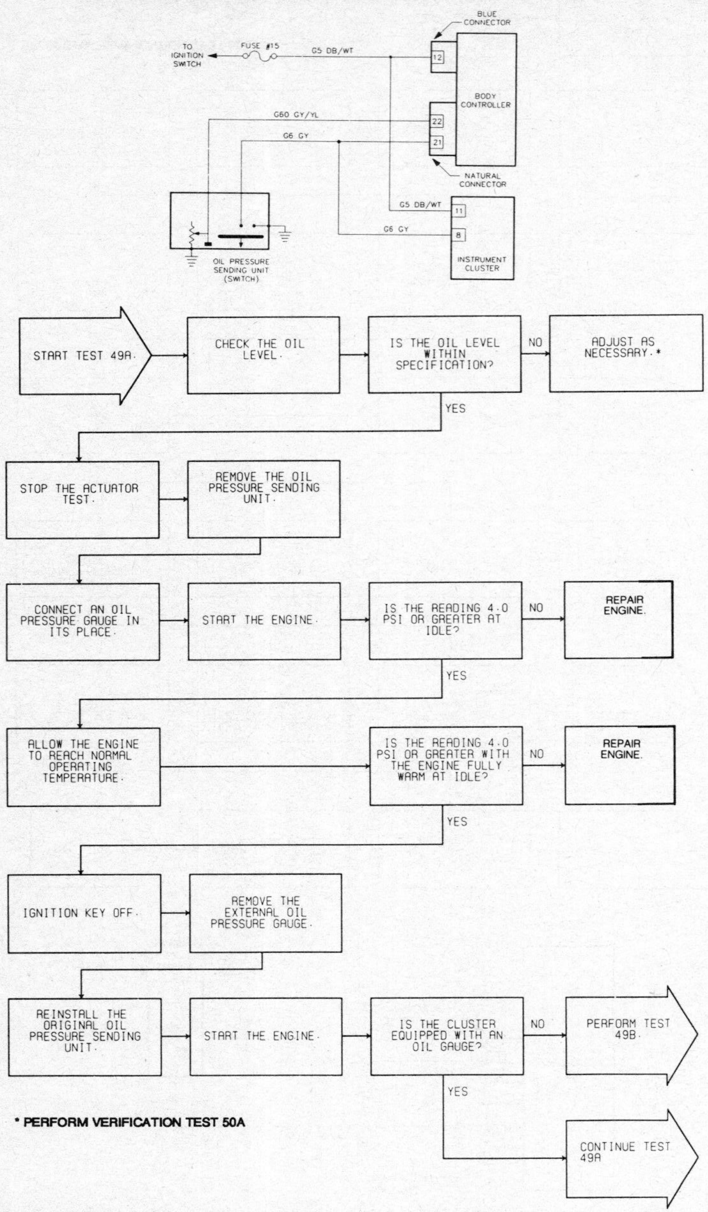
BLUE CONNECTOR
TO IGNITION SWITCH
FUSE #15
G5 DB/WT
12
BODY CONTROLLER
G60 GY/YL
22
G6 GY
21
NATURAL CONNECTOR
G5 DB/WT
11
G6 GY
8
INSTRUMENT CLUSTER
OIL PRESSURE SENDING UNIT (SWITCH)
START TEST 49A.
CHECK THE OIL LEVEL.
IS THE OIL LEVEL WITHIN SPECIFICATION?
NO
ADJUST AS NECESSARY.*
YES
STOP THE ACTUATOR TEST.
REMOVE THE OIL PRESSURE SENDING UNIT.
CONNECT AN OIL PRESSURE GAUGE IN ITS PLACE.
START THE ENGINE.
IS THE READING 4.0 PSI OR GREATER AT IDLE?
NO
REPAIR ENGINE.
YES
ALLOW THE ENGINE TO REACH NORMAL OPERATING TEMPERATURE.
IS THE READING 4.0 PSI OR GREATER WITH THE ENGINE FULLY WARM AT IDLE?
NO
REPAIR ENGINE.
YES
IGNITION KEY OFF.
REMOVE THE EXTERNAL OIL PRESSURE GAUGE.
REINSTALL THE ORIGINAL OIL PRESSURE SENDING UNIT.
START THE ENGINE.
IS THE CLUSTER EQUIPPED WITH AN OIL GAUGE?
NO
PERFORM TEST 49B.
YES
CONTINUE TEST 49A

* PERFORM VERIFICATION TEST 50A

91I14678 91J14679

Fig. 87: Test 49A – Checking Wiring & Sending Unit For Proper Operation (1 of 3)

TEST 49A: CHECKING WIRING & SENDING UNIT FOR PROPER OPERATION (2 OF 3)

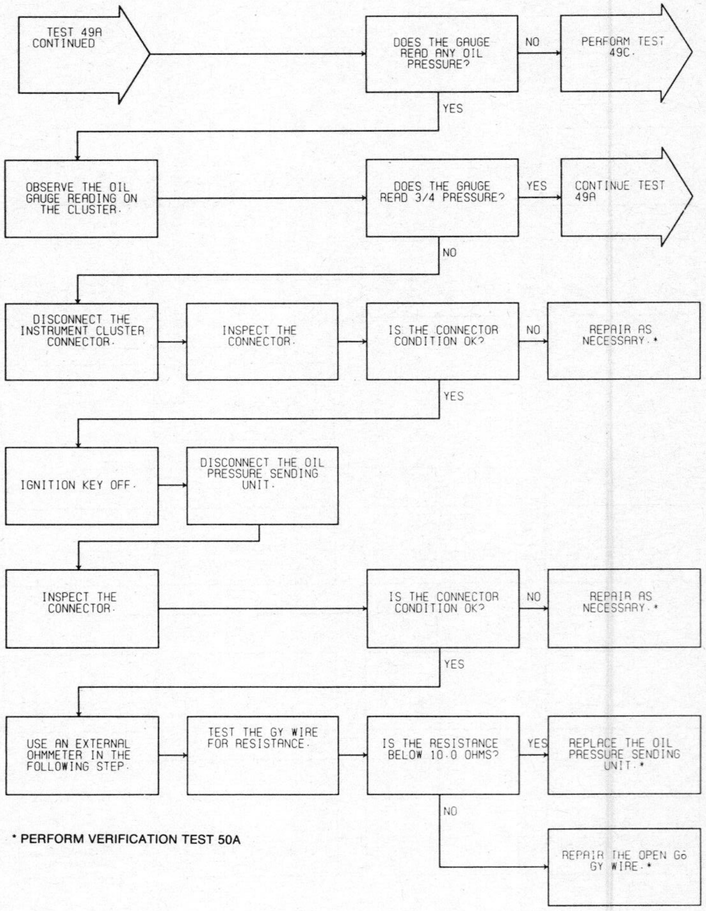
TEST 49A CONTINUED
DOES THE GAUGE READ ANY OIL PRESSURE?
NO
PERFORM TEST 49C.
YES
OBSERVE THE OIL GAUGE READING ON THE CLUSTER.
DOES THE GAUGE READ 3/4 PRESSURE?
YES
CONTINUE TEST 49A
NO
DISCONNECT THE INSTRUMENT CLUSTER CONNECTOR.
INSPECT THE CONNECTOR.
IS THE CONNECTOR CONDITION OK?
NO
REPAIR AS NECESSARY.*
YES
IGNITION KEY OFF.
DISCONNECT THE OIL PRESSURE SENDING UNIT.
INSPECT THE CONNECTOR.
IS THE CONNECTOR CONDITION OK?
NO
REPAIR AS NECESSARY.*
YES
USE AN EXTERNAL OHMMETER IN THE FOLLOWING STEP.
TEST THE GY WIRE FOR RESISTANCE.
IS THE RESISTANCE BELOW 10.0 OHMS?
YES
REPLACE THE OIL PRESSURE SENDING UNIT.*
NO
REPAIR THE OPEN G6 GY WIRE.*

* PERFORM VERIFICATION TEST 50A

91C14680

Fig. 88: Test 49A – Checking Wiring & Sending Unit For Proper Operation (2 of 3)

TEST 49A: CHECKING WIRING & SENDING UNIT FOR PROPER OPERATION (3 OF 3)

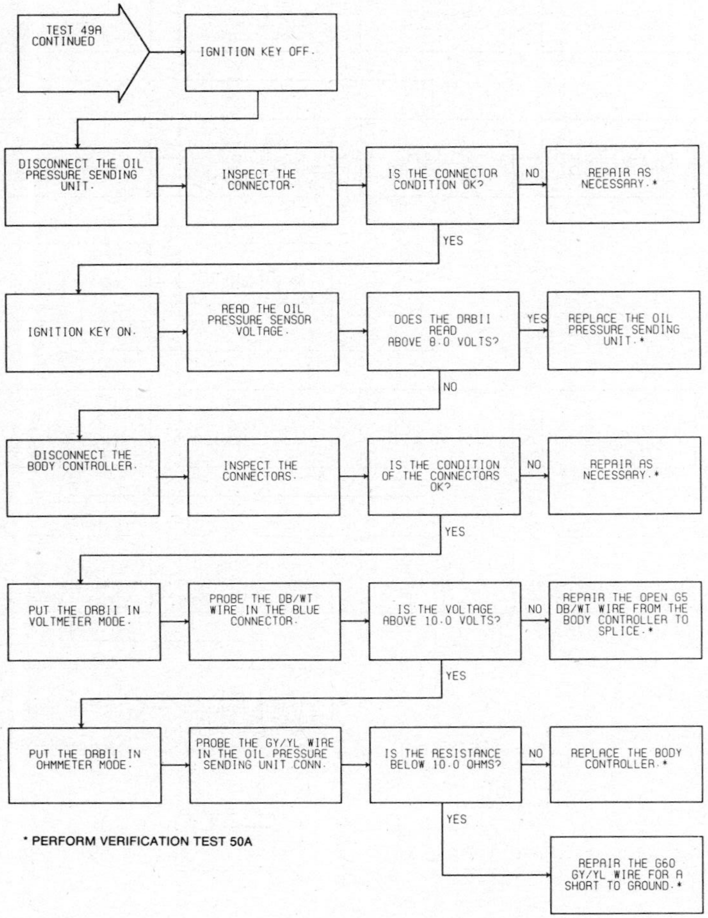
TEST 49A CONTINUED
IGNITION KEY OFF.
DISCONNECT THE OIL PRESSURE SENDING UNIT.
INSPECT THE CONNECTOR.
IS THE CONNECTOR CONDITION OK?
NO
REPAIR AS NECESSARY.*
YES
IGNITION KEY ON.
READ THE OIL PRESSURE SENSOR VOLTAGE.
DOES THE DRBII READ ABOVE 8.0 VOLTS?
YES
REPLACE THE OIL PRESSURE SENDING UNIT.*
NO
DISCONNECT THE BODY CONTROLLER.
INSPECT THE CONNECTORS.
IS THE CONDITION OF THE CONNECTORS OK?
NO
REPAIR AS NECESSARY.*
YES
PUT THE DRBII IN VOLTMETER MODE.
PROBE THE DB/WT WIRE IN THE BLUE CONNECTOR.
IS THE VOLTAGE ABOVE 10.0 VOLTS?
NO
REPAIR THE OPEN G5 DB/WT WIRE FROM THE BODY CONTROLLER TO SPLICE.*
YES
PUT THE DRBII IN OHMMETER MODE.
PROBE THE GY/YL WIRE IN THE OIL PRESSURE SENDING UNIT CONN.
IS THE RESISTANCE BELOW 10.0 OHMS?
NO
REPLACE THE BODY CONTROLLER.*
YES
REPAIR THE G60 GY/YL WIRE FOR A SHORT TO GROUND.*

* PERFORM VERIFICATION TEST 50A

91D14681

Fig. 89: Test 49A – Checking Wiring & Sending Unit For Proper Operation (3 of 3)

TEST 49B: CHECKING WIRING & SENDING UNIT FOR PROPER OPERATION

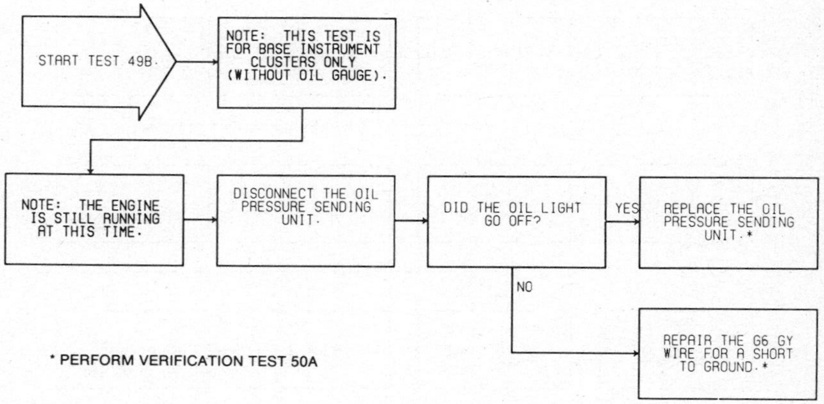
START TEST 49B.
NOTE: THIS TEST IS FOR BASE INSTRUMENT CLUSTERS ONLY (WITHOUT OIL GAUGE).
NOTE: THE ENGINE IS STILL RUNNING AT THIS TIME.
DISCONNECT THE OIL PRESSURE SENDING UNIT.
DID THE OIL LIGHT GO OFF?
YES
REPLACE THE OIL PRESSURE SENDING UNIT.*
NO
REPAIR THE G6 GY WIRE FOR A SHORT TO GROUND.*

* PERFORM VERIFICATION TEST 50A

91E14682

Fig. 90: Test 49B – Checking Wiring & Sending Unit For Proper Operation

1991 ENGINE PERFORMANCE
Body Control Computer (Cont.)

TEST 49C: CHECKING WIRING, CONTROLLER & CLUSTER FOR PROPER OPERATION (1 OF 2)

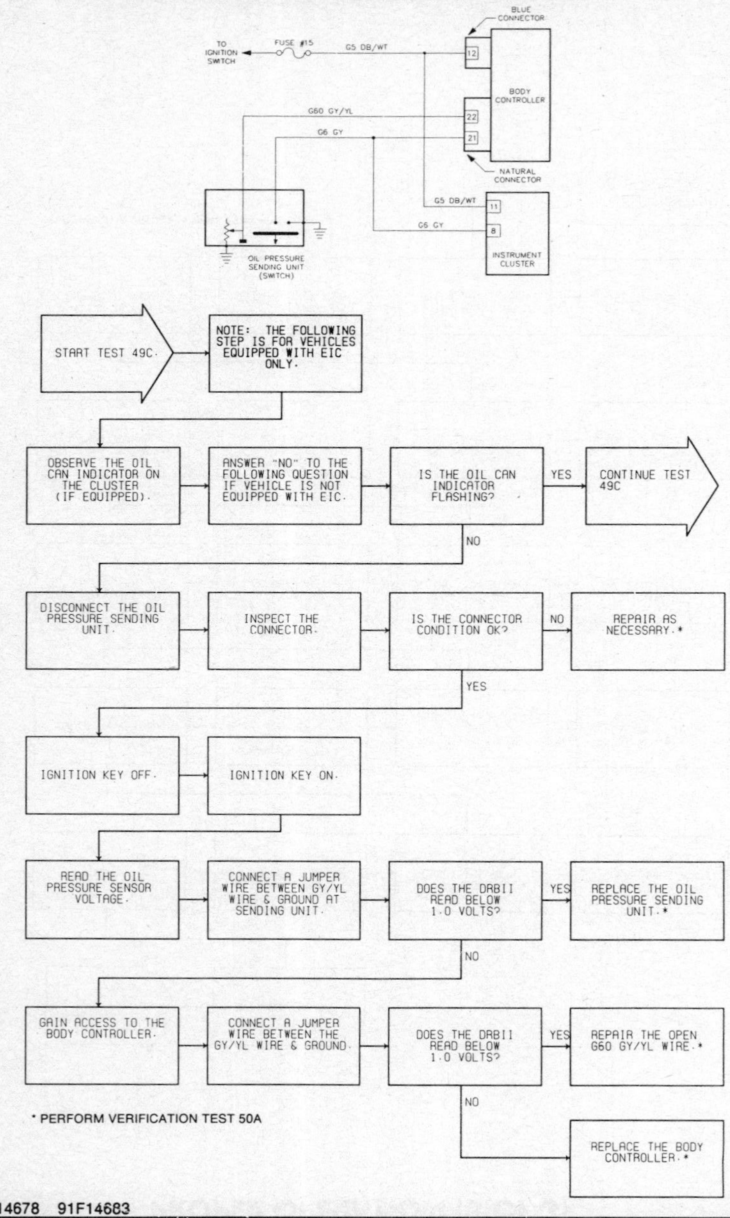
TO IGNITION SWITCH
FUSE #15
G5 DB/WT
BLUE CONNECTOR
12
BODY CONTROLLER
G60 GY/YL
22
G6 GY
21
NATURAL CONNECTOR
G5 DB/WT
11
G6 GY
8
INSTRUMENT CLUSTER
OIL PRESSURE SENDING UNIT (SWITCH)
START TEST 49C.
NOTE: THE FOLLOWING STEP IS FOR VEHICLES EQUIPPED WITH EIC ONLY.
OBSERVE THE OIL CAN INDICATOR ON THE CLUSTER (IF EQUIPPED).
ANSWER "NO" TO THE FOLLOWING QUESTION IF VEHICLE IS NOT EQUIPPED WITH EIC.
IS THE OIL CAN INDICATOR FLASHING?
YES
CONTINUE TEST 49C
NO
DISCONNECT THE OIL PRESSURE SENDING UNIT.
INSPECT THE CONNECTOR.
IS THE CONNECTOR CONDITION OK?
NO
REPAIR AS NECESSARY.*
YES
IGNITION KEY OFF.
IGNITION KEY ON.
READ THE OIL PRESSURE SENSOR VOLTAGE.
CONNECT A JUMPER WIRE BETWEEN GY/YL WIRE & GROUND AT SENDING UNIT.
DOES THE DRBII READ BELOW 1.0 VOLTS?
YES
REPLACE THE OIL PRESSURE SENDING UNIT.*
NO
GAIN ACCESS TO THE BODY CONTROLLER.
CONNECT A JUMPER WIRE BETWEEN THE GY/YL WIRE & GROUND.
DOES THE DRBII READ BELOW 1.0 VOLTS?
YES
REPAIR THE OPEN G60 GY/YL WIRE.*
NO
REPLACE THE BODY CONTROLLER.*

* PERFORM VERIFICATION TEST 50A

91I14678 91F14683

Fig. 91: Test 49C – Checking Wiring, Controller & Cluster For Proper Operation (1 of 2)

TEST 49C: CHECKING WIRING, CONTROLLER & CLUSTER FOR PROPER OPERATION (2 OF 2)

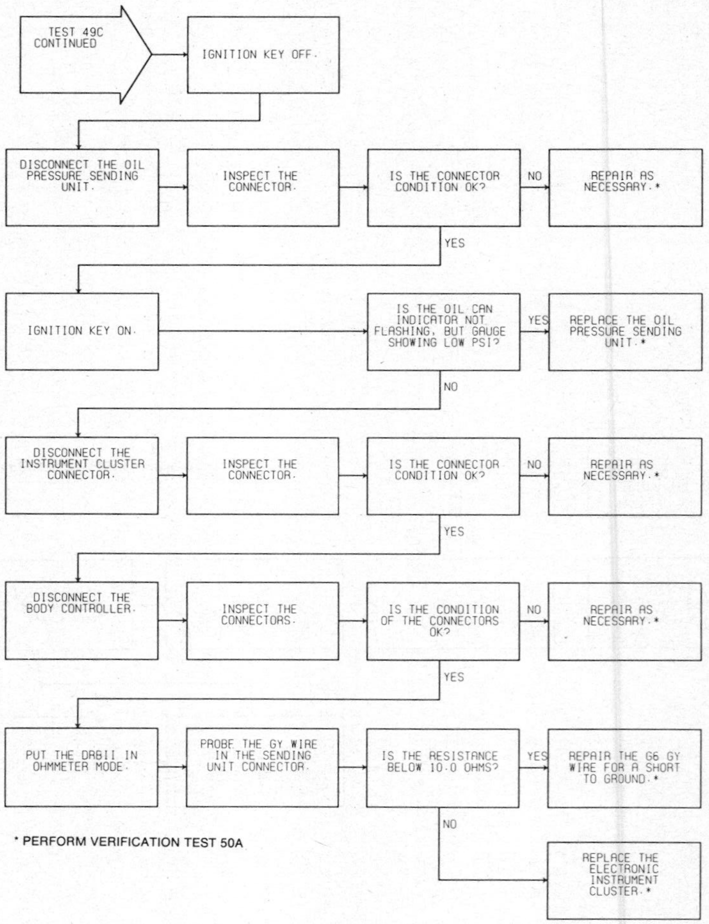
TEST 49C CONTINUED
IGNITION KEY OFF.
DISCONNECT THE OIL PRESSURE SENDING UNIT.
INSPECT THE CONNECTOR.
IS THE CONNECTOR CONDITION OK?
NO
REPAIR AS NECESSARY.*
YES
IGNITION KEY ON.
IS THE OIL CAN INDICATOR NOT FLASHING, BUT GAUGE SHOWING LOW PSI?
YES
REPLACE THE OIL PRESSURE SENDING UNIT.*
NO
DISCONNECT THE INSTRUMENT CLUSTER CONNECTOR.
INSPECT THE CONNECTOR.
IS THE CONNECTOR CONDITION OK?
NO
REPAIR AS NECESSARY.*
YES
DISCONNECT THE BODY CONTROLLER.
INSPECT THE CONNECTORS.
IS THE CONDITION OF THE CONNECTORS OK?
NO
REPAIR AS NECESSARY.*
YES
PUT THE DRBII IN OHMMETER MODE.
PROBE THE GY WIRE IN THE SENDING UNIT CONNECTOR.
IS THE RESISTANCE BELOW 10.0 OHMS?
YES
REPAIR THE G6 GY WIRE FOR A SHORT TO GROUND.*
NO
REPLACE THE ELECTRONIC INSTRUMENT CLUSTER.*

* PERFORM VERIFICATION TEST 50A

91G14684

Fig. 92: Test 49C – Checking Wiring, Controller & Cluster For Proper Operation (2 of 2)

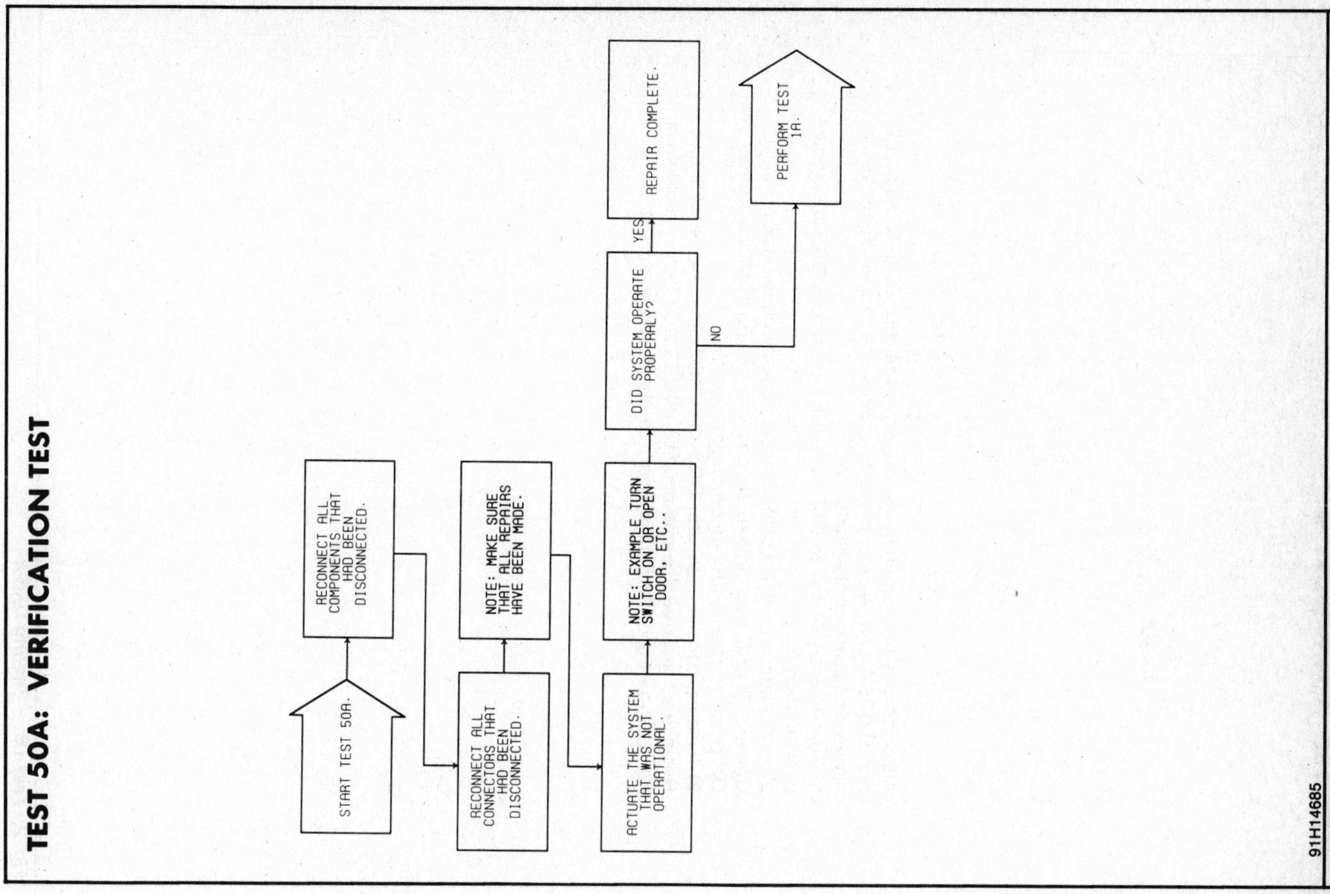
TEST 50A: VERIFICATION TEST
START TEST 50A.
RECONNECT ALL COMPONENTS THAT HAD BEEN DISCONNECTED.
RECONNECT ALL CONNECTORS THAT HAD BEEN DISCONNECTED.
NOTE: MAKE SURE THAT ALL REPAIRS HAVE BEEN MADE.
ACTUATE THE SYSTEM THAT WHS NOT OPERATIONAL.
NOTE: EXAMPLE TURN SWITCH ON OR OPEN DOOR, ETC..
DID SYSTEM OPERATE PROPERALY?
YES
REPAIR COMPLETE.
NO
PERFORM TEST 1A.
91H14685

Fig. 93: Test 50A – Verification Test

TEST 1A: GENERAL FAILURE MESSAGES

Select error message and corresponding test from GENERAL FAILURE MESSAGES table. Proceed to specified VEHICLE COMMUNICATIONS trouble shooting chart. Each specific error message is diagnosed by following a specific testing sequence. It is not necessary to perform all tests to diagnose an individual error message.

GENERAL FAILURE MESSAGES

Message	Test No.
Ram Test Failure Message	2A
Cartridge Error Message	3A
Key Pad Test Failure Message	4A
High Battery Message	5A
Low Battery Message	6A
Bus Failure Message	7A
No Response Message	65A
Blank DRB-II Message Screen	72A

Fig. 1: Test 1A – General Failure Messages

TEST 1B: TESTING DRB-II

Although only the manufacturer can physically test DRB-II, the condition of DRB-II can be determined by using some simple situation techniques and process of elimination.

1) Turn ignition switch to OFF position. Disconnect DRB-II, adapter cable and cartridge.

2) Find a second vehicle with identical equipment as original vehicle. Connect DRB-II assembly to second vehicle. Turn ignition switch to ON position. Use DRB-II as on original vehicle.

3) If same condition occurs, DRB-II or adapter cable is defective. Replace as required. If same condition DOES NOT occur, problem is not DRB-II or adapter cable. Return to diagnostic test chart.

Fig. 2: Test 1B – Testing DRB-II

TEST 2A: TESTING FOR RAM TEST FAILURE

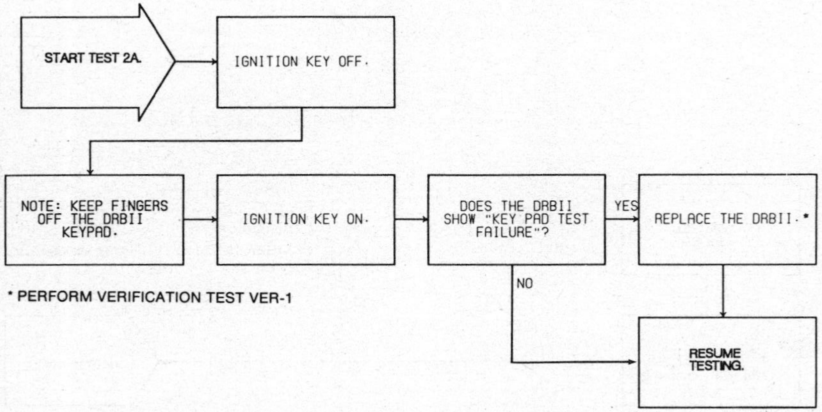
START TEST 2A.
IGNITION KEY OFF.
NOTE: KEEP FINGERS OFF THE DRBII KEYPAD.
IGNITION KEY ON.
DOES THE DRBII SHOW "KEY PAD TEST FAILURE"?
YES
REPLACE THE DRBII.*
NO
RESUME TESTING.
* PERFORM VERIFICATION TEST VER-1

91E11605

Fig. 3: Test 2A – Testing for Ram Test Failure

TEST 3A: TESTING FOR CARTRIDGE ERROR MESSAGE

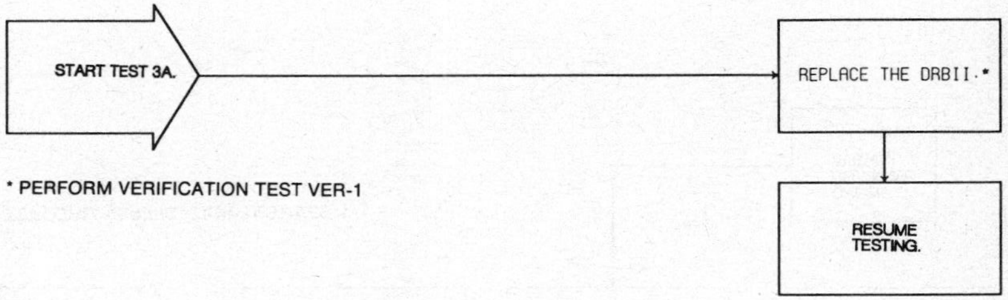
START TEST 3A.
REPLACE THE DRBII.*
RESUME TESTING.
* PERFORM VERIFICATION TEST VER-1

91F11606

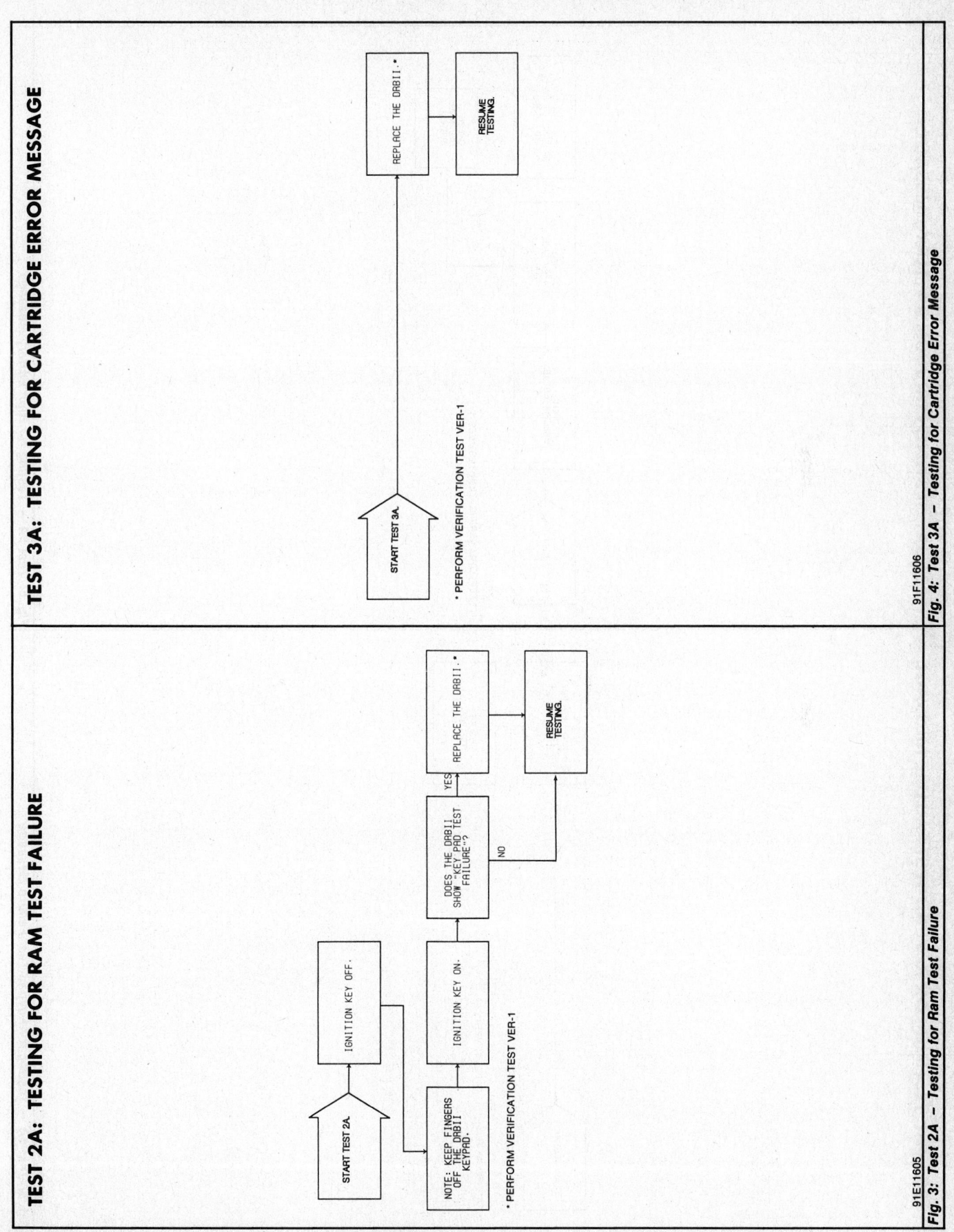

Fig. 4: Test 3A – Testing for Cartridge Error Message

1991 ENGINE PERFORMANCE
Vehicle Communications (Cont.)

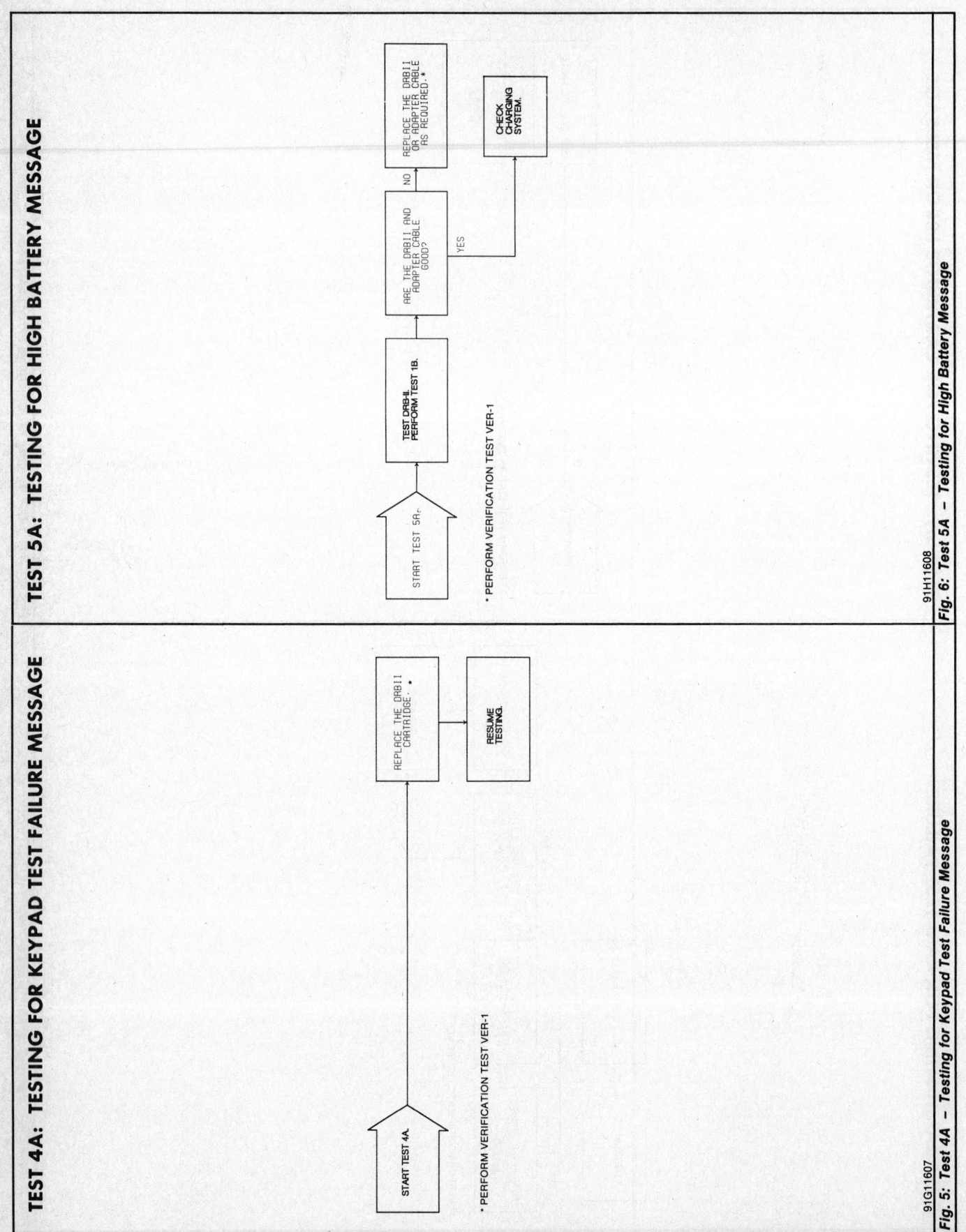

TEST 4A: TESTING FOR KEYPAD TEST FAILURE MESSAGE

START TEST 4A.
REPLACE THE DRBII CARTRIDGE. *
RESUME TESTING.

* PERFORM VERIFICATION TEST VER-1

91G11607

Fig. 5: Test 4A – Testing for Keypad Test Failure Message

TEST 5A: TESTING FOR HIGH BATTERY MESSAGE

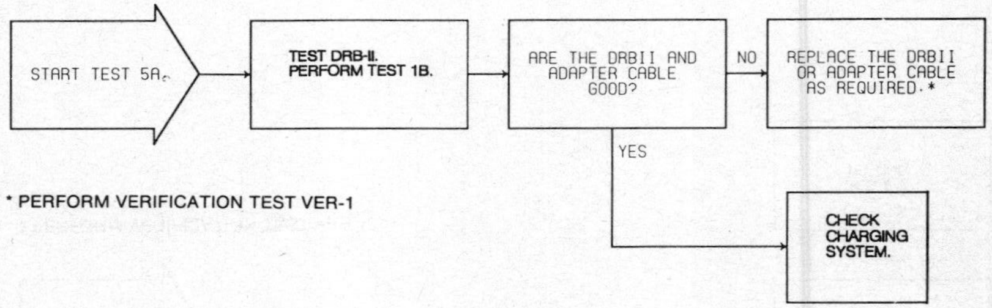
START TEST 5A.
TEST DRB-II.
PERFORM TEST 1B.
ARE THE DRBII AND ADAPTER CABLE GOOD?
NO
REPLACE THE DRBII OR ADAPTER CABLE AS REQUIRED.*
YES
CHECK CHARGING SYSTEM.

* PERFORM VERIFICATION TEST VER-1

91H11608

Fig. 6: Test 5A – Testing for High Battery Message

TEST 6A: TESTING FOR LOW BATTERY MESSAGE

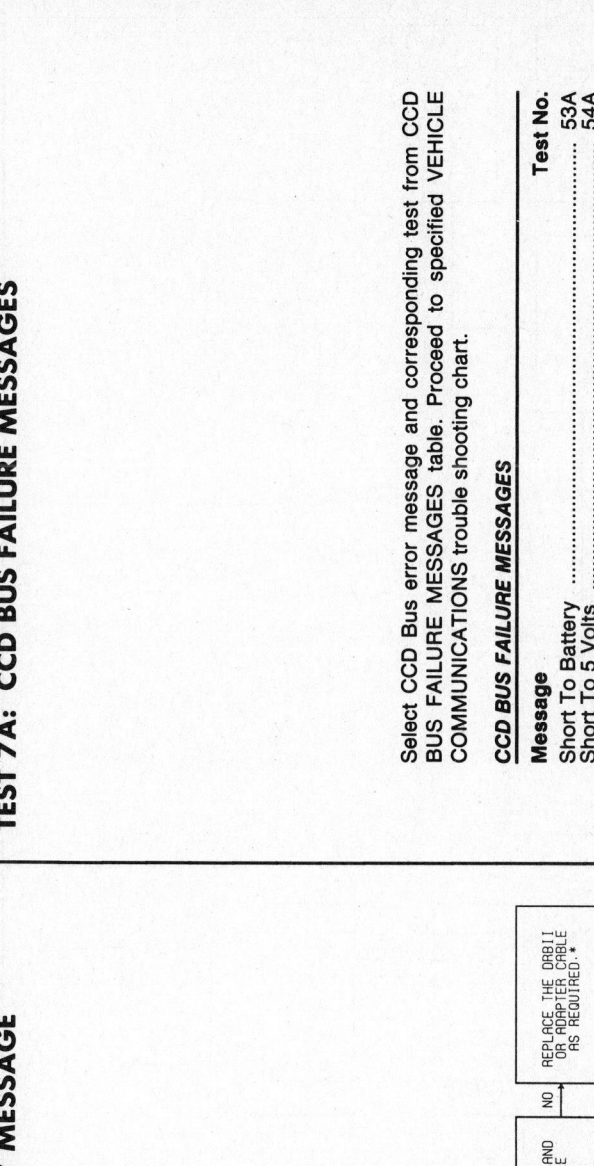

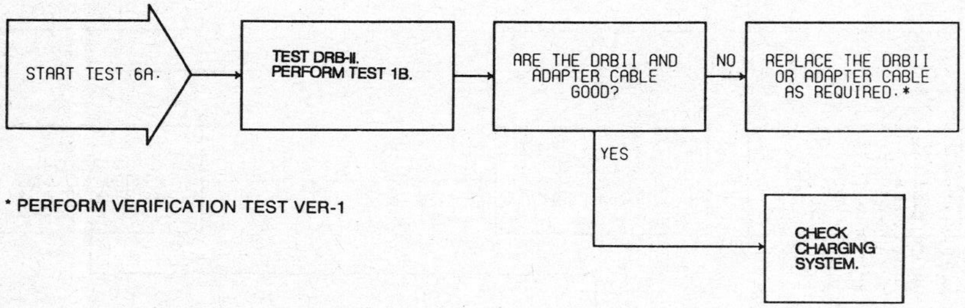
START TEST 6A.
TEST DRB-II. PERFORM TEST 1B.
ARE THE DRBII AND ADAPTER CABLE GOOD?
NO
REPLACE THE DRBII OR ADAPTER CABLE AS REQUIRED.*
YES
CHECK CHARGING SYSTEM.

* PERFORM VERIFICATION TEST VER-1

91I11609

Fig. 7: Test 6A – Testing for Low Battery Message

TEST 7A: CCD BUS FAILURE MESSAGES

Select CCD Bus error message and corresponding test from CCD BUS FAILURE MESSAGES table. Proceed to specified VEHICLE COMMUNICATIONS trouble shooting chart.

CCD BUS FAILURE MESSAGES

Message	Test No.
Short To Battery	53A
Short To 5 Volts	54A
Short To Ground	55A
Bus (+) & Bus (-) Shorted Together	56A
No Termination	57A
Bus Bias Level Too Low	58A
Bus Bias Level Too High	59A
No Bus Bias	60A
Bus (+) Open	61A
Bus (-) Open	62A
Bus (+) Or Bus (-) Open	63A
Not Receiving Bus Messages Correctly	64A

Fig. 8: Test 7A – CCD Bus Failure Messages

1991 ENGINE PERFORMANCE
Vehicle Communications (Cont.)

TEST 53A: TESTING FOR SHORT TO BATTERY ON BUS (1 OF 2)

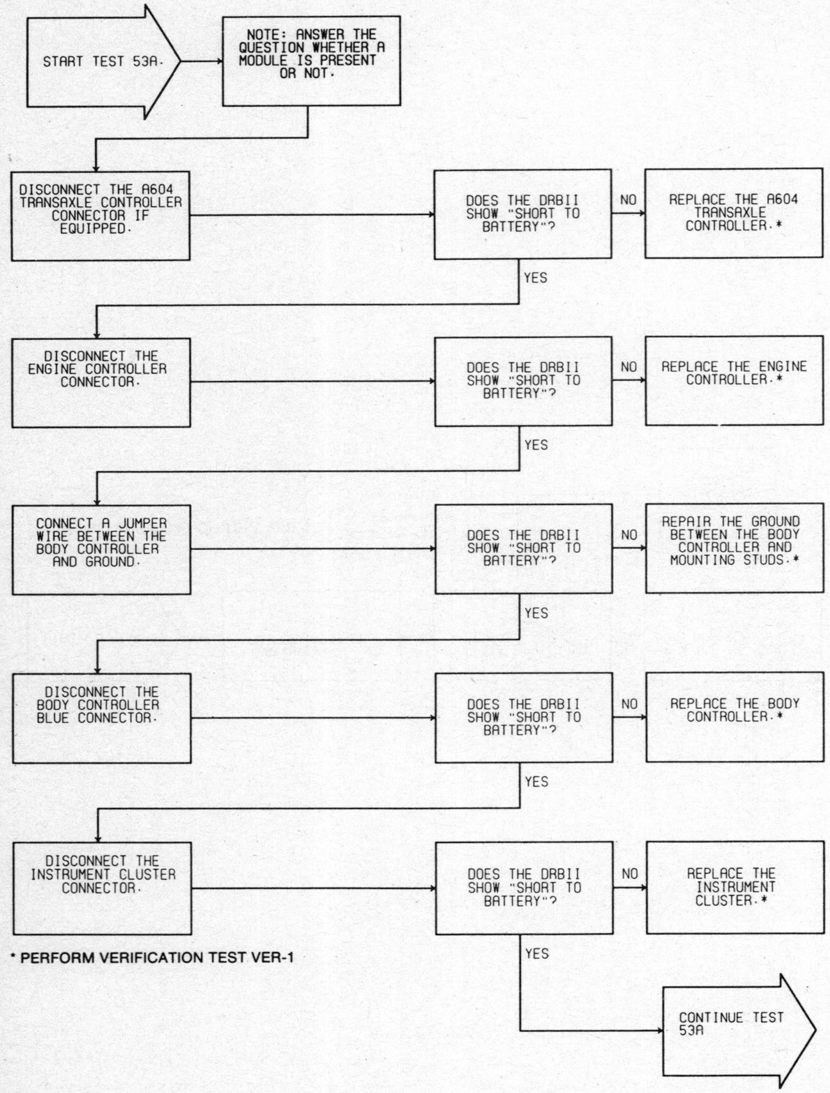
START TEST 53A.
NOTE: ANSWER THE QUESTION WHETHER A MODULE IS PRESENT OR NOT.
DISCONNECT THE A604 TRANSAXLE CONTROLLER CONNECTOR IF EQUIPPED.
DOES THE DRBII SHOW "SHORT TO BATTERY"?
NO
REPLACE THE A604 TRANSAXLE CONTROLLER.*
YES
DISCONNECT THE ENGINE CONTROLLER CONNECTOR.
DOES THE DRBII SHOW "SHORT TO BATTERY"?
NO
REPLACE THE ENGINE CONTROLLER.*
YES
CONNECT A JUMPER WIRE BETWEEN THE BODY CONTROLLER AND GROUND.
DOES THE DRBII SHOW "SHORT TO BATTERY"?
NO
REPAIR THE GROUND BETWEEN THE BODY CONTROLLER AND MOUNTING STUDS.*
YES
DISCONNECT THE BODY CONTROLLER BLUE CONNECTOR.
DOES THE DRBII SHOW "SHORT TO BATTERY"?
NO
REPLACE THE BODY CONTROLLER.*
YES
DISCONNECT THE INSTRUMENT CLUSTER CONNECTOR.
DOES THE DRBII SHOW "SHORT TO BATTERY"?
NO
REPLACE THE INSTRUMENT CLUSTER.*
YES
CONTINUE TEST 53A

* PERFORM VERIFICATION TEST VER-1

91I14686

Fig. 9: Test 53A – Testing for Short to Battery on Bus (1 of 2)

TEST 53A: TESTING FOR SHORT TO BATTERY ON BUS (2 OF 2)

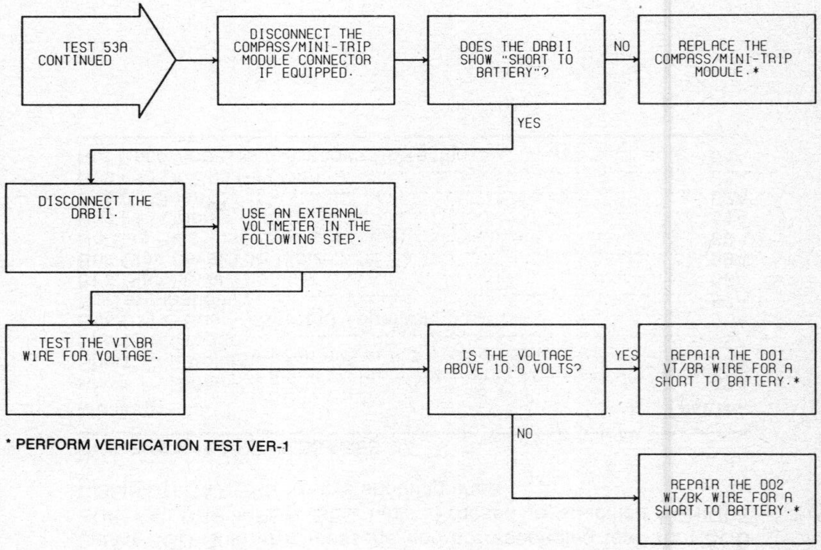
TEST 53A CONTINUED
DISCONNECT THE COMPASS/MINI-TRIP MODULE CONNECTOR IF EQUIPPED.
DOES THE DRBII SHOW "SHORT TO BATTERY"?
NO
REPLACE THE COMPASS/MINI-TRIP MODULE.*
YES
DISCONNECT THE DRBII.
USE AN EXTERNAL VOLTMETER IN THE FOLLOWING STEP.
TEST THE VT\BR WIRE FOR VOLTAGE.
IS THE VOLTAGE ABOVE 10.0 VOLTS?
YES
REPAIR THE D01 VT/BR WIRE FOR A SHORT TO BATTERY.*
NO
REPAIR THE D02 WT/BK WIRE FOR A SHORT TO BATTERY.*

* PERFORM VERIFICATION TEST VER-1

91J14687

Fig. 10: Test 53A – Testing for Ram Test Failure (2 of 2)

TEST 54A: TESTING FOR SHORT TO 5 VOLTS ON BUS

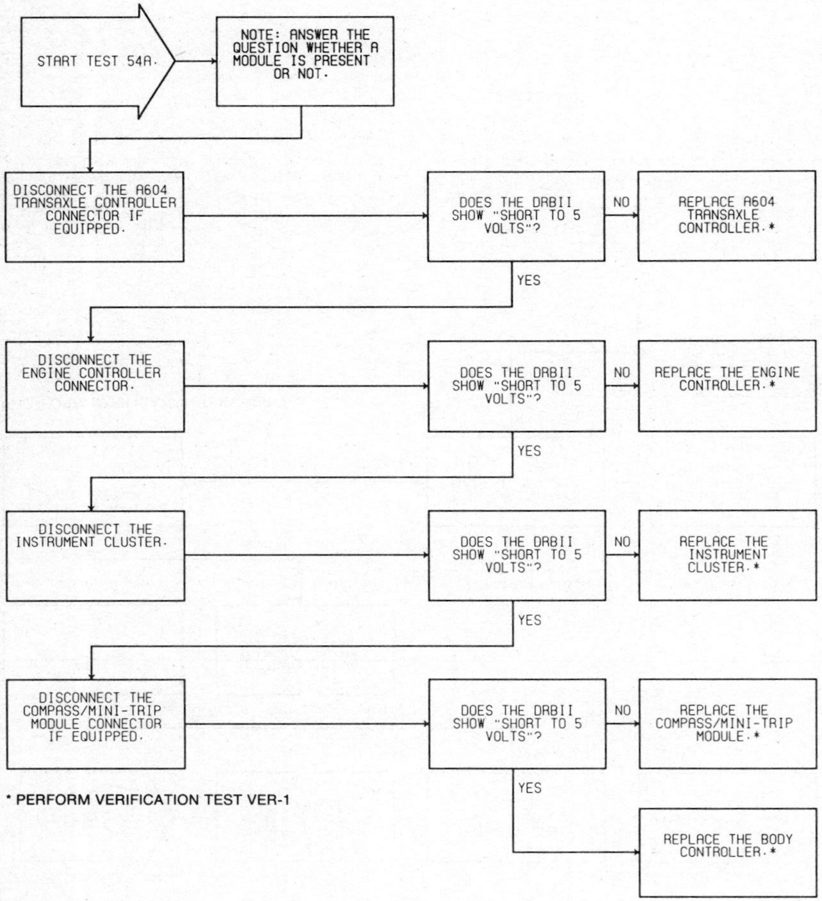
START TEST 54A.
NOTE: ANSWER THE QUESTION WHETHER A MODULE IS PRESENT OR NOT.
DISCONNECT THE A604 TRANSAXLE CONTROLLER CONNECTOR IF EQUIPPED.
DOES THE DRBII SHOW "SHORT TO 5 VOLTS"?
NO
REPLACE A604 TRANSAXLE CONTROLLER.*
YES
DISCONNECT THE ENGINE CONTROLLER CONNECTOR.
DOES THE DRBII SHOW "SHORT TO 5 VOLTS"?
NO
REPLACE THE ENGINE CONTROLLER.*
YES
DISCONNECT THE INSTRUMENT CLUSTER.
DOES THE DRBII SHOW "SHORT TO 5 VOLTS"?
NO
REPLACE THE INSTRUMENT CLUSTER.*
YES
DISCONNECT THE COMPASS/MINI-TRIP MODULE CONNECTOR IF EQUIPPED.
DOES THE DRBII SHOW "SHORT TO 5 VOLTS"?
NO
REPLACE THE COMPASS/MINI-TRIP MODULE.*
YES
REPLACE THE BODY CONTROLLER.*

* PERFORM VERIFICATION TEST VER-1

91A14688

Fig. 11: Test 54A – Testing for Short to 5 Volts on Bus

TEST 55A: TESTING FOR SHORT TO GROUND ON BUS (1 OF 2)

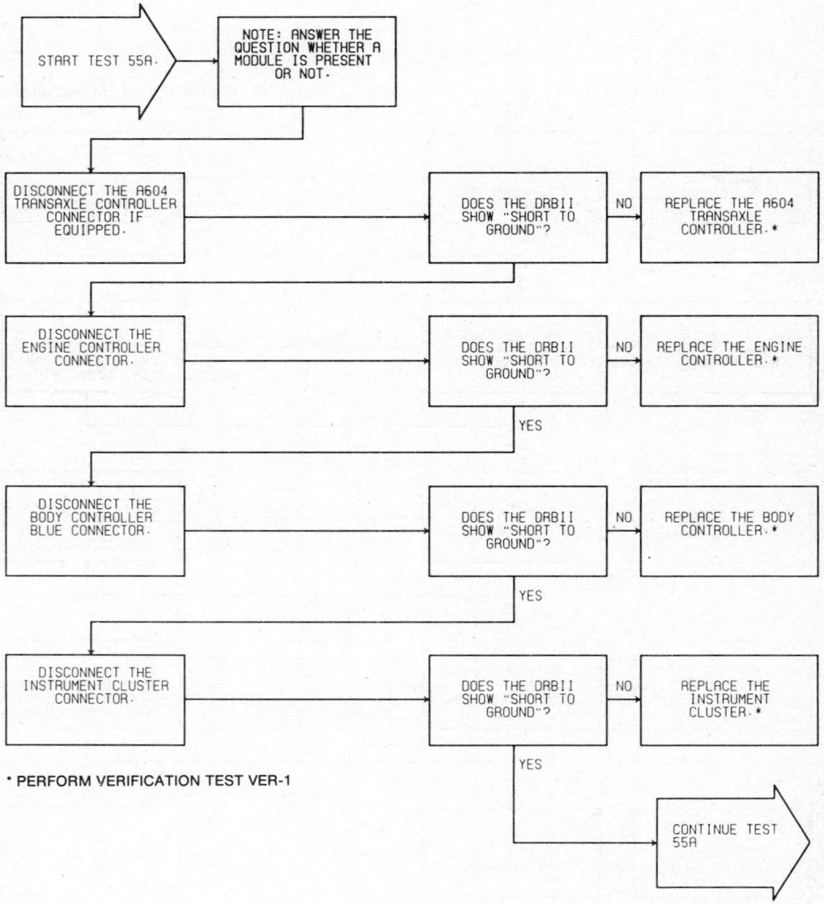
START TEST 55A.
NOTE: ANSWER THE QUESTION WHETHER A MODULE IS PRESENT OR NOT.
DISCONNECT THE A604 TRANSAXLE CONTROLLER CONNECTOR IF EQUIPPED.
DOES THE DRBII SHOW "SHORT TO GROUND"?
NO
REPLACE THE A604 TRANSAXLE CONTROLLER.*
DISCONNECT THE ENGINE CONTROLLER CONNECTOR.
DOES THE DRBII SHOW "SHORT TO GROUND"?
NO
REPLACE THE ENGINE CONTROLLER.*
YES
DISCONNECT THE BODY CONTROLLER BLUE CONNECTOR.
DOES THE DRBII SHOW "SHORT TO GROUND"?
NO
REPLACE THE BODY CONTROLLER.*
YES
DISCONNECT THE INSTRUMENT CLUSTER CONNECTOR.
DOES THE DRBII SHOW "SHORT TO GROUND"?
NO
REPLACE THE INSTRUMENT CLUSTER.*
YES
CONTINUE TEST 55A

* PERFORM VERIFICATION TEST VER-1

91B14689

Fig. 12: Test 55A – Testing for Short to Ground on Bus (1 of 2)

1991 ENGINE PERFORMANCE
Vehicle Communications (Cont.)

TEST 55A: TESTING FOR SHORT TO GROUND ON BUS (2 OF 2)

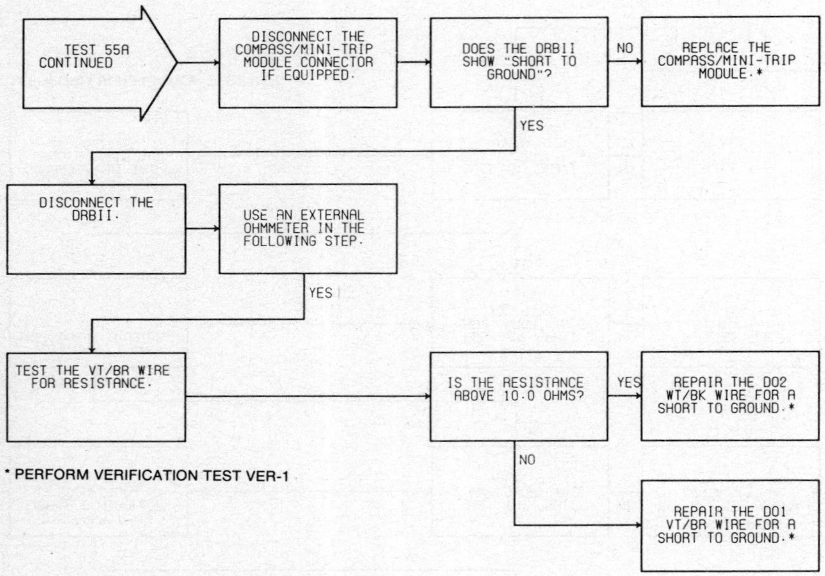
TEST 55A CONTINUED
DISCONNECT THE COMPASS/MINI-TRIP MODULE CONNECTOR IF EQUIPPED.
DOES THE DRBII SHOW "SHORT TO GROUND"?
NO
REPLACE THE COMPASS/MINI-TRIP MODULE.*
YES
DISCONNECT THE DRBII.
USE AN EXTERNAL OHMMETER IN THE FOLLOWING STEP.
YES
TEST THE VT/BR WIRE FOR RESISTANCE.
IS THE RESISTANCE ABOVE 10.0 OHMS?
YES
REPAIR THE D02 WT/BK WIRE FOR A SHORT TO GROUND.*
NO
REPAIR THE D01 VT/BR WIRE FOR A SHORT TO GROUND.*

* PERFORM VERIFICATION TEST VER-1

91E14690

Fig. 13: Test 55A – Testing for Short to Ground on Bus (2 of 2)

TEST 56A: TESTING FOR BUS (+) & BUS (–) SHORTED TOGETHER (1 OF 2)

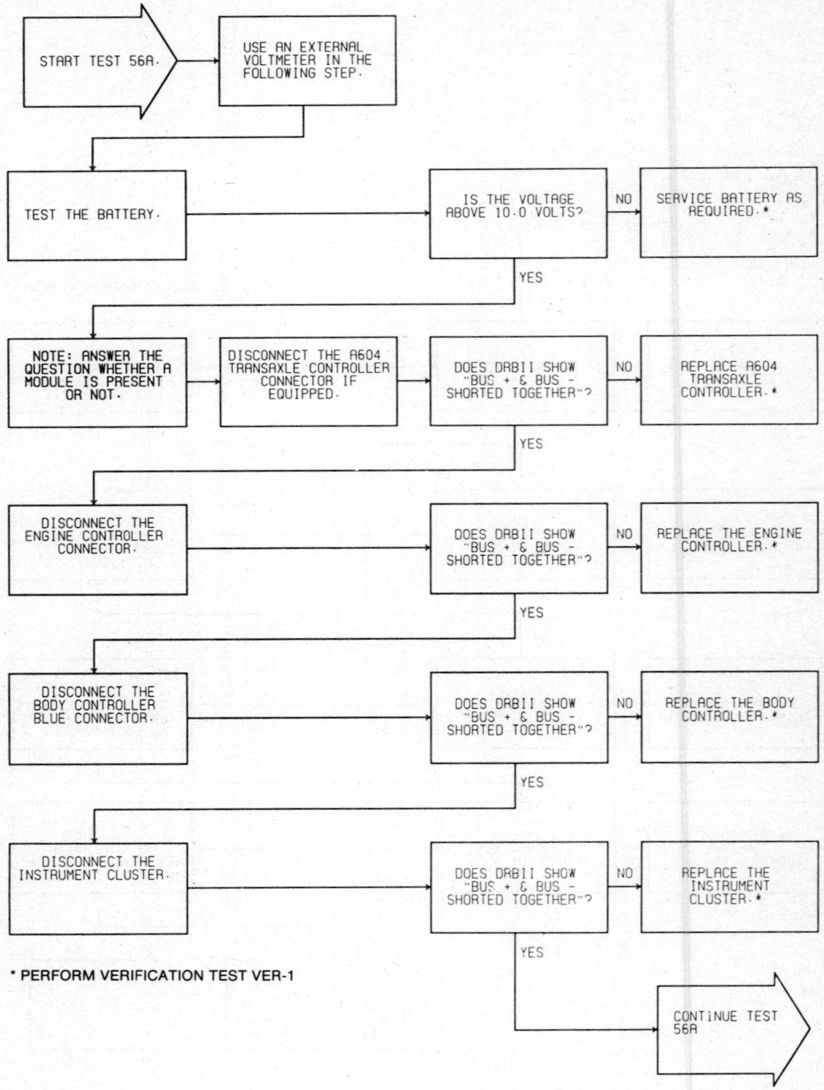
START TEST 56A.
USE AN EXTERNAL VOLTMETER IN THE FOLLOWING STEP.
TEST THE BATTERY.
IS THE VOLTAGE ABOVE 10.0 VOLTS?
NO
SERVICE BATTERY AS REQUIRED.*
YES
NOTE: ANSWER THE QUESTION WHETHER A MODULE IS PRESENT OR NOT.
DISCONNECT THE A604 TRANSAXLE CONTROLLER CONNECTOR IF EQUIPPED.
DOES DRBII SHOW "BUS + & BUS - SHORTED TOGETHER"?
NO
REPLACE A604 TRANSAXLE CONTROLLER.*
YES
DISCONNECT THE ENGINE CONTROLLER CONNECTOR.
DOES DRBII SHOW "BUS + & BUS - SHORTED TOGETHER"?
NO
REPLACE THE ENGINE CONTROLLER.*
YES
DISCONNECT THE BODY CONTROLLER BLUE CONNECTOR.
DOES DRBII SHOW "BUS + & BUS - SHORTED TOGETHER"?
NO
REPLACE THE BODY CONTROLLER.*
YES
DISCONNECT THE INSTRUMENT CLUSTER.
DOES DRBII SHOW "BUS + & BUS - SHORTED TOGETHER"?
NO
REPLACE THE INSTRUMENT CLUSTER.*
YES
CONTINUE TEST 56A

* PERFORM VERIFICATION TEST VER-1

91F14691

Fig. 14: Test 56A – Testing for Bus (+) & Bus (–) Shorted together (1 of 2)

TEST 56A: TESTING FOR BUS (+) & BUS (–) SHORTED TOGETHER (2 OF 2)

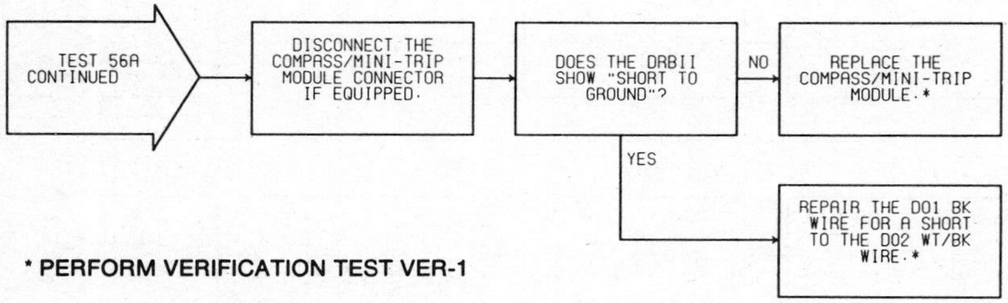

TEST 56A CONTINUED
DISCONNECT THE COMPASS/MINI-TRIP MODULE CONNECTOR IF EQUIPPED.
DOES THE DRBII SHOW "SHORT TO GROUND"?
NO
REPLACE THE COMPASS/MINI-TRIP MODULE.*
YES
REPAIR THE D01 BK WIRE FOR A SHORT TO THE D02 WT/BK WIRE.*

* PERFORM VERIFICATION TEST VER-1

91G14692

Fig. 15: Test 56A – Testing for Bus (+) & Bus (–) Shorted together (2 of 2)

TEST 57A: TESTING FOR NO TERMINATION ON BUS (1 OF 3)

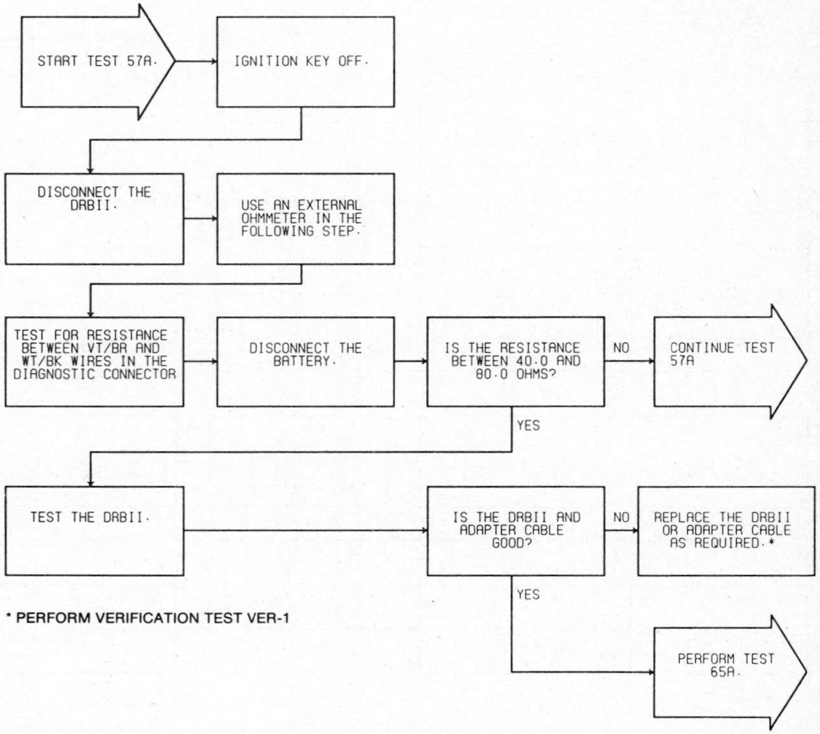

START TEST 57A.
IGNITION KEY OFF.
DISCONNECT THE DRBII.
USE AN EXTERNAL OHMMETER IN THE FOLLOWING STEP.
TEST FOR RESISTANCE BETWEEN VT/BR AND WT/BK WIRES IN THE DIAGNOSTIC CONNECTOR
DISCONNECT THE BATTERY.
IS THE RESISTANCE BETWEEN 40.0 AND 80.0 OHMS?
NO
CONTINUE TEST 57A
YES
TEST THE DRBII.
IS THE DRBII AND ADAPTER CABLE GOOD?
NO
REPLACE THE DRBII OR ADAPTER CABLE AS REQUIRED.*
YES
PERFORM TEST 65A.

* PERFORM VERIFICATION TEST VER-1

91H14693

Fig. 16: Test 57A – Testing for No Termination on Bus (1 of 3)

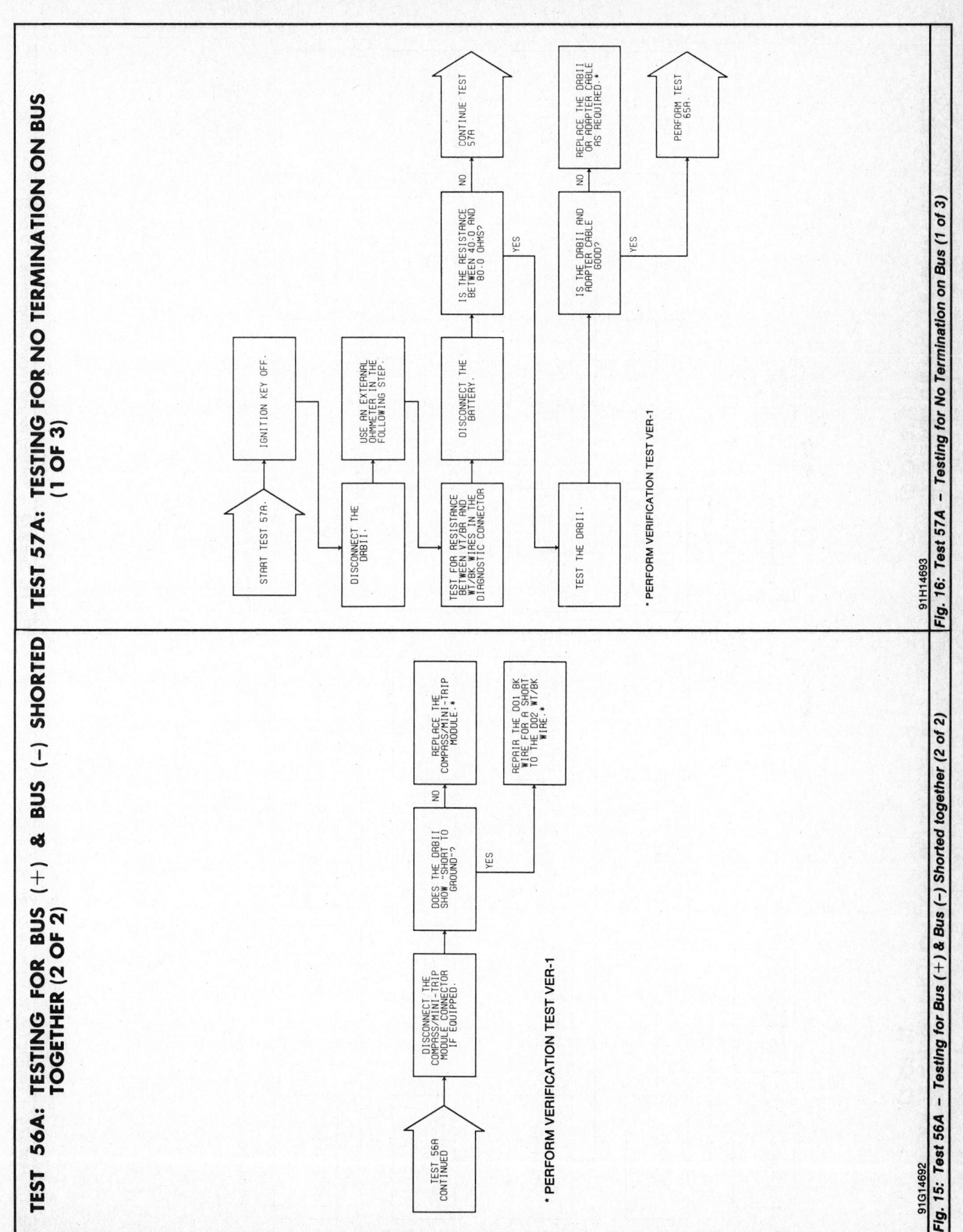

1991 ENGINE PERFORMANCE
Vehicle Communications (Cont.)

TEST 57A: TESTING FOR NO TERMINATION ON BUS (2 OF 3)

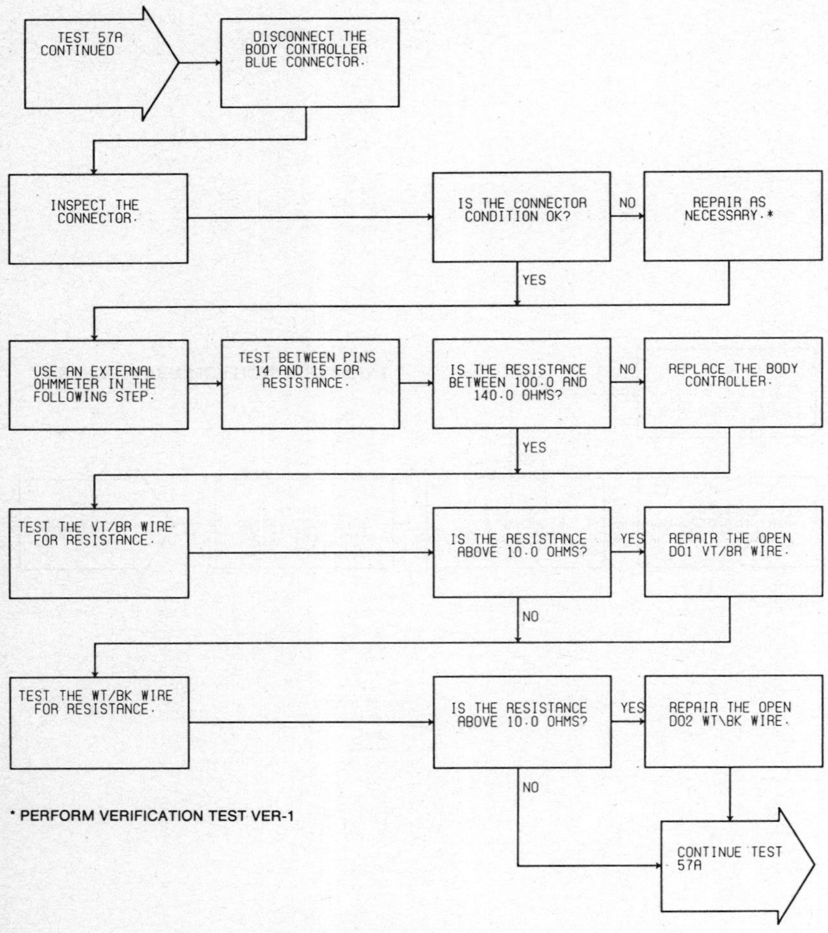
TEST 57A CONTINUED
DISCONNECT THE BODY CONTROLLER BLUE CONNECTOR.
INSPECT THE CONNECTOR.
IS THE CONNECTOR CONDITION OK?
NO
REPAIR AS NECESSARY.*
YES
USE AN EXTERNAL OHMMETER IN THE FOLLOWING STEP.
TEST BETWEEN PINS 14 AND 15 FOR RESISTANCE.
IS THE RESISTANCE BETWEEN 100.0 AND 140.0 OHMS?
NO
REPLACE THE BODY CONTROLLER.
YES
TEST THE VT/BR WIRE FOR RESISTANCE.
IS THE RESISTANCE ABOVE 10.0 OHMS?
YES
REPAIR THE OPEN D01 VT/BR WIRE.
NO
TEST THE WT/BK WIRE FOR RESISTANCE.
IS THE RESISTANCE ABOVE 10.0 OHMS?
YES
REPAIR THE OPEN D02 WT\BK WIRE.
NO
CONTINUE TEST 57A

* PERFORM VERIFICATION TEST VER-1

91I14694

Fig. 17: Test 57A – Testing for No Termination on Bus (2 of 3)

TEST 57A: TESTING FOR NO TERMINATION ON BUS (3 OF 3)

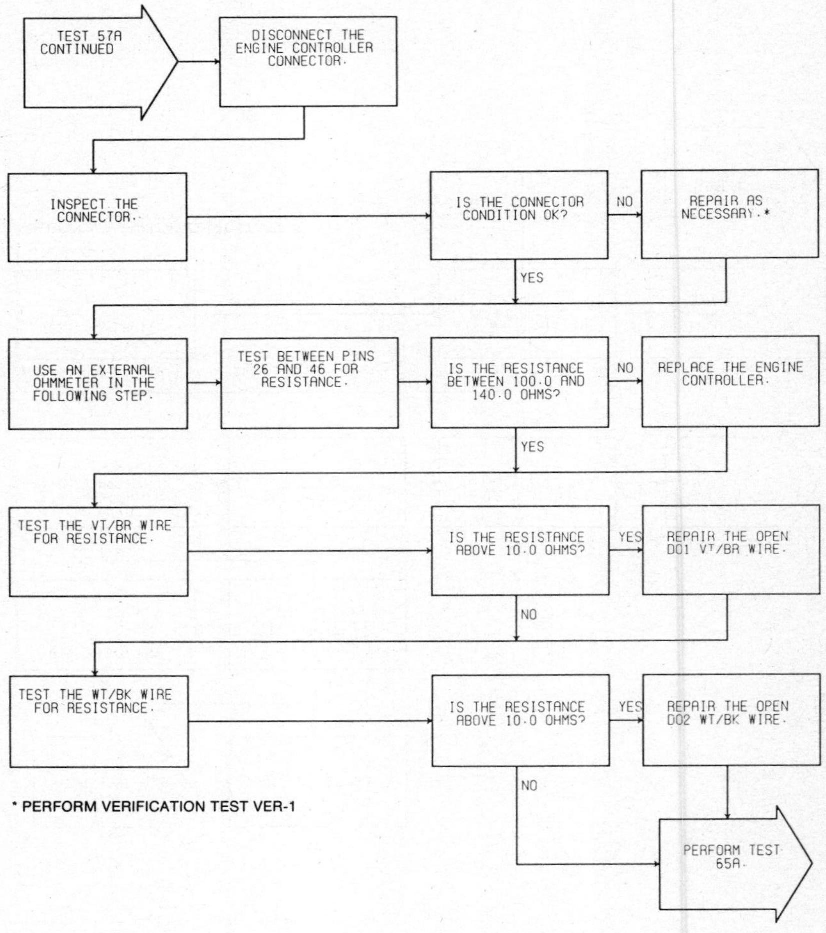
TEST 57A CONTINUED
DISCONNECT THE ENGINE CONTROLLER CONNECTOR.
INSPECT THE CONNECTOR.
IS THE CONNECTOR CONDITION OK?
NO
REPAIR AS NECESSARY.*
YES
USE AN EXTERNAL OHMMETER IN THE FOLLOWING STEP.
TEST BETWEEN PINS 26 AND 46 FOR RESISTANCE.
IS THE RESISTANCE BETWEEN 100.0 AND 140.0 OHMS?
NO
REPLACE THE ENGINE CONTROLLER.
YES
TEST THE VT/BR WIRE FOR RESISTANCE.
IS THE RESISTANCE ABOVE 10.0 OHMS?
YES
REPAIR THE OPEN D01 VT/BR WIRE.
NO
TEST THE WT/BK WIRE FOR RESISTANCE.
IS THE RESISTANCE ABOVE 10.0 OHMS?
YES
REPAIR THE OPEN D02 WT/BK WIRE.
NO
PERFORM TEST 65A.

* PERFORM VERIFICATION TEST VER-1

91J14695

Fig. 18: Test 57A – Testing for No Termination on Bus (3 of 3)

TEST 58A: TESTING FOR BUS BIAS LEVEL TOO LOW (1 OF 3)

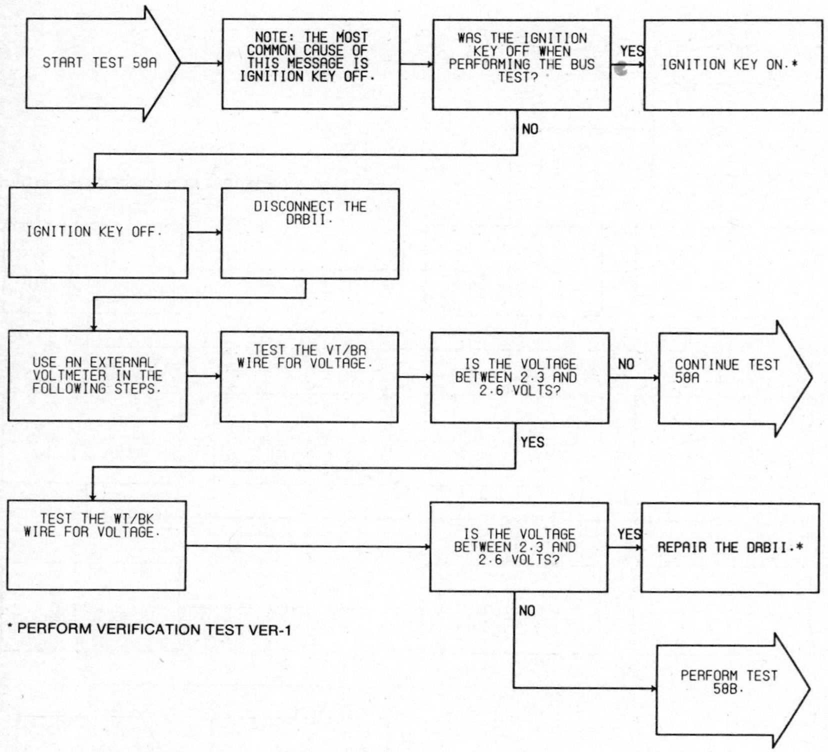
START TEST 58A
NOTE: THE MOST COMMON CAUSE OF THIS MESSAGE IS IGNITION KEY OFF.
WAS THE IGNITION KEY OFF WHEN PERFORMING THE BUS TEST?
YES
IGNITION KEY ON.*
NO
IGNITION KEY OFF.
DISCONNECT THE DRBII.
USE AN EXTERNAL VOLTMETER IN THE FOLLOWING STEPS.
TEST THE VT/BR WIRE FOR VOLTAGE.
IS THE VOLTAGE BETWEEN 2.3 AND 2.6 VOLTS?
NO
CONTINUE TEST 58A
YES
TEST THE WT/BK WIRE FOR VOLTAGE.
IS THE VOLTAGE BETWEEN 2.3 AND 2.6 VOLTS?
YES
REPAIR THE DRBII.*
NO
PERFORM TEST 58B.

* PERFORM VERIFICATION TEST VER-1

91A14696

Fig. 19: Test 58A – Testing for Bus Bias Level Too Low (1 of 3)

TEST 58A: TESTING FOR BUS BIAS LEVEL TOO LOW (2 OF 3)

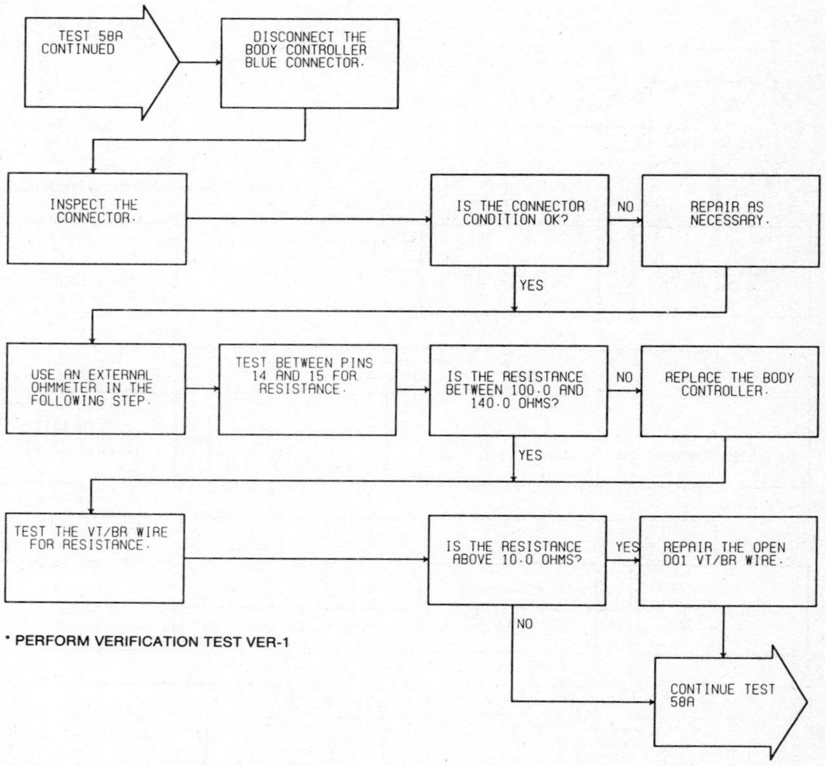
TEST 58A CONTINUED
DISCONNECT THE BODY CONTROLLER BLUE CONNECTOR.
INSPECT THE CONNECTOR.
IS THE CONNECTOR CONDITION OK?
NO
REPAIR AS NECESSARY.
YES
USE AN EXTERNAL OHMMETER IN THE FOLLOWING STEP.
TEST BETWEEN PINS 14 AND 15 FOR RESISTANCE.
IS THE RESISTANCE BETWEEN 100.0 AND 140.0 OHMS?
NO
REPLACE THE BODY CONTROLLER.
YES
TEST THE VT/BR WIRE FOR RESISTANCE.
IS THE RESISTANCE ABOVE 10.0 OHMS?
YES
REPAIR THE OPEN DO1 VT/BR WIRE.
NO
CONTINUE TEST 58A

* PERFORM VERIFICATION TEST VER-1

91B14697

Fig. 20: Test 58A – Testing for Bus Bias Level Too Low (2 of 3)

TEST 58A: TESTING FOR BUS BIAS LEVEL TOO LOW (3 OF 3)

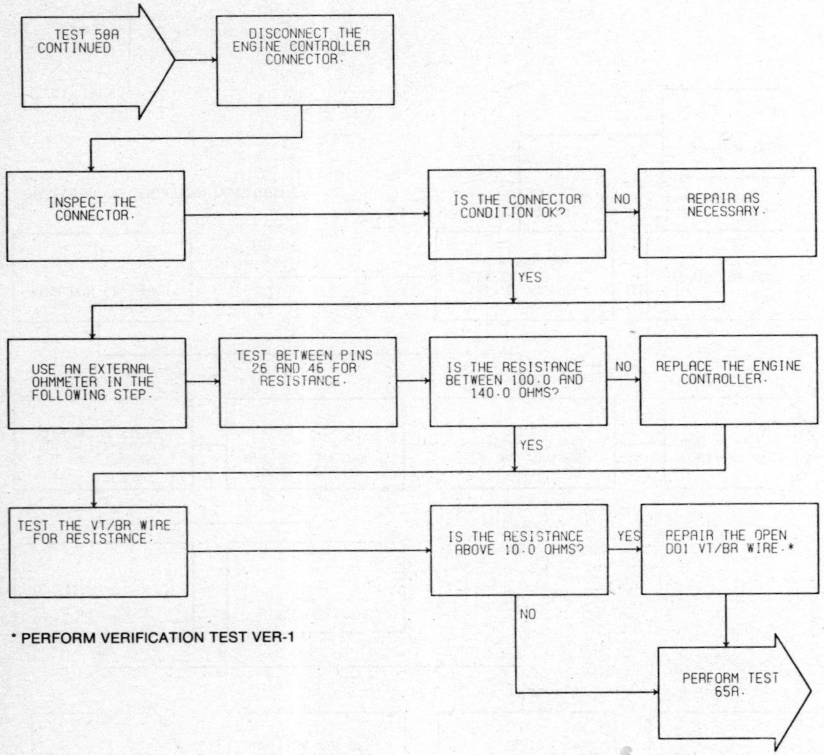
TEST 58A CONTINUED
DISCONNECT THE ENGINE CONTROLLER CONNECTOR.
INSPECT THE CONNECTOR.
IS THE CONNECTOR CONDITION OK?
NO
REPAIR AS NECESSARY.
YES
USE AN EXTERNAL OHMMETER IN THE FOLLOWING STEP.
TEST BETWEEN PINS 26 AND 46 FOR RESISTANCE.
IS THE RESISTANCE BETWEEN 100.0 AND 140.0 OHMS?
NO
REPLACE THE ENGINE CONTROLLER.
YES
TEST THE VT/BR WIRE FOR RESISTANCE.
IS THE RESISTANCE ABOVE 10.0 OHMS?
YES
REPAIR THE OPEN D01 VT/BR WIRE.*
NO
PERFORM TEST 65A.

* PERFORM VERIFICATION TEST VER-1

91C14698

Fig. 21: Test 58A – Testing for Bus Bias Level Too Low (3 of 3)

TEST 58B: TESTING FOR BUS BIAS LEVEL TOO LOW (1 OF 2)

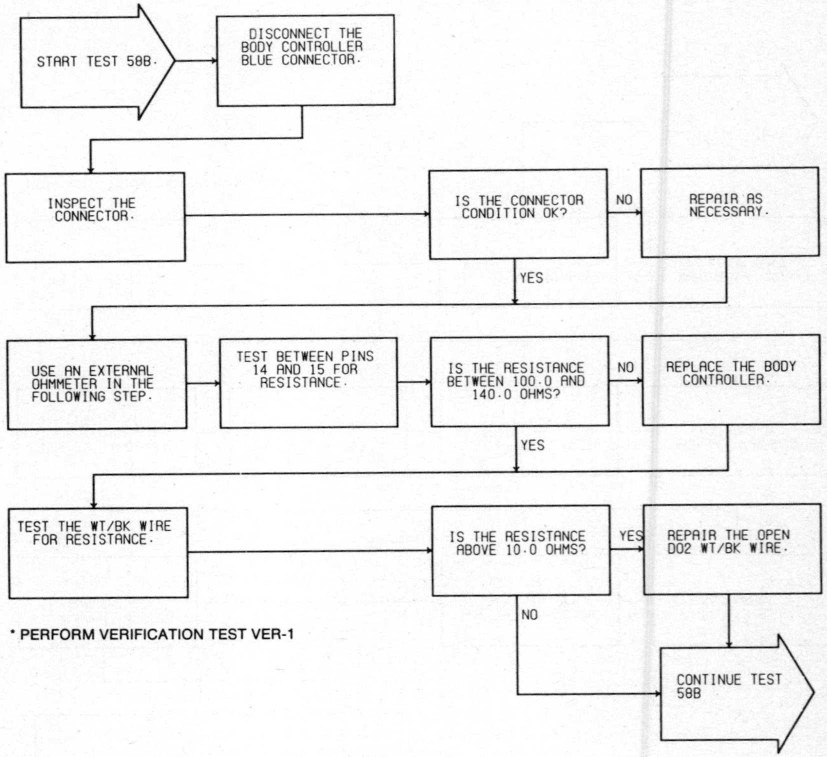
START TEST 58B.
DISCONNECT THE BODY CONTROLLER BLUE CONNECTOR.
INSPECT THE CONNECTOR.
IS THE CONNECTOR CONDITION OK?
NO
REPAIR AS NECESSARY.
YES
USE AN EXTERNAL OHMMETER IN THE FOLLOWING STEP.
TEST BETWEEN PINS 14 AND 15 FOR RESISTANCE.
IS THE RESISTANCE BETWEEN 100.0 AND 140.0 OHMS?
NO
REPLACE THE BODY CONTROLLER.
YES
TEST THE WT/BK WIRE FOR RESISTANCE.
IS THE RESISTANCE ABOVE 10.0 OHMS?
YES
REPAIR THE OPEN D02 WT/BK WIRE.
NO
CONTINUE TEST 58B

* PERFORM VERIFICATION TEST VER-1

91D14699

Fig. 22: Test 58B – Testing for Bus Bias Level Too Low (1 of 2)

TEST 58B: TESTING FOR BUS BIAS LEVEL TOO LOW (2 OF 2)

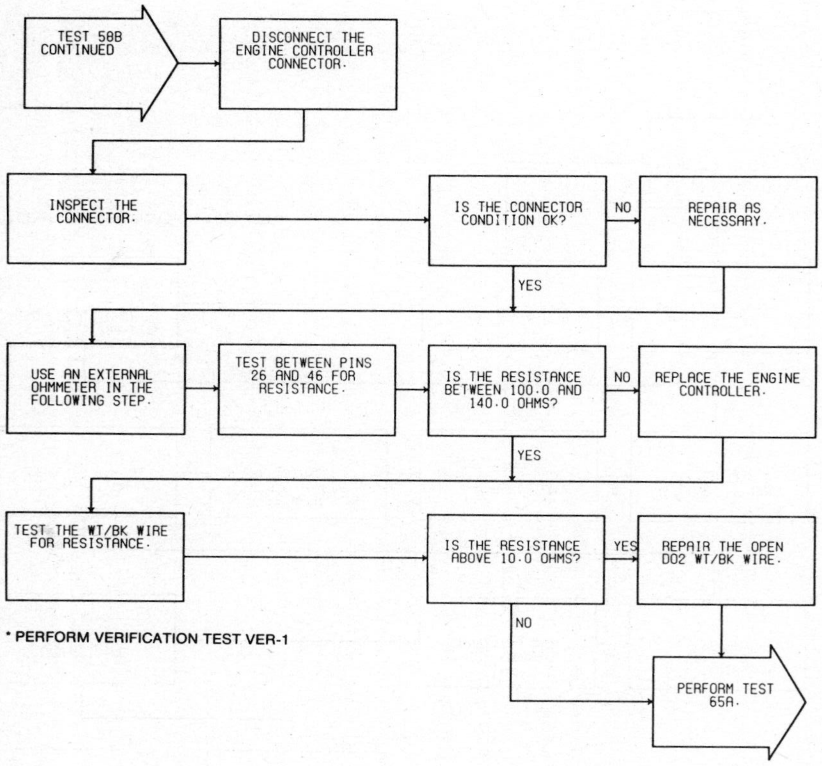
TEST 58B CONTINUED
DISCONNECT THE ENGINE CONTROLLER CONNECTOR.
INSPECT THE CONNECTOR.
IS THE CONNECTOR CONDITION OK?
NO
REPAIR AS NECESSARY.
YES
USE AN EXTERNAL OHMMETER IN THE FOLLOWING STEP.
TEST BETWEEN PINS 26 AND 46 FOR RESISTANCE.
IS THE RESISTANCE BETWEEN 100.0 AND 140.0 OHMS?
NO
REPLACE THE ENGINE CONTROLLER.
YES
TEST THE WT/BK WIRE FOR RESISTANCE.
IS THE RESISTANCE ABOVE 10.0 OHMS?
YES
REPAIR THE OPEN DO2 WT/BK WIRE.
NO
PERFORM TEST 65A.
* PERFORM VERIFICATION TEST VER-1

91G14700

Fig. 23: Test 58B – Testing for Bus Bias Level Too Low (2 of 2)

TEST 59A: TESTING FOR BUS BIAS LEVEL TOO HIGH (1 OF 3)

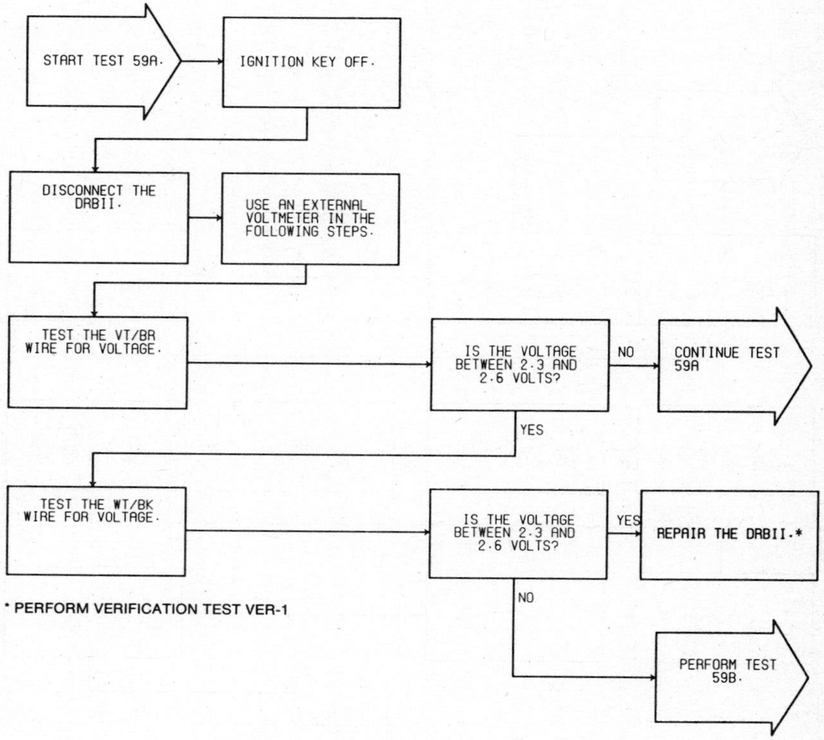
START TEST 59A.
IGNITION KEY OFF.
DISCONNECT THE DRBII.
USE AN EXTERNAL VOLTMETER IN THE FOLLOWING STEPS.
TEST THE VT/BR WIRE FOR VOLTAGE.
IS THE VOLTAGE BETWEEN 2.3 AND 2.6 VOLTS?
NO
CONTINUE TEST 59A
YES
TEST THE WT/BK WIRE FOR VOLTAGE.
IS THE VOLTAGE BETWEEN 2.3 AND 2.6 VOLTS?
YES
REPAIR THE DRBII.*
NO
PERFORM TEST 59B.
* PERFORM VERIFICATION TEST VER-1

91H14701

Fig. 24: Test 59A – Testing for Bus Bias Level Too High (1 of 3)

1991 ENGINE PERFORMANCE
Vehicle Communications (Cont.)

TEST 59A: TESTING FOR BUS BIAS LEVEL TOO HIGH (2 OF 3)

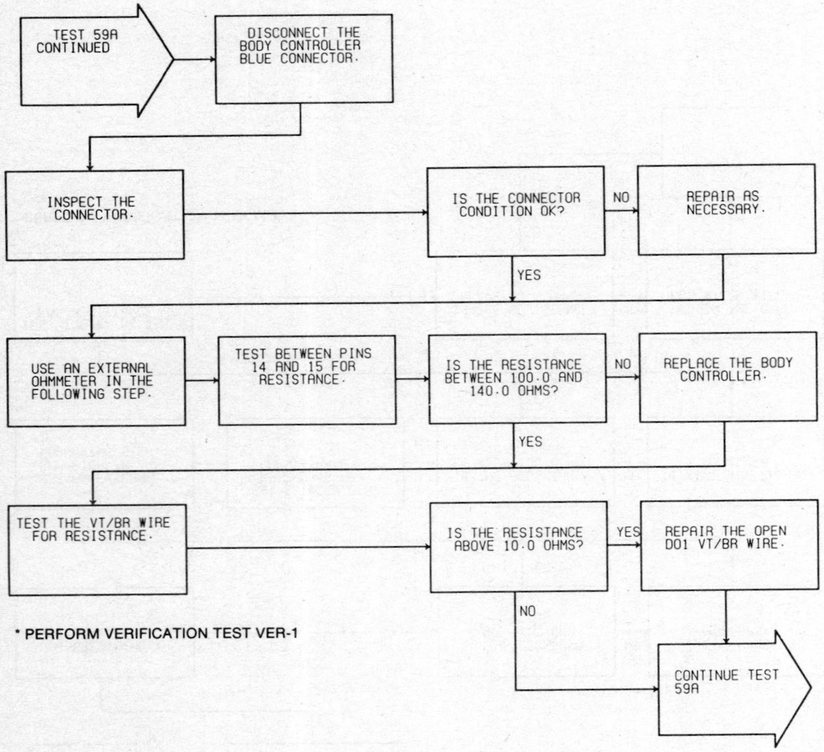
TEST 59A CONTINUED
DISCONNECT THE BODY CONTROLLER BLUE CONNECTOR.
INSPECT THE CONNECTOR.
IS THE CONNECTOR CONDITION OK?
NO
REPAIR AS NECESSARY.
YES
USE AN EXTERNAL OHMMETER IN THE FOLLOWING STEP.
TEST BETWEEN PINS 14 AND 15 FOR RESISTANCE.
IS THE RESISTANCE BETWEEN 100.0 AND 140.0 OHMS?
NO
REPLACE THE BODY CONTROLLER.
YES
TEST THE VT/BR WIRE FOR RESISTANCE.
IS THE RESISTANCE ABOVE 10.0 OHMS?
YES
REPAIR THE OPEN D01 VT/BR WIRE.
NO
CONTINUE TEST 59A

* PERFORM VERIFICATION TEST VER-1

91I14702

Fig. 25: Test 59A – Testing for Bus Bias Level Too High (2 of 3)

TEST 59A – BUS BIAS LEVEL TOO HIGH (3 OF 3)

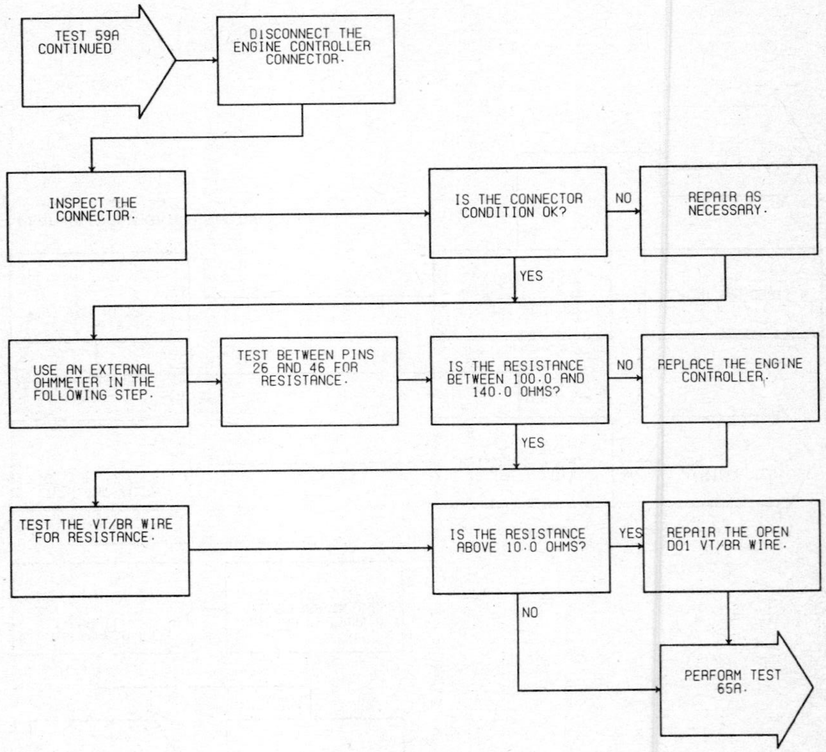
TEST 59A CONTINUED
DISCONNECT THE ENGINE CONTROLLER CONNECTOR.
INSPECT THE CONNECTOR.
IS THE CONNECTOR CONDITION OK?
NO
REPAIR AS NECESSARY.
YES
USE AN EXTERNAL OHMMETER IN THE FOLLOWING STEP.
TEST BETWEEN PINS 26 AND 46 FOR RESISTANCE.
IS THE RESISTANCE BETWEEN 100.0 AND 140.0 OHMS?
NO
REPLACE THE ENGINE CONTROLLER.
YES
TEST THE VT/BR WIRE FOR RESISTANCE.
IS THE RESISTANCE ABOVE 10.0 OHMS?
YES
REPAIR THE OPEN D01 VT/BR WIRE.
NO
PERFORM TEST 65A.

91J14521

Fig. 26: Test 59A – Bus Bias Level Too High (3 of 3)

TEST 59B – BUS BIAS LEVEL TOO HIGH (1 OF 2)

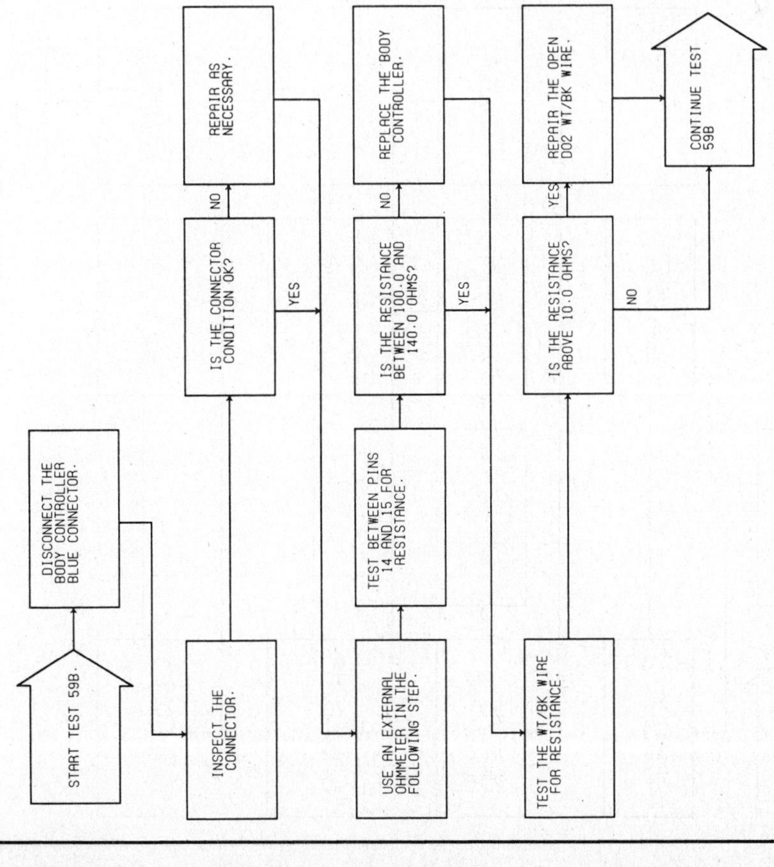

START TEST 59B.
DISCONNECT THE BODY CONTROLLER BLUE CONNECTOR.
INSPECT THE CONNECTOR.
IS THE CONNECTOR CONDITION OK?
NO
REPAIR AS NECESSARY.
YES
USE AN EXTERNAL OHMMETER IN THE FOLLOWING STEP.
TEST BETWEEN PINS 14 AND 15 FOR RESISTANCE.
IS THE RESISTANCE BETWEEN 100.0 AND 140.0 OHMS?
NO
REPLACE THE BODY CONTROLLER.
YES
TEST THE WT/BK WIRE FOR RESISTANCE.
IS THE RESISTANCE ABOVE 10.0 OHMS?
YES
REPAIR THE OPEN D02 WT/BK WIRE.
NO
CONTINUE TEST 59B

91A14522

Fig. 27: Test 59B – Bus Bias Level Too High (1 of 2)

TEST 59B – BUS BIAS LEVEL TOO HIGH (2 OF 2)

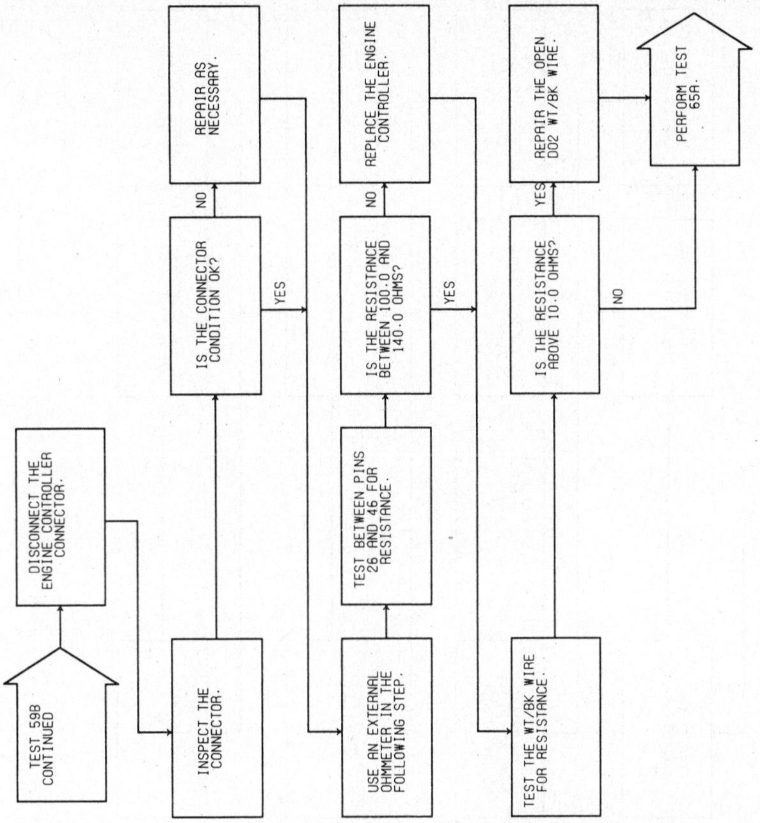

TEST 59B CONTINUED
DISCONNECT THE ENGINE CONTROLLER CONNECTOR.
INSPECT THE CONNECTOR.
IS THE CONNECTOR CONDITION OK?
NO
REPAIR AS NECESSARY.
YES
USE AN EXTERNAL OHMMETER IN THE FOLLOWING STEP.
TEST BETWEEN PINS 26 AND 46 FOR RESISTANCE.
IS THE RESISTANCE BETWEEN 100.0 AND 140.0 OHMS?
NO
REPLACE THE ENGINE CONTROLLER.
YES
TEST THE WT/BK WIRE FOR RESISTANCE.
IS THE RESISTANCE ABOVE 10.0 OHMS?
YES
REPAIR THE OPEN D02 WT/BK WIRE.
NO
PERFORM TEST 65A.

91B14523

Fig. 28: Test 59B – Bus Bias Level Too High (2 of 2)

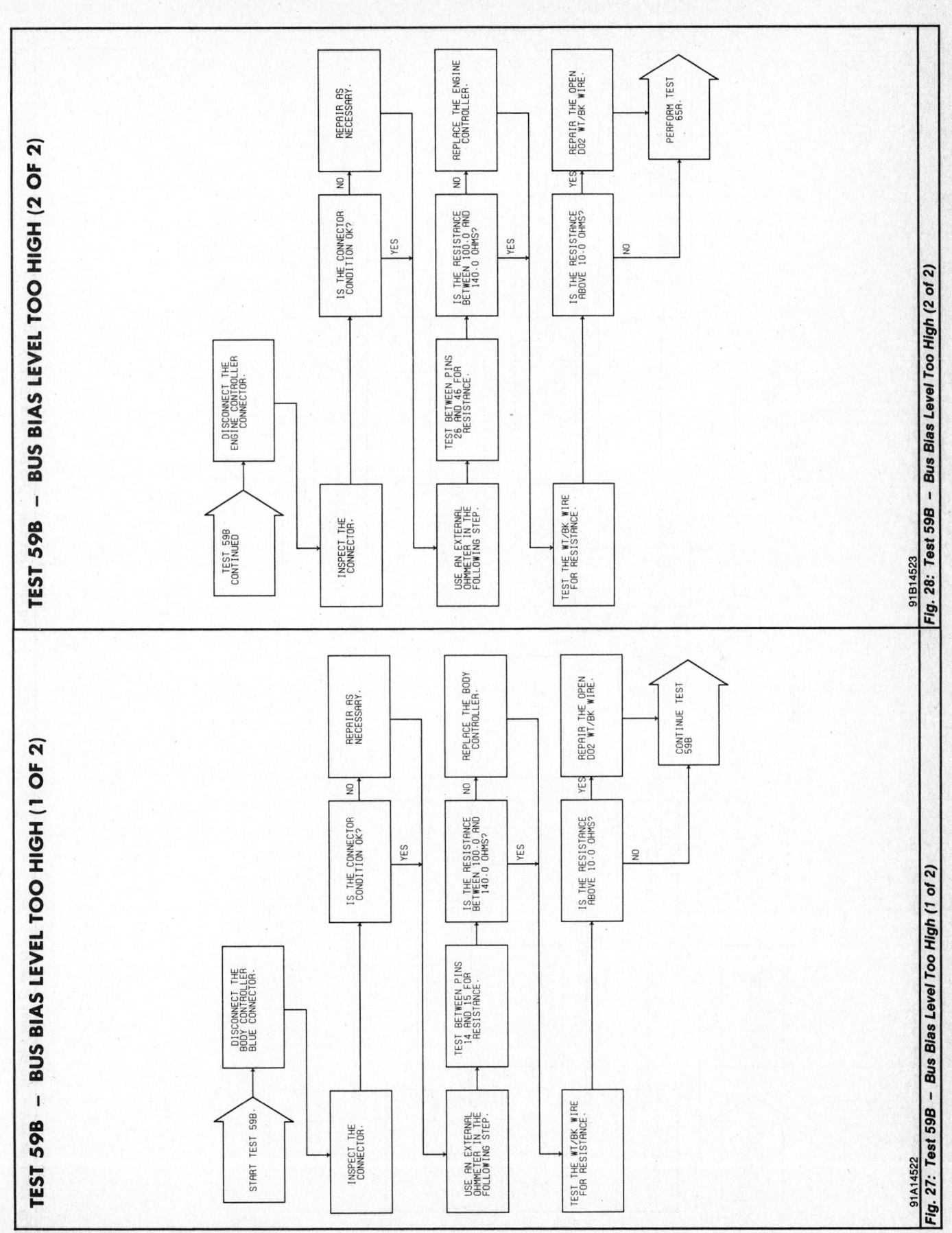

1991 ENGINE PERFORMANCE
Vehicle Communications (Cont.)

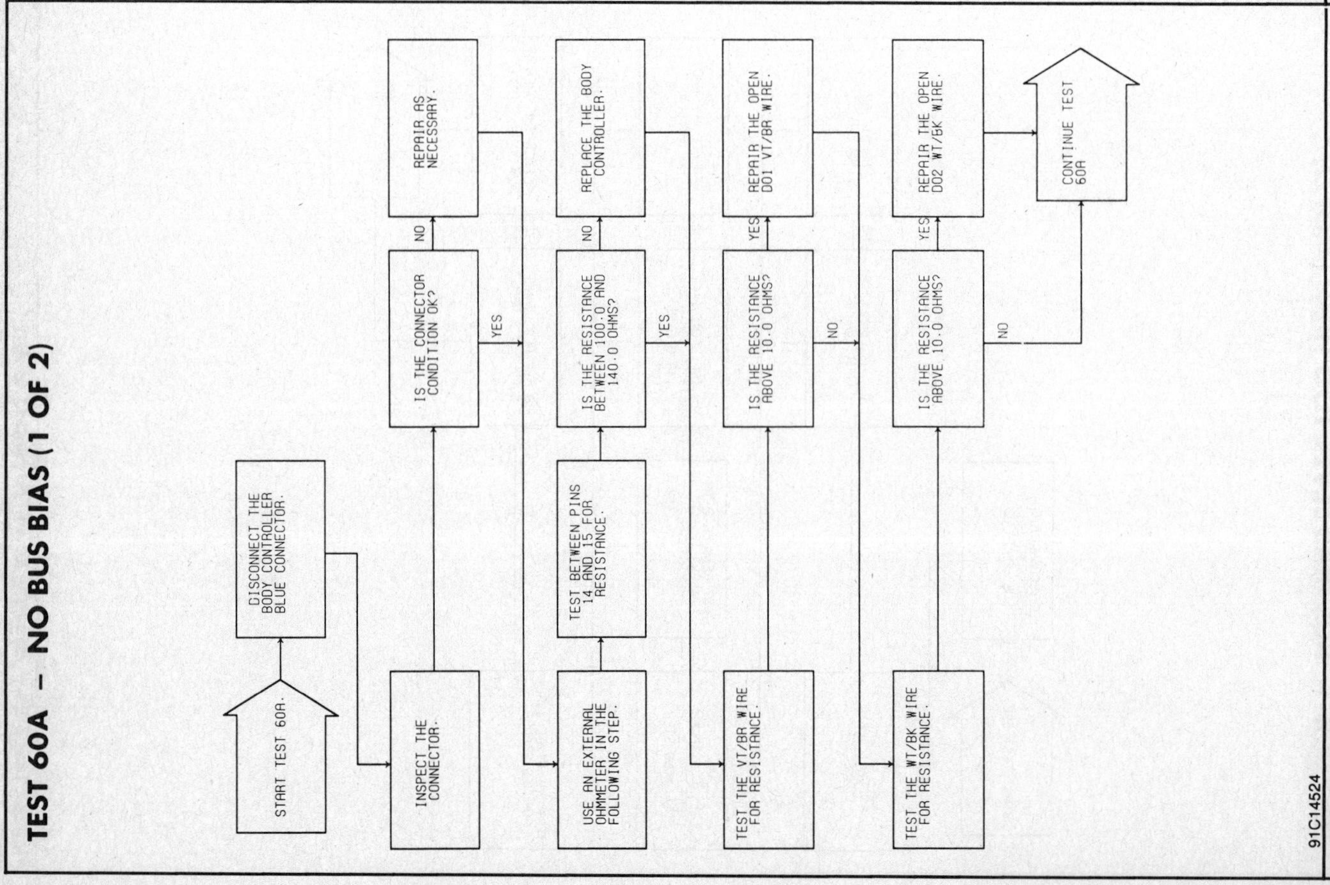
TEST 60A – NO BUS BIAS (1 OF 2)
START TEST 60A.
DISCONNECT THE BODY CONTROLLER BLUE CONNECTOR.
INSPECT THE CONNECTOR.
IS THE CONNECTOR CONDITION OK?
NO
REPAIR AS NECESSARY.
YES
USE AN EXTERNAL OHMMETER IN THE FOLLOWING STEP.
TEST BETWEEN PINS 14 AND 15 FOR RESISTANCE.
IS THE RESISTANCE BETWEEN 100.0 AND 140.0 OHMS?
NO
REPLACE THE BODY CONTROLLER.
YES
TEST THE VT/BR WIRE FOR RESISTANCE.
IS THE RESISTANCE ABOVE 10.0 OHMS?
YES
REPAIR THE OPEN DO1 VT/BR WIRE.
NO
TEST THE WT/BK WIRE FOR RESISTANCE.
IS THE RESISTANCE ABOVE 10.0 OHMS?
YES
REPAIR THE OPEN DO2 WT/BK WIRE.
NO
CONTINUE TEST 60A
91C14524

Fig. 29: Test 60A – No Bus Bias (1 of 2)

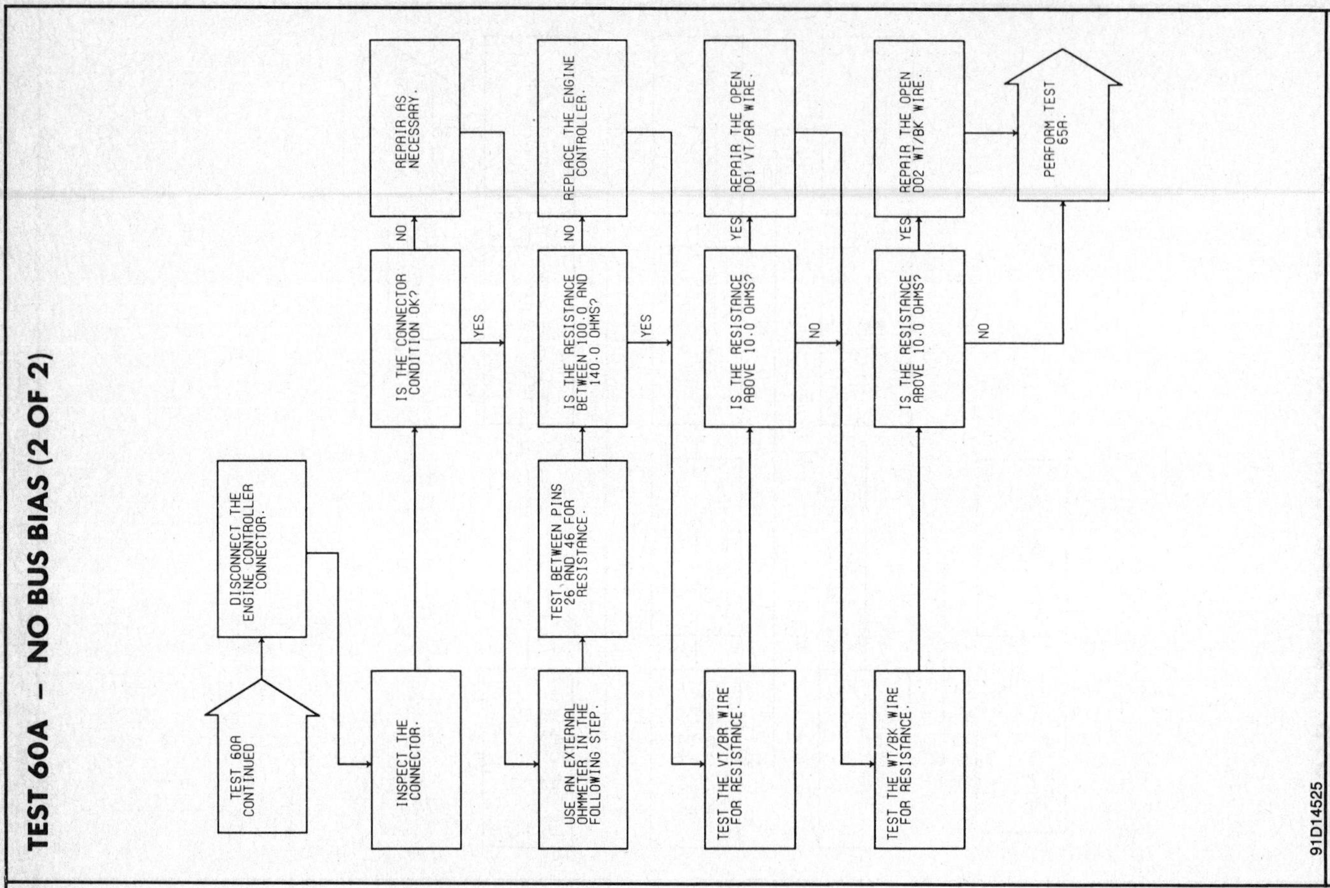
TEST 60A – NO BUS BIAS (2 OF 2)
TEST 60A CONTINUED
DISCONNECT THE ENGINE CONTROLLER CONNECTOR.
INSPECT THE CONNECTOR.
IS THE CONNECTOR CONDITION OK?
NO
REPAIR AS NECESSARY.
YES
USE AN EXTERNAL OHMMETER IN THE FOLLOWING STEP.
TEST BETWEEN PINS 26 AND 46 FOR RESISTANCE.
IS THE RESISTANCE BETWEEN 100.0 AND 140.0 OHMS?
NO
REPLACE THE ENGINE CONTROLLER.
YES
TEST THE VT/BR WIRE FOR RESISTANCE.
IS THE RESISTANCE ABOVE 10.0 OHMS?
YES
REPAIR THE OPEN DO1 VT/BR WIRE.
NO
TEST THE WT/BK WIRE FOR RESISTANCE.
IS THE RESISTANCE ABOVE 10.0 OHMS?
YES
REPAIR THE OPEN DO2 WT/BK WIRE.
NO
PERFORM TEST 65A.
91D14525

Fig. 30: Test 60A – No Bus Bias (2 of 2)

TEST 61A: TESTING FOR BUS (+) OPEN (1 OF 2)

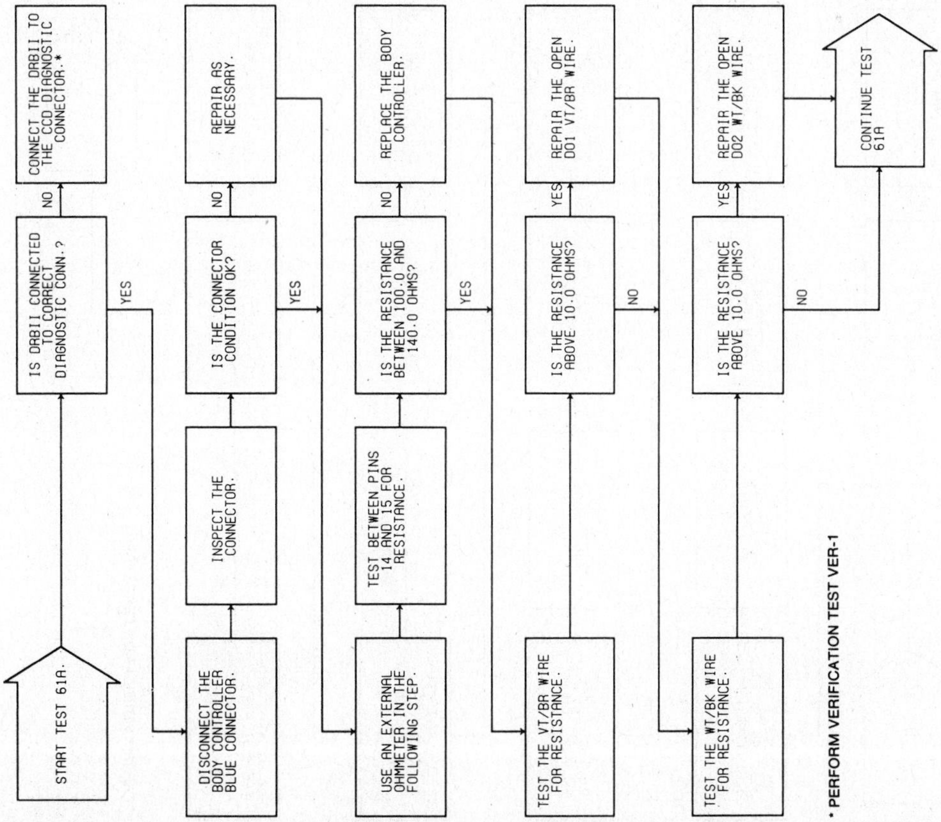

START TEST 61A.
IS DRBII CONNECTED TO CORRECT DIAGNOSTIC CONN.?
NO
CONNECT THE DRBII TO THE CCD DIAGNOSTIC CONNECTOR.*
YES
DISCONNECT THE BODY CONTROLLER BLUE CONNECTOR.
INSPECT THE CONNECTOR.
IS THE CONNECTOR CONDITION OK?
NO
REPAIR AS NECESSARY.
YES
USE AN EXTERNAL OHMMETER IN THE FOLLOWING STEP.
TEST BETWEEN PINS 14 AND 15 FOR RESISTANCE.
IS THE RESISTANCE BETWEEN 100.0 AND 140.0 OHMS?
NO
REPLACE THE BODY CONTROLLER.
YES
TEST THE VT/BR WIRE FOR RESISTANCE.
IS THE RESISTANCE ABOVE 10.0 OHMS?
YES
REPAIR THE OPEN DO1 VT/BR WIRE.
NO
TEST THE WT/BK WIRE FOR RESISTANCE.
IS THE RESISTANCE ABOVE 10.0 OHMS?
YES
REPAIR THE OPEN DO2 WT/BK WIRE.
NO
CONTINUE TEST 61A

* PERFORM VERIFICATION TEST VER-1

91D14715

Fig. 31: Test 61A – Testing for Bus (+) Open (1 of 2)

TEST 61A: TESTING FOR BUS (+) OPEN (2 OF 2)

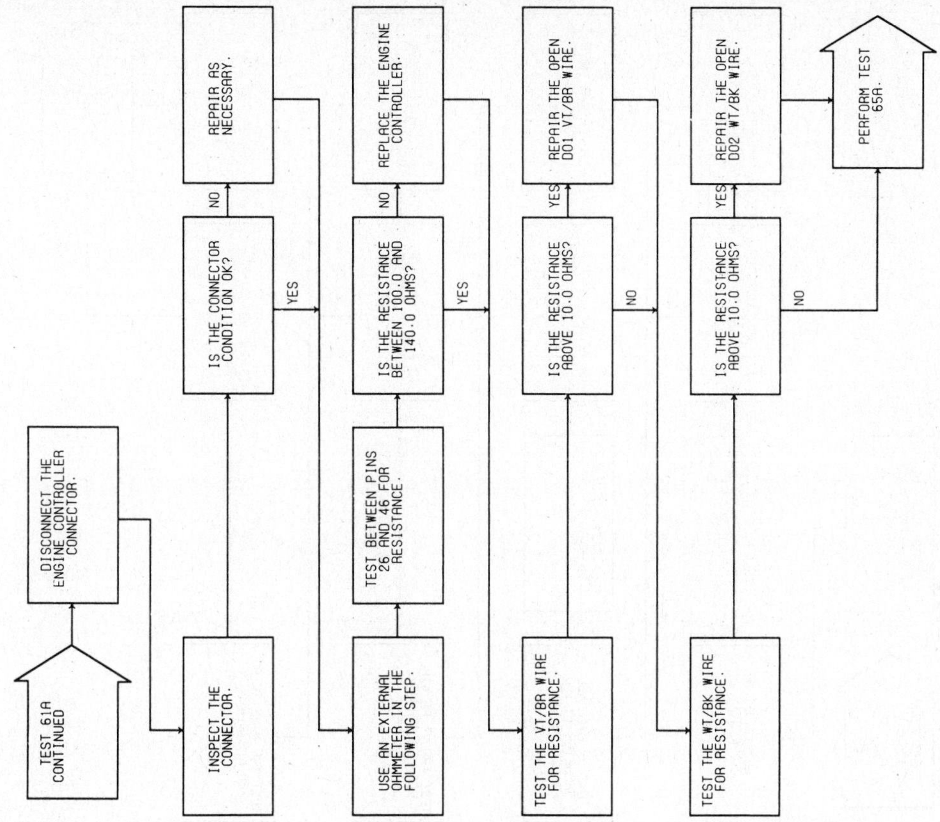

TEST 61A CONTINUED
DISCONNECT THE ENGINE CONTROLLER CONNECTOR.
INSPECT THE CONNECTOR.
IS THE CONNECTOR CONDITION OK?
NO
REPAIR AS NECESSARY.
YES
USE AN EXTERNAL OHMMETER IN THE FOLLOWING STEP.
TEST BETWEEN PINS 26 AND 46 FOR RESISTANCE.
IS THE RESISTANCE BETWEEN 100.0 AND 140.0 OHMS?
NO
REPLACE THE ENGINE CONTROLLER.
YES
TEST THE VT/BR WIRE FOR RESISTANCE.
IS THE RESISTANCE ABOVE 10.0 OHMS?
YES
REPAIR THE OPEN DO1 VT/BR WIRE.
NO
TEST THE WT/BK WIRE FOR RESISTANCE.
IS THE RESISTANCE ABOVE 10.0 OHMS?
YES
REPAIR THE OPEN DO2 WT/BK WIRE.
NO
PERFORM TEST 65A.

91E14716

Fig. 32: Test 61A – Testing for Bus (+) Open (2 of 2)

1991 ENGINE PERFORMANCE
Vehicle Communications (Cont.)

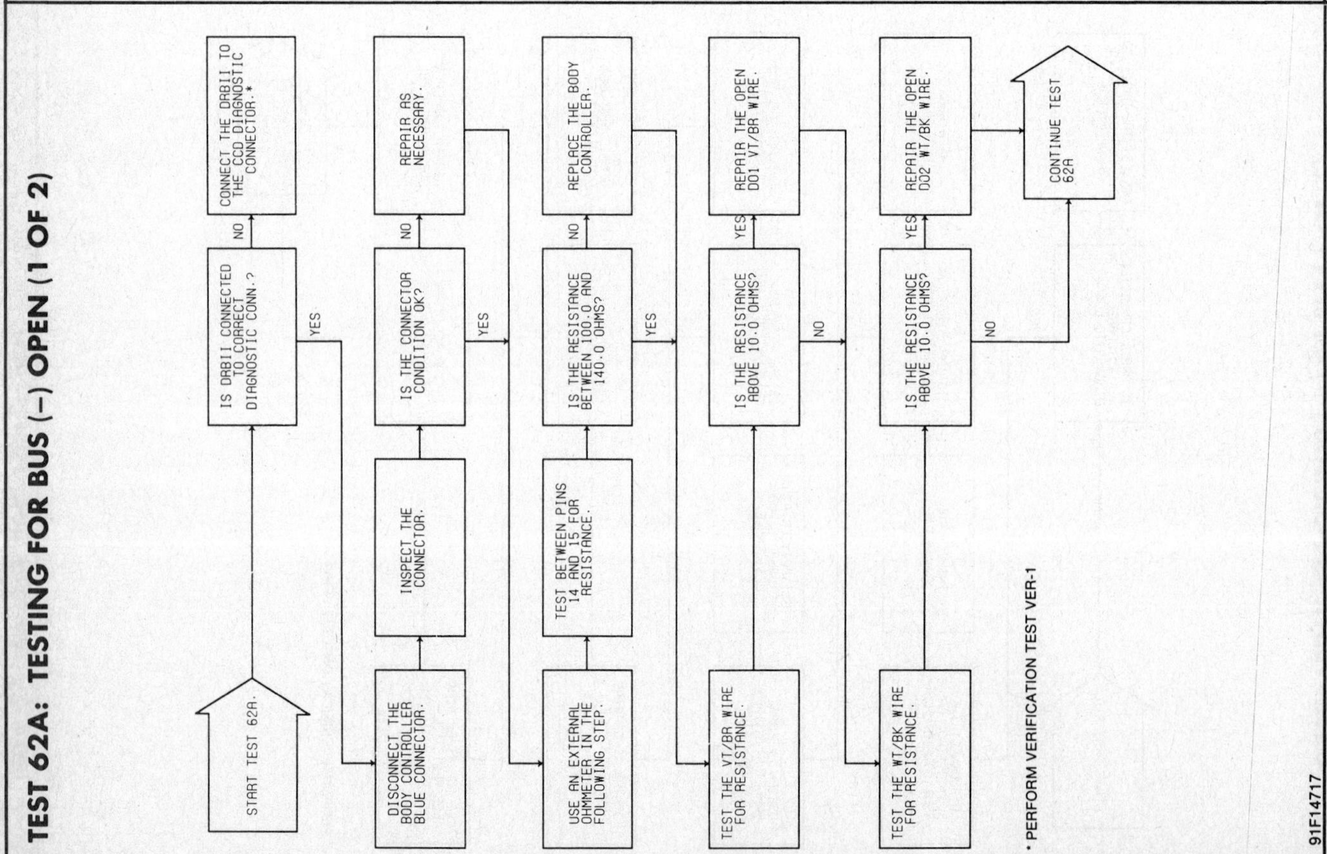
TEST 62A: TESTING FOR BUS (–) OPEN (1 OF 2)
START TEST 62A.
IS DRBII CONNECTED TO CORRECT DIAGNOSTIC CONN.?
NO
CONNECT THE DRBII TO THE CCD DIAGNOSTIC CONNECTOR.*
YES
DISCONNECT THE BODY CONTROLLER BLUE CONNECTOR.
INSPECT THE CONNECTOR.
IS THE CONNECTOR CONDITION OK?
NO
REPAIR AS NECESSARY.
YES
USE AN EXTERNAL OHMMETER IN THE FOLLOWING STEP.
TEST BETWEEN PINS 14 AND 15 FOR RESISTANCE.
IS THE RESISTANCE BETWEEN 100.0 AND 140.0 OHMS?
NO
REPLACE THE BODY CONTROLLER.
YES
TEST THE VT/BR WIRE FOR RESISTANCE.
IS THE RESISTANCE ABOVE 10.0 OHMS?
YES
REPAIR THE OPEN DO1 VT/BR WIRE.
NO
TEST THE WT/BK WIRE FOR RESISTANCE.
IS THE RESISTANCE ABOVE 10.0 OHMS?
YES
REPAIR THE OPEN DO2 WT/BK WIRE.
NO
CONTINUE TEST 62A
* PERFORM VERIFICATION TEST VER-1
91F14717

Fig. 33: Test 62A – Testing for Bus (–) Open (1 of 2)

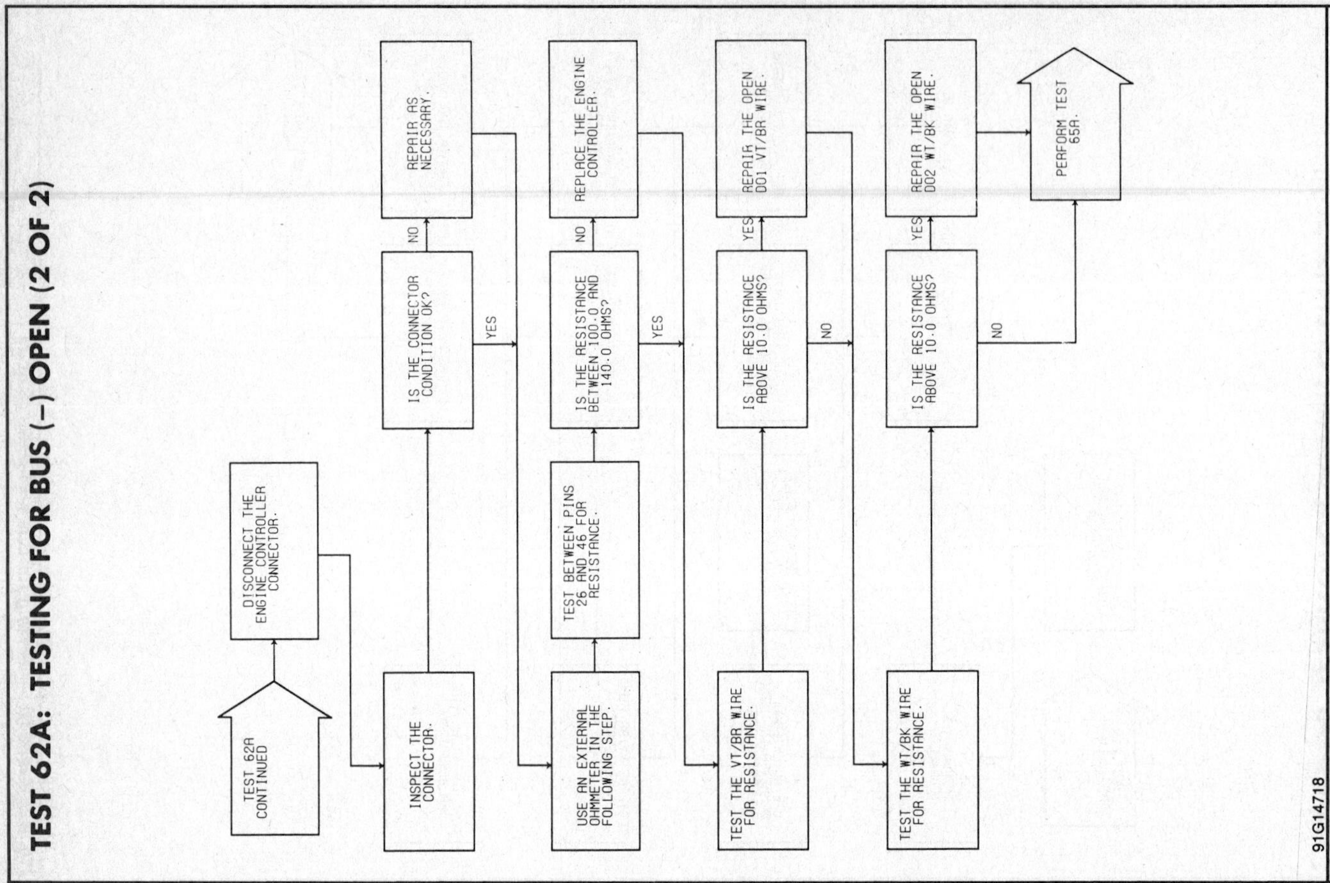
TEST 62A: TESTING FOR BUS (–) OPEN (2 OF 2)
TEST 62A CONTINUED
DISCONNECT THE ENGINE CONTROLLER CONNECTOR.
INSPECT THE CONNECTOR.
IS THE CONNECTOR CONDITION OK?
NO
REPAIR AS NECESSARY.
YES
USE AN EXTERNAL OHMMETER IN THE FOLLOWING STEP.
TEST BETWEEN PINS 26 AND 46 FOR RESISTANCE.
IS THE RESISTANCE BETWEEN 100.0 AND 140.0 OHMS?
NO
REPLACE THE ENGINE CONTROLLER.
YES
TEST THE VT/BR WIRE FOR RESISTANCE.
IS THE RESISTANCE ABOVE 10.0 OHMS?
YES
REPAIR THE OPEN DO1 VT/BR WIRE.
NO
TEST THE WT/BK WIRE FOR RESISTANCE.
IS THE RESISTANCE ABOVE 10.0 OHMS?
YES
REPAIR THE OPEN DO2 WT/BK WIRE.
NO
PERFORM TEST 65A.
91G14718

Fig. 34: Test 62A – Testing for Bus (–) Open (2 of 2)

TEST 63A: TESTING FOR BUS (+) & BUS (–) OPEN (1 OF 2)

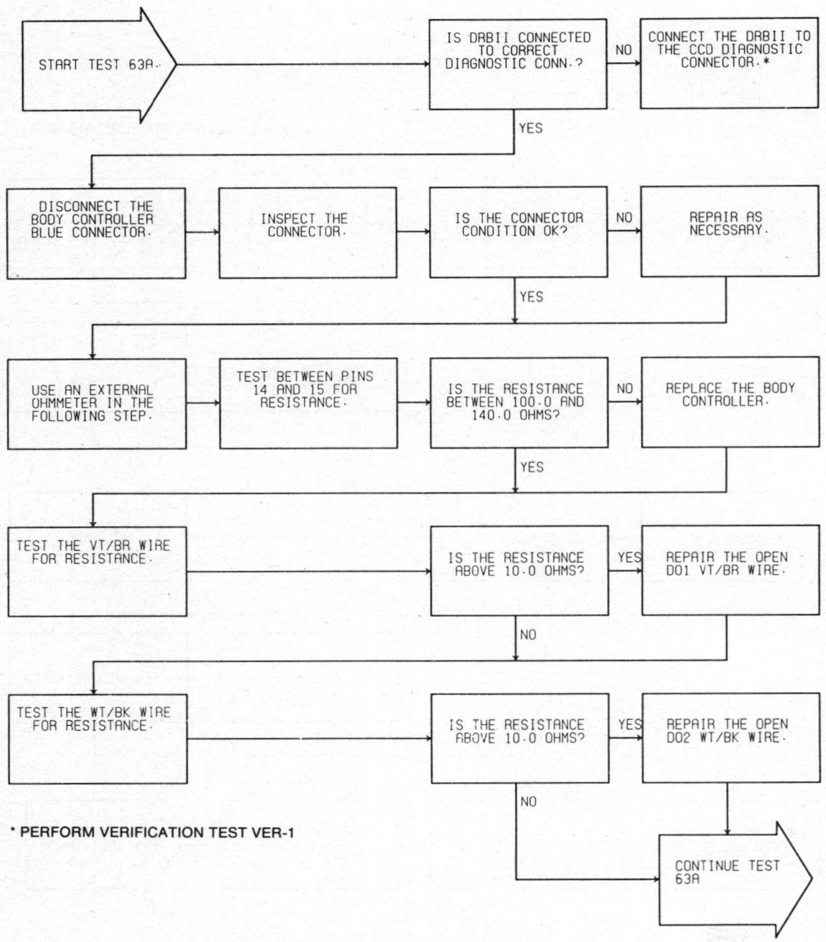
START TEST 63A.
IS DRBII CONNECTED TO CORRECT DIAGNOSTIC CONN.?
NO
CONNECT THE DRBII TO THE CCD DIAGNOSTIC CONNECTOR.*
YES
DISCONNECT THE BODY CONTROLLER BLUE CONNECTOR.
INSPECT THE CONNECTOR.
IS THE CONNECTOR CONDITION OK?
NO
REPAIR AS NECESSARY.
YES
USE AN EXTERNAL OHMMETER IN THE FOLLOWING STEP.
TEST BETWEEN PINS 14 AND 15 FOR RESISTANCE.
IS THE RESISTANCE BETWEEN 100.0 AND 140.0 OHMS?
NO
REPLACE THE BODY CONTROLLER.
YES
TEST THE VT/BR WIRE FOR RESISTANCE.
IS THE RESISTANCE ABOVE 10.0 OHMS?
YES
REPAIR THE OPEN DO1 VT/BR WIRE.
NO
TEST THE WT/BK WIRE FOR RESISTANCE.
IS THE RESISTANCE ABOVE 10.0 OHMS?
YES
REPAIR THE OPEN DO2 WT/BK WIRE.
NO
CONTINUE TEST 63A

* PERFORM VERIFICATION TEST VER-1

91H14719

Fig. 35: Test 63A – Testing for Bus (+) & Bus (–) Open (1 of 2)

TEST 63A: TESTING FOR BUS (+) & BUS (–) OPEN (2 OF 2)

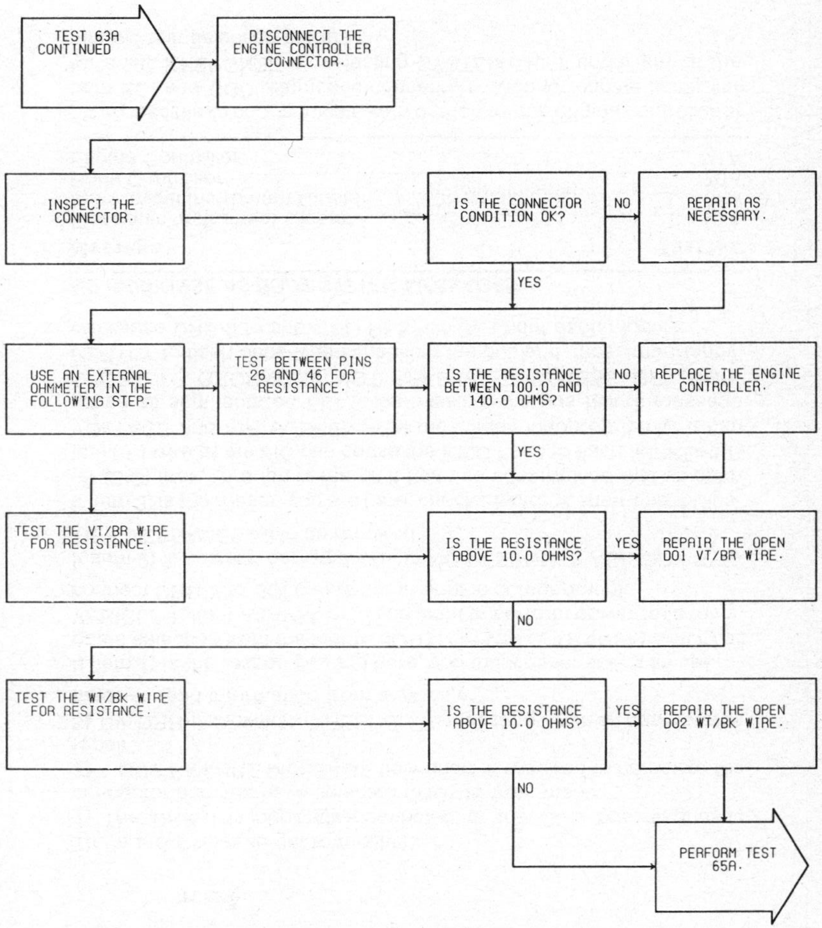
TEST 63A CONTINUED
DISCONNECT THE ENGINE CONTROLLER CONNECTOR.
INSPECT THE CONNECTOR.
IS THE CONNECTOR CONDITION OK?
NO
REPAIR AS NECESSARY.
YES
USE AN EXTERNAL OHMMETER IN THE FOLLOWING STEP.
TEST BETWEEN PINS 26 AND 46 FOR RESISTANCE.
IS THE RESISTANCE BETWEEN 100.0 AND 140.0 OHMS?
NO
REPLACE THE ENGINE CONTROLLER.
YES
TEST THE VT/BR WIRE FOR RESISTANCE.
IS THE RESISTANCE ABOVE 10.0 OHMS?
YES
REPAIR THE OPEN DO1 VT/BR WIRE.
NO
TEST THE WT/BK WIRE FOR RESISTANCE.
IS THE RESISTANCE ABOVE 10.0 OHMS?
YES
REPAIR THE OPEN DO2 WT/BK WIRE.
NO
PERFORM TEST 65A.

91A14720

Fig. 36: Test 63A – Testing for Bus (+) & Bus (–) Open (2 of 2)

TEST 64A: TESTING FOR NOT RECEIVING BUS MESSAGES CORRECTLY ON BUS

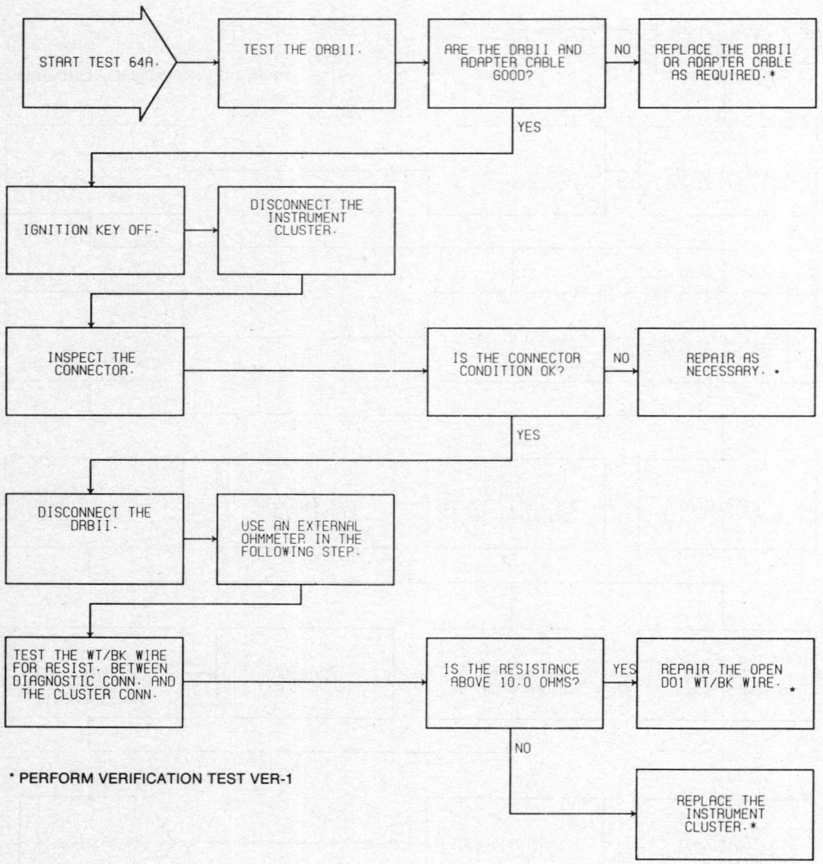
START TEST 64A.
TEST THE DRBII.
ARE THE DRBII AND ADAPTER CABLE GOOD?
NO
REPLACE THE DRBII OR ADAPTER CABLE AS REQUIRED.*
YES
IGNITION KEY OFF.
DISCONNECT THE INSTRUMENT CLUSTER.
INSPECT THE CONNECTOR.
IS THE CONNECTOR CONDITION OK?
NO
REPAIR AS NECESSARY.*
YES
DISCONNECT THE DRBII.
USE AN EXTERNAL OHMMETER IN THE FOLLOWING STEP.
TEST THE WT/BK WIRE FOR RESIST. BETWEEN DIAGNOSTIC CONN. AND THE CLUSTER CONN.
IS THE RESISTANCE ABOVE 10.0 OHMS?
YES
REPAIR THE OPEN D01 WT/BK WIRE.*
NO
REPLACE THE INSTRUMENT CLUSTER.*
* PERFORM VERIFICATION TEST VER-1

91B14721

Fig. 37: Test 64A – Testing for Not Receiving Bus Messages Correctly on Bus

TEST 65A: NO RESPONSE (*) AS-BODY SYSTEM

There are 3 ways to get to this test:
1) The DRB-II is currently connected to the CCD bus diagnostic connector and you have selected ENGINE from menu.
2) A BUS FAILURE MESSAGE flow chart is required to complete the repair.
3) The DRB-II showed NO RESPONSE message when an attempt was made to read information from a module*.

If item **1)** is the reason you are here, you must either select an appropriate selection from the menu (BODY, CHASSIS, TRANSMISSION or VEHICLE THEFT ALARM) or, if you want to perform power train tests, connect DRB-II to SCI connector in engine compartment.

If item **2)** is correct, perform tests in NO RESPONSE AS-BODY SYSTEM MESSAGES table as required.

If item **3)** is the reason you are here, check Electronic Instrument Cluster (EIC) first. Through research it has been determined that an open bus (+) wire at the EIC can cause the EVIC head to flash IMPROPER VOLTAGE and AIR SUSPENSION messages inappropriately. It can cause all segments on EIC to be missing, the bus failure message SHORT TO GROUND or NOT READING BUS MESSAGES CORRECTLY to flash once when checking the bus and, most importantly, will cause DRB-II to show NO RESPONSE under each module.

NO RESPONSE AS-BODY SYSTEM MESSAGES

Message	Test No.
Electronic Instrument Cluster	66A
Mechanical Instrument Cluster	67A
Body Controller	70A
Engine Controller*	71A

* It is possible to communicate with or monitor the engine controller at both SCI and CCD diagnostic connectors. Monitor engine controller for a NO RESPONSE by selecting SYSTEM TEST under any of the module test selection menus.

Fig. 38: Test 65A – No Response (*) AS-Body System

TEST 66A – TESTING FOR ELECTRONIC INSTRUMENT CLUSTER NO RESPONSE (1 OF 3)

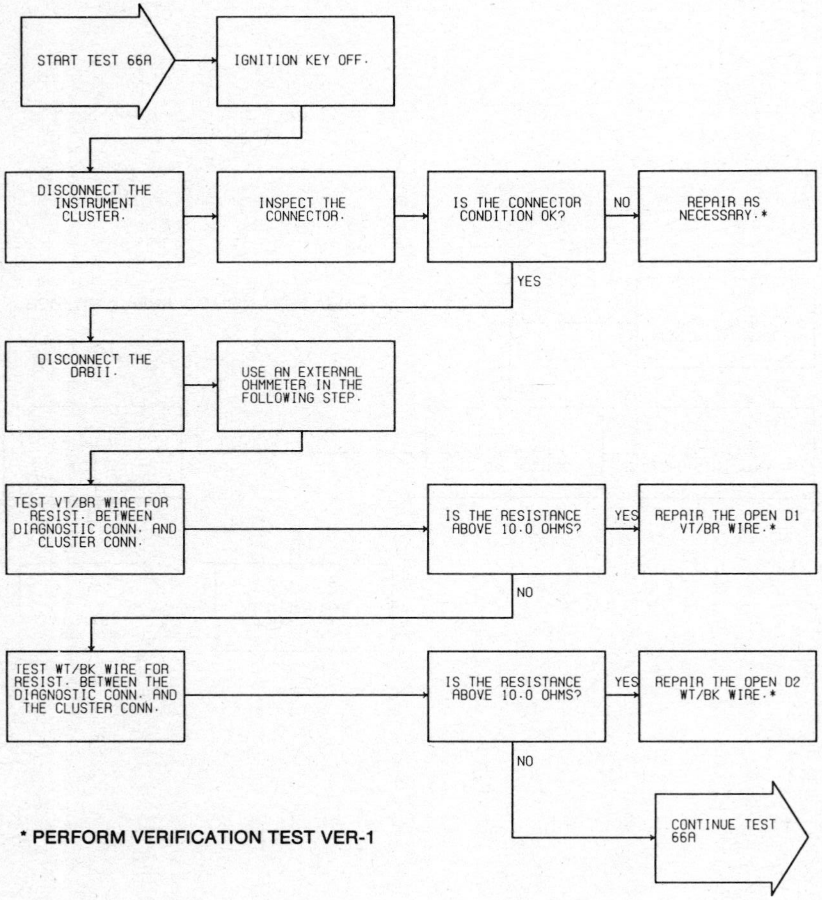
START TEST 66A
IGNITION KEY OFF.
DISCONNECT THE INSTRUMENT CLUSTER.
INSPECT THE CONNECTOR.
IS THE CONNECTOR CONDITION OK?
NO
REPAIR AS NECESSARY.*
YES
DISCONNECT THE DRBII.
USE AN EXTERNAL OHMMETER IN THE FOLLOWING STEP.
TEST VT/BR WIRE FOR RESIST. BETWEEN DIAGNOSTIC CONN. AND CLUSTER CONN.
IS THE RESISTANCE ABOVE 10.0 OHMS?
YES
REPAIR THE OPEN D1 VT/BR WIRE.*
NO
TEST WT/BK WIRE FOR RESIST. BETWEEN THE DIAGNOSTIC CONN. AND THE CLUSTER CONN.
IS THE RESISTANCE ABOVE 10.0 OHMS?
YES
REPAIR THE OPEN D2 WT/BK WIRE.*
NO
CONTINUE TEST 66A

* PERFORM VERIFICATION TEST VER-1

91C14722

Fig. 39: Test 66A – Testing for Electronic Instrument Cluster No Response (1 of 3)

TEST 66A – TESTING FOR ELECTRONIC INSTRUMENT CLUSTER NO RESPONSE (2 OF 3)

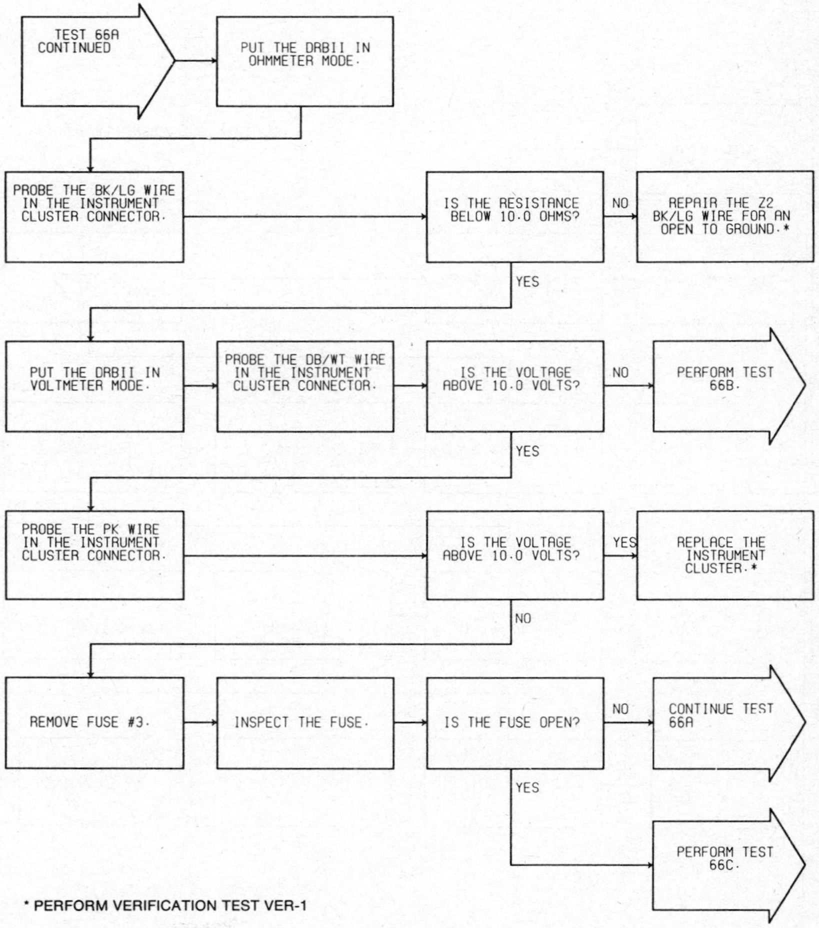
TEST 66A CONTINUED
PUT THE DRBII IN OHMMETER MODE.
PROBE THE BK/LG WIRE IN THE INSTRUMENT CLUSTER CONNECTOR.
IS THE RESISTANCE BELOW 10.0 OHMS?
NO
REPAIR THE Z2 BK/LG WIRE FOR AN OPEN TO GROUND.*
YES
PUT THE DRBII IN VOLTMETER MODE.
PROBE THE DB/WT WIRE IN THE INSTRUMENT CLUSTER CONNECTOR.
IS THE VOLTAGE ABOVE 10.0 VOLTS?
NO
PERFORM TEST 66B.
YES
PROBE THE PK WIRE IN THE INSTRUMENT CLUSTER CONNECTOR.
IS THE VOLTAGE ABOVE 10.0 VOLTS?
YES
REPLACE THE INSTRUMENT CLUSTER.*
NO
REMOVE FUSE #3.
INSPECT THE FUSE.
IS THE FUSE OPEN?
NO
CONTINUE TEST 66A
YES
PERFORM TEST 66C.

* PERFORM VERIFICATION TEST VER-1

91G14528

Fig. 40: Test 66A – Testing for Electronic Instrument Cluster No Response (2 of 3)

1991 ENGINE PERFORMANCE
Vehicle Communications (Cont.)

TEST 66A – TESTING FOR ELECTRONIC INSTRUMENT CLUSTER NO RESPONSE (3 OF 3)

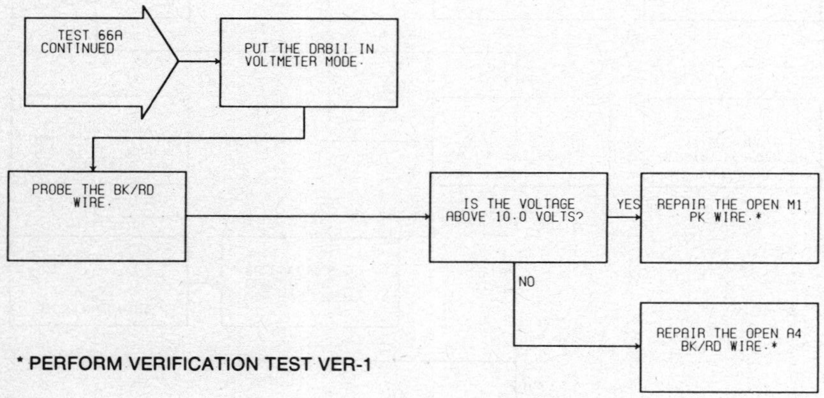
TEST 66A CONTINUED
PUT THE DRBII IN VOLTMETER MODE.
PROBE THE BK/RD WIRE.
IS THE VOLTAGE ABOVE 10.0 VOLTS?
YES
REPAIR THE OPEN M1 PK WIRE.*
NO
REPAIR THE OPEN A4 BK/RD WIRE.*

* PERFORM VERIFICATION TEST VER-1

91H14529

Fig. 41: Test 66A – Testing for Electronic Instrument Cluster No Response (3 of 3)

TEST 66B – TESTING FOR ELECTRONIC INSTRUMENT CLUSTER NO RESPONSE (1 OF 2)

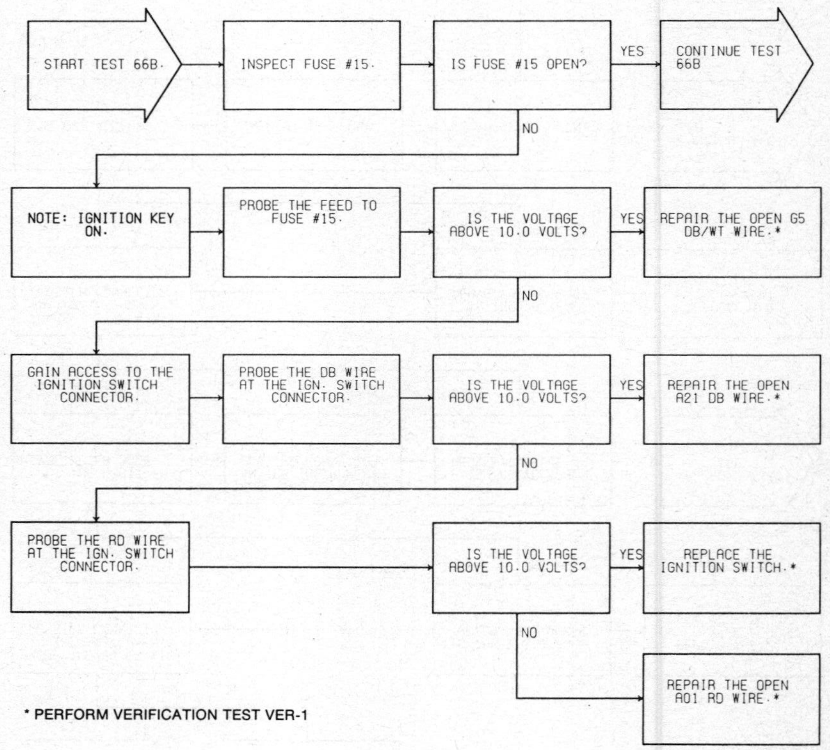
START TEST 66B.
INSPECT FUSE #15.
IS FUSE #15 OPEN?
YES
CONTINUE TEST 66B
NO
NOTE: IGNITION KEY ON.
PROBE THE FEED TO FUSE #15.
IS THE VOLTAGE ABOVE 10.0 VOLTS?
YES
REPAIR THE OPEN G5 DB/WT WIRE.*
NO
GAIN ACCESS TO THE IGNITION SWITCH CONNECTOR.
PROBE THE DB WIRE AT THE IGN. SWITCH CONNECTOR.
IS THE VOLTAGE ABOVE 10.0 VOLTS?
YES
REPAIR THE OPEN A21 DB WIRE.*
NO
PROBE THE RD WIRE AT THE IGN. SWITCH CONNECTOR.
IS THE VOLTAGE ABOVE 10.0 VOLTS?
YES
REPLACE THE IGNITION SWITCH.*
NO
REPAIR THE OPEN A01 RD WIRE.*

* PERFORM VERIFICATION TEST VER-1

91A14530

Fig. 42: Test 66B – Testing for Electronic Instrument Cluster No Response (1 of 2)

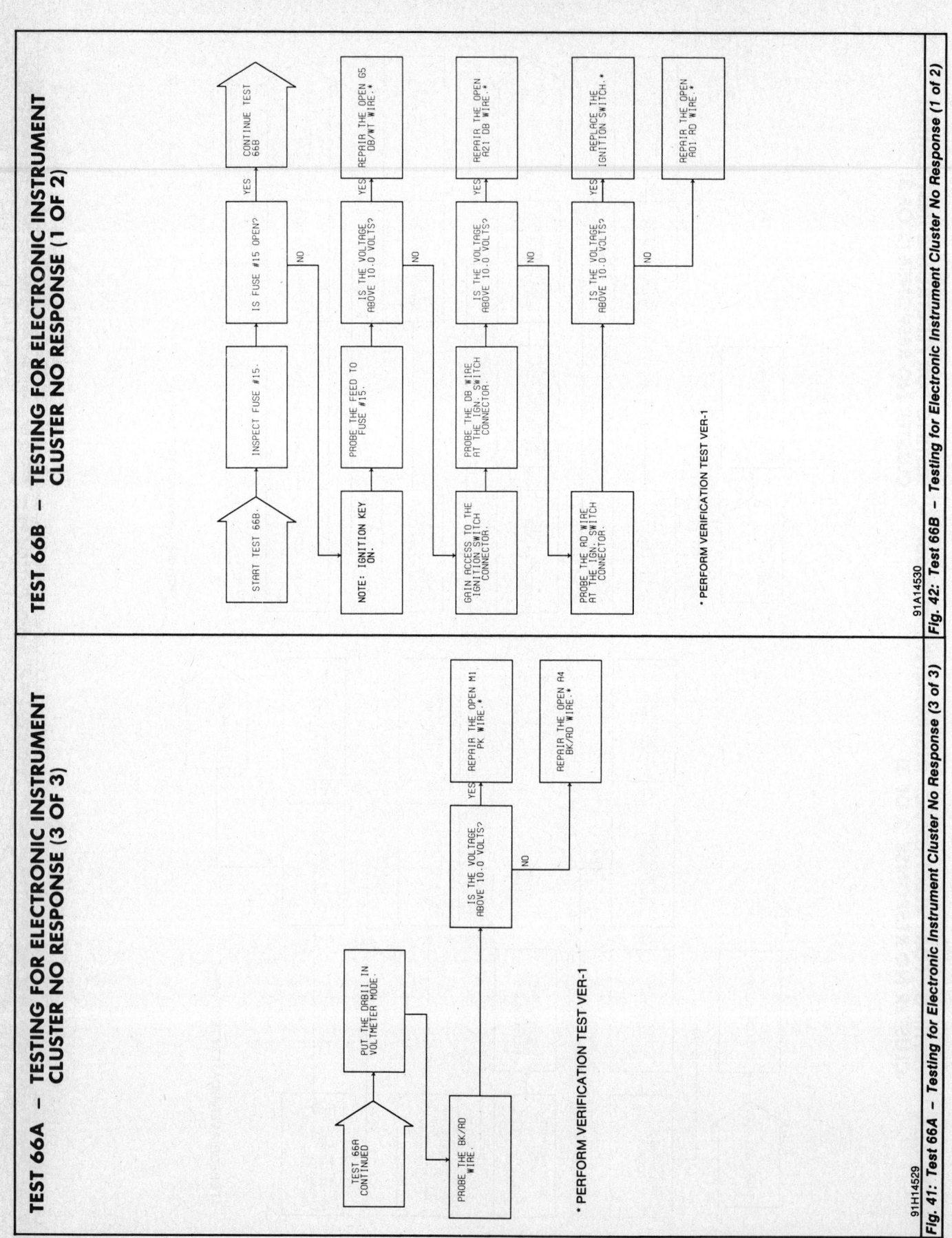

TEST 66B – TESTING FOR ELECTRONIC INSTRUMENT CLUSTER NO RESPONSE (2 OF 2)

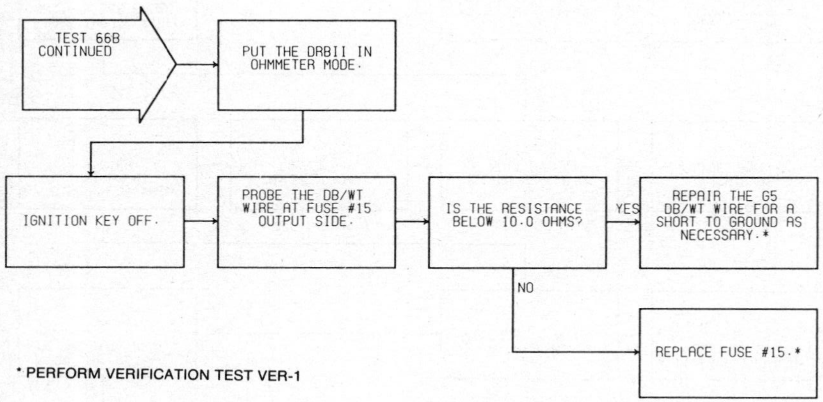
TEST 66B CONTINUED
PUT THE DRBII IN OHMMETER MODE.
IGNITION KEY OFF.
PROBE THE DB/WT WIRE AT FUSE #15 OUTPUT SIDE.
IS THE RESISTANCE BELOW 10.0 OHMS?
YES
REPAIR THE G5 DB/WT WIRE FOR A SHORT TO GROUND AS NECESSARY.*
NO
REPLACE FUSE #15.*

* PERFORM VERIFICATION TEST VER-1

91B14531

Fig. 43: Test 66B – Testing for Electronic Instrument Cluster No Response (2 of 2)

TEST 66C – TESTING ELECTRONIC INSTRUMENT CLUSTER FOR NO RESPONSE (1 OF 2)

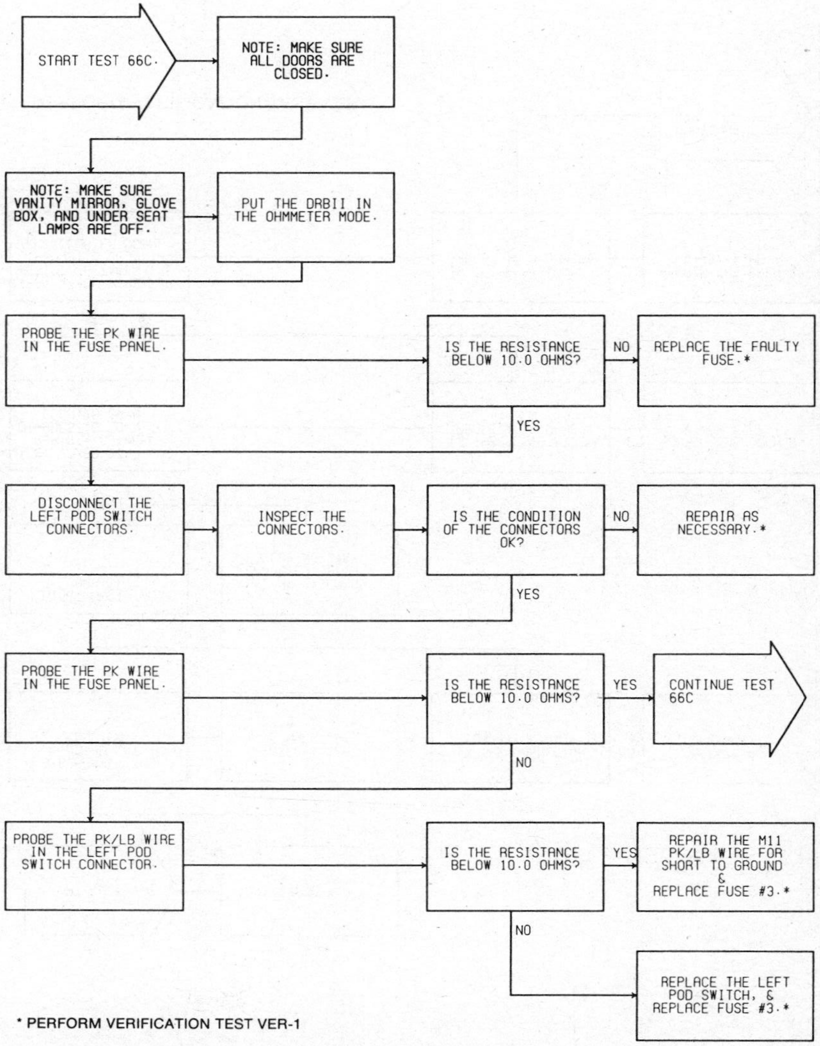
START TEST 66C.
NOTE: MAKE SURE ALL DOORS ARE CLOSED.
NOTE: MAKE SURE VANITY MIRROR, GLOVE BOX, AND UNDER SEAT LAMPS ARE OFF.
PUT THE DRBII IN THE OHMMETER MODE.
PROBE THE PK WIRE IN THE FUSE PANEL.
IS THE RESISTANCE BELOW 10.0 OHMS?
NO
REPLACE THE FAULTY FUSE.*
YES
DISCONNECT THE LEFT POD SWITCH CONNECTORS.
INSPECT THE CONNECTORS.
IS THE CONDITION OF THE CONNECTORS OK?
NO
REPAIR AS NECESSARY.*
YES
PROBE THE PK WIRE IN THE FUSE PANEL.
IS THE RESISTANCE BELOW 10.0 OHMS?
YES
CONTINUE TEST 66C
NO
PROBE THE PK/LB WIRE IN THE LEFT POD SWITCH CONNECTOR.
IS THE RESISTANCE BELOW 10.0 OHMS?
YES
REPAIR THE M11 PK/LB WIRE FOR SHORT TO GROUND & REPLACE FUSE #3.*
NO
REPLACE THE LEFT POD SWITCH, & REPLACE FUSE #3.*

* PERFORM VERIFICATION TEST VER-1

91C14532

Fig. 44: Test 66C – Testing Electronic Instrument Cluster for No Response (1 of 2)

1991 ENGINE PERFORMANCE
Vehicle Communications (Cont.)

TEST 66C – TESTING ELECTRONIC INSTRUMENT CLUSTER FOR NO RESPONSE (2 OF 2)

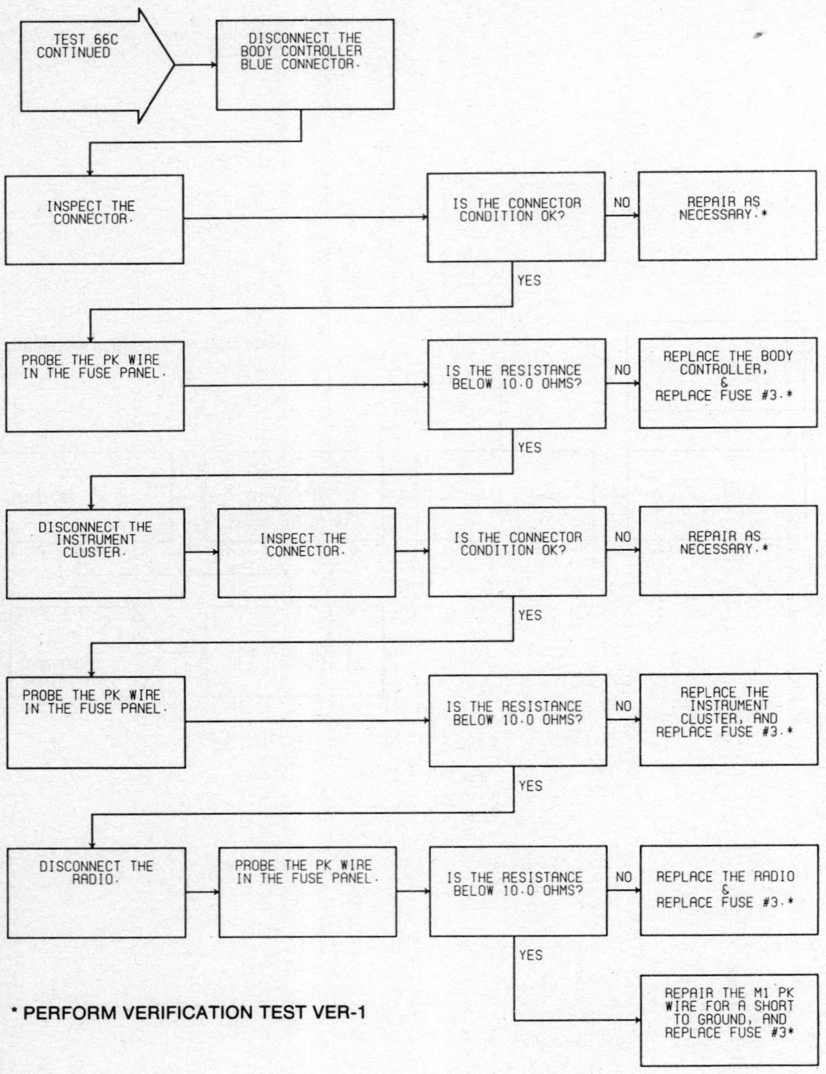
TEST 66C CONTINUED
DISCONNECT THE BODY CONTROLLER BLUE CONNECTOR.
INSPECT THE CONNECTOR.
IS THE CONNECTOR CONDITION OK?
NO
REPAIR AS NECESSARY.*
YES
PROBE THE PK WIRE IN THE FUSE PANEL.
IS THE RESISTANCE BELOW 10.0 OHMS?
NO
REPLACE THE BODY CONTROLLER, & REPLACE FUSE #3.*
YES
DISCONNECT THE INSTRUMENT CLUSTER.
INSPECT THE CONNECTOR.
IS THE CONNECTOR CONDITION OK?
NO
REPAIR AS NECESSARY.*
YES
PROBE THE PK WIRE IN THE FUSE PANEL.
IS THE RESISTANCE BELOW 10.0 OHMS?
NO
REPLACE THE INSTRUMENT CLUSTER, AND REPLACE FUSE #3.*
YES
DISCONNECT THE RADIO.
PROBE THE PK WIRE IN THE FUSE PANEL.
IS THE RESISTANCE BELOW 10.0 OHMS?
NO
REPLACE THE RADIO & REPLACE FUSE #3.*
YES
REPAIR THE M1 PK WIRE FOR A SHORT TO GROUND, AND REPLACE FUSE #3*

* PERFORM VERIFICATION TEST VER-1

91D14533

Fig. 45: Test 66C – Testing Electronic Instrument Cluster for No Response (2 of 2)

TEST 67A – TESTING MECHANICAL INSTRUMENT CLUSTER FOR NO RESPONSE (1 OF 3)

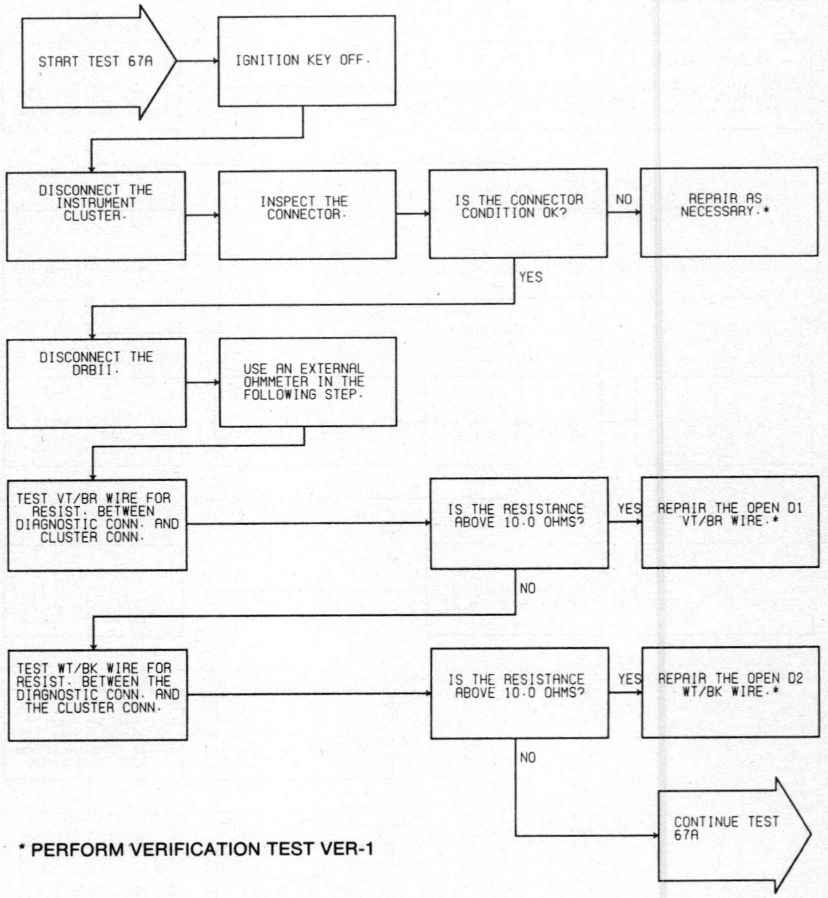
START TEST 67A
IGNITION KEY OFF.
DISCONNECT THE INSTRUMENT CLUSTER.
INSPECT THE CONNECTOR.
IS THE CONNECTOR CONDITION OK?
NO
REPAIR AS NECESSARY.*
YES
DISCONNECT THE DRBII.
USE AN EXTERNAL OHMMETER IN THE FOLLOWING STEP.
TEST VT/BR WIRE FOR RESIST. BETWEEN DIAGNOSTIC CONN. AND CLUSTER CONN.
IS THE RESISTANCE ABOVE 10.0 OHMS?
YES
REPAIR THE OPEN D1 VT/BR WIRE.*
NO
TEST WT/BK WIRE FOR RESIST. BETWEEN THE DIAGNOSTIC CONN. AND THE CLUSTER CONN.
IS THE RESISTANCE ABOVE 10.0 OHMS?
YES
REPAIR THE OPEN D2 WT/BK WIRE.*
NO
CONTINUE TEST 67A

* PERFORM VERIFICATION TEST VER-1

91E14534

Fig. 46: Test 67A – Testing Mechanical Instrument Cluster for No Response (1 of 3)

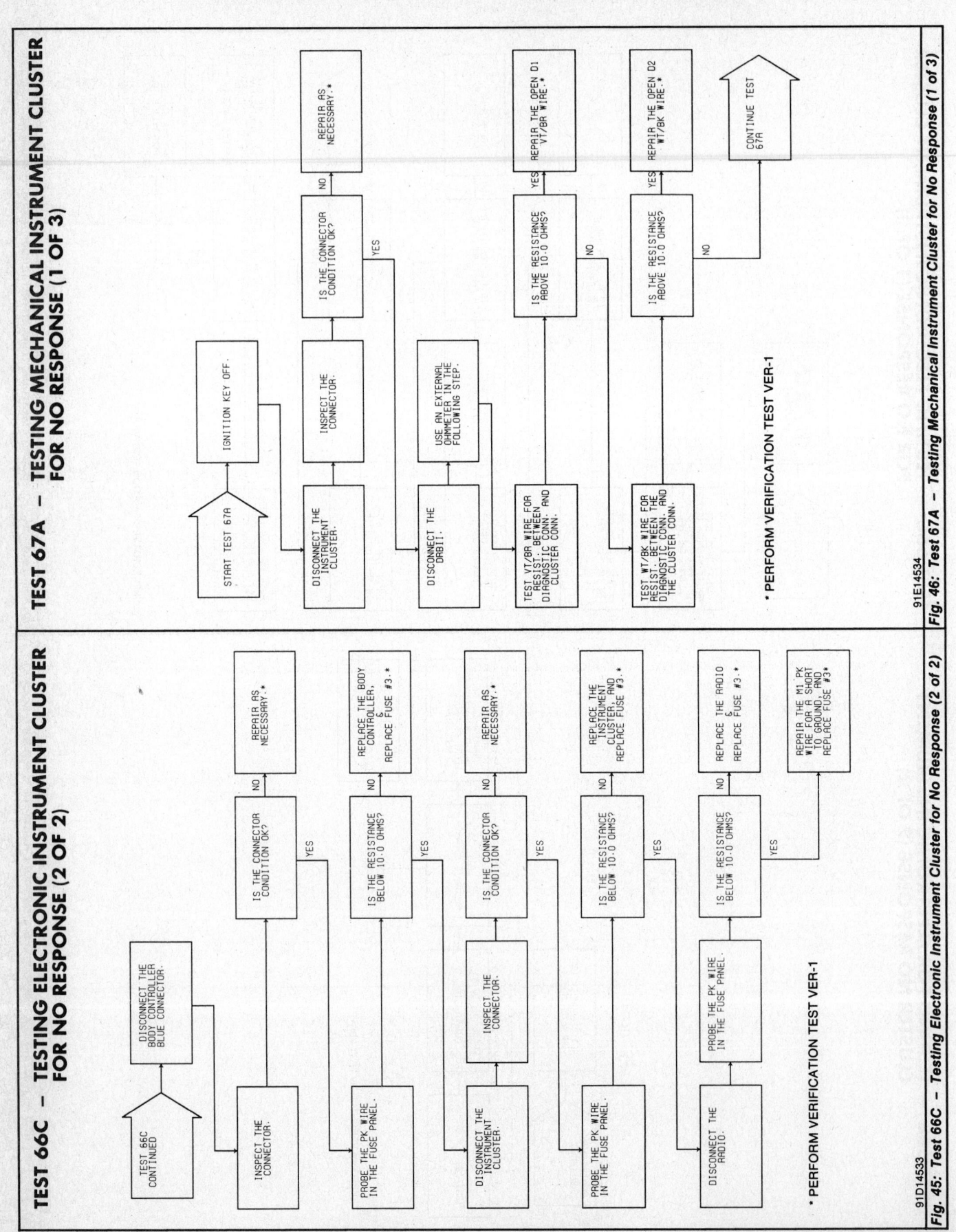

TEST 67A – TESTING MECHANICAL INSTRUMENT CLUSTER FOR NO RESPONSE (2 OF 3)

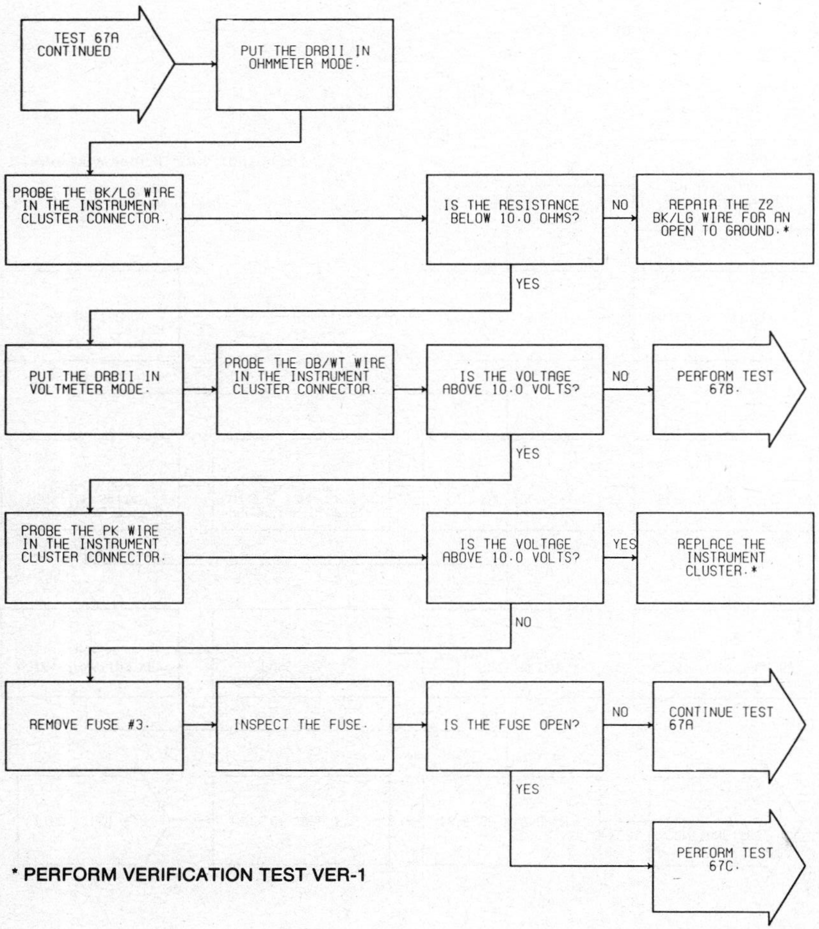
TEST 67A CONTINUED
PUT THE DRBII IN OHMMETER MODE.
PROBE THE BK/LG WIRE IN THE INSTRUMENT CLUSTER CONNECTOR.
IS THE RESISTANCE BELOW 10.0 OHMS?
NO
REPAIR THE Z2 BK/LG WIRE FOR AN OPEN TO GROUND.*
YES
PUT THE DRBII IN VOLTMETER MODE.
PROBE THE DB/WT WIRE IN THE INSTRUMENT CLUSTER CONNECTOR.
IS THE VOLTAGE ABOVE 10.0 VOLTS?
NO
PERFORM TEST 67B.
YES
PROBE THE PK WIRE IN THE INSTRUMENT CLUSTER CONNECTOR.
IS THE VOLTAGE ABOVE 10.0 VOLTS?
YES
REPLACE THE INSTRUMENT CLUSTER.*
NO
REMOVE FUSE #3.
INSPECT THE FUSE.
IS THE FUSE OPEN?
NO
CONTINUE TEST 67A
YES
PERFORM TEST 67C.

* PERFORM VERIFICATION TEST VER-1

91F14535

Fig. 47: Test 67A – Testing Mechanical Instrument Cluster for No Response (2 of 3)

TEST 67A – TESTING MECHANICAL INSTRUMENT CLUSTER FOR NO RESPONSE (3 OF 3)

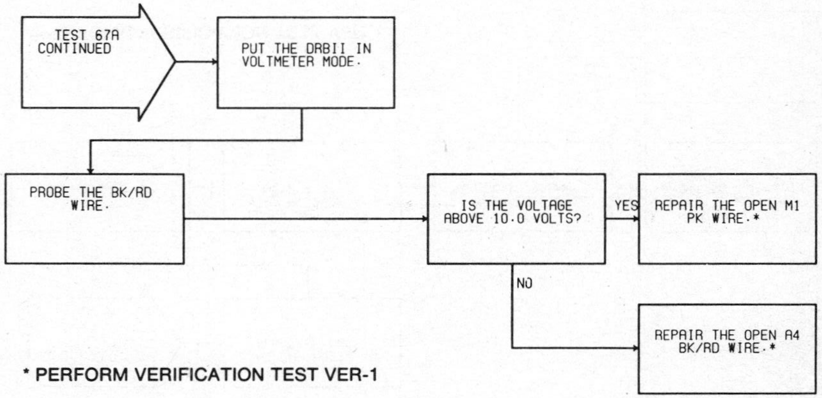
TEST 67A CONTINUED
PUT THE DRBII IN VOLTMETER MODE.
PROBE THE BK/RD WIRE.
IS THE VOLTAGE ABOVE 10.0 VOLTS?
YES
REPAIR THE OPEN M1 PK WIRE.*
NO
REPAIR THE OPEN A4 BK/RD WIRE.*

* PERFORM VERIFICATION TEST VER-1

91G14536

Fig. 48: Test 67A – Testing Mechanical Instrument Cluster for No Response (3 of 3)

TEST 67B – TESTING G5, A21 & A01 WIRES FOR POWER (1 OF 2)

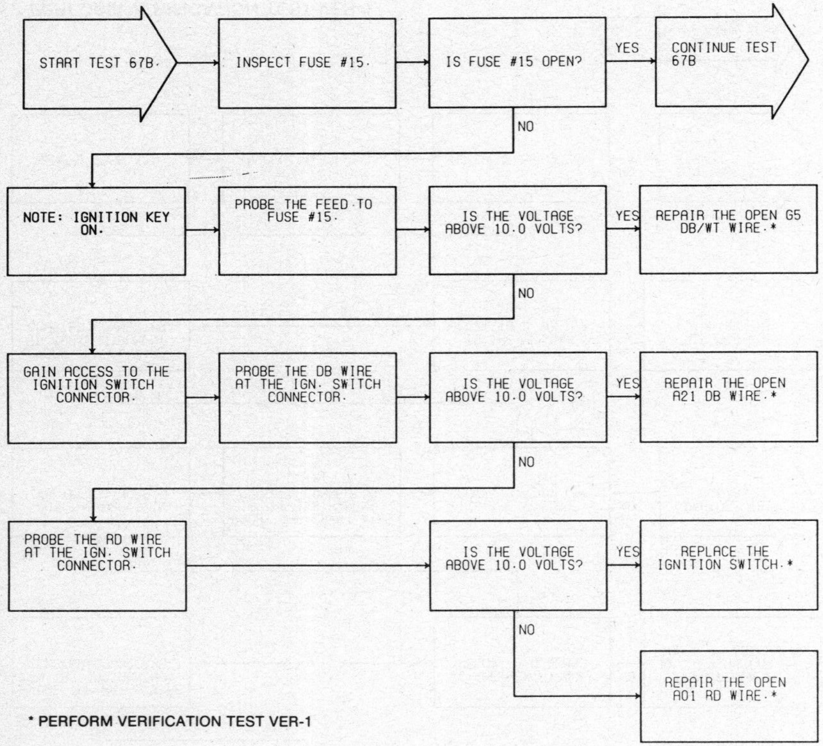
START TEST 67B.
INSPECT FUSE #15.
IS FUSE #15 OPEN?
YES
CONTINUE TEST 67B
NO
NOTE: IGNITION KEY ON.
PROBE THE FEED TO FUSE #15.
IS THE VOLTAGE ABOVE 10.0 VOLTS?
YES
REPAIR THE OPEN G5 DB/WT WIRE.*
NO
GAIN ACCESS TO THE IGNITION SWITCH CONNECTOR.
PROBE THE DB WIRE AT THE IGN. SWITCH CONNECTOR.
IS THE VOLTAGE ABOVE 10.0 VOLTS?
YES
REPAIR THE OPEN A21 DB WIRE.*
NO
PROBE THE RD WIRE AT THE IGN. SWITCH CONNECTOR.
IS THE VOLTAGE ABOVE 10.0 VOLTS?
YES
REPLACE THE IGNITION SWITCH.*
NO
REPAIR THE OPEN A01 RD WIRE.*

* PERFORM VERIFICATION TEST VER-1

91H14537

Fig. 49: Test 67B – Testing G5, A21 & A01 Wires for Power (1 of 2)

TEST 67B – TESTING G5, A21 & A01 WIRES FOR POWER (2 OF 2)

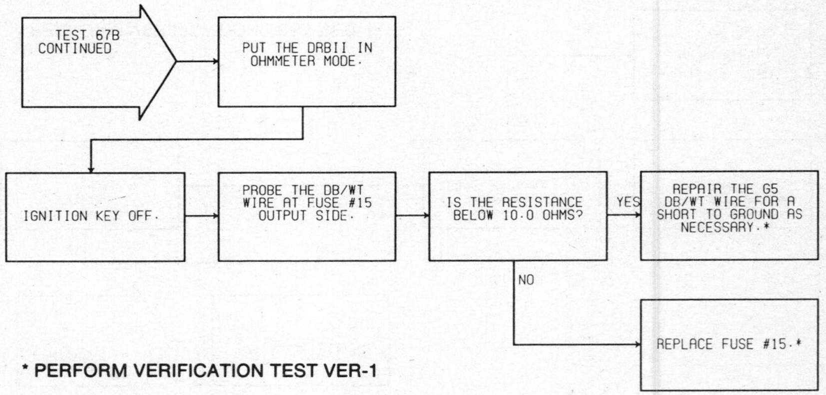
TEST 67B CONTINUED
PUT THE DRBII IN OHMMETER MODE.
IGNITION KEY OFF.
PROBE THE DB/WT WIRE AT FUSE #15 OUTPUT SIDE.
IS THE RESISTANCE BELOW 10.0 OHMS?
YES
REPAIR THE G5 DB/WT WIRE FOR A SHORT TO GROUND AS NECESSARY.*
NO
REPLACE FUSE #15.*

* PERFORM VERIFICATION TEST VER-1

91I14538

Fig. 50: Test 67B – Testing G5, A21 & A01 Wires for Power (2 of 2)

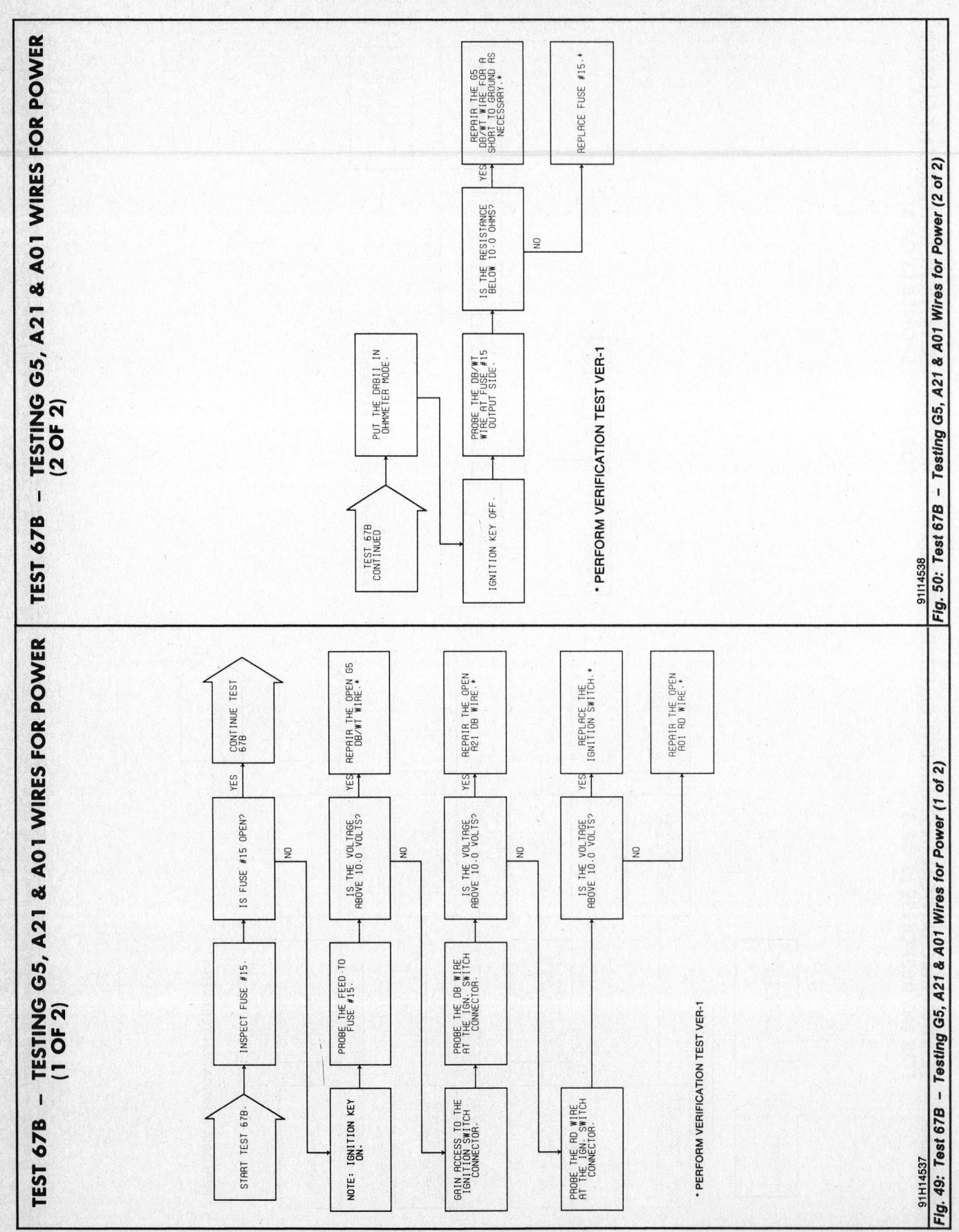

TEST 67C – TESTING M01 CIRCUIT (1 OF 2)

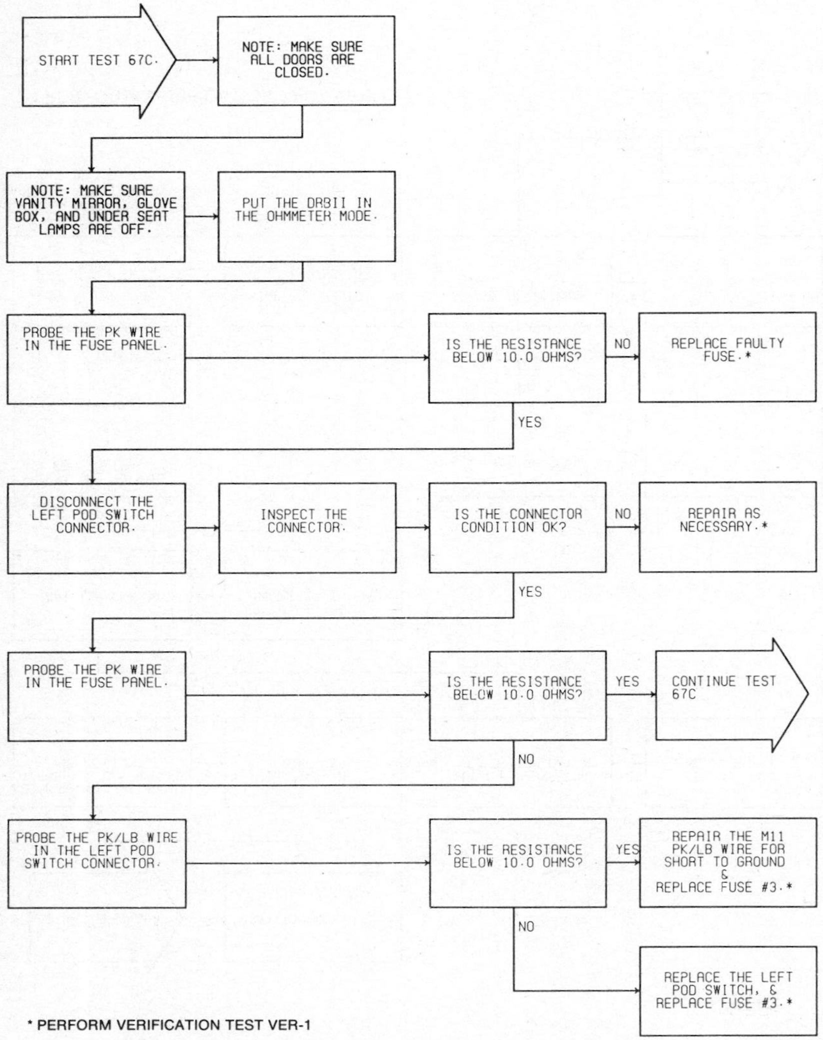
START TEST 67C.
NOTE: MAKE SURE ALL DOORS ARE CLOSED.
NOTE: MAKE SURE VANITY MIRROR, GLOVE BOX, AND UNDER SEAT LAMPS ARE OFF.
PUT THE DRBII IN THE OHMMETER MODE.
PROBE THE PK WIRE IN THE FUSE PANEL.
IS THE RESISTANCE BELOW 10.0 OHMS?
NO
REPLACE FAULTY FUSE.*
YES
DISCONNECT THE LEFT POD SWITCH CONNECTOR.
INSPECT THE CONNECTOR.
IS THE CONNECTOR CONDITION OK?
NO
REPAIR AS NECESSARY.*
YES
PROBE THE PK WIRE IN THE FUSE PANEL.
IS THE RESISTANCE BELOW 10.0 OHMS?
YES
CONTINUE TEST 67C
NO
PROBE THE PK/LB WIRE IN THE LEFT POD SWITCH CONNECTOR.
IS THE RESISTANCE BELOW 10.0 OHMS?
YES
REPAIR THE M11 PK/LB WIRE FOR SHORT TO GROUND & REPLACE FUSE #3.*
NO
REPLACE THE LEFT POD SWITCH, & REPLACE FUSE #3.*

* PERFORM VERIFICATION TEST VER-1

91J14539

Fig. 51: Test 67C – Testing M01 Circuit (1 of 2)

TEST 67C – TESTING M01 CIRCUIT (2 OF 2)

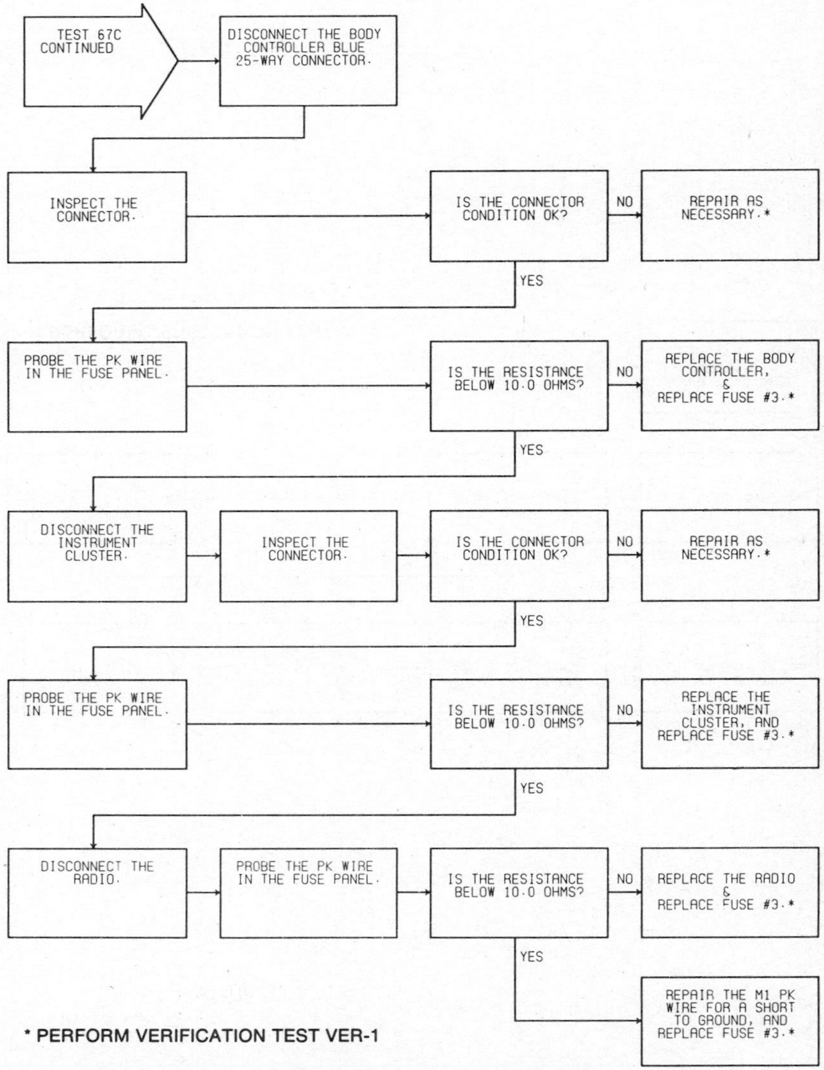
TEST 67C CONTINUED
DISCONNECT THE BODY CONTROLLER BLUE 25-WAY CONNECTOR.
INSPECT THE CONNECTOR.
IS THE CONNECTOR CONDITION OK?
NO
REPAIR AS NECESSARY.*
YES
PROBE THE PK WIRE IN THE FUSE PANEL.
IS THE RESISTANCE BELOW 10.0 OHMS?
NO
REPLACE THE BODY CONTROLLER, & REPLACE FUSE #3.*
YES
DISCONNECT THE INSTRUMENT CLUSTER.
INSPECT THE CONNECTOR.
IS THE CONNECTOR CONDITION OK?
NO
REPAIR AS NECESSARY.*
YES
PROBE THE PK WIRE IN THE FUSE PANEL.
IS THE RESISTANCE BELOW 10.0 OHMS?
NO
REPLACE THE INSTRUMENT CLUSTER, AND REPLACE FUSE #3.*
YES
DISCONNECT THE RADIO.
PROBE THE PK WIRE IN THE FUSE PANEL.
IS THE RESISTANCE BELOW 10.0 OHMS?
NO
REPLACE THE RADIO & REPLACE FUSE #3.*
YES
REPAIR THE M1 PK WIRE FOR A SHORT TO GROUND, AND REPLACE FUSE #3.*

* PERFORM VERIFICATION TEST VER-1

91C14540

Fig. 52: Test 67C – Testing M01 Circuit (2 of 2)

1991 ENGINE PERFORMANCE
Vehicle Communications (Cont.)

TEST 68A – TESTING A-604 CONTROLLER FOR NO RESPONSE (1 OF 2)

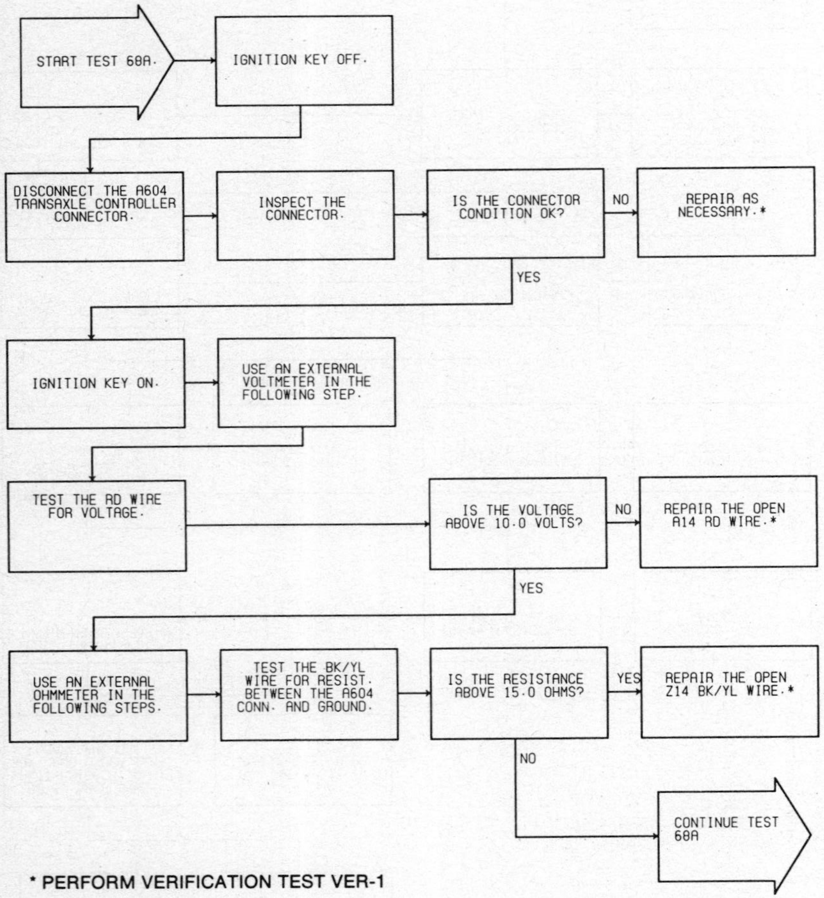
START TEST 68A.
IGNITION KEY OFF.
DISCONNECT THE A604 TRANSAXLE CONTROLLER CONNECTOR.
INSPECT THE CONNECTOR.
IS THE CONNECTOR CONDITION OK?
NO
REPAIR AS NECESSARY.*
YES
IGNITION KEY ON.
USE AN EXTERNAL VOLTMETER IN THE FOLLOWING STEP.
TEST THE RD WIRE FOR VOLTAGE.
IS THE VOLTAGE ABOVE 10.0 VOLTS?
NO
REPAIR THE OPEN A14 RD WIRE.*
YES
USE AN EXTERNAL OHMMETER IN THE FOLLOWING STEPS.
TEST THE BK/YL WIRE FOR RESIST. BETWEEN THE A604 CONN. AND GROUND.
IS THE RESISTANCE ABOVE 15.0 OHMS?
YES
REPAIR THE OPEN Z14 BK/YL WIRE.*
NO
CONTINUE TEST 68A

* PERFORM VERIFICATION TEST VER-1

91D14541

Fig. 53: Test 68A – Testing A-604 Controller for No Response (1 of 2)

TEST 68A – TESTING A-604 CONTROLLER FOR NO RESPONSE (2 OF 2)

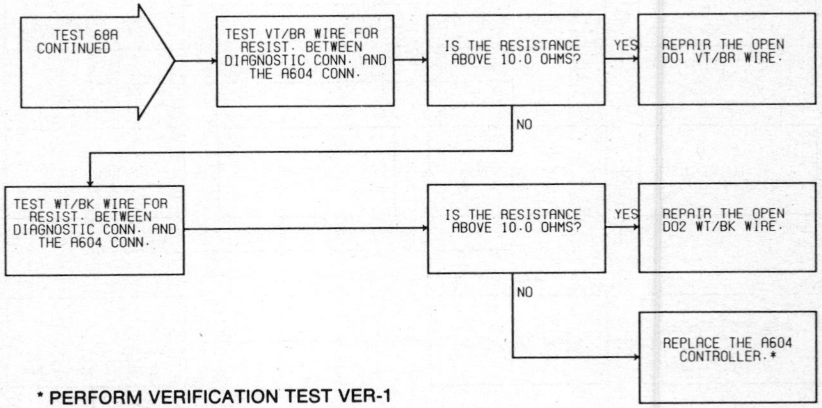
TEST 68A CONTINUED
TEST VT/BR WIRE FOR RESIST. BETWEEN DIAGNOSTIC CONN. AND THE A604 CONN.
IS THE RESISTANCE ABOVE 10.0 OHMS?
YES
REPAIR THE OPEN D01 VT/BR WIRE.
NO
TEST WT/BK WIRE FOR RESIST. BETWEEN DIAGNOSTIC CONN. AND THE A604 CONN.
IS THE RESISTANCE ABOVE 10.0 OHMS?
YES
REPAIR THE OPEN D02 WT/BK WIRE.
NO
REPLACE THE A604 CONTROLLER.*

* PERFORM VERIFICATION TEST VER-1

91E14542

Fig. 54: Test 68A – Testing A-604 Controller for No Response (2 of 2)

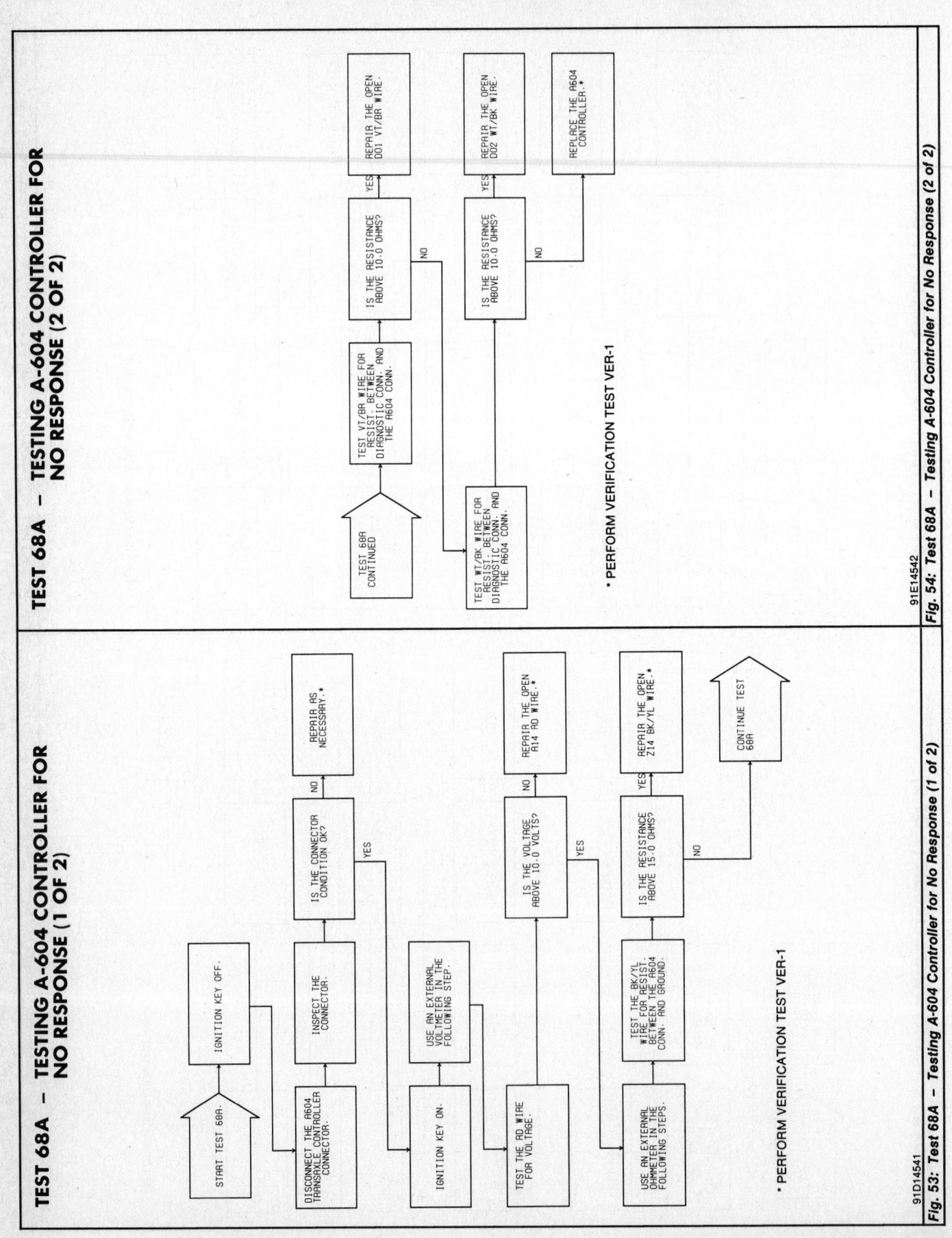

TEST 70A – TESTING BODY CONTROLLER FOR NO RESPONSE (1 OF 3)

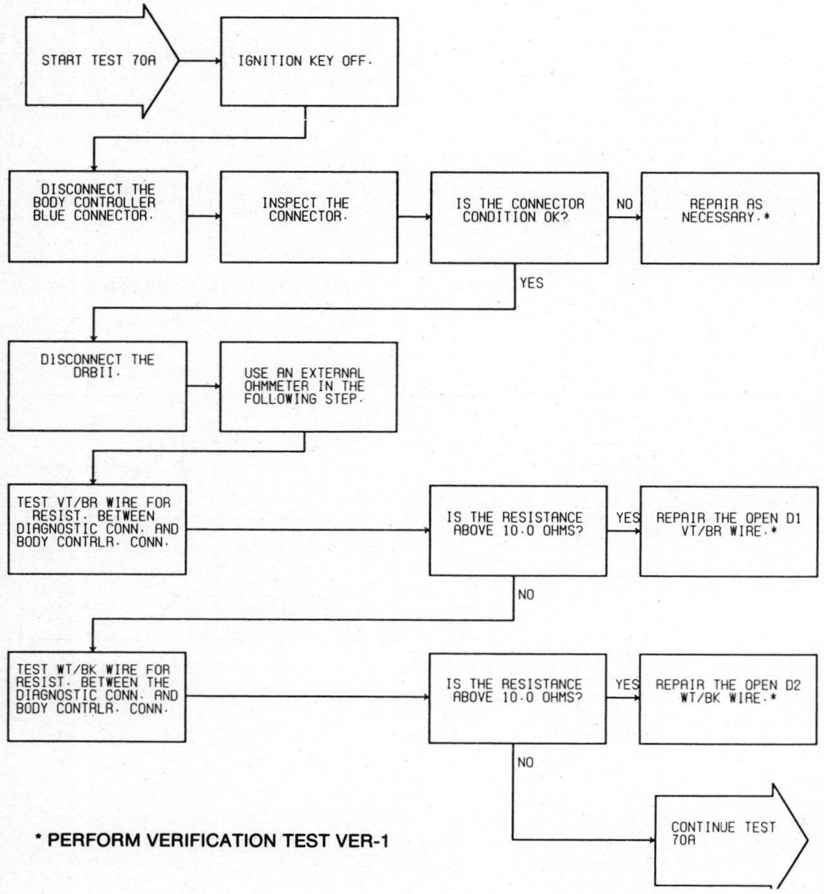
START TEST 70A
IGNITION KEY OFF.
DISCONNECT THE BODY CONTROLLER BLUE CONNECTOR.
INSPECT THE CONNECTOR.
IS THE CONNECTOR CONDITION OK?
NO
REPAIR AS NECESSARY.*
YES
DISCONNECT THE DRBII.
USE AN EXTERNAL OHMMETER IN THE FOLLOWING STEP.
TEST VT/BR WIRE FOR RESIST. BETWEEN DIAGNOSTIC CONN. AND BODY CONTRLR. CONN.
IS THE RESISTANCE ABOVE 10.0 OHMS?
YES
REPAIR THE OPEN D1 VT/BR WIRE.*
NO
TEST WT/BK WIRE FOR RESIST. BETWEEN THE DIAGNOSTIC CONN. AND BODY CONTRLR. CONN.
IS THE RESISTANCE ABOVE 10.0 OHMS?
YES
REPAIR THE OPEN D2 WT/BK WIRE.*
NO
CONTINUE TEST 70A

* PERFORM VERIFICATION TEST VER-1

91B14705

Fig. 55: Test 70A – Testing Body Controller for No Response (1 of 3)

TEST 70A – TESTING BODY CONTROLLER FOR NO RESPONSE (2 OF 3)

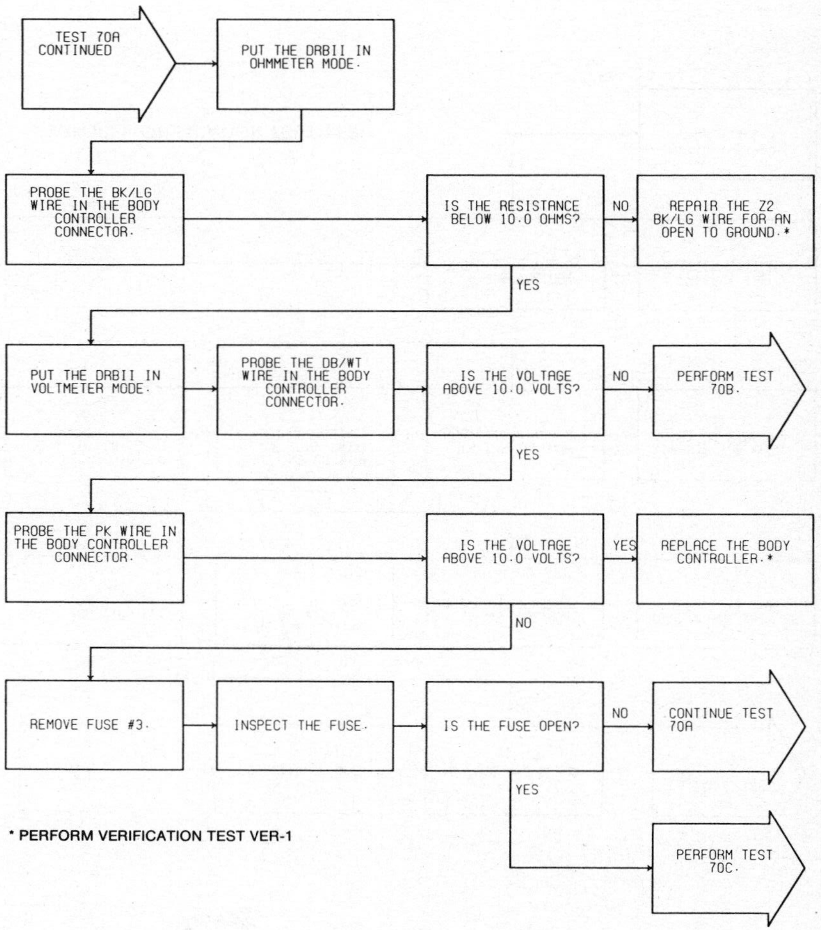
TEST 70A CONTINUED
PUT THE DRBII IN OHMMETER MODE.
PROBE THE BK/LG WIRE IN THE BODY CONTROLLER CONNECTOR.
IS THE RESISTANCE BELOW 10.0 OHMS?
NO
REPAIR THE Z2 BK/LG WIRE FOR AN OPEN TO GROUND.*
YES
PUT THE DRBII IN VOLTMETER MODE.
PROBE THE DB/WT WIRE IN THE BODY CONTROLLER CONNECTOR.
IS THE VOLTAGE ABOVE 10.0 VOLTS?
NO
PERFORM TEST 70B.
YES
PROBE THE PK WIRE IN THE BODY CONTROLLER CONNECTOR.
IS THE VOLTAGE ABOVE 10.0 VOLTS?
YES
REPLACE THE BODY CONTROLLER.*
NO
REMOVE FUSE #3.
INSPECT THE FUSE.
IS THE FUSE OPEN?
NO
CONTINUE TEST 70A
YES
PERFORM TEST 70C.

* PERFORM VERIFICATION TEST VER-1

91C14706

Fig. 56: Test 70A – Testing Body Controller for No Response (2 of 3)

TEST 70A – TESTING BODY CONTROLLER FOR NO RESPONSE (3 OF 3)

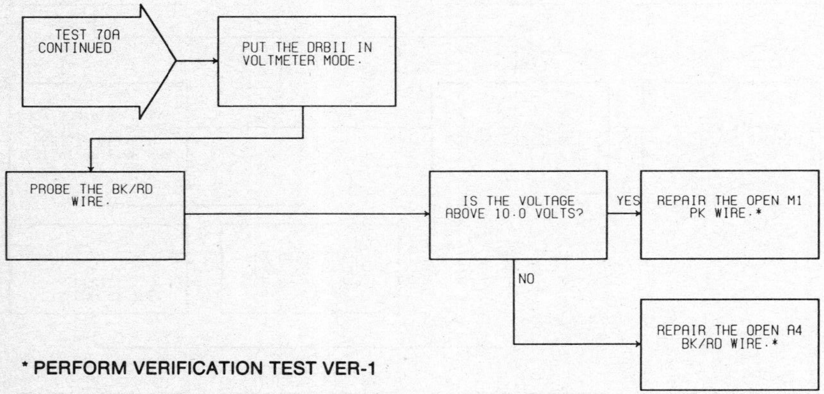
TEST 70A CONTINUED
PUT THE DRBII IN VOLTMETER MODE.
PROBE THE BK/RD WIRE.
IS THE VOLTAGE ABOVE 10.0 VOLTS?
YES
REPAIR THE OPEN M1 PK WIRE.*
NO
REPAIR THE OPEN A4 BK/RD WIRE.*

* PERFORM VERIFICATION TEST VER-1

91D14707

Fig. 57: Test 70A – Testing Body Controller for No Response (3 of 3)

TEST 70B – TESTING G5, A21 & A01 CIRCUITS (1 OF 2)

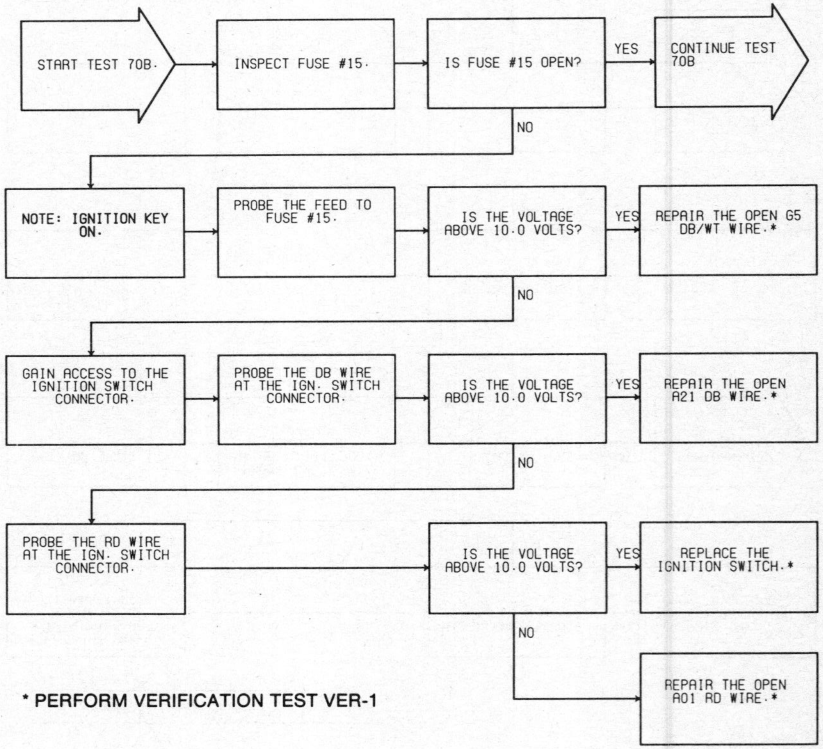
START TEST 70B.
INSPECT FUSE #15.
IS FUSE #15 OPEN?
YES
CONTINUE TEST 70B
NO
NOTE: IGNITION KEY ON.
PROBE THE FEED TO FUSE #15.
IS THE VOLTAGE ABOVE 10.0 VOLTS?
YES
REPAIR THE OPEN G5 DB/WT WIRE.*
NO
GAIN ACCESS TO THE IGNITION SWITCH CONNECTOR.
PROBE THE DB WIRE AT THE IGN. SWITCH CONNECTOR.
IS THE VOLTAGE ABOVE 10.0 VOLTS?
YES
REPAIR THE OPEN A21 DB WIRE.*
NO
PROBE THE RD WIRE AT THE IGN. SWITCH CONNECTOR.
IS THE VOLTAGE ABOVE 10.0 VOLTS?
YES
REPLACE THE IGNITION SWITCH.*
NO
REPAIR THE OPEN A01 RD WIRE.*

* PERFORM VERIFICATION TEST VER-1

91E14708

Fig. 58: Test 70B – Testing G5, A21 & A01 Circuits (1 of 2)

TEST 70B – TESTING G5, A21 & A01 CIRCUITS (2 OF 2)

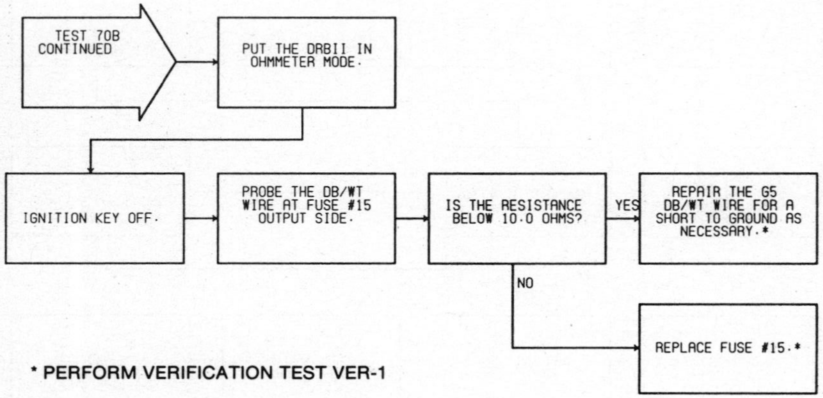
TEST 70B CONTINUED
PUT THE DRBII IN OHMMETER MODE.
IGNITION KEY OFF.
PROBE THE DB/WT WIRE AT FUSE #15 OUTPUT SIDE.
IS THE RESISTANCE BELOW 10.0 OHMS?
YES
REPAIR THE G5 DB/WT WIRE FOR A SHORT TO GROUND AS NECESSARY.*
NO
REPLACE FUSE #15.*

* PERFORM VERIFICATION TEST VER-1

91F14709

Fig. 59: Test 70B – Testing G5, A21 & A01 Circuits (2 of 2)

TEST 70C – TESTING M01 CIRCUIT (1 OF 2)

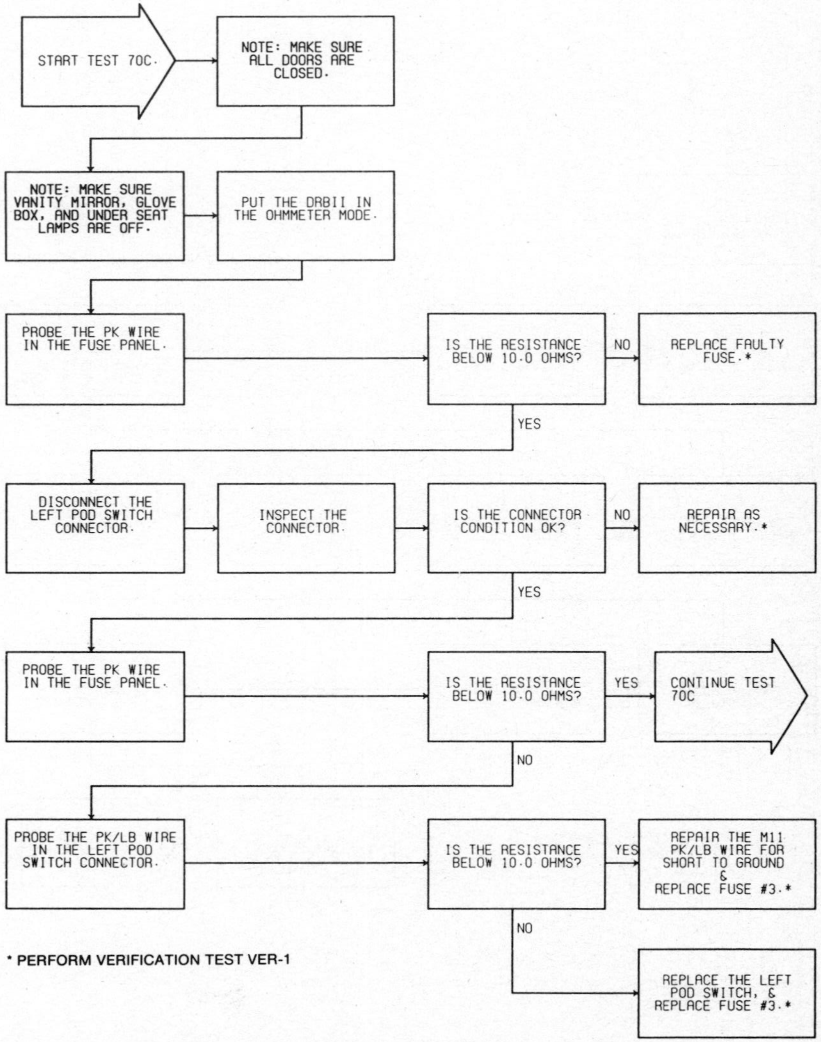
START TEST 70C.
NOTE: MAKE SURE ALL DOORS ARE CLOSED.
NOTE: MAKE SURE VANITY MIRROR, GLOVE BOX, AND UNDER SEAT LAMPS ARE OFF.
PUT THE DRBII IN THE OHMMETER MODE.
PROBE THE PK WIRE IN THE FUSE PANEL.
IS THE RESISTANCE BELOW 10.0 OHMS?
NO
REPLACE FAULTY FUSE.*
YES
DISCONNECT THE LEFT POD SWITCH CONNECTOR.
INSPECT THE CONNECTOR.
IS THE CONNECTOR CONDITION OK?
NO
REPAIR AS NECESSARY.*
YES
PROBE THE PK WIRE IN THE FUSE PANEL.
IS THE RESISTANCE BELOW 10.0 OHMS?
YES
CONTINUE TEST 70C
NO
PROBE THE PK/LB WIRE IN THE LEFT POD SWITCH CONNECTOR.
IS THE RESISTANCE BELOW 10.0 OHMS?
YES
REPAIR THE M11 PK/LB WIRE FOR SHORT TO GROUND & REPLACE FUSE #3.*
NO
REPLACE THE LEFT POD SWITCH, & REPLACE FUSE #3.*

* PERFORM VERIFICATION TEST VER-1

91I14710

Fig. 60: Test 70C – Testing M01 Circuit (1 of 2)

1991 ENGINE PERFORMANCE
Vehicle Communications (Cont.)

TEST 70C – TESTING M01 CIRCUIT (2 OF 2)

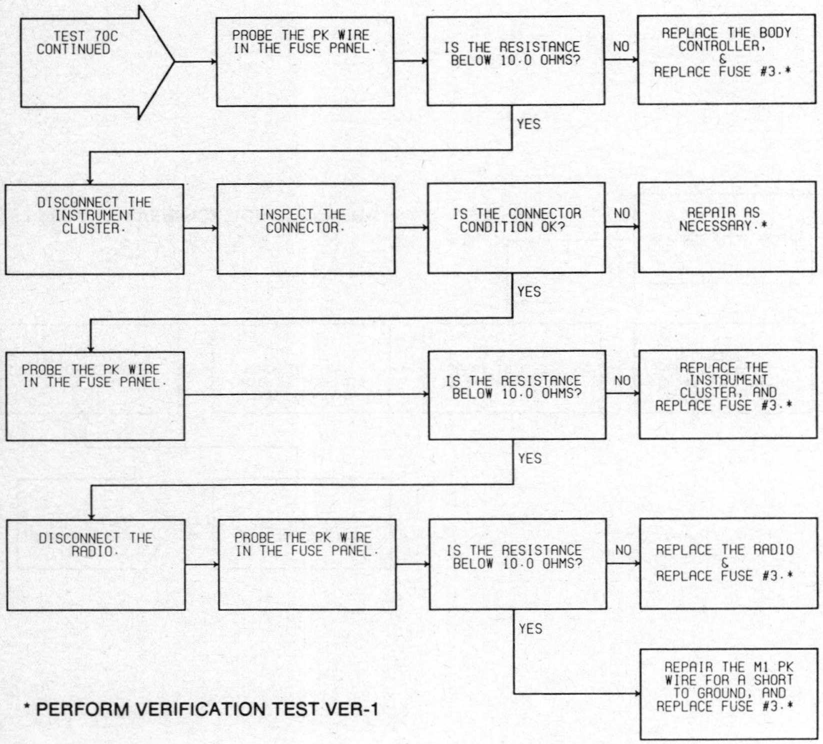
TEST 70C CONTINUED
PROBE THE PK WIRE IN THE FUSE PANEL.
IS THE RESISTANCE BELOW 10.0 OHMS?
NO
REPLACE THE BODY CONTROLLER, & REPLACE FUSE #3.*
YES
DISCONNECT THE INSTRUMENT CLUSTER.
INSPECT THE CONNECTOR.
IS THE CONNECTOR CONDITION OK?
NO
REPAIR AS NECESSARY.*
YES
PROBE THE PK WIRE IN THE FUSE PANEL.
IS THE RESISTANCE BELOW 10.0 OHMS?
NO
REPLACE THE INSTRUMENT CLUSTER, AND REPLACE FUSE #3.*
YES
DISCONNECT THE RADIO.
PROBE THE PK WIRE IN THE FUSE PANEL.
IS THE RESISTANCE BELOW 10.0 OHMS?
NO
REPLACE THE RADIO & REPLACE FUSE #3.*
YES
REPAIR THE M1 PK WIRE FOR A SHORT TO GROUND, AND REPLACE FUSE #3.*

* PERFORM VERIFICATION TEST VER-1

91J14711

Fig. 61: Test 70C – Testing M01 Circuit (2 of 2)

TEST 71A – TESTING ENGINE CONTROLLER FOR NO RESPONSE

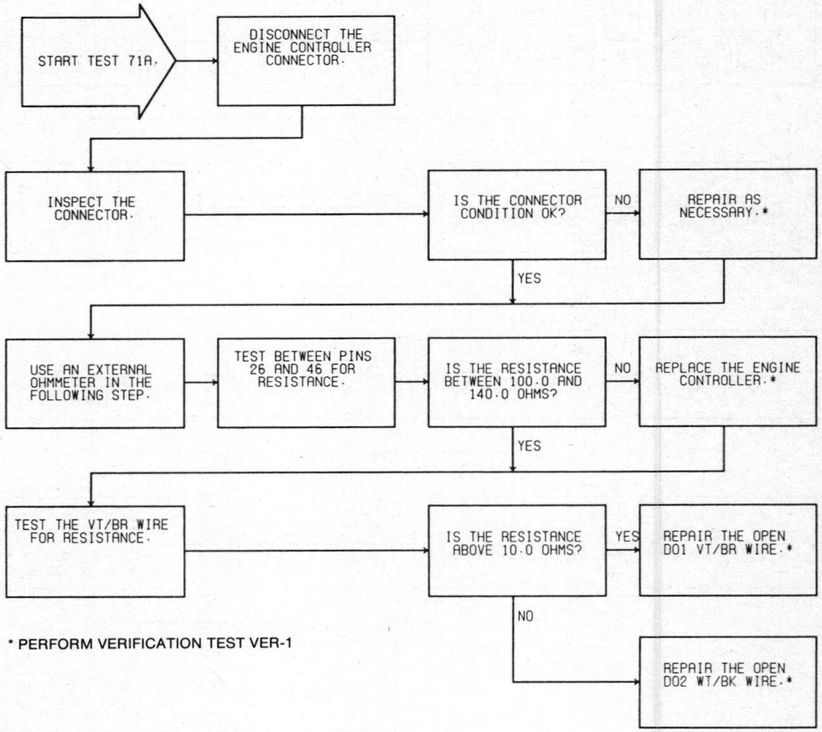
START TEST 71A.
DISCONNECT THE ENGINE CONTROLLER CONNECTOR.
INSPECT THE CONNECTOR.
IS THE CONNECTOR CONDITION OK?
NO
REPAIR AS NECESSARY.*
YES
USE AN EXTERNAL OHMMETER IN THE FOLLOWING STEP.
TEST BETWEEN PINS 26 AND 46 FOR RESISTANCE.
IS THE RESISTANCE BETWEEN 100.0 AND 140.0 OHMS?
NO
REPLACE THE ENGINE CONTROLLER.*
YES
TEST THE VT/BR WIRE FOR RESISTANCE.
IS THE RESISTANCE ABOVE 10.0 OHMS?
YES
REPAIR THE OPEN DO1 VT/BR WIRE.*
NO
REPAIR THE OPEN DO2 WT/BK WIRE.*

* PERFORM VERIFICATION TEST VER-1

91A14712

Fig. 62: Test 71A – Testing Engine Controller for No Response

TEST 72A – TESTING FOR BLANK DRB-II MESSAGE SCREEN (1 OF 2)

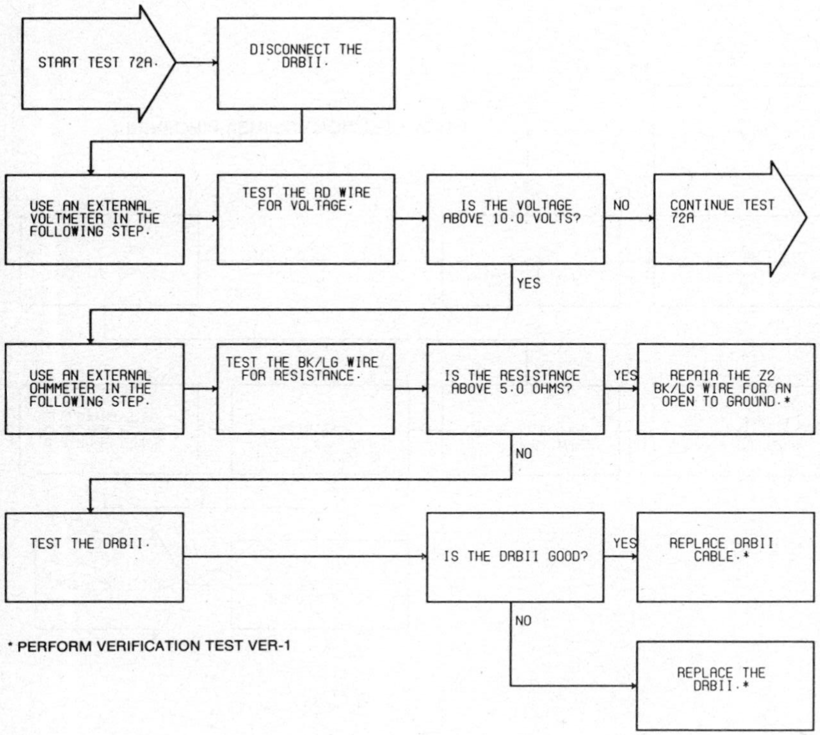
START TEST 72A.
DISCONNECT THE DRBII.
USE AN EXTERNAL VOLTMETER IN THE FOLLOWING STEP.
TEST THE RD WIRE FOR VOLTAGE.
IS THE VOLTAGE ABOVE 10.0 VOLTS?
NO
CONTINUE TEST 72A
YES
USE AN EXTERNAL OHMMETER IN THE FOLLOWING STEP.
TEST THE BK/LG WIRE FOR RESISTANCE.
IS THE RESISTANCE ABOVE 5.0 OHMS?
YES
REPAIR THE Z2 BK/LG WIRE FOR AN OPEN TO GROUND.*
NO
TEST THE DRBII.
IS THE DRBII GOOD?
YES
REPLACE DRBII CABLE.*
NO
REPLACE THE DRBII.*

* PERFORM VERIFICATION TEST VER-1

91B14713

Fig. 63: Test 72A – Testing for Blank DRB-II Message Screen (1 of 2)

TEST 72A – TESTING FOR BLANK DRB-II MESSAGE SCREEN (2 OF 2)

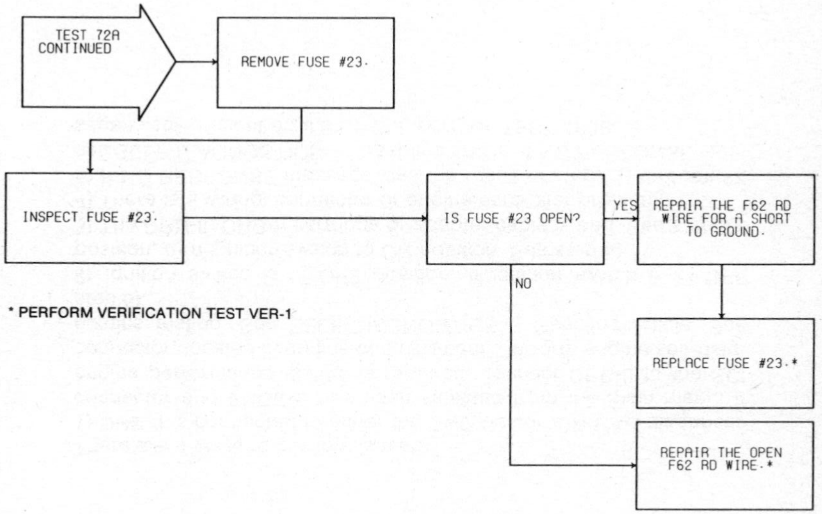
TEST 72A CONTINUED
REMOVE FUSE #23.
INSPECT FUSE #23.
IS FUSE #23 OPEN?
YES
REPAIR THE F62 RD WIRE FOR A SHORT TO GROUND.
REPLACE FUSE #23.*
NO
REPAIR THE OPEN F62 RD WIRE.*

* PERFORM VERIFICATION TEST VER-1

91C14714

Fig. 64: Test 72A – Testing for Blank DRB-II Message Screen (2 of 2)

TEST 108A – TESTING ENGINE DIAGNOSTIC CONNECTOR GROUND & DRB-II FOR CORRECT OPERATION

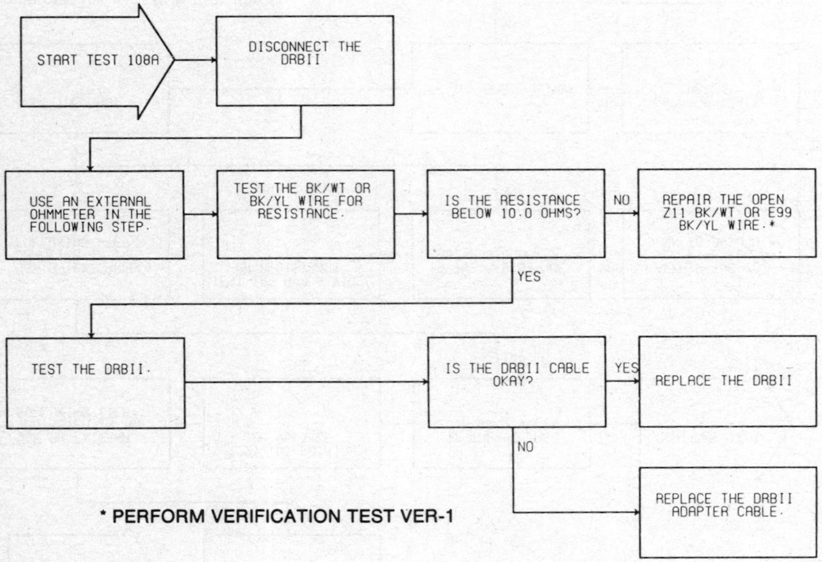
START TEST 108A
DISCONNECT THE DRBII
USE AN EXTERNAL OHMMETER IN THE FOLLOWING STEP.
TEST THE BK/WT OR BK/YL WIRE FOR RESISTANCE.
IS THE RESISTANCE BELOW 10.0 OHMS?
NO
REPAIR THE OPEN Z11 BK/WT OR E99 BK/YL WIRE.*
YES
TEST THE DRBII.
IS THE DRBII CABLE OKAY?
YES
REPLACE THE DRBII
NO
REPLACE THE DRBII ADAPTER CABLE.

* PERFORM VERIFICATION TEST VER-1

91F14543

Fig. 65: TEST 108A – Testing Engine Diagnostic Connector for Ground & DRB-II for Correct Operation

TEST 109A – TESTING FOR NO RESPONSE ON THE DRB-II SCREEN

There are 4 ways to get to this test:

1) DRB-II is connected to either the CCD bus or AIR BAG diagnostic connector and ENGINE has been selected from the main menu. If engine performance testing is required, connect DRB-II to the SCI connector, located in engine compartment. Perform engine self-diagnostics testing. See SELF-DIAGNOSTICS – Gasoline article. See step **5)**.

2) Ignition switch is in OFF position. If ignition switch is in OFF position, turn ignition switch to ON position. See step **5)**.

3) The DRB-II, DRB-II cartridge or adapter cable is bad. See step **5)**.

4) There is a wiring, connector or engine controller problem.

5) If NO RESPONSE message was the result of steps **1)** through **3)**, see SELF-DIAGNOSTICS – Gasoline article. If NO RESPONSE message is still present on the DRB-II, perform TEST 109B.

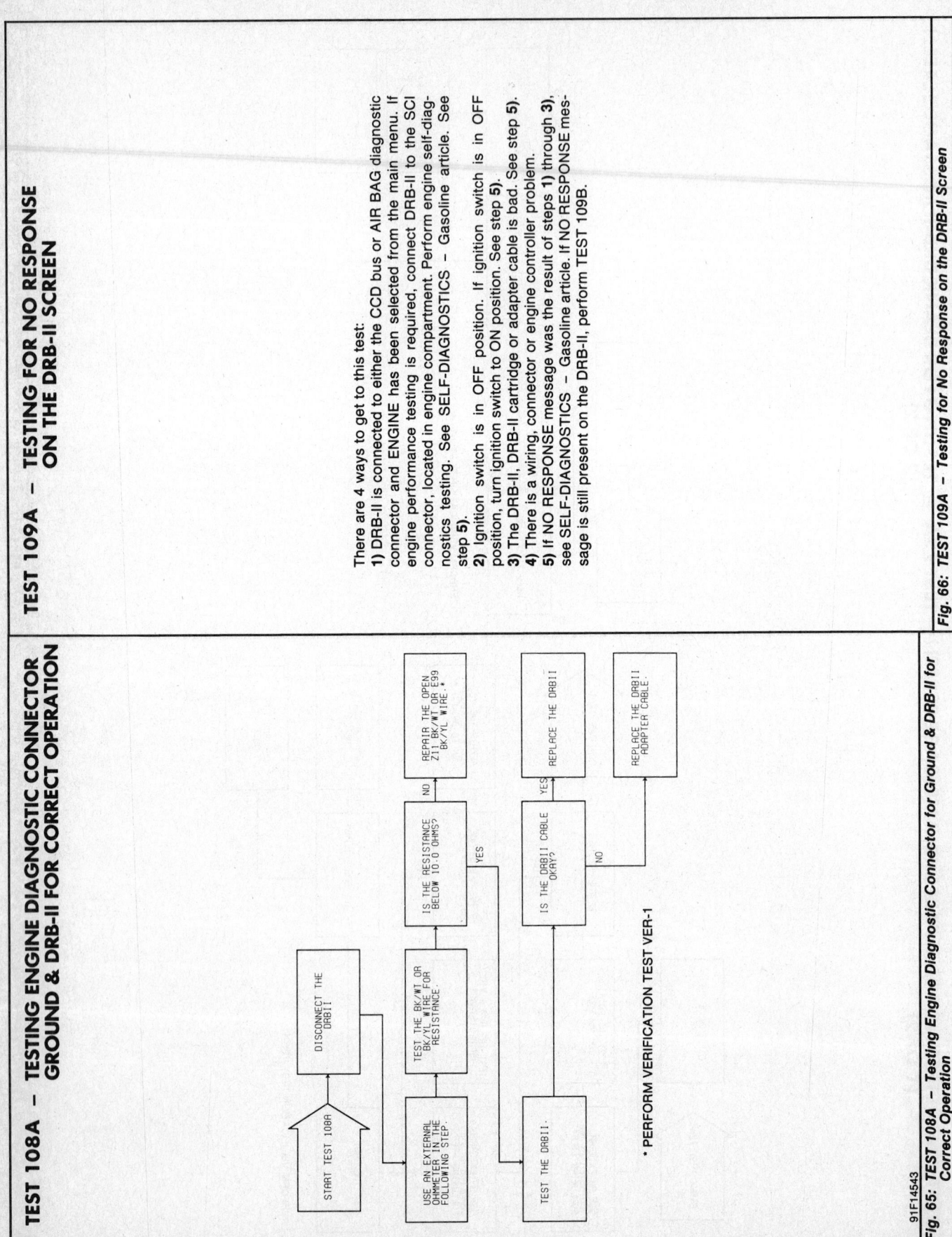

Fig. 66: TEST 109A – Testing for No Response on the DRB-II Screen

TEST 109B – TESTING FOR NO RESPONSE ON THE DRB-II SCREEN

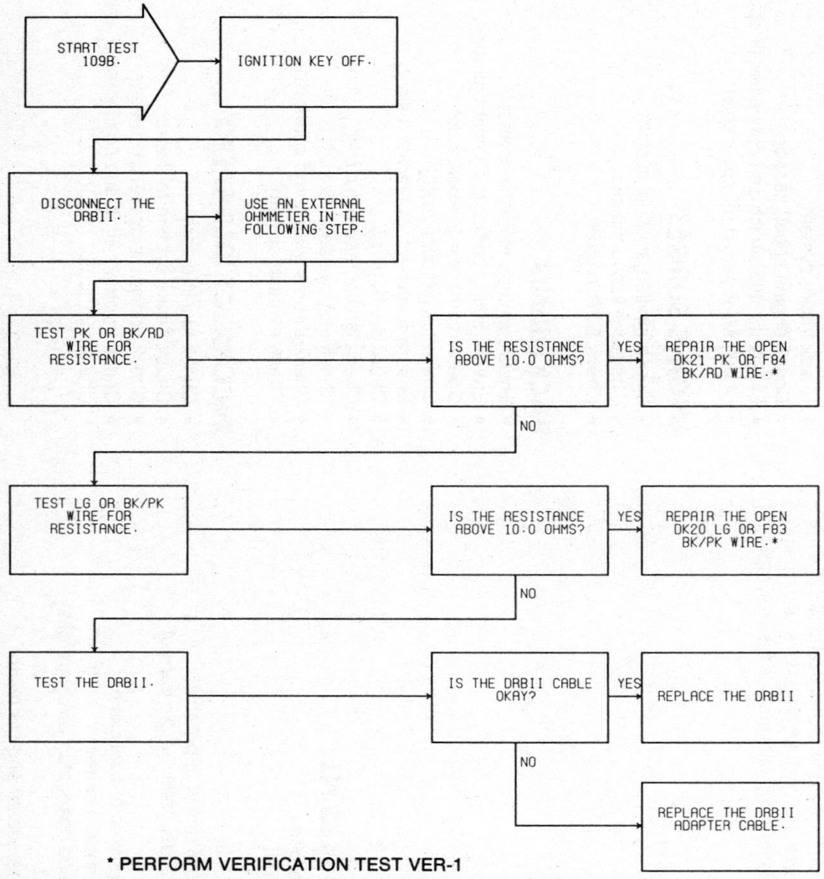
START TEST 109B.
IGNITION KEY OFF.
DISCONNECT THE DRBII.
USE AN EXTERNAL OHMMETER IN THE FOLLOWING STEP.
TEST PK OR BK/RD WIRE FOR RESISTANCE.
IS THE RESISTANCE ABOVE 10.0 OHMS?
YES
REPAIR THE OPEN DK21 PK OR F84 BK/RD WIRE.*
NO
TEST LG OR BK/PK WIRE FOR RESISTANCE.
IS THE RESISTANCE ABOVE 10.0 OHMS?
YES
REPAIR THE OPEN DK20 LG OR F83 BK/PK WIRE.*
NO
TEST THE DRBII.
IS THE DRBII CABLE OKAY?
YES
REPLACE THE DRBII
NO
REPLACE THE DRBII ADAPTER CABLE.
* PERFORM VERIFICATION TEST VER-1

91G14544

Fig. 67: TEST 109B – Testing for No Response on the DRB-II Screen

TEST VER-1 – VERIFICATION TEST

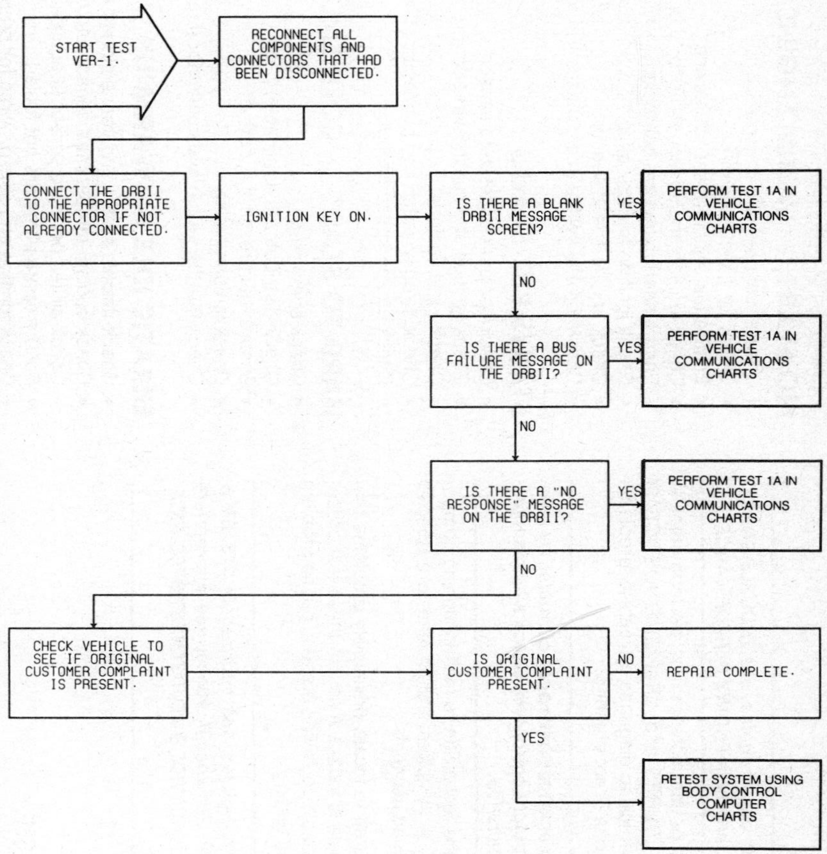
START TEST VER-1.
RECONNECT ALL COMPONENTS AND CONNECTORS THAT HAD BEEN DISCONNECTED.
CONNECT THE DRBII TO THE APPROPRIATE CONNECTOR IF NOT ALREADY CONNECTED.
IGNITION KEY ON.
IS THERE A BLANK DRBII MESSAGE SCREEN?
YES
PERFORM TEST 1A IN VEHICLE COMMUNICATIONS CHARTS
NO
IS THERE A BUS FAILURE MESSAGE ON THE DRBII?
YES
PERFORM TEST 1A IN VEHICLE COMMUNICATIONS CHARTS
NO
IS THERE A "NO RESPONSE" MESSAGE ON THE DRBII?
YES
PERFORM TEST 1A IN VEHICLE COMMUNICATIONS CHARTS
NO
CHECK VEHICLE TO SEE IF ORIGINAL CUSTOMER COMPLAINT IS PRESENT.
IS ORIGINAL CUSTOMER COMPLAINT PRESENT.
NO
REPAIR COMPLETE.
YES
RETEST SYSTEM USING BODY CONTROL COMPUTER CHARTS

91A14738

Fig. 68: TEST VER-1 – Verification Test

1991 ENGINE PERFORMANCE
Trouble Shooting – No Codes – Gasoline

Caravan, Dakota, Pickup, Ramcharger
RWD Van, Town & Country, Voyager

INTRODUCTION

NOTE: For Pickup models with diesel engine, see TROUBLE SHOOTING – NO CODES – DIESEL article in ENGINE PERFORMANCE.

Before diagnosing symptoms or intermittent faults, perform steps in BASIC DIAGNOSTIC PROCEDURES and SELF-DIAGNOSTICS (if applicable) articles. Use this article to diagnose driveability problems that exist when a hard fault code is not present.

NOTE: Some driveability problems may have been corrected by manufacturer with a revised computer control unit. Check with manufacturer for latest computer application.

Symptom checks can direct the technician to malfunctioning component(s) for further diagnosis. A symptom should lead to a specific component, system test or an adjustment.

Use intermittent test procedures to locate driveability problems that DO NOT occur when the vehicle is tested. Also use these test procedures if a soft (intermittent) trouble code was present, but no problem is found during self-diagnostic testing.

NOTE: For specific testing procedures, see appropriate SYSTEM & COMPONENT TESTING article. For specifications, see appropriate ON-VEHICLE ADJUSTMENTS or SERVICE & ADJUSTMENT SPECIFICATIONS article.

SYMPTOMS

SYMPTOM DIAGNOSIS

Symptom checks cannot be used properly unless problem occurs while vehicle is tested. To reduce diagnostic time, ensure steps in appropriate BASIC DIAGNOSTIC PROCEDURES and SELF-DIAGNOSTICS (if applicable) articles are performed before diagnosing a symptom. Symptoms available for diagnosis include these symptoms.

- No Start – Cold Engine
- No Start – Warm Engine
- Starts But Stalls
- Hard To Start – Cold Engine
- Erratic Idle – Warm-Up
- Engine Surges
- Backfiring
- Incorrect Idle Speed
- Hesitation – Acceleration
- Hesitation – Coasting
- Knocking
- Engine Misfire – All Conditions
- Insufficient Engine Power
- Poor Fuel Economy
- Excessive HC & NOx

NO START – COLD ENGINE

- Ensure battery is fully charged
- Check for contaminated fuel
- Check spark plugs
- Check fuel pump fuse(s)
- Check in-line fuse to control unit (if applicable)
- Ensure ignition timing and fuel pressure are correct
- Check fuel injectors
- Ensure timing belt is not broken (if applicable)
- Ensure ignition coil resistance is correct
- Ensure rotor, distributor and spark plug wires are okay
- Check ignition control unit
- Check coolant temperature sensor and connector
- Check throttle switch and connector (if applicable)
- Check engine speed sensor
- Check airflow sensor

NO START – WARM ENGINE

- Ensure fuel pressure is correct
- Check for gasoline in oil
- Ensure fuel injectors are not leaking
- Check ignition and sensor wires for proper connection
- Ensure spark plugs are not fouled
- Check ignition and coil circuit
- Check engine speed sensor
- Check throttle switch and connector (if applicable)

STARTS BUT STALLS

- Check coolant temperature sensor
- Check ignition and sensor wires for proper connection
- Check fuel injectors
- Check throttle switch and connector (if applicable)
- Check engine speed sensor

HARD TO START – COLD ENGINE

- Check spark plugs
- Check distributor (if applicable)
- Ensure fuel pressure is correct
- Check ignition timing
- Check throttle switch and connector (if applicable)

ERRATIC IDLE – WARM-UP

- Check throttle switch and connection (if applicable)
- Check coolant temperature sensor and connection
- Check air temperature sensor (if applicable)
- Ensure spark plugs are not fouled
- Check ignition and sensor wires for proper connection
- Check distributor (if applicable)
- Check ignition and coil circuit
- Check intake system
- Check engine speed sensor
- Check throttle switch and connector (if applicable)
- Check MAP sensor (if applicable)

ENGINE SURGES

- Check ignition and fuel system
- Check for vacuum leaks
- Check EGR system

BACKFIRING

- Ensure ignition timing is correct.
- Ensure timing belt/chain has not jumped.
- Check distributor (if applicable)
- Check for gasoline in oil
- Ensure fuel injectors are not leaking
- Check spark plugs
- Check ignition and coil circuit
- Check engine speed sensor
- Check throttle switch and connector
- Check exhaust system

INCORRECT IDLE SPEED

- Check fuel injectors
- Check intake system for leaks
- Check coolant temperature sensor
- Check throttle switch and connector (if applicable)
- Check distributor (if applicable)

1991 ENGINE PERFORMANCE
Trouble Shooting – No Codes – Gasoline (Cont.)

HESITATION – ACCELERATION

- Check ignition and sensor wires for proper connection
- Check distributor cap for moisture or carbon tracking (if applicable)
- Ensure spark plug wires are okay
- Ensure spark plugs are not fouled
- Check MAP sensor (if applicable)
- Check throttle switch and connector (if applicable)
- Check ignition and coil circuit
- Check engine speed sensor

HESITATION – COASTING

- Check fuel injectors
- Check ignition and sensor wires for proper connection
- Check throttle switch and connector
- Check engine speed sensor
- Check for gasoline in oil

KNOCKING

- Check ignition and coil circuit
- Check for defect in throttle body power system
- Check for restrictions at throttle body air inlet
- Check EGR system
- Ensure spark plugs fire
- Check knock sensor (if applicable)
- Check throttle switch and connector (if applicable)
- Check engine speed sensor
- Check MAP sensor (if applicable)

ENGINE MISFIRE – ALL CONDITIONS

- Check fuel injectors
- Check ignition and sensor wires for proper connection
- Check ignition and coil circuit
- Check for gasoline in oil
- Check intake and exhaust system
- Check throttle switch and connector (if applicable)
- Check for vacuum leaks
- Check engine speed sensor
- Check MAP sensor (if applicable)

INSUFFICIENT ENGINE POWER

- Check fuel injectors
- Check for air inlet restriction
- Ensure fuel pressure is correct
- Check airflow sensor
- Check for restricted exhaust
- Check coolant temperature sensor
- Check air temperature sensor (if applicable)
- Check throttle switch and connector (if applicable)
- Check ignition and coil circuit
- Check MAP sensor (if applicable)
- Check engine speed sensor
- Check intake and exhaust system
- Check EGR system

POOR FUEL ECONOMY

- Check for leaky fuel injectors
- Ensure spark plugs are not fouled
- Check for faulty oxygen sensor
- Check throttle switch and connector
- Check for poor wire connections
- Check engine speed sensor
- Check for gasoline in oil
- Check MAP sensor (if applicable)

EXCESSIVE HC & NOx

- Check for gasoline in oil
- Check for leaky fuel injectors
- Check for faulty oxygen sensor
- Check ignition and sensor wires for poor connection
- Check engine speed sensor
- Check throttle switch and connector (if applicable)
- Check for vacuum leaks

INTERMITTENTS

INTERMITTENT PROBLEM DIAGNOSIS

Intermittent fault testing requires duplicating circuit or component failure to identify the problem. These procedures may lead to the computer setting a fault code (on some systems), which may help in diagnosis.

If problem vehicle does not produce fault codes, monitor voltage or resistance values using a digital volt-ohmmeter (DVOM) while attempting to reproduce conditions causing intermittent fault. A status change on DVOM indicates a fault has been located.

Use a DVOM to pinpoint faults. When monitoring voltage, ensure ignition switch is in ON position or engine is running. Ensure ignition switch is in OFF position or negative battery cable is disconnected when monitoring circuit resistance. Status changes on DVOM during test procedures indicate area of fault.

TEST PROCEDURES

Intermittent Simulation – To reproduce the conditions creating an intermittent fault, use the following methods:

- Lightly vibrate component
- Heat component
- Wiggle or bend wiring harness
- Spray component with water
- Remove/apply vacuum source

Monitor circuit/component voltage or resistance while simulating intermittent. If engine is running, monitor for self-diagnostic codes. Use test results to identify a faulty component or circuit.

1991 ENGINE PERFORMANCE
Trouble Shooting – No Codes – Diesel

Pickup

NOTE: In mid-year, an intercooler was installed in front of the radiator and was connected to turbocharger and intake manifold. Note if vehicle contains an intercooler. Intercooled models contain a Single Board Engine Controller (SBEC) with a self-diagnostic system.

On intercooled models, before diagnosing symptoms, perform steps in BASIC DIAGNOSTIC PROCEDURES - DIESEL - INTERCOOLED and SELF-DIAGNOSTICS - DIESEL - INTERCOOLED articles.

On all models, use this article to diagnose driveability problems existing when a trouble code (intercooled models) is not present or vehicle is not equipped with a self-diagnostic system (non-intercooled models).

Symptom checks can direct the technician to malfunctioning component(s) for further diagnosis. A symptom should lead to a specific component, system test or an adjustment.

NOTE: For specific testing procedures, refer to SYSTEM & COMPONENT TESTING - DIESEL article. For specifications, see ON-VEHICLE ADJUSTMENTS - DIESEL or SERVICE & ADJUSTMENT SPECIFICATIONS - DIESEL article.

SYMPTOMS

SYMPTOM DIAGNOSIS

Symptom checks cannot be used properly unless problem occurs while vehicle is being tested. On intercooled models, reduce diagnostic time by ensuring steps in BASIC DIAGNOSTIC PROCEDURES - DIESEL - INTERCOOLED and SELF-DIAGNOSTICS -DIESEL - INTERCOOLED articles are performed before diagnosing a symptom. On all models, symptoms available for diagnosis include these symptoms.

- Engine Hard To Start
- Engine Surges At Idle
- Engine Has Rough Idle When Warm
- Engine Misfiring Under Load
- Engine Has Low Power
- Excessive Fuel Consumption
- Engine Will Not Shut Off
- White Or Blue Exhaust Smoke
- Incorrect Idle Speed
- Engine Speed Will Not Increase
- Fuel Injection Pump Runs Hot

ENGINE HARD TO START

- Air in fuel system
- Clogged fuel filter
- Poor fuel quality
- Electrical shutoff solenoid not operating
- Fuel tank empty or fuel tank vent blocked
- Restricted, blocked or leaking fuel injection or supply lines
- Incorrect timing or defective fuel injection pump
- Malfunctioning intake manifold heater system
- Malfunctioning KSB valve
- Low or uneven engine compression
- Injection sequence does not correspond with firing order
- Restricted or damaged air filter

ENGINE SURGES AT IDLE

- Air in fuel system
- Fuel tank empty or fuel tank vent blocked
- Low idle speed
- Incorrect timing or defective fuel injection pump

ENGINE HAS ROUGH IDLE WHEN WARM

- Air in fuel system
- Poor fuel quality
- Low idle speed
- Restricted or damaged fuel injector
- Injection sequence does not correspond with firing order
- Low or uneven engine compression
- Incorrect timing or defective fuel injection pump

ENGINE MISFIRING UNDER LOAD

- Air in fuel system
- Poor fuel quality
- Fuel tank empty or fuel tank vent blocked
- Clogged or defective fuel filter
- Restricted, blocked or leaking fuel injection or supply lines
- Incorrect timing or defective fuel injection pump
- Restricted or damaged fuel injector
- Restricted or damaged air filter

ENGINE HAS LOW POWER

- Air in fuel system
- Poor fuel quality
- Fuel tank empty or fuel tank vent blocked
- Fuel control lever not obtaining full throttle
- Clogged or defective fuel filter
- Clogged or leaking intercooler
- Restricted, blocked or leaking fuel injection or supply lines
- Improper fuel line banjo bolts at fuel injection pump
- Incorrect timing or defective fuel injection pump
- Restricted or damaged fuel injector
- Restricted or damaged air filter
- Turbocharger boost control line broken or leaking
- Low manifold pressure
- Injection sequence does not correspond with firing order
- Low or uneven engine compression

EXCESSIVE FUEL CONSUMPTION

- Poor fuel quality
- Incorrect timing or defective fuel injection pump
- Damaged fuel injector
- Restricted or damaged air filter
- Injection sequence does not correspond with firing order
- Clogged or leaking intercooler
- Improper idle speed
- Malfunctioning KSB valve

ENGINE WILL NOT SHUT OFF

- Electrical shutoff solenoid not operating
- Voltage always exists at electrical shutoff solenoid

WHITE OR BLUE EXHAUST SMOKE

- Air in fuel system
- Poor fuel quality
- Clogged or defective fuel filter
- Restricted or blocked fuel injection or supply lines
- Improper fuel line banjo bolts at fuel injection pump
- Incorrect timing or defective fuel injection pump

INCORRECT IDLE SPEED

- Improper idle speed adjustment
- Defective fuel injection pump

ENGINE SPEED WILL NOT INCREASE

- Air in fuel system
- Poor fuel quality
- Fuel tank empty or fuel tank vent blocked
- Fuel control lever not obtaining full throttle
- Clogged or defective fuel filter
- Clogged or leaking intercooler
- Restricted, blocked or leaking fuel injection or lines
- Incorrect timing or defective fuel injection pump
- Improper fuel line banjo bolts at fuel injection pump
- Low or uneven engine compression

FUEL INJECTION PUMP RUNS HOT

- Fuel injection pump return line restricted

1991 ENGINE PERFORMANCE
System & Component Testing – Gasoline

Caravan, Dakota, Pickup, Ramcharger, RWD Van, Town & Country, Voyager

NOTE: Testing procedures not covered in this article require a Chrysler Diagnostic Readout Box-II (DRB-II). See appropriate SELF-DIAGNOSTICS article.

INTRODUCTION

Before testing individual components or systems, perform procedures in appropriate BASIC DIAGNOSTIC PROCEDURES article. Since many computer controlled and monitored components set a trouble code if they malfunction, also perform procedures in appropriate SELF-DIAGNOSTICS article.

NOTE: Testing of individual components does not isolate possible shorts or opens in the wiring harness of electronically controlled systems. Perform all voltage tests with a Digital Volt-Ohmmeter (DVOM) with a minimum 10-megohm input impedance, unless stated otherwise in procedure. Use an ohmmeter to isolate wiring harness shorts or opens.

COMPUTERIZED ENGINE CONTROLS

SINGLE BOARD ENGINE CONTROLLER (SBEC)

Harness Check – 1) If during SELF-DIAGNOSTICS testing, SBEC is found to be faulty, perform the following steps to confirm diagnosis. Most components are incorrectly diagnosed due to faulty electrical connectors or poor connections between component and vehicle. Sometimes, simply disconnecting and connecting an electrical component will provide a good electrical connection.

2) Before replacing an SBEC, check all components in suspected circuit. If components are okay, carefully disconnect SBEC from vehicle harness.

3) Inspect SBEC harness connector and SBEC contact pins for corrosion. Clean harness connector and SBEC contact pins with contact cleaner.

4) Inspect SBEC harness connector for bent pins, missing pins and broken wires. Repair or replace as necessary.

5) Connect SBEC harness connector to SBEC and retest system with Diagnostic Readout Box (DRB-II) or similar scan tool. See appropriate SELF-DIAGNOSTICS article. If vehicle does not pass test and fails with the same message, replace SBEC.

ENGINE SENSORS & SWITCHES

Air Temperature Sensor – See THERMOSTATIC AIR CLEANER under EMISSION SYSTEMS & SUB-SYSTEMS.

Coolant Temperature Sensor (CTS) – Sensor is mounted in intake manifold, next to thermostat housing. With key off, disconnect wire connector from sensor. Connect ohmmeter between sensor terminals. See COOLANT TEMPERATURE SENSOR RESISTANCE table. If ohmmeter readings are not within specification, replace CTS.

COOLANT TEMPERATURE SENSOR RESISTANCE

Temperature	Resistance
200°F (93°C)	700-1000 ohms
70°F (21°C)	7000-13,000 ohms

Idle Position Switch – 1) Idle position switch is located on throttle body. Disconnect idle position switch connector. Using an ohmmeter, check continuity between switch terminal and ground.

2) With accelerator pedal depressed, no continuity should exist. With accelerator pedal released, continuity should exist. Replace idle position switch if it does not test as specified.

Oxygen Sensor – Oxygen sensor is located at outlet of exhaust manifold. Warm engine until coolant temperature reaches 185-205°F (85-95°C). Disconnect oxygen sensor connector and connect a voltmeter to connector. With engine speed more than 1300 RPM, measure oxygen sensor output voltage. Output voltage should be .6-1.0 volt. If output voltage is not within specification, replace oxygen sensor.

Park/Neutral Switch – 1) Park/Neutral switch is located on transmission. Turn ignition off. Put shift selector in Park position. Disconnect Single Board Engine Controller (SBEC) connector. Disconnect starter relay connector (located in engine compartment).

2) Using an ohmmeter, backprobe cavity No. 30 in SBEC connector while moving shift selector in and out of Park and Reverse. *See Fig. 1.* If ohmmeter reading varies from less than 5 ohms to more than 5 ohms, replace ignition switch. If ohmmeter reading is less than 5 ohms at all times, check Brown/Yellow wire for short to ground.

3) If ohms reading is more than 5 ohms at all times, disconnect Park/Neutral switch connector. Check resistance in Brown/Yellow wire. If resistance is less than 10 ohms, replace Park/Neutral switch. If resistance is more than 10 ohms, check Brown/Yellow wire for open.

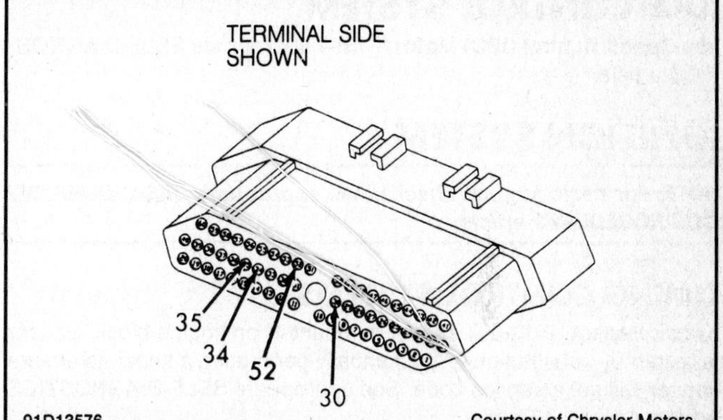
TERMINAL SIDE
SHOWN
35
34
52
30
91D13576
Courtesy of Chrysler Motors.

Fig. 1: Identifying SBEC 60-Pin Connector Cavities

Throttle Position Sensor (TPS) – 1) TPS is located on throttle body. Disconnect and inspect TPS connector. Repair as necessary. Measure resistance between TPS terminals No. 3 (sensor ground) and No. 1 (sensor power).

2) Resistance should be approximately 3500-6500 ohms. If resistance is not within specification, replace TPS. If resistance is within specification, go to next step.

3) Connect an ohmmeter between terminals No. 3 (sensor ground) and No. 2 (sensor output). Operate throttle valve slowly from idle position to fully open position. Resistance should change smoothly in proportion to throttle valve opening angle. Replace TPS if it does not test as specified.

MODULES, MOTORS, RELAYS & SOLENOIDS

MODULES

Ignition Module – See IGNITION SYSTEM.

MOTORS

Idle Speed Control (ISC) Motor – See IDLE CONTROL SYSTEM.

RELAYS

A/C Clutch Relay – See MISCELLANEOUS CONTROLS.
Lock-Up Relay – See MISCELLANEOUS CONTROLS.

SOLENOIDS

Lock-Up Solenoid – See MISCELLANEOUS CONTROLS.
EGR Solenoid – See EMISSION SYSTEMS & SUB-SYSTEMS.

1991 ENGINE PERFORMANCE
System & Component Testing – Gasoline (Cont.)

FUEL SYSTEM

FUEL DELIVERY

NOTE: For fuel system pressure testing, see appropriate BASIC DIAGNOSTIC PROCEDURES article.

FUEL CONTROL

Fuel Injector – Disconnect fuel injector connector. Using a DVOM in ohmmeter position, test between pins of injector for resistance. If resistance is less than 10 ohms, replace throttle body injector wiring. If resistance is more than 10 ohms, replace fuel injector.

Fuel Pressure Regulator – See appropriate BASIC DIAGNOSTIC PROCEDURES article.

IDLE CONTROL SYSTEM

Idle Speed Control (ISC) Motor – See appropriate SELF-DIAGNOSTICS article.

IGNITION SYSTEM

NOTE: For basic ignition checks, see appropriate BASIC DIAGNOSTIC PROCEDURES article.

TIMING CONTROL SYSTEMS

Knock Sensor – Knock sensor is mounted on engine block. Sensor is tested by substitution or by manually generating a knock to ensure sensor will set a service code. See appropriate SELF-DIAGNOSTICS article.

EMISSION SYSTEMS & SUB-SYSTEMS

NOTE: To locate emission components, refer to emission control information label in engine compartment.

AIR INJECTION

No Air Supply – **1)** Start engine and raise speed to 1500 RPM. Check air supply at rubber hoses. If air supply increases with RPM, air pump operation is okay. If air pump is okay, check for leakage at hoses and fittings. Repair or replace as necessary.

2) If hoses are okay, check diverter valve for leakage. If air is expelled through diverter exhaust with vehicle at idle, replace valve. If diverter valve is okay, remove check valve. Blow air through check valve in direction of air pump. Air should not pass through. Blow air through opposite direction. Air should pass freely.

Air Supply Pump – Check and adjust belt tension (if necessary). Disconnect air supply hose from by-pass control valve. Start engine. Pump is operating correctly if airflow is felt at pump outlet and airflow increases as engine speed increases. If this condition is not met, replace pump.

CAUTION: DO NOT pry on the air pump to adjust belt tension, or housing may collapse.

EXHAUST GAS RECIRCULATION (EGR)

NOTE: To ensure proper EGR system operation all passages and moving parts must be free from restrictive deposits. Clean or replace components as necessary.

EGR System Operation Check – **1)** Warm engine to operating temperature. Attach a tachometer to engine. Run engine at idle in Neutral an additional 70 seconds.

2) Accelerate the engine abruptly to 2000-3000 RPM and check EGR valve stem for movement. Repeat test to confirm stem movement, indicating EGR control system is functioning correctly.

3) If EGR valve stem does not move, check for cracked, leaking, disconnected or plugged vacuum hoses. Verify correct hose routing. Disconnect hose harness from EGR valve/transducer, and connect a vacuum pump to harness.

4) Start engine and raise engine speed to 2000 RPM and hold. Apply 10 In. Hg. vacuum to EGR, while checking for EGR valve movement. If no movement occurs, replace EGR valve/transducer assembly.

5) If valve opens approximately 1/8", hold vacuum constant and check for valve diaphragm leakage. Valve should remain open for at least 30 seconds. If leakage occurs, replace valve/transducer assembly. If valve is okay, check control system.

6) If EGR valve stem did not move in step **2)**, but operates normally on external vacuum source, remove throttle body and check port in throttle bore for blockage. Use a solvent to remove deposits and check flow with light air pressure. Normal operation should be restored.

7) If engine will not idle correctly or stalls, check for leaking EGR valve. With engine running, remove vacuum hose from EGR valve. If removing the vacuum hose does not correct rough idle, remove EGR valve/transducer assembly. Check valve for proper seating. Replace assembly as necessary.

8) Also check EGR-to-intake manifold tube for leak. Remove tube and inspect gasket. Tube end should be uniformly indented on gasket, without signs of leakage. If there are signs of leakage, replace gaskets and tighten flange nuts to 17 ft. lbs. (23 N.m). If leak persists, replace EGR tube and gaskets.

NOTE: DO NOT use drills or wires to clean passages for EGR control system. Calibration of precision orifices could be altered, resulting in unsatisfactory vehicle operation.

EGR Solenoid – **1)** EGR solenoid is located in engine compartment. With ignition switch in OFF position, disconnect and inspect solenoid connector. Repair as necessary. If connector is okay, turn ignition switch to ON position.

2) Using a DVOM in voltmeter mode, backprobe Dark Brown wire. If voltage is less than 10 volts, check for open in Dark Brown wire. If voltage is more than 10 volts, turn ignition switch to OFF position. Connect EGR solenoid connector. Disconnect and inspect SBEC connector. Repair as necessary.

3) Turn ignition switch to ON position. With DVOM in voltmeter mode, backprobe cavity No. 35 on SBEC. *See Fig. 1*. If voltage is more than 10 volts, replace SBEC. If voltage is less than 10 volts, turn ignition switch to OFF position. Disconnect EGR solenoid connector.

4) Using an ohmmeter, backprobe cavity No. 35 on SBEC. If resistance is less than 10 ohms, check Green/Yellow wire for short to ground. If resistance is more than 10 volts, test resistance in Green/Yellow wire. If resistance is less than 10 ohms, replace EGR solenoid. If resistance is more than 10 ohms, check Green/Yellow wire for open.

FUEL EVAPORATION

EVAP Canister – EVAP canister is located in engine compartment. There are no moving parts in canister. Check for loose, missing, cracked or broken connections or parts. Repair or replace as necessary. There should not be liquid in canister.

EVAP Solenoid – **1)** EVAP solenoid is located in engine compartment. Turn ignition switch to OFF position. Disconnect and inspect solenoid connector. Repair as necessary.

2) Turn ignition switch to ON position. Using a DVOM in voltmeter mode, backprobe Dark Brown wire at connector. If voltage is less than 10 volts, check for open in Dark Brown wire. If voltage is more than 10 volts, turn ignition switch to OFF position. Connect solenoid connector. Disconnect and inspect SBEC connector. Repair as necessary.

3) Turn ignition switch to ON position. With DVOM in voltage mode, backprobe cavity No. 52 on SBEC connector. *See Fig. 1*. If voltage is more than 10 volts, replace SBEC. If voltage is less than 10 volts, turn ignition switch to OFF position. Disconnect solenoid connector. Using an ohmmeter, backprobe cavity No. 52 on SBEC connector.

4) If resistance is less than 10 ohms, check Pink/Black wire for short to ground. If resistance is more than 10 ohms, test Pink/Black wire for resistance. If resistance is less than 10 ohms, replace EVAP solenoid. If resistance is more than 10 ohms, check Pink/Black wire for open.

POSITIVE CRANKCASE VENTILATION (PCV)

PCV Valve – 1) With engine running at curb idle, remove PCV valve from grommet. If valve is functioning properly, a hissing sound will be heard as air passes through valve.
2) With engine running, place finger over valve inlet. Strong vacuum should be felt at valve inlet. Stop engine. Remove and shake PCV valve to ensure a metallic clicking noise can be heard, indicating valve is free. Reinstall PCV valve.
3) Remove the crankcase ventilation filter or oil filler cap from the valve cover. Hold a piece of stiff paper over the opening. After allowing about one minute for crankcase pressure stabilization, the paper should be drawn against opening.
4) If paper is held against opening, performance is okay. If not, replace PCV valve and retest. If performance does not improve, inspect system for restrictions, and clean as necessary.

THERMOSTATIC AIR CLEANER

NOTE: With engine cold, heat control door in air cleaner snorkel should be closed. With engine running at normal operating temperature, door should be open.

Air Temperature Sensor – Ensure all vacuum hoses are in good condition. Using external vacuum source, apply 20 in. Hg vacuum to air temperature sensor. Door should be in open position. If not, check vacuum diaphragm for leaks or restrictions. If diaphragm is okay, but proper temperature is not maintained, replace temperature sensor.
Air Control Door – Apply 20 in. Hg vacuum to diaphragm. Diaphragm should not bleed down more than 10 in. Hg in 5 minutes. Door should not lift off bottom at less than 2 in. Hg. Door should be fully open at no more than 4 in. Hg. If vacuum diaphragm does not operate properly, replace vacuum diaphragm and repeat test.

MISCELLANEOUS CONTROLS

NOTE: Although some of the controlled devices listed here are not technically engine performance components, they can affect driveability if they malfunction.

A/C CLUTCH RELAY

A/C Clutch Relay (Except Dakota) – 1) A/C clutch relay is located in engine compartment. Turn ignition switch to ON position. Using a DVOM in voltmeter mode, backprobe Dark Brown/Orange wire at A/C clutch relay. *See Fig. 2.* If voltage is more than 10 volts, see appropriate SELF-DIAGNOSTICS article. If voltage is less than 10 volts, turn ignition switch to OFF position. Disconnect and inspect clutch relay connector. Repair as necessary.

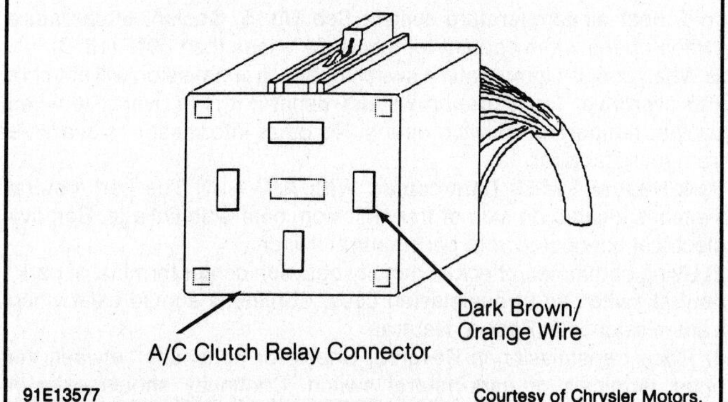
Dark Brown/
Orange Wire
A/C Clutch Relay Connector
91E13577
Courtesy of Chrysler Motors.

Fig. 2: Identifying A/C Clutch Relay Connector

2) If connector is okay, backprobe Dark Brown wire in clutch relay connector. If voltage is less than 10 volts, check for open in Dark Brown wire. If voltage is more than 10 volts, using an ohmmeter, backprobe Dark Brown/Orange wire in clutch relay connector. If resistance is less than 10 volts, check Dark Brown/Orange wire for short to ground. If resistance is more than 10 volts, replace A/C clutch relay.

A/C Clutch Relay (Dakota) – 1) A/C Clutch Relay is located at power distribution center in engine compartment. Turn ignition switch to ON position. Actuate A/C switch on dash panel. If A/C clutch relay clicks, see appropriate SELF-DIAGNOSTICS article.
2) If A/C clutch relay does not click, disconnect and inspect clutch relay connector. Repair as necessary. If connector is okay, replace clutch relay. Actuate A/C switch on dash. If clutch relay clicks, repair is complete. If clutch relay does not click, remove clutch relay.
3) Using DVOM in voltage mode, backprobe cavity "A" in relay connector. *See Fig. 3.* If voltage is less than 10 volts, check for open in Dark Brown wire. If voltage is more than 10 volts, turn ignition switch to OFF position.
4) Reconnect A/C clutch relay. Disconnect and inspect SBEC connector. Repair as necessary. If connector is okay, turn ignition switch to ON position. Using DVOM in voltage mode, backprobe cavity No. 34 on SBEC connector. *See Fig. 1.* If voltage is more than 10 volts, replace SBEC. If voltage is less than 10 volts, check for open in Dark Brown/Orange wire.

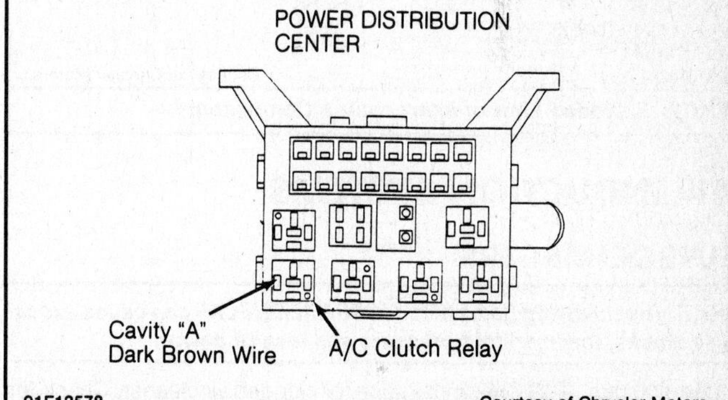
POWER DISTRIBUTION
CENTER
Cavity "A"
Dark Brown Wire
A/C Clutch Relay
91F13578
Courtesy of Chrysler Motors.

Fig. 3: Identifying A/C Clutch Relay Location (Dakota)

TRANSMISSION

Lock-Up Relay – 1) Lock-up relay is located in engine compartment. Turn ignition switch to ON position. Using a DVOM in voltmeter mode, backprobe Orange/Black wire at relay. If voltage is more than 10 volts, see appropriate SELF-DIAGNOSTICS article. If voltage is less than 10 volts, disconnect and inspect relay connector. Repair as necessary.
2) If connector is okay, backprobe Dark Brown wire at relay. If voltage is more than 10 volts, replace lock-up relay. If voltage is less than 10 volts, repair open in Dark Brown wire.
Lock-Up Solenoid – 1) Lock-up solenoid is located on left side of transmission. Turn ignition switch to OFF position. Disconnect solenoid connector from transmission. Inspect connector and repair as necessary.
2) If connector is okay, turn ignition switch to ON position. Using a DVOM in voltage mode, backprobe Dark Brown wire on connector. If voltage is less than 10 volts, check for open in Dark Brown wire. If voltage is more than 10 volts, see appropriate SELF-DIAGNOSTICS article.

1991 ENGINE PERFORMANCE
System & Component Testing – Diesel

Pickup

***NOTE:** In mid-year, an intercooler was installed in front of the radiator. See Fig. 1. Note if vehicle contains an intercooler before servicing engine components. Service procedures may vary on models with intercooler.*

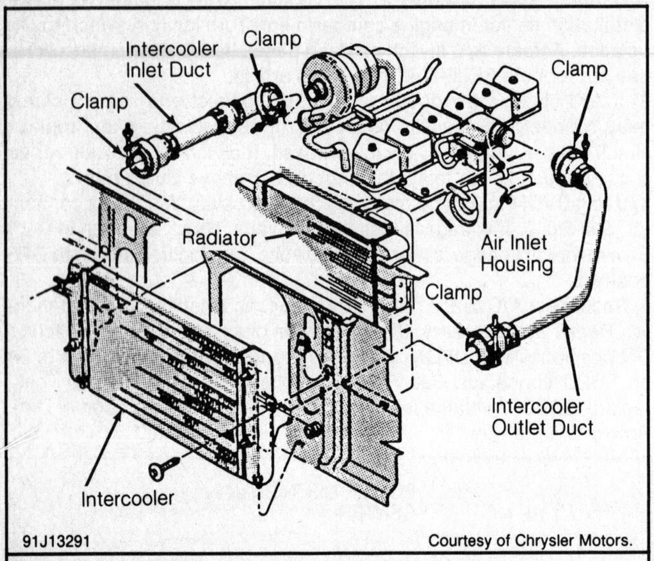
Intercooler
Inlet Duct
Clamp
Clamp
Clamp
Radiator
Air Inlet
Housing
Clamp
Intercooler
Outlet Duct
Intercooler
91J13291
Courtesy of Chrysler Motors.

Fig. 1: Exploded View of Intercooler & Components

AIR INDUCTION SYSTEMS

TURBOCHARGERS

***NOTE:** The following items listed in INITIAL CHECKS can cause excessive smoke, low manifold pressure and loss of power.*

Initial Checks – **1)** Check air intake for clogged air cleaner. Check for loose connections or cracks on suction (intake) side of turbocharger. Check for damage to compressor blades causing an imbalance and resulting in bearing failure.

2) Check for pressurized air leaking from loose connections and cracks in crossover tube from turbocharger to intake manifold cover on non-intercooled models. On intercooled models, check for air leaks at intercooler and intercooler ducts from turbocharger to intercooler and from intercooler to air inlet on intake manifold cover on intercooled models.

3) On all models, a soapy solution may be used to check for pressurized air leaks at intake manifold cover, crossover tube or intercooler and connections.

4) Check for exhaust leaks at exhaust manifold and turbocharger. Check for exhaust pipe restrictions and restricted or damaged turbocharger oil return line.

5) To verify a bearing failure or damaged compressor, remove intake and exhaust piping, and check for compressor or turbine wheel-to-housing contact. Compressor or turbine wheel must rotate freely. Measure shaft end play and radial clearance. See SHAFT END PLAY & RADIAL CLEARANCE.

Boost Pressure – Boost pressure testing information is not available from manufacturer.

Shaft End Play & Radial Clearance – Shaft end play and radial clearance can be checked to determine if turbocharger repairs are required. Using a dial indicator, check shaft end play and radial clearance. *See Fig. 2.* Turbocharger must be repaired if clearances are not within specification. See TURBOCHARGER SPECIFICATIONS table.

***CAUTION:** Turbochargers used on intercooled models and non-intercooled models are different and cannot be interchanged.*

TURBOCHARGER SPECIFICATIONS

Application	In. (mm)
Shaft Clearances	
End Play	[1]
Radial Clearance	.012-.018 (.30-.46)
Turbine Shaft Minimum O.D.	.432 (10.97)

[1] – On turbochargers with serial No. 840637 and earlier, end play should be .004-.006" (.10-.15 mm). On turbochargers with serial No. 840638 and later end play should be .001-.003" (.03-.08 mm).

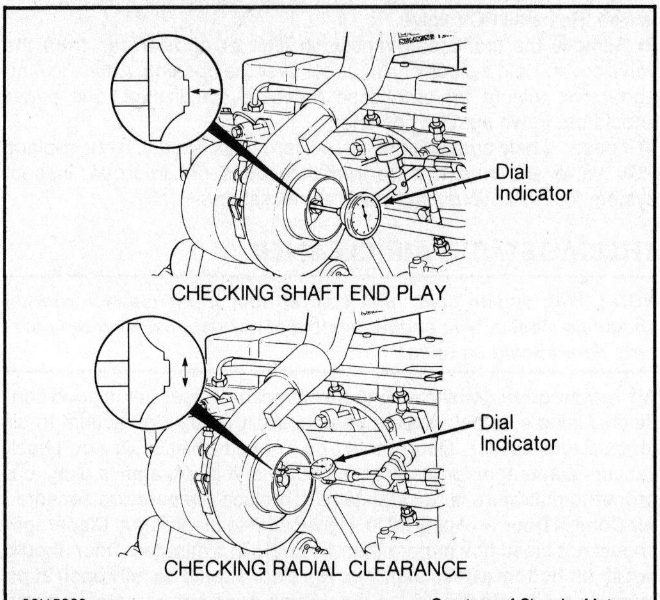
Dial
Indicator
CHECKING SHAFT END PLAY
Dial
Indicator
CHECKING RADIAL CLEARANCE
90I15329
Courtesy of Chrysler Motors.

Fig. 2: Checking Shaft End Play & Radial Clearance

ENGINE SENSORS & SWITCHES

Air Temperature Switch (Intercooled) – **1)** Air temperature switch is located in the intake manifold cover. *See Fig. 5.* Air temperature switch is used for controlling KSB valve.

2) Air temperature switch is open when intake manifold air temperature is more than 60°F (16°C) and fully closed when temperature is less than 54°F (12°C). When air temperature switch is closed, voltage is applied to KSB valve. No other information is available from manufacturer.

Charge Air Temperature Sensor – See CHARGE AIR TEMPERATURE SENSOR under INTAKE MANIFOLD HEATER SYSTEM (INTERCOOLED MODELS) under EMISSION SYSTEMS & SUB-SYSTEMS.

Coolant Temperature Switch (Intercooled With A/T) – **1)** Coolant temperature switch is located in the cylinder head, below intake manifold, near air temperature switch. *See Fig. 5.* Coolant temperature switch opens when coolant temperature is less than 60°F (16°C).

2) When coolant temperature switch opens, transmission will not shift into overdrive. Transmission will downshift if it is in overdrive when coolant temperature switch opens. No other information is available from manufacturer.

Park/Neutral Switch (Intercooled With A/T) – **1)** The park/neutral switch is located on side of transmission, near shift linkage. Remove electrical connector from park/neutral switch.

2) Using ohmmeter, check continuity between center terminal of park/neutral switch and transmission case. Continuity should exist when transmission is in Park or Neutral.

3) Place transmission in Reverse. Check for continuity between the outer terminals of park/neutral switch. Continuity should exist in Reverse only. Continuity should not exist between outer terminals and transmission case. Replace park/neutral switch if defective.

Thermistor (Non-Intercooled) – Thermistor is used for controlling the intake manifold heater system. See THERMISTOR under INTAKE

MANIFOLD HEATER SYSTEM (NON-INTERCOOLED MODELS) under EMISSION SYSTEMS & SUB-SYSTEMS.

Throttle Position Sensor (Intercooled With A/T) – 1) Before checking TPS, ensure cable rod is adjusted so control lever contacts low-speed screw when in idle position.

2) Ensure control lever moves over center position and rests against breakover spring when in full throttle position. If adjustment is required, see THROTTLE LINKAGE in ON-VEHICLE ADJUSTMENTS - DIESEL article.

3) Connect negative probe of voltmeter to ground. Turn ignition on. Backprobe center wire terminal at TPS electrical connector. With control lever contacting low-speed screw (idle position), voltage should be at least one volt. If voltage is not at least one volt, adjust TPS to obtain correct voltage using 10 mm wrench. *See Fig. 3.*

4) Open throttle to full throttle position. Backprobe center wire terminal at TPS electrical connector. Voltage should be at least 2.25 volts higher than voltage obtained with throttle in idle position. If voltage is not at least 2.25 volts more than idle position voltage, adjust TPS to obtain correct voltage. Replace TPS if it cannot be adjusted.

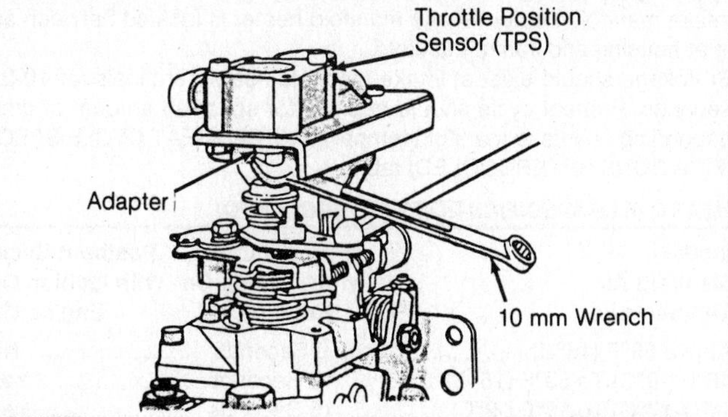
Throttle Position
Sensor (TPS)
Adapter
10 mm Wrench

91I13290 Courtesy of Chrysler Motors.

Fig. 3: Adjusting TPS

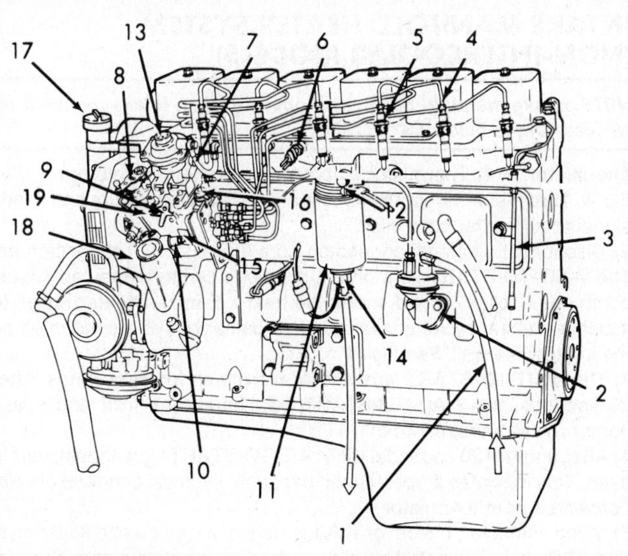
17
13
7
6
5
4
8
9
19
18
16
12
3
15
14
2
10
11
1

1. Fuel Supply Line
2. Fuel Lift Pump
3. Fuel Drain Line
4. High-Pressure Fuel Line
5. Fuel Injector
6. Thermistor (Non-Intercooled)
7. Turbo Boost Control Line
8. Fuel Control Lever
9. Manual Shutdown Lever
10. KSB Valve
11. Fuel/Water Separator Filter
12. Fuel Heater
13. Air Fuel Control (AFC) Valve
14. Water-In-Fuel Sensor
15. Pump Data Plate
16. Shutoff Solenoid Valve
17. Oil Fill Tube
18. Timing Pin Location
19. Fuel Injection Pump

91H13299 Courtesy of Chrysler Motors.

Fig. 4: Identifying Fuel System Components

Water-In-Fuel Sensor – 1) Water-in-fuel sensor is located in bottom of fuel/water separator filter. *See Fig. 4.* The water-in-fuel sensor sends an input signal to SBEC (intercooled models) or air heater controller (non-intercooled models) when water exists in fuel/water separator filter.

2) SBEC or air heater controller will then turn on the WATER-IN-FUEL light on the message center in the cab. No other information is available from manufacturer.

Vehicle Speed Sensor (Intercooled Models) – Vehicle speed sensor is mounted on rear of transmission. No other information is available from manufacturer.

CONTROLLERS

AIR HEATER CONTROLLER

Non-Intercooled Models – Air heater controller is located in left rear corner of engine compartment, on driver's side of dash panel, near bulkhead wiring connector. No other information is available from manufacturer.

SINGLE BOARD ENGINE CONTROLLER (SBEC)

Intercooled Models – SBEC is located on left front corner of engine compartment, near horns on left fender. No other information is available from manufacturer.

FUEL SYSTEM

FUEL DELIVERY

Fuel Heater – 1) Fuel heater is located between fuel/water separator filter and filter adapter on cylinder head. *See Fig. 4.* Voltage to operate fuel heater is provided from ignition switch.

2) A minimum of 7 volts is required for fuel heater operation. Fuel heater will operate when temperature is approximately 43°F (6°C) and shut off at approximately 53°F (13°C). Fuel heater resistance is 2.5-3.0 ohms. No other information is available from manufacturer.

Fuel Injector – 1) To determine which fuel injector is defective, operate engine and loosen high-pressure fuel line nut at fuel injector.

CAUTION: Carefully loosen high-pressure fuel line nut. Fuel is under excessive pressure and will spray out around fuel line nut.

2) Listen for a change in engine RPM. If engine RPM decreases, fuel injector is operating properly. If engine RPM stays the same, fuel injector or engine components are defective. Ensure all high-pressure fuel line nuts are tightened to 18 ft. lbs. (24 N.m).

Fuel Lift Pump – 1) Fuel lift pump is located on left rear side of engine. *See Fig. 4.* To check lift pump vacuum, disconnect fuel supply line at fuel lift pump. Install vacuum gauge on a fitting between fuel supply line and fuel lift pump.

2) Operate engine at approximately 1500 RPM for 30 seconds, and note vacuum reading. If vacuum reading exceeds 3.75 in. Hg, check for restriction in fuel/water separator filter or fuel supply line.

3) Check fuel lift pump output pressure and volume at cranking speed. Replace fuel lift pump if not within specification. See FUEL LIFT PUMP SPECIFICATIONS table.

FUEL LIFT PUMP SPECIFICATIONS

Application	Output
Pump Pressure	3 psi Minimum (.2 kg/cm²)
Volume Within 30 Seconds	.7 qts. (.6L)

CAUTION: Defective fuel lift pump can create low engine power and long cranking periods. Hand lever must be in upward position to provide proper engine operation.

Shutoff Solenoid Valve – 1) Shutoff solenoid valve is located on rear side of fuel injection pump. *See Fig. 4.* Using voltmeter, ensure at least 10 volts exists at shutoff solenoid valve.

2) If at least 10 volts exists, remove shutoff solenoid valve from fuel injection pump.

1991 ENGINE PERFORMANCE
System & Component Testing – Diesel (Cont.)

CAUTION: DO NOT attach power supply to shutoff solenoid valve with plunger removed, or valve assembly will be damaged.

3) Remove plunger and spring from fuel injection pump. Reinstall shutoff solenoid valve with electrical connector disconnected. If engine starts, replace shutoff solenoid valve.

NOTE: Engine must be shut off using manual shutdown lever when plunger and spring are removed. See Fig. 4.

4) If engine does not start, shutoff solenoid valve is not the problem, fuel system or engine should be checked for proper operation. Reinstall plunger, spring and shutoff solenoid valve. Tighten shutoff solenoid valve to 32 ft. lbs. (43 N.m).

EMISSION SYSTEMS & SUB-SYSTEMS

INTAKE MANIFOLD HEATER SYSTEM (INTERCOOLED MODELS)

NOTE: Intake manifold heater will operate when intake manifold air temperature is less than 59°F (15°C).

Charge Air Temperature Sensor – Charge air temperature sensor is located in intake manifold cover. *See Fig. 5.* Charge air temperature sensor monitors intake manifold air temperature and sends signal to Single Board Engine Controller (SBEC). SBEC controls intake manifold heater. No other information is available from manufacturer.

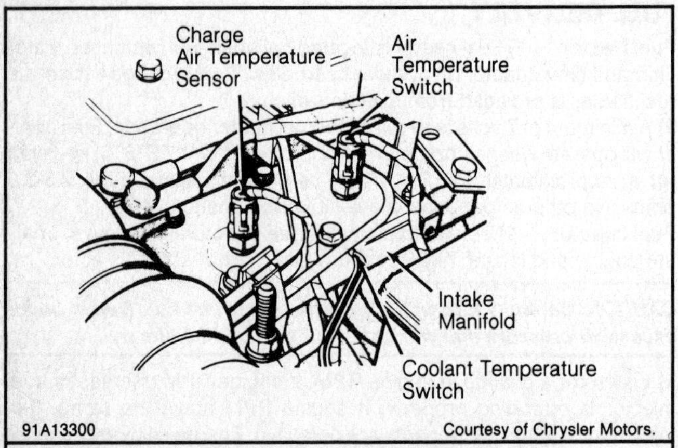
Charge Air Temperature Sensor
Air Temperature Switch
Intake Manifold
Coolant Temperature Switch
91A13300
Courtesy of Chrysler Motors.

Fig. 5: Identifying Charge Air Temperature Sensor & Air Temperature Switch

Intake Manifold Heater – 1) Disconnect electrical leads from intake manifold heater. Intake manifold heater is located between air inlet housing and intake manifold. Isolate electrical leads from contacting other components.
2) Using ohmmeter, measure continuity to ground from each terminal on intake manifold heater. Replace intake manifold heater if continuity exists.
Intake Manifold Heater Relays – 1) Intake manifold heater relays are mounted on the inner wheelwell. *See Fig. 6.* Intake manifold heater relays are energized by SBEC depending on intake manifold air temperature monitored by the charge air temperature sensor.
2) Intake manifold heater relays are not energized during engine cranking. A clicking sound will be heard when relays are energized. No other information is available from manufacturer.

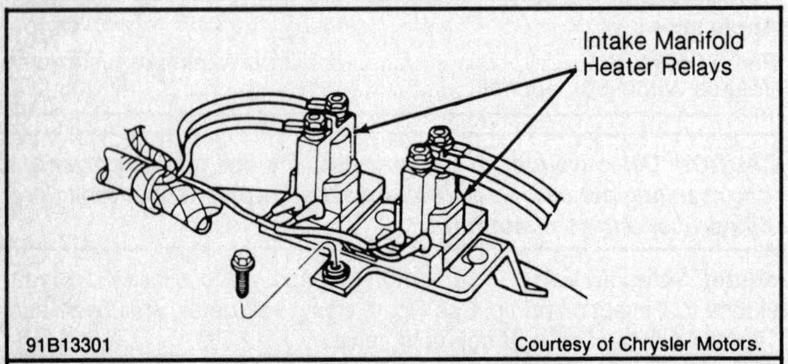
Intake Manifold Heater Relays
91B13301
Courtesy of Chrysler Motors.

Fig. 6: Identifying Intake Manifold Heater Relays

CAUTION: Intake manifold heater relays should not be cycled (ignition turned off and then on) more than once within 15 minutes. Wait 15 minutes before turning ignition on.

NOTE: During preheat/postheat cycle, if intake manifold air temperature is less than 59°F (15°C), intake manifold heater will preheat before engine starts. For normal preheat/postheat cycle operating ranges, see HEAT CYCLE SPECIFICATIONS (INTERCOOLED) table.

Preheat/Postheat Cycle – 1) With intake manifold air temperature less than 60°F (16°C), turn ignition on. The WAIT-TO-START light on the message center in the cab should come on. A "click" sound should be heard at intake heater relays to indicate preheat cycle.
2) Using voltmeter, check for battery voltage at both terminals on intake manifold heater. Intake manifold heater is located between air inlet housing and intake manifold.
3) Voltage should exist at intake manifold heater terminals for 10-20 seconds. Preheat cycle should operate for specified amount of time depending on intake manifold temperature. See HEAT CYCLE SPECIFICATIONS (INTERCOOLED) table.

HEAT CYCLE SPECIFICATIONS (INTERCOOLED)

Intake Manifold Air Temperature	Preheat Cycle With Ignition On Engine Off	Postheat Cycle With Ignition On Engine On
Above 59°F (15°C)	0 Seconds	No
18°F (-8°C) To 59°F (15°C)	10 Seconds	Yes
1°F (-17°C) To 16°F (-9°C)	15 Seconds	Yes
-15°F (-26°C) To 0°F (-18°C)	17.5 Seconds	Yes
Below -15°F (-26°C)	20 Seconds	Yes

INTAKE MANIFOLD HEATER SYSTEM (NON-INTERCOOLED MODELS)

NOTE: Intake manifold heater will operate when intake manifold air temperature is below 59°F (15°C).

Thermistor – 1) Thermistor is located in intake manifold cover. *See Fig. 4.* Thermistor monitors intake manifold air temperature and sends signal to air heater controller.
2) Disconnect electrical connector from thermistor. Turn ignition on. The WAIT-TO-START light on the message center in the cab should come on. A "click" sound should be heard at intake heater relays to indicate preheat cycle. Intake manifold heater relays are mounted on the inner wheelwell. *See Fig. 6.*
3) The WAIT-TO-START light should remain on for 20 seconds. After 20 seconds, the WAIT-TO-START light should turn off and intake heater relays should shut off.
4) After another 20 seconds, the WAIT-TO-START light should start to flash. This indicates a open circuit because electrical connector is disconnected from thermistor.
5) Using voltmeter, check for voltage between ground and KSB valve. The KSB valve is located on side of the fuel injection pump. *See Fig. 4.* No voltage should exist at the KSB valve. Reconnect electrical connector on thermistor.
Intake Manifold Heater – 1) Disconnect electrical leads from intake manifold heater. Isolate electrical leads from contacting other components. Intake manifold heater is located between crossover tube from turbocharger and the intake manifold.
2) Using ohmmeter, measure continuity to ground from each terminal on intake manifold heater. Replace intake manifold heater if continuity exists.
Intake Manifold Heater Relays – 1) Intake manifold heater relays are mounted on the inner wheelwell. *See Fig. 6.* Intake manifold heater

relays are energized by the air heater controller depending on intake manifold air temperature monitored by the thermistor.
2) Intake manifold heater relays are not energized during engine cranking. A clicking sound will be heard when relays are energized.

CAUTION: Intake manifold heater relays should not be cycled (ignition turned off and then on) more than once within 15 minutes. Wait 15 minutes before turning ignition on.

NOTE: During preheat/postheat cycle, if intake manifold air temperature is less than 59°F (15°C), intake manifold heater will preheat before engine starts. For normal preheat/postheat cycle operating ranges, see HEAT CYCLE SPECIFICATIONS (NON-INTERCOOLED) table.

Preheat/Postheat Cycle – 1) With intake manifold air temperature less than 59°F (15°C), turn ignition on. The WAIT-TO-START light on the message center in the cab should come on. A "click" sound should be heard at intake heater relays to indicate preheat cycle.
2) Using voltmeter, check for battery voltage at both terminals on intake manifold heater. Intake manifold heater is located between crossover tube from turbocharger and intake manifold.
3) Voltage should exist at intake manifold heater terminals for 10-20 seconds. Preheat cycle should operate for specified amount of time depending on intake manifold temperature. See HEAT CYCLE SPECIFICATIONS (NON-INTERCOOLED) table.
4) Using voltmeter, check for voltage between ground and KSB valve. The KSB valve is located on side of the fuel injection pump. *See Fig. 4.* No voltage should exist at the KSB valve.

KSB VALVE

Intercooled – 1) KSB valve is located on side of the fuel injection pump. *See Fig. 4.* KSB valve wiring circuit contains a 3-ohm resistor and air temperature switch. Air temperature switch is located in the intake manifold cover. *See Fig. 5.*

2) Air temperature switch is open when intake manifold air temperature is more than 60°F (16°C) and fully closed when temperature is less than 54°F (12°C). The KSB valve should "click" when 10 volts is applied to KSB valve when air temperature switch is fully closed.

CAUTION: DO NOT apply 12 volts to KSB valve. Wiring circuit contains a 3-ohm resistor to decrease voltage to KSB valve to 10 volts.

HEAT CYCLE SPECIFICATIONS (NON-INTERCOOLED)

Intake Manifold Air Temperature	Preheat Cycle With Ignition On Engine Off	Postheat Cycle With Ignition On Engine On
Above 59°F (15°C)	0 Seconds	No
15°F (-9°C) To 59°F (15°C)	10 Seconds	Yes
0°F (-18°C) To 15°F (-9°C)	15 Seconds	Yes
-15°F (-26°C) To 0°F (-18°C)	17.5 Seconds	Yes
Below -15°F (-26°C)	20 Seconds	Yes

Non-Intercooled – 1) The KSB valve is located on side of the fuel injection pump. *See Fig. 4.*
2) The KSB valve is activated by air heater controller when thermistor determines that intake manifold air temperature is more than 59°F (15°C). Thermistor is located in intake manifold cover. *See Fig. 4.*

MISCELLANEOUS CONTROLS

Coolant Temperature Switch (Intercooled With A/T) – 1) Coolant temperature switch is located in the cylinder head, below intake manifold, near air temperature switch. *See Fig. 5.*
2) Coolant temperature switch opens when coolant temperature is less than 60°F (16°C).
3) When coolant temperature switch opens, transmission will not shift into overdrive. Transmission will downshift if it was in overdrive when coolant temperature switch opens. No other information is available from manufacturer.

Transmission Overdrive Override Switch (Intercooled With A/T) – 1) Switch is mounted in instrument panel. The switch is normally closed. If switch is depressed and switch opens, transmission will not go into overdrive.
2) Transmission will downshift if transmission is in overdrive and switch is depressed. No other information is available from manufacturer.

Transmission Thermoswitch (Intercooled With A/T) – 1) Transmission thermoswitch is located in transmission-to-radiator oil cooler line. Transmission thermoswitch opens when transmission fluid temperature is more than 273°F (134°C) and closes at 240°F (116°C).
2) If transmission is in overdrive and thermoswitch opens, transmission will downshift. Once switch closes, SBEC will send a signal to transmission to shift into overdrive. No other information is available from manufacturer.

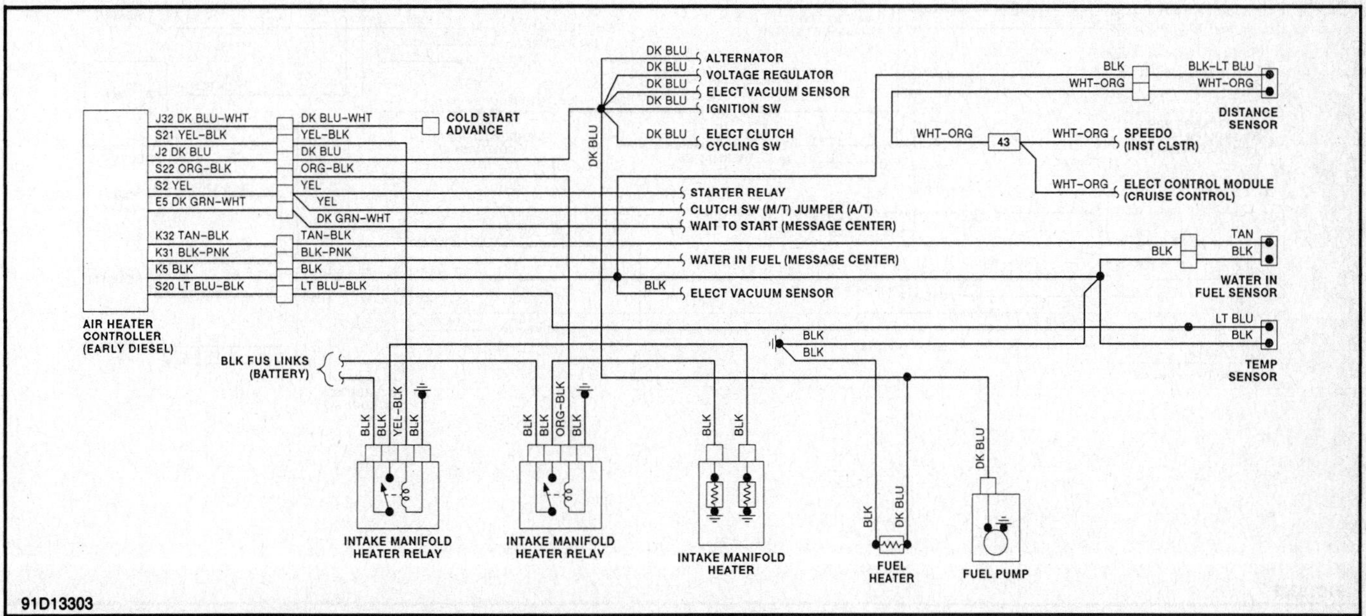
AIR HEATER CONTROLLER (EARLY DIESEL)
J32 DK BLU-WHT
S21 YEL-BLK
J2 DK BLU
S22 ORG-BLK
S2 YEL
E5 DK GRN-WHT
K32 TAN-BLK
K31 BLK-PNK
K5 BLK
S20 LT BLU-BLK
COLD START ADVANCE
ALTERNATOR
VOLTAGE REGULATOR
ELECT VACUUM SENSOR
IGNITION SW
ELECT CLUTCH CYCLING SW
STARTER RELAY
CLUTCH SW (M/T) JUMPER (A/T)
WAIT TO START (MESSAGE CENTER)
WATER IN FUEL (MESSAGE CENTER)
ELECT VACUUM SENSOR
DISTANCE SENSOR
SPEEDO (INST CLSTR)
ELECT CONTROL MODULE (CRUISE CONTROL)
WATER IN FUEL SENSOR
TEMP SENSOR
BLK FUS LINKS (BATTERY)
INTAKE MANIFOLD HEATER RELAY
INTAKE MANIFOLD HEATER RELAY
INTAKE MANIFOLD HEATER
FUEL HEATER
FUEL PUMP
91D13303

Fig. 7: Intake Manifold Heater System Wiring Diagram (Non-Intercooled Models)

1991 ENGINE PERFORMANCE
System & Component Testing – Diesel (Cont.)

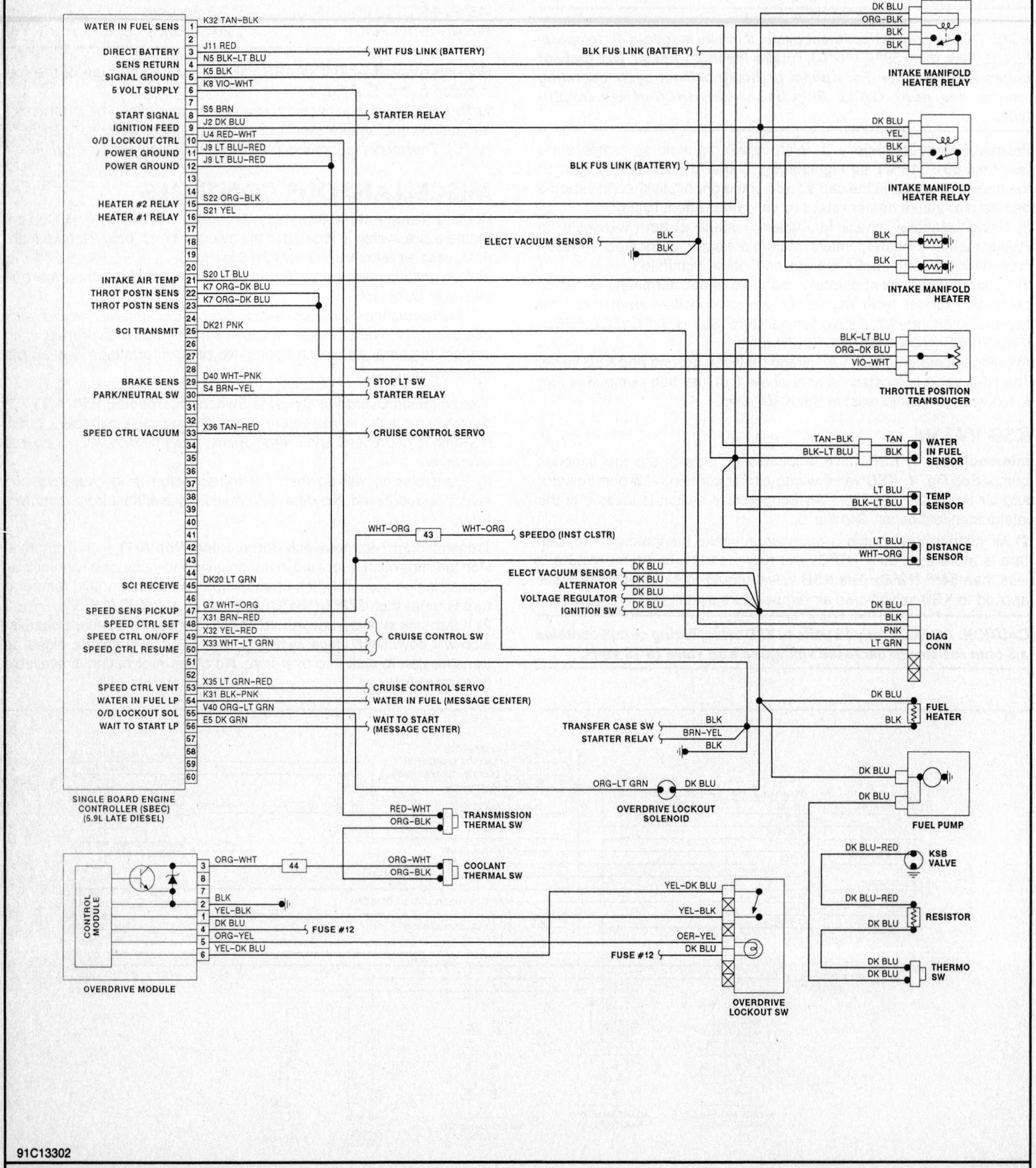
WATER IN FUEL SENS
DIRECT BATTERY
SENS RETURN
SIGNAL GROUND
5 VOLT SUPPLY
START SIGNAL
IGNITION FEED
O/D LOCKOUT CTRL
POWER GROUND
POWER GROUND
HEATER #2 RELAY
HEATER #1 RELAY
INTAKE AIR TEMP
THROT POSTN SENS
THROT POSTN SENS
SCI TRANSMIT
BRAKE SENS
PARK/NEUTRAL SW
SPEED CTRL VACUUM
SCI RECEIVE
SPEED SENS PICKUP
SPEED CTRL SET
SPEED CTRL ON/OFF
SPEED CTRL RESUME
SPEED CTRL VENT
WATER IN FUEL LP
O/D LOCKOUT SOL
WAIT TO START LP
K32 TAN-BLK
J11 RED
N5 BLK-LT BLU
K5 BLK
K8 VIO-WHT
S5 BRN
J2 DK BLU
U4 RED-WHT
J9 LT BLU-RED
J9 LT BLU-RED
S22 ORG-BLK
S21 YEL
S20 LT BLU
K7 ORG-DK BLU
K7 ORG-DK BLU
DK21 PNK
D40 WHT-PNK
S4 BRN-YEL
X36 TAN-RED
DK20 LT GRN
G7 WHT-ORG
X31 BRN-RED
X32 YEL-RED
X33 WHT-LT GRN
X35 LT GRN-RED
K31 BLK-PNK
V40 ORG-LT GRN
E5 DK GRN
WHT FUS LINK (BATTERY)
STARTER RELAY
STOP LT SW
STARTER RELAY
CRUISE CONTROL SERVO
WHT-ORG
43
WHT-ORG
SPEEDO (INST CLSTR)
CRUISE CONTROL SW
CRUISE CONTROL SERVO
WATER IN FUEL (MESSAGE CENTER)
WAIT TO START (MESSAGE CENTER)
SINGLE BOARD ENGINE CONTROLLER (SBEC) (5.9L LATE DIESEL)
BLK FUS LINK (BATTERY)
DK BLU
ORG-BLK
BLK
BLK
INTAKE MANIFOLD HEATER RELAY
DK BLU
YEL
BLK
BLK
BLK FUS LINK (BATTERY)
INTAKE MANIFOLD HEATER RELAY
ELECT VACUUM SENSOR
BLK
BLK
INTAKE MANIFOLD HEATER
BLK-LT BLU
ORG-DK BLU
VIO-WHT
THROTTLE POSITION TRANSDUCER
TAN-BLK
BLK-LT BLU
TAN
BLK
WATER IN FUEL SENSOR
LT BLU
BLK-LT BLU
TEMP SENSOR
LT BLU
WHT-ORG
DISTANCE SENSOR
ELECT VACUUM SENSOR
ALTERNATOR
VOLTAGE REGULATOR
IGNITION SW
DK BLU
DK BLU
DK BLU
DK BLU
DK BLU
BLK
PNK
LT GRN
DIAG CONN
DK BLU
BLK
FUEL HEATER
TRANSFER CASE SW
STARTER RELAY
BLK
BRN-YEL
BLK
ORG-LT GRN
DK BLU
OVERDRIVE LOCKOUT SOLENOID
DK BLU
DK BLU
FUEL PUMP
RED-WHT
ORG-BLK
TRANSMISSION THERMAL SW
ORG-WHT
44
ORG-WHT
ORG-BLK
COOLANT THERMAL SW
CONTROL MODULE
ORG-WHT
BLK
YEL-BLK
DK BLU
ORG-YEL
YEL-DK BLU
FUSE #12
OVERDRIVE MODULE
YEL-DK BLU
YEL-BLK
OER-YEL
DK BLU
FUSE #12
OVERDRIVE LOCKOUT SW
DK BLU-RED
KSB VALVE
DK BLU-RED
DK BLU
RESISTOR
DK BLU
DK BLU
THERMO SW
91C13302

Fig. 8: Intake Manifold Heater System Wiring Diagram (Intercooled Models)

1991 ENGINE PERFORMANCE
Sensor Operating Range Charts

Caravan, Dakota, Pickup, Ramcharger, RWD Van, Town & Country, Voyager

INTRODUCTION

Sensor operating range information can help determine if a sensor is out of calibration. An out-of-calibration sensor may not set a trouble code, but it may cause driveability problems.

NOTE: Unless otherwise stated in test procedure, perform all voltage tests using a Digital Volt-Ohmmeter (DVOM) with a minimum 10-megohm input impedance.

For testing, turn ignition switch to OFF position. Disconnect sensor electrical connector. Connect an ohmmeter lead to one of the sensor connector terminals. Connect other ohmmeter lead to remaining sensor connector terminal. See appropriate sensor resistance table. If readings from sensor are not within specification, replace sensor.

NOTE: Sensor information not covered in this article can be found in appropriate SELF-DIAGNOSTICS article.

CHARGE TEMPERATURE SENSOR RESISTANCE

Temperature °F (°C)	Ohms
200 (93)	700-1000
70 (21)	7000-13,000

COOLANT TEMPERATURE SENSOR RESISTANCE

Temperature °F (°C)	Ohms
200 (93)	700-1000
70 (21)	7000-13,000

THROTTLE BODY TEMPERATURE SENSOR RESISTANCE

Temperature °F (°C)	Ohms
200 (93)	400-1500
70 (21)	5600-14,600

1991 ENGINE PERFORMANCE
Wiring Diagrams

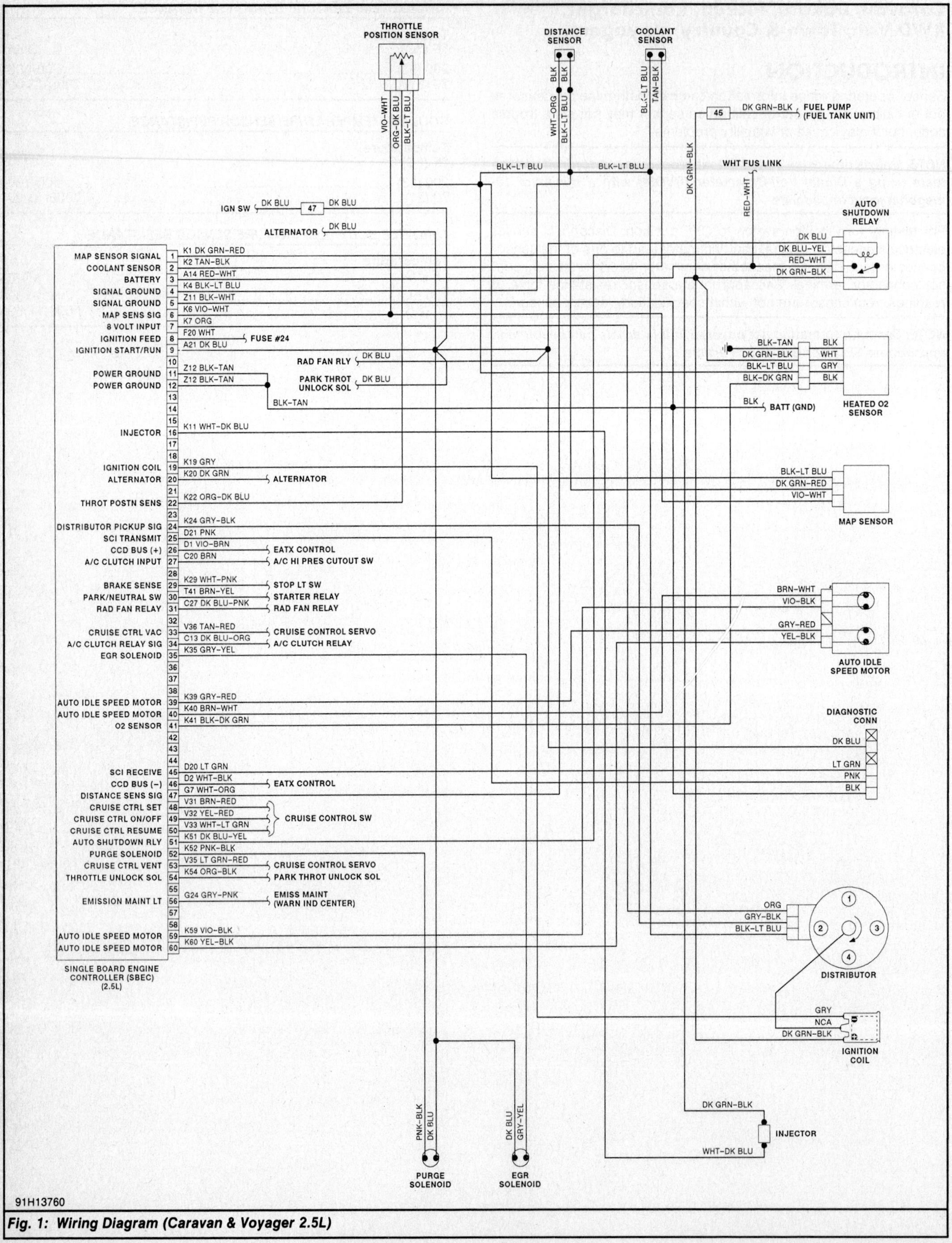
THROTTLE POSITION SENSOR
DISTANCE SENSOR
COOLANT SENSOR
VIO-WHT
ORG-DK BLU
BLK-LT BLU
BLK
WHT-ORG
TAN-BLK
45
DK GRN-BLK
FUEL PUMP (FUEL TANK UNIT)
BLK-LT BLU
WHT FUS LINK
RED-WHT
AUTO SHUTDOWN RELAY
IGN SW
DK BLU
47
ALTERNATOR
DK BLU-YEL
MAP SENSOR SIGNAL
COOLANT SENSOR
BATTERY
SIGNAL GROUND
SIGNAL GROUND
MAP SENS SIG
8 VOLT INPUT
IGNITION FEED
IGNITION START/RUN
POWER GROUND
POWER GROUND
INJECTOR
IGNITION COIL
ALTERNATOR
THROT POSTN SENS
DISTRIBUTOR PICKUP SIG
SCI TRANSMIT
CCD BUS (+)
A/C CLUTCH INPUT
BRAKE SENSE
PARK/NEUTRAL SW
RAD FAN RELAY
CRUISE CTRL VAC
A/C CLUTCH RELAY SIG
EGR SOLENOID
AUTO IDLE SPEED MOTOR
AUTO IDLE SPEED MOTOR
O2 SENSOR
SCI RECEIVE
CCD BUS (–)
DISTANCE SENS SIG
CRUISE CTRL SET
CRUISE CTRL ON/OFF
CRUISE CTRL RESUME
AUTO SHUTDOWN RLY
PURGE SOLENOID
CRUISE CTRL VENT
THROTTLE UNLOCK SOL
EMISSION MAINT LT
AUTO IDLE SPEED MOTOR
AUTO IDLE SPEED MOTOR
SINGLE BOARD ENGINE CONTROLLER (SBEC) (2.5L)
K1 DK GRN-RED
K2 TAN-BLK
A14 RED-WHT
K4 BLK-LT BLU
Z11 BLK-WHT
K6 VIO-WHT
K7 ORG
F20 WHT
A21 DK BLU
FUSE #24
RAD FAN RLY
PARK THROT UNLOCK SOL
Z12 BLK-TAN
Z12 BLK-TAN
BLK-TAN
K11 WHT-DK BLU
K19 GRY
K20 DK GRN
K22 ORG-DK BLU
K24 GRY-BLK
D21 PNK
D1 VIO-BRN
C20 BRN
EATX CONTROL
A/C HI PRES CUTOUT SW
K29 WHT-PNK
T41 BRN-YEL
C27 DK BLU-PNK
STOP LT SW
STARTER RELAY
RAD FAN RELAY
V36 TAN-RED
C13 DK BLU-ORG
K35 GRY-YEL
CRUISE CONTROL SERVO
A/C CLUTCH RELAY
K39 GRY-RED
K40 BRN-WHT
K41 BLK-DK GRN
D20 LT GRN
D2 WHT-BLK
G7 WHT-ORG
EATX CONTROL
V31 BRN-RED
V32 YEL-RED
V33 WHT-LT GRN
K51 DK BLU-YEL
CRUISE CONTROL SW
K52 PNK-BLK
V35 LT GRN-RED
K54 ORG-BLK
CRUISE CONTROL SERVO
PARK THROT UNLOCK SOL
G24 GRY-PNK
EMISS MAINT (WARN IND CENTER)
K59 VIO-BLK
K60 YEL-BLK
BLK-TAN
BLK
WHT
GRY
BLK-DK GRN
BATT (GND)
HEATED O2 SENSOR
DK GRN-RED
MAP SENSOR
BRN-WHT
VIO-BLK
GRY-RED
YEL-BLK
AUTO IDLE SPEED MOTOR
DIAGNOSTIC CONN
LT GRN
PNK
ORG
GRY-BLK
DISTRIBUTOR
GRY
NCA
IGNITION COIL
INJECTOR
WHT-DK BLU
PNK-BLK
GRY-YEL
PURGE SOLENOID
EGR SOLENOID
91H13760

Fig. 1: Wiring Diagram (Caravan & Voyager 2.5L)

1991 ENGINE PERFORMANCE
Wiring Diagrams (Cont.)

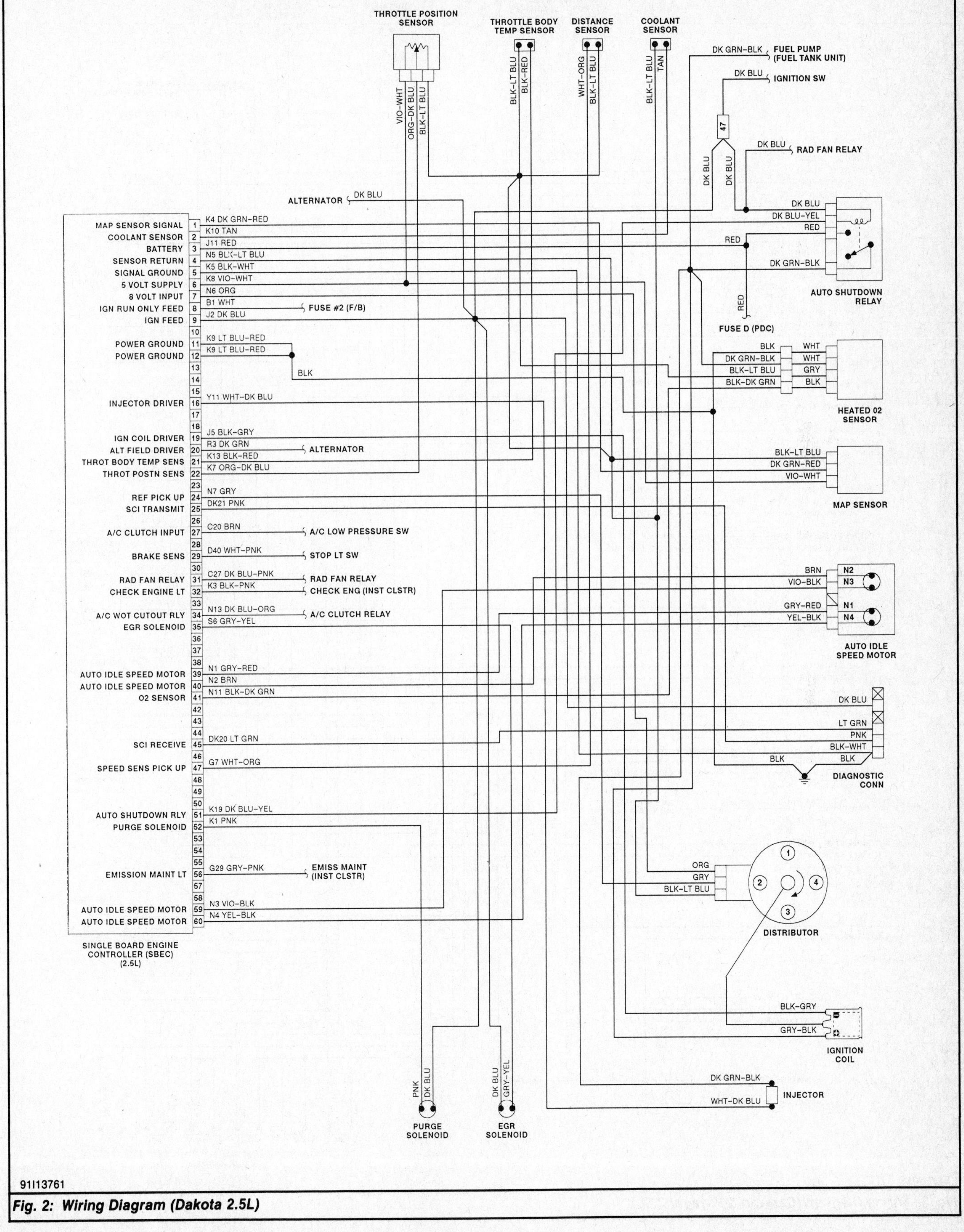

THROTTLE POSITION SENSOR
THROTTLE BODY TEMP SENSOR
DISTANCE SENSOR
COOLANT SENSOR
FUEL PUMP (FUEL TANK UNIT)
IGNITION SW
RAD FAN RELAY
ALTERNATOR
MAP SENSOR SIGNAL
COOLANT SENSOR
BATTERY
SENSOR RETURN
SIGNAL GROUND
5 VOLT SUPPLY
8 VOLT INPUT
IGN RUN ONLY FEED
IGN FEED
POWER GROUND
POWER GROUND
INJECTOR DRIVER
IGN COIL DRIVER
ALT FIELD DRIVER
THROT BODY TEMP SENS
THROT POSTN SENS
REF PICK UP
SCI TRANSMIT
A/C CLUTCH INPUT
BRAKE SENS
RAD FAN RELAY
CHECK ENGINE LT
A/C WOT CUTOUT RLY
EGR SOLENOID
AUTO IDLE SPEED MOTOR
AUTO IDLE SPEED MOTOR
O2 SENSOR
SCI RECEIVE
SPEED SENS PICK UP
AUTO SHUTDOWN RLY
PURGE SOLENOID
EMISSION MAINT LT
AUTO IDLE SPEED MOTOR
AUTO IDLE SPEED MOTOR
K4 DK GRN-RED
K10 TAN
J11 RED
N5 BLK-LT BLU
K5 BLK-WHT
K8 VIO-WHT
N6 ORG
B1 WHT
J2 DK BLU
K9 LT BLU-RED
K9 LT BLU-RED
Y11 WHT-DK BLU
J5 BLK-GRY
R3 DK GRN
K13 BLK-RED
K7 ORG-DK BLU
N7 GRY
DK21 PNK
C20 BRN
D40 WHT-PNK
C27 DK BLU-PNK
K3 BLK-PNK
N13 DK BLU-ORG
S6 GRY-YEL
N1 GRY-RED
N2 BRN
N11 BLK-DK GRN
DK20 LT GRN
G7 WHT-ORG
K19 DK BLU-YEL
K1 PNK
G29 GRY-PNK
N3 VIO-BLK
N4 YEL-BLK
FUSE #2 (F/B)
ALTERNATOR
A/C LOW PRESSURE SW
STOP LT SW
RAD FAN RELAY
CHECK ENG (INST CLSTR)
A/C CLUTCH RELAY
EMISS MAINT (INST CLSTR)
SINGLE BOARD ENGINE CONTROLLER (SBEC) (2.5L)
AUTO SHUTDOWN RELAY
FUSE D (PDC)
HEATED O2 SENSOR
MAP SENSOR
AUTO IDLE SPEED MOTOR
DIAGNOSTIC CONN
DISTRIBUTOR
IGNITION COIL
INJECTOR
PURGE SOLENOID
EGR SOLENOID
91I13761

Fig. 2: Wiring Diagram (Dakota 2.5L)

1991 ENGINE PERFORMANCE
Wiring Diagrams (Cont.)

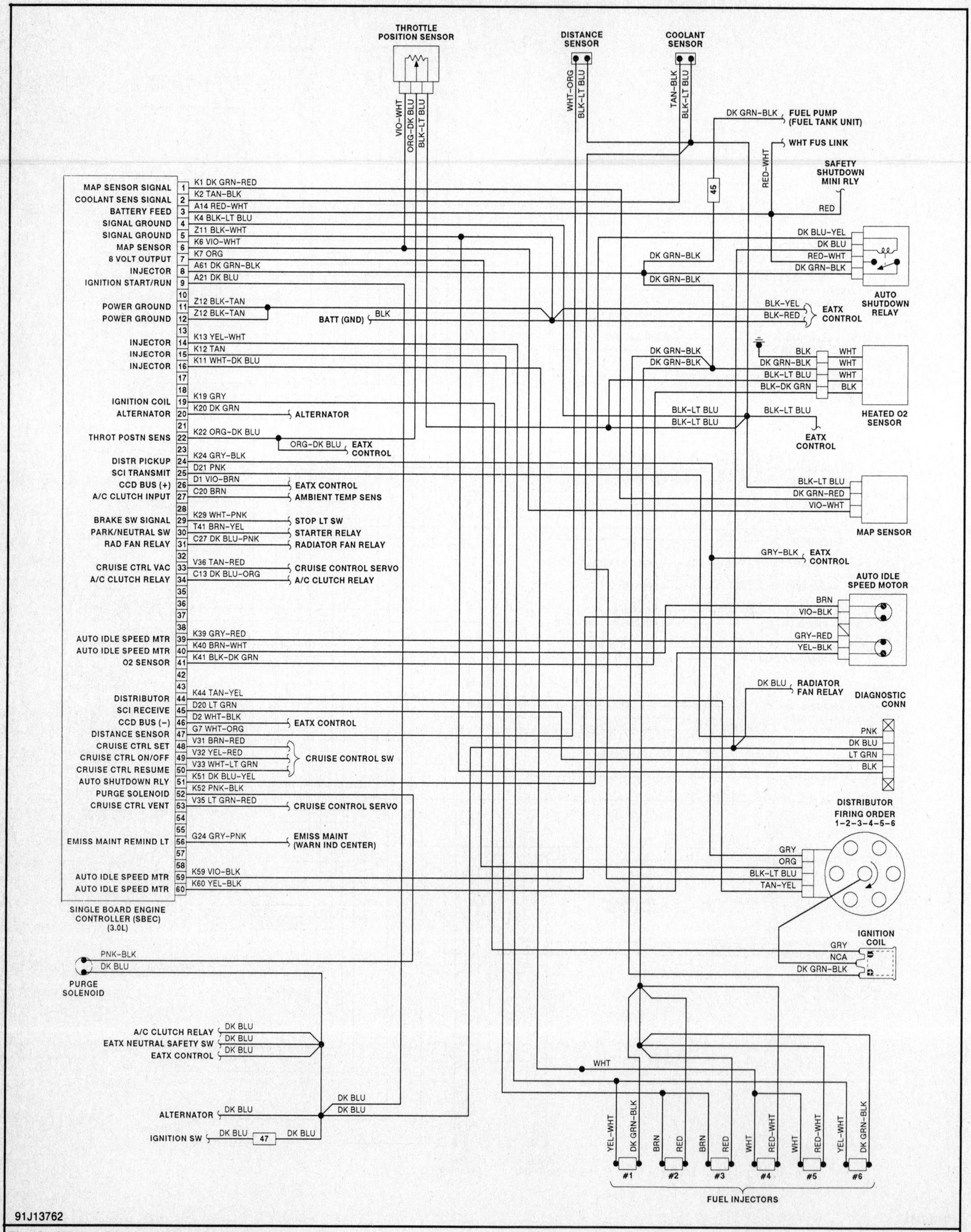
THROTTLE POSITION SENSOR
DISTANCE SENSOR
COOLANT SENSOR
FUEL PUMP (FUEL TANK UNIT)
WHT FUS LINK
SAFETY SHUTDOWN MINI RLY
AUTO SHUTDOWN RELAY
EATX CONTROL
HEATED O2 SENSOR
MAP SENSOR
AUTO IDLE SPEED MOTOR
RADIATOR FAN RELAY
DIAGNOSTIC CONN
DISTRIBUTOR FIRING ORDER 1-2-3-4-5-6
IGNITION COIL
FUEL INJECTORS
MAP SENSOR SIGNAL
COOLANT SENS SIGNAL
BATTERY FEED
SIGNAL GROUND
SIGNAL GROUND
MAP SENSOR
8 VOLT OUTPUT
INJECTOR
IGNITION START/RUN
POWER GROUND
POWER GROUND
INJECTOR
INJECTOR
INJECTOR
IGNITION COIL
ALTERNATOR
THROT POSTN SENS
DISTR PICKUP
SCI TRANSMIT
CCD BUS (+)
A/C CLUTCH INPUT
BRAKE SW SIGNAL
PARK/NEUTRAL SW
RAD FAN RELAY
CRUISE CTRL VAC
A/C CLUTCH RELAY
AUTO IDLE SPEED MTR
AUTO IDLE SPEED MTR
O2 SENSOR
DISTRIBUTOR
SCI RECEIVE
CCD BUS (-)
DISTANCE SENSOR
CRUISE CTRL SET
CRUISE CTRL ON/OFF
CRUISE CTRL RESUME
AUTO SHUTDOWN RLY
PURGE SOLENOID
CRUISE CTRL VENT
EMISS MAINT REMIND LT
AUTO IDLE SPEED MTR
AUTO IDLE SPEED MTR
SINGLE BOARD ENGINE CONTROLLER (SBEC) (3.0L)
K1 DK GRN-RED
K2 TAN-BLK
A14 RED-WHT
K4 BLK-LT BLU
Z11 BLK-WHT
K6 VIO-WHT
K7 ORG
A61 DK GRN-BLK
A21 DK BLU
Z12 BLK-TAN
Z12 BLK-TAN
BATT (GND)
K13 YEL-WHT
K12 TAN
K11 WHT-DK BLU
K19 GRY
K20 DK GRN
K22 ORG-DK BLU
ORG-DK BLU
K24 GRY-BLK
D21 PNK
D1 VIO-BRN
C20 BRN
AMBIENT TEMP SENS
K29 WHT-PNK
STOP LT SW
T41 BRN-YEL
STARTER RELAY
C27 DK BLU-PNK
V36 TAN-RED
CRUISE CONTROL SERVO
C13 DK BLU-ORG
A/C CLUTCH RELAY
K39 GRY-RED
K40 BRN-WHT
K41 BLK-DK GRN
K44 TAN-YEL
D20 LT GRN
D2 WHT-BLK
G7 WHT-ORG
V31 BRN-RED
V32 YEL-RED
V33 WHT-LT GRN
CRUISE CONTROL SW
K51 DK BLU-YEL
K52 PNK-BLK
V35 LT GRN-RED
G24 GRY-PNK
EMISS MAINT (WARN IND CENTER)
K59 VIO-BLK
K60 YEL-BLK
PURGE SOLENOID
PNK-BLK
DK BLU
A/C CLUTCH RELAY
EATX NEUTRAL SAFETY SW
EATX CONTROL
ALTERNATOR
IGNITION SW
47
45
WHT
#1 #2 #3 #4 #5 #6

91J13762

Fig. 3: Wiring Diagram (Caravan & Voyager 3.0L)

1991 ENGINE PERFORMANCE
Wiring Diagrams (Cont.)

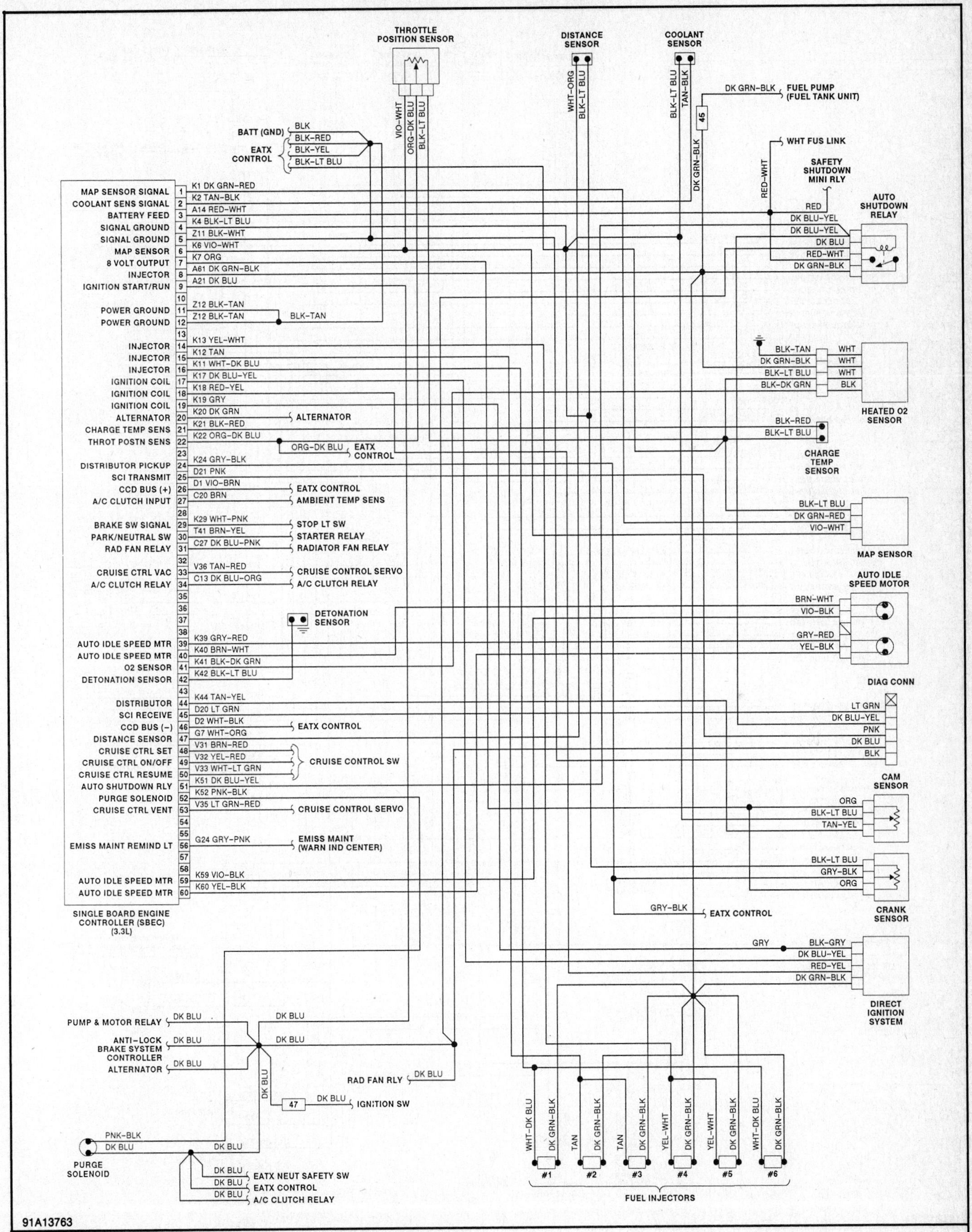
THROTTLE POSITION SENSOR
DISTANCE SENSOR
COOLANT SENSOR
VIO-WHT
ORG-DK BLU
BLK-LT BLU
WHT-ORG
BLK-LT BLU
BLK-LT BLU
TAN-BLK
DK GRN-BLK
FUEL PUMP (FUEL TANK UNIT)
45
DK GRN-BLK
WHT FUS LINK
RED-WHT
SAFETY SHUTDOWN MINI RLY
BATT (GND)
BLK
BLK-RED
EATX CONTROL
BLK-YEL
BLK-LT BLU
MAP SENSOR SIGNAL 1 K1 DK GRN-RED
COOLANT SENS SIGNAL 2 K2 TAN-BLK
BATTERY FEED 3 A14 RED-WHT
SIGNAL GROUND 4 K4 BLK-LT BLU
SIGNAL GROUND 5 Z11 BLK-WHT
MAP SENSOR 6 K6 VIO-WHT
8 VOLT OUTPUT 7 K7 ORG
INJECTOR 8 A61 DK GRN-BLK
IGNITION START/RUN 9 A21 DK BLU
10
POWER GROUND 11 Z12 BLK-TAN
POWER GROUND 12 Z12 BLK-TAN
BLK-TAN
13
INJECTOR 14 K13 YEL-WHT
INJECTOR 15 K12 TAN
INJECTOR 16 K11 WHT-DK BLU
IGNITION COIL 17 K17 DK BLU-YEL
IGNITION COIL 18 K18 RED-YEL
IGNITION COIL 19 K19 GRY
ALTERNATOR 20 K20 DK GRN
ALTERNATOR
CHARGE TEMP SENS 21 K21 BLK-RED
THROT POSTN SENS 22 K22 ORG-DK BLU
ORG-DK BLU
EATX CONTROL
23
DISTRIBUTOR PICKUP 24 K24 GRY-BLK
SCI TRANSMIT 25 D21 PNK
CCD BUS (+) 26 D1 VIO-BRN
EATX CONTROL
A/C CLUTCH INPUT 27 C20 BRN
AMBIENT TEMP SENS
28
BRAKE SW SIGNAL 29 K29 WHT-PNK
STOP LT SW
PARK/NEUTRAL SW 30 T41 BRN-YEL
STARTER RELAY
RAD FAN RELAY 31 C27 DK BLU-PNK
RADIATOR FAN RELAY
32
CRUISE CTRL VAC 33 V36 TAN-RED
CRUISE CONTROL SERVO
A/C CLUTCH RELAY 34 C13 DK BLU-ORG
A/C CLUTCH RELAY
35
36
37
DETONATION SENSOR
38
AUTO IDLE SPEED MTR 39 K39 GRY-RED
AUTO IDLE SPEED MTR 40 K40 BRN-WHT
O2 SENSOR 41 K41 BLK-DK GRN
DETONATION SENSOR 42 K42 BLK-LT BLU
43
DISTRIBUTOR 44 K44 TAN-YEL
SCI RECEIVE 45 D20 LT GRN
CCD BUS (-) 46 D2 WHT-BLK
EATX CONTROL
DISTANCE SENSOR 47 G7 WHT-ORG
CRUISE CTRL SET 48 V31 BRN-RED
CRUISE CTRL ON/OFF 49 V32 YEL-RED
CRUISE CONTROL SW
CRUISE CTRL RESUME 50 V33 WHT-LT GRN
AUTO SHUTDOWN RLY 51 K51 DK BLU-YEL
PURGE SOLENOID 52 K52 PNK-BLK
CRUISE CTRL VENT 53 V35 LT GRN-RED
CRUISE CONTROL SERVO
54
55
EMISS MAINT REMIND LT 56 G24 GRY-PNK
EMISS MAINT (WARN IND CENTER)
57
58
AUTO IDLE SPEED MTR 59 K59 VIO-BLK
AUTO IDLE SPEED MTR 60 K60 YEL-BLK
SINGLE BOARD ENGINE CONTROLLER (SBEC) (3.3L)
RED
DK BLU-YEL
DK BLU-YEL
DK BLU
RED-WHT
DK GRN-BLK
AUTO SHUTDOWN RELAY
BLK-TAN WHT
DK GRN-BLK WHT
BLK-LT BLU WHT
BLK-DK GRN BLK
HEATED O2 SENSOR
BLK-RED
BLK-LT BLU
CHARGE TEMP SENSOR
BLK-LT BLU
DK GRN-RED
VIO-WHT
MAP SENSOR
AUTO IDLE SPEED MOTOR
BRN-WHT
VIO-BLK
GRY-RED
YEL-BLK
DIAG CONN
LT GRN
DK BLU-YEL
PNK
DK BLU
BLK
CAM SENSOR
ORG
BLK-LT BLU
TAN-YEL
BLK-LT BLU
GRY-BLK
ORG
CRANK SENSOR
GRY-BLK
EATX CONTROL
GRY
BLK-GRY
DK BLU-YEL
RED-YEL
DK GRN-BLK
DIRECT IGNITION SYSTEM
PUMP & MOTOR RELAY
DK BLU
DK BLU
ANTI-LOCK BRAKE SYSTEM CONTROLLER
DK BLU
DK BLU
ALTERNATOR
DK BLU
DK BLU
RAD FAN RLY
DK BLU
47
DK BLU
IGNITION SW
PNK-BLK
DK BLU
DK BLU
PURGE SOLENOID
DK BLU
EATX NEUT SAFETY SW
DK BLU
EATX CONTROL
DK BLU
A/C CLUTCH RELAY
WHT-DK BLU
DK GRN-BLK
TAN
DK GRN-BLK
TAN
DK GRN-BLK
YEL-WHT
DK GRN-BLK
YEL-WHT
DK GRN-BLK
WHT-DK BLU
DK GRN-BLK
#1
#2
#3
#4
#5
#6
FUEL INJECTORS
91A13763

Fig. 4: Wiring Diagram (Caravan, Town & Country & Voyager 3.3L)

1991 ENGINE PERFORMANCE
Wiring Diagrams (Cont.)

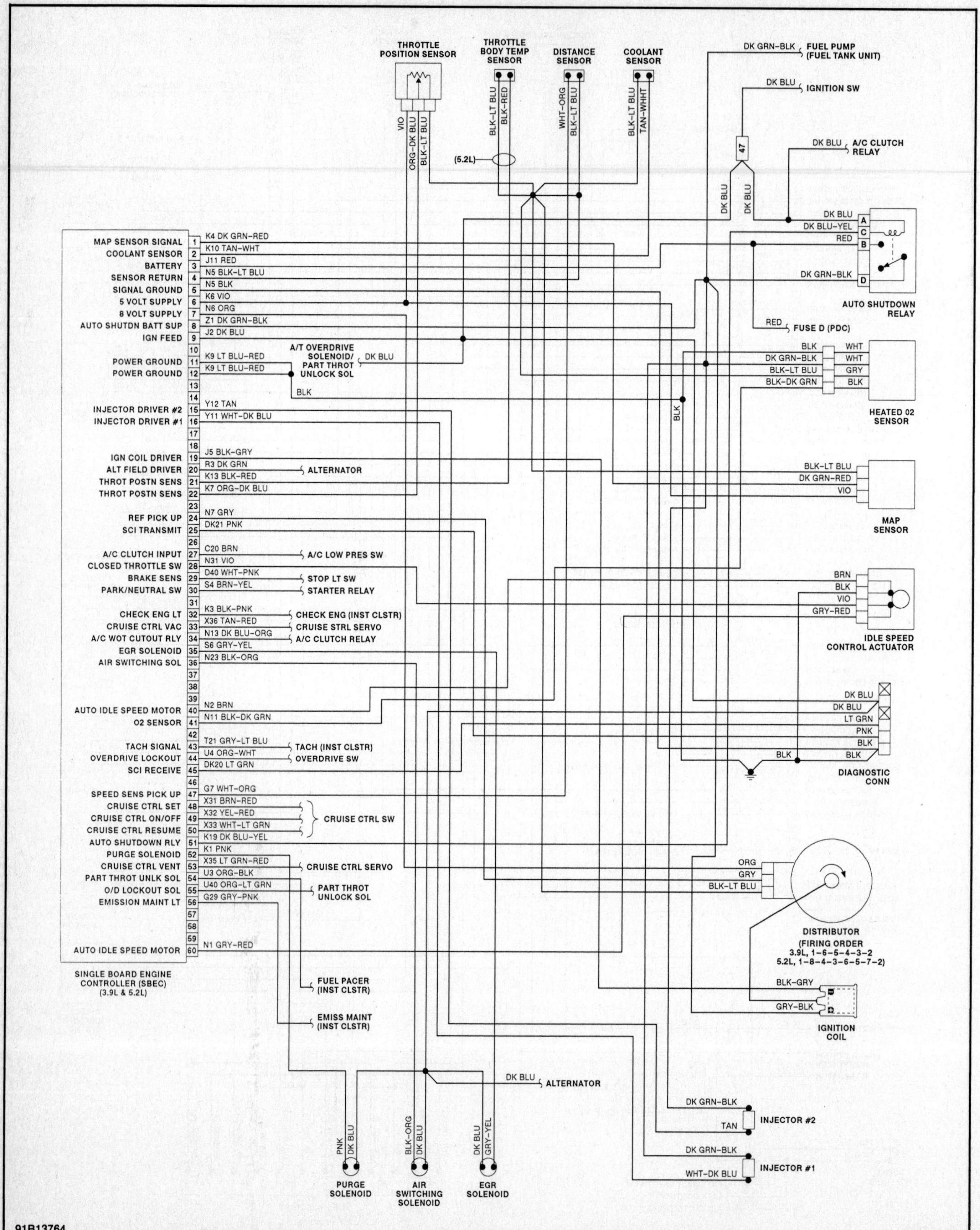
THROTTLE POSITION SENSOR
THROTTLE BODY TEMP SENSOR
DISTANCE SENSOR
COOLANT SENSOR
FUEL PUMP (FUEL TANK UNIT)
IGNITION SW
A/C CLUTCH RELAY
AUTO SHUTDOWN RELAY
FUSE D (PDC)
HEATED 02 SENSOR
MAP SENSOR
IDLE SPEED CONTROL ACTUATOR
DIAGNOSTIC CONN
DISTRIBUTOR (FIRING ORDER 3.9L, 1-6-5-4-3-2 5.2L, 1-8-4-3-6-5-7-2)
IGNITION COIL
INJECTOR #2
INJECTOR #1
PURGE SOLENOID
AIR SWITCHING SOLENOID
EGR SOLENOID
ALTERNATOR
SINGLE BOARD ENGINE CONTROLLER (SBEC) (3.9L & 5.2L)
1 MAP SENSOR SIGNAL K4 DK GRN-RED
2 COOLANT SENSOR K10 TAN-WHT
3 BATTERY J11 RED
4 SENSOR RETURN N5 BLK-LT BLU
5 SIGNAL GROUND N5 BLK
6 5 VOLT SUPPLY K6 VIO
7 8 VOLT SUPPLY N6 ORG
8 AUTO SHUTDN BATT SUP Z1 DK GRN-BLK
9 IGN FEED J2 DK BLU
11 POWER GROUND K9 LT BLU-RED
12 POWER GROUND K9 LT BLU-RED
A/T OVERDRIVE SOLENOID/ PART THROT UNLOCK SOL
15 INJECTOR DRIVER #2 Y12 TAN
16 INJECTOR DRIVER #1 Y11 WHT-DK BLU
19 IGN COIL DRIVER J5 BLK-GRY
20 ALT FIELD DRIVER R3 DK GRN
21 THROT POSTN SENS K13 BLK-RED
22 THROT POSTN SENS K7 ORG-DK BLU
24 REF PICK UP N7 GRY
25 SCI TRANSMIT DK21 PNK
27 A/C CLUTCH INPUT C20 BRN
28 CLOSED THROTTLE SW N31 VIO
29 BRAKE SENS D40 WHT-PNK
30 PARK/NEUTRAL SW S4 BRN-YEL
A/C LOW PRES SW
STOP LT SW
STARTER RELAY
32 CHECK ENG LT K3 BLK-PNK
33 CRUISE CTRL VAC X36 TAN-RED
34 A/C WOT CUTOUT RLY N13 DK BLU-ORG
35 EGR SOLENOID S6 GRY-YEL
36 AIR SWITCHING SOL N23 BLK-ORG
CHECK ENG (INST CLSTR)
CRUISE STRL SERVO
A/C CLUTCH RELAY
40 AUTO IDLE SPEED MOTOR N2 BRN
41 O2 SENSOR N11 BLK-DK GRN
43 TACH SIGNAL T21 GRY-LT BLU
44 OVERDRIVE LOCKOUT U4 ORG-WHT
45 SCI RECEIVE DK20 LT GRN
TACH (INST CLSTR)
OVERDRIVE SW
47 SPEED SENS PICK UP G7 WHT-ORG
48 CRUISE CTRL SET X31 BRN-RED
49 CRUISE CTRL ON/OFF X32 YEL-RED
50 CRUISE CTRL RESUME X33 WHT-LT GRN
51 AUTO SHUTDOWN RLY K19 DK BLU-YEL
52 PURGE SOLENOID K1 PNK
53 CRUISE CTRL VENT X35 LT GRN-RED
54 PART THROT UNLK SOL U3 ORG-BLK
55 O/D LOCKOUT SOL U40 ORG-LT GRN
56 EMISSION MAINT LT G29 GRY-PNK
CRUISE CTRL SW
CRUISE CTRL SERVO
PART THROT UNLOCK SOL
60 AUTO IDLE SPEED MOTOR N1 GRY-RED
FUEL PACER (INST CLSTR)
EMISS MAINT (INST CLSTR)
91B13764

Fig. 5: Wiring Diagram (Dakota 3.9L & 5.2L)

1991 ENGINE PERFORMANCE
Wiring Diagrams (Cont.)

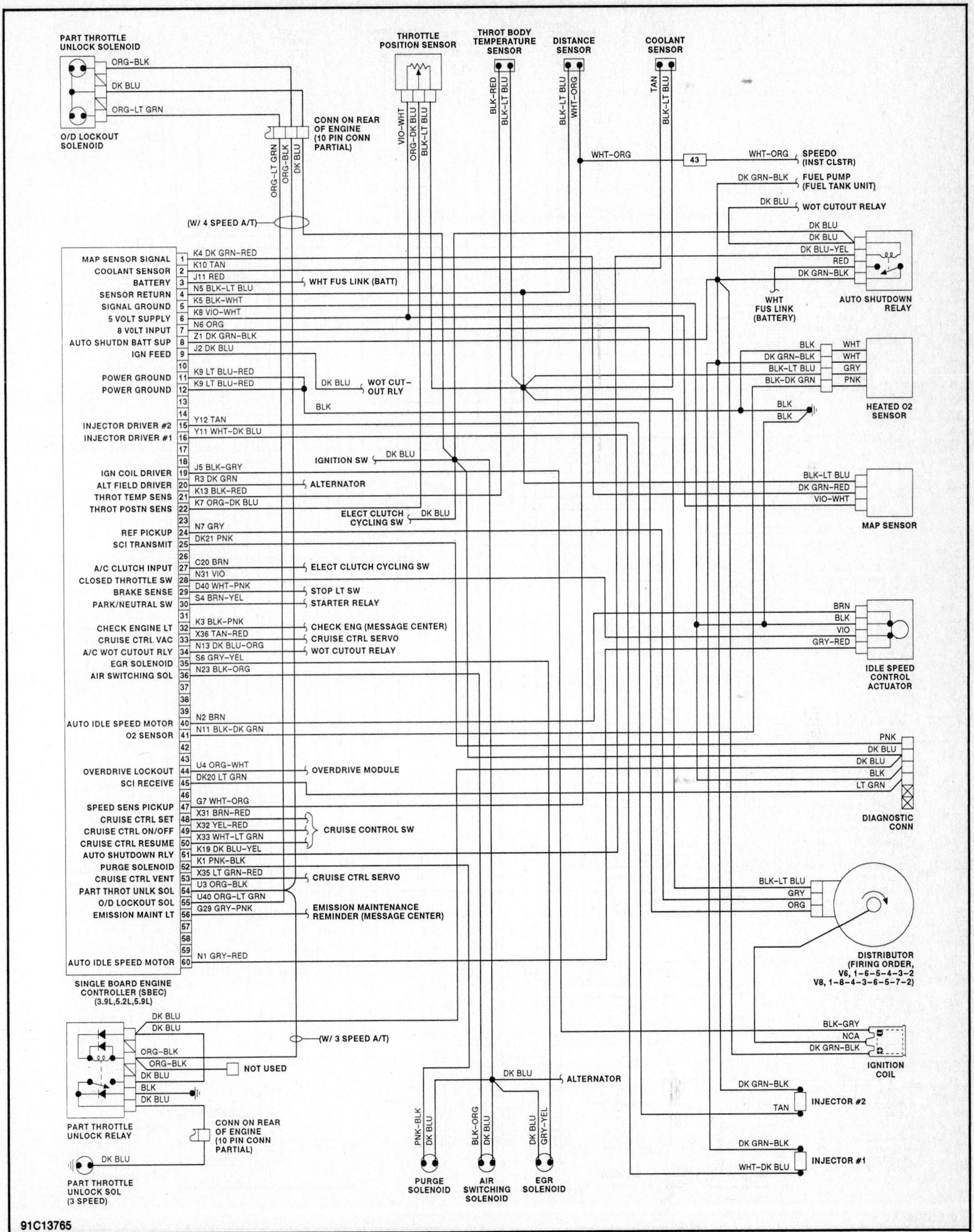
PART THROTTLE UNLOCK SOLENOID
O/D LOCKOUT SOLENOID
ORG-BLK
DK BLU
ORG-LT GRN
CONN ON REAR OF ENGINE (10 PIN CONN PARTIAL)
THROTTLE POSITION SENSOR
THROT BODY TEMPERATURE SENSOR
DISTANCE SENSOR
COOLANT SENSOR
SPEEDO (INST CLSTR)
FUEL PUMP (FUEL TANK UNIT)
WOT CUTOUT RELAY
(W/ 4 SPEED A/T)
AUTO SHUTDOWN RELAY
WHT FUS LINK (BATTERY)
MAP SENSOR SIGNAL
COOLANT SENSOR
BATTERY
SENSOR RETURN
SIGNAL GROUND
5 VOLT SUPPLY
8 VOLT INPUT
AUTO SHUTDN BATT SUP
IGN FEED
POWER GROUND
POWER GROUND
INJECTOR DRIVER #2
INJECTOR DRIVER #1
IGN COIL DRIVER
ALT FIELD DRIVER
THROT TEMP SENS
THROT POSTN SENS
REF PICKUP
SCI TRANSMIT
A/C CLUTCH INPUT
CLOSED THROTTLE SW
BRAKE SENSE
PARK/NEUTRAL SW
CHECK ENGINE LT
CRUISE CTRL VAC
A/C WOT CUTOUT RLY
EGR SOLENOID
AIR SWITCHING SOL
AUTO IDLE SPEED MOTOR
O2 SENSOR
OVERDRIVE LOCKOUT
SCI RECEIVE
SPEED SENS PICKUP
CRUISE CTRL SET
CRUISE CTRL ON/OFF
CRUISE CTRL RESUME
AUTO SHUTDOWN RLY
PURGE SOLENOID
CRUISE CTRL VENT
PART THROT UNLK SOL
O/D LOCKOUT SOL
EMISSION MAINT LT
AUTO IDLE SPEED MOTOR
K4 DK GRN-RED
K10 TAN
J11 RED
N5 BLK-LT BLU
K5 BLK-WHT
K8 VIO-WHT
N6 ORG
Z1 DK GRN-BLK
J2 DK BLU
K9 LT BLU-RED
K9 LT BLU-RED
Y12 TAN
Y11 WHT-DK BLU
J5 BLK-GRY
R3 DK GRN
K13 BLK-RED
K7 ORG-DK BLU
N7 GRY
DK21 PNK
C20 BRN
N31 VIO
D40 WHT-PNK
S4 BRN-YEL
K3 BLK-PNK
X36 TAN-RED
N13 DK BLU-ORG
S6 GRY-YEL
N23 BLK-ORG
N2 BRN
N11 BLK-DK GRN
U4 ORG-WHT
DK20 LT GRN
G7 WHT-ORG
X31 BRN-RED
X32 YEL-RED
X33 WHT-LT GRN
K19 DK BLU-YEL
K1 PNK-BLK
X35 LT GRN-RED
U3 ORG-BLK
U40 ORG-LT GRN
G29 GRY-PNK
N1 GRY-RED
WHT FUS LINK (BATT)
WOT CUT-OUT RLY
IGNITION SW
ALTERNATOR
ELECT CLUTCH CYCLING SW
ELECT CLUTCH CYCLING SW
STOP LT SW
STARTER RELAY
CHECK ENG (MESSAGE CENTER)
CRUISE CTRL SERVO
WOT CUTOUT RELAY
OVERDRIVE MODULE
CRUISE CONTROL SW
CRUISE CTRL SERVO
EMISSION MAINTENANCE REMINDER (MESSAGE CENTER)
HEATED O2 SENSOR
MAP SENSOR
IDLE SPEED CONTROL ACTUATOR
DIAGNOSTIC CONN
DISTRIBUTOR (FIRING ORDER, V6, 1-6-5-4-3-2 V8, 1-8-4-3-6-5-7-2)
IGNITION COIL
INJECTOR #2
INJECTOR #1
SINGLE BOARD ENGINE CONTROLLER (SBEC) (3.9L,5.2L,5.9L)
(W/ 3 SPEED A/T)
NOT USED
PART THROTTLE UNLOCK RELAY
CONN ON REAR OF ENGINE (10 PIN CONN PARTIAL)
PART THROTTLE UNLOCK SOL (3 SPEED)
PURGE SOLENOID
AIR SWITCHING SOLENOID
EGR SOLENOID
ALTERNATOR
91C13765

Fig. 6: Wiring Diagram (Pickup & Ramcharger 3.9L, 5.2L & 5.9L)

1991 ENGINE PERFORMANCE
Wiring Diagrams (Cont.)

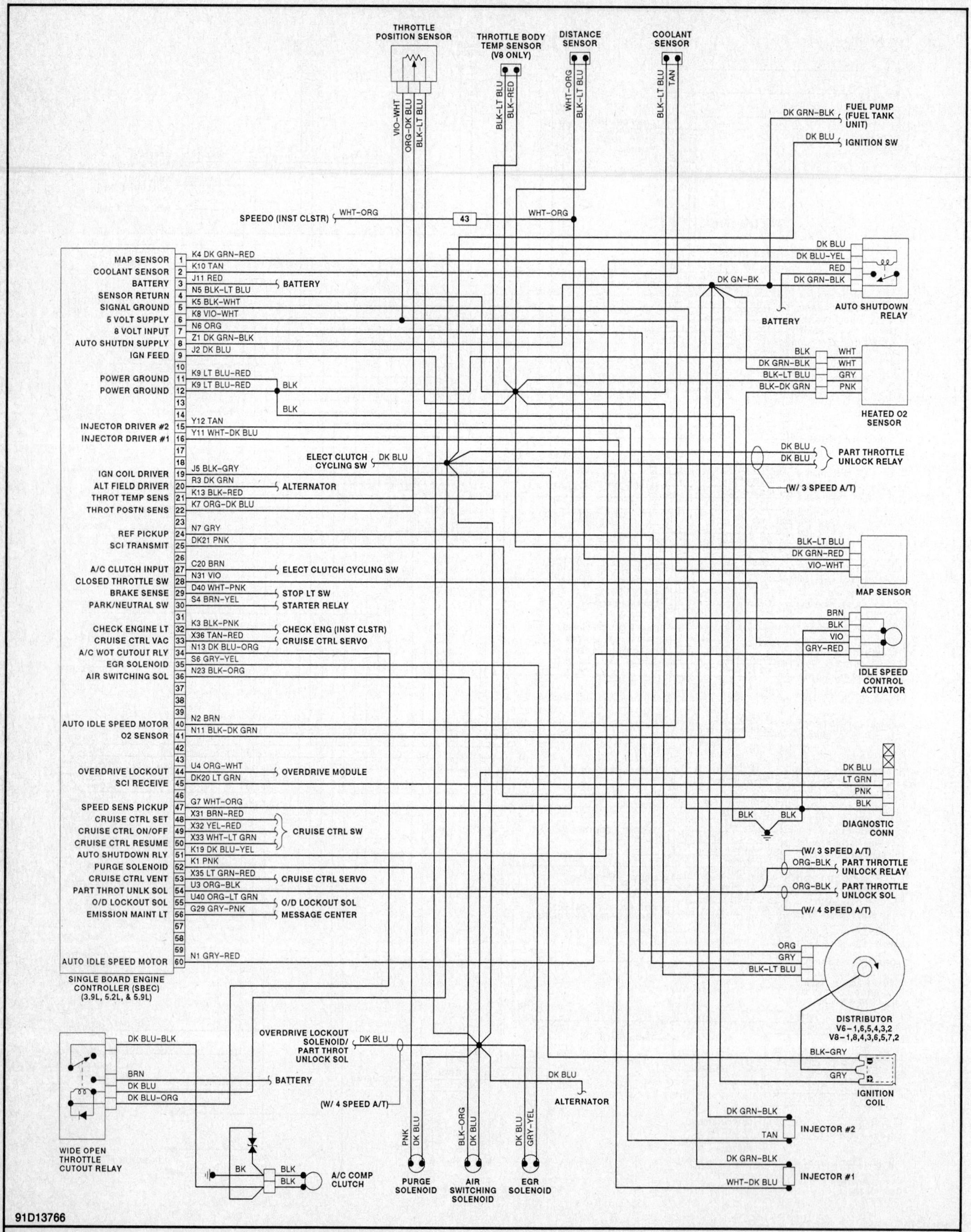
THROTTLE POSITION SENSOR
THROTTLE BODY TEMP SENSOR (V8 ONLY)
DISTANCE SENSOR
COOLANT SENSOR
VIO-WHT
ORG-DK BLU
BLK-LT BLU
BLK-RED
WHT-ORG
TAN
FUEL PUMP (FUEL TANK UNIT)
DK GRN-BLK
DK BLU
IGNITION SW
SPEEDO (INST CLSTR)
43
MAP SENSOR
COOLANT SENSOR
BATTERY
SENSOR RETURN
SIGNAL GROUND
5 VOLT SUPPLY
8 VOLT INPUT
AUTO SHUTDN SUPPLY
IGN FEED
POWER GROUND
POWER GROUND
INJECTOR DRIVER #2
INJECTOR DRIVER #1
IGN COIL DRIVER
ALT FIELD DRIVER
THROT TEMP SENS
THROT POSTN SENS
REF PICKUP
SCI TRANSMIT
A/C CLUTCH INPUT
CLOSED THROTTLE SW
BRAKE SENSE
PARK/NEUTRAL SW
CHECK ENGINE LT
CRUISE CTRL VAC
A/C WOT CUTOUT RLY
EGR SOLENOID
AIR SWITCHING SOL
AUTO IDLE SPEED MOTOR
O2 SENSOR
OVERDRIVE LOCKOUT
SCI RECEIVE
SPEED SENS PICKUP
CRUISE CTRL SET
CRUISE CTRL ON/OFF
CRUISE CTRL RESUME
AUTO SHUTDOWN RLY
PURGE SOLENOID
CRUISE CTRL VENT
PART THROT UNLK SOL
O/D LOCKOUT SOL
EMISSION MAINT LT
AUTO IDLE SPEED MOTOR
K4 DK GRN-RED
K10 TAN
J11 RED
N5 BLK-LT BLU
K5 BLK-WHT
K8 VIO-WHT
N6 ORG
Z1 DK GRN-BLK
J2 DK BLU
K9 LT BLU-RED
K9 LT BLU-RED
Y12 TAN
Y11 WHT-DK BLU
J5 BLK-GRY
R3 DK GRN
K13 BLK-RED
K7 ORG-DK BLU
N7 GRY
DK21 PNK
C20 BRN
N31 VIO
D40 WHT-PNK
S4 BRN-YEL
K3 BLK-PNK
X36 TAN-RED
N13 DK BLU-ORG
S6 GRY-YEL
N23 BLK-ORG
N2 BRN
N11 BLK-DK GRN
U4 ORG-WHT
DK20 LT GRN
G7 WHT-ORG
X31 BRN-RED
X32 YEL-RED
X33 WHT-LT GRN
K19 DK BLU-YEL
K1 PNK
X35 LT GRN-RED
U3 ORG-BLK
U40 ORG-LT GRN
G29 GRY-PNK
N1 GRY-RED
BATTERY
BLK
ALTERNATOR
ELECT CLUTCH CYCLING SW
ELECT CLUTCH CYCLING SW
STOP LT SW
STARTER RELAY
CHECK ENG (INST CLSTR)
CRUISE CTRL SERVO
OVERDRIVE MODULE
CRUISE CTRL SW
CRUISE CTRL SERVO
O/D LOCKOUT SOL
MESSAGE CENTER
SINGLE BOARD ENGINE CONTROLLER (SBEC) (3.9L, 5.2L, & 5.9L)
DK BLU-YEL
RED
DK GN-BK
AUTO SHUTDOWN RELAY
BATTERY
WHT
GRY
PNK
BLK-DK GRN
HEATED O2 SENSOR
PART THROTTLE UNLOCK RELAY
(W/ 3 SPEED A/T)
DK GRN-RED
VIO-WHT
BRN
VIO
GRY-RED
IDLE SPEED CONTROL ACTUATOR
LT GRN
DIAGNOSTIC CONN
ORG-BLK
PART THROTTLE UNLOCK SOL
(W/ 4 SPEED A/T)
ORG
DISTRIBUTOR
V6-1,6,5,4,3,2
V8-1,8,4,3,6,5,7,2
BLK-GRY
IGNITION COIL
DK BLU-BLK
DK BLU-ORG
WIDE OPEN THROTTLE CUTOUT RELAY
OVERDRIVE LOCKOUT SOLENOID/ PART THROT UNLOCK SOL
BK
A/C COMP CLUTCH
GRY-YEL
PURGE SOLENOID
AIR SWITCHING SOLENOID
EGR SOLENOID
INJECTOR #2
INJECTOR #1
WHT-DK BLU
91D13766

Fig. 7: Wiring Diagram (RWD Van 3.9L, 5.2L & 5.9L)

1991 ENGINE PERFORMANCE
Vacuum Diagrams

Caravan, Dakota, Pickup, Ramcharger, RWD Van, Town & Country, Voyager

INTRODUCTION

This article contains underhood views or schematics of vacuum hose routing. Use these vacuum diagrams during the visual inspection in BASIC DIAGNOSTIC PROCEDURES article. This will assist in identifying improperly routed vacuum hoses, which cause driveability and/or computer-indicated malfunctions.

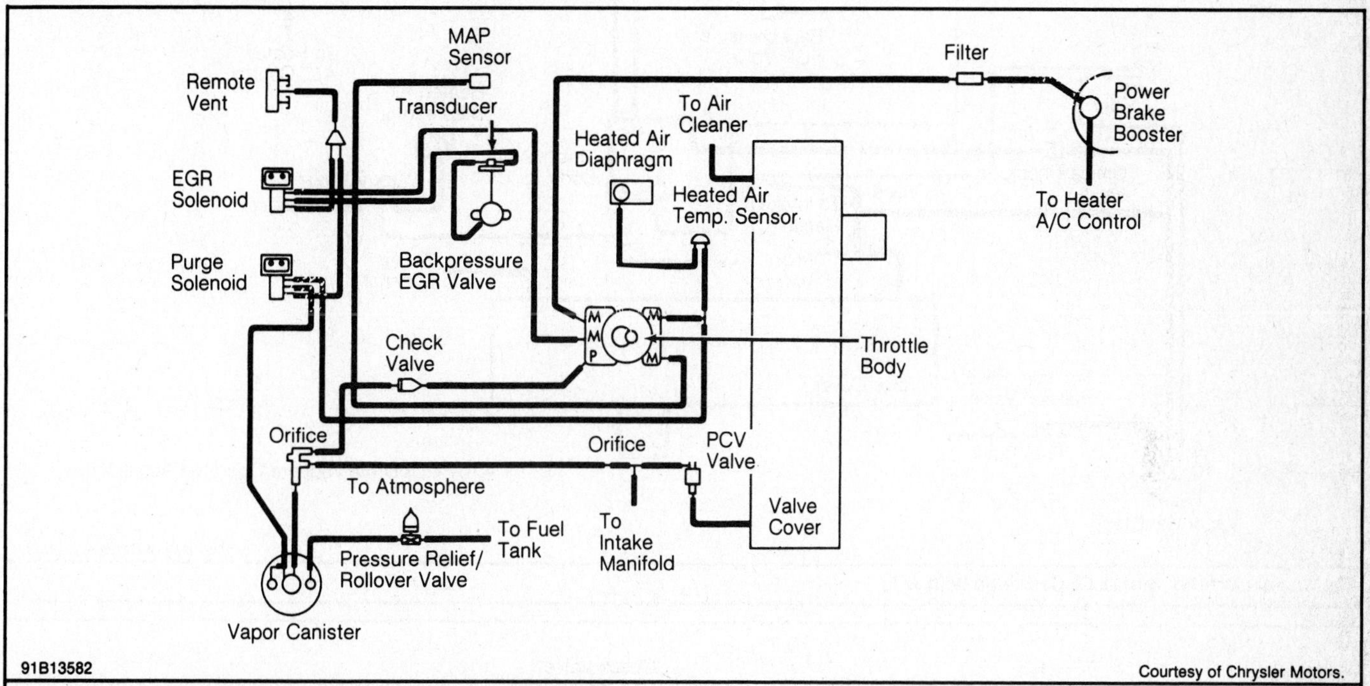
MAP Sensor
Filter
Remote Vent
Transducer
To Air Cleaner
Power Brake Booster
Heated Air Diaphragm
EGR Solenoid
Heated Air Temp. Sensor
To Heater A/C Control
Purge Solenoid
Backpressure EGR Valve
Check Valve
Throttle Body
Orifice
Orifice
PCV Valve
To Atmosphere
Valve Cover
To Fuel Tank
To Intake Manifold
Pressure Relief/ Rollover Valve
Vapor Canister
91B13582
Courtesy of Chrysler Motors.

Fig. 1: Vacuum Diagram (2.5L California & Federal with M/T)

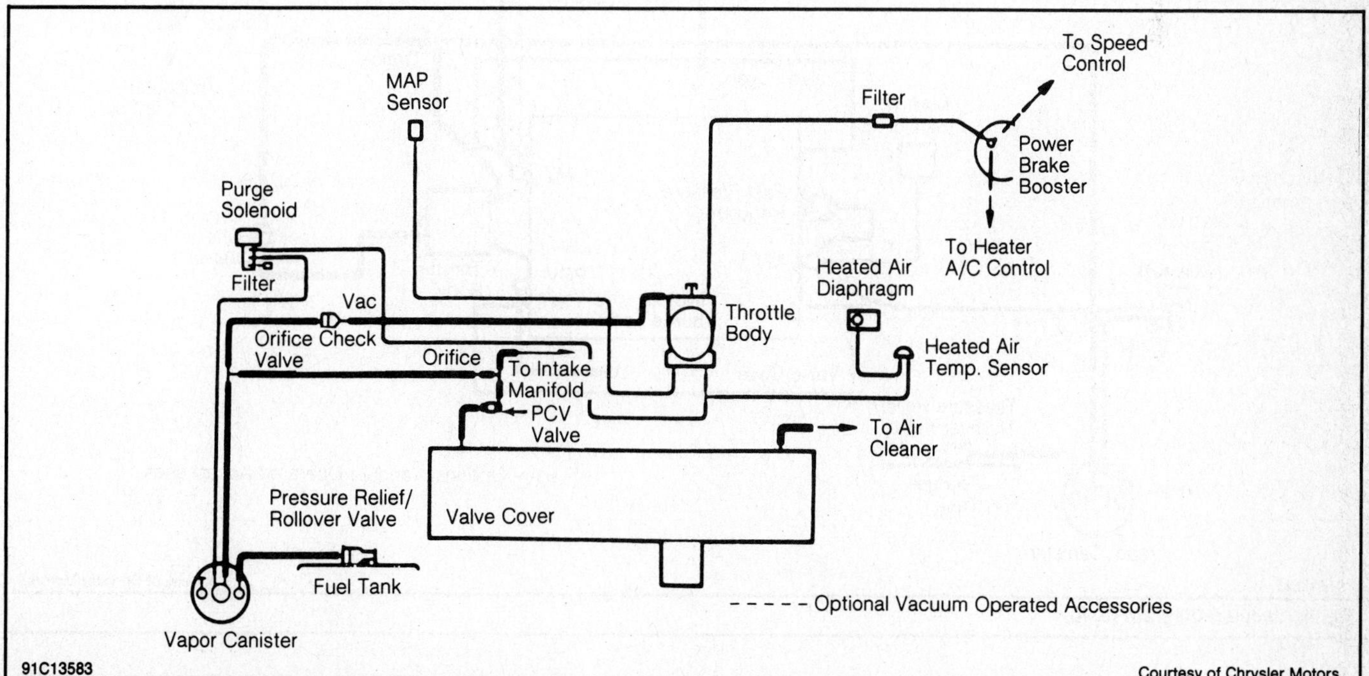
To Speed Control
MAP Sensor
Filter
Power Brake Booster
Purge Solenoid
Filter
To Heater A/C Control
Heated Air Diaphragm
Vac
Throttle Body
Orifice Check Valve
Orifice
To Intake Manifold
Heated Air Temp. Sensor
PCV Valve
To Air Cleaner
Pressure Relief/ Rollover Valve
Valve Cover
Fuel Tank
Vapor Canister
- - - - - Optional Vacuum Operated Accessories
91C13583
Courtesy of Chrysler Motors.

Fig. 2: Vacuum Diagram (2.5L Canada & Federal with A/T)

1991 ENGINE PERFORMANCE
Vacuum Diagrams (Cont.)

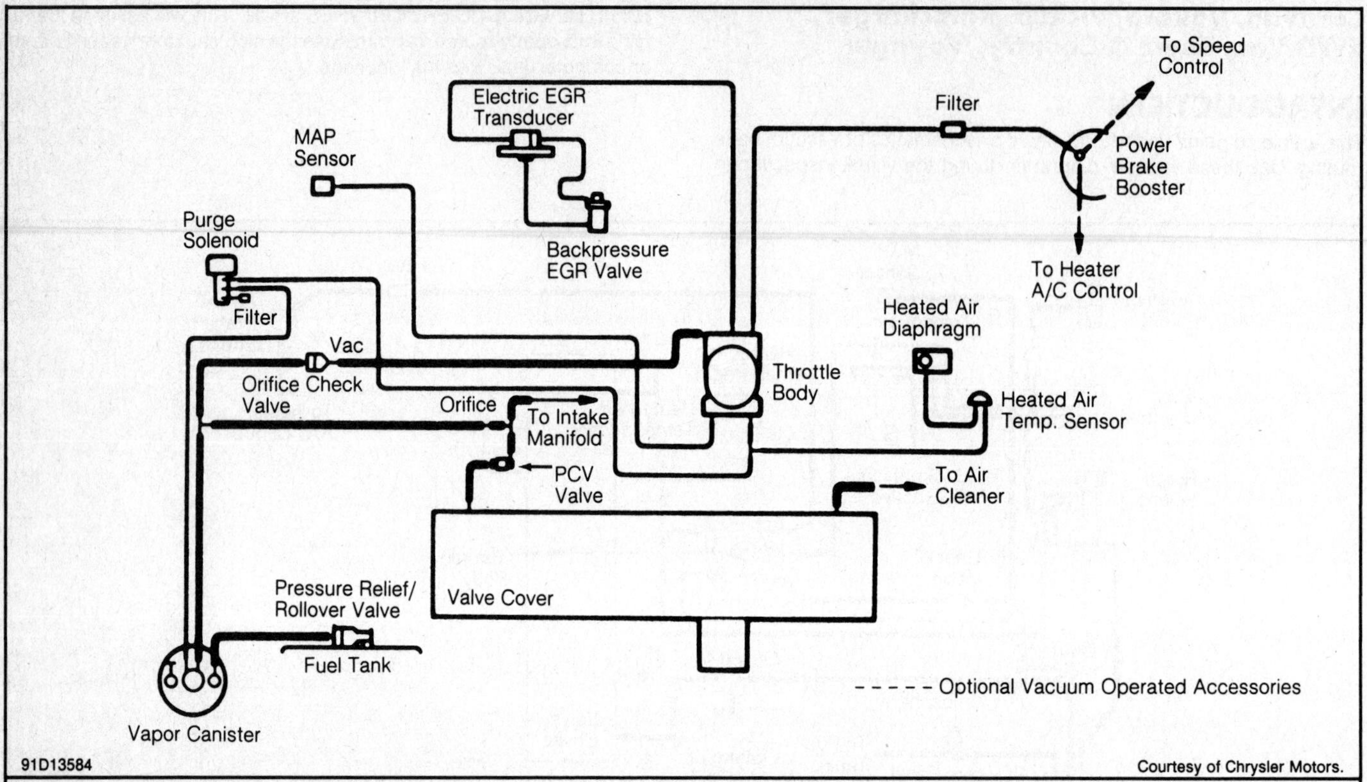
To Speed Control
Electric EGR Transducer
Filter
MAP Sensor
Power Brake Booster
Purge Solenoid
Backpressure EGR Valve
To Heater A/C Control
Filter
Heated Air Diaphragm
Vac
Orifice Check Valve
Throttle Body
Orifice
To Intake Manifold
Heated Air Temp. Sensor
PCV Valve
To Air Cleaner
Pressure Relief/ Rollover Valve
Valve Cover
Fuel Tank
Vapor Canister
- - - - - Optional Vacuum Operated Accessories
91D13584
Courtesy of Chrysler Motors.

Fig. 3: Vacuum Diagram (2.5L California with A/T)

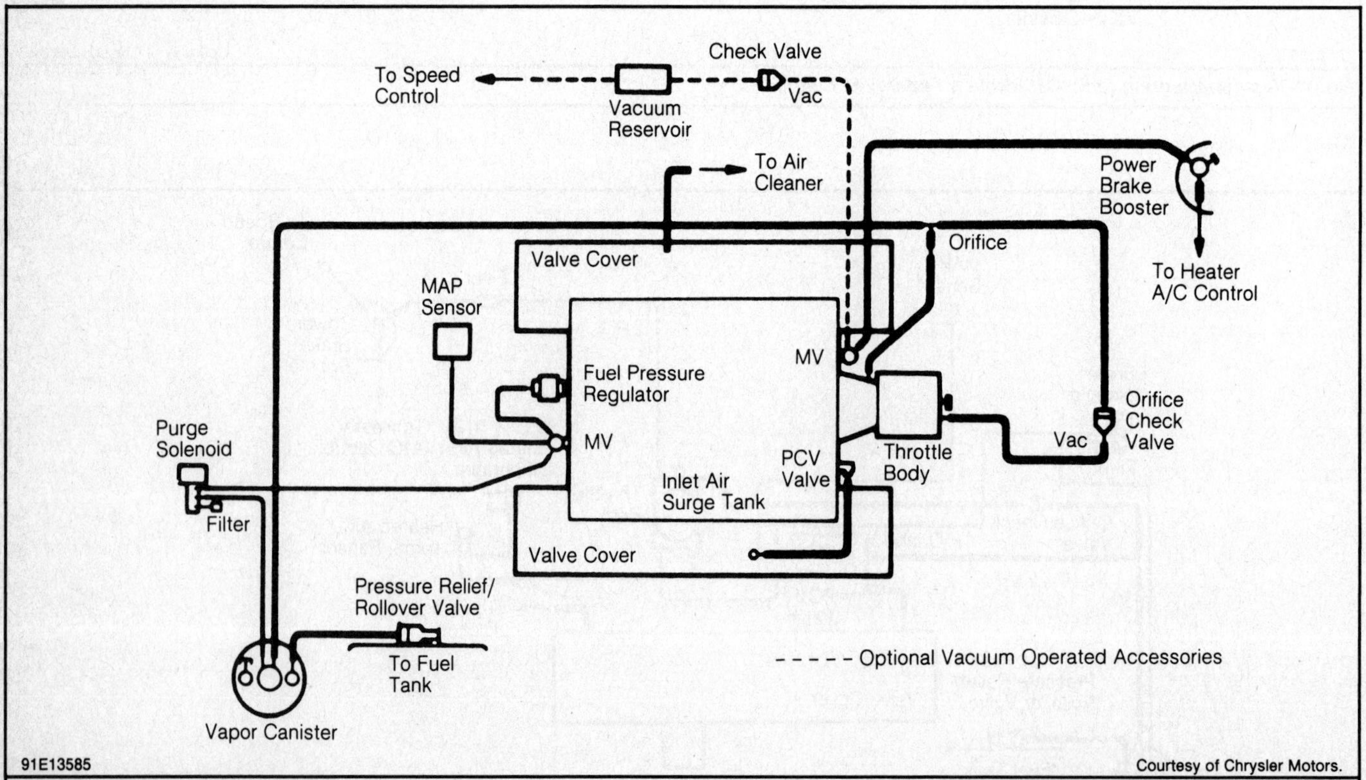
Check Valve
To Speed Control
Vac
Vacuum Reservoir
To Air Cleaner
Power Brake Booster
Orifice
Valve Cover
To Heater A/C Control
MAP Sensor
MV
Fuel Pressure Regulator
Orifice Check Valve
Purge Solenoid
MV
Vac
Throttle Body
PCV Valve
Inlet Air Surge Tank
Filter
Valve Cover
Pressure Relief/ Rollover Valve
To Fuel Tank
- - - - - Optional Vacuum Operated Accessories
Vapor Canister
91E13585
Courtesy of Chrysler Motors.

Fig. 4: Vacuum Diagram (3.0L)

1991 ENGINE PERFORMANCE
Vacuum Diagrams (Cont.)

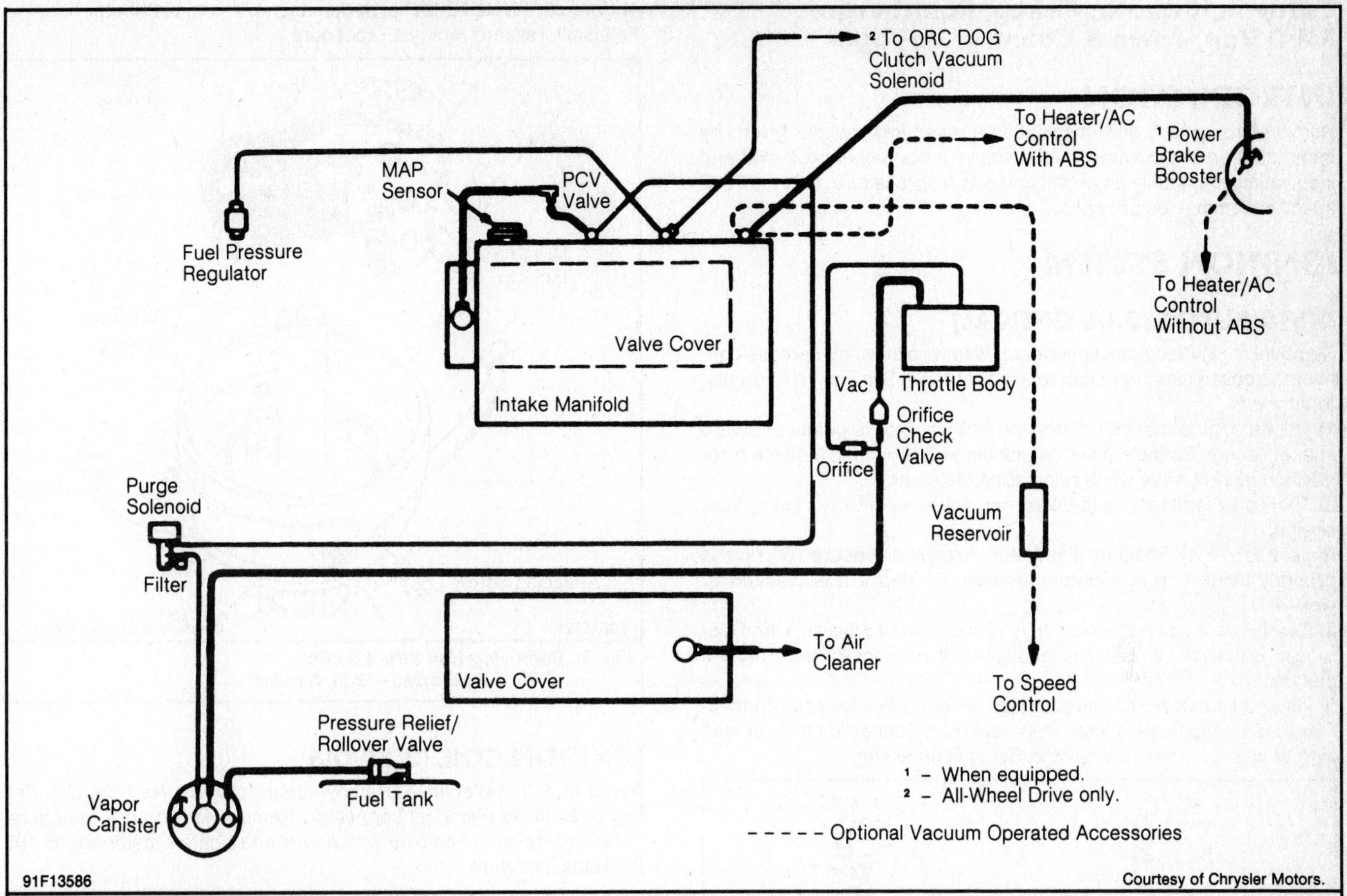
² To ORC DOG Clutch Vacuum Solenoid
To Heater/AC Control With ABS
¹ Power Brake Booster
MAP Sensor
PCV Valve
Fuel Pressure Regulator
To Heater/AC Control Without ABS
Valve Cover
Intake Manifold
Vac
Throttle Body
Orifice Check Valve
Orifice
Purge Solenoid
Vacuum Reservoir
Filter
To Air Cleaner
Valve Cover
To Speed Control
Pressure Relief/ Rollover Valve
Fuel Tank
Vapor Canister
¹ – When equipped.
² – All-Wheel Drive only.
----- Optional Vacuum Operated Accessories
91F13586
Courtesy of Chrysler Motors.

Fig. 5: Vacuum Diagram (3.3L)

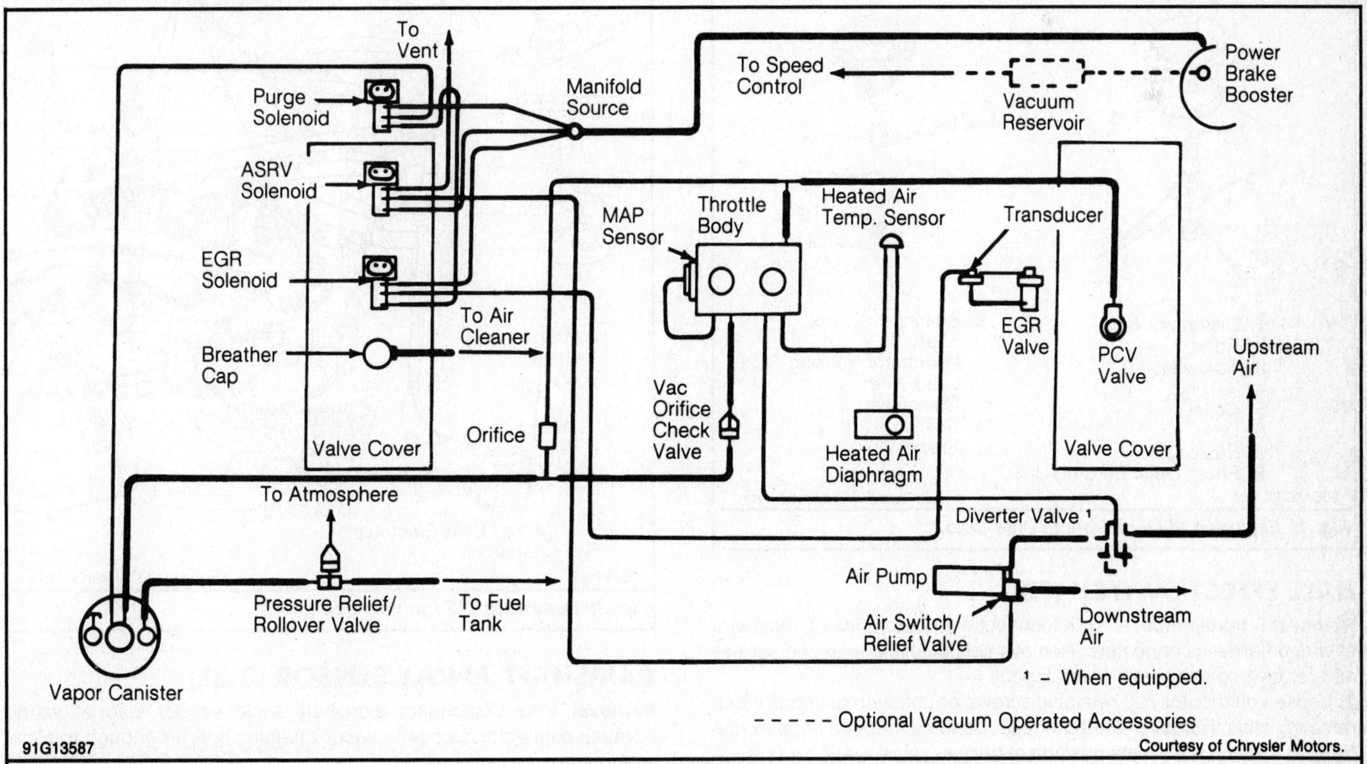
To Vent
Purge Solenoid
Manifold Source
To Speed Control
Vacuum Reservoir
Power Brake Booster
ASRV Solenoid
MAP Sensor
Throttle Body
Heated Air Temp. Sensor
Transducer
EGR Solenoid
To Air Cleaner
Breather Cap
EGR Valve
PCV Valve
Upstream Air
Vac Orifice Check Valve
Orifice
Valve Cover
Heated Air Diaphragm
Valve Cover
To Atmosphere
Diverter Valve ¹
Air Pump
Pressure Relief/ Rollover Valve
To Fuel Tank
Air Switch/ Relief Valve
Downstream Air
Vapor Canister
¹ – When equipped.
----- Optional Vacuum Operated Accessories
91G13587
Courtesy of Chrysler Motors.

Fig. 6: Vacuum Diagram (3.9L, 5.2L & 5.9L)

1991 ENGINE PERFORMANCE
Removal, Overhaul & Installation – Gasoline

Caravan, Dakota, Pickup, Ramcharger, RWD Van, Town & Country, Voyager

INTRODUCTION

Removal, overhaul and installation procedures (when given by manufacturer) are covered in this article. If component removal and installation is primarily an unbolt and bolt-on procedure, only a torque specification may be provided.

IGNITION SYSTEM

DISTRIBUTOR (3.0L OPTICAL)

Removal – 1) Disconnect distributor lead wire at wiring harness connector. Loosen distributor cap retaining screws. *See Fig. 1*. Lift off distributor cap.

2) Rotate engine crankshaft until distributor rotor is pointing toward intake plenum. Scribe a mark on plenum at this point to indicate rotor position as reference when reinstalling distributor.

3) Remove distributor hold-down nut. Carefully lift distributor from engine.

Installation – 1) Position distributor in engine. Ensure "O" ring is properly seated on distributor. Replace "O" ring if it is cracked or nicked.

2) Carefully engage distributor drive with camshaft drive so, when distributor is installed properly, rotor aligns with reference mark on intake plenum.

3) Install distributor cap. Check all high tension wires for good connections. Install and finger tighten hold-down nut. Connect distributor lead wire at wiring harness connector. Set ignition timing.

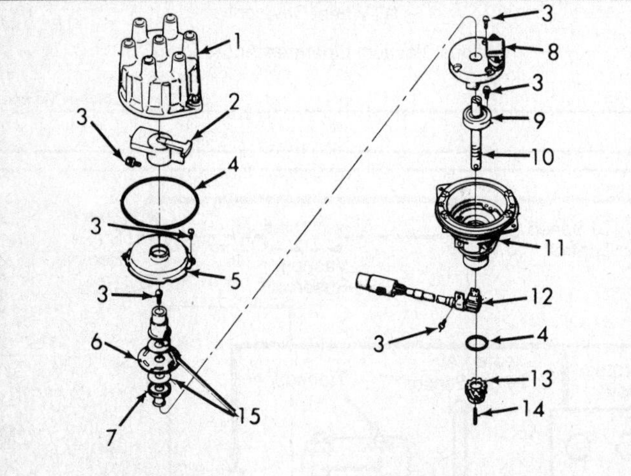
1
2
3
4
3
5
3
6
7
15
3
8
3
9
10
11
12
3
4
13
14

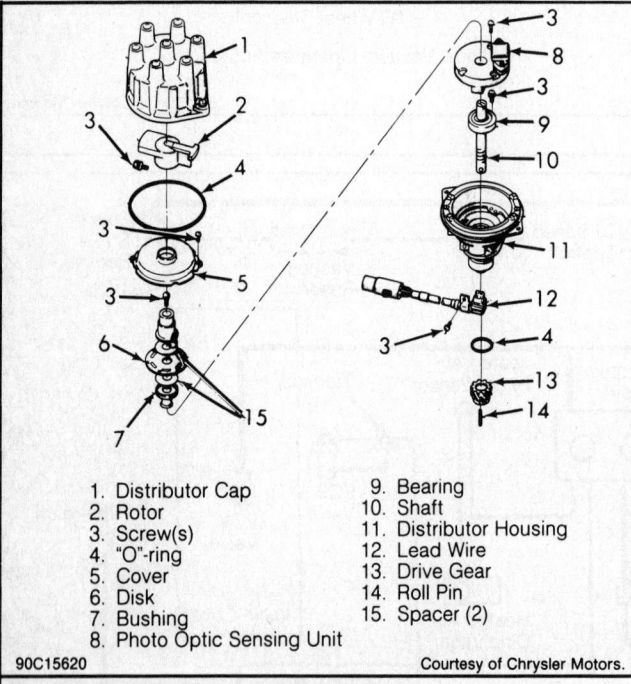

1. Distributor Cap
2. Rotor
3. Screw(s)
4. "O"-ring
5. Cover
6. Disk
7. Bushing
8. Photo Optic Sensing Unit
9. Bearing
10. Shaft
11. Distributor Housing
12. Lead Wire
13. Drive Gear
14. Roll Pin
15. Spacer (2)

90C15620 Courtesy of Chrysler Motors.

Fig. 1: Exploded View of Optical Distributor

HALL EFFECT SWITCH (TBI)

Removal & Installation – 1) Disconnect distributor pick-up lead wire at wiring harness connectors. Remove splash shield retaining screws and remove splash shield (if equipped).

2) Loosen distributor cap retaining screws or unfasten distributor cap retaining clips. Remove distributor cap. Scribe a mark on edge of distributor housing to indicate position of rotor as reinstallation reference when.

3) Remove ignition rotor from distributor shaft. On 3.9L, 5.2L and 5.9L, remove Hall Effect pick-up attaching screws on opposite sides of distributor housing. *See Fig. 2*.

4) Carefully lift Hall Effect pick-up assembly from distributor housing. To install, reverse removal procedure.

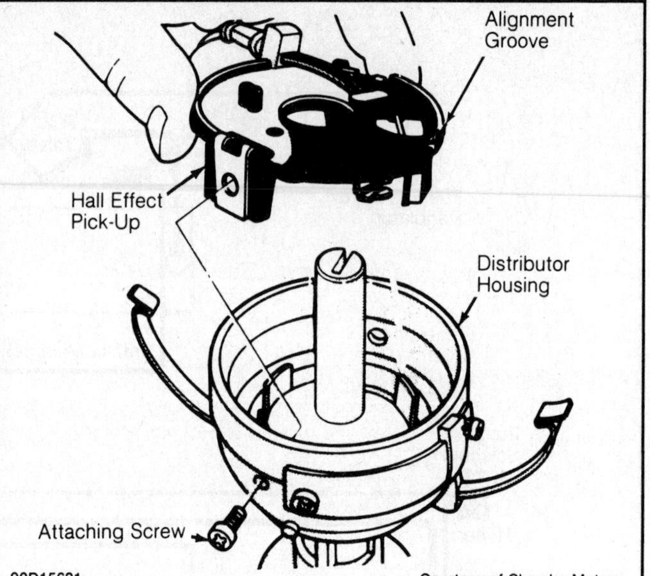
Alignment
Groove
Hall Effect
Pick-Up
Distributor
Housing
Attaching Screw

90D15621 Courtesy of Chrysler Motors.

Fig. 2: Removing Hall Effect Switch (3.9L, 5.2L & 5.9L – 2.5L Similar)

IGNITION COIL (3.3L DIS)

Removal & Installation – Remove spark plug cables from coil. *See Fig. 3*. Remove electrical connector. Remove ignition coil fasteners. To install, reverse removal procedure and tighten fasteners to 105 INCH lbs. (12 N.m).

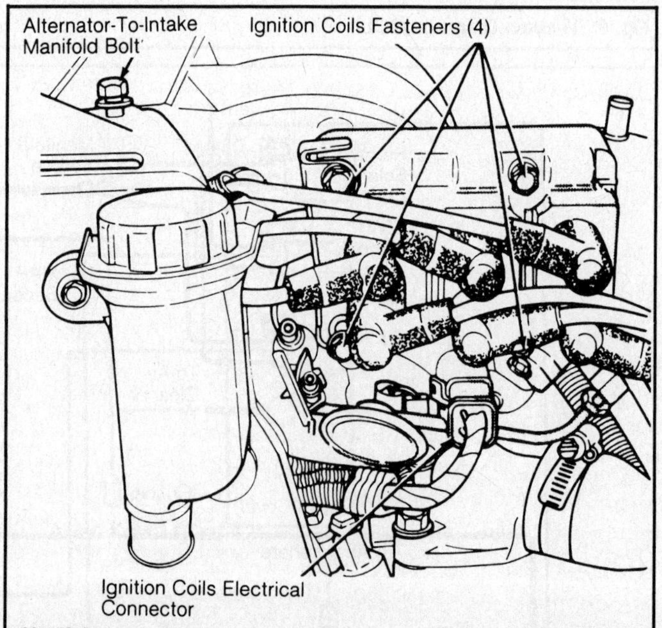
Alternator-To-Intake
Manifold Bolt
Ignition Coils Fasteners (4)
Ignition Coils Electrical
Connector

90J15619 Courtesy of Chrysler Motors.

Fig. 3: Removing DIS Ignition Coil (3.3L)

CAMSHAFT ANGLE SENSOR (3.3L)

Removal – 1) Disconnect camshaft angle sensor lead at wiring harness connector. Loosen sensor retaining bolt far enough to allow slot in sensor to slide past bolt.

2) Pull sensor up out of chain case cover. DO NOT pull on sensor lead. Removal effort will be high due to "O" ring seal on sensor. A light tap to top of sensor prior to removal may reduce removal effort.

Installation – 1) If reinstalling removed sensor, clean off old spacer on sensor face. A new spacer must be attached to face before installation. Inspect "O" ring for damage and replace if necessary.
2) If replacing sensor, confirm paper spacer is attached to sensor face and "O" ring is positioned in groove of new sensor. Apply a couple drops of clean engine oil to "O" ring prior to installation.
3) Install sensor in chain case cover. Push sensor down until it contacts cam timing gear. Hold sensor in this position and tighten retaining bolt to 105 INCH lbs. (12 N.m).
4) Connect sensor lead wire at wiring harness connector. Position lead wire away from accessory belt.

CRANKSHAFT ANGLE SENSOR (3.3L)

Removal – 1) Disconnect crankshaft angle sensor pick-up lead at wiring harness connector. *See Fig. 4.* Remove sensor retaining bolt. Pull sensor straight up out of transaxle housing.
2) If reinstalling removed sensor, clean off old spacer on sensor face. A new spacer MUST be attached to sensor face before installation. If replacing sensor, paper spacer is attached to face of new sensor.
Installation – Install sensor in transaxle and push sensor down until it contacts drive plate. Hold in this position and install retaining bolt. While still holding sensor down, tighten bolt to 105 INCH lbs. (12 N.m). Connect sensor lead wire to wiring harness connector.

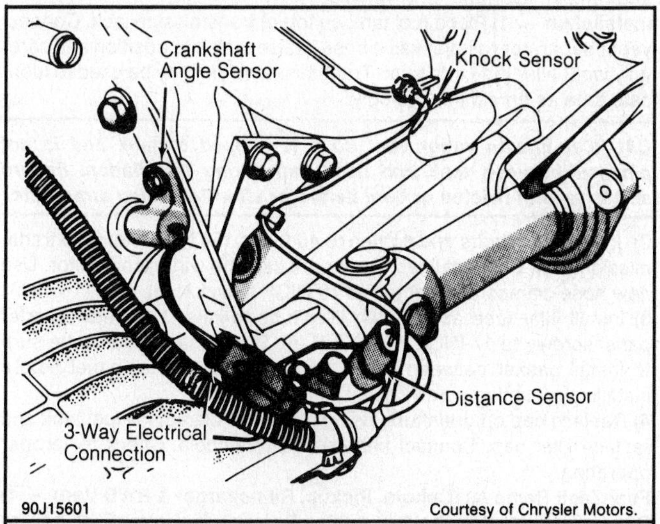
Crankshaft
Angle Sensor
Knock Sensor
Distance Sensor
3-Way Electrical
Connection
90J15601
Courtesy of Chrysler Motors.
Fig. 4: Locating Crankshaft Angle Sensor (3.3L)

FUEL SYSTEM

FUEL SYSTEM PRESSURE RELEASE

CAUTION: ALWAYS relieve pressure before disconnecting any fuel injection-related component. DO NOT allow fuel to contact engine or electrical components.

1) Loosen fuel filler cap to release tank pressure. Disconnect injector wiring harness from engine harness. Connect a jumper wire between terminal No. 1 of injector harness and engine ground. *See Fig. 5.*
2) Connect one end of a second jumper wire to terminal No. 2 of injector harness and touch other end to battery positive for no more than 5 seconds. This releases system pressure. Remove jumper wires. Continue fuel system service.

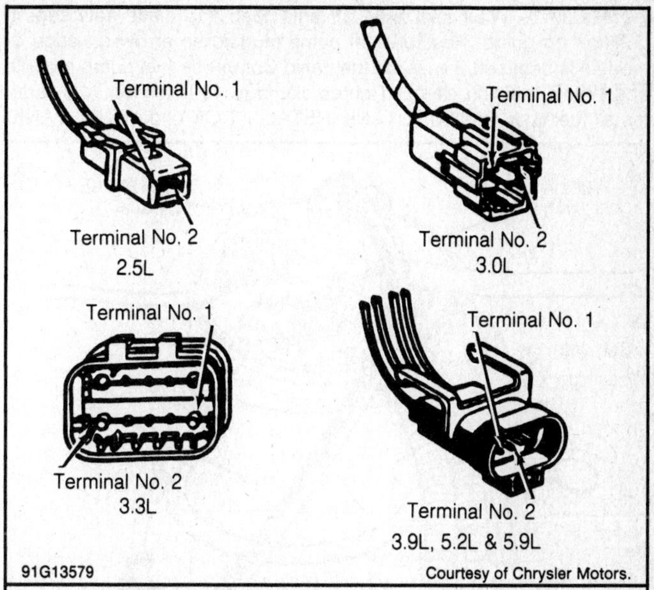
Terminal No. 1
Terminal No. 2
2.5L
Terminal No. 1
Terminal No. 2
3.0L
Terminal No. 1
Terminal No. 2
3.3L
Terminal No. 1
Terminal No. 2
3.9L, 5.2L & 5.9L
91G13579
Courtesy of Chrysler Motors.
Fig. 5: Identifying Injector Harness Connector Terminals

FUEL PUMP

Removal (Caravan, Town & Country, & Voyager) – Remove fuel tank. See FUEL TANK REMOVAL under FUEL TANK. Using a hammer and a brass drift punch, carefully tap lock ring counterclockwise to release pump. Remove fuel pump from tank. *See Fig. 6.*
Installation – Wipe seal area of tank clean. Install a new "O" ring seal in position on pump. Position fuel pump in tank so fuel return hose is not kinked. Install lock ring. Using a hammer and brass drift punch, drive ring around clockwise to lock pump in place. DO NOT overtighten pump lock ring as it may leak. Install fuel tank. See FUEL TANK INSTALLATION under FUEL TANK.

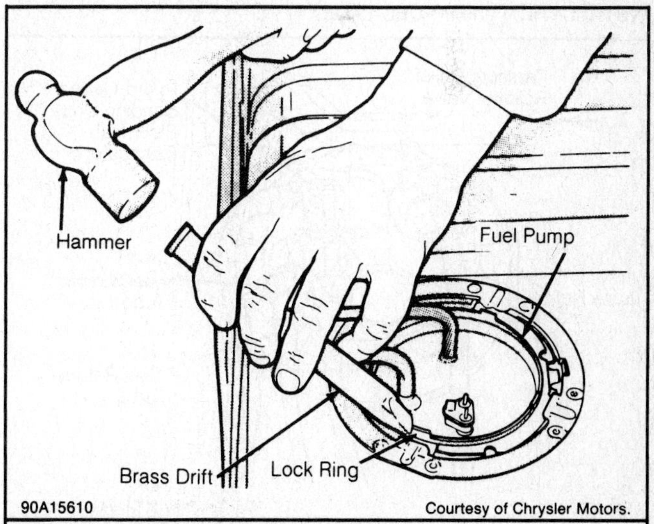
Hammer
Fuel Pump
Brass Drift
Lock Ring
90A15610
Courtesy of Chrysler Motors.
Fig. 6: Removing Fuel Pump Lock Ring (Caravan, Town & Country, & Voyager)

FUEL PUMP MODULE

Removal (All-Wheel Drive) – Release fuel system pressure. See FUEL SYSTEM PRESSURE RELEASE. Disconnect negative battery cable. Remove fuel tank. See FUEL TANK REMOVAL under FUEL TANK. Unclip fuel vapor hose and fuel drain hose from fuel tank. Remove fuel pump module retaining clamp. *See Fig. 7.* Remove fuel pump module.

Installation – Wipe seal area of tank clean and place new seal in position on pump. Position fuel pump module so arrow on edge of module is between 2 lines on fuel tank. Compress fuel pump module and install retaining clamp. Tighten clamp to 40 INCH lbs. (4.5 N.m). Install fuel tank. See FUEL TANK INSTALLATION under FUEL TANK.

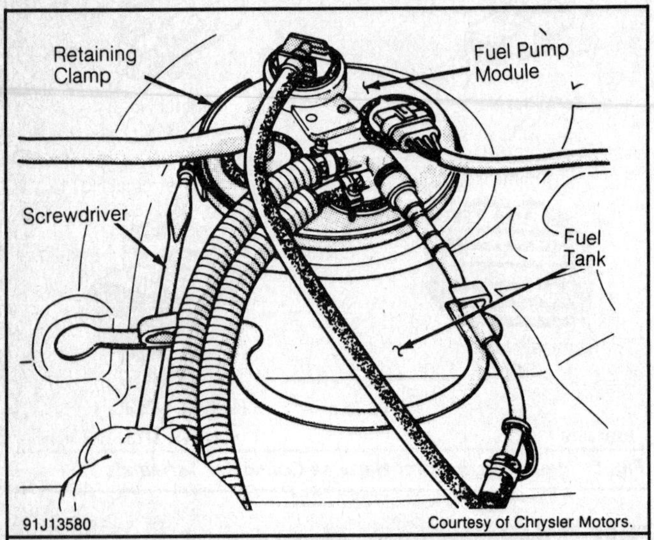
Retaining
Clamp
Fuel Pump
Module
Screwdriver
Fuel
Tank
91J13580
Courtesy of Chrysler Motors.

Fig. 7: Servicing Fuel Pump Module (All-Wheel Drive Caravan, Town & Country, & Voyager)

Removal (Except All-Wheel Drive) – Release fuel system pressure. See FUEL SYSTEM PRESSURE RELEASE. Disconnect negative battery cable. Remove fuel tank. See FUEL TANK REMOVAL under FUEL TANK. Remove fuel pump module lock nut. Lock nut is threaded onto fuel tank. *See Fig. 8*. Fuel pump module will spring up from its position when lock nut is removed. Remove module from tank.

Installation – Install fuel pump module into fuel tank. Push module down and install lock nut. Install fuel tank. See FUEL TANK INSTALLATION under FUEL TANK.

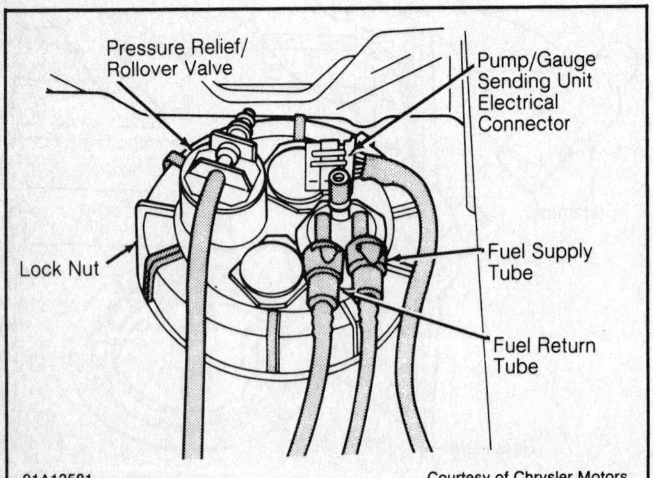
Pressure Relief/
Rollover Valve
Pump/Gauge
Sending Unit
Electrical
Connector
Lock Nut
Fuel Supply
Tube
Fuel Return
Tube
91A13581
Courtesy of Chrysler Motors.

Fig. 8: Servicing Fuel Pump Module (Except All-Wheel Drive)

FUEL TANK

Draining Fuel Tank (Caravan, Town & Country, & Voyager) – 1) Remove fuel filler cap to release fuel tank pressure. Release fuel system pressure. See FUEL SYSTEM PRESSURE RELEASE. Disconnect negative battery cable. Raise vehicle on hoist.

2) Remove drain tube rubber cap located on left frame rail and connect either a portable holding tank or a siphon hose to drain tube. Drain fuel into an appropriate gasoline safety container.

Draining Fuel Tank (Dakota, Pickup, Ramcharger & RWD Van) – 1) Remove fuel filler cap to release fuel tank pressure. Release fuel system pressure. See FUEL SYSTEM PRESSURE RELEASE. Disconnect negative battery cable. Raise vehicle on hoist.

2) Drain fuel into an appropriate gasoline safety container. If fuel pump operates, fuel can be drained through fuel supply hose. If fuel pump does not operate, but fuel level in tank is below fuel filler hose, fuel can be siphoned through fuel filler hose. Disconnect hose from filler neck. If fuel tank is full and fuel pump does not operate, drain fuel from filler neck.

3) To drain fuel tank from filler neck, support fuel tank with transmission jack. Loosen fuel tank mounting straps with passenger side strap loosened more than driver side strap. Lower tank slightly. Loosen filler neck to filler hose clamp. Slide clamp back on hose. Wrap shop towels around filler hose to absorb any spilled fuel. Disconnect filler hose from filler neck. Drain fuel tank through filler hose.

Fuel Tank Removal (Caravan, Town & Country, & Voyager) – 1) Disconnect negative battery cable. Remove fuel tank filler cap to release any tank pressure. Drain fuel tank into a suitable holding tank. See DRAINING FUEL TANK. Position vehicle on hoist. Remove screws that hold filler tube to inner and outer quarter panel.

2) Raise vehicle on hoist. Disconnect all wiring and lines from tank. Use a transmission jack to support fuel tank and remove bolts from fuel tank straps. Lower tank slightly and carefully work filler tube from tank. Lower fuel tank. Disconnect vapor separator rollover valve hose and remove fuel tank from vehicle.

Installation – 1) Place fuel tank on top of transmission jack. Connect vapor separator rollover valve hose. Raise tank into position and carefully work filler tube into tank. Transmission fluid may be used to lubricate tube as an aid in assembly.

CAUTION: Ensure vapor vent hose is clipped to tank and is not pinched between tank and floor pan during installation. Ensure straps are not twisted or bent before or after tightening strap nuts.

2) Install strap bolts and tighten to 40 ft. lbs. (54 N.m). Remove transmission jack. Connect lines, drain tube cap and wiring connector. Use new hose clamps and tighten to 10 INCH lbs. (1 N.m).

3) Install filler tube and tighten filler tube-to-inner and outer quarter panel screws to 17 INCH lbs. (1.9 N.m). On affected models, be sure to install gasket between filler tube and inner quarter panel before installing mounting screws.

4) Replace cap on drain tube using new hose clamp. Fill fuel tank and replace filler cap. Connect negative battery cable. Check for proper operation.

Fuel Tank Removal (Dakota, Pickup, Ramcharger & RWD Van) – 1) Disconnect negative battery cable. Remove fuel tank filler cap to release fuel tank pressure. Drain fuel tank into a suitable holding tank. See DRAINING FUEL TANK. Raise vehicle on hoist. Disconnect all vent hoses and filler hose.

2) Place a transmission jack under center of fuel tank and apply slight pressure. Remove fuel tank retaining straps. Lower tank on transmission jack far enough to access fuel pump module connectors.

3) Disconnect fuel tubes and fuel gauge sending unit connections from fuel pump module. Remove ground strap (if equipped). Remove fuel tank.

Installation – 1) Place fuel tank on top of transmission jack and raise high enough to connect fuel tubes and fuel gauge wire to fuel pump module. Connect fuel tubes and fuel gauge wire to fuel pump module.

2) Raise tank into position. Install ground strap (if equipped). Install fuel tank mounting straps. On Ramcharger, connect and tighten nuts to end of threads on "J" bolts. On all other models, tighten straps to 35 ft. lbs. (47 N.m). Remove transmission jack.

3) Connect vent hoses, filler tube and drain tube cap. Install new hose clamps and tighten securely. Connect fuel line if disconnected earlier. Refill tank and inspect all hoses and lines for leaks. Reconnect negative battery cable. Pressurize system and check for leaks.

FUEL INJECTOR RAILS (PFI)

Removal (3.0L) – 1) Release fuel system pressure. See FUEL SYSTEM PRESSURE RELEASE. Disconnect negative battery cable.

2) Remove air cleaner-to-throttle body hose. Remove throttle cable and transaxle kickdown linkage (if equipped). Remove wiring connectors for automatic idle speed motor and throttle position sensor from throttle body.

3) Remove vacuum/vapor harness from throttle body. Remove brake booster hose from air intake plenum. Remove ignition coil from air intake plenum. Disconnect coolant temperature sensor.

4) Remove vacuum connections from air intake plenum vacuum connector. Remove fuel hoses from fuel rail. Remove fasteners attaching air intake plenum to intake manifold. Remove air intake plenum.

5) Cover intake manifold with suitable cover when servicing. Remove vacuum hoses from fuel rail. Disconnect fuel injector wiring harness from engine wiring harness.

6) Remove fuel pressure regulator attaching bolts. Remove regulator from rail. Remove fuel rail attaching bolts and lift fuel rail assembly from intake manifold.

CAUTION: Carefully remove fuel injectors and fuel pressure regulator. DO NOT damage rubber "O" rings.

Installation – 1) Ensure injectors are seated into receiver cups on rail with lock rings in place. See FUEL INJECTORS. Ensure injector holes are clean and all plugs have been removed.

2) Lubricate injector "O" rings with a drop of clean engine oil to ease installation. Push the tip of each injector into its port. Push entire assembly into place until injectors are seated in ports.

3) Install 3 fuel rail attaching bolts and tighten to 115 INCH lbs. (13 N.m). Lubricate fuel pressure regulator "O" ring with a drop of clean engine oil. Install fuel pressure regulator onto fuel rail.

4) Install fuel pressure regulator attaching bolts and tighten to 77 INCH lbs. (8.7 N.m). Install fuel supply and return tube hold-down bolt. Install vacuum crossover tube hold-down bolt. Tighten both bolts to 95 INCH lbs. (10 N.m).

5) Tighten fuel pressure regulator hose clamps to 10 INCH lbs. (1 N.m). Connect fuel injector wiring harness to engine wiring harness. Connect vacuum harness to fuel rail assembly. Remove covering from lower intake manifold. Clean manifold surface.

6) Place intake manifold gaskets with beaded sealer up on lower manifold. Place air intake plenum in position. Loosely install ignition coil to intake manifold. Install manifold attaching fasteners.

7) Tighten the 8 manifold fasteners to 115 INCH lbs. (13 N.m). Tighten the 2 ignition coil fasteners to 96 INCH lbs. (10 N.m). Connect fuel line to fuel rail. Tighten hose clamps to 10 INCH lbs. (1 N.m).

8) Connect vacuum harness to air intake plenum and fuel pressure regulator. Reconnect coolant temperature sensor electrical connector. Connect brake booster supply hose to intake plenum.

9) Reconnect automatic idle speed motor and throttle position sensor wiring connectors. Connect vacuum/vapor hose harness to throttle body.

10) Install throttle cable and transaxle kickdown linkage (if equipped). Install air inlet hose assembly. Connect negative battery cable. Pressure test system for leaks.

Removal (3.3L) – 1) Release fuel system pressure. See FUEL SYSTEM PRESSURE RELEASE. Disconnect negative battery cable.

2) Remove air cleaner-to-throttle body hose. Remove throttle cable. Remove wiring harness from throttle cable bracket and intake manifold water tube. Remove wiring connectors for automatic idle speed motor and throttle position sensor from throttle body.

3) Remove vacuum hose harness from throttle body. Remove PCV and brake booster hoses from air intake plenum. Remove EGR tube flange from intake plenum. Disconnect charge temperature sensor.

4) Remove vacuum harness connections from air intake plenum. Remove cylinder head-to-intake plenum strut. Disconnect MAP sensor and oxygen sensor electrical connectors.

5) Remove engine-mounted ground strap. Remove fuel hose quick-connect fitting from fuel rail by pushing in on plastic ring located on end of fittings. Gently pull fittings from fuel rail.

WARNING: Wrap a shop towel around hoses to catch any spilled gasoline.

6) Remove direct ignition system coils. See IGNITION COIL under IGNITION SYSTEM. Remove alternator bracket-to-intake manifold bolt. Remove intake manifold bolts, and rotate manifold back over rear valve cover.

7) Cover intake manifold with a suitable cover when servicing. Remove vacuum hose harness connector from fuel pressure regulator. Remove fuel tube retainer bracket screw and fuel rail attaching bolts. Spread the retainer bracket to allow fuel tube removal clearance.

8) Remove fuel rail injector wiring clip from alternator bracket. Disconnect cam sensor, coolant temperature sensor and engine temperature sensor connectors.

9) Remove fuel rail. DO NOT damage rubber "O" rings on injectors when removing injectors from their ports. Replace "O" rings if damaged.

Installation – 1) Ensure injectors are seated into receiver cups on rail with lock rings in place. See FUEL INJECTORS. Ensure injector holes are clean and all plugs have been removed. Replace "O" rings if damaged.

2) Lubricate injector "O" rings with a drop of clean engine oil to ease installation. Push the tip of each injector into its port. Push entire assembly into place until injectors are seated in ports.

3) Install 4 fuel rail attaching bolts and tighten to 17 ft. lbs. (22 N.m). Install fuel tube retaining bracket screw and tighten to 35 INCH lbs. (4 N.m). Reconnect cam sensor, coolant temperature sensor and engine temperature sensor.

4) Reconnect fuel injector wiring harness to engine harness. Install fuel injector wiring harness wiring clips on alternator bracket and intake manifold water tube. Connect fuel pressure regulator vacuum hose. Remove covering on lower intake manifold, and clean manifold surface.

5) Place intake manifold gasket on lower manifold. Put upper manifold into place and install bolts finger tight. Install and finger tighten alternator bracket-to-intake manifold bolt and cylinder head-to-intake manifold strut bolts.

6) Tighten upper-to-lower intake manifold bolts to 21 ft. lbs. (28 N.m) following torque sequence. *See Fig. 9*. Tighten alternator bracket-to-intake manifold bolt to 40 ft. lbs. (54 N.m). Tighten cylinder head-to-intake manifold strut bolts to 40 ft. lbs. (54 N.m).

7) Install ground strap. Reconnect MAP sensor, oxygen sensor and charge temperature sensor electrical connectors. Connect vacuum hose harness to intake plenum.

8) Connect PCV system. Using a new gasket, connect EGR tube flange to intake manifold and tighten to 17 ft. lbs. (22 N.m).

9) Clip wiring harness into hole in throttle cable bracket. Connect wiring connectors to throttle position sensor and automatic idle speed motor. Connect vacuum harness to throttle body.

10) Install direct ignition system coils. See IGNITION COIL under IGNITION SYSTEM. Tighten fasteners to 105 INCH lbs. (12 N.m). Install fuel hose quick-connect fittings to fuel rail. Push each fitting onto rail until it clicks into place. Fuel supply fitting is 5/16" and fuel return fitting is 1/4".

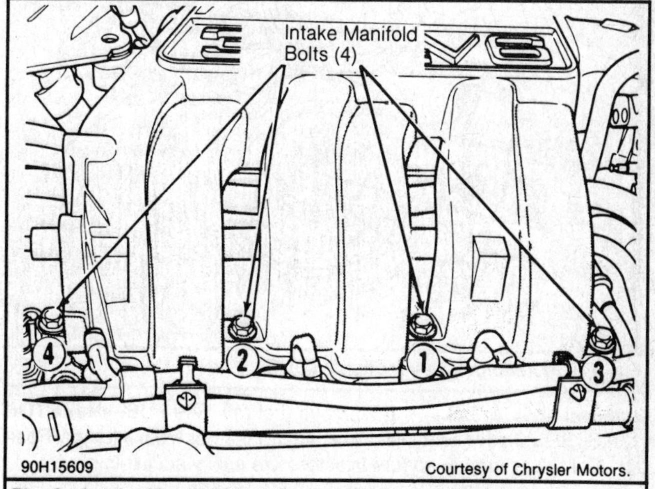

Intake Manifold
Bolts (4)
4
2
1
3

90H15609 Courtesy of Chrysler Motors.

Fig. 9: Intake Manifold Bolt Torque Sequence (3.3L)

11) Install throttle cable. Install air cleaner and hose assembly. Connect negative battery cable. Pressure test system for leaks.

FUEL INJECTORS

Removal (2.5L) – 1) Remove air cleaner assembly. Release fuel system pressure. See FUEL SYSTEM PRESSURE RELEASE. Disconnect negative battery cable. Remove injector hold-down clamp Torx screw.

2) With 2 small screwdrivers, lift the top off injector using slots provided. *See Fig. 10.* Using a small screwdriver placed in hole in the front of electrical connector, gently pry injector from pod. Ensure lower "O" ring has been removed from pod.

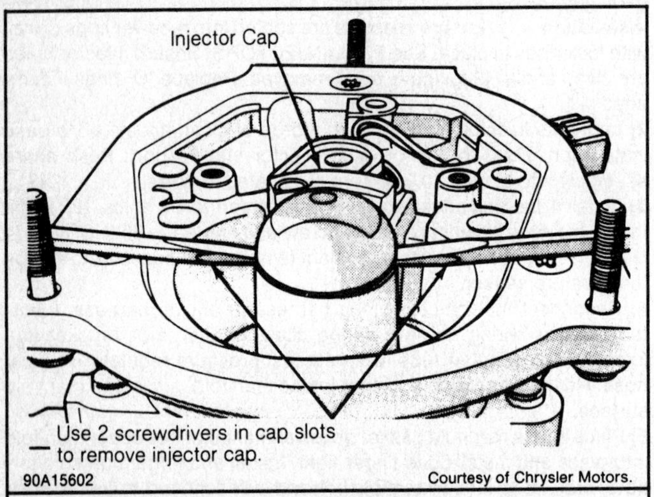
Injector Cap
Use 2 screwdrivers in cap slots to remove injector cap.
90A15602
Courtesy of Chrysler Motors.

Fig. 10: Removing Fuel Injector Cap (2.5L)

Installation – 1) Place a new "O" ring on injector cap. New injector has new upper and lower "O" ring already installed. Apply a light coating of clean engine oil on "O" rings.

2) Place assembly in pod and align injector wiring terminals with injector cap fastener hole. *See Fig. 11.* Install injector cap with locating notch aligned with locating lobe on injector.

3) Push down on cap to ensure a good seal. Rotate cap and injector to line up attachment hole. Install Torx screw and tighten to 35-45 INCH lbs. (4-5 N.m). Reconnect negative battery cable. Pressure test system for leaks. Reinstall air cleaner assembly.

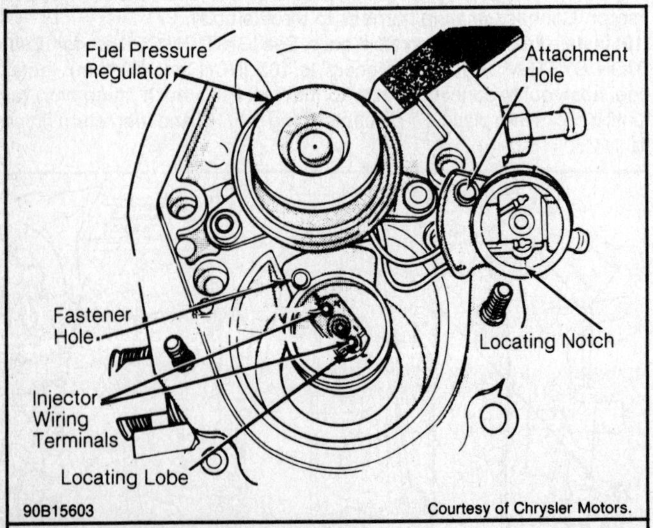
Fuel Pressure Regulator
Attachment Hole
Fastener Hole
Locating Notch
Injector Wiring Terminals
Locating Lobe
90B15603
Courtesy of Chrysler Motors.

Fig. 11: Installing Fuel Injector (2.5L)

Removal (3.0L & 3.3L) – 1) Remove fuel rail. See FUEL INJECTOR RAILS (PFI). Disconnect injector wiring connector from injector. Position fuel rail assembly so fuel injectors are easily accessible.

2) Remove injector lock ring from fuel rail. *See Fig. 12.* Remove injector. Inspect injector "O" ring for damage. Replace "O" ring if damaged. If injector is to be reused, a protective cap must be installed on injector tip to prevent damage. Repeat for remaining injectors.

Installation – 1) Lubricate "O" ring of each injector with a drop of clean engine oil to aid in installation. Install injector top end into fuel rail receiver cup. Be careful not to damage "O" ring during installation. Install injector lock ring.

2) Repeat for remaining injectors. Install wiring harness to injectors. Fasten wiring harness into wiring clips (if equipped).

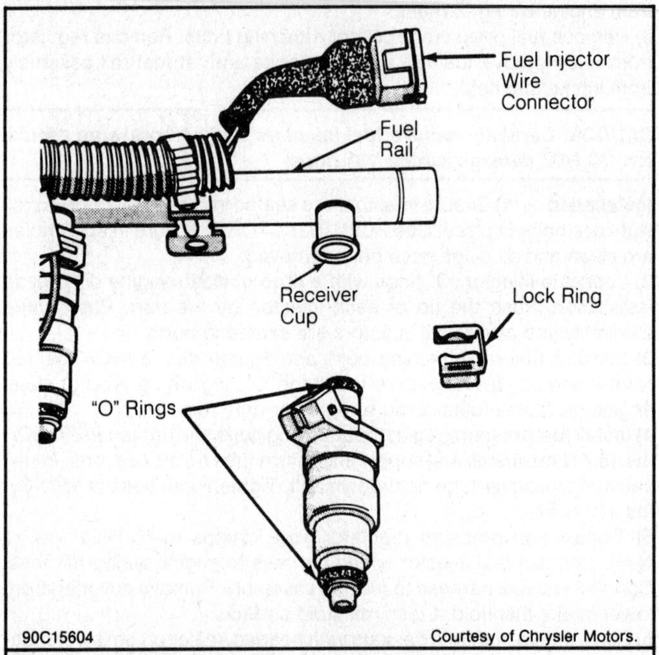
Fuel Injector Wire Connector
Fuel Rail
Receiver Cup
Lock Ring
"O" Rings
90C15604
Courtesy of Chrysler Motors.

Fig. 12: Servicing Fuel Injectors (3.0L & 3.3L)

Removal (3.9L, 5.2L & 5.9L) – 1) Remove air cleaner assembly. Release fuel system pressure. See FUEL SYSTEM PRESSURE RELEASE. Disconnect negative battery cable. Remove injector hold-down clamp Torx screw. *See Fig. 13.*

CAUTION: DO NOT damage loose spacer under clamp.

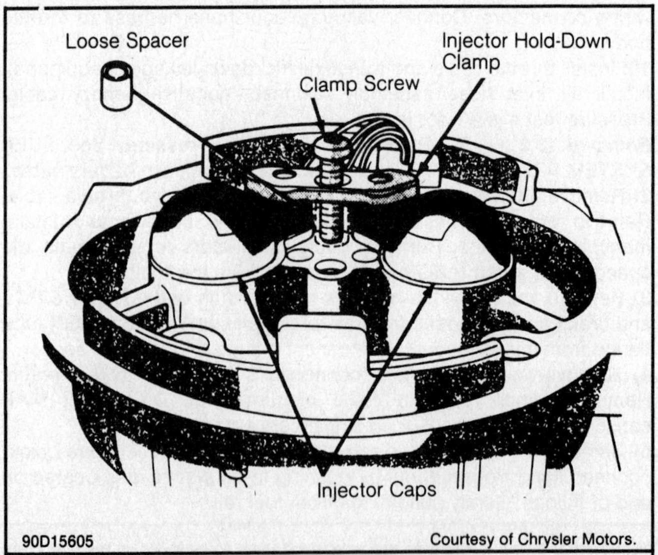
Loose Spacer
Injector Hold-Down Clamp
Clamp Screw
Injector Caps
90D15605
Courtesy of Chrysler Motors.

Fig. 13: Removing Fuel Injector Cap Hold-Down (3.9L, 5.2L & 5.9L)

2) Using a small screwdriver and the area in front of hold-down clamp for leverage, lift the caps off injectors. Using a small screwdriver placed in hole in front of electrical connector, gently pry the injectors from pods. *See Fig. 14*. Ensure each injector lower "O" ring has been removed from pod.

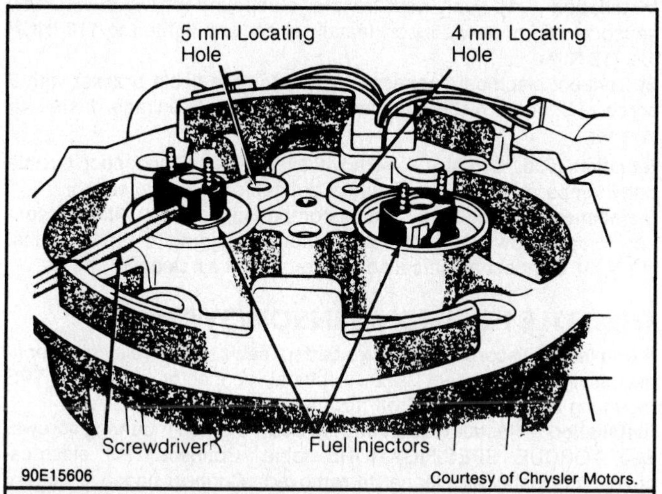

5 mm Locating Hole
4 mm Locating Hole
Screwdriver
Fuel Injectors
90E15606
Courtesy of Chrysler Motors.

Fig. 14: Removing Fuel Injector (3.9L, 5.2L & 5.9L)

Installation – 1) Install lower "O" ring on injector. "O" ring should butt against plastic filter assembly. Inspect both "O" rings for cuts or tears and replace if necessary. Align injector terminal housing with locating socket in injector cap.

2) Press injector into cap so upper "O" ring flange is flush with lower surface of cap. Spray inner surfaces of injector pod with Mopar Brake and Carburetor Parts Cleaner to remove residual gasoline.

3) Lightly lubricate upper and lower "O" rings with petroleum jelly. Place injector and cap in injector pod and align cap locating pin with locating hole in casting. *See Fig. 14*.

CAUTION: Passenger side cap locating pin is 5 mm in diameter and will only fit in passenger side locating hole. Driver side locating pin is 4 mm in diameter.

4) Repeat steps **1)-3)** for other injector and cap. Press firmly on injector caps until flush with casting surface. Place injector hold-down clamp with spacer on rear portion of caps, aligning holes in clamp with pins on caps. Install clamp screw. Ensure spacer is in place.

CAUTION: Because "O" ring may cause caps to lift up, press firmly on both caps with one hand to ensure caps are flush while installing clamp screw.

5) Tighten screw to 35 INCH lbs. (4 N.m). Connect negative battery cable. Pressure test system for leaks. Reinstall air cleaner assembly.

FUEL PRESSURE DAMPENER (3.3L)

WARNING: Place a shop towel under all quick-connect fittings before disconnecting to absorb any spilled fuel.

Removal – 1) Release fuel system pressure. See FUEL SYSTEM PRESSURE RELEASE. Remove Direct Ignition System (DIS) coil pack electrical connector.

2) Remove DIS coil fasteners and rotate to access fuel pressure dampener. *See Fig. 15*. Disconnect fuel hose quick-connect fitting by pushing in on plastic ring located at end of fitting. Slide fitting off fuel tube.

3) Disconnect coolant temperature sensor electrical connector. Remove fuel rail retainer bracket screw.

4) Using 2 open-end wrenches, one on return tube nut and other on fuel rail hex, loosen tube nut. Use 2 wrenches to avoid damaging tube nut. Remove fuel pressure dampener.

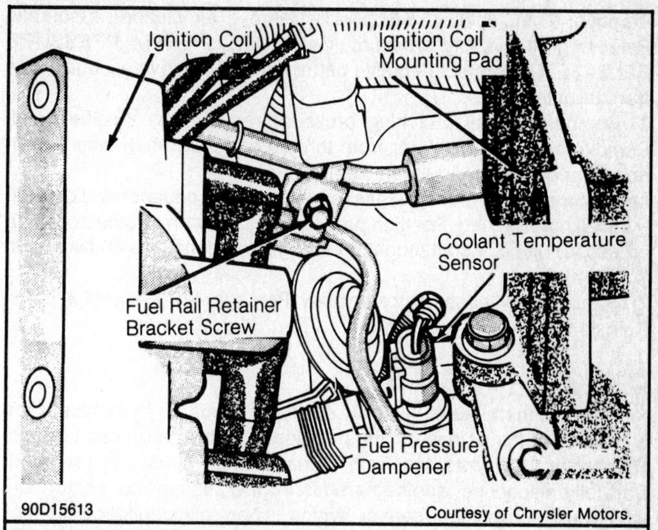

Ignition Coil
Ignition Coil Mounting Pad
Coolant Temperature Sensor
Fuel Rail Retainer Bracket Screw
Fuel Pressure Dampener
90D15613
Courtesy of Chrysler Motors.

Fig. 15: Accessing Fuel Pressure Dampener (3.3L)

Installation – 1) Insert and finger tighten return tube nut into fuel rail hex. Place fuel return tube into fuel rail retainer bracket. Insert fuel rail retainer bracket screw and tighten to 35 INCH lbs. (4 N.m).

2) Connect coolant temperature sensor electrical connector. Place DIS coils in position and install fasteners. Tighten to 105 INCH lbs. (12 N.m). Connect DIS coil 4-way electrical connector.

3) Insert fuel hose quick-connect fitting onto fuel tube until a click is heard. Pressure test system for leaks.

FUEL PRESSURE REGULATOR

Removal & Installation (3.0L) – See FUEL INJECTOR RAILS (PFI).

Removal (3.3L) – 1) Release fuel system pressure. See FUEL SYSTEM PRESSURE RELEASE. Disconnect negative battery cable. Remove fuel pressure regulator vacuum connector.

2) Remove regulator retainer screw. Remove fuel pressure regulator retainer. Remove fuel pressure regulator.

Installation – 1) Ensure fuel pressure regulator has 2 plastic spacers. Ensure fuel rail has 2 "O" rings installed in fuel pressure regulator cavity. *See Fig. 16*.

2) Lubricate "O" rings with clean engine oil. Insert fuel pressure regulator into fuel rail. Install fuel pressure regulator retainer.

3) Install retainer screw. Tighten to 50 INCH lbs. (5.6 N.m). Connect fuel pressure regulator vacuum connection. Pressure test system for leaks.

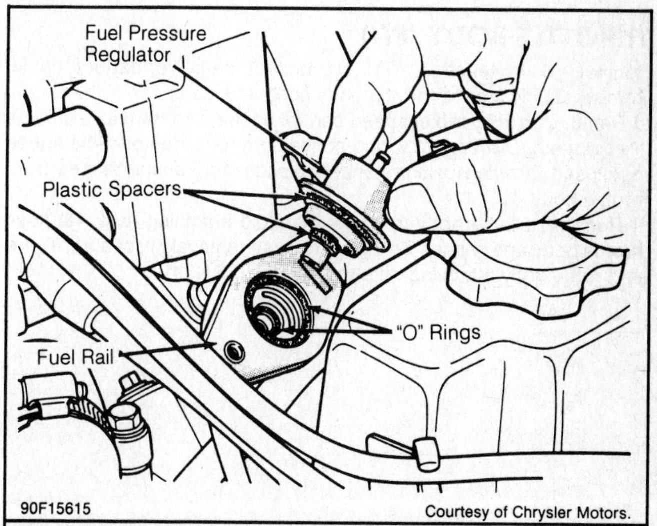

Fuel Pressure Regulator
Plastic Spacers
"O" Rings
Fuel Rail
90F15615
Courtesy of Chrysler Motors.

Fig. 16: Servicing Fuel Pressure Regulator (3.3L)

1991 ENGINE PERFORMANCE
Removal, Overhaul & Installation – Gasoline (Cont.)

Removal (3.9L, 5.2L & 5.9L) – 1) Remove air cleaner assembly. Release fuel system pressure. See FUEL SYSTEM PRESSURE RELEASE. Disconnect negative battery cable. Remove vacuum hose from throttle body.
2) Remove screws attaching pressure regulator to throttle body. Remove pressure regulator from throttle body. Carefully remove "O" ring from pressure regulator. Remove gasket.
Installation – 1) Place new gasket on pressure regulator and carefully install new "O" ring. Position pressure regulator on throttle body and press into place. Install mounting screws and tighten to 40 INCH lbs. (4.5 N.m).
2) Install vacuum hose to throttle body. Pressure test system for leaks. Reinstall air cleaner assembly.

OXYGEN (O_2) SENSOR

Removal & Installation – 1) O_2 sensor is mounted in exhaust pipe just below exhaust header. It is equipped with a permanent pigtail, which must be protected from damage when sensor is removed. Carefully disconnect engine harness from O_2 sensor connector. DO NOT pull on oxygen sensor wiring when disconnecting sensor connector. Remove O_2 sensor with Socket (C-4907). Sensor may be difficult to remove when engine temperature is less than 120°F (48°C).
2) Ensure sensor is free of contaminants; avoid using cleaning solvents of any type. Clean the threads in exhaust manifold with an 18 mm x 1.5 x 6E tap. If installing original sensor, the sensor threads must be coated with an anti-seize compound. New O_2 sensors are packaged with compound already on threads. Tighten sensor to 20 ft. lbs. (27 N.m).

THROTTLE BODY (TBI)

Removal – 1) Remove air cleaner. Release fuel system pressure. See FUEL SYSTEM PRESSURE RELEASE. Disconnect negative battery cable. Disconnect vacuum hoses and electrical connectors from throttle body.
2) Remove throttle cable, speed control cable and transmission kickdown cables (if equipped). Remove throttle return spring. Remove fuel intake and return hoses.
3) Remove throttle body mounting screws, and lift throttle body from vehicle. Remove throttle body gasket from intake manifold.
Installation – 1) Using a new gasket, install throttle body and tighten mounting screws to 15 ft. lbs. (20 N.m). Install fuel intake and return hoses using new original-equipment type clamps.
2) Install throttle return spring. Install throttle cable. Install speed control and transmission kickdown cables (if equipped). Install wiring connectors and vacuum hoses. Install air cleaner. Reconnect negative battery cable.

THROTTLE BODY (PFI)

Removal & Installation – 1) Disconnect negative battery cable. Remove air cleaner-to-throttle body hose and clamp.
2) Remove throttle cable, speed control cables and transaxle linkage (if equipped). Disconnect wiring connectors for automatic idle speed motor and throttle position sensor. Disconnect vacuum hoses from throttle body.
3) Remove throttle body-to-intake manifold attaching nuts. Remove throttle body and gasket. To install, reverse removal procedure. Tighten throttle body attaching nuts to 19 ft. lbs (26 N.m).

THROTTLE BODY TEMPERATURE SENSOR

Removal (2.5L) – Remove air cleaner. Disconnect throttle cables from throttle body linkage. Remove 2 screws from throttle cable bracket and lay bracket aside. Disconnect wiring connector by pulling downward. Unscrew sensor.
Installation – 1) Apply heat transfer compound (provided with new sensor) to tip of new sensor. Install sensor and tighten to 110 INCH lbs. (12 N.m).
2) Connect electrical connector. Install throttle cable bracket with 2 screws. Connect throttle cables to throttle body linkage. Install air cleaner.
Removal (5.2L & 5.9L) – Remove air cleaner. Disconnect throttle body temperature sensor electrical connector. Remove sensor.
Installation – Apply heat transfer compound (provided with new sensor) to tip of new sensor. Install sensor and tighten to 110 INCH lbs. (12 N.m). Connect electrical connector. Install air cleaner.

THROTTLE POSITION SENSOR/SWITCH

Removal – Disconnect negative battery cable. Remove air cleaner (if necessary). Disconnect TPS electrical connector. Remove TPS mounting screws. Lift TPS off throttle shaft.
Installation – Install TPS on throttle body. Tighten mounting screws. See TORQUE SPECIFICATIONS table. Connect TPS electrical connector. Install air cleaner (if removed). Connect negative battery cable.

TORQUE SPECIFICATIONS

TORQUE SPECIFICATIONS

Application	Ft. Lbs. (N.m)
Alternator Bracket-To-Intake Manifold Bolt	40 (54)
Cylinder Head-To-Intake Manifold Strut Bolts	40 (54)
EGR Tube Flange-To-Manifold	17 (22)
Fuel Rail Attaching Bolts (3.3L)	17 (22)
Fuel Tank Attaching Bolts	
Caravan, Town & Country, & Voyager	40 (54)
Fuel Tank Attaching Nuts	
Dakota, Pickup & RWD Van	35 (47)
Intake Manifold Bolts (3.3L)	21 (28)
Oxygen Sensor	20 (27)
Throttle Body Mounting Nuts	
3.0L & 3.3L	19 (26)
2.5L, 3.9L, 5.2L & 5.9L	15 (20)
	INCH Lbs. (N.m)
Camshaft Angle Sensor Bolt	105 (12)
Crankshaft Angle Sensor Bolt	105 (12)
Crossover Tube Hold-down Bolt	95 (10)
Fuel Injector Torx Screws (2.5L)	35-45 (4-5)
Fuel Pressure Regulator Attaching Bolts (3.0L)	77 (8.7)
Fuel Pressure Regulator Retaining Screw	50 (5.6)
Fuel Pump Module Retaining Clamp	40 (54)
Fuel Rail Attaching Bolts (3.0L)	115 (13)
Ignition Coil Fasteners (3.0L)	96 (10)
Ignition Coil Fasteners (3.3L)	105 (12)
Manifold Fasteners (3.0L)	115 (13)
Throttle Body Temperature Sensor	110 (12)
Throttle Position Sensor Screws	
2.5L	20 (2.3)
3.0L & 3.3L	17 (2.0)
3.9L, 5.2L & 5.9L	27 (3.0)

Pickup

INTRODUCTION

Removal, overhaul and installation procedures are covered in this article. If component removal and installation is primarily an unbolt and bolt-on procedure, only a torque specification may be furnished.

AIR INDUCTION SYSTEM

TURBOCHARGER ASSEMBLY

Removal - 1) Disconnect negative battery cable. Remove air intake piping and exhaust pipe at turbocharger. On intercooled models, remove intercooler inlet duct from turbocharger. *See Fig. 4.* On non-intercooled models, remove air crossover tube between turbocharger and intake manifold.

2) Remove and plug turbocharger oil lines. Remove turbocharger retaining nuts and turbocharger. Plug all air intake and oil line openings.

NOTE: Compressor and turbine assembly is a balanced unit. If, during disassembly, compressor or turbine wheel are damaged, turbine shaft and wheel, and compressor wheel MUST be replaced as an assembly.

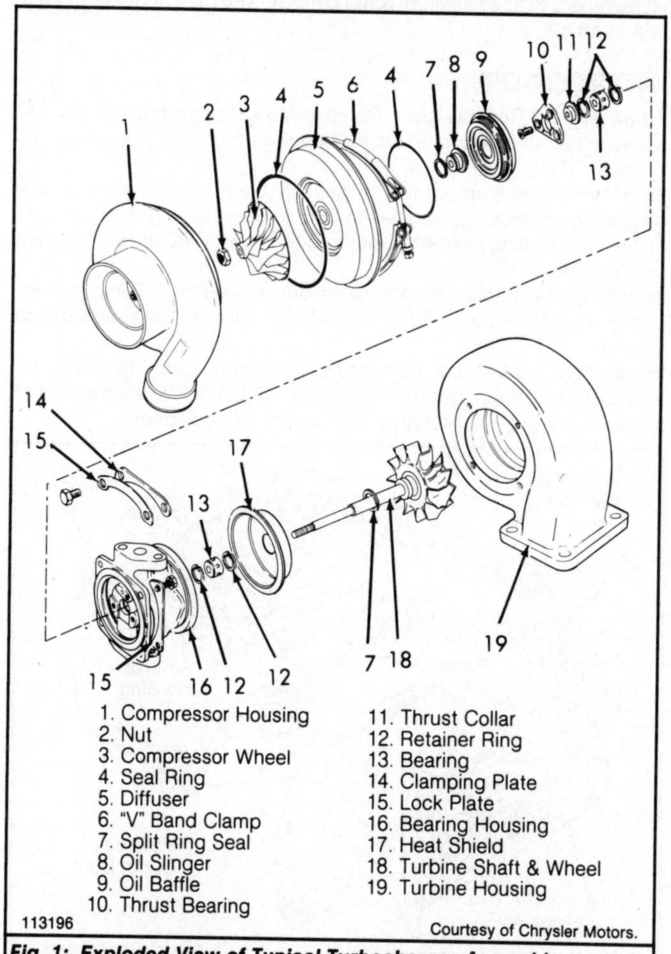
1
2
3
4
5
6
4
7
8
9
10
11
12
13
14
15
17
13
15
16
12
12
7
18
19
1. Compressor Housing
2. Nut
3. Compressor Wheel
4. Seal Ring
5. Diffuser
6. "V" Band Clamp
7. Split Ring Seal
8. Oil Slinger
9. Oil Baffle
10. Thrust Bearing
11. Thrust Collar
12. Retainer Ring
13. Bearing
14. Clamping Plate
15. Lock Plate
16. Bearing Housing
17. Heat Shield
18. Turbine Shaft & Wheel
19. Turbine Housing
113196
Courtesy of Chrysler Motors.

Fig. 1: Exploded View of Typical Turbocharger Assembly

Disassembly - 1) Place reference mark on turbine housing, bearing housing and compressor housing for reassembly reference. Clamp turbocharger housing in soft-jawed vise. Remove "V" band clamp. *See Fig. 1.* Remove compressor housing and seal ring.

CAUTION: Turbine shaft and nut have left-hand threads.

2) Hold turbine shaft and wheel from turning while removing compressor wheel nut. Note alignment marks on turbine shaft and compressor wheel. *See Fig. 2.*

3) Remove left-hand thread retaining nut and compressor wheel. Bend out diffuser retaining bolt lock plates, and remove bolts. Remove diffuser and seal ring. Note alignment marks on oil slinger and turbine shaft. *See Fig. 2.* Remove oil slinger and split ring seal. Remove oil baffle.

4) Remove thrust bearing. Note alignment marks on thrust collar and turbine shaft. *See Fig. 2.* Remove thrust collar. Inspect thrust collar for wear. Thrust bearing must be replaced and cannot be reused. Remove turbine housing, lock plates and clamping plates.

5) Remove bearing housing from turbine housing. Remove turbine shaft and wheel along with heat shield from bearing housing. Remove split ring seals from shaft.

6) Remove outer retainer rings from bearing housing, and remove bearings. Remove inner retainer rings from bearing housing.

Cleaning & Inspection - 1) Using nylon brush and solvent, clean all components. Clean carbon from turbine housing. Turbine shaft and wheel bearing surfaces can be polished with crocus cloth and kerosene.

CAUTION: DO NOT bead blast components or use wire brush to clean compressor wheel.

2) Inspect compressor housing and compressor wheel for contact. Inspect oil slinger and diffuser for cracks. Inspect thrust collar for wear. Inspect turbine shaft and wheel for cracks or damaged blades.

3) Measure O.D. of turbine shaft. Turbine shaft and wheel and compressor wheel must be replaced as an assembly if not within specification. See TURBOCHARGER SPECIFICATIONS table. Replace damaged components.

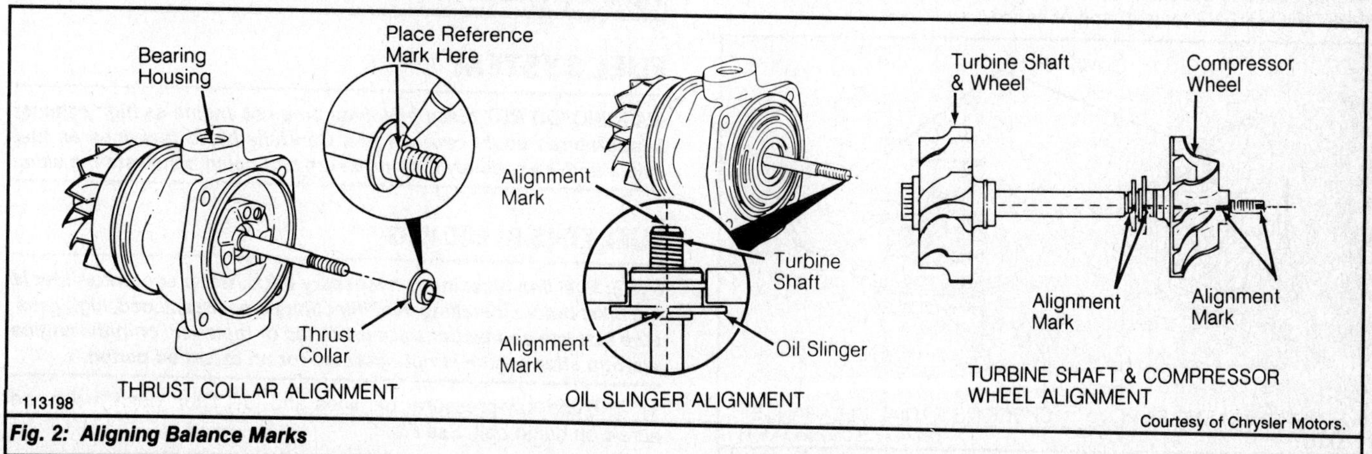
Bearing Housing
Place Reference Mark Here
Thrust Collar
THRUST COLLAR ALIGNMENT
113198
Alignment Mark
Turbine Shaft
Alignment Mark
Oil Slinger
OIL SLINGER ALIGNMENT
Turbine Shaft & Wheel
Compressor Wheel
Alignment Mark
Alignment Mark
TURBINE SHAFT & COMPRESSOR WHEEL ALIGNMENT
Courtesy of Chrysler Motors.

Fig. 2: Aligning Balance Marks

1991 ENGINE PERFORMANCE
Removal, Overhaul & Installation – Diesel (Cont.)

TURBOCHARGER SPECIFICATIONS

Application	In. (mm)
Turbine Shaft Clearances	
End Play	[1]
Radial Clearance	.012-.018 (.30-.46)
Turbine Shaft Minimum O.D.	.432 (10.97)

[1] – On turbochargers with serial No. 840637 and earlier, end play should be .004-.006" (.10-.15 mm). On turbochargers with serial No. 840638 and later, end play should be .001-.003" (.03-.08 mm).

CAUTION: During reassembly, thrust bearing, all split ring seals, seal rings, retainer rings and bearings MUST be replaced. DO NOT reuse these components.

Reassembly – 1) Install split ring seal on turbine shaft and lubricate with oil. Install heat shield. Place turbine shaft and wheel in socket, and clamp in soft-jawed vise. Install inner retainer rings in bearing housing with chamfered edge toward bearing.

CAUTION: Inner and outer bearing retainer rings must be installed with chamfered edge toward bearing. Rotate bearing housing during installation on turbine shaft to seat split ring seals.

2) Lubricate bearings with oil and install. Install outer retainer rings with chamfered edge toward bearing. Install bearing housing over turbine shaft and wheel. Rotate bearing housing during installation to seat split ring seals.

3) Install thrust collar. Ensure alignment marks on thrust collar and turbine shaft are aligned. *See Fig. 2.* Place reference mark on thrust collar so alignment can be verified with thrust bearing installed. *See Fig. 2.*

4) Lubricate thrust bearing with oil and install. Tighten retaining bolts to specification. See TORQUE SPECIFICATIONS table at end of article. Install oil baffle. Ensure thrust collar is aligned with turbine shaft. Install split ring seal on oil slinger.

5) Note alignment mark on oil slinger. Place alignment mark on shaft end of oil slinger to verify alignment once installed. Lubricate oil slinger and install in diffuser.

CAUTION: Ensure bearing housing DOES NOT rotate during compressor wheel installation.

6) Install seal ring in diffuser. Install diffuser. Ensure alignment mark on oil slinger is aligned with turbine shaft. *See Fig. 2.* Install compressor wheel. Ensure alignment mark on compressor wheel aligns with mark on turbine shaft. *See Fig. 2.*

7) Install left-hand nut on shaft and tighten to specification. See TORQUE SPECIFICATIONS table at end of article. Install bearing housing assembly in turbine housing with reference marks aligned.

8) Apply anti-seize compound to all bolts. Install clamp plate, lock plates and bolts to retain bearing housing. Tighten bolts to specification. See TORQUE SPECIFICATIONS table at end of article.

9) Install lock plates and bolts to retain diffuser on bearing housing. Tighten bolts to specification and bend over lock tabs. See TORQUE SPECIFICATIONS table at end of article.

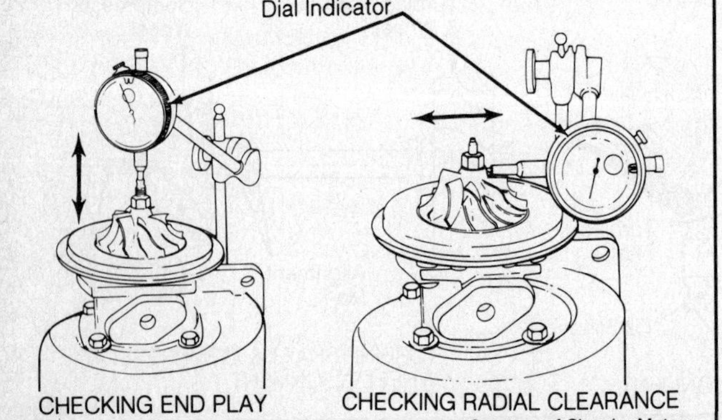
Dial Indicator
CHECKING END PLAY
CHECKING RADIAL CLEARANCE
113197
Courtesy of Chrysler Motors.

Fig. 3: Checking Shaft End Play & Radial Clearance

10) Using dial indicator, check shaft end play and radial clearance. *See Fig. 3.* Clearance should be within specification. See TURBOCHARGER SPECIFICATIONS table. Install seal ring and compressor housing. Ensure reference mark is aligned on compressor housing and bearing housing.

11) Install "V" band clamp. Apply anti-seize compound to "V" band bolt threads. Install nut and tighten to specification. Tap on "V" band clamp in 4 equal areas and retighten nut to specification. See TORQUE SPECIFICATIONS table at end of article.

Installation – To install, reverse removal procedure using new gaskets. Coat all bolts and studs with anti-seize compound. Install oil drain tube on turbocharger. Pour 3 oz. (60 cc) of clean oil in oil inlet while spinning turbocharger. Install remaining components and tighten fasteners to specification. See TORQUE SPECIFICATIONS table at end of article.

INTERCOOLER

Removal – 1) Remove grille. Remove front support bracket, located above center of intercooler. On A/C-equipped models, discharge A/C system.

2) Remove bolt from center of sealing plate on A/C lines at the condenser. Remove condenser-to-intercooler retaining nuts. Lift condenser and sealing plate from intercooler. Plug all A/C lines to prevent contamination.

3) Remove intercooler inlet and outlet ducts. *See Fig. 4.* Remove intercooler retaining bolts. Pivot intercooler forward and upward to remove.

Installation – To install, reverse removal procedure. Tighten bolts/nuts to specification. See TORQUE SPECIFICATIONS table at end of article. Evacuate and recharge A/C system (if equipped).

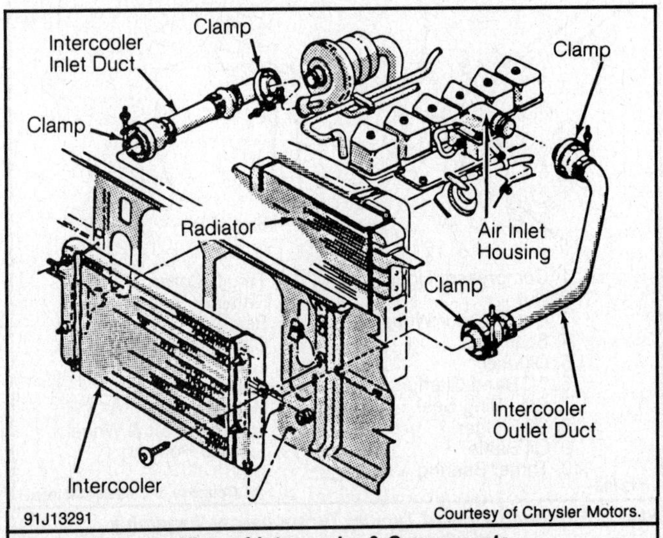
Clamp
Intercooler
Inlet Duct
Clamp
Clamp
Radiator
Air Inlet
Housing
Clamp
Intercooler
Outlet Duct
Intercooler
91J13291
Courtesy of Chrysler Motors.

Fig. 4: Exploded View of Intercooler & Components

FUEL SYSTEM

WARNING: DO NOT bleed fuel lines on a hot engine as high exhaust temperatures could cause a fire. Carefully bleed fuel lines as fuel exists under extremely high pressure and could penetrate the skin.

FUEL LINE BLEEDING

NOTE: Fuel line bleeding is necessary if fuel/water separator filter is not filled before installing, fuel injection pump is replaced, high-pressure fuel line connections are loosened or replaced, or initial engine start-up after engine is not operated for an extended period.

1) To bleed low-pressure fuel lines and fuel filter, open fuel bleed screw on banjo bolt. *See Fig. 5.*

2) Operate hand lever on fuel lift pump until steady fuel stream flows from fuel bleed screw. Tighten fuel bleed screw to 72 INCH lbs. (8 N.m). If hand lever feels like pump is not operating, rotate engine 90 degrees and repeat procedure. Position hand lever in upward position once fuel line is bled.

CAUTION: Fuel lift pump hand lever must be in upward position once fuel lines are bled to provide proper engine operation.

3) To bleed high-pressure fuel lines, carefully loosen high-pressure fuel line nut at fuel injector. Operate starter until fuel flows steadily, and tighten high-pressure fuel line nut to specification. See TORQUE SPECIFICATIONS table at end of article.

CAUTION: DO NOT operate starter for more than 30 seconds. Allow 2 minute intervals between starter operations.

4) Start engine and repeat procedure on all fuel lines, one at a time, until engine operates smoothly.

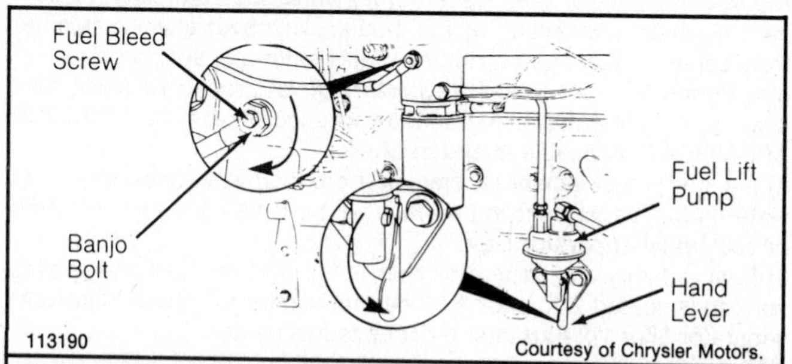
Fuel Bleed Screw
Fuel Lift Pump
Banjo Bolt
Hand Lever
113190
Courtesy of Chrysler Motors.

Fig. 5: Bleeding Fuel Lines

HIGH-PRESSURE FUEL LINES

CAUTION: High-pressure fuel lines must be clamped securely and routed so they do not contact each other or any other component. DO NOT weld or substitute lines. High-pressure lines are the same length, and proper line must be installed in specified area for proper engine operation.

Removal - 1) Disconnect negative battery cable. Disconnect control linkage and remove control linkage bracket from fuel injection pump (if necessary). Mark high-pressure fuel line location for reassembly reference.

2) Disconnect high-pressure fuel lines at fuel injectors and fuel injection pump. Remove high-pressure fuel line clamp retaining bolts. Remove high-pressure fuel lines.

CAUTION: Use wrench to hold delivery valves on fuel injection pump while removing high-pressure lines. Mark fuel line location before removing.

Installation - To install, reverse removal procedure. Bleed high-pressure fuel lines. See FUEL LINE BLEEDING under FUEL SYSTEM.

FUEL INJECTION PUMP

CAUTION: Fuel injection pumps for intercooled and non-intercooled models are different and cannot be interchanged.

Removal - 1) Disconnect negative battery cable. Disconnect necessary electrical connections at fuel injection pump. Disconnect control linkages from control lever on fuel injection pump. DO NOT remove control lever from fuel injection pump.

2) Disconnect control linkage bracket. Remove and cap high-pressure fuel lines. Use wrench to hold delivery valves on fuel injection pump, while removing high-pressure lines. Mark fuel line location for reassembly reference.

3) Disconnect air fuel control tube. This is the tube from fuel injection pump to cylinder head. Disconnect drain tube from fuel injection pump. Disconnect fuel supply line from fuel injection pump.

4) On intercooled models, remove bolt from rear support bracket on fuel injection pump. Remove rear support bracket-to-cylinder block bolts. Loosen center bolt on rear support bracket. Pivot rear support bracket toward rear of engine.

5) On non-intercooled models, remove retaining bolts and rear support bracket on fuel injection pump. On all models, remove oil fill tube from front timing gear cover. Place shop towel in front of fuel pump drive gear to prevent retaining nut and washer from falling during removal. Remove fuel pump drive gear retaining nut and washer.

CAUTION: DO NOT allow fuel pump drive gear retaining nut or washer to fall into front timing gear cover.

6) Rotate engine clockwise so No. 1 cylinder is at TDC of compression stroke. Engine can be rotated by removing dust cover from transmission adapter plate and installing Engine Barring Tool (3377462) in transmission adapter plate. *See Fig. 6.*

7) When No. 1 cylinder is at TDC, key of fuel injection pump shaft should be pointing toward bottom of engine. Ensure timing pin will engage. *See Fig. 6.* Timing pin is located below fuel injection pump.

CAUTION: Carefully engage timing pin to avoid breaking tip of timing pin. DO NOT rotate engine with timing pin engaged.

8) Note if timing marks on fuel injection pump flange and gear housing are aligned for reassembly reference, if original fuel injection pump is installed. *See Fig. 7.* These timing marks apply to each engine and fuel injection pump. Timing marks cannot be used to exchange fuel injection pumps.

9) Loosen lock bolt on fuel injection pump and remove special washer. *See Fig. 7.* Tighten lock bolt to 22 ft. lbs. (30 N.m). This will lock fuel injection pump shaft from rotating. Retain special washer for reassembly.

10) Using gear puller and two 8 mm X 1.25" bolts, pull fuel pump drive gear free from fuel injection pump shaft. Remove retaining nuts, fuel injection pump and gasket.

CAUTION: DO NOT allow key to fall from fuel injection pump shaft during removal.

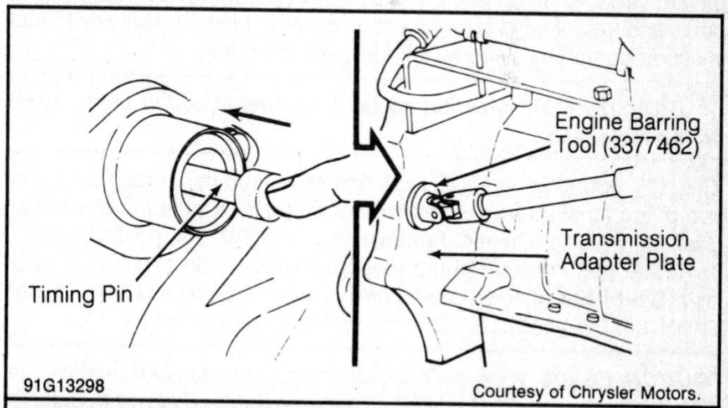
Engine Barring Tool (3377462)
Transmission Adapter Plate
Timing Pin
91G13298
Courtesy of Chrysler Motors.

Fig. 6: Rotating Engine & Engaging Timing Pin

Installation (Original Fuel Injection Pump) - 1) Ensure gasket surfaces are clean. Ensure No. 1 cylinder is at TDC and timing pin is engaged. Install new gasket on cylinder block. Install key in fuel injection pump shaft and install fuel injection pump. DO NOT allow key to drop from fuel injection pump shaft.

CAUTION: DO NOT allow key to fall from fuel injection pump shaft during installation.

2) Install mounting nuts. DO NOT tighten nuts at this time. Fuel injection pump must be free to rotate in slots. Install fuel pump drive gear retaining nut and washer. Tighten retaining nut to 11-15 ft. lbs. (15-20 N.m).

3) If fuel injection pump timing marks on fuel injection flange and gear housing were aligned at removal, fuel injection pump timing does not require adjustment. If marks were not aligned, check fuel injection

1991 ENGINE PERFORMANCE
Removal, Overhaul & Installation – Diesel (Cont.)

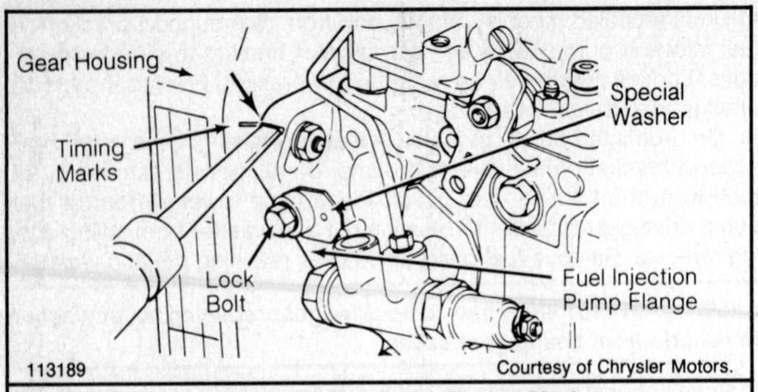
Gear Housing
Timing Marks
Special Washer
Lock Bolt
Fuel Injection Pump Flange
113189
Courtesy of Chrysler Motors.

Fig. 7: Identifying Fuel Injection Pump Timing Marks

pump timing. See FUEL INJECTION PUMP TIMING in ON-VEHICLE ADJUSTMENTS - DIESEL article.

4) If timing marks were aligned at removal, rotate fuel injection pump to align timing marks. Tighten mounting nuts to 18 ft. lbs. (24 N.m). Loosen lock bolt and install special washer under lock bolt. Tighten lock bolt to 10 ft. lbs. (14 N.m). Tighten fuel pump drive gear nut to specification. See TORQUE SPECIFICATIONS table at end of article.

5) Disengage timing pin if not previously disengaged. To install remaining components, reverse removal procedure. Loosely install all bolts in rear support bracket.

6) On intercooled models, tighten rear support bracket bolts to vacuum pump, cylinder block and then to fuel injection pump. On non-intercooled models, tighten rear support bracket bolts to cylinder block and then to fuel injection pump. Tighten bolts to specification. See TORQUE SPECIFICATIONS table at end of article.

7) Install and bleed fuel lines. See FUEL LINE BLEEDING under FUEL SYSTEM. Ensure cable rod is adjusted so control lever contacts low-speed screw when in idle position. Cable rod is located between control linkage and control lever on fuel injection pump.

8) Ensure control lever on fuel injection pump moves over center position and rests against breakover spring (located in center of control lever) when in full throttle position.

Installation (New Or Rebuilt Fuel Injection Pump) – 1) Ensure gasket surfaces are clean. Ensure No. 1 cylinder is at TDC and timing pin is engaged. Install new gasket on cylinder block. Install key in fuel injection pump shaft and install fuel injection pump.

CAUTION: DO NOT allow key to fall from fuel injection pump shaft during installation.

2) Install mounting nuts. DO NOT tighten nuts at this time. Fuel injection pump must be free to rotate in slots. Install fuel pump drive gear retaining nut and washer. Tighten nut to 11-15 ft. lbs. (15-20 N.m).

3) Rotate fuel injection pump toward cylinder head to take up gear lash. Check fuel injection pump timing. See FUEL INJECTION PUMP TIMING in ON-VEHICLE ADJUSTMENTS – DIESEL article.

CAUTION: Ensure lock bolt is loosened and special washer is installed under lock bolt. Lock bolt must be tightened to 10 ft. lbs. (14 N.m).

4) Once correct timing is obtained and mounting nuts are tightened, place timing mark on fuel injection pump flange to align with mark on gear housing. *See Fig. 7.*

5) Disengage timing pin if not previously disengaged. To install remaining components, reverse removal procedure. Install all bolts in rear support.

6) On intercooled models, tighten rear support bracket bolts to vacuum pump, cylinder block and then to fuel injection pump. On non-intercooled models, tighten rear support bracket bolts to cylinder block and then to fuel injection pump. Tighten bolts to specification. See TORQUE SPECIFICATIONS table at end of article.

7) Install and bleed fuel lines. See FUEL LINE BLEEDING under FUEL SYSTEM. Ensure ensure cable rod is adjusted so control lever contacts low-speed screw when in idle position. Cable rod is located between control linkage and control lever on fuel injection pump.

8) Ensure control lever on fuel injection pump moves over center position and rests against breakover spring (located in center of control lever) when in full throttle position.

FUEL LIFT PUMP

Removal & Installation – 1) Disconnect negative battery cable. Disconnect fuel lines at fuel lift pump. Remove retaining bolts, fuel lift pump and gasket.

2) To install, reverse removal procedure using new pump mounting gasket and fuel line banjo bolt sealing washers. Bleed low-pressure fuel lines. See FUEL LINE BLEEDING under FUEL SYSTEM.

FUEL HEATER

Removal – 1) Fuel heater is located between fuel/water separator filter and filter adapter on cylinder head. Ensure area is clean around fuel heater.

2) Disconnect water-in-fuel sensor electrical connection at bottom of fuel/water separator filter. Remove fuel/water separator filter. Disconnect electrical connection at fuel heater. Remove retaining adapter from center of fuel heater. Remove fuel heater and seal rings.

Installation – 1) To install, reverse removal procedure using new seal rings. Tighten retaining adapter to specification. See TORQUE SPECIFICATIONS table at end of article.

2) If water-in-fuel sensor is removed from fuel/water separator, coat water-in-fuel sensor sealing surface with engine oil before installing on fuel/water separator filter.

3) Ensure fuel/water separator filter is full of diesel fuel and sealing surface is coated with engine oil before installing. Tighten fuel/water separator filter 1/2 turn after it contacts fuel heater.

FUEL INJECTOR

Removal – 1) Disconnect negative battery cable. Remove throttle linkage and bracket. Remove high-pressure fuel lines and mark location for reassembly reference. Remove fuel drain lines from fuel injectors, and plug all fuel openings.

2) Clean around fuel injector. Hold fuel injector body with wrench while loosening hold-down nut. Using Fuel Injector Puller (3823276), pull fuel injectors from cylinder head. Remove sealing ring (located below fuel injector) from cylinder head.

Installation – 1) Install new sealing ring on fuel injector. Coat fuel injector retaining nut and top of fuel injector body with anti-seize compound. Install fuel injector in original position.

2) Ensure protrusion side of fuel injector aligns with notch area of cylinder head. Tighten fuel injector retaining nut to specification. See TORQUE SPECIFICATIONS table at end of article. Once fuel injector retaining nut is tightened, push "O" ring on top of fuel injector into groove.

CAUTION: Ensure protruding side of fuel injector aligns with notch area of cylinder head.

3) To install remaining components, reverse removal procedure using new sealing washers. Install and bleed high-pressure fuel lines. See FUEL LINE BLEEDING under FUEL SYSTEM.

INTAKE MANIFOLD HEATER

Removal & Installation (Intercooled Models) – 1) Disconnect negative battery cable. Intake manifold heater is located between air inlet housing and intake manifold cover. Disconnect intercooler outlet duct from air inlet housing. *See Fig. 4.*

2) Remove high-pressure fuel lines (if necessary). Hold delivery valves on fuel injection pump with wrench while removing high-pressure lines. Mark fuel line location for reassembly reference.

3) Disconnect intake manifold heater electrical connector. Disconnect fuel heater ground wire (located above fuel filter) from intake manifold cover. Remove retaining bolts, air inlet housing and gasket. Remove intake manifold heater and gasket.

4) To install, reverse removal procedure. Tighten fasteners to specification. See TORQUE SPECIFICATIONS table at end of article. Install and bleed high-pressure fuel lines (if removed). See FUEL LINE BLEEDING under FUEL SYSTEM.

Removal & Installation (Non-Intercooled Models) – 1) Disconnect negative battery cable. Disconnect control linkage at fuel injection pump.

2) Disconnect electrical connections at intake manifold heater. Intake manifold heater is located below air crossover tube from turbocharger and intake manifold.

3) Loosen air crossover tube clamps at turbocharger. Remove retaining bolts and air crossover tube from intake manifold. Remove intake manifold heater and gaskets.

4) To install, reverse removal procedure. Tighten fasteners to specification. See TORQUE SPECIFICATIONS table at end of article.

INTAKE MANIFOLD HEATER RELAYS

Removal & Installation – Disconnect negative battery cable. Disconnect electrical connections for intake manifold heater relays, located on inner fenderwell. *See Fig. 8.* Remove retaining bolts and intake manifold heater relays. To install, reverse removal procedure.

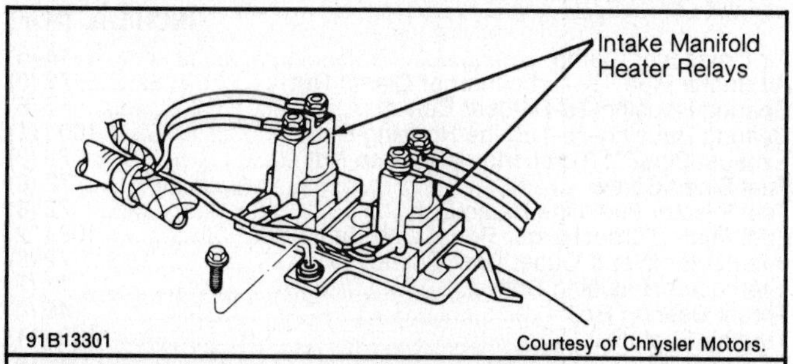
Intake Manifold
Heater Relays
91B13301
Courtesy of Chrysler Motors.

Fig. 8: Identifying Intake Manifold Heater Relays

SHUTOFF SOLENOID VALVE

Removal & Installation – 1) Disconnect wire from shutoff solenoid valve, located on rear of fuel injection pump. Ensure area around shutoff solenoid valve is clean. Remove shutoff solenoid valve, plunger and spring.

CAUTION: DO NOT allow plunger and spring to fall in fuel injection pump while servicing shutoff solenoid valve.

2) To install, reverse removal procedure using new "O" ring. Tighten shutoff solenoid valve to specification. See TORQUE SPECIFICATIONS table at end of article.

CHARGE AIR TEMPERATURE SENSOR & AIR TEMPERATURE SWITCH

Removal & Installation (Intercooled Models) – Charge air temperature sensor and air temperature switch are located in intake manifold cover. *See Fig. 9.* No other information is available from manufacturer.

THERMISTOR

Removal & Installation (Non-Intercooled Models) – Thermistor is located in air intake above fuel/water separator filter. Disconnect electrical connection and remove thermistor. To install, reverse removal procedure. Tighten thermistor to specification. See TORQUE SPECIFICATIONS table at end of article.

THROTTLE POSITION SENSOR (TPS)

Removal (Intercooled Models) – TPS is located above control lever on fuel injection pump. *See Fig. 10.* Disconnect electrical connector at TPS. Remove TPS retaining screws. Lift TPS straight upward from fuel injection pump.

Installation – 1) Install TPS in bracket on fuel injection pump. Ensure adapter on TPS aligns with opening in fuel injection pump shaft. *See Fig. 10.*

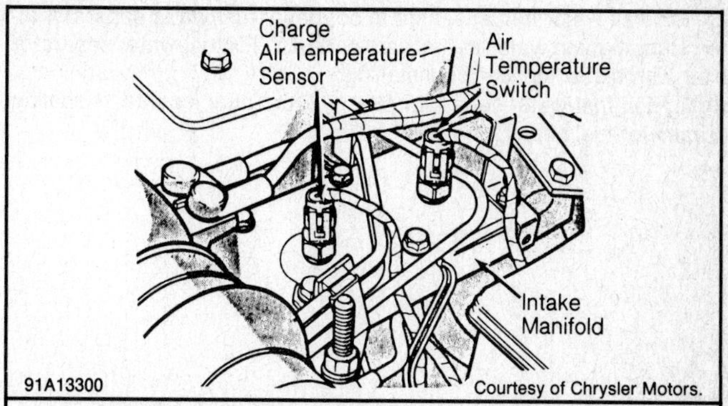
Charge
Air Temperature
Sensor
Air
Temperature
Switch
Intake
Manifold
91A13300
Courtesy of Chrysler Motors.

Fig. 9: Identifying Charge Air Temperature Sensor & Air Temperature Switch

2) If adapter does not align with fuel injection pump shaft, remove TPS bracket retaining screws. Place adapter on fuel injection pump shaft so TPS bracket must be rotated clockwise to align retaining screw holes.

3) Ensure adapter is even or slightly above top of fuel injection pump shaft. To adjust adapter position, hold nylon shaft in place and rotate adapter.

4) Tighten bracket retaining screws. Adjust TPS. See THROTTLE POSITION SENSOR (TPS) in ON-VEHICLE ADJUSTMENTS - DIESEL article in ENGINE PERFORMANCE.

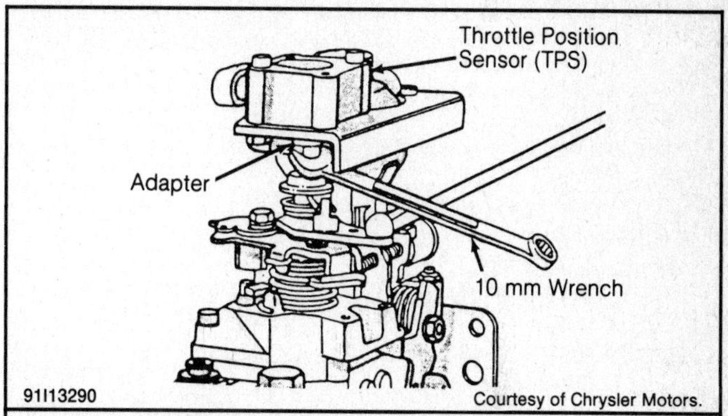
Throttle Position
Sensor (TPS)
Adapter
10 mm Wrench
91I13290
Courtesy of Chrysler Motors.

Fig. 10: Installing & Adjusting Throttle Position Sensor

WATER-IN-FUEL SENSOR

Removal & Installation – 1) Disconnect water-in-fuel sensor electrical connection at bottom of fuel/water separator filter. Remove fuel/water separator filter and drain fuel. Unscrew water-in-fuel sensor from bottom of fuel/water separator filter.

2) To install, reverse removal procedure using new "O" rings. Lubricate "O" rings and fuel/water separator filter sealing surface with engine oil before installing. Only hand tighten water-in-fuel sensor. Fill fuel/water separator filter with diesel fuel and install. Tighten fuel/water separator filter 1/2 turn after it contacts sealing surface of fuel heater.

FUEL/WATER SEPARATOR FILTER

Removal – 1) Disconnect water-in-fuel sensor electrical connection at bottom of fuel/water separator filter. Remove fuel/water separator filter. Ensure electrical connection on fuel heater (located above filter) is not rotated against cylinder block when removing fuel/water separator filter.

2) Remove square cut "O" ring from fuel/water separator filter-to-fuel heater contact area. Drain fuel/water separator filter. Unscrew water-in-fuel sensor from bottom of filter.

Installation – 1) To install, reverse removal procedure using new "O" rings. Lubricate "O" rings and fuel/water separator filter sealing surface with engine oil before installing.

1991 ENGINE PERFORMANCE
Removal, Overhaul & Installation – Diesel (Cont.)

2) Reinstall water-in-fuel sensor in bottom of fuel/water separator filter. Hand tighten water-in-fuel sensor ONLY. Fill fuel/water separator filter with diesel fuel before installing.

3) Tighten fuel/water separator filter 1/2 turn after it contacts sealing surface of fuel heater.

TORQUE SPECIFICATIONS

TORQUE SPECIFICATIONS

Application	Ft. Lbs. (N.m)
Air Crossover Tube Bolt	18 (24)
Air Inlet Housing Bolt	18 (24)
Fuel Heater Retaining Adapter	24 (33)
Fuel Injector Retaining Nut	44 (60)
Fuel Lift Pump Bolt	18 (24)
Fuel Line Banjo Bolt	
At Cylinder Head	18 (24)
At Fuel Pump	24 (33)
Fuel Pump Drive Gear Nut	48 (65)
Fuel Pump Mounting Nut	18 (24)
Fuel Pump Rear Support Bracket Bolt	18 (24)
High-Pressure Fuel Line Nut	18 (24)
Shutoff Solenoid Valve	32 (43)
Thermistor	18 (24)
Turbocharger Mounting Nut	24 (33)
Turbocharger Oil Lines	
Drain Line	18 (24)
Supply Line	11 (15)
	INCH Lbs. (N.m)
Air Crossover Clamp	44 (5)
Air Intake Pipe-To-Turbocharger Clamp Nut	72 (8)
Bearing Housing-To-Diffuser Bolt	50 (6)
Bearing Housing-To-Turbine Housing Bolt	100 (11)
Exhaust Pipe-To-Turbocharger Clamp Nut	72 (8)
Fuel Bleed Screw	72 (8)
Fuel Injector Fuel Line Banjo Bolt	72 (8)
Fuel Pump Turbocharger Boost Line Banjo Bolt	108 (12)
Intercooler Inlet & Outlet Duct Clamp Nut	72 (8)
Intercooler Retaining Bolt	17 (2)
Thrust Bearing Bolt	40 (4)
Turbine Shaft Nut [1]	129 (14)
"V" Clamp Nut [2]	72 (8)

[1] – Nut is left-hand thread.

[2] – Apply anti-seize compound to threads. Tighten nut to specification. Tap equally on "V" clamp in 4 places and retighten to specification.

1991 ELECTRICAL
Alternators & Regulators

Caravan, Dakota, Pickup, Ramcharger, RWD Van, Town & Country, Voyager

DESCRIPTION

Chrysler Motors light trucks use either a Bosch or a Denso alternator. The alternator consists of a rotor, stator, rectifiers, front and rear covers and drive pulley. Voltage regulation is controlled by the Single Board Engine Controller (SBEC) on all models except diesel. On diesel models, voltage regulation is controlled by a transistorized voltage regulator.

OPERATION

The SBEC monitors critical input to control fuel injection, ignition, emission and other engine management functions. The SBEC has also been programmed to monitor several charging system related circuits:

- Battery feed to SBEC
- Alternator field control
- Battery charging voltage (high and low)

If a problem is sensed in a monitored circuit, a fault code is stored in the SBEC's memory and the CHECK ENGINE light will be turned on (with a few exceptions). Fault codes can be read using the CHECK ENGINE light or with the Chrysler Diagnostic Readout Box-II (DRB-II).

NOTE: Fault codes remain in memory for 50 engine starts. Fault is erased from memory if failure does not reoccur .

For certain fault codes, CHECK ENGINE light will illuminate and engine controller will enter limp-in mode. In limp-in mode, engine controller attempts to compensate for particular component failure by substituting information from other sources. This allows vehicle operation until proper repairs are made.

ALTERNATOR APPLICATION

Application	[1] Case Number	Pulley Grooves
Caravan, Town & Country, & Voyager		
Bosch 90 Amp	4557431	4
	5234231	4
Denso 90 Amp	5234031	4
	5234032	6
Denso 120 Amp	5234208	4
	5234033	6
Dakota		
Bosch 90 Amp	5234231	4
	5235028	2
Denso 75 Amp	4557301	4
	5234026	2
	5234027	6
Denso 90 Amp	5234031	4
	5234028	2
	5234032	6
Denso 120 Amp	5234199	2
	5234208	4
	5234033	6
Pickup & Ramcharger		
Bosch 90 Amp	5235028	2
Denso 75 Amp	5234026	2
Denso 90 Amp	5234028	2
Denso 120 Amp	5234199	2
	5234374	8
RWD Van		
Denso 75 Amp	5234026	2
Denso 90 Amp	5234028	2
Denso 120 Amp	5234199	2

[1] – Located on tag on bottom of alternator case.

ADJUSTMENTS

BELT TENSION

BELT TENSION

Application	New Belt Lbs. (kg)	[1] Used Belt Lbs. (kg)
Caravan, Town & Country, & Voyager		
2.5L	125 (57)	80 (36)
3.0L	[2]	[2]
3.3L	[2]	[2]
Dakota		
2.5L	160 (73)	80 (36)
3.9L	100-140 (45-64)	60-90 (27-41)
5.2L	[2]	[2]
Pickup & Ramcharger		
3.9L & 5.2L	100-140 (45-64)	60-90 (27-41)
5.9L		
Gas	100-140 (45-64)	60-90 (27-41)
Diesel	[2]	[2]
RWD Van		
3.9L, 5.2L & 5.9L	100-140 (45-64)	60-90 (27-41)

[1] – Any belt operated for 15 minutes.
[2] – Dynamic tensioner used, no adjustment is required.

TROUBLE SHOOTING

INITIAL CHECKS

Before proceeding with charging system diagnosis, ensure:

- Battery is fully charged and in good condition
- Battery cables are in good condition with connections clean and secure
- Alternator belt is in good condition and properly tightened
- Alternator and SBEC wiring harness connections are clean and tight
- Engine ground strap is in place

UNSTEADY OR LOW CHARGING

Check for loose alternator belt, charging resistance too high, defective alternator, loose alternator ground wire or corroded battery terminals.

OVERCHARGING

Check for grounded alternator field wiring or faulty alternator.

NOISY ALTERNATOR

Check for worn alternator bearings or loose alternator mounting.

SELF-DIAGNOSTIC SYSTEM

SYSTEM DIAGNOSIS

The self-diagnostic capabilities of this system, if properly used, can simplify testing. SBEC monitors several different engine control system circuits.

If a problem is sensed with a monitored circuit, a fault code is stored in SBEC, CHECK ENGINE light illuminates and SBEC enters limp-in mode. In limp-in mode, SBEC compensates for component failure by substituting information from other sources. This allows vehicle operation until repairs can be made.

Once codes are known, refer to CHARGING SYSTEM FAULT CODES table to determine the questionable circuit. Test circuits and repair or replace components as required. If problem is repaired or ceases to exist, the SBEC cancels that fault code after 50 ignition on/off cycles. To clear codes, refer to ERASING FAULT CODES under ENTERING ON-BOARD DIAGNOSTICS.

1991 ELECTRICAL
Alternators & Regulators (Cont.)

A specific fault code results from a particular system failure. Components in that system are NOT necessarily the reason for that failure. The fault code does not condemn a specific component, it calls out a CIRCUIT malfunction.

Hard Failures – Hard failures cause CHECK ENGINE light to illuminate and remain on until the malfunction is repaired. If light comes on and remains on (light may flash) during vehicle operation, cause of malfunction must be determined using diagnostic (code) charts. If a sensor fails, SBEC will use a substitute value in its calculations, allowing engine operation in limp-in mode. In this condition, vehicle will run, but driveability may be poor.

Intermittent Failures – Intermittent failures may cause CHECK ENGINE light to flicker or stay on until the intermittent fault goes away. The corresponding trouble code will be retained in SBEC memory, however. If fault does not reoccur within a certain time frame, corresponding trouble code will be erased from SBEC memory. Intermittent failures can be caused by faulty sensor, bad connector or wiring related problems. See INTERMITTENTS in TROUBLE SHOOTING - NO CODES article in ENGINE PERFORMANCE.

DIAGNOSTIC PROCEDURE

Refer to ENTERING ON-BOARD DIAGNOSTICS to retrieve fault codes. If fault codes are NOT present and/or DRB-II (Diagnostic Readout Box-II) is used, proceed to TEST CH-1, BATTERY TEST.

NOTE: When using trouble shooting charts for diagnosis, DO NOT skip any steps in chart or incorrect diagnosis may result.

Before proceeding with diagnosis, the following precautions must be followed:

- Vehicle must have a fully charged battery and functional charging system. See TROUBLE SHOOTING and ON-VEHICLE TESTING.
- Probe SBEC connector from pin side. DO NOT backprobe SBEC connector.
- DO NOT cause short circuits when performing electrical tests. This will set additional fault codes, making diagnosis of original problem more difficult.
- DO NOT use a test light in place of a voltmeter.
- Always repair lowest fault code number (CHECK ENGINE light) or first fault displayed (DRB-II) first.
- Always perform verification procedure test after repairs are made.
- Always disconnect DRB-II after use.
- Always disconnect DRB-II before charging battery.

ENTERING ON-BOARD DIAGNOSTICS

CAUTION: Before entering on-board diagnostics, check charging system for other problems. See INITIAL CHECKS under TROUBLE SHOOTING. DO NOT connect DRB-II to vehicle with battery charger connected, as damage to DRB-II may result.

Reading Trouble Codes – Trouble codes may be read by using the CHECK ENGINE light on the instrument panel or with the DRB-II. See CHECK ENGINE LIGHT DIAGNOSTIC MODE and DIAGNOSIS USING DRB-II. A more complete diagnosis is possible using the DRB-II.

NOTE: The SBEC CANNOT diagnose every charging system problem. If a fault still exists after performing self-diagnostic procedures, proceed to ON-VEHICLE TESTING.

Trouble Code Explanation – **1)** See CHARGING SYSTEM FAULT CODES table for charging-related faults.

2) Code 12 will set if battery feed to the SBEC has been disconnected within last 50-100 starts. SBEC monitors this circuit whenever ignition is on.

3) Code 41 will set if the alternator field control fails to switch properly. SBEC monitors this circuit whenever ignition is on.

4) If battery temperature sense voltage goes out of range, Code 44 will be set in memory. The SBEC monitors this circuit any time ignition is on.

5) If battery sense voltage is more than one volt above desired control voltage for more than 20 seconds, a Code 46 will be set in memory. SBEC monitors this signal whenever the engine is running.

6) If battery sense voltage is more than one volt below desired control voltage for more than 20 seconds and no significant change in voltage is detected during active test of alternator, Code 47 will be set. The SBEC monitors this signal whenever engine speed is more than 1500 RPM.

CHARGING SYSTEM FAULT CODES

Code	Circuit	CHECK ENGINE Light On?
12	Battery Feed to SBEC	No
41 [1]	Alternator Field Control	Yes
44 [1]	[2] Battery Temp. Sensor	Yes
46 [1]	High Battery Voltage	Yes
47 [1]	Low Battery Voltage	No
55	End of Diagnostic Mode	No

[1] – This code will cause limp-in mode.
[2] – Sensor inside SBEC. If failed, replace SBEC.

NOTE: Only charging system-related codes are listed here. For engine-related codes, see appropriate SELF-DIAGNOSTICS article in ENGINE PERFORMANCE.

CHECK ENGINE Light Diagnostic Mode – **1)** Start engine (if possible). On models equipped with automatic transmission, place foot on brake and cycle transmission shift lever through all positions, ending in Park. On all models, turn A/C switch on and then off (if equipped).

2) Turn engine off. Without starting engine again, turn ignition on, off, on, off and on. CHECK ENGINE light will come on for 2 seconds as a bulb check, followed by fault codes. Record 2-digit fault codes as displayed by flashing CHECK ENGINE light.

3) For example, Code 23 is displayed as flash, flash, 4 second pause, then flash, flash, flash. After a slightly longer pause, any other codes stored are displayed in numerical order.

4) Once check engine light begins to flash fault codes, it cannot be stopped. Go to step **1)** to enter diagnostic mode again. Code 55 indicates end of fault code display. For more information on vehicle self-diagnostics, see appropriate SELF-DIAGNOSTICS article in ENGINE PERFORMANCE.

5) Refer to CHARGING SYSTEM FAULT CODES table to translate trouble code number to a system fault description (DRB-II display). Once trouble area is identified, refer to appropriate charging system test procedures.

NOTE: CHECK ENGINE light CANNOT be used to perform actuation test mode, sensor test modes or engine running test. Fault codes can only be erased using DRB-II. Fault codes will be erased from SBEC memory after 50 key starts if fault does not reoccur.

Diagnosis Using DRB-II – The DRB-II is used as part of a charging system diagnostic procedure. Perform tests CH-1, BATTERY TEST through CH-VER, CHARGING VERIFICATION.

DRB-II Diagnostic Mode – **1)** Turn ignition off. Attach DRB-II to engine diagnostic connector. Connector is located in engine compartment, near SBEC.

2) Start engine (if possible). On models equipped with automatic transmission, place foot on brake pedal and cycle transmission shift lever through all positions, ending in Park. On all models, turn A/C switch on and then off (if equipped).

3) Turn engine off. Without starting engine again, turn ignition on. Enter CHARGING MENU. To enter CHARGING MENU see DRB-II TEST FUNCTIONS. At CHARGING MENU, press "2" (READ FAULTS) key. Press ENTER key. After fault codes are accessed, refer to TEST CH-1, BATTERY TESTING under ON-VEHICLE TESTING.

Erasing Fault Codes – **1)** To erase faults, press ATM key. At DRB-II display, press "2" (ERASE) key. DRB-II will display ERASE FAULTS ARE YOU SURE? (ENTER TO ERASE). Press ENTER key.

1991 ELECTRICAL
Alternators & Regulators (Cont.)

2) When DRB-II is finished erasing fault codes, it will display FAULTS ERASED. This display will remain until ATM key is pressed. After ATM key is pressed, display will return to CHARGING MENU screen.

DRB-II TEST FUNCTIONS

NOTE: DO NOT touch DRB-II keypad during DRB-II power-up sequence, or an error message will result.

1) To perform diagnostic tests using DRB-II, DRB-II must be in the CHARGING MENU. At the CHARGING MENU, fault codes and DRB-II test functions can be accessed.

2) To reach CHARGING MENU, turn ignition off. Attach DRB-II to engine diagnostic connector. Connector is located in engine compartment, near SBEC. Turn ignition switch to RUN position.

3) All DRB-II character positions will illuminate and copyright information will appear on screen for several seconds. If DRB-II screen is blank or any error messages appear, see DRB-II PROBLEMS & ERROR MESSAGES.

4) After several seconds DRB-II menu will appear. At DRB-II menu, press "4" (SELECT SYSTEM) key. Press ENTER key. At SELECT SYSTEM menu, press "1" (ENGINE) key. Press ENTER key. DRB-II menu will appear, indicating engine year and size, type of transmission and SBEC part number.

5) After several seconds AIR COND menu will appear. Press "1" (WITH A/C) or press "2" (WITHOUT A/C). DRB-II display will change to ENGINE SYSTEMS menu. At ENGINE SYSTEMS menu, press "2" (CHARGING) key. Press ENTER key.

6) Display will change to CHARGING MENU. At CHARGING menu of engine diagnostic program, specific test functions programmed into DRB-II can be performed. The following DRB-II modes can be accessed: SYSTEM TEST, READ FAULTS, STATE DISPLAYS, ACTUATOR TEST and ADJUSTMENTS.

SYSTEM TEST Mode – This function is not available in the engine diagnostics program.

READ FAULTS Mode – 1) This function allows the user to read and erase fault codes. A fault counter will appear along with fault displayed on DRB-II. As an example, DRB-II will display 1 OF 2 FAULTS. SBEC will store up to 8 fault messages. Faults are numbered in reverse order of setting. The most recent fault to occur will be number one. Vehicles without A/C will always have A/C CLUTCH RELAY CKT (circuit) stored in memory. This fault will always be number one if vehicle is not equipped with A/C. If no fault messages are stored, DRB-II will display NO FAULTS DETECTED and start counter will show 0 STARTS SINCE ERS.

2) A start counter will appear below DRB-II fault counter display. Start counter counts the number of times vehicle is started since faults were last set, erased, or battery was disconnected. This helps determine if fault is intermittent. Memory space limits start counter to first 3 faults. Start counter of zero equals a hard fault. Start counter of more than zero indicates an intermittent fault. Start counter will count up to 255 starts. If no fault messages are stored, DRB-II will display NO FAULTS DETECTED and start counter will show 0 STARTS SINCE ERS.

STATE DISPLAYS Mode – 1) This function allows user to read states or values of a variety of sensors, inputs/outputs and components.

2) The SBEC can only recognize high and low states on switch circuits. SBEC cannot differentiate between an open or short circuit or a defective switch. If DRB-II displays a change between INPUT HIGH and INPUT LOW, it can be assumed that the entire switch circuit to the SBEC is functioning.

ACTUATOR TEST Mode – 1) This function allows the user to check for proper operation of output circuits or devices, which the SBEC cannot internally recognize. DRB-II allows SBEC to activate these outputs or devices, allowing an observer to verify proper operation.

2) Most of the tests available in this mode provide an audible or visual indication of device operation (click of relay contacts, spray fuel, etc.). With the exception of an intermittent condition, if a device functions properly during its test, it can be assumed that the device, wiring and its driver circuit are functioning properly.

ADJUSTMENTS Mode – This function allows the user to erase fault codes. Function also allows user to reset Emission Maintenance Reminder (EMR) light and mileage (trucks only).

DRB-II Volt/Ohmmeter Mode – 1) To access volt/ohmmeter mode of DRB-II, connect Red volt/ohmmeter test lead to Red port, located on right-top side of DRB-II.

NOTE: Because DRB-II is grounded through engine diagnostic connector, only one volt/ohmmeter test lead is required when using volt/ohmmeter option. DRB-II volt/ohmmeter should only be used when diagnostic procedures require the use of this option.

2) To access voltmeter, press VOLT/OHM key once. DRB-II is now in voltmeter mode. Touch test probe to connector or wire to be measured. Read voltage on DRB-II display. When voltage testing is complete, press VOLT/OHM key 3 times to exit voltmeter mode.

3) To access ohmmeter, press VOLT/OHM key twice. DRB-II is now in ohmmeter mode. Touch test probe to connector or wire to be measured. Read resistance to circuit ground on DRB-II display. When resistance testing is complete, press VOLT/OHM key twice to exit ohmmeter mode.

DRB-II Continuity Meter Mode – Press VOLT/OHM key 3 times. Display will read NO CONTINUITY. Touch test probe to connector or wire to be measured. Read continuity on DRB-II display. When continuity testing is complete, press VOLT/OHM key once to exit continuity meter mode.

VEHICLES TESTED Mode – 1) Mode is used to show what vehicles are covered by DRB-II cartridge. To access vehicles tested mode, turn ignition off. Attach DRB-II to engine diagnostic connector. Connector is located in engine compartment, near SBEC.

2) Turn ignition switch to RUN position. All DRB-II character positions will illuminate and copyright information will appear on screen for several seconds. After several seconds DRB-II menu will appear.

3) At DRB-II menu, press "1" (VEHICLES TESTED) key. Press ENTER key. DRB-II will display vehicles covered by cartridge. Screen will display for 5 seconds and return to DRB-II menu.

HOW TO USE Mode – Enter DRB-II menu display. Refer to steps **1)** and **2)** under VEHICLES TESTED MODE. At DRB-II menu, press "2" (HOW TO USE) key. Press ENTER key. A series of screens will be displayed explaining the use of DRB-II keys used to move through engine diagnostic program.

CONFIGURE Mode – 1) Configure option allows user to customize DRB-II display. For example, if metric system is more useful to use, simply select METRIC from the appropriate menu.

2) All selections made under CONFIGURE option remain active until user changes selection. To enter configure mode, enter DRB-II menu display. Refer to steps **1)** and **2)** under VEHICLES TESTED MODE. At DRB-II menu, press "3" (CONFIGURE) key. Press ENTER key. DRB-II will display CONFIGURE menu.

DRB-II PROBLEMS & ERROR MESSAGES

Blank Message Screen – 1) Connect DRB-II to a different vehicle. If message screen is still blank, DRB-II or cable adapter is faulty. Substitute to find faulty component.

2) If message screen is not blank, DRB-II and cable adapter are functioning properly. Inspect diagnostic connector for proper wire placement, damaged terminals or pushed out pins. Repair as necessary.

3) If diagnostic connector is okay, using an ohmmeter, check resistance between Black/White or Black/Yellow wire and ground at engine diagnostic connector. If resistance is greater than 10 ohms, repair open in Black/White or Black/Yellow wire.

NO RESPONSE Message – 1) Connect DRB-II to another vehicle. If DRB-II displays NO RESPONSE message again, DRB-II or cable adapter is faulty. Substitute to find faulty component. If message screen does not display NO RESPONSE, DRB-II and cable adapter are functioning properly. Go to next step.

2) Turn ignition off. Disconnect DRB-II. Using an ohmmeter, check Pink or Black/Red wire for resistance between SBEC and engine diagnostic connectors. If resistance is more than 10 ohms, repair open in Pink or Black/Red wire.

1991 ELECTRICAL
Alternators & Regulators (Cont.)

3) If resistance is less than 10 ohms, check Light Green/Orange or Black/Pink wire for resistance between SBEC and engine diagnostic connectors. If resistance is more than 10 ohms, repair open in Light Green/Orange or Black/Pink wire.

RAM TEST FAILURE Message – Replace DRB-II.

CARTRIDGE ERROR Message – Replace DRB-II cartridge.

KEY PAD TEST FAILURE Message – Power up DRB-II again with fingers off the keypad. If error message returns, replace DRB-II.

HIGH OR LOW BATTERY Message – Correct condition of vehicle battery and reconnect DRB-II.

NOTE: For more information on SBEC diagnostic capabilities and using DRB-II, see appropriate SELF-DIAGNOSTICS article in ENGINE PERFORMANCE.

ON-VEHICLE TESTING

NOTE: ALTERNATOR OUTPUT WIRE RESISTANCE TEST will show amount of voltage drop across alternator output wire between alternator BAT terminal and positive battery post.

Alternator Output Wire Resistance Test – 1) Charge battery as necessary. Turn ignition off. Disconnect negative battery cable. Disconnect alternator output wire from alternator BAT terminal.

2) Using a 0-150-ampere scale DC ammeter, connect positive ammeter lead to alternator BAT terminal and negative lead to disconnected alternator output wire. *See Fig. 1 and 2.*

3) Using a voltmeter (0-18 volts minimum), connect positive voltmeter lead to disconnected alternator output wire and negative lead to positive battery cable.

CAUTION: Alternator has 2 field terminals. One field terminal has Dark Green wire and other field terminal has Dark Blue wire. DO NOT connect jumper wire to alternator field terminal Dark Blue wire.

4) On Caravan, Town & Country and Voyager, remove air hose between SBEC and air cleaner. On all models, connect one end of jumper wire to ground and other end to alternator field terminal Dark Green wire on rear side of alternator.

5) Connect engine tachometer and reconnect negative battery cable. Connect carbon pile rheostat between battery terminals. Ensure carbon pile is in OFF position before connecting leads.

6) Start engine. Reduce engine speed to idle. Adjust engine speed and carbon pile to maintain 20 amps flowing in circuit. Observe voltmeter reading. Voltage drop should be .5 volt or less.

7) If voltage drop is more than .5 volt, inspect, clean and tighten all connections between alternator BAT terminal and positive battery post. Voltage drop test may be performed at each connection to locate connection with excessive resistance. If resistance tests satisfactorily, reduce engine speed, turn off carbon pile and ignition switch.

8) Disconnect negative battery cable. Remove test ammeter, voltmeter, carbon pile and tachometer. Remove jumper wire between alternator Dark Green field wire and ground. Connect alternator output wire to alternator BAT terminal. Reconnect negative battery cable and hose between SBEC and air cleaner.

NOTE: CURRENT OUTPUT TEST determines if alternator is capable of delivering its rated current output.

Current Output Test – 1) Charge battery as necessary. Disconnect negative battery cable. Disconnect alternator output wire at alternator BAT terminal. *See Fig. 3.* Using a 0-150-ampere scale DC ammeter, connect positive ammeter lead to alternator BAT terminal and negative lead to disconnected alternator output wire. *See Fig. 4 and 5.*

2) Using a voltmeter (0-18 volts range minimum), connect positive voltmeter lead to disconnected alternator BAT terminal and negative lead to good ground.

3) Connect engine tachometer and reconnect negative battery cable. Connect carbon pile rheostat between battery terminals. Ensure carbon pile is in OFF position before connecting leads.

CAUTION: Alternator has 2 field terminals. One field terminal has Dark Green wire and other field terminal has Dark Blue wire. DO NOT connect jumper wire to alternator field terminal Dark Blue wire.

4) On Caravan, Town & Country and Voyager, remove air hose between SBEC and air cleaner. On all models, connect one end of jumper wire to ground and other end to alternator field terminal Dark Green wire on back of alternator.

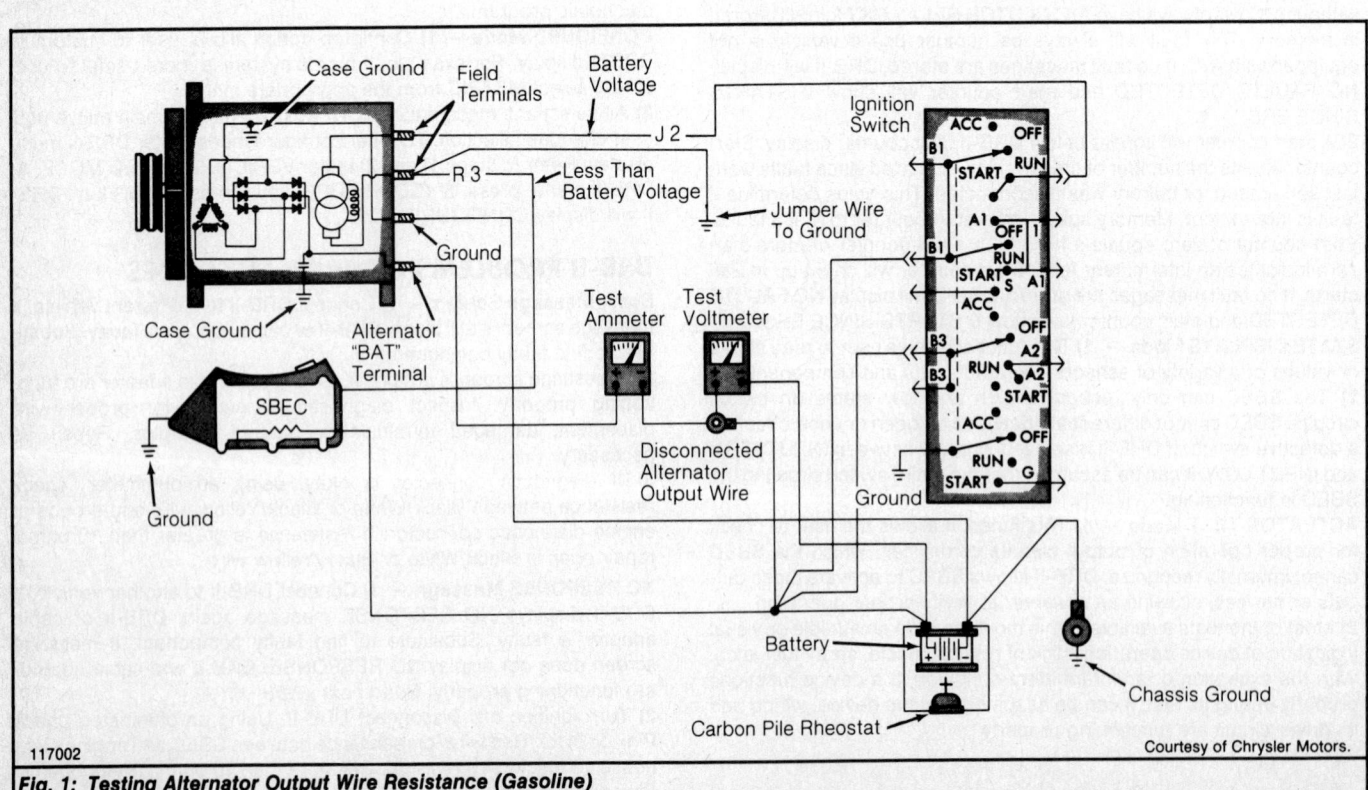

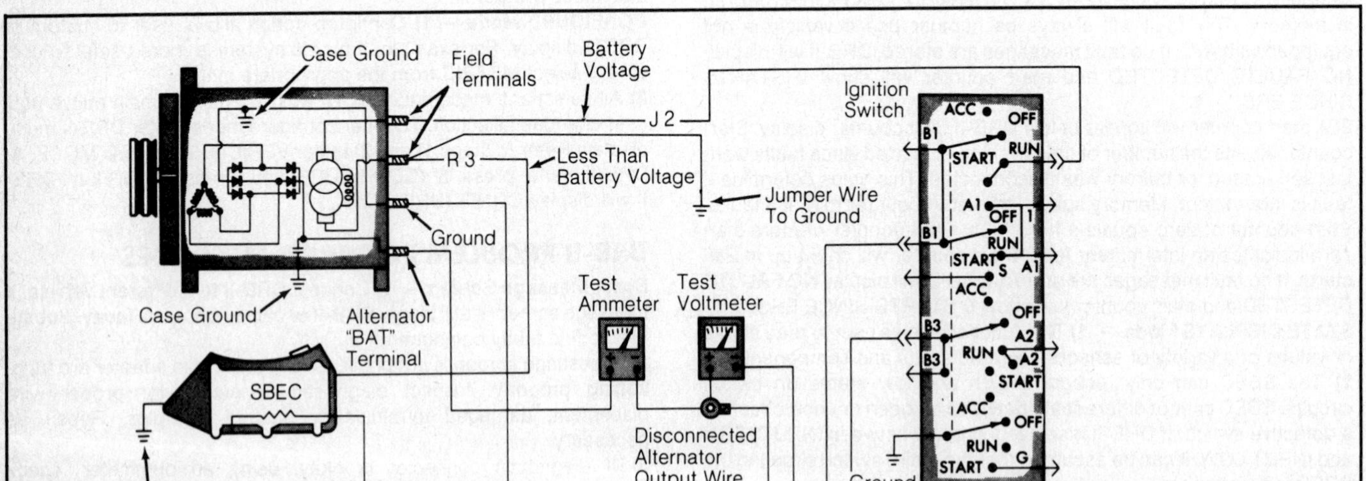
Case Ground
Field Terminals
Battery Voltage
J 2
R 3
Less Than Battery Voltage
Ground
Case Ground
Alternator "BAT" Terminal
SBEC
Ground
Test Ammeter
Test Voltmeter
Jumper Wire To Ground
Disconnected Alternator Output Wire
Ignition Switch
ACC
OFF
B1
START
RUN
A1
OFF
1
RUN
START
S
A1
ACC
B3
OFF
A2
RUN
A2
START
ACC
OFF
RUN
G
START
Ground
Battery
Chassis Ground
Carbon Pile Rheostat
117002
Courtesy of Chrysler Motors.

Fig. 1: Testing Alternator Output Wire Resistance (Gasoline)

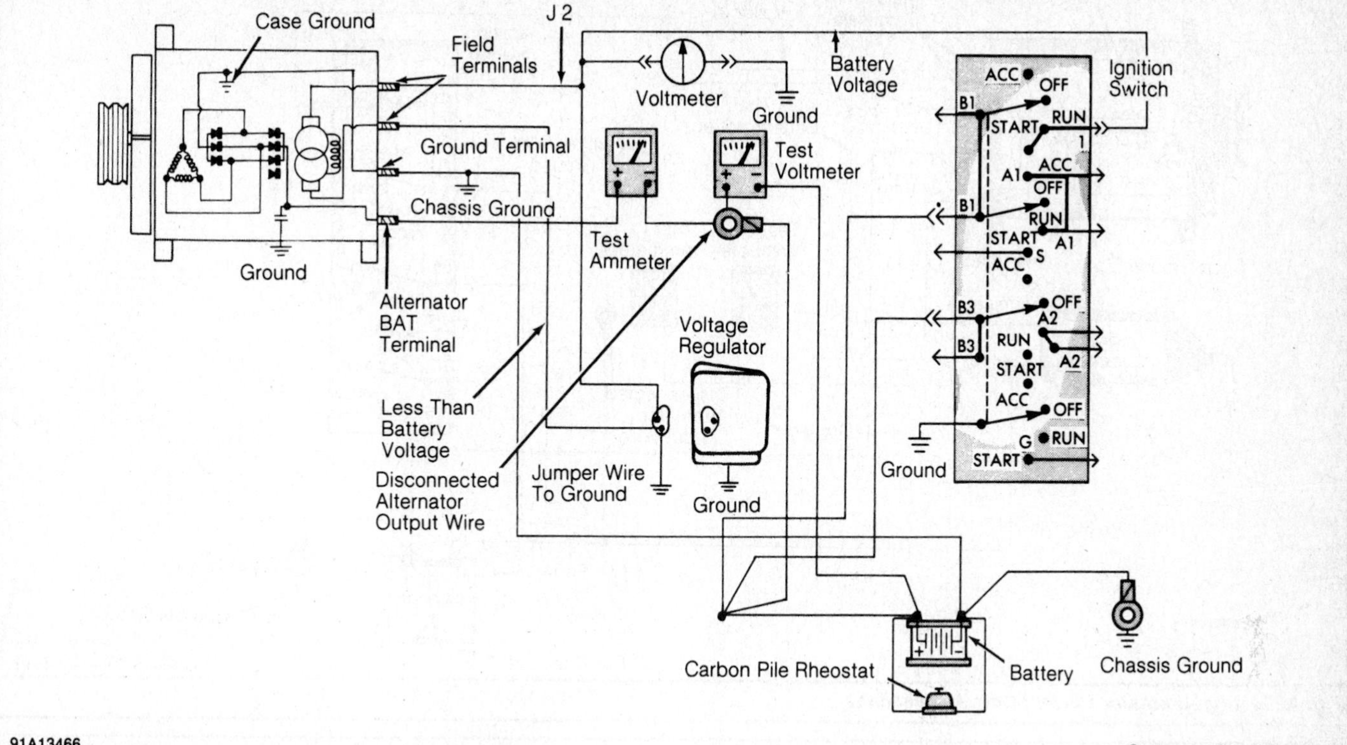
Case Ground
J 2
Field Terminals
Battery Voltage
Ignition Switch
Voltmeter
Ground
Ground Terminal
Test Voltmeter
Chassis Ground
Test Ammeter
Ground
Alternator BAT Terminal
Voltage Regulator
Less Than Battery Voltage
Disconnected Alternator Output Wire
Jumper Wire To Ground
Ground
ACC
OFF
RUN
START
B1
A1
B3
A2
S
G
Carbon Pile Rheostat
Battery
Chassis Ground
91A13466
Courtesy of Chrysler Motors.

Fig. 2: Testing Alternator Output Wire Resistance (Diesel)

5) Start engine and reduce engine speed to idle. Adjust carbon pile and engine speed in increments until engine speed is 1250 RPM and voltmeter reads 15 volts. DO NOT allow voltage to read more than 16 volts.

6) Ammeter should read within specification. See ALTERNATOR MINIMUM OUTPUT table. If alternator amperage reads less than specified and alternator output wire resistance is not excessive, replace alternator. After CURRENT OUTPUT TEST is completed, reduce engine speed, turn off carbon pile and ignition switch.

7) Disconnect negative battery cable. Remove test ammeter, voltmeter, tachometer and carbon pile. Remove jumper wire between alternator field terminal Dark Green wire and ground. Reconnect alternator output wire to alternator BAT terminal. Reconnect negative battery cable and hose between SBEC and air cleaner.

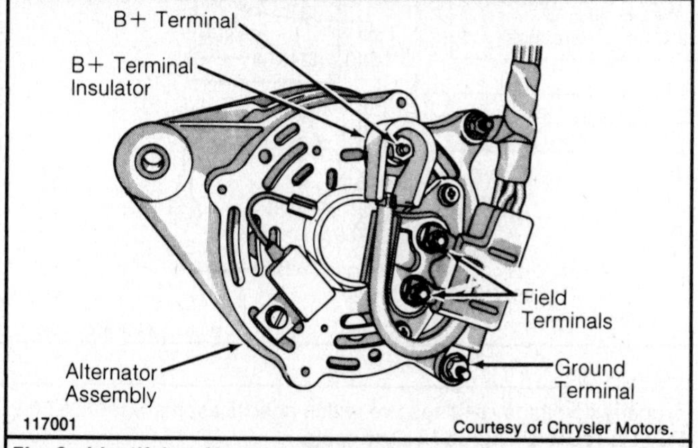
B+ Terminal
B+ Terminal Insulator
Field Terminals
Alternator Assembly
Ground Terminal
117001
Courtesy of Chrysler Motors.

Fig. 3: Identifying Alternator Terminals

ALTERNATOR MINIMUM OUTPUT

Application	[1] Case Number	[2] Minimum Amperage
Caravan, Town & Country, & Voyager		
Bosch 90 Amp	4557431	84
	5234231	88
Denso 90 Amp	5234031	86
	5234032	90
Denso 120 Amp	5234208	98
	5234033	102
Dakota		
Bosch 90 Amp	5234231	90
	5235028	90
Denso 75 Amp	4557301	75
	5234026	75
	5234027	75
Denso 90 Amp	5234031	90
	5234028	90
	5234032	90
Denso 120 Amp	5234199	90
	5234208	120
	5234033	120
Pickup & Ramcharger		
Bosch 90 Amp	5235028	90
Denso 75 Amp	5234026	75
Denso 90 Amp	5234028	90
Denso 120 Amp	5234199	120
	5234374	120
RWD Van		
Denso 75 Amp	5234026	75
Denso 90 Amp	5234028	90
Denso 120 Amp	5234199	120

[1] – Located on tag on bottom of alternator case.
[2] – Full-fielded at 1250 RPM.

1991 ELECTRICAL
Alternators & Regulators (Cont.)

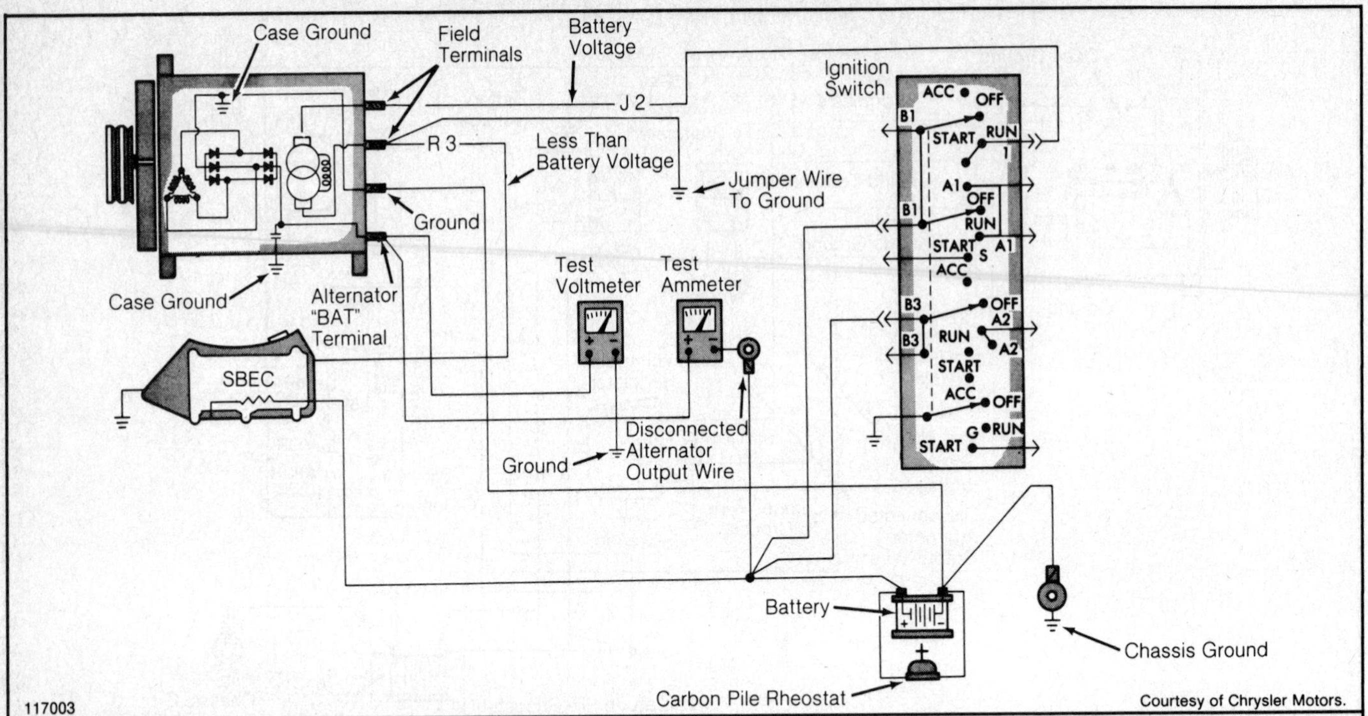
Case Ground
Field Terminals
Battery Voltage
J 2
R 3
Less Than Battery Voltage
Jumper Wire To Ground
Ground
Ignition Switch
Case Ground
Alternator "BAT" Terminal
Test Voltmeter
Test Ammeter
SBEC
Disconnected Alternator Output Wire
Ground
Battery
Chassis Ground
Carbon Pile Rheostat
117003
Courtesy of Chrysler Motors.

Fig. 4: Testing Alternator Current Output (Gasoline)

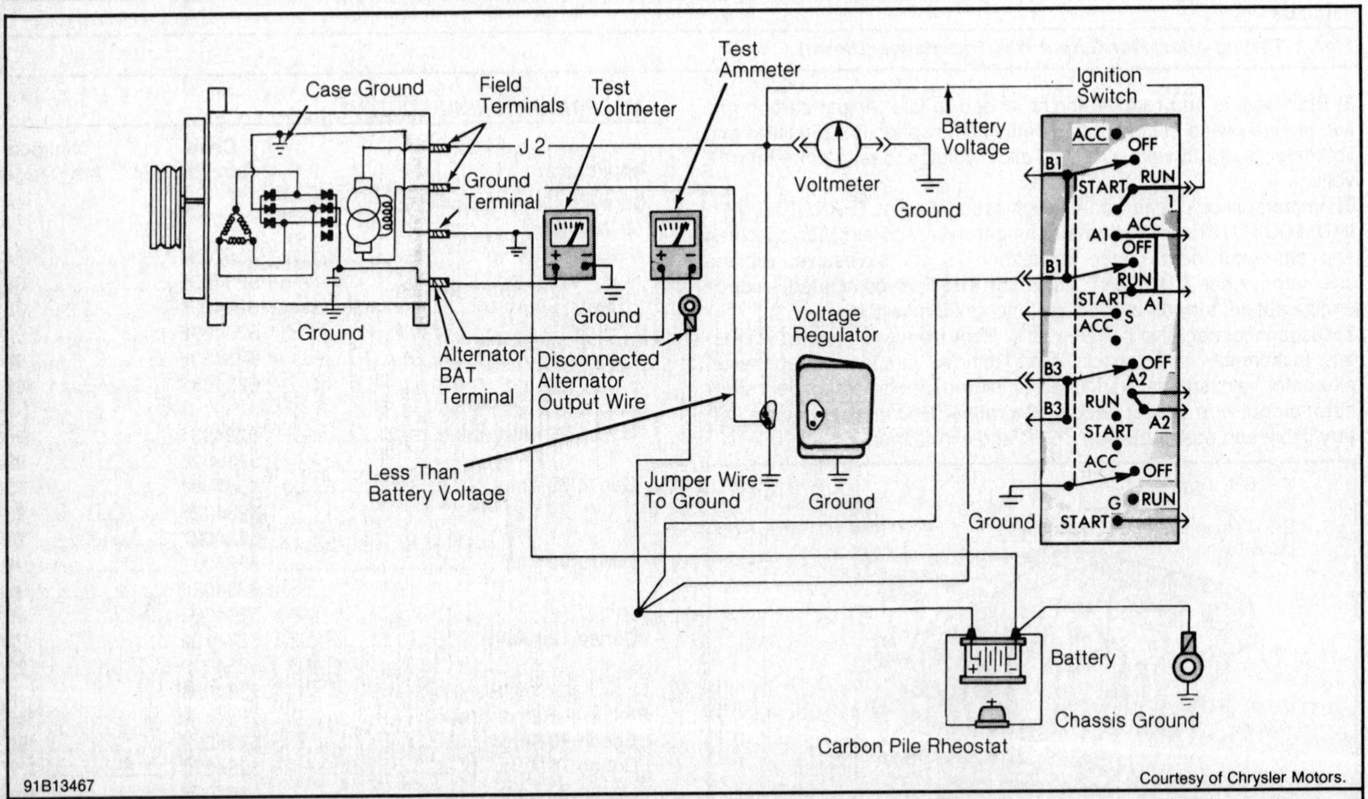
Test Ammeter
Case Ground
Field Terminals
Test Voltmeter
J 2
Ground Terminal
Battery Voltage
Voltmeter
Ground
Ignition Switch
Ground
Ground
Alternator BAT Terminal
Disconnected Alternator Output Wire
Voltage Regulator
Less Than Battery Voltage
Jumper Wire To Ground
Ground
Ground
Battery
Chassis Ground
Carbon Pile Rheostat
91B13467
Courtesy of Chrysler Motors.

Fig. 5: Testing Alternator Current Output (Diesel)

Voltage Regulator Test (Diesel) – **1)** Charge battery as necessary. Turn ignition off. Using a voltmeter with a minimum of a 0-18 volt scale, connect the positive lead to the positive battery post. Connect voltmeter negative lead to chassis ground. Connect a tachometer to the engine *See Fig. 6*.

2) Start engine and adjust idle to 1250 RPM. Turn all lights and accessories off. Observe voltmeter readings. Voltage regulator is working properly if voltage readings are within specifications. See VOLTAGE REGULATOR SPECIFICATIONS table.

3) If voltage is out of range, or is fluctuating, check the following:

- Voltage regulator is properly grounded
- Voltage regulator terminals are not spread causing an open
- Battery voltage is present at both terminals with ignition on

4) If voltage regulator ground connection and wiring check okay, replace regulator.

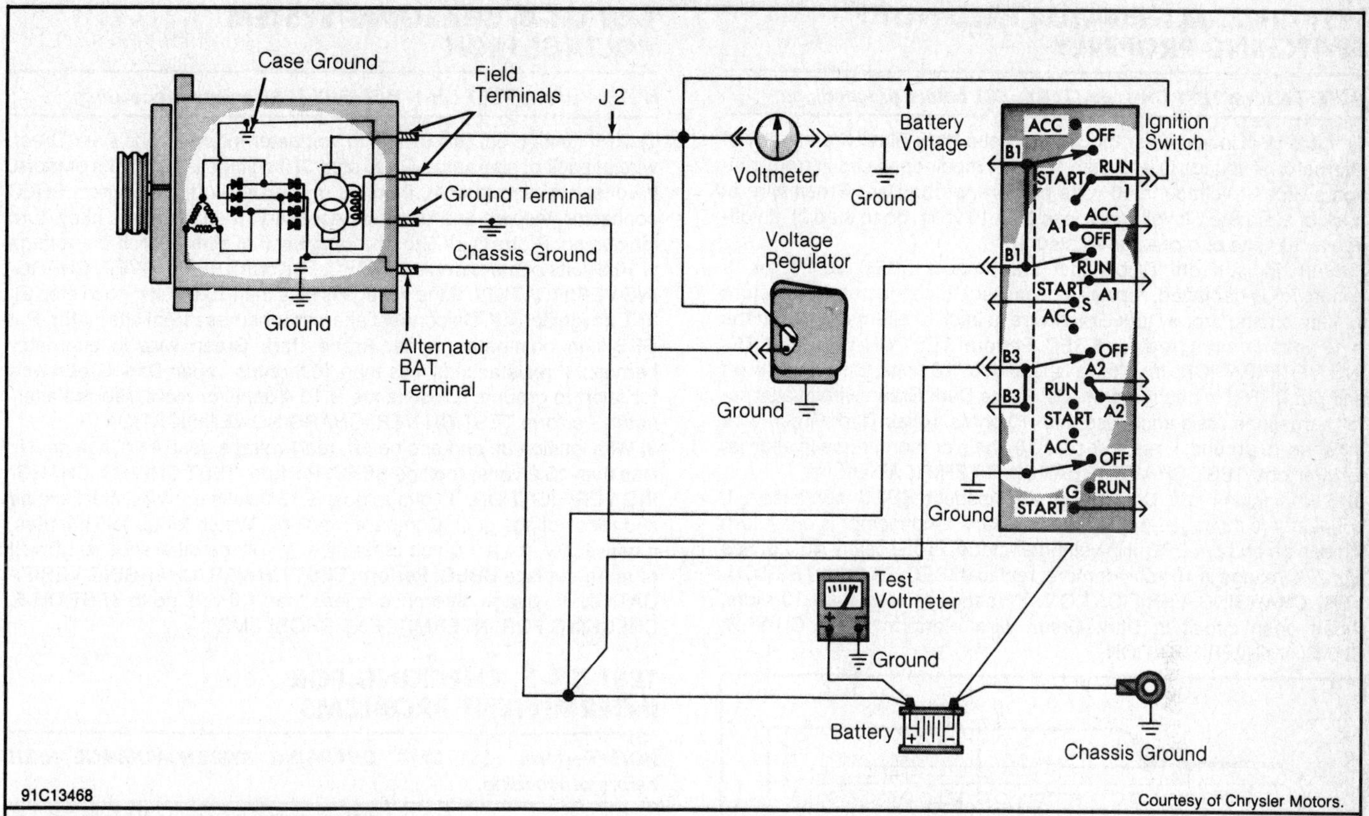

Case Ground
Field Terminals
J 2
Ground Terminal
Chassis Ground
Ground
Alternator BAT Terminal
Voltmeter
Battery Voltage
Ground
Voltage Regulator
Ground
Ignition Switch
ACC
OFF
RUN
START
B1
A1
S
B3
A2
G
Ground
Test Voltmeter
Ground
Battery
Chassis Ground
91C13468
Courtesy of Chrysler Motors.

Fig. 6: Testing Voltage Regulator (Diesel)

VOLTAGE REGULATOR SPECIFICATIONS

Temperature [1]	Volts
20° (-30°C)	14.6-15.8
80° (27°C)	13.9-14.4
140° (60°C)	13.0-13.7
Above 140° (60°)	Less than 13.7

1 – Ambient at voltage regulator.

TEST CH-1, BATTERY TEST

NOTE: Perform visual check before proceeding.

CAUTION: If battery shows signs of freezing or leakage, battery posts are loose or battery has low electrolyte level, DO NOT test.

1) If battery has a built-in hydrometer, go to step **2)**. Turn ignition and all accessories off. Using a voltmeter, check battery voltage across battery posts. If voltage is 12.3 volts or more, go to step **3)**. If voltage is less than 12.3 volts, charge battery and go to step **3)**.

2) If battery hydrometer is Green, go to step **3)**. If battery hydrometer is Yellow or a bright color, replace battery and perform TEST CH-VER, CHARGING VERIFICATION. If battery hydrometer is dark in color, charge battery and go to step **3)**.

3) Disconnect battery cables and check terminals and posts. Clean terminals and posts as necessary and retest. Connect a load tester to battery posts. Apply 300-amp load for 15 seconds. Wait 15 seconds to allow battery to stabilize. Apply a load equal to 50 percent of battery cold cranking rating for 15 seconds and record minimum voltage reading.

4) Determine battery operating temperature and check battery minimum voltage specification. See MINIMUM VOLTAGE SPECIFICATION table. If voltage is not to specification, replace battery and perform TEST CH-VER, CHARGING VERIFICATION. If voltage reading is to specification, go to step **5)**.

MINIMUM VOLTAGE SPECIFICATION

Battery Temperature	Minimum Volts
70°F (21°C) Or More	9.6
60°F (16°C)	9.5
50°F (12°C)	9.4
40°F (4°C)	9.3
30°F (-1°C)	9.1
20°F (-7°C)	8.9
10°F (-12°C)	8.7
0°F (-18°C)	8.5

5) Reconnect battery cables. Inspect alternator belt tension and condition. Replace belt as necessary. Start engine. Set engine speed to 2000 RPM for 30 seconds. Turn ignition off. Connect DRB-II. Turn ignition on with engine off. Read faults.

6) If DRB-II displays BATTERY TEMP SENSOR OUT OF LIMIT, replace SBEC and perform TEST CH-VER, CHARGING VERIFICATION. If DRB-II displays ALTERNATOR FIELD NOT SWITCHING PROPERLY, go to TEST CH-2, ALTERNATOR FIELD NOT SWITCHING PROPERLY. If DRB-II does not display either message, go to next step.

7) If DRB-II displays CHARGING SYSTEM VOLTAGE TOO LOW, go to TEST CH-3, CHARGING SYSTEM VOLTAGE LOW. If DRB-II displays CHARGING SYSTEM VOLTAGE TOO HIGH, go to TEST CH-4, CHARGING SYSTEM VOLTAGE HIGH. If DRB-II does not display any faults, there are either no fault messages or faults are intermittent.

8) Actuate the alternator field. Put DRB-II in voltmeter mode. Probe Dark Green wire at rear of alternator. Voltage reading should fluctuate between zero and battery voltage every 1.4 seconds. While watching DRB-II, wiggle wires between alternator harness and SBEC.

9) If there is no interruption in normal voltage cycle, test is complete. Perform TEST CH-VER, CHARGING VERIFICATION. If normal voltage cycle is interrupted, repair harness as necessary. Perform TEST CH-VER, CHARGING VERIFICATION.

1991 ELECTRICAL
Alternators & Regulators (Cont.)

TEST CH-2, ALTERNATOR FIELD NOT SWITCHING PROPERLY

NOTE: Perform TEST CH-1, BATTERY TEST before proceeding.

1) Put DRB-II in voltmeter mode and probe Dark Blue wire at back of alternator. If voltage is less than 10 volts, repair open circuit from ignition switch. If voltage is 10 volts or more, probe Dark Green wire at back of alternator. If voltage is less than 10 volts, go to step **2)**. If voltage is 10 volts or more , go to step **3)**.
2) Turn ignition off. Disconnect and inspect SBEC connector. If connector is damaged, repair as necessary. If connector is okay, turn ignition on and probe Dark Green wire at back of alternator. If voltage is 10 volts or more, replace SBEC. Perform TEST CH-VER, CHARGING VERIFICATION. If voltage is less than 10 volts, turn ignition off and put DRB-II in ohmmeter mode. Probe Dark Green wire in alternator harness. If resistance less than 10 ohms, repair Dark Green wire for short to ground. If resistance is 10 ohms or more, replace alternator. Perform TEST CH-VER, CHARGING VERIFICATION.
3) Turn ignition off. Disconnect and inspect SBEC connector. If connector is damaged, repair as necessary. If connector is okay, turn ignition on and put DRB-II in voltmeter mode. Probe cavity No. 20. *See Fig. 7*. If voltage is 10 volts or more, replace SBEC. Perform TEST CH-VER, CHARGING VERIFICATION. If voltage is less than 10 volts, repair open circuit in Dark Green wire. Perform TEST CH-VER, CHARGING VERIFICATION.

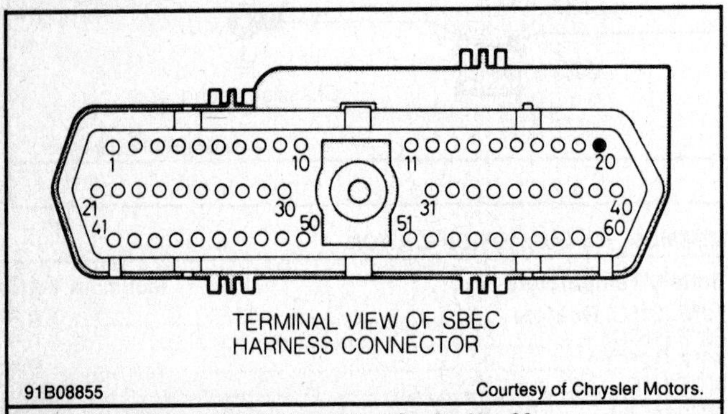
1
10
11
20
21
30
31
40
41
50
51
60
TERMINAL VIEW OF SBEC
HARNESS CONNECTOR
91B08855
Courtesy of Chrysler Motors.

Fig. 7: Identifying SBEC Connector Cavity No. 20

TEST CH-3, CHARGING SYSTEM VOLTAGE LOW

NOTE: Perform TEST CH-1, BATTERY TEST before proceeding.

1) Read voltage goal. If voltage goal is 15.1 volts or more, replace SBEC. If voltage goal is less than 15.1 volts, use an external voltmeter and connect positive lead to the alternator BAT (B+) and negative lead to battery positive terminal.

CAUTION: Ensure all wires are clear of moving parts.

2) Start engine. If voltage is 0.4 volt or more, repair Black or Red wire for high resistance between alternator and battery. If voltage is less than 0.4 volt, turn ignition off. Using an external voltmeter, connect positive lead to alternator case and negative lead to negative battery terminal.
3) Start engine. If voltage is 0.1 volt or more, repair high resistance between alternator and negative battery cable. If the voltage is less than 0.1 volt, manually set engine speed to 1600 RPM. Compare voltage goal on DRB-II and reading on external meter. If difference is 1.0 volt or more, replace alternator. If difference is less than 1.0 volt, go to TEST CH-5, CHECKING FOR INTERMITTENT PROBLEMS.

TEST CH-4, CHARGING SYSTEM VOLTAGE HIGH

NOTE: Perform TEST CH-1, BATTERY TEST before proceeding.

1) Turn ignition on. Put DRB-II in voltmeter mode. Probe Dark Green wire at back of alternator. Go to step **3)** if voltage is 10.0 volts or more. If voltage is less than 10.0 volts, turn ignition off. Disconnect SBEC connector, inspect and repair if necessary. If connector is okay, turn ignition on. Probe Dark Green wire at back of alternator. If the voltage is 10.0 volts or more, replace SBEC. Perform TEST CH-VER, CHARGING VERIFICATION. If the voltage is less than 10.0 volts, go to step **2)**.
2) Turn ignition off. Disconnect alternator harness from alternator. Put DRB-II in ohmmeter mode. Probe Dark Green wire in alternator harness. If resistance is less than 10.0 ohms, repair Dark Green wire for short to ground. If resistance is 10.0 ohms or more, replace alternator. Perform TEST CH-VER, CHARGING VERIFICATION.
3) With ignition on and engine off, read voltage goal. If voltage goal is less than 13.0 volts, replace SBEC. Perform TEST CH-VER, CHARGING VERIFICATION. If voltage goal is 13.0 volts or more, start engine and read voltage goal. Compare readings. Watch for up to 5 minutes, if necessary, for a 1.0-volt difference. If voltage difference is 1.0 volt or more, replace SBEC. Perform TEST CH-VER, CHARGING VERIFICATION. If voltage difference is less than 1.0 volt, go to TEST CH-5, CHECKING FOR INTERMITTENT PROBLEMS.

TEST CH-5, CHECKING FOR INTERMITTENT PROBLEMS

NOTE: Perform TEST CH-4, CHARGING SYSTEM VOLTAGE HIGH before proceeding.

1) Actuate the alternator field. Put DRB-II in voltmeter mode. Probe the Dark Green wire at back of alternator.

NOTE: Voltage should cycle from zero to battery voltage every 1.4 seconds.

2) While watching the DRB-II, wiggle wires between alternator and SBEC. If there is any interruption in the voltage cycle, repair wire at point cycle at which was interrupted. If there is no interruption of voltage cycle, test is complete. Perform TEST CH-VER, CHARGING VERIFICATION.

TEST CH-VER, CHARGING VERIFICATION

1) Inspect and ensure that all engine components are connected.
2) If the SBEC has been changed and if vehicle is equipped with a factory theft alarm, start vehicle at least 20 times so alarm will activate when desired. If the vehicle is a minivan or truck body, write the Emission Maintenance Reminder (EMR) mileage into the new SBEC.
3) Connect DRB-II to engine diagnostic and erase faults.
4) Ensure no other charging system problems remain by doing the following:

- Start engine.
- Raise engine speed to 2000 RPM for at least 30 seconds.
- Allow engine to idle.
- Turn engine off.
- Turn ignition on.
- With DRB-II, read fault messages.

5) If repaired fault has reset, repair is incomplete. Check all pertinent MITCHELL TECHNICAL SERVICE BULLETINS and return to TEST CH-1, BATTERY TEST if necessary. If there are no other faults, repair is complete.

BENCH TESTING

NOTE: Alternators are non-serviceable and must be replaced as complete units.

TORQUE SPECIFICATIONS

TORQUE SPECIFICATIONS

Application	Ft. Lbs. (N.m)
Alternator Mounting Bolts	
2.5L	40 (54)
3.0L	
Upper	18 (24)
Lower	21 (28)
3.3L	40 (54)
3.9L & 5.2L	30 (41)
5.9L	
Gas	[1]
Diesel	
Upper	18 (24)
Lower	32 (43)

[1] Information not available from manufacturer.

1991 ELECTRICAL
Starters – Bosch & Nippondenso

Caravan, Dakota, Pickup, Ramcharger, RWD Van, Town & Country, Voyager

DESCRIPTION

Bosch starter is a permanent magnet motor design. A planetary gear system between the armature and pinion shaft makes it possible to increase torque and reduce starter size. The planetary gear drive is splined to both the armature shaft and overrunning clutch. Starter torque is transmitted to the overrunning clutch pinion through the planetary gears which provide higher rotational speeds. Starter has serviceable solenoid and gear and clutch assembly.

Nippondenso starter is a 4-field, 4-brush 12-volt motor with a solenoid mounted within the housing. The unit has a 2-to-1 reduction gear set in a die cast aluminum housing. Starter has serviceable gear and clutch assembly only. If starter solenoid fails, entire starter motor must be replaced.

STARTER APPLICATIONS

Model	Type
Caravan, Town & Country & Voyager	
2.5L	Bosch
3.0L	[1]
3.3L	Nippondenso
Dakota	
2.5L	Bosch
3.9L & 5.2L	Nippondenso
Pickup & Ramcharger	
3.9L, 5.2L, 5.9L & 5.9L Diesel	Nippondenso
RWD Van	
3.9L, 5.2L & 5.9L	Nippondenso

[1] – May be equipped with either Bosch or Nippondenso starter.

TROUBLE SHOOTING

STARTER DOES NOT CRANK OR CRANKS SLOWLY

1) Ensure battery is fully charged. Turn on headlights. Crank engine using ignition key. If starter fails to crank or cranks slowly then stops and headlights dim way down, proceed to AMPERAGE DRAW TEST under ON-VEHICLE TESTING.
2) If starter fails to crank or cranks slowly and headlights dim slightly, proceed to STARTER RESISTANCE TEST under ON-VEHICLE TESTING. If starter fails to crank engine and headlights do not dim, proceed to RELAY TEST under ON-VEHICLE TESTING.

ON-VEHICLE TESTING

AMPERAGE DRAW TEST

NOTE: Ensure battery is fully charged and terminals are clean and tight. Perform a battery load test before proceeding.

1) Using an inductive volt/ammeter type battery tester, clamp ammeter probe to positive battery cable. Connect positive voltmeter lead to positive battery post and negative lead to negative battery post. On 3.3L engine, disconnect coil pack harness connector. On 5.9L diesel engine, disconnect both wires at fuel solenoid on injection pump. On all other models, disconnect coil wire from distributor cap and attach to ground.
2) Ensure that all vehicle accessories are off and transmission is in Neutral or Park. Crank engine using ignition key and observe exact reading on volt/ammeter. Readings should be as specified. See STARTER SPECIFICATIONS table in this article.
3) If amperage is greater than specified or voltage is less than specified, check and repair wiring between battery and starter. If wiring is okay, turn engine by hand and check for ease of turning. If engine turns okay, proceed to STARTER RESISTANCE TEST.

STARTER RESISTANCE TEST

1) Using a voltmeter that will indicate tenths of a volt, perform the following voltage drop tests. Crank engine and observe voltmeter readings with voltmeter connected at following locations:
- Positive lead to battery positive post and negative lead to battery terminal on starter.
- Positive lead to starter housing and negative lead to negative post on battery.
- Positive lead to battery negative post and negative lead to battery cable engine ground connection.

2) If voltage reading is greater than .2 volt at any connection, repair or replace wiring, or repair starter-to-engine ground. If voltage readings are less than .2 volt at all connections, proceed to step **3)**.
3) Connect voltmeter at following locations and observe readings:
- Positive lead to battery positive post and negative lead to positive cable clamp.
- Positive lead to battery negative post and negative lead to negative cable clamp.

If either reading is greater than zero, repair or replace battery cables. If both readings are zero, proceed to step **4)**.
4) Connect positive voltmeter lead to battery positive post and negative lead to starter solenoid battery terminal. If voltage reading is greater than .3 volt, repair or replace cable between starter and battery. If voltage reading is less than .3 volt, starter circuitry is okay and test is complete. Repair or replace starter.

RELAY TEST

1) On automatic transmission/transaxle vehicles, put gear selector in Neutral or Park. On manual transmission/transaxle vehicles, put gear selector in Neutral. Set parking brake and block wheels. DO NOT remove relay connector. Using a 12-volt test light, check for power between starter relay battery terminal and ground. If power does not exist, repair wiring. If power exists, proceed to step **2)**.
2) Using test light, check for power at ignition terminal on stater relay while a helper holds key in START position. If power does not exist, repair wiring between ignition switch and starter relay. If power exists, proceed to step **3)**.
3) Reconnect jumper wire between battery and ignition terminals. Connect a second jumper wire between starter relay ground terminal and chassis ground. If engine cranks, starter relay is good. Check and repair poor ground connection between relay housing and mounting surface. On models with automatic transmission, inspect neutral safety switch for malfunction and transmission linkage for improper adjustment.

SOLENOID TEST

1) Connect a heavy jumper wire between battery and starter solenoid terminals on starter relay. If engine cranks, solenoid is okay. Proceed to RELAY TEST.
2) If engine does not crank, check and repair wiring between starter relay and starter. Repeat test. If engine still fails to crank, repair or replace starter.

BENCH TESTING

CAUTION: Starters are extremely sensitive to hammering, shocks and external pressure. DO NOT clamp starter in a vise by field housing. Starter can be clamped in vise by mounting flange.

INSPECTION

1) Check pinion gear for freedom of movement by turning it on shaft. Check armature for freedom of movement by prying on pinion gear to engage it with shaft.
2) If gear and armature do not rotate freely, starter should be disassembled. If pinion gear and armature rotate freely, proceed to NO-LOAD TEST.
3) No rotation and high current draw indicates that bearings are seized or connecting terminal or armature windings are shorted to ground.

4) No rotation or current flow indicates one or both of the following:

- Open armature windings (inspect commutator for burned commutator bars after disassembly).
- Broken brush springs, worn brushes, protruding insulation between commutator bars, or other causes that could prevent good contact between brushes and commutator.

NO-LOAD TEST

1) Mount starter in soft-jawed vise by mounting flange. Install voltmeter between solenoid terminal and starter frame.
2) Connect a switch, ammeter and fully charged battery in series with starter motor. Ensure switch is in the OPEN position prior to connecting battery.
3) Close switch and note voltage and amperage. Reading should be within specification. See STARTER SPECIFICATIONS table at end of article.
4) Disconnect electrical connections with switch in OPEN position only. Repair or replace starter if not within specification.

CAUTION: DO NOT operate starter for more than 30 seconds at a time without allowing starter to cool for at least 2 minutes.

OVERHAUL

STARTER GEAR AND CLUTCH

Bosch – Remove starter. Remove 2 starter solenoid field terminal nuts. Remove 3 solenoid mounting screws and remove solenoid. Remove 2 through bolts securing starter drive end housing to the motor housing. Remove rubber seal and pull gear and clutch assembly from drive housing. To install, reverse removal procedure
Nippondenso – Remove starter. Remove 2 gear housing attaching screws and separate gear housing from solenoid housing. Remove pinion gear, pinion gear bearing, and drive gear from gear housing. Remove starter gear and clutch assembly from solenoid housing. Clean and lubricate pinion gear, bearing and drive gear and reinstall in gear housing. Install starter gear and clutch assembly in solenoid. To install starter, reverse removal procedure.

STARTER SPECIFICATIONS

STARTER SPECIFICATIONS

Application	Specification
Cranking Amps [1]	
Gas	150-220 Amps
Diesel	450-550 Amps
Cranking Voltage	
Gas	7.5 Volts
Diesel	8 Volts
No-Load Test	
Amperage	
2.5L	69 @ 3447 RPM
3.0L	73 @ 3473 RPM
3.3L, 3.9L, 5.2L & 5.9L (Gas)	@ 3601 RPM
5.9L (Diesel)	220 @ 4200 RPM
Voltage	
Gas & Diesel	11 Volts

[1] – Engine at full operating temperature.

TORQUE SPECIFICATIONS

TORQUE SPECIFICATIONS

Application	Ft. Lbs. (N.m)
Mounting Bolts	
2.5L, 3.0L & 3.8L	40 (54)
3.9L, 5.2L & 5.9L (Gas)	50 (68)
5.9L (Diesel)	32 (43)

1991 WIRING DIAGRAMS
Caravan, Town & Country, & Voyager

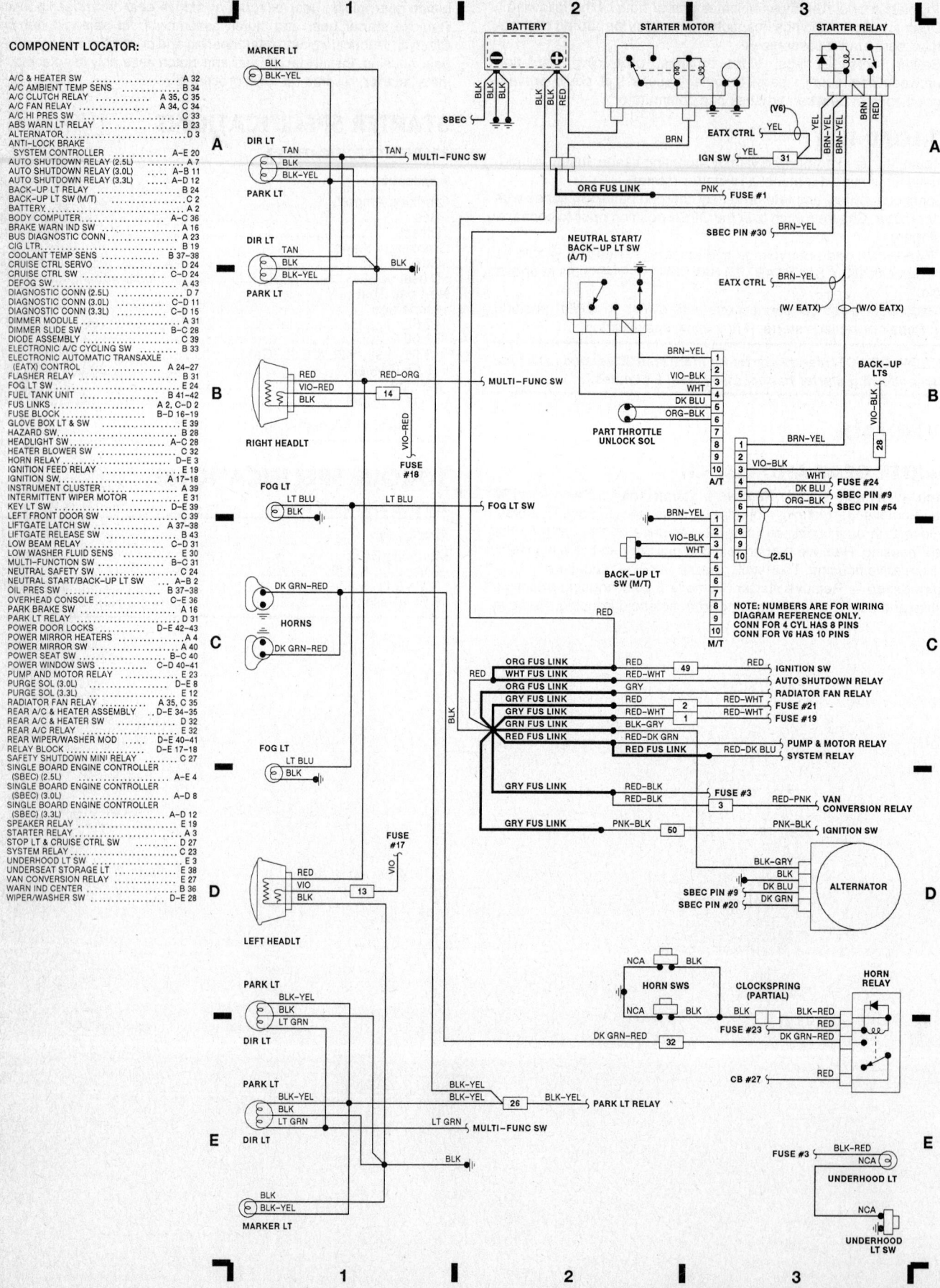

COMPONENT LOCATOR:

A/C & HEATER SW	A 32
A/C AMBIENT TEMP SENS	B 34
A/C CLUTCH RELAY	A 35, C 35
A/C FAN RELAY	A 34, C 34
A/C HI PRES SW	C 33
ABS WARN LT RELAY	B 23
ALTERNATOR	D 3
ANTI-LOCK BRAKE SYSTEM CONTROLLER	A-E 20
AUTO SHUTDOWN RELAY (2.5L)	A 7
AUTO SHUTDOWN RELAY (3.0L)	A-B 11
AUTO SHUTDOWN RELAY (3.3L)	A-D 12
BACK-UP LT RELAY	B 24
BACK-UP LT SW (M/T)	C 2
BATTERY	A 2
BODY COMPUTER	A-C 36
BRAKE WARN IND SW	A 16
BUS DIAGNOSTIC CONN	A 23
CIG LTR	B 19
COOLANT TEMP SENS	B 37-38
CRUISE CTRL SERVO	D 24
CRUISE CTRL SW	C-D 24
DEFOG SW	A 43
DIAGNOSTIC CONN (2.5L)	D 7
DIAGNOSTIC CONN (3.0L)	C-D 11
DIAGNOSTIC CONN (3.3L)	C-D 15
DIMMER MODULE	A 31
DIMMER SLIDE SW	B-C 28
DIODE ASSEMBLY	C 39
ELECTRONIC A/C CYCLING SW	B 33
ELECTRONIC AUTOMATIC TRANSAXLE (EATX) CONTROL	A 24-27
FLASHER RELAY	B 31
FOG LT SW	E 24
FUEL TANK UNIT	B 41-42
FUS LINKS	A 2, C-D 2
FUSE BLOCK	B-D 16-19
GLOVE BOX LT & SW	E 39
HAZARD SW	B 28
HEADLIGHT SW	A-C 28
HEATER BLOWER SW	C 32
HORN RELAY	D-E 3
IGNITION FEED RELAY	E 19
IGNITION SW	A 17-18
INSTRUMENT CLUSTER	A 39
INTERMITTENT WIPER MOTOR	E 31
KEY LT SW	D-E 39
LEFT FRONT DOOR SW	C 39
LIFTGATE LATCH SW	A 37-38
LIFTGATE RELEASE SW	B 43
LOW BEAM RELAY	C-D 31
LOW WASHER FLUID SENS	E 30
MULTI-FUNCTION SW	B-C 31
NEUTRAL SAFETY SW	C 24
NEUTRAL START/BACK-UP LT SW	A-B 2
OIL PRES SW	B 37-38
OVERHEAD CONSOLE	C-E 36
PARK BRAKE SW	A 16
PARK LT RELAY	D 31
POWER DOOR LOCKS	D-E 42-43
POWER MIRROR HEATERS	A 4
POWER MIRROR SW	A 40
POWER SEAT SW	B-C 40
POWER WINDOW SWS	C-D 40-41
PUMP AND MOTOR RELAY	E 23
PURGE SOL (3.0L)	D-E 8
PURGE SOL (3.3L)	E 12
RADIATOR FAN RELAY	A 35, C 35
REAR A/C HEATER ASSEMBLY	D-E 34-35
REAR A/C & HEATER SW	D 32
REAR A/C RELAY	E 32
REAR WIPER/WASHER MOD	D-E 40-41
RELAY BLOCK	D-E 17-18
SAFETY SHUTDOWN MINI RELAY	C 27
SINGLE BOARD ENGINE CONTROLLER (SBEC) (2.5L)	A-E 4
SINGLE BOARD ENGINE CONTROLLER (SBEC) (3.0L)	A-D 8
SINGLE BOARD ENGINE CONTROLLER (SBEC) (3.3L)	A-D 12
SPEAKER RELAY	E 19
STARTER RELAY	A 3
STOP LT & CRUISE CTRL SW	D 27
SYSTEM RELAY	C 23
UNDERHOOD LT SW	E 3
UNDERSEAT STORAGE LT	E 38
VAN CONVERSION RELAY	E 27
WARN IND CENTER	B 36
WIPER/WASHER SW	D-E 28

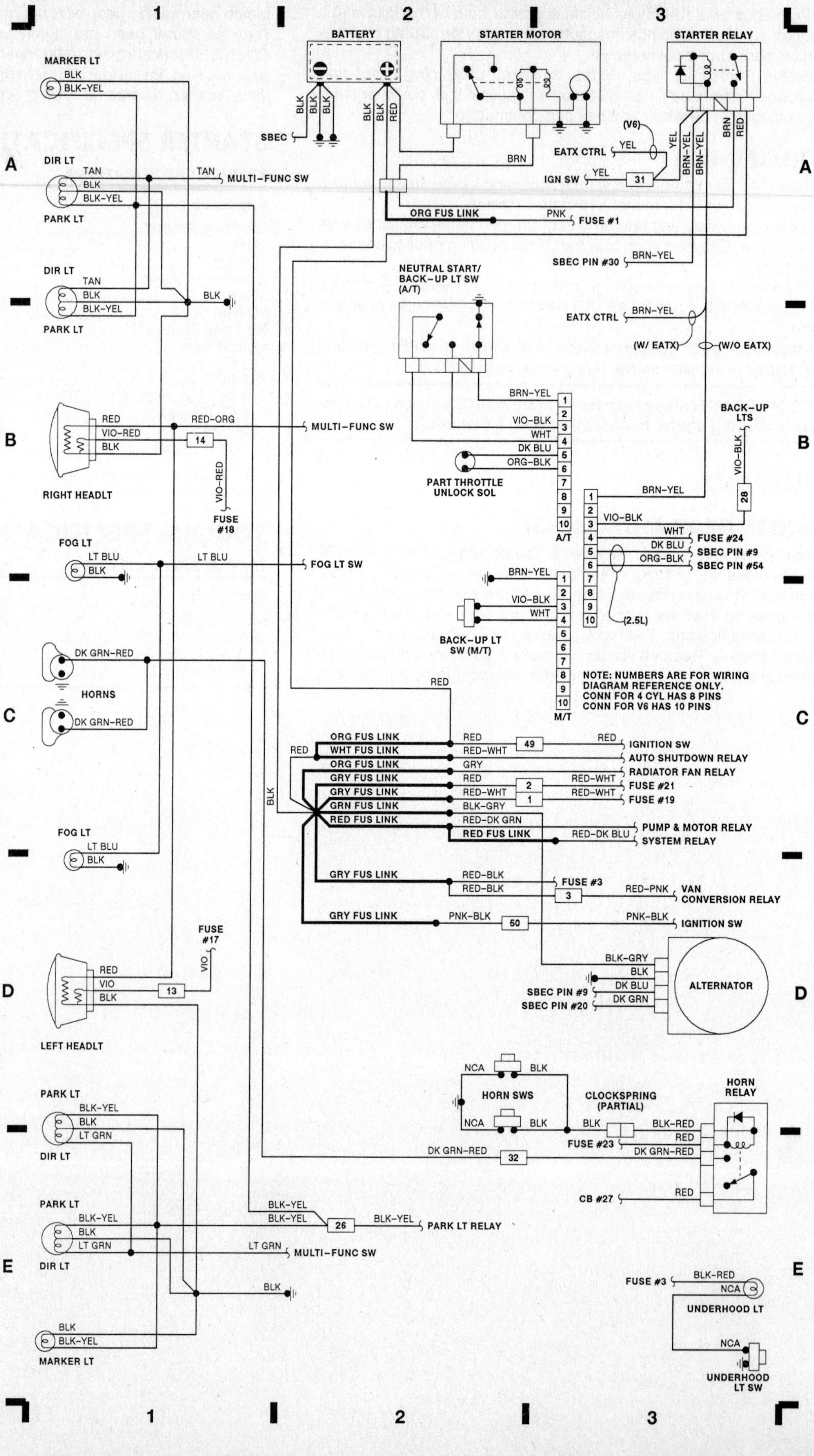
1
2
3
A
B
C
D
E
BATTERY
STARTER MOTOR
STARTER RELAY
MARKER LT
DIR LT
PARK LT
MULTI-FUNC SW
SBEC
EATX CTRL
IGN SW
ORG FUS LINK
FUSE #1
SBEC PIN #30
NEUTRAL START/
BACK-UP LT SW
(A/T)
(W/ EATX)
(W/O EATX)
BACK-UP
LTS
RIGHT HEADLT
FUSE
#18
PART THROTTLE
UNLOCK SOL
FUSE #24
SBEC PIN #9
SBEC PIN #54
FOG LT
FOG LT SW
BACK-UP LT
SW (M/T)
HORNS
NOTE: NUMBERS ARE FOR WIRING
DIAGRAM REFERENCE ONLY.
CONN FOR 4 CYL HAS 8 PINS
CONN FOR V6 HAS 10 PINS
WHT FUS LINK
GRY FUS LINK
GRN FUS LINK
RED FUS LINK
IGNITION SW
AUTO SHUTDOWN RELAY
RADIATOR FAN RELAY
FUSE #21
FUSE #19
PUMP & MOTOR RELAY
SYSTEM RELAY
FUSE #3
VAN
CONVERSION RELAY
FUSE
#17
ALTERNATOR
SBEC PIN #20
LEFT HEADLT
HORN SWS
CLOCKSPRING
(PARTIAL)
HORN
RELAY
FUSE #23
CB #27
PARK LT RELAY
UNDERHOOD LT
UNDERHOOD
LT SW

1991 WIRING DIAGRAMS
Caravan, Town & Country, & Voyager (Cont.)

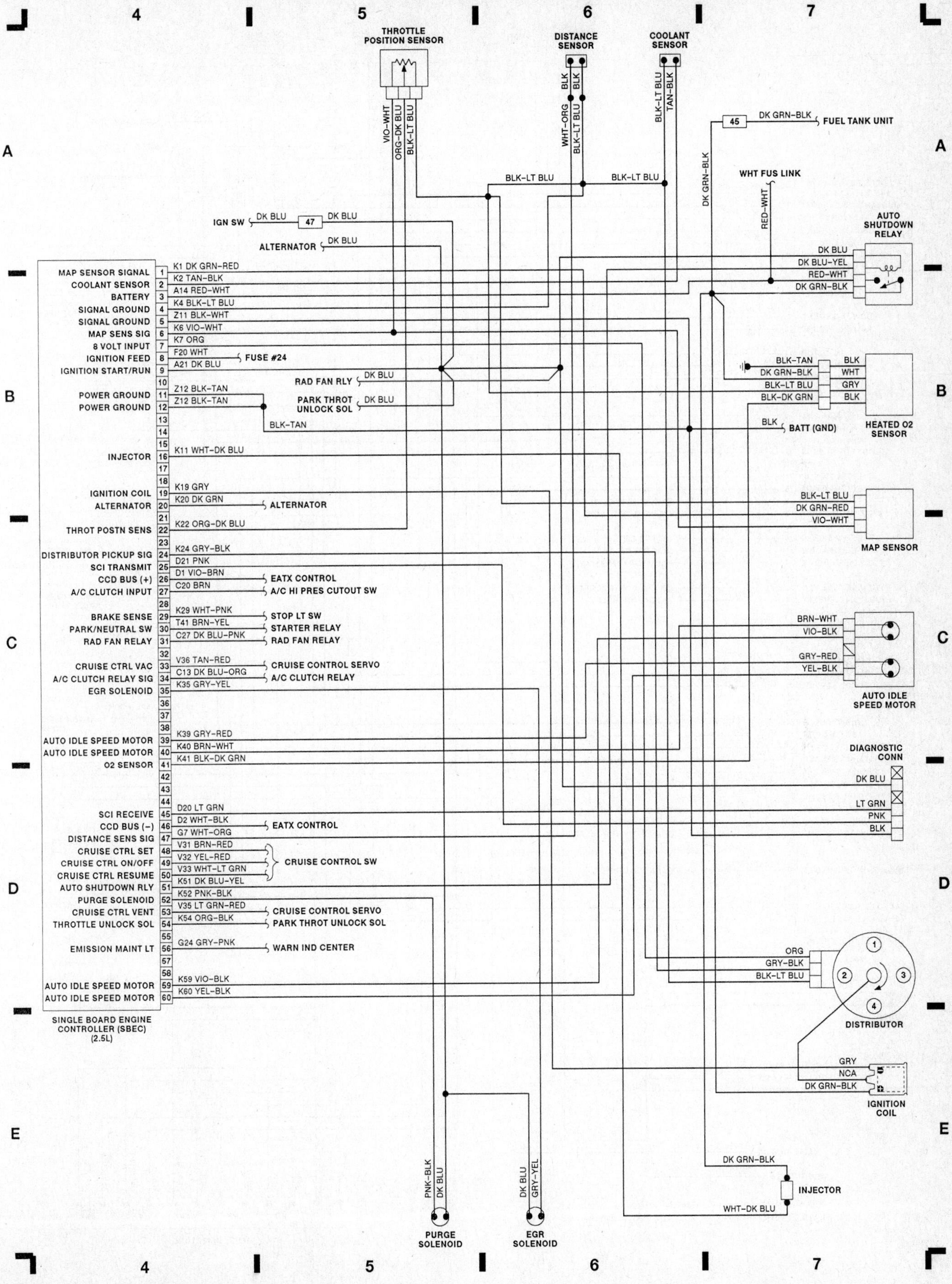
THROTTLE POSITION SENSOR
VIO-WHT
ORG-DK BLU
BLK-LT BLU
DISTANCE SENSOR
BLK
BLK
WHT-ORG
BLK-LT BLU
COOLANT SENSOR
BLK-LT BLU
TAN-BLK
45
DK GRN-BLK
FUEL TANK UNIT
DK GRN-BLK
WHT FUS LINK
RED-WHT
BLK-LT BLU
BLK-LT BLU
IGN SW
DK BLU
47
DK BLU
ALTERNATOR
DK BLU
AUTO SHUTDOWN RELAY
DK BLU
DK BLU-YEL
RED-WHT
DK GRN-BLK
MAP SENSOR SIGNAL 1 K1 DK GRN-RED
COOLANT SENSOR 2 K2 TAN-BLK
BATTERY 3 A14 RED-WHT
SIGNAL GROUND 4 K4 BLK-LT BLU
SIGNAL GROUND 5 Z11 BLK-WHT
MAP SENS SIG 6 K6 VIO-WHT
8 VOLT INPUT 7 K7 ORG
IGNITION FEED 8 F20 WHT
FUSE #24
IGNITION START/RUN 9 A21 DK BLU
10
RAD FAN RLY
DK BLU
POWER GROUND 11 Z12 BLK-TAN
POWER GROUND 12 Z12 BLK-TAN
PARK THROT UNLOCK SOL
DK BLU
13
BLK-TAN
14
15
INJECTOR 16 K11 WHT-DK BLU
17
18
IGNITION COIL 19 K19 GRY
ALTERNATOR 20 K20 DK GRN
ALTERNATOR
21
THROT POSTN SENS 22 K22 ORG-DK BLU
23
DISTRIBUTOR PICKUP SIG 24 K24 GRY-BLK
SCI TRANSMIT 25 D21 PNK
CCD BUS (+) 26 D1 VIO-BRN
EATX CONTROL
A/C CLUTCH INPUT 27 C20 BRN
A/C HI PRES CUTOUT SW
28
BRAKE SENSE 29 K29 WHT-PNK
STOP LT SW
PARK/NEUTRAL SW 30 T41 BRN-YEL
STARTER RELAY
RAD FAN RELAY 31 C27 DK BLU-PNK
RAD FAN RELAY
32
CRUISE CTRL VAC 33 V36 TAN-RED
CRUISE CONTROL SERVO
A/C CLUTCH RELAY SIG 34 C13 DK BLU-ORG
A/C CLUTCH RELAY
EGR SOLENOID 35 K35 GRY-YEL
36
37
38
AUTO IDLE SPEED MOTOR 39 K39 GRY-RED
AUTO IDLE SPEED MOTOR 40 K40 BRN-WHT
O2 SENSOR 41 K41 BLK-DK GRN
42
43
44
SCI RECEIVE 45 D20 LT GRN
CCD BUS (-) 46 D2 WHT-BLK
EATX CONTROL
DISTANCE SENS SIG 47 G7 WHT-ORG
CRUISE CTRL SET 48 V31 BRN-RED
CRUISE CTRL ON/OFF 49 V32 YEL-RED
CRUISE CONTROL SW
CRUISE CTRL RESUME 50 V33 WHT-LT GRN
AUTO SHUTDOWN RLY 51 K51 DK BLU-YEL
PURGE SOLENOID 52 K52 PNK-BLK
CRUISE CTRL VENT 53 V35 LT GRN-RED
CRUISE CONTROL SERVO
THROTTLE UNLOCK SOL 54 K54 ORG-BLK
PARK THROT UNLOCK SOL
55
EMISSION MAINT LT 56 G24 GRY-PNK
WARN IND CENTER
57
58
AUTO IDLE SPEED MOTOR 59 K59 VIO-BLK
AUTO IDLE SPEED MOTOR 60 K60 YEL-BLK
SINGLE BOARD ENGINE CONTROLLER (SBEC) (2.5L)
BLK-TAN
DK GRN-BLK
BLK-LT BLU
BLK-DK GRN
BLK
WHT
GRY
BLK
HEATED O2 SENSOR
BLK
BATT (GND)
BLK-LT BLU
DK GRN-RED
VIO-WHT
MAP SENSOR
BRN-WHT
VIO-BLK
GRY-RED
YEL-BLK
AUTO IDLE SPEED MOTOR
DIAGNOSTIC CONN
DK BLU
LT GRN
PNK
BLK
ORG
GRY-BLK
BLK-LT BLU
1
2
3
4
DISTRIBUTOR
GRY
NCA
DK GRN-BLK
IGNITION COIL
DK GRN-BLK
INJECTOR
WHT-DK BLU
PNK-BLK
DK BLU
PURGE SOLENOID
DK BLU
GRY-YEL
EGR SOLENOID
4
5
6
7
A
B
C
D
E

1991 WIRING DIAGRAMS
Caravan, Town & Country, & Voyager (Cont.)

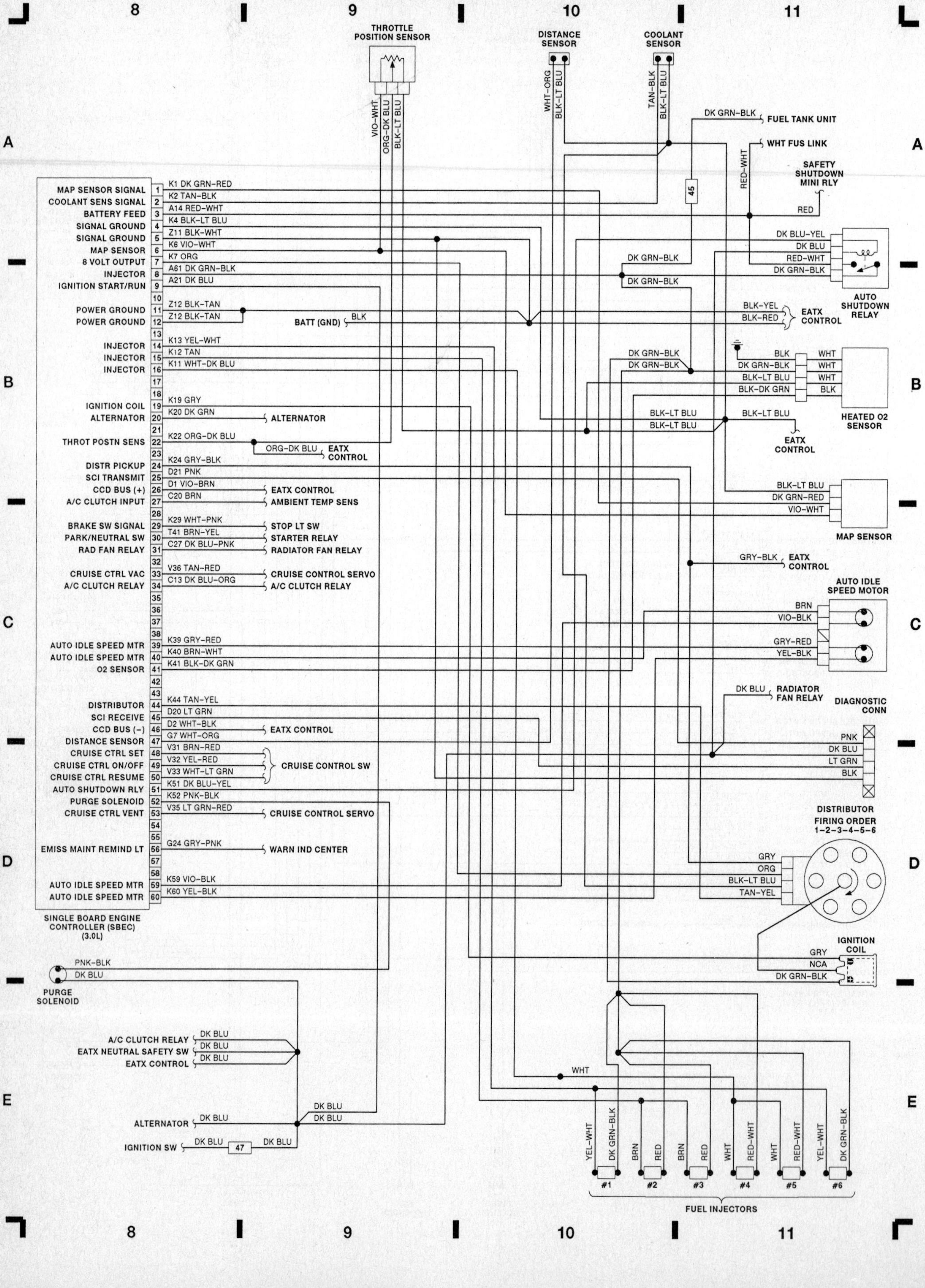
8
9
10
11
A
B
C
D
E
THROTTLE POSITION SENSOR
VIO-WHT
ORG-DK BLU
BLK-LT BLU
DISTANCE SENSOR
WHT-ORG
BLK-LT BLU
COOLANT SENSOR
TAN-BLK
BLK-LT BLU
DK GRN-BLK
FUEL TANK UNIT
WHT FUS LINK
RED-WHT
SAFETY SHUTDOWN MINI RLY
45
RED
MAP SENSOR SIGNAL 1 K1 DK GRN-RED
COOLANT SENS SIGNAL 2 K2 TAN-BLK
BATTERY FEED 3 A14 RED-WHT
SIGNAL GROUND 4 K4 BLK-LT BLU
SIGNAL GROUND 5 Z11 BLK-WHT
MAP SENSOR 6 K6 VIO-WHT
8 VOLT OUTPUT 7 K7 ORG
INJECTOR 8 A61 DK GRN-BLK
IGNITION START/RUN 9 A21 DK BLU
10
POWER GROUND 11 Z12 BLK-TAN
POWER GROUND 12 Z12 BLK-TAN
13
INJECTOR 14 K13 YEL-WHT
INJECTOR 15 K12 TAN
INJECTOR 16 K11 WHT-DK BLU
17
18
IGNITION COIL 19 K19 GRY
ALTERNATOR 20 K20 DK GRN
21
THROT POSTN SENS 22 K22 ORG-DK BLU
23
DISTR PICKUP 24 K24 GRY-BLK
SCI TRANSMIT 25 D21 PNK
CCD BUS (+) 26 D1 VIO-BRN
A/C CLUTCH INPUT 27 C20 BRN
28
BRAKE SW SIGNAL 29 K29 WHT-PNK
PARK/NEUTRAL SW 30 T41 BRN-YEL
RAD FAN RELAY 31 C27 DK BLU-PNK
32
CRUISE CTRL VAC 33 V36 TAN-RED
A/C CLUTCH RELAY 34 C13 DK BLU-ORG
35
36
37
38
AUTO IDLE SPEED MTR 39 K39 GRY-RED
AUTO IDLE SPEED MTR 40 K40 BRN-WHT
O2 SENSOR 41 K41 BLK-DK GRN
42
43
DISTRIBUTOR 44 K44 TAN-YEL
SCI RECEIVE 45 D20 LT GRN
CCD BUS (-) 46 D2 WHT-BLK
DISTANCE SENSOR 47 G7 WHT-ORG
CRUISE CTRL SET 48 V31 BRN-RED
CRUISE CTRL ON/OFF 49 V32 YEL-RED
CRUISE CTRL RESUME 50 V33 WHT-LT GRN
AUTO SHUTDOWN RLY 51 K51 DK BLU-YEL
PURGE SOLENOID 52 K52 PNK-BLK
CRUISE CTRL VENT 53 V35 LT GRN-RED
54
55
EMISS MAINT REMIND LT 56 G24 GRY-PNK
57
58
AUTO IDLE SPEED MTR 59 K59 VIO-BLK
AUTO IDLE SPEED MTR 60 K60 YEL-BLK
SINGLE BOARD ENGINE CONTROLLER (SBEC) (3.0L)
ALTERNATOR
ORG-DK BLU
EATX CONTROL
EATX CONTROL
AMBIENT TEMP SENS
STOP LT SW
STARTER RELAY
RADIATOR FAN RELAY
CRUISE CONTROL SERVO
A/C CLUTCH RELAY
EATX CONTROL
CRUISE CONTROL SW
CRUISE CONTROL SERVO
WARN IND CENTER
BATT (GND)
BLK
DK BLU-YEL
DK BLU
RED-WHT
DK GRN-BLK
AUTO SHUTDOWN RELAY
DK GRN-BLK
DK GRN-BLK
BLK-YEL
BLK-RED
EATX CONTROL
DK GRN-BLK
DK GRN-BLK
BLK
DK GRN-BLK
BLK-LT BLU
BLK-DK GRN
WHT
WHT
WHT
BLK
HEATED O2 SENSOR
BLK-LT BLU
BLK-LT BLU
BLK-LT BLU
EATX CONTROL
BLK-LT BLU
DK GRN-RED
VIO-WHT
MAP SENSOR
GRY-BLK
EATX CONTROL
AUTO IDLE SPEED MOTOR
BRN
VIO-BLK
GRY-RED
YEL-BLK
DK BLU
RADIATOR FAN RELAY
DIAGNOSTIC CONN
PNK
DK BLU
LT GRN
BLK
DISTRIBUTOR FIRING ORDER 1-2-3-4-5-6
GRY
ORG
BLK-LT BLU
TAN-YEL
IGNITION COIL
GRY
NCA
DK GRN-BLK
PNK-BLK
DK BLU
PURGE SOLENOID
A/C CLUTCH RELAY
DK BLU
EATX NEUTRAL SAFETY SW
DK BLU
EATX CONTROL
DK BLU
ALTERNATOR
DK BLU
DK BLU
DK BLU
IGNITION SW
DK BLU
47
DK BLU
WHT
YEL-WHT
DK GRN-BLK
BRN
RED
BRN
RED
WHT
RED-WHT
WHT
RED-WHT
YEL-WHT
DK GRN-BLK
#1
#2
#3
#4
#5
#6
FUEL INJECTORS
8
9
10
11

1991 WIRING DIAGRAMS
Caravan, Town & Country, & Voyager (Cont.)

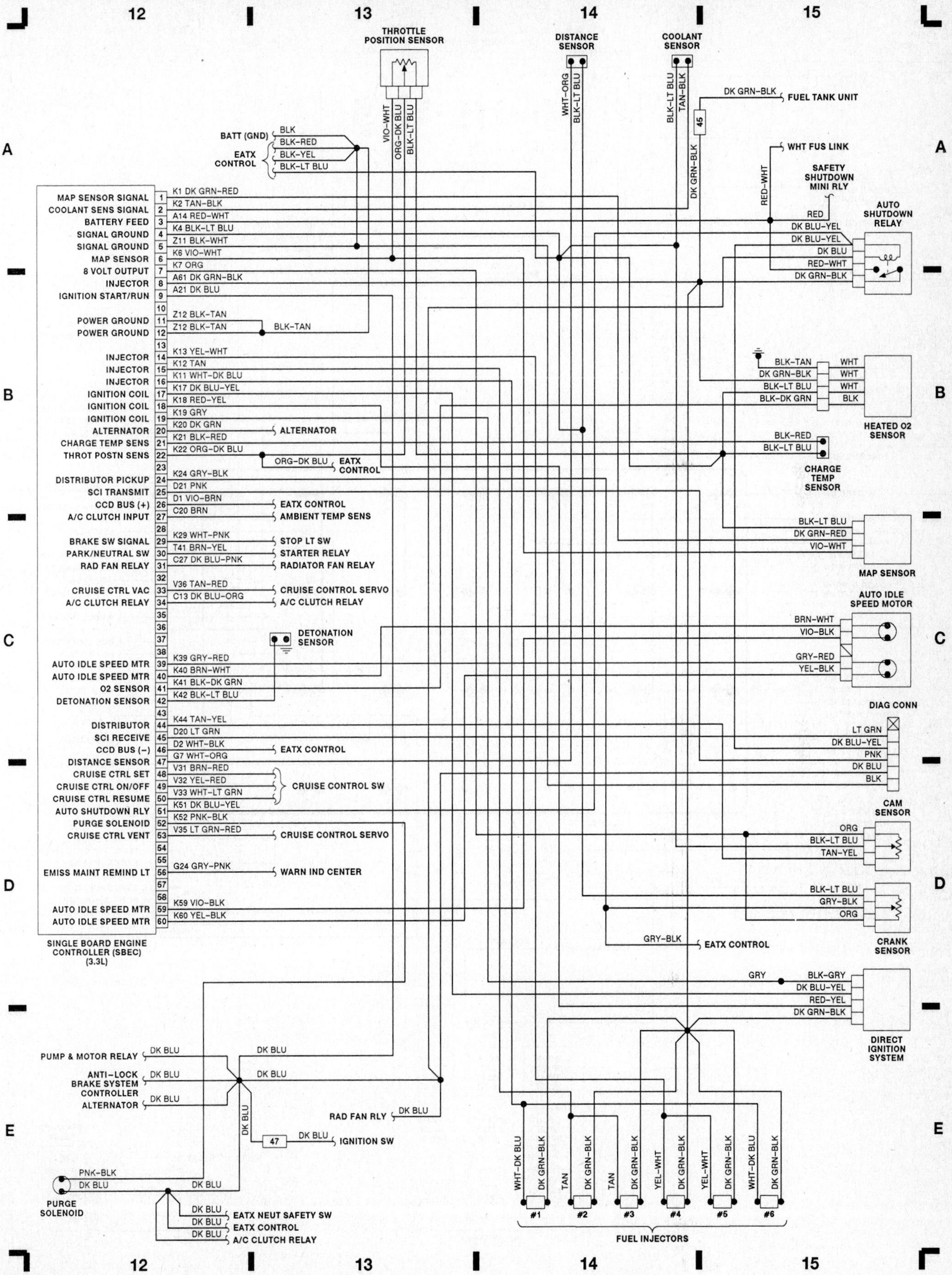
12
13
14
15
A
B
C
D
E
THROTTLE POSITION SENSOR
VIO-WHT
ORG-DK BLU
BLK-LT BLU
DISTANCE SENSOR
WHT-ORG
BLK-LT BLU
COOLANT SENSOR
BLK-LT BLU
TAN-BLK
DK GRN-BLK
FUEL TANK UNIT
45
DK GRN-BLK
WHT FUS LINK
RED-WHT
SAFETY SHUTDOWN MINI RLY
AUTO SHUTDOWN RELAY
RED
DK BLU-YEL
DK BLU-YEL
DK BLU
RED-WHT
DK GRN-BLK
BATT (GND)
BLK
BLK-RED
EATX CONTROL
BLK-YEL
BLK-LT BLU
MAP SENSOR SIGNAL 1 K1 DK GRN-RED
COOLANT SENS SIGNAL 2 K2 TAN-BLK
BATTERY FEED 3 A14 RED-WHT
SIGNAL GROUND 4 K4 BLK-LT BLU
SIGNAL GROUND 5 Z11 BLK-WHT
MAP SENSOR 6 K6 VIO-WHT
8 VOLT OUTPUT 7 K7 ORG
INJECTOR 8 A61 DK GRN-BLK
IGNITION START/RUN 9 A21 DK BLU
10
POWER GROUND 11 Z12 BLK-TAN
POWER GROUND 12 Z12 BLK-TAN
BLK-TAN
13
INJECTOR 14 K13 YEL-WHT
INJECTOR 15 K12 TAN
INJECTOR 16 K11 WHT-DK BLU
IGNITION COIL 17 K17 DK BLU-YEL
IGNITION COIL 18 K18 RED-YEL
IGNITION COIL 19 K19 GRY
ALTERNATOR 20 K20 DK GRN
ALTERNATOR
CHARGE TEMP SENS 21 K21 BLK-RED
THROT POSTN SENS 22 K22 ORG-DK BLU
ORG-DK BLU
EATX CONTROL
23
DISTRIBUTOR PICKUP 24 K24 GRY-BLK
SCI TRANSMIT 25 D21 PNK
CCD BUS (+) 26 D1 VIO-BRN
EATX CONTROL
A/C CLUTCH INPUT 27 C20 BRN
AMBIENT TEMP SENS
28
BRAKE SW SIGNAL 29 K29 WHT-PNK
STOP LT SW
PARK/NEUTRAL SW 30 T41 BRN-YEL
STARTER RELAY
RAD FAN RELAY 31 C27 DK BLU-PNK
RADIATOR FAN RELAY
32
CRUISE CTRL VAC 33 V36 TAN-RED
CRUISE CONTROL SERVO
A/C CLUTCH RELAY 34 C13 DK BLU-ORG
A/C CLUTCH RELAY
35
36
37
DETONATION SENSOR
38
AUTO IDLE SPEED MTR 39 K39 GRY-RED
AUTO IDLE SPEED MTR 40 K40 BRN-WHT
O2 SENSOR 41 K41 BLK-DK GRN
DETONATION SENSOR 42 K42 BLK-LT BLU
43
DISTRIBUTOR 44 K44 TAN-YEL
SCI RECEIVE 45 D20 LT GRN
CCD BUS (–) 46 D2 WHT-BLK
EATX CONTROL
DISTANCE SENSOR 47 G7 WHT-ORG
CRUISE CTRL SET 48 V31 BRN-RED
CRUISE CTRL ON/OFF 49 V32 YEL-RED
CRUISE CONTROL SW
CRUISE CTRL RESUME 50 V33 WHT-LT GRN
AUTO SHUTDOWN RLY 51 K51 DK BLU-YEL
PURGE SOLENOID 52 K52 PNK-BLK
CRUISE CTRL VENT 53 V35 LT GRN-RED
CRUISE CONTROL SERVO
54
55
EMISS MAINT REMIND LT 56 G24 GRY-PNK
WARN IND CENTER
57
58
AUTO IDLE SPEED MTR 59 K59 VIO-BLK
AUTO IDLE SPEED MTR 60 K60 YEL-BLK
SINGLE BOARD ENGINE CONTROLLER (SBEC) (3.3L)
BLK-TAN
WHT
DK GRN-BLK
WHT
BLK-LT BLU
WHT
BLK-DK GRN
BLK
HEATED O2 SENSOR
BLK-RED
BLK-LT BLU
CHARGE TEMP SENSOR
BLK-LT BLU
DK GRN-RED
VIO-WHT
MAP SENSOR
AUTO IDLE SPEED MOTOR
BRN-WHT
VIO-BLK
GRY-RED
YEL-BLK
DIAG CONN
LT GRN
DK BLU-YEL
PNK
DK BLU
BLK
CAM SENSOR
ORG
BLK-LT BLU
TAN-YEL
BLK-LT BLU
GRY-BLK
ORG
CRANK SENSOR
GRY-BLK
EATX CONTROL
GRY
BLK-GRY
DK BLU-YEL
RED-YEL
DK GRN-BLK
DIRECT IGNITION SYSTEM
PUMP & MOTOR RELAY
DK BLU
DK BLU
ANTI-LOCK BRAKE SYSTEM CONTROLLER
DK BLU
DK BLU
ALTERNATOR
DK BLU
DK BLU
RAD FAN RLY
DK BLU
47
DK BLU
IGNITION SW
PNK-BLK
DK BLU
DK BLU
PURGE SOLENOID
DK BLU
EATX NEUT SAFETY SW
DK BLU
EATX CONTROL
DK BLU
A/C CLUTCH RELAY
WHT-DK BLU
DK GRN-BLK
TAN
DK GRN-BLK
TAN
DK GRN-BLK
YEL-WHT
DK GRN-BLK
YEL-WHT
DK GRN-BLK
WHT-DK BLU
DK GRN-BLK
#1
#2
#3
#4
#5
#6
FUEL INJECTORS
12
13
14
15

1991 WIRING DIAGRAMS
Caravan, Town & Country, & Voyager (Cont.)

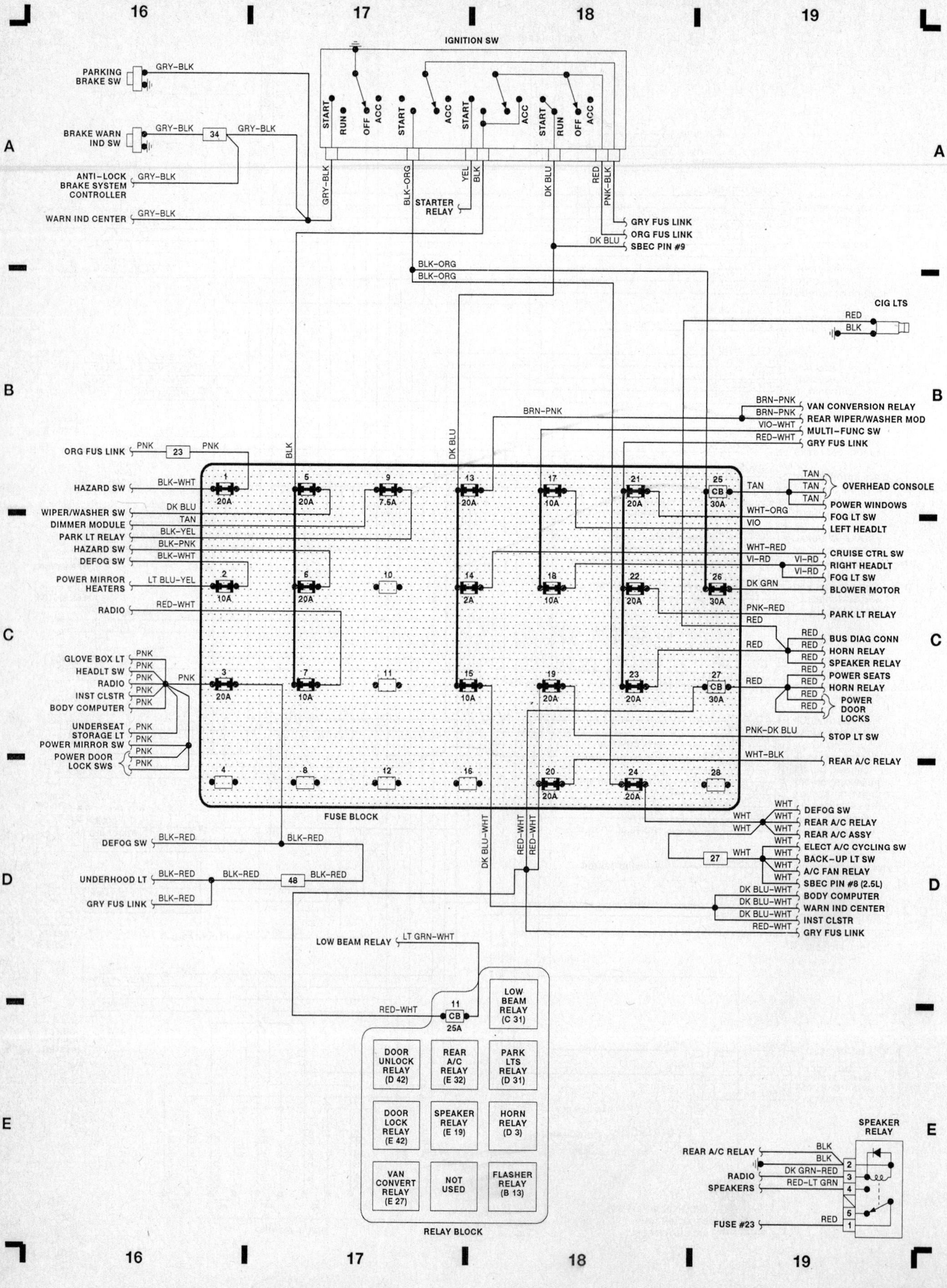
IGNITION SW
PARKING BRAKE SW
BRAKE WARN IND SW
ANTI-LOCK BRAKE SYSTEM CONTROLLER
WARN IND CENTER
STARTER RELAY
GRY FUS LINK
ORG FUS LINK
SBEC PIN #9
CIG LTS
VAN CONVERSION RELAY
REAR WIPER/WASHER MOD
MULTI-FUNC SW
GRY FUS LINK
ORG FUS LINK
HAZARD SW
WIPER/WASHER SW
DIMMER MODULE
PARK LT RELAY
HAZARD SW
DEFOG SW
POWER MIRROR HEATERS
RADIO
GLOVE BOX LT
HEADLT SW
RADIO
INST CLSTR
BODY COMPUTER
UNDERSEAT STORAGE LT
POWER MIRROR SW
POWER DOOR LOCK SWS
OVERHEAD CONSOLE
POWER WINDOWS
FOG LT SW
LEFT HEADLT
CRUISE CTRL SW
RIGHT HEADLT
FOG LT SW
BLOWER MOTOR
PARK LT RELAY
BUS DIAG CONN
HORN RELAY
SPEAKER RELAY
POWER SEATS
HORN RELAY
POWER DOOR LOCKS
STOP LT SW
REAR A/C RELAY
FUSE BLOCK
DEFOG SW
REAR A/C RELAY
REAR A/C ASSY
ELECT A/C CYCLING SW
BACK-UP LT SW
A/C FAN RELAY
SBEC PIN #8 (2.5L)
BODY COMPUTER
WARN IND CENTER
INST CLSTR
GRY FUS LINK
DEFOG SW
UNDERHOOD LT
GRY FUS LINK
LOW BEAM RELAY
LOW BEAM RELAY (C 31)
DOOR UNLOCK RELAY (D 42)
REAR A/C RELAY (E 32)
PARK LTS RELAY (D 31)
DOOR LOCK RELAY (E 42)
SPEAKER RELAY (E 19)
HORN RELAY (D 3)
VAN CONVERT RELAY (E 27)
NOT USED
FLASHER RELAY (B 13)
RELAY BLOCK
SPEAKER RELAY
REAR A/C RELAY
RADIO
SPEAKERS
FUSE #23

1991 WIRING DIAGRAMS
Caravan, Town & Country, & Voyager (Cont.)

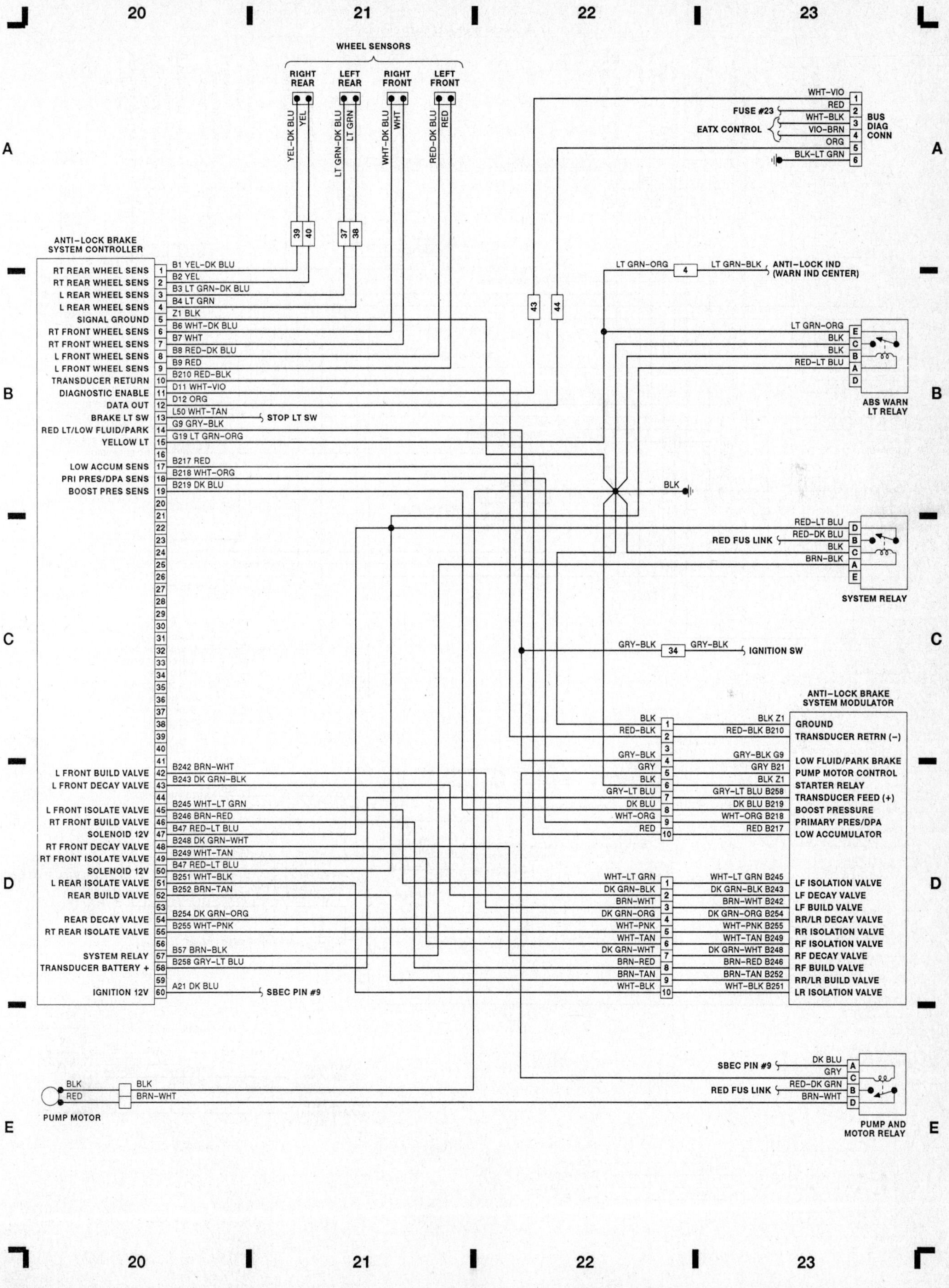

20
21
22
23
A
B
C
D
E
WHEEL SENSORS
RIGHT REAR
LEFT REAR
RIGHT FRONT
LEFT FRONT
YEL-DK BLU
YEL
LT GRN-DK BLU
LT GRN
WHT-DK BLU
WHT
RED-DK BLU
RED
39
40
37
38
43
44
ANTI-LOCK BRAKE SYSTEM CONTROLLER
RT REAR WHEEL SENS
RT REAR WHEEL SENS
L REAR WHEEL SENS
L REAR WHEEL SENS
SIGNAL GROUND
RT FRONT WHEEL SENS
RT FRONT WHEEL SENS
L FRONT WHEEL SENS
L FRONT WHEEL SENS
TRANSDUCER RETURN
DIAGNOSTIC ENABLE
DATA OUT
BRAKE LT SW
RED LT/LOW FLUID/PARK
YELLOW LT
LOW ACCUM SENS
PRI PRES/DPA SENS
BOOST PRES SENS
L FRONT BUILD VALVE
L FRONT DECAY VALVE
L FRONT ISOLATE VALVE
RT FRONT BUILD VALVE
SOLENOID 12V
RT FRONT DECAY VALVE
RT FRONT ISOLATE VALVE
SOLENOID 12V
L REAR ISOLATE VALVE
REAR BUILD VALVE
REAR DECAY VALVE
RT REAR ISOLATE VALVE
SYSTEM RELAY
TRANSDUCER BATTERY +
IGNITION 12V
B1 YEL-DK BLU
B2 YEL
B3 LT GRN-DK BLU
B4 LT GRN
Z1 BLK
B6 WHT-DK BLU
B7 WHT
B8 RED-DK BLU
B9 RED
B210 RED-BLK
D11 WHT-VIO
D12 ORG
L50 WHT-TAN
STOP LT SW
G9 GRY-BLK
G19 LT GRN-ORG
B217 RED
B218 WHT-ORG
B219 DK BLU
B242 BRN-WHT
B243 DK GRN-BLK
B245 WHT-LT GRN
B246 BRN-RED
B47 RED-LT BLU
B248 DK GRN-WHT
B249 WHT-TAN
B47 RED-LT BLU
B251 WHT-BLK
B252 BRN-TAN
B254 DK GRN-ORG
B255 WHT-PNK
B57 BRN-BLK
B258 GRY-LT BLU
A21 DK BLU
SBEC PIN #9
WHT-VIO
RED
FUSE #23
WHT-BLK
EATX CONTROL
VIO-BRN
ORG
BLK-LT GRN
BUS DIAG CONN
LT GRN-ORG
4
LT GRN-BLK
ANTI-LOCK IND (WARN IND CENTER)
LT GRN-ORG
BLK
BLK
RED-LT BLU
ABS WARN LT RELAY
BLK
RED-LT BLU
RED FUS LINK
RED-DK BLU
BLK
BRN-BLK
SYSTEM RELAY
GRY-BLK
34
GRY-BLK
IGNITION SW
ANTI-LOCK BRAKE SYSTEM MODULATOR
BLK
RED-BLK
GRY-BLK
GRY
BLK
GRY-LT BLU
DK BLU
WHT-ORG
RED
BLK Z1
RED-BLK B210
GRY-BLK G9
GRY B21
BLK Z1
GRY-LT BLU B258
DK BLU B219
WHT-ORG B218
RED B217
GROUND
TRANSDUCER RETRN (-)
LOW FLUID/PARK BRAKE
PUMP MOTOR CONTROL
STARTER RELAY
TRANSDUCER FEED (+)
BOOST PRESSURE
PRIMARY PRES/DPA
LOW ACCUMULATOR
WHT-LT GRN
DK GRN-BLK
BRN-WHT
DK GRN-ORG
WHT-PNK
WHT-TAN
DK GRN-WHT
BRN-RED
BRN-TAN
WHT-BLK
WHT-LT GRN B245
DK GRN-BLK B243
BRN-WHT B242
DK GRN-ORG B254
WHT-PNK B255
WHT-TAN B249
DK GRN-WHT B248
BRN-RED B246
BRN-TAN B252
WHT-BLK B251
LF ISOLATION VALVE
LF DECAY VALVE
LF BUILD VALVE
RR/LR DECAY VALVE
RR ISOLATION VALVE
RF ISOLATION VALVE
RF DECAY VALVE
RF BUILD VALVE
RR/LR BUILD VALVE
LR ISOLATION VALVE
BLK
RED
BLK
BRN-WHT
PUMP MOTOR
SBEC PIN #9
DK BLU
GRY
RED FUS LINK
RED-DK GRN
BRN-WHT
PUMP AND MOTOR RELAY

1991 WIRING DIAGRAMS
Caravan, Town & Country, & Voyager (Cont.)

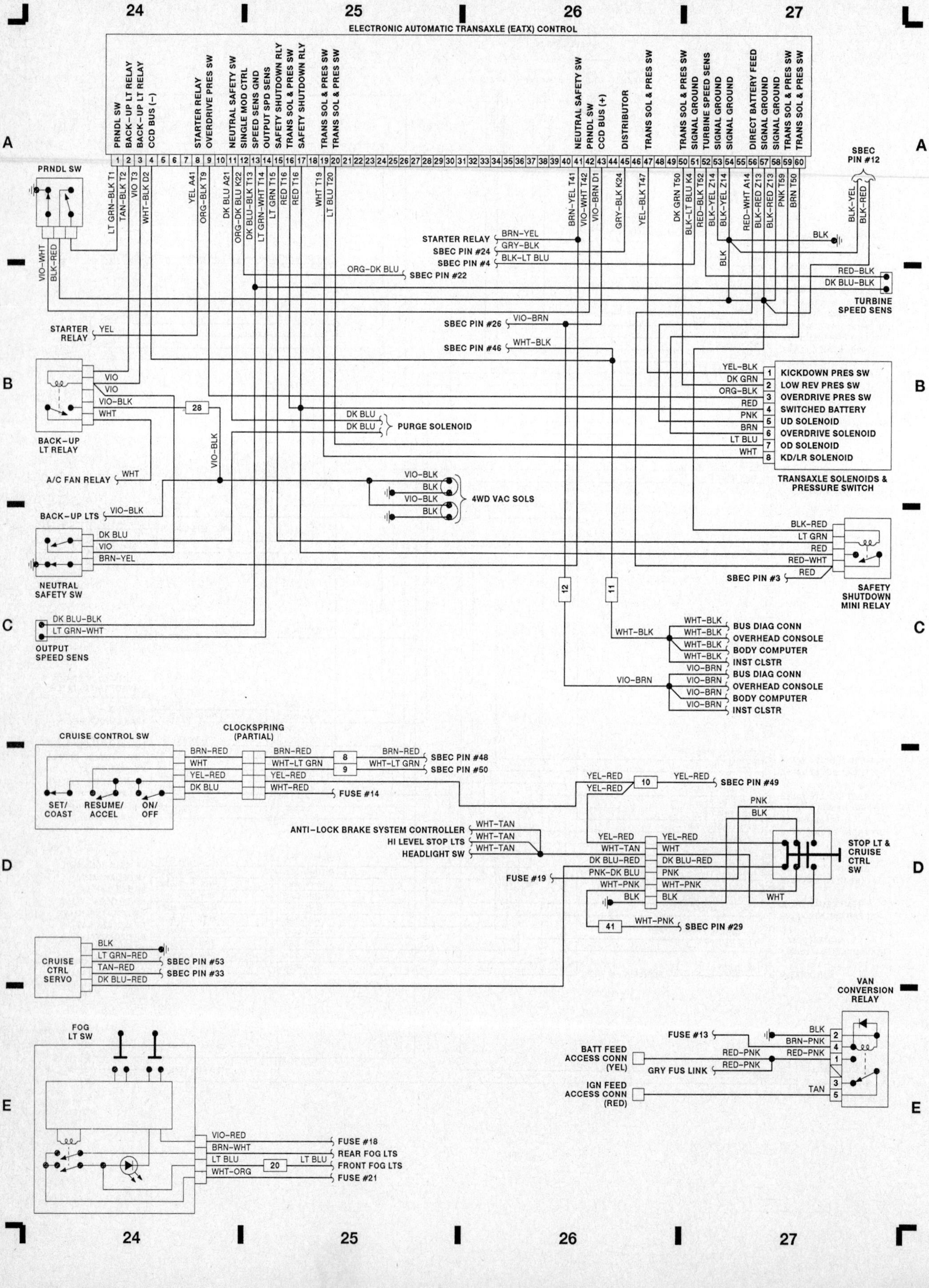
ELECTRONIC AUTOMATIC TRANSAXLE (EATX) CONTROL
PRNDL SW
BACK-UP LT RELAY
CCD BUS (-)
STARTER RELAY
OVERDRIVE PRES SW
NEUTRAL SAFETY SW
SINGLE MOD CTRL
SPEED SENS GND
OUTPUT SPD SENS
SAFETY SHUTDOWN RLY
TRANS SOL & PRES SW
DISTRIBUTOR
CCD BUS (+)
TURBINE SPEED SENS
SIGNAL GROUND
DIRECT BATTERY FEED
PRNDL SW
STARTER RELAY
SBEC PIN #24
SBEC PIN #4
SBEC PIN #22
SBEC PIN #26
SBEC PIN #46
SBEC PIN #12
TURBINE SPEED SENS
BACK-UP LT RELAY
PURGE SOLENOID
A/C FAN RELAY
4WD VAC SOLS
BACK-UP LTS
NEUTRAL SAFETY SW
KICKDOWN PRES SW
LOW REV PRES SW
OVERDRIVE PRES SW
SWITCHED BATTERY
UD SOLENOID
OVERDRIVE SOLENOID
OD SOLENOID
KD/LR SOLENOID
TRANSAXLE SOLENOIDS & PRESSURE SWITCH
SBEC PIN #3
SAFETY SHUTDOWN MINI RELAY
OUTPUT SPEED SENS
BUS DIAG CONN
OVERHEAD CONSOLE
BODY COMPUTER
INST CLSTR
CRUISE CONTROL SW
CLOCKSPRING (PARTIAL)
SET/COAST
RESUME/ACCEL
ON/OFF
SBEC PIN #48
SBEC PIN #50
FUSE #14
SBEC PIN #49
ANTI-LOCK BRAKE SYSTEM CONTROLLER
HI LEVEL STOP LTS
HEADLIGHT SW
FUSE #19
STOP LT & CRUISE CTRL SW
SBEC PIN #29
CRUISE CTRL SERVO
SBEC PIN #53
SBEC PIN #33
FOG LT SW
VAN CONVERSION RELAY
FUSE #13
BATT FEED ACCESS CONN (YEL)
GRY FUS LINK
IGN FEED ACCESS CONN (RED)
FUSE #18
REAR FOG LTS
FRONT FOG LTS
FUSE #21

1991 WIRING DIAGRAMS
Caravan, Town & Country, & Voyager (Cont.)

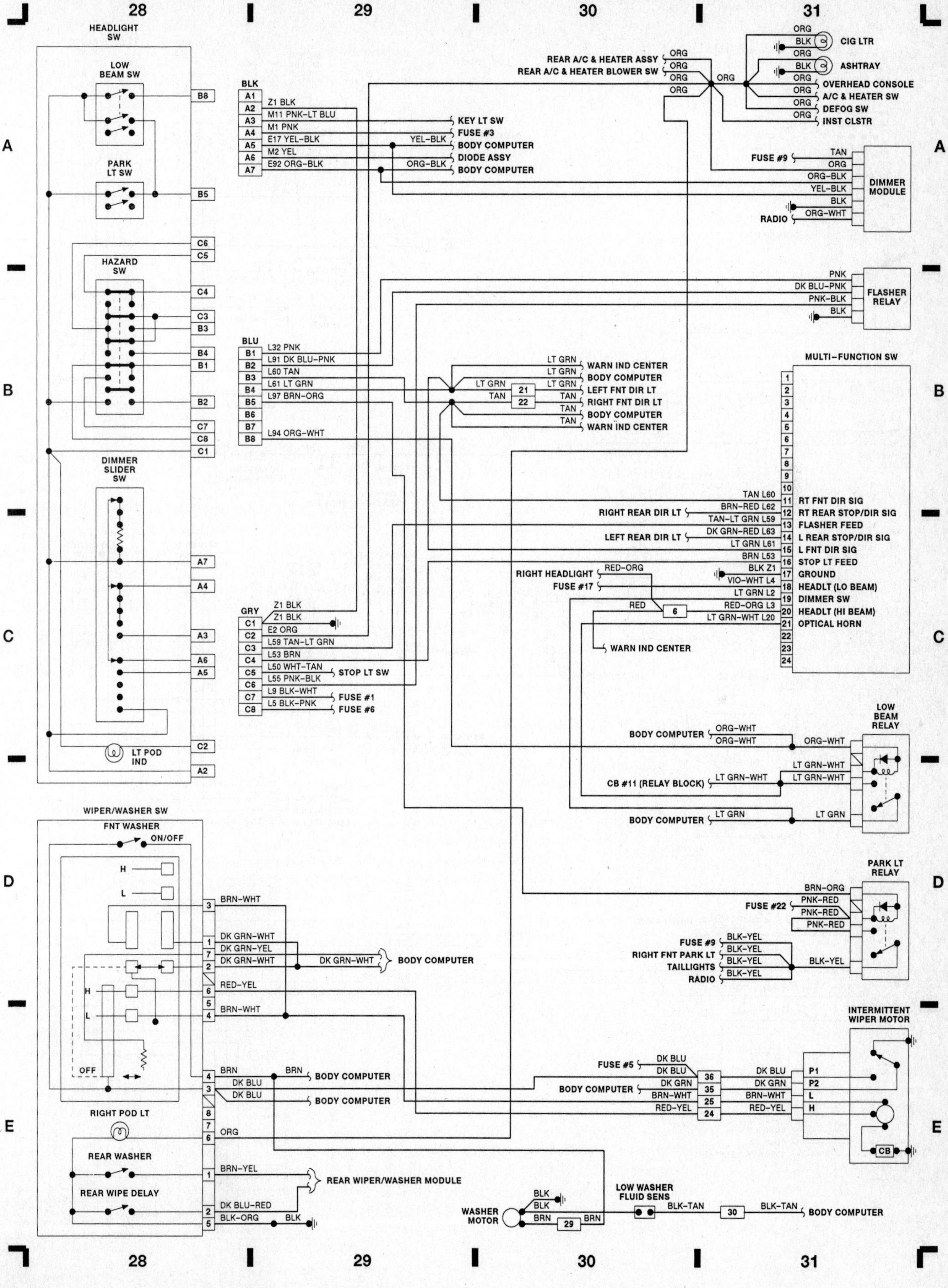
28
29
30
31
A
B
C
D
E
HEADLIGHT SW
LOW BEAM SW
PARK LT SW
HAZARD SW
DIMMER SLIDER SW
LT POD IND
B8
B5
C6
C5
C4
C3
B3
B4
B1
B2
C7
C8
C1
A7
A4
A3
A6
A5
C2
A2
BLK
A1 Z1 BLK
A2 M11 PNK-LT BLU
A3 M1 PNK
A4 E17 YEL-BLK
A5 M2 YEL
A6 E92 ORG-BLK
A7
KEY LT SW
FUSE #3
BODY COMPUTER
DIODE ASSY
BODY COMPUTER
YEL-BLK
ORG-BLK
REAR A/C & HEATER ASSY
REAR A/C & HEATER BLOWER SW
ORG
BLK
CIG LTR
ASHTRAY
OVERHEAD CONSOLE
A/C & HEATER SW
DEFOG SW
INST CLSTR
FUSE #9
TAN
ORG-BLK
YEL-BLK
ORG-WHT
RADIO
DIMMER MODULE
PNK
DK BLU-PNK
PNK-BLK
FLASHER RELAY
BLU
B1 L32 PNK
B2 L91 DK BLU-PNK
B3 L60 TAN
B4 L61 LT GRN
B5 L97 BRN-ORG
B6
B7
B8 L94 ORG-WHT
LT GRN
21
22
WARN IND CENTER
BODY COMPUTER
LEFT FNT DIR LT
RIGHT FNT DIR LT
BODY COMPUTER
WARN IND CENTER
MULTI-FUNCTION SW
TAN L60
BRN-RED L62
TAN-LT GRN L59
DK GRN-RED L63
LT GRN L61
BRN L53
BLK Z1
VIO-WHT L4
LT GRN L2
RED-ORG L3
LT GRN-WHT L20
RIGHT REAR DIR LT
LEFT REAR DIR LT
RIGHT HEADLIGHT
FUSE #17
RED-ORG
RED
6
WARN IND CENTER
11 RT FNT DIR SIG
12 RT REAR STOP/DIR SIG
13 FLASHER FEED
14 L REAR STOP/DIR SIG
15 L FNT DIR SIG
16 STOP LT FEED
17 GROUND
18 HEADLT (LO BEAM)
19 DIMMER SW
20 HEADLT (HI BEAM)
21 OPTICAL HORN
GRY
C1 Z1 BLK
Z1 BLK
C2 E2 ORG
C3 L59 TAN-LT GRN
C4 L53 BRN
C5 L50 WHT-TAN
C6 L55 PNK-BLK
C7 L9 BLK-WHT
C8 L5 BLK-PNK
STOP LT SW
FUSE #1
FUSE #6
LOW BEAM RELAY
BODY COMPUTER
ORG-WHT
CB #11 (RELAY BLOCK)
LT GRN-WHT
LT GRN
PARK LT RELAY
BRN-ORG
FUSE #22
PNK-RED
FUSE #9
RIGHT FNT PARK LT
TAILLIGHTS
BLK-YEL
WIPER/WASHER SW
FNT WASHER
ON/OFF
H
L
OFF
BRN-WHT
DK GRN-WHT
DK GRN-YEL
RED-YEL
BRN
DK BLU
ORG
BRN-YEL
DK BLU-RED
BLK-ORG
RIGHT POD LT
REAR WASHER
REAR WIPE DELAY
REAR WIPER/WASHER MODULE
INTERMITTENT WIPER MOTOR
FUSE #5
DK GRN
36
35
25
24
P1
P2
CB
WASHER MOTOR
29
LOW WASHER FLUID SENS
BLK-TAN
30

1991 WIRING DIAGRAMS
Caravan, Town & Country, & Voyager (Cont.)

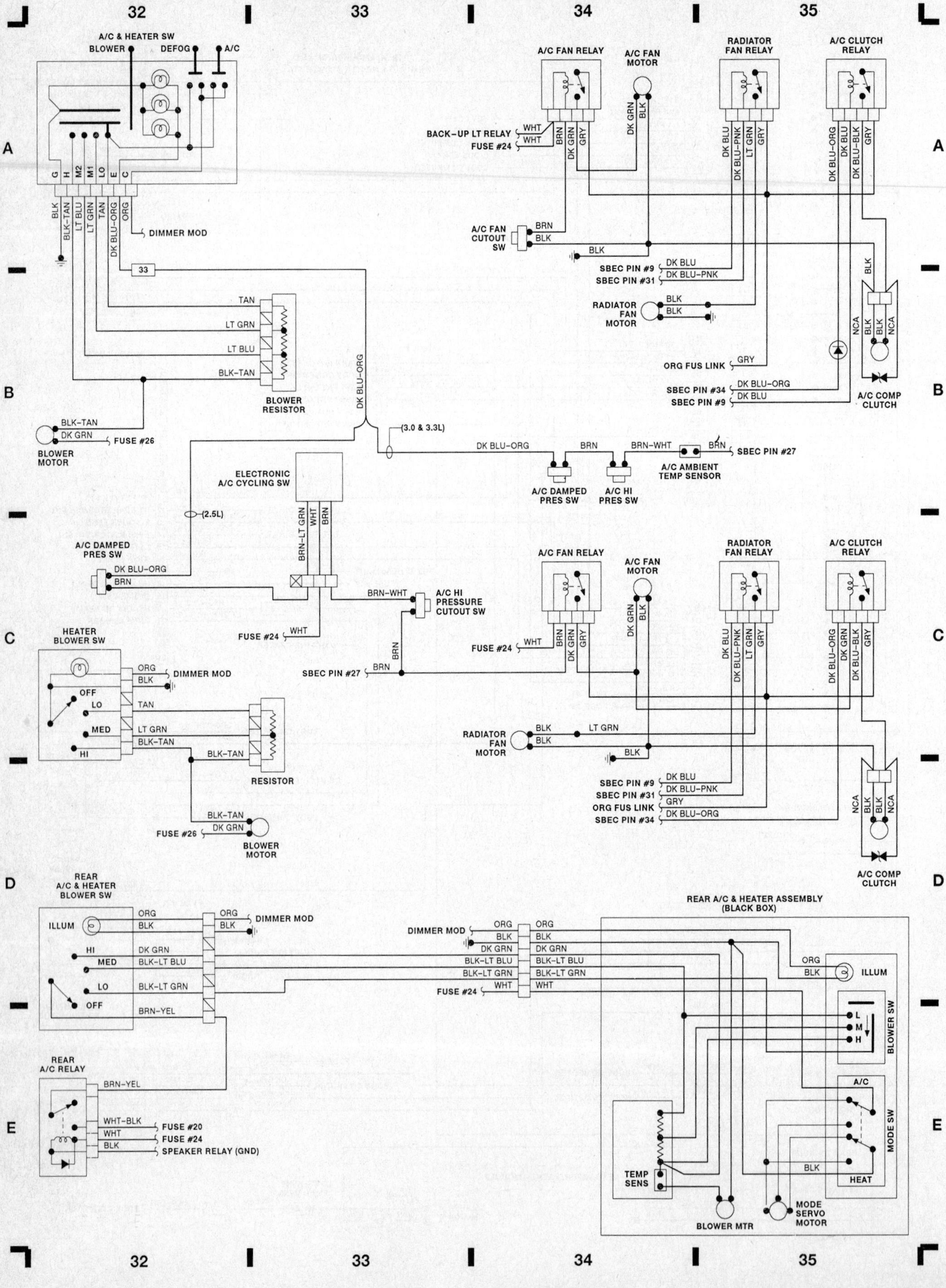
A/C & HEATER SW
BLOWER
DEFOG
A/C
G H M2 M1 LO E C
BLK
BLK-TAN
LT BLU
LT GRN
TAN
DK BLU-ORG
ORG
DIMMER MOD
33
BLOWER RESISTOR
BLOWER MOTOR
FUSE #26
A/C FAN RELAY
A/C FAN MOTOR
RADIATOR FAN RELAY
A/C CLUTCH RELAY
BACK-UP LT RELAY
FUSE #24
A/C FAN CUTOUT SW
SBEC PIN #9
SBEC PIN #31
RADIATOR FAN MOTOR
ORG FUS LINK
SBEC PIN #34
A/C COMP CLUTCH
(3.0 & 3.3L)
(2.5L)
A/C DAMPED PRES SW
A/C HI PRES SW
A/C AMBIENT TEMP SENSOR
SBEC PIN #27
ELECTRONIC A/C CYCLING SW
A/C HI PRESSURE CUTOUT SW
HEATER BLOWER SW
OFF
LO
MED
HI
RESISTOR
REAR A/C & HEATER BLOWER SW
ILLUM
REAR A/C RELAY
FUSE #20
SPEAKER RELAY (GND)
REAR A/C & HEATER ASSEMBLY (BLACK BOX)
BLOWER SW
MODE SW
A/C
HEAT
TEMP SENS
BLOWER MTR
MODE SERVO MOTOR

1991 WIRING DIAGRAMS
Caravan, Town & Country, & Voyager (Cont.)

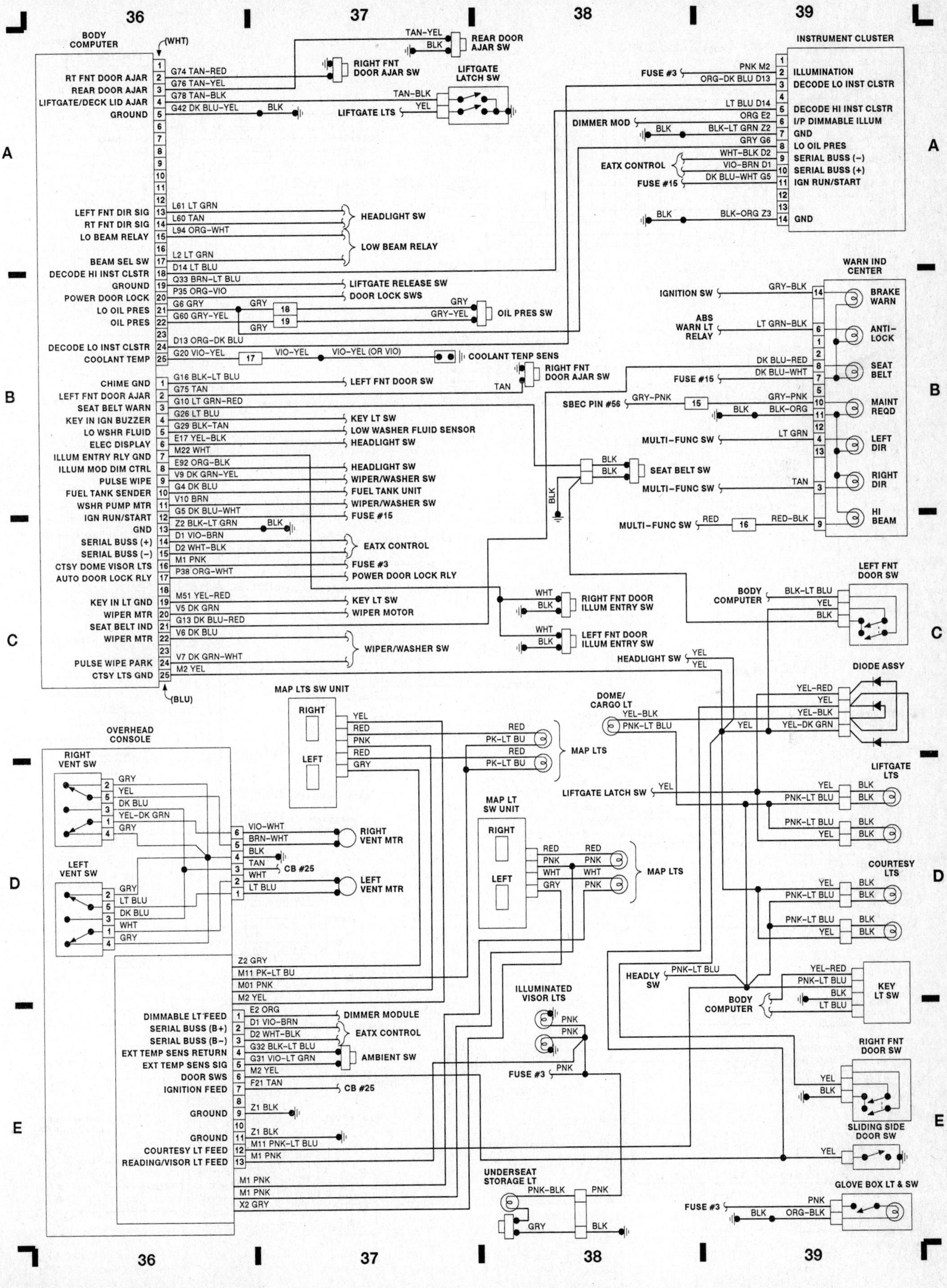
36
37
38
39
A
B
C
D
E
BODY COMPUTER
(WHT)
RT FNT DOOR AJAR
REAR DOOR AJAR
LIFTGATE/DECK LID AJAR
GROUND
G74 TAN-RED
G76 TAN-YEL
G78 TAN-BLK
G42 DK BLU-YEL
BLK
TAN-YEL
REAR DOOR AJAR SW
RIGHT FNT DOOR AJAR SW
LIFTGATE LATCH SW
TAN-BLK
YEL
LIFTGATE LTS
LEFT FNT DIR SIG
RT FNT DIR SIG
LO BEAM RELAY
BEAM SEL SW
DECODE HI INST CLSTR
GROUND
POWER DOOR LOCK
LO OIL PRES
OIL PRES
DECODE LO INST CLSTR
COOLANT TEMP
L61 LT GRN
L60 TAN
L94 ORG-WHT
L2 LT GRN
D14 LT BLU
Q33 BRN-LT BLU
P35 ORG-VIO
G6 GRY
G60 GRY-YEL
D13 ORG-DK BLU
G20 VIO-YEL
HEADLIGHT SW
LOW BEAM RELAY
LIFTGATE RELEASE SW
DOOR LOCK SWS
OIL PRES SW
VIO-YEL
VIO-YEL (OR VIO)
COOLANT TENP SENS
CHIME GND
LEFT FNT DOOR AJAR
SEAT BELT WARN
KEY IN IGN BUZZER
LO WSHR FLUID
ELEC DISPLAY
ILLUM ENTRY RLY GND
ILLUM MOD DIM CTRL
PULSE WIPE
FUEL TANK SENDER
WSHR PUMP MTR
IGN RUN/START
GND
SERIAL BUSS (+)
SERIAL BUSS (–)
CTSY DOME VISOR LTS
AUTO DOOR LOCK RLY
KEY IN LT GND
WIPER MTR
SEAT BELT IND
WIPER MTR
PULSE WIPE PARK
CTSY LTS GND
(BLU)
G16 BLK-LT BLU
G75 TAN
G10 LT GRN-RED
G26 LT BLU
G29 BLK-TAN
E17 YEL-BLK
M22 WHT
E92 ORG-BLK
V9 DK GRN-YEL
G4 DK BLU
V10 BRN
G5 DK BLU-WHT
Z2 BLK-LT GRN
D1 VIO-BRN
D2 WHT-BLK
M1 PNK
P38 ORG-WHT
M51 YEL-RED
V5 DK GRN
G13 DK BLU-RED
V6 DK BLU
V7 DK GRN-WHT
M2 YEL
LEFT FNT DOOR SW
KEY LT SW
LOW WASHER FLUID SENSOR
HEADLIGHT SW
WIPER/WASHER SW
FUEL TANK UNIT
FUSE #15
EATX CONTROL
FUSE #3
POWER DOOR LOCK RLY
WIPER MOTOR
RIGHT FNT DOOR AJAR SW
RIGHT FNT DOOR ILLUM ENTRY SW
LEFT FNT DOOR ILLUM ENTRY SW
INSTRUMENT CLUSTER
PNK M2
ORG-DK BLU D13
LT BLU D14
ORG E2
BLK-LT GRN Z2
GRY G6
WHT-BLK D2
VIO-BRN D1
DK BLU-WHT G5
BLK-ORG Z3
DIMMER MOD
ILLUMINATION
DECODE LO INST CLSTR
DECODE HI INST CLSTR
I/P DIMMABLE ILLUM
GND
LO OIL PRES
SERIAL BUSS (–)
SERIAL BUSS (+)
IGN RUN/START
GND
WARN IND CENTER
IGNITION SW
GRY-BLK
BRAKE WARN
ABS WARN LT RELAY
LT GRN-BLK
ANTI-LOCK
DK BLU-RED
DK BLU-WHT
SEAT BELT
SBEC PIN #56
GRY-PNK
BLK-ORG
MAINT REQD
MULTI-FUNC SW
LT GRN
LEFT DIR
SEAT BELT SW
TAN
RIGHT DIR
RED
RED-BLK
HI BEAM
LEFT FNT DOOR SW
BODY COMPUTER
BLK-LT BLU
YEL
BLK
HEADLIGHT SW
DIODE ASSY
DOME/ CARGO LT
YEL-BLK
PNK-LT BLU
YEL-RED
YEL-DK GRN
LIFTGATE LATCH SW
LIFTGATE LTS
COURTESY LTS
MAP LTS SW UNIT
RIGHT
LEFT
MAP LTS
PK-LT BU
OVERHEAD CONSOLE
RIGHT VENT SW
LEFT VENT SW
GRY
YEL
DK BLU
YEL-DK GRN
LT BLU
WHT
VIO-WHT
BRN-WHT
CB #25
RIGHT VENT MTR
LEFT VENT MTR
MAP LT SW UNIT
Z2 GRY
M11 PK-LT BU
M01 PNK
M2 YEL
DIMMABLE LT FEED
SERIAL BUSS (B+)
SERIAL BUSS (B–)
EXT TEMP SENS RETURN
EXT TEMP SENS SIG
DOOR SWS
IGNITION FEED
GROUND
COURTESY LT FEED
READING/VISOR LT FEED
E2 ORG
G32 BLK-LT BLU
G31 VIO-LT GRN
F21 TAN
Z1 BLK
M11 PNK-LT BLU
M1 PNK
X2 GRY
DIMMER MODULE
AMBIENT SW
ILLUMINATED VISOR LTS
HEADLY SW
KEY LT SW
RIGHT FNT DOOR SW
SLIDING SIDE DOOR SW
UNDERSEAT STORAGE LT
PNK-BLK
GLOVE BOX LT & SW
ORG-BLK

1991 WIRING DIAGRAMS
Caravan, Town & Country, & Voyager (Cont.)

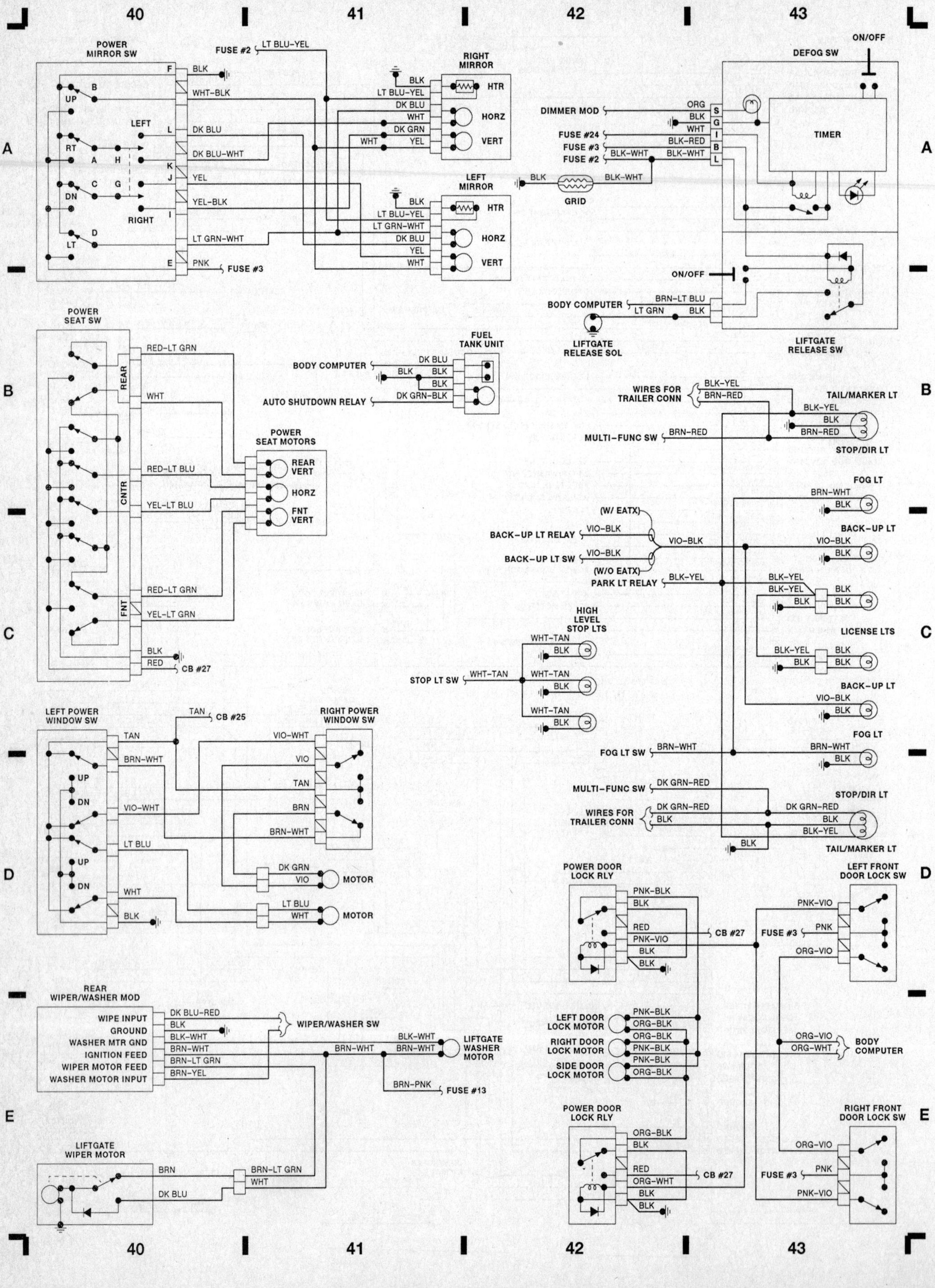
40
41
42
43
A
B
C
D
E
POWER MIRROR SW
FUSE #2
LT BLU-YEL
BLK
WHT-BLK
DK BLU
DK BLU-WHT
YEL
YEL-BLK
LT GRN-WHT
PNK
FUSE #3
UP
RT
DN
LT
LEFT
RIGHT
RIGHT MIRROR
HTR
HORZ
VERT
LEFT MIRROR
DK GRN
WHT
ON/OFF
DEFOG SW
DIMMER MOD
FUSE #24
FUSE #3
FUSE #2
ORG
BLK-RED
BLK-WHT
TIMER
GRID
BODY COMPUTER
BRN-LT BLU
LT GRN
LIFTGATE RELEASE SOL
LIFTGATE RELEASE SW
POWER SEAT SW
REAR
CNTR
FNT
RED-LT GRN
RED-LT BLU
YEL-LT BLU
YEL-LT GRN
RED
CB #27
POWER SEAT MOTORS
REAR VERT
FNT VERT
FUEL TANK UNIT
AUTO SHUTDOWN RELAY
DK GRN-BLK
WIRES FOR TRAILER CONN
BLK-YEL
BRN-RED
TAIL/MARKER LT
MULTI-FUNC SW
STOP/DIR LT
FOG LT
BRN-WHT
BACK-UP LT
(W/ EATX)
(W/O EATX)
BACK-UP LT RELAY
BACK-UP LT SW
VIO-BLK
PARK LT RELAY
LICENSE LTS
HIGH LEVEL STOP LTS
WHT-TAN
STOP LT SW
FOG LT SW
DK GRN-RED
LEFT POWER WINDOW SW
RIGHT POWER WINDOW SW
TAN
CB #25
VIO-WHT
VIO
BRN
LT BLU
MOTOR
POWER DOOR LOCK RLY
PNK-BLK
PNK-VIO
LEFT FRONT DOOR LOCK SW
ORG-VIO
REAR WIPER/WASHER MOD
WIPE INPUT
GROUND
WASHER MTR GND
IGNITION FEED
WIPER MOTOR FEED
WASHER MOTOR INPUT
DK BLU-RED
BLK-WHT
BRN-LT GRN
BRN-YEL
WIPER/WASHER SW
LIFTGATE WASHER MOTOR
BRN-PNK
FUSE #13
LEFT DOOR LOCK MOTOR
RIGHT DOOR LOCK MOTOR
SIDE DOOR LOCK MOTOR
ORG-BLK
ORG-WHT
RIGHT FRONT DOOR LOCK SW
LIFTGATE WIPER MOTOR

COMPONENT LOCATOR:

A/C CLUTCH RELAY	E 19
A/C CONTROL SW	C–D 18–19
A/C LOW PRESSURE SW	D 18
A/T O/D SOL/PART THROTTLE UNLOCK SOL	E 2
ALTERNATOR	B 3
AUTO SHUTDOWN RELAY (2.5L)	A–B 7
AUTO SHUTDOWN RELAY (3.9L & 5.2L)	A–B 11
BACK–UP LT SW (M/T)	D 2
BATTERY	A 3
CRUISE CONTROL SERVO	C–D 25
CRUISE CONTROL SW	D 24–27
DIR FLASHER	B 14
DIR SW	A 18–19
ELECTRONIC CYCLING CLUTCH SW	D–E 19
FOG LT SW	D 2
FUEL TANK UNIT	A 23
FUSE BLOCK	A–C 12–15
FUSE F1	A 2
FUSE F2	A 2
HAZARD FLASHER	A 14
HEADLIGHT SW	C–D 12
HEADLT DIMMER SW	E 12
HEATER CONTROL SW	D–E 16
HORN RELAY	A 12
IGNITION SW	B–C 15
INSTRUMENT CLUSTER	A–E 20–23
INTERIOR LTS	D 13–14
INTERMITTENT WIPER CONTROL UNIT	D 16
INTERMITTENT WIPER SW	B–C 16
NEUTRAL START & BACK–UP LT SW	E 2
OIL PRESSURE SW/SENDING UNIT	E 23
OVERDRIVE SW	B–C 19
PARK BRAKE SW	A–B 15
POWER DISTRIBUTION CENTER (PDC) FUSES	A–B 2–3
POWER DISTRIBUTION CENTER (PDC) LAYOUT	E 15
POWER DOOR LOCKS	E 24–25
POWER MIRROR SW	A–B 24–26
POWER WINDOW SW	E 26–27
RADIATOR FAN RELAY (2.5L)	E 19
REAR WHEEL ANTI–LOCK MODULE	B–C 24–25
SEAT BELT/HEADLT ON/KEY IN WARNING BUZZER	B 12
SINGLE BOARD ENGINE CONTROLLER (SBEC) (2.5L)	A–E 4–7
SINGLE BOARD ENGINE CONTROLLER (SBEC) (3.9L & 5.2L)	A–E 8–11
STARTER	C 2
STARTER RELAY	C 3
STOP LT SW	C–D 24
TIME DELAY RELAY	D 15
UNDERHOOD LT	D 1
WASHER LOW FLUID LEVEL SENSOR (INTERMITTENT)	B 17
WASHER LOW FLUID LEVEL SENSOR (STANDARD)	A 17
WIPER SW (STANDARD)	A 16
2 SPEED WIPER MOTOR	A 17–18
4WD IND	D 26–27

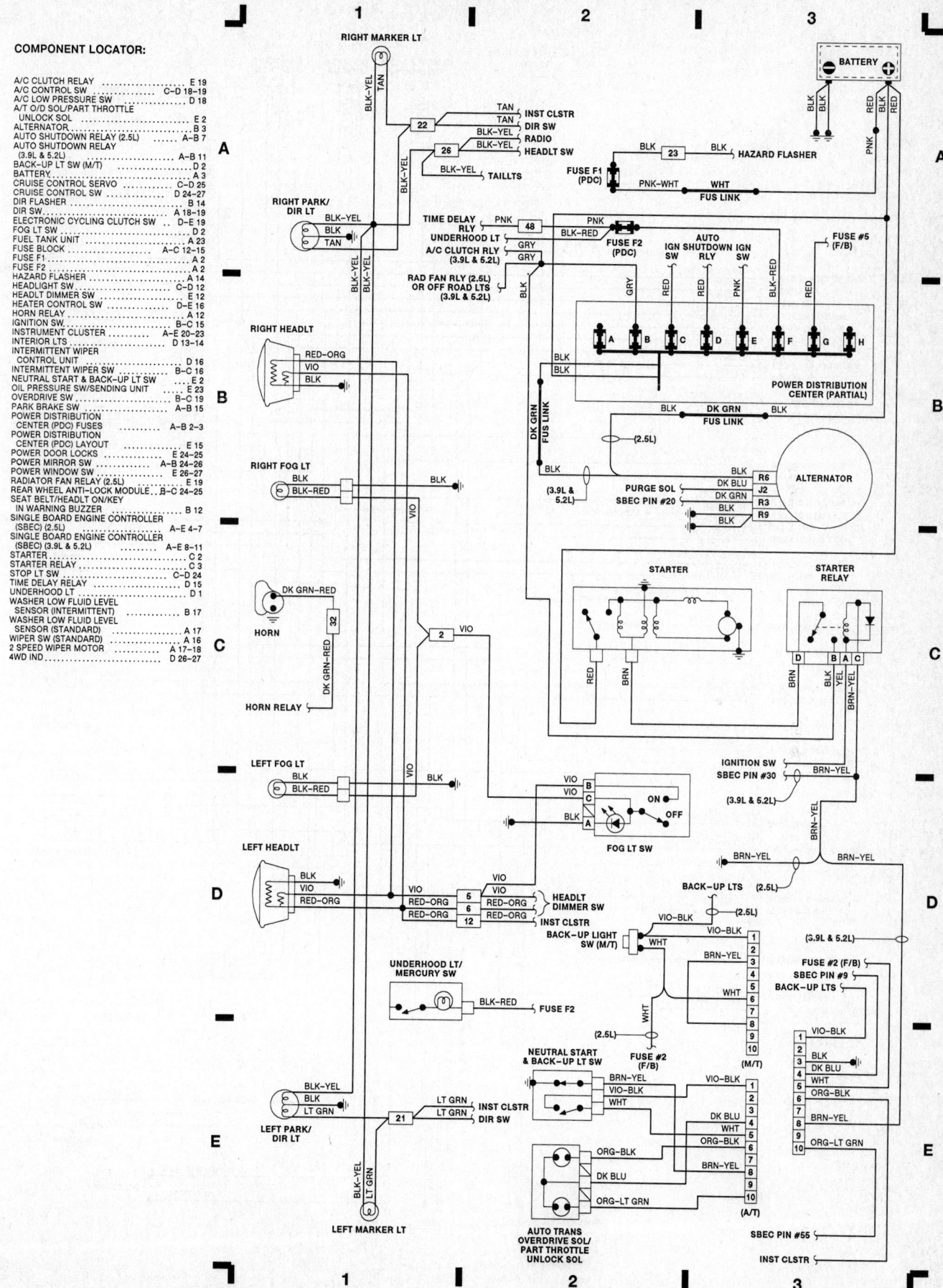

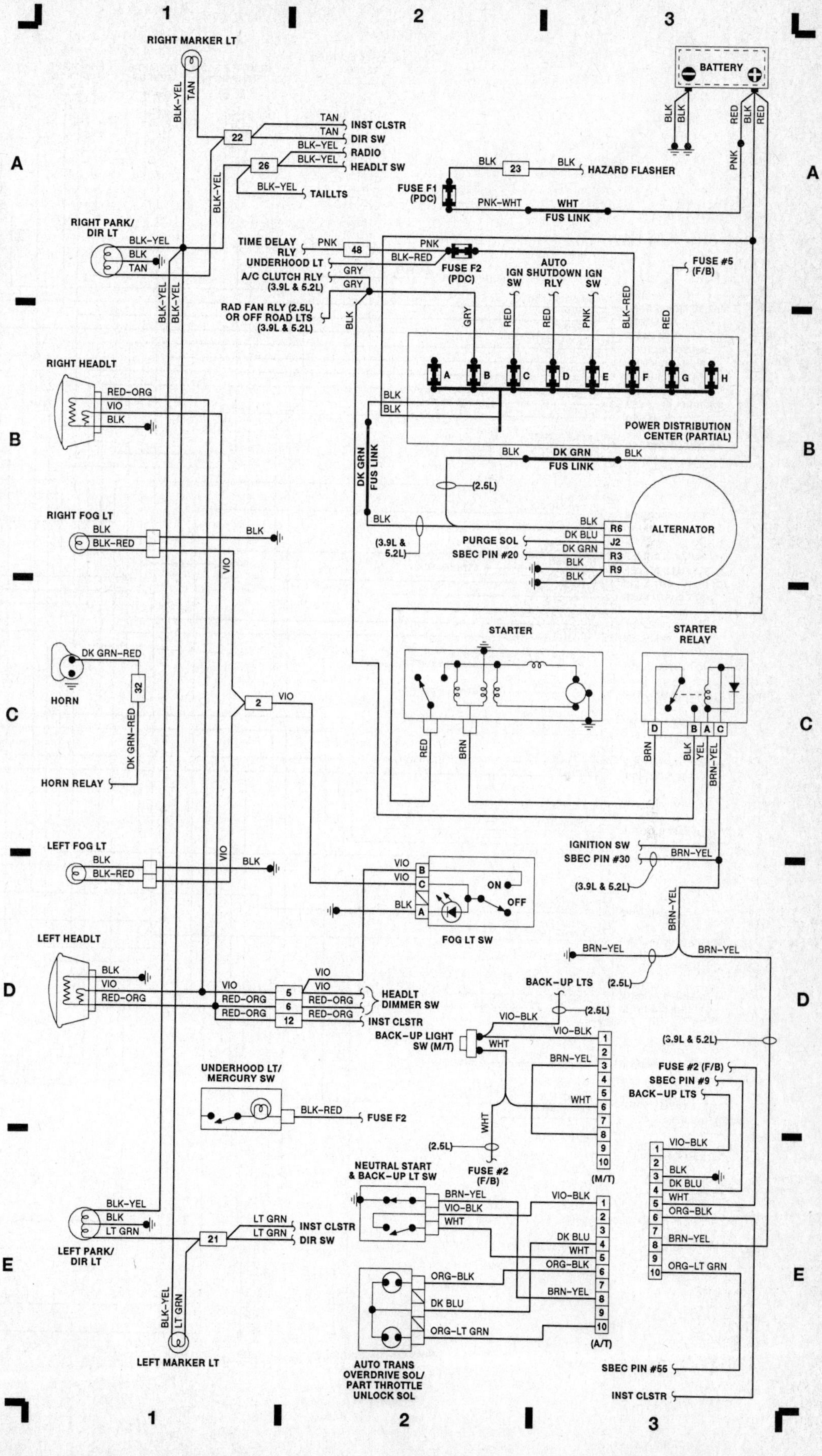
1
2
3
A
B
C
D
E
RIGHT MARKER LT
BATTERY
INST CLSTR
DIR SW
RADIO
HEADLT SW
TAILLTS
HAZARD FLASHER
FUSE F1 (PDC)
FUS LINK
RIGHT PARK/ DIR LT
TIME DELAY RLY
UNDERHOOD LT
A/C CLUTCH RLY (3.9L & 5.2L)
RAD FAN RLY (2.5L) OR OFF ROAD LTS (3.9L & 5.2L)
FUSE F2 (PDC)
AUTO IGN SHUTDOWN RLY
IGN SW
FUSE #5 (F/B)
RIGHT HEADLT
POWER DISTRIBUTION CENTER (PARTIAL)
RIGHT FOG LT
PURGE SOL
SBEC PIN #20
ALTERNATOR
STARTER
STARTER RELAY
HORN
HORN RELAY
LEFT FOG LT
IGNITION SW
SBEC PIC #30
FOG LT SW
ON
OFF
LEFT HEADLT
BACK-UP LTS
HEADLT DIMMER SW
BACK-UP LIGHT SW (M/T)
FUSE #2 (F/B)
SBEC PIN #9
BACK-UP LTS
UNDERHOOD LT/ MERCURY SW
FUSE F2
NEUTRAL START & BACK-UP LT SW
(M/T)
LEFT PARK/ DIR LT
(A/T)
LEFT MARKER LT
AUTO TRANS OVERDRIVE SOL/ PART THROTTLE UNLOCK SOL
SBEC PIN #55
INST CLSTR

1991 WIRING DIAGRAMS
Dakota (Cont.)

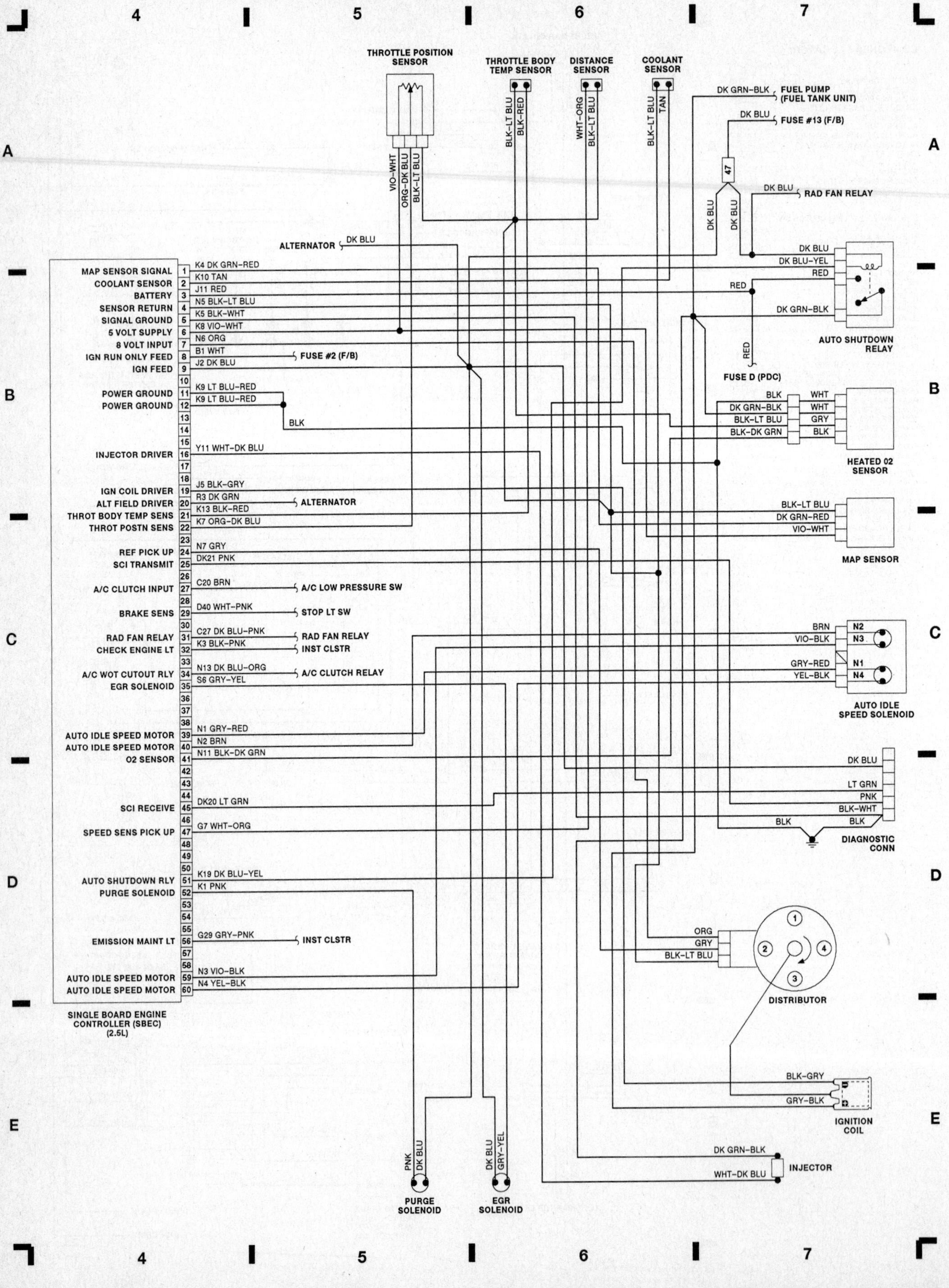
THROTTLE POSITION SENSOR
THROTTLE BODY TEMP SENSOR
DISTANCE SENSOR
COOLANT SENSOR
VIO-WHT
ORG-DK BLU
BLK-LT BLU
BLK-RED
WHT-ORG
TAN
DK GRN-BLK
FUEL PUMP (FUEL TANK UNIT)
DK BLU
FUSE #13 (F/B)
47
RAD FAN RELAY
ALTERNATOR
DK BLU-YEL
RED
AUTO SHUTDOWN RELAY
FUSE D (PDC)
MAP SENSOR SIGNAL
COOLANT SENSOR
BATTERY
SENSOR RETURN
SIGNAL GROUND
5 VOLT SUPPLY
8 VOLT INPUT
IGN RUN ONLY FEED
IGN FEED
POWER GROUND
POWER GROUND
INJECTOR DRIVER
IGN COIL DRIVER
ALT FIELD DRIVER
THROT BODY TEMP SENS
THROT POSTN SENS
REF PICK UP
SCI TRANSMIT
A/C CLUTCH INPUT
BRAKE SENS
RAD FAN RELAY
CHECK ENGINE LT
A/C WOT CUTOUT RLY
EGR SOLENOID
AUTO IDLE SPEED MOTOR
AUTO IDLE SPEED MOTOR
O2 SENSOR
SCI RECEIVE
SPEED SENS PICK UP
AUTO SHUTDOWN RLY
PURGE SOLENOID
EMISSION MAINT LT
AUTO IDLE SPEED MOTOR
AUTO IDLE SPEED MOTOR
K4 DK GRN-RED
K10 TAN
J11 RED
N5 BLK-LT BLU
K5 BLK-WHT
K8 VIO-WHT
N6 ORG
B1 WHT
J2 DK BLU
FUSE #2 (F/B)
K9 LT BLU-RED
K9 LT BLU-RED
BLK
Y11 WHT-DK BLU
J5 BLK-GRY
R3 DK GRN
K13 BLK-RED
K7 ORG-DK BLU
N7 GRY
DK21 PNK
C20 BRN
A/C LOW PRESSURE SW
D40 WHT-PNK
STOP LT SW
C27 DK BLU-PNK
K3 BLK-PNK
INST CLSTR
N13 DK BLU-ORG
A/C CLUTCH RELAY
S6 GRY-YEL
N1 GRY-RED
N2 BRN
N11 BLK-DK GRN
DK20 LT GRN
G7 WHT-ORG
K19 DK BLU-YEL
K1 PNK
G29 GRY-PNK
N3 VIO-BLK
N4 YEL-BLK
SINGLE BOARD ENGINE CONTROLLER (SBEC) (2.5L)
BLK
WHT
DK GRN-BLK
BLK-LT BLU
GRY
BLK-DK GRN
HEATED O2 SENSOR
DK GRN-RED
MAP SENSOR
BRN
VIO-BLK
GRY-RED
YEL-BLK
N1
N2
N3
N4
AUTO IDLE SPEED SOLENOID
LT GRN
PNK
BLK-WHT
DIAGNOSTIC CONN
ORG
DISTRIBUTOR
BLK-GRY
GRY-BLK
IGNITION COIL
DK GRN-BLK
WHT-DK BLU
INJECTOR
PURGE SOLENOID
GRY-YEL
EGR SOLENOID

1991 WIRING DIAGRAMS
Dakota (Cont.)

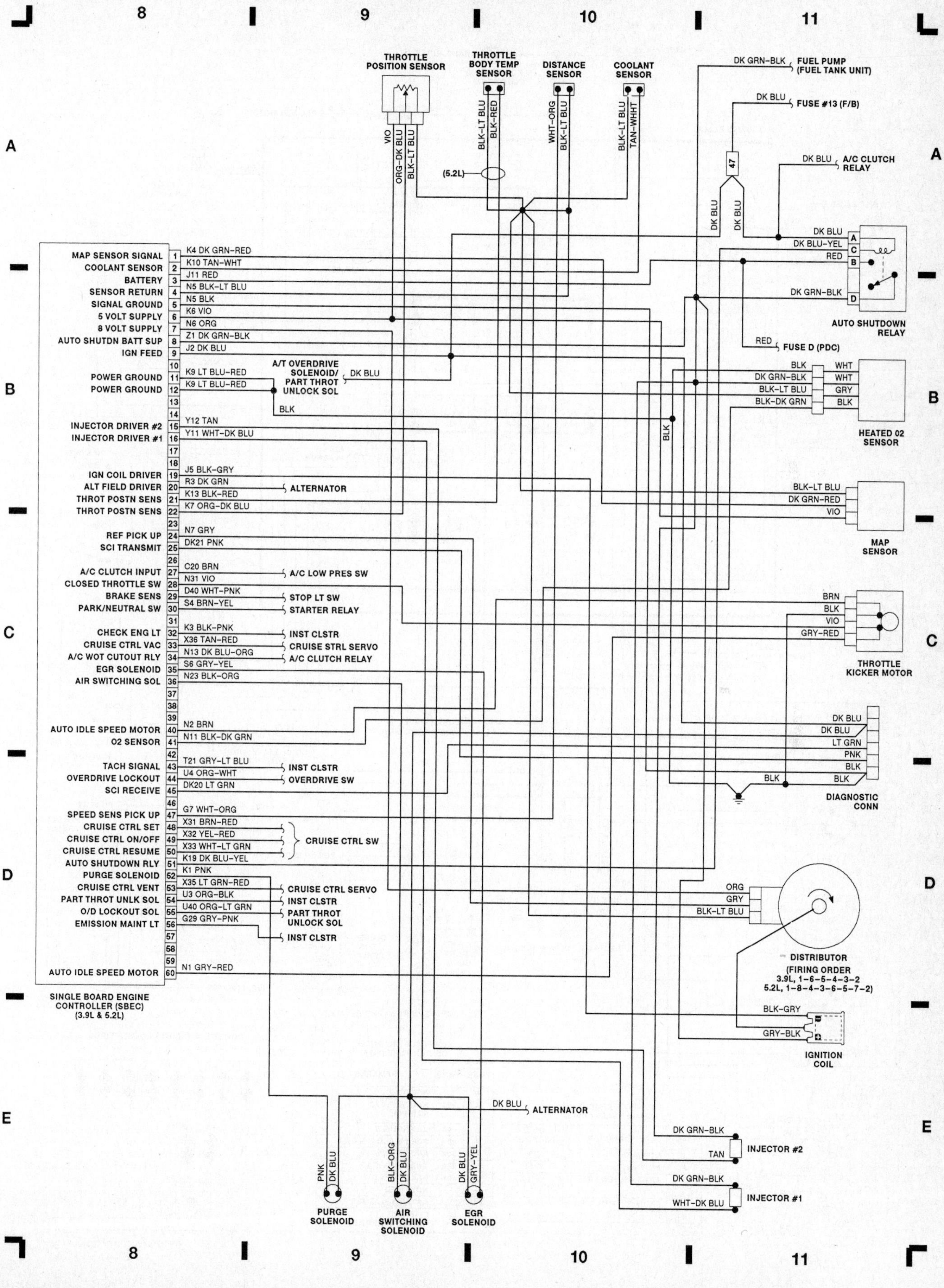
THROTTLE POSITION SENSOR
THROTTLE BODY TEMP SENSOR
DISTANCE SENSOR
COOLANT SENSOR
FUEL PUMP (FUEL TANK UNIT)
FUSE #13 (F/B)
A/C CLUTCH RELAY
AUTO SHUTDOWN RELAY
FUSE D (PDC)
(5.2L)
MAP SENSOR SIGNAL 1 K4 DK GRN-RED
COOLANT SENSOR 2 K10 TAN-WHT
BATTERY 3 J11 RED
SENSOR RETURN 4 N5 BLK-LT BLU
SIGNAL GROUND 5 N5 BLK
5 VOLT SUPPLY 6 K6 VIO
8 VOLT SUPPLY 7 N6 ORG
AUTO SHUTDN BATT SUP 8 Z1 DK GRN-BLK
IGN FEED 9 J2 DK BLU
POWER GROUND 11 K9 LT BLU-RED
POWER GROUND 12 K9 LT BLU-RED
A/T OVERDRIVE SOLENOID/ PART THROT UNLOCK SOL
INJECTOR DRIVER #2 15 Y12 TAN
INJECTOR DRIVER #1 16 Y11 WHT-DK BLU
IGN COIL DRIVER 19 J5 BLK-GRY
ALT FIELD DRIVER 20 R3 DK GRN
THROT POSTN SENS 21 K13 BLK-RED
THROT POSTN SENS 22 K7 ORG-DK BLU
ALTERNATOR
REF PICK UP 24 N7 GRY
SCI TRANSMIT 25 DK21 PNK
A/C CLUTCH INPUT 27 C20 BRN
CLOSED THROTTLE SW 28 N31 VIO
BRAKE SENS 29 D40 WHT-PNK
PARK/NEUTRAL SW 30 S4 BRN-YEL
A/C LOW PRES SW
STOP LT SW
STARTER RELAY
CHECK ENG LT 32 K3 BLK-PNK
CRUISE CTRL VAC 33 X36 TAN-RED
A/C WOT CUTOUT RLY 34 N13 DK BLU-ORG
EGR SOLENOID 35 S6 GRY-YEL
AIR SWITCHING SOL 36 N23 BLK-ORG
INST CLSTR
CRUISE STRL SERVO
A/C CLUTCH RELAY
AUTO IDLE SPEED MOTOR 40 N2 BRN
O2 SENSOR 41 N11 BLK-DK GRN
TACH SIGNAL 43 T21 GRY-LT BLU
OVERDRIVE LOCKOUT 44 U4 ORG-WHT
SCI RECEIVE 45 DK20 LT GRN
OVERDRIVE SW
SPEED SENS PICK UP 47 G7 WHT-ORG
CRUISE CTRL SET 48 X31 BRN-RED
CRUISE CTRL ON/OFF 49 X32 YEL-RED
CRUISE CTRL RESUME 50 X33 WHT-LT GRN
AUTO SHUTDOWN RLY 51 K19 DK BLU-YEL
PURGE SOLENOID 52 K1 PNK
CRUISE CTRL SW
CRUISE CTRL VENT 53 X35 LT GRN-RED
PART THROT UNLK SOL 54 U3 ORG-BLK
O/D LOCKOUT SOL 55 U40 ORG-LT GRN
EMISSION MAINT LT 56 G29 GRY-PNK
CRUISE CTRL SERVO
PART THROT UNLOCK SOL
AUTO IDLE SPEED MOTOR 60 N1 GRY-RED
SINGLE BOARD ENGINE CONTROLLER (SBEC) (3.9L & 5.2L)
HEATED 02 SENSOR
MAP SENSOR
THROTTLE KICKER MOTOR
DIAGNOSTIC CONN
DISTRIBUTOR (FIRING ORDER 3.9L, 1-6-5-4-3-2 5.2L, 1-8-4-3-6-5-7-2)
IGNITION COIL
ALTERNATOR
INJECTOR #2
INJECTOR #1
PURGE SOLENOID
AIR SWITCHING SOLENOID
EGR SOLENOID

1991 WIRING DIAGRAMS
Dakota (Cont.)

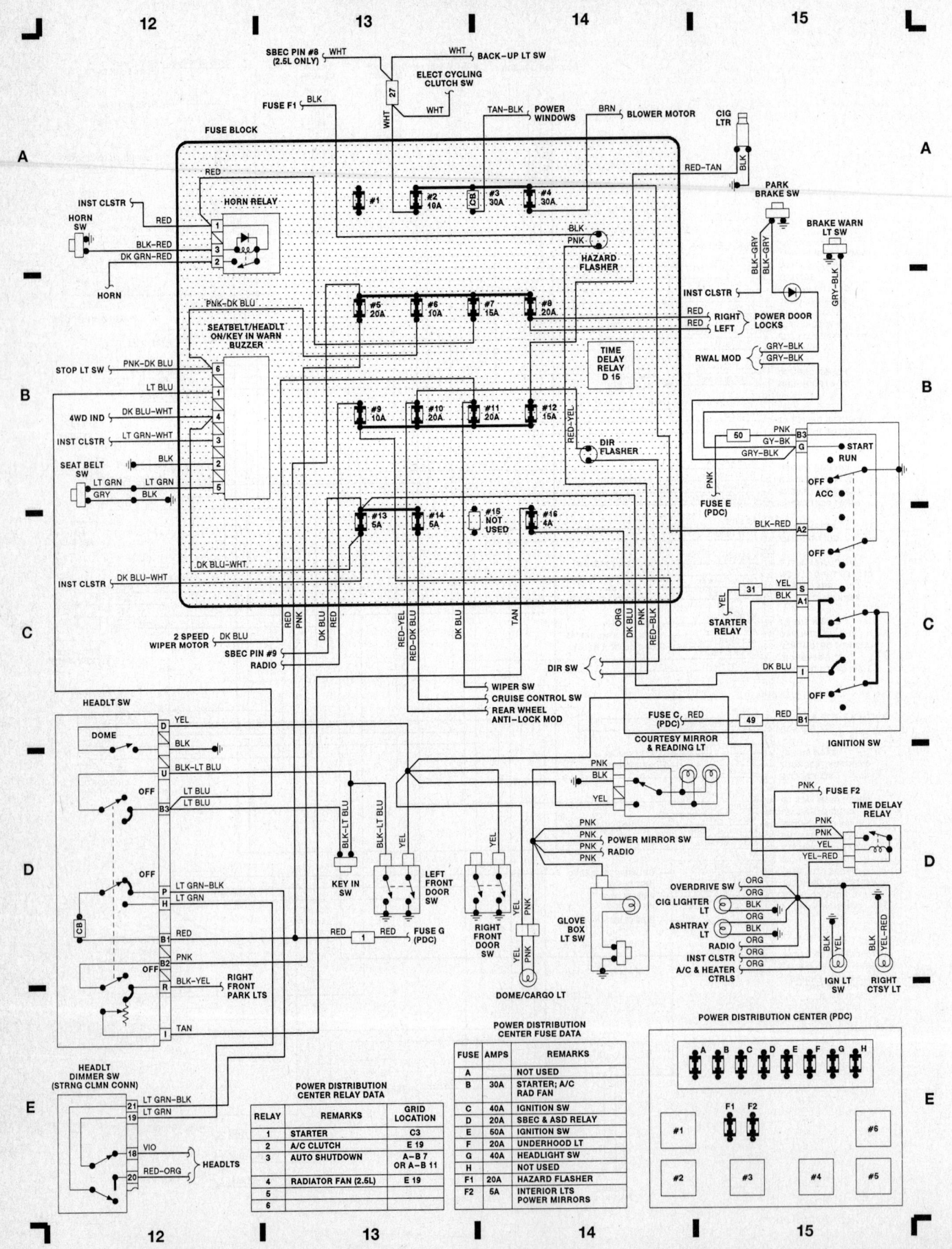

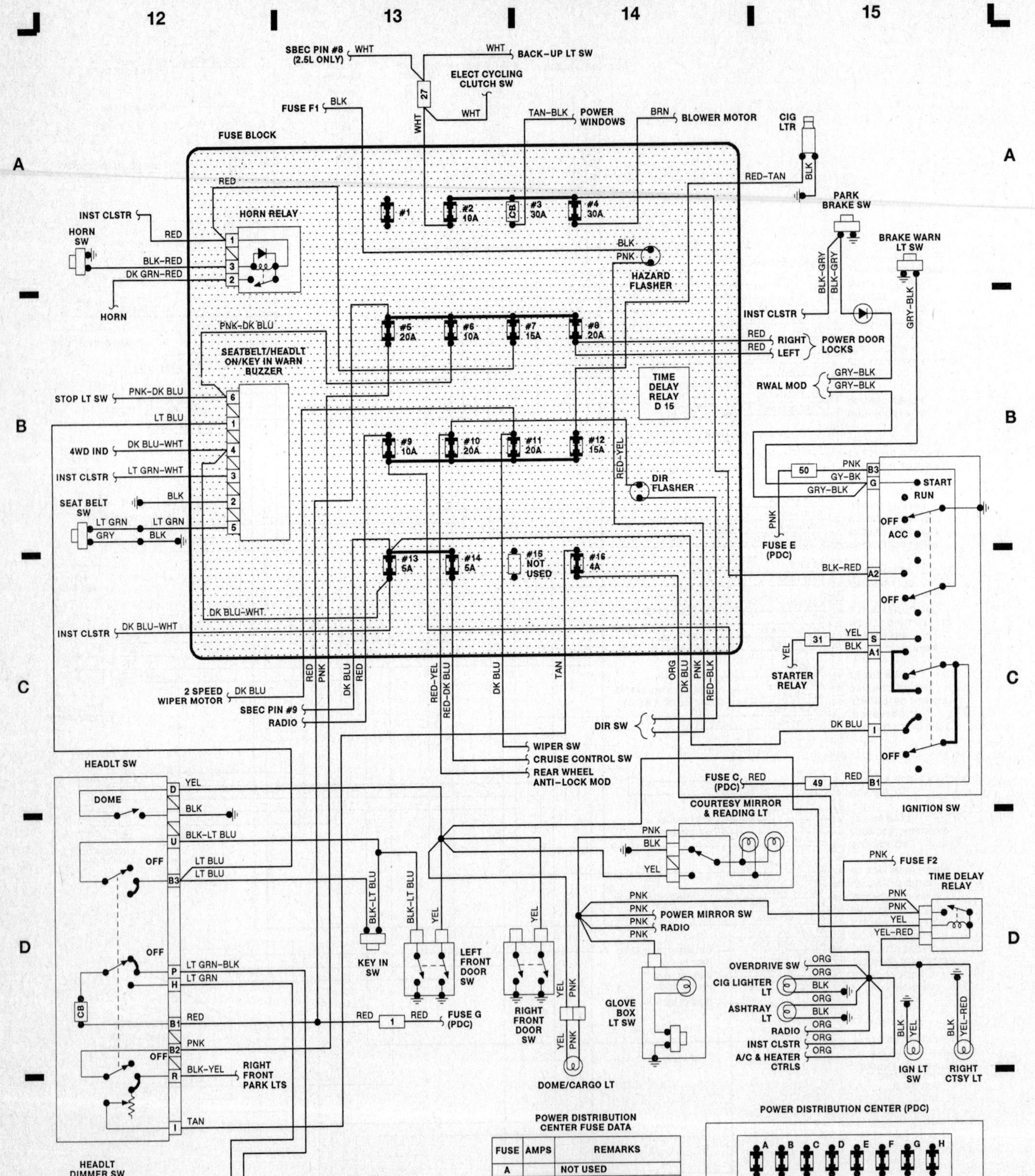
12
13
14
15
A
B
C
D
E
SBEC PIN #8 (2.5L ONLY)
WHT
BACK-UP LT SW
ELECT CYCLING CLUTCH SW
27
FUSE F1
BLK
TAN-BLK
POWER WINDOWS
BRN
BLOWER MOTOR
CIG LTR
FUSE BLOCK
RED-TAN
PARK BRAKE SW
INST CLSTR
HORN RELAY
HORN SW
RED
BLK-RED
DK GRN-RED
HORN
#1
#2 10A
CB #3 30A
#4 30A
HAZARD FLASHER
PNK
BRAKE WARN LT SW
BLK-GRY
GRY-BLK
#5 20A
#6 10A
#7 15A
#8 20A
RIGHT
LEFT
POWER DOOR LOCKS
PNK-DK BLU
SEATBELT/HEADLT ON/KEY IN WARN BUZZER
TIME DELAY RELAY D 15
RWAL MOD
STOP LT SW
LT BLU
4WD IND
DK BLU-WHT
INST CLSTR
LT GRN-WHT
#9 10A
#10 20A
#11 20A
#12 15A
RED-YEL
DIR FLASHER
50
GY-BK
GRY-BLK
START
RUN
OFF
ACC
SEAT BELT SW
LT GRN
GRY
FUSE E (PDC)
#13 5A
#14 5A
#15 NOT USED
#16 4A
DK BLU-WHT
INST CLSTR
31
YEL
STARTER RELAY
IGNITION SW
2 SPEED WIPER MOTOR
DK BLU
SBEC PIN #9
RADIO
RED-DK BLU
TAN
ORG
RED-BLK
DIR SW
WIPER SW
CRUISE CONTROL SW
REAR WHEEL ANTI-LOCK MOD
FUSE C (PDC)
49
HEADLT SW
DOME
BLK-LT BLU
COURTESY MIRROR & READING LT
FUSE F2
TIME DELAY RELAY
YEL-RED
POWER MIRROR SW
RADIO
KEY IN SW
LEFT FRONT DOOR SW
RIGHT FRONT DOOR SW
GLOVE BOX LT SW
LT GRN-BLK
OVERDRIVE SW
CIG LIGHTER LT
ASHTRAY LT
RADIO
INST CLSTR
A/C & HEATER CTRLS
FUSE G (PDC)
1
BLK-YEL
RIGHT FRONT PARK LTS
DOME/CARGO LT
IGN LT SW
RIGHT CTSY LT
HEADLT DIMMER SW (STRNG CLMN CONN)
VIO
RED-ORG
HEADLTS

POWER DISTRIBUTION CENTER RELAY DATA

RELAY	REMARKS	GRID LOCATION
1	STARTER	C3
2	A/C CLUTCH	E 19
3	AUTO SHUTDOWN	A–B 7 OR A–B 11
4	RADIATOR FAN (2.5L)	E 19
5		
6		

POWER DISTRIBUTION CENTER FUSE DATA

FUSE	AMPS	REMARKS
A		NOT USED
B	30A	STARTER; A/C RAD FAN
C	40A	IGNITION SW
D	20A	SBEC & ASD RELAY
E	50A	IGNITION SW
F	20A	UNDERHOOD LT
G	40A	HEADLIGHT SW
H		NOT USED
F1	20A	HAZARD FLASHER
F2	5A	INTERIOR LTS POWER MIRRORS

POWER DISTRIBUTION CENTER (PDC)

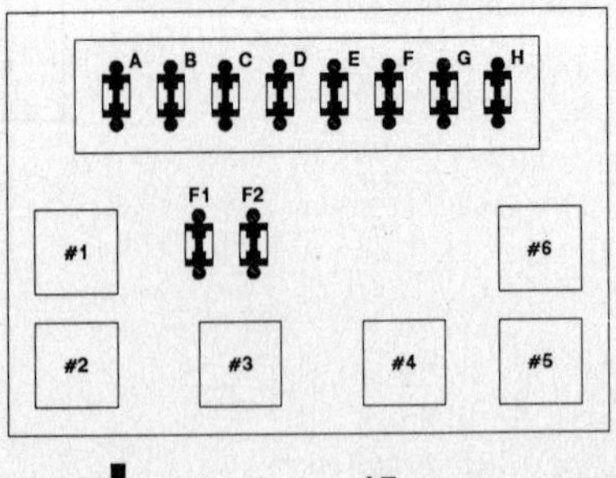
A
B
C
D
E
F
G
H
F1
F2
#1
#2
#3
#4
#5
#6

12 13 14 15

1991 WIRING DIAGRAMS
Dakota (Cont.)

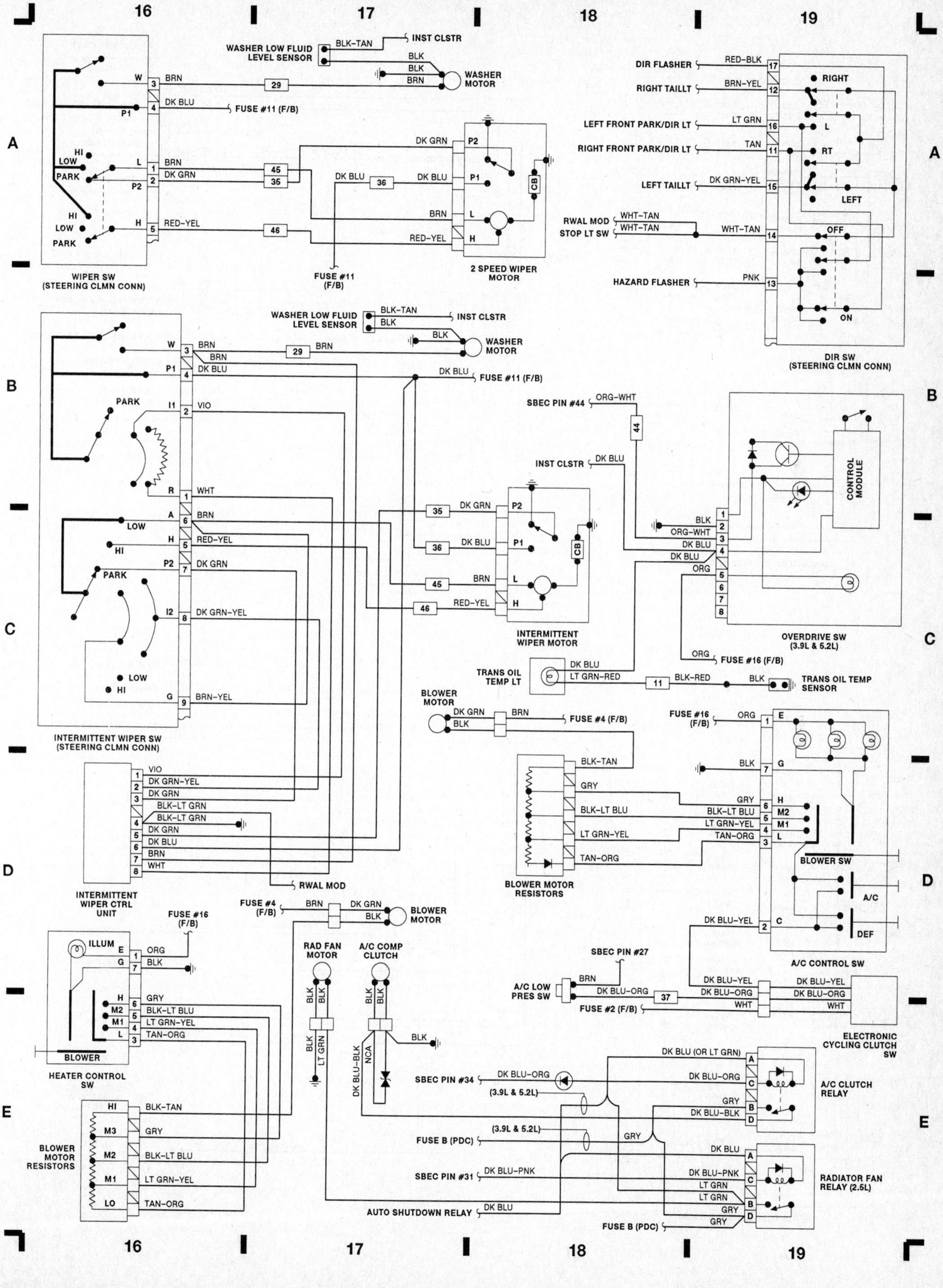
16
17
18
19
A
B
C
D
E
WASHER LOW FLUID LEVEL SENSOR
BLK-TAN
INST CLSTR
BLK
BRN
WASHER MOTOR
W
P1
DK BLU
FUSE #11 (F/B)
HI
LOW
PARK
L
P2
H
DK GRN
RED-YEL
DK BLU
FUSE #11 (F/B)
2 SPEED WIPER MOTOR
CB
WIPER SW (STEERING CLMN CONN)
DIR FLASHER
RED-BLK
RIGHT TAILLT
BRN-YEL
LEFT FRONT PARK/DIR LT
LT GRN
RIGHT FRONT PARK/DIR LT
TAN
LEFT TAILLT
DK GRN-YEL
RWAL MOD
STOP LT SW
WHT-TAN
HAZARD FLASHER
PNK
RIGHT
RT
LEFT
OFF
ON
DIR SW (STEERING CLMN CONN)
I1
VIO
R
WHT
A
I2
DK GRN-YEL
G
BRN-YEL
INTERMITTENT WIPER SW (STEERING CLMN CONN)
SBEC PIN #44
ORG-WHT
INST CLSTR
ORG
CONTROL MODULE
OVERDRIVE SW (3.9L & 5.2L)
INTERMITTENT WIPER MOTOR
FUSE #16 (F/B)
TRANS OIL TEMP LT
LT GRN-RED
BLK-RED
TRANS OIL TEMP SENSOR
BLOWER MOTOR
FUSE #4 (F/B)
BLK-LT BLU
LT GRN-YEL
TAN-ORG
GRY
BLOWER MOTOR RESISTORS
E
M2
M1
BLOWER SW
A/C
DEF
C
DK BLU-YEL
A/C CONTROL SW
INTERMITTENT WIPER CTRL UNIT
BLK-LT GRN
RWAL MOD
ILLUM
HEATER CONTROL SW
BLOWER
HI
M3
LO
RAD FAN MOTOR
A/C COMP CLUTCH
NCA
DK BLU-BLK
LT GRN
SBEC PIN #27
A/C LOW PRES SW
DK BLU-ORG
FUSE #2 (F/B)
ELECTRONIC CYCLING CLUTCH SW
DK BLU (OR LT GRN)
SBEC PIN #34
(3.9L & 5.2L)
A/C CLUTCH RELAY
FUSE B (PDC)
SBEC PIN #31
DK BLU-PNK
RADIATOR FAN RELAY (2.5L)
AUTO SHUTDOWN RELAY
FUSE B (PDC)

1991 WIRING DIAGRAMS
Dakota (Cont.)

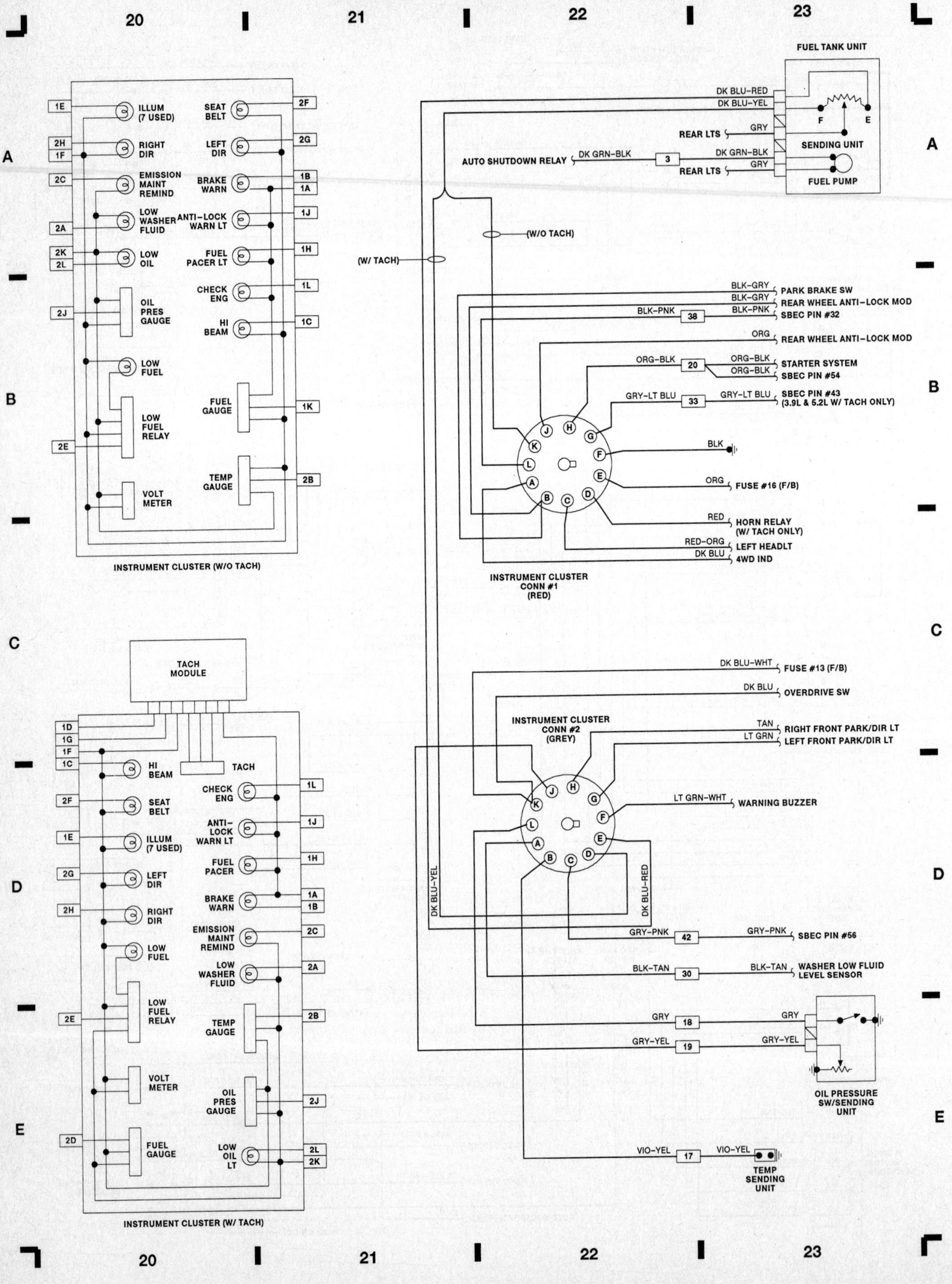
20
21
22
23
A
B
C
D
E
FUEL TANK UNIT
DK BLU-RED
DK BLU-YEL
GRY
REAR LTS
SENDING UNIT
AUTO SHUTDOWN RELAY
DK GRN-BLK
3
FUEL PUMP
(W/O TACH)
(W/ TACH)
BLK-GRY
PARK BRAKE SW
REAR WHEEL ANTI-LOCK MOD
BLK-PNK
38
SBEC PIN #32
ORG
ORG-BLK
20
STARTER SYSTEM
SBEC PIN #54
GRY-LT BLU
33
SBEC PIN #43
(3.9L & 5.2L W/ TACH ONLY)
BLK
FUSE #16 (F/B)
RED
HORN RELAY
(W/ TACH ONLY)
RED-ORG
LEFT HEADLT
DK BLU
4WD IND
INSTRUMENT CLUSTER
CONN #1
(RED)
INSTRUMENT CLUSTER (W/O TACH)
ILLUM
(7 USED)
SEAT
BELT
RIGHT
DIR
LEFT
DIR
EMISSION
MAINT
REMIND
BRAKE
WARN
LOW
WASHER
FLUID
ANTI-LOCK
WARN LT
LOW
OIL
FUEL
PACER LT
CHECK
ENG
OIL
PRES
GAUGE
HI
BEAM
LOW
FUEL
FUEL
GAUGE
LOW
FUEL
RELAY
TEMP
GAUGE
VOLT
METER
TACH
MODULE
TACH
INSTRUMENT CLUSTER (W/ TACH)
DK BLU-WHT
FUSE #13 (F/B)
OVERDRIVE SW
INSTRUMENT CLUSTER
CONN #2
(GREY)
TAN
RIGHT FRONT PARK/DIR LT
LT GRN
LEFT FRONT PARK/DIR LT
LT GRN-WHT
WARNING BUZZER
DK BLU-YEL
DK BLU-RED
GRY-PNK
42
SBEC PIN #56
BLK-TAN
30
WASHER LOW FLUID
LEVEL SENSOR
18
GRY-YEL
19
OIL PRESSURE
SW/SENDING
UNIT
VIO-YEL
17
TEMP
SENDING
UNIT

1991 WIRING DIAGRAMS
Dakota (Cont.)

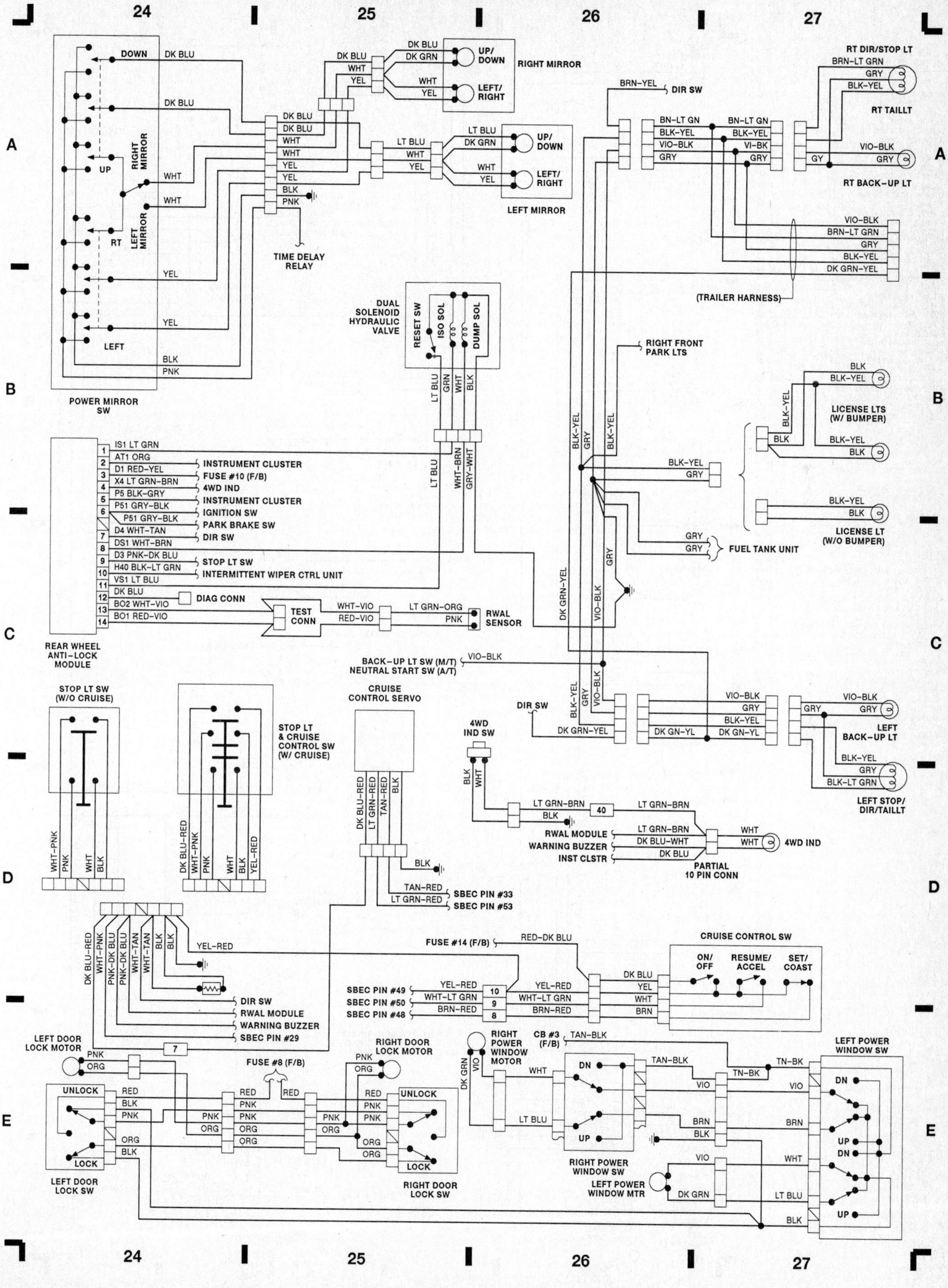
24
25
26
27
A
B
C
D
E
DOWN
UP
RT
LEFT
RIGHT MIRROR
LEFT MIRROR
POWER MIRROR SW
DK BLU
DK GRN
WHT
YEL
BLK
PNK
LT BLU
UP/ DOWN
LEFT/ RIGHT
RIGHT MIRROR
LEFT MIRROR
TIME DELAY RELAY
DUAL SOLENOID HYDRAULIC VALVE
RESET SW
ISO SOL
DUMP SOL
BRN-YEL
DIR SW
BN-LT GN
BLK-YEL
VIO-BLK
GRY
VI-BK
RT DIR/STOP LT
BRN-LT GRN
RT TAILLT
RT BACK-UP LT
VIO-BLK
BRN-LT GRN
DK GRN-YEL
(TRAILER HARNESS)
RIGHT FRONT PARK LTS
LICENSE LTS (W/ BUMPER)
LICENSE LT (W/O BUMPER)
FUEL TANK UNIT
IS1 LT GRN
AT1 ORG
D1 RED-YEL
X4 LT GRN-BRN
P5 BLK-GRY
P51 GRY-BLK
P51 GRY-BLK
D4 WHT-TAN
DS1 WHT-BRN
D3 PNK-DK BLU
H40 BLK-LT GRN
VS1 LT BLU
DK BLU
BO2 WHT-VIO
BO1 RED-VIO
INSTRUMENT CLUSTER
FUSE #10 (F/B)
4WD IND
INSTRUMENT CLUSTER
IGNITION SW
PARK BRAKE SW
DIR SW
STOP LT SW
INTERMITTENT WIPER CTRL UNIT
DIAG CONN
TEST CONN
WHT-VIO
RED-VIO
LT GRN-ORG
RWAL SENSOR
REAR WHEEL ANTI-LOCK MODULE
BACK-UP LT SW (M/T)
NEUTRAL START SW (A/T)
STOP LT SW (W/O CRUISE)
STOP LT & CRUISE CONTROL SW (W/ CRUISE)
CRUISE CONTROL SERVO
DIR SW
4WD IND SW
DK GRN-YEL
DK GN-YL
LEFT BACK-UP LT
BLK-LT GRN
LEFT STOP/ DIR/TAILLT
LT GRN-BRN
40
RWAL MODULE
WARNING BUZZER
INST CLSTR
DK BLU-WHT
PARTIAL 10 PIN CONN
4WD IND
WHT-PNK
DK BLU-RED
YEL-RED
LT GRN-RED
TAN-RED
SBEC PIN #33
SBEC PIN #53
FUSE #14 (F/B)
RED-DK BLU
CRUISE CONTROL SW
ON/ OFF
RESUME/ ACCEL
SET/ COAST
SBEC PIN #49
SBEC PIN #50
SBEC PIN #48
WHT-LT GRN
BRN-RED
10
9
8
PNK-DK BLU
WHT-TAN
DIR SW
RWAL MODULE
WARNING BUZZER
SBEC PIN #29
7
LEFT DOOR LOCK MOTOR
RIGHT DOOR LOCK MOTOR
FUSE #8 (F/B)
UNLOCK
LOCK
LEFT DOOR LOCK SW
RIGHT DOOR LOCK SW
RED
ORG
RIGHT POWER WINDOW MOTOR
CB #3 (F/B)
TAN-BLK
TN-BK
DN
UP
RIGHT POWER WINDOW SW
LEFT POWER WINDOW MTR
LEFT POWER WINDOW SW
VIO
BRN
WHT
LT BLU
DK GRN

1991 WIRING DIAGRAMS
Pickup & Ramcharger

COMPONENT LOCATOR:

A/C/HEATER SW	A 20-22
AIR HEATER CONTROLLER (EARLY DIESEL)	E 12
ALTERNATOR	E 3
AUTO SHUTDOWN RELAY	B 7
BACK-UP LT SW	C 2
BATTERY	A 2
BRAKE WARNING LT SW	D 24
COURTESY LTS	D-E 16-19
CRUISE CONTROL SERVO (GAS & LATE DIESEL)	C 12
CRUISE CONTROL SW (EARLY DIESEL)	A 12
CRUISE CONTROL SW (GAS & LATE DIESEL)	C 12
DIODE/MOLD ASSY	E 19
DIR/HAZARD SW	A 18-19
DISTANCE SENSOR	D 15
ELECT CLUTCH CYCLING SW	B 22
ELECT VACUUM SENSOR (DIESEL)	C 24
ELECTRONIC CONTROL MODULE (EARLY DIESEL)	A 15
FRONT AXLE SW	E 31
FUEL TANK UNIT (DIESEL)	C 32
FUEL TANK UNIT (GAS)	D 32
FUS LINKS	A-D 2-3
FUSE BLOCK	C 16-18
HEADLT DIMMER SW	B 26
HEADLT SW	A-B 24
HEATER BLOWER MOTOR SW	C 23
IGNITION SW	A-B 16
INSTRUMENT CLUSTER	B-C 28-29
INTAKE MANIFOLD HEATER RELAYS (EARLY DIESEL)	E 13
INTAKE MANIFOLD HEATER RELAYS (LATE DIESEL)	A 11
INTERMITTENT WIPER CONTROL UNIT	D 21
LEFT DOOR SW	E 17
MESSAGE CENTER (DIESEL)	D-E 28
MESSAGE CENTER (GAS)	A 28
NEUTRAL START & BACK-UP LT SW (A/T)	B 2
OVERDRIVE LOCKOUT SW (LATE DIESEL)	E 8
OVERDRIVE MODULE (EX LATE DIESEL)	E 11
OVERDRIVE MODULE (LATE DIESEL)	D 8
PART THROTTLE UNLOCK RELAY	E 4
POWER DOOR LOCKS	B 32
POWER MIRROR SW	D-E 27
POWER WINDOWS	A 32-33
REAR WHEEL ANTI-LOCK MODULE	E 24
REAR WINDOW DEFOG SW	C 27
SEAT BELT SW	A 27
SEAT BELT WARNING MODULE	A 27
SINGLE BOARD ENGINE CONTROLLER (SBEC) (3.9L,5.2L,5.9L)	B-D 4
SINGLE BOARD ENGINE CONTROLLER (SBEC) (5.9L LATE DIESEL)	A-D 8
STARTER RELAY	A 3
STOP LT SW (W/ CRUISE CONTROL)	B 15
STOP LT SW (W/O CRUISE CONTROL)	B 15
TRANSFER CASE SW	E 31
UNDERHOOD LT	C 1
VOLTAGE REGULATOR (DIESEL)	E 3
WIDE OPEN THROTTLE CUTOUT RELAY (GAS)	C 20
WIPER/WASHER SW (INTERMITTENT)	E 20
WIPER/WASHER SW (STANDARD)	D 23

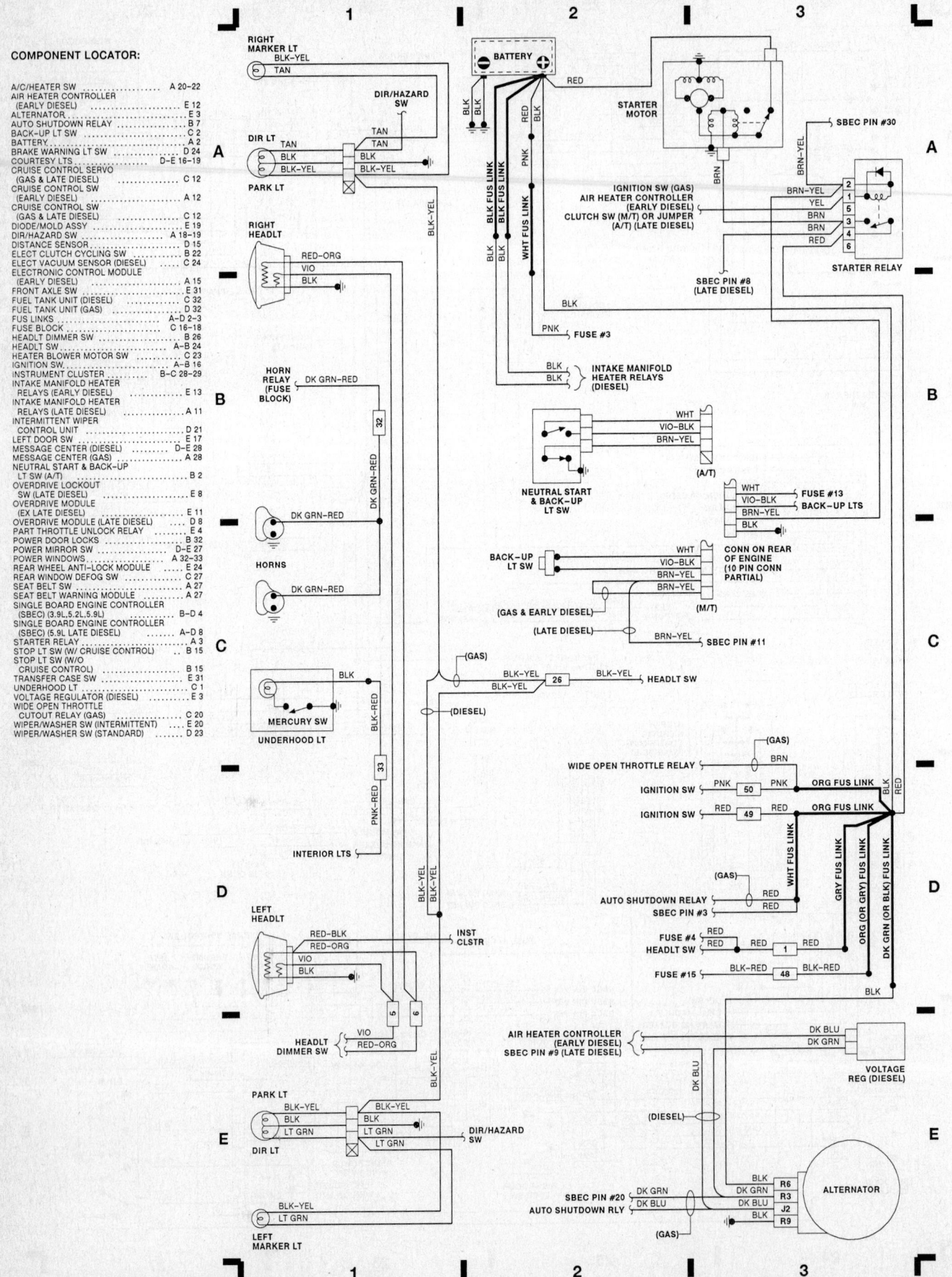

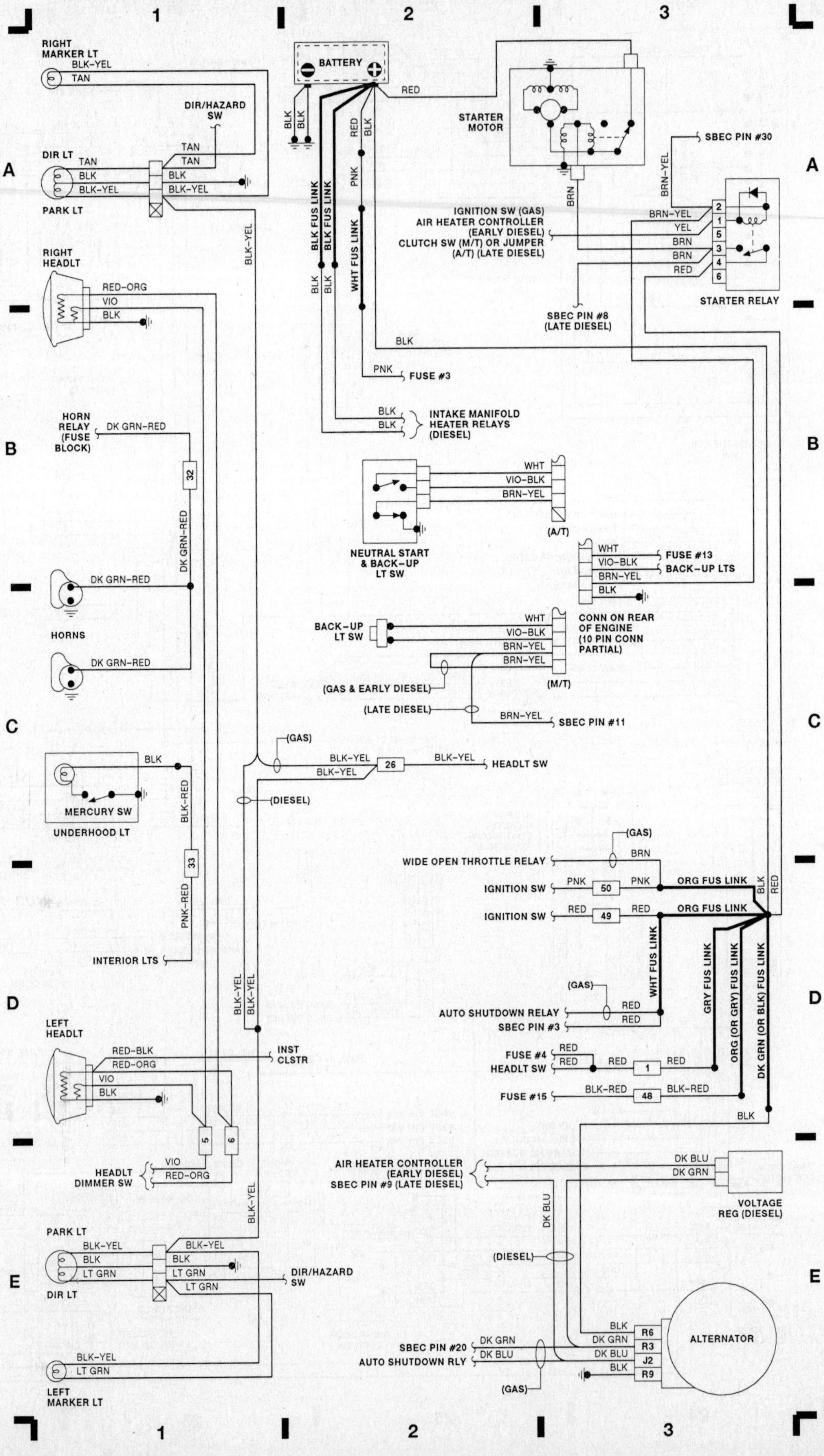
1
2
3
A
B
C
D
E
RIGHT MARKER LT
BATTERY
STARTER MOTOR
DIR/HAZARD SW
DIR LT
PARK LT
SBEC PIN #30
IGNITION SW (GAS)
AIR HEATER CONTROLLER (EARLY DIESEL)
CLUTCH SW (M/T) OR JUMPER (A/T) (LATE DIESEL)
STARTER RELAY
SBEC PIN #8 (LATE DIESEL)
RIGHT HEADLT
BLK FUS LINK
WHT FUS LINK
FUSE #3
HORN RELAY (FUSE BLOCK)
INTAKE MANIFOLD HEATER RELAYS (DIESEL)
NEUTRAL START & BACK-UP LT SW
(A/T)
FUSE #13
BACK-UP LTS
HORNS
BACK-UP LT SW
CONN ON REAR OF ENGINE (10 PIN CONN PARTIAL)
(M/T)
(GAS & EARLY DIESEL)
(LATE DIESEL)
SBEC PIN #11
(GAS)
HEADLT SW
MERCURY SW
UNDERHOOD LT
(DIESEL)
WIDE OPEN THROTTLE RELAY
IGNITION SW
ORG FUS LINK
INTERIOR LTS
AUTO SHUTDOWN RELAY
SBEC PIN #3
GRY FUS LINK
ORG (OR GRY) FUS LINK
DK GRN (OR BLK) FUS LINK
LEFT HEADLT
INST CLSTR
FUSE #4
FUSE #15
HEADLT DIMMER SW
AIR HEATER CONTROLLER (EARLY DIESEL)
SBEC PIN #9 (LATE DIESEL)
VOLTAGE REG (DIESEL)
ALTERNATOR
SBEC PIN #20
AUTO SHUTDOWN RLY
LEFT MARKER LT

1991 WIRING DIAGRAMS
Pickup & Ramcharger (Cont.)

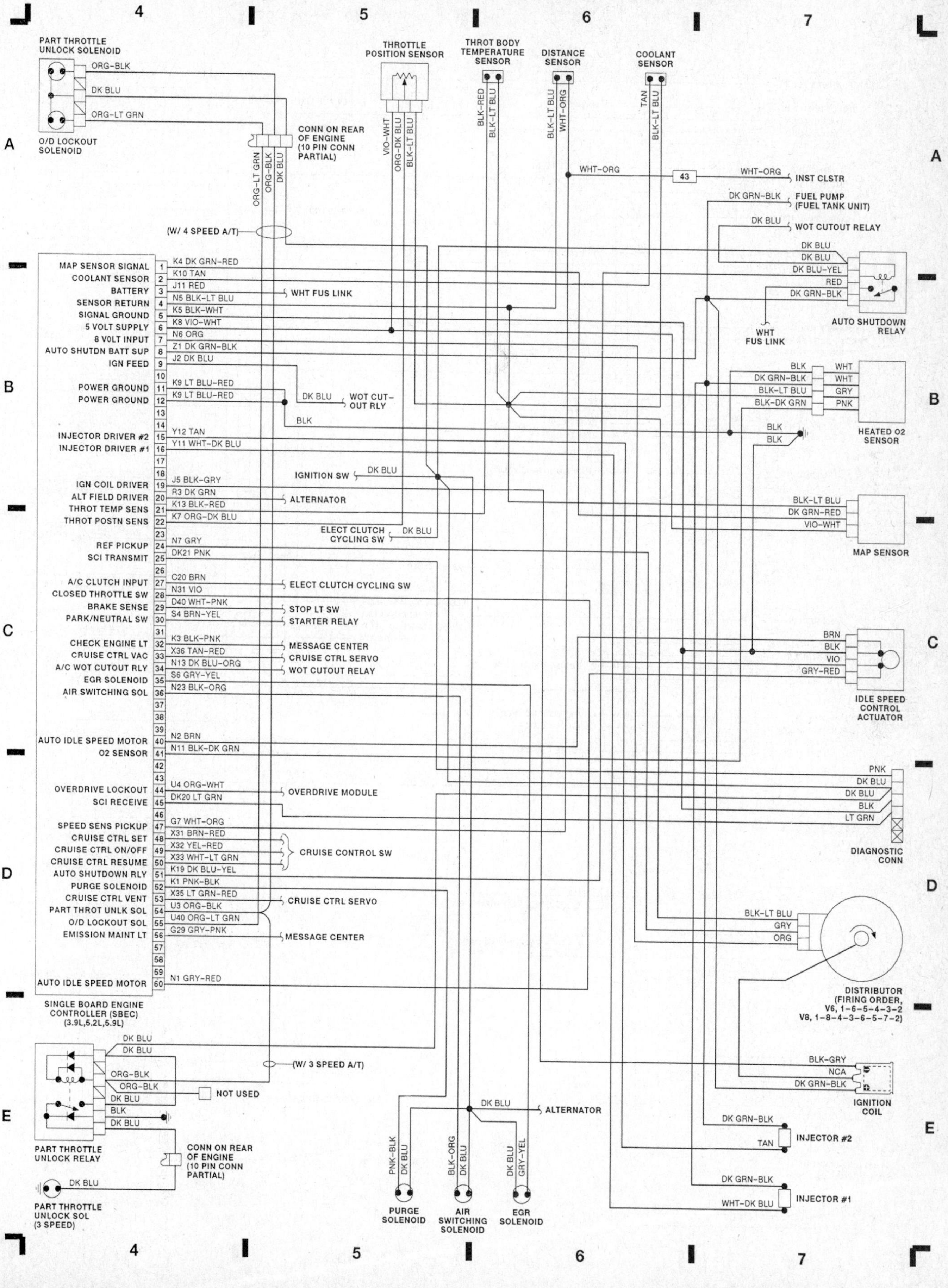
4
5
6
7
A
B
C
D
E
PART THROTTLE UNLOCK SOLENOID
ORG-BLK
DK BLU
ORG-LT GRN
O/D LOCKOUT SOLENOID
CONN ON REAR OF ENGINE (10 PIN CONN PARTIAL)
ORG-LT GRN
ORG-BLK
DK BLU
(W/ 4 SPEED A/T)
THROTTLE POSITION SENSOR
VIO-WHT
ORG-DK BLU
BLK-LT BLU
THROT BODY TEMPERATURE SENSOR
BLK-RED
BLK-LT BLU
DISTANCE SENSOR
BLK-LT BLU
WHT-ORG
COOLANT SENSOR
TAN
BLK-LT BLU
WHT-ORG
43
WHT-ORG
INST CLSTR
DK GRN-BLK
FUEL PUMP (FUEL TANK UNIT)
DK BLU
WOT CUTOUT RELAY
DK BLU
DK BLU
DK BLU-YEL
RED
DK GRN-BLK
WHT FUS LINK
AUTO SHUTDOWN RELAY
MAP SENSOR SIGNAL 1 K4 DK GRN-RED
COOLANT SENSOR 2 K10 TAN
BATTERY 3 J11 RED
WHT FUS LINK
SENSOR RETURN 4 N5 BLK-LT BLU
SIGNAL GROUND 5 K5 BLK-WHT
5 VOLT SUPPLY 6 K8 VIO-WHT
8 VOLT INPUT 7 N6 ORG
AUTO SHUTDN BATT SUP 8 Z1 DK GRN-BLK
IGN FEED 9 J2 DK BLU
10
POWER GROUND 11 K9 LT BLU-RED
POWER GROUND 12 K9 LT BLU-RED
DK BLU
WOT CUT-OUT RLY
13
BLK
14
INJECTOR DRIVER #2 15 Y12 TAN
INJECTOR DRIVER #1 16 Y11 WHT-DK BLU
17
18
IGNITION SW
DK BLU
IGN COIL DRIVER 19 J5 BLK-GRY
ALT FIELD DRIVER 20 R3 DK GRN
ALTERNATOR
THROT TEMP SENS 21 K13 BLK-RED
THROT POSTN SENS 22 K7 ORG-DK BLU
23
ELECT CLUTCH CYCLING SW
DK BLU
REF PICKUP 24 N7 GRY
SCI TRANSMIT 25 DK21 PNK
26
A/C CLUTCH INPUT 27 C20 BRN
ELECT CLUTCH CYCLING SW
CLOSED THROTTLE SW 28 N31 VIO
BRAKE SENSE 29 D40 WHT-PNK
STOP LT SW
PARK/NEUTRAL SW 30 S4 BRN-YEL
STARTER RELAY
31
CHECK ENGINE LT 32 K3 BLK-PNK
MESSAGE CENTER
CRUISE CTRL VAC 33 X36 TAN-RED
CRUISE CTRL SERVO
A/C WOT CUTOUT RLY 34 N13 DK BLU-ORG
WOT CUTOUT RELAY
EGR SOLENOID 35 S6 GRY-YEL
AIR SWITCHING SOL 36 N23 BLK-ORG
37
38
39
AUTO IDLE SPEED MOTOR 40 N2 BRN
O2 SENSOR 41 N11 BLK-DK GRN
42
43
OVERDRIVE LOCKOUT 44 U4 ORG-WHT
OVERDRIVE MODULE
SCI RECEIVE 45 DK20 LT GRN
46
SPEED SENS PICKUP 47 G7 WHT-ORG
CRUISE CTRL SET 48 X31 BRN-RED
CRUISE CTRL ON/OFF 49 X32 YEL-RED
CRUISE CTRL RESUME 50 X33 WHT-LT GRN
CRUISE CONTROL SW
AUTO SHUTDOWN RLY 51 K19 DK BLU-YEL
PURGE SOLENOID 52 K1 PNK-BLK
CRUISE CTRL VENT 53 X35 LT GRN-RED
CRUISE CTRL SERVO
PART THROT UNLK SOL 54 U3 ORG-BLK
O/D LOCKOUT SOL 55 U40 ORG-LT GRN
EMISSION MAINT LT 56 G29 GRY-PNK
MESSAGE CENTER
57
58
59
AUTO IDLE SPEED MOTOR 60 N1 GRY-RED
SINGLE BOARD ENGINE CONTROLLER (SBEC) (3.9L,5.2L,5.9L)
BLK
WHT
DK GRN-BLK
WHT
BLK-LT BLU
GRY
BLK-DK GRN
PNK
HEATED O2 SENSOR
BLK
BLK
BLK-LT BLU
DK GRN-RED
VIO-WHT
MAP SENSOR
BRN
BLK
VIO
GRY-RED
IDLE SPEED CONTROL ACTUATOR
PNK
DK BLU
DK BLU
BLK
LT GRN
DIAGNOSTIC CONN
BLK-LT BLU
GRY
ORG
DISTRIBUTOR (FIRING ORDER, V6, 1-6-5-4-3-2 V8, 1-8-4-3-6-5-7-2)
BLK-GRY
NCA
DK GRN-BLK
IGNITION COIL
DK GRN-BLK
TAN
INJECTOR #2
DK GRN-BLK
WHT-DK BLU
INJECTOR #1
DK BLU
DK BLU
(W/ 3 SPEED A/T)
ORG-BLK
ORG-BLK
NOT USED
DK BLU
BLK
DK BLU
PART THROTTLE UNLOCK RELAY
CONN ON REAR OF ENGINE (10 PIN CONN PARTIAL)
DK BLU
PART THROTTLE UNLOCK SOL (3 SPEED)
DK BLU
ALTERNATOR
PNK-BLK
DK BLU
BLK-ORG
DK BLU
DK BLU
GRY-YEL
PURGE SOLENOID
AIR SWITCHING SOLENOID
EGR SOLENOID

1991 WIRING DIAGRAMS
Pickup & Ramcharger (Cont.)

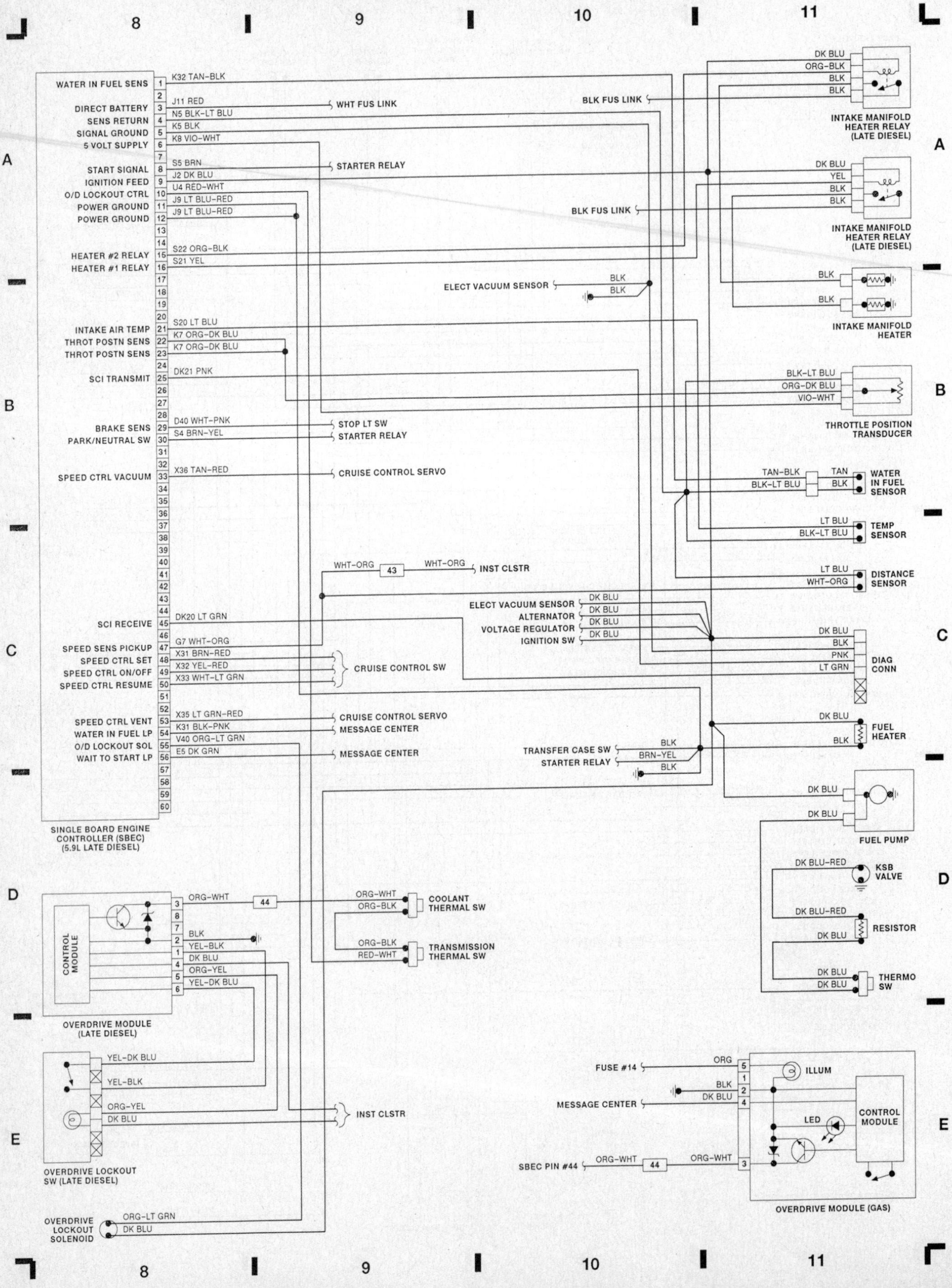
8
9
10
11
A
B
C
D
E
WATER IN FUEL SENS
DIRECT BATTERY
SENS RETURN
SIGNAL GROUND
5 VOLT SUPPLY
START SIGNAL
IGNITION FEED
O/D LOCKOUT CTRL
POWER GROUND
POWER GROUND
HEATER #2 RELAY
HEATER #1 RELAY
INTAKE AIR TEMP
THROT POSTN SENS
THROT POSTN SENS
SCI TRANSMIT
BRAKE SENS
PARK/NEUTRAL SW
SPEED CTRL VACUUM
SCI RECEIVE
SPEED SENS PICKUP
SPEED CTRL SET
SPEED CTRL ON/OFF
SPEED CTRL RESUME
SPEED CTRL VENT
WATER IN FUEL LP
O/D LOCKOUT SOL
WAIT TO START LP
K32 TAN-BLK
J11 RED
N5 BLK-LT BLU
K5 BLK
K8 VIO-WHT
S5 BRN
J2 DK BLU
U4 RED-WHT
J9 LT BLU-RED
J9 LT BLU-RED
S22 ORG-BLK
S21 YEL
S20 LT BLU
K7 ORG-DK BLU
K7 ORG-DK BLU
DK21 PNK
D40 WHT-PNK
S4 BRN-YEL
X36 TAN-RED
DK20 LT GRN
G7 WHT-ORG
X31 BRN-RED
X32 YEL-RED
X33 WHT-LT GRN
X35 LT GRN-RED
K31 BLK-PNK
V40 ORG-LT GRN
E5 DK GRN
SINGLE BOARD ENGINE CONTROLLER (SBEC) (5.9L LATE DIESEL)
WHT FUS LINK
STARTER RELAY
STOP LT SW
STARTER RELAY
CRUISE CONTROL SERVO
WHT-ORG
43
INST CLSTR
CRUISE CONTROL SW
CRUISE CONTROL SERVO
MESSAGE CENTER
MESSAGE CENTER
BLK FUS LINK
BLK FUS LINK
ELECT VACUUM SENSOR
DK BLU
ORG-BLK
BLK
YEL
INTAKE MANIFOLD HEATER RELAY (LATE DIESEL)
INTAKE MANIFOLD HEATER
BLK-LT BLU
ORG-DK BLU
VIO-WHT
THROTTLE POSITION TRANSDUCER
TAN-BLK
TAN
WATER IN FUEL SENSOR
LT BLU
TEMP SENSOR
WHT-ORG
DISTANCE SENSOR
ELECT VACUUM SENSOR
ALTERNATOR
VOLTAGE REGULATOR
IGNITION SW
PNK
LT GRN
DIAG CONN
FUEL HEATER
TRANSFER CASE SW
STARTER RELAY
BRN-YEL
FUEL PUMP
DK BLU-RED
KSB VALVE
RESISTOR
THERMO SW
CONTROL MODULE
ORG-WHT
44
COOLANT THERMAL SW
TRANSMISSION THERMAL SW
ORG-BLK
RED-WHT
YEL-BLK
ORG-YEL
YEL-DK BLU
OVERDRIVE MODULE (LATE DIESEL)
OVERDRIVE LOCKOUT SW (LATE DIESEL)
INST CLSTR
OVERDRIVE LOCKOUT SOLENOID
ORG-LT GRN
FUSE #14
ORG
ILLUM
MESSAGE CENTER
LED
SBEC PIN #44
OVERDRIVE MODULE (GAS)

1991 WIRING DIAGRAMS
Pickup & Ramcharger (Cont.)

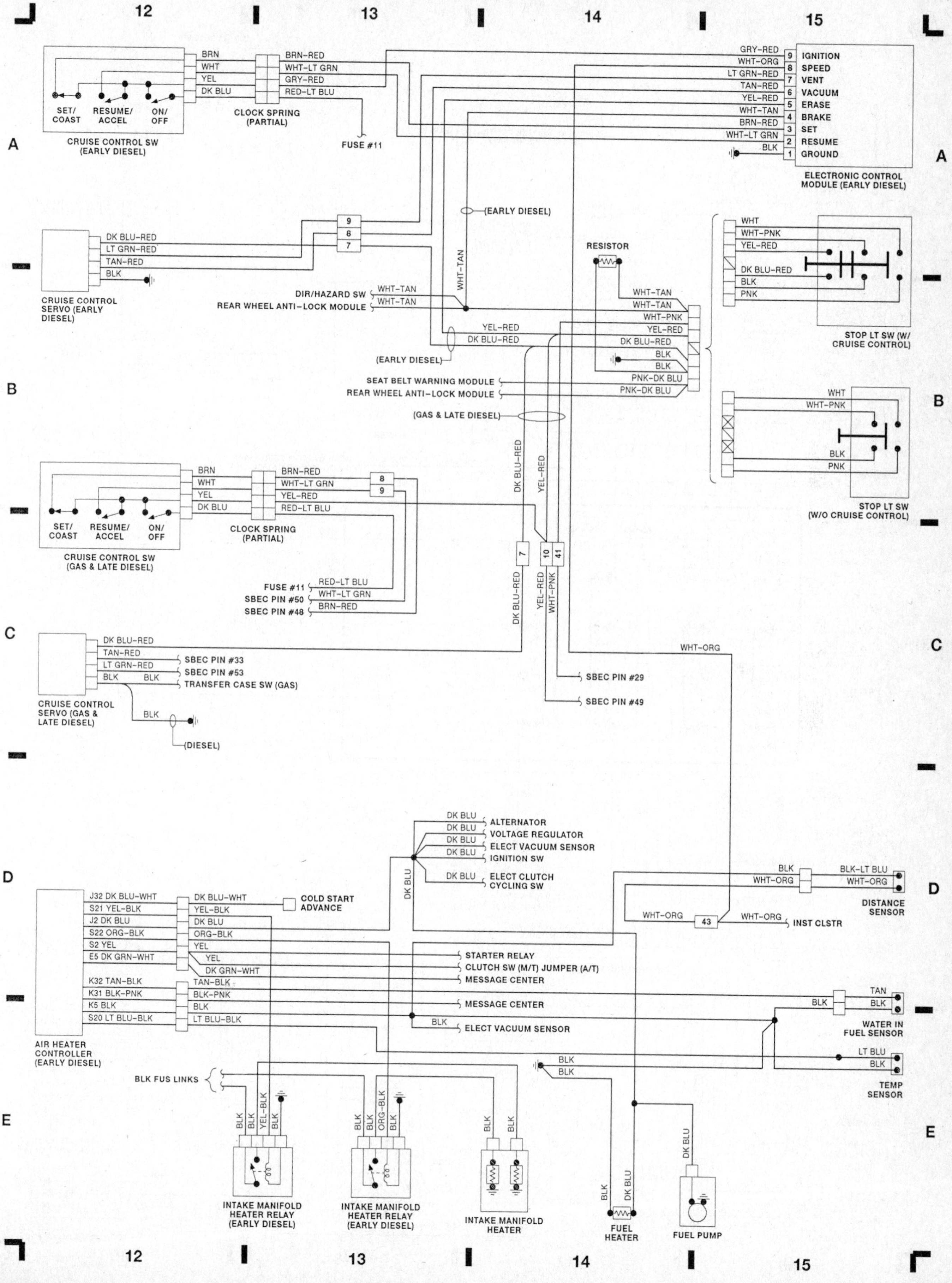
12
13
14
15
A
B
C
D
E
SET/ COAST
RESUME/ ACCEL
ON/ OFF
CRUISE CONTROL SW (EARLY DIESEL)
BRN
WHT
YEL
DK BLU
CLOCK SPRING (PARTIAL)
BRN-RED
WHT-LT GRN
GRY-RED
RED-LT BLU
FUSE #11
GRY-RED
WHT-ORG
LT GRN-RED
TAN-RED
YEL-RED
WHT-TAN
BRN-RED
WHT-LT GRN
BLK
9 IGNITION
8 SPEED
7 VENT
6 VACUUM
5 ERASE
4 BRAKE
3 SET
2 RESUME
1 GROUND
ELECTRONIC CONTROL MODULE (EARLY DIESEL)
(EARLY DIESEL)
DK BLU-RED
LT GRN-RED
TAN-RED
BLK
CRUISE CONTROL SERVO (EARLY DIESEL)
WHT-TAN
RESISTOR
DIR/HAZARD SW
REAR WHEEL ANTI-LOCK MODULE
WHT-PNK
YEL-RED
DK BLU-RED
PNK-DK BLU
SEAT BELT WARNING MODULE
REAR WHEEL ANTI-LOCK MODULE
(GAS & LATE DIESEL)
WHT
WHT-PNK
PNK
STOP LT SW (W/ CRUISE CONTROL)
STOP LT SW (W/O CRUISE CONTROL)
CRUISE CONTROL SW (GAS & LATE DIESEL)
FUSE #11
SBEC PIN #50
SBEC PIN #48
CRUISE CONTROL SERVO (GAS & LATE DIESEL)
SBEC PIN #33
SBEC PIN #53
TRANSFER CASE SW (GAS)
(DIESEL)
WHT-ORG
SBEC PIN #29
SBEC PIN #49
DK BLU
ALTERNATOR
VOLTAGE REGULATOR
ELECT VACUUM SENSOR
IGNITION SW
ELECT CLUTCH CYCLING SW
BLK-LT BLU
DISTANCE SENSOR
INST CLSTR
J32 DK BLU-WHT
S21 YEL-BLK
J2 DK BLU
S22 ORG-BLK
S2 YEL
E5 DK GRN-WHT
K32 TAN-BLK
K31 BLK-PNK
K5 BLK
S20 LT BLU-BLK
AIR HEATER CONTROLLER (EARLY DIESEL)
COLD START ADVANCE
STARTER RELAY
CLUTCH SW (M/T) JUMPER (A/T)
MESSAGE CENTER
ELECT VACUUM SENSOR
TAN
WATER IN FUEL SENSOR
LT BLU
TEMP SENSOR
BLK FUS LINKS
INTAKE MANIFOLD HEATER RELAY (EARLY DIESEL)
INTAKE MANIFOLD HEATER
FUEL HEATER
FUEL PUMP

1991 WIRING DIAGRAMS
Pickup & Ramcharger (Cont.)

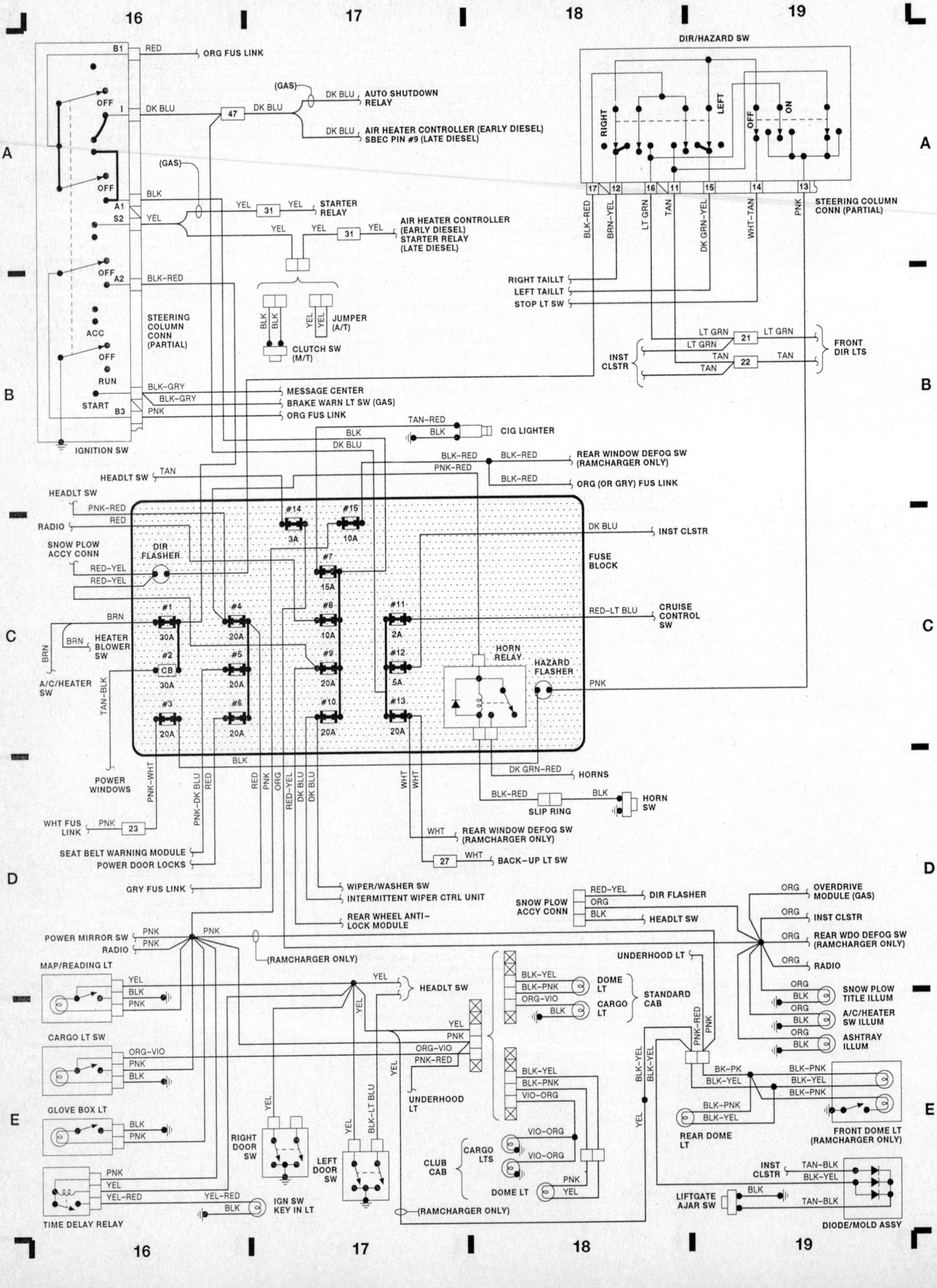
16
17
18
19
A
B
C
D
E
IGNITION SW
STEERING COLUMN CONN (PARTIAL)
ORG FUS LINK
AUTO SHUTDOWN RELAY
AIR HEATER CONTROLLER (EARLY DIESEL)
SBEC PIN #9 (LATE DIESEL)
STARTER RELAY
AIR HEATER CONTROLLER (EARLY DIESEL)
STARTER RELAY (LATE DIESEL)
JUMPER (A/T)
CLUTCH SW (M/T)
DIR/HAZARD SW
STEERING COLUMN CONN (PARTIAL)
RIGHT TAILLT
LEFT TAILLT
STOP LT SW
INST CLSTR
FRONT DIR LTS
MESSAGE CENTER
BRAKE WARN LT SW (GAS)
ORG FUS LINK
CIG LIGHTER
REAR WINDOW DEFOG SW (RAMCHARGER ONLY)
ORG (OR GRY) FUS LINK
HEADLT SW
RADIO
SNOW PLOW ACCY CONN
DIR FLASHER
HEATER BLOWER SW
A/C/HEATER SW
FUSE BLOCK
INST CLSTR
CRUISE CONTROL SW
HORN RELAY
HAZARD FLASHER
POWER WINDOWS
HORNS
SLIP RING
HORN SW
WHT FUS LINK
REAR WINDOW DEFOG SW (RAMCHARGER ONLY)
BACK-UP LT SW
SEAT BELT WARNING MODULE
POWER DOOR LOCKS
GRY FUS LINK
WIPER/WASHER SW
INTERMITTENT WIPER CTRL UNIT
REAR WHEEL ANTI-LOCK MODULE
SNOW PLOW ACCY CONN
DIR FLASHER
HEADLT SW
OVERDRIVE MODULE (GAS)
INST CLSTR
REAR WDO DEFOG SW (RAMCHARGER ONLY)
RADIO
POWER MIRROR SW
RADIO
(RAMCHARGER ONLY)
UNDERHOOD LT
MAP/READING LT
HEADLT SW
DOME LT
CARGO LT
STANDARD CAB
SNOW PLOW TITLE ILLUM
A/C/HEATER SW ILLUM
ASHTRAY ILLUM
CARGO LT SW
UNDERHOOD LT
REAR DOME LT
FRONT DOME LT (RAMCHARGER ONLY)
GLOVE BOX LT
RIGHT DOOR SW
LEFT DOOR SW
CARGO LTS
CLUB CAB
DOME LT
INST CLSTR
LIFTGATE AJAR SW
TIME DELAY RELAY
IGN SW KEY IN LT
(RAMCHARGER ONLY)
DIODE/MOLD ASSY

1991 WIRING DIAGRAMS
Pickup & Ramcharger (Cont.)

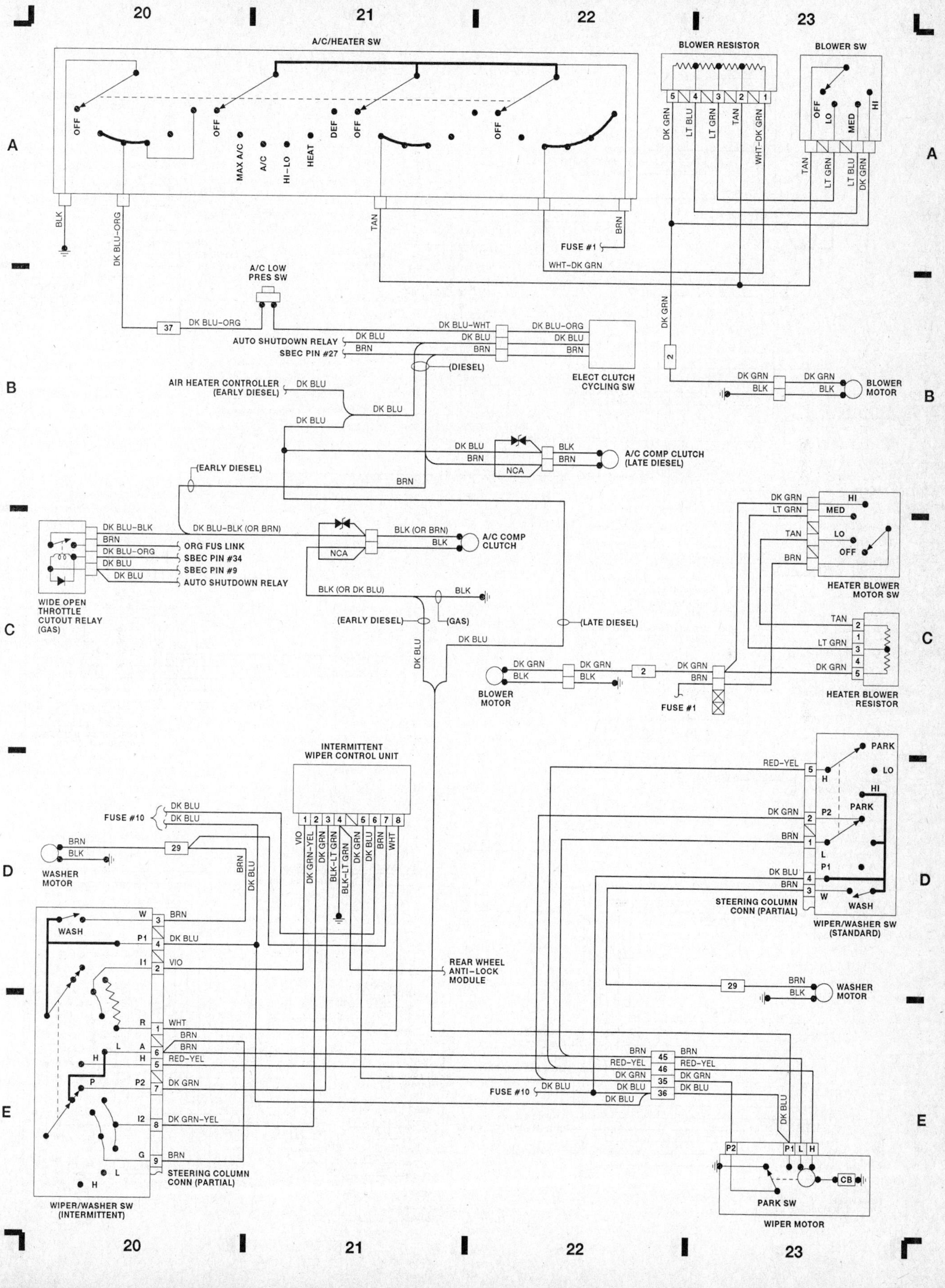
A/C/HEATER SW
BLOWER RESISTOR
BLOWER SW
A/C LOW PRES SW
AUTO SHUTDOWN RELAY
SBEC PIN #27
(DIESEL)
ELECT CLUTCH CYCLING SW
BLOWER MOTOR
AIR HEATER CONTROLLER (EARLY DIESEL)
A/C COMP CLUTCH (LATE DIESEL)
(EARLY DIESEL)
ORG FUS LINK
SBEC PIN #34
SBEC PIN #9
AUTO SHUTDOWN RELAY
WIDE OPEN THROTTLE CUTOUT RELAY (GAS)
A/C COMP CLUTCH
HEATER BLOWER MOTOR SW
(EARLY DIESEL)
(GAS)
(LATE DIESEL)
HEATER BLOWER RESISTOR
BLOWER MOTOR
FUSE #1
INTERMITTENT WIPER CONTROL UNIT
FUSE #10
WASHER MOTOR
REAR WHEEL ANTI-LOCK MODULE
STEERING COLUMN CONN (PARTIAL)
WIPER/WASHER SW (STANDARD)
WASHER MOTOR
WIPER/WASHER SW (INTERMITTENT)
PARK SW
WIPER MOTOR

1991 WIRING DIAGRAMS
Pickup & Ramcharger (Cont.)

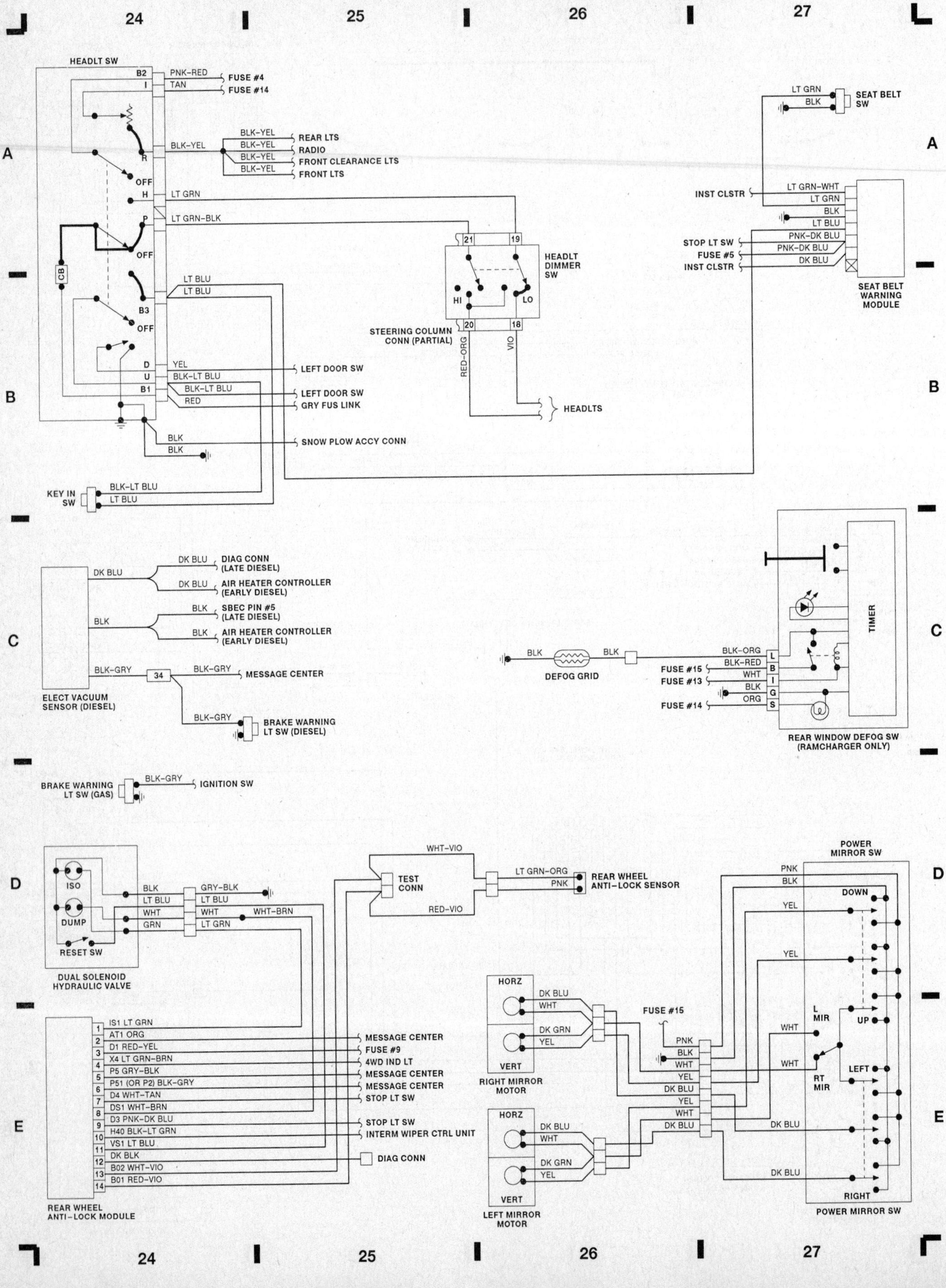
24
25
26
27
A
B
C
D
E
HEADLT SW
B2
I
PNK-RED
TAN
FUSE #4
FUSE #14
BLK-YEL
REAR LTS
RADIO
FRONT CLEARANCE LTS
FRONT LTS
R
OFF
H
LT GRN
P
LT GRN-BLK
CB
OFF
LT BLU
B3
OFF
D
U
B1
YEL
BLK-LT BLU
RED
LEFT DOOR SW
GRY FUS LINK
BLK
SNOW PLOW ACCY CONN
KEY IN SW
HEADLT DIMMER SW
HI
LO
21
19
20
18
STEERING COLUMN CONN (PARTIAL)
RED-ORG
VIO
HEADLTS
LT GRN
SEAT BELT SW
INST CLSTR
LT GRN-WHT
LT BLU
STOP LT SW
FUSE #5
PNK-DK BLU
DK BLU
SEAT BELT WARNING MODULE
DK BLU
DIAG CONN (LATE DIESEL)
AIR HEATER CONTROLLER (EARLY DIESEL)
SBEC PIN #5 (LATE DIESEL)
BLK-GRY
34
MESSAGE CENTER
ELECT VACUUM SENSOR (DIESEL)
BRAKE WARNING LT SW (DIESEL)
BRAKE WARNING LT SW (GAS)
IGNITION SW
DEFOG GRID
BLK-ORG
BLK-RED
WHT
ORG
FUSE #15
FUSE #13
FUSE #14
L
B
I
G
S
TIMER
REAR WINDOW DEFOG SW (RAMCHARGER ONLY)
ISO
DUMP
RESET SW
DUAL SOLENOID HYDRAULIC VALVE
GRY-BLK
GRN
LT GRN
WHT-BRN
WHT-VIO
TEST CONN
RED-VIO
LT GRN-ORG
PNK
REAR WHEEL ANTI-LOCK SENSOR
IS1 LT GRN
AT1 ORG
D1 RED-YEL
X4 LT GRN-BRN
P5 GRY-BLK
P51 (OR P2) BLK-GRY
D4 WHT-TAN
DS1 WHT-BRN
D3 PNK-DK BLU
H40 BLK-LT GRN
VS1 LT BLU
DK BLK
B02 WHT-VIO
B01 RED-VIO
MESSAGE CENTER
FUSE #9
4WD IND LT
STOP LT SW
INTERM WIPER CTRL UNIT
DIAG CONN
REAR WHEEL ANTI-LOCK MODULE
HORZ
VERT
DK GRN
RIGHT MIRROR MOTOR
LEFT MIRROR MOTOR
POWER MIRROR SW
DOWN
UP
LEFT
RIGHT
L MIR
RT MIR

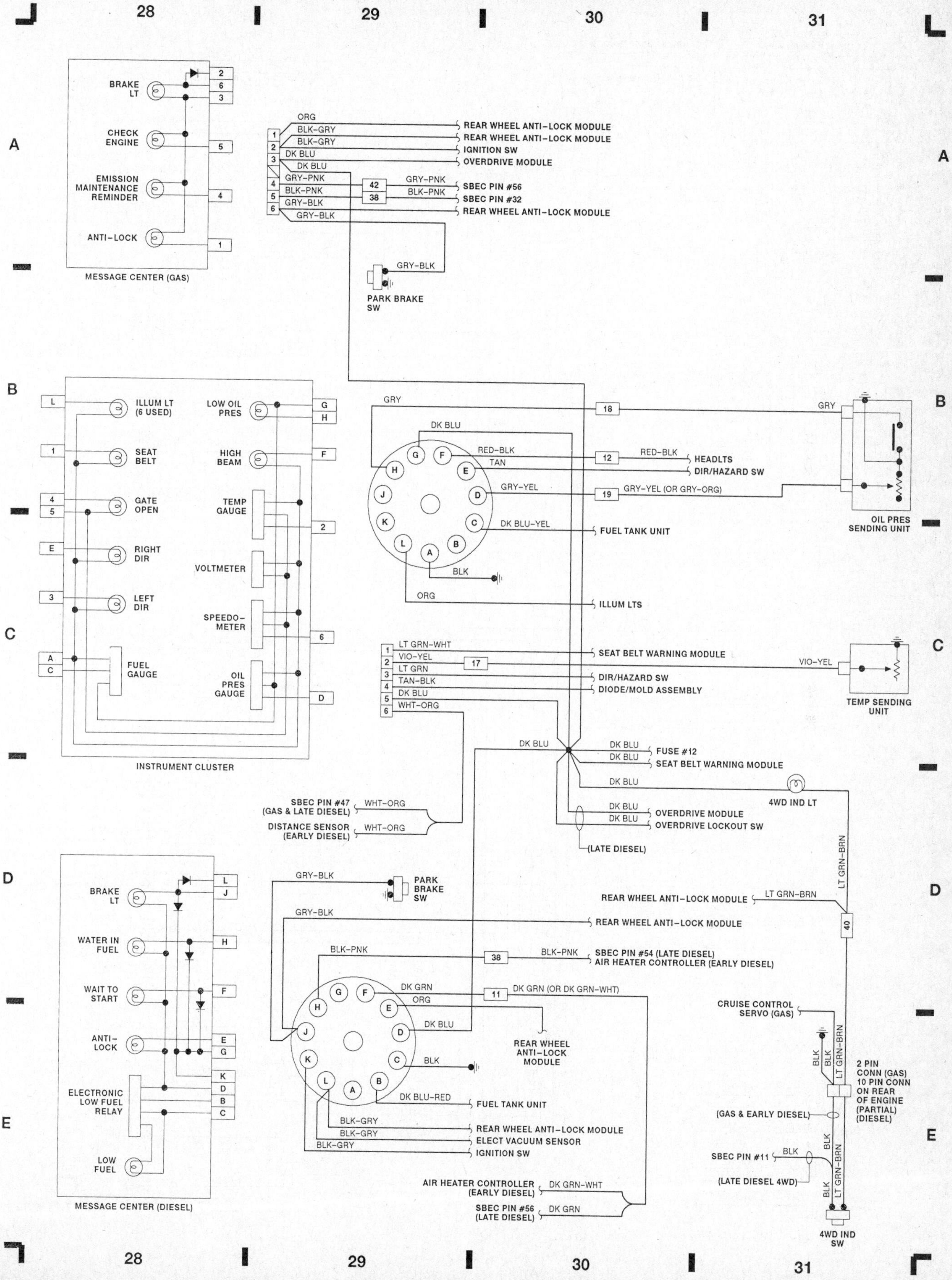
BRAKE LT
CHECK ENGINE
EMISSION MAINTENANCE REMINDER
ANTI-LOCK
MESSAGE CENTER (GAS)
ORG
BLK-GRY
DK BLU
GRY-PNK
BLK-PNK
GRY-BLK
REAR WHEEL ANTI-LOCK MODULE
IGNITION SW
OVERDRIVE MODULE
SBEC PIN #56
SBEC PIN #32
PARK BRAKE SW
ILLUM LT (6 USED)
SEAT BELT
GATE OPEN
RIGHT DIR
LEFT DIR
FUEL GAUGE
LOW OIL PRES
HIGH BEAM
TEMP GAUGE
VOLTMETER
SPEEDO-METER
OIL PRES GAUGE
INSTRUMENT CLUSTER
GRY
RED-BLK
TAN
GRY-YEL
DK BLU-YEL
BLK
HEADLTS
DIR/HAZARD SW
GRY-YEL (OR GRY-ORG)
FUEL TANK UNIT
ILLUM LTS
OIL PRES SENDING UNIT
LT GRN-WHT
VIO-YEL
LT GRN
TAN-BLK
WHT-ORG
SEAT BELT WARNING MODULE
DIODE/MOLD ASSEMBLY
TEMP SENDING UNIT
FUSE #12
4WD IND LT
SBEC PIN #47 (GAS & LATE DIESEL)
DISTANCE SENSOR (EARLY DIESEL)
OVERDRIVE LOCKOUT SW
(LATE DIESEL)
LT GRN-BRN
WATER IN FUEL
WAIT TO START
ELECTRONIC LOW FUEL RELAY
LOW FUEL
MESSAGE CENTER (DIESEL)
SBEC PIN #54 (LATE DIESEL)
AIR HEATER CONTROLLER (EARLY DIESEL)
DK GRN
DK GRN (OR DK GRN-WHT)
REAR WHEEL ANTI-LOCK MODULE
DK BLU-RED
ELECT VACUUM SENSOR
CRUISE CONTROL SERVO (GAS)
2 PIN CONN (GAS) 10 PIN CONN ON REAR OF ENGINE (PARTIAL) (DIESEL)
(GAS & EARLY DIESEL)
SBEC PIN #11
(LATE DIESEL 4WD)
DK GRN-WHT
AIR HEATER CONTROLLER (EARLY DIESEL)
SBEC PIN #56 (LATE DIESEL)
4WD IND SW

1991 WIRING DIAGRAMS
Pickup & Ramcharger (Cont.)

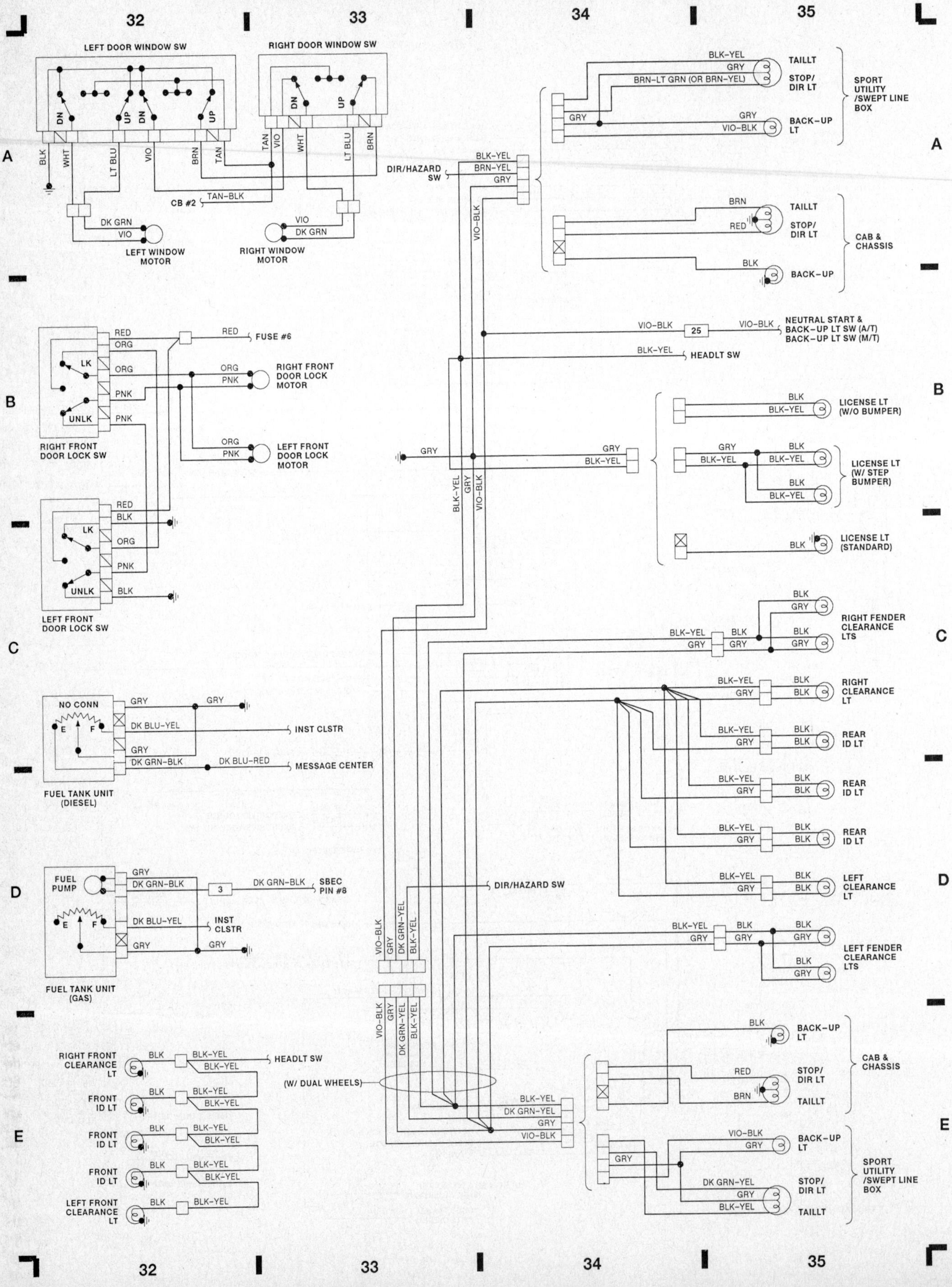
32
33
34
35
A
B
C
D
E
LEFT DOOR WINDOW SW
RIGHT DOOR WINDOW SW
LEFT WINDOW MOTOR
RIGHT WINDOW MOTOR
CB #2
TAN-BLK
DIR/HAZARD SW
FUSE #6
RIGHT FRONT DOOR LOCK SW
LEFT FRONT DOOR LOCK SW
RIGHT FRONT DOOR LOCK MOTOR
LEFT FRONT DOOR LOCK MOTOR
NO CONN
INST CLSTR
MESSAGE CENTER
FUEL TANK UNIT (DIESEL)
FUEL PUMP
SBEC PIN #8
FUEL TANK UNIT (GAS)
TAILLT
STOP/ DIR LT
BACK-UP LT
SPORT UTILITY /SWEPT LINE BOX
CAB & CHASSIS
NEUTRAL START & BACK-UP LT SW (A/T)
BACK-UP LT SW (M/T)
HEADLT SW
LICENSE LT (W/O BUMPER)
LICENSE LT (W/ STEP BUMPER)
LICENSE LT (STANDARD)
RIGHT FENDER CLEARANCE LTS
RIGHT CLEARANCE LT
REAR ID LT
LEFT CLEARANCE LT
LEFT FENDER CLEARANCE LTS
RIGHT FRONT CLEARANCE LT
FRONT ID LT
LEFT FRONT CLEARANCE LT
(W/ DUAL WHEELS)
BRN-LT GRN (OR BRN-YEL)

1991 WIRING DIAGRAMS
RWD Van

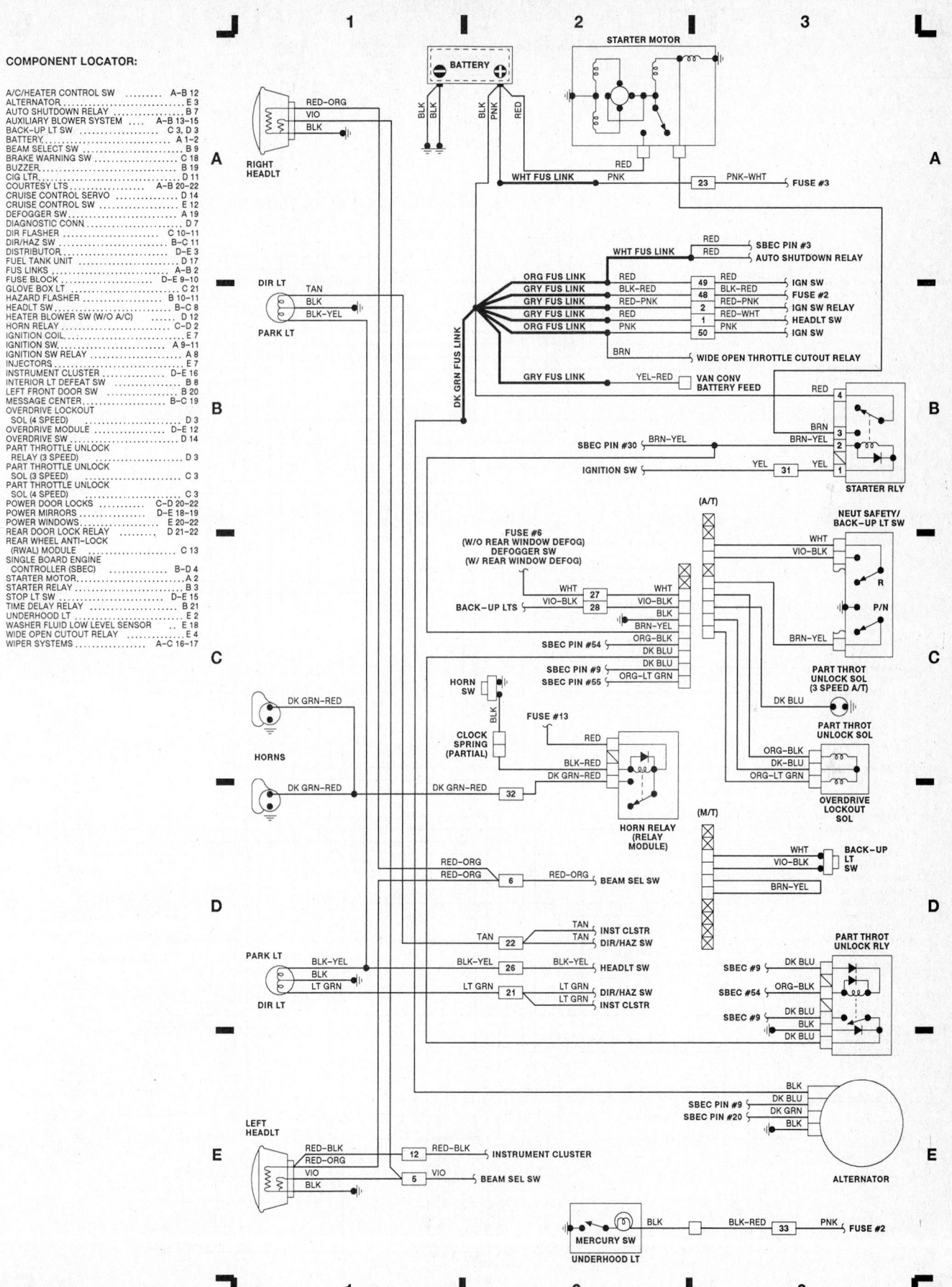

COMPONENT LOCATOR:

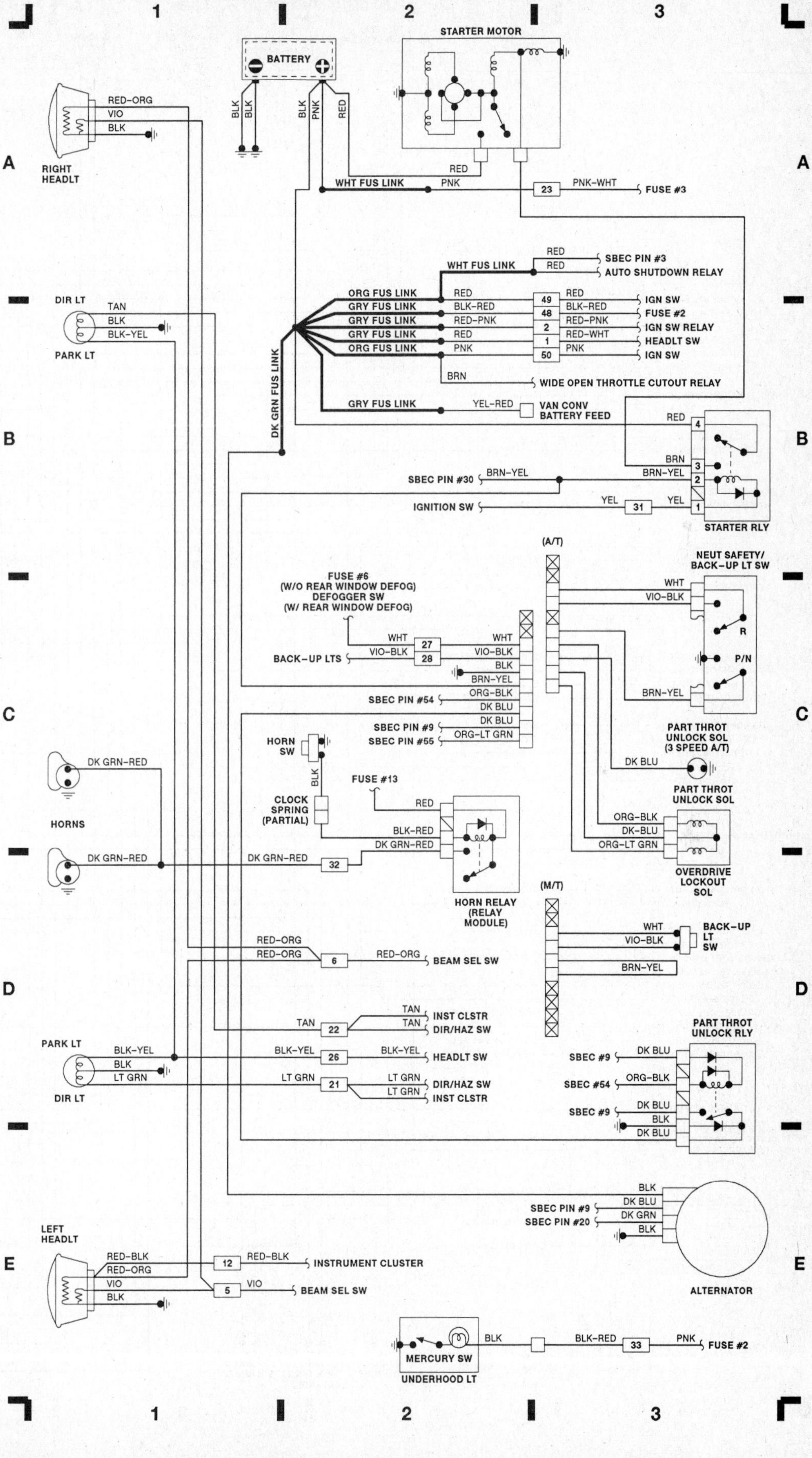
1
2
3
A
B
C
D
E
BATTERY
STARTER MOTOR
RIGHT HEADLT
RED-ORG
VIO
BLK
RED
PNK
WHT FUS LINK
23
PNK-WHT
FUSE #3
SBEC PIN #3
AUTO SHUTDOWN RELAY
ORG FUS LINK
GRY FUS LINK
DK GRN FUS LINK
49
48
2
1
50
IGN SW
FUSE #2
IGN SW RELAY
HEADLT SW
BLK-RED
RED-PNK
RED-WHT
BRN
WIDE OPEN THROTTLE CUTOUT RELAY
YEL-RED
VAN CONV BATTERY FEED
DIR LT
TAN
BLK-YEL
PARK LT
SBEC PIN #30
BRN-YEL
IGNITION SW
YEL
31
STARTER RLY
(A/T)
NEUT SAFETY/ BACK-UP LT SW
WHT
VIO-BLK
R
P/N
FUSE #6 (W/O REAR WINDOW DEFOG) DEFOGGER SW (W/ REAR WINDOW DEFOG)
27
28
BACK-UP LTS
SBEC PIN #54
ORG-BLK
DK BLU
SBEC PIN #9
SBEC PIN #55
ORG-LT GRN
PART THROT UNLOCK SOL (3 SPEED A/T)
PART THROT UNLOCK SOL
DK-BLU
OVERDRIVE LOCKOUT SOL
HORN SW
CLOCK SPRING (PARTIAL)
FUSE #13
DK GRN-RED
HORNS
32
HORN RELAY (RELAY MODULE)
(M/T)
BACK-UP LT SW
6
BEAM SEL SW
22
INST CLSTR
DIR/HAZ SW
26
21
LT GRN
PART THROT UNLOCK RLY
SBEC #9
SBEC #54
SBEC PIN #20
DK GRN
ALTERNATOR
LEFT HEADLT
RED-BLK
12
INSTRUMENT CLUSTER
5
MERCURY SW
UNDERHOOD LT
33

1991 WIRING DIAGRAMS
RWD Van (Cont.)

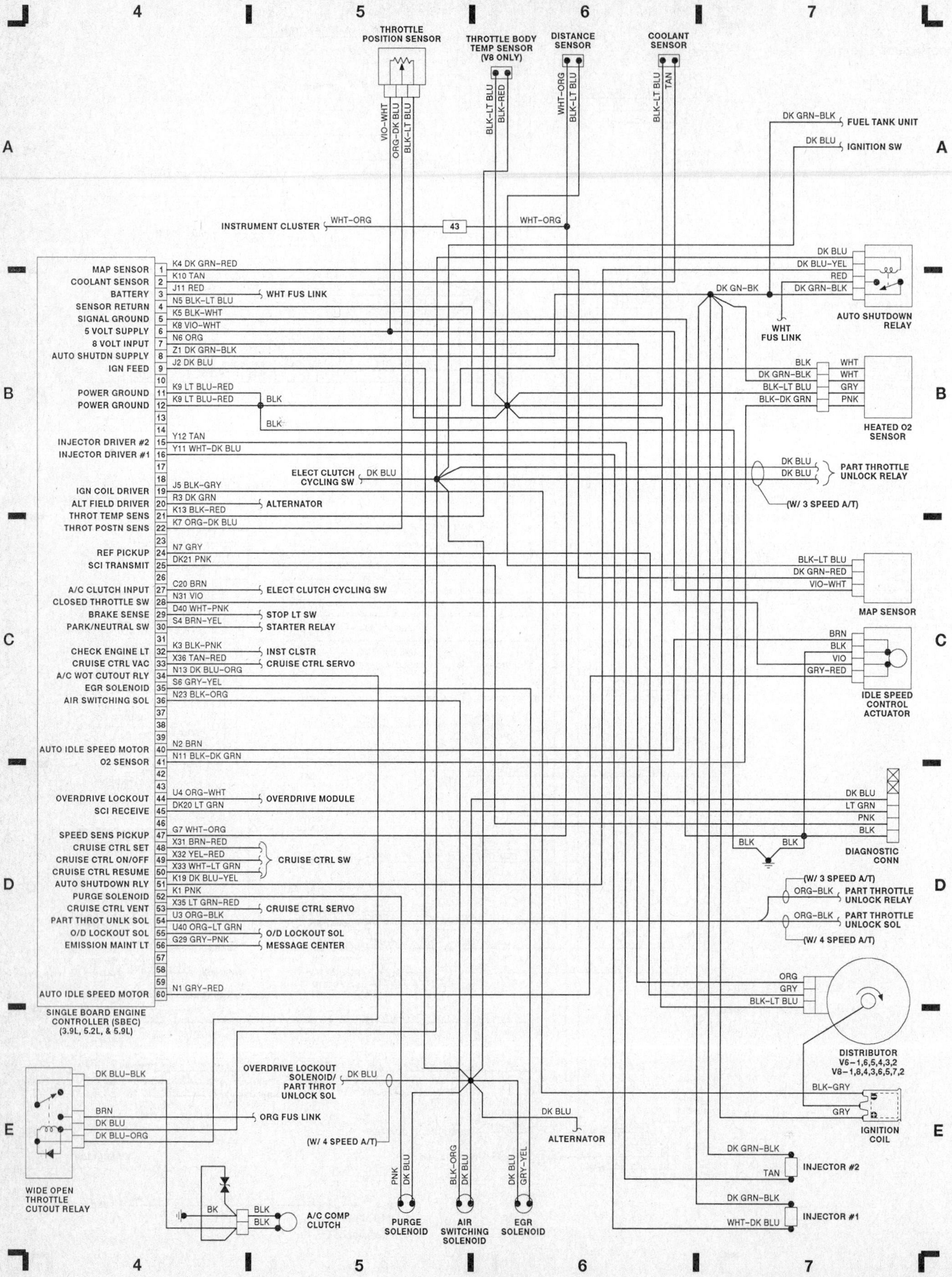
4
5
6
7
A
B
C
D
E
THROTTLE POSITION SENSOR
VIO-WHT
ORG-DK BLU
BLK-LT BLU
THROTTLE BODY TEMP SENSOR (V8 ONLY)
BLK-LT BLU
BLK-RED
DISTANCE SENSOR
WHT-ORG
BLK-LT BLU
COOLANT SENSOR
BLK-LT BLU
TAN
DK GRN-BLK
FUEL TANK UNIT
DK BLU
IGNITION SW
INSTRUMENT CLUSTER
WHT-ORG
43
WHT-ORG
MAP SENSOR 1 K4 DK GRN-RED
COOLANT SENSOR 2 K10 TAN
BATTERY 3 J11 RED
WHT FUS LINK
SENSOR RETURN 4 N5 BLK-LT BLU
SIGNAL GROUND 5 K5 BLK-WHT
5 VOLT SUPPLY 6 K8 VIO-WHT
8 VOLT INPUT 7 N6 ORG
AUTO SHUTDN SUPPLY 8 Z1 DK GRN-BLK
IGN FEED 9 J2 DK BLU
10
POWER GROUND 11 K9 LT BLU-RED
POWER GROUND 12 K9 LT BLU-RED
BLK
13
BLK
14
INJECTOR DRIVER #2 15 Y12 TAN
INJECTOR DRIVER #1 16 Y11 WHT-DK BLU
17
18
ELECT CLUTCH CYCLING SW
DK BLU
IGN COIL DRIVER 19 J5 BLK-GRY
ALT FIELD DRIVER 20 R3 DK GRN
ALTERNATOR
THROT TEMP SENS 21 K13 BLK-RED
THROT POSTN SENS 22 K7 ORG-DK BLU
23
REF PICKUP 24 N7 GRY
SCI TRANSMIT 25 DK21 PNK
26
A/C CLUTCH INPUT 27 C20 BRN
CLOSED THROTTLE SW 28 N31 VIO
ELECT CLUTCH CYCLING SW
BRAKE SENSE 29 D40 WHT-PNK
STOP LT SW
PARK/NEUTRAL SW 30 S4 BRN-YEL
STARTER RELAY
31
CHECK ENGINE LT 32 K3 BLK-PNK
INST CLSTR
CRUISE CTRL VAC 33 X36 TAN-RED
CRUISE CTRL SERVO
A/C WOT CUTOUT RLY 34 N13 DK BLU-ORG
EGR SOLENOID 35 S6 GRY-YEL
AIR SWITCHING SOL 36 N23 BLK-ORG
37
38
39
AUTO IDLE SPEED MOTOR 40 N2 BRN
O2 SENSOR 41 N11 BLK-DK GRN
42
43
OVERDRIVE LOCKOUT 44 U4 ORG-WHT
OVERDRIVE MODULE
SCI RECEIVE 45 DK20 LT GRN
46
SPEED SENS PICKUP 47 G7 WHT-ORG
CRUISE CTRL SET 48 X31 BRN-RED
CRUISE CTRL ON/OFF 49 X32 YEL-RED
CRUISE CTRL RESUME 50 X33 WHT-LT GRN
CRUISE CTRL SW
AUTO SHUTDOWN RLY 51 K19 DK BLU-YEL
PURGE SOLENOID 52 K1 PNK
CRUISE CTRL VENT 53 X35 LT GRN-RED
CRUISE CTRL SERVO
PART THROT UNLK SOL 54 U3 ORG-BLK
O/D LOCKOUT SOL 55 U40 ORG-LT GRN
O/D LOCKOUT SOL
EMISSION MAINT LT 56 G29 GRY-PNK
MESSAGE CENTER
57
58
59
AUTO IDLE SPEED MOTOR 60 N1 GRY-RED
SINGLE BOARD ENGINE CONTROLLER (SBEC) (3.9L, 5.2L, & 5.9L)
DK BLU
DK BLU-YEL
RED
DK GN-BK
DK GRN-BLK
WHT FUS LINK
AUTO SHUTDOWN RELAY
BLK
DK GRN-BLK
BLK-LT BLU
BLK-DK GRN
WHT
WHT
GRY
PNK
HEATED O2 SENSOR
DK BLU
DK BLU
PART THROTTLE UNLOCK RELAY
(W/ 3 SPEED A/T)
BLK-LT BLU
DK GRN-RED
VIO-WHT
MAP SENSOR
BRN
BLK
VIO
GRY-RED
IDLE SPEED CONTROL ACTUATOR
DK BLU
LT GRN
PNK
BLK
BLK
BLK
DIAGNOSTIC CONN
(W/ 3 SPEED A/T)
ORG-BLK
PART THROTTLE UNLOCK RELAY
ORG-BLK
PART THROTTLE UNLOCK SOL
(W/ 4 SPEED A/T)
ORG
GRY
BLK-LT BLU
DISTRIBUTOR
V6–1,6,5,4,3,2
V8–1,8,4,3,6,5,7,2
BLK-GRY
GRY
IGNITION COIL
DK BLU-BLK
BRN
DK BLU
DK BLU-ORG
ORG FUS LINK
WIDE OPEN THROTTLE CUTOUT RELAY
OVERDRIVE LOCKOUT SOLENOID/ PART THROT UNLOCK SOL
DK BLU
(W/ 4 SPEED A/T)
DK BLU
ALTERNATOR
BK
BLK
BLK
A/C COMP CLUTCH
PNK
DK BLU
PURGE SOLENOID
BLK-ORG
DK BLU
AIR SWITCHING SOLENOID
DK BLU
GRY-YEL
EGR SOLENOID
DK GRN-BLK
TAN
INJECTOR #2
DK GRN-BLK
WHT-DK BLU
INJECTOR #1

1991 WIRING DIAGRAMS
RWD Van (Cont.)

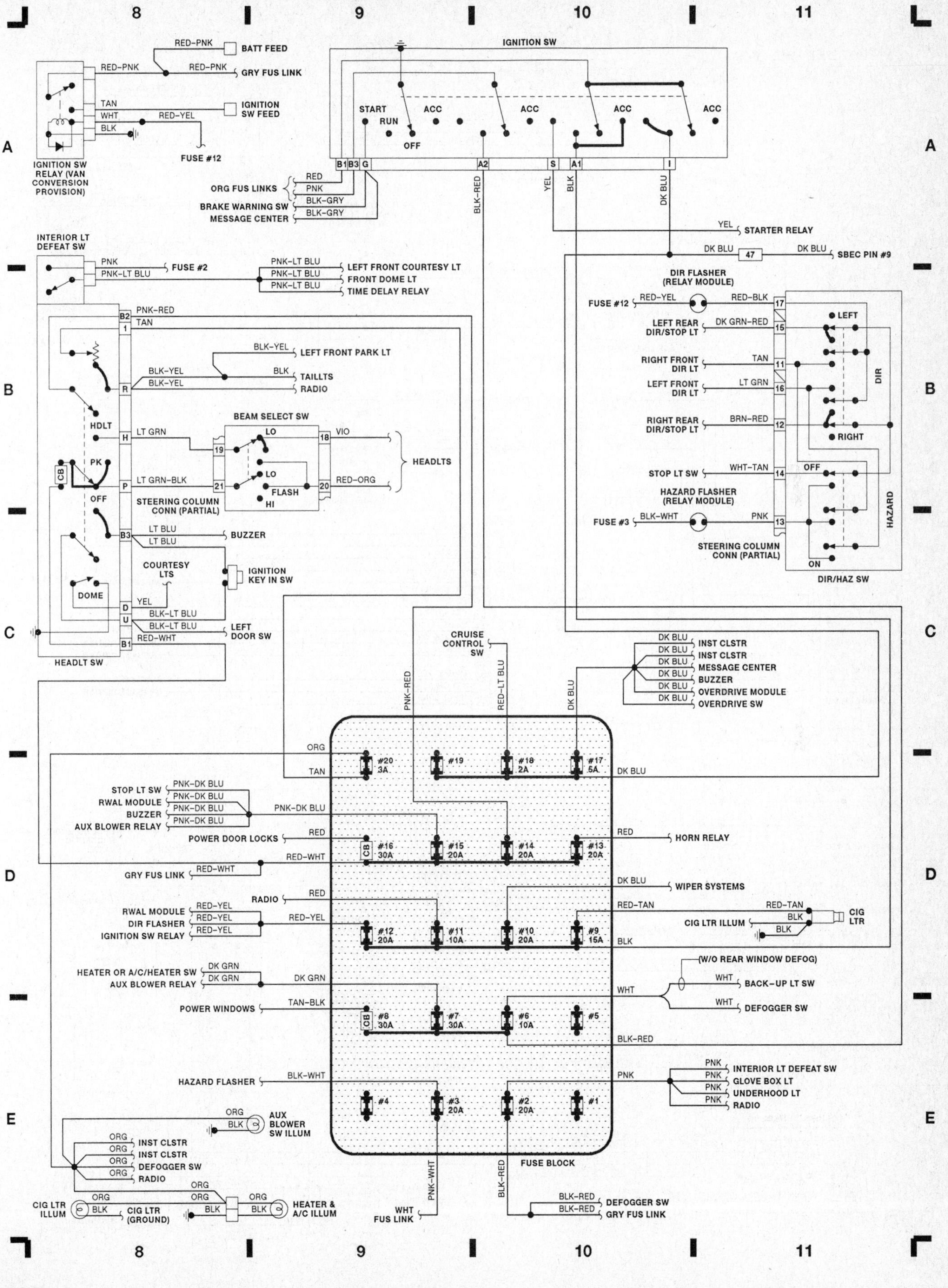
8
9
10
11
A
B
C
D
E
BATT FEED
GRY FUS LINK
IGNITION SW FEED
FUSE #12
IGNITION SW RELAY (VAN CONVERSION PROVISION)
IGNITION SW
START
RUN
OFF
ACC
ORG FUS LINKS
BRAKE WARNING SW
MESSAGE CENTER
STARTER RELAY
SBEC PIN #9
DIR FLASHER (RELAY MODULE)
INTERIOR LT DEFEAT SW
FUSE #2
LEFT FRONT COURTESY LT
FRONT DOME LT
TIME DELAY RELAY
LEFT FRONT PARK LT
TAILLTS
RADIO
HDLT
PK
OFF
BEAM SELECT SW
LO
FLASH
HI
HEADLTS
STEERING COLUMN CONN (PARTIAL)
BUZZER
COURTESY LTS
IGNITION KEY IN SW
DOME
LEFT DOOR SW
HEADLT SW
LEFT REAR DIR/STOP LT
RIGHT FRONT DIR LT
LEFT FRONT DIR LT
RIGHT REAR DIR/STOP LT
STOP LT SW
HAZARD FLASHER (RELAY MODULE)
FUSE #3
LEFT
RIGHT
DIR
HAZARD
ON
DIR/HAZ SW
CRUISE CONTROL SW
INST CLSTR
MESSAGE CENTER
OVERDRIVE MODULE
OVERDRIVE SW
RWAL MODULE
AUX BLOWER RELAY
POWER DOOR LOCKS
GRY FUS LINK
HORN RELAY
WIPER SYSTEMS
DIR FLASHER
IGNITION SW RELAY
CIG LTR ILLUM
CIG LTR
(W/O REAR WINDOW DEFOG)
BACK-UP LT SW
DEFOGGER SW
HEATER OR A/C/HEATER SW
POWER WINDOWS
HAZARD FLASHER
GLOVE BOX LT
UNDERHOOD LT
AUX BLOWER SW ILLUM
FUSE BLOCK
CIG LTR (GROUND)
HEATER & A/C ILLUM
WHT FUS LINK
#20 3A
#19
#18 2A
#17 5A
#16 30A
#15 20A
#14 20A
#13 20A
#12 20A
#11 10A
#10 20A
#9 15A
#8 30A
#7 30A
#6 10A
#5
#4
#3 20A
#2 20A
#1

1991 WIRING DIAGRAMS
RWD Van (Cont.)

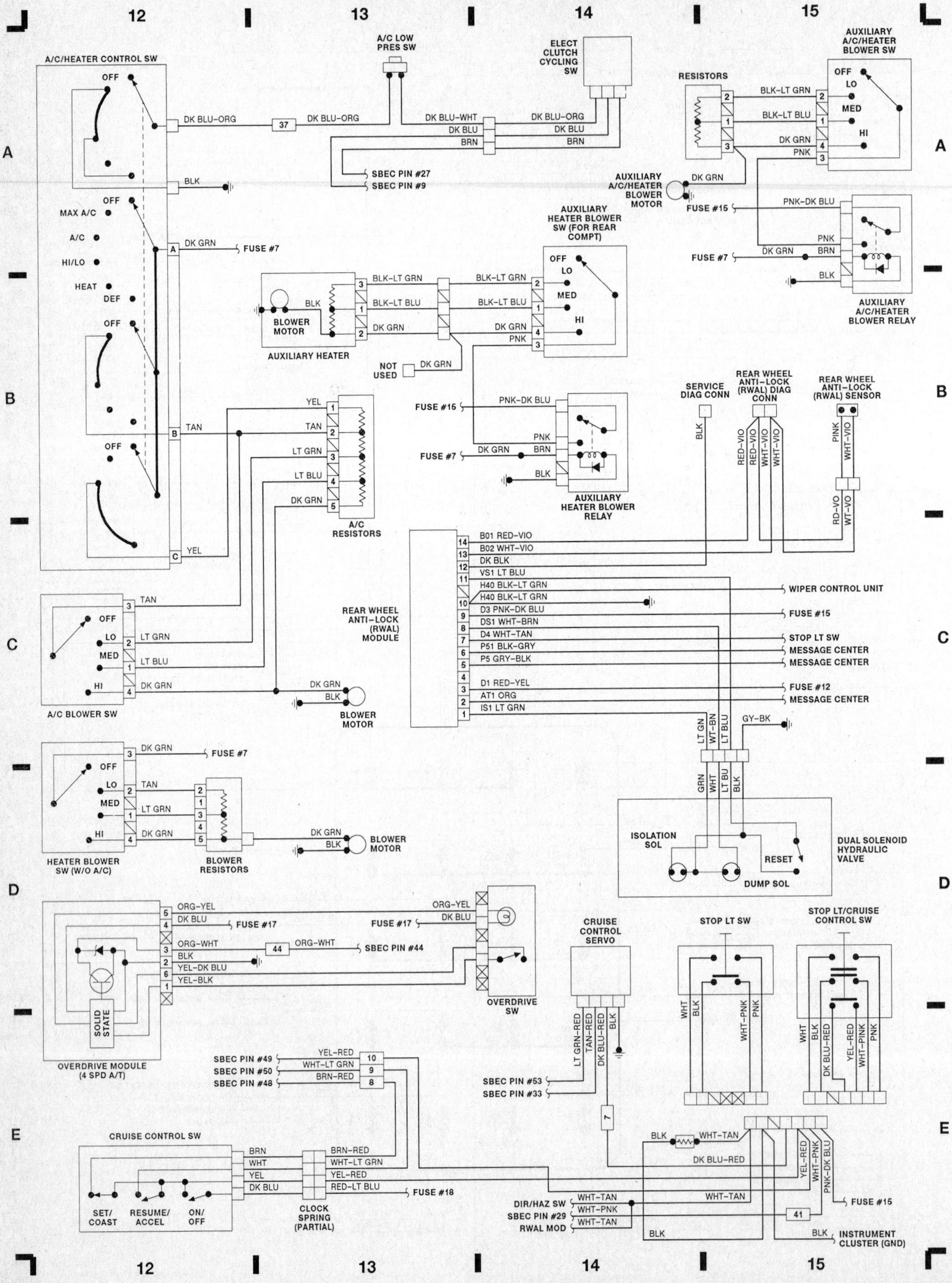
12
13
14
15
A
B
C
D
E
A/C HEATER CONTROL SW
OFF
MAX A/C
A/C
HI/LO
HEAT
DEF
DK BLU-ORG
37
A/C LOW PRES SW
DK BLU-WHT
DK BLU
BRN
ELECT CLUTCH CYCLING SW
SBEC PIN #27
SBEC PIN #9
BLK
DK GRN
FUSE #7
TAN
YEL
RESISTORS
BLK-LT GRN
BLK-LT BLU
DK GRN
PNK
AUXILIARY A/C/HEATER BLOWER SW
LO
MED
HI
AUXILIARY A/C/HEATER BLOWER MOTOR
FUSE #15
PNK-DK BLU
AUXILIARY A/C/HEATER BLOWER RELAY
AUXILIARY HEATER BLOWER SW (FOR REAR COMPT)
BLOWER MOTOR
AUXILIARY HEATER
NOT USED
AUXILIARY HEATER BLOWER RELAY
LT GRN
LT BLU
A/C RESISTORS
SERVICE DIAG CONN
REAR WHEEL ANTI-LOCK (RWAL) DIAG CONN
REAR WHEEL ANTI-LOCK (RWAL) SENSOR
RED-VIO
WHT-VIO
RD-VO
WT-VO
REAR WHEEL ANTI-LOCK (RWAL) MODULE
B01 RED-VIO
B02 WHT-VIO
DK BLK
VS1 LT BLU
H40 BLK-LT GRN
D3 PNK-DK BLU
DS1 WHT-BRN
D4 WHT-TAN
P51 BLK-GRY
P5 GRY-BLK
D1 RED-YEL
AT1 ORG
IS1 LT GRN
WIPER CONTROL UNIT
STOP LT SW
MESSAGE CENTER
FUSE #12
A/C BLOWER SW
GY-BK
ISOLATION SOL
RESET
DUMP SOL
DUAL SOLENOID HYDRAULIC VALVE
HEATER BLOWER SW (W/O A/C)
BLOWER RESISTORS
ORG-YEL
FUSE #17
ORG-WHT
44
SBEC PIN #44
YEL-DK BLU
YEL-BLK
SOLID STATE
OVERDRIVE MODULE (4 SPD A/T)
OVERDRIVE SW
CRUISE CONTROL SERVO
LT GRN-RED
TAN-RED
DK BLU-RED
SBEC PIN #53
SBEC PIN #33
STOP LT SW
STOP LT/CRUISE CONTROL SW
WHT-PNK
YEL-RED
SBEC PIN #49
SBEC PIN #50
SBEC PIN #48
WHT-LT GRN
BRN-RED
CRUISE CONTROL SW
SET/ COAST
RESUME/ ACCEL
ON/ OFF
CLOCK SPRING (PARTIAL)
RED-LT BLU
FUSE #18
WHT-TAN
DIR/HAZ SW
SBEC PIN #29
RWAL MOD
41
INSTRUMENT CLUSTER (GND)
12
13
14
15

1991 WIRING DIAGRAMS
RWD Van (Cont.)

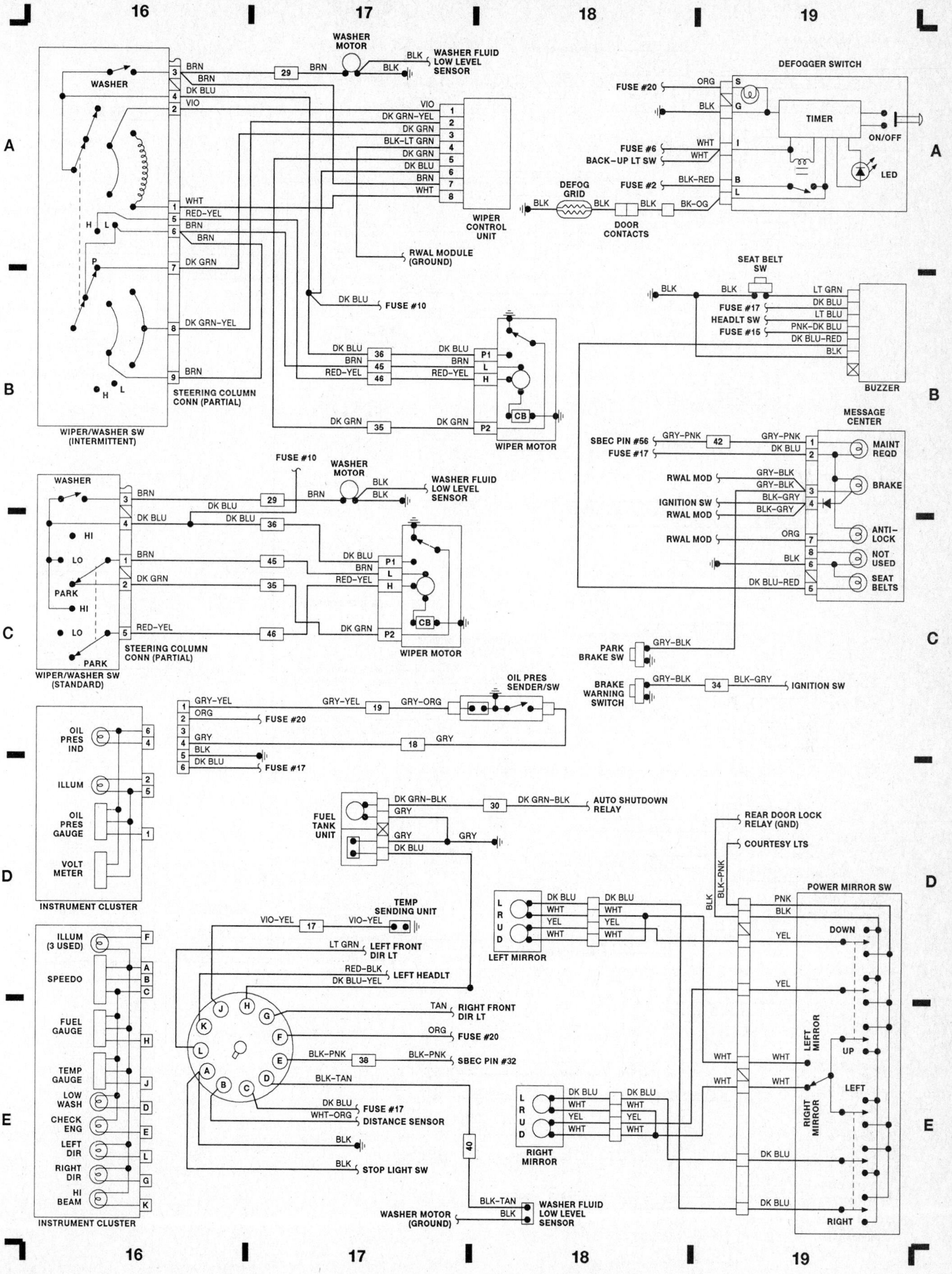
16
17
18
19
A
B
C
D
E
WASHER MOTOR
WASHER FLUID LOW LEVEL SENSOR
WASHER
DEFOGGER SWITCH
FUSE #20
TIMER
ON/OFF
FUSE #6
BACK-UP LT SW
LED
FUSE #2
DEFOG GRID
DOOR CONTACTS
WIPER CONTROL UNIT
RWAL MODULE (GROUND)
SEAT BELT SW
FUSE #17
HEADLT SW
FUSE #15
FUSE #10
BUZZER
STEERING COLUMN CONN (PARTIAL)
WIPER/WASHER SW (INTERMITTENT)
WIPER MOTOR
MESSAGE CENTER
SBEC PIN #56
MAINT REQD
RWAL MOD
BRAKE
IGNITION SW
ANTI-LOCK
NOT USED
SEAT BELTS
PARK
HI
LO
WIPER/WASHER SW (STANDARD)
PARK BRAKE SW
BRAKE WARNING SWITCH
OIL PRES SENDER/SW
OIL PRES IND
ILLUM
OIL PRES GAUGE
VOLT METER
INSTRUMENT CLUSTER
FUEL TANK UNIT
AUTO SHUTDOWN RELAY
REAR DOOR LOCK RELAY (GND)
COURTESY LTS
POWER MIRROR SW
LEFT MIRROR
TEMP SENDING UNIT
LEFT FRONT DIR LT
LEFT HEADLT
RIGHT FRONT DIR LT
SBEC PIN #32
DISTANCE SENSOR
STOP LIGHT SW
ILLUM (3 USED)
SPEEDO
FUEL GAUGE
TEMP GAUGE
LOW WASH
CHECK ENG
LEFT DIR
RIGHT DIR
HI BEAM
DOWN
UP
LEFT
RIGHT
RIGHT MIRROR
WASHER MOTOR (GROUND)

1991 WIRING DIAGRAMS
RWD Van (Cont.)

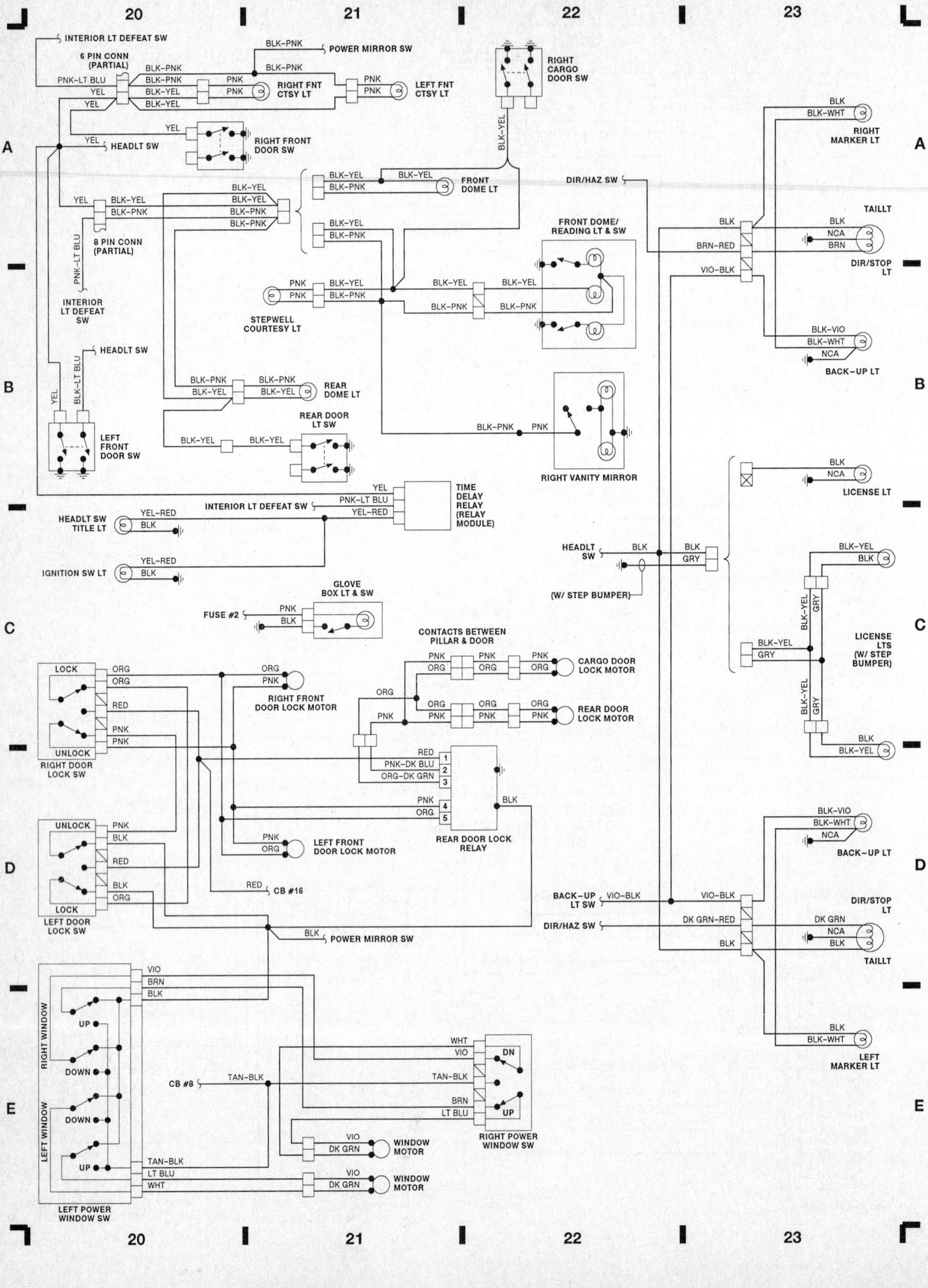
20
21
22
23
A
B
C
D
E
INTERIOR LT DEFEAT SW
6 PIN CONN (PARTIAL)
POWER MIRROR SW
RIGHT FNT CTSY LT
LEFT FNT CTSY LT
RIGHT CARGO DOOR SW
HEADLT SW
RIGHT FRONT DOOR SW
FRONT DOME LT
DIR/HAZ SW
8 PIN CONN (PARTIAL)
INTERIOR LT DEFEAT SW
STEPWELL COURTESY LT
FRONT DOME/ READING LT & SW
RIGHT MARKER LT
TAILLT
DIR/STOP LT
BACK-UP LT
REAR DOME LT
REAR DOOR LT SW
LEFT FRONT DOOR SW
RIGHT VANITY MIRROR
LICENSE LT
TIME DELAY RELAY (RELAY MODULE)
HEADLT SW TITLE LT
IGNITION SW LT
(W/ STEP BUMPER)
LICENSE LTS (W/ STEP BUMPER)
GLOVE BOX LT & SW
FUSE #2
CONTACTS BETWEEN PILLAR & DOOR
CARGO DOOR LOCK MOTOR
REAR DOOR LOCK MOTOR
RIGHT FRONT DOOR LOCK MOTOR
LOCK
UNLOCK
RIGHT DOOR LOCK SW
REAR DOOR LOCK RELAY
LEFT FRONT DOOR LOCK MOTOR
LEFT DOOR LOCK SW
CB #16
BACK-UP LT SW
POWER MIRROR SW
LEFT MARKER LT
RIGHT WINDOW
LEFT WINDOW
UP
DOWN
DN
CB #8
RIGHT POWER WINDOW SW
WINDOW MOTOR
LEFT POWER WINDOW SW

1991 SAFETY EQUIPMENT
Air Bag Restraint System

Caravan, Town & Country, Voyager

***WARNING:** To avoid injury from accidental air bag deployment, read and carefully follow all WARNINGS and SERVICE PRECAUTIONS.*

DESCRIPTION & OPERATION

The Air Bag Restraint System (ABRS) is a supplemental restraint system, designed to work in conjunction with seat belts. ABRS increases driver protection from serious injury during a front-end collision. The air bag, stored in a module in the steering wheel hub, begins to inflate in 1/10 second when impact sensors close. This creates a cushion of air between driver and steering wheel.

The system consists of an AIR BAG light, clockspring, air bag module, Air Bag System Diagnostic Module (ASDM) and 3 impact sensors. *See Fig. 1.* The ASDM contains one of the impact sensors, which is called the safing sensor. The ASDM monitors system, stores fault codes and provides information to AIR BAG light and diagnostic connector. A fault code is stored when AIR BAG light is activated for more than 12 seconds.

During a front-end collision, impact sensors receive the impact force and complete the circuit through ASDM and clockspring to air bag module on steering wheel. The inflator, located inside air bag module, uses electrical current to quickly produce a large quantity of nitrogen gas, which inflates air bag.

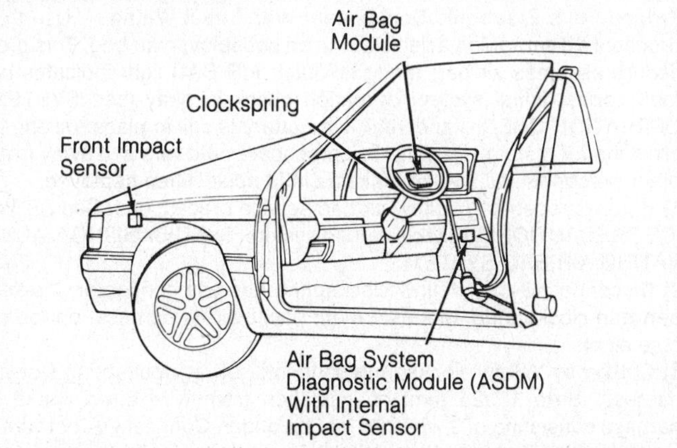
Air Bag
Module
Clockspring
Front Impact
Sensor
Air Bag System
Diagnostic Module (ASDM)
With Internal
Impact Sensor

91J12319 Courtesy of Chrysler Motors.

Fig. 1: Identifying Air Bag Restraint System Components

AIR BAG LIGHT

Whenever ignition switch is in RUN or START position, AIR BAG light on instrument panel will illuminate for 6-8 seconds and then turn off. This signifies ASDM has checked the system and found it free of problems. If air bag light illuminates for 12 seconds or more, stays on all the time or does not come on, a system malfunction exists.

IMPACT SENSORS

Three impact sensors are used. Two impact sensors are mounted on left and right radiator closure panels. The third sensor, called the safing sensor, is located inside ASDM. Impact sensors are inertia switches, which complete an electrical circuit when impact provides sufficient "G" force. Sensors close during crashes equivalent to a 14-MPH or more front-end collision. For air bag to deploy, safing sensor and at least one impact sensor must activate at the same time.

AIR BAG MODULE

The air bag module is mounted on front face of steering wheel. *See Figs. 1 and 3.* The module's inflator assembly produces nitrogen gas to fill air bag. When a small amount of current from ASDM is applied, the ignitor assembly (also known as squib or initiator) starts a thermal reaction that spreads an ignitor charge. Surrounding the ignitor charge is a pellet-filled area, which produces nitrogen gas. Gas pressure builds and discharges from inflator through a diffuser and screen assembly, forcing steering wheel cover to burst along its seams until air bag is fully inflated. Once air bag is fully inflated, gas escapes from air bag through vents, away from driver.

AIR BAG SYSTEM DIAGNOSTIC MODULE (ASDM)

ASDM is located behind center console, at center of instrument panel. *See Fig. 2.* The ASDM stores fault codes and provides system information to AIR BAG light and diagnostic connector. A fault code is stored whenever AIR BAG light stays on, or if light is activated for 12 seconds or more. Safing sensor is an integral part of ASDM.

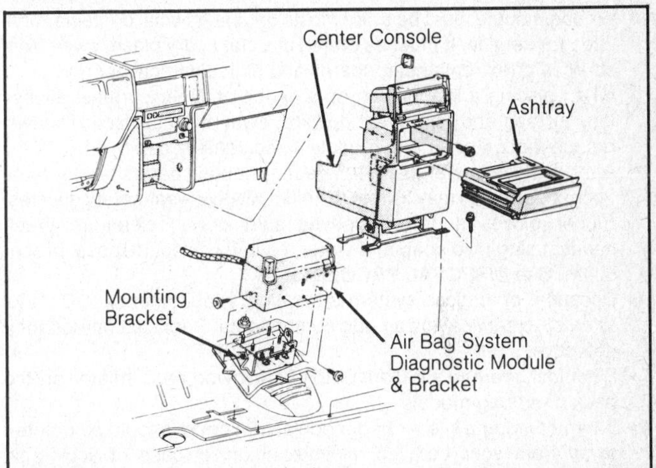
Center Console
Ashtray
Mounting
Bracket
Air Bag System
Diagnostic Module
& Bracket

91C12320 Courtesy of Chrysler Motors.

Fig. 2: Locating Air Bag System Diagnostic Module

CLOCKSPRING

Clockspring connects air bag module to steering column wiring, completing ABRS circuit. *See Fig. 3.* Inside clockspring is a flat, ribbon-like tape of conductive material, which winds and unwinds with steering wheel movement. Clockspring is the most fragile part in system. Clockspring must be centered properly to allow 1 1/2 steering wheel turns in either direction. If clockspring is not centered properly, it can break from stretching or fatigue.

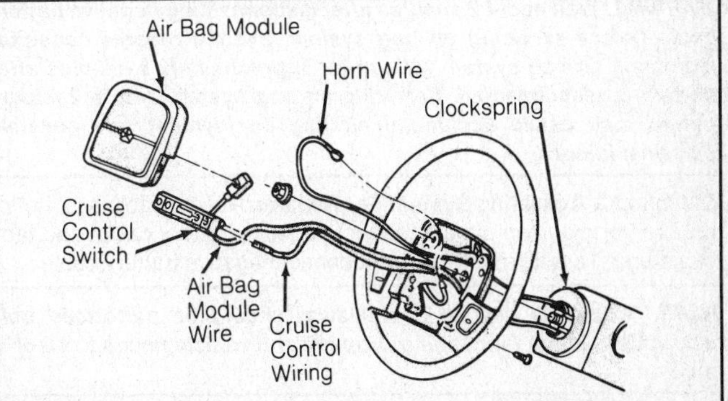
Air Bag Module
Horn Wire
Clockspring
Cruise
Control
Switch
Air Bag
Module
Wire
Cruise
Control
Wiring

91D12321 Courtesy of Chrysler Motors.

Fig. 3: Identifying ABRS Steering Column Components

SYSTEM OPERATION CHECK

***WARNING:** After repairs, turn ignition on from passenger side of vehicle in case of accidental air bag deployment.*

Turn ignition on and observe AIR BAG light. It should come on for 6-8 seconds, then go out, indicating system is functioning okay. If AIR

1991 SAFETY EQUIPMENT
Air Bag Restraint System (Cont.)

BAG light either fails to illuminate or comes on and stays on, a system malfunction exists.

SERVICE PRECAUTIONS

These precautions should be observed when working with air bag systems:

- Disable air bag system before servicing any air bag system or steering column component. Failure to do this could result in accidental air bag deployment and possible personal injury. See DISABLING & ACTIVATING AIR BAG SYSTEM.
- After repairs, turn ignition on from passenger side of vehicle in case of accidental air bag deployment. Ensure AIR BAG light is working properly. See SYSTEM OPERATION CHECK.
- Always wear safety glasses when servicing or handling an air bag.
- Air bag module must be stored in its original special container until used for service. It must be stored in a clean, dry place, away from sources of extreme heat, sparks and high electrical energy.
- When placing a live air bag on a bench or other surface, always face air bag and trim cover upward, away from surface. This will reduce motion of air bag module if accidentally deployed.
- After deployment, air bag surface may contain deposits of sodium hydroxide, which may irritate the skin. Always wear safety glasses, rubber gloves and long-sleeved shirt during clean-up. Wash hands, using mild soap and water. Follow correct disposal procedures. See DISPOSAL PROCEDURES.
- Because of critical system operating requirements, DO NOT attempt to service any air bag components. Replace component if defective.
- Electrical sources should NEVER be allowed near inflator on the back of air bag module.
- When carrying a live air bag module, trim cover should be pointed away from your body to minimize injury in case of accidental deployment.
- Clockspring must be replaced whenever air bag deploys.
- If air bag system is not fully functional for any reason, vehicle should not be driven until system is repaired and again becomes operational. DO NOT remove bulbs, modules, sensors or other components or in any way disable system from operating normally. If air bag system is not functional, park vehicle until it is repaired and functions properly.

DISABLING & ACTIVATING AIR BAG SYSTEM

WARNING: Wait about 2 minutes after disconnecting negative battery cable before servicing air bag system. System reserve capacitor maintains air bag system voltage for approximately 2 minutes after battery is disconnected. Servicing air bag system before 2-minute period may cause accidental air bag deployment and possible personal injury.

Disabling & Activating System For Repairs – To disable system for repairs, turn ignition off. Disconnect negative battery cable, and tape cable end. To activate system, reconnect negative battery cable.

NOTE: Complete system deactivation should be performed only when ABRS is not functioning properly and vehicle needs to be driven.

Complete System Deactivation – 1) Disconnect negative battery cable, and tape cable end. Disconnect 2-way Yellow clockspring harness connector, located between clockspring and instrument panel wiring harness, on top of fuse block.
2) Clockspring connector may also be disconnected at ASDM. Reconnect battery, and drive vehicle to repair area. Disconnect negative battery cable, and tape cable end.
3) Reconnect clockspring connector. Reconnect negative battery cable. Repair as required.

DISPOSAL PROCEDURES

WARNING: Vehicle interior will contain sodium hydroxide powder, a by-product of air bag deployment. Since powder can irritate the skin, eyes, nose, or throat, be sure to wear safety glasses, rubber gloves and long-sleeved shirt during clean-up.

DEPLOYED AIR BAG

1) Begin clean-up by putting tape over air bag exhaust vent, so no additional powder will escape into vehicle interior. Use vacuum cleaner to remove residual powder from A/C-heater outlets and vehicle interior.
2) Turn blower motor on low speed for a few minutes and exit vehicle. Turn blower off. Vacuum additional powder expelled from plenum. Vacuum interior again to recover all powder. Avoid kneeling or sitting on uncleaned surfaces. Dispose of deployed air bag as any part.

UNDEPLOYED AIR BAG

WARNING: Failure to follow service precautions may result in air bag deployment and personal injury. See SERVICE PRECAUTIONS.

In some accidents, such as side or rear-end collisions, air bag may not deploy. If damage results in scrapping vehicle or selling it for junk, air bag must be deployed. Air bag module should never be sold as a used component. Follow appropriate procedure for deployment of air bags.
Procedure 1: Electronic Deployment With Intact Wiring – Use this procedure if scrapping a vehicle with an undeployed air bag. This procedure assumes air bag wiring is intact: AIR BAG light indicates no fault codes, initial system operation check is okay (see SYSTEM OPERATION CHECK) and vehicle's battery is still in place (or one is provided for testing). Perform this procedure outdoors and away from other personnel, as air bag makes a loud noise when deployed.
1) Before proceeding, follow air bag service precautions. See SERVICE PRECAUTIONS. Disable air bag system. See DISABLING & ACTIVATING AIR BAG SYSTEM.
2) Disconnect 2-way Yellow clockspring harness connector, located between clockspring and instrument panel wiring harness, on top of fuse block.
3) Cut 2-way Yellow clockspring connector off at clockspring side of harness. Strip 1" (25 mm) of insulation from wire ends. Make a harness consisting of 2 wires 20 feet or longer. Connect 20-foot wires to clockspring harness. Ensure there are no loose parts in passenger compartment and that no one is within 20 feet of vehicle.
4) Stay at least 20 feet away from vehicle. Connect the other 2 ends of 20-foot wires to terminals of a 12-volt battery. When deployment is achieved, loud bang will be heard and air bag will inflate. After air bag module deploys, allow air bag module to cool and dust settle before approaching vehicle. If air bag fails to deploy, go to PROCEDURE 2.
Procedure 2: Remote Deployment Of Air Bag – Use this procedure if scrapping a vehicle with live air bag, but a problem in electrical system prevents deployment with air bag still installed in vehicle. Also use this procedure if PROCEDURE 1 was unsuccessful.

WARNING: Perform remote deployment outdoors. NEVER attempt to deploy air bag module inside a building, within 20 feet of personnel, or with air bag module trim cover facing downward.

1) Before proceeding, follow air bag service precautions. See SERVICE PRECAUTIONS. Disable air bag system. See DISABLING & ACTIVATING AIR BAG SYSTEM. Remove air bag module. See AIR BAG MODULE & STEERING WHEEL under REMOVAL & INSTALLATION.
2) Cut pigtail wiring harness between clockspring and air bag as close to clockspring housing as possible. Reconnect other end of pigtail harness back into air bag module.
3) Strip 1" (25 mm) of insulation from cut ends of harness. Position air bag module with trim cover facing upward. Connect 2 20-foot wires to end of harness wires. Move 20 feet away. Connect other end of 20 foot wires to terminals of a 12-volt battery. After air bag module deploys, let air bag module cool and dust settle before approaching.

REMOVAL & INSTALLATION

WARNING: Failure to follow air bag service precautions may result in air bag deployment and personal injury. See SERVICE PRECAUTIONS. Always use new parts and correct part number for vehicle being worked on. After component replacement, always perform a system operation check to ensure proper system operation. See SYSTEM OPERATION CHECK.

LEFT & RIGHT IMPACT SENSORS

CAUTION: Always replace impact sensors if faulty. NEVER repair or disassemble impact sensors. Handle impact sensors carefully. Replace impact sensors if they are dented, cracked, deformed rusted, or after air bag has deployed.

Removal – 1) Before proceeding, follow air bag service precautions. See SERVICE PRECAUTIONS. Disable air bag system. See DISABLING & ACTIVATING AIR BAG SYSTEM.

2) Impact sensors are mounted on left and right side of radiator closure panels. *See Fig. 1.* Disconnect impact sensor electrical connector. Remove impact sensor-to-radiator closure panel retaining screws. Remove impact sensor.

Installation – 1) Mount impact sensor with arrow pointing toward front of vehicle, on engine side of radiator closure panel. Install new screws and tighten to specification. See TORQUE SPECIFICATIONS table at end of article. Use only screws supplied with new impact sensor.

2) Install electrical connector on impact sensor, ensuring locking tab is engaged. Check AIR BAG indicator light to ensure system is functioning properly. See SYSTEM OPERATION CHECK.

AIR BAG SYSTEM DIAGNOSTIC MODULE (ASDM)

WARNING: ASDM contains safing sensor which enables ABRS system to activate air bag. To avoid accidental air bag deployment, NEVER connect ASDM electrically to system unless it is bolted to vehicle.

Removal – 1) Before proceeding, follow air bag service precautions. See SERVICE PRECAUTIONS. Disable air bag system. See DISABLING & ACTIVATING AIR BAG SYSTEM.

2) ASDM is located behind center console, at center of instrument panel. *See Fig. 2.* Remove forward console or cover as necessary. Remove ASDM module and bracket mounting screws. Carefully lift module up and rearward. Disconnect wiring at ASDM, and remove ASDM module.

Installation – 1) Install ASDM module with arrow pointing toward front of vehicle. Install electrical connectors, ensuring connectors are locked into position. Place ASDM module and bracket on lower mounting bracket, using locating tab to position ASDM module.

2) Install ASDM module and bracket with new screws and tighten to specification. See TORQUE SPECIFICATIONS table at end of article. Use only screws supplied with new ASDM module. Check AIR BAG indicator light to ensure system is functioning properly. See SYSTEM OPERATION CHECK.

AIR BAG MODULE & STEERING WHEEL

NOTE: Clockspring must be replaced whenever replacing a deployed air bag. See CLOCKSPRING under REMOVAL & INSTALLATION.

Removal – 1) Before proceeding, follow air bag service precautions. See SERVICE PRECAUTIONS. Disable air bag system. See DISABLING & ACTIVATING AIR BAG SYSTEM.

CAUTION: Failure to position wheels in straight-ahead position with steering wheel locked when removing steering wheel could damage clockspring and/or require clockspring to be readjusted.

2) Air bag module is mounted on face of steering wheel. *See Figs. 1 and 3.* Ensure wheels are in straight-ahead position and steering wheel is locked. Remove air bag module-to-steering wheel nuts from back side of steering wheel.

3) Lift air bag module and disconnect electrical connector. Remove cruise control switch and connectors (if equipped) or cover.

4) Remove steering wheel retaining nut. Using Puller (C3428B), remove steering wheel. Self-centering clockspring will automatically lock in place when steering wheel is removed.

Installation – 1) If replacing a deployed air bag module, clockspring must be replaced. See CLOCKSPRING under REMOVAL & INSTALLATION. Position steering wheel on column. Ensure flats on steering wheel hub fit formations on inside of clockspring.

2) Pull clockspring, cruise control switch (if equipped) and horn wires through lower large holes and upper small holes in steering wheel.

3) Install steering wheel retaining nut and tighten to specification. See TORQUE SPECIFICATIONS table at end of article. Connect horn and cruise control wiring.

4) Attach cruise control switch to steering wheel (if equipped). Connect air bag wire connector to air bag module, and secure air bag module to steering wheel.

5) Tighten air bag module-to-steering wheel nuts to specification. See TORQUE SPECIFICATIONS table at end of article. Check AIR BAG indicator light to ensure system is functioning properly. See SYSTEM OPERATION CHECK.

CLOCKSPRING

CAUTION: Failure to position wheels in the straight-ahead position with steering wheel locked when removing steering wheel could damage clockspring and/or require clockspring readjustment.

NOTE: Clockspring is self-centering and will automatically lock in the centered position when steering wheel is removed. Adjustment is only required if centering position is disturbed.

Removal – 1) If replacing a deployed air bag, clockspring must be replaced. Before proceeding, follow air bag service precautions. See SERVICE PRECAUTIONS. Disable air bag system. See DISABLING & ACTIVATING AIR BAG SYSTEM.

2) Clockspring is located behind steering wheel. *See Figs. 1 and 4.* Remove air bag module and steering wheel. See AIR BAG MODULE & STEERING WHEEL under REMOVAL & INSTALLATION. When steering wheel is removed, self-centering clockspring will automatically lock in place.

3) Remove upper and lower steering column shrouds to gain access to clockspring wiring.

4) Disconnect 2-way Yellow clockspring harness connector between clockspring and instrument panel wiring harness, on top of fuse block.

5) Remove clockspring by releasing 2 tabs on side of clockspring. *See Fig. 4.* Clocksprings CANNOT be repaired and must be replaced if faulty.

Installation – 1) Snap clockspring onto steering column. If clockspring centering adjustment is disturbed, adjust clockspring. See CLOCKSPRING CENTERING under ADJUSTMENTS before installing steering wheel. Connect clockspring wiring connectors. Install steering column covers.

2) Install steering wheel. Ensure flats on steering wheel hub fit the formations on inside of clockspring. Pull horn wire through small upper hole and clockspring and cruise control wires (if equipped) through larger bottom hole in steering wheel. *See Fig. 4.*

3) Tighten retaining nut to specification. See TORQUE SPECIFICATIONS table at end of article.

4) Install electrical connectors on horn and cruise control wires (if equipped). Connect clockspring wire to air bag module, ensuring latching arms on connector are visible on top of connector housing. Tighten nuts to specification. See TORQUE SPECIFICATIONS table at end of article.

5) Check AIR BAG indicator light to ensure system is functioning properly. See SYSTEM OPERATION CHECK.

1991 SAFETY EQUIPMENT
Air Bag Restraint System (Cont.)

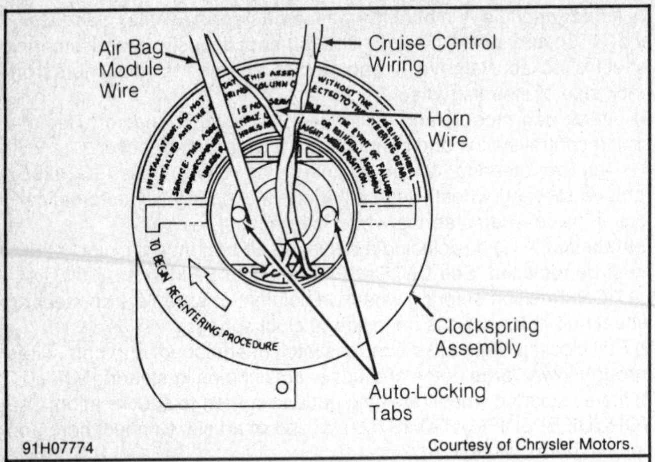
Air Bag Module Wire
Cruise Control Wiring
Horn Wire
Clockspring Assembly
Auto-Locking Tabs
TO BEGIN RECENTERING PROCEDURE
91H07774
Courtesy of Chrysler Motors.

Fig. 4: Identifying Clockspring Components

ADJUSTMENTS

CLOCKSPRING CENTERING

CAUTION: If rotating part of clockspring is not positioned properly with steering column and front wheels, clockspring failure may result. The following procedure must be used to center clockspring.

1) Before proceeding, follow air bag service precautions. See SERVICE PRECAUTIONS. Disable air bag system. See DISABLING & ACTIVATING AIR BAG SYSTEM.

2) Place front wheels in straight-ahead position. Remove air bag module and steering wheel. See AIR BAG MODULE & STEERING WHEEL under REMOVAL & INSTALLATION. Depress 2 plastic auto-locking tabs. *See Fig. 4.* Rotate clockspring rotor in clockwise direction to the end of its travel.

3) From the end of its travel, rotate rotor 2 1/2 turns in counterclockwise direction. The horn wire should end up at the top and air bag module wire at the bottom. *See Fig. 4.*

4) Install steering wheel and air bag module. Tighten retaining nuts to specification. See TORQUE SPECIFICATIONS table at end of article. Check AIR BAG indicator light to ensure system is functioning properly. See SYSTEM OPERATION CHECK.

TORQUE SPECIFICATIONS

TORQUE SPECIFICATIONS

Application	Ft. Lbs. (N.m)
Steering Wheel Nut	45 (61)
	INCH Lbs. (N.m)
Air Bag Diagnostic Module Screw	35 (4)
Air Bag Module Nut	80-100 (9-11)
Impact Sensor Screw	40-60 (4.5-7.0)

Caravan, Town & Country, Voyager

DESCRIPTION & OPERATION

Vehicles are equipped with either an analog or electronic instrument cluster. The body computer, which receives input from various sensors, sends display information to the cluster.

On analog clusters, this information is used to drive the magnetic gauges. Cluster also incorporates warning lights for low fuel, check gauges, door ajar, low washer fluid, check engine and liftgate ajar. On non-gauge equipped models, there are also warning lights for low oil pressure and charging system malfunction.

Electronic cluster uses analog bar gauge displays for oil pressure, coolant temperature, charging voltage, engine RPM and fuel level. Cluster also contains LED message center for door ajar, liftgate ajar and low washer fluid. Odometer mileage memory is not in cluster, but in the body computer instead.

MAINTENANCE REMINDER LIGHT

For information about maintenance reminder lights, see MAINTENANCE REMINDER LIGHTS article in GENERAL INFORMATION.

TESTING

NOTE: Testing of analog and electronic instrument clusters requires usage of tester (DRB-II) and special service publication.

REMOVAL & INSTALLATION

NOTE: Disconnect negative battery cable before servicing instrument panel, cluster or gauges.

INSTRUMENT CLUSTER

Removal & Installation – 1) Using a flat-blade screwdriver, pry up and remove warning indicator grille. Remove warning indicator retaining screws. Disconnect harness connector, and remove indicator. Remove lower steering column cover. Apply parking brake. Shift gear selector to Low.

2) Remove cluster bezel. Disconnect harness connectors. Remove cluster retaining screws. *See Fig. 1.*

3) Pull cluster rearward and disconnect harness connectors. Rotate cluster for access to shift indicator retaining screws. Remove shift indicator and cluster. To install cluster, reverse removal procedure. DO NOT bend shift indicator guide tube during installation. *See Fig. 2.*

4) Check shift indicator adjustment in Drive, Low and Park. If necessary, adjust center needle in Neutral. *See Fig. 3.*

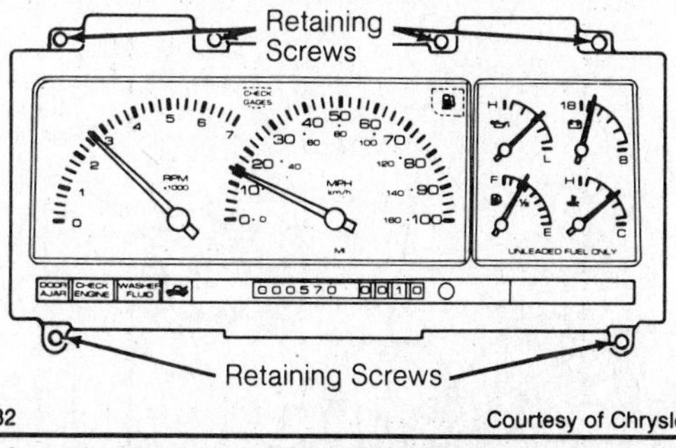

Retaining Screws
Retaining Screws

91A14332 Courtesy of Chrysler Motors.

Fig. 1: Locating Instrument Cluster Retaining Screws (Caravan, Town & Country, Voyager)

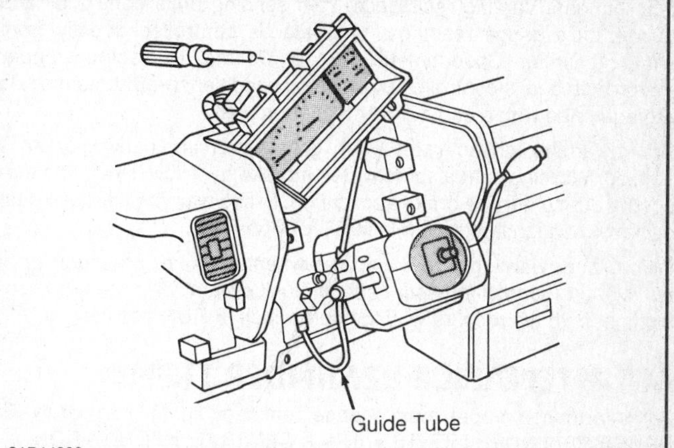

Guide Tube

91B14333 Courtesy of Chrysler Motors.

Fig. 2: Installing Instrument Cluster (Caravan, Town & Country, Voyager)

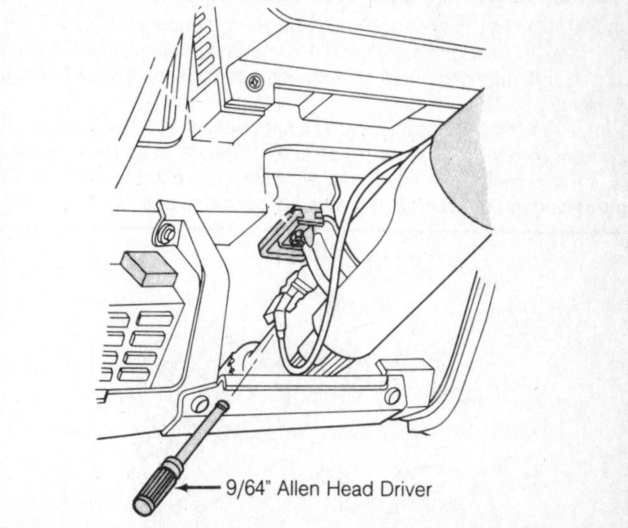

9/64" Allen Head Driver

91C14334 Courtesy of Chrysler Motors.

Fig. 3: Adjusting Shift Indicator (Caravan, Town & Country, Voyager)

GAUGES

Removal & Installation – 1) Using a flat-blade screwdriver, pry up and remove warning indicator grille. Remove warning indicator retaining screws. Disconnect harness connector, and remove indicator. Remove lower steering column cover. Apply parking brake. Shift gear selector to Low.

2) Remove cluster bezel. Disconnect harness connectors. Remove cluster lens. Remove gauge attaching screws. Pull gauge straight out so as not to damage gauge pins. To install gauge, reverse removal procedure.

1991 SAFETY EQUIPMENT
Instrument Panels

Dakota, Pickup, Ramcharger, RWD Van

DESCRIPTION & OPERATION

Analog instrument panel includes either warning lights or magnetic-type gauges. Varying resistance from sending units control oil and temperature gauge readings. Voltmeter is controlled directly from charging circuit. Speedometer (except Dakota) is electric stepper motor-type and is controlled by vehicle speed sensor. Dakota models are equipped with a cable-driven speedometer.

Brake warning light activates when ignition is on and parking brake is applied. Warning light also activates if brake hydraulic system failure occurs during service brake application. Brake warning light bulb test occurs when ignition switch is in START position.

Oil pressure warning light illuminates when engine oil pressure is not sufficient to open oil pressure sending unit switch. Oil pressure warning light bulb test occurs with ignition switch in RUN position.

MAINTENANCE REMINDER LIGHT

For information about maintenance reminder lights, see MAINTENANCE REMINDER LIGHTS article in GENERAL INFORMATION.

TESTING

FUEL GAUGE & FUEL TANK SENDING UNIT

Dakota - 1) Test fuel gauge and wiring by grounding fuel tank sending unit lead. Turn ignition on, and note gauge reading. DO NOT leave sending unit lead grounded for extended periods, as gauge damage will result.

2) If gauge indicates maximum reading, wiring and fuel gauge are operating properly. Proceed to step **4)**. If gauge does NOT indicate maximum reading, remove gauge. Using a voltmeter, check for battery voltage between B+ pin and ground pin. *See Fig. 1.*

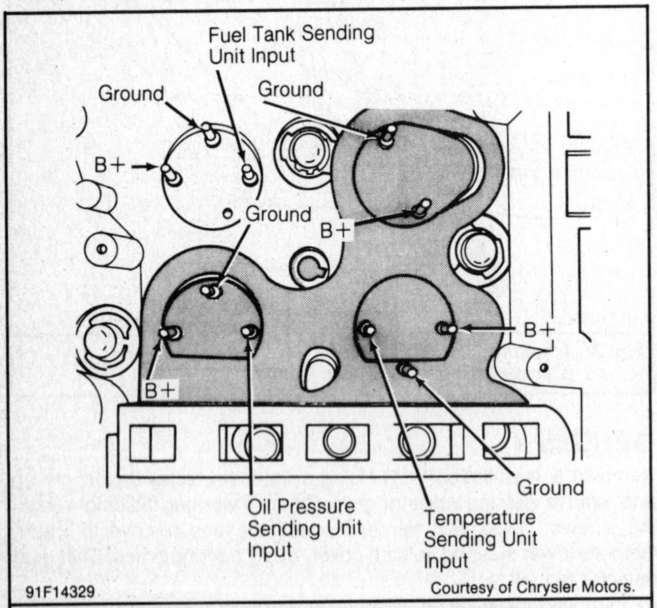
Fuel Tank Sending Unit Input
Ground
Ground
B+
Ground
B+
B+
B+
Oil Pressure Sending Unit Input
Temperature Sending Unit Input
Ground
91F14329
Courtesy of Chrysler Motors.

Fig. 1: Identifying Instrument Panel Gauge Pins (Dakota)

3) If voltage reading is not as specified, check wiring connections and instrument panel printed circuit board continuity. If wiring and circuit board test okay, replace fuel gauge.

4) Remove fuel tank sending unit. Connect a jumper wire between sending unit body and chassis ground. Install sending unit harness connector. Move float arm to FULL, then EMPTY stop positions. Note fuel gauge readings at each float arm position. Allow at least 2 minutes at each test point for gauge to stabilize.

5) If no reading or improper reading is obtained at either test position, replace sending unit. If sending unit tests okay, check for damaged ground wire or poor connection. Ensure float assembly does not bind in fuel tank and tank is not damaged. Repair as required.

Pickup, Ramcharger & RWD Van - 1) Disconnect wire from fuel tank sending unit. Attach wire to known good sending unit. Install jumper wire between sending unit body and chassis ground.

2) Turn ignition on. Move sending unit float arm to EMPTY position, and note fuel gauge reading. Gauge should read EMPTY plus one pointer width or minus 2 pointer widths. Allow at least 2 minutes to allow gauge to stabilize.

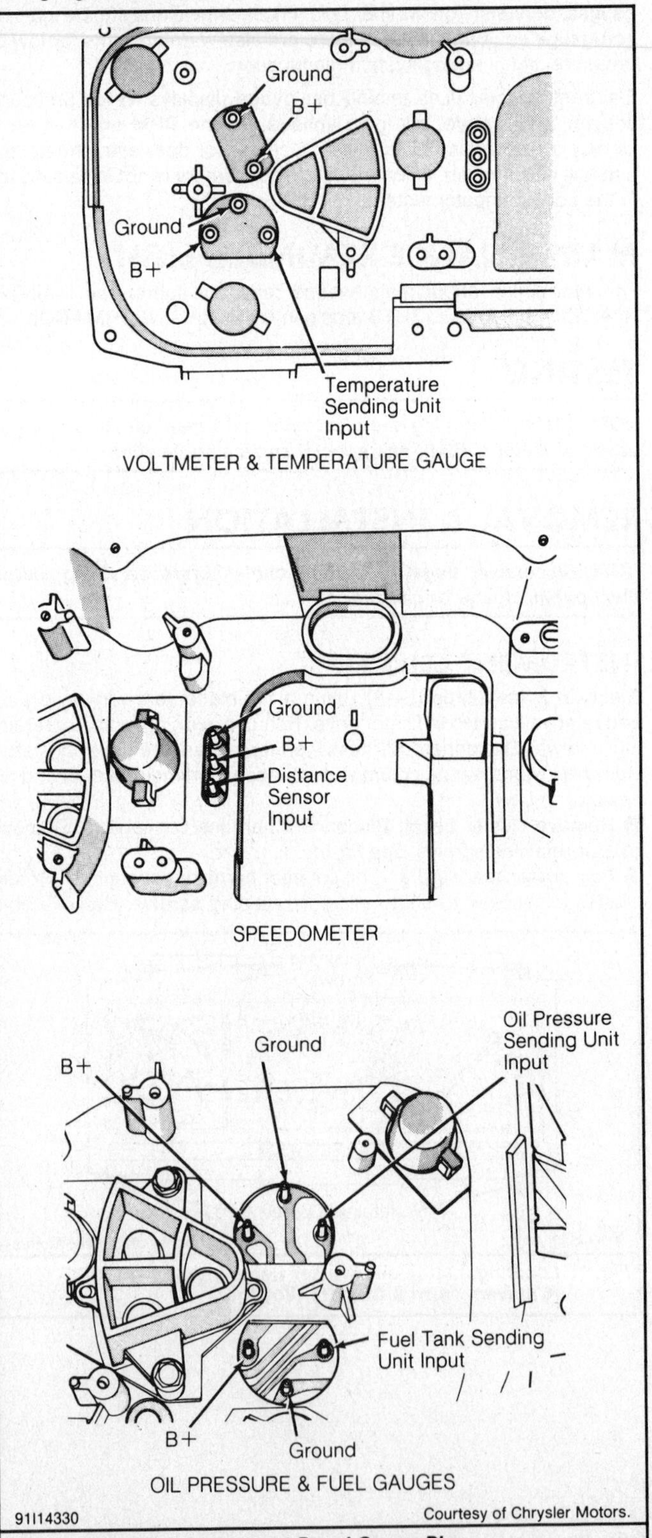
Ground
B+
Ground
B+
Temperature Sending Unit Input
VOLTMETER & TEMPERATURE GAUGE
Ground
B+
Distance Sensor Input
SPEEDOMETER
B+
Ground
Oil Pressure Sending Unit Input
Fuel Tank Sending Unit Input
B+
Ground
OIL PRESSURE & FUEL GAUGES
91I14330
Courtesy of Chrysler Motors.

Fig. 2: Identifying Instrument Panel Gauge Pins (Pickup & Ramcharger)

3) Move float arm to FULL position. Gauge should read FULL plus 2 pointer widths or minus one pointer width. Allow at least 2 minutes to allow gauge to stabilize. If correct reading is obtained, proceed to step **5)**. If correct reading is not obtained, remove gauge. Using a voltmeter, check for battery voltage between B+ pin and ground pin. *See Figs. 2 and 3.*

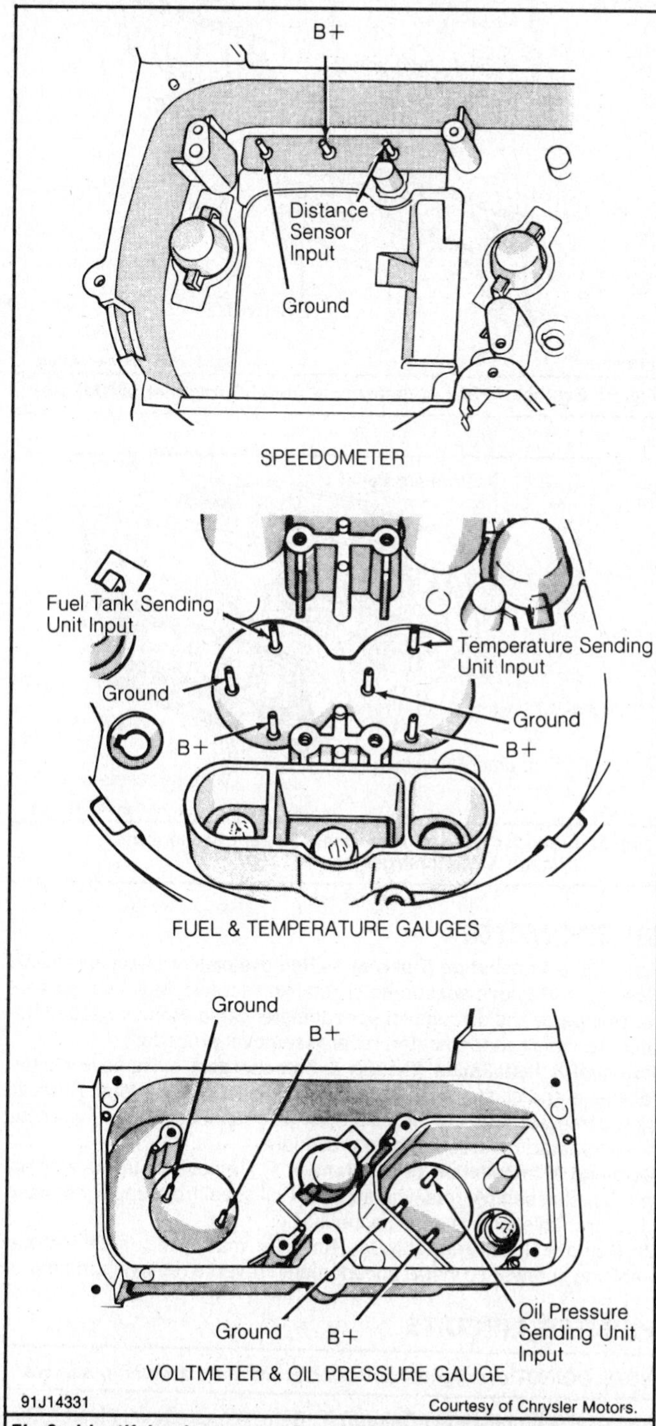

B+
Distance Sensor Input
Ground
SPEEDOMETER
Fuel Tank Sending Unit Input
Temperature Sending Unit Input
Ground
Ground
B+
B+
FUEL & TEMPERATURE GAUGES
Ground
B+
Ground
B+
Oil Pressure Sending Unit Input
VOLTMETER & OIL PRESSURE GAUGE
91J14331
Courtesy of Chrysler Motors.

Fig 3: Identifying Instrument Panel Gauge Pins (RWD Van)

4) If voltage reading is not as specified, check wiring connections and instrument panel printed circuit board continuity. If wiring and circuit board test okay, replace fuel gauge.
5) Remove fuel tank sending unit. Install sending unit harness connector. Move float arm to FULL, then EMPTY stop positions. Note fuel gauge readings at each float arm position. Allow at least 2 minutes at each test point for gauge to stabilize.
6) If no reading or improper reading is obtained at either test position, replace sending unit. If sending unit tests okay, check for poor ground or damaged ground wire. Ensure float assembly does not bind in fuel tank and tank is not damaged. Repair as required.

TEMPERATURE & OIL PRESSURE GAUGES

Temperature Gauge – 1) Test temperature gauge and wiring by grounding temperature sending unit lead. Turn ignition on, and note gauge reading. DO NOT leave sending unit lead grounded for extended periods, as gauge damage will result.
2) If gauge indicates maximum reading, wiring and temperature gauge are operating properly. Proceed to step **4)**. If gauge does NOT indicate maximum reading, remove gauge. See GAUGES under REMOVAL & INSTALLATION. Using a voltmeter, check for battery voltage between B+ pin and ground pin. *See Figs. 1-3.*
3) If voltage reading is not as specified, check wiring connections and instrument panel printed circuit board continuity. If wiring and circuit board test okay, replace temperature gauge.
4) Disconnect temperature sending unit harness connector. Using an ohmmeter, test resistance between sending unit terminal and engine block. If resistance reading is zero or infinity, replace sending unit. If resistance reading is between zero and infinity and gauge does not read correctly, sending unit may be faulty. Compare with known good unit. Replace as required.
Oil Pressure Gauge – 1) Test oil pressure gauge and wiring by grounding oil pressure sending unit lead. Turn ignition on, and note gauge reading. DO NOT leave sending unit lead grounded for extended periods, as gauge damage will result.
2) If gauge indicates maximum reading, wiring and oil pressure gauge are operating properly. Proceed to step **4)**. If gauge does NOT indicate maximum reading, remove gauge. Using a voltmeter, check for battery voltage between B+ pin and ground pin. *See Figs. 1-3.*
3) If voltage reading is not as specified, check wiring connections and instrument panel printed circuit board continuity. If wiring and circuit board test okay, replace oil pressure gauge.
4) Disconnect oil pressure sending unit harness connector. Using an ohmmeter, test resistance between sending unit terminal and engine block. If resistance reading is zero or infinity, replace sending unit. If resistance reading is between zero and infinity and gauge does not read correctly, sending unit may be faulty. Replace as required.
5) Oil pressure should be checked with a mechanical gauge to ensure correct oil pressure is available. If correct oil pressure is available and correct gauge reading was obtained in step **1)**, replace sending unit. If correct oil pressure is not available, repair engine.

VOLTMETER

1) Remove voltmeter gauge and seat belt indicator (if equipped). Using a voltmeter, connect positive lead to "B+" terminal and negative lead to chassis ground. *See Figs. 1-3.*
2) Turn ignition on, and note reading. If voltage reading obtained is battery voltage, replace voltmeter gauge. If voltage reading is less than battery voltage, check wiring and printed circuit board for continuity.

OIL PRESSURE WARNING LIGHT

1) Turn ignition on. If warning light does not glow, check fuse. If fuse is blown, replace fuse, and retest. If fuse is okay, proceed to step **3)**. If light glows, start engine.
2) If light remains on, immediately turn engine off. Check oil pressure using mechanical gauge. If pressure reading is correct, check wiring for short to ground. If wiring tests okay, replace oil pressure switch.
3) Remove molded or single lead connector at oil pressure switch. Ground oil pressure signal wire (center terminal on 3-wire molded connector).
4) If warning light glows, replace oil pressure switch. If warning light does not glow, check bulb, socket, wiring and connections. Repair as required.

1991 SAFETY EQUIPMENT
Instrument Panels (Cont.)

BRAKE WARNING LIGHT

1) Turn ignition on. Apply parking brake. If brake warning light glows, proceed to step **3)**. If brake warning light does not glow, check fuse. If fuse is blown, replace fuse, and retest. If fuse is okay, proceed to next step.
2) Using a test light, check for power at parking brake switch. If power does not exist, repair open circuit between fuse block and parking brake switch. If power exists, replace switch.
3) Raise and support vehicle. Have an assistant depress brake pedal and observe warning light. Open bleeder screw on wheel cylinder. Brake pedal should fall to floor and warning light should glow. If warning light glows, test is complete. If warning light does not glow, proceed to next step.
4) Inspect bulb, socket, wiring and brake warning light switch on proportioning valve. Repair as required. Check master cylinder reservoir, and add fluid if necessary.

REMOVAL & INSTALLATION

NOTE: Disconnect negative battery cable before servicing instrument panel, cluster or gauges.

INSTRUMENT CLUSTER

Removal & Installation (Dakota) – 1) Remove silencer pad (if equipped). Remove steering column cover. Remove cluster bezel. *See Fig. 4*. On A/T equipped vehicles, place shift lever in "D" position. Remove gearshift indicator cable retaining clip at steering column, and disconnect indicator cable.
2) Remove instrument cluster retaining screws. Move cluster rearward. Disconnect speedometer cable and cluster wiring. Remove cluster assembly. To install cluster, reverse removal procedure.

Removal & Installation (Pickup & Ramcharger) – 1) Tape or cover steering column to protect paint. Remove bezel. Remove 4 steering column lower cover retaining screws. Spread upper steering column cover from locking tangs, and slide cover downward. Disconnect shift actuator cable from steering column.
2) Loosen heater and A/C control assembly. Pull control assembly rearward to clear forward mount on instrument cluster housing. Remove 6 cluster retaining screws. Remove instrument cluster. *See Fig. 5*. To install cluster, reverse removal procedure.

Removal & Installation (RWD Van) – 1) Remove instrument cluster hood and bezel assembly retaining screws. *See Fig. 6*. Pull bezel from upper retaining clips. Remove cluster retaining screws. Disconnect message center connector.
2) Disconnect gearshift indicator cable from column. Remove connectors from printed circuit board. Remove instrument cluster assembly. To install, reverse removal procedure.

GAUGES

Removal & Installation (Dakota) – Remove silencer pad (if equipped) and steering column cover. Remove cluster bezel, mask and lens. Remove gauge retaining screws, and pull gauge straight out so as not to damage gauge pins. On some models, it is necessary to remove 2 gauges as an assembly, such as temperature/oil pressure gauges. To install gauge(s), reverse removal procedure.
Removal & Installation (Pickup & Ramcharger) – Remove faceplate, cluster mask and lens. Remove gauge retaining screws, and pull gauge straight out so as not to damage gauge pins. To install gauge, reverse removal procedure.
Removal & Installation (RWD Van) – 1) Remove instrument panel hood and bezel retaining screws. Pull bezel from upper retaining clips.
2) Remove lens retaining screws, and remove lens and shroud. Remove mask. Remove gauge retaining screws, and pull gauge straight out so as not to damage gauge pins. To install gauge, reverse removal procedure.

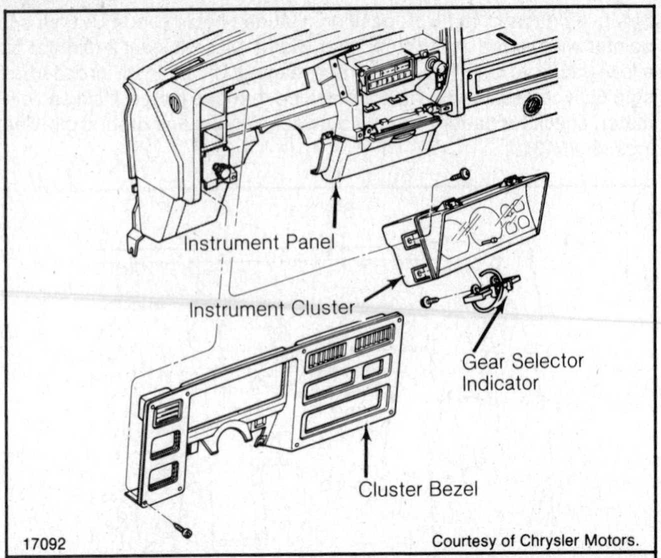
Instrument Panel
Instrument Cluster
Gear Selector
Indicator
Cluster Bezel
17092
Courtesy of Chrysler Motors.

Fig. 4: Exploded View of Instrument Panel Components (Dakota)

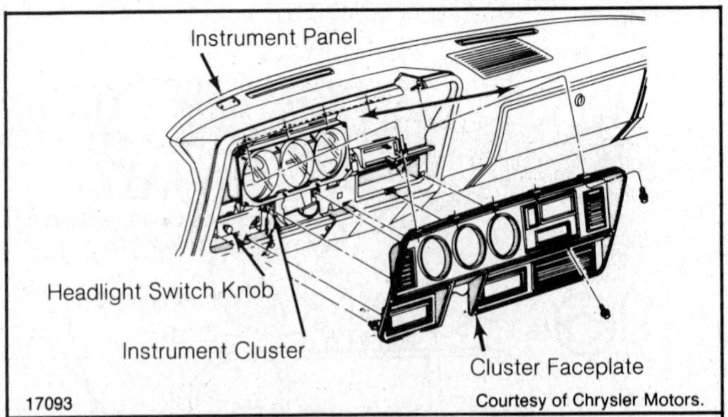
Instrument Panel
Headlight Switch Knob
Instrument Cluster
Cluster Faceplate
17093
Courtesy of Chrysler Motors.

Fig. 5: Exploded View of Instrument Panel Components (Pickup & Ramcharger)

SPEEDOMETER

Removal & Installation (Dakota) – Remove cluster bezel and mask. *See Fig. 4*. Remove speedometer retaining screws. Move speedometer rearward, and disconnect speedometer cable. Remove speedometer. To install speedometer, reverse removal procedure.
Removal & Installation (Pickup & Ramcharger) – Remove cluster faceplate and cluster assembly. Remove cluster mask lens. Remove speedometer retaining screws. Remove speedometer. To install speedometer, reverse removal procedure.
Removal & Installation (RWD Van) – 1) Remove instrument panel and bezel assembly retaining screws. Pull bezel from upper retaining clips. Remove lens retaining screws.
2) Remove lens and shroud. Remove mask and speedometer retaining screws. To install speedometer, reverse removal procedure.

PRINTED CIRCUITS

NOTE: DO NOT overtighten printed circuit board attaching screws.

Removal & Installation (Dakota) – Remove instrument cluster. Disconnect low fuel relay. Remove light sockets. Remove printed circuit retaining screws. Remove printed circuit. To install, reverse removal procedure.

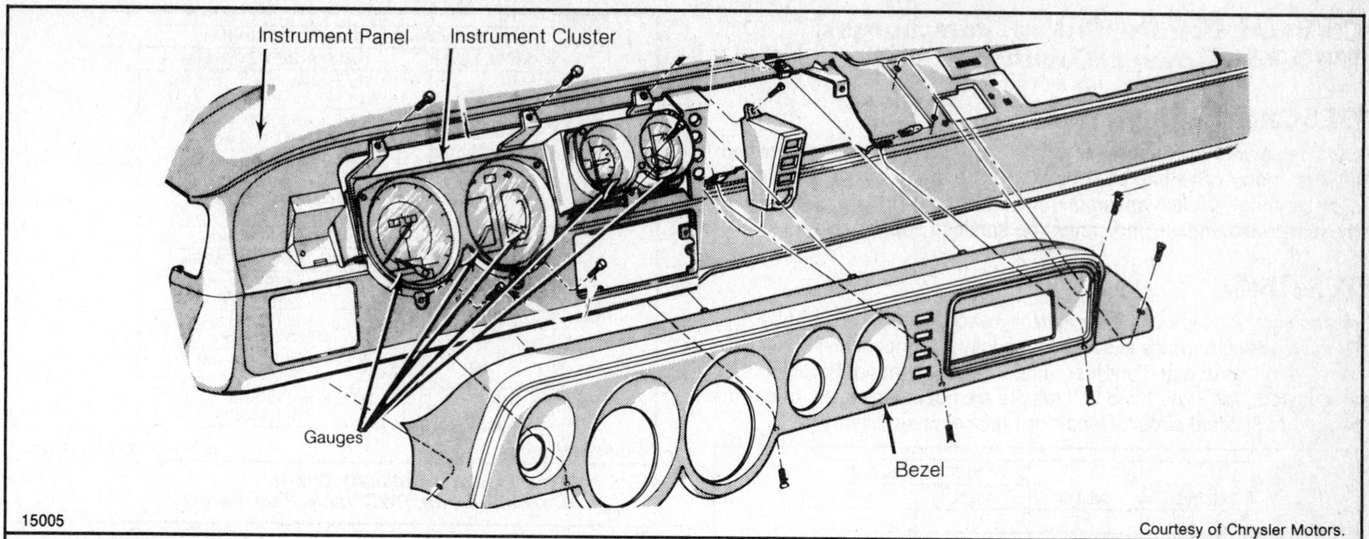
Instrument Panel
Instrument Cluster
Gauges
Bezel
15005
Courtesy of Chrysler Motors.

Fig. 6: Exploded View of Instrument Panel Components (RWD Van)

Removal & Installation (Pickup & Ramcharger) – 1) Remove cluster mask and lens. Remove instrument cluster. Remove voltmeter, and fuel, temperature and oil gauges. Remove speedometer.

2) Remove light socket assemblies. Rotate light sockets counterclockwise to remove. Remove circuit board retaining screws, and remove circuit board. To install circuit board, reverse removal procedure.

Removal & Installation (RWD Van) – 1) Remove instrument cluster. Remove lens and shroud retaining screws. Remove lens and shroud. Remove voltage limiter and light socket assemblies. Remove all gauges. Speedometer does not require removal.

2) Remove circuit board retaining screws, and remove circuit board. To install circuit board, reverse removal procedure.

HEADLIGHT SWITCH

Removal & Installation (Dakota) – 1) Remove silencer pad (if equipped). Remove steering column cover and cluster bezel. Remove headlight bezel retaining screws. Move headlight switch rearward, and disconnect wiring.

2) Pull headlight knob outward. Push release button on right side of switch inward and pull knob outward. Remove retaining spanner nut. Remove headlight switch. To install switch, reverse removal procedure.

Removal & Installation (Pickup & Ramcharger) – 1) Remove cluster faceplate. From under instrument panel, depress release button located on bottom of switch. Pull knob and stem from front panel.

2) Remove power mirror switch knob. Remove bezel. Remove switch retaining spanner nut. Lower switch down far enough to disconnect wiring harness. Remove switch. To install switch, reverse removal procedure.

Removal & Installation (RWD Van) – 1) From under instrument panel, depress stem locking button located on bottom of switch. Pull knob and stem from switch while locking button is depressed.

2) Remove instrument panel hood and bezel assembly. Remove switch bezel attaching screws. Remove headlight switch retaining nut. Remove switch, and disconnect wiring harness. To install switch, reverse removal procedure.

1991 SAFETY EQUIPMENT
Power Mirrors

Caravan, Dakota, Pickup, Ramcharger, RWD Van, Town & Country, Voyager

DESCRIPTION

Outside power rear view mirrors consist of door-mounted mirrors with internal motor drive and backing plate. The mirrors are controlled by a single toggle switch assembly. The mirror motors are integral with the mirror assemblies and cannot be serviced separately.

TESTING

Motor Test – Remove power mirror switch from mounting position. Remove wiring harness at switch connector. Connect one jumper wire to a 12-volt source and another jumper wire to ground. Perform tests as outlined. *See Figs. 1 and 2.* If results are not as specified, check for broken or shorted circuit. Repair or replace as necessary.

12 Volts	Ground	MIRROR REACTION Right	MIRROR REACTION Left
YL	WT	UP	
YL/BK	WT/BK		UP
WT	YL	DOWN	
WT/BK	YL/BK		DOWN
DB	WT	RIGHT	
DB/WT	WT/BK		RIGHT
WT	DB	LEFT	
WT/BK	DB/WT		LEFT

DAKOTA

12 Volts	Ground	MIRROR REACTION Right	MIRROR REACTION Left
YL/BK	WT/BK	UP	
YL	WT		UP
WT/BK	YL/BK	DOWN	
WT	YL		DOWN
WT/BK	DB/WT	RIGHT	
WT	DB		RIGHT
DB/WT	WT/BK	LEFT	
DB	WT		LEFT

PICKUP, RAMCHARGER & RWD VAN

91H13489 Courtesy of Chrysler Motors.

Fig. 1: Mirror Test Charts (Dakota, Pickup, RWD Van & Ramcharger)

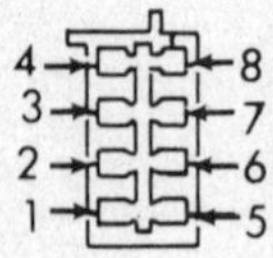
4
3
2
1
8
7
6
5

MIRROR TEST

SWITCH CONNECTOR

12 Volts	Ground	MIRROR REACTION Right	MIRROR REACTION Left
PIN 5	PIN 8	UP	
PIN 5	PIN 4		UP
PIN 8	PIN 5	DOWN	
PIN 4	PIN 5		DOWN
PIN 7	PIN 6	RIGHT	
PIN 3	PIN 6		RIGHT
PIN 6	PIN 7	LEFT	
PIN 6	PIN 3		LEFT

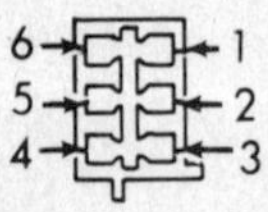
6
5
4
1
2
3

DOOR CONNECTOR

12 Volts	Ground	MIRROR REACTION
PIN 4	PIN 2	UP
PIN 2	PIN 4	DOWN
PIN 6	PIN 5	RIGHT
PIN 5	PIN 6	LEFT
PIN 1	PIN 3	HEATER

91F13487 Courtesy of Chrysler Motors.

Fig. 2: Mirror Test Chart (Caravan, Town & Country and Voyager)

Mirror Switch Test – Remove switch, and disconnect wiring connector. Using an ohmmeter, check for continuity between switch terminals. *See Figs. 3 and 4.* If ohmmeter readings are not as specified, replace switch.

Mirror Selector Knob in "L" Position	
MOVE LEVER	CONTINUITY BETWEEN
▲	YL/BK and PK, WT and BK YL and PK
►	WT and PK, DB and BK DB/WT and BK
▼	WT and PK, YL and BK YL/BK and BK
◄	WT and BK, DB and PK DB/WT and PK
Mirror Selector Knob in "R" Position	
MOVE LEVER	CONTINUITY BETWEEN
▲	WT/BK and BK, YL and PK YL/BK and PK
►	WT/BK and PK, DB and BK DB/WT and BK
▼	WT/BK and PK, YL and BK YL/BK and BK
◄	WT/BK and BK, DB and PK DB/WT and PK

90J04352 Courtesy of Chrysler Motors.

Fig. 3: Mirror Switch Continuity Charts (Dakota, Pickup, RWD Van & Ramcharger)

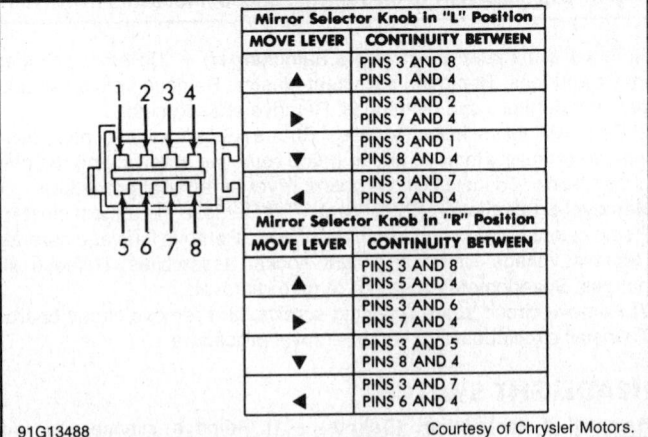

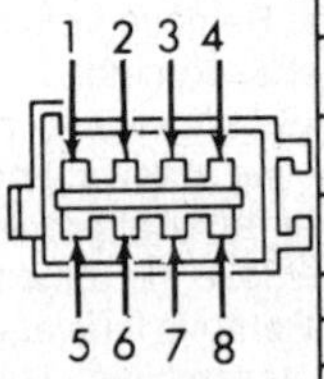
1 2 3 4
5 6 7 8

Mirror Selector Knob in "L" Position	
MOVE LEVER	CONTINUITY BETWEEN
▲	PINS 3 AND 8 PINS 1 AND 4
►	PINS 3 AND 2 PINS 7 AND 4
▼	PINS 3 AND 1 PINS 8 AND 4
◄	PINS 3 AND 7 PINS 2 AND 4
Mirror Selector Knob in "R" Position	
MOVE LEVER	CONTINUITY BETWEEN
▲	PINS 3 AND 8 PINS 5 AND 4
►	PINS 3 AND 6 PINS 7 AND 4
▼	PINS 3 AND 5 PINS 8 AND 4
◄	PINS 3 AND 7 PINS 6 AND 4

91G13488 Courtesy of Chrysler Motors.

Fig. 4: Mirror Switch Continuity Charts (Caravan, Town & Country and Voyager)

REMOVAL & INSTALLATION

MIRROR SWITCH

Removal & Installation (Dakota) – **1)** Remove 3 steering column cover and 10 instrument cluster bezel screws. Remove cover and cluster bezel. Remove 5 headlight and accessory switch bezel screws. Disconnect wiring connectors.

2) Remove power mirror switch knob by pulling straight back from switch. Remove 2 switch mounting plate screws on back of switch bezel. Remove switch-to-mounting plate retaining ring. Remove switch. To install, reverse removal procedure.

Removal & Installation (Caravan, Town & Country and Voyager) – Remove driver door trim panel and weathershield. Reach inside door and disconnect mirror switch connector. Remove mirror control knob and bezel retaining screws. Pull bezel away from door. Loosen Allen head lock screw on back side of bezel. Remove switch. To install, reverse removal procedure.

Removal & Installation (Pickup, Ramcharger & RWD Van) – Remove instrument panel lower steering column cover. Remove mirror control knob by pulling straight out. Reach under instrument panel and disconnect switch connector. Remove 2 switch mounting plate screws, and pull switch from panel. Remove switch-to-mounting plate retaining nut, and remove switch. To install, reverse removal procedure.

WIRING DIAGRAMS

See appropriate chassis wiring diagram in WIRING DIAGRAMS.

1991 SAFETY EQUIPMENT
Rear Window Defogger

Caravan, Ramcharger, RWD Van, Town & Country, Voyager

DESCRIPTION & OPERATION

The heated rear window defogger system consists of a window with 2 vertical bus bars electrically connected to a set of grid lines baked on the inside surface of the glass. A fusible link protects the rear grid, and a fuse protects the relay control circuit.

When control switch is in the ON position, current is directed to the grid. Actuating control switch energizes the relay circuit. Relay circuit will remain energized for approximately 10 minutes or until ignition is turned off. Relay is integral in control switch/timer relay module. An indicator light on module indicates when system is operating.

TROUBLE SHOOTING

Ensure ignition switch is in the ON position. Ensure defogger pigtail is connected to wiring harness and ground is secure. Ensure fuse is okay and all wiring and relay connectors are securely attached. If all conditions are okay, one or more of the following conditions exist.

- Defective control switch
- Defective control switch relay
- Broken grid line(s)
- Loose connector(s)

To test the above components, proceed to individual tests under TESTING.

TESTING

SYSTEM TEST

1) Turn ignition on and place control switch in ON position. Vehicle ammeter (voltmeter on Caravan, Town & Country and Voyager) should indicate current draw. If vehicle is not equipped with an ammeter, defogger operation can be checked by feeling glass. Glass should be warm in 3-4 minutes.

2) Connect a DC voltmeter between the right and left vertical grids. It should indicate 10-14 volts. If no current draw is indicated, ensure power feed wire is connected to rear window grid. Ensure ground wire is properly grounded.

3) If turning control switch produces severe ammeter (voltmeter) deflections, check system for short circuit. If system operation has been verified, but indicator bulb does not light, check and replace bulb.

CONTROL SWITCH/TIMER RELAY MODULE TEST

1) Remove switch assembly, leaving harness connected. Turn ignition on. Using a voltmeter, backprobe connector and check voltage at terminals No. 2, 4 and 1. Terminals No. 2 and 4 should read battery voltage. Terminal No. 1 should read zero volt. If readings are as specified, proceed to step **3)**. If readings are not as specified, proceed to next step.

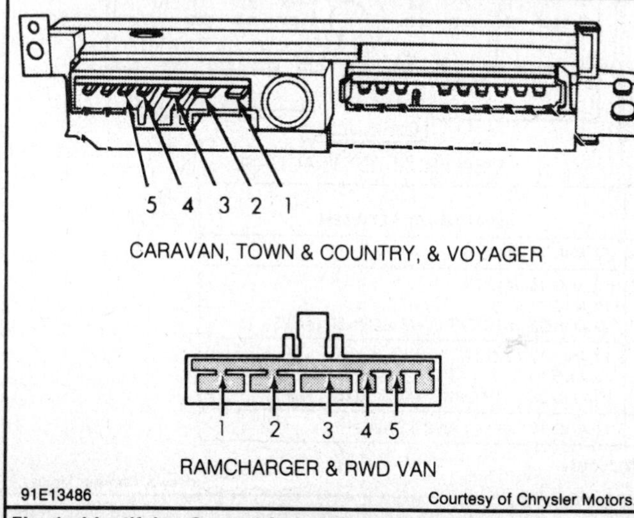
5 4 3 2 1
CARAVAN, TOWN & COUNTRY, & VOYAGER
1 2 3 4 5
RAMCHARGER & RWD VAN
91E13486
Courtesy of Chrysler Motors.

Fig. 1: Identifying Control Switch/Timer Relay Terminal

2) If voltage does not exist at terminals No. 2 and 4, check for wiring problems, burnt out fusible links or inoperative circuit breaker. If terminal No. 1 voltage reads more than zero, turn ignition off and recheck terminal. If voltage reading is still more than zero, replace module.

3) Turn defogger on. Check for voltage at terminal No. 1. Voltage should read battery voltage for approximately 10 minutes and then drop to zero. Indicator light should illuminate when defogger is turned on, and remain on for same time period. If indicator light fails to illuminate, or voltage reading is not as specified, replace module.

GRID TEST

1) Using a voltmeter with a 0-15 volt range, contact bus bar connecting grid lines on passenger's side of glass with negative lead of voltmeter. Contact driver's side bus bar with positive lead. *See Fig. 2.*

2) Turn ignition and control switches to ON position. Reading should be 10-14 volts. Lower voltage indicates a poor ground. Attach negative voltmeter lead to ground. Voltage reading should not vary.

3) Contact negative lead to passenger's side bus bar. Probe each grid line at midpoint with positive lead. A 6-volt reading indicates line is good. A zero volt reading indicates a break between midpoint and driver's side bus bar line.

4) A 10-14 volt reading indicates a break between midpoint and passenger's side bus bar line. Move positive lead toward break, and voltage will change when break is crossed.

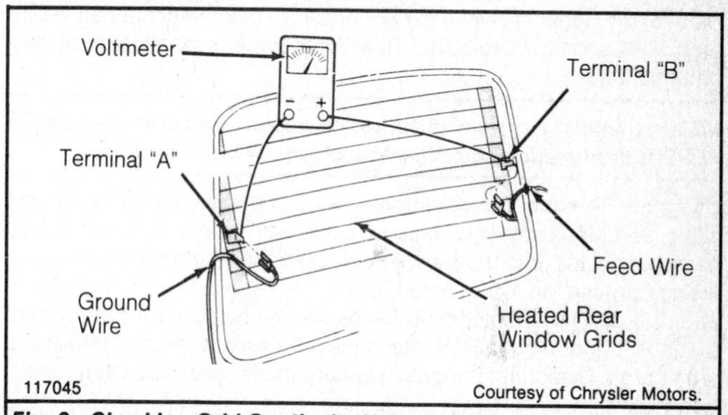
Voltmeter
Terminal "B"
Terminal "A"
Feed Wire
Ground Wire
Heated Rear Window Grids
117045
Courtesy of Chrysler Motors.

Fig. 2: Checking Grid Continuity Voltage Drop

GRID REPAIR

1) Gently clean repair area with fine steel wool. Finish cleaning repair area with alcohol or similar solvent. Using Mopar Repair Kit (3744970) for grid(s) or Mopar Repair Kit (4267922) for terminal(s), prepare conductive epoxy.

2) For grid line repair, mask damaged area with tape. Apply conductive epoxy over damaged area overlapping both ends of break. Allow epoxy to dry for 24 hours at room temperature, or use heat gun for 15 minutes.

3) For grid terminal repair, apply conductive epoxy over damaged area overlapping both ends of terminal break. Position terminal in the desired location and secure to prevent from falling. Allow epoxy to dry for 24 hours at room temperature, or use heat gun for 15 minutes.

WIRING DIAGRAMS

See appropriate chassis wiring diagram in WIRING DIAGRAMS.

1991 SAFETY EQUIPMENT
Steering Column Switches

Caravan, Dakota, Pickup, Ramcharger, RWD Van, Town & Country, Voyager

DESCRIPTION

Ignition switch and lock cylinder are incorporated into an assembly which attaches to side of steering column. Lock cylinder can be serviced as a separate unit, but requires removal of ignition switch assembly. Turn signal and hazard flasher systems use a common turn signal/hazard light switch assembly (multifunction switch), mounted within upper steering column housing.

WARNING: If vehicle is equipped with a driver-side air bag, use extreme caution while servicing steering column. Ensure battery is disconnected before attempting any repair. See SERVICE PRECAUTIONS in AIR BAG RESTRAINT SYSTEM article.

DISABLING & ACTIVATING AIR BAG SYSTEM

WARNING: Wait about 2 minutes after disconnecting negative battery cable before servicing air bag system. System reserve capacitor maintains air bag system voltage for about 2 minutes after battery is disconnected. Servicing air bag system before 2 minutes may cause accidental air bag deployment and possible personal injury.

Disabling & Activating System For Repairs – To disable system for repairs, turn ignition switch to OFF position. Disconnect negative battery cable, and tape cable end. To activate system, reconnect negative battery cable.

NOTE: Complete system deactivation should be performed only if ABRS is not functioning properly and vehicle must be driven.

Complete System Deactivation – **1)** Disconnect negative battery cable, and tape cable end. Disconnect 2-way Yellow clockspring harness connector, located between clockspring and instrument panel wiring harness, on top of fuse block.

2) Clockspring connector may also be disconnected at Air Bag System Diagnostic Module (ASDM). Reconnect battery, and drive vehicle to repair area. Disconnect negative battery cable, and tape cable end.

TROUBLE SHOOTING

Hazard Flashers Inoperative – Blown fuse. Faulty hazard flasher. Open circuit in feed wire to hazard switch. Faulty turn signal/hazard switch. Open or grounded circuit in wiring to external lights.

Indicator Light Inoperative, External Lights Okay – Burned out indicator bulb in instrument cluster.

Indicator Light Okay, External Lights Inoperative – Open circuit in wire to external light(s).

Indicator Light Okay, External Lights Glow Dimly Or Do Not Flash – Loose or corroded external light connections. Poor ground circuit at external light(s).

Turn Signals Do Not Cancel After Turn – Broken canceling finger on turn signal switch. Improperly aligned canceling cam. Broken or loose canceling cam.

Turn Signals Inoperative (Both Sides) – Blown fuse. Faulty turn signal flasher. Loose bulkhead connector. Loose or faulty rear wiring harness or terminals. Open circuit to turn signal flasher. Open circuit in feed wire to turn signal switch. Faulty switch connections. Open or grounded circuit in wiring to external lights.

Turn Signal Inoperative (One Side) – Faulty external bulb. Poor ground at external light. Open circuit in wiring to external light(s). Faulty turn signal/hazard switch.

TESTING

MULTIFUNCTION SWITCH

Disconnect negative battery cable. Remove multifunction switch. See MULTIFUNCTION SWITCH under REMOVAL & INSTALLATION. Use an ohmmeter to check continuity between switch terminals. *See Fig. 1.* If continuity is not as specified, replace multifunction switch.

REMOVAL & INSTALLATION

WARNING: If vehicle is equipped with a driver-side air bag, use extreme caution while servicing steering column. Ensure battery is disconnected before attempting any repair. See SERVICE PRECAUTIONS in AIR BAG RESTRAINT SYSTEM article.

HORN PAD

Removal & Installation (Caravan, Town & Country and Voyager) – **1)** Disconnect and isolate negative battery cable. Remove 4 air bag retaining nuts, and remove air bag module. Disconnect air bag initiator harness connector.

SWITCH POSITIONS TURN SIGNAL	CONTINUITY BETWEEN
NEUTRAL	12 AND 14 AND 16
LEFT	13 AND 14 AND 15
LEFT	12 AND 16
RIGHT	11 AND 12 AND 13
RIGHT	14 AND 16

CARAVAN, TOWN & COUNTRY AND VOYAGER

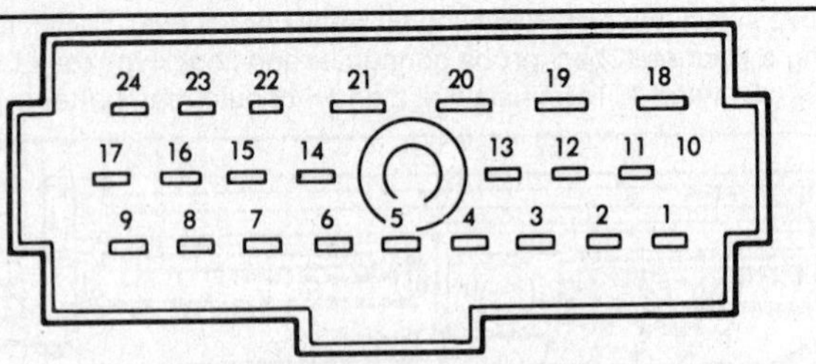
24 23 22 21 20 19 18
17 16 15 14 13 12 11 10
9 8 7 6 5 4 3 2 1

VIEW FROM TERMINAL CASE

SWITCH POSITIONS TURN SIGNAL	HAZARD WARNING	CONTINUITY BETWEEN
NEUTRAL	OFF	12 AND 14 AND 15
LEFT	OFF	15 AND 16 AND 17
LEFT	OFF	12 AND 14
LEFT	OFF	22 AND 23 WITH OPTIONAL CORNER LAMPS
RIGHT	OFF	11 AND 12 AND 17
RIGHT	OFF	14 AND 15
RIGHT	OFF	23 AND 24 WITH OPTIONAL CORNER LAMPS
NEUTRAL	ON	11 AND 12 AND 13 AND 15 AND 16

DAKOTA, PICKUP, RAMCHARGER & RWD VAN

91A13490

Courtesy of Chrysler Motors.

Fig. 1: Testing Multifunction Switch

1991 SAFETY EQUIPMENT
Steering Column Switches (Cont.)

2) Place air bag module face up on a clean level surface. Remove horn switch retaining screws, and remove switch. To install switch, reverse removal procedure.

Removal & Installation (All Others) – Remove horn pad mounting screws located on underside of steering wheel. Pull pad from wheel, and disconnect harness connector(s). Remove pad. To install pad, reverse removal procedure.

MULTIFUNCTION SWITCH

Removal & Installation – Disconnect negative battery cable. On tilt columns, remove tilt lever. On all models, remove upper and lower steering column covers. Remove tamper proof mounting screws. Pull switch away from column, and loosen connector screw (screw remains in connector). Remove switch. To install switch, reverse removal procedure.

IGNITION SWITCH & LOCK CYLINDER

CAUTION: Special care must be taken to avoid bumping, jolting or hammering on the steering shaft and gearshift tube.

Ignition Switch (Removal & Installation) – Remove negative battery cable. On tilt columns, remove tilt lever. On all models, remove upper and lower steering column covers. Remove 3 (tamper proof Torx) mounting screws. *See Fig. 2.* Gently pull switch away from column. Release connector locks on ignition, Key In switch and Halo light connectors, and remove switch from connectors. To install switch, reverse removal procedure.

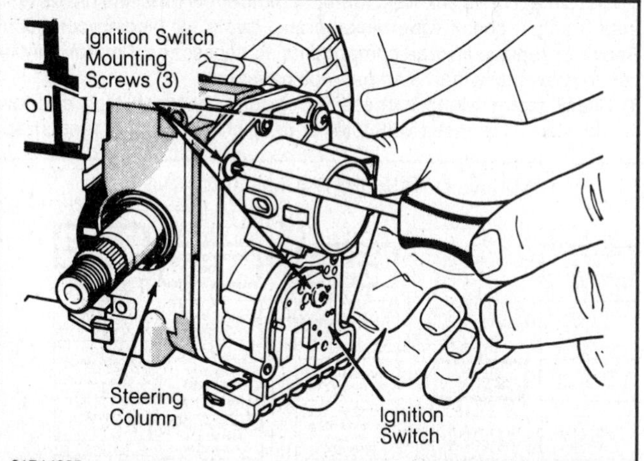
Ignition Switch
Mounting
Screws (3)
Steering
Column
Ignition
Switch

91B14325 Courtesy of Chrysler Motors.

Fig. 2: Removing Ignition Switch Mounting Screws

Lock Cylinder (Removal) – Remove ignition switch. With key inserted and ignition switch in LOCK position, depress lock cylinder retaining pin using a small screwdriver. *See Fig. 3.* Rotate cylinder to OFF position. Lock cylinder should now be unseated from ignition switch assembly. Rotate cylinder back to LOCK position and remove key. Remove lock cylinder.

Installation – **1)** Install electrical connectors on switch assembly. Position park lock slider linkage in mid-travel. *See Fig. 4.*

NOTE: On column shift vehicles, shifter must be in Park. Ignition switch must be in LOCK position (column lock flag parallel with ignition switch terminals. See Fig. 5.

2) Mount ignition switch to column. Tighten mounting screws to 17 INCH lbs. (2 N.m). Install upper and lower steering column covers. Install tilt lever (if equipped). Reconnect negative battery cable.

3) With lock cylinder and ignition switch in LOCK position, insert lock cylinder into switch assembly until it bottoms. Insert key. Gently push in on key while rotating key clockwise to end of travel. Check for proper operation of ignition switch in all positions.

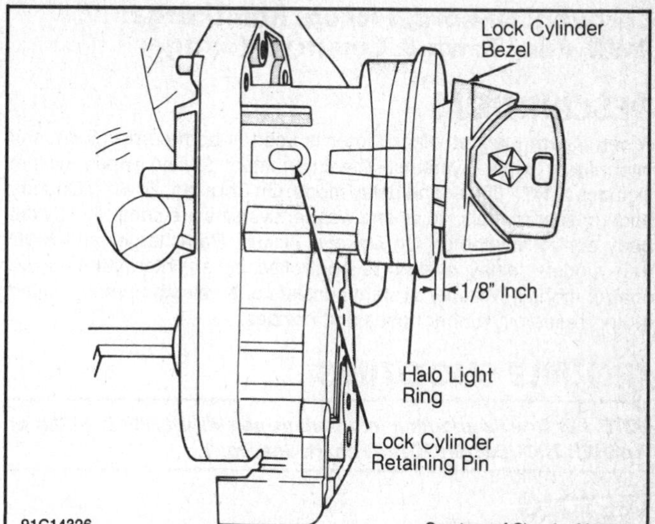
Lock Cylinder
Bezel
1/8" Inch
Halo Light
Ring
Lock Cylinder
Retaining Pin

91C14326 Courtesy of Chrysler Motors.

Fig. 3: Removing Lock Cylinder

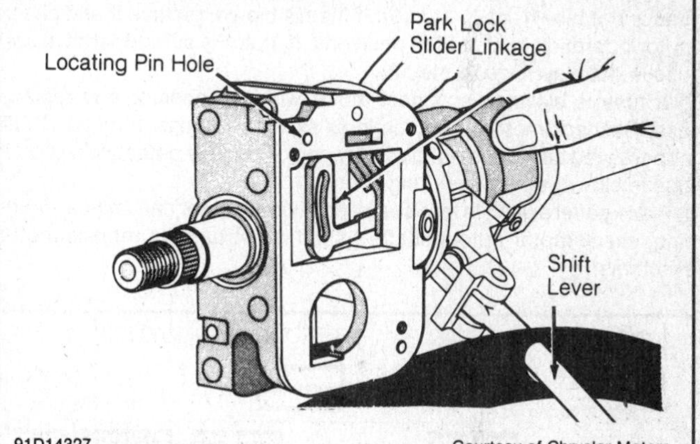
Park Lock
Slider Linkage
Locating Pin Hole
Shift
Lever

91D14327 Courtesy of Chrysler Motors.

Fig 4: Positioning Park Lock Slider Linkage

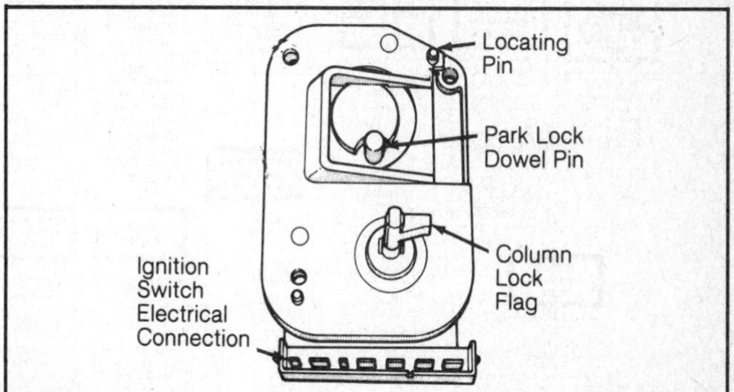
Locating
Pin
Park Lock
Dowel Pin
Column
Lock
Flag
Ignition
Switch
Electrical
Connection

91E14328 Courtesy of Chrysler Motors.

Fig. 5: Positioning Column Lock Flag

WIRING DIAGRAMS

See appropriate chassis wiring diagram in WIRING DIAGRAMS.

TORQUE SPECIFICATIONS

TORQUE SPECIFICATIONS

Application	INCH. Lbs. (N.m)
Air Bag Retaining Nuts	80-100 (9-11)
Ignition Switch Mounting Screws	17 (2)

1991 SAFETY EQUIPMENT
Wiper/Washer Systems

Caravan, Dakota, Pickup, Ramcharger RWD Van, Town & Country, Voyager

DESCRIPTION

A permanent magnet wiper motor is used in both conventional and intermittent wiper systems. The intermittent (delay) wiper system includes a 1/2 - 30 second delay mode. On Caravan, Town & Country and Voyager models, delay and washer systems are controlled by the body control computer. On Dakota, Pickup, Ramcharger and RWD Van models, delay system is controlled by an intermittent wiper control module. Washer system consists of an electric pump, sealed motor, reservoir, rubber hoses and nozzles.

TROUBLE SHOOTING

NOTE: For trouble shooting information, see WINDSHIELD WIPER or WASHER TROUBLE SHOOTING chart. See Fig. 1.

TESTING

WINDSHIELD WIPER/WASHER SYSTEM

Windshield Wiper Motor Will Not Run – 1) Check for blown fuse. If fuse is not blown, go to step **3)**. If fuse is blown, replace it and check motor operation in all switch positions. If motor is still inoperative and fuse is not blown, go to step **3)**.

2) If fuse is blown, disconnect motor wiring connector and replace fuse. Recheck motor operation in all switch positions. If motor is still inoperative and fuse is not blown, repair or replace defective motor. If fuse is blown, switch or wiring is faulty.

3) Place panel switch in low-speed position. If motor can be heard running, check motor output shaft. If shaft is not turning, replace motor assembly.

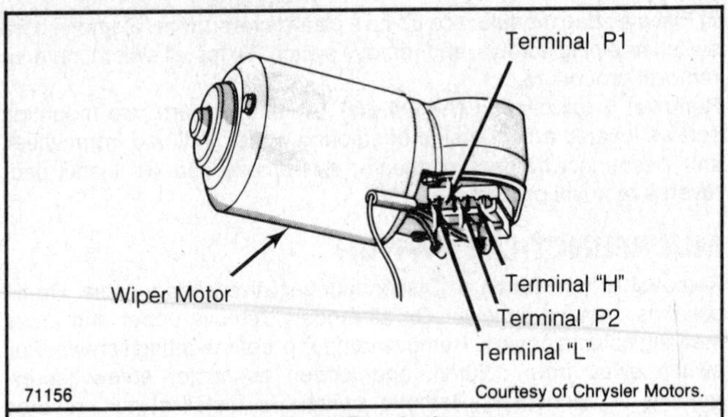
Terminal P1
Wiper Motor
Terminal "H"
Terminal P2
Terminal "L"
71156
Courtesy of Chrysler Motors.

Fig. 2: Identifying Wiper Motor Terminals

4) If shaft is turning, check drive link to output shaft for worn parts or disconnected components. If motor cannot be heard running, connect a voltmeter between motor terminal "L" and ground strap. *See Fig. 2.*

5) If battery voltage does not exist, move voltmeter negative probe to negative battery terminal. If battery voltage now exists, fault is open ground circuit. Ensure mount is free of paint, and mounting nuts are tight.

Windshield Wiper Motor Slow At All Speeds – 1) Disconnect wiring harness at motor. Remove wiper arms and blades. Connect ammeter between battery and terminal "L" on motor. *See Fig. 2.* If motor runs and average ammeter reading is more than 6 amps, go to next step. If reading is less than 6 amps, go to step **3)**.

2) Disconnect drive link from motor. If motor now runs and draws less than 3 amps, check wiper linkage and pivots for binding condition. Repair or replace linkage components as necessary. If motor continues to draw more than 3 amps, replace motor.

3) Check motor wiring harness for shorting between high and low speed wires. Connect a voltmeter or test light to motor ground strap.

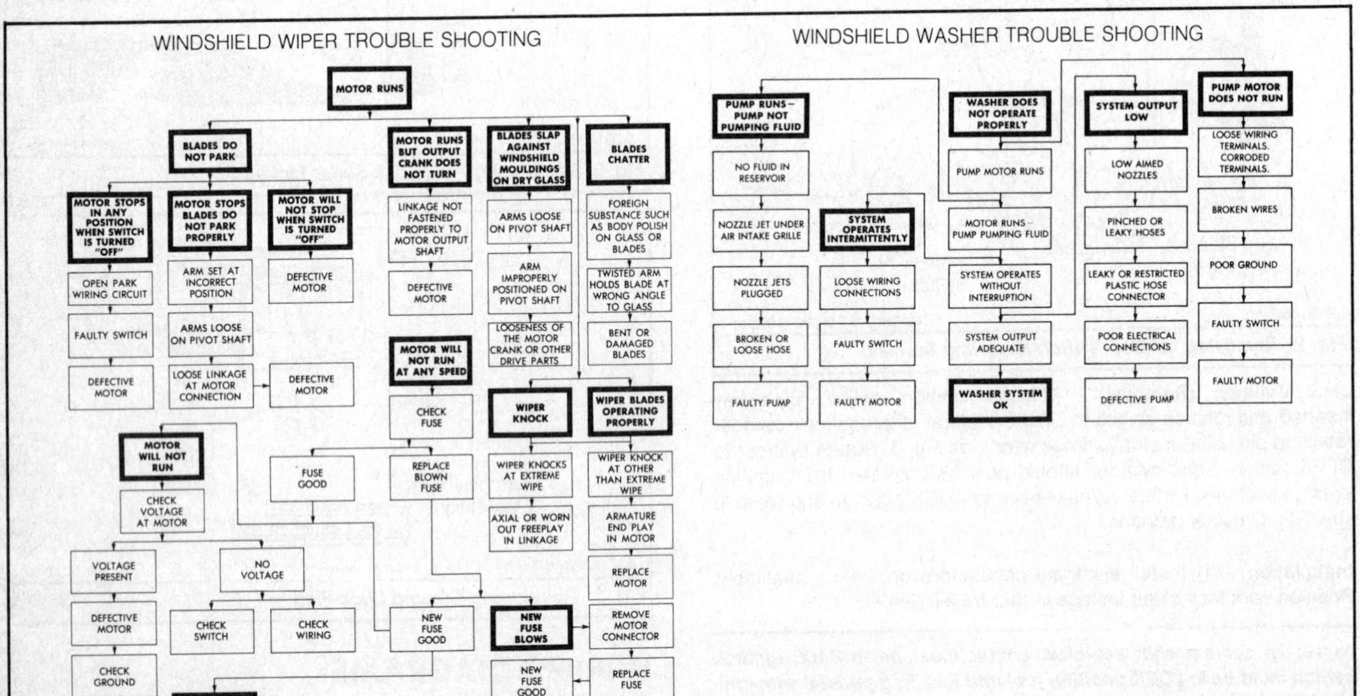
WINDSHIELD WIPER TROUBLE SHOOTING
MOTOR RUNS
BLADES DO NOT PARK
MOTOR STOPS IN ANY POSITION WHEN SWITCH IS TURNED "OFF"
OPEN PARK WIRING CIRCUIT
FAULTY SWITCH
DEFECTIVE MOTOR
MOTOR STOPS BLADES DO NOT PARK PROPERLY
ARM SET AT INCORRECT POSITION
ARMS LOOSE ON PIVOT SHAFT
LOOSE LINKAGE AT MOTOR CONNECTION
MOTOR WILL NOT STOP WHEN SWITCH IS TURNED "OFF"
DEFECTIVE MOTOR
DEFECTIVE MOTOR
MOTOR RUNS BUT OUTPUT CRANK DOES NOT TURN
LINKAGE NOT FASTENED PROPERLY TO MOTOR OUTPUT SHAFT
DEFECTIVE MOTOR
BLADES SLAP AGAINST WINDSHIELD MOULDINGS ON DRY GLASS
ARMS LOOSE ON PIVOT SHAFT
ARM IMPROPERLY POSITIONED ON PIVOT SHAFT
LOOSENESS OF THE MOTOR CRANK OR OTHER DRIVE PARTS
BLADES CHATTER
FOREIGN SUBSTANCE SUCH AS BODY POLISH ON GLASS OR BLADES
TWISTED ARM HOLDS BLADE AT WRONG ANGLE TO GLASS
BENT OR DAMAGED BLADES
MOTOR WILL NOT RUN AT ANY SPEED
CHECK FUSE
FUSE GOOD
REPLACE BLOWN FUSE
NEW FUSE GOOD
NEW FUSE BLOWS
NEW FUSE GOOD
REPLACE MOTOR
CHECK WIRING
REMOVE MOTOR CONNECTOR
REPLACE FUSE
FUSE BLOWS
CHECK SWITCH
WIPER KNOCK
WIPER KNOCKS AT EXTREME WIPE
AXIAL OR WORN OUT FREEPLAY IN LINKAGE
WIPER BLADES OPERATING PROPERLY
WIPER KNOCK AT OTHER THAN EXTREME WIPE
ARMATURE END PLAY IN MOTOR
REPLACE MOTOR
MOTOR WILL NOT RUN
CHECK VOLTAGE AT MOTOR
VOLTAGE PRESENT
DEFECTIVE MOTOR
CHECK GROUND
NO VOLTAGE
CHECK SWITCH
CHECK WIRING
MOTOR RUNS BLADES DO NOT MOVE
OUTPUT SHAFT STATIONARY
REPLACE MOTOR
OUTPUT SHAFT ROTATES
LOOSE MOTOR CRANK
BAD LINKAGE CONNECTION
ARMS LOOSE ON PIVOT SHAFT
WINDSHIELD WASHER TROUBLE SHOOTING
PUMP RUNS – PUMP NOT PUMPING FLUID
NO FLUID IN RESERVOIR
NOZZLE JET UNDER AIR INTAKE GRILLE
NOZZLE JETS PLUGGED
BROKEN OR LOOSE HOSE
FAULTY PUMP
SYSTEM OPERATES INTERMITTENTLY
LOOSE WIRING CONNECTIONS
FAULTY SWITCH
FAULTY MOTOR
WASHER DOES NOT OPERATE PROPERLY
PUMP MOTOR RUNS
MOTOR RUNS – PUMP PUMPING FLUID
SYSTEM OPERATES WITHOUT INTERRUPTION
SYSTEM OUTPUT ADEQUATE
WASHER SYSTEM OK
SYSTEM OUTPUT LOW
LOW AIMED NOZZLES
PINCHED OR LEAKY HOSES
LEAKY OR RESTRICTED PLASTIC HOSE CONNECTOR
POOR ELECTRICAL CONNECTIONS
DEFECTIVE PUMP
PUMP MOTOR DOES NOT RUN
LOOSE WIRING TERMINALS. CORRODED TERMINALS.
BROKEN WIRES
POOR GROUND
FAULTY SWITCH
FAULTY MOTOR
71154, 71155
Courtesy of Chrysler Motors.

Fig. 1: Windshield Wiper/Washer System Trouble Shooting Charts

Place wiper switch in LOW position. Connect other lead of voltmeter or test light to terminal "H" of wiring harness. *See Fig. 2.* If voltage is present or test light illuminates, short exists in wiring or wiper switch.
4) If voltage is not present or test light does not light, place wiper switch in HIGH position. Move voltmeter/test light lead from terminal "H" to terminal "L" of wiring harness. If voltage is present or test light illuminates short exists in wiring or wiper switch.

Windshield Wiper Motor Runs In LOW Position Only – Place switch in HIGH position and connect test light or voltmeter between terminal "H" and ground. If test light does not light or voltage is not present, an open exists in wiring or switch. If test light illuminates or voltage exists, replace motor.

Windshield Wiper Motor Runs In HIGH Position Only – Place switch in LOW position and connect test light or voltmeter between terminal "L" and ground. If test light does not illuminate or voltage is not present, an open exists in wiring or switch. If test light glows or voltage is present, replace motor.

Windshield Wiper Motor Runs With Switch In OFF Or PARK Position – Remove wiring harness and connect a jumper wire from terminal P2 to terminal "L". Connect another jumper wire from terminal P1 to battery. *See Fig. 2.* If wiper motor runs to park position and stops, instrument panel switch is defective. If motor continues to run and does not park, replace motor.

Windshield Wiper Motor Will Not Park When Switch Is In OFF Position – **1)** Remove wiper motor wiring connector and clean terminals. Reconnect connector and test motor. If problem continues, place switch in OFF position.
2) Disconnect motor wiring connector. Connect a voltmeter or test light to motor ground. Connect other lead to terminal P1 of wiring connector. If voltage is not present or test light does not illuminate, check for an open circuit in wiring harness or wiper control switch.
3) If voltage is present or test light illuminates, connect an ohmmeter between terminals "L" and P2. *See Fig. 2.* If continuity exists, motor is faulty. If continuity does not exist, open circuit is present in wiper control switch or wiring harness.

DELAY WIPER SYSTEM

NOTE: Wiper/washer system is controlled by body control computer. Test procedure requires use of DRB-II tester

Delay Wiper System Inoperative (Caravan, Town & Country, & Voyager) – **1)** Turn ignition on. Operate wipers in all speeds. If wipers will not operate in HIGH or LOW position, go to WINDSHIELD WIPER/WASHER SYSTEM. If wipers operate in HIGH and LOW position but not in DELAY, proceed to next step. If wipers operate in HIGH and LOW, but do not operate correctly in DELAY, proceed to TESTING POWER & GROUND SUPPLY.
2) Turn wiper switch to DELAY position. Connect DRB-II to vehicle body diagnostic connector located near fuse block.
3) Actuate wiper motor test. If wiper motor operates, proceed to TESTING BODY CONTROL COMPUTER & WIPER/WASHER SWITCH. If wiper motor does not operate, proceed to next step.
4) Stop wiper motor test. Turn ignition off. Disconnect body control computer harness connectors. Inspect connectors for damaged or pushed out pins. Repair as necessary. Turn ignition on. With DRB-II in voltmeter mode, probe Dark Blue wire in Blue 25-way connector. If voltage reading is less than 10 volts, repair open in Dark Blue wire. Perform VERIFICATION TEST. If voltage reading is 10 volts or more, proceed to next step.
5) Turn ignition off. Remove windshield wiper/washer pod switch. SEE WINDSHIELD WIPER/WASHER SWITCH under REMOVAL & INSTALLATION. Check harness connector and repair as necessary. With DRB-II in ohmmeter mode, probe cavity A1. *See Fig. 4.* If resistance reading is less than 10 ohms, repair Dark Green/White wire for short to ground. Perform VERIFICATION TEST. If resistance reading is 10 ohms or more, proceed to next step.
6) Ensure switch is still in DELAY position. Using an external ohmmeter, probe terminals A1 and B5 on wiper/washer switch. If resistance reading is less than 10 ohms, replace switch. Perform VERIFICATION TEST. If the resistance reading is 10 ohms or more, probe terminals A1 and A3. If resistance reading is less than 10 ohms, replace switch. If resistance reading is 10 ohms or more, proceed to next step.
7) Using external ohmmeter, check continuity between cavity A1 in wiper/washer switch harness connector and Dark Green/White wire in Blue 25-way body control computer harness connector. If resistance reading is 10 ohms or more, repair Dark Green/White wire between body control computer and wiper/washer switch. Perform VERIFICATION TEST. If resistance reading is less than 10 ohms, proceed to next step.
8) Using external ohmmeter, check continuity between cavities A3 and A4. *See Fig. 4.* If resistance reading is 10 ohms or more, repair Brown/White for open condition to splice. Perform VERIFICATION TEST. If resistance is less than 10 ohms, replace body control computer. Perform VERIFICATION TEST.

TESTING BODY CONTROL COMPUTER & WIPER/WASHER SWITCH

Wiper Motor Operative in HIGH & LOW, Inoperative in DELAY (Caravan, Town & Country, & Voyager) – **1)** With DRB-II connected, ensure wiper motor actuator test is off and wiper switch is in DELAY position. Turn ignition on. Put DRB-II in voltmeter mode. Read delay wiper sensor voltage. If voltage reading is 1-12 volts, replace body control computer. Perform VERIFICATION TEST. If voltage is not as specified, proceed to next step.
2) Turn ignition off. Disconnect body controller and inspect connectors for damage. Repair as required. With DRB-II in voltmeter mode, and wiper switch in DELAY position, probe Dark Green/Yellow in blue body controller connector. If voltage reading is 1-12 volts, replace body control computer. Perform VERIFICATION TEST. If voltage is not as specified, proceed to next step.
3) Remove wiper/washer switch. Backprobe cavity A7 with DRB-II voltmeter probe. *See Fig. 4.* If voltage reading is 1-12 volts, repair Dark Green/Yellow wire for open between body controller and wiper switch. Perform VERIFICATION TEST. If voltage reading is not as specified, proceed to next step.
4) Turn ignition off. Disconnect wiper/washer switch assembly. Inspect connectors and repair as required. Perform VERIFICATION TEST. If connectors are okay, place DRB-II in ohmmeter mode. Probe Dark Green/Yellow wire in cavity A7. *See Fig. 4.* If resistance reading is less than 10 ohms, repair Dark Green/Yellow wire for short to ground. If resistance reading is 10 ohms or more, replace wiper/washer switch. Perform VERIFICATION TEST.

TESTING POWER & GROUND SUPPLY

Wipers Operative in HIGH & LOW, Operate Incorrectly in DELAY – **1)** Turn ignition on. Turn wiper switch off. If wipers park correctly, proceed to TESTING WASHER PUMP OPERATION. If wipers do not park correctly, proceed to next step.
2) Remove wiper/washer switch. With DRB-II in voltmeter mode and wiper switch in DELAY position, backprobe cavity A7 of wiper switch. *See Fig. 4.* If voltage reading obtained during wiper sweep is less than 10 volts, repair Dark Green/White wire for open condition between cavity and splice. Perform VERIFICATION TEST. If voltage reading is 10 volts or more, proceed to next step.
3) Remove but do not disconnect body control computer. Turn wiper switch to LOW position. Using an analog voltmeter, backprobe Dark Green wire in body controller Blue connector. If voltage reading does not switch from 10 volts or more to less than 3 volts, proceed to next step. If voltage reading is as specified, disconnect body control computer connectors and inspect. Repair as required. If connectors are okay, replace body control computer, Perform VERIFICATION TEST.
4) Turn ignition off. Disconnect wiper motor harness connector and inspect connector for damage. Repair as required. Perform VERIFICATION TEST. If connector is okay, turn ignition on. Turn wiper switch off. With DRB-II in voltmeter mode, probe Dark Blue wire in wiper motor connector. If voltage reading is less than 10 volts, repair open condition. If voltage reading is 10 volts or more, proceed to next step.
5) Probe Dark Green wire in wiper motor connector with DRB-II voltmeter probe. If voltage reading is 10 volts or more, repair Dark Green

1991 SAFETY EQUIPMENT
Wiper/Washer Systems (Cont.)

wire for short to ground. If voltage reading is less than 10 volts, proceed to next step.
6) Turn ignition off. Disconnect body controller and inspect connectors. Repair as required. Using an external ohmmeter, test resistance of Dark Green wire between wiper motor connector and body controller connector. If resistance reading is less than 10 ohms, replace wiper motor. If resistance reading is 10 ohms or more, repair Dark Green wire for open condition. Perform VERIFICATION TEST.

TESTING WASHER PUMP OPERATION

Wipers Operative in HIGH & LOW, Operate Incorrectly in DELAY (Caravan, Town & Country, & Voyager) – 1) Push washer button on wiper/washer switch. If washer does not operate, proceed to step **3)**. If washer operates okay, disconnect body control computer and inspect connectors. Repair as required. Perform VERIFICATION TEST. If connectors are okay, proceed to next step.
2) With DRB-II in voltmeter mode, probe Brown wire in Blue connector. Push washer button and observe DRB-II screen. If voltage reading is 10 volts or more, replace body controller. If voltage reading is less than 10 volts, repair Brown wire for open condition. Perform VERIFICATION TEST.
3) Remove, but do not disconnect, wiper/washer switch. With DRB-II in voltmeter mode, backprobe B4 cavity of wiper/washer switch. *See Fig. 4.* Push washer button and observe DRB-II. If voltage is less than 10 volts, replace wiper/washer switch. Perform VERIFICATION TEST. If voltage is 10 volts or more, proceed to next step.
4) Disconnect washer pump harness connector and insect for damage. Repair as required. If connector is okay, probe Brown wire with DRB-II voltmeter probe. Push washer button and observe DRB-II. If voltage is less than 10 volts, repair Brown wire for open condition to splice. If voltage is 10 volts or more, proceed to next step.
5) Place DRB-II in ohmmeter mode. Probe Black wire in washer pump connector. If resistance reading is 10 ohms or more, repair Black wire for open condition. If resistance is less than 10 ohms, replace washer pump. Perform VERIFICATION TEST.

VERIFICATION TEST

Caravan, Town & Country, & Voyager – Reconnect all components. Actuate wiper/washer system and ensure all modes operate correctly. If system operates okay, repair is complete. If system is still inoperative, return to start of testing.

DELAY WIPER SYSTEM

Wipers Do Not Delay With Switch In DELAY Position (Dakota, Pickup, Ramcharger & RWD Van) – 1) Ensure motor will park when switch is in OFF or PARK position. Place switch in LOW position. Disconnect 8-wire connector from intermittent wipe control unit. Check contacts for damage or corrosion.

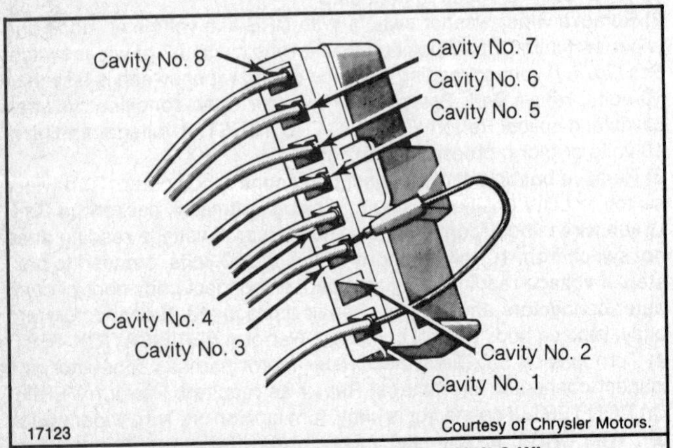
Cavity No. 8
Cavity No. 7
Cavity No. 6
Cavity No. 5
Cavity No. 4
Cavity No. 3
Cavity No. 2
Cavity No. 1
17123
Courtesy of Chrysler Motors.

Fig. 3: Identifying Intermittent Wipe Control Unit 8-Wire Connector Terminals

2) Connect test light between connector cavity No. 1 and cavity No. 3. *See Fig. 3.* Test light should glow once every cycle. If test light glows erratically, replace defective control unit.
3) If test light does not glow at all, check for voltage between motor terminals P1 and P2. *See Fig. 2.* If test light glows when connected at wiper motor terminals, check wiring.
Wipers Do Not Operate With Switch In DELAY Position (Dakota, Pickup, Ramcharger & RWD Van) – 1) Disconnect 8-wire connector from intermittent wipe control unit. Place switch in maximum DELAY position. Connect voltmeter between connector cavities No. 4 and No. 6. If voltmeter reads zero volt, check switch and wiring. *See Fig. 3.*
2) If voltage is 10-15 volts, place column switch in LOW position. Connect positive lead of voltmeter to cavity No. 3 and negative lead to cavity No. 4. If voltmeter reads 10-15 volts, replace wipe control unit. If voltmeter reads zero volt, check and repair wiring.
Wipers Do Not Operate In Intermittent Mode (Dakota, Pickup, Ramcharger & RWD Van) – 1) Disconnect 8-wire connector from intermittent wipe control unit. Inspect contacts for damaged or corroded terminals. Place switch in maximum DELAY position.
2) Connect voltmeter between connector cavity No. 4 and cavity No. 8. *See Fig. 3.* If voltmeter reads zero volt, check switch and wiring. If voltmeter reads 10-15 volts, replace wipe control unit.
Excessive Delay Or Inadequate Variation In DELAY Mode (Dakota, Pickup, Ramcharger & RWD Van) – Minimum delay (delay control at extreme counterclockwise position, before LOW speed detent) should be 1/2 - 2 seconds. Maximum delay (first position after OFF detent, in counterclockwise direction) should be 10-30 seconds. If there is excessive delay or no variation in delay, replace switch.
Wipers Do Not Operate With Wash Control Operated During DELAY Mode (Dakota, Pickup, Ramcharger & RWD Van) – Disconnect 8-wire connector from intermittent wipe control unit. Connect voltmeter between connector cavity No. 4 and cavity No. 7. *See Fig. 3.* Depress wash switch. If voltmeter reads zero volt, check switch and wiring. If voltage is 10-15 volts, replace wipe control unit.
Wipers Start Erratically During DELAY Mode (Dakota, Pickup, Ramcharger & RWD Van) – Ensure ground connection at instrument panel is tight and making good contact. Ensure wiper motor ground strap is making good contact and mounting bolts are tight. Ensure wiring ground connections for intermittent wipe control unit and wiper switch are tight. If problem still exists, replace wipe control unit.

NOTE: For switch testing purposes, terminal identification is molded into switch at plug connection.

REAR WIPER MOTOR

Caravan, Town & Country, & Voyager – 1) Remove liftgate wiper motor. With ignition on, check for battery voltage at Blue wire. With ignition and liftgate wiper switch in ON position, check for battery voltage at Blue and Brown wires. If voltage does not exist in either step, check fuse, liftgate wiper switch and wiring.
2) With ignition on and liftgate wiper switch in OFF position, check for battery voltage between Blue and Brown wires. If voltage does not exist, check ground wire to liftgate switch. If battery voltage exists, replace liftgate wiper motor.

WINDSHIELD WIPER/WASHER SWITCH

Caravan, Town & Country, & Voyager – Remove windshield wiper/washer pod switch. See WINDSHIELD WIPER/WASHER SWITCH under REMOVAL & INSTALLATION. Disconnect harness connectors. Using an ohmmeter, test for continuity between specified terminals. See WINDSHIELD WIPER/WASHER POD SWITCH CONTINUITY table. If continuity is not as specified in any test, replace switch. *See Fig. 4.*

Dakota, Pickup, Ramcharger & RWD Van – Remove windshield wiper/washer switch. See WINDSHIELD WIPER/WASHER SWITCH under REMOVAL & INSTALLATION. Using an ohmmeter, test windshield wiper/washer switch continuity. *See Fig. 5.*

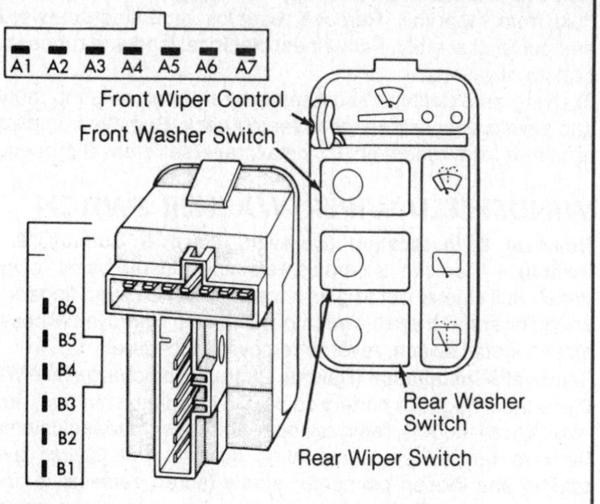
A1 A2 A3 A4 A5 A6 A7
Front Wiper Control
Front Washer Switch
B6
B5
B4
B3
B2
B1
Rear Washer Switch
Rear Wiper Switch

91B13491 Courtesy of Chrysler Motors.

Fig. 4: Identifying Windshield Wiper/Washer POD Switch (Caravan, Town & Country, & Voyager)

WINDSHIELD WIPER/WASHER POD SWITCH CONTINUITY

Switch Position	Terminals
Front Wiper/Washer	
Off	A6 & A4
Maximum Delay	A7 & A5, A3 & B3, [1] A1 & B3
Minimum Delay	A7 & A5, A3 & B3, [2] A1 & B3
Maximum-To-Minimum Delay	A7 & A5, A3 & B3, [3] A1 & B3
Minimum-To-Maximum Delay	A7 & A5, A3 & B3, [4] A1 & B3
Low	A4 & B3
High	A2 & B3
Washer	B3 & B4
Rear Wiper/Washer	
Wiper	B2 & B5
Washer	B5 & B1

[1] – 210,000-390,000 ohms.
[2] – 350-650 ohms.
[3] – Resistance decreases as control is moved from maximum to minimum delay.
[4] – Resistance increases as control is moved from minimum to maximum delay.

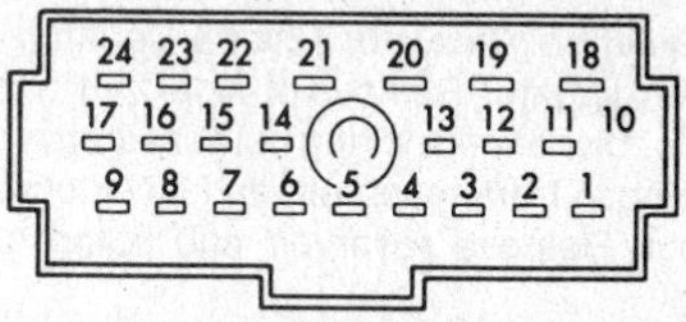
24 23 22 21 20 19 18
17 16 15 14 13 12 11 10
9 8 7 6 5 4 3 2 1

WINDSHIELD WIPER/WASHER SWITCH PINS

TWO SPEED WIPER SWITCH CONTINUITY CHART

SWITCH POSITION	CONTINUITY BETWEEN
OFF & PARK	PIN 1 & PIN 2
LOW	PIN 1 & PIN 4
HIGH	PIN 4 & PIN 5
WASH	PIN 3 & PIN 4

SWITCH POSITION	CONTINUITY BETWEEN
OFF	PIN 6 AND PIN 7
DELAY	PIN 8 AND PIN 9 PIN 2 AND PIN 4 PIN 1 AND PIN 2 PIN 1 AND PIN 4
LOW	PIN 4 AND PIN 6
HIGH	PIN 4 AND PIN 5
WASH	PIN 3 AND PIN 4

*RESISTANCE AT MAXIMUM DELAY POSITION SHOULD BE BETWEEN 270,000 OHMS AND 330,000 OHMS.

*RESISTANCE AT MINIMUM DELAY POSITION SHOULD BE ZERO WITH OHMMETER SET ON HIGH OHM SCALE.

91A14324 Courtesy of Chrysler Motors.

Fig. 5: Windshield Wiper/Washer Switch Continuity Test Charts (Dakota, Pickup, Ramcharger & RWD Van)

REMOVAL & INSTALLATION

REAR WIPER MOTOR

Removal (Caravan, Town & Country, & Voyager) – Disconnect battery negative cable. Install Wiper Arm Remover (C-3982) on wiper arm. Lift and remove arm from output shaft. Raise liftgate. Remove liftgate trim panel. Remove 5 rear wiper motor mounting screws. Disconnect wiring harness from rear wiper motor. Remove rear wiper motor.

Installation – To install, reverse removal procedure. Mount rear wiper arm so that tip of wiper blade is parallel to and is about 1.5" (38 mm) away from lower edge of liftgate glass. Operate rear wiper. Tip of wiper blade should be .88-2.38" (22-60 mm) above lower edge of liftgate glass.

WINDSHIELD WIPER MOTOR

Removal & Installation (Caravan, Town & Country, & Voyager) – 1) Disconnect negative battery cable. With wipers in park position, remove wiper arms. Open hood and remove cowl top plenum grille. Disconnect washer hoses from connectors.

2) Remove cowl plenum chamber plastic screen. Remove hose connectors and wiper pivot retaining bolts. Push pivots down into plenum chamber. Remove nut from wiper motor output shaft and remove linkage assembly.

3) Disconnect wiper motor wiring harness. Remove mounting bolt and nuts from wiper motor. Remove wiper motor. Clamp motor crank in a vise and remove nut from end of motor shaft. Be careful NOT to rotate motor from PARK position.

4) Remove crank from motor. To install, reverse removal procedure. Position left and right wiper arms at least 1" (25 mm) above cowl, with wiper motor in park position.

Removal & Installation (Dakota) – 1) Disconnect negative battery cable. Disconnect wiring from wiper motor. Remove nuts securing wiper motor. Remove cowl screen. Hold drive crank with a wrench and remove crank nut.

2) Remove drive crank. Remove wiper motor. To install, reverse removal procedure. Position right tip of left wiper arm 3.19" (81 mm) and right tip of right wiper arm 3.7" (94 mm) above cowl, with wiper motor in PARK position.

Removal & Installation (Pickup, Ramcharger & RWD Van) – 1) Disconnect battery negative cable. Disconnect wiring connector from motor. Remove wiper motor mounting screws. Lower motor far enough to gain access to crank arm-to-drive link retainer bushing. Remove crank arm by prying retainer bushing from crank arm pin.

2) Remove wiper motor. Remove crank arm-to-motor drive shaft nut. Remove crank arm from motor. To install, reverse removal procedure. Position right tip of left wiper blade at least 1.61" (41 mm) and right tip of right wiper blade 2.12" (54 mm) from lower windshield weather stripping when motor is in park position.

1991 SAFETY EQUIPMENT
Wiper/Washer Systems (Cont.)

REAR WASHER PUMP

Removal & Installation (Caravan, Town & Country, & Voyager) – 1) Unlock and open liftgate. Remove 2 side trim panel and reservoir mounting screws. Disconnect wiring harness from washer pump. Disconnect washer hose from reservoir, and block outlet to prevent fluid from running out. Remove reservoir and pump assembly through access hole.

2) Work filler tube off reservoir and empty reservoir. Loosen pump filter and nut through reservoir neck. Disconnect outside portion of pump. Remove inner and outer portions of pump and remove pump. To install, reverse removal procedure.

WINDSHIELD WASHER PUMP

Removal & Installation (Caravan, Town & Country, & Voyager) – 1) Drain fluid from reservoir. Remove reservoir mounting screws, reservoir and pump assembly. Disconnect electrical lead and rubber hose from bottom of pump.

2) Note position of pump. Loosen pump filter and nut by reaching through reservoir neck using an extension and deep socket. Disconnect outside portion of pump. Remove inner and outer portions of pump and remove pump. To install, reverse removal procedure.

Removal & Installation (Dakota) – 1) Drain fluid from reservoir. Remove reservoir mounting screws, reservoir and pump assembly.

2) Disconnect electrical lead and rubber hose from bottom of pump. Pry pump away from reservoir, being careful not to puncture reservoir. Remove and discard grommet. To install, reverse removal procedure.

Removal & Installation (Pickup, Ramcharger & RWD Van) – 1) Drain fluid from reservoir. Remove reservoir mounting screws, reservoir and pump assembly. Disconnect electrical lead and rubber hose from bottom of pump.

2) Using an extension and deep socket, remove pump mounting nut and plastic washer through reservoir neck. Remove pump and rubber grommet from reservoir. To install, reverse removal procedure.

WINDSHIELD WIPER/WASHER SWITCH

Removal & Installation (Caravan, Town & Country, & Voyager Switch) – Remove 8 screws retaining cluster bezel to instrument panel. Pull cluster out to gain access to switch snap fingers. Depress snap fingers and push switch out of bezel. Remove harness connector. To install switch, reverse removal procedure.

Removal & Installation (Dakota, Pickup, Ramcharger & RWD Van) – Disconnect negative battery cable. On tilt column models, remove tilt lever. On all models, remove upper and lower steering column covers. Remove tamper proof mounting screws. Pull switch away from column and loosen connector screw (screw remains in connector). Remove switch. To install switch, reverse removal procedure.

OVERHAUL

WIPER MOTORS

Windshield and rear wiper motors are serviced as a complete units. If either motor is defective, replace entire assembly.

WIRING DIAGRAMS

See appropriate chassis wiring diagram in WIRING DIAGRAMS.

1991 ENGINES
2.5L 4-Cylinder

Caravan, Dakota, Voyager

***NOTE:* For engine repair procedures not covered in this article, see ENGINE OVERHAUL PROCEDURES article in GENERAL INFORMATION.**

ENGINE IDENTIFICATION

Engine may be identified by eighth character of Vehicle Identification Number (VIN) stamped on a plate on top of instrument panel, at lower left corner of windshield.

ENGINE IDENTIFICATION CODE

Engine	Code
2.5L TBI	K

SPECIAL ENGINE MARKS

Information identifying undersize and oversize components will be found at various locations on engine. It is decoded as follows:

- Oversize camshaft journals are indicated by Green camshaft bearing caps, and "O/S J" stamped behind oil gallery plug on rear of cylinder head.
- Green camshaft, with "O/S J" stamped on end of camshaft, indicates oversize camshaft journal diameter.

ADJUSTMENTS

VALVE CLEARANCE ADJUSTMENT

Hydraulic lash adjusters are used. No valve adjustment is required.

DRY LASH

***NOTE:* Dry lash should be checked when valve components are serviced.**

1) Dry lash is amount of clearance between camshaft base circle and rocker arm pad. Lash adjuster must be completely collapsed and free of oil when checking clearance.
2) Remove retainer cap from lash adjuster. Disassemble and drain oil. Install lash adjuster when completely collapsed. Using feeler gauge, measure clearance between camshaft base circle and rocker arm pad.
3) Clearance should be .024-.060" (.61-1.52 mm). If clearance is not within specification, check for wear on related parts and replace as necessary. Fill lash adjuster with engine oil. Reassemble using NEW retainer cap. Allow 10 minutes for lash adjuster to bleed down before rotating camshaft.

REMOVAL & INSTALLATION

***NOTE:* For reassembly reference, label all electrical connectors, vacuum hoses and fuel lines before removal. Also place mating marks on engine hood and other major assemblies before removal.**

FUEL PRESSURE RELEASE

***CAUTION:* Fuel system is under pressure. Pressure must be released before servicing fuel system components.**

1) Loosen fuel tank cap to release pressure. Disconnect injector wiring harness from engine wiring harness. Connect jumper wire from terminal No. 1 of injector harness to ground. *See Fig. 1.*
2) Connect another jumper wire to terminal No. 2 of injector harness. Touch jumper wire to positive battery terminal for no more than 5 seconds to release fuel pressure. Remove jumper wires and reconnect wiring harness.

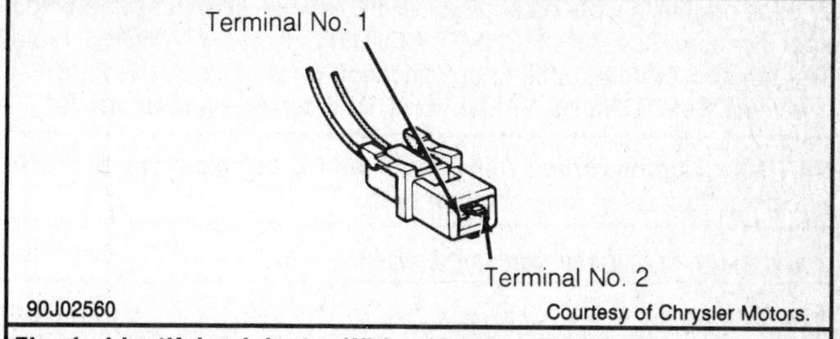
Terminal No. 1
Terminal No. 2
90J02560
Courtesy of Chrysler Motors.

Fig. 1: Identifying Injector Wiring Harness Terminals

COOLING SYSTEM BLEEDING

Remove vent plug from top of thermostat housing. Fill cooling system. Allow air to bleed from cooling system. Install vent plug once coolant reaches thermostat housing level. Tighten vent plug to specification. See TORQUE SPECIFICATIONS table at end of article. Finish filling cooling system.

ENGINE

***NOTE:* Remove engine with transaxle or transmission remaining in the vehicle.**

Removal (Caravan & Voyager) – 1) Release fuel pressure. See FUEL PRESSURE RELEASE under REMOVAL & INSTALLATION. Disconnect battery. Scribe hood hinge location on hood for reassembly. Remove hood. Drain cooling system. Disconnect necessary coolant hoses, fuel lines, electrical connections and vacuum hoses.
2) Remove radiator, shroud and fan. Remove air cleaner with hoses. Remove A/C compressor and power steering pump with hoses attached and set aside (if equipped).
3) Remove oil filter, alternator and starter. Disconnect accelerator cable. Remove alternator. Remove transaxle lower case cover. Disconnect exhaust pipe at manifold.
4) Reference mark flexplate to torque converter. Remove torque converter-to-flexplate bolts. Attach "C" clamp to bottom front edge of torque converter housing to secure torque converter.
5) Support transaxle and attach lifting hoist to engine. Remove right inner splash shield. Disconnect ground strap. To lower engine from engine compartment, separate right (timing belt side) mount bracket from bracket at front of cylinder block. To raise engine from engine compartment, remove long through bolt from right (timing belt side) mount bracket. Separate insulator from right side rail.

***CAUTION:* If removing insulator from right side rail, mark insulator-to-side rail position for reassembly reference. Insulator must be installed in original position.**

6) Remove transaxle-to-cylinder block bolts. Remove front engine mount bolt. Remove insulator through bolt of left mount from inside fenderwell. Insulator bracket-to-transaxle bolts may be removed instead of through bolt. Remove engine from vehicle.
Installation – 1) To install, reverse removal procedure. DO NOT tighten engine mount bolts until all bolts are installed. If vertical bolts on right or left upper mount on frame rail were loosened, axle shaft length must be checked.
2) To determine axle shaft length, measure distance between inner edge of outboard boot and inner edge of inboard boot at 6 o'clock position. *See Fig. 2.*

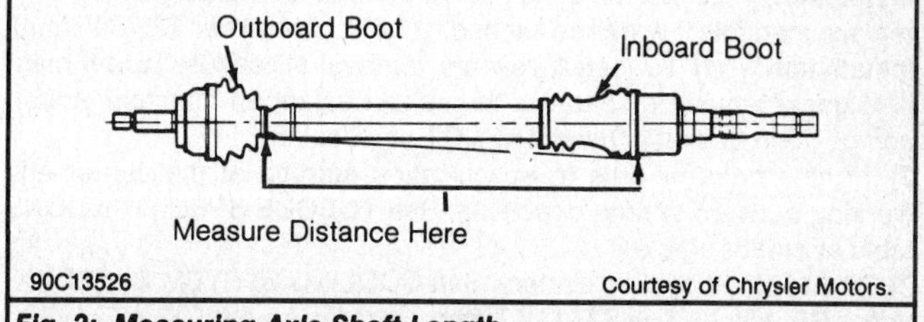
Outboard Boot
Inboard Boot
Measure Distance Here
90C13526
Courtesy of Chrysler Motors.

Fig. 2: Measuring Axle Shaft Length

1991 ENGINES
2.5L 4-Cylinder (Cont.)

3) Slide engine in slots on engine mounts so axle shaft length is within specification. See AXLE SHAFT LENGTH SPECIFICATIONS table. Tighten all mounting bolts to specification once correct axle length is obtained. See TORQUE SPECIFICATIONS table at end of article.

CAUTION: Tighten vertical bolt in right (timing belt side) mount bracket before tightening long through bolt.

AXLE SHAFT LENGTH SPECIFICATIONS

Application	In. (mm)
Right Axle Shaft	20.5-20.9 (521-531)
Left Axle Shaft	9.0-9.4 (229-239)

4) Ensure reference mark is aligned on torque converter and flexplate. Fill and bleed cooling system. See COOLING SYSTEM BLEEDING under REMOVAL & INSTALLATION.

CAUTION: Fuel system is under pressure. Pressure must be released before disconnecting fuel system components.

Removal (Dakota) - 1) Release fuel pressure. See FUEL PRESSURE RELEASE under REMOVAL & INSTALLATION. Remove battery and air cleaner. Scribe hood hinge location on hood for reassembly reference. Remove hood. Drain cooling system. Disconnect necessary coolant hoses, fuel lines, electrical connections and vacuum hoses.
2) Remove radiator and shroud. Discharge A/C system and remove necessary A/C hoses. Plug A/C hoses to prevent contamination. Remove throttle body and linkage. Disconnect power steering hoses.
3) Remove starter, alternator, charcoal canister and horns. Raise and support vehicle. Disconnect exhaust pipe at manifold. Remove engine mount bolts. Install lifting fixture. Raise engine until front engine insulators clear crossmember retaining brackets. Support transmission with floor jack.
4) Disconnect clutch release assembly. Remove transmission-to-clutch housing bolts. Move engine forward until transmission shaft clears clutch disc. Lift engine from vehicle.
Installation - To install, reverse removal procedure. Tighten bolts to specification. See TORQUE SPECIFICATIONS table at end of article. Fill and bleed cooling system. See COOLING SYSTEM BLEEDING under REMOVAL & INSTALLATION.

INTAKE & EXHAUST MANIFOLDS

NOTE: Exhaust and intake manifolds use a one-piece mounting gasket. Both manifolds must be removed to perform service on either manifold.

Removal (Caravan & Voyager) - 1) Release fuel pressure. See FUEL PRESSURE RELEASE under REMOVAL & INSTALLATION. Disconnect negative battery cable. Drain cooling system. Remove air cleaner. Disconnect necessary wiring, fuel lines and linkage at throttle body.
2) Remove drive belt from power steering. Remove brake booster vacuum hose from intake manifold. Disconnect EGR tube from intake manifold. Disconnect coolant hoses from coolant crossover.
3) Raise and support vehicle. Disconnect exhaust pipe from exhaust manifold. Remove power steering pump with hoses attached and secure aside. Remove intake manifold bolts.
4) Lower vehicle. Remove exhaust manifold nuts. Remove intake and exhaust manifolds.
Inspection - Check manifold gasket surface for warpage. Repair or replace manifold if warpage exceeds .006" (.15 mm) per 12" (305 mm).
Installation - 1) To install, reverse removal procedure. Steel manifold gasket must be coated with gasket sealant on manifold side. If composition gasket is used, DO NOT use sealant.
2) Tighten bolts or nuts to specification starting at the center and working outward in both directions. See TORQUE SPECIFICATIONS table at end of article.
3) Fill and bleed cooling system. See COOLING SYSTEM BLEEDING under REMOVAL & INSTALLATION.

Removal (Dakota) - 1) Release fuel pressure. See FUEL PRESSURE RELEASE under REMOVAL & INSTALLATION. Disconnect negative battery cable. Drain cooling system. Remove air cleaner. Disconnect necessary wiring, fuel lines and linkage at throttle body.
2) Remove throttle body. Remove power steering and air pump support bracket. Remove brake booster vacuum hose from intake manifold. Remove diverter valve assembly. Disconnect air injection tube from exhaust manifold. Disconnect coolant hoses from coolant crossover.
3) Raise and support vehicle. Remove EGR tube. Disconnect exhaust pipe from exhaust manifold. Remove intake manifold bolts. Lower vehicle. Remove exhaust manifold nuts. Remove intake and exhaust manifolds.
Inspection - Check manifold gasket surface for warpage. Repair or replace manifold if warpage exceeds .006" (.15 mm) per 12" (305 mm).
Installation - 1) To install, reverse removal procedure. Install new manifold gaskets; coat gaskets with gasket sealant on manifold side. If composition gasket is used, DO NOT use sealant.
2) Tighten bolts or nuts to specification starting at the center and working outward in both directions. See TORQUE SPECIFICATIONS table at end of article.
3) Fill and bleed cooling system. See COOLING SYSTEM BLEEDING under REMOVAL & INSTALLATION.

CYLINDER HEAD

NOTE: Camshaft sprocket must be separated from camshaft when removing and installing camshaft or cylinder head. To maintain camshaft, intermediate shaft and crankshaft timing during service procedures, timing belt must remain installed on camshaft sprocket while assembly is suspended under a continuous light tension. See Fig. 3.

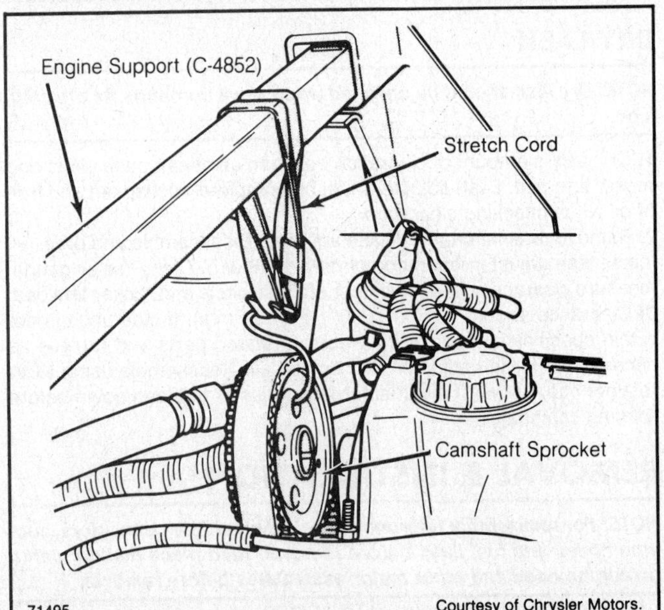
Engine Support (C-4852)
Stretch Cord
Camshaft Sprocket
71495
Courtesy of Chrysler Motors.

Fig. 3: Maintaining Timing with Camshaft Sprocket Disconnected

Removal - 1) Release fuel pressure. See FUEL PRESSURE RELEASE under REMOVAL & INSTALLATION. Disconnect negative battery cable. Drain cooling system.
2) Remove air cleaner. Disconnect necessary vacuum hoses, linkages, coolant hoses and electrical connections. On Caravan and Voyager, remove power steering pump and secure aside.
3) On all models, disconnect exhaust pipe from exhaust manifold. Disconnect dipstick tube from thermostat housing and rotate bracket from stud. Remove all drive belts. On A/C-equipped models, remove A/C compressor with lines connected and secure aside.
4) On all models, remove alternator pivot bolt. Disconnect wiring and remove alternator. Remove A/C compressor idler pulley (if equipped). Remove side mounting bolts No. 1, 4, 5, 6 and 7 from the solid mount A/C compressor bracket. *See Fig. 4.*

1991 ENGINES
2.5L 4-Cylinder (Cont.)

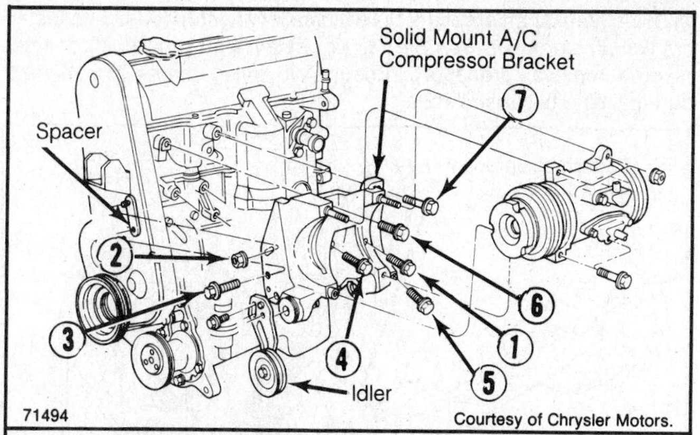
Solid Mount A/C
Compressor Bracket
Spacer
Idler
71494
Courtesy of Chrysler Motors.

Fig. 4: Removing & Installing Solid Mount A/C Compressor Bracket

5) Remove front mounting nut No. 2 and remove (or loosen) front bolt No. 3. Coolant will leak from bolt hole. Rotate solid mount A/C compressor bracket away from engine, and slide on stud (No. 2 mounting stud) until free.

6) Front mounting bolt and spacer will be removed with bracket. Remove upper timing belt cover. Using Sprocket Holder (C-4687) with Adapter (C-4687-1), hold camshaft sprocket and remove sprocket bolt. *See Fig. 5.*

7) Remove camshaft sprocket, maintaining camshaft, intermediate shaft, and crankshaft timing with timing belt. It may be necessary to remove timing belt. See TIMING BELT under REMOVAL & INSTALLATION.

8) Remove valve cover and curtain (if equipped). *See Fig. 7.* Remove cylinder head bolts in proper sequence. *See Fig. 6.* Remove cylinder head and gasket.

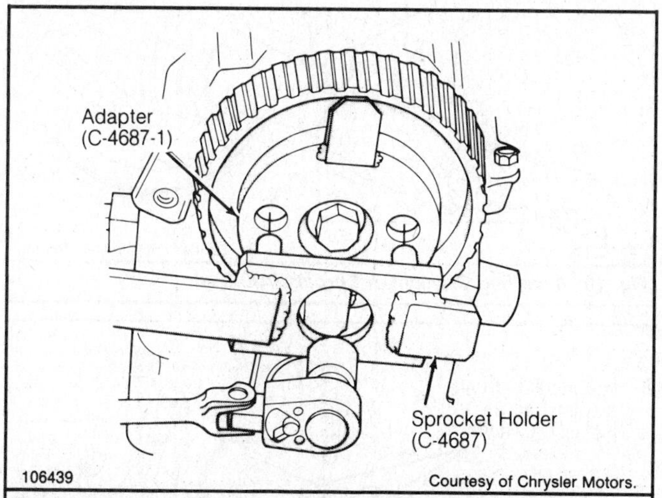
Adapter
(C-4687-1)
Sprocket Holder
(C-4687)
106439
Courtesy of Chrysler Motors.

Fig. 5: Removing Camshaft or Intermediate Shaft Sprocket

Inspection – Check cylinder head warpage. Warpage must not exceed specification. See CYLINDER HEAD table under ENGINE SPECIFICATIONS at end of article. If cylinder head or camshaft is serviced, ensure oversized camshaft is used in cylinder head with oversized bores. See SPECIAL ENGINE MARKS at beginning of article.

CAUTION: Use proper cylinder head bolts when installing cylinder head. Cylinder head bolt diameter is 11 millimeters and is identified by "11" on bolt head. Ten-millimeter bolts will thread into 11-mm bolt hole, but cylinder block threads will be stripped if used.

Installation – 1) Hold a straightedge across threads of cylinder head bolts. Ensure cylinder head bolt threads contact straightedge in all areas. If threads fail to contact straightedge, cylinder head bolts are stretched and must be replaced.

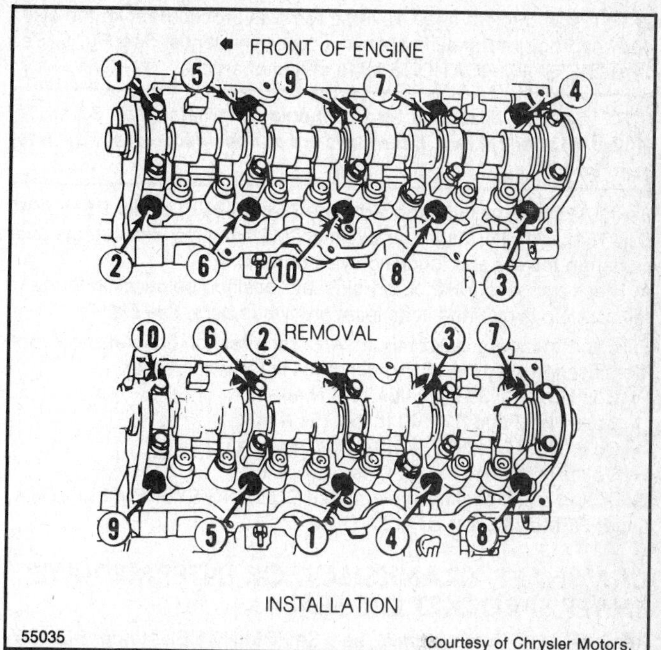
FRONT OF ENGINE
REMOVAL
INSTALLATION
55035
Courtesy of Chrysler Motors.

Fig. 6: Cylinder Head Bolt Removal & Installation Sequence

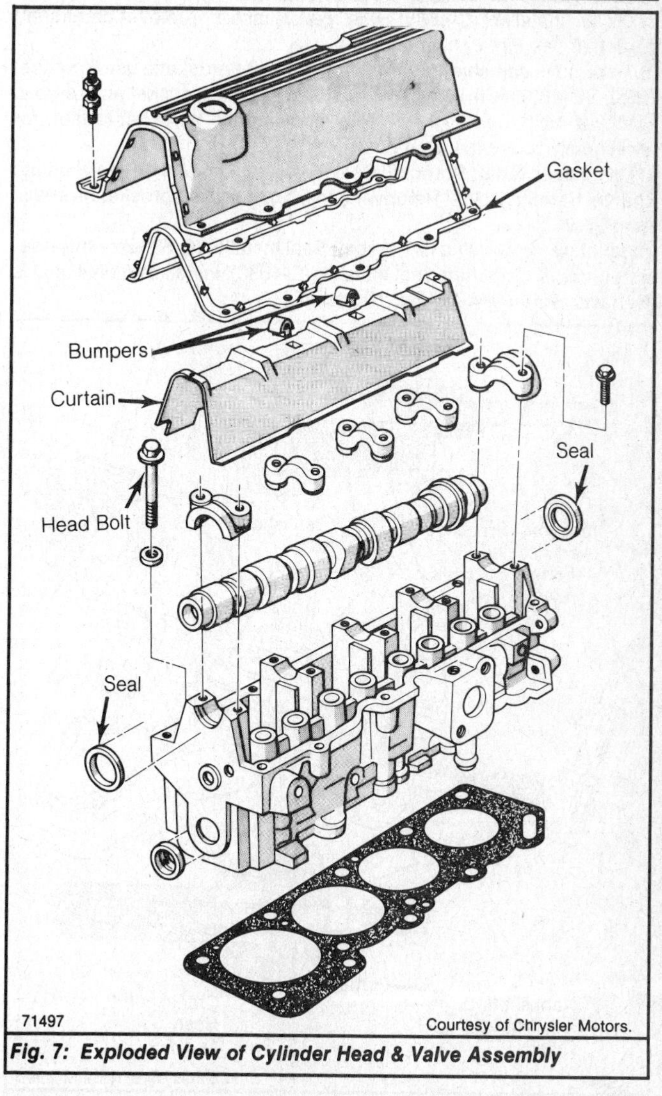
Gasket
Bumpers
Curtain
Seal
Head Bolt
Seal
71497
Courtesy of Chrysler Motors.

Fig. 7: Exploded View of Cylinder Head & Valve Assembly

1991 ENGINES
2.5L 4-Cylinder (Cont.)

2) To install cylinder head, reverse removal procedure. Tighten cylinder head bolts to specification in proper sequence. *See Fig. 6.* See TORQUE SPECIFICATIONS table at end of article.

NOTE: Cylinder head bolt torque should be greater than 90 ft. lbs. (122 N.m) after 1/4 turn. If torque is not as specified, replace cylinder head bolt.

3) Adjust timing belt (if removed). See TIMING BELT under REMOVAL & INSTALLATION. Install curtain, manifold side first, with cutouts over camshaft towers and touching cylinder head.

4) Press opposite (distributor) side into position below cylinder head rail. Curtain is retained in its location by bumpers. *See Fig. 7.*

5) When installing solid mount A/C compressor bracket, note bolt identification. *See Fig. 4.* Tighten bolts in following order:

- Bolt No. 1 - 30 INCH lbs. (3.3 N.m)
- Bolts No. 2 and 3 - 40 ft. lbs. (54 N.m)
- Bolts No. 1, 4 and 5 - 40 ft. lbs. (54 N.m)
- Bolts No. 6 and 7 - 40 ft. lbs. (54 N.m)

6) Fill and bleed cooling system. See COOLING SYSTEM BLEEDING under REMOVAL & INSTALLATION.

CAMSHAFT, CRANKSHAFT OR INTERMEDIATE SHAFT SPROCKET OIL SEAL

Removal - 1) Remove timing belt. See TIMING BELT under REMOVAL & INSTALLATION. For crankshaft sprocket seal replacement, remove crankshaft sprocket retaining bolt. Using Crankshaft Sprocket Puller/Installer (C-4685) with puller insert, remove crankshaft sprocket. *See Fig. 8.*

2) To remove camshaft or intermediate shaft sprockets, use Sprocket Holder (C-4687) with Adapter (C-4687-1) to hold sprocket and remove sprocket bolt. *See Fig. 5.* Note direction of sprocket offset for reassembly reference. Remove sprocket.

3) Using Crankshaft Sprocket Seal Remover (C-6341) or Intermediate Shaft & Camshaft Seal Remover (C-4679), remove sprocket oil seals. *See Fig. 9.*

Installation - 1) Using Crankshaft Seal Installer (C-6342) or Intermediate Shaft & Camshaft Seal Installer (C-4680), install seal until seal is even with surface. *See Figs. 10 and 11.*

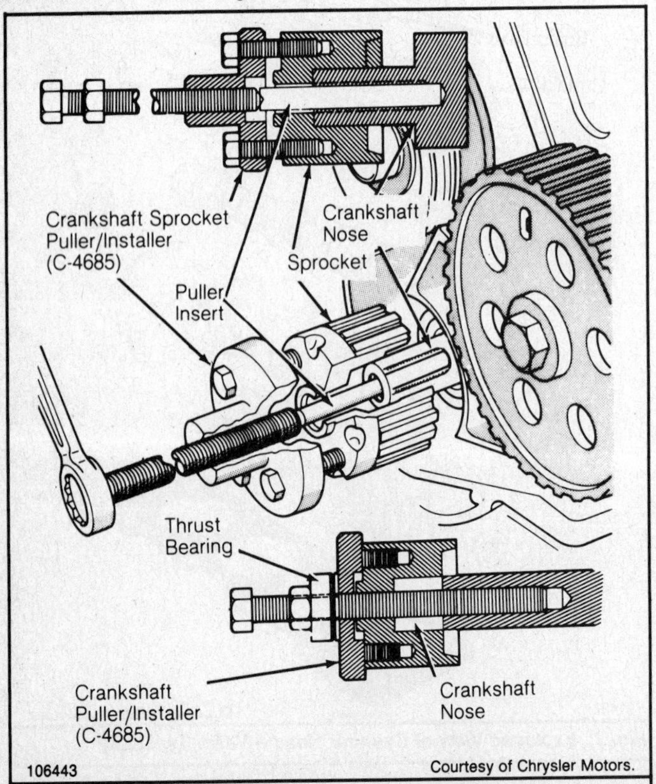
Crankshaft Sprocket Puller/Installer (C-4685)
Crankshaft Nose
Sprocket
Puller Insert
Thrust Bearing
Crankshaft Puller/Installer (C-4685)
Crankshaft Nose
106443
Courtesy of Chrysler Motors.

Fig. 8: Removing & Installing Crankshaft Sprocket

2) Using crankshaft sprocket puller/installer and thrust bearing, install crankshaft sprocket. *See Fig. 8.* To install remaining components, reverse removal procedure. Ensure all timing marks are aligned during timing belt installation.

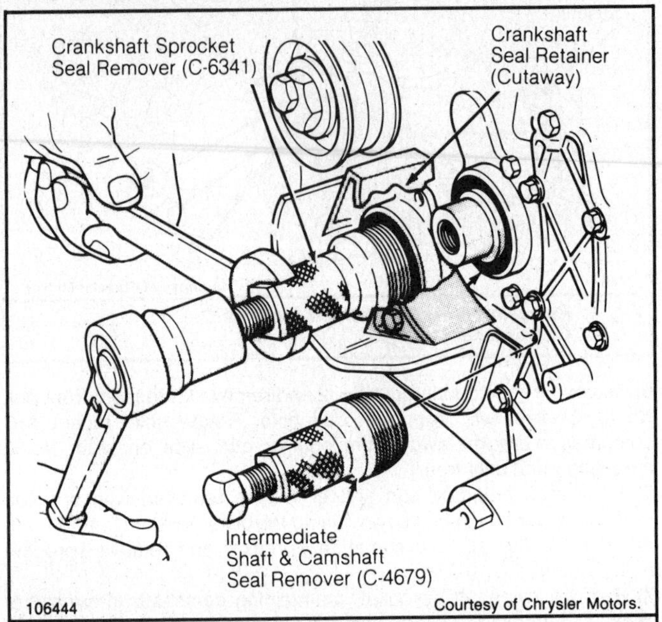
Crankshaft Sprocket Seal Remover (C-6341)
Crankshaft Seal Retainer (Cutaway)
Intermediate Shaft & Camshaft Seal Remover (C-4679)
106444
Courtesy of Chrysler Motors.

Fig. 9: Removing Sprocket Oil Seals

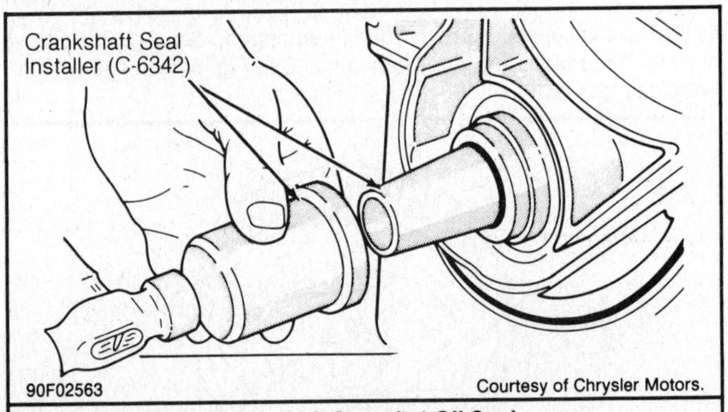
Crankshaft Seal Installer (C-6342)
90F02563
Courtesy of Chrysler Motors.

Fig. 10: Installing Crankshaft Sprocket Oil Seal

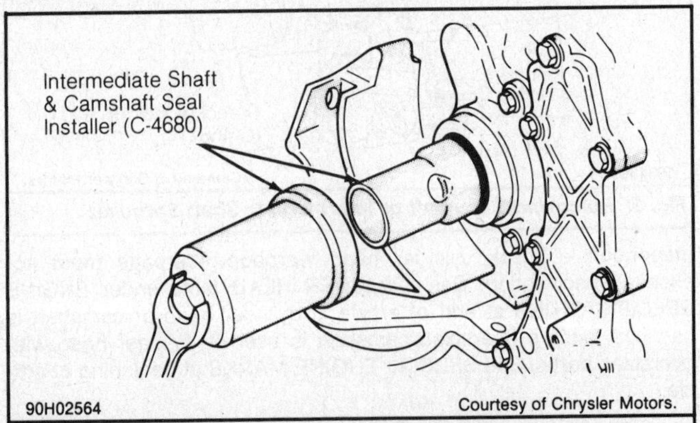
Intermediate Shaft & Camshaft Seal Installer (C-4680)
90H02564
Courtesy of Chrysler Motors.

Fig. 11: Installing Intermediate or Camshaft Sprocket Oil Seal

TIMING BELT

Removal - 1) Disconnect negative battery cable. On Caravan and Voyager, remove right inner splash shield. On all models, remove accessory drive belts.

2) Remove water pump and crankshaft pulleys. Remove upper and lower timing belt covers. *See Fig. 12.* Support engine with a floor jack.

3) Remove right engine mount bolt and raise engine slightly. Loosen timing belt tensioner bolt. Rotate hex area on timing belt tensioner, and remove timing belt.

CAUTION: If timing belt is to be reused, mark timing belt for direction of rotation for reassembly reference.

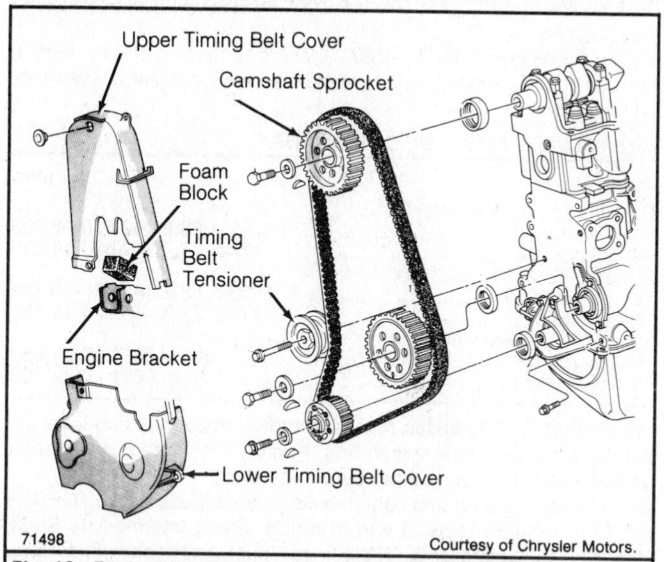
Upper Timing Belt Cover
Camshaft Sprocket
Foam Block
Timing Belt Tensioner
Engine Bracket
Lower Timing Belt Cover
71498
Courtesy of Chrysler Motors.

Fig. 12: Exploded View of Timing Belt & Components

Installation - 1) Remove spark plugs. Place No. 1 cylinder on TDC. Align timing marks on crankshaft and intermediate shaft sprockets. *See Fig. 13.* Rotate camshaft sprocket until 2 holes on sprocket hub align with camshaft bearing cap-to-cylinder head parting line. Small hole on camshaft sprocket must be at 12 o'clock position.

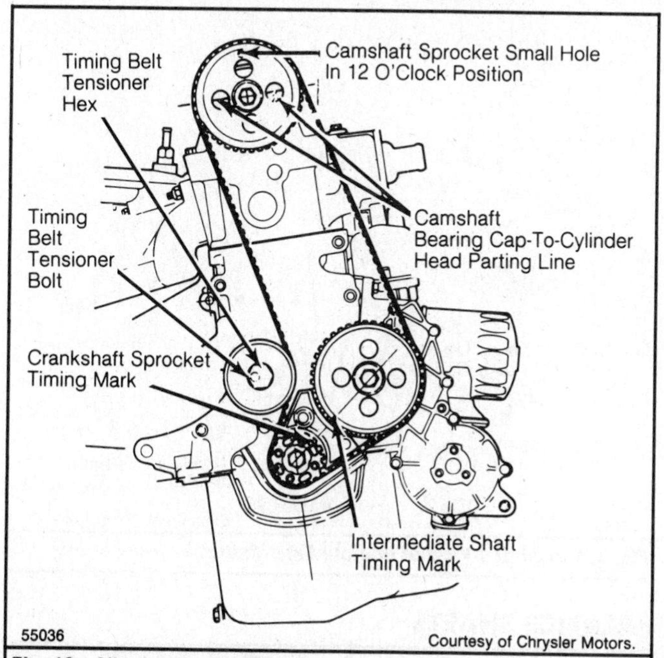
Timing Belt Tensioner Hex
Camshaft Sprocket Small Hole In 12 O'Clock Position
Timing Belt Tensioner Bolt
Camshaft Bearing Cap-To-Cylinder Head Parting Line
Crankshaft Sprocket Timing Mark
Intermediate Shaft Timing Mark
55036
Courtesy of Chrysler Motors.

Fig. 13: Aligning Timing Marks

2) Install timing belt. Ensure timing belt is installed in original direction of rotation. Install Timing Belt Tensioner Wrench (C-4703) horizontally on large hex of timing belt tensioner.

3) Loosen timing belt tensioner bolt (if necessary) to reset timing belt tensioner to within a 15-degree axis of timing belt tensioner wrench horizontal position. *See Fig. 14.*

4) Rotate crankshaft clockwise 2 complete revolutions to TDC. Tighten timing belt tensioner bolt to specification while holding timing belt tensioner wrench in position. See TORQUE SPECIFICATIONS table at end of article.

5) Ensure all timing marks align. To install remaining components, reverse removal procedure.

CAUTION: DO NOT rotate crankshaft counterclockwise, or rotate engine using camshaft or intermediate shaft sprocket bolts.

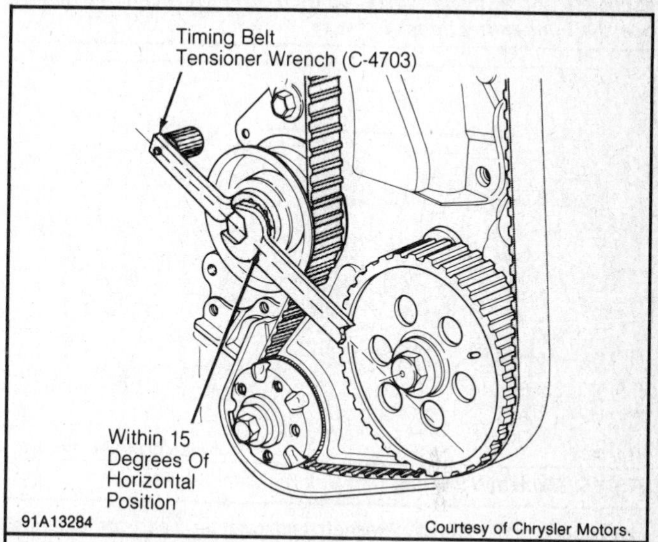
Timing Belt Tensioner Wrench (C-4703)
Within 15 Degrees Of Horizontal Position
91A13284
Courtesy of Chrysler Motors.

Fig. 14: Adjusting Timing Belt Tension

ROCKER ARM & LASH ADJUSTER

Removal — Remove valve cover. Rotate camshaft until base circle contacts rocker arm. Using Spring Compressor (C-4682), compress valve spring. Note location of rocker arm and lash adjuster for reassembly reference. Remove rocker arm and lash adjuster.

NOTE: If rocker arm or camshaft are changed, check dry lash to ensure proper clearance exists. See DRY LASH under ADJUSTMENTS.

Installation - 1) To install, reverse removal procedure. Ensure lash adjusters are at least partially full of oil before installing. Little or no plunger travel should exist when lash adjuster is depressed.

2) Ensure components are installed in original location. Check clearance between rocker arm ear and valve spring retainer. *See Fig. 21.* Clearance must be at least .050" (1.27 mm). If insufficient clearance exists, grind rocker arm ears to correct clearance. Install valve cover.

CAUTION: Ensure valve spring retainer locks are fully seated after servicing rocker arms.

CAMSHAFT

NOTE: Camshaft can be removed while supporting camshaft sprocket in timing belt, with tension applied to timing belt. See Fig. 3. If camshaft sprocket cannot be supported, timing belt must be removed.

Removal - 1) Remove timing belt if camshaft sprocket cannot be supported. See TIMING BELT under REMOVAL & INSTALLATION. Remove valve cover and curtain. If camshaft sprocket is to be removed, use Sprocket Holder (C-4687) with Adapter (C-4687-1) to hold camshaft sprocket and remove sprocket bolt. *See Fig. 5.* Remove camshaft sprocket. Support timing belt and camshaft sprocket. *See Fig. 3.*

2) Using Intermediate Shaft/Camshaft Seal Remover (C-4679), remove camshaft seal. *See Fig. 9.* Place reference mark on rocker arm for reassembly reference.

3) Note that arrow on camshaft bearing caps is toward camshaft sprocket, and camshaft bearing caps are numbered for location with

1991 ENGINES
2.5L 4-Cylinder (Cont.)

No. 1 at timing belt end of engine. Loosen camshaft bearing cap bolts several turns in proper sequence. *See Fig. 15.*

4) Using soft-faced mallet, tap rear of camshaft to loosen camshaft bearing caps. Remove bolts, camshaft bearing caps and camshaft. Remove rocker arms (if necessary).

CAUTION: Camshaft bearing cap bolts must be removed in sequence, or camshaft may bind in cylinder head, damaging camshaft or bearing thrust surfaces.

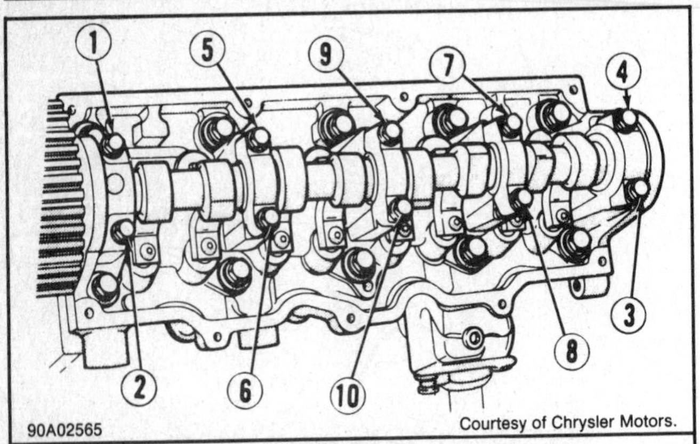
1
5
9
7
4
3
8
2
6
10
90A02565
Courtesy of Chrysler Motors.

Fig. 15: Camshaft Bearing Cap Bolt Removal Sequence

Inspection – 1) Inspect camshaft and cylinder head for damage. Measure journal O.D. Replace camshaft if O.D. is not within specification. See CAMSHAFT table under ENGINE SPECIFICATIONS at end of article.

2) Measure camshaft lobe on outer edges, and in rocker contact surface areas. Replace camshaft if camshaft lobe wear exceeds .010" (.25 mm).

NOTE: If an oversized camshaft is used, cylinder head must also have oversized camshaft bores. Oversized camshafts are identified by Green barrel, and "O/S J" stamped on end of camshaft. Oversized cylinder head is identified by Green bearing caps, and "O/S J" stamped behind oil gallery plug on rear of cylinder head.

Installation – 1) Install rocker arms in original location. Install camshaft on cylinder head. Apply anaerobic sealer to camshaft bearing caps No. 1 and 5 at camshaft bearing cap-to-cylinder head surfaces.

2) Install No. 1 camshaft bearing cap at timing belt end, and No. 5 at rear of cylinder head. Ensure arrows on camshaft bearing caps No. 1 through 4 point toward timing belt. Install bolts and tighten alternately, working outward from middle, to specification. See TORQUE SPECIFICATIONS table at end of article.

3) Check camshaft end play. If end play exceeds specification, replace camshaft and/or cylinder head. See CAMSHAFT table under ENGINE SPECIFICATIONS at end of article.

4) Coat camshaft oil seal lip with oil. Using Intermediate Shaft/Camshaft Seal Installer (C-4680), install camshaft oil seal even with camshaft bearing cap. To install remaining components, reverse removal procedure. Tighten bolts to specification. See TORQUE SPECIFICATIONS table at end of article.

INTERMEDIATE SHAFT

CAUTION: Remove oil pump and distributor before removing intermediate shaft.

Removal – 1) Remove timing belt. See TIMING BELT under REMOVAL & INSTALLATION. Using Sprocket Holder (C-4687) with Adapter (C-4687-1), hold intermediate sprocket and remove sprocket retaining bolt. *See Fig. 5.* Note direction of sprocket offset for reassembly reference. Remove intermediate shaft sprocket.

2) Using Intermediate Shaft/Camshaft Seal Remover (C-4679), remove sprocket oil seals. *See Fig. 9.* Remove retaining bolts. Remove seal retainer and intermediate shaft. *See Fig. 16.*

Inspection – 1) Inspect bearing journals and bushings for damage. Measure bearing journal diameters and intermediate shaft bushing bore diameters. Determine maximum oil clearance. Replace shaft and/or bushings if measurements are not within specification. See INTERMEDIATE SHAFT SPECIFICATIONS table.

2) If intermediate shaft bushings require replacement, remove using Bushing Remover (C-4697-2) for front bushing, and (C-4686-2) for rear bushing.

3) Use Bushing Installer (C-4697-1) for front bushing and (C-4686-1) for rear bushing. Install bushings until bushing installer is even with cylinder block.

INTERMEDIATE SHAFT SPECIFICATIONS

Application	In. (mm)
Bearing Journal Diameter	
Large Journal	1.6799-1.6809 (42.670-42.695)
Small Journal	.7744-.7753 (19.670-19.695)
Bushing Bore Diameter	
Large Bushing	1.6823-1.6830 (42.730-42.750)
Small Bushing	.7764-.7776 (19.720-19.750)
Maximum Oil Clearance	
Large Journal	.0014-.0031 (.035-.080)
Small Journal	.0010-.0031 (.025-.080)

Installation – 1) To install, reverse removal procedure. Lubricate distributor drive gear before installing. Apply a 1/16" bead of anaerobic gasket sealer on seal retainer before installing.

2) Install seal retainer and tighten bolts to specification. See TORQUE SPECIFICATIONS table at end of article. Using Intermediate Shaft/Camshaft Seal Installer (C-4680), install seal until even with surface. *See Fig. 11.* To install remaining components, reverse removal procedure.

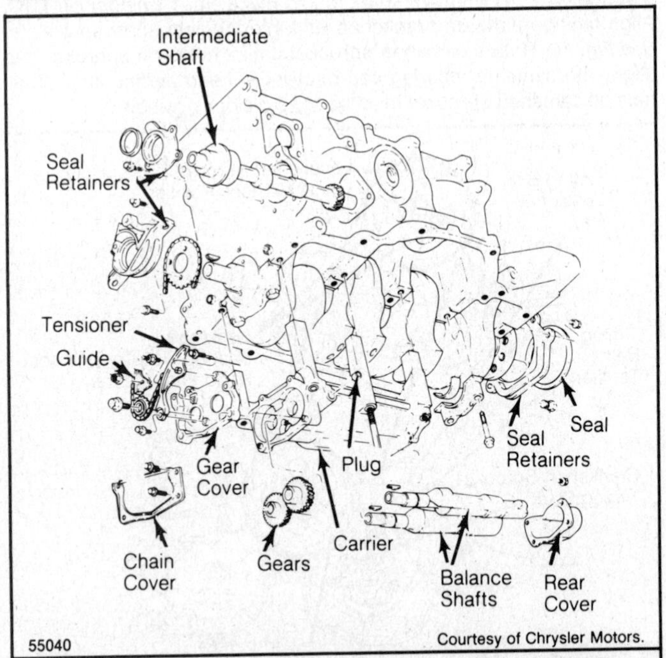
Intermediate Shaft
Seal Retainers
Tensioner
Guide
Gear Cover
Plug
Seal Retainers
Seal
Chain Cover
Gears
Carrier
Balance Shafts
Rear Cover
55040
Courtesy of Chrysler Motors.

Fig. 16: Exploded View of Intermediate Shaft & Balance Shafts

BALANCE SHAFTS

NOTE: Balance shafts are used on Caravan and Voyager only.

Removal & Installation (Gears & Shafts) – 1) Remove oil pan and oil pick-up. See OIL PAN under REMOVAL & INSTALLATION. Remove timing belt. See TIMING BELT under REMOVAL & INSTALLATION.

2) Remove crankshaft sprocket bolt. Using Crankshaft Sprocket Puller/Installer (C-4685) and puller insert, remove crankshaft sprocket. *See Fig. 8.* Remove crankshaft seal retainer.

3) Remove chain cover, guide and tensioner. *See Fig. 16.* Remove balance shaft chain sprocket bolts, and crankshaft balance shaft chain sprocket Torx bolts. Remove chain and sprocket assembly. Remove gear cover retaining stud.

4) Remove gear cover and balance shaft gears. Remove rear cover and remove balance shafts from carrier.

5) To install, reverse removal procedure. See ALIGNING BALANCE SHAFTS procedure under BALANCE SHAFTS to ensure correct timing of balance shafts and crankshaft.

Removal (Carrier Assembly & Balance Shafts) - 1) The following components will remain intact during carrier assembly removal: gear cover, gears, balance shafts and rear cover.

2) Remove oil pan and oil pick-up. See OIL PAN under REMOVAL & INSTALLATION. Remove timing belt. See TIMING BELT under REMOVAL & INSTALLATION.

3) Remove crankshaft sprocket bolt. Using Crankshaft Sprocket Puller/Installer (C-4685) and puller insert, remove crankshaft sprocket. *See Fig. 8.* Remove crankshaft seal retainer.

4) Remove chain cover. Remove balance shaft sprocket bolt. Loosen tensioner pivot and adjusting bolts. Move chain-driven balance shaft inboard through chain sprocket. Sprocket should remain hanging in lower chain loop. Remove carrier-to-cylinder block bolts, and remove carrier assembly.

Installation - To install, reverse removal procedure. See ALIGNING BALANCE SHAFTS procedure under BALANCE SHAFTS to ensure correct timing of balance shafts.

Aligning Balance Shafts - 1) With balance shafts installed in carrier, position carrier (if removed) on cylinder block, and install carrier bolts. Tighten bolts to specification. See TORQUE SPECIFICATIONS table at end of article.

2) Rotate both balance shafts until shaft keyways are facing upward (parallel to vertical center line of engine). Install short hub gear on (sprocket) driven shaft. Install long hub gear on (gear) driven shaft. After installing, ensure balance shaft keyways remain facing upward when alignment marks are together. *See Fig. 17.*

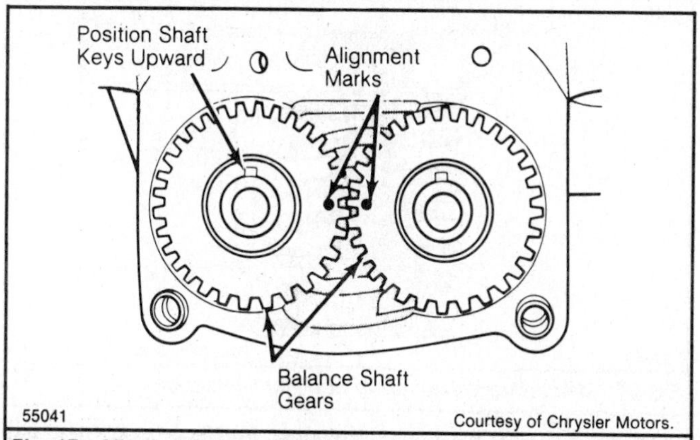
Position Shaft
Keys Upward
Alignment
Marks
Balance Shaft
Gears
55041
Courtesy of Chrysler Motors.

Fig. 17: Aligning Balance Shafts

3) Install gear cover and tighten double-ended stud to specification. Install crankshaft balance shaft chain sprocket. Tighten bolt to specification. See TORQUE SPECIFICATIONS table at end of article. Rotate crankshaft until No. 1 cylinder is at TDC. Ensure crankshaft sprocket timing mark aligns with No. 1 main bearing cap parting line. *See Fig. 18.*

4) Install chain over crankshaft sprocket, with upper nickel-plated link of chain aligned with timing mark on crankshaft sprocket. *See Fig. 18.*

5) Install balance shaft chain (lower) sprocket into timing chain, with timing mark (Yellow dot) of sprocket aligned with lower nickel-plated link on chain. *See Fig. 18.*

NOTE: Upper and lower nickel-plated chain links should align with timing marks of upper and lower chain sprockets, respectively.

6) With balance shaft keyways at 12 o'clock position, install balance shaft chain sprocket on nose of left balance shaft. Balance shaft may have to be pushed slightly inward to allow for clearance.

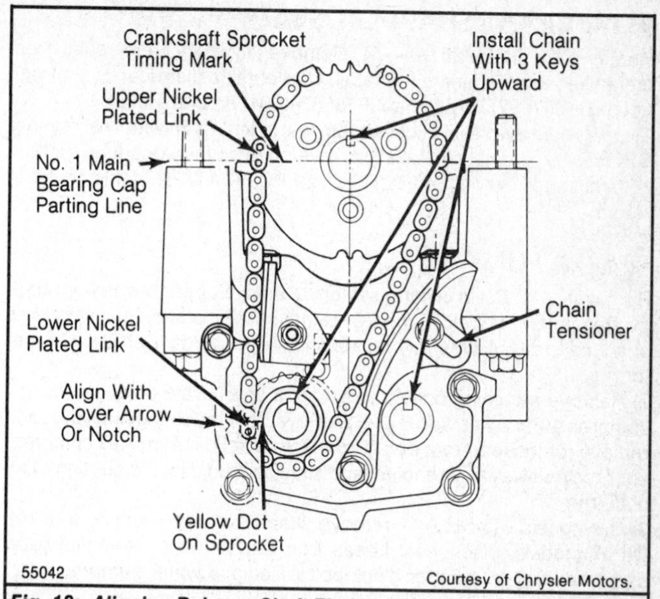
Crankshaft Sprocket
Timing Mark
Install Chain
With 3 Keys
Upward
Upper Nickel
Plated Link
No. 1 Main
Bearing Cap
Parting Line
Chain
Tensioner
Lower Nickel
Plated Link
Align With
Cover Arrow
Or Notch
Yellow Dot
On Sprocket
55042
Courtesy of Chrysler Motors.

Fig. 18: Aligning Balance Shaft Timing Marks

NOTE: Balance shaft timing is correctly set when timing mark (Yellow dot) on balance shaft chain (lower) sprocket and lower nickel-plated chain link are aligned with cover arrow or notch. See Fig. 18.

7) Install sprocket retaining bolts and tighten to specification. See TORQUE SPECIFICATIONS table at end of article. Adjust chain tension. See CHAIN TENSIONING.

Chain Tensioning - 1) Loosely install chain tensioner. Install guide on double-ended stud on gear cover. Ensure guide tab on guide engages with slot in gear cover.

2) Install guide retaining nut and tighten to specification. See TORQUE SPECIFICATIONS table at end of article. Install a .039" (.99 mm) thick by 2.75" (69.8 mm) long shim between chain tensioner and chain.

3) Push chain tensioner and shim against chain. Apply firm pressure directly behind chain tensioner adjusting slot to take up all the slack. *See Fig. 19.*

4) With pressure applied on chain tensioner, tighten chain tensioner adjusting bolt first, then tighten pivot bolt to specification. See TORQUE SPECIFICATIONS table at end of article. *See Fig. 19.* Remove shim. Install chain cover. Tighten bolts to specification. See TORQUE SPECIFICATIONS table.

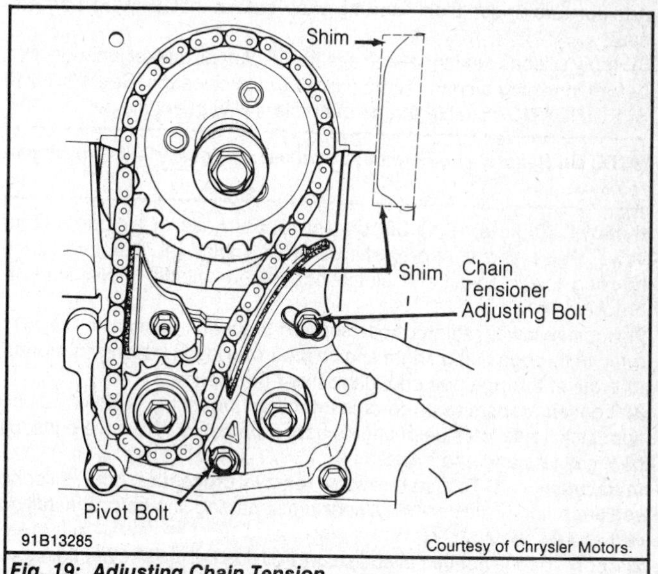
Shim
Shim
Chain
Tensioner
Adjusting Bolt
Pivot Bolt
91B13285
Courtesy of Chrysler Motors.

Fig. 19: Adjusting Chain Tension

1991 ENGINES
2.5L 4-Cylinder (Cont.)

REAR CRANKSHAFT OIL SEAL

Removal & Installation – 1) Remove flywheel. Pry seal from crankshaft seal retainer. To install, coat outside diameter of seal with Loctite (4057987). Install Seal Pilot (C-4681) on crankshaft.

2) Install seal over seal pilot and tap seal in until even with seal retainer surface. To complete installation, reverse removal procedure. Tighten bolts to specification. See TORQUE SPECIFICATIONS table at end of article.

WATER PUMP

Removal – 1) Drain cooling system. Remove upper and lower radiator hoses. On models with A/C, remove A/C compressor with lines attached from solid mount bracket and secure aside. Remove alternator.

2) Remove mounting bolts No. 1, 4, 5, 6 and 7 from solid mount A/C compressor bracket. *See Fig. 4.* Remove front mounting nut No. 2, and remove (or loosen) front bolt No. 3. Rotate solid mount A/C compressor bracket away from engine, and slide on stud (No. 2 mounting stud) until free.

3) On models without A/C, remove alternator and mounting bracket. On all models, disconnect hoses from water pump. Remove water pump housing-to-cylinder block bolts. Remove water pump housing, water pump and "O" ring.

4) Remove water pump pulley. Remove water pump-to-housing bolts. Separate water pump from housing. Remove "O" ring from housing groove.

Installation – 1) Install water pump on housing with a new gasket and "O" ring. Tighten retaining bolts to specification. See TORQUE SPECIFICATIONS table at end of article. Install new "O" ring in housing groove.

2) Install water pump pulley. Ensure pump rotates freely. Install water pump and housing on engine. Tighten bolts to specification. See TORQUE SPECIFICATIONS table at end of article. When installing solid mount A/C compressor bracket, tighten bolts in following order:

- Bolt No. 1 – 30 INCH lbs. (3.3 N.m)
- Bolts No. 2 and 3 – 40 ft. lbs. (54 N.m)
- Bolts No. 1, 4 and 5 – 40 ft. lbs. (54 N.m)
- Bolts No. 6 and 7 – 40 ft. lbs. (54 N.m)

3) Fill cooling system. See COOLING SYSTEM BLEEDING under REMOVAL & INSTALLATION.

OIL PAN

Removal & Installation (Caravan & Voyager) – 1) Drain engine oil. Remove retaining bolts, oil pan, gaskets and end seals.

2) To install, reverse removal procedure. Apply silicone sealant at seal retainer-to-cylinder block parting lines before installing oil pan end seals.

3) Apply silicone sealant at end seal-to-oil pan rail gasket junction area before installing oil pan. Tighten bolts to specification. See TORQUE SPECIFICATIONS table at end of article. Fill with engine oil.

NOTE: On Dakota, engine must be raised on driver's side for oil pan removal.

Removal (Dakota) – 1) Disconnect rubber hose at air pump relief valve. Raise and support vehicle. Drain engine oil. Remove clutch housing lower cover and clutch housing-to-cylinder block support brackets.

2) Remove lower radiator hose support bracket. Loosen but DO NOT remove through bolt on right engine mount. Loosen left engine mount-to-bracket through bolt enough to clear bracket.

3) Loosen transmission-to-crossmember mounting bracket. Using floor jack, raise left side of engine approximately 2". Remove bolts, oil pan, gaskets and end seals.

Installation – 1) To install, reverse removal procedure. Apply silicone sealant at seal retainer-to-cylinder block parting line before installing oil pan end seals.

2) Apply silicone sealant at end seal-to-oil pan rail gasket junction area before installing oil pan. Tighten bolts to specification. See TORQUE SPECIFICATIONS table at end of article. Fill with engine oil.

OVERHAUL

Cylinder Head – 1) Check cylinder head warpage. Warpage must not exceed specification. See CYLINDER HEAD table under ENGINE SPECIFICATIONS at end of article.

2) If cylinder head or camshaft is serviced, ensure oversized camshaft is used in cylinder head with oversized bores. See SPECIAL ENGINE MARKS.

3) After grinding valves or valve seats, install valve into cylinder. Measure valve stem installed height from spring seat of cylinder head to tip of valve. *See Fig. 20.* Distance should be 1.960-2.009" (49.78-51.03 mm). Grind valve tip if necessary.

CAUTION: If valve tip is ground more than .020" (.51 mm), check clearance between rocker arm ear and valve spring retainer. See Fig. 21. Clearance must be at least .050" (1.27 mm). If clearance is insufficient, grind rocker arm ears to obtain correct clearance.

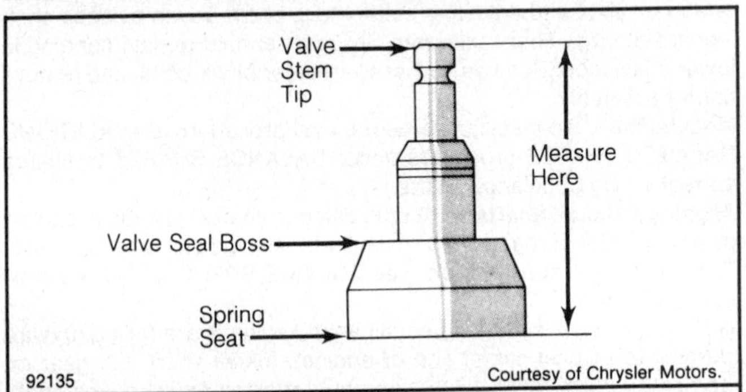
Valve
Stem
Tip
Measure
Here
Valve Seal Boss
Spring
Seat
92135
Courtesy of Chrysler Motors.

Fig. 20: Measuring Valve Stem Installed Height

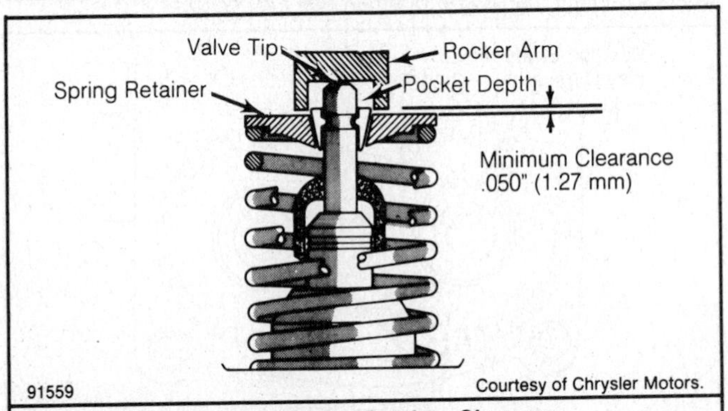
Valve Tip
Rocker Arm
Spring Retainer
Pocket Depth
Minimum Clearance
.050" (1.27 mm)
91559
Courtesy of Chrysler Motors.

Fig. 21: Measuring Valve Spring Retainer Clearance

Valve Springs – 1) Measure valve spring free length, out-of-square and pressure. Replace valve spring if measurements are not within specification. See VALVES & VALVE SPRINGS table under ENGINE SPECIFICATIONS at end of article.

2) Measure valve spring installed height from lower edge of valve spring to upper edge. DO NOT include spring seat or retainer flange. Ensure valve spring installed height is within specification. See VALVES & VALVE SPRINGS table. If valve spring installed height is not within specification, add an additional spring seat.

Valve Stem Oil Seals – Oversize valve stem seals must be used with oversize valves. Ensure lower edge of valve stem oil seal is against valve guide after installation.

Valve Guides — 1) Check valve stem oil clearance. Ensure valve stem diameter is within specification. Valve guide must be reamed for oversize valve stem if clearance exceeds specification. See CYLINDER HEAD table under ENGINE SPECIFICATIONS at end of article.

2) Valves are available with oversize valve stems of .006" (.15 mm), .016" (.40 mm) and .031" (.80 mm). Replace cylinder head if valve guide cannot be reamed using a .031" (.80 mm) reamer, or if valve guide is loose.

NOTE: DO NOT ream valve guides from standard to maximum oversize in one step. Ream valve guides to oversize in gradual steps, so valve guides are reamed in relation to valve seat.

Valve Seats — 1) Ensure valve seat angle, seat width and seat runout are within specification. See CYLINDER HEAD table under ENGINE SPECIFICATIONS at end of article.

2) If valve face and/or valve seats have been ground, measure valve stem installed height from spring seat of cylinder head to tip of valve. *See Fig. 20.* Distance should be 1.960-2.009" (49.78-51.03 mm). Grind valve tip if necessary.

Valves - 1) Check head diameter, valve margin and stem diameter. Replace valve if measurements are not within specification. See VALVES & VALVE SPRINGS table under ENGINE SPECIFICATIONS at end of article.

2) After grinding valves, install valve into cylinder and measure valve stem installed height from spring seat of cylinder head to tip of valve. *See Fig. 20.* Distance should be 1.960-2.009" (49.78-51.03 mm). Grind valve tip if necessary.

CAUTION: If valve tip is ground more than .020" (.51 mm), check clearance between rocker arm ear and valve spring retainer. See Fig. 21. Clearance must be at least .050" (1.27 mm). If clearance is insufficient, grind rocker arm ears to obtain correct clearance.

3) Valves are available with oversize valve stems of .006" (.15 mm), .016" (.40 mm) and .031" (.80 mm). Valve tip diameter should be no less than .275" (6.99 mm) after grinding. If necessary, tip chamfer should be reground to prevent seal damage when valve is installed.

Seat Correction Angles - After grinding, if seat width is too wide, use a 15-degree or 65-degree stone to alter seat width. A 15-degree stone will lower valve seat and a 65-degree stone will raise valve seat.

VALVE TRAIN

Rocker Arm - Replace rocker arms if damaged.

Lash Adjusters - 1) No adjustment is required on lash adjusters. If lash adjuster is disassembled for cleaning purposes, reassemble with NEW cap.

2) Ensure lash adjusters are partially full of oil before installing. Little or no plunger travel should exist when lash adjuster is depressed.

NOTE: Always service lash adjusters as complete assemblies. Lash adjuster internal components are not interchangeable.

CYLINDER BLOCK ASSEMBLY

Piston & Rod Assembly - Valve clearance cutout(s) on top of piston should face manifold side of engine. Oiling hole on connecting rod must face toward front (timing belt end) of engine. *See Fig. 22.*

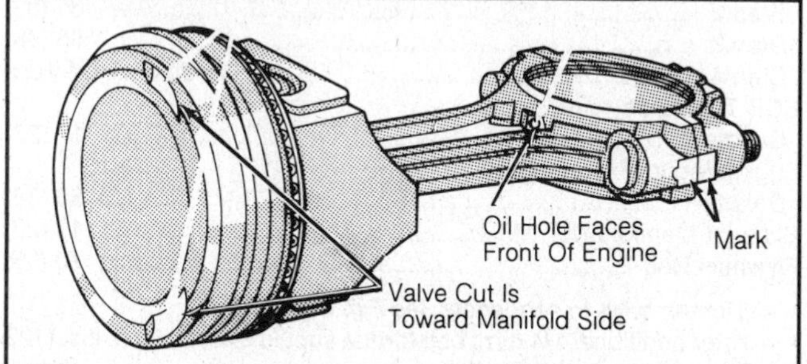

Oil Hole Faces
Front Of Engine
Mark
Valve Cut Is
Toward Manifold Side
71506
Courtesy of Chrysler Motors.

Fig. 22: Installing Piston on Connecting Rod

Fitting Pistons - Measure piston diameter at 1.87" (47.4 mm) below top of piston, at 90-degree angle to piston pin. Measure cylinder bore diameter at center of cylinder bore. Ensure piston diameter and piston clearance are within specification. See PISTONS, PINS & RINGS table under ENGINE SPECIFICATIONS at end of article.

Piston Rings - Ensure ring end gap and side clearances are within specification. See PISTON, PINS & RINGS table under ENGINE SPECIFICATIONS at end of article. Ensure piston ring end gaps are properly positioned. *See Fig. 23.*

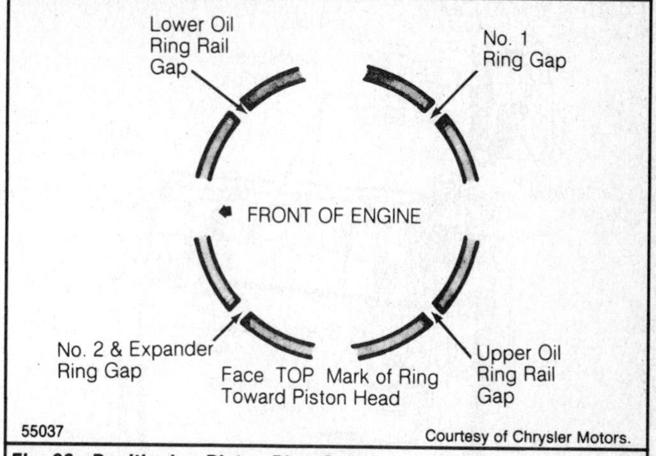

Lower Oil
Ring Rail
Gap
No. 1
Ring Gap
FRONT OF ENGINE
No. 2 & Expander
Ring Gap
Face TOP Mark of Ring
Toward Piston Head
Upper Oil
Ring Rail
Gap
55037
Courtesy of Chrysler Motors.

Fig. 23: Positioning Piston Ring Gaps

Rod Bearings - 1) Before installing connecting rod bearings, hold a straightedge across connecting rod bolt threads. Ensure threads contact straightedge in all areas. If threads fail to contact straightedge, rod bolts are stretched and must be replaced.

2) Lightly coat rod bolts with engine oil before installing nuts. Ensure connecting rod is installed so oiling hole on connecting rod faces toward front (timing belt end) of engine. *See Fig. 22.*

3) Tighten connecting rod nuts to specification. See TORQUE SPECIFICATIONS table at end of article. Ensure bearing oil clearance and side play are within specification. See CRANKSHAFT, MAIN & CONNECTING ROD BEARINGS and CONNECTING RODS tables under ENGINE SPECIFICATIONS at end of article.

Crankshaft & Main Bearings - 1) Main bearing caps are numbered with No. 1 at timing belt end, and No. 5 at flywheel end. Arrow on main bearing cap must point toward timing belt end of engine.

2) Before installing main bearings, hold a straightedge across threads of main bearing cap bolts. Ensure threads contact straightedge in all areas. If threads fail to contact straightedge, bolts are stretched and must be replaced.

3) Lightly coat bolt threads with engine oil before installing. Tighten main bearing cap bolts to specification. See TORQUE SPECIFICATIONS table at end of article.

4) Ensure main bearing oil clearance and crankshaft end play are within specification. See CRANKSHAFT, MAIN & CONNECTING ROD BEARINGS table under ENGINE SPECIFICATIONS at end of article. Replace thrust bearing if end play is not within specification.

Thrust Bearing - Thrust bearing is located on No. 3 main bearing. Replace thrust bearing if crankshaft end play is not within specification. See CRANKSHAFT, MAIN & CONNECTING ROD BEARINGS table under ENGINE SPECIFICATIONS at end of article.

Cylinder Block - 1) Using a feeler gauge and straightedge, check cylinder block head surface for warpage. Measure cylinder bore, taper and out-of-round. Measure at .375" (9.52 mm) below top surface of cylinder bore, middle of bore and .375" (9.52 mm) from bottom of cylinder bore.

2) Repair or replace cylinder block if measurements are not within specification. See CYLINDER BLOCK table under ENGINE SPECIFICATIONS at end of article.

ENGINE OILING

ENGINE LUBRICATION SYSTEM

A crankshaft-driven oil pump provides pressurized lubrication to main oil gallery. *See Fig. 24.*

Crankcase Capacity - Oil capacity with oil filter is 4.5 qts. (4.2L).

Oil Pressure - Oil pressure is 4 psi (.28 kg/cm²) at curb idle, and 25-80 psi (1.75-5.6 kg/cm²) at 3000 RPM with engine at normal operating temperature.

1991 ENGINES
2.5L 4-Cylinder (Cont.)

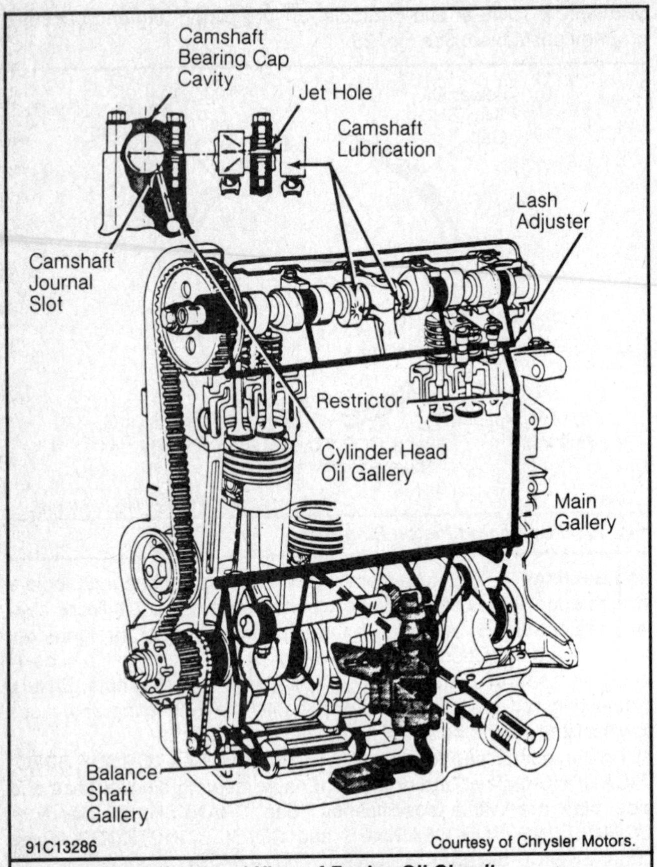
Camshaft
Bearing Cap
Cavity
Jet Hole
Camshaft
Lubrication
Lash
Adjuster
Camshaft
Journal
Slot
Restrictor
Cylinder Head
Oil Gallery
Main
Gallery
Balance
Shaft
Gallery
91C13286
Courtesy of Chrysler Motors.

Fig. 24: Cross-Sectional View of Engine Oil Circuit

OIL PUMP

Removal & Disassembly – 1) Remove oil pan. See OIL PAN under REMOVAL & INSTALLATION. Remove oil pick-up tube-to-oil pump bolt. Remove pick-up tube and "O" ring. Remove oil pump-to-cylinder block bolts. Remove oil pump.

2) Remove pump cover-to-pump housing bolts. Remove pump cover. Note direction of rotor installation. Remove inner and outer rotors. *See Fig. 25.* Remove pin, cap, spring and pressure relief valve from oil pump housing. Clean all components in solvent and blow dry with compressed air.

Inspection – 1) Install inner rotor (drive gear) and outer rotor (driven gear) into pump housing. Place straightedge across pump housing and both gears. Using feeler gauge, check rotor-to-housing clearance between rotor and straightedge.

2) With rotors installed, check outer rotor-to-inner rotor clearance. Check outer rotor-to-housing clearance. Remove rotors. Measure outer rotor O.D. and thickness. Measure inner rotor thickness. Check pump cover flatness.

3) Measure free length of pressure relief valve spring. Using spring pressure tester, check pressure of pressure relief valve spring. Replace oil pump assembly if measurements are not within specification. See OIL PUMP SPECIFICATIONS table.

OIL PUMP SPECIFICATIONS

Application	Specification
Inner Rotor Thickness	.9435" (23.965 mm)
Outer Rotor O.D.	2.469" (62.71 mm)
Outer Rotor Thickness	.9435" (23.965 mm)
Outer Rotor-To-Housing Clearance	.014" (.35 mm)
Outer Rotor-To-Inner Rotor Clearance	.008" (.20 mm)
Pressure Relief Valve Spring	
Free Length	1.95" (49.5 mm)
Pressure	20 Lbs. @ 1.34" (9 kg @ 34.0 mm
Pump Cover Flatness	.003" (.07 mm)
Rotor-To-Housing Clearance [1]	.0010-.0035" (.025-.088 mm)

[1] – Measured by placing straightedge across pump housing.

Reassembly & Installation – 1) To reassemble, reverse disassembly procedure. Install outer rotor in pump housing, with large chamfered edge toward pump housing.

2) To install, apply Loctite Sealer (515) to oil pump housing-to-cylinder block surface. Align slot in oil pump drive gear. Install oil pump. Rotate pump back and forth to ensure proper seating while tightening retaining bolts to specification. See TORQUE SPECIFICATIONS table at end of article.

3) Install new "O" ring on pick-up tube. To install remaining components, reverse removal procedure.

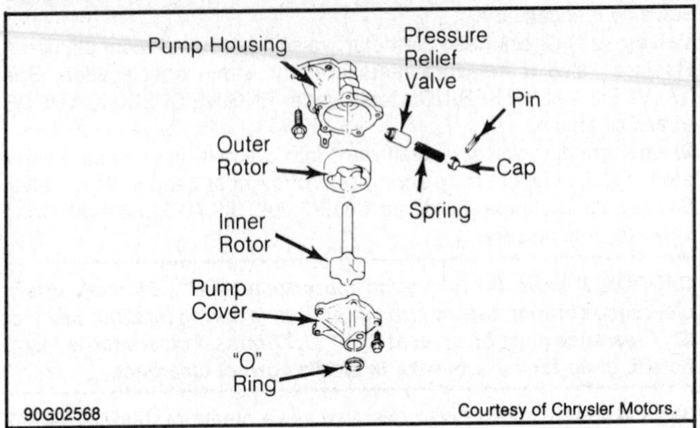
Pump Housing
Pressure
Relief
Valve
Pin
Outer
Rotor
Cap
Spring
Inner
Rotor
Pump
Cover
"O"
Ring
90G02568
Courtesy of Chrysler Motors.

Fig. 25: Exploded View of Oil Pump

TORQUE SPECIFICATIONS

TORQUE SPECIFICATIONS

Application	Ft. Lbs. (N.m)
Balance Shaft Carrier-To-Cylinder Block Bolt	40 (54)
Balance Shaft Chain Sprocket Bolt	21 (29)
Balance Shaft Sprocket-To-Crankshaft Bolt	11 (15)
Camshaft Bearing Cap Bolt	18 (24)
Camshaft Sprocket Bolt	65 (88)
Clutch Housing-To-Cylinder Block	
Support Bracket Bolt	
Dakota	70 (95)
Connecting Rod Cap Nut	
Step 1	40 (54)
Step 2	Additional 1/4 Turn
Coolant Tube-To-Thermostat Housing	30 (41)
Crankshaft Belt Sprocket Bolt	85 (115)
Crankshaft Pulley Bolt	20 (27)
Cylinder Head Bolt [1]	
Step 1	45 (61)
Step 2	65 (88)
Step 3	65 (88)
Step 4	[2] Additional 1/4 Turn
EGR Tube Bolt	
Dakota	17 (23)
Engine Mount Through Bolt	
Dakota	50 (68)
Exhaust Manifold Nut	17 (23)
Flywheel Bolt	70 (95)

[1] – Tighten bolts in sequence. *See Fig. 6.*

[2] – After additional 1/4 turn, bolt torque should exceed 90 ft. lbs. (122 N.m). If not, replace bolt.

1991 ENGINES
2.5L 4-Cylinder (Cont.)

TORQUE SPECIFICATIONS (Cont.)

Application	Ft. Lbs. (N.m)
Front Mount Through Bolt	
Caravan & Voyager	50 (68)
Front Mount-To-Cylinder Block Bolt	
Caravan & Voyager	75 (102)
Fuel Rail Bolt	21 (29)
Insulator-To-Side Rail Bolt	
Caravan & Voyager	27 (37)
Intake Manifold Bolt	17 (23)
Intermediate Shaft Sprocket Bolt	65 (88)
Main Bearing Cap Bolt	
Step 1	30 (41)
Step 2	Additional 1/4 Turn
Oil Pump Pick-Up Tube Bolt	21 (29)
Oil Pump-To-Cylinder Block Bolt	17 (23)
Right (Timing Belt Side) Mount Through Bolt	
Caravan & Voyager	100 (136)
Right (Timing Belt Side) Mount Vertical Bolt	
Caravan & Voyager	75 (102)
Solid Mount A/C Compressor Bracket	[3]
Throttle Body Bolt	17 (23)
Timing Belt Tensioner Bolt	45 (61)
Torque Converter-To-Flexplate Bolt	
Caravan & Voyager	40 (54)
Transaxle-To-Cylinder Block Bolt	
Caravan & Voyager	70 (95)
Transmission-To-Clutch Housing Bolt	
Dakota	30 (41)
Water Pump Housing Bolt	
Lower	40 (54)
Upper	21 (29)
Vent Plug	15 (20)
	INCH Lbs. (N.m)
Balance Shaft Chain Guide Nut	105 (12)
Balance Shaft Chain Pivot & Tensioner Bolt	105 (12)
Balance Shaft Cover Bolt	105 (12)
Crankshaft Balance Shaft Chain Sprocket Torx Bolt	130 (15)
Crankshaft Front & Rear Seal Retainer Bolt	105 (12)
Fuel Pressure Regulator Nut	65 (7)
Gear Cover Stud/Bolt	105 (12)
Intermediate Shaft Seal Retainer Bolt	105 (12)
Oil Pan Bolt	[4]
Oil Pump Cover Bolt	105 (12)
Timing Belt Cover Bolt	40 (5)
Valve Cover Bolt	105 (12)
Water Pump Pulley Bolt	105 (12)
Water Pump-To-Housing Bolt	105 (12)

[3] – *See Fig. 4* for bolt identification. Tighten bolts in sequence as follows.
- Bolt No. 1 to 30 INCH lbs. (3.3 N.m)
- Bolts No. 2 & 3 to 40 ft. lbs. (54 N.m)
- Bolts No. 1, 4 & 5 to 40 ft. lbs. (54 N.m)
- Bolts No. 6 & 7 to 40 ft. lbs. (54 N.m)

[4] – Tighten 8-mm bolts to 17 ft. lbs. (23 N.m), and 6-mm bolts to 105 INCH lbs. (12 N.m).

ENGINE SPECIFICATIONS

GENERAL SPECIFICATIONS

Application	Specification
2.5L	
Displacement	153 Cu. In. (2.5L)
Bore	3.44" (87.4 mm)
Stroke	4.09" (103.8 mm)
Compression Ratio	8.9:1
Fuel System	TBI
Horsepower @ RPM	
Caravan & Voyager	100 @ 4800
Dakota	117 @ 5250
Torque Ft. Lbs. @ RPM	
Caravan & Voyager	135 @ 2800
Dakota	139 @ 3500

CRANKSHAFT, MAIN & CONNECTING ROD BEARINGS

Application	In. (mm)
2.5L	
Crankshaft End Play	
Standard	.002-.007 (.05-.18)
Wear Limit	.014 (.36)
Main Bearings	
Journal Diameter	2.362-2.363 (59.99-60.02)
Journal Out-Of-Round	.0005 (.013)
Journal Taper	.0004 (.010)
Oil Clearance	
Caravan & Voyager	
Standard	.0004-.0028 (.010-.071)
Wear Limit	.004 (.10)
Dakota	
Standard	.0003-.0031 (.008-.079)
Wear Limit	.004 (.10)
Connecting Rod Bearings	
Journal Diameter	1.968-1.969 (49.99-50.01)
Journal Out-Of-Round	.0005 (.013)
Journal Taper	.0004 (.010)
Oil Clearance	
Standard	.0008-.0034 (.020-.086)
Wear Limit	.004 (.10)

CONNECTING RODS

Application	In. (mm)
2.5L	
Maximum Bend	.003 (.08)
Maximum Twist	.003 (.08)
Side Play	.005-.013 (.13-.33)

CYLINDER BLOCK

Application	In. (mm)
2.5L	
Cylinder Bore	
Standard Diameter	3.44 (87.4)
Maximum Taper	.005 (.13)
Maximum Out-Of-Round	.002 (.05)

1991 ENGINES
2.5L 4-Cylinder (Cont.)

PISTONS, PINS & RINGS

Application	In. (mm)
2.5L	
Pistons	
Clearance	
Standard	.0010-.0020 (.025-.051)
Wear Limit	.0027 (.069)
Diameter	3.442-3.444 (87.43-87.48)
Rings	
No. 1	
End Gap	
Standard	.010-.020 (.25-.51)
Wear Limit	.039 (.99)
Side Clearance	
Standard	.0015-.0031 (.038-.079)
Wear Limit	.004 (.10)
No. 2	
End Gap	
Standard	.011-.021 (.28-.53)
Wear Limit	.039 (.99)
Side Clearance	
Standard	.0015-.0037 (.038-.094)
Wear Limit	.004 (.10)
No. 3 (Oil)	
End Gap	
Standard	.015-.055 (.38-1.40)
Wear Limit	.074 (1.88)

VALVES & VALVE SPRINGS

Application	Specification
2.5L	
Intake Valves	
Face Angle	45°
Head Diameter	1.60" (40.6 mm)
Minimum Margin	.031" (.79 mm)
Stem Diameter	.3124" (7.935 mm)
Exhaust Valves	
Face Angle	45°
Head Diameter	1.39" (35.3 mm)
Minimum Margin	.047" (1.19 mm)
Stem Diameter	.3103" (7.882 mm)
Valve Springs	
Free Length	
Caravan & Voyager	2.39" (60.7 mm)
Dakota	2.16" (54.9 mm)
Installed Height	1.62-1.68" (41.1-42.7 mm)
Out-Of-Square	.079" (2.01 mm)
Pressure	Lbs. @ In. (kg @ mm)
Valve Closed	108-120 @ 1.65 (49-54 @ 42)
Valve Open	
Caravan & Voyager	195-215 @ 1.22 (89-97 @ 31)
Dakota	221-235 @ 1.22 (100-107 @ 31)

CYLINDER HEAD

Application	Specification
2.5L	
Maximum Warpage	.004" (.10 mm)
Valve Seats	
Intake Valve	
Seat Angle	45°
Seat Width	.069-.088" (1.75-2.24 mm)
Maximum Seat Runout	.002" (.05 mm)
Seat Bore Diameter	1.593" (40.46 mm)
Exhaust Valve	
Seat Angle	45°
Seat Width	.059-.078" (1.50-1.98 mm)
Maximum Seat Runout	.002" (.05 mm)
Seat Bore Diameter	1.371" (34.82 mm)
Valve Guides	
Intake Valve	
Valve Stem-To-Guide	
Oil Clearance	.0009-.0026" (.023-.066 mm)
Exhaust Valve	
Valve Stem-To-Guide	
Oil Clearance	.0030-.0047" (.076-.119 mm)

CAMSHAFT

Application	In. (mm)
2.5L	
Cam Lobe Wear	.010 (.25)
End Play	
Standard	.005-.013 (.13-.33)
Wear Limit	.020 (.51)
Journal Diameter	
Standard	1.375-1.376 (34.93-34.95)
Oversized	1.395-1.396 (35.43-35.46)

Caravan, Voyager

NOTE: For engine repair procedures not covered in this article, see ENGINE OVERHAUL PROCEDURES in GENERAL INFORMATION.

ENGINE IDENTIFICATION

Engine may be identified by eighth character of Vehicle Identification Number (VIN). The VIN is stamped on a plate on top of instrument panel at lower left of windshield.

ENGINE IDENTIFICATION CODE

Application	Code
3.0L PFI	3

ADJUSTMENTS

VALVE CLEARANCE ADJUSTMENT

Hydraulic lash adjusters are used. No valve adjustment is required.

REMOVAL & INSTALLATION

NOTE: For reassembly reference, label all electrical connectors, vacuum hoses and fuel lines before removal. Also place mating marks on engine hood and other major assemblies before removal.

FUEL PRESSURE RELEASE

CAUTION: Fuel system is under pressure. Pressure must be released before servicing any fuel system components.

1) Loosen fuel tank cap to release pressure. Disconnect injector wiring harness from engine wiring harness. Connect jumper wire from terminal No. 1 of injector harness to ground. *See Fig. 1.*
2) Connect a second jumper wire to terminal No. 2 of injector harness. Touch jumper wire to positive battery terminal for no more than 5 seconds to release fuel pressure. Remove jumper wires and reconnect wiring harness.

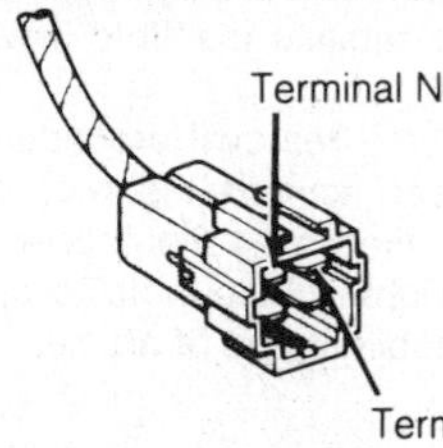

Terminal No. 1
Terminal No. 2

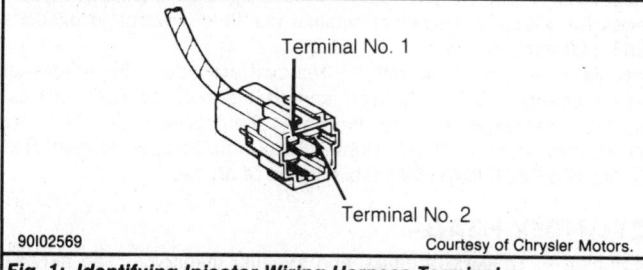

90I02569 Courtesy of Chrysler Motors.

Fig. 1: Identifying Injector Wiring Harness Terminals

ENGINE

NOTE: Remove engine with transaxle remaining in the vehicle.

Removal – 1) Release fuel pressure. See FUEL PRESSURE RELEASE under REMOVAL & INSTALLATION. Disconnect battery. Scribe hood hinge location on hood for reassembly. Remove hood. Drain cooling system and engine oil. Disconnect necessary coolant hoses, control cables, fuel lines, electrical connections and vacuum hoses.
2) Remove air cleaner and radiator/fan assembly. Raise and support vehicle. Remove A/C compressor and power steering pump with hoses attached and set aside (if equipped).
3) Remove starter. Disconnect exhaust pipe at exhaust manifold. Remove torque converter cover. Reference mark flexplate to torque converter for reassembly reference.
4) Remove torque converter-to-flexplate bolts. Attach "C" clamp to bottom front edge of torque converter housing to secure torque converter.
5) Remove lower transaxle-to-cylinder block bolts. Lower vehicle. Support transaxle with floor jack. Attach lifting hoist to engine. Remove remaining transaxle-to-cylinder block bolts.
6) Place reference mark on side rail to indicate right insulator (timing belt side) position for reassembly reference. Remove right insulator-to-side rail bolts.

CAUTION: To ensure proper positioning of the engine, right insulator position on side rail must be marked before removal for reassembly reference. Insulator must be installed in original position.

7) Remove through bolt from left engine mount from inside fenderwell. Insulator bracket-to-transaxle bolts may be removed instead of through bolt. Remove front engine mount bolts. Lift engine from vehicle.
Installation – 1) To install, reverse removal procedure. DO NOT tighten engine mount bolts until all bolts are installed. If vertical bolts on right or left mount was loosened, axle shaft length must be checked.
2) To determine axle shaft length, measure distance between inner edge of outboard boot and inner edge of inboard boot at 6 o'clock position. *See Fig. 2.*

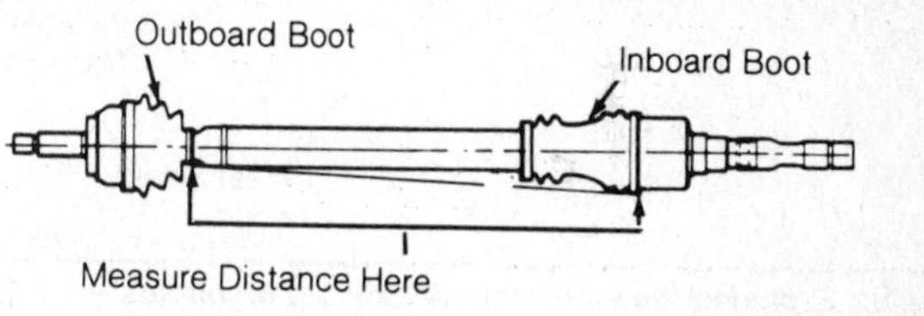

Outboard Boot
Inboard Boot
Measure Distance Here

90C13526 Courtesy of Chrysler Motors.

Fig. 2: Measuring Axle Shaft Length

3) Axle shaft length must be within specification. See AXLE SHAFT LENGTH SPECIFICATIONS table.

AXLE SHAFT LENGTH SPECIFICATIONS

Application	In. (mm)
Right Axle Shaft	20.5-20.9 (521-531)
Left Axle Shaft	9.0-9.4 (229-239)

4) Adjust axle shaft length to specification by sliding engine in slots on engine mounts. Tighten all engine mount bolts once correct axle shaft length is obtained.

CAUTION: Tighten vertical bolt in right mount bracket (timing belt side) before tightening through bolt.

5) Ensure reference mark is aligned on torque converter and flexplate. Tighten bolts to specification. See TORQUE SPECIFICATIONS table at end of article.

INTAKE MANIFOLD

CAUTION: Fuel system is under pressure. Fuel pressure must be released before disconnecting fuel lines.

Removal – 1) Release fuel pressure. See FUEL PRESSURE RELEASE under REMOVAL & INSTALLATION. Disconnect negative battery cable. Drain cooling system. Remove air cleaner hose from throttle body. Remove throttle cable and transaxle kickdown linkage. Disconnect necessary electrical connections and vacuum hoses at throttle body and intake manifold.
2) Remove ignition coil from upper intake manifold. Wrap fuel lines with shop towel and disconnect from fuel rail. Remove retaining bolts, upper air intake and gaskets. *See Fig. 3.* Cover intake manifold openings with shop towel.

1991 ENGINES
3.0L V6 (Cont.)

3) Disconnect vacuum hoses from fuel rail and pressure regulator. Disconnect fuel injector wiring harness from engine wiring harness. Remove retaining bolts and pressure regulator from fuel rail.

4) Remove retaining bolts and fuel rail assembly from intake manifold. Disconnect radiator and heater hoses. Remove retaining bolts, intake manifold and gaskets. *See Fig. 3.*

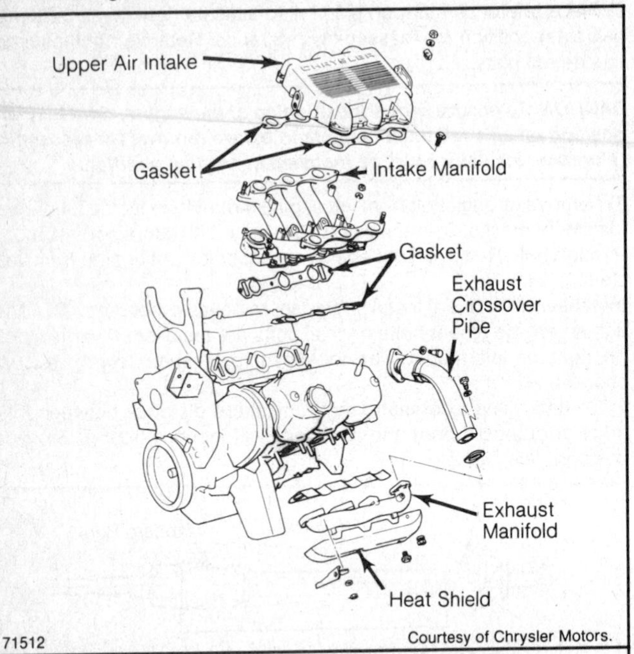
Upper Air Intake
Gasket
Intake Manifold
Gasket
Exhaust
Crossover
Pipe
Exhaust
Manifold
Heat Shield
71512
Courtesy of Chrysler Motors.

Fig. 3: Exploded View of Intake & Exhaust Manifolds

Inspection – Inspect for clogged coolant passages in end crossovers. Check mounting surfaces for warpage. Ensure warpage does not exceed specification. See INTAKE MANIFOLD WARPAGE table.

INTAKE MANIFOLD WARPAGE

Application	In. (mm)
Cylinder Head Mounting Surface	
Standard	.003 (.08)
Maximum	.005 (.13)
Upper Air Intake Mounting Surface	
Standard	.004 (.10)
Maximum	.008 (.20)

Installation – **1)** Install gaskets and intake manifold. Tighten intake manifold nuts to specification in sequence. *See Fig. 4.* See TORQUE SPECIFICATIONS table at end of article.

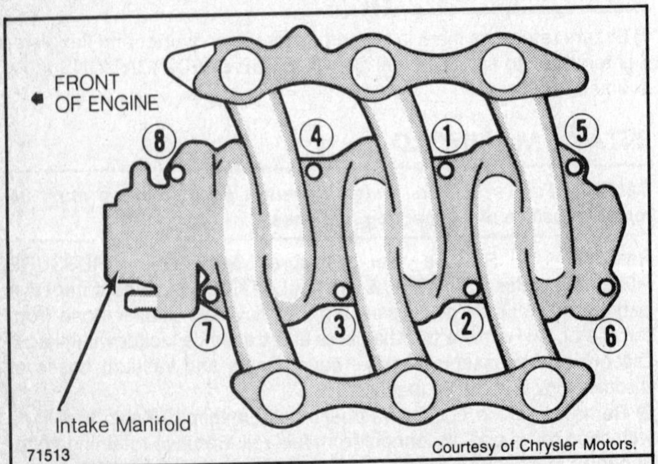
FRONT
OF ENGINE
8
4
1
5
7
3
2
6
Intake Manifold
71513
Courtesy of Chrysler Motors.

Fig. 4: Intake Manifold Nut Tightening Sequence

2) Ensure injector holes are clean. Lubricate injector "O" rings with engine oil before installing. Install fuel rail and injectors until injectors firmly seated in port. Install fuel rail retaining bolts. Install pressure regulator. Tighten bolts/nuts to specification. See TORQUE SPECIFICATIONS table.

3) Install upper air intake gaskets on intake manifold with beaded sealant side upward, away from intake manifold. Install upper air intake. Tighten upper air bolts in sequence to specification. *See Fig. 5.* See TORQUE SPECIFICATIONS table.

4) To install remaining components, reverse removal procedure. Fill cooling system.

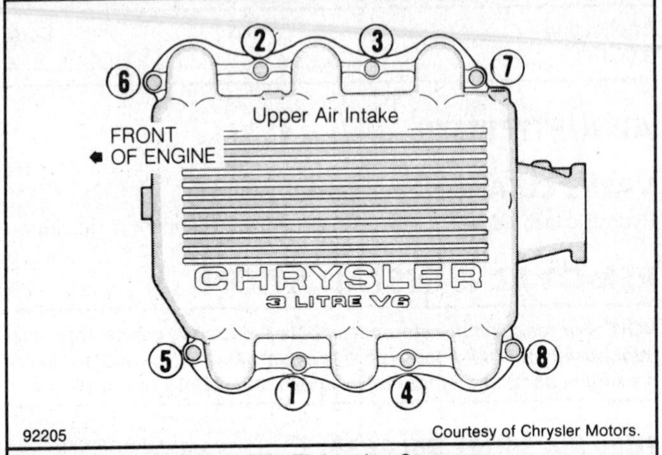
2
3
6
7
Upper Air Intake
FRONT
OF ENGINE
CHRYSLER
3 LITRE V6
5
8
1
4
92205
Courtesy of Chrysler Motors.

Fig. 5: Upper Air Intake Bolt Tightening Sequence

EXHAUST MANIFOLD

Removal – **1)** Raise and support vehicle. Disconnect exhaust pipe from rear exhaust manifold flange. Disconnect O_2 sensor wiring. Remove exhaust crossover pipe mounting bolts. *See Fig. 3.* Remove rear exhaust manifold retaining nuts, and remove exhaust manifold.

2) Lower vehicle. Remove heat shield-to-front exhaust manifold bolts. Disconnect exhaust crossover pipe at front exhaust manifold. Remove retaining nuts and front exhaust manifold.

Inspection – Check manifolds for cracks, damage and mounting surfaces for warpage. Repair or replace manifold if warpage exceeds .008" (.20 mm).

Installation – To install, reverse removal procedure. Install gasket with numbers 1-3-5 embossed toward the top, on rear exhaust manifold. Install gasket with numbers 2-4-6 embossed toward the top, on front exhaust manifold. Tighten bolts/nuts to specification. See TORQUE SPECIFICATIONS table at end of article.

CYLINDER HEAD

Removal – **1)** Remove intake and exhaust manifolds. See INTAKE MANIFOLD and EXHAUST MANIFOLD under REMOVAL & INSTALLATION. Remove timing belt and camshaft sprockets. See TIMING BELT under REMOVAL & INSTALLATION. Remove distributor and adapter housing from cylinder head.

2) Remove rocker arm shaft assembly. See ROCKER ARM & LASH ADJUSTER under REMOVAL & INSTALLATION. Remove camshaft. Remove cylinder head bolts in sequence. *See Fig. 6.* Remove cylinder head and gasket.

CAUTION: Note location of 10 mm Allen hex cylinder head bolt and washer for reassembly reference. See Fig. 6.

Inspection – Check cylinder head for warpage. Resurface head if warpage exceeds specification. See CYLINDER HEAD table under ENGINE SPECIFICATIONS at end of article.

CAUTION: DO NOT grind more than .008" (.20 mm) combined total from surface of cylinder head and deck surface of cylinder block.

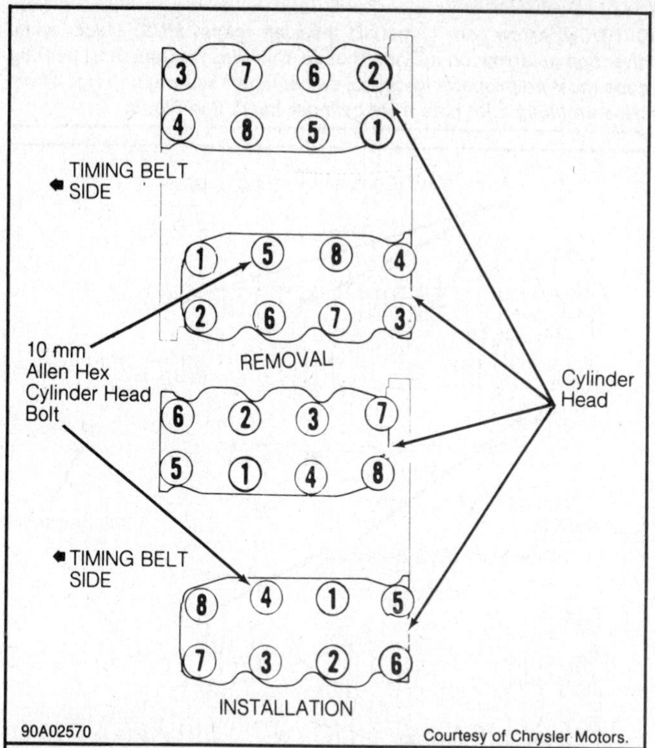
TIMING BELT SIDE
10 mm Allen Hex Cylinder Head Bolt
REMOVAL
Cylinder Head
TIMING BELT SIDE
INSTALLATION
90A02570
Courtesy of Chrysler Motors.

Fig. 6: Cylinder Head Bolt Removal & Installation Sequence

Installation - **1)** To install, reverse removal procedure. Ensure 10 mm Allen hex cylinder head bolts and washers are installed in correct location. See Fig. 6. Tighten cylinder head bolts to specification in sequence, using 2-3 steps. *See Fig. 6.* See TORQUE SPECIFICATIONS table at end of article.

2) Lubricate camshaft with engine oil before installing. To install remaining components, reverse removal procedure. Tighten bolts to specification. See TORQUE SPECIFICATIONS table at end of article.

CRANKSHAFT FRONT SEAL

Removal & Installation - **1)** Crankshaft front seal is located in oil pump housing. Timing belt and crankshaft sprocket must be removed for access to crankshaft front seal. Manufacturer does not indicate procedure for seal removal.

2) To install, apply light coat of engine oil on circumference of crankshaft front seal. Use Seal Installer (MB998306) to install crankshaft front seal.

TIMING BELT

Removal - **1)** Disconnect negative battery cable. Remove accessory drive belts. Remove A/C compressor with hoses attached and secure aside. Remove A/C compressor mounting bracket and drive belt tensioner. Remove power steering/alternator belt tensioner. Remove power steering pump with hoses attached and secure aside.

2) Raise and support vehicle. Remove right inner fender shield. Remove crankshaft pulley and vibration damper. Lower vehicle and support engine with floor jack. Separate engine mount from engine mount bracket located in front of timing belt cover. Raise engine slightly. Remove engine mount bracket.

3) Remove timing belt covers, noting bolt length for reassembly reference. Rotate engine and align timing marks on front and rear camshaft sprockets, and on crankshaft sprocket. *See Fig. 7.* Mark direction of timing belt rotation for reassembly reference.

4) Loosen timing belt tensioner. Remove timing belt. Note direction of flange installation on front of crankshaft and remove (if necessary). If camshaft sprocket removal is required, use Camshaft Sprocket Holder (MB990775) to hold sprocket. Remove retaining bolt and camshaft sprocket.

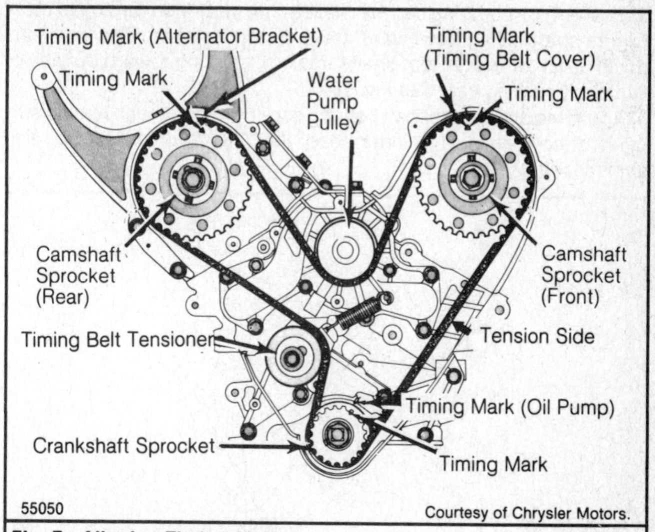
Timing Mark (Alternator Bracket)
Timing Mark
Water Pump Pulley
Timing Mark (Timing Belt Cover)
Timing Mark
Camshaft Sprocket (Rear)
Camshaft Sprocket (Front)
Timing Belt Tensioner
Tension Side
Timing Mark (Oil Pump)
Crankshaft Sprocket
Timing Mark
55050
Courtesy of Chrysler Motors.

Fig. 7: Aligning Timing Marks

Installation - **1)** Install camshaft sprockets (if removed). Using camshaft sprocket holder, tighten camshaft sprocket retaining bolt to specification. See TORQUE SPECIFICATIONS table at end of article.

2) Ensure all timing marks are aligned. *See Fig. 7.* Rotate timing belt tensioner fully counterclockwise and temporarily tighten retaining bolt. Install timing belt on crankshaft sprocket while holding belt tight on tension side.

CAUTION: When installing timing belt, ensure it will turn in original direction.

3) Install timing belt on front (radiator side) camshaft sprocket. *See Fig. 7.* Install timing belt on water pump pulley, rear camshaft sprocket and then on timing belt tensioner.

4) Apply rotating force on front (radiator side) camshaft sprocket in opposite direction to apply pressure on tension side of timing belt. Ensure all timing marks align. *See Fig. 7.*

5) Install flange on front of crankshaft sprocket (if removed) with flat side against timing belt and offset side toward front of crankshaft. Loosen timing belt tensioner bolt, allowing spring tension to be applied on timing belt. Rotate crankshaft clockwise 2 full revolutions.

CAUTION: Rotate crankshaft in a clockwise direction. DO NOT rotate crankshaft counterclockwise.

6) Realign all timing marks and tighten timing belt tensioner to specification. See TORQUE SPECIFICATIONS table at end of article. To install remaining components, reverse removal procedure. Ensure timing belt cover bolts are installed in original location. Tighten to specification. See TORQUE SPECIFICATIONS table at end of article.

ROCKER ARM & LASH ADJUSTER

NOTE: Lash adjuster operation should be checked before removing rocker arm.

Removal - **1)** Remove air cleaner assembly. Disconnect spark plug wires. Remove valve covers.

2) To check lash adjuster operation, insert a small wire through air bleed hole at top of rocker arm, directly above lash adjuster. Lightly push check ball downward in lash adjuster and check rocker arm for free play. If free play does not exist, replace lash adjuster.

3) Install Lash Adjuster Retainers (MD998443) on rocker arms. *See Fig. 8.* Loosen, but DO NOT remove, camshaft bearing cap bolts. Mark location of rocker arms for reassembly reference. Camshaft bearing caps are numbered for location. *See Fig. 10.* Remove rocker arms, shafts and camshaft bearing caps as an assembly.

Installation - **1)** Ensure rocker arm shaft for intake valves contains an additional oil feed hole in the bottom of the shaft. *See Fig. 9.*

1991 ENGINES
3.0L V6 (Cont.)

2) Ensure No. 1 bearing cap is installed with machined portion of rocker arm shaft facing downward, toward cylinder head. This positions notch areas of rocker arm shafts upward, pointing toward outside of camshaft bearing cap. *See Fig. 10.*

3) Apply sealant on camshaft bearing cap-to-cylinder head mating surfaces at both ends of cylinder head. *See Fig. 11.* Install rocker arm shaft assembly.

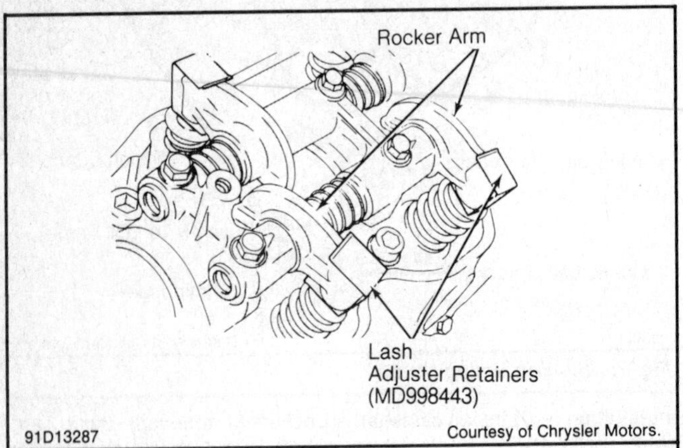
Rocker Arm
Lash
Adjuster Retainers
(MD998443)
91D13287
Courtesy of Chrysler Motors.

Fig. 8: Installing Lash Adjuster Retainers

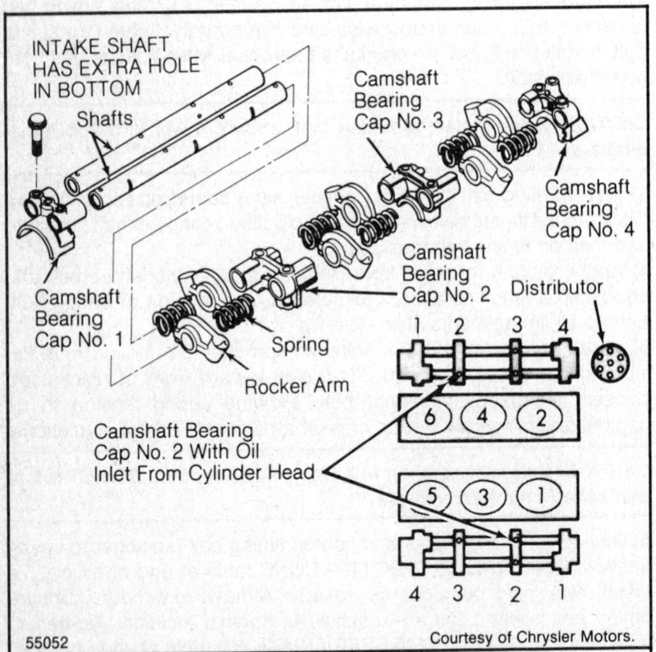
INTAKE SHAFT
HAS EXTRA HOLE
IN BOTTOM
Shafts
Camshaft
Bearing
Cap No. 3
Camshaft
Bearing
Cap No. 4
Camshaft
Bearing
Cap No. 2
Distributor
Camshaft
Bearing
Cap No. 1
Spring
Rocker Arm
Camshaft Bearing
Cap No. 2 With Oil
Inlet From Cylinder Head
1 2 3 4
6 4 2
5 3 1
4 3 2 1
55052
Courtesy of Chrysler Motors.

Fig. 9: Exploded View of Rocker Arm Components

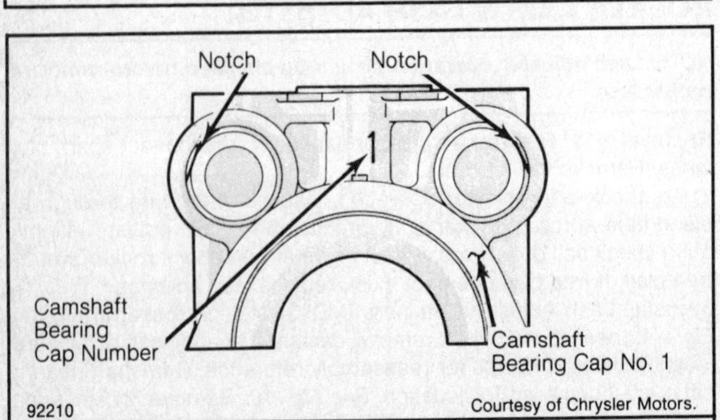
Notch
Notch
1
Camshaft
Bearing
Cap Number
Camshaft
Bearing Cap No. 1
92210
Courtesy of Chrysler Motors.

Fig. 10: Identifying No. 1 Camshaft Bearing Cap

CAUTION: Arrow on camshaft bearing caps MUST face same direction as arrow on cylinder heads. See Fig. 11. Camshaft bearing caps must be properly installed, as camshaft bearing cap No. 2 contains an oiling inlet hole from cylinder head. See Fig. 9.

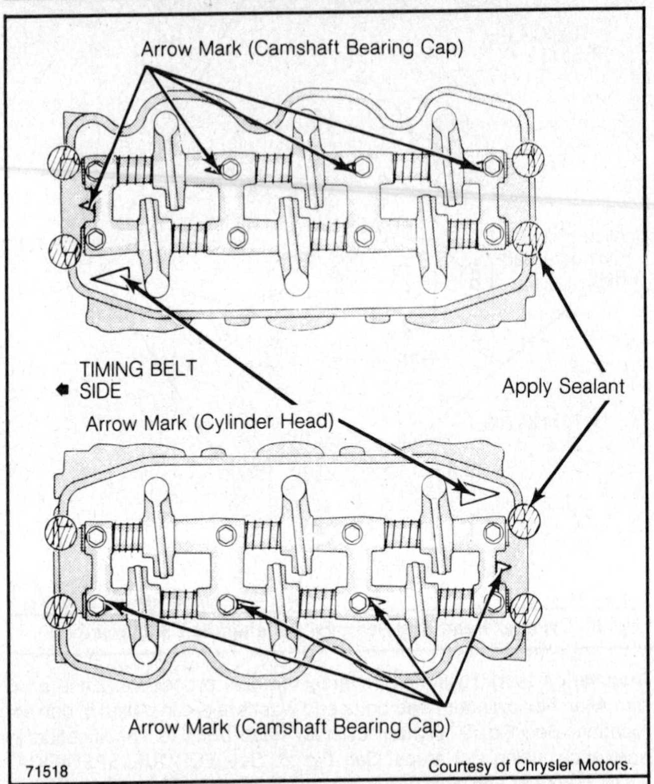
Arrow Mark (Camshaft Bearing Cap)
TIMING BELT
SIDE
Apply Sealant
Arrow Mark (Cylinder Head)
Arrow Mark (Camshaft Bearing Cap)
71518
Courtesy of Chrysler Motors.

Fig. 11: Positioning Camshaft Bearing Caps

4) Tighten camshaft bearing caps bolts to specification in 2 steps in the following order: No. 3, No. 2, No. 1 and then No. 4 camshaft bearing caps. See TORQUE SPECIFICATIONS table at end of article.

5) Install distributor adapter (if removed). Tighten bolts to specification. See TORQUE SPECIFICATIONS table at end of article. Coat camshaft oil seal lip with grease.

6) Thread Seal Installer (MD998713) into camshaft and install camshaft oil seal. Using Plug Installer (MD998306), install camshaft plug. Before installing valve cover, apply RTV sealant at front and rear camshaft bearing cap-to-valve cover gasket contact areas.

7) To install remaining components, reverse removal procedure. Tighten bolts to specification. See TORQUE SPECIFICATIONS table at end of article.

CAMSHAFT

Removal – 1) Remove distributor and distributor adapter (if necessary). Remove timing belt. See TIMING BELT under REMOVAL & INSTALLATION.

2) Remove rocker arm and lash adjuster. See ROCKER ARM & LASH ADJUSTER under REMOVAL & INSTALLATION. Remove camshaft and oil seals.

Inspection – Inspect components for damage. Replace if damaged. Ensure all oil holes are not restricted. Inspect camshaft and cylinder head journal areas for damage. Inspect distributor drive gear for damage. Measure lobe height. Replace camshaft if not within specification. See CAMSHAFT table under ENGINE SPECIFICATIONS at end of article.

Installation – To install, reverse removal procedure. Lubricate camshaft with engine oil before installing.

CAUTION: Ensure proper procedure is used when installing rocker arms, as camshaft bearing caps must be properly installed. See ROCKER ARM & LASH ADJUSTER under REMOVAL & INSTALLATION.

REAR CRANKSHAFT OIL SEAL

NOTE: Rear crankshaft oil seal is a one-piece oil seal mounted in seal retainer. Manufacturer lists procedure with seal retainer removed from cylinder block.

Removal & Installation - 1) Remove flywheel for access to seal retainer. Remove seal retainer. It may be necessary to remove oil pan, as oil pan seals against seal retainer. Remove oil seal from seal retainer.

2) Using Seal Installer (MD998718), install rear crankshaft oil seal into seal retainer. Before installing seal retainer, apply RTV sealant on seal retainer-to-cylinder block surface. Install seal retainer. To install remaining components, reverse removal procedure. Tighten bolts to specification. See TORQUE SPECIFICATIONS table at end of article.

WATER PUMP

Removal & Installation - 1) Remove timing belt. See TIMING BELT under REMOVAL & INSTALLATION. Drain cooling system. Remove retaining bolts, water pump, gasket and "O" ring on coolant inlet pipe.

2) To install, reverse removal procedure. Install new "O" ring on coolant inlet pipe. Apply water to "O" ring before installing water pump. DO NOT apply grease to "O" ring. Tighten bolts to specification. See TORQUE SPECIFICATIONS table at end of article. To install remaining components, reverse removal procedure. Fill cooling system.

OIL PAN

Removal & Installation - 1) Removal procedure is not available from manufacturer. To install, apply a .12" (3.0 mm) diameter bead of RTV sealant around edge of oil pan before installing.

2) Ensure sealant is applied in sealing surface groove and on outside of bolt holes. DO NOT allow sealant to be forced from flange area toward flywheel.

3) Install oil pan. Tighten bolts to specification in sequence. *See Fig. 12.* See TORQUE SPECIFICATIONS table at end of article.

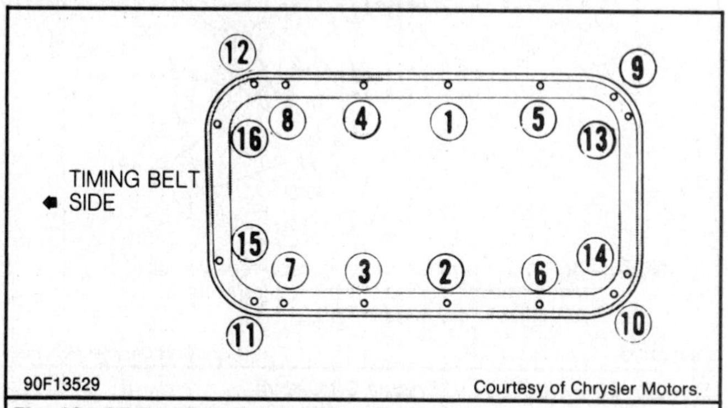

12
9
8
4
1
5
16
13
TIMING BELT
SIDE
15
7
3
2
6
14
11
10
90F13529
Courtesy of Chrysler Motors.

Fig. 12: Oil Pan Bolt Tightening Sequence

OVERHAUL

CYLINDER HEAD

Cylinder Head - Check cylinder head warpage. Resurface cylinder head if warpage exceeds specification. See CYLINDER HEAD table under ENGINE SPECIFICATIONS at end of article.

CAUTION: DO NOT grind more than .008" (.20 mm) combined total from surface of cylinder head and deck surface of cylinder block.

Valve Springs - Check valve spring free length, out-of-square and pressure. Replace valve spring if not within specification. See VALVES & VALVE SPRINGS table under ENGINE SPECIFICATIONS at end of article.

CAUTION: Valve spring must be installed with enamel-coated end toward spring retainer.

Valve Stem Oil Seals - Umbrella-type oil seals are used on all valves. Seals must be replaced if removed for any reason. When reinstalling valves, DO NOT overcompress valve springs or valve stem oil seal may be damaged.

Valve Guides - Check valve guide I.D. and valve stem-to-valve guide clearance. Clearance must be within specification. See CYLINDER HEAD table under ENGINE SPECIFICATIONS at end of article. No service procedure is available from manufacturer.

Valve Seats - Check valve seat width. Grind valve seat if width is not within specification. See CYLINDER HEAD table under ENGINE SPECIFICATIONS at end of article.

Valves - Check margin and stem diameter. Replace valve if not within specification. See VALVES & VALVE SPRINGS table under ENGINE SPECIFICATIONS at end of article.

Seat Correction Angles - Use a 15 degree stone to lower valve seat or a 65 degree stone to raise valve seat.

VALVE TRAIN

Rocker Arm Shaft Assembly - 1) Note location and direction of rocker arm components and camshaft bearing caps. Remove camshaft bearing cap bolts. Disassemble rocker arm shaft assembly. *See Fig. 9.*

2) Ensure intake valve rocker arm shaft has a .12" (3 mm) oil hole in bottom of shaft. *See Fig. 9.* Exhaust valve rocker shaft does not have oil hole. Oil hole supplies oil to exhaust valve rocker arm shaft through camshaft bearing cap.

3) Inspect components for damage. Replace if damaged. Ensure all oil holes are not clogged. Reassemble rocker arm shaft assembly.

CAUTION: The No. 1 camshaft bearing cap must be installed with machined portion of rocker arm shaft facing downward, toward cylinder head. This positions notch areas of rocker arm shafts upward, pointing toward outside of camshaft bearing cap. See Fig. 10. Ensure No. 2 camshaft bearing cap contains oil inlet for from cylinder head. See Fig. 9.

Lash Adjuster - Lash adjuster is located in rocker arm. Lash adjuster must not be disassembled.

CYLINDER BLOCK ASSEMBLY

Piston & Rod Assembly - For cylinders No. 1, 3 and 5, install pistons with "R" front mark on top of piston toward timing belt side of engine. For cylinders No. 2, 4 and 6, install piston with "L" front mark toward timing belt side of engine. Ensure front mark "72" on connecting rod is facing toward timing belt side of engine. *See Fig. 13.*

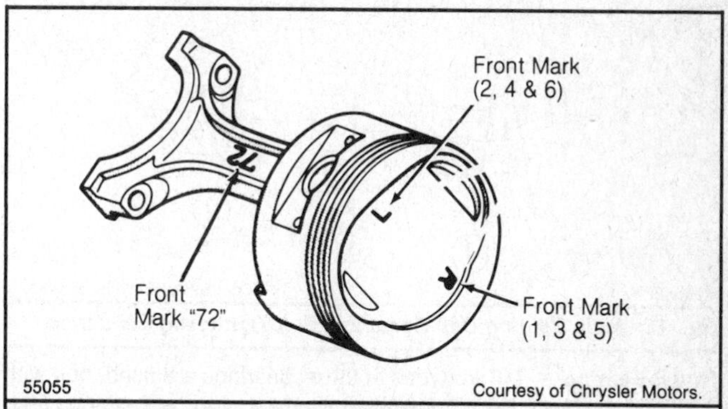

Front Mark
(2, 4 & 6)
72
Front
Mark "72"
Front Mark
(1, 3 & 5)
55055
Courtesy of Chrysler Motors.

Fig. 13: Installing Piston & Connecting Rod

CAUTION: Pistons are not interchangeable from side-to-side.

Fitting Pistons — Measure cylinder bore diameter and taper at .50" (12.7 mm) below top surface of cylinder bore, middle of bore and .38" (9.6 mm) from bottom of cylinder bore. Measure piston diameter at .08" (2.0 mm) from bottom of piston skirt at right angle to piston pin. Piston diameter and clearance must be within specification. See PISTONS, PINS & RINGS table under ENGINE SPECIFICATIONS at end of article.

1991 ENGINES
3.0L V6 (Cont.)

Piston Rings – Ensure ring end gap and side clearances are within specification. See PISTON, PINS & RINGS table under ENGINE SPECIFICATIONS at end of article. Ensure piston ring end gaps are properly positioned. *See Fig. 14.*

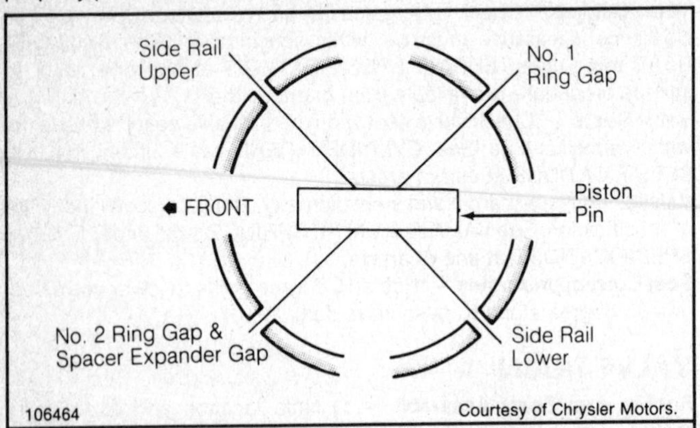
Side Rail
Upper
No. 1
Ring Gap
FRONT
Piston
Pin
No. 2 Ring Gap &
Spacer Expander Gap
Side Rail
Lower
106464
Courtesy of Chrysler Motors.

Fig. 14: Positioning Piston Rings

Rod Bearings – **1)** When replacing rod bearings, ensure front mark "72" on connecting rod faces toward timing belt side of engine. *See Fig. 13.*

2) Tighten connecting rod nuts to specification. See TORQUE SPECIFICATIONS table at end of article. Ensure bearing oil clearance and side play are within specifications. See CRANKSHAFT, MAIN & CONNECTING ROD BEARINGS and CONNECTING RODS tables under ENGINE SPECIFICATIONS at end of article.

Crankshaft & Main Bearings – **1)** Upper main bearings contain oil grooves, while lower bearings installed in main bearing cap assembly do not.

2) Main bearing cap assembly must be installed with arrow toward front (timing belt end) of engine. Coat bolts with oil before installing. Tighten bolts to specification in sequence. *See Fig. 15.* See TORQUE SPECIFICATIONS table at end of article.

3) Ensure main bearing oil clearance and crankshaft end play are within specification. See CRANKSHAFT, MAIN & CONNECTING ROD BEARINGS table under ENGINE SPECIFICATIONS at end of article. Replace thrust bearing if end play is not within specification.

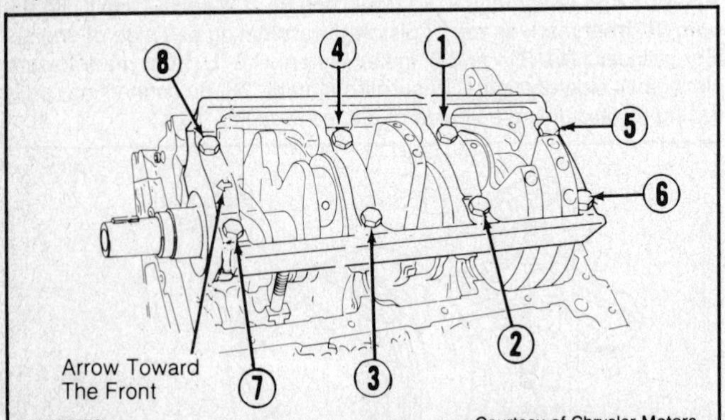
8
4
1
5
6
2
3
7
Arrow Toward
The Front
90E02572
Courtesy of Chrysler Motors.

Fig. 15: Main Bearing Cap Assembly Bolt Tightening Sequence

Thrust Bearing – **1)** Two types of thrust bearings are used, one with positioning tabs and another without. One set of thrust bearings (one with positioning tab and one without tab) fit in cylinder block and another set in main bearing cap assembly at No. 3 main bearing.

2) Thrust bearing without positioning tab fits on front (timing belt side) of cylinder block and rear (flywheel side) of main bearing cap assembly. Thrust bearing with positioning tab fits on rear (flywheel side) of cylinder block and on front (timing belt side) of main bearing cap assembly. Groove side on thrust bearing goes toward crankshaft.

3) Replace thrust bearing if crankshaft end play is not within specification. See CRANKSHAFT, MAIN & CONNECTING ROD BEARINGS table under ENGINE SPECIFICATIONS at end of article.

Cylinder Block – **1)** Using a feeler gauge and straightedge, check cylinder block deck surface for warpage. Surface cylinder block if warpage exceeds specification. See CYLINDER BLOCK table under ENGINE SPECIFICATIONS at end of article.

CAUTION: DO NOT grind more than .008" (.20 mm) combined total from surface of cylinder head and deck surface of cylinder block.

2) Check cylinder bore, taper and out-of-round. Measurements should be taken at .50" (12.7 mm) below top surface of cylinder bore, middle of bore and .38" (9.6 mm) from bottom of cylinder bore. Bore cylinder block if not within specification. See CYLINDER BLOCK table under ENGINE SPECIFICATIONS at end of article.

ENGINE OILING

ENGINE LUBRICATION SYSTEM

A crankshaft-driven oil pump provides pressurized lubrication to main oil gallery. *See Fig. 16.*

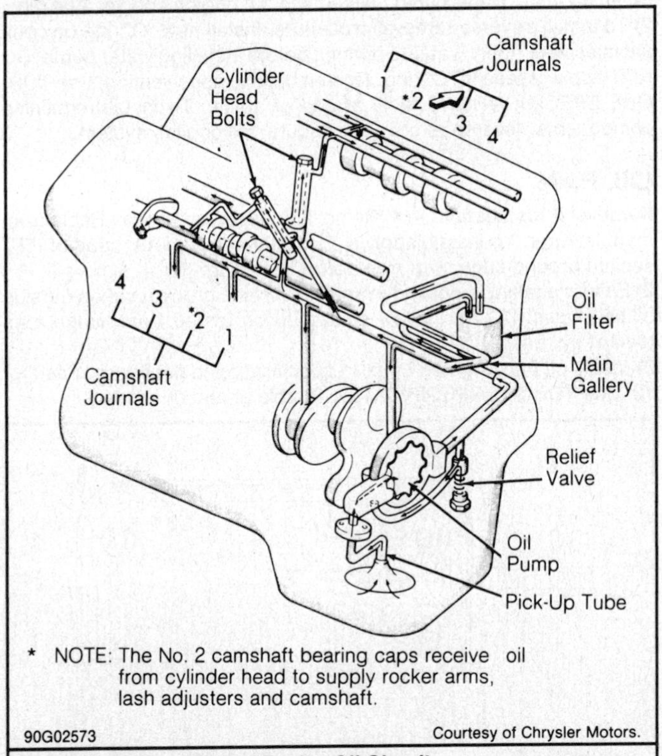
Camshaft
Journals
Cylinder
Head
Bolts
1
*2
3
4
4
3
*2
1
Camshaft
Journals
Oil
Filter
Main
Gallery
Relief
Valve
Oil
Pump
Pick-Up Tube
* NOTE: The No. 2 camshaft bearing caps receive oil
from cylinder head to supply rocker arms,
lash adjusters and camshaft.
90G02573
Courtesy of Chrysler Motors.

Fig. 16: Cutaway View of Engine Oil Circuit

Crankcase Capacity – Oil capacity with oil filter is 4.5 qts. (4.2L).

Oil Pressure – Oil pressure is 30-100 psi (2.1-7.0 kg/cm²) at 3000 RPM with engine at normal operating temperature.

OIL PUMP

Removal & Disassembly – **1)** Remove timing belt and crankshaft sprocket. See TIMING BELT under REMOVAL & INSTALLATION. Remove oil pan and pick-up tube.

2) Remove oil pump-to-cylinder block bolts. Note bolt location and length for reassembly. Remove oil pump. Disassemble oil pump. *See Fig. 17.* Remove oil seal from oil pump case.

Inspection – **1)** Inspect components for damage. Measure clearance between small area of inner rotor and oil pump case. Measure clearance between outer rotor and oil pump case.

2) With inner and outer rotors installed in oil pump case, place straightedge across oil pump case and both rotors. Using feeler gauge, check rotor end clearance between rotors and straightedge. Ensure relief plunger slides freely in bore. Replace oil pump assembly if clearance exceeds specification. See OIL PUMP SPECIFICATIONS table.

OIL PUMP SPECIFICATIONS

Application	In. (mm)
Inner Rotor Small Diameter-To-Pump Case Clearance	.006 (.15)
Outer Rotor-To-Pump Case Clearance	.004-.007 (.10-.18)
Rotor End Clearance	.0015-.0035 (.038-.089)

Reassembly & Installation – 1) To reassemble, reverse disassembly procedure. Ensure components are installed in original location. If oil seal was removed from oil pump case, use Seal Installer (MB998306) to install new seal. Lubricate seal lip with oil before installing.
2) To install, reverse removal procedure. Ensure bolts are installed in original location. *See Fig. 17.* Tighten bolts to specification. See TORQUE SPECIFICATIONS table at end of article.

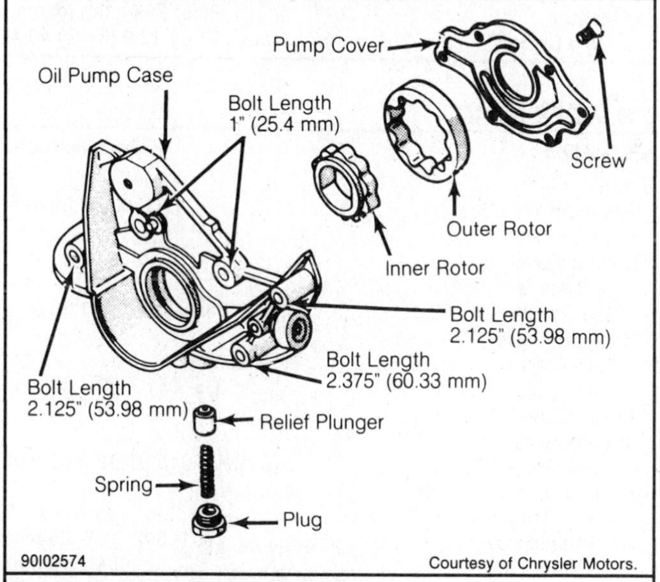
Pump Cover
Oil Pump Case
Bolt Length
1" (25.4 mm)
Screw
Outer Rotor
Inner Rotor
Bolt Length
2.125" (53.98 mm)
Bolt Length
2.375" (60.33 mm)
Bolt Length
2.125" (53.98 mm)
Relief Plunger
Spring
Plug
90I02574
Courtesy of Chrysler Motors.

Fig. 17: Exploded View of Oil Pump

TORQUE SPECIFICATIONS

TORQUE SPECIFICATIONS

Application	Ft. Lbs. (N.m)
A/C Compressor Mount Bolt	40 (54)
Camshaft Bearing Cap Bolt	1
Camshaft Sprocket Bolt	70 (95)
Connecting Rod Nut	38 (52)
Crankshaft Belt Pulley Bolt	21 (29)
Cylinder Head Bolt	2 70 (95)
Distributor Adapter Bolt	10 (14)
Engine Bracket-To-Cylinder Block Bolt	35 (47)
Exhaust Crossover Pipe Bolt	51 (69)
Exhaust Manifold Heat Shield Bolt	11 (15)
Exhaust Manifold Nut	15 (20)
Flexplate Bolt	70 (95)
Front Mount-To-Cylinder Block Bolt/Nut	
Lower Nut	75 (102)
Upper Bolt	125 (170)
Front Mount-To-Frame Rail Bolt/Nut	40 (54)
Fuel Rail Bolt	10 (14)
Intake Manifold Nut	3 14 (19)
Left Mount Through Bolt	50 (68)
Left Mount-To-Frame Rail Bolt	50 (68)
Main Bearing Cap Bolt	4 60 (81)
Oil Pick-Up Tube Bolt	16 (22)
Oil Pump Bolt	11 (15)
Oil Pump Relief Plunger Plug	36 (49)

TORQUE SPECIFICATIONS (Cont.)

Application	Ft. Lbs. (N.m)
Right Mount (Timing Belt Side)	
Through Bolt	100 (136)
Mount-To-Frame Bolt	50 (68)
Vertical Bolt/Nut	75 (102)
Timing Belt Tensioner Bolt	21 (29)
Torque Converter-To-Flexplate Bolt	55 (75)
Transaxle-To-Cylinder Block Bolt	75 (102)
Upper Air Intake Bolt	5 10 (14)
Vibration Damper Bolt	112 (152)
Water Pump Bolt	20 (27)
	INCH Lbs. (N.m)
Fuel Pressure Regulator Bolt	95 (11)
Oil Pan Bolt	51 (6)
Oil Pump Cover Screw	104 (12)
Rear Crankshaft Seal Retainer Bolt	104 (12)
Timing Belt Cover Bolt	115 (13)
Valve Cover Bolt	88 (10)

1 – Tighten camshaft bearing cap bolts to 85 INCH lbs. (10 (N.m) in the following sequence: No. 3, No. 2, No. 1, No. 4. Repeat procedure and tighten bolts to 15 ft. lbs. (20 N.m).
2 – Tighten bolts in sequence. *See Fig. 6.*
3 – Tighten nuts in sequence. *See Fig. 4.*
4 – Coat bolts with oil before installing. Tighten bolts in sequence. *See Fig. 15.*
5 – Tighten bolts in sequence. *See Fig. 5.*

ENGINE SPECIFICATIONS

GENERAL SPECIFICATIONS

Application	Specification
3.0L	
Displacement	181 Cu. In. (3.0L)
Bore	3.59" (91.1 mm)
Stroke	2.99" (75.9 mm)
Compression Ratio	8.9:1
Fuel System	PFI
Horsepower @ RPM	142 @ 5000
Torque Ft. Lbs. @ RPM	173 @ 2800

CRANKSHAFT, MAIN & CONNECTING ROD BEARINGS

Application	In. (mm)
3.0L	
Crankshaft End Play	
Standard	.002-.010 (.05-.25)
Wear Limit	.012 (.30)
Main Bearings	
Journal Diameter	2.361-2.362 (59.97-59.99)
Journal Out-Of-Round	.001 (.02)
Journal Taper	.0002 (.005)
Oil Clearance	.0006-.0020 (.015-.051)
Connecting Rod Bearings	
Journal Diameter	1.968-1.969 (49.99-50.01)
Journal Out-Of-Round	.001 (.02)
Journal Taper	.0002 (.005)
Oil Clearance	.0008-.0026 (.020-.066)

1991 ENGINES
3.0L V6 (Cont.)

CONNECTING RODS

Application	In. (mm)
3.0L	
Center-To-Center Length	5.547-5.551 (140.89-140.99)
Maximum Bend & Twist	.0019 (.048)
Side Play	
Standard	.004-.010 (.10-.25)
Wear Limit	.016 (.41)

PISTONS, PINS & RINGS

Application	In. (mm)
3.0L	
Pistons	
Clearance	.0012-.0020 (.030-.051)
Diameter	3.585-3.586 (91.06-91.08)
Rings	
No. 1	
End Gap	
Standard	.012-.018 (.30-.46)
Wear Limit	.031 (.79)
Side Clearance	
Standard	.0020-.0035 (.051-.089)
Wear Limit	.0039 (.099)
No. 2	
End Gap	
Standard	.010-.016 (.25-.41)
Wear Limit	.031 (.79)
Side Clearance	
Standard	.0008-.0020 (.020-.051)
Wear Limit	.0039 (.099)
No. 3 (Oil)	
End Gap	
Standard	.012-.035 (.30-.89)
Wear Limit	.039 (.99)

CYLINDER BLOCK

Application	In. (mm)
3.0L	
Cylinder Bore	
Standard Diameter	3.586-3.587 (91.08-91.10)
Maximum Taper & Out-Of-Round	.0008 (.020)
Maximum Deck Warpage	[1] .0020 (.051)

[1] – Service limit is .0039" (.099 mm). Combined maximum total grind limit of cylinder head and cylinder block is .008" (.20 mm).

VALVES & VALVE SPRINGS

Application	Specification
3.0L	
Intake Valves	
Face Angle	45°
Minimum Margin	.027" (.69 mm)
Stem Diameter	.313-.314" (7.95-7.98 mm)
Exhaust Valves	
Face Angle	45°
Minimum Margin	.059" (1.50 mm)
Stem Diameter	.3120-.3125" (7.92-7.94 mm)
Valve Springs	
Free Length	1.921-1.960" (48.79-49.48 mm)
Out-Of-Square	4°
Pressure	Lbs. @ In. (kg @ mm)
Valve Closed	73 @ 1.59 (33 @ 40.4)

CYLINDER HEAD

Application	Specifications
3.0L	
Maximum Warpage	[1] .002" (.05 mm)
Valve Seats	
Intake Valve	
Seat Angle	44°
Seat Width	.035-.051" (.89-1.30 mm)
Exhaust Valve	
Seat Angle	44°
Seat Width	.035-.051" (.89-1.30 mm)
Valve Guides	
Intake Valve	
Valve Guide I.D.	.314-.315" (7.98-8.00 mm)
Valve Stem-To-Guide	
Oil Clearance	
Standard	.001-.002" (.02-.05 mm)
Wear Limit	.004" (.10 mm)
Exhaust Valve	
Valve Guide I.D.	.314-.315" (7.98-8.00 mm)
Valve Stem-To-Guide	
Oil Clearance	
Standard	.0019-.0030" (.048-.076 mm)
Wear Limit	.006" (.15 mm)

[1] – Combined maximum total grind limit of cylinder head and cylinder block is .008" (.20 mm)

CAMSHAFT

Application	In. (mm)
3.0L	
Lobe Height	1.604-1.624 (40.74-41.25)

Caravan, Town & Country, Voyager

NOTE: For repair procedures not covered in this article, see ENGINE OVERHAUL PROCEDURES article in GENERAL INFORMATION.

ENGINE IDENTIFICATION

Engine may be identified by eighth character of Vehicle Identification Number (VIN). The VIN is stamped on a plate on top of instrument panel at lower left of windshield.

ENGINE IDENTIFICATION CODE

Engine	Code
3.3L PFI	R

ADJUSTMENTS

VALVE CLEARANCE ADJUSTMENT

Hydraulic valve lifters are used. No valve adjustment is required.

REMOVAL & INSTALLATION

NOTE: For reassembly reference, label all electrical connectors, vacuum hoses and fuel lines before removal. Also place mating marks on engine hood and other major assemblies before removal.

FUEL PRESSURE RELEASE

CAUTION: Fuel system is under pressure. Pressure must be released before servicing any fuel system component.

1) Loosen fuel tank cap to release pressure. Disconnect injector wiring harness from engine wiring harness. Connect jumper wire from terminal No. 1 of injector harness to ground. *See Fig. 1.*

2) Connect another jumper wire to terminal No. 2 of injector harness. *See Fig. 1.* Touch jumper wire to positive battery terminal for no more than 5 seconds to release fuel pressure. Remove jumper wires and reconnect wiring harness.

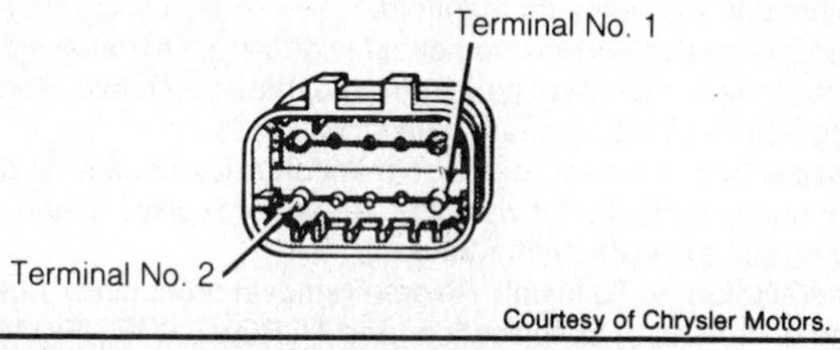
Terminal No. 1
Terminal No. 2
90B02575
Courtesy of Chrysler Motors.

Fig. 1: Identifying Injector Wiring Harness Terminals

COOLING SYSTEM BLEEDING

1) To bleed cooling system, remove engine temperature sending unit. Sending unit is located in front of cylinder head, near thermostat housing, just below spark plug wire holder.

2) Fill cooling system until coolant reaches sending unit level. Install sending unit and tighten to 60 INCH lbs. (7 N.m). Finish filling cooling system.

ENGINE

NOTE: Remove engine with transaxle remaining in vehicle.

Removal - 1) Release fuel pressure. See FUEL PRESSURE RELEASE under REMOVAL & INSTALLATION. Disconnect negative battery cable. Scribe hood hinge location on hood for reassembly. Remove hood. Drain cooling system and engine oil. Disconnect necessary coolant hoses, control cables, electrical connections and vacuum hoses.

2) Remove air cleaner and radiator/fan assembly. Wrap shop towel around fuel lines. Remove fuel lines from fuel rail by pushing inward on plastic ring, located at end of fuel line fitting, and pull fuel line from fitting.

3) Raise and support vehicle. Remove A/C compressor and power steering pump with hoses attached and secure aside.

4) Remove starter. Disconnect exhaust pipe at exhaust manifold. Remove torque converter cover. Reference mark flexplate to torque converter for reassembly reference.

5) Remove torque converter-to-flexplate bolts. Attach "C" clamp at bottom front edge of torque converter housing to secure torque converter.

6) Remove lower transaxle-to-cylinder block bolts. Lower vehicle. Support transaxle with floor jack. Attach lifting hoist to engine. Remove remaining transaxle-to-cylinder block bolts.

7) Place reference mark on side rail to indicate right insulator (timing chain side) position for reassembly reference. Remove right insulator-to-side rail bolts.

CAUTION: Right insulator position on side rail must be marked before removal for reassembly reference to ensure proper positioning of the engine. Insulator must be installed in original position.

8) Remove through bolt from left engine mount from inside fenderwell. Insulator bracket-to-transaxle bolts may be removed instead of through bolt. Remove front engine mount bolts. Lift engine from vehicle.

Installation - 1) To install, reverse removal procedure. DO NOT tighten engine mount bolts until all bolts are installed. If vertical bolts on right or left mount were loosened, axle shaft length must be checked.

2) To determine axle shaft length, measure distance between inner edge of outboard boot and inner edge of inboard boot at 6 o'clock position. *See Fig. 2.*

3) Axle shaft length must be within specification. See AXLE SHAFT LENGTH SPECIFICATIONS table.

AXLE SHAFT LENGTH SPECIFICATIONS

Application	In. (mm)
AWD Models	
Right Axle Shaft	11.5-11.9 (292-302)
Left Axle Shaft	9.0-9.4 (229-239)
2WD Models	
Right Axle Shaft	20.5-20.9 (521-531)
Left Axle Shaft	9.0-9.4 (229-239)

4) Adjust axle shaft length to specification by sliding engine in slots on engine mounts. Tighten all engine mount bolts once correct axle shaft length is obtained.

CAUTION: Tighten vertical bolt in right (timing chain side) mount bracket before tightening through bolt.

5) Ensure reference mark is aligned on torque converter and flexplate. Tighten bolts/nuts to specification. See TORQUE SPECIFICATIONS table at end of article.

6) Lubricate fuel lines with 30W engine oil before reconnecting. Ensure fuel lines are installed until a "click" sound is heard.

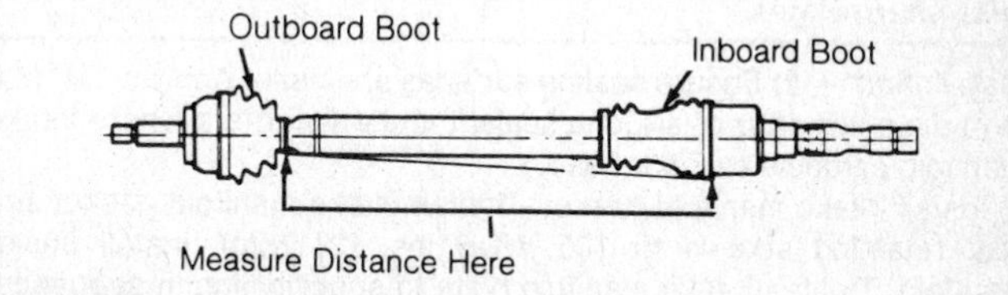
Outboard Boot
Inboard Boot
Measure Distance Here
90C13526
Courtesy of Chrysler Motors.

Fig. 2: Measuring Axle Shaft Length

1991 ENGINES
3.3L V6 (Cont.)

NOTE: Fuel supply line is a 5/16" diameter fitting, and fuel return line is a 1/4" diameter fitting.

7) Fill and bleed cooling system. See COOLING SYSTEM BLEEDING under REMOVAL & INSTALLATION.

INTAKE MANIFOLD

Removal – 1) Release fuel pressure. See FUEL PRESSURE RELEASE under REMOVAL & INSTALLATION. Disconnect negative battery cable. Drain cooling system. Remove air cleaner-to-throttle body hose.

2) Disconnect control cables and linkages at throttle body. Disconnect Automatic Idle Speed (AIS) motor and Throttle Position Sensor (TPS) wiring harness connectors at throttle body. Remove vacuum hoses from throttle body and intake manifold.

3) Disconnect vacuum hoses and EGR tube flange from air intake plenum (upper intake manifold). Disconnect wiring connectors at charge temperature sensor, MAP sensor and O_2 sensor heater. Remove cylinder head-to-air intake plenum support brace.

4) Wrap shop towel around fuel lines. Remove fuel lines from fuel rail by pushing inward on plastic ring, located at end of fuel line fitting, and pull fuel line from fitting.

5) Remove ignition coils and alternator bracket from air intake plenum. Remove air intake plenum bolts in sequence. *See Fig. 3.* Rotate air intake plenum back over the valve cover. Cover intake manifold ports with shop towels.

6) Disconnect vacuum hose at pressure regulator. Disconnect fuel injector wiring harness from engine wiring harness. Disconnect necessary sensor wiring connectors, near fuel rail and intake manifold.

7) Remove fuel rail retaining bolts and fuel rail. Disconnect coolant hoses at intake manifold. Remove intake manifold retaining bolts in sequence, and remove intake manifold. *See Fig. 4.* Remove intake manifold gasket end seal retaining screws, and remove gasket.

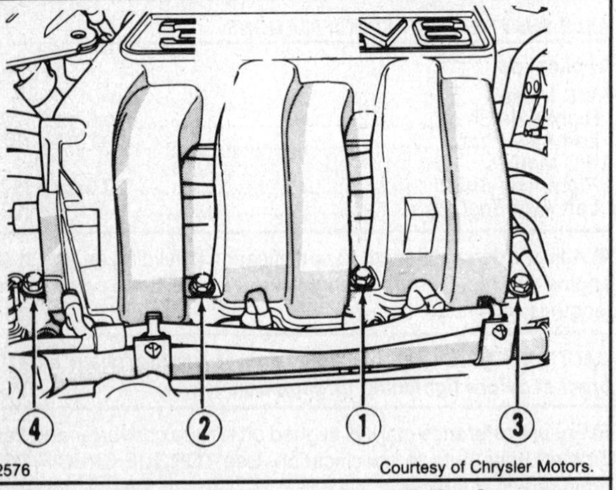
4
2
1
3

90D02576 Courtesy of Chrysler Motors.

Fig. 3: Air Intake Plenum Bolt Removal & Installation Sequence

CAUTION: Handle intake manifold gasket seal carefully, as seal contains sharp edges.

Installation – 1) Ensure sealing surfaces are clean. Apply a 1/4" (6.4 mm) diameter drop of silicone sealant in the 4 corners where intake manifold contacts cylinder head.

2) Install intake manifold gasket. Tighten intake manifold gasket end seal retaining screws to 105 INCH lbs. (12 N.m). Install intake manifold. Tighten intake manifold bolts to specification in sequence. *See Fig. 4.* See TORQUE SPECIFICATIONS table at end of article.

3) To install remaining components, reverse removal procedure. Ensure injector holes are clean. Lubricate injector "O" rings with engine oil before installing. Install injector until firmly seated in port.

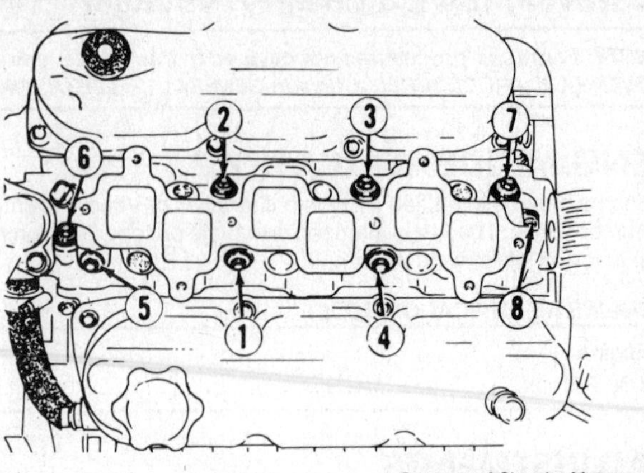
2
3
7
6
5
1
4
8

90F02577 Courtesy of Chrysler Motors.

Fig. 4: Intake Manifold Bolt Removal & Installation Sequence

4) Install air intake plenum with bolts finger tight. Loosely install alternator bracket-to-intake manifold bolt and cylinder head-to-intake manifold brace bolts.

5) Tighten air intake plenum bolts to specification in sequence. *See Fig. 3.* See TORQUE SPECIFICATIONS table at end of article. Tighten alternator bracket and intake manifold brace bolts.

6) Lubricate fuel lines with 30W engine oil before reconnecting. Ensure fuel lines are installed until a "click" sound is heard.

NOTE: Fuel supply line is a 5/16" diameter fitting, and fuel return line is a 1/4" diameter fitting.

7) Fill and bleed cooling system. See COOLING SYSTEM BLEEDING under REMOVAL & INSTALLATION.

EXHAUST MANIFOLD

Removal – 1) Raise and support vehicle. Disconnect exhaust pipe from rear exhaust manifold flange. Disconnect EGR tube from rear exhaust manifold. Disconnect O_2 sensor wiring.

2) Remove alternator assembly support brace at front of exhaust manifold. Remove crossover pipe mounting bolts. Remove retaining bolts and rear exhaust manifold.

3) Lower vehicle. Remove heat shield-to-front exhaust manifold bolts. Disconnect crossover pipe at front exhaust manifold. Remove retaining bolts and front exhaust manifold.

Inspection – Check exhaust manifolds for cracks or damage and mounting surfaces for warpage. Repair or replace exhaust manifold if warpage exceeds .008" (.20 mm).

Installation – To install, reverse removal procedure. Tighten mounting bolts/nuts to specification. See TORQUE SPECIFICATIONS table at end of article.

CYLINDER HEAD

Removal – 1) Remove intake manifold and exhaust manifold. See INTAKE MANIFOLD and EXHAUST MANIFOLD under REMOVAL & INSTALLATION. Disconnect necessary wiring and coolant hoses.

2) Remove rocker arm assembly. See ROCKER ARMS & PUSH RODS under REMOVAL & INSTALLATION. Mark push rod location for reassembly reference. Remove push rods. Remove cylinder head bolts in sequence. *See Fig. 5.* Remove cylinder head.

Inspection – 1) Check cylinder head warpage. Resurface head if warpage exceeds specification. See CYLINDER HEAD table under ENGINE SPECIFICATIONS at end of article.

CAUTION: DO NOT grind more than .008" (.20 mm) total from cylinder head surface and cylinder block deck surface.

2) Hold a straightedge across cylinder head bolt threads. If threads fail to contact straightedge in all areas, cylinder head bolts are stretched and must be replaced.

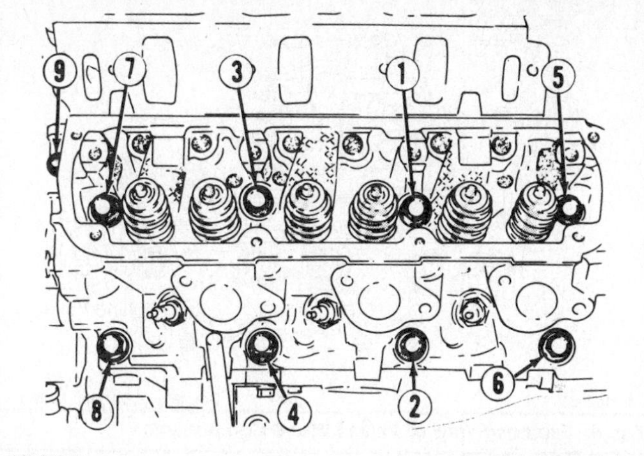
9
7
3
1
5
8
4
2
6

90H02578 Courtesy of Chrysler Motors.

Fig. 5: Cylinder Head Bolt Removal & Installation Sequence

Installation – **1)** To install, reverse removal procedure. Ensure cylinder head gasket is installed with identification number facing away from cylinder block. Tighten cylinder head bolts to specification in sequence using 4 steps. *See Fig. 5.* See TORQUE SPECIFICATIONS table at end of article.

CAUTION: The No. 9 cylinder head bolt is an 8-mm bolt and must be tightened to specification after 11-mm bolts are tightened in sequence to specification.

2) When tightening cylinder head bolts the required additional 1/4 turn, torque should exceed 90 ft. lbs. (122 N.m). Replace cylinder head bolt if torque DOES NOT exceed specification.
3) To install remaining components, reverse removal procedure. Ensure proper procedure is followed when installing rocker arm assembly and push rods. See ROCKER ARMS & PUSH RODS under REMOVAL & INSTALLATION.
4) Fill and bleed cooling system. See COOLING SYSTEM BLEEDING under REMOVAL & INSTALLATION.

FRONT CRANKSHAFT OIL SEAL

Removal – Raise and support vehicle. Remove right wheel inner splash shield. Remove drive belt. Remove retaining bolt and vibration damper. Using Seal Remover (C-4991), remove seal from timing chain cover. *See Fig. 6.*
Installation – Using Seal Installer (C-4992), install seal until seal is even with timing chain cover surface. Using Plate (L-4524), thrust bearing/washer and bolt, install vibration damper. Tighten bolt to specification. See TORQUE SPECIFICATIONS table at end of article. To install remaining components, reverse removal procedure.

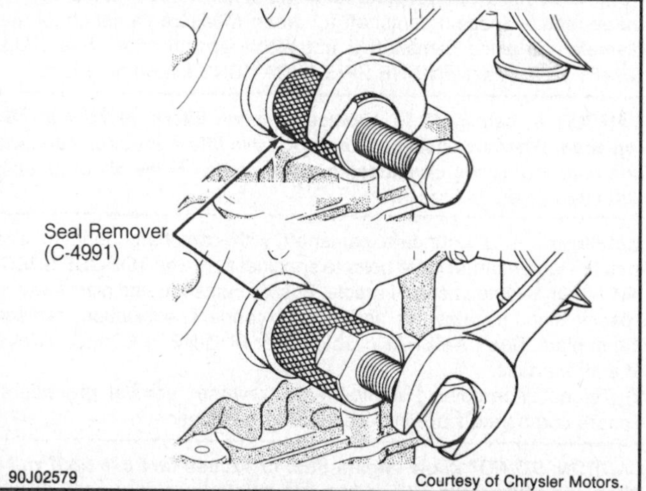
Seal Remover
(C-4991)

90J02579 Courtesy of Chrysler Motors.

Fig. 6: Removing Front Crankshaft Oil Seal

TIMING CHAIN COVER

Removal – **1)** Disconnect battery cables. Drain cooling system. Disconnect coolant hoses from timing chain cover. Support engine and remove right engine mount at timing chain cover. Remove oil pan. See OIL PAN under REMOVAL & INSTALLATION.
2) Remove oil pump pick-up tube. Remove transaxle inspection cover (if necessary). Raise and support vehicle. Remove right wheel and inner splash shield. Remove drive belt.
3) Remove A/C compressor with hoses attached and secure aside. Remove A/C compressor mounting bracket. Remove retaining bolt and vibration damper. Remove idler pulley from front engine bracket on front of cylinder block. Remove engine bracket from cylinder block.
4) Note location of cam sensor, located in top of timing chain cover. Disconnect electrical connector at cam sensor. Loosen cam sensor retaining bolt enough for slot in cam sensor to slide past bolt. Pull cam sensor from timing chain cover. Remove timing chain cover retaining bolts, cover, gasket and "O" rings.

NOTE: Tap lightly on top of cam sensor to loosen it (if necessary). DO NOT pull on wiring harness during cam sensor removal.

NOTE: Install front crankshaft oil seal after installing timing chain cover to ensure oil pump engages properly.

Installation – **1)** Install new gasket and "O" rings on cylinder block. Rotate crankshaft so oil pump drive areas (flat areas) of crankshaft are positioned vertically.
2) Align flat areas of oil pump in timing chain cover with flat areas on crankshaft. Install timing chain cover. Ensure oil pump engages with crankshaft. Install timing chain cover retaining bolts and tighten to specification. See TORQUE SPECIFICATIONS table at end of article.
3) Using Seal Installer (C-4992), install front crankshaft oil seal until seal is even with timing chain cover surface. Using Plate (L-4524), thrust bearing/washer and bolt, install vibration damper. Tighten retaining bolt to specification. See TORQUE SPECIFICATIONS table.
4) When installing cam sensor, ensure cam sensor and mounting surface is clean. If original cam sensor is installed, use NEW spacer and "O" ring. If replacement cam sensor is installed, ensure paper spacer and "O" ring are installed on cam sensor.
5) Apply engine oil to cam sensor "O" ring, and install cam sensor in timing chain cover. Hold cam sensor downward until cam sensor contacts camshaft timing gear. Tighten retaining bolt to specification while cam sensor is held downward. See TORQUE SPECIFICATIONS table. Reconnect electrical connector at cam sensor.
6) To install remaining components, reverse removal procedure. Tighten bolts to specification. See TORQUE SPECIFICATIONS table.
7) Fill and bleed cooling system. See COOLING SYSTEM BLEEDING under REMOVAL & INSTALLATION.

TIMING CHAIN

Removal – **1)** Remove timing chain cover. See TIMING CHAIN COVER under REMOVAL & INSTALLATION. Check timing chain stretch to determine if chain requires replacement.
2) Position measuring scale near link on timing chain at camshaft sprocket so movement can be measured. Place torque wrench on camshaft sprocket bolt. Apply 30 ft. lbs. (41 N.m) torque with cylinder heads installed or 15 ft. lbs. (20 N.m) with cylinder heads removed on camshaft sprocket bolt in direction of engine rotation. Note reading on measuring scale.

NOTE: When applying torque to camshaft sprocket bolt, DO NOT allow crankshaft to move. It may be necessary to hold crankshaft.

3) Apply the same amount of torque in the opposite direction and note amount of timing chain movement on measuring scale. If movement exceeds 1/8" (3.17 mm), replace timing chain.

1991 ENGINES
3.3L V6 (Cont.)

4) To remove timing chain, rotate crankshaft so timing marks are aligned. *See Fig. 7.* Remove camshaft sprocket retaining bolt, washer, camshaft sprocket, timing chain and crankshaft sprocket.

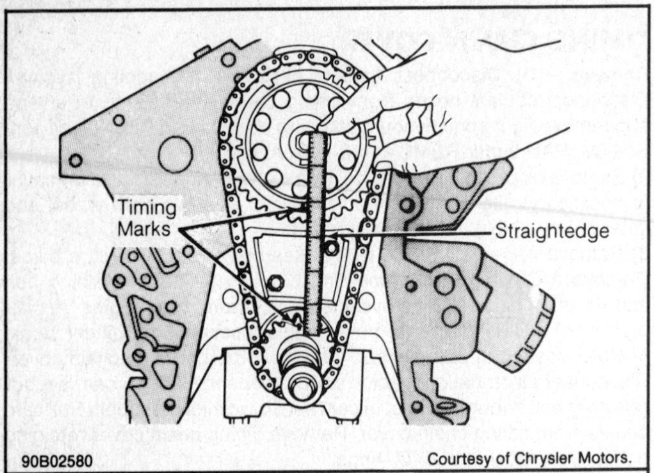
Timing
Marks
Straightedge
90B02580
Courtesy of Chrysler Motors.

Fig. 7: Aligning Timing Marks

Installation - 1) Install crankshaft sprocket on crankshaft. Rotate crankshaft so timing mark on crankshaft sprocket is at 12 o'clock position.
2) Install timing chain on camshaft sprocket. Position camshaft sprocket so timing mark is at 6 o'clock position. Install timing chain on crankshaft sprocket.
3) Install camshaft sprocket on camshaft. Ensure timing marks are aligned. *See Fig. 7.* Install washer and camshaft sprocket bolt. Tighten camshaft sprocket bolt to specification. See TORQUE SPECIFICATIONS table at end of article.
4) Ensure camshaft end play is within specification. See CAMSHAFT table under ENGINE SPECIFICATIONS at end of article. If camshaft end play is not within specification, replace thrust plate, located between camshaft sprocket and camshaft. To install remaining components, reverse removal procedure.

ROCKER ARMS & PUSH RODS

Removal - 1) Remove air intake plenum (upper intake manifold). See INTAKE MANIFOLD under REMOVAL & INSTALLATION. Disconnect spark plug wires. Disconnect closed ventilation system and evaporation control system components from valve cover (if necessary).
2) Remove valve cover. Remove rocker arm and shaft assembly retaining bolts. Remove rocker arm assembly. If removing push rods, mark component location for reassembly reference.

NOTE: If disassembling rocker arm assemblies, mark component location for reassembly reference. Components must be installed in original location.

Installation - 1) Ensure push rods are seated in valve lifters. Install rocker arm assembly in original location. Ensure steel retainers are located on retaining bolt area of rocker arm shafts.
2) Slowly tighten rocker arm shaft bolts to specification, starting at the center and working outward. See TORQUE SPECIFICATIONS table at end of article. To install remaining components, reverse removal procedure.

CAUTION: DO NOT operate engine until 20 minutes after rocker arm installation and until valve lifters have bled down.

VALVE LIFTERS

Removal - 1) Remove cylinder head. See CYLINDER HEAD under REMOVAL & INSTALLATION. Remove retaining bolts, yoke retainer and aligning yoke. *See Fig. 8.*
2) Using Valve Lifter Remover (C-4129), remove valve lifter. Mark component location for reassembly reference.

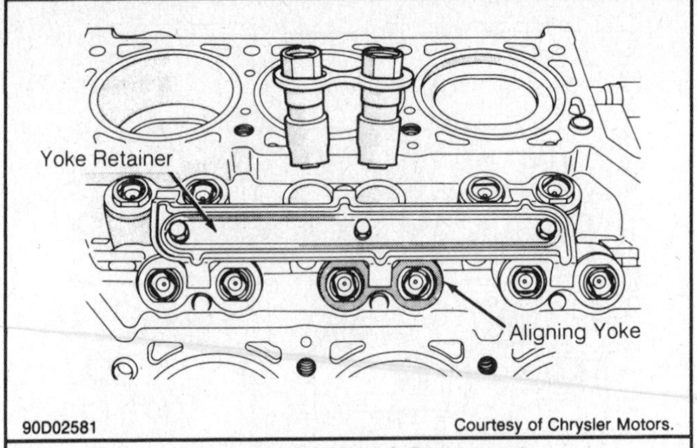
Yoke Retainer
Aligning Yoke
90D02581
Courtesy of Chrysler Motors.

Fig. 8: Exploded View of Valve Lifter & Components

Inspection - 1) Inspect valve lifter roller for damage. Ensure valve lifter O.D. and oil clearance are within specification. See VALVE LIFTERS table under ENGINE SPECIFICATIONS at end of article. Inspect valve lifter bore in cylinder block and outside surface of lifter for scoring.
2) If scoring exists, ream cylinder block bore for the next oversize valve lifter. Oversize valve lifters are available in .001" (.02 mm), .008" (.20 mm) and .030" (.76 mm).

CAUTION: If camshaft is replaced, valve lifters must also be replaced. Whenever new camshaft or valve lifters are replaced, add one pint of Chrysler crankcase conditioner to engine oil for at least 500 miles to aid break-in.

Installation - To install, reverse removal procedure. Ensure components are installed in original location. Lubricate valve lifters with engine oil before installing. Tighten bolts to specification. See TORQUE SPECIFICATIONS table at end of article.

CAUTION: DO NOT allow engine RPM to exceed fast idle until valve lifters have filled with oil and become quiet.

CAMSHAFT

NOTE: Manufacturer lists camshaft service procedure with engine removed only.

Removal - Remove engine. See ENGINE under REMOVAL & INSTALLATION. Remove valve lifters and timing chain. See VALVE LIFTERS and TIMING CHAIN under REMOVAL & INSTALLATION. Remove camshaft thrust plate retaining bolts. Remove camshaft.
Inspection - Inspect camshaft for wear. Measure camshaft journal diameter. Replace camshaft if not within specification. See CAMSHAFT table under ENGINE SPECIFICATIONS at end of article.

CAUTION: If camshaft is replaced, valve lifters must also be replaced. Whenever new camshaft or valve lifters are replaced, add one pint of Chrysler crankcase conditioner to engine oil for at least 500 miles to aid in break-in.

Installation - 1) Lubricate camshaft with camshaft lubricant and install. Tighten thrust plate bolts to specification. See TORQUE SPECIFICATIONS table at end of article. Ensure camshaft end play is within specification. If camshaft end play exceeds specification, replace thrust plate. See CAMSHAFT table under ENGINE SPECIFICATIONS at end of article.
2) To install remaining components, reverse removal procedure. Ensure components are installed in original location.

CAUTION: DO NOT allow engine RPM to exceed fast idle until valve lifters have filled with oil and become quiet.

CAMSHAFT BEARINGS

Removal & Installation - 1) Inspect camshaft bearing for damage. Replace camshaft bearing if damaged or I.D. is not within specification. See CAMSHAFT table under ENGINE SPECIFICATIONS at end of article.

2) Use Camshaft Bearing Remover/Installer (C-3132-A) for camshaft bearing replacement. Ensure all oil holes are aligned.

CAUTION: Ensure No. 2 camshaft bearing aligns with oil passage to left cylinder head and No. 3 camshaft bearing aligns with oil passage to right cylinder head.

REAR CRANKSHAFT OIL SEAL

Removal & Installation - 1) Remove transaxle and flexplate. Using screwdriver, pry oil seal from seal retainer.

2) To install, place Oil Seal Installer (C-4681) on crankshaft. Coat oil seal O.D. with Loctite. Install oil seal over oil seal installer. Tap oil seal into seal retainer. Install flexplate and transaxle. Tighten bolts to specification. See TORQUE SPECIFICATIONS table at end of article.

WATER PUMP

Removal & Installation - 1) Drain cooling system. Remove drive belt. Remove right front lower fender shield. Remove water pump pulley. Remove retaining bolts, water pump and "O" ring.

2) To install, reverse removal procedure using new "O" ring. Tighten bolts to specification. See TORQUE SPECIFICATIONS table at end of article.

3) Fill and bleed cooling system. See COOLING SYSTEM BLEEDING under REMOVAL & INSTALLATION.

OIL PAN

Removal & Installation - 1) Disconnect negative battery cable. Remove engine oil dipstick. Raise and support vehicle. Drain engine oil. Remove retaining bolts, oil pan and gasket.

2) To install, reverse removal procedure. Apply silicone sealant at timing chain cover and rear crankshaft seal retainer-to-cylinder block junction areas before installing gasket. Tighten bolts to specification. See TORQUE SPECIFICATIONS table at end of article.

OVERHAUL

CYLINDER HEAD

Cylinder Head - Inspect cylinder head for cracks and warpage. Repair or replace cylinder head if warpage exceeds specification. See CYLINDER HEAD table under ENGINE SPECIFICATIONS at end of article.

CAUTION: DO NOT grind more than .008" (.20 mm) total from cylinder head surface and cylinder block deck surface.

Valve Springs - 1) Check valve spring free length and pressure. Replace valve spring if not within specification. See VALVES & VALVE SPRINGS table under ENGINE SPECIFICATIONS at end of article.

2) Measure valve spring installed height from spring seat to bottom of spring retainer. If spacers are installed, measure from top of spacer. If height exceeds 1.594" (40.5 mm), install a .031" (.80 mm) thick spacer in cylinder head counterbore to obtain correct installed height. See VALVES & VALVE SPRINGS table under ENGINE SPECIFICATIONS.

Valve Stem Oil Seals - Ensure oversize valve stem seals are used when oversize valves are installed.

Valve Guides - 1) Check valve stem oil clearance. Ensure valve stem diameter is within specification. Valve guide must be reamed for valve with oversize valve stem if oil clearance exceeds specification. See CYLINDER HEAD table under ENGINE SPECIFICATIONS at end of article.

2) Valves are available with oversize valve stems of .006" (.15 mm), .016" (.40 mm) and .031" (.80 mm). Cylinder head must be replaced if guide cannot be cleaned using a .031" (.80 mm) reamer.

NOTE: DO NOT ream valve guides from standard to maximum oversize in one step. Ream valve guides to oversize in gradual steps, so guides are reamed true in relation to valve seat. After reaming valve guides, valve seat runout must be checked.

Valve Seat - Check valve seat width and runout. Grind valve seat if not within specification. See CYLINDER HEAD table under ENGINE SPECIFICATIONS at end of article. Cylinder head must be replaced if valve seat cannot be corrected.

Valves - Ensure valve margin, head diameter, refinish length and stem diameter are within specification. See VALVES & VALVE SPRINGS table under ENGINE SPECIFICATIONS at end of article. Valves are available with oversize valve stems of .006" (.15 mm), .016" (.40 mm) and .031" (.80 mm).

Seat Correction Angles - Use a 15-degree stone to lower valve seat and a 65-degree stone to raise valve seat.

CYLINDER BLOCK ASSEMBLY

Piston & Rod Assembly - Install piston must be installed with notch or groove on top of piston toward front (timing chain end) of engine. Note direction of connecting rod installation on piston before removal. Connecting rod must be installed in original direction. No other information for connecting rod-to-piston installation is available from manufacturer.

Fitting Pistons - 1) Measure piston diameter at 1.65" (41.9 mm) from top of piston at 90-degree angle to piston pin. Measure cylinder bore diameter at .50" (12.7 mm) below top surface of cylinder bore, middle of bore and .50" (12.7 mm) from bottom of cylinder bore.

2) Ensure piston diameter and clearance are within specification. See PISTONS, PINS & RINGS table under ENGINE SPECIFICATIONS at end of article.

NOTE: Piston diameter and cylinder bore should be measured at room temperature of approximately 70°F (21°C).

Piston Rings - Ensure ring end gap and side clearances are within specification. See PISTONS, PINS & RINGS table under ENGINE SPECIFICATIONS at end of article. Ensure piston ring end gaps are properly positioned. *See Fig. 9.*

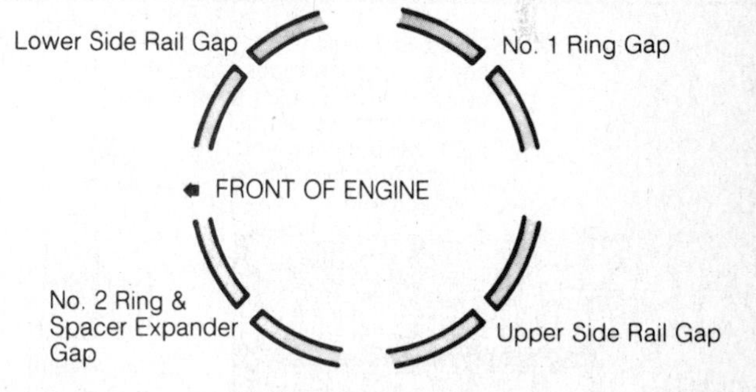

Lower Side Rail Gap
No. 1 Ring Gap
FRONT OF ENGINE
No. 2 Ring & Spacer Expander Gap
Upper Side Rail Gap

90F02582 Courtesy of Chrysler Motors.

Fig. 9: Positioning Piston Rings

Rod Bearings - 1) Before installing rod bearings, hold a straightedge across threads of connecting rod bolts. If threads fail to contact straightedge in all areas, bolts are stretched and must be replaced.

2) Apply light coat of engine oil to connecting rod bolt threads before tightening nut to specification. See TORQUE SPECIFICATIONS table at end of article. Ensure oil clearance and side play are within specification. See CRANKSHAFT, MAIN & CONNECTING ROD BEARINGS and CONNECTING RODS tables under ENGINE SPECIFICATIONS at end of article.

Crankshaft & Main Bearings - 1) Before installing main bearings, hold a straightedge across threads of main bearing cap bolts. If threads fail to contact straightedge in all areas, bolts are stretched and must be replaced.

2) Apply light coat of engine oil to threads before tightening bolt to specification. See TORQUE SPECIFICATIONS table at end of article.

1991 ENGINES
3.3L V6 (Cont.)

Ensure oil clearance and end play are within specification. See CRANKSHAFT, MAIN & CONNECTING ROD BEARINGS table under ENGINE SPECIFICATIONS at end of article.

CAUTION: Crankshaft journal grinding should not exceed .012" (.30 mm) undersize. DO NOT grind thrust surfaces of No. 2 main bearing. With cast iron crankshafts, final paper or cloth polishing after regrind must be done in same direction as engine rotation.

Thrust Bearing – Thrust bearing is located on No. 2 main bearing. Replace thrust bearing if crankshaft end play is not within specification. See CRANKSHAFT, MAIN & CONNECTING ROD BEARINGS table under ENGINE SPECIFICATIONS at end of article.

Cylinder Block – **1)** Check cylinder bore, out-of-round and taper. Measurements should be taken at .50" (12.7 mm) below top surface of cylinder bore, middle of bore and .50" (12.7 mm) from bottom of cylinder bore.

NOTE: Cylinder bore should be measured at room temperature of approximately 70°F (21°C).

2) Bore cylinder block if not within specification. See CYLINDER BLOCK table under ENGINE SPECIFICATIONS at end of article. Cylinder block warpage information not available from manufacturer.

3) Check valve lifter bore diameter and for signs of scoring. If scoring exists or lifter bore diameter is not within specification, ream cylinder block bore for the next oversize valve lifter. See VALVE LIFTERS table under ENGINE SPECIFICATIONS at end of article.

4) Oversize valve lifters are available in .001" (.02 mm), .008" (.20 mm) and .030" (.76 mm).

ENGINE OILING

ENGINE LUBRICATION SYSTEM

The crankshaft-driven oil pump provides lubrication to the main gallery. *See Fig. 10.*

Crankcase Capacity – Crankcase capacity with oil filter is 4.5 qts. (4.3L).

Normal Oil Pressure – Oil pressure should be 5 psi (.35 kg/cm²) at curb idle and 30-80 psi (2.1-5.6 kg/cm²) at 3000 RPM.

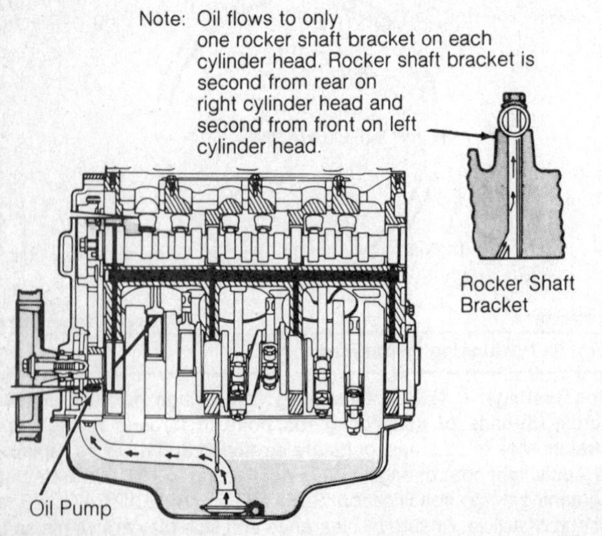
Note: Oil flows to only one rocker shaft bracket on each cylinder head. Rocker shaft bracket is second from rear on right cylinder head and second from front on left cylinder head.
Rocker Shaft Bracket
Oil Pump

90H02583 Courtesy of Chrysler Motors.

Fig. 10: Engine Oil Circuit

OIL PUMP

NOTE: Oil pan and timing chain cover must be removed to service oil pump. Pressure relief valve can be serviced by removing oil pan and pick-up tube only.

Removal & Disassembly – **1)** If servicing oil pump, remove oil pan. See OIL PAN under REMOVAL & INSTALLATION. Remove pick-up tube. Remove timing chain cover. See TIMING CHAIN COVER under REMOVAL & INSTALLATION.

2) To service pressure relief valve, drill a 1/8" (3.175 mm) hole in relief valve retainer cap. Retainer cap is located at oil pan surface of timing chain cover, near oil pan stud.

3) Install a self-tapping screw into the hole. If timing chain cover is installed, pull self-tapping screw to remove retainer cap.

4) If timing chain cover is removed, clamp self-tapping screw in a vise. Support timing chain cover while lightly tapping on timing chain cover with soft-faced hammer until retainer cap is removed.

5) Remove spring and pressure relief valve. Remove retaining bolts and pump cover. Note direction of rotor installation for reassembly reference. Remove inner and outer rotors. *See Fig. 11.*

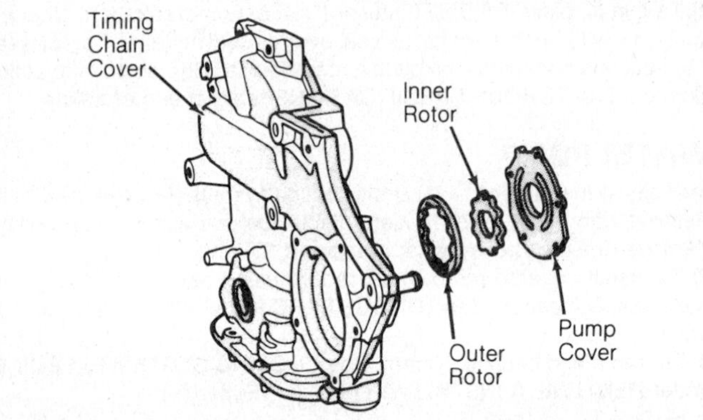
Timing Chain Cover
Inner Rotor
Pump Cover
Outer Rotor

90J02584 Courtesy of Chrysler Motors.

Fig. 11: Exploded View of Oil Pump

Inspection – **1)** Inspect components for damage. Using straightedge and feeler gauge, check pump cover warpage. Replace pump cover if clearance equals or exceeds specification. See OIL PUMP SPECIFICATIONS table.

2) Measure thickness of both rotors and outer rotor O.D. Replace rotors if not within specification.

3) Install outer rotor in timing chain cover. Measure clearance between outer rotor and timing chain cover. If clearance equals or exceeds specification, but outer rotor O.D. is within specification, replace timing chain cover.

4) Install inner rotor and measure clearance between inner and outer rotors. Replace pump assembly if clearance is equal to or exceeds specification.

5) Place straightedge across timing chain cover surface. Using feeler gauge, check rotor end clearance between rotors and straightedge. Replace pump assembly if clearance is equal to or exceeds specification.

6) Ensure pressure relief valve slides freely in bore. Check pressure relief valve spring free length and pressure. Replace spring if not within specification.

OIL PUMP SPECIFICATIONS

Application	Specification
Inner Rotor-To-Outer Rotor Clearance	.008" (.20 mm)
Outer Rotor O.D.	3.141" (79.78 mm)
Outer Rotor-To-Timing Chain Cover Clearance	.002" (.05 mm)
Pressure Relief Valve Spring	
Free Length	1.95" (49.5 mm)
Pressure	19.5-20.5 lbs. @ 1.031" (8.8-9.3 kg @ 26.19 mm)
Pump Cover Warpage	.003" (.08 mm)
Rotor End Clearance	.004" (.10 mm)
Rotor Thickness	
Inner Rotor	.301" (7.65 mm)
Outer Rotor	.3005" (7.633 mm)

Reassembly & Installation – To reassemble, reverse disassembly procedure. Install new retainer cap. Tighten pump cover bolts to specification. See TORQUE SPECIFICATIONS table at end of article. Fill rotor cavity with engine oil before installing. To install, reverse removal procedure.

TORQUE SPECIFICATIONS

TORQUE SPECIFICATIONS

Application	Ft. Lbs. (N.m)
Air Compressor Bolt	50 (68)
Air Intake Plenum Bolt	[1] 21 (29)
Alternator Bracket-To-Manifold Bolt	34 (41)
Camshaft Sprocket Bolt	40 (54)
Connecting Rod Nut	
Step 1	40 (54)
Step 2	Additional 1/4 Turn
Cylinder Head Bolt [2]	
Step 1	45 (61)
Step 2	65 (88)
Step 3	65 (88)
Step 4	[3] Additional 1/4 Turn
EGR Tube Bolt	17 (23)
Engine Bracket Bolt	40 (54)
Exhaust Crossover Pipe Bolt	25 (34)
Exhaust Manifold Bolt	17 (23)
Flexplate Bolt	70 (95)
Front Mount Through Bolt	50 (68)
Front Mount-To-Cylinder Block Bolt	
Lower Bolt	40 (54)
Upper Bolt	75 (102)
Front Mount-To-Frame Rail Bolt/Nut	40 (54)
Fuel Rail Bolt	17 (23)
Intake Manifold Bolt [4]	
Step 1	[5]
Step 2	17 (23)
Step 3	17 (23)
Intake Manifold Brace-To-Cylinder Head Bolt	40 (54)
Left Mount Through Bolt	50 (68)
Left Mount-To-Frame Rail Bolt	50 (68)
Main Bearing Cap Bolt	
Step 1	30 (41)
Step 2	Additional 1/4 Turn
Oil Pump Pick-Up Bolt	21 (29)
Right Mount (Timing Chain Side) Through Bolt	100 (136)
Right Mount (Timing Chain Side)-To-Frame Bolt	50 (68)
Right Mount (Timing Chain Side) Vertical Bolt/Nut	75 (102)
Rocker Arm Shaft Bolt	21 (29)
Timing Chain Cover	
8 mm Bolt	20 (27)
10 mm Bolt	40 (54)
Torque Converter-To-Flexplate Bolt	55 (75)
Transaxle-To-Cylinder Block Bolt	75 (102)
Vibration Damper Bolt	40 (54)
Water Pump Pulley Bolt	21 (29)
Wheel Lug Nut	95 (129)

[1] – Tighten bolts in sequence. *See Fig. 3.*

[2] – All bolts except No. 9 (8 mm) bolt must be tightened to specification in sequence. *See Fig. 5.* The No. 9 bolt should be tightened to 25 ft. lbs. (34 N.m) after all other bolts are tightened to specification.

[3] – After additional 1/4 turn, bolt torque should exceed 90 ft. lbs. (122 N.m). If torque is not exceeded, replace cylinder head bolt.

[4] – Tighten bolts in sequence. *See Fig. 4.*

[5] – Tighten bolts in sequence to 10 INCH lbs. (1 N.m). *See Fig. 4.*

TORQUE SPECIFICATIONS (Cont.)

Application	INCH Lbs. (N.m)
Cam Sensor Retaining Bolt	105 (12)
Camshaft Thrust Plate Bolt	105 (12)
Ignition Coil Mounting Bolt	105 (12)
Intake Manifold Gasket End Seal Bolt	105 (12)
Oil Pan Bolt	105 (12)
Oil Pump Cover Bolt	105 (12)
Rear Crankshaft Seal Retainer Bolt	105 (12)
Timing Chain Snubber Bolt	105 (12)
Valve Cover Bolt	105 (12)
Valve Lifter Yoke Retainer Bolt	105 (12)
Water Pump Bolt	105 (12)

ENGINE SPECIFICATIONS

GENERAL SPECIFICATIONS

Application	Specification
3.3L	
Displacement	201 Cu. In.
Bore	3.66" (92.9 mm)
Stroke	3.19" (81.0 mm)
Compression Ratio	8.9:1
Fuel System	PFI
Horsepower @ RPM	147 @ 4800
Torque Ft. Lbs. @ RPM	185 @ 3600

CRANKSHAFT, MAIN & CONNECTING ROD BEARINGS

Application	In. (mm)
3.3L	
Crankshaft End Play	
Standard	.003-.009 (.08-.23)
Wear Limit	.015 (.38)
Main Bearings	
Journal Diameter	2.519 (63.98)
Journal Out-Of-Round	.001 (.03)
Journal Taper	.002 (.05)
Oil Clearance	.0007-.0022 (.018-.056)
Connecting Rod Bearings	
Journal Diameter	2.2830 (57.998)
Journal Out-Of-Round	.001 (.03)
Journal Taper	.001 (.03)
Oil Clearance	.0007-.0022 (.018-.056)

CONNECTING RODS

Application	In. (mm)
3.3L	
Side Play	.005-.015 (.13-.38)

1991 ENGINES
3.3L V6 (Cont.)

PISTONS, PINS & RINGS

Application	In. (mm)
3.3L	
Pistons	
Clearance	.0010-.0022 (.025-.056)
Diameter	3.6594-3.6602 (92.949-92.969)
Pins	
Diameter	.9007-.9009 (22.878-22.883)
Piston Fit	.0002-.0007 (.005-.018)
Rod Fit	Interference Fit
Rings	
No. 1 & No. 2	
End Gap	
Standard	.012-.022 (.30-.56)
Wear Limit	.039 (.99)
Side Clearance	
Standard	.001-.003 (.03-.08)
Wear Limit	.004 (.10)
No. 3 (Oil)	
End Gap	
Standard	.010-.039 (.25-.99)
Wear Limit	.074 (1.88)
Side Clearance	.0006-.0089 (.015-.226)

CYLINDER BLOCK

Application	In. (mm)
3.3L	
Cylinder Bore	
Standard Diameter	3.6610-3.6617 (92.989-93.007)
Maximum Taper	.002 (.05)
Maximum Out-Of-Round	.003 (.08)

VALVES & VALVE SPRINGS

Application	Specification
3.3L	
Intake Valves	
Face Angle	44 1/2°
Head Diameter	1.79" (45.5 mm)
Minimum Margin	.031" (.79 mm)
Minimum Refinish Length	4.916" (124.87 mm)
Stem Diameter	.312-.313" (7.92-7.95 mm)
Exhaust Valves	
Face Angle	44 1/2°
Head Diameter	1.476" (37.49 mm)
Minimum Margin	.047" (1.19 mm)
Minimum Refinish Length	4.941" (125.50 mm)
Stem Diameter	.3112-.3119" (7.905-7.922 mm)
Valve Springs	
Free Length	1.909" (48.49 mm)
Installed Height	1.531-1.594" (38.89-40.49 mm)
Pressure	Lbs. @ In. (kg @ mm)
Valve Closed	58-63 @ 1.57 (26-29 @ 39.8)
Valve Open	136-145 @ 1.14 (62-66 @ 28.9)

CYLINDER HEAD

Application	Specification
3.3L	
Maximum Warpage	[1] .00075" Per 1" (.0191 mm Per 25 mm)
Valve Seats	
Intake Valve	
Seat Angle	45°
Seat Width	.069-.088" (1.75-2.24 mm)
Maximum Seat Runout	.002" (.05 mm)
Exhaust Valve	
Seat Angle	45°
Seat Width	.059-.078" (1.49-1.98 mm)
Maximum Seat Runout	.002" (.05 mm)
Valve Guides	
Intake Valve	
Valve Guide I.D.	.3130-.3149" (7.950-7.998 mm)
Valve Stem-To-Guide Oil Clearance	
Standard	.001-.003" (.03-.08 mm)
Wear Limit	[2] .010" (.25 mm)
Exhaust Valve	
Valve Guide I.D.	.3130-.3149" (7.950-7.998 mm)
Valve Stem-To-Guide Oil Clearance	
Standard	.002-.006" (.05-.15 mm)
Wear Limit	[2] .016" (.41 mm)

1 – Combined maximum total grind limit of cylinder head and cylinder block is .008" (.20 mm).

2 – Specification applies to measurement obtained by rocking valve stem in valve guide.

CAMSHAFT

Application	In. (mm)
3.3L	
Camshaft Bearing I.D. [1]	
No. 1	2.000-2.001 (50.80-50.83)
No. 2	1.984-1.985 (50.39-50.42)
No. 3	1.969-1.970 (50.01-50.04)
No. 4	1.953-1.954 (49.61-49.63)
End Play	.005-.012 (.13-.30)
Journal Diameter	
No. 1	1.997-1.999 (50.72-50.77)
No. 2	1.980-1.982 (50.29-50.34)
No. 3	1.965-1.967 (49.91-49.96)
No. 4	1.949-1.952 (49.50-49.58)
Oil Clearance	
Standard	.001-.004 (.03-.10)
Wear Limit	.005 (.13)

1 – Bearings are numbered from the front of camshaft.

VALVE LIFTERS

Application	In. (mm)
3.3L	
Bore Diameter	.9051-.9059 (22.990-23.010)
Lifter Diameter	[1] .9035-.9040 (22.949-22.962)
Oil Clearance	.0011-.0024 (.028-.061)

1 – Standard diameter valve lifter is listed. Oversize valve lifters are available in .001" (.03 mm), .008" (.20 mm) and .030" (.76 mm).

1991 ENGINES
3.9L V6, 5.2L & 5.9L V8

Dakota, Pickup, Ramcharger, RWD Van

NOTE: For repair procedures not covered in this article, see ENGINE OVERHAUL PROCEDURES article in GENERAL INFORMATION.

ENGINE IDENTIFICATION

Engine may be identified by eighth character of Vehicle Identification Number (VIN) stamped on metal tab, located near lower left corner of windshield.

Engine serial number may be required when ordering replacement parts. On the 3.9L, engine serial number is located on pad on right side of cylinder block. On 5.2L and 5.9L, engine serial number is located on left front corner of cylinder block just below cylinder head.

ENGINE IDENTIFICATION CODES

Engine	Code
3.9L TBI	X
5.2L TBI	Y
5.9L TBI	
Light Duty Emissions	W Or Z
Heavy Duty Emissions	5

SPECIAL ENGINE MARKS

Information identifying undersize and oversize components is found at various engine locations and decoded as follows:

Crankshaft & Rod Journals

- "M" or "R" followed by number indicates which main or rod bearing journal is .001" (.02 mm) undersize. Mark is stamped on No. 6 crankshaft counterweight on 3.9L, No. 8 crankshaft counterweight on 5.2L and No. 3 crankshaft counterweight on 5.9L engines.
- "MX" or "RX" indicates all main or rod bearing journals are .010" (.25 mm) undersize. Mark is stamped on No. 6 crankshaft counterweight on 3.9L, No. 8 crankshaft counterweight on 5.2L and No. 3 crankshaft counterweight on 5.9L engines.

Cylinder Block

- Letter "A" following engine serial number indicates .020" (.51 mm) oversize cylinder bores.
- A diamond-shaped stamp located on top pad at front of engine and stamped on flat area of each oversize lifter bore indicates .008" (.20 mm) oversize lifters.
- A stamp "X" indicates .005" (.13 mm) oversize valve stems. Stamp is found on machined pad, near two 3/8" tapped holes on each end of cylinder head.

ADJUSTMENTS

VALVE CLEARANCE ADJUSTMENT

Hydraulic valve lifters are used. No valve adjustment is required.

REMOVAL & INSTALLATION

NOTE: For reassembly reference, label all electrical connectors, vacuum hoses and fuel lines before removal. Also place mating marks on engine hood and other major assemblies before removal.

FUEL PRESSURE RELEASE

CAUTION: Fuel system is under pressure. Pressure must be released before servicing fuel system components.

1) Loosen fuel tank cap to release pressure. Disconnect injector wiring harness from engine wiring harness. Connect jumper wire between terminal No. 1 of injector harness and ground. *See Fig. 1.*

2) Connect another jumper wire to terminal No. 2 of injector harness. Touch jumper wire to positive battery terminal for no more than 5 seconds to release fuel pressure. Remove jumper wires, and reconnect wiring harness.

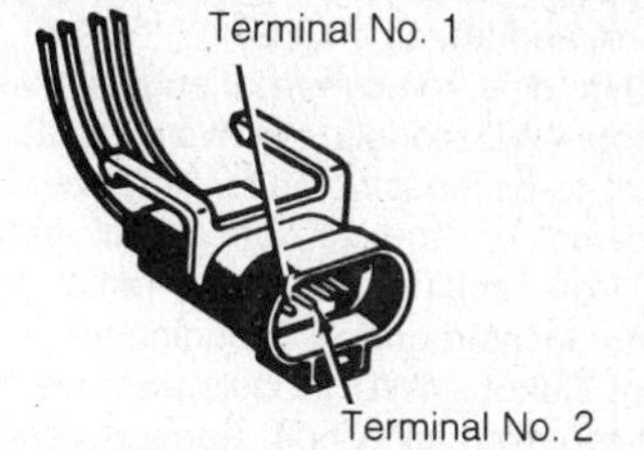
Terminal No. 1
Terminal No. 2

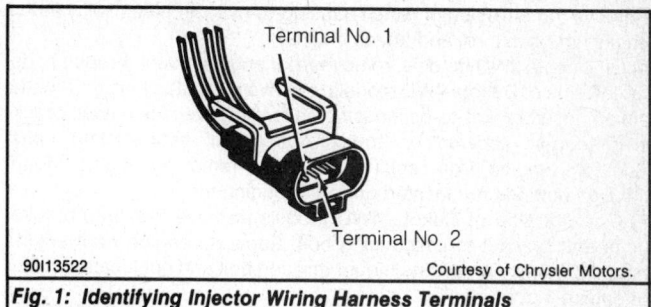

90I13522 Courtesy of Chrysler Motors.

Fig. 1: Identifying Injector Wiring Harness Terminals

ENGINE

Removal (RWD Van) – 1) Release fuel pressure. See FUEL PRESSURE RELEASE under REMOVAL & INSTALLATION. Disconnect negative battery cable. Scribe hood hinges, and remove hood. Drain cooling system and engine oil.

2) Remove engine cover and oil dipstick. On A/C equipped models, discharge A/C system, and disconnect A/C lines at condenser. Plug all A/C line openings to prevent contamination, and remove A/C compressor.

3) On all models, remove front bumper, grille and support brace. Disconnect coolant hoses, and remove radiator, condenser and support as an assembly.

4) Remove power steering pump with hoses attached, and secure aside. Remove air pump, spark plug wires and distributor cap. Disconnect necessary electrical connections, fuel lines, coolant hoses and vacuum hoses. Remove air cleaner, throttle body, drive belts, alternator, fan and fan pulley.

5) Raise and support vehicle. Disconnect exhaust crossover pipe. Remove left exhaust manifold and heat shield. Remove starter, oil pan, oil pump and pick-up tube.

6) On A/T models, remove transmission inspection cover. Mark torque converter-to-flexplate for reassembly reference. Remove torque converter-to-flexplate bolts. On M/T models, disconnect clutch release mechanism at clutch housing.

7) On all models, support transmission using a floor jack. Remove transmission or clutch housing-to-cylinder block bolts. Remove engine mount bolts. Remove engine out front of vehicle.

Installation – 1) To install, reverse removal procedure. Install engine with oil pan removed. Before installing oil pan, place a small amount of RTV sealant at corners where side and front oil pan gaskets meet.

2) Tighten bolts/nuts to specification. See TORQUE SPECIFICATIONS table at end of article. On A/T models, ensure reference marks on torque converter and flexplate are aligned. Evacuate and recharge A/C system.

Removal (All Others) – 1) Release fuel pressure. See FUEL PRESSURE RELEASE under REMOVAL & INSTALLATION. Disconnect and remove battery. Scribe hood hinges, and remove hood. Drain cooling system.

2) Disconnect coolant hoses. Remove radiator, fan and shroud. On A/C equipped models, discharge A/C system, and disconnect A/C lines. Plug A/C lines to prevent contamination. On all models, remove air cleaner, vacuum lines, distributor cap and wiring.

3) Disconnect necessary electrical connections and fuel lines. Remove throttle body and linkage. Remove starter, alternator, charcoal canister and horns. Disconnect power steering hoses (if equipped). Raise and support vehicle. Disconnect exhaust pipe at exhaust manifold.

4) On A/T models, remove transmission housing inspection plate. Attach "C" clamp to front of housing to secure torque converter. Mark torque converter-to-flexplate for reassembly reference. Remove torque converter-to-flexplate bolts.

NOTE: It may be necessary to remove manual transmission if transmission cannot be supported using floor jack.

5) On M/T models, disconnect clutch release mechanism at clutch housing. On all models, support transmission using a floor jack.

1991 ENGINES
3.9L V6, 5.2L & 5.9L V8 (Cont.)

Remove transmission or clutch housing-to-cylinder block bolts. Install engine lifting fixture, and attach chain.

6) On Dakota 2WD models, remove front engine mount through bolts. On left side of Dakota 4WD models, remove bolts attaching differential pinion nose bracket-to-bellhousing bolts. Remove pinion nose bracket-to-adapter (located on top of differential near pinion) bolts. Separate engine from engine mount by removing engine mount through bolt and nut located on top of engine mount.

7) On right side of Dakota 4WD models, remove 2 axle-to-bracket bolts and bracket-to-bellhousing bolt. Separate engine from engine mount by removing engine mount through bolt and nut located on top of engine mount.

8) On Pickup and Ramcharger, remove front engine mount bolts. On all models, remove engine.

Installation – To install, reverse removal procedure. Tighten bolts/nuts to specifications. See TORQUE SPECIFICATIONS table at end of article. On A/T models, ensure reference marks on torque converter and flexplate are aligned. Evacuate and recharge A/C system.

INTAKE MANIFOLD

Removal – 1) Release fuel pressure. See FUEL PRESSURE RELEASE under REMOVAL & INSTALLATION. Disconnect negative battery cable. Drain cooling system. Disconnect accelerator cable, control cables and fuel lines at throttle body. Remove air cleaner and alternator.

2) Disconnect necessary electrical connections, coolant hoses and vacuum hoses. Remove distributor cap and wires. Remove valve cover (if necessary).

3) Remove intake manifold bolts, intake manifold and gaskets. Separate throttle body from intake manifold (if necessary).

CAUTION: Intake manifold side gaskets are identified by a cutout "RT" (right side) or "LT" (left side). Ensure gaskets are installed in proper location.

Installation – 1) Install side gaskets on cylinder head. Place a 1/4" (6.4 mm) bead of RTV sealant at all cylinder block-to-cylinder head corners. Coat front and rear intake manifold end gaskets and cylinder block with a quick-dry cement, and allow to dry 4-5 minutes.

2) Install front and rear gaskets. Ensure center hole in front and rear gaskets engage with dowel in cylinder block and ends of gaskets engage with cylinder head gasket.

3) Install intake manifold, and install all bolts finger tight. Tighten bolts to specifications in sequence. *See Fig. 2.* See TORQUE SPECIFICATIONS table at end of article. To install remaining components, reverse removal procedure.

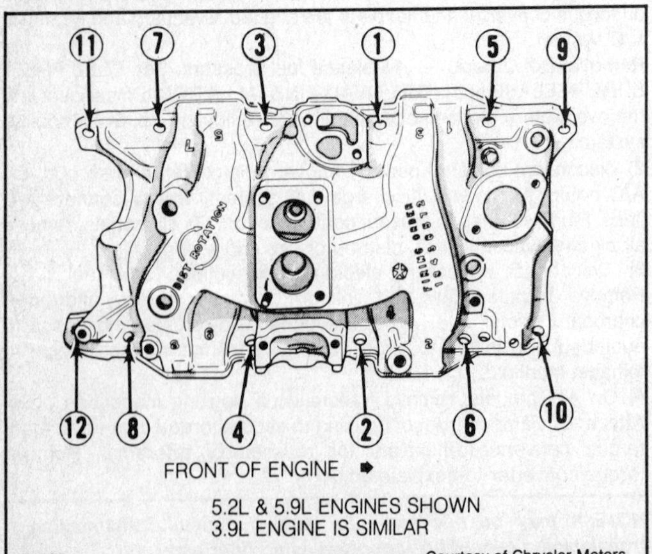
11
7
3
1
5
9
12
8
4
2
6
10
FRONT OF ENGINE
5.2L & 5.9L ENGINES SHOWN
3.9L ENGINE IS SIMILAR
71523
Courtesy of Chrysler Motors.

Fig. 2: Intake Manifold Bolt Tightening Sequence

EXHAUST MANIFOLD

Removal – Disconnect negative battery cable. Raise and support vehicle. Disconnect exhaust pipe from exhaust manifold. Remove retaining bolts, nuts, washers and exhaust manifold. Note location of conical washer on bolts. Remove manifold.

Inspection – Check exhaust manifold mating surface warpage. Repair or replace exhaust manifold if warpage exceeds .008" (.20 mm) per 12" (305 mm).

CAUTION: Install new studs in cylinder head if studs came out when removing exhaust manifold. Apply sealant to coarse threads of studs before installing.

Installation – 1) To install, reverse removal procedure. Tighten bolts/nuts to specifications, starting at center and working outward. See TORQUE SPECIFICATIONS table at end of article.

2) Ensure conical washers are installed on end studs on 3.9L and on bolt and stud for front and rear cylinders on 5.2L. DO NOT use conical washers on center bolts.

NOTE: Information is not available from manufacturer on conical washers for 5.9L.

CYLINDER HEAD

Removal – Remove intake and exhaust manifold. See INTAKE MANIFOLD and EXHAUST MANIFOLD under REMOVAL & INSTALLATION. Remove rocker arm shaft assembly. See ROCKER ARM SHAFT ASSEMBLY under REMOVAL & INSTALLATION. Remove cylinder head bolts, cylinder head and gasket.

Inspection – Check cylinder head warpage. Repair or replace cylinder head if warpage exceeds specification. See CYLINDER HEAD table under ENGINE SPECIFICATIONS at end of article.

Installation – To install, reverse removal procedure. Tighten cylinder head bolts to specifications in sequence using 3 steps. *See Fig. 3.* See TORQUE SPECIFICATIONS table at end of article. To install remaining components, reverse removal procedure.

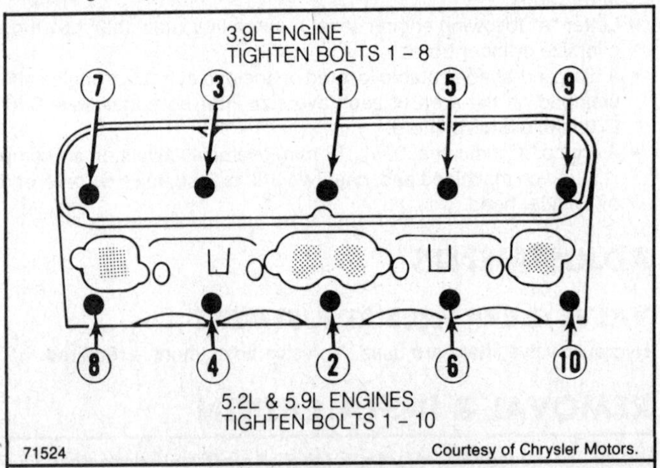
3.9L ENGINE
TIGHTEN BOLTS 1 – 8
7
3
1
5
9
8
4
2
6
10
5.2L & 5.9L ENGINES
TIGHTEN BOLTS 1 – 10
71524
Courtesy of Chrysler Motors.

Fig. 3: Cylinder Head Bolt Tightening Sequence

FRONT COVER OIL SEAL

Removal – Disconnect negative battery cable. Remove drive belts from crankshaft pulley. Remove fan and shroud. Remove crankshaft pulley and vibration damper. Pry oil seal from front cover.

Installation – 1) Use Seal Installer (C-4251) for seal installation. Install threaded shaft of seal installer into crankshaft threads. Install oil seal in front cover with spring facing rear of engine.

2) Position Installing Adapter (C-4251-3) with thrust bearing and nut on shaft. *See Fig. 4.* Tighten nut until installing adapter is even with front cover. Remove installing adapter. To install remaining components, reverse removal procedure. Tighten bolts to specification. See TORQUE SPECIFICATIONS table at end of article.

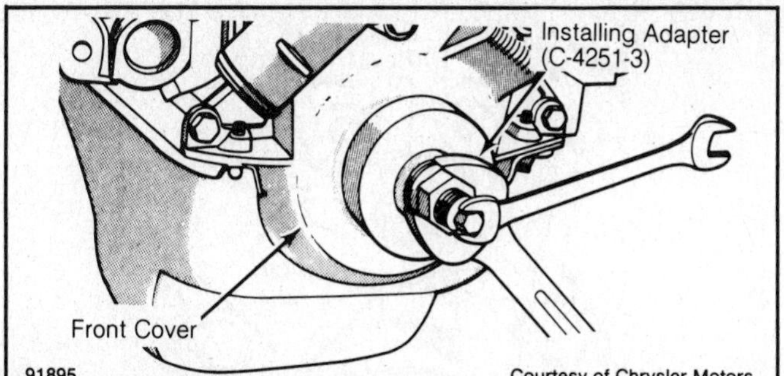

Installing Adapter
(C-4251-3)
Front Cover

91895 Courtesy of Chrysler Motors.

Fig. 4: Installing Front Cover Seal

FRONT COVER

Removal - 1) Remove water pump. See WATER PUMP under REMOVAL & INSTALLATION. Remove power steering pump (if equipped). Remove drive belts. Remove crankshaft pulley and vibration damper.

2) Loosen oil pan bolts. Remove oil pan-to-front cover bolts on each side of oil pan. Remove retaining bolts, front cover and gasket. Use care not to damage oil pan gasket.

Installation - 1) Ensure sealing surfaces are clean. Apply a 1/8" (3.2 mm) bead of RTV sealant to oil pan gasket. Lubricate front cover oil seal lip with Lubriplate. Install gasket, front cover and retaining bolts, but DO NOT tighten yet.

2) Install vibration damper onto crankshaft to align front cover oil seal. Tighten front cover, oil pan and then vibration damper bolts to specifications. See TORQUE SPECIFICATIONS table at end of article. To install remaining components, reverse removal procedure.

TIMING CHAIN

Removal - 1) Remove front cover. See FRONT COVER under REMOVAL & INSTALLATION. Check timing chain stretch to determine if it requires replacement.

2) Position measuring scale near link on timing chain at camshaft sprocket so movement can be measured. Place torque wrench on camshaft sprocket bolt. Apply 30 ft. lbs. (41 N.m) torque with cylinder heads installed or 15 ft. lbs. (20 N.m) with cylinder heads removed on camshaft sprocket bolt in direction of engine rotation. Note reading on measuring scale.

NOTE: When applying torque to camshaft sprocket bolt, DO NOT allow crankshaft to move. It may be necessary to hold crankshaft.

3) Apply same amount of torque in opposite direction, and note amount of timing chain movement on measuring scale. If movement exceeds 1/8" (3.17 mm), replace timing chain.

4) To remove timing chain, rotate crankshaft so timing marks are aligned. *See Fig. 5.* Remove camshaft sprocket retaining bolt, camshaft sprocket, timing chain and crankshaft sprocket.

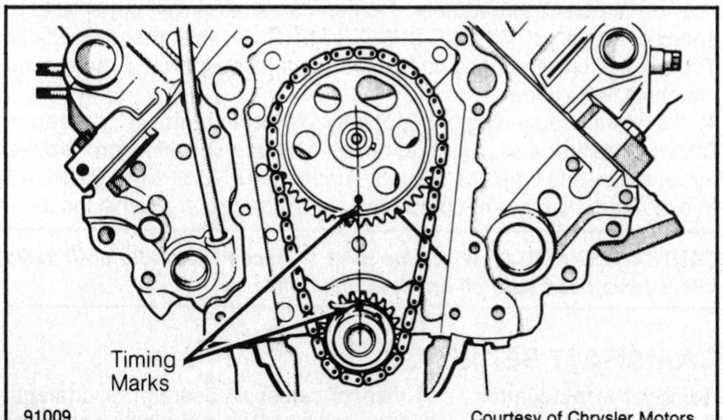

Timing
Marks

91009 Courtesy of Chrysler Motors.

Fig. 5: Aligning Timing Marks

Installation - 1) Install timing chain and sprockets. Use straightedge to ensure timing marks are aligned. *See Fig. 5.* Install camshaft sprocket retaining bolt, and tighten to specification. See TORQUE SPECIFICATIONS table at end of article.

2) Ensure camshaft end play is within specifications. See CAMSHAFT table under ENGINE SPECIFICATIONS at end of article. If end play is not within specifications, replace thrust plate, located between camshaft sprocket and camshaft. To install remaining components, reverse removal procedure.

ROCKER ARM SHAFT ASSEMBLY

Removal - 1) Disconnect spark plug wires, PCV and fuel evaporation hoses. Remove valve covers. Remove bolts and retainers attaching rocker arm shaft assembly to cylinder head.

2) Remove rocker arms and shaft as an assembly. Mark push rod location, and remove (if necessary). If rocker arm components are to be separated, note rocker arm identification. *See Figs. 6 and 7.*

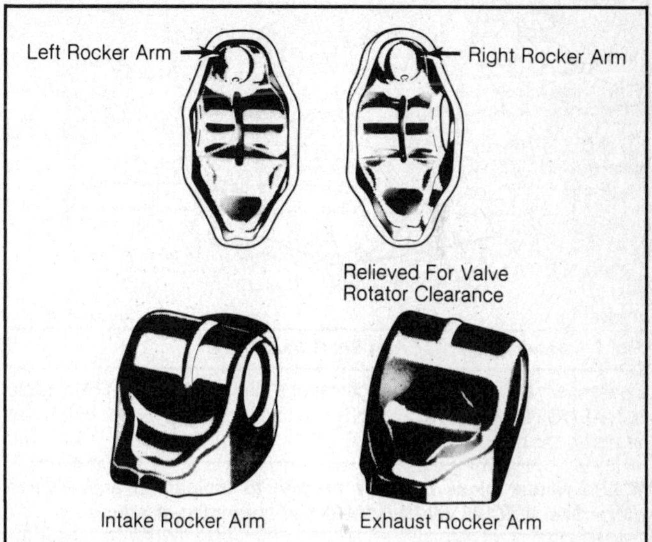

Left Rocker Arm
Right Rocker Arm
Relieved For Valve
Rotator Clearance
Intake Rocker Arm
Exhaust Rocker Arm

91596 Courtesy of Chrysler Motors.

Fig. 6: Identifying Rocker Arms

CAUTION: On engines with exhaust valve rotators, ensure rocker arm for exhaust valve contains relieved area for valve rotator clearance. See Fig. 6.

Installation - 1) Install push rods in original location. Install rocker arm and shaft assembly with notch on end of rocker arm shaft on bottom and toward front of engine (left bank) or rear of engine (right bank).

2) Ensure long, stamped-steel retainers are installed on No. 2 and No. 4 rocker arm shaft retaining bolts. *See Fig. 7.* Slowly tighten rocker arm shaft bolts to specification, starting at center and working outward. See TORQUE SPECIFICATIONS table at end of article. To install remaining components, reverse removal procedure.

CAUTION: Wait 20 minutes before starting engine to allow valve lifters to bleed down after rocker arm installation.

VALVE LIFTERS

Removal - 1) Remove air cleaner. Remove rocker arm shaft assembly. See ROCKER ARM SHAFT ASSEMBLY under REMOVAL & INSTALLATION. Mark push rod location, and remove.

2) Remove intake manifold. See INTAKE MANIFOLD under REMOVAL & INSTALLATION. Remove yoke retainer and aligning yoke. Note if aligning yoke contains an arrow which points toward camshaft.

3) Using Valve Lifter Remover/Installer (C-4129), remove valve lifter through opening of cylinder head.

Inspection - Inspect components for damage. Measure lifter O.D and bore diameter in cylinder block. Determine oil clearance.

1991 ENGINES
3.9L V6, 5.2L & 5.9L V8 (Cont.)

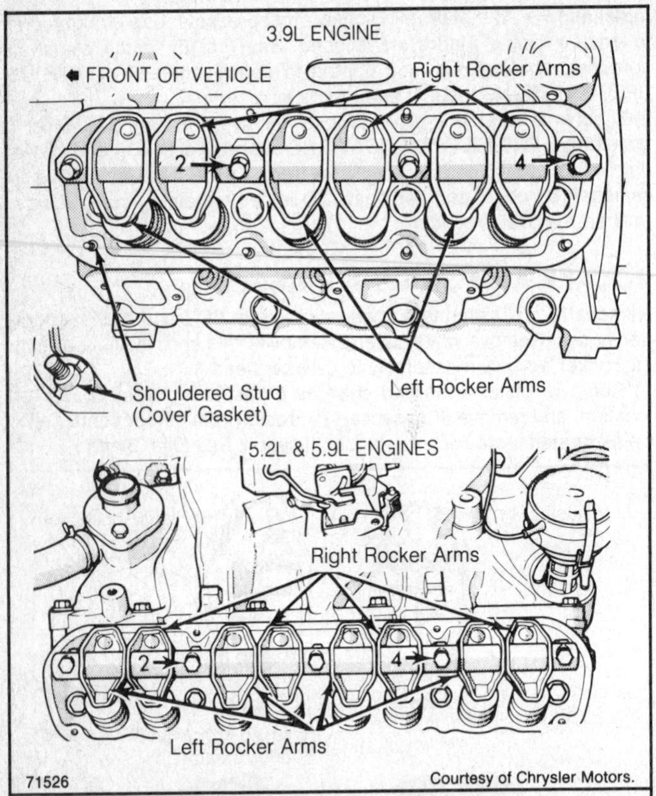
3.9L ENGINE
FRONT OF VEHICLE
Right Rocker Arms
2
4
Shouldered Stud
(Cover Gasket)
Left Rocker Arms
5.2L & 5.9L ENGINES
Right Rocker Arms
2
4
Left Rocker Arms
71526
Courtesy of Chrysler Motors.

Fig. 7: Installing Rocker Arm Shaft Assembly

Clearance must be within specifications. See VALVE LIFTERS table under ENGINE SPECIFICATIONS at end of article. Cylinder block can be bored for oversize lifters.

NOTE: Cylinder block must be marked to indicate oversize valve lifters. See SPECIAL ENGINE MARKS at beginning of article.

CAUTION: If camshaft is replaced, valve lifters must also be replaced. Whenever new camshaft or valve lifters are installed, add one pint of Chrysler crankcase conditioner to engine oil for at least 500 miles to aid break-in.

Installation – To install, reverse removal procedure. Lubricate valve lifter before installing. Ensure components are installed in original location. Tighten bolts to specifications. See TORQUE SPECIFICATIONS table at end of article.

CAUTION: Ensure valve lifter is installed so oil feed hole in side of valve lifter is facing upward, away from crankshaft. If aligning yoke contains an arrow, ensure aligning yoke is installed with arrow pointing toward camshaft.

CAUTION: DO NOT allow engine RPM to exceed fast idle until valve lifters have filled with oil and become quiet.

CAMSHAFT

NOTE: Manufacturer lists camshaft service procedure with engine removed.

Removal – 1) Remove engine. See ENGINE under REMOVAL & INSTALLATION. Remove front cover and timing chain. See FRONT COVER and TIMING CHAIN under REMOVAL & INSTALLATION. Remove valve lifters. See VALVE LIFTERS under REMOVAL & INSTALLATION.

2) Remove distributor and distributor drive shaft. Remove camshaft thrust plate retaining screws. Note direction of oil tab installation on camshaft thrust plate. *See Fig. 8.* Remove camshaft.

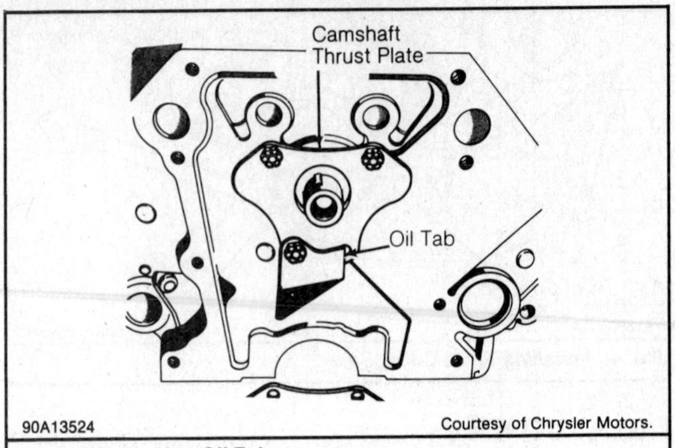
Camshaft
Thrust Plate
Oil Tab
90A13524
Courtesy of Chrysler Motors.

Fig. 8: Positioning Oil Tab

Inspection – Inspect camshaft and camshaft bearings for wear. Measure camshaft journal diameter and camshaft bearing I.D. Replace camshaft or camshaft bearings if not within specifications. See CAMSHAFT table under ENGINE SPECIFICATIONS at end of article.

CAUTION: If camshaft is replaced, valve lifters must also be replaced. Whenever new camshaft or valve lifters are installed, add one pint of Chrysler crankcase conditioner to engine oil for at least 500 miles to aid break-in.

Installation – 1) Ensure cup plugs are installed in oil passages behind thrust plate. Lubricate camshaft with camshaft lubricant, and install within approximately 2" (50.8 mm) of final installation location.

2) Install Camshaft Installer (C-3509) with long area behind distributor drive gear. *See Fig. 9.* This prevents camshaft from contacting plug, located in rear of cylinder block. Install distributor lock bolt to retain camshaft installer.

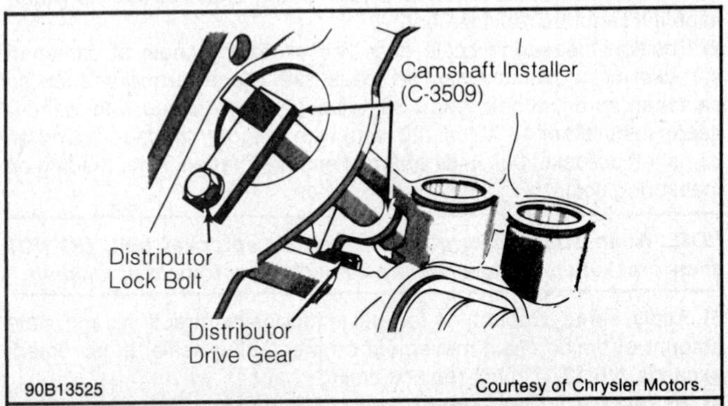
Camshaft Installer
(C-3509)
Distributor
Lock Bolt
Distributor
Drive Gear
90B13525
Courtesy of Chrysler Motors.

Fig. 9: Installing Camshaft

3) Install camshaft thrust plate. Ensure tang engages with lower right hole of camshaft thrust plate. Tighten camshaft thrust plate bolts to specification. See TORQUE SPECIFICATIONS table at end of article. Top edge of oil tab should be flat against camshaft thrust plate for timing chain lubrication.

4) To install remaining components, reverse removal procedure. Check camshaft end play. If end play exceeds specification, replace thrust plate. See CAMSHAFT table under ENGINE SPECIFICATIONS at end of article. Ensure components are installed in original location.

CAUTION: DO NOT allow engine RPM to exceed fast idle until valve lifters have filled with oil and become quiet.

CAMSHAFT BEARINGS

Removal & Installation – 1) Inspect camshaft bearing for damage. Replace camshaft bearing if damaged or I.D. is not within specifications. See CAMSHAFT table under ENGINE SPECIFICATIONS at end of article.

2) Use Camshaft Bearing Remover/Installer (C-3132-A) for camshaft bearing replacement. Ensure all oil holes are aligned. Install new camshaft plug at rear of cylinder block.

CAUTION: Ensure No. 2 bearing aligns with oil hole to left cylinder head and No. 3 bearing (3.9L) or No. 4 bearing (5.2L and 5.9L) aligns with oil hole to right cylinder head.

DISTRIBUTOR DRIVE SHAFT BUSHING

Removal – 1) Rotate crankshaft so No. 1 cylinder is at TDC on compression stroke. Remove distributor and distributor drive shaft. Insert Bushing Puller (C-3502) into bushing, and thread down until obtaining a tight fit.

2) Hold bushing puller bolt, and rotate bushing puller nut until distributor drive shaft bushing is removed.

Installation – 1) Install new distributor drive shaft bushing over burnishing end of Bushing Installer (C-3503). Insert bushing installer and distributor drive shaft bushing into cylinder block.

2) Using hammer, drive bushing installer and distributor drive shaft bushing into cylinder block. Tighten nut to pull bushing installer through distributor drive shaft bushing. Tightening nut expands bushing tight in cylinder block and burnishes it to correct size.

NOTE: DO NOT ream distributor drive shaft bushing.

3) Ensure No. 1 cylinder is at TDC on compression stroke. Install distributor drive shaft so slot is aligned toward left front intake manifold bolt as viewed from rear of engine on 3.9L or is aligned from front to rear of engine on 5.2L and 5.9L. Install distributor with rotor positioned to No. 1 cylinder in distributor cap.

REAR CRANKSHAFT OIL SEAL

NOTE: The 3.9L and 5.2L use a rope-type rear crankshaft oil seal; 5.9L uses a rubber-type oil seal. Rear crankshaft oil seal can be changed with crankshaft installed.

Removal (3.9L & 5.2L W/Crankshaft Installed) – Remove oil pan. See OIL PAN under REMOVAL & INSTALLATION. Remove oil pump and rear main bearing cap. Using Oil Seal Remover/Installer (KD-492), remove rear crankshaft oil seal using instructions provided with oil seal remover/installer.

Installation – 1) Install new upper rear crankshaft oil seal in cylinder block. Trim edges of oil seal even with cylinder block surface. Install new rear crankshaft oil seal in main bearing cap with both ends of seal protruding above main bearing cap surface.

2) Using Oil Seal Installer (C-3511), tap rear crankshaft oil seal downward until oil seal installer is seated in main bearing bore. Hold oil seal installer in this position and cut ends of rear crankshaft oil seal even with main bearing cap surface.

3) Install end seals in main bearing cap. Seals extend from rope oil seal to end of main bearing cap. Coat oil seal with engine oil. Install main bearing cap, and tighten bolts to specification. See TORQUE SPECIFICATIONS table at end of article. To install remaining components, reverse removal procedure.

Removal & Installation (3.9L & 5.2L W/Crankshaft Removed) – 1) Remove rear crankshaft oil seals from cylinder block and main bearing cap. Install new rear crankshaft oil seal in cylinder block and main bearing cap.

2) Using Oil Seal Installer (C-3511), tap oil seal downward until oil seal installer is seated in main bearing bore in cylinder block and main bearing cap. Hold oil seal installer in this position and cut ends of oil seal even with main bearing cap or cylinder block surface.

3) Install end seals in main bearing cap. Seals extend from rope oil seal to end of main bearing cap. Coat oil seal with engine oil.

Removal & Installation (5.9L W/Crankshaft Installed) – 1) Remove oil pan. See OIL PAN under REMOVAL & INSTALLATION. Remove oil pump and rear main bearing cap. Using small screwdriver, press on rear crankshaft oil seals to remove from cylinder block and main bearing cap.

CAUTION: Clean crankshaft, and lightly oil crankshaft surface and oil seal lips before installing. Rear crankshaft oil seal must be installed with paint stripe toward rear of engine. RTV sealant MUST be applied next to oil seal on main bearing cap surface to prevent oil leakage.

2) Rotate rear crankshaft oil seal in cylinder block with paint stripe toward rear of engine. Install rear crankshaft oil seal in main bearing cap with paint stripe toward rear of engine.

3) To prevent oil leakage, apply RTV sealant next to oil seal on main bearing cap surface before installing. Install main bearing cap, and tighten bolts to specification. See TORQUE SPECIFICATIONS table at end of article. To install remaining components, reverse removal procedure.

Removal & Installation (5.9L W/Crankshaft Removed) – Remove rear crankshaft oil seals from cylinder block and main bearing cap. Install rear crankshaft oil seals with paint stripe toward rear of engine. To prevent oil leakage, apply RTV sealant next to oil seal on main bearing cap surface before installing.

WATER PUMP

CAUTION: After removing fan clutch assembly, DO NOT place fan clutch with rear of shaft pointing downward. Silicone fluid from fan clutch may drain into fan drive bearing, causing lubricant failure.

Removal (Dakota 3.9L) – 1) Drain cooling system. Remove drive belts, alternator, fan and fan clutch assembly, pulley and bolts.

2) Remove alternator and alternator bracket bolts, and position alternator aside. Remove air pump and power steering pump, and secure aside.

3) Remove crankshaft pulley. Disconnect necessary coolant hoses. Remove retaining bolts, water pump and gasket.

Installation – To install, reverse removal procedure using new gasket. Tighten bolts to specification. See TORQUE SPECIFICATIONS table at end of article. Fill system with coolant.

Removal (Dakota 5.2L) – 1) Drain cooling system. Note direction of drive belt installation for reassembly reference.

CAUTION: Note direction of accessory drive belt routing. Belt must be installed in correct direction or engine will overheat due to water pump rotating in wrong direction.

2) Remove fan clutch assembly bolts. Remove fan shroud bolts. Remove fan clutch assembly, fan shroud and water pump pulley. Disconnect necessary coolant hoses. Remove retaining bolts, water pump and gasket.

Installation – To install, reverse removal procedure using new gasket. Tighten bolts to specification. See TORQUE SPECIFICATIONS table at end of article. Fill system with coolant. Ensure accessory drive belt in installed in original direction to ensure proper rotation of water pump.

Removal (Pickup, Ramcharger & RWD Vans) – 1) Drain cooling system. On models equipped with A/C, remove radiator. On all models, remove drive belts, fan and spacer or fan clutch assembly (if equipped), pulley and bolts.

2) Remove front bracket supporting alternator and A/C compressor or idler pulley (if equipped). Position alternator aside. Remove air pump.

3) Remove power steering pump with hoses attached, and secure aside. Disconnect necessary coolant hoses. Remove retaining bolts, water pump and gasket.

Installation – To install, reverse removal procedure using new gasket. Tighten bolts to specification. See TORQUE SPECIFICATIONS table at end of article. Fill system with coolant.

OIL PAN

Removal (Dakota 3.9L – 2WD) – 1) Disconnect negative battery cable. Remove oil dipstick and distributor cap. Raise and support vehicle. Drain engine oil.

1991 ENGINES
3.9L V6, 5.2L & 5.9L V8 (Cont.)

2) Remove exhaust pipe crossover. Remove side engine mount bolts. Slightly raise engine. When engine is at adequate height, install bolts in side engine mount-to-frame bracket holes to support engine.

3) Lower engine, and allow it to rest on bolts installed in side engine mounts. Remove retaining bolts, oil pan and gaskets.

Installation – To install, reverse removal procedure. Before installing oil pan, apply RTV sealant where front cover contacts cylinder block, oil pan side gaskets meet end seals and end seals contact cylinder block. *See Fig. 10.* Tighten bolts to specification. To install remaining components, reverse removal procedure.

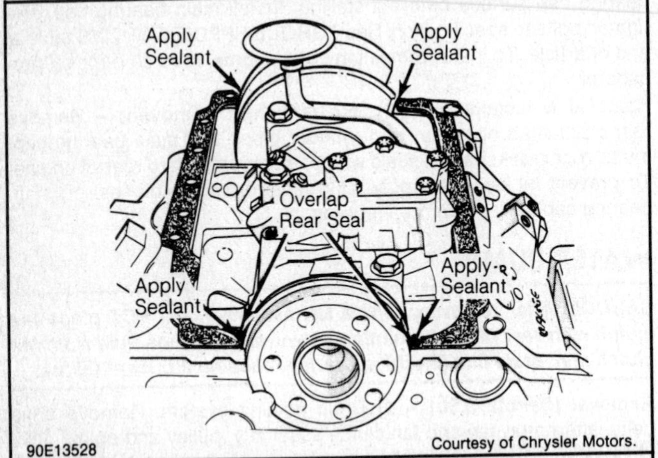
Apply
Sealant
Apply
Sealant
Overlap
Rear Seal
Apply
Sealant
Apply
Sealant
90E13528
Courtesy of Chrysler Motors.

Fig. 10: Applying Sealant on Oil Pan Sealing Surfaces

Removal (Dakota 3.9L – 4WD) – 1) Disconnect negative battery cable. Remove oil dipstick. Drain engine oil. Remove exhaust pipe crossover and lower transmission cover.

NOTE: Remove front drive axle for access to oil pan (if necessary). Axle shaft is splined into wheel hub and is retained by a nut.

2) For front drive axle removal, loosen wheel lug nuts. Remove cotter pin, lock nut and spring washer. Loosen axle shaft nut with vehicle on floor and brakes applied. Raise and support vehicle.

3) Remove wheels and skid plate. Remove axle shaft nut. Remove axle shaft-to-differential flange bolts at front drive axle. Support axle shaft, and separate axle splines from wheel hub by pulling inward at outer CV joint.

CAUTION: DO NOT pull on rubber boot during axle shaft removal. Pull on outer CV joint only.

4) Remove remaining axle shaft. Mark front drive shaft and transfer case yoke for reassembly reference. Remove front drive shaft from transfer case. Disconnect vacuum hoses from shift motor and electrical connections at shift indicator switch.

5) Support front drive axle using a floor jack. Remove front drive axle and shift motor retaining bolts. Lower floor jack, and remove front drive axle with drive shaft. Remove retaining bolts, oil pan and gaskets.

Installation – 1) To install, reverse removal procedure. Before installing oil pan, apply RTV sealant where front cover contacts cylinder block, oil pan side gaskets meet end seals and end seals contact cylinder block. *See Fig. 10.*

2) When installing front drive axle, loosely install all retaining bolts before tightening to specifications. Tighten axle shaft nut to specification with vehicle on ground. See TORQUE SPECIFICATIONS table at end of article. Ensure reference marks on transfer case yoke and front drive shaft are aligned.

Removal (Dakota 5.2L) – 1) Disconnect negative battery cable. Remove oil dipstick. Raise and support vehicle. Drain engine oil. Remove exhaust crossover pipe.

2) Remove left transmission-to-engine brace. Remove retaining bolts, oil pan and gaskets.

Installation – To install, reverse removal procedure. Before installing oil pan, apply RTV sealant where front cover contacts cylinder block, oil pan side gaskets meet end seals and end seals contact cylinder block. *See Fig. 10.* Tighten bolts to specification. To install remaining components, reverse removal procedure.

Removal (Pickup, Ramcharger & RWD Van 3.9L) – 1) Disconnect negative battery cable. Remove oil dipstick, engine cover (RWD Van) and air cleaner assembly. Remove engine controller. Raise and support vehicle. Drain engine oil.

2) Remove transmission-to-engine braces. Loosen exhaust pipe support bracket. Remove starter, transmission dust shield, O_2 sensor and air injection tube.

3) Disconnect exhaust pipe. Remove right engine mount nut. Loosen but DO NOT remove left engine mount nut. Support right side of engine using jack stand. Remove transmission mount through bolt, and support transmission using jack stand.

4) Raise engine and transmission enough for oil pan removal. Remove retaining bolts, oil pan and gaskets.

Installation – To install, reverse removal procedure. Before installing oil pan, apply RTV sealant where front cover contacts cylinder block, oil pan side gaskets meet end seals and end seals contact cylinder block. *See Fig. 10.* Tighten bolts to specification. To install remaining components, reverse removal procedure.

Removal (Pickup, Ramcharger & RWD Van 5.2L & 5.9L) – Disconnect negative battery cable. Remove oil dipstick. Raise and support vehicle. Drain engine oil. Remove exhaust crossover pipe. Remove left engine-to-transmission brace. Remove retaining bolts, oil pan and gaskets.

Installation – To install, reverse removal procedure. Before installing oil pan, apply RTV sealant where front cover contacts cylinder block, oil pan side gaskets meet end seals and end seals contact cylinder block. *See Fig. 10.* Tighten bolts to specification. To install remaining components, reverse removal procedure.

OVERHAUL

CYLINDER HEAD

Cylinder Head – Check cylinder head warpage. Repair or replace cylinder head if warpage exceeds specification. See CYLINDER HEAD table under ENGINE SPECIFICATIONS at end of article.

Valve Springs – 1) Check valve spring free length, out-of-square and pressure. Replace valve spring if not within specifications. See VALVES & VALVE SPRINGS table under ENGINE SPECIFICATIONS at end of article.

CAUTION: Installation of wrong spring on exhaust valves with valve rotators can cause severe engine damage. See VALVE SPRING IDENTIFICATION table.

VALVE SPRING IDENTIFICATION

Application	Spring Color Code
3.9L & 5.2L	
Exhaust Valve	White
Intake Valve	Blue
5.9L	
Exhaust Valve	Yellow
Intake Valve	Blue

2) Measure valve spring installed height from bottom of spring seat (cylinder head surface) to bottom of spring retainer. If spacers are installed, measure from top of spacer.

3) If height exceeds 1.688" (42.86 mm), install a .063" (1.58 mm) thick spacer in cylinder head counterbore to obtain correct installed spring height. See VALVES & VALVE SPRINGS table under ENGINE SPECIFICATIONS at end of article.

Valve Stem Oil Seals – Cup-type oil seals are used on all valves. Ensure oversize valve stem oil seals are used when oversize valves are installed. When installing valves, DO NOT overcompress valve springs or damage to valve stem oil seal may result.

Valve Guides – 1) Check valve stem oil clearance. Ensure valve stem diameter is within specifications. Valve guide must be reamed for valve with oversize valve stem if oil clearance exceeds specification. See CYLINDER HEAD table under ENGINE SPECIFICATIONS at end of article.

2) Valves are available with oversize valve stems of .005" (.13 mm), .015" (.38 mm) and .030" (.76 mm).

NOTE: DO NOT ream valve guides from standard to maximum oversize in one step. Ream valve guides to oversize in gradual steps so guides are reamed true in relation to valve seat. After reaming valve guides, valve seat runout must be checked.

Valve Seat – Check valve seat width and runout. Grind valve seat if not within specifications. See CYLINDER HEAD table under ENGINE SPECIFICATIONS at end of article.

CAUTION: If valve seat is ground, valve stem installed height must be checked. See VALVE STEM INSTALLED HEIGHT.

Valve Stem Installed Height – Valve stem installed height should be checked if valves or valve seats are serviced. Measure valve stem installed height using Valve Stem Installed Height Gauge (C-3968). *See Fig. 11.* Grind off tip of valve stem if too long.

CAUTION: DO NOT grind tip of valve stem on models equipped with exhaust valve rotators.

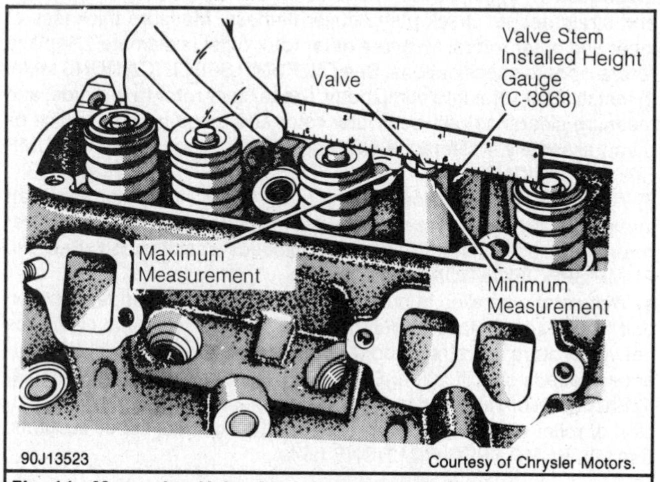
Valve Stem
Installed Height
Gauge
(C-3968)
Valve
Maximum
Measurement
Minimum
Measurement
90J13523
Courtesy of Chrysler Motors.

Fig. 11: Measuring Valve Stem Installed Height

Valves – Ensure valve margin, head diameter and stem diameter are within specifications. See VALVES & VALVE SPRINGS table under ENGINE SPECIFICATIONS at end of article. Valves are available with oversize valve stems of .005" (.13 mm), .015" (.38 mm) and .030" (.76 mm).

CAUTION: If valves are serviced, valve stem installed height must be checked. See VALVE STEM INSTALLED HEIGHT.

Seat Correction Angles – Use a 15-degree stone to lower valve seat and a 65-degree stone to raise valve seat.

VALVE TRAIN

Rocker Arm Shaft Assembly – **1)** If rocker arm components are to be separated, note rocker arm identification. *See Figs. 6 and 7.*

CAUTION: On engines with exhaust valve rotators, ensure rocker arm for exhaust valve contains relieved area for valve rotator clearance. See Fig. 6.

2) Install rocker arm and shaft assembly with notch on end of rocker arm shaft on bottom and toward front of engine (left bank) or rear of engine (right bank). Ensure long, stamped-steel retainers are installed on No. 2 and No. 4 rocker arm shaft retaining bolts. *See Fig. 7.*

Valve Lifters – Measure valve lifter diameter and bore diameter in cylinder block. Determine oil clearance. Clearance must be within specifications. See VALVE LIFTERS table under ENGINE SPECIFICATIONS at end of article. Cylinder block can be bored for oversize lifters.

NOTE: Cylinder block must be marked to indicate oversize valve lifters. See SPECIAL ENGINE MARKS at beginning of this article.

CYLINDER BLOCK ASSEMBLY

Piston & Rod Assembly – Install piston with notch on top of piston toward front of engine (timing chain end) with larger chamfer of connecting rod bore toward crankshaft journal fillet.

Fitting Pistons – **1)** Measure piston diameter at top of piston skirt at 90-degree angle to piston pin. Measure cylinder bore diameter below top surface of cylinder bore, middle of bore and bottom of cylinder bore.

2) Ensure piston diameter and clearance are within specifications. See PISTONS, PINS & RINGS table under ENGINE SPECIFICATIONS at end of article.

NOTE: Piston diameter and cylinder bore should be measured at room temperature of approximately 70°F (21°C).

Piston Rings – **1)** Ensure ring end gap and side clearances are within specifications. See PISTONS, PINS & RINGS table under ENGINE SPECIFICATIONS at end of article.

2) Position ring gaps in proper location. Compression ring gaps must be staggered so they do not align with oil ring rail gap. Ensure identification marks on compression rings face upward.

3) Oil ring expander ends should be butted under notch on front of piston. Oil ring rail gaps should be facing middle of engine when installed, and spread 3" (76 mm) apart. *See Fig. 12.*

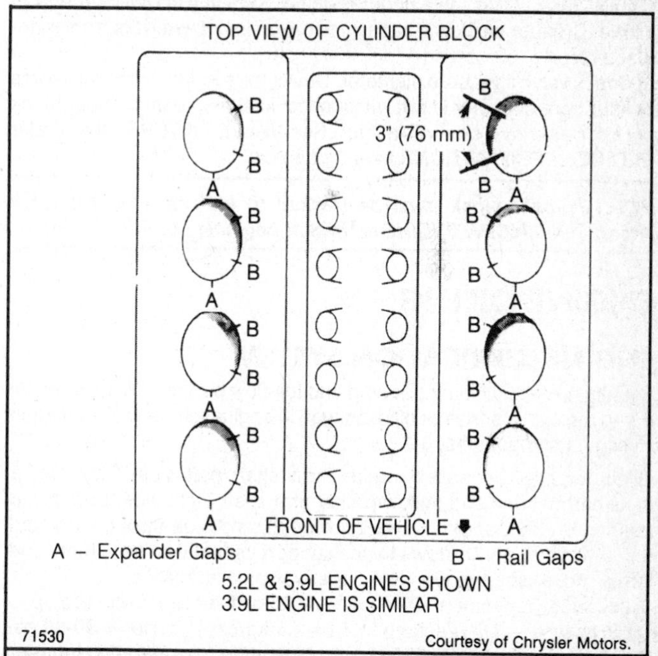
TOP VIEW OF CYLINDER BLOCK
3" (76 mm)
A
B
FRONT OF VEHICLE
A - Expander Gaps
B - Rail Gaps
5.2L & 5.9L ENGINES SHOWN
3.9L ENGINE IS SIMILAR
71530
Courtesy of Chrysler Motors.

Fig. 12: Positioning Oil Rings

Rod Bearings – **1)** Crankshaft is marked to indicate undersize rod bearings. See SPECIAL ENGINE MARKS. When replacing connecting rod bearings, ensure connecting rod is installed with larger chamfer of connecting rod bore toward crankshaft journal fillet.

2) Apply light coat of engine oil to connecting rod bolt threads before tightening nut to specification. See TORQUE SPECIFICATIONS table at end of article. Ensure oil clearance and side play are within specifications. See CRANKSHAFT, MAIN & CONNECTING ROD BEARINGS and CONNECTING RODS tables under ENGINE SPECIFICATIONS at end of article.

Crankshaft & Main Bearings – **1)** Crankshaft is marked to indicate undersize main bearings. See SPECIAL ENGINE MARKS. Main bear-

1991 ENGINES
3.9L V6, 5.2L & 5.9L V8 (Cont.)

ing cap location and direction of installation should be marked before removal.
2) Ensure journal diameter, taper and out-of-round are within specifications. See CRANKSHAFT, MAIN & CONNECTING ROD BEARINGS table under ENGINE SPECIFICATIONS at end of article. Upper main bearings contain oil holes while lower bearings installed in main bearing cap do not.
3) Apply light coat of engine oil to threads before tightening bolt to specification. See TORQUE SPECIFICATIONS table at end of article.
4) Ensure oil clearance and end play are within specifications. See CRANKSHAFT, MAIN & CONNECTING ROD BEARINGS table under ENGINE SPECIFICATIONS at end of article.

CAUTION: Crankshaft journal grinding should not exceed .012" (.30 mm) under standard size. DO NOT grind thrust surfaces of No. 2 main bearing (3.9L) or No. 3 main bearing (5.2L and 5.9L). With cast iron crankshafts, final paper or cloth polishing after regrind must be done in same direction as engine rotation.

Thrust Bearing – Thrust bearing is located on No. 2 main bearing on 3.9L or No. 3 main bearing on 5.2L and 5.9L. Replace thrust bearing if crankshaft end play is not within specifications. See CRANKSHAFT, MAIN & CONNECTING ROD BEARINGS table under ENGINE SPECIFICATIONS at end of article.
Cylinder Block – **1)** Check cylinder bore, out-of-round and taper. Measure cylinder bore diameter below top surface of cylinder bore, middle of bore and bottom of cylinder bore.

NOTE: Cylinder bore should be measured at room temperature of approximately 70°F (21°C).

2) Bore cylinder block if bore diameter is not within specifications. See CYLINDER BLOCK table under ENGINE SPECIFICATIONS at end of article. Cylinder block warpage information is not available from manufacturer.
3) Check valve lifter bore diameter. Check for scoring. If scoring exists or lifter bore diameter is not within specifications, ream cylinder block bore for next oversize valve lifter. See VALVE LIFTERS table under ENGINE SPECIFICATIONS at end of article.

NOTE: Cylinder block must be marked to indicate oversize valve lifters. See SPECIAL ENGINE MARKS at beginning of this article.

ENGINE OILING

ENGINE LUBRICATION SYSTEM

System has a rotor-type oil pump and full-flow oil filter. Oil is forced by pump through a series of oil passages in engine to provide lubrication to engine components.

Oil is supplied to hollow rocker arm shaft (left side) from No. 2 camshaft bearing and hollow rocker arm shaft (right side) from No. 3 bearing on 3.9L or No. 4 bearing on 5.2L and 5.9L through indexed holes in camshaft. Oil flows to one support pedestal on each head and into a rocker shaft to lubricate upper valve components.
Crankcase Capacity – Oil capacity with oil filter is 4.5 qts. (4.3L).
Oil Pressure – Oil pressure is 6 psi (.4 kg/cm²) at idle or 30-80 psi (2.1-5.6 kg/cm²) at 3000 RPM with engine at normal operating temperature.

OIL PUMP

Removal & Disassembly – **1)** Remove oil pan. See OIL PAN under REMOVAL & INSTALLATION. Remove retaining bolts and oil pump from rear main bearing cap.
2) Remove cotter pin, drill a 1/8" (3.2 mm) hole into relief valve retainer cap and insert a self-tapping sheet metal screw into cap. Clamp screw into vise. While supporting pump, remove retainer cap by tapping pump body using soft-faced hammer.
3) Discard retainer cap, and remove spring and relief valve. Remove pump cover, and discard oil seal ring. Remove inner rotor and shaft and outer rotor. *See Fig. 13.*

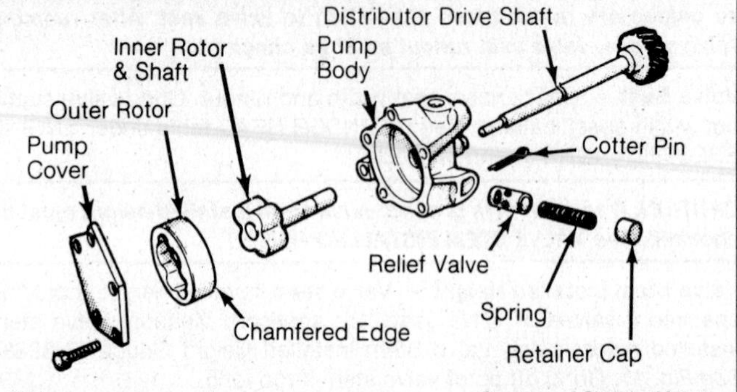
Distributor Drive Shaft
Inner Rotor & Shaft
Pump Body
Outer Rotor
Pump Cover
Cotter Pin
Relief Valve
Spring
Chamfered Edge
Retainer Cap
92161
Courtesy of Chrysler Motors.

Fig. 13: Exploded View of Oil Pump Assembly

Inspection – **1)** Inspect components for damage. Using feeler gauge and straightedge, check pump cover flatness. Measure thickness of inner and outer rotors. Measure outer rotor outside diameter. Replace rotors if not to specifications. See OIL PUMP SPECIFICATIONS table.
2) Install outer rotor into pump body. Press outer rotor to one side, and measure clearance between outer rotor and pump body. Replace oil pump assembly if clearance exceeds specifications. See OIL PUMP SPECIFICATIONS table.
3) With outer rotor installed in pump body, install inner rotor and shaft into pump body. Measure rotor tip clearance between inner and outer rotors. Replace rotors if clearance exceeds specification. See OIL PUMP SPECIFICATIONS table.
4) With rotors installed in pump body, place a straightedge (between bolt holes) across face of pump body. Measure rotor end clearance between rotors and straightedge. Replace oil pump assembly if clearance exceeds specification. See OIL PUMP SPECIFICATIONS table.
5) Ensure relief valve slides freely in bore. Check free length and tension of relief valve spring. Replace spring if not within specifications. See OIL PUMP SPECIFICATIONS table.

OIL PUMP SPECIFICATIONS

Application	Specification
Inner & Outer Rotor Thickness	.825" (20.96 mm) Min.
Outer Rotor Diameter	2.47" (62.7 mm) Min.
Outer Rotor-To-Pump Body Clearance	.014" (.36 mm) Max.
Pump Cover Flatness	.0015" (.038 mm) Max.
Rotor End Clearance	.004" (.10 mm)
Rotor Tip Clearance	.008" (.20 mm) Max.
Spring Free Length	1.95" (49.5 mm)
Spring Tension	19.5-20.5 lbs. @ 1.34" (8.8-9.3 kg @ 34.0 mm)

Reassembly & Installation – To reassemble, reverse disassembly procedure. Install new retainer cap. Tighten pump cover bolts to specification. See TORQUE SPECIFICATIONS table at end of article. Fill rotor cavity with engine oil before installing. To install, reverse removal procedure.

CAUTION: Ensure oil pump fully engages with distributor drive shaft before tightening retaining bolt. It may be necessary to slightly rotate oil pump during installation to align with distributor drive shaft.

1991 ENGINES
3.9L V6, 5.2L & 5.9L V8 (Cont.)

TORQUE SPECIFICATIONS

TORQUE SPECIFICATIONS

Application	Ft. Lbs. (N.m)
Axle Bracket-To-Bellhousing Bolt	
Dakota 4WD	65 (88)
Axle Shaft Nut	
Dakota 4WD	190 (258)
Axle Shaft-To-Differential Flange Bolt	
Dakota 4WD	65 (88)
Axle-To-Insulator Bolt	
Dakota 4WD	75 (102)
Camshaft Sprocket Bolt	35 (47)
Camshaft Thrust Plate Bolt	18 (24)
Clutch Housing-To-Cylinder Block Bolt	
Dakota	30 (41)
All Others	40 (54)
Connecting Rod Nut	45 (61)
Crankshaft Pulley Bolt	17 (23)
Cylinder Head Bolt [1]	
Step 1	50 (68)
Step 2	105 (142)
Step 3	Recheck At 105 (142)
Differential Pinion Nose Bracket-To-Adapter Bolt	
Dakota 4WD	65 (88)
Differential Pinion Nose Bracket-To-Bellhousing Bolt	
Dakota 4WD	65 (88)
Engine Mount Bracket-To-Frame Rail Bolt	
Dakota 2WD	30 (41)
Engine Mount Through Bolt	
Dakota 2WD	50 (68)
Dakota 4WD	75 (102)
Engine Mount-To-Cylinder Block Bolt	
Dakota	30 (41)
Engine Mount-To-Frame Bracket Bolt/Nut	
Pickup & Ramcharger	75 (102)
RWD Van	68 (92)
Exhaust Manifold	
Bolt	20 (27)
Nut	15 (20)
Flywheel/Flexplate-To-Crankshaft Bolt	55 (75)
Front Cover Bolt	30 (41)
Intake Manifold Bolt [2]	
Step 1	All Bolts Finger Tight
Step 2	25 (34)
Step 3	40 (54)
Step 4	Recheck At 40 (54)
Main Bearing Cap Bolt	85 (115)
Oil Filter Adapter Stud	50 (68)
Oil Pan Bolt	17 (23)
Oil Pump Bolt	30 (41)
Rocker Arm Shaft Bolt	17 (23)
Shift Motor Bolt	
Dakota 4WD	65 (88)
Spark Plug	30 (41)
Transfer Case Yolk Bolt	
Dakota 4WD	20 (27)
Transmission-To-Cylinder Block Bolt	30 (41)
Vibration Damper Bolt	135 (183)
Water Pump Bolt	30 (41)
Wheel Lug Nut	
Dakota	85 (115)
	INCH Lbs. (N.m)
Oil Pump Cover Bolt	95 (11)
Valve Cover Bolts	80 (9)

[1] – Tighten bolts in sequence. *See Fig. 3.*
[2] – Tighten bolts in sequence. *See Fig. 2.*

ENGINE SPECIFICATIONS

GENERAL SPECIFICATIONS

Application	Specification
3.9L	
Displacement	239 Cu. In. (3.9L)
Bore	3.91" (99.3 mm)
Stroke	3.31" (84.1 mm)
Compression Ratio	9.0:1
Fuel System	TBI
Horsepower @ RPM	125 @ 4000
Torque Ft. Lbs. @ RPM	195 @ 2000
5.2L	
Displacement	318 Cu. In. (5.2L)
Bore	3.91" (99.3 mm)
Stroke	3.31" (84.1 mm)
Compression Ratio	9.0:1
Fuel System	TBI
Horsepower @ RPM	170 @ 4000
Torque Ft. Lbs. @ RPM	260 @ 2500
5.9L	
Displacement	360 Cu. In. (5.9L)
Bore	4.00" (101.6 mm)
Stroke	3.58" (90.9 mm)
Compression Ratio	8.1:1
Fuel System	TBI
Horsepower @ RPM	190 @ 4000
Torque Ft. Lbs. @ RPM	292 @ 2400

CRANKSHAFT, MAIN & CONNECTING ROD BEARINGS

Application	In. (mm)
3.3L, 5.2L & 5.9L	
Crankshaft End Play	
3.9L & 5.2L	
Standard	.002-.007 (.05-.18)
Wear Limit	.010 (.25)
5.9L	
Standard	.002-.009 (.05-.22)
Wear Limit	.010 (.25)
Main Bearings	
Journal Diameter	
3.9L & 5.2L	2.4495-2.5005 (62.217-63.513)
5.9L	2.8095-2.8105 (71.361-71.387)
Journal Out-Of-Round	.001 (.03)
Journal Taper	.001 (.03)
Oil Clearance	
Journal No. 1	
Standard	.0005-.0015 (.013-.038)
Wear Limit	.0015 (.038)
All Others	
Standard	.0005-.0020 (.013-.051)
Wear Limit	.0025 (.064)
Connecting Rod Bearings	
Journal Diameter	2.124-2.125 (53.950-53.975)
Journal Out-Of-Round	.001 (.03)
Journal Taper	.001 (.03)
Oil Clearance	
3.9L & 5.2L	
Standard	.0005-.0022 (.013-.056)
Wear Limit	.0022 (.056)
5.9L	
Standard	.0005-.0022 (.013-.056)
Wear Limit	.0025 (.064)

1991 ENGINES
3.9L V6, 5.2L & 5.9L V8 (Cont.)

CONNECTING RODS

Application	In. (mm)
3.9L, 5.2L & 5.9L	
Center-To-Center Length	
3.9L	Information Not Available
5.2L & 5.9L	6.121 (155.47)
Side Play	.006-.014 (.15-.36)

PISTONS, PINS & RINGS

Application	In. (mm)
3.9L, 5.2L & 5.9L	
Pistons	
Clearance	.0005-.0015 (.013-.038)
Pins	
Piston Fit	
3.9L & 5.2L	0-.0005 (0-.013)
5.9L	.00025-.00075 (.0064-.0191)
Rod Fit	Press Fit
Rings	
No. 1 & No. 2	
End Gap	.010-.020 (.25-.51)
Side Clearance	.0015-.0030 (.038-.076)
No. 3 (Oil)	
End Gap	.015-.055 (.38-1.40)
Side Clearance	.0002-.0050 (.005-.127)

VALVES & VALVE SPRINGS

Application	Specification
3.9L, 5.2L & 5.9L	
Intake Valves	
Face Angle	45°
Head Diameter	
3.9L & 5.2L	1.780" (45.21 mm)
5.9L	1.880" (47.75 mm)
Minimum Margin	.047" (1.19 mm)
Stem Diameter	.372-.373" (9.45-9.47 mm)
Exhaust Valves	
Face Angle	45°
Head Diameter	
3.9L & 5.2L	1.517" (38.53 mm)
5.9L	1.617" (41.07 mm)
Minimum Margin	.047" (1.19 mm)
Stem Diameter	.371-.372" (9.42-9.45 mm)
Valve Springs	
Free Length	
Intake	2.00" (50.1 mm)
Exhaust	1.81" (45.9 mm)
Installed Height	
Intake	1.625-1.687" (41.23-42.85 mm)
Exhaust	1.453-1.516" (36.91-38.51 mm)
Out-Of-Square	.063" (1.60 mm)
	Lbs. @ In. (kg @ mm)
Pressure	
Valve Closed	
Intake	78-88 @ 1.687 (35-40 @ 42.85)
Exhaust	80-90 @ 1.203 (36-41 @ 30.56)
Valve Open	
Intake	170-184 @ 1.313 (77-83 @ 33.35)
Exhaust	
3.9L	180-194 @ 1.063 (81-88 @ 27.00)
5.2L	180-194 @ 1.078 (81-88 @ 27.38)
5.9L	181-197 @ 1.063 (82-89 @ 27.00)

CYLINDER BLOCK

Application	In. (mm)
3.9L, 5.2L & 5.9L	
Cylinder Bore	
Standard Diameter	
3.9L & 5.2L	3.910-3.912 (99.31-99.36)
5.9L	4.000-4.002 (101.60-101.61)
Maximum Taper	.010 (.25)
Maximum Out-Of-Round	.005 (.13)

CYLINDER HEAD

Application	Specification
3.9L, 5.2L & 5.9L	
Maximum Warpage	.00075" Per 1" (.0191 mm Per 25 mm)
Valve Seats	
Intake Valve	
Seat Angle	45°
Seat Width	.065-.085" (1.65-2.16 mm)
Maximum Seat Runout	.003" (.08 mm)
Exhaust Valve	
Seat Angle	45°
Seat Width	.080-.100" (2.03-2.54 mm)
Maximum Seat Runout	.003" (.08 mm)
Valve Guides	
Intake Valve	
Valve Guide I.D.	.374-.375" (9.50-9.53 mm)
Valve Stem-To-Guide	
Oil Clearance	
Standard	.001-.003" (.02-.08 mm)
Wear Limit	[1] .017" (.43 mm)
Exhaust Valve	
Valve Guide I.D.	.374-.375" (9.50-9.53 mm)
Valve Stem-To-Guide	
Oil Clearance	
Standard	.002-.004" (.05-.10 mm)
Wear Limit	[1] .017" (.43 mm)

[1] – Specification applies to method obtained by rocking valve stem in valve guide.

VALVE LIFTERS

Application	In. (mm)
3.9L, 5.2L & 5.9L	
Bore Diameter	.9051-.9059 (22.990-23.010)
Lifter Diameter	[1] .9035-.9040 (22.949-22.962)
Oil Clearance	.0011-.0024 (.028-.061)

[1] – Standard diameter valve lifter is listed. Oversize valve lifters are available in .001" (.02 mm), .008" (.20 mm) and .030" (.76 mm).

1991 ENGINES
3.9L V6, 5.2L & 5.9L V8 (Cont.)

CAMSHAFT

Application [1]	In. (mm)
3.9L, 5.2L & 5.9L	
End Play	.002-.010 (.05-.25)
Camshaft Bearing Bore I.D.	
3.9L	
No. 1	2.000-2.001 (50.80-50.82)
No. 2	1.984-1.985 (50.39-50.42)
No. 3	1.953-1.954 (49.61-49.63)
No. 4	1.5625-1.5635 (39.688-39.713)
5.2L & 5.9L	
No. 1	2.000-2.001 (50.80-50.82)
No. 2	1.984-1.985 (50.39-50.42)
No. 3	1.969-1.970 (50.01-50.03)
No. 4	1.953-1.954 (49.61-49.63)
No. 5	1.5625-1.5635 (39.688-39.713)
Journal Diameter	
3.9L	
No. 1	1.998-1.999 (50.75-50.77)
No. 2	1.982-1.983 (50.34-50.37)
No. 3	1.951-1.952 (49.56-49.58)
No. 4	1.5605-1.5615 (39.637-39.662)
5.2L & 5.9L	
No. 1	1.998-1.999 (50.75-50.77)
No. 2	1.982-1.983 (50.34-50.37)
No. 3	1.967-1.968 (49.97-49.99)
No. 4	1.951-1.952 (49.56-49.58)
No. 5	1.5605-1.5615 (39.637-39.662)
Oil Clearance	
Standard	.001-.003 (.02-.08)
Wear Limit	.005 (.13)

[1] – Bearings are numbered from front of camshaft.

1991 ENGINES
Cummins Diesel "B" Series 5.9L 6-Cylinder

D250/350 Pickup, W250/350 Pickup

***NOTE:** In mid-year, an intercooler was installed in front of the radiator. See Fig. 7. Note if vehicle contains an intercooler before servicing engine components. Service procedures may vary on models with intercooler.*

***NOTE:** For repair procedures not covered in this article, see ENGINE OVERHAUL PROCEDURES article in GENERAL INFORMATION.*

ENGINE IDENTIFICATION

Engine may be identified by eighth character of Vehicle Identification Number (VIN), stamped on metal tab located near lower left corner of windshield.

Engine model code, serial number and Control Parts List (CPL) number are listed on engine data plate. Engine data plate is mounted on fuel injection pump side of timing gear cover. *See Fig. 1.* Serial number and CPL may be required when ordering replacement engine components.

ENGINE IDENTIFICATION CODES

Application	Code
5.9L 6-Cylinder Turbo Diesel	
VIN Code	8
Data Plate Model Code	6BT

ADJUSTMENTS

VALVE CLEARANCE ADJUSTMENT

***NOTE:** Valve clearance must be adjusted with engine temperature less than 140°F (60°C).*

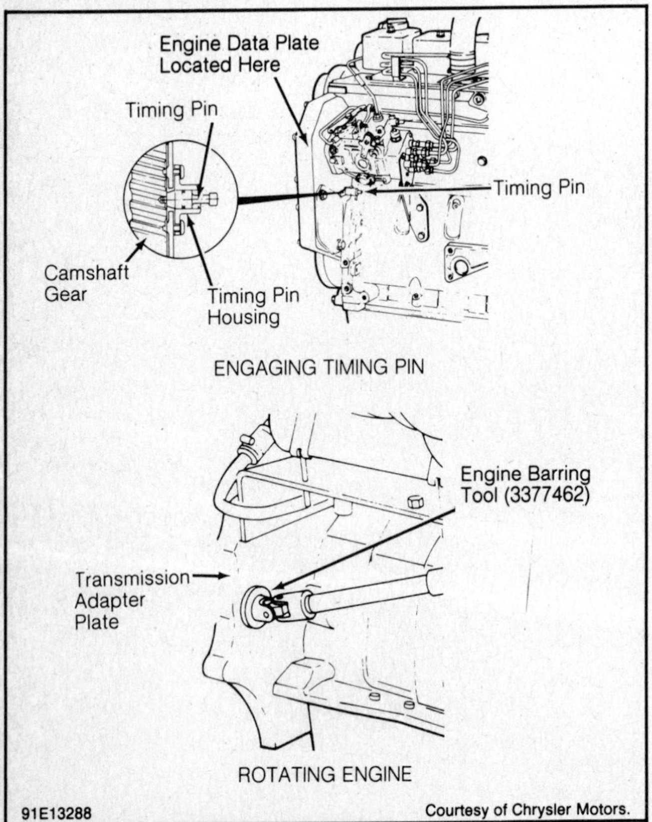
Engine Data Plate
Located Here
Timing Pin
Timing Pin
Camshaft
Gear
Timing Pin
Housing
ENGAGING TIMING PIN
Engine Barring
Tool (3377462)
Transmission
Adapter
Plate
ROTATING ENGINE
91E13288
Courtesy of Chrysler Motors.

Fig. 1: Rotating Engine & Engaging Timing Pin

1) Engine can be rotated by removing dust cover from transmission adapter plate and installing Engine Barring Tool (3377462) in adapter plate. *See Fig. 1.* Rotate engine clockwise until No. 1 cylinder is at TDC. Engage timing pin.

***CAUTION:** Use care when engaging timing pin to avoid breaking tip of timing pin. Ensure timing pin is disengaged before rotating engine.*

2) Remove rocker lever covers, and ensure No. 1 cylinder push rods are loose and valves are closed. If cylinder push rods are not loose or valves are not closed, disengage timing pin and rotate engine 360 degrees. With No. 1 cylinder at TDC, check clearance on proper valves. See VALVE ADJUSTING SEQUENCE table. Adjust clearance using rocker lever adjusting screw if clearance is not to specifications. See VALVE CLEARANCE SPECIFICATIONS table.
3) Once correct valves are checked and adjusted, place reference marks on vibration damper and front timing gear cover. Disengage timing pin, rotate engine 360 degrees and realign reference marks.
4) Clearance must be checked on proper valves. See VALVE ADJUSTING SEQUENCE table. Adjust clearance if not to specifications. See VALVE CLEARANCE SPECIFICATIONS table.

VALVE ADJUSTING SEQUENCE

Procedure	Cylinder Number
Step 1 [1]	
Exhaust Valves	1, 3 & 5
Intake Valves	1, 2 & 4
Step 2 [2]	
Exhaust Valves	2, 4 & 6
Intake Valves	3, 5 & 6

[1] – Adjust with engine cold, timing pin engaged and No. 1 cylinder at TDC.
[2] – Engine rotated 360 degrees from TDC of No. 1 cylinder and reference marks aligned.

VALVE CLEARANCE SPECIFICATIONS

Application	[1] In. (mm)
Exhaust Valves	.020 (.51)
Intake Valves	.010 (.25)

[1] – Adjust with engine temperature below 140°F (60°C).

FUEL INJECTION PUMP TIMING

***CAUTION:** Special washer must be located under lock bolt before rotating engine to allow fuel injection pump to rotate. If special washer is not installed, loosen lock bolt and install special washer. Tighten lock bolt to 10 ft. lbs. (14 N.m). See Fig. 17.*

1) Ensure special washer is located under lock bolt. *See Fig. 17.* Rotate engine clockwise until No. 1 cylinder is at TDC. Engage timing pin. *See Fig. 1.* Engine can be rotated by removing dust cover from transmission adapter plate and installing Engine Barring Tool (3377462) in adapter plate.

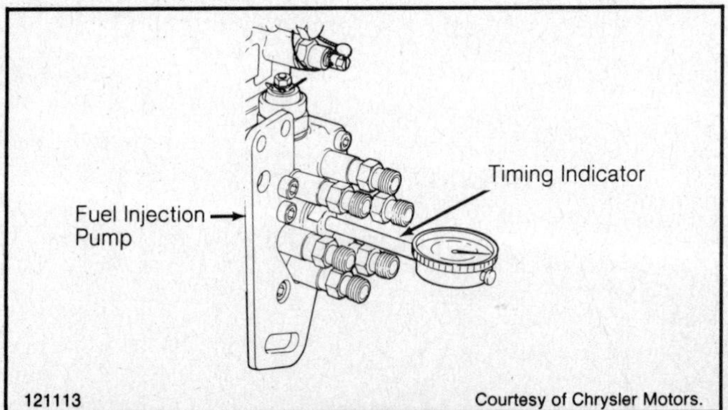
Timing Indicator
Fuel Injection
Pump
121113
Courtesy of Chrysler Motors.

Fig. 2: Checking Fuel Injection Pump Timing

2) Remove plug from end of fuel injection pump. Install timing indicator in end of fuel injection pump. *See Fig. 2.* It may be necessary to remove some high-pressure fuel lines for timing indicator installation.

NOTE: Note timing indicator range and amount of travel in one revolution. This reading may vary with type of timing indicator used.

3) Ensure timing indicator has at least .079" (2.00 mm) of travel. Disengage timing pin. Rotate engine in opposite direction of rotation until dial indicator stops moving. Adjust dial indicator to zero.
4) Rotate engine in direction of rotation to TDC of No. 1 cylinder while counting number of revolutions of dial indicator. Ensure timing pin engages. Reading is plunger lift.
5) Plunger lift should be 1.25 mm on intercooled models and 1.4 mm on non-intercooled models. If plunger lift is not as specified, loosen mounting nuts, and rotate fuel injection pump on mounting studs to obtain correct plunger lift. Tighten mounting nuts to 18 ft. lbs. (24 N.m).
6) If new or replacement fuel injection pump is installed, place timing mark on fuel injection pump flange to align with timing mark on gear housing. *See Fig. 17.*
7) Remove timing indicator, and install plug. Tighten plug to 84 INCH lbs. (10 N.m). Ensure timing pin is disengaged. Bleed high-pressure fuel lines if fuel lines were disconnected. See FUEL LINE BLEEDING.

THROTTLE POSITION SENSOR (TPS)

NOTE: Throttle Position Sensor (TPS) is used only on intercooled models with A/T.

CAUTION: Before adjusting TPS, ensure cable rod is adjusted so control lever contacts low-speed screw when in idle position. Ensure control lever moves over center position and rests against breakover spring when in full throttle position. See Fig. 3.

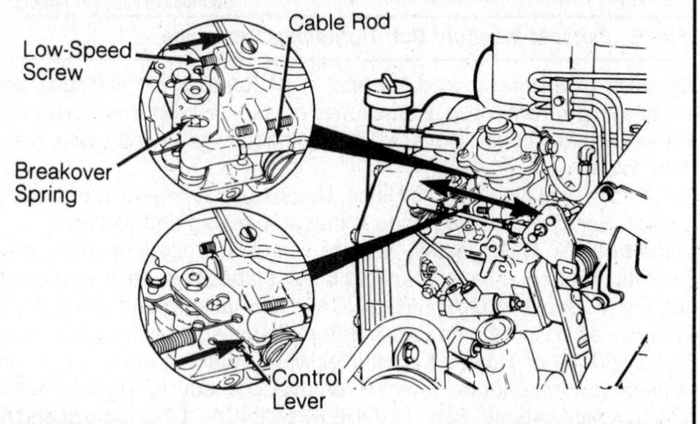
Cable Rod
Low-Speed Screw
Breakover Spring
Control Lever
91F13289
Courtesy of Chrysler Motors.

Fig. 3: Adjusting Throttle Linkage

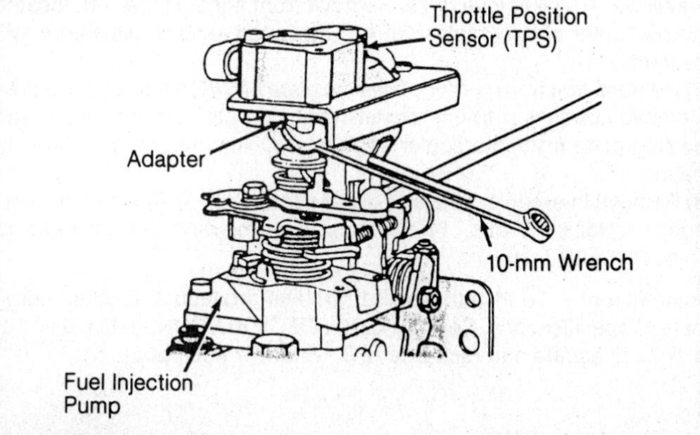
Throttle Position Sensor (TPS)
Adapter
10-mm Wrench
Fuel Injection Pump
91I13290
Courtesy of Chrysler Motors.

Fig. 4: Adjusting TPS

1) Connect negative probe of voltmeter to ground. Turn ignition on. Backprobe center wire terminal of TPS electrical connector. With control lever contacting low-speed screw (idle position), voltage should be at least one volt. If voltage is not at least one volt, use 10-mm wrench to adjust TPS to obtain correct voltage. *See Fig. 4.*
2) Open throttle to full throttle position. Ensure control lever moves over center position and rests against breakover spring when in full throttle position. *See Fig. 3.* Backprobe center wire terminal at TPS electrical connector.
3) Voltage should be at least 2.25 volts higher than voltage obtained with throttle in idle position. If voltage is not at least 2.25 volts higher than idle position voltage, adjust TPS to obtain correct voltage. *See Fig. 4.*

FUEL LINE BLEEDING

WARNING: DO NOT bleed fuel lines on a hot engine as high exhaust temperatures could cause a fire. Use care when bleeding fuel lines as fuel is under extreme pressure and could penetrate skin, causing personal injury.

1) To bleed low-pressure fuel lines and fuel filter, open fuel bleed screw on banjo bolt. *See Fig. 5.*

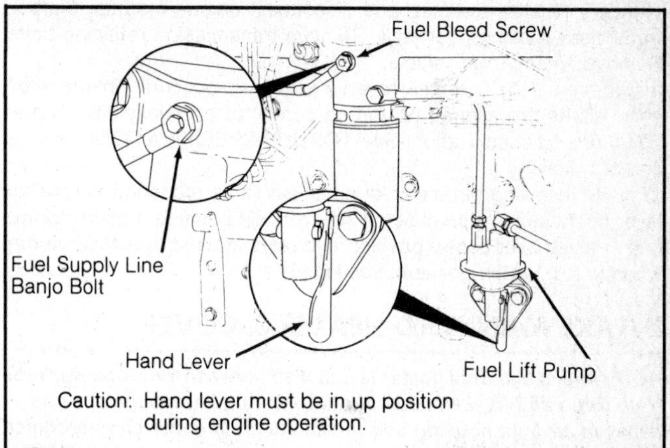
Fuel Bleed Screw
Fuel Supply Line Banjo Bolt
Hand Lever
Fuel Lift Pump
Caution: Hand lever must be in up position during engine operation.
121114
Courtesy of Chrysler Motors.

Fig. 5: Bleeding Fuel Lines

2) Operate hand lever on fuel lift pump until steady fuel stream flows from fuel bleed screw. Tighten fuel bleed screw to 72 INCH lbs. (8 N.m). If hand lever feels like fuel lift pump is not operating, rotate engine 90 degrees, and repeat procedure. Position hand lever in upward position once fuel line is bled.

CAUTION: Fuel lift pump hand lever must be in upward position once fuel lines are bled.

3) To bleed high-pressure fuel lines, cautiously loosen fuel line nut at fuel injector. Operate starter until steady fuel flow exists, and then tighten fuel line nut to specification. See TORQUE SPECIFICATIONS table at end of article.

CAUTION: DO NOT operate starter for more than 30 seconds. Allow 2 minute intervals between starter operations.

4) Start engine, and repeat procedure on all fuel lines individually until engine operates smoothly.

REMOVAL & INSTALLATION

NOTE: For reassembly reference, label all electrical connectors, vacuum hoses and fuel lines before removal. Also place mating marks on engine hood and other major assemblies before removal.

1991 ENGINES
Cummins Diesel "B" Series 5.9L 6-Cylinder (Cont.)

ENGINE

Removal - 1) Remove battery. Scribe hood hinges, and remove hood. Drain cooling system and engine oil. Remove fan and fan clutch as an assembly. Remove fan shroud and radiator.

2) Disconnect necessary electrical connections and coolant hoses. On intercooled models, disconnect and remove intercooler outlet duct from intercooler and intake manifold. Disconnect and remove intercooler inlet tube from turbo and intercooler. *See Fig. 7.*

3) On all models, disconnect air inlet tube from turbo. Disconnect control linkages from control lever on fuel injection pump. DO NOT remove control lever from fuel injection pump. *See Fig. 3.*

4) Disconnect exhaust pipe at turbo. On A/C equipped models, remove A/C compressor with lines attached, and secure aside. On all models, disconnect necessary electrical connections. Disconnect power steering lines, vacuum pump lines and fuel lines.

5) On A/T models, remove torque converter cover. Mark torque converter-to-flexplate for reassembly reference. Attach "C" clamp on front of torque converter housing to hold torque converter in place. Remove torque converter-to-flexplate bolts. Disconnect transmission oil cooler lines.

6) On all models, connect engine hoist to engine lifting eyes. It may be necessary to remove lifting eyes and turn so eye on lifting bracket is facing upward. Tighten lifting bracket bolt to 57 ft. lbs. (77 N.m).

7) Apply tension to hoist, and disconnect engine mounts. Support transmission using floor jack. Remove transmission retaining bolts. Remove engine from vehicle.

Installation - 1) To install, reverse removal procedure. Ensure reference marks are aligned on torque converter and flexplate. Tighten bolts/nuts to specification. See TORQUE SPECIFICATIONS table at end of article.

2) When installing throttle linkage, adjust cable rod length so control lever contacts low-speed screw when in idle position. Ensure control lever moves over center position and rests against breakover spring when in full throttle position. *See Fig. 3.*

INTAKE MANIFOLD HEATER & COVER

NOTE: Intake manifold heater is installed between air crossover tube from turbo and intake manifold cover on non-intercooled models or between air inlet housing and intake manifold cover on intercooled models.

Removal (Intercooled Models) - 1) Disconnect intercooler outlet duct from air inlet housing. *See Fig. 7.* Remove high-pressure fuel lines. Hold delivery valves on fuel injection pump using wrench while removing high-pressure lines. Mark fuel line location for reassembly reference.

2) Disconnect intake manifold heater electrical connector. Disconnect fuel heater ground wire (located above fuel filter) from intake manifold cover. Remove retaining.bolts, air inlet housing and gasket.

3) Remove intake manifold heater and gasket. Disconnect electrical connectors from charge air temperature sensor and air temperature switch on intake manifold cover. Remove retaining bolts, intake manifold cover and gasket.

Installation - To install, reverse removal procedure using new gaskets. Apply thread sealant to intake manifold cover bolts before installing. Tighten bolts to specification. See TORQUE SPECIFICATIONS table at end of article. Install and bleed high-pressure fuel lines. See FUEL LINE BLEEDING.

Removal (Non-Intercooled Models) - 1) Remove air crossover tube retaining bolts. Loosen throttle cable bracket lower mounting bolts, and move bracket from engine. Loosen air crossover tube clamps at turbo. Remove air crossover tube.

2) Remove high-pressure fuel lines. Hold delivery valves on fuel injection pump using wrench while removing high-pressure lines. Mark fuel line location for reassembly reference.

3) Disconnect intake manifold heater electrical connector. Disconnect fuel heater ground wire (located above fuel filter) from intake manifold cover. Remove intake manifold heater. Remove retaining bolts, intake manifold cover and gasket.

Installation - To install, reverse removal procedure using new gasket. Apply thread sealant to intake manifold cover bolts before installing. Tighten bolts to specification. See TORQUE SPECIFICATIONS table at end of article. Install and bleed high-pressure fuel lines. See FUEL LINE BLEEDING.

EXHAUST MANIFOLD & TURBO

Removal (Intercooled Models) - 1) Disconnect air inlet tube and exhaust pipe from turbo. Remove and plug turbo oil lines. Remove intercooler inlet tube from turbo and intercooler. *See Fig. 7.*

2) Remove retaining nuts, turbo and gasket. Remove coolant line bracket-to-exhaust manifold bolts. Remove retaining bolts, exhaust manifold and gasket.

Installation - 1) To install, reverse removal procedure using new gaskets. Tighten exhaust manifold bolts to specification in sequence. *See Fig. 6.* See TORQUE SPECIFICATIONS table at end of article.

2) Install oil drain tube on turbo. Before installing oil supply line, pour 3 ozs. (60 cc) of clean oil in oil inlet while spinning turbo. To install remaining components, reverse removal procedure. Tighten bolts/nuts to specification. See TORQUE SPECIFICATIONS table at end of article.

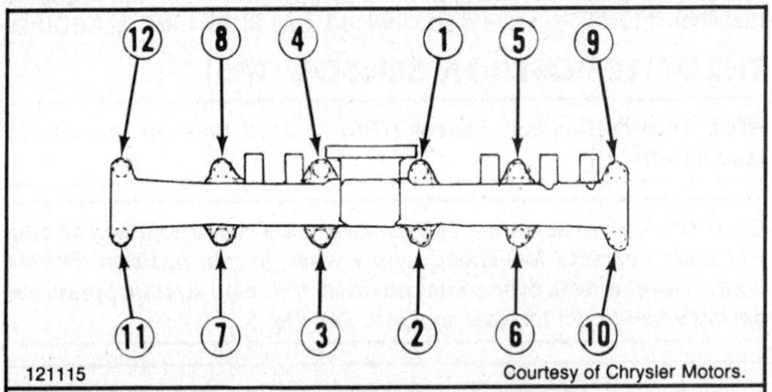
12
8
4
1
5
9
11
7
3
2
6
10
121115
Courtesy of Chrysler Motors.

Fig. 6: Exhaust Manifold Bolt Tightening Sequence

Removal (Non-Intercooled Models) - 1) Remove air inlet tube and exhaust pipe from turbo. Remove air crossover tube from turbo and intake manifold cover. Cover inlet openings on turbo and intake manifold cover.

2) Remove and plug turbo oil lines. Remove retaining nuts, turbo and gasket. Remove retaining bolts, exhaust manifold and gasket.

Installation - 1) To install, reverse removal procedure using new gaskets. Tighten exhaust manifold bolts to specification in sequence. *See Fig. 6.* See TORQUE SPECIFICATIONS table at end of article.

2) Install oil drain tube on turbo. Before installing oil supply line, pour 3 ozs. (60 cc) of clean oil in oil inlet while spinning turbo. To install remaining components, reverse removal procedure. Tighten bolts/nuts to specifications. See TORQUE SPECIFICATIONS table at end of article.

INTERCOOLER

Removal - 1) Remove grille. Remove front support bracket, located above center of intercooler. On A/C equipped models, discharge A/C system.

2) Remove bolt from center of sealing plate on A/C lines at condenser. Remove condenser-to-intercooler retaining nuts. Lift condenser and sealing plate from intercooler. Plug all A/C lines to prevent contamination.

3) Remove intercooler inlet and outlet ducts. *See Fig. 7.* Remove intercooler retaining bolts. Pivot intercooler forward and upward to remove.

Installation - To install, reverse removal procedure. Tighten bolts/nuts to specifications. See TORQUE SPECIFICATIONS table at end of article. Evacuate and recharge A/C system (if equipped).

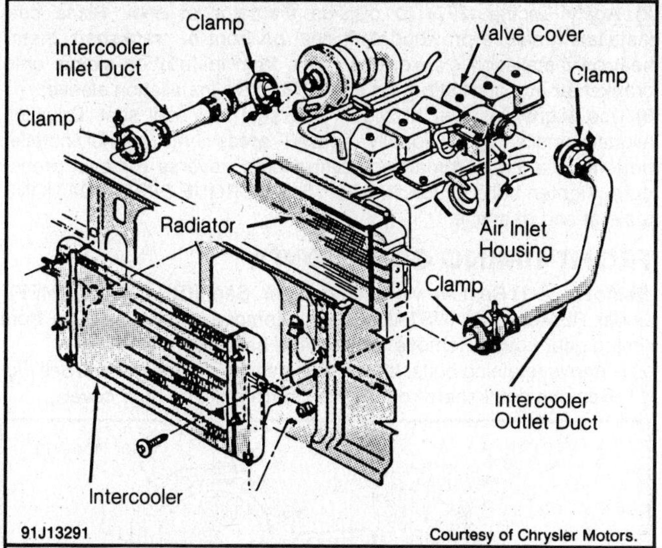
Clamp
Intercooler Inlet Duct
Valve Cover
Clamp
Clamp
Radiator
Air Inlet Housing
Clamp
Intercooler Outlet Duct
Intercooler
91J13291
Courtesy of Chrysler Motors.

Fig. 7: Exploded View of Intercooler & Components

CYLINDER HEAD

CAUTION: Intercooled and non-intercooled cylinder heads are different and cannot be interchanged.

Removal - 1) Drain cooling system and engine oil. Disconnect necessary coolant hoses and electrical connections. Remove exhaust manifold and turbo. See EXHAUST MANIFOLD & TURBO under REMOVAL & INSTALLATION. Remove throttle linkage and bracket (if necessary).

2) Remove high-pressure fuel lines. Hold delivery valves on fuel injection pump using wrench while removing high-pressure lines. Mark fuel line location for reassembly reference.

3) Disconnect air fuel control tube. Tube is from fuel injection pump to cylinder head. Remove fuel drain lines from fuel injectors, and plug all fuel openings.

CAUTION: Mark location of fuel supply line banjo bolts at fuel filter head before removing. See Fig. 5.

4) Remove fuel banjo fittings at fuel filter head. Remove fuel filter. Remove fuel lines from fuel lift pump. Fuel injectors should be removed to prevent damage during cylinder head removal.

5) Clean around fuel injector. Hold fuel injector body using wrench while loosening hold-down nut. Using Fuel Injector Puller (3823276), pull fuel injectors from cylinder head. Remove sealing ring (located below fuel injector) from cylinder head.

6) Remove rocker lever assembly and push rods. See ROCKER LEVER ASSEMBLY & PUSH RODS under REMOVAL & INSTALLATION. Remove cylinder head bolts in sequence. *See Fig. 8.* Remove cylinder head and gasket.

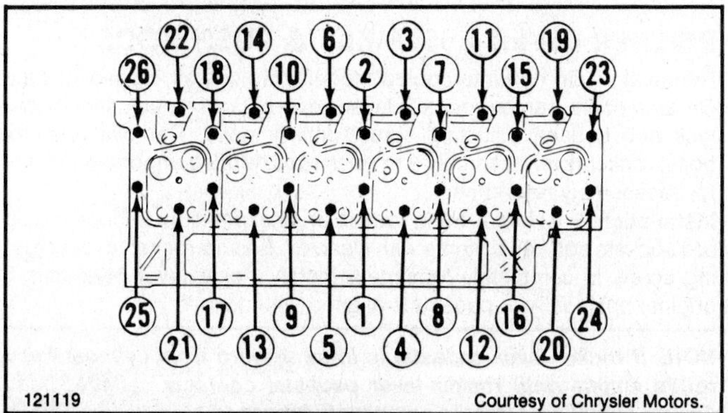
22 14 6 3 11 19
26 18 10 2 7 15 23
25 17 9 1 8 16 24
21 13 5 4 12 20
121119
Courtesy of Chrysler Motors.

Fig. 8: Cylinder Head Bolt Removal & Installation Sequence

Inspection - 1) Inspect cylinder head for warpage at deck surface. Resurface cylinder head if warpage exceeds specifications. See CYLINDER HEAD table under ENGINE SPECIFICATIONS at end of article. Replace cylinder head if total metal removed exceeds .0393" (.998 mm).

NOTE: Amount of material removed from cylinder head should be stamped on lower right rear corner of cylinder head above deck surface.

2) Inspect cylinder block warpage. Warpage should not exceed specifications. See CYLINDER BLOCK table under ENGINE SPECIFICATIONS at end of article.

CAUTION: Proper head gasket must be installed in accordance with cylinder block height. Different thickness gaskets are used as deck surface is resurfaced.

Installation - 1) Note if marking exists on upper right corner of cylinder block. *See Fig. 9.* If no mark exists, cylinder block has not been resurfaced. Cylinder block can only be resurfaced twice: once .0059" (.149 mm), and then an additional .0138" (.350 mm) for total limit of .0197" (.500 mm).

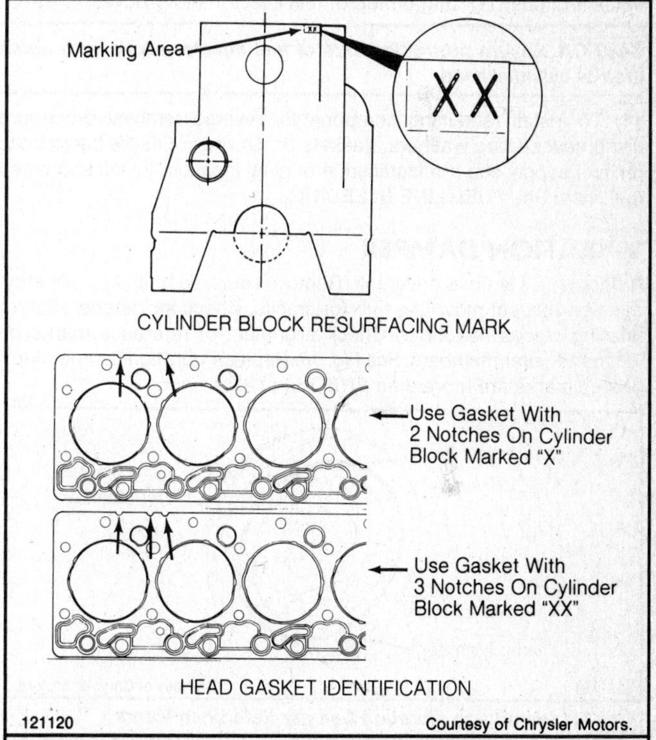
Marking Area
XX
CYLINDER BLOCK RESURFACING MARK
Use Gasket With 2 Notches On Cylinder Block Marked "X"
Use Gasket With 3 Notches On Cylinder Block Marked "XX"
HEAD GASKET IDENTIFICATION
121120
Courtesy of Chrysler Motors.

Fig. 9: Identifying Cylinder Block Resurfacing Mark

2) If "X" appears, this indicates cylinder block was resurfaced .0059" (.149 mm), while a marking of "XX" indicates block was resurfaced to total of .0197" (.500 mm).

3) Head gasket with 2 notches is used on cylinder block marked "X"; head gasket with 3 notches is used with "XX" cylinder block marking. *See Fig. 9.* Determine proper head gasket usage.

NOTE: Consult parts department for proper gasket application to provide proper piston-to-valve clearance.

4) Ensure sealing surfaces, cylinder head bolts and holes are clean and dry. Install dowels in cylinder block (if removed). Install new head gasket. Ensure all holes are aligned.

5) Install cylinder head. Ensure cylinder head properly seats on dowels in cylinder block. Lubricate cylinder head bolts with oil. Install all bolts EXCEPT those for rocker lever pedestals. DO NOT tighten bolts yet. Rocker levers must be installed before tightening cylinder head bolts.

1991 ENGINES
Cummins Diesel "B" Series 5.9L 6-Cylinder (Cont.)

6) Install push rods in original position. Lubricate push rod sockets and valve stems with clean oil. Ensure rocker lever adjusting screw is completely loosened. Install rocker lever pedestals in original position with pedestals aligned with dowels.

NOTE: If rocker lever pedestal is lifted upward from cylinder head, rotate engine until rocker lever pedestal contacts cylinder head. Ensure adjusting screw is completely loosened.

7) Lubricate remaining bolts with oil, and install. Tighten cylinder head bolts to specifications using proper sequence. See TORQUE SPECIFICATIONS table at end of article. *See Fig. 8.* Tighten remaining rocker lever pedestal bolts to specifications. See TORQUE SPECIFICATIONS table.

8) Adjust valve clearance. See VALVE CLEARANCE ADJUSTMENT under ADJUSTMENTS. Replace seal rings on rocker lever cover bolts. Install rocker lever cover, gasket and bolts.

9) Ensure fuel injector sleeve is clean. Install new sealing ring on fuel injector. Coat fuel injector retaining nut and top of fuel injector body with anti-seize. Install fuel injector in original position.

10) Ensure protruding side of fuel injector aligns with notch area of cylinder head. Tighten fuel injector retaining nut to specification. See TORQUE SPECIFICATIONS table. Once fuel injector retaining nut is tightened, push "O" ring on top of fuel injector into groove.

CAUTION: Ensure protruding side of fuel injector aligns with notch area of cylinder head.

11) To install remaining components, reverse removal procedure using new sealing washers, gaskets or "O" rings. Ensure banjo bolts for fuel supply line are installed in original location. Install and bleed fuel lines. See FUEL LINE BLEEDING.

VIBRATION DAMPER

Removal – Remove drive belt. Remove retaining bolts and vibration damper. Inspect mounting hub for cracks. Check for deterioration or missing pieces of rubber. Check alignment of reference marks on inner and outer members. *See Fig. 10.* Replace vibration damper if reference marks are more than 1/16" out of alignment.

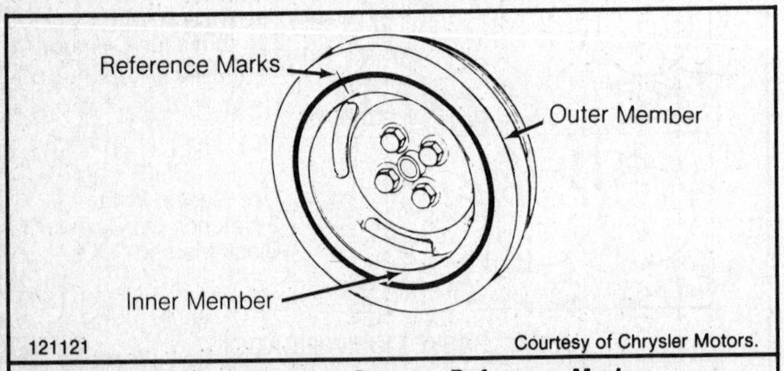
Reference Marks
Outer Member
Inner Member
121121
Courtesy of Chrysler Motors.

Fig. 10: Identifying Vibration Damper Reference Marks

Installation – To install, reverse removal procedure. Tighten vibration damper bolts to specification. See TORQUE SPECIFICATIONS table at end of article. Install drive belt.

CRANKSHAFT FRONT SEAL

Removal – Remove vibration damper. See VIBRATION DAMPER under REMOVAL & INSTALLATION. Drill two 1/8" holes in face of seal 180 degrees apart. Install sheet metal screws in holes. Using slide hammer, remove crankshaft front seal.

Installation – **1)** Ensure seal seating surfaces of crankshaft and front timing gear cover are clean. If front timing gear cover has been recently removed, install aligner/installer provided with crankshaft front seal on front of crankshaft, and ensure alignment of front timing gear cover and crankshaft.

CAUTION: Crankshaft and seal must be free of oil during installation to prevent seal leakage.

2) Apply Loctite (277) to outside diameter of seal. Place seal installation sleeve provided with seal on front of crankshaft. Install seal on installation sleeve, push seal from installation sleeve onto crankshaft and start into gear cover. Remove installation sleeve.

3) Use aligner/installer provided with seal to install seal. Drive on aligner/installer in 4 equally spaced areas until aligner/installer bottoms. To install remaining components, reverse removal procedure. Tighten bolts to specification. See TORQUE SPECIFICATIONS table at end of article.

FRONT TIMING GEAR COVER

Removal – **1)** Remove vibration damper. See VIBRATION DAMPER under REMOVAL & INSTALLATION. Remove oil fill tube from front timing gear cover. Remove fan hub and belt tensioner.

2) Remove retaining bolts, front timing gear cover and gasket. *See Fig. 11.* Remove crankshaft front seal from front timing gear cover.

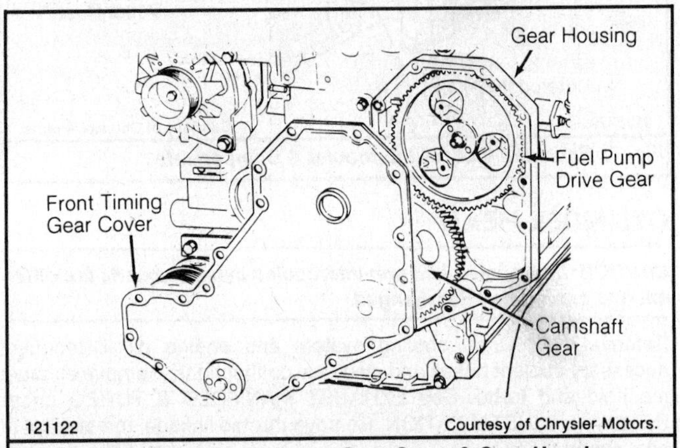
Gear Housing
Fuel Pump
Drive Gear
Front Timing
Gear Cover
Camshaft
Gear
121122
Courtesy of Chrysler Motors.

Fig. 11: Identifying Front Timing Gear Cover & Gear Housing

Installation – **1)** Lubricate gear train with oil. Ensure gasket and crankshaft seal surfaces are clean and dry. Install gasket, front timing gear cover and retaining bolts. DO NOT tighten bolts yet.

CAUTION: Crankshaft and seal must be free of oil during installation to prevent seal leakage.

2) Install aligner/installer provided with crankshaft front seal on front of crankshaft. Tighten front timing gear cover retaining bolts to specification, and remove aligner/installer. See TORQUE SPECIFICATIONS table at end of article.

3) Apply Loctite (277) to outside diameter of seal. Place seal installation sleeve provided with seal on front of crankshaft. Install seal on installation sleeve, push seal from installation sleeve onto crankshaft and start into gear cover. Remove installation sleeve.

4) Use aligner/installer provided with seal to install seal. Drive on aligner/installer in 4 equally spaced areas until aligner/installer bottoms. To install remaining components, reverse removal procedure. Tighten bolts to specification. See TORQUE SPECIFICATIONS table.

ROCKER LEVER ASSEMBLY & PUSH RODS

Removal – On non-intercooled models, remove air crossover tube. On all models, remove rocker lever covers. Loosen adjusting screw lock nut. Loosen adjusting screw until it stops. Remove retaining bolts, rocker lever assembly and push rods. Mark component location for reassembly reference.

Installation – **1)** Install push rods in original position. Lubricate push rod sockets and valve stems with clean oil. Ensure rocker lever adjusting screw is completely loosened. Install rocker lever pedestals in original position with pedestals aligned with dowels.

NOTE: If rocker lever pedestal is lifted upward from cylinder head, rotate engine until rocker lever pedestal contacts cylinder head. Ensure adjusting screw is completely loosened.

2) Lubricate retaining bolts with oil, and install. Tighten rocker lever assembly 12-mm bolts to specifications in sequence. *See Fig. 12.* See TORQUE SPECIFICATIONS table at end of article.
3) Tighten 8-mm bolts to specification. See TORQUE SPECIFICATIONS table. Adjust valve clearance. See VALVE CLEARANCE ADJUSTMENT under ADJUSTMENTS. Replace seal rings on rocker cover bolts. Install rocker lever cover, gasket and bolts.

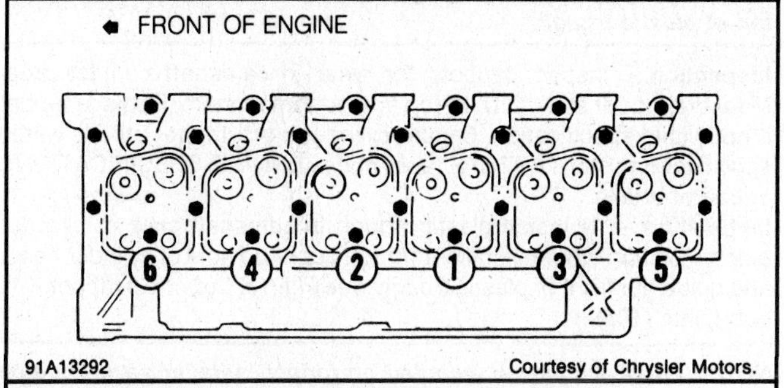
FRONT OF ENGINE
6
4
2
1
3
5
91A13292
Courtesy of Chrysler Motors.

Fig. 12: Rocker Lever 12-mm Bolt Tightening Sequence

CAMSHAFT

Removal - 1) Remove rocker lever assembly and push rods. See ROCKER LEVER ASSEMBLY & PUSH RODS under REMOVAL & INSTALLATION. Remove front timing gear cover. See FRONT TIMING GEAR COVER under REMOVAL & INSTALLATION.
2) Remove fuel lift pump. Install Dowel (3822513) through push rod hole. Using plastic hammer, lightly tap dowel into each tappet. *See Fig. 13.* Raise tappets upward and away from camshaft, and install rubber band around both intake and exhaust tappet dowels to retain tappets from camshaft.
3) Rotate crankshaft, and align timing marks on camshaft gear, crankshaft gear and fuel pump drive gear. *See Fig. 14.* Remove bolts, camshaft and thrust plate.
4) Inspect camshaft gear for damage. If camshaft gear requires replacement, see CAMSHAFT GEAR under REMOVAL & INSTALLATION. Inspect tappet-to-camshaft contact areas for wear. If tappets require replacement, see TAPPETS under REMOVAL & INSTALLATION.

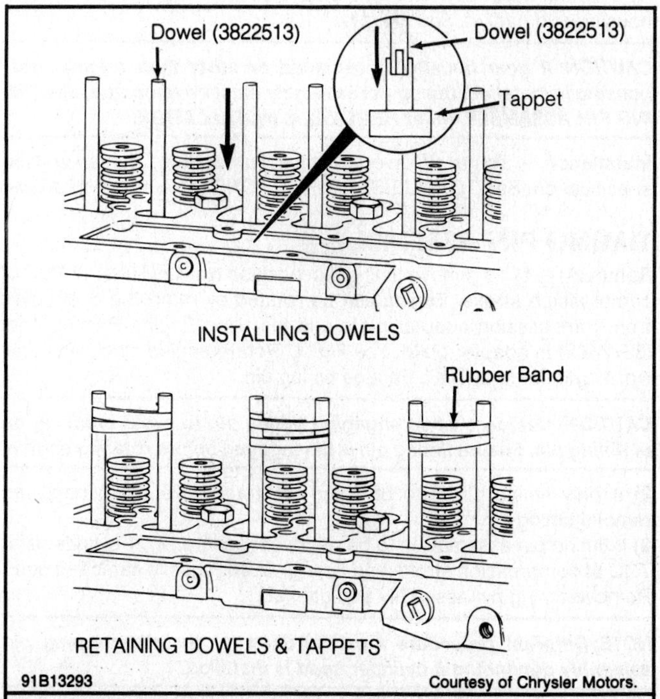
Dowel (3822513)
Dowel (3822513)
Tappet
INSTALLING DOWELS
Rubber Band
RETAINING DOWELS & TAPPETS
91B13293
Courtesy of Chrysler Motors.

Fig. 13: Retaining Tappet In Cylinder Block

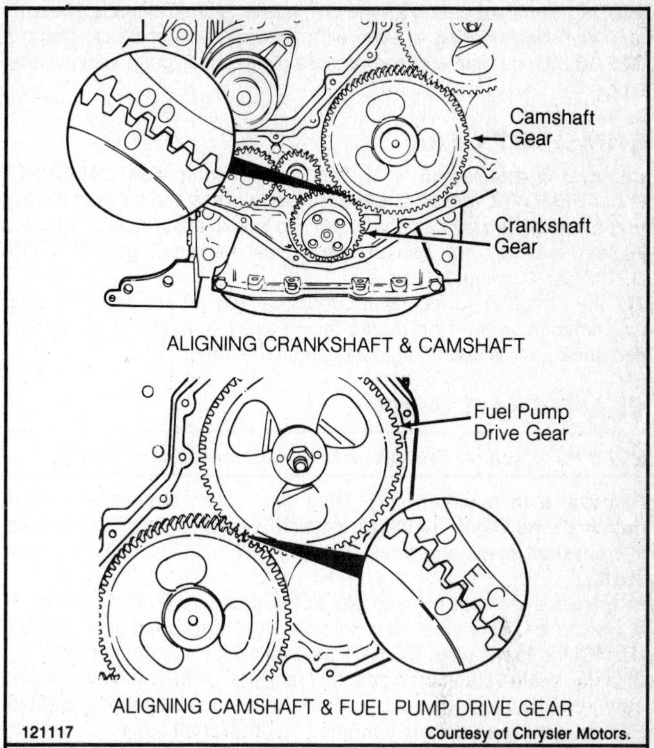
Camshaft Gear
Crankshaft Gear
ALIGNING CRANKSHAFT & CAMSHAFT
Fuel Pump Drive Gear
ALIGNING CAMSHAFT & FUEL PUMP DRIVE GEAR
121117
Courtesy of Chrysler Motors.

Fig. 14: Aligning Timing Marks

Inspection - Inspect camshaft bearings. See CAMSHAFT BEARINGS under REMOVAL & INSTALLATION. Measure camshaft journals and camshaft lobes. Replace camshaft if damaged or not within specifications. See CAMSHAFT table under ENGINE SPECIFICATIONS at end of article.
Installation - 1) Coat camshaft bearings, camshaft journals and thrust plate with Lubriplate (105). Install camshaft with all timing marks aligned. *See Fig. 14.*

CAUTION: DO NOT push camshaft inward beyond area for thrust plate. Excessive inward movement of camshaft will dislodge plug in rear of cylinder block, causing an oil leak.

2) Install thrust plate, and tighten retaining bolts to specification. See TORQUE SPECIFICATIONS table at end of article. Using dial indicator, check gear backlash between camshaft gear, crankshaft gear and fuel pump drive gear. Check camshaft end play.
3) Gear backlash and camshaft end play should be within specifications. See CAMSHAFT table under ENGINE SPECIFICATIONS at end of article.
4) To install remaining components, reverse removal procedure. Adjust valve clearance. See VALVE CLEARANCE ADJUSTMENT under ADJUSTMENTS.

CAMSHAFT BEARINGS

NOTE: Camshaft bearing is used only on front camshaft journal. All other camshaft journal bores should be same I.D. as front camshaft bearing. Front camshaft bearing can be replaced. If remaining bores exceed specification, camshaft bores must be machined to accommodate service bearings.

Inspection - Inspect camshaft bearing for scratches or damage. Measure I.D. of camshaft bearing and journal bores. Replace camshaft bearing or machine bores for service bearing if bore I.D. exceeds specification. See CAMSHAFT table under ENGINE SPECIFICATIONS at end of article.
Removal & Installation - 1) Using camshaft bearing remover/installer, drive camshaft bearing from cylinder block. To install, mark camshaft bearing and cylinder block for oil hole alignment.

1991 ENGINES
Cummins Diesel "B" Series 5.9L 6-Cylinder (Cont.)

2) Using camshaft bearing remover/installer, install camshaft bearing until camshaft bearing is even with front of cylinder block. Using a .128" (3.25 mm) diameter rod, ensure oil hole is aligned with cylinder block.

CAMSHAFT GEAR

Removal & Installation - 1) Remove camshaft. See CAMSHAFT under REMOVAL & INSTALLATION. Using press and support blocks, press camshaft from camshaft gear. To install, ensure camshaft gear keyway and key are free of burrs. Heat camshaft gear to 250°F (121°C) for 45 minutes.
2) Coat camshaft surface with Lubriplate (105). Press camshaft gear on camshaft with timing marks facing away from camshaft. Ensure camshaft gear is seated against camshaft shoulder.

CRANKSHAFT GEAR

NOTE: Manufacturer lists procedure with crankshaft removed.

Removal & Installation - 1) Using gear puller, remove crankshaft gear from crankshaft. To install, install NEW alignment pin (if removed) in crankshaft so pin protrudes .063-.094" (1.60-2.38 mm) above crankshaft.
2) Ensure alignment pin and pin slot in crankshaft gear are free of burrs and end of crankshaft is smooth. Heat crankshaft gear at 250°F (121°C) for 45 minutes. DO NOT heat for longer than 45 minutes.
3) Install heated crankshaft gear on crankshaft with timing mark facing outward. Ensure alignment pin and slot in crankshaft gear are aligned. Ensure crankshaft gear is bottomed on crankshaft.

TAPPETS

Removal - 1) Remove camshaft. See CAMSHAFT under REMOVAL & INSTALLATION. Install plastic trough from Tappet Changing Set (3822513) full length of camshaft bore area of cylinder block. *See Fig. 15.* Ensure plastic trough is positioned under tappet to retain tappet when dowel is removed.

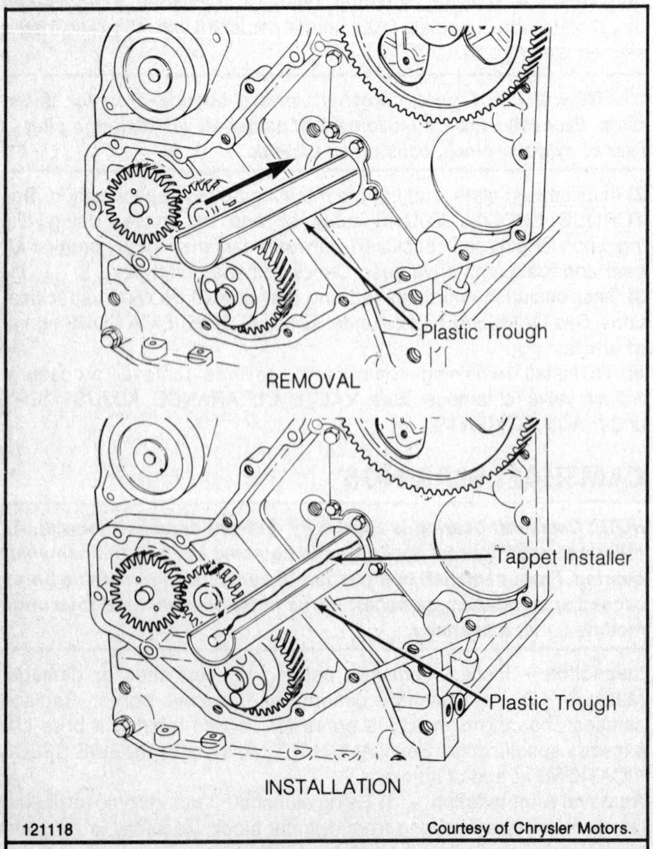
Plastic Trough
REMOVAL
Tappet Installer
Plastic Trough
INSTALLATION
121118
Courtesy of Chrysler Motors.

Fig. 15 Removing & Installing Tappets

2) Remove rubber band and dowel (installed during camshaft removal) from tappet. Allow tappet to fall into plastic trough. Ensure tappet falls over in plastic trough. Remove trough and tappet. Mark tappet for location.

CAUTION: DO NOT remove more than one tappet at a time. Ensure tappet falls over in plastic trough before removing. Use care when removing tappets from No. 6 cylinder, as not to shake tappets over top of plastic trough.

Inspection - Inspect tappets for wear in camshaft contact area. Measure tappet stem O.D. at top and bottom of stem. Replace tappet if not within specification. Ensure cylinder block tappet bore is within specification. See TAPPETS table under ENGINE SPECIFICATIONS at end of article.
Installation - 1) Install plastic trough in camshaft area of cylinder block. Position tappet installer through push rod hole of cylinder head, and guide out front of plastic trough. *See Fig. 15.* Lubricate tappet with Lubriplate (105).

NOTE: Tappet should be installed on tappet installer several times before installing to aid in tappet installer removal from tappet once installed in cylinder block.

2) Install tappet on tappet installer. Pull tappet up plastic trough, and align with original installation location. It may be necessary to pull plastic trough toward front of cylinder block to allow tappet to drop down and align with tappet bore.
3) Once tappet is installed in cylinder block bore, rotate plastic trough so rounded side of trough is against bottom of tappet. This will hold tappet in place. Install dowel and rubber band to retain tappet. Install camshaft and remaining components.

GEAR HOUSING

NOTE: Manufacturer lists procedure with engine removed.

Removal - 1) Remove engine. See ENGINE under REMOVAL & INSTALLATION. Remove camshaft. See CAMSHAFT under REMOVAL & INSTALLATION. Remove fuel injection pump. See FUEL INJECTION PUMP under REMOVAL & INSTALLATION.
2) Disconnect necessary hoses, and remove power steering and vacuum pump assembly. Remove gear housing retaining bolts, gear housing and gasket. *See Fig. 11.*

CAUTION: If gear housing is replaced or other than original gear housing is installed, timing pin assembly must be relocated. See TIMING PIN ASSEMBLY under REMOVAL & INSTALLATION.

Installation - To install, reverse removal procedure. Tighten bolts to specification. See TORQUE SPECIFICATIONS table at end of article.

TIMING PIN ASSEMBLY

Removal - 1) To remove timing pin, position No. 1 cylinder at TDC of compression stroke. Engine can be rotated by removing dust cover from transmission adapter plate and installing Engine Barring Tool (3377462) in adapter plate. *See Fig. 1.* Rotate engine clockwise until No. 1 cylinder is at TDC. Engage timing pin.

CAUTION: Use care when engaging timing pin to avoid breaking tip of timing pin. Ensure timing pin is disengaged before rotating engine.

2) If only timing pin is to be removed, remove retaining ring, and remove timing pin.
3) If timing pin assembly is to be removed, ensure No. 1 cylinder is at TDC of compression stroke and timing pin engages in camshaft gear. Remove timing pin assembly and gasket.

NOTE: Different procedure must be used for installing timing pin assembly depending if cylinder head is installed.

Installation (With Cylinder Head Installed) – 1) If only timing pin was removed, lubricate new "O" ring and timing pin with oil, and install in housing. Install retaining ring.

2) If timing pin assembly was removed, timing pin must be accurately located. Look through hole of gear housing, and rotate engine until timing pin hole in camshaft gear can be seen.

3) Remove rocker lever cover. Adjust exhaust valve rocker lever to zero clearance on No. 1 cylinder. Fuel injectors should be removed on all cylinders to provide smooth engine rotation.

4) Clean around fuel injectors. Disconnect fuel lines from fuel injectors. Hold fuel injector body using wrench while loosening hold-down nut. Remove fuel injector, and mark cylinder location for reassembly reference.

5) Temporarily install vibration damper (if removed). Fabricate and install pointer to align with vibration damper. Rotate crankshaft 1/4 turn counterclockwise in opposite direction of rotation. *See Fig. 16.* Tighten adjusting screw for exhaust valve 2 complete turns, and tighten lock nut.

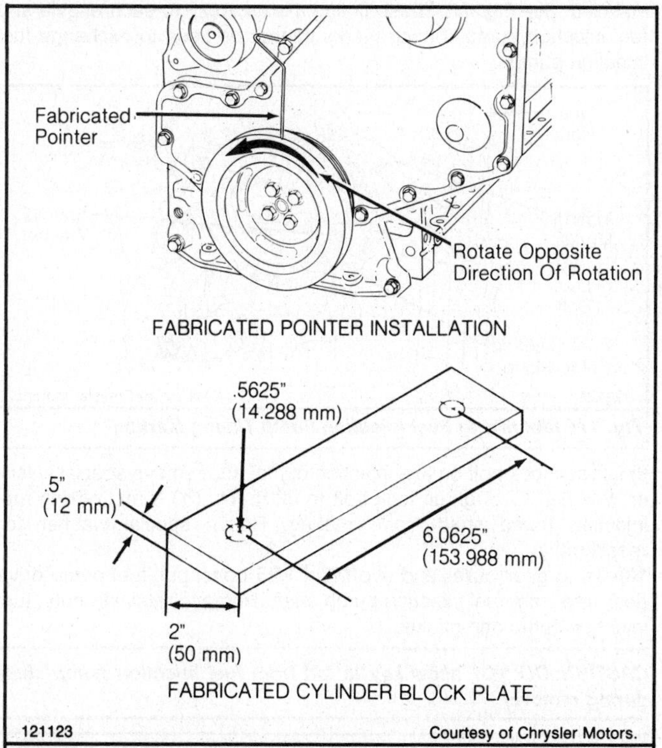
Fabricated Pointer
Rotate Opposite Direction Of Rotation
FABRICATED POINTER INSTALLATION
.5625" (14.288 mm)
.5" (12 mm)
6.0625" (153.988 mm)
2" (50 mm)
FABRICATED CYLINDER BLOCK PLATE
121123
Courtesy of Chrysler Motors.

Fig. 16: Installing Fabricated Pointer

CAUTION: Use care when rotating engine so piston does not contact exhaust valve.

6) Slowly rotate crankshaft clockwise in direction of rotation until piston slightly contacts exhaust valve. Place reference mark on vibration damper at fabricated pointer.

7) Slowly rotate crankshaft counterclockwise in opposite direction of rotation until piston contacts valve with same amount of force. Place reference mark on vibration damper at fabricated pointer.

8) Measure distance between reference marks. Place reference mark on vibration damper at a point halfway between reference marks. This is TDC mark. Completely loosen exhaust valve adjusting screw on No. 1 cylinder.

9) Rotate crankshaft clockwise in direction of rotation approximately 180 degrees until fabricated pointer is aligned with TDC mark. Look through back side of gear housing and note timing pin hole in camshaft gear. If timing pin hole is not visible, rotate crankshaft one revolution.

10) Install timing pin assembly and gasket. Hold timing pin in camshaft gear hole, and align housing with bolt holes. Coat bolts with thread sealant, and install. Tighten bolts to specification. See TORQUE SPECIFICATIONS table at end of article. Remove fabricated pointer.

CAUTION: Ensure timing pin is disengaged before rotating engine.

11) Adjust valve clearance on No. 1 cylinder. See VALVE CLEARANCE ADJUSTMENT under ADJUSTMENTS. Replace seal rings on rocker cover bolts. Install gasket, rocker lever cover and retaining bolts.

12) Ensure injector sleeve is clean. Install new sealing ring on fuel injector. Coat fuel injector retaining nut and top of fuel injector body with anti-seize. Install fuel injectors in original position.

13) Ensure protruding side of fuel injector aligns with notch area of cylinder head. Tighten fuel injector retaining nuts to specification. See TORQUE SPECIFICATIONS table. Once fuel injector retaining nut is tightened, push "O" ring on top of fuel injector into groove. To install remaining components, reverse removal procedure.

CAUTION: Ensure protruding side of fuel injector nozzle aligns with notch area of cylinder head.

14) Install and bleed high-pressure fuel lines. See FUEL LINE BLEEDING. To install remaining components, reverse removal procedure.

Installation (With Cylinder Head Removed) – 1) If only timing pin was removed, coat new "O" ring and timing pin with oil, and install in housing. Install retaining ring.

2) If timing pin assembly was removed, timing pin must be accurately located. Temporarily install vibration damper (if removed). Fabricate and install pointer to align with vibration damper. *See Fig. 16.* If front timing gear cover is removed, install flat washer between gear housing and fabricated pointer to prevent damage to gear housing.

3) Fabricate cylinder block plate. *See Fig. 16.* Install cylinder block plate over No. 1 cylinder. Rotate crankshaft clockwise in direction of rotation until piston contacts cylinder block plate. Place reference mark on vibration damper at fabricated pointer.

4) Slowly rotate crankshaft counterclockwise in opposite direction of rotation until piston contacts cylinder block plate. Place reference mark on vibration damper at fabricated pointer.

5) Measure distance between reference marks. Place reference mark on vibration damper at a point halfway between reference marks. This is TDC mark.

6) Remove cylinder block plate. Rotate crankshaft clockwise in direction of rotation until fabricated pointer aligns with TDC mark. Look through back side of gear housing, and note timing pin hole in camshaft gear. If pin hole is not visible, rotate crankshaft one revolution.

7) Install timing pin assembly and gasket. Hold timing pin in camshaft gear hole, and align housing with bolt holes. Coat bolts with thread sealant, and install. Tighten bolts to specification. See TORQUE SPECIFICATIONS table at end of article. Remove fabricated pointer.

CAUTION: Ensure timing pin is disengaged before rotating engine.

REAR CRANKSHAFT OIL SEAL

NOTE: Crankshaft and oil seal must be free of oil during installation to prevent seal leakage.

Removal & Installation – 1) Remove transmission, clutch pressure plate and disc (if equipped) and flywheel. Drill two 1/8" holes in seal face 180 degrees apart. Install sheet metal screws in holes. Using slide hammer, remove oil seal.

2) To install, ensure all sealing surfaces are clean and dry. Install oil seal pilot provided with rear crankshaft oil seal on rear of crankshaft. Install oil seal on pilot, and push oil seal from oil seal pilot onto crankshaft. Remove oil seal pilot.

3) On oil seals with rubber coating on outer diameter, coat rubber area with soapy water. On oil seals without rubber coating, apply Loctite (277) sealant to outside diameter of oil seal.

4) Use oil seal aligner/installer provided with oil seal to install oil seal. Drive on oil seal aligner/installer in 4 equally spaced areas until oil seal aligner/installer bottoms. Remove oil seal aligner/installer.

5) To install remaining components, reverse removal procedure. Tighten flywheel bolts in a crisscross pattern to specification. See TORQUE SPECIFICATIONS table at end of article.

REAR CRANKSHAFT OIL SEAL HOUSING

NOTE: Procedure listed from manufacturer with transmission, flywheel and oil pan removed.

Removal - Remove retaining bolts, oil seal housing and gasket from rear of cylinder block. Support oil seal housing, and drive oil seal from oil seal housing.

NOTE: Crankshaft and oil seal must be free of oil during installation to prevent seal leakage. Ensure oil seal housing is even with bottom of cylinder block surface to prevent oil leakage.

Installation - 1) Ensure all sealing surfaces are clean and dry. Install gasket and oil seal housing on cylinder block. DO NOT tighten bolts yet.
2) Install oil seal aligner/installer provided with rear crankshaft oil seal on rear of crankshaft. Ensure oil seal housing is even with bottom of cylinder block surface. Tighten retaining bolts to specification. See TORQUE SPECIFICATIONS table at end of article.
3) Trim oil seal housing gasket even with cylinder block surface. Remove oil seal aligner/installer. Install oil seal pilot provided with rear crankshaft oil seal on rear of crankshaft. Install oil seal on pilot, and push oil seal from oil seal pilot onto crankshaft. Remove oil seal pilot.
4) On oil seals with rubber coating on outer diameter, coat rubber area with soapy water. On oil seals without rubber coating, apply Loctite (277) sealant to outside diameter of oil seal.
5) Use oil seal aligner/installer provided with oil seal to install oil seal. Drive on oil seal aligner/installer in 4 equally spaced areas until oil seal aligner/installer bottoms. Remove oil seal aligner/installer.

FLYWHEEL RING GEAR

Removal & Installation - 1) Remove transmission, clutch pressure plate and disc (if equipped) and flywheel. Note direction of flywheel ring gear installation. Using brass drift and hammer, drive ring gear from flywheel.
2) To install, heat ring gear in oven at 250°F (121°C) for 20 minutes. Install flywheel ring gear with chamfered edge on teeth toward crankshaft side of flywheel.

CAUTION: Ring gear must be installed with chamfered edge on teeth toward crankshaft side of flywheel.

FUEL INJECTION PUMP

CAUTION: Fuel injection pump for intercooled and non-intercooled models are different and cannot be interchanged.

Removal - 1) Disconnect negative battery cable. Disconnect necessary electrical connections at fuel injection pump. Disconnect control linkages from control lever on fuel injection pump. DO NOT remove control lever from fuel injection pump. *See Fig. 3.*
2) Disconnect control linkage bracket. Remove and cap high-pressure fuel lines. Hold delivery valves on fuel injection pump using wrench while removing high-pressure lines. Mark fuel line location for reassembly reference.
3) Disconnect air fuel control tube. Tube is from fuel injection pump to cylinder head. Disconnect drain tube from fuel injection pump. Disconnect fuel supply line from fuel injection pump.
4) On intercooled models, remove bolt from rear support bracket on fuel injection pump. Remove rear support bracket-to-cylinder block bolts. Loosen center bolt on rear support bracket. Pivot rear support bracket toward rear of engine.
5) On non-intercooled models, remove retaining bolts and rear support bracket on fuel injection pump. On all models, remove oil fill tube from front timing gear cover. Place shop towel in front of fuel pump drive gear to prevent retaining nut and washer from falling during removal. Remove fuel pump drive gear retaining nut and washer.

CAUTION: DO NOT allow fuel pump drive gear retaining nut or washer to fall into front timing gear cover.

6) Rotate engine clockwise so No. 1 cylinder is at TDC of compression stroke. Engine can be rotated by removing dust cover from transmission adapter plate and installing Engine Barring Tool (3377462) in adapter plate. *See Fig. 1.*
7) When No. 1 cylinder is at TDC, key of fuel injection pump shaft should be pointing toward bottom of engine. Ensure timing pin will engage. *See Fig. 1.*

CAUTION: Use care when engaging timing pin to avoid breaking tip of timing pin. DO NOT rotate engine with timing pin engaged.

8) Note if timing marks on fuel injection pump flange and gear housing are aligned for reassembly reference if original fuel injection pump is installed. *See Fig. 17.* These timing marks apply to each engine and fuel injection pump. Timing marks cannot be used to exchange fuel injection pumps.

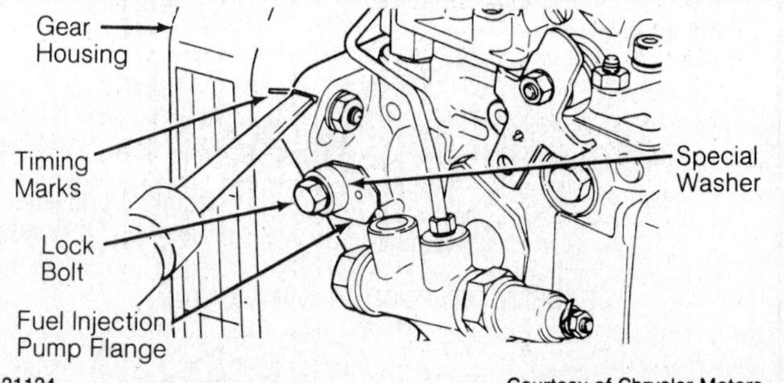
Gear Housing
Timing Marks
Lock Bolt
Fuel Injection Pump Flange
Special Washer
121124
Courtesy of Chrysler Motors.

Fig. 17: Identifying Fuel Injection Pump Timing Marks

9) Loosen lock bolt on fuel injection pump, and remove special washer. *See Fig. 17.* Tighten lock bolt to 22 ft. lbs. (30 N.m), locking fuel injection pump shaft from rotating. Retain special washer for reassembly.
10) Using gear puller and two M8 X 1.25 bolts, pull fuel pump drive gear free from fuel injection pump shaft. Remove retaining nuts, fuel injection pump and gasket.

CAUTION: DO NOT allow key to fall from fuel injection pump shaft during removal.

NOTE: Different procedure must be used depending on whether component is original or is new or rebuilt.

Installation (Original Fuel Injection Pump) - 1) Ensure gasket surfaces are clean. Ensure No. 1 cylinder is at TDC and timing pin is engaged. Install new gasket on cylinder block. Install key in fuel injection pump shaft, and install fuel injection pump. DO NOT allow key to drop from fuel injection pump shaft.

CAUTION: Use care when installing fuel injection pump to prevent key from dropping from fuel injection pump shaft.

2) Install mounting nuts. DO NOT tighten nuts yet. Fuel injection pump must be free to rotate in slots. Install fuel pump drive gear retaining nut and washer. Tighten fuel pump drive gear retaining nut to 11-15 ft. lbs. (15-20 N.m).
3) If fuel injection pump timing marks on fuel injection flange and gear housing were aligned at removal, fuel injection pump timing does not require adjustment. If marks were not aligned, fuel injection pump timing must be checked. See FUEL INJECTION PUMP TIMING under ADJUSTMENTS.
4) If timing marks were aligned at removal, rotate fuel injection pump to align timing marks. Tighten mounting nuts to 18 ft. lbs. (24 N.m). On all applications, loosen lock bolt, and install special washer under lock

bolt. Tighten lock bolt to 10 ft. lbs. (14 N.m). Tighten fuel pump drive gear nut to specification. See TORQUE SPECIFICATIONS table at end of article.

5) Disengage timing pin if not previously done. To install remaining components, reverse removal procedure. Loosely install all bolts in rear support bracket.

6) On intercooled models, tighten rear support bracket bolts to vacuum pump, cylinder block and then to fuel injection pump. On non-intercooled models, tighten rear support bracket bolts to cylinder block and then to fuel injection pump. Tighten bolts to specification. See TORQUE SPECIFICATIONS table at end of article.

7) Install and bleed fuel lines. See FUEL LINE BLEEDING. Ensure cable rod is adjusted so control lever contacts low-speed screw when in idle position. Ensure control lever moves over center position and rests against breakover spring when in full throttle position. *See Fig. 3.*

Installation (New Or Rebuilt Fuel Injection Pump) - 1) Ensure gasket surfaces are clean. Ensure No. 1 cylinder is at TDC and timing pin is engaged. Install new gasket on cylinder block. Install key in fuel injection pump shaft, and install fuel injection pump.

CAUTION: Use care when installing fuel injection pump to prevent key from dropping from fuel injection pump shaft.

2) Install mounting nuts. DO NOT tighten nuts yet. Fuel injection pump must be free to rotate in slots. Install fuel pump drive gear retaining nut and washer. Tighten nut to 11-15 ft. lbs. (15-20 N.m).

3) Rotate fuel injection pump toward cylinder head to take up gear lash. Fuel injection pump timing should be checked. See FUEL INJECTION PUMP TIMING under ADJUSTMENTS.

CAUTION: Ensure lock bolt is loosened and special washer is installed under lock bolt. Lock bolt must be tightened to 10 ft. lbs. (14 N.m).

4) Once correct timing is obtained and mounting nuts are tightened, place timing mark on fuel injection pump flange to align with mark on gear housing. *See Fig. 17.*

5) Disengage timing pin if not previously done. To install remaining components, reverse removal procedure. Install all bolts in rear support.

6) On intercooled models, tighten rear support bracket bolts to vacuum pump, cylinder block and then to fuel injection pump. On non-intercooled models, tighten rear support bracket bolts to cylinder block and then to fuel injection pump. Tighten bolts to specifications. See TORQUE SPECIFICATIONS table at end of article.

7) Install and bleed fuel lines. See FUEL LINE BLEEDING. Ensure cable rod is adjusted so control lever contacts low-speed screw when in idle position. Ensure control lever moves over center position and rests against breakover spring when in full throttle position. *See Fig. 3.*

THROTTLE POSITION SENSOR (TPS)

Removal - Disconnect electrical connector at TPS. Remove TPS retaining screws. Lift TPS straight upward from fuel injection pump.

Installation - 1) Install TPS in bracket on fuel injection pump. Ensure adapter on TPS aligns with opening in fuel injection pump shaft. *See Fig. 4.*

2) If adapter does not align with fuel injection pump shaft, remove TPS bracket retaining screws. Place adapter on fuel injection pump shaft so TPS bracket must be rotated clockwise to align retaining screw holes.

3) Ensure adapter is even or slightly above top of fuel injection pump shaft. To adjust adapter position, hold nylon shaft in place, and rotate adapter. Tighten bracket retaining screws. Adjust TPS. See THROTTLE POSITION SENSOR (TPS) under ADJUSTMENTS.

FAN HUB

NOTE: Fan assembly uses left-hand threads.

Removal & Disassembly - 1) Remove drive belt and fan assembly. Remove fan hub retaining bolts and fan hub. Inspect for signs of lubrication leakage between mounting hub and bearing housing. Replace bearing if leakage exists.

2) To disassemble, remove fan hub bearing retaining bolt and washer from rear of fan hub. Using press and a 1 3/8" pin, support bearing housing, and press shaft from bearing.

3) Using press and a Black pipe approximately 2 3/8" O.D. and 4" long, support bearing housing, and press bearing from bearing housing.

Reassembly & Installation - 1) Using press and flat plate, install bearing in bearing housing from front side until bearing is even with bearing housing. Support inner race of bearing from back side of bearing housing.

2) Press shaft into bearing until inner shoulder of shaft contacts bearing. Install bearing retaining bolt and washer. Tighten to specification. See TORQUE SPECIFICATIONS table at end of article.

WATER PUMP

Removal & Installation - Drain cooling system. Remove drive belt. Remove water pump retaining bolts, water pump and "O" ring. To install, reverse removal procedure using new "O" ring. Tighten bolts to specification. See TORQUE SPECIFICATIONS table at end of article. Fill cooling system.

THERMOSTAT

CAUTION: Engine MUST NOT be operated without a thermostat. With no thermostat, coolant passes through by-pass to water pump inlet and causes engine overheating. Thermostat and rubber seal must be installed in correct direction. See Fig. 18.

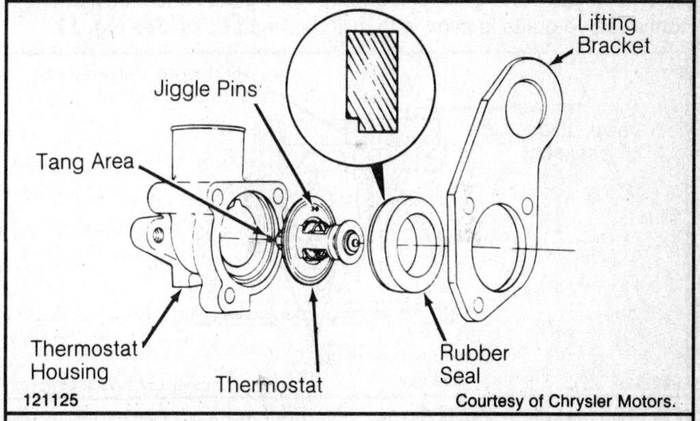
Lifting Bracket
Jiggle Pins
Tang Area
Thermostat Housing
Thermostat
Rubber Seal
121125
Courtesy of Chrysler Motors.

Fig. 18: Installing Thermostat

Removal - Disconnect negative battery cable. Drain cooling system. Remove drive belt and upper radiator hose. Remove alternator bolt, and rotate alternator aside. Remove retaining bolts, thermostat housing, lifting bracket and thermostat. *See Fig. 18.*

Installation - To install, reverse removal procedure. Thermostat must be installed in housing so tang on thermostat aligns with notch of housing. *See Fig. 18.* Rubber seal must be installed in proper direction. Tighten bolts to specification. See TORQUE SPECIFICATIONS table at end of article. Fill cooling system.

OIL PAN

Removal & Installation - 1) Remove engine. See ENGINE under REMOVAL & INSTALLATION. Remove retaining bolts, oil pan and gasket.

2) To install, reverse removal procedure. Apply sealant at crankshaft rear seal housing and front timing gear cover-to-cylinder block junction areas before installing gasket. Tighten bolts to specification. See TORQUE SPECIFICATIONS table at end of article.

OVERHAUL

CYLINDER HEAD

Cylinder Head - Inspect cylinder head warpage at deck surface. Resurface cylinder head if warpage exceeds specifications. See CYLINDER HEAD table under ENGINE SPECIFICATIONS at end of article. Replace cylinder head if total metal removed exceeds .0393" (.998 mm).

NOTE: Amount of material removed from cylinder head should be stamped on lower right rear corner of cylinder head above deck surface.

Valve Springs - Check valve spring free length, out-of-square and pressure. Replace valve spring if not to specifications. See VALVES & VALVE SPRINGS table under ENGINE SPECIFICATIONS at end of article.

Valve Stem Oil Seals - Intake and exhaust valve stem oil seals are same. Ensure valve stem oil seals are seated on cylinder head.

NOTE: Valve guides may be either thick wall or thin wall. Note wall thickness before servicing valve guides.

Valve Guides - **1)** Cylinder head valve guide bore must be reamed if service valve guide I.D. exceeds specification. See CYLINDER HEAD table under ENGINE SPECIFICATIONS at end of article. Ream cylinder head to proper dimension. See VALVE GUIDE INSTALLATION SPECIFICATIONS table.

2) Service valve guides must be centered with valve seats within .01378" (.3500 mm) and be square with deck surface with .004" (.10 mm) within a 1.9685" (49.999 mm) radius.

3) On thin wall valve guides, lubricate valve guide, and install until bottom of valve guide is even with cylinder head boss. *See Fig. 19.*

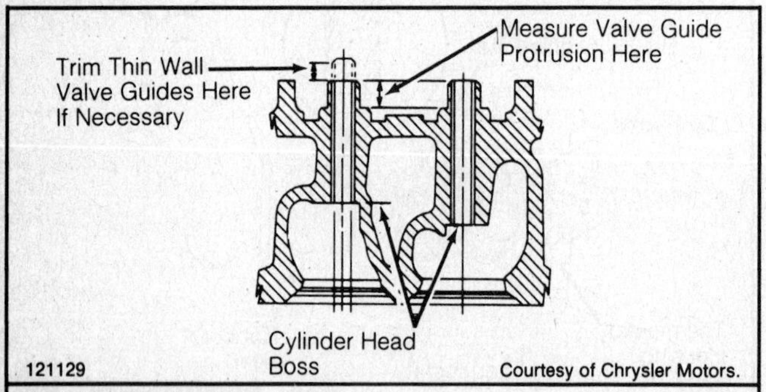
Measure Valve Guide
Protrusion Here
Trim Thin Wall
Valve Guides Here
If Necessary
Cylinder Head
Boss
121129
Courtesy of Chrysler Motors.

Fig. 19: Installing Valve Guide

4) Valve guide may require trimming so top of valve guide is even with cylinder head boss. Ream valve guide to specification. See VALVE GUIDE INSTALLATION SPECIFICATIONS table.

5) On thick wall valve guides, lubricate valve guide, and install until valve guide protrusion above cylinder head is correct. *See Fig. 19.* Valve guide protrusion must be within specifications. Ream valve guide to specification. See VALVE GUIDE INSTALLATION SPECIFICATIONS table.

VALVE GUIDE INSTALLATION SPECIFICATIONS

Application	In. (mm)
Cylinder Head Bore Reaming Dimension	
Thick Wall Valve Guide	.5507-.5517 (13.988-14.013)
Thin Wall Valve Guide	.4375-.4385 (11.113-11.138)
Valve Guide Protrusion	
Thick Wall Valve Guide	.4623-.5023 (11.742-12.758)
Valve Guide Reaming Dimension	.3157-.3165 (8.019-8.039)

Valve Seats - **1)** On cylinder heads containing integral valve seats, valve seats can be reground only once. Integral valve seats which have been reground must be replaced with service valve seats. Reground valve seats should be identified by an "X" stamped on cylinder head. *See Fig. 20.* Cylinder head should be stamped twice if service valve seats have been installed. *See Fig. 20.*

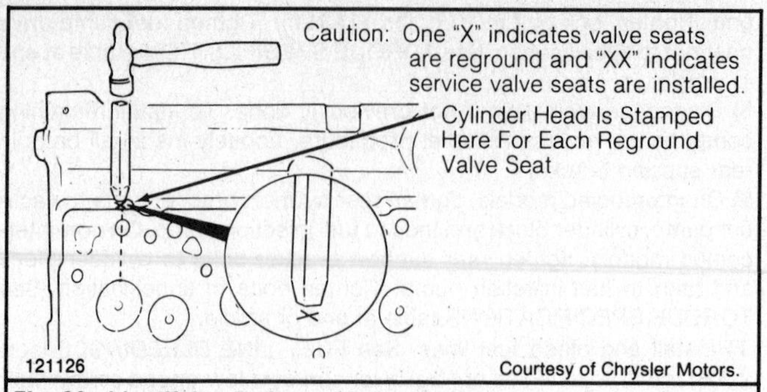
Caution: One "X" indicates valve seats are reground and "XX" indicates service valve seats are installed.
Cylinder Head Is Stamped Here For Each Reground Valve Seat
121126
Courtesy of Chrysler Motors.

Fig. 20: Identifying Reground Valve Seats

CAUTION: On integral valve seats, if material removed from cylinder head is .010" (.25 mm) or more, service valve seats must be installed.

2) To determine if cylinder head has been resurfaced before determining valve grind depth, inspect lower right rear corner of cylinder head above deck surface for marking indicating amount of material removed.

3) If no marking exists, measure cylinder head height from deck surface to rocker cover surface. If cylinder head height is 3.730" (94.75 mm) or greater, valve seats can be reground if not previously done.

4) On integral valve seats only, check valve grind depth. Install resurfaced valve in original location of cylinder head. Using dial indicator, measure distance from cylinder head surface to face of valve. *See Fig. 21.* Record this depth measurement as "A".

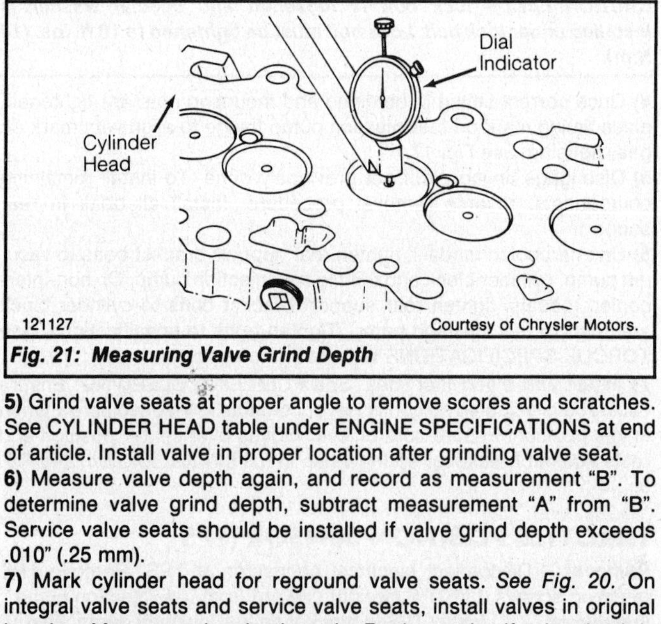
Dial
Indicator
Cylinder
Head
121127
Courtesy of Chrysler Motors.

Fig. 21: Measuring Valve Grind Depth

5) Grind valve seats at proper angle to remove scores and scratches. See CYLINDER HEAD table under ENGINE SPECIFICATIONS at end of article. Install valve in proper location after grinding valve seat.

6) Measure valve depth again, and record as measurement "B". To determine valve grind depth, subtract measurement "A" from "B". Service valve seats should be installed if valve grind depth exceeds .010" (.25 mm).

7) Mark cylinder head for reground valve seats. *See Fig. 20.* On integral valve seats and service valve seats, install valves in original location. Measure valve depth again. Replace valve if valve depth is not within .039-.060" (.99-1.52 mm).

8) Lap each valve, and measure valve seat width. Valve seat must be ground if not within specifications. See CYLINDER HEAD table.

Valve Seat Replacement - **1)** Ensure valve guide I.D. is within specifications. Defective valve guides must be replaced before replacing valve seats. See CYLINDER HEAD table under ENGINE SPECIFICATIONS at end of article. Valve seat must be machined to specification for service valve seat installation. *See Fig. 22.*

2) Press service valve seats into cylinder head, and stake valve seats in position. Grind valve seats at proper angle. See CYLINDER HEAD table. Install valve in proper location.

3) Using dial indicator, measure distance from cylinder head surface to face of valve to determine valve depth. Replace valve if valve depth is not within .039-.060" (.99-1.52 mm).

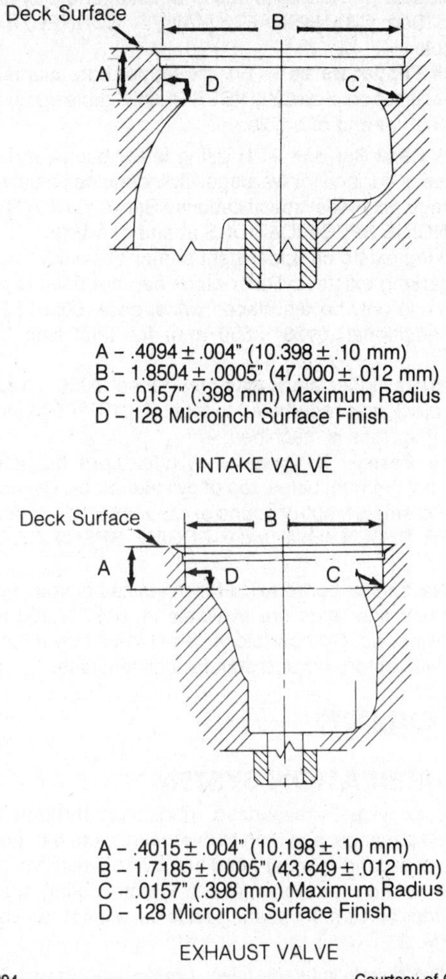
Deck Surface
B
A
D
C
A - .4094 ± .004" (10.398 ± .10 mm)
B - 1.8504 ± .0005" (47.000 ± .012 mm)
C - .0157" (.398 mm) Maximum Radius
D - 128 Microinch Surface Finish
INTAKE VALVE
Deck Surface
B
A
D
C
A - .4015 ± .004" (10.198 ± .10 mm)
B - 1.7185 ± .0005" (43.649 ± .012 mm)
C - .0157" (.398 mm) Maximum Radius
D - 128 Microinch Surface Finish
EXHAUST VALVE

91C13294 Courtesy of Chrysler Motors.

Fig. 22: Machining Cylinder Head for Valve Seat Installation

4) Lap each valve, and measure valve seat width. Valve seat must be ground if not within specifications. See CYLINDER HEAD table.

Valves - Ensure valve stem diameter and margin are within specifications. See VALVES & VALVE SPRINGS table under ENGINE SPECIFICATIONS at end of article. When installing valves, valve spring collets must always be replaced. DO NOT reuse valve spring collets.

Seat Correction Angles - Use a 15 degree stone to lower valve seat or a 65 degree stone to raise valve seat.

VALVE TRAIN

Rocker Levers - **1)** To disassemble, remove retaining rings from ends of rocker lever assembly. Remove thrust washers. Mark component location for reassembly reference.

2) Remove rocker levers. DO NOT remove rocker lever shaft from pedestal. Rocker lever shaft and pedestal are serviced as an assembly. Remove adjusting screw and lock nut from rocker lever.

3) Inspect components for damage or wear. Ensure adjusting screw rotates freely in rocker lever. Measure rocker lever bore I.D. and rocker lever shaft O.D. Replace components if not within specification. See ROCKER LEVER SPECIFICATIONS table.

ROCKER LEVER SPECIFICATIONS

Application	In. (mm)
Maximum Rocker Lever Bore I.D.	.750 (19.05)
Minimum Rocker Lever Shaft O.D.	.746 (18.94)

4) To reassemble, coat components with oil, and reverse disassembly procedure. Ensure components are installed in original location. *See Fig. 23.*

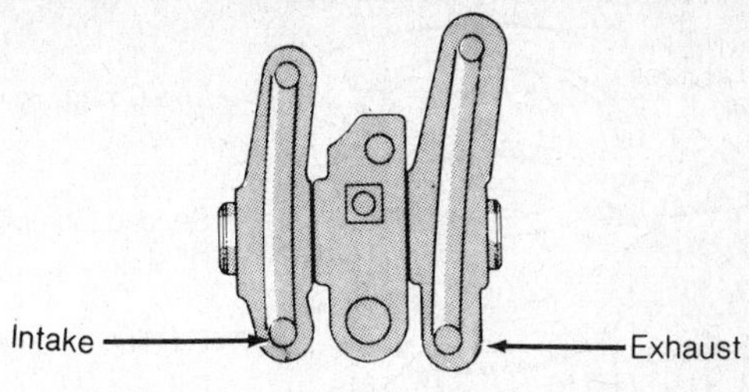
Intake
Exhaust

121130 Courtesy of Chrysler Motors.

Fig. 23: Identifying Rocker Levers

CYLINDER BLOCK ASSEMBLY

Piston & Rod Assembly - Piston must be installed on connecting rod with arrow and connecting rod number properly located. *See Fig. 24.* Piston and connecting rod assembly must be installed with arrow on top of piston toward front of engine.

CAUTION: Four digit number on connecting rod cap and connecting rod must match and be installed toward oil cooler side of engine. See Fig. 24.

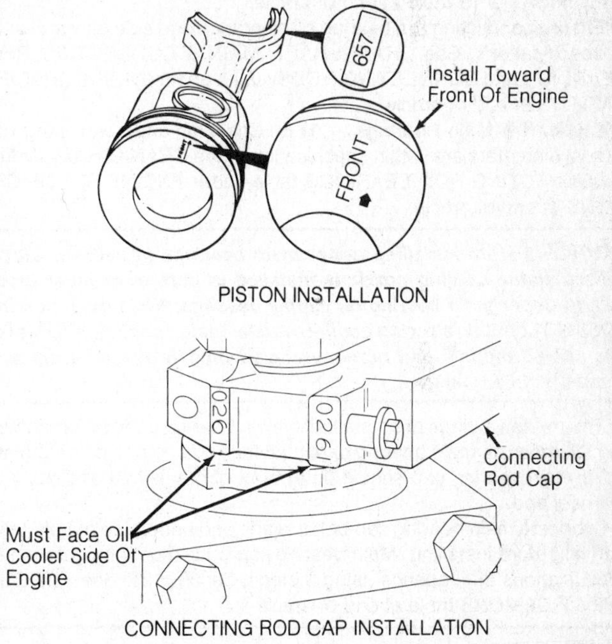
657
Install Toward
Front Of Engine
FRONT
PISTON INSTALLATION
026
026
Connecting
Rod Cap
Must Face Oil
Cooler Side Of
Engine
CONNECTING ROD CAP INSTALLATION

121132 Courtesy of Chrysler Motors.

Fig. 24: Installing Piston & Connecting Rod

Fitting Pistons - Piston diameter should be measured .50" (12.7 mm) from bottom of piston skirt at 90 degree angle to piston pin. Replace piston if piston diameter is not within specifications. See PISTONS, PINS & RINGS table under ENGINE SPECIFICATIONS at end of article.

CAUTION: Pistons for intercooled and non-intercooled models are different and cannot be interchanged.

Piston Rings - **1)** Ensure piston ring end gap and side clearance are within specifications. See PISTONS, PINS & RINGS table under ENGINE SPECIFICATIONS at end of article.

2) Piston rings must be installed with identification mark toward top of piston and rings properly positioned. *See Fig. 25.* Ensure expander in oil control ring is installed with ends of expander ring opposite ends of oil control ring.

Cummins Diesel "B" Series 5.9L 6-Cylinder (Cont.)

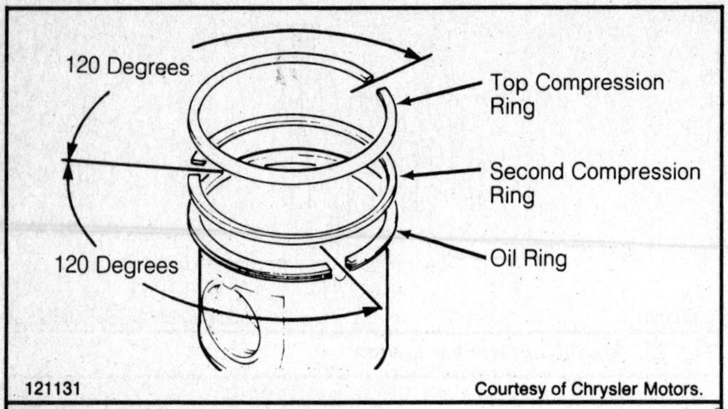
120 Degrees
Top Compression Ring
Second Compression Ring
120 Degrees
Oil Ring
121131
Courtesy of Chrysler Motors.

Fig. 25: Positioning Piston Rings

Rod Bearings – 1) Before installing rod bearings, lubricate connecting rod bolt threads and head of bolts with engine oil. Install connecting rod so arrow on top of piston is toward front of engine.

CAUTION: Four digit number on connecting rod cap and connecting rod must match and be installed toward oil cooler side of engine. See Fig. 24.

2) Tighten connecting rod bolts to specifications. See TORQUE SPECIFICATIONS table at end of article.

3) Ensure connecting rod bearing oil clearance and side play are within specifications. See CRANKSHAFT, MAIN & CONNECTING ROD BEARINGS and CONNECTING RODS tables under ENGINE SPECIFICATIONS at end of article.

Crankshaft & Main Bearings – 1) Ensure main and connecting rod journal diameters are within specifications. See CRANKSHAFT, MAIN & CONNECTING ROD BEARINGS table under ENGINE SPECIFICATIONS at end of article.

CAUTION: Before installing upper main bearings in cylinder block, ensure piston cooling nozzle is installed in bore of cylinder block next to upper main bearing oil supply passage. No. 1 main bearing DOES NOT contain a piston cooling nozzle. Piston cooling nozzles for intercooled models and non-intercooled models are different and cannot be interchanged.

2) Ensure dowel rings are installed in main bearing caps before installing. Number on main bearing cap must face oil cooler side of engine. No. 1 main bearing cap should be at front of crankshaft and No. 7 at flywheel end.

3) Lubricate main bearing cap bolt threads and underside of bolt head with oil before installing. Main bearing cap bolts must be tightened to specifications in sequence using 3 steps. *See Fig. 26.* See TORQUE SPECIFICATIONS table at end of article.

CAUTION: Ensure main bearing caps are installed with number on main bearing cap facing oil cooler side of engine. No. 1 main bearing cap should be at front of crankshaft and No. 7 at flywheel end.

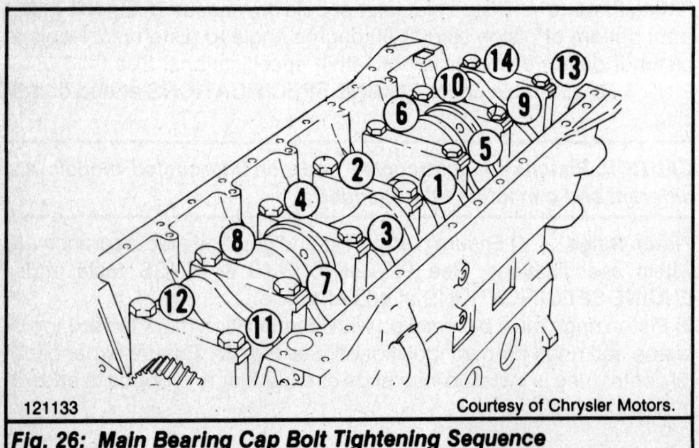
14
13
10
9
6
5
2
1
4
3
8
7
12
11
121133
Courtesy of Chrysler Motors.

Fig. 26: Main Bearing Cap Bolt Tightening Sequence

4) Ensure main bearing clearance and crankshaft end play are within specifications. See CRANKSHAFT, MAIN & CONNECTING ROD BEARINGS table.

Cylinder Block Tappet Bores – Ensure tappet bore diameter does not exceed specification. See CYLINDER BLOCK table under ENGINE SPECIFICATIONS at end of article.

Cylinder Block Deck Surface – 1) Using feeler gauge and straightedge, inspect deck surface for warpage. Cylinder block must be resurfaced if warpage exceeds specifications. See CYLINDER BLOCK table under ENGINE SPECIFICATIONS at end of article.

2) Note if marking exists on upper right corner of cylinder block. *See Fig. 9.* If no marking exists, cylinder block has not been resurfaced. Cylinder block can only be resurfaced twice: once .0059" (.149 mm), and then an additional .0138" (.350 mm) for total limit of .0197" (.500 mm).

3) If "X" appears, cylinder block was resurfaced .0059" (.149 mm); if "XX" appears, block was resurfaced to total of .0197" (.500 mm). Mark cylinder block if surface is machined.

Cylinder Block Bore – 1) Measure cylinder bore diameter at 1" (25 mm) and 4.5" (114 mm) below top of cylinder block. Cylinder block can be bored if diameter, out-of-round or taper exceeds specification. See CYLINDER BLOCK table under ENGINE SPECIFICATIONS at end of article.

2) Cylinder block can be bored twice for oversized pistons and rings. Oversized pistons and rings are available in .0197" (.500 mm) and .0393" (.998 mm) sizes. Cylinder block can also be bored for a repair sleeve, which will restore bore to standard dimensions.

ENGINE OILING

ENGINE LUBRICATION SYSTEM

Gerotor pump provides pressurized lubrication through a cross passage to main passage, and then to overhead, camshaft and crankshaft. Oil passes around cylinder head bolts, into passages of rocker lever pedestals and out to rocker levers. Piston cooling nozzles are located in cylinder block main bearing saddles, except for No. 1 main bearing. *See Fig. 27.*

No piston cooling nozzle is used on No. 1 main bearing saddle. Oil for cylinder No. 1 piston is received from No. 2 main bearing saddle, No. 2 piston is supplied from No. 3 bearing, etc. Oil cooler housing contains an oil pressure regulator valve.

Crankcase Capacity – Oil capacity is approximately 12 qts. (11.4L) with oil filter.

Oil Pressure – Minimum oil pressure at idle is 10 psi (.7 kg/cm²) and 30 psi (2.1 kg/cm²) at governor rated speed.

PISTON COOLING NOZZLES

Removal & Installation – 1) Remove crankshaft and upper main bearings. Using a 3/16" pin punch, remove piston cooling nozzle from cylinder block.

2) Inspect piston cooling nozzles for damaged spray tip or cracks. Use pin punch to install piston cooling nozzle until it is even or slightly below main bearing saddle surface.

CAUTION: Use only hand force to install piston cooling nozzles. DO NOT use hammer or piston cooling nozzle will be damaged. Piston cooling nozzles for intercooled models and non-intercooled models are different and cannot be interchanged.

OIL PUMP

Removal & Disassembly – 1) Remove front timing gear cover. See FRONT TIMING GEAR COVER under REMOVAL & INSTALLATION. Remove oil pump bolts and oil pump. *See Fig. 27.*

2) Remove rear sealing plate from rear of oil pump. Mark TOP side of gerotors for reassembly reference.

Inspection – 1) Inspect components for damage or excessive wear. With inner and outer gerotors installed, use feeler gauge to measure gerotor tip clearance between tip of inner and outer gerotor.

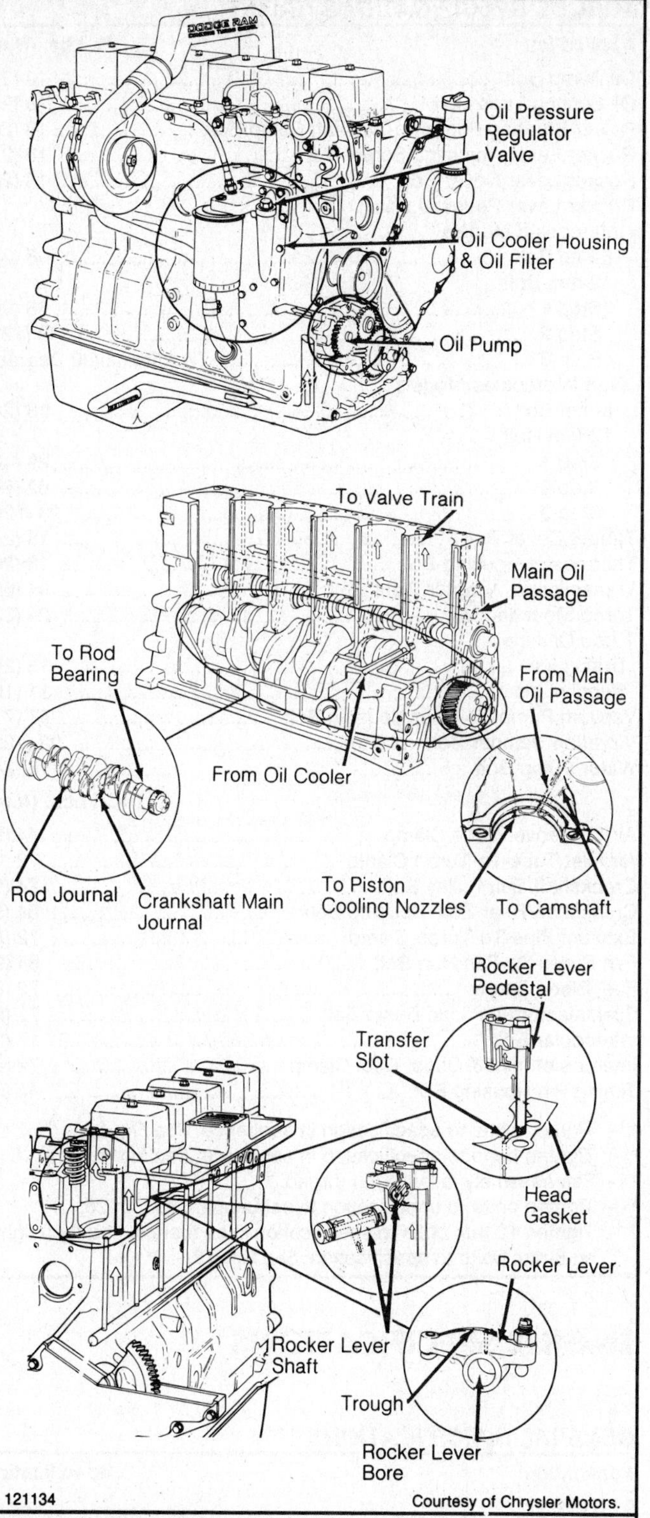

Oil Pressure Regulator Valve
Oil Cooler Housing & Oil Filter
Oil Pump
To Valve Train
Main Oil Passage
To Rod Bearing
From Main Oil Passage
From Oil Cooler
Rod Journal
Crankshaft Main Journal
To Piston Cooling Nozzles
To Camshaft
Rocker Lever Pedestal
Transfer Slot
Head Gasket
Rocker Lever
Rocker Lever Shaft
Trough
Rocker Lever Bore
121134
Courtesy of Chrysler Motors.

Fig. 27: Engine Oil Circuit

2) Place straightedge on oil pump housing in place of rear sealing plate. Measure gerotor-to-sealing plate clearance between gerotors and straightedge.

3) Measure distance between outer gerotor and oil pump housing. Measure backlash between gears on oil pump drive. Replace oil pump if not within specifications. See OIL PUMP SPECIFICATIONS table.

OIL PUMP SPECIFICATIONS

Application	In. (mm)
Drive Gear Backlash	.003-.015 (.08-.38)
Gerotor Tip Clearance	.007 (.17)
Gerotor-To-Pump Housing Clearance	.015 (.38)
Gerotor-To-Sealing Plate Clearance	.005 (.13)

CAUTION: Oil pumps from intercooled models can be used on non-intercooled models, but oil pumps from non-intercooled models cannot be used on intercooled models.

Reassembly & Installation – **1)** To reassemble, reverse disassembly procedure. Ensure gerotors are installed in original location. Lubricate oil pump with engine oil.

2) Install oil pump. Tighten oil pump bolts to specification in sequence. *See Fig. 28.* See TORQUE SPECIFICATIONS table at end of article.

CAUTION: Ensure idler gear locating pin is aligned with cylinder block during installation. When oil pump is correctly installed, flange on oil pump will not contact cylinder block, as rear sealing plate contacts bottom of bore in cylinder block.

3) Using dial indicator, check oil pump gear backlash on both oil pump gears. Ensure adjoining gear does not rotate while measuring gear backlash. Backlash must be within specifications. *See Fig. 28.* Install remaining components.

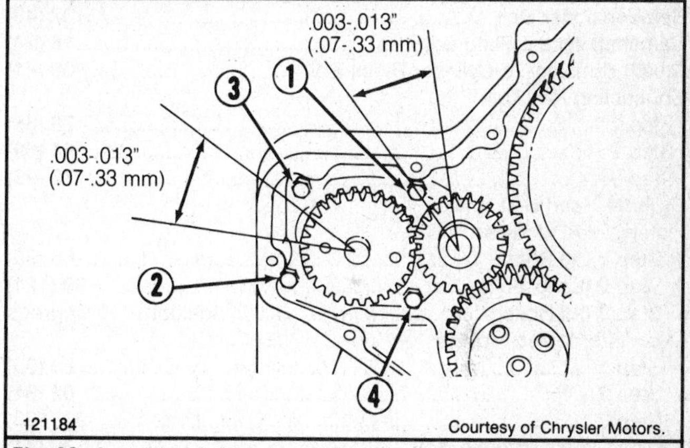

.003-.013"
(.07-.33 mm)
.003-.013"
(.07-.33 mm)
1
2
3
4
121184
Courtesy of Chrysler Motors.

Fig. 28: Installing & Checking Oil Pump Gear Backlash

OIL COOLER

Removal – Drain cooling system. Remove oil filter. Disconnect turbo oil supply line. Remove oil cooler bolts, oil cooler housing, gaskets and cooler element. *See Fig. 27.*

Testing – **1)** Plug outlet fitting of oil cooler element. Install air hose fitting in inlet fitting. Install pressure regulator and air hose. Apply air pressure to oil cooler element. Place oil cooler element in container of water. Element must be covered by water level.

2) Adjust air pressure to 70 psi (4.9 kg/cm²). Check for air bubbles indicating leak. Turn off air pressure, and remove test equipment. Replace oil cooler element if leaks exist.

CAUTION: Oil cooler assembly from intercooled models can be used on non-intercooled models, but oil cooler assembly from non-intercooled models cannot be used on intercooled models. On replacement oil coolers, ensure plastic caps are removed from inlet and outlet ports before installing.

Installation – To install, reverse removal procedure. Fill oil filter with oil before installing.

OIL PRESSURE REGULATOR VALVE

Removal – Remove plug and sealing washer from lower edge of oil cooler housing. *See Fig. 27.* Remove plunger and spring.

1991 ENGINES
Cummins Diesel "B" Series 5.9L 6-Cylinder (Cont.)

Inspection – Inspect plunger for scoring or wear. Ensure plunger moves freely in bore. Using spring tension tester, check spring tension. Replace spring if not to specifications. See OIL PRESSURE REGULATOR VALVE SPRING SPECIFICATIONS table.

OIL PRESSURE REGULATOR VALVE SPRING SPECIFICATIONS

Application	Pressure Lbs. @ In. (kg @ mm)
Valve Closed	13.5 @ 1.77 (6.12 @ 44.9)
Valve Open	20.5 @ 1.574 (9.30 @ 39.98)

Installation – To install, reverse removal procedure using new sealing washer on plug. Tighten plug to specification. See TORQUE SPECIFICATIONS table at end of article.

TORQUE SPECIFICATIONS

TORQUE SPECIFICATIONS

Application	Ft. Lbs. (N.m)
A/C Compressor Bolt	35 (47)
Air Inlet Housing Bolt	18 (24)
Air Intake Heater Power Supply Nut	10 (14)
Air Crossover Tube Bolt	18 (24)
A/T Transmission-To-Cylinder Block Bolt	30 (41)
Belt Tensioner Bolt	32 (43)
Camshaft Thrust Plate Bolt	18 (24)
Clutch Housing-To-Cylinder Block Bolt	30 (41)
Connecting Rod Bolt	
Step 1	26 (35)
Step 2	51 (69)
Step 3	73 (99)
Cylinder Head Bolt [1]	
Intercooled Models	
Step 1 (All Bolts)	66 (90)
Step 2 (Long Bolts)	89 (121)
Step 3 (All Bolts)	Additional 90 Degrees
Non-Intercooled Models	
Step 1	29 (90)
Step 2	62 (84)
Step 3	93 (126)
Engine Mount Through Bolt	30 (41)
Exhaust Manifold Bolt [2]	32 (43)
Fan Assembly [3]	42 (57)
Fan Hub Bearing Retaining Bolt	57 (77)
Fan Hub Mounting Bolt	18 (24)
Flywheel/Flexplate Bolt	101 (137)
Front Timing Gear Cover Bolt	18 (24)
Fuel Heater Mounting Bolt	24 (33)
Fuel High-Pressure Line Nut	18 (24)
Fuel Injection Pump Mounting Nut	18 (24)
Fuel Injection Pump Rear Support Bolt	18 (24)
Fuel Injector Retaining Nut	44 (60)
Fuel Lift Pump Bolt	18 (24)
Fuel Line Banjo Bolt	
At Cylinder Head	18 (24)
At Fuel Injection Pump	24 (33)
Fuel Pump Drive Gear Nut	48 (65)
Gear Housing-To-Cylinder Block Bolt	18 (24)
Intake Manifold Cover Bolt	18 (24)
Lifting Bracket Bolt	57 (77)
Main Bearing Cap Bolt [4]	
Step 1	45 (61)
Step 2	88 (119)
Step 3	129 (175)
Oil Cooler Cover Bolt	18 (24)
Oil Pan Bolt	18 (24)
Oil Pressure Regulator Valve Plug	60 (81)

TORQUE SPECIFICATIONS (Cont.)

Application	Ft. Lbs. (N.m)
Oil Pump Bolt	18 (24)
Oil Suction Tube Bolt	18 (24)
Power Steering Pump-To-Vacuum Pump Bolt	18 (24)
Rocker Lever Adjusting Screw Nut	18 (24)
Rocker Lever Cover Bolt	18 (24)
Rocker Lever Pedestal Bolt [5]	
Intercooled Models	
8-mm Bolt	18 (24)
12-mm Bolt	
Step 1	66 (90)
Step 2	89 (121)
Step 3	Additional 90 Degrees
Non-Intercooled Models	
8-mm Bolt	18 (24)
12-mm Bolt	
Step 1	29 (40)
Step 2	62 (84)
Step 3	93 (126)
Tappet Cover Bolt	18 (24)
Thermostat Housing Bolt	18 (24)
Transmission Adapter Plate Bolt	44 (60)
Turbo Mounting Nut	24 (33)
Turbo Oil Line	
Drain Line	18 (24)
Supply Line	11 (15)
Vacuum Pump-To-Gear Housing Bolt	57 (77)
Vibration Damper Bolt	92 (125)
Water Pump Bolt	18 (24)
	INCH Lbs. (N.m)
Air Crossover Tube Clamp	44 (5)
Air Inlet Tube-To-Turbo Clamp	72 (8)
Crankshaft Belt Pulley Bolt	84 (9)
Crankshaft Rear Seal Housing Bolt	84 (9)
Exhaust Pipe-To-Turbo Clamp	72 (8)
Fan Pulley-To-Fan Hub Bolt	84 (9)
Fuel Bleed Screw	72 (8)
Fuel Injector Fuel Line Banjo Bolt	72 (8)
Intercooler Bolt	17 (2)
Intercooler Inlet & Outlet Duct Clamp	72 (8)
Timing Pin Housing Bolt	44 (5)

[1] – Tighten bolts to specification in sequence. *See Fig. 8.*
[2] – Tighten bolts to specification in sequence. *See Fig. 6.*
[3] – Fan assembly is left-hand thread.
[4] – Tighten bolts to specification in sequence. *See Fig. 26.*
[5] – Tighten 12-mm bolts to specification in sequence, and then tighten 8-mm bolts to specification. *See Fig. 12.*

ENGINE SPECIFICATIONS

GENERAL SPECIFICATIONS

Application	Specification
5.9L Diesel	
Displacement	360 Cu. In. (5.9L)
Bore	4.02" (102.1 mm)
Stroke	4.72" (119.8 mm)
Compression Ratio	17.5:1
Fuel System	Mechanical Fuel Injection
Horsepower @ RPM	160 @ 2500
Torque Ft. Lbs. @ RPM	400 @ 1750

CRANKSHAFT, MAIN & CONNECTING ROD BEARINGS

Application	In. (mm)
5.9L Diesel	
Crankshaft End Play	.005-.012 (.13-.30)
Main Bearings	
Journal Diameter	3.2662-3.2682 (82.961-83.012)
Journal Out-Of-Round	.002 (.05)
Journal Taper	.0005 (.013)
Oil Clearance	.0047 (.119) Maximum
Connecting Rod Bearings	
Journal Diameter	2.7150-2.7170 (68.961-69.012)
Journal Out-Of-Round	.002 (.05)
Journal Taper	.0005 (.013)
Oil Clearance	.0035 (.089) Maximum

CONNECTING RODS

Application	In. (mm)
5.9L Diesel	
Bore Diameter	
Pin Bore	1.5769 (40.053) Maximum
Side Play	.004-.012 (.10-.30)

PISTONS, PINS & RINGS

Application	In. (mm)
5.9L Diesel	
Pistons	
Diameter	4.009-4.011 (101.83-101.88)
Pin Bore	1.5758 (40.025) Maximum
Pins	
Diameter	1.5744 (39.989) Minimum
Rings	
No. 1	
End Gap	.0160-.0275 (.409-.698)
Side Clearance	[1]
No. 2	
End Gap	.0100-.0215 (.254-.546)
Side Clearance	.006 (.15) Maximum
No. 3 (Oil)	
End Gap	.0100-.0215 (.254-.546)
Side Clearance	.005 (.13) Maximum

[1] – Inspect for damage only. No specification is available from manufacturer.

CYLINDER BLOCK

Application	In. (mm)
5.9L Diesel	
Cylinder Bore	
Maximum Diameter	4.0203 (102.116)
Maximum Taper	.003 (.08)
Maximum Out-Of-Round	.0015 (.038)
Maximum Deck Warpage	[1]
Maximum Tappet Bore Diameter	.632 (16.05)

[1] – Warpage should not exceed .0004" (.010 mm) per 2" (51 mm) area or .012" (.30 mm) overall or side-to-side. See CYLINDER BLOCK DECK SURFACE under CYLINDER BLOCK ASSEMBLY under OVERHAUL for cylinder block marking areas.

VALVES & VALVE SPRINGS

Application	Specification
5.9L Diesel	
Intake Valves	
Face Angle	30°
Minimum Margin	.031" (.79 mm)
Stem Diameter	.3126-.3134" (7.940-7.960 mm)
Installed Valve Depth	.039-.060" (.99-1.52 mm)
Exhaust Valves	
Face Angle	45°
Minimum Margin	.031" (.79 mm)
Stem Diameter	.3126-.3134" (7.940-7.960 mm)
Installed Valve Depth	.039-.060" (.99-1.52 mm)
Valve Springs	
Free Length	2.19" (55.6 mm)
Out-Of-Square	.039" (.99 mm)
Pressure	
Valve Closed	65 Lbs. @ 1.94" (29 kg @ 49.3 mm)

CYLINDER HEAD

Application	Specification
5.9L Diesel	
Cylinder Head Height	3.730" (94.75 mm)
Maximum Warpage	[1]
Valve Seats	
Intake Valve	
Seat Angle	30°
Seat Width	.060-.080" (1.52-2.03 mm)
Exhaust Valve	
Seat Angle	45°
Seat Width	.060-.080" (1.52-2.03 mm)
Valve Guides	
Valve Guide I.D.	.3157-.3185" (8.019-8.089 mm)
Valve Guide Installed Height	[2]
Valve Stem-To-Guide	
Oil Clearance	.002-.006" (.05-.15 mm)

[1] – Warpage should not exceed .0004" (.010 mm) per 2" (51 mm) area or .012" (.30 mm) overall or side-to-side.

[2] – See VALVE GUIDES under CYLINDER HEAD under OVERHAUL.

CAMSHAFT

Application	In. (mm)
5.9L Diesel	
Maximum Camshaft Bearing Or Bore I.D.	
No. 1 Bearing	2.1312 (54.132)
No. 1 Bearing Bore	2.2543 (57.259)
All Other Bores	2.1312 (54.132)
End Play	.006-.010 (.15-.25)
Gear Backlash	.003-.013 (.08-.33)
Minimum Journal Diameter	2.1245 (53.962)
Minimum Lobe Height	
Exhaust	1.841 (46.76)
Intake	1.852 (47.04)
Lift Pump	1.398 (35.51)

TAPPETS

Application	In. (mm)
5.9L Diesel	
Bore Diameter	.632 (16.05) Maximum
Tappet Diameter	.627 (15.93) Minimum

1991 ENGINE COOLING
Specifications & Electric Cooling Fans

Caravan, Dakota, Pickup, Ramcharger, RWD Van, Town & Country, Voyager

SPECIFICATIONS

BELT ADJUSTMENT

Belts should be adjusted to proper tension using belt tension gauge. See BELT ADJUSTMENT SPECIFICATIONS table. Some models may be equipped with automatic belt tensioner to maintain belt tension. Ensure serpentine drive belts are routed properly. *See Figs. 1-5.*

NOTE: Cracking across belt rib surfaces is considered normal wear. Belt must be replaced if cracks run parallel to rib area.

BELT ADJUSTMENT SPECIFICATIONS

Application	Tension Lbs. (kg)
2.5L	
Caravan & Voyager	
A/C Compressor Belt	
New Belt	125 (56.7)
Used Belt	80 (36.3)
Alternator/Water Pump Belt	
New Belt	130 (59.0)
Used Belt	80 (36.3)
Power Steering Pump Belt	
New Belt	105 (47.6)
Used Belt	80 (36.3)
Dakota	
A/C Compressor Belt	
New Belt	160 (72.6)
Used Belt	80 (36.3)
Alternator/Water Pump Belt	
New Belt	160 (72.6)
Used Belt	80 (36.3)
Power Steering Pump Belt	
New Belt	120 (54.4)
Used Belt	80 (36.3)
3.0L	
A/C Compressor Belt	
New Belt	125 (56.7)
Used Belt	80 (36.3)
Alternator/Water & Power Steering Pump Belt	Automatic Belt Tensioner
3.3L	
A/C Compressor, Alternator Water Pump & Power Steering Pump Belt	Automatic Belt Tensioner
3.9L	
All Belts	
New Belt	100-140 (45.4-63.5)
Used Belt	60-90 (27.2-40.9)
5.2L	
Dakota	Automatic Belt Tensioner
All Others	
All Belts	
New Belt	100-140 (45.4-63.5)
Used Belt	60-90 (27.2-40.9)
5.9L	
Gasoline Engines	
All Belts	
New Belt	100-140 (45.4-63.5)
Used Belt	60-90 (27.2-40.9)
Diesel Engines	Automatic Belt Tensioner

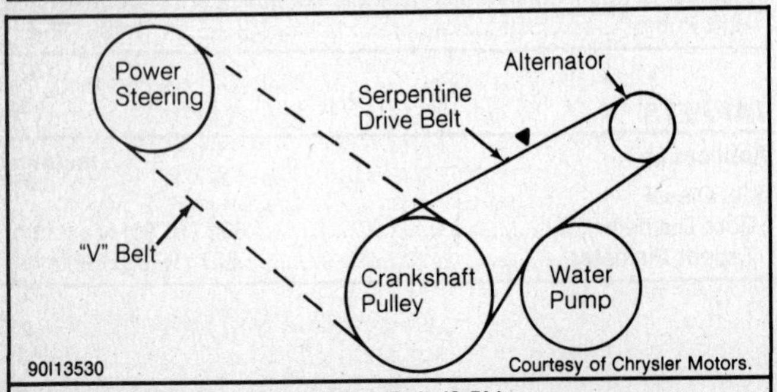
Power Steering
Alternator
Serpentine Drive Belt
"V" Belt
Crankshaft Pulley
Water Pump

90I13530 Courtesy of Chrysler Motors.

Fig. 1: Routing Serpentine Drive Belt (2.5L)

COOLING SYSTEM SPECIFICATIONS

COOLING SYSTEM SPECIFICATIONS

Model	Specification
Coolant Replacement Interval	
5.9L Diesel	24 Months Or 24,000 miles
All Others	[1]
Coolant Capacity [2]	
Caravan, Town & Country, & Voyager	
2.5L	[3] 8.5 (8.1)
3.0L & 3.3L	[3] 10.0 (9.5)
Dakota	
2.5L	9.8 (9.3)
3.9L	14.0 (13.2)
5.2L	14.3 (13.5)
Pickup & Ramcharger	
3.9L	15.1 (14.3)
5.2L	17.0 (16.1)
5.9L	
Gasoline Engines	15.5 (14.7)
Diesel Engines	
A/T Models	[4] 16.5 (15.6)
M/T Models	[4] 15.5 (14.7)
RWD Van	
3.9L	14.6 (13.8)
5.2L	16.5 (15.6)
5.9L	
With Rear Heater	16.0 (15.1)
Without Rear Heater	15.0 (14.2)
Pressure Cap	16 psi
Thermostat Temperature Rating	
Caravan, Town & Country, & Voyager	195°F (90°C)
Dakota	195°F (90°C)
Pickup & Ramcharger	
Gasoline Engines	Information Is Not Available
Diesel Engines	[5]
RWD Van	Information Is Not Available

[1] – Drain and flush cooling system every 36 months or 52,500 miles, and then every 24 months or 30,000 miles thereafter.
[2] – Capacities listed are approximates.
[3] – Capacity includes one pt. (.4L) for coolant recovery tank. Add one qt. (.9L) for models with rear heater.
[4] – Add one qt. (.9L) for coolant recovery bottle.
[5] – Thermostat starts to open at 181°F (83°C), then fully opens at 203°F (95°C).

COOLING SYSTEM BLEEDING

2.5L – Remove vent plug from top of thermostat housing. Fill cooling system and allow air to bleed from cooling system. Install vent plug once coolant reaches thermostat housing level. Tighten vent plug to 15 ft. lbs. (20 N.m).

3.3L – 1) Remove engine temperature sending unit. Engine temperature sending unit is located in front of cylinder head, near thermostat housing, just below spark plug wire holder.

2) Fill cooling system until coolant reaches engine temperature sending unit. Install engine temperature sending unit and tighten to 60 INCH lbs. (7 N.m). Finish filling cooling system.

ELECTRIC COOLING FAN

OPERATION

Caravan, Dakota (2.5L), Town & Country, & Voyager – Electric cooling fan should not operate during engine cranking. Fan should operate whenever A/C compressor clutch is engaged. If vehicle is not equipped with A/C or if A/C is off, fan should turn on or off as coolant temperature sensor senses the following changes in coolant temperatures. See COOLING FAN OPERATING TEMPERATURES table.

COOLING FAN OPERATING TEMPERATURES

Vehicle Speed	Coolant Temp. °F (°C)	Cooling Fan Status
40 MPH Or More	230 (110) Or More	Turns On
40 MPH Or More	220 (104) Or Less	Shuts Off
40 MPH Or Less	210 (99) Or More	Turns On
40 MPH Or Less	200 (93) Or Less	Shuts Off

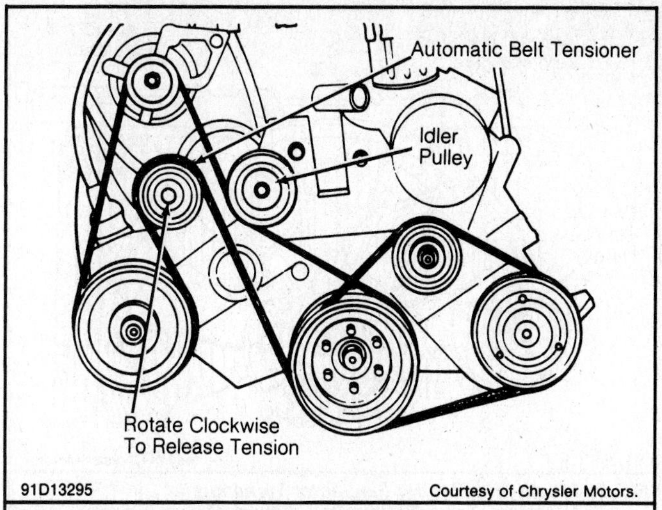

Automatic Belt Tensioner
Idler Pulley
Rotate Clockwise To Release Tension
91D13295
Courtesy of Chrysler Motors.

Fig. 2: Routing Serpentine Drive Belt (3.0L)

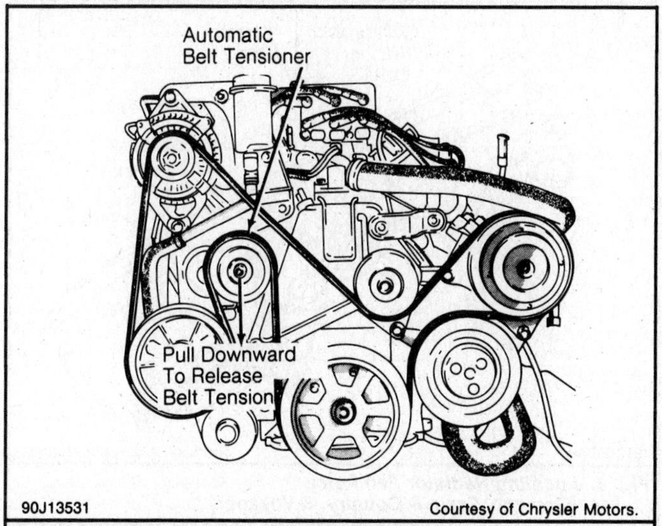

Automatic Belt Tensioner
Pull Downward To Release Belt Tension
90J13531
Courtesy of Chrysler Motors.

Fig. 3: Routing Serpentine Drive Belt (3.3L)

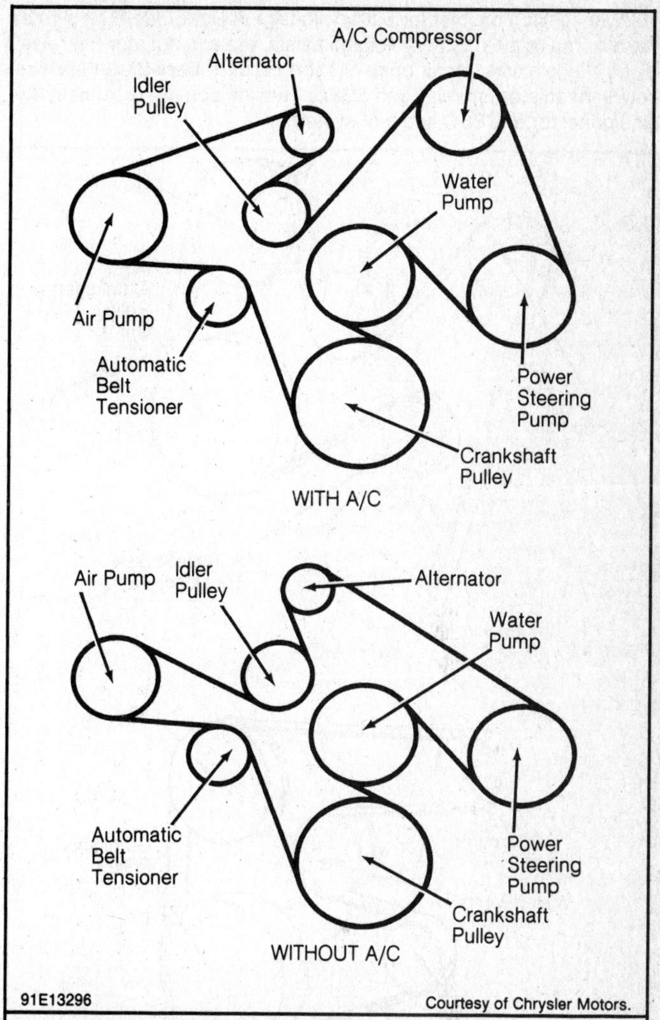

A/C Compressor
Alternator
Idler Pulley
Water Pump
Air Pump
Automatic Belt Tensioner
Power Steering Pump
Crankshaft Pulley
WITH A/C
Air Pump
Idler Pulley
Alternator
Water Pump
Automatic Belt Tensioner
Power Steering Pump
Crankshaft Pulley
WITHOUT A/C
91E13296
Courtesy of Chrysler Motors.

Fig. 4: Routing Serpentine Drive Belt (5.2L Dakota)

Coolant temperature sensor sends a signal to the Single-Board Engine Controller (SBEC), which controls cooling fan operation through a radiator fan relay.

On Caravan, Town & Country and Voyager, fan will operate to prevent steaming water vapor from outside of radiator. Fan will operate for 3 minutes when vehicle is stopped with engine idling, coolant temperature is 100-195°F (38-97°C), and ambient temperature is less than 60°F (16°C).

TROUBLE SHOOTING & TESTING

Electric Fan Motor – To check electric fan motor, disconnect fan motor electrical connector. Ensure correct polarity, and connect a 12-volt battery source and ground to fan motor electrical connector. *See Figs. 6 and 7.* Replace fan motor if it fails to operate.

NOTE: If fan motor is noticeably overheated, it indicates system voltage may be excessive. Check charging system.

NOTE: Check electric fan motor operation before checking fan relay and SBEC.

Radiator Fan Relay & SBEC – **1)** With ignition on, check for voltage at Gray wire of radiator fan relay. Radiator fan relay is located in power distribution center (Dakota 2.5L), or in front of left strut tower (all other models). *See Figs. 8 and 9.*

2) If battery voltage exists at Gray wire, proceed to step **3)**. If battery voltage does not exist, check for open or short circuit in Gray wire.

3) Install jumper wire between Gray and Light Green wires on radiator fan relay. If fan operates, proceed to step **4)**. If fan fails to operate, check for open or short circuit in Light Green wire between radiator fan relay and fan motor connector.

4) If fan operates, warm engine to normal operating temperature. Check for loose connections at fan motor and radiator fan relay. If all connections are okay, fault codes must be checked.

5) Fault codes can be checked by using diagnostic connector. See SELF-DIAGNOSTICS article in ENGINE PERFORMANCE for complete instructions on connecting diagnostic tester and checking fault codes.

6) If fault code indicates 88-12-35-55 (RADIATOR FAN RELAY), turn ignition on and check for battery voltage at Dark Blue wire of radiator fan relay. If battery voltage exists, proceed to step **7)**. If voltage is 0-1 volt, proceed to step **9)**.

7) With ignition off, disconnect 60-pin connector from SBEC. The SBEC is located on right wheelwell of engine compartment (Dakota 2.5L), or left front corner of engine compartment (all other models).

8) Turn ignition on. Check for battery voltage at cavity No. 31 (Dark Blue/Pink) wire of connector. *See Fig. 10.* If battery voltage exists and female terminal is not damaged, replace the SBEC. If no voltage exists, repair open or short in Dark Blue/Pink wire from radiator fan relay to SBEC.

9) With ignition off, disconnect 60-pin connector from SBEC. Turn ignition on. Check for battery voltage at Dark Blue wire of radiator fan relay. If battery voltage exists, replace SBEC. If voltage is 0-1 volt, proceed to step **10)**.

1991 ENGINE COOLING
Specifications & Electric Cooling Fans (Cont.)

10) With ignition on, test for battery voltage at Dark Blue/Pink wire at radiator fan relay. If battery voltage exists, replace radiator fan relay. If no voltage exists, repair open or short circuit in Dark Blue/Pink wire between radiator fan relay and SBEC. Turn ignition off, reconnect 60-pin connector to SBEC and test system.

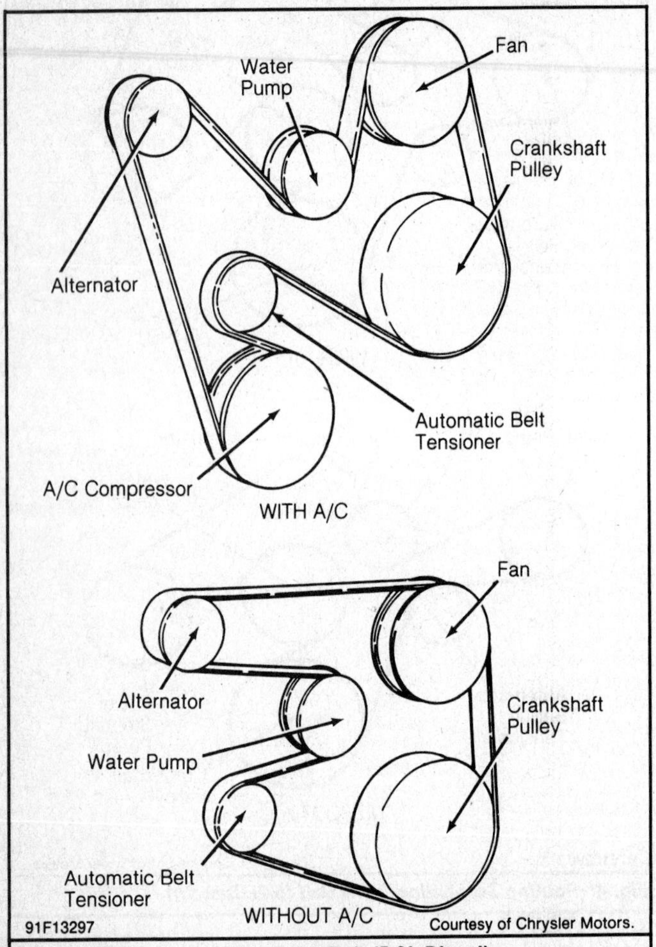
Fan
Water Pump
Crankshaft Pulley
Alternator
Automatic Belt Tensioner
A/C Compressor
WITH A/C
Fan
Alternator
Crankshaft Pulley
Water Pump
Automatic Belt Tensioner
WITHOUT A/C

91F13297 Courtesy of Chrysler Motors.

Fig. 5: Routing Serpentine Drive Belt (5.9L Diesel)

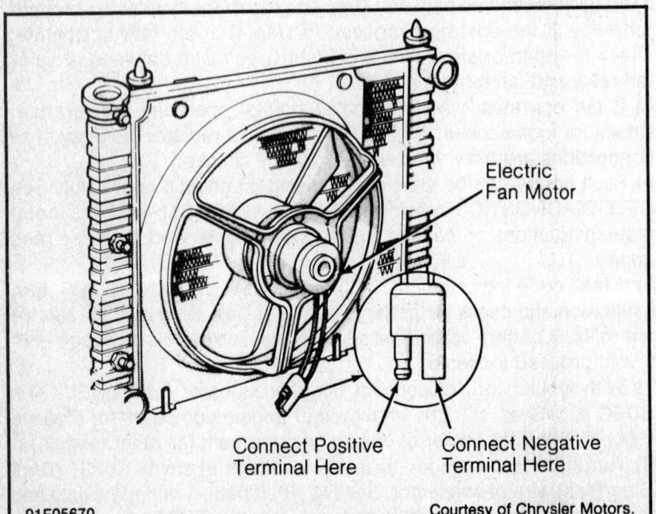
Electric Fan Motor
Connect Positive Terminal Here
Connect Negative Terminal Here

91F05670 Courtesy of Chrysler Motors.

Fig. 6: Identifying Electric Fan Motor Terminals (Dakota 2.5L)

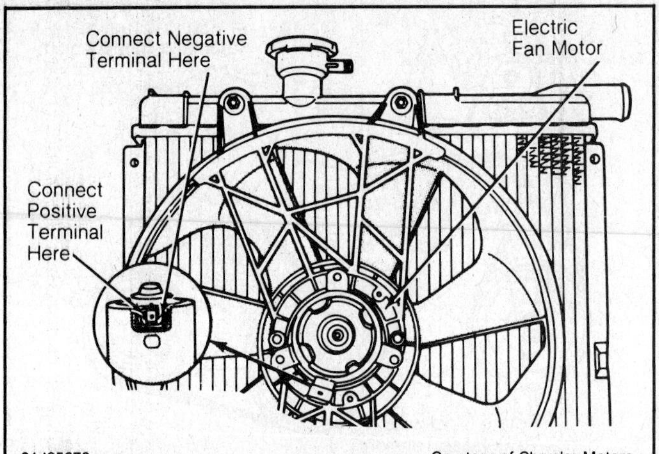
Connect Negative Terminal Here
Electric Fan Motor
Connect Positive Terminal Here

91J05672 Courtesy of Chrysler Motors.

Fig. 7: Identifying Electric Fan Motor Terminals (Caravan, Town & Country, & Voyager)

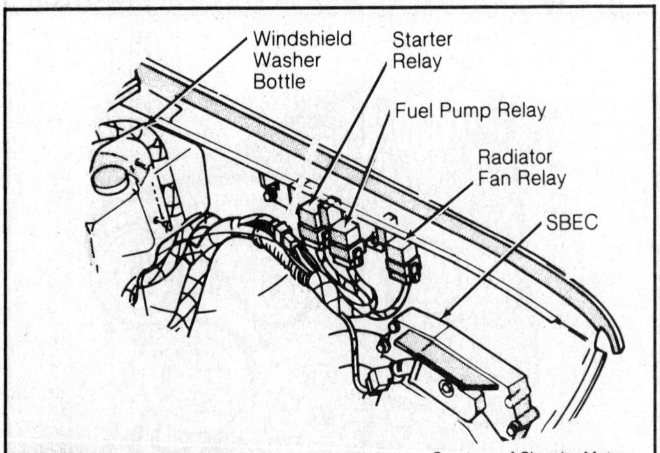
Windshield Washer Bottle
Starter Relay
Fuel Pump Relay
Radiator Fan Relay
SBEC

91D05674 Courtesy of Chrysler Motors.

Fig. 8: Locating Radiator Fan Relay (Caravan, Town & Country, & Voyager)

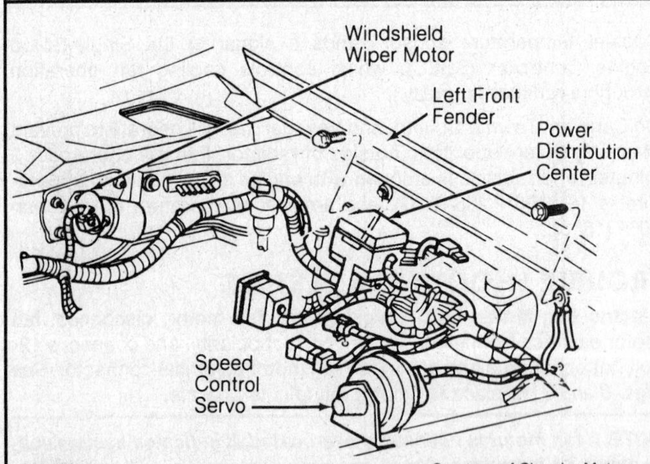
Windshield Wiper Motor
Left Front Fender
Power Distribution Center
Speed Control Servo

91B05673 Courtesy of Chrysler Motors.

Fig. 9: Locating Radiator Fan Relay (Dakota 2.5L)

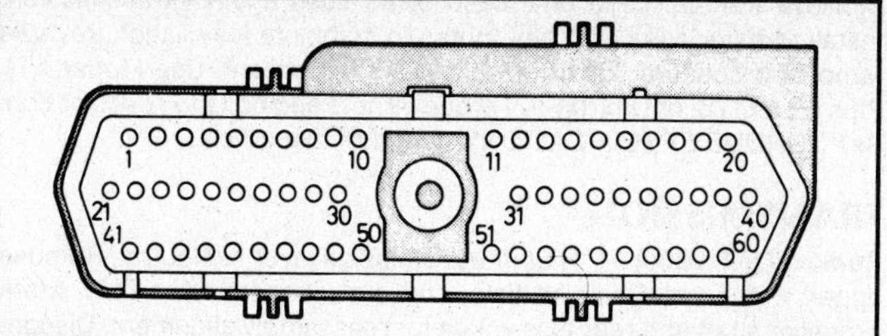

1
10
11
20
21
30
31
40
41
50
51
60

104279 Courtesy of Chrysler Motors.

Fig. 10: Identifying SBEC 60-Pin Connector Terminals

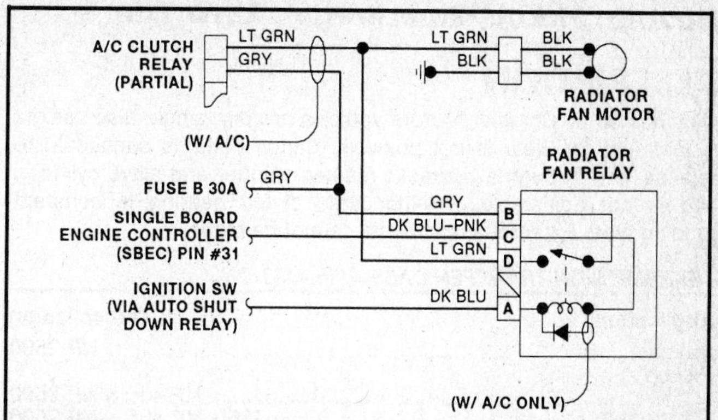

A/C CLUTCH
RELAY
(PARTIAL)
LT GRN
GRY
LT GRN
BLK
BLK
BLK
RADIATOR
FAN MOTOR
(W/ A/C)
RADIATOR
FAN RELAY
GRY
FUSE B 30A
GRY
SINGLE BOARD
ENGINE CONTROLLER
(SBEC) PIN #31
DK BLU-PNK
LT GRN
B
C
D
IGNITION SW
(VIA AUTO SHUT
DOWN RELAY)
DK BLU
A
(W/ A/C ONLY)

91G05359

Fig. 12: Electric Cooling Fan Wiring Diagram (Dakota 2.5L)

WIRING DIAGRAMS

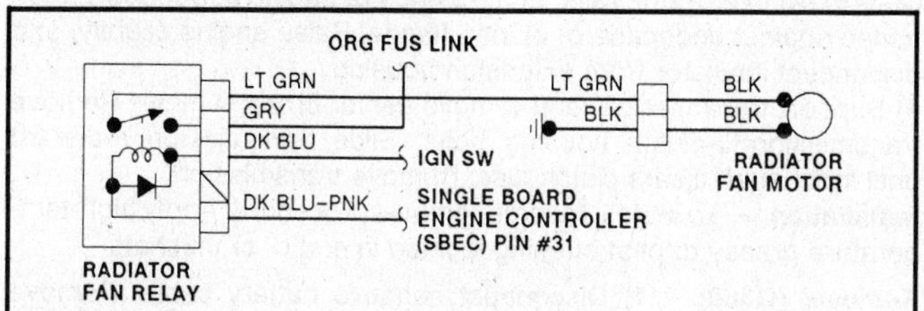

ORG FUS LINK
LT GRN
GRY
DK BLU
DK BLU-PNK
LT GRN
BLK
BLK
BLK
IGN SW
SINGLE BOARD
ENGINE CONTROLLER
(SBEC) PIN #31
RADIATOR
FAN MOTOR
RADIATOR
FAN RELAY

91I05394

Fig. 11: Electric Cooling Fan Wiring Diagram (Caravan, Town & Country, & Voyager)

1991 CLUTCHES
Single Disc

Dakota, Pickup, Ramcharger, RWD Van

DESCRIPTION

Clutches on all Chrysler Motors vehicles are dry, single disc design. Adjustment for wear is not possible. Clutch pedal is connected to release fork through a hydraulic master cylinder and slave cylinder, and is not adjustable. Pre-lubricated clutch bearing is constant running type. External adjustments cannot be made.

TRANSMISSION/TRANSFER CASE APPLICATION

Application	Transmission
Dakota	NP 2500
Pickup	
D150	NP 435 & NP 2500
D250/350	G360, NP 435 & NP 2500
W150	NP 435
W250/350	G360, NP 435 & NP 2500
Ramcharger	NP 435
RWD Van	NP 2500
	Transfer Case
Dakota	NP 231
Pickup	
W150	NP 241
W250/350	NP 205
Ramcharger	NP 241

ADJUSTMENTS

CLUTCH PEDAL FREE PLAY

NOTE: Clutches are a single, dry disc type. Adjustment for wear is not possible. Clutch is actuated through a hydraulic master cylinder and slave cylinder, and is self-adjusting.

REMOVAL & INSTALLATION

TRANSFER CASE

CAUTION: When removing transfer case, DO NOT allow propeller shafts to hang free, as damage to universal joints may result.

Removal (NP 205) - 1) Raise and support vehicle. Drain transfer case. Disconnect vehicle speed sensor harness connector. Mark front and rear propeller shaft yokes for installation reference. Disconnect propeller shafts at transfer case and support to one side.

2) Disconnect shift lever rod from shift lever on transfer case. Support transfer case. Remove transfer case-to-transmission adapter bolts. Move transfer case to rear until input shaft clears adapter. Lower transfer case from vehicle.

Installation - To install transfer case, reverse removal procedure. Torque all nuts and bolts to specification. See TORQUE SPECIFICATIONS at end of this article. Fill transfer case with lubricant. Use API Service SG or SG/CD SAE 30 viscosity grade oil.

Removal (NP 231 & NP 241) - 1) Raise and support vehicle, remove drain plug and drain transfer case. Mark front and rear output shaft yokes and propeller shafts for installation reference. Disconnect vehicle speed sensor harness and vacuum switch hoses. Disconnect shift lever link from operating lever.

2) Support transfer case with transmission jack. On NP 241 models, remove skid plate and skid plate crossmember. On all models, remove rear crossmember. Disconnect front and rear propeller shafts at yokes and support to one side. Remove nuts attaching transfer case to transmission adapter.

3) Move transfer case assembly to rear until clear of transmission adapter. Remove transfer case from vehicle. Remove all gasket material from rear of transmission adapter housing.

Installation - 1) Install new transmission-to-transfer case gasket with sealer on both sides. Align transfer case with transmission. Rotate transfer case output shaft until transmission output shaft engages transfer case input shaft.

2) Move transfer case until case seats flush against transmission. Install transfer case attaching nuts. To complete installation, reverse removal procedure. Fill transfer case with lubricant. Use Mopar ATF Plus type 7176, or Dexron-II. Torque all nuts and bolts to specification. See TORQUE SPECIFICATIONS at end of this article.

TRANSMISSION

Removal (NP 2500) - 1) Shift transmission lever to Neutral. Remove upper shift lever. Raise vehicle, and drain transmission fluid. Mark propeller shaft and rear axle yokes for reassembly alignment. Disconnect and remove propeller shaft.

2) Disconnect wires from distance sensor. Loosen sensor coupling, and remove sensor from speedometer adapter. Remove speedometer adapter and pinion gear.

3) Disconnect back-up light switch wires. Install Engine Support (C-3487-A) over frame rails. Ensure ends of engine support are positioned against underside of oil pan flange. Raise engine slightly, and disconnect insulator from extension housing.

4) Support transmission, and remove center crossmember. Remove transmission-to-clutch housing bolts. Slide transmission rearward until input shaft clears clutch disc. Remove transmission.

Installation - To install, reverse removal procedure. Apply high-temperature grease to pilot bushing located in end of crankshaft.

Removal (G360) - 1) Disconnect negative battery cable. Remove upper shift boot attaching screws and upper shift boot. Remove shift lever extension by unthreading it from shift lever stub shaft. Remove lower boot attaching screws and lower boot. Remove shift tower boot. Remove 2 shifter alignment bolts from side of shift tower. Remove snap ring securing stub shaft in tower. Remove stub shaft.

2) Raise and support vehicle. Mark propeller shaft and axle yokes for installation reference, and remove propeller shaft(s). Disconnect speed sensor connector. Support transmission with suitable jackstand. On 4WD vehicles, remove skid plates (if equipped) and transfer case crossmember. Disconnect shift rods at transfer case. Support transfer case with jack. Remove transfer case bolts. Move transfer case rearward, and disengage front input spline.

3) Lower transfer case from vehicle. Remove bolts attaching transmission rear mount to crossmember. Support transmission with suitable transmission jack, and move jackstand underneath engine. Remove crossmember-to-frame braces and crossmember. Remove clutch slave cylinder shield. Remove slave cylinder, and secure aside. Disconnect back-up light switch connector.

4) Remove transmission-to-clutch housing bolts. Using safety chains, secure transmission to transmission jack. Slide transmission rearward until input shaft clears clutch disc, and lower transmission from vehicle.

Installation - To install, reverse removal procedure. Apply high-temperature grease to pilot bushing located in end of crankshaft.

Removal (NP 435) - 1) Disconnect negative battery cable. Remove shift lever retainer by pressing downward, rotating retainer counterclockwise and releasing retainer. On 4WD models, remove transfer case and transmission skid plates (if equipped). On all models, mark propeller shafts and shaft yokes for installation reference.

2) Remove front and rear output shaft(s). On 4WD models, disconnect shift rods at transfer case. Support transfer case with jack. Remove transfer case bolts. Move transfer case rearward, and disengage front input spline. Lower transfer case from vehicle.

3) On all models, disconnect back-up light switch. Install Engine Support (C-3487-A) with Adapter (DD-1279) over frame rails. Ensure ends of engine support are positioned against underside of oil pan flange.

4) Support transmission, and remove center crossmember. Remove transmission-to-clutch housing bolts. Slide transmission rearward until input shaft clears clutch disc. Remove transmission.

Installation - To install, reverse removal procedure. Apply high-temperature grease to pilot bushing located in end of crankshaft.

CLUTCH ASSEMBLY

CAUTION: Clutch disc may contain asbestos fibers which can cause serious health risk. DO NOT sand clutch components. DO NOT clean components with compressed air. To clean components, use a water dampened cloth.

Removal - With transmission and clutch housing removed, mark pressure plate and flywheel for reassembly reference. Install clutch alignment tool in clutch disc to prevent disc from falling. Loosen pressure plate bolts evenly to avoid warping pressure plate. Remove pressure plate and disc from flywheel. *See Fig. 1.*

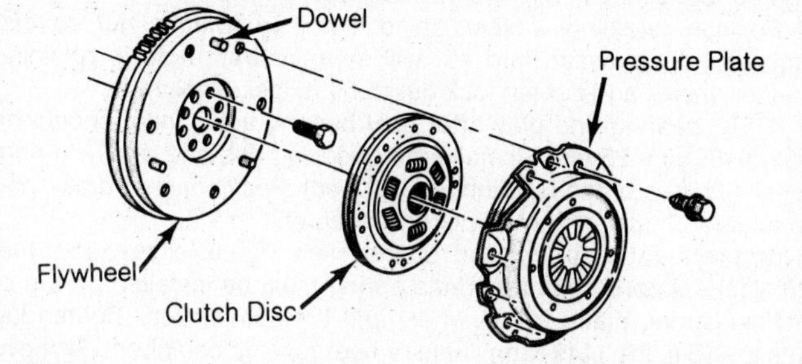
Dowel
Pressure Plate
Flywheel
Clutch Disc
121001
Courtesy of Chrysler Motors.

Fig. 1: Exploded View Of Clutch Assembly

Installation - To install, reverse removal procedure using clutch alignment tool. Ensure reference marks are aligned. Tighten pressure plate bolts evenly to prevent warpage. See TORQUE SPECIFICATIONS table at end of article.

CLUTCH RELEASE BEARING & FORK

Removal - **1)** Remove transmission and clutch housing as an assembly. Disconnect release bearing from fork, and remove bearing. *See Fig. 2.* Remove release fork.

2) Inspect bearing. Bearing should turn smoothly under a light thrust load. Bearing is pre-lubricated, sealed and should not be immersed in solvent. Inspect release fork and fork ball pivot for distortion and wear.

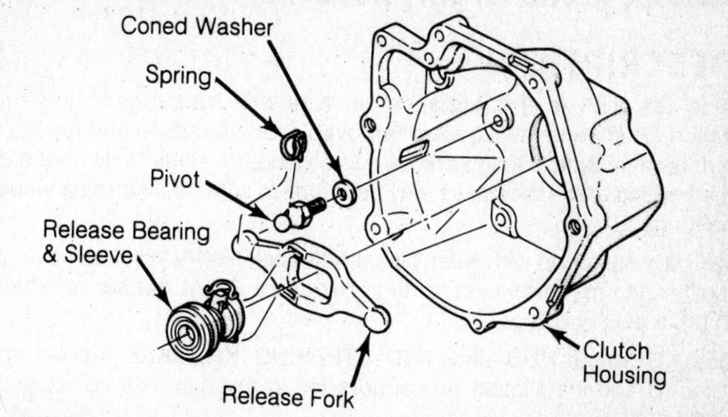
Coned Washer
Spring
Pivot
Release Bearing & Sleeve
Clutch Housing
Release Fork
90H04450
Courtesy of Chrysler Motors.

Fig. 2: Exploded View of RWD Clutch Release Bearing Assembly

Installation - **1)** Lubricate crankshaft pilot bushing, input shaft splines, bearing retainer slide surface, fork pivot and release fork pivot surface with high-temperature wheel bearing grease.

2) Install release fork and release bearing. Ensure fork and bearing are properly secured. Install transmission and clutch housing.

TORQUE SPECIFICATIONS

TORQUE SPECIFICATIONS

Application	Ft. Lbs. (N.m)
Clutch Fork Pivot Bolt	17 (23)
Clutch Housing Bolt	
3/8"	30 (41)
7/16"	50 (68)
Flywheel Bolt	55 (75)
Pressure Plate Bolt	
5/16"	17 (23)
3/8"	30 (41)
Transfer Case Attaching Nuts	35 (47)
Transmission-To-Clutch Housing Bolts (NP 2500)	50 (68)

1991 DRIVE AXLES
Dana Full-Floating Axles

Pickup, Ramcharger, RWD Van

DESCRIPTION

Axle assembly is an integral carrier type with hypoid gear ring and pinion. Stamped steel cover is removable for inspection and repair of differential. Vehicle loads are carried by axle housings. Axle shafts of full-floating rear assemblies may be removed without disturbing wheel bearings.

Vehicles equipped with Rear Wheel Anti-Lock (RWAL) brakes have an exciter ring mounted next to ring gear and a RWAL sensor mounted in drive axle housing.

See LOCKING HUB and 4WD STEERING KNUCKLE articles for removal and installation procedures for front drive axle component parts.

AXLE RATIO & IDENTIFICATION

A metal tag on axle is stamped with gear ratio, part numbers and limited slip identification. Use the following tables to determine drive axle ratio.

NOTE: Unless specified otherwise, references to Model 60 and Model 70 axles include Model 60M and Model 70HD, respectively.

MODEL IDENTIFICATION BY RING GEAR SIZE

Application	Ring Gear Diameter
Model 44 Axle	8.50"
Model 60 Axle	9.75"
Model 70 Axle	10.50"

FRONT AXLE RATIO IDENTIFICATION

Application	Ratio
Model 44 (8.5" Ring Gear)	3.54:1, 3.92:1, 4.09:1
Model 60 (9.75" Ring Gear)	[1] 3.07:1, 3.54:1, 4.10:1, 4.56:1

[1] - Diesel only.

REAR AXLE RATIO IDENTIFICATION

Application	Ratio
Model 60 (9.75" Ring Gear)	3.54:1, 4.10:1
Model 60M (9.75" Ring Gear)	4.10:1
Model 70 (10.50" Ring Gear)	4.10:1, 4.56:1
Model 70HD (10.50" Ring Gear)	4.88:1

LUBRICATION

CAUTION: If rear axle is submerged in water, axle lubricant MUST be replaced immediately to avoid premature failure due to contamination.

Use Multipurpose Gear Lubricant (MIL-L-2105-B/API GL-5). Four ounces of Mopar Hypoid Gear Oil Additive Friction Modifier (4318060) MUST be used with every fluid change if equipped with Trac-Lok.

REMOVAL & INSTALLATION

FRONT HUB, BEARING, SPINDLE & AXLE SHAFT

Removal (Model 44 Axle) – 1) Raise and support vehicle. Remove tire and wheel assembly. Remove caliper retainer and anti-rattle spring. Remove brake caliper and support out of the way. Remove inner brake pad. Remove hub cap and snap ring.

2) Remove driving hub and retaining spring. Use Wheel Bearing Lock Nut Adjuster (C-4170-A) to remove wheel bearing nut lock. Remove retaining washer and wheel bearing adjusting nut. Remove hub assembly. Remove brake caliper adapter from steering knuckle. Remove spindle attaching nuts. Remove splash shield and spindle.

3) Clamp spindle in soft-jawed vise and remove bearing seals. Remove needle bearings with Bearing Puller (D-131) and a slide hammer. Carefully remove axle shaft from shaft tube. Remove axle shaft from axle shaft tube. Remove seal and stone shield from shaft.

Installation – 1) Install seal on axle shaft shield with lip facing toward axle shaft splines. Carefully insert right axle shaft into axle shaft tube. Avoid damaging differential housing seal. Install intermediate axle shaft. See INTERMEDIATE AXLE SHAFT.

2) Install replacement needle bearings in spindle with Installer (D-360) and Drive Handle (C-4171). Install replacement brake hub seal with Seal Tool (D-155) and Drive Handle (C-4171). Position replacement spacer on axle shaft. Install spindle and splash shield. Install nuts and tighten to 25-30 ft. lbs. (34-41 N.m).

3) Position hub assembly and outer wheel bearing on spindle. Install lock nut and tighten to 50 ft. lbs. (68 N.m) to seat wheel bearings. Loosen lock nut and retighten to 30-40 ft. lbs. (41-54 N.m) while rotating hub. Loosen lock nut 135-150 degrees.

4) Position retaining washer on lock nut by rotating nut so that alignment pin pressed into nut will enter nearest hole in retaining washer. Install and tighten lock nut to 50 ft. lbs. (68 N.m).

5) Wheel bearing end play after final bearing adjustment should be .001-.010" (.03-.25 mm). Install spring, driving hub and retaining ring. Install hub cap or locking hub (if equipped). Position inner brake pad on adapter. Install brake caliper and adapter.

6) Install anti-rattle springs and retainer clips. Tighten clips to 15 ft. lbs. (20 N.m). Inboard shoe anti-rattle spring must be installed on top of retainer spring plate. Install wheel and tire assemblies. Tighten lug nuts to 110 ft. lbs. (149 N.m). Install wheel cover (if equipped). Remove supports and lower vehicle.

Removal (Model 60 Axle) – 1) Raise and support vehicle. Remove tire and wheel assembly. Remove caliper-to-adapter hex-head screw. Tap adapter lock and spring with a punch to remove. Separate caliper from adapter. Support caliper out of the way. Remove hub cap and snap ring.

2) Remove flange nuts and lock washers. Remove drive flange or locking hub (if equipped). Discard drive flange gasket. Straighten lock ring tangs and remove outer lock nut and lock ring. Remove inner lock nut and outer wheel bearing. Remove hub assembly. Remove seal and inner wheel bearing from hub.

Installation – 1) Lubricate hub bore. Install inner wheel bearing in hub bore and install replacement seal. Lubricate spindle and install hub onto spindle. Install outer wheel bearing and inner lock nut. Using Wheel Bearing Lock Nut Adjuster (DD-1241-JD), tighten inner lock nut to 50 ft. lbs. (68 N.m).

2) Loosen lock nut and retighten to 30-40 ft. lbs. (41-54 N.m) while rotating hub. Loosen lock nut 135-150 degrees. Install lock ring and outer lock nut. Tighten lock nut to at least 65 ft. lbs. (88 N.m). Bend one lock ring tang over inner lock nut and one tang over outer lock nut. Wheel bearing end play after final bearing adjustment should be .001-.010" (.03-.25 mm).

3) Install replacement gasket on hub. Install drive flange, lock washers and nuts. Tighten nuts to 30-40 ft. lbs. (41-54 N.m). Install snap ring. Install hub cap or locking hub (if equipped). Install brake caliper and adapter. Install adapter lock and spring and tighten hex-head screw to 12-18 ft. lbs. (16-24 N.m). Install wheel and tire assemblies. Tighten lug nuts to 75 ft. lbs. (102 N.m). Lubricate all fittings. Remove supports and lower vehicle.

INTERMEDIATE AXLE SHAFT

Removal (Disconnect Axle Models) – 1) Remove outer axle. See FRONT HUB, BEARING, SPINDLE & AXLE SHAFT in this article.

2) Remove axle assembly inspection cover and drain fluid. Remove vacuum and electrical connections at shift motor housing. Remove bolts. Pull disconnect housing from axle tube. *See Fig. 1.*

3) Remove intermediate shaft retaining clip on inner end of axle shaft. Carefully slide intermediate axle shaft through seal and out end of axle tube. Remove shift collar.

4) Inspect intermediate shaft bearings and seals for wear. If replacement of bearings or seal is necessary, use recommended tools.

5) Using Adapter Shaft (D-354-4) and Adapter (D-354-1) with Puller (C-637), remove axle shaft bearing. Use Adapter Shaft (D-354-4) and Adapter (D-354-2) with Puller (C-637) to install new bearing.

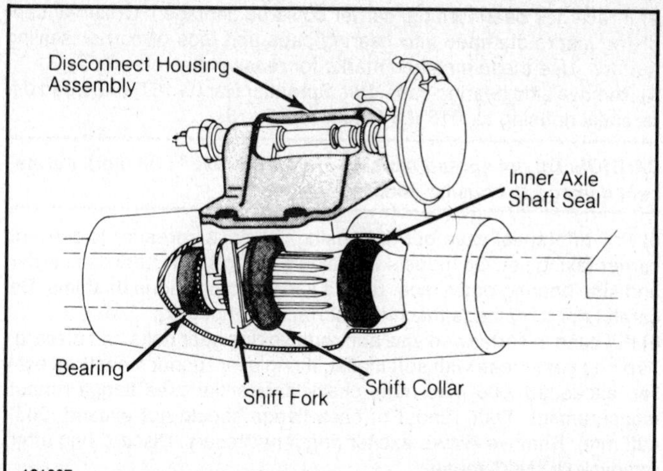
Disconnect Housing Assembly
Inner Axle Shaft Seal
Bearing
Shift Fork
Shift Collar
121007

Courtesy of Chrysler Motors.

Fig. 1: Cutaway View Of Disconnect Axle Assembly

6) To install new seal, use Installer (5041-1), Adapter Handle (5041-2) and Adapter (5041-3) to press new axle seal into housing. Use Adapter (D-328) and Driver Handle (C-4171) to install needle bearing on axle shaft.

Installation – 1) Coat intermediate shaft with lubricant and carefully slide through seal and engage in drive axle splines. Install retaining clip.

2) Install shift collar on axle shaft. Install outer axle shaft and check for smooth operation of shift collar.

3) Apply a bead of silicone sealer to inspection cover and install cover. Fill axle housing with 2.5 pts. (1.2L) of 75W-90 gear oil. Pour a small amount of gear oil on shift collar and install disconnect housing. Ensure shifting fork is properly positioned in shift collar.

4) To complete installation, reverse removal procedure. Tighten all bolts and nuts to specification. See TORQUE SPECIFICATIONS table at end of this article.

PINION FLANGE & SEAL

Removal – 1) Raise and support vehicle. Disconnect propeller shaft and support to one side. Using Flange Holder (C-3281), remove pinion nut.

2) Remove flange using Flange Puller (C-542). Remove oil seal from housing using Pinion Seal Puller (C-748). Use care to avoid damage to housing seal surface.

NOTE: DO NOT drive flange on with hammer. Hammering could result in damage to ring and pinion gear.

Installation – 1) Lubricate seal lip with grease. Place seal in axle housing and drive seal in using appropriate seal installer. See SEAL INSTALLATION TOOL SPECIFICATION table.

2) Install flange on pinion shaft. Install flange holder and install pinion washer and nut. Tighten pinion nut to specification. See TORQUE SPECIFICATIONS table at end of this article.

SEAL INSTALLATION TOOL SPECIFICATION

Application	Seal Installation Tool
Model 44 Axle	W-147
Model 60 Axles	C-3719
Model 70 Axle	C-359

FRONT AXLE ASSEMBLY

Removal – 1) Raise and support vehicle. Remove tire and wheel assembly. Remove hubs, spindles and axles. See FRONT HUB, BEARING, SPINDLE & AXLE SHAFT. Disconnect vacuum hoses and harness connector from shift motor housing.

2) Remove left and right tie rod ends. Remove stabilizer bar links, lower shock mounts and track bar bolt. Disconnect drag link. Mark propeller shaft and front pinion yoke for reinstallation reference. Disconnect front propeller shaft at front pinion yoke and support to one side. Disconnect axle housing vent tube and plug opening.

3) Support axle housing with floor jack. Remove spring "U" bolt nuts and remove. Carefully lower axle assembly from vehicle and remove.

Installation – 1) Place axle assembly on floor jack. Position assembly under vehicle and raise until assembly contacts springs. Ensure leaf spring center pin is engaged with hole in axle housing spring plate.

2) Check all bushings and mounting hardware for wear or damage. To complete installation, reverse removal procedure. Tighten all bolts and nuts to specification. See TORQUE SPECIFICATIONS table at end of this article. Fill axle assembly with gear oil. Check wheel alignment. See SPECIFICATIONS & PROCEDURES article in WHEEL ALIGNMENT.

REAR HUB, BEARINGS & AXLE SHAFTS

Removal & Installation – 1) Raise and support vehicle. Remove tire and wheel assembly. Remove axle flange nuts or bolts. If nuts are used, rap center of axle flange sharply with hammer to loosen tapered dowels. Remove bolts or dowels and pull axle shaft out of hub.

2) Remove locking wedge from nut. Remove bearing adjusting nut and remove hub assembly.

3) Remove inner hub seal and bearing. Inspect bearings and races for wear. To replace bearing, drive outer race from bearing hub using a punch and hammer. Install new race being careful not to chip or dent race. Ensure new race is seated in hub.

4) Pack bearings with multipurpose grease. Install new seal. Carefully install hub on axle spindle; DO NOT damage seal lip and spindle threads.

5) Install outer bearing and adjusting nut. Tighten bearing adjusting nut in steps. See REAR HUB BEARING ADJUSTING SPECIFICATIONS table. Rear hub end play should be .001-.008" (.03-.20 mm). Install spindle nut lock.

6) Install new axle flange gasket or apply silicone sealer. Install axle and tighten bolts or nuts to specification. See TORQUE SPECIFICATIONS table at end of this article.

REAR HUB BEARING ADJUSTING SPECIFICATIONS

Application	[1] Ft. Lbs. (N.m)
Adjusting Nut	
Step 1	120-140 (163-190)
Step 2	Back Off 120 Degrees

[1] – While rotating hub.

REAR AXLE ASSEMBLY

Removal – 1) Raise and support vehicle. Remove wheels, hubs and axles. See REAR HUB, BEARINGS & AXLE SHAFTS.

2) Remove lower shock mounts and stabilizer bar mount. Disconnect propeller shaft and support to one side. Remove hydraulic brake line at junction block and plug to prevent fluid loss. Disconnect RWAL electrical connector (if equipped).

3) Disconnect park brake cables and hydraulic brake lines to wheel cylinders. Remove brake backing plates. Support axle housing with floor jack and remove leaf spring "U" bolts. Carefully lower axle housing and remove from vehicle.

Installation – Place axle housing on floor jack. Raise axle and install "U" bolts and nuts. To complete installation, reverse removal procedure. Tighten all bolts and nuts to specification. See TORQUE SPECIFICATIONS table at end of article and REAR HUB BEARING ADJUSTING SPECIFICATIONS table.

1991 DRIVE AXLES
Dana Full-Floating Axles (Cont.)

OVERHAUL

AXLE SHAFT

***NOTE:** All front axle shafts use Cardan "U" joints and should be overhauled in same manner as propeller shaft "U" joints.*

AXLE ASSEMBLY

***NOTE:** Use extreme care when removing differential case from vehicle to avoid damage to RWAL exciter ring.*

Disassembly – 1) Drain lubricant. Remove RWAL sensor (if equipped). Remove axle shafts and housing cover. If no side play is found in the differential case assembly, mount dial indicator on pilot stud with tip against back of ring gear. *See Fig. 2.* Measure runout of ring gear, marking ring gear and case at point of maximum runout.

2) If runout total exceeds .006" (.15 mm), ring gear could be loose or case could be damaged. Using .003" (.08 mm) feeler gauge, try to force feeler gauge between cap and race. If gauge does fit, bearing race may have been turning in carrier.

3) If race has been turning, carrier could be damaged. Observe identifying marks stamped into bearing caps and face of carrier sealing surface. Use these matched marks for reassembly reference.

4) Remove side bearing caps. Use Spreader Bar (D-167) to spread differential housing to .015" (.38 mm). *See Fig. 3.*

***CAUTION:** Do not spread housing more than .015" (.38 mm). Permanent damage to housing could result.*

5) Pry differential case out of housing. Remove spreader to prevent carrier taking set. On models with side bearing shims between carrier and side bearing outer race, record sizes and positions of shims. Be careful not to damage machined surfaces of housing.

6) Put case in soft-jawed vise and remove ring gear bolts and discard. Tap ring gear loose with soft mallet. If ring gear runout measured earlier, exceeded .006" (.15 mm), check differential case flange runout measurement. Total runout of case flange should not exceed .003" (.08 mm). Remove RWAL exciter ring if necessary. Discard ring after removal, DO NOT reuse.

7) Using Flange Holder (C-3281), remove drive pinion nut and washer. Using holder wrench and Flange Puller (C-452), remove drive pinion

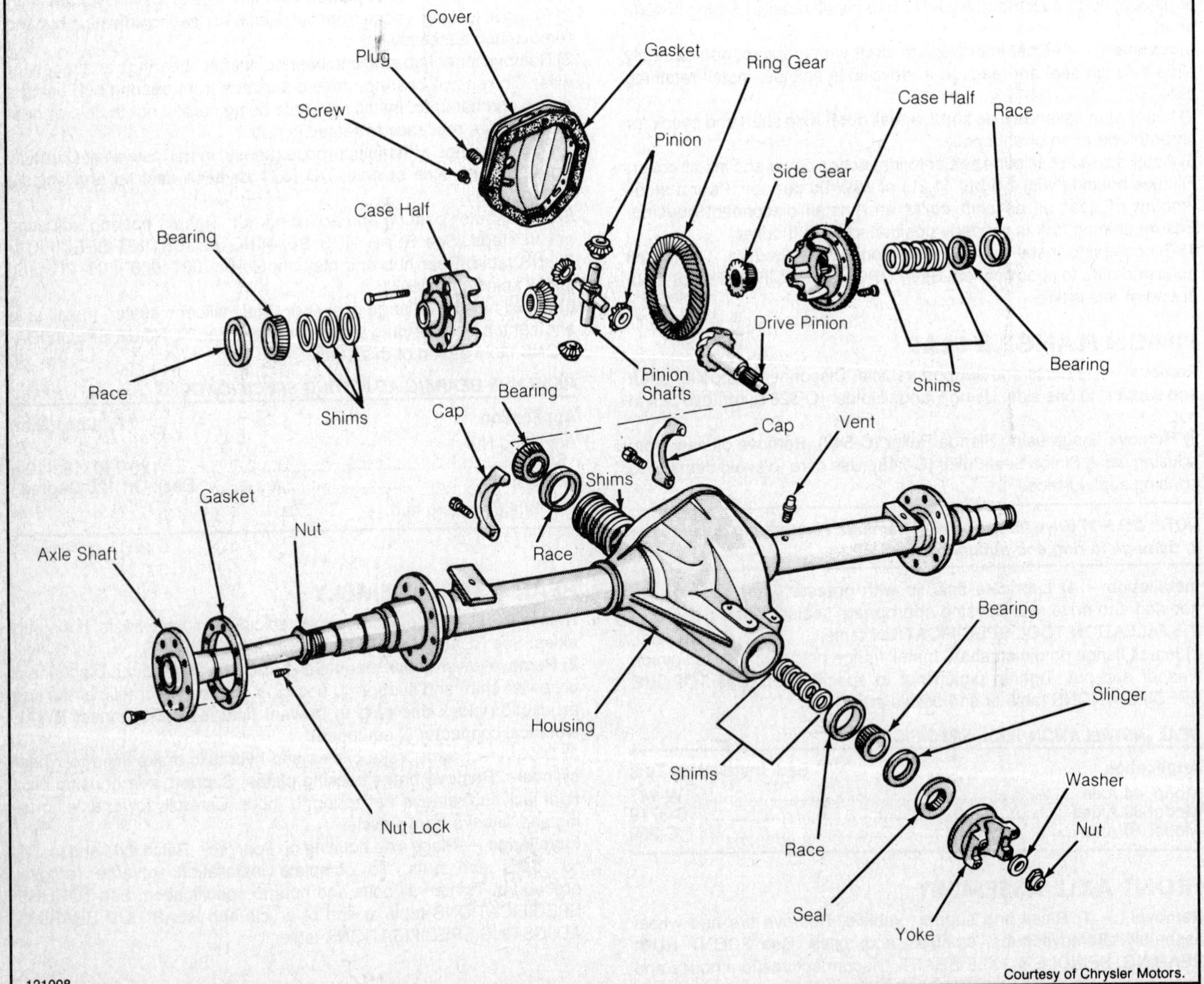
Cover
Plug
Gasket
Ring Gear
Case Half
Race
Screw
Pinion
Side Gear
Case Half
Bearing
Drive Pinion
Bearing
Race
Shims
Pinion
Shafts
Shims
Cap
Bearing
Cap
Vent
Shims
Gasket
Nut
Axle Shaft
Race
Bearing
Slinger
Housing
Shims
Washer
Nut Lock
Race
Nut
Seal
Yoke
121008
Courtesy of Chrysler Motors.

Fig. 2: Exploded View Of Dana Model 70 Full-Floating Axle Assembly

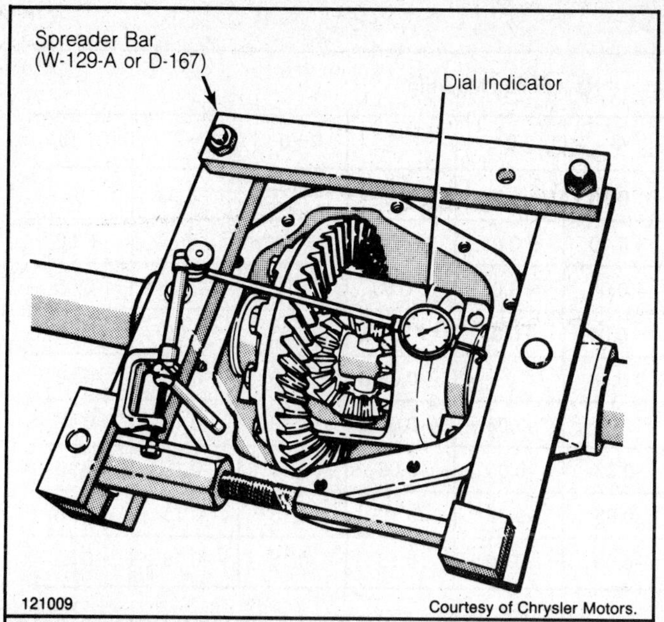

Spreader Bar
(W-129-A or D-167)
Dial Indicator
121009
Courtesy of Chrysler Motors.

Fig. 3: Spreading Differential Housing

flange. Using Pinion Seal Puller (C-748), remove pinion oil seal. Remove slinger, gasket, outer pinion bearing and preload shim pack.

8) Remove drive pinion with inner bearing. Remove inner and outer pinion bearing races. Remove and note thickness of shim pack behind inner bearing race. Remove inner pinion bearing from pinion shaft using Puller Press (DD-914-P) with Adapter Ring (DD-914-9) and appropriate pinion bearing puller. See BEARING PULLER TOOL SPECIFICATION table.

BEARING PULLER TOOL SPECIFICATION

Application	Bearing Puller
Model 44 Axle	C-293-39
Model 60 Axles	DD-914-37
Model 70 Axle	DD-914-95

NOTE: Pinion bearing adjusting shims may remain on pinion shaft, stick to bearing or fall loose. Collect and save them for reassembly.

9) Remove side bearings with Bearing Puller (DD-914-P), Adapter Ring (DD-914-8), Plate (DD-914-62) Screw Extension (DD-914-7) and Button (DD-914-42). Record shim thickness and location for reassembly reference.

10) Drive out lock pin holding differential pinion shaft to case. Remove differential pinion shaft, gears and thrust washers (one for each gear).

Inspection – 1) Use cleaning solvent to rinse gears and bearings. Check large end of bearing rollers for wear. Check pinion and flange splines for excessive wear. Ensure ring gear teeth are undamaged.

2) Check differential case for cracks, scoring of side gears, thrust washers and pinion thrust faces. Check fit of side gears to case and to axle shaft splines. Examine pinion shaft and spacer for scoring or excessive wear.

Reassembly & Adjustments – 1) When reassembling ring and pinion assembly, pinion depth, pinion bearing preload, side bearing preload and backlash between ring and pinion must be adjusted.

2) If only pinion shaft and ring gear are to be replaced and carrier housing can be reused, compare pinion depth adjustment numbers etched in faces of old and new pinion heads. *See Fig. 4.* Using PINION DEPTH SHIM ADJUSTMENT CHART, correct shims can be selected for new pinion shaft depth adjustment.

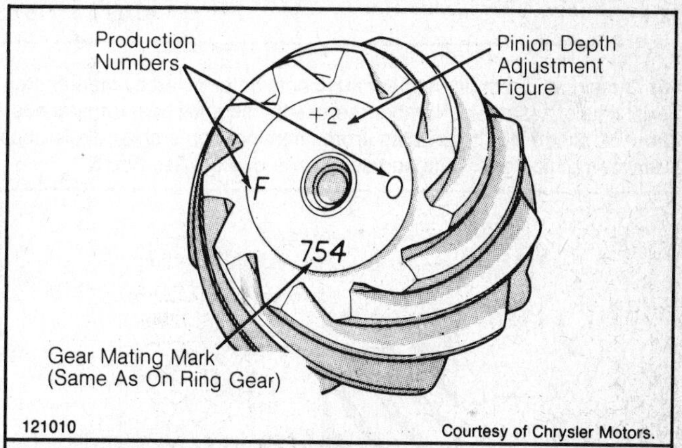

Production
Numbers
Pinion Depth
Adjustment
Figure
+2
F
0
754
Gear Mating Mark
(Same As On Ring Gear)
121010
Courtesy of Chrysler Motors.

Fig. 4: Locating Pinion Gear Markings

NOTE: In order to use PINION DEPTH SHIM ADJUSTMENT CHART procedure, old pinion shaft shim pack dimensions MUST be determined accurately. If original pinion shaft shim pack dimension cannot be determined accurately, Pinion Depth Gauge Set (D-271) must be used to properly determine pinion depth setting. Depth gauge set must also be used if new carrier housing is to be used.

PINION DEPTH SHIM ADJUSTMENT CHART (INCHES)

Old Pinion Marking	New Pinion Marking								
	-4	-3	-2	-1	0	+1	+2	+3	+4
+4	+0.008	+0.007	+0.006	+0.005	+0.004	+0.003	+0.002	+0.001	0
+3	+0.007	+0.006	+0.005	+0.004	+0.003	+0.002	+0.001	0	-0.001
+2	+0.006	+0.005	+0.004	+0.003	+0.002	+0.001	0	-0.001	-0.002
+1	+0.005	+0.004	+0.003	+0.002	+0.001	0	-0.001	-0.002	-0.003
0	+0.004	+0.003	+0.002	+0.001	0	-0.001	-0.002	-0.003	-0.004
-1	+0.003	+0.002	+0.001	0	-0.001	-0.002	-0.003	-0.004	-0.005
-2	+0.002	+0.001	0	-0.001	-0.002	-0.003	-0.004	-0.005	-0.006
-3	+0.001	0	-0.001	-0.002	-0.003	-0.004	-0.005	-0.006	-0.007
-4	0	-0.001	-0.002	-0.003	-0.004	-0.005	-0.006	-0.007	-0.008

1991 DRIVE AXLES
Dana Full-Floating Axles (Cont.)

PINION DEPTH SHIM ADJUSTMENT CHART (MILLIMETERS)

Old Pinion Marking	New Pinion Marking								
	-10	-8	-5	-3	0	+3	+5	+8	+10
+10	+0.20	+0.18	+0.15	+0.13	+0.10	+0.08	+0.05	+0.03	0
+8	+0.18	+0.15	+0.13	+0.10	+0.08	+0.05	+0.03	0	-0.03
+5	+0.15	+0.13	+0.10	+0.08	+0.05	+0.03	0	-0.03	-0.05
+3	+0.13	+0.10	+0.08	+0.05	+0.03	0	-0.03	-0.05	-0.08
0	+0.10	+0.08	+0.05	+0.03	0	-0.03	-0.05	-0.08	-0.10
-3	+0.08	+0.05	+0.03	0	-0.03	-0.05	-0.08	-0.10	-0.13
-5	+0.05	+0.03	0	-0.03	-0.05	-0.08	-0.10	-0.13	-0.15
-8	+0.03	0	-0.03	-0.05	-0.08	-0.10	-0.13	-0.15	-0.18
-10	0	-0.03	-0.05	-0.08	-0.10	-0.13	-0.15	-0.18	-0.20

3) The pinion depth adjustment number is determined by manufacturer at time of assembly. Number represents distance best running position of pinion shaft deviates from "nominal" or standard distance between pinion gear face and center line of axle. *See Fig. 5.*

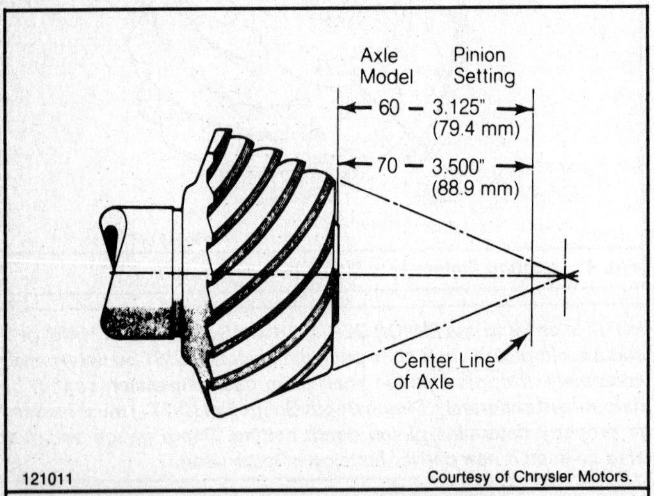
Axle
Model
Pinion
Setting
60 – 3.125"
(79.4 mm)
70 – 3.500"
(88.9 mm)
Center Line
of Axle
121011
Courtesy of Chrysler Motors.

Fig. 5: Identifying Pinion Setting Standard Dimension

4) Pinion Depth Gauge Set (D-271) allows shim pack adjustments to be made without having to remove and replace differential bearings.

5) Place differential case in holding fixture or vise. Lubricate all parts with gear oil. Place side gears and new thrust washers in case. Place differential pinions and new thrust washers in case. Rotate side gears until holes in pinion gears and washers line up with holes in case. Install differential pinion shaft. Install lock pin after aligning hole in shaft with hole in case. Peen edge of hole to keep pin in place.

6) Inspect ring gear and case for any burrs or nicks. If replacing RWAL exciter ring, align exciter ring tab with slot on differential case. Install 2 NEW ring gear bolts to maintain bolt hole alignment. Mount assembly onto hydraulic press and press exciter ring onto case using ring gear as a pilot. Install remaining ring gear bolts and tighten evenly in alternating pattern to specification. See TORQUE SPECIFICATIONS table at end of article.

7) Install Master Bearings into case. Use (D-343) for Model 44 or (D-117) for Models 60 and 70. Install differential case in carrier. Install and tighten side bearing caps finger tight over master bearings. Caps must be in same location as marked during disassembly. Mount dial indicator on carrier with indicator tip against back of ring gear.

8) Pry case assembly to one side of carrier. Zero dial indicator and pry case in opposite direction. *See Fig. 6.* Record reading. This indicates thickness of shim pack necessary to eliminate clearance between case and side bearing races.

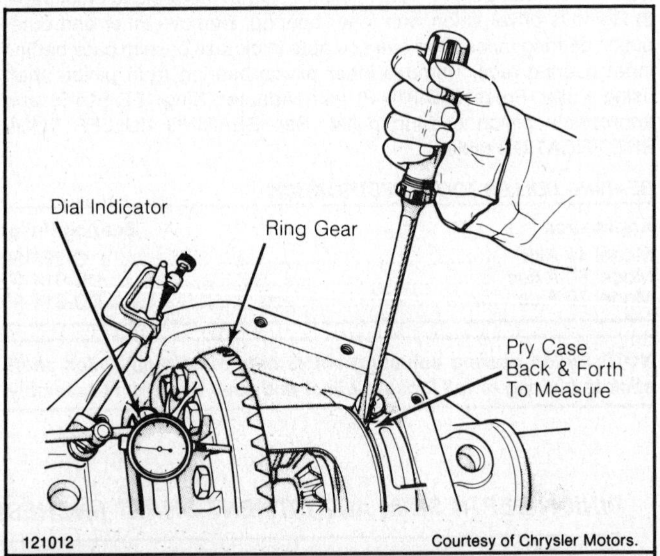
Dial Indicator
Ring Gear
Pry Case
Back & Forth
To Measure
121012
Courtesy of Chrysler Motors.

Fig. 6: Measuring Differential Case End Play

9) Actual placement of shim pack and necessary preload will be calculated after drive pinion is installed and pinion depth has been determined. Remove dial indicator. Remove bearing caps and differential case from carrier.

NOTE: If new differential side and pinion gears are used with new washers, gear backlash should be correct due to close machine tolerances. If old gears and/or washers are used, gear backlash must be checked.

NOTE: If original ring and pinion are to be used, measure old shim packs and make up packs of same dimensions with new shims. Baffles are considered part of shim pack.

Pinion Depth – 1) Depth Gauge Set (D-271) is used to determine pinion depth. Place Master Pinion Block (D-139 for Model 44, D-120 for Models 60, or D-137 for Model 70) in pinion bore of carrier. Put Arbor Discs (D-115-4-44 for Model 44, or D-116-2 for Models 60 and 70) on Arbor (D-115-3). Install arbor in carrier with discs riding in bearing bore.

1991 DRIVE AXLES
Dana Full-Floating Axles (Cont.)

2) Put Pinion Height Block (D-116-1) on top of master pinion block with side against arbor. Place Scooter Block (D-115-2) with Dial Indicator (D-106-5) on lowest step of pinion height block. Zero dial indicator with scooter block flat on pinion height block.
3) Move scooter block so dial indicator tip touches arbor. Move block back and forth (perpendicular to arbor) to get highest reading. This reading, plus or minus value etched on pinion head, is thickness of shim pack necessary for pinion bearing.
4) Measure shims separately with micrometer. If baffle is used, its thickness must be included in shim pack. This is also true if slinger is used between inner bearing and head of pinion shaft. Place pinion height shim pack in carrier bore for inner bearing race. Drive bearing race into carrier, making sure cup is fully seated.
Pinion Bearing Preload - 1) Drive outer pinion bearing into carrier housing. Press inner pinion bearing onto pinion shaft using Press Tube (C-3095-A). Ensure bearings seat fully. Insert pinion shaft into carrier. Install outer bearing, slinger (if equipped), flange, washer and nut.

NOTE: Pinion preload shims and oil seal should NOT be installed at this time.

2) Using an INCH lb. torque wrench, tighten pinion nut until 10 INCH lbs. (1.13 N.m) rotational torque is required to move pinion shaft. Recheck pinion depth with arbor and discs at this time. Place pinion height block on face of pinion shaft.
3) Place dial indicator on small step of height block. Zero dial indicator and move it across arbor to get highest reading. If reading is within .002" (.05 mm) of etching on pinion face, pinion depth is correct.

NOTE: If pinion depth is not with .002" (.05 mm) of etched number on face of pinion, shim pack under inner bearing race must be changed before proceeding with differential settings.

4) Remove pinion nut, washer, flange, slinger and outer bearing. Place preload shims (removed during disassembly) on pinion. Install bearing and slinger. After lightly coating lips with gear oil, install pinion seal in carrier housing. Install flange, washer and NEW pinion nut. Tighten nut to specification. See TORQUE SPECIFICATIONS table at end of this article.

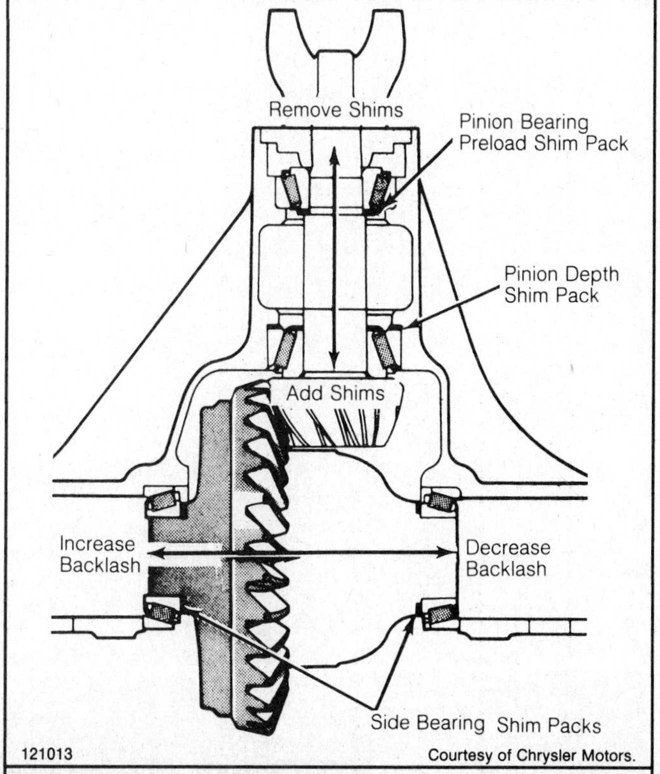
Remove Shims
Pinion Bearing Preload Shim Pack
Pinion Depth Shim Pack
Add Shims
Increase Backlash
Decrease Backlash
Side Bearing Shim Packs
121013
Courtesy of Chrysler Motors.

Fig. 7: Positioning Carrier Housing Shim

5) Using an INCH lb. torque wrench, measure preload (rotational torque) of pinion shaft. Rotational torque required to keep pinion shaft turning freely and smoothly should be 20-40 INCH lbs. (2.3-4.5 N.m). If preload needs to be increased, remove a few shims and recheck. To decrease preload, add a few shims and recheck. *See Fig. 7.*
Differential Bearing Preload - 1) Install differential case in housing with master bearings on case. Set up dial indicator in same position as when case end play was checked. *See Fig. 6.* Press ring gear toward pinion head while rocking ring gear so teeth mesh fully. Zero dial indicator while holding ring gear into pinion gear.
2) Press differential case (ring gear) away from pinion gear. Repeat until dial indicator gives same reading each time. This figure is shim pack thickness necessary between case and side bearing on ring gear side. Remove dial indicator and differential from carrier. Remove master bearings from case.
3) Put calculated shim pack on hub of case at ring gear side. Place side bearing on hub. Use Bearing Installer (C-4025A) and Handle (C-4171) to drive bearing onto case until it is seated. Take remaining shim pack as determined from case end play measurement and install pack on opposite side of case from ring gear.
4) Add .015" (.38 mm) thickness to shim pack opposite ring gear to provide side bearing preload. Drive side bearing onto case with installer and handle. Install spreader and dial indicator on carrier housing. Spread housing .015" (.38 mm). Put side bearing races onto side bearings. Install differential case into carrier.
Ring & Pinion Backlash - 1) Install side bearing caps, making sure reference marks made on caps and carrier match. Tighten cap bolts to 80 ft. lbs. (108 N.m). Check backlash between ring and pinion gears at 3 points spaced equal distance on ring gear. *See Fig. 8.*

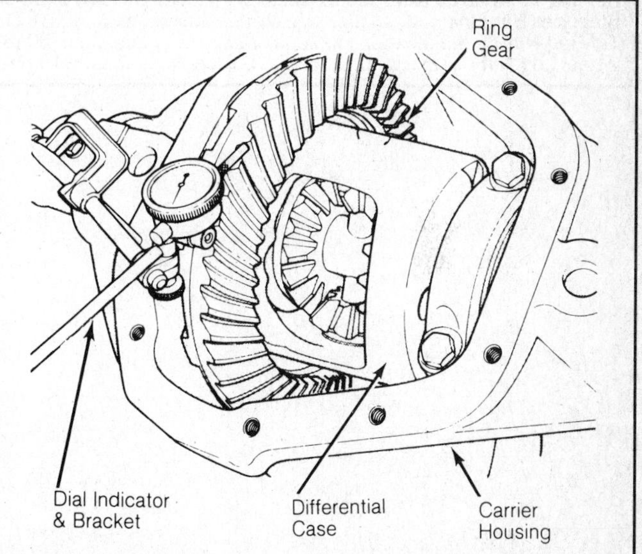
Ring Gear
Dial Indicator & Bracket
Differential Case
Carrier Housing
121014
Courtesy of Chrysler Motors.

Fig. 8: Measuring Backlash Between Ring & Pinion Gears

2) Backlash reading between ring and pinion gears should be .005-.009" (.13-.23 mm) for Model 44, and .004-.009" (.10-.23 mm) for Models 60 and 70. Maximum variation between readings at 3 points is .003" (.08 mm) for Model 44 and .002" (.05 mm) for all others. If backlash is too high, move ring gear closer to pinion gear. If backlash is too low, move ring gear away from pinion gear.
3) To change backlash readings, move shims from one side of differential case to other. When backlash adjustment is completed, check tooth contact pattern. See GEAR TOOTH CONTACT PATTERNS article in GENERAL INFORMATION. Pattern should be correct if assembly and adjustments have been done properly.
4) When differential is complete and correctly adjusted, install new cover gasket and cover. Tighten cover bolts to 35 ft. lbs. (47 N.m). Fill assembly with hypoid lubricant.

1991 DRIVE AXLES
Dana Full-Floating Axles (Cont.)

AXLE ASSEMBLY SPECIFICATIONS

AXLE ASSEMBLY SPECIFICATIONS

Application	Specifications
Pinion Gear Depth (Nominal Dimension)	
Model 44	2.625" (66.68 mm)
Model 60	3.125" (79.38 mm)
Model 70	3.500" (88.90 mm)
Ring Gear Backlash	.004-.009" (.10-.23 mm)
Side Bearing Preload	.015" (.38 mm)
Pinion Bearing Preload	
New Bearings	20-40 INCH lbs. (2.3-4.5 N.m)
Used Bearings	10-20 INCH lbs. (1.1-2.3 N.m)

TORQUE SPECIFICATIONS

TORQUE SPECIFICATIONS

Applications	Ft. Lbs. (N.m)
Front Axle	
Differential Cap Bearing Bolt	80 (108)
Disconnect Housing Bolt	10 (14)
Drag Link Nut	60 (81)
Housing Cover Bolts	35 (47)
Leaf Spring "U" Bolt Nut	110 (149)
Lower Shock Mount Bolt	55 (75)
Pinion Shaft Flange Nut	
Model 44	210 (285)
Model 60	260 (352)
Propeller Shaft Nut	25 (34)
Ring Gear-To-Case Bolt	
Model 44	45-60 (61-81)
Spindle-To-Knuckle Nut	50-70 (68-95)
Stabilizer Bar Link	10 (14)
Tie Rod Nut	60 (81)
Wheel Lug Nut	110 (149)

TORQUE SPECIFICATIONS (Cont.)

Applications	Ft. Lbs. (N.m)
Rear Axle	
Axle Flange-To-Hub Bolt	
Models 60 & 70	72 (98)
Housing Cover Bolts	35 (47)
Pinion Shaft Flange Nut	
Models 60 & 70	260 (352)
Ring Gear-To-Case Bolt	
Models 60	113 (153)
Model 70	105 (142)
Leaf Spring "U" Bolt Nut	180 (244)
Lower Shock Mount Nut	50 (68)
Propeller Shaft Bolt	16 (21)
Side Bearing Cap Bolt	
Model 60	85 (115)
Model 70	88 (119)
Wheel Lug Nut	
Coned	200 (271)
Flanged 5/8 x 18	325 (441)
Flanged 1 1/8 x 16	475 (644)

1991 DRIVE AXLES
Dana Trac-Lok

Pickup, RWD Van

DESCRIPTION

Trac-Lok differential has the same internal components as a standard differential, plus 2 clutch disc packs to provide limited slip action. The multiple disc clutches permit differential action when required for turning corners and transmit equal torque to both wheels when driving straight ahead.

When one wheel tries to spin because of reduced traction, clutch packs automatically provide more torque to wheel with greater traction. Trac-Lok has a one-piece differential case and 2 differential pinion gears.

Vehicles equipped with Rear Wheel Anti-Lock (RWAL) brakes have an exciter ring mounted next to ring gear, and a RWAL sensor mounted in drive axle housing.

REAR AXLE RATIO IDENTIFICATION

Application	Ratio
Model 60M (9.75" Ring Gear)	4.10:1
Model 70HD (10.50" Ring Gear)	4.88:1

LUBRICATION

CAUTION: If rear axle is submerged in water, replace axle lubricant immediately to avoid premature failure due to contamination.

Use Multipurpose Gear Lubricant (MIL-L-2105-B/API GL-5). Four ounces of Mopar Hypoid Gear Oil Additive Friction Modifier (4318060) MUST be used with every fluid change.

TROUBLE SHOOTING

DIFFERENTIAL NOISE

1) Operate vehicle for 10 minutes or more to bring differential lubricant to operating temperature. If noise is still evident, raise vehicle on hoist and drain differential lubricant.

2) Fill differential with MOPAR Hypoid Lubricant (4318058). With rear wheels off ground, start vehicle and operate rear wheels at approximately 40 MPH for at least 10 minutes.

3) Stop vehicle. Remove differential filler plug. Using a suction gun, remove as much lubricant as possible. Add 4 ounces of MOPAR Hypoid Friction Modifier (4318060). Refill differential housing to correct fluid level with MOPAR hypoid gear lubricant. Install filler plug and tighten to 25 ft. lbs. (35 N.m).

4) Manufacturer recommends driving vehicle for at least 100 miles before re-evaluating differential noise. If noise is still evident, replace entire differential case assembly. The ring gear, differential side gears and RWAL exciter ring are the only serviceable parts. Differential case and internal parts are serviced as a unit.

TESTING

1) Drive vehicle for a minimum of 10 minutes. Place a piece of Kraft paper over a smooth Formica board. Place Formica board with paper under a rear wheel. Block the front tires with a 2" wood block.

2) Start vehicle. With gradual throttle pressure, attempt to drive vehicle over wood block. If paper slips out from under wheel before vehicle drives over wood block, move Formica and paper under other rear wheel.

3) Attempt to drive over wood block again. If vehicle drives over wood block with Formica and paper under either wheel, drive axle is considered normal.

REMOVAL & INSTALLATION

Removal and installations procedures are the same as Dana 60 and 60M rear drive axles. See DANA FULL-FLOATING AXLES article.

OVERHAUL

NOTE: The ring gear, differential side gears and RWAL exciter ring are the only parts replaceable. Differential case and internal parts are serviced as a unit.

For overhaul procedures, see DANA FULL-FLOATING AXLES article.

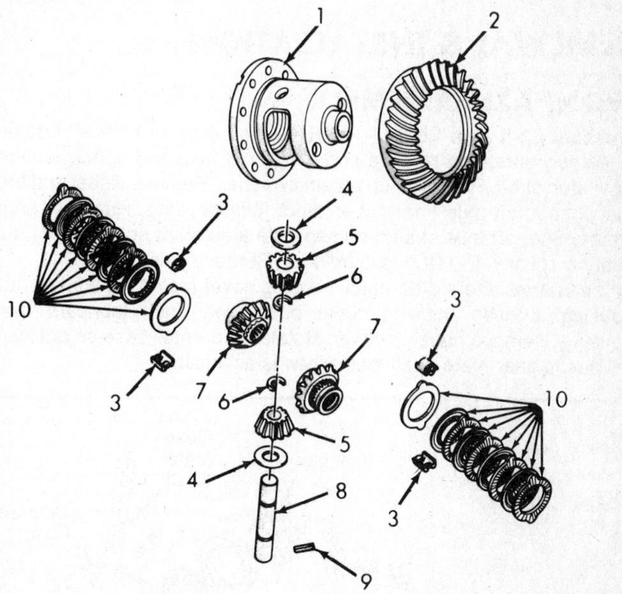
1
2
3
4
5
6
7
8
9
10

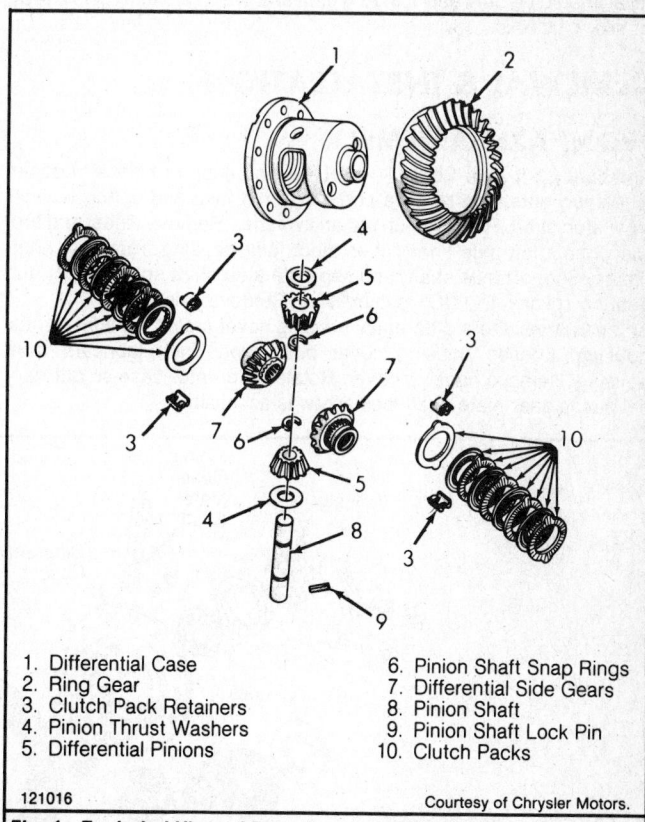

1. Differential Case
2. Ring Gear
3. Clutch Pack Retainers
4. Pinion Thrust Washers
5. Differential Pinions
6. Pinion Shaft Snap Rings
7. Differential Side Gears
8. Pinion Shaft
9. Pinion Shaft Lock Pin
10. Clutch Packs

121016 Courtesy of Chrysler Motors.

Fig. 1: Exploded View of Dana Trac-Lok Differential

1991 DRIVE AXLES
7 1/4" Ring Gear

Dakota

DESCRIPTION

On 4WD models, front axle assembly is hypoid gear type. Assembly has a vacuum-operated shift motor for engaging and disengaging front driving axles. A small metal tag attached to axle housing cover identifies axle ratio.

On 2WD and 4WD models, rear axle assembly is hypoid gear type. Models equipped with Rear Wheel Anti-Lock (RWAL) brakes use a sensor mounted on the differential housing and an exciter ring pressed onto the differential case for speed sensing.

FRONT & REAR AXLE RATIO IDENTIFICATION

Application	Ratio
7 1/4" Ring Gear	2.76:1, 2.94:1, 3.23:1, 3.55:1

LUBRICATION

CAUTION: If front or rear axle is submerged in water, axle lubricant MUST be replaced immediately to avoid premature failure due to contamination.

Use Multipurpose Gear Lubricant (MIL-L-2105-B/API GL-5). Lubricant level should be between 1/4" (6.4 mm) and 1/2" (12.8 mm) below level of filler plug hole.

REMOVAL & INSTALLATION

FRONT AXLE ASSEMBLY

Removal (Left Axle Shaft) – 1) Raise and support vehicle. Loosen wheel lug nuts, and remove cotter pin, nut lock and spring washer from stub shaft. Remove hub nut and washer. Remove wheel and tire. Disconnect left axle shaft inner tripot joint housing from axle shaft flange. Support axle shaft, and separate stub shaft splines from hub bearing splines. DO NOT pull on boot. Remove axle shaft.

2) Clean area where differential housing cover mates with differential housing. Loosen housing cover bolts, and drain lubricant from housing. Remove housing cover. Rotate differential case so differential pinion gear mate shaft lock screw is accessible.

3) Remove lock screw and pinion gear mate shaft from differential case. *See Fig. 1.* Force left axle shaft toward center of vehicle, and remove axle shaft "C" lock from recessed groove in axle shaft. Remove axle shaft from differential housing. DO NOT damage axle shaft bearing, which remains in housing.

4) Inspect axle shaft bearing contact surfaces for brinelling, excessive wear or damage. If any of these conditions exist, replace axle shaft and bearing. Remove axle shaft seal from end of housing bore. Remove axle shaft bearing if it appears damaged or excessively worn. Remove axle shaft bearing using Bearing Remover (C-4167) and a slide hammer.

Installation – 1) Install new seal and bearing in housing with Bearing Installer (C-4203). When installer contacts housing flange face, seal is positioned at correct depth in bore. Lubricate bearing bore and seal lip.

2) Insert axle shaft into housing bore, and engage splines with differential side gear splines. DO NOT damage axle shaft seal lip. With axle shaft in place, insert "C" lock in recessed groove of axle shaft.

3) Force axle shaft outward to seat "C" lock in differential side gear counterbore. Insert differential pinion gear mate shaft into case and through thrust washers and pinion gears. Align hole in shaft with lock screw hole in differential case, and install lock screw. Tighten lock screw to 98 INCH lbs. (11 N.m).

4) Remove residual sealant material from differential housing and cover. Thoroughly clean contact surfaces with mineral spirits, and dry surfaces completely. Apply a 1/16" to 3/32" thick bead of silicone rubber sealant around bolt circle on housing.

5) Install housing cover. Install axle gear ratio identification tag with one cover bolt. Tighten cover bolts to 35 ft. lbs. (47 N.m).

6) Install axle shaft by reversing removal procedure. Remove supports, and lower vehicle until level. Fill differential housing with lubricant, and install fill plug. Lower vehicle, and test axle for correct operation.

Removal (Right & Intermediate Axle Shaft) – 1) Raise and support vehicle. Loosen wheel lug nuts, and remove cotter pin, nut lock and spring washer from stub shaft. Remove hub nut and washer. Remove wheel and tire. Disconnect right axle shaft inner tripot joint housing from axle shaft flange. Support axle shaft, and separate stub shaft splines from hub bearing splines. DO NOT pull on boot. Remove axle shaft.

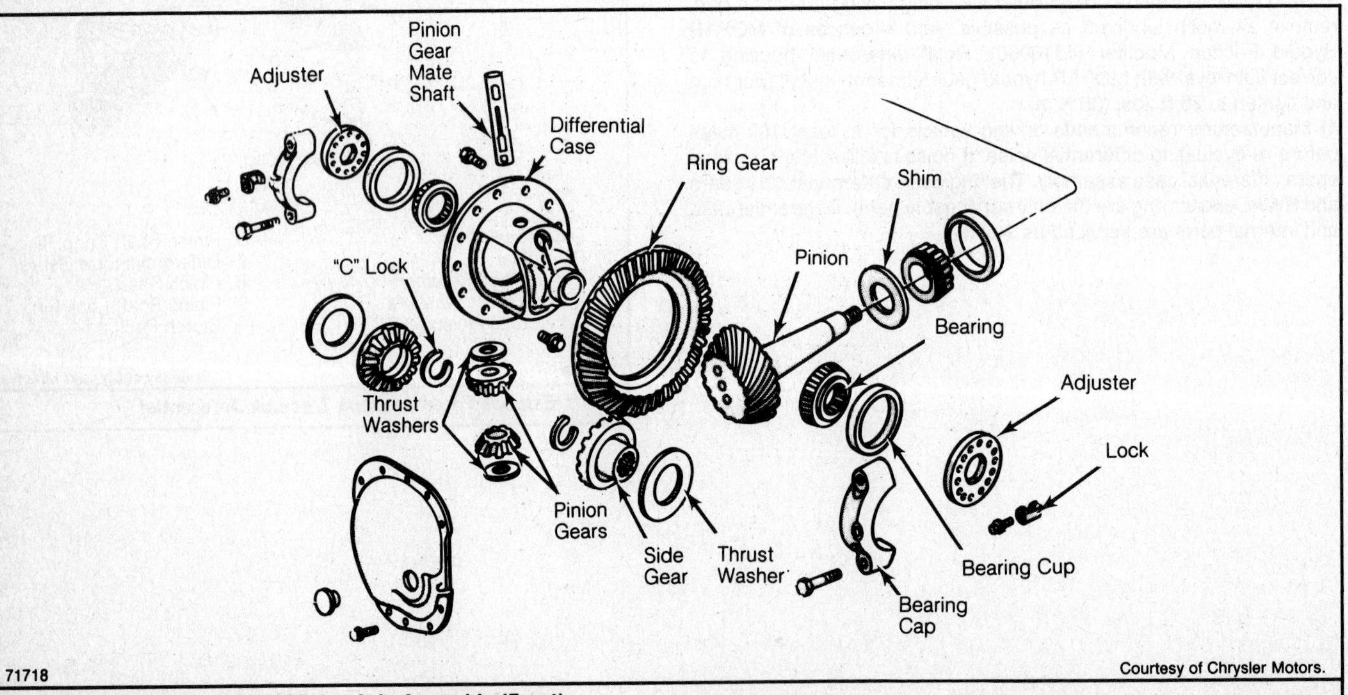
Pinion Gear Mate Shaft
Adjuster
Differential Case
Ring Gear
Shim
"C" Lock
Pinion
Bearing
Thrust Washers
Adjuster
Lock
Pinion Gears
Side Gear
Thrust Washer
Bearing Cup
Bearing Cap
71718
Courtesy of Chrysler Motors.

Fig. 1: Exploded View of 7 1/4" Drive Axle Assembly (Front)

2) Disconnect right axle shaft inner tripot joint housing from axle shaft flange. Clean area where differential housing mates with differential housing cover. Loosen housing cover bolts, and drain lubricant. Remove housing cover. Remove shift motor and housing cover from housing. See REMOVAL (SHIFT MOTOR).

3) Remove bearing seal/retainer attaching screws. Remove outer axle shaft from differential housing. Remove snap ring and splined gear from outer axle shaft. Separate bearing and seal from outer axle shaft. Remove shift collar from shift motor housing. *See Fig. 2*.

4) Rotate differential case so differential pinion gear mate shaft lock screw is accessible. Remove lock screw and pinion gear mate shaft from differential case. Force right axle shaft toward center of vehicle, and remove axle shaft "C" lock from recessed groove in axle shaft.

5) Remove intermediate axle shaft from differential housing and tube. Remove needle bearing from end of intermediate axle shaft using Needle Bearing Remover (D-330). Remove intermediate axle shaft bearing using Bearing Removers (D-354-4 and D-354-1) and Puller (C-637).

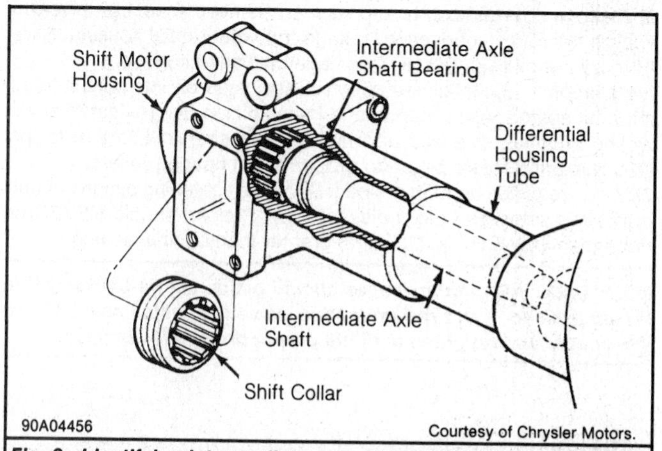

Shift Motor Housing
Intermediate Axle Shaft Bearing
Differential Housing Tube
Intermediate Axle Shaft
Shift Collar
90A04456
Courtesy of Chrysler Motors.

Fig. 2: Identifying Intermediate Axle Shaft, Bearing & Shift Collar

Installation – 1) Install intermediate axle shaft bearing with Bearing Installer (D-354-2) and Driver Handle (C-4171). Install needle bearing in end of intermediate axle shaft with Bearing Installer (D-328) and Driver Handle (C-4171). Lubricate bearing. Insert axle shaft into tube and housing bore, and engage splines with differential side gear splines.

2) With axle shaft in place, insert "C" lock in recessed groove of axle shaft. Force axle shaft outward to seat "C" lock in differential side gear counterbore. Insert differential pinion gear mate shaft into case and through thrust washers and pinion gears. Align hole in shaft with lock screw hole in differential case, and install lock screw. Tighten lock screw to 98 INCH lbs. (11 N.m).

3) Install shift collar on splined end of intermediate axle shaft. Install seal/retainer onto outer axle shaft. Press on replacement bearing. Install splined gear and retaining snap ring. Insert outer axle shaft into shift motor housing. Tighten attaching screws to 17 ft. lbs. (23 N.m). Install shift motor. See REMOVAL (SHIFT MOTOR). Ensure shift fork is correctly engaged in shift collar groove.

4) Remove residual sealant material from differential housing and cover. Thoroughly clean contact surfaces with mineral spirits, and dry surfaces completely. Apply a 1/16" to 3/32" thick bead of silicone rubber sealant around bolt circle on housing cover.

5) Install housing cover. Install axle gear ratio identification tag with one cover bolt. Tighten cover bolts to 35 ft. lbs. (47 N.m). Install axle shaft by reversing removal procedure. Remove supports, and lower vehicle until level. Fill differential housing with lubricant, and install fill plug. Lower vehicle, and test axle for correct operation.

Removal (Shift Motor) – 1) Disconnect vacuum hoses to shift motor. Disconnect indicator light harness connector. Remove shift motor housing cover and gasket. *See Fig. 3*. Remove "E" clips from shift motor armature.

2) Remove shift motor and shift fork from cover. Remove "O" ring seal from shift motor. Remove pads from shift fork. Clean and inspect all components. Replace any worn or damaged component.

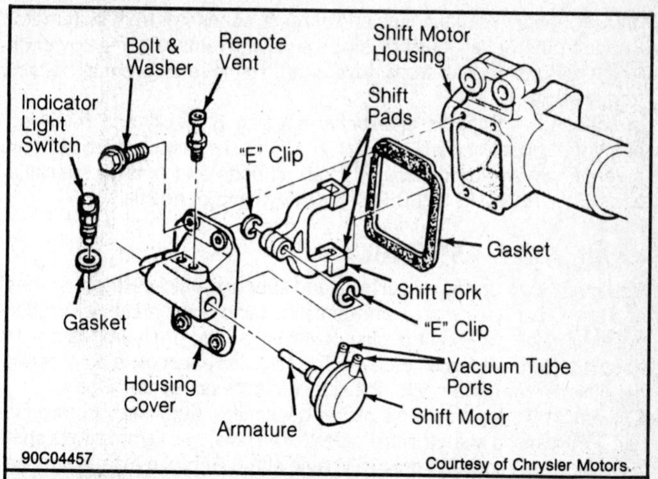

Bolt & Washer
Remote Vent
Shift Motor Housing
Indicator Light Switch
Shift Pads
"E" Clip
Gasket
Shift Fork
Gasket
"E" Clip
Vacuum Tube Ports
Housing Cover
Shift Motor
Armature
90C04457
Courtesy of Chrysler Motors.

Fig. 3: Exploded View of Shift Motor Components

Installation – 1) Install a replacement "O" ring seal on shift motor. Install replacement pads on shift fork bore. Install "E" clips on shift motor. Install shift motor cover using a new gasket. Ensure shift fork is correctly engaged in shift collar groove.

2) Install and tighten cover attaching screws to 10 ft. lbs. (14 N.m). Connect vacuum hoses to shift motor ports and harness connector to indicator light switch on shift motor housing cover.

Removal (Drive Pinion Gear Shaft & Seal) – 1) Raise and support vehicle. Mark front propeller shaft, front propeller shaft "U" joint, drive pinion gear shaft yoke and pinion stem for reassembly reference. Disconnect propeller shaft, and support aside.

2) Shift axle to 2WD operation to prevent any wheel or brake drag from causing a possible false bearing preload measurement. Using an INCH lb. torque wrench, turn pinion in both directions for several revolutions. Measure and record pinion bearing preload.

3) Remove drive pinion nut and washer. Remove yoke. Lower front of vehicle to prevent lubrication leakage from differential housing. Carefully pry out oil seal; DO NOT damage machined surface.

Installation – 1) Install new pinion oil seal squarely into bore in housing until seated. Align marks, and install pinion flange. Install pinion washer (convex side out) and nut. Tighten shaft nut to 210 ft. lbs. (286 N.m), and rotate pinion to properly seat bearing rollers.

2) Measure pinion bearing preload. Continue tightening pinion nut until preload is same as before disassembly. Preload should NEVER be more than 10 INCH lbs. (1.1 N.m) greater than original setting.

NOTE: Under NO circumstances should pinion nut be backed off to lessen preload. If desired preload is exceeded, install new collapsible spacer and retighten nut until proper preload is obtained.

3) Install front propeller shaft with reference marks aligned. Tighten "U" joint yoke clamp screws to 14 ft. lbs. (19 N.m). Check differential housing lubricant level, adding lubricant if necessary. Road test vehicle.

Removal (CV Boots) – Remove axle shafts from vehicle. Remove clamps holding boot to CV joint and shaft. Remove CV joint from axle shaft. See INNER CV JOINT and OUTER CV JOINT under OVERHAUL. Remove boot from axle shaft.

Installation – 1) CV joint boot uses 2 sizes of ladder-type clamps. Clamp Installer (C-4124) is used to tighten and cut strap clamps.

2) Slide small clamp onto axle shaft. Slide small end of boot onto axle shaft. Position small end of boot at same position on axle as old boot. Position clamp evenly in groove on axle boot. Crimp using installer.

3) Fill boot with lubricant included in boot kit. Install CV joint onto end of axle shaft. Slide boot over edge of CV joint, and clean off excess lubricant. Position clamp into groove on boot. Crimp using installer.

Removal (Differential Housing) – 1) Raise and support vehicle. Remove skid plate. Disconnect axle shafts from axle shaft flanges. Remove front drive shaft from transfer case output shaft flange.

1991 DRIVE AXLES
7 1/4" Ring Gear (Cont.)

2) Disconnect vacuum hoses and harness connector from shift motor. Support differential housing using a jack, and remove bolts. Lower differential housing with front drive shaft. Remove differential housing from vehicle.

Installation – Support differential housing on jack, and raise into position. Loosely install all bolts and nuts. To complete installation, reverse removal procedure. Tighten all bolts and nuts to specifications. See TORQUE SPECIFICATIONS at end of article.

REAR AXLE ASSEMBLY

Removal (Axle Shaft) – 1) Raise and support vehicle. Remove wheel and tire. Clean area where differential housing cover mates with differential housing. Loosen housing cover bolts, and drain lubricant from housing. Remove housing cover. Rotate differential case so differential pinion gear mate shaft lock screw is accessible. *See Fig. 4.*

2) Remove lock screw and pinion gear mate shaft from differential case. Force axle shaft toward center of vehicle, and remove axle shaft "C" lock from recessed groove in axle shaft. Remove axle shaft from differential housing. DO NOT damage axle shaft bearing, which remains in housing.

3) Inspect axle shaft bearing contact surfaces for brinelling, excessive wear or damage. If any of these conditions exist, replace axle shaft and bearing. Remove axle shaft seal from end of housing bore. Remove axle shaft bearing if it appears damaged or excessively worn. Remove axle shaft bearing using Bearing Remover (C-4167) and a slide hammer.

Installation – 1) Install new seal and bearing in housing using Bearing Installer (C-4203). When installer contacts housing flange face, seal will be positioned at correct depth in bore. Lubricate bearing bore and seal lip.

2) Insert axle shaft into housing bore, and engage splines with differential side gear splines. DO NOT damage axle shaft seal lip. With axle shaft in place, insert "C" lock in recessed groove of axle shaft.

3) Force axle shaft outward to seat "C" lock in differential side gear counterbore. Insert differential pinion gear mate shaft into case and through thrust washers and pinion gears. Align hole in shaft with lock screw hole in differential case, and install lock screw. Tighten lock screw to 98 INCH lbs. (11 N.m).

4) Remove residual sealant material from differential housing and cover. Thoroughly clean contact surfaces with mineral spirits, and dry surfaces completely. Apply a 1/16" to 3/32" thick bead of silicone rubber sealant around bolt circle on housing.

5) Install housing cover. Install axle gear ratio identification tag with one cover bolt. Tighten cover bolts to 35 ft. lbs. (47 N.m). Remove supports, and lower vehicle until level. Fill differential housing with lubricant, and install fill plug. Lower vehicle, and test axle for correct operation.

Removal (Drive Pinion Gear Shaft & Seal) – 1) Raise and support vehicle. Mark propeller shaft, drive pinion gear shaft yoke and pinion stem for reassembly reference. Disconnect propeller shaft, and support aside.

2) Using an INCH lb. torque wrench, turn pinion several revolutions in both directions. Measure and record pinion bearing preload.

3) Remove drive pinion nut and washer. Remove yoke. Lower rear of vehicle to prevent lubrication leakage from differential housing. Carefully pry out oil seal; DO NOT damage machined surface.

Installation – 1) Install new pinion oil seal squarely into bore in housing until seated. Align marks, and install pinion flange. Install pinion washer (convex side out) and nut. Tighten shaft nut to 210 ft. lbs. (286 N.m), and rotate pinion to properly seat bearing rollers.

2) Measure pinion bearing preload. Continue tightening pinion nut until preload is same as before disassembly. Preload should NEVER be more than 10 INCH lbs. (1.1 N.m) greater than original setting.

NOTE: Under NO circumstances should pinion nut be backed off to lessen preload. If desired preload is exceeded, install new collapsible spacer and retighten nut until proper preload is obtained.

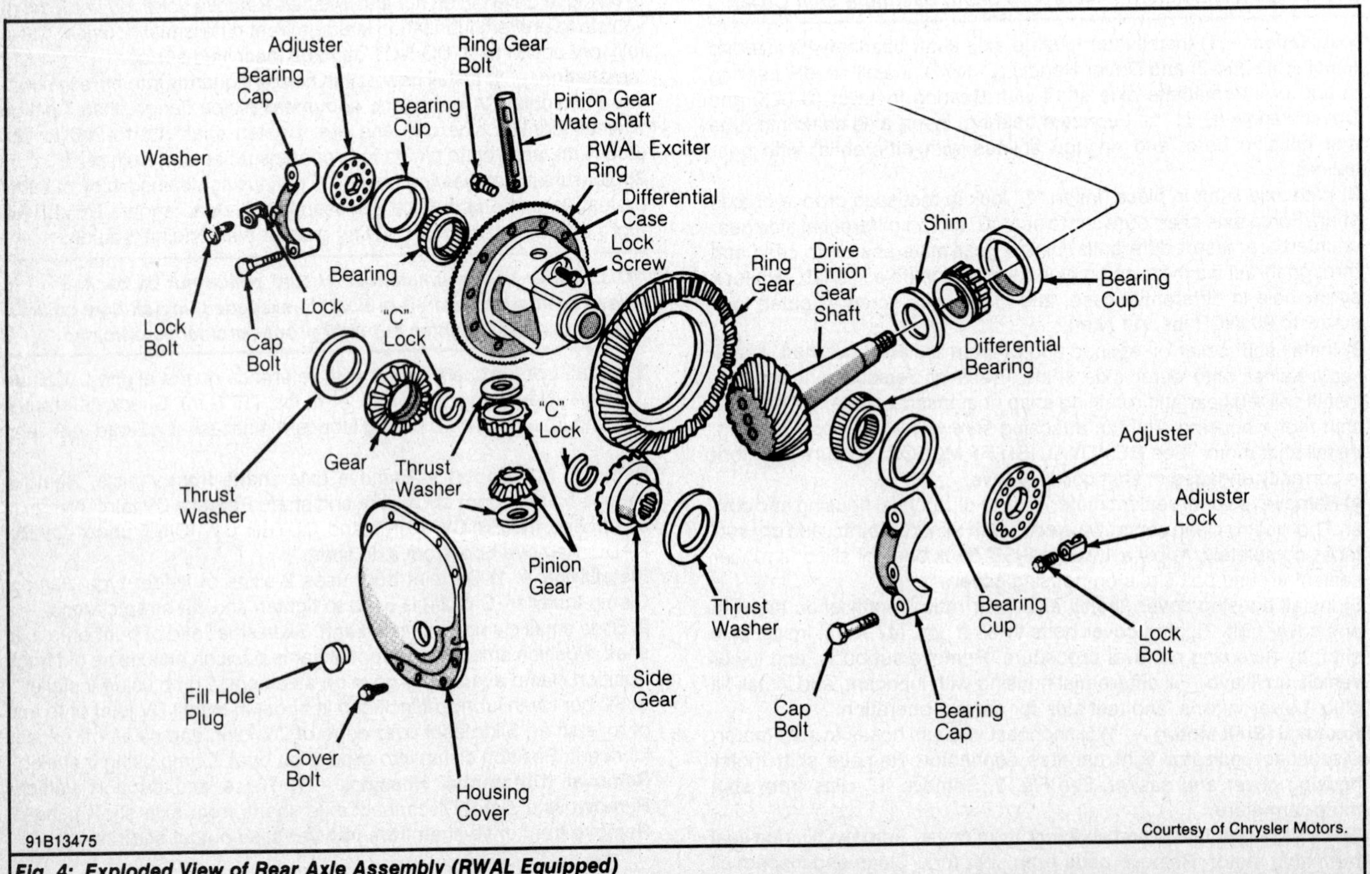
Adjuster
Bearing Cap
Ring Gear Bolt
Bearing Cup
Pinion Gear Mate Shaft
RWAL Exciter Ring
Washer
Differential Case
Lock Screw
Bearing
Lock
Lock Bolt
Cap Bolt
"C" Lock
Ring Gear
Drive Pinion Gear Shaft
Shim
Bearing Cup
Differential Bearing
Gear
"C" Lock
Thrust Washer
Thrust Washer
Adjuster
Adjuster Lock
Pinion Gear
Thrust Washer
Bearing Cup
Lock Bolt
Side Gear
Cap Bolt
Bearing Cap
Fill Hole Plug
Cover Bolt
Housing Cover
91B13475
Courtesy of Chrysler Motors.

Fig. 4: Exploded View of Rear Axle Assembly (RWAL Equipped)

3) Install drive shaft with reference marks aligned. Tighten "U" joint yoke clamp screws to 14 ft. lbs. (19 N.m). Check differential housing lubricant level; add lubricant if necessary. Road test vehicle.

Removal & Installation (Differential Housing) – 1) Raise and support vehicle. Block brake pedal in up position. Remove rear wheels. DO NOT remove brake drums. Disconnect brake lines at wheel cylinders and cap lines to prevent fluid loss. Remove differential vent hose from brake tee fitting.

2) Remove brake tee fitting bolt, and disengage brake lines from axle housing clips. Disconnect parking brake cables. Disconnect propeller shaft, and support aside. Remove shock absorber attaching bolts.

3) Remove rear spring "U" bolt nuts. Remove "U" bolts and spring brackets. Carefully lower axle assembly from vehicle.

4) To install axle, reverse removal procedure. On 2WD vehicles, tighten "U"bolt nuts to 65 ft. lbs. (88 N.m). On 4WD vehicles, tighten "U" bolt nuts to 110 ft. lbs. (149 N.m). Bleed and adjust brakes. Check differential fluid level; add fluid if necessary.

OVERHAUL

INNER CV JOINT

Disassembly – 1) Remove CV axle shaft. Clamp axle shaft in vise. Remove and discard boot clamps. Pull boot back to reach tripot retainer assembly. Move axle shaft toward end of CV housing, and use hammer to tap axle to remove end cap.

2) Remove outer snap ring from axle shaft groove. Remove tripot by hand. If necessary, use brass punch to tap tripot body. Remove housing and boot.

Reassembly – 1) Install new boot on axle shaft. Install CV housing. Slide tripot onto axle shaft, chamfered side first. Flat side of tripot should be next to retaining ring groove. Using grease in boot kit, put 2 of 3 packets into boot. Third packet will go into CV housing.

2) Install retaining ring. Place boot over retaining groove in housing. Clamp boot in position using Clamp Installer (C-4653). Install end cap.

OUTER CV JOINT

Disassembly – 1) Remove CV axle shaft from vehicle. Remove and discard boot clamps. Wipe away grease so CV joint body edge is visible. Hold axle shaft in soft jaws of vise. Using soft hammer, give top of CV joint body a sharp blow to break body loose from internal circlip in groove at end of shaft.

2) Wear sleeve on outer CV housing is a wiping surface for hub bearing seal. If wear sleeve is bent or damaged, pry sleeve away from machined ledge of CV joint. Remove and discard circlip from shaft groove.

3) If shaft is damaged, remove heavy spacer ring from inner groove. If joint was operating properly, replace boots only. If joint was noisy or badly worn, replace complete joint. Replace boot whenever joint is replaced.

4) Wipe grease off outer CV joint, and mark inner race (cross), cage and housing with paint. Position joint vertically in vise, using soft jaws to clamp on splined shaft. Press down on one side of inner race to tilt cage, and remove ball from opposite side. Remove all balls.

CAUTION: DO NOT hit cage when using hammer and drift to loosen CV joint.

5) If joint is tight, use brass drift and hammer to tap inner race and remove balls. Tilt cage and inner race assembly to vertical position.

6) Remove inner race and cage assembly by pulling up and away from housing. Turn inner race 90 degrees to cage. Align elongated cage window with one of spherical lands on race. Raise land to cage window, and remove inner race by swinging it out of cage.

Inspection – Check grease for contamination. Wash all parts in solvent, and dry with compressed air. Inspect races, splined shaft and nut threads for damage. Inspect balls and cage for damage.

Reassembly – 1) Position new wear sleeve on joint housing machined ledge. Lightly oil all components before reassembly. Align parts according to paint markings.

2) Insert one inner race (cross) into cage window, and feed race into cage. Pivot inner race to fully assemble cage and race. Align opposing elongated cage windows with housing land. Feed cage assembly into housing. Pivot cage 90 degrees to complete installation.

3) Counterbore of inner race should face outward from joint. Apply lubricant to ball races from packet in boot kit.

4) Distribute grease equally between all sides of ball grooves. Insert balls into raceways by tilting cage and inner race assembly. Fasten boot to shaft. Insert new circlip from shaft groove kit.

5) Position outer joint on splined end of axle shaft. Put hub nut on stub axle. Engage splines, and use mallet to tap sharply on hub nut. Ensure circlip is properly seated by trying to pull joint off shaft.

6) Install large end of boot over joint housing, ensuring boot is not twisted. Clamp boot to housing using Clamp Installer (C-4653).

DIFFERENTIAL

NOTE: Differential overhaul procedures for front and rear axle are identical. It is not necessary to remove complete front axle assembly to overhaul differential.

Disassembly – 1) Mark propeller shaft and "U" joint for reassembly. Remove propeller shaft, and support aside. Drain lubricant, and remove housing cover.

2) Remove differential pinion lock bolt and pinion. On rear axle, push left axle shaft inward, and remove "C" lock. Pull left axle shaft out of differential housing. Remove right axle in same manner.

3) On front axle, remove shift motor and housing cover. Remove bearing seal retainer attaching screws. Remove right axle shaft from differential. Remove snap ring and splined gear from right axle shaft. Separate bearing and seal from right axle shaft. Remove shift collar from shift motor housing.

4) Force intermediate shaft toward center of vehicle, and remove axle shaft "C" lock. Install pinion gear mate shaft and lock screw. Remove intermediate axle shaft.

5) On front and rear axles, measure and record differential side play, ring gear runout and pinion gear shaft preload. Mark differential gear and case at point of maximum runout. Side play should not exist and ring gear runout should not exceed .005" (.13 mm). If ring gear runout exceeds .005" (.13 mm), check differential case flange runout.

6) To check case flange runout, use Hex Adjuster (C-4164). Tighten adjusters until all case side play is eliminated. Remove and discard ring gear bolts (left-hand threads). Using a hammer and brass drift, force ring gear from differential case flange, and remove ring gear.

7) Mount dial indicator to housing, and place dial indicator pointer on ring gear flange of differential case. *See Fig. 5.* Rotate case several times, checking reading on dial indicator. If reading varies more than .003" (.08 mm), replace differential case.

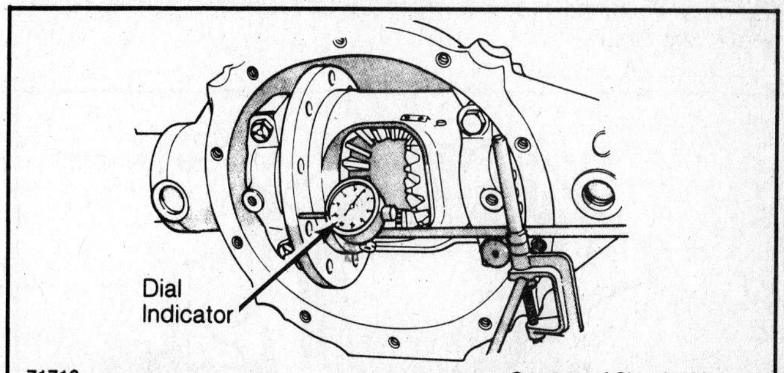

Dial
Indicator

71716 Courtesy of Chrysler Motors.

Fig. 5: Checking Differential Case Flange Runout

8) Remove drive pinion flange using Flange Holder (C-3281), and pry out seal. Mark side bearing caps and axle housing for reassembly reference. Remove adjuster locks. Loosen, but DO NOT remove, bearing caps. Insert hex adjuster through axle tube, and loosen hex adjuster on each side.

9) Remove bearing caps, adjusters and differential case assembly. Keep all bearing races and adjusters with their respective bearings. Using soft drift punch and hammer, drive pinion shaft out of housing.

1991 DRIVE AXLES
7 1/4" Ring Gear (Cont.)

NOTE: Bearings, races, collapsible spacer and shim(s) must be replaced after driving out pinion.

10) Using Bearing Remover (C-4306) and Driver Handle (C-4171), drive bearing races out of housing. Remove bearings from pinion shaft using Puller (C-293-PA) and Adapter (C-293-42). Remove shim(s) from behind rear bearing, and record thickness.
11) Mount differential case assembly in soft-jawed vise. Remove and discard ring gear bolts (left-hand thread). Using soft-faced hammer, drive ring gear off differential case.

NOTE: DO NOT remove ring gear from differential case unless case or gear set is replaced.

Cleaning & Inspection - Clean all components, and inspect for wear. Inspect all bearings and races for wear and pitting, and replace as set. Inspect all gear teeth for wear and chipping, and replace as matched set.
Reassembly & Adjustment - 1) Install thrust washers on differential side gears, and position gears in differential case. Place thrust washers on differential pinion gears, and position gears in case so gears are 180 degrees apart when meshed with side gears.
2) Rotate side gears until holes in pinion gears are in alignment with pinion shaft holes in case. Install differential pinion shaft. Ensure hole in pinion shaft is aligned with lock bolt hole in case. Install lock bolt, and tighten to 90 INCH lbs. (10 N.m).
3) Ensure contact surface of ring gear and case flange is clean and free of all nicks and burrs. Using an Arkansas stone, remove any sharp areas from chamfer on inside diameter of ring gear.
4) Heat ring gear using heat lamp, hot oil or water. Temperature of ring gear must not exceed 300°F (149°C). DO NOT use torch to heat ring gear. Install 3 equally spaced pilot studs on ring gear. Place heated ring gear on jaws of vise, and install case using new left-hand threaded bolts.
5) Tighten ring gear-to-case bolts alternately and evenly to specifications. Install side bearings on case using Bearing Installer (C-3716-A) and Driver Handle (C-4171). See TORQUE SPECIFICATIONS table at end of article.
Drive Pinion Depth - 1) Install both drive pinion bearing races into axle housing bores. Assemble Pinion Locating Spacer (SP-3244) over body of Main Stem (SP-5385) followed by rear pinion bearing cone. Insert assembly into axle carrier from rear.
2) Position bearing and tools in housing. Install Locating Sleeve (SP-3245) and drive pinion gear shaft front bearing. Install Compression Sleeve (SP-3194-B), Centralizing Washer (SP-534) and Compression Nut (SP-3193).
3) Install Gauge Block (SP-3250) on end of main body (SP-5385). Install Cap Screw (SP-536), and tighten securely using Wrench (SP-531). Position Cross Bar Arbor (SP-3243) in axle housing bearing seats. *See Fig. 6.*

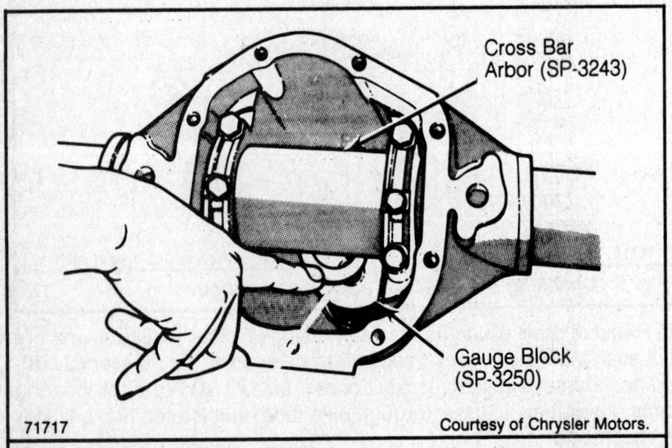
Cross Bar
Arbor (SP-3243)
Gauge Block
(SP-3250)
71717
Courtesy of Chrysler Motors.

Fig. 6: Measuring Pinion Depth

4) Use feeler gauge to determine proper thickness of shims so they will fit snugly between arbor and gauge block. Fit must be snug, but not excessively tight.
5) To select correct shim pack, read markings on end of pinion head. When marking is minus, add that amount to feeler gauge thickness to obtain thickness of correct shim pack. When marking is plus, subtract that amount of thickness. Remove all tools.

Pinion Bearing Preload - 1) Place selected shim on pinion shaft. Press bearing on pinion shaft using Press Sleeve (C-3717) and an arbor press. Lubricate pinion and bearing with gear oil.
2) Insert drive pinion assembly through axle housing. Install new collapsible spacer and front pinion bearing onto stem of gear. Install pinion flange using Installer (C-3718) and Holder (C-3281).

NOTE: DO NOT collapse spacer. If spacer is collapsed, new spacer must be installed.

3) Remove pinion flange. Install new pinion oil seal using Seal Installer (C-4076). Align marks, and install pinion flange, washer (convex side out) and nut. While rotating pinion assembly to ensure proper bearing seating, tighten pinion flange nut until all end play is removed.
4) Tighten drive pinion nut to specification. See TORQUE SPECIFICATIONS at end of article. Measure pinion bearing preload by rotating pinion through several revolutions using INCH lb. torque wrench. Continue tightening pinion flange nut in small increments until correct bearing preload is obtained. DO NOT back off nut to lessen bearing preload. If desired preload is exceeded, install new collapsible spacer, and retighten nut until proper preload is obtained.
Backlash & Side Bearing Preload - 1) Observe 2 precautions when checking and adjusting ring gear backlash and differential bearing preload:

- Index gears so same teeth are meshed during all backlash measurements. Permissible backlash variation is .003" (.08 mm). For example, if backlash at minimum point is .006" (.15 mm) and backlash at maximum point is .009" (.23 mm), variation is correct.
- Maintain specified adjuster torque to obtain accurate differential bearing preload.

2) Using Hex Adjuster (C-4164), turn each adjuster until bearing free play is eliminated with approximately .01" (.25 mm) backlash. Seat differential roller bearings, as bearings do not always move with adjusters. To ensure accurate adjustment, bearings must be seated by oscillating drive pinion 1/2 turn in each direction 5-10 times each time adjusters are moved.
3) Install dial indicator on cover flange . Position indicator stem against drive side of ring gear. Check backlash every 90 degrees to find point of minimum backlash. Mark each position so backlash readings will be taken with same teeth meshed. Rotate ring gear to point of minimum backlash.
4) Loosen right adjuster and tighten left adjuster until backlash is .003-.004" (.08-.10 mm) with each adjuster tightened to 10 ft. lbs. (14 N.m). Seat bearings as before. Tighten bearing cap bolts to 45 ft. lbs. (61 N.m). Using hex adjuster, tighten right adjuster to 70 ft. lbs. (95 N.m). Seat bearings, and continue to tighten right adjuster until torque remains constant at 70 ft. lbs. (95 N.m).
5) Check backlash again using indicator. If backlash is not between .003-.006" (.08-.15 mm), increase torque on right adjuster, and seat bearings. Continue operation until backlash is .003-.006" (.08-.15 mm). Tighten left adjuster to 70 ft. lbs. (95 N.m), and seat bearings. With adjustments completed, install adjuster locks. Ensure lock teeth are engaged in adjuster threads. Tighten lock bolts to 90 INCH lbs. (10 N.m).
Final Inspection & Assembly - With pinion bearing preload and ring gear backlash properly adjusted, check tooth pattern contact. When pattern is satisfactory, install axle shafts, wheels, tires and axle housing cover. Refill with hypoid gear lubricant.

1991 DRIVE AXLES
7 1/4" Ring Gear (Cont.)

AXLE ASSEMBLY SPECIFICATIONS

AXLE ASSEMBLY SPECIFICATIONS

Application	Specifications
Maximum Ring Gear Runout	.005" (.13 mm)
Maximum Differential Case Flange Runout	.003" (.08 mm)
Pinion Bearing Preload	
New Bearings	10-20 INCH lbs. (1.1-2.3 N.m)
Used Rear & New Front Bearings	[1] 10 INCH lbs. (1.1 N.m)
Ring Gear Backlash	.003-.006" (.08-.15 mm)

[1] – Maximum increase over original preload before disassembly.

TORQUE SPECIFICATIONS

TORQUE SPECIFICATIONS

Application	Ft. Lbs. (N.m)
Axle Housing Cover Bolt	35 (47)
Axle Shaft Nut	190 (258)
Axle "U" Bolt Nut	
2WD	65 (88)
4WD	110 (149)
Drive Pinion Nut (Minimum)	210 (286)
Inner Axle Flange Bolt	65 (88)
Insulator-To-Differential Housing Nut	75 (102)
Insulator-To-Shift Motor Housing Nut	75 (102)
Propeller Shaft Nut	65 (88)
Ring Gear-To-Differential Case Bolt [1]	70 (95)
Side Bearing Cap Bolt	45 (61)
Skid Plate Bolts	17 (23)
Support Bracket-To-Adapter Bolt	65 (88)
Support Bracket-To-Shift Motor Housing Bolt	65 (88)
"U" Joint Yoke Clamp Screws	14 (19)
Wheel Lug Nut	85 (115)
	INCH Lbs.
Adjuster Lock Bolt	90 (10)
Differential Case Lock Screw	98 (11)

[1] – Left-hand threaded bolt.

1991 DRIVE AXLES
8 1/4", 8 3/8" & 9 1/4" Ring Gear

Dakota, Pickup, Ramcharger, RWD Van

DESCRIPTION

Axle assembly is hypoid gear type with an integral carrier housing. It is used on light-duty vehicles with semi-floating axles. Pinion bearing preload adjustment is made with collapsible spacer. Differential bearing preload adjustment is made with adjusting nuts seated on the bearing races. Removable housing cover permits inspection and minor servicing of differential without removal from vehicle.

NOTE: If vehicle is equipped with Dana axle assembly, see DANA FULL-FLOATING AXLES article.

Vehicles equipped with Rear Wheel Anti-Lock (RWAL) brakes have an exciter ring pressed onto differential case next to ring gear, and a RWAL sensor mounted in differential housing. A small metal tag attached to rear axle housing cover bolt identifies axle ratio.

REAR AXLE RATIO IDENTIFICATION

Application	Ratio
8 1/4" Ring Gear	2.94:1, 3.21:1, 3.55:1, 3.90:1, 4.10:1
8 3/8" Ring Gear	2.94:1, 3.21:1, 3.55:1, 3.90:1
9 1/4" Ring Gear	3.21:1, 3.55:1, 3.90:1

LUBRICATION

CAUTION: If axle has been submerged in water, axle lubricant MUST be replaced immediately to avoid premature failure due to contamination.

Use Multipurpose Gear Lubricant (MIL-L-2105-B/API GL-5). Lubricant level should be 1/4-1/2" (6.4-12.8 mm) below level of filler hole.

REMOVAL & INSTALLATION

AXLE SHAFTS & BEARINGS

NOTE: During repairs, DO NOT heat (with torch) or hammer on bearing cones, cups, bores or journals.

Removal – 1) Raise vehicle and remove wheel, tire and brake drum. Clean all dirt and foreign material from area of housing cover. Loosen housing cover attaching bolts to drain lubricant. Remove housing cover. Remove pinion gear mate shaft lock bolt and differential pinion gear mate shaft.

2) Force axle shaft toward center of vehicle. Remove "C" lock from groove in axle shaft. Pull axle shaft out of housing, using care not to damage roller bearing. Remove oil seal from housing bore.

3) To remove axle shaft bearing on 8 1/4" and 8 3/8", use Bearing Puller (C-4167). On 9 1/4" models, use Bearing Puller (C-4828). On 8 1/4" and 8 3/8" models, attach slide hammer to puller and remove axle shaft bearing. On 9 1/4" models, use a wrench to turn threaded shaft through puller bar and remove axle shaft bearing. On all models, if either axle or bearing shows any signs of brinnelling, spalling or pitting, replace component.

Installation – 1) Clean all parts thoroughly. Install axle shaft bearing using Bearing Installer (C-4198) for 8 1/4" and 8 3/8". Use Bearing Installer (C-4826) with Handle (C-4171) for 9 1/4". Make sure bearing is bottomed against shoulder in bore. Lubricate and install a new oil seal in housing bore.

2) Slide axle shaft into place. Install "C" lock into groove in axle shaft. Pull outward on axle shaft so that "C" lock seats in counterbore of differential side gear.

3) Install differential pinion gear mate shaft. Align hole in shaft with lock bolt hole in case. Install pinion gear mate shaft lock bolt and tighten to 100 INCH lbs. (11 N.m). Apply a 1/16" bead of Silicone Rubber Sealant (4318025) to housing cover sealing surface. Install housing

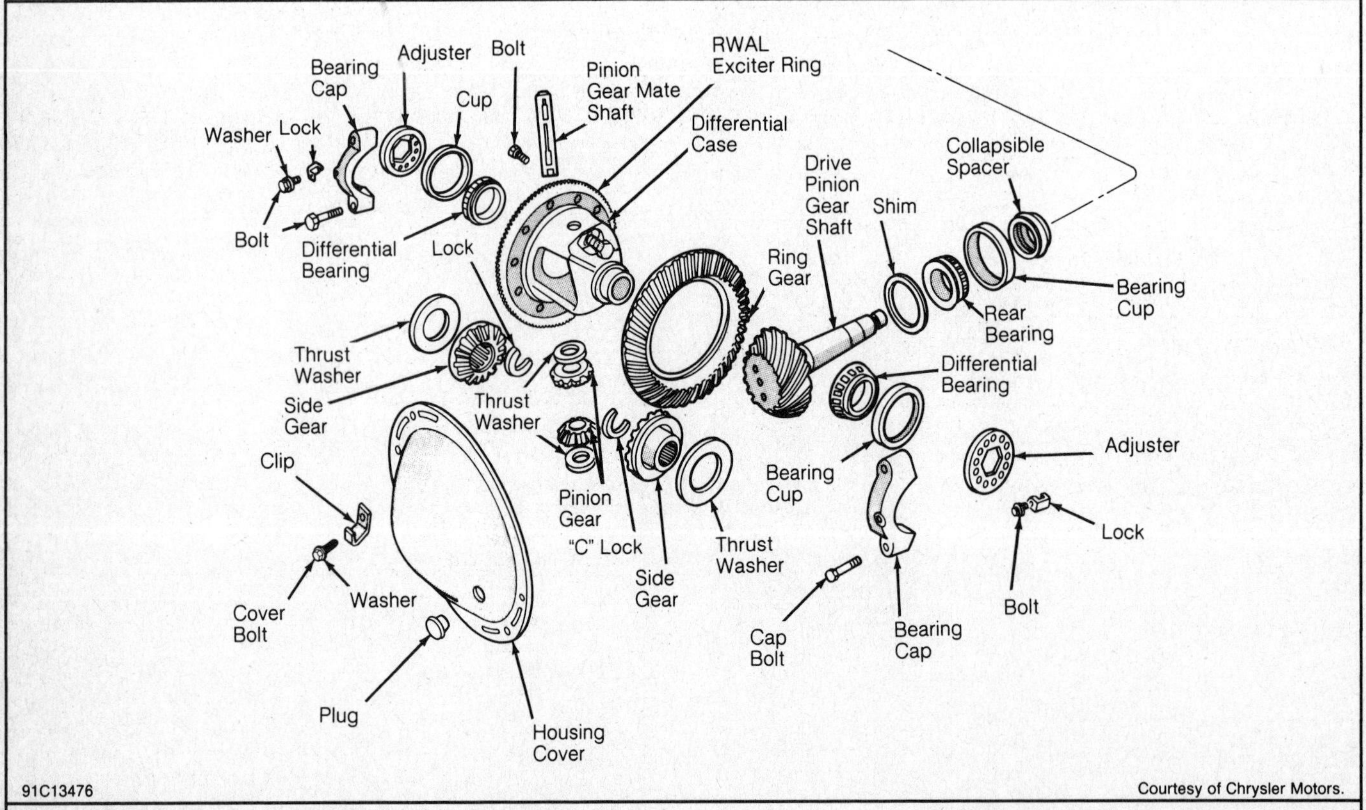
Bearing Cap
Adjuster
Bolt
Cup
Pinion Gear Mate Shaft
RWAL Exciter Ring
Differential Case
Washer
Lock
Bolt
Differential Bearing
Lock
Drive Pinion Gear Shaft
Shim
Collapsible Spacer
Ring Gear
Bearing Cup
Rear Bearing
Thrust Washer
Side Gear
Thrust Washer
Differential Bearing
Clip
Pinion Gear
"C" Lock
Side Gear
Thrust Washer
Bearing Cup
Adjuster
Lock
Bolt
Cover Bolt
Washer
Plug
Housing Cover
Cap Bolt
Bearing Cap
91C13476
Courtesy of Chrysler Motors.

Fig. 1: Exploded View of 8 1/4", 8 3/8" & 9 1/4" Drive Axle Assembly

1991 DRIVE AXLES
8 1/4", 8 3/8" & 9 1/4" Ring Gear (Cont.)

cover and identification tag. Tighten bolts to specification. See TORQUE SPECIFICATIONS table at end of article.

PINION FLANGE & SEAL

Removal - 1) Raise vehicle, mark propeller shaft universal joint, drive pinion flange and pinion stem for reassembly. Disconnect propeller shaft and tie out of way. Remove rear wheels and brake drums to prevent false preload reading.

2) Using INCH lb. torque wrench, rotate pinion nut to measure pinion bearing preload. Record preload reading. Using Pinion Flange Holder (C-3281), remove drive pinion nut and washer. Pull off flange using 2-jaw puller. Pry out oil seal, taking care not to damage machined surface.

Installation - 1) Examine drive pinion for any burrs or excessive wear. Remove burrs with crocus cloth and replace drive pinion gear if excessively worn. Install new pinion oil seal using Seal Installer (C-4076) for 8 1/4" and 8 3/8". Use Seal Installer (C-3980 or C-4109) for 9 1/4".

2) Align marks and install pinion flange. Install pinion washer (convex side out) and nut. Use pinion flange holder and tighten nut to specifications. See TORQUE SPECIFICATIONS table at end of article. Rotate pinion to properly seat bearing rollers.

3) Measure pinion bearing preload. Continue tightening pinion nut until preload is the same as that noted before disassembly. Preload should NEVER be more than 10 INCH lbs. (1.1 N.m) greater than original setting.

CAUTION: Under NO circumstances should pinion nut be backed off to lessen preload. If desired preload is exceeded, install new collapsible spacer, and retighten nut until proper preload is obtained.

AXLE ASSEMBLY

Removal & Installation - 1) Raise vehicle and remove wheels, tires and brake drums. Disconnect brake lines at wheel cylinders and cap to prevent fluid loss. Disconnect differential vent hose. Disconnect parking brake cables. Disconnect RWAL sensor electrical connection (if equipped).

2) Mark propeller shaft universal joint, drive pinion flange and pinion stem for reassembly reference. Disconnect propeller shaft and support to one side. Remove shock absorbers and rear spring "U" bolts. Remove rear axle assembly. To install, reverse removal procedure. Bleed brakes.

OVERHAUL

DISASSEMBLY

NOTE: It is not necessary to remove complete rear axle assembly to overhaul differential.

Differential - 1) Remove wheels and brake drums. Mark propeller shaft and universal joint for reassembly. Remove propeller shaft and support to one side. Drain lubricant and remove housing cover. Remove pinion gear mate shaft lock screw. Remove pinion gear mate shaft.

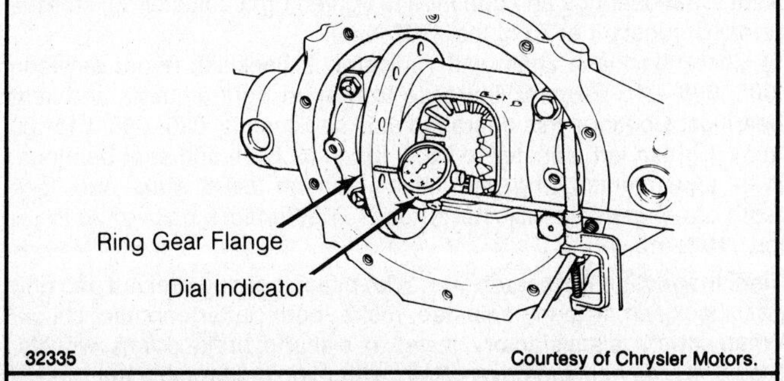
Ring Gear Flange
Dial Indicator
32335
Courtesy of Chrysler Motors.

Fig. 2: Checking Differential Case Flange Runout

2) Force both axle shafts toward center of vehicle and remove "C" locks. Remove axles. Measure and record differential side play, ring gear runout and pinion gear shaft preload. Mark differential gear and case at point of maximum runout. There should be no side play and ring gear runout should not exceed .005" (.13 mm). If ring gear runout exceeded .005" (.13 mm), differential case flange runout must be checked.

3) Tighten adjusters until all case side play is eliminated. Remove ring gear bolts from differential case flange and discard bolts (left-hand thread). Mount dial indicator to housing and place dial indicator pointer on ring gear flange of differential case. *See Fig. 2.*

4) Rotate case several times, checking reading on dial indicator. If reading varies more than .003" (.08 mm), replace differential case. Remove drive pinion flange and seal as previously described. Mark side bearing caps and axle housing for reassembly. Remove adjuster locks. Loosen, but do not remove, bearing caps. Insert hex adjuster through axle tube and loosen hex adjuster on each side.

CAUTION: Use extreme care when removing differential case from vehicle to avoid damage to RWAL exciter ring.

5) Remove bearing caps, adjusters and differential case assembly. Be sure to keep all bearing races and adjusters with their respective bearings. Using soft drift punch and hammer, drive pinion shaft out of housing.

6) Drive bearing races out of housing using hammer and soft drift punch. Remove shim(s) from behind rear race and record thickness. Remove bearing cones from pinion shaft using Puller and Adapter (C-293-PA and C-293-42).

NOTE: DO NOT remove ring gear from differential case unless case, gear set or RWAL exciter ring is being replaced.

7) Mount differential case assembly in soft-jawed vise. Remove and discard ring gear bolts (left-hand thread), if not removed previously. Using soft-faced hammer, drive ring gear off differential case.

8) If RWAL exciter ring is being replaced, use a hammer and punch to drive exciter ring from differential case.

CLEANING & INSPECTION

Differential - Clean all components and inspect for wear. Inspect all bearings and races for wear or pitting and replace as set. Inspect all gear teeth for wear or chipping and replace as matched set only.

REASSEMBLY & ADJUSTMENT

Differential Case Assembly - 1) Install thrust washers on differential side gears and position gears in differential case. Place thrust washers on differential pinion gears and position gears in case so that they are 180 degrees apart when meshed with side gears.

2) Rotate side gears until holes in pinion gears are in alignment with pinion gear mate shaft holes in case. Install differential pinion gear mate shaft. Ensure hole in shaft is aligned with lock bolt hole in case.

3) Ensure contact surface of ring gear and case flange is clean and free of all nicks and burrs. Using an Arkansas stone, remove any sharp areas from chamfer on inside diameter of ring gear.

NOTE: RWAL exciter ring is installed using same heating procedures as ring gear.

4) Heat ring gear using heat lamp, hot oil or water. Temperature of ring gear must not exceed 300°F (149°C). DO NOT use torch to heat ring gear. Install 3 equally spaced pilot studs on ring gear. Place heated ring gear on jaws of vise and install case using new left-hand threaded bolts.

5) Tighten ring gear-to-case bolts alternately and evenly to specification. See TORQUE SPECIFICATIONS table at end of article. Install side bearings on case using Bearing Installer (C-4340 for 8 1/4" and 8 3/8" ring gear, or C-4213 for 9 1/4" ring gear) and Driver (C-4171). Use these tools in conjunction with an arbor press. Lubricate assembly with hypoid gear lubricant.

1991 DRIVE AXLES
8 1/4", 8 3/8" & 9 1/4" Ring Gear (Cont.)

Drive Pinion Depth – 1) Install both drive pinion bearing races into axle housing bores. Assemble Pinion Locating Spacer (SP-6030) over body of Main Stem (SP-5385) followed by rear pinion bearing. Insert assembly into axle housing from rear.

NOTE: All tool numbers indicated in procedure apply to 8 1/4" and 8 3/8" ring gear axles. For equivalent tool numbers for 9 1/4" ring gear axles, see EQUIVALENT TOOL NUMBERS table.

EQUIVALENT TOOL NUMBERS

Application	8 1/4" & 8 3/8"	9 1/4"
Bearing Installer	C-4340	C-4213
Centralizing Washer	SP-534	SP-534
Compression Sleeve	SP-3194-B	SP-535A
Cross Bore Arbor	SP-6029	SP-6018
Gauge Block	SP-5383	SP-6020
Holding Tool	C-3281	C-3281
Main Stem	SP-5385	SP-526
Nut	SP-3193	SP-533
Spacer	SP-5382	SP-1730
Spacer	SP-6030	SP-6017
Washer	SP-6022	SP-6022

2) On 8 1/4" and 8 3/8" assembly, hold spacer and main stem assembly in position. Install front pinion bearing over Spacer (SP-5382) and position over main stem of tool. On 9 1/4" and 9 1/4" HD assemblies, position spacer and main stem assembly in housing. Install front pinion bearing and Washer (SP-6022).

3) Procedure from this point is same for both assemblies, except for tool numbers. See EQUIVALENT TOOL NUMBERS table. Position compression sleeve, centralizing washer, and main screw nut on main stem. Hold compression sleeve with companion flange wrench and tighten nut. Allow tool to rotate as nut is being tightened to prevent damaging bearings and races. *See Fig. 3.*

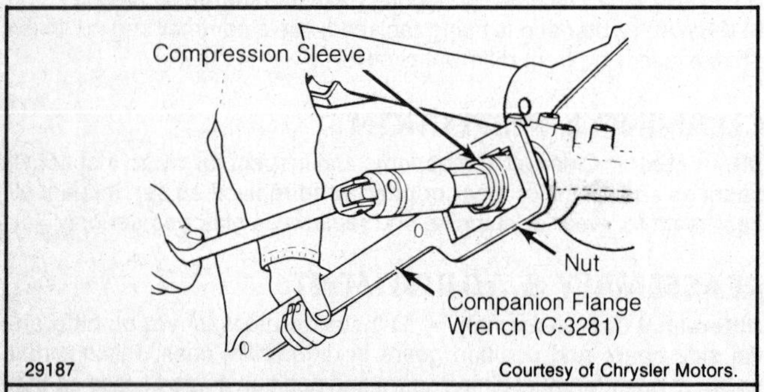
Compression Sleeve
Nut
Companion Flange
Wrench (C-3281)
29187
Courtesy of Chrysler Motors.

Fig. 3: Seating Pinion Bearing Races

4) Loosen tool nut, then retighten to obtain appropriate pinion bearing preload. See AXLE ASSEMBLY SPECIFICATIONS table. Rotate tool after tightening to properly seat pinion bearings. Install Gauge Block (SP-5383 or SP-6020) on main tool and tighten screw.

5) Position Cross Bore Arbor (SP-6029 or SP-6018) in housing side bearing seats and center arbor in bore. *See Fig. 4.* Position bearing caps on carrier pedestals and insert .002" (.051 mm) spacer between arbor and each cap. Install cap bolts and tighten to 10 ft. lbs. (14 N.m).

6) Use feeler gauge to determine proper thickness of shims that will fit snugly between arbor and gauge block. This fit must be snug, but not excessively tight.

7) To select correct shim pack, read markings on end of pinion head. When marking is minus, add that amount of thickness to feeler gauge thickness to obtain thickness of correct shim pack. When marking is plus, subtract that amount of thickness. Remove all tools and rear pinion bearing race from housing.

Pinion Bearing Preload – 1) Place selected shim in pinion shaft bore and reinstall rear pinion bearing cup. Lubricate rear pinion bearing and press into position on drive pinion stem.

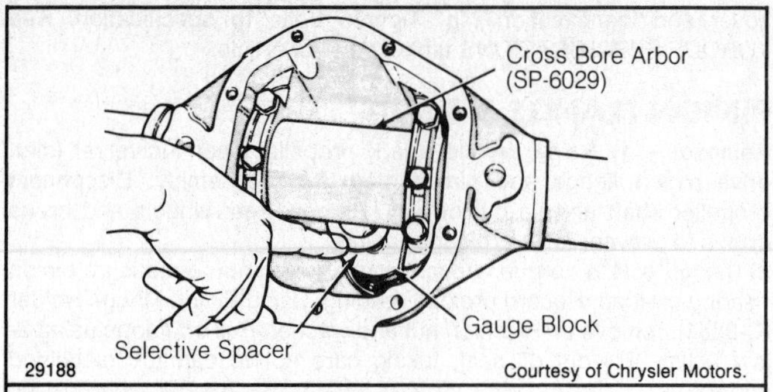
Cross Bore Arbor
(SP-6029)
Gauge Block
Selective Spacer
29188
Courtesy of Chrysler Motors.

Fig. 4: Measuring Shim Pack Thickness

2) Insert drive pinion assembly through axle housing. Install collapsible spacer and front pinion bearing onto stem of gear. Install pinion flange and tighten nut until front bearing is seated.

NOTE: Use care not to collapse spacer. If spacer is collapsed, new spacer must be installed.

3) With front bearing fully seated, remove pinion flange. Install new pinion oil seal. Align marks and install pinion flange, washer (convex side out) and nut. While rotating pinion assembly (to ensure proper bearing seating), tighten pinion flange nut until all end play is removed.

4) Tighten pinion nut to specified torque and measure pinion bearing preload by rotating pinion through several revolutions with INCH lb. torque wrench. Continue tightening pinion flange nut in small increments until correct bearing preload is obtained.

CAUTION: DO NOT back off nut to lessen bearing preload. If desired preload is exceeded, new collapsible spacer must be installed and nut retightened until proper preload is obtained.

Backlash & Side Bearing Preload – 1) There are 2 precautions that must be observed when checking and adjusting ring gear backlash and differential bearing preload.

- Index gears so same teeth are meshed during all backlash measurements. Permissible backlash variation is .003" (.08 mm).
- It is also important to maintain specified adjuster torque to obtain accurate differential bearing preload.

2) Using hex adjuster, turn each adjuster until bearing free play is eliminated with approximately .010" (.25 mm) backlash. Seat differential roller bearings, as bearings do not always move with adjusters. To ensure accurate adjustment, bearings must be seated by oscillating drive pinion 1/2 turn in each direction 5-10 times each time adjusters are moved.

3) Install dial indicator on cover flange. Position indicator stem against drive side of ring gear. Check backlash every 90 degrees to find point of minimum backlash. Mark each position so backlash readings will be taken with same teeth meshed. Rotate ring gear to point of minimum backlash.

4) Loosen right adjuster and tighten left adjuster until backlash is .003-.004" (.08-.10 mm) with each adjuster tightened to 10 ft. lbs. (14 N.m). Seat bearings as previously described. Tighten bearing cap bolts to 70 ft. lbs. (95 N.m) for 8 3/8", and to 100 ft. lbs. (136 N.m) for 8 1/4" and 9 1/4". Using hex adjuster, tighten right adjuster to 75 ft. lbs. (102 N.m). Seat bearings and continue to tighten right adjuster until torque remains constant at 75 ft. lbs. (102 N.m).

5) Check backlash again with indicator. If backlash is not between .006-.008" (.15-.20 mm), increase torque on right adjuster and seat bearings. Continue this operation until backlash is .006-.008" (.15-.20 mm). Tighten left adjuster to 75 ft. lbs. (102 N.m) and seat bearings. With adjustments completed, install adjuster locks. Make sure lock teeth are engaged in adjuster threads. Tighten lock bolts to 90 INCH lbs. (10 N.m).

Final Inspection & Assembly – With pinion bearing preload and ring gear backlash properly adjusted, make tooth pattern contact check. When pattern is satisfactory, install axle shafts, brake drums, wheels, tires and axle housing cover. Refill with hypoid gear lubricant.

1991 DRIVE AXLES
8 1/4", 8 3/8" & 9 1/4" Ring Gear (Cont.)

AXLE ASSEMBLY SPECIFICATIONS

AXLE ASSEMBLY SPECIFICATIONS

Application	Specifications
Maximum Ring Gear Runout	.005" (.13 mm)
Maximum Differential Case	
Flange Runout	.003" (.08 mm)
Pinion Bearing Preload	
New Bearings	
Except 8 1/4"	20-35 INCH lbs. (2.3-4 N.m)
8 1/4"	10-20 INCH lbs. (1.3-2.3 N.m)
Used Rear & New Front Bearing	[1] 10 INCH lbs. (1.3 N.m)
Ring Gear Backlash	.006-.008" (.15-.20 mm)

[1] – Maximum increase over original preload reading before disassembly.

TORQUE SPECIFICATIONS

TORQUE SPECIFICATIONS

Application	Ft. Lbs. (N.m)
Differential Bearing Cap Bolts	
8 3/8" Ring Gear	70 (95)
8 1/4" & 9 1/4" Ring Gear	100 (136)
Drive Pinion Nut (Minimum)	210 (285)
Housing Cover Bolts	35 (47)
Propeller Shaft Bolts	14-17 (19-23)
Ring Gear-To-Differential Case Bolts [1]	70 (95)
RWAL Brake Sensor Cover Screw	18 (24)
Shock Absorber Nuts	
8 1/4" Ring Gear	60 (81)
8 3/8" & 9 1/4" Ring Gear	50 (68)
Spring "U" Bolt Nuts	
8 3/8" Ring Gear	45 (61)
8 1/4" & 9 1/4" Ring Gear	65 (88)
Dakota 4WD	110 (149)
Wheel Lug Nuts	
8 1/4"	85 (115)
8 3/8" & 9 1/4" Ring Gear	105 (142)
	INCH Lbs. (N.m)
Bearing Adjuster Lock Screws	90 (10)
Pinion Gear Mate Shaft Lock Bolt	100 (11)

[1] – Left-hand threaded bolts.

1991 DRIVE AXLES
Sure-Grip Differential

Dakota, Pickup, Ramcharger, RWD Van

DESCRIPTION

The cone clutch Sure-Grip is a positive traction, limited slip type differential. It is similar in operation to conventional type differentials, except for helical-grooved clutch cones that grip side gears to differential case. These grooves assure maximum lubrication of clutch surface during operation.

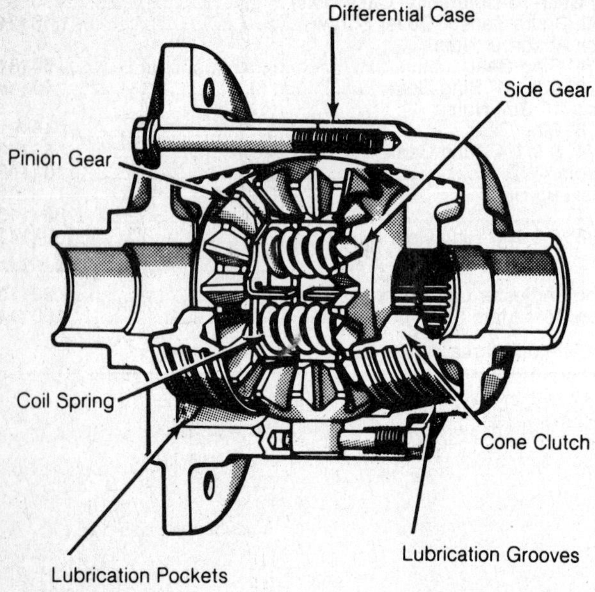
Differential Case
Side Gear
Pinion Gear
Coil Spring
Cone Clutch
Lubrication Grooves
Lubrication Pockets
121015
Courtesy of Chrysler Motors.

Fig. 1: Cross-Sectional View of Chrysler Motors Sure-Grip Differential Assembly

REAR AXLE RATIO IDENTIFICATION

Application	Ratio
8.375" Ring Gear	3.21:1, 3.55:1, 3.90:1
9.25" Ring Gear	3.21:1, 3.55:1, 3.90:1

LUBRICATION

CAUTION: If rear axle is submerged in water, axle lubricant MUST be replaced immediately to avoid premature failure due to contamination.

Use Multipurpose Gear Lubricant (MIL-L-2105-B/API GL-5). Four ounces of Mopar Hypoid Gear Oil Additive Friction Modifier (4318060) MUST be used with every fluid change.

TROUBLE SHOOTING

WARNING: Whenever axle assembly is to be rotated using engine, both rear wheels must be raised off the ground to avoid vehicle jumping which could result in personal injury

NOTE: If road test produces noise in turns but not during straight-ahead driving, the probable cause is incorrect or dissipated rear axle lubricant. Perform the following procedure before tear-down.

1) With lubricant of rear axle assembly at operating temperature, raise vehicle so rear wheels are free to turn. Remove axle cover and drain lubricant. Rotate differential so hole in case is facing down. Wipe out all accessible areas of carrier.

2) Scrape gasket material from housing and cover. Thoroughly clean surface with mineral spirits and dry completely. Apply a 1/16-3/32" bead of Mopar Silicone Rubber Sealant (4318025) along bolt circle of cover. Install housing cover on differential housing with attaching bolts. Install axle gear ratio identification tag under one bolt. Tighten bolts to 35 ft. lbs. (47 N.m).

3) Remove filler plug. Add 4 ounces of Mopar Hypoid Gear Oil Additive Friction Modifier (4318060). Refill axle to proper level with Mopar Hypoid Lubricant (4318058). Install filler plug and lower vehicle. Road test vehicle to see if condition is cured. If noise persists, replace carrier assembly. See 8 1/4", 8 3/8" & 9 1/4" RING GEAR article.

TESTING

1) Raise rear wheels off ground. Ensure engine is off. On models with automatic transmission, place shift lever in Park. On models with manual transmission, place shift lever in 1st gear. Grip tread of tire and attempt to rotate wheel.

2) If rotation is extremely difficult or impossible, differential is performing correctly. If either wheel turns relatively easily or continuously, differential is not performing correctly and should be replaced.

REMOVAL & INSTALLATION

Procedure is same as used to remove and install standard differential. See 8 1/4", 8 3/8" & 9 1/4" RING GEAR article.

NOTE: During removal and installation of axle shafts, DO NOT rotate one axle shaft unless both are in position. Rotation of one axle shaft without other in place may result in misalignment of 2 spline segments with which axle shaft splines engage. This would require difficult realignment procedures when axle shaft is reinstalled.

OVERHAUL

Sure-Grip differential is serviced as an assembly. Under NO circumstances should Sure-Grip differential be disassembled.

1991 DRIVE AXLES
4WD Steering Knuckles

Dakota, Pickup, Ramcharger

DESCRIPTION

Open type steering knuckles are used on all models. Open type knuckles provide sharper turning angle, decreasing turning radius. Axle shafts are free floating. Depending upon vehicle model, steering knuckles can be attached to axle housing by either ball joints or roller bearings and king (pivot) pins.

NOTE: References to Model 44 and Model 60 refer to axle models used on Pickup and Ramcharger models.

REMOVAL & INSTALLATION

BALL JOINT TYPE

Removal (Dakota) - 1) Remove cotter pin, nut lock, and spring washer from end stub shaft. Raise and support vehicle. Remove wheel hub nut and washer from end of stub shaft. Remove wheel and tire assembly. Remove brake caliper and support out of the way.

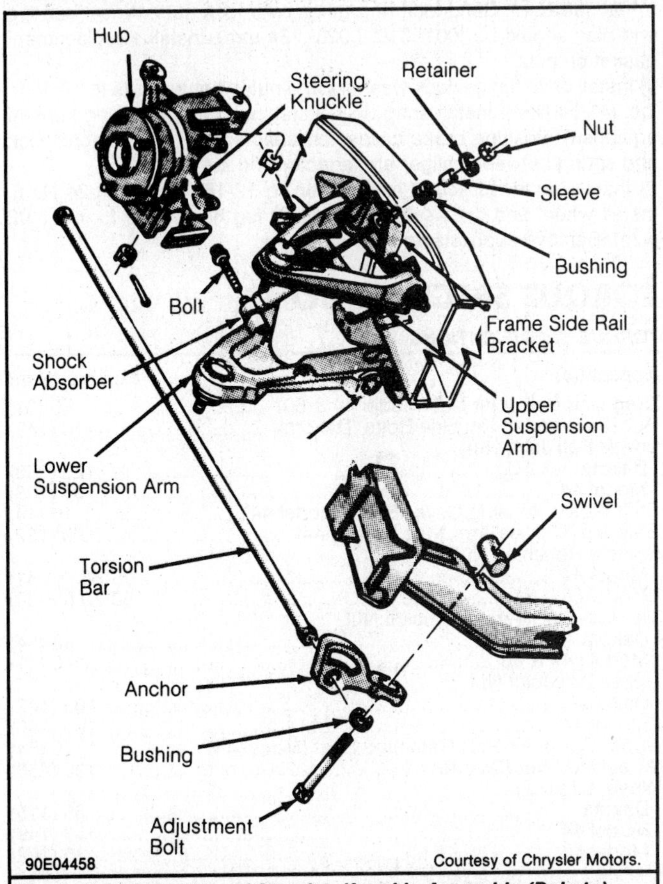
Hub
Steering Knuckle
Retainer
Nut
Sleeve
Bushing
Bolt
Frame Side Rail Bracket
Shock Absorber
Upper Suspension Arm
Lower Suspension Arm
Swivel
Torsion Bar
Anchor
Bushing
Adjustment Bolt
90E04458
Courtesy of Chrysler Motors.

Fig. 1: Exploded View of Steering Knuckle Assembly (Dakota)

2) Remove brake rotor. Remove bolts that attach wheel hub to steering knuckle and remove wheel hub. *See Fig. 1.* Remove cotter pin and nut from tie rod end at steering knuckle arm. Using Puller Tool (C-3894-A), loosen tie rod end ball joint from steering knuckle. Remove torsion bar. Remove front shock absorber lower bolt.

3) Disconnect stabilizer bar. Remove cotter pin and nut from lower and upper ball joints. Separate lower ball joint from steering knuckle arm bore. Using Ball Joint Remover (C-3564-A) between steering knuckle arms, apply force on upper ball joint.

4) Strike steering knuckle with hammer to loosen ball joint. Separate upper ball joint from steering knuckle arm bore. Remove steering knuckle. Remove bearing seal from steering knuckle.

Installation - 1) Install replacement wheel hub on steering knuckle. Tighten bolts to 110 ft. lbs. (149 N.m). Fill cavity between replacement seal lip and steering knuckle and lubricate lip with multi-purpose lubricant. Position replacement seal in bore at inner side of steering knuckle and seal with Installer (C-4698).

2) Lubricate outer surface area around perimeter of CV drive shaft wear sleeve with multi-purpose lubricant. Position steering knuckle adjacent to suspension arms. Insert ball joints into steering knuckle arm bores. Install ball joint retaining nuts and tighten to specification. See TORQUE SPECIFICATIONS at end of article.

3) Install replacement cotter pins. Install torsion bar. Attach stabilizer bar and tighten bolts to 20 ft. lbs. (27 N.m). Install shock absorber lower bolt and tighten to 100 ft. lbs. (136 N.m). Install wheel hub on steering knuckle and tighten attaching bolts to 110 ft. lbs. (149 N.m).

4) Insert tie rod end into steering knuckle arm bore. Install and tighten retaining nut to 40 ft. lbs. (54 N.m). Install a replacement cotter pin. Install brake rotor. Install brake caliper and tighten pins to 22 ft. lbs. (30 N.m).

5) Install wheel hub washer and nut on stub shaft. Tighten wheel hub nut to 190 ft. lbs. (258 N.m). Install spring washer, nut lock, and replacement cotter pin. Install wheel and tire assembly. Remove supports and lower vehicle. Tighten lug nuts in correct sequence to 85 ft. lbs. (115 N.m). Adjust front suspension height. See SPECIFICATIONS & PROCEDURES article in WHEEL ALIGNMENT.

Removal (Model 44 Axle) - 1) Raise vehicle and support securely. Remove wheels. Remove brake caliper and support out of the way. Remove inner brake pad. Remove dust cap and driving hub snap ring. Remove wheel bearing lock nut with Wheel Bearing Lock Nut Socket (C-4170-A). Remove retaining washer and wheel bearing adjusting nut. Remove hub.

2) Remove brake caliper adapter. Remove spindle nuts and lightly tap spindle with soft face hammer to free it from steering knuckle. Remove bearing seal and needle bearings from spindle. Pull out axle shaft assembly. Remove seal from axle shaft. Disconnect right side tie rod. Disconnect left side drag link ball.

3) Remove nuts and washers from left side steering knuckle arm. Tap steering knuckle with soft faced hammer and remove. Remove ball joint cotter keys and nuts. Break ball joints loose from steering knuckle. Clamp steering knuckle upside down and remove snap ring from lower ball joint.

4) Clean all components with solvent and dry with compressed air. Inspect all parts for burrs, chips, wear, flat spots or cracks. Replace all damaged or worn parts.

NOTE: When aligning upper ball joint nut to install cotter pin, always tighten nut to align holes. Never loosen nut to align holes.

Installation - 1) Press upper and lower ball joints into steering knuckle. Install snap ring on lower ball joint. Install replacement rubber boots over both ball joints. Thread replacement sleeve into axle shaft tube yoke upper arm bore. Leave 2 threads exposed at top of arm.

2) Position steering knuckle on axle shaft arms and install replacement ball joint nut. Tighten nut to 80 ft. lbs. (108 N.m). Tighten sleeve in yoke arm bore to 40 ft. lbs. (54 N.m) with Wrench (C-4169). Install upper ball joint nut and tighten to 100 ft. lbs. (136 N.m). Install a new cotter pin.

3) Position left steering knuckle arm on steering knuckle. Install washers and nuts and tighten to 90 ft. lbs. (122 N.m). Connect drag link ball joint to steering knuckle arm. Install retaining nut and tighten to 60 ft. lbs. (81 N.m). Install a new cotter pin.

4) Connect tie rod end ball joint to steering knuckle arm. Install retaining nut and tighten to 45 ft. lbs. (61 N.m). Install a new cotter pin. Install seal on axle shaft shield. Lubricate seal. On right side, carefully insert axle shaft into shaft tube.

5) On left side only, remove shift motor housing cover. Position shift collar on splined end of shaft, insert intermediate shaft through axle shaft seal. Install shift motor housing cover and gasket. Tighten bolts to 10 ft. lbs. (14 N.m). Connect vacuum hoses and electrical connector to shift motor housing.

6) Install replacement needle bearings in spindle with Installer (D-360) and Handle (C-4171). Install replacement brake hub seal with Installer (D-155). Lubricate seal. Position replacement spacer on axle shaft.

1991 DRIVE AXLES
4WD Steering Knuckles (Cont.)

Install spindle and brake splash shield. Install replacement nuts and tighten to 25-35 ft. lbs. (34-41 N.m).

7) Position hub and outer wheel on spindle. Install adjusting nut and tighten to 50 ft. lbs. (68 N.m) with Tool (C-4170). Loosen adjusting nut and retighten to 30-40 ft. lbs. (41-54 N.m) while rotating hub. Loosen adjusting nut 135-150°. Install and tighten nut lock to 50 ft. lbs. (68 N.m). Wheel bearing end play after final bearing adjustment should be .001-.010" (.03-.25 mm).

8) Install retaining spring, driving hub, and retaining ring. Install dust cap on hub. Position inboard brake pad on brake caliper adapter with pad flanges engaged with adapter rails. Slowly slide caliper into position in adapter and over brake rotor. Align caliper on adapter rails.

9) Install anti-rattle springs and retainer clips and tighten to 15 ft. lbs. (20 N.m). Install wheel and tire assembly. Tighten lug nuts to 110 ft. lbs. (149 N.m). Remove supports and lower vehicle.

ROLLER BEARING & KING PIN TYPE

Removal (Model 60 Axle) – 1) Raise vehicle and support securely. Remove wheels. Remove brake caliper-to-adapter hex screw. Remove adapter lock and spring from between brake caliper and adapter. Separate brake caliper from adapter and support aside.

2) Remove hub cap. Remove flange nuts and lock washers. Remove drive flange and discard gasket or remove locking hub (if equipped). See LOCKING HUBS article. Remove outer lock nut and lock ring. Remove inner lock nut and outer wheel bearing.

3) Slide hub from steering knuckle spindle. Remove inner brake pad from adapter. Remove nuts and washers that attach splash shield, brake adapter, and spindle to steering knuckle. Remove spindle. Slide inner and outer axle shaft with bronze spacer, seal and slinger from axle shaft tube and steering knuckle.

4) Remove cotter pin and retaining nut from tie rod end ball joint. Loosen ball joint with Puller (C-3894-A). Remove tie rod end from steering knuckle. Remove cotter pin and retaining nut from left side drag link ball stud. Loosen ball stud with Puller (C-4150) and remove drag link from steering knuckle arm. Remove nuts and steering knuckle upper cap. Discard gasket.

5) Remove spring and upper socket sleeve. Remove cap screws from steering knuckle lower cap. Dislodge cap from steering knuckle and axle shaft tube yoke. Remove steering knuckle from axle shaft tube yoke. Remove seal. Press out lower ball socket from axle shaft tube yoke lower arm bore.

6) Clean all components with solvent and dry with compressed air. Inspect all parts for burrs, chips, wear, flat spots or cracks. Replace all damaged or worn parts.

NOTE: When aligning upper ball joint nut to install cotter pin, always tighten nut to align holes. Never loosen nut to align holes.

Installation – 1) Lubricate lower ball socket. Press lower bearing cup into axle shaft tube yoke lower arm bore. Press lower bearing and seal into axle shaft tube yoke lower arm bore. Install upper socket pin in axle shaft yoke upper arm bore. Tighten socket pin to 500-600 ft. lbs. (668-813 N.m).

2) Install seal over socket pin. Position steering knuckle over socket pin. Fill socket lower cavity with MOPAR Multi-Mileage Lubricant or equivalent. Maneuver lower cap into place on steering knuckle and axle shaft tube yoke. Install cap screws and tighten to 70-90 ft. lbs. (95-122 N.m).

3) Liberally lubricate upper socket pin. Align upper socket sleeve keyway with steering knuckle and slide it into position. Install new gasket over steering knuckle upper studs. Position spring over sleeve. Install cap on left side steering knuckle arm. Install nuts and tighten to 70-90 ft. lbs. (95-122 N.m).

4) On left side only, connect drag link ball joint to steering knuckle arm and install retaining nut. Tighten nut to 60 ft. lbs. (81 N.m). Install a new cotter pin.

5) Connect tie rod end ball joint to steering knuckle and install retaining nut. Tighten nut to 45 ft. lbs. (61 N.m). Install new cotter pin. Position bronze spacer on axle shaft with chamfer facing toward "U" joint. Slide axle shaft into steering knuckle and axle shaft tube.

6) Install spindle, brake adapter and brake splash shield. Install washers and nuts, and tighten to 50-70 ft. lbs. (68-95 N.m). Position inner brake pad on adapter. Install hub on spindle. Install outer wheel bearing and inner lock nut. Tighten inner lock nut to 50 ft. lbs. (68 N.m) using Wrench (DD-1241-JD). Loosen lock nut and then retighten to 30-40 ft. lbs. (41-54 N.m) while rotating hub. Loosen lock nut 135-150°.

7) Install a lock ring and outer lock nut. Tighten lock nut to at least 65 ft. lbs. (88 N.m). Bend lock ring tangs over lock nuts. Wheel bearing end play should be .001-.010" (.025-.254 mm). Install a replacement gasket on hub.

8) Install drive flange, lock washers and nuts. Tighten nuts to 30-40 ft. lbs. (41-54 N.m). Install snap ring. Install hub cap or locking hubs (if equipped). Position brake caliper on adapter. Position adapter lock and spring between caliper and adapter and tap in place.

9) Install hex-head screw and tighten to 12-18 ft. lbs. (16-24 N.m). Install wheel and tire assembly. Tighten lug nuts to 75 ft. lbs. (102 N.m). Remove supports and lower vehicle.

TORQUE SPECIFICATIONS

TORQUE SPECIFICATIONS

Application	Ft. Lbs. (N.m)
Drag Link Ball Joint Nut (Model 44 & 60)	60 (81)
Hub-To-Steering Knuckle Bolts (Dakota)	110 (149)
Lower Ball Joint Nut	
Dakota	120 (163)
Model 44	80 (108)
Shift Motor Housing Cover Bolts (Model 44)	10 (14)
Steering Knuckle Arm Nuts (Model 44)	90 (122)
Spindle Retaining Nuts	
Model 44	25-35 (34-41)
Model 60	50-70 (68-90)
Tie Rod-To-Steering Knuckle Nut	
Dakota	40 (54)
Models 44 & 60	45 (61)
Upper Ball Joint Nut	
Dakota	105 (142)
Model 44	100 (136)
Upper Ball Joint Split Retaining Seat (Model 44)	40 (54)
Wheel Hub Nut (Dakota)	190 (258)
Wheel Lug Nuts	
Dakota	85 (115)
Model 44	110 (149)
Model 60	75 (102)

1991 DRIVE AXLES
FWD Axle Shafts

Caravan, Town & Country, Voyager

DESCRIPTION

Front Wheel Drive (FWD) vans use 2 types of axle shaft systems, equal and unequal length. *See Fig. 1.* Components from systems are not interchangeable. The equal length system uses an intermediate shaft on the right side. Unequal length system has a long axle shaft on right side and short axle shaft on left side. Except for a rubber washer seal attached to right inner CV joint of the equal length system, axle shafts are serviced in the same manner.

LUBRICATION

CV joints require special lubrication. Joints are enclosed in a boot to contain lubricant and prevent contamination. Periodic lubrication of CV joints is not required, but boots should be inspected at regular intervals.

When adding fluid to transaxle, use Mopar ATF Plus (7176). If Mopar ATF is not available, Dexron-II may be used.

ADJUSTMENTS

AXLE SHAFT POSITIONING

NOTE: Check axle shaft positioning if engine/transaxle is loosened or moved or if front structural damage has occurred. Incorrect axle shaft positioning may result in premature failure of components.

1) Engine mount bolt holes are slotted for side-to-side positioning of engine. With vehicle completely assembled, ensure front wheels are in straight ahead position. Vehicle should be on platform hoist or alignment rack.

2) Using a tape measure, measure distance from inner edge of outer boot to inner edge of inner boot on both axle shafts. *See Fig. 2.* This measurement must be taken at bottom of axle shaft only.

3) If both axle shafts are within specifications, no further service is necessary. If either left or right axle shaft is not within specification, support engine/transaxle assembly using a floor jack. See AXLE SHAFT POSITIONING SPECIFICATIONS table.

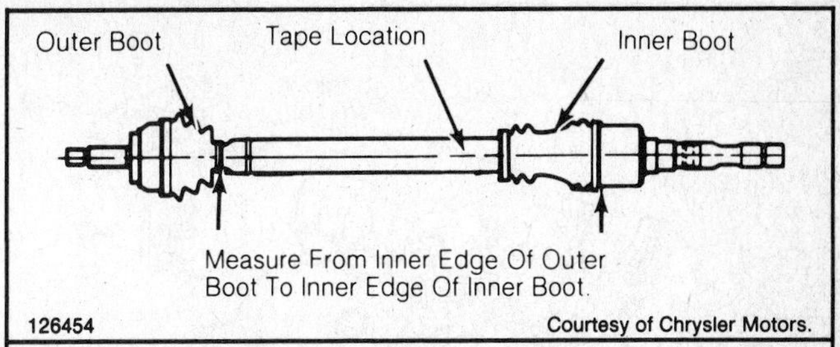
Outer Boot
Tape Location
Inner Boot
Measure From Inner Edge Of Outer Boot To Inner Edge Of Inner Boot.
126454
Courtesy of Chrysler Motors.

Fig. 2: Measuring Axle Shaft Position

4) Loosen right engine mount fasteners, front engine mount bracket and front crossmember fasteners. Pry engine right or left as required to obtain correct axle shaft length. See AXLE SHAFT POSITIONING SPECIFICATIONS table.

5) Tighten mounting bolts/nuts to specifications. *See Fig. 3.* Recheck axle shaft length. Install damper weight (if equipped), and tighten to specification. See TORQUE SPECIFICATIONS table at end of article.

AXLE SHAFT POSITIONING SPECIFICATIONS

Application	Right Side Length In. (mm)	Left Side Length In. (mm)
2.5L, 3.0L & 3.3L	20.5-20.9 (520-530)	9.0-9.4 (228-238)

REMOVAL & INSTALLATION

AXLE SHAFTS

Removal – 1) Remove axle nut. Raise and support vehicle. If removing right axle shaft, remove speedometer pinion assembly from transaxle. Using brass hammer, lightly tap axle shaft end to free axle shaft from hub splines. Remove lower ball joint clamp bolt. Separate lower ball joint from steering knuckle.

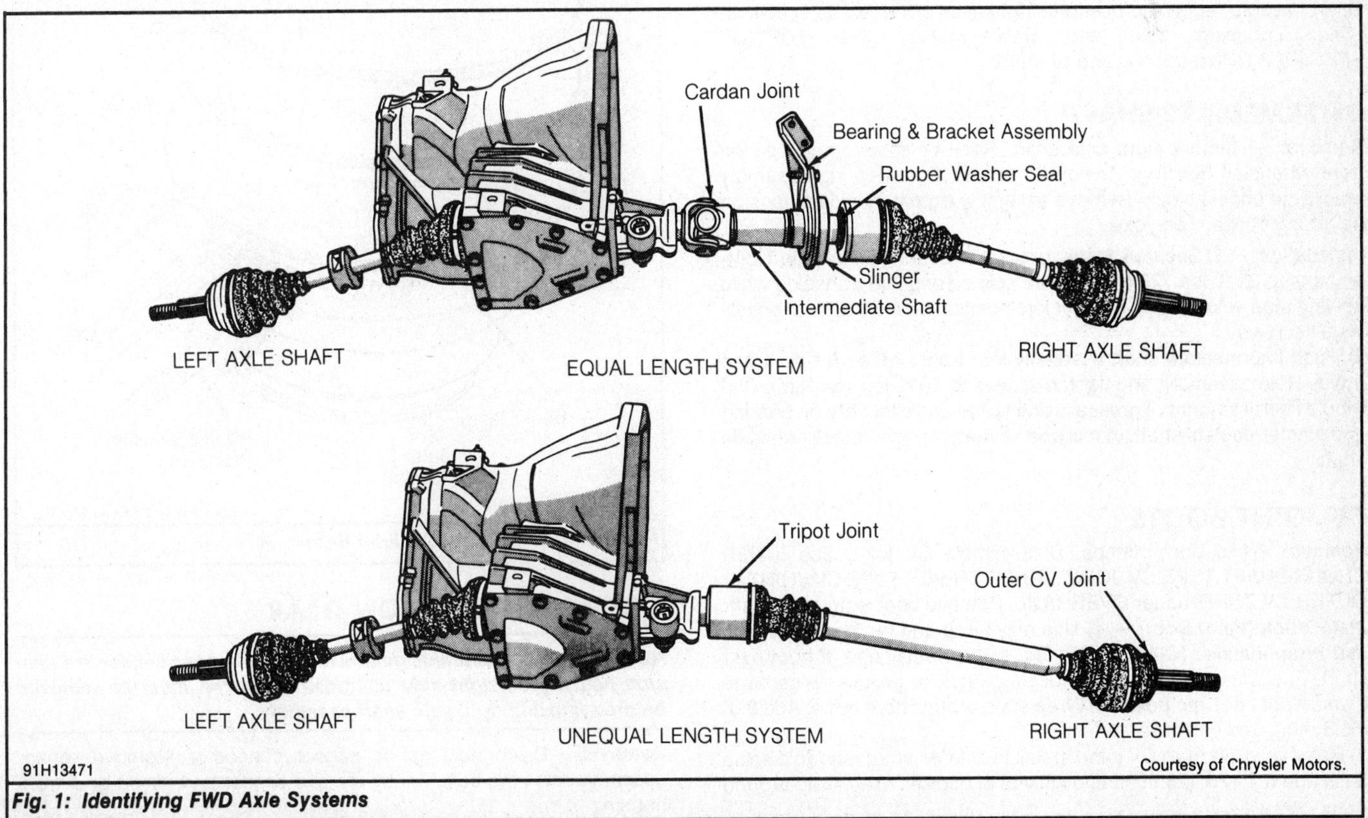
Cardan Joint
Bearing & Bracket Assembly
Rubber Washer Seal
Slinger
Intermediate Shaft
LEFT AXLE SHAFT
EQUAL LENGTH SYSTEM
RIGHT AXLE SHAFT
Tripot Joint
Outer CV Joint
LEFT AXLE SHAFT
UNEQUAL LENGTH SYSTEM
RIGHT AXLE SHAFT
91H13471
Courtesy of Chrysler Motors.

Fig. 1: Identifying FWD Axle Systems

1991 DRIVE AXLES
FWD Axle Shafts (Cont.)

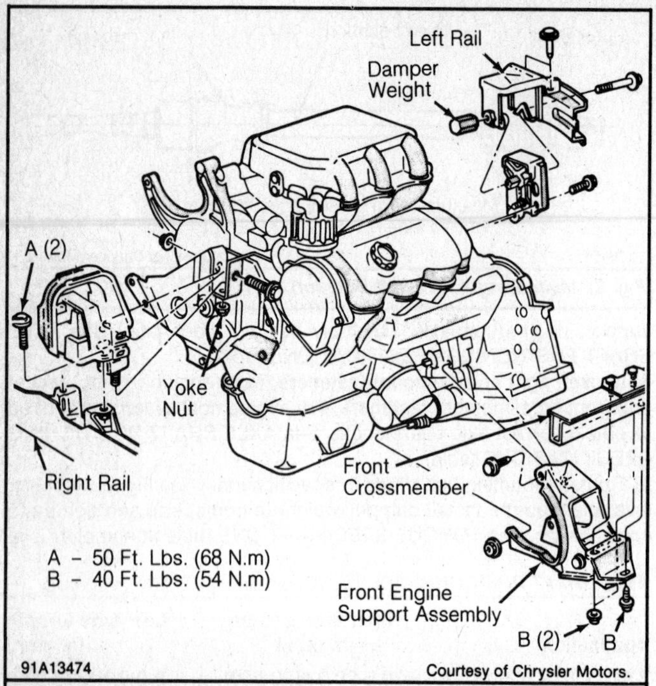
Left Rail
Damper
Weight
A (2)
Yoke
Nut
Right Rail
Front
Crossmember
A - 50 Ft. Lbs. (68 N.m)
B - 40 Ft. Lbs. (54 N.m)
Front Engine
Support Assembly
B (2)
B
91A13474
Courtesy of Chrysler Motors.

Fig. 3: Identifying Engine Mounting Bolts/Nuts (Typical)

NOTE: Remove speedometer drive pinion before removing right axle shaft. See SPEEDOMETER PINION GEAR under REMOVAL & INSTALLATION.

2) Pull out on hub/steering knuckle assembly, and separate axle shaft from hub. Grasp both CV joints at outer housings to prevent separation, and pull axle shaft out of transaxle or intermediate shaft. Remove axle shaft from vehicle.

Installation - Grasp both CV joints at outer housings, and insert inner CV joint into transaxle or intermediate shaft. To complete installation, reverse removal procedure. Tighten all bolts/nuts to specifications. Lubricate seal and wear sleeve. See TORQUE SPECIFICATIONS table at end of article.

INTERMEDIATE SHAFT

Removal - Remove right axle shaft. Remove speedometer pinion from extension housing. Remove 2 screws from bearing assembly bracket to engine block. Remove assembly from transaxle extension by pulling outward on yoke.

Installation - **1)** Securely fasten bracket to bearing assembly. Tighten bolts to 21 ft. lbs. (28 N.m). Guide splined end into transaxle while holding stub yoke. Swing bracket into position on engine, and loosely install screws.

2) Push intermediate shaft assembly into transaxle as far as it can travel. Hold assembly, and tighten screws to 40 ft. lbs. (54 N.m). Distribute liberal amount of grease inside spline and pilot bore on bearing end of intermediate shaft. Install speedometer pinion. Install right axle shaft.

CV JOINT BOOTS

Removal - Cut boot clamps. Disassemble CV joint. See INNER CROSS SHAFT TYPE CV JOINT, INNER TRIPOT TYPE CV JOINT or OUTER CV JOINT under OVERHAUL. Remove boot from axle shaft.

Installation (Inner Boot) - **1)** Use only strap and buckle type clamp and Strap Installer (C-4653). *See Fig. 4.* Slide small end of boot over shaft. Position boot to edge of locating mark or groove. Slide large diameter of boot into position. Wrap strap around boot twice. Add 2.5" (63.5 mm), and cut strap.

2) Remove strap from CV joint. Install buckle on strap, and fold strap back about 1.125" (28.58 mm) on inside of buckle. Wrap strap around CV joint twice, passing strap through buckle on each wrap. Using Strap Installer (C-4653), tighten strap.

3) DO NOT pull installer downward to tighten strap, as strap can break. If necessary, disconnect and reinstall installer to retighten strap. With strap tightened sufficiently, remove installer to side and cut strap .125" (3.18 mm) beyond buckle. Complete by folding strap under buckle.

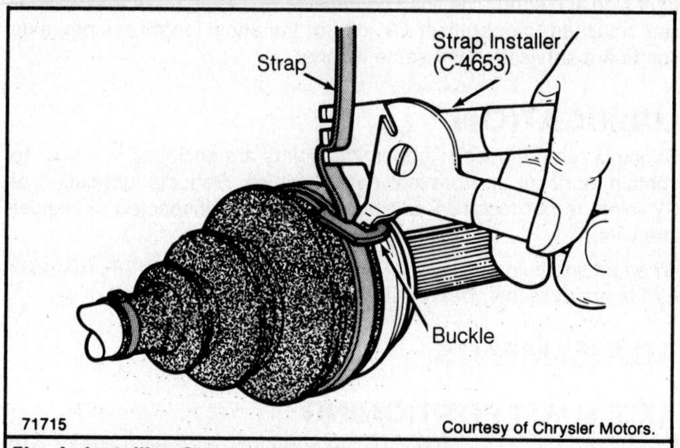
Strap
Strap Installer
(C-4653)
Buckle
71715
Courtesy of Chrysler Motors.

Fig. 4: Installing Strap on Inner CV Joint Boot

Installation (Outer Boot) - Slide small diameter boot clamp onto axle shaft. Slide boot onto axle shaft until small end of boot is seated in boot groove on shaft. Position boot clamp evenly in clamp groove on boot. Position tabs on boot clamp in jaws of Clamp Installer (C-4975). *See Fig. 5.* Tighten bolt on clamp installer until tabs on boot clamp interlock.

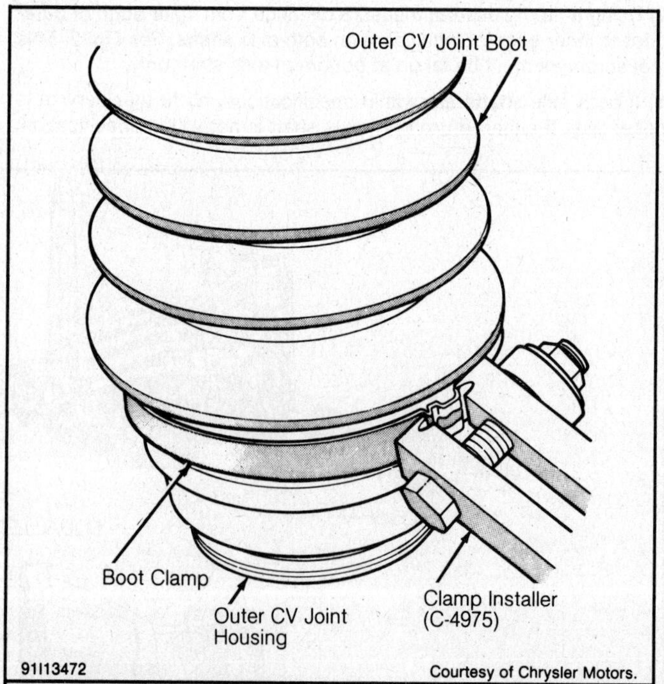
Outer CV Joint Boot
Boot Clamp
Outer CV Joint
Housing
Clamp Installer
(C-4975)
91I13472
Courtesy of Chrysler Motors.

Fig 5: Clamping Outer CV Joint Boot

SPEEDOMETER PINION GEAR

NOTE: Speedometer pinion gear is located on speed sensor in extension housing on right side of transaxle. Pinion must be removed before removing right axle shaft assembly.

Removal - Disconnect speed sensor connector. Remove sensor assembly retaining bolt. Gently remove sensor and pinion gear from housing.

Installation - To install, reverse removal procedure. Ensure adapter and transaxle housing area are clean. Install and tighten retaining bolt.

AXLE SHAFT DAMPER WEIGHTS

Removal & Installation - Damper weights are attached to axle shaft between inner and outer CV joints. Damper weights should be removed from axle shaft during axle shaft positioning procedure. Ensure damper weight bolts are tightened to specification. See TORQUE SPECIFICATIONS table at end of article.

OVERHAUL

INNER CROSS SHAFT TYPE CV JOINT

Disassembly - Mark shafts for reassembly reference. Apply penetrating oil to bushings, and remove snap rings. Support yoke in a vise. Press out bushings.

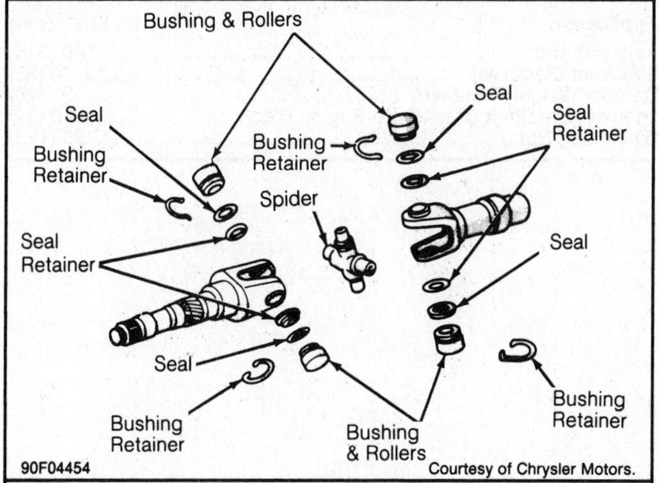

Bushing & Rollers
Seal
Seal
Seal Retainer
Bushing Retainer
Bushing Retainer
Spider
Seal Retainer
Seal
Seal
Bushing Retainer
Bushing Retainer
Bushing & Rollers
90F04454
Courtesy of Chrysler Motors.

Fig. 6: Exploded View of Inner Cross Shaft Type CV Joint

Reassembly - Hold spider in position between yoke ears, and position one bushing assembly into yoke. *See Fig. 6.* Hammer bushing assembly into yoke, and install snap ring. Install opposite bushing. Install stub shaft yoke.

INNER TRIPOT TYPE CV JOINT

Disassembly - **1)** Remove boot clamps. *See Fig. 7.* Pull boot back to reach tripot retainer assembly. Clamp axle shaft in vise. Push CV housing toward axle shaft to compress retention spring. Use pliers to bend back retaining tabs (part of housing) while spring is compressed.

2) Support housing in horizontal plane while retention spring pressure forces housing off tripot. Remove outer snap ring from axle shaft groove. Remove tripot by hand. If necessary, use brass punch to tap tripot body.

Reassembly - **1)** Install new axle boot on axle shaft. Slide tripot onto axle shaft, chamfered side first. Flat side of tripot should be next to retaining ring groove. Using grease supplied in boot kit, put 2 of 3 packets into boot. Third packet will go into CV housing.

2) Position retention spring in housing spring pocket. Install spring cup onto exposed end of spring. Lubricate concave surface of spring cup with grease.

NOTE: Ensure spring stays centered in housing spring pocket as tripot seats in spring cup.

3) Install housing over tripot, and bend retaining tabs into original position. Ensure tabs can hold tripot in housing. Place boot over retaining groove in housing. Clamp boot in position.

OUTER CV JOINT

CAUTION: DO NOT hit cage when using hammer and drift to loosen CV joint.

Disassembly - **1)** Remove and discard boot clamps. Wipe away grease so CV joint body edge is visible. Hold axle shaft in soft jaws of vise. Using soft hammer, give top of CV joint body sharp blow to break joint loose from internal circlip in groove at end of shaft.

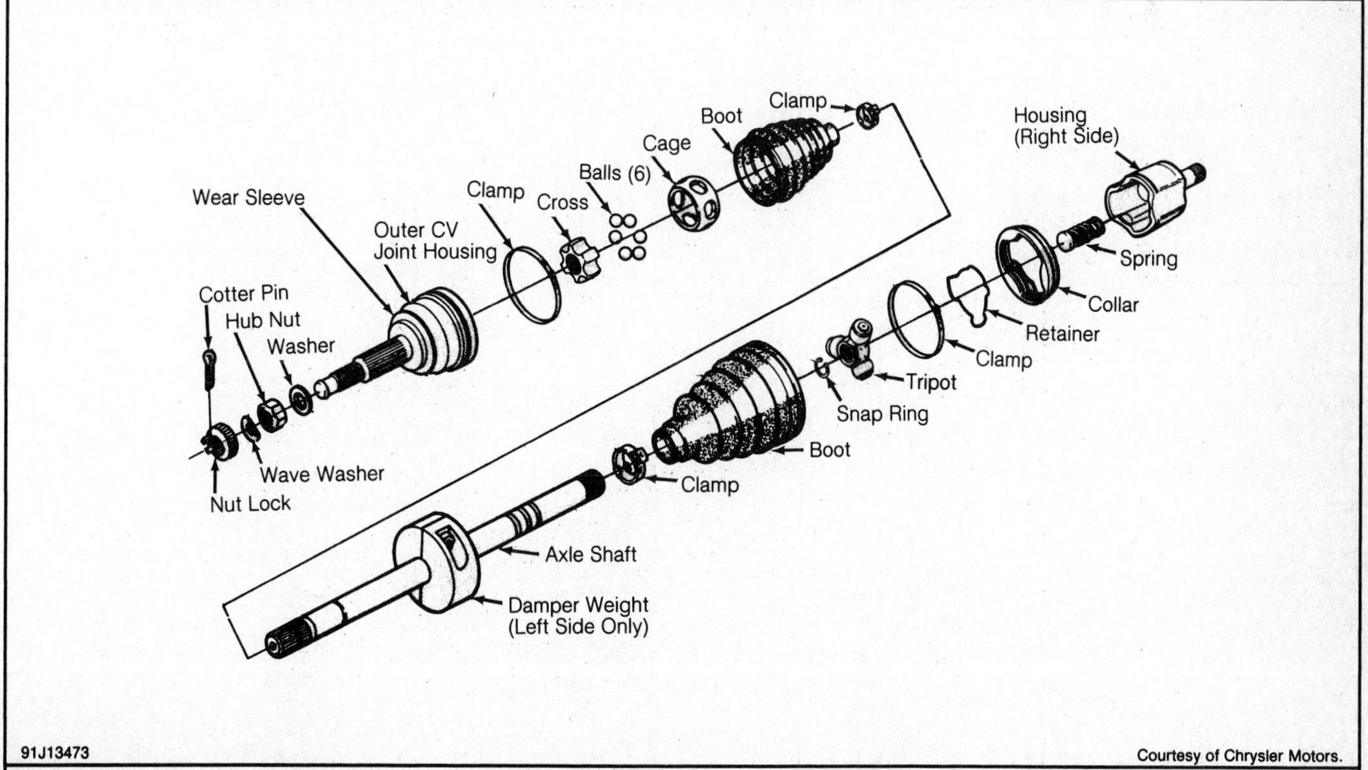

Clamp
Boot
Housing
(Right Side)
Cage
Balls (6)
Wear Sleeve
Clamp
Cross
Outer CV
Joint Housing
Spring
Cotter Pin
Hub Nut
Collar
Washer
Retainer
Clamp
Tripot
Snap Ring
Boot
Wave Washer
Clamp
Nut Lock
Axle Shaft
Damper Weight
(Left Side Only)
91J13473
Courtesy of Chrysler Motors.

Fig. 7: Exploded View Of Axle Assembly

1991 DRIVE AXLES
FWD Axle Shafts (Cont.)

2) Wear sleeve on outer CV housing is a wiping surface for hub bearing seal. *See Fig. 7.* If wear sleeve is bent or damaged, pry sleeve away from machined ledge of CV joint. Remove and discard circlip from shaft groove. New circlip is supplied in replacement boot kit.
3) If shaft is damaged, remove heavy spacer ring from inner groove. If joint was operating properly, only replace boots. If joint was noisy or badly worn, replace complete joint. Replace boot whenever joint is replaced.
4) Wipe grease off outer CV joint, and mark inner race (cross), cage and housing with paint. Position joint vertically in vise, using soft jaws to clamp on splined shaft. Press down on one side of inner race to tilt cage, and remove ball from opposite side. Remove all balls.
5) If joint is very tight, use brass drift and hammer to tap inner race and remove balls. Tilt cage and inner race assembly to vertical.
6) Remove inner race and cage assembly by pulling upward away from housing. Turn inner race 90 degrees to cage. Align elongated cage window with one of spherical lands on race. Raise land to cage window, and remove inner race by swinging it out of cage.
Inspection – Check grease for contamination. Wash all parts in solvent, and dry with compressed air. Inspect races, splined shaft and nut threads for damage. Inspect balls and cage for excessive wear or damage. If excessive wear or damage is found, replace CV joint.
Reassembly – 1) Position new wear sleeve on joint housing machined ledge. Lightly oil all components before reassembly. Align parts according to paint markings.
2) Insert one inner race (cross) into cage window, and feed race into cage. Pivot inner race to fully assemble cage and race. Align opposing elongated cage windows with housing land. Feed cage assembly into housing. Pivot cage 90 degrees to complete installation.
3) Counterbore of inner race should face outward from joint. Apply lubricant to ball races from packet in boot kit.
4) Distribute grease equally between all sides of ball grooves. Insert balls into raceways by tilting cage and inner race assembly. Fasten boot to shaft. Insert new circlip from shaft groove kit.
5) Position outer joint on splined end of axle shaft. Put hub nut on stub axle. Engage splines, and tap sharply on hub nut using mallet. Ensure circlip is properly seated by trying to pull joint off shaft.
6) Install large end of boot over joint housing, ensuring boot is not twisted. Clamp boot to housing.

TORQUE SPECIFICATIONS

TORQUE SPECIFICATIONS

Application	Ft. Lbs. (N.m)
Axle Hub Nut	180 (245)
Ball Joint Clamp Nut	70 (95)
Damper Weight Fasteners	21 (28)
Intermediate Shaft Bracket-To-Engine Block	40 (54)
Wheel Lug Nut	95 (129)

1991 DRIVE AXLES
All-Wheel Drive Axle

Caravan, Town & Country, Voyager

DESCRIPTION

All-Wheel Drive (AWD) is available on all models equipped with 3.3L engine and A604 transaxle. AWD system consists of rear carrier, torque tube, overrunning clutch assembly, a vacuum operated dog clutch and a viscous coupling in one unit called the Rear Driveline Module (RDLM) . Power is supplied by a Power Transfer Unit (PTU) that sits in place of the extension housing on the transmission.

Rear carrier contains conventional open differential with hypoid ring and pinion gear set. *See Fig. 1*. Hypoid gears are lubricated by SAE 85W-90 gear oil.

Torque tube assembly attaches to overrunning clutch case. *See Fig. 2*. A propeller shaft and a sealed front bearing assembly are located inside torque tube housing. A vacuum reservoir and solenoid assembly are bolted to top of torque tube.

Overrunning clutch allows rear wheels to overrun front wheels during rapid front wheel braking. Overrunning clutch prevents feedback of front wheel braking torque to rear wheels and allows braking behavior similar to FWD models. Overrunning clutch has separate oil sump and is filled independently from differential. See LUBRICATION.

Dog clutch provides AWD action in reverse by bridging and locking out overrunning clutch. Dog clutch is operated by double-acting servo using manifold vacuum. Two vacuum solenoids, controlled by back-up light switch, engage and disengage dog clutch. Spring in servo disengages dog clutch if vacuum supply is lost.

Viscous coupling controls and distributes torque to rear wheels. Coupling is similar to a multi-plate clutch. Alternating plates are indexed to front and rear drive units and operate in a silicone fluid. Unit is sealed and requires no maintenance or adjustment.

Rear axle shafts are similar to FWD axle and are serviced using FWD procedures. See. FWD AXLE SHAFTS article in DRIVE AXLES.

AWD AXLE RATIO IDENTIFICATION

Application	Ratio
Power Transfer Unit	3.45:1
Rear Carrier Assembly	3.42:1

LUBRICATION

When adding fluid to overrunning clutch, use Mopar ATF Plus (7176). If Mopar ATF is not available, Dexron-II may be used.

FLUID CAPACITIES

Application	Pts. (L)
Carrier Assembly	4.0 (1.90)
Overrunning Clutch	.8 (.37)
PTU	2.4 (1.15)

TROUBLE SHOOTING

FLUID LEAK DIAGNOSIS

Two weep holes are provided on bottom of rear drive assembly to assist in fluid leakage diagnosis. *See Fig. 3*. If leak is detected from either hole, seal replacement is necessary. Red fluid leaking from weep hole "A" indicates front overrunning clutch seal failure. Red fluid leaking from weep hole "B" indicates rear overrunning clutch seal failure. Brown fluid leaking from weep hole "B" indicates input pinion seal failure.

ON-VEHICLE TESTING

SYSTEM TESTS

Rear Wheels Not Overrunning – 1) If rear wheels are not overrunning, check that dog clutch is stuck engaged. If dog clutch is stuck engaged, proceed to next step. If dog clutch is not stuck engaged, check overrunning clutch for reverse mounted or failed sprags. If sprags are reversed, disassemble overrunning clutch and remount sprags. If sprags have failed, repair or replace overrunning clutch.

2) Using a vacuum gauge, check vacuum system for proper operation. If vacuum system if functioning properly, proceed to next step. If vacuum system is not functioning properly, check and repair misrouted or kinked vacuum lines. If vacuum lines are okay, proceed to step **4)**.

3) Check dog clutch for jammed on spline condition. If dog clutch is jammed on spline, inspect for burrs or nicks, and repair as required. If dog clutch is not jammed on spline, check for torsional bind-up con-

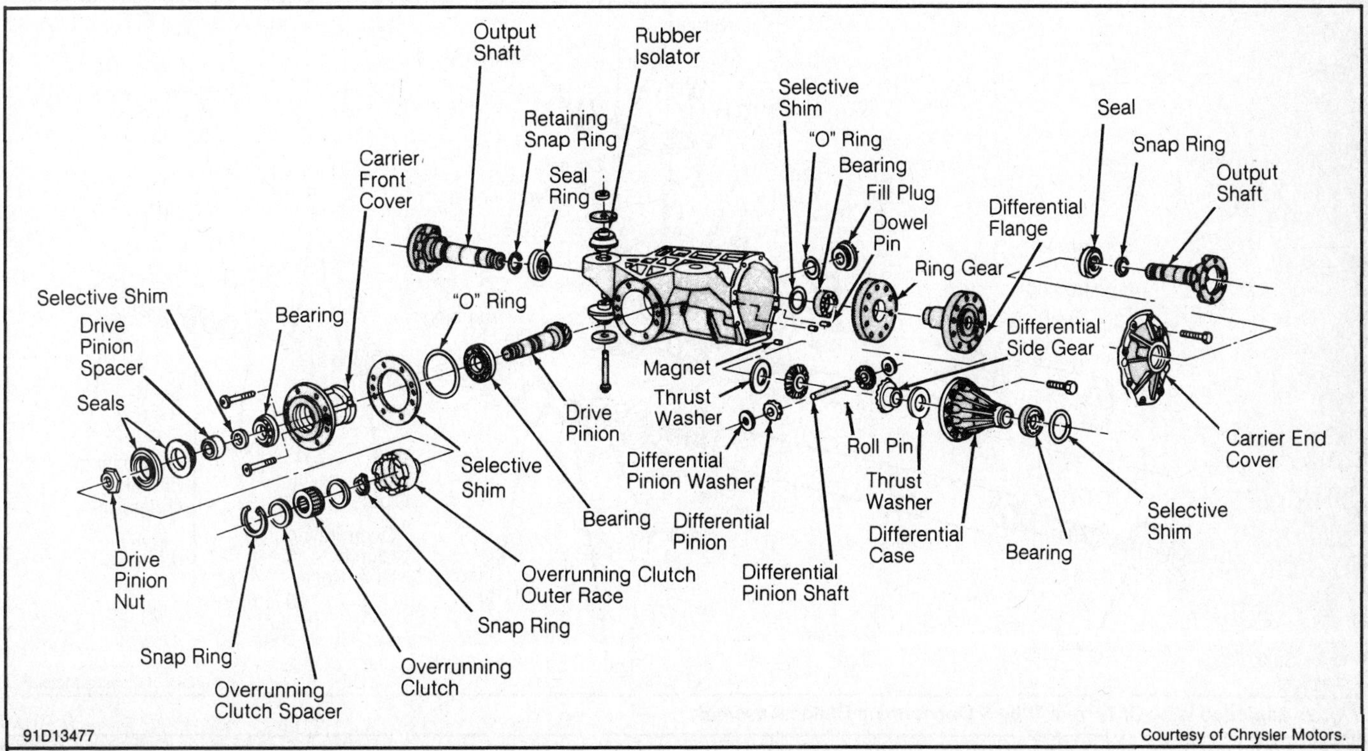
Output Shaft
Rubber Isolator
Selective Shim
Seal
Retaining Snap Ring
"O" Ring
Snap Ring
Carrier Front Cover
Seal Ring
Bearing
Output Shaft
Fill Plug
Differential Flange
Dowel Pin
Ring Gear
Selective Shim
"O" Ring
Drive Pinion Spacer
Bearing
Differential Side Gear
Magnet
Seals
Thrust Washer
Drive Pinion
Roll Pin
Carrier End Cover
Differential Pinion Washer
Selective Shim
Thrust Washer
Selective Shim
Bearing
Differential Pinion
Differential Case
Bearing
Drive Pinion Nut
Overrunning Clutch Outer Race
Differential Pinion Shaft
Snap Ring
Snap Ring
Overrunning Clutch
Overrunning Clutch Spacer
91D13477
Courtesy of Chrysler Motors.

Fig. 1: Exploded View Of Rear Carrier Assembly

1991 DRIVE AXLES
All-Wheel Drive Axle (Cont.)

dition. If dog clutch is bound up, repair binding condition. If dog clutch is not bound up, check for shift fork interference. If shift fork is interfering, repair or replace as required.

4) Turn ignition on. Place gearshift lever in Park. Using a test light, backprobe Purple/Black wire at vacuum solenoids. If power does not exist, proceed to next step. If power exists, check for failed back-up light relay. If relay has failed, replace relay. If relay is okay, check for shorted back-up light switch. If switch is shorted, replace switch. If switch is okay, check and repair short circuit in back-up light wiring.

5) With ignition on, place gearshift lever in Reverse. Using test light, once again backprobe Purple/Black wire at solenoid connector. If power exists, disconnect vacuum solenoid harness connector and connect test light between Purple/Black wire and Black wire in harness half of connector. If power exists, proceed to next step. If power does not exist, repair Black wire between harness connector and chassis ground.

6) Using a helper, check vacuum solenoids for proper operation. Listen and feel for solenoids to activate while a helper moves shift lever between Park and Reverse. If solenoids are not functioning properly, replace solenoids. If solenoids are functioning properly, check vent system for proper operation. If vent system is plugged, repair as necessary. If vent system is not plugged, proceed to next step.

7) Check dog clutch for combination of vacuum motor and overrunning clutch failure. If both components have failed, repair or replace as necessary. If spring is okay and vacuum motor has failed, replace vacuum motor.

AWD Inoperative In Forward Gear With Propeller Shaft Turning – Check for reverse-mounted overrunning clutch sprags. If sprags are reversed, disassemble overrunning clutch and install sprags correctly. If sprags are not reversed, check for missing sprags. If sprags are missing, replace as required. If sprags are not missing, check for overrunning clutch failure and repair or replace as required.

AWD Inoperative In Forward Or Reverse Gear – Check PTU. If PTU has failed, replace PTU. If PTU is okay, Check viscous coupling, propeller shaft and rear carrier. If any component has failed, replace component. If all components are okay, check rear half-shafts and replace as required.

AWD Inoperative In Reverse With Propeller Shaft Turning – 1) Check for missing dog clutch. If dog clutch is missing, install missing parts. If dog clutch is present and inoperative, check vacuum actuation system. If vacuum actuation system is not functioning properly, proceed to step **3)**.

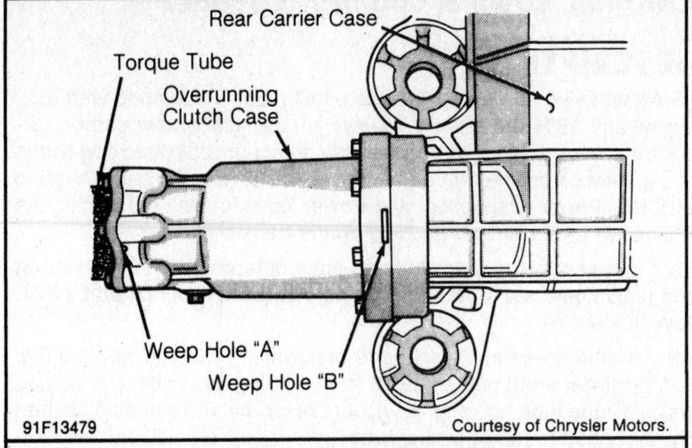
Rear Carrier Case
Torque Tube
Overrunning Clutch Case
Weep Hole "A"
Weep Hole "B"
91F13479
Courtesy of Chrysler Motors.

Fig 3: Identifying Overrunning Clutch Weep Holes

2) If vacuum actuation system is functioning properly, check for dog clutch jammed disengaged, shift fork "E" clip(s) missing, broken shift fork, shift fork interference, or overrunning clutch spring jammed or too strong. If any condition exists, repair or replace as required.

3) Using a test light, backprobe Purple/Black wire at solenoid connector. If power does not exist, proceed to next step. If power exists, check vacuum system to solenoids and solenoid switching. To test solenoid switching, listen and feel for solenoid clicking while a helper moves shift lever between Park and Reverse. If solenoids fail to operate correctly, replace solenoids. If solenoids operate correctly, proceed to step **5)**.

4) Check harness and connector for damage or pushed out terminals. If harness is damaged, or terminals are damaged or pushed out, repair as required. If harness and connectors are okay, check back-up light relay and back-up light switch. If either component is faulty, replace component. If components are okay, check harness between switch, relay and solenoids. If harness is okay check solenoids as described in step **2)**. Repair or replace as necessary.

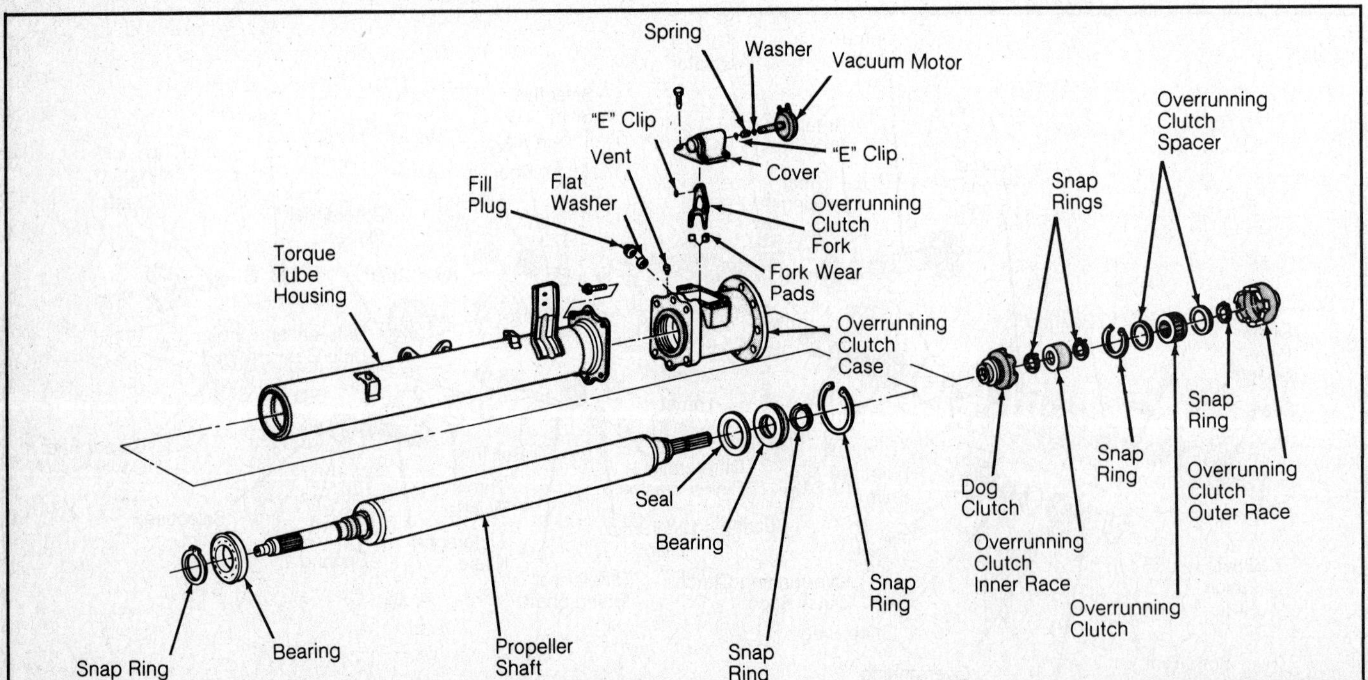
Spring
Washer
Vacuum Motor
"E" Clip
Vent
"E" Clip
Cover
Fill Plug
Flat Washer
Overrunning Clutch Fork
Fork Wear Pads
Torque Tube Housing
Overrunning Clutch Case
Overrunning Clutch Spacer
Snap Rings
Snap Ring
Snap Ring
Overrunning Clutch Outer Race
Dog Clutch
Overrunning Clutch Inner Race
Overrunning Clutch
Seal
Bearing
Snap Ring
Snap Ring
Snap Ring
Bearing
Propeller Shaft
91E13478
Courtesy of Chrysler Motors.

Fig. 2: Exploded View Of Torque Tube & Overrunning Clutch Assembly

1991 DRIVE AXLES
All-Wheel Drive Axle (Cont.)

5) Check that vacuum valve is installed correctly. If valve is incorrectly installed, replace vacuum reservoir. If vacuum valve is installed correctly, check for leaking vacuum reservoir. If reservoir is leaking, replace reservoir. If vacuum reservoir is okay, check front and rear vacuum harnesses. If vacuum harnesses are okay, proceed to next step. If vacuum harnesses are faulty, repair or replace as required.
6) Check for plugged vacuum filter. If filter is plugged, replace filter. If filter is okay, check vacuum motor for leaks. If vacuum motor is leaking, replace motor. If vacuum motor is not leaking, check for motor shaft jammed condition. If vacuum motor shaft is jammed, replace vacuum motor.

REMOVAL & INSTALLATION

REAR DRIVELINE MODULE (RDLM)

Removal & Installation - 1) Raise and support vehicle. Remove left and right inner half-shaft joint mounting bolts and support half-shafts to one side. Remove propeller shaft-to-viscous coupling bolts and support propeller shaft to one side. Remove viscous coupling retaining nut and slide coupling off RDLM assembly.
2) Disconnect RDLM main vacuum harness. Support RDLM with suitable transmission jack and chain RDLM to jack to prevent assembly falling. Remove RDLM rear mounting bolts. Remove RDLM front mounting bolts. Partially lower RDLM and disconnect remote solenoid vent and remote carrier vent. Carefully lower RDLM from vehicle.
3) To install RDLM, reverse removal procedure. Tighten mounting bolts to specification. See TORQUE SPECIFICATIONS at end of article.

REAR CARRIER UNIT

Removal & Installation - 1) Remove RDLM. See REAR DRIVELINE MODULE (RDLM). Drain oil from overrunning clutch assembly. Remove overrunning clutch-to-rear carrier case bolts. Separate rear carrier case from overrunning clutch case.
2) To install rear carrier, reverse removal procedure. Tighten mounting bolts to specification. See TORQUE SPECIFICATIONS table at end of article.

TORQUE TUBE

Removal & Installation - 1) Remove RDLM. See REAR DRIVELINE MODULE (RDLM). Remove viscous coupling. Remove snap ring and torque tube bearing shield. Remove torque tube-to-overrunning clutch bolts. Slide torque tube off of propeller shaft.
2) To install torque tube, reverse removal procedure. Tighten bolts to specifications. See TORQUE SPECIFICATIONS table at end of article.

PROPELLER SHAFT & REAR HALF-SHAFTS

NOTE: Propeller shaft and rear half-shafts may be removed without removing RDLM from vehicle.

Removal & Installation (Propeller Shaft) - Raise and support vehicle. Remove propeller shaft rear mounting bolts and support shaft. Remove propeller shaft front mounting bolts and remove propeller shaft. To install propeller shaft, reverse removal procedure. Tighten bolts to specification. See TORQUE SPECIFICATIONS at end of article.
Removal & Installation (Rear Half-Shaft) - Raise and support vehicle so that rear wheels hang freely. Remove rear wheel assembly. Remove cotter pin, nut lock and spring washer. Remove hub nut and washer. Remove inner half-shaft mounting bolts. Compress inner half-shaft joint slightly, pull downward to clear differential and remove half-shaft. To install half-shaft, reverse removal procedure. Tighten retaining bolts and axle nut to specifications. See TORQUE SPECIFICATIONS at end of article.

OVERHAUL

NOTE: All overhaul procedures except REAR CARRIER OUTPUT SHAFT SEALS and DIFFERENTIAL SIDE GEARS require removal of RDLM.

REAR CARRIER OUTPUT SHAFT SEALS

Removal & Installation - 1) Remove appropriate inner half-shaft retaining bolts and support shaft to one side. Using 2 pry bars and 2 wooden support blocks, pop out output shaft. *See Fig. 4.* Carefully pry oil seal from rear carrier case so as not to damage bearing race.

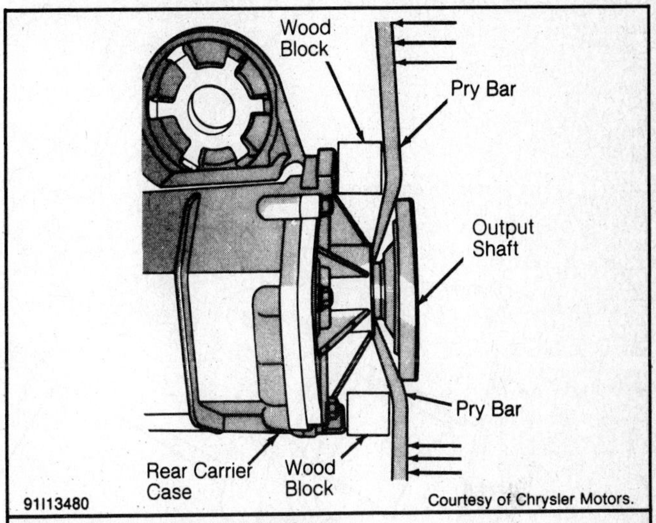
Wood
Block
Pry Bar
Output
Shaft
Pry Bar
Rear Carrier
Case
Wood
Block
91I13480
Courtesy of Chrysler Motors.

Fig. 4: Removing Output Shaft

2) Clean and inspect shaft and seal area. Install seal using Seal Installer (MD998334). Install output shaft. Using a soft-face mallet, tap output shaft into rear carrier assembly until retainer ring seats. Check and top off differential fluid.

FRONT OVERRUNNING CLUTCH SEAL

Removal - 1) Remove RDLM and viscous coupling unit. See REAR DRIVELINE MODULE (RDLM) under REMOVAL & INSTALLATION. Remove overrunning clutch cover assembly. *See Fig. 5.* Drain fluid from overrunning clutch. Remove overrunning clutch case-to-rear carrier bolts. Separate overrunning clutch case from rear carrier case.
2) Remove overrunning clutch inner race snap ring. Slide overrunning clutch inner race off of shaft. Remove shaft snap ring and slide dog clutch off shaft. Remove propeller shaft snap ring and torque tube bearing shield.
3) Remove torque tube retaining bolts. Remove inner propeller shaft bearing snap ring. Separate overrunning clutch case from torque tube. Remove rear propeller shaft bearing retaining outer snap ring in overrunning clutch case. Remove rear propeller shaft bearing. Remove seal using Seal Driver (C-4967).
Installation - 1) Clean and inspect sealing surface for nicks or grooves. Replace as required. Using Seal Installer (MD998334), install seal flush with outer edge of case. Install rear propeller shaft bearing and outer snap ring. Install overrunning clutch case onto torque tube and tighten bolts to specification. See TORQUE SPECIFICATIONS table at end of article.
2) Install propeller shaft inner snap ring. Install dog clutch and snap ring. Slide overrunning clutch inner race onto shaft with tapered end of inner race facing outward. Install inner race retaining snap ring.
3) Clean sealing surfaces, apply a bead of Mopar Gasket Maker (4318083), and reinstall overrunning clutch housing to rear carrier case. Install bolts and tighten to specification.
4) Clean sealing surfaces, apply a bead of Mopar Gasket Maker (4318083), and reinstall overrunning clutch cover. Ensure that overrunning clutch fork engages clutch dog. Install RDLM into vehicle. Check and fill fluid levels as required.

DRIVE PINION SEAL & REAR OVERRUNNING CLUTCH SEAL

NOTE: Overrunning clutch seal must be removed to gain access to input pinion seal. DO NOT reuse overrunning clutch seal.

1991 DRIVE AXLES
All-Wheel Drive Axle (Cont.)

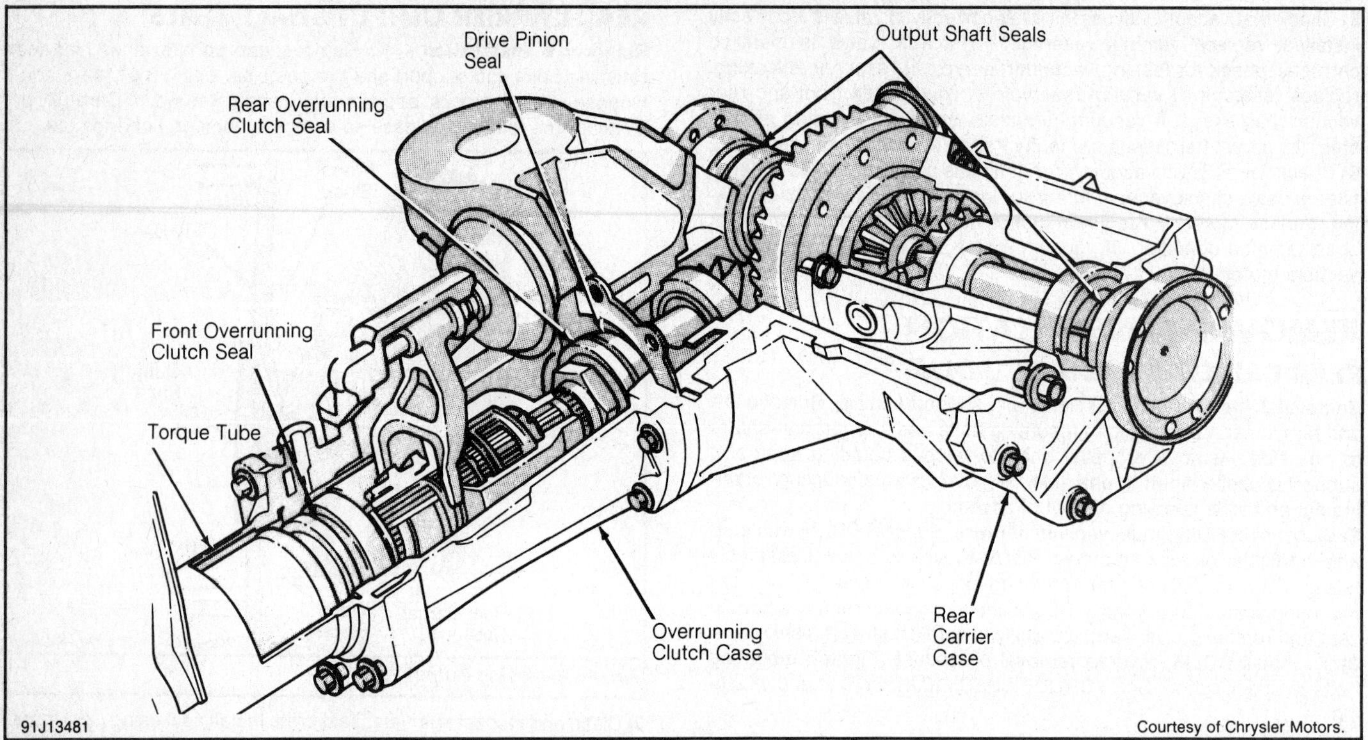
Drive Pinion
Seal
Output Shaft Seals
Rear Overrunning
Clutch Seal
Front Overrunning
Clutch Seal
Torque Tube
Overrunning
Clutch Case
Rear
Carrier
Case
91J13481
Courtesy of Chrysler Motors.

Fig. 5: Identifying Rear Carrier Assembly & Overrunning Clutch Assembly Seals

Removal - 1) Remove RDLM. Remove overrunning clutch case-to-rear carrier bolts. Separate overrunning clutch case from differential carrier case. Remove overrunning clutch outer race snap ring. Slide overrunning clutch off of shaft.

2) Using Spline Tool (6534) and a wrench, remove drive pinion nut. Remove front carrier cover retaining screws and remove cover. Remove pinion spacer and bearing shim from pinion shaft by inverting carrier cover and tapping pinion shaft on a block of wood. *See Fig. 6.* Reinstall front carrier cover into carrier case and tighten retaining bolts to 105 INCH lbs. (12 N.m)

CAUTION: Install bearing shim along with cover to avoid possibility of cutting "O" ring.

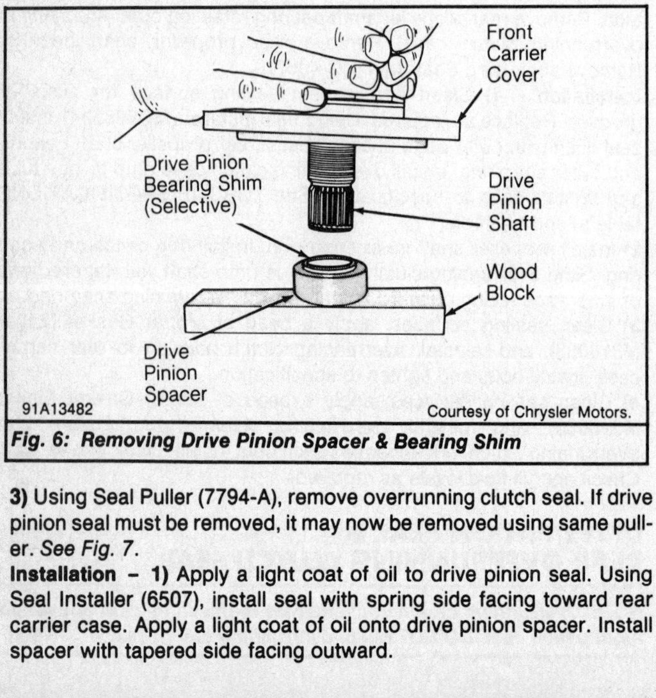
Front
Carrier
Cover
Drive Pinion
Bearing Shim
(Selective)
Drive
Pinion
Shaft
Wood
Block
Drive
Pinion
Spacer
91A13482
Courtesy of Chrysler Motors.

Fig. 6: Removing Drive Pinion Spacer & Bearing Shim

3) Using Seal Puller (7794-A), remove overrunning clutch seal. If drive pinion seal must be removed, it may now be removed using same puller. *See Fig. 7.*

Installation - 1) Apply a light coat of oil to drive pinion seal. Using Seal Installer (6507), install seal with spring side facing toward rear carrier case. Apply a light coat of oil onto drive pinion spacer. Install spacer with tapered side facing outward.

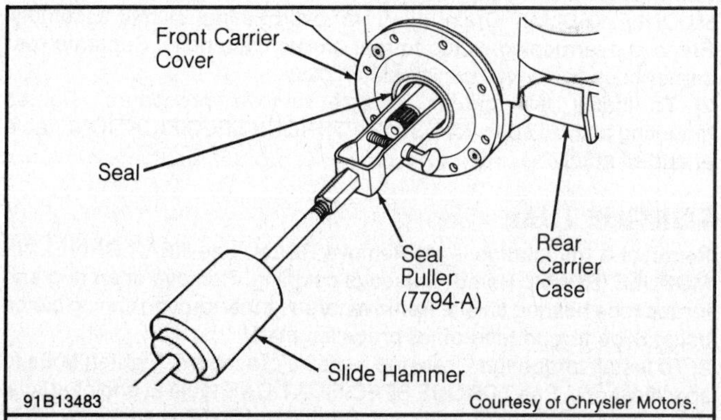
Front Carrier
Cover
Seal
Seal
Puller
(7794-A)
Rear
Carrier
Case
Slide Hammer
91B13483
Courtesy of Chrysler Motors.

Fig. 7: Removing Overrunning Clutch & Drive Pinion Seals

CAUTION: If drive pinion spacer is grooved or damaged, it must be replaced. Replacement spacer may require different size bearing shim. See DRIVE PINION BEARING SHIM SELECTION.

2) Apply a light coat of oil onto overrunning clutch seal. Using Seal Installer (6508), install seal with spring side facing AWAY from rear carrier case. Install drive pinion nut and tighten to 155 ft. lbs. (210 N.m). Install overrunning clutch outer race and snap ring.

3) Apply sealer to overrunning clutch sealing surface and reinstall overrunning clutch case to rear carrier case. Install RDLM into vehicle. Check and fill all fluids as required.

DRIVE PINION BEARING SHIM SELECTION

NOTE: This procedure MUST be performed whenever drive pinion spacer requires replacement.

1) Using a one inch micrometer, measure thickness of ORIGINAL spacer. *See Fig. 8.* Measure NEW spacer in same manner. If new spacer is same thickness as old spacer, reuse original shim. If new pinion spacer measurement is less than original pinion spacer measurement, a thicker shim is required. If new pinion spacer measurement is greater than original pinion spacer measurement, a thinner shim is required.

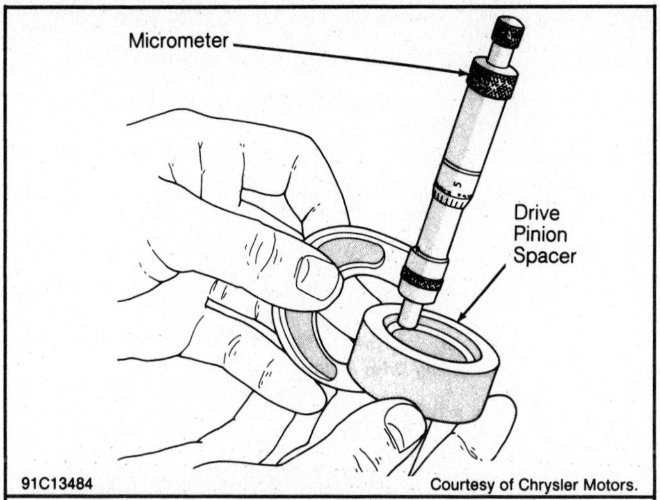

Micrometer
Drive
Pinion
Spacer
91C13484
Courtesy of Chrysler Motors.

Fig. 8: Measuring Drive Pinion Spacer

2) Record difference in measurements between new spacer and original spacer. Measure and record thickness of original shim. Add or subtract difference in spacer measurements to shim measurement to determine correct shim size.

DIFFERENTIAL SIDE GEARS

Removal – Disconnect both half-shafts from RDLM and support to one side. Using 2 pry bars, pop out output shafts. *See Fig. 4*. Remove differential end cover bolts and remove cover. Remove differential assembly from case.

Disassembly & Inspection – Remove ring gear bolts and separate differential case from differential body. Using a hammer and punch, remove differential pinion shaft roll pin. Remove differential pinion shaft from differential case. Inspect and replace pinion gears, pinion shaft and pinion washers as required.

Installation – To reassemble differential carrier assembly, reverse disassembly procedure. To complete overhaul, install differential assembly into case. Clean sealer surfaces, apply a bead of Mopar Gasket Maker (4318083) and install end cover. Tighten bolts, in sequence, to specification. *See Fig. 9*. See TORQUE SPECIFICATIONS at end of article.

TORQUE TUBE BEARINGS

Removal & Installation (Front Bearing) – **1)** Remove RDLM. Remove viscous coupling. Remove overrunning clutch cover assembly and drain fluid. Remove overrunning clutch case-to-rear carrier case bolts and separate overrunning clutch case from carrier case.

2) Remove overrunning clutch inner race snap ring. Slide overrunning clutch inner race off of shaft. Remove shaft snap ring and slide dog clutch off of shaft. Remove propeller shaft rear bearing snap ring.

3) Remove overrunning clutch case-to-torque tube bolts. Separate torque tube from overrunning clutch case. Remove front snap ring and torque tube bearing shield. Slide propeller shaft out of torque tube. Drive bearing out of housing.

4) To install torque tube front bearing, reverse removal procedure. Tighten bolts to specifications.

Removal & Installation (Rear Bearing) – **1)** Remove RDLM. Remove viscous coupling. Remove overrunning clutch cover assembly and drain fluid. Remove overrunning clutch case-to-rear carrier case bolts and separate overrunning clutch case from carrier case.

2) Remove overrunning clutch inner race snap ring. Slide overrunning clutch inner race off of shaft. Remove shaft snap ring and slide dog clutch off of shaft. Remove propeller shaft rear bearing snap ring.

3) Remove overrunning clutch case-to-torque tube bolts. Separate torque tube from overrunning clutch case. Remove rear bearing retaining snap ring in overrunning clutch case. Remove rear torque tube bearing.

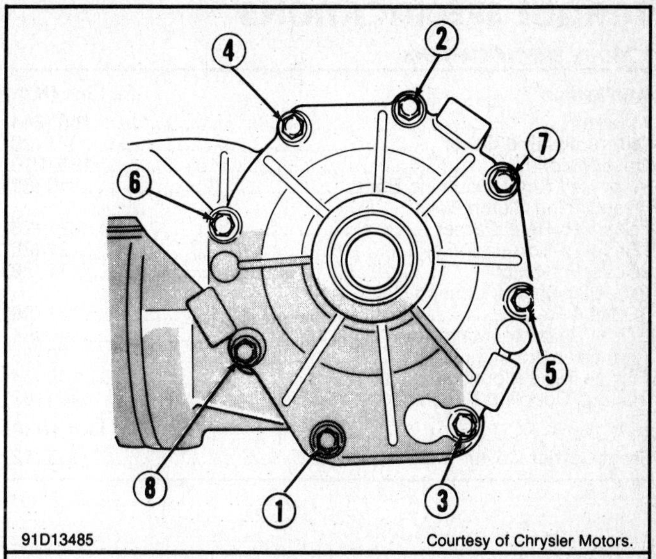

4
2
7
6
5
8
1
3
91D13485
Courtesy of Chrysler Motors.

Fig. 9: Identifying Rear Carrier Cover Bolt Tightening Sequence

4) To install torque tube rear bearing, reverse removal procedure. Tighten bolts to specifications.

OVERRUNNING CLUTCH

Removal (Vacuum Motor)– **1)** Remove RDLM. Disconnect hoses to vacuum motor. Remove overrunning clutch cover assembly mounting bolts. Lift overrunning clutch cover assembly off of overrunning clutch case.

2) Clamp assembly in soft-jawed vise. Remove 2 "E" clips from vacuum motor shaft. While holding overrunning clutch shift fork, slide vacuum motor out of housing. Clean and inspect all parts and sealing surfaces. Replace worn or damaged parts.

CAUTION: Note position of shift fork before removing vacuum motor as it is possible to install fork backwards. Offset on fork must angle AWAY from vacuum motor.

Installation – Slide vacuum motor into housing and through shift fork. Install 2 "E" clips: one on vacuum motor shaft and one on vacuum motor bushing. Apply a bead of Mopar Gasket Maker (4318083) and reinstall cover assembly. Ensure that shift fork engages overrunning clutch dog. Install RDLM into vehicle. Check and fill fluid levels as required.

Removal (Overrunning Clutch Assembly) – **1)** Remove RDLM. Remove overrunning clutch assembly cover and drain fluid. Separate overrunning clutch case from rear carrier case. Remove overrunning clutch snap ring. Remove spacers and overrunning clutch.

CAUTION: Keep overrunning clutch components in order as removed to prevent reassembling backward.

2) Remove overrunning clutch outer race snap ring. Slide outer race off of shaft. Remove overrunning clutch inner snap ring. Slide inner race off of shaft. Remove dog clutch snap ring and slide dog clutch off of shaft. Clean and inspect all parts and repair or replace as necessary.

Installation – **1)** Install outer overrunning clutch race and snap ring. Install overrunning clutch spacers and snap ring. To test for proper installation, temporarily install the inner race into the overrunning clutch, tapered end first. Inner race should spin when turned counterclockwise and grab when turned clockwise.

2) Install dog clutch onto shaft and reinstall snap ring. Install overrunning onto the shaft with the tapered end facing outward and install snap ring. Apply Mopar Gasket Maker (4318083) sealer and reinstall overrunning clutch case to rear carrier case. Apply sealer and reinstall overrunning clutch cover making sure that shift fork engages clutch dog. Install RDLM into vehicle. Check and fill fluid levels as required.

1991 DRIVE AXLES
All-Wheel Drive Axle (Cont.)

TORQUE SPECIFICATIONS

TORQUE SPECIFICATIONS

Application	Ft. Lbs. (N.m)
Axle Nut	180 (244)
Differential End Cover	21 (28)
Drive Pinion Nut	155 (210)
Inner Half Shaft Mounting Bolts	45 (61)
Overrunning Clutch Bolts	
Case-To-Rear Carrier	21 (28)
Case-To-Torque Tube	21 (28)
Cover Assembly	21 (28)
Propeller Shaft Mounting Bolts	
Front & Rear	21 (28)
RDLM Rear Mounting Bolts	40 (54)
Ring Gear Bolts	70 (95)
Torque Tube Mounting Bolts	40 (54)
Viscous Coupling Retaining Nut	120 (163)
	INCH Lbs. (N.m)
Front Carrier Cover	105 (12)

1991 DRIVE AXLES
Locking Hubs

Pickup, Ramcharger

DESCRIPTION

Locking hubs provide a means of engaging and disengaging front wheels from the front transfer case. When locking hubs and transfer case are engaged, power is transmitted to front wheels. When hubs are disengaged and transfer case is not in 4WD, front wheels are free wheeling and axle shafts and differential remain idle.

Engagement is accomplished through gears within the hub. With hub engaged, the inner clutch gear locks with the outer clutch and engages the axle shaft with wheel hub.

REMOVAL & INSTALLATION

Removal - 1) Turn shift knob to ENGAGE position. Apply downward pressure to face of shift knob and remove 3 shift knob retaining screws nearest to flange. With an outward pull, remove shift knob from mounting base.

2) Remove snap ring from axle shaft. Remove cam screws and lock washers from mounting base flange. Separate and remove locking hub assembly from rotor hub. Remove and discard gasket.

Inspection - Wash parts in mineral spirits and blow dry with compressed air. Examine gear splines, shift knob, cam, sliding gear, drive shaft gear and mounting base for damage. Replace as necessary.

Installation - 1) Lubricate parts lightly with multipurpose lubricant. Position new gasket and locking hub onto rotor hub. Install attaching cap screws and lock washers. Tighten to 30-40 ft. lbs. (41-54 N.m). Install axle shaft snap ring.

2) Position shift knob on mounting base. Align splines by pushing inward on shift knob. Turn clockwise to lock in position. Install and tighten 3 shift knob retaining screws.

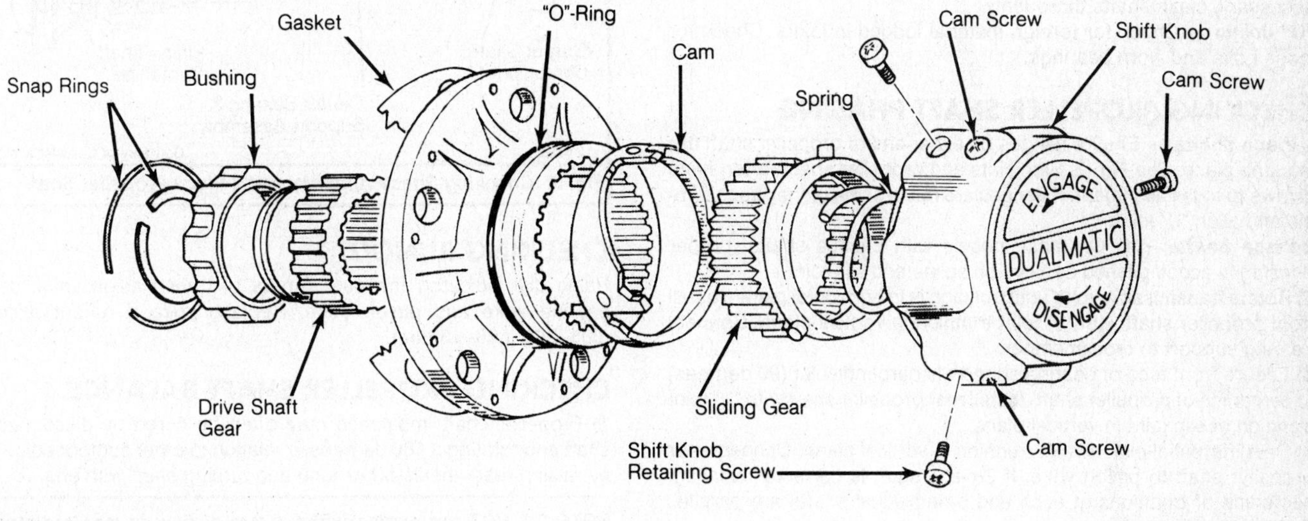
Gasket
"O"-Ring
Cam Screw
Shift Knob
Cam
Cam Screw
Snap Rings
Bushing
Spring
ENGAGE
DUALMATIC
DISENGAGE
Drive Shaft
Gear
Sliding Gear
Shift Knob
Retaining Screw
Cam Screw
121019
Courtesy of Chrysler Motors.

Fig. 1: Exploded View of Locking Hub Assembly

1991 DRIVE AXLES
Propeller Shafts

Dakota, Pickup, Ramcharger, RWD Van

DESCRIPTION

Propeller shafts are balanced, tubular shafts with "U" joints at each end. Number of shafts used in vehicle varies: single shaft, 2 shafts with center bearing, or 3 shafts. *See Fig. 1.* Most 4WD applications use 3 shafts. Location of slip joints varies with model application.

CHECKING & ADJUSTING

Vibration can come from many sources. Before overhauling driveline, check other sources of possible vibration.

Tires & Wheels – Check tire inflation and wheel balance. Check for foreign objects in tread, damaged tread, mismatched tread patterns or incorrect tire size.

Center Bearing – Tighten propeller shaft center bearing mounting bolts. If bearing insulator is deteriorated or oil-soaked, replace it.

Engine & Transmission Mountings – Tighten mounting bolts. If mountings are deteriorated, replace them.

Propeller Shaft – Check propeller shaft for missing weights or for dents affecting balance. Check for undercoating adhering to shafts. If necessary, clean shafts thoroughly.

"U" Joints – Check for foreign material lodged in joints. Check for loose bolts and worn bearings.

CHECKING PROPELLER SHAFT PHASING

1-Piece Shafts – Ensure flanges on either end of propeller shaft are in same plane. *See Fig. 2.* Slip joints and propeller shafts often have arrows to aid in alignment. If flanges are not in same plane, disassemble and align "U" joint.

2-Piece Shafts – **1)** On most models with 2-piece shafts, proper phasing is accomplished by keys on spline and slip joint.

2) Rotate transmission yoke until trunnion is in horizontal plane. Install front propeller shaft with "U" joint trunnion in vertical plane. Connect bearing support to crossmember.

3) Ensure front face of bearing support is perpendicular (90 degrees) to centerline of propeller shaft. Install rear propeller shaft with "U" joint trunnion of slip joint in vertical plane.

4) Set differential pinion yoke trunnion in vertical plane. Connect rear propeller shaft to pinion yoke. If 2-piece shaft is correctly installed, centerline of trunnions at each end of individual shafts are parallel. *See Fig. 3.*

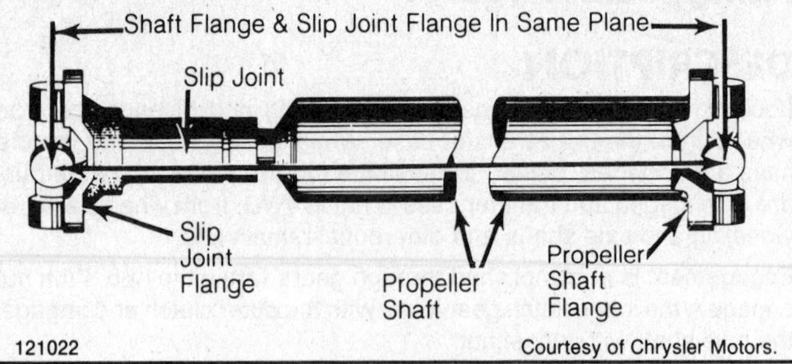
Shaft Flange & Slip Joint Flange In Same Plane
Slip Joint
Slip Joint Flange
Propeller Shaft
Propeller Shaft Flange
121022
Courtesy of Chrysler Motors.

Fig. 2: Checking Phase Alignment of 1-Piece Propeller Shaft

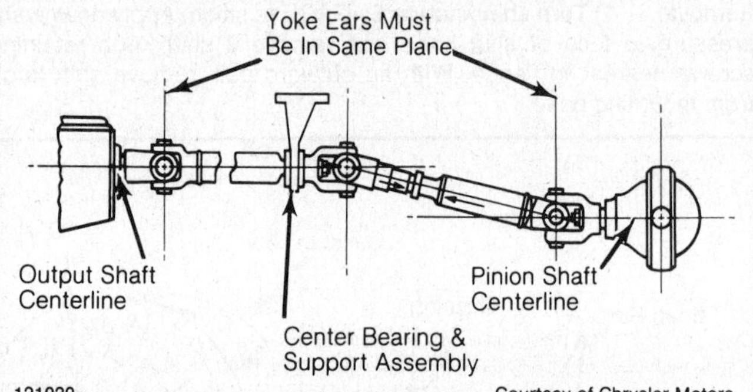
Yoke Ears Must Be In Same Plane
Output Shaft Centerline
Pinion Shaft Centerline
Center Bearing & Support Assembly
121020
Courtesy of Chrysler Motors.

Fig. 3: Checking Phase Alignment of 2-Piece Propeller Shaft

CHECKING RUNOUT

Using dial indicator, measure runout of transmission yoke, center bearing yoke and pinion yoke. Replace yoke if runout exceeds .003-.005" (.08-.13 mm).

CHECKING PROPELLER SHAFT BALANCE

1) Propeller shaft imbalance may often be cured by disconnecting shaft and rotating it 180 degrees in relation to other components. Test by raising rear wheels off ground and turning shaft with engine.

NOTE: DO NOT run engine without ram airflow across radiator for prolonged periods, as engine or transmission may overheat.

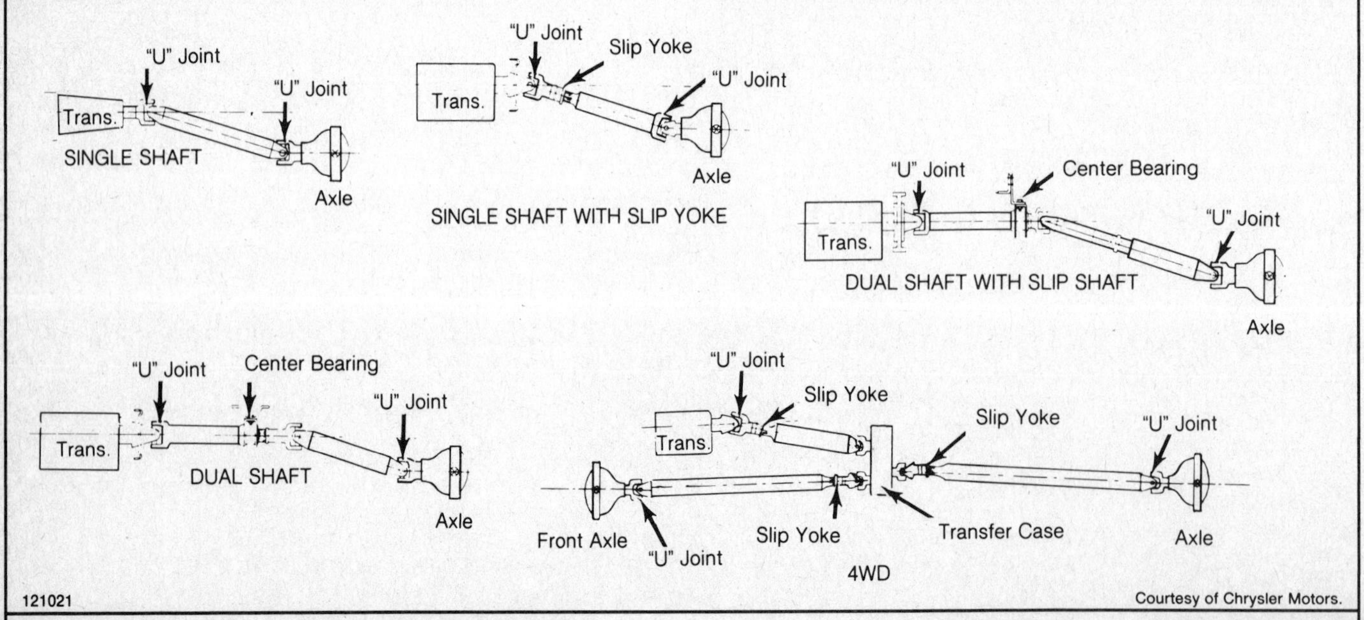
"U" Joint
"U" Joint
Trans.
SINGLE SHAFT
Axle
"U" Joint
Slip Yoke
"U" Joint
Trans.
Axle
SINGLE SHAFT WITH SLIP YOKE
"U" Joint
Center Bearing
"U" Joint
Trans.
DUAL SHAFT WITH SLIP SHAFT
Axle
"U" Joint
Center Bearing
"U" Joint
Trans.
DUAL SHAFT
Axle
"U" Joint
Slip Yoke
Trans.
Slip Yoke
"U" Joint
Front Axle
"U" Joint
Slip Yoke
Transfer Case
Axle
4WD
121021
Courtesy of Chrysler Motors.

Fig. 1: Identifying 5 Common Propeller Shaft Combinations

2) On most models, balance testing may be done by marking shaft in 4 positions, 90 degrees apart. Place marks approximately 6" forward of weld, at rear end of shaft. Number marks 1-4.

3) Place screw-type hose clamp so clamp head is in No. 1 position, and rotate shaft with engine. If there is little or no change in vibration intensity, move clamp head to No. 2 position, and repeat test.

4) Continue procedure until vibration is at lowest level. If no difference is noted with clamp head moved to all 4 positions, vibrations may not be propeller shaft imbalance.

5) If vibration decreases but is not completely eliminated, place a second clamp at same position, and repeat test. Combined weight of both clamps in one position may increase vibration. If so, rotate clamps 1/2" apart, above and below best position, and repeat test.

6) Continue to rotate clamps as necessary, until vibration is at lowest point. If vibration level is still unacceptable, leave rear clamp(s) in place, and repeat procedure at front end of propeller shaft. If vibration can be eliminated or reduced to acceptable level, bend back slack end of clamp so screw cannot loosen. Road test vehicle. On 4WD models, procedure may be used on each shaft.

CHECKING VERTICAL ANGLE

1-Piece Shafts – 1) Using Inclinometer (C-4224), measure propeller shaft vertical angle. *See Fig. 4.*

2) Raise and support vehicle so rear wheels can be rotated. Rotate propeller shaft so a PINION YOKE bearing cap faces downward. Attach inclinometer magnet to bearing cap, and note angle.

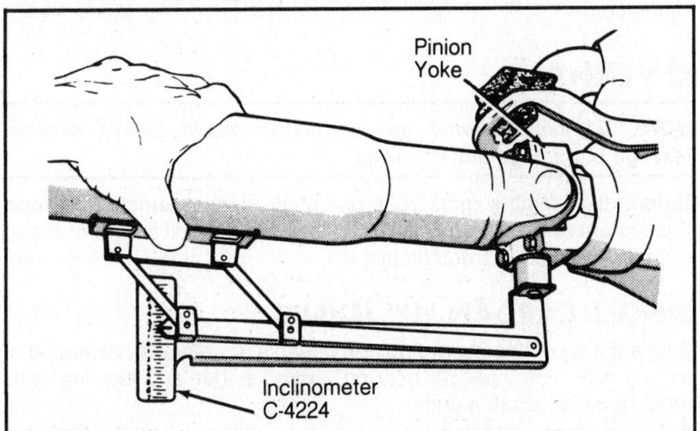
Pinion
Yoke
Inclinometer
C-4224

91D13469 Courtesy of Chrysler Motors.

Fig 4: Measuring Propeller Shaft Vertical Angle

3) Rotate propeller shaft until a REAR YOKE bearing cap faces downward. Attach inclinometer magnet to bearing cap, and note angle. Difference between 2 measured angles is propeller shaft rear angle. *See Fig. 5.*

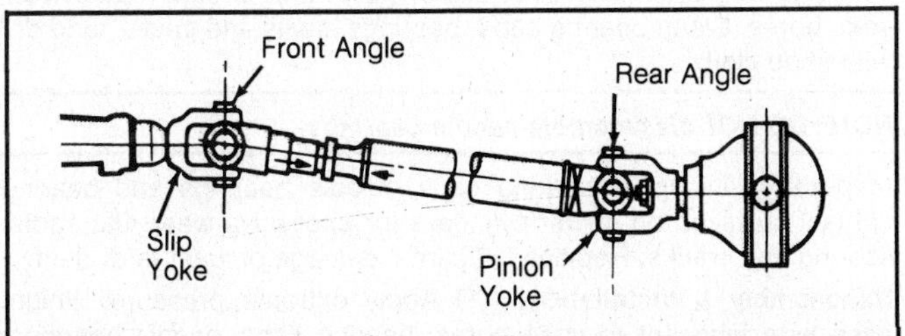
Front Angle
Rear Angle
Slip
Yoke
Pinion
Yoke

91G13470 Courtesy of Chrysler Motors.

Fig 5: Identifying Front & Rear Vertical Angle

4) Rotate propeller shaft until a SLIP YOKE bearing cap faces downward. Attach inclinometer magnet to bearing cap, and note angle. Rotate propeller shaft until FRONT YOKE bearing cap faces downward. Attach inclinometer magnet to bearing cap, and note angle.

5) Difference between 2 measured angles is propeller shaft front angle. *See Fig. 5.* Compare front and rear angles. Allowable difference between angles is plus or minus one degree. If difference of angles is greater than specified, adjustment is necessary.

2-Piece Shafts ("Broken Back" Type) – 1) All yokes must be perpendicular in both vertical and horizontal planes to engine crankshaft. Only exception is "broken back" type driveline, in which yokes are not perpendicular in vertical plane. *See Fig. 6.*

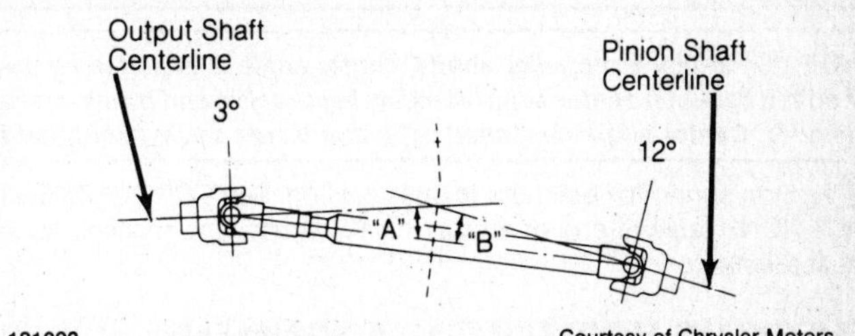
Output Shaft
Centerline
3°
Pinion Shaft
Centerline
12°
"A"
"B"

121023 Courtesy of Chrysler Motors.

Fig. 6: Identifying "Broken Back" Type Propeller Shaft

2) With non-parallel or "broken back" type installation, working angles of "U" joints of given propeller shaft are equal. Angle "A" = angle "B".

3) Calculate by subtracting angle of output shaft centerline from angle of propeller shaft. Difference should equal front shaft angle subtracted from rear shaft angle.

2-Piece Shafts (Except "Broken Back" Type) – 1) Using Inclinometer (C-4224), measure propeller shaft vertical angle.

2) Raise and support vehicle so rear wheels can be rotated. Rotate propeller shaft so a PINION YOKE bearing cap faces downward. Attach inclinometer magnet to bearing cap, and note angle. *See Fig. 4.*

3) Rotate propeller shaft until a REAR YOKE bearing cap faces downward. Attach inclinometer magnet to bearing cap, and note angle. Difference between 2 measured angles is propeller shaft rear angle.

4) Rotate propeller shaft until a SLIP YOKE bearing cap faces downward. Attach inclinometer magnet to bearing cap, and note angle. Rotate propeller shaft until a FRONT YOKE bearing cap faces downward. Attach inclinometer magnet to bearing cap, and note angle. Difference between 2 measured angles is propeller shaft front angle.

5) Rotate propeller shaft until FRONT yoke of rear shaft faces downward. Attach inclinometer magnet to bearing cap, and note angle. Rotate propeller shaft until REAR yoke of front propeller shaft faces downward. Attach inclinometer magnet to bearing cap, and note angle. Difference between 2 measured angles is propeller shaft center angle. Compare front, center and rear angles. Vertical alignment of 2-piece propeller shafts at yokes should be greater than 1/2 degree and must be retained as close to one degree as possible. *See Fig. 7.* If difference of angles is greater than specified, adjustment is necessary.

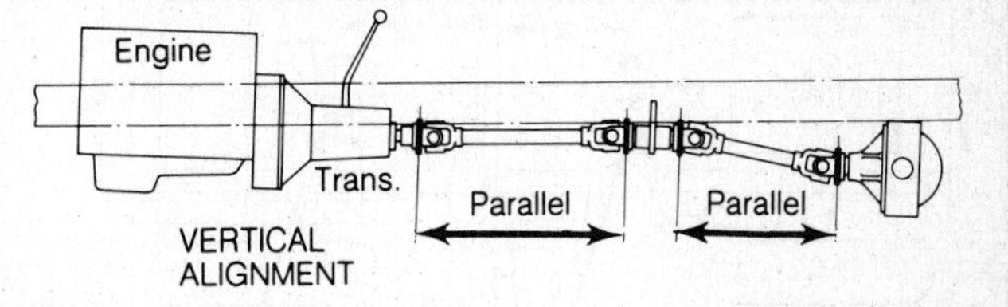
Engine
Trans.
Parallel
Parallel
VERTICAL
ALIGNMENT

121024 Courtesy of Chrysler Motors.

Fig. 7: Checking Vertical Alignment of 2-Piece Propeller Shaft

ADJUSTING VERTICAL ANGLE

1) If front angle minus rear angle is greater than one degree positive (+1 degree), rear angle is too small and must be increased. If front angle minus rear angle is greater than one degree negative (-1 degree), rear angle is too large and must be decreased. To adjust angle, proceed to step **2)**.

2) Raise and support rear of vehicle using jackstands under frame. Position a hydraulic jack under differential housing. Remove rear wheel assemblies. Loosen rear spring "U" bolt nuts. Insert tapered shim between spring and axle spring pad. If increasing angle, insert shim with taper facing front of vehicle. If decreasing angle, insert shim with taper facing rear of vehicle.

1991 DRIVE AXLES
Propeller Shafts (Cont.)

NOTE: If encountering difficulty in making propeller shaft vertical adjustments on 1-piece propeller shafts, propeller shaft may be out of horizontal alignment. See CHECKING HORIZONTAL ALIGNMENT under CHECKING & ADJUSTMENTS.

NOTE: On 2-piece propeller shafts, center angle is adjusted by use of shims between center support mounting bracket and frame cross-member. Center angle may need adjusting if rear angle is changed.

3) Tighten spring "U" bolt nuts to specification. See TORQUE SPECIFICATIONS table at end of article. Install wheels, and recheck angle measurements.

CHECKING HORIZONTAL ALIGNMENT

1) Propeller shaft horizontal alignment should be checked if collision damage is suspected or when major components have been replaced. *See Fig. 8.*

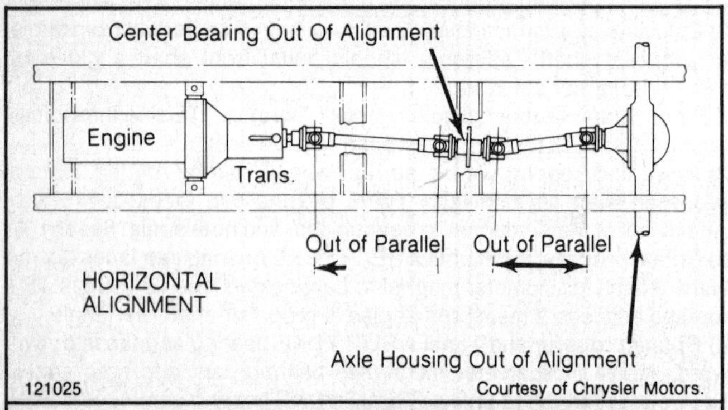
Center Bearing Out Of Alignment
Engine
Trans.
Out of Parallel
Out of Parallel
HORIZONTAL ALIGNMENT
Axle Housing Out of Alignment
121025
Courtesy of Chrysler Motors.

Fig. 8: Identifying Horizontal Misalignment of Propeller Shaft

2) Clamp a straightedge (12" longer than width of rear wheel track) at 90 degrees to frame side rails. *See Fig. 9.* Use large framing squares to align straightedge with side rails.

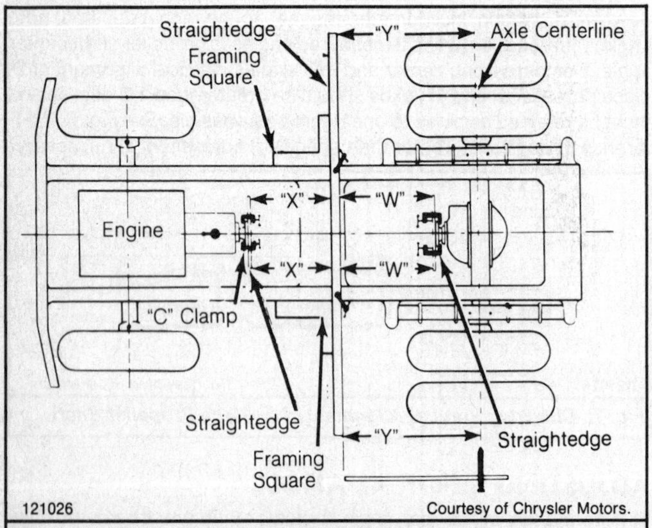
Straightedge
Framing Square
"Y"
Axle Centerline
Engine
"X"
"W"
"X"
"W"
"C" Clamp
Straightedge
Framing Square
"Y"
Straightedge
121026
Courtesy of Chrysler Motors.

Fig. 9: Checking Horizontal Alignment

3) To make horizontal alignment checks, set up straightedges. *See Fig. 9.* Set transmission output yoke horizontal, and clamp straightedge to yoke in a horizontal plane. Repeat procedure with drive pinion yoke. Ensure yokes are horizontal by checking angle of straightedge using a machinist spirit level.

4) Measure distance "X" at each side. If measurements are not within 1/16" (1.6 mm) of each other, transmission flange is horizontally misaligned.

5) Measure distance "Y" (edge of straightedge to axle shaft centerline) at each side. If measurements are not within 1/8" (3.2 mm) of each other, axle housing is misaligned.

6) Measure distance "W" at each side. If measurements are not within 1/16" (1.6 mm) of each other, pinion flange is horizontally misaligned.

ADJUSTING HORIZONTAL ALIGNMENT

NOTE: Excessive difference in measurements may indicate frame damage. DO NOT attempt to correct for more than slight horizontal misalignment.

Minute adjustment of propeller shaft horizontal alignment may be made by loosening axle housing "U" bolts and moving either side of axle housing forward or back. Only move axle slightly to make "W" measurements equal. *See Fig. 9.*

REMOVAL & INSTALLATION

CENTER BEARING

Removal – Disconnect propeller shaft from pinion yoke. Support shaft while removing center bearing mounting bolts. Slide propeller shaft from transmission extension housing.

Disassembly – Clamp front half-shaft in a vise. Remove and discard center bearing support and rubber insulator. Bend slinger away from center bearing to provide clearance for bearing puller. Using bearing puller, remove center bearing from front half-shaft.

Reassembly & Installation – To install, reverse disassembly and removal procedures. Ensure angle adjustment shims are replaced if removed.

OVERHAUL

NOTE: "U" joints should not be disassembled unless external leakage or damage has occurred.

Before disassembly, mark yoke and shaft for reassembly reference. If joints are rusted or corroded, apply penetrating oil before pressing out bearing cups or trunnion pin.

SINGLE CARDAN "U" JOINTS

Single cardan "U" joints are not serviceable. If defective, damaged or excessively worn, needle bearing, seals, spider and bearing cups must be replaced as a unit.

Removal & Disassembly – Remove propeller shaft. *See Fig. 10.* Remove bearing cap retainers. Press out bearing caps. Remove bearings, seals and spider from yoke bore.

NOTE: Saturate bearing caps with penetrating oil before removal.

Cleaning – Clean yoke arm bores using an appropriate cleaning solvent and wire brush. Remove all corrosion and foreign matter from yoke bores. Clean bearing caps, bearings, seals and spider, and dry with shop cloth.

NOTE: DO NOT disassemble needle bearings.

Inspection – Inspect bearing caps, needle bearings and bearing contact surfaces on spider cylinders for excessive wear, flat spots, scoring and cracks. Replace "U" joint if damage or wear is evident.

Reassembly & Installation – **1)** Apply extreme pressure, lithium base type lubricant to yoke bores, bearing caps, needle bearings, seals and bearing contact surfaces on spider cylinders. Position spider in yoke bores.

2) Insert seals into yoke bores and against spider cylinders. Tap bearing caps into yoke bore far enough to retain spider in place.

CAUTION: DO NOT clamp propeller shaft tube or slip yoke tube in a vise. Clamp only forged portion of each yoke in vise. To avoid distorting yoke, DO NOT overtighten vise jaws.

3) Carefully press bearing caps into yoke bores until retainers can be installed, keeping spider aligned in center of bearing caps. Install bearing cap retainers. If applicable, attach slip yoke to fixed yoke. Install propeller shaft, and tighten "U" joint clamp bolts to 14 ft. lbs. (19 N.m). Remove supports, and lower vehicle.

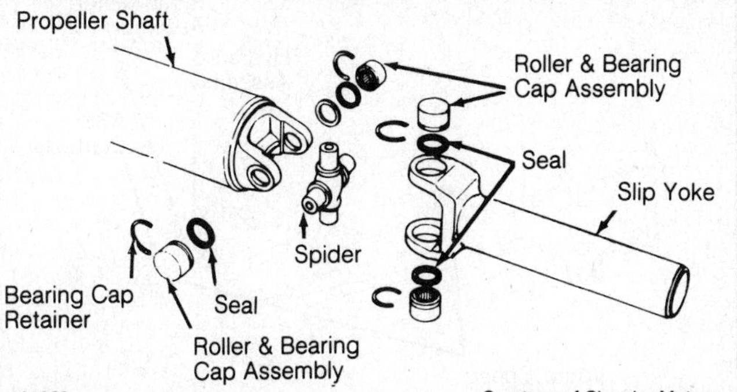
Propeller Shaft
Roller & Bearing
Cap Assembly
Seal
Slip Yoke
Spider
Bearing Cap
Retainer
Seal
Roller & Bearing
Cap Assembly

121028 Courtesy of Chrysler Motors.

Fig. 10: Exploded View of Sliding Yoke "U" Joint

DOUBLE CARDAN CONSTANT VELOCITY (CV) TYPE "U" JOINTS (4WD)

***NOTE:** To prevent damage to joints, center ball when removing propeller shaft assembly. When handling propeller shaft after removal, support shafts on both sides of constant velocity joint if propeller shaft is being moved horizontally. DO NOT allow one end to hang free or one shaft to bend at sharp angle. After removal, shaft may be carried vertically without damage.*

Removal & Disassembly (Dakota) – 1) Disconnect yoke attaching bolts and flange attaching bolts, and remove propeller shaft from vehicle. Mark propeller shaft, link and flange yokes for installation reference. *See Fig. 11.* Remove bearing cap snap rings.

2) Disassemble components in this order.

- Bearing caps retaining FRONT spider in link yoke.
- Separate link yoke from propeller shaft yoke.
- Bearing caps retaining REAR spider in link yoke.
- Separate link yoke from socket yoke.
- Bearing caps and spider from socket yoke.
- Bearing caps and spider from propeller shaft yoke.

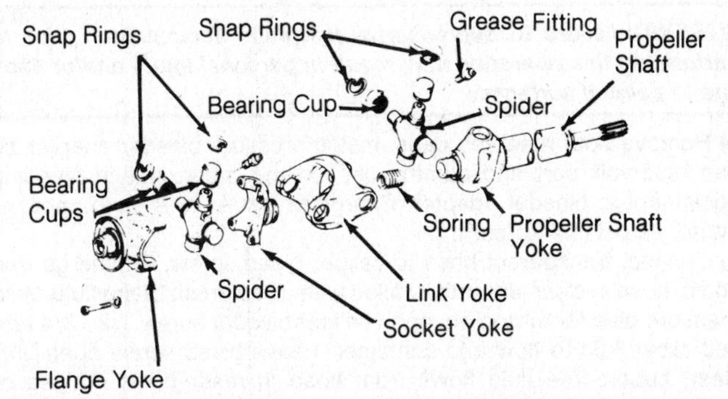
Snap Rings
Snap Rings
Grease Fitting
Propeller
Shaft
Bearing Cup
Spider
Bearing
Cups
Spring
Propeller Shaft
Yoke
Spider
Link Yoke
Socket Yoke
Flange Yoke

121027 Courtesy of Chrysler Motors.

Fig. 11: Exploded View of Double Cardan Constant Velocity "U" Joint (Pickup & Ramcharger)

Reassembly & Installation – Clean dirt and rust from all contact areas. Reassemble components in reverse order of disassembly, ensuring reference marks align. Install propeller shaft in vehicle, and tighten clamp bolts to 14 ft. lbs. (19 N.m).

Removal & Disassembly (Pickup & Ramcharger) – 1) Disconnect yoke attaching bolts and flange attaching bolts. Remove propeller shaft from vehicle. Mark center yoke, end yoke and spiders for installation reference.

2) Remove bearing cups in order. *See Fig. 12.* Support propeller shaft horizontally in line with base plate of press. Place rear ear of link yoke over a 1 1/8" socket. Place Press Remover (C-4365-1) on bearing cup in yoke. Press bearing cup out of link yoke ear.

3) If bearing cup is not completely removed, insert Spacer (C-4365-4), and complete removal of bearing cup. Rotate propeller shaft 180 degrees. Shear opposite plastic retaining ring. Press bearing cup out of link yoke.

4) Disengage trunnions of spider, still attached to flange yoke, from link yoke. Pull flange yoke and spider from centering ball on ball support on yoke tube. Ball socket is part of flange yoke. Pry seal from ball socket. Remove washers, spring and 3 shoes.

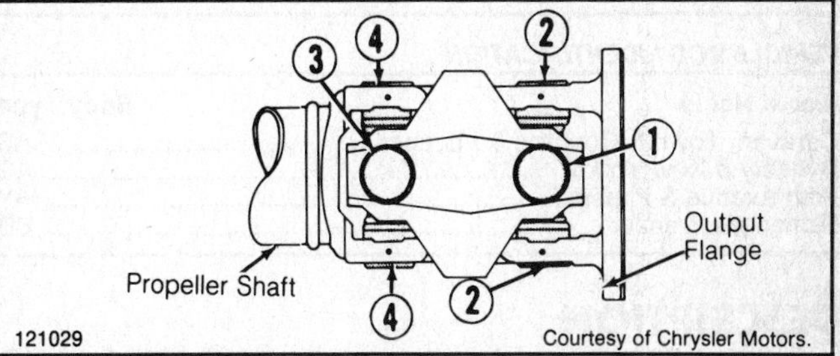
3
4
2
1
Output
Flange
Propeller Shaft
4
2

121029 Courtesy of Chrysler Motors.

Fig. 12: Identifying Bearing Cup Removal Sequence

Reassembly – 1) Using Ball Installer (C-4365-3), drive centering ball onto stud. Ensure ball seats firmly against shoulder at stud base.

2) To install spider, install one bearing cup part way into one side of yoke, and turn this yoke to bottom. Insert spider into yoke so trunnion seats into bearing cup.

3) Install opposite bearing cup part way. Press bearing cups, working spider to ensure free movement of trunnions in bearings. When one retaining ring groove clears inside of yoke, stop pressing, and snap retaining ring in place.

4) Continue to press until opposite retaining ring can be snapped into place. If encountering difficulty, strike yoke ear firmly using a hammer to seat retaining rings.

5) Lubricate center ball and socket. Assemble other half of "U" joint the same way. Lubricate all parts with grease provided with ball seat kit, and insert into clean ball seat in this order: spring, small O.D. washer, 3 ball seats with large opening outward, and large O.D. washer.

6) Lubricate seal lip, and press in seal until flush. Sealing lip should tip inward. Fill cavity with grease provided in service kit.

***NOTE:** Propeller shaft assembly, with spider and bearings installed, must have its yoke ears at each end of shaft on same plane.*

Installation – 1) Before installing propeller shaft, clean yoke, and inspect machined surface for scratches, nicks and burrs.

2) Support propeller shaft during installation to prevent damage to "U" joints. Position front end of shaft, aligning reference marks.

3) Attach 2 clamps to pinion yoke, and tighten attaching bolts to 14 ft. lbs. (19 N.m). Install 4 screws and lock washer assemblies on CV joint at transfer case. Use press bar to prevent assembly from rotating while attaching screw assemblies.

TORQUE SPECIFICATIONS

TORQUE SPECIFICATIONS

Application	Ft. Lbs. (N.m)
Center Bearing Bracket-To-Frame Bolts	50 (68)
Center Bearing Support-To-Bracket Bolts	50 (68)
Spring "U" Bolt Nuts	
Dakota	
2WD	65 (88)
4WD	110 (149)
Pickup, Ramcharger & RWD Van	
2WD (1/2" x 20")	45 (61)
4WD (1/2" x 20")	65 (88)
4WD (9/16" x 18")	180 (244)
"U" Joint Clamp Bolts	
1/4"	14 (19)
5/16"	25 (34)
Transfer Case	14 (19)
Wheel Lug Nuts	100 (136)

1991 BRAKES
Anti-Lock – Bendix-10

Caravan, Town & Country, Voyager

MODEL IDENTIFICATION

Throughout code charts, references to model designations will be made. Use the following VEHICLE BODY IDENTIFICATION table to determine the vehicle on which you are working.

NOTE: Diagnostic procedures and code charts include several references to AC, AY and BB bodies. For detailed coverage of those models, see 1991 Mitchell DOMESTIC CARS SERVICE & REPAIR manual.

VEHICLE BODY IDENTIFICATION

Model Name	Body Type
Caravan, Town & Country, & Voyager	AS
Dynasty & New Yorker	AC
Fifth Avenue & Imperial	AY
Monaco & Premier	BB

DESCRIPTION

Bendix-10 Anti-Lock Brake System (ABS) is designed to prevent wheel lock-up during heavy braking. This allows operator to maintain steering control, while stopping vehicle in shortest distance possible. Major components consist of hydraulic assembly, 4 wheel speed sensors, Anti-Lock Brake Controller (CAB), 2 warning lights (Red BRAKE and Amber ANTI-LOCK) and pump/motor assembly. *See Fig. 1*. ABS has a self-diagnostic system to warn of system malfunction and for trouble shooting.

NOTE: For more information on brake system, see appropriate DISC & DRUM article.

OPERATION

Each wheel sensor sends an AC electrical signal to the CAB. The CAB translates this information as wheel speed. When any decelerating wheel speed rate is determined to be excessive in comparison to other wheels, the CAB cycles hydraulic brake pressure to each wheel to equalize speed of all wheels. ABS turns itself off at 3-5 MPH. Minor lock-up may occur at this point.

Red BRAKE warning light will come on when ignition switch is in START position. Light should go off when ignition is released. If light does not go off, the following problems are possible: parking brake not fully released, low brake fluid, low accumulator pressure or low hydraulic pressure.

Amber ANTI-LOCK warning light will come on for 1-30 seconds after ignition is turned on. This indicates system is performing a self-diagnostic test. If light does not go off after indicated time, system has found a fault. ABS is deactivated during this period. Normal braking is unaffected. Testing should be done to find and correct fault.

CAUTION: See ANTI-LOCK BRAKE SAFETY PRECAUTIONS article in GENERAL INFORMATION.

SYSTEM PRECAUTIONS

1) DO NOT unplug or plug in CAB connector with ignition on. Before bleeding brake system or before disconnecting any hydraulic brake component (including brake lines), depressurize system by turning ignition switch to OFF position and depressing brake pedal 40 or more times.

2) Unplug CAB and sensor block connectors before using an arc welder on vehicle. When painting vehicle, CAB and sensor block should be insulated or removed before placing vehicle in oven.

3) Visually inspect ABS system before performing any test. Ensure hydraulic system, normal brake system, charging system and battery are okay. Low battery voltage can cause faulty reading. If necessary, connect a battery charger and apply slow charge. DO NOT fast charge battery.

4) Ensure parking brake switch, all related electrical wiring, electrical connections and electrical grounds appear okay.

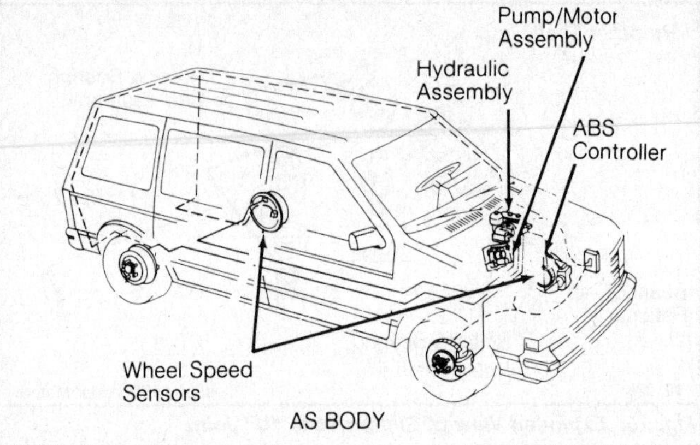
Pump/Motor
Assembly
Hydraulic
Assembly
ABS
Controller
Wheel Speed
Sensors
AS BODY
91J10883
Courtesy of Chrysler Motors.

Fig. 1: Locating ABS Components

BLEEDING BRAKE SYSTEM

ABS must be bled anytime air enters system while lines, hoses, calipers or hydraulic assembly are disconnected for service. It is important to note that air in the brake system may set a primary pressure/delta "P" fault in the Anti-Lock Brake Controller (CAB). Refer to DIAGNOSIS & TESTING in this article.

NOTE: During bleeding operations, ensure fluid level remains close to full. Check fluid level periodically while bleeding and add DOT 3 brake fluid as required.

PRESSURE BLEEDING

NOTE: Use only diaphragm-type pressure bleeding equipment to prevent air, moisture and other contaminants from entering system.

1) Ensure ignition is off and remains off during bleeding procedure. Depressurize accumulator by pumping brake pedal a minimum of 40 times.

WARNING: Failure to depressurize hydraulic accumulator prior to performing this operation may result in personal injury and/or damage to painted surfaces.

2) Remove both reservoir caps. Install pressure bleeder adapter on one reservoir port and dummy cap on the other. Attach bleeding equipment to bleeder adapter. Charge pressure bleeder to approximately 20 psi (1.4 kg/cm²).

3) Connect transparent hose to caliper bleed screw. Submerge free end of hose in clear jar partially filled with clean, fresh brake fluid. With pressure bleeder turned on, open caliper bleeder screw 1/2 - 3/4 turn and allow fluid to flow into container. Leave bleed screw open until clear, bubble-free fluid flows from hose. If reservoir is drained or hydraulic assembly removed prior to bleeding, slowly pump brake pedal one or 2 times while bleed screw is open and fluid is flowing. This will help purge air from hydraulic assembly. Torque bleeder screw to 80-170 INCH lbs. (9-19 N.m).

4) After bleeding all calipers in order, LR, RR, LF and RF, remove pressure bleeding equipment and bleeder adapter by closing pressure bleeder valve and slowly unscrewing bleeder adapter from hydraulic assembly reservoir.

WARNING: Failure to release pressure slowly from reservoir will cause spillage of fluid and could result in injury or damage to painted surfaces.

5) Using a syringe, remove excess fluid from reservoir down to normal full level. Install reservoir caps and turn on ignition to allow ABS pump to charge accumulator.

1991 BRAKES
Anti-Lock – Bendix-10 (Cont.)

MANUAL BLEEDING

NOTE: Manual bleeding requires assistance from a second technician.

1) Ensure ignition is off and remains off during bleeding procedure. Depressurize accumulator by pumping brake pedal a minimum of 40 times.

WARNING: Failure to depressurize hydraulic accumulator prior to performing this operation may result in personal injury and/or damage to painted surfaces.

2) Connect transparent hose to caliper bleed screw. Submerge free end of hose in clear jar partially filled with clean, fresh brake fluid. Slowly pump brake pedal several times, using full strokes of pedal and allowing approximately 5 seconds between pedal strokes. After 2 or 3 strokes, continue holding pressure with pedal at bottom of travel.
3) With pressure on pedal, open bleed screw 1/2 - 3/4 turn. Leave bleed screw open until fluid no longer flows from hose. Tighten bleed screw and release pedal. Repeat until clear, bubble-free fluid flows from hose. Bleed all calipers in order, LR, RR, LF and RF.

ADJUSTMENTS

PARKING BRAKE ADJUSTMENT

NOTE: Ensure operating cables are properly assembled to equalizer bracket prior to cable adjustment.

Using a 7/32" Allen wrench, turn hex socket adjuster on parking brake lever assembly counterclockwise approximately 15 degrees. While turning adjuster, self adjuster release is a loud snapping noise followed by a felt detent. Very slight effort is required to seat lock-out arm into detent. Follow through to detent is important to prevent lock-out rod from rattling. Cycle lever to position cables. Rear wheels should rotate freely.

STOPLIGHT SWITCH ADJUSTMENT

Install switch in retaining bracket and push switch forward as far as possible. The brake pedal will move forward slightly. Gently pull back on pedal, bringing striker back toward switch until pedal will go no further. This ratchets the switch to its correct position and no other adjustment is necessary.

REMOVAL & INSTALLATION

NOTE: Depressurize hydraulic system before removing any component. To do so, turn ignition off and depress brake pedal a minimum of 40 times. When a definite increase in pedal effort is felt, pump pedal a few more times before disconnecting any hydraulic line or component.

PUMP/MOTOR ASSEMBLY

Removal & Installation – 1) Disconnect negative battery cable. Depressurize hydraulic accumulator by pumping brake pedal a minimum of 40 times. Remove fresh air intake ducts from engine induction system.
2) Disconnect electrical connectors that run across engine compartment, near pump/motor high and low pressure hoses. Disconnect high and low pressure hoses from hydraulic assembly and cap reservoir outlet. Disconnect pump/motor electrical connector from engine mount.
3) Remove pump heat shield bolt from front of pump bracket. Remove heat shield. Lift pump/motor assembly from bracket and remove from vehicle. To install, reverse removal procedure.

PRESSURE & RETURN HOSES

Removal & Installation – 1) Disconnect negative battery cable. Depressurize hydraulic accumulator by pumping brake pedal a minimum of 40 times. Remove fresh air intake ducts from engine induction system.
2) Remove pump/motor assembly. Cut 2 tie straps securing hoses and wiring harness. Remove banjo bolt from pump/motor. Remove pressure and return hoses.
3) To install, reverse removal procedure. Install NEW rubber "O" rings on high and low pressure hoses. Position hose assemblies on pump/motor and install banjo bolt. Carefully route wiring harness along side hoses. Install 2 tie straps around hoses and wiring harness. Install pump/motor assembly in vehicle.

HYDRAULIC ASSEMBLY

Removal & Installation – 1) Disconnect negative battery cable. Turn ignition off. Depress brake pedal 40 or more times to depressurize brake system. Remove air intake ducts. Unplug all electrical connectors from hydraulic assembly.
2) With a syringe, remove as much brake fluid as possible from reservoir. Remove high pressure hose fitting from hydraulic assembly. Disconnect pump return hose from filter nipple, and cap fitting on filter. Disconnect all brake lines from hydraulic assembly.
3) From under instrument panel, remove clip and brake pedal pin. Discard clip. Remove 4 hydraulic assembly mounting nuts. Remove hydraulic assembly. To install, reverse removal procedure. Install new clip. Bleed brake system. See BLEEDING BRAKE SYSTEM.

RESERVOIR

Removal – 1) Disconnect negative battery cable. Turn ignition off. Depress brake pedal 40 or more times to depressurize brake system. With a syringe, remove as much brake fluid as possible from reservoir.
2) Remove accumulator and high pressure pump hose banjo fitting. Remove 3 locking pins from hydraulic assembly. Remove reservoir by carefully prying between reservoir and hydraulic assembly with blunt tool.

CAUTION: DO NOT damage or puncture reservoir during removal.

Installation – To install, reverse removal procedure. Lubricate new reservoir grommets with clean brake fluid, and press reservoir into hydraulic assembly. Bleed brake system. See BLEEDING BRAKE SYSTEM.

CAUTION: DO NOT attempt to pound reservoir into hydraulic assembly using a hammer. Press in by hand using a rocking motion to fully seat hydraulic assembly into 3 grommets.

ACCUMULATOR

Removal – Disconnect negative battery cable. Turn ignition off. Depress brake pedal 40 or more times to depressurize brake system. Loosen accumulator fitting and remove accumulator from hydraulic assembly.
Installation – Install accumulator onto hydraulic assembly and torque to 30 ft. lbs. (40 N.m). Turn ignition on. Let hydraulic system pressurize. Check for leaks at hydraulic assembly-to-accumulator fitting.

PROPORTIONING VALVES

CAUTION: NEVER disassemble proportioning valves.

Removal – Disconnect negative battery cable. Turn ignition off. Depress brake pedal 40 or more times to depressurize brake system. Remove brake tube and fitting from proportioning valve. Remove proportioning valve.
Installation – Install proportioning valve on hydraulic assembly and torque to 30 ft. lbs. (40 N.m). Install brake tube on proportioning valve. Torque to 11 ft. lbs. (15 N.m). Bleed affected brake line. See BRAKE BLEEDING in this article.

1991 BRAKES
Anti-Lock – Bendix-10 (Cont.)

ANTI-LOCK BRAKE CONTROLLER (CAB)

Removal & Installation – Ensure ignition is off. Raise vehicle on hoist. Remove transaxle oil cooler line routing clip. Disconnect wiring harness 60-way connector from controller. Remove 3 mounting bolts securing controller to left frame rail. Remove controller. To install, reverse removal procedure.

SYSTEM RELAY, ANTI-LOCK WARNING LIGHT RELAY & PUMP/MOTOR RELAY

***NOTE:* See Figs. 2, 3 and 4 to locate and identify ABS relay, fuse cartridge and connector circuits.**

Removal & Installation – Locate power distribution center on left inner fender, next to strut tower. Open cover, locate relay and remove by pulling upward. *See Fig. 2.* To install, push relay firmly into position.

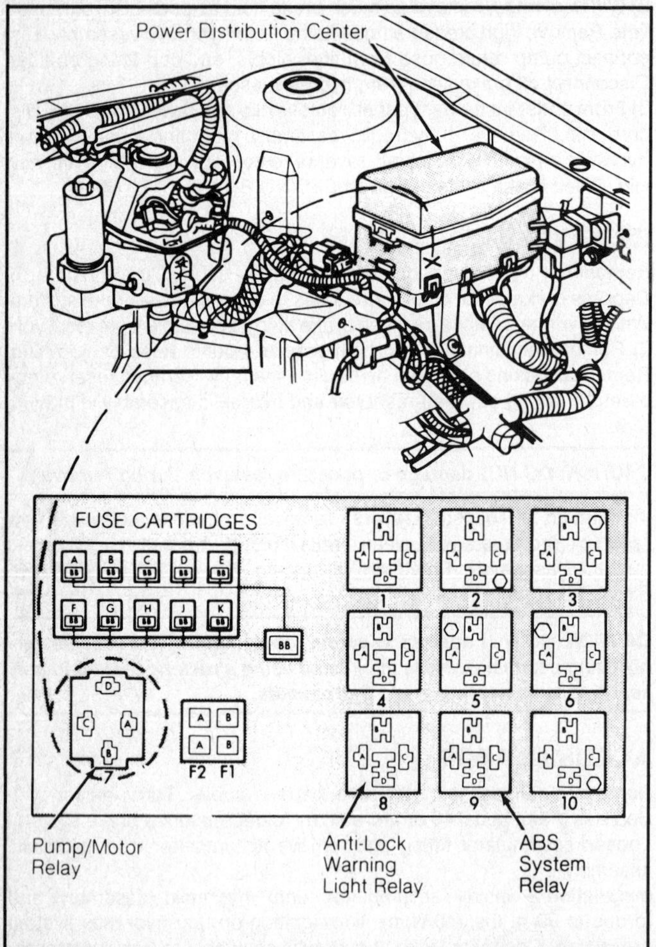
Power Distribution Center
FUSE CARTRIDGES
A B C D E
F G H J K
BB
1 2 3
4 5 6
7 8 9 10
F2 F1
Pump/Motor Relay
Anti-Lock Warning Light Relay
ABS System Relay

90B08308 Courtesy of Chrysler Motors.

Fig. 2: Locating Anti-Lock Relays

FRONT WHEEL SPEED SENSOR

Removal & Installation – **1)** Raise vehicle and remove wheel and tire assembly. Remove screw and clip securing sensor to fender shield. Carefully pull sensor assembly grommet from fender shield. Unplug connector from harness. Remove retainer clip from bracket on strut. Remove grommets from retainer brackets.

2) Remove sensor retaining screw. Carefully remove sensor from steering knuckle. If sensor is frozen, DO NOT use pliers. Use a hammer and punch to tap edge of sensor ear, rocking sensor from side to side until free.

3) To install, reverse removal procedure. Coat sensor with high-temperature multipurpose grease before installing. Tighten sensor screw to 60 INCH lbs. (7 N.m). There is no air gap adjustment.

CAUTION: Proper installation of wheel speed sensor cables is critical to system operation. Ensure cables are installed in retainers. Failure to install cables in retainers may result in contact with moving parts and/or over-extension of cables, causing an open circuit.

REAR WHEEL SPEED SENSOR

Removal – **1)** Raise vehicle and remove wheel and tire assembly. Remove sensor assembly grommet from underbody, and pull harness through hole in underbody. Unplug connector from harness. Remove sensor grommet screw from body hose bracket, just forward of trailing arm bushing.

2) Remove sensor assembly clip, located on inboard side of trailing arm. Remove sensor wire fastener from rear brake hose bracket. Remove outboard sensor assembly retainer nut.

3) Remove sensor head screw. Carefully remove sensor. If sensor is frozen, DO NOT use pliers. Use a hammer and punch to tap edge of sensor ear, rocking sensor from side to side until free.

Installation – To install, reverse removal procedure. Be sure to coat sensor with high-temperature multipurpose grease before installing. Tighten sensor screw to 60 INCH lbs. (7 N.m). There is no air gap adjustment.

CAUTION: Proper installation of wheel speed sensor cables is critical to system operation. Ensure cables are installed in retainers. Failure to install cables in retainers may result in contact with moving parts and/or over-extension of cables, causing an open circuit.

TORQUE SPECIFICATIONS

TORQUE SPECIFICATIONS

Application	Ft. Lbs. (N.m)
Accumulator	30 (40)
Adapter Mounting Bolt	130-190 (176-258)
Banjo Bolt	19-29 (26-40)
Brake Tube-To-Proportioning Valve	11 (15)
Guide Pins	25-35 (34-47)
Proportioning Valve	30 (40)
	INCH Lbs. (N.m)
Caliper Bleed Screw	80-170 (9-19)
Tubes To Fittings	115-175 (13-20)
Wheel Speed Sensor Screw	60 (7)

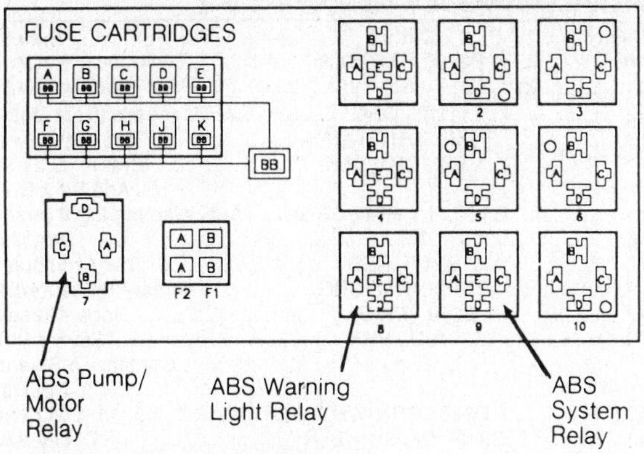
FUSE CARTRIDGES
A
B
C
D
E
F
G
H
J
K
BB
F2 F1
ABS Pump/ Motor Relay
ABS Warning Light Relay
ABS System Relay

FUSE CARTRIDGES (AC/AY BODIES)

Cavity	Circuit	Function
A		ABS System Cartridge-Power
BB		Bus Bar
B		ABS Pump/Motor Cartridge-Power

ABS PUMP/MOTOR RELAY (AC/AY BODIES)

Cavity	Circuit	Function
A	A21J...DK BLU	Ignition Switch
B	A10...RED/WHT	Battery 12 Volt
C	B21...GRN	Pump Switch/Dual Function Pressure Switch
D	B10...BRN/WHT	Pump/Motor

ABS WARNING LIGHT RELAY (AC/AY BODIES)

Cavity	Circuit	Function
A	B47A...RED/LT BLU	System Relay Voltage
B	Z01V...BLK	Ground
C	Z01W...BLK	Ground
D		Not Used
E	G19...LT GRN/ORG	CAB-Anti-lock Warning Light/Bulb
	G19A...LT GRN/ORG	(Double Crimp At Relay Terminal)

ABS SYSTEM RELAY (AC/AY BODIES)

Cavity	Circuit	Function
A	B57...BRN/BLK	System Relay Actuation
B	A20...RED/LT GRN	Battery 12 Volt
C	Z01T...BLK	Ground
D	B47...RED/LT BLU	System Relay Voltage
E		Not Used

ABS PUMP/MOTOR RELAY (AS BODY)

Cavity	Circuit	Function
A	A21...DK BLU	System Relay Voltage
B	A10...RED/DK GRN	Battery 12 Volt
C	B21...GRY	Pump/Motor Ground CAB Controlled
D	B82...BRN/WHT	Pump/Motor & CAB Motor Monitor

ABS WARNING LIGHT RELAY (AS BODY)

Cavity	Circuit	Function
A	B47...RED/LT BLU	System Relay Voltage
B	Z1...LT BLK	CAB-Anti-lock Warning Light Anti-Lock Warning Light Bulb
C	Z1W...BLK	Ground
D		Not Used
E	G19...LT GRN/ORG	ABS Warning Light AMBER Anti-Lock

ABS SYSTEM RELAY (AS BODY)

Cavity	Circuit	Function
A	B57...BRN/BLK	System Relay Actuation
B	A20...RED/DK BLU	Battery 12 Volt
C	Z1...BLK	Ground
D	B47...RED/LT BLU	System Relay Voltage
E		Not Used

FUSE CARTRIDGES (BB BODY)

Cavity	Circuit	Function
F2		ABS System Cartridge-Power
BB		Bus Bar
G		ABS Pump/Motor Cartridge-Power

ABS PUMP/MOTOR RELAY (BB BODY)

Cavity	Circuit	Function
A	A21D...DK BLU	Ignition Start/Run
B	A10...RED/DK GRN	Battery 12 Volt
	A12A... RED/DK GRN	BAttery 12 Volt (Relay C)
C	B10...GRY	Pump Switch - Dual Function Pressure Switch (DFPS)
D	B10...BRN/WHT	Pump/Motor Feed

ABS WARNING LIGHT RELAY (BB BODY)

Cavity	Circuit	Function
A	B47...RED/LT BLU	System Relay Voltage
B	Z1BG...BLK	Ground
C	Z1BC...BLK	Ground
	Z1BG...BLK	Ground
D		Not Used
E	G19...LT GRN/ORG	Anti-Lock Warning Light

ABS SYSTEM RELAY (BB BODY)

Cavity	Circuit	Function
A	B57...BRN/BLK	System Relay Coil Feed
B	F101...RED/LT GRN	Battery 12 Volt
C	Z1BB...BLK	Ground
D	B47...RED/LT BLU	System Relay Voltage
E		Not Used

91I10882

Courtesy of Chrysler Motors.

Fig. 3: Identifying ABS Relay Circuits

1991 BRAKES
Anti-Lock – Bendix-10 (Cont.)

CAB 60-WAY CONNECTOR

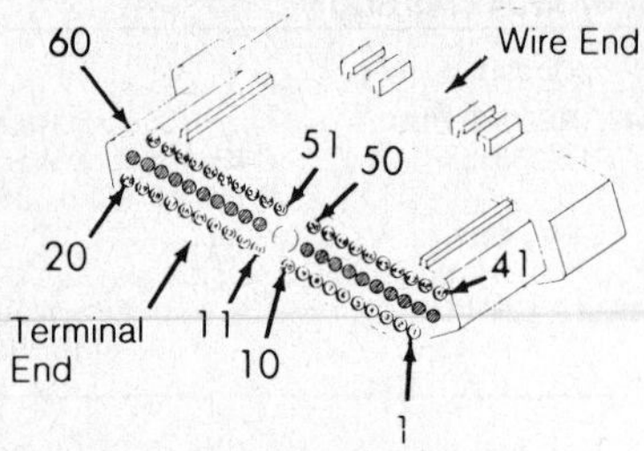
60
Wire End
51
50
20
41
Terminal End
11
10
1

CAB 60-WAY CONNECTOR (AC/AY BODIES)

CAVITY	CIRCUIT	FUNCTION
1.	B1...YEL/DK BLU	RR ABS Wheel Sensor
2.	B2...YEL	RR ABS Wheel Sensor
3.	B3...LT GRN/DK BLU	LR Wheel Sensor
4.	B4...LT GRN	LR Wheel Sensor
5.	Z1...BLK	Ground
6.	B6...WHT/DK BLU	RF ABS Wheel Sensor
7.	B7...WHT	RF ABS Wheel Sensor
8.	B8...RED/DK BLU	LF ABS Wheel Sensor
9.	B9...RED	LF ABS Wheel Sensor
10.	B210...RED/BLK	Transducer Return (-)
11.	D11...WHT/VIO	Diagnostic ABS (Signal Data In)
12.	D12...ORG	Diagnostic ABS (Signal Data Out)
13.	L50...WHT/TAN	StopLamp Signal To Lamps
14.	G09A...GRY/BLK	Brake Fluid Level/ Park Brake
15.	G19...DK BLU	Boost Pressure
16. [1]	B16...BLK/LT BLU	Low Fluid Output Sense
17.	B217...RED	Low Accumulator
18.	B218...WHT/ORG	Primary Pressure/DPA
19.	B219...DK BLU	Boost Pressure
20. [2]	T40B...BRN	Starter Relay Contact To Solenoid
21-41.		Not Used
42.	B242...BRN/WHT	Left Front Build Valve
43.	B243...DK GRN/BLK	Left Front Decay Valve
44.		Not Used
45.	B245...WHT/LT GRN	Left Front Isolation Valve
46.	B246...BRN/RED	Right Front Build Valve
47.	B247...RED/LT BLU	12 Volt ABS Solenoid Signal
48.	B248...DK GRN/WHT	Right Front Decay Valve
49.	B249...WHT/TAN	Right Front Isolation Valve
50.	B47B...RED/LT BLU	Solenoid 12 Volt
51.	B251...WHT/BLK	Left Rear Isolation Valve
52.	B252...BRN/TAN	RR/LR Build Valve
53.		Not Used
54.	B254...DK GRN/ORG	RR/LR Decay Valve
55.	B255...WHT/PNK	Right Rear Isolation Valve
56.		Not Used
57.	B57...BRN/BLK	ABS System Relay Control
58.	B258...GRY/LT BLU	Transducer Feed (+)
59.		Not Used
60.	A21G..DK BLU	Ignition Start/Run

[1] – Wired only if vehicle equipped with Electronic Vehicle Information Center (EVIC).
[2] – May not be wired.

CAB 60-WAY CONNECTOR (AS BODY)

Cavity	Circuit	Function
1.	B1...YEL/DK BLU	RR Wheel Sensor –
2.	B2...YEL	RR Wheel Sensor +
3.	B3..LT GRN/DK BLU	LR Wheel Sensor –
4.	B4...LT GRN	LR Wheel Sensor +
5.	Z1...BLK	Ground
6.	B6...WHT/DK BLU	RF Wheel Sensor –
7.	B7...WHT	RF Wheel Sensor +
8.	B8...RED/DK BLU	LF Wheel Sensor –
9.	B9...RED	LF Wheel Sensor +

CAB 60-WAY CONNECTOR (AS BODY – Cont.)

Cavity	Circuit	Function
10.	B210...RED/BLK	Transducer Return (-)
11.	D11...WHT/VIO	Diagnostic (Data Input)
12.	D12...ORG	Diagnostic (Data Output)
13.	L50...WHT/TAN	Stop Light Switch
14.	G9B...GRY/BLK	Brake Fluid Level And Park Brake
15.	G19C...LT GRN/ORG	ABS Warning Light (Amber)
16.		Not Used
17.	B217...RED	Low Accumulator
19.	B218...WHT/ORG	Primary Pressure/DPA
19.	B219...DK BLU	Boost Pressure
20. [1]	T40D...BRN	Starter Relay Contact To Solenoid
21.-41.		Not Used
42.	B242...BRN/WHT	LF Build Valve
43.	B243...DK GRN/BLK	LF Decay Valve
44.		Not Used
45.	B245...WHT/LT GRN	LF Isolation Valve
46.	B246...BRN/RED	RF Build Valve
47.	B47A...RED/LT BLU	Solenoid +12 Volt
48.	B248...DK GRN/WHT	RF Decay Valve
49.	B249...WHT/TAN	RF Isolation Valve
50.	B47B...RED/LT BLU	ABS Solenoid
51.	B251...WHT/BLK	LR Isolation Valve
52.	B252...BRN/TAN	RR/LR Build Valve
53.		Not Used
54.	B254...DK GRN/ORG	RR/LR Decay Valve
55.	B255...WHT/PNK	RR Isolation Valve
56.		Not Used
57.	B57...BRN/BLK	System Relay
58.	B258...GRY/LT BLU	Transducer feed (+)
59.		Not Used
60.	A21...DK/BLU	Ignition Start/Run

[1] May not be wired.

CAB 60 WAY CONNECTOR (BB BODY)

Cavity	Circuit	Function
1.	B01...YEL/DK BLU	RR Wheel Sensor –
2.	B02...YEL	RR Wheel Sensor +
3.	B03..LT BLU/DK BLU	LR Wheel Sensor –
4.	B04...LT GRN	LR Wheel Sensor +
5.	Z01...BLK	Ground
6.	B06...WHT/DK BLU	RF Wheel Sensor –
7.	B07...WHT	RF Wheel Sensor +
8.	B08...RED/DK BLU	LF Wheel Sensor –
9.	B09...RED	LF Wheel Sensor +
10.	B210...RED/BLK	Transducer Return (-)
11.	D11...WHT/VIO	Diagnostic (Data Input)
12.	D12...ORG	Diagnostic (Data Output)
13.	L50...WHT/TAN	Stop Light Switch
14.	G09...GRY/BLK	Fluid Level & Park Brake
15.	G19...LT GRN/ORG	ABS (Amber) Warning Light
16.		Not Used
17.	B217...RED	Low Accumulator
18.	B218...WHT/ORG	Primary Pressure/DPA
19.	B219...DK BLU	Boost Pressure
20.-41.		Not Used
42.	B242...BRN/WHT	LF Build Valve
43.	B243...DK GRN/BLK	LF Decay Valve
44.		Not Used
45.	B245...WHT/LT GRN	LF Isolation Valve
46.	B246...BRN/RED	RF Build Valve
47.	B47...RED/LT BLU	Solenoid +12 Volt
48.	B248...DK GRN/WHT	RF Decay Valve
49.	B249...WHT/TAN	RF Valve
50.	B47B...RED/LT BLU	Solenoid Signal
51.	B251...WHT/BLK	Left Rear Isolation Valve
52.	B252...BRN/TAN	RR/LR Build Valve
53.		Not Used
54.	B254...DK GRN/ORG	RR/LR Decay Valve
55.	B255...WHT/PNK	RR Isolation Valve
56		Not Used
57.	B57...RED/BLK	System Relay
58.	B57...BRN/BLK	System Relay Control
59.		Not Used
60.	F20C...WHT	Ignition Start/Run

91A10884

Courtesy of Chrysler Motors.

Fig. 4: Identifying ABS Connector Circuits

DIAGNOSIS & TESTING

SELF-DIAGNOSTIC SYSTEM

The Bendix Anti-Lock Brake System (ABS) is controlled and monitored by the Anti-Lock Brake Controller (CAB). In addition to controlling ABS system, CAB has several useful diagnostic capabilities.

First, fault codes are stored in memory until erased by a technician using the Chrysler's DRB-II (Diagnostic Readout Box-II), or erased automatically after 50 ignition (key) cycles.

Second, more than one fault code can be stored at a time. The number of fault codes stored is displayed by the DRB-II. The number of key cycles since the most recent fault was stored is also displayed.

Third, using DRB-II, most functions of the CAB and ABS system can be accessed by a technician for testing and diagnostic purposes.

Start-Up Cycle - The start-up cycle takes place immediately after ignition switch is turned on. It is an electrical check of ABS relay and anti-lock warning light relay. During this check, the instrument cluster ANTI-LOCK warning light comes on and then goes out at completion of start-up cycle test. Test cycle is 1-2 seconds.

Drive-Off Cycle - The drive-off cycle takes place when vehicle reaches about 3 MPH the first time after an ignition reset.

Latching & Non-Latching Faults - Some faults detected by CAB are "latching", meaning the fault is set and ABS is disabled until ignition switch is reset. ABS is disabled even if the original fault has disappeared.

Other faults are "non-latching". Any illuminated warning lights are only illuminated as long as the fault condition exists. As soon as the condition does not exist, the light(s) are turned off, although a fault code will be set in most cases. See ABS SYSTEM FAULT MESSAGES table.

ABS SYSTEM FAULT MESSAGES

Component/ System Fault	Warning Light	Fault Type
ANTI-LOCK Light	None	....
ANTI-LOCK Light Relay	None	....
Boost Pressure	[1]	Non-Latching
CAB	[2]	Latching
Excess Decay	[2]	Non-Latching
Low Accumulator	[1]	Non-Latching
Low Fluid/Parking Brake	[3]	
Modulator	[2]	Latching
Primary/Delta Pressure	....	Non-Latching
Wheel Speed Sensor(s)	[2]	Latching
Solenoid Undervoltage	[2]	Non-Latching
ABS System Relay	[2]	Latching

[1] - The BRAKE and ANTI-LOCK warning lights come on during brake application.

[2] - The ANTI-LOCK warning light comes on.

[3] - The BRAKE warning light comes on immediately; the ANTI-LOCK warning light comes on when vehicle speed is above 3 MPH.

DRB-II TEST FUNCTIONS

NOTE: DO NOT touch DRB-II keypad during DRB-II power-up sequence or an error message will result.

1) In order to perform diagnostic tests using the DRB-II, the DRB-II must be in the ABS MENU. At the ABS MENU, fault codes and DRB-II test functions can be accessed.

2) To reach ABS MENU, turn ignition off. Attach DRB-II to Chrysler Collision Detection (CCD) bus diagnostic connector. Connector is located under driver's side of instrument cluster. Turn ignition switch to RUN position.

3) All DRB-II character positions will illuminate and copyright information will appear on screen for a few seconds. If DRB-II screen is blank or any error messages appear, refer to DRB-II PROBLEMS & ERROR MESSAGES.

4) After a few seconds, the DRB-II menu will appear. At DRB-II menu, press "4" (SELECT SYSTEM) key to enter diagnostic test program. Press down arrow 3 times to change menu display.

5) Select "5" (ABS) key to enter ABS part of the DRB-II program. After a few seconds, the ABS MENU will appear. The screen will display a menu of the DRB-II test categories for the anti-lock brake system. Press down arrow 3 times to view rest of menu.

6) At this point, you have reached the ABS menu. At ABS menu of anti-lock brake system diagnostic program, specific test functions programmed into DRB-II cartridge can be performed. The following DRB-II modes can be accessed: SYSTEM TEST, READ FAULTS, STATE DISPLAY, ACTUATOR TEST and ADJUSTMENTS.

SYSTEM TEST Mode - This function is not available in the anti-lock brake system diagnostic program.

READ FAULTS Mode - This function allows user to read and erase fault codes.

STATE DISPLAY Mode - This function allows user to read states or values of a variety of sensors, inputs/outputs and components.

ACTUATOR TEST Mode - This function allows user to activate various outputs, valves, and hydraulics to verify proper operation.

ADJUSTMENTS Mode - This function allows user to erase fault codes.

DRB-II Volt-Ohmmeter Mode - **1)** To access volt-ohmmeter mode of DRB-II, connect Red volt-ohmmeter test lead to Red port, located on top right side of DRB-II.

NOTE: Because DRB-II is grounded through diagnostic connector, only one volt-ohmmeter test lead is required when using volt-ohmmeter option. DRB-II volt-ohmmeter should only be used when required by diagnostic flow charts.

2) To access voltmeter, press VOLT/OHM key once. DRB-II is now in voltmeter mode. Touch test probe to connector or wire to be measured. Read voltage on DRB-II display. When voltage testing is complete, press VOLT/OHM key 3 times to exit voltmeter mode.

3) To access ohmmeter, press VOLT/OHM key twice. DRB-II is now in ohmmeter mode. Touch test probe to connector or wire to be measured. Read resistance to circuit ground on DRB-II display. When resistance testing is complete, press VOLT/OHM key twice to exit ohmmeter mode.

DRB-II Continuity Meter Mode - Press VOLT/OHM key 3 times. Display will read NO CONTINUITY. Touch test probe to connector or wire to be measured. Read continuity on DRB-II display. When continuity testing is complete, press VOLT/OHM key once to exit continuity meter mode.

VEHICLES TESTED Mode - **1)** Vehicles tested mode is used to show what vehicles are covered by DRB-II cartridge. To access VEHICLES TESTED mode, turn ignition off. Attach DRB-II to BUS diagnostic connector. Connector is located under driver's side of instrument cluster.

2) Turn ignition switch to RUN position. All DRB-II character positions will illuminate and copyright information will appear on screen. After a few seconds DRB-II menu will appear.

3) At DRB-II menu, press "1" (VEHICLES TESTED) key. Press ENTER key. DRB-II will display vehicles covered by cartridge. Screen will display for 5 seconds and return to DRB-II menu.

HOW TO USE Mode - Enter DRB-II menu display. Refer to steps **1)** and **2)** under VEHICLES TESTED MODE. At DRB-II menu, press "2" (HOW TO USE) key. Press ENTER key. A series of screens will be displayed explaining the use of DRB-II keys used to move through diagnostic program.

CONFIGURE Mode - **1)** Configure option allows user to customize DRB-II display. For example, if metric system is more useful, simply select METRIC from the appropriate menu.

2) All selections made under CONFIGURE option remain active until user changes selection. To enter configure mode, enter DRB-II menu display. Refer to steps **1)** and **2)** under VEHICLES TESTED MODE. At DRB-II menu, press "3" (CONFIGURE) key. Press ENTER key. DRB-II will display CONFIGURE menu.

1991 BRAKES
Anti-Lock - Bendix-10 (Cont.)

DRB-II PROBLEMS & ERROR MESSAGES

Blank Message Screen - 1) Turn ignition off and disconnect DRB-II, adapter cable 'and cartridge. Find a second vehicle with equipment identical to the original vehicle.

2) Connect DRB-II to substitute (second) vehicle and use DRB-II as on original vehicle. If message screen is still blank, adapter cable or DRB-II is faulty. Substitute adapter cable with a known good cable to find faulty component.

3) If message screen is not blank, DRB-II and cable adapter are functioning properly. Inspect diagnostic connector for proper wire placement, corrosion, damaged terminals or pushed-out pins. Repair as necessary.

4) If diagnostic connector is okay, use an external voltmeter to check Red wire at CCD bus diagnostic connector for voltage. CCD bus diagnostic connector is located under driver's side of instrument cluster.

5) If voltmeter reading at Red wire is at least 9 volts, repair open in CCD bus diagnostic connector Black/Light Green (ground) wire. If voltage is not 9 volts, repair open in Red wire back to battery.

NO RESPONSE Message - 1) Disconnect Anti-Lock Brake Controller (CAB) 60-pin connector. Inspect connector for proper wire placement, corrosion, damaged terminals, or pushed out pins. Repair as necessary.

2) Place DRB-II in voltmeter mode and probe cavity No. 60 of CAB 60-pin connector. *See Fig. 4*. If reading is at least 9 volts, go to next step. If voltage is not 9 volts, repair open in Dark Blue or Dark Blue/White wire.

3) Place DRB-II in ohmmeter mode and probe cavity No. 5 of CAB 60-pin connector. *See Fig. 4*. If resistance is below 10 ohms, go to next step. If resistance is NOT below 10 ohms, repair open Black (ground) wire.

4) Disconnect DRB-II from CCD bus diagnostic connector. Inspect connector for proper wire placement, corrosion, damaged terminals, or pushed out pins. Repair as necessary.

5) If diagnostic connector is okay, use an external ohmmeter to check resistance of White/Violet wire terminal of CCD bus diagnostic connector. If resistance is above 10 ohms, go to next step. If resistance is NOT above 10 ohms, repair short circuit to ground in White/Violet wire.

6) Use an external ohmmeter to check resistance of Orange wire terminal of CCD bus diagnostic connector. If resistance is above 10 ohms, go to next step. If resistance is NOT above 10 ohms, repair short circuit to ground in Orange wire.

7) Connect a jumper wire between ground and cavities No. 11 and 12 of CAB 60-pin connector. *See Fig. 4*. Use an external ohmmeter to check resistance of White/Violet wire terminal of CCD bus diagnostic connector. If resistance is below 10 ohms, go to next step. If resistance is NOT below 10 ohms, repair open White/Violet wire.

8) With jumper wire still connected, use an external ohmmeter to check resistance of Orange wire terminal of CCD bus diagnostic connector. If resistance is below 10 ohms, replace anti-lock brake controller. If resistance is NOT below 10 ohms, repair open Orange wire.

RAM TEST FAILURE Message - Replace DRB-II.

CARTRIDGE ERROR Message - Replace DRB-II diagnostic cartridge.

KEY PAD TEST FAILURE Message - Power-up DRB-II again with fingers off the keypad. If error message returns, replace DRB-II.

HIGH Or LOW BATTERY Message - Correct condition of vehicle battery and reconnect DRB-II.

DIAGNOSTIC PROCEDURE

Visual Inspection - A careful and thorough visual inspection of components may quickly identify cause of malfunction and eliminate the need for diagnostic testing. Perform visual inspection using the following procedure:

1) Completely depress brake pedal 40 times and check brake fluid level. Inspect hydraulic assembly for leaks and for damaged or unplugged connectors. Inspect all brake fluid lines for any leaks or damage.

2) Ensure all ABS relays are properly installed in power distribution center. Power distribution center is located in engine compartment, next to strut tower.

3) Inspect all 4 wheel speed sensors and their 2-way connectors for damage or disconnection. Inspect Anti-Lock Brake Controller (CAB) for secure mounting and CAB connector for damage or loose connection. CAB is located under battery tray or on right front strut tower.

Test Equipment Required - In order to perform diagnostic tests, the following equipment is required:

- DRB-II (Diagnostic Readout Box-II)
- 1991 Diagnostic Program Cartridge
- Body Diagnostic Cable
- High Impedance Volt/Ohmmeter
- Jumper Wires

Diagnostic Procedure - To properly diagnose and test anti-lock brake system, ALWAYS start diagnosis with TEST 1A: READING FAULT MESSAGES chart. Starting with any other chart may result in incorrect diagnosis.

NOTE: When using trouble shooting charts for diagnosis, DO NOT skip any steps in chart or incorrect diagnosis may result.

Before proceeding with diagnosis, the following precautions must be followed:

- Vehicle must have a fully charged battery and functional charging system.
- Probe Anti-Lock Brake Controller (CAB) connector from pin side. DO NOT backprobe CAB connector. Probe connector cavity carefully. DO NOT spread terminal. This could cause an intermittent problem.
- DO NOT cause short circuits when performing electrical tests. This will set additional fault codes, making diagnosis of original problem more difficult.
- Use DRB-II voltmeter, unless instructed to use an "external" voltmeter. DO NOT use a test light in place of a voltmeter.
- Use DRB-II ohmmeter, unless instructed to use an "external" ohmmeter.
- Always perform TEST VER-1: SYSTEM VERIFICATION TEST after repairs are made.
- Always disconnect DRB-II after use.
- Always disconnect DRB-II before charging battery.

CODE CHARTS

NOTE: The following trouble shooting charts and illustrations are courtesy of Chrysler Motors.

TEST 1A: READING FAULT MESSAGES

Perform Visual Inspection First

Read faults. If there are no fault messages present, perform TEST 23A.

In some instances the cause of one fault message may trigger the setting of an additional fault message. If multiple fault messages appear on the DRBII when reading faults, fault repairs must be performed in the order in which they are displayed in the chart below. If only one fault has occurred, perform the indicated test for that fault message.

NOTE: If a fault has occurred more than 2 key cycles ago, perform the Verification Test procedure (TEST VER-1) before any attempt is made to diagnose that particular fault message.

FAULT MESSAGES

CAB FAULT	PERFORM TEST 2A
MODULATOR FAULT	PERFORM TEST 3A
SOLENOID UNDERVOLTAGE FAULT	PERFORM TEST 4A
LOW FLUID/PARKING BRAKE FAULT	PERFORM TEST 5A
SYSTEM RELAY FAULT	PERFORM TEST 6A
LOW ACCUMULATOR FAULT	PERFORM TEST 7A
PRIMARY PRESSURE/DELTA PRESSURE FAULT	PERFORM TEST 17A
BOOST PRESSURE FAULT	PERFORM TEST 8A
RR WHEEL SPEED SENS CONTINUITY FAULT	PERFORM TEST 9A
LR WHEEL SPEED SENS CONTINUITY FAULT	PERFORM TEST 10A
RF WHEEL SPEED SENS CONTINUITY FAULT	PERFORM TEST 11A
LF WHEEL SPEED SENS CONTINUITY FAULT	PERFORM TEST 12A
RIGHT REAR WHEEL SPEED SENSOR FAULT	PERFORM TEST 13A
LEFT REAR WHEEL SPEED SENSOR FAULT	PERFORM TEST 14A
RIGHT FRONT WHEEL SPEED SENSOR FAULT	PERFORM TEST 15A
LEFT FRONT WHEEL SPEED SENSOR FAULT	PERFORM TEST 16A
ANTILOCK LAMP FAULT	PERFORM TEST 18A
ANTILOCK LAMP RELAY FAULT	PERFORM TEST 19A
EXCESS DECAY FAULT	PERFORM TEST 20A

91D09163

Fig. 5: Anti-Lock Brake Test 1A – Reading Fault Messages

TEST 2A: CAB FAULT

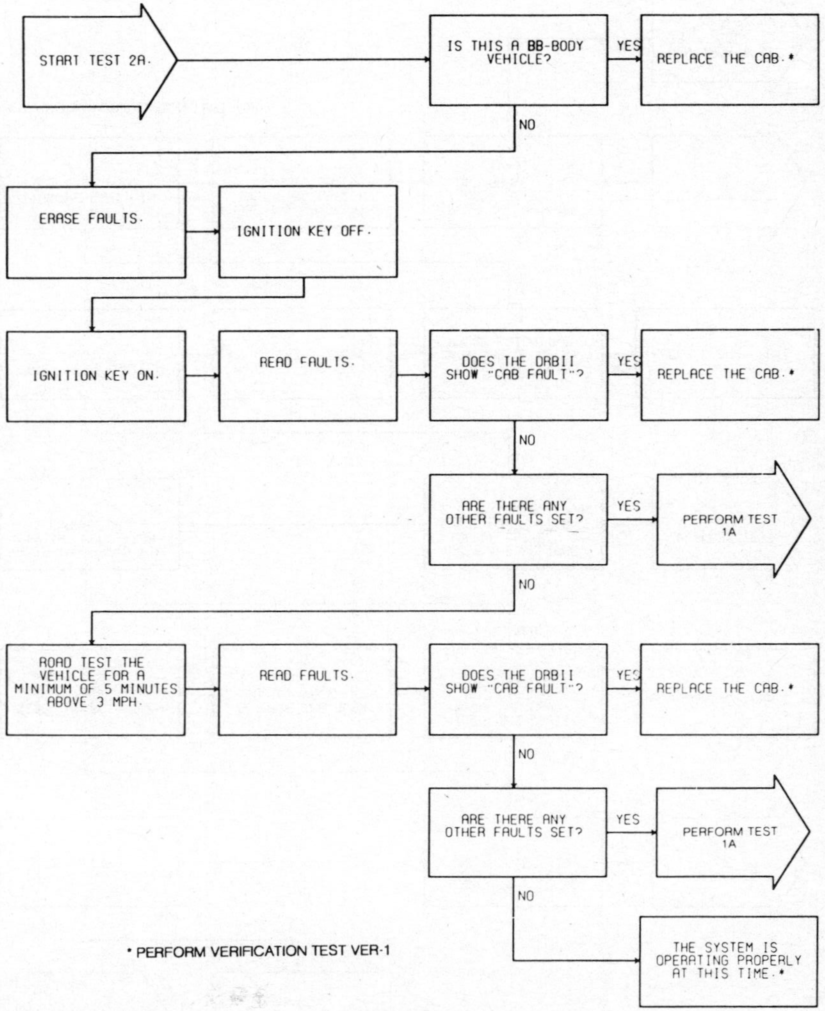
START TEST 2A.
IS THIS A BB-BODY VEHICLE?
YES
REPLACE THE CAB.*
NO
ERASE FAULTS.
IGNITION KEY OFF.
IGNITION KEY ON.
READ FAULTS.
DOES THE DRBII SHOW "CAB FAULT"?
YES
REPLACE THE CAB.*
NO
ARE THERE ANY OTHER FAULTS SET?
YES
PERFORM TEST 1A
NO
ROAD TEST THE VEHICLE FOR A MINIMUM OF 5 MINUTES ABOVE 3 MPH.
READ FAULTS.
DOES THE DRBII SHOW "CAB FAULT"?
YES
REPLACE THE CAB.*
NO
ARE THERE ANY OTHER FAULTS SET?
YES
PERFORM TEST 1A
NO
THE SYSTEM IS OPERATING PROPERLY AT THIS TIME.*
* PERFORM VERIFICATION TEST VER-1

91F09164

Fig. 6: Anti-Lock Brake Test 2A – CAB Fault

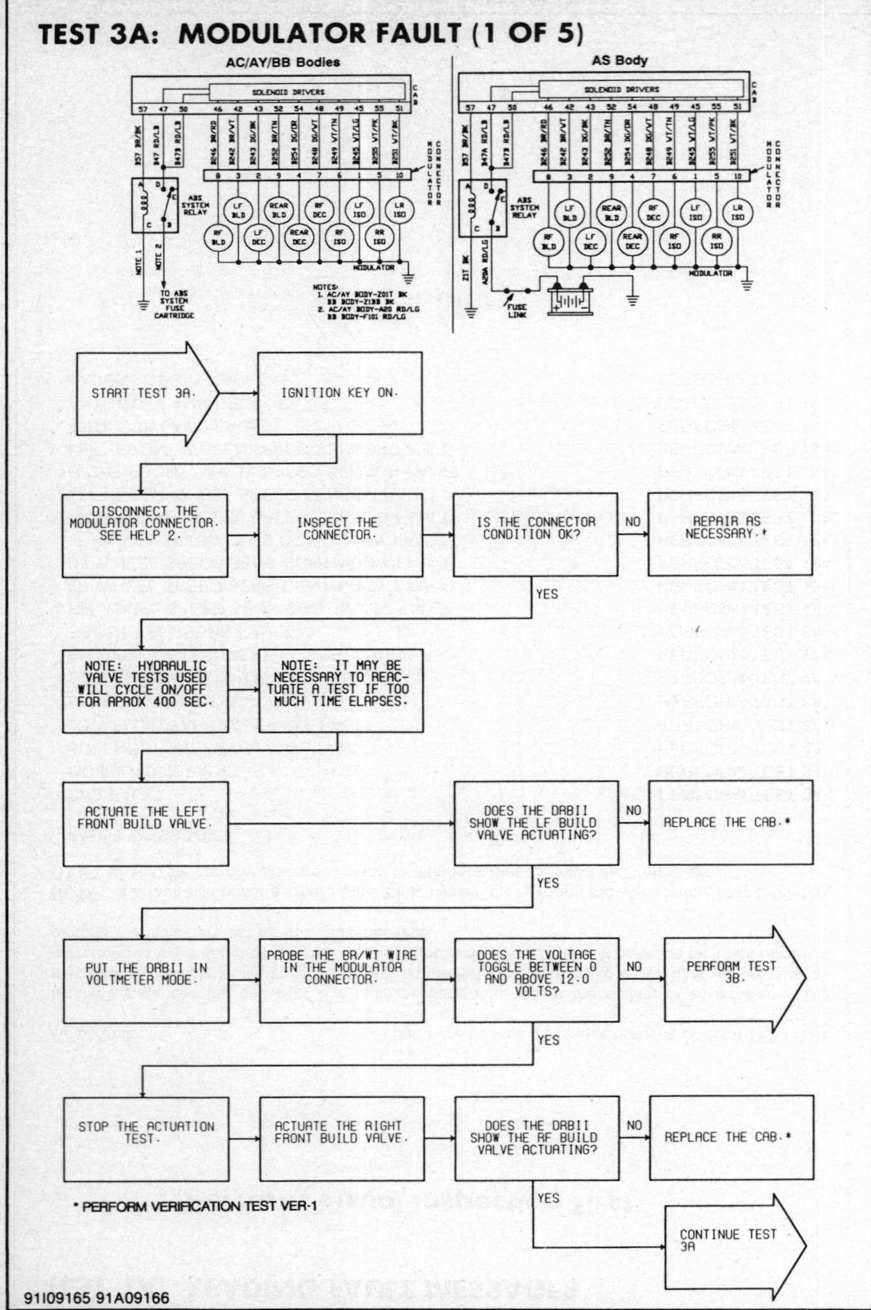
TEST 3A: MODULATOR FAULT (1 OF 5)
AC/AY/BB Bodies
AS Body
SOLENOID DRIVERS
ABS SYSTEM RELAY
MODULATOR
TO ABS SYSTEM FUSE CARTRIDGE
FUSE LINK
START TEST 3A.
IGNITION KEY ON.
DISCONNECT THE MODULATOR CONNECTOR. SEE HELP 2.
INSPECT THE CONNECTOR.
IS THE CONNECTOR CONDITION OK?
NO
REPAIR AS NECESSARY.*
YES
NOTE: HYDRAULIC VALVE TESTS USED WILL CYCLE ON/OFF FOR APROX 400 SEC.
NOTE: IT MAY BE NECESSARY TO REACTUATE A TEST IF TOO MUCH TIME ELAPSES.
ACTUATE THE LEFT FRONT BUILD VALVE.
DOES THE DRBII SHOW THE LF BUILD VALVE ACTUATING?
NO
REPLACE THE CAB.*
YES
PUT THE DRBII IN VOLTMETER MODE.
PROBE THE BR/WT WIRE IN THE MODULATOR CONNECTOR.
DOES THE VOLTAGE TOGGLE BETWEEN 0 AND ABOVE 12.0 VOLTS?
NO
PERFORM TEST 3B.
YES
STOP THE ACTUATION TEST.
ACTUATE THE RIGHT FRONT BUILD VALVE.
DOES THE DRBII SHOW THE RF BUILD VALVE ACTUATING?
NO
REPLACE THE CAB.*
YES
CONTINUE TEST 3A
* PERFORM VERIFICATION TEST VER-1
91I09165 91A09166

Fig. 7: Anti-Lock Brake Test 3A – Modulator Fault (1 of 5)

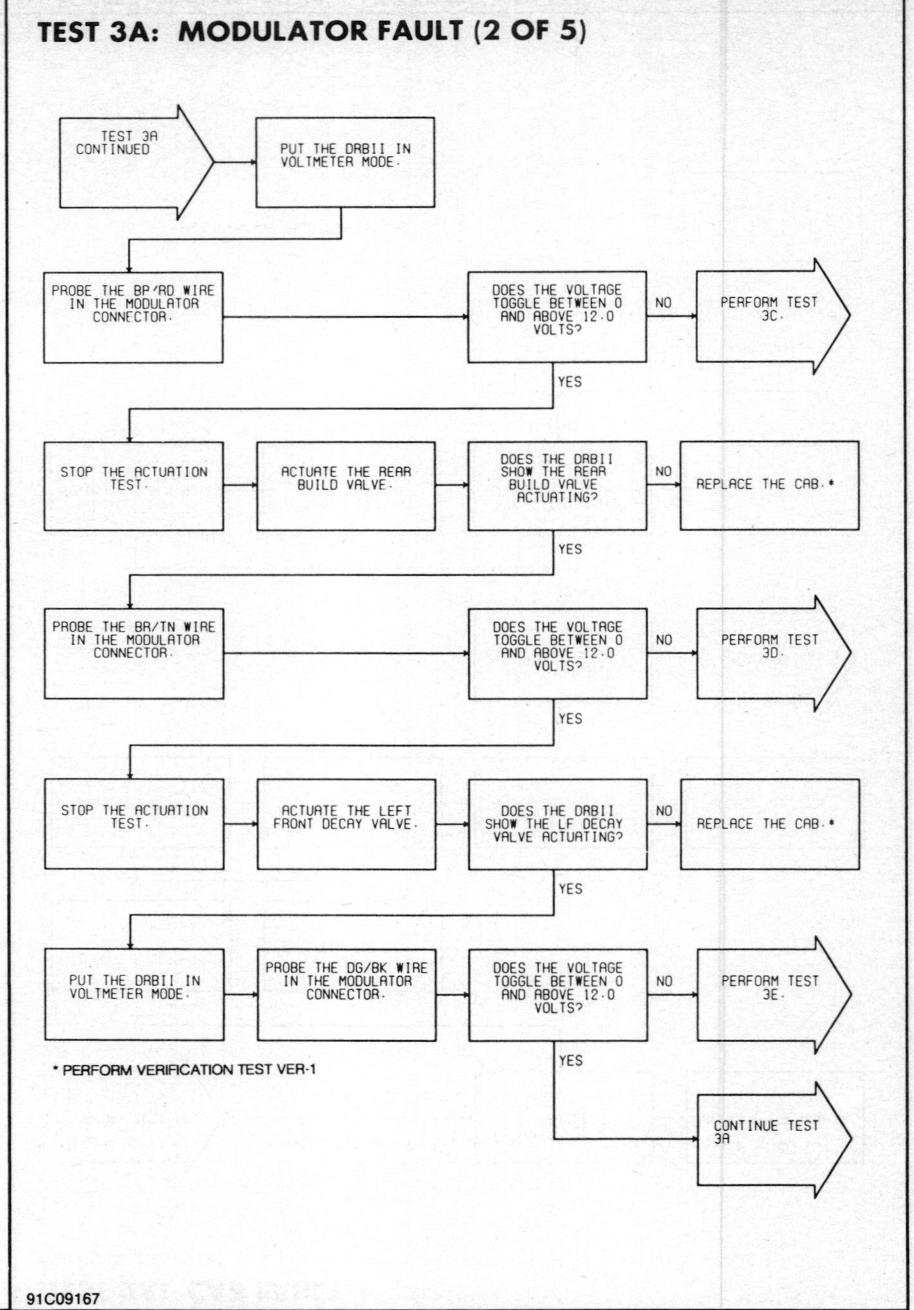
TEST 3A: MODULATOR FAULT (2 OF 5)
TEST 3A CONTINUED
PUT THE DRBII IN VOLTMETER MODE.
PROBE THE BP/RD WIRE IN THE MODULATOR CONNECTOR.
DOES THE VOLTAGE TOGGLE BETWEEN 0 AND ABOVE 12.0 VOLTS?
NO
PERFORM TEST 3C.
YES
STOP THE ACTUATION TEST.
ACTUATE THE REAR BUILD VALVE.
DOES THE DRBII SHOW THE REAR BUILD VALVE ACTUATING?
NO
REPLACE THE CAB.*
YES
PROBE THE BR/TN WIRE IN THE MODULATOR CONNECTOR.
DOES THE VOLTAGE TOGGLE BETWEEN 0 AND ABOVE 12.0 VOLTS?
NO
PERFORM TEST 3D.
YES
STOP THE ACTUATION TEST.
ACTUATE THE LEFT FRONT DECAY VALVE.
DOES THE DRBII SHOW THE LF DECAY VALVE ACTUATING?
NO
REPLACE THE CAB.*
YES
PUT THE DRBII IN VOLTMETER MODE.
PROBE THE DG/BK WIRE IN THE MODULATOR CONNECTOR.
DOES THE VOLTAGE TOGGLE BETWEEN 0 AND ABOVE 12.0 VOLTS?
NO
PERFORM TEST 3E.
YES
CONTINUE TEST 3A
* PERFORM VERIFICATION TEST VER-1
91C09167

Fig. 8: Anti-Lock Brake Test 3A – Modulator Fault (2 of 5)

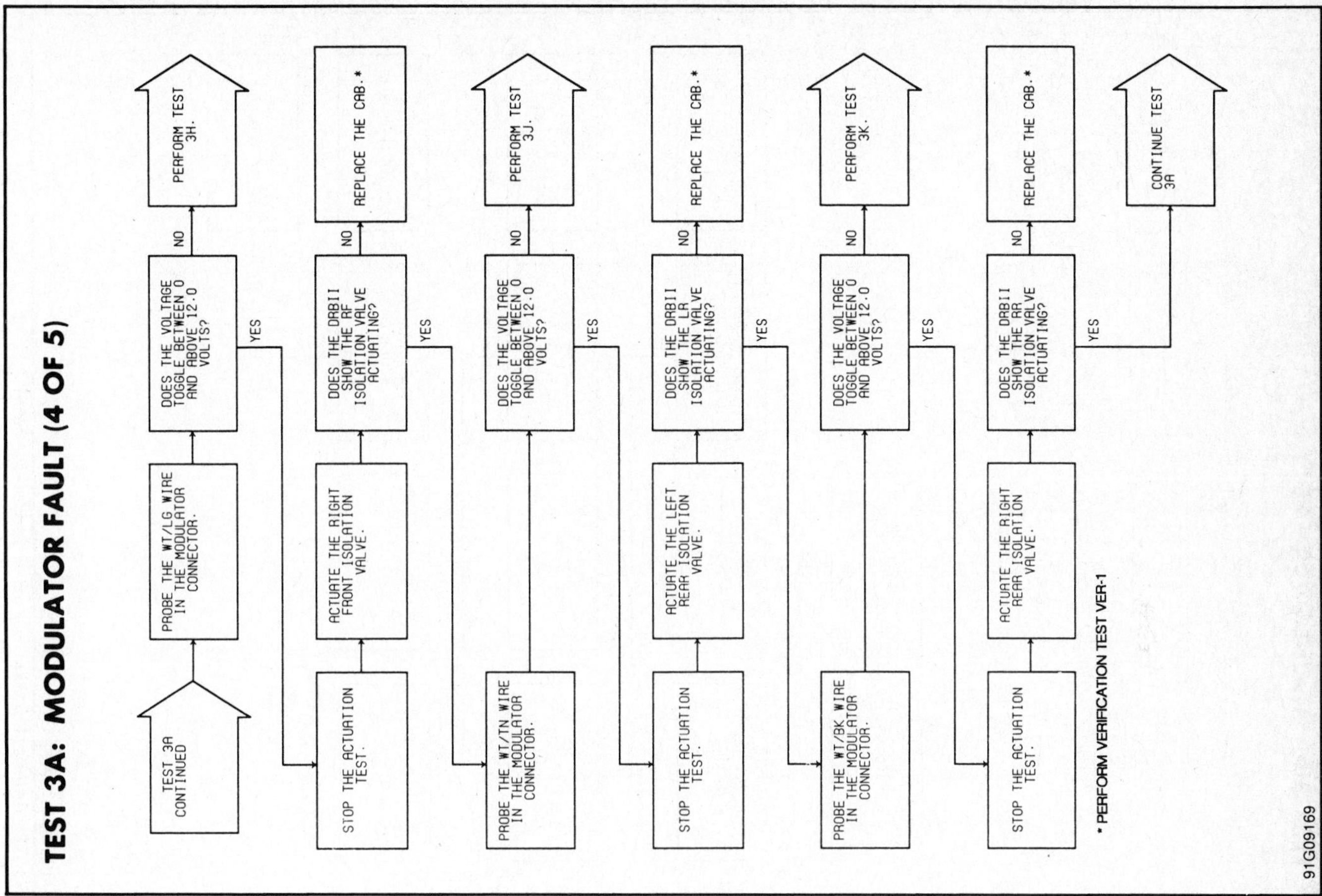

TEST 3A: MODULATOR FAULT (4 OF 5)
TEST 3A CONTINUED
PROBE THE WT/LG WIRE IN THE MODULATOR CONNECTOR.
DOES THE VOLTAGE TOGGLE BETWEEN 0 AND ABOVE 12.0 VOLTS?
NO
PERFORM TEST 3H.
YES
STOP THE ACTUATION TEST.
ACTUATE THE RIGHT FRONT ISOLATION VALVE.
DOES THE DRBII SHOW THE RF ISOLATION VALVE ACTUATING?
NO
REPLACE THE CAB.*
YES
PROBE THE WT/TN WIRE IN THE MODULATOR CONNECTOR.
DOES THE VOLTAGE TOGGLE BETWEEN 0 AND ABOVE 12.0 VOLTS?
NO
PERFORM TEST 3J.
YES
STOP THE ACTUATION TEST.
ACTUATE THE LEFT REAR ISOLATION VALVE.
DOES THE DRBII SHOW THE LR ISOLATION VALVE ACTUATING?
NO
REPLACE THE CAB.*
YES
PROBE THE WT/BK WIRE IN THE MODULATOR CONNECTOR.
DOES THE VOLTAGE TOGGLE BETWEEN 0 AND ABOVE 12.0 VOLTS?
NO
PERFORM TEST 3K.
YES
STOP THE ACTUATION TEST.
ACTUATE THE RIGHT REAR ISOLATION VALVE.
DOES THE DRBII SHOW THE RR ISOLATION VALVE ACTUATING?
NO
REPLACE THE CAB.*
YES
CONTINUE TEST 3A
* PERFORM VERIFICATION TEST VER-1
91G09169

Fig. 10: Anti-Lock Brake Test 3A – Modulator Fault (4 of 5)

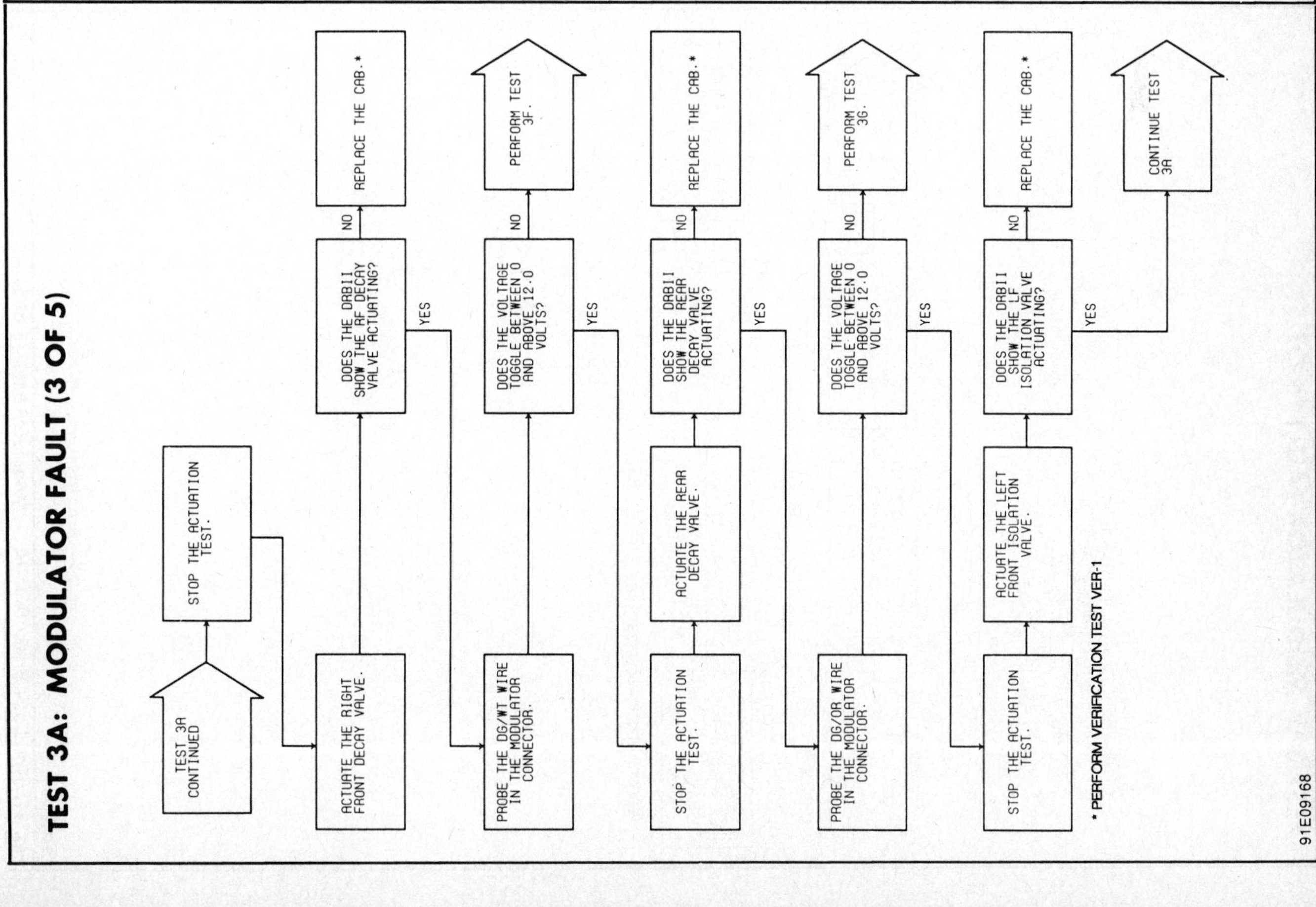

TEST 3A: MODULATOR FAULT (3 OF 5)
TEST 3A CONTINUED
STOP THE ACTUATION TEST.
ACTUATE THE RIGHT FRONT DECAY VALVE.
DOES THE DRBII SHOW THE RF DECAY VALVE ACTUATING?
NO
REPLACE THE CAB.*
YES
PROBE THE DG/WT WIRE IN THE MODULATOR CONNECTOR.
DOES THE VOLTAGE TOGGLE BETWEEN 0 AND ABOVE 12.0 VOLTS?
NO
PERFORM TEST 3F.
YES
STOP THE ACTUATION TEST.
ACTUATE THE REAR DECAY VALVE.
DOES THE DRBII SHOW THE REAR DECAY VALVE ACTUATING?
NO
REPLACE THE CAB.*
YES
PROBE THE DG/OR WIRE IN THE MODULATOR CONNECTOR.
DOES THE VOLTAGE TOGGLE BETWEEN 0 AND ABOVE 12.0 VOLTS?
NO
PERFORM TEST 3G.
YES
STOP THE ACTUATION TEST.
ACTUATE THE LEFT FRONT ISOLATION VALVE.
DOES THE DRBII SHOW THE LF ISOLATION VALVE ACTUATING?
NO
REPLACE THE CAB.*
YES
CONTINUE TEST 3A
* PERFORM VERIFICATION TEST VER-1
91E09168

Fig. 9: Anti-Lock Brake Test 3A – Modulator Fault (3 of 5)

1991 BRAKES
Anti-Lock – Bendix-10 (Cont.)

TEST 3A: MODULATOR FAULT (5 OF 5)

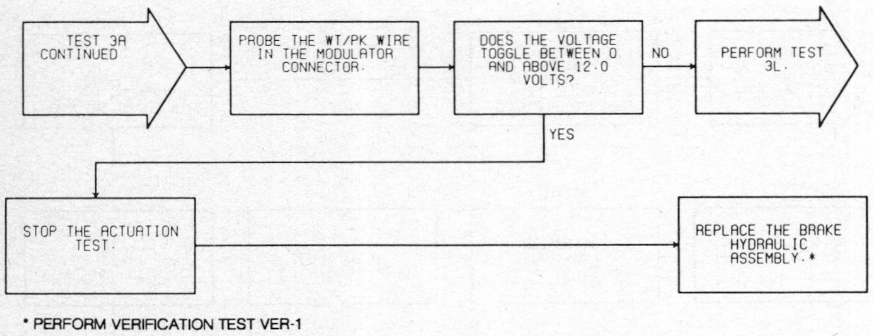
TEST 3A CONTINUED
PROBE THE WT/PK WIRE IN THE MODULATOR CONNECTOR.
DOES THE VOLTAGE TOGGLE BETWEEN 0 AND ABOVE 12.0 VOLTS?
NO
PERFORM TEST 3L.
YES
STOP THE ACTUATION TEST.
REPLACE THE BRAKE HYDRAULIC ASSEMBLY.*

* PERFORM VERIFICATION TEST VER-1

91I09170

Fig. 11: Anti-Lock Brake Test 3A – Modulator Fault (5 of 5)

TEST 3B: MODULATOR FAULT

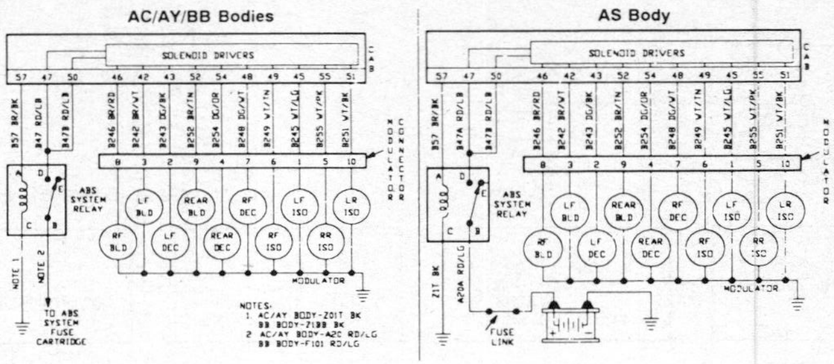
AC/AY/BB Bodies
AS Body
SOLENOID DRIVERS
ABS SYSTEM RELAY
MODULATOR
TO ABS SYSTEM FUSE CARTRIDGE
FUSE LINK
NOTES:
1 AC/AY BODY-Z01T BK
BB BODY-Z138 BK
2 AC/AY BODY-A2C RD/LG
BB BODY-F101 RD/LG

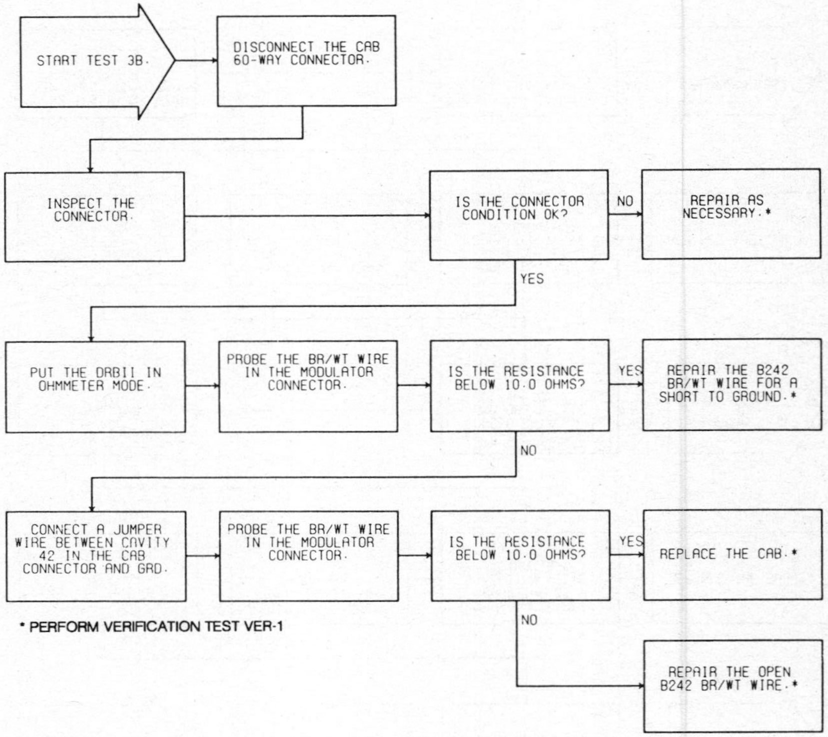
START TEST 3B.
DISCONNECT THE CAB 60-WAY CONNECTOR.
INSPECT THE CONNECTOR.
IS THE CONNECTOR CONDITION OK?
NO
REPAIR AS NECESSARY.*
YES
PUT THE DRBII IN OHMMETER MODE.
PROBE THE BR/WT WIRE IN THE MODULATOR CONNECTOR.
IS THE RESISTANCE BELOW 10.0 OHMS?
YES
REPAIR THE B242 BR/WT WIRE FOR A SHORT TO GROUND.*
NO
CONNECT A JUMPER WIRE BETWEEN CAVITY 42 IN THE CAB CONNECTOR AND GRD.
PROBE THE BR/WT WIRE IN THE MODULATOR CONNECTOR.
IS THE RESISTANCE BELOW 10.0 OHMS?
YES
REPLACE THE CAB.*
NO
REPAIR THE OPEN B242 BR/WT WIRE.*

* PERFORM VERIFICATION TEST VER-1

91I09165 91C09172

Fig. 12: Anti-Lock Brake Test 3B – Modulator Fault

TEST 3C: MODULATOR FAULT

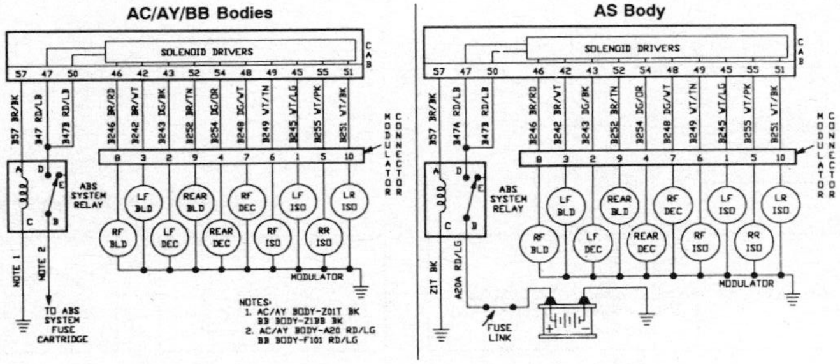
AC/AY/BB Bodies
AS Body
SOLENOID DRIVERS
CAB
MODULATOR CONNECTOR
ABS SYSTEM RELAY
MODULATOR
NOTE 1
NOTE 2
TO ABS SYSTEM FUSE CARTRIDGE
FUSE LINK

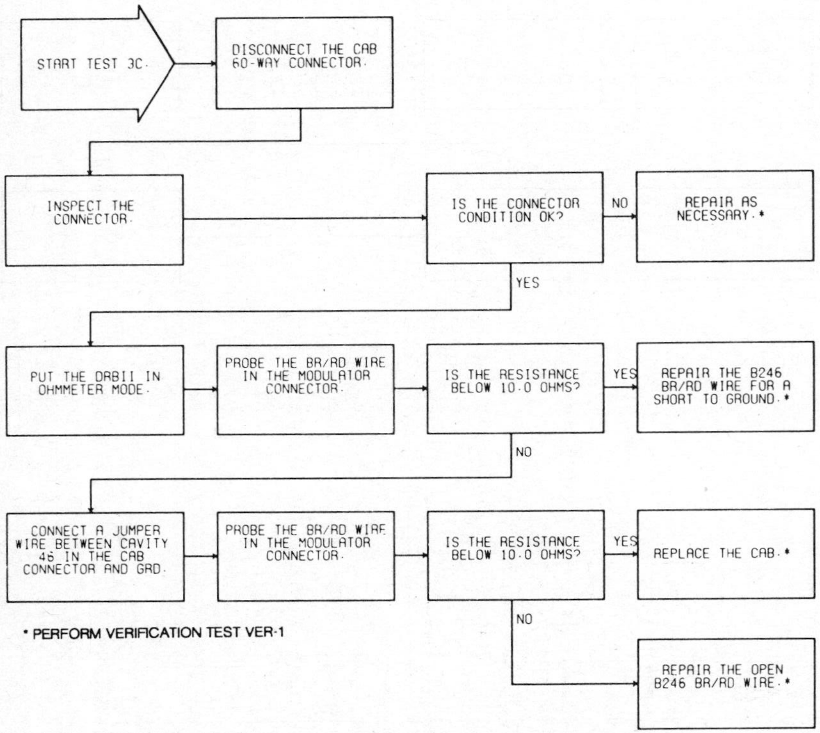
START TEST 3C.
DISCONNECT THE CAB 60-WAY CONNECTOR.
INSPECT THE CONNECTOR.
IS THE CONNECTOR CONDITION OK?
NO
REPAIR AS NECESSARY.*
YES
PUT THE DRBII IN OHMMETER MODE.
PROBE THE BR/RD WIRE IN THE MODULATOR CONNECTOR.
IS THE RESISTANCE BELOW 10.0 OHMS?
YES
REPAIR THE B246 BR/RD WIRE FOR A SHORT TO GROUND.*
NO
CONNECT A JUMPER WIRE BETWEEN CAVITY 46 IN THE CAB CONNECTOR AND GRD.
PROBE THE BR/RD WIRE IN THE MODULATOR CONNECTOR.
IS THE RESISTANCE BELOW 10.0 OHMS?
YES
REPLACE THE CAB.*
NO
REPAIR THE OPEN B246 BR/RD WIRE.*

* PERFORM VERIFICATION TEST VER-1

91I09165 91E09173

Fig. 13: Anti-Lock Brake Test 3C – Modulator Fault

TEST 3D: MODULATOR FAULT

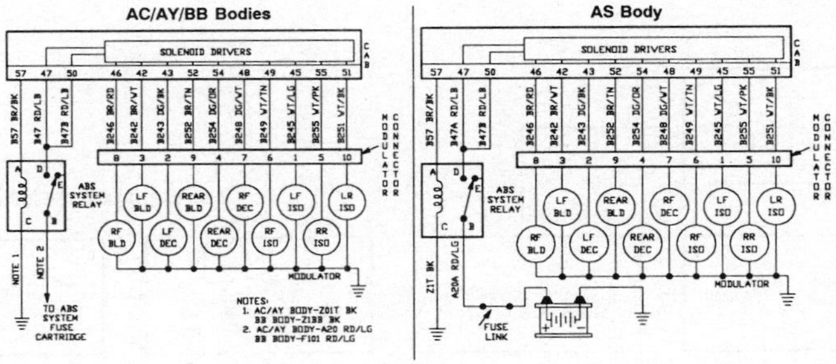
AC/AY/BB Bodies
AS Body
SOLENOID DRIVERS
CAB
MODULATOR CONNECTOR
ABS SYSTEM RELAY
MODULATOR
NOTE 1
NOTE 2
TO ABS SYSTEM FUSE CARTRIDGE
FUSE LINK

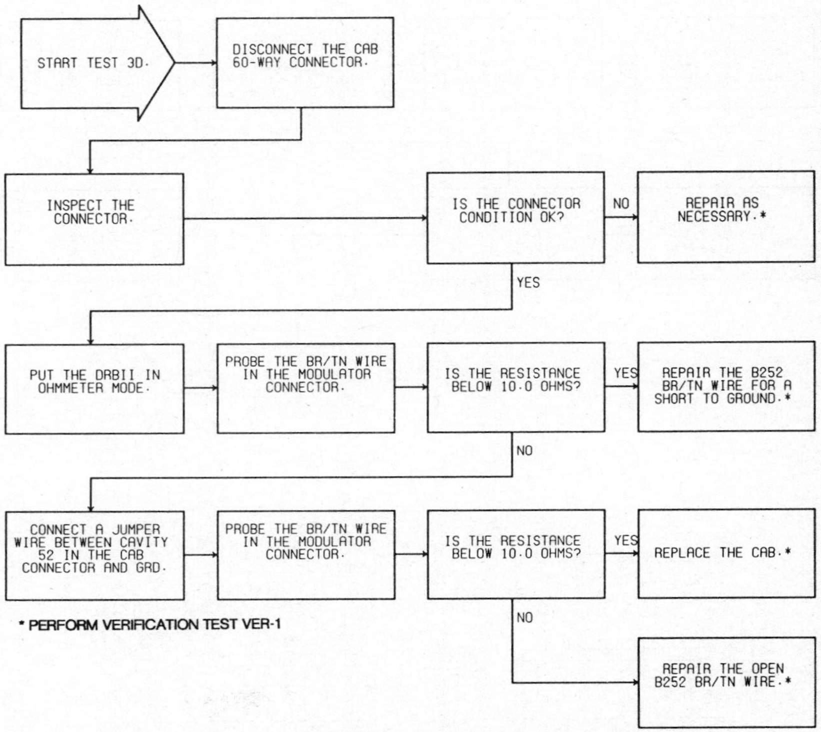
START TEST 3D.
DISCONNECT THE CAB 60-WAY CONNECTOR.
INSPECT THE CONNECTOR.
IS THE CONNECTOR CONDITION OK?
NO
REPAIR AS NECESSARY.*
YES
PUT THE DRBII IN OHMMETER MODE.
PROBE THE BR/TN WIRE IN THE MODULATOR CONNECTOR.
IS THE RESISTANCE BELOW 10.0 OHMS?
YES
REPAIR THE B252 BR/TN WIRE FOR A SHORT TO GROUND.*
NO
CONNECT A JUMPER WIRE BETWEEN CAVITY 52 IN THE CAB CONNECTOR AND GRD.
PROBE THE BR/TN WIRE IN THE MODULATOR CONNECTOR.
IS THE RESISTANCE BELOW 10.0 OHMS?
YES
REPLACE THE CAB.*
NO
REPAIR THE OPEN B252 BR/TN WIRE.*

* PERFORM VERIFICATION TEST VER-1

91I09165 91G09174

Fig. 14: Anti-Lock Brake Test 3D – Modulator Fault

1991 BRAKES
Anti-Lock – Bendix-10 (Cont.)

TEST 3E: MODULATOR FAULT

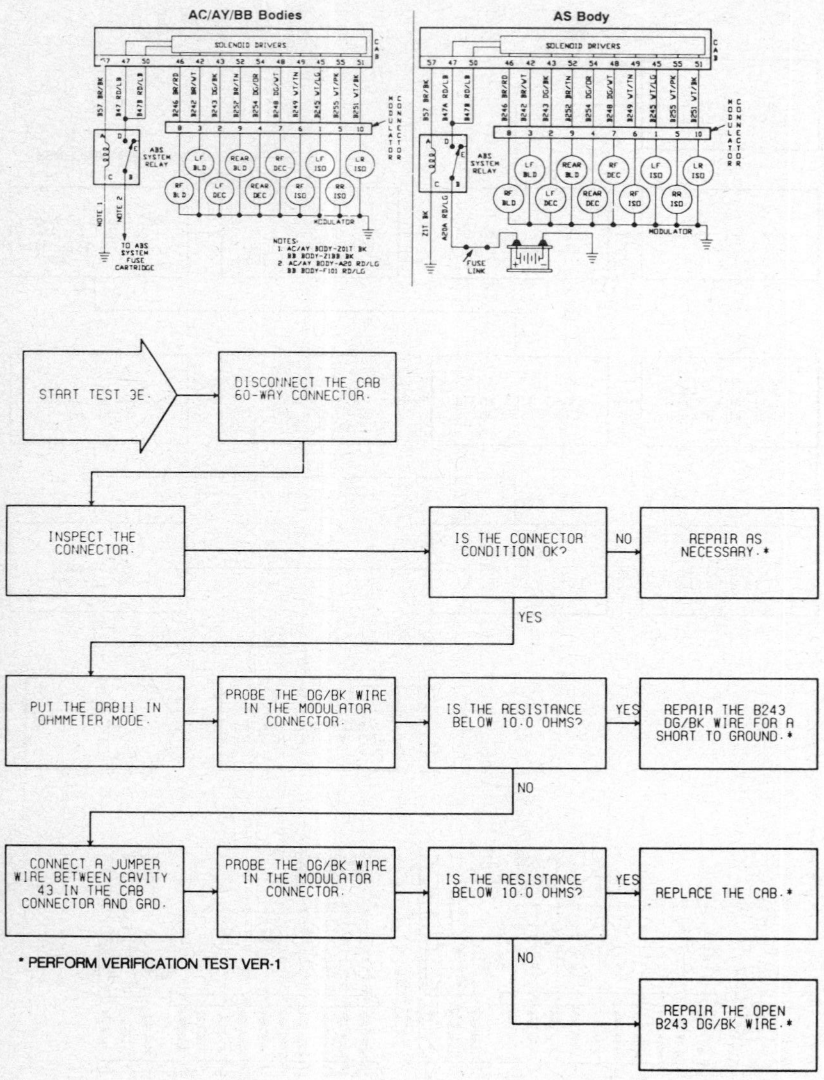
AC/AY/BB Bodies
AS Body
START TEST 3E.
DISCONNECT THE CAB 60-WAY CONNECTOR.
INSPECT THE CONNECTOR.
IS THE CONNECTOR CONDITION OK?
NO
REPAIR AS NECESSARY.*
YES
PUT THE DRBII IN OHMMETER MODE.
PROBE THE DG/BK WIRE IN THE MODULATOR CONNECTOR.
IS THE RESISTANCE BELOW 10.0 OHMS?
YES
REPAIR THE B243 DG/BK WIRE FOR A SHORT TO GROUND.*
NO
CONNECT A JUMPER WIRE BETWEEN CAVITY 43 IN THE CAB CONNECTOR AND GRD.
PROBE THE DG/BK WIRE IN THE MODULATOR CONNECTOR.
IS THE RESISTANCE BELOW 10.0 OHMS?
YES
REPLACE THE CAB.*
NO
REPAIR THE OPEN B243 DG/BK WIRE.*
* PERFORM VERIFICATION TEST VER-1

91I09165 91J09175

Fig. 15: Anti-Lock Brake Test 3E – Modulator Fault

TEST 3F: MODULATOR FAULT

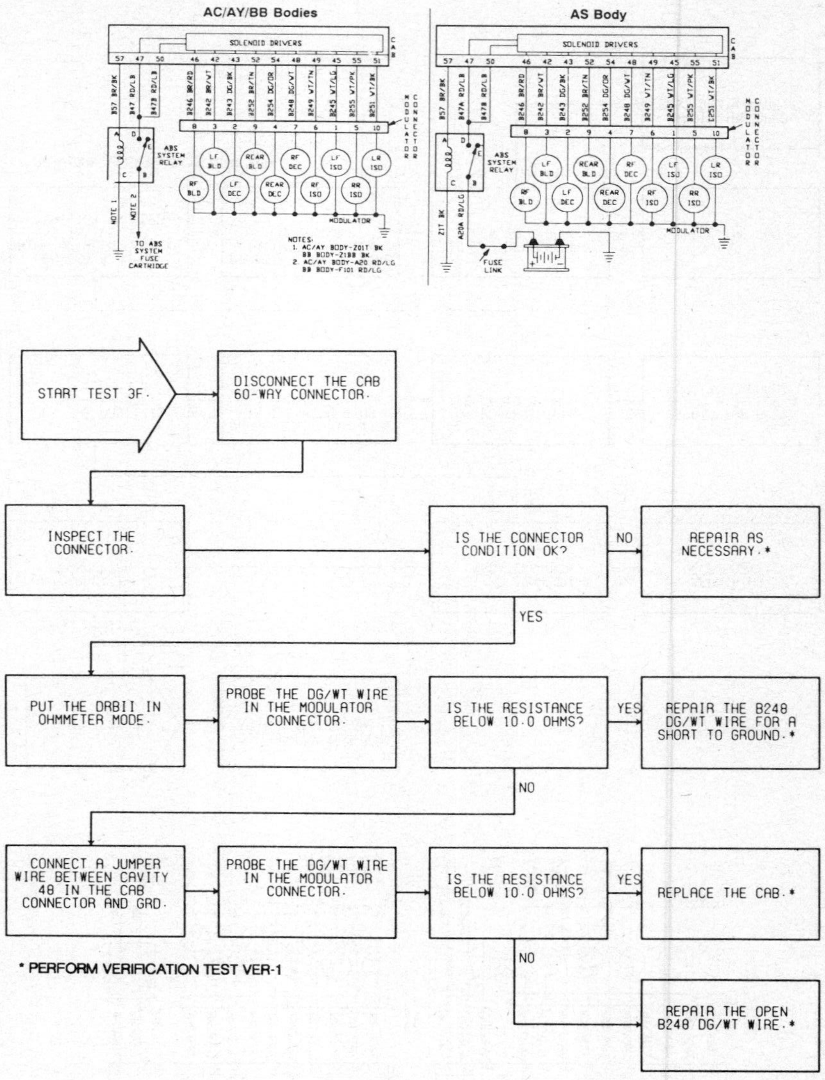
AC/AY/BB Bodies
AS Body
START TEST 3F.
DISCONNECT THE CAB 60-WAY CONNECTOR.
INSPECT THE CONNECTOR.
IS THE CONNECTOR CONDITION OK?
NO
REPAIR AS NECESSARY.*
YES
PUT THE DRBII IN OHMMETER MODE.
PROBE THE DG/WT WIRE IN THE MODULATOR CONNECTOR.
IS THE RESISTANCE BELOW 10.0 OHMS?
YES
REPAIR THE B248 DG/WT WIRE FOR A SHORT TO GROUND.*
NO
CONNECT A JUMPER WIRE BETWEEN CAVITY 48 IN THE CAB CONNECTOR AND GRD.
PROBE THE DG/WT WIRE IN THE MODULATOR CONNECTOR.
IS THE RESISTANCE BELOW 10.0 OHMS?
YES
REPLACE THE CAB.*
NO
REPAIR THE OPEN B248 DG/WT WIRE.*
* PERFORM VERIFICATION TEST VER-1

91I09165 91B09176

Fig. 16: Anti-Lock Brake Test 3F – Modulator Fault

TEST 3G: MODULATOR FAULT

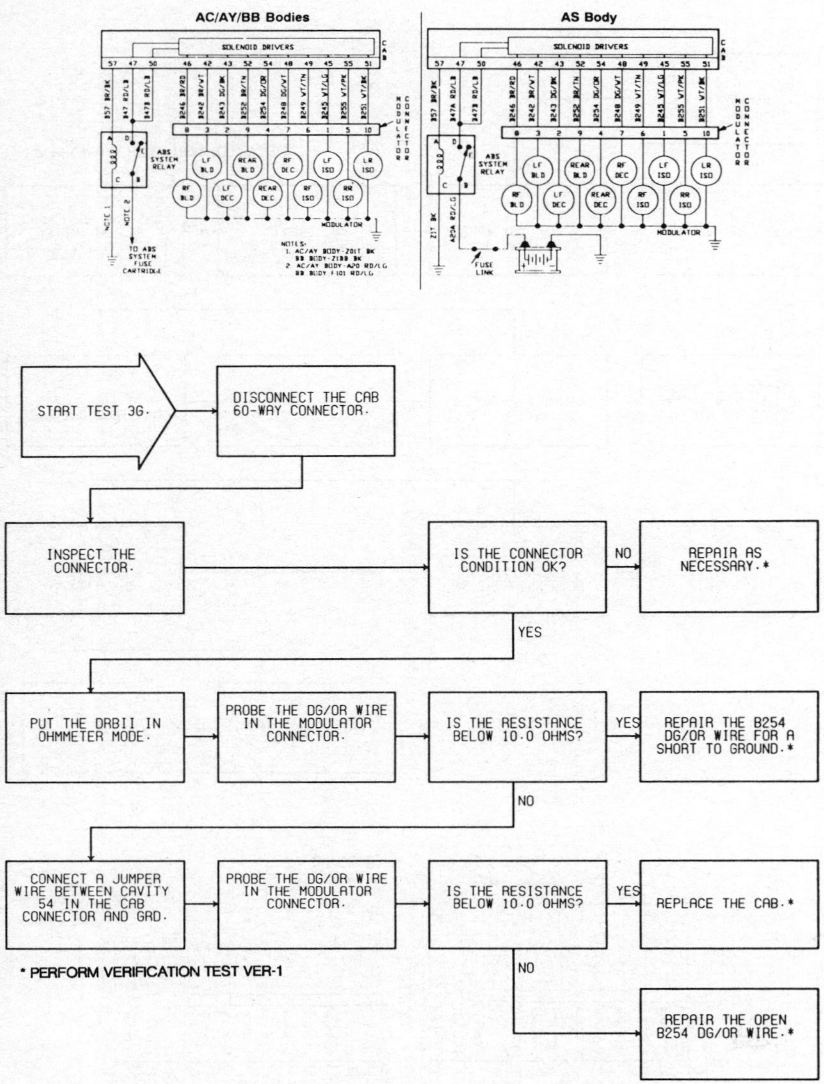
AC/AY/BB Bodies
AS Body
SOLENOID DRIVERS
MODULATOR
START TEST 3G.
DISCONNECT THE CAB 60-WAY CONNECTOR.
INSPECT THE CONNECTOR.
IS THE CONNECTOR CONDITION OK?
NO
REPAIR AS NECESSARY.*
YES
PUT THE DRBII IN OHMMETER MODE.
PROBE THE DG/OR WIRE IN THE MODULATOR CONNECTOR.
IS THE RESISTANCE BELOW 10.0 OHMS?
YES
REPAIR THE B254 DG/OR WIRE FOR A SHORT TO GROUND.*
NO
CONNECT A JUMPER WIRE BETWEEN CAVITY 54 IN THE CAB CONNECTOR AND GRD.
PROBE THE DG/OR WIRE IN THE MODULATOR CONNECTOR.
IS THE RESISTANCE BELOW 10.0 OHMS?
YES
REPLACE THE CAB.*
NO
REPAIR THE OPEN B254 DG/OR WIRE.*
* PERFORM VERIFICATION TEST VER-1

91I09165 91D09177

Fig. 17: Anti-Lock Brake Test 3G – Modulator Fault

TEST 3H: MODULATOR FAULT

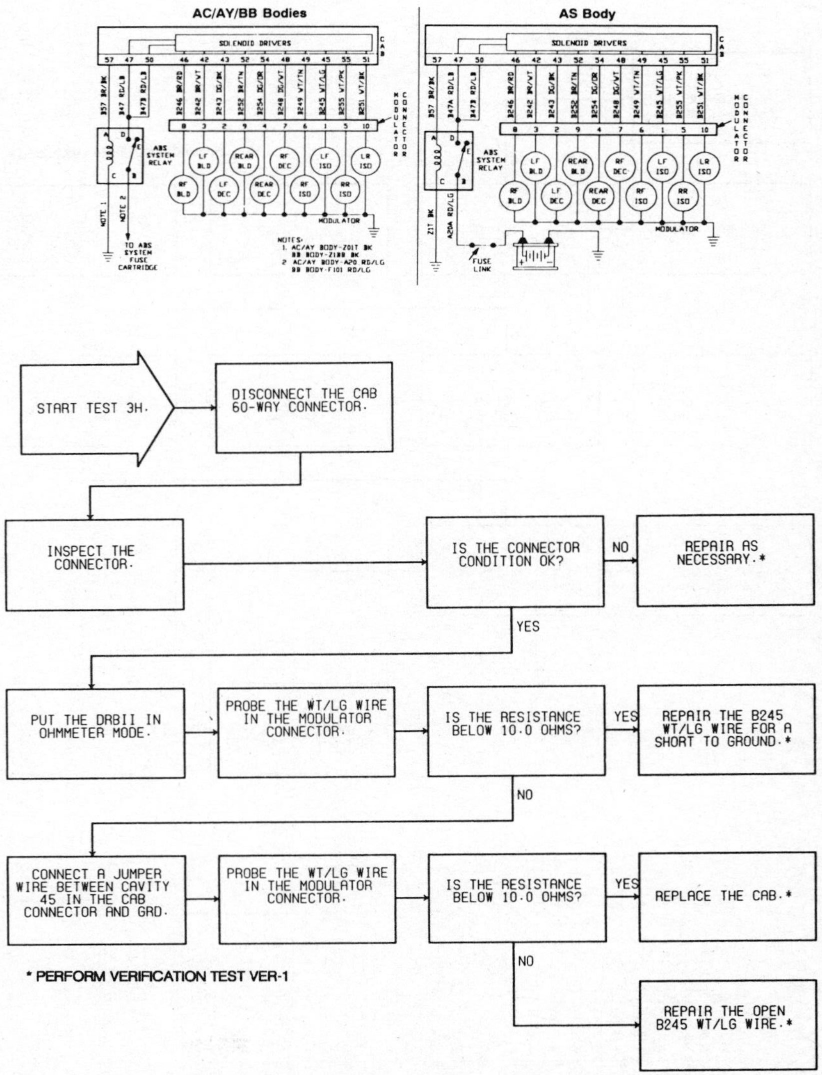
AC/AY/BB Bodies
AS Body
SOLENOID DRIVERS
MODULATOR
START TEST 3H.
DISCONNECT THE CAB 60-WAY CONNECTOR.
INSPECT THE CONNECTOR.
IS THE CONNECTOR CONDITION OK?
NO
REPAIR AS NECESSARY.*
YES
PUT THE DRBII IN OHMMETER MODE.
PROBE THE WT/LG WIRE IN THE MODULATOR CONNECTOR.
IS THE RESISTANCE BELOW 10.0 OHMS?
YES
REPAIR THE B245 WT/LG WIRE FOR A SHORT TO GROUND.*
NO
CONNECT A JUMPER WIRE BETWEEN CAVITY 45 IN THE CAB CONNECTOR AND GRD.
PROBE THE WT/LG WIRE IN THE MODULATOR CONNECTOR.
IS THE RESISTANCE BELOW 10.0 OHMS?
YES
REPLACE THE CAB.*
NO
REPAIR THE OPEN B245 WT/LG WIRE.*
* PERFORM VERIFICATION TEST VER-1

91I09165 91F09178

Fig. 18: Anti-Lock Brake Test 3H – Modulator Fault

1991 BRAKES
Anti-Lock – Bendix-10 (Cont.)

TEST 3J: MODULATOR FAULT

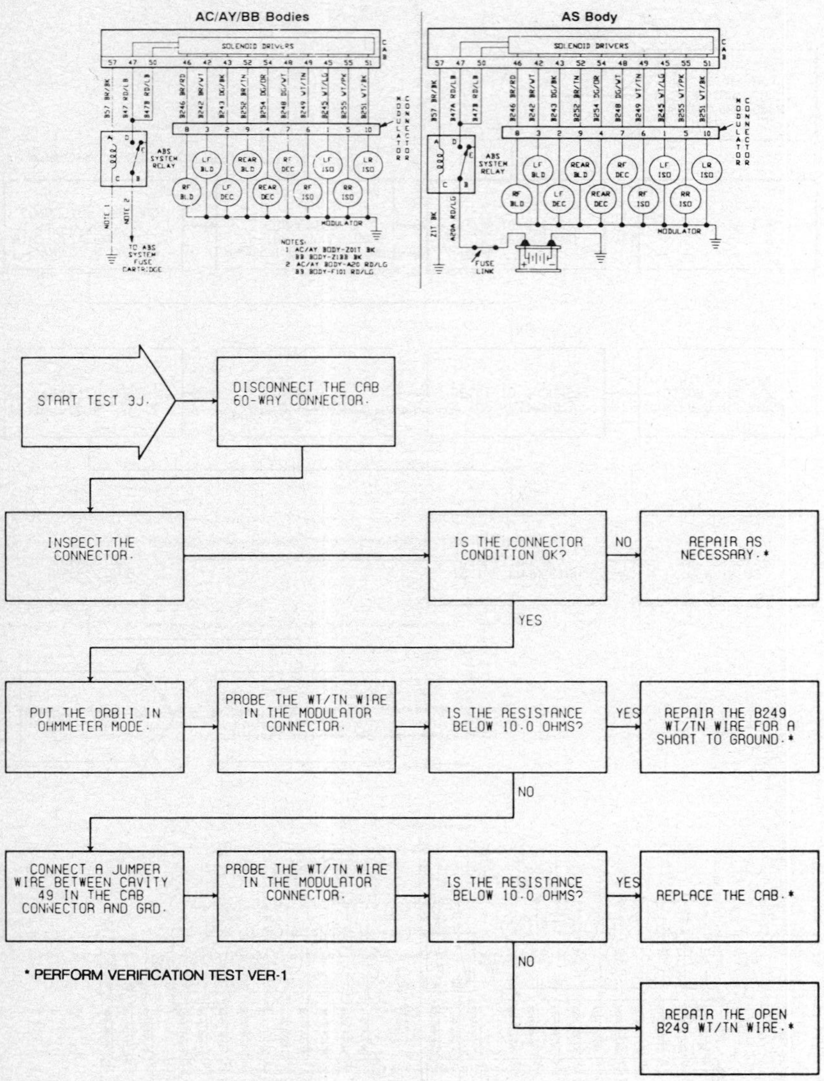
AC/AY/BB Bodies
AS Body
SOLENOID DRIVERS
ABS SYSTEM RELAY
MODULATOR
FUSE LINK
TO ABS SYSTEM FUSE CARTRIDGE
START TEST 3J.
DISCONNECT THE CAB 60-WAY CONNECTOR.
INSPECT THE CONNECTOR.
IS THE CONNECTOR CONDITION OK?
NO
REPAIR AS NECESSARY.*
YES
PUT THE DRBII IN OHMMETER MODE.
PROBE THE WT/TN WIRE IN THE MODULATOR CONNECTOR.
IS THE RESISTANCE BELOW 10.0 OHMS?
YES
REPAIR THE B249 WT/TN WIRE FOR A SHORT TO GROUND.*
NO
CONNECT A JUMPER WIRE BETWEEN CAVITY 49 IN THE CAB CONNECTOR AND GRD.
PROBE THE WT/TN WIRE IN THE MODULATOR CONNECTOR.
IS THE RESISTANCE BELOW 10.0 OHMS?
YES
REPLACE THE CAB.*
NO
REPAIR THE OPEN B249 WT/TN WIRE.*

* PERFORM VERIFICATION TEST VER-1

91I09165 91H09179

Fig. 19: Anti-Lock Brake Test 3J – Modulator Fault

TEST 3K: MODULATOR FAULT

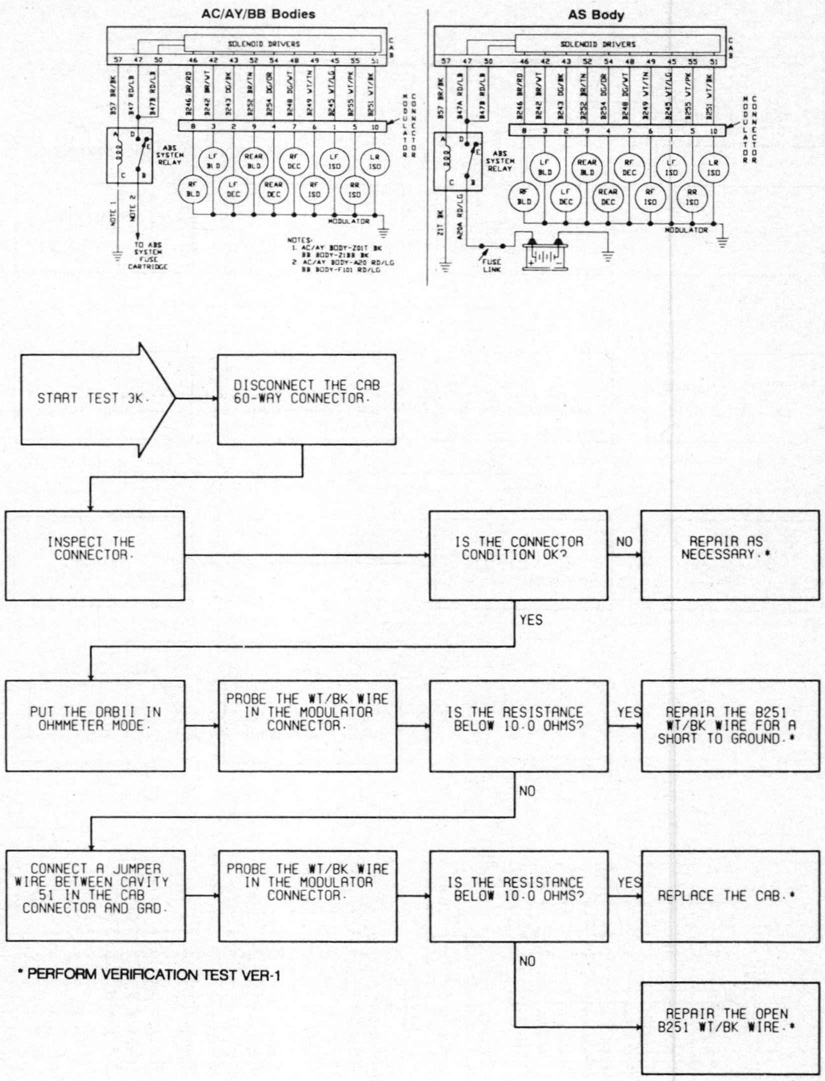
AC/AY/BB Bodies
AS Body
SOLENOID DRIVERS
ABS SYSTEM RELAY
MODULATOR
FUSE LINK
TO ABS SYSTEM FUSE CARTRIDGE
START TEST 3K.
DISCONNECT THE CAB 60-WAY CONNECTOR.
INSPECT THE CONNECTOR.
IS THE CONNECTOR CONDITION OK?
NO
REPAIR AS NECESSARY.*
YES
PUT THE DRBII IN OHMMETER MODE.
PROBE THE WT/BK WIRE IN THE MODULATOR CONNECTOR.
IS THE RESISTANCE BELOW 10.0 OHMS?
YES
REPAIR THE B251 WT/BK WIRE FOR A SHORT TO GROUND.*
NO
CONNECT A JUMPER WIRE BETWEEN CAVITY 51 IN THE CAB CONNECTOR AND GRD.
PROBE THE WT/BK WIRE IN THE MODULATOR CONNECTOR.
IS THE RESISTANCE BELOW 10.0 OHMS?
YES
REPLACE THE CAB.*
NO
REPAIR THE OPEN B251 WT/BK WIRE.*

* PERFORM VERIFICATION TEST VER-1

91I09165 91J09180

Fig. 20: Anti-Lock Brake Test 3K – Modulator Fault

TEST 3L: MODULATOR FAULT

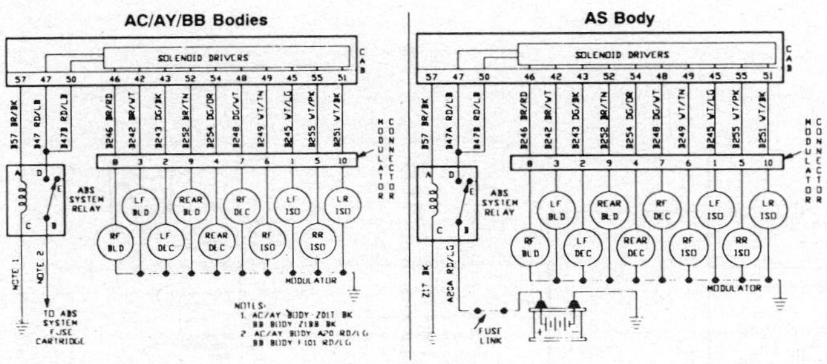
AC/AY/BB Bodies
AS Body

- START TEST 3L. → DISCONNECT THE CAB 60-WAY CONNECTOR.
- INSPECT THE CONNECTOR. → IS THE CONNECTOR CONDITION OK?
  - NO → REPAIR AS NECESSARY.*
  - YES → PUT THE DRBII IN OHMMETER MODE. → PROBE THE WT/PK WIRE IN THE MODULATOR CONNECTOR. → IS THE RESISTANCE BELOW 10.0 OHMS?
    - YES → REPAIR THE B255 WT/PK WIRE FOR A SHORT TO GROUND.*
    - NO → CONNECT A JUMPER WIRE BETWEEN CAVITY 55 IN THE CAB CONNECTOR AND GRD. → PROBE THE WT/PK WIRE IN THE MODULATOR CONNECTOR. → IS THE RESISTANCE BELOW 10.0 OHMS?
      - YES → REPLACE THE CAB.*
      - NO → REPAIR THE OPEN B255 WT/PK WIRE.*

* PERFORM VERIFICATION TEST VER-1

91I09165 91B09181

Fig. 21: Anti-Lock Brake Test 3L – Modulator Fault

TEST 4A: SOLENOID UNDERVOLTAGE FAULT (1 OF 2)

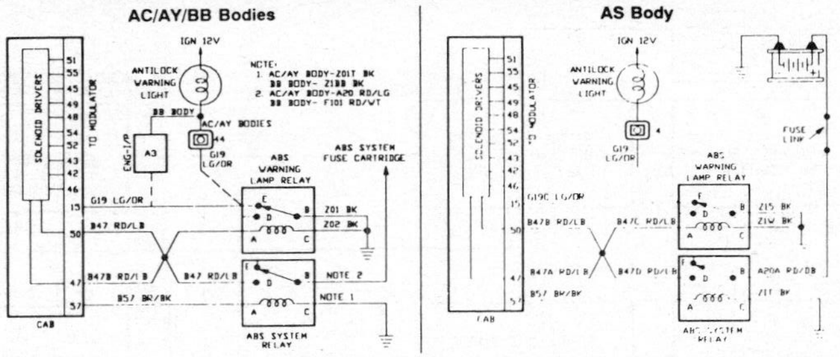
AC/AY/BB Bodies
AS Body

- START TEST 4A. → INSPECT THE ABS SYSTEM FUSE CARTRIDGE OR FUSE LINK. → IS THE ABS SYSTEM FUSE CARTRIDGE OR FUSE LINK BLOWN?
  - NO → PERFORM TEST 4B.
  - YES → DISCONNECT THE CAB 60-WAY CONNECTOR. → INSPECT THE CONNECTOR. → IS THE CONNECTOR CONDITION OK?
    - NO → REPAIR AS NECESSARY. → REPLACE THE ABS SYSTEM FUSE CARTRIDGE.*
    - YES → REMOVE ABS SYSTEM FUSE CARTRIDGE (AC/AY/BB BODIES). → REMOVE THE ABS WARNING LAMP RELAY. → REMOVE THE ABS SYSTEM RELAY. → PUT THE DRBII IN THE OHMMETER MODE. → PROBE CAVITY B OF THE ABS SYSTEM RELAY SOCKET/CONNECTOR. → IS THE RESISTANCE BELOW 10.0 OHMS?
      - YES → REPAIR THE WIRE BETW CAV B AND FUSE FOR A SHORT TO GROUND.*
      - NO → PROBE CAVITY D OF THE ABS SYSTEM RELAY SOCKET/CONNECTOR. → IS THE RESISTANCE BELOW 10.0 OHMS?
        - YES → REPAIR THE B47 RD/LB WIRE FOR A SHORT TO GROUND.*
        - NO → CONTINUE TEST 4A

* PERFORM VERIFICATION TEST VER-1

91D09182 91F09183

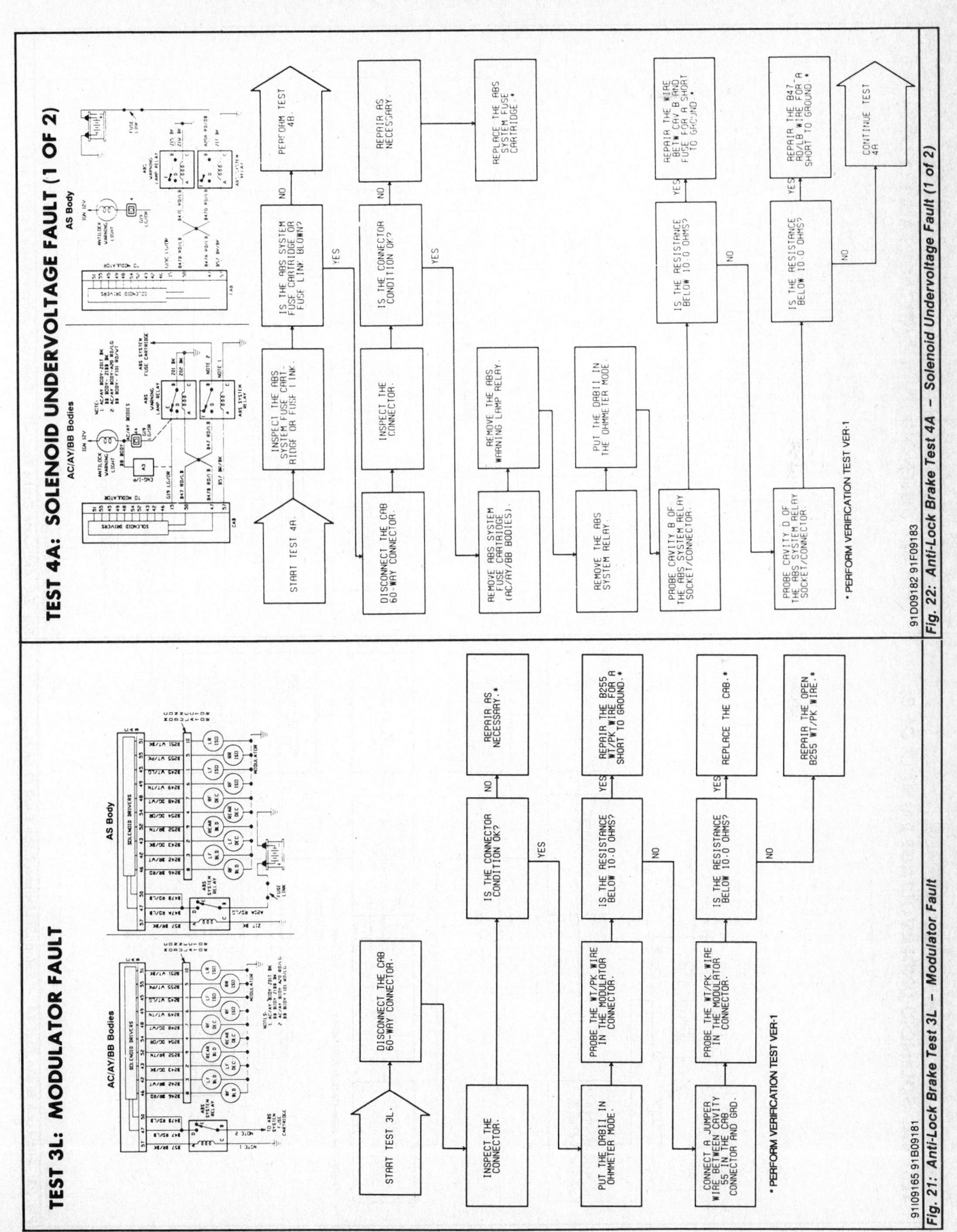

Fig. 22: Anti-Lock Brake Test 4A – Solenoid Undervoltage Fault (1 of 2)

TEST 4A: SOLENOID UNDERVOLTAGE FAULT (2 OF 2)

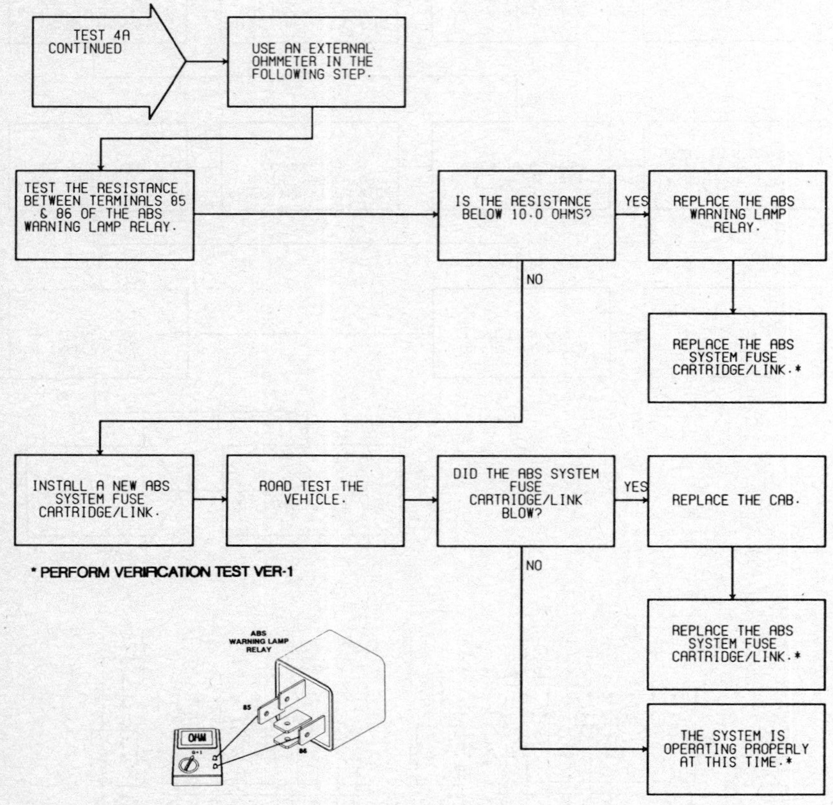
TEST 4A CONTINUED
USE AN EXTERNAL OHMMETER IN THE FOLLOWING STEP.
TEST THE RESISTANCE BETWEEN TERMINALS 85 & 86 OF THE ABS WARNING LAMP RELAY.
IS THE RESISTANCE BELOW 10.0 OHMS?
YES
NO
REPLACE THE ABS WARNING LAMP RELAY.
REPLACE THE ABS SYSTEM FUSE CARTRIDGE/LINK.*
INSTALL A NEW ABS SYSTEM FUSE CARTRIDGE/LINK.
ROAD TEST THE VEHICLE.
DID THE ABS SYSTEM FUSE CARTRIDGE/LINK BLOW?
YES
NO
REPLACE THE CAB.
REPLACE THE ABS SYSTEM FUSE CARTRIDGE/LINK.*
THE SYSTEM IS OPERATING PROPERLY AT THIS TIME.*
* PERFORM VERIFICATION TEST VER-1
ABS WARNING LAMP RELAY
85
86
OHM

91H09184

Fig. 23: Anti-Lock Brake Test 4A – Solenoid Undervoltage Fault (2 of 2)

TEST 4B: SOLENOID UNDERVOLTAGE FAULT (1 OF 6)

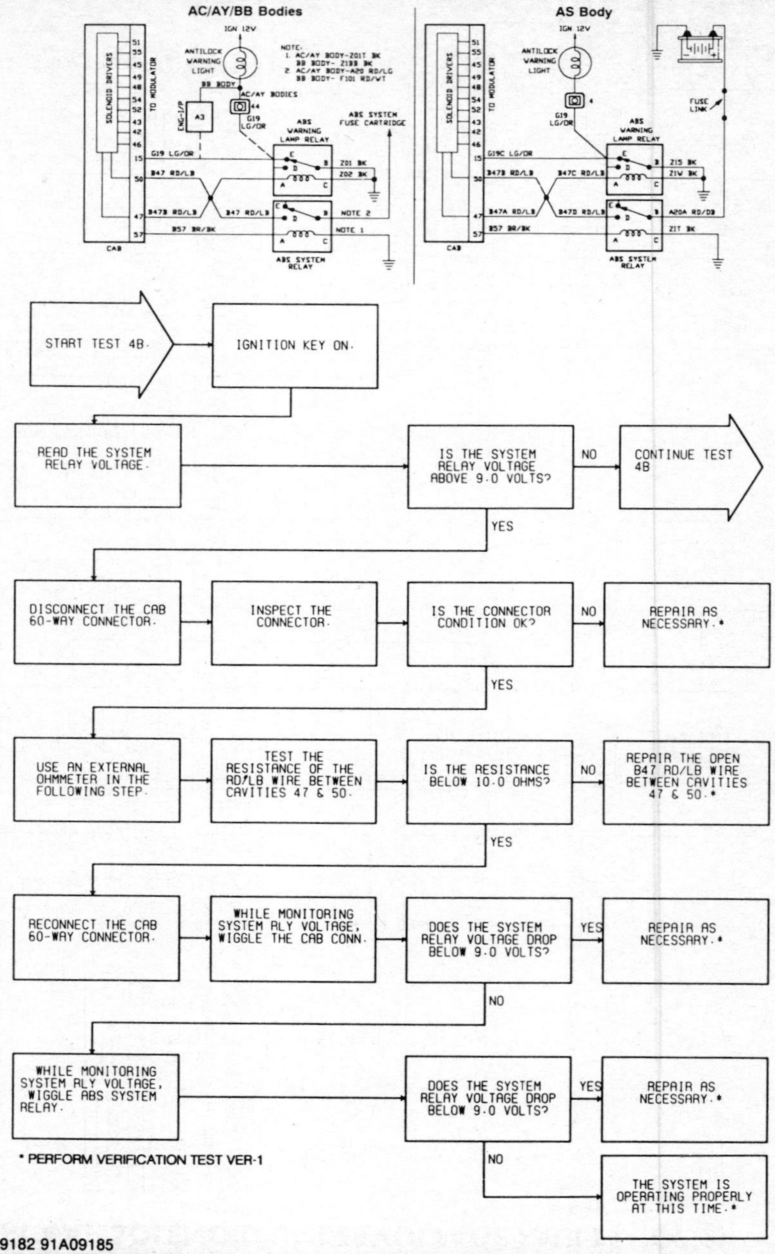
AC/AY/BB Bodies
AS Body
SOLENOID DRIVERS
TO MODULATOR
CAB
ANTILOCK WARNING LIGHT
IGN 12V
ABS WARNING LAMP RELAY
ABS SYSTEM RELAY
ABS SYSTEM FUSE CARTRIDGE
FUSE LINK
START TEST 4B.
IGNITION KEY ON.
READ THE SYSTEM RELAY VOLTAGE.
IS THE SYSTEM RELAY VOLTAGE ABOVE 9.0 VOLTS?
NO
CONTINUE TEST 4B
YES
DISCONNECT THE CAB 60-WAY CONNECTOR.
INSPECT THE CONNECTOR.
IS THE CONNECTOR CONDITION OK?
NO
REPAIR AS NECESSARY.*
YES
USE AN EXTERNAL OHMMETER IN THE FOLLOWING STEP.
TEST THE RESISTANCE OF THE RD/LB WIRE BETWEEN CAVITIES 47 & 50.
IS THE RESISTANCE BELOW 10.0 OHMS?
NO
REPAIR THE OPEN B47 RD/LB WIRE BETWEEN CAVITIES 47 & 50.*
YES
RECONNECT THE CAB 60-WAY CONNECTOR.
WHILE MONITORING SYSTEM RLY VOLTAGE, WIGGLE THE CAB CONN.
DOES THE SYSTEM RELAY VOLTAGE DROP BELOW 9.0 VOLTS?
YES
REPAIR AS NECESSARY.*
NO
WHILE MONITORING SYSTEM RLY VOLTAGE, WIGGLE ABS SYSTEM RELAY.
DOES THE SYSTEM RELAY VOLTAGE DROP BELOW 9.0 VOLTS?
YES
REPAIR AS NECESSARY.*
NO
THE SYSTEM IS OPERATING PROPERLY AT THIS TIME.*
* PERFORM VERIFICATION TEST VER-1

91D09182 91A09185

Fig. 24: Anti-Lock Brake Test 4B – Solenoid Undervoltage Fault (1 of 6)

TEST 4B: SOLENOID UNDERVOLTAGE FAULT (2 OF 6)

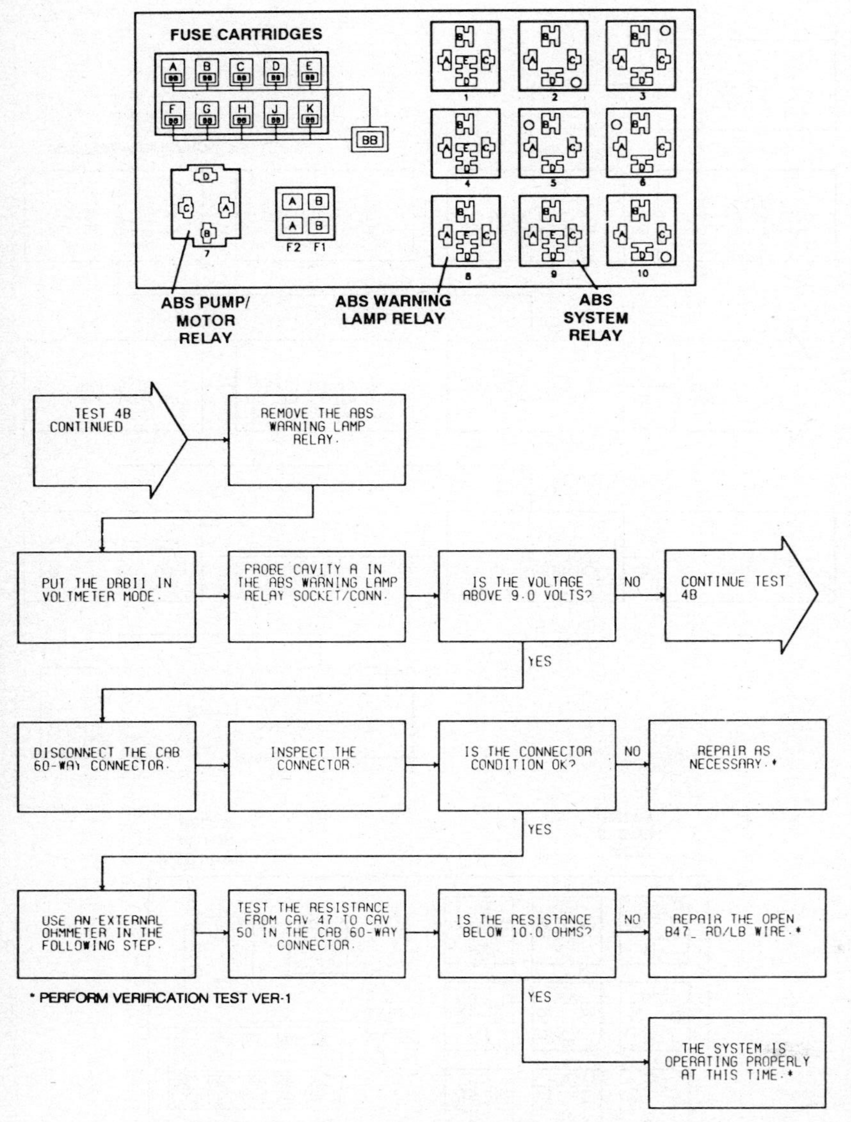
FUSE CARTRIDGES
ABS PUMP/
MOTOR
RELAY
ABS WARNING
LAMP RELAY
ABS
SYSTEM
RELAY
TEST 4B CONTINUED
REMOVE THE ABS WARNING LAMP RELAY.
PUT THE DRBII IN VOLTMETER MODE.
PROBE CAVITY A IN THE ABS WARNING LAMP RELAY SOCKET/CONN.
IS THE VOLTAGE ABOVE 9.0 VOLTS?
NO
CONTINUE TEST 4B
YES
DISCONNECT THE CAB 60-WAY CONNECTOR.
INSPECT THE CONNECTOR.
IS THE CONNECTOR CONDITION OK?
NO
REPAIR AS NECESSARY.*
YES
USE AN EXTERNAL OHMMETER IN THE FOLLOWING STEP.
TEST THE RESISTANCE FROM CAV 47 TO CAV 50 IN THE CAB 60-WAY CONNECTOR.
IS THE RESISTANCE BELOW 10.0 OHMS?
NO
REPAIR THE OPEN B47_ RD/LB WIRE.*
YES
THE SYSTEM IS OPERATING PROPERLY AT THIS TIME.*
* PERFORM VERIFICATION TEST VER-1

91J10883 91C09186

Fig. 25: Anti-Lock Brake Test 4B – Solenoid Undervoltage Fault (2 of 6)

TEST 4B: SOLENOID UNDERVOLTAGE FAULT (3 OF 6)

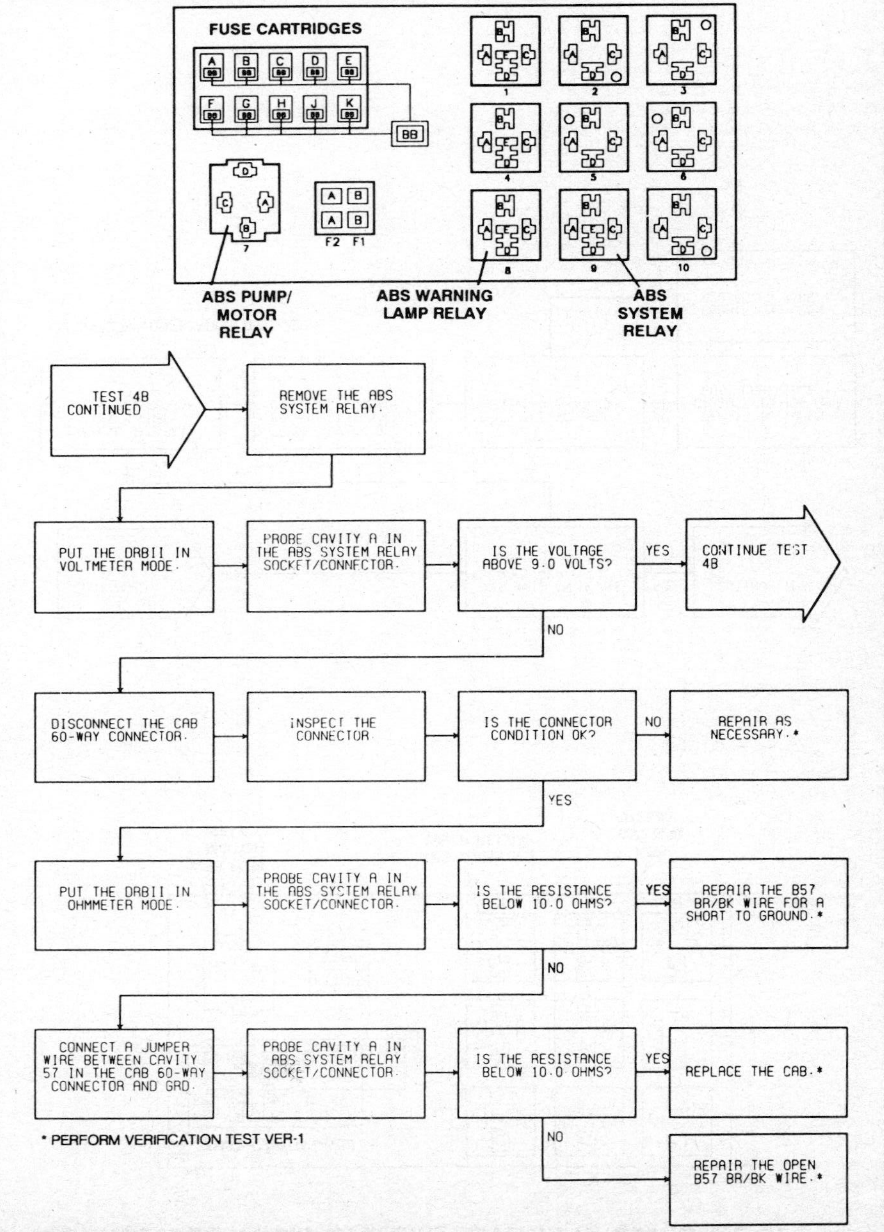
FUSE CARTRIDGES
ABS PUMP/
MOTOR
RELAY
ABS WARNING
LAMP RELAY
ABS
SYSTEM
RELAY
TEST 4B CONTINUED
REMOVE THE ABS SYSTEM RELAY.
PUT THE DRBII IN VOLTMETER MODE.
PROBE CAVITY A IN THE ABS SYSTEM RELAY SOCKET/CONNECTOR.
IS THE VOLTAGE ABOVE 9.0 VOLTS?
YES
CONTINUE TEST 4B
NO
DISCONNECT THE CAB 60-WAY CONNECTOR.
INSPECT THE CONNECTOR.
IS THE CONNECTOR CONDITION OK?
NO
REPAIR AS NECESSARY.*
YES
PUT THE DRBII IN OHMMETER MODE.
PROBE CAVITY A IN THE ABS SYSTEM RELAY SOCKET/CONNECTOR.
IS THE RESISTANCE BELOW 10.0 OHMS?
YES
REPAIR THE B57 BR/BK WIRE FOR A SHORT TO GROUND.*
NO
CONNECT A JUMPER WIRE BETWEEN CAVITY 57 IN THE CAB 60-WAY CONNECTOR AND GRD.
PROBE CAVITY A IN ABS SYSTEM RELAY SOCKET/CONNECTOR.
IS THE RESISTANCE BELOW 10.0 OHMS?
YES
REPLACE THE CAB.*
NO
REPAIR THE OPEN B57 BR/BK WIRE.*
* PERFORM VERIFICATION TEST VER-1

91J10883 91E09187

Fig. 26: Anti-Lock Brake Test 4B – Solenoid Undervoltage Fault (3 of 6)

1991 BRAKES
Anti-Lock – Bendix-10 (Cont.)

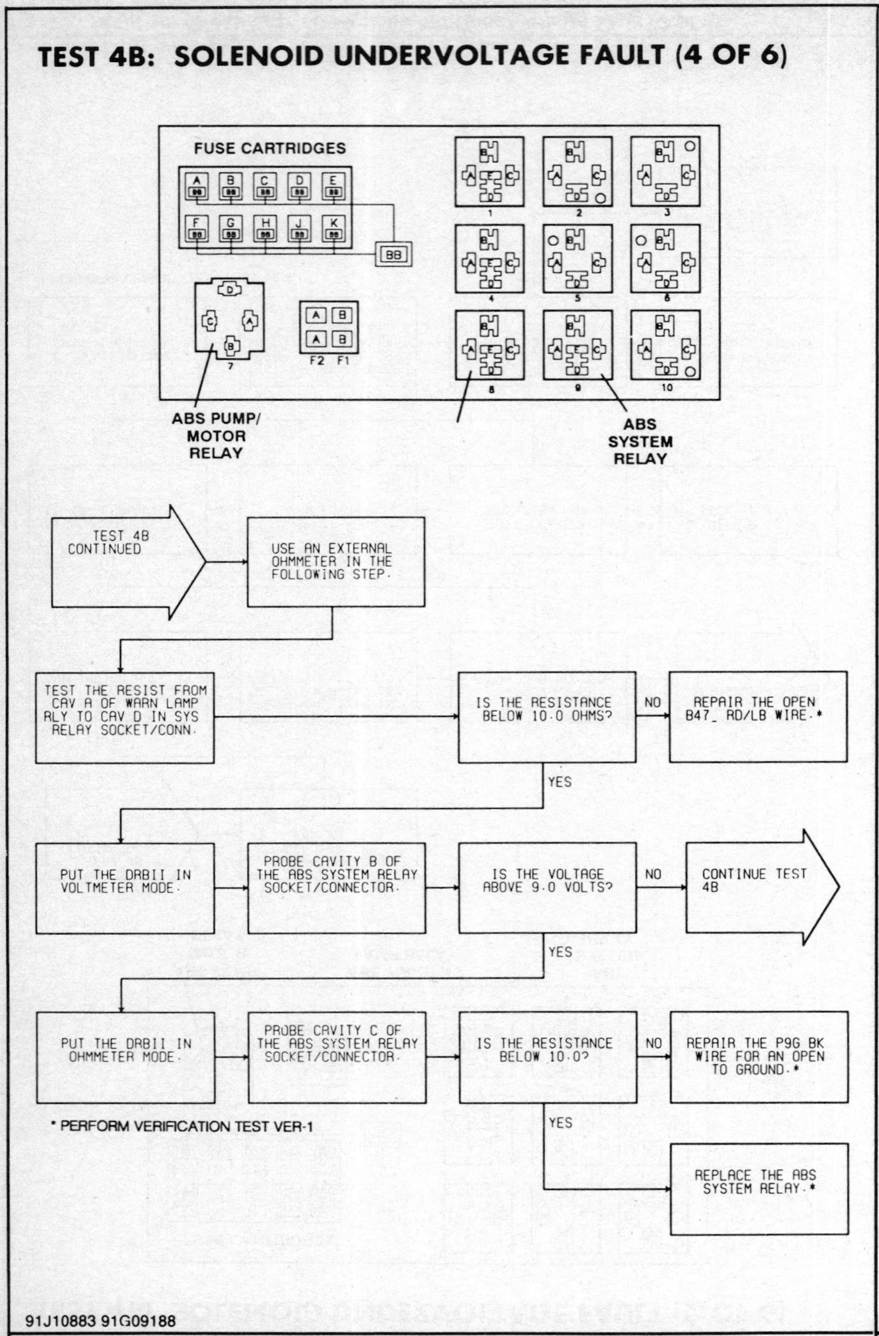
TEST 4B: SOLENOID UNDERVOLTAGE FAULT (4 OF 6)
FUSE CARTRIDGES
ABS PUMP/ MOTOR RELAY
ABS SYSTEM RELAY
TEST 4B CONTINUED
USE AN EXTERNAL OHMMETER IN THE FOLLOWING STEP.
TEST THE RESIST FROM CAV A OF WARN LAMP RLY TO CAV D IN SYS RELAY SOCKET/CONN.
IS THE RESISTANCE BELOW 10.0 OHMS?
NO
REPAIR THE OPEN B47_ RD/LB WIRE.*
YES
PUT THE DRBII IN VOLTMETER MODE.
PROBE CAVITY B OF THE ABS SYSTEM RELAY SOCKET/CONNECTOR.
IS THE VOLTAGE ABOVE 9.0 VOLTS?
NO
CONTINUE TEST 4B
YES
PUT THE DRBII IN OHMMETER MODE.
PROBE CAVITY C OF THE ABS SYSTEM RELAY SOCKET/CONNECTOR.
IS THE RESISTANCE BELOW 10.0?
NO
REPAIR THE P9G BK WIRE FOR AN OPEN TO GROUND.*
YES
REPLACE THE ABS SYSTEM RELAY.*
* PERFORM VERIFICATION TEST VER-1
91J10883 91G09188

Fig. 27: Anti-Lock Brake Test 4B – Solenoid Undervoltage Fault (4 of 6)

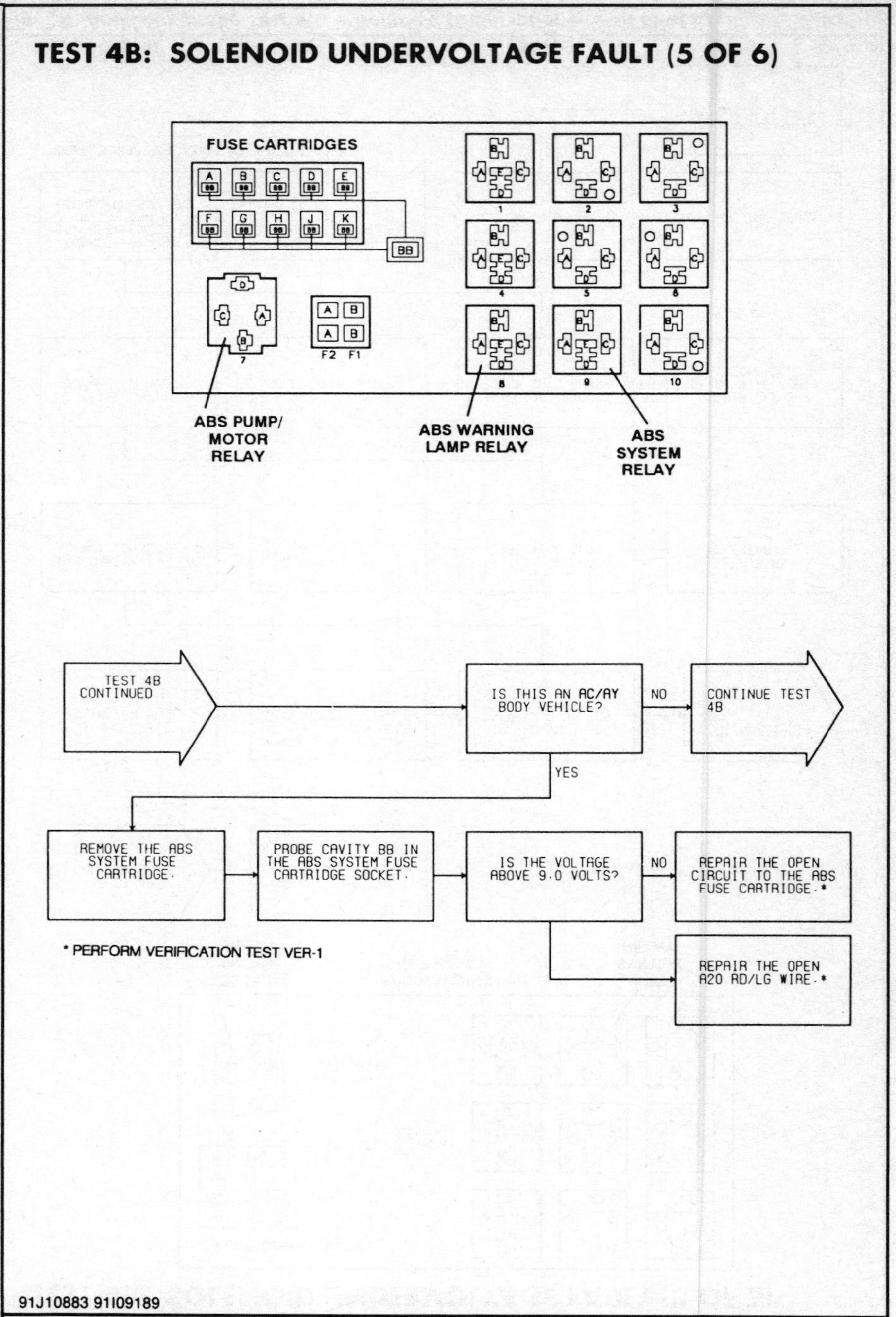
TEST 4B: SOLENOID UNDERVOLTAGE FAULT (5 OF 6)
FUSE CARTRIDGES
ABS PUMP/ MOTOR RELAY
ABS WARNING LAMP RELAY
ABS SYSTEM RELAY
TEST 4B CONTINUED
IS THIS AN AC/AY BODY VEHICLE?
NO
CONTINUE TEST 4B
YES
REMOVE THE ABS SYSTEM FUSE CARTRIDGE.
PROBE CAVITY BB IN THE ABS SYSTEM FUSE CARTRIDGE SOCKET.
IS THE VOLTAGE ABOVE 9.0 VOLTS?
NO
REPAIR THE OPEN CIRCUIT TO THE ABS FUSE CARTRIDGE.*
REPAIR THE OPEN A20 RD/LG WIRE.*
* PERFORM VERIFICATION TEST VER-1
91J10883 91I09189

Fig. 28: Anti-Lock Brake Test 4B – Solenoid Undervoltage Fault (5 of 6)

TEST 4B: SOLENOID UNDERVOLTAGE FAULT (6 OF 6)

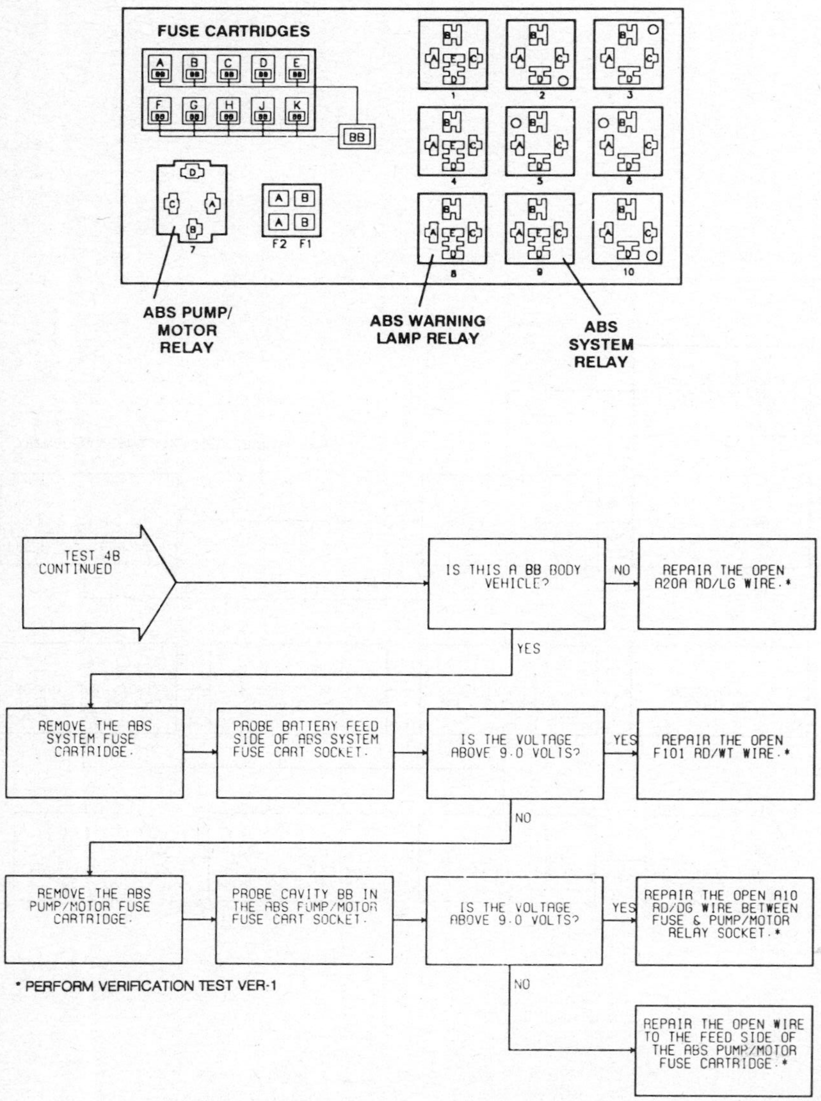
FUSE CARTRIDGES
A B C D E
F G H J K
BB
F2 F1
ABS PUMP/ MOTOR RELAY
ABS WARNING LAMP RELAY
ABS SYSTEM RELAY
TEST 4B CONTINUED
IS THIS A BB BODY VEHICLE?
NO
REPAIR THE OPEN A20A RD/LG WIRE.*
YES
REMOVE THE ABS SYSTEM FUSE CARTRIDGE.
PROBE BATTERY FEED SIDE OF ABS SYSTEM FUSE CART SOCKET.
IS THE VOLTAGE ABOVE 9.0 VOLTS?
YES
REPAIR THE OPEN F101 RD/WT WIRE.*
NO
REMOVE THE ABS PUMP/MOTOR FUSE CARTRIDGE.
PROBE CAVITY BB IN THE ABS PUMP/MOTOR FUSE CART SOCKET.
IS THE VOLTAGE ABOVE 9.0 VOLTS?
YES
REPAIR THE OPEN A10 RD/DG WIRE BETWEEN FUSE & PUMP/MOTOR RELAY SOCKET.*
NO
REPAIR THE OPEN WIRE TO THE FEED SIDE OF THE ABS PUMP/MOTOR FUSE CARTRIDGE.*

* PERFORM VERIFICATION TEST VER-1

91J10883 91A09190

Fig. 29: Anti-Lock Brake Test 4B – Solenoid Undervoltage Fault (6 of 6)

TEST 5A: LOW FLUID/PARKING BRAKE FAULT (1 OF 3)

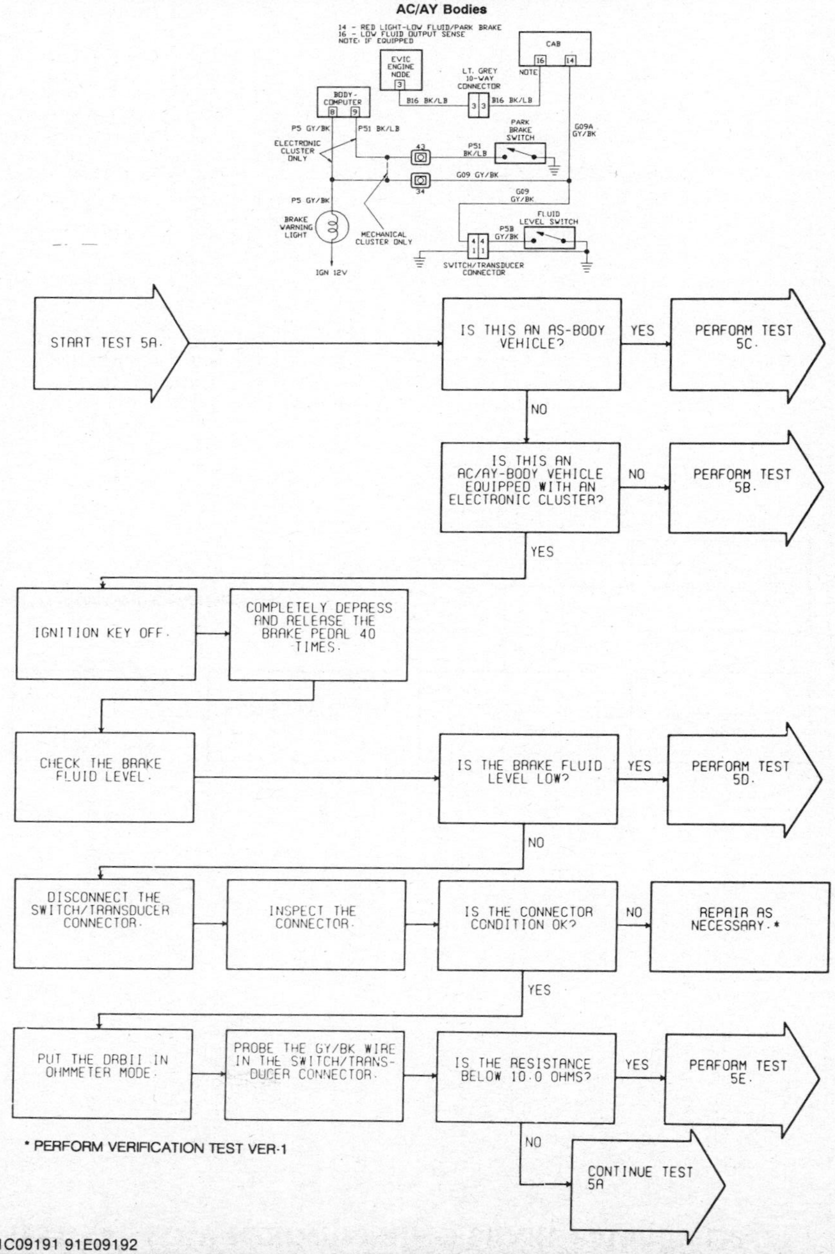
AC/AY Bodies
14 - RED LIGHT-LOW FLUID/PARK BRAKE
16 - LOW FLUID OUTPUT SENSE
NOTE: IF EQUIPPED
CAB
EVIC ENGINE NODE
LT. GREY 10-WAY CONNECTOR
BODY-COMPUTER
B16 BK/LB
P5 GY/BK
P51 BK/LB
ELECTRONIC CLUSTER ONLY
PARK BRAKE SWITCH
G09A GY/BK
G09 GY/BK
BRAKE WARNING LIGHT
MECHANICAL CLUSTER ONLY
FLUID LEVEL SWITCH
P5B GY/BK
SWITCH/TRANSDUCER CONNECTOR
IGN 12V
START TEST 5A.
IS THIS AN AS-BODY VEHICLE?
YES
PERFORM TEST 5C.
NO
IS THIS AN AC/AY-BODY VEHICLE EQUIPPED WITH AN ELECTRONIC CLUSTER?
NO
PERFORM TEST 5B.
YES
IGNITION KEY OFF.
COMPLETELY DEPRESS AND RELEASE THE BRAKE PEDAL 40 TIMES.
CHECK THE BRAKE FLUID LEVEL.
IS THE BRAKE FLUID LEVEL LOW?
YES
PERFORM TEST 5D.
NO
DISCONNECT THE SWITCH/TRANSDUCER CONNECTOR.
INSPECT THE CONNECTOR.
IS THE CONNECTOR CONDITION OK?
NO
REPAIR AS NECESSARY.*
YES
PUT THE DRBII IN OHMMETER MODE.
PROBE THE GY/BK WIRE IN THE SWITCH/TRANSDUCER CONNECTOR.
IS THE RESISTANCE BELOW 10.0 OHMS?
YES
PERFORM TEST 5E.
NO
CONTINUE TEST 5A

* PERFORM VERIFICATION TEST VER-1

91C09191 91E09192

Fig. 30: Anti-Lock Brake Test 5A – Low Fluid/Parking Brake Fault (1 of 3)

TEST 5A: LOW FLUID/PARKING BRAKE FAULT (2 OF 3)

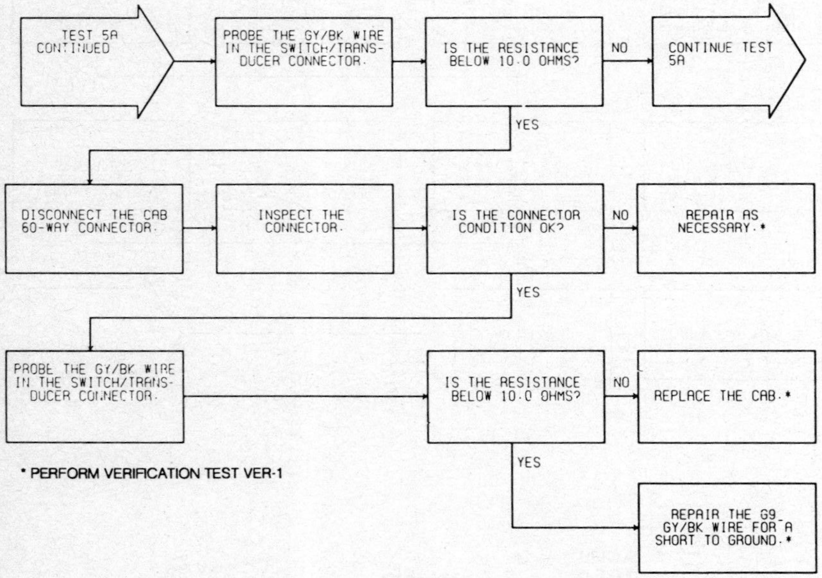
TEST 5A CONTINUED
PROBE THE GY/BK WIRE IN THE SWITCH/TRANSDUCER CONNECTOR.
IS THE RESISTANCE BELOW 10.0 OHMS?
NO
CONTINUE TEST 5A
YES
DISCONNECT THE CAB 60-WAY CONNECTOR.
INSPECT THE CONNECTOR.
IS THE CONNECTOR CONDITION OK?
NO
REPAIR AS NECESSARY.*
YES
PROBE THE GY/BK WIRE IN THE SWITCH/TRANSDUCER CONNECTOR.
IS THE RESISTANCE BELOW 10.0 OHMS?
NO
REPLACE THE CAB.*
YES
REPAIR THE G9 GY/BK WIRE FOR A SHORT TO GROUND.*
* PERFORM VERIFICATION TEST VER-1

91G09193

Fig. 31: Anti-Lock Brake Test 5A – Low Fluid/Parking Brake Fault (2 of 3)

TEST 5A: LOW FLUID/PARKING BRAKE FAULT (3 OF 3)

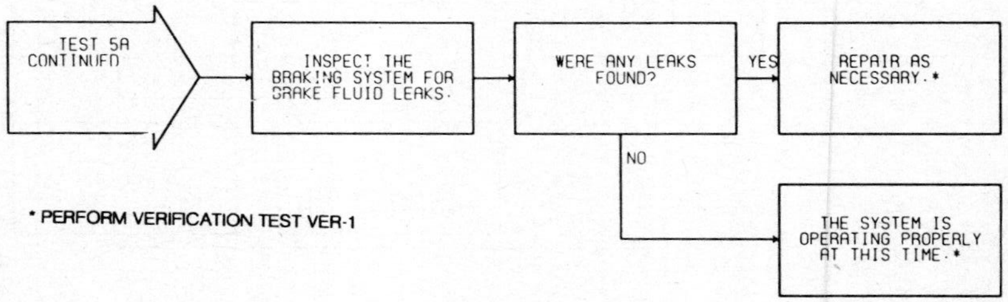
TEST 5A CONTINUED
INSPECT THE BRAKING SYSTEM FOR BRAKE FLUID LEAKS.
WERE ANY LEAKS FOUND?
YES
REPAIR AS NECESSARY.*
NO
THE SYSTEM IS OPERATING PROPERLY AT THIS TIME.*
* PERFORM VERIFICATION TEST VER-1

91I09194

Fig. 32: Anti-Lock Brake Test 5A – Low Fluid/Parking Brake Fault (3 of 3)

TEST 5B: LOW FLUID/PARKING BRAKE FAULT (1 OF 3)

AC Body (without electronic cluster)

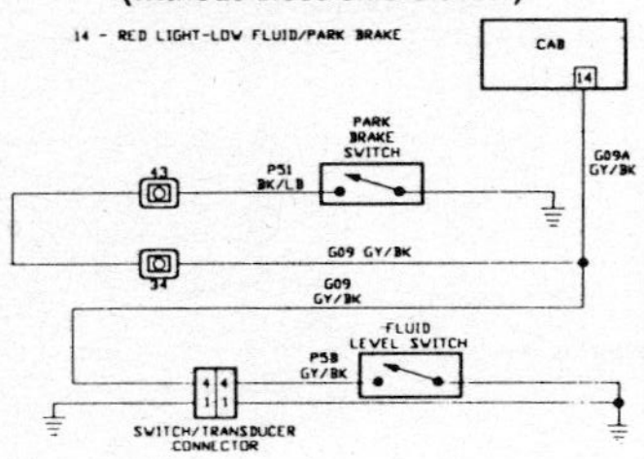
14 - RED LIGHT-LOW FLUID/PARK BRAKE
CAB
14
G09A GY/BK
PARK BRAKE SWITCH
P51 BK/LB
43
34
G09 GY/BK
G09 GY/BK
FLUID LEVEL SWITCH
P58 GY/BK
SWITCH/TRANSDUCER CONNECTOR

BB Body

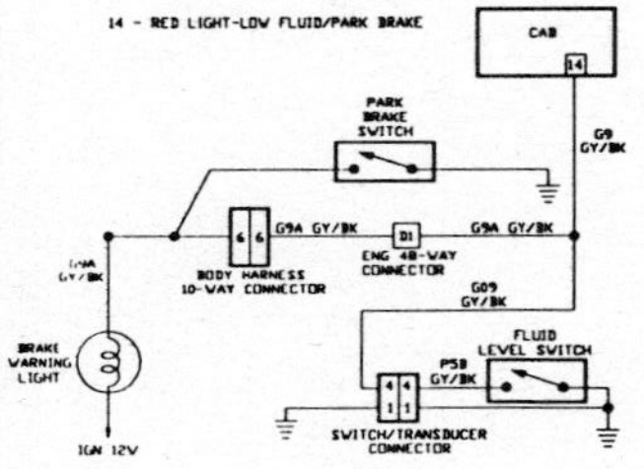
14 - RED LIGHT-LOW FLUID/PARK BRAKE
CAB
14
G9 GY/BK
PARK BRAKE SWITCH
G9A GY/BK
G9A GY/BK
BODY HARNESS 10-WAY CONNECTOR
ENG 48-WAY CONNECTOR
G09 GY/BK
BRAKE WARNING LIGHT
IGN 12V
FLUID LEVEL SWITCH
P58 GY/BK
SWITCH/TRANSDUCER CONNECTOR

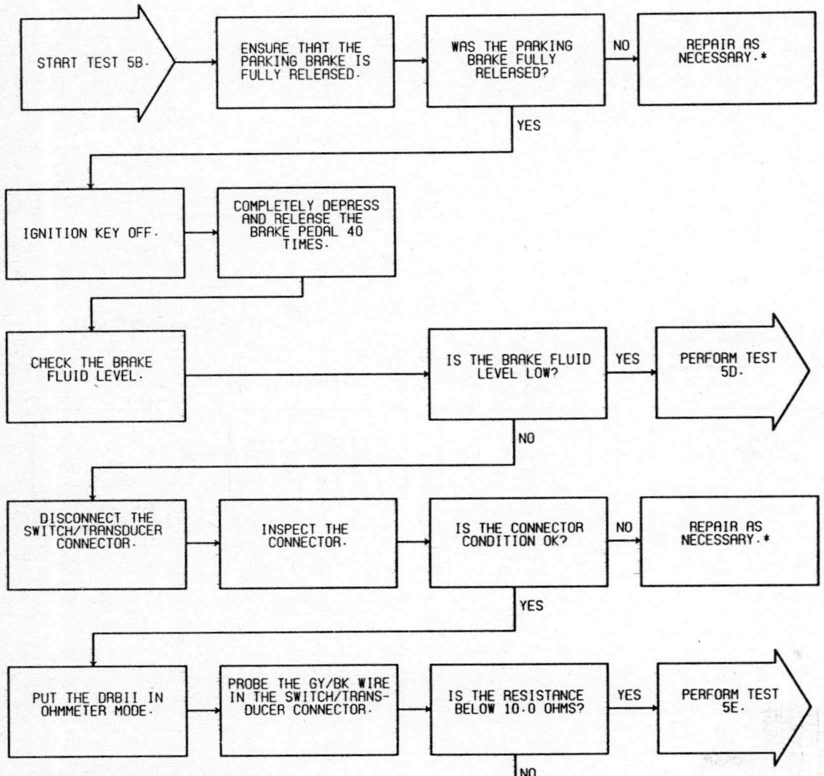
START TEST 5B.
ENSURE THAT THE PARKING BRAKE IS FULLY RELEASED.
WAS THE PARKING BRAKE FULLY RELEASED?
NO
REPAIR AS NECESSARY.*
YES
IGNITION KEY OFF.
COMPLETELY DEPRESS AND RELEASE THE BRAKE PEDAL 40 TIMES.
CHECK THE BRAKE FLUID LEVEL.
IS THE BRAKE FLUID LEVEL LOW?
YES
PERFORM TEST 5D.
NO
DISCONNECT THE SWITCH/TRANSDUCER CONNECTOR.
INSPECT THE CONNECTOR.
IS THE CONNECTOR CONDITION OK?
NO
REPAIR AS NECESSARY.*
YES
PUT THE DRBII IN OHMMETER MODE.
PROBE THE GY/BK WIRE IN THE SWITCH/TRANSDUCER CONNECTOR.
IS THE RESISTANCE BELOW 10.0 OHMS?
YES
PERFORM TEST 5E.
NO
CONTINUE TEST 5B

* PERFORM VERIFICATION TEST VER-1

91B09195 91D09196

Fig. 33: Anti-Lock Brake Test 5B – Low Fluid/Parking Brake Fault (1 of 3)

TEST 5B: LOW FLUID/PARKING BRAKE FAULT (2 OF 3)

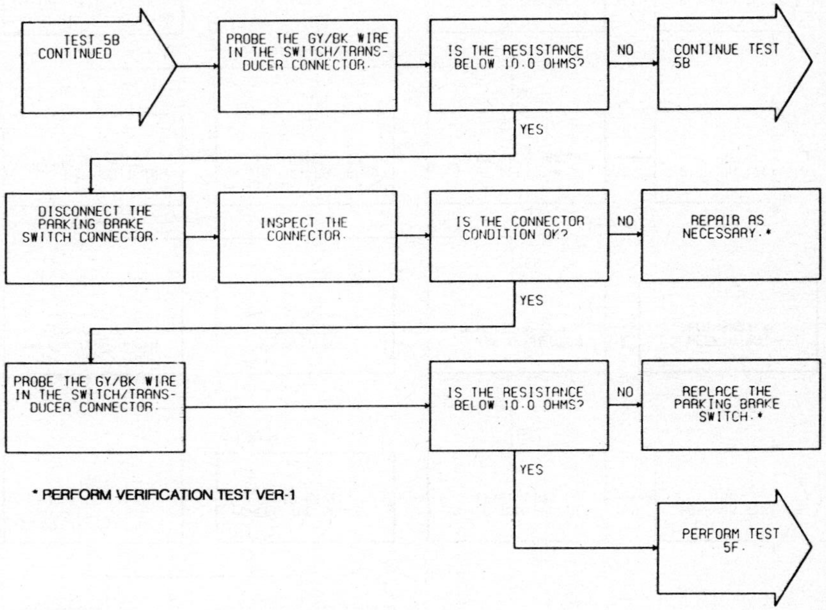
TEST 5B CONTINUED
PROBE THE GY/BK WIRE IN THE SWITCH/TRANSDUCER CONNECTOR.
IS THE RESISTANCE BELOW 10.0 OHMS?
NO
CONTINUE TEST 5B
YES
DISCONNECT THE PARKING BRAKE SWITCH CONNECTOR.
INSPECT THE CONNECTOR.
IS THE CONNECTOR CONDITION OK?
NO
REPAIR AS NECESSARY.*
YES
PROBE THE GY/BK WIRE IN THE SWITCH/TRANSDUCER CONNECTOR.
IS THE RESISTANCE BELOW 10.0 OHMS?
NO
REPLACE THE PARKING BRAKE SWITCH.*
YES
PERFORM TEST 5F.

* PERFORM VERIFICATION TEST VER-1

91F09197

Fig. 34: Anti-Lock Brake Test 5B – Low Fluid/Parking Brake Fault (2 of 3)

1991 BRAKES
Anti-Lock – Bendix-10 (Cont.)

TEST 5B: LOW FLUID/PARKING BRAKE FAULT (3 OF 3)

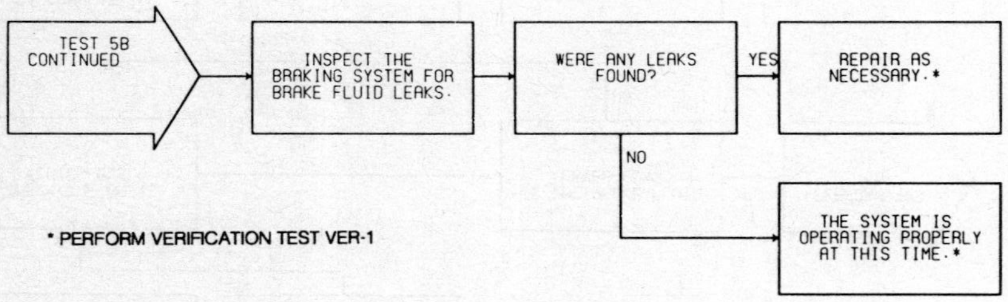
TEST 5B CONTINUED
INSPECT THE BRAKING SYSTEM FOR BRAKE FLUID LEAKS.
WERE ANY LEAKS FOUND?
YES
REPAIR AS NECESSARY.*
NO
THE SYSTEM IS OPERATING PROPERLY AT THIS TIME.*

* PERFORM VERIFICATION TEST VER-1

91H09198

Fig. 35: Anti-Lock Brake Test 5B – Low Fluid/Parking Brake Fault (3 of 3)

TEST 5C: LOW FLUID/PARKING BRAKE FAULT

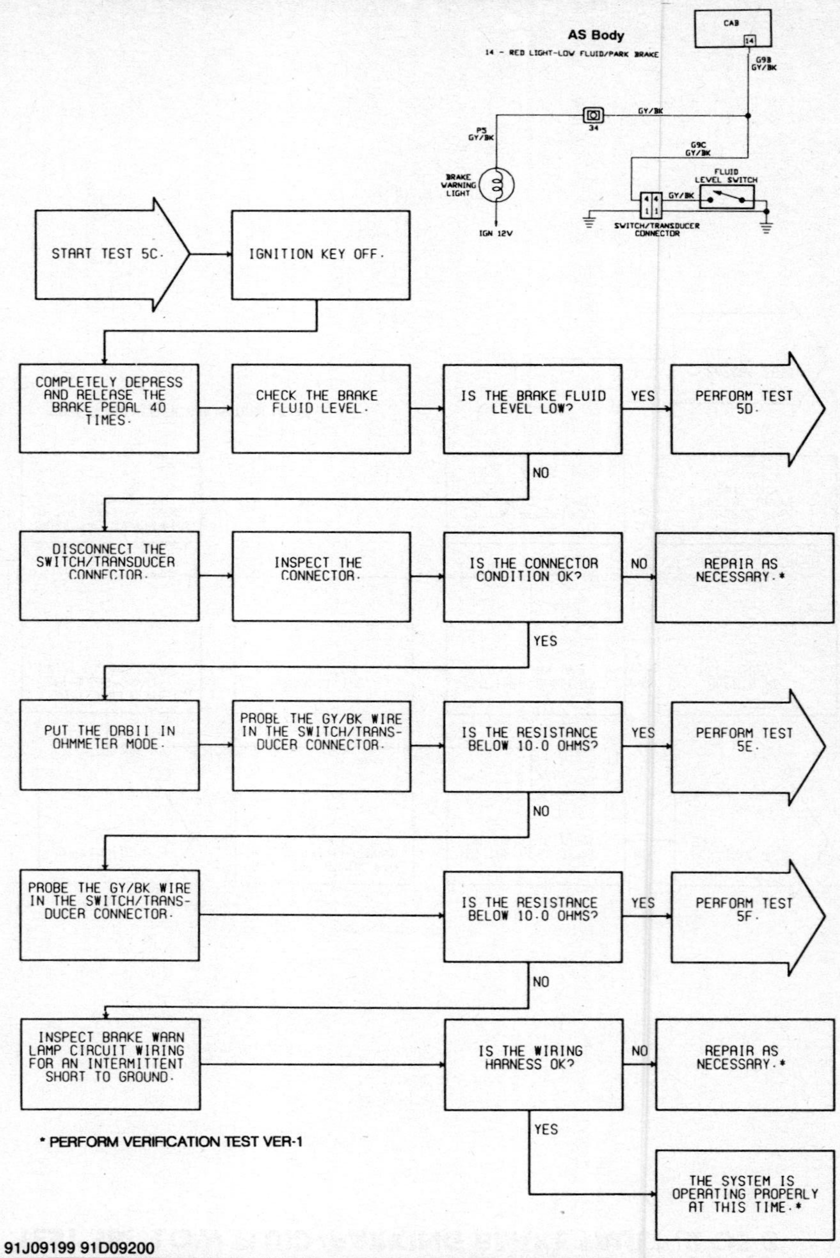
AS Body
14 – RED LIGHT-LOW FLUID/PARK BRAKE
CAB
14
G9B GY/BK
GY/BK
34
P5 GY/BK
G9C GY/BK
BRAKE WARNING LIGHT
IGN 12V
FLUID LEVEL SWITCH
GY/BK
SWITCH/TRANSDUCER CONNECTOR
START TEST 5C.
IGNITION KEY OFF.
COMPLETELY DEPRESS AND RELEASE THE BRAKE PEDAL 40 TIMES.
CHECK THE BRAKE FLUID LEVEL.
IS THE BRAKE FLUID LEVEL LOW?
YES
PERFORM TEST 5D.
NO
DISCONNECT THE SWITCH/TRANSDUCER CONNECTOR.
INSPECT THE CONNECTOR.
IS THE CONNECTOR CONDITION OK?
NO
REPAIR AS NECESSARY.*
YES
PUT THE DRBII IN OHMMETER MODE.
PROBE THE GY/BK WIRE IN THE SWITCH/TRANS- DUCER CONNECTOR.
IS THE RESISTANCE BELOW 10.0 OHMS?
YES
PERFORM TEST 5E.
NO
PROBE THE GY/BK WIRE IN THE SWITCH/TRANS- DUCER CONNECTOR.
IS THE RESISTANCE BELOW 10.0 OHMS?
YES
PERFORM TEST 5F.
NO
INSPECT BRAKE WARN LAMP CIRCUIT WIRING FOR AN INTERMITTENT SHORT TO GROUND.
IS THE WIRING HARNESS OK?
NO
REPAIR AS NECESSARY.*
YES
THE SYSTEM IS OPERATING PROPERLY AT THIS TIME.*

* PERFORM VERIFICATION TEST VER-1

91J09199 91D09200

Fig. 36: Anti-Lock Brake Test 5C – Low Fluid/Parking Brake Fault

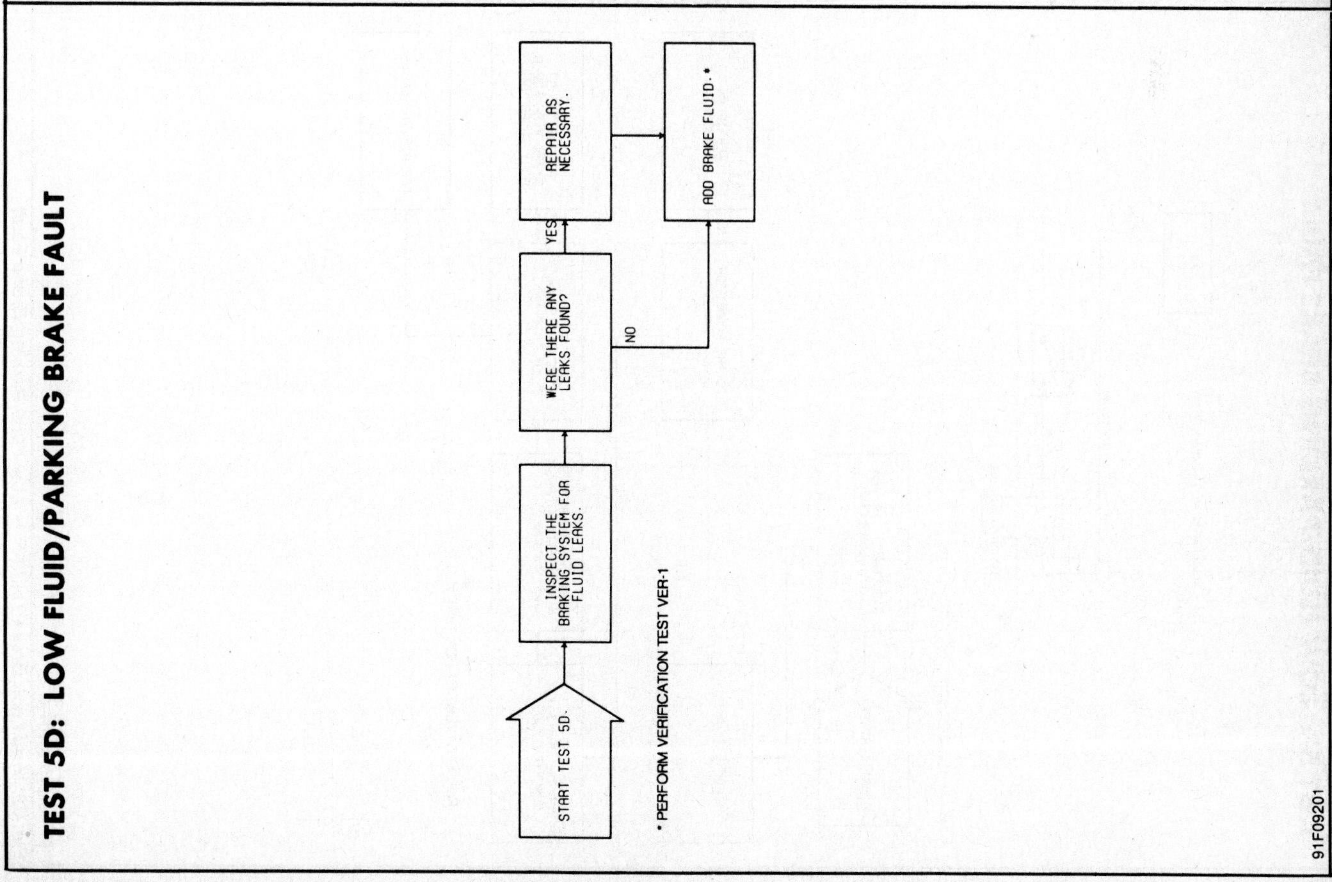

TEST 5D: LOW FLUID/PARKING BRAKE FAULT
START TEST 5D.
INSPECT THE BRAKING SYSTEM FOR FLUID LEAKS.
WERE THERE ANY LEAKS FOUND?
YES
REPAIR AS NECESSARY.
NO
ADD BRAKE FLUID.*
* PERFORM VERIFICATION TEST VER-1
91F09201

Fig. 37: Anti-Lock Brake Test 5D – Low Fluid/Parking Brake Fault

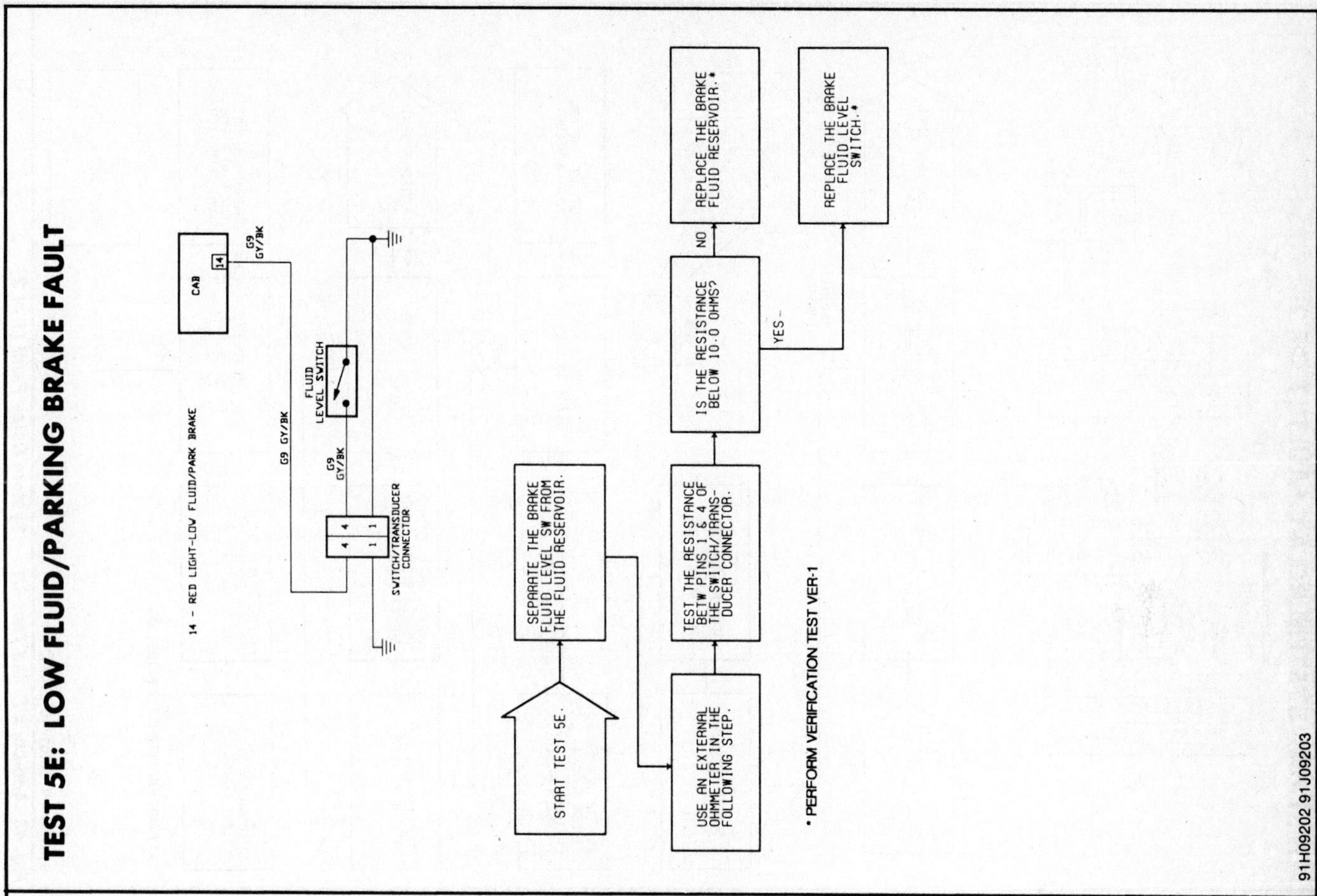

TEST 5E: LOW FLUID/PARKING BRAKE FAULT
14 - RED LIGHT-LOW FLUID/PARK BRAKE
CAB
14
G9 GY/BK
G9 GY/BK
FLUID LEVEL SWITCH
G9 GY/BK
4 4
1 1
SWITCH/TRANSDUCER CONNECTOR
START TEST 5E.
SEPARATE THE BRAKE FLUID LEVEL SW FROM THE FLUID RESERVOIR.
USE AN EXTERNAL OHMMETER IN THE FOLLOWING STEP.
TEST THE RESISTANCE BETW PINS 1 & 4 OF THE SWITCH/TRANSDUCER CONNECTOR.
IS THE RESISTANCE BELOW 10.0 OHMS?
NO
REPLACE THE BRAKE FLUID RESERVOIR.*
YES
REPLACE THE BRAKE FLUID LEVEL SWITCH.*
* PERFORM VERIFICATION TEST VER-1
91H09202 91J09203

Fig. 38: Anti-Lock Brake Test 5E – Low Fluid/Parking Brake Fault

1991 BRAKES
Anti-Lock – Bendix-10 (Cont.)

TEST 5F: LOW FLUID/PARKING BRAKE FAULT

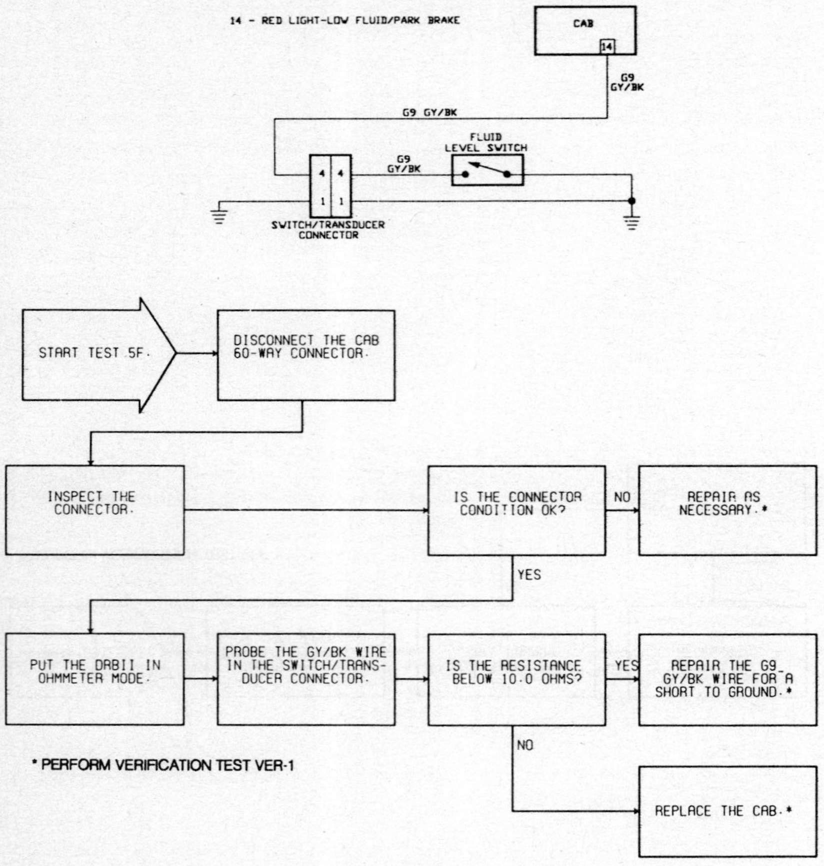
14 - RED LIGHT-LOW FLUID/PARK BRAKE
CAB
14
G9 GY/BK
G9 GY/BK
FLUID LEVEL SWITCH
G9 GY/BK
SWITCH/TRANSDUCER CONNECTOR
START TEST 5F.
DISCONNECT THE CAB 60-WAY CONNECTOR.
INSPECT THE CONNECTOR.
IS THE CONNECTOR CONDITION OK?
NO
REPAIR AS NECESSARY.*
YES
PUT THE DRBII IN OHMMETER MODE.
PROBE THE GY/BK WIRE IN THE SWITCH/TRANSDUCER CONNECTOR.
IS THE RESISTANCE BELOW 10.0 OHMS?
YES
REPAIR THE G9 GY/BK WIRE FOR A SHORT TO GROUND.*
NO
REPLACE THE CAB.*
* PERFORM VERIFICATION TEST VER-1

91H09202 91H10790

Fig. 39: Anti-Lock Brake Test 5F – Low Fluid/Parking Brake Fault

TEST 6A: SYSTEM RELAY FAULT (1 OF 2)

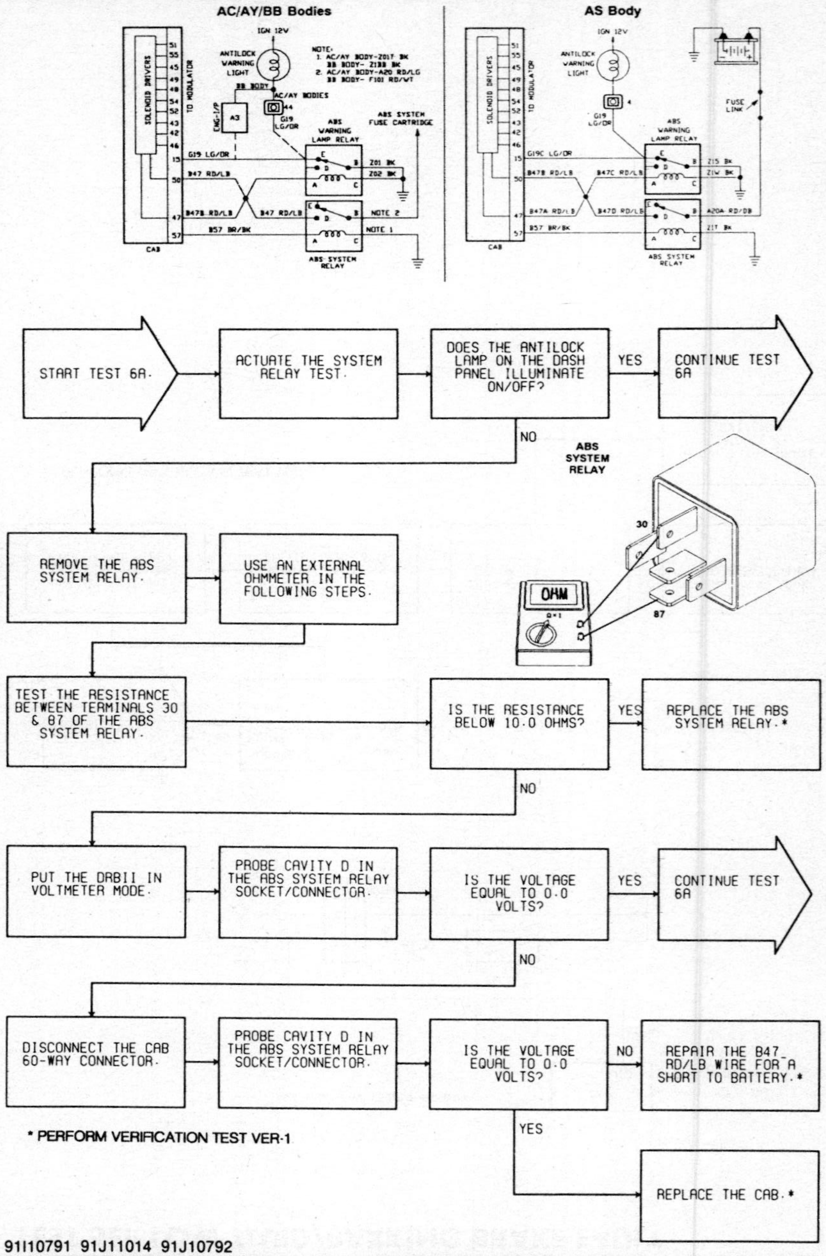
AC/AY/BB Bodies
AS Body
IGN 12V
ANTILOCK WARNING LIGHT
NOTE:
1. AC/AY BODY-Z01T BK BB BODY- Z13B BK
2. AC/AY BODY-A20 RD/LG BB BODY- F101 RD/WT
AC/AY BODIES
ABS WARNING LAMP RELAY
ABS SYSTEM FUSE CARTRIDGE
ABS SYSTEM RELAY
SOLENOID DRIVERS
TO MODULATOR
CAB
FUSE LINK
START TEST 6A.
ACTUATE THE SYSTEM RELAY TEST.
DOES THE ANTILOCK LAMP ON THE DASH PANEL ILLUMINATE ON/OFF?
YES
CONTINUE TEST 6A
NO
ABS SYSTEM RELAY
30
87
OHM
REMOVE THE ABS SYSTEM RELAY.
USE AN EXTERNAL OHMMETER IN THE FOLLOWING STEPS.
TEST THE RESISTANCE BETWEEN TERMINALS 30 & 87 OF THE ABS SYSTEM RELAY.
IS THE RESISTANCE BELOW 10.0 OHMS?
YES
REPLACE THE ABS SYSTEM RELAY.*
NO
PUT THE DRBII IN VOLTMETER MODE.
PROBE CAVITY D IN THE ABS SYSTEM RELAY SOCKET/CONNECTOR.
IS THE VOLTAGE EQUAL TO 0.0 VOLTS?
YES
CONTINUE TEST 6A
NO
DISCONNECT THE CAB 60-WAY CONNECTOR.
PROBE CAVITY D IN THE ABS SYSTEM RELAY SOCKET/CONNECTOR.
IS THE VOLTAGE EQUAL TO 0.0 VOLTS?
NO
REPAIR THE B47 RD/LB WIRE FOR A SHORT TO BATTERY.*
YES
REPLACE THE CAB.*
* PERFORM VERIFICATION TEST VER-1

91I10791 91J11014 91J10792

Fig. 40 Anti-Lock Brake Test 6A – System Relay Fault (1 of 2)

TEST 6A: SYSTEM RELAY FAULT (2 OF 2)

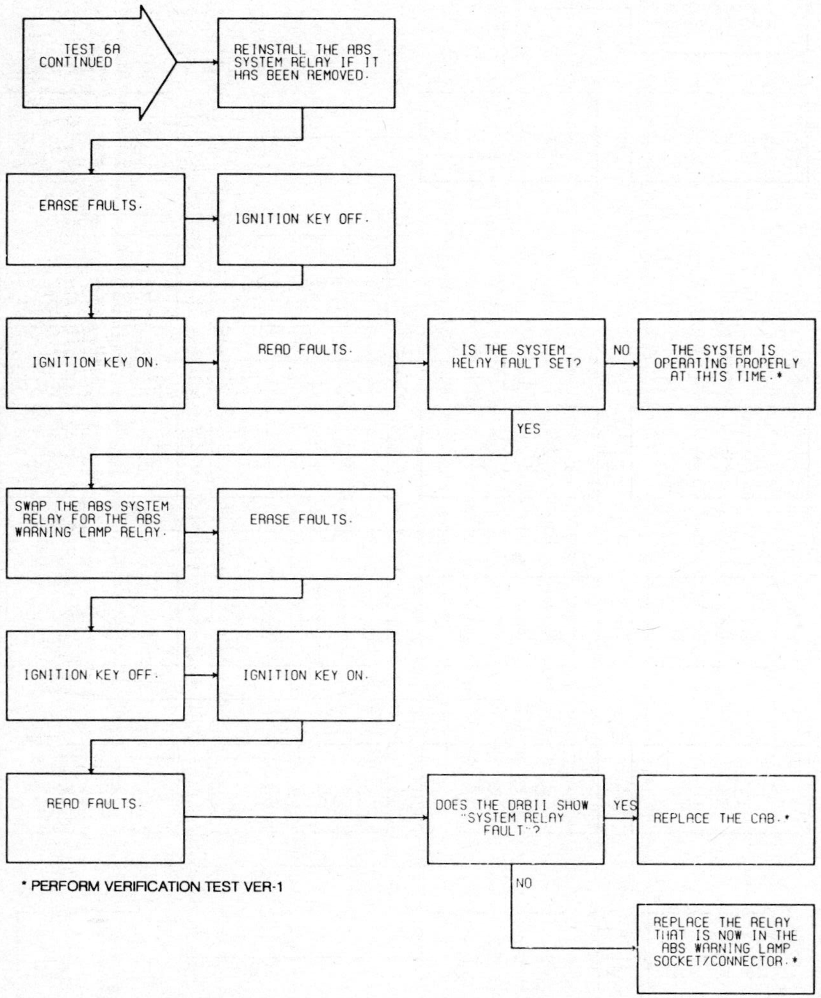
TEST 6A CONTINUED
REINSTALL THE ABS SYSTEM RELAY IF IT HAS BEEN REMOVED.
ERASE FAULTS.
IGNITION KEY OFF.
IGNITION KEY ON.
READ FAULTS.
IS THE SYSTEM RELAY FAULT SET?
NO
THE SYSTEM IS OPERATING PROPERLY AT THIS TIME.*
YES
SWAP THE ABS SYSTEM RELAY FOR THE ABS WARNING LAMP RELAY.
ERASE FAULTS.
IGNITION KEY OFF.
IGNITION KEY ON.
READ FAULTS.
DOES THE DRBII SHOW "SYSTEM RELAY FAULT"?
YES
REPLACE THE CAB.*
NO
REPLACE THE RELAY THAT IS NOW IN THE ABS WARNING LAMP SOCKET/CONNECTOR.*

* PERFORM VERIFICATION TEST VER-1

91A10793

Fig. 41: Anti-Lock Brake Test 6A – System Relay Fault (2 of 2)

TEST 7A: LOW ACCUMULATOR FAULT (1 OF 2)

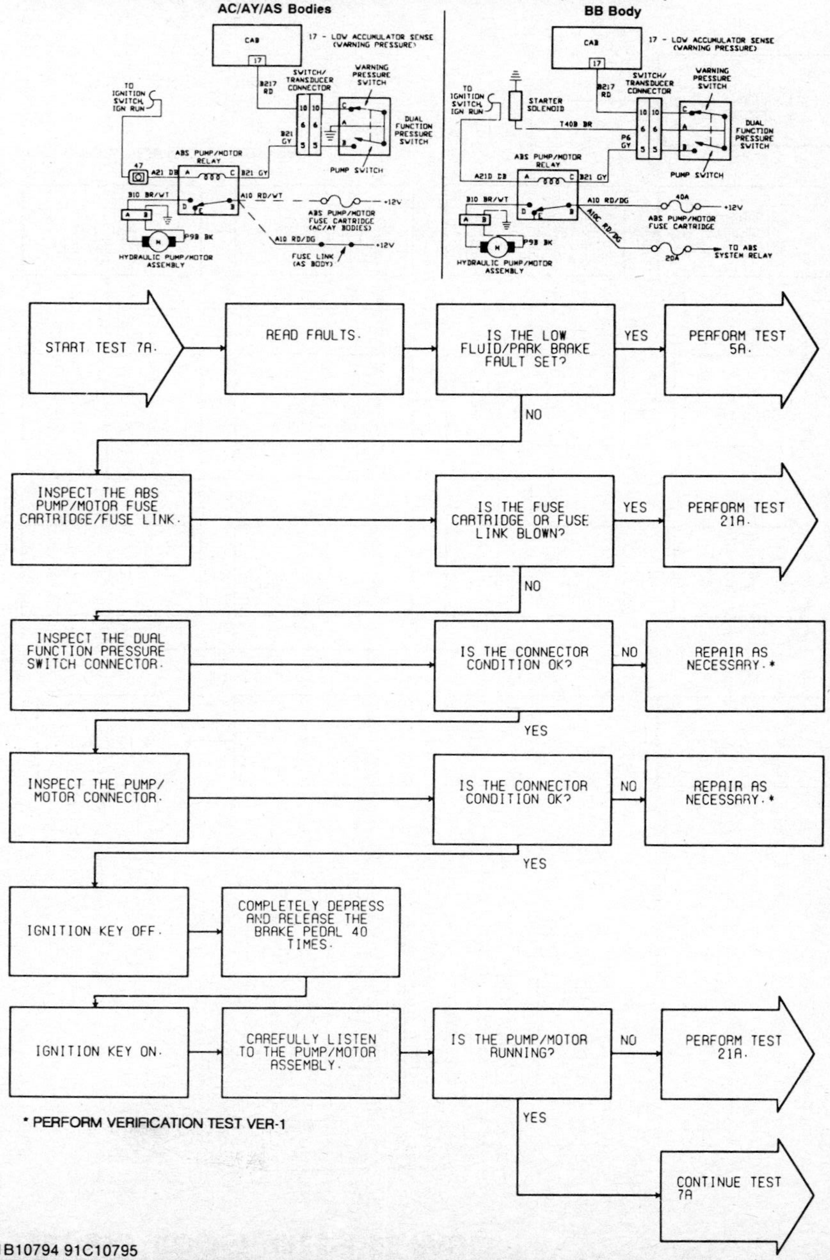
AC/AY/AS Bodies
BB Body
START TEST 7A.
READ FAULTS.
IS THE LOW FLUID/PARK BRAKE FAULT SET?
YES
PERFORM TEST 5A.
NO
INSPECT THE ABS PUMP/MOTOR FUSE CARTRIDGE/FUSE LINK.
IS THE FUSE CARTRIDGE OR FUSE LINK BLOWN?
YES
PERFORM TEST 21A.
NO
INSPECT THE DUAL FUNCTION PRESSURE SWITCH CONNECTOR.
IS THE CONNECTOR CONDITION OK?
NO
REPAIR AS NECESSARY.*
YES
INSPECT THE PUMP/MOTOR CONNECTOR.
IS THE CONNECTOR CONDITION OK?
NO
REPAIR AS NECESSARY.*
YES
IGNITION KEY OFF.
COMPLETELY DEPRESS AND RELEASE THE BRAKE PEDAL 40 TIMES.
IGNITION KEY ON.
CAREFULLY LISTEN TO THE PUMP/MOTOR ASSEMBLY.
IS THE PUMP/MOTOR RUNNING?
NO
PERFORM TEST 21A.
YES
CONTINUE TEST 7A

* PERFORM VERIFICATION TEST VER-1

91B10794 91C10795

Fig. 42: Anti-Lock Brake Test 7A – Low Accumulator Fault (1 of 2)

1991 BRAKES
Anti-Lock – Bendix-10 (Cont.)

TEST 7A: LOW ACCUMULATOR FAULT (2 OF 2)

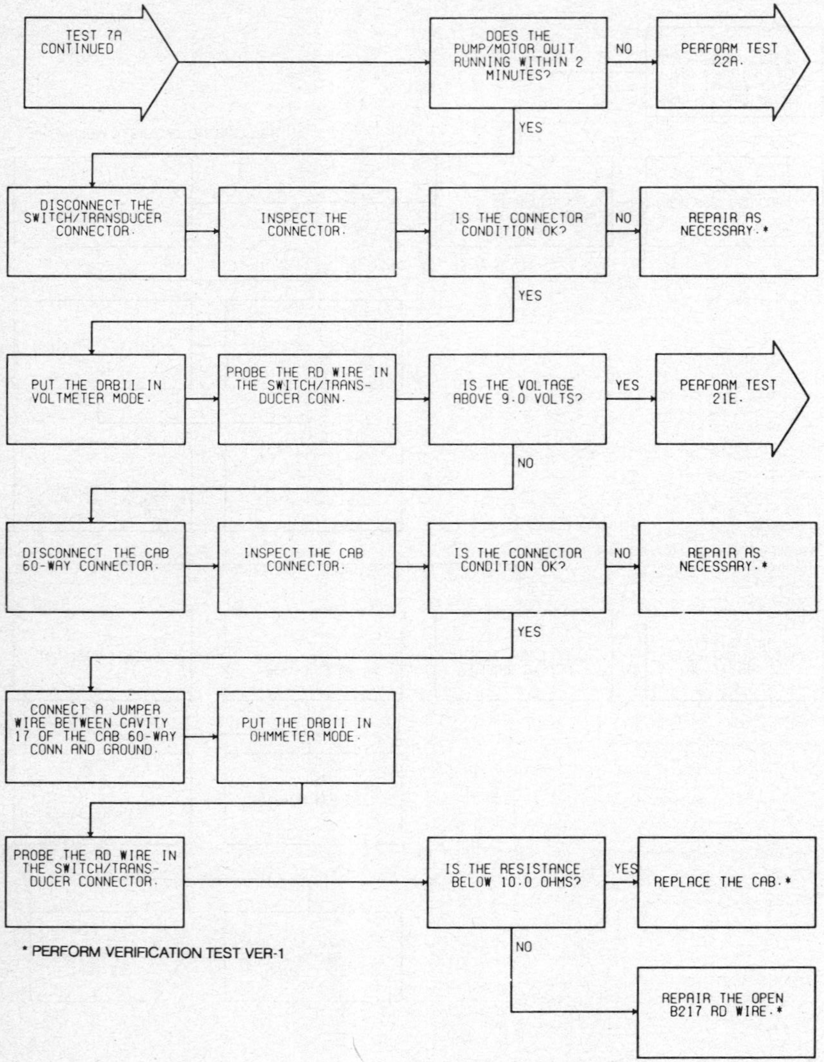
TEST 7A CONTINUED
DOES THE PUMP/MOTOR QUIT RUNNING WITHIN 2 MINUTES?
NO
PERFORM TEST 22A.
YES
DISCONNECT THE SWITCH/TRANSDUCER CONNECTOR.
INSPECT THE CONNECTOR.
IS THE CONNECTOR CONDITION OK?
NO
REPAIR AS NECESSARY.*
YES
PUT THE DRBII IN VOLTMETER MODE.
PROBE THE RD WIRE IN THE SWITCH/TRANS-DUCER CONN.
IS THE VOLTAGE ABOVE 9.0 VOLTS?
YES
PERFORM TEST 21E.
NO
DISCONNECT THE CAB 60-WAY CONNECTOR.
INSPECT THE CAB CONNECTOR.
IS THE CONNECTOR CONDITION OK?
NO
REPAIR AS NECESSARY.*
YES
CONNECT A JUMPER WIRE BETWEEN CAVITY 17 OF THE CAB 60-WAY CONN AND GROUND.
PUT THE DRBII IN OHMMETER MODE.
PROBE THE RD WIRE IN THE SWITCH/TRANS-DUCER CONNECTOR.
IS THE RESISTANCE BELOW 10.0 OHMS?
YES
REPLACE THE CAB.*
NO
REPAIR THE OPEN B217 RD WIRE.*

* PERFORM VERIFICATION TEST VER-1

91D10796

Fig. 43: Anti-Lock Brake Test 7A – Low Accumulator Fault (2 of 2)

TEST 8A: BOOST PRESSURE FAULT

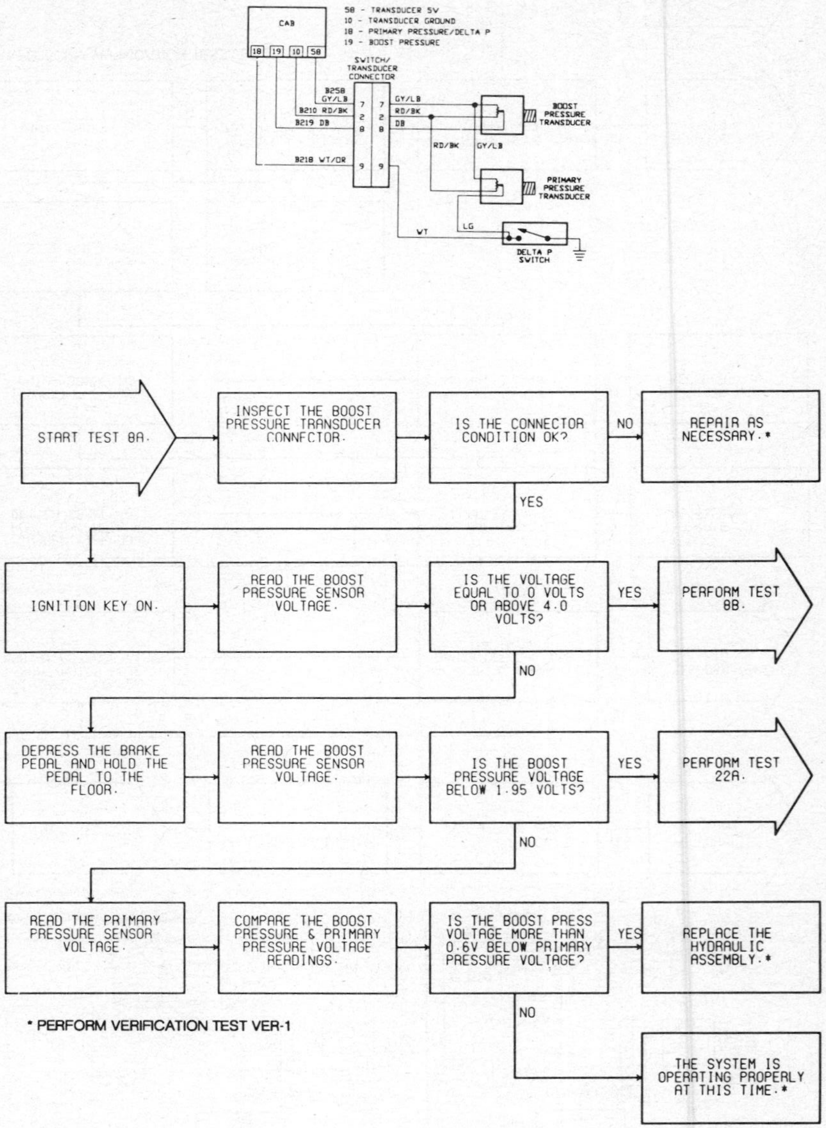
CAB
18 19 10 58
58 - TRANSDUCER 5V
10 - TRANSDUCER GROUND
18 - PRIMARY PRESSURE/DELTA P
19 - BOOST PRESSURE
SWITCH/ TRANSDUCER CONNECTOR
B258 GY/LB
B210 RD/BK
B219 DB
B218 WT/OR
GY/LB
RD/BK
DB
RD/BK
GY/LB
WT
LG
BOOST PRESSURE TRANSDUCER
PRIMARY PRESSURE TRANSDUCER
DELTA P SWITCH
START TEST 8A.
INSPECT THE BOOST PRESSURE TRANSDUCER CONNECTOR.
IS THE CONNECTOR CONDITION OK?
NO
REPAIR AS NECESSARY.*
YES
IGNITION KEY ON.
READ THE BOOST PRESSURE SENSOR VOLTAGE.
IS THE VOLTAGE EQUAL TO 0 VOLTS OR ABOVE 4.0 VOLTS?
YES
PERFORM TEST 8B.
NO
DEPRESS THE BRAKE PEDAL AND HOLD THE PEDAL TO THE FLOOR.
READ THE BOOST PRESSURE SENSOR VOLTAGE.
IS THE BOOST PRESSURE VOLTAGE BELOW 1.95 VOLTS?
YES
PERFORM TEST 22A.
NO
READ THE PRIMARY PRESSURE SENSOR VOLTAGE.
COMPARE THE BOOST PRESSURE & PRIMARY PRESSURE VOLTAGE READINGS.
IS THE BOOST PRESS VOLTAGE MORE THAN 0.6V BELOW PRIMARY PRESSURE VOLTAGE?
YES
REPLACE THE HYDRAULIC ASSEMBLY.*
NO
THE SYSTEM IS OPERATING PROPERLY AT THIS TIME.*

* PERFORM VERIFICATION TEST VER-1

91E10797 91F10798

Fig. 44: Anti-Lock Brake Test 8A – Boost Pressure Fault

TEST 8B: BOOST PRESSURE FAULT (1 OF 3)

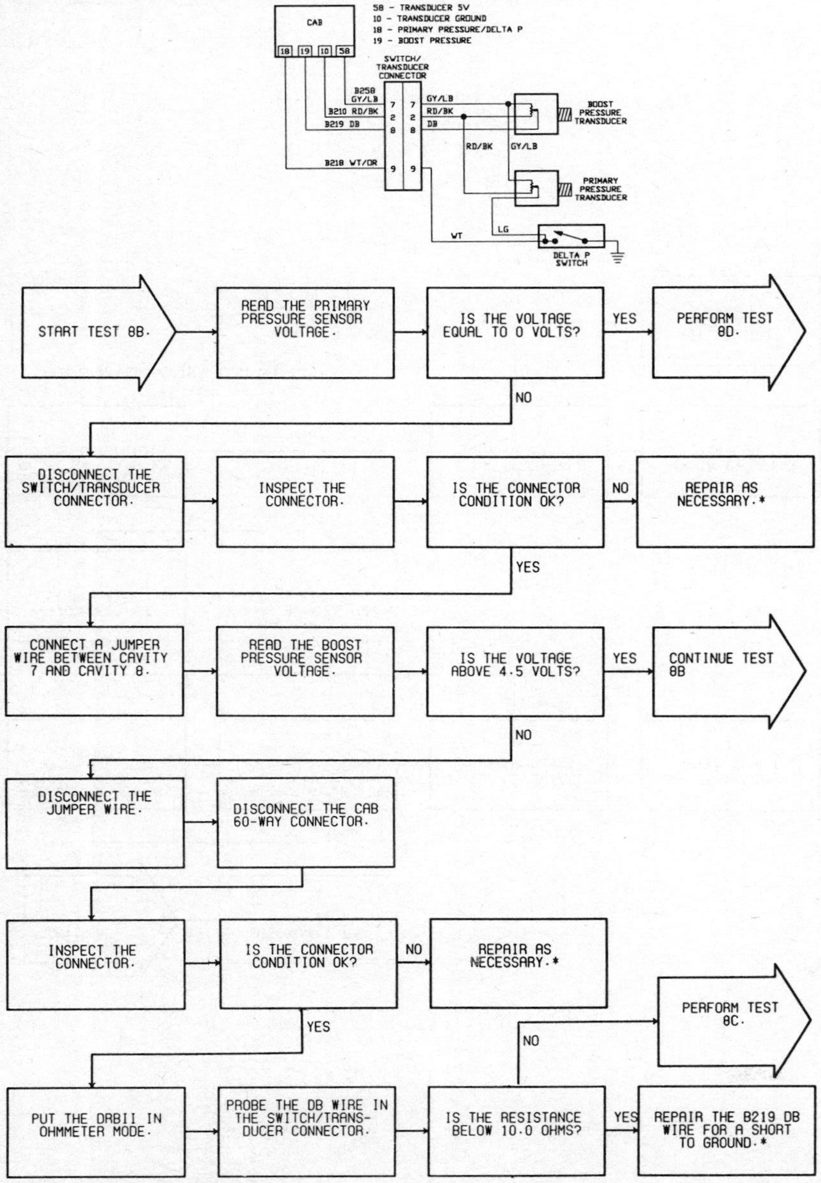
CAB
58 - TRANSDUCER 5V
10 - TRANSDUCER GROUND
18 - PRIMARY PRESSURE/DELTA P
19 - BOOST PRESSURE
SWITCH/TRANSDUCER CONNECTOR
B258 GY/LB
B210 RD/BK
B219 DB
B218 WT/OR
GY/LB
RD/BK
DB
BOOST PRESSURE TRANSDUCER
PRIMARY PRESSURE TRANSDUCER
DELTA P SWITCH
WT
LG
START TEST 8B.
READ THE PRIMARY PRESSURE SENSOR VOLTAGE.
IS THE VOLTAGE EQUAL TO 0 VOLTS?
YES
PERFORM TEST 8D.
NO
DISCONNECT THE SWITCH/TRANSDUCER CONNECTOR.
INSPECT THE CONNECTOR.
IS THE CONNECTOR CONDITION OK?
NO
REPAIR AS NECESSARY.*
YES
CONNECT A JUMPER WIRE BETWEEN CAVITY 7 AND CAVITY 8.
READ THE BOOST PRESSURE SENSOR VOLTAGE.
IS THE VOLTAGE ABOVE 4.5 VOLTS?
YES
CONTINUE TEST 8B
NO
DISCONNECT THE JUMPER WIRE.
DISCONNECT THE CAB 60-WAY CONNECTOR.
INSPECT THE CONNECTOR.
IS THE CONNECTOR CONDITION OK?
NO
REPAIR AS NECESSARY.*
YES
PUT THE DRBII IN OHMMETER MODE.
PROBE THE DB WIRE IN THE SWITCH/TRANSDUCER CONNECTOR.
IS THE RESISTANCE BELOW 10.0 OHMS?
NO
PERFORM TEST 8C.
YES
REPAIR THE B219 DB WIRE FOR A SHORT TO GROUND.*

* PERFORM VERIFICATION TEST VER-1

91E10797 91G10799

Fig. 45: Anti-Lock Brake Test 8B – Boost Pressure Fault (1 of 3)

TEST 8B: BOOST PRESSURE FAULT (2 OF 3)

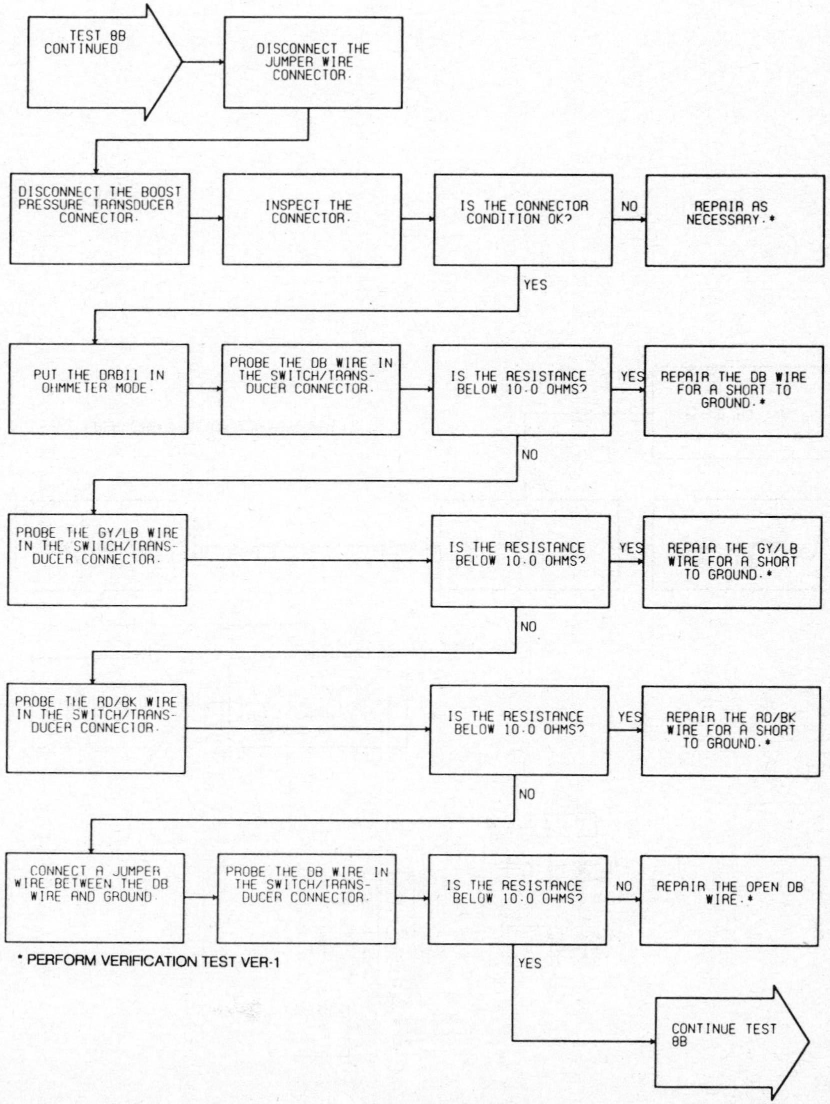
TEST 8B CONTINUED
DISCONNECT THE JUMPER WIRE CONNECTOR.
DISCONNECT THE BOOST PRESSURE TRANSDUCER CONNECTOR.
INSPECT THE CONNECTOR.
IS THE CONNECTOR CONDITION OK?
NO
REPAIR AS NECESSARY.*
YES
PUT THE DRBII IN OHMMETER MODE.
PROBE THE DB WIRE IN THE SWITCH/TRANSDUCER CONNECTOR.
IS THE RESISTANCE BELOW 10.0 OHMS?
YES
REPAIR THE DB WIRE FOR A SHORT TO GROUND.*
NO
PROBE THE GY/LB WIRE IN THE SWITCH/TRANSDUCER CONNECTOR.
IS THE RESISTANCE BELOW 10.0 OHMS?
YES
REPAIR THE GY/LB WIRE FOR A SHORT TO GROUND.*
NO
PROBE THE RD/BK WIRE IN THE SWITCH/TRANSDUCER CONNECTOR.
IS THE RESISTANCE BELOW 10.0 OHMS?
YES
REPAIR THE RD/BK WIRE FOR A SHORT TO GROUND.*
NO
CONNECT A JUMPER WIRE BETWEEN THE DB WIRE AND GROUND
PROBE THE DB WIRE IN THE SWITCH/TRANSDUCER CONNECTOR.
IS THE RESISTANCE BELOW 10.0 OHMS?
NO
REPAIR THE OPEN DB WIRE.*
YES
CONTINUE TEST 8B

* PERFORM VERIFICATION TEST VER-1

91J10800

Fig. 46: Anti-Lock Brake Test 8B – Boost Pressure Fault (2 of 3)

TEST 8B: BOOST PRESSURE FAULT (3 OF 3)

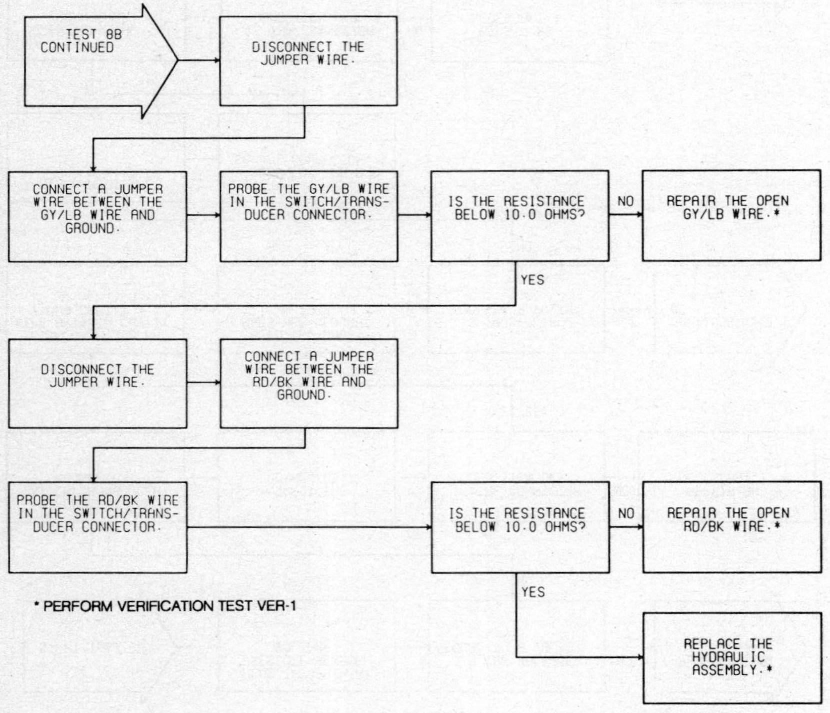
TEST 8B CONTINUED
DISCONNECT THE JUMPER WIRE.
CONNECT A JUMPER WIRE BETWEEN THE GY/LB WIRE AND GROUND.
PROBE THE GY/LB WIRE IN THE SWITCH/TRANSDUCER CONNECTOR.
IS THE RESISTANCE BELOW 10.0 OHMS?
NO
REPAIR THE OPEN GY/LB WIRE.*
YES
DISCONNECT THE JUMPER WIRE.
CONNECT A JUMPER WIRE BETWEEN THE RD/BK WIRE AND GROUND.
PROBE THE RD/BK WIRE IN THE SWITCH/TRANSDUCER CONNECTOR.
IS THE RESISTANCE BELOW 10.0 OHMS?
NO
REPAIR THE OPEN RD/BK WIRE.*
YES
REPLACE THE HYDRAULIC ASSEMBLY.*
* PERFORM VERIFICATION TEST VER-1

91A10801

Fig. 47: Anti-Lock Brake Test 8B – Boost Pressure Fault (3 of 3)

TEST 8C: BOOST PRESSURE FAULT

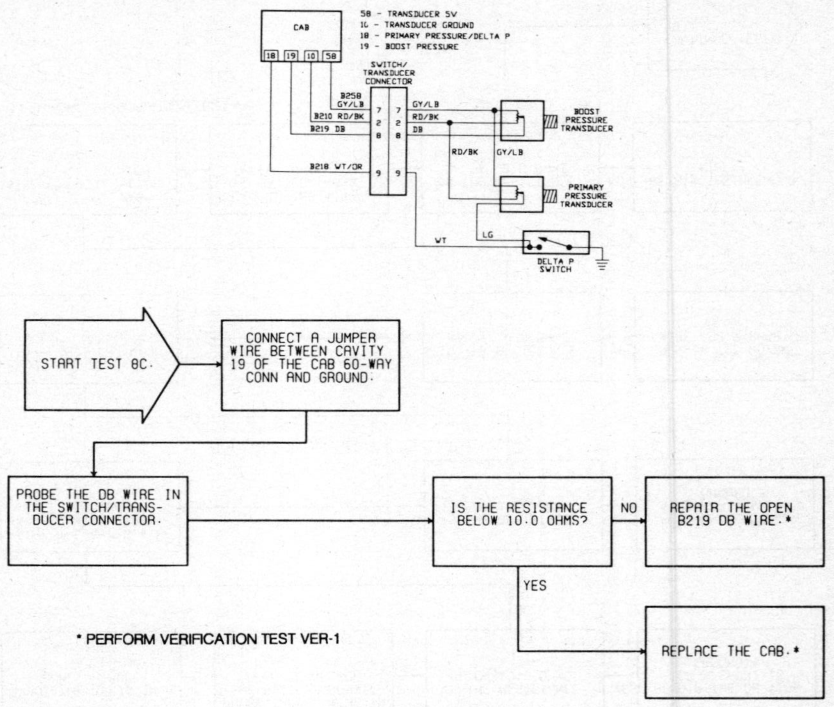
CAB
18 19 10 58
58 - TRANSDUCER 5V
1L - TRANSDUCER GROUND
18 - PRIMARY PRESSURE/DELTA P
19 - BOOST PRESSURE
SWITCH/TRANSDUCER CONNECTOR
B258 GY/LB
B210 RD/BK
B219 DB
B218 WT/OR
GY/LB
RD/BK
DB
BOOST PRESSURE TRANSDUCER
PRIMARY PRESSURE TRANSDUCER
WT
LG
DELTA P SWITCH
START TEST 8C.
CONNECT A JUMPER WIRE BETWEEN CAVITY 19 OF THE CAB 60-WAY CONN AND GROUND.
PROBE THE DB WIRE IN THE SWITCH/TRANSDUCER CONNECTOR.
IS THE RESISTANCE BELOW 10.0 OHMS?
NO
REPAIR THE OPEN B219 DB WIRE.*
YES
REPLACE THE CAB.*
* PERFORM VERIFICATION TEST VER-1

91E10797 91B10802

Fig. 48: Anti-Lock Brake Test 8C – Boost Pressure Fault

TEST 8D: BOOST PRESSURE FAULT

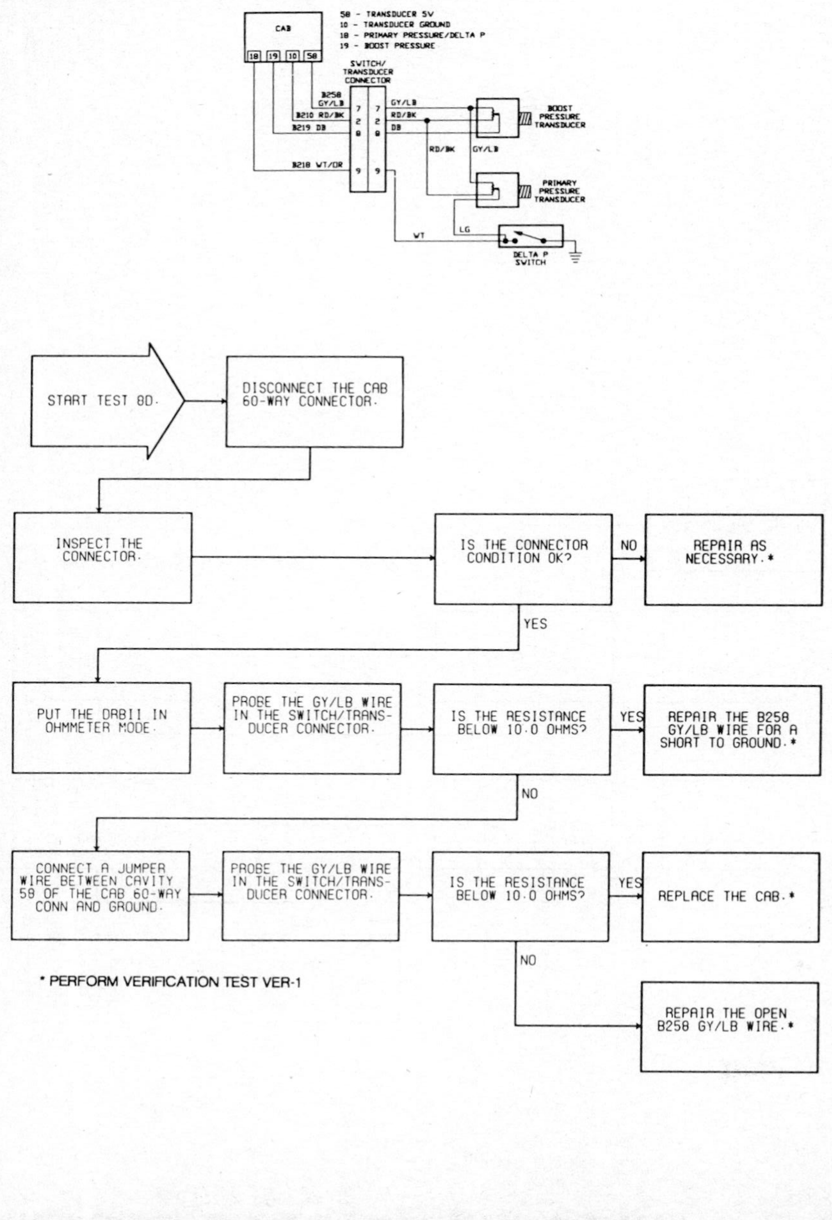
58 - TRANSDUCER 5V
10 - TRANSDUCER GROUND
18 - PRIMARY PRESSURE/DELTA P
19 - BOOST PRESSURE
CAB
SWITCH/TRANSDUCER CONNECTOR
BOOST PRESSURE TRANSDUCER
PRIMARY PRESSURE TRANSDUCER
DELTA P SWITCH
START TEST 8D.
DISCONNECT THE CAB 60-WAY CONNECTOR.
INSPECT THE CONNECTOR.
IS THE CONNECTOR CONDITION OK?
NO
REPAIR AS NECESSARY.*
YES
PUT THE DRBII IN OHMMETER MODE.
PROBE THE GY/LB WIRE IN THE SWITCH/TRANSDUCER CONNECTOR.
IS THE RESISTANCE BELOW 10.0 OHMS?
YES
REPAIR THE B258 GY/LB WIRE FOR A SHORT TO GROUND.*
NO
CONNECT A JUMPER WIRE BETWEEN CAVITY 58 OF THE CAB 60-WAY CONN AND GROUND.
PROBE THE GY/LB WIRE IN THE SWITCH/TRANSDUCER CONNECTOR.
IS THE RESISTANCE BELOW 10.0 OHMS?
YES
REPLACE THE CAB.*
NO
REPAIR THE OPEN B258 GY/LB WIRE.*
* PERFORM VERIFICATION TEST VER-1

91E10797 91C10803

Fig. 49: Anti-Lock Brake Test 8D – Boost Pressure Fault

TEST 9A: RR WHEEL SPEED SENSOR CONTINUITY FAULT (1 OF 2)

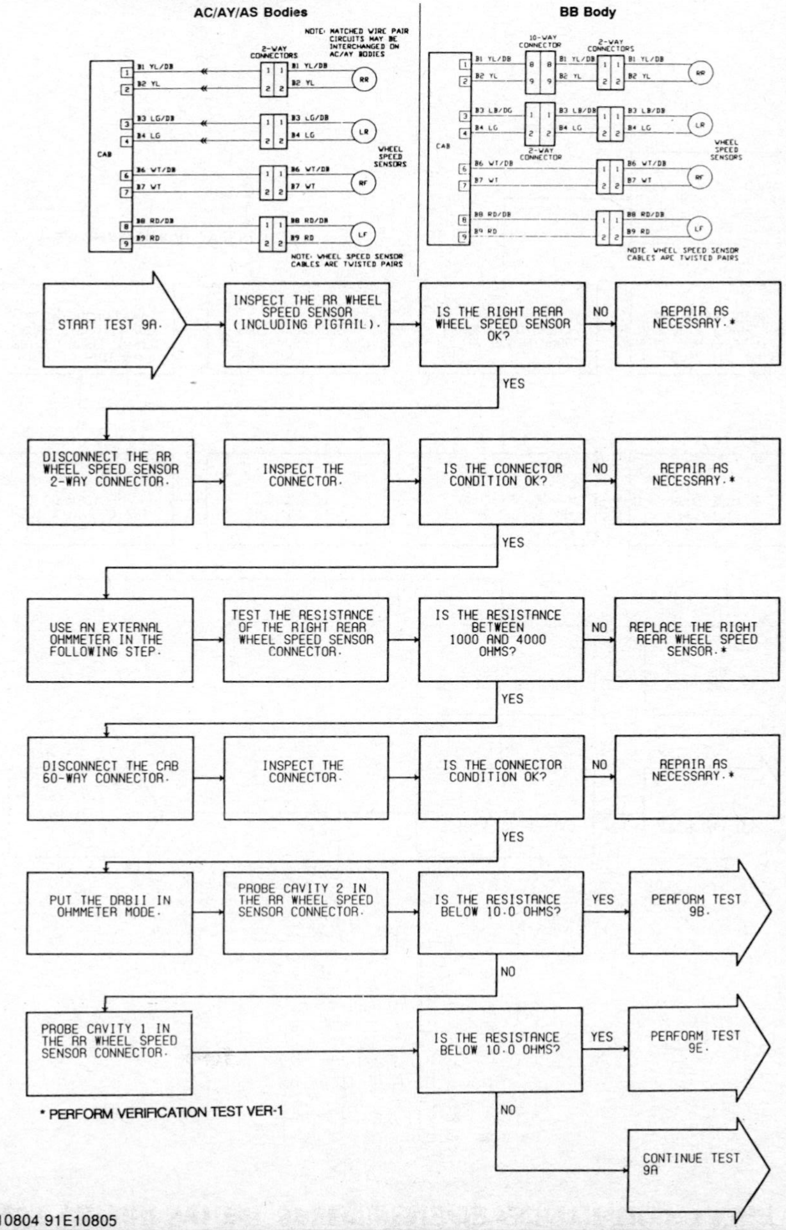
AC/AY/AS Bodies
BB Body
NOTE: MATCHED WIRE PAIR CIRCUITS MAY BE INTERCHANGED ON AC/AY BODIES
NOTE: WHEEL SPEED SENSOR CABLES ARE TWISTED PAIRS
WHEEL SPEED SENSORS
START TEST 9A.
INSPECT THE RR WHEEL SPEED SENSOR (INCLUDING PIGTAIL).
IS THE RIGHT REAR WHEEL SPEED SENSOR OK?
NO
REPAIR AS NECESSARY.*
YES
DISCONNECT THE RR WHEEL SPEED SENSOR 2-WAY CONNECTOR.
INSPECT THE CONNECTOR.
IS THE CONNECTOR CONDITION OK?
NO
REPAIR AS NECESSARY.*
YES
USE AN EXTERNAL OHMMETER IN THE FOLLOWING STEP.
TEST THE RESISTANCE OF THE RIGHT REAR WHEEL SPEED SENSOR CONNECTOR.
IS THE RESISTANCE BETWEEN 1000 AND 4000 OHMS?
NO
REPLACE THE RIGHT REAR WHEEL SPEED SENSOR.*
YES
DISCONNECT THE CAB 60-WAY CONNECTOR.
INSPECT THE CONNECTOR.
IS THE CONNECTOR CONDITION OK?
NO
REPAIR AS NECESSARY.*
YES
PUT THE DRBII IN OHMMETER MODE.
PROBE CAVITY 2 IN THE RR WHEEL SPEED SENSOR CONNECTOR.
IS THE RESISTANCE BELOW 10.0 OHMS?
YES
PERFORM TEST 9B.
NO
PROBE CAVITY 1 IN THE RR WHEEL SPEED SENSOR CONNECTOR.
IS THE RESISTANCE BELOW 10.0 OHMS?
YES
PERFORM TEST 9E.
NO
CONTINUE TEST 9A
* PERFORM VERIFICATION TEST VER-1

91D10804 91E10805

Fig. 50: Anti-Lock Brake Test 9A – RR Wheel Speed Sensor Continuity Fault (1 of 2)

TEST 9A: RR WHEEL SPEED SENSOR CONTINUITY FAULT (2 OF 2)

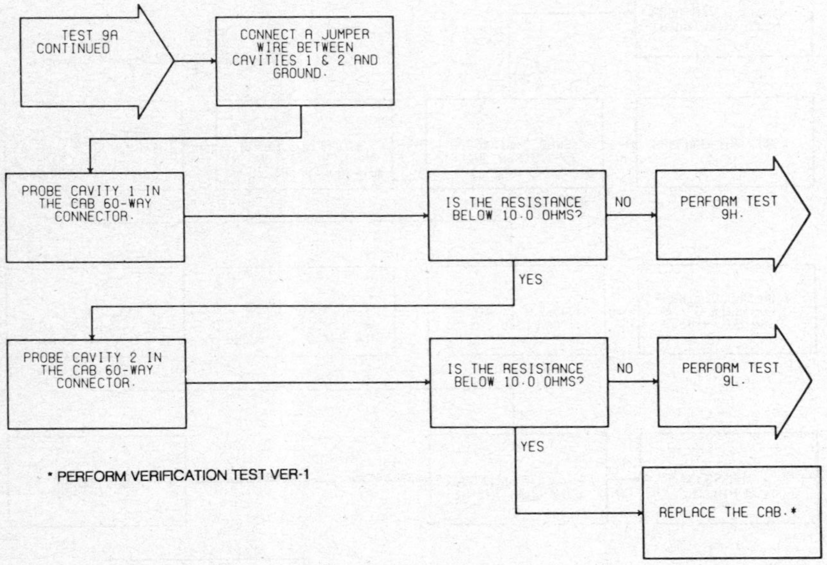
TEST 9A CONTINUED
CONNECT A JUMPER WIRE BETWEEN CAVITIES 1 & 2 AND GROUND.
PROBE CAVITY 1 IN THE CAB 60-WAY CONNECTOR.
IS THE RESISTANCE BELOW 10.0 OHMS?
NO
PERFORM TEST 9H.
YES
PROBE CAVITY 2 IN THE CAB 60-WAY CONNECTOR.
IS THE RESISTANCE BELOW 10.0 OHMS?
NO
PERFORM TEST 9L.
YES
REPLACE THE CAB.*

* PERFORM VERIFICATION TEST VER-1

91F10806

Fig. 51: Anti-Lock Brake Test 9A – RR Wheel Speed Sensor Continuity Fault (2 of 2)

TEST 9B: RR WHEEL SPEED SENSOR CONTINUITY FAULT

AC/AY Bodies

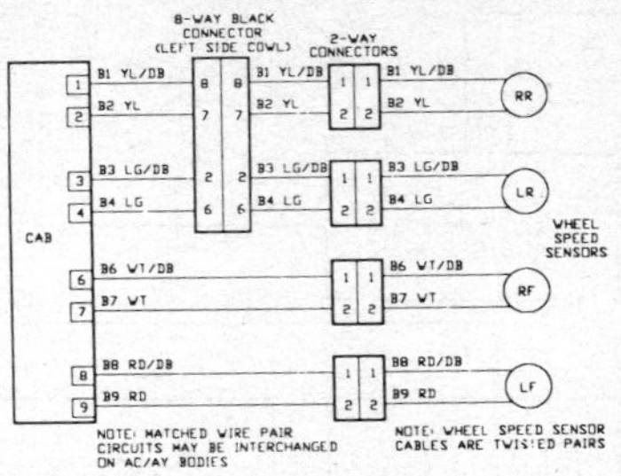
8-WAY BLACK CONNECTOR (LEFT SIDE COWL)
2-WAY CONNECTORS
CAB
B1 YL/DB
B2 YL
B3 LG/DB
B4 LG
B6 WT/DB
B7 WT
B8 RD/DB
B9 RD
RR
LR
RF
LF
WHEEL SPEED SENSORS
NOTE: MATCHED WIRE PAIR CIRCUITS MAY BE INTERCHANGED ON AC/AY BODIES
NOTE: WHEEL SPEED SENSOR CABLES ARE TWISTED PAIRS

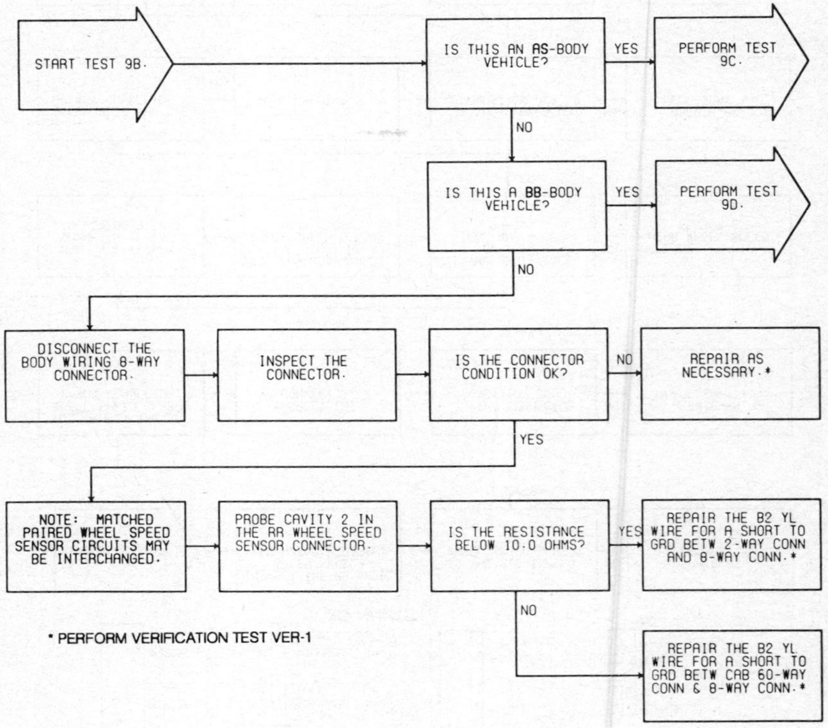
START TEST 9B.
IS THIS AN AS-BODY VEHICLE?
YES
PERFORM TEST 9C.
NO
IS THIS A BB-BODY VEHICLE?
YES
PERFORM TEST 9D.
NO
DISCONNECT THE BODY WIRING 8-WAY CONNECTOR.
INSPECT THE CONNECTOR.
IS THE CONNECTOR CONDITION OK?
NO
REPAIR AS NECESSARY.*
YES
NOTE: MATCHED PAIRED WHEEL SPEED SENSOR CIRCUITS MAY BE INTERCHANGED.
PROBE CAVITY 2 IN THE RR WHEEL SPEED SENSOR CONNECTOR.
IS THE RESISTANCE BELOW 10.0 OHMS?
YES
REPAIR THE B2 YL WIRE FOR A SHORT TO GRD BETW 2-WAY CONN AND 8-WAY CONN.*
NO
REPAIR THE B2 YL WIRE FOR A SHORT TO GRD BETW CAB 60-WAY CONN & 8-WAY CONN.*

* PERFORM VERIFICATION TEST VER-1

91G10807 91H10808

Fig. 52: Anti-Lock Brake Test 9B – RR Wheel Speed Sensor Continuity Fault

TEST 9C: RR WHEEL SPEED SENSOR CONTINUITY FAULT

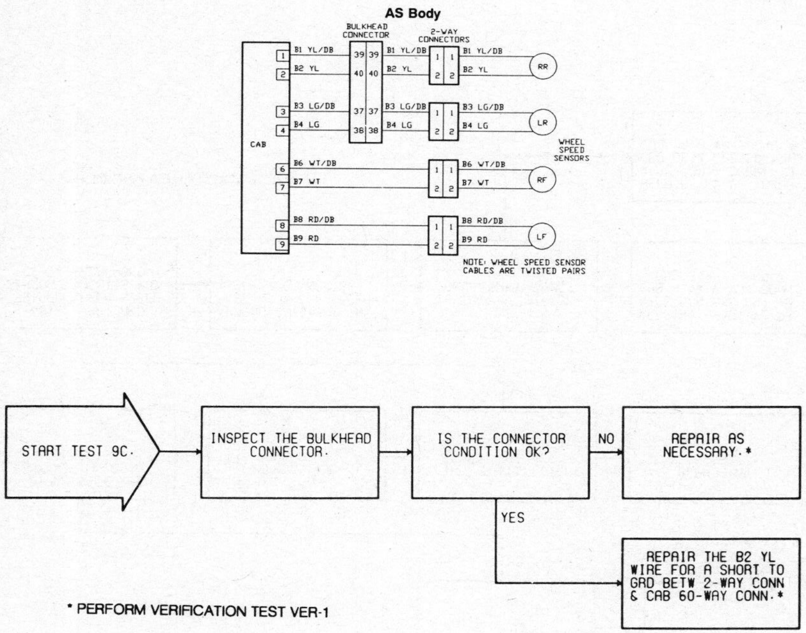
AS Body
BULKHEAD CONNECTOR
2-WAY CONNECTORS
CAB
B1 YL/DB
B2 YL
B3 LG/DB
B4 LG
B6 WT/DB
B7 WT
B8 RD/DB
B9 RD
RR
LR
RF
LF
WHEEL SPEED SENSORS
NOTE: WHEEL SPEED SENSOR CABLES ARE TWISTED PAIRS
START TEST 9C.
INSPECT THE BULKHEAD CONNECTOR.
IS THE CONNECTOR CONDITION OK?
NO
REPAIR AS NECESSARY.*
YES
REPAIR THE B2 YL WIRE FOR A SHORT TO GRD BETW 2-WAY CONN & CAB 60-WAY CONN.*

* PERFORM VERIFICATION TEST VER-1

91I10809 91B10810

Fig. 53: Anti-Lock Brake Test 9C – RR Wheel Speed Sensor Continuity Fault

TEST 9D: RR WHEEL SPEED SENSOR CONTINUITY FAULT

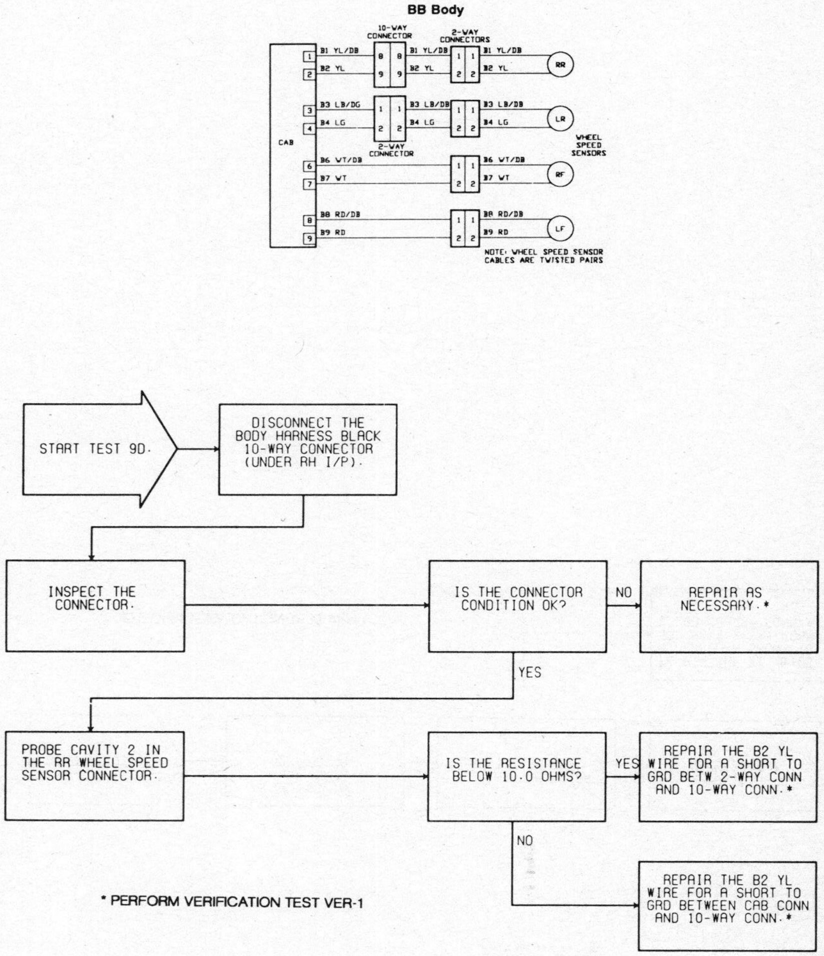
BB Body
10-WAY CONNECTOR
2-WAY CONNECTORS
2-WAY CONNECTOR
CAB
B1 YL/DB
B2 YL
B3 LB/DG
B3 LB/DB
B4 LG
B6 WT/DB
B7 WT
B8 RD/DB
B9 RD
RR
LR
RF
LF
WHEEL SPEED SENSORS
NOTE: WHEEL SPEED SENSOR CABLES ARE TWISTED PAIRS
START TEST 9D.
DISCONNECT THE BODY HARNESS BLACK 10-WAY CONNECTOR (UNDER RH I/P).
INSPECT THE CONNECTOR.
IS THE CONNECTOR CONDITION OK?
NO
REPAIR AS NECESSARY.*
YES
PROBE CAVITY 2 IN THE RR WHEEL SPEED SENSOR CONNECTOR.
IS THE RESISTANCE BELOW 10.0 OHMS?
YES
REPAIR THE B2 YL WIRE FOR A SHORT TO GRD BETW 2-WAY CONN AND 10-WAY CONN.*
NO
REPAIR THE B2 YL WIRE FOR A SHORT TO GRD BETWEEN CAB CONN AND 10-WAY CONN.*

* PERFORM VERIFICATION TEST VER-1

91C10811 91D10812

Fig. 54: Anti-Lock Brake Test 9D – RR Wheel Speed Sensor Continuity Fault

1991 BRAKES
Anti-Lock – Bendix-10 (Cont.)

TEST 9E: RR WHEEL SPEED SENSOR CONTINUITY FAULT

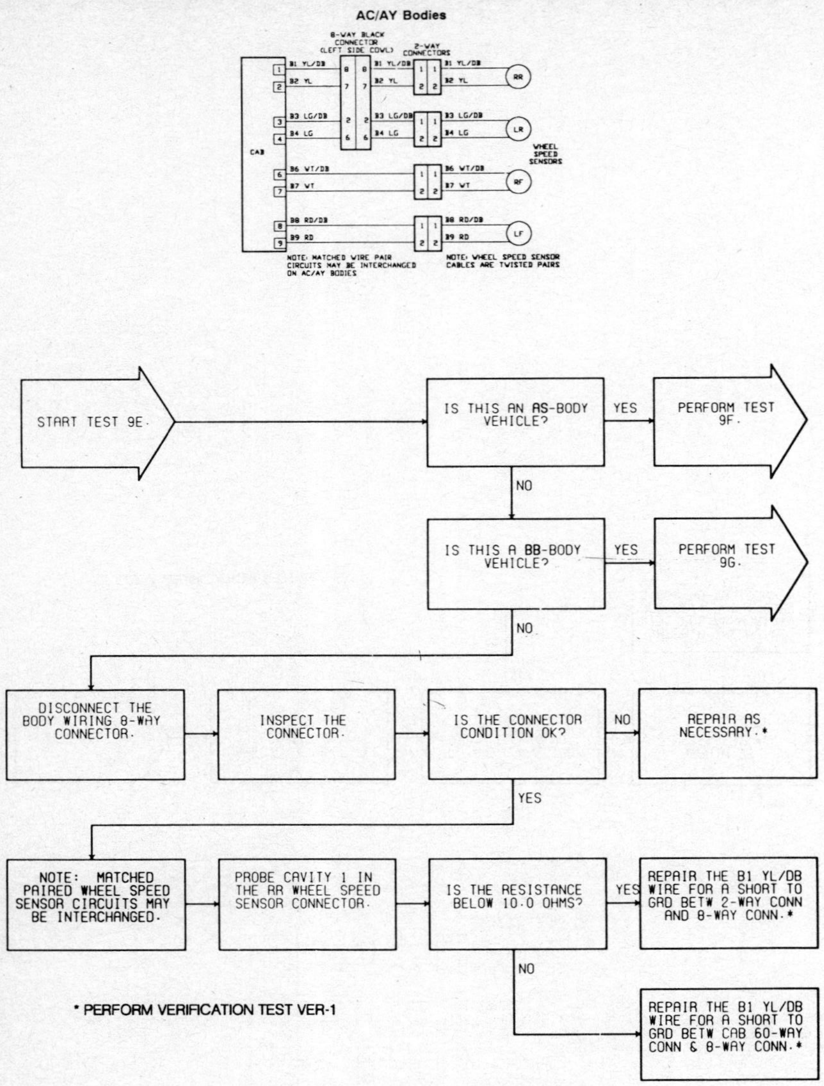
AC/AY Bodies
8-WAY BLACK CONNECTOR (LEFT SIDE COWL)
2-WAY CONNECTORS
CAB
B1 YL/DB
B2 YL
B3 LG/DB
B4 LG
B6 WT/DB
B7 WT
B8 RD/DB
B9 RD
RR
LR
RF
LF
WHEEL SPEED SENSORS
NOTE: MATCHED WIRE PAIR CIRCUITS MAY BE INTERCHANGED ON AC/AY BODIES
NOTE: WHEEL SPEED SENSOR CABLES ARE TWISTED PAIRS
START TEST 9E.
IS THIS AN AS-BODY VEHICLE?
YES
PERFORM TEST 9F.
NO
IS THIS A BB-BODY VEHICLE?
YES
PERFORM TEST 9G.
NO
DISCONNECT THE BODY WIRING 8-WAY CONNECTOR.
INSPECT THE CONNECTOR.
IS THE CONNECTOR CONDITION OK?
NO
REPAIR AS NECESSARY.*
YES
NOTE: MATCHED PAIRED WHEEL SPEED SENSOR CIRCUITS MAY BE INTERCHANGED.
PROBE CAVITY 1 IN THE RR WHEEL SPEED SENSOR CONNECTOR.
IS THE RESISTANCE BELOW 10.0 OHMS?
YES
REPAIR THE B1 YL/DB WIRE FOR A SHORT TO GRD BETW 2-WAY CONN AND 8-WAY CONN.*
NO
REPAIR THE B1 YL/DB WIRE FOR A SHORT TO GRD BETW CAB 60-WAY CONN & 8-WAY CONN.*

* PERFORM VERIFICATION TEST VER-1

91G10807 91B10885

Fig. 55: Anti-Lock Brake Test 9E – RR Wheel Speed Sensor Continuity Fault

TEST 9F: RR WHEEL SPEED SENSOR CONTINUITY FAULT

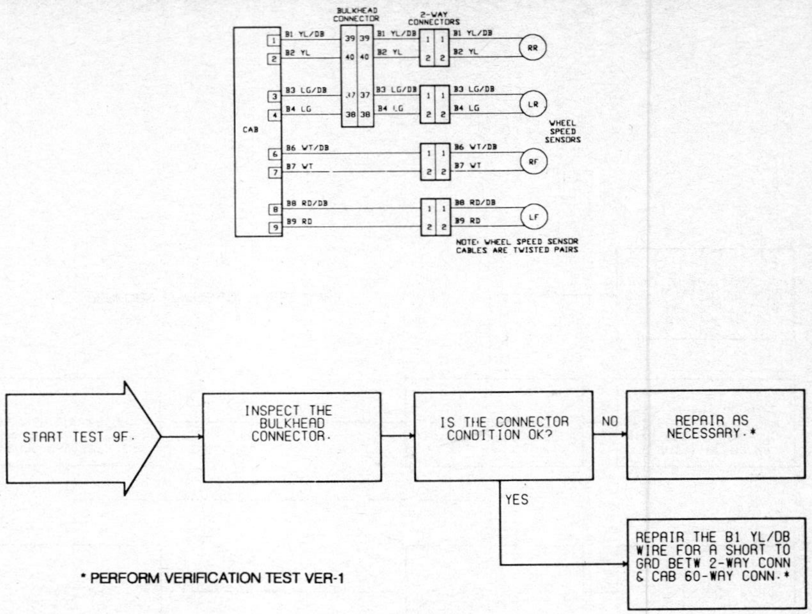
BULKHEAD CONNECTOR
2-WAY CONNECTORS
CAB
B1 YL/DB
B2 YL
B3 LG/DB
B4 LG
B6 WT/DB
B7 WT
B8 RD/DB
B9 RD
RR
LR
RF
LF
WHEEL SPEED SENSORS
NOTE: WHEEL SPEED SENSOR CABLES ARE TWISTED PAIRS
START TEST 9F.
INSPECT THE BULKHEAD CONNECTOR.
IS THE CONNECTOR CONDITION OK?
NO
REPAIR AS NECESSARY.*
YES
REPAIR THE B1 YL/DB WIRE FOR A SHORT TO GRD BETW 2-WAY CONN & CAB 60-WAY CONN.*

* PERFORM VERIFICATION TEST VER-1

91I10809 91C10886

Fig. 56: Anti-Lock Brake Test 9F – RR Wheel Speed Sensor Continuity Fault

TEST 9G: RR WHEEL SPEED SENSOR CONTINUITY FAULT

BB Body

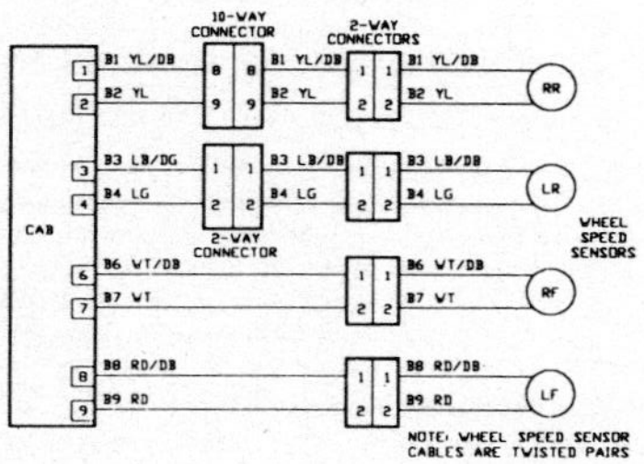
10-WAY CONNECTOR
2-WAY CONNECTORS
2-WAY CONNECTOR
CAB
B1 YL/DB
B2 YL
B3 LB/DG
B4 LG
B3 LB/DB
B6 WT/DB
B7 WT
B8 RD/DB
B9 RD
RR
LR
RF
LF
WHEEL SPEED SENSORS
NOTE: WHEEL SPEED SENSOR CABLES ARE TWISTED PAIRS

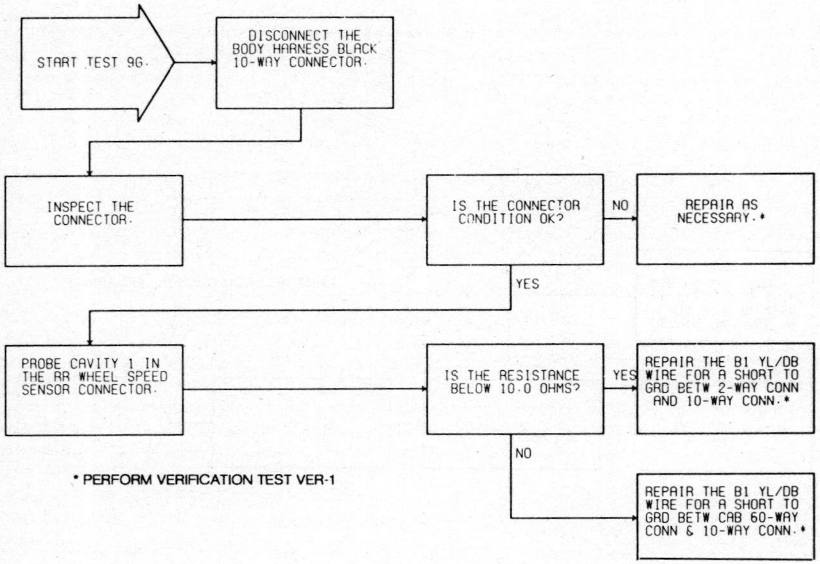
START TEST 9G.
DISCONNECT THE BODY HARNESS BLACK 10-WAY CONNECTOR.
INSPECT THE CONNECTOR.
IS THE CONNECTOR CONDITION OK?
NO
REPAIR AS NECESSARY.*
YES
PROBE CAVITY 1 IN THE RR WHEEL SPEED SENSOR CONNECTOR.
IS THE RESISTANCE BELOW 10.0 OHMS?
YES
REPAIR THE B1 YL/DB WIRE FOR A SHORT TO GRD BETW 2-WAY CONN AND 10-WAY CONN.*
NO
REPAIR THE B1 YL/DB WIRE FOR A SHORT TO GRD BETW CAB 60-WAY CONN & 10-WAY CONN.*

* PERFORM VERIFICATION TEST VER-1

91C10811 91E10813

Fig. 57: Anti-Lock Brake Test 9G – RR Wheel Speed Sensor Continuity Fault

TEST 9H: RR WHEEL SPEED SENSOR CONTINUITY FAULT

AC/AY Body

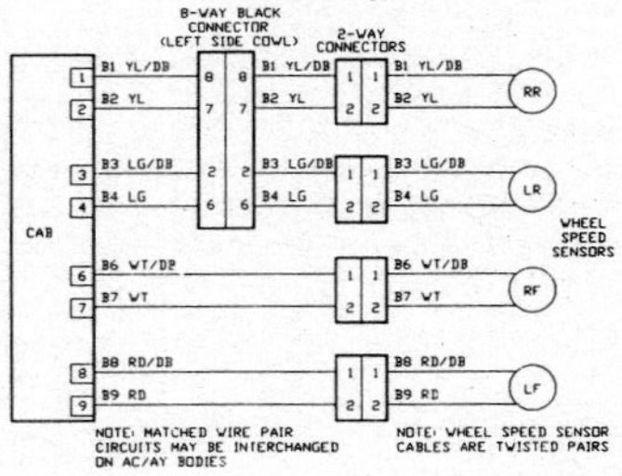
8-WAY BLACK CONNECTOR (LEFT SIDE COWL)
2-WAY CONNECTORS
CAB
B1 YL/DB
B2 YL
B3 LG/DB
B4 LG
B6 WT/DB
B7 WT
B8 RD/DB
B9 RD
RR
LR
RF
LF
WHEEL SPEED SENSORS
NOTE: MATCHED WIRE PAIR CIRCUITS MAY BE INTERCHANGED ON AC/AY BODIES
NOTE: WHEEL SPEED SENSOR CABLES ARE TWISTED PAIRS

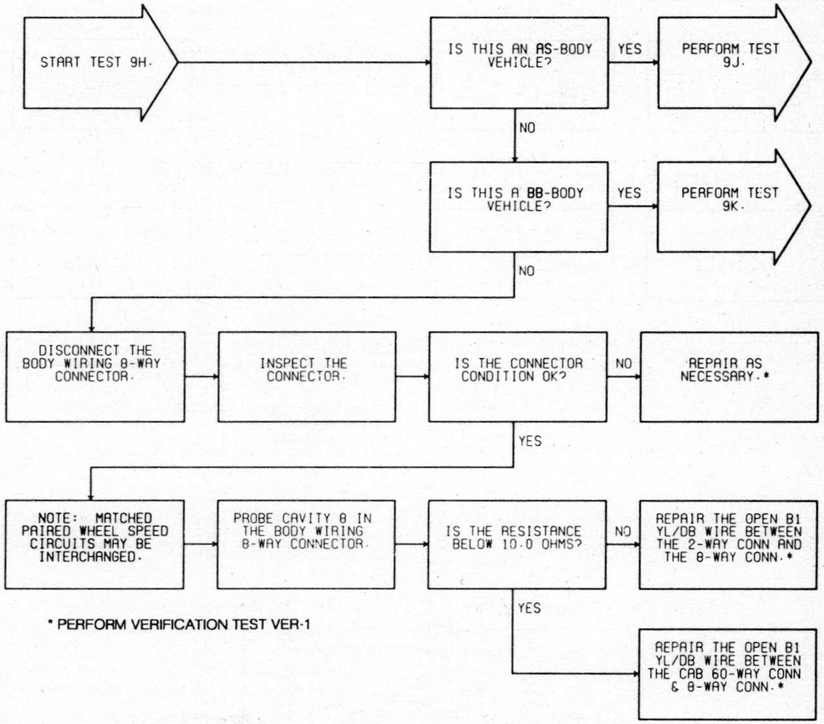
START TEST 9H.
IS THIS AN AS-BODY VEHICLE?
YES
PERFORM TEST 9J.
NO
IS THIS A BB-BODY VEHICLE?
YES
PERFORM TEST 9K.
NO
DISCONNECT THE BODY WIRING 8-WAY CONNECTOR.
INSPECT THE CONNECTOR.
IS THE CONNECTOR CONDITION OK?
NO
REPAIR AS NECESSARY.*
YES
NOTE: MATCHED PAIRED WHEEL SPEED CIRCUITS MAY BE INTERCHANGED.
PROBE CAVITY 8 IN THE BODY WIRING 8-WAY CONNECTOR.
IS THE RESISTANCE BELOW 10.0 OHMS?
NO
REPAIR THE OPEN B1 YL/DB WIRE BETWEEN THE 2-WAY CONN AND THE 8-WAY CONN.*
YES
REPAIR THE OPEN B1 YL/DB WIRE BETWEEN THE CAB 60-WAY CONN & 8-WAY CONN.*

* PERFORM VERIFICATION TEST VER-1

91G10807 91F10814

Fig. 58: Anti-Lock Brake Test 9H – RR Wheel Speed Sensor Continuity Fault

1991 BRAKES
Anti-Lock – Bendix-10 (Cont.)

TEST 9J: RR WHEEL SPEED SENSOR CONTINUITY FAULT

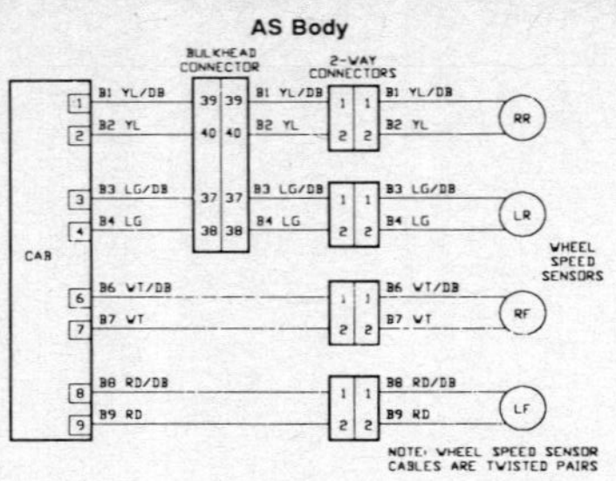
AS Body
BULKHEAD CONNECTOR
2-WAY CONNECTORS
CAB
B1 YL/DB
B2 YL
B3 LG/DB
B4 LG
B6 WT/DB
B7 WT
B8 RD/DB
B9 RD
RR
LR
RF
LF
WHEEL SPEED SENSORS
NOTE: WHEEL SPEED SENSOR CABLES ARE TWISTED PAIRS

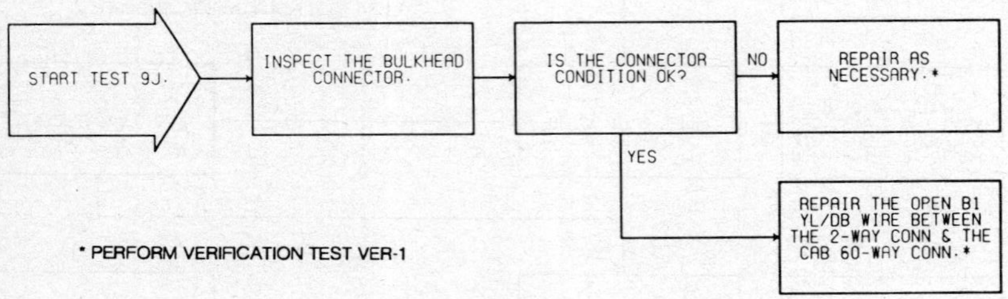
START TEST 9J.
INSPECT THE BULKHEAD CONNECTOR.
IS THE CONNECTOR CONDITION OK?
NO
REPAIR AS NECESSARY.*
YES
REPAIR THE OPEN B1 YL/DB WIRE BETWEEN THE 2-WAY CONN & THE CAB 60-WAY CONN.*

* PERFORM VERIFICATION TEST VER-1

91I10809 91G10815

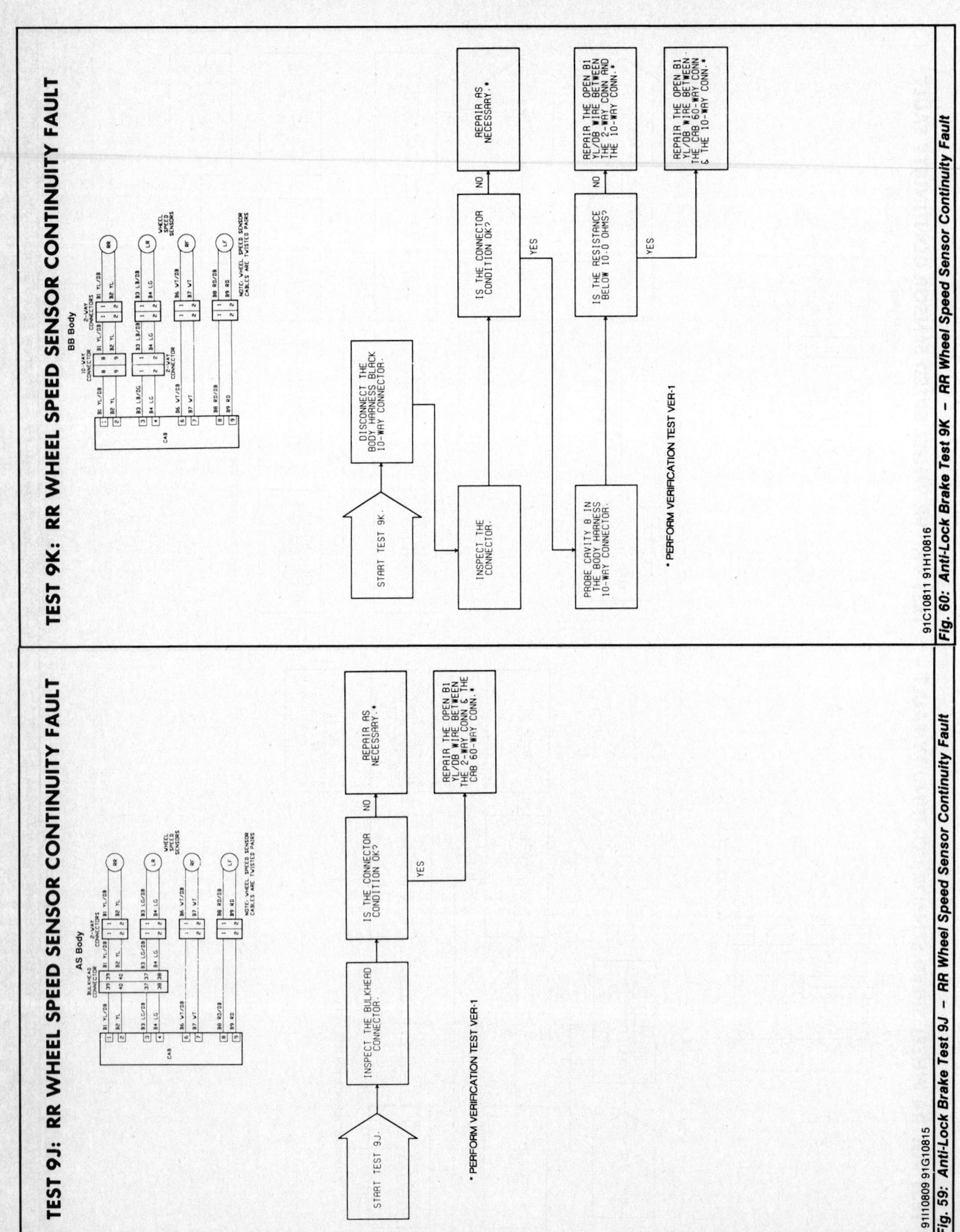

Fig. 59: Anti-Lock Brake Test 9J – RR Wheel Speed Sensor Continuity Fault

TEST 9K: RR WHEEL SPEED SENSOR CONTINUITY FAULT

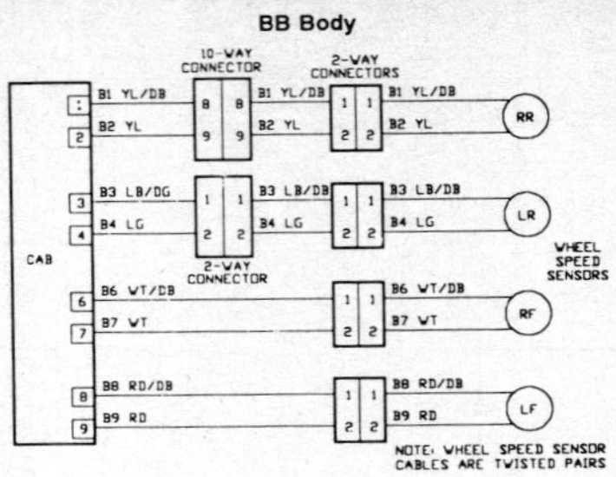
BB Body
10-WAY CONNECTOR
2-WAY CONNECTORS
2-WAY CONNECTOR
CAB
B1 YL/DB
B2 YL
B3 LB/DG
B3 LB/DB
B4 LG
B6 WT/DB
B7 WT
B8 RD/DB
B9 RD
RR
LR
RF
LF
WHEEL SPEED SENSORS
NOTE: WHEEL SPEED SENSOR CABLES ARE TWISTED PAIRS

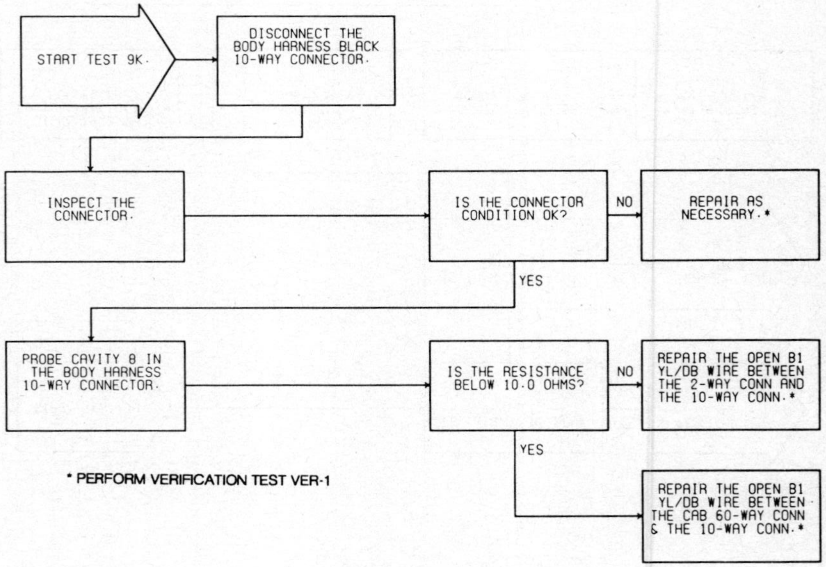
START TEST 9K.
DISCONNECT THE BODY HARNESS BLACK 10-WAY CONNECTOR.
INSPECT THE CONNECTOR.
IS THE CONNECTOR CONDITION OK?
NO
REPAIR AS NECESSARY.*
YES
PROBE CAVITY 8 IN THE BODY HARNESS 10-WAY CONNECTOR.
IS THE RESISTANCE BELOW 10.0 OHMS?
NO
REPAIR THE OPEN B1 YL/DB WIRE BETWEEN THE 2-WAY CONN AND THE 10-WAY CONN.*
YES
REPAIR THE OPEN B1 YL/DB WIRE BETWEEN THE CAB 60-WAY CONN & THE 10-WAY CONN.*

* PERFORM VERIFICATION TEST VER-1

91C10811 91H10816

Fig. 60: Anti-Lock Brake Test 9K – RR Wheel Speed Sensor Continuity Fault

TEST 9L: RR WHEEL SPEED SENSOR CONTINUITY FAULT

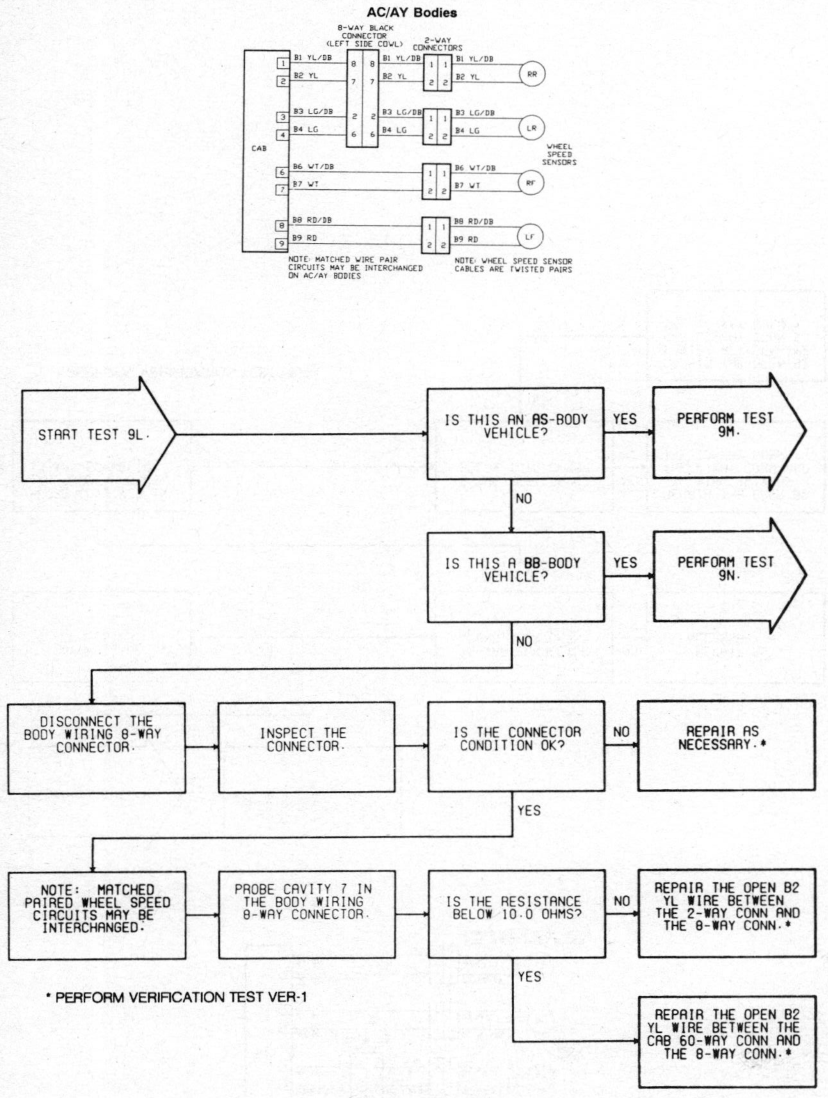
AC/AY Bodies
8-WAY BLACK CONNECTOR (LEFT SIDE COWL)
2-WAY CONNECTORS
CAB
WHEEL SPEED SENSORS
NOTE: MATCHED WIRE PAIR CIRCUITS MAY BE INTERCHANGED ON AC/AY BODIES
NOTE: WHEEL SPEED SENSOR CABLES ARE TWISTED PAIRS
START TEST 9L.
IS THIS AN AS-BODY VEHICLE?
YES
PERFORM TEST 9M.
NO
IS THIS A BB-BODY VEHICLE?
YES
PERFORM TEST 9N.
NO
DISCONNECT THE BODY WIRING 8-WAY CONNECTOR.
INSPECT THE CONNECTOR.
IS THE CONNECTOR CONDITION OK?
NO
REPAIR AS NECESSARY.*
YES
NOTE: MATCHED PAIRED WHEEL SPEED CIRCUITS MAY BE INTERCHANGED.
PROBE CAVITY 7 IN THE BODY WIRING 8-WAY CONNECTOR.
IS THE RESISTANCE BELOW 10.0 OHMS?
NO
REPAIR THE OPEN B2 YL WIRE BETWEEN THE 2-WAY CONN AND THE 8-WAY CONN.*
YES
REPAIR THE OPEN B2 YL WIRE BETWEEN THE CAB 60-WAY CONN AND THE 8-WAY CONN.*
* PERFORM VERIFICATION TEST VER-1

91G10807 91I10817

Fig. 61: Anti-Lock Brake Test 9L – RR Wheel Speed Sensor Continuity Fault

TEST 9M: RR WHEEL SPEED SENSOR CONTINUITY FAULT

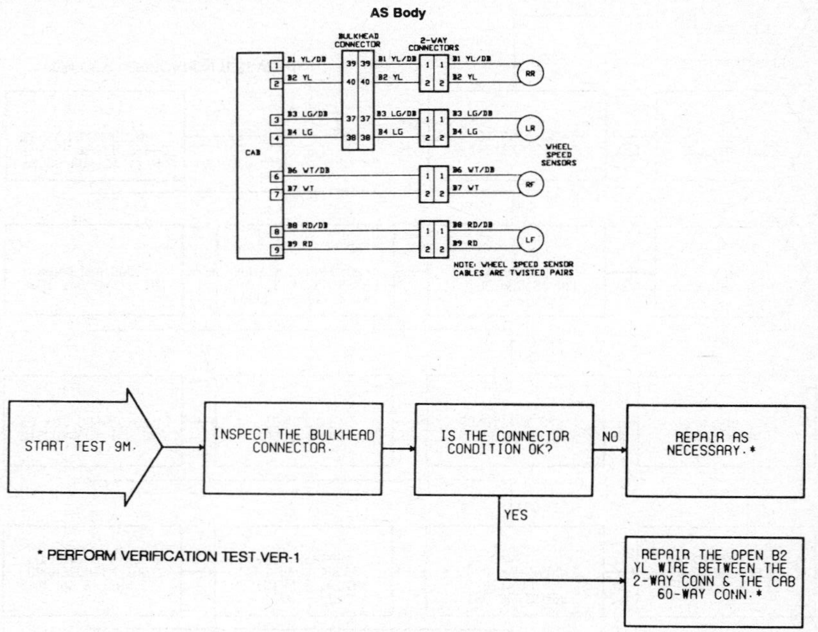
AS Body
BULKHEAD CONNECTOR
2-WAY CONNECTORS
CAB
WHEEL SPEED SENSORS
NOTE: WHEEL SPEED SENSOR CABLES ARE TWISTED PAIRS
START TEST 9M.
INSPECT THE BULKHEAD CONNECTOR.
IS THE CONNECTOR CONDITION OK?
NO
REPAIR AS NECESSARY.*
YES
REPAIR THE OPEN B2 YL WIRE BETWEEN THE 2-WAY CONN & THE CAB 60-WAY CONN.*
* PERFORM VERIFICATION TEST VER-1

91I10809 91J10818

Fig. 62: Anti-Lock Brake Test 9M – RR Wheel Speed Sensor Continuity Fault

TEST 9N: RR WHEEL SPEED SENSOR CONTINUITY FAULT

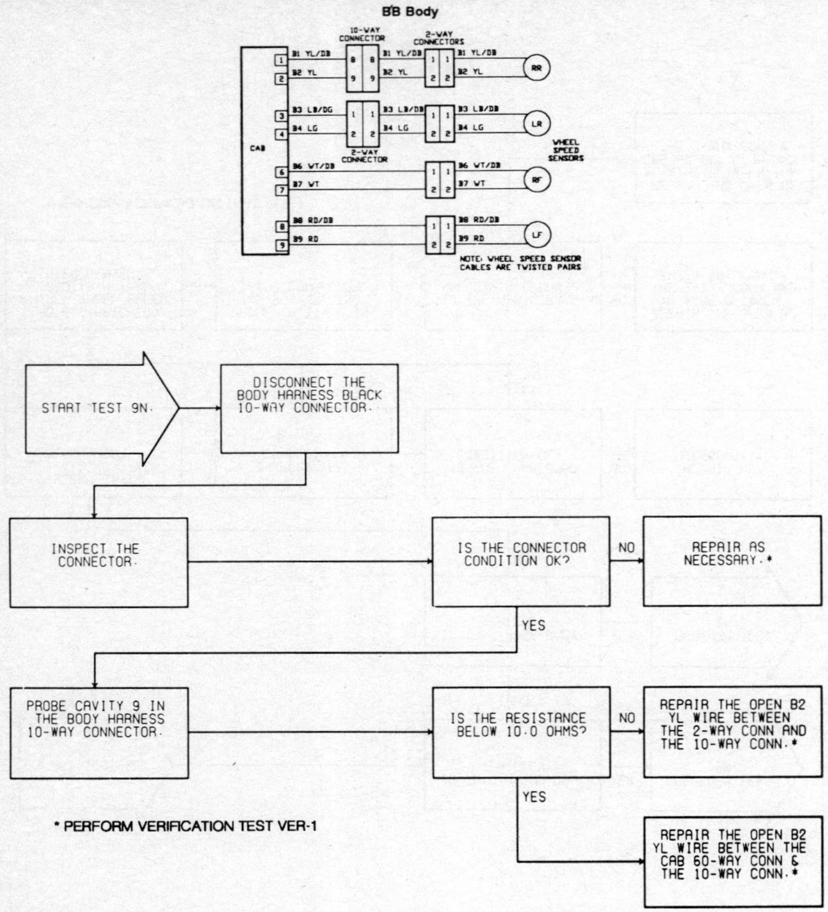
BB Body
10-WAY CONNECTOR
2-WAY CONNECTORS
2-WAY CONNECTOR
CAB
WHEEL SPEED SENSORS
RR
LR
RF
LF
NOTE: WHEEL SPEED SENSOR CABLES ARE TWISTED PAIRS
START TEST 9N.
DISCONNECT THE BODY HARNESS BLACK 10-WAY CONNECTOR.
INSPECT THE CONNECTOR.
IS THE CONNECTOR CONDITION OK?
NO
REPAIR AS NECESSARY.*
YES
PROBE CAVITY 9 IN THE BODY HARNESS 10-WAY CONNECTOR.
IS THE RESISTANCE BELOW 10.0 OHMS?
NO
REPAIR THE OPEN B2 YL WIRE BETWEEN THE 2-WAY CONN AND THE 10-WAY CONN.*
YES
REPAIR THE OPEN B2 YL WIRE BETWEEN THE CAB 60-WAY CONN & THE 10-WAY CONN.*
* PERFORM VERIFICATION TEST VER-1

91C10811 91A10819

Fig. 63: Anti-Lock Brake Test 9N – RR Wheel Speed Sensor Continuity Fault

TEST 10A: LR WHEEL SPEED SENSOR CONTINUITY FAULT (1 OF 2)

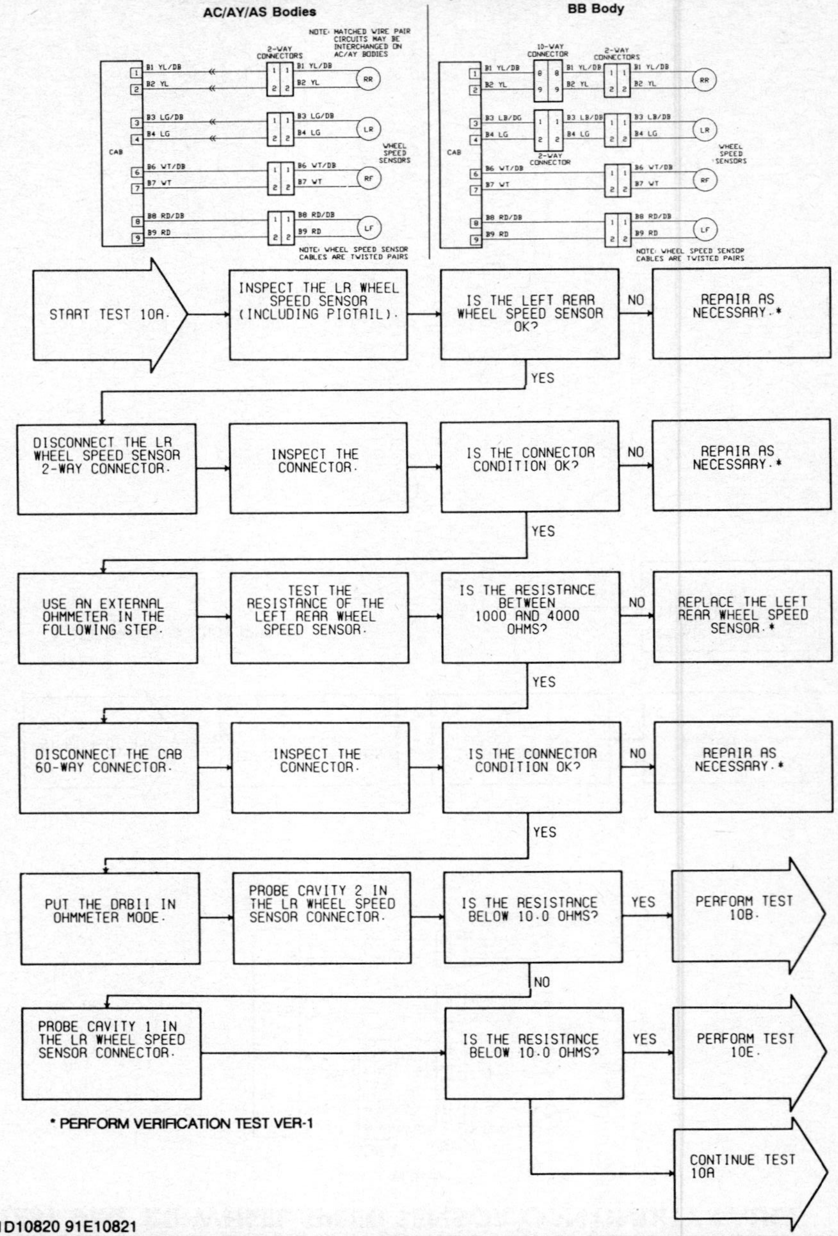
AC/AY/AS Bodies
BB Body
NOTE: MATCHED WIRE PAIR CIRCUITS MAY BE INTERCHANGED ON AC/AY BODIES
2-WAY CONNECTORS
10-WAY CONNECTOR
2-WAY CONNECTOR
CAB
WHEEL SPEED SENSORS
RR
LR
RF
LF
NOTE: WHEEL SPEED SENSOR CABLES ARE TWISTED PAIRS
START TEST 10A.
INSPECT THE LR WHEEL SPEED SENSOR (INCLUDING PIGTAIL).
IS THE LEFT REAR WHEEL SPEED SENSOR OK?
NO
REPAIR AS NECESSARY.*
YES
DISCONNECT THE LR WHEEL SPEED SENSOR 2-WAY CONNECTOR.
INSPECT THE CONNECTOR.
IS THE CONNECTOR CONDITION OK?
NO
REPAIR AS NECESSARY.*
YES
USE AN EXTERNAL OHMMETER IN THE FOLLOWING STEP.
TEST THE RESISTANCE OF THE LEFT REAR WHEEL SPEED SENSOR.
IS THE RESISTANCE BETWEEN 1000 AND 4000 OHMS?
NO
REPLACE THE LEFT REAR WHEEL SPEED SENSOR.*
YES
DISCONNECT THE CAB 60-WAY CONNECTOR.
INSPECT THE CONNECTOR.
IS THE CONNECTOR CONDITION OK?
NO
REPAIR AS NECESSARY.*
YES
PUT THE DRBII IN OHMMETER MODE.
PROBE CAVITY 2 IN THE LR WHEEL SPEED SENSOR CONNECTOR.
IS THE RESISTANCE BELOW 10.0 OHMS?
YES
PERFORM TEST 10B.
NO
PROBE CAVITY 1 IN THE LR WHEEL SPEED SENSOR CONNECTOR.
IS THE RESISTANCE BELOW 10.0 OHMS?
YES
PERFORM TEST 10E.
CONTINUE TEST 10A
* PERFORM VERIFICATION TEST VER-1

91D10820 91E10821

Fig. 64: Anti-Lock Brake Test 10A – LR Wheel Speed Sensor Continuity Fault (1 of 2)

TEST 10A: LR WHEEL SPEED SENSOR CONTINUITY FAULT (2 OF 2)

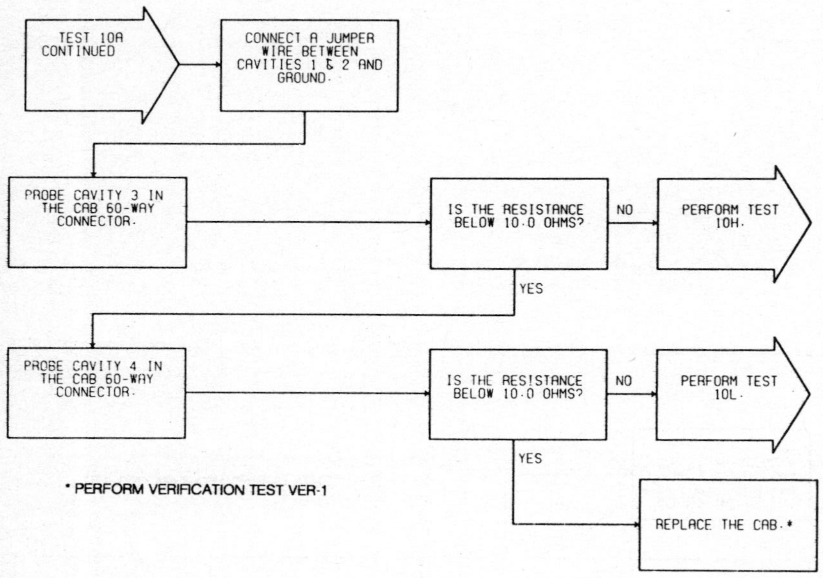
TEST 10A CONTINUED
CONNECT A JUMPER WIRE BETWEEN CAVITIES 1 & 2 AND GROUND.
PROBE CAVITY 3 IN THE CAB 60-WAY CONNECTOR.
IS THE RESISTANCE BELOW 10.0 OHMS?
NO
PERFORM TEST 10H.
YES
PROBE CAVITY 4 IN THE CAB 60-WAY CONNECTOR.
IS THE RESISTANCE BELOW 10.0 OHMS?
NO
PERFORM TEST 10L.
YES
REPLACE THE CAB.*

* PERFORM VERIFICATION TEST VER-1

91F10822

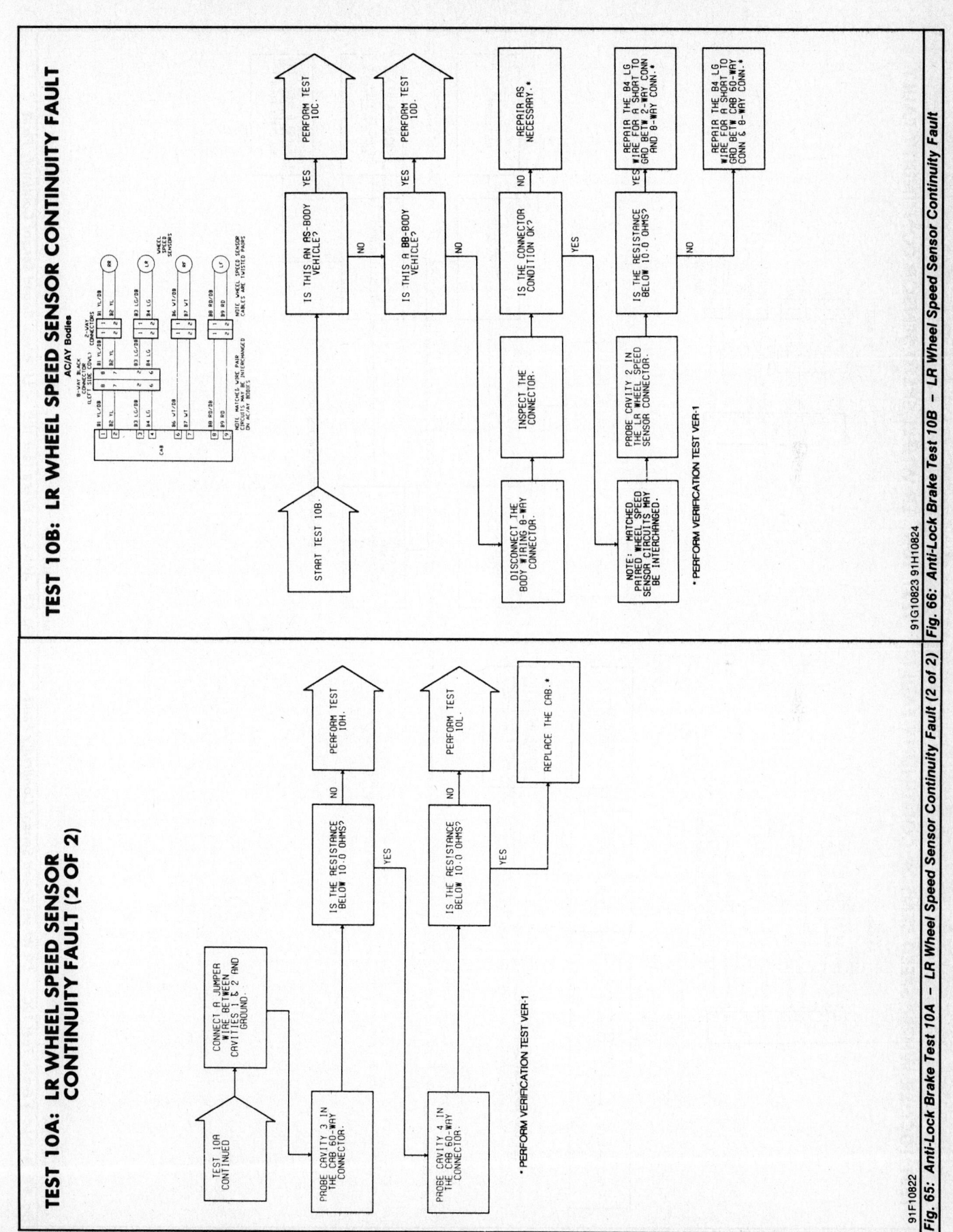

Fig. 65: Anti-Lock Brake Test 10A – LR Wheel Speed Sensor Continuity Fault (2 of 2)

TEST 10B: LR WHEEL SPEED SENSOR CONTINUITY FAULT

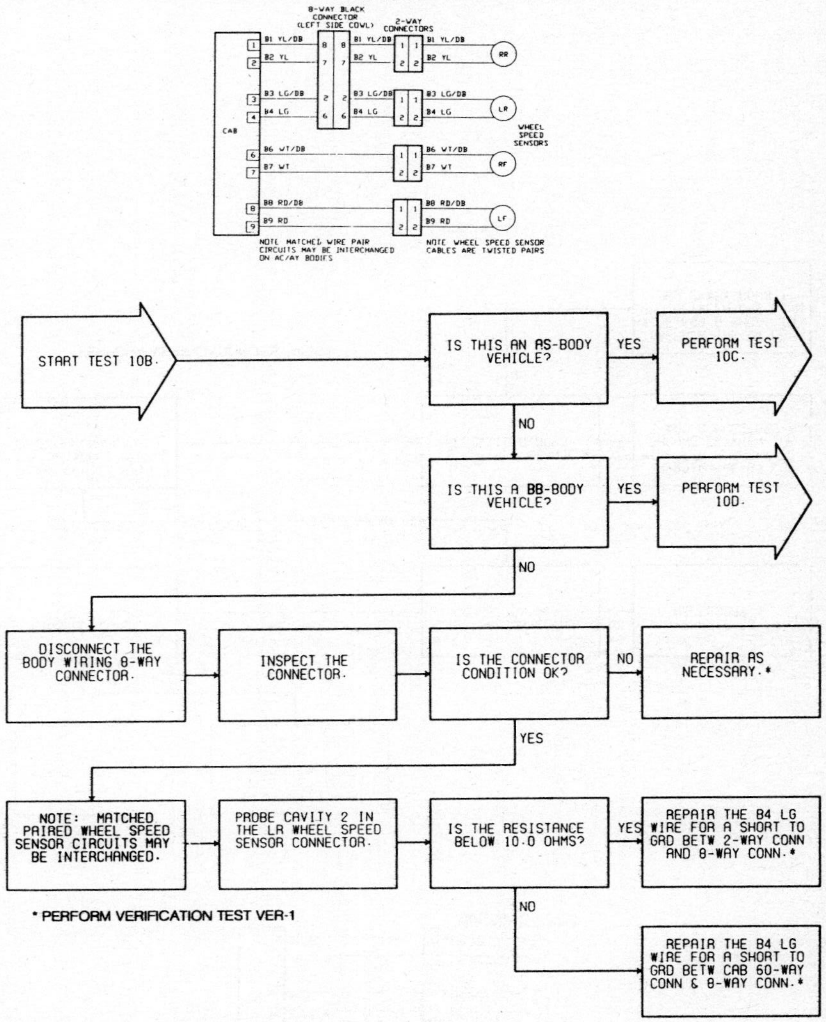
AC/AY Bodies
8-WAY BLACK CONNECTOR (LEFT SIDE COWL)
2-WAY CONNECTORS
CAB
B1 YL/DB
B2 YL
B3 LG/DB
B4 LG
B6 WT/DB
B7 WT
B8 RD/DB
B9 RD
RR
LR
RF
LF
WHEEL SPEED SENSORS
NOTE: MATCHED WIRE PAIR CIRCUITS MAY BE INTERCHANGED ON AC/AY BODIES
NOTE: WHEEL SPEED SENSOR CABLES ARE TWISTED PAIRS
START TEST 10B.
IS THIS AN AS-BODY VEHICLE?
YES
PERFORM TEST 10C.
NO
IS THIS A BB-BODY VEHICLE?
YES
PERFORM TEST 10D.
NO
DISCONNECT THE BODY WIRING 8-WAY CONNECTOR.
INSPECT THE CONNECTOR.
IS THE CONNECTOR CONDITION OK?
NO
REPAIR AS NECESSARY.*
YES
NOTE: MATCHED PAIRED WHEEL SPEED SENSOR CIRCUITS MAY BE INTERCHANGED.
PROBE CAVITY 2 IN THE LR WHEEL SPEED SENSOR CONNECTOR.
IS THE RESISTANCE BELOW 10.0 OHMS?
YES
REPAIR THE B4 LG WIRE FOR A SHORT TO GRD BETW 2-WAY CONN AND 8-WAY CONN.*
NO
REPAIR THE B4 LG WIRE FOR A SHORT TO GRD BETW CAB 60-WAY CONN & 8-WAY CONN.*

* PERFORM VERIFICATION TEST VER-1

91G10823 91H10824

Fig. 66: Anti-Lock Brake Test 10B – LR Wheel Speed Sensor Continuity Fault

1991 BRAKES
Anti-Lock – Bendix-10 (Cont.)

TEST 10C: LR WHEEL SPEED SENSOR CONTINUITY FAULT

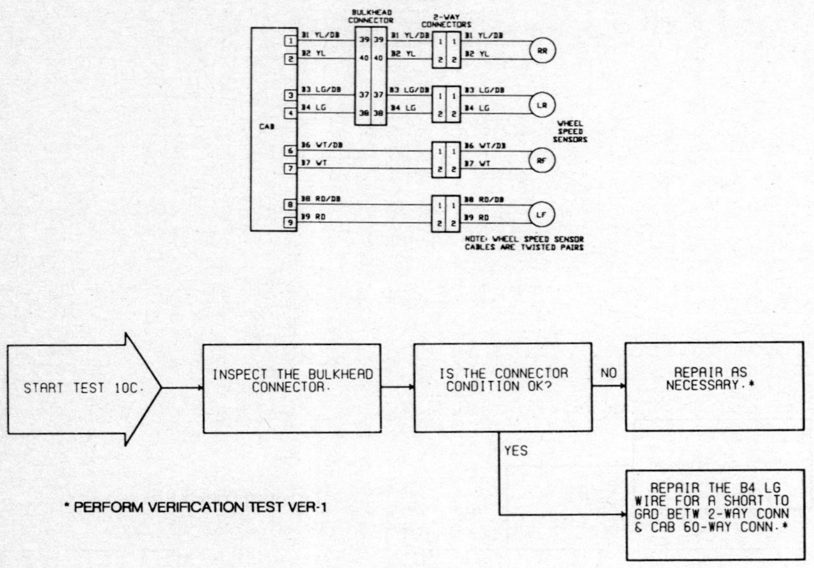
AS Body
CAB
BULKHEAD CONNECTOR
2-WAY CONNECTORS
WHEEL SPEED SENSORS
RR
LR
RF
LF
NOTE: WHEEL SPEED SENSOR CABLES ARE TWISTED PAIRS
START TEST 10C.
INSPECT THE BULKHEAD CONNECTOR.
IS THE CONNECTOR CONDITION OK?
NO
REPAIR AS NECESSARY.*
YES
REPAIR THE B4 LG WIRE FOR A SHORT TO GRD BETW 2-WAY CONN & CAB 60-WAY CONN.*
* PERFORM VERIFICATION TEST VER-1

91I10825 91J10826

Fig. 67: Anti-Lock Brake Test 10C – LR Wheel Speed Sensor Continuity Fault

TEST 10D: LR WHEEL SPEED SENSOR CONTINUITY FAULT

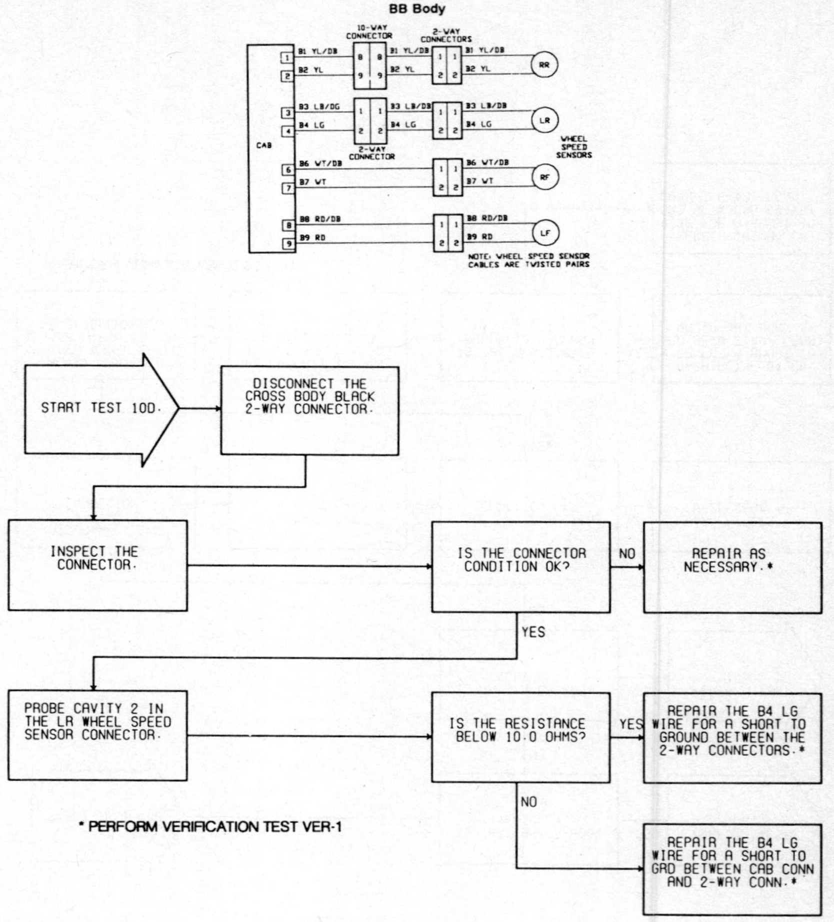
BB Body
CAB
10-WAY CONNECTOR
2-WAY CONNECTORS
2-WAY CONNECTOR
WHEEL SPEED SENSORS
RR
LR
RF
LF
NOTE: WHEEL SPEED SENSOR CABLES ARE TWISTED PAIRS
START TEST 10D.
DISCONNECT THE CROSS BODY BLACK 2-WAY CONNECTOR.
INSPECT THE CONNECTOR.
IS THE CONNECTOR CONDITION OK?
NO
REPAIR AS NECESSARY.*
YES
PROBE CAVITY 2 IN THE LR WHEEL SPEED SENSOR CONNECTOR.
IS THE RESISTANCE BELOW 10.0 OHMS?
YES
REPAIR THE B4 LG WIRE FOR A SHORT TO GROUND BETWEEN THE 2-WAY CONNECTORS.*
NO
REPAIR THE B4 LG WIRE FOR A SHORT TO GRD BETWEEN CAB CONN AND 2-WAY CONN.*
* PERFORM VERIFICATION TEST VER-1

91C10811 91A10827

Fig. 68: Anti-Lock Brake Test 10D – LR Wheel Speed Sensor Continuity Fault

TEST 10E: LR WHEEL SPEED SENSOR CONTINUITY FAULT

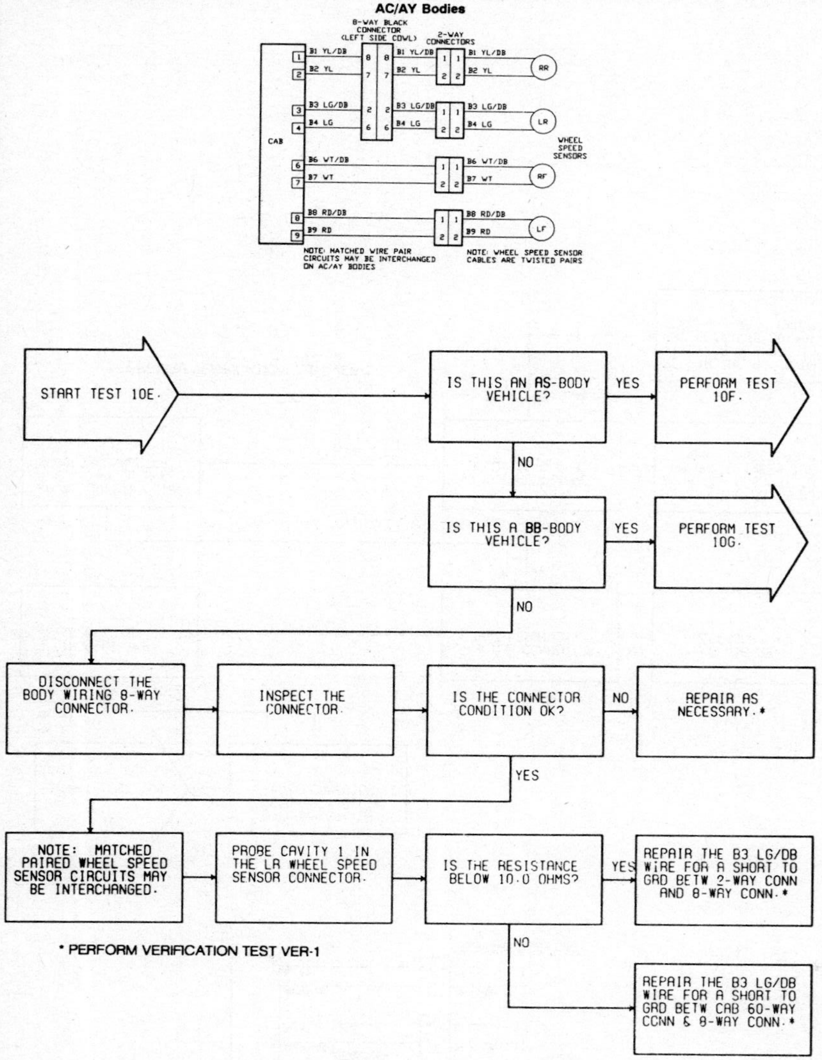
AC/AY Bodies
8-WAY BLACK CONNECTOR (LEFT SIDE COWL)
2-WAY CONNECTORS
CAB
WHEEL SPEED SENSORS
NOTE: MATCHED WIRE PAIR CIRCUITS MAY BE INTERCHANGED ON AC/AY BODIES
NOTE: WHEEL SPEED SENSOR CABLES ARE TWISTED PAIRS
START TEST 10E.
IS THIS AN AS-BODY VEHICLE?
YES
PERFORM TEST 10F.
NO
IS THIS A BB-BODY VEHICLE?
YES
PERFORM TEST 10G.
NO
DISCONNECT THE BODY WIRING 8-WAY CONNECTOR.
INSPECT THE CONNECTOR.
IS THE CONNECTOR CONDITION OK?
NO
REPAIR AS NECESSARY.*
YES
NOTE: MATCHED PAIRED WHEEL SPEED SENSOR CIRCUITS MAY BE INTERCHANGED.
PROBE CAVITY 1 IN THE LR WHEEL SPEED SENSOR CONNECTOR.
IS THE RESISTANCE BELOW 10.0 OHMS?
YES
REPAIR THE B3 LG/DB WIRE FOR A SHORT TO GRD BETW 2-WAY CONN AND 8-WAY CONN.*
NO
REPAIR THE B3 LG/DB WIRE FOR A SHORT TO GRD BETW CAB 60-WAY CCNN & 8-WAY CONN.*
* PERFORM VERIFICATION TEST VER-1

91G10807 91B10828

Fig. 69 Anti-Lock Brake Test 10E – LR Wheel Speed Sensor Continuity Fault

TEST 10F: LR WHEEL SPEED SENSOR CONTINUITY FAULT

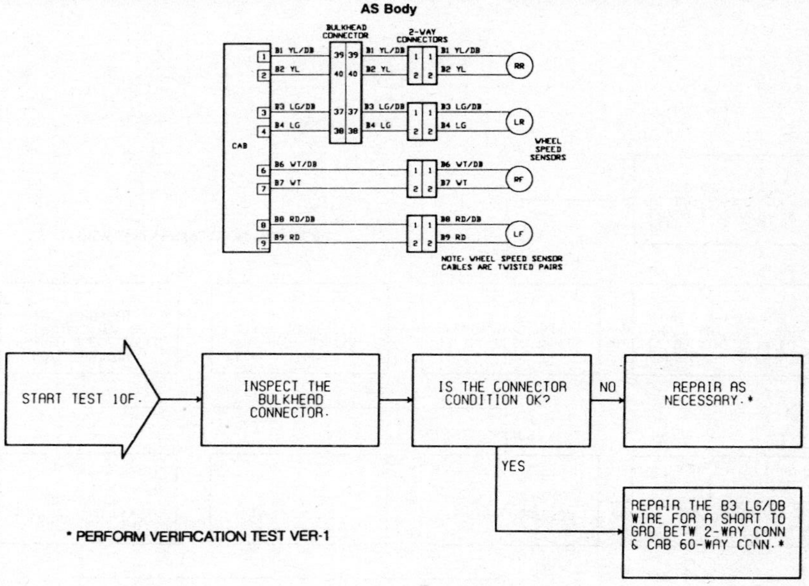
AS Body
BULKHEAD CONNECTOR
2-WAY CONNECTORS
CAB
WHEEL SPEED SENSORS
NOTE: WHEEL SPEED SENSOR CABLES ARE TWISTED PAIRS
START TEST 10F.
INSPECT THE BULKHEAD CONNECTOR.
IS THE CONNECTOR CONDITION OK?
NO
REPAIR AS NECESSARY.*
YES
REPAIR THE B3 LG/DB WIRE FOR A SHORT TO GRD BETW 2-WAY CONN & CAB 60-WAY CCNN.*
* PERFORM VERIFICATION TEST VER-1

91I100809 91C10829

Fig. 70: Anti-Lock Brake Test 10F – LR Wheel Speed Sensor Continuity Fault

TEST 10G: LR WHEEL SPEED SENSOR CONTINUITY FAULT

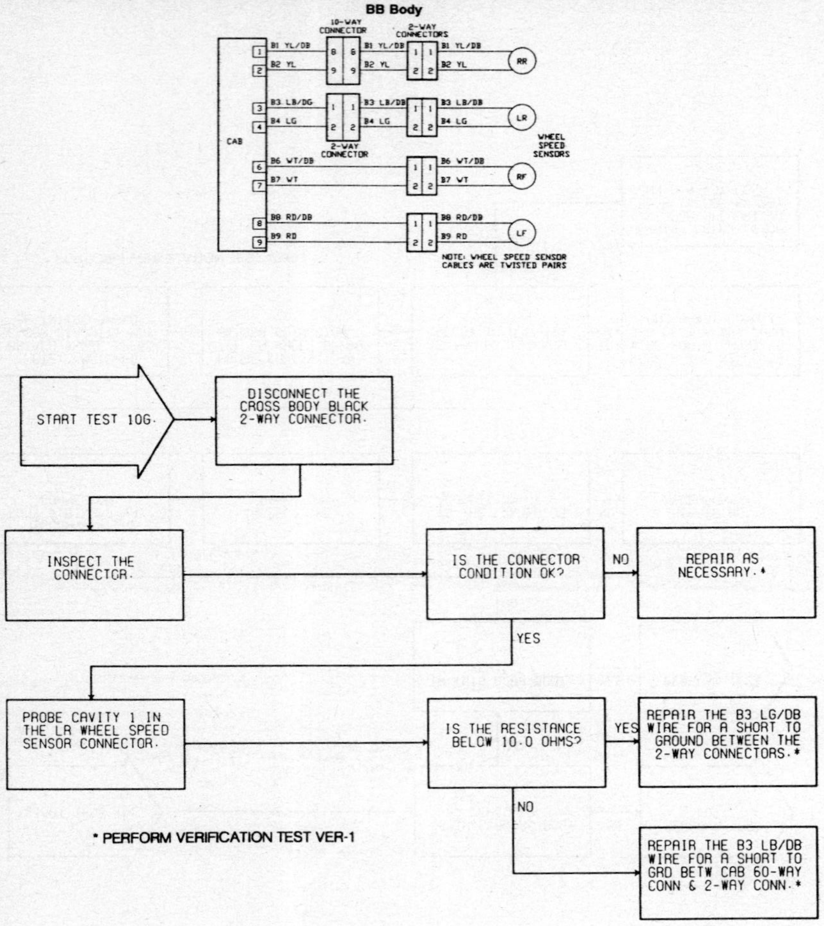
BB Body
10-WAY CONNECTOR
2-WAY CONNECTORS
2-WAY CONNECTOR
CAB
B1 YL/DB
B2 YL
B3 LB/DG
B4 LG
B3 LB/DB
B6 WT/DB
B7 WT
B8 RD/DB
B9 RD
RR
LR
RF
LF
WHEEL SPEED SENSORS
NOTE: WHEEL SPEED SENSOR CABLES ARE TWISTED PAIRS
START TEST 10G.
DISCONNECT THE CROSS BODY BLACK 2-WAY CONNECTOR.
INSPECT THE CONNECTOR.
IS THE CONNECTOR CONDITION OK?
NO
REPAIR AS NECESSARY.*
YES
PROBE CAVITY 1 IN THE LR WHEEL SPEED SENSOR CONNECTOR.
IS THE RESISTANCE BELOW 10.0 OHMS?
YES
REPAIR THE B3 LG/DB WIRE FOR A SHORT TO GROUND BETWEEN THE 2-WAY CONNECTORS.*
NO
REPAIR THE B3 LB/DB WIRE FOR A SHORT TO GRD BETW CAB 60-WAY CONN & 2-WAY CONN.*
* PERFORM VERIFICATION TEST VER-1

91C10811 91F10830

Fig. 71: Anti-Lock Brake Test 10G – LR Wheel Speed Sensor Continuity Fault

TEST 10H: LR WHEEL SPEED SENSOR CONTINUITY FAULT

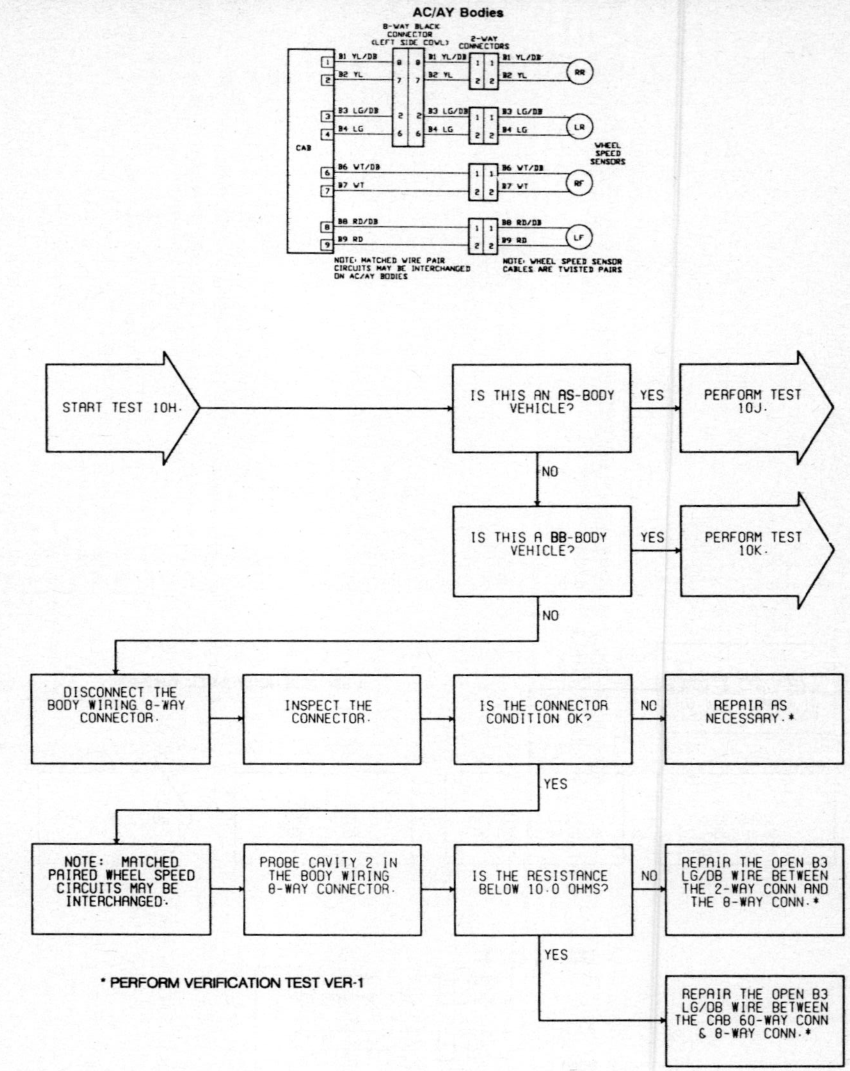
AC/AY Bodies
8-WAY BLACK CONNECTOR (LEFT SIDE COWL)
2-WAY CONNECTORS
CAB
B1 YL/DB
B2 YL
B3 LG/DB
B4 LG
B6 WT/DB
B7 WT
B8 RD/DB
B9 RD
RR
LR
RF
LF
WHEEL SPEED SENSORS
NOTE: MATCHED WIRE PAIR CIRCUITS MAY BE INTERCHANGED ON AC/AY BODIES
NOTE: WHEEL SPEED SENSOR CABLES ARE TWISTED PAIRS
START TEST 10H.
IS THIS AN AS-BODY VEHICLE?
YES
PERFORM TEST 10J.
NO
IS THIS A BB-BODY VEHICLE?
YES
PERFORM TEST 10K.
NO
DISCONNECT THE BODY WIRING 8-WAY CONNECTOR.
INSPECT THE CONNECTOR.
IS THE CONNECTOR CONDITION OK?
NO
REPAIR AS NECESSARY.*
YES
NOTE: MATCHED PAIRED WHEEL SPEED CIRCUITS MAY BE INTERCHANGED.
PROBE CAVITY 2 IN THE BODY WIRING 8-WAY CONNECTOR.
IS THE RESISTANCE BELOW 10.0 OHMS?
NO
REPAIR THE OPEN B3 LG/DB WIRE BETWEEN THE 2-WAY CONN AND THE 8-WAY CONN.*
YES
REPAIR THE OPEN B3 LG/DB WIRE BETWEEN THE CAB 60-WAY CONN & 8-WAY CONN.*
* PERFORM VERIFICATION TEST VER-1

91G10807 91G10831

Fig. 72: Anti-Lock Brake Test 10H – LR Wheel Speed Sensor Continuity Fault

TEST 10J: LR WHEEL SPEED SENSOR CONTINUITY FAULT

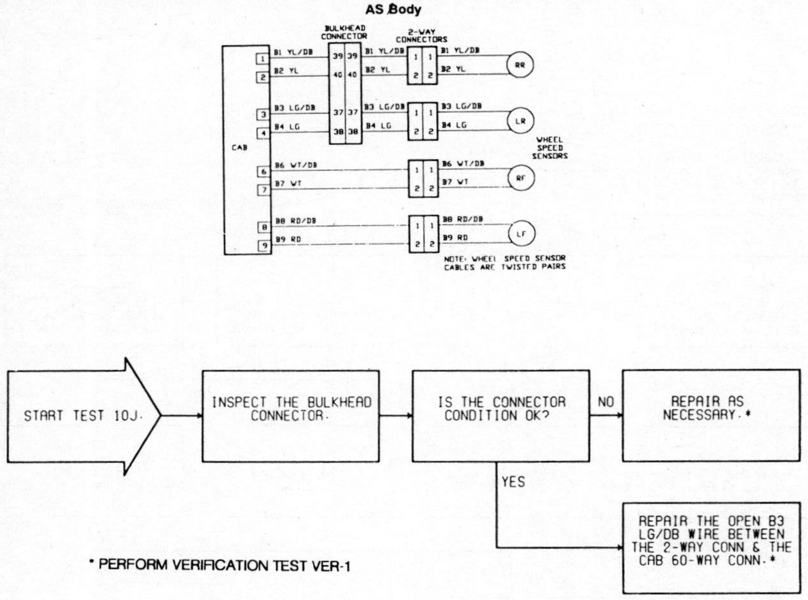
AS Body
BULKHEAD CONNECTOR
2-WAY CONNECTORS
CAB
B1 YL/DB
B2 YL
B3 LG/DB
B4 LG
B6 WT/DB
B7 WT
B8 RD/DB
B9 RD
RR
LR
RF
LF
WHEEL SPEED SENSORS
NOTE: WHEEL SPEED SENSOR CABLES ARE TWISTED PAIRS
START TEST 10J.
INSPECT THE BULKHEAD CONNECTOR.
IS THE CONNECTOR CONDITION OK?
NO
REPAIR AS NECESSARY.*
YES
REPAIR THE OPEN B3 LG/DB WIRE BETWEEN THE 2-WAY CONN & THE CAB 60-WAY CONN.*
* PERFORM VERIFICATION TEST VER-1

91I10809 91H10832

Fig. 73: Anti-Lock Brake Test 10J – LR Wheel Speed Sensor Continuity Fault

TEST 10K: LR WHEEL SPEED SENSOR CONTINUITY FAULT

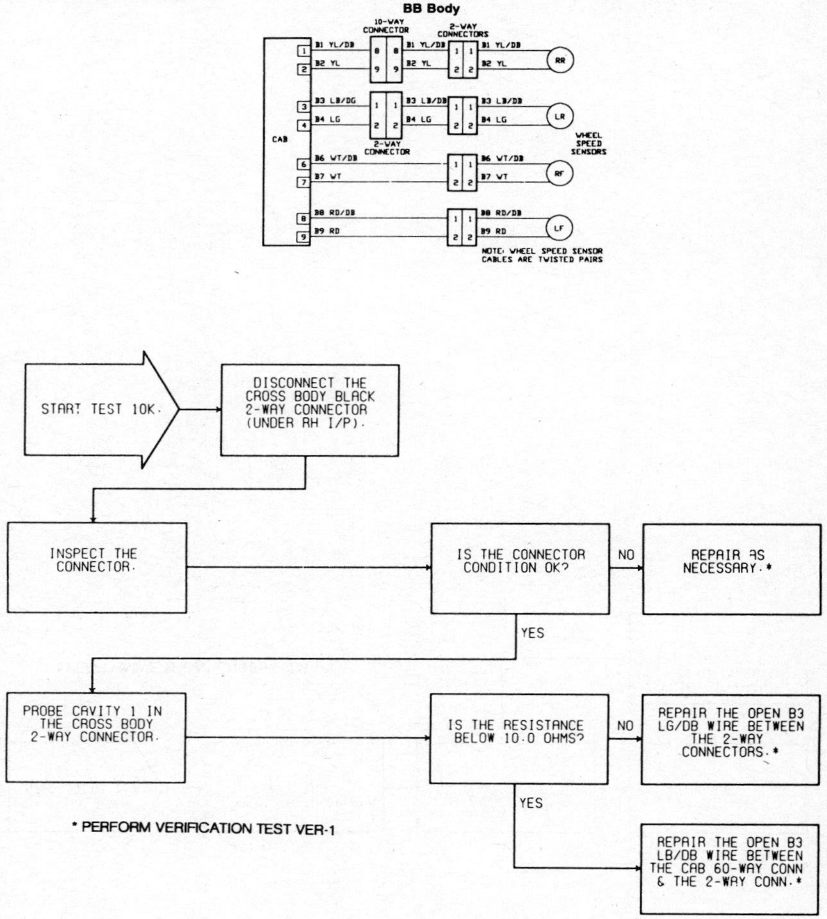
BB Body
10-WAY CONNECTOR
2-WAY CONNECTORS
2-WAY CONNECTOR
CAB
B1 YL/DB
B2 YL
B3 LB/DG
B3 LB/DB
B4 LG
B6 WT/DB
B7 WT
B8 RD/DB
B9 RD
RR
LR
RF
LF
WHEEL SPEED SENSORS
NOTE: WHEEL SPEED SENSOR CABLES ARE TWISTED PAIRS
START TEST 10K.
DISCONNECT THE CROSS BODY BLACK 2-WAY CONNECTOR (UNDER RH I/P).
INSPECT THE CONNECTOR.
IS THE CONNECTOR CONDITION OK?
NO
REPAIR AS NECESSARY.*
YES
PROBE CAVITY 1 IN THE CROSS BODY 2-WAY CONNECTOR.
IS THE RESISTANCE BELOW 10.0 OHMS?
NO
REPAIR THE OPEN B3 LG/DB WIRE BETWEEN THE 2-WAY CONNECTORS.*
YES
REPAIR THE OPEN B3 LB/DB WIRE BETWEEN THE CAB 60-WAY CONN & THE 2-WAY CONN.*
* PERFORM VERIFICATION TEST VER-1

91C10811 91I10833

Fig. 74: Anti-Lock Brake Test 10K – LR Wheel Speed Sensor Continuity Fault

TEST 10L: LR WHEEL SPEED SENSOR CONTINUITY FAULT

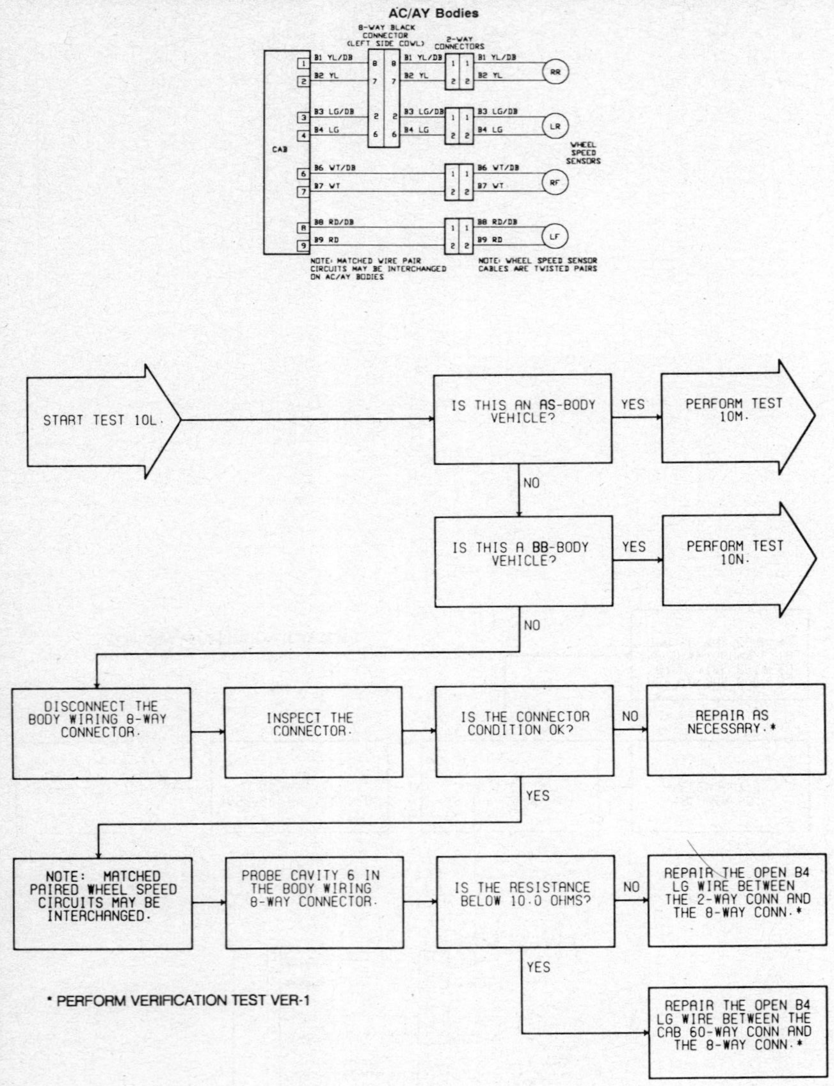
AC/AY Bodies
8-WAY BLACK CONNECTOR (LEFT SIDE COWL)
2-WAY CONNECTORS
CAB
B1 YL/DB
B2 YL
B3 LG/DB
B4 LG
B6 WT/DB
B7 WT
B8 RD/DB
B9 RD
RR
LR
RF
LF
WHEEL SPEED SENSORS
NOTE: MATCHED WIRE PAIR CIRCUITS MAY BE INTERCHANGED ON AC/AY BODIES
NOTE: WHEEL SPEED SENSOR CABLES ARE TWISTED PAIRS
START TEST 10L.
IS THIS AN AS-BODY VEHICLE?
YES
PERFORM TEST 10M.
NO
IS THIS A BB-BODY VEHICLE?
YES
PERFORM TEST 10N.
NO
DISCONNECT THE BODY WIRING 8-WAY CONNECTOR.
INSPECT THE CONNECTOR.
IS THE CONNECTOR CONDITION OK?
NO
REPAIR AS NECESSARY.*
YES
NOTE: MATCHED PAIRED WHEEL SPEED CIRCUITS MAY BE INTERCHANGED.
PROBE CAVITY 6 IN THE BODY WIRING 8-WAY CONNECTOR.
IS THE RESISTANCE BELOW 10.0 OHMS?
NO
REPAIR THE OPEN B4 LG WIRE BETWEEN THE 2-WAY CONN AND THE 8-WAY CONN.*
YES
REPAIR THE OPEN B4 LG WIRE BETWEEN THE CAB 60-WAY CONN AND THE 8-WAY CONN.*
* PERFORM VERIFICATION TEST VER-1

91G10807 91J10834

Fig. 75: Anti-Lock Brake Test 10L – LR Wheel Speed Sensor Continuity Fault

TEST 10M: LR WHEEL SPEED SENSOR CONTINUITY FAULT

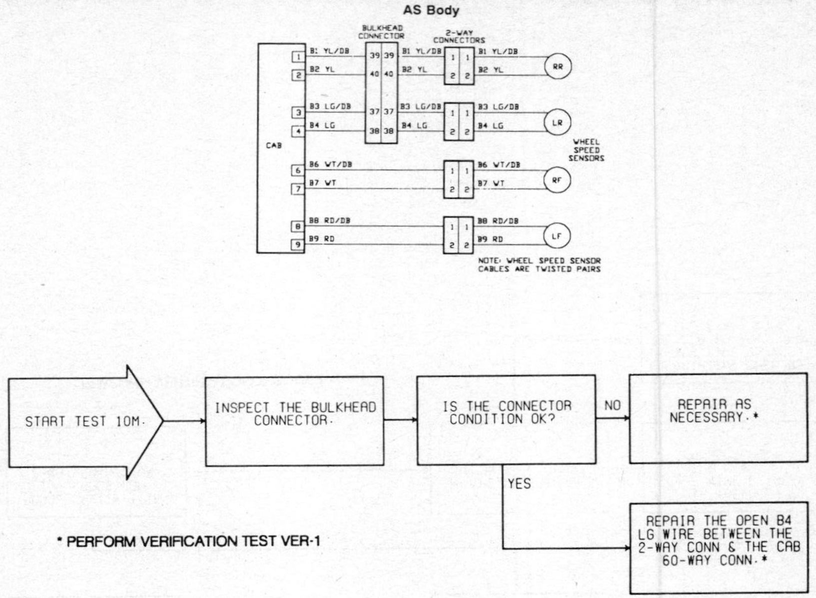
AS Body
BULKHEAD CONNECTOR
2-WAY CONNECTORS
CAB
B1 YL/DB
B2 YL
B3 LG/DB
B4 LG
B6 WT/DB
B7 WT
B8 RD/DB
B9 RD
RR
LR
RF
LF
WHEEL SPEED SENSORS
NOTE: WHEEL SPEED SENSOR CABLES ARE TWISTED PAIRS
START TEST 10M.
INSPECT THE BULKHEAD CONNECTOR.
IS THE CONNECTOR CONDITION OK?
NO
REPAIR AS NECESSARY.*
YES
REPAIR THE OPEN B4 LG WIRE BETWEEN THE 2-WAY CONN & THE CAB 60-WAY CONN.*
* PERFORM VERIFICATION TEST VER-1

91I10809 91A10835

Fig. 76: Anti-Lock Brake Test 10M – LR Wheel Speed Sensor Continuity Fault

TEST 10N: LR WHEEL SPEED SENSOR CONTINUITY FAULT

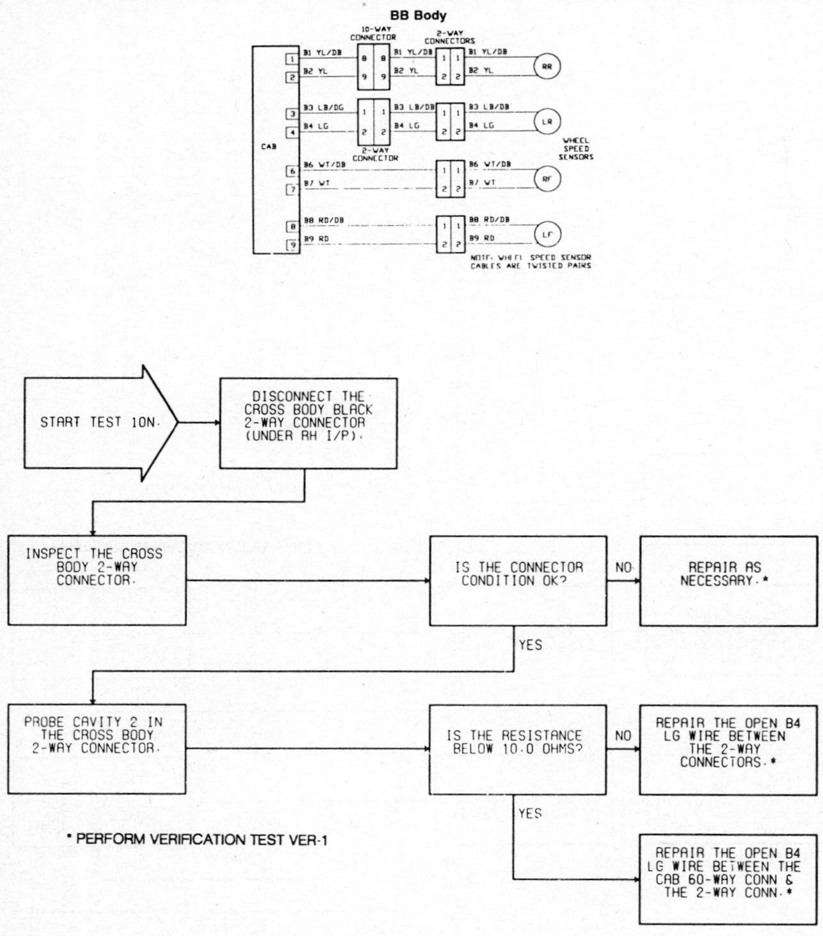
BB Body
10-WAY CONNECTOR
2-WAY CONNECTORS
2-WAY CONNECTOR
CAB
B1 YL/DB
B2 YL
B3 LB/DG
B3 LB/DB
B4 LG
B6 WT/DB
B7 WT
B8 RD/DB
B9 RD
RR
LR
RF
LF
WHEEL SPEED SENSORS
NOTE: WHEEL SPEED SENSOR CABLES ARE TWISTED PAIRS
START TEST 10N.
DISCONNECT THE CROSS BODY BLACK 2-WAY CONNECTOR (UNDER RH I/P).
INSPECT THE CROSS BODY 2-WAY CONNECTOR.
IS THE CONNECTOR CONDITION OK?
NO
REPAIR AS NECESSARY.*
YES
PROBE CAVITY 2 IN THE CROSS BODY 2-WAY CONNECTOR.
IS THE RESISTANCE BELOW 10.0 OHMS?
NO
REPAIR THE OPEN B4 LG WIRE BETWEEN THE 2-WAY CONNECTORS.*
YES
REPAIR THE OPEN B4 LG WIRE BETWEEN THE CAB 60-WAY CONN & THE 2-WAY CONN.*
* PERFORM VERIFICATION TEST VER-1

91C10811 91B10836

Fig. 77: Anti-Lock Brake Test 10N – LR Wheel Speed Sensor Continuity Fault

TEST 11A: RF WHEEL SPEED SENSOR CONTINUITY FAULT (1 OF 2)

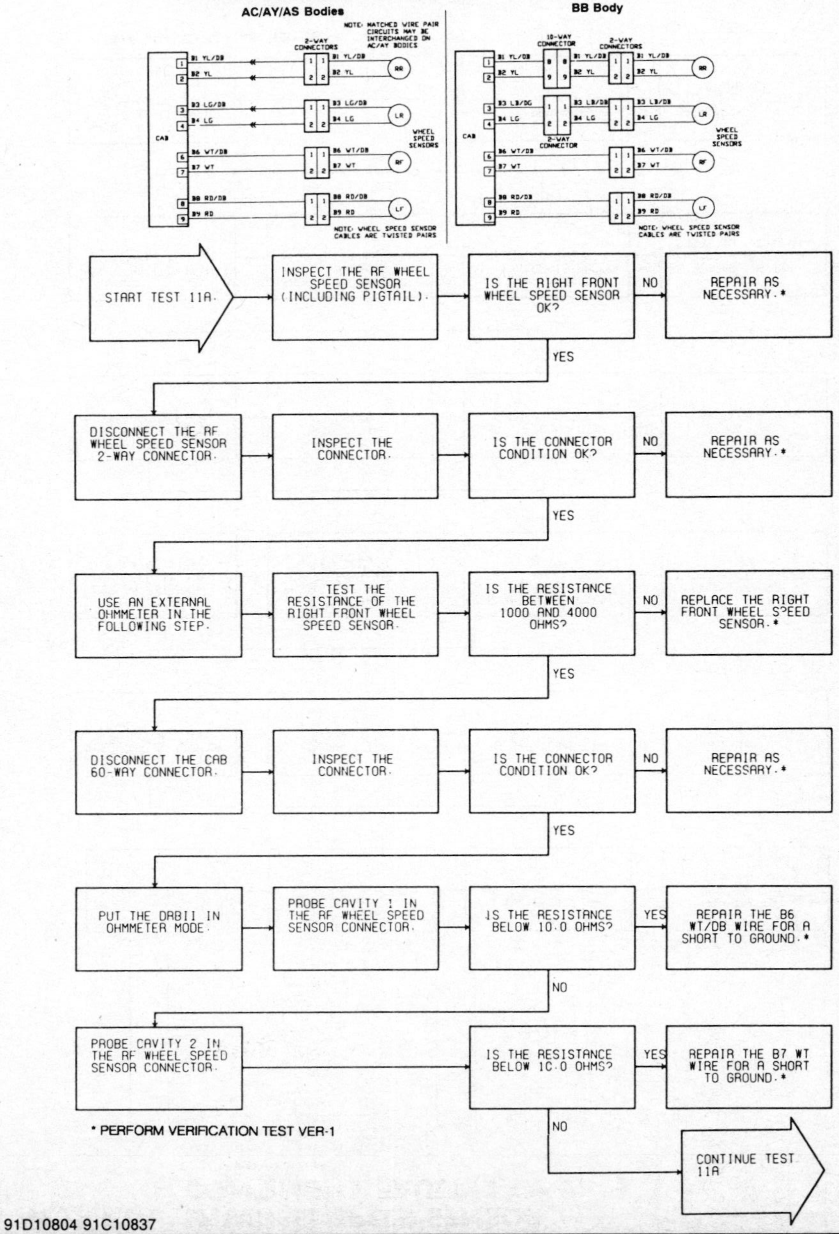
AC/AY/AS Bodies
BB Body
NOTE: MATCHED WIRE PAIR CIRCUITS MAY BE INTERCHANGED ON AC/AY BODIES
2-WAY CONNECTORS
10-WAY CONNECTOR
2-WAY CONNECTOR
CAB
B1 YL/DB
B2 YL
B3 LG/DB
B3 LB/DG
B4 LG
B6 WT/DB
B7 WT
B8 RD/DB
B9 RD
RR
LR
RF
LF
WHEEL SPEED SENSORS
NOTE: WHEEL SPEED SENSOR CABLES ARE TWISTED PAIRS
START TEST 11A.
INSPECT THE RF WHEEL SPEED SENSOR (INCLUDING PIGTAIL).
IS THE RIGHT FRONT WHEEL SPEED SENSOR OK?
NO
REPAIR AS NECESSARY.*
YES
DISCONNECT THE RF WHEEL SPEED SENSOR 2-WAY CONNECTOR.
INSPECT THE CONNECTOR.
IS THE CONNECTOR CONDITION OK?
NO
REPAIR AS NECESSARY.*
YES
USE AN EXTERNAL OHMMETER IN THE FOLLOWING STEP.
TEST THE RESISTANCE OF THE RIGHT FRONT WHEEL SPEED SENSOR.
IS THE RESISTANCE BETWEEN 1000 AND 4000 OHMS?
NO
REPLACE THE RIGHT FRONT WHEEL SPEED SENSOR.*
YES
DISCONNECT THE CAB 60-WAY CONNECTOR.
INSPECT THE CONNECTOR.
IS THE CONNECTOR CONDITION OK?
NO
REPAIR AS NECESSARY.*
YES
PUT THE DRBII IN OHMMETER MODE.
PROBE CAVITY 1 IN THE RF WHEEL SPEED SENSOR CONNECTOR.
IS THE RESISTANCE BELOW 10.0 OHMS?
YES
REPAIR THE B6 WT/DB WIRE FOR A SHORT TO GROUND.*
NO
PROBE CAVITY 2 IN THE RF WHEEL SPEED SENSOR CONNECTOR.
IS THE RESISTANCE BELOW 10.0 OHMS?
YES
REPAIR THE B7 WT WIRE FOR A SHORT TO GROUND.*
NO
CONTINUE TEST 11A
* PERFORM VERIFICATION TEST VER-1

91D10804 91C10837

Fig. 78: Anti-Lock Brake Test 11A – RF Wheel Speed Sensor Continuity Fault (1 of 2)

1991 BRAKES
Anti-Lock – Bendix-10 (Cont.)

TEST 11A: RF WHEEL SPEED SENSOR CONTINUITY FAULT (2 OF 2)

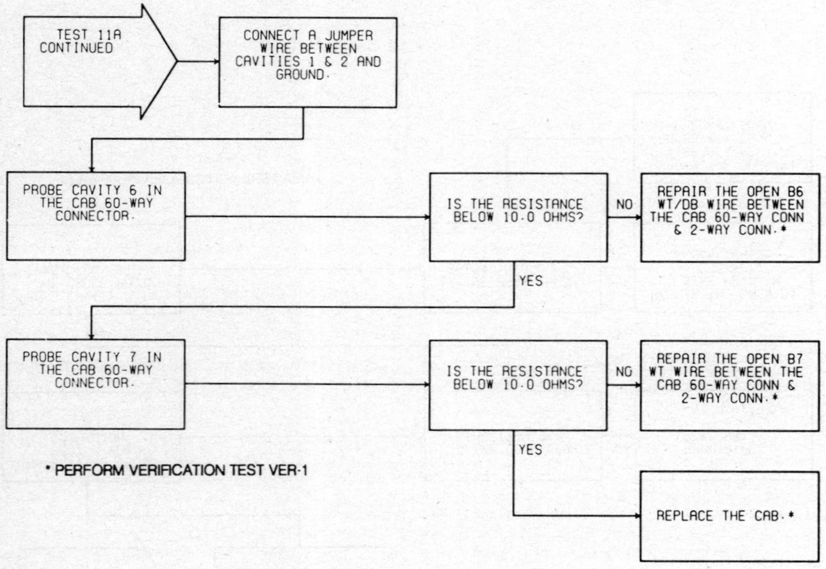
TEST 11A CONTINUED
CONNECT A JUMPER WIRE BETWEEN CAVITIES 1 & 2 AND GROUND.
PROBE CAVITY 6 IN THE CAB 60-WAY CONNECTOR.
IS THE RESISTANCE BELOW 10.0 OHMS?
NO
REPAIR THE OPEN B6 WT/DB WIRE BETWEEN THE CAB 60-WAY CONN & 2-WAY CONN.*
YES
PROBE CAVITY 7 IN THE CAB 60-WAY CONNECTOR.
IS THE RESISTANCE BELOW 10.0 OHMS?
NO
REPAIR THE OPEN B7 WT WIRE BETWEEN THE CAB 60-WAY CONN & 2-WAY CONN.*
YES
REPLACE THE CAB.*

* PERFORM VERIFICATION TEST VER-1

91D10838

Fig. 79: Anti-Lock Brake Test 11A – RF Wheel Speed Sensor Continuity Fault (2 of 2)

TEST 12A: LF WHEEL SPEED SENSOR CONTINUITY FAULT (1 OF 2)

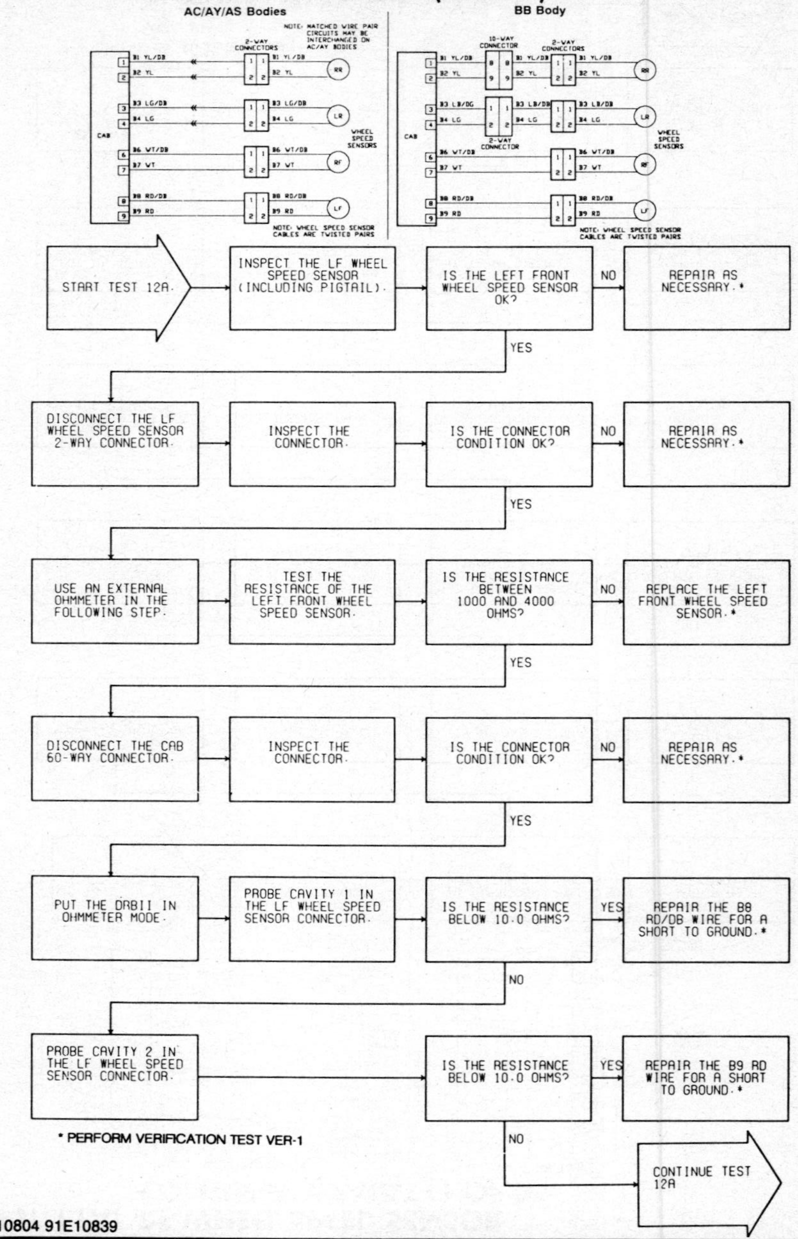
AC/AY/AS Bodies
BB Body
CAB
2-WAY CONNECTORS
10-WAY CONNECTOR
WHEEL SPEED SENSORS
NOTE: WHEEL SPEED SENSOR CABLES ARE TWISTED PAIRS
START TEST 12A.
INSPECT THE LF WHEEL SPEED SENSOR (INCLUDING PIGTAIL).
IS THE LEFT FRONT WHEEL SPEED SENSOR OK?
NO
REPAIR AS NECESSARY.*
YES
DISCONNECT THE LF WHEEL SPEED SENSOR 2-WAY CONNECTOR.
INSPECT THE CONNECTOR.
IS THE CONNECTOR CONDITION OK?
NO
REPAIR AS NECESSARY.*
YES
USE AN EXTERNAL OHMMETER IN THE FOLLOWING STEP.
TEST THE RESISTANCE OF THE LEFT FRONT WHEEL SPEED SENSOR.
IS THE RESISTANCE BETWEEN 1000 AND 4000 OHMS?
NO
REPLACE THE LEFT FRONT WHEEL SPEED SENSOR.*
YES
DISCONNECT THE CAB 60-WAY CONNECTOR.
INSPECT THE CONNECTOR.
IS THE CONNECTOR CONDITION OK?
NO
REPAIR AS NECESSARY.*
YES
PUT THE DRBII IN OHMMETER MODE.
PROBE CAVITY 1 IN THE LF WHEEL SPEED SENSOR CONNECTOR.
IS THE RESISTANCE BELOW 10.0 OHMS?
YES
REPAIR THE B8 RD/DB WIRE FOR A SHORT TO GROUND.*
NO
PROBE CAVITY 2 IN THE LF WHEEL SPEED SENSOR CONNECTOR.
IS THE RESISTANCE BELOW 10.0 OHMS?
YES
REPAIR THE B9 RD WIRE FOR A SHORT TO GROUND.*
NO
CONTINUE TEST 12A

* PERFORM VERIFICATION TEST VER-1

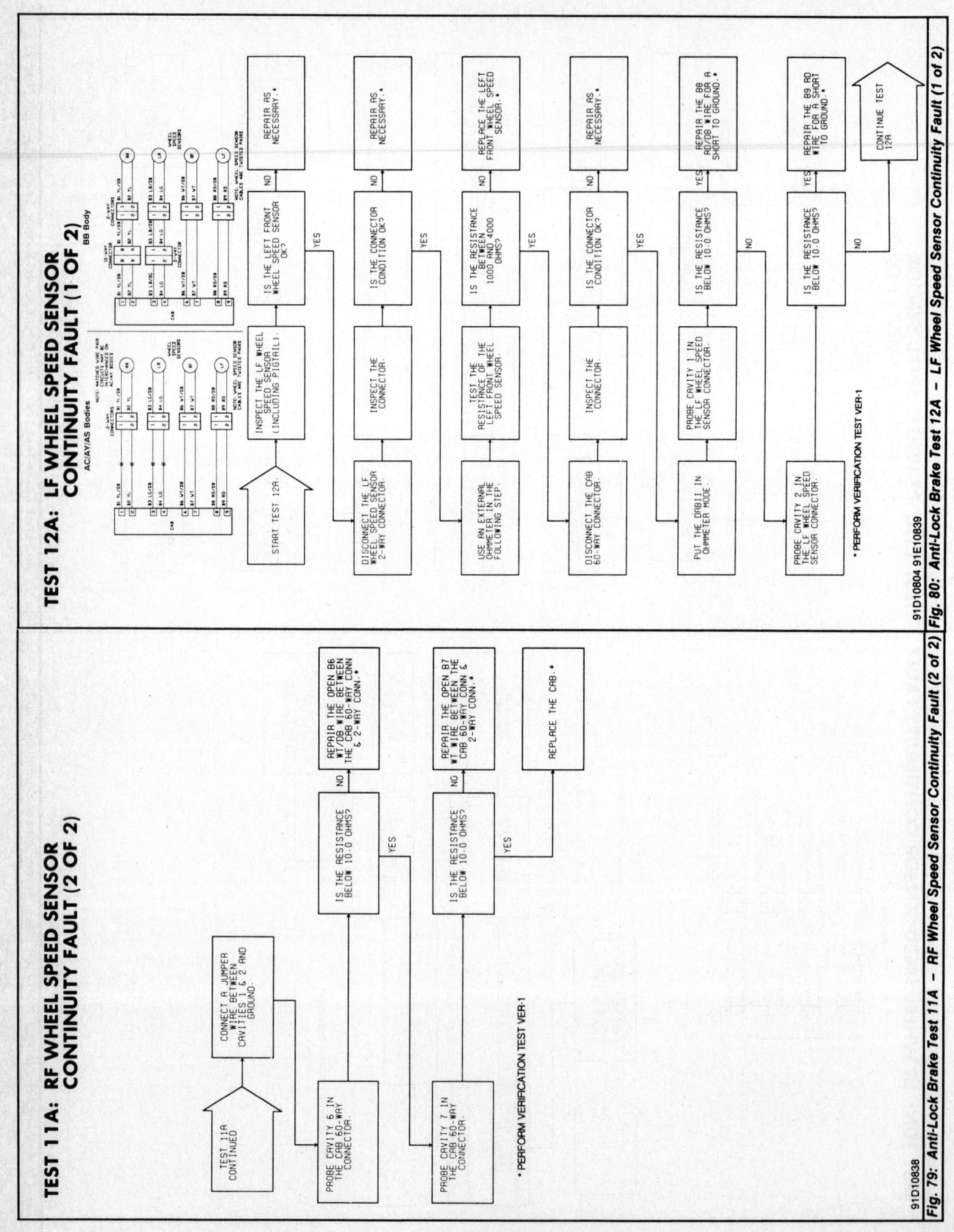

91D10804 91E10839

Fig. 80: Anti-Lock Brake Test 12A – LF Wheel Speed Sensor Continuity Fault (1 of 2)

TEST 12A: LF WHEEL SPEED SENSOR CONTINUITY FAULT (2 OF 2)

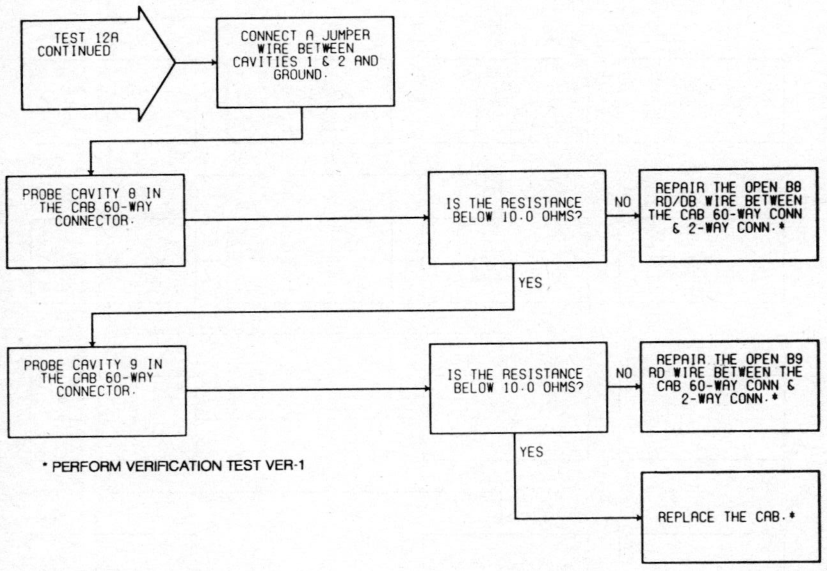
TEST 12A CONTINUED
CONNECT A JUMPER WIRE BETWEEN CAVITIES 1 & 2 AND GROUND.
PROBE CAVITY 8 IN THE CAB 60-WAY CONNECTOR.
IS THE RESISTANCE BELOW 10.0 OHMS?
NO
REPAIR THE OPEN B8 RD/DB WIRE BETWEEN THE CAB 60-WAY CONN & 2-WAY CONN.*
YES
PROBE CAVITY 9 IN THE CAB 60-WAY CONNECTOR.
IS THE RESISTANCE BELOW 10.0 OHMS?
NO
REPAIR THE OPEN B9 RD WIRE BETWEEN THE CAB 60-WAY CONN & 2-WAY CONN.*
YES
REPLACE THE CAB.*

* PERFORM VERIFICATION TEST VER-1

91H10840

Fig. 81: Anti-Lock Brake Test 12A – LF Wheel Speed Sensor Continuity Fault (2 of 2)

TEST 13A: RR WHEEL SPEED SENSOR FAULT

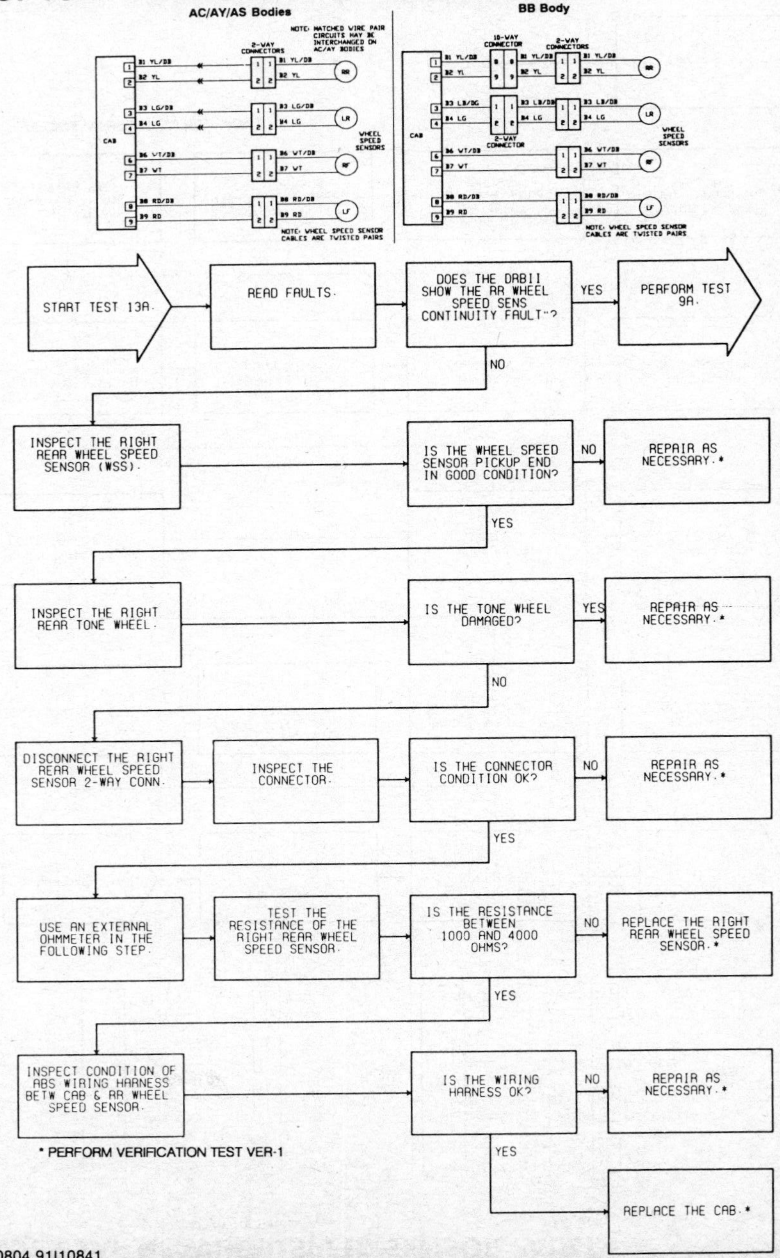
AC/AY/AS Bodies
BB Body
CAB
2-WAY CONNECTORS
10-WAY CONNECTOR
WHEEL SPEED SENSORS
NOTE: MATCHED WIRE PAIR CIRCUITS MAY BE INTERCHANGED ON AC/AY BODIES
NOTE: WHEEL SPEED SENSOR CABLES ARE TWISTED PAIRS
START TEST 13A.
READ FAULTS.
DOES THE DRBII SHOW THE RR WHEEL SPEED SENS CONTINUITY FAULT"?
YES
PERFORM TEST 9A.
NO
INSPECT THE RIGHT REAR WHEEL SPEED SENSOR (WSS).
IS THE WHEEL SPEED SENSOR PICKUP END IN GOOD CONDITION?
NO
REPAIR AS NECESSARY.*
YES
INSPECT THE RIGHT REAR TONE WHEEL.
IS THE TONE WHEEL DAMAGED?
YES
REPAIR AS NECESSARY.*
NO
DISCONNECT THE RIGHT REAR WHEEL SPEED SENSOR 2-WAY CONN.
INSPECT THE CONNECTOR.
IS THE CONNECTOR CONDITION OK?
NO
REPAIR AS NECESSARY.*
YES
USE AN EXTERNAL OHMMETER IN THE FOLLOWING STEP.
TEST THE RESISTANCE OF THE RIGHT REAR WHEEL SPEED SENSOR.
IS THE RESISTANCE BETWEEN 1000 AND 4000 OHMS?
NO
REPLACE THE RIGHT REAR WHEEL SPEED SENSOR.*
YES
INSPECT CONDITION OF ABS WIRING HARNESS BETW CAB & RR WHEEL SPEED SENSOR.
IS THE WIRING HARNESS OK?
NO
REPAIR AS NECESSARY.*
YES
REPLACE THE CAB.*

* PERFORM VERIFICATION TEST VER-1

91D10804 91I10841

Fig. 82: Anti-Lock Brake Test 13A – RR Wheel Speed Sensor Fault

1991 BRAKES
Anti-Lock – Bendix-10 (Cont.)

TEST 14A: LR WHEEL SPEED SENSOR FAULT

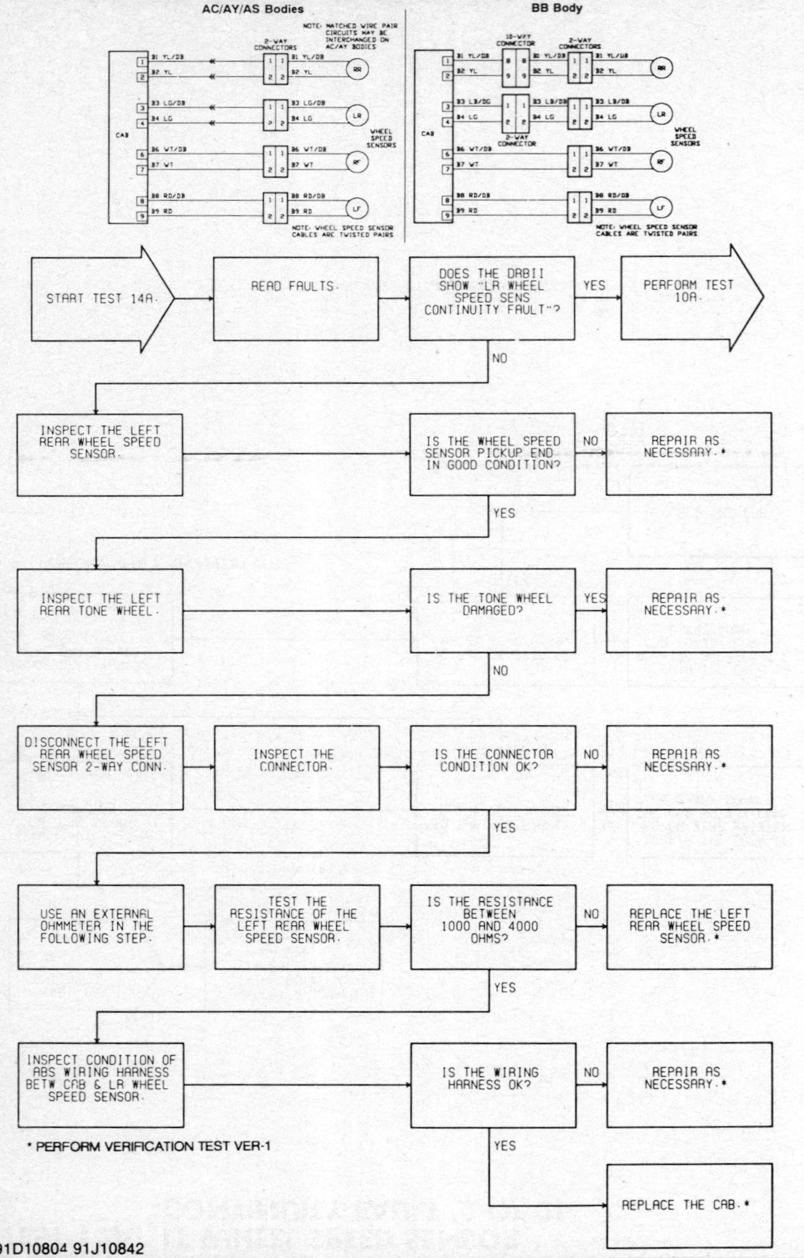
AC/AY/AS Bodies
BB Body
START TEST 14A.
READ FAULTS.
DOES THE DRBII SHOW "LR WHEEL SPEED SENS CONTINUITY FAULT"?
YES
PERFORM TEST 10A.
NO
INSPECT THE LEFT REAR WHEEL SPEED SENSOR.
IS THE WHEEL SPEED SENSOR PICKUP END IN GOOD CONDITION?
NO
REPAIR AS NECESSARY.*
YES
INSPECT THE LEFT REAR TONE WHEEL.
IS THE TONE WHEEL DAMAGED?
YES
REPAIR AS NECESSARY.*
NO
DISCONNECT THE LEFT REAR WHEEL SPEED SENSOR 2-WAY CONN.
INSPECT THE CONNECTOR.
IS THE CONNECTOR CONDITION OK?
NO
REPAIR AS NECESSARY.*
YES
USE AN EXTERNAL OHMMETER IN THE FOLLOWING STEP.
TEST THE RESISTANCE OF THE LEFT REAR WHEEL SPEED SENSOR.
IS THE RESISTANCE BETWEEN 1000 AND 4000 OHMS?
NO
REPLACE THE LEFT REAR WHEEL SPEED SENSOR.*
YES
INSPECT CONDITION OF ABS WIRING HARNESS BETW CAB & LR WHEEL SPEED SENSOR.
IS THE WIRING HARNESS OK?
NO
REPAIR AS NECESSARY.*
YES
REPLACE THE CAB.*
* PERFORM VERIFICATION TEST VER-1

91D10804 91J10842

Fig. 83: Anti-Lock Brake Test 14A – LR Wheel Speed Sensor Fault

TEST 15A: RF WHEEL SPEED SENSOR FAULT

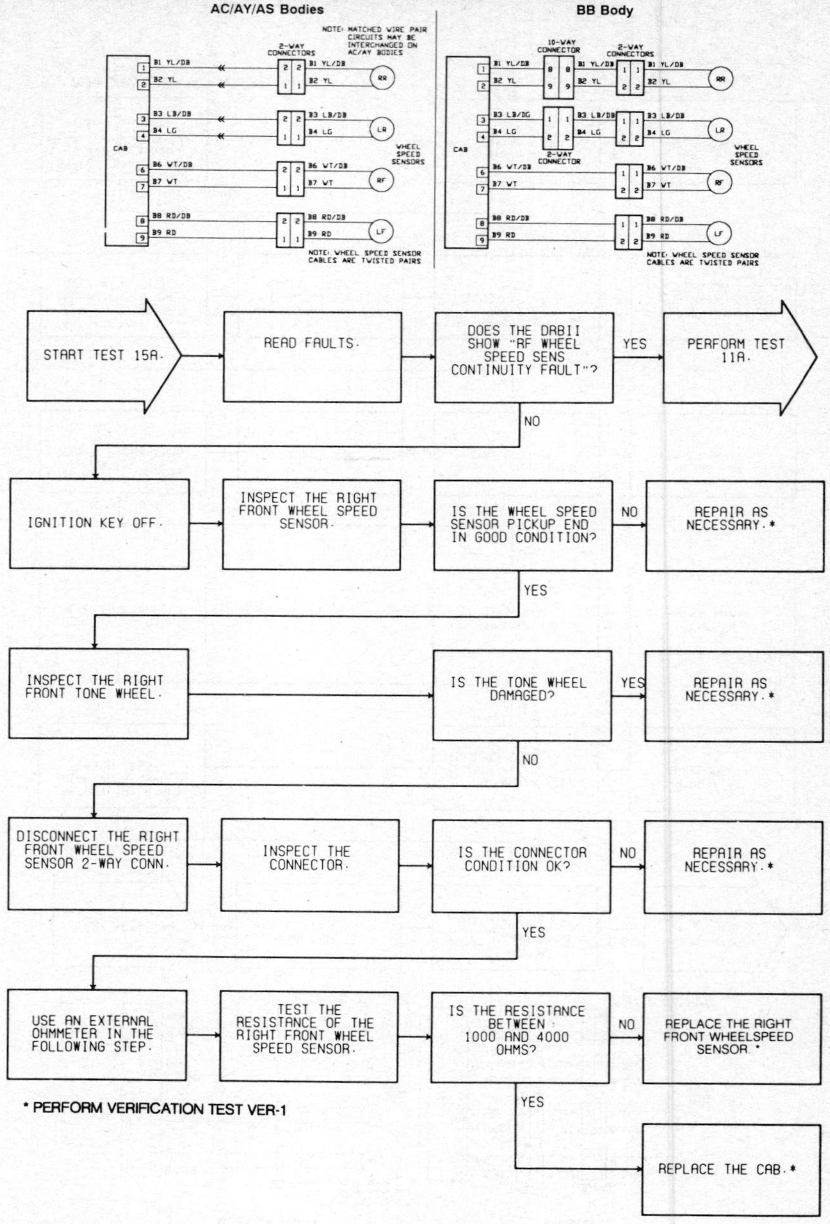
AC/AY/AS Bodies
BB Body
START TEST 15A.
READ FAULTS.
DOES THE DRBII SHOW "RF WHEEL SPEED SENS CONTINUITY FAULT"?
YES
PERFORM TEST 11A.
NO
IGNITION KEY OFF.
INSPECT THE RIGHT FRONT WHEEL SPEED SENSOR.
IS THE WHEEL SPEED SENSOR PICKUP END IN GOOD CONDITION?
NO
REPAIR AS NECESSARY.*
YES
INSPECT THE RIGHT FRONT TONE WHEEL.
IS THE TONE WHEEL DAMAGED?
YES
REPAIR AS NECESSARY.*
NO
DISCONNECT THE RIGHT FRONT WHEEL SPEED SENSOR 2-WAY CONN.
INSPECT THE CONNECTOR.
IS THE CONNECTOR CONDITION OK?
NO
REPAIR AS NECESSARY.*
YES
USE AN EXTERNAL OHMMETER IN THE FOLLOWING STEP.
TEST THE RESISTANCE OF THE RIGHT FRONT WHEEL SPEED SENSOR.
IS THE RESISTANCE BETWEEN 1000 AND 4000 OHMS?
NO
REPLACE THE RIGHT FRONT WHEELSPEED SENSOR.*
YES
REPLACE THE CAB.*
* PERFORM VERIFICATION TEST VER-1

91D10804 91A10843

Fig. 84: Anti-Lock Brake Test 15A – RF Wheel Speed Sensor Fault

1991 BRAKES
Anti-Lock – Bendix-10 (Cont.)

TEST 16A: LF WHEEL SPEED SENSOR FAULT

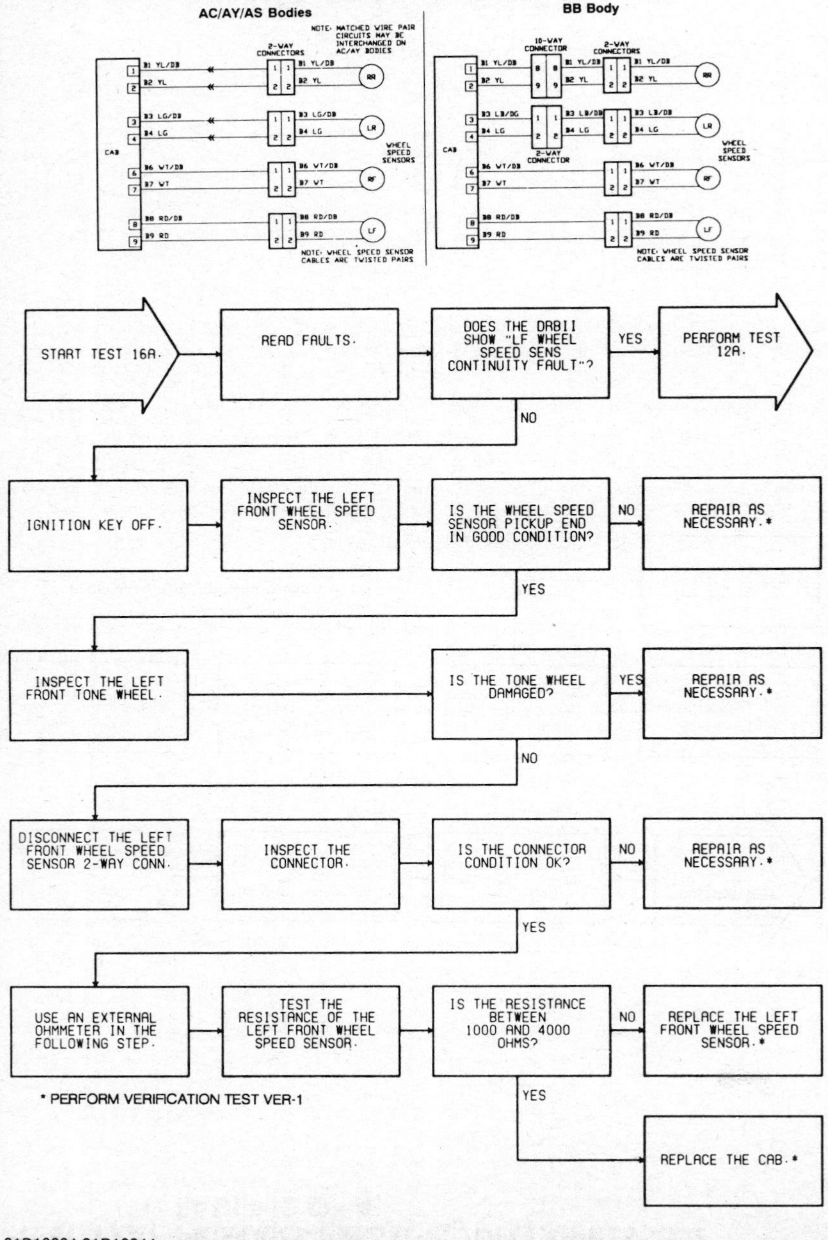
AC/AY/AS Bodies
BB Body
CAB
2-WAY CONNECTORS
10-WAY CONNECTOR
WHEEL SPEED SENSORS
NOTE: MATCHED WIRE PAIR CIRCUITS MAY BE INTERCHANGED ON AC/AY BODIES
NOTE: WHEEL SPEED SENSOR CABLES ARE TWISTED PAIRS
START TEST 16A.
READ FAULTS.
DOES THE DRBII SHOW "LF WHEEL SPEED SENS CONTINUITY FAULT"?
YES
PERFORM TEST 12A.
NO
IGNITION KEY OFF.
INSPECT THE LEFT FRONT WHEEL SPEED SENSOR.
IS THE WHEEL SPEED SENSOR PICKUP END IN GOOD CONDITION?
NO
REPAIR AS NECESSARY.*
YES
INSPECT THE LEFT FRONT TONE WHEEL.
IS THE TONE WHEEL DAMAGED?
YES
REPAIR AS NECESSARY.*
NO
DISCONNECT THE LEFT FRONT WHEEL SPEED SENSOR 2-WAY CONN.
INSPECT THE CONNECTOR.
IS THE CONNECTOR CONDITION OK?
NO
REPAIR AS NECESSARY.*
YES
USE AN EXTERNAL OHMMETER IN THE FOLLOWING STEP.
TEST THE RESISTANCE OF THE LEFT FRONT WHEEL SPEED SENSOR.
IS THE RESISTANCE BETWEEN 1000 AND 4000 OHMS?
NO
REPLACE THE LEFT FRONT WHEEL SPEED SENSOR.*
YES
REPLACE THE CAB.*
* PERFORM VERIFICATION TEST VER-1

91D10804 91B10844

Fig. 85: Anti-Lock Brake Test 16A – LF Wheel Speed Sensor Fault

TEST 17A: PRIMARY PRESSURE/DELTA PRESSURE FAULT (1 OF 4)

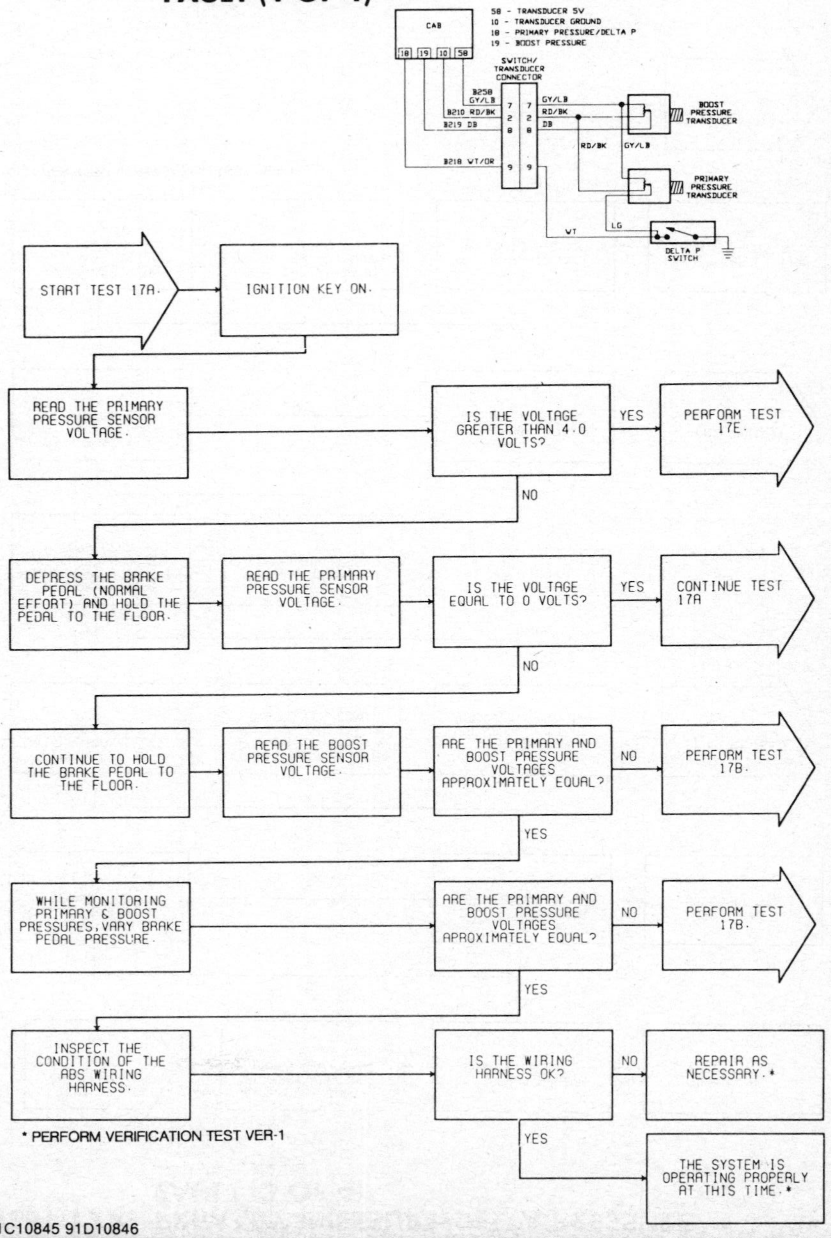
CAB
58 - TRANSDUCER 5V
10 - TRANSDUCER GROUND
18 - PRIMARY PRESSURE/DELTA P
19 - BOOST PRESSURE
SWITCH/ TRANSDUCER CONNECTOR
BOOST PRESSURE TRANSDUCER
PRIMARY PRESSURE TRANSDUCER
DELTA P SWITCH
START TEST 17A.
IGNITION KEY ON.
READ THE PRIMARY PRESSURE SENSOR VOLTAGE.
IS THE VOLTAGE GREATER THAN 4.0 VOLTS?
YES
PERFORM TEST 17E.
NO
DEPRESS THE BRAKE PEDAL (NORMAL EFFORT) AND HOLD THE PEDAL TO THE FLOOR.
READ THE PRIMARY PRESSURE SENSOR VOLTAGE.
IS THE VOLTAGE EQUAL TO 0 VOLTS?
YES
CONTINUE TEST 17A
NO
CONTINUE TO HOLD THE BRAKE PEDAL TO THE FLOOR.
READ THE BOOST PRESSURE SENSOR VOLTAGE.
ARE THE PRIMARY AND BOOST PRESSURE VOLTAGES APPROXIMATELY EQUAL?
NO
PERFORM TEST 17B.
YES
WHILE MONITORING PRIMARY & BOOST PRESSURES, VARY BRAKE PEDAL PRESSURE.
ARE THE PRIMARY AND BOOST PRESSURE VOLTAGES APROXIMATELY EQUAL?
NO
PERFORM TEST 17B.
YES
INSPECT THE CONDITION OF THE ABS WIRING HARNESS.
IS THE WIRING HARNESS OK?
NO
REPAIR AS NECESSARY.*
YES
THE SYSTEM IS OPERATING PROPERLY AT THIS TIME.*
* PERFORM VERIFICATION TEST VER-1

91C10845 91D10846

Fig. 86: Anti-Lock Brake Test 17A – Primary Pressure/Delta Pressure Fault (1 of 4)

TEST 17A: PRIMARY PRESSURE/DELTA PRESSURE FAULT (2 OF 4)

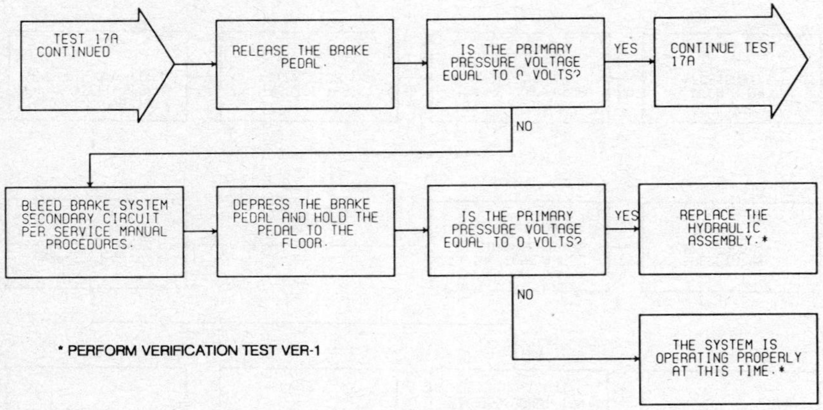
TEST 17A CONTINUED
RELEASE THE BRAKE PEDAL.
IS THE PRIMARY PRESSURE VOLTAGE EQUAL TO 0 VOLTS?
YES
CONTINUE TEST 17A
NO
BLEED BRAKE SYSTEM SECONDARY CIRCUIT PER SERVICE MANUAL PROCEDURES.
DEPRESS THE BRAKE PEDAL AND HOLD THE PEDAL TO THE FLOOR.
IS THE PRIMARY PRESSURE VOLTAGE EQUAL TO 0 VOLTS?
YES
REPLACE THE HYDRAULIC ASSEMBLY.*
NO
THE SYSTEM IS OPERATING PROPERLY AT THIS TIME.*

* PERFORM VERIFICATION TEST VER-1

91E10847

Fig. 87: Anti-Lock Brake Test 17A – Primary Pressure/Delta Pressure Fault (2 of 4)

TEST 17A: PRIMARY PRESSURE/DELTA PRESSURE FAULT (3 OF 4)

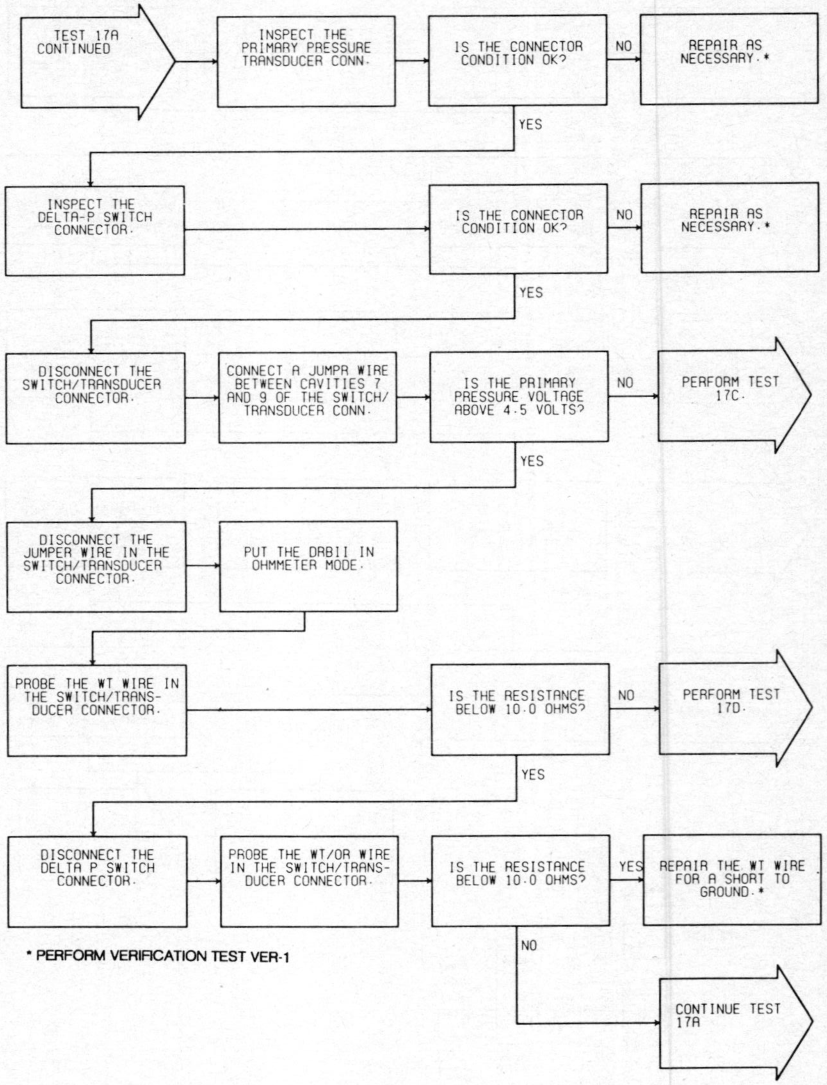
TEST 17A CONTINUED
INSPECT THE PRIMARY PRESSURE TRANSDUCER CONN.
IS THE CONNECTOR CONDITION OK?
NO
REPAIR AS NECESSARY.*
YES
INSPECT THE DELTA-P SWITCH CONNECTOR.
IS THE CONNECTOR CONDITION OK?
NO
REPAIR AS NECESSARY.*
YES
DISCONNECT THE SWITCH/TRANSDUCER CONNECTOR.
CONNECT A JUMPR WIRE BETWEEN CAVITIES 7 AND 9 OF THE SWITCH/TRANSDUCER CONN.
IS THE PRIMARY PRESSURE VOLTAGE ABOVE 4.5 VOLTS?
NO
PERFORM TEST 17C.
YES
DISCONNECT THE JUMPER WIRE IN THE SWITCH/TRANSDUCER CONNECTOR.
PUT THE DRBII IN OHMMETER MODE.
PROBE THE WT WIRE IN THE SWITCH/TRANS-DUCER CONNECTOR.
IS THE RESISTANCE BELOW 10.0 OHMS?
NO
PERFORM TEST 17D.
YES
DISCONNECT THE DELTA P SWITCH CONNECTOR.
PROBE THE WT/OR WIRE IN THE SWITCH/TRANS-DUCER CONNECTOR.
IS THE RESISTANCE BELOW 10.0 OHMS?
YES
REPAIR THE WT WIRE FOR A SHORT TO GROUND.*
NO
CONTINUE TEST 17A

* PERFORM VERIFICATION TEST VER-1

91F10848

Fig. 88: Anti-Lock Brake Test 17A – Primary Pressure/Delta Pressure Fault (3 of 4)

TEST 17A: PRIMARY PRESSURE/DELTA PRESSURE FAULT (4 OF 4)

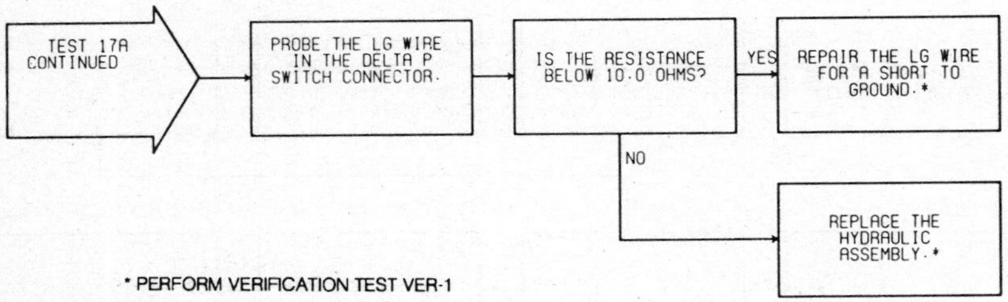
TEST 17A CONTINUED
PROBE THE LG WIRE IN THE DELTA P SWITCH CONNECTOR.
IS THE RESISTANCE BELOW 10.0 OHMS?
YES
REPAIR THE LG WIRE FOR A SHORT TO GROUND.*
NO
REPLACE THE HYDRAULIC ASSEMBLY.*

* PERFORM VERIFICATION TEST VER-1

91G10849

Fig. 89: Anti-Lock Brake Test 17A – Primary Pressure/Delta Pressure Fault (4 of 4)

TEST 17B: PRIMARY PRESSURE/DELTA PRESSURE FAULT

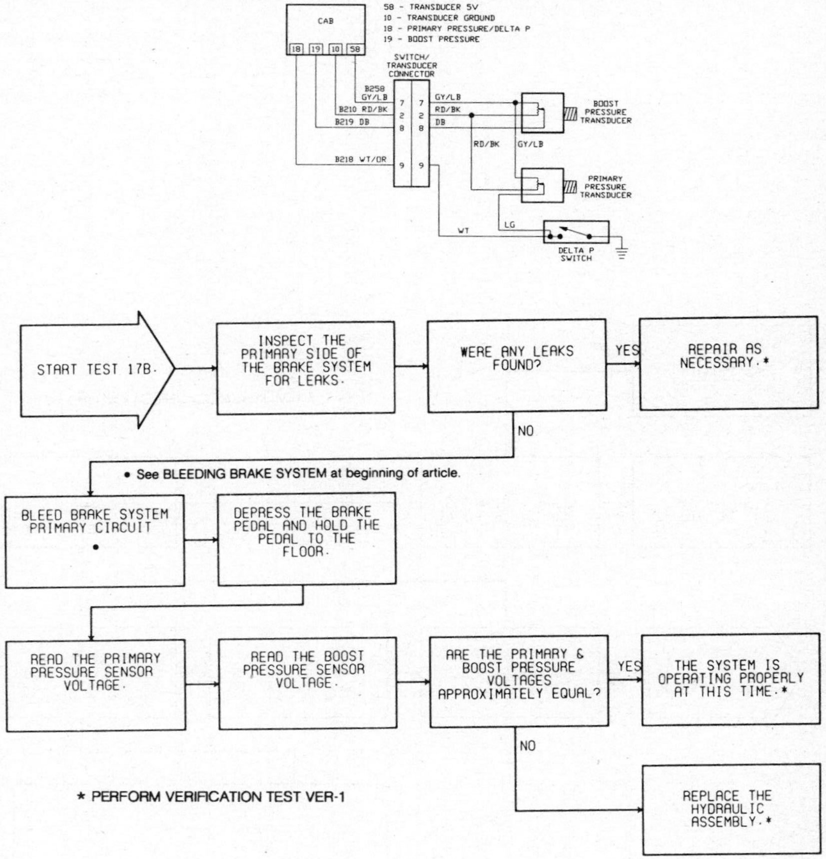
CAB
58 - TRANSDUCER 5V
10 - TRANSDUCER GROUND
18 - PRIMARY PRESSURE/DELTA P
19 - BOOST PRESSURE
18 19 10 58
SWITCH/ TRANSDUCER CONNECTOR
B258 GY/LB
B210 RD/BK
B219 DB
B218 WT/OR
GY/LB
RD/BK
DB
RD/BK
GY/LB
WT
LG
BOOST PRESSURE TRANSDUCER
PRIMARY PRESSURE TRANSDUCER
DELTA P SWITCH
START TEST 17B.
INSPECT THE PRIMARY SIDE OF THE BRAKE SYSTEM FOR LEAKS.
WERE ANY LEAKS FOUND?
YES
REPAIR AS NECESSARY.*
NO
BLEED BRAKE SYSTEM PRIMARY CIRCUIT •
DEPRESS THE BRAKE PEDAL AND HOLD THE PEDAL TO THE FLOOR.
READ THE PRIMARY PRESSURE SENSOR VOLTAGE.
READ THE BOOST PRESSURE SENSOR VOLTAGE.
ARE THE PRIMARY & BOOST PRESSURE VOLTAGES APPROXIMATELY EQUAL?
YES
THE SYSTEM IS OPERATING PROPERLY AT THIS TIME.*
NO
REPLACE THE HYDRAULIC ASSEMBLY.*

• See BLEEDING BRAKE SYSTEM at beginning of article.

* PERFORM VERIFICATION TEST VER-1

91C10845 91A10850

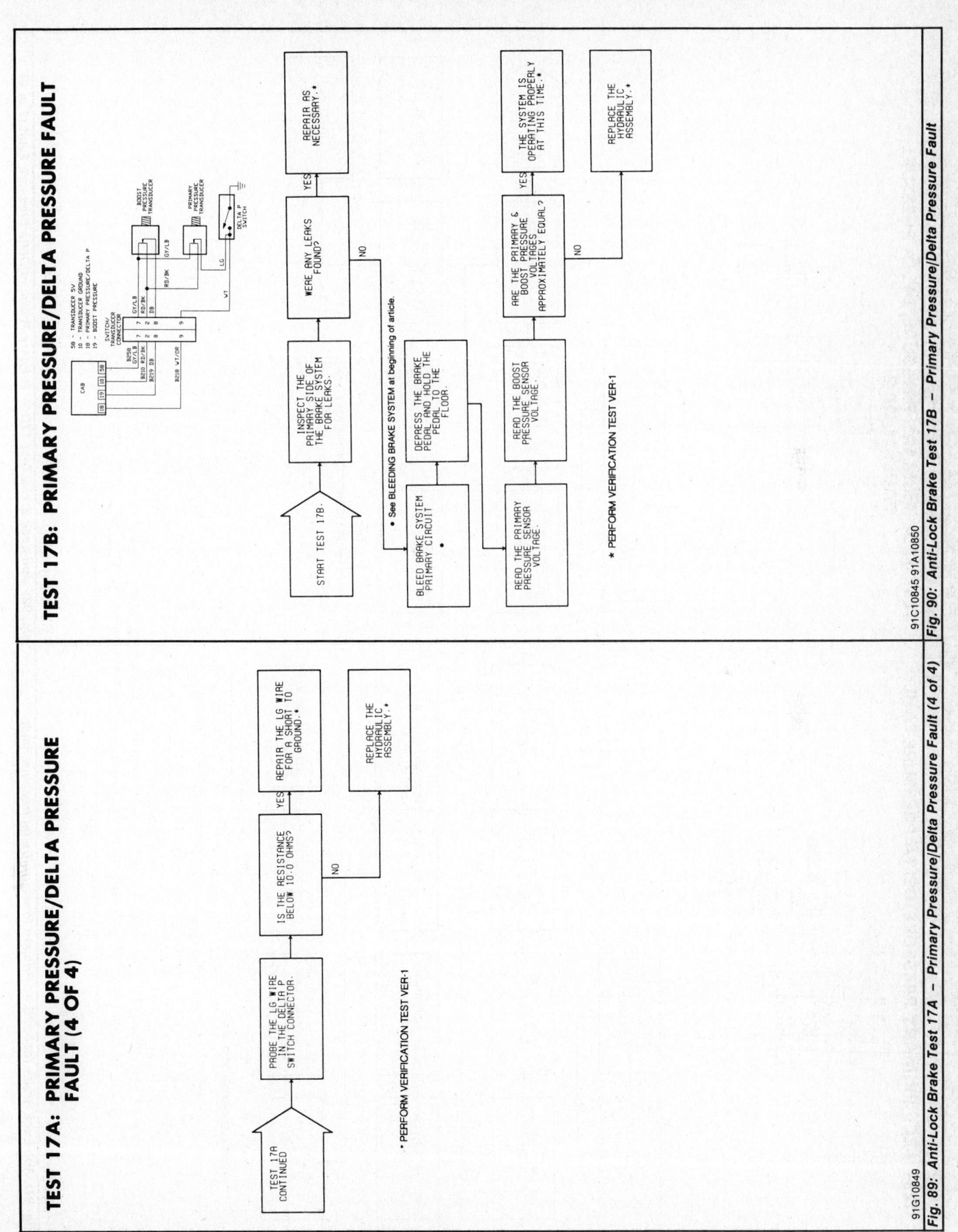

Fig. 90: Anti-Lock Brake Test 17B – Primary Pressure/Delta Pressure Fault

1991 BRAKES
Anti-Lock – Bendix-10 (Cont.)

TEST 17C: PRIMARY PRESSURE/DELTA PRESSURE FAULT

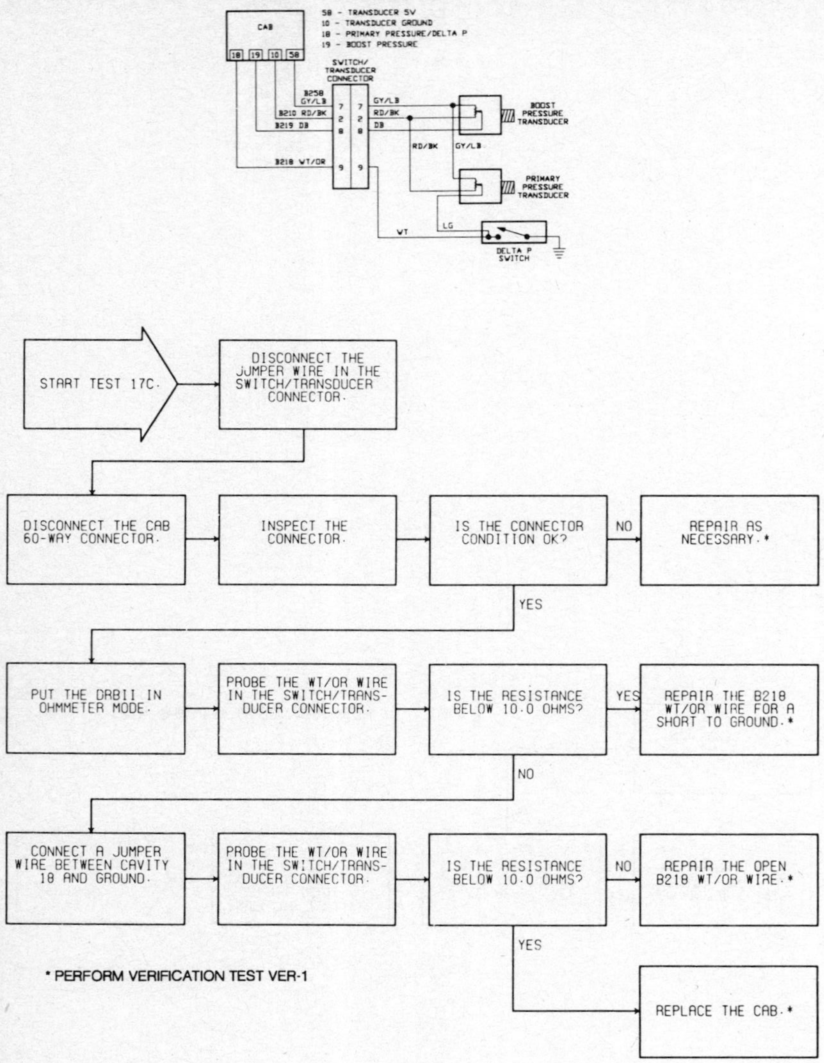
CAB
18
19
10
58
58 - TRANSDUCER 5V
10 - TRANSDUCER GROUND
18 - PRIMARY PRESSURE/DELTA P
19 - BOOST PRESSURE
SWITCH/TRANSDUCER CONNECTOR
B258 GY/LB
B210 RD/BK
B219 DB
B218 WT/OR
GY/LB
RD/BK
DB
BOOST PRESSURE TRANSDUCER
PRIMARY PRESSURE TRANSDUCER
WT
LG
DELTA P SWITCH
START TEST 17C.
DISCONNECT THE JUMPER WIRE IN THE SWITCH/TRANSDUCER CONNECTOR.
DISCONNECT THE CAB 60-WAY CONNECTOR.
INSPECT THE CONNECTOR.
IS THE CONNECTOR CONDITION OK?
NO
REPAIR AS NECESSARY.*
YES
PUT THE DRBII IN OHMMETER MODE.
PROBE THE WT/OR WIRE IN THE SWITCH/TRANS-DUCER CONNECTOR.
IS THE RESISTANCE BELOW 10.0 OHMS?
YES
REPAIR THE B218 WT/OR WIRE FOR A SHORT TO GROUND.*
NO
CONNECT A JUMPER WIRE BETWEEN CAVITY 18 AND GROUND.
PROBE THE WT/OR WIRE IN THE SWITCH/TRANS-DUCER CONNECTOR.
IS THE RESISTANCE BELOW 10.0 OHMS?
NO
REPAIR THE OPEN B218 WT/OR WIRE.*
YES
REPLACE THE CAB.*

* PERFORM VERIFICATION TEST VER-1

91C10845 91B10851

Fig. 91: Anti-Lock Brake Test 17C – Primary Pressure/Delta Pressure Fault

TEST 17D: PRIMARY PRESSURE/DELTA PRESSURE FAULT (1 OF 2)

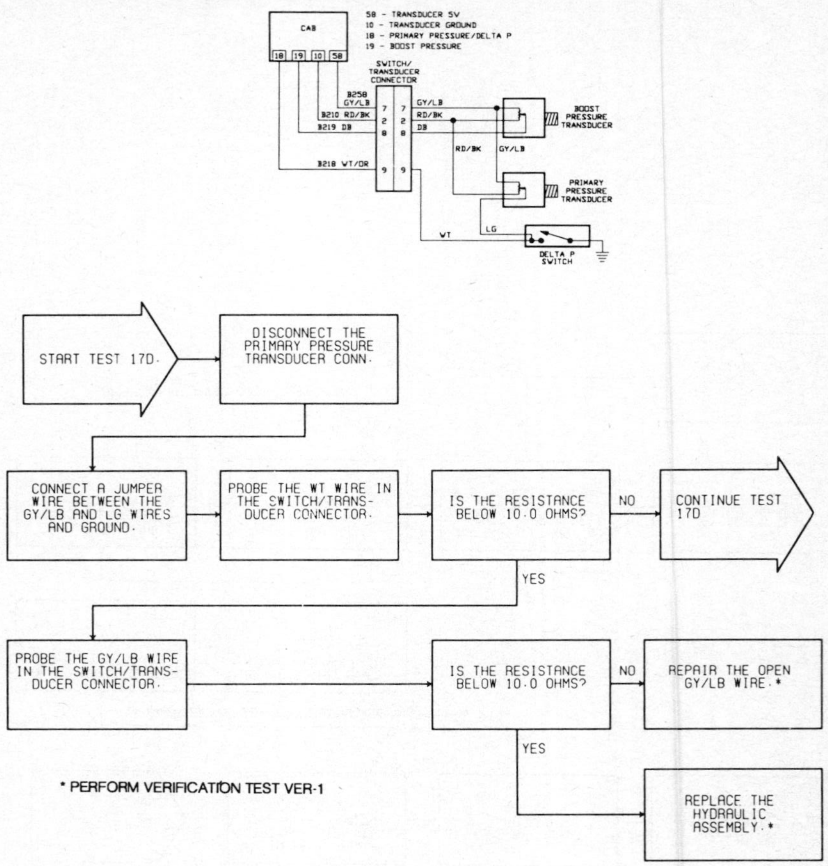
CAB
18
19
10
58
58 - TRANSDUCER 5V
10 - TRANSDUCER GROUND
18 - PRIMARY PRESSURE/DELTA P
19 - BOOST PRESSURE
SWITCH/TRANSDUCER CONNECTOR
B258 GY/LB
B210 RD/BK
B219 DB
B218 WT/OR
GY/LB
RD/BK
DB
BOOST PRESSURE TRANSDUCER
PRIMARY PRESSURE TRANSDUCER
WT
LG
DELTA P SWITCH
START TEST 17D.
DISCONNECT THE PRIMARY PRESSURE TRANSDUCER CONN.
CONNECT A JUMPER WIRE BETWEEN THE GY/LB AND LG WIRES AND GROUND.
PROBE THE WT WIRE IN THE SWITCH/TRANS-DUCER CONNECTOR.
IS THE RESISTANCE BELOW 10.0 OHMS?
NO
CONTINUE TEST 17D
YES
PROBE THE GY/LB WIRE IN THE SWITCH/TRANS-DUCER CONNECTOR.
IS THE RESISTANCE BELOW 10.0 OHMS?
NO
REPAIR THE OPEN GY/LB WIRE.*
YES
REPLACE THE HYDRAULIC ASSEMBLY.*

* PERFORM VERIFICATION TEST VER-1

91C10845 91C10852

Fig. 92: Anti-Lock Brake Test 17D – Primary Pressure/Delta Pressure Fault (1 of 2)

TEST 17D: PRIMARY PRESSURE/DELTA PRESSURE FAULT (2 OF 2)

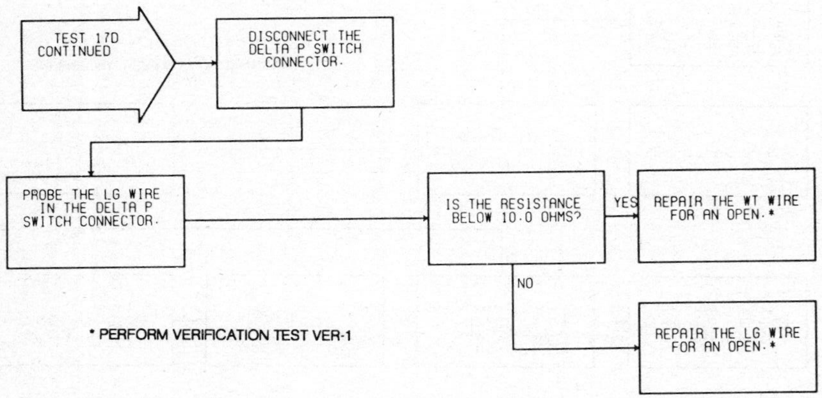
TEST 17D CONTINUED
DISCONNECT THE DELTA P SWITCH CONNECTOR.
PROBE THE LG WIRE IN THE DELTA P SWITCH CONNECTOR.
IS THE RESISTANCE BELOW 10.0 OHMS?
YES
REPAIR THE WT WIRE FOR AN OPEN.*
NO
REPAIR THE LG WIRE FOR AN OPEN.*

* PERFORM VERIFICATION TEST VER-1

91D10853

Fig. 93: Anti-Lock Brake Test 17D – Primary Pressure/Delta Pressure Fault (2 of 2)

TEST 17E: PRIMARY PRESSURE/DELTA PRESSURE FAULT

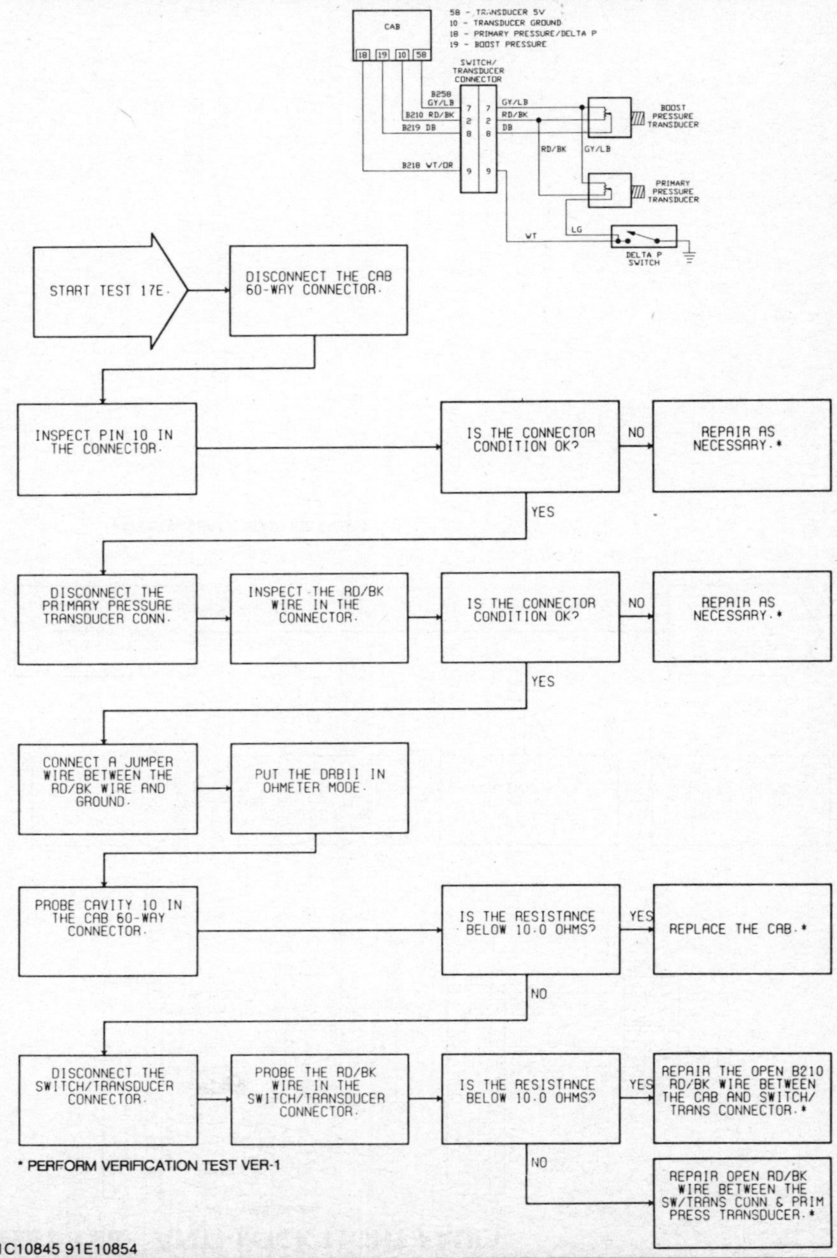
CAB
58 - TRANSDUCER 5V
10 - TRANSDUCER GROUND
18 - PRIMARY PRESSURE/DELTA P
19 - BOOST PRESSURE
SWITCH/ TRANSDUCER CONNECTOR
B258 GY/LB
B210 RD/BK
B219 DB
B218 WT/OR
GY/LB
RD/BK
DB
BOOST PRESSURE TRANSDUCER
PRIMARY PRESSURE TRANSDUCER
LG
WT
DELTA P SWITCH
START TEST 17E.
DISCONNECT THE CAB 60-WAY CONNECTOR.
INSPECT PIN 10 IN THE CONNECTOR.
IS THE CONNECTOR CONDITION OK?
NO
REPAIR AS NECESSARY.*
YES
DISCONNECT THE PRIMARY PRESSURE TRANSDUCER CONN.
INSPECT THE RD/BK WIRE IN THE CONNECTOR.
IS THE CONNECTOR CONDITION OK?
NO
REPAIR AS NECESSARY.*
YES
CONNECT A JUMPER WIRE BETWEEN THE RD/BK WIRE AND GROUND.
PUT THE DRBII IN OHMETER MODE.
PROBE CAVITY 10 IN THE CAB 60-WAY CONNECTOR.
IS THE RESISTANCE BELOW 10.0 OHMS?
YES
REPLACE THE CAB.*
NO
DISCONNECT THE SWITCH/TRANSDUCER CONNECTOR.
PROBE THE RD/BK WIRE IN THE SWITCH/TRANSDUCER CONNECTOR.
IS THE RESISTANCE BELOW 10.0 OHMS?
YES
REPAIR THE OPEN B210 RD/BK WIRE BETWEEN THE CAB AND SWITCH/ TRANS CONNECTOR.*
NO
REPAIR OPEN RD/BK WIRE BETWEEN THE SW/TRANS CONN & PRIM PRESS TRANSDUCER.*

* PERFORM VERIFICATION TEST VER-1

91C10845 91E10854

Fig. 94: Anti-Lock Brake Test 17E – Primary Pressure/Delta Pressure Fault

1991 BRAKES
Anti-Lock – Bendix-10 (Cont.)

TEST 18A: ANTI-LOCK LIGHT FAULT

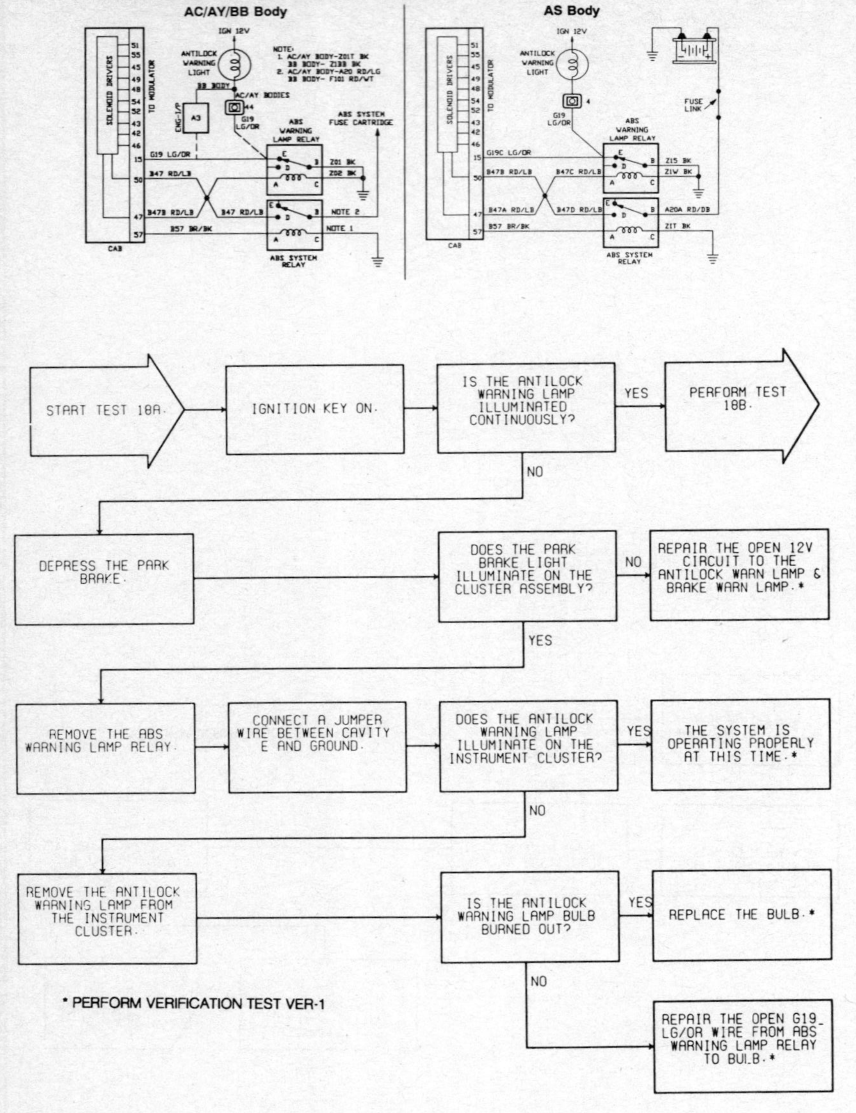
AC/AY/BB Body
AS Body
START TEST 18A.
IGNITION KEY ON.
IS THE ANTILOCK WARNING LAMP ILLUMINATED CONTINUOUSLY?
YES
PERFORM TEST 18B.
NO
DEPRESS THE PARK BRAKE.
DOES THE PARK BRAKE LIGHT ILLUMINATE ON THE CLUSTER ASSEMBLY?
NO
REPAIR THE OPEN 12V CIRCUIT TO THE ANTILOCK WARN LAMP & BRAKE WARN LAMP.*
YES
REMOVE THE ABS WARNING LAMP RELAY.
CONNECT A JUMPER WIRE BETWEEN CAVITY E AND GROUND.
DOES THE ANTILOCK WARNING LAMP ILLUMINATE ON THE INSTRUMENT CLUSTER?
YES
THE SYSTEM IS OPERATING PROPERLY AT THIS TIME.*
NO
REMOVE THE ANTILOCK WARNING LAMP FROM THE INSTRUMENT CLUSTER.
IS THE ANTILOCK WARNING LAMP BULB BURNED OUT?
YES
REPLACE THE BULB.*
NO
REPAIR THE OPEN G19 LG/OR WIRE FROM ABS WARNING LAMP RELAY TO BULB.*
* PERFORM VERIFICATION TEST VER-1

91D09182 91F10855

Fig. 95: Anti-Lock Brake Test 18A – ANTI-LOCK Light Fault

TEST 18B: ANTI-LOCK LIGHT FAULT

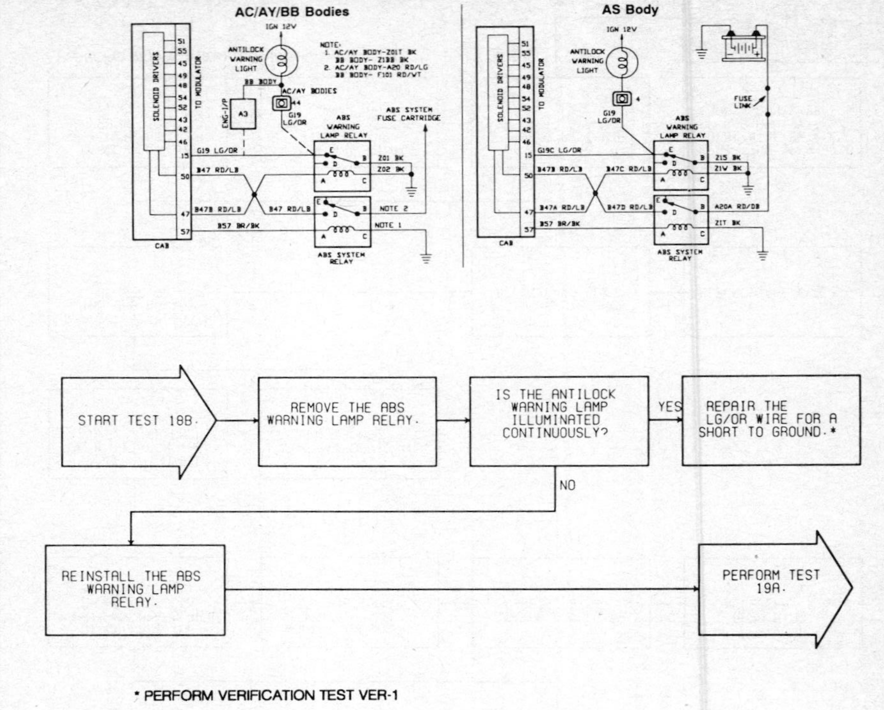
AC/AY/BB Bodies
AS Body
START TEST 18B.
REMOVE THE ABS WARNING LAMP RELAY.
IS THE ANTILOCK WARNING LAMP ILLUMINATED CONTINUOUSLY?
YES
REPAIR THE LG/OR WIRE FOR A SHORT TO GROUND.*
NO
REINSTALL THE ABS WARNING LAMP RELAY.
PERFORM TEST 19A.
* PERFORM VERIFICATION TEST VER-1

91D09182 91G10856

Fig. 96: Anti-Lock Brake Test 18B – ANTI-LOCK Light Fault

TEST 19A: ANTI-LOCK LIGHT RELAY FAULT (1 OF 2)

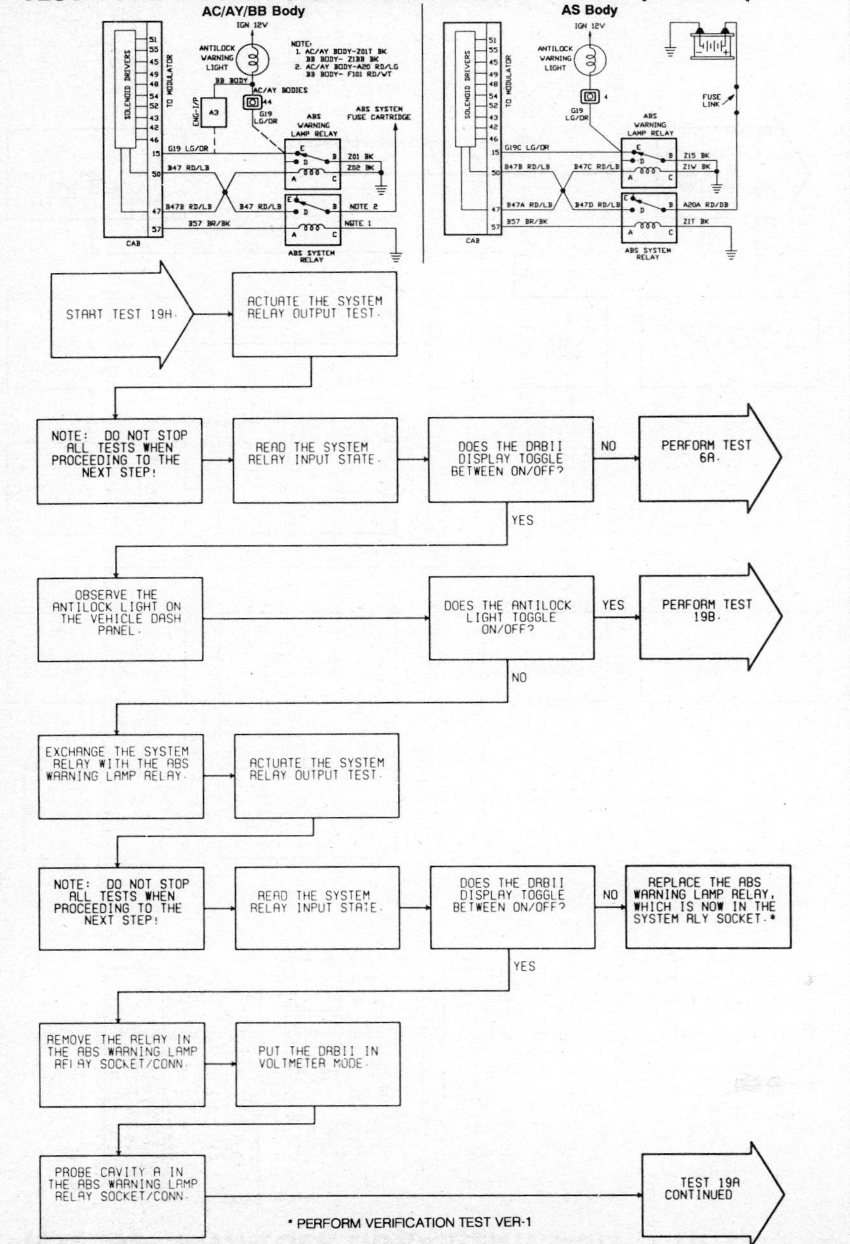
AC/AY/BB Body
AS Body
SOLENOID DRIVERS
TO MODULATOR
CAB
ANTILOCK WARNING LIGHT
IGN 12V
ABS WARNING LAMP RELAY
ABS SYSTEM RELAY
ABS SYSTEM FUSE CARTRIDGE
FUSE LINK
NOTE:
1. AC/AY BODY-Z01T BK
BB BODY- Z1BB BK
2. AC/AY BODY-A20 RD/LG
BB BODY- F101 RD/WT
START TEST 19H.
ACTUATE THE SYSTEM RELAY OUTPUT TEST.
NOTE: DO NOT STOP ALL TESTS WHEN PROCEEDING TO THE NEXT STEP!
READ THE SYSTEM RELAY INPUT STATE.
DOES THE DRBII DISPLAY TOGGLE BETWEEN ON/OFF?
NO
PERFORM TEST 6A.
YES
OBSERVE THE ANTILOCK LIGHT ON THE VEHICLE DASH PANEL.
DOES THE ANTILOCK LIGHT TOGGLE ON/OFF?
YES
PERFORM TEST 19B.
NO
EXCHANGE THE SYSTEM RELAY WITH THE ABS WARNING LAMP RELAY.
ACTUATE THE SYSTEM RELAY OUTPUT TEST.
NOTE: DO NOT STOP ALL TESTS WHEN PROCEEDING TO THE NEXT STEP!
READ THE SYSTEM RELAY INPUT STATE.
DOES THE DRBII DISPLAY TOGGLE BETWEEN ON/OFF?
NO
REPLACE THE ABS WARNING LAMP RELAY, WHICH IS NOW IN THE SYSTEM RLY SOCKET.*
YES
REMOVE THE RELAY IN THE ABS WARNING LAMP RELAY SOCKET/CONN.
PUT THE DRBII IN VOLTMETER MODE.
PROBE CAVITY A IN THE ABS WARNING LAMP RELAY SOCKET/CONN.
TEST 19A CONTINUED
* PERFORM VERIFICATION TEST VER-1

91D09182 91H10857

Fig. 97: Anti-Lock Brake Test 19A – ANTI-LOCK Light Relay Fault (1 of 2)

TEST 19A: ANTI-LOCK LIGHT RELAY FAULT (2 OF 2)

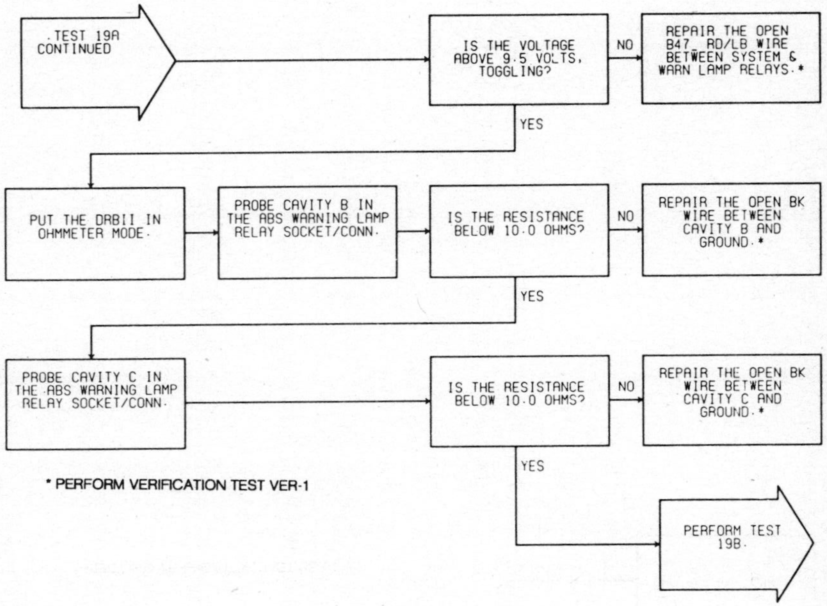
TEST 19A CONTINUED
IS THE VOLTAGE ABOVE 9.5 VOLTS, TOGGLING?
NO
REPAIR THE OPEN B47 RD/LB WIRE BETWEEN SYSTEM & WARN LAMP RELAYS.*
YES
PUT THE DRBII IN OHMMETER MODE.
PROBE CAVITY B IN THE ABS WARNING LAMP RELAY SOCKET/CONN.
IS THE RESISTANCE BELOW 10.0 OHMS?
NO
REPAIR THE OPEN BK WIRE BETWEEN CAVITY B AND GROUND.*
YES
PROBE CAVITY C IN THE ABS WARNING LAMP RELAY SOCKET/CONN.
IS THE RESISTANCE BELOW 10.0 OHMS?
NO
REPAIR THE OPEN BK WIRE BETWEEN CAVITY C AND GROUND.*
YES
PERFORM TEST 19B.
* PERFORM VERIFICATION TEST VER-1

91I10858

Fig. 98: Anti-Lock Brake Test 19A – ANTI-LOCK Light Relay Fault (2 of 2)

1991 BRAKES
Anti-Lock – Bendix-10 (Cont.)

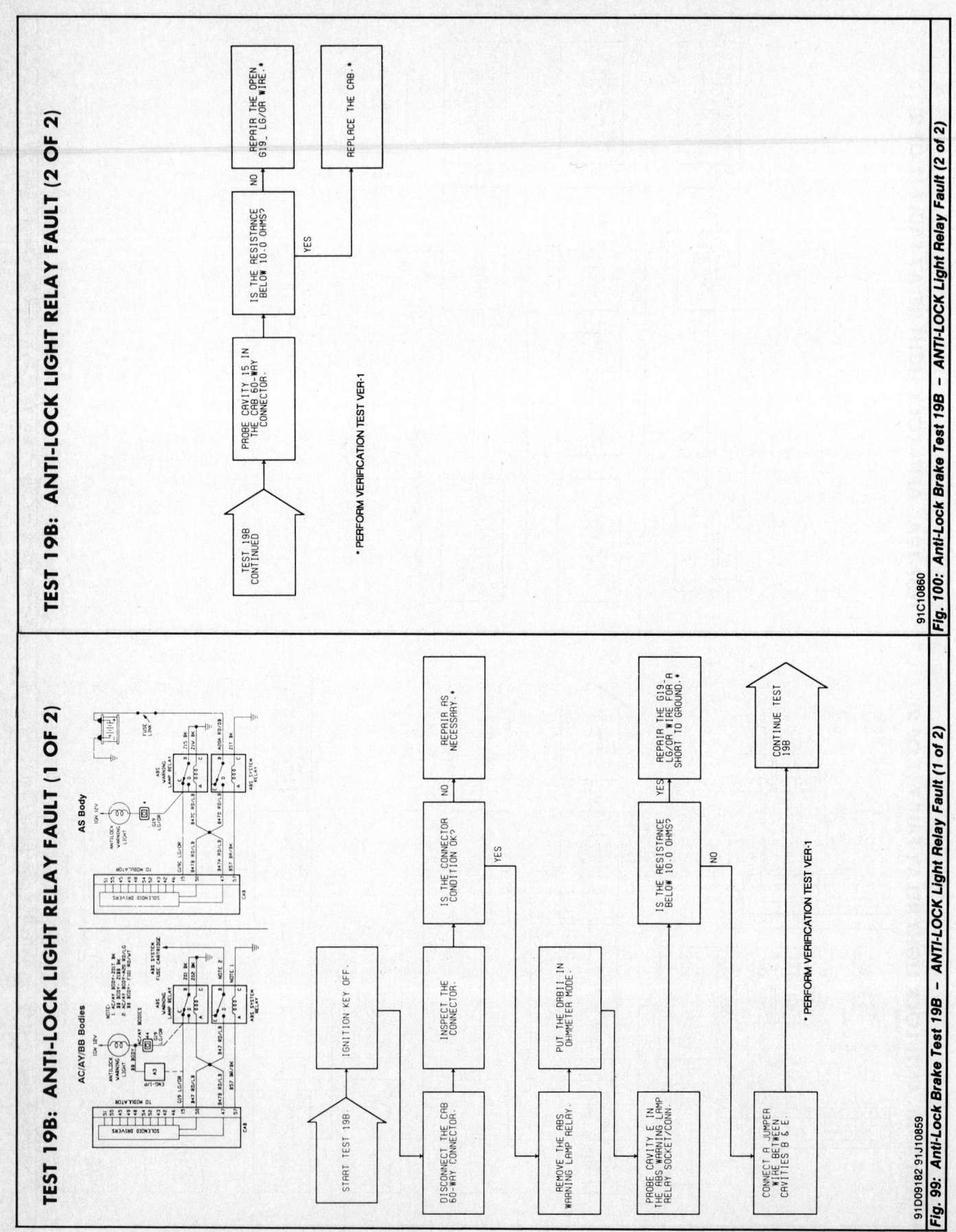

TEST 19B: ANTI-LOCK LIGHT RELAY FAULT (1 OF 2)

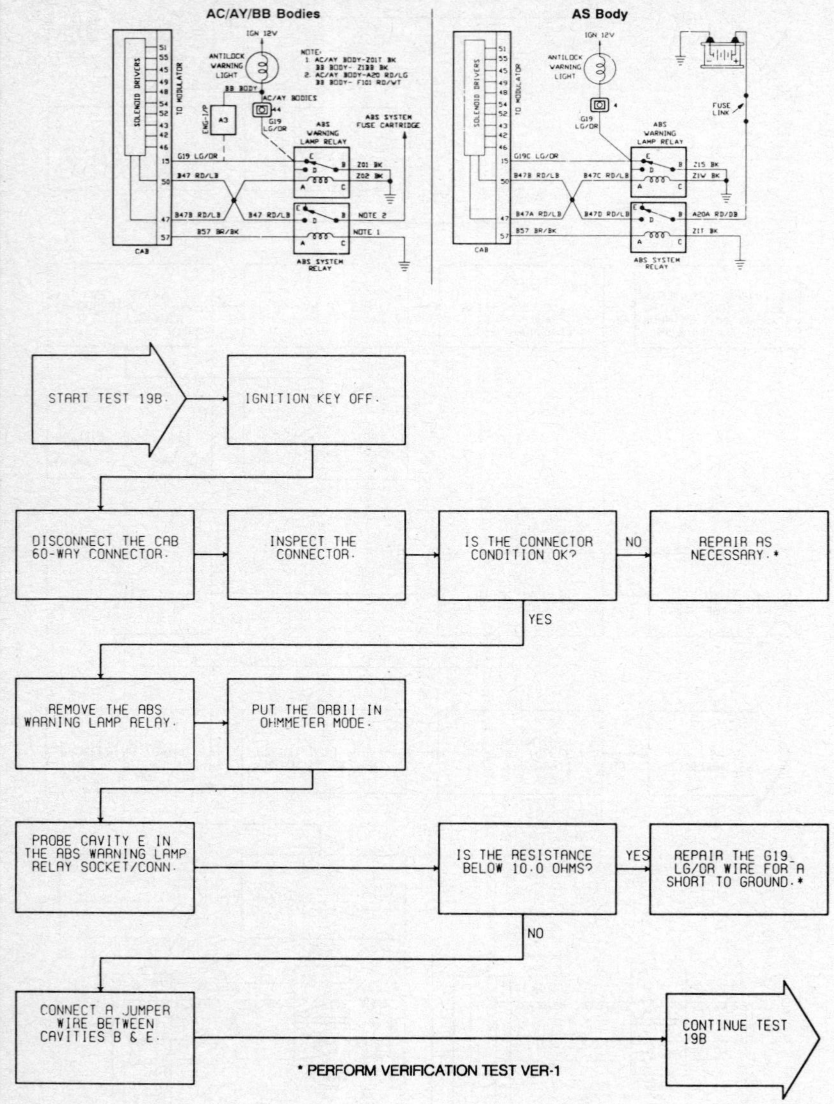
AC/AY/BB Bodies
AS Body
START TEST 19B.
IGNITION KEY OFF.
DISCONNECT THE CAB 60-WAY CONNECTOR.
INSPECT THE CONNECTOR.
IS THE CONNECTOR CONDITION OK?
NO
REPAIR AS NECESSARY.*
YES
REMOVE THE ABS WARNING LAMP RELAY.
PUT THE DRBII IN OHMMETER MODE.
PROBE CAVITY E IN THE ABS WARNING LAMP RELAY SOCKET/CONN.
IS THE RESISTANCE BELOW 10.0 OHMS?
YES
REPAIR THE G19_ LG/OR WIRE FOR A SHORT TO GROUND.*
NO
CONNECT A JUMPER WIRE BETWEEN CAVITIES B & E.
CONTINUE TEST 19B
* PERFORM VERIFICATION TEST VER-1

91D09182 91J10859

Fig. 99: Anti-Lock Brake Test 19B – ANTI-LOCK Light Relay Fault (1 of 2)

TEST 19B: ANTI-LOCK LIGHT RELAY FAULT (2 OF 2)

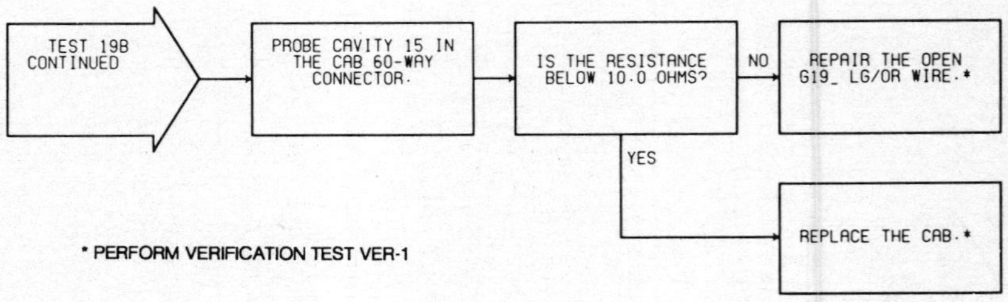
TEST 19B CONTINUED
PROBE CAVITY 15 IN THE CAB 60-WAY CONNECTOR.
IS THE RESISTANCE BELOW 10.0 OHMS?
NO
REPAIR THE OPEN G19_ LG/OR WIRE.*
YES
REPLACE THE CAB.*
* PERFORM VERIFICATION TEST VER-1

91C10860

Fig. 100: Anti-Lock Brake Test 19B – ANTI-LOCK Light Relay Fault (2 of 2)

TEST 20A: EXCESS DECAY FAULT (1 OF 2)

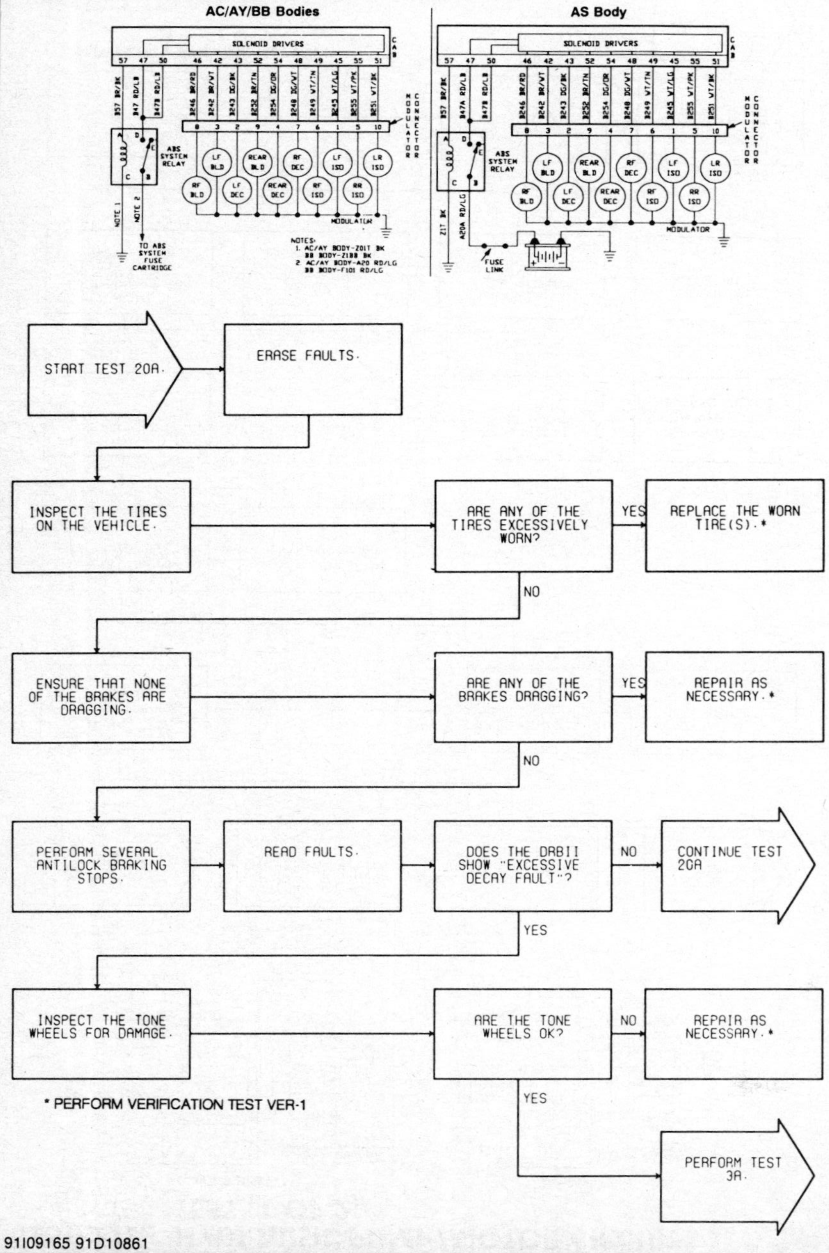
AC/AY/BB Bodies
AS Body
SOLENOID DRIVERS
ABS SYSTEM RELAY
MODULATOR
MODULATOR CONNECTOR
START TEST 20A.
ERASE FAULTS.
INSPECT THE TIRES ON THE VEHICLE.
ARE ANY OF THE TIRES EXCESSIVELY WORN?
YES
REPLACE THE WORN TIRE(S).*
NO
ENSURE THAT NONE OF THE BRAKES ARE DRAGGING.
ARE ANY OF THE BRAKES DRAGGING?
YES
REPAIR AS NECESSARY.*
NO
PERFORM SEVERAL ANTILOCK BRAKING STOPS.
READ FAULTS.
DOES THE DRBII SHOW "EXCESSIVE DECAY FAULT"?
NO
CONTINUE TEST 20A
YES
INSPECT THE TONE WHEELS FOR DAMAGE.
ARE THE TONE WHEELS OK?
NO
REPAIR AS NECESSARY.*
YES
PERFORM TEST 3A.

* PERFORM VERIFICATION TEST VER-1

91I09165 91D10861

Fig. 101: Anti-Lock Brake Test 20A – Excess Decay Fault (1 of 2)

TEST 20A: EXCESS DECAY FAULT (2 OF 2)

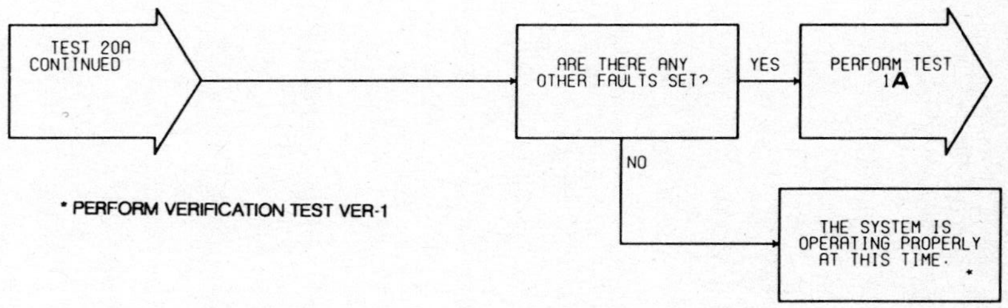
TEST 20A CONTINUED
ARE THERE ANY OTHER FAULTS SET?
YES
PERFORM TEST 1A
NO
THE SYSTEM IS OPERATING PROPERLY AT THIS TIME.*

* PERFORM VERIFICATION TEST VER-1

91E10862

Fig. 102: Anti-Lock Brake Test 20A – Excess Decay Fault (2 of 2)

1991 BRAKES
Anti-Lock – Bendix-10 (Cont.)

TEST 21A: HYDRAULIC PUMP/MOTOR CIRCUIT TEST (1 OF 2)

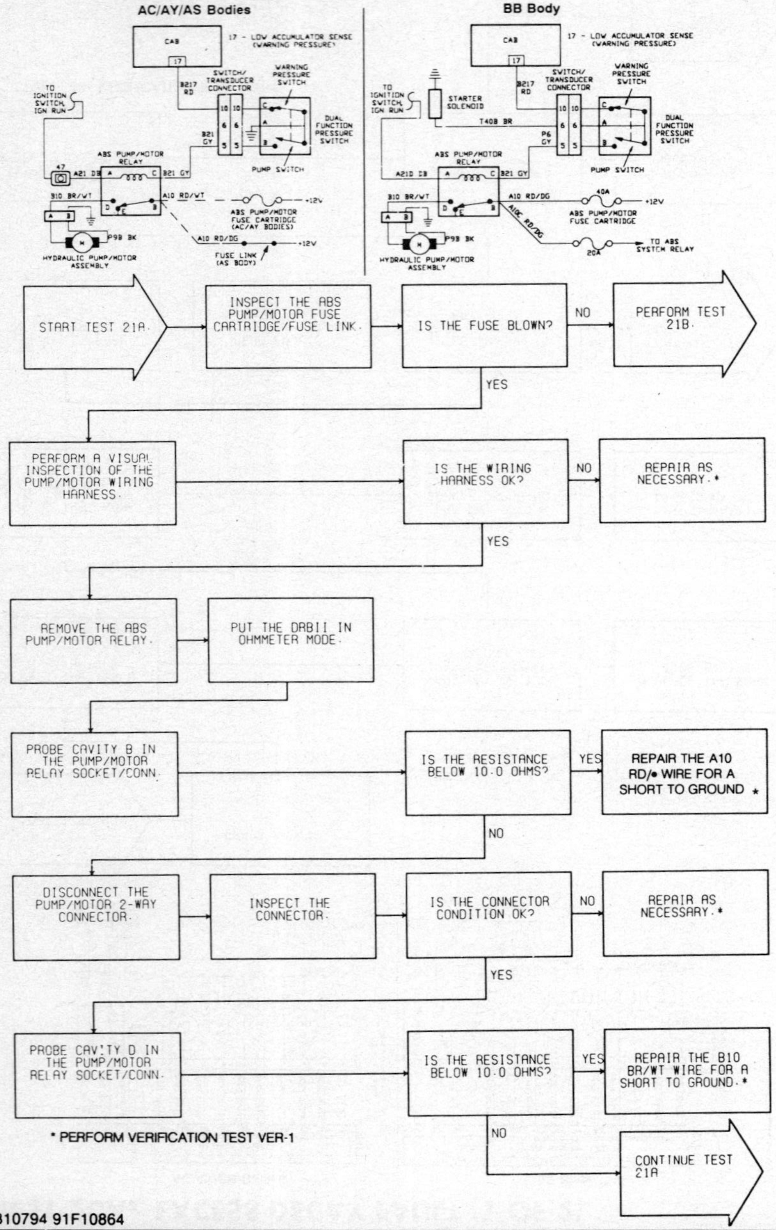
AC/AY/AS Bodies
BB Body
START TEST 21A.
INSPECT THE ABS PUMP/MOTOR FUSE CARTRIDGE/FUSE LINK.
IS THE FUSE BLOWN?
NO
PERFORM TEST 21B.
YES
PERFORM A VISUAL INSPECTION OF THE PUMP/MOTOR WIRING HARNESS.
IS THE WIRING HARNESS OK?
NO
REPAIR AS NECESSARY.*
YES
REMOVE THE ABS PUMP/MOTOR RELAY.
PUT THE DRBII IN OHMMETER MODE.
PROBE CAVITY B IN THE PUMP/MOTOR RELAY SOCKET/CONN.
IS THE RESISTANCE BELOW 10.0 OHMS?
YES
REPAIR THE A10 RD/• WIRE FOR A SHORT TO GROUND *
NO
DISCONNECT THE PUMP/MOTOR 2-WAY CONNECTOR.
INSPECT THE CONNECTOR.
IS THE CONNECTOR CONDITION OK?
NO
REPAIR AS NECESSARY.*
YES
PROBE CAVITY D IN THE PUMP/MOTOR RELAY SOCKET/CONN.
IS THE RESISTANCE BELOW 10.0 OHMS?
YES
REPAIR THE B10 BR/WT WIRE FOR A SHORT TO GROUND.*
NO
CONTINUE TEST 21A
* PERFORM VERIFICATION TEST VER-1

91B10794 91F10864

Fig. 103: Anti-Lock Brake Test 21A – Hydraulic Pump/Motor Circuit Test (1 of 2)

TEST 21A: HYDRAULIC PUMP/MOTOR CIRCUIT TEST (2 OF 2)

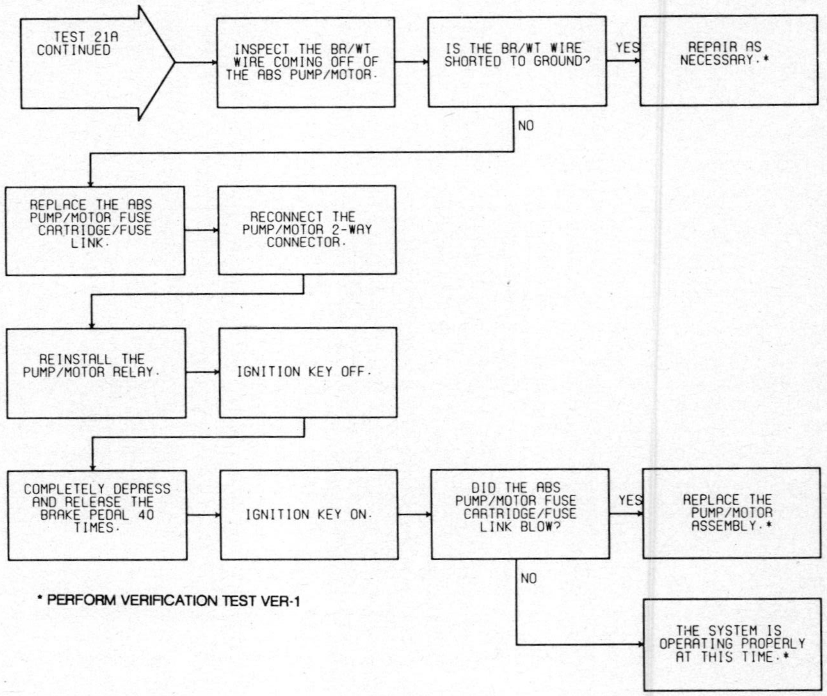
TEST 21A CONTINUED
INSPECT THE BR/WT WIRE COMING OFF OF THE ABS PUMP/MOTOR.
IS THE BR/WT WIRE SHORTED TO GROUND?
YES
REPAIR AS NECESSARY.*
NO
REPLACE THE ABS PUMP/MOTOR FUSE CARTRIDGE/FUSE LINK.
RECONNECT THE PUMP/MOTOR 2-WAY CONNECTOR.
REINSTALL THE PUMP/MOTOR RELAY.
IGNITION KEY OFF.
COMPLETELY DEPRESS AND RELEASE THE BRAKE PEDAL 40 TIMES.
IGNITION KEY ON.
DID THE ABS PUMP/MOTOR FUSE CARTRIDGE/FUSE LINK BLOW?
YES
REPLACE THE PUMP/MOTOR ASSEMBLY.*
NO
THE SYSTEM IS OPERATING PROPERLY AT THIS TIME.*
* PERFORM VERIFICATION TEST VER-1

91H10865

Fig. 104: Anti-Lock Brake Test 21A – Hydraulic Pump/Motor Circuit Test (2 of 2)

TEST 21B: HYDRAULIC PUMP/MOTOR CIRCUIT TEST (1 OF 3)

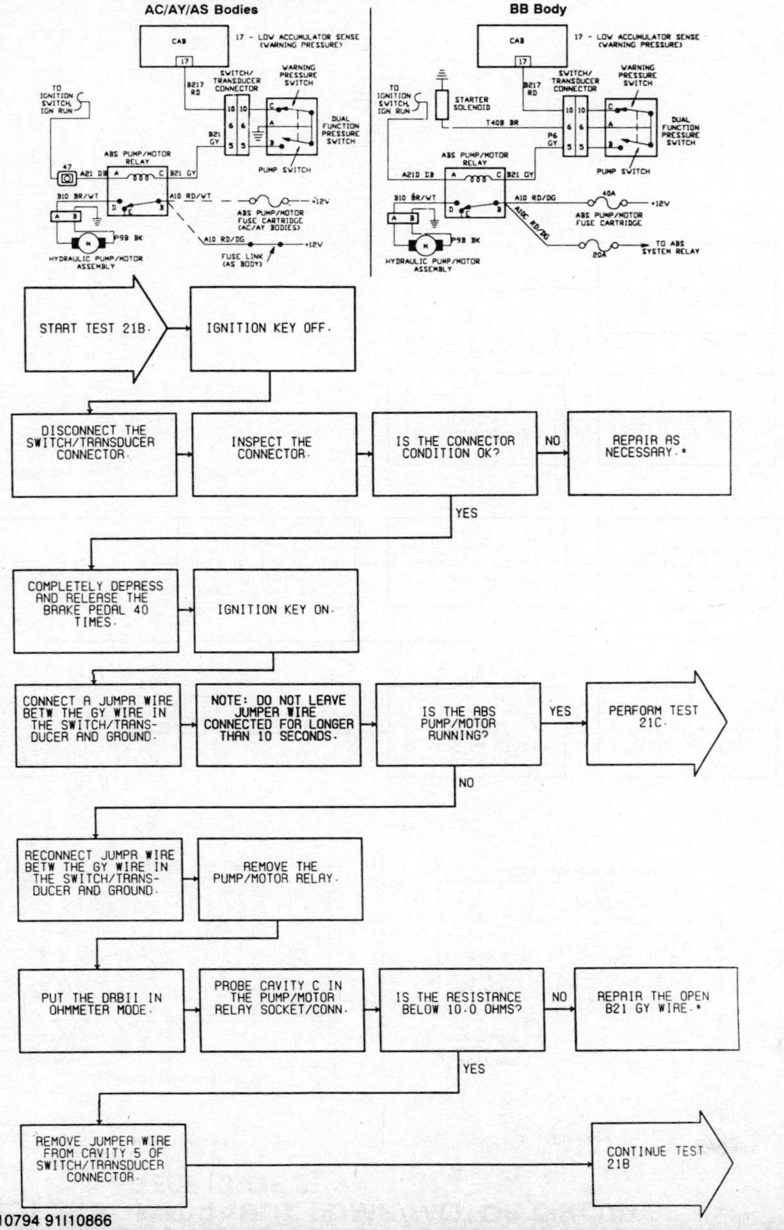
AC/AY/AS Bodies
BB Body
CAB
17 - LOW ACCUMULATOR SENSE (WARNING PRESSURE)
SWITCH/TRANSDUCER CONNECTOR
WARNING PRESSURE SWITCH
DUAL FUNCTION PRESSURE SWITCH
PUMP SWITCH
ABS PUMP/MOTOR RELAY
ABS PUMP/MOTOR FUSE CARTRIDGE
HYDRAULIC PUMP/MOTOR ASSEMBLY
TO IGNITION SWITCH, IGN RUN
STARTER SOLENOID
TO ABS SYSTEM RELAY
START TEST 21B.
IGNITION KEY OFF.
DISCONNECT THE SWITCH/TRANSDUCER CONNECTOR.
INSPECT THE CONNECTOR.
IS THE CONNECTOR CONDITION OK?
NO
REPAIR AS NECESSARY.*
YES
COMPLETELY DEPRESS AND RELEASE THE BRAKE PEDAL 40 TIMES.
IGNITION KEY ON.
CONNECT A JUMPR WIRE BETW THE GY WIRE IN THE SWITCH/TRANSDUCER AND GROUND.
NOTE: DO NOT LEAVE JUMPER WIRE CONNECTED FOR LONGER THAN 10 SECONDS.
IS THE ABS PUMP/MOTOR RUNNING?
YES
PERFORM TEST 21C.
NO
RECONNECT JUMPR WIRE BETW THE GY WIRE IN THE SWITCH/TRANSDUCER AND GROUND.
REMOVE THE PUMP/MOTOR RELAY.
PUT THE DRBII IN OHMMETER MODE.
PROBE CAVITY C IN THE PUMP/MOTOR RELAY SOCKET/CONN.
IS THE RESISTANCE BELOW 10.0 OHMS?
NO
REPAIR THE OPEN B21 GY WIRE.*
YES
REMOVE JUMPER WIRE FROM CAVITY 5 OF SWITCH/TRANSDUCER CONNECTOR.
CONTINUE TEST 21B

91B10794 91I10866

Fig. 105: Anti-Lock Brake Test 21B – Hydraulic Pump/Motor Circuit Test (1 of 3)

TEST 21B: HYDRAULIC PUMP/MOTOR CIRCUIT TEST (2 OF 3)

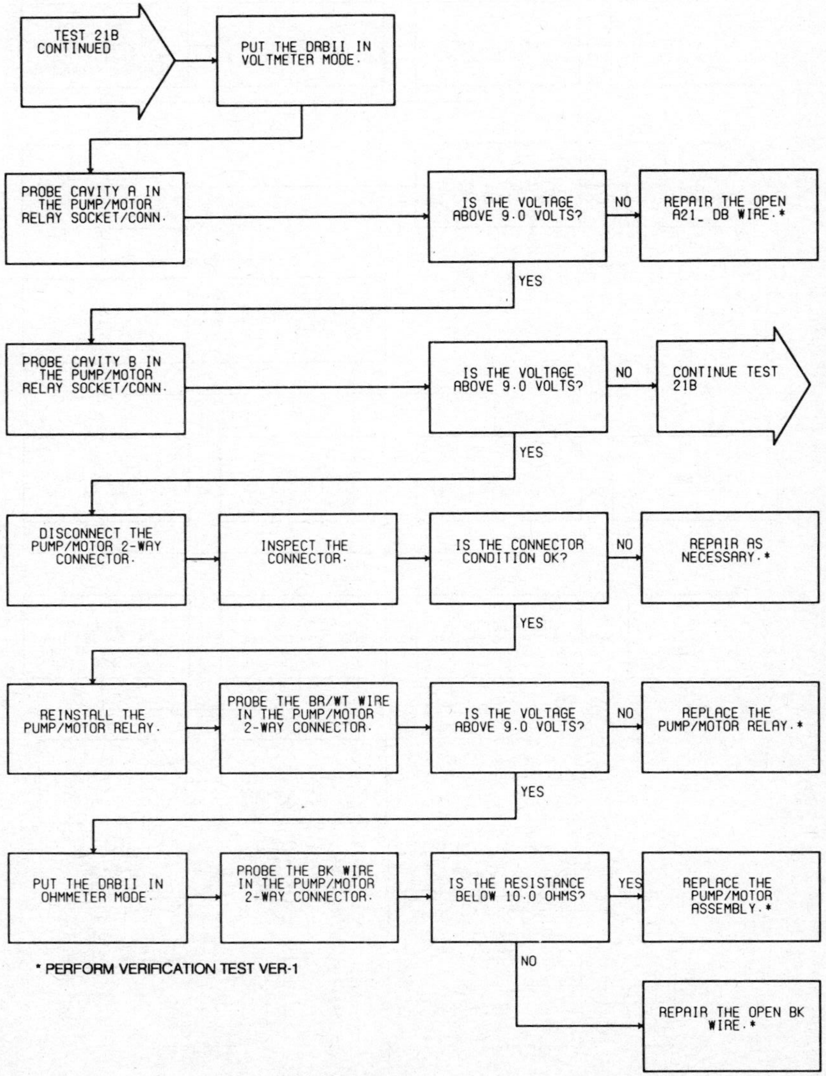
TEST 21B CONTINUED
PUT THE DRBII IN VOLTMETER MODE.
PROBE CAVITY A IN THE PUMP/MOTOR RELAY SOCKET/CONN.
IS THE VOLTAGE ABOVE 9.0 VOLTS?
NO
REPAIR THE OPEN A21_ DB WIRE.*
YES
PROBE CAVITY B IN THE PUMP/MOTOR RELAY SOCKET/CONN.
IS THE VOLTAGE ABOVE 9.0 VOLTS?
NO
CONTINUE TEST 21B
YES
DISCONNECT THE PUMP/MOTOR 2-WAY CONNECTOR.
INSPECT THE CONNECTOR.
IS THE CONNECTOR CONDITION OK?
NO
REPAIR AS NECESSARY.*
YES
REINSTALL THE PUMP/MOTOR RELAY.
PROBE THE BR/WT WIRE IN THE PUMP/MOTOR 2-WAY CONNECTOR.
IS THE VOLTAGE ABOVE 9.0 VOLTS?
NO
REPLACE THE PUMP/MOTOR RELAY.*
YES
PUT THE DRBII IN OHMMETER MODE.
PROBE THE BK WIRE IN THE PUMP/MOTOR 2-WAY CONNECTOR.
IS THE RESISTANCE BELOW 10.0 OHMS?
YES
REPLACE THE PUMP/MOTOR ASSEMBLY.*
NO
REPAIR THE OPEN BK WIRE.*

* PERFORM VERIFICATION TEST VER-1

91J10867

Fig. 106: Anti-Lock Brake Test 21B – Hydraulic Pump/Motor Circuit Test (2 of 3)

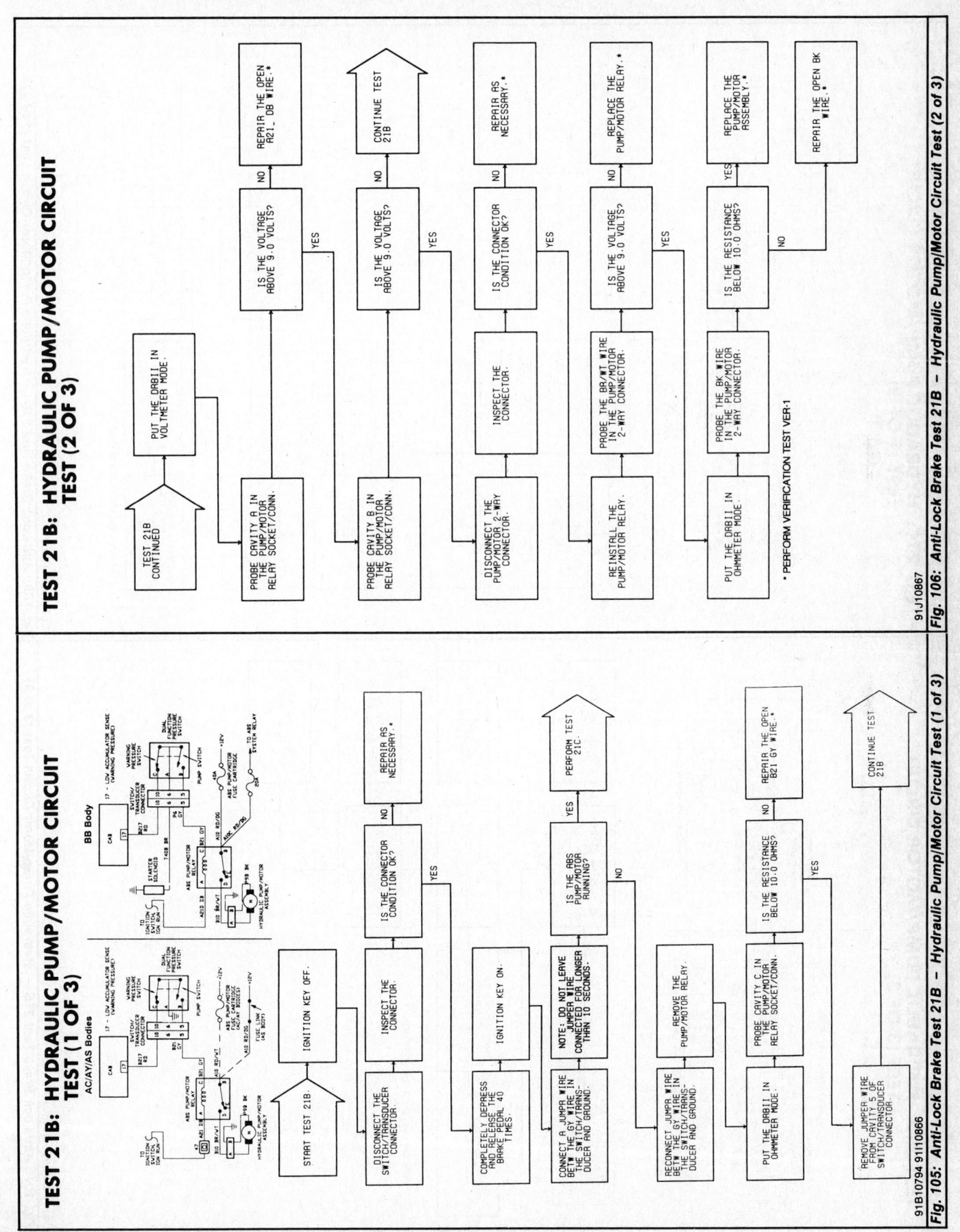

TEST 21B: HYDRAULIC PUMP/MOTOR CIRCUIT TEST (3 OF 3)

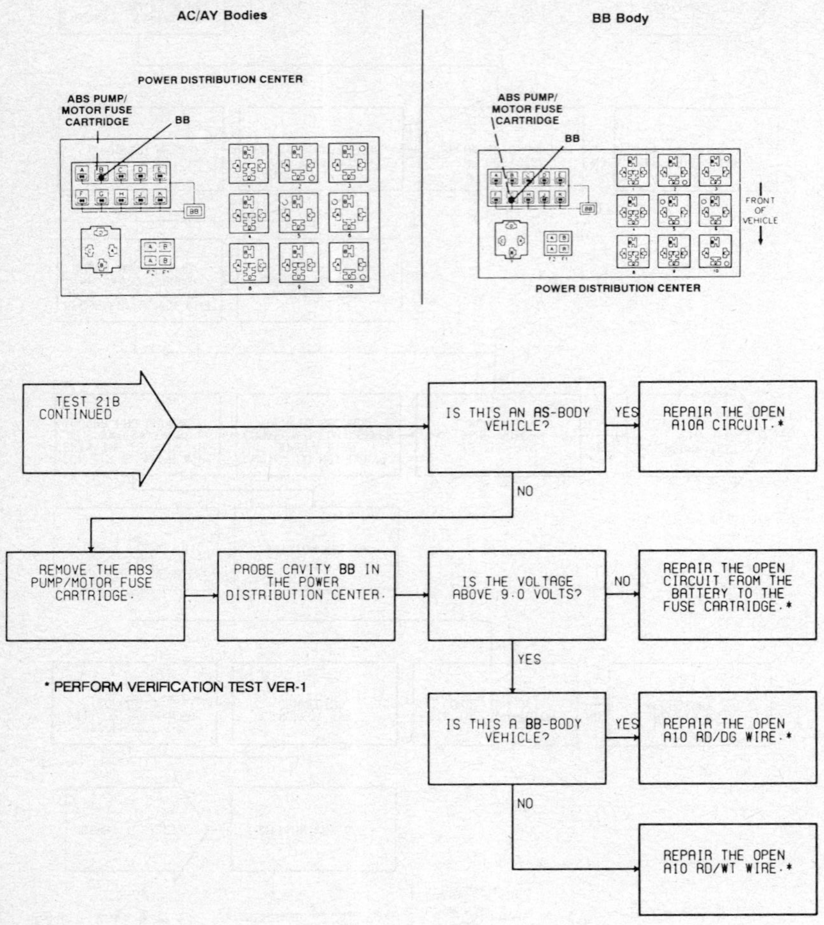
AC/AY Bodies
POWER DISTRIBUTION CENTER
ABS PUMP/ MOTOR FUSE CARTRIDGE
BB
BB Body
ABS PUMP/ MOTOR FUSE CARTRIDGE
BB
FRONT OF VEHICLE
POWER DISTRIBUTION CENTER
TEST 21B CONTINUED
IS THIS AN AS-BODY VEHICLE?
YES
REPAIR THE OPEN A10A CIRCUIT.*
NO
REMOVE THE ABS PUMP/MOTOR FUSE CARTRIDGE.
PROBE CAVITY BB IN THE POWER DISTRIBUTION CENTER.
IS THE VOLTAGE ABOVE 9.0 VOLTS?
NO
REPAIR THE OPEN CIRCUIT FROM THE BATTERY TO THE FUSE CARTRIDGE.*
YES
IS THIS A BB-BODY VEHICLE?
YES
REPAIR THE OPEN A10 RD/DG WIRE.*
NO
REPAIR THE OPEN A10 RD/WT WIRE.*

* PERFORM VERIFICATION TEST VER-1

91A11015 91B11016 91A10868

Fig. 107: Anti-Lock Brake Test 21B – Hydraulic Pump/Motor Circuit Test (3 of 3)

TEST 21C: HYDRAULIC PUMP/MOTOR CIRCUIT TEST (1 OF 2)

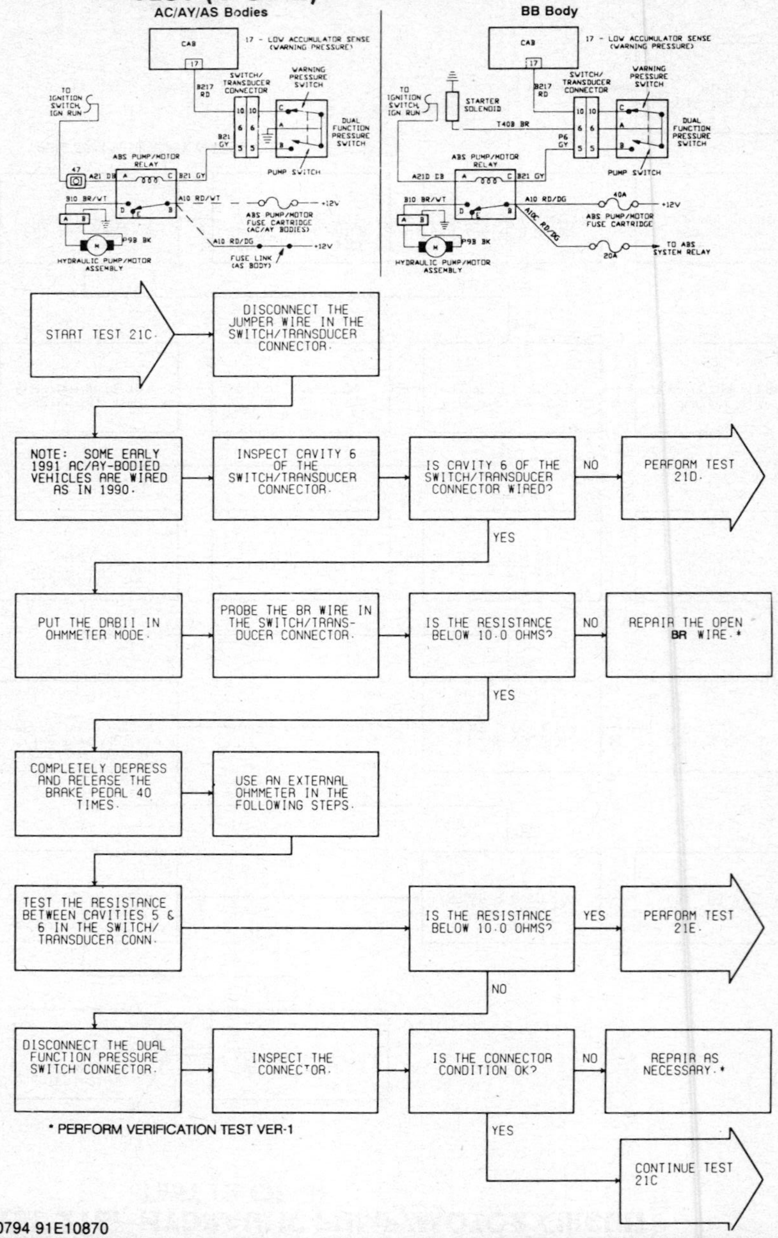
AC/AY/AS Bodies
BB Body
CAB
17 - LOW ACCUMULATOR SENSE (WARNING PRESSURE)
SWITCH/ TRANSDUCER CONNECTOR
WARNING PRESSURE SWITCH
DUAL FUNCTION PRESSURE SWITCH
PUMP SWITCH
ABS PUMP/MOTOR RELAY
TO IGNITION SWITCH, IGN RUN
HYDRAULIC PUMP/MOTOR ASSEMBLY
ABS PUMP/MOTOR FUSE CARTRIDGE (AC/AY BODIES)
FUSE LINK (AS BODY)
STARTER SOLENOID
TO ABS SYSTEM RELAY
START TEST 21C.
DISCONNECT THE JUMPER WIRE IN THE SWITCH/TRANSDUCER CONNECTOR.
NOTE: SOME EARLY 1991 AC/AY-BODIED VEHICLES ARE WIRED AS IN 1990.
INSPECT CAVITY 6 OF THE SWITCH/TRANSDUCER CONNECTOR.
IS CAVITY 6 OF THE SWITCH/TRANSDUCER CONNECTOR WIRED?
NO
PERFORM TEST 21D.
YES
PUT THE DRBII IN OHMMETER MODE.
PROBE THE BR WIRE IN THE SWITCH/TRANS-DUCER CONNECTOR.
IS THE RESISTANCE BELOW 10.0 OHMS?
NO
REPAIR THE OPEN BR WIRE.*
YES
COMPLETELY DEPRESS AND RELEASE THE BRAKE PEDAL 40 TIMES.
USE AN EXTERNAL OHMMETER IN THE FOLLOWING STEPS.
TEST THE RESISTANCE BETWEEN CAVITIES 5 & 6 IN THE SWITCH/ TRANSDUCER CONN.
IS THE RESISTANCE BELOW 10.0 OHMS?
YES
PERFORM TEST 21E.
NO
DISCONNECT THE DUAL FUNCTION PRESSURE SWITCH CONNECTOR.
INSPECT THE CONNECTOR.
IS THE CONNECTOR CONDITION OK?
NO
REPAIR AS NECESSARY.*
YES
CONTINUE TEST 21C

* PERFORM VERIFICATION TEST VER-1

91B10794 91E10870

Fig. 108: Anti-Lock Brake Test 21C – Hydraulic Pump/Motor Circuit Test (1 of 2)

TEST 21C: HYDRAULIC PUMP/MOTOR CIRCUIT TEST (2 OF 2)

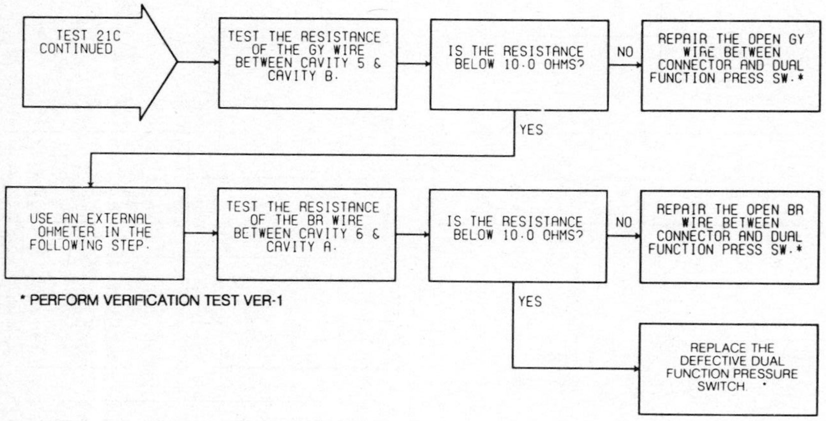

TEST 21C CONTINUED
TEST THE RESISTANCE OF THE GY WIRE BETWEEN CAVITY 5 & CAVITY B.
IS THE RESISTANCE BELOW 10.0 OHMS?
NO
REPAIR THE OPEN GY WIRE BETWEEN CONNECTOR AND DUAL FUNCTION PRESS SW.*
YES
USE AN EXTERNAL OHMETER IN THE FOLLOWING STEP.
TEST THE RESISTANCE OF THE BR WIRE BETWEEN CAVITY 6 & CAVITY A.
IS THE RESISTANCE BELOW 10.0 OHMS?
NO
REPAIR THE OPEN BR WIRE BETWEEN CONNECTOR AND DUAL FUNCTION PRESS SW.*
YES
REPLACE THE DEFECTIVE DUAL FUNCTION PRESSURE SWITCH *

* PERFORM VERIFICATION TEST VER-1

91E10871

Fig. 109: Anti-Lock Brake Test 21C – Hydraulic Pump/Motor Circuit Test (2 of 2)

TEST 21D: HYDRAULIC PUMP/MOTOR CIRCUIT TEST (1 OF 2)

AC/AY/AS Bodies

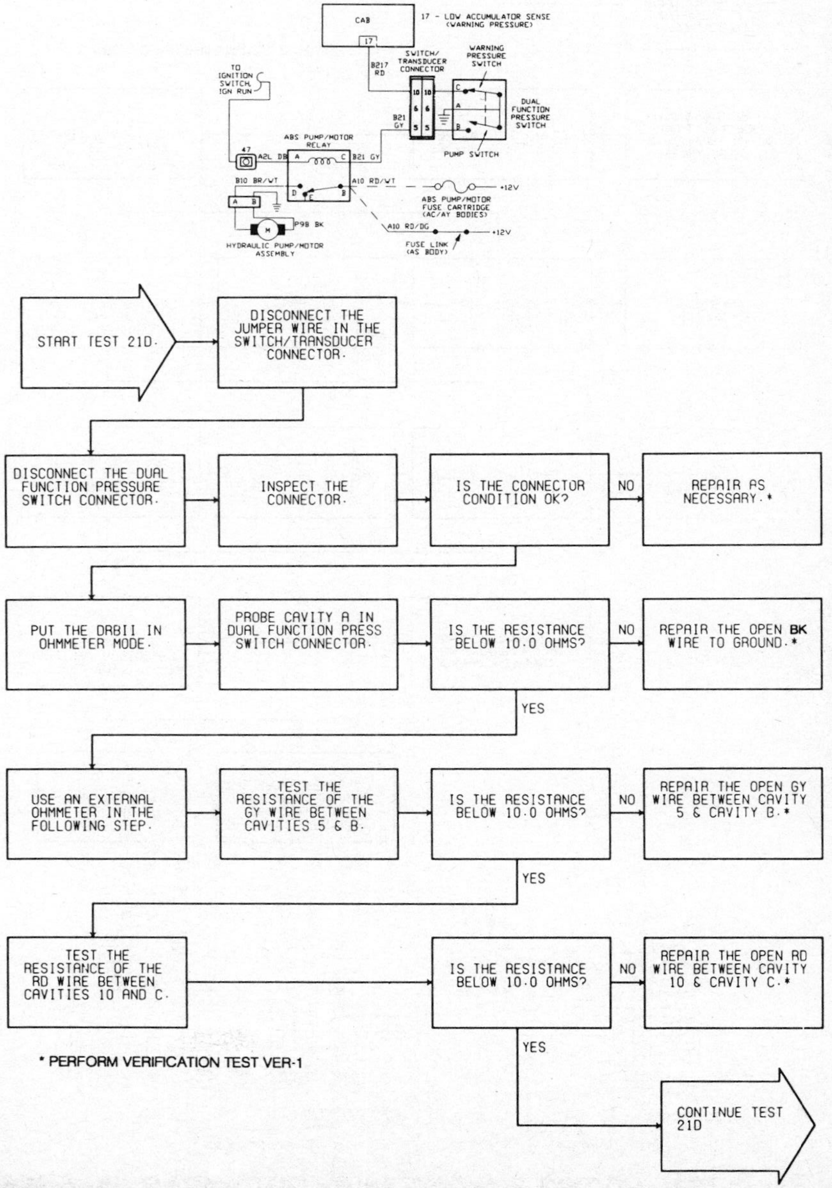

CAB
17 - LOW ACCUMULATOR SENSE (WARNING PRESSURE)
SWITCH/TRANSDUCER CONNECTOR
WARNING PRESSURE SWITCH
DUAL FUNCTION PRESSURE SWITCH
PUMP SWITCH
TO IGNITION SWITCH, IGN RUN
B217 RD
B21 GY
ABS PUMP/MOTOR RELAY
A2L DB
B21 GY
B10 BR/WT
A10 RD/WT
+12V
ABS PUMP/MOTOR FUSE CARTRIDGE (AC/AY BODIES)
A10 RD/DG
+12V
FUSE LINK (AS BODY)
P98 BK
HYDRAULIC PUMP/MOTOR ASSEMBLY
START TEST 21D.
DISCONNECT THE JUMPER WIRE IN THE SWITCH/TRANSDUCER CONNECTOR.
DISCONNECT THE DUAL FUNCTION PRESSURE SWITCH CONNECTOR.
INSPECT THE CONNECTOR.
IS THE CONNECTOR CONDITION OK?
NO
REPAIR AS NECESSARY.*
PUT THE DRBII IN OHMMETER MODE.
PROBE CAVITY A IN DUAL FUNCTION PRESS SWITCH CONNECTOR.
IS THE RESISTANCE BELOW 10.0 OHMS?
NO
REPAIR THE OPEN BK WIRE TO GROUND.*
YES
USE AN EXTERNAL OHMMETER IN THE FOLLOWING STEP.
TEST THE RESISTANCE OF THE GY WIRE BETWEEN CAVITIES 5 & B.
IS THE RESISTANCE BELOW 10.0 OHMS?
NO
REPAIR THE OPEN GY WIRE BETWEEN CAVITY 5 & CAVITY B.*
YES
TEST THE RESISTANCE OF THE RD WIRE BETWEEN CAVITIES 10 AND C.
IS THE RESISTANCE BELOW 10.0 OHMS?
NO
REPAIR THE OPEN RD WIRE BETWEEN CAVITY 10 & CAVITY C.*
YES
CONTINUE TEST 21D

* PERFORM VERIFICATION TEST VER-1

91G10872 91H10873

Fig. 110: Anti-Lock Brake Test 21D – Hydraulic Pump/Motor Circuit Test (1 of 2)

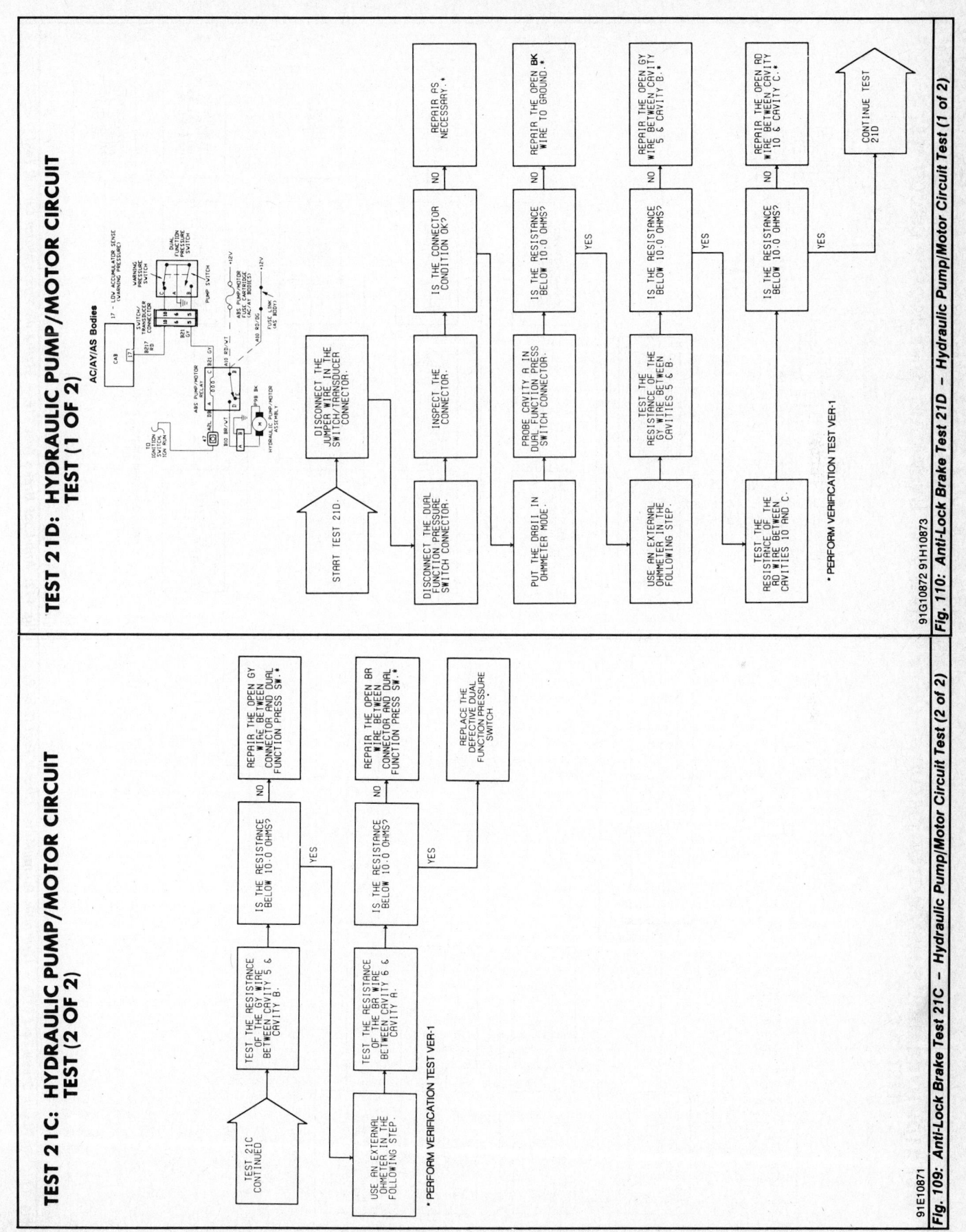

1991 BRAKES
Anti-Lock – Bendix-10 (Cont.)

TEST 21D: HYDRAULIC PUMP/MOTOR CIRCUIT TEST (2 OF 2)

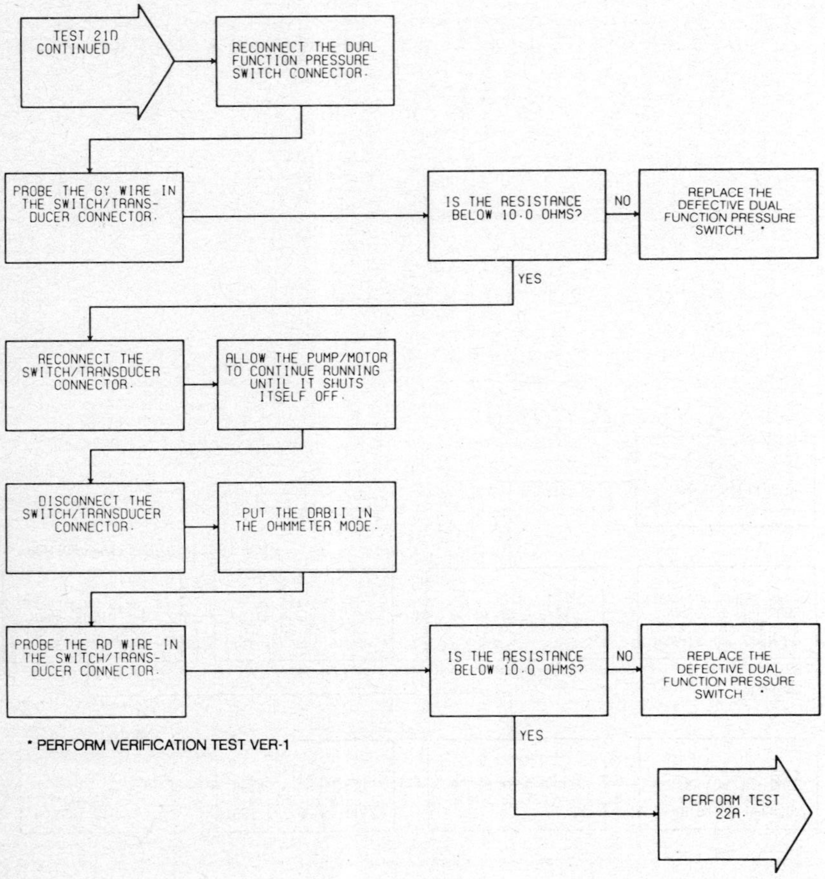
TEST 21D CONTINUED
RECONNECT THE DUAL FUNCTION PRESSURE SWITCH CONNECTOR.
PROBE THE GY WIRE IN THE SWITCH/TRANSDUCER CONNECTOR.
IS THE RESISTANCE BELOW 10.0 OHMS?
NO
REPLACE THE DEFECTIVE DUAL FUNCTION PRESSURE SWITCH *
YES
RECONNECT THE SWITCH/TRANSDUCER CONNECTOR.
ALLOW THE PUMP/MOTOR TO CONTINUE RUNNING UNTIL IT SHUTS ITSELF OFF.
DISCONNECT THE SWITCH/TRANSDUCER CONNECTOR.
PUT THE DRBII IN THE OHMMETER MODE.
PROBE THE RD WIRE IN THE SWITCH/TRANSDUCER CONNECTOR.
IS THE RESISTANCE BELOW 10.0 OHMS?
NO
REPLACE THE DEFECTIVE DUAL FUNCTION PRESSURE SWITCH *
YES
PERFORM TEST 22A.

* PERFORM VERIFICATION TEST VER-1

91I10874

Fig. 111: Anti-Lock Brake Test 21D – Hydraulic Pump/Motor Circuit Test (2 of 2)

TEST 21E: HYDRAULIC PUMP/MOTOR CIRCUIT TEST

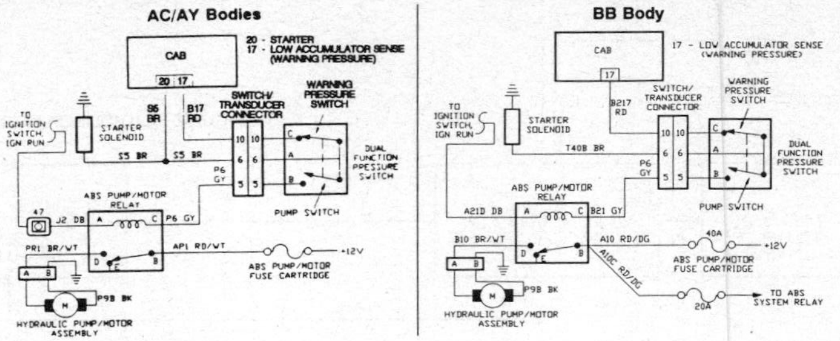
AC/AY Bodies
BB Body
CAB
20 - STARTER
17 - LOW ACCUMULATOR SENSE (WARNING PRESSURE)
SWITCH/TRANSDUCER CONNECTOR
WARNING PRESSURE SWITCH
DUAL FUNCTION PRESSURE SWITCH
PUMP SWITCH
STARTER SOLENOID
TO IGNITION SWITCH IGN RUN
ABS PUMP/MOTOR RELAY
ABS PUMP/MOTOR FUSE CARTRIDGE
HYDRAULIC PUMP/MOTOR ASSEMBLY
TO ABS SYSTEM RELAY
+12V

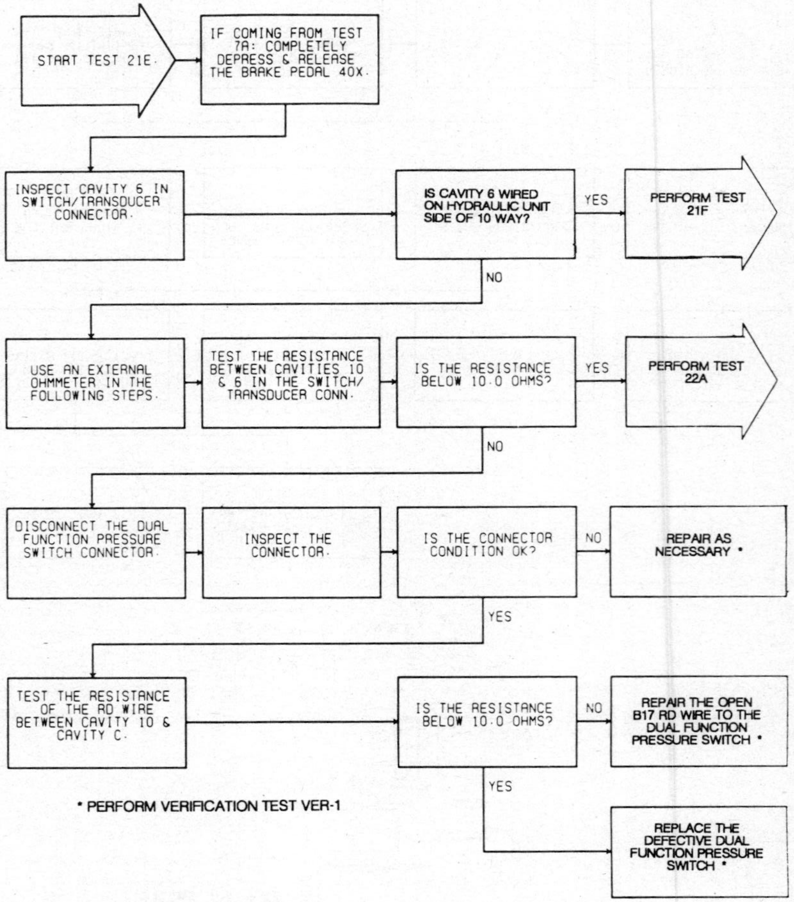
START TEST 21E.
IF COMING FROM TEST 7A: COMPLETELY DEPRESS & RELEASE THE BRAKE PEDAL 40X.
INSPECT CAVITY 6 IN SWITCH/TRANSDUCER CONNECTOR.
IS CAVITY 6 WIRED ON HYDRAULIC UNIT SIDE OF 10 WAY?
YES
PERFORM TEST 21F
NO
USE AN EXTERNAL OHMMETER IN THE FOLLOWING STEPS.
TEST THE RESISTANCE BETWEEN CAVITIES 10 & 6 IN THE SWITCH/TRANSDUCER CONN.
IS THE RESISTANCE BELOW 10.0 OHMS?
YES
PERFORM TEST 22A
NO
DISCONNECT THE DUAL FUNCTION PRESSURE SWITCH CONNECTOR.
INSPECT THE CONNECTOR.
IS THE CONNECTOR CONDITION OK?
NO
REPAIR AS NECESSARY *
YES
TEST THE RESISTANCE OF THE RD WIRE BETWEEN CAVITY 10 & CAVITY C.
IS THE RESISTANCE BELOW 10.0 OHMS?
NO
REPAIR THE OPEN B17 RD WIRE TO THE DUAL FUNCTION PRESSURE SWITCH *
YES
REPLACE THE DEFECTIVE DUAL FUNCTION PRESSURE SWITCH *

* PERFORM VERIFICATION TEST VER-1

91F10863 91C11512

Fig. 112: Anti-Lock Brake Test 21E – Hydraulic Pump/Motor Circuit Test

TEST 21F: HYDRAULIC PUMP/MOTOR CIRCUIT TEST

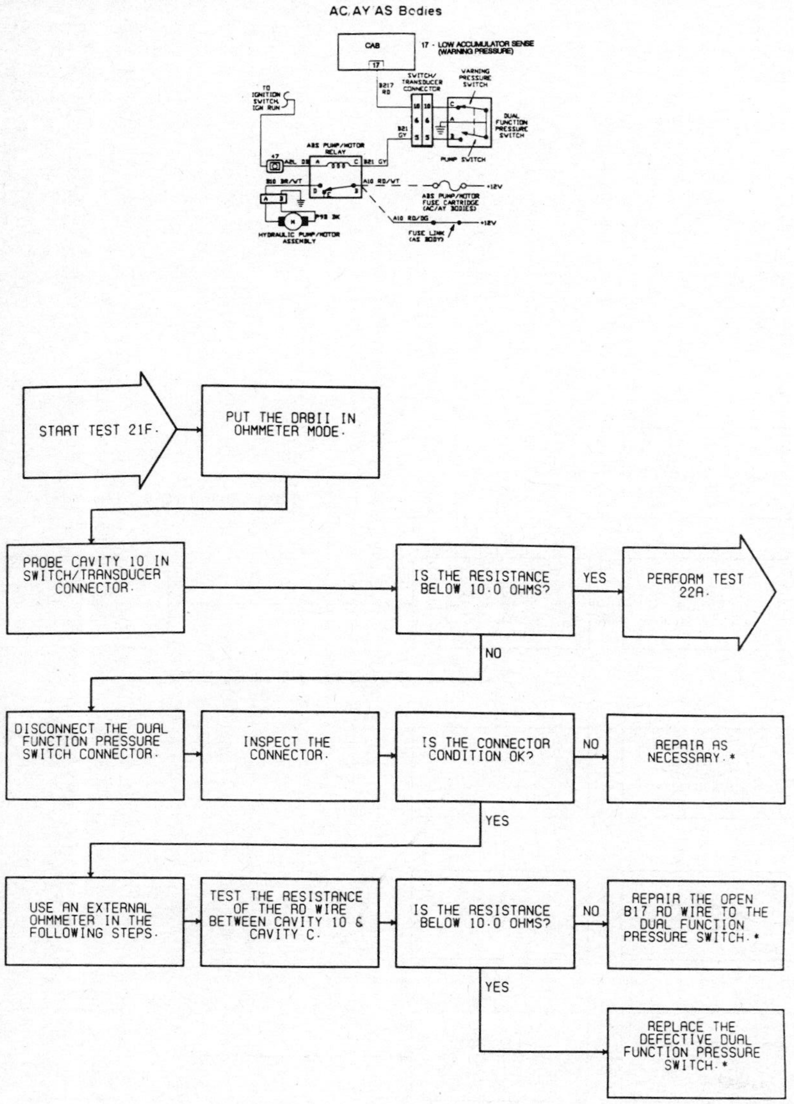
AC/AY/AS Bodies
CAB
17 - LOW ACCUMULATOR SENSE (WARNING PRESSURE)
SWITCH/TRANSDUCER CONNECTOR
WARNING PRESSURE SWITCH
DUAL FUNCTION PRESSURE SWITCH
PUMP SWITCH
ABS PUMP/MOTOR RELAY
ABS PUMP/MOTOR FUSE CARTRIDGE (AC/AY BODIES)
FUSE LINK (AS BODY)
HYDRAULIC PUMP/MOTOR ASSEMBLY
+12V
START TEST 21F.
PUT THE DRBII IN OHMMETER MODE.
PROBE CAVITY 10 IN SWITCH/TRANSDUCER CONNECTOR.
IS THE RESISTANCE BELOW 10.0 OHMS?
YES
PERFORM TEST 22A.
NO
DISCONNECT THE DUAL FUNCTION PRESSURE SWITCH CONNECTOR.
INSPECT THE CONNECTOR.
IS THE CONNECTOR CONDITION OK?
NO
REPAIR AS NECESSARY.*
YES
USE AN EXTERNAL OHMMETER IN THE FOLLOWING STEPS.
TEST THE RESISTANCE OF THE RD WIRE BETWEEN CAVITY 10 & CAVITY C.
IS THE RESISTANCE BELOW 10.0 OHMS?
NO
REPAIR THE OPEN B17 RD WIRE TO THE DUAL FUNCTION PRESSURE SWITCH.*
YES
REPLACE THE DEFECTIVE DUAL FUNCTION PRESSURE SWITCH.*

91F11002 91G11003

Fig. 113: Anti-Lock Brake Test 21F – Hydraulic Pump/Motor Circuit Test

TEST 22A: HYDRAULIC PRESSURE PERFORMANCE TEST (1 OF 2)

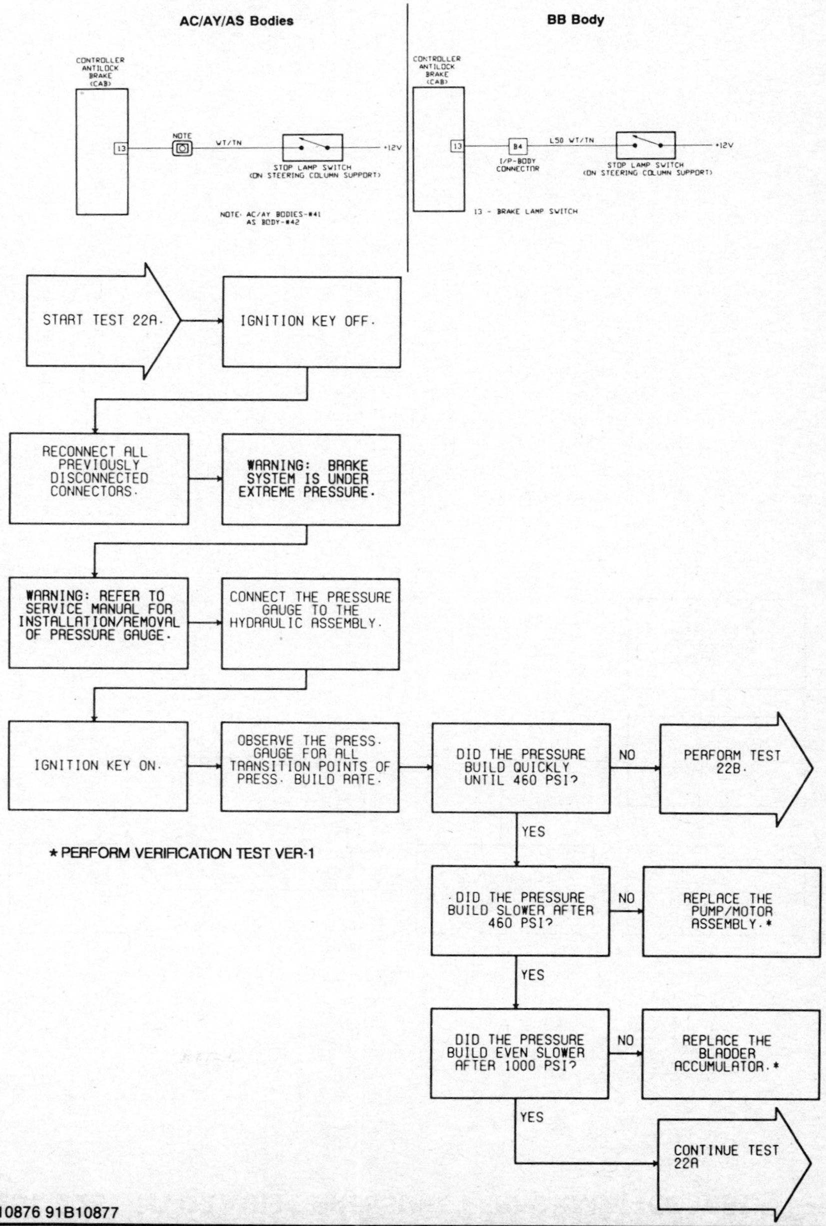
AC/AY/AS Bodies
BB Body
CONTROLLER ANTILOCK BRAKE (CAB)
13
NOTE
VT/TN
STOP LAMP SWITCH (ON STEERING COLUMN SUPPORT)
+12V
NOTE: AC/AY BODIES-#41 AS BODY-#42
B4
L50 VT/TN
I/P-BODY CONNECTOR
13 - BRAKE LAMP SWITCH
START TEST 22A.
IGNITION KEY OFF.
RECONNECT ALL PREVIOUSLY DISCONNECTED CONNECTORS.
WARNING: BRAKE SYSTEM IS UNDER EXTREME PRESSURE.
WARNING: REFER TO SERVICE MANUAL FOR INSTALLATION/REMOVAL OF PRESSURE GAUGE.
CONNECT THE PRESSURE GAUGE TO THE HYDRAULIC ASSEMBLY.
IGNITION KEY ON.
OBSERVE THE PRESS. GAUGE FOR ALL TRANSITION POINTS OF PRESS. BUILD RATE.
DID THE PRESSURE BUILD QUICKLY UNTIL 460 PSI?
NO
PERFORM TEST 22B.
YES
DID THE PRESSURE BUILD SLOWER AFTER 460 PSI?
NO
REPLACE THE PUMP/MOTOR ASSEMBLY.*
YES
DID THE PRESSURE BUILD EVEN SLOWER AFTER 1000 PSI?
NO
REPLACE THE BLADDER ACCUMULATOR.*
YES
CONTINUE TEST 22A
* PERFORM VERIFICATION TEST VER-1

91A10876 91B10877

Fig. 114: Anti-Lock Brake Test 22A – Hydraulic Pressure Performance Test (1 of 2)

TEST 22A: HYDRAULIC PRESSURE PERFORMANCE TEST (2 OF 2)

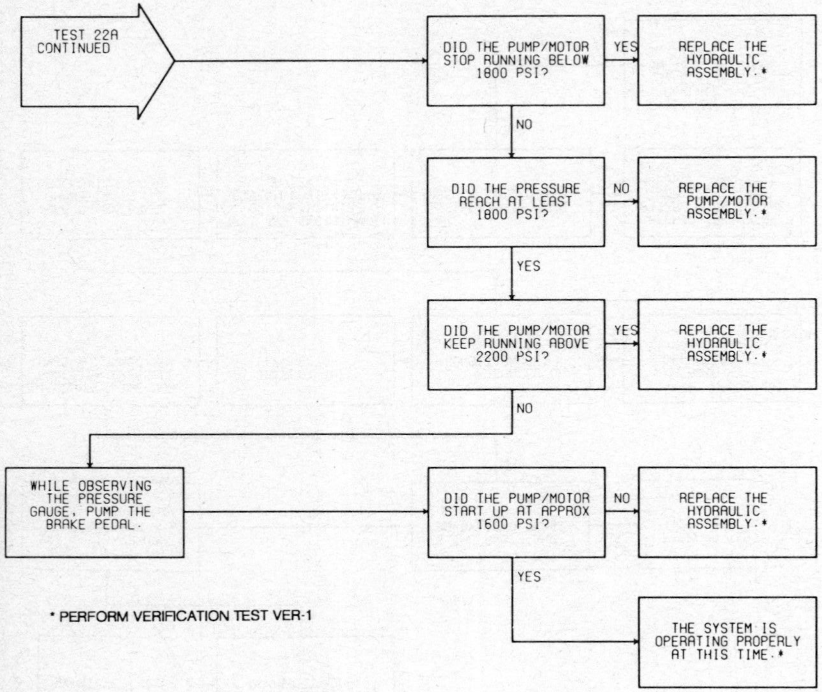
TEST 22A CONTINUED
DID THE PUMP/MOTOR STOP RUNNING BELOW 1800 PSI?
YES
REPLACE THE HYDRAULIC ASSEMBLY.*
NO
DID THE PRESSURE REACH AT LEAST 1800 PSI?
NO
REPLACE THE PUMP/MOTOR ASSEMBLY.*
YES
DID THE PUMP/MOTOR KEEP RUNNING ABOVE 2200 PSI?
YES
REPLACE THE HYDRAULIC ASSEMBLY.*
NO
WHILE OBSERVING THE PRESSURE GAUGE, PUMP THE BRAKE PEDAL.
DID THE PUMP/MOTOR START UP AT APPROX 1600 PSI?
NO
REPLACE THE HYDRAULIC ASSEMBLY.*
YES
THE SYSTEM IS OPERATING PROPERLY AT THIS TIME.*

* PERFORM VERIFICATION TEST VER-1

91C10878

Fig. 115: Anti-Lock Brake Test 22A – Hydraulic Pressure Performance Test (2 of 2)

TEST 22B: HYDRAULIC PRESSURE PERFORMANCE TEST

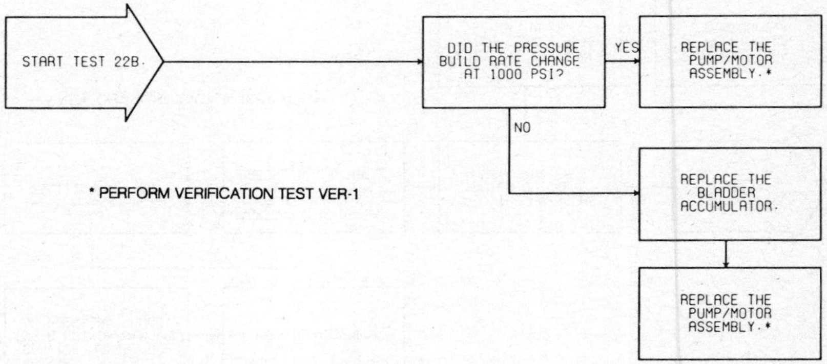
START TEST 22B.
DID THE PRESSURE BUILD RATE CHANGE AT 1000 PSI?
YES
REPLACE THE PUMP/MOTOR ASSEMBLY.*
NO
REPLACE THE BLADDER ACCUMULATOR.
REPLACE THE PUMP/MOTOR ASSEMBLY.*

* PERFORM VERIFICATION TEST VER-1

91D10879

Fig. 116: Anti-Lock Brake Test 22B – Hydraulic Pressure Performance Test

TEST 23A: STOPLIGHT SWITCH INPUT TEST

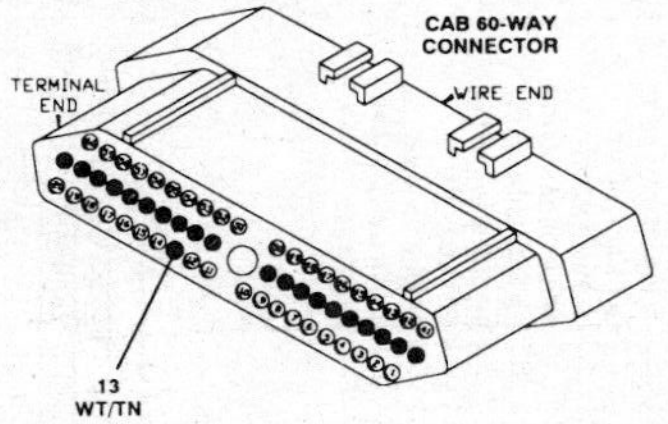
CAB 60-WAY CONNECTOR
WIRE END
TERMINAL END
13
WT/TN

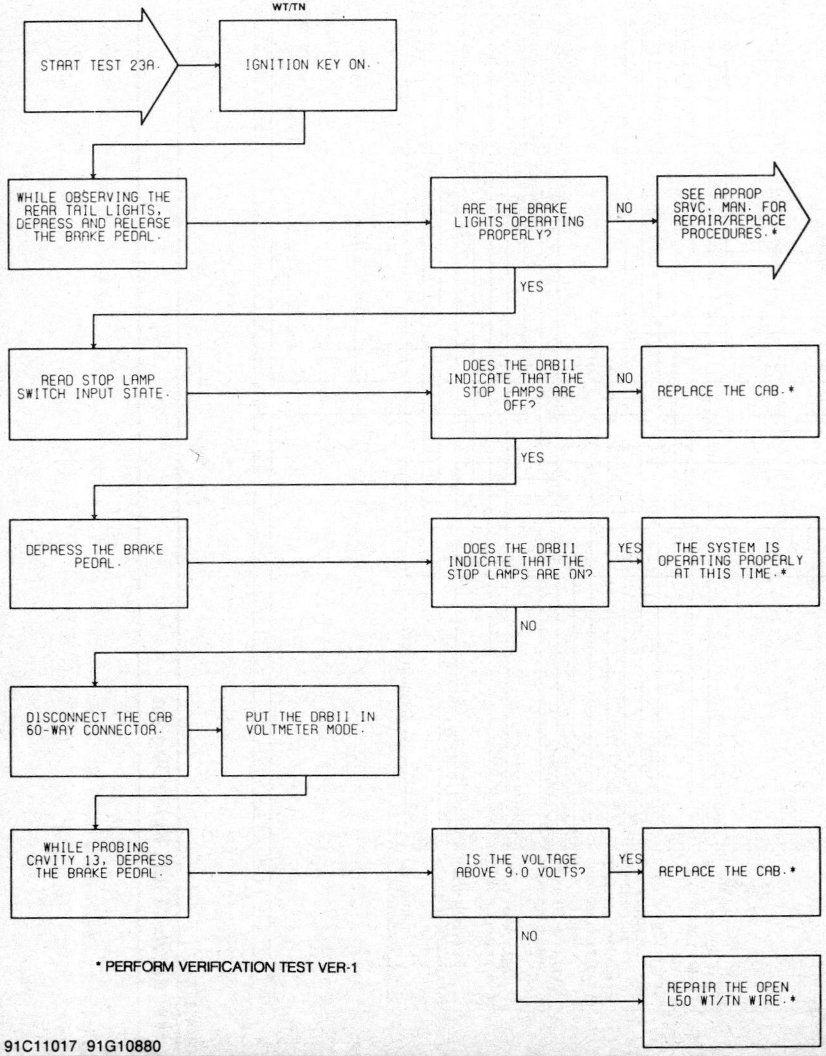
START TEST 23A.
IGNITION KEY ON.
WHILE OBSERVING THE REAR TAIL LIGHTS, DEPRESS AND RELEASE THE BRAKE PEDAL.
ARE THE BRAKE LIGHTS OPERATING PROPERLY?
NO
SEE APPROP SRVC. MAN. FOR REPAIR/REPLACE PROCEDURES.*
YES
READ STOP LAMP SWITCH INPUT STATE.
DOES THE DRBII INDICATE THAT THE STOP LAMPS ARE OFF?
NO
REPLACE THE CAB.*
YES
DEPRESS THE BRAKE PEDAL.
DOES THE DRBII INDICATE THAT THE STOP LAMPS ARE ON?
YES
THE SYSTEM IS OPERATING PROPERLY AT THIS TIME.*
NO
DISCONNECT THE CAB 60-WAY CONNECTOR.
PUT THE DRBII IN VOLTMETER MODE.
WHILE PROBING CAVITY 13, DEPRESS THE BRAKE PEDAL.
IS THE VOLTAGE ABOVE 9.0 VOLTS?
YES
REPLACE THE CAB.*
NO
REPAIR THE OPEN L50 WT/TN WIRE.*

* PERFORM VERIFICATION TEST VER-1

91C11017 91G10880

Fig. 117: Anti-Lock Brake Test 23A – Stoplight Switch Input Test

TEST VER-1: SYSTEM VERIFICATION TEST

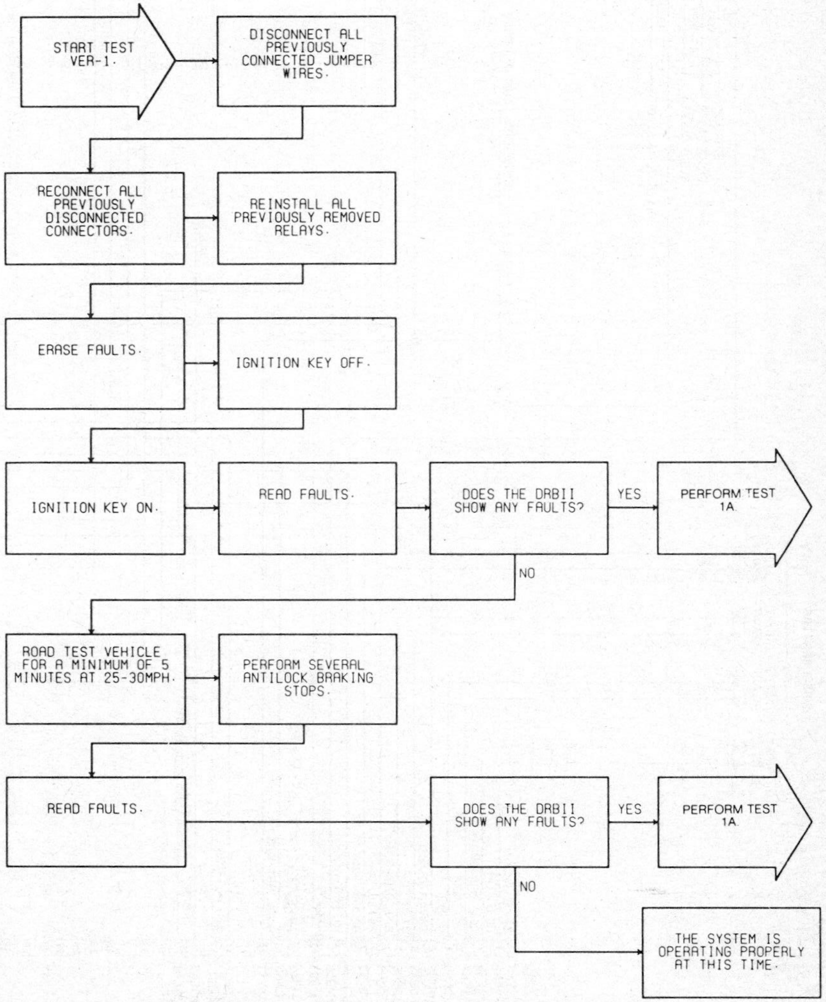
START TEST VER-1.
DISCONNECT ALL PREVIOUSLY CONNECTED JUMPER WIRES.
RECONNECT ALL PREVIOUSLY DISCONNECTED CONNECTORS.
REINSTALL ALL PREVIOUSLY REMOVED RELAYS.
ERASE FAULTS.
IGNITION KEY OFF.
IGNITION KEY ON.
READ FAULTS.
DOES THE DRBII SHOW ANY FAULTS?
YES
PERFORM TEST 1A.
NO
ROAD TEST VEHICLE FOR A MINIMUM OF 5 MINUTES AT 25-30MPH.
PERFORM SEVERAL ANTILOCK BRAKING STOPS.
READ FAULTS.
DOES THE DRBII SHOW ANY FAULTS?
YES
PERFORM TEST 1A.
NO
THE SYSTEM IS OPERATING PROPERLY AT THIS TIME.

91H10881

Fig. 118: Anti-Lock Brake Test VER-1 – System Verification Test

1991 BRAKES
Anti-Lock – Bendix-10 (Cont.)

WIRING DIAGRAM

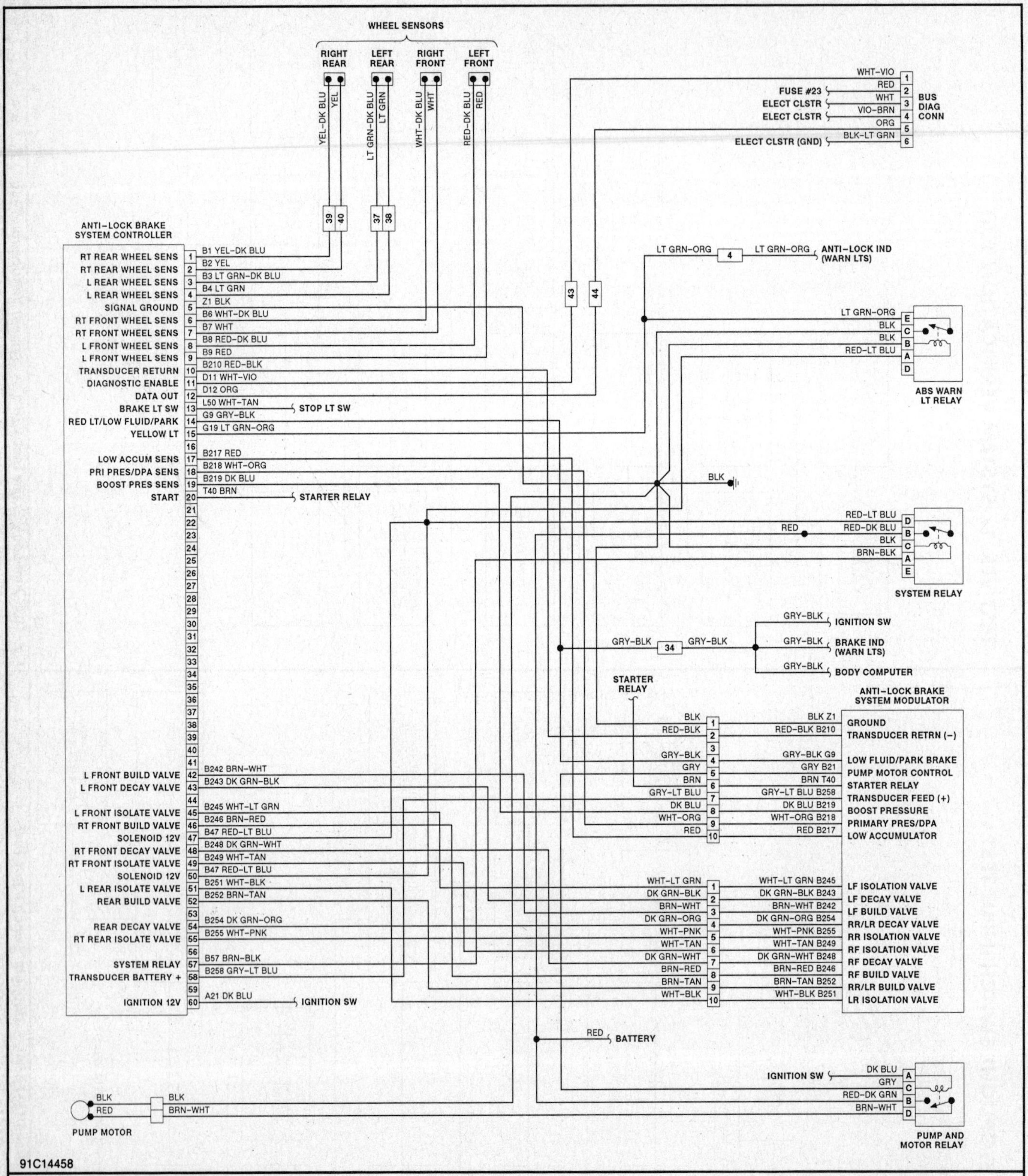
WHEEL SENSORS
RIGHT REAR
LEFT REAR
RIGHT FRONT
LEFT FRONT
ANTI-LOCK BRAKE SYSTEM CONTROLLER
RT REAR WHEEL SENS
L REAR WHEEL SENS
SIGNAL GROUND
RT FRONT WHEEL SENS
L FRONT WHEEL SENS
TRANSDUCER RETURN
DIAGNOSTIC ENABLE
DATA OUT
BRAKE LT SW
RED LT/LOW FLUID/PARK
YELLOW LT
LOW ACCUM SENS
PRI PRES/DPA SENS
BOOST PRES SENS
START
STOP LT SW
STARTER RELAY
BUS DIAG CONN
FUSE #23
ELECT CLSTR
ELECT CLSTR (GND)
ANTI-LOCK IND (WARN LTS)
ABS WARN LT RELAY
SYSTEM RELAY
IGNITION SW
BRAKE IND (WARN LTS)
BODY COMPUTER
ANTI-LOCK BRAKE SYSTEM MODULATOR
GROUND
TRANSDUCER RETRN (–)
LOW FLUID/PARK BRAKE
PUMP MOTOR CONTROL
TRANSDUCER FEED (+)
BOOST PRESSURE
PRIMARY PRES/DPA
LOW ACCUMULATOR
L FRONT BUILD VALVE
L FRONT DECAY VALVE
L FRONT ISOLATE VALVE
RT FRONT BUILD VALVE
SOLENOID 12V
RT FRONT DECAY VALVE
RT FRONT ISOLATE VALVE
L REAR ISOLATE VALVE
REAR BUILD VALVE
REAR DECAY VALVE
RT REAR ISOLATE VALVE
SYSTEM RELAY
TRANSDUCER BATTERY +
IGNITION 12V
LF ISOLATION VALVE
LF DECAY VALVE
LF BUILD VALVE
RR/LR DECAY VALVE
RR ISOLATION VALVE
RF ISOLATION VALVE
RF DECAY VALVE
RF BUILD VALVE
RR/LR BUILD VALVE
LR ISOLATION VALVE
BATTERY
PUMP MOTOR
PUMP AND MOTOR RELAY
91C14458

Fig. 119: Bendix-10 ABS Wiring Diagram

Dakota, Pickup, Ramcharger, RWD Van

DESCRIPTION

The Kelsey-Hayes Rear Wheel Anti-Lock (RWAL) Brake System is designed to prevent rear wheel lock-up during heavy braking conditions, no matter what type of road surface vehicle is on. Preventing rear wheel lock-up allows driver to maintain vehicle directional stability during braking. System components include an Electronic Control Module (ECM), speed sensor, 2 warning lights and dual solenoid control valve. System has the capability to self-diagnose and store trouble codes to detect problems within the system. Benefit of the RWAL system is limited when vehicle is operating in 4WD mode.

OPERATION

When ignition is turned on, the Electronic Control Module (ECM) performs a self-diagnosis on the system. ECM is located on lower right side cowl panel on Dakota or behind glove box on all others. *See Figs. 1-3.* If ECM detects a problem, the Amber ANTI-LOCK warning light, located on instrument panel, will stay on after engine is started. If ECM stores a trouble code, the Red BRAKES warning light will also come on. If system is okay, both lights will go out in approximately 2 seconds.

As vehicle is moving, speed sensor, located on top of rear differential housing, sends a AC voltage signal to the ECM. ECM translates this signal into wheel speed. Using this signal, ECM detects deceleration from a reduction in wheel speed and electronic signal from stoplight switch. ECM then signals the dual solenoid hydraulic valve to increase, decrease or maintain rear wheel brake hydraulic pressure to prevent rear wheel lock-up. Dual solenoid hydraulic valve is located on frame rail.

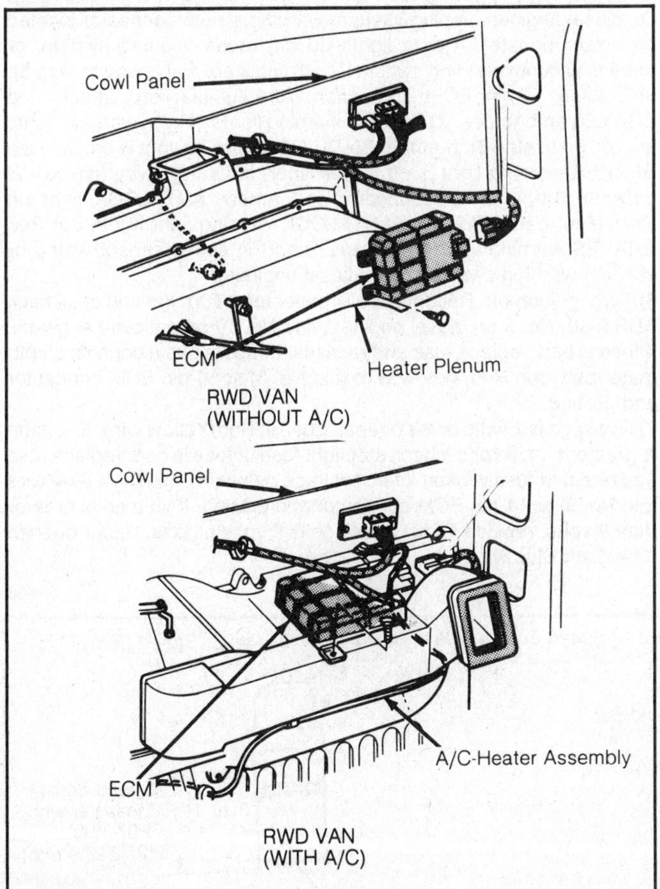
Cowl Panel
ECM
Heater Plenum
RWD VAN
(WITHOUT A/C)
Cowl Panel
A/C-Heater Assembly
ECM
RWD VAN
(WITH A/C)

NOTE: Diagnostic connector is located on lower right side cowl.

90E06363 Courtesy of Chrysler Motors.

Fig. 1: Locating Electronic Control Module (RWD Van)

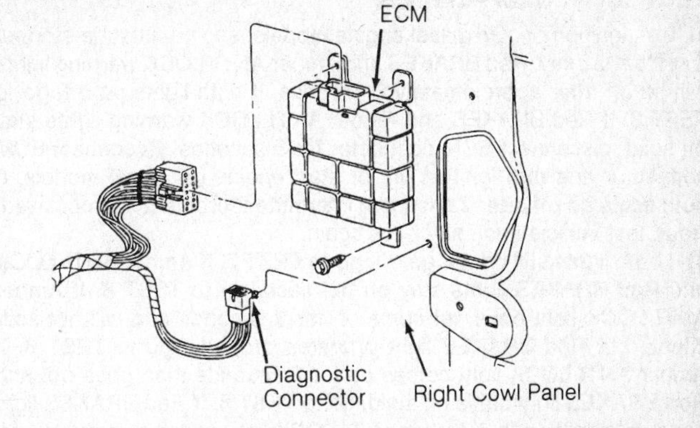
ECM
Diagnostic
Connector
Right Cowl Panel

90F13420 Courtesy of Chrysler Motors.

Fig. 2: Locating Electronic Control Module (Dakota)

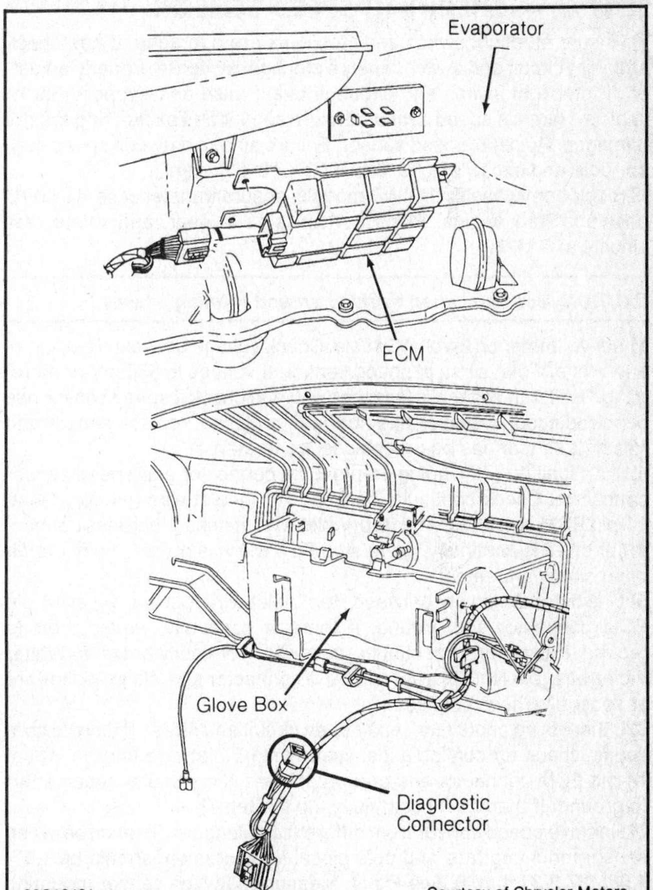
Evaporator
ECM
Glove Box
Diagnostic
Connector

90G13421 Courtesy of Chrysler Motors.

Fig. 3: Locating Electronic Control Module (Pickup & Ramcharger)

BLEEDING BRAKE SYSTEM

Bleed brake system, using pressure bleeder or depressing brake pedal, in the following sequence: dual solenoid hydraulic valve, right rear, left rear, right front and left front. Use DOT 3 brake fluid.

TESTING

TEST 1 – VISUAL INSPECTION

Check all electrical connectors and terminals, and instrument panel ground before continuing test. Faulty terminals or connectors can lead to misdiagnosis. Loose or faulty instrument panel ground can also lead to misdiagnosis.

1991 BRAKES
Anti-Lock (Cont.)

TEST 2 – SELF-CHECK

1) Turn ignition on. On diesel engine models, engine must be started. If system is okay, Red BRAKES and Amber ANTI-LOCK warning lights will go off after approximately 2 seconds. If both lights go off, go to TEST 3. If Red BRAKES and Amber ANTI-LOCK warning lights stay on solid, disconnect ECM connector for 5 seconds. Reconnect ECM connector and turn ignition on, or start engine on diesel models. If both lights go off after 2 seconds, intermittent problem has occurred. Road test vehicle and self-check again.

2) If both lights still do not go off, go to TEST 5. If Amber ANTI-LOCK and Red BRAKES lights stay on but flash, go to TEST 8. If Amber ANTI-LOCK light does not come on for 2 seconds and will not self-check, but Red BRAKES light operates properly, go to TEST 6. If Amber ANTI-LOCK light comes on for 2 seconds then goes off, and Red BRAKES light stays on solid, go to TEST 6. If Red BRAKES light does not come on, but Amber ANTI-LOCK light operates properly, go to TEST 7.

TEST 3 – CHECKING SPEED SENSOR

1) Ensure stoplight switch and stoplights are operating. If not, check stoplight circuit and switch. Ensure stoplight switch is properly adjusted. If stoplight switch and circuit is okay, raise and support rear of vehicle. Remove speed sensor. Ensure sensor and exciter ring are not damaged. Reinstall speed sensor. Ensure air gap between speed sensor pole and exciter ring is .005-.050" (.13-1.27 mm).

2) Block front wheels. On 4WD models, ensure transfer case is in 2WD position. Start engine. Place transmission in gear, and rotate rear wheels at 5 MPH.

CAUTION: Use care when working around rotating wheels.

3) Set voltmeter on 2-volt AC scale. Check voltage between Red/Violet and White/Violet wires at speed sensor. If voltage is 650 mV or more, go to TEST 4. If voltage is less than 650 mV, check if speed sensor has been replaced. If sensor has not been replaced, replace sensor and retest. If sensor has been replaced, go to step **4)**.

4) Turn ignition off. Unplug 14-pin ECM connector and speed sensor connector. Check continuity between Red/Violet wire (pin No. 14) at 14-pin ECM connector and Red/Violet wire at sensor harness connector. If there is continuity, go to step **5)**. If there is no continuity, repair open circuit and retest.

5) Check for continuity between Red/Violet wire (pin No. 14) at 14-pin ECM connector and ground. If there is continuity, repair short to ground. If there is no continuity, check for continuity between White/Violet wire (pin No. 13) at 14-pin ECM connector and White/Violet wire at sensor harness connector.

6) If there is no continuity, repair open circuit and retest. If there is continuity, check for continuity between White/Violet wire (pin No. 13) at 14-pin ECM connector and ground. If there is continuity, repair short to ground. If there is no continuity, go to step **7)**.

7) Remove speed sensor from differential. Measure distance between sensor mounting face and pole piece. Measurement should be 1.07-1.08" (27.2-27.4 mm). *See Fig. 4.* Measure between sensor mounting face on differential and exciter ring. Measurement should be 1.085-1.120" (27.56-28.45 mm).

8) Subtract sensor measurement from differential-to-exciter ring measurement. Difference should be .005-.050" (.13-1.27 mm). If difference is not as specified, recheck measurements. If component measurement is not as specified, replace sensor or disassemble differential and replace exciter ring. If speed sensor gap is correct, go to TEST 4.

TEST 4 – MECHANICAL PROBLEMS CHECK

Drive vehicle and check rear brake operation. If rear brakes are grabbing, locking or pulling, remove brake drum. Check components for wear or damage. If rear brake components are okay, recheck rear brake operation. If mechanical components of rear brakes are operating okay, replace ECM and retest system.

TEST 5 – DIAGNOSTIC CONNECTOR CHECK

1) With all connectors plugged in, turn ignition on. Ground diagnostic connector to ground. *See Figs. 1-3.* Amber ANTI-LOCK warning light should flash a code starting with one long flash, and followed by short flashes. If a code is flashed, count flashes, including first long flash, and go to TROUBLE CODES.

2) If no code is flashed, turn ignition off. Unplug 14-pin connector from ECM. Using an ohmmeter, check for continuity between Black wire (pin No. 12) at 14-pin ECM connector and Black wire at diagnostic connector. If there is no continuity, repair open circuit and retest.

3) If there is continuity, ensure master cylinder reservoir fluid level is correct. If reservoir fluid level is not correct, check for hydraulic leak. Repair leak and retest system. If reservoir fluid level is correct, reconnect 14-pin ECM connector. Unplug proportioning valve switch connector. Turn ignition on. Check if Amber ANTI-LOCK and Red BRAKES warning lights are on. If lights are not on, check for air in brake system, or damage to brake system.

4) If lights are on, turn ignition off. On gasoline engines, go to step **5)**. On diesel engines, unplug vacuum warning switch connector located on power booster. If both lights go off, repair vacuum system, or replace vacuum warning switch. If both lights are still on, go to step **5)**.

5) Unplug 14-pin ECM connector. Turn ignition on. Check Red BRAKES and Amber ANTI-LOCK warning lights. If both warning lights are off, go to step **6)**. If Amber ANTI-LOCK warning light is on, but Red BRAKES warning light is off, repair short in Orange wire (pin No. 2) between 14-pin ECM connector and Amber ANTI-LOCK light on instrument panel. If Amber ANTI-LOCK warning light is off, but Red BRAKES warning light is on, repair short in speed sensor wiring or vacuum warning switch circuit (diesel engines).

6) Turn ignition off. Reconnect all connectors. Turn ignition on. Check ABS fuse (No. 5 on diesel engines, and No. 10 on gasoline engines). If fuse is bad, replace fuse and recheck. If fuse is okay, connect a voltmeter between Red/Yellow wire (pin No. 3) at 14-pin ECM connector and ground.

7) If voltage is 9 volts or less, repair open in Red/Yellow wire. If voltage is greater than 9 volts, check stoplight fuse. If fuse is bad, replace fuse and retest. If fuse is okay, check voltage between Pink/Dark Blue wire (pin No. 9) at 14-pin ECM connector and ground. If voltage is greater than 9 volts, replace ECM. If voltage is 9 volts or less, repair open in Pink/Dark Blue wire.

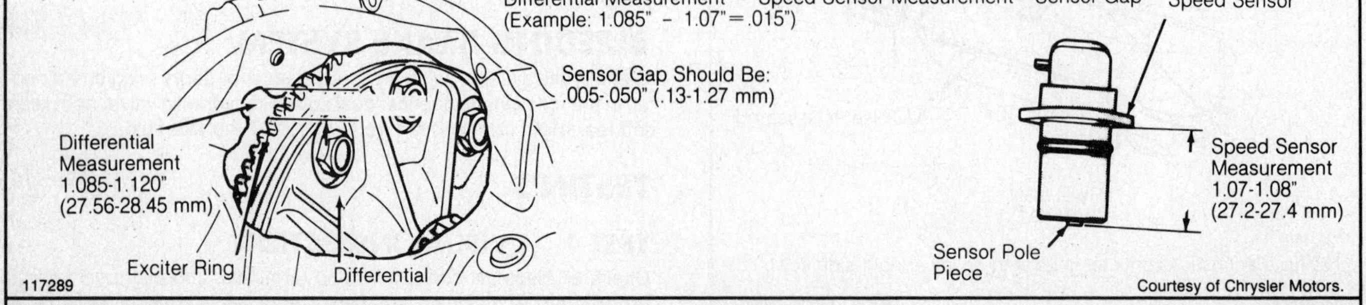
Differential Measurement - Speed Sensor Measurement = Sensor Gap
(Example: 1.085" - 1.07" = .015")
Speed Sensor
Sensor Gap Should Be:
.005-.050" (.13-1.27 mm)
Differential
Measurement
1.085-1.120"
(27.56-28.45 mm)
Speed Sensor
Measurement
1.07-1.08"
(27.2-27.4 mm)
Exciter Ring
Differential
Sensor Pole
Piece
117289
Courtesy of Chrysler Motors.

Fig. 4: Measuring Speed Sensor & Gap

TEST 6 – ECM POWER & GROUND

1) Ensure 14-pin ECM connector is connected fully. Insufficient connection can cause faulty or intermittent ABS failure. If insufficient connection is found, retest system. If connection is okay, disconnect battery. Unplug 14-pin ECM connector. Check resistance between Black/Light Green wire (pin No. 10) at ECM connector and ground.
2) If resistance is one ohm or more, repair open in Black/Light Green wire. Ensure connector terminals are mating properly. If resistance is less than one ohm, check Amber ANTI-LOCK light fuse. If fuse is bad, replace fuse and retest system. If fuse is okay, reconnect battery. Turn ignition on.
3) Check voltage between Orange wire (pin No. 2) at 14-pin ECM connector and ground. If is 9 volts or more, replace ECM and retest system. If voltage is less than 9 volts, check Amber ANTI-LOCK warning light bulb. If bulb is bad, replace bulb and retest system. If bulb is okay, repair open in Orange wire between pin No. 2 at 14-pin ECM connector and Amber ANTI-LOCK warning light. Retest system.

TEST 7 – PARKING BRAKE CIRCUIT

1) To check parking brake circuit for short, turn ignition off. Ensure all connectors are plugged in. Turn ignition on. Block wheels. Release parking brake and check Red BRAKES warning light operation. If Red BRAKES warning light goes off after releasing parking brake, turn ignition off.
2) Retest ABS system and self-diagnosis. If Red BRAKES warning light does not go off, pull parking brake release lever and pull up on parking brake pedal. If Red BRAKES warning light goes off, repair parking brake switch or mechanism. If Red BRAKES warning light does not go off, unplug parking brake switch connector.
3) If Red BRAKES warning light goes off, adjust or replace parking brake switch and retest system. If Red BRAKES warning light does not go off, unplug 14-pin ECM connector. If Red BRAKES warning light is off, replace ECM and retest system. If Red BRAKES warning light does not go off, check for short in Black/Gray wire. If no short can be found, check for air in hydraulic system or mechanical problem.
4) To check parking brake circuit for open, ensure all connectors are plugged in. If Red BRAKES warning light does not operate, unplug parking brake switch connector. Unplug 11-pin Red connector from instrument panel. Check continuity in Black/Gray wire between 11-pin Red connector and parking brake switch.
5) If continuity is not present, repair open in Black/Gray wire and retest system. If continuity exists, check Red BRAKES warning light bulb and connectors. Replace bulb or repair connectors (if necessary). If bulb and connector are okay, replace instrument panel printed circuit board.

TEST 8 – INTERMITTENT PROBLEMS

1) Turn ignition off. Unplug 14-pin ECM connector. Turn ignition on. Check for voltage between Red/Yellow wire (pin No. 3) at 14-pin ECM connector and ground. Shake instrument panel harness while measuring voltage. If voltage is not a steady 9 volts, repair open in Red/Yellow wire.
2) If voltage is a steady 9 volts, turn ignition off. Disconnect battery. Check resistance between Black wire (pin No. 12) at 14-pin ECM connector and ground. Shake instrument panel harness while measuring resistance. If resistance is not 100,000 ohms or more, and steady, repair short to ground in Black wire.
3) If resistance is 100,000 ohms or more, and steady, check resistance between Black/Light Green wire (pin No. 10) at 14-pin ECM connector and ground. Shake instrument panel harness while measuring resistance. If resistance is a steady one ohm, replace ECM and retest system. If resistance is not a steady one ohm, repair open in Black/Light Green wire.

TROUBLE CODES

RETRIEVING TROUBLE CODES

To retrieve trouble codes, momentarily ground RWAL diagnostic connector located at ECM. Count the number of flashes by Amber ANTI-

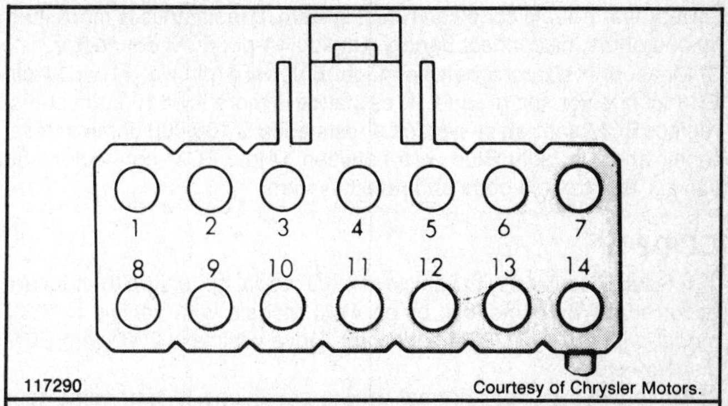
1
2
3
4
5
6
7
8
9
10
11
12
13
14
117290
Courtesy of Chrysler Motors.

Fig. 5: Identifying 14-Pin ECM Connector Terminals

LOCK warning light. The first flash will be a long flash, followed by a number of short flashes. To accurately diagnose the system, count all flashes, including long flash. Long flash indicates starting of code sequence. Proceed to appropriate test after flashes have been counted.

CLEARING TROUBLE CODES

To clear trouble codes, turn ignition off. Unplug 14-pin ECM connector, or remove battery voltage for 5 seconds. Reconnect battery or connector. During system retest, wait approximately 30 seconds before reading codes.

CODE 1

Code 1 is not a valid code. Retest system and ensure proper code is being read. If Code 1 returns, go to TEST 4 under TESTING.

CODE 2

1) Disconnect battery. Unplug 14-pin ECM connector. Check resistance between Light Green wire (pin No. 1) at 14-pin ECM connector and ground. If resistance is 6 ohms or less, replace ECM and retest system. If resistance is more than 6 ohms, unplug dual solenoid hydraulic valve connector.
2) Check resistance between Gray/Black wire (Dakota and RWD Van), or Gray/White wire (all others), at dual solenoid hydraulic valve harness connector and ground. If resistance is more than one ohm, repair Gray/Black or Gray/White wire, or connector terminal. If resistance is one ohm or less, reconnect 14-pin ECM connector.
3) Measure resistance between Green wire and Black wire at dual solenoid hydraulic valve connector. If resistance is more than 6 ohms, replace dual solenoid hydraulic valve and retest system. If resistance is 6 ohms or less, repair Light Green wire between valve and 14-pin ECM connector (pin No. 1). Retest system.

CODE 3

1) Disconnect battery. Unplug 14-pin ECM connector. Measure resistance between White/Brown wire (pin No. 8) at 14-pin ECM connector and ground. If resistance is 3 ohms or less, replace ECM and retest system. If resistance is more than 3 ohms, unplug dual solenoid hydraulic valve connector.
2) Measure resistance between White wire and Black wire at valve connector. If resistance is more than 3 ohms, replace dual solenoid hydraulic valve. If resistance is 3 ohms or less, repair White/Brown wire between valve and 14-pin ECM connector (pin No. 8).

CODE 4

1) Unplug dual solenoid hydraulic valve connector. Measure resistance between Light Blue wire on valve connector and ground. If resistance is 10,000 ohms or less, replace dual solenoid hydraulic valve. Clear trouble code and retest system.
2) If resistance is more than 10,000 ohms, measure resistance between Light Blue wire and Black wire at valve connector. If resistance is 10,000 ohms or less, replace dual solenoid hydraulic

1991 BRAKES
Anti-Lock (Cont.)

valve. Clear trouble code and retest system. If resistance is more than 10,000 ohms, disconnect battery. Unplug 14-pin ECM connector.
3) Measure resistance between Light Blue wire (pin No. 11) at 14-pin ECM connector and ground. If resistance is more than 100,000 ohms, replace ECM and retest system. If resistance is 100,000 ohms or less, repair short in Light Blue wire between 14-pin ECM connector and valve. Clear trouble code and retest system.

CODE 5

1) If failure occurred with vehicle in 4WD mode, go to step **3)**. If failure occurred on 2WD models, or on 4WD models with vehicle in 2WD mode, unplug 14-pin ECM connector. Drive vehicle in 2WD with ECM disconnected.
2) Drive vehicle under normal driving conditions to determine rear brake operation. If brakes are operating normally, replace dual valve hydraulic solenoid and retest system. If brakes do not operate properly, repair brake as necessary.
3) Unplug 14-pin ECM connector. Start engine. Place transfer case in 4WD mode. Move vehicle a short distance. Measure voltage between Light Green/Brown wire (pin No. 4) at 14-pin ECM connector and ground. If voltage is more than one volt, repair open in Light Green/ Brown wire, or 4WD indicator switch located on transfer case. Retest system. If voltage is one volt or less, replace dual solenoid hydraulic valve. Clear trouble code and retest system.

CODE 6

1) Recheck code after driving vehicle. If Code 6 does not appear after driving vehicle, clear codes and retest. If Code 6 is reset, disconnect battery. Unplug 14-pin ECM connector. Measure resistance between White/Violet wire (pin No. 13) and Red/Violet wire (pin No. 14) at 14-pin connector.
2) Shake ABS wiring harness from ECM to speed sensor while measuring resistance. If resistance is not a constant 1000-2000 ohms, repair wiring or connector and retest system. If resistance is a constant 1000-2000 ohms, remove speed sensor from differential. Check for metal chips on sensor pole.
3) If chips are found, disassemble differential and replace exciter ring. Check exciter ring for damage. Replace exciter ring if damaged. If exciter ring and sensor are okay, reinstall speed sensor. Locate speed sensor test connector on right of steering column (RWD Van), or on left side cowl panel (all others). Connect a voltmeter between Red/Violet wire and White/Violet wire at test connector.

CAUTION: Use care when working around rotating wheels.

4) Raise and support rear of vehicle. Block front wheels. Ensure vehicle is in 2WD mode. Start engine and place transmission in gear. With vehicle operating at 5 MPH, measure voltage. If voltage is more than 650 mV and steady, replace ECM and retest system. If voltage is 650 mV or lower, and/or is not steady, replace speed sensor and retest system.

CODE 7

1) Unplug dual solenoid hydraulic valve connector. Measure resistance between Green wire and Black wire at valve connector. If resistance is less than 3 ohms, replace valve. Clear trouble code and retest system. If resistance is 3 ohms or more, disconnect battery.
2) Unplug 14-pin ECM connector. Measure resistance between Light Green wire (pin No. 1) and ground at 14-pin ECM connector. If resistance is 20,000 ohms or less, repair short in Light Green wire to ground. Clear trouble code and retest system. If resistance is more than 20,000 ohms, replace ECM. Clear trouble code and retest system.

CODE 8

1) Unplug dual solenoid hydraulic valve connector. Measure resistance between White wire and Black wire at valve connector. If resistance is less than one ohm, replace dual solenoid hydraulic valve. Clear trouble code and retest system. If resistance is one ohm or more, disconnect battery.
2) Unplug 14-pin ECM connector. Measure resistance between White/ Brown wire (pin No. 8) and ground at 14-pin ECM connector. If resistance is more than 20,000 ohms, replace ECM. If resistance is 20,000 ohms or less, repair short to ground in White/Brown wire. Clear trouble code and retest system.

CODE 9

NOTE: Ensure seal is placed between sensor and connector whenever separated.

1) Unplug speed sensor connector at differential. Measure resistance between Pink wire and Light Green/Orange wire at sensor connector. If resistance is 2500 ohms or less, replace speed sensor. Clear trouble code and retest system.
2) If resistance is more than 2500 ohms, reconnect speed sensor connector. Disconnect battery. Unplug 14-pin ECM connector. Measure resistance between White/Violet wire (pin No. 13) and Red/Violet wire (pin No. 14) at 14-pin ECM connector.
3) If resistance is 2500 ohms or less, replace ECM. Clear trouble code and retest system. If resistance is more than 2500 ohms, repair open in White/Violet wire or Red/Violet wire. Also ensure connector terminals are mating properly and are not damaged. Clear trouble code and retest system.

CODE 10

NOTE: Ensure seal is placed between sensor and connector whenever separated.

1) Unplug speed sensor connector at differential. Measure resistance between Pink wire and Light Green/Orange wire at sensor connector. If resistance is less than 1000 ohms, replace sensor. Clear trouble code and retest system.
2) If resistance is 1000 ohms or more, disconnect battery. Unplug 14-pin ECM connector. Measure resistance between Red/Violet wire (pin No. 14) and ground at 14-pin ECM connector. If resistance is 20,000 ohms or less, repair open circuit in Red/Violet wire between ECM and sensor. Clear trouble code and retest system.
3) If resistance is more than 20,000 ohms, measure resistance between White/Violet wire (pin No. 13) and Red/Violet wire (pin No. 14) at 14-pin ECM connector. If resistance is more than 20,000 ohms, replace ECM and retest system. If resistance is 20,000 ohms or less, repair short between White/Violet wire and Red/Violet wire. Clear trouble code and retest system.

CODE 11

1) Recheck for Code 11 after driving vehicle at 35 MPH or more. If trouble code reappears after driving 35 MPH or more, apply brake pedal and check stoplight operation.
2) If stoplights do not work, repair stoplight circuit. Clear trouble code and retest system. If stoplights work, turn ignition off. Unplug 14-pin ECM connector. Measure voltage between White or White/Tan wire (pin No. 7) at 14-pin ECM connector and ground while depressing brake pedal.
3) If voltage is less than 9 volts, repair open circuit in White/Pink or White/Tan wire between stoplight switch and ECM. Clear trouble code and retest system. If voltage is 9 volts or more, ensure 4-way flasher, turn signals, cruise control (if equipped) and stoplight circuits are okay. If circuits are okay, ensure Amber ANTI-LOCK and Red BRAKES warning lights operate properly. Clear trouble code and retest system.

CODES 12 OR MORE

Ensure codes are read correctly. Clear trouble code and retest system. If Codes 12, 13, 14, etc. are still recorded, replace ECM and retest system.

REMOVAL & INSTALLATION

SPEED SENSOR

Removal & Installation – Raise and support rear of vehicle. Remove speed sensor mounting bolt. Unplug speed sensor connector. Remove speed sensor. To install, reverse removal procedure. Ensure seal between sensor and connector is in place.

ELECTRONIC CONTROL MODULE (ECM)

Removal & Installation (Dakota) – Remove right side sill plate and cowl cover. Ensure ignition is off. Unplug 14-pin ECM connector. Remove ECM. To install, reverse removal procedure.

Removal & Installation (All Others) – Remove glove box. Ensure ignition is off. Unplug 14-pin ECM connector. Remove ECM. To install, reverse removal procedure.

DUAL SOLENOID HYDRAULIC VALVE

Removal & Installation – Raise and support vehicle. Disconnect and plug hydraulic lines from valve. Unplug valve connector. Remove valve from vehicle. To install, reverse removal procedure. Bleed brake system.

WIRING DIAGRAMS

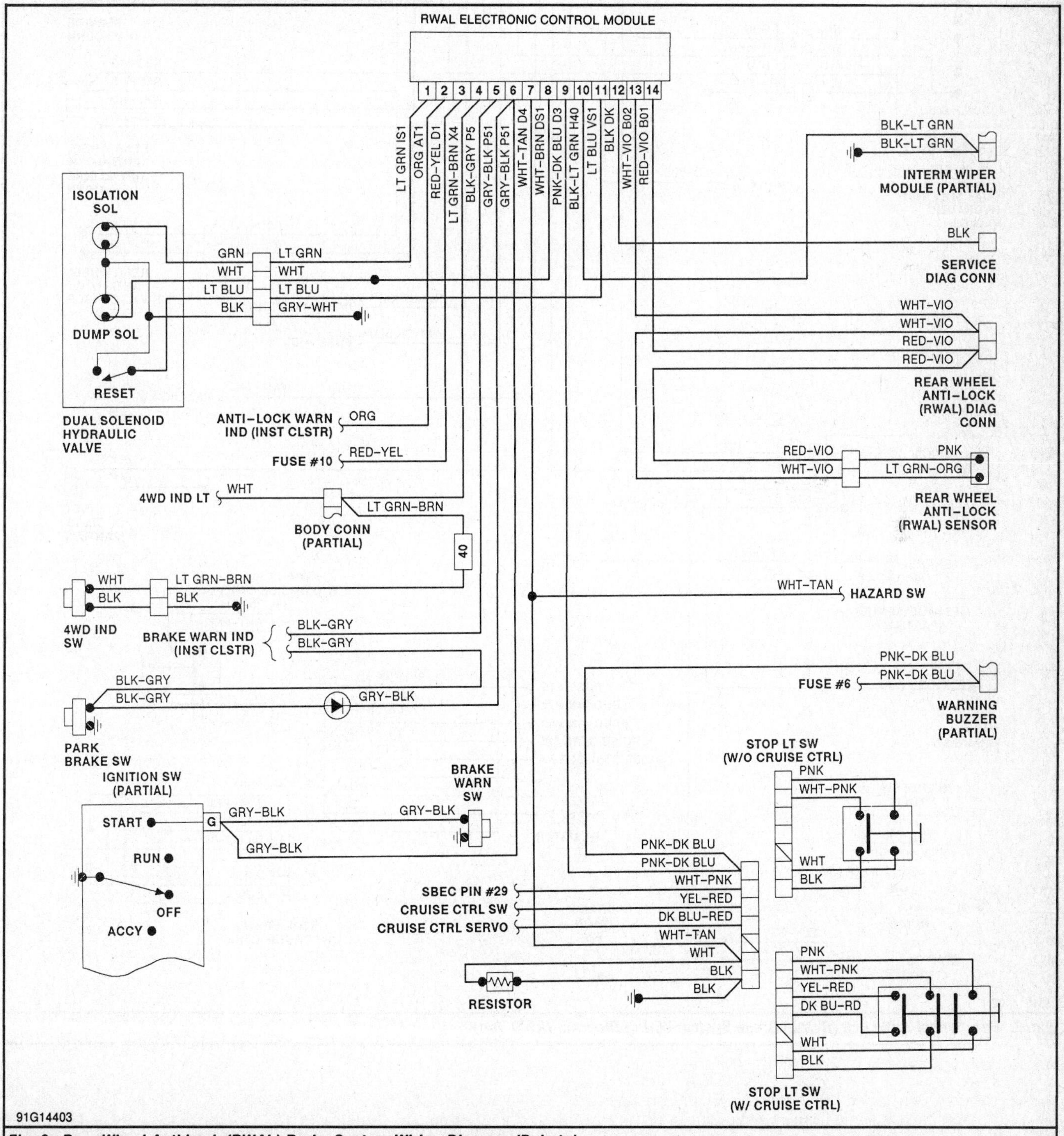
RWAL ELECTRONIC CONTROL MODULE
LT GRN IS1
ORG AT1
RED-YEL D1
LT GRN-BRN X4
BLK-GRY P5
GRY-BLK P51
GRY-BLK P51
WHT-TAN D4
WHT-BRN DS1
PNK-DK BLU D3
BLK-LT GRN H40
LT BLU VS1
BLK DK
WHT-VIO B02
RED-VIO B01
ISOLATION SOL
DUMP SOL
RESET
DUAL SOLENOID HYDRAULIC VALVE
GRN
WHT
LT BLU
BLK
LT GRN
GRY-WHT
INTERM WIPER MODULE (PARTIAL)
BLK-LT GRN
SERVICE DIAG CONN
REAR WHEEL ANTI-LOCK (RWAL) DIAG CONN
WHT-VIO
RED-VIO
REAR WHEEL ANTI-LOCK (RWAL) SENSOR
PNK
LT GRN-ORG
ANTI-LOCK WARN IND (INST CLSTR)
ORG
FUSE #10
RED-YEL
4WD IND LT
BODY CONN (PARTIAL)
LT GRN-BRN
40
4WD IND SW
BRAKE WARN IND (INST CLSTR)
BLK-GRY
GRY-BLK
PARK BRAKE SW
HAZARD SW
WHT-TAN
FUSE #6
PNK-DK BLU
WARNING BUZZER (PARTIAL)
IGNITION SW (PARTIAL)
START
RUN
OFF
ACCY
G
BRAKE WARN SW
STOP LT SW (W/O CRUISE CTRL)
PNK
WHT-PNK
WHT
SBEC PIN #29
CRUISE CTRL SW
CRUISE CTRL SERVO
YEL-RED
DK BLU-RED
DK BU-RD
RESISTOR
STOP LT SW (W/ CRUISE CTRL)
91G14403

Fig. 6: Rear Wheel Anti-Lock (RWAL) Brake System Wiring Diagram (Dakota)

1991 BRAKES
Anti-Lock (Cont.)

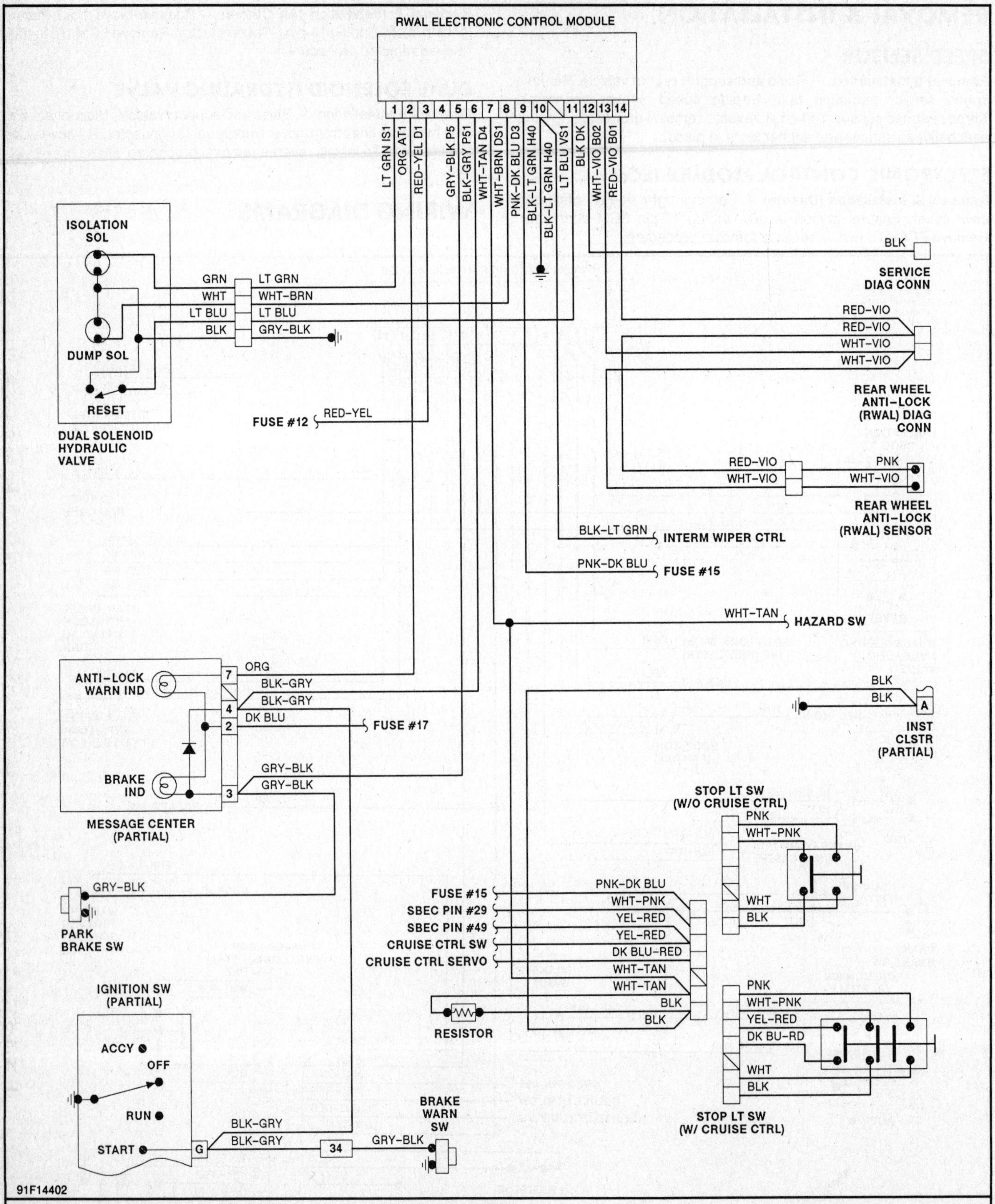
RWAL ELECTRONIC CONTROL MODULE
1 2 3 4 5 6 7 8 9 10 11 12 13 14
LT GRN IS1
ORG AT1
RED-YEL D1
GRY-BLK P5
BLK-GRY P51
WHT-TAN D4
WHT-BRN DS1
PNK-DK BLU D3
BLK-LT GRN H40
BLK-LT GRN H40
LT BLU VS1
BLK DK
WHT-VIO B02
RED-VIO B01
ISOLATION SOL
GRN
LT GRN
WHT
WHT-BRN
LT BLU
LT BLU
BLK
GRY-BLK
DUMP SOL
RESET
DUAL SOLENOID HYDRAULIC VALVE
FUSE #12
RED-YEL
BLK
SERVICE DIAG CONN
RED-VIO
RED-VIO
WHT-VIO
WHT-VIO
REAR WHEEL ANTI-LOCK (RWAL) DIAG CONN
RED-VIO
WHT-VIO
PNK
WHT-VIO
REAR WHEEL ANTI-LOCK (RWAL) SENSOR
BLK-LT GRN
INTERM WIPER CTRL
PNK-DK BLU
FUSE #15
WHT-TAN
HAZARD SW
ANTI-LOCK WARN IND
ORG
BLK-GRY
BLK-GRY
DK BLU
FUSE #17
BRAKE IND
GRY-BLK
GRY-BLK
MESSAGE CENTER (PARTIAL)
BLK
BLK
A
INST CLSTR (PARTIAL)
STOP LT SW (W/O CRUISE CTRL)
PNK
WHT-PNK
WHT
BLK
GRY-BLK
PARK BRAKE SW
FUSE #15
SBEC PIN #29
SBEC PIN #49
CRUISE CTRL SW
CRUISE CTRL SERVO
PNK-DK BLU
WHT-PNK
YEL-RED
YEL-RED
DK BLU-RED
WHT-TAN
WHT-TAN
BLK
BLK
RESISTOR
PNK
WHT-PNK
YEL-RED
DK BU-RD
WHT
BLK
IGNITION SW (PARTIAL)
ACCY
OFF
RUN
START
G
BLK-GRY
BLK-GRY
34
GRY-BLK
BRAKE WARN SW
STOP LT SW (W/ CRUISE CTRL)
91F14402

Fig. 7: Rear Wheel Anti-Lock (RWAL) Brake System Wiring Diagram (RWD Van)

1991 BRAKES
Anti-Lock (Cont.)

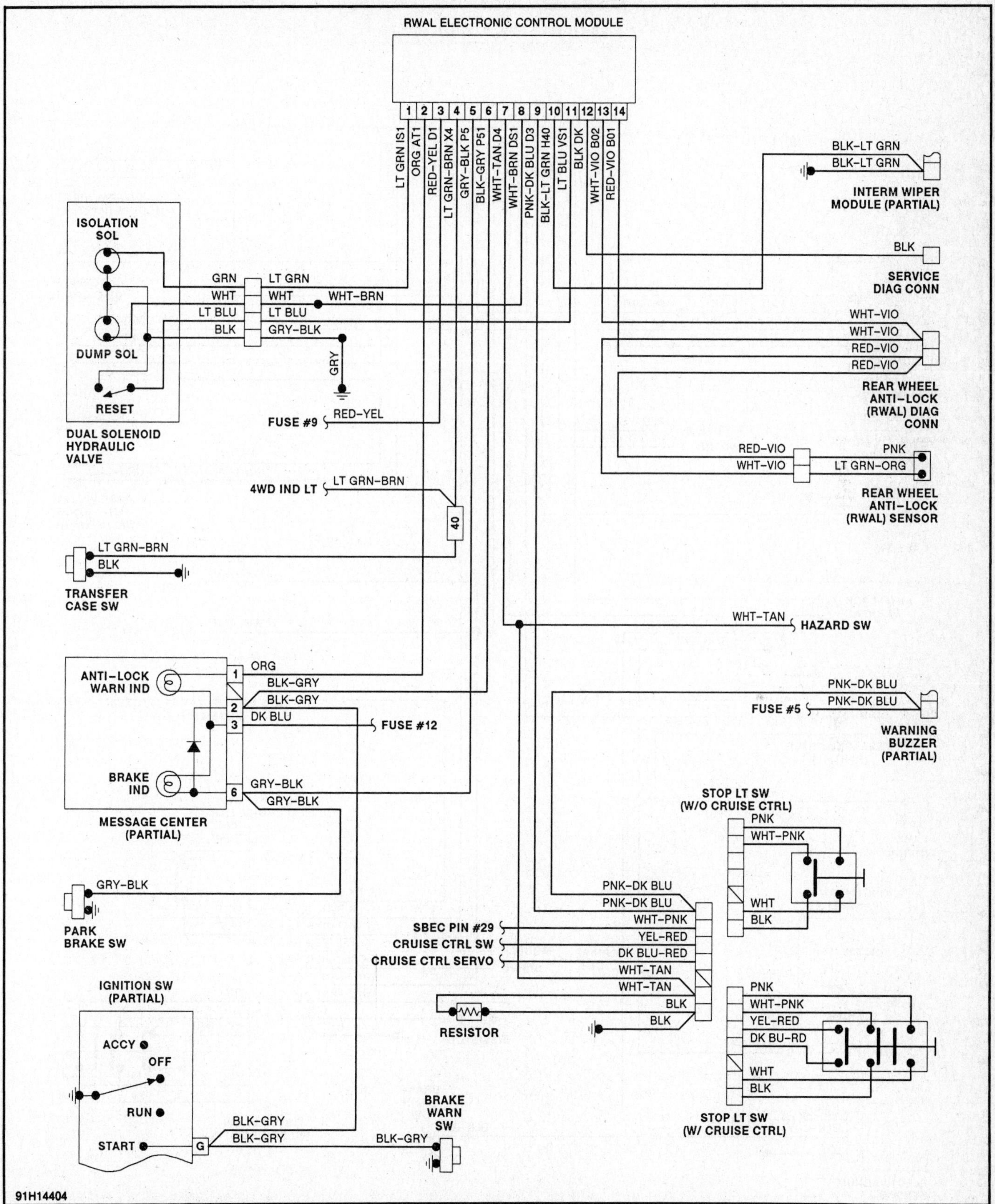
RWAL ELECTRONIC CONTROL MODULE
1 2 3 4 5 6 7 8 9 10 11 12 13 14
LT GRN IS1
ORG AT1
RED-YEL D1
LT GRN-BRN X4
GRY-BLK P5
BLK-GRY P51
WHT-TAN D4
WHT-BRN DS1
PNK-DK BLU D3
BLK-LT GRN H40
LT BLU VS1
BLK DK
WHT-VIO B02
RED-VIO B01
ISOLATION SOL
DUMP SOL
RESET
DUAL SOLENOID HYDRAULIC VALVE
GRN
WHT
LT BLU
BLK
LT GRN
WHT
LT BLU
GRY-BLK
WHT-BRN
GRY
FUSE #9
RED-YEL
4WD IND LT
LT GRN-BRN
40
LT GRN-BRN
BLK
TRANSFER CASE SW
BLK-LT GRN
BLK-LT GRN
INTERM WIPER MODULE (PARTIAL)
BLK
SERVICE DIAG CONN
WHT-VIO
WHT-VIO
RED-VIO
RED-VIO
REAR WHEEL ANTI-LOCK (RWAL) DIAG CONN
RED-VIO
WHT-VIO
PNK
LT GRN-ORG
REAR WHEEL ANTI-LOCK (RWAL) SENSOR
WHT-TAN
HAZARD SW
ANTI-LOCK WARN IND
BRAKE IND
MESSAGE CENTER (PARTIAL)
ORG
BLK-GRY
BLK-GRY
DK BLU
GRY-BLK
GRY-BLK
1
2
3
6
FUSE #12
PNK-DK BLU
PNK-DK BLU
FUSE #5
WARNING BUZZER (PARTIAL)
GRY-BLK
PARK BRAKE SW
STOP LT SW (W/O CRUISE CTRL)
PNK
WHT-PNK
WHT
BLK
PNK-DK BLU
PNK-DK BLU
WHT-PNK
YEL-RED
DK BLU-RED
WHT-TAN
WHT-TAN
BLK
BLK
SBEC PIN #29
CRUISE CTRL SW
CRUISE CTRL SERVO
RESISTOR
PNK
WHT-PNK
YEL-RED
DK BU-RD
WHT
BLK
STOP LT SW (W/ CRUISE CTRL)
IGNITION SW (PARTIAL)
ACCY
OFF
RUN
START
G
BLK-GRY
BLK-GRY
BLK-GRY
BRAKE WARN SW
91H14404

Fig. 8: Rear Wheel Anti-Lock (RWAL) Brake System Wiring Diagram (Pickup & Ramcharger – Gasoline)

1991 BRAKES
Anti-Lock (Cont.)

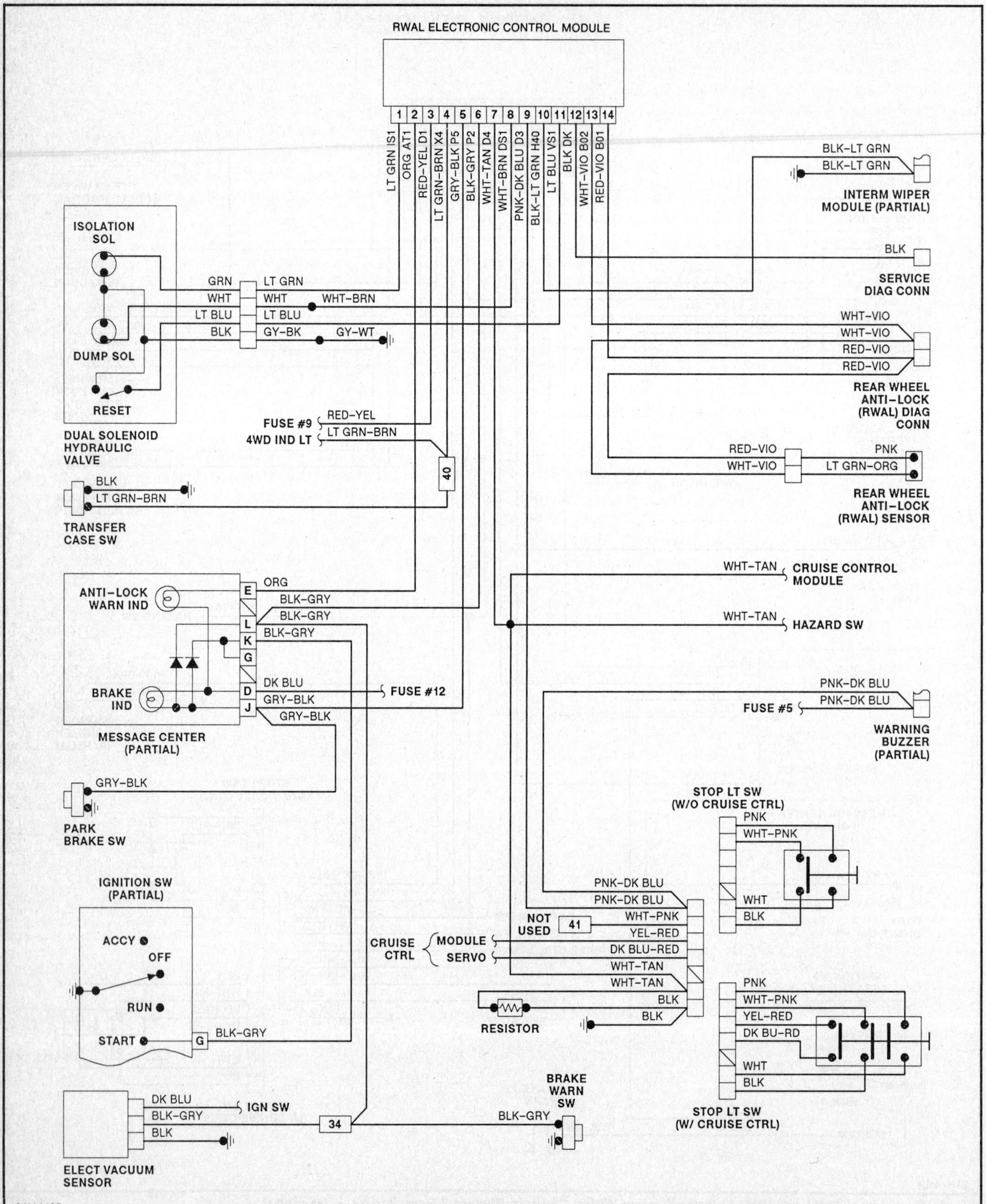
RWAL ELECTRONIC CONTROL MODULE
1 2 3 4 5 6 7 8 9 10 11 12 13 14
LT GRN IS1
ORG AT1
RED-YEL D1
LT GRN-BRN X4
GRY-BLK P5
BLK-GRY P2
WHT-TAN D4
WHT-BRN DS1
PNK-DK BLU D3
BLK-LT GRN H40
LT BLU VS1
BLK DK
WHT-VIO B02
RED-VIO B01
BLK-LT GRN
BLK-LT GRN
INTERM WIPER MODULE (PARTIAL)
BLK
SERVICE DIAG CONN
WHT-VIO
WHT-VIO
RED-VIO
RED-VIO
REAR WHEEL ANTI-LOCK (RWAL) DIAG CONN
RED-VIO
PNK
WHT-VIO
LT GRN-ORG
REAR WHEEL ANTI-LOCK (RWAL) SENSOR
ISOLATION SOL
GRN
WHT
LT BLU
BLK
LT GRN
WHT
WHT-BRN
LT BLU
GY-BK
GY-WT
DUMP SOL
RESET
DUAL SOLENOID HYDRAULIC VALVE
FUSE #9
RED-YEL
4WD IND LT
LT GRN-BRN
40
BLK
LT GRN-BRN
TRANSFER CASE SW
WHT-TAN
CRUISE CONTROL MODULE
WHT-TAN
HAZARD SW
ANTI-LOCK WARN IND
BRAKE IND
E
L
K
G
D
J
ORG
BLK-GRY
BLK-GRY
BLK-GRY
DK BLU
FUSE #12
GRY-BLK
GRY-BLK
MESSAGE CENTER (PARTIAL)
PNK-DK BLU
PNK-DK BLU
FUSE #5
WARNING BUZZER (PARTIAL)
GRY-BLK
PARK BRAKE SW
STOP LT SW (W/O CRUISE CTRL)
PNK
WHT-PNK
WHT
BLK
IGNITION SW (PARTIAL)
ACCY
OFF
RUN
START
G
BLK-GRY
PNK-DK BLU
PNK-DK BLU
NOT USED
41
WHT-PNK
YEL-RED
CRUISE CTRL
MODULE
SERVO
DK BLU-RED
WHT-TAN
WHT-TAN
BLK
BLK
RESISTOR
PNK
WHT-PNK
YEL-RED
DK BU-RD
WHT
BLK
STOP LT SW (W/ CRUISE CTRL)
BRAKE WARN SW
DK BLU
BLK-GRY
BLK
IGN SW
34
BLK-GRY
ELECT VACUUM SENSOR
91I14405

Fig. 9: Rear Wheel Anti-Lock (RWAL) Brake System Wiring Diagram (Pickup & Ramcharger – Diesel)

1991 BRAKES
Disc & Drum

Caravan, Dakota, Pickup, Ramcharger, RWD Van, Town & Country, Voyager

DESCRIPTION & OPERATION

All models are equipped with single piston, sliding caliper front disc brakes with ventilated cast iron rotors. Rear brakes are equipped with anti-lock drum brakes. System also includes a power brake booster, a dual reservoir master cylinder, wheel cylinders, brake lines, hoses and a combination valve. Combination valve consists of a metering valve and a pressure differential switch. Caravan, Town & Country and Voyager also include a height sensing proportioning valve.

The disc brake caliper is free to move laterally on adapter slide surfaces. On brake application, fluid pressure is exerted equally against caliper piston and all surfaces of caliper piston bore. Piston pressure is transmitted directly to inboard disc pad, which presses against disc rotor. Pressure applied to inboard pad makes the caliper slide inward. The inward movement presses the outboard pad against opposite side of disc rotor to complete braking action. On brake release, piston and caliper return to normal, non-applied position.

All models without full floating rear axle use 9", 10" or 11" single anchor rear brakes. All 3 sizes are of the same design. *See Fig. 9.*

All models with full floating rear axle use 12" single anchor rear brakes of slightly different design than 9", 10" and 11" brakes. *See Fig. 10.*

NOTE: For information on Anti-Lock Brake Systems (ABS), see ANTI-LOCK BRAKES article.

BLEEDING BRAKE SYSTEM

BLEEDING PROCEDURES

Master Cylinder (Bench Bleeding) - 1) To prevent excessive amount of air from entering the brake system, creating poor brake operation, bleed master cylinder before installation.

2) Place master cylinder in soft-jawed vise. DO NOT tighten vise enough to damage master cylinder. Install bleeder tubes in both outlets of master cylinder. *See Fig. 1.*

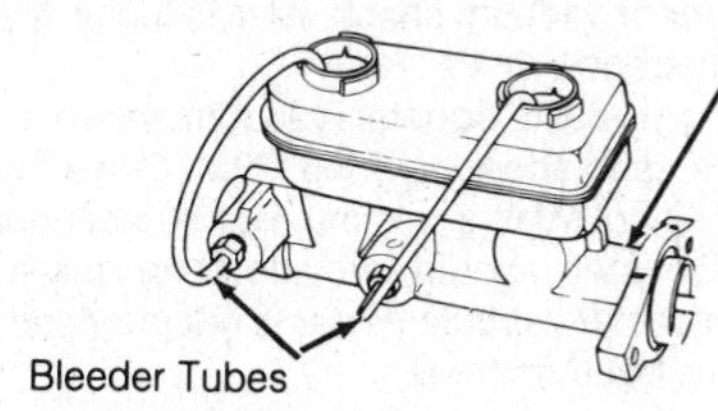
Master Cylinder
Bleeder Tubes
30000
Courtesy of Chrysler Motors.

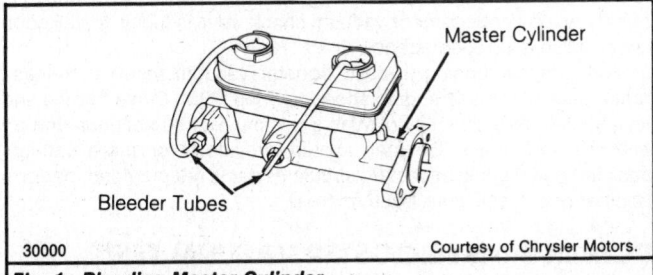

Fig. 1: Bleeding Master Cylinder

3) Fill master cylinder with clean brake fluid that meets DOT 3 specifications. Ensure that the end of bleeder tubes are submerged in the brake fluid.

4) Using proper sized rod, apply and release master cylinder until no air bubbles exist in brake fluid flow. Once all air bubbles are gone from master cylinder, secure cap and install on vehicle.

5) Leave bleeder tubes installed on master cylinder until master cylinder is installed. Bleed brake system after installation.

Master Cylinder (On-Vehicle Bleeding) - 1) After bench bleeding, install master cylinder on vehicle. Remove bleeder lines and install brake lines. DO NOT fully tighten brake lines at this time.

2) Slowly force brake pedal to the floor, and hold pedal in this position. Tighten brake lines and release brake pedal. Repeat procedure until no air bubbles exist at brake lines. Wheel cylinders and calipers may also require bleeding.

POSITIONING METERING VALVE BEFORE BLEEDING SYSTEM

Dakota, Pickup, Ramcharger & RWD Van - 1) Before using pressure tank bleeding procedure, correctly position the metering valve (incorporated in the combination valve) to allow brake fluid to flow through the valve to the entire brake system.

2) The valve stem may be retained in the metering valve during bleeding procedure, using Valve Retainer (C-4121). *See Fig. 2.* Remove valve retainer once brake bleeding procedure is complete.

CAUTION: DO NOT use rigid clamp to position valve stem. Damage to the valve assembly may result causing brake failure.

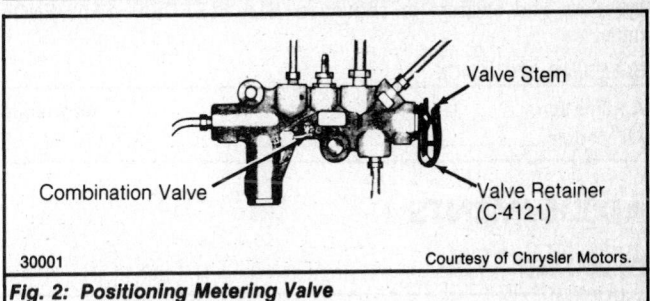

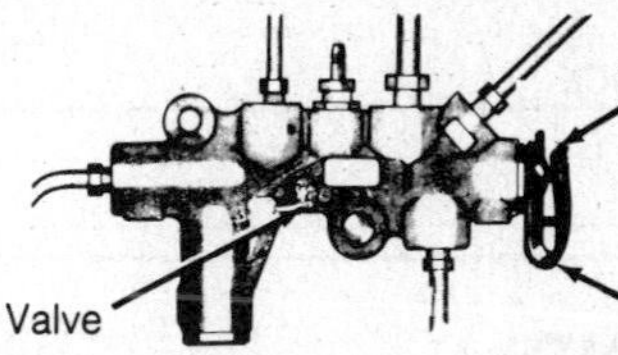
Valve Stem
Combination Valve
Valve Retainer
(C-4121)
30001
Courtesy of Chrysler Motors.

Fig. 2: Positioning Metering Valve

VACUUM BLEEDING

Fill master cylinder. Install vacuum bleed equipment to first bleeder valve to be serviced. Open bleeder valve 3/4-1 turn. Depress vacuum pump, and pull fluid into reservoir jar. Bleed each bleeder valve in sequence. See BLEEDING SEQUENCE table.

PRESSURE BLEEDING

CAUTION: When using pressure bleeding method on Dakota, Pickup, Ramcharger and RWD Van models, valve stem on combination valve must be pressed in and held in to properly bleed brake system. See POSITIONING METERING VALVE BEFORE BLEEDING SYSTEM.

1) Clean master cylinder cap and surrounding area. Remove cap. With pressure tank at least 1/2 full, connect to master cylinder with adapters. Attach bleeder hose to first bleeder valve to be serviced. See BLEEDING SEQUENCE table.

2) Place other end of hose in clean glass jar partially filled with clean brake fluid so end of hose is submerged in fluid. The metering valve must be positioned properly before pressure bleeding. See POSITIONING METERING VALVE BEFORE BLEEDING SYSTEM.

3) Open release valve on pressure bleeder. Follow equipment manufacturer's pressure instructions or see PRESSURE BLEEDER SETTINGS table. Open bleeder screw 3/4-1 turn and note fluid flow.

4) Close bleeder screw when fluid flowing is free of bubbles. Repeat procedure on remaining wheels in proper sequence. Check brake pedal operation after bleeding has been completed.

5) Remove pressure bleeding equipment and valve retainer from metering valve. Ensure that master cylinder is full of fluid.

PRESSURE BLEEDER SETTINGS

Application	psi (kg/cm^2)
All Models	35 (2.5)

MANUAL BLEEDING

NOTE: When bleeding disc brakes, air may tend to cling to caliper walls. Lightly tap caliper, while bleeding, to aid in removal of air.

1) Fill master cylinder. Install bleeder hose to first bleeder valve to be serviced. See BLEEDING SEQUENCE table. Submerge other end of hose in clean glass jar partially filled with clean brake fluid.

1991 BRAKES
Disc & Drum (Cont.)

2) Open bleeder valve 3/4-1 turn. Depress brake pedal slowly through full travel. Close bleeder valve and release pedal. Repeat procedure until flow of fluid shows no signs of air bubbles.

NOTE: When bleeding brake system manually, ensure bleeder valve is closed when brake pedal is released.

BLEEDING SEQUENCE

Before bleeding system, exhaust all vacuum from power unit by depressing brake pedal several times. Bleed master cylinder with bleeder screws (if equipped). Bleed slave cylinder on vehicles equipped with remote mount power assist units. Bleed wheel cylinders and calipers in sequence. See BLEEDING SEQUENCE table.

BLEEDING SEQUENCE

Application	Sequence
All Models	RR, LR, RF, LF

ADJUSTMENTS

DISC PAD

NOTE: When replacing pads, ALWAYS replace inner and outer pads on both front wheels.

Pad wear is automatically compensated by piston moving outward in caliper bore. Disc pad adjustment is not required. Inspect disc pads whenever wheels are removed.

HEIGHT SENSING PROPORTIONING VALVE

Caravan, Town & Country, & Voyager – 1) Premature rear wheel skid may be caused by incorrect adjustment of the height sensing proportioning valve. Before making adjustment, inspect brake system and bleed entire system using appropriate method. See BLEEDING PROCEDURES under BLEEDING BRAKE SYSTEM.

2) Raise vehicle on hoist and allow rear suspension to hang free with rear wheels removed. Ensure hoist does not contact rear springs. Disconnect shock absorbers. Loosen adjustment nut on actuator assembly. *See Fig. 3.* Ensure actuator assembly hook is correctly seated on proportioning valve lever.

3) Pull actuator assembly toward spring hanger until proportioning valve lever bottoms. Hold proportioning valve lever in this position. Tighten adjustment nut to 25 INCH lbs. (2.8 N.m). Install shock absorbers and rear wheels.

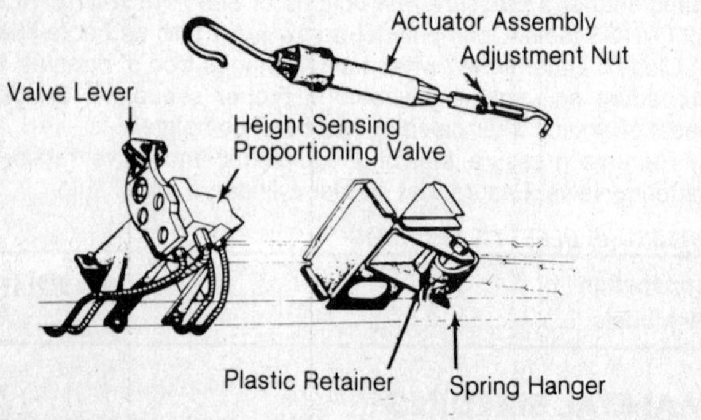
Actuator Assembly
Adjustment Nut
Valve Lever
Height Sensing
Proportioning Valve
Plastic Retainer
Spring Hanger
30005
Courtesy of Chrysler Motors.

Fig. 3: Height Sensing Proportioning Valve (Caravan, Town & Country, & Voyager)

PARKING BRAKE

1) Release parking brake and loosen cable adjusting nut to allow slack in cable. Adjust rear brakes. Tighten cable adjusting nut until a slight drag is felt while rotating rear wheels.

2) Loosen cable adjusting nut until both rear wheels can be rotated freely. Back off adjusting nut an additional 2 turns. Apply and release parking brake several times, checking for free rotation at rear wheels.

REAR BRAKE SHOES

1) Raise and support vehicle. Ensure parking brake lever is fully released. Back off parking brake cable adjustment to ensure cable has slack. Remove adjusting hole cover.

2) Using a brake adjuster, expand brake shoes until slight drag is felt when wheel assembly is rotated. Using thin screwdriver, hold automatic adjusting lever away from adjustment star wheel.

3) Back off adjustment star wheel until wheel assembly rotates freely and brake shoe drag is eliminated. Repeat adjustment for remaining wheels. Adjustment must be equal at all wheels. Replace adjusting hole covers and adjust parking brake.

STOPLIGHT SWITCH

The stoplight switch is attached to the brake pedal support. Push stoplight switch through clip in mounting bracket until switch seats in bracket. Pull brake pedal backward as far as pedal will travel. Brake pedal will ratchet stoplight switch to correct position. Verify full brake pedal return and that stoplights glow when brake pedal is applied.

TESTING

POWER BRAKE BOOSTER FUNCTIONAL TEST

1) Start engine and check booster vacuum hose connections. A hissing noise indicates a vacuum leak. Repair any vacuum leaks before proceeding. Stop engine and shift transmission into Neutral. Pump brake pedal until all vacuum reserve in booster is depleted.

2) Hold brake pedal under light foot pressure. If pedal does not hold firm and falls away, master cylinder is faulty. If pedal holds firm, start engine and observe pedal action. If pedal falls away slightly under light foot pressure and then holds firm, go to step **3)**. If no pedal action is observed, power booster or vacuum check valve is faulty. Install good check valve and repeat steps.

3) With engine running, rebuild booster vacuum reserve. Release brake pedal. Increase engine speed to 1500 RPM. Close throttle and immediately turn off ignition. Wait a minimum of 90 seconds and try brake action again. Booster should provide 2 or more vacuum assisted pedal applications. If vacuum assist is not provided, perform booster and check valve vacuum tests.

POWER BRAKE BOOSTER VACUUM TEST

Connect vacuum gauge to booster check valve with "T" fitting. Start engine and run at idle speed for one minute. Clamp hose shut between vacuum source and check valve. Stop engine and observe vacuum gauge. If vacuum drops more than one in. Hg within 15 seconds, booster diaphragm or check valve is faulty.

POWER BRAKE BOOSTER CHECK VALVE TEST

Disconnect vacuum hose from check valve. Remove check valve and valve seal from booster. Use a hand operated vacuum pump for testing. Apply 15-20 in. Hg vacuum at large end of check valve. Vacuum should hold steady. If gauge on pump indicates vacuum loss, check valve is faulty and should be replaced.

HEIGHT SENSING PROPORTIONING VALVE TEST

Caravan, Town & Country, & Voyager – 1) Remove actuator assembly adjustment nut. Disconnect actuator assembly hook from height sensing proportioning valve. Install one gauge and "T" of Height Sensing Proportioning Valve Test Set (C-4007-A) in either line of master cylinder outlet port between master cylinder and brake warning switch.

2) Install other gauge and "T" of test set in either line of proportioning valve outlet port between proportioning valve and rear wheel cylinder. Bleed brake system and gauges.

3) Have an assistant press and hold brake pedal. Note reading on both gauges. Pressure on inlet gauge (at master cylinder) should be 500 psi (35 kg/cm²). Pressure on outlet gauge (at proportioning valve) should be 100-200 psi (7-14 kg/cm²).

4) If pressures are not to specification, replace height sensing proportioning valve. If pressures are okay, remove test equipment. Install actuator and adjust. See HEIGHT SENSING PROPORTIONING VALVE under ADJUSTMENTS. Bleed brake system.

COMBINATION VALVE METERING VALVE TEST

Metering valve operation can be checked visually with the aid of an assistant. While an assistant applies and releases the brake pedal, observe metering valve stem. If valve is operating correctly, stem will extend slightly when brakes are applied and contract when brakes are released. If valve is faulty, replace combination valve assembly.

COMBINATION VALVE PRESSURE DIFFERENTIAL SWITCH TEST

1) Have an assistant in vehicle to observe brake warning light and apply brake pedal. Raise and support vehicle and connect a bleed hose to one of the rear wheel cylinders. Submerge other end of hose into a container partially filled with brake fluid. Have an assistant press and hold brake pedal all the way down while observing brake warning light. If warning light glows, switch is operating properly.

2) If warning light fails to glow, check circuit fuse, bulb and wiring. Repair as necessary. Repeat step **1)**. If warning light fails to glow, check brakelight, parking brake switches and related wiring. Repair as necessary. Repeat step **1)**. If warning light fails to glow, pressure differential switch is faulty. Replace combination valve assembly, bleed brake system and verify proper valve operation.

REMOVAL & INSTALLATION

CALIPER

Removal (Bendix) – 1) Raise and support vehicle. Remove wheels. Remove support key retaining screw. *See Fig. 4.* Using drift punch, drive out support key and spring. Remove caliper from adapter and pry outer pad from caliper.

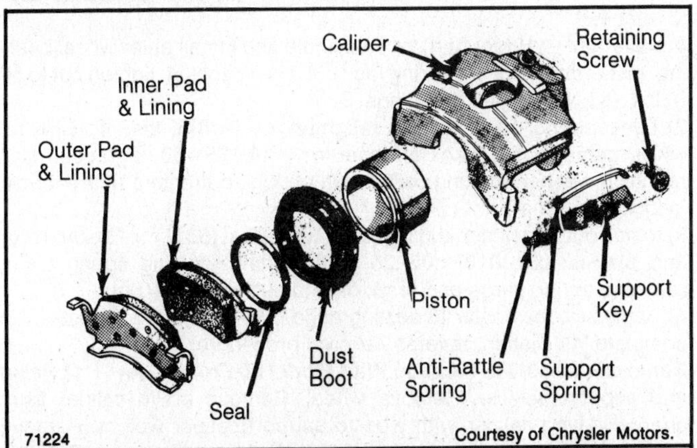
Caliper
Retaining Screw
Inner Pad & Lining
Outer Pad & Lining
Piston
Support Key
Dust Boot
Anti-Rattle Spring
Support Spring
Seal
71224
Courtesy of Chrysler Motors.

Fig. 4: Exploded View of Single-Piston Sliding Caliper (Bendix)

2) Hang caliper with wire. DO NOT allow caliper to hang by brake hose. Remove inner pad and anti-rattle spring from adapter. Note position of anti-rattle spring for installation. If pads are to be reused, mark pads for installation to original position.

3) Replace pads if lining is worn to within 1/16" (1.6 mm) of rivet heads. Inspect rotor. See inspection procedure for ROTOR under REMOVAL & INSTALLATION. Check piston seal for leaks and piston boot for cuts. If piston seal leaks or if boot is damaged, overhaul caliper assembly. Disconnect and plug hydraulic brake hose at caliper

Installation – 1) Clean caliper and adapter slide surfaces with wire brush. Lubricate with multipurpose grease. Install anti-rattle spring on inner pad, ensuring loop portion of spring is away from rotor. Install inner pad in adapter, ensuring spring remains in position.

2) Install outer pad in caliper. Free play should not exist between pad flange (tab) and caliper flange. If free play exists, bend pad flange (tab) until interference fit with caliper is obtained. If disc pad cannot be installed by hand, press into place using a block of wood and "C" clamp. Place caliper into position over rotor and seat caliper in adapter.

3) Place support spring over support key. Install assembly between adapter and lower caliper machined surfaces. Tap assembly into place using drift punch. Install support key retaining screw, ensuring boss on screw fits into cut-out on key.

4) If caliper overhaul was necessary, install brake hose. Bleed brake system. See BLEEDING PROCEDURES under BLEEDING BRAKE SYSTEM. Install wheels. Fill reservoir to proper level. Slowly pump brake pedal until it is firm. Check reservoir fluid level. Road test vehicle.

Removal (Chrysler Motors) – 1) Raise and support vehicle. Remove wheels. Remove caliper retainer bolts, anti-rattle springs and clips. *See Fig. 5.* Carefully lift caliper assembly away from rotor. Pry between outer pad and caliper to remove outer pad. Hang caliper with wire. DO NOT allow caliper to hang by brake hose. Remove inner pad from adapter.

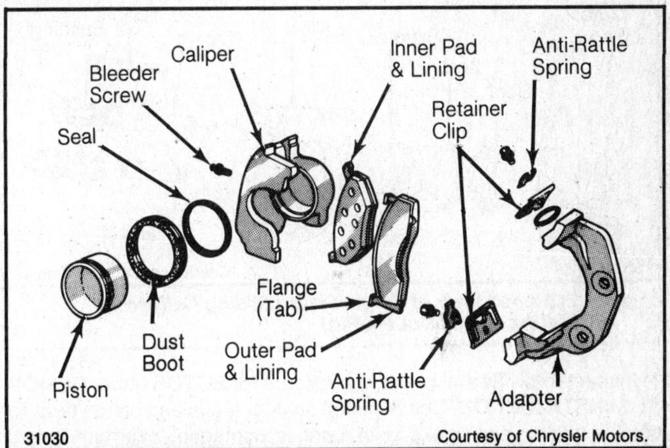
Caliper
Bleeder Screw
Inner Pad & Lining
Anti-Rattle Spring
Retainer Clip
Seal
Flange (Tab)
Dust Boot
Outer Pad & Lining
Piston
Anti-Rattle Spring
Adapter
31030
Courtesy of Chrysler Motors.

Fig. 5: Exploded View of Single-Piston Sliding Caliper (Chrysler Motors)

2) Measure pad lining thickness. If pad lining is worn to a thickness of 1/8" (3.2 mm) or less, replace pads. Inspect rotor. See inspection procedure for ROTOR under REMOVAL & INSTALLATION. Check piston seal for leaks and piston boot for cuts. If piston seal leaks or if boot is damaged, overhaul caliper assembly. Disconnect and plug hydraulic brake hose at caliper

Installation – 1) Install inner pad into adapter. Remove protective paper from noise suppression gasket on outer pad. Install outer pad in caliper. Free play should not exist between pad flange (tab) and caliper flange. If free play exists, bend pad flange (tab) until interference fit with caliper is obtained. Lubricate slide surfaces of adapter and caliper with multipurpose grease.

2) Carefully install caliper over rotor. Align caliper in adapter. Install retainer clips and anti-rattle springs. If caliper overhaul was necessary, install brake hose. Bleed brake system. See BLEEDING PROCEDURES under BLEEDING BRAKE SYSTEM. Install wheels. Fill master cylinder to proper level. Slowly pump brake pedal to obtain firm pedal. Check master cylinder fluid level. Road test vehicle.

Removal (Kelsey-Hayes Single & Double Pin) – 1) Raise and support vehicle. Remove front wheels. Remove caliper guide pin(s). On single pin caliper, pry caliper away from adapter and pads. *See Fig. 6.* Remove caliper. Hang caliper with wire. DO NOT allow caliper to hang by brake hose. Remove outer pad, rotor and inner pad.

1991 BRAKES
Disc & Drum (Cont.)

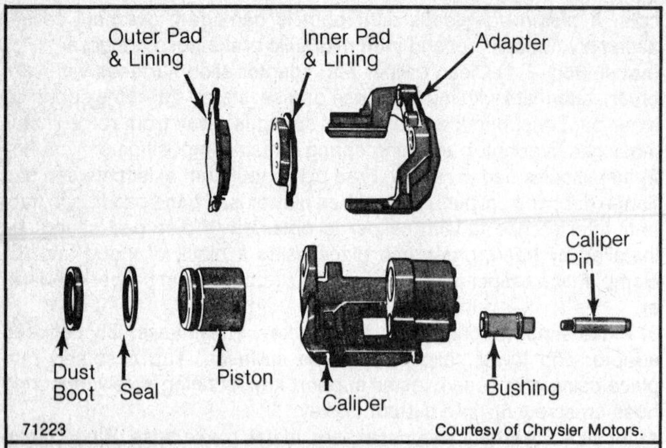
Outer Pad
& Lining
Inner Pad
& Lining
Adapter
Caliper
Pin
Dust
Boot
Seal
Piston
Caliper
Bushing
71223
Courtesy of Chrysler Motors.

Fig. 6: Exploded View of Single-Piston Sliding Caliper (Kelsey-Hayes Single Pin)

2) On double pin caliper, pull lower end of caliper out from machined abutment on steering knuckle. *See Fig. 7.* Remove caliper and pads as an assembly. Remove pads from caliper. Remove rotor. On all models, measure combined thickness of pad and backing at thinnest part of pad. If combined thickness is 1/4" (6.35 mm) or less, replace pads.

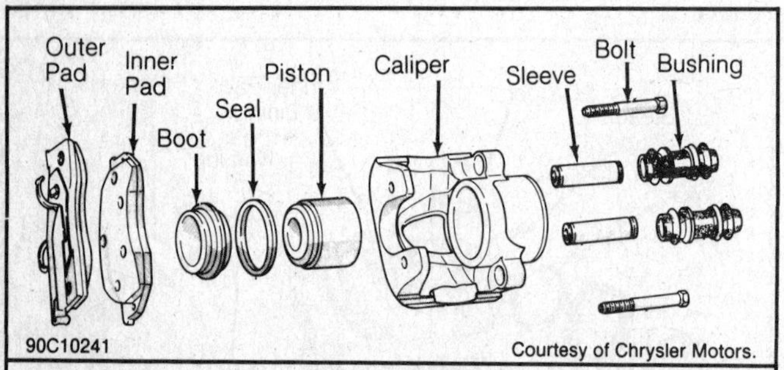
Outer
Pad
Inner
Pad
Boot
Seal
Piston
Caliper
Sleeve
Bolt
Bushing
90C10241
Courtesy of Chrysler Motors.

Fig. 7: Exploded View of Single-Piston Sliding Caliper (Kelsey-Hayes Double Pin)

3) Inspect rotor. See inspection procedure for ROTOR under REMOVAL & INSTALLATION. Check piston seal for leaks and piston boot for cuts. If piston seal leaks or if boot is damaged, overhaul caliper assembly. Disconnect and plug hydraulic brake hose at caliper

Installation – 1) Clean caliper and adapter slide surfaces with wire brush. Lubricate with multipurpose grease. On single pin caliper, remove protective paper from noise suppression gasket on inner and outer pads. Install anti-rattle clips on top of inner pad, on bottom of outer pad, and on top finger of caliper. Install inner pad, rotor and outer pad. Install caliper assembly.

2) Install caliper guide pin and tighten. On double pin caliper, inner pads are interchangeable. Outer pads are marked "L" or "R", denoting left or right side. Remove protective paper from noise suppression gasket on outer pad. Install inner and outer pads into caliper. Carefully lower caliper and pads over rotor, guiding hold-down spring under machined abutment on steering knuckle.

3) Install caliper guide pins and tighten. On all models, if caliper overhaul was necessary, install brake hose. Bleed brake system. See BLEEDING PROCEDURES under BLEEDING BRAKE SYSTEM. Install wheels. Fill master cylinder to proper level. Slowly pump brake pedal until firm. Check master cylinder fluid level. Road test vehicle.

ROTOR

Inspection – 1) Raise and support vehicle. Remove wheels. On Caravan, Dakota 4WD, Town & Country and Voyager, install and torque wheel lug nuts to secure rotor. On Dakota 2WD, Pickup, Ramcharger and RWD Van, remove dust cap and temporarily adjust wheel bearings to zero end play.

2) On all models, mount dial indicator on steering arm, with plunger contacting rotor approximately 1" (25 mm) from edge of rotor. Slowly rotate rotor and note lateral runout. Lateral runout on either side of rotor should not exceed specification. See DISC BRAKE ROTOR SPECIFICATIONS table.

3) On Caravan, Dakota, Town & Country and Voyager, if runout exceeds specification, check runout of hub face. Before removing rotor, make a chalk mark across rotor and one wheel stud. Make mark on high side of runout.

4) Remove rotor from hub. Install dial indicator on steering arm, with stem contacting hub face near outer diameter. Place dial indicator stem outside stud circle but inside chamfer on hub rim. If runout is not within specification, hub must be replaced.

5) If hub runout is within specification, install rotor on hub with chalk marks 180 degrees apart. Install wheel lug nuts and recheck rotor runout. If runout is not within specification, resurface or replace rotor.

6) On all models, measure rotor parallelism. To measure parallelism, measure rotor thickness with micrometer at 12 equal points around rotor radius approximately 1" (25 mm) from edge of rotor. If thickness varies more than parallelism specification, resurface or replace rotor.

Removal (Dakota 2WD, Pickup 2WD, Ramcharger 2WD & RWD Van) – Raise and support vehicle. Remove wheels. Remove brake caliper from adapter. Hang caliper with wire to support caliper weight. Remove grease cap, cotter pin, nut lock, nut, thrust washer and outer wheel bearing. Pull rotor assembly off spindle.

Installation – 1) Slide rotor assembly into position on spindle. Install outer wheel bearing, thrust washer and nut. While rotating rotor and hub assembly, tighten wheel bearing nut to 20-25 ft. lbs. (27-34 N.m) on RWD Van, and 90 INCH lbs. (10 N.m) on all other 2WD models.

2) Back off nut to release preload. Retighten nut finger tight. Install nut lock and cotter pin. Coat inside of cap with grease and install. To complete installation, reverse removal procedure.

Removal & Installation (Caravan, Dakota 4WD, Town & Country, & Voyager) – Raise and support vehicle. Remove wheels. Remove brake caliper. Hang caliper with wire to support caliper weight. Remove rotor from drive flange. To install, reverse removal procedure.

Removal (Ramcharger 4WD & W150/250 Pickups With Model 44 Front Axle) – 1) Raise and support vehicle. Remove wheel. Remove brake caliper from adapter. Hang caliper with wire to support caliper weight. Remove grease cap and driving hub snap ring. Remove driving hub and retaining spring.

2) Using Socket (C-4170), remove outer wheel bearing lock nut. Remove retaining washer and inner lock nut. Remove rotor. Outer wheel bearing and retainer spring plate will slide off of spindle as rotor is removed.

Installation – 1) Mount rotor on spindle and install outer wheel bearing. Install inner wheel bearing lock nut. Using socket, tighten nut to 50 ft. lbs. (68 N.m) to seat bearings.

2) Loosen inner lock nut and retighten to 30-40 ft. lbs. (41-54 N.m) while rotating rotor. Back off inner lock nut 135-150 degrees. Install retaining washer, making certain pin on lock nut enters nearest hole in locking washer.

3) Install outer lock nut and tighten to 50 ft. lbs. (68 N.m). Ensure rotor end play is .001-.010" (.03-.25 mm). Install retaining spring plate, retaining spring (large end first), driving hub and snap ring.

4) Apply silicone sealer to sealing edge of grease cap and install. To complete installation, reverse removal procedure.

Removal (W250/350 Pickups With Model 60 Front Axle) – 1) Raise and support vehicle. Remove wheel. Remove brake caliper from adapter. Hang caliper with wire to support caliper weight. Remove inner pad. Remove grease cap and drive flange snap ring. Remove drive flange nuts and lock washers and remove drive flange. Discard flange gasket.

2) On models with locking hubs, turn locking hub shift knob to ENGAGE position. Apply pressure to face of shift knob. Remove 3 screws spaced 120 degrees apart and nearest to flange. *See Fig. 8.*

3) Pull shift knob from mounting base. Remove snap ring from axle shaft. Remove cap screws and lock washers from flange. Remove locking hubs.

1991 BRAKES
Disc & Drum (Cont.)

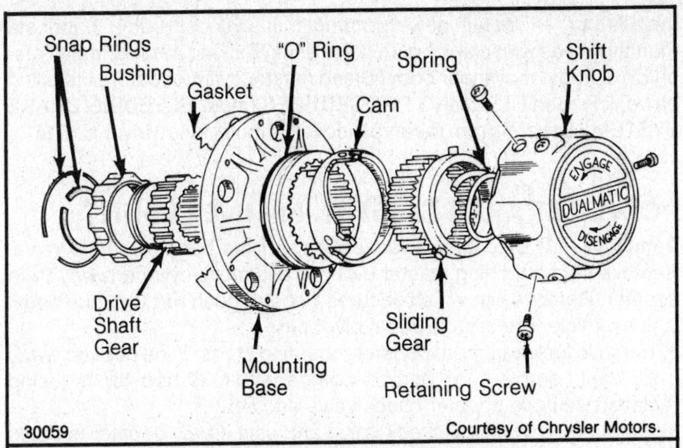
Snap Rings
Bushing
Gasket
"O" Ring
Spring
Cam
Shift Knob
ENGAGE
DUALMATIC
DISENGAGE
Drive Shaft Gear
Mounting Base
Sliding Gear
Retaining Screw
30059
Courtesy of Chrysler Motors.

Fig. 8: Exploded View of Locking Hub Assembly

4) On all models, straighten lock tab on outer wheel bearing lock ring. Using Socket (DD-1241-JD), remove outer wheel bearing lock nut. Remove lock ring, inner lock nut and outer bearing. Remove rotor.

Installation – 1) Mount rotor on spindle and install outer wheel bearing. Install inner wheel bearing lock nut. Using socket, tighten nut to 50 ft. lbs. (68 N.m) to seat bearings.

2) Loosen inner lock nut and retighten to 30-40 ft. lbs. (41-54 N.m) while rotating rotor. Back off inner lock nut 135-150 degrees. Install lock ring and outer lock nut and tighten to 65 ft. lbs. (88 N.m). Ensure rotor end play is .001-.010" (.03-.25 mm).

3) Bend one tang of lock ring over adjusting nut and another tang over lock nut to secure nuts. Install new gasket on hub and install drive flange, lock washers and nuts. Tighten nuts to 30-40 ft. lbs. (41-54 N.m). Install snap ring. On models without locking hubs, reverse removal procedure to complete installation.

4) On models with locking hubs, lubricate hub interior parts with multipurpose grease. Position new gasket and locking hub onto rotor hub. Install cap screws and lock washers. Tighten screws to 30-40 ft. lbs. (41-54 N.m). Install axle shaft snap ring.

5) Position shift knob on mounting base. Align splines by pushing in on shift knob and turning clockwise to lock in position. Install and tighten shift knob retaining screws.

REAR BRAKE SHOES

Removal (9", 10" & 11" Drum) – 1) Remove drum. Note how secondary spring overlaps primary spring. Remove brake shoe return springs using spring remover. Slide automatic adjuster cable off anchor. Disconnect cable from adjusting lever.

2) Remove cable, cable guide, and anchor plate. *See Fig. 9.* Disconnect adjusting lever return spring from lever. Remove lever and return spring from pivot pin. Remove shoe-to-shoe spring. Spread shoes and remove adjustment star wheel.

3) Remove shoe retainers, springs and nails. Remove parking brake lever from secondary shoe. Remove shoes and parking brake strut with anti-rattle spring. Detach parking brake lever from cable.

Installation – 1) Apply thin coat of multipurpose grease to 6 shoe contact pads on support plate. Attach parking brake lever to cable and connect lever to secondary shoe. Install primary shoe on support plate with shoe nail, spring and retainer.

2) Install spring on parking brake strut and engage strut into primary shoe. Install secondary shoe on support plate with shoe nail, spring and retainer. Insert strut into slot in parking brake lever.

3) Install anchor plate and eye of adjusting cable over anchor. Install primary return spring. Position cable guide over hole in secondary shoe and install secondary return spring.

NOTE: To identify left and right adjustment star wheels, unscrew threaded rod from star wheel. Note stamped "L" or "R" on end of threaded rod.

4) Install adjustment star wheel with wheel closest to secondary shoe. Install shoe-to-shoe spring, engaging in primary shoe first with coil on

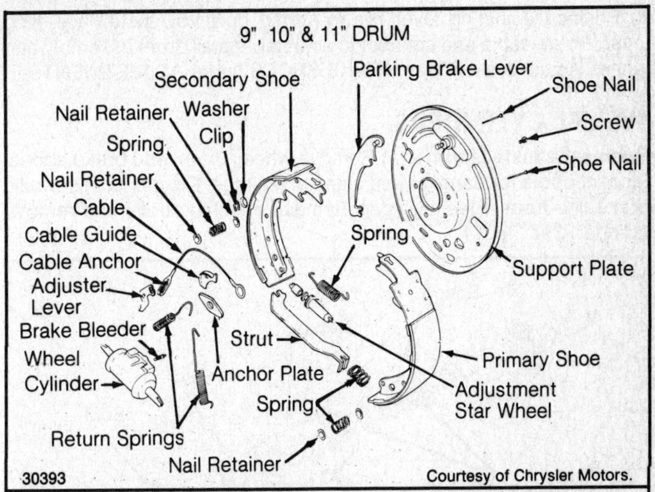
9", 10" & 11" DRUM
Secondary Shoe
Parking Brake Lever
Shoe Nail
Nail Retainer
Washer
Screw
Spring
Clip
Shoe Nail
Nail Retainer
Cable
Cable Guide
Spring
Cable Anchor
Support Plate
Adjuster Lever
Brake Bleeder
Strut
Wheel Cylinder
Primary Shoe
Anchor Plate
Adjustment Star Wheel
Spring
Return Springs
Nail Retainer
30393
Courtesy of Chrysler Motors.

Fig. 9: Exploded View of Rear Drum Brake Assembly (9", 10" & 11")

opposite side of adjusting lever. Install lever spring and adjusting lever over pivot pin.

5) Slide lever rearward to lock in position. Thread adjuster cable over guide and hook end of cable in lever. Verify adjuster operation. Pull adjuster cable upward. Cable should lift lever and rotate star wheel. Be sure adjuster lever properly engages star wheel teeth. Adjust brakes. See REAR BRAKE SHOES under ADJUSTMENTS.

Removal (12" Drum) – 1) Remove drum. See AXLE BEARING & SEAL (FULL FLOATING AXLE) under REMOVAL & INSTALLATION. Disconnect adjusting lever from cable. Disconnect adjusting lever return spring from lever. Remove lever and return spring from pivot pin. Remove upper shoe-to-shoe spring.

2) Disconnect and remove shoe retainers, springs and nails. Disconnect parking brake cable from lever. Remove lower shoe-to-shoe spring. Remove shoes and adjustment star wheel as an assembly. *See Fig. 10.*

NOTE: Adjustment star wheel on left brake assembly has left-hand threads. Right side assembly has right-hand threads.

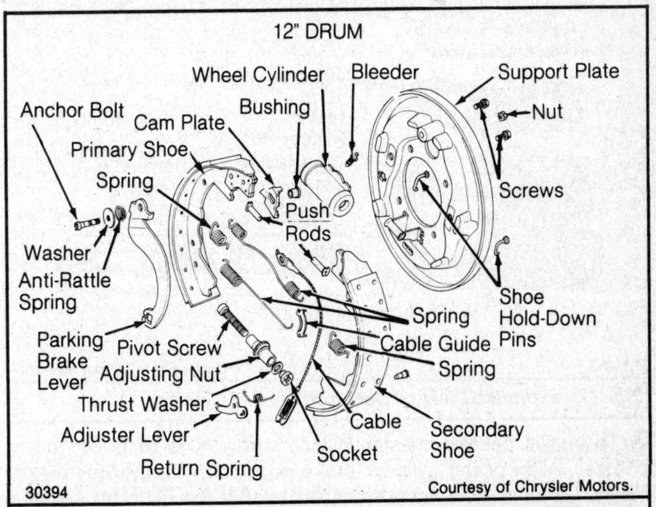
12" DRUM
Wheel Cylinder
Bleeder
Support Plate
Anchor Bolt
Bushing
Nut
Cam Plate
Primary Shoe
Spring
Screws
Push Rods
Washer
Anti-Rattle Spring
Shoe Hold-Down Pins
Spring
Parking Brake Lever
Pivot Screw
Cable Guide
Adjusting Nut
Spring
Thrust Washer
Cable
Adjuster Lever
Secondary Shoe
Socket
Return Spring
30394
Courtesy of Chrysler Motors.

Fig. 10: Exploded View of Rear Drum Brake Assembly (12")

Installation – 1) Lubricate and assemble adjustment star wheel. Apply thin film of multipurpose grease to shoe contact pads on support plate. Assemble lower shoe-to-shoe spring, adjustment star wheel and both shoes.

2) Position shoe assembly on support plate. Attach parking brake cable to lever. Install shoe nails, springs and retainers. Install upper shoe-to-shoe spring.

1991 BRAKES
Disc & Drum (Cont.)

3) Position adjusting lever return spring on pivot. Install adjusting lever. Route cable and connect to adjuster. Install drum assembly and wheel. Adjust brakes. See BRAKE SHOES under ADJUSTMENTS.

WHEEL CYLINDERS

Removal & Installation – 1) Remove wheel, drum, and brake shoes. Inspect boots for damage and signs of leakage. Disconnect hydraulic brake line from wheel cylinder. Remove attaching bolts and remove cylinder. *See Fig. 11.*

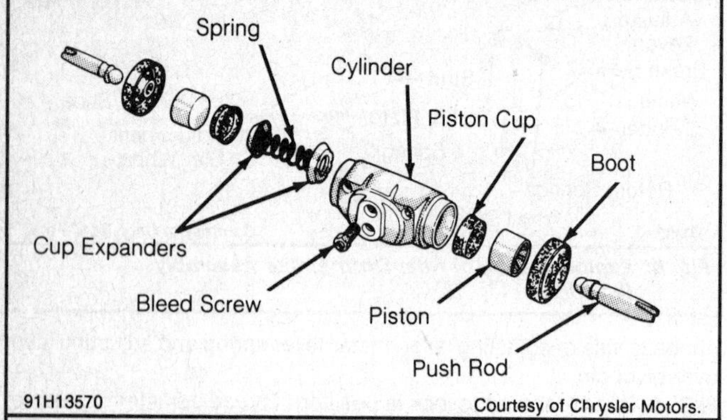
Spring
Cylinder
Piston Cup
Boot
Cup Expanders
Bleed Screw
Piston
Push Rod
91H13570
Courtesy of Chrysler Motors.

Fig. 11: Exploded View of Rear Wheel Cylinder

2) Apply silicone sealer to cylinder mounting surface and position cylinder on support plate. Start brake line fitting in wheel cylinder. Install mounting bolts and tighten. Tighten brake line fitting. To complete installation, reverse removal procedure. Fill brake fluid reservoir and bleed hydraulic system. See BLEEDING PROCEDURES under BLEEDING BRAKE SYSTEM.

MASTER CYLINDER

Removal & Installation – 1) Disconnect and plug primary and secondary brake lines from master cylinder. Remove master cylinder-to-power brake booster nuts. Slide master cylinder straight out and away from brake unit. *See Fig. 12.*

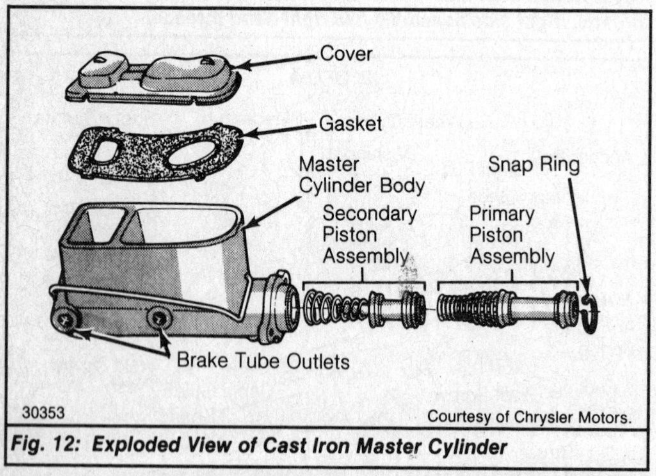
Cover
Gasket
Master
Cylinder Body
Snap Ring
Secondary
Piston
Assembly
Primary
Piston
Assembly
Brake Tube Outlets
30353
Courtesy of Chrysler Motors.

Fig. 12: Exploded View of Cast Iron Master Cylinder

2) To install, position master cylinder over studs of power brake booster. Align power cylinder brake push rod with cylinder piston. Install master cylinder nuts and tighten to 16 ft. lbs. (21 N.m). Connect both brake lines and bleed system. See BLEEDING PROCEDURES under BLEEDING BRAKE SYSTEM.

RESERVOIR REPLACEMENT (ALUMINUM MASTER CYLINDER)

Removal – Empty brake fluid from reservoir. Position cylinder body in vise. Clean reservoir exterior and master cylinder body. Rock reservoir from side-to-side, removing reservoir. Remove grommets from cylinder body.

Installation – Install new grommets in cylinder body. Lubricate mounting area with clean brake fluid. Using rocking motion, install reservoir on master cylinder body. Bleed master cylinder before installing on vehicle. See BLEEDING PROCEDURES under BLEEDING BRAKE SYSTEM. Lettering on reservoir cover should face driver's side of vehicle.

POWER BRAKE BOOSTER IN-LINE MOUNT

Removal – 1) Disconnect vacuum hose from booster check valve. Remove nuts attaching master cylinder and move cylinder away from booster. Remove clip which secures booster push rod to brake pedal inside vehicle. Pry clip off pedal pivot pin.

2) Remove lock nuts from booster mounting studs. Slide booster away from dash and out of engine compartment. If booster is being replaced, remove booster check valve and seal.

Installation – 1) Install check valve and seal if new booster is being installed. Position booster on dash and install lock nuts on booster mounting studs finger tight. Install booster push rod on brake pedal pin and secure rod with a new retaining clip.

2) Tighten booster lock nuts to 18 ft. lbs. (25 N.m). Install master cylinder on booster and tighten mounting nuts to 16 ft. lbs. (21 N.m). Connect vacuum hose to booster check valve. Start vehicle and ensure proper booster operation.

POWER BRAKE BOOSTER TRANSVERSE MOUNT

Removal – Disconnect vacuum hose from booster check valve. Remove nuts attaching master cylinder to booster studs. Move master cylinder away from booster. Remove pivot bolt, "O" ring and nut attaching booster rod to bellcrank. Remove lock nuts attaching booster to mounting bracket. Slide booster off mounting bracket and out of engine compartment. If booster is being replaced, remove booster check valve and seal.

Installation – 1) Install check valve and seal if new booster is being installed. Position booster on mounting bracket and install lock nuts on booster mounting studs finger tight. Align booster rod with bellcrank arm and install pivot pin, "O" ring and nut.

2) Tighten booster lock nuts and pivot pin nut to 30 ft. lbs. (41 N.m). Install master cylinder on booster and tighten mounting nuts to 16 ft. lbs. (21 N.m). Connect vacuum hose to booster check valve. Start vehicle and ensure proper booster operation.

HEIGHT SENSING PROPORTIONING VALVE

Removal & Installation (Caravan, Town & Country, & Voyager) – Raise and support vehicle. Disconnect actuator assembly and brake lines from valve. Cap brake lines to prevent dirt from entering system. Remove screws securing valve and remove valve. Install new valve. Bleed brake system. See BLEEDING PROCEDURE under BLEEDING BRAKE SYSTEM. Adjust valve. See HEIGHT SENSING PROPORTIONING VALVE under ADJUSTMENTS.

COMBINATION VALVE

Removal & Installation – Raise and support vehicle. Mark brake lines for assembly reference. Disconnect parking brake cable from clip on valve. Disconnect brake warning light connection at switch. Disconnect all brake hydraulic lines at valve. Cap brake lines to prevent dirt from entering system. Remove valve mounting bolts. Remove valve from vehicle. To install, reverse removal procedures. Bleed brake system. See BLEEDING PROCEDURES under BLEEDING BRAKE SYSTEM.

AXLE BEARING & SEAL (FULL FLOATING AXLE)

Removal & Installation (12" Drum) – 1) Raise and support vehicle. Remove wheel assembly. Remove axle shaft nuts, washers and cones. Using hammer, sharply strike center of axle flange to free cones. Remove axle shaft and gasket.

2) Remove nut lock. Remove adjustment nut and outer bearing. Carefully remove drum assembly. Remove seal and inner bearing from drum assembly.

1991 BRAKES
Disc & Drum (Cont.)

3) Install inner bearing and seal in drum. Install drum assembly, outer bearing and adjustment nut. Tighten adjustment nut to 120-140 ft. lbs. (163-190 N.m) while rotating drum.

4) Back off adjustment nut approximately 1/3 turn (120 degrees) to obtain .001-.008" (0.03-0.20 mm) end play. Tap nut lock into spindle keyway. Install gasket and axle shaft. Install wheel assembly and lower vehicle.

OVERHAUL

NOTE: When overhauling components, refer to Figs. 4-12.

TORQUE SPECIFICATIONS

TORQUE SPECIFICATIONS

Application	Ft. Lbs. (N.m)
Axle Shaft Flange or Support Plate Mounting Nuts	
3/8"	25-60 (34-81)
7/16"	40-70 (54-95)
1/2"	65-105 (88-142)
Caliper	
Guide Pin(s) (Kelsey-Hayes)	25-35 (34-47)
Retaining Bolt (Chrysler Motors)	17 (22)
Retaining Screw (Bendix)	15 (20)
Caliper Adapter Bolts	
1/2" Bolts	95-125 (129-170)
5/8" Bolts	140-180 (190-245)
Drive Flange Lock Nuts (4WD)	30-40 (41-54)
Master Cylinder Nuts	16 (21)
Pivot Pin	30 (41)
Power Booster Lock Nuts	
In-Line Mount	18 (25)
Transverse Mount	30 (41)
Wheel Bearing Outer Lock Nut (4WD)	65 (88)
Wheel Lug Nuts	
Caravan, Town & Country, & Voyager	95 (129)
Dakota	85 (115)
Pickup, Ramcharger & RWD Van	
Cone 1/2" x 20	105 (142)
Cone 5/8" x 18	200 (271)
Flanged 5/8" x 18	325 (440)
	INCH Lbs. (N.m)
Proportioning Valve Adjusting Nut	25 (2.8)

DISC BRAKE SPECIFICATIONS

DISC BRAKE SPECIFICATIONS

Application	In. (mm)
Disc Diameter	
Caravan, Town & Country, & Voyager	
Standard	10.24 (260)
Heavy Duty	11.14 (283)
Dakota	
Standard	10.70 (272)
Heavy Duty	11.40 (290)
Pickup 2WD	
D100/150	11.75 (298)
D250/350	12.88 (327)
Pickup 4WD	
W100/150	11.63 (295)
W250	12.82 (326)
W250/350 with Model 60 Front Axle	12.88 (327)
Ramcharger	
AD100/150	11.75 (298)
AW100/150	11.63 (295)
RWD Van	
B150/250	11.75 (298)
B350	12.82 (326)

DISC BRAKE SPECIFICATIONS (Cont.)

Application	In. (mm)
Lateral Runout	
Caravan, Town & Country, & Voyager	.005 (.13)
Dakota, Pickup [1], Ramcharger & RWD Van	.004 (.10)
Parallelism	
All Models Except W250/350	.0005 (.013)
W250/350	.001 (.025)
Original Thickness	
Caravan, Town & Country, & Voyager	.870 (22.10)
Dakota	
Standard & Heavy Duty	.871 (22.12)
Pickup [2] & Ramcharger	1.25 (31.75)
RWD Van	[3]
Min. Refinish Thickness	
Caravan, Town & Country, & Voyager	
Standard & Heavy Duty	.833 (21.16)
Dakota	
Standard & Heavy Duty	.811 (20.6)
Pickup & Ramcharger	[4]
RWD Van	
B150/250	1.18 (29.97)
B350	1.25 (31.75)
Discard Thickness	
Caravan, Town & Country, & Voyager	
Standard & Heavy Duty	.803 (20.4)
Dakota	
Standard & Heavy Duty	.811 (20.6)
Pickup & Ramcharger	[5]
RWD Van	
B150/250	1.18 (29.97)
B350	1.125 (28.58)

[1] – On Pickup W250/350, lateral runout is .005" (.127 mm).
[2] – On Pickup W250/350 with Model 60 front axle, original thickness is 1.19" (30.23).
[3] – Information is not available from manufacturer.
[4] – Discard thickness plus .030" (76 mm) equals minimum refinish thickness.
[5] – Discard thickness is marked on rotor hub.

DRUM BRAKE SPECIFICATIONS

DRUM BRAKE SPECIFICATIONS

Application	In. (mm)
9" Drum	
Drum Width	2.50 (63.5)
Max. Allowable Diameter	9.060 (230.12)
Wheel Cylinder Diameter	3/4 (19.05)
10" Drum	
Drum Width	2.50 (63.5)
Max. Allowable Diameter	10.060 (255.52)
Wheel Cylinder Diameter	13/16 (20.64)
11" Drum	
Drum Width	2.50 (63.5)
Max. Allowable Diameter	11.060 (280.92)
Wheel Cylinder Diameter	15/16 (23.81)
12" Drum	
Drum Width	[1] 2.50 (63.5)
Max. Allowable Diameter	12.060 (306.32)
Wheel Cylinder Diameter	[2]

[1] – On Pickup and RWD Van B350 with Model 60 front axle, drum width is 3.00" (76.2 mm).
[2] – Wheel cylinder diameter is 1.00" (25.40 mm) on Pickup W250/350, 1 1/8" (28.58 mm) on Pickup W350 with Model 60 front axle, and 15/16" (23.81 mm) on RWD Van.

1991 WHEEL ALIGNMENT
Specifications & Procedures

Caravan, Dakota, Pickup, Ramcharger RWD Van, Town & Country, Voyager

NOTE: Prior to performing wheel alignment, perform visual and mechanical inspection of wheels, tires and suspension components. See PRE-ALIGNMENT INSTRUCTIONS in WHEEL ALIGNMENT THEORY & OPERATION article in GENERAL INFORMATION.

RIDING HEIGHT ADJUSTMENT

Dakota (4WD) – 1) Height differential from side-to-side of vehicle should not differ more than .25" (6.4 mm). Measure inner height from floor surface to underside surface of lower control arm rear pivot bores. Outer measurement is from floor surface to underside surface of lower control arm rear edge, at area that is immediately inboard of steering stop.

2) Check inner and outer measurements and adjust height differential to specifications. See ALIGNMENT SPECIFICATIONS at end of article. Adjust each front suspension arm by rotating the torsion bar anchor adjustment bolt. After each adjustment, jounce vehicle before measuring to determine effects of adjustment.

JACKING & HOISTING

FLOOR JACK

Dakota, Pickup & Ramcharger – 1) For 2WD, raise front by centering floor jack under inner edge of lower control arm pivot bolt mounting bracket. To raise rear end, position floor jack under rear axle next to leaf spring mount. *See Fig. 1.*

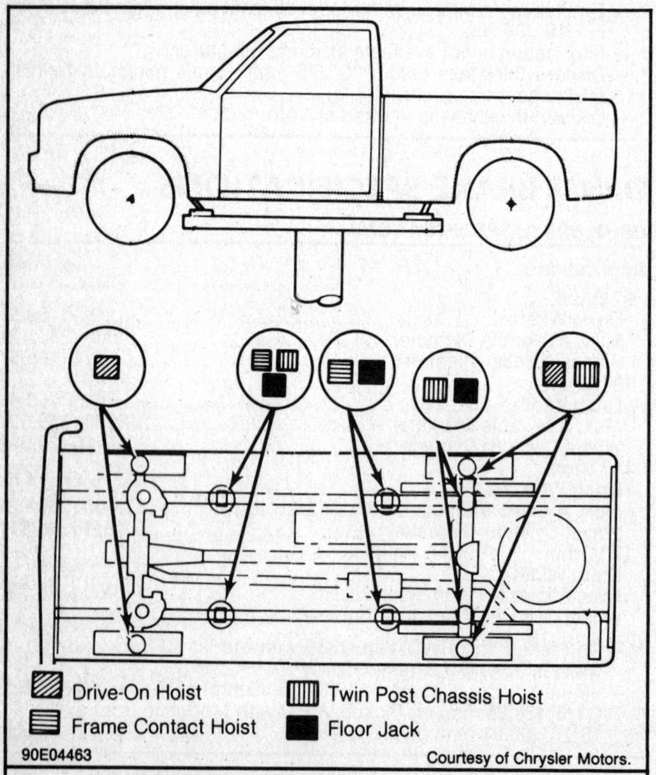
Drive-On Hoist
Frame Contact Hoist
Twin Post Chassis Hoist
Floor Jack
90E04463
Courtesy of Chrysler Motors.

Fig. 1: Hoisting & Jacking Locations (Dakota, Pickup & Ramcharger)

2) For 4WD, raise front end by placing floor jack under outside of front leaf spring mount and center it under front axle. To raise rear end, place floor jack under rear axle next to leaf spring mount. *See Fig. 1.*

CAUTION: Never place jack under any part of vehicle underbody. DO NOT attempt to raise one entire side of vehicle by placing a jack midway between front and rear wheels, as permanent body damage could occur.

Caravan, Town & Country, & Voyager – To raise front end, place floor jack under front crossmember forward flange, inboard of lower control arm pivot. To raise rear end, place floor jack under rear axle, next to leaf spring mount. *See Fig. 2.*

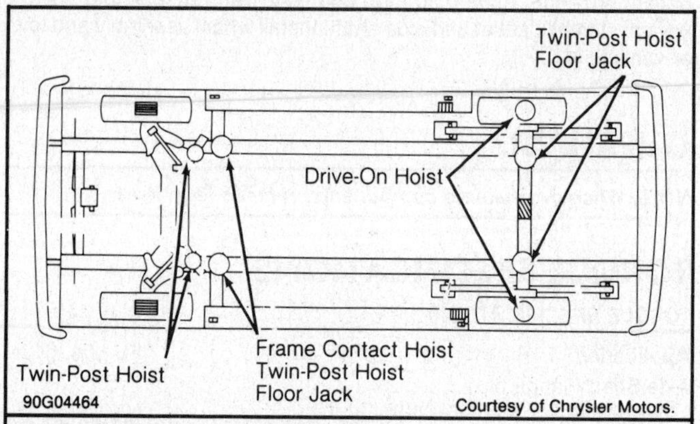
Twin-Post Hoist
Floor Jack
Drive-On Hoist
Frame Contact Hoist
Twin-Post Hoist
Floor Jack
Twin-Post Hoist
90G04464
Courtesy of Chrysler Motors.

Fig. 2: Hoisting & Jacking Locations (Caravan, Town & Country, & Voyager)

CAUTION: Never place jack under any part of vehicle underbody. DO NOT attempt to raise one entire side of vehicle by placing a jack midway between front and rear wheels, as permanent body damage could occur.

RWD Van – To raise front end, place floor jack under center of front crossmember, inboard of lower control arm pivot. *See Fig. 3.* To raise rear end, place floor jack under rear axle, next to leaf spring "U" bolt mount.

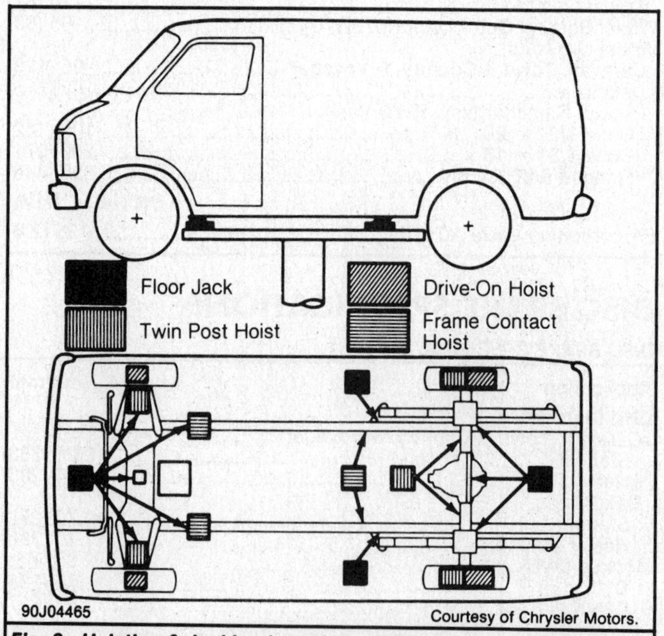
Floor Jack
Twin Post Hoist
Drive-On Hoist
Frame Contact Hoist
90J04465
Courtesy of Chrysler Motors.

Fig. 3: Hoisting & Jacking Locations (RWD Van)

HOIST

CAUTION: DO NOT raise vehicle by hoisting or jacking against front lower control arms. If rear axle, fuel tank, spare tire and liftgate will be removed for service, place additional weight on rear end of vehicle. This will prevent tipping as center of gravity changes.

Dakota, Pickup & Ramcharger – 1) Vehicle may be raised on single or twin-post swiveling arm, or ramp-type drive hoists. If using swiveling arm hoist, ensure lifting arms, pads or ramps are positioned evenly on frame rails, and adequate clearance is maintained for transfer case (4WD models) or skid plate. *See Figs. 1 and 4.*

1991 WHEEL ALIGNMENT
Specifications & Procedures (Cont.)

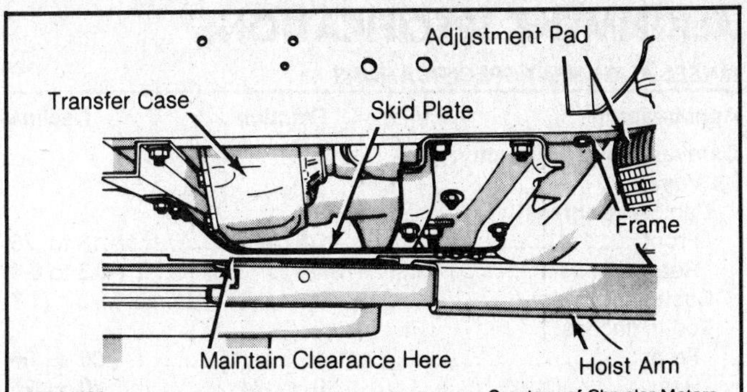
Adjustment Pad
Transfer Case
Skid Plate
Frame
Maintain Clearance Here
Hoist Arm

90B04466 Courtesy of Chrysler Motors.

Fig. 4: Hoist Precautions (Dakota, Pickup & Ramcharger)

2) On all models except Dakota, if twin-post hoist is used, a 4" x 4" x 12" wooden spacer may be required to maintain level vehicle. Position spacer under front axle tube (opposite differential housing). All hoists must be equipped with adapters to support vehicle properly.

Caravan, RWD Van, Town & Country, & Voyager – To raise vehicle on single and twin post type hoists, ensure hoist pads contact vehicle frame behind front control arm pivots and inside rear wheels on rear axle housing. Always use appropriate hoist adapters. *See Fig. 2 or 3.*

WHEEL ALIGNMENT PROCEDURES

CAMBER & CASTER ADJUSTMENT

Dakota – Completely loosen pivot bar attaching bolts and move ends of upper control arm either in or out to obtain proper camber and caster angles. *See Fig. 5.* See ALIGNMENT SPECIFICATIONS table at end of article. Tighten pivot retaining bolts. See TORQUE SPECIFICATIONS table at end of article.

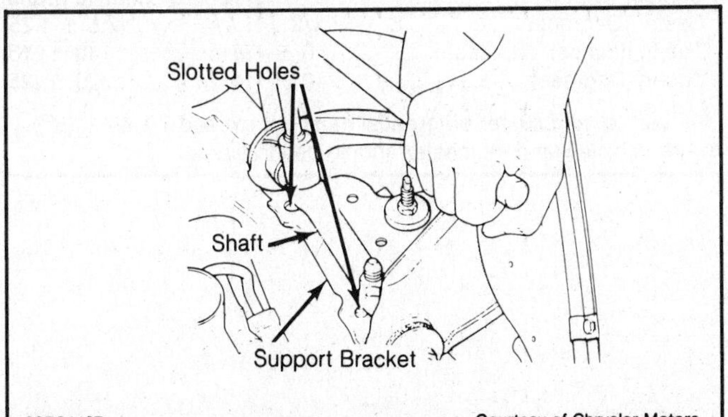
Slotted Holes
Shaft
Support Bracket

90D04467 Courtesy of Chrysler Motors.

Fig. 5: Adjusting Camber & Caster (Dakota)

Pickup & Ramcharger (2WD) – Clean eccentric cam bolt threads. Record camber and caster measurements. Loosen cam bolt retaining nuts. *See Fig. 6.* Adjust camber and caster to specification. See ALIGNMENT SPECIFICATIONS table at end of article. Tighten cam bolt retaining nuts to specification. See TORQUE SPECIFICATIONS table at end of article.

Pickup & Ramcharger (4WD) – Camber is not adjustable on 4WD models. Caster angle may be adjusted using shims. Record caster measurements. Remove original caster shims from spring pads and add or delete shims to meet specifications. See ALIGNMENT SPECIFICATIONS table at end of article.

Caravan, Town & Country, & Voyager – Caster is not adjustable on FWD vehicles. Loosen cam and through bolts on each side. *See Fig. 7.* Rotate cam bolt to move top of wheel in or out to specified camber. See ALIGNMENT SPECIFICATIONS table at end of article. Tighten through bolt nuts to specification. See TORQUE SPECIFICATIONS table at end of article.

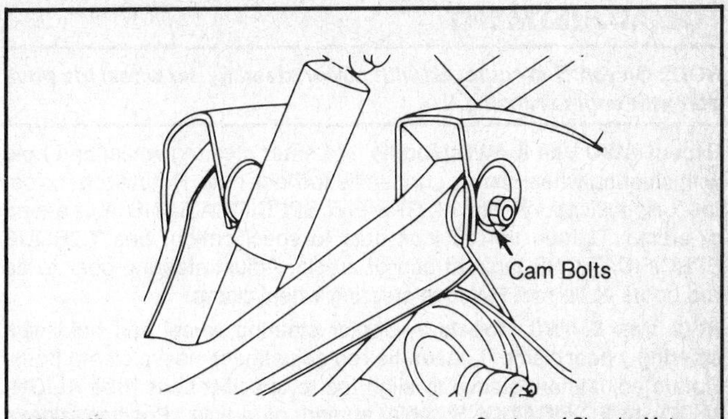
Cam Bolts

90H04469 Courtesy of Chrysler Motors.

Fig. 6: Adjusting Camber & Caster (Pickup & Ramcharger)

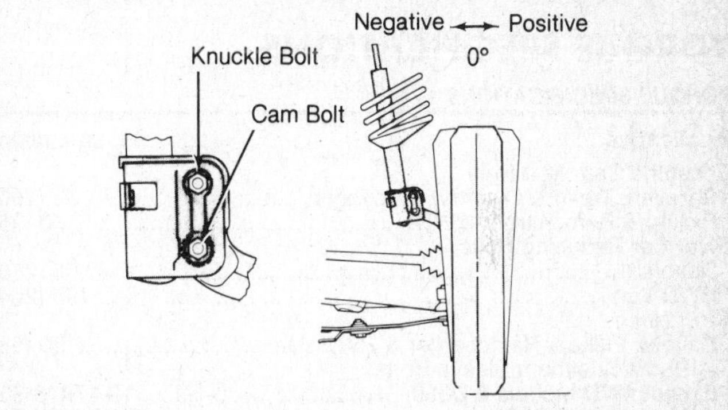
Negative ←→ Positive
0°
Knuckle Bolt
Cam Bolt

90F04468 Courtesy of Chrysler Motors.

Fig. 7: Adjusting Camber (Caravan, Town & Country, & Voyager)

RWD Van – **1)** Use Tool Set (C-4581) for this procedure. *See Fig. 8.* Position each tool with small hook attached to upper control arm frame bracket and large hook around pivot bar. Tighten adjustment nut on each tool until large hook is snug against pivot bar. Loosen both upper control arm retaining bolts completely.

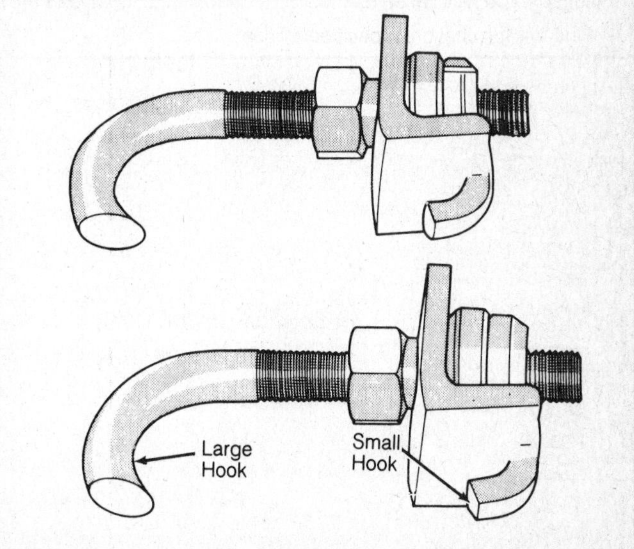
Large Hook
Small Hook

90J04470 Courtesy of Chrysler Motors.

Fig. 8: Camber & Caster Angle Adjustment Tool Set (C-4581)

2) To obtain proper camber and caster angles, tighten or loosen tool adjustment nuts on each tool to move one or both ends of upper control arm. See ALIGNMENT SPECIFICATIONS table at end of article. Tighten pivot retaining bolts. See TORQUE SPECIFICATIONS table at end of article.

1991 WHEEL ALIGNMENT Specifications & Procedures (Cont.)

TOE ADJUSTMENT

NOTE: On vehicles equipped with power steering, set wheel toe position with engine running.

Except RWD Van & 4WD Models - Center steering wheel and hold with steering wheel clamp. Loosen tie rod lock nuts. Rotate rods to set toe to specifications. See ALIGNMENT SPECIFICATIONS table at end of article. Tighten tie rod lock nuts to specification. See TORQUE SPECIFICATIONS table at end of article. Adjust steering gear to tie rod boots at tie rod. Remove steering wheel clamp.

RWD Van & 4WD Models - Center steering wheel and hold with steering wheel clamp. Loosen tie rod adjustment sleeve clamp bolts. Rotate adjustment sleeve to align toe to specifications. See ALIGNMENT SPECIFICATIONS table at end of article. Position sleeve clamps on underside of sleeve so that clamp ends are not over sleeve slot. Tighten adjustment sleeve clamp bolts to specification. See TORQUE SPECIFICATIONS table. Remove steering wheel clamp.

TORQUE SPECIFICATIONS

TORQUE SPECIFICATIONS

Application	Ft. Lbs. (N.m)
Eccentric Cam Bolt Nuts	
Caravan, Town & Country, & Voyager	[1] 75 (100)
Pickup & Ramcharger (2WD)	70 (95)
Pivot Bar Retaining Bolts	
Dakota	155 (210)
RWD Van	195 (264)
Strut Nut	
Dakota, Pickup, Ramcharger & RWD Van	50 (68)
Tie Rod Adjustment Sleeve Bolts	
Except 4WD Models & D350	13-17 (18-23)
4WD Models & D350	25-26 (34-35)
Tie Rod Lock Nut(s)	
Caravan, Town & Country, & Voyager	55 (75)
All Other Models	13 (18)
Wheel Lug Nuts	
Caravan, Town & Country, & Voyager	95 (129)
Dakota	85 (115)
All Other Models	
1/2" x 20	105 (142)
5/8" x 18	200 (271)
Flanged Type Nut	325 (441)

[1] - Plus 1/4 turn beyond specified torque.

ALIGNMENT SPECIFICATIONS

WHEEL ALIGNMENT SPECIFICATIONS

Application	Fraction	Decimal
Caravan, Town & Country, & Voyager		
Camber (Degrees)		
Front	-1/8 to 3/4	(-.13 to .75)
Rear	-13/16 to 13/32	(-0.8 to 0.4)
Caster (Degrees) [1]	1 11/16	(1.7)
Toe-in (Inches)		
Front	1/16 ± 1/16	(.06 ± .06)
Rear	0 ± 1/4	(0 ± .25)
Toe-in (Degrees)		
Front	1/8 ± 1/8	(.13 ± .13)
Rear	1/4 ± 1/4	(.25 ± .26)
Dakota		
Camber (Degrees)	1/2 ± 1/2	(0.5 ± 0.5)
Caster (Degrees) [1 2]	1 1/2 ± 1	(1.5 ± 1.0)
Height Differential (Inches)	1 1/4 ± 1/4	(1.25 ± .25)
Toe-in (Inches)	1/8 ± 1/16	(.13 ± .06)
Toe-in (Degrees)	1/4 ± 3/32	(.25 ± 0.1)
Pickup & Ramcharger		
Camber (Degrees)		
2WD	1/2 ± 1/2	(0.5 ± 0.5)
4WD	0 ± 1	(0 ± 1.0)
Caster (Degrees) [2]		
2WD	1/2 ± 1 1/2	(0.5 ± 1.5)
4WD	2 ± 1 1/2	(2.0 ± 1.5)
Toe-in (Degrees)		
2WD	1/8 ± 1/8	(.13 ± .13)
4WD	13/64 ± 1/4	(0.2 ± .25)
RWD Van		
Camber (Degrees)	0 ± 19/32	(0 ± 0.6)
Caster (Degrees) [1]	2 1/2 ± 1 1/4	(2.5 ± 1.25)
Toe-in (Inches)	0 ± 1/8	(0 ± .13)
Toe-in (Degrees)	0 ± 1/4	(0 ± .25)

[1] - Left to right caster differential must not exceed 1 1/4" (1.25°).
[2] - If vehicle wanders, caster should be increased.

1991 SUSPENSION
Front – FWD

Caravan, Town & Country, Voyager

DESCRIPTION

The front suspension is an independent MacPherson strut type. The struts are attached to upper fender reinforcements and steering knuckle. Lower control arms are attached to crossmember through bushings, and steering knuckle through ball joint. Working through a pivot bearing in upper retainer, the upper strut and steering knuckle turn as an assembly during steering maneuvers. *See Fig. 1.*

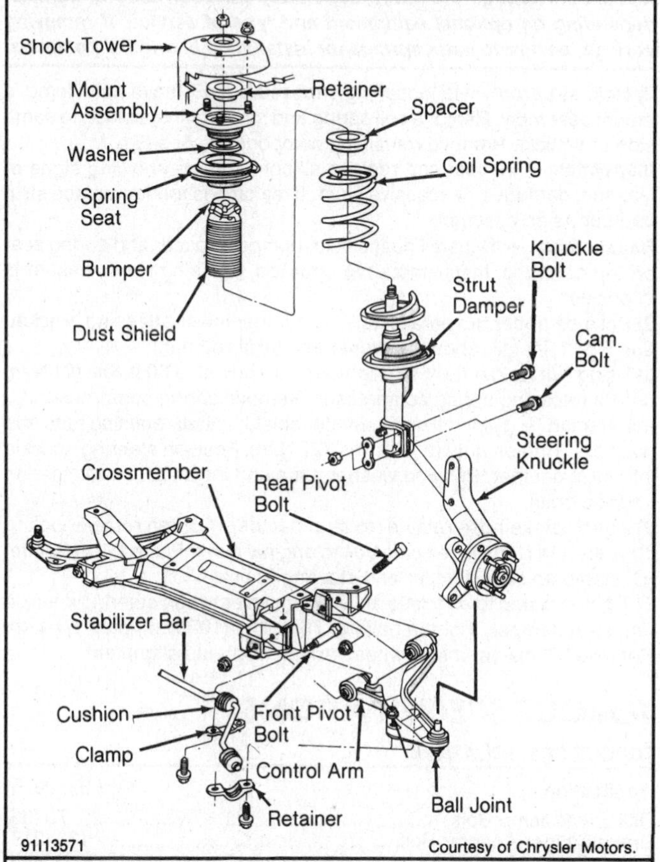
Shock Tower
Mount Assembly
Retainer
Spacer
Washer
Coil Spring
Spring Seat
Bumper
Knuckle Bolt
Strut Damper
Dust Shield
Cam Bolt
Steering Knuckle
Crossmember
Rear Pivot Bolt
Stabilizer Bar
Cushion
Front Pivot Bolt
Clamp
Control Arm
Retainer
Ball Joint
91I13571
Courtesy of Chrysler Motors.

Fig. 1: Exploded View of Suspension & Strut Damper Assembly

ADJUSTMENTS & INSPECTION

WHEEL ALIGNMENT SPECIFICATIONS & PROCEDURES

NOTE: See SPECIFICATIONS & PROCEDURES article in WHEEL ALIGNMENT.

WHEEL BEARING

Front wheel bearings are permanently sealed; lubrication and adjustment are not required. The hub and bearing unit is replaced as a complete assembly. With brakes applied, tighten hub nut to 180 ft. lbs. (244 N.m).

BALL JOINT CHECKING

NOTE: Lower ball joint operates with no free play. Lower ball joint is not a serviceable component. Replace lower control arm assembly if lower ball joint has free play.

Lower Ball Joint – With weight of vehicle resting on wheels in normal driving position, grasp ball joint grease fitting and attempt to move it. Replace lower control arm assembly if fitting moves freely.

REMOVAL & INSTALLATION

HUB & BEARING ASSEMBLY

NOTE: If service procedures require front hub removal, replace grease seal.

Removal – 1) Remove cotter pin, nut lock and spring washer. *See Fig. 2.* Loosen hub nut with vehicle on ground and brakes applied. Raise and support vehicle. Remove wheel.

2) Remove hub nut. Ensure drive shaft is free to separate from spline in hub. Remove brake hose retainer from strut, and remove brake caliper from steering knuckle. Using wire, support caliper aside. Remove rotor from hub studs.

3) Remove cotter pin and nut from tie rod. Using Puller (C-3894-A), disconnect tie rod end from steering arm. Remove clamp bolt securing ball joint stud in steering knuckle. *See Fig. 2.* Separate ball joint stud from steering knuckle assembly.

4) Pull steering knuckle out and away from drive shaft. Remove 4 hub bolts attaching hub and bearing assembly to steering knuckle. Remove hub and bearing assembly.

NOTE: Knuckle and bearing mounting surfaces must be smooth and completely free of foreign material and nicks.

Installation – 1) Install new hub and bearing assembly, and tighten bolts to 45 ft. lbs. (61 N.m). Position new seal in recess. Using Seal Installer (C-4698), install seal.

2) Lubricate full circumference of seal and wear sleeve with multipurpose grease. Install drive shaft through hub. Install steering knuckle to suspension. To install remaining components, reverse removal procedure.

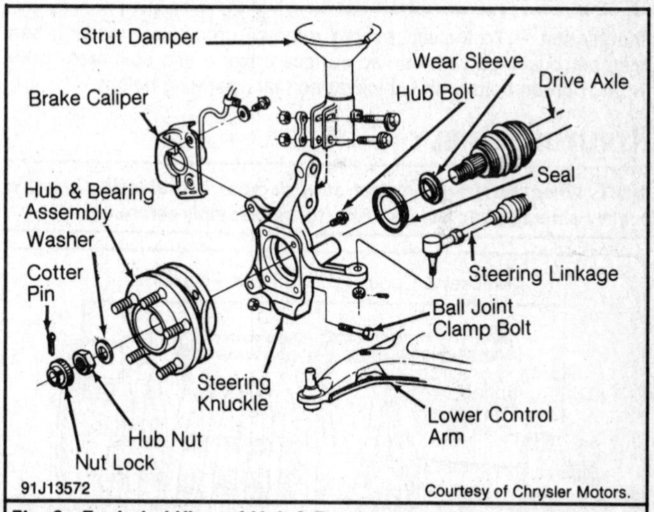
Strut Damper
Wear Sleeve
Drive Axle
Brake Caliper
Hub Bolt
Seal
Hub & Bearing Assembly
Washer
Cotter Pin
Steering Linkage
Ball Joint Clamp Bolt
Steering Knuckle
Lower Control Arm
Hub Nut
Nut Lock
91J13572
Courtesy of Chrysler Motors.

Fig. 2: Exploded View of Hub & Bearing Assembly

STEERING KNUCKLE

Removal – 1) Remove cotter pin, nut lock and spring washer. Loosen hub nut with vehicle on ground and brakes applied. Raise and support vehicle. Remove wheel. Remove hub nut. Ensure splined drive shaft is free from hub. If necessary, drive shaft may be tapped lightly with soft brass punch.

2) Remove cotter pin and nut from tie rod. Using Puller (C-3894-A), separate tie rod from steering knuckle. Remove brake hose retaining clamp. Remove ball joint clamp stud bolt. Remove caliper adapter bolts with washers attached. Remove caliper and support with wire. DO NOT hang by brake flex hose. Remove rotor.

3) Mark camber position on upper cam bolt, then remove both bolts. Remove steering knuckle from strut damper and from ball joint stud. *See Fig. 2.* Ensure drive shaft is supported during removal of steering knuckle to prevent damage to constant velocity joints.

Installation – To install, reverse removal procedure.

1991 SUSPENSION
Front – FWD (Cont.)

LOWER CONTROL ARM & BALL JOINT

***NOTE:** Lower ball joint is not a serviceable component. Lower control arm is serviced as a complete assembly which includes lower ball joint and pivot bushings.*

Removal – 1) Raise and support vehicle. Remove front inner pivot bolt. *See Fig. 1.* Remove rear stub strut nut, retainer and bushings. Remove ball joint-to-steering knuckle clamp bolt. Separate ball joint from steering knuckle.

***NOTE:** DO NOT pull steering knuckle from vehicle after releasing ball joint, or inner constant velocity joint will separate.*

2) Remove stabilizer bar-to-control arm end bushing retainer nuts, and rotate control arm over stabilizer bar. Remove stub strut retainer. Check control arm for distortion, and bushings for deterioration. Replace component as necessary.

Installation – To install, reverse removal procedure. Ensure control arm mount bolts are tightened with vehicle at normal operating height. Tighten pivot bolts to 125 ft. lbs. (169 N.m).

STABILIZER BAR

Removal – Raise and support vehicle. Remove nuts, bolts and retainers from control arms. Remove bolts at crossmember clamps. Remove clamps and remove stabilizer bar. Inspect components for cracks, damage or rubber deterioration.

Bushing Replacement – Inner bushing can be removed by opening split and removing bushing. Outer bushing must be cut or hammered off. Install new outer bushing until 1/2" of sway bar protrudes.

***NOTE:** Control arm retainers will bend slightly upon installation.*

Installation – To install, reverse removal procedure. Install cross-member bushings with curved surface upward and split area to the front. Tighten bolts with vehicle at normal operating height.

STRUT ASSEMBLY

***NOTE:** When servicing original strut damper and steering knuckle, mark cam adjusting bolt position for reassembly reference.*

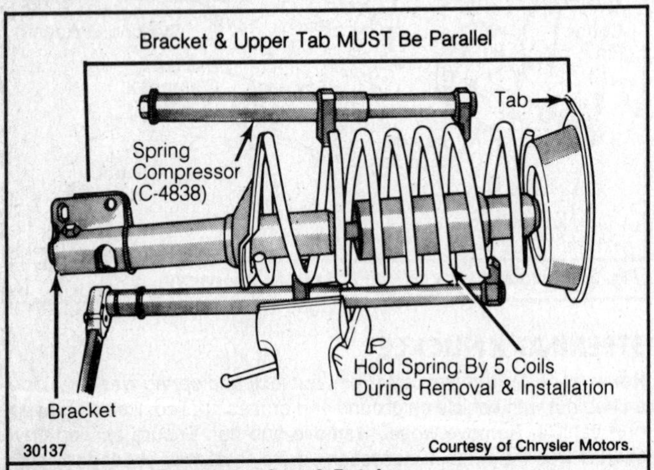
Bracket & Upper Tab MUST Be Parallel
Tab
Spring Compressor (C-4838)
Hold Spring By 5 Coils During Removal & Installation
Bracket
30137
Courtesy of Chrysler Motors.

***Fig. 3:** Positioning Spring Seat & Retainer*

Removal – 1) Raise and support vehicle. Remove wheel. Remove cam adjusting bolt and steering knuckle bolt from strut damper assembly. *See Fig. 1.* Remove brake hose-to-damper bracket retaining screw.

2) Remove strut damper-to-fender shield mounting nuts. Remove strut damper assembly from vehicle.

Disassembly – 1) Compress coil spring in Spring Compressor (C-4838), with at least 5 coils of spring between its jaws. *See Fig. 3.*

***NOTE:** Coil springs are rated separately for each side of vehicle, depending on optional equipment and type of service. If removing springs, ensure to mark springs for installation in original positions.*

2) Hold strut rod while loosening strut rod nut. Remove nut. Remove mount assembly. Remove coil spring and mark for installation to same side of vehicle. Remove remaining components. *See Fig. 1.*

Inspection – Inspect and replace all components showing signs of leakage, damage or excessive wear. If leakage is found, replace strut damper as an assembly.

Reassembly – 1) Install dust shield, bumper, spacer and spring seat on top of spring. Install mount to strut rod, ensuring lower washer is in position.

2) Position upper tab parallel to strut damper lower attaching bracket. *See Fig. 3.* Install rebound retainer and strut rod nut.

3) Using Nut Holder (L-4558), tighten strut rod nut to 60 ft. lbs. (81 N.m) before releasing spring compressor. Remove spring compressor.

Installation – 1) Install unit in fender shield. Install retaining nuts and washers. Tighten nuts to 20 ft. lbs. (27 N.m). Position steering knuckle into strut damper. Position washer plate and install cam and steering knuckle bolts.

2) Attach brake hose retainer to strut damper. Tighten retainer bolt to 10 ft. lbs. (14 N.m). Index cam bolt to original mark. Place a 4" (102 mm) "C" clamp on strut damper and steering knuckle.

3) Tighten clamp to eliminate any looseness between steering knuckle and strut damper. Tighten bolts to 75 ft. lbs. (102 N.m) plus 1/4 turn. Remove "C" clamp. Install wheel. Adjust front end alignment.

TORQUE SPECIFICATIONS

TORQUE SPECIFICATIONS

Application	Ft. Lbs. (N.m)
Ball Joint Clamp Bolt	70 (95)
Brake Caliper Adapter Bolt	160 (217)
Brake Caliper Guide Pins	18-26 (25-35)
Brake Hose-To-Strut Retainer Bolt	10 (14)
Control Arm Pivot Bolt	125 (169)
Hub & Bearing Assembly Bolts	45 (61)
Stabilizer Bar-To-Control Arm Bolt	50 (70)
Stabilizer Bar-To-Crossmember Bolt	50 (70)
Strut Damper Rod Nut	60 (81)
Strut Damper-To-Fender Shield Nut	20 (27)
Strut Damper-To-Steering Knuckle	
Cam & Knuckle Bolt	[1] 75 (102)
Tie Rod End Nut	35 (47)
Wheel Hub Mount Nut	180 (244)
Wheel Nut	95 (129)

[1] – Tighten an additional 1/4 turn.

1991 SUSPENSION
Front – 2WD Coil Spring

Dakota, Pickup, Ramcharger, RWD Vans

DESCRIPTION

All models are equipped with independent front suspension, which consists of upper and lower control arms, steering knuckles, coil springs and shock absorbers. Upper control arms are mounted to frame side rails, while lower control arms are mounted to crossmember. Steering knuckles are mounted between upper and lower control arms by conventional ball joints. Coil springs are mounted between seat in frame and lower control arm.

ADJUSTMENTS & INSPECTION

WHEEL ALIGNMENT SPECIFICATIONS & PROCEDURES

NOTE: See SPECIFICATIONS & PROCEDURES article in WHEEL ALIGNMENT.

WHEEL BEARING

1) While rotating wheel, tighten wheel bearing adjusting nut to 30-40 ft. lbs. (40-53 N.m). Stop rotation, and back off adjusting nut to release all preload. Retighten nut finger tight.
2) Check bearing end play. End play should be .0001-.0030" (.003-.076 mm). Install nut lock and cotter pin. Coat grease cap lightly with grease, and install.

BALL JOINT CHECKING

Ball joints are preloaded. Replace ball joint if vertical movement exceeds .02" (.5 mm).

REMOVAL & INSTALLATION

COIL SPRING

Removal – 1) Raise vehicle, position safety stands under frame and remove wheels. Remove brake caliper retainer and brake caliper (if necessary). Support caliper aside. On 2WD Pickup and Ramcharger, remove hub.

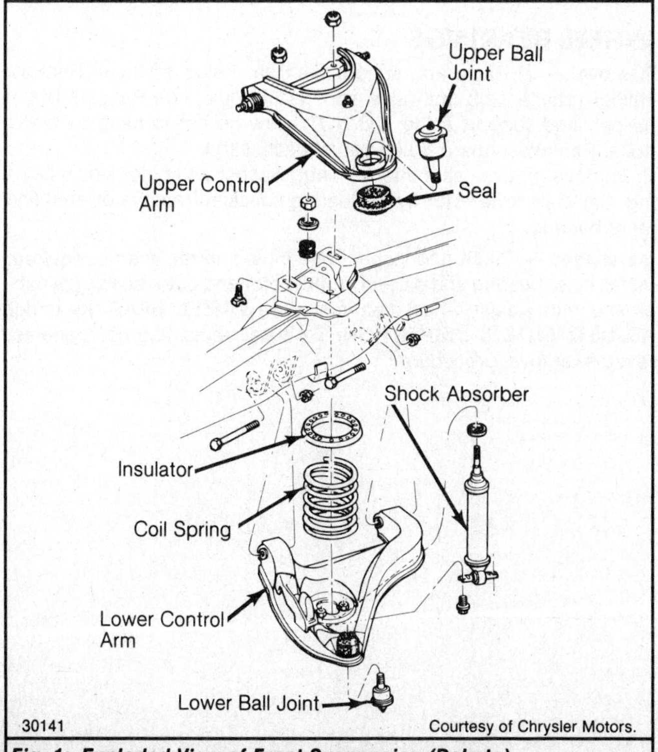
Upper Ball Joint
Upper Control Arm
Seal
Shock Absorber
Insulator
Coil Spring
Lower Control Arm
Lower Ball Joint
30141
Courtesy of Chrysler Motors.

Fig. 1: Exploded View of Front Suspension (Dakota)

2) Remove shock absorber. *See Figs. 1-3.* Remove lower control strut rod. Disconnect sway bar (if equipped). Install Spring Compressor (DD-1278), tighten compressor finger tight and then back off 1/2 turn.

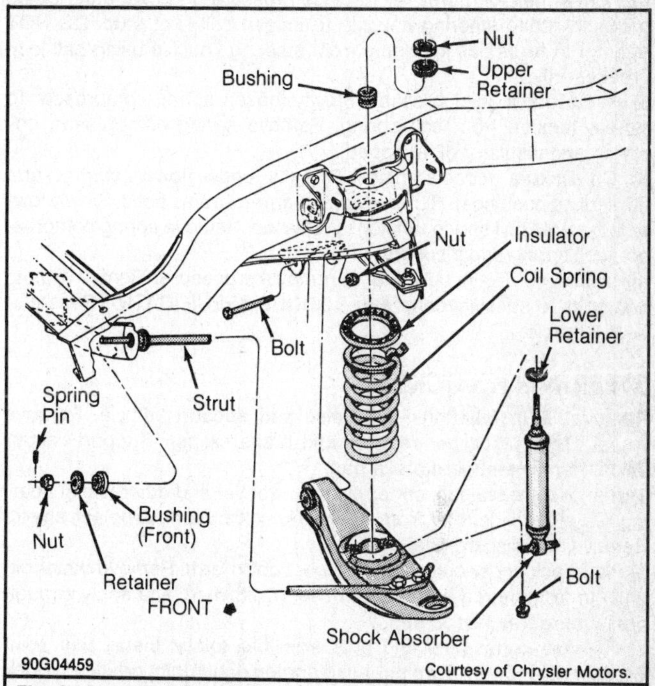
Nut
Upper Retainer
Bushing
Nut
Insulator
Coil Spring
Lower Retainer
Bolt
Spring Pin
Strut
Bushing (Front)
Nut
Retainer
FRONT
Bolt
Shock Absorber
90G04459
Courtesy of Chrysler Motors.

Fig. 2: Exploded View of Front Suspension (2WD Pickup & Ramcharger)

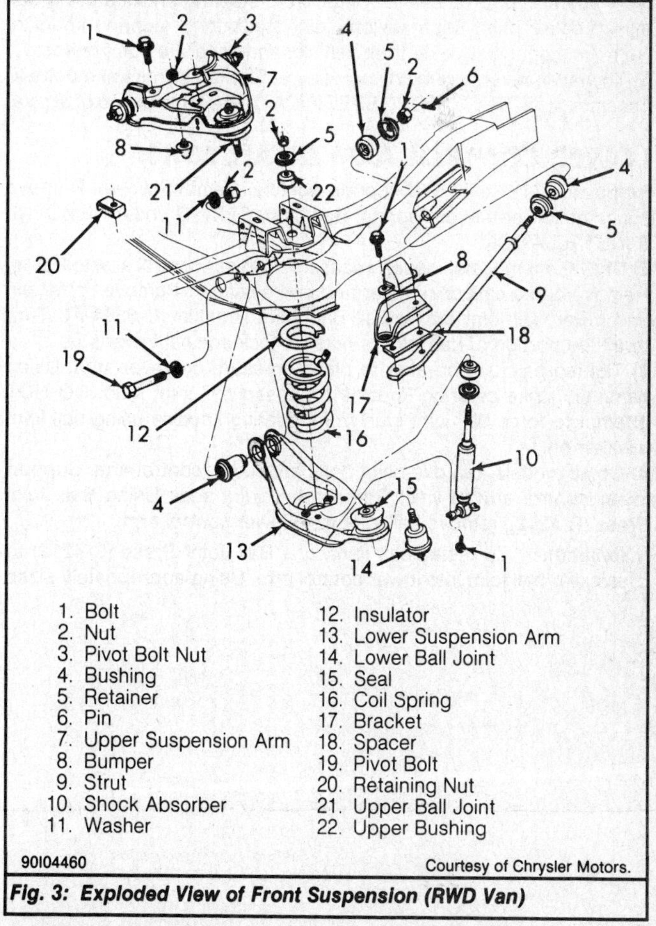
1. Bolt
2. Nut
3. Pivot Bolt Nut
4. Bushing
5. Retainer
6. Pin
7. Upper Suspension Arm
8. Bumper
9. Strut
10. Shock Absorber
11. Washer
12. Insulator
13. Lower Suspension Arm
14. Lower Ball Joint
15. Seal
16. Coil Spring
17. Bracket
18. Spacer
19. Pivot Bolt
20. Retaining Nut
21. Upper Ball Joint
22. Upper Bushing
90I04460
Courtesy of Chrysler Motors.

Fig. 3: Exploded View of Front Suspension (RWD Van)

1991 SUSPENSION
Front – 2WD Coil Spring (Cont.)

3) On all models except Dakota, remove cotter pins and ball joint nuts. Install Ball Joint Breaker (C-3564-A). Turn threaded portion of ball joint breaker to lock against lower stud.
4) Tighten ball joint breaker to place pressure on lower stud. Using hammer, strike steering knuckle to loosen ball joint stud. DO NOT attempt to force ball joint stud from steering knuckle using ball joint breaker only.
5) Remove ball joint breaker. Slowly loosen spring compressor to relieve tension from coil spring. Remove spring compressor, coil spring and insulator (if equipped).
6) On Dakota models, place 2 jacks under lower control arm (straddling bushings). Remove control arm-to-frame bolts. Slowly lower jacks until coil spring tension is released. Remove spring compressor, coil spring and insulator.
Installation – To install, reverse removal procedure. Tighten all nuts and bolts to specifications. See TORQUE SPECIFICATIONS table at end of article.

STEERING KNUCKLE

Removal & Installation – **1)** Raise and support vehicle. Remove wheel. Remove caliper retainer and brake caliper. Support caliper aside. Remove inboard brake pad.
2) Remove grease cap, cotter pin, nut, washer and outer wheel bearing. Carefully slide rotor from steering knuckle. Remove splash shield. Remove and discard dust seal.
3) Place jack under outer end of lower control arm. Remove cotter pin and nut from tie rod end. Install Puller (C-3894-A), and apply enough pressure to free tie rod end.
4) Remove cotter pins and nuts from ball joints. Install Ball Joint Breaker (C-3564-A). Turn threaded portion of ball joint breaker to lock against lower stud. Tighten ball joint breaker to place pressure on lower stud.
5) Using hammer, strike steering knuckle to loosen ball joint stud. DO NOT attempt to force ball joint stud from steering knuckle using ball joint breaker only. Separate ball joint studs from steering knuckle. Remove steering knuckle from vehicle, and separate components.
6) To install, reverse removal procedure. Tighten all nuts and bolts to specifications. See TORQUE SPECIFICATIONS table at end of article.

LOWER CONTROL ARM & BALL JOINT

Removal – **1)** Raise and support vehicle. Remove wheel. Remove shock absorber and coil spring. See COIL SPRING under REMOVAL & INSTALLATION.
2) On Dakota models, loosely reassemble lower control arm to frame. Remove brake caliper retainer and brake caliper. Remove cotter pin and lower ball joint nut. Install Ball Joint Breaker (C-3564-A). Turn threaded portion of ball joint breaker to lock against lower stud.
3) Tighten ball joint breaker to place pressure on lower stud. Using hammer, strike steering knuckle to loosen ball joint stud. DO NOT attempt to force ball joint stud from steering knuckle using ball joint breaker only.
4) On all models, remove pivot bolts and lower control arm. Support lower control arm in vise. Remove ball joint seal. Using Ball Joint Press (C-4212), remove ball joint from lower control arm.
Installation – To install ball joint, use Ball Joint Press (C-4212) to press new ball joint into lower control arm. Using appropriately sized socket, seat ball joint seal until firmly locked. To install remaining components, reverse removal procedure. With vehicle at normal operating height, tighten all nuts and bolts to specifications. See TORQUE SPECIFICATIONS table at end of article.
Bushing Replacement – If bushings are worn, remove lower control arm. Using a sleeve and press, remove and replace bushings.

STABILIZER BAR

Removal & Installation – Raise and support vehicle. Remove link rod retaining nut at each end of stabilizer bar. Remove outer retainers and rubber bushings from link rods. Remove bolts from "U"-shaped support brackets. Remove stabilizer bar from vehicle. To install, reverse removal procedure. Tighten all nuts and bolts to specifications. See TORQUE SPECIFICATIONS table at end of article.

STRUT ASSEMBLY

Removal & Installation – Raise and support vehicle. Remove stabilizer bar from strut bracket. Using a hammer and punch, remove spring pin from rear end of strut rod. Remove strut rod front retaining nuts and bolts from lower control arm. Remove strut assembly. Replace bushings (if necessary). To install, reverse removal procedure. Tighten all nuts and bolts to specifications. See TORQUE SPECIFICATIONS table at end of article.

UPPER CONTROL ARM & BALL JOINT

Removal – **1)** Raise vehicle, and position safety stands under frame. Remove wheel. Remove shock absorber and coil spring. See COIL SPRING under REMOVAL & INSTALLATION.
2) On Dakota models, remove brake caliper retainer and brake caliper. Disconnect ball joint. See steps **2)** and **3)** of LOWER CONTROL ARM & BALL JOINT under REMOVAL & INSTALLATION.
3) On all models, remove pivot bolts and control arm. Support control arm in vise. Using Ball Joint Wrench (C-3561), unscrew ball joint from control arm.
Installation – To install, reverse removal procedure. Ensure ball joint is fully seated against control arm. With vehicle at normal operating height, tighten all nuts and bolts to specifications. See TORQUE SPECIFICATIONS table at end of article.
Bushing Replacement – If bushings are worn, remove upper control arm. Using a sleeve and press, remove and replace bushings.

WHEEL BEARINGS

Removal – **1)** Raise and support vehicle. Remove wheel. Remove caliper retainer and anti-rattle springs (if equipped). Remove brake caliper, and support aside. DO NOT allow caliper to hang by brake hose. Remove inboard brake pad (if necessary).
2) Remove grease cap, cotter pin, nut, washer and outer wheel bearing. Carefully slide rotor from steering knuckle. Remove oil seal and inner bearing.

Installation – Clean and inspect bearings, and replace as required. Install inner bearing and oil seal. Install rotor and outer bearing, washer and nut. Adjust wheel bearings. See WHEEL BEARING under ADJUSTMENTS & INSPECTION. To install remaining components, reverse removal procedure.

1991 SUSPENSION
Front – 2WD Coil Spring (Cont.)

TORQUE SPECIFICATIONS

TORQUE SPECIFICATIONS

Application	Ft. Lbs. (N.m)
Ball Joint Nuts	
Upper	
Dakota	105 (142)
2WD Pickup, Ramcharger & RWD Van	135 (183)
Lower	
Dakota	135 (183)
2WD Pickup, Ramcharger & RWD Van	
11/16"	135 (183)
3/4"	175 (237)
Brake Caliper Anti-Rattle Spring Retainer Clips	
2WD Pickup, Ramcharger & RWD Van	18 (25)
Lower Control Arm-To-Frame Nut	
Dakota	
Front	130 (176)
Rear	80 (108)
Lower Control Arm-To-Crossmember Bolt	
2WD Pickup & Ramcharger	210 (285)
RWD Van	175 (237)
Lower Control Arm Strut	
2WD Pickup & Ramcharger	
Mounting Bolt	95 (129)
Mounting Nut	50 (68)
RWD Van	
Mounting Bolt	100 (136)
Mounting Nut	52 (70)
Lower Shock Absorber Mounting Bolt	17 (23)
Sway Bar Bolts/Nuts	
Frame End	
Dakota	40 (54)
2WD Pickup, Ramcharger & RWD Van	23 (31)
Link End	
Dakota	17 (23)
2WD Pickup, Ramcharger & RWD Van	[1]

TORQUE SPECIFICATIONS (Cont.)

Application	Ft. Lbs. (N.m)
Tie Rod End Nut	
Dakota, 2WD Pickup & Ramcharger	40 (54)
RWD Van	
9/16"-18	55 (75)
9/16"-20	75 (102)
Upper Ball Joint-To-Control Arm Nut	125 (169)
Upper Control Arm Eccentric Cam Bolt	
2WD Pickup & Ramcharger	70 (95)
Upper Control Arm Pivot Bar Bolt	
Dakota	155 (210)
RWD Van	195 (264)
Upper Shock Absorber Mounting Bolt	25 (34)
Wheel Lug Nuts	
Dakota	85 (115)
2WD Pickup & Ramcharger	
Coned	
1/2"-20	105 (142)
5/8"-18	200 (271)
Flanged	
5/8"-18	325 (440)
RWD Van	
Except 350 H/D Axle	85-110 (115-149)
350 H/D Axle	
Coned	175-225 (217-305)
Flanged	300-350 (407-475)

[1] – Tighten to 100 INCH lbs. (11 N.m).

1991 SUSPENSION
Front – 4WD Leaf Spring

4WD Pickup, Ramcharger

DESCRIPTION

Front suspension uses leaf springs which are mounted to frame rail brackets and shackles to provide support for axle housing. Shock absorbers are attached to brackets on frame rails and axle assembly. *See Fig. 1.* Sway bar is mounted to frame rail by brackets and to axle assembly by link assembly. Steering knuckles are mounted at each end of axle assembly.

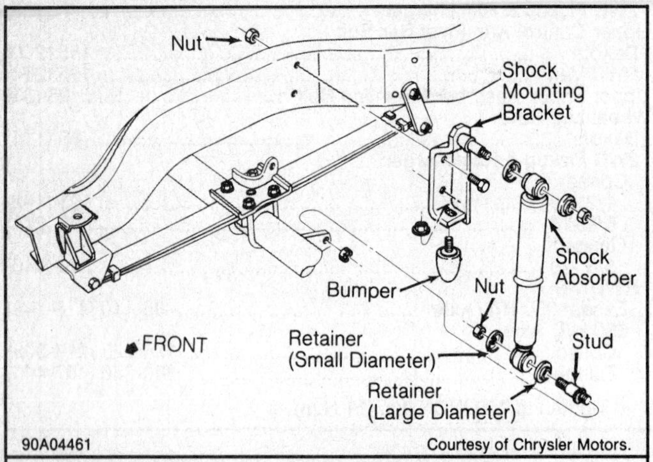
Nut
Shock
Mounting
Bracket
Shock
Absorber
Bumper
Nut
FRONT
Retainer
(Small Diameter)
Stud
Retainer
(Large Diameter)
90A04461
Courtesy of Chrysler Motors.

Fig. 1: Exploded View of Front Suspension Assembly

ADJUSTMENTS & INSPECTION

WHEEL ALIGNMENT SPECIFICATIONS & PROCEDURES

NOTE: *See* ***SPECIFICATIONS & PROCEDURES*** *article in* ***WHEEL ALIGNMENT.***

WHEEL BEARING

1) Raise and support vehicle. Remove wheel. On Model 44 axle, remove grease cap and driving hub snap ring. Remove driving hub and retaining spring.

2) On Model 60 axle, remove hub cap. Using snap ring pliers, remove snap ring. Remove flange nuts and lock washers. Remove drive flange. Discard gasket. Remove locking hub (if equipped). See LOCKING HUB under REMOVAL & INSTALLATION. Straighten tang on lock ring.

3) On all models, remove wheel bearing lock nut using Socket (C-4170-A on Model 44 axle or DD-1241-JD on Model 60 axle). Using socket and Adapter (C-4170 on Model 44 axle or C-3952 on Model 60 axle), tighten inner lock nut to 50 ft. lbs. (68 N.m). Loosen lock nut. Retighten to 30-40 ft. lbs. (41-54 N.m) while rotating hub. Back lock nut off 135-150 degrees.

4) Install lock ring. Install outer lock nut, and tighten to 50 ft. lbs. (68 N.m) for Model 44 axle or 65 ft. lbs. (88 N.m) for Model 60 axle. On all models, end play should be .001-.010" (.03-.25 mm) after adjustment. To install remaining components, reverse removal procedure.

REMOVAL & INSTALLATION

AXLE SHAFTS

Removal (Model 44) – 1) Raise and support vehicle. Remove wheel. Remove rotor. See WHEEL BEARINGS under REMOVAL & INSTALLATION. Remove caliper adapter from steering knuckle.

2) Remove 6 torque retaining nuts and washers from spindle-to-steering knuckle bolts. Remove brake splash shield. Using soft-faced mallet, strike spindle lightly to loosen from steering knuckle.

3) To remove right axle shaft, carefully extract axle shaft from axle housing. Remove seal and stone shield from shaft.

4) To remove left axle, disconnect vacuum lines and electrical connector from switch on disconnect housing assembly. *See Fig. 2.* Remove cover assembly, gasket and shield. Remove intermediate axle shaft from axle without damaging axle shaft seal.

5) Using Bearing Extractor (D-330), remove bearing from inside axle. Remove shift collar from axle. Remove differential cover. Drain gear oil into container.

6) Push inner axle shaft toward center of vehicle. Remove "C" lock from recessed groove on shaft. Using Bar (D-354-4) and Adapter (D-354-3), drive out inner shaft. *See Figs. 3 and 4.*

7) Using Bar (D-354-4), Remover (D-354-1) and Puller (C-637), remove inner axle shaft bearing. Using Puller (C-637), remove outer axle bearing and seal.

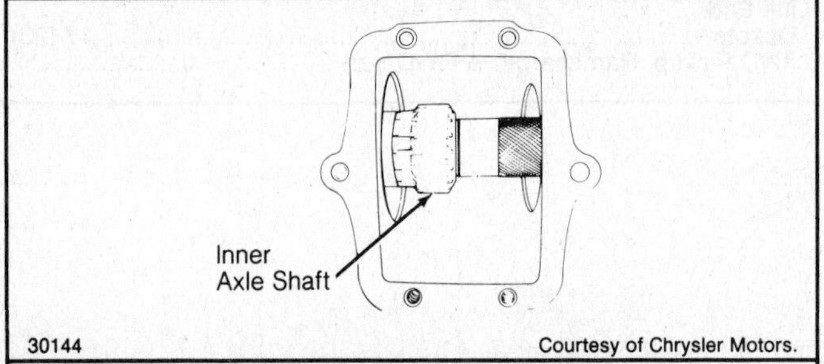
Inner
Axle Shaft
30144
Courtesy of Chrysler Motors.

Fig. 3: Removing Inner Axle Shaft from Model 44 Axle

Installation (Left Side) – 1) Using Bar (D-354-4), Installer (D-354-2) and Puller (C-637), install inner axle shaft bearing. *See Fig. 4.* Using bar and Adapter (D-354-3), install and seat inner axle shaft. Insert "C" lock in recessed groove in shaft. Position shift collar on splined end of inner axle shaft.

2) Using Installer (D-360) and Handle (C-4171), install outer axle shaft bearing and seal. Using handle and Installer (D-328), install bearing into intermediate axle shaft. Install intermediate axle shaft through seal into housing without damaging shaft seal.

3) Install disconnect housing assembly and gasket while guiding shift fork into groove of shift collar. Install and tighten disconnect housing assembly bolts.

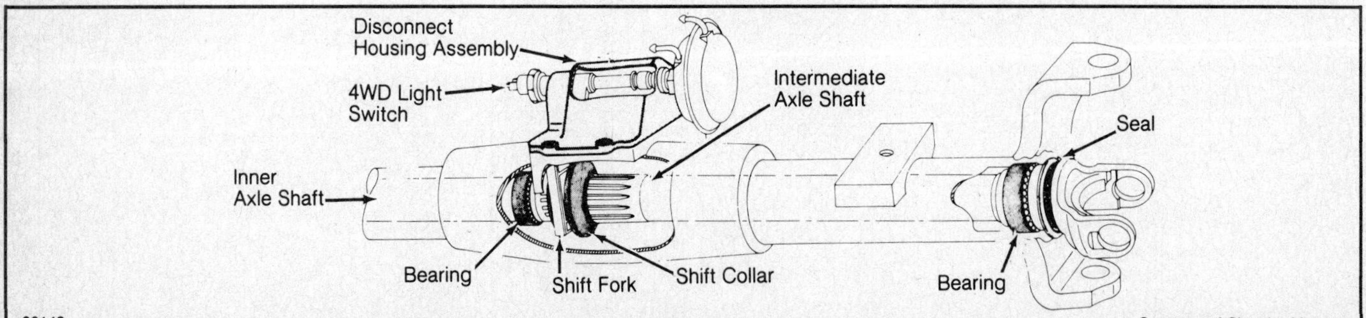
Disconnect
Housing Assembly
4WD Light
Switch
Intermediate
Axle Shaft
Seal
Inner
Axle Shaft
Bearing
Shift Fork
Shift Collar
Bearing
30143
Courtesy of Chrysler Motors.

Fig. 2: Cut-Away View of Model 44 Axle Disconnect Housing Assembly

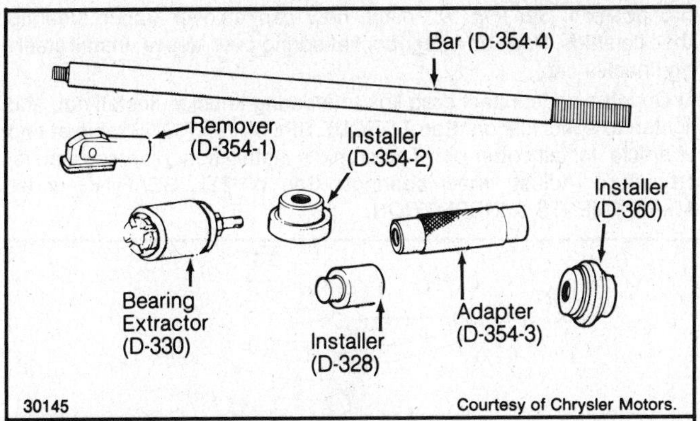

Bar (D-354-4)
Remover (D-354-1)
Installer (D-354-2)
Installer (D-360)
Bearing Extractor (D-330)
Adapter (D-354-3)
Installer (D-328)
30145
Courtesy of Chrysler Motors.

Fig. 4: Identifying Model 44 Axle Tool Set

4) To complete installation, reverse removal procedure. Apply RTV sealant to edge of grease cap. Apply 1/16-3/32" bead of silicone rubber sealant along bolt circle of differential housing cover before installing.

5) Install inner pad anti-rattle spring on top of retainer spring plate. Adjust wheel bearings. See WHEEL BEARING under ADJUSTMENTS & INSPECTION. Tighten bolts to specification. See TORQUE SPECIFICATIONS table at end of article.

Installation (Right Side) – 1) Position seal on stone shield with seal lip facing toward shaft spline. Install axle shaft into housing without damaging differential seal at side gear.

2) To complete installation, reverse removal procedure. Apply RTV sealant to edge of grease cap. Inner pad anti-rattle spring must be installed on top of retainer spring plate. Adjust wheel bearings. See WHEEL BEARING under ADJUSTMENTS & INSPECTION. Tighten bolts to specification. See TORQUE SPECIFICATIONS table at end of article.

Removal (Model 60) – 1) Block brake pedal in up position. Raise and support vehicle. Remove wheel. Remove rotor. See WHEEL BEARINGS under REMOVAL & INSTALLATION.

2) Remove brake splash shield, brake adapter and spindle-to-steering knuckle nuts and washers. Remove spindle from steering knuckle. Remove axle shaft, Bronze spacer, seal and slinger from housing.

Installation – Install axle shaft. Place Bronze spacer on axle shaft with chamfered edge facing inward. To complete installation, reverse removal procedure. Adjust wheel bearings. See WHEEL BEARING under ADJUSTMENTS & INSPECTION. Tighten bolts to specification. See TORQUE SPECIFICATIONS table at end of article.

STEERING KNUCKLE, SPINDLE & BALL JOINT

Removal (Model 44 Axle) – 1) Raise and support vehicle. Remove wheel. Remove brake rotor. See WHEEL BEARINGS under REMOVAL & INSTALLATION. Remove caliper adapter from steering knuckle.

2) Remove and discard 6 nuts and washers from spindle-to-knuckle attaching bolts. Remove brake splash shield. Using soft-faced mallet, strike spindle lightly to loosen from knuckle.

3) Place spindle in soft-jawed vise. DO NOT clamp bearing surfaces. Remove seal. On right side, use Puller (D-131) to remove needle bearings from right spindle. Remove axle shaft. Remove seal from axle shaft.

4) Remove cotter pin and nut from tie rod end. Loosen clamp bolt nut. Using Puller (C-3894-A), remove tie rod end from steering knuckle. Mark tie rod end and tie rod for reassembly reference. Remove tie rod end.

5) On left side, remove cotter pin and nut from drag link. Using Puller (C-4150), remove drag link from steering knuckle arm and steering gear arm. Lower drag link from vehicle. Remove nuts and cone washers from steering knuckle arm. Tap steering knuckle arm to loosen. Remove steering knuckle arm.

6) On both sides, remove cotter pin from upper ball joint nut. Remove upper and lower ball joint nut. Discard lower ball joint nut. Using brass drift and hammer, separate steering knuckle from axle housing yoke. Using Sleeve Tool (C-4169), remove and discard sleeve from upper ball joint yoke on axle housing.

7) Position steering knuckle upside-down in vise. Using Snap Ring Pliers (C-4020), remove snap ring from lower ball joint. Using Ball Joint Stand (C-4212-L), Adapter (D-150-3), Screw (D-150-2) and Block (D-150-1), press lower ball joint from steering knuckle. *See Fig. 5.* Reposition stand. Press upper ball joint from steering knuckle.

8) Replace ball joints if any looseness or play exists. Clean all components with solvent, and dry with compressed air. Inspect all parts for burrs, chips, wear or cracks. Replace as required.

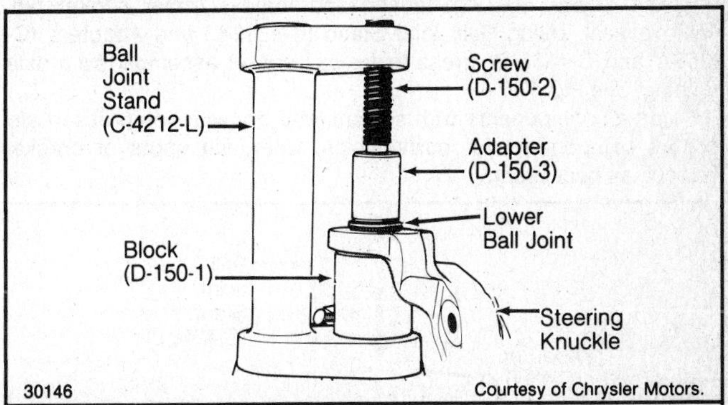

Ball Joint Stand (C-4212-L)
Screw (D-150-2)
Adapter (D-150-3)
Lower Ball Joint
Block (D-150-1)
Steering Knuckle
30146
Courtesy of Chrysler Motors.

Fig. 5: Removing Model 44 Lower Ball Joint

Installation – 1) Place steering knuckle in vise. Press ball joints into position with stand and components. *See Fig. 6.* Install new boots on ball joints. Remove steering knuckle from vise. Insert new sleeve into upper ball joint yoke of axle housing, allowing 2 threads to be exposed at top of housing.

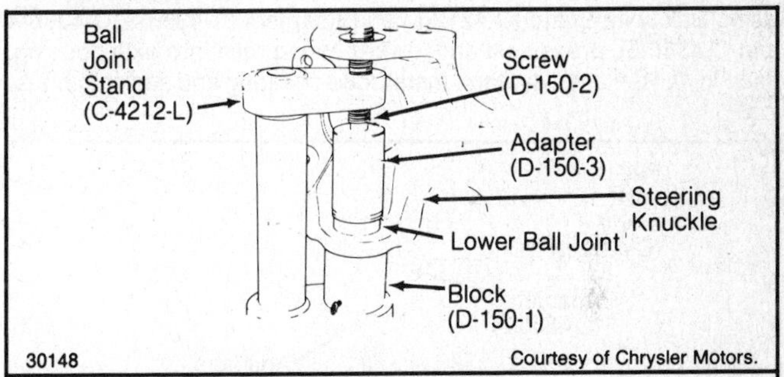

Ball Joint Stand (C-4212-L)
Screw (D-150-2)
Adapter (D-150-3)
Steering Knuckle
Lower Ball Joint
Block (D-150-1)
30148
Courtesy of Chrysler Motors.

Fig. 6: Installing Model 44 Lower Ball Joint

2) Place steering knuckle on axle housing yoke. Install and tighten NEW lower ball joint nut. Using Sleeve Tool (C-4169) and torque wrench, tighten upper ball joint yoke sleeve to 40 ft. lbs. (54 N.m). Install upper ball joint nut, and tighten to 100 ft. lbs. (136 N.m).

3) Align cotter pin hole in stud with slot in castellated nut. Tighten nut to align hole and slot. DO NOT loosen. Insert cotter pin. Install steering knuckle arm, cone washer and drag link on left side of vehicle.

4) Install tie rod ends. Apply multipurpose grease to seal lip. Install seal on stone shield with seal lip facing axle shaft spline. Install right axle shaft into housing without damaging seal.

5) On left axle shaft, remove disconnect housing assembly. Install shaft. Install disconnect housing assembly. Using Installer (D-360) and Handle (C-4171), install new needle bearings in RIGHT spindle.

6) Using Installer (D-155) and handle, install new brake hub seals. Grease full circumference of seal and spindle thrust surface. Install new spacer on axle shaft. Install spindle and brake splash shield.

7) To complete installation, reverse removal procedure. Ensure inboard brake pad anti-rattle spring is on top of retainer spring plate. Adjust wheel bearings. See WHEEL BEARING under ADJUSTMENTS & INSPECTION. Tighten bolts to specification. See TORQUE SPECIFICATIONS table at end of article.

Removal (Model 60 Axle) – 1) Remove axle shafts. See AXLE SHAFTS under REMOVAL & INSTALLATION. Remove cotter pin and

1991 SUSPENSION
Front – 4WD Leaf Spring (Cont.)

nut from tie rod end. Loosen clamp bolt nut. Using Puller (C-3894-A), remove tie rod end.

2) On left side, remove cotter pin and nut from drag link. Using Puller (C-4150), remove tie rod end from steering knuckle arm. Disconnect drag link from steering knuckle. Remove steering knuckle arm bolts and arm.

3) On left side, remove upper steering knuckle cap, and discard gasket. Remove spring and upper socket sleeve. Remove lower steering knuckle cap bolts and cap. To separate steering knuckle from axle housing, swing steering knuckle outward at bottom while lifting up and off upper socket pin.

4) Using Socket (D-192), loosen and remove upper socket pin. Remove seal. Using Ball Joint Stand (C-4212-L) and Adapters (C-4366-1 and C-4366-2), press lower ball socket assembly from axle housing. *See Fig. 7.*

5) Clean all components with solvent, and dry with compressed air. Inspect components for burrs, chips, wear, flat spots or cracks. Replace as necessary.

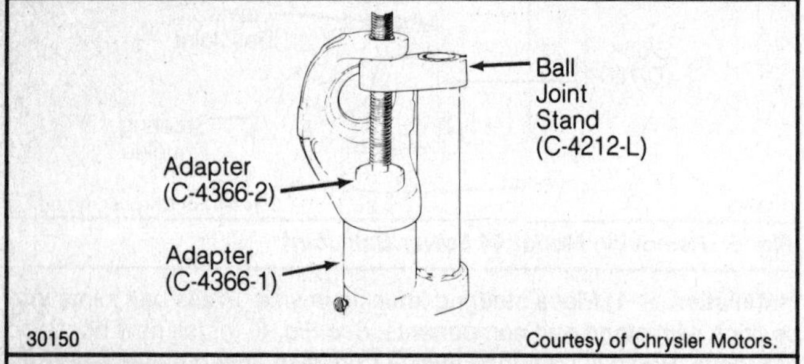
Ball
Joint
Stand
(C-4212-L)
Adapter
(C-4366-2)
Adapter
(C-4366-1)
30150
Courtesy of Chrysler Motors.

Fig. 7: Removing Model 60 Lower Ball Socket

Installation – 1) Apply multipurpose lubricant to lower ball socket. Using Ball Joint Stand (C-4212-L) and Adapters (C-4366-3, C-4366-4 and C-4366-5), press seal and lower bearing race into axle housing. *See Fig. 8.* Replace adapters. Install lower bearing and seal into housing.

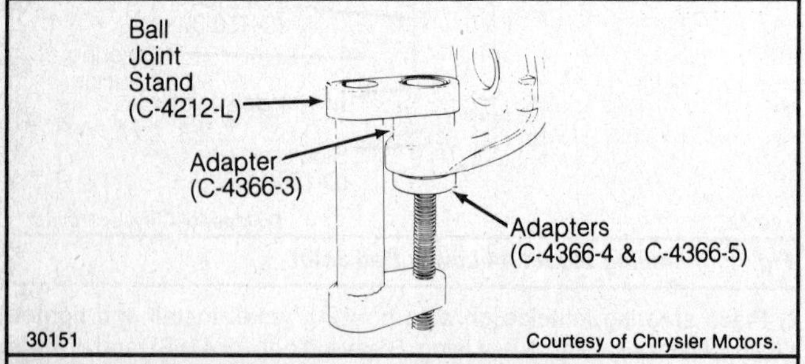
Ball
Joint
Stand
(C-4212-L)
Adapter
(C-4366-3)
Adapters
(C-4366-4 & C-4366-5)
30151
Courtesy of Chrysler Motors.

Fig. 8: Installing Model 60 Lower Bearing & Seal

2) Using Socket (D-192) and torque wrench, install and tighten upper socket pin. Install seal over pin. Position steering knuckle over socket pin. Fill lower socket cavity with multipurpose lubricant. Install lower steering knuckle cap.

3) Apply generous amount of multipurpose lubricant to upper socket pin. Align upper socket sleeve in keyway of steering knuckle, and slide into position. *See Fig. 9.* Install new gasket over upper steering knuckle studs. Position upper socket spring over sleeve. Install steering knuckle cap.

4) On left side, connect drag link to steering knuckle. Install nut, and tighten to specification. See TORQUE SPECIFICATIONS table at end of article. Install cotter pin. To complete installation, reverse removal procedure. Adjust wheel bearings. See WHEEL BEARING under ADJUSTMENTS & INSPECTION.

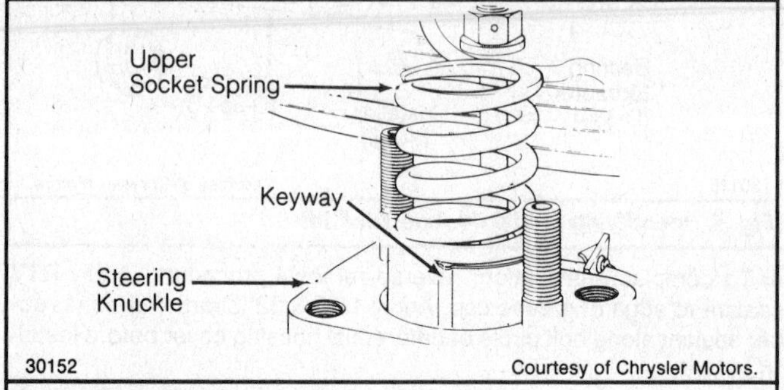
Upper
Socket Spring
Keyway
Steering
Knuckle
30152
Courtesy of Chrysler Motors.

Fig. 9: Aligning Keyway & Steering Knuckle

LOCKING HUB

Removal – 1) Turn shift knob to ENGAGE position. Apply downward pressure to face of shift knob, and remove 3 shift knob retaining screws nearest to flange. With an outward pull, remove shift knob from mounting base.

2) Remove snap ring from axle shaft. Remove cam screws and lock washers from mounting base flange. Separate and remove locking hub assembly from rotor hub. Remove and discard gasket.

Inspection – Wash parts in mineral spirits, and blow dry with compressed air. Examine gear splines, shift knob, cam, sliding gear, drive shaft gear and mounting base for damage. Replace components as necessary.

Installation – 1) Lightly lubricate parts with multipurpose lubricant. Position new gasket and locking hub onto rotor hub. Install attaching cam screws and lock washers. Tighten to 30-40 ft. lbs. (41-54 N.m). Install axle shaft snap ring.

2) Position shift knob on mounting base. Align splines by pushing inward on shift knob. Turn clockwise to lock in position. Install and tighten 3 shift knob retaining screws.

WHEEL BEARINGS

Removal (Model 44 Axle) – 1) Raise and support vehicle. Remove wheel. Remove caliper retainer and anti-rattle spring assemblies. Remove caliper from rotor. Wire caliper aside. DO NOT allow caliper to hang by hose.

2) Remove inner brake pad. Remove grease cap and driving hub snap ring. Remove driving hub and retaining spring. Using Socket (C-4170-A), remove bearing lock nut.

3) Remove retaining washer and adjusting nut. Remove rotor. Outer bearing and retainer spring will also slide out. Pry inner seal from hub. Remove bearing.

Installation - 1) Lubricate and install inner bearing. Using Seal Installer (D-359) and Handle (C-4171), install inner seal. Install rotor and outer wheel bearing.

2) Install adjusting nut. Adjust wheel bearings. See WHEEL BEARING under ADJUSTMENTS & INSPECTION. Apply RTV sealer on edge of grease cap. Install grease cap. Position inner pad on adapter, with shoe flanges in adapter guides.

3) Slide caliper into position in adapter and over rotor. Align caliper on machined faces of adapter without pulling dust boot from groove on caliper as piston and boot are slid over inner pad.

4) Install anti-rattle springs and retaining clips. Tighten to 15 ft. lbs. (20 N.m). Inner pad anti-rattle spring must be installed on top of retainer spring plate.

Removal & Installation (Model 60 Axle) - 1) Block brake pedal in up position. Raise and support vehicle. Remove wheel. Remove caliper-to-adapter Allen screw. Tap adapter lock and spring from between brake caliper and adapter. Separate brake caliper from adapter.

2) Wire caliper aside. DO NOT allow brake caliper to hang by hose. Inner pad will remain on adapter. Remove hub cap. Using Snap Ring Pliers (C-4020), remove snap ring. Remove flange nuts and lock washers. Remove drive flange. Discard gasket. Remove locking hub (if equipped). See LOCKING HUB under REMOVAL & INSTALLATION.

3) Straighten tangs on lock ring. Using Socket (DD-1241-JD), loosen outer lock nut. Remove lock nut, lock ring, inner lock nut and outer bearing. Slide hub and rotor from spindle knuckle. Remove oil seal and inner bearing.

4) Clean bearings. Inspect for damage. If necessary, replace bearings and races as an assembly. To install, reverse removal procedure. Inner pad anti-rattle spring must be installed on top of retainer spring plate. Adjust wheel bearings. See WHEEL BEARING under ADJUSTMENTS & INSPECTION.

TORQUE SPECIFICATIONS

TORQUE SPECIFICATIONS

Application	Ft. Lbs. (N.m)
Anti-Rattle Springs & Clips	15 (20)
Ball Joint Nut	
Lower (Except 350)	135 (183)
Lower (350)	175 (237)
Upper (Except 350)	135 (183)
Upper (350)	225 (305)
Brake Adapter Allen Screw	12-18 (16-24)
Differential Cover Bolt	20 (27)
Disconnect Housing Assembly Bolt	10 (14)
Drag Link Nut	60 (81)
Drive Flange Nut (Model 60)	30-40 (41-54)
Locking Hub Cam Screws	30-40 (41-54)
Shock Absorber Upper & Lower Mounting Nuts	55 (75)
Spindle Nut	
Model 44	25-35 (34-41)
Model 60	50-70 (68-95)
Spring Eye Pivot Bolt Nut	80 (108)
Spring Plate Stud Nut	
9/16"-18 Stud	95 (129)
Model 44 Axle	105 (142)
Model 60 Axle	115 (156)
Spring Shackle Bolt	80 (108)
Spring "U" Bolt Nut	95 (129)
Steering Knuckle Arm Nut	90 (122)
Steering Knuckle Cap Bolt (Model 60)	70-90 (95-122)
Steering Knuckle Cone Washer Nut (Model 44)	90 (122)
Sway Bar Bracket-To-Frame Nuts	17 (23)
Sway Bar Link-To-Spring Bracket Nut	75 (102)
Tie Rod Clamp Bolt	25-30 (34-41)
Tie Rod End Nut	
Model 44	45 (61)
Model 60	55 (75)
Upper Ball Joint Yoke Sleeve (Model 44)	40 (54)
Upper Socket Pin (Model 60)	500-600 (678-813)
Wheel Lug Nuts	
Model 44	110 (149)
Model 60	75 (102)
	INCH Lbs. (N.m)
Sway Bar Link Rod Nut	100 (11)

1991 SUSPENSION
Front – Torsion Bar

Dakota (4WD)

DESCRIPTION

The front suspension consists of upper and lower control arms, sway bar, shock absorbers and left and right torsion bars. The front end of torsion bar is connected to lower control arm. The rear end of torsion bar is mounted to an adjustable arm at crossmember. *See Fig. 1.*

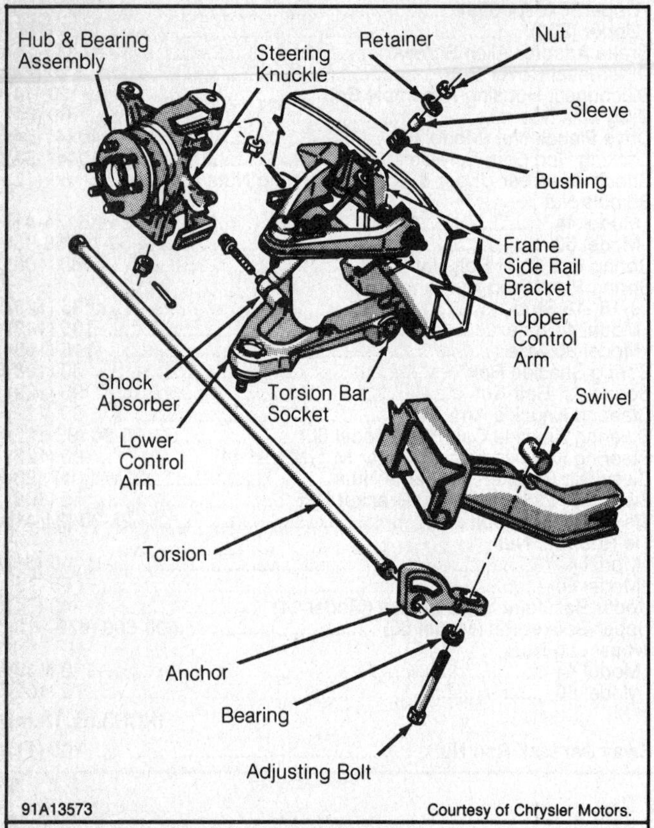
Hub & Bearing
Assembly
Steering
Knuckle
Retainer
Nut
Sleeve
Bushing
Frame
Side Rail
Bracket
Upper
Control
Arm
Shock
Absorber
Torsion Bar
Socket
Swivel
Lower
Control
Arm
Torsion
Anchor
Bearing
Adjusting Bolt
91A13573
Courtesy of Chrysler Motors.

Fig. 1: Exploded View of Front Suspension

ADJUSTMENTS & INSPECTION

WHEEL ALIGNMENT SPECIFICATIONS & PROCEDURES

NOTE: See SPECIFICATIONS & PROCEDURES article in WHEEL ALIGNMENT.

WHEEL BEARING

Front wheel bearings are permanently sealed, and require no lubrication or adjustment. Hub and bearing unit is replaced as an assembly. With brakes applied, tighten hub nut to 190 ft. lbs. (258 N.m).

RIDING HEIGHT

Vehicle height is adjusted by rotating torsion bar anchor adjusting bolt. Turning adjusting bolt clockwise increases vehicle height; turning adjusting bolt counterclockwise decreases vehicle height. Adjust ride height with vehicle on a level surface and its tires properly inflated. Measure inner height from floor surface to underside surface of lower control arm rear pivot bores.

Measure outer height from floor surface to underside surface of lower control arm rear edge, at area immediately inboard of steering stop. Check inner and outer measurements, and adjust height differential to specification. Height differential from side-to-side of vehicle should not be more than .25" (6.4 mm). See SPECIFICATIONS & PROCEDURES article in WHEEL ALIGNMENT. After each adjustment, jounce vehicle before measuring to determine effects of adjustment.

BALL JOINT CHECKING

Ball joints are preloaded. Replace ball joint if vertical movement exceeds .02" (.5 mm).

REMOVAL & INSTALLATION

WHEEL HUB & BEARING ASSEMBLY

Removal – 1) Remove cotter pin, nut lock and spring washer. Loosen hub nut, and then raise and support vehicle. Remove hub nut, washer and wheel. Remove brake caliper guide pins, and remove caliper. Mark brake rotor and hub, and remove brake rotor.

2) Remove hub and bearing assembly mounting bolts from rear of steering knuckle. *See Fig. 1.* Slide hub and bearing assembly off front axle shaft splines. Inspect steering knuckle grease seal and hub and bearing assembly for excessive wear or damage. Replace components as necessary.

Installation – 1) Install hub and bearing assembly onto steering knuckle, guiding axle shaft through spline in hub. Tighten mounting bolts to 110 ft. lbs. (150 N.m).

2) Align marks, and install brake rotor and caliper. Install caliper pins, and tighten to 22 ft. lbs. (30 N.m). With brakes applied, tighten hub retainer nut to 190 ft. lbs. (258 N.m). Install spring washer, nut lock and new cotter pin. DO NOT back off nut to install cotter pin. To complete installation, reverse removal procedure. For tightening specifications, see TORQUE SPECIFICATIONS at end of article.

STEERING KNUCKLE

Removal – 1) Remove wheel hub. See WHEEL HUB & BEARING ASSEMBLY under REMOVAL & INSTALLATION. Remove tie rod end nut. Using Tie Rod Puller (C-3894-A), disconnect tie rod end from steering knuckle.

2) Unload torsion bar completely by turning adjusting bolt counterclockwise. *See Fig. 2.* Remove lower shock absorber mounting bolt. Disconnect sway bar from lower control arm.

3) Place Ball Joint Remover (C-3564-A) over top of lower control arm with tool nut up against upper ball joint stud. *See Fig. 3.* Loosen ball joint stud nut. Tighten ball joint remover to apply pressure to ball joint stud, and strike steering knuckle sharply using hammer to loosen stud. Detach opposite ball joint in same manner. DO NOT attempt to force stud out using ball joint remover pressure only.

4) Separate lower ball joint stud from steering knuckle. Remove steering knuckle from vehicle. Inspect steering knuckle grease seal for cuts, distortion and wear. Check steering knuckle and hub and bearing assembly for damage. Replace components as necessary.

Installation – 1) Install new steering knuckle grease seal. Position new grease seal in recess of steering knuckle, and install using Seal Installer (C-4698). Lubricate seal lip with multipurpose grease. Install steering knuckle onto ball joint studs.

2) Install hub and bearing assembly onto steering knuckle, guiding axle shaft through spline in hub. Install tie rod end. Install brake rotor and caliper. Tighten caliper guide pins to 22 ft. lbs. (30 N.m).

3) With brakes applied, tighten hub retainer nut to 190 ft. lbs. (258 N.m). Install spring washer, nut lock and new cotter pin. DO NOT back off nut to install cotter pin. To complete installation, reverse removal procedure. Check and adjust ride height. For tightening specifications, see TORQUE SPECIFICATIONS at end of article.

LOWER CONTROL ARM & BALL JOINT

Removal – 1) Loosen hub nut. Raise and support vehicle. Remove wheel. Remove mounting bolts from inner CV joint, and remove axle shaft. Unload torsion bar completely by turning adjusting bolt counterclockwise. *See Fig. 2.* Remove torsion bar. See TORSION BARS under REMOVAL & INSTALLATION.

2) Remove lower shock absorber mounting bolt. Disconnect sway bar from lower control arm. Disconnect lower ball joint. Separate lower control arm from steering knuckle. Remove lower control arm pivot bolts, and remove lower control arm. Pry retainer off ball joint. Remove ball joint from lower control arm.

Installation – **1)** Install new ball joint in lower control arm. Install new ball joint grease seal. Position control arm on vehicle, and install nuts on pivot bolts finger tight.
2) To complete installation, reverse removal procedure. Lubricate ball joint. With vehicle on floor, tighten lower control arm pivot bolts to specifications. See TORQUE SPECIFICATIONS at end of article. Check and adjust ride height and front end alignment.
Bushing Replacement – If bushings are worn, remove lower control arm. Use a sleeve and press to remove and replace bushings.

TORSION BARS

NOTE: Left and right torsion bars are NOT interchangeable. Torsion bars may be installed with either end facing forward.

Removal – **1)** Remove upper control arm rebound bumper, and then raise and support vehicle. Unload torsion bar completely by turning adjusting bolt counterclockwise. *See Fig. 2.*

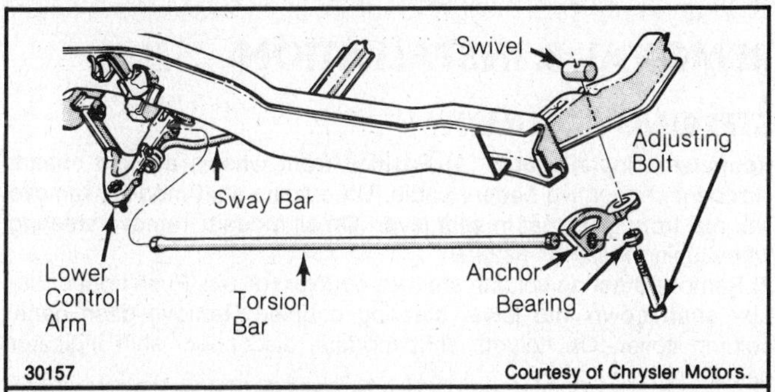

Swivel
Adjusting Bolt
Sway Bar
Lower Control Arm
Torsion Bar
Anchor Bearing
30157
Courtesy of Chrysler Motors.

Fig. 2: Removing Torsion Bar

2) Remove adjusting bolt from anchor, and remove torsion bar and anchor as an assembly from control arm. Separate torsion bar from anchor and bearing.
3) Inspect torsion bars, anchors, swivels, bearings and crossmember support for bend, cracks, deterioration or damage. Check adjusting bolt and nut for damage or stripped threads. Replace components as necessary.
Installation – **1)** Install torsion bar through anchor, and slide torsion bar forward into control arm. Position anchor bearing into frame crossmember, and thread adjusting bolt into swivel.
2) Turn adjusting bolt clockwise to place load on torsion bar. Lower vehicle, and install upper control arm rebound bumper. Check and adjust ride height and front end alignment.

UPPER CONTROL ARM & BALL JOINT

Removal – **1)** Remove hub nut. Raise and support vehicle. Remove wheel. Remove mounting bolts from inner CV joint, and remove axle shaft. Unload torsion bar completely by turning adjusting bolt counterclockwise. *See Fig. 2.* Remove cotter pin, and loosen ball joint stud nut.
2) Position Ball Joint Remover (C-3564-A) over top of lower control arm with tool nut up against upper ball joint stud. *See Fig. 3.* Tighten ball joint remover to apply pressure to ball joint stud, and strike steering knuckle sharply using hammer to loosen stud.
3) DO NOT attempt to force stud out using ball joint remover pressure only. Separate upper control arm from steering knuckle. Remove ball joint seal. Using Ball Joint Wrench (C-3561), unscrew upper ball joint from control arm. Remove upper control arm pivot bolts. Remove control arm from mounting bracket.

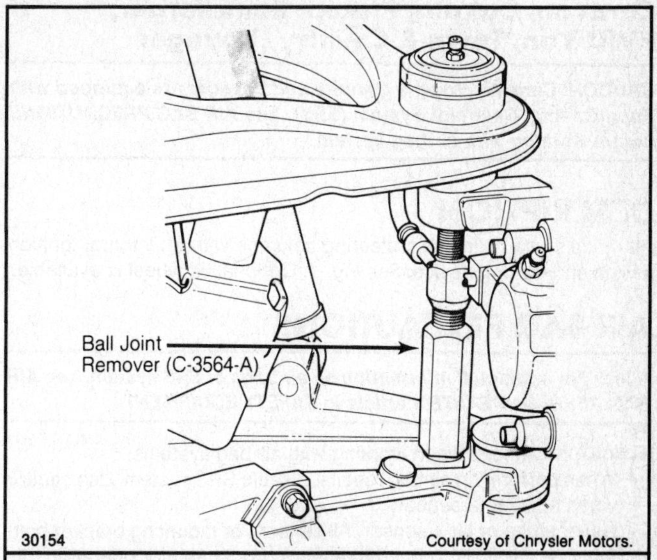

Ball Joint Remover (C-3564-A)
30154
Courtesy of Chrysler Motors.

Fig. 3: Removing Upper Ball Joint Stud

Installation – **1)** Position upper control arm onto mounting bracket. Install upper control arm pivot bolts. Tighten bolts finger tight. Using Ball Joint Wrench (C-3561), screw upper ball joint into control arm. Tighten ball joint to 125 ft. lbs. (170 N.m). Install new ball joint grease seal. Connect steering knuckle to ball joint.
2) To complete installation, reverse removal procedure. With vehicle on floor, tighten upper control arm pivot bolts to specification. See TORQUE SPECIFICATIONS at end of article. Lubricate ball joint. Check and adjust ride height and front end alignment.
Bushing Replacement – If bushings are worn, remove upper control arm. Use a sleeve and press to remove and replace bushings.

TORQUE SPECIFICATIONS

TORQUE SPECIFICATIONS

Application	Ft. Lbs. (N.m)
Ball Joint Stud Nut	
Lower	120 (163)
Upper	105 (142)
Brake Caliper Guide Pins	22 (30)
CV Joint Flange-To-Axle Flange Bolt	65 (88)
Hub & Bearing Assembly-To-Drive Axle	
Retainer Nut	[1] 190 (258)
Hub & Bearing Assembly-To-Steering Knuckle	
Mounting Bolt	110 (150)
Lower Control Arm-To-Frame Pivot Bolt	
Front	80 (108)
Rear	130 (176)
Shock Absorber Bolt	
Lower	100 (136)
Upper	25 (34)
Sway Bar Mounting Bolt	20 (27)
Tie Rod End Nut	50 (68)
Upper Ball Joint-To-Control Arm	125 (170)
Upper Control Arm-To-Frame Pivot Bolt	155 (210)
Wheel Lug Nut	85 (115)

[1] – Do not back off retainer nut to install new cotter pin. After reaching proper torque, tighten nut only enough to align slot.

1991 STEERING
Steering Columns

Caravan, Dakota, Pickup, Ramcharger, RWD Van, Town & Country, Voyager

CAUTION: Caravan, Town & Country and Voyager are equipped with Supplemental Restraint System (SRS). See AIR BAG PRECAUTIONS before working with air bag system.

DESCRIPTION

All models use collapsible steering columns with an integral ignition switch and locking device. *See Fig. 1*. Optional tilt wheel is available.

AIR BAG PRECAUTIONS

NOTE: For additional information on air bags or SRS system, see AIR BAG RESTRAINT SYSTEM article in SAFETY EQUIPMENT.

Follow precautions when working with air bag systems:

- When performing air bag repairs, disable SRS system. Use caution when handing a sensor.
- Never strike or jar a sensor. All sensors or mounting bracket bolts must be carefully torqued to ensure proper sensor operation.
- Never apply power to SRS system if a sensor is not rigidly attached to vehicle.
- To avoid accidental air bag deployment while trouble shooting SRS system, DO NOT use electrical test equipment, such as battery-powered or AC-powered voltmeter, ohmmeter, etc.
- Always carry air bag module with trim cover away from body. Always place inflatable module on workbench with trim cover up, away from loose objects.
- DO NOT install used air bag part from another vehicle. Use new parts only. DO NOT disassemble or tamper with air bag assembly.
- Wait at least 30 seconds after disconnecting battery before proceeding with repairs or trouble shooting system. Some manufacturers recommend waiting up to 20 minutes before making SRS repairs. For a short time after battery is disconnected, SRS system retains enough voltage to deploy air bag.

WARNING: Wait about 2 minutes after disconnecting negative battery cable before servicing air bag system. System reserve capacitor maintains air bag system voltage for about 2 minutes after battery is disconnected. Servicing air bag system before 2 minutes may cause accidental air bag deployment and possible personal injury.

NOTE: Complete system deactivation should be performed only when Air Bag Restraint System (ABRS) is not functioning properly and vehicle needs to be driven.

Complete System Deactivation – Disconnect negative battery cable, and tape end. Disconnect 2-way Yellow clockspring harness connector, located on top of fuse block between clockspring and instrument panel wiring harness. Clockspring connector may also be disconnected at Air Bag System Diagnostic Module (ASDM).

REMOVAL & INSTALLATION

STEERING COLUMN

Removal & Installation – 1) Position front wheels straight ahead. Disconnect negative battery cable. On column shift models, remove link rod from grommet in shift lever. On all models, remove steering wheel using Puller (C-3428-B).

2) Remove steering column shaft-to-coupler roll pin. Push upper coupler shaft down into lower steering coupler. Remove dash panel column cover. On column shift models, disconnect shift indicator cable.

3) On all models, remove tilt lever (if equipped). Remove upper and lower shroud. Remove lower fixed shroud. Disconnect multifunction switch harness connector. Disconnect harness connectors from ignition switch, key-in light, horn and speed control (if equipped).

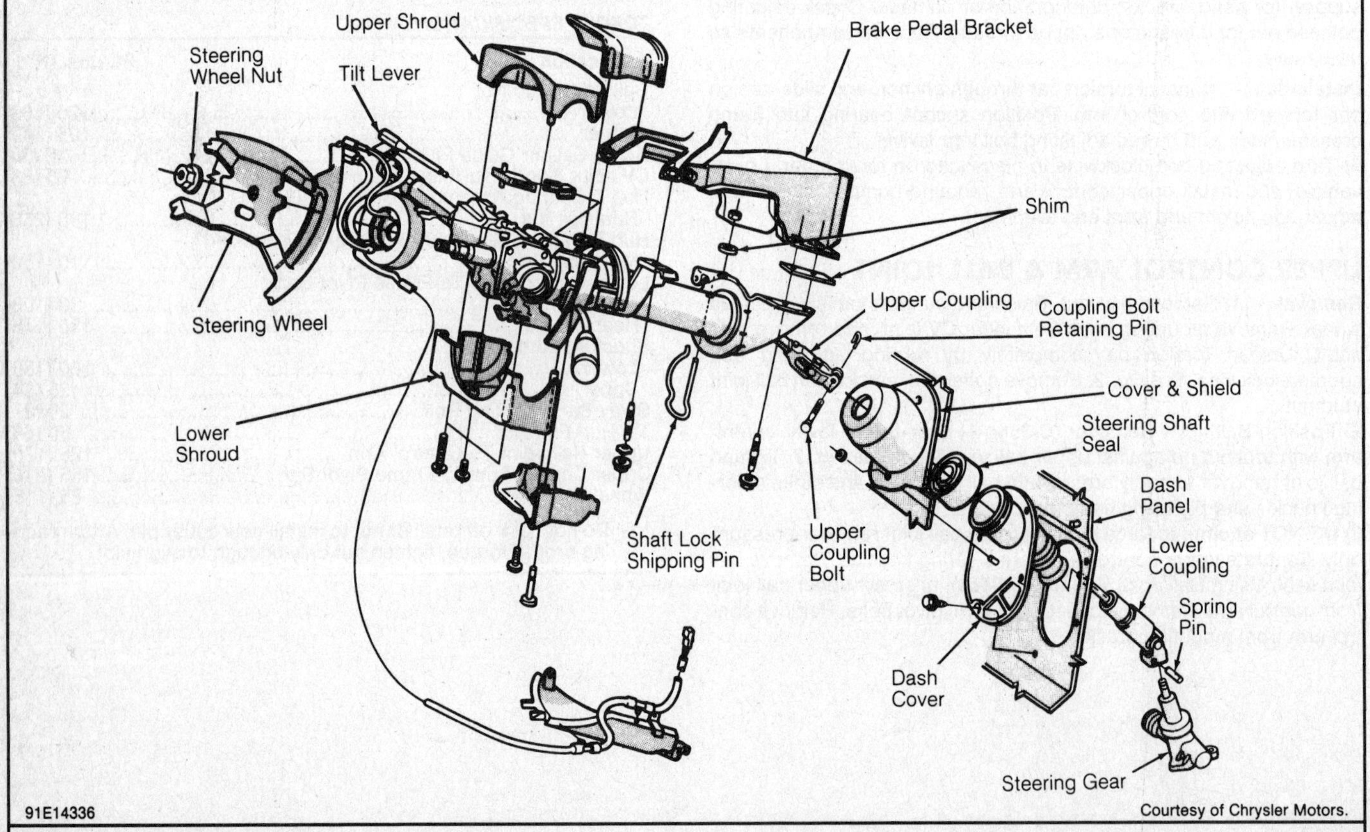
Upper Shroud
Steering Wheel Nut
Tilt Lever
Brake Pedal Bracket
Shim
Upper Coupling
Coupling Bolt Retaining Pin
Steering Wheel
Cover & Shield
Steering Shaft Seal
Lower Shroud
Dash Panel
Shaft Lock Shipping Pin
Upper Coupling Bolt
Lower Coupling
Spring Pin
Dash Cover
Steering Gear
91E14336
Courtesy of Chrysler Motors.

Fig. 1: Exploded View of Steering Column

1991 STEERING
Steering Columns (Cont.)

4) Loosen upper support bracket nuts and allow column to drop slightly. Remove upper fixed shroud. Disconnect wiring harness retainers from column, and move harness to one side. Remove lower dash panel. Remove lower steering column retaining nuts. Remove column.
5) To install column, reverse removal procedure. Reconnect clockspring connector. Reconnect negative battery cable.

CAUTION: DO NOT reuse bushing in shift rod lever once shift rod is removed. Always install a NEW bushing.

NOTE: On column shift models, whenever steering column is removed or loosened, shift rod adjustment must be checked.

OVERHAUL

NOTE: Steering column is not serviceable except for trim, switches and steering wheel. If service is required, replace column.

TORQUE SPECIFICATIONS

TORQUE SPECIFICATIONS

Application	Ft. Lbs. (N.m)
Steering Wheel Retaining Nut	45 (61)
	INCH Lbs. (N.m)
Steering Column-To-Instrument Panel Bracket Bolt/Nut	
Caravan, Town & Country and Voyager	105 (12)
All Others	110 (12)

1991 STEERING
Manual Rack & Pinion

Dakota (2WD)

DESCRIPTION

Steering gear assembly is not serviceable. Service is limited to replacement of outer tie rod ends or boot seals.

REMOVAL & INSTALLATION

OUTER TIE ROD END

NOTE: If part replacement is necessary, check part number carefully, as 1991 models use a larger diameter ball stud on the outer tie rod end. Parts are NOT interchangeable with previous model years.

Removal - 1) Place reference mark on outer tie rod end and inner tie rod end for reassembly reference. Loosen lock nut at inner tie rod end. Remove cotter pin and nut from tie rod end at steering knuckle.

2) Separate tie rod end from steering knuckle. Unscrew tie rod end from inner tie rod end. It may be necessary to expand or remove outer boot seal clamp.

Installation - 1) To install, reverse removal procedure. Expand or remove outer clamp on boot seal while installing tie rod end. Lubricate groove of boot seal with silicone lubricant.

2) Install tie rod to reference mark made during removal. Adjust toe-in. See SPECIFICATIONS & PROCEDURES article in WHEEL ALIGNMENT. Install and tighten outer clamp on boot seal. Ensure boot seal is not twisted. Tighten lock nut and tie rod end-to-steering knuckle nut to specification. See TORQUE SPECIFICATIONS table at end of article.

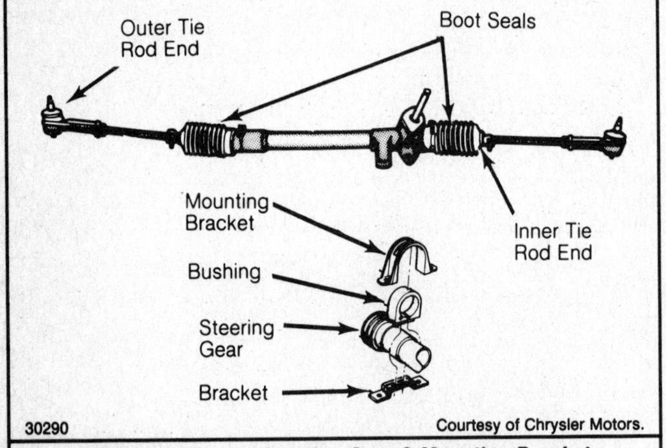
Outer Tie
Rod End
Boot Seals
Mounting
Bracket
Inner Tie
Rod End
Bushing
Steering
Gear
Bracket
30290
Courtesy of Chrysler Motors.

Fig. 1: Exploded View Of Steering Gear & Mounting Bracket

BOOT SEAL

NOTE: Boot seal replacement procedure is with steering gear removed from vehicle.

Removal & Installation - 1) Remove outer tie rod end. See OUTER TIE ROD END under REMOVAL & INSTALLATION.

2) Expand outer boot seal clamp and remove. Cut inner boot seal clamp and remove. *See Fig. 1.* Place reference mark for breather tube location on steering gear housing before removing boot seal. Using a small screwdriver, remove boot seal from groove in steering gear housing and remove boot seal.

3) To install, ensure all surfaces are clean. Lubricate tie rod boot seal groove with silicone lubricant before installing outer clamp. Install boot seal, aligning reference mark with breather tube. Install new boot seal clamps and tighten. Ensure boot seal is not twisted. To complete installation, reverse removal procedure.

STEERING GEAR

Removal - 1) Raise and support vehicle. Remove front wheels. Separate tie rod ends from steering knuckles.

2) Remove pin from steering shaft coupling at the steering gear shaft. Remove steering gear-to-crossmember bolts. Remove steering gear.

Installation - To install, reverse removal procedure. Adjust toe-in. See SPECIFICATIONS & PROCEDURES article in WHEEL ALIGNMENT.

TORQUE SPECIFICATIONS

TORQUE SPECIFICATIONS

Application	Ft. Lbs. (N.m)
Steering Gear-To-Crossmember Bolt	150 (203)
Tie Rod End-To-Steering Knuckle Nut	40 (54)
Tie Rod Lock Nut	55 (75)
Wheel Lug Nut	85 (115)

1991 STEERING
Power Rack & Pinion

Caravan, Dakota (2WD), Town & Country, Voyager

DESCRIPTION & OPERATION

Two kinds of power steering pumps are used, Saginaw and ZF. See POWER STEERING PUMP APPLICATION table.

POWER STEERING PUMP APPLICATION

Application	Pump Type
Caravan, Town & Country, & Voyager	
2.5L & 3.0L	Saginaw
3.3L	ZF
Dakota	
2.5L, 3.9L & [1] 5.2L	Saginaw

[1] - Vane-nonsubmerged type pump.

The Saginaw power steering pump is a constant displacement, vane-type pump with an integral fluid reservoir. Rectangular pumping vanes, carried by a shaft-driven rotor, move fluid from intake to pressure cavities of the cam ring. As the rotor begins to rotate, centrifugal force throws the vanes against the inside surface of the cam ring to pick up residual oil, which is then forced into the high pressure area. Oil is forced into cavities of the thrust plate and through 2 crossover holes in the cam ring and pressure plate. This oil empties into the high pressure area between the pressure plate and housing end plate (thrust plate on vane-nonsubmerged type pump).

Filling the high pressure area causes oil to flow under the vanes in the rotor slots. The vanes are forced to follow the inside oval surface of cam ring. As the vanes rotate to the small area of the cam ring, oil is forced out from between the vanes, creating high pressure. When pressure exceeds set limits, the flow control valve opens and allows fluid to return to the inlet side of the pump.

The ZF pump is non-serviceable. If the pump, reservoir or cap fails or leaks, it should be replaced.

A rotary valve in pinion assembly directs fluid to either side of integral rack piston. Tie rods connect steering gear (rack and pinion) to steering knuckles. Loosely fitted pinion drive-tangs will provide manual steering control in the event of a system malfunction.

Steering wheel movement is transmitted by shaft to the pinion through 2 universal joint couplings. Steering gear rack and pinion assembly converts rotational movement of the pinion to transverse movement of the rack.

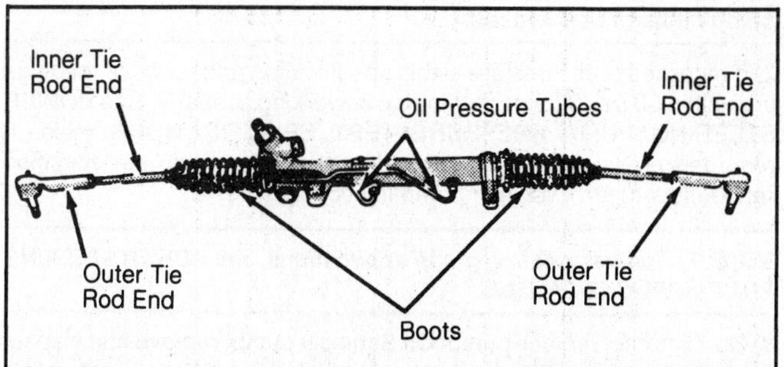
Inner Tie
Rod End
Oil Pressure Tubes
Inner Tie
Rod End
Outer Tie
Rod End
Outer Tie
Rod End
Boots

91G14338 Courtesy of Chrysler Motors.

Fig. 1: Power Rack & Pinion Steering Gear (Typical)

LUBRICATION

CAPACITY

Power steering system capacity is 1.7 pts. (.81L).

FLUID TYPE

Use Mopar Power Steering Fluid (4318055).

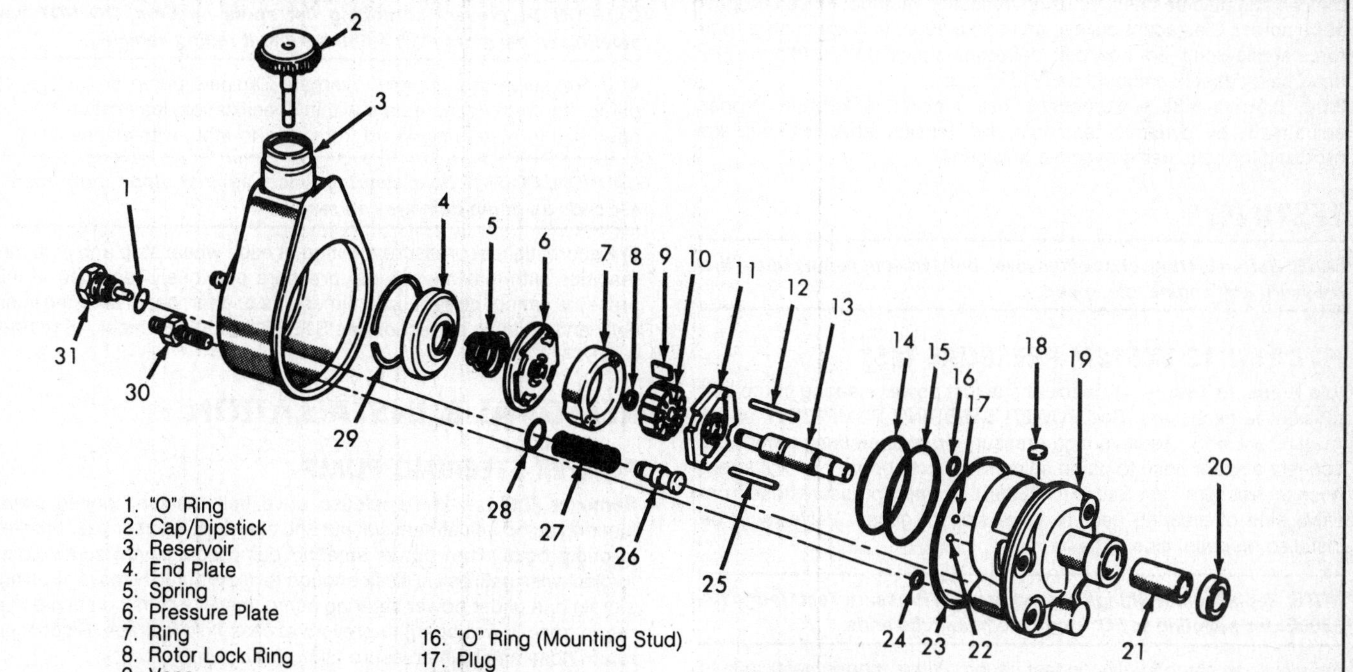

1. "O" Ring
2. Cap/Dipstick
3. Reservoir
4. End Plate
5. Spring
6. Pressure Plate
7. Ring
8. Rotor Lock Ring
9. Vane
10. Rotor
11. Thrust Plate
12. Dowel Pin
13. Shaft
14. "O" Ring (End Plate)
15. "O" Ring (Pressure Plate)
16. "O" Ring (Mounting Stud)
17. Plug
18. Plug
19. Pump Housing
20. Shaft Seal
21. Bushing
22. Plug
23. "O" Ring (Reservoir)
24. "O" Ring (Mounting Stud)
25. Dowel Pin
26. Flow Control Valve
27. Spring
28. "O" Ring (Valve)
29. Retaining Ring
30. Mounting Stud
31. Fitting (Pressure Hose)

91F14337 Courtesy of Chrysler Motors.

Fig. 2: Exploded View of Vane-Submerged Type Power Steering Pump

1991 STEERING
Power Rack & Pinion (Cont.)

FLUID LEVEL CHECK

Check fluid level with engine cold and not running. Remove fluid level dipstick on pump reservoir. Dipstick should indicate FULL COLD with fluid temperature of 70-80°F (21-27°C). If needed, add fluid through dipstick opening, and recheck. DO NOT overfill.

HYDRAULIC SYSTEM BLEEDING

Fill power steering pump reservoir to specified level. Start engine and slowly turn steering wheel to the left and right but DO NOT contact steering stops in either direction. Stop engine. Inspect reservoir fluid level and add fluid if necessary. Bleeding process may have to be repeated several times to completely purge all air from system.

ADJUSTMENTS

POWER STEERING PUMP BELT

2.5L & 3.9L - 1) Power steering belt tension is adjusted by adjusting power steering pump position. To check belt tension, use a Poly-V Burroughs gauge or similar gauge. See POWER STEERING BELT TENSION SPECIFICATIONS table.

POWER STEERING BELT TENSION SPECIFICATIONS

Application	New Belt Lbs. (kg)	Used Belt Lbs. (kg)
2.5L		
Caravan, Town & Country, & Voyager	105 (48)	80 (36)
Dakota	120 (54)	80 (36)
3.0L & 3.3L	[1]	[1]
3.9L	100-140 (45-64)	60-90 (27-41)
5.2L	[1]	[1]

[1] - Dynamic tensioner equipped, no adjustment required.

2) On Caravan, Town & Country and Voyager 2.5L models, belt tension can also be checked using deflection method. Place straight-edge across 2 adjacent pulleys and use a 10 lb. (4.5 kg) push or pull force at mid-point. For new belt, deflection should be 1/4" (6 mm). For used belt, deflection should be 7/16" (11 mm).

3.0L, 3.3L & 5.2L - Serpentine belt tension is kept in proper adjustment by dynamic tensioner. No tension specifications are provided for belts using dynamic tensioner.

TESTING

NOTE: Before testing, check fluid level, belt tension, pump pulley, tire pressure and engine idle speed.

HYDRAULIC SYSTEM PRESSURE TEST

Idle Pressure Test - 1) Check and adjust power steering pump belt tension as necessary. See POWER STEERING PUMP BELT under ADJUSTMENTS. Remove high pressure hose at steering pump and connect a spare hose to pump fitting. Connect opposite end of spare hose to Pressure Test Gauge (C-3309E). Connect pressure hose from valve side of steering gear to valve side of gauge. Valve must be installed on outlet side of gauge.

NOTE: Replacement fittings are required on Pressure Test Gauge (C-3309E) for adapting to "O" ring type hose tube ends.

2) Fully open shutoff valve on test gauge. With a thermometer in fluid reservoir, start engine and warm fluid to 150-170°F (66-77°C). Turning wheels from stop-to-stop will aid in warming fluid. DO NOT hold wheels against stop.

3) With engine at idle speed and gauge valve open, check initial pressure. See POWER STEERING PUMP PRESSURE TEST SPECIFICATIONS table. On Dakota models, if pressure is greater than 125 psi (8.8 kg/cm²), or on all other models, if pressure is greater than 100 psi (7.0 kg/cm²), check for restricted hoses or crimped lines.

POWER STEERING PUMP PRESSURE TEST SPECIFICATIONS

Application	Pressure psi (kg/cm²)
Idle Pressure	
Caravan, Town & Country & Voyager	30-50 (2.1-3.5)
Dakota	50-80 (3.5-5.7)
Relief Pressure	
Caravan, Town & Country & Voyager	1175-1225 (83-86)
Dakota	
2.5L	1250 (88)
3.9L	1500 (105)
5.2L	1450 (102)

Relief Pressure Test - 1) Close gauge shutoff valve completely 3 times. Record highest pressure attained each time.

CAUTION: DO NOT leave shutoff valve closed more 5 seconds, as pump damage could result.

2) If recorded pressures are within specification and range of readings are within 50 psi (3.5 kg/cm²), pump is working properly. See POWER STEERING PUMP PRESSURE TEST SPECIFICATIONS table. If recorded pressures are high but do not repeat within the specified range, flow control valve in pump is sticking.

NOTE: For power steering pump applications, see POWER STEERING PUMP APPLICATION table.

3) On ZF pump, replace pump. On Saginaw pump, remove and inspect flow control valve. Check flow control valve for nicks or burrs. See POWER STEERING PUMP under OVERHAUL. Gently smooth flow control valve defects with crocus cloth. Install valve and retest.

CAUTION: To prevent scrubbing flat spots on tires, DO NOT turn steering wheel more than 5 times without rolling vehicle.

4) If pressures are still low, overhaul Saginaw pump or replace ZF pump. If pump pressures are within specification, leave shutoff valve open and turn steering wheel from stop-to-stop, with engine idling.

CAUTION: DO NOT hold steering wheel against stops more than 4 seconds as pump damage can result

5) Record highest pressure attained at each wheel stop and compare readings with maximum pump pressure previously recorded. If this pressure cannot be built up in either side of gear, gear is leaking internally and must be replaced. See STEERING GEAR under REMOVAL & INSTALLATION.

REMOVAL & INSTALLATION

POWER STEERING PUMP

Removal (2.5L) - 1) To release drive belt tension, loosen power steering pump adjustment slot nut and pivot bolt. Loosen rear bracket-to-pump bolts. Turn power steering pump adjustment screw counterclockwise until belt is slack enough to allow pump removal. Position a drain pan under power steering pump. Install a clamp on pump fluid return hose (if equipped) to prevent excess fluid leakage. Disconnect return hose and high pressure fitting from pump.

2) Remove rear bracket-to-pump bolts. Remove adjustment bracket-to-rear bracket bolts and pivot bolt. Remove power steering pump, front bracket and adjustment bracket.

Installation - To install, reverse removal procedure. Ensure "O" ring at end of high pressure fitting (if equipped) is replaced before connecting fitting to power steering pump. Fill and bleed system. See HYDRAULIC SYSTEM BLEEDING under LUBRICATION.

1991 STEERING
Power Rack & Pinion (Cont.)

Removal (3.0L & 3.3L) – 1) Rotate belt tensioner and remove drive belt. Position a drain pan under power steering pump. Install a clamp on pump fluid return line to prevent excessive fluid leakage. Disconnect fluid line hose from pump.

2) Remove lower stud nut and pivot screw. Remove right side splash shield. Remove power steering pump.

Installation – To install, reverse removal procedure. Ensure "O" ring at end of high pressure fitting is replaced before connecting fitting to power steering pump. Fill and bleed system. See HYDRAULIC SYSTEM BLEEDING under LUBRICATION.

Removal & Installation (3.9L) – Loosen pump and remove drive belt. Place drain pan under pump and drain pump. Disconnect and cap hoses. Remove attaching bolts and remove pump. To install pump, reverse removal procedure. Fill and bleed system. See HYDRAULIC SYSTEM BLEEDING under LUBRICATION.

Removal & Installation (5.2L) – Rotate belt tensioner and remove drive belt. Place drain pan under pump and drain pump. Disconnect and cap hoses. Remove attaching bolts and remove pump. To install pump, reverse removal procedure. Fill and bleed system. See HYDRAULIC SYSTEM BLEEDING under LUBRICATION.

CAUTION: Excessive belt tension can cause the pump shaft bushing to fail. DO NOT pry on the reservoir. When filling pump reservoir, DO NOT use ATF.

PUMP PULLEY

CAUTION: Examine exposed end of rotor drive shaft before removal. If it is corroded, clean the surface with crocus cloth to prevent damage to the shaft bushing during removal.

Removal & Installation – Remove pulley using Puller (C-4068) and Puller Adapter (C-4068-1). *See Fig. 3.* Replace pulley if bent, cracked or loose. Install Saginaw and ZF pump pulleys using Installer (C-4063). Press pulley until flush with shaft end.

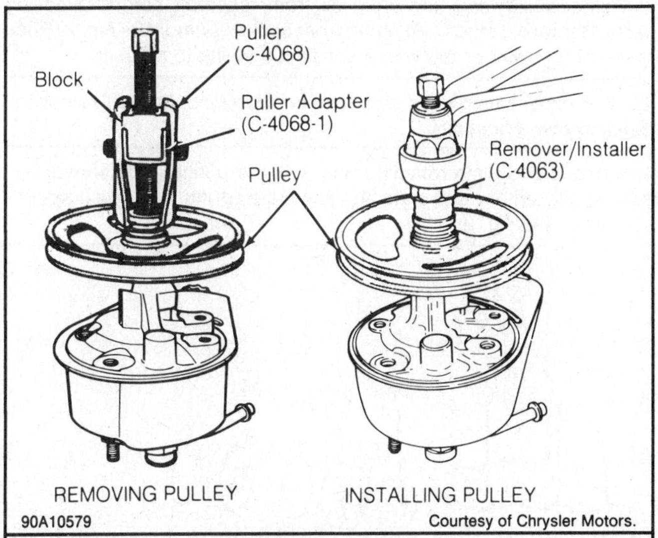
Puller
(C-4068)
Block
Puller Adapter
(C-4068-1)
Pulley
Remover/Installer
(C-4063)
REMOVING PULLEY
INSTALLING PULLEY
90A10579
Courtesy of Chrysler Motors.

Fig. 3: Removing & Installing Pump Pulley

ZF PUMP RESERVOIR

Removal – Remove 2 bolts "A" and 2 pin retaining plates "B". *See Fig. 4.* Drive pins "C" out from front. Lift reservoir off. Inspect pump inlet. Replace pump if inlet is damaged or worn. Clean all parts.

Installation – 1) To install, reverse removal procedure. Use new "O" rings and seals. Carefully snap reservoir in place. Install new pins "C" from rear. Push in until even with back plate.

2) Install pin retaining plates "B" and bolts "A". Tighten bolts "A" to 90 INCH lbs. (10 N.m). Refill reservoir. Fill system, start engine and turn steering wheel several times from between stops to bleed system. Stop engine, check fluid level, and inspect for leaks.

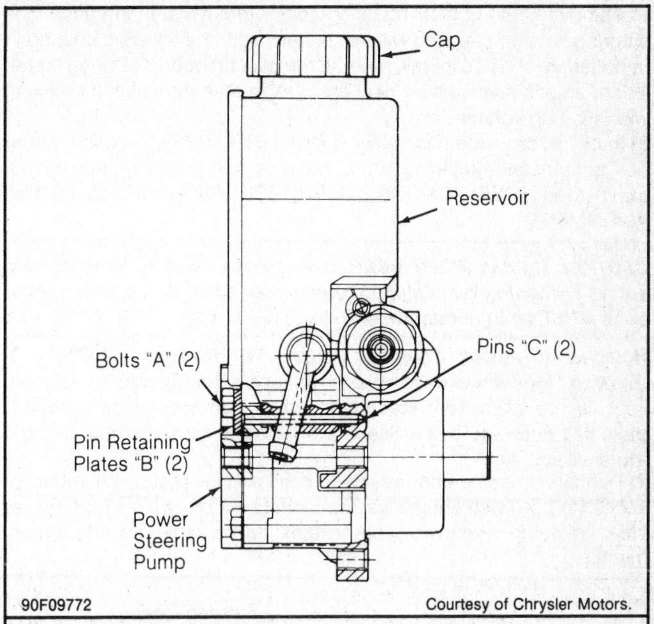
Cap
Reservoir
Pins "C" (2)
Bolts "A" (2)
Pin Retaining
Plates "B" (2)
Power
Steering
Pump
90F09772
Courtesy of Chrysler Motors.

Fig. 4: Removing ZF Power Steering Pump Reservoir

OUTER TIE ROD END

Removal – 1) Place reference mark on outer tie rod end and inner tie rod end for reassembly reference. Loosen lock nut at inner tie rod end. Remove cotter pin and nut from tie rod end at steering knuckle.

2) Separate tie rod end from steering knuckle. Unscrew tie rod end from inner tie rod end. It may be necessary to expand or remove outer boot seal clamp.

Installation – 1) To install, reverse removal procedure. Expand or remove outer clamp on boot seal while installing tie rod end. Lubricate groove of boot seal with silicone lubricant.

2) Install tie rod to reference mark made during removal. Adjust toe-in. See SPECIFICATIONS & PROCEDURES article in WHEEL ALIGNMENT. Install and tighten outer clamp on boot seal. Ensure boot seal is not twisted. Tighten lock nut and tie rod end-to-steering knuckle nut to specification. See TORQUE SPECIFICATIONS table at end of article.

BOOT SEAL

NOTE: Boot seal replacement procedure is with steering gear removed from vehicle.

Removal & Installation – 1) Remove outer tie rod end. See OUTER TIE ROD END under REMOVAL & INSTALLATION. Expand outer boot seal clamp and remove. Cut inner boot seal clamp and remove.

2) Place reference mark for breather tube location on steering gear housing before removing boot seal. Using a small screwdriver, remove boot seal from groove in steering gear housing and remove boot seal.

3) To install, ensure all surfaces are clean. Lubricate tie rod end boot seal groove with silicone lubricant before installing outer clamp. Install boot seal, aligning reference mark with breather tube. Install new boot seal clamps and tighten. Ensure boot seal is not twisted. To complete installation, reverse removal procedure.

STEERING GEAR

Removal (Caravan, Town & Country, & Voyager – FWD) – 1) Raise and support vehicle. Disconnect hoses from steering gear. Remove front wheels. Separate tie rod ends from steering knuckles. Disconnect engine damper strut from crossmember (if equipped).

2) Support front suspension crossmember with floor jack. Remove front suspension crossmember bolts. Lower front suspension crossmember so steering gear can be disconnected from steering column.

1991 STEERING
Power Rack & Pinion (Cont.)

3) Remove steering gear retaining bolts. Remove steering gear. The steering column coupling will disconnect from the steering column.
Installation - 1) To install, reverse removal procedure. During installation, an assistant will be needed to align steering column coupling with steering column.
2) Install all crossmember bolts. Tighten RIGHT REAR crossmember bolt first. Install remaining components and fill steering gear. Adjust toe-in. See SPECIFICATIONS & PROCEDURES article in WHEEL ALIGNMENT.

CAUTION: Tighten RIGHT REAR crossmember bolt to specification before tightening remaining crossmember bolts. ALL crossmember bolts MUST be tightened to 90 ft. lbs. (122 N.m).

Removal (Caravan, Town & Country, & Voyager - AWD) - 1) Remove front wheel assemblies. Remove steering column. Disconnect tie rod ends from steering knuckle. Remove bridge assembly attaching nuts and bolts. *See Fig. 5.* Support crossmember using a transmission jack.
2) Remove crossmember attaching bolts and lower crossmember for access to power steering lines. Disconnect hydraulic lines from power steering pump. Remove bracket retaining hydraulic lines to crossmember.

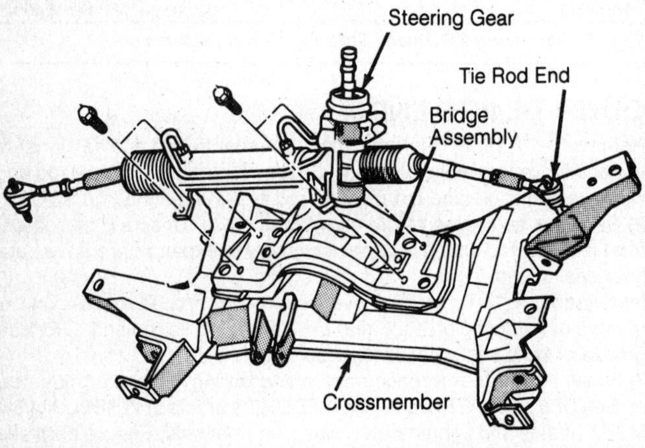
Steering Gear
Tie Rod End
Bridge
Assembly
Crossmember
91H14339
Courtesy of Chrysler Motors.

Fig. 5: Exploded View of Steering Gear Mounting (Caravan, Town & Country, & Voyager AWD Models)

3) Remove 4 bolts attaching steering gear to crossmember. Note location of bolts for reassembly reference. Using a drift, drive roll pin from steering gear lower coupling. Remove coupling from steering gear stub shaft.

NOTE: Pin and coupling MUST be removed to obtain clearance for steering gear removal.

4) Slide gear toward left side of vehicle. Rotate gear housing to clear frame rail and remove gear assembly. To install gear, reverse removal procedure. During installation, an assistant will be needed to align steering column coupling with steering column. Adjust toe-in. See SPECIFICATIONS & PROCEDURES article in WHEEL ALIGNMENT.
Removal (Dakota) - 1) Disconnect hoses from steering gear. Raise and support vehicle. Remove front wheels. Separate tie rod ends from steering knuckles.
2) Remove pin from steering shaft coupling at the steering gear shaft. Remove steering gear-to-crossmember bolts. Remove steering gear.
Installation - To install, reverse removal procedure. Install remaining components and fill steering gear. Adjust toe-in. See SPECIFICATIONS & PROCEDURES under WHEEL ALIGNMENT.

OVERHAUL

NOTE: Overhaul is possible only on Saginaw vane-submerged type pump. Saginaw vane-nonsubmerged type pump may be disassembled for inspection only. If components are damaged, replace pump. ZF pumps are non-serviceable. If pump is faulty, remove reservoir and replace pump. See ZF PUMP RESERVOIR under REMOVAL & INSTALLATION.

POWER STEERING PUMP

Disassembly (Vane-Submerged Type) - 1) Remove pump pulley using Pulley Remover (C-4068) and Pulley Adapter (C-4068-1). *See Fig. 3.*
2) Remove filler cap and drain oil from reservoir before removing parts. Remove 2 studs and fitting from back of pump. *See Fig. 2.* Rock reservoir by hand or tap with a soft-faced mallet to remove.

NOTE: If expansion plug is deformed or dislodged, DO NOT remove it. Replace pump housing.

3) Remove end plate retaining ring, using a punch and screwdriver. *See Fig. 7.* Remove end plate and end plate spring. Remove flow control valve. *See Fig. 2.*

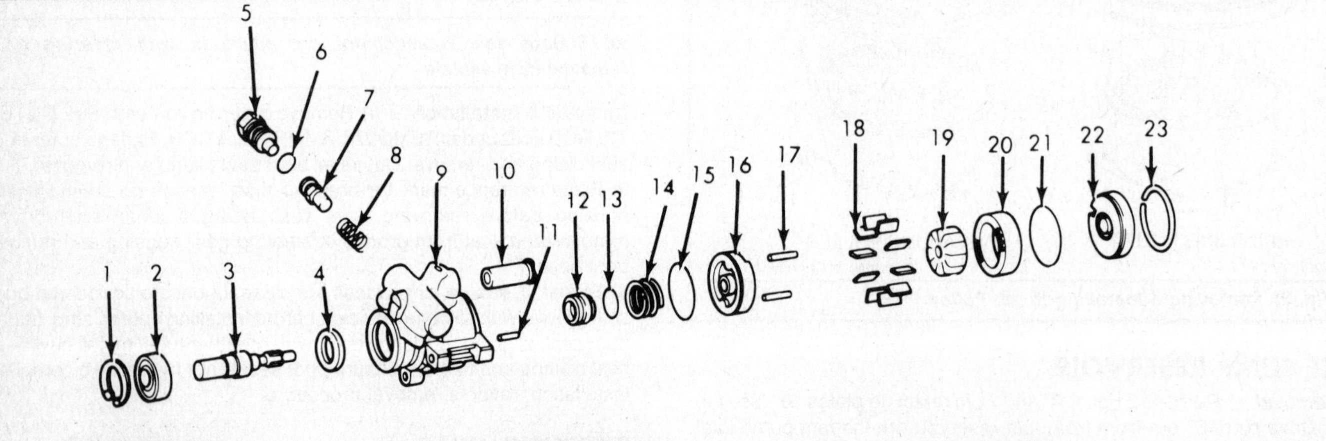
1
2
3
4
5
6
7
8
9
10
11
12
13
14
15
16
17
18
19
20
21
22
23

1. Retaining Ring
2. Pump Shaft Bearing
3. Pump Shaft
4. Pump Shaft Seal
5. Flow Control Fitting
6. "O" Ring
7. Flow Control Valve
8. Flow Control Spring
9. Pump Housing
10. Return Tube
11. Dowel Pin
12. Sleeve
13. "O" Ring
14. Pressure Plate Spring
15. "O" Ring
16. Pressure Plate
17. Dowel Pins
18. Pump Vanes (10)
19. Pump Rotor
20. Cam Ring
21. "O" Ring
22. Thrust Plate
23. Retaining Ring

56730 Courtesy of Chrysler Motors.

Fig. 6: Exploded View of Vane-Nonsubmerged Type Saginaw Power Steering Pump

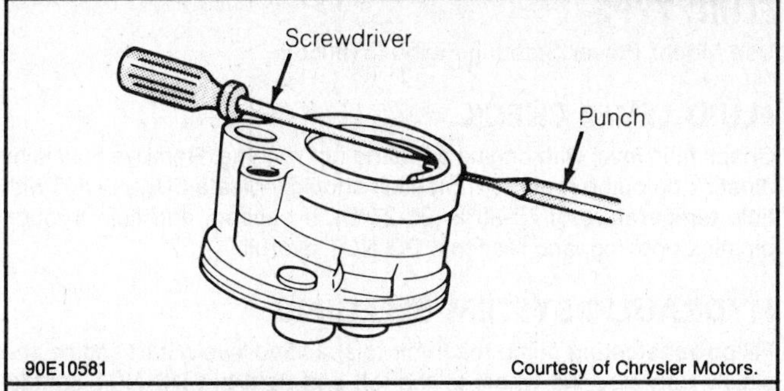
Screwdriver
Punch
90E10581
Courtesy of Chrysler Motors.

Fig. 7: Removing Retaining Ring

4) Using soft-faced hammer, tap end of pump shaft lightly until pressure plate, ring and rotor, thrust plate and shaft can be removed as a unit. Remove rotor assembly dowel pins, pump seals, and drive shaft seal. Put assembly in a vise, being careful to protect pump shaft from damage. Remove rotor lock ring. *See Fig. 8.*

5) Remove rotor and thrust plate from shaft. Clean and inspect all wear surfaces. Replace parts that have excessive wear, scuffing and scoring.

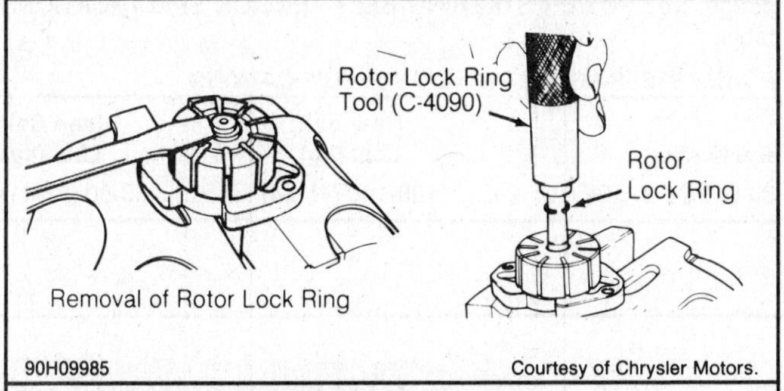
Rotor Lock Ring
Tool (C-4090)
Rotor
Lock Ring
Removal of Rotor Lock Ring
90H09985
Courtesy of Chrysler Motors.

Fig. 8: Removing & Installing Rotor Lock Ring

Reassembly – 1) Install pump shaft seal. Lubricate pressure plate "O" ring seal with power steering fluid and install in inner-most housing groove. Clamp housing in soft-jawed vise. Assemble pump shaft, thrust plate and rotor. Using Lock Ring Installer (C-4090), install new rotor lock ring. *See Fig. 8.*

2) Insert assembled components into pump housing being careful not to damage shaft seal. Install ring with directional arrow (stamped in ring), facing upward. Install 10 rotor vanes into rotor slots. Ensure vanes slide into slots easily.

3) Lubricate chamfered edge of pressure plate and install on dowel pins with spring groove facing upward. Using a large socket, force pressure plate downward to seat it. Lubricate end plate "O" ring and install in middle groove of pump housing.

4) Lubricate end plate. Install end plate and spring on pressure plate. Force end plate downward and install retaining ring. Install flow control valve and spring.

5) Install mounting stud, flow control valve and reservoir "O" rings. Lubricate inner edge of reservoir and install reservoir onto pump housing. Recheck alignment of "O" rings after reservoir is seated. Install mounting studs and tighten to 35 ft. lbs. (48 N.m).

6) Using Installer (C-4063), install pump pulley. *See Fig. 3.* Install pump and bleed hydraulic system. See HYDRAULIC SYSTEM BLEEDING under LUBRICATION.

Disassembly (Vane-Nonsubmerged Type) – 1) Remove pump pulley using Pulley Remover (C-4068) and Pulley Adapter (C-4068-1). *See Fig. 3.* Remove reservoir from pump by prying and sliding retaining clips from pump. Remove flow control valve fitting, flow control valve and spring.

2) Remove and discard pump shaft retaining ring. Remove pump shaft and bearing. Using a small screwdriver, pry pump shaft seal from pump body. Remove thrust plate retaining ring, using a punch and screwdriver. *See Fig. 7.*

3) Using a brass drift, press thrust plate from pump body. Remove thrust plate "O" ring. Remove ring, rotor, vanes, dowel pins and pressure plate. Remove pressure plate "O" ring.

Inspection – Clean all metal parts with mineral spirits and dry with compressed air. Inspect for scoring or burning of internal pump components. Replace pump if any damage is apparent. If pump is okay, reassemble using new gasket set.

Reassembly – To reassemble pump, reverse disassembly procedure. Ensure vanes move freely in rotor slots. Replace thrust plate retaining ring if bent or distorted. Install pump shaft retaining ring beveled side outward (small lug on left and large lug on right). Install pump and bleed hydraulic system. See HYDRAULIC SYSTEM BLEEDING under LUBRICATION.

STEERING GEAR

NOTE: DO NOT attempt to service or adjust the power steering gear. If a malfunction or oil leak occurs, replace steering gear as a complete assembly.

TORQUE SPECIFICATIONS

TORQUE SPECIFICATIONS

Application	Ft. Lbs. (N.m)
Bridge Assembly Nuts and Bolts	
Caravan, Town & Country, & Voyager	50 (68)
Crossmember Bolt [1]	
Caravan, Town & Country, & Voyager	90 (122)
Pressure Hose Fitting	25 (34)
Pump Bracket Nut	30 (41)
Steering Gear-To-Crossmember Bolt	
Caravan, Town & Country, & Voyager	50 (68)
Dakota	150 (203)
Tie Rod End-To-Steering Knuckle Nut	
Caravan, Town & Country, & Voyager	35 (47)
Dakota	40 (54)
Tie Rod Lock Nut	55 (75)
Wheel Lug Nut	
Caravan, Town & Country, & Voyager	95 (129)
Dakota	85 (115)
	INCH Lbs. (N.m)
Ball Seat	50 (6)
ZF Pump, "A" Bolts [2]	90 (10)

[1] – Tighten right rear bolt to specification before tightening all other bolts.

[2] – *See Fig. 3.*

1991 STEERING
Power – Constant Control

RWD Van

DESCRIPTION & OPERATION

The Saginaw power steering pump is a constant displacement, vane-type pump with an integral fluid reservoir. Rectangular pumping vanes, carried by a shaft-driven rotor, move fluid from intake to pressure cavities of the cam ring. As the rotor begins to rotate, centrifugal force throws the vanes against the inside surface of the cam ring to pick up residual oil, which is then forced into the high pressure area.

Oil is forced into cavities of the thrust plate and through 2 crossover holes in the cam ring and pressure plate. This oil empties into the high pressure area between the pressure plate and housing end plate.

Filling the high pressure area causes oil to flow under the vanes in the rotor slots. The vanes are forced to follow the inside oval surface of cam ring. As the vanes rotate to the small area of the cam ring, oil is forced out from between the vanes, creating high pressure. When pressure exceeds set limits, the flow control valve opens and allows fluid to return to the inlet side of the pump.

Power steering gear contains a sector shaft with sector gear, a worm/piston with gear teeth on side of piston, and a worm shaft. Worm/piston teeth and sector gear constantly mesh with each other. Steering control valve, mounted on top of steering gear housing, directs fluid flow through system.

LUBRICATION

CAPACITY

CAPACITY

Application	Pts. (L)
RWD Van	2.7 (1.3)

FLUID TYPE

Use Mopar Power Steering Fluid (4318055).

FLUID LEVEL CHECK

Check fluid level with engine cold and not running. Remove fluid level dipstick on pump reservoir. Dipstick should indicate FULL COLD with fluid temperature of 70-80°F (21-27°C). If needed, add fluid through dipstick opening, and recheck. DO NOT overfill.

HYDRAULIC SYSTEM BLEEDING

Fill power steering pump reservoir to specified level. Start engine and slowly turn steering wheel to the left and right but DO NOT contact steering stops in either direction. Stop engine. Inspect reservoir fluid level and add fluid if necessary. Bleeding process may have to be repeated several times to completely purge all air from system.

ADJUSTMENTS

POWER STEERING PUMP BELT

Power steering belt tension is adjusted by adjusting power steering pump position. To check belt tension, use a Poly-V Burroughs type gauge. See POWER STEERING BELT TENSION SPECIFICATIONS table.

POWER STEERING BELT TENSION SPECIFICATIONS

Application	New Belt Lbs. (kg)	Used Belt Lbs. (kg)
3.9L, 5.2L & 5.9L	100-140 (45-64)	60-90 (27-41)

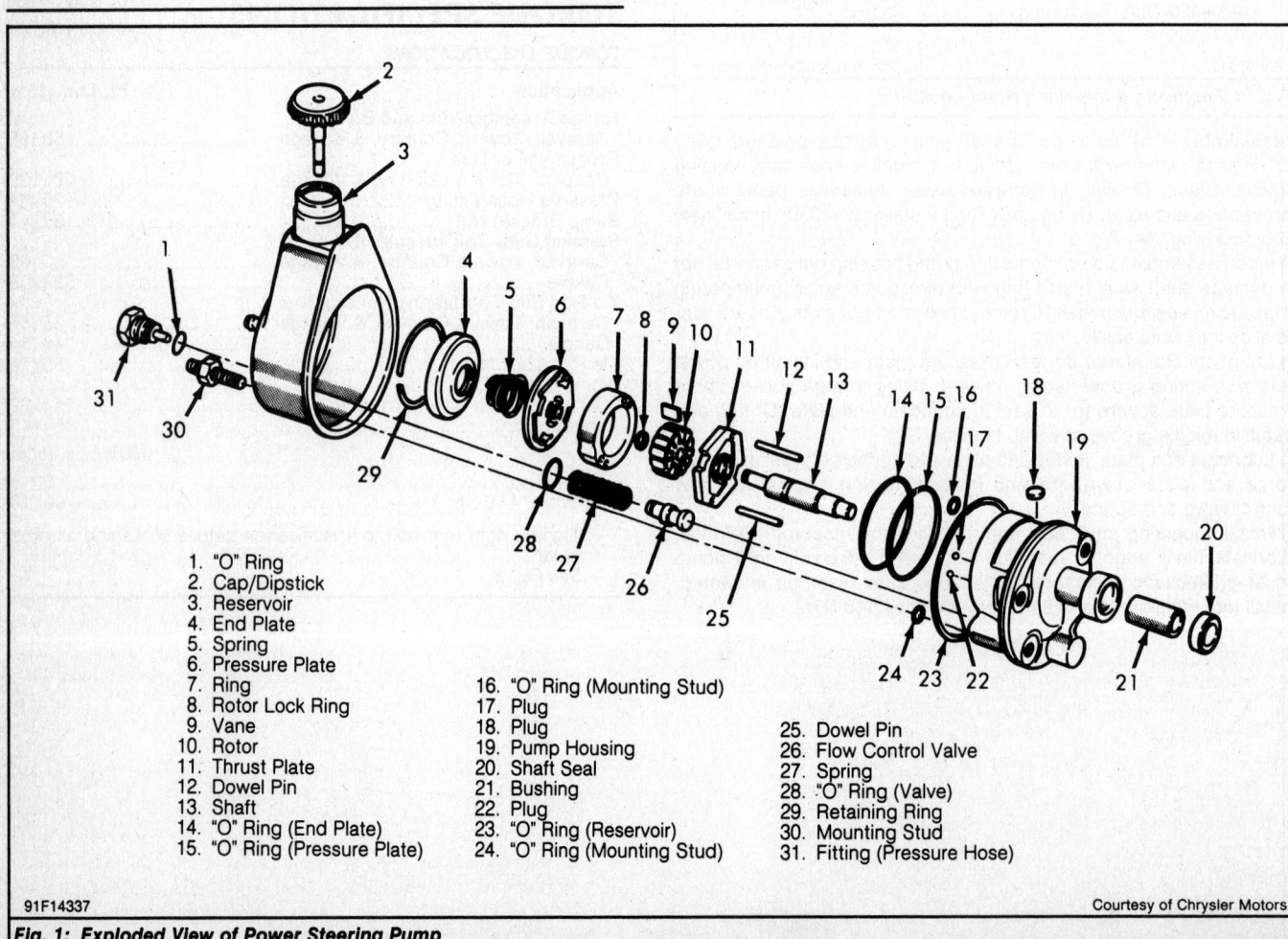

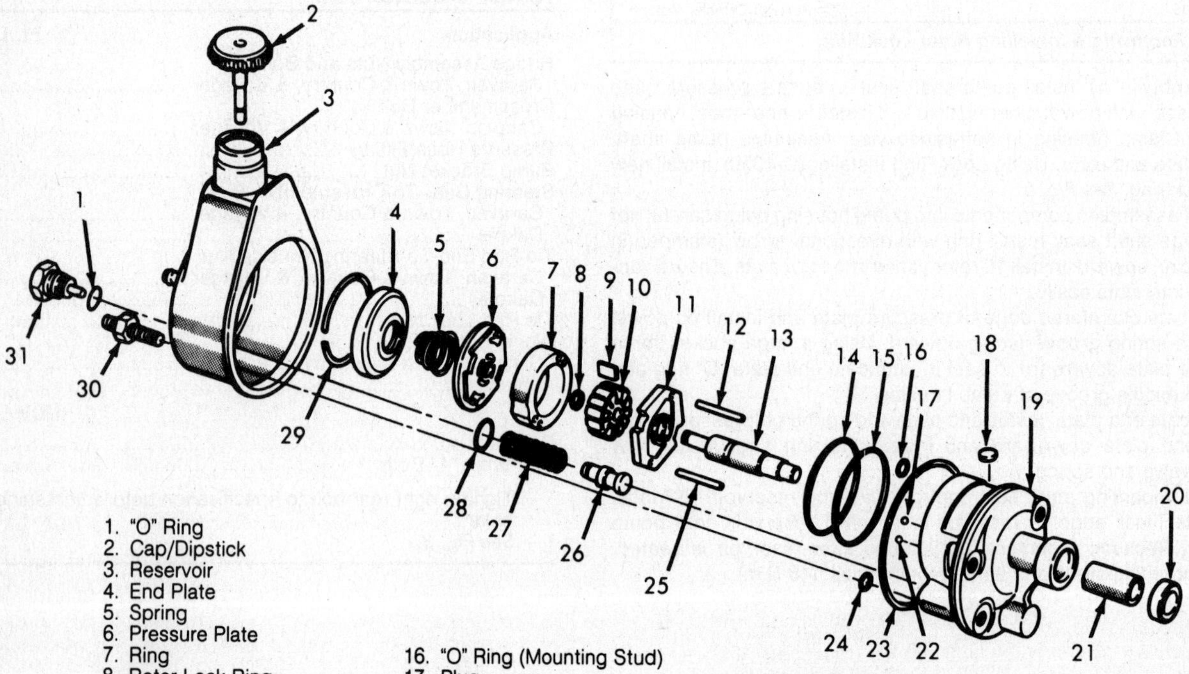
1. "O" Ring
2. Cap/Dipstick
3. Reservoir
4. End Plate
5. Spring
6. Pressure Plate
7. Ring
8. Rotor Lock Ring
9. Vane
10. Rotor
11. Thrust Plate
12. Dowel Pin
13. Shaft
14. "O" Ring (End Plate)
15. "O" Ring (Pressure Plate)
16. "O" Ring (Mounting Stud)
17. Plug
18. Plug
19. Pump Housing
20. Shaft Seal
21. Bushing
22. Plug
23. "O" Ring (Reservoir)
24. "O" Ring (Mounting Stud)
25. Dowel Pin
26. Flow Control Valve
27. Spring
28. "O" Ring (Valve)
29. Retaining Ring
30. Mounting Stud
31. Fitting (Pressure Hose)
91F14337
Courtesy of Chrysler Motors.

Fig. 1: Exploded View of Power Steering Pump

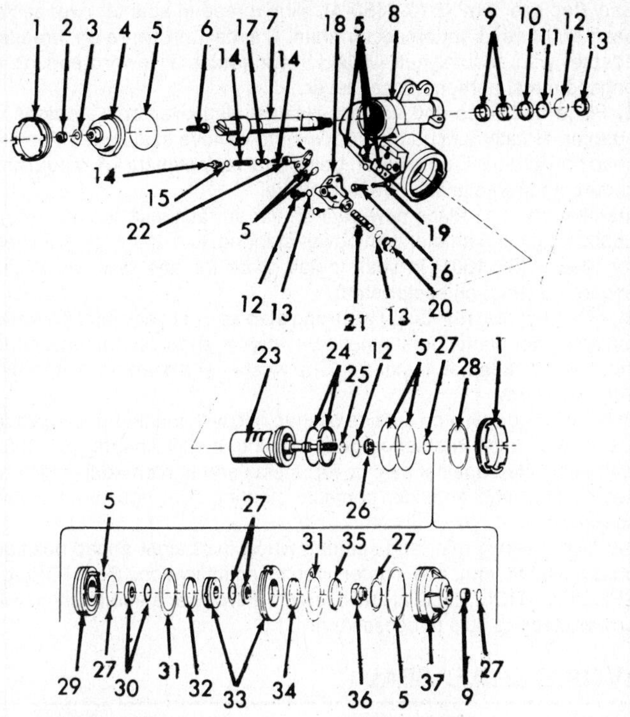

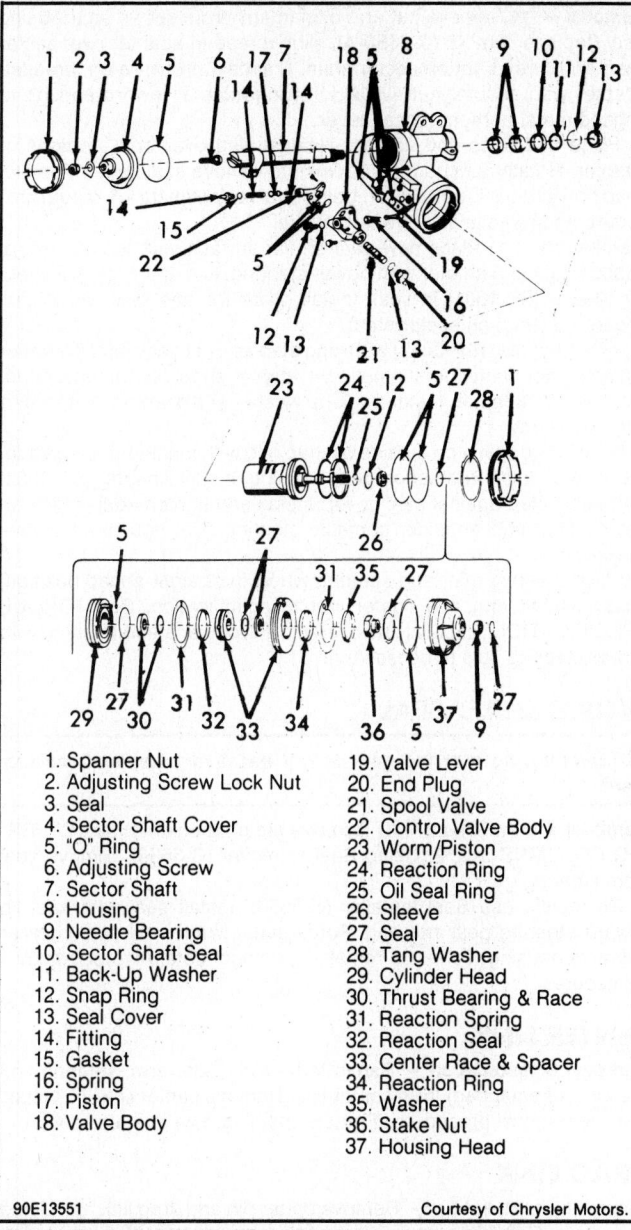

1. Spanner Nut
2. Adjusting Screw Lock Nut
3. Seal
4. Sector Shaft Cover
5. "O" Ring
6. Adjusting Screw
7. Sector Shaft
8. Housing
9. Needle Bearing
10. Sector Shaft Seal
11. Back-Up Washer
12. Snap Ring
13. Seal Cover
14. Fitting
15. Gasket
16. Spring
17. Piston
18. Valve Body
19. Valve Lever
20. End Plug
21. Spool Valve
22. Control Valve Body
23. Worm/Piston
24. Reaction Ring
25. Oil Seal Ring
26. Sleeve
27. Seal
28. Tang Washer
29. Cylinder Head
30. Thrust Bearing & Race
31. Reaction Spring
32. Reaction Seal
33. Center Race & Spacer
34. Reaction Ring
35. Washer
36. Stake Nut
37. Housing Head

90E13551 Courtesy of Chrysler Motors.

Fig. 2: Exploded View of Constant Control Steering Gear

VALVE BODY CENTERING

NOTE: Valve body centering should only be performed when steering wheel movement is noticed when engine starts or if valve body is removed from steering gear.

1) Start engine and check for steering wheel movement. If movement exists, loosen valve body mounting bolts. Tighten bolts to 84 INCH lbs. (10 N.m) to allow for valve body centering.
2) Tap control valve up or down until steering wheel movement upon engine start-up stops. To move valve downward, tap on end plug of valve body. To move valve upward, tap on valve body retaining bolt. Turn steering wheel from stop-to-stop several times to bleed air from system.

CAUTION: DO NOT turn steering wheel tightly against stops with valve body mounting bolts loose or excessive pressure may blow out valve body "O" rings.

3) Check power steering fluid level and fill as necessary. With front wheels in straight-ahead position, start and stop engine several times. If steering wheel moves, repeat steps **1)** and **2)**. If steering wheel does not move, tighten valve body bolts to specification. See TORQUE SPECIFICATIONS table at end of article.

SECTOR SHAFT PRELOAD

1) Ensure that valve body is centered before adjusting sector shaft preload. See VALVE BODY CENTERING under ADJUSTMENTS. Disconnect drag link from pitman arm. Start engine and run at idle. Turn steering wheel from stop-to-stop and note number of turns. Turn wheel back 1/2 number of turns to center the gear.
2) Loosen sector shaft adjuster screw until backlash exists. Tighten adjuster screw until no backlash exists. Tighten adjuster screw an additional 3/8 to 1/2 turn. Tighten lock nut to specification. See TORQUE SPECIFICATIONS table at end of article.

TESTING

NOTE: Before testing, check fluid level, belt tension, pump pulley, tire pressure and engine idle speed.

HYDRAULIC SYSTEM PRESSURE TEST

Idle Pressure Test – 1) Check and adjust power steering pump belt tension as necessary. See POWER STEERING PUMP BELT under ADJUSTMENTS. Remove high pressure hose at steering pump and connect a spare hose to pump fitting. Connect opposite end of spare hose to Pressure Test Gauge (C-3309E). Connect pressure hose from valve side of steering gear to valve side of gauge. Valve must be installed on outlet side of gauge.

NOTE: Replacement fittings are required on Pressure Test Gauge (C-3309E) for adapting to "O" ring type hose tube ends.

2) Fully open shutoff valve on test gauge. With a thermometer in fluid reservoir, start engine and warm fluid to 150-170°F (66-77°C). Turning wheels from stop-to-stop will aid in warming fluid. DO NOT hold wheels against stop.
3) With engine at idle speed and gauge valve open, check initial pressure. See POWER STEERING PUMP PRESSURE TEST SPECIFICATIONS table. If pressure is greater than 125 psi (8.8 kg/cm²), check for restricted hoses or crimped lines.

POWER STEERING PUMP PRESSURE TEST SPECIFICATIONS

Application	Pressure psi (kg/cm²)
Idle Pressure	30-50 (2.1-3.5)
Relief Pressure	1400 (98)

Relief Pressure Test – 1) Close gauge shutoff valve completely 3 times. Record highest pressure attained each time.

CAUTION: DO NOT leave shutoff valve closed more 5 seconds, as pump damage could result.

2) If recorded pressures are within specification and range of readings are within 50-80 psi (3.5-5.6 kg/cm²), pump is working properly. See POWER STEERING PUMP PRESSURE TEST SPECIFICATIONS table. If recorded pressures are high or do not read within the specified range, flow control valve in pump is sticking.
3) If recorded pressures are constant but less than specified, clean or replace flow control valve assembly. Remove and inspect flow control valve for nicks or burrs. See POWER STEERING PUMP under OVERHAUL. Gently smooth flow control valve defects with crocus cloth. Install valve and retest.

CAUTION: To prevent scrubbing flat spots on tires, DO NOT turn steering wheel more than 5 times without rolling vehicle.

4) If pressures are still low, overhaul pump. If pump pressures are within specification, leave shutoff valve open and turn steering wheel from stop-to-stop, with engine idling.

1991 STEERING
Power – Constant Control (Cont.)

5) Record highest pressure attained at each wheel stop and compare readings with maximum pump pressure previously recorded. If this pressure cannot be built up in either side of gear, gear is leaking internally and must be repaired or replaced. Shut off engine, remove test gauge and connect pressure hose.

REMOVAL & INSTALLATION

POWER STEERING PUMP

Removal & Installation – Loosen pump and remove drive belt. Place drain pan under pump and drain pump. Disconnect and cap hoses. Remove attaching bolts and remove pump. To install pump, reverse removal procedure.

PUMP PULLEY

CAUTION: Examine exposed end of rotor drive shaft before removal. If it is corroded, clean the surface with crocus cloth to prevent damage to the shaft bushing during removal.

Removal & Installation – Using Puller (C-4068) and Puller Adapter (C-4068-1), remove pump pulley. *See Fig. 3.* Replace pulley if bent, cracked or loose. Using Installer (C-4063), Press pulley until flush with shaft end.

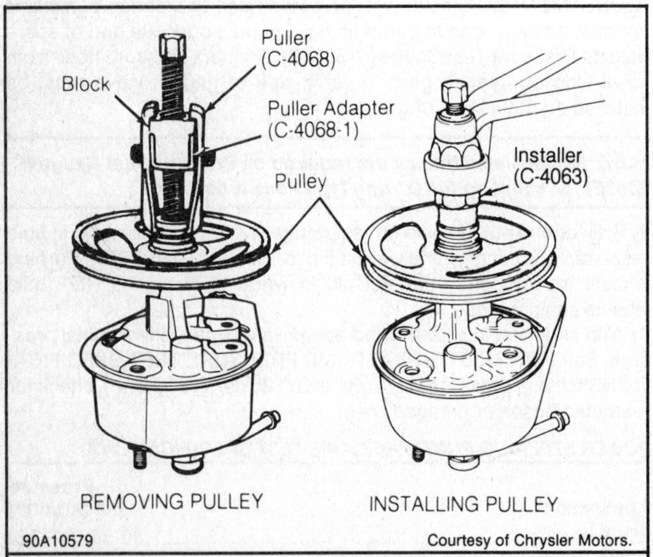
Puller
(C-4068)
Block
Puller Adapter
(C-4068-1)
Pulley
Installer
(C-4063)
REMOVING PULLEY
INSTALLING PULLEY
90A10579
Courtesy of Chrysler Motors.

Fig. 3: Removing & Installing Pump Pulley

STEERING GEAR

NOTE: To avoid damaging collapsible steering column, disconnect steering column from floor panel and instrument panel. See STEERING COLUMNS article.

Removal – **1)** Disconnect negative battery cable. Detach steering column from floor panel and instrument panel. Disconnect and cap pressure and return hoses at steering gear.
2) Remove nut and pitman arm from sector shaft. Remove steering gear-to-frame bolts and remove steering gear.
Installation – To install, reverse removal procedure. Tighten bolts to specification. See TORQUE SPECIFICATIONS table at end of article. Fill pump with fluid and start engine. Turn steering wheel from stop-to-stop several times to bleed system. Stop engine and refill pump (if necessary).

SECTOR SHAFT OIL SEAL

NOTE: Removing steering gear is not necessary for seal replacement.

Removal – **1)** Remove nut and pitman arm from sector shaft. Using Seal Replacement Kit (C-3350-A), slide threaded adapter over sector shaft and thread nut on sector shaft. Maintain pressure on threaded adapter with adapter nut, while screwing adapter inward enough to engage metal portion of seal cover.
2) Place half rings and adapter retainer ring over both portions of adapter. Rotate nut counterclockwise to remove seal cover. Remove snap ring and back-up washer. Using seal replacement kit, repeat procedure and remove sector shaft oil seal.
Installation – **1)** Place new seal on flat surface with lip downward. Lubricate inner diameter with power steering fluid. Install Seal Protector Sleeve (SP-1601) in seal. Install protector and seal (lip of seal toward housing) on sector shaft.
2) Install Adapter (SP-3052) with long step against seal. Install adapter nut on sector shaft. Tighten nut until adapter shoulder contacts housing. Remove adapter. Install back-up washer and snap ring with sharp edge outward.
3) Fill housing cavity on outside of snap ring with multipurpose grease. Install seal cover in steering gear housing. Install Adapter (SP-3052) with short step against seal cover. Install and tighten adapter nut on sector shaft until shoulder contacts steering gear housing. Remove adapter.
4) Place steering gear and steering wheel in straight-ahead position. Install pitman arm and tighten nut to specification. See TORQUE SPECIFICATIONS table at end of article. Fill power steering pump with power steering fluid (if necessary).

WORM SHAFT SEAL

NOTE: Removing steering gear is not necessary for seal replacement.

Removal & Installation – **1)** Remove steering column. See STEERING COLUMNS article. Using Seal Remover (C-3638), remove seal from steering gear.
2) To install, use Seal Installer (C-3650). Install seal with seal lip toward steering gear housing. Force seal inward until seal installer contacts housing. To install remaining components, reverse removal procedure.

CENTER LINK

Removal & Installation – Separate tie rods, idler arm, steering and drag link (if equipped) from center link. Remove center link. To install, reverse removal procedure. Tighten retaining nuts to specification.

DRAG LINK

Removal & Installation – Remove cotter pin and drag link nut. Using Separator (C-4150), separate drag link from center link and steering arm. Remove drag link. To install drag link, reverse removal procedure. Install drag link retaining nuts and new cotter pins.

IDLER ARM

Removal & Installation – Remove cotter pin and nut from idler arm. Separate idler arm from center link. Remove idler arm retaining bolt(s). Remove idler arm. To install, reverse removal procedure. Tighten bolts to specification. Install new cotter pin.

STEERING ARM

Removal & Installation – **1)** Remove cotter pin and nut at steering arm-to-center link or drag link. Separate steering arm from center link or drag link. Mark location of steering arm on steering gear shaft. Remove steering arm-to-steering gear shaft nut. Separate steering arm from steering gear.
2) To install, reverse removal procedure. Ensure reference marks are aligned. Tighten bolts and nuts to specification. Install new cotter pin.

CAUTION: Stake steering arm nut against steering gear shaft to ensure proper retention.

TIE ROD END

Removal – 1) Remove cotter pin and nut from tie rod end. Using Tie Rod End Puller (C-3894-A), remove tie rod end from steering knuckle or center link. *See Fig. 4*.

2) Loosen lock nut or clamp bolt. Remove tie rod end. Note number of turns required for removal.

NOTE: Use Tie Rod End Puller (C-3894-A) to prevent tie rod end seal damage.

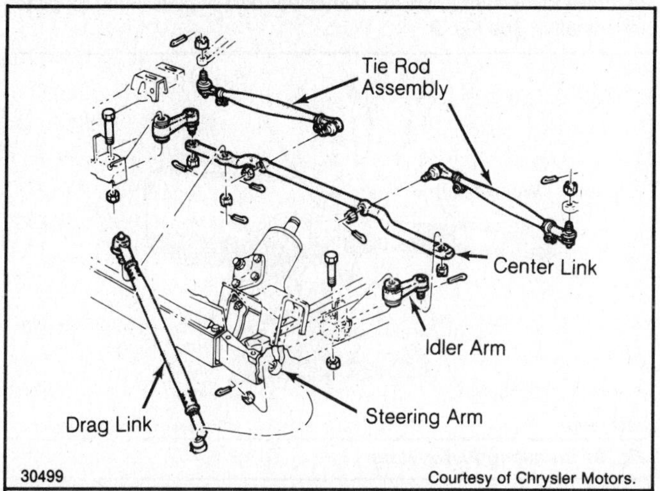
Tie Rod
Assembly
Center Link
Idler Arm
Steering Arm
Drag Link
30499
Courtesy of Chrysler Motors.

Fig. 4: Exploded View of Steering Linkage

Installation – 1) To install, reverse removal procedure. Ensure tie rod end is installed at the same location. Position clamp sleeve with bolt located on the bottom. Clamp opening should be aligned with slot in sleeve.

2) Tighten tie rod end nut to specification. Install cotter pin. Check and adjust toe-in. See SPECIFICATIONS & PROCEDURES article in WHEEL ALIGNMENT. Tighten clamp bolt to specification.

OVERHAUL

POWER STEERING PUMP

Disassembly – 1) Remove pump pulley using Pulley Remover (C-4068) and Pulley Adapter (C-4068-1). *See Fig. 3*.

2) Remove filler cap and drain oil from reservoir before removing parts. Remove 2 studs and fitting from the back of pump. *See Fig. 1*. Rock reservoir by hand or tap with a soft-faced mallet to remove.

NOTE: If expansion plug is deformed or dislodged, DO NOT remove it. Replace pump housing.

3) Remove end plate retaining ring using a punch and screwdriver. *See Fig. 5*. Remove end plate and end plate spring. Remove flow control valve. *See Fig. 1*.

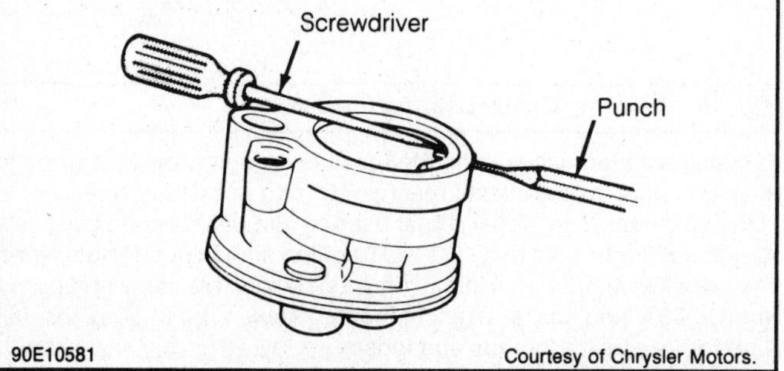
Screwdriver
Punch
90E10581
Courtesy of Chrysler Motors.

Fig. 5: Removing Retaining Ring

4) Using soft-faced hammer, tap end of pump shaft lightly until pressure plate, ring and rotor, thrust plate and shaft can be removed as a unit. Remove rotor assembly dowel pins, pump seals, and drive shaft seal. Put assembly in a vise, being careful to protect pump shaft from damage. Remove rotor lock ring. *See Fig. 6*.

5) Remove rotor and thrust plate from shaft. Clean and inspect all wear surfaces. Replace parts that have excessive wear, scuffing and scoring.

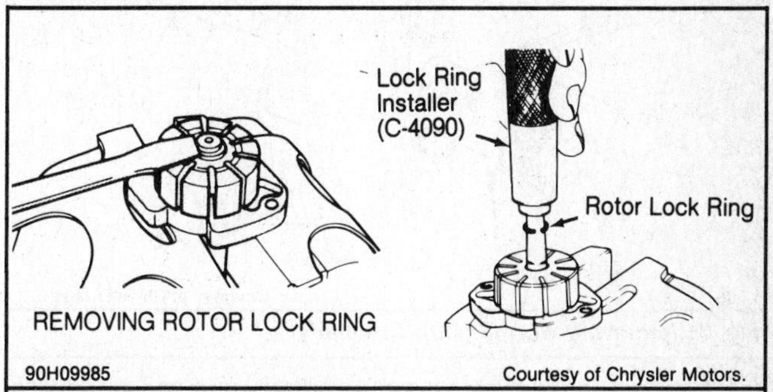
Lock Ring
Installer
(C-4090)
Rotor Lock Ring
REMOVING ROTOR LOCK RING
90H09985
Courtesy of Chrysler Motors.

Fig. 6: Removing & Installing Rotor Lock Ring

Reassembly – 1) Install pump shaft seal. Lubricate pressure plate "O" ring seal with power steering fluid and install in inner-most housing groove. Clamp housing in soft jawed vise. Assemble pump shaft, thrust plate and rotor. Using Lock Ring Installer (C-4090), install new rotor lock ring. *See Fig. 6*.

2) Insert assembled components into pump housing being careful not to damage shaft seal. Install ring with directional arrow (stamped in ring), facing upward. Install 10 rotor vanes into rotor slots. Ensure vanes slide into slots easily.

3) Lubricate chamfered edge of pressure plate and install on dowel pins with spring groove facing upward. Using a large socket, force pressure plate downward to seat it. Lubricate end plate "O" ring and install in middle groove of pump housing.

4) Lubricate end plate. Install end plate and spring down on pressure plate. Force end plate downward and install retaining ring. Install flow control valve and spring.

5) Install mounting stud, flow control valve and reservoir "O" rings. Lubricate inner edge of reservoir and install reservoir onto pump housing. Recheck alignment of "O" rings after reservoir is seated. Install mounting studs and tighten to 35 ft. lbs. (48 N.m).

6) Using Installer (C-4063), install pump pulley. *See Fig. 3*. Install pump and bleed hydraulic system. See HYDRAULIC SYSTEM BLEEDING under LUBRICATION.

STEERING GEAR

Disassembly – 1) Clean exterior of steering gear and clamp it in a soft-jawed vise. Rotate worm and piston assembly shaft from stop-to-stop several times to drain fluid. Remove valve body and "O" rings from valve body housing. *See Figs. 2 and 12*. Remove spring. Using a screwdriver, pry valve lever up and then outward.

CAUTION: DO NOT collapse slotted valve lever end. This will destroy bearing tolerances of spherical head.

2) Loosen sector shaft adjusting screw lock nut. Using Spanner Wrench (C-3988), remove spanner nut from sector shaft cover. Position sector shaft teeth at center of travel. Using Spanner Wrench (C-3989), loosen worm and piston spanner nut. Install Arbor (C-3786) on threaded end of sector shaft. *See Fig. 7*. Slide arbor into housing until both arbor and shaft engage with bearings.

CAUTION: Keep worm and piston firmly compressed to keep retaining rings from dislodging.

3) Compress housing head components by rotating worm shaft to full left turn position. Using spanner wrench, remove spanner nut and tang washer. Remove worm and piston assembly cover nut and tang washer. Using a screwdriver and sector shaft as fulcrum, pry on worm and piston teeth and remove assembly. *See Fig. 7*.

1991 STEERING
Power – Constant Control (Cont.)

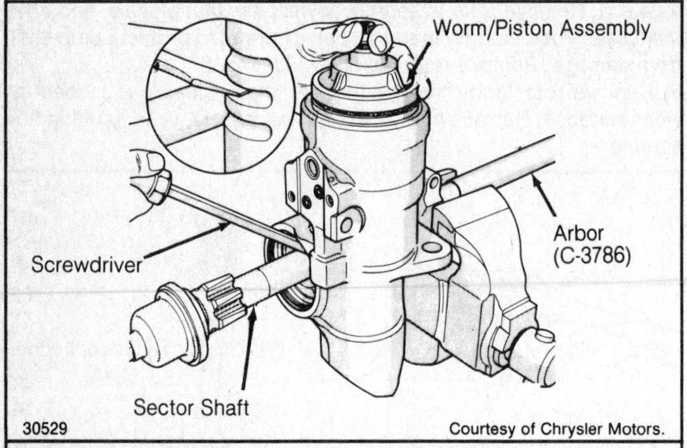
Worm/Piston Assembly
Arbor
(C-3786)
Screwdriver
Sector Shaft
30529
Courtesy of Chrysler Motors.

Fig. 7: Removing Worm/Piston Assembly

4) Place worm and piston assembly vertically in a soft-jawed vise. Raise housing head until worm shaft oil seal clears worm shaft. Position Arbor (C-3929) on top of worm shaft and extend into oil seal. Arbor retains needle bearings in place.

CAUTION: Arbor must be inserted into housing head during removal to hold needle bearings in place. If replacing worm shaft oil seal, remove seal with housing head assembled in steering gear housing.

5) With arbor installed, pull upward on housing head until arbor is fully engaged in bearing. Remove housing head and arbor as a unit. If needle bearings dislodge, use wheel bearing grease to hold in position during installation.
6) Remove large "O" ring from housing head. Apply air to chamber of housing head and remove reaction seal from groove. *See Fig. 8.* Remove reaction spring, reaction ring, balancing ring and spacer. Hold worm shaft and remove staked nut.

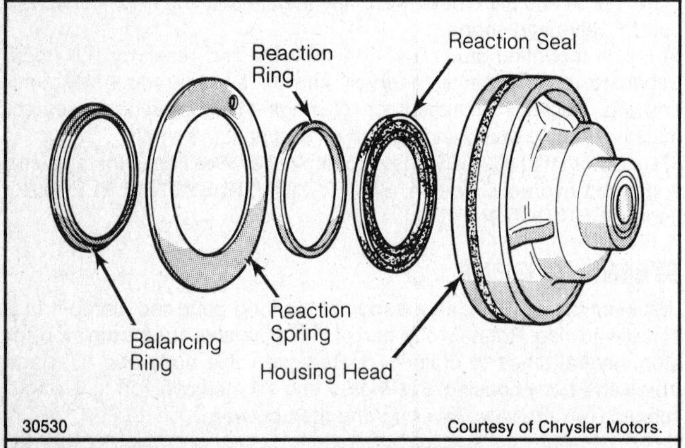
Reaction
Ring
Reaction Seal
Reaction
Spring
Balancing
Ring
Housing Head
30530
Courtesy of Chrysler Motors.

Fig. 8: Exploded View of Housing Head & Seals

7) Remove upper thrust bearing race and bearing from worm shaft. Remove center race from worm shaft. Remove lower thrust bearing and race from worm shaft. Remove reaction ring and reaction spring.
8) Remove cylinder head assembly. Remove "O" rings from outside of cylinder head. Apply air to oil hole between "O" ring grooves of cylinder head to remove reaction ring "O" ring from cylinder head.

NOTE: Worm and piston are serviced as an assembly only. DO NOT disassemble.

9) Remove snap ring, sleeve and rectangular oil seal from cylinder head counterbore. Using INCH lb. torque wrench, check torque required to rotate worm shaft through its travel. Torque should not exceed 1.50 INCH lbs. (.17 N.m).
Inspection – 1) Place worm and piston in a soft-jawed vise with rack teeth facing upward and worm centered. Attach a dial indicator and position pointer on worm shaft at 2.313" (58.75 mm) from piston flange.

2) Vertical side play should not exceed .008" (.20 mm) with a lifting force of 1 lb. (2.2 kg) at end of worm shaft. Inspect Teflon piston ring for wear and cuts. Replace with cast iron piston ring and sealing ring (if necessary).

NOTE: Lubricate all seals and "O" rings with power steering fluid before installing.

Reassembly – 1) If replacing piston ring, replace rubber seal ring and cast iron ring in piston groove. Place piston and ring assembly into Piston Ring Installer (C-3676), with lower part of piston ring on piston ring installer. *See Fig. 9.*

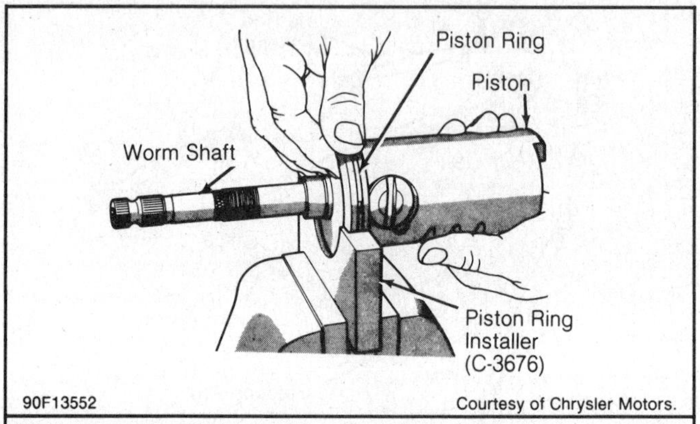
Piston Ring
Piston
Worm Shaft
Piston Ring
Installer
(C-3676)
90F13552
Courtesy of Chrysler Motors.

Fig. 9: Installing Piston Ring

2) Press downward on piston and rotate to seat ring in groove, forcing ends of ring out for ease of locking. Place worm/piston assembly in a soft-jawed vise with worm shaft upward.
3) Ensure cylinder head oil passage is not restricted. Lubricate large "O" rings and install in cylinder head grooves.
4) Install rectangular oil seal, sleeve and snap ring in cylinder head. Install reaction ring "O" ring in cylinder head.

CAUTION: Ensure piston ring end gap is closed before installing cylinder head to avoid damaging "O" ring.

5) Slide cylinder head assembly on worm shaft with ferrule end upward. *See Fig. 10.* Install lower (thick) thrust bearing race, bearing and reaction spring (with small hole over ferrule).

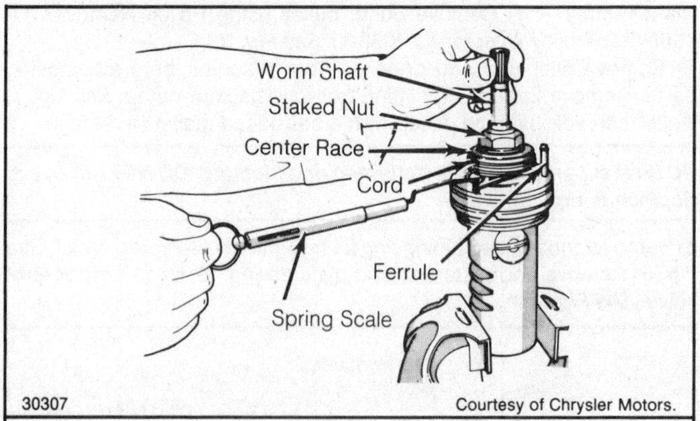
Worm Shaft
Staked Nut
Center Race
Cord
Ferrule
Spring Scale
30307
Courtesy of Chrysler Motors.

Fig. 10: Checking Center Bearing Preload

6) Install reaction ring with flange upward, so ring protrudes through reaction spring and contacts reaction "O" ring in cylinder head.
7) Install center race, upper thrust bearing and thin race. Install a new staked nut finger tight only. DO NOT tighten staked nut. Rotate worm shaft clockwise 1/2 turn. Hold worm shaft in this position with Splined Nut (C-3637) and socket wrench. Tighten staked nut to 50 ft. lbs. (68 N.m) to pre-stretch threads and loosen.
8) Place several rounds of cord around center race. Attach a spring scale. Pull on cord to rotate bearing. *See Fig. 10.* Tighten nut while pulling cord. Adjustment is correct when reading on spring scale is 16-24 oz. (4.4-6.7 N) with race rotating.

9) Using a 1/4" punch, stake upper portion of stake nut into knurled area of worm shaft. If nut moves while staking, tap in opposite direction to regain proper adjustment. Recheck center bearing preload adjustment.
10) If adjustment is correct, stake nut in 3 areas and recheck adjustment. Check nut for proper staking by applying 20 ft. lbs. (27 N.m) torque in both directions. If nut does not move, staking is proper.
11) Install spacer over center race, so dowel pin of spacer engages in center race slot, and spacer slot is centered over cylinder head ferrule. This aligns valve lever hole in center race with valve lever hole in the spacer.

NOTE: Small "O" ring for ferrule groove should not be installed until after reaction spring and spacer have been installed.

12) Install upper reaction ring on center race and spacer with flange down against spacer. Install upper reaction spring over reaction ring. Ensure ferrule goes through hole in reaction spring. Install worm balancing ring (without flange) inside upper reaction ring.
13) Lubricate and install ferrule "O" ring. Using Seal Installer (C-3650), install seal in housing head with seal lip toward needle bearing (if removed) until seal installer bottoms.
14) Lubricate and install reaction seal in housing head face with seal flat side out. *See Fig. 8.* Install "O" ring on housing head.
15) Slide housing head over worm shaft, engaging cylinder head ferrule and "O" ring. Ensure reaction rings enter groove in housing head. Lubricate worm/piston bore of housing. Rotate worm shaft fully counterclockwise to retain reaction rings in place. Install worm/piston assembly.

CAUTION: Ensure cylinder head is bottomed on housing shoulder.

16) Ensure piston teeth face right and valve lever hole in spacer faces upward. Align valve lever hole in center race and spacer with valve lever hole in gear housing.
17) Install valve lever with double bearing end first, through hole in housing. *See Fig. 11.* Ensure slots in lever are parallel to worm shaft.

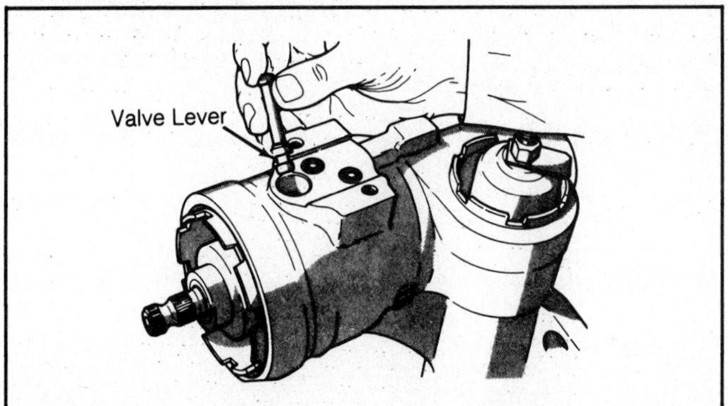
Valve Lever

90G13553 Courtesy of Chrysler Motors.

Fig. 11: Installing Valve Lever

18) Lightly tap end of valve lever to seat lower pivot point in center race. Center valve lever in steering gear by tapping on reinforcing to slightly rotate housing head.
19) Align tang washer with groove in housing and install. Install spanner nut. Using spanner wrench, tighten spanner nut to specification.
20) Ensure valve lever remains centered in hole. Rotate worm shaft until piston bottoms in both directions and note valve lever action. Valve lever must center in hole and snap back to center position when worm tension is relieved. Install valve lever spring, small end first.
21) Position piston at center of travel. Install sector shaft and center sector teeth with piston teeth. Ensure "O" ring is properly installed on sector shaft cover. Install spanner nut. Using spanner wrench, tighten spanner nut to specification. Install valve body and "O" rings.
22) Ensure lever enters hole of spool valve. Tighten bolts to specification. See TORQUE SPECIFICATIONS table at end of article. Place new seal on flat surface with lip downward. Lubricate inner diameter with power steering fluid. Install Seal Protector Sleeve (SP-1601) in seal. Install protector and seal (lip of seal toward housing) on sector shaft.
23) Install Adapter (SP-3052) with long step against seal. Install adapter nut on sector shaft. Tighten nut until adapter shoulder contacts housing. Remove adapter. Install back-up washer and snap ring with sharp edge outward.
24) Fill housing cavity on outside of snap ring with multipurpose grease. Install seal cover in steering gear housing. Install Adapter (SP-3052) with short step against seal cover. Install and tighten adapter nut on sector shaft until shoulder contacts steering gear housing. Remove adapter.
25) Adjust sector shaft preload. See SECTOR SHAFT PRELOAD under ADJUSTMENTS.

VALVE BODY

Disassembly – 1) Disconnect and cap pressure and return hoses from valve body. Tie hoses above power steering pump fluid level to prevent drainage. Remove mounting bolts and lift valve body assembly from steering gear. Remove control body-to-valve body bolts.

NOTE: DO NOT remove end plug from valve unless gasket is leaking.

2) Separate both bodies. *See Fig. 12.* Remove pump inlet fitting, washer, spring, piston and piston spring. Remove spool valve from steering body and inspect for nicks, burrs and scores. Replace complete assembly if damage exists.

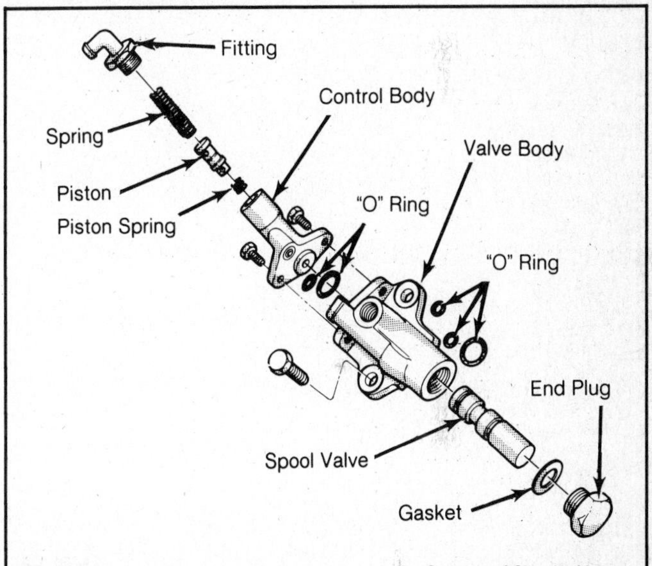
Fitting
Control Body
Spring
Valve Body
Piston
"O" Ring
Piston Spring
"O" Ring
End Plug
Spool Valve
Gasket

90H13554 Courtesy of Chrysler Motors.

Fig. 12: Exploded View of Valve Body

Reassembly – 1) Install spool valve in valve body so valve lever hole is aligned with lever opening of valve body. Ensure valve slides freely in valve body. Install a new gasket on end plug (if removed). Install and tighten end plug to specification.
2) Install piston spring in control body. Ensure spring seats in counterbore at bottom of housing. Lubricate piston and properly install piston in control body. *See Fig. 12.* Ensure piston slides freely in bore. Install other spring on top of piston.
3) Install new washer and pump inlet fitting. Tighten fitting to specification. See TORQUE SPECIFICATIONS table at end of article. Install new "O" rings between control body and valve body. Install and tighten attaching bolts to specification. Align lever hole in spool valve with lever opening in valve body. Install valve body on steering gear.
4) Install valve body-to-steering gear bolts. Tighten bolts to 84 INCH lbs. (10 N.m). Valve body must be centered. See VALVE BODY CENTERING under ADJUSTMENTS. With valve body centered, tighten mounting bolts to final specification. See TORQUE SPECIFICATIONS table.

1991 STEERING
Power – Constant Control (Cont.)

TORQUE SPECIFICATIONS

TORQUE SPECIFICATIONS

Application	Ft. Lbs. (N.m)
Drag Link-To-Center Link Nut	55 (75)
Housing Head Spanner Nut	162 (220)
Idler Arm-To-Center Link Nut	47 (64)
Idler Arm-To-Frame Bolt	70 (95)
Pump Inlet Fitting	40 (55)
Sector Shaft Adjuster Screw Lock Nut	28 (38)
Sector Shaft Spanner Nut	155 (210)
Steering Arm-To-Steering Gear Nut	175 (237)
Steering Arm Nut	175 (237)
Steering Gear Assembly-To-Frame Bolt	100 (136)
Tie Rod Clamp Bolt	
B150/250	17 (23)
B350	26 (35)
Tie Rod Nut	
9/16"	55 (75)
5/8"	75 (102)
Valve Body End Plug	25 (34)
Valve Body-To-Steering Gear Housing Bolt	17 (23)
	INCH Lbs. (N.m)
Control Valve Body-To-Valve Body Bolt	95 (11)

1991 STEERING
Power Recirculating Ball

Dakota (4WD), Pickup, Ramcharger

DESCRIPTION

The Saginaw power steering pump is a constant displacement, vane-type pump with an integral fluid reservoir. Dakota 5.2L models use a vane-nonsubmerged type pump. All other models use vane-submerged type pumps. *See Figs. 1 and 2*. The power steering pump of diesel models is incorporated into a vacuum/power steering pump assembly.

Rectangular pumping vanes, carried by a shaft driven rotor, move fluid from intake to pressure cavities of the cam ring. As the rotor begins to rotate, centrifugal force throws the vanes against the inside surface of the cam ring to pick up residual oil, which is then forced into the high pressure area. Oil is forced into cavities of the thrust plate and through 2 cross-over holes in the cam ring and pressure plate. This oil empties into the high pressure area between the pressure plate and housing end plate (thrust plate on vane-nonsubmerged type).

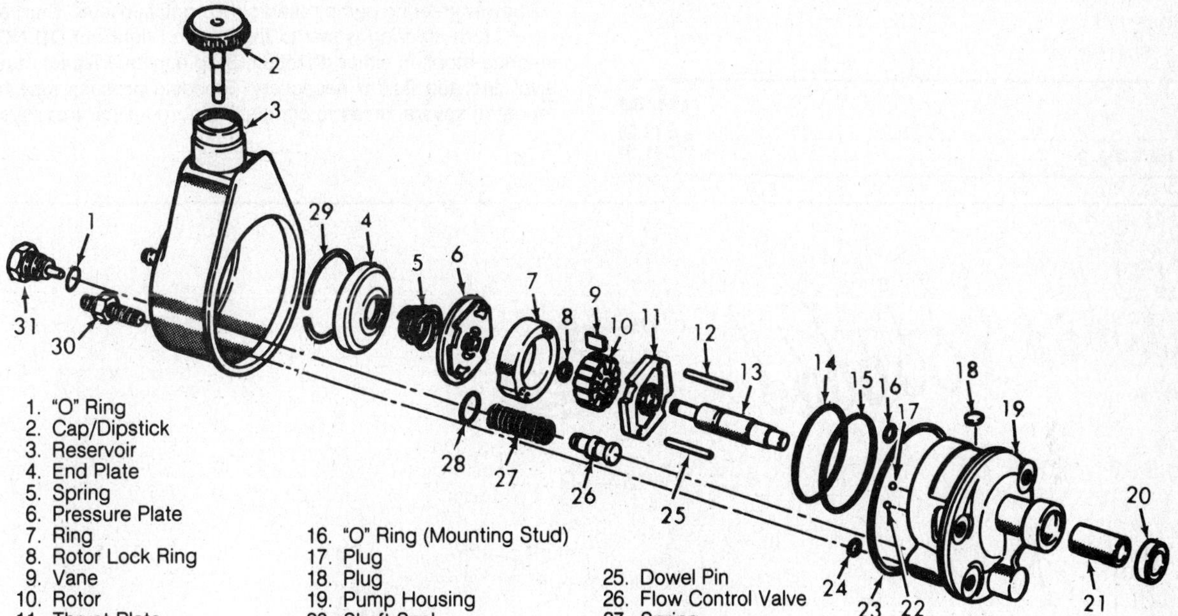

1. "O" Ring
2. Cap/Dipstick
3. Reservoir
4. End Plate
5. Spring
6. Pressure Plate
7. Ring
8. Rotor Lock Ring
9. Vane
10. Rotor
11. Thrust Plate
12. Dowel Pin
13. Shaft
14. "O" Ring (End Plate)
15. "O" Ring (Pressure Plate)
16. "O" Ring (Mounting Stud)
17. Plug
18. Plug
19. Pump Housing
20. Shaft Seal
21. Bushing
22. Plug
23. "O" Ring (Reservoir)
24. "O" Ring (Mounting Stud)
25. Dowel Pin
26. Flow Control Valve
27. Spring
28. "O" Ring (Valve)
29. Retaining Ring
30. Mounting Stud
31. Fitting (Pressure Hose)

91F14337

Courtesy of Chrysler Motors.

Fig. 1: Exploded View of Vane-Submerged Type Power Steering Pump

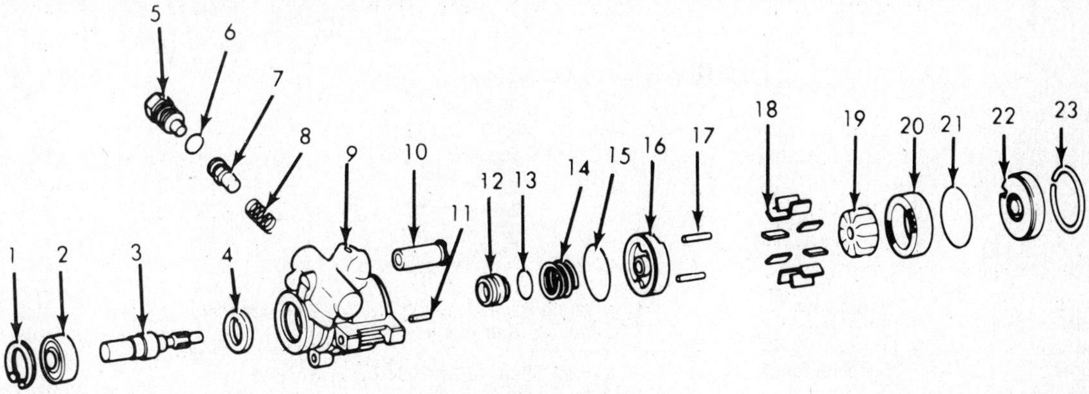

1. Retaining Ring
2. Pump Shaft Bearing
3. Pump Shaft
4. Pump Shaft Seal
5. Flow Control Fitting
6. "O" Ring
7. Flow Control Valve
8. Flow Control Spring
9. Pump Housing
10. Return Tube
11. Dowel Pin
12. Sleeve
13. "O" Ring
14. Pressure Plate Spring
15. "O" Ring
16. Pressure Plate
17. Dowel Pins
18. Pump Vanes (10)
19. Pump Rotor
20. Cam Ring
21. "O" Ring
22. Thrust Plate
23. Retaining Ring

56730

Courtesy of Chrysler Motors.

Fig. 2: Exploded View of Vane-Nonsubmerged Type Saginaw Power Steering Pump (Dakota 5.2L)

1991 STEERING
Power Recirculating Ball (Cont.)

Filling the high pressure area causes oil to flow under the vanes in the rotor slots. The vanes are forced to follow the inside oval surface of cam ring. As the vanes rotate to the small area of the cam ring, oil is forced out from between the vanes, creating high pressure. When pressure exceeds set limits, the flow control valve opens and allows fluid to return to the inlet side of the pump.

Steering gear a variable ratio, recirculating ball type. Control valves are located inside steering gear housing.

LUBRICATION

CAPACITY

CAPACITY

Models	Pts. (L)
Dakota	2.5 (1.2)
Pickup & Ramcharger	2.7 (1.3)

FLUID TYPE

Use Mopar Power Steering Fluid (4318055).

FLUID LEVEL CHECK

Check fluid level with engine cold and not running. Remove fluid level dipstick on pump reservoir. Dipstick should indicate FULL COLD with fluid temperature of 70-80°F (21-27°C). If needed, add fluid through dipstick opening, and recheck. DO NOT overfill.

HYDRAULIC SYSTEM BLEEDING

Fill power steering pump reservoir to specified level. Start engine and slowly turn steering wheel to the left and right but DO NOT contact steering stops in either direction. Stop engine. Inspect reservoir fluid level and add fluid if necessary. Bleeding process may have to be repeated several times to completely purge all air from system.

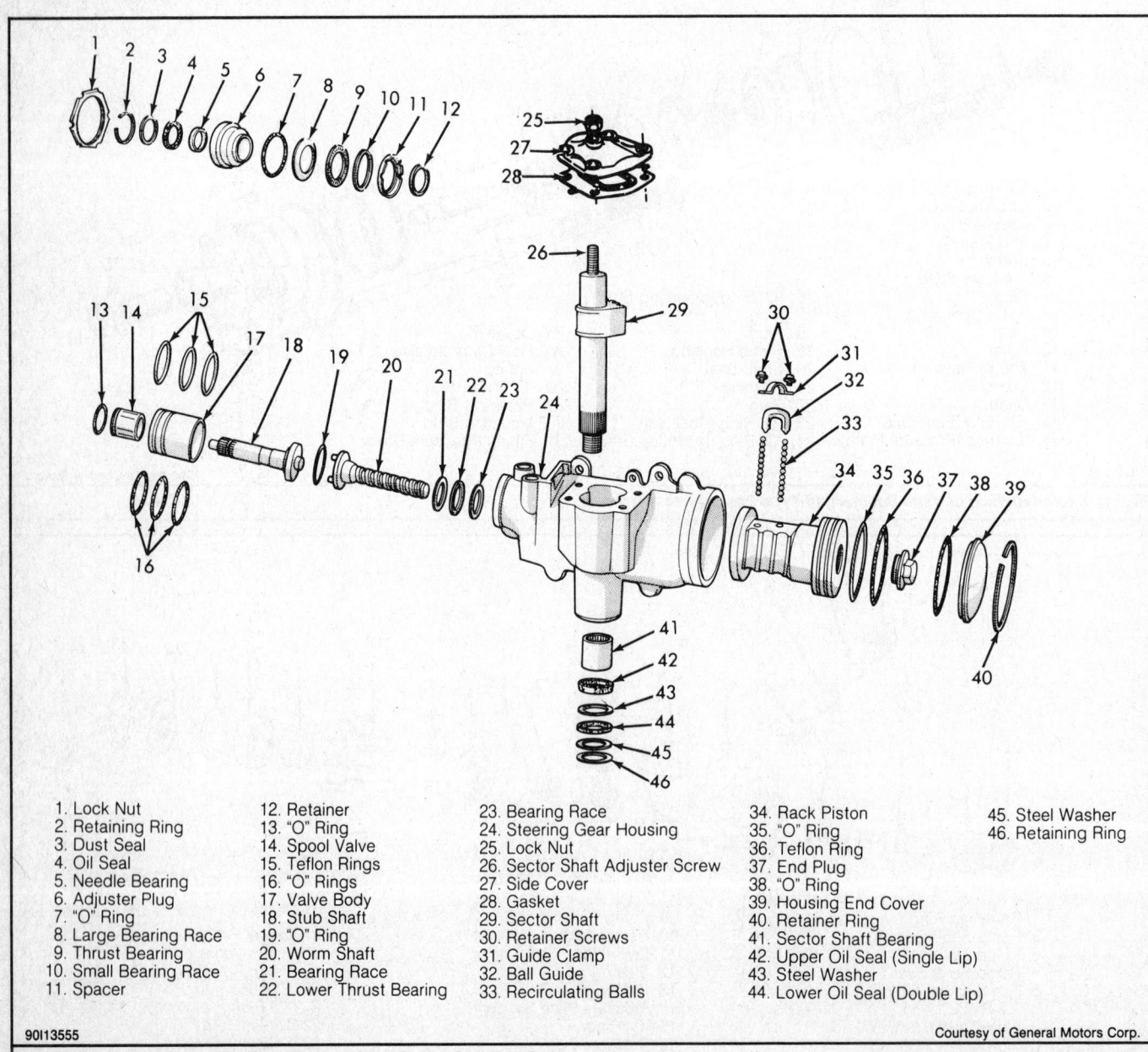

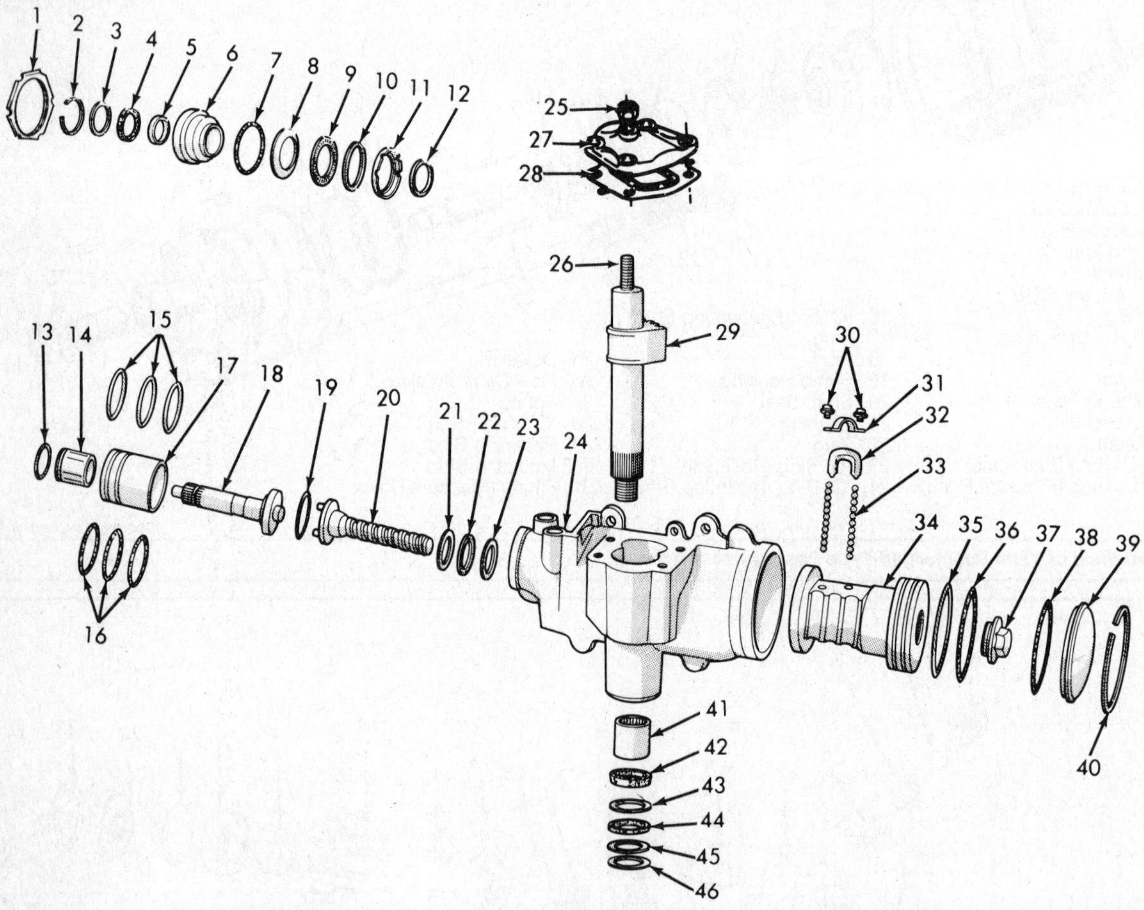
1
2
3
4
5
6
7
8
9
10
11
12
13
14
15
16
17
18
19
20
21
22
23
24
25
26
27
28
29
30
31
32
33
34
35
36
37
38
39
40
41
42
43
44
45
46

1. Lock Nut
2. Retaining Ring
3. Dust Seal
4. Oil Seal
5. Needle Bearing
6. Adjuster Plug
7. "O" Ring
8. Large Bearing Race
9. Thrust Bearing
10. Small Bearing Race
11. Spacer
12. Retainer
13. "O" Ring
14. Spool Valve
15. Teflon Rings
16. "O" Rings
17. Valve Body
18. Stub Shaft
19. "O" Ring
20. Worm Shaft
21. Bearing Race
22. Lower Thrust Bearing
23. Bearing Race
24. Steering Gear Housing
25. Lock Nut
26. Sector Shaft Adjuster Screw
27. Side Cover
28. Gasket
29. Sector Shaft
30. Retainer Screws
31. Guide Clamp
32. Ball Guide
33. Recirculating Balls
34. Rack Piston
35. "O" Ring
36. Teflon Ring
37. End Plug
38. "O" Ring
39. Housing End Cover
40. Retainer Ring
41. Sector Shaft Bearing
42. Upper Oil Seal (Single Lip)
43. Steel Washer
44. Lower Oil Seal (Double Lip)
45. Steel Washer
46. Retaining Ring

90I13555

Courtesy of General Motors Corp.

Fig. 3: Exploded View of Saginaw Rotary Valve Power Steering Gear

1991 STEERING
Power Recirculating Ball (Cont.)

ADJUSTMENTS

POWER STEERING PUMP BELT

3.9L, 5.2L & 5.9L – Power steering belt tension is adjusted by adjusting power steering pump position. To check belt tension, use a Poly-V Burroughs gauge or similar gauge. See POWER STEERING BELT TENSION SPECIFICATIONS table.

POWER STEERING BELT TENSION SPECIFICATIONS

Application	New Belt Lbs. (kg)	Used Belt Lbs. (kg)
3.9L, 5.2L [1] & 5.9L	100-140 (45-64)	60-90 (27-41)

[1] – Dakota models are equipped with dynamic tensioner. No adjustment is required

NOTE: Manufacturer recommends removing steering gear from vehicle before performing any adjustments.

THRUST BEARING PRELOAD

1) Remove steering gear from vehicle. See STEERING GEAR under REMOVAL & INSTALLATION. Ensure steering gear is empty of hydraulic fluid. Rotate steering from stop-to-stop several times to drain fluid. Loosen lock nut on adjuster plug. *See Fig. 4.* Using spanner wrench, rotate adjuster plug clockwise until plug is seated in housing. Torque will be approximately 20 ft. lbs. (27 N.m).

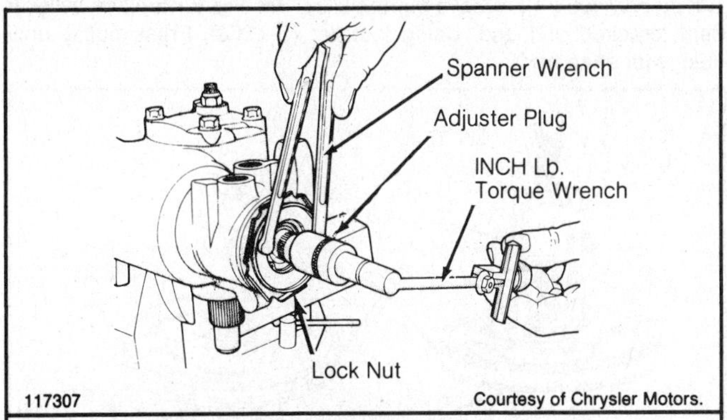
Spanner Wrench
Adjuster Plug
INCH Lb.
Torque Wrench
Lock Nut
117307
Courtesy of Chrysler Motors.

Fig. 4: Measuring Thrust Bearing Preload

2) Place reference mark on steering gear housing adjacent to one hole in adjuster plug. Measure counterclockwise approximately 1/4" from reference mark and place a second reference mark on steering gear housing. Rotate adjuster plug counterclockwise until hole in adjuster plug aligns with second mark on steering gear housing.

3) Tighten lock nut on adjuster plug to 85 ft. lbs. (115 N.m). Ensure adjuster plug DOES NOT move while tightening lock nut. Using an INCH lb. torque wrench, rotate stub shaft clockwise to the stop, then back 1/4 turn.

4) Using torque wrench, measure rotational torque required to rotate stub shaft. Reading should be checked with torque wrench handle nearly vertical, while rotating stub shaft counterclockwise at an even rate. Reading should be 4-10 INCH lbs. (.4-1.1 N.m). *See Fig. 4.*

5) If reading is not within specification, ensure adjuster plug did not rotate while tightening lock nut. Check for defective thrust bearing and races or improperly installed components. Correct as necessary and readjust.

OVER-CENTER PRELOAD

CAUTION: Thrust bearing preload MUST be adjusted before adjusting over-center preload. Note thrust bearing preload reading for use in over-center preload adjustment.

1) Loosen lock nut on sector shaft adjuster screw. *See Fig. 3.* Rotate sector shaft adjuster screw counterclockwise until fully extended and rotate clockwise 180 degrees.

2) Rotate stub shaft and count turns required to go from stop-to-stop. Turn stub shaft back 1/2 the number of turns to center the steering gear. Steering gear is centered when flat side of stub shaft is facing upward, toward pressure line fitting holes on steering gear. Master spline for pitman arm on sector shaft should be aligned with sector shaft adjuster screw.

3) Attach INCH lb. torque wrench to end of stub shaft. Position torque wrench handle in a vertical position. Rotate stub shaft 45 degrees in each direction from vertical and note highest reading. *See Fig. 5.*

4) The over-center preload reading should be within designated amount above the thrust bearing preload and the total of over-center preload and thrust bearing preload should not exceed the total limit. See OVER-CENTER PRELOAD SPECIFICATIONS table.

5) If not within specification, rotate sector shaft adjuster screw clockwise until specification is obtained. Hold adjuster screw and tighten lock nut to specification. See TORQUE SPECIFICATIONS table at end of article.

OVER-CENTER PRELOAD SPECIFICATIONS

Application	Over-Center INCH Lbs. (N.m)	[1] Total INCH Lbs. (N.m)
New Gears	4-8 (.5-.9)	18 (2.0)
Used Gears [2]	4-5 (.5-.6)	18 (2.0)

[1] – Total preload is sum of thrust bearing preload and over-center preload.

[2] – Used steering gears are those in service more than 400 miles.

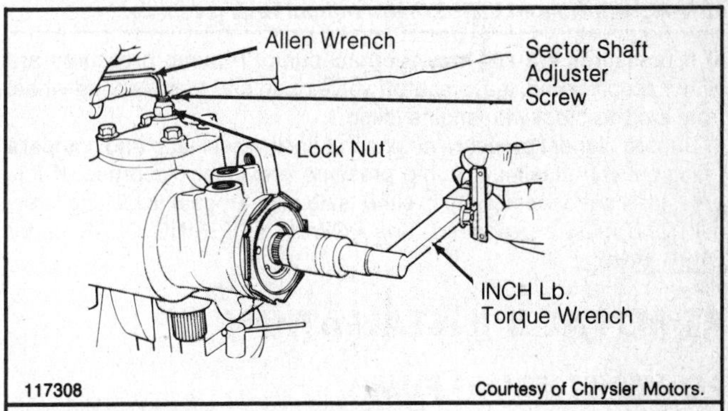
Allen Wrench
Sector Shaft
Adjuster
Screw
Lock Nut
INCH Lb.
Torque Wrench
117308
Courtesy of Chrysler Motors.

Fig. 5: Adjusting Over-Center Preload

TESTING

NOTE: Before testing, check fluid level, belt tension, pump pulley, tire pressure and engine idle speed.

HYDRAULIC SYSTEM PRESSURE TEST

Idle Pressure Test – 1) Remove high pressure hose at steering pump and connect a spare hose to pump fitting. Connect opposite end of spare hose to Pressure Test Gauge (C-3309E). Connect pressure hose from valve side of steering gear to valve side of gauge. Valve must be installed on outlet side of gauge.

NOTE: Replacement fittings are required on Pressure Test Gauge (C-3309E) for adapting to "O" ring type hose tube ends.

2) Fully open shutoff valve on test gauge. With a thermometer in fluid reservoir, start engine and warm fluid to 150-170°F (66-77°C). Turning wheels from stop-to-stop will aid in warming fluid. DO NOT hold wheels against stop.

3) With engine at idle speed and gauge valve open, check initial pressure. See POWER STEERING PUMP PRESSURE TEST SPECIFICATIONS table. If pressure is greater than 125 psi (8.8 kg/cm²), check for restricted hoses or crimped lines.

1991 STEERING
Power Recirculating Ball (Cont.)

POWER STEERING PUMP PRESSURE TEST SPECIFICATIONS

Application	Pressure psi (kg/cm^2)
Idle Pressure	
Dakota	50-80 (3.5-5.6)
Pickup & Ramcharger	30-50 (2.1-3.5)
Relief Pressure	
Dakota	
3.9L	1500 (105)
5.2L	1450 (102)
Pickup & Ramcharger	1400 (98)

Relief Pressure Test - 1) Close gauge shutoff valve completely 3 times. Record highest pressure attained each time.

CAUTION: DO NOT leave shutoff valve closed more 5 seconds, as pump damage could result.

2) If recorded pressures are within specification and range of readings are within 50-80 psi (3.5-5.6 kg/cm^2), pump is working properly. See POWER STEERING PUMP PRESSURE TEST SPECIFICATIONS table. If recorded pressures are high but do not repeat within the specified range, flow control valve in pump is sticking.

3) Remove and inspect flow control valve for nicks or burrs. See POWER STEERING PUMP under OVERHAUL. Gently smooth flow control valve defects with crocus cloth. Install valve and retest.

CAUTION: To prevent scrubbing flat spots on tires, DO NOT turn steering wheel more than 5 times without rolling vehicle.

4) If pressures are still low, overhaul pump. If pump pressures are within specification, leave shutoff valve open and turn steering wheel from stop-to-stop, with engine idling.

5) Record highest pressure attained at each wheel stop and compare readings with maximum pump pressure previously recorded. If this pressure cannot be built up in either side of gear, gear is leaking internally and must be repaired. See POWER STEERING GEAR under OVERHAUL.

REMOVAL & INSTALLATION

POWER STEERING PUMP

Removal & Installation (Gasoline) - On Dakota 5.2L models, rotate belt tensioner and remove pump drive belt. On all other models, loosen pump and remove drive belt. Place drain pan under pump and drain pump. Disconnect and cap hoses. Remove attaching bolts and remove pump. To install pump, reverse removal procedure.

VACUUM/POWER STEERING PUMP

Removal (Diesel) - 1) Disconnect negative battery cable. Disconnect power brake booster hose at upper vacuum pump. Disconnect hydraulic lines at power steering pump and cap to prevent contamination. Remove bolts attaching vacuum/power steering pump to engine block. Drain fluid from steering pump reservoir.

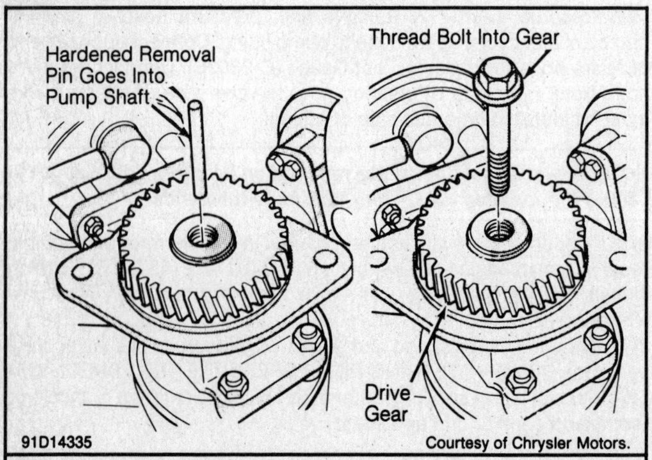
Hardened Removal
Pin Goes Into
Pump Shaft
Thread Bolt Into Gear
Drive
Gear
91D14335
Courtesy of Chrysler Motors.

Fig. 6: Removing Power Steering Pump Drive Gear (Diesel)

2) Fabricate drive gear removal pin from .312" (8 mm) hardened drill rod or similar diameter SAE grade 8 bolt. Pin should be 2" (50.8 mm) long. Insert pin into threaded hole in shaft of pump eccentric. Pin will pass through eccentric shaft and bottom against steering pump shaft. *See Fig. 6.*

3) Thread a hardened 14 mm bolt into threaded shaft until bolt contacts pin. Tighten bolt against pin until drive gear, eccentric and bearing assembly come free of shaft. Remove nuts retaining power steering pump to vacuum pump and separate assemblies.

Installation - 1) To install pump, reverse removal procedure. Start drive gear onto pump shaft by hand. Thread a 3/8 x 18 bolt and flat washer through gear and into pump shaft. Tighten bolt to draw drive gear down onto pump shaft.

2) Assemble power steering pump to vacuum pump and tighten nuts to specification. Use a new gasket between vacuum/power steering pump assembly and engine block. See TORQUE SPECIFICATIONS table at end of article.

PUMP PULLEY

CAUTION: Examine exposed end of rotor drive shaft before removal. If it is corroded, clean the surface with crocus cloth to prevent damage to the shaft bushing during removal.

Removal & Installation (Gasoline) - Using Puller (C-4068) and Puller Adapter (C-4068-1), remove pump pulley. *See Fig. 7.* Replace pulley if bent, cracked or loose. Using Installer (C-4063), Press pulley until flush with shaft end.

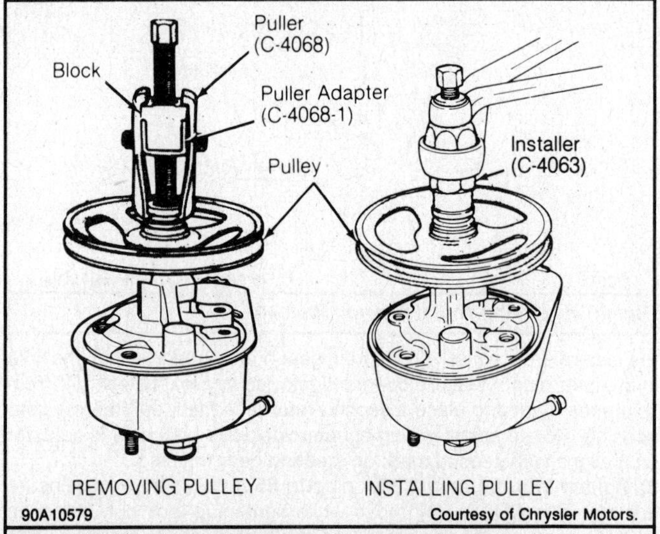
Block
Puller
(C-4068)
Puller Adapter
(C-4068-1)
Pulley
Installer
(C-4063)
REMOVING PULLEY
INSTALLING PULLEY
90A10579
Courtesy of Chrysler Motors.

Fig. 7: Removing & Installing Pump Pulley (Gasoline)

STEERING GEAR

Removal - 1) Place wheels in straight-ahead position. Place drain pan under steering gear assembly. Disconnect and cap pressure and return hoses from steering gear. Disconnect steering column shaft coupling from steering gear stub shaft.

2) Raise and support vehicle. Disconnect steering linkage (center link) from pitman arm. Disconnect stabilizer bar (if necessary). Place reference mark on pitman arm and sector shaft. Remove nut and pitman arm from sector shaft. Remove steering gear-to-frame bolts. Remove steering gear.

Installation - 1) Install steering gear with retaining bolts finger tight. Center steering gear and align stub shaft with steering column. Install steering column shaft coupling bolt and tighten to specification. See TORQUE SPECIFICATIONS table at end of article.

1991 STEERING
Power Recirculating Ball (Cont.)

2) Reposition steering gear to eliminate binding and tighten retaining bolts to specification. Install pitman arm on sector shaft with reference marks aligned. Install lock washer and nut. Tighten nut to specification.

CAUTION: Stake pitman arm retaining nut against pitman arm to ensure proper retention.

3) To install, remaining components, reverse removal procedure. Fill pump reservoir. Bleed air from system. See HYDRAULIC SYSTEM BLEEDING under LUBRICATION.

SECTOR SHAFT OIL SEAL

Removal - 1) Raise and support vehicle. Place wheels in straight-ahead position. Disconnect steering linkage (center link) from pitman arm. Disconnect stabilizer bar (if necessary).
2) Place reference mark on pitman arm and sector shaft. Remove nut and pitman arm from sector shaft. Place drain pan under steering gear. Remove retaining ring and steel washer. *See Fig. 3.*
3) Start engine and momentarily hold steering wheel in extreme left turn. When pressure develops, this should force upper oil seal, steel washer and lower oil seal from steering gear housing. Stop engine and remove seals.

CAUTION: DO NOT hold wheels in left turn for more than 2-second intervals.

Installation - 1) Ensure seal bore of steering gear is free of burrs and sector shaft is free of pitting or roughness. Lubricate replacement seals and steel washers with power steering fluid.
2) Wrap sector shaft with plastic tape or .005" (.13 mm) thick shim stock. Install upper oil seal (single lip seal) and steel washer first. Oil seal must be installed only deep enough to allow for remaining oil seal, steel washer and retaining ring.

CAUTION: DO NOT install upper oil seal against the inner bore surface of steering gear housing. Oil seals must be installed so each oil seal is separately seated in the shaft bore.

3) Install lower oil seal (double lip seal) and steel washer. Oil seal must be installed only deep enough to allow for steel washer and retaining ring. Remove tape or shim stock and install retaining ring.
4) Install pitman arm. Install pitman arm on sector shaft with reference marks aligned. Install lock washer and nut. Tighten nut to specification. See TORQUE SPECIFICATIONS table at end of article.

CAUTION: Stake pitman arm retaining nut against pitman arm to ensure proper retention.

5) To install, remaining components, reverse removal procedure. Fill pump reservoir. Allow engine to idle for at least 3 minutes. DO NOT turn wheels during this time. Rotate wheels both directions and check for leaks. Refill pump reservoir.

HOUSING END COVER SEAL

Removal - 1) Raise and support vehicle. Place wheels in straight-ahead position. Place drain pan under steering gear.
2) Rotate housing end cover retainer ring until one end of ring is under small hole in steering gear housing. Insert punch through small hole and depress retainer ring. Remove retainer ring.
3) Rotate steering wheel to left until rack piston forces housing end cover from steering gear housing. Turn steering wheel back to center position. Remove housing end cover and "O" ring.

CAUTION: DO NOT rotate steering wheel any more than necessary, as recirculating balls may fall from the rack piston.

Installation - Lubricate "O" ring with power steering fluid and install on housing end cover. Install housing end cover and retainer ring. Fill pump reservoir. Allow engine to idle for at least 3 minutes. DO NOT turn wheels during this time. Rotate wheels both directions and check for leaks. Refill pump reservoir.

CENTER LINK

Removal & Installation - Separate tie rods, idler arm, steering and drag link (if equipped) from center link. Remove center link. To install, reverse removal procedure. Tighten retaining nuts to specification.

CAUTION: Ensure center link is installed so when viewed from front of vehicle, center link ends turn upward.

DRAG LINK

Removal - Remove cotter pin and drag link nut. Using Separator (C-4150), separate drag link from steering knuckle or center link and steering arm.

Installation - On Pickup and Ramcharger 4WD models, drag link must be installed to steering knuckle with the short distance ("A") attached to the steering knuckle. *See Fig. 8.* On all models, install drag link and retaining nuts. Tighten nuts to specification. See TORQUE SPECIFICATIONS table at end of article. Install cotter pin.

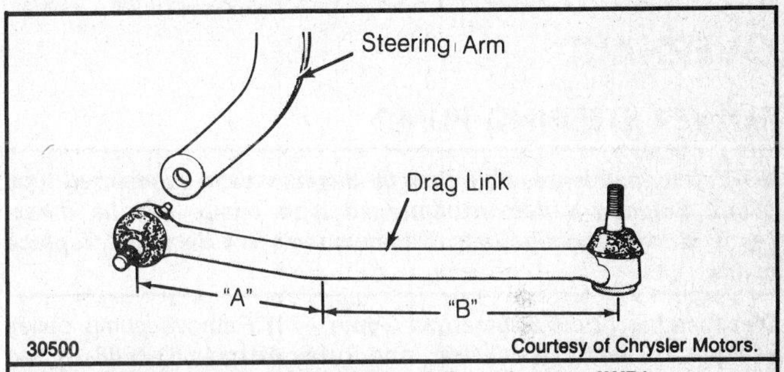
Steering Arm
Drag Link
"A"
"B"
30500
Courtesy of Chrysler Motors.

Fig. 8: Installing Drag Link (Pickup & Ramcharger 4WD)

IDLER ARM

Removal & Installation - Remove cotter pin and nut from idler arm. Separate idler arm from center link. Remove idler arm retaining bolt(s). Remove idler arm. To install, reverse removal procedure. Tighten bolts to specification. See TORQUE SPECIFICATIONS table at end of article. Install new cotter pin.

STEERING ARM

Removal & Installation - 1) Remove cotter pin and nut at steering arm-to-center link or drag link. Separate steering arm from center link or drag link. Mark location of steering arm on steering gear shaft. Remove steering arm-to-steering gear shaft nut. Separate steering arm from steering gear.
2) To install, reverse removal procedure. Ensure reference marks are aligned. Tighten bolts and nuts to specification. Install new cotter pin.

CAUTION: Stake steering arm nut against steering gear shaft to ensure proper retention.

TIE ROD END

Removal - 1) Remove cotter pin and nut from tie rod end. Using Tie Rod End Puller (C-3894-A), remove tie rod end from steering knuckle or center link.
2) Loosen lock nut or clamp bolt. Remove tie rod end. Note number of turns required for removal.

NOTE: Use Tie Rod End Puller (C-3894-A) to prevent tie rod end seal damage.

Installation - 1) To install, reverse removal procedure. Ensure tie rod end is installed at the same location. Position clamp sleeve with bolt located on the bottom. Clamp opening should be aligned with slot in sleeve.
2) Tighten tie rod end nut to specification. Install cotter pin. Check and adjust toe-in. See SPECIFICATIONS & PROCEDURES article in WHEEL ALIGNMENT. Tighten clamp bolt to specification. See TORQUE SPECIFICATIONS table at end of article.

1991 STEERING
Power Recirculating Ball (Cont.)

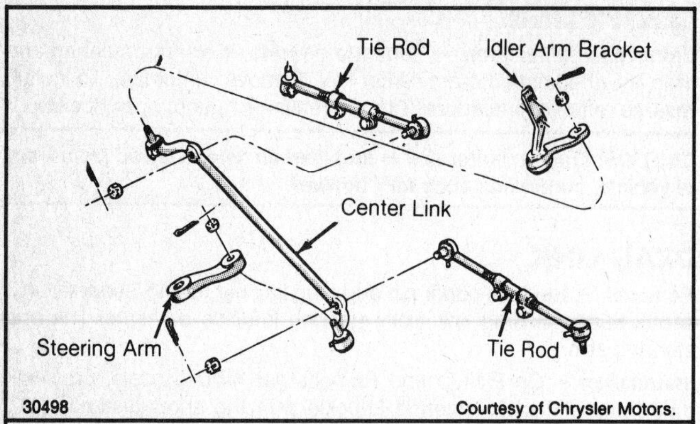
Tie Rod
Idler Arm Bracket
Center Link
Steering Arm
Tie Rod
30498
Courtesy of Chrysler Motors.

Fig. 9: Exploded View of Steering Linkage (Dakota 4WD, Pickup & Ramcharger 2WD)

OVERHAUL

POWER STEERING PUMP

NOTE: Overhaul is possible only on Saginaw vane-submerged type pump. Saginaw vane-nonsubmerged type pump may be disassembled for inspection only. If components are damaged, replace pump.

Disassembly (Vane-Submerged Type) - 1) Remove pump pulley using Pulley Remover (C-4068) and Pulley Adapter (C-4068-1). *See Fig. 3.*

2) Remove filler cap and drain oil from reservoir before removing parts. Remove 2 studs and fitting from the back of pump. *See Fig. 1.* Rock reservoir by hand or tap with a soft-faced mallet to remove.

NOTE: If expansion plug is deformed or dislodged, DO NOT remove it. Replace pump housing.

3) Remove end plate retaining ring, using a punch and screwdriver. *See Fig. 10.* Remove end plate and end plate spring. Remove flow control valve. *See Fig. 2.*

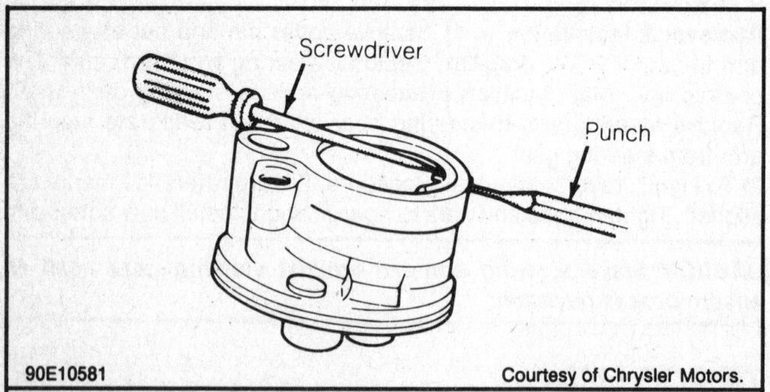
Screwdriver
Punch
90E10581
Courtesy of Chrysler Motors.

Fig. 10: Removing Retaining Ring

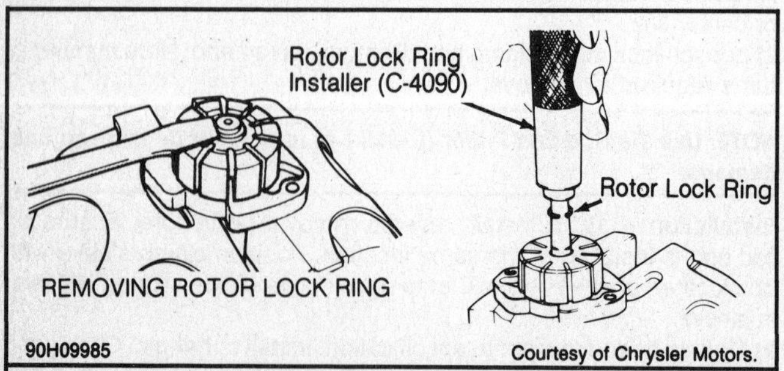
Rotor Lock Ring Installer (C-4090)
Rotor Lock Ring
REMOVING ROTOR LOCK RING
90H09985
Courtesy of Chrysler Motors.

Fig. 11: Removing & Installing Rotor Lock Ring

4) Using soft hammer, tap end of pump shaft lightly until pressure plate, ring and rotor, thrust plate and shaft can be removed as a unit. Remove rotor assembly dowel pins, pump seals, and drive shaft seal. Put assembly in a vise, being careful to protect pump shaft from damage. Remove rotor lock ring. *See Fig. 11.*

5) Remove rotor and thrust plate from shaft. Clean and inspect all wear surfaces. Replace parts that have excessive wear, scuffing and scoring.

Reassembly - 1) Install pump shaft seal. Lubricate pressure plate "O" ring seal with power steering fluid and install in inner-most housing groove. Clamp housing in soft jawed vise. Assemble pump shaft, thrust plate and rotor. Using Lock Ring Installer (C-4090), install new rotor lock ring. *See Fig. 11.*

2) Insert assembled components into pump housing, being careful not to damage shaft seal. Install ring with directional arrow (stamped in ring), facing upward. Install 10 rotor vanes into rotor slots. Ensure vanes slide into slots easily.

3) Lubricate chamfered edge of pressure plate and install on dowel pins with spring groove facing upward. Using a large socket, force pressure plate downward to seat it. Lubricate end plate "O" ring and install in middle groove of pump housing.

4) Lubricate end plate. Install end plate and spring on pressure plate. Force end plate downward and install retaining ring. Install flow control valve and spring.

5) Install mounting stud, flow control valve and reservoir "O" rings. Lubricate inner edge of reservoir and install reservoir onto pump housing. Recheck alignment of "O" rings after reservoir is seated. Install mounting studs and tighten to 35 ft. lbs. (48 N.m).

6) Using Installer (C-4063), install pump pulley. *See Fig. 7.* Install pump and bleed hydraulic system. See HYDRAULIC SYSTEM BLEEDING under LUBRICATION.

Disassembly (Vane-Nonsubmerged Type) - 1) Remove pump pulley using Pulley Remover (C-4068) and Pulley Adapter (C-4068-1). *See Fig. 7.* Remove reservoir from pump by prying and sliding retaining clips from pump. Remove flow control valve fitting, flow control valve and spring.

2) Remove and discard pump shaft retaining ring. Remove pump shaft and bearing. Using a small screwdriver, pry pump shaft seal from pump body. Remove thrust plate retaining ring, using a punch and screwdriver. *See Fig. 10.*

3) Using a brass drift, press thrust plate from pump body. Remove thrust plate "O" ring. Remove ring, rotor, vanes, dowel pins and pressure plate. Remove pressure plate "O" ring.

Inspection - Clean all metal parts with mineral spirits and dry with compressed air. Inspect for scoring or burning of internal pump components. Replace pump if any damage is apparent. If pump is okay, reassemble using new gasket set.

Reassembly - To reassemble pump, reverse disassembly procedure. Ensure vanes move freely in rotor slots. Replace thrust plate retaining ring if bent or distorted. Install pump shaft retaining ring beveled side outward (small lug on left and large lug on right). Install pump and bleed hydraulic system. See HYDRAULIC SYSTEM BLEEDING under LUBRICATION.

STEERING GEAR

Disassembly - 1) Mount steering gear in vise so sector shaft is pointing downward. Rotate housing end cover retainer ring until one end of plug is over hole in steering gear housing.

2) Force end of retainer ring from groove in steering gear housing and remove ring. Rotate stub shaft counterclockwise to force housing end cover from steering gear housing. Rotate stub shaft clockwise 1/2 turn to move rack piston inward.

CAUTION: DO NOT rotate stub shaft any more than necessary, as recirculating balls may fall from rack piston.

3) Using soft-faced hammer, tap on end plug. *See Fig. 3.* Hit end plug with a soft-faced hammer to unseat it. Remove end plug. Remove lock nut from sector shaft adjuster screw. Remove side cover bolts.

4) Rotate sector shaft adjuster screw while holding side cover until side cover and gasket can be removed. Rotate stub shaft until sector shaft teeth are centered in steering gear housing.
5) Using a soft-faced hammer, tap end of sector shaft to free it from steering gear housing. Remove sector shaft. Remove retainer adjuster plug lock nut. *See Fig. 3.* Using a spanner wrench, remove adjuster plug.
6) Insert Rack Piston Arbor (C-4175) into end of rack piston assembly until arbor just contacts worm shaft. Rack piston arbor will retain recirculating balls in rack piston. Rotate stub shaft counterclockwise to force rack piston onto rack piston arbor. Remove rack piston and arbor as an assembly.
7) Remove stub shaft and valve body from steering gear housing by pulling outward on stub shaft splined end. Remove worm shaft, lower thrust bearing and bearing races from steering gear housing.

Cleaning – 1) Clean all internal parts in solvent and dry with compressed air. Avoid wiping valve parts with cloth. Lint may cause binding of mechanism.
2) DO NOT steam clean hydraulic parts. If further disassembly is required, see appropriate sub-assembly heading under OVERHAUL.

Reassembly – 1) Lubricate all parts with power steering fluid before reassembly. Mount steering gear in vise so sector shaft points downward. Install lower thrust bearing and bearing races on worm shaft. *See Fig. 12.*

NOTE: Bearing races must be installed so the cone (raised area) faces toward the steering gear housing. See Fig. 4.

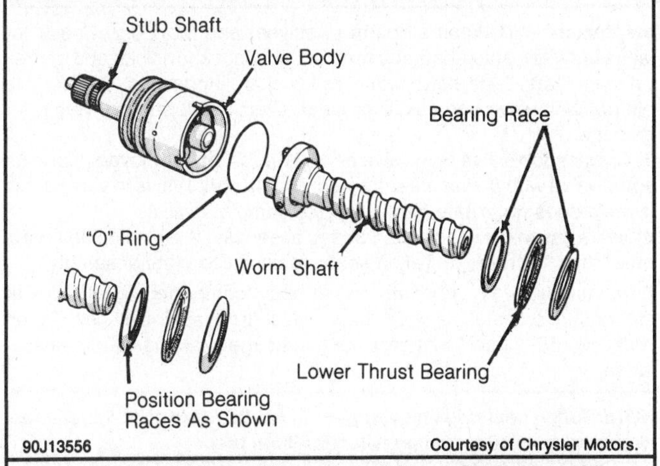
Stub Shaft
Valve Body
Bearing Race
"O" Ring
Worm Shaft
Lower Thrust Bearing
Position Bearing
Races As Shown
90J13556
Courtesy of Chrysler Motors.

Fig. 12: Exploded View of Valve Body & Worm Shaft Assembly

2) Place worm shaft in valve body. Install "O" ring in valve body. Ensure "O" ring is seated against inner edge of stub shaft. Align notch in valve body with drive pin in worm shaft.
3) Install valve body and worm shaft assembly into steering gear housing. Seat valve body in steering gear housing by pressing on outer diameter surface of valve body with fingertips.
4) Ensure Teflon rings do not bind in steering gear housing. Valve body is seated when all or most of fluid return port in steering gear housing is fully visible.

CAUTION: DO NOT press against stub shaft while seating valve body in steering gear housing. This may cause stub shaft to separate from valve body and allow spool valve "O" ring to fall into fluid passages.

5) Place Seal Protector (C-4182) over stub shaft. Using new "O" ring, install adjuster plug on stub shaft. Using spanner wrench, tighten adjuster plug until it seats against valve body. Approximately 20 ft. lbs. (27 N.m) is required to seat adjuster plug.
6) Remove seal protector. Loosely install adjuster plug lock nut. Install rack piston (with rack piston arbor to retain recirculating balls) into steering gear housing until worm shaft engages with valve body and stub shaft. Rotate stub shaft clockwise to force rack piston into steering gear housing. Maintain pressure on rack piston arbor until worm shaft is fully engaged.
7) Rotate stub shaft clockwise to align center groove of rack piston is aligned with center of sector shaft bearing bore. Remove arbor. Lubricate rubber portion of sector shaft cover gasket with petroleum jelly.
8) Install gasket on sector shaft cover. Ensure rubber portion is seated in groove of sector shaft cover. Install sector shaft cover on sector shaft adjuster screw.
9) Thread sector shaft cover onto adjuster screw until cover contacts the sector shaft. Install sector shaft so center gear tooth meshes with center groove in rack piston. Install sector shaft cover bolts and tighten to specification.
10) Install NEW lock nut half-way on sector shaft adjuster screw. Install end plug in rack piston and tighten to specification. Install housing end cover, end plug and retainer ring.
11) Ensure end of retainer ring is not aligned with hole in steering gear housing. Lightly tap on housing end cover to ensure retainer ring is fully seated. Adjust worm bearing preload and over-center preload. See THRUST BEARING PRELOAD and OVER-CENTER PRELOAD under ADJUSTMENTS.

ADJUSTER PLUG

Disassembly – 1) Using a screwdriver, carefully remove and discard retainer. *See Fig. 13.* Remove spacer, thrust bearing and bearing races. Note direction of bearing race installation for reassembly. Remove and discard "O" ring.
2) Remove retaining ring. Remove dust seal. Pry oil seal from adjuster plug. Inspect needle bearing. Remove needle bearing by pressing bearing out of adjuster plug from spacer end of adjuster plug (if necessary). *See Fig. 13.*

Inspection – Inspect thrust bearing for cracks. Check rollers for pitting, scoring, or cracking. Check bearing races and spacer for damage. Replace components as necessary.

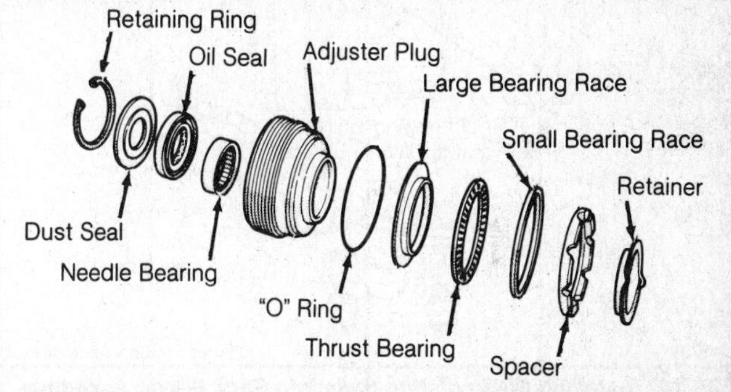
Retaining Ring
Oil Seal
Adjuster Plug
Large Bearing Race
Small Bearing Race
Retainer
Dust Seal
Needle Bearing
"O" Ring
Thrust Bearing
Spacer
90A13557
Courtesy of Chrysler Motors.

Fig. 13: Exploded View of Adjuster Plug Assembly

Reassembly – 1) Lubricate components with power steering fluid. Press needle bearing into adjuster plug with identification number away from adjuster plug until bearing bottoms in bore. Install oil seal with seal lip toward the adjuster plug.
2) Lubricate dust seal with petroleum jelly. Install dust seal with rubber side away from adjuster plug. Install retaining ring. Ensure retaining ring is fully seated.
3) Lubricate "O" ring with petroleum jelly and install on adjuster plug. Assemble thrust bearing, bearing races, and spacer on adjuster plug. Ensure bearing races are installed in correct location. *See Fig. 13.* Using a punch, tap NEW retainer into adjuster plug.

RACK PISTON & WORM SHAFT

Disassembly – 1) Remove clamp for ball guide. Place assembly over container to catch recirculating balls. Remove ball guides, worm shaft with arbor and recirculating balls. Ensure 24 recirculating balls are removed.
2) Remove rack piston arbor (if installed). Remove Teflon and "O" rings from rack piston.

1991 STEERING
Power Recirculating Ball (Cont.)

Inspection - 1) Clean and dry all parts. Inspect worm shaft and rack piston grooves for scoring. Inspect ball bearings for damage. If any ball bearings are damaged, replace entire set. Check ball guides for pinching of ends.
2) Inspect lower thrust bearing and races for cracking, scoring, or pitting. Inspect rack piston teeth for chips, cracks, dents or scoring. Replace components as necessary.
Reassembly - 1) Lubricate all components with power steering fluid. Install new Teflon seal and "O" ring onto rack piston. Ensure "O" ring is not twisted. Install worm shaft completely into rack piston.
2) Install recirculating balls in rack piston by alternately installing one Black ball and then a Silver ball. *See Fig. 14.* Press each ball downward to allow for installation of the next ball.

NOTE: Ensure a Black ball is installed first, and then a Silver ball is alternately installed in rack piston.

3) A total of 18 balls should be installed in the rack piston. Rotate worm shaft counterclockwise as viewed from steering shaft end to install recirculating balls in rack piston.
4) Apply petroleum jelly to one ball guide and install 6 recirculating balls. Ensure a Black ball is followed by a Silver ball and is in sequence with those installed in rack piston.
5) Install remaining ball guide and install both ball guides in rack piston. Install clamp and tighten bolts to specification. Insert Rack Piston Arbor (C-4175) into rack piston until it contacts the worm shaft.

CAUTION: DO NOT allow rack piston arbor to separate from worm shaft until rack piston is fully installed on worm shaft.

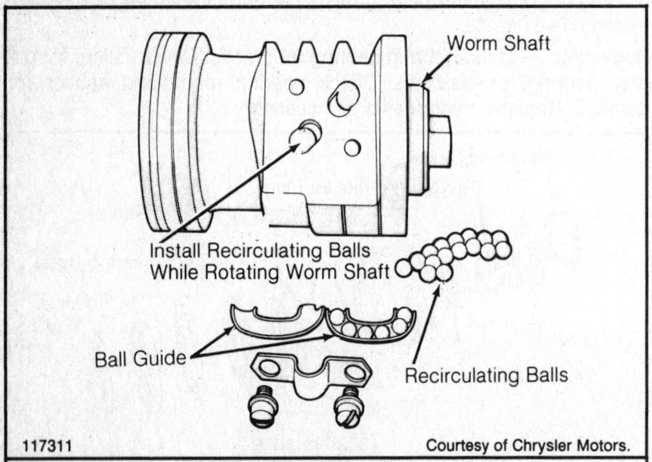
Worm Shaft
Install Recirculating Balls
While Rotating Worm Shaft
Ball Guide
Recirculating Balls
117311
Courtesy of Chrysler Motors.
Fig. 14: Installing Recirculating Balls Into Rack Piston Assembly

VALVE BODY & STUB SHAFT

NOTE: Valve body and stub shaft should not be disassembled unless necessary. If components are defective, valve body and stub shaft must be replaced as a unit.

Disassembly - 1) Lightly tap end of stub shaft against wooden block until cap (large end) of stub shaft is free of valve body. Remove "O" ring from stub shaft cap. This is the "O" ring that fits between stub shaft and worm shaft. Pull stub shaft outward from valve body until drive pin hole is visible. *See Fig. 15.*

CAUTION: DO NOT pull stub shaft outward more than 1/4" (6 mm) or spool valve may become cocked in valve body.

2) Disengage drive pin. Remove stub shaft from valve body. Remove spool valve from valve body. If spool valve becomes cocked, realign spool valve and remove. Remove and discard all "O" rings and Teflon rings. *See Fig. 16.*

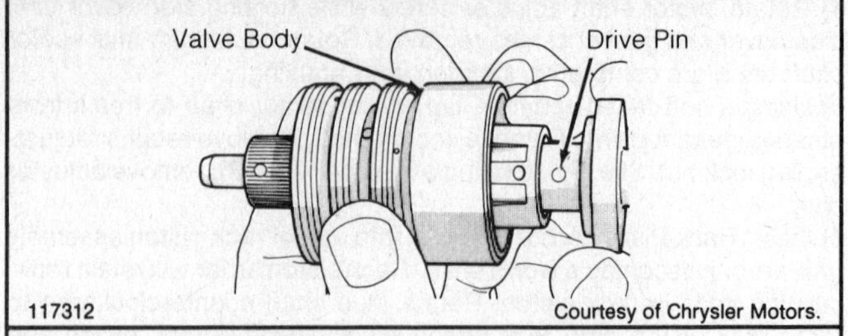
Valve Body
Drive Pin
117312
Courtesy of Chrysler Motors.
Fig. 15: Removing Stub Shaft From Valve Body

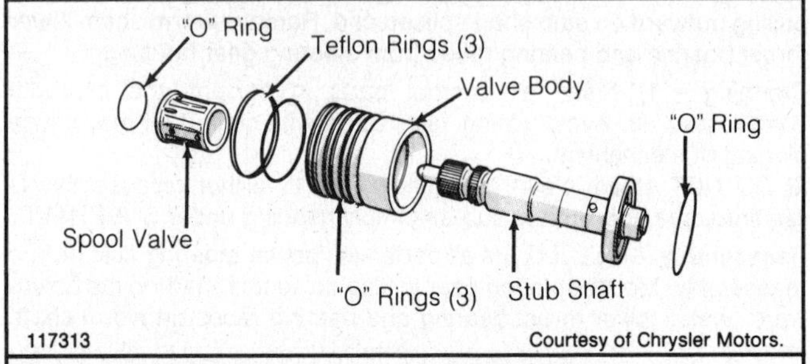
"O" Ring
Teflon Rings (3)
Valve Body
"O" Ring
Spool Valve
"O" Rings (3)
Stub Shaft
117313
Courtesy of Chrysler Motors.
Fig. 16: Exploded View of Valve Body Assembly

CAUTION: DO NOT force stub shaft or spool valve out of valve body.

Inspection - 1) Wash all parts in solvent and blow dry. Check for leaks between stub shaft and torsion bar. Check for nicks and scores on stub shaft. Sand down with Crocus cloth, if possible. Check drive pin notch in valve body skirt for wear. Check stub shaft drive pin for damage.
2) Check spool valve fit in valve body. With "O" ring removed, lubricate spool valve with power steering fluid. Rotate spool valve in valve body. If valve does not rotate freely, replace complete valve.
3) Valve assembly is balanced during assembly. If replacing any parts other than "O" rings or Teflon seals, replace complete assembly.
Reassembly - 1) Lubricate valve body components with power steering fluid. Install new "O" rings in seal grooves. Install new Teflon rings over "O" rings. Take care not to damage seal rings during installation.

NOTE: Teflon seal rings may appear to be distorted after installation. However, heat of operation will straighten them.

2) Lubricate replacement "O" ring for spool valve with petroleum jelly and install on spool valve. Carefully install spool valve in valve body.
3) Push spool valve through valve body until stub shaft drive pin hole is visible on valve body and spool valve is even with notched end of valve body. Install stub shaft into spool valve and valve body.
4) Align notch at top of stub shaft with pin in valve body. *See Fig. 17.* Press stub shaft and spool valve into valve body. Install "O" ring in groove on stub shaft.

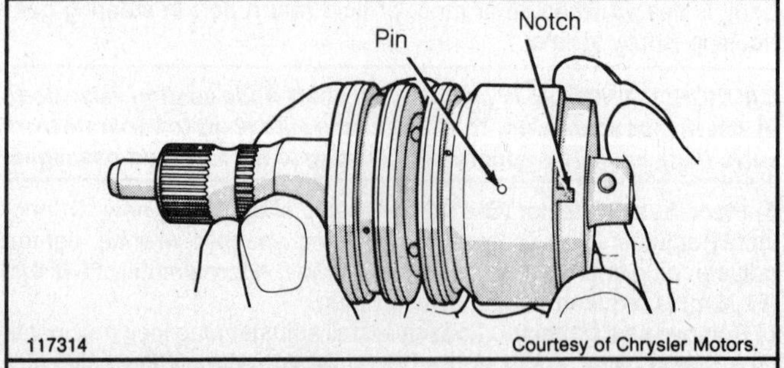
Notch
Pin
117314
Courtesy of Chrysler Motors.
Fig. 17: Aligning Stub Shaft

1991 STEERING
Power Recirculating Ball (Cont.)

STEERING GEAR HOUSING

Disassembly – Remove retaining ring for sector shaft seals. *See Fig. 3.* Remove steel washer, lower oil seal, steel washer and upper oil seal from housing. Press sector shaft bearing from steering gear housing.

Reassembly – **1)** Lubricate steering housing bore, steel washers and oil seals with power steering fluid. Install sector shaft bearing in steering gear housing using Handle (C-4171) and Adapter (C-4178). Bearing should be installed until bearing is .030" (.76 mm) below shoulder of inner bore.

2) Install upper oil seal (single lip seal) and steel washer. Oil seal lip should face toward steering gear housing, and must be installed only deep enough to allow for remaining oil seal, steel washer and retaining ring to be installed.

CAUTION: DO NOT install upper oil seal against the inner bore surface of steering gear housing. Oil seals must be installed so each oil seal is separately seated in the shaft bore.

3) Install lower oil seal (double lip seal) and steel washer. Oil seal must be installed only deep enough to allow for steel washer and retaining ring. Lips of both seals should face toward steering gear housing bore. Install retaining ring.

TORQUE SPECIFICATIONS

TORQUE SPECIFICATIONS

Application	Ft. Lbs. (N.m)
Adjuster Plug Lock Nut	85 (115)
Ball Guide Clamp Bolt	10 (14)
Center Link-To-Steering Arm Nut	
Dakota	38 (52)
Pickup & Ramcharger	40 (54)
Drag Link Nut	60 (81)
Flow Control Valve Fitting	40 (54)
Idler Arm-To-Center Link Nut	38 (52)
Idler Arm-To-Frame Bolt	
Dakota	65 (88)
Pickup & Ramcharger	40 (54)
Mounting Studs	35 (48)
Rack Piston End Plug	50 (68)
Sector Shaft Adjuster Screw Lock Nut	20 (27)
Side Cover Bolt	28 (38)
Steering Arm Nut [1]	
Dakota	185 (251)
Pickup & Ramcharger	175 (238)
Steering Gear Housing-To-Frame Bolt	100 (136)
Tie Rod Clamp Bolt	
Dakota	17 (23)
Pickup & Ramcharger	15 (20)
Tie Rod Nut	
2WD Models	40 (54)
4WD Models	60 (81)
Vacuum/Power Steering Pump Assembly-To-Engine Bolts	57 (77)
Vacuum Pump-To-Power Steering Pump Attaching Nuts	18 (24)

[1] – Retaining nut must be staked against pitman arm threads.

1991 TRANSMISSION SERVICING
Automatic Transaxle – FWD

Caravan, Town & Country, Voyager

IDENTIFICATION

TRANSAXLE APPLICATION

Application	Model
2.5L	A-413 3-Speed
3.0L	A-670 3-Speed & A-604 4-Speed
3.3L	A-604 4-Speed

LUBRICATION

SERVICE INTERVALS

Light duty service requires no transaxle servicing. Vehicles subjected to severe heavy-duty conditions should have transaxle serviced (fluid drained and refilled, bands adjusted) every 15,000 miles.

CHECKING FLUID LEVEL

1) Check fluid level with vehicle parked on level surface, engine idling at normal operating temperature for a minimum of 60 seconds and parking brake applied. Move selector lever through all gear ranges, ending in "P".
2) Fluid level should be in WARM crosshatched area of dipstick with transaxle fluid temperature about 100°F (38°C) and in HOT cross-hatched area of dipstick with transaxle temperature about 180°F (82°C). Check condition of fluid for contamination or burned smell.

RECOMMENDED FLUID

It is important that proper lubricant be used in transaxle. Mopar ATF Plus automatic transaxle fluid Type 7176 should be used to aid in assuring optimum transaxle performance. Fluids of the type labeled Dexron-II should be used only if recommended fluid is not available.

FLUID CAPACITIES

NOTE: Transaxle total refill capacities listed in table should only be used as a guide. Correct fluid level should always be determined by marks on dipstick. See DRAINING & REFILLING when performing regular servicing.

TRANSAXLE TOTAL REFILL CAPACITIES [1]

Application	Qts. (L)
A-413 & A-670	8.9 (8.4)
A-604	9.1 (8.6)

[1] – Includes torque converter.

DRAINING & REFILLING

NOTE: Torque converter is not equipped with a drain.

1) Loosen oil pan bolts. Break pan loose by tapping lightly on one corner of pan and allow fluid to drain. Remove pan. Install new filter on bottom of valve body and tighten retaining screws to 40 INCH lbs. (5 N.m). Clean oil pan. Clean magnet (if equipped), and place over boss

121158

Fig. 1: A-413 & A-670 Oil Pan Gasket Identification

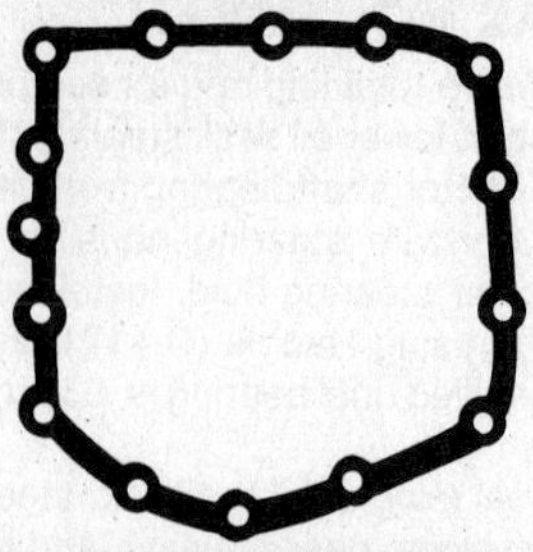

107125

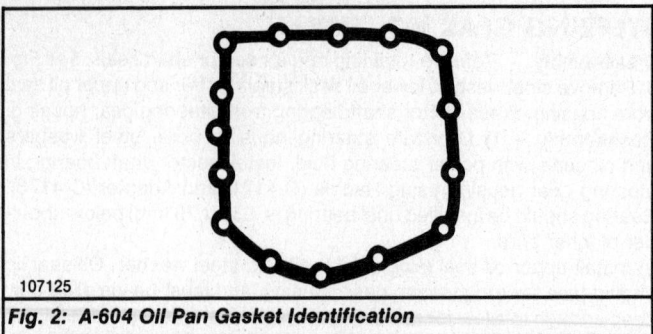

Fig. 2: A-604 Oil Pan Gasket Identification

in right rear corner of pan. Install pan with new gasket. *See Figs. 1 and 2.* Tighten pan bolts to 165 INCH lbs. (19 N.m).

2) Add 4 qts. (3.8L) ATF to transaxle. Start engine and run at idle for at least one minute. Apply parking brake and move shift selector lever through all ranges, ending in "P". Add fluid to 1/8" below middle hole on dipstick. DO NOT overfill. Recheck fluid level when transaxle reaches normal operating temperature.

ADJUSTMENTS

NOTE: The A-604 transaxle does not have any bands.

KICKDOWN (FRONT) BAND

A-413 & A-670 Transaxle – 1) Locate kickdown band adjusting screw on left side (top front) of transaxle case. Loosen adjusting screw lock nut and back off screw 5 turns. Ensure adjusting screw turns freely in case.
2) Using Wrench (C-3380-A) with Adapter (C-3705), tighten adjusting screw to 48 INCH lbs. (5 N.m). If adapter is not used, tighten adjusting screw to 72 INCH lbs. (8 N.m).
3) Back off front adjusting screw 2 1/2 turns. Hold adjusting screw and tighten lock nut to 35 ft. lbs. (47 N.m).

LOW-REVERSE (REAR) BAND

A-413 & A-670 Transaxle – 1) Drain transaxle fluid and remove oil pan. Apply 30 psi (2.1 kg/cm²) air pressure to low-reverse servo and measure gap between band ends. If gap is less than .080" (2.0 mm), band is excessively worn and should be replaced.
2) To adjust band, loosen lock nut approximately 5 turns and tighten adjusting screw to 44 INCH lbs. (5 N.m). Back off adjusting screw 3 1/2 turns. Hold screw in position and tighten lock nut to 10 ft. lbs. (14 N.m).

THROTTLE PRESSURE CABLE

A-413 Transaxle – 1) Start and run engine to normal operating temperature. Loosen adjustment bracket lock screw. Position bracket with both bracket alignment tabs touching transaxle case. Tighten lock screw to 105 INCH lbs. (12 N.m).
2) Release cable assembly cross-lock by pulling upward. Ensure that cable is free to slide all the way toward engine, against its stop, after cross-lock is released. Move throttle lever fully clockwise against its internal stop and press cross-lock downward into locked position. This completes adjustment. Cable backlash is automatically removed.
3) To check cable operation, move transaxle throttle lever forward and release slowly. Ensure cable returns to full rear position.

THROTTLE PRESSURE LINKAGE ROD

A-670 Transaxle – 1) Start and run engine to normal operating temperature. Loosen adjustment swivel lock screw. Ensure that swivel is free to slide along flat end of throttle rod and that preload spring is unrestricted.
2) Hold transaxle throttle lever firmly against its internal stop (toward engine). Tighten swivel screw to 100 INCH lbs. (11 N.m). Linkage rod adjustment is complete. Linkage backlash is removed by preload spring.

1991 TRANSMISSION SERVICING
Automatic Transaxle – FWD (Cont.)

GEARSHIFT LINKAGE

NOTE: If gearshift linkage cable is disconnected from transaxle lever for any reason, always use a new plastic grommet when reassembling linkage.

1) Place shift selector in "P" position. Loosen lock screw on cable adjusting bracket on transaxle.
2) On models with column shift, ensure preload adjusting spring engages fork on transaxle bracket. Move shift lever on transaxle all the way to rear detent ("P") position and hold. Tighten lock screw.
3) On A-413 and A-670 transaxles, tighten lock screw to 105 INCH lbs. (12 N.m). On A-604 transaxle, tighten lock screw to 100 INCH lbs. (11 N.m). To check adjustment, gearshift lever should be within limits of gate stops when shifted through gear positions. Vehicle must only start in Park or Neutral.

NEUTRAL SAFETY SWITCH

A combination neutral safety and back-up light switch is screwed into side of transaxle case. Switch is nonadjustable. Switch may be tested for continuity using following method.

NOTE: Ensure gearshift linkage is properly adjusted before replacing a switch that tests bad.

Testing – 1) With transaxle linkage properly adjusted, switch should allow starter operation in "P" and "N" only. To test switch, remove wire connector and test for continuity between switch center pin and transaxle case. Continuity should exist only when transaxle is in "P" or "N".
2) Check for continuity between 2 outer pins. Continuity should exist with transaxle in "R" position only. There should be no continuity between either outside pin and the transaxle case.
3) To replace neutral safety switch, remove switch from case and allow fluid to drain. Move selector lever to "P" and "N" positions and check that switch operating fingers are centered in switch opening. Install new switch and seal. Tighten to 25 ft. lbs. (34 N.m). Retest switch for continuity and add transaxle fluid as required.

TORQUE SPECIFICATIONS

TORQUE SPECIFICATIONS

Application	Ft. Lbs. (N.m)
Kickdown (Front) Band Adjustment Lock Nut	35 (47)
Neutral Safety Switch	25 (34)
Rear Band Adjustment Lock Nut	10 (14)
	INCH Lbs. (N.m)
Band Adjusting Screws [1]	
Kickdown (Front)	
With Adapter	48 (5)
Without Adapter	72 (8)
Rear [2]	44 (5)
Filter Retaining Screws	40 (5)
Gearshift Linkage Lock Screw	
A-413 & A-670	105 (12)
A-604	100 (11)
Pan Bolts	165 (19)
Throttle Pressure Cable-To-Transaxle Lock Screw	105 (12)
Throttle Pressure Linkage Rod Swivel Screw	100 (11)

[1] – Tighten to specification; then back off 2 1/2 turns.
[2] – Tighten to specification; then back off 3 1/2 turns.

Manual Transmission – RWD

Dakota, Pickup, Ramcharger, RWD Van

IDENTIFICATION

TRANSMISSION/TRANSFER CASE APPLICATION

Application	Transmission
Dakota	NP-2500
Pickup	
D150	NP-435 & NP-2500
D250/350	G-360, NP-435 & NP-2500
W150	NP-435
W250/350	G-360, NP-435 & NP-2500
Ramcharger	NP-435
RWD Van	NP-2500
	Transfer Case
Dakota	NP-231
Pickup	
W150	NP-241
W250/350	NP-205
Ramcharger	NP-241

LUBRICATION

SERVICE INTERVALS

Transmission – Light-duty service requires transmission servicing (fluid drained and refilled) every 37,500 miles. Under normal heavy-duty conditions, service transmission every 36,000 miles. Vehicles subjected to severe heavy-duty conditions should have transmission serviced every 18,000 miles.
Shift Linkage – Gearshift control mechanism should be lubricated every 2 years or 22,500 miles with multipurpose grease. Lubricate if shift effort or noise is apparent.
Transfer Case – Light-duty service requires transfer case servicing (fluid drained and refilled) every 37,500 miles. Under normal heavy-duty conditions, service transmission every 36,000 miles.

CHECKING FLUID LEVEL

Transmission – With vehicle in level position, check lubricant level at filler plug hole on side of transmission. Lubricant should be level with bottom of filler plug hole. Add lubricant as needed to bring to correct level.
Transfer Case – With vehicle in level position remove filler plug and check fluid level. If level is below bottom of filler plug hole, add lubricant to bottom of filler hole.

RECOMMENDED FLUID

Transmission (G-360 5-Speed) – Use API SG or SG-CD SAE 5W-30 engine oil.
Transmission (NP-2500 5-Speed & NP-435 4-Speed) – Use API SG or SG/CD SAE 10W-30 engine oil. Dexron-II ATF may be used if high shift effort is experienced during warm-up in cold weather. Drain 10W-30 engine oil from transmission and refill with Dexron-II ATF.
Transfer Case (NP-205) – Engine oils labeled for API Service SG or SG/CD with a SAE 30 viscosity grade should be used.
Transfer Case (NP-241 & NP-231) – Fluids of the type labeled Mopar ATF Plus type 7176, or Dexron-II are recommended.

FLUID CAPACITIES

REFILL CAPACITIES

Application	Pts. (L)
Transmission	
NP-435 4-Speed & G-360 5-Speed	7.0 (3.3)
NP-2500 5-Speed	4.0 (1.9)
Transfer Case	
NP-205	4.5 (2.1)
NP-231	2.5 (1.2)
NP-241	6.0 (2.8)

1991 TRANSMISSION SERVICING
Automatic Transmission – RWD

Dakota, Pickup, Ramcharger, RWD Van

IDENTIFICATION

TRANSMISSION/TRANSFER CASE APPLICATION

Application	Transmission
Dakota	
3.9L & 5.2L	A-500 4-Speed
Pickup, Ramcharger & RWD Van	
3.9L & 5.2L [1]	A-999 3-Speed & A-500 4-Speed
5.9L Gas & Diesel	A-727 3-Speed & A-518 4-Speed
	Transfer Case
Dakota	NP-231
Pickup	
W150	NP-241
W250/350	NP-205
Ramcharger	NP-241

[1] – Some 5.2L models are equipped with either A-727 3-Speed or A-518 4-Speed

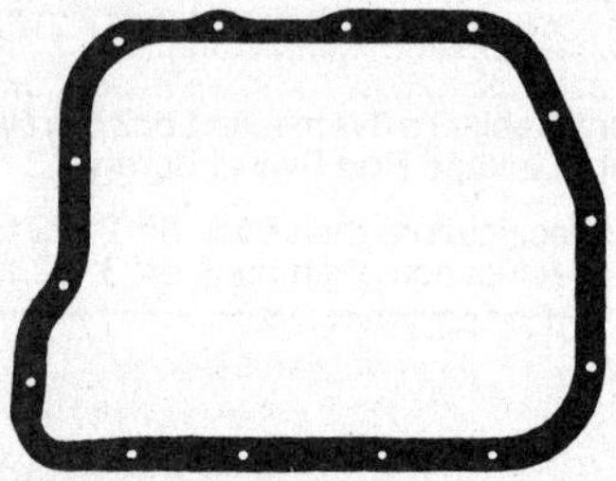
121156

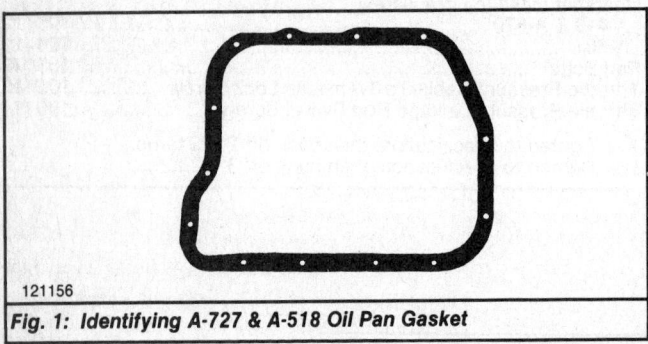

Fig. 1: Identifying A-727 & A-518 Oil Pan Gasket

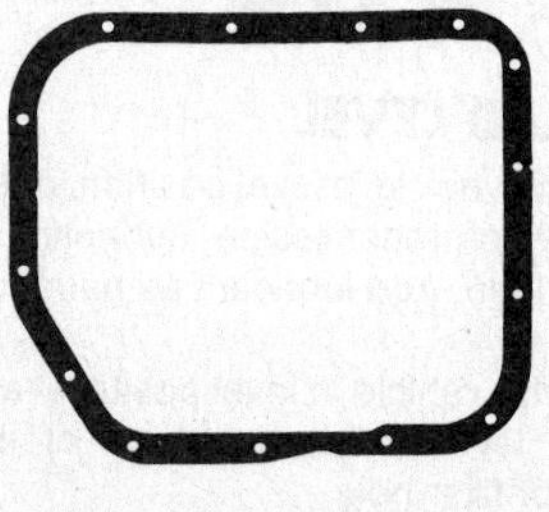
121157

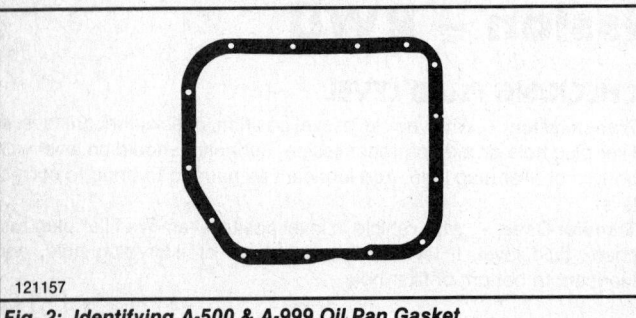

Fig. 2: Identifying A-500 & A-999 Oil Pan Gasket

LUBRICATION

SERVICE INTERVALS

Transmission – Light-duty service requires transmission servicing (fluid drained and refilled, bands adjusted) every 37,500 miles. Under normal heavy-duty conditions, service transmission every 24,000 miles. Vehicles subjected to severe heavy-duty conditions should have transmission serviced every 12,000 miles.

Transfer Case – Light-duty service requires transfer case servicing (fluid drained and refilled) every 37,500 miles. Under normal heavy-duty conditions, service transmission every 36,000 miles.

CHECKING FLUID LEVEL

Transmission – **1)** Check fluid level with vehicle parked on level surface, engine idling at normal operating temperature and parking brake applied. Move selector lever through all gear ranges, ending in "N".

2) Fluid level when warm, 85-125°F (29-52°C), should be between 2 dimples on dipstick. Fluid level when hot, 180°F (82°C), should be in the "OK" crosshatched area of dipstick. Check condition of fluid for contamination or burned smell.

Transfer Case – With vehicle in level position, remove filler plug and check fluid level. Add lubricant If level is below bottom of filler plug hole.

RECOMMENDED FLUID

Transmission – It is important that the proper lubricant be used in transmission. Mopar ATF Plus automatic transmission fluid Type 7176 should be used. Fluids of the type labeled Dexron-II should be used only if the recommended fluid is not available.

Transfer Case (NP-205) – Engine oils labeled for API Service SG or SG/CD with a SAE 30 viscosity grade should be used.

Transfer Case (NP-241 & NP-231) – Fluids of the type labeled Mopar ATF Plus type 7176, or Dexron-II are recommended.

FLUID CAPACITIES

NOTE: Use capacities listed in TOTAL REFILL CAPACITIES table only as a guide. Correct fluid level should always be determined by marks on dipstick. Capacities listed are total system capacity including torque converter. See DRAINING & REFILLING when performing regular servicing.

TOTAL REFILL CAPACITIES

Application	Qts. (L)
Transmission [1]	
A-500	10.2 (9.6)
A-518	8.42 (7.9)
A-727	8.4 (7.9)
A-999	8.6 (8.1)
	Pts. (L)
Transfer Case	
NP-205	4.5 (2.4)
NP-231	2.5 (1.2)
NP-241	6.0 (2.8)

[1] – Includes torque converter.

DRAINING & REFILLING

NOTE: Converter is not equipped with a drain. No attempt should be made to drain torque converter.

Transmission – **1)** Raise and support vehicle. Loosen oil pan bolts. Tap lightly on one corner of pan to break loose, and allow fluid to drain. Remove pan. Install new filter on bottom of valve body. Torque filter retaining screws to 35 INCH lbs. (4 N.m).

2) Clean oil pan. Ensure magnet (if equipped) is over boss in right front corner of pan. Install pan with new gasket. Torque oil pan bolts to 150 INCH lbs. (17 N.m).

3) Refill transmission with 4 qts. (3.8L) of recommended fluid. See RECOMMENDED FLUID. Start engine and allow to run at idle for at least 2 minutes. With engine at curb idle and parking brake applied, move shift selector lever through all ranges, ending in "N".

4) Add fluid up to 2 dimples on dipstick. DO NOT overfill. Recheck fluid level when transmission reaches normal operating temperature. See CHECKING FLUID LEVEL.

Transfer Case – Raise and support vehicle. Position drain pan under transfer case. Remove drain and fill plugs. Drain lubricant. Install drain plug. Tighten drain plug to 40 ft. lbs. (54 N.m). Remove drain pan. Using recommended lubricant, fill transfer case to bottom edge of fill plug opening. See RECOMMENDED FLUID. Lower vehicle.

ADJUSTMENTS

KICKDOWN (FRONT) BAND

1) Locate kickdown band adjusting screw on left side of transmission case, near throttle lever shaft. *See Fig. 3.* Loosen adjusting screw lock nut and back off screw 5 turns. Ensure adjusting screw turns freely in case.
2) Using Wrench (C-3380-A) with Adapter (C-3705), tighten adjusting screw to 48 INCH lbs. (5 N.m). If adapter is not used, tighten adjusting screw to 72 INCH lbs. (8 N.m).
3) Back off front adjusting screw 2 1/2 turns. Hold adjusting screw in position and tighten lock nut to 35 ft. lbs. (47 N.m).

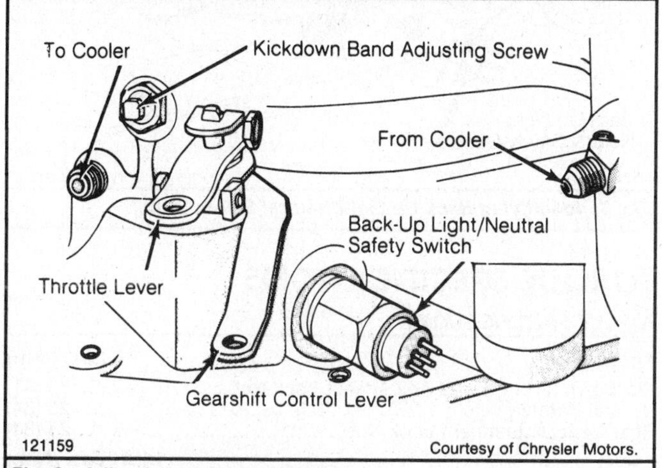

To Cooler
Kickdown Band Adjusting Screw
From Cooler
Back-Up Light/Neutral Safety Switch
Throttle Lever
Gearshift Control Lever
121159
Courtesy of Chrysler Motors.

Fig. 3: Adjusting Kickdown Band

LOW-REVERSE (REAR) BAND

1) Drain transmission and remove oil pan. Locate low-reverse band adjusting screw on rear servo lever. *See Fig. 4.* Loosen adjusting screw lock nut and back off screw about 5 turns. Ensure screw turns freely in lever. Using Wrench (C-3380-A), tighten adjusting screw to 72 INCH lbs. (8 N.m).
2) Back off rear adjusting screw specified number of turns. See LOW-REVERSE (REAR) BAND ADJUSTMENT table. Hold adjusting screw in position and tighten lock nut to 35 ft. lbs. (47 N.m). Clean oil pan, install new gasket with pan and fill transmission with fluid. See DRAINING & REFILLING under LUBRICATION.

LOW-REVERSE (REAR) BAND ADJUSTMENT

Application	Back Off Screw
A-727	2 Turns
A-999	4 Turns

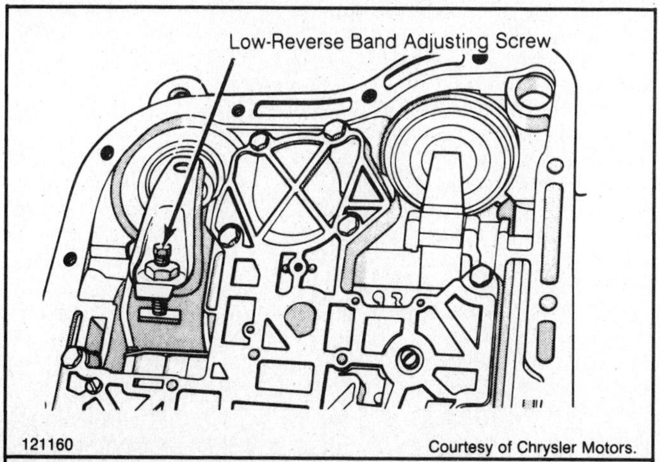

Low-Reverse Band Adjusting Screw
121160
Courtesy of Chrysler Motors.

Fig. 4: Locating Low-Reverse Band Adjusting Screw

THROTTLE PRESSURE CABLE

NOTE: A .180" (4.57 mm) diameter gauge is required to check and adjust throttle pressure cable on diesel models. Use a drill of correct diameter or fabricate gauge from metal stock.

A-727 (5.9L Diesel) – 1) Start engine and let it warm to operating temperature. Adjust idle speed if necessary. Using gauge, check clearance between rear of cable actuating pin and end of slot in throttle pressure cable.
2) Clearance should be .180" (4.57 mm). If clearance is okay, cable adjustment is correct. If clearance is not as specified, proceed to next step.
3) Release cable lock pawl. Insert gauge between cable actuating pin and end of slot in cable. Slide cable forward or rearward to obtain specified clearance. Press cable lock pawl down until it snaps into locked position. Recheck clearance.

THROTTLE PRESSURE LINKAGE ROD

Except A-727 (5.9L Diesel) – 1) Start engine and let it warm to operating temperature. Retract Idle Speed Control (ISC) actuator with Chrysler's Diagnostic Readout Box (DRB-II), or with jumper wires. If DRB-II is not available, go to step **3)**. If DRB-II is used, connect tester to diagnostic connector in engine compartment.
2) Start engine and place DRB-II in THROTTLE BODY MINIMUM AIR-FLOW test. Disconnect electrical connector on ISC actuator. Turn engine off and disconnect DRB-II tester. DO NOT leave DRB-II connected to diagnostic connector. Actuator is now fully retracted and transmission throttle rod may be adjusted. Go to step **4)**.
3) If DRB-II is not available and jumper wires are used, turn engine off. Disconnect electrical connector at ISC actuator. Connect one jumper wire between negative battery terminal and top pin on ISC actuator. Connect other jumper wire between positive battery terminal and second pin on ISC actuator. Disconnect jumper wires after 5 seconds. ISC actuator is now fully retracted. Go to next step.
4) Raise and support vehicle. Loosen swivel lock screw. *See Fig. 5.* Ensure swivel is free to slide along flat end of throttle rod so preload spring action is not restricted. Disassemble and clean parts to assure free action, if necessary.
5) Hold transmission lever firmly forward against internal stop and tighten swivel lock screw. Adjustment is complete. Linkage backlash is automatically removed by preload spring.
6) Lower vehicle. Reconnect ISC actuator electrical connector. Reposition ISC actuator for normal operation. Turn ignition on for a minimum of 5 seconds. DO NOT start engine. Turn ignition off. Actuator is now positioned for normal operation.

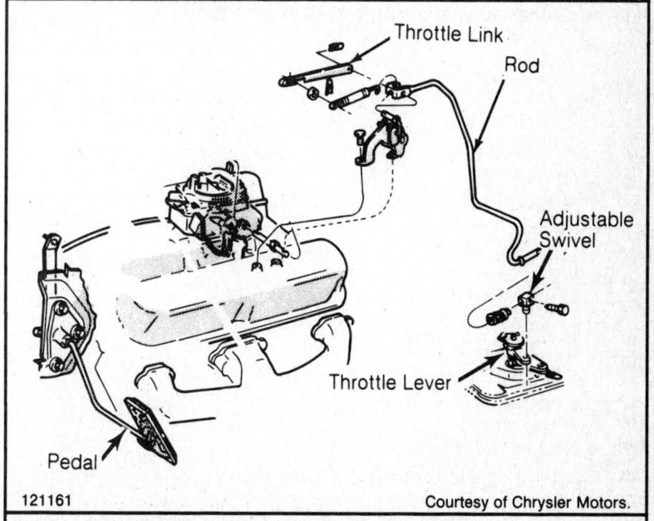

Throttle Link
Rod
Adjustable Swivel
Throttle Lever
Pedal
121161
Courtesy of Chrysler Motors.

Fig. 5: Adjusting Throttle Pressure Linkage Rod

1991 TRANSMISSION SERVICING
Automatic Transmission – RWD (Cont.)

GEARSHIFT LINKAGE

1) With column shift lever in "P" position, loosen adjustable swivel lock screw. *See Fig. 6.* Ensure swivel is free to move on shift rod. Disassemble and clean components if required.

2) Move shift lever on transmission to full rear detent ("P") position and tighten swivel lock screw. When linkage is properly adjusted, detent positions for "N" and "D" will be within limits of shift lever gate stops and engine will start only in "P" or "N".

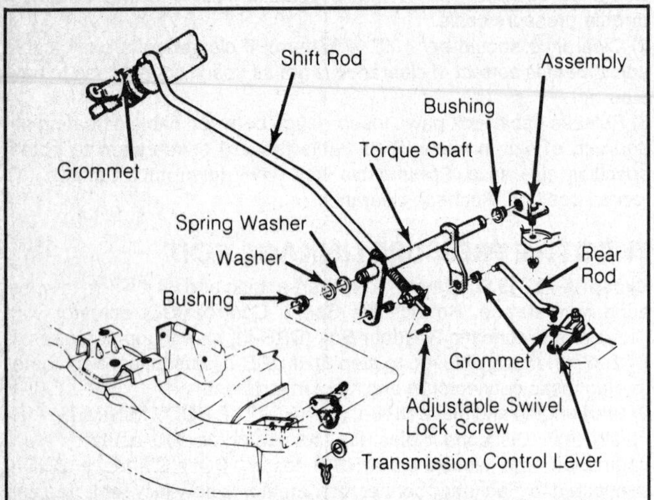
Shift Rod
Assembly
Bushing
Torque Shaft
Grommet
Spring Washer
Washer
Rear
Rod
Bushing
Grommet
Adjustable Swivel
Lock Screw
Transmission Control Lever
121162
Courtesy of Chrysler Motors.

Fig. 6: Adjusting Column Shift Linkage

NEUTRAL SAFETY SWITCH

A combination neutral safety and back-up light switch is screwed into side of transmission case. Switch is not adjustable. Switch may be tested for continuity using following method.

NOTE: Before replacing a switch that tests bad, ensure gearshift linkage is properly adjusted.

Testing – 1) With transmission linkage properly adjusted, switch should allow starter operation in "P" and "N" only. To test switch, remove wire connector. Using an ohmmeter, test for continuity between center pin of switch and case. Continuity should exist only with transmission in "P" or "N".

2) Check for continuity between 2 outer pins. Continuity should exist with transmission in Reverse, only. There should be no continuity between either outside pin or transmission case.

3) To replace neutral safety switch, remove switch from case and allow fluid to drain. Move selector lever to "P" and "N" positions and check that switch operating fingers are centered in switch opening. Install new switch and seal. Tighten to 25 ft. lbs. (34 N.m). Retest switch for continuity and add transmission fluid.

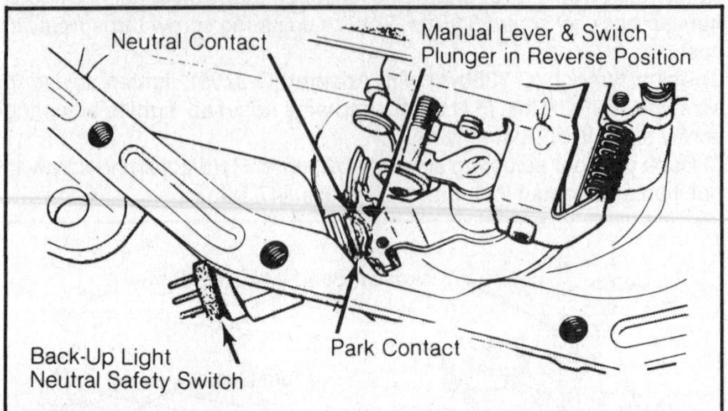
Neutral Contact
Manual Lever & Switch
Plunger in Reverse Position
Back-Up Light
Neutral Safety Switch
Park Contact
121163
Courtesy of Chrysler Motors.

Fig. 7: Identifying Back-Up Light/Neutral Safety Switch

TORQUE SPECIFICATIONS

TORQUE SPECIFICATIONS

Application	Ft. Lbs. (N.m)
Kickdown (Front) Band Adjustment Lock Nut	30 (41)
Neutral Safety Switch	25 (34)
Rear Band Adjustment Lock Nut	25 (34)
	INCH Lbs. (N.m)
Band Adjusting Screws [1]	
Kickdown (Front)	
With Adapter	48 (5)
Without Adapter	72 (8)
Low-Reverse (Rear) [2]	44 (5)
Filter Retaining Screws	35 (4)
Gearshift Linkage Lock Screw	90 (10)
Pan Bolts	150 (17)
Throttle Pressure Linkage Rod Swivel Screw	90 (10)

[1] – Tighten to specification; then back off 2 1/2 turns.
[2] – Tighten to specification; then back off 2 turns on A-727 or 4 turns on A-999.

1991 TRANSMISSION SERVICING
Transaxle Removal & Installation – FWD

Caravan, Town & Country, Voyager

POWER TRANSFER UNIT (PTU)

Removal & Installation – 1) Raise and support vehicle. Remove front wheel assemblies. Remove propeller shaft. Remove crossmember bridge attaching bolts. Remove power steering hose bracket attaching bolt. Using tie wraps, secure steering gear assembly to frame rails.
2) Disconnect ball joints from steering knuckles. Remove lower transaxle-to-crossmember strut bolt. Support crossmember with suitable transmission jack. Remove crossmember attaching bolts and remove crossmember from vehicle.
3) Remove right front drive axle. Remove PTU support bracket and strut assembly. Remove rear PTU brace attaching bolts. Remove speed sensor. Remove PTU remote vent from left engine mount Remove 4 PTU mounting bolts and remove PTU. To install PTU, reverse removal procedure.

AUTOMATIC TRANSAXLE

NOTE: Transaxle removal does not require engine removal.

CAUTION: Transaxle and torque converter must be removed as an assembly to avoid damage to torque converter drive plate, pump bushing or oil seal. Transaxle weight should not be allowed to rest on drive plate during removal.

Removal & Installation – 1) Disconnect negative battery cable. Disconnect throttle linkage and shift linkage from transaxle. Remove upper and lower oil cooler hoses. Support engine using engine support fixture. Remove bellhousing upper bolts.
2) Remove wheel hub cotter pin, nut lock and spring washer. Loosen hub nut and wheel nuts with vehicle on ground. Raise and support vehicle. Remove hub nut, washer and tire.
3) Remove speedometer adapter and pinion as an assembly. Remove ball joint-to-steering knuckle clamp bolt.
4) Separate ball joint stud from steering knuckle by prying against knuckle leg and control arm. Separate outer Constant Velocity (CV) joint splined shaft from hub by holding CV housing while moving knuckle (hub) assembly away.

CAUTION: DO NOT pull on shaft when removing drive shaft assembly.

5) Support drive shaft at CV joint housings. Remove drive shaft by pulling outward on inner joint CV joint housing. DO NOT pull on shaft. Remove left splash shield.
6) Remove torque converter dust cover. Mark torque converter and drive plate for installation reference. Remove torque converter mounting bolts. Remove access plug in right splash shield to rotate engine crankshaft.
7) Disconnect neutral safety switch. Remove engine mount bracket from front crossmember. Remove front mount insulator through-bolt and bellhousing bolts. Position transmission jack under transaxle. Remove left engine mount. Remove starter. Remove lower bellhousing bolts.
8) Attach a small "C" clamp to edge of bellhousing to hold torque converter in place during transaxle removal. Slowly lower transaxle.
9) To install, reverse removal procedure. Adjust gearshift and throttle cables. Torque all nuts and bolts to specification. Refill transaxle with Mopar ATF Plus Type 7176 or if not available, use Dexron-II automatic transmission fluid.

TORQUE SPECIFICATIONS

TORQUE SPECIFICATIONS

Application	Ft. Lbs. (N.m)
Ball Joint-To-Steering Knuckle Clamp Bolt	70 (95)
Crossmember-To-Frame Bolts & Nuts	90 (122)
Drive Plate-To-Crankshaft Bolts	70 (95)
Drive Plate-To-Torque Converter Bolts	40 (54)
Front Motor Mount Bolts	40 (54)
Hub Nut	180 (245)
Left Motor Mount Bolts	40 (54)
Manual Cable-To-Transaxle Case Bolts	21 (28)
PTU-To-Transaxle attaching Bolts	21 (28)
Starter-To-Transaxle Bellhousing Bolts	40 (54)
Transaxle-To-Cylinder Block Bolts	70 (95)
Wheel Lug Nuts	95 (129)
	INCH Lbs. (N.m)
Bellhousing Cover Bolts	108 (12)
Lower Bellhousing Cover Bolts	108 (12)
Manual Control Lever Bolts	108 (12)
Power Steering Line Bracket Bolt	70 (8)
Speedometer-To-Extension Bolts	60 (7)
Throttle Cable-To-Transaxle Case Bolts	108 (12)
Throttle Lever-To-Transaxle Shaft Bolts	108 (12)

1991 TRANSMISSION SERVICING
Transmission Removal & Installation – RWD

Dakota, Pickup, Ramcharger, RWD Van

MANUAL TRANSMISSION

NOTE: For manual transmission replacement procedures, see appropriate CLUTCHES article.

TRANSFER CASE (A/T)

MODEL NP-205

Removal – 1) Raise and support vehicle. Drain transfer case. Disconnect speedometer cable (if equipped). Mark front and rear propeller shaft yokes for installation reference. Disconnect propeller shaft at transfer case and support to one side. Disconnect shift lever rod from shift rail link.

CAUTION: DO NOT allow propeller shaft to hang free, as damage to universal joints may result.

2) Support transfer case with transmission jack. Remove transfer case-to-transmission adapter bolts and nuts. Move transfer case to rear until input shaft clears adapter. Lower transfer case from vehicle.
Installation – To install transfer case, reverse removal procedure. Torque all nuts and bolts to specification. See TORQUE SPECIFICATIONS table. With vehicle in level position, remove filler plug and add lubricant until fluid level reaches bottom of filler hole. Use engine oil labeled API Service SG or SG/CD SAE 30 viscosity grade.

MODELS NP-231 & NP-241

Removal – 1) Raise and support vehicle. Drain transfer case. Mark front and rear output shaft yokes and propeller shaft for installation reference. Disconnect speedometer cable (if equipped) and vacuum switch hoses.
2) Disconnect shift lever link from operating lever. Support transfer case with transmission jack. Remove crossmember. Disconnect front and rear propeller shaft yokes and support to one side.
3) Remove transfer case-to-transmission nuts. Move transfer case assembly to rear until clear of transmission output shaft. Lower transfer case from vehicle. Remove all gasket material from rear of transmission adapter housing.
Installation – 1) Install new transmission-to-transfer case gasket with sealer on both sides. Align transfer case with transmission. Rotate transfer case output shaft until transmission output shaft engages transfer case input shaft.
2) Move transfer case until case seats flush against transmission. Install transfer case attaching bolts. To complete installation, reverse removal procedure. With vehicle in level position, remove filler plug and add lubricant until fluid level reaches bottom of filler hole.
3) Use Mopar ATF Plus type 7176, or Dexron-II transmission fluid. Torque all nuts and bolts to specification. See TORQUE SPECIFICATIONS table.

OVERDRIVE UNIT

Removal & Installation – 1) Shift transmission to Park. Raise and support vehicle. Remove transmission pan. Drain fluid. Reinstall pan.

NOTE: If overdrive unit has failed or fluid is contaminated, remove entire transmission. If clutch or governor problems exist, remove only overdrive unit.

2) Mark propeller shaft(s) for installation reference. Remove propeller shaft(s). Remove transfer case (if equipped). See TRANSFER CASE. Remove overdrive unit attaching bolts.
3) Carefully pull overdrive unit off intermediate shaft. Remove and retain overdrive piston thrust bearing. Bearing may be located on piston or in clutch hub. To install overdrive unit, reverse removal procedure.

AUTOMATIC TRANSMISSION

CAUTION: Transmission and converter must be removed and installed as an assembly to prevent damage to converter drive plate, front pump bushing, and oil seal. DO NOT allow weight of transmission to rest on drive plate during removal or installation.

Removal – 1) Remove transfer case from 4WD vehicles. See TRANSFER CASE. Disconnect negative battery cable. Disconnect and lower exhaust system as needed for removal clearance. Remove engine-to-transmission struts (if equipped). Disconnect cooler lines at transmission. Remove starter, cooler line bracket and converter access cover.

NOTE: Crankshaft flange bolt circle, inner and outer circle of holes in drive plate and tapped holes in converter all have one hole offset so parts can only be installed in original position.

2) Loosen oil pan bolts. Tap pan to break loose and allow fluid to drain. Reinstall pan. Mark torque converter and drive plate for installation reference. Rotate crankshaft clockwise with socket on vibration damper bolt to access converter-to-drive plate bolts. Remove bolts. Mark propeller shaft for installation reference. Remove from vehicle.
3) Disconnect wiring connector from back-up light/neutral safety switch. Disconnect gearshift rod and torque shaft assembly from transmission. Disconnect transmission throttle rod from lever. Remove linkage bellcrank assembly (if equipped). Remove oil filler tube. Disconnect speedometer cable if equipped.
4) Install engine support fixture under rear of engine. Raise transmission with service jack to relieve load on supports. Remove bolts securing crossmember to transmission and frame. Remove crossmember. Remove all converter housing-to-engine attaching bolts.
5) Carefully work transmission and converter assembly rearward off engine block dowel pins, disengaging converter hub from end of crankshaft. Attach a small "C" clamp on edge of converter housing to hold converter in place while transmission is being removed. Lower transmission and remove from vehicle.
Inspection – 1) Before installing converter, rotate front pump rotors with Aligner (C-3881) until 2 holes in tool handle are vertical. Slide torque converter over input and reaction shafts. Ensure converter hub slots are vertical and fully engage pump inner rotor lugs.
2) Test for full engagement by placing a straightedge across face of transmission case. Surface of converter front cover lug should be at least 1/2" to rear of straightedge when converter is fully engaged. Attach small "C" clamp to edge of converter housing to hold converter in place while installing transmission.
3) Inspect converter drive plate for distortion or cracks and replace if necessary. Install drive plate and tighten bolts to specification.
Installation – 1) Coat converter hub hole in crankshaft with multipurpose grease. Place transmission assembly on jack and position under vehicle. Make sure marks on converter and drive plate (made during removal) are aligned.
2) Carefully work transmission assembly into position over dowels. Install all converter housing-to-engine bolts and tighten to specification.
3) To complete installation, reverse removal procedure. Adjust shift and throttle linkages and fill transmission with fluid. Use Mopar ATF Plus Type 7176 or Dexron-II automatic transmission fluid. On 4WD models, install transfer case.

TORQUE SPECIFICATIONS

TORQUE SPECIFICATIONS

Application	Ft. Lbs. (N.m)
Converter Drive Plate-To-Engine Bolts	55 (75)
Converter-To-Drive Plate Bolts	23 (31)
Converter Housing-To-Engine Bolts	30 (41)
Cooler Line Fitting	13 (18)
Drain & Fill Plugs	40 (54)
Oil Pan Bolts	12 (17)
Overdrive Unit-To-Transmission Bolts	25 (34)
Propeller Shaft Clamp Bolts (1/4")	14 (19)
Propeller Shaft Clamp Bolts (5/16")	25 (34)
Transfer Case-To-Transmission Bolts	40 (54)

FORD MOTOR CO.

1991 FORD MOTOR CO. CONTENTS

GENERAL INFORMATION [1]

[1] – For all GENERAL INFORMATION, see front of this manual.

ENGINE PERFORMANCE

ENGINE PERFORMANCE (Cont.)

ENGINE PERFORMANCE (Cont.)

PIN VOLTAGE CHARTS

SENSOR OPERATING RANGE CHARTS

WIRING DIAGRAMS

VACUUM DIAGRAMS

REMOVAL, OVERHAUL & INSTALLATION

ELECTRICAL

ALTERNATORS – WITH INTERNAL REGULATOR

ALTERNATORS – LEECE/NEVILLE 165-AMP

ALTERNATORS – WITH EXTERNAL REGULATOR

ALTERNATORS – WITH INTERNAL FAN & REGULATOR

STARTERS – MOTORCRAFT GEAR REDUCTION

STARTERS – MOTORCRAFT POSITIVE ENGAGEMENT

1991 FORD MOTOR CO. CONTENTS (Cont.)

ELECTRICAL (Cont.)

STARTERS – MITSUBISHI GEAR REDUCTION Page

WIRING DIAGRAMS

CHASSIS WIRING DIAGRAMS

SAFETY EQUIPMENT

INSTRUMENT PANELS

REAR WINDOW DEFOGGER

STEERING COLUMN SWITCHES

SAFETY EQUIPMENT (Cont.)

WIPER/WASHER SYSTEMS

Page

ENGINES

2.3L 4-CYLINDER

2.9L V6

3.0L V6

ENGINES (Cont.)

ENGINE COOLING

CLUTCHES

DRIVE AXLES

1991 FORD MOTOR CO. CONTENTS (Cont.)

DRIVE AXLES (Cont.)

DRIVE AXLES (Cont.)

BRAKES

WHEEL ALIGNMENT

1991 FORD MOTOR CO. CONTENTS (Cont.)

SUSPENSION

STEERING

STEERING (Cont.)

TRANSMISSION SERVICING

1991 ENGINE PERFORMANCE
Ford Motor Co. Introduction

1991 MODEL COVERAGE

MODEL	ENGINE	ENGINE ID	FUEL SYSTEM	IGNITION SYSTEM
Aerostar	3.0L	U	PFI	TFI-IV
	4.0L	X	MA PFI	EDIS
Bronco	4.9L	Y	PFI	TFI-IV
	5.0L	N	PFI	TFI-IV
	5.8L	H	PFI	TFI-IV
"E" Series Van (E150/350)	4.9L	Y	PFI	TFI-IV
	5.0L	N	PFI	TFI-IV
	5.8L	H	PFI	TFI-IV
	[1] 7.3L	M	Diesel	
	7.5L	G	PFI	TFI-IV
Explorer	4.0L	X	MA PFI	EDIS
"F" Series Pickup (F150/350)	4.9L	Y	PFI	TFI-IV
	5.0L	N	PFI	TFI-IV
	5.8L	H	PFI	TFI-IV
	[1] 7.3L	M	Diesel	
	7.5L	G	PFI	TFI-IV
Ranger	2.3L	A	PFI	DIS
	2.9L	T	MA PFI	TFI-IV
	3.0L	U	MA PFI	TFI-IV
	4.0L	X	MA PFI	EDIS

[1] – Available only with F250 Heavy Duty, F350 and E350.

VIN DEFINITION

1 F T B F 2 5 X 5 M L A 0 0 0 0 1
① ② ③ ④ ⑤ ⑥ ⑦ ⑧ ⑨ ⑩ ⑪ ⑫ ⑬ ⑭ ⑮ ⑯ ⑰

①②③ Indicates Manufacturer, Make and Type.
④ Indicates Brake System/GVWR Class.
⑤⑥⑦ Indicates Model or Line.
⑧ **Indicates Engine Code.**
⑨ Indicates Check Digit.
⑩ **Indicates Model Year.**
⑪ Indicates Assembly Plant.
⑫ Constant A.
⑬⑭⑮⑯⑰ Indicates Plant Sequential Number.

MODEL YEAR VIN CODE APPLICATION

VIN Code	Model Year
K	1989
L	1990
M	1991

ENGINE CODE LOCATION

NOTE: Emission calibration number label is located on driver's door or door post pillar as well as engine. It also identifies engine code number and revision number. Engine code and calibration number may be needed when ordering parts.

ENGINE CODE LOCATION

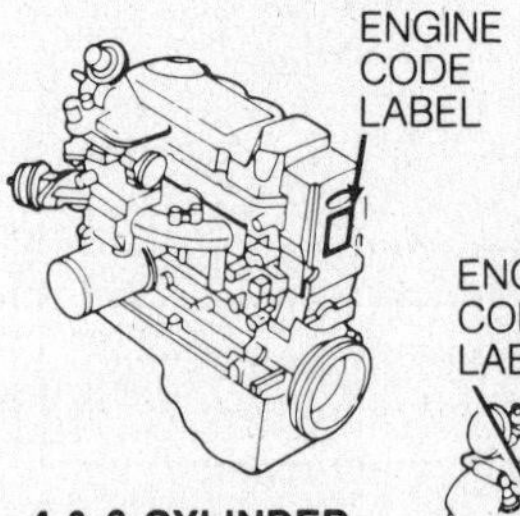
ENGINE
CODE
LABEL

4 & 6-CYLINDER

ENGINE
CODE
LABEL

V6

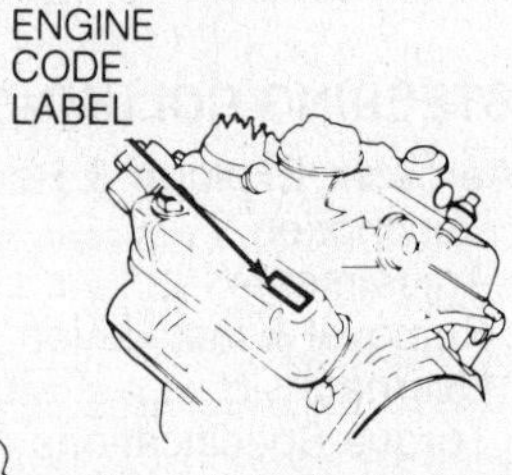
ENGINE
CODE
LABEL

V8

90J14448 90E10037 90F10038

Courtesy of Ford Motor Co.

1991 ENGINE PERFORMANCE
Emission Applications

1991 FORD MOTOR CO.

Engine & Fuel System	Emission Control Systems & Devices	Remarks
Light Duty		
2.3L (140") 4-Cyl. MA PFI	**PCV, EVAP, TWC, EGR** [1], **AP, O_2, CEC,** AP-BPV	[1] - M/T only.
2.9L (177") V6 PFI	**PCV, EVAP, TWC, AP, O_2, CEC,** AP-BPV	
3.0L (183") V6 MA PFI	**PCV, EVAP, TWC, AP, O_2, CEC,** AP-BPV	
3.0L (183") V6 PFI	**PCV, EVAP, TWC, AP, O_2, CEC,** AP-BPV	
4.0L (244") V6 MA PFI	**PCV, EVAP, TWC, AP, O_2, CEC,** AP-BPV	
4.9L (300") 6-Cyl. PFI	**PCV, EVAP, TWC/OC, EGR, AP, O_2, CEC,** EGR-EVR	
5.0L (302") V8 PFI	**PCV, EVAP, TWC/OC, EGR, AP, O_2, CEC,** AP-BPV, EGR-EVR	
5.8L (351") V8 PFI	**PCV, EVAP, TWC, EGR, AP, O_2, CEC**	
Heavy Duty		
4.9L (300") 6-Cyl. PFI	**PCV, EVAP, TWC/OC, EGR, AP, O_2, CEC,** AP-BPV, EGR-EVR	
5.8L (351") V8 PFI	**PCV, EVAP, EGR, AP, O_2, CEC,** AP-BPV, EGR-EVR	
7.3L (446") V8 Diesel	**PCV**	
7.5L (460") V8 PFI	**PCV, EVAP, OC, EGR, AP, O_2, CEC,** EGR-EVR	

NOTE: Major emission control systems are listed in bold type; components are listed in light type.

AP-BPV - Air By-Pass Valve
AP - Air Pump
CEC - Computerized Engine Control
EGR - Exhaust Gas Recirculation
EGR-EVR - EGR Electronic Vacuum Regulator
EVAP - Fuel Evaporative System
MA PFI - Mass Air PFI
M/T - Manual Transmission
OC - Oxidation Catalyst
O_2 - Oxygen Sensor
PCV - Positive Crankcase Ventilation
PFI - Port Fuel Injection
TWC - Three-Way Catalyst
TWC/OC - Three-Way Catalyst/Oxidation Catalyst

1991 ENGINE PERFORMANCE
Service & Adjustment Specifications

Aerostar, Bronco, Explorer, Ranger, "E" & "F" Series, "F" Series Super Duty

NOTE: Unless otherwise specified, references to "F" Series include "F" Series Super Duty. For engine repair procedures not covered in this article, see ENGINE OVERHAUL PROCEDURES article in GENERAL INFORMATION.

INTRODUCTION

Use this article to find specifications related to servicing and on-vehicle adjustments. This article may be used as a quick reference when you are familiar with proper adjustment procedures but need a specification.

CAPACITIES

AXLE CAPACITIES

Application	Pts. (L)
Aerostar	
Front	2.2 (1.0)
Rear	
7.5" Ford [1]	[2] 3.5 (1.65)
8.8" Ford [1]	[2] 5.0 (2.4)
Bronco	
Front	3.8 (1.8)
Rear (8.8" Ford [1])	[2] 5.5 (2.6)
Explorer	
Front (Dana 35)	3.5 (1.65)
Rear (8.8" Ford [1])	[2] 5.5 (2.6)
Ranger	
Front	
Dana 28	1.1 (.5)
Dana 35	3.5 (1.65)
Rear	
7.5" & 8.8" Ford [1]	[2] 5.0 (2.4)
"E" Series	
Rear	
8.8" Ford [1]	[2]5.5 (2.6)
9.75" Dana M60-1U	6.3 (3.0)
10.5" Dana M70-2U	6.6 (3.1)
"F" Series	
Front	
Dana 44-IFS L.D.	3.6 (1.7)
Dana 50-IFS H.D.	3.8 (1.8)
Dana 60 Monobeam	5.8 (2.8)
Rear	
8.8" Ford	5.5 (2.6)
10.25" Ford [3]	7.5 (3.5)
11.25" Dana 80	8.3 (3.9)

[1] – Conventional and Traction-Lok.
[2] – Add 4 oz. Friction Modifier for Traction-Lok Axles.
[3] – Conventional and Traction-Lok, Semi and Full Float.

BATTERY SPECIFICATIONS

Application & Group	Amp Hr. Rating
Aerostar, Bronco, Explorer & "F" Series	
Standard BXT-65	650
Optional BXT-65	850
Ranger	
Regular Cab 2.3, 2.9L & 3.0L BX-58C	N/A
Optional BXT-65	650
Regular Cab 4.0L BXT-65	650
Optional BXT-65	850
Super Cab All Engines BXT-65	650
Optional BXT-65	850
"E" Series	
Standard BXT-64A	N/A
Auxiliary BH-27A	N/A

COOLING SYSTEM CAPACITIES

Application	Qts. (L)
Aerostar, Explorer & Ranger	
2.3L	
Manual or Automatic Transmission	7.2 (6.8)
2.9L	
Manual or Automatic Transmission [1]	7.2 (6.8)
Manual or Automatic Transmission [2]	7.8 (7.4)
3.0L	
Manual or Automatic Transmission	11.8 (11.2)
4.0L	
Automatic Transmission [2 3]	8.5 (8.0)
Manual or Automatic Transmission [1]	8.1 (7.6)
Bronco & "F" Series	
4.9L	
Manual or Automatic Transmission [1]	13 (12)
Manual Transmission [4]	14 (13)
Manual Transmission [2 3]	15 (14)
Automatic Transmission [2 5]	15 (14)
Automatic Transmission [5]	14 (13)
5.0L	
Manual Transmission [1]	13 (12)
Automatic Transmission [1]	14 (13)
Manual or Automatic Transmission [2]	14 (13)
Manual or Automatic Transmission [3]	15 (14)
5.8L	
Manual Transmission [1]	15 (14)
Automatic Transmission [1]	16 (15)
Manual or Automatic Transmission [2]	16 (15)
Manual or Automatic Transmission [3]	17 (16)
7.3L	[6] 29 (27)
7.5L	18 (17)
"E" Series	
4.9L	
Manual or Automatic Transmission [1]	15 (14)
Manual or Automatic Transmission [4]	18 (17)
5.0L	
Manual or Automatic Transmission [1 2]	17.5 (16.6)
Manual or Automatic Transmission [3]	18.5 (17.5)
5.8L	
Manual or Automatic Transmission [1]	20 (19)
Manual or Automatic Transmission [4]	21 (20)
7.3L	[6] 31 (29)
7.5L	28 (26)

[1] – With Standard Cooling.
[2] – With A/C.
[3] – With Super Cooling.
[4] – With A/C or Super Cooling.
[5] – With Standard or Super Cooling.
[6] – Include 5 qts. (4.7L) in reservoir bottle.

CRANKCASE CAPACITIES

Application	[1] Qts. (L)
All Engines Except 3.0L & 7.3L	[2] 5.0 (4.7)
3.0L	4.5 (4.25)
7.3L	10.0 (9.5)

[1] – Add 1/2 qt. if equipped with oil cooler.
[2] – "F" Series, 6 qts. (5.6L).

1991 ENGINE PERFORMANCE
Service & Adjustment Specifications (Cont.)

TRANSMISSION & TRANSFER CASE CAPACITIES

Application	Specification	Quantity
Aerostar		
A4LD Auto.	Mercon	9.7 qts. (9.2L)
E4WD Auto.	Mercon	10.0 qts. (9.5L)
5-Speed Overdrive (Mazda R-1)	Mercon	5.6 pts. (2.65L)
Transfer Case (TC-28 Dana)	Mercon	4.5 qts. (4.3L)
Bronco		
AOD Auto.	Mercon	12.3 qts. (11.6L)
C-6 Auto. (4X4)	Mercon	13.5 qts. (12.7L)
E4OD Auto. (4X2)	Mercon	16.2 qts. (15.3L)
4-Speed (Warner T-18)	SAE 80W-90	3.5 qts. (3.3L)
5-Speed Overdrive (Mazda R-2)	Mercon	3.8 qts. (3.6L)
5-Speed Overdrive (ZF S5-42)	Mercon	3.4 qts. (3.2L)
Transfer Case (1356 Warner)	Mercon	2.0 qts. (1.9L)
Explorer		
A4LD Auto. (4X2)	Mercon	9.7 qts. (9.2L)
A4LD Auto. (4X4)	Mercon	10.0 qts. (9.5L)
5-Speed Overdrive (Mazda R-1)	Mercon	5.6 pts. (2.65L)
Transfer Case 13-54 Warner	Mercon	2.5 pts. (1.2L)
Ranger		
A4LD Auto. (4X2)	Mercon	9.7 qts. (9.2L)
A4LD Auto. (4X4)	Mercon	10.0 qts. (9.5L)
5-Speed Overdrive (Mazda R-1)	Mercon	5.6 pts. (2.65L)
5-Speed Overdrive (Mitsubishi)	SAE 80W-85	4.8 pts. (2.3L)
Transfer Case 13-54 Warner	Mercon	2.5 pts. (1.2L)
"E" Series		
AOD Auto.	Mercon	12.3 qts. (11.6L)
C-6 Auto.	Mercon	12.0 qts. (11.4L)
E4OD Auto.	Mercon	15.7 qts. (14.8L)
5-Speed Overdrive (ZF HD)	Mercon	3.4 qts. (3.2L)
"F" Series		
AOD Auto. (4X2)	Mercon	12.3 qts. (11.6L)
C-6 Auto. (4X2)	Mercon	12.0 qts. (11.4L)
C-6 Auto. (4X4)	Mercon	13.5 qts. (12.7L)
E4OD Auto. (4X2)	Mercon	15.7 qts. (14.8L)
E4OD Auto. (4X4)	Mercon	16.2 qts. (15.3L)
4-Speed (Warner T-18)	SAE 80W-90	3.5 qts. (3.3L)
5-Speed Overdrive (Mazda R-2)	Mercon	3.8 qts. (3.6L)
5-Speed Overdrive (ZF S5-42)	Mercon	3.4 qts. (3.2L)
Transfer Case (1345 Warner)	Mercon	3.25 qts. (3.0L)
Transfer Case (1356 Warner)	Mercon	2.0 qts. (1.9L)

QUICK-SERVICE

SERVICE INTERVALS & SPECIFICATIONS

REPLACEMENT INTERVALS

Component	Interval (Miles)
Gasoline Engines	
Air Filter	30,000
Cam Timing Belt	60,000
Coolant	30,000
Crankcase Ventilation Filter	30,000
Fuel Filter	30,000
Oil & Filter	7500
PCV Valve	30,000
Spark Plugs (Standard)	30,000
Spark Plugs (Platinum)	60,000
Spark Plug Wires	60,000
Transfer Case Oil	60,000
Transmission Oil	60,000
Diesel Engines	
Air Filter	30,000
Coolant	30,000
Fuel Filter	[1] 60,000
Oil & Filter	5000
Transfer Case Oil	60,000
Transmission Oil	60,000

[1] – Drain water from fuel filter bowl every 5000 miles.

BELT ADJUSTMENT

Application	New Belt Lbs. (kg)	[1] Used Belt Lbs. (kg)
2.3L		
Fixed	150-190 (68-86)	140-160 (64-73)
With Tensioner [2]	150-190 (68-86)	140-160 (64-73)
2.9L	120-160 (54-73)	110-130 (50-59)
3.0L		
Fixed	120-160 (54-73)	110-130 (50-59)
With Tensioner [2]	150-190 (68-86)	140-160 (64-73)
4.0L With Tensioner [2]	108-132 (49-60)	108-132 (49-60)
4.9L With Tensioner [2]	[3]	[3]
5.0L With Tensioner [2]	[4]	[4]
5.8L With Tensioner [2]	[4]	[4]
7.3L Except Ambulance		
Vac. Pump W/ 3/8" Belt	90-130 (41-59)	65-85 (30-39)
Vac. Pump W/ 1/2" Belt	110-150 (50-68)	75-95 (34-43)
All Other W/ 1/2" Belt	140-180 (64-82)	95-115 (43-52)
7.3L Ambulance		
Alternator	140-160 (64-73)	140-160 (64-73)
Vac. Pump	90-130 (41-59)	65-85 (30-39)
A/C & P/S	140-180 (64-82)	95-115 (43-52)
7.5L		
With Tensioner [2]	[5]	[5]
Alt. & Air Pump	160-200 (73-91)	110-130 (50-59)

[1] – Any belt operated for 10 minutes.

[2] – Tension is correct if tensioner is within indicator marks.

[3] – 90 Lbs. (41 kg) minimum for vehicles with 60 & 75 Amp Alternators. 117 Lbs. (53 kg) minimum for vehicles with 100 Amp Alternators.

[4] – 77 Lbs. (35 kg) minimum for vehicles with 60 & 75 Amp Alternators. 111 Lbs. (50 kg) minimum for vehicles with 100 Amp Alternators.

[5] – 94 Lbs. (43 kg) minimum tension.

1991 ENGINE PERFORMANCE
Service & Adjustment Specifications (Cont.)

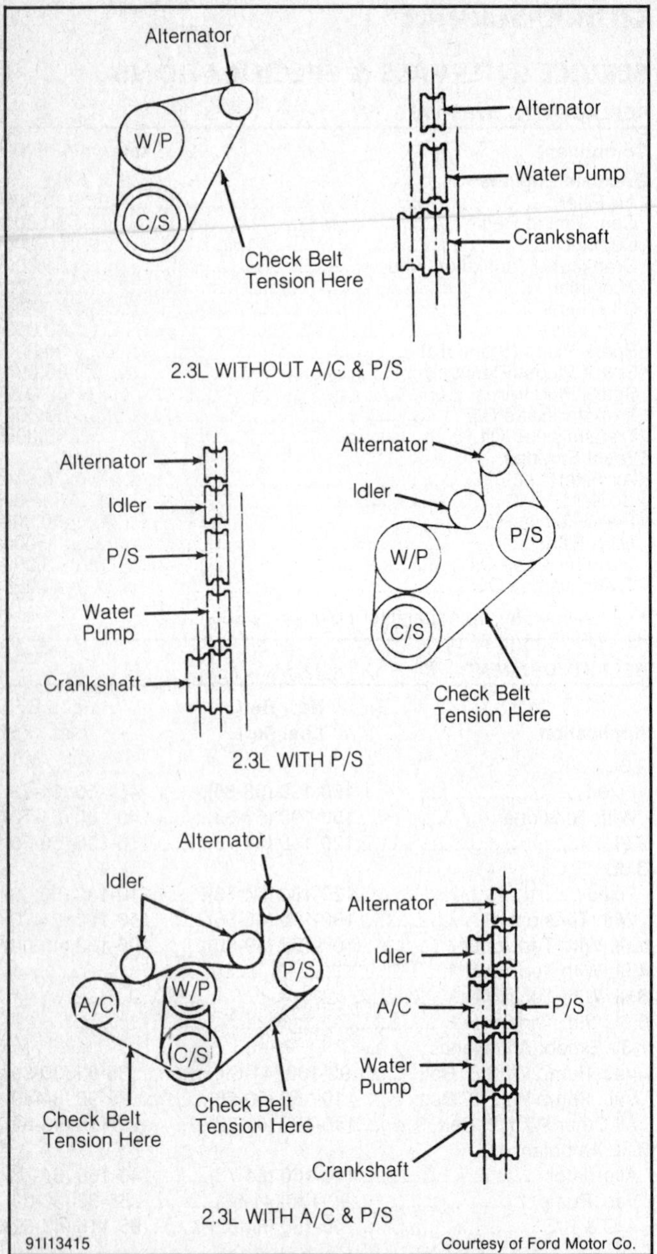
Alternator
W/P
C/S
Check Belt
Tension Here
Alternator
Water Pump
Crankshaft
2.3L WITHOUT A/C & P/S
Alternator
Idler
P/S
Water
Pump
Crankshaft
Alternator
Idler
W/P
P/S
C/S
Check Belt
Tension Here
2.3L WITH P/S
Alternator
Idler
A/C
W/P
P/S
C/S
Check Belt
Tension Here
Check Belt
Tension Here
Alternator
Idler
A/C
P/S
Water
Pump
Crankshaft
2.3L WITH A/C & P/S
91I13415
Courtesy of Ford Motor Co.

Fig. 1: Checking Belt Routing & Tension (2.3L)

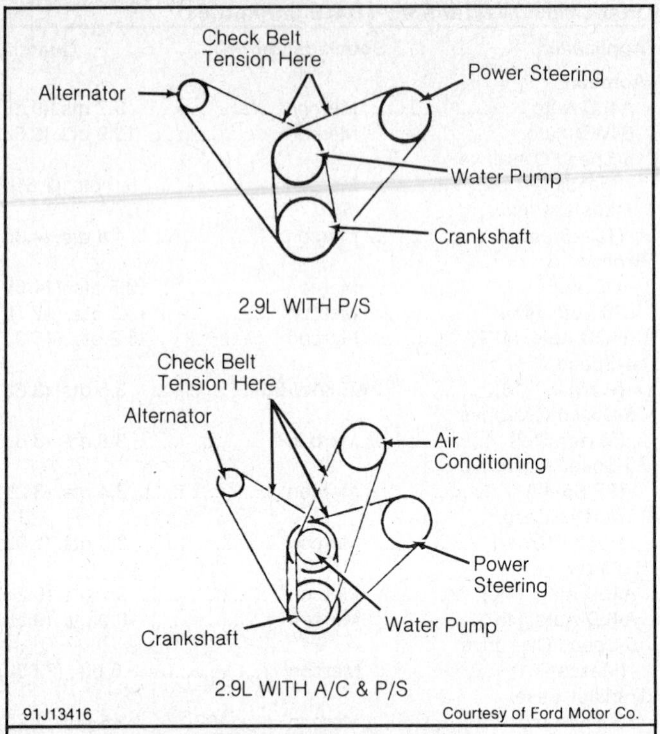
Check Belt
Tension Here
Alternator
Power Steering
Water Pump
Crankshaft
2.9L WITH P/S
Check Belt
Tension Here
Alternator
Air
Conditioning
Power
Steering
Water Pump
Crankshaft
2.9L WITH A/C & P/S
91J13416
Courtesy of Ford Motor Co.

Fig. 2: Checking Belt Routing & Tension (2.9L)

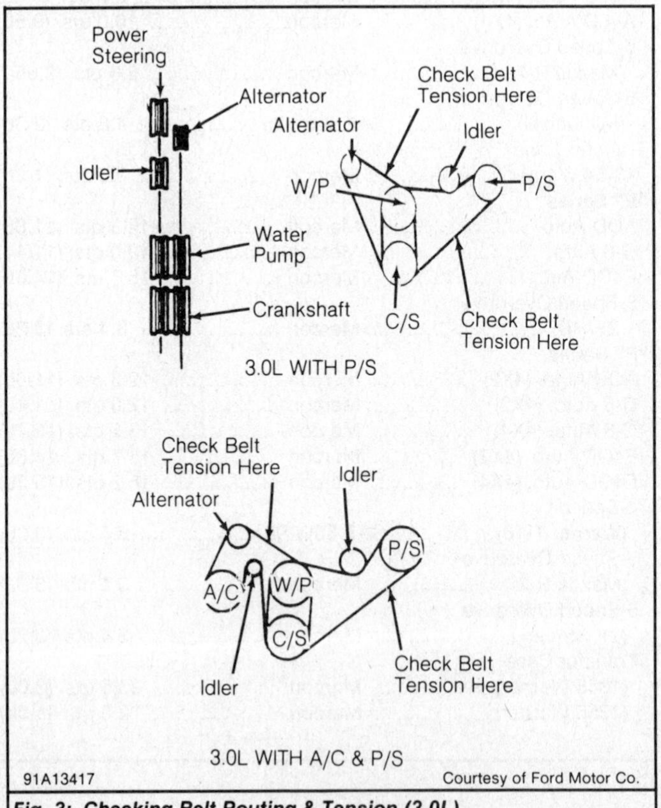
Power
Steering
Alternator
Idler
Water
Pump
Crankshaft
3.0L WITH P/S
Check Belt
Tension Here
Alternator
Idler
W/P
P/S
C/S
Check Belt
Tension Here
Check Belt
Tension Here
Idler
Alternator
P/S
A/C
W/P
C/S
Idler
Check Belt
Tension Here
3.0L WITH A/C & P/S
91A13417
Courtesy of Ford Motor Co.

Fig. 3: Checking Belt Routing & Tension (3.0L)

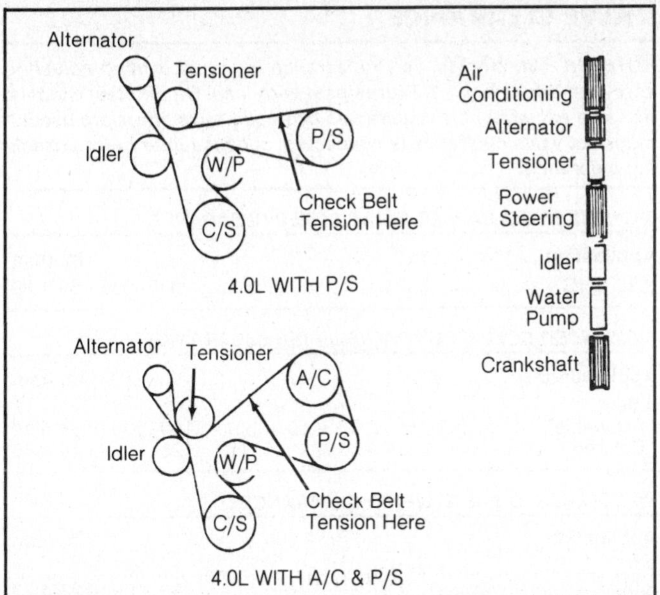
Alternator
Tensioner
Air Conditioning
Alternator
Tensioner
Power Steering
Idler
Water Pump
Crankshaft
P/S
Idler
W/P
C/S
Check Belt Tension Here
4.0L WITH P/S
Alternator
Tensioner
A/C
P/S
Idler
W/P
C/S
Check Belt Tension Here
4.0L WITH A/C & P/S

91B13418 Courtesy of Ford Motor Co.

Fig. 4: Checking Belt Routing & Tension (4.0L)

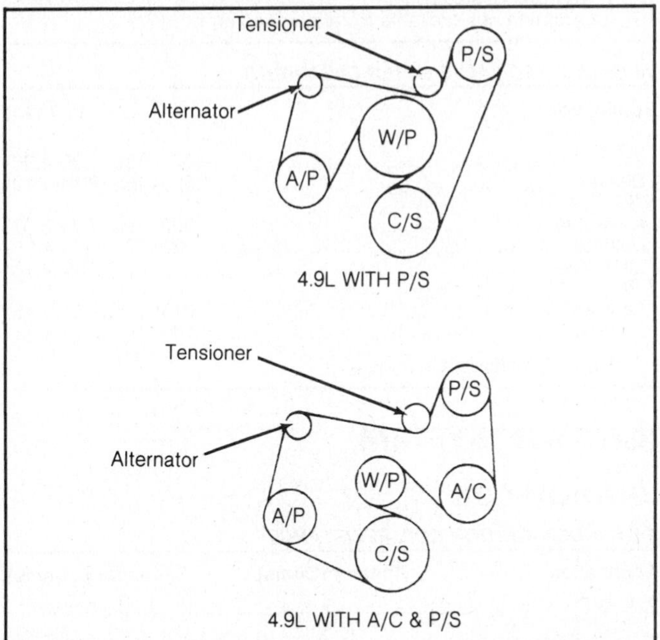
Tensioner
P/S
Alternator
W/P
A/P
C/S
4.9L WITH P/S
Tensioner
P/S
Alternator
W/P
A/C
A/P
C/S
4.9L WITH A/C & P/S

91C13419 Courtesy of Ford Motor Co.

Fig. 5: Checking Belt Routing (4.9L)

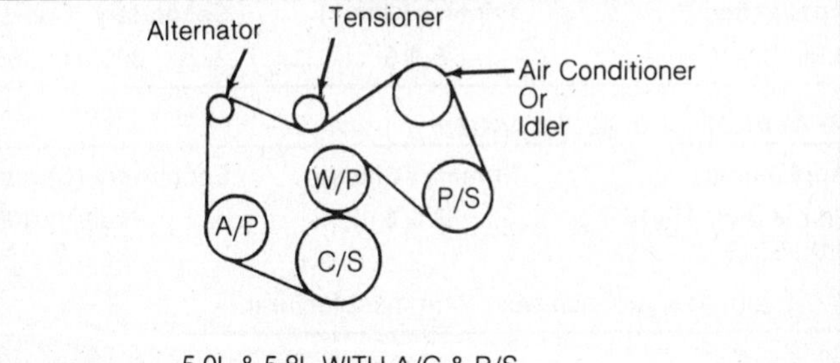
Alternator
Tensioner
Air Conditioner Or Idler
W/P
P/S
A/P
C/S
5.0L & 5.8L WITH A/C & P/S

91F13420 Courtesy of Ford Motor Co.

Fig. 6: Checking Belt Routing (5.0L & 5.8L)

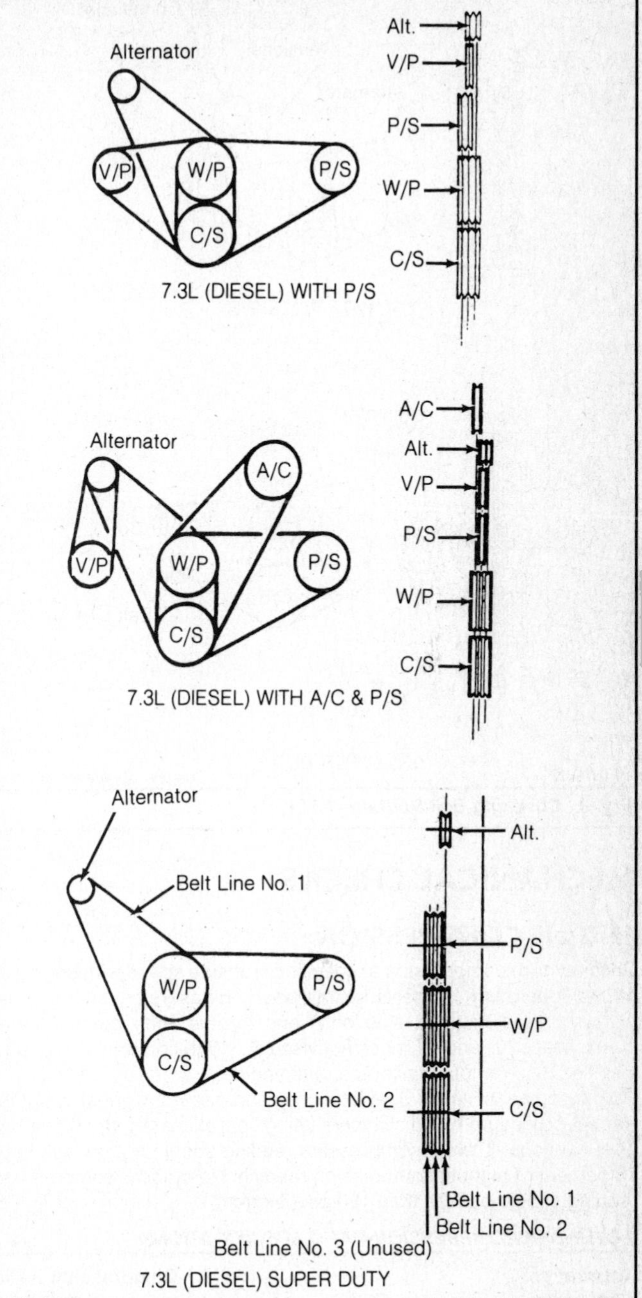
Alt.
V/P
P/S
W/P
C/S
Alternator
V/P
W/P
P/S
C/S
7.3L (DIESEL) WITH P/S
A/C
Alt.
V/P
P/S
W/P
C/S
Alternator
A/C
V/P
W/P
P/S
C/S
7.3L (DIESEL) WITH A/C & P/S
Alternator
Belt Line No. 1
Alt.
P/S
W/P
P/S
W/P
C/S
Belt Line No. 2
C/S
Belt Line No. 1
Belt Line No. 2
Belt Line No. 3 (Unused)
7.3L (DIESEL) SUPER DUTY

91G13421 Courtesy of Ford Motor Co.

Fig. 7: Checking Belt Routing (7.3L Diesel)

1991 ENGINE PERFORMANCE
Service & Adjustment Specifications (Cont.)

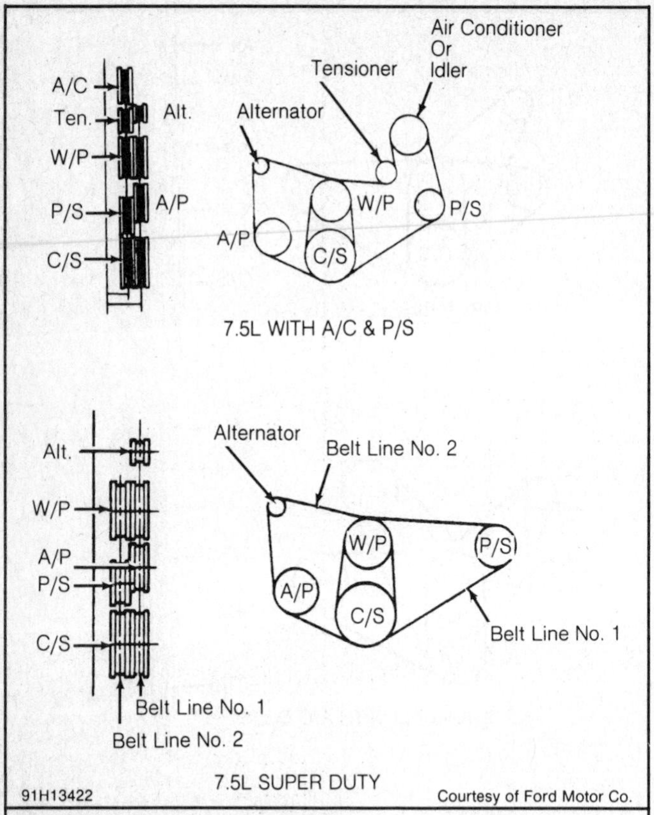
A/C
Ten.
Alt.
W/P
P/S
A/P
C/S
Air Conditioner Or Idler
Tensioner
Alternator
W/P
P/S
A/P
C/S
7.5L WITH A/C & P/S
Alt.
W/P
A/P
P/S
C/S
Alternator
Belt Line No. 2
W/P
P/S
A/P
C/S
Belt Line No. 1
Belt Line No. 1
Belt Line No. 2
7.5L SUPER DUTY
91H13422
Courtesy of Ford Motor Co.

Fig. 8: Checking Belt Routing (7.5L)

MECHANICAL CHECKS

ENGINE COMPRESSION

Check engine compression at specified cranking speed with engine at normal operating temperature, all spark plugs removed (on dual plugs, remove exhaust side only) and throttle wide open. Ensure crankcase is full and oil is correct viscosity. With compression gauge installed, use remote starter to crank engine.

Crank engine at least 5 revolutions, and record highest reading. Repeat procedure for all cylinders using approximately same number of revolutions. Lowest compression reading should not be less than 75 percent of highest compression reading. No cylinder compression reading should be less than 100 psi (7 kg/cm²).

4-CYLINDER COMPRESSION RATIO SPECIFICATIONS

Application	Compression Ratio
2.3L	9.2:1

6-CYLINDER COMPRESSION RATIO SPECIFICATIONS

Application	Compression Ratio
4.9L	8.8:1

V6 COMPRESSION RATIO SPECIFICATIONS

Application	Compression Ratio
2.9L & 4.0L	9.0:1
3.0L	9.3:1

V8 COMPRESSION RATIO SPECIFICATIONS

Application	Compression Ratio
5.0L	9.0:1
5.8L	8.8:1
7.5L	8.5:1
7.3L (Diesel)	21.5:1

VALVE CLEARANCE

***NOTE:** On 2.9L models, valve clearance is set by turning adjusting screw an additional 1 1/2 turns past zero lash. On all other models, no valve adjustment is required as hydraulic valve lifters are used. If incorrect valve clearance is suspected, collapse lifter before checking clearance.*

4-CYLINDER COLLAPSED VALVE LIFTER CLEARANCE

Application	In. (mm)
2.3L OHC	.035-.055 (.89-1.39)

6-CYLINDER COLLAPSED VALVE LIFTER CLEARANCE

Application	In. (mm)
4.9L	
Allowable	.100-.200 (2.54-5.10)
Desired	.125-.175 (3.18-4.45)

V6 COLLAPSED VALVE LIFTER CLEARANCE

Application	In. (mm)
2.9L	[1]
3.0L	.088-.189 (2.23-4.77)
4.0L	[2]

[1] – Valve clearance is set by turning adjusting screw an additional 1 1/2 turns past zero lash.
[2] – Information not available from manufacturer.

V8 COLLAPSED VALVE LIFTER CLEARANCE

Application	In. (mm)
5.0L	
Allowable	.071-.193 (1.80-4.90)
Desired	.096-.165 (2.44-4.19)
5.8L	
Allowable	.098-.198 (2.48-5.03)
Desired	.123-.173 (3.12-4.39)
7.3L (Diesel)	[1] .185 (4.70)
7.5L	
Allowable	.075-.175 (1.91-4.45)
Desired	.100-.150 (2.54-4.81)

[1] – Maximum clearance value.

IGNITION SYSTEM

IGNITION COIL

4-CYLINDER IGNITION COIL RESISTANCE

Application	Primary (Ohms)	Secondary (Ohms)
2.3L DIS	.5	[1]

[1] – Information not available from manufacturer.

6-CYLINDER IGNITION COIL RESISTANCE

Application	Primary (Ohms)	Secondary (Ohms)
4.9L TFI-IV	.8-1.6	8000-11,500

V6 IGNITION COIL RESISTANCE

Application	Primary (Ohms)	Secondary (Ohms)
2.9L & 3.0L TFI-IV	.8-1.6	8000-11,500
4.0L EDIS	.5	[1]

[1] – Information not available from manufacturer.

V8 IGNITION COIL RESISTANCE

Application	Primary Ohms	Secondary Ohms
5.0L & 5.8L TFI-IV	.8-1.6	8000-11,500
7.5L TFI-IV/(CBD)	.8-1.6	8000-11,500

1991 ENGINE PERFORMANCE
Service & Adjustment Specifications (Cont.)

HIGH TENSION WIRE RESISTANCE

HIGH TENSION WIRE RESISTANCE

Application	Ohms
DIS, EDIS & TFI-IV	7000 Per Foot

SPARK PLUGS

SPARK PLUG TYPE

Application	Motorcraft No.
2.3L	AWSF-32C
2.9L	AWSF-42C
3.0L	AWSF-32P
4.0L	
Aerostar & Ranger	AWSF-42P
Explorer	AWSF-42C
4.9L	BSF-44C
5.0L	ASF-42C
5.8L	ASF-32C
7.5L	ASF-44P

FIRING ORDER & TIMING MARKS

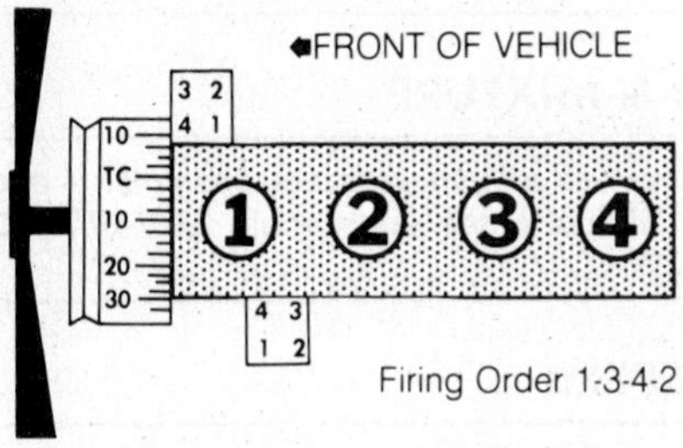
FRONT OF VEHICLE
10
TC
10
20
30
3 2
4 1
4 3
1 2
1 2 3 4
Firing Order 1-3-4-2

120009

Fig. 9: 2.3L Firing Order & Timing Marks

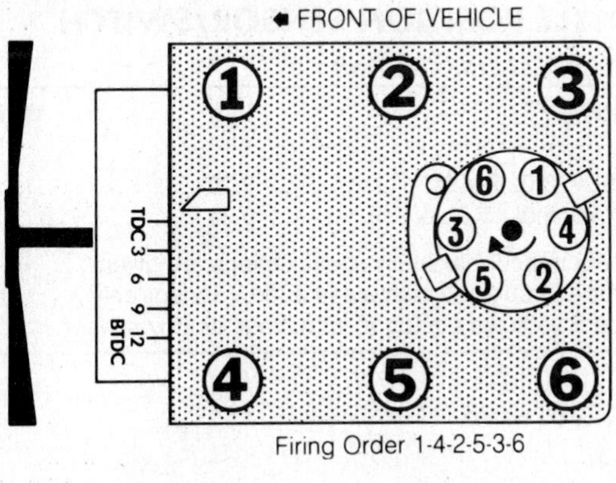
FRONT OF VEHICLE
1 2 3
4 5 6
TDC 3 6 9 12 BTDC
Firing Order 1-4-2-5-3-6

9049

Fig. 10: 2.9L & 3.0L Firing Order & Timing Marks

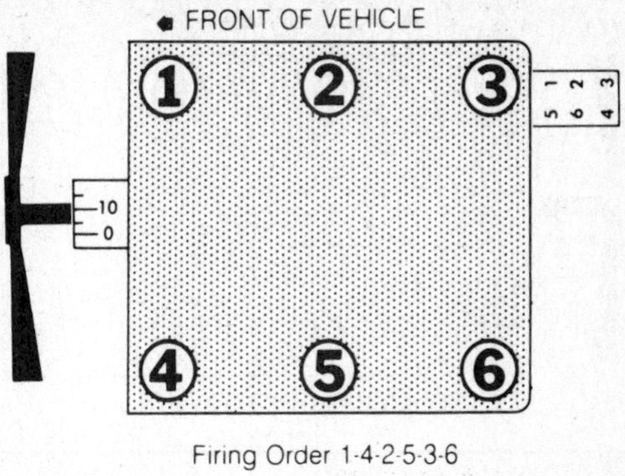
FRONT OF VEHICLE
1 2 3
4 5 6
10
0
Firing Order 1-4-2-5-3-6

91F13438

Fig. 11: 4.0L Firing Order & Timing Marks

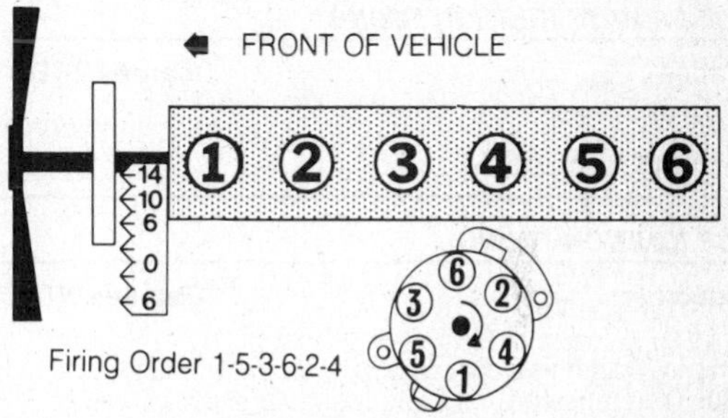
FRONT OF VEHICLE
1 2 3 4 5 6
14
10
6
0
6
Firing Order 1-5-3-6-2-4

8330

Fig. 12: 4.9L Firing Order & Timing Marks

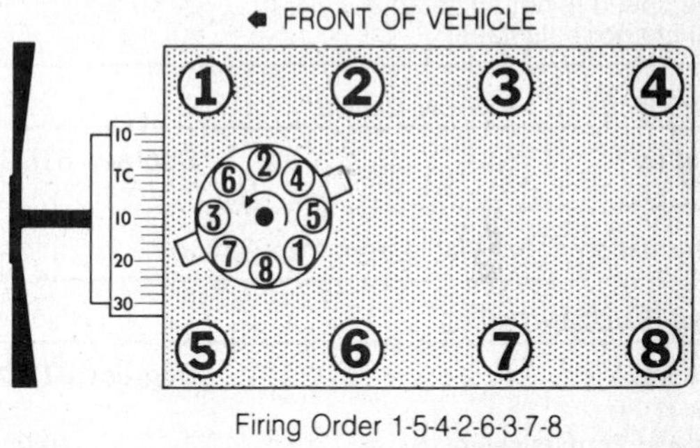
FRONT OF VEHICLE
1 2 3 4
5 6 7 8
10
TC
10
20
30
Firing Order 1-5-4-2-6-3-7-8

8339

Fig. 13: 5.0L & 7.5L Firing Order & Timing Marks

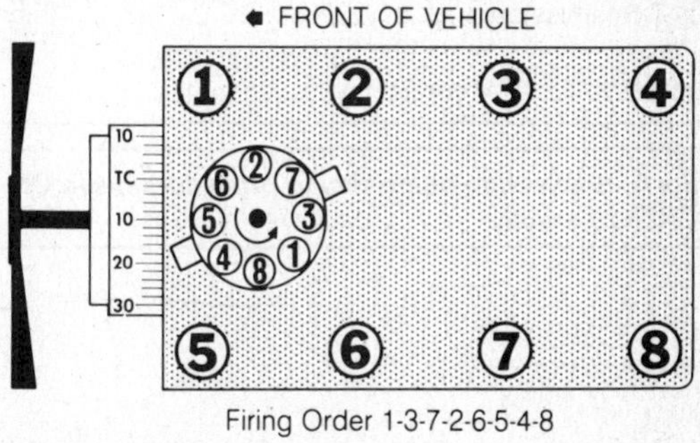
FRONT OF VEHICLE
1 2 3 4
5 6 7 8
10
TC
10
20
30
Firing Order 1-3-7-2-6-5-4-8

8340

Fig. 14: 5.8L Firing Order & Timing Marks

1991 ENGINE PERFORMANCE
Service & Adjustment Specifications (Cont.)

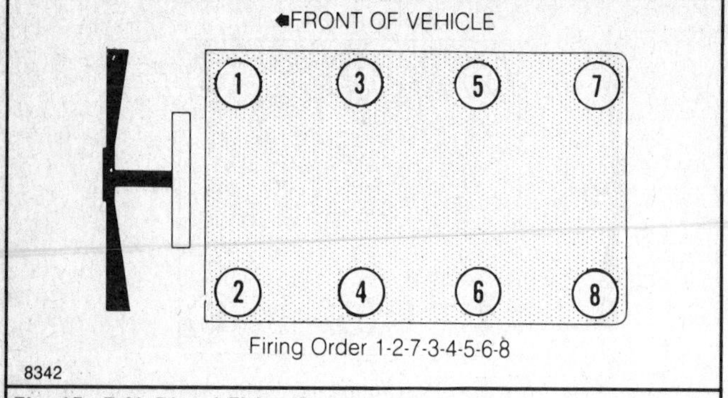
FRONT OF VEHICLE
1
3
5
7
2
4
6
8
Firing Order 1-2-7-3-4-5-6-8
8342

Fig. 15: 7.3L Diesel Firing Order

IGNITION TIMING

4-CYLINDER BASE IGNITION TIMING

Application	Degrees BTDC @ RPM
2.3L	[1]

[1] – Timing not adjustable.

V6 BASE IGNITION TIMING

Application [1]	Degrees BTDC @ RPM
2.9L	
Automatic Transmission	10 @ 800
Manual Transmission	10 @ 850
3.0L	10 @ [2]
4.0L	[3]

[1] – With SPOUT in-line connector disconnected.
[2] – Idle speed is not adjustable.
[3] – Timing not adjustable.

6-CYLINDER BASE IGNITION TIMING

Application [1]	Degrees BTDC @ RPM
4.9L	10 @ [1]

[1] – Information not available from manufacturer.

V8 BASE IGNITION TIMING

Application	[1] Degrees BTDC @ RPM
5.0L	
Automatic Transmission	10 @ 525-825
Manual Transmission	10 @ 550-850
5.8L	
C6 Automatic Transmission	10 @ 630-930
E4OD Automatic Transmission	10 @ 580-880
Manual Transmission	10 @ 580-880
7.5L	10 @ 500-800

[1] – With SPOUT in-line connector disconnected.

***NOTE:** For 7.3L injection pump timing procedures, see ON-VEHICLE ADJUSTMENTS article.*

FUEL SYSTEM

FUEL PUMP

***NOTE:** Fuel pump performance is a measurement of fuel pressure and volume availability, not regulated fuel pressure.*

FUEL PUMP PERFORMANCE

Application	Specification
Gasoline Engines	
Fuel Line Pressure	
4.9L [1]	[2] 50-60 psi (3.5-4.2 kg/cm²)
All Others [1]	[2] 35-45 psi (2.5-3.2 kg/cm²)
Volume	1.5 pts. (.72L) in 30 seconds.
Diesel Engines	
Fuel Line Pressure	
Filter Inlet	[3] 2 psi (.14 kg/cm²)
Filter Outlet	[4] 1 psi (.07 kg/cm²)
Return Line	[4] 2 psi (.14 kg/cm²)
Volume	1 pt. (.5L) in 30 seconds.

[1] – Key on, engine off.
[2] – Engine running pressure may be 5 psi (.4 kg/cm²) less.
[3] – At idle.
[4] – At 3300 RPM.

IDLE SPEED & MIXTURE

***NOTE:** No idle mixture adjustments are possible. If engine performance is unsatisfactory, see appropriate SELF-DIAGNOSTICS article.*

FAST IDLE SPEED

***NOTE:** Refer to underhood engine decal for engine fast idle RPM specification.*

THROTTLE POSITION SENSOR/SWITCH

TPS VOLTAGE SPECIFICATIONS [1]

Application	Idle	Wide Open Throttle
2.3L, 2.9L [2], 3.0L & 4.0L	0.20	4.84
2.9L [3], 4.9L, 5.0L, 5.8L & 7.5L	0.34	4.84

[1] – Minimum and maximum specifications are given.
[2] – Vehicles equipped with mass airflow sensor only.
[3] – Except vehicles equipped with mass airflow sensor.

1991 ENGINE PERFORMANCE
On-Vehicle Adjustments

Aerostar, Bronco, Explorer, Ranger, "E" & "F" Series, "F" Series Super Duty

ENGINE MECHANICAL

Before performing any on-vehicle adjustments to fuel or ignition systems, ensure engine mechanical condition is okay.

VALVE CLEARANCE

***NOTE:** Valve cover(s) must be removed before performing valve adjustment. See appropriate article in ENGINES for removal and installation procedures.*

2.3L VALVE CLEARANCE ADJUSTMENT

***NOTE:** Valve clearance is nonadjustable, but clearance can be checked to determine if worn components exist.*

1) Rotate camshaft so base circle of camshaft lobe is positioned on valve to be checked. Using Valve Spring Compressor (T88T-6565-BH), apply pressure on cam follower until lash adjuster is fully collapsed.
2) While holding lash adjuster fully collapsed, use feeler gauge to measure clearance between base circle of camshaft and camshaft follower. Desired clearance is .040-.050" (1.01-1.27 mm), with an allowable clearance of .035-.055" (.89-1.40 mm).
3) If clearance is not within specification, inspect camshaft follower for damage. If camshaft follower is not damaged, check for sticking valve, worn valve spring or camshaft lobe(s). If components are okay, check for defective lash adjuster. Replace components as necessary.

2.9L VALVE CLEARANCE ADJUSTMENT

1) Position camshaft lobe on cylinder to be adjusted so that rocker arm is on the base circle area. Loosen adjusting screw on rocker arm until a distinct lash between rocker arm pad and valve tip can be noticed. Plunger of lash adjuster should be fully extended.
2) Carefully screw in the adjusting screw until rocker arm slightly touches valve stem. To achieve nominal working position of the plunger, screw in adjusting screw an additional 1 1/2 turns, which is equivalent to .07" (2 mm).

3.0L VALVE CLEARANCE ADJUSTMENT

***NOTE:** Hydraulic valve lifters are used; no valve adjustment is required. If incorrect valve clearance is suspected, lifter must be collapsed before clearance can be checked.*

1) Position No. 1 piston at TDC of compression stroke. Slowly apply pressure until valve lifter is completely collapsed on No. 1 intake.
2) Holding lifter in collapsed position, measure clearance between rocker arm and tip of valve stem. If clearance is not within specification, repair or replace components as necessary. See 3.0L COLLAPSED VALVE LIFTER SPECIFICATIONS table.
3) Repeat procedure for exhaust valves No. 1, No. 2 and No. 4, and intake valves No. 3 and No. 6. Rotate crankshaft 360 degrees (one revolution). Repeat procedure for exhaust valves No. 3, No. 5 and No. 6, and intake valves No. 2, No. 4 and No. 5.

3.0L COLLAPSED VALVE LIFTER SPECIFICATIONS

Application	In. (mm)
All Valves	.088-.189 (2.23-4.77)

4.0L VALVE CLEARANCE ADJUSTMENT

***NOTE:** Hydraulic roller valve lifters and nonadjustable rocker arms are used; valve adjustment is not possible. If valve lifters are found to be excessively worn or noisy, test and repair or replace as necessary.*

5.0L VALVE CLEARANCE ADJUSTMENT

***NOTE:** Hydraulic valve lifters are used; no valve adjustment is required. If valve clearance is incorrect, use oversize or undersize push rods to correct clearance.*

1) Rotate crankshaft in normal operation direction until No. 1 cylinder is at TDC of compression stroke. Using Tappet Bleed Down Wrench (T71P-6513-B), apply pressure to No. 1 intake tappet until lifter is completely bottomed.
2) Hold tappet in this position while measuring clearance between tappet and valve stem. Record measurement. Repeat this procedure for intake valves No. 7 and No. 8, and exhaust valves No. 1, No. 5 and No. 4.
3) Rotate crankshaft 180 degrees (1/2 turn). Bleed lifter and check intake valves No. 5 and No. 4, and exhaust valves No. 2 and No. 6. Rotate crankshaft 270 degrees (3/4 turn). Bleed lifter down and check intake valves No. 2, No. 3 and No. 6, and exhaust valves No. 7, No. 3 and No. 8. Record measurement and compare it to specification. See 5.0L COLLAPSED VALVE LIFTER CLEARANCE table. If clearance is not within specification, use shorter or longer push rod to obtain correct clearance.

5.0L COLLAPSED VALVE LIFTER CLEARANCE

Application	In. (mm)
5.8L	
Allowable	.071-.193 (1.80-4.90)
Desired	.096-.165 (2.44-4.19)

5.8L VALVE CLEARANCE ADJUSTMENT

***NOTE:** Hydraulic valve lifters are used; no valve adjustment is required. If valve clearance is incorrect, use oversize or undersize push rod to obtain correct clearance.*

1) Rotate crankshaft in normal operation direction until No. 1 cylinder is at TDC of compression stroke. Using Tappet Bleed Down Wrench (T71P-6513-B), apply pressure to No. 1 intake tappet until lifter is completely bottomed.
2) Hold tappet in this position while measuring clearance between tappet and valve stem. Record measurement. Repeat this procedure for intake valves No. 4 and No. 8, and exhaust valves No. 1, No. 3 and No. 7.
3) Rotate crankshaft 180 degrees (1/2 turn). Bleed lifter and check intake valves No. 3 and No. 7, and exhaust valves No. 2 and No. 6. Rotate crankshaft 270 degrees (3/4 turn). Bleed lifter down and check intake valves No. 2, No. 5 and No. 6, and exhaust valves No. 4, No. 5 and No. 8. Record measurement and compare it to specification. See 5.8L COLLAPSED VALVE LIFTER CLEARANCE table. If clearance is not within specification, use shorter or longer push rod to obtain correct clearance.

5.8L COLLAPSED VALVE LIFTER CLEARANCE

Application	In. (mm)
5.8L	
Allowable	.098-.198 (2.48-5.03)
Desired	.123-.173 (3.12-4.39)

7.5L VALVE CLEARANCE ADJUSTMENT

***NOTE:** Hydraulic valve lifters are used and no valve adjustment is required. If valve clearance is incorrect, use oversize or undersize push rod to obtain correct clearance.*

1) Rotate crankshaft in normal operation direction until No. 1 cylinder is at TDC of compression stroke. Using Tappet Bleed Down Wrench (T71P-6513-B), apply pressure to No. 1 intake tappet until lifter is completely bottomed.
2) Hold tappet in this position while measuring clearance between tappet and valve stem. Record measurement. Repeat this procedure for intake valves No. 3, No. 7 and No. 8, and exhaust valves No. 1, No. 4, No. 5 and No. 8.

1991 ENGINE PERFORMANCE
On-Vehicle Adjustments (Cont.)

3) Rotate crankshaft 360 degrees (one turn). Bleed lifter and check intake valves No. 2, No. 4, No. 5 and No. 6, and exhaust valves No. 2, No. 3, No. 6 and No. 7. Record measurement and compare it to specification. See 7.5L COLLAPSED VALVE LIFTER CLEARANCE table. If clearance is not within specification, use shorter or longer push rod to obtain correct clearance.

7.5L COLLAPSED VALVE LIFTER CLEARANCE

Application	In. (mm)
7.5L	
Allowable	.075-.175 (1.91-4.45)
Desired	.100-.150 (2.54-4.81)

7.3L (DIESEL) VALVE CLEARANCE ADJUSTMENT

NOTE: Hydraulic valve lifters are used; no valve adjustment is required. If incorrect valve clearance is suspected, lifter must be collapsed before clearance can be checked.

Position each piston at TDC of compression stroke so both valves are closed. Using Lifter Bleed Down Wrench (T83T-6500-A), bleed down lifters until lifter plunger bottoms. Check valve clearance. If clearances are not correct, check valve train components for wear and damage. Maximum valve clearance is .185" (4.70 mm).

IGNITION TIMING

GASOLINE ENGINES

NOTE: Ignition timing on 2.3L with DIS and 4.0L with EDIS is not adjustable.

Initial Timing (TFI-IV) – 1) Place transmission in Park or Neutral. Ensure A/C and heater are off. Connect inductive timing light and tachometer to engine. With engine off, disconnect the single-wire in-line spout (Yellow/Light Green wire near distributor) connector or remove shorting bar from the double-wire spout connector. Start and warm engine to normal operating temperature.
2) With engine at idle speed, check/adjust initial timing to 10 degrees BTDC. Turn engine off and reconnect the single-wire in-line spout connector or reinstall shorting bar on double-wire spout connector. Start engine and check timing advance to verify distributor is advancing beyond initial setting. Remove test equipment and reconnect all disconnected components.

7.3L DIESEL INJECTION TIMING

STATIC TIMING

1) Remove fast idle bracket and solenoid from injection pump. Using Pump Mounting Wrench (T83T-9000-B), loosen nuts holding injection pump to pump mounting adapter. Install Rotating Wrench (T83T-9000-C) on front of pump, and rotate to align timing mark on pump mounting flange with timing mark on pump mounting adapter. *See Fig. 1.*
2) Align timing marks to within .030". Remove rotating wrench and tighten nuts to 84 INCH lbs. (9.5 N.m). Ensure timing marks are aligned. Install fast idle bracket and solenoid.

DYNAMIC TIMING

NOTE: Engine must be at normal operating temperature of 192-212°F (89-100°C) when checking/setting dynamic timing.

1) Bring engine to normal operating temperature. Stop engine and install Dynamic Timing Meter (078-00200) into timing probe hole until it almost touches vibration damper. *See Fig. 2.*
2) Attach clamp from Timing Meter Adapter (078-00201) to line pressure sensor on No. 1 injector nozzle ("F" Series) or No. 4 injector nozzle ("E" Series), and connect to dynamic timing meter. Connect dynamic timing meter to battery and dial in minus 20 degrees offset on meter.

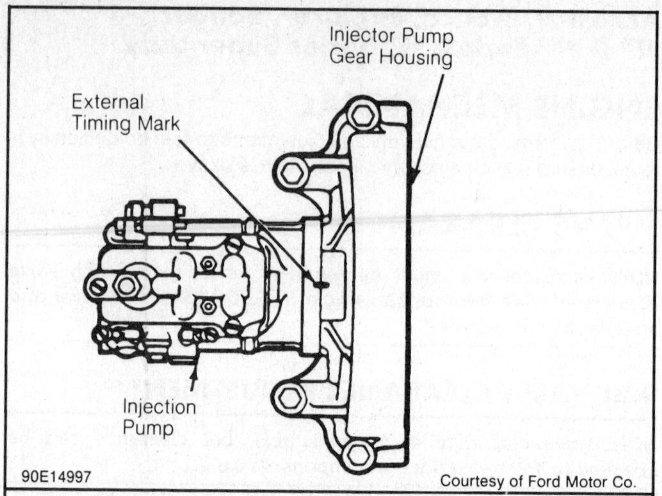
Injector Pump
Gear Housing
External
Timing Mark
Injection
Pump
90E14997
Courtesy of Ford Motor Co.

Fig. 1: Aligning Injection Pump Timing Marks

3) Disconnect cold start advance terminal connector from solenoid terminal. *See Fig. 3.* With transmission in Neutral and rear wheels raised, start engine. Using Throttle Control Tool (D83T-9000-E), set engine speed to 2000 RPM with no accessory load.
4) Observe injection timing on dynamic timing meter. Injection timing should be 8.5 degrees BTDC at 2000 RPM. Apply battery voltage to cold start advance solenoid. Activating cold start advance solenoid terminal can increase engine speed. Adjust throttle if necessary.
5) Timing at 2000 RPM should be at least one degree before the timing obtained in first timing check. If the advance is less than one degree, replace fuel injection pump top cover assembly. If dynamic timing is not within ±2 degrees of specification, adjust pump timing.

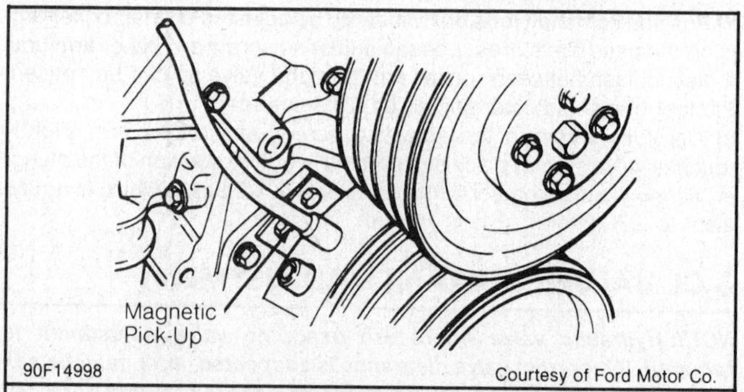
Magnetic
Pick-Up
90F14998
Courtesy of Ford Motor Co.

Fig. 2: Positioning Magnetic Pick-Up

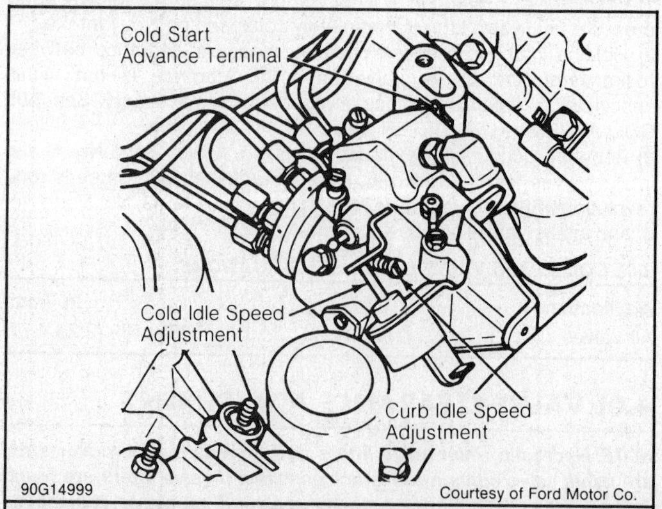
Cold Start
Advance Terminal
Cold Idle Speed
Adjustment
Curb Idle Speed
Adjustment
90G14999
Courtesy of Ford Motor Co.

Fig. 3: Locating Idle Speed Adjusting Screw

1991 ENGINE PERFORMANCE
On-Vehicle Adjustments (Cont.)

IDLE SPEED & MIXTURE

COLD (FAST) IDLE

Gasoline Engines – Fast idle speed is computer controlled. Adjustment procedures are not supplied by manufacturer.

7.3L Diesel – **1)** Connect tachometer. Place transmission in Neutral or Park. Start engine and bring to normal operating temperature. Disconnect fast idle solenoid from harness and apply battery voltage to activate solenoid.

2) Rev engine momentarily to set solenoid. Fast idle should be 800-850 RPM. Adjust by turning solenoid plunger. *See Fig. 3*. Recheck fast idle and adjust if necessary. Reconnect solenoid connector.

IDLE ADJUSTMENT PROCEDURES (GASOLINE ENGINES)

Idle Adjustment Precautions – Idle speed, on all engines, is controlled by ECA and idle speed control air by-pass valve. If control system is operating properly, engine idle RPM is fixed and cannot be changed by standard adjustments. Many engines do not provide an RPM specification. A Scan tool must be used on these systems because control strategy and idle speed specification are controlled by ECA.

Before performing idle speed adjustment procedure, complete a thorough basic inspection and self-test (KOEO, KOER, Continuous Memory self-tests) to confirm operation of sub-systems contributing to idle speed control problems. See appropriate SELF-DIAGNOSTICS article.

Before performing idle speed check and adjustment procedures, ensure throttle bore and both sides of throttle plate(s) are clean. Ensure throttle plate does not stick in bore and/or linkage is not limiting throttle plate operation. Throttle lever MUST be resting on throttle stop screw. When idle speed control device (air by-pass solenoid or DC motor) is disconnected to set minimum air rate, engine may stall. This is acceptable only if throttle plate and linkage are not stuck.

Some throttle bodies use sludge tolerant throttle plate designs. See THROTTLE PLATE COATING INDEX chart for application.

THROTTLE PLATE COATING INDEX [1]

Application	Engine Equipped with Protective Coating
4-Cylinder Engines	2.3L
6-Cylinder Engines	4.9L
V6 Engines	3.0L & [1] 4.0L
V8 Engines	5.0L, 5.8L & [1] 7.5L

[1] – Sludge tolerant throttle body introduced 1991 1/2.

These units must not be cleaned because a protective coating is applied to the lip of throttle plate(s). *See Fig. 4* for location of identification label.

Turn off all accessories before checking and adjusting idle speed. Ensure cooling system is filled to correct level. Ensure there are no vacuum leaks or unmetered air entering the throttle chamber on mass airflow design systems. If vehicle is equipped with electric cooling fan, check and adjust idle speed when fan is off.

2.3L OHC, 3.0L, 4.0L & 7.5L W/ Sludge Tolerant Throttle Body – **1)** With engine off, disconnect negative battery cable for at least 5 minutes then reconnect it. Start engine and allow idle speed to stabilize for 2 minutes. Snap throttle open and return to idle. Lightly depress and release accelerator and allow engine to idle. If engine idles properly, idle speed adjustment is not required.

2) If engine does not idle properly, disconnect the SPOUT in-line connector and verify base ignition timing is correct (2.3L only). With ignition off, disconnect idle speed control air by-pass solenoid. Start engine and run at 2500 RPM for 30 seconds. Place A/T in Park (Neutral on M/T) and apply parking brake. Check idle speed. If idle speed is less than 475-575 RPM (2.3L), 550-675 RPM (3.0L), 555-725 RPM (4.0L) or 500-800 RPM (7.5L), go to next step. If idle speed is greater than specified, go to step **5)**.

3) If idle speed is too low, check throttle body for presence of throttle plate orifice plug. *See Fig. 5*. If there is no plug, turn idle adjusting

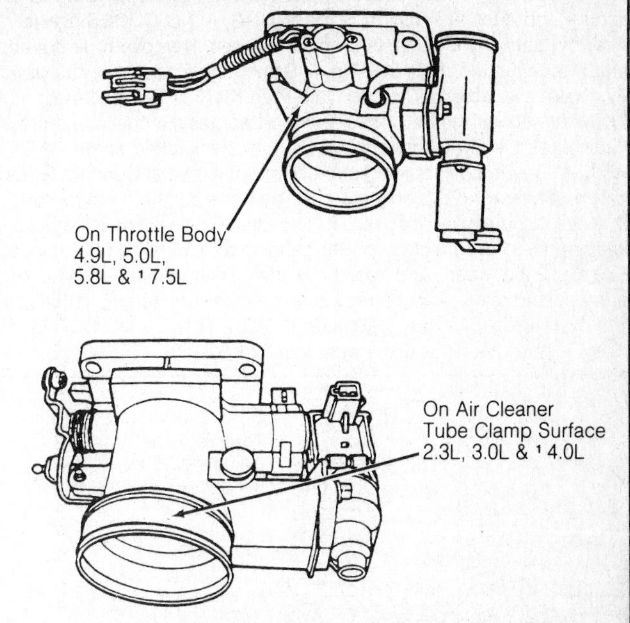
On Throttle Body
4.9L, 5.0L,
5.8L & [1] 7.5L
On Air Cleaner
Tube Clamp Surface
2.3L, 3.0L & [1] 4.0L
[1] – Sludge tolerant throttle body introduced 1991 1/2.
91G13439
Courtesy of Ford Motor Co.

Fig. 4: Locating Sludge Tolerant Throttle Plate Labels

screw CLOCKWISE only to adjust idle speed. If there is a plug from previous service, remove it and turn screw to obtain correct idle speed. After adjustment, idle adjusting screw MUST be in contact with lever pad.

4) Turn engine off and disconnect battery for 5 minutes. Reconnect SPOUT in-line connector and ISC by-pass solenoid power lead. Move throttle plate to ensure it is not stuck in bore. Start engine and stabilize for 2 minutes. Snap throttle open and let it return to idle. With engine idling, lightly depress and release accelerator to exercise the ISC solenoid.

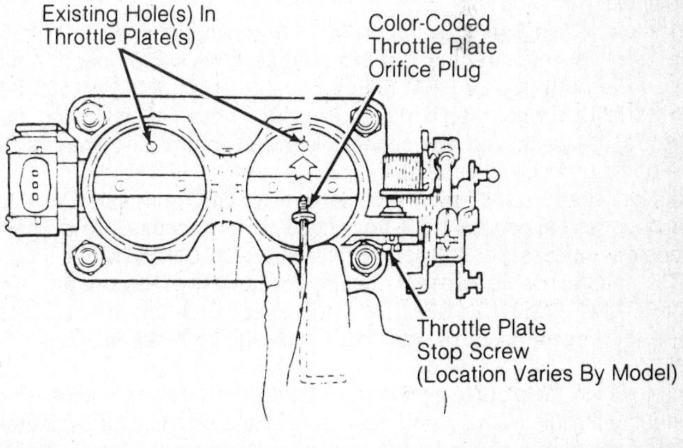
Existing Hole(s) In
Throttle Plate(s)
Color-Coded
Throttle Plate
Orifice Plug
Throttle Plate
Stop Screw
(Location Varies By Model)
91J13440
Courtesy of Ford Motor Co.

Fig. 5: Locating Throttle Plate Orifices & Installing Plug

5) If idle speed is too high, turn ignition off. Disconnect air cleaner hose. Using tape, block off orifice in throttle plate. *See Fig. 5*. If orifice is already plugged, go to next step. On mass airflow engines, reconnect air cleaner hose. On all models, restart engine and check idle speed. If engine stalls, crack throttle plate open using throttle plate stop screw. *See Fig. 6*. If idle speed is still too high, go next step. If idle speed drops to specification, drops lower than specification, or engine stalls, go to step **7)**.

6) Perform a KOEO self-test. Check for fault codes, especially TPS fault code. If fault codes are present, repair as necessary. See appropriate SELF-DIAGNOSTICS article. If TPS fault code is present, check for proper TPS output. See THROTTLE POSITION SENSOR (TPS) at

1991 ENGINE PERFORMANCE
On-Vehicle Adjustments (Cont.)

end of article. If no fault codes are present, remove tape. Exit this procedure and refer to TROUBLE SHOOTING - NO CODES article.
7) Turn ignition off. Remove air cleaner hose. Remove tape covering the throttle plate orifice. *See Fig. 5.* Select correct plug for the orifice. Plugs are available in Throttle Plate Plug Kit (FOPE-9F652-AA).
8) Reconnect air cleaner hose and start engine. Recheck idle speed. If idle speed is not within specification, turn adjusting screw CLOCKWISE to obtain correct idle speed. Turn ignition off. Connect SPOUT in-line connector (2.3L only) and ISC by-pass solenoid power lead.
9) Move throttle plate to ensure it is not stuck in bore and linkage is not keeping throttle from closing. Start engine and stabilize for 2 minutes. Snap throttle open and return to idle. With engine idling, lightly depress and release accelerator to exercise ISC solenoid. If idle problem is still present, refer to TROUBLE SHOOTING - NO CODES article to locate other possible causes of high idle.

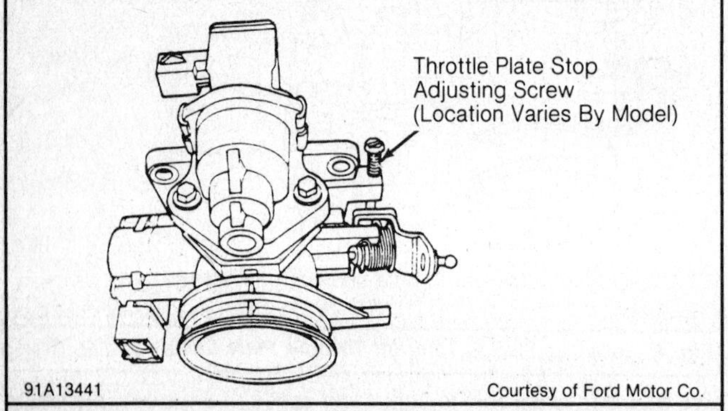
Throttle Plate Stop
Adjusting Screw
(Location Varies By Model)
91A13441
Courtesy of Ford Motor Co.

Fig. 6: Locating Throttle Plate Stop Adjusting Screw (Typical)

2.9L, 4.0L & 7.5L W/O Sludge Tolerant Throttle Body - 1) With engine off, disconnect negative battery cable for at least 5 minutes then reconnect it. Start engine and allow idle speed to stabilize for 2 minutes. Snap throttle open and return to idle. Lightly depress and release accelerator.
2) Allow engine to idle. Ensure electric cooling fan is off. If engine idle is okay, idle speed adjustment is not required. If engine does not idle properly, turn ignition off. Disconnect idle speed control air by-pass solenoid.
3) Place A/T in Park (Neutral on M/T). Start engine and run at 2500 RPM for 30 seconds. Apply parking brake. Check idle speed. If idle speed is not 600-725 RPM (2.9L), 550-725 RPM (4.0L) or 500-800 RPM (7.5L), turn throttle plate stop screw to obtain specification. *See Fig. 6.* Turn ignition off. Reconnect idle speed control air by-pass solenoid and recheck idle speed.
4) If idle speed is still not correct, perform a KOEO self-test. Check for fault codes, especially TPS fault code. If fault codes are present, repair as necessary. See appropriate SELF-DIAGNOSTICS article. If TPS fault code is present, check for proper TPS output. See THROTTLE POSITION SENSOR (TPS) at end of article. If fault codes are not present, exit this procedure and refer to TROUBLE SHOOTING - NO CODES article.
5) Move throttle plate to ensure it is not stuck in bore and linkage is not keeping throttle from closing. Start engine and stabilize for 2 minutes. Snap throttle open and return to idle. With engine idling, lightly depress and release accelerator. If idle problem is still present, refer to TROUBLE SHOOTING - NO CODES article to locate other possible causes of high idle.
5.0L (Except E4OD), 5.8L (Over 8500 GVW) & E250 W/O 0-64K Calibration - 1) With engine off, disconnect negative battery cable for at least 5 minutes then reconnect it. Start engine and allow idle speed to stabilize for 2 minutes. Snap throttle open and return to idle. Lightly depress and release accelerator, and allow engine to idle. If engine idles properly, idle speed adjustment is not required.
2) If engine does not idle properly, turn engine off. Install a .050" (1.27 mm) feeler gauge (A/T) or .030" (.76 mm) feeler gauge (M/T) between throttle plate stop screw and throttle lever. Disconnect the SPOUT in-line connector and verify base ignition timing is correct. With ignition off, disconnect idle speed control air by-pass solenoid. Start engine and allow to idle for 120 seconds. Place A/T in Park (Neutral on M/T) and apply parking brake. Check idle speed. If idle speed is less than 525-825 RPM (5.0L A/T), 550-850 RPM (5.0L M/T), 780 RPM (5.8L w/ C-6 trans.), or 580-880 RPM (5.8L w/ E4OD or M/T), go to next step. If idle speed is greater than specified, go to step **5)**.
3) If idle speed is too low, check throttle body for presence of throttle plate orifice plug. *See Fig. 5.* If there is no plug, turn idle adjusting screw CLOCKWISE only to adjust idle speed. If there is a plug from previous service, remove it and turn screw to obtain correct idle speed. After adjustment, idle adjusting screw MUST be in contact with lever pad.
4) Turn engine off and disconnect battery for 5 minutes. Reconnect SPOUT in-line connector and ISC by-pass solenoid power lead. Move throttle plate to ensure it is not stuck in bore. Start engine and stabilize for 2 minutes. Snap throttle open and let it return to idle. With engine idling, lightly depress and release accelerator to activate the ISC solenoid.
5) If idle speed is too high, turn ignition off. Disconnect air cleaner hose. Using tape, block off orifice in throttle plate. *See Fig. 5.* If orifice is already plugged, go to next step. On mass airflow engines, reconnect air cleaner hose. On all models, restart engine and check idle speed. If engine stalls, crack throttle plate open using throttle plate stop screw. *See Fig. 6.* If idle speed is still too high, go to next step. If idle speed drops to specification, drops lower than specification, or engine stalls, go to step **7)**.
6) Perform a KOEO self-test. Check for fault codes, especially TPS fault code. If fault codes are present, repair as necessary. See appropriate SELF-DIAGNOSTICS article. If TPS fault code is present, check for proper TPS output. See THROTTLE POSITION SENSOR (TPS) at end of article. If fault codes are not present, remove tape. Exit this procedure and refer to TROUBLE SHOOTING - NO CODES article.
7) Turn ignition off. Remove air cleaner hose. Remove tape covering the throttle plate orifice. *See Fig. 5.* Select correct plug for orifice. Plugs are available in Throttle Plate Plug Kit (FOPE-9F652-AA).
8) Reconnect air cleaner hose, remove feeler gauge and start engine. Recheck idle speed. If idle speed is not within specification, turn adjusting screw CLOCKWISE to obtain correct idle speed. Turn ignition off. Connect SPOUT in-line connector and ISC by-pass solenoid power lead.
9) Move throttle plate to ensure it is not stuck in bore and linkage is not keeping throttle from closing. Start engine and stabilize for 2 minutes. Snap throttle open and return to idle. With engine idling, lightly depress and release accelerator to activate ISC solenoid. If idle problem is still present, refer to TROUBLE SHOOTING - NO CODES article to locate other possible causes of high idle.
10) On vehicles equipped with AOD transmission, check throttle valve pressure adjustment.

NOTE: Engine RPM oscillations may occur if throttle plate is open far enough to expose canister purge port. To verify, disconnect and plug purge port on throttle body. If problem no longer exists, close throttle plate just enough to eliminate oscillations.

4.9L, 5.0L (W/ E4OD), 5.8L (Under 8500 GVW), E250 W/ 0-64K Calibration & All 1991 1/2 5.8L - 1) Connect Scan tool to diagnostic connector. Enter KOER self-test. A single-pulse tone indicates entry mode has been successfully entered. Observe "Scan" tool read-out.
2) If a constant tone, solid light or STO LO is displayed, base idle speed is within range and adjustment is not necessary. Exit self-test.
3) If a beeping tone, flashing light or STO LO at 8 Hz is displayed, TPS is out of range and adjustment may be required. Perform adjustment and repeat test.
4) If a beeping tone, flashing light or STO LO at 4 Hz is displayed, base idle speed is too high. Go to step **8)**.
5) If a beeping tone, flashing light or STO LO at one Hz is displayed, base idle speed is too low. Go to next step.
6) DO NOT clean throttle bore. Check throttle plate for presence of throttle plate orifice plug. *See Fig. 5.* If there is no plug, turn idle adjusting screw CLOCKWISE only to adjust idle speed until conditions in step **2)** are obtained. If there is a plug from previous service, remove

it and turn screw to obtain conditions in step **2)**. After adjustment, screw MUST be in contact with lever pad.

7) Perform a KOEO Self-Test to ensure TPS fault code is not present. Move throttle plate to ensure it is not stuck in bore and linkage is not keeping throttle from closing. On models with automatic overdrive transmissions, check throttle valve adjustment.

8) If idle speed is too high, turn engine off. Using tape, block off orifice in throttle plate. *See Fig. 5.*

9) If orifice is already plugged, go to next step. On mass airflow engines, reconnect air cleaner hose. On all models, restart engine and check idle speed. If engine stalls, crack throttle plate open using throttle plate stop screw. If idle speed is still too high, go to next step. If idle speed drops to specification or drops lower than specification, go to step **11)**.

10) Perform KOEO self-test. If fault codes are present, repair as necessary. See appropriate SELF-DIAGNOSTICS article. If TPS fault code is present, check for proper TPS output. See THROTTLE POSITION SENSOR (TPS) at end of article. Ensure adjustment screw is in contact with lever pad. If fault codes are not present, see TROUBLE SHOOTING - NO CODES article.

11) Turn ignition off. Remove air cleaner hose and remove tape covering throttle plate orifice. Select correct color plug for orifice. Plugs are available in Throttle Plate Plug Kit (FOPE-9F652-AA).

12) Reconnect air cleaner hose and start engine. Recheck idle speed. If idle speed is not within specification, turn adjusting screw CLOCKWISE to obtain correct idle speed. After adjustment, screw MUST be in contact with lever pad.

13) On all models, perform a KOEO self-test to ensure TPS fault code is not present. Move throttle plate to ensure it is not stuck in bore and linkage is not keeping throttle from closing. On models with automatic overdrive transmissions, check throttle valve pressure adjustment.

7.3L Diesel - 1) Place transmission in Neutral or Park and bring engine up to normal operating temperature. Check idle speed with transmission in Neutral (M/T) or Drive (A/T). Ensure curb idle adjustment screw is against the stop. If adjustment screw is not against the stop, correct linkage.

2) Connect tachometer and check curb idle speed. Idle speed should be 600-700 RPM. Adjust idle speed using curb idle speed adjustment screw. *See Fig. 3.* Repeat check and adjust again if necessary.

THROTTLE POSITION SENSOR (TPS)

GASOLINE ENGINES

NOTE: Throttle Position Sensor (TPS) on gasoline engines is not adjustable. Replace TPS if sensor is not within specification.

1) Disconnect ECA 60-pin connector. Inspect connector for damaged pins, corrosion or loose wires; repair as necessary. Connect Breakout Box (T83L-50-EEC-IV) and reconnect ECA to breakout box. Connect digital voltmeter positive lead to pin No. 47 and negative lead to pin No. 46. Turn ignition on. Observe voltmeter reading while moving throttle slowly to wide open throttle (WOT) position. Release throttle slowly to closed position. See TPS VOLTAGE SPECIFICATIONS table.

2) If voltage is not as specified, ensure throttle stop screw and linkage are adjusted correctly. Remove sensor and check for damaged, corroded or misadjusted pins. If pins are okay, install sensor. Ensure sensor is seated correctly. Repeat step **1)**. If voltage is not as specified, perform KOEO self-test. See appropriate SELF-DIAGNOSTICS article.

TPS VOLTAGE SPECIFICATIONS [1]

Application	Idle	Wide Open Throttle
2.3L	0.20	4.84
2.9L	0.34	4.84
2.9L [2]	0.20	4.84
3.0L	0.20	4.84
4.0L	0.20	4.84
4.9L	0.34	4.84
5.0L	0.34	4.84
5.8L	0.34	4.84
7.5L	0.34	4.84

1 - Minimum and maximum specifications are given.
2 - Vehicles equipped with mass airflow sensor only.

FUEL INJECTION PUMP LEVER (FIPL) SENSOR

7.3L DIESEL ENGINES

1) Install Scan tool and enter Key On Engine Off (KOEO) self-test while holding throttle in Wide Open Throttle (WOT) position. After last service code has been displayed, remain in self-test. Place a 0.515" (13.08 mm) Gauge Block (T83T-7B200-AH) between fuel pump lever travel screw and gauge boss. *See Fig. 7.*

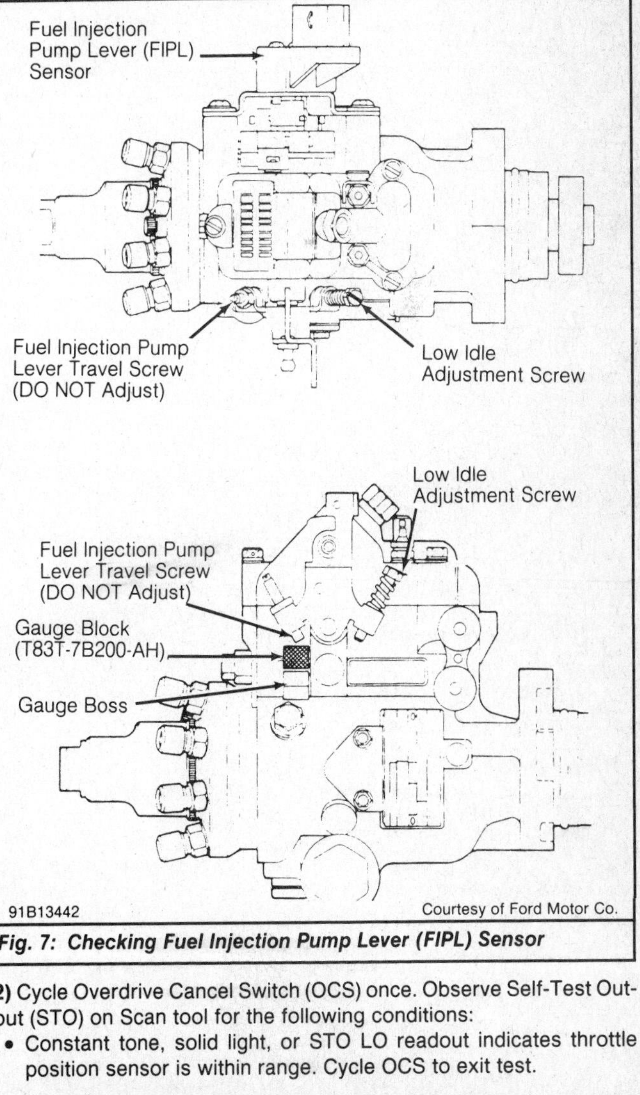

Fuel Injection Pump Lever (FIPL) Sensor
Fuel Injection Pump Lever Travel Screw (DO NOT Adjust)
Low Idle Adjustment Screw
Low Idle Adjustment Screw
Fuel Injection Pump Lever Travel Screw (DO NOT Adjust)
Gauge Block (T83T-7B200-AH)
Gauge Boss

91B13442 Courtesy of Ford Motor Co.

Fig. 7: Checking Fuel Injection Pump Lever (FIPL) Sensor

2) Cycle Overdrive Cancel Switch (OCS) once. Observe Self-Test Output (STO) on Scan tool for the following conditions:

- Constant tone, solid light, or STO LO readout indicates throttle position sensor is within range. Cycle OCS to exit test.

1991 ENGINE PERFORMANCE
On-Vehicle Adjustments (Cont.)

- Fast beeping tone, flashing light, or STO LO erratic readout (4 per second) indicates throttle position sensor requires adjustment.
- Slow beeping tone, flashing light, or STO LO erratic readout (one per second) indicates throttle position sensor requires adjustment.
- No tone, solid light, or STO LO readout indicates throttle position sensor may have worn internal components. Check by trying to move sensor.

3) If FIPL sensor and bracket screws are tight and there are no signs of wear between mounted parts, loosen FIPL sensor attachment screws. *See Fig. 8*. Rotate sensor one way or the other until a constant tone, solid light, or STO LO readout is obtained. Tighten FIPL sensor attachment screws. Remove gauge block. Cycle throttle lever to WOT 5 times. Reinsert gauge block to verify setting.

4) If FIPL sensor bracket shows signs of wear due to movement or vibration, remove epoxy from FIPL sensor bracket screw head. *See Fig. 8*. Loosen screws and turn FIPL sensor/bracket assembly to get within range (indicated by constant tone, solid light or STO LO readout). Retighten screws and apply epoxy to screw heads. Remove gauge block. Cycle throttle lever to WOT 5 times. Reinsert gauge block to verify setting.

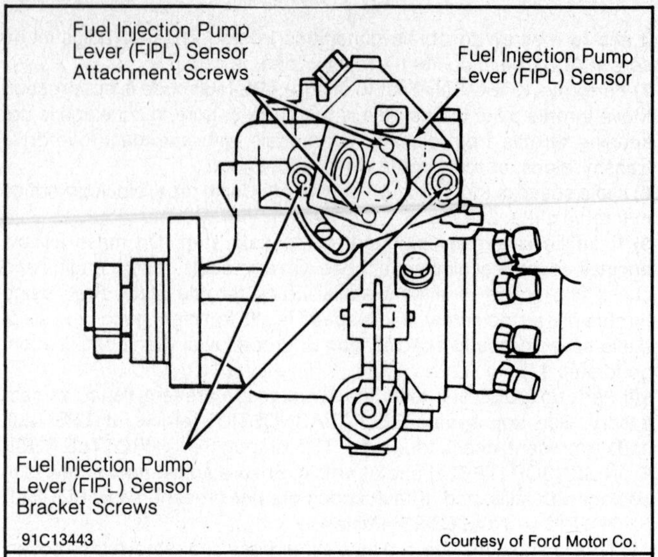
Fuel Injection Pump
Lever (FIPL) Sensor
Attachment Screws
Fuel Injection Pump
Lever (FIPL) Sensor
Fuel Injection Pump
Lever (FIPL) Sensor
Bracket Screws
91C13443
Courtesy of Ford Motor Co.

Fig. 8: Adjusting Fuel Injection Pump Lever (FIPL) Sensor

Aerostar, Bronco, Explorer, Ranger, "E" & "F" Series, "F" Series Super Duty

NOTE: Unless otherwise specified, references to "F" Series include "F" Series Super Duty. For engine repair procedures not covered in this article, see ENGINE OVERHAUL PROCEDURES article in GENERAL INFORMATION.

INTRODUCTION

This article covers basic description and operation of engine performance-related systems and components. Read this article before diagnosing vehicles or systems with which you are not completely familiar.

COMPUTERIZED ENGINE CONTROLS

ELECTRONIC CONTROL ASSEMBLY (ECA)

During system operation, ECA transmits electrical reference signals to engine sensors and analyzes return signals to determine engine operating conditions. *See Fig. 1.* If a sensor or actuator fails, ECA initiates an alternative strategy, allowing vehicle to maintain driveability. This strategy is called Failure Mode Effects Management (FMEM).

The CHECK ENGINE light will illuminate and remain on whenever FMEM is in operation. The ECA, overriding failed component with a FMEM substitute operation value, continues to monitor failed sensor. Should signals from faulty sensor return to within operational limits, ECA will cancel FMEM and resume control based on sensor signals.

ECA LOCATION

Application	Location
Aerostar	Under Left Instrument Panel
Bronco & "F" Series	Behind Left Kick Panel
"E" Series	Under Right Instrument Panel
Explorer & Ranger	Behind Right Kick Panel

NOTE: Components are grouped into 2 categories. The first category is INPUT DEVICES, covering components which control or produce voltage signals monitored by the ECA. The second category is OUTPUT SIGNALS, covering components controlled by the ECA.

INPUT DEVICES

Vehicles are equipped with different combinations of input devices. Not all devices are used on all models. To determine the input device usage on a specific model, see WIRING DIAGRAMS article in ENGINE PERFORMANCE. The available input signals include:

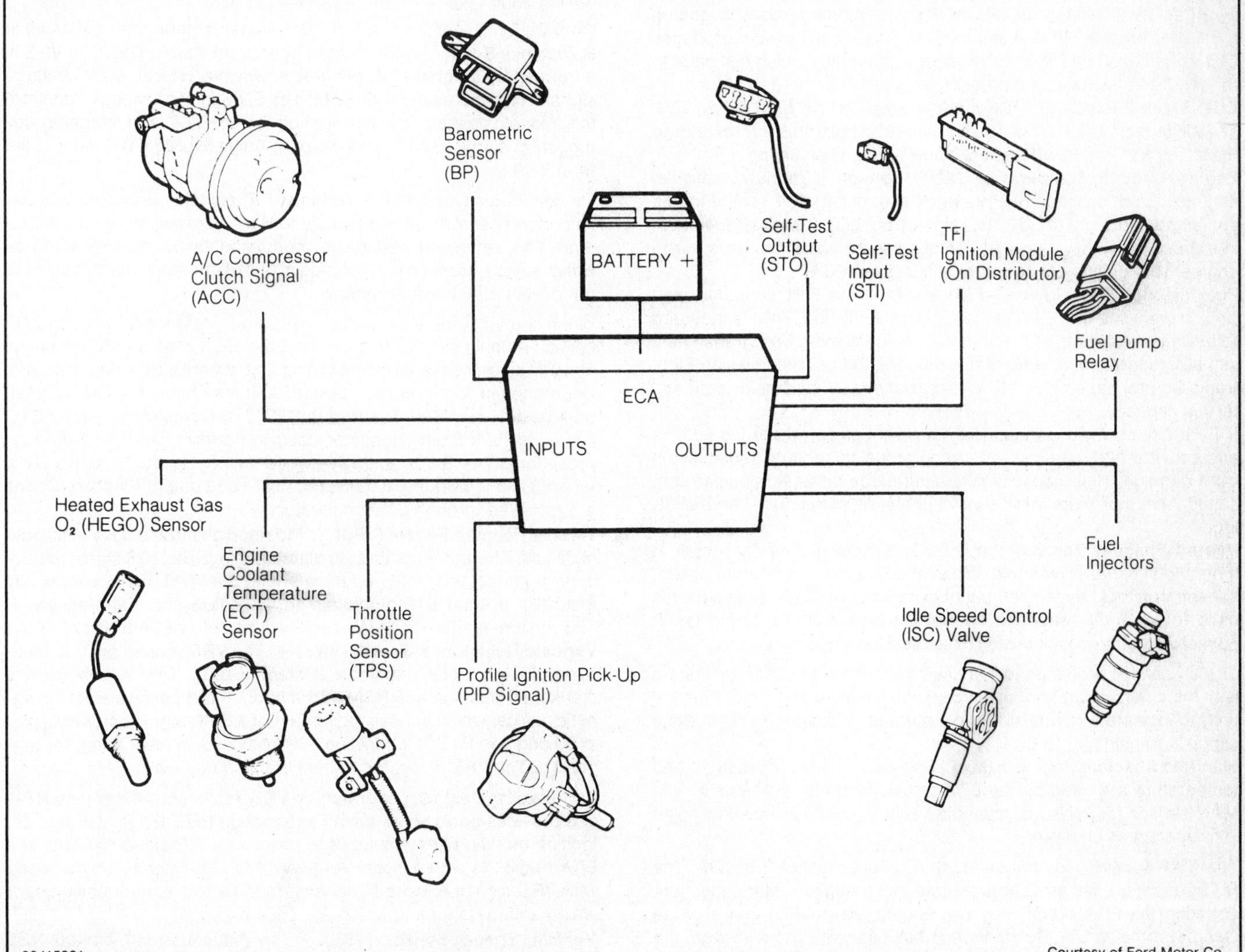
Barometric Sensor (BP)
A/C Compressor Clutch Signal (ACC)
BATTERY +
Self-Test Output (STO)
Self-Test Input (STI)
TFI Ignition Module (On Distributor)
Fuel Pump Relay
ECA
INPUTS
OUTPUTS
Heated Exhaust Gas O_2 (HEGO) Sensor
Engine Coolant Temperature (ECT) Sensor
Throttle Position Sensor (TPS)
Profile Ignition Pick-Up (PIP Signal)
Idle Speed Control (ISC) Valve
Fuel Injectors
90J15981
Courtesy of Ford Motor Co.

Fig. 1: EEC-IV System Component Diagram (Typical)

1991 ENGINE PERFORMANCE
Theory & Operation (Cont.)

A/C Compressor Clutch Signal - When battery voltage is supplied to A/C compressor clutch, ECA receives a signal, which it uses to increase engine idle speed to compensate for A/C compressor load.

Air Charge Temperature (ACT) Sensor - Threaded into a cylinder runner of intake manifold, the ACT sensor provides electronic fuel injection system with mixture temperature information. The ACT sensor is used both as a density corrector for airflow calculation and to proportion cold enrichment fuel flow.

Barometric Pressure (BP) Sensor - BP sensor measures barometric pressure of atmosphere. Variations in atmospheric pressure (changes in altitude) modify an electrical signal monitored by ECA. The BP sensor input affects spark advance, EGR flow and air/fuel mixture adjustments by ECA. Sensor input is updated during key-on and wide open throttle applications. The sensor looks identical to Manifold Absolute Pressure (MAP) sensor, except tubing nipple on BP sensor is open to atmosphere, while tubing nipple on MAP sensor is connected to intake manifold.

Brake On-Off (BOO) Switch - The BOO switch is mounted on brake pedal. It signals deceleration for air/fuel ratio adjustment.

Clutch Engage Switch - This switch is mounted at clutch pedal and signals ECA when transmission is in gear. Clutch engage switch signal to ECA affects air/fuel ratio and idle speed.

Coolant Temperature Sensor - See ENGINE COOLANT TEMPERATURE (ECT) SENSOR.

Crankshaft Sensor - A dual Hall Effect crankshaft sensor, mounted at crankshaft pulley, is used on 2.3L dual-plug Distributorless Ignition System (DIS). Sensor signals are generated when 2 trigger wheels, mounted on pulley assembly, pass through air gap of 2 Hall Effect switches. One switch produces a PIP signal, monitored by DIS ignition module to provide RPM signal to ECA. The second switch produces CID signal, used by DIS ignition module to identify which coil pack to trigger. If CID signal is not present, vehicle will be hard to start.

EGR Valve Position (EVP) Sensor - Mounted on EGR valve, EVP sensor detects EGR valve position and transmits this information to ECA. The EVP signal affects EGR flow and ignition timing.

Engine Coolant Temperature (ECT) Sensor - Threaded into an engine coolant passage near thermostat housing, ECT sensor inputs coolant temperature to ECA. The signal from ECT affects air/fuel ratio, idle speed, EGR flow, purge flow, fuel pressure, boost pressure (turbo engine) and ignition timing output signal from ECA.

Fuel Injection Pump Lever (FIPL) Sensor - The FIPL sensor is used on 7.3L vehicles with E40D automatic transmission. FIPL is mounted to fuel injection pump and actuated by throttle lever. FIPL transmits a signal, proportional to level of fuel delivery, to the Transmission Electronic Control Assembly (TECA) for assisting in transmission shift and torque capacity.

If FIPL circuit malfunctions, TECA will recognize erroneous signals and provide high capacity operating mode to protect transmission from damage. High capacity operating mode includes singular shift schedule at maximum throttle valve pressure, resulting in harsh shifting.

Heated Exhaust Gas Oxygen (HEGO) Sensor - The O_2 sensor is mounted in exhaust manifold. When at operating temperature, the O_2 sensor monitors oxygen content of exhaust gases. A heating circuit is used to warm O_2 sensor to operating temperature, enabling faster conversion of feedback system to closed loop operation.

The O_2 sensor produces low voltage (less than .4 volt) to indicate a lean mixture (high amount of oxygen) and a high voltage (more than .6 volt) to indicate a rich mixture (low amount of oxygen). This voltage signal is transmitted to ECA.

Manifold Absolute Pressure (MAP) Sensor - Manifold pressure and temperature are used by the ECA to calculate the airflow rate. The MAP sensor responds to manifold vacuum changes due to engine load and speed changes.

The MAP sensor uses frequency to measure manifold vacuum. The MAP sensor is used as a barometric sensor for altitude compensation, updating the ECA during Key On, Engine Off (KOEO) and at Wide Open Throttle (WOT). By monitoring MAP sensor output voltage, the ECA can determine correct rate of spark advance, EGR flow and air/fuel ratio. If MAP sensor fails, the ECA will supply a fixed MAP value and use the Throttle Position Sensor (TPS) to control fuel distribution.

Mass Airflow (MAF) Sensor - MAF sensor measures flow of air entering the engine. This measurement of airflow is a reflection of engine load (throttle opening). The sensing element (hot wire) is a thin platinum wire wound on a ceramic bobbin and coated with glass. The hot wire is maintained at 392°F (200°C) above cold wire (ambient) temperature. Cold wire is located downstream of hot wire. As air passes through the airflow sensor, the air temperature is measured as air passes over the cold wire sensor. The ECA uses this information to control fuel delivery.

Neutral Gear Switch (NGS) - The NGS monitors in-gear conditions and signals ECA. This signal affects air/fuel ratio, idle speed and ignition timing.

Neutral Safety Switch (NSS) - Mounted on side of transmission, this switch monitors gear position on automatic transmission vehicles. The signal affects air/fuel ratio, idle speed and EGR flow.

Power Steering (P/S) Pressure Switch - The P/S pressure switch monitors power steering pressure, signaling ECA to adjust engine idle speed under load conditions. The switch is located in high pressure line from P/S pump to steering rack assembly.

Profile Ignition Pick-Up (PIP) - On 2.3L DIS ignition systems, modulated PIP and CID signals are produced by dual Hall Effect crankshaft sensor and monitored by DIS ignition module. See CRANKSHAFT SENSOR under INPUT DEVICES. Ignition module relays the PIP signal to ECA, which uses it as an RPM reference to determine timing adjustments.

ECA timing control returns to ignition module in form of a Spark Output (SPOUT) signal. The leading edge of SPOUT signal fires coil, and trailing edge controls dwell on-time.

On 4.0L EDIS ignition systems, PIP signal is generated by Variable Reluctance Sensor (VRS), located near crankshaft pulley. The VRS is a Permanent Magnet (PM) generator, which produces an AC voltage signal which increases with RPM. The EDIS ignition module monitors this signal, passes this information on to ECA and modifies coil triggering signal based upon a Spark Angle Word (SAW) signal sent from ECA.

On distributor-type ignition systems, PIP signal is provided by a 12-volt reference from ignition module to Hall Effect switch, inside distributor. This reference voltage is modulated by window/shutter Hall Effect switch. Monitored reference is pulled low when shutter blade is out of Hall Effect switch window.

When shutter blade enters window, 12-volt reference returns, and TFI ignition module sends PIP signal to ECA. ECA uses the PIP signal as an RPM reference to calculate timing adjustments. ECA timing control returns to ignition module in form of a Spark Output (SPOUT) signal.

Self-Test Output/Self-Test Input (STO/STI) Connectors - The STO connector is a 6-pin connector used to perform self-test diagnostic procedure. The STI is a single-pin connector, located next to STO. When STI is grounded, it activates fault code output function. Codes are retrieved through STO connector.

Throttle Position Sensor (TPS) - Mounted on throttle body at throttle plate rod, TPS monitors throttle plate opening. The TPS signal to ECA is proportional to throttle opening angle. The TPS signal affects air/fuel ratio, injector timing, idle speed, EGR flow and fuel pressure. If TPS system malfunctions, Code 12 will be set in ECA memory.

Variable Reluctance Sensor (VRS) - The VRS is used on 4.0L Electronic Distributorless Ignition System (EDIS). The VRS transmits crankshaft position and RPM information. It is a passive electromagnetic device, which senses movement of a 35-tooth wheel (with a gap at 60 degrees BTDC, where the 36th tooth would have been, for triggering). The VRS is located behind crankshaft pulley.

An AC voltage signal, generated by VRS, increases with engine RPM and provides basic spark timing information to EDIS ignition module. Ignition module uses this input to produce a PIP signal to ECA. The ECA responds with a Spark Angle Word (SAW) signal, which, along with VRS signal, is used by ignition module to compute basic spark timing and to determine which coil pack to trigger.

Vehicle Speed Sensor (VSS) - The transmission-mounted VSS sends a pulsing signal to ECA when vehicle is moving. The VSS gen-

erates pulses with axle shaft revolution. The ECA interprets speed sensor input along with TPS closed throttle input.
This input enables ECA to differentiate between closed throttle deceleration and closed throttle idle (vehicle stopped) conditions. During deceleration, ECA controls Idle Speed Control (ISC) Valve to maintain a desired manifold pressure. During idle, ECA controls ISC motor to maintain a desired idle speed.

OUTPUT SIGNALS

NOTE: Vehicles are equipped with different combinations of computer-controlled components. Not all components listed below are used on every vehicle. For theory and operation on components, refer to indicated system.

A/C Clutch Cycling Switch – See MISCELLANEOUS CONTROLS.
Canister Purge Solenoid Valve – See EMISSION SYSTEMS.
CHECK ENGINE Light – See SELF-DIAGNOSTIC SYSTEM.
Cooling Fan – See MISCELLANEOUS CONTROLS.
EGR System – See EMISSION SYSTEMS.
Fuel Injectors – See FUEL SYSTEMS.
Fuel Pump – See FUEL SYSTEMS.
Fuel Pressure Regulator – See FUEL SYSTEMS.
Idle Speed Control (ISC) Valve – See FUEL SYSTEMS.
Self-Diagnostic – See SELF-DIAGNOSTIC SYSTEM.
Self-Test Output/Self-Test Input Connectors – See SELF-DIAGNOSTIC SYSTEM.
Wide Open Throttle Cut-Off – See MISCELLANEOUS CONTROLS.

FUEL SYSTEMS

FUEL DELIVERY

System Types – Fuel delivery systems differ in design depending upon model. System designs use one of the following configurations:
- Single tank with single pump.
- Single tank with dual pump.
- Dual tank with mechanical selector valve/reservoir.

Low Pressure Fuel Pump – All vehicles are equipped with a high pressure pump, but some vehicles use multiple pump systems. These systems have a primary, low pressure in-tank pump for supplying fuel to reservoir. The low pressure pump rests in a sump (depression) in fuel tank. A nylon screen protects low pressure pump inlet from contaminating particles, but allows passage of small amounts of water which may accumulate in fuel tank sump.

When dual tanks are used, each tank is equipped with a low pressure pump. Such a system has a total of 3 pumps: 2 low pressure and one high pressure.
High Pressure Fuel Pump – The high pressure fuel pump is positioned inside fuel tank. A reservoir is built onto pump and sender assembly, instead of as part of tank.

In a 2-tank system, sender assembly handles switching of high pressure fuel through internal valves. Should one tank overfill during use (return line returns fuel to wrong tank), pump and sender unit in overfilling tank need replacement.
The high pressure fuel pump is capable of pumping over 33 gallons (125 liters) of fuel per hour at a working pressure of 39.2 psi (2.75 kg/cm²). This pump also has internal pressure relief and discharge check valves.
Mechanical Fuel Pump – The 7.3L diesel engine uses a mechanical fuel pump to pump fuel from fuel tank to a combination fuel filter/fuel heater/water separator.
Mechanical Selector Valve – A driver-operated selector switch controls selector valve for switching fuel supply from one tank to other. The mechanical selector valve is contained within 6-port reservoir assembly. This valve switches fuel supply and return lines from one tank to other in response to fuel pressure from in-tank pumps acting on its actuating diaphragm.

The diaphragm switches tank connection when less than 2 psi of fuel pressure is acting on upper side of front tank and lower side of rear tank. Valve functioning depends upon proper operation of in-tank low pressure pumps. In all dual tank vehicles, excess fuel not used by engine is returned to same tank from which it was pumped.
Reservoirs & Filters – Fuel reservoirs are used to prevent fuel flow interruptions during extreme vehicle maneuvers with low tank fill levels. Models using multiple pumps use in-line reservoirs, frame mounted between low and high pressure pumps. On models using one pump, reservoir is either molded or welded into either tank or fuel pump and sender plastic housing.

There are 2 types of in-line reservoirs: single function and dual function. Both contain a fine mesh in-filter; the dual function contains a mechanical selector valve.
Fuel Supply Manifold Assembly – Fuel supply manifold assembly (fuel rail) delivers high pressure fuel from fuel pump supply line to fuel injectors. Fuel rail consists of tubular rail or stamping with injector connectors. Fuel pressure regulator is mounted on flange attached to rail. Rail also has mounting attachments which secure fuel injectors in intake manifold.
Fuel Pressure Regulator – The fuel pressure regulator is attached to fuel supply manifold assembly, downstream of fuel injectors. It regulates fuel pressure supplied to injectors. Regulator is a diaphragm-operated valve with one side responding to fuel pressure and the other side to intake manifold vacuum.

When intake manifold vacuum is low, an internal spring increases pressure on diaphragm, blocking off fuel return passage and increasing fuel pressure. When manifold pressure is high, spring pressure is overcome by vacuum, opening fuel return passage and lowering fuel pressure. Excess fuel is by-passed through regulator and returned to fuel tank.

The regulator also controls fuel line vapor formation, allowing for rapid restarts, assistance in engine idle stabilization and maintenance of fuel pressure when engine is turned off. Pressure is adjusted at factory to compensate for fuel flow differences between injectors.
Fuel Pump Shut-Off (Inertia) Switch – All models use an electrical interrupt switch in fuel system. During a collision or vehicle roll-over, electrical contacts within inertia switch open, shutting off fuel supply to electric fuel pump. Fuel supply is interrupted even when engine is running.

A reset button is located on switch assembly. If electrical circuit trips, vehicle will not re-start until switch is reset. Fuel system should be inspected before resetting switch.

On Aerostar models, inertia switch is located in right kick panel. On "E" Series models, inertia switch is located on right cowl panel, near front of door. On Bronco and "F" Series models, inertia switch is located on left toe board, near parking brake assembly. On Ranger and Explorer models, inertia switch is located on toe board, near right side of transmission hump.

NOTE: DO NOT reset fuel pump shut-off (inertia) switch after an accident until inspecting entire fuel system for leaks.

FUEL CONTROL (GASOLINE ENGINES)

Precise fuel metering is accomplished with EEC-IV system. The ECA continually monitors engine operating conditions based on information received from various sensors and switches. In response to information received, ECA calculates optimum air/fuel mixture in relation to present engine operating conditions and affects required metering adjustments through output actuators control.

When ignition switch is turned to START position, ECA operates fuel pump relay to provide fuel for starting engine. ECA senses engine speed and shuts off fuel pump by opening ground circuit to fuel pump relay when engine stops or speed drops to less than 120 RPM. When ignition switch is in ON position, EEC power relay is energized (contacts closed). Power is provided to fuel pump relay and timer in ECA. Fuel pump receives power through fuel pump relay contacts.
Fuel Injection – The ECA controls fuel injectors to meter pulse width or time each injector is energized. Each injector receives battery voltage through ignition switch circuit. The ECA-controlled ground circuit

1991 ENGINE PERFORMANCE
Theory & Operation (Cont.)

completes circuit to energize injector. The ECA receives inputs from engine sensors to compute fuel flow necessary to maintain air/fuel mixture ratio throughout entire engine operational range.

Each cylinder has a solenoid-operated injector which sprays fuel toward back of each intake valve. Injector bodies consist of solenoid-actuated pintle and needle valve assembly. Injector flow orifice is fixed, and fuel pressure at injector tip is constant. Atomizing spray is obtained by shape of pintle.

Throttle Body Assembly – The throttle body assembly controls air-flow to engine through a butterfly valve. Throttle position is controlled by either linkage or cable/cam mechanism. Body is one-piece aluminum casting with single bore and air by-pass channel.

FUEL CONTROL (7.3L DIESEL)

The fuel pump delivers fuel from fuel tank to the fuel filter. After being filtered, fuel enters the injection pump and is delivered under high pressure through injection nozzles into cylinders. Injectors are equipped with a fuel return outlet. Excess fuel collected at the injectors and injector pump are recirculated back to the fuel tank.

IDLE SPEED (GASOLINE ENGINES)

Idle Speed Control (ISC) Valve – The ISC valve, mounted on the throttle body, controls idle smoothness by regulating throttle plate by-pass air. ISC valve consists of an air by-pass valve, which functions during cold engine conditions below 122°F (50°C), and the idle speed control solenoid valve, which works throughout the entire temperature range. The air by-pass valve is affected by the engine coolant temperature. The idle speed control solenoid is controlled by ECA.

Idle is controlled by idle speed control air by-pass valve. The throttle air by-pass valve is a solenoid-operated valve controlled by ECA. The valve allows air to by-pass throttle plates to control cold engine fast idle, no-touch start, dashpot, overtemperature idle boost and engine load idle correction.

Air by-pass channel carries idle airflow regulated by air by-pass valve. Air by-pass valve is controlled by ECA to adjust both cold and warm idle speeds. Air by-pass valve uses solenoid valve to vary idle airflow volume allowed to enter engine.

IDLE SPEED (7.3L DIESEL)

Idle is controlled by curb idle speed adjustment screw, located on injection pump. Fast (cold) idle is controlled by cold idle solenoid, located by curb idle speed adjustment screw. For additional information, see ON-VEHICLE ADJUSTMENTS article.

IGNITION SYSTEMS

Distributorless Ignition System (DIS) – The DIS system, used on 4-cylinder engines, is a dual plug system consisting of a crankshaft-mounted dual Hall Effect sensor, two 4-tower DIS coil packs and a DIS ignition module.

The DIS eliminates distributor by using multiple coils, each of which simultaneously fires 2 paired spark plugs. The first time a pair of spark plugs is fired, one fires during compression stroke and other during exhaust stroke. The next time same pair of spark plugs is fired, the roles are reversed. Although spark in exhaust stroke is wasted, little of coil's energy is lost.

Two ignition coils are mounted together in a coil pack. Since there are 2 plugs per cylinder, 2 coil packs are required. The right coil pack operates continuously, whereas left coil pack may be switched on or off by ECA.

The ECA computes spark angle and dwell for ignition system. The crankshaft-mounted dual Hall Effect sensor is a dual digital output device, which responds to 2 rotating metallic shutters mounted on crankshaft. One output from Hall Effect sensor, Profile Ignition Pick-Up (PIP), is a 50 percent duty cycle signal, providing base spark timing information. The other output signal, Cylinder Identification (CID) signal, is required for DIS module to know which coil to fire. CID is high (battery voltage) for half of crankshaft revolution (180 degrees) and low (zero volts) for other half of revolution.

The ECA determines Spark Output (SPOUT) by using PIP signal to establish base timing. The SPOUT signal is produced and sent by ECA to DIS module and serves 2 purposes: the leading edge of signal fires coil, and trailing edge of signal controls dwell on-time. This feature is called Computer Controlled Dwell (CCD).

Another feature of system is Ignition Diagnostic Monitor (IDM). This is an output from DIS module to ECA which provides diagnostic information about ignition system for self-test.

Dual Plug Inhibit (DPI), another system feature, allows ECA processor to switch ignition system from single-to-dual plug operation. During cranking, vehicle is in single plug mode: only plugs on right side of engine fire. When engine starts, ECA sends a command to DIS module to switch to dual plug operation.

If CID circuit fails, DIS module will randomly select one of 2 coils to fire. If hard starting results, turning key off and then cranking again will result in another random selection. Several attempts may be needed before DIS module selects proper coil, which will allow vehicle to start and be driven until repairs can be made.

The Failure Mode Effects Management (FMEM) system will keep vehicle drivable in event of an EEC-IV system or ignition failure, which would otherwise prevent spark angle or dwell commands. During FMEM, ECA opens SPOUT line and DIS module fires coils directly from PIP output. This results in a fixed spark angle of 10 degrees and a fixed dwell.

Electronic Distributorless Ignition System (EDIS) – System is used on 4.0L engines and consists of a Variable Reluctance Sensor (VRS), an EDIS ignition module, an ECA and one 6-tower coil pack.

During system operation, EDIS ignition module receives crankshaft position information from VRS. In turn, EDIS ignition module generates a Profile Ignition Pick-Up (PIP) signal and sends it to ECA. The ECA responds with a Spark Angle Word (SAW) signal containing advance or retard timing information, which it sends to EDIS module. The EDIS ignition module then processes VRS and SAW signals to decide which coils to fire. In addition, EDIS ignition module generates an Ignition Diagnostic Monitor (IDM) signal and sends it to ECA, which uses it during failure mode to provide a tach output signal.

The EDIS ignition module is a microprocessor and makes decisions about spark timing and coil firing. The EDIS ignition module turns coils on and off at correct times and in proper sequence, based on VRS and SAW signals. The EDIS ignition module, upon receiving VRS and SAW signals, produces PIP and IDM output signals and sends these signals to ECA.

The ECA receives IGN GND and PIP signals from EDIS ignition module, and then generates a SAW output signal, based upon fuel, air and other sensor information. ECA also receives an IDM signal from EDIS ignition module to determine if a failure mode should be recorded.

The coil pack receives active low signals from EDIS ignition module and fires 2 spark plugs at a time. One plug is for cylinder which is to be fired (on compression stroke) and other goes to mating cylinder (on exhaust stroke). The next time coil is fired, situation is reversed. Coils are fired according to engine firing order.

Thick Film Ignition (TFI) – All engines, except those with distributorless ignition systems, use TFI ignition systems. The TFI distributor is a gear-driven, die-cast unit. A Hall Effect stator assembly is used to trigger ignition coil. This distributor does not use conventional centrifugal/vacuum advance mechanisms. The TFI ignition module may be mounted in base of distributor bowl or on cowl behind engine. Vehicles which have a remotely mounted module are often referred to as Closed Bowl Distributor (CBD) TFI systems.

The TFI distributor uses a Hall Effect switch mechanism to switch primary voltage and send a Profile Ignition Pick-Up (PIP) signal to ECA. The ECA uses PIP input signal to produce a Spark Output signal (SPOUT), which is sent to TFI ignition module to trigger coil secondary voltage discharge.

On manual transaxle vehicles, the TFI ignition module features a push start mode, which allows vehicle to be push started if necessary. An "E" core ignition coil is used.

EMISSION SYSTEMS

Several systems and components are used to control emissions. Operation and actuation method is provided for most devices. For testing procedures, refer to specific system in SYSTEM & COMPONENT TESTING article.

Temperature Vacuum Switch (TVS) – The TVS incorporates a bimetallic disc which opens and closes vacuum ports. TVS may be used in conjunction with distributor, canister purge or EGR systems.

Vacuum Control Valve – This temperature-operated vacuum switch has 2 or more ports. Valve uses a wax pellet or bimetallic material to open or close vacuum ports at normal engine operating temperatures. Vacuum control valve is usually mounted in some part of cooling system with its base immersed in coolant. Valve may be either normally open or closed.

Vacuum Delay Valve – Vacuum delay valve is inserted in vacuum lines to provide gradual application or vacuum release to engine or emission control devices. One-way or two-way valve may be used, depending on function and system.

Vacuum Reservoir – The vacuum reservoir stores vacuum and provides an amplified vacuum signal, preventing rapid fluctuations or sudden drops in a vacuum signal during such conditions as acceleration.

Vacuum Restrictor – This orifice-type flow restrictor is used as an emission calibration to control flow rate and/or actuation timing of components and systems.

Vacuum Vent Valve – Vacuum vent valve controls induction of fresh air into system, preventing accumulation of fuel vapors which could cause decay of vacuum diaphragms. Valve may be vent only or combined vent and delay valve. Valve should always be mounted with ports pointing downward.

AIR INJECTION SYSTEM

The air injection system reduces carbon monoxide (CO) and hydrocarbon (HC) content of exhaust gases. It injects fresh air into exhaust gas stream, which continues combustion of unburned gases. Air can be by-passed to atmosphere by a thermactor air by-pass valve and/or directed near exhaust manifold or catalytic converter.

Depending upon engine size and application, individual systems may vary in number and type of components. All systems use same basic components: air supply pump, air by-pass valve, filter, check valve(s), air control valve, air manifold and air hoses. Some models may use a combined air by-pass/air control valve.

Air By-Pass Valve – Valve directs airflow from thermactor air pump to exhaust system or atmosphere as required. Valve may be mounted on air pump or in-line (remote). Air by-pass valve is vacuum operated and may be either normally open or closed.

Normally closed valve supplies air to exhaust system with medium and high applied vacuum signals during normal modes, short idles and some acceleration. With low or no vacuum applied, pump air is dumped through silencer valve ports.

Normally open valve with a vacuum vent provides a timed air dump during deceleration. Valve also dumps when a vacuum pressure difference is maintained between signal and vent ports.

Air Pump – The air pump is a belt-driven, positive displacement, vane-type pump which provides air for air injection system. Air is received from a remote silencer/filter, attached to air inlet nipple of pump, or through a centrifugal fan on front of pump. The by-pass valve performs pressure relief.

The air pump supplies air under pressure to exhaust port near exhaust valve by either an external air manifold or through an internal drilled passage in cylinder head or exhaust manifold. This pressurized air, combined with hot exhaust gases, creates a secondary combustion stage, which produces carbon dioxide and water.

Air Supply Control Valve – Operated by vacuum, this valve directs air pump output upstream to exhaust manifold or downstream to catalytic converter.

Check Valves – Check valves are used on all thermactor systems in various locations. These valves allow airflow in one direction only.

Combination Air By-Pass & Air Control Valve – By-pass valve routes thermactor air to either the exhaust system or atmosphere. When air is routed to exhaust system, control valve routes air either upstream to exhaust manifolds or downstream to catalytic converter.

Both valves are normally closed and come in either a bleed or non-bleed type. Bleed-type valves will have bleed percentage molded into plastic case.

Dual Thermactor Air Control Solenoid Valve – The dual thermactor air control solenoid valve assembly consists of 2 normally closed solenoid valves with vents. One valve controls thermactor air by-pass valve and other controls thermactor air diverter valve. Both valves pass air when deactivated and do not pass air when activated.

Thermactor Idle Vacuum (TIV) Valve – The TIV valve vents vacuum signal to atmosphere when preset manifold vacuum or pressure is exceeded. During periods of extended idle, this valve is used to divert thermactor airflow to limit exhaust temperature. This prevents excessive underbody temperature. TIV valve also cuts EGR in a heavy boost mode for turbocharged applications.

EGR SYSTEM

NOTE: Not all vehicles use EGR systems. EGR system usage depends on engine application.

The Exhaust Gas Recirculation (EGR) system distributes exhaust gas into intake mixture. This lowers combustion temperatures due to lower concentrations of oxygen. Lowering combustion temperatures reduces NOx emissions.

Electronic EGR Valve – The Electronic EGR valve is required in EEC systems where EGR flow is controlled according to computer demands of EGR Valve Position (EVP) sensor. The EGR valve is operated by a vacuum signal from EGR Vacuum Regulator (EVR).

EGR valve is mounted on top of an intake and exhaust gas port. The EGR pintle blocks exhaust gas from entering intake system. When vacuum is applied to EGR valve, the diaphragm is actuated. This lifts EGR pintle (attached to diaphragm) and allows exhaust gas to recirculate into intake system.

EGR Vacuum Regulator (EVR) – The vacuum regulator is an electromagnetic device controlling vacuum to EGR valve. Regulator operation is measured as a duty cycle: increased duty means increased vacuum to EGR.

EGR Valve Position (EVP) Sensor – This sensor is attached to EGR valve assembly and indicates EGR valve position to ECA.

EVAPORATIVE EMISSION CONTROL

NOTE: Not all listed components are used on every vehicle system. Component usage depends on calibration of vehicle.

The function of evaporative emission control system is to store gasoline fumes from fuel system in a carbon canister when engine is not running. During engine operation, fumes are drawn into engine for burning during combustion process, purging canister.

Three basic components are used in evaporative emission system:

- Activated carbon canister.
- Computer-controlled solenoid.
- Tank pressure control cap.

For specific component application and vacuum hose routing, see VACUUM DIAGRAMS article.

Carbon Canister – Carbon canister storage is used for evaporative fuel control on all vehicles.

Canister Purge Solenoid Valve – This normally closed solenoid valve controls fuel vapor flow from canister to intake manifold. It is opened or closed by a signal from ECA during various engine operating modes.

Fill Control/Vent System – Fill limiting is accomplished through configuration of fill neck and/or internal vent lines. Vent system is designed to permit air space in 10-12 percent of tank to allow for thermal expansion.

1991 ENGINE PERFORMANCE
Theory & Operation (Cont.)

Vapor generated in fuel supply line is continuously vented back to fuel tank. Venting prevents engine surging from fuel enrichment and assists in hydrocarbon (HC) emission control.

Pressure/Vacuum Relief Fuel Cap – This system consists of a sealed filler cap with an integral pressure/vacuum relief valve. Fuel system vacuum relief is provided after 1.0 in. Hg of vacuum. Pressure relief is provided after 1.8 psi (.13 kg/cm²). Under normal conditions, fill cap allows air to enter fuel tank as fuel is used, without allowing fuel vapors to escape.

Vapor Vent System – System provides a vapor space above gasoline surface in fuel tank. This area is sufficient to permit adequate breathing room for tank vapor valve assembly.

All vapor valves are mounted on fuel tank and use a small orifice which allows vapor (but not liquid) fuel to pass into line running to canister. Fuel vapors in fuel tank are vented though vapor valve assembly on top of fuel tank. Vapors are routed through a vapor line to carbon canister in engine compartment.

POSITIVE CRANKCASE VENTILATION (PCV)

The PCV system uses intake manifold vacuum to eliminate blow-by gases from crankcase. Manifold vacuum draws gases from crankcase, through PCV hose, into combustion chamber. The PCV valve is positioned in hose through which blow-by gases flow on their way to combustion chamber.

By opening and closing in direct relation to engine vacuum, the PCV valve meters blow-by gas flow to combustion chamber. During periods of high manifold vacuum, such as at idle and deceleration, valve is almost completely closed, limiting flow of gases. During cruise speeds, valve permits greatest flow of gases.

Under conditions in which excessively high amounts of blow-by gases are produced (such as worn cylinders or rings), system allows excess gases to flow back through crankcase vent hose and into intake manifold.

SELF-DIAGNOSTIC SYSTEM

NOTE: All systems have self-diagnostic capabilities. For information on procedures for entering self-test modes and reading service codes, see appropriate SELF-DIAGNOSTICS article.

CHECK ENGINE LIGHT

The CHECK ENGINE light (if equipped) will illuminate whenever ignition is turned to the ON position (bulb check) or systems related to the EEC-IV system malfunction during normal engine operation. For additional information, see appropriate SELF-DIAGNOSTICS article.

SELF-TEST OUTPUT/SELF-TEST INPUT (STO/STI) CONNECTORS

The STO connector is a 6-pin connector used to perform self-test diagnostic procedure. The STI is a single-pin connector, located next to STO. When STI is grounded, it activates fault code output function. Codes are retrieved through STO connector.

MISCELLANEOUS CONTROLS

A/C CLUTCH CYCLING PRESSURE SWITCH (CCPS)

On models with manual A/C system, the CCPS is mounted on top of the receiver-drier. Based on refrigerant system pressure, a signal is sent to the ECA. The ECA uses this signal to maintain system pressure within the programmed range.

COOLING FAN

The ECA regulates operation of the electric cooling fan through an ECA-controlled relay, which controls the ground or power circuit of the cooling fan. This allows the ECA to operate the cooling fan based on engine temperature. A malfunction of the cooling fan will cause engine overheating and possible detonation.

WIDE OPEN THROTTLE A/C (WAC) CUT-OFF

During wide open throttle, WAC circuit interrupts power to A/C compressor clutch. The A/C remains off for about 3 seconds after returning from WOT.

WAIT TO START INDICATOR LIGHT

On 7.3L models, this light comes on when engine is cold and ignition is in the RUN position. The light will remain on for 5-10 seconds, depending on time required for glow plugs to warm.

WATER IN FUEL INDICATOR LIGHT

On 7.3L models, this light comes on when engine is in the START position. The light will remain on if fuel filter water separator has a water level that exceeds predetermined level.

1991 ENGINE PERFORMANCE
Basic Diagnostic Procedures

Aerostar, Bronco, Explorer, Ranger, "E" & "F" Series, "F" Series Super Duty

***NOTE:** Unless otherwise specified, references to "F" Series include "F" Series Super Duty.*

INTRODUCTION

The following diagnostic steps help prevent overlooking simple problems and begin diagnosis for no-start conditions.

The first step in diagnosing any driveability problem is verifying the customer's complaint by test driving vehicle under the conditions in which the problem reportedly occurred.

Before entering self-diagnostics, perform a careful and complete visual inspection. Most engine control problems result from mechanical breakdowns, poor electrical connections or damaged/misrouted vacuum hoses. Before condemning the computerized system, perform each test listed in this article.

***NOTE:** Unless otherwise instructed in test procedure, perform all voltage tests using a Digital Volt-Ohmmeter (DVOM) with a minimum 10-megohm input impedance.*

PRELIMINARY INSPECTION & ADJUSTMENTS

VISUAL INSPECTION

Visually inspect all electrical wiring. Look for chafed, stretched, cut or pinched wiring. Ensure electrical connectors fit tightly and are not corroded. Ensure vacuum hoses are properly routed and are not pinched or cut. If necessary, see VACUUM DIAGRAMS article to verify routing and connections. Inspect air induction system for possible vacuum leaks.

MECHANICAL INSPECTION

Compression – Check engine mechanical condition using a compression gauge, vacuum gauge or engine analyzer. If using engine analyzer, see engine analyzer manual for specific instructions. Compression pressures are considered within specifications if lowest reading cylinder is within 75 percent of highest reading cylinder.

***WARNING:** Because fuel injectors on many models are triggered by ignition switch, DO NOT use ignition switch during compression tests on fuel injected vehicles. Use a remote starter to crank engine to prevent fire hazard or engine oiling system contamination.*

Exhaust System Backpressure – Using a vacuum or pressure gauge, check exhaust system. Remove O_2 sensor or air injection check valve (if equipped). Connect a 0-5 psi pressure gauge, and run engine at 2500 RPM. If exhaust system backpressure is greater than 1 3/4 - 2 psi, exhaust system or catalytic converter is plugged.

If using a vacuum gauge, connect vacuum gauge hose to intake manifold vacuum port, and start engine. Observe vacuum gauge. Open throttle part way and hold steady. If vacuum gauge reading slowly drops after stabilizing, check exhaust system for restrictions.

NO-START DIAGNOSIS

***NOTE:** For diesel information, see TROUBLE SHOOTING – NO CODES article.*

Definition – No-start is defined as engine cranks okay, but does not start. Engine may fire a few times.

PRELIMINARY CHECKS

Before diagnosing problems in ignition system, ensure following systems and components are in good condition and operating properly.

- Battery
- State of tune
- Fuel delivery and injection system
- All wiring and vacuum connections
- Air cleaner and ducts
- Cooling system

DISTRIBUTORLESS IGNITION SYSTEM (DIS) – 2.3L

***NOTE:** Following diagnostic tests are sequential. Beginning with first test, complete each successive test. DO NOT skip tests unless so directed.*

Test 1, Check ECA For Fault Codes – Repair any fault codes as necessary. See SELF-DIAGNOSTICS article. If no fault codes are retrieved, proceed to next test.

Test 2, Check For Spark During Crank – Using Neon Bulb Spark Tester (D89P-6666-A), check for spark at each right side spark plug wire while cranking. If spark is present and consistent (one spark per crank revolution) on all right side spark plug wires, go to next test. If spark is not present or is inconsistent, go to TEST 5.

Test 3, Check DIS Module PIP Out – Install DIS Diagnostic Cable (007-00044). Connect diagnostic cable to Breakout Box (T83L-50-EEC-IV). *See Fig. 1.* Use 2.3L overlay. Connect LED test light between breakout box pins No. (+) J31 (PIP EEC) and (-) J60 (BAT -). Crank engine. If test light blinks continuously during cranking, go to next test. If test light does not blink continuously during cranking, replace DIS module, and check for fault codes.

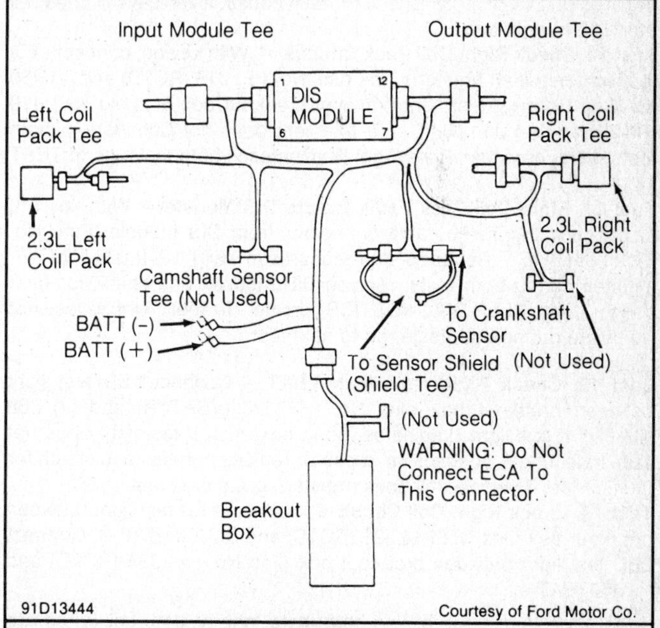
Input Module Tee
Output Module Tee
DIS MODULE
1
12
6
7
Left Coil Pack Tee
Right Coil Pack Tee
2.3L Left Coil Pack
2.3L Right Coil Pack
Camshaft Sensor Tee (Not Used)
BATT (-)
BATT (+)
To Crankshaft Sensor
To Sensor Shield (Shield Tee)
(Not Used)
(Not Used)
WARNING: Do Not Connect ECA To This Connector.
Breakout Box
91D13444
Courtesy of Ford Motor Co.

***Fig. 1:** Installing DIS Diagnostic Cable*

Test 4, Check PIP Out Continuity – With key off, disconnect ECA. Using ohmmeter, measure resistance between vehicle harness connector pin No. 56 and breakout box pin No. J31 (PIP EEC). *See Fig. 2.* If resistance is less than 5 ohms, see CIRCUIT TEST A in SELF-DIAGNOSTICS article. If resistance is more than 5 ohms, repair open circuit, reconnect ECA and retest system. If vehicle still does not start, go to next test.

Test 5, Determine Missing Spark Combination – If during cranking spark is missing from both cylinders No. 1 and 4 plug wires or both cylinders No. 2 and 3 plug wires, go to next test. If spark is present, go to TEST 7.

1991 ENGINE PERFORMANCE
Basic Diagnostic Procedures (Cont.)

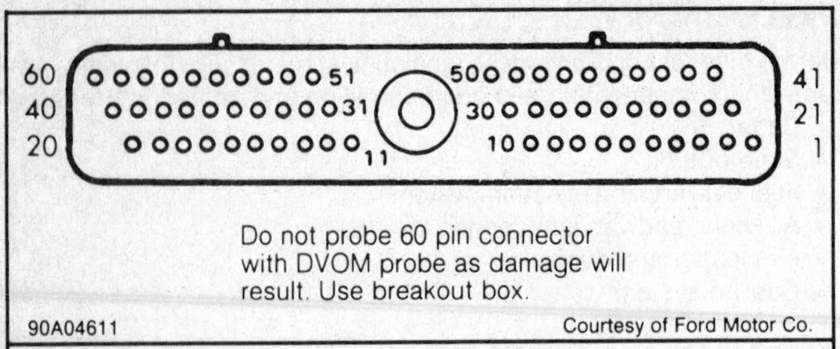
60
40
20
51
31
11
50
30
10
41
21
1
Do not probe 60 pin connector with DVOM probe as damage will result. Use breakout box.
90A04611
Courtesy of Ford Motor Co.

Fig. 2: Identifying ECA Connector Pin Locations

Test 6, Check Plugs & Wires – Check spark plug wires for insulation damage, looseness, shorting or other damage. Remove and check spark plugs for damage, wear, carbon deposits and proper plug gap. If spark plug wires and spark plugs are good, reinstall, and go to next test. If components are faulty, service or replace as required. If vehicle still does not start, go to next test.

Test 7, Check DIS Module VBAT – Install diagnostic cable. Connect diagnostic cable to breakout box. Use 2.3L overlay. Connect LED test light between breakout box pins No. (-) J2 (IGND D) and (+) J5 (VBAT D). Turn key on. If test light is on, go to next test. If test light is not on, check connectors, repair or replace harness and check for fault codes. If vehicle still does not start, go to next test.

Test 8, Check DIS Module Ignition Ground – With key off, check resistance between breakout box pins No. J2 (IGND D) and J60 (BAT -). If resistance is more than 5 ohms, go to next test. If resistance is less than 5 ohms, go to TEST 10.

Test 9, Check DIS Module Mounting Screws – Check DIS module mounting screws for corrosion or looseness. If mounting screws are clean and tight, replace DIS module, and check for fault codes. If screws are not clean and tight, clean or replace screws. Clean mounting area on DIS module. Check for fault codes. If vehicle still does not start, go to next test.

Test 10, Check Right Coil Pack Circuits – With key on, connect LED test light between breakout box pins No. (+) J18 (RC1D) and (-) J60 (BAT -). Connect test light between breakout box pins No. (+) J10 (RC2D) and (-) J60 (BAT -). If test light does not illuminate in both tests, go to next test. If test light illuminates in both tests, go to TEST 14.

Test 11, Right Coil Pack Fault, Isolate DIS Module – With key off, disconnect diagnostic cable connector from DIS module (Pins No. 7-12). *See Fig. 3.* Repeat test procedures in TEST 10. If test light illuminates during both tests, replace DIS module, and check for fault codes. See SELF-DIAGNOSTICS article. If test light does not illuminate during both tests, go to next test.

Test 12, Check Right Coil Pack VBAT – Connect LED test light between breakout box pins No. (+) J26 (VBAT R) and (-) J60 (BAT -). If test light illuminates, go to next test. If test light does not illuminate, check connectors, repair or replace harness and check for fault codes. If vehicle still does not start, go to next test.

Test 13, Check Right Coil Circuit – Connect LED test light between breakout box pins No. (+) J23 (RC1C) and (-) J60 (BAT -). Connect LED test light between breakout box pins No. (+) J24 (RC2C) and (-) J60 (BAT -).

If test light illuminates during both tests, one or both coil wires are shorted to VBAT. Repair connectors and harness, and check for fault codes. If test light does not illuminate during both tests, replace right coil pack, and check for fault codes. If vehicle still does not start, go to next test.

Test 14, Check PIP D At DIS Module – Connect LED test light between breakout box pins No. (+) J32 (PIP D) and (-) J60 (BAT -). Crank engine. If test light blinks continuously during crank, go to next test. If test light does not blink continuously during crank, go to TEST 19.

Test 15, Check DIS Module Coil Drivers – Connect LED test light between breakout box pins No. (+) J18 (RC1D) and (-) J60 (BAT -). Crank engine. Connect test light between breakout box pins No. (+) J10 (RC2D) and (-) J60 (BAT -). Crank engine.

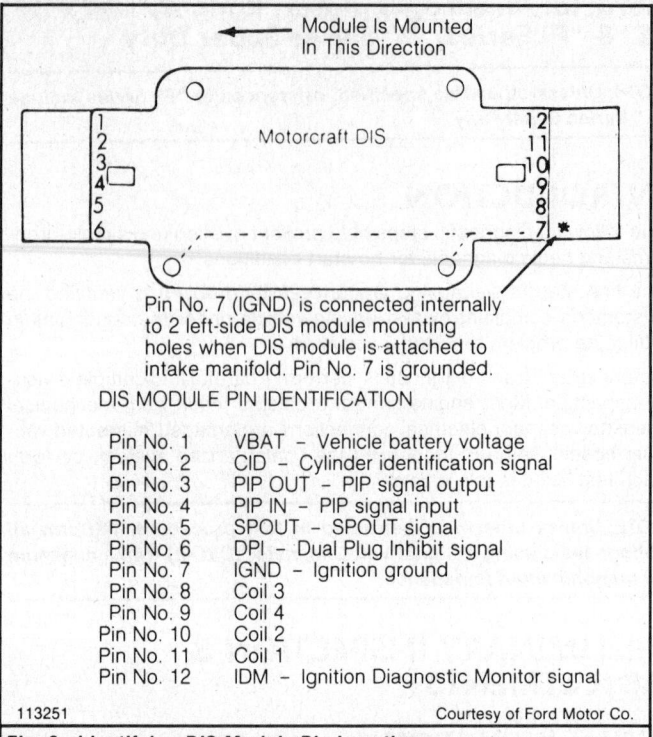

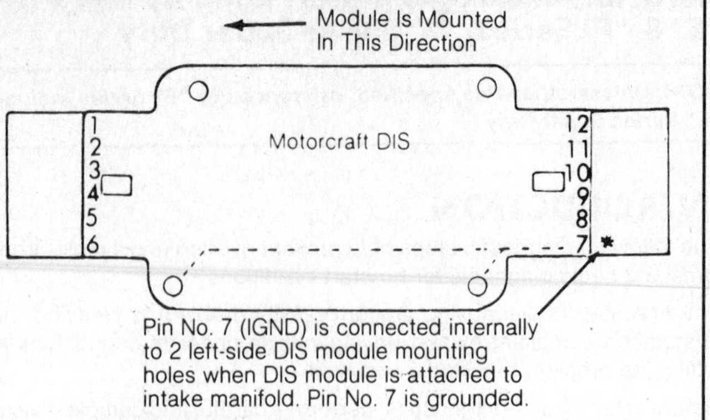
Module Is Mounted In This Direction
Motorcraft DIS
1
2
3
4
5
6
12
11
10
9
8
7
*
Pin No. 7 (IGND) is connected internally to 2 left-side DIS module mounting holes when DIS module is attached to intake manifold. Pin No. 7 is grounded.

DIS MODULE PIN IDENTIFICATION

Pin No. 1	VBAT - Vehicle battery voltage
Pin No. 2	CID - Cylinder identification signal
Pin No. 3	PIP OUT - PIP signal output
Pin No. 4	PIP IN - PIP signal input
Pin No. 5	SPOUT - SPOUT signal
Pin No. 6	DPI - Dual Plug Inhibit signal
Pin No. 7	IGND - Ignition ground
Pin No. 8	Coil 3
Pin No. 9	Coil 4
Pin No. 10	Coil 2
Pin No. 11	Coil 1
Pin No. 12	IDM - Ignition Diagnostic Monitor signal

113251 Courtesy of Ford Motor Co.

Fig. 3: Identifying DIS Module Pin Locations

If test light blinks continuously during both tests, go to next test. If test light does not blink continuously during both tests, replace DIS module, and check for fault codes. If vehicle still does not start, go to next test.

Test 16, Check Right Coil Pack VBAT – Connect LED test light between breakout box pins No. (+) J26 (BAT R) and (-) J60 (BAT -). If test light illuminates, go to next test. If test light does not illuminate, check connectors, repair or replace harness and check for fault codes. If vehicle still does not start, go to next test.

Test 17, Check Right Coil Circuit – Connect LED test light between breakout box pins No. (+) J23 (RC1C) and (-) J60 (BAT -). Connect test light between breakout box pins No. (+) J24 (RC2C) and (-) J60 (BAT -).

If test light illuminates in both tests, go to next test. If test light does not illuminate in both tests, one or both coil wires is shorted to ground or coil pack may be damaged. Check connectors, and repair or replace harness. Check for fault codes. If vehicle still does not start, go to next test.

Test 18, Check Right Coil Circuit – Repeat test procedures in TEST 17, but crank engine during each test connection. If test light blinks continuously during each test, replace right coil pack, and check for fault codes. If test light does not blink continuously during each test connection, one or both coil wires are open. Check connectors, and service or replace harness. Check for fault codes. If vehicle still does not start, go to next test.

Test 19, Isolate DIS Module From PIP D – With key off, disconnect diagnostic cable connector from DIS module (Pins No. 1-6). *See Fig. 3.* Connect LED test light between breakout box pins No. (+) J32 (PIP D) and (-) J55 (IGND S). Crank engine. If test light does not blink continuously, go to next test. If test light blinks continuously, go to TEST 26.

Test 20, Check Crankshaft Sensor VBAT – With key on, connect LED test light between breakout box pins No. (+) J56 (VBAT S) and (-) J2 (IGND D). If test light illuminates, go to next test. If test light does not illuminate, check connectors. Repair or replace harness. Check for fault codes. If vehicle still does not start, go to next test.

Test 21, Check Crankshaft Sensor Ignition Ground – With key off, disconnect ECA. Disconnect diagnostic cable connector from crankshaft sensor. Connect an ohmmeter between breakout box pins No. J55 (IGND S) and J60 (BAT -).

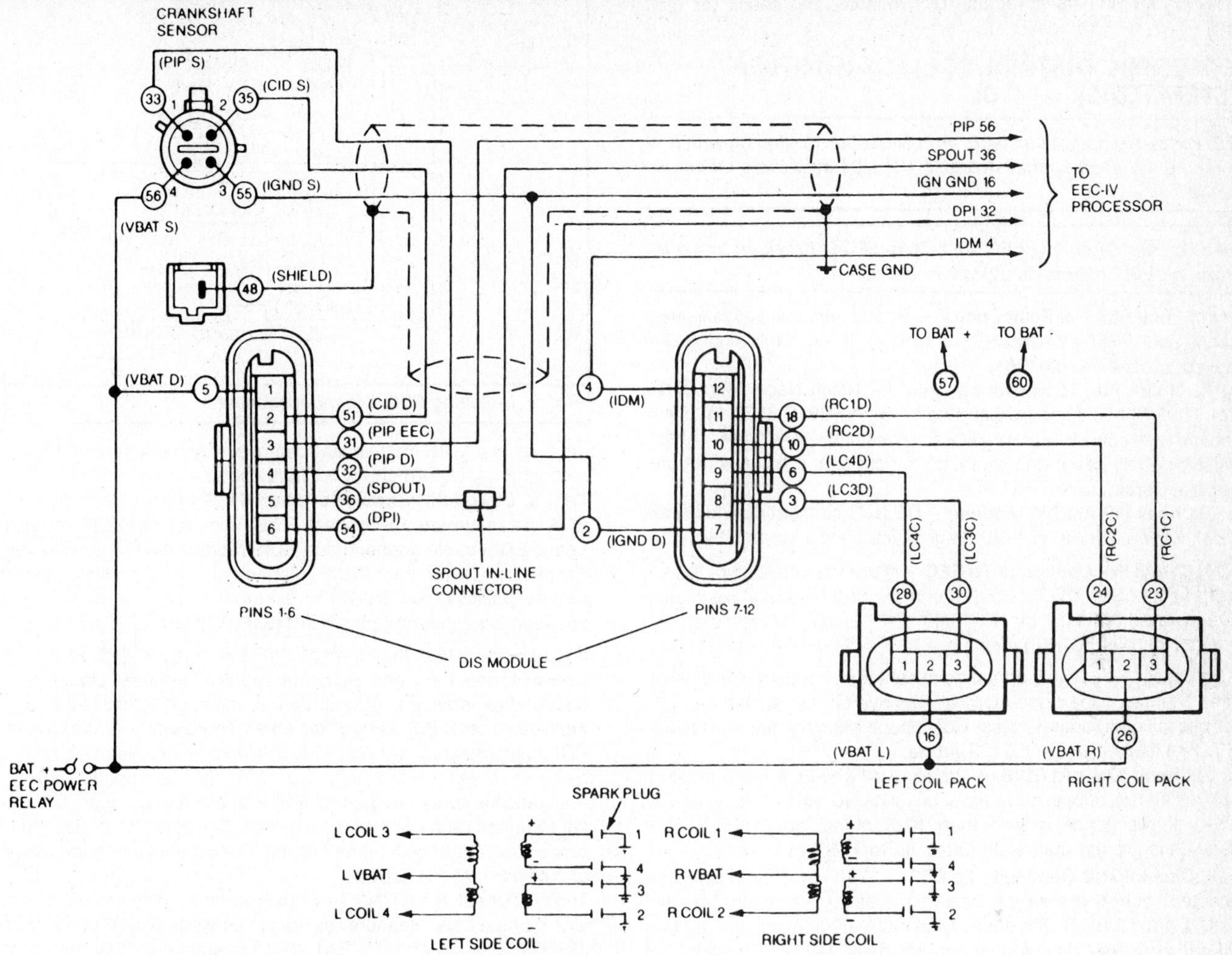

CRANKSHAFT SENSOR
(PIP S)
(CID S)
(IGND S)
(VBAT S)
(SHIELD)
PIP 56
SPOUT 36
IGN GND 16
DPI 32
IDM 4
CASE GND
TO EEC-IV PROCESSOR
TO BAT +
TO BAT -
(VBAT D)
(CID D)
(PIP EEC)
(PIP D)
(SPOUT)
(DPI)
SPOUT IN-LINE CONNECTOR
(IDM)
(IGND D)
(RC1D)
(RC2D)
(LC4D)
(LC3D)
(LC4C)
(LC3C)
(RC2C)
(RC1C)
PINS 1-6
PINS 7-12
DIS MODULE
(VBAT L)
(VBAT R)
LEFT COIL PACK
RIGHT COIL PACK
BAT +
EEC POWER RELAY
SPARK PLUG
L COIL 3
L VBAT
L COIL 4
R COIL 1
R VBAT
R COIL 2
LEFT SIDE COIL
RIGHT SIDE COIL

NOTE: Connections are shown looking into the wiring harness.
IGN GND is a low current reference for the EEC-IV ECA and DIS module.
It is connected to battery negative via the DIS module metal base plate.
Proper system operation depends on a low resistance path to ground.

91F13446

Courtesy of Ford Motor Co.

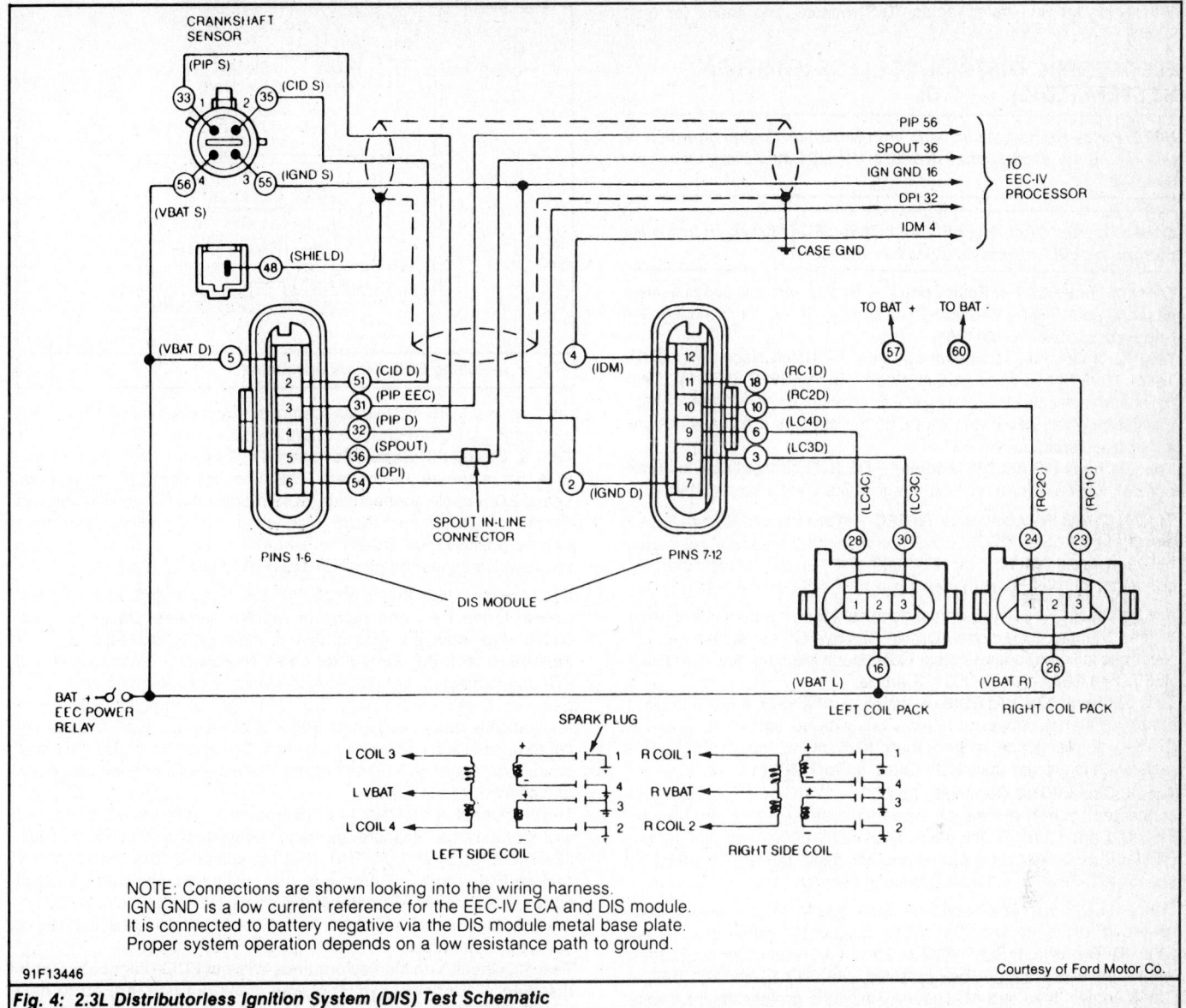

Fig. 4: 2.3L Distributorless Ignition System (DIS) Test Schematic

If resistance is less than 5 ohms, go to next test. If resistance is not less than 5 ohms, check connectors, repair or replace harness and check for fault codes. If vehicle still does not start, go to next test.

Test 22, Check Crankshaft Sensor PIP S – Connect ECA. Connect diagnostic cable connector to crankshaft sensor. Connect LED test light between breakout box pins No. (+) J33 (PIP S) and (-) J2 (IGND D). Crank engine.

If test light blinks continuously, PIP is open between sensor and DIS module. Check connectors, and repair or replace harness. Check for fault codes. If vehicle still does not start, go to next test. If test light does not blink continuously, go to next test.

Test 23, Check PIP Circuit For Short To Ground – With key off, disconnect diagnostic cable connector from crankshaft sensor. Disconnect diagnostic cable connector from DIS module (Pins No. 1-6). *See Fig. 3.* Connect LED test light between breakout box pins No. (-) J33 (PIP S) and (+) J57 (BAT +). Turn key on.

If test light does not illuminate, go to next test. If test light illuminates, PIP is shorted to ground between sensor and DIS module. Check connectors, repair or replace harness and check for fault codes. If vehicle still does not start, go to next test.

Test 24, Check PIP Circuit For Short To VBAT – Connect LED test light between breakout box pins No. (+) J33 (PIP S) and (-) J60 (BAT -). If test light does not illuminate, go to next test. If test light illuminates, PIP is shorted to VBAT between sensor and DIS connectors. Repair or replace harness. Check for fault codes. If vehicle still does not start, go to next test.

Test 25, Check Crankshaft Vane – Crank engine. If crankshaft vane moves through sensor air gap, replace crankshaft sensor, and check for fault codes. If crankshaft vane does not move through sensor air gap, inspect components contributing to operation of crankshaft vane and sensor. Repair as necessary.

Test 26, Isolate EEC-IV Processor (ECA) From PIP Circuit – With key off, reconnect diagnostic cable connector to DIS module (Pins No. 1-6). *See Fig. 3.* Disconnect ECA. Crank engine. If test light does not blink continuously, go to next test. If test light blinks continuously, replace ECA. Check for fault codes. If vehicle still does not start, go to next test.

Test 27, Check PIP EEC Circuit For Short To VBAT – With key off, disconnect diagnostic cable connector from DIS module (Pins No. 1-6). *See Fig. 3.* Connect LED test light between breakout box pins No. (+) J31 (PIP EEC) and (-) J60 (BAT -). Turn key on. If test light does not illuminate, go to next test. If test light illuminates, PIP EEC is shorted to BAT. Check connectors, repair or replace harness and check for fault codes. If vehicle still does not start, go to next test.

Test 28, Check PIP EEC Circuit For Short To Ground – Connect LED test light between breakout box pins No. (-) J31 (PIP EEC) and (+) J57 (BAT +). If test light illuminates, PIP EEC is shorted to ground. Check connectors, repair or replace harness and check for fault codes. If test

1991 ENGINE PERFORMANCE
Basic Diagnostic Procedures (Cont.)

light does not illuminate, replace DIS module, and check for fault codes.

ELECTRONIC DISTRIBUTORLESS IGNITION SYSTEM (EDIS) – 4.0L

NOTE: Following diagnostic tests are sequential. Beginning with first test, complete each successive test. DO NOT skip tests unless so directed.

CAUTION: DO NOT connect EEC-IV ECA to EEC-IV breakout box while performing EDIS diagnosis unless so instructed.

Test 1, Check ECA For Fault Codes – Repair any fault codes as necessary. See SELF-DIAGNOSTICS article. If no fault codes are retrieved, proceed to next test.

Test 2, Check For Spark During Crank – Using Neon Bulb Spark Tester (D89P-6666-A) or Air Gap Spark Tester (D81P-6666-A), check for spark at all spark plug wires while cranking. If spark is present and consistent on all spark plug wires, go to next test. If spark is not present on all wires, go to TEST 7.

Test 3, Check PIP At EDIS Module – DO NOT connect ECA to breakout box while performing EDIS diagnostics unless so directed. Turn

Test 4, Check PIP Continuity To EEC – Turn key off. Ensure ECA is disconnected. Set DVOM to 2-k/ohm scale. Measure resistance between breakout box pin No. J43 (PIP E) and vehicle harness connector pin No. 56 (PIP). *See Fig. 2.*

If resistance is less than 5 ohms, go to next test. If resistance is greater than 5 ohms, repair open circuit. Remove all test equipment, and reconnect all components. Clear Continuous Memory, and run QUICK TEST. See SELF-DIAGNOSTICS article.

Test 5, Check IGND At EDIS – With key off and ECA disconnected, check resistance between breakout box pins No. J47 (IGND E) and J7 (BAT –). If resistance is less than 1025 ohms, go to TEST 6. If resistance is greater than 1025 ohms, go to TEST 11.

Test 6, Check IGND Continuity To EEC – With key off and ECA disconnected, check resistance between breakout box pin No. J47 key off. Connect EDIS Diagnostic Cable (007-00059) to breakout box (T83L-50-EEC-IV), EDIS module and coil pack. DO NOT connect VR sensor tee. *See Fig. 5.* Use EDIS No. 6 overlay.

Connect EDIS diagnostic cable negative lead to battery, leaving positive lead disconnected. Set EDIS diagnostic cable box to 4/6 CYLINDER position. Set DVOM to 20-volt AC scale. Connect DVOM leads between breakout box pins No. J43 (PIP E) and J7 (BAT –). Crank engine. If settled AC voltage reading is greater than 0.4 volts, go to next test. If settled AC voltage reading is less than 0.4 volts, go to TEST 8.

(IGND E) and vehicle harness connector pin No. 16 (IGN GND). *See Fig. 2.* If resistance is less than 1025 ohms, remove all test equipment. Reconnect all components. Clear Continuous Memory, and run QUICK TEST. See SELF-DIAGNOSTICS article.

If Continuous Memory Code 16 or 18 is present, go to TEST 32. If no codes are present, go to TROUBLE SHOOTING – NO CODES article for other possible causes of no-start. If resistance is greater than 1025 ohms, repair open circuit, and remove all test equipment. Reconnect all components, and check for fault codes.

Test 7, Check Plugs & Wires – Check spark plug wires for insulation damage, looseness, shorting or other damage. Remove spark plugs, and check plugs for damage, wear, carbon deposits and proper plug gap. If spark plugs and spark plug wires are good, reinstall, and go to TEST 12. If any components are not good, repair or replace as required. Remove all test equipment, and check for fault codes.

Test 8, Isolate EDIS Module/PIP Fault – With key off, connect EDIS diagnostic cable positive lead to battery positive. Set DVOM to 20-volt AC scale. Hold EDIS diagnostic cable PIP push button down. Crank engine, and measure voltage breakout box pins No. J43 (PIP E) and J7 (BAT –).

If settled AC voltage is greater than one volt, go to next test. If settled AC voltage is less than one volt, there is no PIP output from EDIS mod-

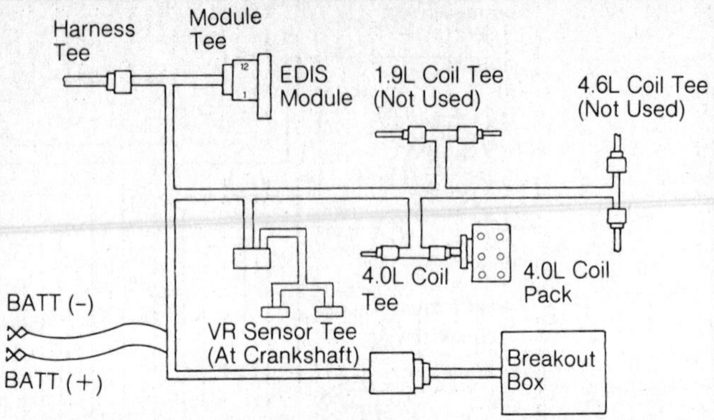
Harness Tee
Module Tee
EDIS Module
1.9L Coil Tee (Not Used)
4.6L Coil Tee (Not Used)
4.0L Coil Tee
4.0L Coil Pack
BATT (–)
BATT (+)
VR Sensor Tee (At Crankshaft)
Breakout Box

91E13445 Courtesy of Ford Motor Co.

Fig. 5: Installing EDIS Diagnostic Cable

ule. Replace EDIS module, and remove all test equipment. Reconnect all components, and check for fault codes.

Test 9, Check PIP Circuit For Short To Ground – With key off and ECA disconnected, disconnect EDIS module from EDIS module tee. Leave EDIS cable connected to EDIS module side of vehicle harness connector. Disconnect EDIS diagnostic cable positive lead from battery positive. Set DVOM to 2-k/ohm scale. Measure resistance between breakout box pins No. J43 (PIP E) and J7 (BAT –).

If resistance is less than 5 ohms, PIP is shorted to ground in harness. Check connectors, and repair or replace harness. Check for fault codes. If resistance is greater than 5 ohms, go to next test.

Test 10, Check PIP Circuit For Short To Power – With key off and ECA disconnected, set DVOM to 2-k/ohm scale. Measure resistance between breakout box pins No. J43 (PIP E) and J1 (BAT +). If resistance is less than 5 ohms, PIP is shorted in harness. Check connectors, and repair or replace harness. Check for fault codes. If resistance is greater than 5 ohms, replace ECA. Clear Continuous Memory, and check for fault codes.

Test 11, Check PWR GND To EDIS Module – With key off, set DVOM to 2-k/ohm scale. Measure resistance between breakout box pins No. J27 (PWR GND) and J7 (BAT –). If resistance is less than 5 ohms, replace EDIS module. Remove all test equipment, and check for fault codes. If resistance is greater than 5 ohms, repair open circuit, reconnect all components and check for fault codes. If vehicle still does not start, go to next test.

Test 12, Check Vehicle Performance Without EDIS Diagnostic Cable Installed – If original symptom was crank but no start, go to next test. If original symptom was not crank but no start, go to TEST 46.

Test 13, Check PWR GND To EDIS Module – Turn key off. Disconnect ECA. Install EDIS diagnostic cable, and connect it to breakout box, EDIS module and coil pack. Do not connect VR sensor tee. Connect diagnostic cable negative lead to battery negative terminal, leaving positive lead disconnected. Set diagnostic cable box switch to 4/6 CYLINDER position. Set DVOM to 2-k/ohm scale. Measure resistance between breakout box pins No. J27 (PWR GND) and J7 (BAT –).

If resistance is less than 5 ohms, go to next test. If resistance is greater than 5 ohms, repair open circuit. Remove all test equipment, and reconnect all components. Check for fault codes. If vehicle still does not start, go to next test.

Test 14, Check For VBAT Open To EDIS Module – With key off and ECA disconnected, set DVOM to 20-volt scale. Measure voltage between breakout box pins No. (+) J51 (VBAT E) and (–) J7 (BAT –). If voltage is greater than 10.5 volts, go to next test. If voltage is less than 10.5 volts, repair open circuit. Remove all test equipment, reconnect all components and check for fault codes.

Test 15, Check VRS+ Bias At EDIS Module – With key off and ECA disconnected, set DVOM to 20-volt scale. Measure voltage between breakout box pins No. (+) J35 (VRS + E) and (–) J7 (BAT –). If voltage is 0.8-2.2 volts, go to next test. If voltage is not 0.8-2.2 volts, go to TEST 17.

Test 16, Check VRS Amplitude At EDIS Module - With key off and ECA connected to breakout box, disconnect diagnostic cable negative lead from battery negative terminal. Set DVOM to 20-volt AC scale. Crank engine, and measure voltage between breakout box pins No. J35 (VRS + E) and J48 (VRS - E). If settled voltage is greater than 0.4 volt, go to TEST 46. If settled voltage is less than 0.4 volt, go to TEST 25.

Test 17, Check VRS+ Bias/Isolate VRS/Bias Fault - With key off and ECA disconnected, disconnect VR sensor from vehicle harness connector. Set DVOM to 20-volt scale. Turn key on, but leave engine off. Measure voltage between breakout box pins No. (+) J35 (VRS + E) and (-) J7 (BAT -). If voltage is not 0.8-2.2 volts, go to next test. If voltage is 0.8-2.2 volts, go to TEST 21.

Test 18, Check VRS+ High Or Low/Bias Fault - If voltage in TEST 17 was less than 0.8 volt, go to next test. If voltage in TEST 17 was greater than 2.2 volts, go to TEST 20.

Test 19, Check VRS+ Circuit For Short To Ground - With key off and ECA disconnected, disconnect EDIS module from EDIS module tee, leaving diagnostic cable connected to vehicle harness connector. Set DVOM to 2-k/ohm scale. Measure resistance between breakout box pins No. J35 (VRS + E) and J7 (BAT -).

If resistance is less than 1025 ohms, repair short circuit. Remove all test equipment, and reconnect all components. Clear Continuous Memory, and check for fault codes. If resistance is greater than 1025 ohms, replace EDIS module. Remove all test equipment, and reconnect all components. Clear Continuous Memory, and check for fault codes.

Test 20, Check VRS+ Circuit For Short To VBAT - With key off and ECA disconnected, disconnect EDIS module from EDIS module tee, leaving diagnostic cable connected to vehicle harness connector. Set DVOM to 20-volt scale. Turn key on, but leave engine off. Measure voltage between breakout box pins No. (+) J35 (VRS + E) and (-) J7 (BAT -).

If voltage is greater than 0.5 volt, repair short in harness. Remove all test equipment, and reconnect all components. Clear Continuous Memory, and check for fault codes. If voltage is less than 0.5 volt, replace EDIS module. Remove all test equipment, and reconnect all components. Clear Continuous Memory, and check for fault codes.

Test 21, Check VRS Bias - With key off and ECA disconnected, set DVOM to 20-volt scale. Turn key on, but leave engine off. Measure voltage between breakout box pins No. (+) J48 (VRS - E) and (-) J7 (BAT -). If voltage is 0.8-2.2 volts, replace VR sensor. Remove all test equipment, and reconnect all components. Clear Continuous Memory, and check for fault codes. If voltage is not 0.8-2.2 volts, go to next test.

Test 22, Check VRS- High Or Low/Bias Fault - If voltage in TEST 21 was less than 0.8 volt, go to next test. If voltage in TEST 21 was greater than 2.2 volts, go to TEST 24.

Test 23, Check VRS- Circuit For Short To Ground - With key off and ECA disconnected, disconnect EDIS module from EDIS module tee, leaving diagnostic cable connected to vehicle harness connector. Set DVOM to 2-k/ohm scale. Measure resistance between breakout box pins No. J48 (VRS - E) and J7 (BAT -).

If resistance is less than 1025 ohms, repair short circuit. Remove all test equipment, and reconnect all components. Clear Continuous Memory, and check for fault codes. If resistance is greater than 1025 ohms, replace EDIS module. Remove all test equipment, and reconnect all components. Clear Continuous Memory, and check for fault codes.

Test 24, Check VRS- Circuit For Short To VBAT - With key off and ECA disconnected, disconnect EDIS module from EDIS module tee, leaving diagnostic cable connected to vehicle harness connector. Set DVOM to 20-volt scale. Turn key on, but leave engine off. Measure voltage between breakout box pins No. J48 (VRS - E) and J7 (BAT -).

If voltage is greater than 0.5 volt, repair short circuit. Remove all test equipment, and reconnect all components. Clear Continuous Memory, and check for fault codes. If voltage is less than 0.5 volt, replace EDIS module. Remove all test equipment, and reconnect all components. Clear Continuous Memory, and check for fault codes.

Test 25, Check VRS Amplitude At EDIS Module - With key off and ECA connected, disconnect EDIS module from EDIS module tee, leaving diagnostic cable connected to vehicle harness connector. Set DVOM to 20-volt AC scale. Crank engine, and measure voltage between breakout box pins No. J35 (VRS + E) and J48 (VRS - E). If settled voltage is greater than 0.4 volt, replace EDIS module. Remove all test equipment, and reconnect all components. Clear Continuous Memory, and check for fault codes. If settled voltage is less than 0.4 volt, go to next test.

Test 26, Check VRS Resistance - With key off and ECA disconnected, connect EDIS diagnostic cable negative lead to negative battery terminal. Set DVOM to 20-k/ohm scale. Measure resistance between breakout box pins No. J48 (VRS - E) and J35 (VRS + E). If resistance is 2580-2700 ohms, go to next test. If resistance is not 2580-2700 ohms, go to TEST 28.

Test 27, Check VRS Air Gap & Trigger Wheel - With key off, inspect trigger wheel for damage. Check VRS air gap. If air gap and trigger wheel are okay, replace VR sensor. Remove all test equipment, and reconnect all components. Clear Continuous Memory, and check for fault codes.

If air gap and trigger wheel are damaged, repair or replace damaged components. Remove all test equipment, and reconnect all components. Clear Continuous Memory, and check for fault codes.

Test 28, Check VRS High Or Low Resistance - With key off and ECA disconnected, disconnect EDIS diagnostic cable negative lead from battery. Set DVOM to 20-k/ohm scale. Measure resistance between breakout box pins No. J48 (VRS - E) and J35 (VRS + E). If resistance is less than 2550 ohms, go to next test. If resistance is greater than 2550 ohms, go to TEST 30.

Test 29, Check VRS+ Shorted To VRS- - With key off and ECA disconnected, disconnect VR sensor from vehicle harness connector. Set DVOM to 20-k/ohm scale. Measure resistance between breakout box pins No. J35 (VRS + E) and J48 (VRS - E).

If resistance is greater than 3 k/ohms, replace VR sensor. Remove all test equipment, and reconnect all components. Clear Continuous Memory, and check for fault codes. If resistance is less than 3 k/ohms, repair short circuit. Remove all test equipment, and reconnect all components. Clear Continuous Memory, and check for fault codes.

Test 30, Check VRS+ For Open Circuit - With key off and ECA disconnected, connect VR sensor tee to VR sensor and vehicle harness connector. Set DVOM to 20-k/ohm scale. Measure resistance between breakout box pins No. J31 (VRS + S) and J35 (VRS + E).

If resistance is less than 2025 ohms, go to next test. If resistance is greater than 2025 ohms, repair open circuit. Remove all test equipment, and reconnect all components. Clear Continuous Memory, and check for fault codes.

Test 31, Check VRS- For Open Circuit - With key off and ECA disconnected, set DVOM to 20-k/ohm scale. Measure resistance between breakout box pins No. J32 (VRS - S) and J48 (VRS - E).

If resistance is less than 2025 ohms, replace VR sensor. Remove all test equipment, and reconnect all components. Clear Continuous Memory, and check for fault codes. If resistance is greater than 2025 ohms, repair open circuit. Remove all test equipment, and reconnect all components. Clear Continuous Memory, and check for fault codes.

NOTE: Tests 32-37 may also be used for diagnosing KOEO Code 16, Continuous Memory Code 18 and/or "CHECK ENGINE" light on: IDM failure.

CAUTION: DO NOT connect EEC-IV ECA to EEC-IV breakout box while performing EDIS diagnosis unless so instructed.

Test 32, Check For IDM Short High - Turn key off. Connect EDIS Diagnostic Cable (007-00059) to breakout box (T83L-50-EEC-IV), EDIS module and coil pack. DO NOT connect VR sensor tee. *See Fig. 5.* Use EDIS No. 6 overlay. Connect EDIS diagnostic cable negative and positive leads to battery. Set EDIS diagnostic cable box switch to 4/6 CYLINDER position. Set DVOM to 20-volt scale.

1991 ENGINE PERFORMANCE
Basic Diagnostic Procedures (Cont.)

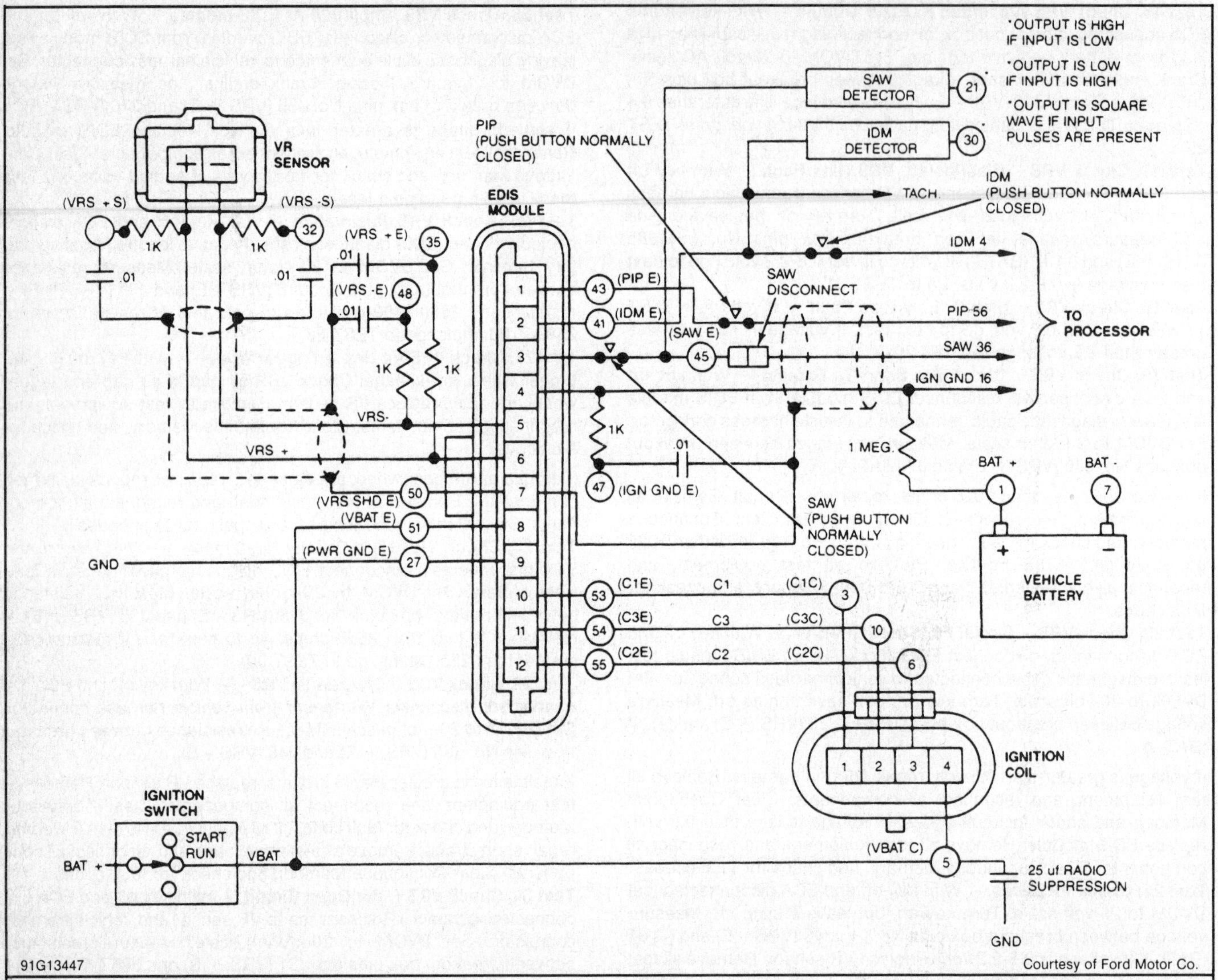
*OUTPUT IS HIGH IF INPUT IS LOW
*OUTPUT IS LOW IF INPUT IS HIGH
*OUTPUT IS SQUARE WAVE IF INPUT PULSES ARE PRESENT
SAW DETECTOR
21
IDM DETECTOR
30
PIP (PUSH BUTTON NORMALLY CLOSED)
IDM (PUSH BUTTON NORMALLY CLOSED)
TACH
VR SENSOR
(VRS + S)
(VRS -S)
1K
1K
32
.01
.01
(VRS + E)
35
(VRS -E)
48
EDIS MODULE
(PIP E)
43
(IDM E)
41
(SAW E)
45
SAW DISCONNECT
IDM 4
PIP 56
SAW 36
IGN GND 16
TO PROCESSOR
VRS-
VRS +
1K
1 MEG.
.01
47
(IGN GND E)
BAT +
BAT -
1
7
(VRS SHD E)
50
(VBAT E)
51
(PWR GND E)
27
GND
SAW (PUSH BUTTON NORMALLY CLOSED)
VEHICLE BATTERY
(C1E)
53
C1
(C1C)
3
(C3E)
54
C3
(C3C)
10
(C2E)
55
C2
(C2C)
6
IGNITION COIL
IGNITION SWITCH
START
RUN
BAT +
VBAT
(VBAT C)
5
25 uf RADIO SUPPRESSION
GND
91G13447
Courtesy of Ford Motor Co.

Fig. 6: 4.0L Electronic Distributorless Ignition System (EDIS) Test Schematic

Crank engine, and measure voltage between breakout box pins No. J30 (EDIS diagnostic cable IDM detector) and J7 (BAT –). If pulses are present, IDM detector output will be 5-7 volts DC. If pulses are present, go to next test. If pulses are not present, go to TEST 34.

Test 33, Check For IDM Open Circuit – With key off and ECA disconnected, disconnect EDIS module from EDIS module tee. Leave EDIS diagnostic cable connected to vehicle harness connector. Set DVOM to 200-ohm scale. Measure resistance between breakout box pin No. J41 (IDM E) and vehicle harness connector pin No. 4. *See Figs. 2 and 6.*

If resistance is less than 5 ohms, replace ECA. Remove all test equipment, and reconnect all components. Clear Continuous Memory, and check for fault codes. If resistance is greater than 5 ohms, repair open circuit. Remove all test equipment, and reconnect all components. Clear Continuous Memory, and check for fault codes.

Test 34, Check IDM Output From EDIS Module – With key off and ECA connected, set DVOM to 20-volt scale. Push EDIS IDM button at EDIS diagnostic cable connector to breakout box. Crank engine, and measure voltage between breakout box pins No. J30 (EDIS diagnostic cable IDM detector) and J7 (BAT –). If voltage is 5-7 volts, go to next test. If voltage is not 5-7 volts, replace EDIS module. Remove all test equipment, and reconnect all components. Clear Continuous Memory, and check for fault codes.

Test 35, Check For IDM Short In ECA – With key off and ECA disconnected, set DVOM to 20-volt scale. Crank engine, and measure voltage between breakout box pins No. J30 (EDIS diagnostic cable IDM detector) and J7 (BAT –). If voltage is 4.5-6.0 volts, replace ECA. Remove all test equipment, and reconnect all components. Clear Continuous Memory, and check for fault codes. If voltage is not 4.5-6.0 volts, go to next test.

Test 36, Check For IDM Short To Ground In Harness – With key off and ECA disconnected, disconnect EDIS module from EDIS module tee. Leave EDIS cable connected to vehicle harness connector. Set DVOM to 20-k/ohm scale. Measure resistance between breakout box pins No. J41 (IDM E) and J7 (BAT –). If resistance is less than 5 ohms, repair short circuit. Remove all test equipment, and reconnect all components. Clear Continuous Memory, and check for fault codes. If resistance is greater than 5 ohms, go to next test.

Test 37, Check For IDM Short To VBAT In Harness – With key off and ECA disconnected, set DVOM to 20-volt scale. Turn key on, leaving engine off. Measure voltage between breakout box pins No. (+) J41 (IDM E) and (–) J7 (BAT –). If voltage is greater than 0.5 volt, IDM is shorted to VBAT between EDIS module and ECA. Repair short circuit. Remove all test equipment, and reconnect all components. Clear Continuous Memory, and check for fault codes.

If voltage is less than 0.5 volt, IDM is shorted to another wire between EDIS module and ECA. Repair short or replace harness. Remove all test equipment, and reconnect all components. Clear Continuous Memory, and check for fault codes.

1991 ENGINE PERFORMANCE
Basic Diagnostic Procedures (Cont.)

NOTE: Tests 38-45 may also be used for diagnosing KOER Code 18.

CAUTION: DO NOT connect EEC-IV ECA to EEC-IV breakout box while performing EDIS diagnosis unless so instructed.

Test 38, Check Base Timing – Turn key off. Connect EDIS Diagnostic Cable (007-00059) to breakout box (T83L-50-EEC-IV), EDIS module and coil pack. DO NOT connect VR sensor tee. *See Fig. 5*. Use EDIS No. 6 overlay. Connect EDIS diagnostic cable negative and positive leads to battery. Set EDIS diagnostic cable box switch to 4/6 CYLINDER position. Connect timing light (must be DIS/EDIS compatible).

Start engine, and bring to normal operating temperature. Check timing. If timing is 10 ± 2 degrees BTDC when EDIS diagnostic cable SAW DETECTOR button is pushed, go to next test. If timing is not 10 ± 2 degrees BTDC when EDIS diagnostic cable SAW DETECTOR button is pushed, go to TEST 45.

Test 39, Check Advance Spark Angle – If engine timing is greater than 15 degrees BTDC when EDIS diagnostic cable SAW DETECTOR button is released, EDIS ignition is functioning normally. Go to TROUBLE SHOOTING–NO CODES article for other possible causes of symptoms. If timing is less than 15 degrees BTDC when EDIS diagnostic cable SAW DETECTOR button is released, go to next test.

Test 40, Check SAW At EDIS Module – With key off, set DVOM to 20-volt scale. Start engine, and measure voltage between breakout box pins No. (+) J21 (EDIS diagnostic cable SAW detector) and (-) J7 (BAT -). If voltage is 5-7 volts, replace EDIS module. If voltage is not 5-7 volts, go to next test.

Test 41, Check SAW For Short In EDIS Module – With key off, connect ECA. Set DVOM to 20-volt scale. Push EDIS diagnostic cable SAW button. Start engine, and measure voltage between breakout box pins No. (+) J21 (EDIS diagnostic cable SAW detector) and (-) J7 (BAT -). If voltage is 5-7 volts, SAW is shorted in EDIS module. Replace EDIS module. Remove all test equipment, and reconnect all components. Clear Continuous Memory, and check for fault codes. If voltage is not 5-7 volts, go to next test.

Test 42, Check For SAW Short To Ground In Harness – Turn key off, and disconnect ECA. Disconnect EDIS module from EDIS module tee, leaving EDIS diagnostic cable connected to vehicle harness connector. Disconnect Heated Exhaust Gas Oxygen Sensor (HEGO) connector. Set DVOM to 200-ohm scale. Measure resistance between breakout box pins No. J45 (SAW E) and J7 (BAT -). If resistance is less than 100 ohms, repair short circuit. Remove all test equipment, and reconnect all components. Clear Continuous Memory, and check for fault codes. If resistance is greater than 100 ohms, reconnect HEGO, and go to next test.

Test 43, Check For SAW Short To VBAT In Harness – With key off and ECA disconnected, set DVOM to 20-volt scale. Turn key on, but leave engine off. Measure voltage between breakout box pins No. (+) J45 (SAW E) and (-) J7 (BAT -). If voltage is less than 0.5 volt, repair short circuit. Remove all test equipment, and reconnect all components. Clear Continuous Memory, and check for fault codes. If voltage is greater than 0.5 volt, go to next test.

Test 44, Check For SAW Open – With key off and ECA disconnected, set DVOM to 2-k/ohm scale. Measure resistance between breakout box pin No. J45 (SAW E) and vehicle harness connector pin No. 36. *See Fig. 2*. If resistance is less than 5 ohms, SAW is not being transmitted by ECA. Replace ECA. Remove all test equipment, and reconnect all components. Clear Continuous Memory, and check for fault codes. If resistance is greater than 5 ohms, repair open circuit. Remove all test equipment, and reconnect all components. Clear Continuous Memory, and check for fault codes.

Test 45, Inspect VR Sensor & Trigger Wheel – If VR sensor or trigger wheel is damaged, loose or misaligned, repair or replace components as necessary. Remove all test equipment, and reconnect all components. Clear Continuous Memory, and check for fault codes. If VR sensor or trigger wheel is not damaged, loose or misaligned, there is no PIP signal output from EDIS module. Replace EDIS module. Remove all test equipment, and reconnect all components. Clear Continuous Memory, and check for fault codes.

NOTE: Tests 46-56 may also be used for diagnosing Continuous Memory Code 45 and/or "CHECK ENGINE" light on: coil failure.

CAUTION: DO NOT connect EEC-IV ECA to EEC-IV breakout box while performing EDIS diagnosis unless so instructed.

Test 46, Check VBAT Open To Coil – Turn key off, and connect ECA. Connect EDIS Diagnostic Cable (007-00059) to breakout box (T83L-50-EEC-IV), EDIS module and coil pack. DO NOT connect VR sensor tee. *See Fig. 5*. Use EDIS No. 6 overlay. Connect EDIS diagnostic cable negative to negative battery terminal, leaving positive lead disconnected. Set EDIS diagnostic cable box switch to 4/6 CYLINDER position. Set DVOM to 20-volt scale.

Turn key on, but leave engine off. Measure voltage between breakout box pins No. (+) J5 (VBAT C) and (-) J7 (BAT -). If voltage is greater than 10.5 volts, go to next test. If voltage is less than 10.5 volts, repair open circuit. Remove all test equipment, and reconnect all components. Clear Continuous Memory, and check for fault codes.

Test 47, Verify Vehicle Operating Mode – If vehicle will not crank and start, go to next test. If vehicle will crank and start, go to TEST 49.

Test 48, Check C1, C2 & C3 At Coil Pack – Turn key off, and connect ECA. Set DVOM to 20-volt AC scale. Crank engine, and measure voltage between breakout box pins No. J7 (BAT -) and J3 (C1), J7 and J6 (C2) and J7 and J10 (C3). If any settled voltage is less than 0.2 volt, replace coil pack. Remove all test equipment, and reconnect all components. Clear Continuous Memory, and check for fault codes. If all settled voltage readings are greater than 0.2 volt, go to TEST 50.

Test 49, Check C1, C2 & C3 At Coil Pack – Turn key off, and connect ECA. Set DVOM to 20-volt AC scale. Start engine, and measure voltage between breakout box pins No. J7 (BAT -) and J3 (C1), J7 and J6 (C2) and J7 and J10 (C3). If any settled voltage is less than one volt, replace coil pack. Remove all test equipment, and reconnect all components. Clear Continuous Memory, and check for fault codes. If all settled voltage readings are greater than one volt, go to next test.

Test 50, Check C1, C2 & C3 At Coil Pack – Turn key off, and disconnect ECA. Set DVOM to 20-volt scale. Turn key on, but leave engine off. Measure voltage between breakout box pins No. J7 (BAT -) and J3 (C1), J7 and J6 (C2) and J7 and J10 (C3). If each voltage reading is greater than 10.5 volts, go to next test. If each voltage reading is less than 10.5 volts, go to TEST 55.

Test 51, Check C1, C2 & C3 At EDIS – Turn key off, and disconnect ECA. Set DVOM to 20-volt scale. Turn key on, but leave engine off. Measure voltage between breakout box pins No. (-) J7 (BAT -) and J3 (C1), J7 and J6 (C2) and J7 and J10 (C3). If each voltage reading is greater than 10.5 volts, go to next test. If each voltage reading is less than 10.5 volts, repair open circuit. Remove all test equipment, and reconnect all components. Clear Continuous Memory, and check for fault codes.

Test 52, Check C1, C2 & C3 At Coil Pack – Turn key off, and disconnect ECA. Disconnect coil pack from coil pack tee, leaving EDIS diagnostic cable connected to vehicle harness connector. Set DVOM to 20-volt scale. Turn key on, but leave engine off. Measure voltage between breakout box pins No. J7 (BAT -) and J3 (C1), J7 and J6 (C2) and J7 and J10 (C3). If each voltage reading is greater than 0.5 volt, go to next test. If each voltage reading is less than 0.5 volt, go to TEST 54.

Test 53, Check C1, C2 & C3 At Coil Pack – Turn key off, and disconnect ECA. Disconnect EDIS module from EDIS module tee, leaving EDIS diagnostic cable connected to vehicle harness connector. Set DVOM to 20-volt scale. Turn key on, but leave engine off. Measure voltage between breakout box pins No. J7 (BAT -) and J3 (C1), J7 and J6 (C2) and J7 and J10 (C3).

If each voltage reading is less than 0.5 volt, replace EDIS module. Remove all test equipment, and reconnect all components. Clear Continuous Memory, and check for fault codes. If each voltage reading is greater than 0.5 volt, repair short circuit. Remove all test equipment, and reconnect all components. Clear Continuous Memory, and check for fault codes.

1991 ENGINE PERFORMANCE
Basic Diagnostic Procedures (Cont.)

Test 54, Check C1, C2 & C3 Coil Primary – Turn key off, and disconnect ECA. Reconnect coil pack to coil tee. Set DVOM to 2-k/ohm scale. Measure resistance between breakout box pins No. J5 (VBAT C) and J3 (C1), J5 and J6 (C2) and J5 and J10 (C3). If each resistance is greater than 0.8 ohms, replace EDIS module. If any resistance is less than 0.8 ohms, replace coil pack. Remove all test equipment, and reconnect all components. Clear Continuous Memory, and check for fault codes.

Test 55, Check C1, C2 & C3 For Short To Ground – Turn key off, and disconnect ECA. Set DVOM to 2-k/ohm scale. Measure resistance between breakout box pins No. J7 (BAT –) and J3 (C1), J7 and J6 (C2) and J7 and J10 (C3). If each resistance is less than 1200 ohms, go to next test. If each resistance is greater than 1200 ohms, replace coil pack. Remove all test equipment, and reconnect all components. Clear Continuous Memory, and check for fault codes.

Test 56, Check C1, C2 & C3 For Short To Ground – Turn key off, and disconnect ECA. Disconnect EDIS coil tee from coil pack and vehicle harness connector. Disconnect EDIS module from EDIS module tee, leaving EDIS diagnostic cable connected to vehicle harness connector. Set DVOM to 2-k/ohm scale. Measure resistance between breakout box pins No. J7 (BAT –) and J3 (C1), J7 and J6 (C2) and J7 and J10 (C3).

If any resistance is less than 5 ohms, repair short circuit. Remove all test equipment, and reconnect all components. Clear Continuous Memory, and check for fault codes. If resistance readings are greater than 5 ohms, replace EDIS module. Remove all test equipment, and reconnect all components. Clear Continuous Memory, and check for fault codes.

THICK FILM IGNITION (TFI) IV

Spark Check – **1)** Using a high output spark tester, check for spark at coil wire while cranking engine. If spark is present, go to step **2)**. If spark is not present, remove distributor cap, and crank engine to check for distributor rotation. If distributor rotation is okay, check coil secondary wire resistance. Resistance should not be greater than 7000 ohms per foot.

2) Place transmission in Neutral. Disconnect TFI wiring harness connector. Attach TFI Ignition Tester (105-000003). Connect Red lead of tester to 12 volts. Attach remote starter to "S" terminal of starter relay. While observing 2 LED lights on tester, use remote starter to crank engine. If PIP light blinks, go to step **4)**. If PIP light does not blink, remove distributor.

3) Remove TFI module from distributor. Using an ohmmeter, ensure all circuit resistance values are correct. See TFI MODULE CIRCUIT RESISTANCE SPECIFICATIONS table. *See Fig. 7*. If readings are incorrect, replace TFI module. If readings are correct, check stator for open winding or short to ground. See SYSTEM & COMPONENT TESTING article.

TFI MODULE CIRCUIT RESISTANCE SPECIFICATIONS

TFI Terminals [1]	Ohms
Ground Pin – PIP	More than 500
Power Pin – PIP Input Pin	Less than 2000
Power Pin – TFI Power	Less than 200
Ground Pin – Ignition Ground	Less than 2
PIP Input Pin – PIP	Less than 200

[1] – See Fig. 7 for terminal identification.

4) If TACH light did not blink in step **2)**, replace TFI module, and repeat step **1)**. If spark is still not present, replace ignition coil and module connector. If TACH light did blink in step **2)**, substitute ignition coil with a known working unit, and repeat step **1)**. If spark is now present, ensure coil secondary wire resistance is not greater than 7000 ohms per foot, and replace ignition coil.

5) If spark was not present in step **4)**, connect original vehicle coil and spark tester. Remove pin-in-line connector located near distributor. Crank engine while checking for spark. If spark is present, inspect PIP and ignition ground circuits to verify continuity, and repair as necessary.

6) If spark was not present in step **5)**, measure battery voltage with negative lead from voltmeter attached to base of distributor. Measure voltage at ignition coil positive (+) terminal. Ignition coil positive (+) terminal voltage should be at least 90 percent of battery voltage. If not, check circuitry between ignition coil and ignition switch for wear or damage. Repair as necessary.

7) If ignition coil positive (+) terminal voltage was at least 90 percent of battery voltage in step **6)**, remove connector from ignition module. Disconnect starter relay "S" terminal. Turn ignition on. Measure voltage at ignition module connector power terminals No. 3 and 4. *See Fig. 7*. See TFI MODULE VOLTAGE TEST TERMINALS table. Voltage should be at least 90 percent of battery voltage.

8) If voltage is not at least 90 percent of battery voltage, check circuitry between ignition coil and ignition switch for wear or damage. Repair as necessary. If voltage was at least 90 percent of battery voltage in step **7)**, inspect wiring between ignition module terminal No. 2 and coil. If okay, check all related circuitry. Replace or repair as necessary.

TFI MODULE VOLTAGE TEST TERMINALS

TFI Terminal	Ignition Switch Position
With CCD [1]	
No. 3	Run & Start
Without CCD [1]	
No. 3	Run & Start
No. 4	Start

[1] – Computer Controlled Dwell.

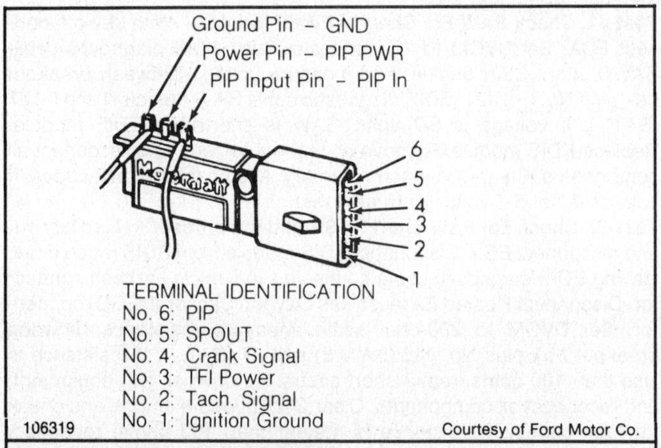
Ground Pin – GND
Power Pin – PIP PWR
PIP Input Pin – PIP In
6
5
4
3
2
1
TERMINAL IDENTIFICATION
No. 6: PIP
No. 5: SPOUT
No. 4: Crank Signal
No. 3: TFI Power
No. 2: Tach. Signal
No. 1: Ignition Ground
106319
Courtesy of Ford Motor Co.

Fig. 7: Identifying TFI Ignition Module Connector Terminals

IGNITION COIL RESISTANCE

IGNITION COIL RESISTANCE – OHMS @ 75°F (24°C)

Application	Primary	Secondary
DIS, EDIS	.5	[1]
TFI-IV	0.8-1.6	8000-11,500

[1] – Resistance values are not provided by manufacturer.

FUEL SYSTEM

PRELIMINARY CHECKS

Ensure following systems and components are in good condition and operating properly before diagnosing problems in fuel injection system.

- Battery
- State of tune
- Fuel delivery system
- All wiring and vacuum connections
- Air cleaner and ducts
- Cooling system

1991 ENGINE PERFORMANCE
Basic Diagnostic Procedures (Cont.)

Engine Does Not Crank - Check for hydrostatic lock (liquid in cylinder). Repair as needed. Check for starting and charging system problems.

Engine Cranks But Will Not Start - **1)** Check fuel tank contents and fuel gauge accuracy. Check for dirt, water or other contamination in fuel.

2) Check ignition system for strong secondary current at spark plugs. If no spark exists or if spark is weak, repair ignition system problem.

3) Check fuel lines and fittings for leaks. If no leaks are found, check fuel delivery system for proper pressure and volumes. Reset inertia switch (if necessary).

4) Check for a defective fuel injector or coolant temperature sensor. Ensure TPS does not stick.

WARNING: ALWAYS relieve fuel pressure before disconnecting any fuel injection-related component. DO NOT allow fuel to contact engine or electrical components.

FUEL PRESSURE RELEASE

Disconnect negative battery cable. Remove fuel cap to release fuel tank pressure. Using EFI Pressure Gauge (T80L-9974-B), release fuel pressure from relief valve. Relief valve is located on fuel supply manifold.

FUEL PRESSURE

Release fuel pressure. Install fuel pressure gauge. Fuel pump may be activated by grounding fuel pump lead at Self-Test connector. Using a jumper lead, ground "FP" terminal with ignition on. This activates fuel pump. *See Fig. 8*. For additional circuit test information, see appropriate SELF-DIAGNOSTICS article.

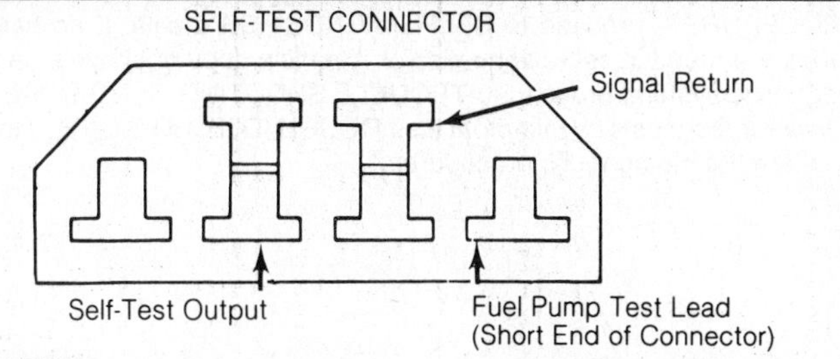
SELF-TEST CONNECTOR
Signal Return
Self-Test Output
Fuel Pump Test Lead
(Short End of Connector)

90I04610 Courtesy of Ford Motor Co.

Fig. 8: Identifying Fuel Pump Self-Test Connector

CAUTION: Inspect fuel system for leaks or damage before testing fuel pump.

FUEL PRESSURE SPECIFICATIONS (GASOLINE)

Engine	Pressure KOER psi (kg/cm²)	Pressure KOEO psi (kg/cm²)
4.9L	45-60 (3.2-4.2)	[1] 50-60 (3.5-4.2)
All Others	30-45 (2.1-4.2)	[1] 35-45 (2.5-4.2)

[1] - Fuel pump outlet pressure (maximum output).

FUEL PRESSURE SPECIFICATIONS (DIESEL)

Application	psi (kg/cm²)
Filter Inlet	[1] 2 (.14)
Filter Outlet	[2] 1 (.07)
Return Line	[2] 2 (.14)

[1] - At idle.
[2] - At 3300 RPM.

FUEL INJECTORS

Fuel Injector Check - **1)** Connect tachometer to engine. Run engine at idle. Disconnect and reconnect injectors individually. If each injector causes a momentary drop in engine speed of at least 100 RPM, injectors are providing proper fuel delivery. RPM drop should only be momentary, as ISC will attempt to re-establish correct idle RPM.

2) Replace any injectors not causing sufficient drop in engine speed. When test is complete, turn engine off. To check curb idle, refer to emission control specifications on decal in engine compartment or IDLE SPEED & MIXTURE in ON-VEHICLE ADJUSTMENTS article.

Fuel Injector Circuit - Disconnect all injector harness connectors. Using digital ohmmeter, check resistance across terminals of each injector. See INDIVIDUAL INJECTOR RESISTANCE table. Disconnect injector bank harness connector, and check resistance of injector bank. See INJECTOR BANK RESISTANCE table. Repair injector bank or any injector not within specifications.

INDIVIDUAL INJECTOR RESISTANCE [1]

Engine	Ohms
2.3L & 3.0L	15-18
All Others	13-16

[1] - Resistance values are for a single injector.

INJECTOR BANK RESISTANCE

Engine	Ohms
2.3L	7.0-9.5
2.9L, 3.0L & 4.9L	5.0-6.5
5.0L, 5.8L & 7.5L	3.0-4.0

NOTE: For further component testing and information, see appropriate SELF-DIAGNOSTICS article.

INERTIA SWITCH

1) In event of a collision, electrical contacts in inertia switch open, automatically shutting off fuel pump. Fuel pump shuts off even if engine does not stop running. Engine eventually stops due to lack of fuel.

2) Engine cannot be restarted until inertia switch is manually reset. To reset inertia switch, depress button on switch. Inertia switches may be found in following locations:

- Aerostar & "E" Series - On right kick panel, just forward of door opening.
- Bronco & "F" Series - On floorboard, left of and above steering column.
- Explorer - Under instrument panel, right of transmission hump.

CAUTION: DO NOT reset inertia switch until inspecting fuel system for leaks.

IDLE SPEED & IGNITION TIMING

BASE IGNITION TIMING

Ensure idle speed and ignition timing are set to specification. For adjustment procedures, see ON-VEHICLE ADJUSTMENTS article. Ensure all accessories are off and transmission is in Park or Neutral. Set parking brake. Disconnect automatic parking brake release (if equipped). Ensure vehicle front wheels are in straight-ahead position and curb idle speed set to specification.

NOTE: Ignition timing is not adjustable on models with DIS or EDIS.

4-CYLINDER BASE IGNITION TIMING

Application	Degrees BTDC @ RPM
2.3L	[1]

[1] - Timing not adjustable.

6-CYLINDER BASE IGNITION TIMING

Application [1]	Degrees BTDC @ RPM
4.9L	10 @ [1]

[1] - Information not available from manufacturer.

1991 ENGINE PERFORMANCE
Basic Diagnostic Procedures (Cont.)

V6 BASE IGNITION TIMING

Application [1]	Degrees BTDC @ RPM
2.9L	
Automatic Transmission	10 @ 800
Manual Transmission	10 @ 850
3.0L	10 @ [2]
4.0L	[3]

[1] – With SPOUT in-line connector disconnected.
[2] – Idle speed is not adjustable.
[3] – Timing not adjustable.

V8 BASE IGNITION TIMING

Application	[1] Degrees BTDC @ RPM
5.0L	
Automatic Transmission	10 @ 525-825
Manual Transmission	10 @ 550-850
5.8L	
C6 Automatic Transmission	10 @ 630-930
E4OD Automatic Transmission	10 @ 580-880
Manual Transmission	10 @ 580-880
7.5L	10 @ 500-800

[1] – With SPOUT in-line connector disconnected.

IDLE SPEED

Idle speed is controlled by ECA and idle speed control air by-pass valve on all engines. If control system is operating properly, engine idle RPM is fixed and cannot be changed by standard adjustments. Manufacturer does not provide RPM specifications for many engines. A Scan tool must be used on these systems because control strategy and idle speed specification are controlled by ECA. See appropriate ON-VEHICLE ADJUSTMENTS article.

Before performing idle speed adjustment procedure, complete a thorough basic inspection and self-test (KOEO, KOER, Continuous Memory self-tests) to confirm operation of sub-systems contributing to idle speed control. See appropriate SELF-DIAGNOSTICS article.

IDLE MIXTURE ADJUSTMENT

NOTE: No idle mixture adjustments are possible on any models. See appropriate SELF-DIAGNOSTICS article for diagnosis of incorrect idle mixture.

THROTTLE POSITION SENSOR (TPS) ADJUSTMENT

NOTE: Throttle Position Sensor (TPS) on gasoline engines is not adjustable. Replace TPS if sensor is not within specifications.

TPS VOLTAGE SPECIFICATIONS [1]

Application	Idle	Wide Open Throttle
2.3L, 2.9L [2], 3.0L & 4.0L	0.20	4.84
2.9L [3], 4.9L, 5.0L, 5.8L & 7.5L	0.34	4.84

[1] – Minimum and maximum specifications are given.
[2] – Vehicles equipped with mass airflow sensor only.
[3] – Except vehicles equipped with mass airflow sensor.

FUEL INJECTION PUMP LEVER (FIPL) SENSOR ADJUSTMENT

For Fuel Injection Pump Lever (FIPL) sensor adjustment, see ON-VEHICLE ADJUSTMENTS article.

SUMMARY

If no faults were found while performing BASIC DIAGNOSTIC PROCEDURES, proceed to SELF-DIAGNOSTICS article. If no hard codes are found in self-diagnostics or if vehicle does not have a self-diagnostic system, proceed to TROUBLE SHOOTING – NO CODES article for diagnosis by symptom (i.e., ROUGH IDLE, NO START, etc.) or intermittent diagnostic procedures.

1991 ENGINE PERFORMANCE
Self-Diagnostics – EEC-IV

Aerostar, Bronco, Explorer, Ranger, "E" & "F" Series

NOTE: Unless otherwise specified, references to "F" Series includes "F" Series Super Duty.

INTRODUCTION

Perform all steps in BASIC DIAGNOSTIC PROCEDURES article in ENGINE PERFORMANCE. If no fault is found while performing BASIC DIAGNOSTIC PROCEDURES, proceed with self-diagnostics. If no service code or only pass codes are found during self-diagnostics, proceed to TROUBLE SHOOTING – NO CODES article in ENGINE PERFORMANCE for diagnosis by symptoms.

SELF-DIAGNOSTIC SYSTEM

DIAGNOSTIC FORMATS

There are 2 diagnostic formats used to test and service the EEC-IV system: QUICK TEST and CIRCUIT TESTS. QUICK TEST allows the technician to identify problems and retrieve and record service codes. CIRCUIT TESTS check circuits, sensors and actuators.

Before starting any CIRCUIT TEST, follow all steps under QUICK TEST to find the correct CIRCUIT TEST. If vehicle passes QUICK TEST, and there are no driveability symptoms or intermittent faults, the EEC-IV system is okay. Problem is in another system.

SERVICE CODES

There are 3 types of service codes retrieved during self-test procedure: Key On Engine Off (KOEO), Key On Engine Running (KOER) and Continuous Memory codes. *See Fig. 1.* See QUICK TEST in this article for self-test procedures. Codes may be cleared from ECA memory by the technician after they have been recorded or repaired. See CLEARING CODES.

KOEO & KOER Codes (Hard Faults) – These codes indicate faults are present at time of testing. A hard fault may cause CHECK ENGINE or SERVICE ENGINE SOON light to illuminate and remain on until fault is repaired. If KOEO or KOER codes are retrieved during KOEO SELF-TEST or KOER SELF-TEST, use appropriate KOEO SELF-TEST CODES or KOER SELF-TEST CODES chart under SERVICE CODE REFERENCE CHARTS to select the correct CIRCUIT TEST for testing and repair.

Continuous Memory Codes (Soft Faults) – Continuous Memory Codes are retrieved during the KOEO SELF-TEST. These codes may cause CHECK ENGINE light to flicker or illuminate. Light will go out after fault goes away. These faults indicate a defect that may or may not be present at the time of testing, however, the corresponding trouble code will be retained in ECA memory.

If the fault does not reoccur within 40 warm-up cycles (80 cycles on some models), code will be erased from ECA memory. Continuous memory failures may be caused by a sensor, connector or wiring related problems. See INTERMITTENTS in TROUBLE SHOOTING – NO CODES article.

CAUTION: Continuous Memory Codes should be recorded when received during KOEO SELF-TEST. These codes may be used to identify intermittent problems that exist after all KOEO and KOER codes have been repaired, and a Code 11 or 111 (pass code) has been obtained. Some Continuous Memory Codes faults may not be valid after KOEO and KOER codes are repaired. Failure to follow this procedure may result in unnecessary testing and replacement of non-faulty components.

CLEARING CODES

To clear codes from ECA memory, start KOEO SELF-TEST. When service codes appear on test equipment or CHECK ENGINE light, disconnect jumper wire from Self-Test Input (STI) connector. If using STAR Series Tester, unlatch center button. This procedure erases Continuous Memory Codes from ECA memory. If problem has not been corrected and fault is still present, hard code will be reset in ECA memory.

NOTE: DO NOT disconnect vehicle battery to clear codes. This will erase stored operating information from the Keep-Alive Memory (KAM). If KAM has been cleared, drive vehicle 10 miles or more to allow ECA to relearn operating conditions and driving style of vehicle. Driveability may be affected during relearning cycle.

READING CODES

KOEO & KOER Self-Test Codes – All service codes are 2 or 3-digit numbers. Codes are outputted, one digit at a time, by ECA. These codes indicate current faults in the system, and should be serviced in the order of appearance. Use appropriate chart under SERVICE CODE REFERENCE CHARTS to find the correct CIRCUIT TEST.

Separator Pulse – A single 1/2-second separator pulse is issued 6-9 seconds after last KOEO code. Then 6-9 seconds after the 1/2-second separator pulse, Continuous Memory Codes (soft faults) are displayed. Some digital test equipment may display the separator code as a 10 or a 1.

Pass Codes – A Code 11 or 111 indicates there are no service codes recorded and system passes that portion of the test. If Code 11 or 111 is not received in KOEO SELF-TEST, codes received during KOER SELF-TEST may not be valid. It is very important that Code 11 or 111 (pass code) be observed in KOEO SELF-TEST. A Code 11-1-11 or 111-1-111 output during KOEO SELF-TEST indicates there is no KOEO code or Continuous Memory Code recorded.

Continuous Memory Codes – These codes result from information stored by ECA during continuous self-test monitoring. Codes are displayed in KOEO SELF-TEST after separator pulse code. Use these codes for diagnosis ONLY when KOEO SELF-TEST and KOER SELF-TEST result in Code 11 or 111 (pass code) and all steps under QUICK TEST are successfully completed. These codes indicate faults recorded within last 40 engine starts. Fault may or may not be currently present. See appropriate chart under SERVICE CODE REFERENCE CHARTS for definitions of codes.

Fast Codes – At the start of KOEO SELF-TEST, and after Wide Open Throttle (WOT) request in KOER SELF-TEST, there is an output from the ECA known as Fast Codes. These are short bursts of information used by manufacturer during assembly. With most equipment, these code bursts are not visible; as the entire code sequence lasts less than 1/2 second. If this fluctuation is visible on test equipment, ignore it.

QUICK TEST

Description – The following procedures are functional tests of EEC-IV system. There are 7 basic test steps. These test steps must be carefully followed in sequence, otherwise misdiagnosis or replacement of non-faulty components may result.

- Visual Check & Vehicle Preparation
- Equipment Hookup
- Key On Engine Off (KOEO) Self-Test
- Computed Timing Check
- Key On Engine Running (KOER) Self-Test
- Continuous Monitor Mode (Wiggle Test)
- Intermittents & Diagnosis By Symptom

Diagnostic Aids – After all tests, servicing or repairs have been completed, repeat QUICK TEST procedure to ensure all EEC-IV systems work properly and service codes are no longer present.

VISUAL CHECK & VEHICLE PREPARATION

Complete all steps in BASIC DIAGNOSTIC PROCEDURES article before proceeding to next test step. Ensure vacuum hoses are connected correctly and EEC-IV wiring harnesses are connected.

EQUIPMENT HOOKUP

Apply parking brake. Place shift lever in Park (A/T) or Neutral (M/T). Block drive wheels. Turn off all electrical loads. Connect appropriate test equipment to vehicle as follows.

1991 ENGINE PERFORMANCE
Self-Diagnostics – EEC-IV (Cont.)

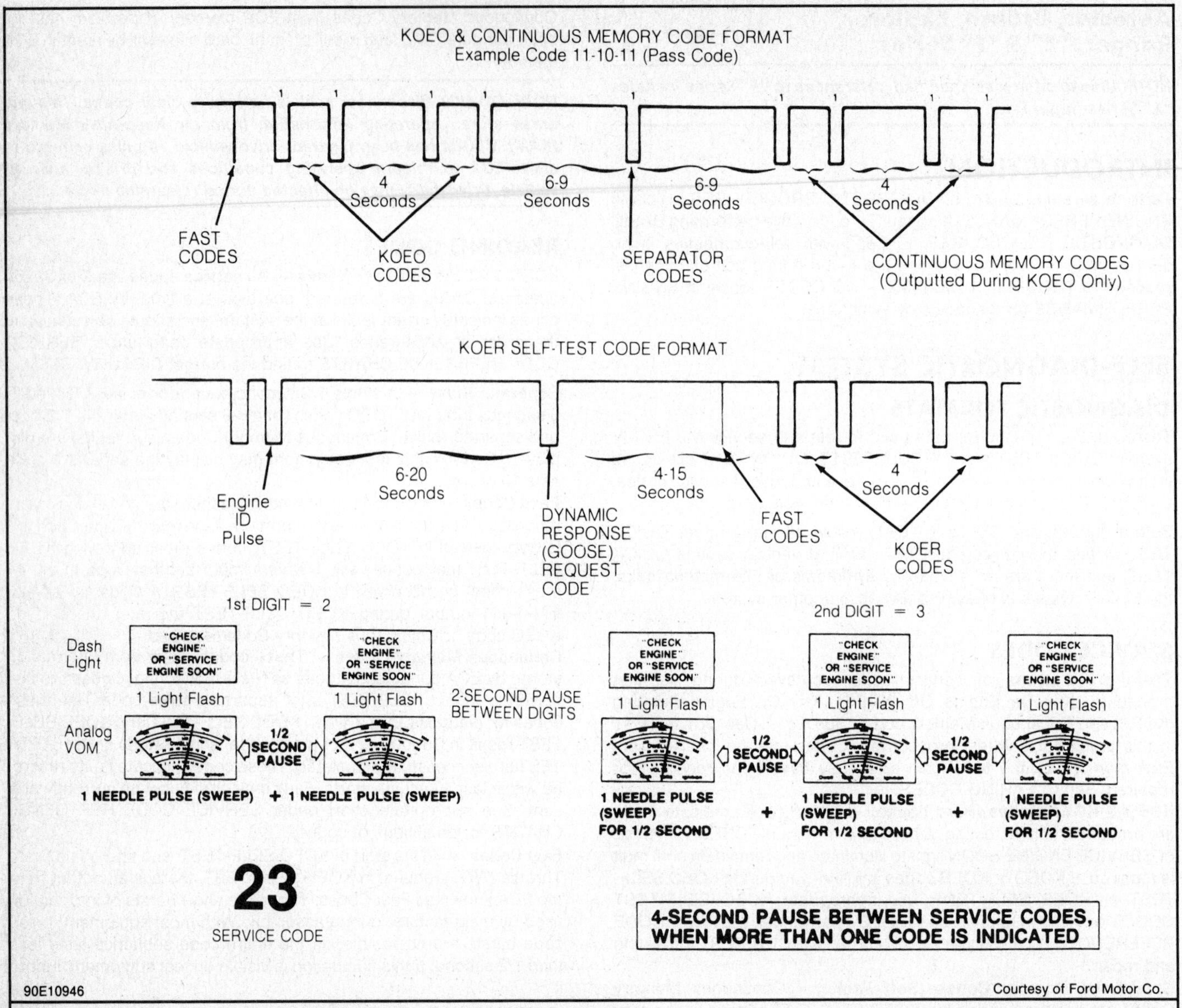
KOEO & CONTINUOUS MEMORY CODE FORMAT
Example Code 11-10-11 (Pass Code)
4 Seconds
6-9 Seconds
6-9 Seconds
4 Seconds
FAST CODES
KOEO CODES
SEPARATOR CODES
CONTINUOUS MEMORY CODES (Outputted During KOEO Only)
KOER SELF-TEST CODE FORMAT
6-20 Seconds
4-15 Seconds
4 Seconds
Engine ID Pulse
DYNAMIC RESPONSE (GOOSE) REQUEST CODE
FAST CODES
KOER CODES
1st DIGIT = 2
2nd DIGIT = 3
Dash Light
"CHECK ENGINE" OR "SERVICE ENGINE SOON"
1 Light Flash
2-SECOND PAUSE BETWEEN DIGITS
Analog VOM
1/2 SECOND PAUSE
1 NEEDLE PULSE (SWEEP) + 1 NEEDLE PULSE (SWEEP)
1 NEEDLE PULSE (SWEEP) FOR 1/2 SECOND
23
SERVICE CODE
4-SECOND PAUSE BETWEEN SERVICE CODES, WHEN MORE THAN ONE CODE IS INDICATED
90E10946
Courtesy of Ford Motor Co.

Fig. 1: Reading Service Codes (2-Digit Codes Shown, 3-Digit Codes Similar)

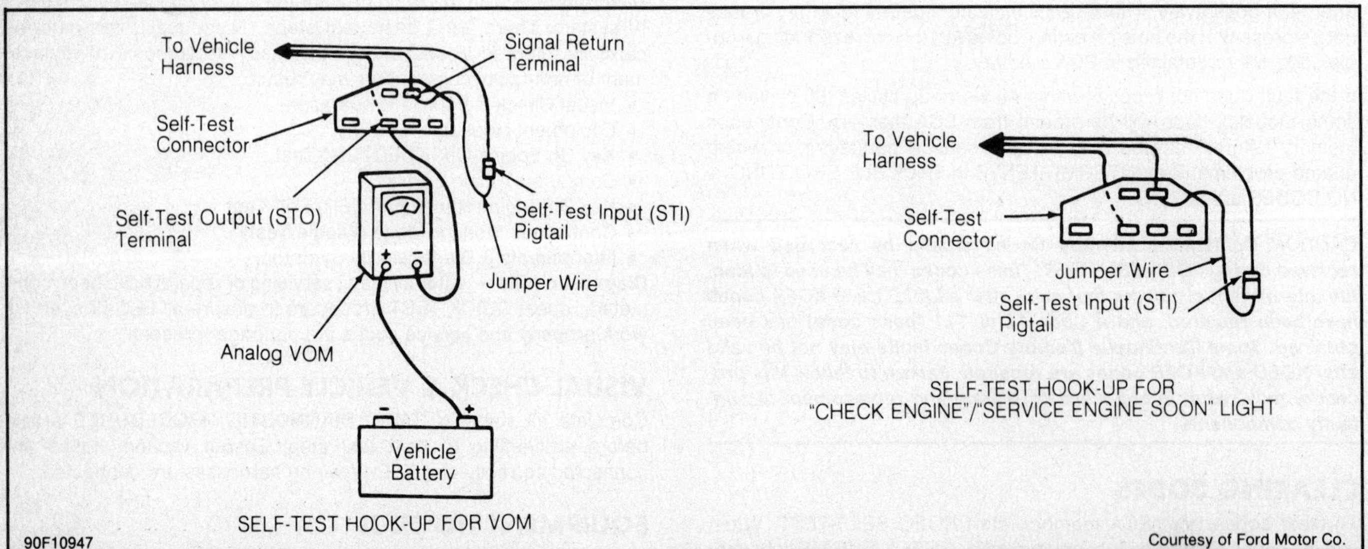
To Vehicle Harness
Signal Return Terminal
Self-Test Connector
Self-Test Output (STO) Terminal
Self-Test Input (STI) Pigtail
Jumper Wire
Analog VOM
Vehicle Battery
SELF-TEST HOOK-UP FOR VOM
To Vehicle Harness
Self-Test Connector
Jumper Wire
Self-Test Input (STI) Pigtail
SELF-TEST HOOK-UP FOR "CHECK ENGINE"/"SERVICE ENGINE SOON" LIGHT
90F10947
Courtesy of Ford Motor Co.

Fig. 2: Self-Test Connector Equipment Hookup

NOTE: The accuracy of service codes depends on correct operation of non-EEC-IV components and systems. All non-EEC problems in the engine must be corrected before attempting to diagnose the EEC-IV system.

Perform Key On Engine Off (KOEO) and Key On Engine Running (KOER) self-test procedures with one of the following: analog volt-ohmmeter (VOM), CHECK ENGINE light, SUPER STAR II tester or appropriate scan tool. After codes have been retrieved, use KOEO SELF-TEST CODES or KOER SELF-TEST CODES chart under SERVICE CODE REFERENCE CHARTS to select the correct CIRCUIT TEST for testing and repair.

Analog Volt-Ohmmeter (VOM) – 1) Turn ignition off. To initiate KOEO self-test, connect a jumper wire from self-test connector STI terminal to ground. *See Fig. 2*.

2) Set VOM at 0-20V DC range. Connect positive (+) lead of VOM to self-test connector STO terminal. Connect the negative (-) test lead to engine ground. Turn ignition on and observe voltmeter.

3) Codes are shown as voltage pulses (needle sweeps). *See Fig. 1*. Pay careful attention to the length of pauses in order to read codes correctly. There is a 1/2-second pause between number of sweeps in a digit, and a 2-second pause between the digits in a code.

4) There is a 4-second pause between each code. KOEO codes are separated from Continuous Memory codes by a 6-second delay, a single 1/2-second sweep (Separator) and another 6-second delay. Record codes in the order received.

NOTE: If no code is present and engine will not start, go to BASIC DIAGNOSTICS PROCEDURES article.

5) Record all codes displayed and repair fault as necessary. Refer to SERVICE CODE REFERENCE CHART table to determine the correct CIRCUIT TEST. If no code is present and engine starts, begin KOER self-test.

CHECK ENGINE Light – 1) Connect a jumper wire between the STI connector and ground. *See Fig. 2*. Turn ignition on. Observe CHECK ENGINE light, and record pulses to determine KOEO codes stored.

NOTE: Reading code from ENGINE LIGHT pulses is similar to reading code from needle sweep of Analog Volt-Ohmmeter (VOM).

2) If no code is present and engine does not start, go to BASIC DIAGNOSTIC PROCEDURES article. If no code is present and engine starts, begin KOER self-test and go to step **3)**.

3) Start engine and run at 2000 RPM for 2 minutes to ensure EGO sensor is operating. Ensure vehicle is at normal operating temperature. Jumper STI connector to ground.

4) Observe CHECK ENGINE light. Record pulses to determine KOER codes stored. Use CODE REFERENCE CHART table to determine the appropriate CIRCUIT TEST.

Scan Tool – Follow manufacturer's instructions to hook up equipment and record service codes.

SUPER STAR II Tester – 1) To initiate KOEO self-test, turn ignition off. Connect color-coded adapter cable leads to SUPER STAR II tester. Connect service adapter cables to vehicle self-test connectors.

2) Slide adapter switch to EEC-IV position. Slide mode selector switch to either Fast or Slow position. Use Fast mode on vehicles using 3 digit codes. Use Slow mode on vehicles using 2 digit codes.

3) Turn SUPER STAR II tester on. The display window should flash 88, indicating display check. When 00 appears in display, tester is ready. Set center button in TEST position. Turn ignition on.

4) After all codes have been received by tester, release center button. Retrieve and record all codes in tester memory. Refer to SERVICE CODE REFERENCE CHART table to determine the appropriate CIRCUIT TEST. If no codes exist and engine starts, begin KOER self-test and go to step **5)**.

NOTE: If no code is present and engine does not start, go to BASIC DIAGNOSTIC PROCEDURES article.

5) To initiate KOER self-test. Ensure center button on SUPER STAR II tester is unlatched. Start engine and run at 2000 RPM for 2 minutes to ensure EGO sensor is operating. Turn ignition off. Ensure SUPER STAR II tester is on. Set center button in TEST position.

6) Start engine and let it idle. On models using 2-digit service codes, engine ID will be displayed. On some models, a dynamic response will appear briefly. On models using 3-digit service codes, only service codes will appear. Record all codes displayed. Refer to SERVICE CODE REFERENCE CHART table to determine appropriate CIRCUIT TEST.

SELF-TEST CONNECTOR LOCATIONS

Application	Location
Aerostar	Left front inner fender panel
Bronco & "F" Series	Left front inner fender panel
"E" Series	Right front inner fender panel
Explorer & Ranger	Right front inner fender panel

KOEO SELF-TEST

1) Start engine and allow to idle until vehicle reaches operating temperature. If engine does not start or stalls after starting, continue KOEO SELF-TEST. DO NOT depress throttle on gasoline-engine vehicles. On 4.9L models, depress clutch pedal for test. On 7.3L Diesel models, depress throttle pedal for test.

2) Turn ignition off and wait 10 seconds. Activate self-test procedure by using a jumper wire or appropriate test equipment. Turn ignition on, leaving engine off. Record all KOEO and Continuous Memory Codes.

3) If a Code 11 or 111 (pass code) is not received in the KOEO portion of the test, service the KOEO codes. See appropriate chart under SERVICE CODE REFERENCE CHARTS. If the ECA will not output codes, go to CIRCUIT TEST QA, step **1)**. If service codes are received, check the following procedures:

- If CHECK ENGINE or SERVICE ENGINE SOON light is on when vehicle arrived for service, use recorded Continuous Memory Codes and appropriate chart under SERVICE CODE REFERENCE CHARTS before addressing any other symptoms.
- On all vehicles, except vehicles with Distributorless Ignition System (DIS) or Electronic Distributorless Ignition System (EDIS), if engine runs rough or idles rough, go to CIRCUIT TEST S, step **2)**. On vehicles with DIS or EDIS, use recorded Continuous Memory Codes and appropriate chart under SERVICE CODE REFERENCE CHARTS.
- On DIS and EDIS vehicles, perform only the following. If Continuous Memory Codes 45, 46, 48, 215, 216, 217, 232 or 238 are received during KOEO SELF-TEST, see appropriate system in SYSTEM & COMPONENT TESTING article. If Codes 45, 46, 48, 215, 216, 217, 232 or 238 were not received, go to CIRCUIT TEST S, step **2)**.
- On all vehicles, except vehicles with EDIS, if vehicle has a no-start condition, go to CIRCUIT TEST A, step **1)**. On vehicles with EDIS, go to CIRCUIT TEST AA, step **1)**.
- If vehicle displays a Code 11 or 111 (pass code) and does not have any of the symptoms described in previous steps, go to COMPUTED TIMING CHECK.

COMPUTED TIMING CHECK

Turn ignition off and wait 10 seconds. Using jumper wire or test equipment, activate KOER SELF-TEST. Start engine and check for the following:

- If engine starts and stalls, or stalls during self-test, go to Circuit Test S, step **1)**.
- If Code 98 or 998 is displayed, it indicates EEC-IV system is operating in Failure Mode Effects Management (FMEM). Vehicle cannot be diagnosed in KOER SELF-TEST; rerun KOEO SELF-TEST.
- Check computed timing after the last service code has been displayed. The timing will remain fixed for 2 minutes after the last code has been received, unless self-test is deactivated.
- Computed timing, at the crankshaft, should equal the base timing (see vehicle emission decal) plus 20 degrees BTDC. This timing may vary 3 degrees. If computed timing is within specification, perform KOER SELF-TEST. If timing is not within specification, go to step **2)** of CIRCUIT TEST PC (vehicles with EDIS), step **2)** of CIR-

1991 ENGINE PERFORMANCE
Self-Diagnostics – EEC-IV (Cont.)

CUIT TEST PB (vehicles with DIS), or step **2)** of CIRCUIT TEST PA (vehicles with TFI).

KOER SELF-TEST

Diagnostic Aids – 1) DO NOT enter this test sequence until a Code 11 or 111 (pass code) has been received in KOEO SELF-TEST. If system has not passed KOEO SELF-TEST, code recorded in KOER SELF-TEST may not be valid.
2) Deactivate self-test by removing and reconnecting jumper wire, or by procedure specified by test equipment in use. Start and run engine for 2 minutes at 2000 RPM to warm-up Heated Exhaust Gas Oxygen (HEGO) sensor. Turn engine off and wait 10 seconds. Activate KOER SELF-TEST using a jumper wire or appropriate procedure for test equipment used. Start engine. Record all service codes displayed. Check the following items:

- If engine starts and stalls, or stalls during self-test, go to CIRCUIT TEST S, step **1)**.
- If vehicle is equipped with a Brake On/Off (BOO) switch, brake pedal MUST be depressed and released AFTER the ID code portion of test.
- On vehicles with Power Steering Pressure Switch (PSPS), turn steering wheel at least 1/2 turn and release within 1-2 seconds after the ID code portion of test.
- On vehicles with E4OD transmissions, the Overdrive Cancel Switch (OCS) MUST be cycled after the ID code portion of the test.
- When the Dynamic Response Code appears, perform a brief Wide Open Throttle (WOT). DO NOT perform WOT unless requested.
- If Code 98 or 998 is displayed, EEC-IV system is operating in Failure Management Effects Mode (FMEM). Vehicle has not passed KOEO SELF-TEST and cannot be diagnosed while in FMEM mode. See Code 98 or 998 in appropriate CONTINUOUS MEMORY CODE chart under SERVICE CODE REFERENCE CHARTS.
- If KOER codes are present, refer to appropriate KOER SELF-TEST CODES chart under SERVICE CODE REFERENCE CHARTS. If system will not output codes, go to CIRCUIT TEST QA, step **1)**.

CONTINUOUS MONITOR MODE (WIGGLE TEST)

The Continuous Monitor Mode allows technician to attempt a recreation of intermittent fault while monitoring the system. This mode, also called the wiggle test, may be used in both KOEO SELF-TEST and KOER SELF-TEST. The CIRCUIT TESTS specify the use of this procedure to identify intermittent faults in specific circuits or components.

KOEO Wiggle Test Procedure – 1) Connect test equipment. Turn ignition on and activate self-test with jumper lead or diagnostic tester. Wait 10 seconds, deactivate, and then reactivate self-test. Wiggle test mode is now activated. Tap, move and wiggle the suspected sensor and/or harness area.
2) If a fault is detected, a service code may be stored in memory and indicated at the diagnostic tester or "Scan" tool. If voltmeter is used, needle will sweep. If using check Engine light, light will come on. Record code and perform test indicated by appropriate CONTINUOUS MEMORY CODES chart under SERVICE CODE REFERENCE CHARTS.

KOER Wiggle Test Procedure – 1) Connect test equipment. *See Fig.* 2. Turn ignition off and wait 10 seconds. Start engine. Activate self-test with jumper lead or diagnostic tester. Wait 10 seconds, deactivate, and then reactivate self-test. DO NOT turn engine off. KOER wiggle test mode is now activated.
2) Tap, move and wiggle the suspected sensor and/or harness area. If a fault is detected, a service code may be stored in memory and indicated at the diagnostic tester or "Scan" tool. If voltmeter is used, needle will sweep. If using check Engine light, light will come on. Record code and perform test indicated in appropriate CONTINUOUS MEMORY CODES chart under SERVICE CODE REFERENCE CHARTS.

INTERMITTENT & DIAGNOSIS BY SYMPTOMS

See TROUBLE SHOOTING – NO CODES article in ENGINE PERFORMANCE.

ADDITIONAL SYSTEM FUNCTIONS

A number of additional diagnostic system features are available to help technicians diagnose driveability problems and test EEC-IV systems.

Output State Check – The Output State Check is used as an aid in servicing output actuators associated with EEC-IV system. It allows technicians to energize and de-energize most of the system output actuators on command. This mode is entered from the KOEO SELF-TEST, after all codes have been received. Leave self-test activated and depress throttle to initiate test sequence. Each time throttle is depressed and released, the output actuators will change state (from on to off, or off to on).

Failure Mode Effects Management (FMEM) – The FMEM mode allows system operation when sensor(s) fails or transmits signals which are out of normal operating range. When this happens, ECA substitutes a mid-range signal for the defective sensor(s) while continuing to monitor the sensor(s). If the faulty sensor's signals return to normal operating range, the ECA will use those signals. A Code 98 or 998 will be displayed when the FMEM mode is in effect.

Hardware Limited Operational Strategy (HLOS) – If a number of system or sensor failures are present, and the ECA is not receiving enough information to operate, ECA will switch to HLOS mode. ECA will output fixed values to allow operation of vehicle. ECA will not output service codes in this mode.

Cylinder Balance Test – This test helps identify a weak or noncontributing cylinder in engines with sequential PFI fuel systems. The ECA shuts off fuel supply to each injector and measures RPM drop. It computes the variation between cylinders and identifies the weak ones.

This test mode is entered from the KOER SELF-TEST, after all codes have been displayed. Within 2 minutes after codes have been displayed, lightly depress throttle (2-3 degree throttle angle). After a brief stabilizing period, ECA will activate the test procedure. The test will be repeated if the throttle is depressed within 2 minutes of the final code output.

Service codes displayed during this test identify the weak or non-contributing cylinder. See CYLINDER BALANCE TEST SERVICE CODES table. Code 90 indicates a passing result. If Code 77 is displayed, repeat cylinder balance test. If throttle is moved during this test, Code 77 will appear, indicating that test is not completed. Total test time is about 3 minutes.

CYLINDER BALANCE TEST SERVICE CODES

Service Code	Application
10	Cylinder No. 1
20	Cylinder No. 2
30	Cylinder No. 3
40	Cylinder No. 4
50	Cylinder No. 5
60	Cylinder No. 6
70	Cylinder No. 7
80	Cylinder No. 8
77	Retest
90	Pass

SUMMARY

If no service code (only pass code) is present, but driveability problem still exists, proceed to TROUBLE SHOOTING – NO CODES article for diagnosis by symptom (i.e. ROUGH IDLE, NO START, etc.), or intermittent diagnosis procedures.

NOTE: The following SERVICE CODE REFERENCE CHARTS are courtesy of Ford Motor Co.

1991 ENGINE PERFORMANCE
Self-Diagnostics – EEC-IV (Cont.)

SERVICE CODE REFERENCE CHARTS

KOEO SELF-TEST CODES (2 DIGITS)

Key On Engine Off Service Code	CIRCUIT TEST and step number									
	2.3L EFI	2.9L EFI	3.0L EFI	3.0L MA EFI	4.0L EFI	4.9L EFI	5.0L EFI	5.8L EFI	7.3L DIESEL	7.5L EFI
15 GO to ▶	QB3	QB3	QB3	QB3	QB3	QB3	QB3	QB3	QB3	QB3
16 GO to ▶	—	—	—	—	NC2	—	—	—	—	—
19 GO to ▶	Replace Processor									
21 GO to ▶	DA1	DA1	DA1	DA1	DA1	DA1	DA1	DA1	—	DA1
22 GO to ▶	DF1	DF1	DF1	DF1	DF1	DF1	DF1	DF1	DF1	DF1
23 GO to ▶	DH2	DH2	DH2	DH2	DH2	DH2	DH2	DH2	DQ1	DH2
24 GO to ▶	DA1	DA1	DA1	DA1	DA1	DA1	DA1	DA1	—	DA1
26 GO to ▶	DC1	—	—	DC1	DC1	TC30	—	TC30	TC30	TC30
31 GO to ▶	DN1	—	—	—	—	DN1	DN1	DN1	—	DN1
32 GO to ▶	DN25	—	—	—	—	DN25	DN25	DN25	—	DN25
34 GO to ▶	DN20	—	—	—	—	DN20	DN20	DN20	—	DN20
35 GO to ▶	DN5	—	—	—	—	DN5	DN5	DN5	—	DN5
47 GO to ▶	—	—	—	—	—	TC10	—	TC10	TC10	TC10
51 GO to ▶	DA10	DA10	DA10	DA10	DA10	DA10	DA10	DA10	—	DA10
52 GO to ▶	FF1	—	FF1	—	—	—	FF1	—	—	—
53 GO to ▶	DH3	DH3	DH3	DH3	DH3	DH3	DH3	DH3	DQ2	DH3
54 GO to ▶	DA10	DA10	DA10	DA10	DA10	DA10	DA10	DA10	—	DA10
56 GO to ▶	DC20	—	—	DC20	DC20	TC40	—	TC40	TC40	TC40
57 GO to ▶	KP1	—	—	—	KP1	—	—	—	—	—
61 GO to ▶	DA20	DA20	DA20	DA20	DA20	DA20	DA20	DA20	—	DA20
63 GO to ▶	DH10	DH10	DH10	DH10	DH10	DH10	DH10	DH10	DQ10	DH10
64 GO to ▶	DA20	DA20	DA20	DA20	DA20	DA20	DA20	DA20	—	DA20
66 GO to ▶	DC10	—	—	DC10	DC10	TC50	—	TC50	TC50	TC50
67 GO to ▶	TA1	TA1	TA1	TA1	TA1	TA1	TA1	TA1	TA1	TA1
79 GO to ▶	KM40	—	—	KM40	KM40	—	—	—	—	—
81 GO to ▶	—	—	—	—	—	KC8	KC8	KC8	—	—
82 GO to ▶	—	—	—	—	—	KC8	KC8	KC8	—	KC8
84 GO to ▶	DN10	—	—	—	—	DN10	DN10	DN10	—	DN10
85 GO to ▶	—	—	KD6	KD6	KD6	KD6	—	KD6	—	KD6
86 GO to ▶	TB1	TB1	TB1	TB1	TB1	—	—	—	—	—
87 GO to ▶	J7	J7	J7	J7	J7	J7	J7	J7	—	J7
89 GO to ▶	TB1	TB1	TB1	TB1	TB1	TC18	TC18	TC18	TC18	TC18
91 GO to ▶	—	—	—	—	—	TC18	TC18	TC18	TC18	TC18
92 GO to ▶	—	—	—	—	—	TC18	TC18	TC18	TC18	TC18
93 GO to ▶	—	—	—	—	—	TC18	TC18	TC18	TC18	TC18
94 GO to ▶	—	—	—	—	—	TC18	TC18	TC18	TC18	TC18
95 GO to ▶	J20	J20	J20	J20	J20	J20	J20	J20	—	J20
96 GO to ▶	J30	J30	J30	J30	J30	J30	J30	J30	—	J30
97 GO to ▶	—	—	—	—	—	TC10	TC10	TC10	TC10	TC10
98 GO to ▶	—	—	—	—	—	TC20	TC20	TC20	TC20	TC20
99 GO to ▶	—	—	—	—	—	TC20	TC20	TC20	TC20	TC20
NO CODES CODES NOT LISTED	Go to CIRCUIT TEST QA, step 1									

91F14246

Courtesy of Ford Motor Co.

1991 ENGINE PERFORMANCE
Self-Diagnostics – EEC-IV (Cont.)

KOEO SELF-TEST CODES (3 DIGITS)

Key On Engine Off Service Code	CIRCUIT TEST and step number				
	4.9L EFI	5.0L EFI	5.8L EFI	7.0L EFI	7.5L EFI
112 GO to ▶	DA20	DA20	DA20	DA20	DA20
113 GO to ▶	DA10	DA10	DA10	DA10	DA10
114 GO to ▶	DA1	DA1	DA1	DA1	DA1
116 GO to ▶	DA1	DA1	DA1	DA1	DA1
117 GO to ▶	DA20	DA20	DA20	DA20	DA20
118 GO to ▶	DA10	DA10	DA10	DA10	DA10
121 GO to ▶	DH2	DH2	DH2	DH2	DH2
122 GO to ▶	DH10	DH10	DH10	DH10	DH10
123 GO to ▶	DH3	DH3	DH3	DH3	DH3
126 GO to ▶	DF1	DF1	DF1	DF1	DF1
327 GO to ▶	DN1	DN1	DN1	DN1	DN1
328 GO to ▶	DN25	DN25	DN25	DN25	DN25
334 GO to ▶	DN20	DN20	DN20	DN20	DN20
337 GO to ▶	DN5	DN5	DN5	DN5	DN5
511 GO to ▶	QB3	QB3	QB3	QB3	QB3
513 GO to ▶	Replace Processor				
525 GO to ▶	—	—	—	TA1	—
539 GO to ▶	KM40	KM40	KM40	KM40	KM40
542 GO to ▶	J20	J20	J20	J20	J20
543 GO to ▶	J30	J30	J30	J30	J30
552 GO to ▶	KC8	KC8	KC8	KC8	KC8
553 GO to ▶	KC8	KC8	KC8	KC8	KC8
556 GO to ▶	J7	J7	J7	J7	J7
558 GO to ▶	DN10	DN10	DN10	DN10	DN10
565 GO to ▶	KD6	KD6	KD6	KD6	KD6
569 GO to ▶	—	—	—	KD6	—
621 GO to ▶	TC18	TC18	TC18	—	TC18
622 GO to ▶	TC18	TC18	TC18	—	TC18
624 GO to ▶	TC20	TC20	TC20	—	TC20
625 GO to ▶	TC20	TC20	TC20	—	TC20
626 GO to ▶	TC18	TC18	TC18	—	TC18
627 GO to ▶	TC18	TC18	TC18	—	TC18
629 GO to ▶	TC18	TC18	TC18	—	TC18
631 GO to ▶	TC10	TC10	TC10	—	TC10
633 GO to ▶	TC10	TC10	TC10	—	TC10
634 GO to ▶	TA1	TA1	TA1	—	TA1
636 GO to ▶	TC30	TC30	TC30	—	TC30
637 GO to ▶	TC40	TC40	TC40	—	TC40
638 GO to ▶	TC50	TC50	TC50	—	TC50
641 GO to ▶	TC18	TC18	TC18	—	TC18
654 GO to ▶	TC1	TC1	TC1	—	TC1
998 GO to ▶	TC20	TC20	TC20	—	TC20
NO CODES/ CODES NOT LISTED	Go to CIRCUIT TEST QA, step 1				

91G14247

Courtesy of Ford Motor Co.

KOER SELF-TEST CODES (2 DIGITS)

Engine Running Service Code	CIRCUIT TEST and step number									
	2.3L EFI	2.9L EFI	3.0L EFI	3.0L MA EFI	4.0L EFI	4.9L EFI	5.0L EFI	5.8L EFI	7.3L DIESEL	7.5L EFI
12 GO to ▶	KE1	KE1	KE1	KE1	KE1	KE1	KE1	KE1	—	KE1
13 GO to ▶	KE15	KE15	KE15	KE15	KE15	KE15	KE15	KE15	—	KE15
16 GO to ▶	KE1	—	—	—	—	—	—	—	—	—
18 GO to ▶	PB1	PA1	PA1	PA1	PC1	PA1	PA1	PA1	—	PA1
21 GO to ▶	DA1	DA1	DA	DA1	DA1	DA1	DA1	DA1	—	DA1
22 GO to ▶	DF1	DF7	DF7	DF1	DF1	DF7	DF7	DF7	DF7	DF7
23 GO to ▶	DH1	DH1	DH1	DH1	DH1	DH1	DH1	DH1	DQ1	DH1
24 GO to ▶	DA1	DA1	DA1	DA1	DA1	DA1	DA1	DA1	—	DA1
25 GO to ▶	—	—	—	—	—	DG1	DG1	—	—	—
26 GO to ▶	DC1	—	—	DC1	DC1	TC30	—	TC30	TC30	TC30
31 GO to ▶	DN1	—	—	—	—	DN1	DN1	DN1	—	DN1
32 GO to ▶	DN25	—	—	—	—	DN25	DN25	DN25	—	DN25
33 GO to ▶	DN40	—	—	—	—	DN40	DN40	DN40	—	DN40
34 GO to ▶	DN50	—	—	—	—	DN50	DN50	DN50	—	DN50
35 GO to ▶	DN5	—	—	—	—	DN5	DN5	DN5	—	DN5
41 GO to ▶	H1	H1	H1	H1	H1	H1	H1	H1	—	H1
42 GO to ▶	H1	H1	H1	H1	H1	H1	H1	H1	—	H1
44 GO to ▶	—	—	—	—	—	KC1	KC1	KC1	—	KC1
45 GO to ▶	—	—	—	—	—	KC1	KC1	KC1	—	KC1
46 GO to ▶	—	—	—	—	—	KC1	KC1	KC1	—	—
52 GO to ▶	FF5	—	FF5	—	—	—	FF5	—	—	—
56 GO to ▶	DC20	—	—	DC20	DC20	—	—	—	—	—
65 GO to ▶	—	—	—	—	—	TC10	—	TC10	TC10	TC10
72 GO to ▶	DF10	DF10	DF10	DF10	DF10	DF10	DF10	DF10	—	DF10
73 GO to ▶	DH20	DH20	DH20	DH20	DH20	DH20	DH20	DH20	—	DH20
74 GO to ▶	FD1	FD1	FD1	FD1	FD1	FD1	—	FD1	FD1	FD1
77 GO to ▶	M1	M1	M1	M1	M1	M1	M1	M1	—	M1
98 GO to ▶	GO TO QUICK TEST									
NO CODES ▶ CODES NOT LISTED ▶	Go to CIRCUIT TEST QA, step 1									

91H14248

Courtesy of Ford Motor Co.

1991 ENGINE PERFORMANCE
Self-Diagnostics – EEC-IV (Cont.)

KOER SELF-TEST CODES (3 DIGITS)

Engine Running Service Code	CIRCUIT TEST and step number				
	4.9L EFI	5.0L EFI	5.8L EFI	7.0L EFI	7.5L EFI
114 GO to ▶	DA1	DA1	DA1	DA1	DA1
116 GO to ▶	DA1	DA1	DA1	DA1	DA1
121 GO to ▶	DH1	DH1	DH1	DH1	DH1
129 GO to ▶	DF10	DF10	DF10	DF10	DF10
136 GO to ▶	H1	H1	H1	H1	H1
137 GO to ▶	H1	H1	H1	H1	H1
167 GO to ▶	DH20	DH20	DH20	DH20	DH20
172 GO to ▶	H1	H1	H1	H1	H1
173 GO to ▶	H1	H1	H1	H1	H1
213 GO to ▶	PA1	PA1	PA1	PA1	PA1
225 GO to ▶	DG1	DG1	—	—	—
311 GO to ▶	KC1	KC1	KC1	KC1	KC1
312 GO to ▶	KC1	KC1	KC1	KC1	KC1
313 GO to ▶	KC1	KC1	KC1	KC1	KC1
327 GO to ▶	DN1	DN1	DN1	DN1	DN1
328 GO to ▶	DN25	DN25	DN25	DN25	DN25
332 GO to ▶	DN40	DN40	DN40	DN40	DN40
334 GO to ▶	DN50	DN50	DN50	DN50	DN50
337 GO to ▶	DN5	DN5	DN5	DN5	DN5
411 GO to ▶	KE15	KE15	KE15	KE15	KE15
412 GO to ▶	KE1	KE1	KE1	KE1	KE1
536 GO to ▶	FD1	FD1	FD1	FD1	FD1
538 GO to ▶	M1	M1	M1	M1	M1
632 GO to ▶	TC10	TC10	TC10	—	TC10
636 GO to ▶	TC30	TC30	TC30	—	TC30
998 GO to ▶	GO TO QUICK TEST				
NO CODES/ CODES NOT LISTED	Go to CIRCUIT TEST QA, step 1				

91I14249

Courtesy of Ford Motor Co.

1991 ENGINE PERFORMANCE
Self-Diagnostics – EEC-IV (Cont.)

CONTINUOUS MEMORY CODES (2 DIGITS)

Continuous Memory Service Code	CIRCUIT TEST and step number									
	2.3L EFI	2.9L EFI	3.0L EFI	3.0L MA EFI	4.0L EFI	4.9L EFI	5.0L EFI	5.8L EFI	7.3L DIESEL	7.5L EFI
14 GO to ▶	NB1	NA1	NA1	NA1	NA1	NA1	NA1	NA1	DJ1	NA1
15 GO to ▶	QB1	QB1	QB1	QB1	QB1	QB1	QB1	QB1	QB1	QB1
18 GO to ▶	[1]	NA3	NA3	NA3	NC2	NA3	NA3	NA3	—	NA3
19 GO to ▶	[1]	—	—	—	—	—	—	—	—	—
22 GO to ▶	DF90	DF90	DF90	DF90	DF90	DF90	DF90	DF90	DF90	DF90
28 GO to ▶	NB3	—	—	—	—	—	—	—	—	—
29 GO to ▶	DP1	DP1	DP1	DP1	DP1	DP1	DP1	DP1	DP1	DP1
31 GO to ▶	DN91	—	—	—	—	DN91	DN91	DN91	—	DN91
32 GO to ▶	DN90	—	—	—	—	DN90	DN90	DN90	—	DN90
33 GO to ▶	DN95	—	—	—	—	DN95	DN95	DN95	—	DN95
34 GO to ▶	DN98	—	—	—	—	DN98	DN98	DN98	—	DN98
35 GO to ▶	DN93	—	—	—	—	DN93	DN93	DN93	—	DN93
41 GO to ▶	H1	H1	H1	H1	H1	H1	H1	H1	—	H1
45 GO to ▶	—	—	—	H1	[2]	—	—	—	—	—
48 GO to ▶	NB3	—	—	—	—	—	—	—	—	—
49 GO to ▶	—	—	—	—	—	TC90	—	TC90	TC90	TC90
51 GO to ▶	DA90	DA90	DA90	DA90	DA90	DA90	DA90	DA90	—	DA90
53 GO to ▶	DH90	DH90	DH90	DH90	DH90	DH90	DH90	DH90	DQ90	DH90
54 GO to ▶	DA90	DA90	DA90	DA90	DA90	DA90	DA90	DA90	—	DA90
56 GO to ▶	DC20	—	—	DC20	DC20	TC90	—	TC90	TC90	TC90
59 GO to ▶	—	—	—	—	—	TC90	—	TC90	TC90	TC90
61 GO to ▶	DA90	DA90	DA90	DA90	DA90	DA90	DA90	DA90	—	DA90
62 GO to ▶	—	—	—	—	—	TC90	—	TC90	TC90	TC90
63 GO to ▶	DH94	DH94	DH94	DH94	DH94	DH94	DH94	DH94	DQ94	DH94
64 GO to ▶	DA90	DA90	DA90	DA90	DA90	DA90	DA90	DA90	—	DA90
66 GO to ▶	DC10	—	—	DC10	DC10	TC90	—	TC90	TC90	TC90
67 GO to ▶	TA1	TA1	TA1	—	TA1	TC90	—	TC90	TC90	TC90
69 GO to ▶	—	—	—	—	—	TC90	—	TC90	TC90	TC90
81 GO to ▶	—	—	—	—	—	—	DF11	—	—	—
87 GO to ▶	J95	J95	J95	J95	J95	J95	J95	J95	—	J95
88 GO to ▶	NB20	—	—	—	—	—	—	—	—	—
95 GO to ▶	J90	J90	J90	J90	J90	J90	J90	J90	—	J90
96 GO to ▶	J93	J93	J93	J93	J93	J93	J93	J93	—	J93
99 GO to ▶	—	—	—	—	—	TC90	—	TC90	TC90	TC90
NO CODES CODES NOT LISTED	Go to CIRCUIT TEST QA, step 1									

91C14250

Courtesy of Ford Motor Co.

[1] – Check air intake for restrictions or defective mass airflow sensor.

[2] – See BASIC DIAGNOSTIC PROCEDURES for EDIS test procedures.

1991 ENGINE PERFORMANCE
Self-Diagnostics – EEC-IV (Cont.)

CONTINUOUS MEMORY CODES (3 DIGITS)

Continuous Memory Service Code	CIRCUIT TEST and step number				
	4.9L EFI	5.0L EFI	5.8L EFI	7.0L EFI	7.5L EFI
112 GO to ▶	DA90	DA90	DA90	DA90	DA90
113 GO to ▶	DA90	DA90	DA90	DA90	DA90
117 GO to ▶	DA90	DA90	DA90	DA90	DA90
118 GO to ▶	DA90	DA90	DA90	DA90	DA90
122 GO to ▶	DH94	DH94	DH94	DH94	DH94
123 GO to ▶	DH90	DH90	DH90	DH90	DH90
126 GO to ▶	DF90	DF90	DF90	DF90	DF90
128 GO to ▶	—	DF11	DF11	—	—
139 GO to ▶	H1	H1	H1	H1	H1
144 GO to ▶	H1	H1	H1	H1	H1
172 GO to ▶	H1	H1	H1	H1	H1
173 GO to ▶	H1	H1	H1	H1	—
174 GO to ▶	H1	H1	H1	H1	H1
175 GO to ▶	H1	H1	H1	H1	H1
176 GO to ▶	H1	H1	H1	H1	H1
177 GO to ▶	H1	H1	H1	H1	H1
178 GO to ▶	H1	H1	H1	H1	H1
179 GO to ▶	HA15	HA15	HA15	HA15	HA15
181 GO to ▶	HA1	HA1	HA1	HA1	HA1
182 GO to ▶	HA15	HA15	HA15	HA15	HA15
183 GO to ▶	HA1	HA1	HA1	HA1	HA1
211 GO to ▶	NA1	NA1	NA1	NA1	NA1
212 GO to ▶	NA4	NA4	NA4	NA1	NA4
327 GO to ▶	DN91	DN91	DN91	DN91	DN91
328 GO to ▶	DN90	DN90	DN90	DN90	DN90
332 GO to ▶	DN95	DN95	DN95	DN95	DN95
334 GO to ▶	DN98	DN98	DN98	DN98	DN98
337 GO to ▶	DN93	DN93	DN93	DN93	DN93
452 GO to ▶	DP1	DP1	DP1	DP1	DP1
512 GO to ▶	QB1	QB1	QB1	QB1	QB1
525 GO to ▶	—	—	—	TA1	—
542 GO to ▶	J90	J90	J90	J90	J90
543 GO to ▶	J93	J93	J93	J93	J93
556 GO to ▶	J95	J95	J95	J95	J95
617 GO to ▶	TC90	TC90	TC90	—	TC90
618 GO to ▶	TC90	TC90	TC90	—	TC90
619 GO to ▶	TC90	TC90	TC90	—	TC90
624 GO to ▶	TC90	TC90	TC90	—	TC90
628 GO to ▶	TC90	TC90	TC90	—	TC90
634 GO to ▶	TC90	TC90	TC90	—	TC90
637 GO to ▶	TC90	TC90	TC90	—	TC90
638 GO to ▶	TC90	TC90	TC90	—	TC90
NO CODES/ CODES NOT LISTED	Go to CIRCUIT TEST QA, step 1				

91D14251

Courtesy of Ford Motor Co.

CIRCUIT TESTS

***NOTE:** A breakout box, connected in series with wiring harness and ECA, is necessary to perform most circuit tests. References to Test Pin No. found in CIRCUIT TEST steps refer to test terminals on the manufacturer's breakout box. Circuit diagrams at the beginning of each test identify circuit and wire colors.*

HOW TO USE CIRCUIT TESTS

1) Ensure all non-EEC related faults found while performing steps in BASIC DIAGNOSTIC PROCEDURES article have been corrected. DO NOT perform any CIRCUIT TEST unless specifically instructed by a QUICK TEST procedure. FOLLOW EACH TEST STEP IN ORDER UNTIL FAULT IS FOUND.

2) When more than one code is received, start with the first code displayed. CIRCUIT TESTS check electrical circuits to make sure they are okay before replacing sensors or any other components. Always test circuits for continuity between sensor and ECA.

3) Test all circuits for short to power, opens, or short to ground. DO NOT measure voltage or resistance at ECA, or connect any test light unless specified in testing procedure. All measurements are made by probing REAR of connector.

4) Isolate both ends of a circuit and turn ignition off whenever checking for shorts or continuity, unless stated otherwise. Disconnect solenoids and switches from harness before measuring continuity or resistance. After each repair, check all component connections and repeat CIRCUIT TEST.

***NOTE:** In the following tests, circuit diagrams and illustrations are courtesy of Ford Motor Co.*

CIRCUIT TESTS are grouped as follows.

- A-C – No Start & Voltage Tests
- DA-DQ – Input Sensor Tests
- FD-FF – Additional Input Component Tests
- G-J Fuel – Control Systems
- KC-TC – ECA (Processor) Output Tests

CIRCUIT TEST A

NO START (TFI & DIS IGNITION SYSTEMS)

CAUTION: Stop this test at first sign of a fuel leak. DO NOT allow smoking or an open flame in the vicinity of the vehicle during these tests.

Diagnostic Aids – Enter this CIRCUIT TEST only when steps in QUICK TEST have been successfully completed but engine still does not start, or when directed here from another test or chart.

This test is intended to diagnose only the following EEC-IV ignition systems and circuits:

- Thick Film Ignition (TFI) Systems
- TFI Systems With Closed Bowl Distributors (CBD) And Cowl-Mounted TFI Modules
- Distributorless Ignition Systems (DIS)
- Spark (ECA Controlled)
- Wiring Harness Circuits (PIP, SPOUT, IGN GND & VPWR)
- ECA

NOTE: Vehicles are equipped with either a Closed Bowl Distributor (CBD) with remotely mounted TFI module, or a standard TFI module (distributor mounted).

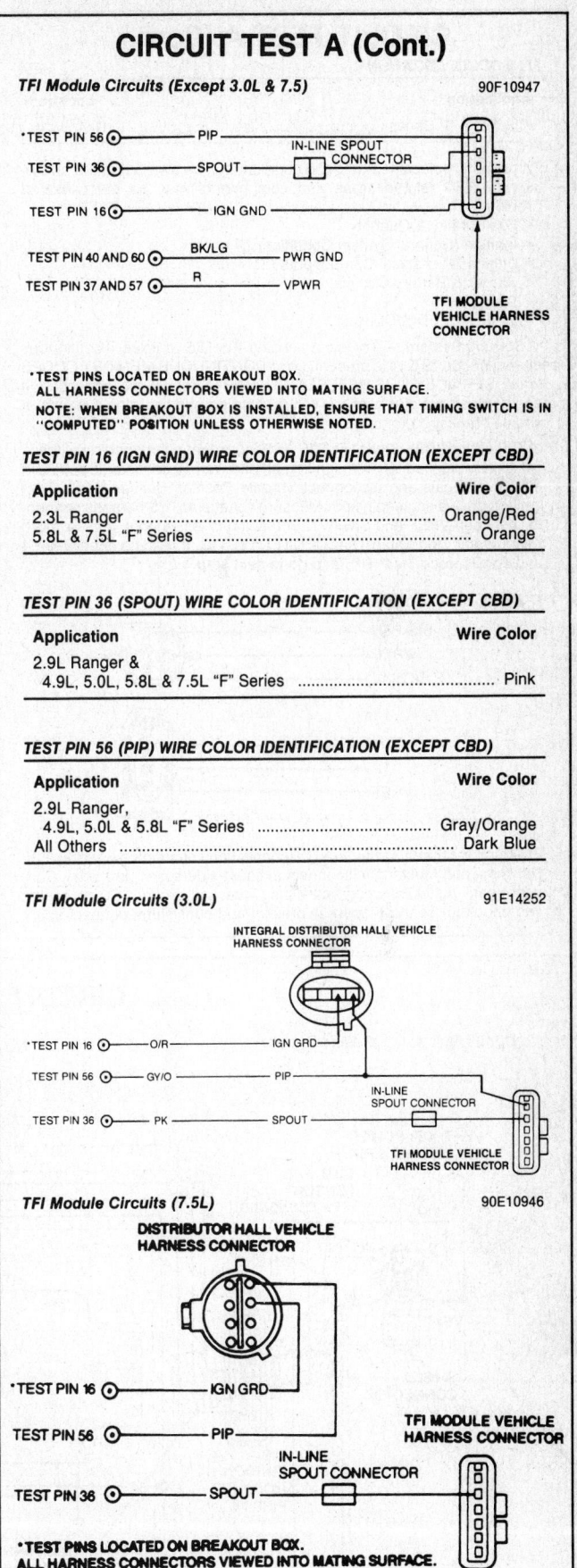

CIRCUIT TEST A (Cont.)

TFI Module Circuits (Except 3.0L & 7.5) 90F10947

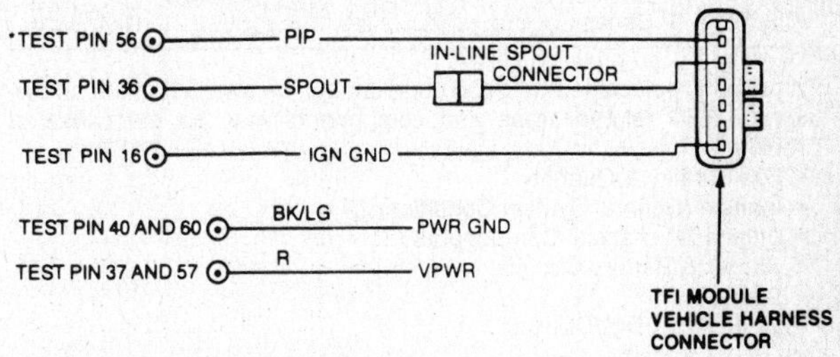
*TEST PIN 56
PIP
TEST PIN 36
SPOUT
IN-LINE SPOUT CONNECTOR
TEST PIN 16
IGN GND
TEST PIN 40 AND 60
BK/LG
PWR GND
TEST PIN 37 AND 57
R
VPWR
TFI MODULE VEHICLE HARNESS CONNECTOR

*TEST PINS LOCATED ON BREAKOUT BOX.
ALL HARNESS CONNECTORS VIEWED INTO MATING SURFACE.
NOTE: WHEN BREAKOUT BOX IS INSTALLED, ENSURE THAT TIMING SWITCH IS IN "COMPUTED" POSITION UNLESS OTHERWISE NOTED.

TEST PIN 16 (IGN GND) WIRE COLOR IDENTIFICATION (EXCEPT CBD)

Application	Wire Color
2.3L Ranger	Orange/Red
5.8L & 7.5L "F" Series	Orange

TEST PIN 36 (SPOUT) WIRE COLOR IDENTIFICATION (EXCEPT CBD)

Application	Wire Color
2.9L Ranger & 4.9L, 5.0L, 5.8L & 7.5L "F" Series	Pink

TEST PIN 56 (PIP) WIRE COLOR IDENTIFICATION (EXCEPT CBD)

Application	Wire Color
2.9L Ranger, 4.9L, 5.0L & 5.8L "F" Series	Gray/Orange
All Others	Dark Blue

TFI Module Circuits (3.0L) 91E14252

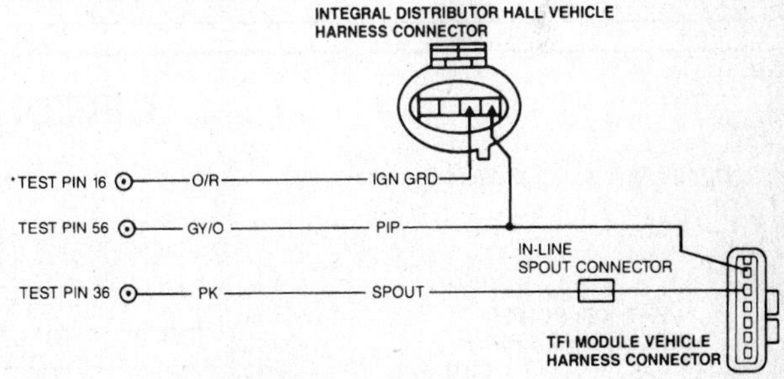
INTEGRAL DISTRIBUTOR HALL VEHICLE HARNESS CONNECTOR
*TEST PIN 16
O/R
IGN GRD
TEST PIN 56
GY/O
PIP
IN-LINE SPOUT CONNECTOR
TEST PIN 36
PK
SPOUT
TFI MODULE VEHICLE HARNESS CONNECTOR

TFI Module Circuits (7.5L) 90E10946

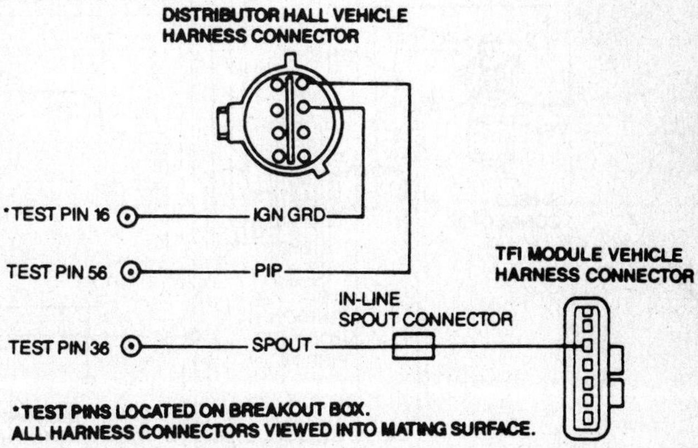
DISTRIBUTOR HALL VEHICLE HARNESS CONNECTOR
*TEST PIN 16
IGN GRD
TEST PIN 56
PIP
TFI MODULE VEHICLE HARNESS CONNECTOR
IN-LINE SPOUT CONNECTOR
TEST PIN 36
SPOUT

*TEST PINS LOCATED ON BREAKOUT BOX.
ALL HARNESS CONNECTORS VIEWED INTO MATING SURFACE.

1991 ENGINE PERFORMANCE
Self-Diagnostics – EEC-IV (Cont.)

CIRCUIT TEST A (Cont.)

TFI MODULE LOCATION

Application	Location
7.5L "E" & "F Series	Distributor

To prevent replacement of good components, be aware that the following non-EEC related areas and components may be the cause of problem:

- Fuel Quality & Quantity
- Ignition (General System Condition)
- Engine Mechanical Components
- Starter & Battery Circuits
- Distributor
- Ignition or EDIS/DIS Coil

1) Starting System – Try to start engine. For DIS vehicles, if continuous memory code 19/214 is present, go to CONTINUOUS MEMORY CODES under SERVICE CODE REFERENCE CHARTS for proper instruction. If engine does not crank, check vehicle starting and charging systems. If engine cranks, go to next step.

2) Checking VREF Signal at TPS – Ensure fuel pump inertia switch is set (button pushed in). Turn ignition off and wait 10 seconds. Set DVOM on 20-volt scale and disconnect Throttle Position Sensor (TPS). Turn ignition on, leaving engine off. Measure voltage at TPS harness connector between VREF and SIG RTN. If reading is less than 4 volts or more than 6 volts, go to step **1)** of CIRCUIT TEST C. If reading is between 4 and 6 volts, reconnect TPS and go to next step.

TPS Harness Connectors 90B10950

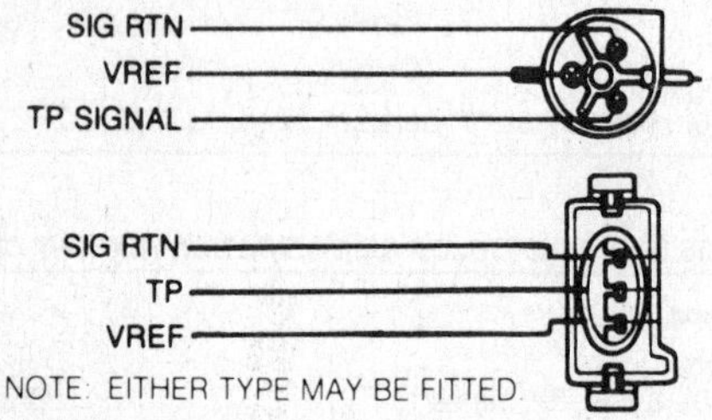
SIG RTN
VREF
TP SIGNAL
SIG RTN
TP
VREF
NOTE: EITHER TYPE MAY BE FITTED.

3) Check for Spark at Plugs – Disconnect any spark plug wire (on 2.3L DIS truck and Mustang, disconnect exhaust-side spark plug only). Connect spark tester between spark plug wire and ground. Crank engine and check for spark. If spark is present and consistent, connect spark plug wire and go to step **12)**. If there is no spark, connect spark plug wire and go to next step (on DIS vehicles, go step **5)**.

CIRCUIT TEST A (Cont.)

4) Check for Spark at Coil – Remove high-tension coil wire from distributor and install spark tester. Check for spark while cranking engine. If spark exists, connect coil wire and service TFI ignition system. If no spark exists, connect coil wire and go to next step.

5) Check Ignition Circuit Ground Continuity – Turn ignition off and wait 10 seconds. Disconnect and inspect ECA 60-pin connector. Install breakout box, leaving ECA disconnected. Set DVOM on 200-ohm scale and disconnect TFI module or DIS module (pins No. 7-12). Disconnect Hall sensor if equipped. Measure resistance between test pin No. 16 at the breakout box and IGN GND circuit of TFI, Hall sensor or DIS harness connector. If reading is more than 5 ohms, repair open in circuit and repeat QUICK TEST. If reading is less than 5 ohms, go to next step.

6) Isolating SPOUT Circuit Fault – Install breakout box. Connect TFI module, DIS module (pins No. 7-12) or distributor Hall sensor as applicable. Connect ECA to breakout box. Set breakout box timing switch to DISTRIBUTOR or DIST position. Try to start vehicle. If vehicle starts, move timing switch to COMPUTED position and go to step **10)**. If vehicle does not start, go to next step.

7) Check SPOUT Signal – With KOEO, install breakout box and connect ECA. Move breakout box timing switch to DIST position. Set DVOM on 20-volt scale and measure voltage between test pin No. 36 at breakout box and battery negative post while cranking engine. If voltage is between 3 and 6 volts, EEC system is NOT at fault. Diagnose TFI or DIS ignition system. See BASIC DIAGNOSTIC PROCEDURES article. If voltage is less than 3 volts or more than 6 volts, go to next step. Switch timing switch on breakout box to COMPUTED position.

8) Check SPOUT & PIP Circuits for Shorts – Turn ignition off and wait 10 seconds. With breakout box installed, disconnect ECA. On 2.3L models, disconnect DIS module (pins No. 1-6). On vehicles with a closed bowl distributor, disconnect TFI and distributor Hall sensor. For all other vehicles, disconnect TFI module. Set DVOM on 200-k/ohm scale.

On SPOUT circuit, measure resistance between test pin No. 36 (SPOUT) and test pins No. 16, 20, 40, 46, and 60 for short to ground. Measure resistance between test pin No. 36 and test pins No. 26, 37 and 57 for short to power (VPWR). Measure resistance between test pins No. 36 and 56 for short to PIP.

On PIP circuit, measure resistance between test pin No. 56 (PIP) and test pins No. 16, 20, 40, 46, and 60 for short to ground. Measure resistance between test pin No. 56 and pins No. 26, 37 and 57 for short to power.

CIRCUIT TEST A (Cont.)

Circuit Test A: DIS Module Circuits 90H10949

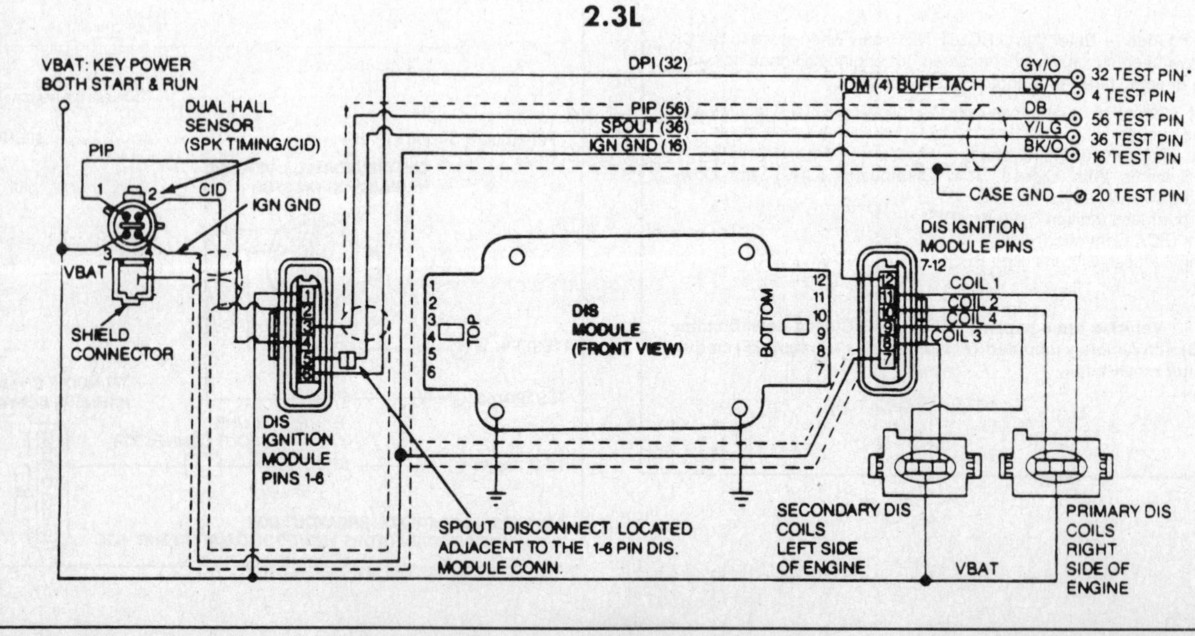
2.3L
VBAT: KEY POWER
BOTH START & RUN
DUAL HALL
SENSOR
(SPK TIMING/CID)
PIP
CID
IGN GND
VBAT
SHIELD
CONNECTOR
DIS
IGNITION
MODULE
PINS 1-6
DPI (32)
PIP (56)
SPOUT (36)
IGN GND (16)
IDM (4) BUFF TACH
GY/O
LG/Y
DB
Y/LG
BK/O
32 TEST PIN*
4 TEST PIN
56 TEST PIN
36 TEST PIN
16 TEST PIN
CASE GND
20 TEST PIN
DIS IGNITION
MODULE PINS
7-12
COIL 1
COIL 2
COIL 4
COIL 3
TOP
DIS
MODULE
(FRONT VIEW)
BOTTOM
SPOUT DISCONNECT LOCATED
ADJACENT TO THE 1-6 PIN DIS.
MODULE CONN.
SECONDARY DIS
COILS
LEFT SIDE
OF ENGINE
VBAT
PRIMARY DIS
COILS
RIGHT
SIDE OF
ENGINE

CIRCUIT TEST A (Cont.)

If any reading is less than 10 k/ohms, repair short in harness and repeat QUICK TEST. If engine still does not start, go to next step. If all readings are 10 k/ohms or more, go to next step.

9) Isolating Shorts in ECA – Turn ignition off and wait 10 seconds. With breakout box installed, reconnect ECA. On 2.3L models, disconnect DIS module (pins No. 1-6). On vehicles with a closed bowl distributor, disconnect TFI and distributor Hall sensor. For all other vehicles, disconnect TFI module. Set DVOM on 200-k/ohm scale.

On SPOUT circuit, measure resistance between test pin No. 36 (SPOUT) and test pins No. 37 and 57 for short to power. Measure resistance between test pin No. 36 and test pins No. 40 and 60 for short to ground.

On PIP circuit, measure resistance between test pin No. 56 (PIP) and test pins No. 37 and 57 for short to power. Measure resistance between test pin No. 56 and test pins No. 40 and 60 for short to ground.

If any reading is less than 500 ohms, replace ECA and repeat QUICK TEST. If all readings are 500 ohms or more, connect TFI and go to next step.

10) Check PIP Signal – With ignition off, install breakout box. Set DVOM on 20-volt scale. On 2.3L models, switch timing switch to DIST position on breakout box. Measure voltage between test pins No. 56 and 16 while cranking engine. If reading is between 3 and 7 volts, remove breakout box. Replace ECA and repeat QUICK TEST. If reading is less than 3 volts or more than 7 volts, go to next step. On 2.3L models, switch timing switch on breakout box to COMPUTED position.

11) Check Continuity of PIP Circuit – Install breakout box, turn ignition off and wait 10 seconds. Set DVOM on 200-ohm scale. Disconnect ECA and TFI (on 2.3L models, disconnect DIS pins No. 1-6). On vehicles with a closed bowl distributor, disconnect distributor Hall sensor and TFI module. Measure resistance between test pin No. 56 and TFI connector PIP circuit. If reading is 5 ohms or more, repair open PIP circuit and repeat QUICK TEST. If readings is less than 5 ohms, remove breakout box, reconnect all components and diagnose TFI or DIS ignition system. See BASIC DIAGNOSTIC PROCEDURES article.

12) Verify SPOUT Signal – Turn ignition off and wait 10 seconds. Disconnect ECA 60-pin connector and inspect for damaged pins, corrosion, or loose wires. Repair as necessary. Install breakout box and connect ECA. Ensure breakout box timing switch is in COMPUTED position. Set DVOM on 20-volt scale and measure voltage between test pin No. 36 and test pins No. 40 and 60 while cranking engine. If reading is between 3 and 6 volts, go to step **20)**. If reading is less than 3 volts or more than 6 volts, return to step **8)**.

NOTE: There is a break in the step numbering sequence at this point, skipping from step 12) to step 20). Break is due to previous chart references to these testing procedures. No test procedures have been omitted.

WARNING: Use safety precautions when working on fuel system. No smoking or open flame is allowed. If fuel starts leaking, turn ignition off immediately.

20) Fuel Pump Check – Connect pressure gauge to vehicle. Note initial pressure reading. Pressurize fuel system by turning ignition on for one second and observe pressure gauge. Turn ignition off and wait 10 seconds. Repeat sequence 5 times. If pressure increases, go to CIRCUIT TEST S, step **1)**. If pressure does not increase, go to next step.

21) Inertia Switch Resistance Check – Turn ignition off. Locate fuel pump inertia switch and ensure push button on switch is pushed down in ON or CLOSED position. Set DVOM on 200-ohm scale. Measure resistance of switch. If resistance is greater than 5 ohms, replace switch. If resistance is less than 5 ohms, go to step **1)** of CIRCUIT TEST J.

CIRCUIT TEST AA

NO START (EDIS IGNITION SYSTEMS)

CAUTION: Stop this test at first sign of a fuel leak. Do not allow smoking or an open flame in the vicinity of the vehicle during these tests.

Diagnostic Aids – Enter this CIRCUIT TEST only when all steps under QUICK TEST have been successfully completed and the engine still does not start, or when directed here from another test or chart.

This test is intended to diagnose only the following EEC-IV ignition systems and circuits:

- Spark (ECA Controlled)
- Wiring Harness Circuits (PIP, IGN GND & VPWR)
- ECA

EDIS Module Circuits (4.0L) 90D10952

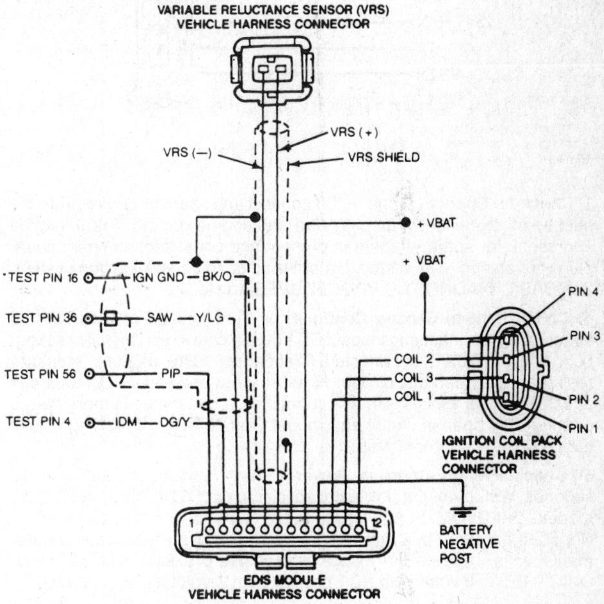
VARIABLE RELUCTANCE SENSOR (VRS)
VEHICLE HARNESS CONNECTOR
VRS (+)
VRS (–)
VRS SHIELD
+ VBAT
+ VBAT
*TEST PIN 16
IGN GND
BK/O
TEST PIN 36
SAW
Y/LG
TEST PIN 56
PIP
TEST PIN 4
IDM
DG/Y
COIL 2
COIL 3
COIL 1
PIN 4
PIN 3
PIN 2
PIN 1
IGNITION COIL PACK
VEHICLE HARNESS
CONNECTOR
1
12
BATTERY
NEGATIVE
POST
EDIS MODULE
VEHICLE HARNESS CONNECTOR

Test Pin 56	PIP
4.0L Aerostar	DB
4.0L Ranger/Bronco II	BK/LB

*TEST PINS LOCATED ON BREAKOUT BOX.
ALL HARNESS CONNECTORS VIEWED INTO MATING SURFACE.

TEST PIN 36 (SAW) WIRE COLOR IDENTIFICATION

Application	Wire Color
4.0L Aerostar	Yellow/Light Green
4.0L Explorer & 4.0L Ranger	Pink

TEST PIN 56 (PIP) WIRE COLOR IDENTIFICATION

Application	Wire Color
4.0L Aerostar	Dark Blue
4.0L Explorer & 4.0L Ranger	Gray/Orange

To prevent replacement of good components, be aware that the following non-EEC related areas and components may be the cause of problem:

- Fuel Quality & Quantity
- Ignition (General Condition)
- Engine Mechanical Components
- Starter & Battery Circuits
- Variable Reluctance Sensor (VRS)
- EDIS Module
- Coil Packs

1991 ENGINE PERFORMANCE
Self-Diagnostics – EEC-IV (Cont.)

CIRCUIT TEST AA (Cont.)

1) Starting System – Ensure fuel pump inertia switch is closed (button pushed in). Try to start engine. If engine does not crank, check vehicle starting and charging systems. If engine cranks, go to next step.

2) Check VREF Signal at TPS – Turn ignition off and wait 10 seconds. Set DVOM on 20-volt scale and disconnect Throttle Position Sensor (TPS). Turn ignition on, leaving engine off. Measure voltage at TPS harness connector between VREF and SIG RTN. If reading is less than 4 volts or more than 6 volts, go to CIRCUIT TEST C, step **1**). If reading is between 4 and 6 volts, reconnect TPS and go to next step.

TPS Harness Connectors 90B10950

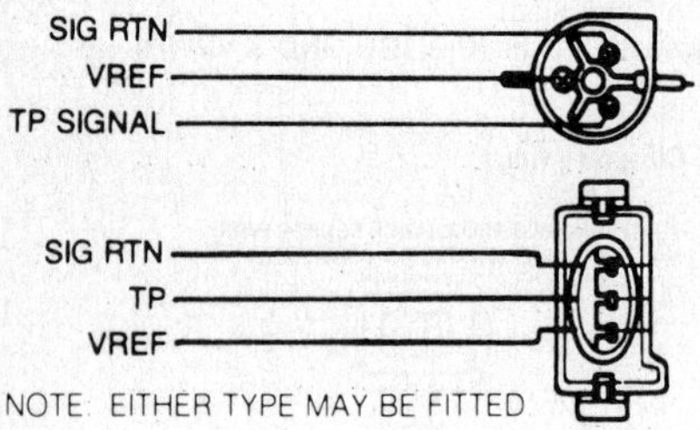
SIG RTN
VREF
TP SIGNAL
SIG RTN
TP
VREF
NOTE: EITHER TYPE MAY BE FITTED

3) Check for Spark at Plugs – Disconnect any spark plug wire and connect spark tester between plug wire and engine ground. Crank engine and check for spark. If spark is present and consistent, connect spark plug wire and go to next step. If there is no spark, check ignition system. See BASIC DIAGNOSTIC PROCEDURES article.

4) Check Ignition Ground Continuity – Turn ignition off and wait 10 seconds. Disconnect and inspect ECA 60-pin connector. Install breakout box, leaving ECA disconnected. Disconnect EDIS module. Measure resistance between test pin No. 16 at breakout box and IGN GND circuit at EDIS module vehicle harness connector. If resistance is more than 5 ohms, repair open in circuit and repeat QUICK TEST. If reading is less than 5 ohms, go to next step.

5) Check PIP for Short to Power – Turn ignition off and wait 10 seconds. With breakout box installed, disconnect ECA. Disconnect EDIS module. Set DVOM on 20-volt scale. Measure voltage between test pin No. 56 at breakout box and battery negative post. If voltage is greater than 7 volts, repair short to power. Remove breakout box and rerun QUICK TEST. If voltage is NOT greater than 7 volts, go to next step.

6) Check PIP Circuit Continuity – Turn ignition off and wait 10 seconds. With breakout box installed, disconnect ECA. Disconnect EDIS module. Measure resistance between test pin No. 56 at breakout box and PIP circuit at EDIS module vehicle harness connector. If resistance is less than 5 ohms, go to next step. If resistance is greater than 5 ohms, repair open circuit. Remove breakout box, reconnect all components and rerun QUICK TEST.

7) Check PIP Circuit for Shorts to Ground – Turn ignition off and wait 10 seconds. With breakout box installed, reconnect ECA. Disconnect EDIS module. Set DVOM on 200-k/ohm scale. Measure resistance between test pin No. 56 (PIP) and test pins No. 16, 40, 46 and 60 for short to ground. If any reading is less than 10 k/ohms, repair short in harness and repeat QUICK TEST. If engine still does not start, go to next step. If all readings are 10 k/ohms or more, go to next step.

8) Isolate Shorts in ECA – Turn ignition off and wait 10 seconds. With breakout box installed, connect ECA to breakout box. Disconnect EDIS module. Set DVOM on 200-k/ohm scale. Measure resistance between test pin No. 56 (PIP) and test pins No. 37 and 57 for short to power. Measure resistance between test pin No. 56 and test pins No. 40 and 60 for short to ground. If all readings are less than 20 k/ohms or greater than 150 k/ohms, problem is in EDIS system. Replace ECA and repeat QUICK TEST. If any reading is 20-150 k/ohms go to next step.

9) Check PIP Signal – Turn ignition off and wait 10 seconds. With breakout box installed, disconnect ECA. Reconnect EDIS module. Set DVOM on 20-volt scale. Measure voltage between test pin No. 56 and test pin No. 16 at breakout box. Crank engine and record reading. If voltage is less than 3 volts or greater than 7 volts, remove breakout box and rerun QUICK TEST. If voltage is 3-7 volts, replace EDIS module and go to next step.

CIRCUIT TEST AA (Cont.)

WARNING: Use safety precautions when working on fuel system. No smoking or open flame is allowed. If fuel starts leaking, turn ignition off immediately.

10) Fuel Pump Check – Connect pressure gauge to vehicle. Note initial pressure reading. Pressurize fuel system by turning ignition on for one second and observe pressure gauge. Turn ignition off and wait 10 seconds. Repeat sequence 5 times. If pressure increases, go to CIRCUIT TEST S, step **1**). If pressure does not increase, check fuel pump and system for mechanical problems.

CIRCUIT TEST B

CHECKING VEHICLE BATTERY

Diagnostic Aids – Enter this CIRCUIT TEST only when directed by CIRCUIT TEST C, CIRCUIT TEST J, CIRCUIT TEST PA, CIRCUIT TEST PB or CIRCUIT TEST PC.

Power Relay Circuits
All Models 90J12376

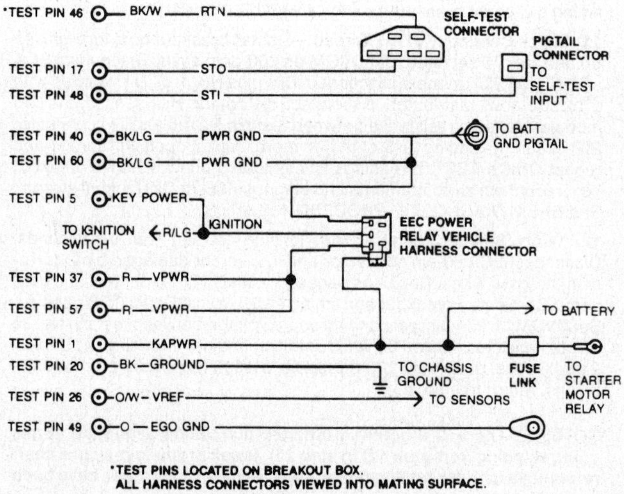
*TEST PIN 46 — BK/W — RTN
SELF-TEST CONNECTOR
PIGTAIL CONNECTOR
TEST PIN 17 — STO
TO SELF-TEST INPUT
TEST PIN 48 — STI
TEST PIN 40 — BK/LG — PWR GND
TO BATT GND PIGTAIL
TEST PIN 60 — BK/LG — PWR GND
TEST PIN 5 — KEY POWER
TO IGNITION SWITCH ← R/LG
IGNITION
EEC POWER RELAY VEHICLE HARNESS CONNECTOR
TEST PIN 37 — R — VPWR
TEST PIN 57 — R — VPWR
TO BATTERY
TEST PIN 1 — KAPWR
TEST PIN 20 — BK — GROUND
TO CHASSIS GROUND
FUSE LINK
TO STARTER MOTOR RELAY
TEST PIN 26 — O/W — VREF
TO SENSORS
TEST PIN 49 — O — EGO GND
*TEST PINS LOCATED ON BREAKOUT BOX.
ALL HARNESS CONNECTORS VIEWED INTO MATING SURFACE.

TEST PIN 1 (KAPWR) WIRE COLOR IDENTIFICATION

Application	Wire Color
"E" Series	Black/Orange
All Others	Yellow

TEST PIN 17 (STO) WIRE COLOR IDENTIFICATION

Application	Wire Color
2.3L, 3.0L, 4.0L & "F" Series	Pink/Light Green
All Others	Tan/Red

TEST PIN 48 (STI) WIRE COLOR IDENTIFICATION

Application	Wire Color
2.3L, 2.9L, 3.0L & 4.0L Ranger	White/Black
"F" Series	White/Purple
All Other Models	White/Red

To prevent replacement of good components, be aware that the following non-EEC related areas may be the cause of problem: battery cables and ground straps, voltage regulator, alternator or ignition switch. This test is intended to diagnose the ECA, power relay, battery voltage and the following harness circuits:

- Signal Return
- STO

CIRCUIT TEST B (Cont.)

- STI
- PWR GND
- VPWR
- KAPWR
- VREF
- IGNITION

1) Battery Voltage Check – Turn ignition on, leaving engine off. Set DVOM on 20-volt scale and measure voltage across battery terminals. If reading is less than 10.5 volts, service or replace discharged battery. If reading is 10.5 volts or more, go to next step.

2) Check Continuity of PWR GND Circuit – Turn ignition off and wait 10 seconds. Install breakout box, leaving ECA connected. Inspect ECA connector and pins. Measure resistance between test pins No. 40 and 60 at breakout box and battery negative post. If readings are greater than 5 ohms, repair open in PWR GND circuit. Remove breakout box, reconnect components and repeat QUICK TEST. If readings are less than 5 ohms, go to next step.

3) Check for Open Between SIG RTN & PWR GND Circuits at ECA – With breakout box installed and ECA connected, turn ignition off and wait 10 seconds. Measure resistance between test pin No. 46 and test pins No. 40 and 60 at breakout box. If both readings are less than 5 ohms, go to next step. If readings are greater than 5 ohms, disconnect ECA connector. Ensure pins are not corroded or damaged. Repair as necessary. If fault is still present, replace ECA and repeat QUICK TEST.

4) Check Continuity of SIG RTN Circuit – With breakout box installed and ECA connected, turn ignition off and wait 10 seconds. Measure resistance between test pin No. 46 at breakout box and SIG RTN circuit at self-test connector. If resistance is greater than 5 ohms, repair open in SIG RTN circuit. Remove breakout box, reconnect components and repeat QUICK TEST. If reading is less than 5 ohms, remove breakout box, connect ECA and go to next step.

5) Check KAPWR Circuit Voltage at EEC Power Relay – Turn ignition on, leaving engine off. With ECA connected, set DVOM on 20-volt scale. Measure voltage between battery negative post and KAPWR circuit at EEC power relay harness connector. If reading is less than 10.5 volts, check KAPWR circuit from EEC power relay to battery positive post for open circuit. If reading is 10.5 volts or more, go to next step.

6) Check Ignition Circuit Voltage at EEC Power Relay – Turn ignition on, leaving engine off. Ensure ECA is connected. Measure voltage between battery negative post and IGNITION circuit at EEC power relay vehicle harness connector. If reading is less than 10.5 volts, check for open in ignition switch circuits. Repair wiring and repeat QUICK TEST. If reading is 10.5 volts or more, go to next step.

7) Check PWR GND Circuit Continuity – Turn ignition off and wait 10 seconds. With ECA connected, measure resistance between battery negative post and PWR GND circuit at EEC power relay vehicle harness connector. If resistance is 5 ohms or more, repair wiring in ground circuit. Repeat QUICK TEST. If reading is less than 5 ohms, go to next step.

8) Check VPWR Circuit at EEC Power Relay – Turn ignition on, leaving engine off. With ECA connected and DVOM on 20-volt scale, measure voltage between battery negative post and VPWR circuit at EEC power relay vehicle harness connector. If reading is 10.5 volts or more, repair open or short to ground in VPWR circuit between ECA and EEC power relay. Reconnect components and repeat QUICK TEST. If reading is less than 10.5 volts, replace EEC power relay. Repeat QUICK TEST.

CIRCUIT TEST C

REFERENCE VOLTAGE

Diagnostic Aids – Perform this test if a check for VREF signal has failed in sensor input CIRCUIT TEST DA–CIRCUIT TEST DQ or if directed by CIRCUIT TEST A or CIRCUIT TEST QA.

This circuit test is intended to diagnose only ECA, SIG RTN, VREF, TPS, EVP, MAP and BP circuits.

CIRCUIT TEST C (Cont.)

Reference Voltage Circuits 90G10955

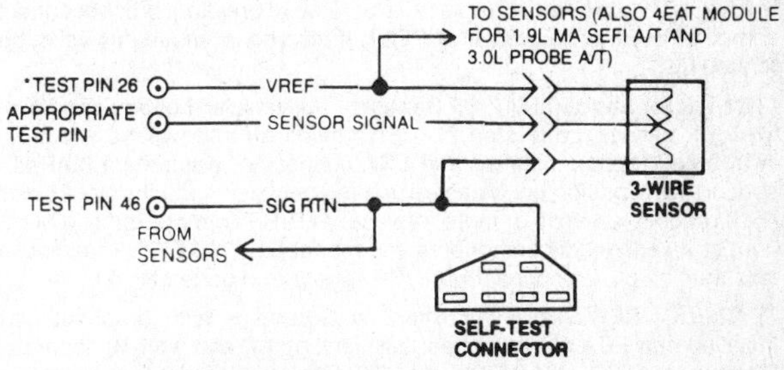
TO SENSORS (ALSO 4EAT MODULE FOR 1.9L MA SEFI A/T AND 3.0L PROBE A/T)
*TEST PIN 26
VREF
APPROPRIATE TEST PIN
SENSOR SIGNAL
3-WIRE SENSOR
TEST PIN 46
SIG RTN
FROM SENSORS
SELF-TEST CONNECTOR
*TEST PINS LOCATED ON BREAKOUT BOX.
ALL HARNESS CONNECTORS VIEWED INTO MATING SURFACE.

Test Pin 26	VREF
Application	Wire Color
1.9L MA SEFI	R/W
F-Series/Bronco	BR/W
3.0L Probe	LG/R
All Others	O/W

Test Pin 46	SIG RTN
Application	Wire Color
1.9L MA SEFI	LG/BK
F-Series/Bronco	GY/R
3.0L Probe	LG/Y
All Others	BK/W

TEST PIN 26 (VREF) WIRE COLOR IDENTIFICATION

Application	Wire Color
All Models	Brown/White

TEST PIN 46 (SIG RTN) WIRE COLOR IDENTIFICATION

Application	Wire Color
All Models	Gray/Red

1) Check Battery Power Circuit – Turn ignition off and wait 10 seconds. Disconnect ECA 60-pin connector. Inspect connector for damaged pins, corrosion, or loose wires. Repair as necessary. Install breakout box, leaving ECA connected. Turn ignition on, leaving engine off. Set DVOM on 20-volt scale. Measure voltage between test pin No. 37 and SIG RTN/PWR GND circuit of self-test connector. Record reading. Measure voltage across battery terminals. Record reading. If both readings are less than 10.5 volts, or if they differ by more than one volt, go to step **1)** of CIRCUIT TEST B. If reading is 10.5 volts or more and does not differ from one another by more than one volt, go to next step.

2) Check VREF Voltage – With breakout box installed and ECA connected, turn ignition on, leaving engine off. Set DVOM on 20-volt scale. Measure voltage between test pins No. 26 and 46 at breakout box. If reading is 6 volts or more, go to step **4)**. If reading is 4 volts or less, go to step **5)**. If reading is 4–6 volts, go to next step.

3) Check VREF & SIG RTN Circuit Continuity – With breakout box installed and ECA disconnected, turn ignition off. If directed here by a sensor test, ensure sensor is disconnected. Measure resistance between test pin No. 26 and VREF circuit terminal at vehicle harness connector of applicable sensor. Measure resistance between test pin No. 46 and SIG RTN circuit terminal at vehicle harness connector of applicable sensor. If both readings are less than 5 ohms, VREF voltage is okay. Remove breakout box, reconnect components and sensor, and repeat QUICK TEST. If any reading is 5 ohms or more, repair open in VREF or SIG RTN circuit. Remove breakout box, reconnect components and repeat QUICK TEST.

4) Check for Excess VREF Circuit Voltage – Turn ignition off and wait 10 seconds. With breakout box installed, disconnect ECA and "Scan" tool or STAR tester (if attached). Turn ignition on, leaving engine off. Set DVOM on 20-volt scale and measure voltage between test pin No. 26 and battery ground. If reading is less than 0.5 volt, replace ECA, remove breakout box, reconnect components and repeat QUICK TEST. If reading is 0.5 volt or more, repair short to battery power in EEC vehicle harness. Remove breakout box, reconnect components and repeat QUICK TEST. Replace ECA if fault still occurs.

1991 ENGINE PERFORMANCE
Self-Diagnostics – EEC-IV (Cont.)

CIRCUIT TEST C (Cont.)

5) Check for Shorted TPS Sensor – Turn ignition off and wait 10 seconds. With breakout box installed and ECA connected, disconnect Throttle Position Sensor (TPS) from vehicle harness. Turn ignition on, leaving engine off. Measure voltage between test pins No. 26 and 46. If reading is 4 volts or more, replace TPS, remove breakout box, reconnect components and repeat QUICK TEST. If reading is less than 4 volts, go to step **6)**.

6) Check for Shorted MAP/BP Sensor – All vehicles not equipped with MAP/BP sensor, go to step **7)**. Turn ignition off and wait 10 seconds. With breakout box installed and ECA connected, disconnect MAP/BP sensor. Turn ignition on. Measure voltage between test pins No. 26 and 46. If reading is 4 volts or more, replace MAP/BP sensor. Remove breakout box, reconnect components and repeat QUICK TEST. If reading is less than 4 volts, reconnect MAP/BP sensor and go to step **7)**.

7) Check VREF Circuit for Short to Ground – With breakout box installed and ECA disconnected, turn ignition off and wait 10 seconds. Disconnect TPS, MAP/BP and EVP sensor. Measure resistance between test pin No. 26 and test pins No. 20, 40, 46 and 60. If any resistance is less than 5 ohms, repair short to ground. Remove breakout box, connect all sensors and repeat QUICK TEST. If original problem still exists, replace ECA and repeat QUICK TEST. If reading is 5 ohms or more, connect sensors, replace ECA and repeat QUICK TEST.

CIRCUIT TEST DA

TEMPERATURE SENSOR TEST (ACT & ECT)

Diagnostic Aids – Perform this test only when directed by QUICK TEST. Ambient air temperature must be at least 50°F (10°C) to receive valid input from ACT sensor. Engine coolant temperature must be greater than 50°F (10°C) to pass KOEO SELF-TEST and greater than 180°F (82°C) to pass KOER SELF-TEST. Voltage values in this test are based on a 5-volt VREF signal. Values may vary up to 15% due to sensor and VREF variations.

This circuit test is intended to diagnose the following components and circuits:

- ACT Sensor
- ECT Sensor
- Vehicle Harness Circuits (ACT, ECT & SIG RTN)
- ECA

Temperature Sensor Circuits 90I10957

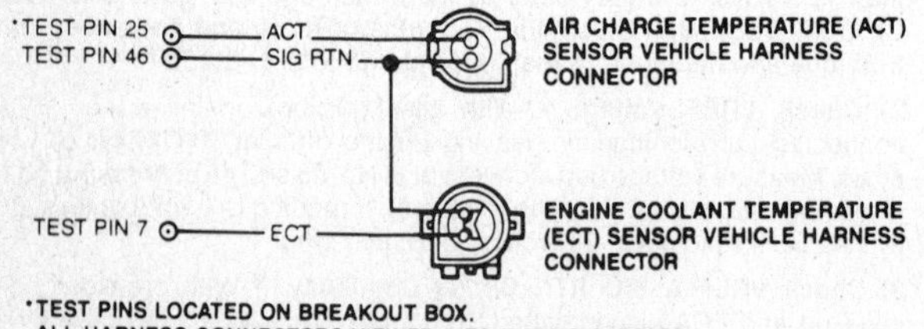
*TEST PIN 25
TEST PIN 46
ACT
SIG RTN
AIR CHARGE TEMPERATURE (ACT) SENSOR VEHICLE HARNESS CONNECTOR
TEST PIN 7
ECT
ENGINE COOLANT TEMPERATURE (ECT) SENSOR VEHICLE HARNESS CONNECTOR

*TEST PINS LOCATED ON BREAKOUT BOX.
ALL HARNESS CONNECTORS VIEWED INTO MATING SURFACE.

TEST PIN 7 (ECT) WIRE COLOR IDENTIFICATION

Application	Wire Color
All Models	Light Green/Red

TEST PIN 25 (ACT) WIRE COLOR IDENTIFICATION

Application	Wire Color
2.3L, 2.9L, 3.0L MA, 4.0L, 4.9L Bronco & "F" Series, 5.0L Bronco & "F" Series & 7.5L "F" Series	Gray
4.9L & 5.0L "E" Series, 5.8L & 7.5L	Red/Black
All Other Models	Light Green/Purple

CIRCUIT TEST DA (Cont.)

TEST PIN 46 (SIG RTN) WIRE COLOR IDENTIFICATION

Application	Wire Color
All Models	Gray/Red

To prevent replacing good components, ensure the following non-EEC areas or components are not the cause of problem:

- Air Cleaner Duct
- Ambient Temperature Too Low
- Coolant Level Low
- Cooling System, Water Pump or Fan
- Electric Cooling Fan
- Engine Operating Temperature Low
- Engine Oil Level Low
- Heat Riser Duct Valve
- Thermostat

1) Code 21/116 or 24/114: Check Installation & Operation of Temperature Sensor – Codes 21/116 (ECT) or 24/114 (ACT) indicates that the corresponding sensor is out of self-test range. Correct range for measurement is .3–3.7 volts. Check for the following possible causes:

- Low Ambient Temperature (Less Than 50°F)
- Low Coolant Level
- Faulty Harness Connector
- Faulty Sensor
- ACT sensor improperly mounted in air cleaner

If vehicle cannot be started, go to step **2)**. If vehicle stalls, or starts then dies, go to CIRCUIT TEST S, step **1)**.

2) Check Temperature Sensor Resistance with Engine Off – Turn ignition off and wait 10 seconds. Disconnect suspected sensor. Set DVOM on 200-k/ohm scale. Measure resistance between sensor signal circuit and SIG RTN circuit at sensor. See ACT & ECT SENSOR SPECIFICATIONS table. If resistance is within specification, perform the following step as applicable.

- For ECT sensor with a no-start condition, go to CIRCUIT TEST A, step **1)**. DO NOT service code 21/116 at this time.
- For all others, go to next step.

If resistance is not within specification, replace sensor. Reconnect vehicle harness and rerun QUICK TEST.

ACT & ECT SENSOR SPECIFICATIONS

Temperature °F (°C)	Voltage	Ohms
50 (10)	3.5	58,750
68 (20)	3.1	37,300
86 (30)	2.6	24,270
104 (40)	2.1	16,150
122 (50)	1.7	10,970
140 (60)	1.3	7700
158 (70)	1.0	5370
176 (80)	.8	384
194 (90)	.6	280
212 (100)	.5	207
230 (110)	.4	155

3) Sensor Resistance Check (Engine Running) – If engine has cooled down, warm engine before measuring sensor resistance. Ensure thermostat is open. Turn ignition off and wait 10 seconds. Disconnect suspected sensor. Run engine at 2000 RPM for 2 minutes. Measure resistance between sensor signal circuit and SIG RTN circuit at sensor. See ACT & ECT SENSOR SPECIFICATIONS table. If resistance is within specification, replace ECA; reconnect components and repeat QUICK TEST. If sensor is not within specification, replace sensor. Reconnect components and repeat QUICK TEST.

NOTE: There is a break in the step numbering sequence at this point, skipping from step 3) to step 10). Break is due to previous chart references to these testing procedures. No test procedures have been omitted.

10) Code 51/118 or 54/113: Induce Opposite Code (61/117 or 64/112) – Code 51/118 (ECT) or 54/113 (ACT) indicate that the corresponding sensor signal is greater than the self-test maximum. Maximum signal voltage for ECT and ACT sensors is 4.6 volts. Possible causes for excess voltage signals are as follows:

- Open Circuit In Vehicle Harness (ACT or ECT)
- Faulty Connection

CIRCUIT TEST DA (Cont.)

- Faulty Sensor
- Faulty ECA

Turn ignition off and wait 10 seconds. Disconnect suspected temperature sensor. Connect a jumper wire between sensor signal circuit and SIG RTN circuit at temperature sensor vehicle harness connector. Perform KOEO SELF-TEST. See KEY ON ENGINE OFF (KOEO) SELF-TEST under QUICK TEST. If Code 61, 64, 112 or 117 is displayed, replace suspected sensor. Remove jumper wire, reconnect vehicle harness and repeat QUICK TEST. If Code 61, 64, 112 or 117 is not displayed, remove jumper wire and go to next step.

11) Check Continuity of Sensor Signal & SIG RTN Circuits - Turn ignition off and wait 10 seconds. Ensure suspected temperature sensor is disconnected. Disconnect ECA 60-pin connector. Check for damaged wiring and repair as necessary. Install breakout box, leaving ECA disconnected. Measure resistance between test pin No. 7 (ECT sensor) or test pin No. 25 (ACT sensor) at breakout box and SIG RTN circuit at sensor vehicle harness connector. Also measure resistance between test pin No. 46 and SIG RTN circuit at sensor vehicle harness connector. If both readings are less than 5 ohms, replace ECA. Remove breakout box, reconnect components and rerun QUICK TEST. If either reading is 5 ohms or more, repair open circuits. Remove breakout box, reconnect components and rerun QUICK TEST.

NOTE: There is a break in the step numbering sequence at this point, skipping from step 11) to step 20). Break is due to previous chart references to these testing procedures. No test procedures have been omitted.

20) Code 61/117 or 64/112: Induce Opposite Code (51/118 or 54/113) - Code 61/117 (ECT) or 64/112 (ACT) indicates that sensor signal is less than the self-test minimum. Minimum signal for ACT and ECT sensor is 0.2 volt. Minimum signal for VAT sensor is 0.35 volt. Possible causes for this fault are as follows:

- Circuit Grounded In Vehicle Harness (ACT or ECT)
- Faulty Sensor
- Faulty ECA
- Faulty Connection

Turn ignition off and wait 10 seconds. Disconnect vehicle harness connector from suspected sensor. Check for damaged wiring and repair as necessary. Repeat KOEO SELF-TEST. If code 51, 54, 113 or 118 is displayed, replace sensor and connect harness. Repeat QUICK TEST. If code 51, 54, 113 or 118 is not displayed, go to next step.

21) Check VREF Circuit Voltage at TPS - Turn ignition off and wait 10 seconds. Set DVOM on 20-volt scale. Disconnect TPS. With ignition on and engine off, measure voltage between VREF and SIG RTN at TPS vehicle harness connector. If reading is less than 4 volts or more than 6 volts, go to CIRCUIT TEST C, step **1**). If reading is 4-6 volts, connect TPS and go to next step.

TPS Connectors 90D10960

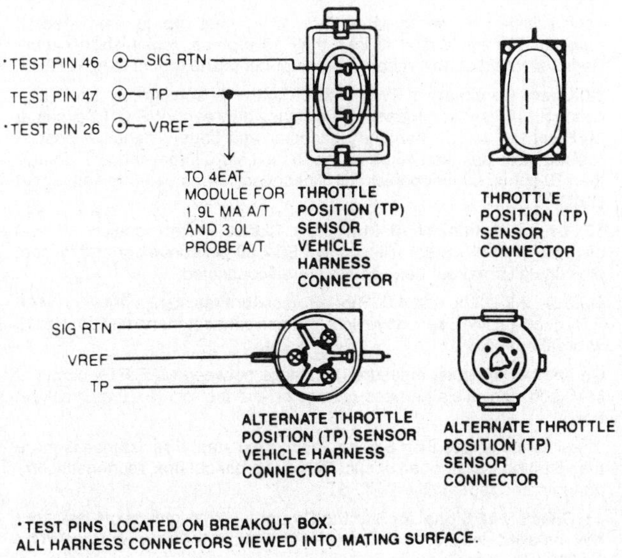
*TEST PIN 46
SIG RTN
TEST PIN 47
TP
*TEST PIN 26
VREF
TO 4EAT MODULE FOR 1.9L MA A/T AND 3.0L PROBE A/T
THROTTLE POSITION (TP) SENSOR VEHICLE HARNESS CONNECTOR
THROTTLE POSITION (TP) SENSOR CONNECTOR
SIG RTN
VREF
TP
ALTERNATE THROTTLE POSITION (TP) SENSOR VEHICLE HARNESS CONNECTOR
ALTERNATE THROTTLE POSITION (TP) SENSOR CONNECTOR
*TEST PINS LOCATED ON BREAKOUT BOX.
ALL HARNESS CONNECTORS VIEWED INTO MATING SURFACE.

CIRCUIT TEST DA (Cont.)

22) Check Temperature Sensor Signal for Shorts to Ground - Turn ignition off and wait 10 seconds. Disconnect suspected sensor. Disconnect ECA 60-pin connector. Check for damaged wiring and repair as necessary. Install breakout box, leaving ECA disconnected. Set DVOM on 200-k/ohm scale. Measure resistance between test pin No. 7 (ECT) or test pin No. 25 (ACT) and test pins No. 40, 46, and 60. If any reading is less than 10 k/ohms, repair short circuit. Remove breakout box, reconnect components and repeat QUICK TEST. If all readings are 10 k/ohms or more, replace ECA. Remove breakout box and reconnect components. Repeat QUICK TEST.

NOTE: There is a break in the step numbering sequence at this point, skipping from step 22) to step 90). Break is due to previous chart references to these testing procedures. No test procedures have been omitted.

90) Continuous Memory Code 51/118, 54/113, 61/117 or 68/112: Check Sensor - A Continuous Memory Code 51/118 and 54/113 indicates that sensor signal is greater than the self-test maximum of 4.6 volts. The code is set during normal driving conditions.

Continuous Memory Code 61/117 and 64/112 indicates that sensor signal is less than the self-test minimum of 0.2 volt. The code is set during normal driving conditions.

Possible causes for these faults are as follows:

- Faulty Sensor
- Open Or Grounded Circuit In Harness
- Faulty ECA

SENSOR CODES

Sensor	Continuous Memory Code
ACT	54/113, 64/112
ECT	51/118, 61/117

Sensor Circuit Fault 90A10959

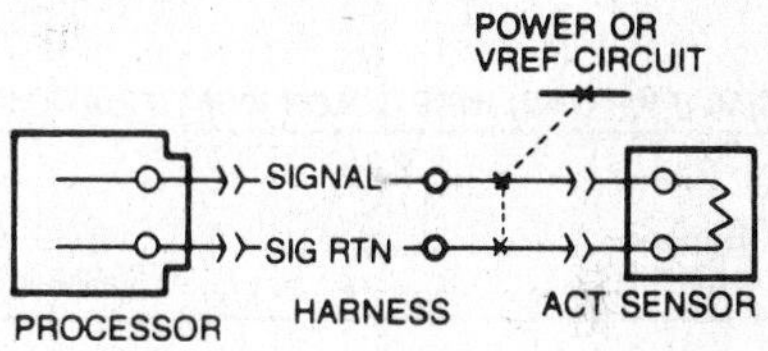
POWER OR VREF CIRCUIT
SIGNAL
SIG RTN
PROCESSOR
HARNESS
ACT SENSOR

Enter KOEO wiggle test mode. See CONTINUOUS MONITOR MODE (WIGGLE TEST) under QUICK TEST. Observe VOM or diagnostic tester for indication of fault while tapping sensor lightly and wiggling sensor connector. If fault is indicated, disconnect and inspect connector and terminals. If connector and terminals are okay, replace sensor, clear continuous memory and repeat QUICK TEST. If fault is not indicated, go to next step.

91) Check EEC-IV Vehicle Harness - While in CONTINUOUS MONITOR MODE (WIGGLE TEST), observe VOM or diagnostic tester while wiggling and bending EEC-IV harness from sensor to cowl, a small section at a time. Also check harness from cowl to ECA. If fault is indicated, isolate fault and repair as necessary. Clear continuous memory and repeat QUICK TEST. If no fault is found, go to next step.

92) Inspecting ECA and Vehicle Harness Connectors - Turn ignition off and wait 10 seconds. Disconnect ECA 60-pin connector. Inspect connector and connector terminals for damage. Repair as necessary and repeat QUICK TEST. If connectors and terminals are okay, and fault cannot be duplicated at this time, clear codes and repeat QUICK TEST. See INTERMITTENTS in TROUBLE SHOOTING - NO CODES article.

1991 ENGINE PERFORMANCE
Self-Diagnostics – EEC-IV (Cont.)

CIRCUIT TEST DC

MASS AIRFLOW SENSOR (MAF)

Diagnostic Aids – Perform this test when directed by QUICK TEST. This test procedure is intended to diagnose only MAF, ECA and vehicle harness circuits (VPWR, PWR GND, MAF and MAF RTN).

To prevent replacement of good components, be aware that the following non-EEC related areas may be the cause of problem:

- Air Cleaner Element
- Inlet Air Duct
- Throttle Body

Mass Airflow Sensor (MAF) Circuits 91C06932

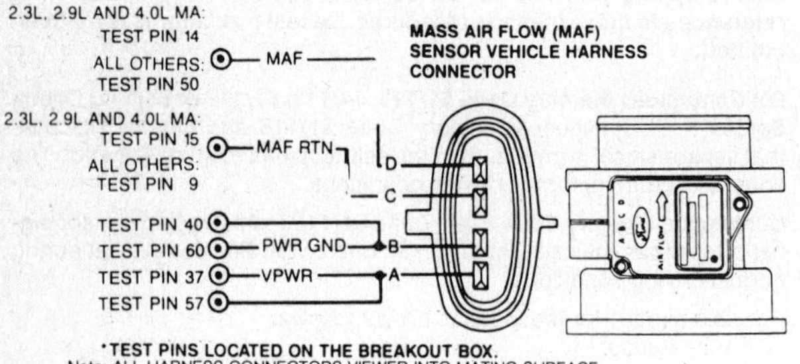
2.3L, 2.9L AND 4.0L MA:
TEST PIN 14
ALL OTHERS:
TEST PIN 50
MAF
MASS AIR FLOW (MAF)
SENSOR VEHICLE HARNESS
CONNECTOR
2.3L, 2.9L AND 4.0L MA:
TEST PIN 15
ALL OTHERS:
TEST PIN 9
MAF RTN
D
C
TEST PIN 40
TEST PIN 60
PWR GND
B
TEST PIN 37
VPWR
A
TEST PIN 57

*TEST PINS LOCATED ON THE BREAKOUT BOX.
Note: ALL HARNESS CONNECTORS VIEWED INTO MATING SURFACE

TEST PIN 50 Or 14 (MAF) WIRE COLOR IDENTIFICATION

Application	Wire Color
All Models	Light Blue/Red

TEST PIN 9 Or 15 (MAF RTN) WIRE COLOR IDENTIFICATION

Application	Wire Color
All Models	Tan/Light Blue

TEST PIN 40/60 (PWR GND) WIRE COLOR IDENTIFICATION

Application	Wire Color
Explorer & Ranger	Black/White
All Other Models	Black/Light Green

TEST PIN 37/57 (VPWR) WIRE COLOR IDENTIFICATION

Application	Wire Color
All Models	Red

MAF SIGNAL VOLTAGE

Application	Volts
Idle	.60
20 MPH	1.10
40 MPH	1.70
60 MPH	2.10

Diagnostic Aids – MAF signal voltage is typical for A/T vehicles at normal operating temperature. Voltage signal may vary due to engine load and temperature.Code 26/159 indicates MAF sensor voltage is out of self-test range. If code is received during KOEO SELF-TEST, it indicates voltage exceeded .70-volt test range. If Code 26/159 is received during KOER SELF-TEST, it indicates voltage is not within .20–1.50 volt operating range.

1) Code 26/159: Check VPWR Circuit Voltage – Turn ignition off and disconnect MAF sensor. Turn ignition on, leaving engine off. Measure voltage between VPWR circuit at MAF sensor vehicle harness connector and battery negative post. If voltage is greater than 10.5 volts, go to next step. If voltage is not greater than 10.5 volts, repair open in VPWR circuit and rerun QUICK TEST.

CIRCUIT TEST DC (Cont.)

NOTE: Code 26/159 may be caused by use of a garage exhaust ventilation system. Ensure vehicle is vented to outside atmosphere before repeating QUICK TEST.

2) Check MAF Sensor Ground – Turn ignition on. Disconnect MAF sensor. Set DVOM on 20-volt scale. Measure voltage between VPWR circuit and PWR GND circuit at MAF sensor connector. If voltage is greater than 10.5 volts, go to next step. If voltage is less than 10.5 volts repair open PWR GND circuit. Connect MAF sensor and rerun QUICK TEST.

NOTE: There is a break in step numbering sequence at this point, skipping from step 2) to step 10). Break is due to previous chart references to these testing procedures. No test procedures have been omitted.

10) Code 66/157 or 72/129: Check Continuity of MAF Signal and VPWR Circuits – Code 66/157 indicates that MAF signal was less than .40 volt sometime during last 80 warm-up cycles. Code 72/129 indicates insufficient MAF change during DYNAMIC RESPONSE TEST. Possible causes for this fault are as follows:

- Open MAF Circuit
- Open VPWR Circuit To MAF Sensor
- Open PWR GND Circuit To MAF Sensor
- Open MAF RTN Circuit To MAF Sensor
- MAF Circuit Shorted To Ground
- Faulty ECA Or MAF Sensor
- Air Leak Before Or After MAF Sensor
- MAF Sensor Disconnected

Ensure ignition is off. Disconnect and inspect 60-pin connector at ECA. Service as necessary. Disconnect MAF sensor and install breakout box; leave ECA disconnected. Set DVOM on 200-ohm scale. Measure resistance between VPWR circuit at MAF sensor vehicle harness connector and test pins No. 37 and 57 at breakout box.

On 2.3L, 2.9L, 3.0L and 4.0L models, measure resistance between MAF circuit at MAF sensor vehicle harness connector and test pin No. 14 at breakout box. On all others, measure resistance between MAF circuit at MAF sensor vehicle harness connector and test pin No. 50 at breakout box.

If both resistances are less than 5 ohms, go to next step. If either resistance is greater than 5 ohms, remove breakout box and repair open circuit. Reconnect all components and rerun QUICK TEST.

11) Check MAF Circuit for Shorts to Ground and MAF RTN Circuit – With ignition off and MAF sensor disconnected, set DVOM on 200-k/ohm scale. Disconnect ECA 60-pin connector. Inspect connector and terminals. Install breakout box, leaving ECA disconnected.

On 2.3L, 2.9L, 3.0L and 4.0L MA, measure resistance between test pin No. 14 and test pins No. 15, 40, and 60 at breakout box. On all others, measure resistance between test pin No. 50 and test pins No. 9, 40, and 60 at breakout box.

If all resistances are greater than 10 k/ohms, go to next step. If resistance in any circuit is less than 10 k/ohms, repair short circuit. Remove breakout box, reconnect components and repeat QUICK TEST.

12) Check Continuity of PWR GND Circuit – Ensure ignition is off. Disconnect MAF sensor. Measure resistance between PWR GND circuit at MAF sensor vehicle harness connector and battery negative post. If resistance is less than 10 ohms, go to next step. If resistance is greater than 10 ohms, repair open circuit. Reconnect all components and repeat QUICK TEST.

13) Check Continuity of MAF RTN Circuit – Turn ignition off and disconnect MAF sensor. Disconnect ECA 60-pin connector and inspect pins. Install breakout box; leave ECA disconnected.

On 2.3L, 2.9L, 3.0L and 4.0L models, measure resistance between MAF RTN circuit at MAF sensor vehicle harness connector and test pin No. 15 at breakout box.

On all other models, measure resistance between MAF RTN circuit at MAF sensor vehicle harness connector and test pin No. 9 at breakout box.

If resistance is less than 5 ohms, go to next step. If resistance is more than 5 ohms, repair open circuit. Remove breakout box, reconnect components and repeat QUICK TEST.

14) Check MAF Signal for Short to Ground – With ignition off, breakout box installed and ECA connected, disconnect MAF sensor. Set DVOM on 200-k/ohm scale.

CIRCUIT TEST DC (Cont.)

On 2.3L, 2.9L, 3.0L and 4.0L models, measure resistance between test pin No. 14 and test pins No. 15, 40 and 60 at breakout box. On all other models, measure resistance between test pin No. 50 and test pins No. 9, 40 and 60 at breakout box.

If resistances are greater than 10 k/ohms, go to next step. If all resistances are less than 10 k/ohms, replace ECA. Remove breakout box, reconnect components and repeat QUICK TEST.

15) Check MAF Circuit Output – With ignition off, install breakout box. Ensure ECA and MAF are connected. Set DVOM on 20-volt scale. Start engine. On 2.3L, 2.9L, 3.0L and 4.0L models, measure voltage between test pin No. 14 at breakout box and battery negative post.

On all other models, measure voltage between test pin No. 50 at breakout box and battery negative post. If voltage is .36-1.5 volts, replace ECA; remove breakout box, reconnect components and repeat QUICK TEST. If voltage is not .36-1.5 volts, replace MAF sensor; remove breakout box, reconnect components and repeat QUICK TEST.

NOTE: There is a break in step numbering sequence at this point, skipping from step 15) to step 20). Break is due to previous chart references to these testing procedures. No test procedures have been omitted.

20) Code 56/158: Repeat Self-Test with MAF Sensor Disconnected – With ignition off, disconnect MAF sensor from vehicle harness. Start engine and allow to idle for one minute. Turn ignition off. Repeat KOEO SELF-TEST. See KEY ON ENGINE OFF (KOEO) SELF-TEST under QUICK TEST. If Code 66 or 157 is present, replace MAF sensor and rerun QUICK TEST. If Code 66 or 157 is not present, go to next step.

21) Check MAF Circuit for Short to VPWR – With ignition off, disconnect MAF sensor and ECA. Disconnect ECA 60-pin connector and inspect for damaged or corroded terminals. Repair as necessary. Set DVOM on 200-k/ohm scale. Measure resistance between MAF and VPWR circuits at MAF sensor vehicle harness connector. If resistance is greater than 10 k/ohms, replace ECA; remove breakout box, reconnect components and repeat QUICK TEST. If resistance is less than 10 k/ohms, repair short circuit; remove breakout box, reconnect components and repeat QUICK TEST.

CIRCUIT TEST DF

MANIFOLD ABSOLUTE PRESSURE (MAP)/ BAROMETRIC PRESSURE (BP) SENSOR

Diagnostic Aids – Perform this test when directed by QUICK TEST or CIRCUIT TEST S. Barometric pressure sensor output is digital and must be measured with an oscilloscope or MAP/BP tester.

To prevent replacement of good components, be aware that the following non-EEC related areas may be the cause of problem:

- Unusually High Or Low Atmosphere Barometric Pressure
- Kinked Or Blocked Vacuum Lines
- Engine Mechanical Condition (Valves, Vacuum Leaks, Valve Timing, EGR Valve, etc.)

This test is intended to diagnose the following:

- MAP/BP Sensor
- Vehicle Harness Circuits (VREF, MAP/BP SIG & SIG RTN)
- MAP Vacuum Line
- ECA

CIRCUIT TEST DF (Cont.)

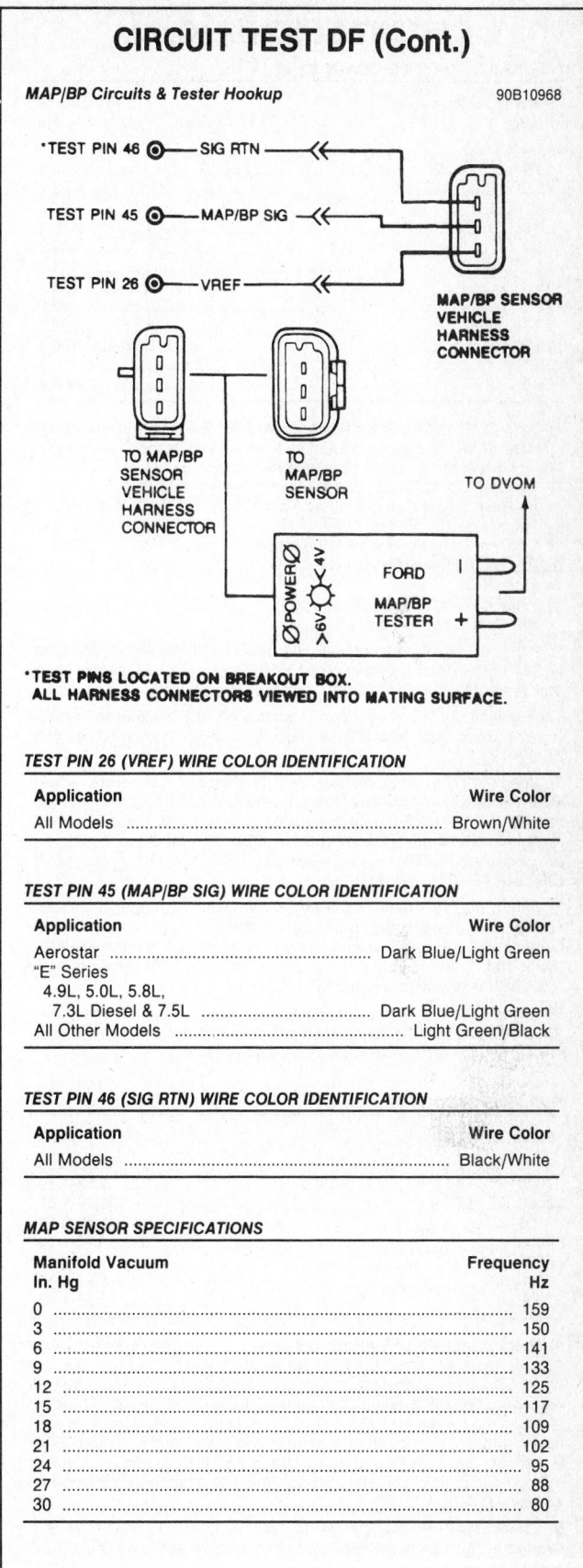

MAP/BP Circuits & Tester Hookup 90B10968

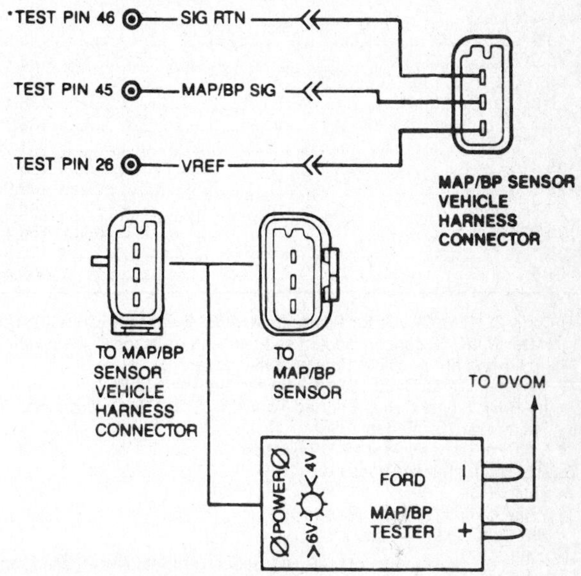
*TEST PIN 46
SIG RTN
TEST PIN 45
MAP/BP SIG
TEST PIN 26
VREF
MAP/BP SENSOR VEHICLE HARNESS CONNECTOR
TO MAP/BP SENSOR VEHICLE HARNESS CONNECTOR
TO MAP/BP SENSOR
TO DVOM
POWER
>6V
<4V
FORD MAP/BP TESTER
–
+

*TEST PINS LOCATED ON BREAKOUT BOX.
ALL HARNESS CONNECTORS VIEWED INTO MATING SURFACE.

TEST PIN 26 (VREF) WIRE COLOR IDENTIFICATION

Application	Wire Color
All Models	Brown/White

TEST PIN 45 (MAP/BP SIG) WIRE COLOR IDENTIFICATION

Application	Wire Color
Aerostar	Dark Blue/Light Green
"E" Series	
4.9L, 5.0L, 5.8L,	
7.3L Diesel & 7.5L	Dark Blue/Light Green
All Other Models	Light Green/Black

TEST PIN 46 (SIG RTN) WIRE COLOR IDENTIFICATION

Application	Wire Color
All Models	Black/White

MAP SENSOR SPECIFICATIONS

Manifold Vacuum In. Hg	Frequency Hz
0	159
3	150
6	141
9	133
12	125
15	117
18	109
21	102
24	95
27	88
30	80

CIRCUIT TEST DF (Cont.)

MAP/BP SENSOR SPECIFICATIONS

Barometric Pressure In. Hg	Frequency Hz
17.1	122.4
18.3	125.5
19.5	128.7
20.7	131.9
21.8	135.1
23.0	138.3
24.2	141.8
25.4	145.4
26.6	148.9
27.7	152.5
28.9	156.1
30.1	159.6
31.0	162.4

1) Code 22/126: Check for Power to MAP/BP Sensor – Code 22/126 indicates MAP/BP sensor is out of self-test voltage range (1.4-1.6 volts). The following are possible causes of this code:

- MAP/BP Signal Circuit Open Between Sensor And ECA
- MAP/BP Signal Circuit Shorted To VREF, SIG RTN Or Ground
- Faulty MAP/BP Sensor
- Vacuum Trapped At MAP/BP Sensor
- High Atmospheric Pressure
- Faulty ECA
- VREF Circuit Open At Sensor
- SIG RTN Open At Sensor

Turn ignition off. Disconnect MAP/BP sensor from vehicle harness. Connect MAP/BP tester between wiring harness and MAP/BP sensor. Connect tester plugs to DVOM. Set DVOM on 20-volt scale.

Turn ignition on. If Red light or no light is on, VREF is either too high or too low. Go to next step. If Green light is on, VREF is okay. Go to step **3)**.

2) Check for Power at Sensor Vehicle Harness Connector – With MAP/BP sensor and MAP/BP tester connected, turn ignition on. Disconnect MAP/BP sensor. If only Green light on tester is lit, VREF is correct; replace MAP/BP sensor and repeat QUICK TEST. If Green light is not on, remove MAP/BP tester; reconnect MAP/BP sensor and go to CIRCUIT TEST C, step **1)**.

3) Check MAP/BP Sensor Output – With MAP/BP tester connected and ignition on, measure sensor output voltage. If output voltage is within range, for altitude in which vehicle is being tested, remove MAP/BP tester and go to next step. If output reading is outside range, remove MAP/BP tester and go to step **5)**.

Diagnostic Aids – If possible, measure output voltage several known good MAP/BP sensors on available vehicles. The average voltage reading will be typical for your location on date of testing.

MAP SENSOR VOLTAGE OUTPUT

Elevation (Feet)	Volts
0	1.55-1.63
1000	1.52-1.60
2000	1.49-1.57
3000	1.46-1.54
4000	1.43-1.51
5000	1.40-1.48
6000	1.37-1.45
7000	1.35-1.43

4) Check Continuity of MAP/BP SIG Circuit – Turn ignition off and wait 10 seconds. Disconnect MAP/BP sensor from vehicle harness. Disconnect ECA 60-pin connector. Inspect for damaged wiring and repair as necessary. Install breakout box, leaving ECA disconnected. Measure resistance between MAP/BP SIG circuit at sensor vehicle harness connector and test pin No. 45. If reading is less than 5 ohms, replace ECA. Reconnect components and repeat QUICK TEST. If reading is 5 ohms or more, repair open circuit. Remove breakout box, reconnect components and repeat QUICK TEST.

5) Check MAP/BP SIG Circuit for Shorts to VREF, SIG RTN and Ground – Turn ignition off and wait 10 seconds. Disconnect ECA 60-pin connector. Inspect for damaged wiring and repair as necessary. Install breakout box, leaving ECA disconnected. Disconnect harness at MAP/BP sensor. Set DVOM on 200-k/ohm scale. Measure resistance between test pin No. 45 and test pins No. 26, 46, 40 and 60. If any reading is less than 10 k/ohms, repair short circuit. Remove breakout box and reconnect all components. Repeat QUICK TEST. If all readings are 10 k/ohms or more, replace MAP/BP sensor. Remove breakout box and connect all wiring. Repeat QUICK TEST.

CIRCUIT TEST DF (Cont.)

NOTE: There is a break in step numbering sequence at this point, skipping from step 5) to step 7). Break is due to previous chart references to these testing procedures. No test procedures have been omitted.

7) KOER Code 22/126: Check for EGR-Related Codes – KOER Code 22/126 indicates MAP/BP signal is out of self-test range during KOER SELF-TEST. Check for Codes 31, 32, 33, 34, 35, 326, 327, 328, 332, 334, 336 or 337. If codes are present, go to appropriate KOER SELF-TEST CODES under SERVICE CODE REFERENCE CHARTS to find the proper CIRCUIT TEST. If codes are not present, go to next step.

8) Check MAP Sensor Operation – Turn ignition off and wait 10 seconds. Disconnect vacuum hose from MAP sensor. Connect vacuum pump to MAP sensor and apply 18 in. Hg to sensor. If sensor does not hold vacuum, replace sensor; connect vacuum line and repeat QUICK TEST. If MAP sensor holds vacuum, release vacuum and go to next step.

9) Attempt to Eliminate Code 22/126 – Turn ignition off. Plug vacuum hose going to MAP sensor. Start engine and run at 1400-1600 RPM. Slowly apply 15 in. Hg to MAP sensor. With engine operating under these conditions, perform KOER SELF-TEST. Check for Code 22/126; disregard any other codes at this time. If Code 22/126 is still present, replace MAP sensor. If Code 22/126 is no longer displayed, inspect vacuum hose going to MAP sensor. If hose is okay, service other codes at this time. If no other code is present, check engine mechanical condition for cause of low vacuum.

10) Code 72/129: Repeat Dynamic Response (Goose) Test – Code 72/129 indicates MAP sensor output did not change enough during dynamic response (Goose) test. Possible causes for this code are as follows.

- System Failed To Detect Partial Wide Open Throttle (WOT)
- Incorrect MAP Sensor Vacuum Line Routing
- Faulty MAP Sensor

Repeat KOER SELF-TEST. Ensure complete WOT is performed during dynamic response portion of test. If KOER Code 72/129 is still present, go to next step. If code is not present, service other codes as necessary.

11) Code 81/128: Check Vacuum Hoses – Continuous memory code 81/128 indicates MAP sensor vacuum has not changed more than 2 in. Hg during normal vehicle operation. Possible causes for this code are as follows:

- MAP Sensor Vacuum Supply Hose Is Improperly Routed, Blocked Or Is Leaking.
- MAP Sensor Is Leaking.

With ignition off, check vacuum lines for correct routing. Refer to Vehicle Emission Control Identification (VECI) decal. Check for disconnections, kinks or blockage. Repair vacuum lines as necessary and repeat QUICK TEST. If vacuum lines are okay, go to next step.

12) Check MAP Sensor Operation – Turn ignition off and wait 10 seconds. Disconnect vacuum supply hose from MAP sensor. Install vacuum pump to MAP sensor. Apply 18 in. Hg to MAP sensor. If MAP sensor holds vacuum, release vacuum and go to next step. If sensor does not hold vacuum, replace MAP sensor; reconnect components and repeat QUICK TEST.

13) MAP Sensor Vacuum Decrease During Dynamic Response (Goose) Test – Turn ignition off and wait 10 seconds. Install "T" fitting and vacuum gauge in intake manifold MAP sensor supply line. Perform KOER SELF-TEST while observing vacuum gauge. If vacuum decreases by more than 10 in. Hg during dynamic response test, remove gauge and replace MAP sensor; rerun QUICK TEST. If vacuum does not decrease by 10 in. Hg or more, EEC-IV system is okay; repair engine mechanical components as necessary to increase engine vacuum.

NOTE: There is a break in step numbering sequence at this point, skipping from step 13) to step 90). Break is due to previous chart references to these testing procedures. No test procedures have been omitted.

CIRCUIT TEST DF (Cont.)

90) Continuous Memory Code 22/126: – Continuous Code 22/126 indicates MAP/BP sensor was out of self-test range (1.4-1.6 volts) during normal driving conditions. Possible causes for this code are as follows:

- Faulty MAP/BP Sensor
- Faulty Wiring Harness Or Connectors
- Unusually High Or Low Barometric Pressure

While in KOEO wiggle test (see CONTINUOUS MONITOR MODE (WIGGLE TEST) under QUICK TEST), observe test equipment while performing the following:

- Connect a vacuum pump to MAP/BP sensor.
- Slowly apply 25 in. Hg to sensor.
- Slowly bleed off vacuum from sensor.
- Lightly tap on sensor (to simulate road shock).
- Wiggle sensor connector.

If a fault is indicated, disconnect sensor and inspect connectors. Repair as necessary. If connectors are okay, replace MAP/BP sensor. Rerun QUICK TEST. If a fault is not indicated, go to next step.

91) Check EEC-IV Vehicle Harness – Stay in KOEO wiggle test. Observe VOM or diagnostic tester for indication of fault while shaking, bending or wiggling small sections of harness from sensor connector to firewall. Check harness from firewall to ECA in same manner. If fault is indicated, isolate fault in harness and repair as necessary. Clear codes and repeat QUICK TEST. If no fault is indicated, go to next step.

92) Check ECA and Vehicle Harness Connectors – Turn ignition off and wait 10 seconds. Disconnect ECA 60-pin connector. Inspect both connectors and terminals for obvious damage. If connectors and terminals are not okay, repair as necessary. Repeat QUICK TEST. If connectors and terminals are okay, fault cannot be duplicated at this time. Continuous Memory Code 22/126 testing is complete. Refer to INTERMITTENTS in TROUBLE SHOOTING – NO CODES article.

CIRCUIT TEST DG

KNOCK SENSOR (KS)

Diagnostic Aids – Perform this test when Code 25/225 is received during QUICK TEST procedure, or when directed by other diagnostic tests.

To prevent replacement of good components, be aware that the following non-EEC related areas may be the cause of problem:

- Poor Fuel Quality
- Engine Mechanical Condition
- Spark Timing

Knock Sensor Circuits 90C10969

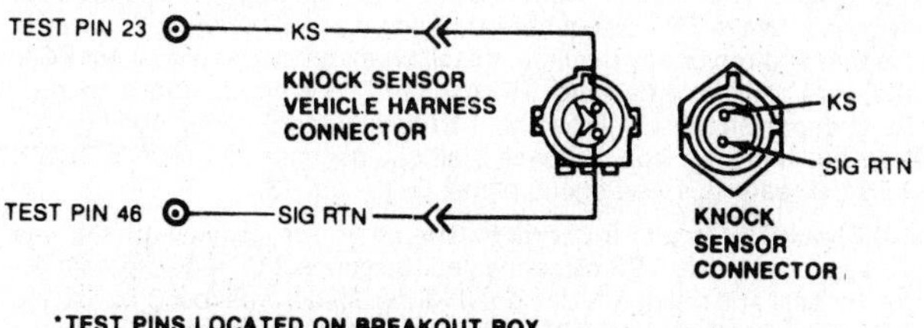
TEST PIN 23
KS
KNOCK SENSOR VEHICLE HARNESS CONNECTOR
KS
SIG RTN
TEST PIN 46
SIG RTN
KNOCK SENSOR CONNECTOR

*TEST PINS LOCATED ON BREAKOUT BOX.
ALL HARNESS CONNECTORS VIEWED INTO MATING SURFACE.

TEST PIN 23 (KS) WIRE COLOR IDENTIFICATION

Application	Wire Color
Bronco & "F" Series 4.9L & 5.0L	Yellow/Red
"E" Series: 4.9L & 5.0L	Light Green/Black

TEST PIN 46 (SIG RTN) WIRE COLOR IDENTIFICATION

Application	Wire Color
Bronco 4.9L & 5.0L	Gray/Red
All Other Models	Black/White

1) Code 25: Generate Knock Signal Manually – Code 25/225 indicates Knock Sensor (KS) signal was not received by ECA during dynamic response (Goose) check (after ID code portion) in KOER SELF-TEST. Possible causes for this fault are as follows:

- Faulty Knock Sensor
- Open Or Shorted Harness
- Faulty ECA

CIRCUIT TEST DG (Cont.)

Ensure engine is at normal operating temperature. Perform KOER SELF-TEST. Immediately after dynamic response check request signal appears, lightly tap above knock sensor with 4-oz. hammer. DO NOT goose throttle. After 15 seconds, check for Code 25/225. Ignore all other codes at this time. If Code 25/225 is displayed, go to next step. If Code 25/225 is not displayed, knock system is okay. Repeat KOER SELF-TEST and service other codes.

2) Check KS Circuit Voltage – Turn ignition off and wait 10 seconds. Disconnect knock sensor. Inspect and repair any damaged wiring. Set DVOM on 20-volt scale. With ignition on and engine off, measure voltage between KS circuit and SIG RTN at sensor vehicle harness connector. If reading is greater than 4 volts, go to step **5)**. If reading is 1-4 volts, go to step **6)**. If reading is less than one volt, go to next step.

3) Check Continuity of KS and SIG RTN Circuits – Turn ignition off and wait 10 seconds. Disconnect ECA 60-pin connector. Inspect and repair any damaged wiring. Install breakout box, leaving ECA and knock sensor disconnected. With DVOM on 200-ohm scale, measure resistance between SIG RTN circuit at KS harness connector and test pin No. 46. Measure resistance between KS circuit at vehicle harness connector and test pin No. 23. If either reading is 5 ohms or more, service open circuit. Remove breakout box, connect all components and repeat QUICK TEST. If both readings are less than 5 ohms, go to next step.

4) Check KS Circuit for Short to Ground – Turn ignition off and wait 10 seconds. With breakout box installed, and ECA and knock sensor disconnected, set DVOM on 200-k/ohm scale. Measure resistance between test pin No. 23 and test pins No. 40, 46 and 60. If all readings are 10 k/ohms or more, remove breakout box; reconnect ECA and go to step **6)**. If any reading is less than 10 k/ohms, repair shorts in harness. Remove breakout box, reconnect all components and repeat QUICK TEST.

5) Check KS Circuit for Short to Voltage – Turn ignition off. Install breakout box. With ECA and KS sensor disconnected, turn ignition on. Measure voltage between test pins No. 23 and 40. If reading is 0.5 volt or more, repair knock sensor harness short to power. Remove breakout box, reconnect all components and repeat QUICK TEST. If reading is less than 0.5 volt, remove breakout box, reconnect ECA and go to next step.

6) Test ECA with Substitute Knock Sensor – Turn ignition off and wait 10 seconds. Remove breakout box and reconnect ECA. Connect substitute knock sensor into harness but do not install sensor on engine. Substitute sensor should be a known good unit with same part number. Ensure engine is at normal operating temperature. Perform KOER SELF-TEST. When dynamic response check signal appears, lightly tap knock sensor with 4-oz. hammer. DO NOT goose throttle. If Code 25/225 is displayed, replace ECA; reconnect original knock sensor and rerun QUICK TEST. Ignore all other codes at this time. If Code 25/225 does not appear, install new knock sensor and repeat QUICK TEST.

CIRCUIT TEST DH

THROTTLE POSITION SENSOR (TPS)

Diagnostic Aids – Perform this test only when directed by QUICK TEST.

TPS Circuits 90F10970

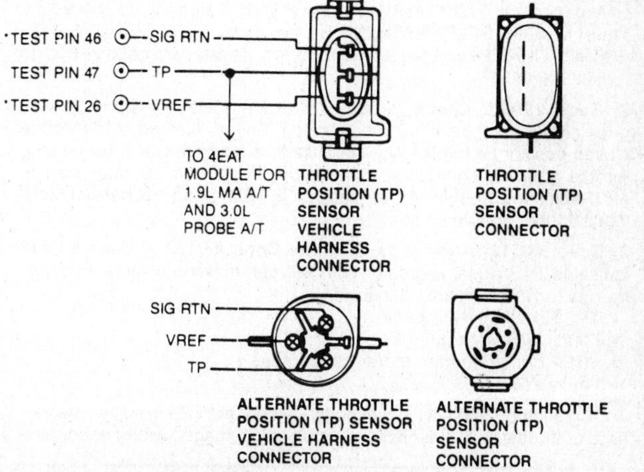
*TEST PIN 46
SIG RTN
TEST PIN 47
TP
*TEST PIN 26
VREF
TO 4EAT MODULE FOR 1.9L MA A/T AND 3.0L PROBE A/T
THROTTLE POSITION (TP) SENSOR VEHICLE HARNESS CONNECTOR
THROTTLE POSITION (TP) SENSOR CONNECTOR
SIG RTN
VREF
TP
ALTERNATE THROTTLE POSITION (TP) SENSOR VEHICLE HARNESS CONNECTOR
ALTERNATE THROTTLE POSITION (TP) SENSOR CONNECTOR

*TEST PINS LOCATED ON BREAKOUT BOX.
ALL HARNESS CONNECTORS VIEWED INTO MATING SURFACE.

1991 ENGINE PERFORMANCE
Self-Diagnostics – EEC-IV (Cont.)

CIRCUIT TEST DH (Cont.)

TEST PIN 26 (VREF) WIRE COLOR IDENTIFICATION

Application	Wire Color
All Models	Brown/White

TEST PIN 46 (SIG RTN) WIRE COLOR IDENTIFICATION

Application	Wire Color
All Models	Gray/Red

TEST PIN 47 (TP) WIRE COLOR IDENTIFICATION

Application	Wire Color
All Models	Gray/White

TPS Specification Chart

Throttle Position Sensor Specifications

Throttle Position Sensor Setting (K.O.E.O. and K.O.E.R.)			TP Circuit (Signal) Voltage Range	
Engine Application	Rotational Degree Range	Voltage Range	Minimum	Maximum
2.3L DIS-EFI	0° - 13.5°	0.59 - 1.22	0.34	4.84
2.9L EFI	0° - 13.5°	0.59 - 1.22	0.34	4.84
3.0L EFI	0° - 13.5°	0.59 - 1.22	0.34	4.84
4.0L EFI	0° - 13.5°	0.59 - 1.22	0.34	4.84
4.9L EFI	3° - 13.5°	0.73 - 1.22	0.20	4.84
5.0L EFI	3° - 13.5°	0.73 - 1.22	0.20	4.84
5.8L EFI	3° - 13.5°	0.73 - 1.22	0.20	4.84
7.5L EFI	3° - 13.5°	0.73 - 1.22	0.20	4.84
5.8L/7.5L EFI E4OD	3° - 13.5°	0.73 - 1.22	0.34	4.84

Diagnostic Aids – The normal range of throttle angle measurement for TPS is 0-85 degrees. To pass QUICK TEST procedure, range of throttle rotation (in degrees) must be within 3% of specification.

To prevent replacement of good components, be aware that the following non-EEC related areas may be at fault.
- Throttle Stop Adjustment
- Binding Throttle Shaft Or Linkage
- Cruise Control Linkage

1) Code 23/121: Check for Other Codes – Code 23/121 indicates TPS rotational setting may be out of self-test range. See TPS SPECIFICATION CHART. Possible causes for this fault are as follows.
- Binding Throttle Linkage
- TPS Not Seated Correctly
- Faulty TPS
- Faulty ECA

Check for Code 31/327 in KOER SELF-TEST. If either code is present, return to KOER SELF-TEST CODES chart under SERVICE CODE REFERENCE CHARTS and proceed as directed. If codes are not present, go to next step.

2) Code 23/121: Check for Stuck Throttle Plate – Inspect throttle body and linkage for binding or sticking. Ensure linkage is in throttle-closed position. If throttle plate or linkage is binding, check for binding throttle or cruise control linkage, vacuum line or harness interference, etc. Repair any problem and repeat QUICK TEST. If no mechanical problem is found, go to next step.

3) Code 53/112: Attempt to Generate Code 63/122 – Code 53/112 indicates TPS signal is greater than self-test maximum value. Possible causes for this fault are as follows.
- TPS Not Seated Properly
- Faulty TPS Sensor
- VREF Circuit Shorted In Vehicle Harness
- Faulty ECA

Turn ignition off and wait 10 seconds. Disconnect TPS from vehicle harness at throttle body. Inspect and repair any damaged wiring or connector pins. Repeat KOEO SELF-TEST. Ignore all other codes at this time. If Code 63/122 is not displayed, go to step **5)**. If Code 63/122 is displayed, go to next step.

CIRCUIT TEST DH (Cont.)

4) Check VREF Circuit Voltage – Turn ignition off and wait 10 seconds. Set DVOM on 20-volt scale. Disconnect TPS vehicle harness connectors. With ignition on and engine off, measure voltage between VREF and SIG RTN at TPS vehicle harness connector. If reading is less than 4 volts or more than 6 volts, reconnect sensor and go to CIRCUIT TEST C, step **1)**. If reading is between 4 and 6 volts, replace TPS and repeat QUICK TEST.

5) Checking TP Circuit for Short to Power – Turn ignition off and wait 10 seconds. Disconnect TPS from harness. Set DVOM on 200-k/ohm scale. Disconnect ECA 60-pin connector. Inspect and repair any damage. Install breakout box, leaving ECA disconnected. Measure resistance between test pin No. 47 and test pins No. 26 and 57. If either reading is less than 10 k/ohms, repair short in harness; connect components and repeat QUICK TEST. If both readings are 10 k/ohms or more, replace ECA; reconnect components and repeat QUICK TEST.

NOTE: There is a break in step numbering sequence at this point, skipping from step 5) to step 10). Break is due to previous chart references to these testing procedures. No test procedures have been omitted.

10) Code 63/122: Attempt to Generate Code 53/123 or 23/121 – Code 63/122 indicates TP signal is less than minimum self-test value. Possible causes for this fault are as follows.
- TPS Not Seated Correctly
- Faulty TPS
- Open Or Ground Circuit In Vehicle Harness
- Faulty ECA

Turn ignition off and wait 10 seconds. Disconnect TPS from harness. Install jumper wire between VREF and TP circuit at TPS harness connector. Perform KOEO SELF-TEST. If no codes are generated, immediately remove jumper wire, and go directly to step **13)**. Check for Codes 53/123 or 23/121 (ignore all other codes at this time). If Codes 53/123 or 23/121 are not present, remove jumper wire, and go to next step. If either Code 53/123 or 23/121 is present, replace TPS, remove jumper and repeat QUICK TEST.

11) Check VREF Circuit Voltage – Turn ignition off and wait 10 seconds. Disconnect TPS from vehicle harness. Inspect and repair any damaged wiring. With ignition on and engine off, measure voltage between VREF and SIG RTN circuits at TPS vehicle harness connector. If reading is less than 4 volts or more than 6 volts, go to CIRCUIT TEST C, step **1)**. If reading is between 4 and 6 volts, reconnect all components and go to next step.

12) Check TPS Circuit Continuity – Turn ignition off and wait 10 seconds. Leave TPS disconnected. Disconnect ECA 60-pin connector. Inspect and repair any damage. Install breakout box and connect ECA. Measure resistance between TP circuit at TPS vehicle harness connector and test pin No. 47. If reading is 5 ohms or more, repair open circuit. Remove breakout box, reconnect all components and repeat QUICK TEST. If reading is less than 5 ohms, go to step **13)**.

13) Check TP Circuit for Shorts to Ground – Turn ignition off and wait 10 seconds. Leave TPS disconnected. Disconnect ECA 60-pin connector. Inspect and repair any damaged wiring. Install breakout box, leaving ECA disconnected. Set DVOM on 200-k/ohm scale. Measure resistance between test pin No. 47 and test pins No. 40, 46 and 60. If any reading is less than 10 k/ohms, repair short circuit; reconnect all components and repeat QUICK TEST. If all readings are 10 k/ohms or more, replace ECA. Remove breakout box, reconnect all components and repeat QUICK TEST.

NOTE: There is a break in step numbering sequence at this point, skipping from step 13) to step 20). Break is due to previous chart references to these testing procedures. No test procedures have been omitted.

20) KOER Code 73/167: Dynamic Response (Goose) Test at Wide Open Throttle (WOT) – KOER Code 73/167 indicates TPS did not exceed 25% of its rotation during dynamic response check portion of KOER SELF-TEST. A complete WOT must be performed during dynamic response check portion.

Run KOER SELF-TEST. Ensure WOT is performed during dynamic response portion of test. If Code 73/167 is still present, go to next step. If code is not present, system is unable to duplicate Code 73/167 at this

CIRCUIT TEST DH (Cont.)

time. Service any other KOER codes. If no other KOER code is present, testing is complete.

21) TPS Movement During Dynamic Response Test – Turn ignition off and disconnect ECA 60-pin connector. Inspect and repair any damage. Install breakout box and connect ECA. Connect DVOM between test pins No. 46 and 47. Perform KOER SELF-TEST and ensure a proper WOT is performed. Monitor DVOM reading during dynamic response check. If reading exceeds 3.5 volts, replace ECA; remove breakout box, reconnect all components and repeat QUICK TEST. If reading does not exceed 3.5 volts, ensure TPS is correctly installed and adjusted. If TPS is correctly installed and adjusted, replace TPS. Repeat QUICK TEST.

NOTE: There is a break in step numbering sequence at this point, skipping from step 21) to step 90). Break is due to previous chart references to these testing procedures. No test procedures have been omitted.

90) Continuous Memory Code 53/123: Monitor TPS Circuit Under Simulated Road Conditions – Enter KOEO wiggle test. See CONTINUOUS MONITOR MODE (WIGGLE TEST) under QUICK TEST. Observe DVOM or diagnostic tester for indication of fault while slowly opening throttle to WOT. Slowly bring throttle to closed position, and lightly tap TPS and wiggle harness connector. This test checks for open or short in TPS, connectors and wiring harness. If no fault is indicated, go to step **92)**. If fault is indicated, go to next step.

91) Measure TP Circuit Voltage While Exercising TPS – Turn ignition off and wait 10 seconds. Disconnect ECA 60-pin connector. Install breakout box, leaving ECA connected. Stay in KOEO wiggle test (as in previous step). Connect DVOM between test pins No. 47 and 46. Set DVOM on 20-volt scale. With ignition on and engine off, observe DVOM and repeat step **90)**. If fault occurs at less than 4.25 volts, inspect TPS connectors and terminals. If connectors and terminals are okay, replace TPS; clear codes and repeat QUICK TEST. If fault does not occur at less than 4.25 volts, TPS over-travel may have caused Continuous Memory Code 53/123. TPS is okay, go to next step to check harness.

92) Check EEC-IV Vehicle Harness – While in KOEO wiggle test, shake, bend and wiggle small sections of EEC-IV harness from TPS vehicle harness connector to firewall, and from firewall to ECA. If fault is indicated, isolate fault in wiring and repair as necessary. Clear codes and repeat QUICK TEST. If no fault is indicated, go to next step.

93) Check ECA and Harness Connectors – Turn ignition off and wait 10 seconds. Disconnect ECA 60-pin connector. Inspect both connectors and terminals for damage. Repair as necessary. Clear Continuous Memory Codes and repeat QUICK TEST. If connectors and terminals are okay, fault cannot be duplicated at this time. Continuous Memory Code 53/123 testing is complete.

94) Continuous Memory Code 63/122: Monitor TP Circuit Under Simulated Road Conditions – Enter KOEO wiggle test. See CONTINUOUS MONITOR MODE (WIGGLE TEST) under QUICK TEST. Check VOM or diagnostic tester for fault while performing the following:

- Slowly open throttle to WOT.
- Slowly bring throttle to closed position.
- Lightly tap TPS and wiggle connector.

This test checks for open or short in TPS, connectors and vehicle harness. If fault is indicated, disconnect TPS. Inspect connectors and terminals. If connectors and terminals are okay, replace TPS. Clear Continuous Memory Codes and repeat QUICK TEST. If no fault is indicated, go to next step.

95) Check EEC-IV Vehicle Harness – While in KOEO wiggle test (CONTINUOUS MONITOR MODE), shake, bend and wiggle small sections of EEC-IV harness from TPS vehicle harness connector to firewall, and from firewall to ECA. If fault is indicated, isolate fault in wiring and repair as necessary. Clear Continuous Memory Codes and repeat QUICK TEST. If no fault is indicated, go to next step.

96) Check ECA and Harness Connectors – Turn ignition off and wait 10 seconds. Disconnect ECA 60-pin connector. Inspect both connectors and terminals for damage. Repair as necessary. Clear Continuous Memory Codes and repeat QUICK TEST. If connectors and terminals are okay, fault cannot be duplicated at this time. Continuous Memory Code 63/122 testing is complete.

CIRCUIT TEST DJ

ENGINE RPM SENSOR (7.3L DIESEL)

NOTE: Perform this test when Code 14 is displayed during QUICK TEST or when directed here by other test procedures. This test is intended to diagnose only the following components:

- **Engine RPM Sensor (RPMS)**
- **ECA**
- **RPMS (+) And RPMS (-) Vehicle Harness Circuits**

To prevent replacement of good components, verify RPM sensor is correctly installed and circuits/connectors are in good condition:

RPM Sensor Circuit 91F14253

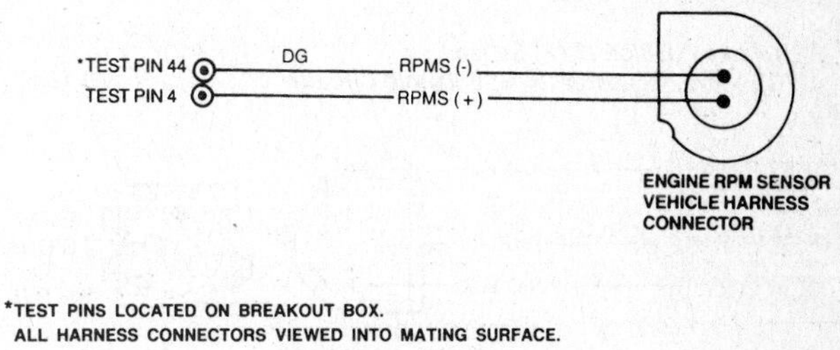
*TEST PIN 44
TEST PIN 4
DG
RPMS (-)
RPMS (+)
ENGINE RPM SENSOR VEHICLE HARNESS CONNECTOR
*TEST PINS LOCATED ON BREAKOUT BOX.
ALL HARNESS CONNECTORS VIEWED INTO MATING SURFACE.

TEST PIN 14 (RPM) WIRE COLOR IDENTIFICATION

Application	Wire Color
"E" Series	Pink/Orange
"F" Series	Tan/Yellow

1) Code 14: Erratic RPM Signal – Code 14 indicates RPM signal output was missing pulses while engine was running. Check EEC-IV system for loose wires or connectors. If vehicle is equipped with 2-way radio or telephone, check for correct installation. Enter KOER CONTINUOUS MONITOR MODE (WIGGLE TEST). See QUICK TEST in this article. Observe VOM or diagnostic tester while lightly tapping engine RPM sensor and wiggling RPM sensor connector. If fault is detected, repair as necessary. Clear memory and repeat QUICK TEST to verify repair. If fault is not detected, go to next step.

2) Remain in KOER CONTINUOUS MONITOR MODE. Observe VOM or diagnostic tester for indication of fault while shaking, bending or wiggling small sections of harness from sensor connector to dash panel and ECA. If fault is detected, repair as necessary. Clear memory and repeat QUICK TEST to verify repair. If fault is not detected, go to next step.

3) Turn ignition off. Disconnect ECA 60-pin connector. Inspect connector for damage, corrosion, loose pins or wires. Repair as necessary. Install breakout box leaving ECA disconnected. Disconnect engine RPM sensor connector. Use ohmmeter to measure resistance between test pin No. 4 and RPMS (+) terminal at sensor. Measure resistance between test pin No. 44 and RPMS (-) terminal at sensor. If each resistance is 5 ohms or more, repair open circuit. Remove breakout box, connect all components and repeat QUICK TEST. If resistance is less than 5 ohms, go to next step.

4) Ensure ignition is off and RPM sensor is disconnected. With breakout box installed and ECA disconnected, measure resistance between test pin No. 4 and test pin Nos. 37/57, 40 and 44 at breakout box. Measure resistance between test pin No. 44 and test pin Nos. 37/57 at breakout box. If each resistance is less than 10,000 ohms, repair short circuit. Remove breakout box, connect all components and repeat QUICK TEST. If resistance is 10,000 ohms or more, go to next step.

5) Ensure ignition is off and RPM sensor is disconnected. Measure resistance between engine RPM sensor terminals. If resistance is 2400-2800 ohms, replace ECA. Remove breakout box, connect all components and repeat QUICK TEST. If resistance is not 2400-2800 ohms, sensor and circuit are okay. Test is complete.

1991 ENGINE PERFORMANCE
Self-Diagnostics – EEC-IV (Cont.)

CIRCUIT TEST DN

EGR VALVE POSITION (EVP) SENSOR & EGR VALVE REGULATOR (EVR) SOLENOID

Diagnostic Aids – Perform this test when instructed by QUICK TEST, or when directed by other test procedures.

To prevent replacement of good components, be aware that a damaged EGR valve may be the cause of problem.

This CIRCUIT TEST is intended to diagnose the following:

- EVP Sensor
- VREF, EVP, SIG RTN, EVR, And VPWR Harness Circuits
- EVR Solenoid
- EGR Valve Assembly
- ECA
- EGR And EVR Vacuum Lines

EGR Valve Position (EVP) Sensor & EGR Valve Regulator (EVR) Solenoid Circuits 90H12382

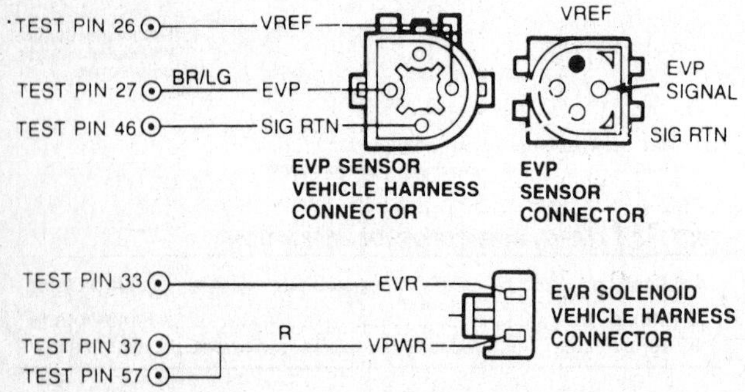
*TEST PIN 26
VREF
TEST PIN 27
BR/LG
EVP
TEST PIN 46
SIG RTN
EVP SENSOR VEHICLE HARNESS CONNECTOR
VREF
EVP SIGNAL
SIG RTN
EVP SENSOR CONNECTOR
TEST PIN 33
EVR
TEST PIN 37
R
VPWR
TEST PIN 57
EVR SOLENOID VEHICLE HARNESS CONNECTOR

*TEST PINS LOCATED ON BREAKOUT BOX.
ALL HARNESS CONNECTORS VIEWED INTO MATING SURFACE.

TEST PIN 26 (VREF) WIRE COLOR IDENTIFICATION

Application	Wire Color
All Models	Brown/White

TEST PIN 27 (EVP) WIRE COLOR IDENTIFICATION

Application	Wire Color
All Models	Brown/Light Green

TEST PIN 33 (EVR) WIRE COLOR IDENTIFICATION

Application	Wire Color
All Models	Brown/Pink

TEST PIN 46 (SIG RTN) WIRE COLOR IDENTIFICATION

Application	Wire Color
All Models	Gray/Red

1) Code 31/327: Generate Code 35/337 – Code 31/327 indicates EVP sensor signal is less than self-test minimum of 0.2 volt. Possible causes for this fault are as follows:

- Faulty EVP Sensor
- Open Or Grounded Harness
- Faulty ECA

Turn ignition off and wait 10 seconds. Disconnect EVP harness at sensor. Install a jumper wire between VREF circuit and EVP circuit at EVP sensor vehicle harness connector. Repeat KOEO SELF-TEST. Check for code 35. Ignore all other codes at this time. If Code 35/337 is displayed, remove jumper and replace EVP sensor. Repeat QUICK TEST. If Code 35/337 is not displayed, remove jumper wire and go to next step.

CIRCUIT TEST DN (Cont.)

2) Check VREF Circuit Voltage – With ignition on and engine off, and EVP sensor disconnected, set DVOM on 20-volt scale. Disconnect ECA 60-pin connector. Inspect and repair any damaged wiring. Measure voltage at EVP sensor vehicle harness connector between VREF circuit and SIG RTN circuit. If reading is NOT 4-6 volts, go to CIRCUIT TEST C, step **1)**. If reading is 4-6 volts, go to next step.

3) Check EVP Circuit Continuity – Turn ignition off and wait 10 seconds. Disconnect EVP sensor and ECA 60-pin connector. Inspect and repair any damaged wiring. Install breakout box, and connect ECA to box. Measure resistance between EVP circuit at EVP sensor connector and test pin No. 27. If reading is 5 ohms or more, repair open circuit. Connect EVP sensor and remove breakout box. Repeat QUICK TEST. If reading is less than 5 ohms, go to next step.

4) Check EVP Circuit for Shorts to Ground – With ignition off and EVP sensor disconnected, leave breakout box installed. Disconnect ECA. Set DVOM on 200-k/ohm scale. Measure resistance between test pin No. 27 and test pins No. 40, 46 and 60. If any reading is less than 10 k/ohms, repair short circuit. Reconnect all components and remove breakout box. Repeat QUICK TEST. If all readings are 10 k/ohms or more, replace ECA. Connect EVP and remove breakout box. Repeat QUICK TEST.

5) Code 35/337: Generate Code 31/327 – Code 35/337 indicates EVP sensor signal is greater than self-test maximum of 4.8 volts. Possible causes for this fault are as follows:

- Faulty EVP Sensor
- Short To Power In Vehicle Harness

Turn ignition off and wait 10 seconds. Disconnect EVP sensor. Inspect and repair any damaged wiring. Perform KOEO SELF-TEST. Check for Code 31/327. Ignore all other codes at this time. If Code 31/327 is not displayed, go to step **7)**. If Code 31/327 is displayed, go to next step.

6) Check VREF Circuit Voltage – With EVP harness disconnected, set DVOM on 20-volt scale. With ignition on and engine off, measure voltage at EVP sensor harness connector between VREF circuit and SIG RTN circuit. If reading is 4-6 volts, replace EVP sensor. Repeat QUICK TEST. If reading is NOT 4-6 volts, go to CIRCUIT TEST C, step **1)**.

7) Check EVP Circuit for Short to Power – Turn ignition off and disconnect EVP sensor. Disconnect ECA 60-pin connector. Inspect and repair any damage. Install breakout box, leaving ECA disconnected. Set DVOM on 200-k/ohm scale. Measure resistance between test pin No. 27 and test pins No. 26 and 57. If either reading is less than 10 k/ohms, repair short in harness. Connect EVP sensor and remove breakout box. Repeat QUICK TEST. If both readings are 10 k/ohms or more, replace ECA. Reconnect EVP sensor and remove breakout box. Repeat QUICK TEST.

NOTE: There is a break in the step numbering sequence at this point, skipping from step 7) to step 10). Break is due to previous chart references to these testing procedures. No test procedures have been omitted.

10) Code 84/558: Check EVR Solenoid Resistance – Code 84/558 indicates fault in EVR solenoid circuit. Possible causes for this fault are as follows:

- Faulty EVR Solenoid
- Shorted Or Open Harness

Turn ignition off and wait 10 seconds. Set DVOM on 200-ohm scale. Disconnect EVR solenoid connector and measure solenoid resistance. If reading is not within specification, replace EVR solenoid assembly and repeat QUICK TEST. See EVR SOLENOID RESISTANCE table for specification. If reading is within specification, go to next step.

EVR SOLENOID RESISTANCE

Application	Ohms
4.9L & 5.8L (under 8500 lbs. GVW)	20-45
7.5L	100-135
All Others	30-70

11) Check VPWR Circuit Voltage – Leave EVR solenoid disconnected and set DVOM on 20-volt scale. Turn ignition on, leaving engine off. Measure voltage between negative battery terminal and VPWR circuit at EVR solenoid wiring harness connector. If reading is less than 10.5 volts, repair VPWR open circuit. Reconnect components and repeat QUICK TEST. If reading is 10.5 volts or more, go to next step.

12) Check EVR Circuit Continuity – With ignition off and EVR solenoid disconnected, disconnect ECA 60-pin connector. Inspect and repair any

CIRCUIT TEST DN (Cont.)

damage. Install breakout box, leaving ECA disconnected. Set DVOM on 200-ohm scale. Measure resistance between test pin No. 33 and EVR circuit at EVR solenoid wiring harness connector. If reading is 5 ohms or more, repair open circuit. Reconnect all components and remove breakout box. Repeat QUICK TEST. If reading is less than 5 ohms, go to next step.

13) Check EVR Circuit for Shorts to Power or Ground – With ignition off, breakout box installed and ECA disconnected, disconnect EVR solenoid. Set DVOM on 200-k/ohm scale. Measure resistance between test pin No. 33 and test pins No. 37, 40, 46, 57 and 60 at breakout box. If any reading is less than 10 k/ohms, repair short circuit. Remove breakout box and reconnect all components. Repeat QUICK TEST; if code is repeated, replace EVR solenoid. If readings are 10 k/ohms or more, replace ECA. Remove breakout box and reconnect all components. Repeat QUICK TEST.

NOTE: There is a break in the step numbering sequence at this point, skipping from step 13) to step 20). Break is due to previous chart references to these testing procedures. No test procedures have been omitted.

20) KOEO Code 34/334: Check for Code 84/558 – KOEO Code 34/334 indicates EGR valve and/or EVP is not fully seated in the closed position. EVP voltage signal, in the closed position, is greater than self-test maximum of 0.67 volt. Because of the preload on the EVP sensor, it is difficult to determine if EGR valve is seated, or EVP sensor is in contact with EGR valve. Possible causes for this fault are as follows:
- Poor Continuity At EVP Sensor
- Non-Seated EGR Valve
- Faulty EGR Valve
- Faulty EVP Sensor

Turn ignition off and wait 10 seconds. Check for Code 84/558 in KOEO SELF-TEST. If Code 84/558 is present, go to step **10)** of this circuit test. If Code 84/558 is not displayed, go to next step.

21) Check EVP Sensor and EGR Valve Operation – Turn ignition off and wait 10 seconds. Disconnect EVP sensor. Inspect harness and connector and service as necessary. Remove vacuum line from EGR valve. To test operation of EGR valve, apply and release vacuum to valve using a vacuum pump, or manually depress and release diaphragm. Connect vacuum line to EGR valve. Connect EVP sensor connector. Repeat KOEO SELF-TEST and KOER SELF-TEST. If Code 34/334 is not displayed, the original code was set by a faulty connection or a sticking EGR valve. Testing of EGR valve is complete. If Code 34/334 is displayed, go to next step.

22) Check EVR Solenoid Operation – Turn ignition off and wait 10 seconds. Install vacuum gauge at EGR valve vacuum hose. Start engine and let idle. If vacuum at EGR valve is less than 2.5 in. Hg at normal operating temperature, remove vacuum gauge and go to next step. If vacuum at EGR valve is greater than 2.5 in. Hg, original code 34/334 is caused by a stuck open EVR solenoid. Replace EVR solenoid and rerun QUICK TEST.

23) Substitute EVP Sensor on Original EGR Valve – Turn ignition off and wait 10 seconds. Install a known good EVP sensor on original EGR valve. Perform KOEO SELF-TEST. If Code 34/334 is present, check EGR valve for mechanical fault. If Code 34/334 is not present, service or replace original EVP sensor. Repeat QUICK TEST.

NOTE: There is a break in the step numbering sequence at this point, skipping from step 23) to step 25). Break is due to previous chart references to these testing procedures. No test procedures have been omitted.

25) KOEO and KOER Code 32/238: Checking EVP Sensor and EGR Valve Operation – Code 32/238 indicates EGR valve and/or EVP sensor signal voltage is less than closed position minimum (0.29 volt). Preload on EVP sensor makes it difficult to determine whether EGR valve has malfunctioned, or EVP sensor has abnormally high resistance. Possible causes for this fault are as follows:
- Poor Continuity At EVP Sensor Connector
- Non-Seated Or Faulty EGR Valve
- Faulty EVP Sensor

Turn ignition off and wait 10 seconds. Disconnect EVP sensor. Inspect connector and harness for damage, and service as necessary. Remove vacuum line from EGR valve. To test operation of EGR valve, apply and release vacuum to valve using vacuum pump, or manually depress and release diaphragm. Connect vacuum line to EGR valve, and connect connector to EVP sensor. Repeat KOEO SELF-TEST and KOER SELF-TEST. If Code 32/328 is still present, go to next step. If Code 32/328 is not displayed, the original code is set by a faulty connection or a sticking EGR valve. Testing of EGR valve is complete.

26) Substitute EVP Sensor on Original EGR Valve – Turn ignition off and wait 10 seconds. Install a known good EVP sensor on original EGR valve. Perform KOEO SELF-TEST. If Code 32/328 is present, check EGR valve for mechanical malfunction. If Code 32/328 is not present, replace original EVP sensor. Repeat QUICK TEST.

NOTE: There is a break in the step numbering sequence at this point, skipping from step 26) to step 40). Break is due to previous chart references to these testing procedures. No test procedures have been omitted.

40) KOER Code 33/332: Check Vacuum at EGR – KOER Code 33/332 indicates EVP sensor input did not change after ECA signaled operation of EGR. Because a Code 84 was not received in KOEO SELF-TEST, EVR solenoid electrical function is okay. The lack of Code 32/328 or 34/334 indicates EVP sensor is within closed position specifications. Possible causes for this fault are as follows:
- Leaking Vacuum Hose
- Restricted Vacuum Hose
- Restricted EVR Solenoid Filter
- Faulty EGR Valve

Turn ignition off. Disconnect vacuum line from EGR valve. Connect a vacuum gauge at open end of line. Perform KOER SELF-TEST and observe vacuum gauge. If reading is greater than 1.5 in. Hg, remove vacuum gauge and go to step **43)**. If reading is not greater than 1.5 in. Hg, remove vacuum gauge and reconnect EGR valve vacuum line; go to next step.

41) Verify Vacuum Supply to EVR Solenoid – Turn ignition off. Disconnect vacuum source to EVR solenoid. Install vacuum gauge at source vacuum hose. Start engine and check vacuum. If reading is 10 in. Hg or more, go to next step. If reading is less than 10 in. Hg, check vacuum hose to EVR solenoid for restriction. Replace if necessary. Repeat QUICK TEST.

42) Check Vacuum Hose Between EVR Solenoid and EGR Valve – Check vacuum line for cracks, loose connections, blockage, kinks and leaks. If vacuum hose is faulty, replace hose. Connect new vacuum hose and repeat QUICK TEST. If vacuum hose is okay, check EVR solenoid filter for obstructions. Replace as necessary. If filter is okay, replace EVR solenoid. Connect all vacuum hoses and repeat QUICK TEST.

43) Check EVP Sensor and EGR Valve Operation – Turn ignition off and wait 10 seconds. Disconnect EVP sensor. Inspect connector and harness for damage and service as necessary. Remove vacuum line from EGR valve. Test EGR valve operation by applying vacuum or manually depressing and releasing diaphragm. Connect vacuum line to EGR valve, and connect connector to EVP sensor. Repeat KOEO SELF-TEST and KOER SELF-TEST. If Code 33/332 is still present, go to next step. If Code 33/332 is not displayed, the original code is set either by poor continuity at EVP sensor connector, or sticking EGR valve. Testing of EGR valve is complete.

44) Verify EGR Valve Vacuum Control – With ignition off, disconnect EGR valve vacuum supply. Connect vacuum gauge to EGR valve and apply 2-3 in. Hg for 2 minutes. If EGR holds vacuum, reconnect supply line and go to next step. If EGR valve does not hold vacuum, service or replace EGR valve.

45) Substitute Known Good EVP Sensor on Original EGR Valve – Turn ignition off and wait 10 seconds. Install a known good EVP sensor on original EGR valve. Perform KOER SELF-TEST. If Code 33/332 is present, check EGR valve and/or system for mechanical malfunction. If Code 33/332 is not present, service or replace original EVP sensor. Repeat QUICK TEST.

NOTE: There is a break in the step numbering sequence at this point, skipping from step 45) to step 50). Break is due to previous chart references to these testing procedures. No test procedures have been omitted.

50) Code 34/334: Check EGR Valve Operation in KOER SELF-TEST with EGR Vacuum Disconnected – KOER Code 34/334 indicates EVP voltage is greater than closed position self-test limit (0.67 volt). Possible causes for this fault are as follows:
- Obstructed EVR Solenoid Filter
- Faulty EVR Solenoid
- Faulty EGR Valve
- Faulty EVP Sensor

1991 ENGINE PERFORMANCE
Self-Diagnostics – EEC-IV (Cont.)

CIRCUIT TEST DN (Cont.)

Turn ignition off. Disconnect and plug EGR valve vacuum hose. Perform KOER SELF-TEST. If Code 34/334 is not present, check EVR solenoid filter for obstructions. Replace as necessary. If filter is okay, replace EVR solenoid. Connect all vacuum hoses and repeat QUICK TEST. If Code 34/334 is present, go to next step.

51) Check EVP Sensor Resistance While Applying Vacuum to EGR Valve – Turn ignition off and wait 10 seconds. Disconnect harness from EVP sensor. Disconnect vacuum hose to EGR valve and connect vacuum pump to valve. Measure resistance at EVP sensor between EVP circuit and VREF circuit while gradually increasing vacuum to 10 in. Hg. If reading decreases from 5500 ohms to 100 ohms, check EGR valve for mechanical malfunction and service as necessary. If reading does not change as indicated, replace EVP sensor. Reconnect vacuum hose and rerun QUICK TEST.

NOTE: There is a break in the step numbering sequence at this point, skipping from step 51) to step 90). Break is due to previous chart references to these testing procedures. No test procedures have been omitted.

90) Continuous Memory Code 32/328: Check EVP Signal Voltage While Operating EVP Sensor – Code 32/328 indicates either EGR valve closed further than normal with engine at idle and at normal operating temperature, or EVP sensor has failed with an intermittent low-voltage spike symptom. Possible causes for this fault are as follows:

- Restricted Vacuum Valve
- Faulty EVP Sensor
- EGR Valve

Turn ignition off and wait 10 seconds. Disconnect ECA 60-pin connector. Inspect and repair any damaged wiring. Install breakout box and connect ECA. Disconnect vacuum hose at EGR valve. Connect a vacuum pump to EGR valve. Set DVOM on 20-volt scale. With ignition on and engine off, measure voltage between test pins No. 27 and 46 while slowly applying 6 in. Hg to EGR valve. Slowly bleed vacuum off EGR valve and lightly tap on EVP sensor to simulate road shock. If voltage drops to less than .24 volt, EGR valve may have caused Code 32/328. Clear continuous memory codes. Check EGR valve for mechanical malfunction. If all readings are greater than .24 volt, go to next step.

91) Continuous Memory Code 32/31 (328/327): Check EVP Sensor While in Continuous Monitor Mode – Code 31/327 indicates that sometime during vehicle operation, EVP signal was out of self-test range. Possible causes for this fault are as follow:

- Faulty EVP Sensor
- Open Or Shorted Circuit

With DVOM connected as in previous step, enter KOEO wiggle test. See CONTINUOUS MONITOR MODE (WIGGLE TEST) under QUICK TEST. Connect vacuum pump to EGR valve. Observe DVOM while performing the following procedures. If a fault is indicated, go to next step. If fault is not indicated, go to step **93)**.

- Very slowly, apply 6 in. Hg to EGR valve.
- Slowly bleed off vacuum from EGR valve while tapping on EVP sensor to simulate road shock.
- Wiggle EVP sensor connector.

Checking EVP Harness Circuit 90I12383

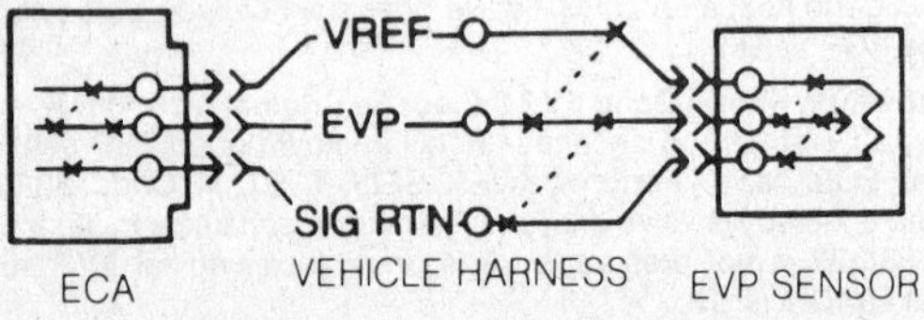
VREF
EVP
SIG RTN
ECA
VEHICLE HARNESS
EVP SENSOR

92) Measure EVP Signal Voltage While Exercising EVP Sensor – Turn ignition off and wait 10 seconds. Disconnect ECA 60-pin connector. Inspect connector and terminals for obvious damage. If connector and terminals are damaged, repair as necessary. Install breakout box and reconnect ECA. Set DVOM on 20-volt scale and connect DVOM between test pins No. 27 and 46. Re-enter KOEO wiggle test. See CONTINUOUS MONITOR MODE (WIGGLE TEST) under QUICK TEST. Observe DVOM while repeating test step **91)**. If fault occurs at less than 4.25 volts, disconnect and inspect connector. If connector is okay, replace EVP sensor. Clear codes and repeat QUICK TEST. If fault does not occur at less than 4.25 volts, go to next step.

93) Continuous Memory Code 31/327 and/or 35/337: Check EEC-IV Harness –Code 31/327 indicates either an open in EVP or VREF

CIRCUIT TEST DN (Cont.)

circuits, or a short to SIG RTN with engine at idle and at normal operating temperature. Code 35/337 indicates a short to VREF and/or VPWR, or an open in SIG RTN with engine at idle and at normal operating temperature.

Enter KOEO wiggle test. See CONTINUOUS MONITOR MODE (WIGGLE TEST) under QUICK TEST. Observe VOM or diagnostic tester for fault indication and grasp harness near sensor; wiggle, shake or bend small section of EEC-IV harness, and work toward dash panel. Wiggle, shake or bend harness from firewall to ECA. If fault is indicated, isolate fault and repair wiring harness as required. Clear codes and repeat QUICK TEST. If fault is not found, go to next step.

EVP Harness Faults 90J12384

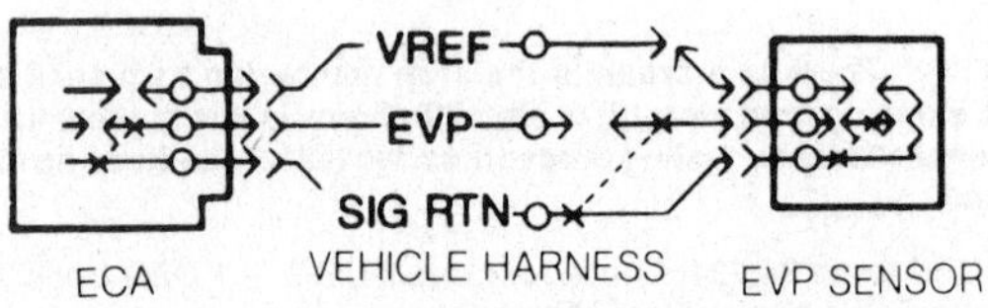
CODE 31
VREF
EVP
SIG RTN
ECA
VEHICLE HARNESS
EVP SENSOR

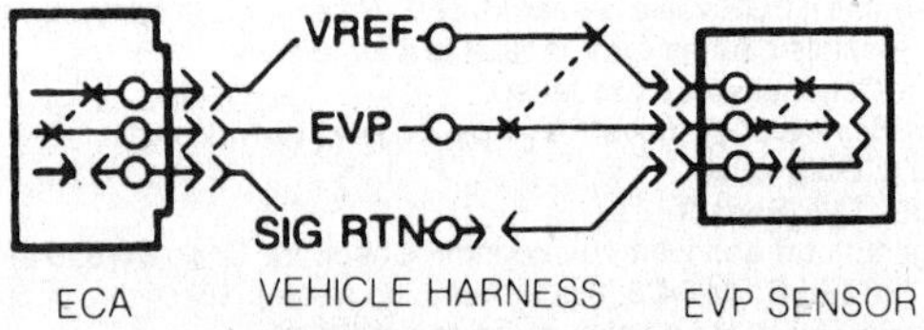
CODE 35
VREF
EVP
SIG RTN
ECA
VEHICLE HARNESS
EVP SENSOR

94) Check ECA and Harness Connectors – Turn ignition off and wait 10 seconds. Disconnect ECA 60-pin connector. Inspect connector and terminals for obvious damage. If connector and terminals are damaged, repair as necessary. Clear codes and repeat QUICK TEST. If connector and terminals are okay, fault cannot be duplicated at this time. Clear codes. Check EGR valve for mechanical fault.

95) Continuous Memory Code 33/332: Leak Test – Code 33/332 indicates EGR valve did not open with engine at normal operating temperature and with EVR solenoid signal present. Possible causes of this fault are as follows:

- Obstructed Or Cracked Vacuum Line
- Open Circuit
- Faulty EGR Valve

Turn ignition off and wait 10 seconds. Disconnect vacuum hose at EGR valve and connect vacuum pump to valve. Apply 20 in. Hg to EGR valve. If EGR valve opens and holds vacuum, remove vacuum pump and reconnect EGR valve; go to next step. If EGR valve does not function as described, remove pump and reconnect EGR valve. Clear codes and service or replace EGR valve as necessary.

96) EVR Solenoid Check – Using Continuous Monitor Mode (Wiggle Test), observe VOM or diagnostic tester for fault indication. Grasp harness close to EVR solenoid connector and wiggle, shake or bend a small section of harness, and work toward ECA. Inspect connectors and terminals for obvious damage. If fault is indicated, isolate fault and repair as necessary. Clear codes and repeat QUICK TEST. If fault is not indicated, fault cannot be duplicated at this time. Clear codes and repeat QUICK TEST.

NOTE: There is a break in the step numbering sequence at this point, skipping from step 96) to step 98). Break is due to previous chart references to these testing procedures. No test procedures have been omitted.

98) Continuous Memory Code 34/334: Check EVP Resistance While Applying Vacuum to EGR Valve – Code 34/334 indicates EGR valve was open with engine idling at normal operating temperature. Possible causes for this fault are as follows:

- Faulty EVR Filter
- Faulty EVR Solenoid
- Faulty EGR Valve

Turn ignition off and disconnect EVP sensor. Inspect connector for obvious damage. Place DVOM on 200-k/ohm scale. Disconnect vacuum hose to EGR valve and connect vacuum pump to valve. Measure resis-

CIRCUIT TEST DN (Cont.)

tance at EVP sensor between EVP circuit and VREF circuit at sensor while increasing vacuum to 10 in. Hg. If reading does not decrease gradually from maximum of 5500 ohms to minimum 100 ohms, remove vacuum pump and reconnect all components. Clear codes and check EGR valve for mechanical malfunction. If reading gradually decreases from maximum of 5500 ohms to minimum of 100 ohms, remove vacuum pump and reconnect all components. Go to next step.

99) EVR Check – Turn ignition off. Disconnect vacuum hose from EGR valve and plug hose. Perform KOER SELF-TEST. If Code 34/334 is present, check EVR filter for obstructions. Replace as necessary. If filter is okay, replace EVR solenoid. Connect all vacuum hoses and repeat QUICK TEST. If Code 34/334 is not present, fault cannot be duplicated at this time. Clear codes and repeat QUICK TEST. Testing is complete.

CIRCUIT TEST DP

VEHICLE SPEED SENSOR (VSS)

Diagnostic Aids – Perform this test when directed by QUICK TEST.

This CIRCUIT TEST is intended to diagnose the following.

- VSS Harness Circuits
- Vehicle Speed Sensor (VSS)
- ECA

Vehicle Speed Sensor Circuit 91J14257

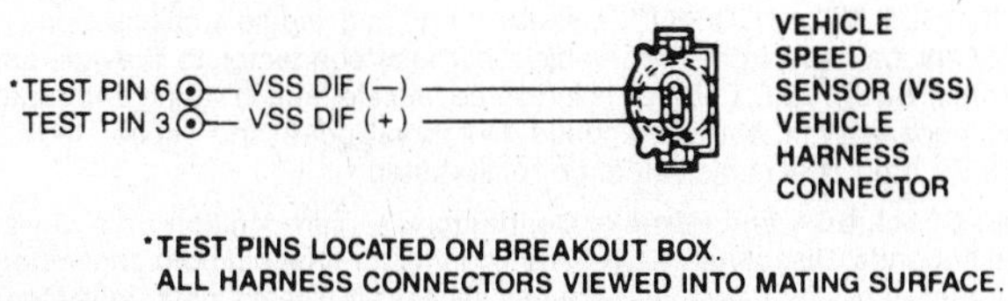

*TEST PIN 6
VSS DIF (–)
TEST PIN 3
VSS DIF (+)
VEHICLE SPEED SENSOR (VSS) VEHICLE HARNESS CONNECTOR
*TEST PINS LOCATED ON BREAKOUT BOX.
ALL HARNESS CONNECTORS VIEWED INTO MATING SURFACE.

TEST PIN 3 (VSS +) WIRE COLOR IDENTIFICATION

Application	Wire Color
Bronco, Explorer, Ranger 3.0L Aerostar, & "F" Series	Gray/Black
All Others	Dark Green/White

TEST PIN 6 (VSS –) WIRE COLOR IDENTIFICATION

Application	Wire Color
"E" Series	Orange/Yellow
All Others	Pink/Orange

Preliminary Instructions (A/T Vehicles) – Record and clear Continuous Memory Codes. Warm engine to normal operating temperature. In Low gear, accelerate hard to 25 MPH and coast down to a stop. Shut off engine. Perform KOEO SELF-TEST. Go to step **1)**.

Preliminary Instructions (M/T Vehicles) – Record and clear Continuous Memory Codes. Warm engine to normal operating temperature. Start in first gear, shift to second gear and accelerate moderately to 40 MPH. Coast down to idle and stop. Shut engine off. Perform KOEO SELF-TEST, and record Continuous Memory Codes. Go to step **1)**.

1) Continuous Memory Code 29/452 – Code 29/452 indicates there is insufficient input to ECA from VSS. Possible causes for this code are as follows.

- Faulty VSS
- Open Or Shorted Circuit
- Faulty ECA

On all vehicles except 3.0L PFI Aerostar, perform appropriate drive cycle procedure. See PRELIMINARY INSTRUCTIONS (A/T VEHICLES) or PRELIMINARY INSTRUCTIONS (M/T VEHICLES). On 3.0L PFI Aerostar, ensure driveability complaint can be verified. If Code 29/452 is still present or driveability complaint can be verified (3.0L PFI Aerostar), go to next step. If code is not present or complaint cannot be verified, fault cannot be duplicated at this time. Clear codes, and see INTERMITTENTS in TROUBLE SHOOTING – NO CODES article.

2) Check VSS Circuit Continuity – Turn ignition off and wait 10 seconds. Remove ECA 60-pin connector and inspect for damaged pins, corrosion, or loose wires. Repair as necessary. Install breakout box. With ECA and VSS disconnected, set DVOM on 200-ohm scale. Measure

CIRCUIT TEST DP (Cont.)

resistance between test pin No. 3 at breakout box and VSS DIF (+) circuit at VSS vehicle harness connector. Also measure resistance between test pin No. 6 at breakout box and VSS DIF (–) circuit vehicle harness connector. If both readings are 5 ohms or less, go to next step. If readings are 5 ohms or more, service open circuit in VSS wiring harness. After repairs, reconnect all components and repeat step **1)**.

Checking VSS Circuits 90H12408

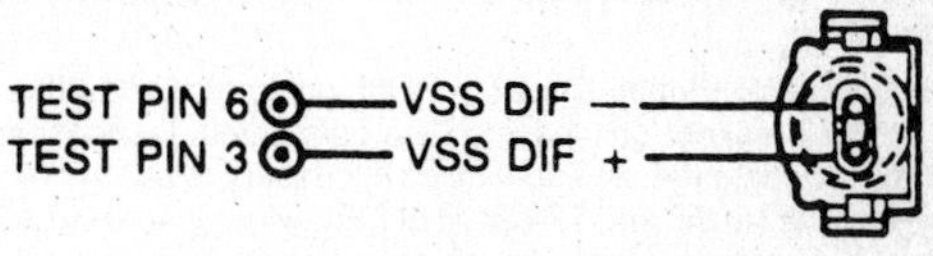

TEST PIN 6
VSS DIF –
TEST PIN 3
VSS DIF +

3) Check VSS Circuits for Shorts to Power or Ground – Turn ignition off. With ECA and VSS disconnected, install breakout box. Set DVOM on 200-k/ohm scale. Measure resistance between test pin No. 3 and test pins No. 37, 40 and 6. If all readings are greater than 500 ohms, remove breakout box and reconnect components; go to step **4)**. If any reading is less than 500 ohms, repair short(s) in VSS wiring harness and reconnect components. After repairs, repeat step **1)**.

4) Checking VSS Resistance – Turn ignition off and wait 10 seconds. Disconnect VSS. Set DVOM on 2-k/ohm scale. Measure resistance across vehicle speed sensor. If reading is 190-250 ohms, replace ECA. Remove breakout box, reconnect components and repeat step **1)**. If reading is NOT 190-250 ohms, replace vehicle speed sensor and repeat appropriate drive cycle procedure.

CIRCUIT TEST DQ

FUEL INJECTION PUMP LEVER (FIPL)

FIPL Connector & Circuits 91G14254

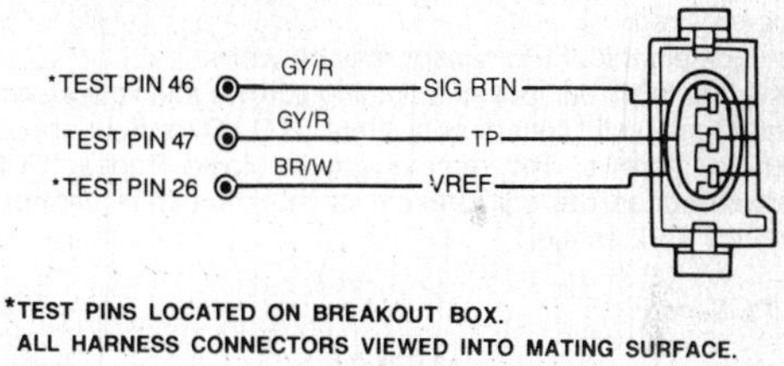

*TEST PIN 46
GY/R
SIG RTN
TEST PIN 47
GY/R
TP
*TEST PIN 26
BR/W
VREF
*TEST PINS LOCATED ON BREAKOUT BOX.
ALL HARNESS CONNECTORS VIEWED INTO MATING SURFACE.

Diagnostic Aids – Enter this CIRCUIT TEST only when instructed during QUICK TEST. If you were directed here from KOEO Code 23 but an engine ID code of 5.0 was not received, go to CIRCUIT TEST DJ.

1) Service Code 23: Throttle Linkage Check – Inspect throttle linkage for binding, sticking or interference. If throttle linkage does not operate smoothly, service as necessary and repeat QUICK TEST. If throttle does operate smoothly, go to next step.

2) Service Code 53: Attempt to Generate Code 63 – With ignition off, and FIPL disconnected, inspect and repair any corroded or damaged pins. Perform KOEO self test. If Code 63 is present, go to next step. If code 63 is not present, go to step **4)**.

3) VREF Circuit Voltage Check – With ignition off and FIPL disconnected, measure voltage at SIG RTN and VREF circuit at connector. If voltage is not 4.0-6.0 volts, connect all components and go to CIRCUIT TEST C, step **1)**. If voltage is 4.0-6.0 volts, connect all components and go to step **14)**.

4) Check for Shorts to Power – With ignition off and FIPL disconnected, install breakout box leaving ECA disconnected. Set DVOM on 200-k/ohm scale. Measure resistance between test pin No. 47 and test pins No. 26 and 57. If resistance is 10,000 ohms or more, replace ECA; remove breakout box and reconnect components. Repeat QUICK TEST. If resistance is less than 10,000 ohms, repair short circuit; remove breakout box and reconnect all components. Repeat QUICK TEST.

NOTE: There is a break in the step numbering sequence at this point, skipping from step 4) to step 10). Break is due to previous chart references to these testing procedures. No test procedures have been omitted.

10) Service Code 63: Attempt to Generate Code 53/23 – With ignition off, disconnect FIPL wiring harness connector. Inspect connector and harness for damage, and service as necessary. Connect jumper wire

1991 ENGINE PERFORMANCE
Self-Diagnostics – EEC-IV (Cont.)

CIRCUIT TEST DQ (Cont.)

between VREF and TP circuit at FIPL wiring harness connector. Perform KOEO SELF TEST. If no codes are present, go to step **13)**. If Codes 23 or 53 are present, remove jumper wire and go to step **14)**. If Codes 23 or 53 are not present, go to next step.

11) VREF Circuit Voltage Check – With ignition off and FIPL disconnected, measure voltage at SIG RTN and VREF circuit at connector. If voltage is not 4.0-6.0 volts, connect all components and go to CIRCUIT TEST C, step **1)**. If voltage is 4.0-6.0 volts, connect all components and go to step **12)**.

12) FIPL Circuit Continuity Check – With ignition off and FIPL disconnected, install breakout box leaving ECA connected. Inspect connector and harness for damage, and service as necessary. Measure resistance between test pin No. 47 and TP circuit at FIPL wiring harness connector. If resistance is 5 ohms or more, repair open circuit; remove breakout box and reconnect components. Repeat QUICK TEST. If resistance is less than 5 ohms, go to next step.

13) Check for Shorts to Ground – With ignition off and FIPL disconnected, install breakout box leaving ECA disconnected. Inspect connector and harness for damage, and service as necessary. Set DVOM on 200-k/ohm scale. Measure resistance between test pin No. 47 and test pins No. 40, 46 and 60 at breakout box. If resistance is 10,000 ohms or more, replace ECA; remove breakout box and reconnect components. Repeat QUICK TEST. If resistance is less than 10,000 ohms, repair short circuit; remove breakout box and reconnect all components. Repeat QUICK TEST.

NOTE: Super Star II Scan tool is required for FIPL adjustment.

14) FIPL Sensor Adjustment – Perform KOEO SELF-TEST while holding throttle fully open. After last service code has been received, remain in self-test. Place 0.515" gauge between FIPL travel screw and gauge boss. Cycle Overdrive Cancel Switch. Observe Super Star II tester for one of the following modes:

- Constant tone, solid light or consistent STO LO readout indicates FIPL sensor is within range. Cycle Overdrive Cancel Switch to exit test.
- Beeping tone, flashing light or erratic STO readout indicates adjustment is required.
- If tone is undetectable, FIPL sensor may be worn.
- If adjustment is required, loosen adjusting screws and rotate sensor until a constant tone, solid light or consistent STO LO readout appears. Tighten adjusting screws, and remove gauge block. Repeat QUICK TEST. If service codes are still present or constant tone cannot be obtained, replace FIPL sensor.

Adjusting FIPL Sensor 91H14255

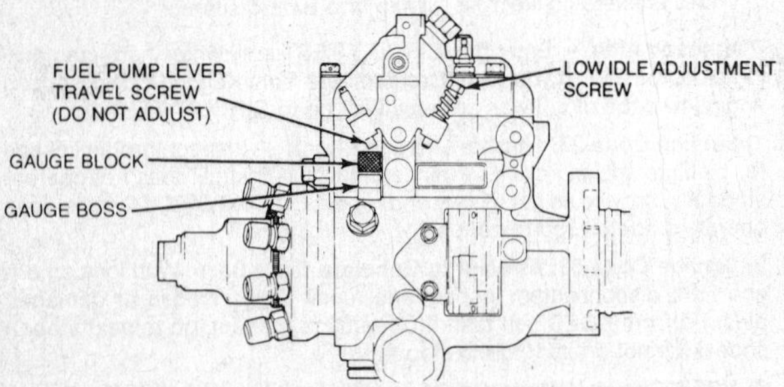
FUEL PUMP LEVER
TRAVEL SCREW
(DO NOT ADJUST)
LOW IDLE ADJUSTMENT
SCREW
GAUGE BLOCK
GAUGE BOSS

NOTE: There is a break in the step numbering sequence at this point, skipping from step 14) to step 90). Break is due to previous chart references to these testing procedures. No test procedures have been omitted.

90) Continuous Memory Code 53: Monitor FIPL Circuit Under Simulated Road Conditions – Enter KOEO wiggle test. See CONTINUOUS MONITOR MODE (WIGGLE TEST) under QUICK TEST. Observe DVOM or diagnostic tester for indication of fault while slowly opening throttle to WOT. Slowly bring throttle to closed position, and lightly tap FIPL and wiggle harness connector. This test checks for open or short in FIPL, connectors and wiring harness. If no fault is indicated, go to step **92)**. If fault is indicated, go to next step.

91) Measure TP Circuit Voltage While Exercising FIPL – Turn ignition off and wait 10 seconds. Disconnect ECA 60-pin connector. Install breakout box, leaving ECA connected. Stay in KOEO wiggle test (as in previous step). Connect DVOM between test pins No. 47 and 46. Set

CIRCUIT TEST DQ (Cont.)

DVOM on 20-volt scale. With ignition on and engine off, observe DVOM and repeat step **90)**. If fault occurs at less than 4.25 volts, inspect FIPL connectors and terminals. If connectors and terminals are okay, go to step **14)**. If fault does not occur at less than 4.25 volts, go to next step to check harness.

92) Check EEC-IV Vehicle Harness – While in KOEO wiggle test, shake, bend and wiggle small sections of EEC-IV harness from FIPL vehicle harness connector to firewall, and from firewall to ECA. If fault is indicated, isolate fault in wiring and repair as necessary. Clear codes and repeat QUICK TEST. If no fault is indicated, go to next step.

93) Check ECA & Harness Connectors – Turn ignition off and wait 10 seconds. Disconnect ECA 60-pin connector. Inspect both connectors and terminals for damage. Repair as necessary. Clear Continuous Memory Codes and repeat QUICK TEST. If connectors and terminals are okay, fault cannot be duplicated at this time. Testing is complete.

94) Continuous Memory Code 63: Monitor TP Circuit Under Simulated Road Conditions – Enter KOEO wiggle test. See CONTINUOUS MONITOR MODE (WIGGLE TEST) under QUICK TEST. Check VOM or diagnostic tester for fault while performing the following:

- Slowly open throttle to WOT.
- Slowly bring throttle to closed position.
- Lightly tap FIPL and wiggle connector.

This test checks for open or short in FIPL, connectors and vehicle harness. If fault is indicated, disconnect FIPL. Inspect connectors and terminals. If connectors and terminals are okay, go to step **14)**. If no fault is indicated, go to next step.

95) Check EEC-IV Vehicle Harness – While in KOEO wiggle test (CONTINUOUS MONITOR MODE), shake, bend and wiggle small sections of EEC-IV harness from FIPL vehicle harness connector to firewall, and from firewall to ECA. If fault is indicated, isolate fault in wiring and repair as necessary. Clear Continuous Memory Codes and repeat QUICK TEST. If no fault is indicated, go to next step.

96) Check ECA and Harness Connectors – Turn ignition off and wait 10 seconds. Disconnect ECA 60-pin connector. Inspect both connectors and terminals for damage. Repair as necessary. Clear Continuous Memory Codes and repeat QUICK TEST. If connectors and terminals are okay, fault cannot be duplicated at this time. Continuous Memory Code 63/122 testing is complete.

CIRCUIT TEST FD

BRAKE ON-OFF SWITCH (BOO)

Diagnostic Aids – Perform this test when directed by QUICK TEST.

To prevent replacement of good components, be aware that the following non-EEC related areas may be at fault: brakelight bulb, brakelight switch or brakelight fuse. This test is intended to diagnose a faulty BOO circuit or ECA.

BOO Circuit 91H06939

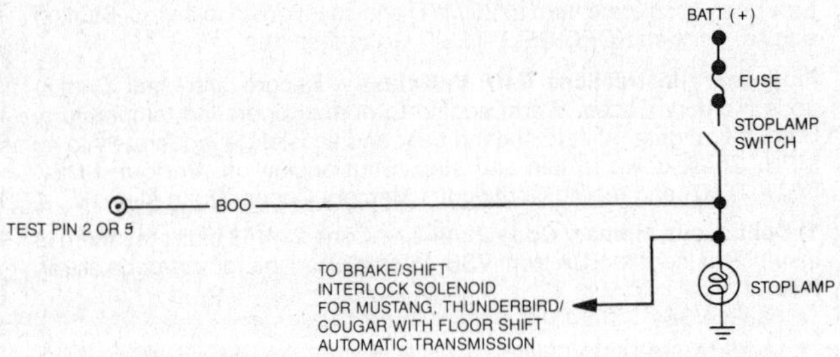
BATT (+)
FUSE
STOPLAMP
SWITCH
BOO
TEST PIN 2 OR 5
TO BRAKE/SHIFT
INTERLOCK SOLENOID
FOR MUSTANG, THUNDERBIRD/
COUGAR WITH FLOOR SHIFT
AUTOMATIC TRANSMISSION
STOPLAMP

* TEST PINS LOCATED ON BREAKOUT BOX.
ALL HARNESS CONNECTORS VIEWED INTO MATING SURFACES.

TEST PIN 2 (BOO) WIRE COLOR IDENTIFICATION

Application	Wire Color
All Models	Light Green

TEST PIN IDENTIFICATION

Application	Test Pin No.
All Models	2

CIRCUIT TEST FD (Cont.)

1) Code 74/536: Verify Brake Pedal Was Depressed – Code 74/536 indicates that when brake pedal is depressed during KOER SELF-TEST, BOO signal did not cycle high and low. Possible causes for this fault are as follows:

- Brake pedal not depressed during entire self-test
- Open brakelight circuit (BATT + side of BOO splice)
- Short to ground or power
- Faulty ECA

If brake was NOT depressed during KOER SELF-TEST, repeat test; depress and release brake pedal ONLY once during test. Depress and release brake pedal AFTER dynamic response code, but BEFORE brief WOT. If pedal was depressed, go to next step.

2) Check Operation of Brakelights – With ignition on, check operation of brakelights. If brakelights operate normally, go to next step. If brakelights do not operate, go to step **4)**. If brakelights are always on, go to step**5)**.

3) Check for BOO Circuit Cycling – Turn ignition off and wait 10 seconds. Disconnect ECA 60-pin connector. Inspect connector for damaged pins, corrosion, and loose wires. Install breakout box, leaving ECA disconnected. Set DVOM on 20-volt scale. Measure voltage between test pins No. 2 or 5 and 40 while applying and releasing brake. If voltage cycles, switch circuit is okay; replace ECA and repeat QUICK TEST. If voltage does not cycle, repair open circuit in BOO circuit between ECA and BOO connection to brakelight circuit.

4) Check for Power to Brake Switch – Ensure related fuses and brakelight bulbs are in good condition. Turn ignition off and wait 10 seconds. Disconnect brakelight switch (located on brake pedal). Set DVOM on 20-volt scale. Measure voltage between BATT (+) input to brakelight switch and chassis ground. If voltage is greater than 10 volts, verify operation of brakelight switch; if brakelight switch is okay, repair open circuit between brakelight switch and brakelight ground. Reconnect components and rerun QUICK TEST. If voltage is less than 10 volts, repair open BATT (+) circuit to brakelight switch. Reconnect all components and rerun QUICK TEST.

5) Verify Brake Switch Is Not Always Closed – With ignition off, disconnect brakelight switch (located on brake pedal). Turn ignition on, leaving engine off. If brakelights are still on, go to next step. If brakelights are not on, verify proper installation of brakelight switch. If installation is okay, replace brakelight switch. Reconnect all components and rerun QUICK TEST.

6) Check for Short to Power in ECA – Turn ignition off. Reconnect BOO circuit harness connector. Disconnect ECA. With ignition on and engine off, check if brakelights are on. If brakelights are on, repair short to power between ECA and harness connector; repeat QUICK TEST. If brakelights are not on, replace ECA and repeat QUICK TEST.

NOTE: There is a break in the step numbering sequence at this point, skipping from step 6) to step 10). Break is due to previous chart references to these testing procedures. No test procedures have been omitted.

10) Code 75/531: Check for Operation of Brakelights – Code 75/531 indicates that while brake pedal was released during KOER SELF-TEST, BOO signal was high. Possible causes for this fault are as follows:

- Brake pedal depressed during entire self-test.
- Open BOO/Brakelight Circuit (Between ECA And Brakelight Ground)
- Short To POWER
- Faulty ECA

Turn ignition on. Check brakelight operation. If brakelights operate normally, go to next step. If brakelights are always on, go to step **5)**. If brakelights are never on, inspect brakelight bulbs. If bulb is okay, repair open circuit between BOO connection to brakelight circuit and brakelight ground.

11) Check Continuity of BOO Circuit – Turn ignition off. Install breakout box, leaving ECA disconnected. Disconnect brakelight switch (located on brake pedal). Measure resistance between test pin No. 2 at breakout box and brakelight switch connector terminal. If resistance is less than 5 ohms, replace ECA; remover breakout box, reconnect all components and rerun QUICK TEST. If resistance is 5 ohms or more, repair open circuit. Remove breakout box, reconnect all components and repeat QUICK TEST.

NOTE: There is a break in the step numbering sequence at this point, skipping from step 11) to step 90). Break is due to previous chart references to these testing procedures. No test procedures have been omitted.

CIRCUIT TEST FD (Cont.)

90) Continuous Memory Code 536: Brakelight Switch Installation Check – Code 536 indicates a BOO circuit failure. If BOO input does not cycle after a predetermined number of transitions from zero MPH to a specific speed, BOO input is assumed to be damaged and code 536 is set. Possible causes for this code are as follows:

- Brakelight Switch Improperly Installed
- Open Brakelight/BOO Circuit
- Damaged Brakelight Switch
- Damaged Brakelight Ground Connection

Inspect brakelight switch for proper installation (alignment with pedal), corrosion or damaged wiring. Repair any problems and rerun QUICK TEST. If all components are in good condition, go to next step.

91) Check Brakelight for Ground – Check brakelight ground connection for corrosion or other damage. Check brakelight connector and wires for corrosion or other damage. If brakelight wires, connector and connection are okay, go to next step. If wires, connector and connection are not okay, repair as necessary; clear codes and rerun QUICK TEST.

92) Check Brakelight/BOO Circuits for Short to Power – Do not depress brake pedal during this test. Turn ignition on, leaving engine off. While watching brakelights, wiggle brakelight/BOO circuit wires and connectors. If brakelights do not flash, go to next step. If brakelights flash, isolate and repair short to power as necessary. Clear codes and rerun QUICK TEST.

93) Check Brakelight Circuit Continuity – With ignition off; depress and hold brake pedal. Wiggle brakelight circuit wires and connectors while observing brakelights. Tap brakelight switch to simulate road shock while observing brakelights. If brakelights are on constantly and do not blink or go off, go to next step. If brakelights blink or go off, isolate and repair open in brakelight circuit. Clear codes and rerun QUICK TEST.

94) Check Continuity of BOO Circuit – Turn ignition off. Release brake pedal. Disconnect ECA 60-pin connector. Inspect connector for damaged pins, corrosion and loose wires. Install breakout box, leaving ECA disconnected. Set DVOM on 200-ohm scale. Measure resistance between test pin No. 2 or No. 5 at breakout box and brakelight circuit at brakelight switch connector. While observing DVOM, wiggle BOO circuit wires and connectors. If resistance is ever greater than 5 ohms, isolate and repair open circuit in BOO circuit; remove breakout box, clear codes rerun QUICK TEST. If resistance is always less than 5 ohms, fault cannot be duplicated at this time. Clear codes and see INTERMITTENTS in TROUBLE SHOOTING – NO CODES article.

CIRCUIT TEST FF

POWER STEERING PRESSURE SWITCH (PSPS)

Diagnostic Aids – Perform this test when instructed during QUICK TEST, or when directed by other test procedures. Some vehicles may not have power steering, but ECA may be equipped with PSPS software strategy. If a KOEO Code 52/519 is displayed, check if vehicle is equipped with power steering. If vehicle is not equipped with power steering, disregard Code 52/519.

This test is intended to diagnose only the following:

- Power Steering Pressure Switch (PSPS)
- Harness Circuits (PSPS And SIG RTN)
- ECA

Power Steering Pressure Switch (PSPS) Circuit 91I14256

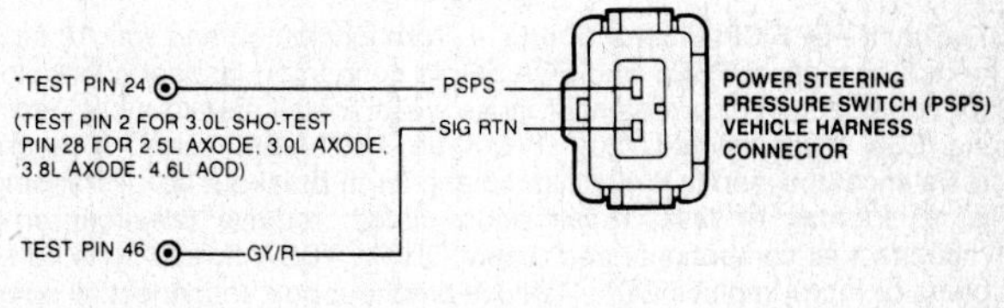
*TEST PIN 24
PSPS
(TEST PIN 2 FOR 3.0L SHO-TEST PIN 28 FOR 2.5L AXODE, 3.0L AXODE, 3.8L AXODE, 4.6L AOD)
SIG RTN
TEST PIN 46
GY/R
POWER STEERING PRESSURE SWITCH (PSPS) VEHICLE HARNESS CONNECTOR

*TEST PINS LOCATED ON BREAKOUT BOX.
ALL HARNESS CONNECTORS VIEWED INTO MATING SURFACE.

1991 ENGINE PERFORMANCE
Self-Diagnostics – EEC-IV (Cont.)

CIRCUIT TEST FF (Cont.)

TEST PIN NUMBER IDENTIFICATION

Application	Test Pin No.
All Models	24

TEST PIN 24 (PSPS) WIRE COLOR IDENTIFICATION

Application	Wire Color
All Models	Yellow/Light Green

TEST PIN 46 (SIG RTN) WIRE COLOR IDENTIFICATION

Application	Wire Color
All Models	Gray/Red

Diagnostic Aids – To prevent replacement of good components, be aware that the following non-EEC related areas may be at fault: idle speed/throttle stop adjustment, binding throttle shaft/linkage or cruise control linkage.

1) Code 52/519 Displayed, Attempt to Eliminate Code – Code 52/519 indicates PSPS circuit is open. Turn ignition off and wait 10 seconds. Disconnect PSPS. Install jumper wire between PSPS circuit and SIG RTN at vehicle harness connector. Repeat KOEO SELF-TEST. If Code 52/519 is not displayed, replace PSPS and repeat QUICK TEST. If Code 52/519 is still displayed, go to next step.

2) Check Continuity of PSPS Circuits – Turn ignition off and wait 10 seconds. Disconnect PSPS and ECA 60-pin connector. Inspect and repair any damaged wiring. Install breakout box, leaving ECA disconnected. Set DVOM on 200-ohm scale, and measure resistance between test pin No. 46 and SIG RTN circuit at PSPS vehicle harness connector. Also measure resistance between test pin No. 24 and PSPS circuit at PSPS vehicle harness connector. If both readings are less than 5 ohms, replace ECA; remove breakout box, reconnect all components and repeat QUICK TEST. If readings are 5 ohms or more, repair open in circuit. Remove breakout box, reconnect all components and repeat QUICK TEST.

3) Check PSPS Operation – Connect tachometer and start engine. Allow engine to idle in Park or Neutral. Disconnect PSPS at switch. If RPM increases, replace PSPS and recheck system. If RPM does not increase, go to next step.

4) Check PSPS Circuits for Shorts – Turn ignition off and wait 10 seconds. Disconnect PSPS and ECA 60-pin connector. Inspect and repair any damaged wiring. Install breakout box, leaving ECA disconnected. Set DVOM on 200-k/ohm scale. Measure resistance between test pin No. 24 and test pin No. 46 at breakout box. If resistance is 10 k/ohms or less, repair short in harness; remove breakout box, reconnect all components and recheck symptom. If reading is 10 k/ohms or more, replace ECA. Repeat QUICK TEST.

5) KOER SELF-TEST Code 52/521 Displayed – Disregard this code if vehicle does not have power steering. Code 52/521 indicates PSPS did not change states due to open or closed switch. If steering wheel was turned 1/2 turn within 1-2 seconds AFTER engine ID code, and front wheels were centered in a no-load condition, go to next step. If steering wheel was not turned, repeat QUICK TEST.

6) Checking ECA Open Circuit Identifying Capabilities – Turn ignition off and wait 10 seconds. Disconnect PSPS. Perform KOEO SELF-TEST. If Code 52/519 is present, go to step **8)**. If Code 52/519 is not present, go to next step.

7) Check PSPS Circuits for Shorts – Turn ignition off and wait 10 seconds. Disconnect PSPS and ECA 60-pin connector. Inspect connector for damaged pins, corrosion, or loose wires. Install breakout box, leaving ECA disconnected. Set DVOM on 200-k/ohm scale. Measure resistance between test pins No. 46 and 24 at breakout box. If reading is 10 k/ohms or less, repair short circuit; remove breakout box, reconnect all components and repeat QUICK TEST. If reading is 10 k/ohms or more, replace ECA. Remove breakout box, reconnect all components and repeat QUICK TEST.

8) Check PSPS Position Comparison – Turn ignition off and wait 10 seconds. Install breakout box, leaving ECA connected. With PSPS connected, set DVOM on 200-ohm scale. Turn ignition on and measure resistance between test pin No. 24 and test pin No. 46. Start engine. If reading remains less than 10 ohms between Key On Engine Off (KOEO)

CIRCUIT TEST FF (Cont.)

and Key On Engine Running (KOER), go to next step. If reading is not as described, go to step **11)**.

9) Check PSPS State with KOER: Load and No Load – Install breakout box and connect ECA. Connect PSPS and set DVOM on 200-ohm scale. Start engine and allow to idle. Measure resistance between test pin No. 24 and test pin No. 46 at breakout box. Turn steering wheel 1/2 turn and return to center position. If resistance changes from less than 10 ohms to infinity (indicating PSPS opening) and then returns to 10 ohms or less (when steering wheel is centered), PSPS system is okay. Remove breakout box and return to QUICK TEST. If reading does not change as indicated, go to next step.

10) Check for PSPS Always Closed Compared to Hydraulic Pressure with Engine Running – At this point, there are only 2 possible causes for original KOER Code 52/521: a PSPS switch that will not open, or low available hydraulic pressure. Turn ignition off and wait 10 seconds. Substitute original switch with a known good PSPS switch. Perform KOER SELF-TEST and turn steering wheel at least 1/2 turn after engine ID code. If Code 52/521 is still present, check power steering system for low hydraulic pressure. If Code 52/521 is not present, replace original PSPS switch. Service other codes as necessary.

11) Check For PSPS Always Open Compared to Hydraulic Pressure with Engine Running – At this point, there are only 2 possible causes for original KOER Code 52/521: a PSPS switch that is always open, or excessively high hydraulic pressure. Turn ignition off and wait 10 seconds. Substitute original PSPS with a known good PSPS. Perform KOER SELF-TEST and turn steering wheel at least 1/2 turn after engine ID code. If Code 52/521 is still present, check power steering system for excessive high hydraulic pressure. If Code 52/521 is not present, replace original PSPS switch. Service other codes as necessary.

CIRCUIT TEST G

IN-RANGE MAF/TPS FUEL INJECTOR PULSE WITH TEST

Diagnostic Aids – Perform this test when instructed during QUICK TEST, or when directed by other test procedures.

This test is intended to diagnose only the following:

- MAP/BP Sensor
- Throttle Position Sensor (TPS)
- Mass Airflow (MAF) Sensor
- Air Charge Temperature (ACT) Sensor
- Fuel Injectors

To prevent replacement of good components, be aware that the following non-EEC related areas may be at fault: excessive blow-by, PCV malfunction, vacuum leak, fuel pressure or throttle linkage sticking or binding.

1) Throttle Position Sensor Integrity – Turn ignition off. Disconnect ECA 60-pin connector. Inspect connector for damaged pins, corrosion, or loose wires. Install breakout box and connect ECA. Set DVOM on 20-volt scale. Connect DVOM to test pins No. 47 and 46. Operate throttle slowly to WOT, and slowly release to closed position. See CIRCUIT TEST DH for schematics and specific engine values. If there are any sudden voltage variations, ensure TPS is properly installed on throttle body. If TPS is properly installed, replace TPS; remove breakout box, reconnect all components and rerun QUICK TEST. If there are no sudden voltage variations, go to next step.

2) Check Throttle Body – Check throttle and/or speed control linkage for binding and smooth operation. Inspect throttle body for contamination. Check engine vacuum hoses. Refer to VECI decal for proper vacuum hose routing. Check for air leak between ISC solenoid and MAF sensor. If all checks reveal no problems, go to next step. If problems are found, repair as necessary; remove breakout box, reconnect all components and rerun QUICK TEST.

3) Check MAP/BP Sensor Output – Refer to CIRCUIT TEST DF for schematic. With MAP/BP tester connected and ignition on, measure sensor output voltage. If voltage output is within range at specific altitude, remove MAP/BP tester and go to next step. See MAP SENSOR VOLTAGE OUTPUT table for specification. If output reading is outside range, replace MAP/BP sensor; remove tester, reconnect all components and rerun QUICK TEST.

Diagnostic Aids – If possible, measure several known good MAP/BP sensors on available vehicles. Average voltage reading will be typical for your location on date of testing.

1991 ENGINE PERFORMANCE
Self-Diagnostics – EEC-IV (Cont.)

CIRCUIT TEST G (Cont.)

MAP SENSOR VOLTAGE OUTPUT

Elevation (Feet)	Volts
0	1.59
1000	1.56
2000	1.53
3000	1.50
4000	1.47
5000	1.44
6000	1.41
7000	1.39

4) Check ACT Sensor – Ensure ambient temperature is greater than 50°F before performing this test. Check and repair any air leaks in front of ACT sensor. Turn ignition off. Install breakout box and connect ECA to breakout box. Set DVOM to 20-volt scale. See CIRCUIT TEST DF for schematic. Connect DVOM to test pins No. 25 and 46. Start engine and let idle. Observe voltage as engine warms up. If voltage does not decrease smoothly and stabilize after engine reaches operating conditions, replace ACT sensor; remove breakout box and rerun QUICK TEST. If voltage decreases smoothly and stabilizes when engine reaches operating conditions, system is operating properly at this time. Reconnect all components and rerun QUICK TEST.

5) Visual Inspection of MAF Sensor – Turn ignition off. Check for air leaks between ISC solenoid and MAF sensor. Inspect MAF sensor for oil contamination caused by excessive blow-by or malfunctioning PCV. If problems are found, repair as necessary; clear codes and rerun QUICK TEST. If all checks are okay, go to step **8)**.

6) Check MAF Sensor – Turn ignition off. Disconnect ECA 60-pin connector. Inspect connector for damaged pins, corrosion, or loose wires. Install breakout box and connect ECA. Set DVOM on 20-volt scale. Start engine and allow to idle until engine reaches normal operating temperature. Measure voltage between MAF signal and test pin 40/60 of breakout box.

If voltage is within acceptable range, system is operating normally at this time. See INTERMITTENTS in TROUBLE SHOOTING – NO CODES article. If voltage is not within acceptable range, replace MAF sensor. See MAF SENSOR DATA table for specification. Reconnect all components and rerun QUICK TEST.

MAF SENSOR DATA

Engine Condition	[1] Voltage
Idle	.8
20 MPH	1.0
40 MPH	1.7
60 MPH	2.1

[1] – Engine at normal operating temperature.

7) Visual Vacuum Checks – Inspect air cleaner and air inlet duct; replace or repair as necessary. Check for unmetered air between MAF sensor and ISC bypass solenoid. Check all engine vacuum hoses for damage, leaks, blockage and proper routing. Make necessary repairs and rerun QUICK TEST. If all items are okay, go to next step.

8) Check Fuel Pressure – Turn ignition off. Install fuel pressure gauge. Ensure fuel pressure regulator is connected to manifold vacuum (if applicable). Start engine and run at idle. If fuel pressure is within specifications, go to next step. See FUEL PRESSURE SPECIFICATIONS table. If fuel pressure is not within specifications, repair fuel pump or fuel pressure regulator as necessary.

FUEL PRESSURE SPECIFICATIONS: psi (kg/cm^2)

Engine	Pressure KOER	Pressure KOEO
4.9L PFI	45-60 (3.16-4.22)	50-60 (3.52-4.22)
All Others	30-45 (2.11-3.16)	35-45 (2.46-3.16)

CIRCUIT TEST G (Cont.)

9) Check Systems Ability to Hold Fuel Pressure – Turn ignition on, leaving engine off. If fuel pressure remains at specification for 60 seconds, go to next step (for SEFI), or go to CIRCUIT TEST H, step **7)** (for EFI). If fuel pressure does not remain at specification, repair fuel delivery system as necessary.

10) Cylinder Balance Test – Run KOER SELF-TEST. After last repeated code, wait 5-10 seconds then "goose" throttle lightly (not wide-open throttle). This will activate cylinder balance test. If code 90 is present after test, go back to step **5)**. If code 90 is not present after test, go to CIRCUIT TEST H, step **4)**.

CIRCUIT TEST H

FUEL CONTROL

Diagnostic Aids – Perform this test when instructed during QUICK TEST, or when directed by other test procedures.

See HOW TO USE CIRCUIT TESTS under CIRCUIT TESTS before performing this test. Fuel contaminated engine oil may affect Codes 41/172, 91/136, 42/173 or 92/137. If this is suspected, remove PCV valve from valve cover and repeat QUICK TEST. If problem is corrected, change engine oil and filter.

Use this test to diagnose only the following components:

- HEGO Sensor
- HEGO Signal And Ground Circuit
- HEGO Sensor Connection
- Vacuum Systems
- Fuel Injector
- ECA
- Electrical Circuits (HEGO GND, HEGO, INJ 1-8, VPWR And SIG RTN)

To prevent replacement of good components, be aware that the following non-EEC areas may be the cause of driveability concerns:

- Ignition System
- Faulty CANP System
- EGR Valve And Gasket
- Air Intake System
- Fuel Or Engine Oil Contamination
- Poor Electrical Ground
- Fuel Pressure
- Intake Or Exhaust System Leaks
- Engine Below Normal Operating Temperature

INDIVIDUAL INJECTOR RESISTANCE [1]

Engine	Ohms
2.3L & 3.0L	15.0-18.0
4.0L	4.0-17.5
All Others	13.0-16.0

[1] – Resistance values are for a single injector.

INJECTOR BANK RESISTANCE

Engine	Ohms
2.3L	7.0-9.5
2.9L, 3.0L & 4.9L	5.0-6.5
4.0L	4.5-6.0
5.0L, 5.8L & 7.5L	3.0-4.0

FUEL PRESSURE SPECIFICATIONS – psi (kg/cm^2)

Engine	Pressure KOER	Pressure KOEO
4.9L PFI	45-60 (3.16-4.22)	50-60 (3.52-4.22)
All Others	30-45 (2.11-3.16)	35-45 (2.46-3.16)

1991 ENGINE PERFORMANCE
Self-Diagnostics – EEC-IV (Cont.)

CIRCUIT TEST H (Cont.)

Test Schematic

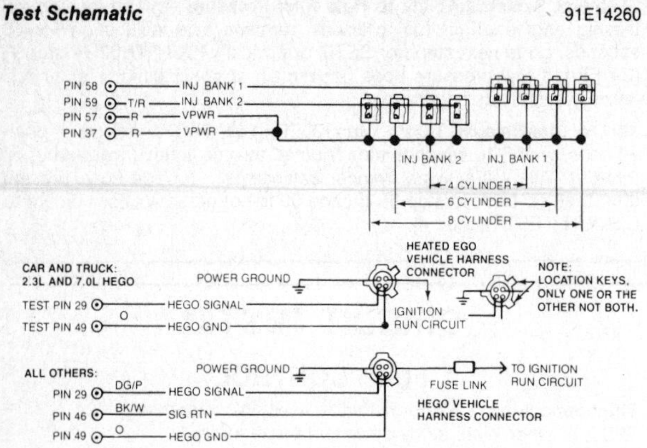
91E14260
PIN 58
INJ BANK 1
PIN 59
T/R
INJ BANK 2
PIN 57
R
VPWR
PIN 37
R
VPWR
INJ BANK 2
INJ. BANK 1
4 CYLINDER
6 CYLINDER
8 CYLINDER
CAR AND TRUCK:
2.3L AND 7.0L HEGO
POWER GROUND
HEATED EGO
VEHICLE HARNESS
CONNECTOR
NOTE:
LOCATION KEYS,
ONLY ONE OR THE
OTHER NOT BOTH.
TEST PIN 29
HEGO SIGNAL
O
TEST PIN 49
HEGO GND
IGNITION
RUN CIRCUIT
ALL OTHERS:
POWER GROUND
TO IGNITION
RUN CIRCUIT
FUSE LINK
PIN 29
DG/P
HEGO SIGNAL
HEGO VEHICLE
HARNESS CONNECTOR
PIN 46
BK/W
SIG RTN
PIN 49
O
HEGO GND

*TEST PINS LOCATED ON BREAKOUT BOX.
ALL HARNESS CONNECTORS VIEWED INTO MATING SURFACE.

TEST PIN 58 (INJ BANK 1) WIRE COLOR IDENTIFICATION

Application	Wire Color
2.3L MA & 2.9L MA	Light Green/White
All Other Models	Tan/Orange

TEST PIN 44 (RIGHT HEGO No. 1) WIRE COLOR IDENTIFICATION

Application	Wire Color
All Models	Tan/Orange

1) Check for Contaminated Engine Oil – Turn ignition off. Remove PCV valve from valve cover. Inspect valve cover hole and PCV for damage, sludge build up, blockage and movement of valve plunger. Repair as necessary. Perform KOER SELF-TEST. If vehicle is a no start, KOER codes 41/172, 91/136, 42/173 or 92/137, or Continuous Memory Codes 176, 177, 144/41, 91/139, 171, 175, 174 or 178 are set, reinstall PCV valve and go to next step. If no code is set, change engine oil and filter; reinstall PCV valve. Drive vehicle for 5 miles at 55 MPH. Rerun QUICK TEST.

2) Check Fuel Pressure – Turn ignition off and wait 10 seconds. Install fuel pressure gauge. Ensure manifold vacuum supply is connected to fuel pressure regulator (if equipped). Run engine at idle and check fuel pressure. If vehicle will not start, cycle ignition on and off several times. See appropriate FUEL PRESSURE SPECIFICATIONS table in this circuit test. If vehicle is a no start, cycle ignition on and off several times. If fuel pressure is within specification, go to next step. If pressure is not to specification, remove fuel pressure gauge. Repair electric fuel pump or fuel pressure regulator.

3) Check Systems Ability to Hold Fuel Pressure – Turn ignition on, leaving engine off. If fuel pressure remains at specification for 60 seconds, go to next step (for no starts), go to step **5)**. If fuel pressure is not as described, repair fuel delivery system as necessary.

4) Fuel Delivery Test – Ensure fuel is of good quality. With ignition off, install fuel pressure gauge and pressurize fuel system as in step **1)**. Disconnect inertia switch. Crank engine for 5 seconds. If fuel pressure drop is greater than 5 psi after 5 seconds of cranking, EEC-IV system is not the cause of no-start condition. Check additional no-start tests in TROUBLE SHOOTING – NO CODES article. If fuel pressure drop is less than 5 psi, remove fuel pressure gauge and reconnect inertia switch; go to step **6)**.

5) Cylinder Balance Test (EFI Engines) – Connect a tachometer to engine. Start engine and run at idle. Disconnect and reconnect injectors one at a time, noting RPM drop as each injector is disconnected. Note that ISC motor will attempt to re-establish RPM. If each injector does not

CIRCUIT TEST H (Cont.)

produce a momentary drop in RPM, go to step **6)**. If each injector produces a momentary drop in RPM, go to step **11)** (for symptoms or codes 41/172, 91/136 or 176), step **22)** (for codes 42/173, 92/137 or 177), or step **12)** (for all others).

6) Check Injector and Harness Resistance – Turn ignition off and wait 10 seconds. Disconnect ECA 60-pin connector. Inspect pins for damage. Install breakout box, leaving ECA disconnected. Set DVOM on 200-ohm scale. Measure resistance of injector banks between test pins No. 37 and 58 (injector bank No. 1) or 59 (injector bank No. 2) at breakout box. Record resistance. Refer to appropriate INJECTOR BANK RESISTANCE table in this circuit test. If each resistance is within specifications for appropriate engine, go to step **10)**. If resistance is not as specified, repair open circuit on VPWR circuit (for no start), or go to step **7** (for all other conditions).

7) Check Continuity of Fuel Injector Harness – Turn ignition off and wait 10 seconds. Install breakout box, leaving ECA disconnected. Disconnect injector vehicle harness connector at injectors. Set DVOM to 200-ohm scale. Measure resistance between test pin No. 37/57 at breakout box and VPWR pin at each injector vehicle harness connector. See appropriate TEST SCHEMATIC in this circuit test. Measure resistance between injector test pin(s) at breakout box and the same injector circuit signal pin at each injector vehicle harness connector. If each resistance is less than 5 ohms, go to next step. If each resistance is 5 ohms or more, repair open circuit. Remove breakout box, reconnect all components and drive vehicle for 5 miles at 55 MPH. Rerun QUICK TEST.

8) Check Injector Harness Circuit for Short to Power or Ground –Turn ignition off and wait for 10 seconds. With breakout box installed and ECA disconnected, disconnect fuel injector vehicle harness. See appropriate TEST SCHEMATIC in this circuit test. Set DVOM to 200-k/ohm scale. Measure resistance between injector test pin(s) and test pins No. 37/57, 40, 46 and 60. Measure resistance between injector test pin(s) at breakout box and chassis ground. If each resistance is 10 k/ohms or more, replace injector per cylinder balance test service code and rerun QUICK TEST (for SEFI), or go to next step (for EFI). If each resistance is less than 10 k/ohms, repair short. Remove breakout box, reconnect all components and drive vehicle for 5 miles at 55 MPH. Rerun QUICK TEST.

9) Isolate Faulty Injector Circuit – Turn ignition off. Install breakout box and disconnect ECA. Disconnect all injectors on suspected bank. With DVOM set on 200-ohm scale, connect one injector and measure resistance between test pins No. 37 and 58 or 59. Disconnect injector and repeat process for all other injectors. See appropriate INDIVIDUAL INJECTOR RESISTANCE table for specifications. If all injectors are within specifications, go to step **12)**. If injectors are not as specified, remove breakout box. Reconnect ECA and injectors. Repair open or short in injector harness. If circuit is okay, replace injector. Drive vehicle for 5 miles at 55 MPH. Rerun QUICK TEST.

10) Check Injector Drive Signal – With ignition off and breakout box installed, connect ECA to breakout box. Use a non-powered 12-volt test light and connect as follows:

- EFI Engines – Connect test light between test pins No. 37 and 58 at breakout box. Connect light between test pins No. 37 and 59 at breakout box.
- Sequential PFI Engines – Connect test light between test pin No. 37 and the suspected injector(s) test pin at breakout box.

Crank or start engine. If test light glows dimly, system is operating properly. remove breakout box and reconnect ECA. Clean and test injectors. Drive vehicle for 5 miles at 55 MPH. Rerun QUICK TEST and CYLINDER BALANCE TEST.

If test light does not glow dimly (no light/bright light), check injector circuit for shorts to ground. If system is okay, remove breakout box and replace ECA. Remove breakout box and reconnect all components. Drive vehicle for 5 miles at 55 MPH. Rerun QUICK TEST.

11) Check Thermactor Operation – If vehicle is equipped with Pulse-Air or does not have Thermactor System, ignore this step and go to next step. With dual HEGO, code 41/172 refers to right or rear HEGO, and code 91/136 or 176 refers to left or front HEGO. A HEGO that is always lean could be caused by Thermactor air being diverted upstream from HEGO sensor. Turn ignition off and wait 10 second. Disconnect Thermactor air hose(s) from Thermactor pump. Run KOER SELF-TEST. If codes 41/172, 91/136 or 176 are present, reconnect Thermactor air hose(s) and go to next step. If codes 41/172, 91/136 or 176 are not present, repair thermactor system as necessary.

CIRCUIT TEST H (Cont.)

12) Check HEGO Integrity – A HEGO sensor that is always lean, slow to switch or does not switch could be caused by the following:

- Moisture Inside HEGO Sensor, Or Harness Connector Causing A Short To Ground
- HEGO Sensor Coated With Containments
- HEGO Circuit Open
- HEGO Circuit Shorted To Ground

Turn ignition off and wait 10 seconds. Inspect HEGO harness for chaffing, burns or other indications of damage; repair or replace as necessary. Inspect HEGO sensor and connector for signs of water entry; repair or replace as necessary. Start engine and run at 2000 RPM for 2 minutes. Turn ignition off and wait 10 seconds. Run KOER SELF-TEST. If fault codes are present, go to next step (for MAP sensor-equipped vehicles), or step **14)** (for MAF sensor-equipped vehicles). If no code is present, go to step **19)**.

13) Checking HEGO Sensor on Engines with MAP Sensors – Turn ignition off and set DVOM on 20-volt scale. Disconnect appropriate HEGO sensor from vehicle harness. Connect DVOM to HEGO SIGNAL lead at sensor connector and battery negative terminal (3-wire HEGO). Connect DVOM to HEGO SIGNAL and HEGO GND leads at sensor connector (4-wire HEGO). Disconnect and plug vacuum line MAP sensor. Start engine and apply 10-14 in Hg to Manifold Absolute Pressure (MAP) sensor. Run engine at 2000 RPM for 2 minutes. If reading is .5 volt or more within 2 minutes, go to step **15)**. If reading is less than .5 volt within 2 minutes, replace HEGO sensor; reconnect MAP and rerun QUICK TEST.

Diagnostic Aids – Vacuum or air leaks in non-EEC-IV related areas may cause Code 41 or 91. Check the following areas: leaking vacuum actuator (A/C control motor, etc.) engine seals, EGR system, PCV system and lead contamination of HEGO sensor.

Identifying HEGO Sensor Terminals 91A14258

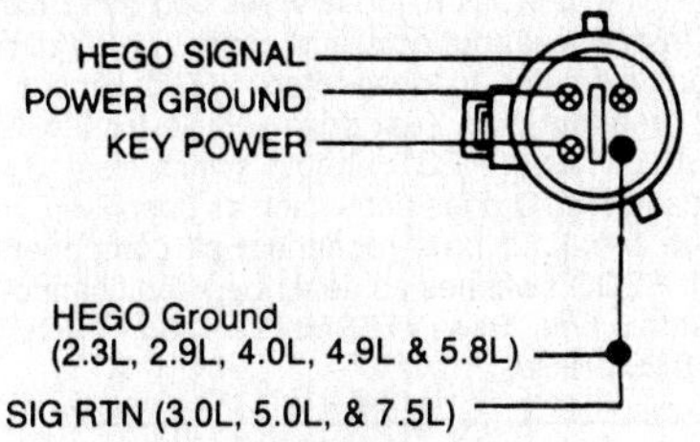

HEGO SIGNAL
POWER GROUND
KEY POWER
HEGO Ground
(2.3L, 2.9L, 4.0L, 4.9L & 5.8L)
SIG RTN (3.0L, 5.0L, & 7.5L)

HEGO SENSOR CONNECTOR

14) Check HEGO Sensor on Engines with MAF Sensor – The purpose of this test is to verify HEGO sensor can generate a voltage signal of greater than .5 volt during KOER SELF-TEST. With ignition off and DVOM set on 20-volt scale, disconnect appropriate HEGO sensor from harness. Depending on type of sensor (3 wires or 4 wires), connect DVOM as follows:

- 4-Wire HEGO Sensors – Connect DVOM between HEGO SIGNAL and HEGO GND at HEGO sensor connector.
- 3-Wire HEGO Sensors – Connect DVOM to HEGO SIGNAL at sensor and battery negative terminal.

Rerun KOER SELF-TEST and monitor HEGO sensor voltage. If voltage is .5 volt or more, go to next step. If voltage is less than .5 volt, replace HEGO sensor and rerun QUICK TEST.

Diagnostic Aids – Vacuum or air leaks in non-EEC-IV related areas may cause Code 41 or 91. Check the following areas: leaking vacuum actuator (A/C control motor, etc.) engine seals, EGR system, PCV system and lead contamination of HEGO sensor.

15) Check Continuity of HEGO SIGNAL and HEGO GROUND Circuits – Turn ignition off. Install breakout box, leaving ECA disconnected. Disconnect suspected HEGO sensor from vehicle harness. Inspect both ends of connector for damage or pushed-out pins, moisture, corrosion, loose wires or other damage. Repair as necessary. Set DVOM on 200-ohm scale. Measure resistance between HEGO SIGNAL (test pin No. 29) at breakout box and HEGO SIGNAL at vehicle harness connector.

On 3-Wire HEGO sensors, measure resistance between HEGO GROUND test pin at breakout box and battery negative terminal.

On 4-Wire HEGO sensors, measure resistance between HEGO GROUND test pin at breakout box and HEGO GND at vehicle harness connector. Where applicable, measure resistance between HEGO GND and SIG RTN at breakout box.

CIRCUIT TEST H (Cont.)

If each resistance is less than 5 ohms, go to next step. If each resistance is 5 ohms or more, repair open circuit. Remove breakout box and reconnect all components. Drive vehicle for 5 minutes at 55 MPH. Rerun QUICK TEST.

16) Check HEGO Circuit for Short to Ground – Turn ignition off. Leave breakout box installed and ECA disconnected. Disconnect HEGO sensor and set DVOM on 200-k/ohm scale. Measure resistance between HEGO SIGNAL (test pin No. 29) and test pins No. 40, 46 and 49 at breakout box. If any reading is less than 10 k/ohms, repair short to ground; remove breakout box, reconnect all components and repeat QUICK TEST. If reading is 10 k/ohms or more, go to next step.

17) Check HEGO Sensor for Short to Ground – With ignition off, breakout box installed and ECA disconnected, set DVOM to 200-k/ohm scale. Disconnect HEGO sensor. Measure resistance between PWR GND and HEGO SIGNAL at HEGO sensor connector. For trucks with 4-wire sensors, measure resistance between PWR GND, HEGO GND, SIG RTN and HEGO SIG at HEGO sensor connector. If resistance is less than 10 k/ohms, replace HEGO sensor and remove breakout box; reconnect all components, drive vehicle for 5 miles at 55 MPH and repeat QUICK TEST. If resistance is 10 k/ohms or more, perform the following procedure as applicable.

- For codes 144/41, 139/91, 171, 174, 175 or 178, go to step **90)**.
- On engines with MAP sensor, go to step **20)**.
- On engines with MAF sensor, remove breakout box. Reconnect HEGO sensor and replace ECA. Drive vehicle for 5 miles at 55 MPH. Rerun QUICK TEST.

18) Attempt to Eliminate Code 41/172, 91/136 or 176: Engines with MAP Sensor – Turn ignition off. Install breakout box; reconnect ECA and HEGO sensor. Ensure MAP sensor vacuum hose is disconnected and plugged. Apply 10-14 in. Hg to MAP sensor. Start and run engine at 2000 RPM for 2 minutes. Allow engine to return to idle. Perform KOER SELF-TEST. If you are here for Continuous Memory Codes, vehicle has to be driven 5 miles at 55 MPH. If Code 41/172, 91/136 or 176 is still present, remove breakout box. Reconnect ECA and MAP sensor vacuum line. If engine still runs rough, go to CIRCUIT TEST S, step **2)**. If engine does not run rough, replace ECA; drive vehicle 5 miles at 55 MPH then repeat QUICK TEST.
If Code 41/172, 91/136 or 176 is not present, remove breakout box and reconnect ECA and MAP sensor vacuum hose. HEGO input circuit and fuel delivery are okay; fault is in area common to all areas. Service as necessary.

19) Check Resistance of HEGO Heating Element – Turn ignition off. Disconnect suspected HEGO sensor. Inspect both ends of connector for damaged or pushed-out pins, moisture, corrosion, loose wires or other damage. Repair as necessary. Set DVOM on 200-ohm scale. Measure resistance between KPWR circuit and PWR GND circuit at HEGO sensor connector. Hot to warm resistance should be 5.0-30.0 ohms. Room temperature resistance is 2.0-5.0 ohms. If resistance is within specification, go to next step. If resistance is not as specified, replace HEGO sensor and repeat QUICK TEST.

Identifying HEGO Wiring Harness Connector Terminals 91B14259

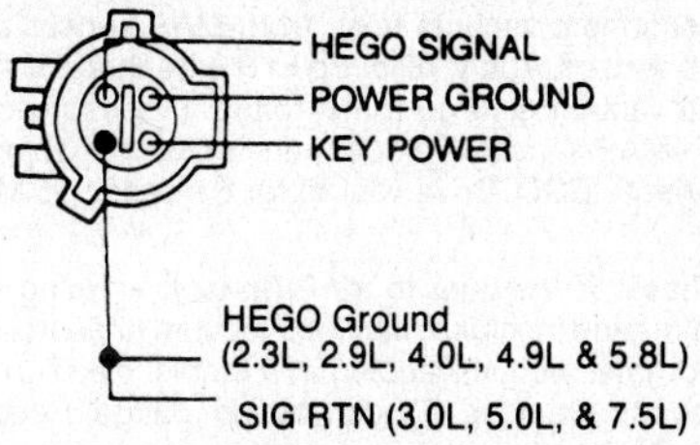

HEGO SIGNAL
POWER GROUND
KEY POWER
HEGO Ground
(2.3L, 2.9L, 4.0L, 4.9L & 5.8L)
SIG RTN (3.0L, 5.0L, & 7.5L)

HEGO VEHICLE HARNESS CONNECTOR

20) Check for Power at HEGO Harness Connector – With ignition on and engine off, and HEGO disconnected, set DVOM on 20-volt scale. Measure voltage between KEY POWER circuit and PWR GND circuit at HEGO vehicle harness connector. If voltage is 10.5 volts or more, HEGO system and fuel delivery are okay; HEGO sensor may have cooled before KOER SELF-TEST. If driveability symptom persists, fault is in area common to all cylinders, such as air or vacuum leaks, fuel contamination, EGR, MAP, etc. If voltage is less than 10.5 volts, go to next step.

21) Check Continuity Of Power Ground Circuit – Turn ignition off and wait 10 seconds. Disconnect HEGO sensor and set DVOM on 200-ohm

1991 ENGINE PERFORMANCE
Self-Diagnostics – EEC-IV (Cont.)

CIRCUIT TEST H (Cont.)

scale. Measure resistance between PWR GND circuit at HEGO vehicle harness connector and battery negative post. If resistance is less than 5 ohms, repair open in KEY POWER circuit. Reconnect HEGO and rerun QUICK TEST. If resistance is 5 ohms or more, reconnect HEGO sensor and repair open in PWR GND circuit. Reconnect HEGO sensor and rerun QUICK TEST.

22) Check HEGO SIGNAL for Short to Power – On dual HEGO systems, Code 42/173 refers to right (or rear) side HEGO, and Code 92/137 or 177 refers to left (or front) side HEGO. Turn ignition off and wait 10 seconds. Disconnect appropriate HEGO sensor. Set DVOM on 20-volt scale. With ignition on and engine off, measure voltage between HEGO SIG and PWR GND at HEGO vehicle harness connector. If reading is less than .5 volt, go to step **26)**. If reading is .5 volt or more, go to next step.

23) Check for Short to Power – Turn ignition off. Disconnect HEGO sensor. Inspect both ends of connector for damaged or pushed-out pins, moisture, corrosion, loose wires or other damage. Repair as necessary. Set DVOM on 200-k/ohm scale. Disconnect ECA 60-pin connector. Install breakout box, leaving ECA disconnected. Measure resistance between KEY POWER circuit and HEGO SIG circuit at breakout box.

If reading is 10 k/ohms or more, replace ECA. Remove breakout box and reconnect all components. Drive vehicle for 5 miles at 55 MPH. Rerun QUICK TEST.

If reading is less than 10 k/ohms, repair short circuit. Remove breakout box and reconnect all components. Drive vehicle for 5 miles at 55 MPH. Rerun QUICK TEST.

24) Check HEGO Sensor for Short to Ignition Run Circuit – Turn ignition off and wait 10 seconds. Disconnect HEGO. Set DVOM to 200-k/ohm scale. Measure resistance between KEY POWER circuit and HEGO SIG circuit at HEGO sensor connector.

If resistance is 10 k/ohms or more, go to next step for codes 42/173, 92/137 or 177. For codes 171, 174, 175 or 178, go to step **28)**.

If resistance is less than 10 k/ohms, replace HEGO sensor. Drive vehicle for 5 miles at 55 MPH, and rerun QUICK TEST.

25) Attempt to Generate Code 41/172, 91/136 or 176 – The following non-EEC areas may cause these codes: fuel-contaminated engine oil, ignition misfire and faulty CANP system. Turn ignition off and wait 10 seconds. Disconnect appropriate HEGO sensor. Using jumper wire, connect HEGO SIG circuit at HEGO vehicle harness connector to battery negative terminal. Repeat KOER SELF-TEST.

If Code 41/172, 91/136 or 176 is present, remove jumper wire and go to next step for engines with MAP. For all other engines, go to step **28)**.

If Codes 41/172, 91/136 or 176 is not present, remove jumper wire. Disconnect ECA connector and inspect for damage. If connector is okay, replace ECA. Drive vehicle for 5 miles at 55 MPH. Repeat QUICK TEST.

Diagnostic Aids – Because MAP sensor has a large influence on fuel control, Code 42/172 or 91/136 may be caused by a faulty MAP sensor, even though Code 22/126 has not been set. The next 2 steps test the MAP vacuum circuit.

26) Check MAP Sensor for Vacuum Leaks – Turn ignition off and wait 10 seconds. Disconnect vacuum hose from MAP sensor and connect vacuum pump to sensor. Apply 18 in. Hg to MAP sensor. If sensor holds vacuum, release vacuum and go to next step. If sensor does not hold vacuum, replace MAP sensor. Remove vacuum pump. Connect vacuum hose and reconnect HEGO. Drive vehicle for 5 miles at 55 MPH. Repeat QUICK TEST.

27) Check for Loss of Vacuum to MAP Sensor – Using vacuum "T", connect vacuum gauge in intake manifold vacuum hose at MAP sensor. Start engine and note vacuum reading at a stable idle. Turn ignition off and wait 10 seconds. Remove "T" and vacuum gauge. Reconnect hose to MAP sensor. Connect vacuum gauge at a different intake manifold location. Start engine and note vacuum reading. If readings do not differ by more than 1 in. Hg, go to next step. If readings differ by more than 1 in. Hg, inspect vacuum hoses for leaks, kinks, or blockage. Repair as necessary. Reconnect all components and drive vehicle for 5 miles at 55 MPH. Rerun QUICK TEST.

28) HEGO Sensor Check – Turn ignition off and wait 10 seconds. Disconnect HEGO sensor. Set DVOM on 20-volt scale. For 4-Wire HEGO, connect DVOM to HEGO SIGNAL and HEGO GND at HEGO sensor connector. For 3-Wire HEGO, connect DVOM to HEGO SIGNAL at HEGO sensor connector and battery negative post. Remove a vacuum hose to create vacuum leak, which will cause HEGO sensor to go lean. Start engine and run at approximately 2000 RPM. DVOM should indicate less than .4 volt within 30 seconds. If voltage is not as specified, replace HEGO sensor. Reconnect vacuum hoses and drive vehicle for 5 miles at 55 MPH. Repeat QUICK TEST. If voltage is as specified, go to next step.

NOTE: There is a break in the step numbering sequence at this point, skipping from step 28) to step 90). Break is due to previous chart references to these testing procedures. No test procedures have been omitted.

90) Check Continuous Monitor Mode – Turn ignition off and wait 10 seconds. Ensure engine is at normal operating temperature. Start engine and run at 2000 RPM for 2 minutes then return to idle. Enter KOER wiggle test. See CONTINUOUS MONITOR MODE (WIGGLE TEST) under QUICK TEST. While observing DVOM or Scan tool, wiggle, shake or bend small sections of EEC-IV wiring harness from HEGO sensor to ECA. Wiggle, shake or bend small sections of EEC-IV wiring harness from HEGO GND to ECA. If no fault is indicated, remain in CONTINUOUS MONITOR MODE and go to next step. If fault is indicated, isolate and repair fault as necessary. Clear codes, remove breakout box and reconnect all components. Rerun QUICK TEST.

91) Continuous Monitor Test Drive Check – While still in KOER wiggle test, test drive vehicle for 5 miles at 55 MPH with minimum road load. Drive an additional 5 miles at 55 MPH over rough roads. If possible, drive vehicle through a pool of water to shower HEGO sensor and connector. If fault is indicated, isolate fault and repair as necessary. Clear codes and remove breakout box. Rerun QUICK TEST. If no codes are indicated, exit KOER wiggle test and go to next step.

92) Check HEGO Switching – Turn ignition off and wait 10 seconds. Inspect EEC-IV wire harness for proper routing and insulation. Check for burnt, chaffed and intermittently shorted or open wires. Repair as necessary. Disconnect ECA 60-pin connector, and inspect for damaged and pushed-out pins, corrosion, loose wires and other damage. Repair as necessary. Install breakout box, and connect ECA to breakout box. Connect analog voltmeter to suspected HEGO sensor test pin and HEGO GND at breakout box. Test drive vehicle for 5 miles at 55 MPH while observing voltmeter. HEGO should switch from .3 volt to .9 volt within 3 seconds. If HEGO does not switch as described, replace HEGO sensor. Remove breakout box, reconnect all components and rerun QUICK TEST. If HEGO switches as described, fault cannot be identified or duplicated at this time. See INTERMITTENTS in TROUBLE SHOOTING – NO CODES article.

CIRCUIT TEST HA

ADAPTIVE FUEL

Diagnostic Aids – Perform this test when directed by QUICK TEST.

The ECA uses Adaptive Fuel logic primarily to compensate for normal variability in fuel system components. If fuel system appears to be too rich or too lean, adaptive fuel will make a corresponding shift in fuel delivery calculations to compensate and remove bias.

FUEL PRESSURE SPECIFICATIONS – psi (kg/cm²)

Engine	Pressure KOER	Pressure KOEO
4.9L PFI	45-60 (3.16-4.22)	50-60 (3.52-4.22)
All Others	30-45 (2.11-3.16)	35-45 (2.46-3.16)

MAP SENSOR VOLTAGE OUTPUT

Elevation (Feet)	Volts
0	1.55-1.63
1000	1.52-1.60
2000	1.49-1.57
3000	1.46-1.54
4000	1.43-1.51
5000	1.40-1.48
6000	1.37-1.45
7000	1.35-1.43

CIRCUIT TEST HA (Cont.)

Diagnostic Aids – If possible, measure several known good MAP/BP sensors on available vehicles. Average voltage reading will be typical for location on date of testing.

1) Continuous Memory Codes 181 or 183 – This test identifies areas that could cause HEGO sensor to detect excessive oxygen, resulting in adaptive fuel enriching the system to compensate. Excessive oxygen will be detected with lean conditions and certain rich conditions.

For vehicles with dual HEGO sensors, a related fuel code from both HEGO sensors could indicate a problem that is common to all cylinders. If a code is present from only one HEGO, this may help isolate a problem or be an early indication of a common problem.

- Code 181 – Indicates the single right or rear HEGO detected a problem, and adaptive fuel rich limit has been reached.
- Code 183 – Indicates the single right or rear HEGO detected a problem, and adaptive fuel rich limit has been reached at idle.

Ensure a pass code (111) is received during both KOEO SELF-TEST and KOER SELF-TEST. Whenever a repair is made, clear Keep-Alive Memory (KAM). If driveability symptoms are not present, be aware of other temporary conditions that may have set this code, such as vehicle is out of fuel or fuel is contaminated.

2) Check for Vacuum/Air Induction Leaks – Check all vacuum hose and connections for leaks or damage. Check air induction system for leak or damage. If leak or damage is found, repair as necessary; clear KAM and rerun QUICK TEST. If leak or damage is not found, go to next step.

3) Check for Low Fuel Pressure – Turn ignition off and wait 10 seconds. Install fuel pressure gauge. Cycle ignition from off to run 2 to 3 times. Observe KOEO fuel pressure. Start engine, observe and record KOER fuel pressure. Compare fuel pressure readings with appropriate FUEL PRESSURE SPECIFICATIONS table in this circuit test. If fuel pressure is within specifications, go to next step. If fuel pressure is not within specifications, repair fuel system as necessary. Clear KAM and rerun QUICK TEST.

4) Check Systems Ability to Hold Fuel Pressure – With fuel pressure gauge installed, cycle ignition from off to on 2 to 3 times to pressurize fuel system (do not start engine). If fuel pressure remains at specifications for 60 seconds, go to next step (MAP/BP-equipped vehicles), or step **7)** (all other vehicles). If fuel pressure does not remain at specifications for 60 seconds, visually inspect fuel system for leaks and repair as necessary. Clear KAM and rerun QUICK TEST.

5) Check MAP/BP Frequency – Turn ignition off and wait 10 seconds. Connect MAP/BP tester to MAP/BP sensor. Turn ignition on. Refer to MAP SENSOR VOLTAGE OUTPUT table at beginning of this circuit test. If MAP/BP voltage is within specifications, go to next step. If voltage is not within specifications, check wiring to MAP/BP sensor for corrosion, high resistance or other damage; repair as necessary. Clear KAM and rerun QUICK TEST. If wiring is okay, replace MAP/BP sensor; clear KAM and rerun QUICK TEST.

6) Check for Proper Battery Voltage to Fuel Injectors – Turn ignition on, leaving engine off. Set DVOM to 20-volt scale. Measure and record voltage across battery terminals. Disconnect any fuel injector harness connector. Measure and record voltage between VPWR circuit at fuel injector vehicle harness connector and battery negative terminal. If both voltage readings are within one volt of each other, go to step **8)** (4.9L E4OD), or next step (all others). If voltage readings differ by more than one volt, fuel injectors are not getting proper battery voltage. Isolate and repair problem. Clear KAM and rerun QUICK TEST.

7) Ensure CANP Solenoid Is Not Stuck Closed – Enter Output State Check. Disconnect hose to manifold vacuum at CANP solenoid. Check for blockage and repair or replace hose as necessary. With outputs off, apply 16 in. Hg vacuum to manifold vacuum side of CANP. Depress throttle to cycle outputs on. If vacuum releases, reconnect vacuum hose to CANP and go to next step (thermactor-equipped vehicles), or step **26)** (all other vehicles). If vacuum does not release, repeat this step to verify results. If vacuum will not release, check canister and vacuum hose to canister for blockage; repair as necessary. If canister and hose are okay, replace CANP solenoid; clear KAM and rerun QUICK TEST.

8) Check Thermactor System for Upstream Air Leak – Check thermactor air control and vacuum control valves. See SYSTEM & COMPONENT TESTING article. If air control valve is operating properly, go to step **25)**. If air control valve is not operating properly, repair or replace valve as necessary. Clear KAM and rerun QUICK TEST.

CIRCUIT TEST HA (Cont.)

NOTE: There is a break in the step numbering sequence at this point, skipping from step 8) to step 15). Break is due to previous chart references to these testing procedures. No test procedures have been omitted.

15) Continuous Memory Codes 179 or 182 – This test identifies areas that could cause engine to run rich, resulting in adaptive fuel reducing the system to compensate.

For vehicles with dual HEGO sensors, a related fuel code from both HEGO sensors could indicate a problem that is common to all cylinders. If a code is present from only one HEGO, this may help isolate a problem or it may be an early indication of a common problem.

- Code 179 – Indicates the single, right or rear HEGO detected a problem, and adaptive fuel lean limit has been reached.
- Code 182 – Indicates the single right or rear HEGO detected a problem, and adaptive fuel lean limit has been reached at idle.

Ensure a pass code (111) is received during both KOEO SELF-TEST and KOER SELF-TEST. Whenever a repair is made, clear Keep-Alive Memory (KAM).

16) Check for Low Fuel Pressure – Turn ignition off and wait 10 seconds. Install fuel pressure gauge. Cycle ignition from off to run 2 to 3 times. Observe KOEO fuel pressure. Start engine, observe and record KOER fuel pressure. Compare fuel pressure readings with appropriate FUEL PRESSURE SPECIFICATIONS table in this circuit test. If fuel pressure is within specifications, go to next step. If fuel pressure is not within specifications, check condition of fuel pressure regulator vacuum hose, fuel return line and fuel pressure regulator. Repair fuel system as necessary. Clear KAM and rerun QUICK TEST.

17) Check Systems Ability to Hold Fuel Pressure – With fuel pressure gauge installed, cycle ignition from off to on 2 to 3 times to pressurize fuel system (do not start engine). If fuel pressure remains at specifications for 60 seconds, go to next step (MAP/BP-equipped vehicles), or step **19)** (all other vehicles). If fuel pressure does not remain at specifications for 60 seconds, visually inspect fuel system for leaks and repair as necessary. Clear KAM and rerun QUICK TEST.

18) Check MAP/BP Frequency – Turn ignition off and wait 10 seconds. Connect MAP/BP tester to MAP/BP sensor. Turn ignition on. Refer to MAP SENSOR VOLTAGE OUTPUT table in this circuit test. If MAP/BP voltage is within specifications, go to next step. If voltage is not within specifications, check wiring to MAP/BP sensor for corrosion, high resistance or other damage; repair as necessary. Clear KAM and rerun QUICK TEST. If wiring is okay, replace MAP/BP sensor; clear KAM and rerun QUICK TEST.

19) Check Throttle Body and Air Induction System – Check throttle body and air induction system for contamination, obstruction, etc. Repair or clean as necessary. Clear KAM and rerun QUICK TEST. If throttle body and air induction system are okay, go to step **25)** (4.9L E4OD-equipped vehicles), or go to next step (all other vehicles).

20) Ensure CANP will Hold Vacuum – Turn ignition off and wait 10 seconds. Disconnect vacuum hose to manifold vacuum at CANP solenoid. Apply 16 in. Hg vacuum to manifold side of CANP solenoid. If solenoid holds vacuum for 20 seconds, reconnect vacuum hose and go to next step. If solenoid does not hold vacuum for 20 seconds, replace CANP solenoid. Clear KAM and rerun QUICK TEST.

NOTE: There is a break in the step numbering sequence at this point, skipping from step 21) to step 25). Break is due to previous chart references to these testing procedures. No test procedures have been omitted.

25) Check PCV Valve – Turn ignition off and wait 10 seconds. Remove PCV valve and shake. If PCV valve rattles freely when shaken, go to next step. If PCV valve does not rattle, replace PCV valve. Clear KAM and rerun QUICK TEST.

26) Check HEGO Heater Circuit – Turn ignition off and wait 10 seconds. Disconnect HEGO sensor(s). Set DVOM to 200-ohm scale. measure resistance between KEY POWER circuit and PWR GND circuit at HEGO sensor connector(s). Resistance should be 2 ohms (room temperature), or 35 ohms (hot).

Turn ignition on, leaving engine off. Set DVOM to 20-volt scale. Measure voltage between KEY POWER circuit and PWR GND circuit at HEGO sensor connector(s). Voltage should be 10.5 volts. If HEGO circuits check okay, go to next step. If HEGO circuits are not okay, isolate problem and repair as necessary. Clear KAM and rerun QUICK TEST.

1991 ENGINE PERFORMANCE
Self-Diagnostics – EEC-IV (Cont.)

CIRCUIT TEST HA (Cont.)

27) Inspect HEGO Sensor for Contamination – Remove HEGO sensor(s) from exhaust manifold. Visually inspect for contamination or other damage. If HEGO sensor(s) appears okay, go to next step (vehicles with EGR), or step **30)** (all other vehicles). If HEGO sensor(s) is not okay, replace HEGO sensor; clear KAM and rerun QUICK TEST.

28) Verify Excessive Vacuum Is Not at EGR Valve During Idle –Disconnect vacuum line at EGR valve. Connect vacuum gauge to EGR vacuum line. Start engine and let idle. If vacuum reading is less than 2.5 in. Hg, go to next step. If vacuum reading is 2.5 in. Hg or more, check EVR solenoid filter for obstructions and repair as necessary. If EVR filter is okay, replace EVR solenoid; reconnect all components, clear KAM and rerun QUICK TEST.

29) Verify EGR Valve Is Fully Seated – Inspect EGR valve to ensure proper seating. If EGR valve is fully seated, reconnect vacuum line to EGR valve and go to next step. If EGR Valve is not fully seated, service or replace EGR valve as necessary; clear KAM and rerun QUICK TEST.

30) Check Cooling System – Ensure cooling system is in good condition and all components are operating properly. If cooling system is okay, go to next step. If system is not okay, repair as necessary. Clear KAM and rerun QUICK TEST.

NOTE: There is a break in the step numbering sequence at this point, skipping from step 30) to step 35). Break is due to previous chart references to these testing procedures. No test procedures have been omitted.

35) Check Ignition System – Ensure ignition system is operating properly. Scope check engine spark plug, coil, secondary wires, distributor cap, rotor, timing, etc. If ignition system is operating properly, go to next step. If system is not operating properly, make necessary repairs. Clear KAM and rerun QUICK TEST.

36) Flow Check Injectors – Flow check fuel injectors. See FUEL CONTROL in SYSTEM & COMPONENT TESTING article. If injectors are okay, go to next step. If injectors are not okay, clean or replace injectors as necessary. Clear KAM and rerun QUICK TEST.

37) Check Cylinder Compression – Check cylinder compression. See MECHANICAL INSPECTION in BASIC DIAGNOSTIC PROCEDURES article. If cylinder compression is not within specifications, service or replace engine as necessary. After servicing engine, clear KAM and rerun QUICK TEST. If cylinder compression is within specifications, go to next step.

NOTE: There is a break in the step numbering sequence at this point, skipping from step 37) to step 40). Break is due to previous chart references to these testing procedures. No test procedures have been omitted.

CIRCUIT TEST HA (Cont.)

WARNING: The following road test is a suggested optional procedure. Follow all applicable safety procedures and traffic laws. This road test requires another person to accompany the driver. The accompanying person can make measurements, observe changes and record notes. If for some reason this test is not performed, go to TROUBLE SHOOTING – NO CODES article for other possible causes.

40) Road Test Vehicle – The purpose of this test is to identify areas of concern by monitoring certain controlled parameters, while trying to recreate a driveability or MIL light symptom. To prepare for road test, do the following:

- Install fuel pressure gauge.
- Install MAP/BP tester.
- Disconnect ECA 60-pin connector; install breakout box and reconnect ECA to breakout box.
- Connect "T" vacuum gauge into manifold vacuum line.
- Have DVOM, writing materials and appropriate schematics or pin voltage charts on hand.

With ignition on and negative lead of DVOM connected to battery negative terminal, ensure the following signals are correct:

- POWERS: KAPWR (pin No. 1) is 10.5 volts or more, VPWR (pins No. 37/57) is 10.5 volts or more and VREF (pin No. 26) is 4-6 volts.
- GROUNDS: PWR GND (pins No. 40/60), SIG RTN (pin No. 46) and IGN GND (pin No. 16) are 0-.5 volt.
- OPTIONAL GROUNDS: HEGO GND (pin No. 49), CSE GND (pin No. 20) and MAF RTN (pin No. 9 or 15).

Drive vehicle and attempt to induce symptom. Information provided by vehicle operator may help when trying to recreate symptom. When symptom occurs, the accompanying passenger should observe and record changes in EEC-IV signals. Information about the symptom, operating condition value of EEC-IV signal and any other information available should be recorded on paper for analysis. If unable to duplicate symptom during road test, it is still useful to verify that EEC-IV values are in expected range.

Once road test has been completed, analyze results to locate and repair exact fault causing symptom. If problem cannot be identified, go to TROUBLE SHOOTING – NO CODES article for other possible causes of symptom.

CIRCUIT TEST J

FUEL PUMP CIRCUIT (RELAY & INERTIA SWITCH)

Diagnostic Aids – Perform this test when instructed by QUICK TEST, or when directed by other test procedures.

This test is intended to diagnose only the following:

- Fuel Pump Relay
- Inertia Switch
- Harness Circuits (BATT +, VPWR, FUEL PUMP, GND & POWER To PUMP)
- ECA

Fuel Pump Circuit Diagram (Ranger, Explorer & Aerostar) 91C06951

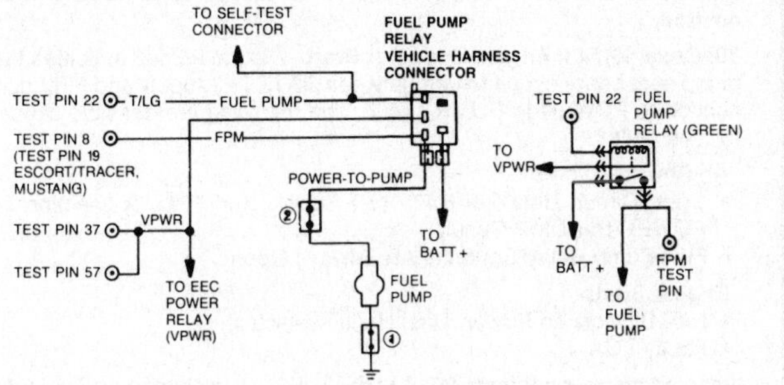
TO SELF-TEST CONNECTOR
FUEL PUMP RELAY VEHICLE HARNESS CONNECTOR
TEST PIN 22
T/LG
FUEL PUMP
TEST PIN 8 (TEST PIN 19 ESCORT/TRACER, MUSTANG)
FPM
POWER-TO-PUMP
TEST PIN 37
VPWR
TEST PIN 57
TO EEC POWER RELAY (VPWR)
TO BATT +
FUEL PUMP
TEST PIN 22
FUEL PUMP RELAY (GREEN)
TO VPWR
TO BATT +
FPM TEST PIN
TO FUEL PUMP

TEST PIN 8 (FPM) WIRE COLOR IDENTIFICATION

Application	Wire Color
2.3L, 2.9L & 4.0L	Orange/Light Blue
All Other Models	Pink/Black

TEST PIN 37/57 (VPWR) WIRE COLOR IDENTIFICATION

Application	Wire Color
All Models	Red

Fuel Pump Circuit Diagram (Bronco, "E" & "F" Series) 91E06952

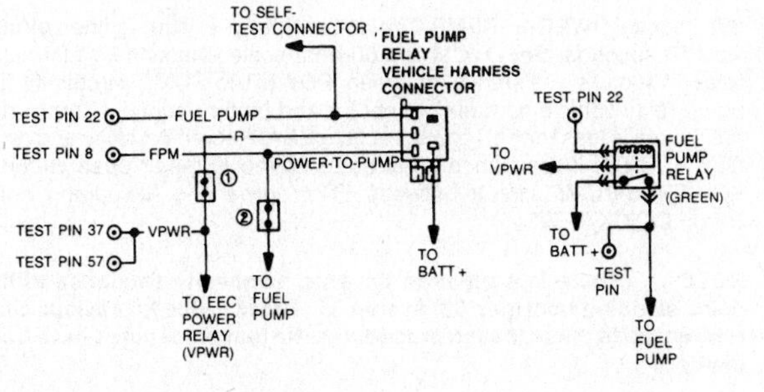
TO SELF-TEST CONNECTOR
FUEL PUMP RELAY VEHICLE HARNESS CONNECTOR
TEST PIN 22
FUEL PUMP
R
TEST PIN 8
FPM
POWER-TO-PUMP
TEST PIN 37
VPWR
TEST PIN 57
TO EEC POWER RELAY (VPWR)
TO FUEL PUMP
TO BATT +
TEST PIN 22
TO VPWR
FUEL PUMP RELAY (GREEN)
TO BATT +
TEST PIN
TO FUEL PUMP

TEST PIN 8 (POWER-TO-PUMP) WIRE COLOR IDENTIFICATION

Application	Wire Color
Bronco, "E" & "F" Series	Dark Green/Yellow

TEST PIN 22 (FP) WIRE COLOR IDENTIFICATION

Application	Wire Color
Bronco & "F" Series	Light Blue/Orange
All Other Models	Tan/Light Green

CIRCUIT TEST J (Cont.)

1) No Fuel Pump Pressure: Check Fuel Pump Electrical Operation – Turn ignition from OFF to RUN position several times (DO NOT turn to START position). If fuel pumps run briefly each time ignition is turned to RUN position, fuel pump circuit is okay. If fuel pumps do not run, go to next step.

2) Check for VPWR to ECA – With ignition off, install breakout box and reconnect ECA. Set DVOM on 20-volt scale. Turn ignition on, leaving engine off. Measure voltage between test pins No. 37 and 40 at breakout box. Measure voltage between test pins No. 57 and 60 at breakout box. If both voltage readings are 10.5 volts or more, go to step **3**). If voltage is less than 10.5 volts, go to CIRCUIT TEST B, step **1**).

3) Check Voltage to POWER-to-PUMP(s) Circuit – With Key On Engine Off (KOEO), breakout box installed and ECA connected, set DVOM on 20-volt scale. Measure voltage between chassis ground and POWER-to-PUMP circuit at fuel pump relay while cranking engine. If reading is less than 8 volts, go to next step. If reading is 8 volts or more, check the following: open in POWER-to-PUMP circuit, open in fuel pump, and open fuel pump ground circuit.

4) Checking BATT (+) Circuit to Fuel Pump Relay – Turn ignition on, leaving engine off. Leave breakout box installed and ECA connected. Locate fuel pump relay. Set DVOM on 20-volt scale. Measure voltage between chassis ground and BATT (+) circuit at fuel pump relay. If reading is less than 10.5 volts, repair open in BATT (+) circuit between fuel pump relay and battery positive post. Repeat QUICK TEST. If reading is 10.5 volts or more, go to next step.

5) Check Voltage at POWER-to-PUMP(s) Circuit – With ignition off, breakout box installed and ECA connected, set DVOM on 20-volt scale. Connect jumper wire from test pin No. 22 to test pin No. 40 or 60 at breakout box. Turn ignition on, leaving engine off. Measure voltage between chassis ground and POWER-to-PUMP circuit at fuel pump relay. If voltage is 10.5 volts or more, replace ECA. Remove breakout box and rerun QUICK TEST. If voltage is less than 10.5 volts, replace fuel pump relay. Remove breakout box, reconnect ECA and rerun QUICK TEST.

NOTE: There is a break in the step numbering sequence at this point, skipping from step 5) to step 7). Break is due to previous chart references to these testing procedures. No test procedures have been omitted.

7) Code 87/556: Checking VPWR Circuit to Fuel Pump Relay – Code 87/556 indicates a fuel pump primary circuit failure. Possible causes for this fault are as follows:

- Inertia Switch Not Reset Or Electrically Open
- Open Or Shorted Circuit
- Faulty Fuel Pump Relay
- Faulty ECA

Turn ignition on, leaving engine off. Set DVOM on 20-volt scale. Disconnect fuel pump relay. Measure voltage between chassis ground and VPWR circuit at fuel pump relay. If reading is 10.5 volts or more, go to next step. If reading is less than 10.5 volts, ensure inertia switch is on. If inertia switch will not reset, replace switch. If switch is okay, repair open in VPWR circuit between EEC power relay and fuel pump relay. Reconnect fuel pump relay and repeat QUICK TEST.

8) Check Fuel Pump Relay – Turn ignition off and wait 10 seconds. Disconnect fuel pump relay. With DVOM on 200-ohm scale, measure resistance between VPWR pin and Fuel Pump circuit pin at fuel pump relay. Resistance should be 40-85 ohms.

Set DVOM to 20-k/ohm scale. Measure resistance between Fuel Pump circuit pin and both POWER-to-PUMP and BATT (+) pins at fuel pump relay. Both resistances should be 10 k/ohms or more. If all resistances are as specified, go to next step. If resistances are not as specified, replace fuel pump relay and rerun QUICK TEST.

Fuel Pump Relay Connector 91B06955

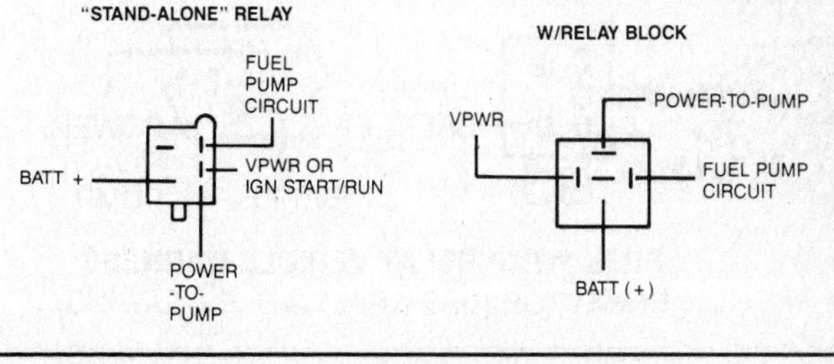
"STAND-ALONE" RELAY
FUEL PUMP CIRCUIT
BATT +
VPWR OR IGN START/RUN
POWER -TO- PUMP
W/RELAY BLOCK
VPWR
POWER-TO-PUMP
FUEL PUMP CIRCUIT
BATT (+)

1991 ENGINE PERFORMANCE
Self-Diagnostics – EEC-IV (Cont.)

CIRCUIT TEST J (Cont.)

9) Check for Short to Power – With ignition off, disconnect 60-pin ECA connector and fuel pump relay. Install breakout box and leave ECA disconnected. Set DVOM on 20-volt scale. Turn ignition on. Measure voltage between test pin No. 22 and battery negative terminal. If voltage is less than one volt, go to next step. If voltage is one volt or more, repair short circuit. Reconnect ECA and attempt to start vehicle. If vehicle fails to start, replace ECA. Rerun QUICK TEST.

10) Check for Shorts to Ground – Turn ignition off and wait 10 seconds. Leave breakout box installed and ECA disconnected. Disconnect fuel pump relay. With DVOM on 200-k/ohm scale, measure resistance between test pin No. 22 and test pins No. 40 and 60. If reading is less than 10 k/ohms, repair short in FUEL PUMP circuit. Remove breakout box and reconnect all components. Repeat QUICK TEST. If reading is 10 k/ohms or more, go to next step.

11) Check Fuel Pump Circuit Continuity – Turn ignition off. Leave breakout box installed and ECA disconnected. Set DVOM to 200-ohm scale. Disconnect fuel pump relay. Measure resistance between fuel pump circuit at fuel pump relay vehicle harness connector and test pin No. 22 at breakout box. If resistance is less than 5 ohms, replace ECA. Reconnect fuel pump relay and rerun QUICK TEST. If resistance is 5 ohms or more, repair open circuit. Remove breakout box, reconnect all components and rerun QUICK TEST.

NOTE: There is a break in the step numbering sequence at this point, skipping from step 11) to step 20). Break is due to previous chart references to these testing procedures. No test procedures have been omitted.

20) Code 95/542: Does Engine Start? – A KOEO Code 95/542 indicates one of the following conditions has occurred:

No Starts
- Inertia Switch Not Reset Or Electrically Open
- Open Circuit In Or Between ECA And Fuel Pump
- Faulty Ground Connection At Fuel Pump

Vehicle Starts
- Fuel Pump Secondary Circuit Shorted To Power
- Fuel Pump Relay Contacts Always Closed
- Open In Fuel Pump Monitor (FPM) Circuit Between ECA And Connection To POWER-to-PUMP Circuit
- HEGO Short To Power (Dual HEGO Applications)
- Faulty ECA

If engine starts, go to next step. If engine does not start, go to step **25)**.

21) Verify Fuel Pump Is Off – Turn ignition on and wait 5 seconds. Listen for fuel pump noise. If fuel pump is off, go to step **23)**. If fuel pump is on, go to next step.

22) Check for Fuel Pump Relay Always Closed – Turn ignition off. Disconnect fuel pump relay. Turn ignition on. If fuel pump is off with relay disconnected, replace fuel pump relay and rerun QUICK TEST. If Fuel pump is on with relay disconnected, repair short to power in POWER-to-PUMP/FPM circuit. (For vehicles with relay block, also check fuel pump prime plug circuit.) Rerun QUICK TEST.

23) Check Continuity of Fuel Pump Monitor (FPM) Circuit – Turn ignition off and wait 10 seconds. Disconnect ECA 60-pin connector. Inspect connector for damaged pins, corrosion, or loose wires. Install breakout box and leave ECA disconnected. Disconnect fuel pump relay. Set DVOM on 200-ohm scale and measure resistance between test pin No. 8 at breakout box and POWER-to-PUMP circuit at fuel pump relay vehicle harness connector. If resistance is less than 5 ohms, go to step **35)** (dual HEGO vehicles), or replace ECA, remove breakout box, reconnect fuel pump relay and rerun QUICK TEST (all other vehicles). If resistance is 5 ohms or more, repair open circuit; remove breakout box, reconnect all components and rerun QUICK TEST.

Fuel Pump Relay Vehicle Harness Connector 90E13130

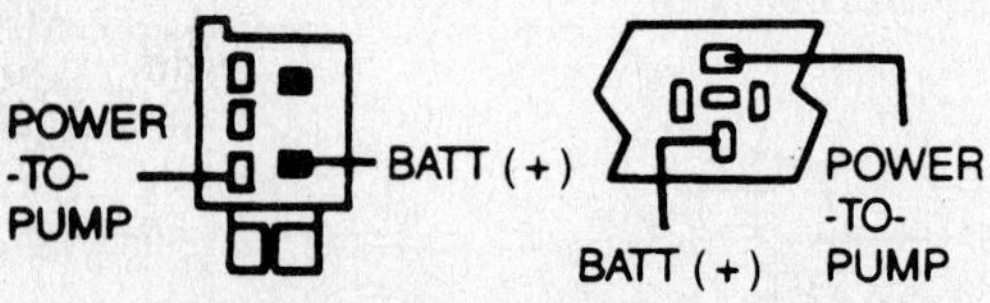
POWER
-TO-
PUMP
BATT (+)
BATT (+)
POWER
-TO-
PUMP

FUEL PUMP RELAY VEHICLE HARNESS CONNECTOR (USE APPLICABLE DRAWING)

CIRCUIT TEST J (Cont.)

NOTE: There is a break in the step numbering sequence at this point, skipping from step 23) to step 25). Break is due to previous chart references to these testing procedures. No test procedures have been omitted.

25) Check Inertia Switch – Turn ignition off and wait 10 seconds. Locate and disconnect fuel pump inertia switch. Ensure switch is reset. Set DVOM on 200-ohm scale. Measure resistance of fuel pump inertia switch. If resistance is less than 5 ohms, reconnect switch and check for open in POWER-to-PUMP circuit, poor fuel pump ground or open in fuel pump. If resistance is 5 ohms or more, replace or reset inertia switch. Repeat QUICK TEST.

NOTE: There is a break in the step numbering sequence at this point, skipping from step 25) to step 30). Break is due to previous chart references to these testing procedures. No test procedures have been omitted.

30) Code 96/543: Engine Does Not Start – Code 96/543 indicates fuel pump secondary circuit failure between BATT (+) supply and FPM connection to POWER-to-PUMP circuit. The following are possible causes for this fault.

No Start
- Open Circuit Between BATT (+) Supply And FPM Connection To POWER-to-PUMP Circuit
- Fuel Pump Relay Contacts Are Always Open

Engine Starts
- HEGO Short To Power (Dual HEGO vehicles)
- Faulty ECA

If engine starts, go to step **35)** (for dual HEGO vehicles) or replace ECA and rerun QUICK TEST (for all other vehicles). If engine does not start, go to next step.

31) Check for BATT (+) to Fuel Pump Relay – With ignition off, set DVOM on 20-volt scale. Connect DVOM between BATT (+) circuit at fuel pump relay and battery negative post. If voltage is 10.5 volts or more, go to next step. If voltage is less than 10.5 volts, check integrity of fuse/fusible link for BATT (+) supply to fuel pump relay. If fuse/fusible is okay, repair open circuit in BATT (+) circuit. Rerun QUICK TEST.

32) Check for Voltage at POWER-to-PUMP Circuit – Turn ignition off and wait 10 seconds. Set DVOM to 20-volt scale. Connect DVOM between POWER-to-PUMP circuit at fuel pump relay and battery negative terminal. Observe DVOM while activating fuel pump relay (turn ignition to RUN position for one second, then turn ignition off for 10 seconds; repeat 5 times). If voltage is 10.5 volts or more for about one second after key is turned to RUN position, go to next step. If voltage is not as specified, disconnect fuel pump relay. Inspect for damaged pins, corrosion, loose pins or other damage. Repair as necessary. If okay, replace fuel pump relay and rerun QUICK TEST.

33) Check POWER-to-PUMP Circuit Continuity – Turn ignition off and wait 10 seconds. Set DVOM to 200-ohm scale. Disconnect fuel pump relay. Measure resistance between POWER-to-PUMP circuit at fuel pump relay vehicle harness connector and battery negative terminal. If resistance is less than 10 ohms, replace ECA. Reconnect relay and rerun QUICK TEST. If resistance is 10 ohms or more, repair open circuit in POWER-to-PUMP circuit between FPM splice and fuel pump relay. Rerun QUICK TEST.

NOTE: There is a break in the step numbering sequence at this point, skipping from step 33) to step 35). Break is due to previous chart references to these testing procedures. No test procedures have been omitted.

Diagnostic Aids – Due to the internal circuitry of ECA, a left/front HEGO signal short to power could produce a code 95/542 or 96/543.

35) Check Left/Front HEGO Sensor for Short to Power – Turn ignition off and wait 10 seconds. Set DVOM to 200-k/ohm scale. Disconnect left

HEGO Sensor Connector 91D06956

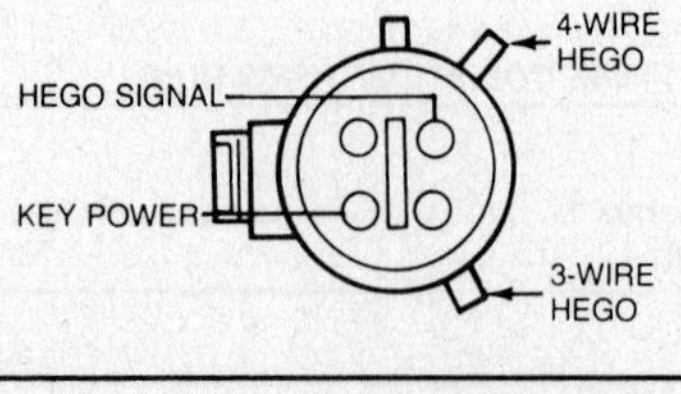
4-WIRE
HEGO
HEGO SIGNAL
KEY POWER
3-WIRE
HEGO

1991 ENGINE PERFORMANCE
Self-Diagnostics – EEC-IV (Cont.)

CIRCUIT TEST J (Cont.)

or front HEGO sensor. Measure resistance between HEGO signal pin and KEY POWER pin at HEGO sensor connector. Is resistance is 10 k/ohms or more, go to next step. If resistance is less than 10 k/ohms, replace HEGO sensor and rerun QUICK TEST. Clear Keep-Alive Memory (KAM).

36) Check HEGO Circuit for Short to Power – Turn ignition off and wait 10 seconds. Set DVOM to 20-volt scale. Disconnect left or front HEGO. Disconnect ECA 60-pin connector and inspect for damaged or pushed-out pins, corrosion, loose wire ore other damage. Leave ECA disconnected. Turn ignition on and measure voltage between HEGO signal at HEGO vehicle harness connector and chassis ground. If voltage is less than 2 volts, replace ECA; reconnect HEGO sensor and rerun QUICK TEST. If voltage is 2 volts or more, repair short circuit. Reconnect ECA and HEGO sensor. Rerun QUICK TEST and clear KAM.

HEGO Sensor Vehicle Harness Connector 91F06957

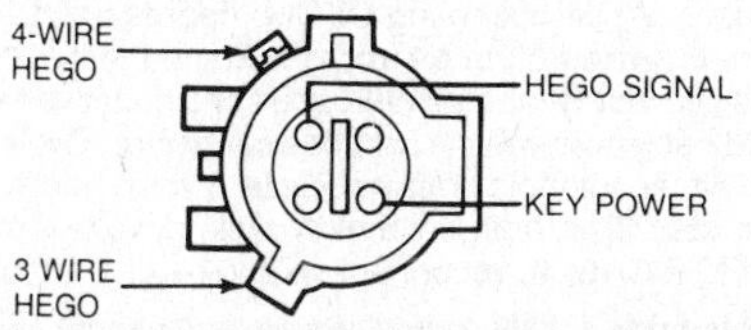
4-WIRE HEGO
HEGO SIGNAL
KEY POWER
3 WIRE HEGO

NOTE: There is a break in the step numbering sequence at this point, skipping from step 36) to step 90). Break is due to previous chart references to these testing procedures. No test procedures have been omitted.

90) Continuous Memory Code 95/542: Check EEC-IV Harness – Code 95/542 indicates one of the following conditions has occurred intermittently:

- Open Circuit In Or Between Fuel Pump And FPM Circuit At ECA
- Faulty Ground Circuit At Fuel Pump
- FPM Or POWER-To-PUMP Circuit Short To Power
- Fuel Pump Relay Contacts Stuck Open
- FUEL PUMP Circuit Is Activated When ECA Expects Circuit To Be Off

Start engine and perform wiggle test on vehicle harness to fuel pump, and to pump ground circuit harness. See CONTINUOUS MONITOR MODE (WIGGLE TEST) under QUICK TEST. Lightly tap inertia switch and pump to simulate road shock. Check for engine miss or stumble while performing test. With ignition off, check harness connectors for corrosion or damage. Isolate and repair any faults; clear Code 95/542 and rerun QUICK TEST. If no fault is found, go to next step.

91) Check FPM Circuit – Turn ignition off. Disconnect ECA 60-pin connector. Inspect connector for damaged pins, corrosion, or loose wires. Install breakout box and leave ECA disconnected. With Key On Engine Off (KOEO), connect a test light between test pin No. 8 and test pin No. 37 at breakout box. With test light on, perform wiggle test on FPM circuit between pump and monitor. Light should go out if fault is found during wiggle test. Isolate and repair any faults found; remove test set-up and rerun QUICK TEST. If no fault is found, go to next step.

92) Check for Shorts to Power – With KOEO, breakout box installed and ECA disconnected, connect a test light between test pin No. 8 and test pin No. 40. Observe test light; perform wiggle test on FPM circuit and POWER-to-PUMP circuit. Lightly tap fuel pump relay to simulate road shock. If light comes on, fault is indicated; isolate and repair as necessary. Remove test set-up and rerun QUICK TEST. If no fault is found, go to step **96)** (dual HEGO-equipped vehicles), or step **99)** (all others).

93) Continuous Memory Code 96/543: Check for Continuous Memory Code 87/556 – If Code 87 or 556 is present, go to step **95)**. If code 87 or 556 is not displayed, go to next step.

94) Check EEC-IV Harness – A Continuous Memory Code 96/543, without an accompanying Continuous Memory Code 87/556, indicates that during vehicle operation, one of the following conditions has occurred:

- An Open In BATT (+) Circuit Between BATT (+) And Fuel Pump Relay
- Fuel Pump Relay Contacts Open
- Open In POWER-To-PUMP Circuit From Fuel Pump Relay To FPM Splice (If Applicable)
- Left/front HEGO Circuit Short To Power (Dual HEGO)

With engine running, attempt to cause a miss or stumble while performing wiggle test on pump harness and connectors. With ignition off, inspect all fuel pump connectors and BATT (+) for damage or corrosion.

CIRCUIT TEST J (Cont.)

If fault is found, isolate and repair as necessary. Clear Continuous Memory Codes and rerun QUICK TEST. If no fault is found, under certain conditions, a Continuous Memory Code 95/543 may have been set without a Continuous Memory Code 87/556, even though a fault has occurred in fuel pump primary circuit. Go to next step.

95) Continuous Code 87/556: Check EEC-IV Harness – A Continuous Memory Code 87 or 556 indicates primary fuel pump circuit has failed during vehicle operation. Possible causes for this fault are as follows:

- Open In VPWR Circuit Between EEC Power Relay And Fuel Pump Relay
- Open Coil In Fuel Pump Relay
- Open In Fuel Pump Circuit (Pin 22)
- Faulty Inertia Switch

With engine running, attempt to cause a miss or stumble while performing wiggle test on VPWR circuit between EEC power relay and fuel pump relay. Wiggle fuel pump circuit harness (test pin No. 22) between ECA and fuel pump relay. Lightly tap fuel pump relay to simulate road shock. With ignition off, inspect ECA 60-pin connector for damage or corrosion. If fault is found, isolate and repair as necessary. Rerun QUICK TEST. If no fault is found, go to next step (dual HEGO-equipped vehicles), or if fault may not be duplicated at this time (all others), go to step **99)**.

Diagnostic Aids – Due to internal circuitry of ECA, an intermittent left/front HEGO signal short to power could produce a Continuous Memory Code 95/542 or 96/543.

96) Check Left/Front HEGO Circuit for Short to Power – Turn ignition off. Install breakout box and leave ECA disconnected. Connect test light between left/front HEGO test pin and pin No. 40 at breakout box. See schematic at beginning of CIRCUIT TEST H for appropriate HEGO test pin No. Perform wiggle test on left/front HEGO circuit to ECA. Lightly tap HEGO sensor to simulate road shock. If light goes on, it indicates fault exists; isolate and repair as necessary. Remove test set-up, clear Keep-Alive Memory (KAM) and rerun QUICK TEST. If no fault is indicated, go to next step.

NOTE: There is a break in the step numbering sequence at this point, skipping from step 96) to step 99). Break is due to previous chart references to these testing procedures. No test procedures have been omitted.

WARNING: This road test is a suggested optional procedure. Follow all applicable safety procedures and traffic laws. This road test requires another person to accompany the driver. The accompanying person can make measurements, observe changes and record notes. If for some reason this test is not performed, go to TROUBLE SHOOTING – NO CODES article for other possible causes.

99) Road Test Vehicle – This test identifies areas of concern by monitoring certain controlled parameters while trying to recreate a driveability or MIL light symptom. To prepare for road test, do the following:

- Install fuel pressure gauge.
- Install MAP/BP tester.
- Disconnect ECA 60-pin connector; install breakout box and reconnect ECA to breakout box.
- Connect "T" vacuum gauge into manifold vacuum line.
- Have DVOM, writing materials and appropriate schematics or pin voltage charts on hand.

With ignition on and negative lead of DVOM connected to battery negative terminal, ensure the following signals are correct:

- POWERS: KAPWR (pin No. 1) is 10.5 volts or more, VPWR (pins No. 37/57) is 10.5 volts or more, and VREF (pin No. 26) is 4-6 volts.
- GROUNDS: PWR GND (pins No. 40/60), SIG RTN (pin No. 46)and IGN GND (pin No. 16) are 0-.5 volt.
- OPTIONAL GROUNDS: HEGO GND (pin No. 49), CSE GND (pin No. 20) and MAF RTN (pin No. 9 or 15).

Drive vehicle and attempt to induce symptom. Information provided by vehicle operator may help when trying to recreate symptom. When symptom occurs, the accompanying passenger should observe and record changes in EEC-IV signals. Information about the symptom, operating condition value of EEC-IV signal and any other information available should be recorded on paper for analysis. If unable to duplicate symptom during road test, it is still useful to verify that EEC-IV values are in expected range.

Once road test has been completed, analyze results to locate and repair fault causing the symptom. If problem cannot be identified, go to TROUBLE SHOOTING – NO CODES article for other possible causes of symptom.

1991 ENGINE PERFORMANCE
Self-Diagnostics – EEC-IV (Cont.)

CIRCUIT TEST KC

AIR MANAGEMENT SYSTEM (AM1/AM2)

Diagnostic Aids – Perform this test when instructed by QUICK TEST, or when directed by other test procedures. This test is intended to diagnose only the following systems or components:

- AM1 Or AM2 Solenoid Valve Assembly
- Harness Circuits (AM1/AM2, VPWR)
- Vacuum Supply
- ECA

To prevent replacement of good components, be aware that the following non-EEC related areas may be at fault: thermactor air system drive belt, air pump or valve.

Air Management Circuits (4.9L, 5.0L & 5.8L) 91F14261

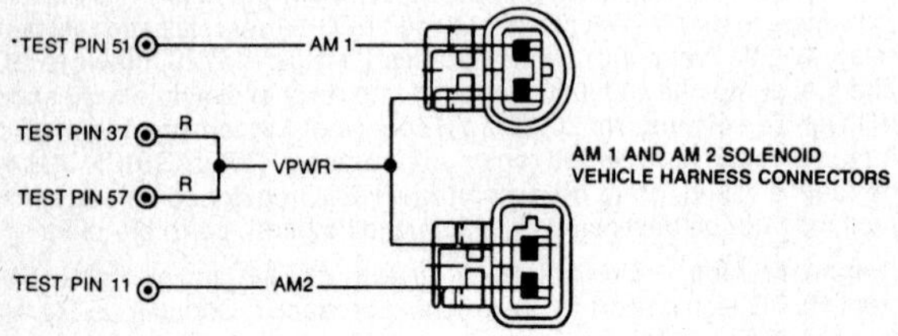
*TEST PIN 51
AM 1
TEST PIN 37
R
VPWR
R
TEST PIN 57
AM 1 AND AM 2 SOLENOID
VEHICLE HARNESS CONNECTORS
TEST PIN 11
AM2

Air Management Circuits (7.5L) 91H06958

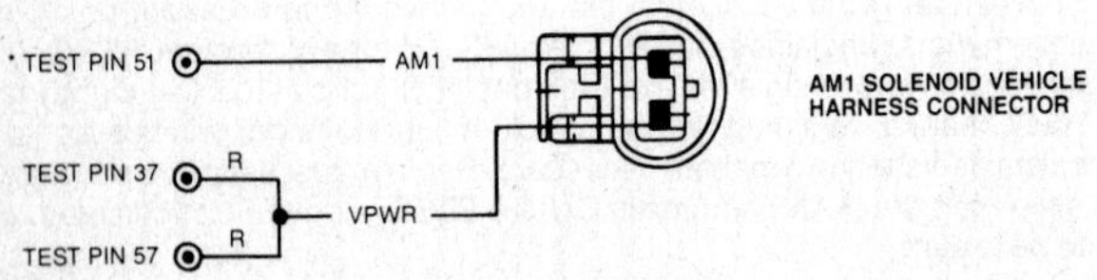
* TEST PIN 51
AM1
AM1 SOLENOID VEHICLE
HARNESS CONNECTOR
TEST PIN 37
R
VPWR
R
TEST PIN 57

TEST PIN 51 (AM1) WIRE COLOR IDENTIFICATION

Application	Wire Color
All Models	White/Orange

TEST PIN 11 (AM2) WIRE COLOR IDENTIFICATION

Application	Wire Color
4.9L, 5.0L & 5.8L: Bronco, "E" & "F" Series	White/Brown

1) Codes 44/311, 45/312, 46/313 & 94/314: Verify Vacuum Line Routing - Code 44/311 or 94/314 indicates thermactor system is inoperative. Code 45/312 indicates thermactor air is flowing upstream when it is NOT signaled to do so by ECA. Code 46/313 indicates thermactor air is NOT by-passed when directed. Possible causes for these faults are as follows:

- Vacuum Hoses Leaked, Blocked Or Kinked
- Diverter Valve Or Thermactor Pump Inoperative
- Am Solenoids Defective Or Blocked

Check for correct vacuum hose routing to AM1/AM2 solenoids and by-pass diverter valve. Use vehicle emissions label as guide. Check for kinked or blocked vacuum hoses. Check for kinked or blocked air hoses. Check for disconnected vacuum hoses. If problems are detected, correct hose routing, repair faults and repeat QUICK TEST. If vacuum routing is okay and Code 44/311 or 94/314 is displayed, go to step **4)**. If Code 46/313 is displayed, go to step **3)**. If Code 45/312 is displayed, go to next step.

2) Attempt to Eliminate Code 45/312 – Disconnect and plug vacuum hose at diverter valve. Turn ignition off and wait 10 seconds. Repeat KOER SELF-TEST and record codes. If Code 45/312 is displayed, EEC-IV system is okay. Inspect diverter valve and check valve for faults. If Code 45/312 is not displayed, go to step **4)**.

3) Attempt to Eliminate Code 46/313 – Disconnect and plug vacuum hose at by-pass valve. Turn ignition off and wait 10 seconds. Repeat KOER SELF-TEST and record codes. If Code 46/313 is displayed, EEC-IV system is okay. Check by-pass valve for problem. If Code 46/313 is not displayed, go to next step.

CIRCUIT TEST KC (Cont.)

4) Output Check – Enter OUTPUT STATE CHECK; see ADDITIONAL SYSTEM FUNCTIONS. Use only a VOM or DVOM for this step; DO NOT use diagnostic tester. Turn ignition off and wait 10 seconds. Disconnect speed control servo (if equipped). With DVOM on 20-volt scale, connect DVOM negative test lead to STO circuit at self-test connector and positive test lead to battery positive terminal. Using jumper wire, connect STI to SIG RTN at self-test connector. Perform KOEO SELF-TEST until end of Continuous Memory Code output (DVOM reads zero volt). Depress and release throttle. DVOM should change to a high-voltage reading. If reading changes, remain in OUTPUT STATE CHECK and go to next step. If reading does not change, depress throttle to WOT and release. If STO voltage does not go high, go to CIRCUIT TEST QC, step **1)**. Leave test equipment hooked up.

5) Check Solenoid Electrical Operation – Set DVOM on 20-volt scale. Disconnect both solenoids. Connect DVOM positive test lead to VPWR circuit and negative test lead to AM1 circuit at AM1 solenoid vehicle harness connector. While observing DVOM, depress and release throttle several times to cycle output on and off. Repeat test for AM2 solenoid. Connect positive test lead to VPWR circuit and negative test lead to AM2 circuit on AM2 solenoid vehicle harness connector. Cycle AM2 solenoid on and off. If either solenoid does not cycle .5 volt or more, remove jumper and go to step **9)**. If both solenoids cycle .5 volt or more, remain in OUTPUT STATE CHECK, reconnect solenoids and go to next step.

6) Check Solenoids for Vacuum Cycling – Connect vacuum pump to AM1 solenoid vacuum supply port. Connect vacuum gauge to output port. Maintain vacuum at source while depressing and releasing throttle to cycle output on and off. Observe vacuum gauge. Repeat for AM2 solenoid. If either output does not cycle on and off, replace solenoid assembly and repeat QUICK TEST. If both outputs cycle on and off, go to next step.

7) Check Solenoids for Internal Vacuum Leaks – Connect a vacuum pump to AM1 solenoid supply port. Connect a vacuum gauge to AM1 solenoid output port. Apply 15 in. Hg vacuum and observe gauge. Repeat test for AM2 solenoid. If vacuum gauge reading holds vacuum for each solenoid, check vacuum source for blockage or leakage from manifold to solenoids and control valves. If vacuum source is okay, inspect thermactor air tube and air passages in cylinder head for carbon blockage. Repeat QUICK TEST. If vacuum gauge does not hold vacuum, replace solenoid assembly and repeat QUICK TEST.

8) Check Voltage of VPWR Circuit – Code 81/553 and 82/552 indicates voltage output for thermactor air solenoid did not change when activated. Possible causes for this fault are as follows:

- Shorted Or Open Circuits
- Solenoid Resistance Out Of Range
- Faulty ECA

Disconnect both solenoid connectors. Turn ignition on, leaving engine off. Set DVOM on 20-volt scale. Measure voltage between AM1 solenoid VPWR circuit and battery ground. Repeat test for AM2 solenoid. If either voltage reading is less than 10.5 volts, repair harness circuit open; reconnect solenoid connectors and repeat QUICK TEST. If both readings are 10.5 volts or more, go to next step.

9) Measure Solenoid Resistance – Turn ignition off and wait 10 seconds. Set DVOM on 200-ohm scale. Disconnect AM1 and AM2 solenoid connectors. Measure resistance of both solenoids. If either reading is NOT 50-100 ohms, replace solenoid assembly and repeat QUICK TEST. If both readings are 50-100 ohms, go to next step.

10) Check Circuit Continuity – Turn ignition off and wait 10 seconds. Disconnect ECA 60-pin connector. Inspect connector for damaged pins, corrosion, or loose wires. Install breakout box, leaving ECA disconnected. With DVOM on 200-ohm scale, measure resistance between test pin No. 51 and AM1 circuit at vehicle harness connector. Measure resistance between test pin No. 11 and AM2 circuit at vehicle harness connector. If either reading is 5 ohms or more, repair harness open circuit and repeat QUICK TEST. If both readings are less than 5 ohms, go to next step.

11) Check for Short to Ground – Turn ignition off and wait 10 seconds. Set DVOM on 200-k/ohm scale. Leave breakout box installed and ECA disconnected. Disconnect AM1/AM2 solenoids. Measure resistance between test pin No. 51 and test pins No. 40, 46 and 60; also measure resistance between test pin No. 11 and test pins No. 40, 46 and 60. If any reading is less than 10 k/ohms, repair short to ground. Remove breakout box, connect harness to ECA and repeat QUICK TEST. If all readings are 10 k/ohms or more, go to next step.

CIRCUIT TEST KC (Cont.)

12) Check for Shorts to Power Circuit – Turn ignition off and wait 10 seconds. Set DVOM on 200-k/ohm scale. Leave breakout box installed with ECA and solenoids disconnected. Measure resistance between test pin No. 51 and test pins No. 37 and 57; also measure resistance between test pin No. 11 and test pins No. 37 and 57.

If any reading is less than 10 k/ohms, repair short to power. Remove breakout box, connect harness to ECA and repeat QUICK TEST. If code is present again, replace ECA.

If all readings are 10 k/ohms or more, replace ECA; remove breakout box, reconnect AM1/AM2 solenoid and repeat QUICK TEST.

CIRCUIT TEST KD

CANISTER PURGE (CANP)

Diagnostic Aids – Perform this test when instructed by QUICK TEST, or when directed by other test procedures. This test is intended to diagnose only the following:

- CANP Solenoid
- Harness Circuits (CANP and VPWR)
- ECA

Canister Purge (CANP) Circuit 91G14262

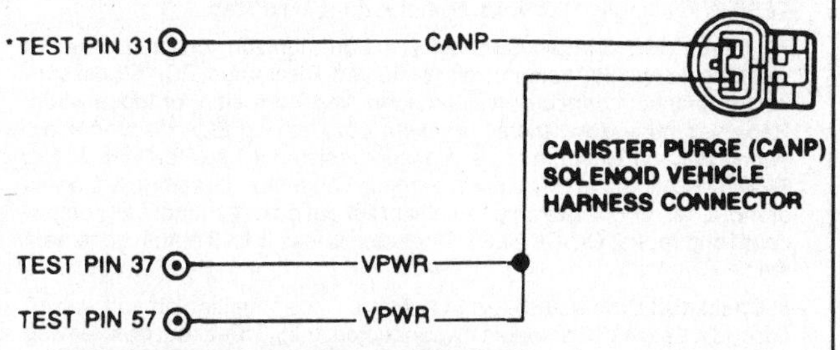

*TEST PIN 31
CANP
CANISTER PURGE (CANP) SOLENOID VEHICLE HARNESS CONNECTOR
TEST PIN 37
VPWR
TEST PIN 57
VPWR

***TEST PINS LOCATED ON BREAKOUT BOX.**
ALL HARNESS CONNECTORS VIEWED INTO MATING SURFACE.

TEST PIN 31 (CANP) WIRE COLOR IDENTIFICATION

Application	Wire Color
All Models	Gray/Yellow

TEST PIN 37/57 (VPWR) WIRE COLOR IDENTIFICATION

Application	Wire Color
All Models	Red

1) Check System Function – Enter OUTPUT STATE CHECK; see ADDITIONAL SYSTEM FUNCTIONS. Use only VOM or DVOM for this step; DO NOT use diagnostic tester. Turn ignition off and wait 10 seconds. Set DVOM on 20-volt scale. Connect DVOM negative test lead to STO and positive test lead to positive battery terminal. Using jumper wire, connect STI circuit to SIG RTN at self-test connector. Perform KOEO SELF-TEST until end of Continuous Memory Codes (DVOM reads zero volt). Depress and release throttle. DVOM should change to a high-voltage reading. If reading changes, remain in OUTPUT STATE CHECK and go to next step. If reading does not change, depress throttle to WOT and release. If STO voltage does not increase, leave test equipment hooked up and go to CIRCUIT TEST QC, step **1)**.

2) Check CANP Solenoid Electrical Function – With Key On Engine Off (KOEO), set DVOM on 20-volt scale. Disconnect CANP solenoid. Connect DVOM positive test lead to VPWR circuit and negative test lead to CANP output circuit on harness connector. While observing DVOM, depress and release throttle several times to cycle output on and off. If CANP circuit does not cycle on and off, remove jumper wire and go to step **6)**. If CANP circuit cycles, remain in OUTPUT STATE CHECK and go to next step.

CIRCUIT TEST KD (Cont.)

3) Check Solenoid for Vacuum Leaks – Turn ignition on. Leave CANP solenoid disconnected. Disconnect vacuum hose at CANP solenoid from manifold vacuum side of solenoid. Apply 16 in. Hg vacuum to manifold vacuum side of CANP solenoid. If CANP solenoid does not hold vacuum for 20 seconds, replace solenoid and repeat QUICK TEST. If fault is still present, service fuel evaporation canister. If CANP holds vacuum for 20 seconds, remain in OUTPUT STATE CHECK, leave vacuum pump attached and go to next step.

4) Check Solenoid Mechanical Operation – While still in OUTPUT STATE CHECK, cycle CANP circuit off (no voltage). Reconnect CANP solenoid connector. Apply 16 in. Hg vacuum to the CANP solenoid as in step **3)**. Depress and release throttle. If vacuum is released, check hose from CANP solenoid to canister for leaks or cracks; if hose is okay, remove jumper wire from STI to SIG RTN and go to next step. If vacuum is not released, check hose from CANP solenoid to canister for leaks or cracks; if hose is okay, replace CANP solenoid and repeat QUICK TEST.

5) Check Vacuum Supply to CANP Solenoid – Disconnect vacuum hose from CANP solenoid on manifold vacuum (PCV) side. Start engine. If vacuum is present at vacuum hose, EEC system is okay; check evaporative canister. If vacuum is not present at hose, check vacuum hose for proper routing, kinks or blockage; if hose is okay, check engine for cause of low vacuum.

6) Code 85/565 or 569: Check CANP Solenoid Resistance – Code 85/565 or 569 indicates fault in CANP solenoid circuit. For vehicles with dual CANP systems, Code 565 refers to CANP 1 while Code 569 refers to CANP 2. Possible causes for this fault are as follows:

- Faulty CANP Solenoid
- Open In Harness Circuit
- Shorted Harness Circuit (Power To Ground)
- Faulty ECA

Turn ignition off and wait 10 seconds. Set DVOM on 200-ohm scale. Disconnect appropriate CANP solenoid connector and measure CANP solenoid resistance. If resistance is 40-90 ohms, go to next step. If reading is NOT 40-90 ohms, replace CANP solenoid and repeat QUICK TEST.

7) Check Voltage of VPWR Circuit – With KOEO and appropriate CANP solenoid disconnected, set DVOM on 20-volt scale. Measure voltage between VPWR circuit at CANP solenoid harness connector and battery negative terminal. If reading is 10.5 volts or more, go to next step. If reading is less than 10.5 volts, repair open in circuit and repeat QUICK TEST.

8) Check Continuity of CANP Circuit – Turn ignition off and wait 10 seconds. Disconnect appropriate CANP solenoid and ECA 60-pin connector. Inspect connector for damaged pins, corrosion, or loose wires. Repair as necessary. Connect breakout box, leaving ECA disconnected. Set DVOM on 200-ohm scale. Measure resistance between test pin No. 11, 31 or 54 (refer to schematic at beginning of this circuit test) and CANP harness connector. If reading is less than 5 ohms, go to next step. If reading is 5 ohms or more, repair open circuit; remove breakout box, reconnect components and repeat QUICK TEST.

9) Check CANP Circuit for Short to Ground – Turn ignition off and wait 10 seconds. Install breakout box, leaving ECA disconnected. Set DVOM on 200-k/ohm scale and disconnect appropriate CANP solenoid. Measure resistance between test pin No. 11, 31 or 54 (refer to schematic at beginning of this circuit test) and test pins No. 40, 46 and 60. If all readings are 10 k/ohms or more, go to next step. If any reading is less than 10 k/ohms, repair short to ground. Remove breakout box, reconnect components and repeat QUICK TEST.

10) Check CANP Circuit for Short to Power – Turn ignition off and wait 10 seconds. Disconnect appropriate CANP solenoid. Install breakout box, leaving ECA disconnected. Set DVOM on 200-k/ohm scale. Measure resistance between test pin No. 11, 31 or 54 (refer to schematic at beginning of this circuit test) and test pins No. 37 and 57. If all reading are 10 k/ohms or more, remove breakout box. Replace ECA and repeat QUICK TEST. If any reading is less than 10 k/ohms, repair short to power; remove breakout box, reconnect components and rerun QUICK TEST. If code is repeated, replace ECA and rerun QUICK TEST.

1991 ENGINE PERFORMANCE
Self-Diagnostics – EEC-IV (Cont.)

CIRCUIT TEST KE

IDLE SPEED CONTROL (AIR BY-PASS)

Diagnostic Aids – Perform this test when instructed by QUICK TEST, or when directed by other test procedures. If engine is running rough or has rough idle, correct these conditions before performing test. Causes may be in ignition system, fuel system or EGR system. This test is intended to diagnose only the following:

- RPM During Self-Test Mode
- ISC Solenoid
- Harness Circuits (ISC And VPWR)
- Faulty ECA

To prevent replacement of good components, be aware that the following non-EEC related areas may be at fault:

- Engine Temperature Not Up To Operating Temperature
- Engine Over Operating Temperature
- A/C Input (Electrical Problem)
- Incorrect Idle Speed Or Throttle Stop Adjustment
- Faulty Cruise Control Linkage

Idle Speed Control (Air By-Pass) Circuit 90G13140

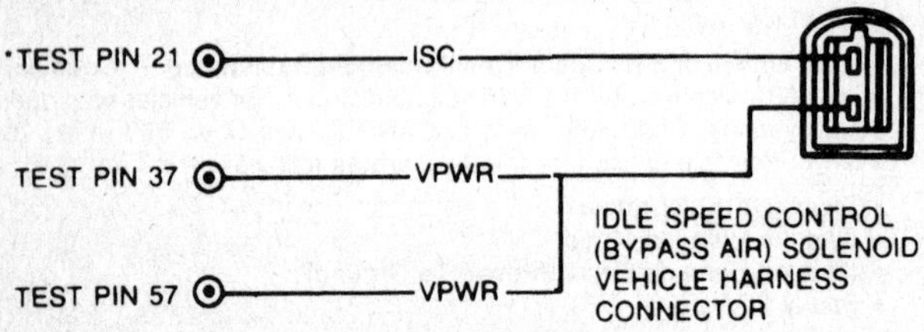
•TEST PIN 21
ISC
TEST PIN 37
VPWR
TEST PIN 57
VPWR
IDLE SPEED CONTROL (BYPASS AIR) SOLENOID VEHICLE HARNESS CONNECTOR

•TEST PINS LOCATED ON BREAKOUT BOX.
ALL HARNESS CONNECTORS VIEWED INTO MATING SURFACE.

TEST PIN 21 (ISC) WIRE COLOR IDENTIFICATION

Application	Wire Color
4.0L Aerostar	Orange/Black
"F" Series	Gray/White
All Others	White/Light Blue

TEST PIN 37/57 (VPWR) WIRE COLOR IDENTIFICATION

Application	Wire Color
All Models	Red

1) Code 12/412: Check for RPM Drop – Code 12/412 indicates that during KOER SELF-TEST, engine RPM could not be controlled within the upper RPM limit of self-test. Possible causes for this fault are as follows:

- Open Or Shorted Circuit
- Sticking Or Binding Throttle Linkage
- Incorrect Idle Adjustment
- Throttle Body Or ISC Solenoid Contaminated
- Faulty ISC Solenoid
- Faulty ECA
- Non-ECC Mechanical Faults That Could Affect RPM

Turn ignition off. Connect engine tachometer and start engine. Disconnect Idle Speed Control (ISC) harness. If RPM drops or engine stalls, go to next step. If RPM doesn't drop or engine doesn't stall, go to step **3)**.

2) Check for EGR Codes – If EGR service codes 31/327, 32/326/328, 33/332 or 34/336/334 are displayed, reconnect ISC solenoid. Go to appropriate KOER SELF-TEST CODES chart under SERVICE CODE REFERENCE CHARTS, and perform appropriate CIRCUIT TEST. If these codes are not displayed, go to next step.

3) Check for Other EEC-IV Codes – If Codes 22/126, 41/172, 42/173, 91/136 or 92/137 are displayed, reconnect ISC solenoid. Go to appropriate KOER SELF-TEST CODES chart under SERVICE CODE REFERENCE CHARTS, and perform appropriate CIRCUIT TEST. If these codes are not displayed, go to next step.

4) Measure ISC Solenoid Resistance – Turn ignition off. Disconnect ISC solenoid. Set DVOM on 200-ohm scale, and measure resistance of

CIRCUIT TEST KE (Cont.)

ISC solenoid. Connect DVOM positive (+) lead to VPWR terminal and DVOM negative lead to ISC terminal, as ISC solenoid is equipped with a diode. If resistance is 7-13 ohms, go to next step. If resistance is NOT 7-13 ohms, replace ISC solenoid and repeat QUICK TEST.

ISC Solenoid Connector 90H13141

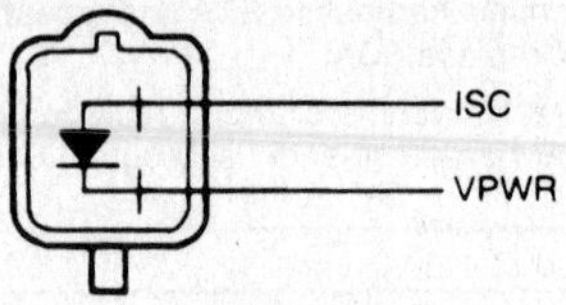
ISC
VPWR

ISC SOLENOID CONNECTOR

5) Check for Internal Short to ISC Solenoid Case – With ignition off and ISC solenoid disconnected, set DVOM on 200-k/ohm scale. Measure resistance from either ISC terminal pin to ISC solenoid housing. If reading is 10 k/ohms or more, go to next step. If reading is less than 10 k/ohms, replace ISC solenoid. Repeat QUICK TEST.

6) Check VPWR Circuit Voltage – Leave ISC harness disconnected. With KOEO, set DVOM on 20-volt scale. Measure voltage between VPWR circuit at ISC harness connector and battery ground terminal. If reading is less than 10.5 volts, repair open in circuit and repeat QUICK TEST. If reading is 10.5 volts or more, go to next step.

7) Check ISC Circuit Continuity – Turn ignition off and wait 10 seconds. Leave ISC solenoid disconnected. Disconnect ECA 60-pin connector. Inspect connector for damaged pins, corrosion, or loose wires. Repair as necessary. Install breakout box, leaving ECA disconnected. With DVOM on 200-ohm scale, measure resistance between test pin No. 21 and ISC circuit at ISC vehicle harness connector. If reading is 5 ohms or more, repair open circuit; remove breakout box, reconnect all components and repeat QUICK TEST. If reading is less than 5 ohms, go to next step.

8) Check ISC Circuit for Short to Ground – Turn ignition off and wait 10 seconds. Leave ISC solenoid disconnected. Install breakout box, leaving ECA disconnected. Set DVOM on 200-k/ohm scale. Measure resistance between test pin No. 21 and test pins No. 40, 46 and 60. If any reading is less than 10 k/ohms, repair short to ground and repeat QUICK TEST. If all readings are 10 k/ohms or more, go to next step.

9) Check ISC Circuit for Short to Power – Turn ignition off and wait 10 seconds. Leave breakout box installed. Leave ECA and ISC solenoid disconnected. Set DVOM on 200-k/ohm scale. Measure resistance by connecting DVOM negative lead to test pin No. 21 and positive lead to test pin No. 37. If reading is 10 k/ohms or more, go to next step. If reading is less than 10 k/ohms, repair short circuit and remove breakout box. Reconnect all components and repeat QUICK TEST. If code or symptom is still present, replace ECA.

10) Check ISC Signal From ECA – With ignition off, reconnect ECA and ISC. Leave breakout box installed and set DVOM on 20-volt scale. Connect DVOM between test pins No. 21 and 40. Start engine and observe DVOM while slowly increasing RPM to 3000 RPM. If DVOM voltage reading is 3.0-11.5 volts, go to next step. If DVOM voltage reading does not vary, replace ECA and repeat QUICK TEST.

11) Check Base Idle – Verify base idle speed. See ON-VEHICLE ADJUSTMENTS article. If base idle speed is within specifications, remove ISC solenoid and inspect for contamination; service as necessary. Rerun QUICK TEST. If code or symptom is still present, replace ISC solenoid.

If curb idle speed is incorrect, reset idle speed to specification. Rerun QUICK TEST. If unable to set idle to specification, go to next step.

12) Check Faults Which Affect Idle Speed – Check the following mechanical items for faults:

- Throttle Linkage And/Or Cruise Control Linkage (Sticking Or Binding)
- Throttle Body (Contamination)
- Vacuum Hoses (Check Emission Decal)
- Leaks Around ISC Solenoid (Gaskets, Etc.)

If all of these items are okay, remove ISC solenoid and inspect for contamination. Service as necessary and rerun QUICK TEST. If code or symptom is still present, replace ISC. If any of these items are faulty, service as necessary. Remove breakout box. Reconnect components and rerun QUICK TEST.

CIRCUIT TEST KE (Cont.)

NOTE: There is a break in the step numbering sequence at this point, skipping from step 12) to step 15). Break is due to previous chart references to these testing procedures. No test procedures have been omitted.

15) Code 13/411: Verify Idle Speed Is Within Specification – Code 13/411 indicates that during KOER SELF-TEST, engine RPM could not be controlled within the lower RPM limit of self-test. Possible causes for this fault are as follows:

- Incorrect Idle Setting
- Vacuum Leaks
- Sticking Or Binding Throttle Linkage
- Throttle Plates Open
- Incorrect Ignition Timing (TFI Ignition Only)
- Throttle Body Or ISC Solenoid Contamination
- ISC Circuit Shorted To Ground
- Faulty ISC Solenoid

If all of the mentioned components are okay and idle is set to specification, remove ISC solenoid and inspect for contamination; service as necessary and rerun QUICK TEST. If code or symptom is still present, replace ISC solenoid. If idle speed is not set to specification, reset and rerun QUICK TEST. If idle speed cannot be reset to specification, go to next step.

16) Check for Conditions Affecting Idle Speed – Check the following mechanical components:

- Engine Vacuum Hoses (Refer To Emission Decal)
- Throttle Linkage And/Or Cruise Control Linkage (Sticking Or Binding)
- Ensure Throttle Plates Are Fully Closed
- Induction System (Vacuum Leaks)
- Throttle Body (Contamination)
- Ensure Base Ignition Timing Is To Specification On Emission Decal (TFI Vehicles Only)

If everything checks okay, go to next step. If fault is found, service as necessary and rerun QUICK TEST.

17) Check for Internal Short to ISC Solenoid Case – With ignition off and ISC solenoid disconnected, set DVOM on 200-k/ohm scale. Measure resistance from either ISC terminal pin to ISC solenoid housing. If reading is 10 k/ohms or more, go to next step. If reading is less than 10 k/ohms, replace ISC solenoid. Repeat QUICK TEST.

18) Check ISC Circuit for Short to Ground – Turn ignition off and wait 10 seconds. Leave ISC solenoid disconnected. Disconnect ECA 60-pin connector. Inspect for damaged or corroded terminal pins; service as necessary. Install breakout box, leaving ECA disconnected. Set DVOM on 200-k/ohm scale. Measure resistance between test pin No. 21 and test pins No. 40, 46 and 60. If any reading is less than 10 k/ohms, repair short to ground and remove breakout box. Reconnect components and repeat QUICK TEST. If all readings are 10 k/ohms or more, go to next step.

19) Check ISC Signal From ECA – With ignition off, connect ECA and ISC. Leave breakout box installed and set DVOM on 20-volt scale. Connect DVOM between test pins No. 21 and 40. Start engine and observe DVOM while slowly increasing and decreasing engine RPM. If DVOM voltage reading varies, remove ISC solenoid and inspect for contamination; service as necessary and rerun QUICK TEST. If code or symptom is still present, replace ISC solenoid. If DVOM voltage does not vary, replace ECA and rerun QUICK TEST.

CIRCUIT TEST KM

WIDE OPEN THROTTLE A/C CUT-OUT (WAC) & A/C DEMAND SWITCH

Diagnostic Aids – Perform this test when diagnosing a symptom. To prevent replacing good components, check the following non-EEC components and systems:

- Refrigerant Charge
- Low Ambient Temperature (Less Than 45°F)

This test is intended to diagnose only the following:

- Harness Circuits (WAC, VPWR, GND, POWER to CLUTCH, and ACD)
- WAC Relay
- A/C Fan Controller
- ECA

CIRCUIT TEST KM (Cont.)

WOT A/C Cut-Out Circuits (Aerostar, Explorer & Ranger) 91E06966

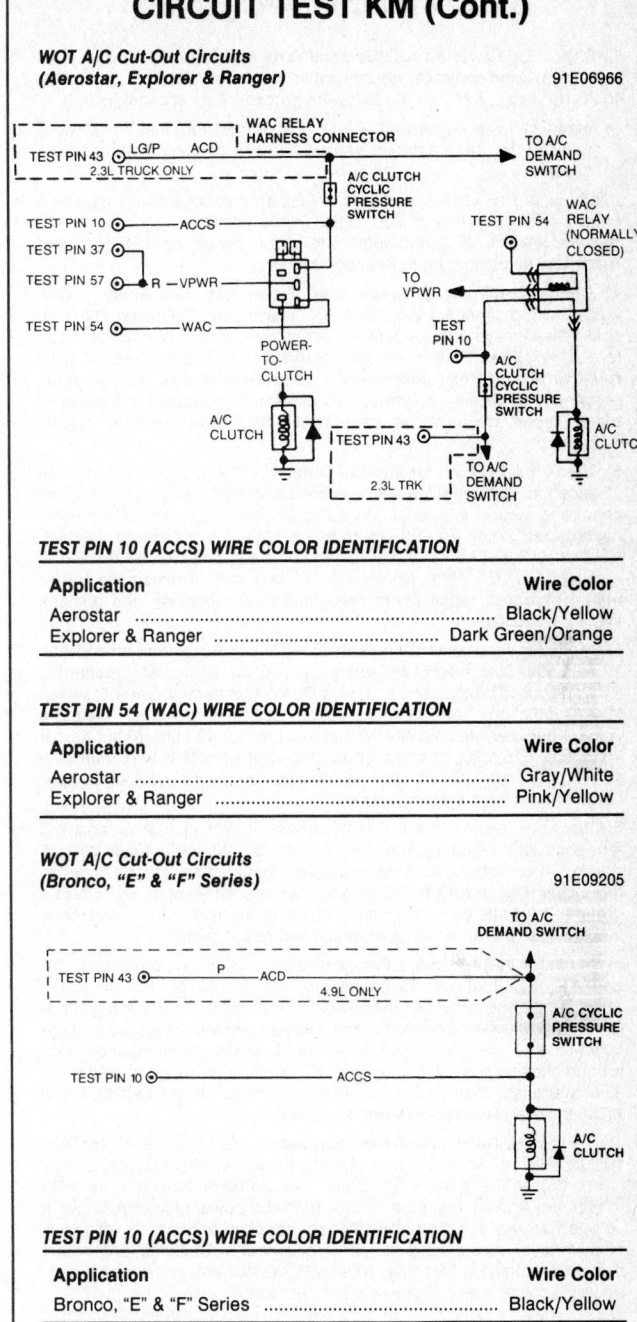

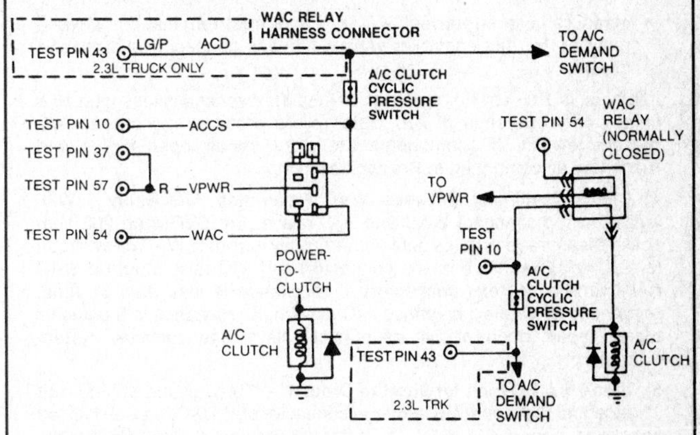
WAC RELAY HARNESS CONNECTOR
TEST PIN 43
LG/P
ACD
2.3L TRUCK ONLY
TO A/C DEMAND SWITCH
A/C CLUTCH CYCLIC PRESSURE SWITCH
TEST PIN 10
ACCS
TEST PIN 37
TEST PIN 57
R – VPWR
TEST PIN 54
WAC
TEST PIN 54
WAC RELAY (NORMALLY CLOSED)
TO VPWR
POWER-TO-CLUTCH
TEST PIN 10
A/C CLUTCH CYCLIC PRESSURE SWITCH
A/C CLUTCH
TEST PIN 43
2.3L TRK
TO A/C DEMAND SWITCH
A/C CLUTCH

TEST PIN 10 (ACCS) WIRE COLOR IDENTIFICATION

Application	Wire Color
Aerostar	Black/Yellow
Explorer & Ranger	Dark Green/Orange

TEST PIN 54 (WAC) WIRE COLOR IDENTIFICATION

Application	Wire Color
Aerostar	Gray/White
Explorer & Ranger	Pink/Yellow

WOT A/C Cut-Out Circuits (Bronco, "E" & "F" Series) 91E09205

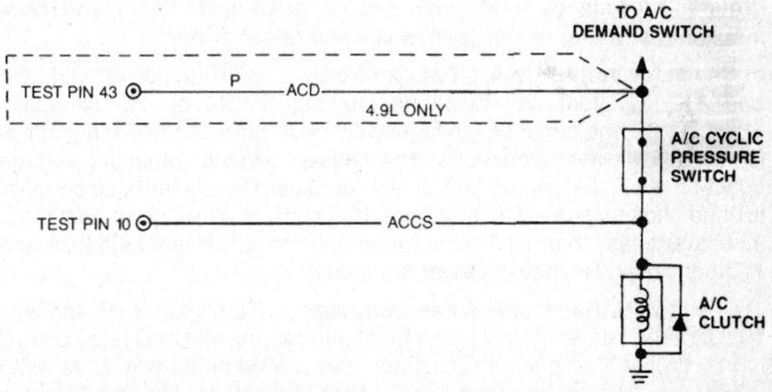
TO A/C DEMAND SWITCH
TEST PIN 43
P
ACD
4.9L ONLY
A/C CYCLIC PRESSURE SWITCH
TEST PIN 10
ACCS
A/C CLUTCH

TEST PIN 10 (ACCS) WIRE COLOR IDENTIFICATION

Application	Wire Color
Bronco, "E" & "F" Series	Black/Yellow

1) No A/C: Check for Voltage at A/C Clutch – Check all A/C related fuses in fuse panel before proceeding with this test. Use only DVOM for this step; DO NOT use diagnostic tester. With ignition off, disconnect A/C clutch harness connector. Turn A/C switch to A/C position. Set DVOM on 20-volt scale. Start engine and wait 10 seconds. Measure voltage between power side of A/C clutch vehicle harness connector and negative battery terminal. If voltage is 10.5 volts or more, EEC-IV system is okay; diagnose A/C system. If voltage is less than 10.5 volts, go to next step.

2) Check Continuity of POWER-to-CLUTCH Circuit – Turn ignition off and wait 10 seconds. Set DVOM on 200-ohm scale. Disconnect A/C clutch harness and harness from WAC relay or A/C fan controller. Measure resistance between power side of A/C clutch vehicle harness connector and POWER-to-CLUTCH circuit terminal pin at WAC relay or A/C fan controller vehicle harness connector. If resistance is less than 5 ohms, reconnect A/C clutch and go to next step. If resistance is 5 ohms or more, service open circuit and retest system.

1991 ENGINE PERFORMANCE
Self-Diagnostics – EEC-IV (Cont.)

CIRCUIT TEST KM (Cont.)

3) Check for Power on A/C Demand Circuit – With KOEO and WAC relay or A/C fan controller disconnected, turn on A/C switch. Set DVOM to 20-volt scale. Perform the following procedure as applicable:

- Measure voltage between A/C demand input terminal pin at WAC relay or A/C fan controller vehicle harness connector and chassis ground.

If voltage is 10.5 volts or more, go to step **5)**. If voltage is less than 10.5 volts, verify operation of A/C clutch cyclic pressure switch and A/C demand switch. If components are okay, repair open circuit and reconnect all components. Recheck system.

4) Check Continuity Between WAC Relay and A/C Relay – With ignition off, disconnect WAC and A/C relays. Set DVOM on 200-ohm scale. Measure resistance between A/C relay output to WAC relay circuit (at A/C relay vehicle harness connector) and A/C relay input (at WAC relay vehicle harness connector). If resistance is less than 5 ohms, reconnect WAC relay; diagnose A/C system. If resistance is 5 ohms or more, repair open circuit; reconnect relays and recheck system operation.

5) Check WAC Circuit for Short to Ground – Turn ignition off and wait 10 seconds. Disconnect ECA 60-pin connector and WAC relay or A/C fan controller. Inspect and repair any damaged wiring. Leaving ECA disconnected, set DVOM on 200-k/ohm scale. Measure resistance between WAC circuit at WAC relay or A/C fan controller and chassis ground. If resistance is 10 k/ohms or more, go to next step. If resistance is less than 10 k/ohms, repair short; reconnect all components and recheck system operation.

6) Check for Voltage at ACCS Input to ECA – Turn ignition off and wait 10 seconds. Disconnect WAC relay and A/C fan controller. Disconnect ECA and install breakout box, leaving ECA disconnected. Set A/C switch to A/C position. Set DVOM to 20-volt scale. With KOEO, measure voltage between test pin No. 10 and test pin No. 40 at breakout box. If voltage is 10.5 volts or more, go to step **9)**. If voltage is less than 10.5 volts, repair open circuit; remove breakout box, reconnect all components and recheck system operation.

7) Check for Ground to A/C Fan Controller – With ignition off and A/C fan controller disconnected, set DVOM on 200-ohm scale. Install breakout box, leaving ECA disconnected. Measure resistance between ground circuit at A/C fan controller harness connector and chassis ground. If resistance is less than 5 ohms, go to next step. If resistance is 5 ohms or more, repair open circuit and retest system.

8) Check for Voltage to A/C Fan Controller – With ignition on and ECA and A/C fan controller disconnected, set DVOM on 20-volt scale. Measure voltage between ignition switch RUN circuit at A/C fan controller vehicle harness connector and chassis ground. Measure voltage between BATT (+) circuit at A/C fan controller vehicle harness connector and chassis ground. If voltage is 10.5 volts or more, go to next step. If voltage is less than 10.5 volts, repair open circuit. Reconnect ECA and A/C controller. Recheck system operation.

9) Check WAC Relay or A/C Fan Controller – Turn ignition off and wait 10 seconds. Leave ECA disconnected and reconnect WAC relay or A/C fan controller. Disconnect A/C clutch. Set DVOM on 20-volt scale. With KOEO and A/C on, measure voltage between power side of A/C clutch vehicle harness connector and battery negative terminal. If voltage is 10.5 volts or more, replace ECA; reconnect A/C clutch and retest system. If voltage is less than 10.5 volts, replace WAC relay or fan controller; reconnect all components and recheck system.

NOTE: There is a break in the step numbering sequence at this point, skipping from step 9) to step 15). Break is due to previous chart references to these testing procedures. No test procedures have been omitted.

15) No A/C Output at WOT – Enter OUTPUT STATE CHECK; see ADDITIONAL SYSTEM FUNCTIONS. Use a VOM or DVOM for this test. Turn ignition off and wait 10 seconds. Disconnect speed control servo electrical connector (if equipped). Set DVOM on 20-volt scale. Connect DVOM negative test lead to STO at self-test connector and positive lead to positive battery terminal. Jumper STI to SIGNAL RETURN at self-test connector. Perform KOEO SELF-TEST until Continuous Memory Code output is completed. Meter will indicate less than one volt when test is complete. Depress and release throttle. If voltage increases to 10.5 volts or more, remain in OUTPUT STATE CHECK and go to next step. If voltage does not increase to 10.5 volts, depress throttle to WOT and release. If STO voltage does not go high, leave test equipment connected and go to CIRCUIT TEST QC, step **2)**.

CIRCUIT TEST KM (Cont.)

16) Check for VPWR to Relay – With vehicle in OUTPUT STATE CHECK, disconnect harness from WAC relay and set DVOM on 20-volt scale. Measure voltage between VPWR circuit at WAC relay vehicle harness connector and chassis ground. If voltage is 10.5 volts or more, go to next step. If voltage is less than 10.5 volts, repair open circuit between power relay and WAC relay. Remove test equipment and retest system.

17) Check WAC System for Cycling – With vehicle in OUTPUT STATE CHECK, reconnect WAC relay and set DVOM on 20-volt scale. Connect positive test lead to VPWR circuit and negative test lead to WAC circuit at WAC relay vehicle harness connector. Check DVOM while depressing and releasing throttle several times to cycle output on and off. If voltage cycles from high to low, replace WAC relay; remove jumper and retest system. If voltage does not cycle, remove test leads; reconnect speed control servo and go to next step.

18) Check Resistance of WAC Relay Coil – Turn ignition off and wait 10 seconds. Disconnect WAC relay. Set DVOM to 200-ohm scale. Measure resistance between WAC pin and VPWR pin on WAC relay. If resistance is 40-100 ohms, go to next step. If resistance is NOT 40-100 ohms, replace WAC relay and retest system.

19) Check Continuity of WAC Circuit – Turn ignition off and wait 10 seconds. Disconnect ECA 60-pin connector. Inspect and repair any damaged wiring. Install breakout box, leaving ECA and WAC relay disconnected. Set DVOM on 200-ohm scale. Measure resistance between test pin No. 54 and WAC circuit at WAC relay vehicle harness connector. If reading is 5 ohms or more, repair open circuit; remove breakout box, reconnect all components and retest system. If reading is less than 5 ohms, go to next step.

20) Check WAC Circuit for Short to Power – Turn ignition off and wait 10 seconds. Leave breakout box installed and ECA and WAC relay disconnected. Set DVOM on 200-k/ohm scale. Measure resistance between test pin No. 54 and test pins No. 37 and 57. If all readings are 10 k/ohms or more, replace ECA; reconnect WAC relay and retest system. If any reading is less than 10 k/ohms, repair short circuit. Reconnect all components and retest system. If symptom is still present, replace ECA.

21) Check WAC Cycling – With vehicle in OUTPUT STATE CHECK, disconnect A/C fan controller and set DVOM on 20-volt scale. Connect DVOM positive test lead to ignition run circuit and negative test lead to WAC circuit at A/C fan controller harness connector. Check DVOM while depressing and releasing throttle several times to cycle system. If voltage does not cycle, remove jumper; reconnect components and go to next step. If voltage cycles from high to low, replace A/C fan controller. Reconnect components and retest system.

22) Check Continuity of WAC Circuit – Turn ignition off and wait 10 seconds. Disconnect ECA 60-pin connector. Inspect and repair any damaged wiring. Install breakout box, leaving ECA and fan controller disconnected. Set DVOM on 200-ohm scale. Measure resistance between test pin No. 54 and WAC circuit at WAC relay vehicle harness connector. If reading is less than 5 ohms, go to next step. If reading is 5 ohms or more, repair open in harness; remove breakout box, reconnect all components and retest system.

23) Check WAC Circuit for Short to Power – Turn ignition off and wait 10 seconds. Install breakout box, leaving ECA and A/C fan controller disconnected. Set DVOM on 200-k/ohm scale. Measure resistance between test pin No. 54 and test pins No. 37 and 57 at breakout box. If all readings are 10 k/ohms or more, replace ECA; reconnect A/C fan controller and retest system. If any reading is 10 k/ohms or less, repair short to power and retest system; if symptom is still present, replace ECA.

NOTE: There is a break in the step numbering sequence at this point, skipping from step 23) to step 30). Break is due to previous chart references to these testing procedures. No test procedures have been omitted.

30) Cycle A/C Demand Switch – Turn ignition off and wait 10 seconds. Disconnect ECA 60-pin connector. Inspect for corroded and damaged connector pins, and repair as necessary. Install breakout box, leaving ECA disconnected. Set DVOM on 20-volt scale. With KOEO, connect DVOM positive test lead to test pin No. 43 and negative test lead to test pin No. 40. If voltage goes high and low as switch is cycled, go to step **44)**. If voltage does not cycle, go to next step.

31) Check Continuity of A/C Demand (ACD) Circuit – Turn ignition off and wait 10 seconds. Install breakout box, leaving ECA disconnected. Set DVOM on 200-ohm scale. Measure resistance between test pin No.

CIRCUIT TEST KM (Cont.)

43 at breakout box and A/C demand switch. If resistance is 5 ohms or more, repair open in ACD circuit and rerun QUICK TEST. If resistance is less than 5 ohms, EEC-IV system is okay. Remove breakout box and reconnect components. Diagnose A/C system.

NOTE: There is a break in the step numbering sequence at this point, skipping from step 31) to step 35). Break is due to previous chart references to these testing procedures. No test procedures have been omitted.

35) Check A/C Demand (ACD) Circuit for Short to Power – With ignition off, disconnect WAC relay or A/C fan controller. Disconnect ECA 60-pin connector. Inspect for corroded or damaged connector pins and repair as necessary. Install breakout box, leaving ECA disconnected. With A/C demand switch in OFF position, set DVOM on 20-volt scale. With KOEO, measure voltage between test pin No. 43 at breakout box and chassis ground. If voltage is less than one volt, EEC-IV system is okay; remove breakout box, reconnect all components and diagnose A/C system. If voltage is one volt or more, check operation of A/C demand switch. If switch operation is okay, repair short circuit. Remove breakout box, reconnect all components and retest system.

NOTE: There is a break in the step numbering sequence at this point, skipping from step 35) to step 40). Break is due to previous chart references to these testing procedures. No test procedures have been omitted.

Diagnostic Aids – Before entering this test, ensure A/C selector is off (and shift selector is in Park for AXODE and E4OD vehicles). If A/C was on, rerun QUICK TEST. If Code 67 or 79/539 is present, continue with this test.

40) Check A/C Input Code 79/539 indicates ACCS input to ECA was high during self-test. Turn ignition off and wait 10 seconds. Disconnect ECA 60-pin connector; inspect for corroded or damaged connector pins and repair as necessary. Install breakout box, leaving ECA disconnected. Set DVOM to 20-volt scale. With KOEO, measure voltage between test pin No. 10 at breakout box and chassis ground. If voltage is one volt or more, repair short to power in A/C circuit. Remove breakout box, reconnect all components and rerun QUICK TEST. If voltage is less than one volt, go to next step for trucks with 2-digit codes and E4OD trans; on all other vehicles, replace ECA, reconnect all components and rerun QUICK TEST.

41) Check for Short to Power In ECA – Turn ignition off and wait 10 seconds. Install breakout box, leaving ECA disconnected. Disconnect A/C clutch connector. Set DVOM to 20-volt scale. With KOEO, measure voltage between test pins No. 10 and 40. If voltage is one volt or more, replace ECA; reconnect A/C clutch and rerun QUICK TEST. If voltage is less than one volt, diagnose transmission.

NOTE: There is a break in the step numbering sequence at this point, skipping from step 41) to step 43). Break is due to previous chart references to these testing procedures. No test procedures have been omitted.

Diagnostic Aids – A low idle with A/C on may be caused by the ECA not receiving or recognizing A/C input from pin No. 10

43) Check A/C Input Circuit – Turn A/C switch to A/C position. Perform KOEO SELF-TEST. If Code 67 or 79/539 is present, ECA is receiving and recognizing A/C input from pin No. 10. Check for other possible cause of low idle. If Code 67 or 79/539 is not present, go to next step.

44) Check A/C Input Circuit – Turn ignition off and wait 10 seconds. Disconnect ECA 60-pin connector. Install breakout box, leaving ECA disconnected. Set DVOM to 20-volt scale. Turn A/C on. With KOEO, measure voltage between test pins No. 10 and 40.

If voltage is 10.5 volts or more, replace ECA. Remove breakout box, reconnect all components and rerun QUICK TEST.

If voltage is less than 10.5 volts, repair open A/C circuit. Remove breakout box, reconnect all components and rerun QUICK TEST.

CIRCUIT TEST KP

OCTANE ADJUST

Diagnostic Aids – Enter this test when directed by QUICK TEST. This test is intended to diagnose only the following systems or components:

- Harness circuits (SIG RTN and OCT ADJ)
- Octane shorting bar connector

Octane Adjust Circuit 91H14263

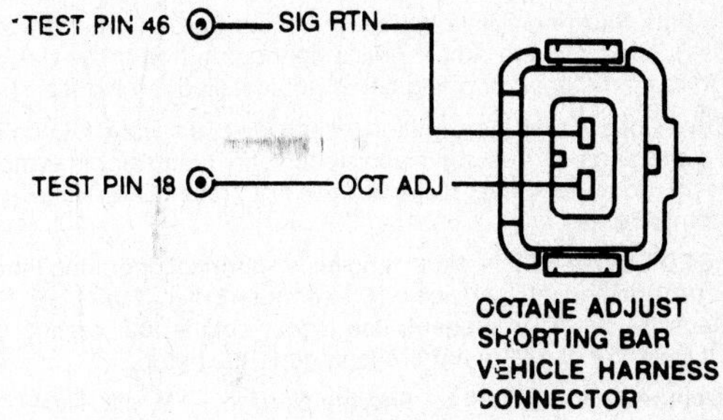
*TEST PIN 46
SIG RTN
TEST PIN 18
OCT ADJ
OCTANE ADJUST SHORTING BAR VEHICLE HARNESS CONNECTOR

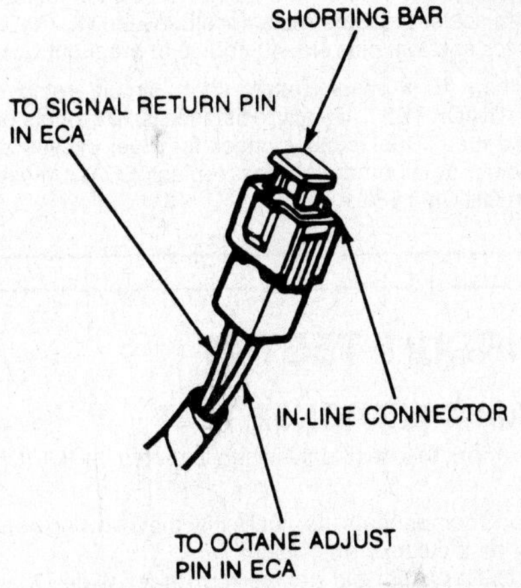
SHORTING BAR
TO SIGNAL RETURN PIN IN ECA
IN-LINE CONNECTOR
TO OCTANE ADJUST PIN IN ECA

***TEST PINS LOCATED ON BREAKOUT BOX.
ALL HARNESS CONNECTORS VIEWED INTO MATING SURFACE.**

TEST PIN 44 (OCT ADJ) WIRE COLOR IDENTIFICATION

Application	Wire Color
2.3L Ranger & 4.0L Explorer	Dark Green
4.0L Ranger	Orange

TEST PIN 46 (SIG RTN) WIRE COLOR IDENTIFICATION

Application	Wire Color
All Models	Gray/Red

The purpose of the Octane Adjust Shorting Bar is to provide optimum spark advance for the fuel used. If vehicle engine detonates (spark knock), remove Octane Shorting Bar. This retards spark advance about 3 to 4 degrees. If vehicle continues to detonate, use fuel with a higher octane rating.

1) Code 57/341: Inspect Octane Adjust In-Line Connector – Code 57/431 indicates Octane Adjust Shorting Bar is not in, or OCT ADJ circuit is open. Turn ignition off and wait 10 seconds. Inspect Octane Adjust in-line connector. If shorting bar has been removed, return to QUICK TEST for complete diagnosis. If shorting bar is in place, go to next step.

2) Check Octane Adjust Circuit Continuity – There should be continuity from OCT ADJ circuit, through in-line connector and shorting bar, to SIG RTN circuit. Turn ignition off and wait 10 seconds. Disconnect ECA 60-pin connector; inspect for corroded or damaged connector pins and repair as necessary. Install breakout box, leaving ECA disconnected. Set DVOM to 200-ohm scale. Measure resistance between test pin No. 46 and OCT ADJ test pin at breakout box. If resistance is less than 5

1991 ENGINE PERFORMANCE
Self-Diagnostics – EEC-IV (Cont.)

CIRCUIT TEST KP (Cont.)

ohms, replace ECA. Remove breakout box and rerun QUICK TEST. If resistance is 5 ohms or more, repair open OCT ADJ circuit, shorting bar or SIG RTN circuit. Remove breakout box and rerun QUICK TEST.

3) Check for Code 11 – Start engine and let idle at operating temperature. Turn ignition off and wait 10 seconds. Enter KOEO SELF-TEST. If Code 11 or 111 is present, go to next step. If Code 11 or 111 is not present, use higher octane fuel or check for other possible causes for Code 57/341; for all other codes, return to QUICK TEST.

4) Verify In-Line Shorting Bar Is Installed – Turn ignition off and wait 10 seconds. Inspect Octane Adjust in-line connector. If shorting bar is installed, go to next step. If shorting bar is not installed, go to step **7)**.

5) Verify Drive Concern – Turn ignition off and wait 10 seconds. Locate and remove shorting bar. Test drive vehicle to verify complaint. If symptom is present, go to next step. If symptom is not present, EEC is okay; testing is complete.

6) Rerun KOEO SELF-TEST – Verify engine is at normal operating temperature. Turn ignition off and wait 10 seconds. Enter KOEO SELF-TEST. If Code 57 or 341 is present, use higher octane fuel; testing is complete. If Code 57 or 341 is not present, go to next step.

7) Check Octane Adjust Circuit for Short to Ground – Turn ignition off and wait 10 seconds. Install breakout box and leave ECA disconnected. Set DVOM to 200-k/ohm scale. Measure resistance between OCT ADJ circuit at in-line connector and test pins No. 40 and 60 at breakout box.

If resistance is less than 10 k/ohms, repair short circuit; remove breakout box and rerun QUICK TEST. If each resistance is 10 k/ohms or more, use higher octane fuel. If fuel is okay, check for other causes of symptoms on 2.3L models; on all other vehicles, replace ECA, remove breakout box and rerun QUICK TEST.

CIRCUIT TEST M

DYNAMIC RESPONSE TEST

Diagnostic Aids - Perform this test only when directed by QUICK TEST.

To prevent replacing good components, be aware that the following non-EEC related areas may be the cause of problem:

- Technician testing EEC system did not perform brief Wide Open Throttle (WOT) after Dynamic Response Code.
- Mechanical engine components are faulty.
- Engine did not go over 2000 RPM during WOT.

This test is intended to diagnose only the following:

- Throttle Movement (Minimum 3/4 Throttle)
- RPM Increase Is Greater Than 2000 RPM

If throttle is snapped open briefly, it may not be sufficient to pass WOT test. Ensure throttle is depressed fully to WOT, and engine speed exceeds 2000 RPM.

Code 77/538 Displayed: System Failed to Recognize WOT Test – Rerun KOER SELF-TEST as follows:

- Start engine.
- Activate KOER SELF-TEST.
- Observe ID Code 2 (Code 0 with STAR tester).
- Observe Dynamic Response Code 1 (Code 0 with STAR tester).
- Perform brief WOT.
- Testing is complete, KOER code output begins.

If Code 77/538 is still displayed, replace ECA and rerun QUICK TEST. If Code 77/538 is no longer present, vehicle has passed dynamic response test; service other codes as necessary.

CIRCUIT TEST ML

SELF-TEST OUTPUT (STO) OR MALFUNCTION INDICATOR LIGHT (MIL)

Diagnostic Aids – Perform this test only when instructed by QUICK TEST, or when directed by CIRCUIT TEST QA.

To prevent replacing good components, be aware that the following non-EEC related areas may be the cause of problem:

- Fuse, Bulb Or Socket

This test is intended to diagnose only the following:

- STO/MIL Circuit
- ECA
- Data Communications Link (DCL)

CHECK ENGINE Light Circuit 90C13286

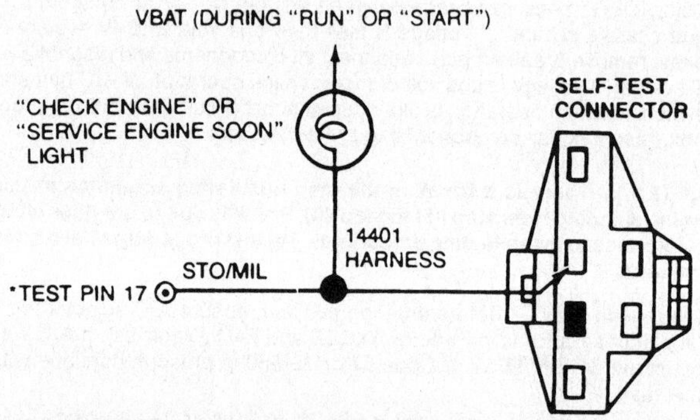
VBAT (DURING "RUN" OR "START")
"CHECK ENGINE" OR "SERVICE ENGINE SOON" LIGHT
SELF-TEST CONNECTOR
14401 HARNESS
STO/MIL
*TEST PIN 17

***TEST PINS LOCATED ON BREAKOUT BOX**
ALL HARNESS CONNECTORS VIEWED INTO MATING SURFACE

Data Communication Link (DCL) Circuit 91I14264

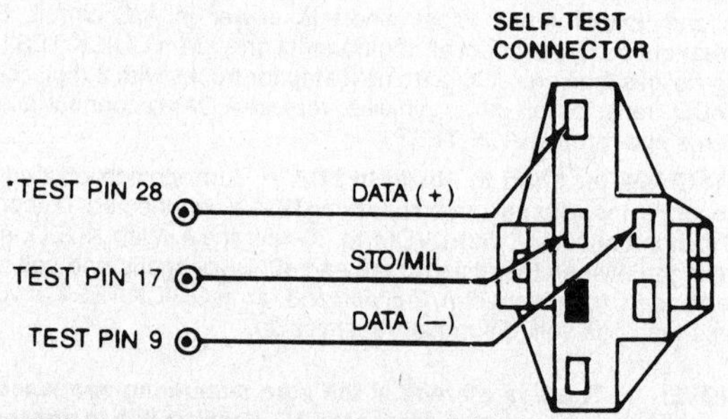
SELF-TEST CONNECTOR
*TEST PIN 28
DATA (+)
STO/MIL
TEST PIN 17
DATA (—)
TEST PIN 9

***TEST PINS LOCATED ON BREAKOUT BOX**
HARNESS CONNECTOR VIEWED INTO MATING SURFACE.

TEST PIN 17 (STO/MIL) WIRE COLOR IDENTIFICATION

Application	Wire Color
Explorer, Bronco, 2.3L Ranger, 2.9L Ranger (49 States), 3.0L MA EFI Ranger & 4.0L MA EFI Ranger	Pink/Light Green
"F" Series 4.9L, 5.0L, 5.8L, 7.3L Diesel (E4OD) & 7.5L	Pink/Light Green
All Others	Tan Red

DATA (+) PIN NO. & WIRE COLOR IDENTIFICATION

Application	Pin No.	Wire Color
4.0L Aerostar	28	Orange/Black
"E" Series 4.9L & 5.0L	28	Orange/Black
Explorer, Ranger 2.3L, 3.0L & 4.0L	28	Tan/Orange
Bronco, "F" Series 4.9L, 5.0L & 5.8L	28	Tan/Orange

1991 ENGINE PERFORMANCE
Self-Diagnostics – EEC-IV (Cont.)

CIRCUIT TEST ML (Cont.)

DATA (-) PIN NO. & WIRE COLOR IDENTIFICATION

Application	Pin No.	Wire Color
4.0L Aerostar	9	Black/Orange
"E" Series 4.9L & 5.0L	9	Black/Orange
Explorer, Ranger 2.3L, 3.0L & 4.0L	9	Pink/Light Blue
Bronco, "F" Series 4.9L, 5.0L & 5.8L	9	Pink/Light Blue

1) Malfunction Indicator Light (MIL) Always On –If vehicle will not start, go to CIRCUIT TEST A, step **1)**. Service all other KOEO and Continuous Memory Codes before proceeding with this test. Turn ignition off. Disconnect ECA 60-pin connector. Inspect connector for damaged pins, corrosion, or loose wires. Install breakout box, leaving ECA disconnected. Set DVOM on 200-ohm scale. Connect DVOM between test pins No. 17 and 40 at breakout box. If resistance is 5 ohms or more, replace ECA; remove breakout box and rerun QUICK TEST. If reading is less than 5 ohms, repair short between test pin No. 17 and self-test connector or CHECK ENGINE light. Remove breakout box, reconnect all components and repeat QUICK TEST.

NOTE: There is a break in the step numbering sequence at this point, skipping from step 1) to step 4). Break is due to previous chart references to these testing procedures. No test procedures have been omitted.

4) Malfunction Indicator Light (MIL) Never On: Check Continuity of STO/MIL Circuit – If vehicle will not start, go to CIRCUIT TEST A, step **1)**. Turn ignition on, leaving engine off. Set DVOM on 20-volt scale. Measure voltage between battery negative terminal to ground side of MIL fuse. If voltage is 10.5 volts or more, go to step **6)**. If voltage is less than 10.5 volts, go to next step.

5) Check for Voltage at Fuse – Set DVOM on 20-volt scale. With Key On Engine Off (KOEO), measure voltage from battery negative post to hot side of MIL fuse. If voltage is 10.5 volts or more, repair fuse or open circuit. Reconnect ECA and verify repair by turning ignition to RUN position. If voltage is less than 10.5 volts, repair MIL/VBAT circuit. Reconnect ECA and verify repair by turning ignition to RUN position.

6) Check Continuity of VBAT Circuit – Turn ignition off. Set DVOM to 200-k/ohm scale. Measure resistance between MIL fuse (at ground side) and MIL bulb socket (VBAT side). If resistance is 10 k/ohms or more, repair open circuit in MIL circuit. Verify repair by turning ignition to RUN position. If resistance is less than 10 k/ohms, go to next step.

7) Check MIL Bulb Response to Grounding – Turn ignition off. Attach one end of jumper wire to negative battery terminal or chassis ground. Attach other end of jumper wire to ground side of MIL bulb socket. Turn ignition to RUN position. If MIL light comes on, turn ignition off. Remove jumper wire and go to next step. If MIL light does not come on, turn ignition off and remove jumper wire. Replace MIL bulb socket. Turn ignition to RUN position to verify operation.

8) Check Continuity of MIL Circuit – Turn ignition off and wait 10 seconds. Disconnect ECA 60-pin connector. Inspect connector for damaged pins, corrosion, or loose wires. Install breakout box and leave ECA disconnected. Set DVOM to 200-ohm scale. Measure resistance between test pin No. 17 at breakout box and MIL. If resistance is less than 5 ohms, replace ECA. Remove breakout box. Verify operation by turning ignition switch to RUN position. If resistance is 5 ohms or more, repair open MIL circuit. Turn ignition switch to RUN position to verify operation.

NOTE: There is a break in the step numbering sequence at this point, skipping from step 8) to step 10). Break is due to previous chart references to these testing procedures. No test procedures have been omitted.

10) CHECK ENGINE or SERVICE ENGINE SOON Light Intermittent, Check for Intermittent Short From STO to Ground – If vehicle does not start, go to CIRCUIT TEST A, step **1)**. The light comes on when a Continuous Memory Code is present. Service all Continuous Memory Codes before proceeding. If no codes are outputted, proceed with this test. Enter KOEO wiggle test. See CONTINUOUS MONITOR MODE (WIGGLE TEST) under QUICK TEST. Observe DVOM for indication of fault while performing wiggle test on harness in the following areas:

- From Self-Test Connector To Dash Panel
- Dash Panel To ECA
- Dash Panel To Malfunction Indicator Light (MIL).

CIRCUIT TEST ML (Cont.)

If a fault is indicated, repair as necessary and rerun QUICK TEST. If a fault is not indicated, then fault cannot be duplicated at this time. Testing for this fault is complete.

NOTE: There is a break in the step numbering sequence at this point, skipping from step 10) to step 15). Break is due to previous chart references to these testing procedures. No test procedures have been omitted.

15) CHECK ENGINE or SERVICE ENGINE SOON Light Flashes with Erratic Idle: Check STI Circuit for Short to Ground – Vehicle symptoms indicate STI is grounded and ECA is performing self-test without tester installed. With ignition off, disconnect ECA 60-pin connector. Inspect connector for damaged pins, corrosion, or loose wires. Repair as necessary. Set DVOM on 200-k/ohm scale. Measure resistance between STI connector and engine block ground. If resistance is less than 10 k/ohms, repair short circuit. Reconnect ECA and retest. If resistance is 10 k/ohms or more, reconnect ECA. Verify symptom and test for other rough idle symptoms.

NOTE: There is a break in the step numbering sequence at this point, skipping from step 15) to step 20). Break is due to previous chart references to these testing procedures. No test procedures have been omitted.

20) CHECK ENGINE Message Displayed – If vehicle will not start, go to CIRCUIT TEST A, step **1)**. Perform KOEO SELF-TEST. If result is Code 11-10-11 (pass code), repair fault in electronic message center Data Communications Link (DCL). If pass code is not displayed, service codes as required in self-test procedures.

CIRCUIT TEST NA

TFI IGNITION
IGNITION DIAGNOSTIC MONITOR (IDM)

Diagnostic Aids – Perform this test when directed by QUICK TEST. This test is intended to diagnose only the EEC-IV portion of ignition system. For additional information on ignition system and component testing, see SYSTEM & COMPONENT TESTING article.

To prevent replacing good components, be aware that the following non-EEC related areas may be the cause of problem:

- Tfi Ignition Module
- Ignition Coil
- Spark Plugs And/Or High Tension Cables
- Distributor
- Secondary Ignition Component Arcing

This test is intended to diagnose the following circuits and components:

- IDM Harness Circuit
- ECA Assembly

IDM Circuit Schematic:
(3.0L Aerostar, 5.8L & 7.5L) 91J14265

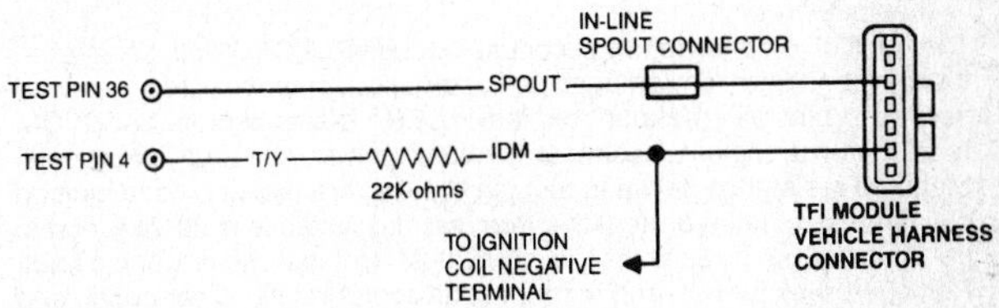
IN-LINE
SPOUT CONNECTOR
TEST PIN 36
SPOUT
TEST PIN 4
T/Y
IDM
22K ohms
TO IGNITION
COIL NEGATIVE
TERMINAL
TFI MODULE
VEHICLE HARNESS
CONNECTOR

IDM Circuit Schematic:
(3.0L Ranger) 91A14266

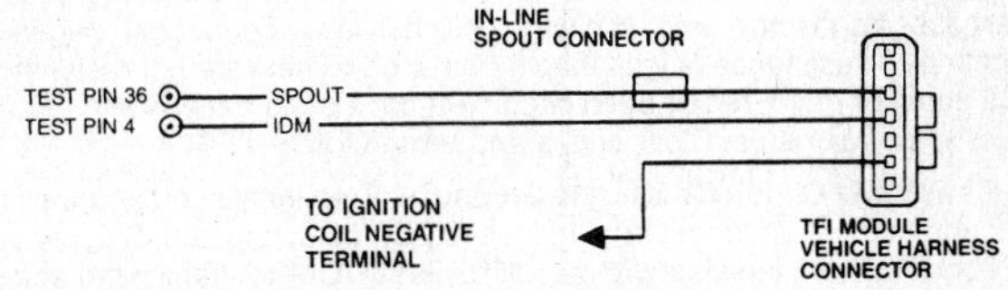
IN-LINE
SPOUT CONNECTOR
TEST PIN 36
SPOUT
TEST PIN 4
IDM
TO IGNITION
COIL NEGATIVE
TERMINAL
TFI MODULE
VEHICLE HARNESS
CONNECTOR

1991 ENGINE PERFORMANCE
Self-Diagnostics – EEC-IV (Cont.)

CIRCUIT TEST NA (Cont.)

TFI MODULE LOCATION TABLE

Application	Location
3.0L	Radiator Support
7.5L	Left Front Fender
All Others	Distributor

TEST PIN 36 (SPOUT) WIRE COLOR IDENTIFICATION

Application	Wire Color
"F" Series & 3.0L Ranger	Pink
All Others	Yellow/Light Green

TEST PIN 4 (IDM) WIRE COLOR IDENTIFICATION

Application	Wire Color
All Models	Tan/Yellow

1) Continuous Memory Code 14/211: Erratic Ignition – Code 14/211 indicates 2 successive erratic Profile Ignition Pick-Up (PIP) pulses occurred, resulting in a possible engine miss or stall. Check for the following possible causes of fault:

- Loose Wires Or Connectors
- Arcing Secondary Ignition Components
- On-Board Transmitter Equipment (2-Way Radio)

Repair any problems in listed items as necessary; clear code and rerun QUICK TEST. If problem is not found in listed items, go to next step for vehicles with Computer-Controlled Dwell (CCD), or go to step **3)** for all others.

2) Code 18/212: Check IDM Circuit Continuity – Continuous Memory Code 18/212 indicates loss of IDM input to ECA. Possible causes for this fault are as follows.

- Open Harness
- Shorted Harness
- Faulty TFI Module
- Faulty ECA

Turn ignition off and wait 10 seconds. Disconnect ECA 60-pin connector. Inspect connector for damaged pins, corrosion and loose wires. Repair as necessary. Install breakout box, leaving ECA disconnected. Disconnect TFI module. Set DVOM to 200-ohm scale. Measure and record resistance between test pin No. 4 at breakout box and pin No. 3 at TFI vehicle harness connector. Measure and record resistance between pin No. 5 at TFI vehicle harness connector and ignition coil harness connector or negative terminal. If each resistance is less than 5 ohms, go to step **5)**. If any resistance is 5 ohms or more, repair open circuit. Remove breakout box, and reconnect all components. Clear codes, and rerun QUICK TEST.

3) Code 18/212: Check IDM Circuit Continuity – Continuous Memory Code 18/212 indicates loss of IDM input to ECA. Possible causes for this fault are as follows:

- Open Harness
- Shorted Harness
- Faulty TFI Module
- Faulty ECA

Turn ignition off and wait 10 seconds. Disconnect ECA 60-pin connector. Inspect connector for damaged pins, corrosion, or loose wires; repair as necessary. Install breakout box, leaving ECA disconnected. Set DVOM to 200-k/ohm scale. Disconnect "E" core ignition coil and TFI module. Measure resistance between test pin No. 4 at breakout box and ignition coil harness connector negative terminal. If resistance is 20-24 k/ohms, go to next step. If resistance is NOT 20-24 k/ohms, repair open circuit. Remove breakout box and reconnect all components. Clear codes and rerun QUICK TEST.

4) Check IDM Circuit Continuity – Turn ignition off and wait 10 seconds. Set DVOM to 200-ohm scale. With breakout box installed and ECA disconnected, measure resistance between pin No. 5 at TFI vehicle harness connector and ignition coil harness connector negative terminal. If resistance is less than 5 ohms, go to next step. If resistance is 5 ohms or more, repair open circuit. Remove breakout box and reconnect all components. Clear codes and rerun QUICK TEST.

5) Check IDM Circuit for Short to Ground – Turn ignition off and wait 10 seconds. Install breakout box and leave ECA disconnected. Disconnect "E" core coil on vehicles without CCD. Set DVOM to 200-k/ohm scale.

CIRCUIT TEST NA (Cont.)

Measure resistance between test pin No. 4 and test pins No. 40, 46 and 60 at breakout box. If each resistance is 10 k/ohms or more, go to next step. If any resistance is less than 10 k/ohms, remove breakout box and repair short to ground in IDM circuit. Reconnect all components, clear codes and rerun QUICK TEST.

6) Check ECA for Short to Ground – Turn ignition off and wait 10 seconds. Install breakout box and connect ECA to breakout box. Disconnect ignition coil and TFI module. Set DVOM to 200-k/ohm scale. Measure voltage between test pin No. 4 and test pins. No. 40 and 60 at breakout box. If resistance is 10 k/ohms or more, reconnect all components and go to next step. If resistance is less than 10 k/ohms, replace ECA. Remove breakout box, reconnect all components and rerun QUICK TEST.

7) Check TFI Module – Turn ignition off and wait 10 seconds. Enter CONTINUOUS MONITOR MODE (WIGGLE TEST). Observe VOM or diagnostic tester for indication of fault while lightly tapping on TFI module to simulate road shock. Wiggle all TFI harness connectors. If fault is indicated, go to next step. If fault is not indicated, disconnect and inspect TFI harness connectors and terminals for damage. If connector and terminals are okay, check ignition system. See BASIC DIAGNOSTIC PROCEDURES article. If ignition is okay, replace ECA.

8) Check EEC-IV Harness – Remain in CONTINUOUS MONITOR MODE (WIGGLE TEST). Wiggle, shake or bend small sections of harness, working from TFI connectors to firewall. Observe VOM or diagnostic tester for indication of fault. Repeat process from firewall to ECA. This test checks for the following circuit faults:

- PIP Open/Shorted To Ground (Check At Test Pin No. 56)
- SPOUT Shorted to Ground (Check At Test Pin No. 36)
- Ignition Ground Open (Check At Test Pin No. 16)
- IDM Open to Ground (Check At Test Pin No. 4)
- IDM Shorted to Power (Check At Test Pin No. 4)

Perform CONTINUOUS MONITOR MODE (WIGGLE TEST) on these circuits, one at a time, to isolate fault. If fault is indicated, isolate fault and repair harness. Repeat QUICK TEST. If no fault is indicated, go to next step.

9) Check ECA and Harness Connectors – Turn ignition off and wait 10 seconds. Disconnect ECA 60-pin connector. Inspect connector for damaged pins, corrosion or loose wires. If connector is damaged, repair as necessary; clear codes and repeat QUICK TEST. If connector is okay, perform the appropriate procedure listed as follows, based on the Continuous Memory Code displayed.

- Code 14/211: Erratic ignition fault in EEC system cannot be duplicated. Remove breakout box and reconnect all components. Diagnose TFI ignition system.
- Code 18/212: Replace ECA, remove breakout box and reconnect all components. Start and run engine for about one minute, then rerun QUICK TEST.

CIRCUIT TEST NB

DIS IGNITION
IGNITION DIAGNOSTIC MONITOR (IDM)

Diagnostic Aids – Perform this test when directed by QUICK TEST. This test is intended to diagnose only the EEC-IV portion of ignition system. For additional information on ignition system and component testing, see BASIC DIAGNOSTIC PROCEDURES article.

To prevent replacing good components, be aware that the following non-EEC related areas may be the cause of problem:

- DIS Ignition Module
- DIS Coil Packs
- Spark Plugs And/Or High Tension Cables
- Crankshaft Sensor
- Camshaft Sensor (If Equipped)
- Secondary Ignition Component Arcing

This test is intended to diagnose the following circuits and components:

- IDM, DPI and SAW Harness Circuit
- ECA Assembly

CIRCUIT TEST NB (Cont.)

IDM Circuit Schematic
(2.3L Ranger)

91I09212

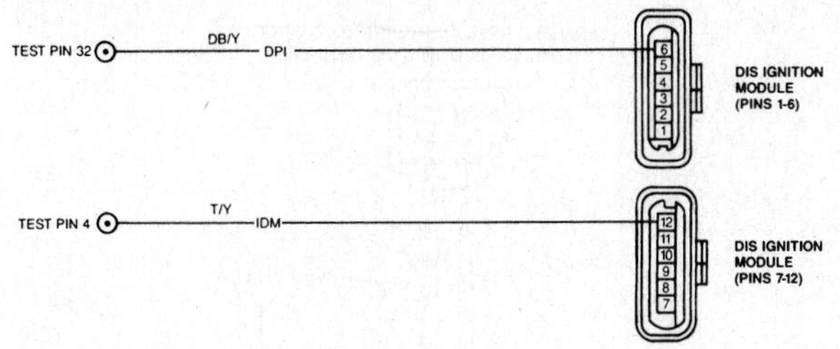

TEST PIN 32
DB/Y
DPI
6
5
4
3
2
1
DIS IGNITION MODULE (PINS 1-6)
TEST PIN 4
T/Y
IDM
12
11
10
9
8
7
DIS IGNITION MODULE (PINS 7-12)

TEST PIN 4 (IDM) WIRE COLOR IDENTIFICATION

Application	Wire Color
2.3L	Tan/Yellow

DIS MODULE LOCATION TABLE

Application	Location
2.3L DPI Ranger	Near Right Fuel Rail

1) Continuous Memory Code 14/211: Erratic Ignition – Code 14/211 indicates 2 successive erratic Profile Ignition Pick-Up (PIP) pulses occurred, resulting in a possible engine miss or stall. Possible causes for this fault are as follows:

- Loose Wires Or Connectors
- Arcing Secondary Ignition Components
- On-Board Transmitter Equipment (2-Way Radio)

Repair any problems in listed items as necessary; clear code and rerun QUICK TEST. If problem is not found in listed items, go to step **4)**.

2) Continuous Memory Code 18/212: Check for Other Codes – Code 18/212 indicates loss of IDM input signal to ECA. Possible causes for this fault are as follows:

- Open Or Shorted Harness
- Faulty DIS Module
- Faulty ECA

If Continuous Memory Code 45, 46, 48, 215, 216 or 217 is present, see testing procedure for DIS in BASIC DIAGNOSTIC PROCEDURES article. If Code 45, 46, 48, 215, 216 or 217 is not present, go to next step.

3) Continuous Memory Codes 18/212, 28/222 or 48/218: Check IDM Circuit Continuity – Code 18/212 indicates loss of IDM input signal. Possible causes are as follows:

- Open Harness Circuit
- Shorted Harness
- Faulty TFI Or DIS Module
- Faulty ECA

Code 28/222 indicates IDM input signal is always low. Possible causes are as follows:

- Open Or Shorted Harness
- Faulty CID Sensor
- VBAT (Battery Voltage) Low At DIS
- Faulty DIS Module
- Faulty ECA

Code 48/218 indicates IDM input signal is always high. Possible causes are as follows:

- Open Signal In Harness
- VBAT Open At Secondary Coil
- VBAT Low At Secondary Coil

Turn ignition off an wait 10 seconds. Disconnect DIS module connector (pins No. 7-12) on DIS-equipped vehicles. Disconnect ECA 60-pin connector. Inspect connector for damaged pins, corrosion, or loose wires. Repair as necessary. Install breakout box, leaving ECA connected. Set DVOM on 200-k/ohm scale.

Measure resistance between test pin No. 4 at breakout box and DIS module harness connector pin No. 12. If resistance is less than 5 ohms, go to next step. If resistance is greater than 5 ohms, repair open circuit; clear codes and rerun QUICK TEST.

4) Check IDM Circuit for Short to Ground – Turn ignition off and wait 10 seconds. Disconnect DIS module connector (pins No. 7-12). Install breakout box and leave ECA disconnected. With DVOM on 200-k/ohm scale, measure resistance between test pin No. 4 and test pins No. 16, 20, 40, 46 and 60. If readings are 10 k/ohms or more, go to next step. If any reading is less than 10 k/ohms, remove breakout box and repair short to ground in IDM circuit. Reconnect all components and rerun QUICK TEST.

5) Check IDM Circuit for Shorts to Power (Except VREF Circuit) –With ignition off, install breakout box. Disconnect ECA and DIS module (pins No. 1-6). Measure voltage between test pin No. 4 and test pins No. 40 and 60. If voltage is less than 10.5 volts, go to next step. If any reading is 10.5 volts or more, repair short circuit. Remove breakout box and reconnect all components. Rerun QUICK TEST.

6) Check IDM Circuit for Short to VREF & PIP – Turn ignition off. Install breakout box, leaving ECA disconnected. Disconnect DIS module (pins No. 1-6). Set DVOM to 200-k/ohm scale.

To test for shorts to VREF, measure resistance between test pins No. 36 and 26 at breakout box. To test for shorts to PIP, measure resistance between test pins No. 36 and 56 at breakout box.

If each resistance is 10 k/ohms or more, go to next step. If resistance is not greater than 10 k/ohms, repair short circuit. Remove breakout box, reconnect all components and repeat QUICK TEST.

7) Check ECA for Short to Ground – Turn ignition off and wait 10 seconds. Disconnect DIS module connector (pins No. 7-12). Install breakout box and connect ECA. With DVOM on 200-k/ohm scale, measure resistance between test pin No. 4 and test pins No. 40, 46 and 60. If readings are 10 k/ohms or more, reconnect components and go to next step. If any reading is less than 10 k/ohms, replace ECA. Reconnect all components and rerun QUICK TEST.

8) Check DIS Module – Turn ignition off and wait 10 seconds. Enter CONTINUOUS MONITOR MODE (WIGGLE TEST). Observe VOM or diagnostic tester for indication of fault while lightly tapping on DIS module to simulate road shock. Wiggle all DIS harness connectors. If fault is indicated, go to next step. If fault is not indicated, disconnect and inspect DIS harness connectors and terminals for damage. If connectors and terminals are okay, check ignition system. See BASIC DIAGNOSTIC PROCEDURES article. If ignition is okay, replace ECA.

9) Check EEC-IV Harness – Remain in CONTINUOUS MONITOR MODE (WIGGLE TEST). Wiggle, shake or bend small sections of harness, working from DIS connectors to firewall. Observe VOM or diagnostic tester for indication of fault. Repeat process from firewall to ECA. This test checks for the following circuit faults.

- PIP Open/Shorted To Ground (Check At Test Pin No. 56)
- SPOUT Shorted To Ground (Check At Test Pin No. 36)
- Ignition Ground Open (Check At Test Pin No. 16)
- IDM Open To Ground (Check At Test Pin No. 4)
- IDM Shorted To Power (Check At Test Pin No. 4)

Perform CONTINUOUS MONITOR MODE (WIGGLE TEST) on these circuits, one at a time, to isolate fault. If fault is indicated, isolate fault and repair harness. Repeat QUICK TEST. If no fault is indicated, go to next step.

10) Check ECA and Harness Connectors – Turn ignition off and wait 10 seconds. Disconnect ECA 60-pin connector. Inspect connector for damaged pins, corrosion or loose wires. If connector is damaged, repair as necessary; clear codes and repeat QUICK TEST. If connector is okay, perform appropriate procedure listed as follows, based on the Continuous Memory Code displayed:

- **Code 14/211:** Erratic ignition fault in EEC system cannot be duplicated. Remove breakout box and reconnect all components. Diagnose DIS ignition system.
- **Code 18/212:** Replace ECA. Remove breakout box and reconnect all components. Start and run engine for about one minute, then rerun QUICK TEST.
- **Code 28/222 and 48/218:** Remove breakout box. Reconnect all components. Diagnose DIS ignition system. If DIS system is okay, replace ECA.

NOTE: There is a break in the step numbering sequence at this point, skipping from step 10) to step 20). Break is due to previous chart references to these testing procedures. No test procedures have been omitted.

20) Continuous Memory Code 88: Check Continuity Of DPI Circuit – Code 88 indicates open in Dual Plug Inhibit (DPI) circuit, or open or short to ground in coil No. 4. Possible causes for this fault are as follows:

- Open Or Short Circuit In Harness
- Faulty ECA
- Faulty DIS Module
- Faulty Coil No. 4

1991 ENGINE PERFORMANCE
Self-Diagnostics – EEC-IV (Cont.)

CIRCUIT TEST NB (Cont.)

Turn ignition off and wait 10 seconds. Disconnect DIS connector (pins No. 1-6). Disconnect ECA 60-pin connector. Inspect connector for damaged pins, corrosion or loose wires. If connector is damaged, repair as necessary. Install breakout box and leave ECA disconnected. Set DVOM on 200-ohm scale. Measure resistance between pin No. 6 at DIS vehicle harness connector and test pin No. 32 at breakout box.
If resistance is less than 5 ohms, remove breakout box. Reconnect all components. Diagnose DIS ignition system. If system is okay, replace ECA.
If resistance is 5 ohms or more, repair open circuit. Remove breakout box, reconnect all components and rerun QUICK TEST.

NOTE: There is a break in the step numbering sequence at this point, skipping from step 20) to step 25). Break is due to previous chart references to these testing procedures. No test procedures have been omitted.

25) Hard to Start: Check for Spark During Crank – Using an Air Gap Spark Tester or Neon Bulb Spark Tester, check for spark at all spark plug wires while cranking engine. If spark is present and consistent (one spark per crankshaft revolution), go to next step. If no spark is present or if spark is inconsistent, replace damaged spark plug or spark plug wire, and rerun QUICK TEST.

26) Hard to Start: Check DPI Circuit for Short to Ground – Turn ignition off and wait 10 seconds. Disconnect DIS module (pins No. 1-6). Disconnect ECA 60-pin connector. Inspect connector for damaged pins, corrosion, or loose wires; repair as necessary. Install breakout box, leaving ECA disconnected. Set DVOM to 200-k/ohm scale. Measure resistance between test pin No. 32 and test pins No. 40 and 60 at breakout box. If resistance is 100 k/ohms or more, go to next step. If resistance is less than 100 k/ohms, repair short circuit. Remove breakout box, reconnect all components and rerun QUICK TEST.

27) Check ECA for Short to Ground – Turn ignition off and wait 10 seconds. Disconnect DIS module (pins No. 1-6). Install breakout box and connect ECA to breakout box. Set DVOM to 200-k/ohm scale. Measure resistance between test pin No. 32 and test pins No. 40 and 60 at breakout box. If resistance is 500 ohms or more, remove breakout box; reconnect all components and diagnose DIS system. If resistance is less than 500 ohms, replace ECA; remove breakout box, reconnect all components and rerun QUICK TEST.

CIRCUIT TEST NC

EDIS IGNITION
IGNITION DIAGNOSTIC MONITOR (IDM)

Diagnostic Aids – Perform this test when directed by QUICK TEST. This test is intended to diagnose only the EEC-IV portion of ignition system. For additional information on ignition system and component testing, see SYSTEM & COMPONENT TESTING article.

To prevent replacing good components, be aware that the following non-EEC related areas may be at fault:

- EDIS Ignition Module
- EDIS Coil Packs
- Spark Plugs And/Or High Tension Cables
- Variable Reluctance Sensor
- Secondary Ignition Component Arcing

This test is intended to diagnose the following circuits and components:

- IDM And SAW Harness Circuit
- ECA Assembly

TEST PIN 56 (PIP) WIRE COLOR IDENTIFICATION

Application	Wire Color
4.0L Aerostar	Dark Blue
4.0L Explorer & 4.0L Ranger	Gray/Orange

TEST PIN 16 (SAW) WIRE COLOR IDENTIFICATION

Application	Wire Color
4.0L Aerostar	Yellow/Light Green
4.0L Explorer & 4.0L Ranger	Pink

CIRCUIT TEST NC (Cont.)

IDM Circuit Schematic (4.0L MA EFI)

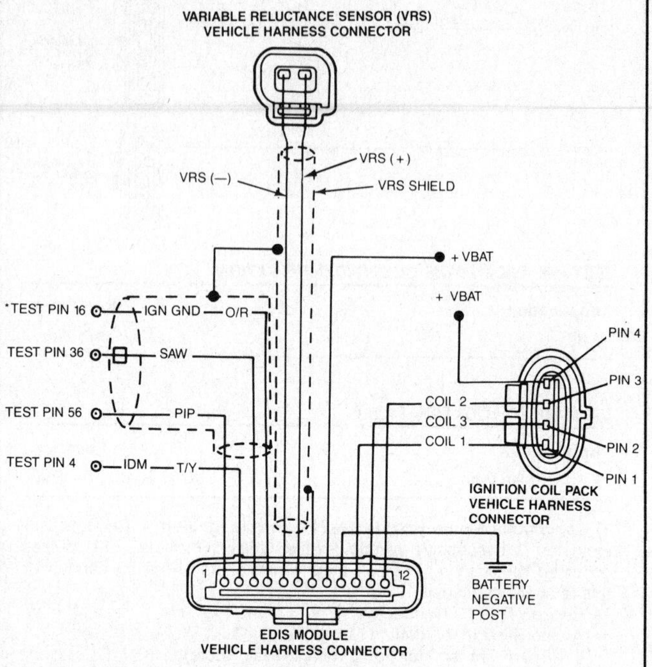
91F09215
VARIABLE RELUCTANCE SENSOR (VRS) VEHICLE HARNESS CONNECTOR
VRS (+)
VRS (—)
VRS SHIELD
+ VBAT
+ VBAT
*TEST PIN 16
IGN GND
O/R
TEST PIN 36
SAW
TEST PIN 56
PIP
TEST PIN 4
IDM
T/Y
PIN 4
PIN 3
PIN 2
PIN 1
COIL 2
COIL 3
COIL 1
IGNITION COIL PACK VEHICLE HARNESS CONNECTOR
1
12
BATTERY NEGATIVE POST
EDIS MODULE VEHICLE HARNESS CONNECTOR

*TEST PINS LOCATED ON BREAKOUT BOX.
ALL HARNESS CONNECTORS VIEWED INTO MATING SURFACE.

TEST PIN 4 (IDM) WIRE COLOR IDENTIFICATION

Application	Wire Color
4.0L	Tan/Yellow

1) Continuous Memory Code 14/211: Erratic Ignition – Code 14/211 indicates 2 successive erratic Profile Ignition Pick-Up (PIP) pulses occurred, resulting in a possible engine miss or stall. Possible causes for this fault are as follows:

- Loose Wires Or Connectors
- Arcing Secondary Ignition Components
- On-Board Transmitter Equipment (2-Way Radio)

Repair any problems in listed items as necessary; clear code and rerun QUICK TEST. If problem is not found in items listed, go to step **4)**.

2) Code 16/226: IDM Circuit Failure – Code 16/226 indicates ECA did not receive IDM signal from EDIS module in KOEO SELF-TEST. Possible causes for this problem are as follows:

- Open Or Short In IDM Or IGN GND Circuit Harness
- Faulty EDIS Module

If engine starts, go to next step. If engine does not start, diagnose EDIS system.

3) Continuous Memory Code 18/212: Check for Other Codes – Code 18/212 indicates loss of IDM input signal to ECA. Possible causes for this fault are as follows:

- Open Or Shorted Harness
- Faulty EDIS Module
- Faulty ECA

If Continuous Memory Code 45, 46, 48, 215, 216 or 217 is present, see testing procedure for EDIS in BASIC DIAGNOSTIC PROCEDURES article. If Code 45, 46, 48, 215, 216 or 217 is not present, go to next step.

4) Continuous Memory Codes 18/212: Check IDM Circuit Continuity – Turn ignition off and wait 10 seconds. Disconnect EDIS module. Disconnect ECA 60-pin connector. Inspect connector for damaged pins, corrosion, or loose wires. Repair as necessary. Install breakout box, leaving ECA disconnected. Set DVOM on 200-ohm scale.
Measure resistance between test pin No. 4 at breakout box and EDIS module harness connector pin No. 2. If resistance is less than 5 ohms, go to next step. If resistance is 5 ohms or more, repair open circuit. Remove breakout box and reconnect all components. Clear codes and rerun QUICK TEST.

1991 ENGINE PERFORMANCE
Self-Diagnostics – EEC-IV (Cont.)

CIRCUIT TEST NC (Cont.)

5) Check IDM Circuit for Short to Ground – Turn ignition off and wait 10 seconds. Disconnect EDIS module connector. Install breakout box and leave ECA disconnected. With DVOM on 200-k/ohm scale, measure resistance between test pin No. 4 and test pins No. 40, 46 and 60. If readings are 10 k/ohms or more, go to next step. If any reading is less than 10 k/ohms, remove breakout box and repair short to ground in IDM circuit. Reconnect all components and rerun QUICK TEST.

6) Check IDM Circuit for Shorts to Power (Except VREF Circuit) –With ignition off, install breakout box. Disconnect ECA and EDIS module. Measure voltage between test pin No. 4 and test pins No. 40 and 60. To check for short to VBAT, turn ignition off. To check for short to VPWR, turn ignition on. If voltage is less than 10.5 volts, go to next step. If any reading is 10.5 volts or more, repair short circuit. Remove breakout box and reconnect all components. Rerun QUICK TEST.

7) Check IDM Circuit for Short to VREF and PIP – Turn ignition off. Install breakout box, leaving ECA disconnected. Disconnect EDIS module. Set DVOM to 200-k/ohm scale.
To check for shorts to VREF, measure resistance between test pins No. 36 and 26 at breakout box. To test for shorts to PIP, measure resistance between test pins No. 36 and 56 at breakout box.
If each resistance is 10 k/ohms or more, go to next step. If resistance is less than 10 k/ohms, repair short circuit. Remove breakout box, reconnect all components and repeat QUICK TEST.

Diagnostic Aids – During this test, when 4-wire HEGO is connected to vehicle harness, a short to SIGRTN (pin No. 46) may be indicated along with an actual short to PWR GND.

8) Check ECA for Short to Ground – Turn ignition off and wait 10 seconds. Disconnect EDIS module. Install breakout box and connect ECA. With DVOM on 200-k/ohm scale, measure resistance between test pin No. 4 and test pins No. 16, 20, 40, 46 and 60. If readings are 10 k/ohms or more, reconnect components and go to next step. If any reading is less than 10 k/ohms, replace ECA. Reconnect all components and rerun QUICK TEST.

9) Check EDIS Module – Turn ignition off and wait 10 seconds. Enter KOER wiggle test. See CONTINUOUS MONITOR MODE (WIGGLE TEST) under QUICK TEST. Observe VOM or diagnostic tester for indication of fault while lightly tapping on EDIS module to simulate road shock. Wiggle all EDIS harness connectors. If fault is indicated, go to next step. If fault is not indicated, disconnect and inspect EDIS harness connectors and terminals for damage. If connectors and terminals are okay, check ignition system. See BASIC DIAGNOSTIC PROCEDURES article. If ignition is okay, replace ECA.

10) Check EEC-IV Harness – Remain in CONTINUOUS MONITOR MODE (WIGGLE TEST). Wiggle, shake or bend small sections of harness, working from EDIS connectors to firewall. Observe VOM or diagnostic tester for indication of fault. Repeat process from firewall to ECA. This test checks for the following circuit faults:

- PIP Open/Shorted To Ground (Check At Test Pin No. 56)
- SAW Shorted To Ground (Check At Test Pin No. 36)
- Ignition Ground Open (Check At Test Pin No. 16)
- IDM Open To Ground (Check At Test Pin No. 4)
- IDM Shorted To Power (Check At Test Pin No. 4)

Perform CONTINUOUS MONITOR MODE (WIGGLE TEST) on these circuits, one at a time, to isolate fault. If fault is indicated, isolate fault and repair harness. Repeat QUICK TEST. If no fault is indicated, go to next step.

11) Check ECA and Harness Connectors – Turn ignition off and wait 10 seconds. Disconnect ECA 60-pin connector. Inspect connector for damaged pins, corrosion or loose wires. If connector is damaged, repair as necessary; clear codes and repeat QUICK TEST. If connector is okay, perform appropriate procedure listed as follows, based on the Continuous Memory Code displayed:

- Code 14/211 – Erratic ignition fault in EEC system cannot be duplicated. Remove breakout box and reconnect all components. Diagnose EDIS ignition system.
- Code 18/212 – Replace ECA. Remove breakout box and reconnect all components. Start and run engine for about one minute, then rerun QUICK TEST.

CIRCUIT TEST PA

SPARK TIMING CHECK (TFI VEHICLES)

Diagnostic Aids – Perform this test when checking computed timing, or when directed by QUICK TEST. This test is intended to diagnose the following:

- Harness Circuit (SPOUT)
- Base Timing
- Faulty ECA

To prevent replacing good components, be aware that the following non-EEC related areas may be at fault:

- Basic Engine Condition (Valves, Vacuum Leaks, Valve Timing, EGR Valve, Etc.)
- Distributor
- TFI Module

TFI Spark Timing Check Circuit 90D13295

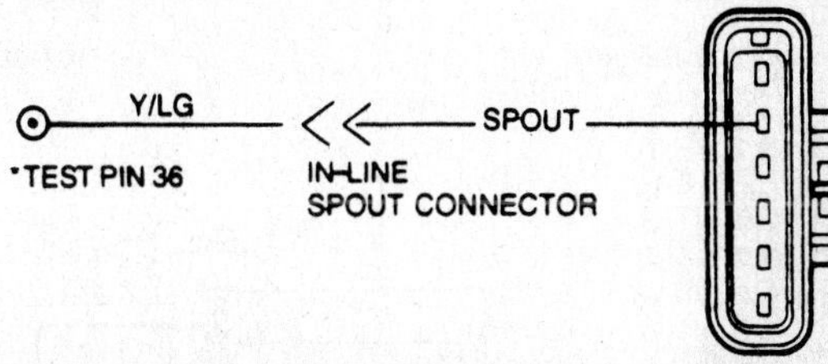
Y/LG
SPOUT
*TEST PIN 36
IN-LINE
SPOUT CONNECTOR

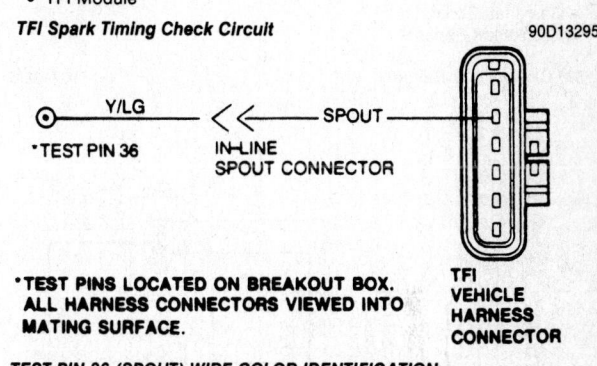

***TEST PINS LOCATED ON BREAKOUT BOX. ALL HARNESS CONNECTORS VIEWED INTO MATING SURFACE.**

TFI VEHICLE HARNESS CONNECTOR

TEST PIN 36 (SPOUT) WIRE COLOR IDENTIFICATION

Application	Wire Color
2.9L, 3.0L & "F" Series	Pink
All Others	Yellow/Light Green

1) KOER Code 18/213: Check Computed Spark Timing – Code 18/213 indicates SPOUT circuit is open. Possible causes for this fault are as follows:

- Open Harness Circuit
- Faulty ECA
- Faulty TFI Module

Activate KOER SELF-TEST. Check and record timing while in KOER SELF-TEST. Self-test locks timing during testing, and during 2 minutes after last code is displayed. Computed timing during these 2 minutes is equal to base timing plus 20 degrees (±3 degrees). If computed timing is correct, restart KOER SELF-TEST. If timing is not to specification, go to next step.

2) Check Base Timing – Turn ignition off and wait 10 seconds. Locate in-line Spark Output (SPOUT) connector, and open connection. Start engine and check base timing. Use specification on VECI decal. If base timing is correct, reconnect SPOUT, and go to next step. If base timing is incorrect, adjust base timing as necessary. See ON-VEHICLE ADJUSTMENTS article. After timing is reset, reconnect SPOUT and perform COMPUTED TIMING CHECK.

3) Check for Power to ECA – Turn ignition off and wait 10 seconds. Disconnect ECA 60-pin connector. Inspect connector for damaged pins, corrosion, or loose wires. Repair as necessary. Install breakout box, leaving ECA disconnected. With Key On Engine Off (KOEO) and DVOM on 20-volt scale, measure voltage between test pins No. 37 and 40, and between test pins No. 57 and 60 at breakout box. If either reading is less than 10.5 volts, go to CIRCUIT TEST B, step **1)**. If both readings are 10.5 volts or more, go to next step.

4) Check SPOUT Circuit for Continuity – Turn ignition off and wait 10 seconds. Install breakout box. Disconnect ECA and TFI module. With DVOM set on 200-ohm scale, measure resistance between test pin No. 36 at breakout box and SPOUT terminal at TFI module vehicle harness connector. If resistance is less than 5 ohms, go to next step. If resistance is 5 ohms or more, repair open circuit. Reconnect all components and check timing as described in step **1)**.

5) Check SPOUT Voltage at ECA – With ignition off and breakout box installed, connect ECA to breakout box. Reconnect TFI module. Ensure timing switch on breakout box is in DIST position. Set DVOM on 20-volt AC scale. With Key On Engine Running (KOER), measure voltage between test pin No. 36 and battery negative post. If voltage is NOT 4-10 volts, replace ECA; remove breakout box and repeat QUICK TEST. If voltage is 4-10 volts, EEC-IV system is okay; remove breakout box, reconnect ECA and check ignition system. See SYSTEM & COMPONENT TESTING article.

1991 ENGINE PERFORMANCE
Self-Diagnostics – EEC-IV (Cont.)

CIRCUIT TEST PB

SPARK TIMING CHECK (DIS VEHICLES)

Diagnostic Aids – Perform this test when checking computed timing, or when directed by QUICK TEST. This test is intended to diagnose the following:

- Harness Circuit (SPOUT)
- Base Timing
- Faulty ECA

To prevent replacing good components, be aware that the following non-EEC related areas may be at fault:

- Basic Engine Condition (Valves, Vacuum Leaks, Valve Timing, EGR Valve, Etc.)
- DIS Module
- Camshaft Sensor
- Crankshaft Sensor

IDM Circuit (2.3L Ranger) 90A13292

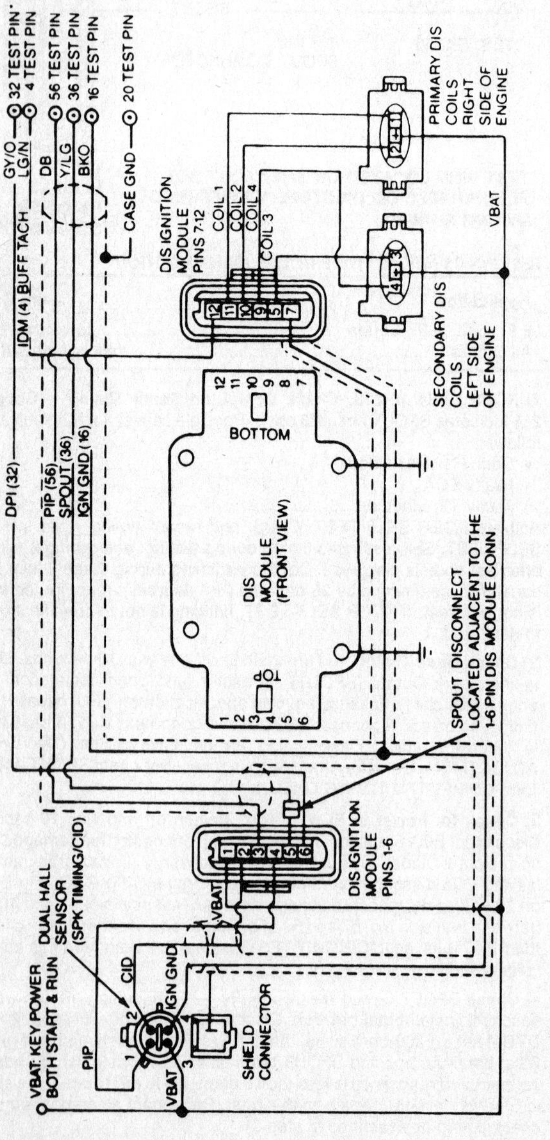
32 TEST PIN
4 TEST PIN
56 TEST PIN
36 TEST PIN
16 TEST PIN
20 TEST PIN
GY/O
LG/N
DB
Y/LG
BKO
CASE GND
IDM (4) BUFF TACH
DIS IGNITION MODULE PINS 7-12
COIL 1
COIL 2
COIL 4
COIL 3
PRIMARY DIS COILS RIGHT SIDE OF ENGINE
VBAT
SECONDARY DIS COILS LEFT SIDE OF ENGINE
BOTTOM
TOP
DIS MODULE (FRONT VIEW)
DPI (32)
PIP (56)
SPOUT (36)
IGN GND (16)
SPOUT DISCONNECT LOCATED ADJACENT TO THE 1-6 PIN DIS MODULE CONN
DIS IGNITION MODULE PINS 1-6
DUAL HALL SENSOR (SPK TIMING/CID)
VBAT: KEY POWER BOTH START & RUN
CID
IGN GND
PIP
VBAT
SHIELD CONNECTOR

TEST PIN 4 (IDM) WIRE COLOR IDENTIFICATION

Application	Wire Color
All Models	Tan/Yellow

CIRCUIT TEST PB (Cont.)

1) KOER Code 18/213: Check Computed Spark Timing – Code 18/213 indicates SPOUT circuit is open. Possible causes for this fault are as follows:

- Open Harness Circuit
- Faulty ECA
- Faulty DIS Module

Activate KOER SELF-TEST. Check and record timing while in KOER SELF-TEST (on 2.3L, use exhaust-side spark plug). Self-test mode locks timing during testing, and during 2 minutes after last code is displayed. Computed timing during these 2 minutes is equal to base timing plus 20 degrees (±3 degrees). If computed timing is correct, restart KOER Self-Test. If timing is not to specification, go to next step.

2) Check Base Timing – Turn ignition off and wait 10 seconds. Locate in-line Spark Output (SPOUT) connector, and open connection. Start engine and check base timing. Use specification on VECI decal. If base timing is correct, reconnect SPOUT and go to next step. If base timing is incorrect, diagnose ignition system, as base timing is not adjustable. See SYSTEM & COMPONENT TESTING article.

3) Check for Power to ECA – Turn ignition off and wait 10 seconds. Disconnect ECA 60-pin connector. Inspect connector for damaged pins, corrosion, or loose wires. Repair as necessary. Install breakout box, leaving ECA disconnected. With KOEO and DVOM set on 20-volt scale, measure voltage between test pins No. 37 and 40, and between test pins No. 57 and 60 at breakout box. If either reading is less than 10.5 volts, go to CIRCUIT TEST B, step **1)** (2.3L). If both readings are 10.5 volts or more, go to next step.

4) Check SPOUT Circuit for Continuity – Turn ignition off and wait 10 seconds. Install breakout box. Disconnect ECA and DIS module. With DVOM set on 200-ohm scale, measure resistance between test pin No. 36 at breakout box and SPOUT terminal at DIS module vehicle harness connector. If resistance is less than 5 ohms, go to next step. If resistance is 5 ohms or more, repair open circuit. Reconnect all components and check timing as described in step **1)**.

Module Connector 91F09220

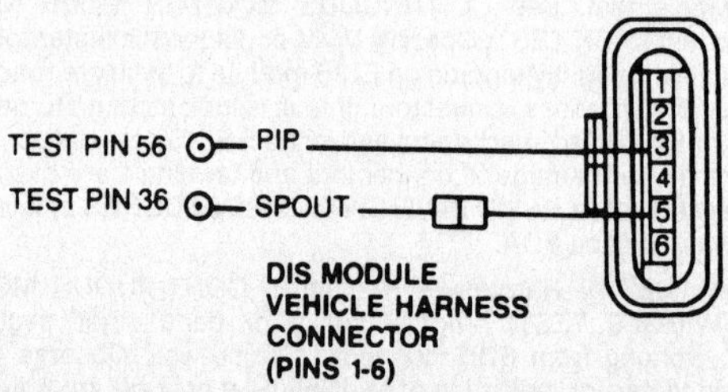
TEST PIN 56
PIP
TEST PIN 36
SPOUT
1
2
3
4
5
6
DIS MODULE VEHICLE HARNESS CONNECTOR (PINS 1-6)

5) Check SPOUT Circuit for Shorts to POWER, GROUND and PIP –Turn ignition off and wait 10 seconds. Set DVOM to 200-k/ohm scale. Install breakout box, leaving ECA and DIS module (pins No. 1-6) disconnected. To check for shorts to ground, measure resistance between test pin 36 and test pins No. 16, 20, 40, 46 and 60. To check for shorts to power, measure resistance between test pin 36 and test pins No. 26, 37 and 57. To check for shorts to PIP circuit, measure resistance between test pin No. 36 and test pin No. 56.

If each resistance is 10 k/ohms or more, go to next step. If resistance is less than 10 k/ohms, repair short circuit. Remove breakout box, reconnect all components and rerun QUICK TEST.

6) Check SPOUT Voltage at ECA – With ignition off and breakout box installed, connect ECA to breakout box. Reconnect DIS module. Ensure timing switch on breakout box is in DIST position. Set DVOM on 20-volt AC scale. With KOER, measure voltage between test pin No. 36 and battery negative post. If AC voltage is NOT 4-10 volts, replace ECA; remove breakout box and repeat QUICK TEST. If AC voltage is 4-10 volts, EEC-IV system is okay; remove breakout box, reconnect ECA and check ignition system. See SYSTEM & COMPONENT TESTING article.

NOTE: There is a break in the step numbering sequence at this point, skipping from step 6) to step 10). Break is due to previous chart references to these testing procedures. No test procedures have been omitted.

10) Continuous Memory Code 49/219: Check SPOUT Circuit Continuity – Code 49/219 indicates spark timing has defaulted to 10 degrees BTDC. SPOUT signal has a variable duty cycle, with amplitude varying from .4 volt to battery voltage. In the event of a SPOUT failure, DIS module will generate a fixed dwell and constant spark angle, based on CID

CIRCUIT TEST PB (Cont.)

and PIP signals (FMEM mode). Possible causes for this fault are as follows:

- Faulty DIS Module
- Faulty SPOUT Circuit

Turn ignition off and wait 10 seconds. Disconnect ECA 60-pin connector. Inspect connector for damaged pins, corrosion, or loose wires; repair as necessary. Install breakout box, leaving ECA disconnected. Disconnect DIS module (pins No. 1-6). Set DVOM to 200-ohm scale. Measure resistance between test pin No. 36 at breakout box and SPOUT circuit at DIS module harness connector. If resistance is less than 5 ohms, go to next step. If resistance is 5 ohms or more, ensure in-line SPOUT connector is correctly connected. If connector is okay, repair open circuit. Reconnect all components and rerun QUICK TEST.

11) Check SPOUT for Short to POWER and GROUND – Turn ignition off and wait 10 seconds. Install breakout box, leaving ECA and DIS module disconnected. Set DVOM to 200-k/ohm scale. Measure resistance between test pin No. 36 and test pins No. 16 and 40. Measure resistance between test pin No. 36 and battery negative terminal. If each resistance is 10 k/ohms or more, EEC system is okay. Remove breakout box, reconnect all components and diagnose ignition system. See SYSTEM & COMPONENT TESTING article. If resistance is less than 10 k/ohms, repair short circuit. Remove breakout box, reconnect all components and rerun QUICK TEST.

CIRCUIT TEST PC

SPARK TIMING CHECK (EDIS VEHICLES)

Diagnostic Aids – Perform this test when checking computed timing, or when directed by QUICK TEST. This test is intended to diagnose the following:

- Harness Circuit (SAW)
- Base Timing
- Faulty ECA

To prevent replacing good components, be aware that the following non-EEC related areas may be at fault:

- Basic Engine Condition (Valves, Vacuum Leaks, Valve Timing, EGR Valve, Etc.)
- EDIS Module
- Distributor

IDM Circuit (4.0L MA EFI) 90C13294

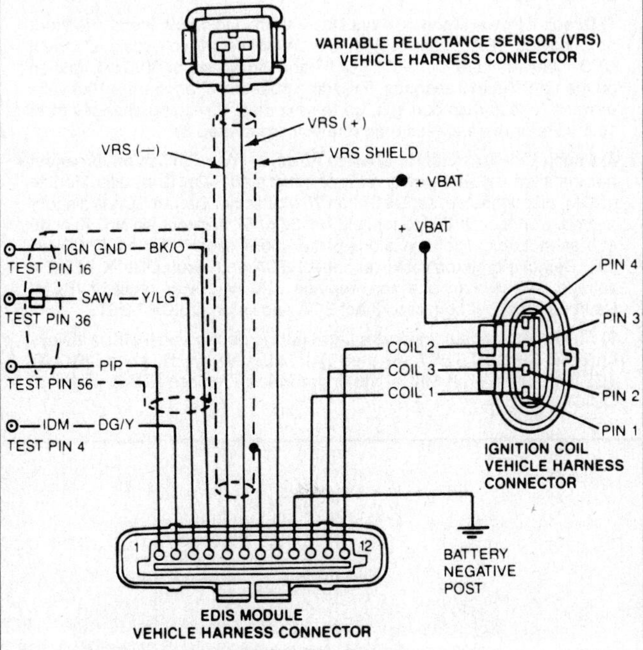

VARIABLE RELUCTANCE SENSOR (VRS)
VEHICLE HARNESS CONNECTOR
VRS (+)
VRS (—)
VRS SHIELD
+ VBAT
+ VBAT
IGN GND — BK/O
TEST PIN 16
SAW — Y/LG
TEST PIN 36
PIP
TEST PIN 56
IDM — DG/Y
TEST PIN 4
PIN 4
PIN 3
PIN 2
PIN 1
COIL 2
COIL 3
COIL 1
IGNITION COIL
VEHICLE HARNESS
CONNECTOR
1
12
BATTERY
NEGATIVE
POST
EDIS MODULE
VEHICLE HARNESS CONNECTOR

*TEST PINS LOCATED ON BREAKOUT BOX.
ALL HARNESS CONNECTORS VIEWED INTO MATING SURFACE.

CIRCUIT TEST PC (Cont.)

TEST PIN 56 (PIP) WIRE COLOR IDENTIFICATION

Application	Wire Color
4.0L Aerostar	Dark Blue
4.0L Explorer & 4.0L Ranger	Gray/Orange

TEST PIN 16 (SAW) WIRE COLOR IDENTIFICATION

Application	Wire Color
4.0L Aerostar	Yellow/Light Green
4.0L Explorer & 4.0L Ranger	Pink

1) KOER Code 18/213: Check Computed Spark Timing – Code 18/213 indicates SAW circuit is open or shorted to ground or VBAT. Possible causes for this fault are as follows:

- Open Or Shorted Harness Circuit
- Faulty ECA
- Faulty EDIS Module

Activate KOER SELF-TEST. Check and record timing while in KOER SELF-TEST. Self-test mode locks timing during testing, and during 2 minutes after last code is displayed. Computed timing during these 2 minutes is equal to base timing plus 20 degrees (±3 degrees). If computed timing is correct, restart KOER SELF-TEST. If timing is not to specification, go to next step.

2) Check Base Timing – Turn ignition off and wait 10 seconds. Locate in-line SAW connector, and open connection. Start engine and check base timing. Use specification on VECI decal. If base timing is correct, reconnect SAW and go to next step. If base timing is incorrect, diagnose ignition system, as base timing is not adjustable. See BASIC DIAGNOSTIC PROCEDURES article.

3) Check for Power to ECA – Turn ignition off and wait 10 seconds. Disconnect ECA 60-pin connector. Inspect connector for damaged pins, corrosion, or loose wires. Repair as necessary. Install breakout box, leaving ECA disconnected. With KOEO and DVOM on 20-volt scale, measure voltage between test pins No. 37 and 40, and between test pins No. 57 and 60 at breakout box. If either reading is less than 10.5 volts, go to CIRCUIT TEST B, step **1)**. If both readings are 10.5 volts or more, go to next step.

4) Check SAW Circuit for Continuity – Turn ignition off and wait 10 seconds. Install breakout box. Disconnect ECA and EDIS module. With DVOM on 200-ohm scale, measure resistance between test pin No. 36 at breakout box and SAW terminal at EDIS module vehicle harness connector. If resistance is less than 5 ohms, go to next step. If resistance is 5 ohms or more, repair open circuit. Reconnect all components and check timing as described in step **1)**.

Module Connector 91B09223

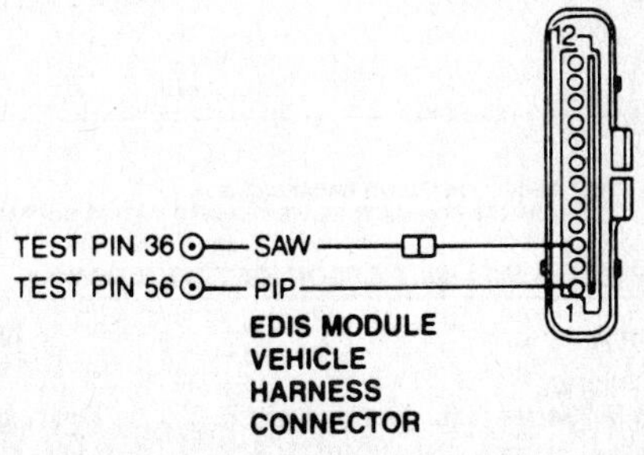

12
1
TEST PIN 36
SAW
TEST PIN 56
PIP
EDIS MODULE
VEHICLE
HARNESS
CONNECTOR

5) Check SAW Circuit for Shorts to Power (Except VREF Circuit) –With ignition off, install breakout box. Disconnect ECA and EDIS module. Measure voltage between test pin No. 36 and test pins No. 40 and 60. To check for short to VBAT, turn ignition off. To check for short to VPWR, turn ignition on.

If voltage is less than 10.5 volts, go to next step. If any reading is 10.5 volts or more, repair short circuit. Remove breakout box and reconnect all components. Rerun QUICK TEST.

6) Check SAW Circuit for Shorts to VREF, GROUND and PIP – Turn ignition off and wait 10 seconds. Set DVOM to 200-k/ohm scale. Install breakout box, leaving ECA and EDIS module disconnected.

To check for shorts to ground, measure resistance between test pin 36 and test pins No. 16, 20, 40, 46 and 60. To check for shorts to VREF,

1991 ENGINE PERFORMANCE
Self-Diagnostics – EEC-IV (Cont.)

CIRCUIT TEST PC (Cont.)

measure resistance between test pin 36 and test pin No. 26. To check for shorts to PIP circuit, measure resistance between test pin No. 36 and test pin No. 56.
If each resistance is 10 k/ohms or more, go to next step. If resistance is less than 10 k/ohms, repair short circuit. Remove breakout box, reconnect all components and rerun QUICK TEST.

Diagnostic Aids – During this test, when 4-wire HEGO is connected to vehicle harness, a short to SIG RTN (pin No. 46) may be indicated along with an actual short to PWR GND.

7) Check SAW Voltage at ECA – With ignition off and breakout box installed, connect ECA to breakout box. Reconnect EDIS module. Ensure timing switch on breakout box is in DIST position. Set DVOM on 20-volt AC scale. With KOER, measure voltage between test pin No. 36 and battery negative post. If AC voltage is NOT .6-1.8 volts replace ECA; remove breakout box and repeat QUICK TEST. If AC voltage is .6-1.8 volts, EEC-IV system is okay; remove breakout box, reconnect ECA and check ignition system. See BASIC DIAGNOSTIC PROCEDURES article.

CIRCUIT TEST QA

NO CODES/CODES NOT LISTED

Diagnostic Aids – Perform this test when directed by QUICK TEST or other test procedures. This test is intended to diagnose only the following:

- ECA
- EEC Power Relay
- Harness Circuits (SIG RTN, STO, STI, VPWR, VREF)

No Codes/Codes Not Listed Circuits 90F13297

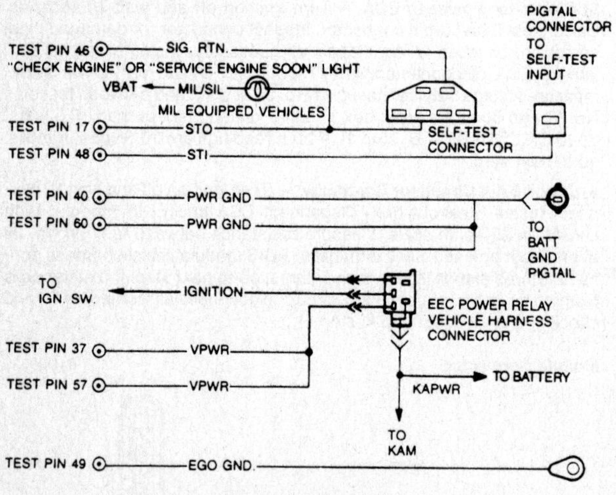
TEST PIN 46
SIG. RTN.
"CHECK ENGINE" OR "SERVICE ENGINE SOON" LIGHT
VBAT
MIL/SIL
MIL EQUIPPED VEHICLES
TEST PIN 17
STO
TEST PIN 48
STI
PIGTAIL CONNECTOR TO SELF-TEST INPUT
SELF-TEST CONNECTOR
TEST PIN 40
PWR GND
TEST PIN 60
PWR GND
TO BATT GND PIGTAIL
TO IGN. SW.
IGNITION
EEC POWER RELAY VEHICLE HARNESS CONNECTOR
TEST PIN 37
VPWR
TEST PIN 57
VPWR
TO BATTERY
KAPWR
TO KAM
TEST PIN 49
EGO GND.

*TEST PINS LOCATED ON BREAKOUT BOX.
ALL HARNESS CONNECTORS VIEWED INTO MATING SURFACE.

TEST PIN 17 (STO & MIL) WIRE COLOR IDENTIFICATION

Application	Wire Color
Bronco, Explorer, Ranger & "F" Series	Pink/Light Green
All Others	Tan/Red

TEST PIN 48 (STI) WIRE COLOR IDENTIFICATION

Application	Wire Color
4.0L Aerostar & "E" Series	White/Red
All Others	White/Purple

TEST PIN 37/57 (VPWR) WIRE COLOR IDENTIFICATION

Application	Wire Color
All Models	Red

CIRCUIT TEST QA (Cont.)

Diagnostic Aids – After-market devices, such as alarm system, may cause self-test to abort if wiring is connected to certain EEC components. If a device is installed, disconnect it completely from EEC system. Before continuing with this circuit test, restore EEC circuits to original and rerun QUICK TEST.

1) Check VREF Voltage at Self-Test Connector – Turn ignition off and wait 10 seconds. Disconnect ECA 60-pin connector. Inspect connector for damaged pins, corrosion, or loose wires. Repair as necessary. Install breakout box and connect ECA. Set DVOM on 20-volt scale. With Key On Engine Off (KOEO), measure voltage between test pin No. 26 and SIG RTN at self-test connector. If reading is NOT 4-6 volts, go to CIRCUIT TEST C, step **1)**. If reading is 4-6 volts, go to next step.

2) Check STI Circuit Continuity – Turn ignition off and wait 10 seconds. With breakout box installed and ECA disconnected, set DVOM on 200-ohm scale. Measure resistance between test pin No. 48 at breakout box and Self-Test Input (STI) at self-test connector pigtail. If reading is less than 5 ohms, go to next step. If resistance is 5 ohms or more, repair open in circuit; remove breakout box and reconnect ECA. Rerun QUICK TEST.

3) Check STO Circuit Continuity – With breakout box installed and ECA disconnected, set DVOM on 200-ohm scale. Measure resistance between test pin No. 17 at breakout box and Self-Test Output (STO) at self-test connector. If reading is less than 5 ohms, go to next step. If reading is 5 ohms or more, repair open circuit; remove breakout box and reconnect ECA. Rerun QUICK TEST.

4) Check EGO Signal for Short to Power – With breakout box installed, ECA disconnected and DVOM on 20-volt scale, measure voltage between HEGO SIGNAL test pin No. 29 or 44 and test pin No. 40 or 60 (refer to schematic at beginning of CIRCUIT TEST H). If voltage is 2 volts or more, go to next step. If voltage is less than 2 volts, go to step **6)**.

5) Isolate Short to Harness or HEGO Sensor – With breakout box installed and ECA disconnected, set DVOM to 20-volt scale. Disconnect HEGO (bank No. 1) sensor connector. With KOEO, measure voltage between HEGO SIGNAL test pin No. 20 or 44 and test pin No. 40 or 60 (refer to schematic at beginning of CIRCUIT TEST H). If voltage is 2 volts or more, repair short to power in HEGO SIGNAL circuit. Remove breakout box, reconnect all components and rerun QUICK TEST. If voltage is less than 2 volts, replace HEGO sensor (bank No. 1). Remove breakout box, reconnect all components and rerun QUICK TEST.

6) Check STO Circuit for Short to Ground – With breakout box installed and ECA disconnected, set DVOM on 200-k/ohm scale. Measure resistance between STO at self-test connector and engine block ground. If reading is 10k/ohms or more, go to next step. If resistance is less than 10 k/ohms, repair STO or MIL/SIL circuit for short to ground. Reconnect ECA and repeat QUICK TEST.

7) Check if Power Relay Always On – With ignition off, install breakout box, leaving ECA disconnected. Set DVOM on 20-volt scale. Connect DVOM between test pin No. 37 or 57 and pin No. 40 or 60. Turn ignition on then off. Wait 10 seconds. If reading does not change from 10.5 volts or more to less than one volt, go to next step. If reading changes from 10.5 volts or more to less than one volt, go to step **8)**.

8) Check VPWR Circuit for Short to Power – With ignition off, breakout box installed and EEC power relay or Integrated Relay Controller Module (IRCM) disconnected, set DVOM on 20-volt scale. Ensure ECA is disconnected. Connect DVOM to test pin No. 37 or 57 and test pin No. 40 or 46 at breakout box. If voltage is one volt or more, repair short to VPWR circuit. Remove breakout box, reconnect ECA and rerun QUICK TEST. If voltage is less than one volt, replace EEC-IV power relay or IRCM. Remove breakout box, reconnect ECA and rerun QUICK TEST.

9) Check Malfunction Indicator Light (MIL) Function – If MIL is always on, go to CIRCUIT TEST ML, step **1)**. If MIL is always off, go to CIRCUIT TEST ML, step **4)**. If MIL is working normally, replace ECA and repeat QUICK TEST.

CIRCUIT TEST QB

CODE 15, 511 OR 512
KOEO OR CONTINUOUS MEMORY CODE

Diagnostic Aids – Perform this test when directed by QUICK TEST. This test is intended to diagnose only the following components or systems:
- ECA
- Harness Circuits (KAPWR)

EEC Power Relay Circuit 91G13298

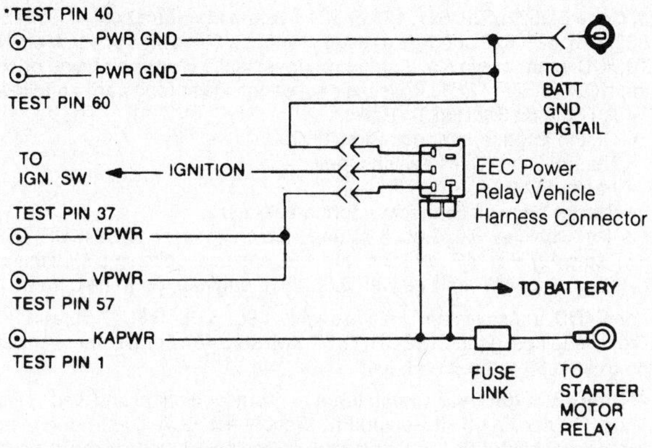

*TEST PIN 40
PWR GND
PWR GND
TEST PIN 60
TO BATT GND PIGTAIL
TO IGN. SW.
IGNITION
EEC Power Relay Vehicle Harness Connector
TEST PIN 37
VPWR
VPWR
TEST PIN 57
TO BATTERY
KAPWR
TEST PIN 1
FUSE LINK
TO STARTER MOTOR RELAY

*TEST PINS LOCATED ON BREAKOUT BOX
ALL HARNESS CONNECTORS VIEWED INTO MATING SURFACE

TEST PIN 1 (KAPWR) WIRE COLOR IDENTIFICATION

Application	Wire Color
"E" Series	Black/Orange
All Others	Yellow

1) Continuous Memory Code 15/512 Displayed – Code 15/512 indicates ECA is experiencing power interruption in its Keep-Alive Memory (KAM) circuit. Clear Continuous Memory Codes. See CLEARING CODES under SELF-DIAGNOSTIC SYSTEM. Wait 5 minutes to allow code to reset. Repeat KOEO SELF-TEST for Continuous Memory Code output. If Continuous Memory Code 15/512 is not displayed, Continuous Memory Code 15/512 testing is complete. Service other codes as necessary. If Continuous Memory Code 15/512 is displayed during retest, go to next step.

Diagnostic Aids – Continuous Memory Code 15/512 may be displayed when power to Keep-Alive Memory (KAM) test pin No. 1 at ECA is interrupted. This code may be set when installing a breakout box, and may be displayed the first time self-test is performed and power is restored to ECA. Repeat self-test to ensure correct diagnosis.

2) Inspect Engine Compartment Wire Routing – Ensure EEC-IV components and wiring are not close to high-tension secondary voltage wires or ignition components. If EEC-IV wiring is close to high-tension wires, reroute EEC wiring. Clear codes and wait 5 minutes. Repeat KOEO SELF-TEST. If Continuous Memory Code 15/512 is no longer displayed, Continuous Memory Code 15/512 testing is complete; service other codes as necessary. If Continuous Memory Code 15/512 is still displayed, go to next step.

3) Code 15/511: Check KAPWR Circuit Voltage – Code 15/511 indicates ECA memory (ROM) failed during KOEO SELF-TEST. Turn ignition off and wait 10 seconds. Disconnect ECA 60-pin connector and inspect for damaged pins and loose wires. Service as necessary. Install breakout box, leaving ECA disconnected. Set DVOM on 20-volt scale. Connect DVOM positive test lead to test pin No. 1 and negative test lead to pin No. 40 or 60 at breakout box. With KOEO, observe voltage reading while wiggling, bending and shaking small sections of EEC harness from EEC to dash. If reading is less than 10.5 volts, repair open circuit; reconnect ECA and repeat QUICK TEST. If reading is 10.5 volts or more, replace ECA; remove breakout box and repeat QUICK TEST.

CIRCUIT TEST QC

OUTPUT STATE CHECK NOT FUNCTIONING

Diagnostic Aids – Perform this circuit test when directed by other CIRCUIT TESTS. This test is intended to diagnose only the following:
- ECA
- Throttle Plate Linkage

1) Check for Codes 23, 53, 63, 121, 122 Or 123 – If vehicle is equipped with speed control, speed control servo must be electrically disconnected. This prevents speed control system from affecting throttle plate movement during Output State Check. Rerun QUICK TEST or Output State Check.

Turn ignition off and wait 10 seconds. Perform KOEO SELF-TEST. If Codes 23, 53, 63, 121, 122 or 123 are displayed, go to appropriate KOEO SELF-TEST CODES chart under SERVICE CODE REFERENCE CHARTS and service code(s) as necessary. If no code is displayed, go to CIRCUIT TEST QA, step **1)**. If Code 11/111 (pass code) is displayed, go to next step.

2) Check Throttle Linkage – Check throttle and linkage for sticking or binding. If throttle and linkage are okay, replace TPS and repeat QUICK TEST. If throttle and linkage are binding, repair as necessary and repeat QUICK TEST.

CIRCUIT TEST S

SYSTEM CHECK

Diagnostic Aids – Perform this test only when directed by CIRCUIT TEST A or CIRCUIT TEST AA.

This test is intended to diagnose the following components or systems:
- ISC By-Pass Air System
- MAP System
- EGR System
- MAF System

To prevent replacing good components, be aware that the following non-EEC-IV areas may be at fault:
- Faulty Power Or Ground Connections
- Ignition System (Distributor Cap, Rotor, Wires, Coil And Plugs)
- Basic Mechanical Engine Components (Cam Timing, Compression, Etc.)

1) ISC-BPA Check – Attempt to start engine at part throttle. If engine starts and runs smoothly at part throttle, go to CIRCUIT TEST KE, step **4)**. If engine does not function as described, go to step **3)**.

2) Check for RPM Drop – Turn ignition off. Connect a tachometer. Start engine and disconnect ISC solenoid. If RPM drops or engine stalls, reconnect ISC solenoid and go to next step. If RPM does not drop, go to step **4)**.

3) Power to MAP/BP Sensor – If vehicle is not equipped with a MAP/BP sensor, go directly to step **8)**. Use Ford Motor Co. MAP/BP tester for this test. If Green light is on, VREF circuit voltage is okay. If Red light (or no light) is on, VREF circuit voltage is either too low or too high. Turn ignition off and disconnect MAP/BP sensor from vehicle harness. Connect MAP/BP tester between vehicle harness and MAP/BP sensor. Connect plugs of tester into DVOM, and set DVOM on 20-volt scale. With tester connected, turn ignition on. If Green light is on, go to next step. If light is not on, repair open in VREF circuit and remove MAP/BP tester. Reconnect components and retest symptom.

4) MAP/BP Tester Output Reading – Measure several known good MAP/BP sensors to obtain average voltage for specific location and date of testing. With MAP/BP tester and DVOM connected, turn ignition on and measure MAP/BP SIG voltage at MAP sensor. If voltage is within specification for the specific altitude, go to step **8)** (vehicles with MA sensors), or go to next step (all others). See MAP VOLTAGE OUTPUT table. If voltage is not within specification for the specific altitude, replace MAP/BP sensor.

5) Check Vacuum Lines – Check vacuum lines for correct routing. Refer to VECI decal. Check MAP sensor vacuum line for leaks or blockage. If vacuum lines are okay, go to next step. If vacuum lines are not okay, repair as necessary. Rerun QUICK TEST.

6) Check MAP Sensor – Turn ignition off and wait 10 seconds. Disconnect vacuum line from MAP sensor. Install vacuum pump to MAP sensor. Apply 18 in. Hg vacuum to MAP sensor. If MAP sensor holds vacuum, release vacuum and remove vacuum pump. Reconnect vacuum line to MAP sensor and go to next step. If MAP sensor does not hold vacuum, replace MAP sensor. Reconnect vacuum line and rerun QUICK TEST.

1991 ENGINE PERFORMANCE
Self-Diagnostics – EEC-IV (Cont.)

CIRCUIT TEST S (Cont.)

MAP/BP Tester & Circuit 90H14511

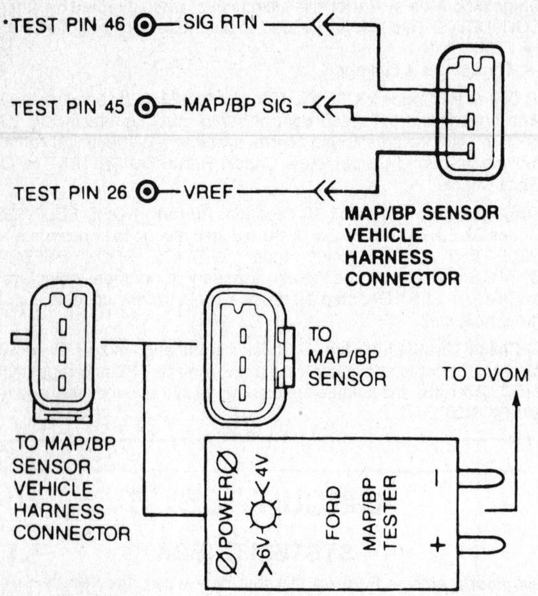
*TEST PIN 46
SIG RTN
TEST PIN 45
MAP/BP SIG
TEST PIN 26
VREF
MAP/BP SENSOR VEHICLE HARNESS CONNECTOR
TO MAP/BP SENSOR
TO DVOM
TO MAP/BP SENSOR VEHICLE HARNESS CONNECTOR
POWER
>6V
<4V
FORD MAP/BP TESTER
–
+

MAP VOLTAGE OUTPUT

Approx. Elevation (Ft.)	Volts
0	1.55-1.63
1000	1.52-1.60
2000	1.49-1.57
3000	1.46-1.54
4000	1.43-1.51
5000	1.40-1.48
6000	1.37-1.45
7000	1.35-1.43

7) Check Vacuum Manifold Source – Turn ignition off. Disconnect MAP sensor vacuum hose from manifold vacuum "T" fitting, and install vacuum gauge in its place. Start engine and observe vacuum gauge. If manifold vacuum is present, remove vacuum gauge; reconnect MAP sensor vacuum hose and go to next step. If vacuum is not present, remove obstruction; reconnect all components and rerun QUICK TEST.

8) Check EGR Vacuum – If vehicle is not equipped with EGR system hardware, go directly to CIRCUIT TEST H, step **2)**. Step **8)** and step **9)** attempt to determine if EGR system is cause of driveability symptom or no-start condition. Disconnect and plug vacuum line at EGR valve. Attempt to start engine. If vehicle could not start previously and still does not start or if vehicle driveability fault is still present, go to next step. If vehicle did not start previously but starts now or if driveability symptoms are eliminated, go to CIRCUIT TEST DN, step **42)** (vehicles with EVP) or go to CIRCUIT TEST DN, step **21)** (all others).

9) Check EGR Valve – Inspect EGR valve for leaks. If valve is fully closed, go to CIRCUIT TEST H, step **2)**. If EGR valve is leaking or is not fully seated, replace or repair valve.

CIRCUIT TEST TA

NEUTRAL DRIVE INPUT

Diagnostic Aids – Perform this test only when directed by QUICK TEST. This test is intended to diagnose only the following circuits or systems:

- Clutch Engage/Interlock Switch
- Neutral Drive/Gear Switch
- ECA
- Harness Circuits: CES, CIS, NDS, NGS and SIG RTN

CIRCUIT TEST TA (Cont.)

TEST PIN 30 (NDS) WIRE COLOR IDENTIFICATION

Application	Wire Color
All Models	Light Blue/Yellow

TEST PIN 48 (SIG RTN) WIRE COLOR IDENTIFICATION

Application	Wire Color
All Models	Gray/Red

1) Code 67/522, 525, 527, 528 or 634 System Identification – Code 67/522, 525, 527, 528 or 634 is a result of voltage being high at either pin No. 10 (A/C input) or pin No. 30 (neutral drive) while cranking engine or during KOEO SELF-TEST. Possible causes for these faults are as follows:

- A/C Circuit Shorted To Power
- Clutch Engage/Interlock Circuits Open
- Neutral Drive/Gear Switch Open
- Faulty ECA
- Starter relay disconnected during self-test

For M/T vehicles with 5.0L, 5.8L and 7.5L engines, go to CIRCUIT TEST KM, step **40)**. For M/T vehicles with 4.9L engines, go to step **7)** of this circuit test. For M/T vehicles with 2.3L, 2.9L engines, go to next step.

For E4OD transmissions vehicles with 4.9L, 5.0L, 5.8L, 7.5L and 7.3L Diesel engines, go to CIRCUIT TEST KM, step **40)**. For all other vehicles, go to step **8)** of this circuit test.

2) Check Neutral Gear/Clutch Input – Turn ignition off and wait 10 seconds. Turn A/C off (if equipped). Disconnect ECA 60-pin connector. Inspect connector for damaged pins, corrosion, or loose wires; repair as necessary. Install breakout box, leaving ECA disconnected. Set DVOM to 200-ohm scale. Measure resistance between test pins No. 30 and 46 with transmission in neutral and clutch pedal up. Measure resistance between test pins No. 30 and 46 with transmission in gear and clutch pedal down. If each resistance is less than 5 ohms, go to next step. If resistance is 5 ohms or more, go to step **5)**.

Neutral Gear/Clutch Input Circuit 91G09230

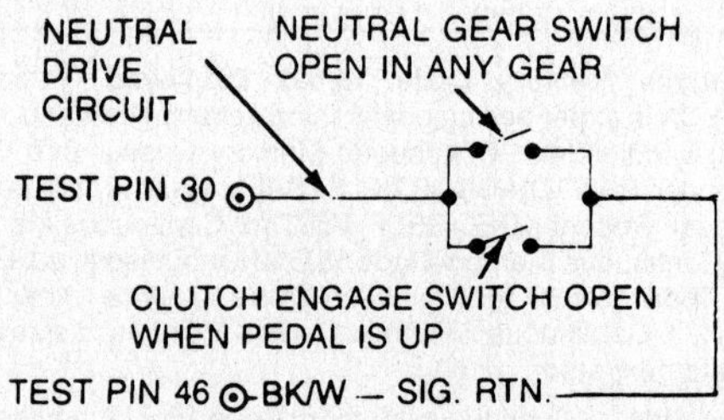
NEUTRAL DRIVE CIRCUIT
NEUTRAL GEAR SWITCH OPEN IN ANY GEAR
TEST PIN 30
CLUTCH ENGAGE SWITCH OPEN WHEN PEDAL IS UP
TEST PIN 46
BK/W – SIG. RTN.

3) Check Neutral Gear/Clutch Input Integrity – Turn ignition off and wait 10 seconds. With breakout box install, ECA disconnected and DVOM set to 200-ohm scale, measure resistance between test pins No. 30 and 46 with transmission in any gear and clutch pedal up. If resistance is less than 5 ohms, go to CIRCUIT TEST KM, step **40)** (vehicles with A/C), or replace ECA, remove breakout box and rerun QUICK TEST (all others). If resistance is 5 ohms or more, go to next step.

4) Check for Short to Ground – Turn ignition off and wait 10 seconds. Install breakout box, leaving ECA disconnected. Disconnect clutch engage switch. Set DVOM to 200-k/ohm scale. Measure resistance between test pins No. 30 and 46. If resistance is 10 k/ohms or more, go to CIRCUIT TEST KM, step **40)** (vehicles with A/C), or replace ECA, remove breakout box and rerun QUICK TEST (all others). If resistance is less than 10 k/ohms, repair short circuit. Remove breakout box, reconnect all components and rerun QUICK TEST.

5) Check Neutral Gear/Clutch Engage Switch – Turn ignition off and wait 10 seconds. Install breakout box, leaving ECA disconnected. Set DVOM to 200-ohm scale. Locate neutral gear switch (on transmission) and clutch engage switch (at clutch pedal linkage). Disconnect vehicle harness at both switches and inspect connectors for pushed-back pins. Measure resistance across neutral gear switch terminals with transmission in neutral, and across clutch engage switch with clutch pedal down. If each resistance is less than 5 ohms, go to next step. If resistance is 5 ohms or more, replace open switch(es). Remove breakout box, reconnect all components and rerun QUICK TEST.

6) Check Neutral Gear/Clutch Harness – Turn ignition off and wait 10 seconds. With breakout box installed, ECA disconnected and DVOM set to 200-ohm scale, disconnect neutral gear and clutch switches. Measure

CIRCUIT TEST TA (Cont.)

resistance between test pin No. 30 and neutral gear switch harness connector, and between test pin No. 30 and clutch engage switch harness connector.

Measure resistance between test pin No. 46 and neutral gear switch harness connector, and between test pin No. 46 and clutch engage switch harness connector. If each resistance is less than 5 ohms, go to CIRCUIT TEST KM, step **40)** (vehicles with A/C), or replace ECA, remove breakout box and rerun QUICK TEST (all others). If resistance is 5 ohms or more, repair open circuit. Remove breakout box, reconnect all components and rerun QUICK TEST.

7) Check Clutch Engage Switch – For vehicles with 4.9L engines, clutch pedal must be down during KOEO SELF-TEST; if not, Code 67/528 will be set. Turn ignition off and wait 10 seconds. Disconnect ECA 60-pin connector. Inspect connector for damaged pins, corrosion, or loose wires; repair as necessary. Install breakout box, leaving ECA disconnected. Set DVOM to 200-ohm scale. Hold clutch pedal down and measure resistance between test pins No. 30 and 40. If resistance is less than 5 ohms, go to CIRCUIT TEST KM, step **40)** (vehicles with A/C), or replace ECA, remove breakout box and rerun QUICK TEST (all others). If each resistance is 5 ohms or more, repair open circuit. Remove breakout box, reconnect all components and rerun QUICK TEST.

Checking Clutch Engage Switch 91I09231

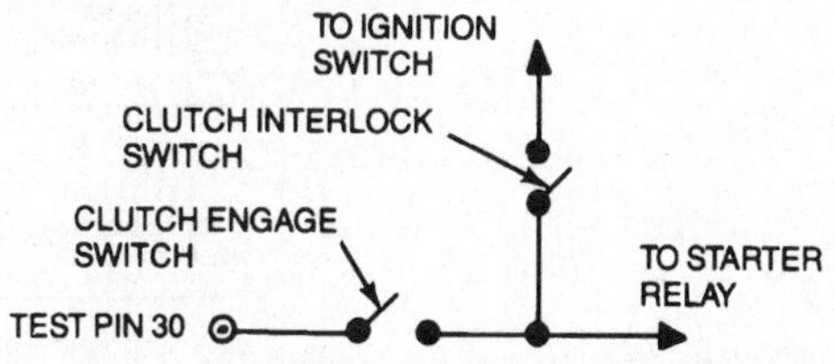
TO IGNITION SWITCH
CLUTCH INTERLOCK SWITCH
CLUTCH ENGAGE SWITCH
TEST PIN 30
TO STARTER RELAY

8) Check Neutral Drive Input – Turn ignition off and wait 10 seconds. Ensure heater control is in OFF position (if equipped). Ensure transmission is in NEUTRAL or PARK position. Disconnect ECA 60-pin connector. Inspect connector for damaged pins, corrosion, or loose wires; repair as necessary. Install breakout box and connect ECA to breakout box. Set DVOM to 20-volt scale. With KOEO, measure voltage between test pin No. 30 and chassis ground. If voltage is less than one volt, go to CIRCUIT TEST KM, step **40)** (vehicles with A/C), or replace ECA, remove breakout box and rerun QUICK TEST (all others). If voltage is one volt or more, go to next step.

Checking Neutral Drive Input 91C09233

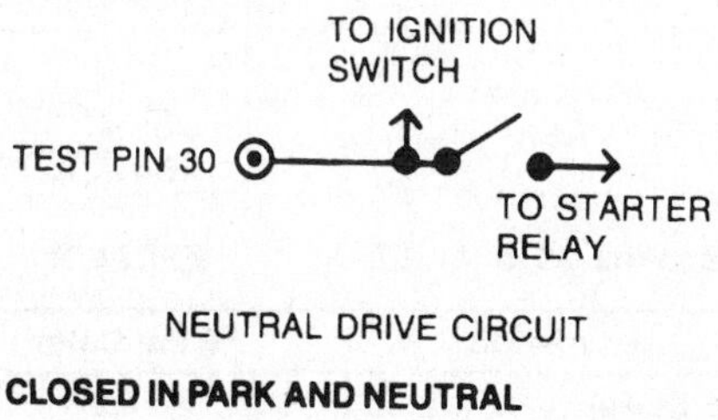
TO IGNITION SWITCH
TEST PIN 30
TO STARTER RELAY
NEUTRAL DRIVE CIRCUIT
CLOSED IN PARK AND NEUTRAL

9) Check Neutral Drive Switch – Turn ignition off and wait 10 seconds. Install breakout box, leaving ECA disconnected. Set DVOM to 200-ohm scale. Disconnect vehicle harness from neutral drive switch and measure resistance across switch. If resistance is less than 5 ohms, repair open circuit in vehicle harness Neutral Drive circuit. Remove breakout box, reconnect all components and rerun QUICK TEST. If resistance is 5 ohms or more, replace neutral drive switch. Remove breakout box, reconnect all components and rerun QUICK TEST.

10) Check NDS Circuit for Short to Ground or Closed Neutral Drive Switch – Turn ignition off and wait 10 seconds. Disconnect ECA 60-pin connector. Inspect connector for damaged pins, corrosion, or loose wires; repair as necessary. Install breakout box and leave ECA disconnected. Set DVOM to 200-k/ohm scale. Place transmission in DRIVE position. Measure resistance between test pins No. 30 and 40/60. If resistance is 10 k/ohms or more, NDS circuit is okay. Diagnose other possible causes. If resistance is less than 10 k/ohms, repair closed neutral drive switch or short circuit. Remove breakout box, reconnect all components and rerun QUICK TEST.

CIRCUIT TEST TB

A4LD TRANSMISSION

Diagnostic Aids – Perform this test only when directed by QUICK TEST. To prevent replacing good components, be aware that the following non-EEC areas may be at fault:

- Hydraulic Or Emergency Brake System
- Transmission Linkage
- Internal Transmission Components

This test is intended to diagnose only the following components or circuits:

- Harness Circuits (CCO, SS 3/4-4/3 And VPWR)
- CCO Solenoid
- Shift Solenoid 3/4-4/3
- ECA

A4LD Transmission Circuits 90I14520

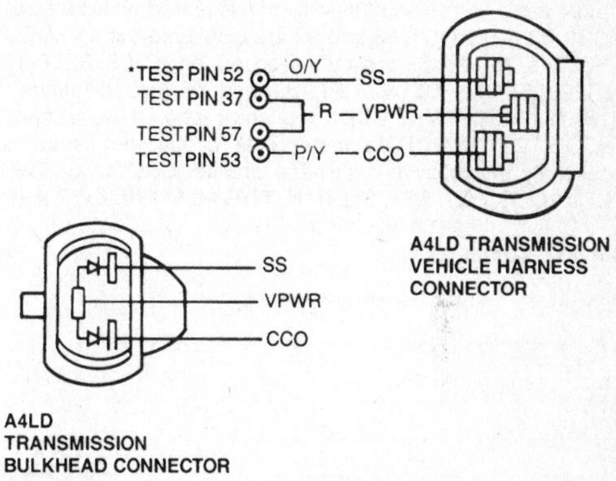
*TEST PIN 52
TEST PIN 37
TEST PIN 57
TEST PIN 53
O/Y
SS
R
VPWR
P/Y
CCO
A4LD TRANSMISSION VEHICLE HARNESS CONNECTOR
SS
VPWR
CCO
A4LD TRANSMISSION BULKHEAD CONNECTOR

1) Code 86/556 or 89/639: Check Solenoid Resistance – Code 86/556 indicates ECA did not detect a voltage drop when Shift Solenoid 3/4 (SS 3/4) was activated. Code 89/626 indicates ECA did not detect a voltage drop when CCO solenoid was activated. Possible causes for this fault are as follows:

- CCO/SS Resistance Out Of Limits
- CCO/SS Circuit Open Or Grounded
- Faulty ECA

Ensure codes match appropriate transmission solenoid circuit. Turn ignition off and wait 10 seconds. Disconnect ECA 60-pin connector. Inspect connector for damaged pins, corrosion, or loose wires. Repair as necessary. Install breakout box, leaving ECA disconnected. Set DVOM on 200-ohm scale. Measure resistance between test pin No. 37/57 and test pins No. 53 (CCO) and 52 (SS 3/4). If resistance is 26-40 ohms, go to step **4)**. If resistance is NOT 26-40 ohms, go to next step.

2) Check Continuity of Vehicle Harness Circuits – With ignition off, install breakout box. Leave ECA and transmission bulkhead connector (A4LD solenoids) disconnected. Set DVOM on 200-ohm scale. Measure resistance between test pin No. 37/ 57 at breakout box and VPWR circuit pin of vehicle harness connector at transmission. Measure resistance between appropriate ECA signal output pin (No. 52 or 53) at breakout box and same circuit at transmission vehicle harness connector. If resistance is less than 5 ohms, go to next step. If resistance is 5 ohms or more, repair open circuit. Remove breakout box, reconnect all components and rerun QUICK TEST.

3) Check Transmission Vehicle Harness Circuits – With ignition off, install breakout box, leaving ECA disconnected. Disconnect transmission bulkhead connector. Set DVOM on 200-k/ohm scale. Measure resistance between appropriate test pin No. 53 (CCO) or 52 (SS 3/4) and test pins No. 37 and 57 at breakout box. Measure resistance between appropriate test pin No. 53 (CCO) or 52 (SS 3/4) and test pins No. 40, 60 and 46 at breakout box and at chassis ground. If all resistances are 10 k/ohms or more, go to next step. If any resistance is less than 10 k/ohms, repair short circuit. Remove breakout box and reconnect components. Rerun QUICK TEST.

4) Check VPWR Voltage to Transmission Solenoids – With ignition off, breakout box installed and ECA connected, set DVOM on 20-volt scale. Disconnect transmission bulkhead connector. Turn ignition on, leaving engine off. Measure voltage between test pins No. 37/57 at bulkhead connector and chassis ground. If voltage is 10.5 volts or more, go to next step. If voltage is less than 10.5 volts, replace ECA. Remove breakout box and reconnect all components. Rerun QUICK TEST.

1991 ENGINE PERFORMANCE
Self-Diagnostics – EEC-IV (Cont.)

CIRCUIT TEST TB (Cont.)

5) Check Output Driver Signal – Turn ignition off. Install breakout box, leaving ECA connected. Disconnect A4LD transmission bulkhead connector. Connect test light between test pin No. 37/57 and appropriate test pin No. 53 (CCO) or 52 (SS 3/4) at breakout box. Enter KOEO SELF-TEST. If test light flashes momentarily and then stays off, fault is internal in transmission. Repair internal electrical fault as necessary. If light does not flash momentarily and then stay off, replace ECA. Remove breakout box and reconnect all components. Repeat QUICK TEST.

CIRCUIT TEST TC

E4OD AUTOMATIC TRANSMISSION

Diagnostic Aids – You should perform this test when Codes 26, 47, 56, 66, 67, 91, 92, 93, 94, 97, 98 and 99 are displayed during KOEO SELF-TEST, Codes 26 and 65 are displayed during KOER SELF-TEST, or Codes 29, 49, 56, 59, 62, 66, 69 and 99 are displayed during CONTINUOUS MONITOR MODE testing or when directed here during DIAGNOSIS BY SYMPTOM tests. This circuit test is intended to diagnose only the following: harness circuits, CCC, CCS, 4WD LOW, EPC, OCIL, OCS, SS1, SS2, SIG RTN, TOT, MLP, EPC PWR and VPWR.

E4OD & MLP Circuit 90HO9315

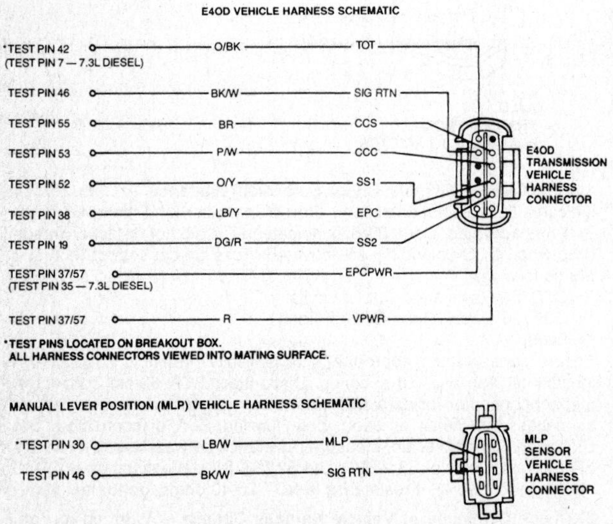
E4OD VEHICLE HARNESS SCHEMATIC
*TEST PIN 42 — O/BK — TOT
(TEST PIN 7 — 7.3L DIESEL)
TEST PIN 46 — BK/W — SIG RTN
TEST PIN 55 — BR — CCS
TEST PIN 53 — P/W — CCC
TEST PIN 52 — O/Y — SS1
TEST PIN 38 — LB/Y — EPC
TEST PIN 19 — DG/R — SS2
TEST PIN 37/57 — EPCPWR
(TEST PIN 35 — 7.3L DIESEL)
TEST PIN 37/57 — R — VPWR
E4OD TRANSMISSION VEHICLE HARNESS CONNECTOR
*TEST PINS LOCATED ON BREAKOUT BOX.
ALL HARNESS CONNECTORS VIEWED INTO MATING SURFACE.
MANUAL LEVER POSITION (MLP) VEHICLE HARNESS SCHEMATIC
*TEST PIN 30 — LB/W — MLP
TEST PIN 46 — BK/W — SIG RTN
MLP SENSOR VEHICLE HARNESS CONNECTOR

1) Code 67: Check Resistance Through MLP Sensor – Code 67 indicates that total resistance in the MLP sensor is out of Self-Test range when the selector lever is in "P" (correct range is 3770-4607 ohms). Possible causes for this fault are: faulty MLP sensor, open or shorted harness, faulty ECA.

Turn key off and wait 10 seconds. Disconnect ECA 60-pin connector and inspect for corroded or damaged pins. Service or repair as necessary. Install breakout box, leaving ECA disconnected. With KOEO, measure resistance between test pins No. 30 and 46 at the breakout box while moving the selector from "P" to "L" and back to "P". Record specifications and compare to specification table. If resistance is within specification, go to step **3)**. If resistance is not as specified, go to next step.

MLP RESISTANCE SPECIFICATIONS

Gear Position	Min. Ohms	Max. Ohms
"P"	3770	4607
"R"	1304	1593
"N"	660	807
"D"	361	442
"2"	190	232
"1"	78	95

CIRCUIT TEST TC (Cont.)

4WD Low & Overdrive Cancel Harness Schematic 91B14267

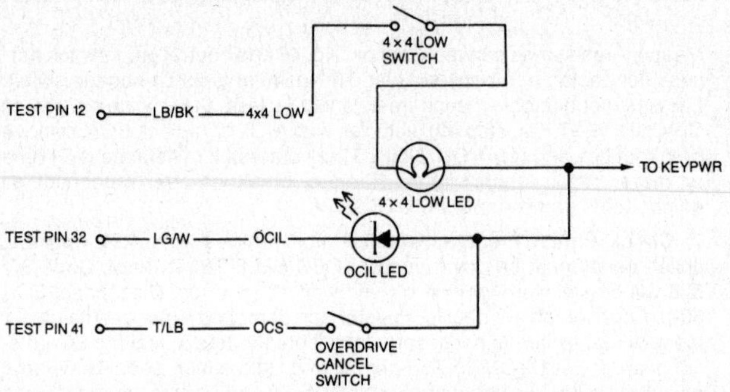
4 x 4 LOW SWITCH
TEST PIN 12 — LB/BK — 4x4 LOW
TO KEYPWR
4 x 4 LOW LED
TEST PIN 32 — LG/W — OCIL
OCIL LED
TEST PIN 41 — T/LB — OCS
OVERDRIVE CANCEL SWITCH

TEST PINS LOCATED ON BREAKOUT BOX.
ALL HARNESS CONNECTORS VIEWED INTO MATING SURFACE.

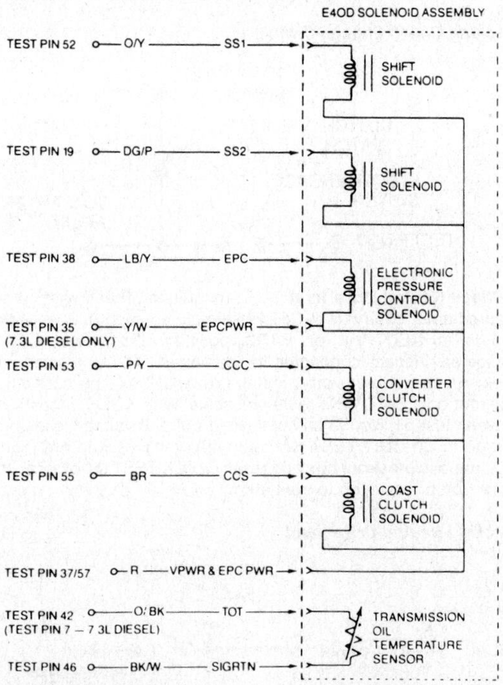
E4OD SOLENOID ASSEMBLY
TEST PIN 52 — O/Y — SS1
SHIFT SOLENOID
TEST PIN 19 — DG/P — SS2
SHIFT SOLENOID
TEST PIN 38 — LB/Y — EPC
ELECTRONIC PRESSURE CONTROL SOLENOID
TEST PIN 35 — Y/W — EPCPWR
(7.3L DIESEL ONLY)
TEST PIN 53 — P/Y — CCC
CONVERTER CLUTCH SOLENOID
TEST PIN 55 — BR — CCS
COAST CLUTCH SOLENOID
TEST PIN 37/57 — R — VPWR & EPC PWR
TEST PIN 42 — O/BK — TOT
(TEST PIN 7 — 7.3L DIESEL)
TRANSMISSION OIL TEMPERATURE SENSOR
TEST PIN 46 — BK/W — SIGRTN

Test Pins 35 & 37/57 EPCPWR

Application	Wire Color
7.3L Diesel	Y/W
5.8L & 7.5L	R or R/W

2) Checking Continuity of MLP Harness – Ensure key is off and MLP sensor is disconnected from harness. Use a mirror to inspect ends of transmission harness connector at MLP sensor for damage or corrosion. Repair as necessary. Install breakout box, leaving ECA disconnected. Measure resistance between test pin No. 30 at the breakout box and corresponding pin at the MLP sensor vehicle harness connector. Measure resistance between test pin No. 46 at the breakout box and corresponding pin at the MLP sensor vehicle harness connector. If both resistances are less than 5 ohms, go to next step. If resistances are not as specified, repair open circuit, remove breakout box, reconnect components and rerun QUICK TEST.

3) Check MLP Harness for Short to Power or Ground – Turn key off. Ensure MLP sensor harness is disconnected. Install breakout box leaving ECA disconnected. Set DVOM on 200-k/ohm scale. Measure

CIRCUIT TEST TC (Cont.)

resistance between test pin No. 30 and test pins No. 37 and 57 at the breakout box. Measure resistance between test pin No. 30 and test pins No. 40, 46 and 60 at the breakout box. Measure resistance between test pin No. 30 at the breakout box and chassis ground. If all resistances are 10 k/ohms or more, go to next step. If resistances are less than 10 k/ohms, repair short circuits, remove breakout box, reconnect components and rerun QUICK TEST.

4) Checking ECA Output Voltage – Ensure key is off. Disconnect MLP sensor from harness. Install breakout box and connect ECA. With KOEO, set DVOM on 20-volt scale. Measure voltage between test pins No. 30 and 46 at the breakout box. If voltage is 4.75-5.25 volts, service or adjust MLP sensor. If voltage is not as specified, replace ECA, reconnect components and rerun QUICK TEST.

5) Code 47, 65 or 97: Verify Self-Test Mode – Code 47 indicates 4WD LOW selector lever is not in 2WD or 4WD High position during KOEO Self-Test. This condition may be accompanied by an early shift in the 4WD High range. Code 65 indicates that Overdrive Cancel Switch (OCS) is not cycled between the engine I.D. code and "Goose Test" in the KOER Self-Test. Code 97 indicates an Overdrive Cancel Light (OCL) fault during KOER Self-Test. Possible causes for this fault are: faulty 4WD LOW switch, faulty OCS switch, burned out bulb, open harness, shorted harness or faulty ECA. Rerun QUICK TEST. If none of the above codes are present, fault cannot be duplicated at this time, testing is complete. If Code 97 is present, go to step **7)**. If any other codes are present, go to next step.

6) Cycle 4WD LOW or Overdrive Cancel Switch Circuit – Turn key off and wait 10 seconds. Disconnect ECA 60-pin connector and inspect for corroded or damaged pins. Service or repair as necessary. Install breakout box, leaving ECA disconnected. With KOEO, set DVOM on 20-volt scale.

4WD LOW Circuit – Measure voltage between test pin No. 12 and test pins No. 40 and 60 at the breakout box while cycling the Overdrive Cancel Switch (OCS). Move transfer case lever between 4WD and 2WD positions several times.

Overdrive Cancel Switch (OCS) Circuit – Measure voltage between test pin No. 41 and test pins No. 40 and 60 at the breakout box while cycling the Overdrive Cancel Switch. Toggle the switch on the dash several times.

If voltage cycles, remove breakout box. Replace ECA and rerun QUICK TEST. If voltage does not cycle, go to step **9)** for driveability faults or next step for other faults.

7) Checking Circuits for Shorts to Ground – Ensure key is off, breakout box is installed and ECA is disconnected. Set DVOM on 200-k/ohm scale.
4WD LOW Circuit – Disconnect 4WD LOW switch. Measure resistance between test pin No. 12 and test pins No. 40 and 60 at the breakout box.
Overdrive Cancel Switch (OCS) Circuit – Disconnect Overdrive Cancel Switch. Measure resistance between test pin No. 41 and test pins No. 40 and 60 at the breakout box.

If resistance(s) is 10 k/ohms or more, go to step **10)** for Code 47 or 65. Go to next step for Code 97. If resistance is less than 10 k/ohms, for Code 47, repair short circuit and rerun KOEO Self-Test; for Code 65, repair short circuit and rerun KOER Self-Test, if Code 65 is still present, go to step **9)**. For Code 97, repair short circuit and rerun KOEO Self-Test.

8) Checking Key Power Through OCIL Circuit – With KOEO, ensure breakout box is installed and ECA is disconnected. Set DVOM on 20-volt scale. Measure voltage between test pin No. 32 and test pins No. 40 and 60 at the breakout box. If voltage is 10.5 volts or more, remove the breakout box, replace ECA and rerun QUICK TEST. If voltage is less than 10.5 volts, go to next step.

9) Checking Continuity of LED Harness (4WD LOW or Overdrive Cancel) – With KOEO, disconnect ECA 60-pin connector and inspect for corroded or damaged pins. Service or repair as necessary. Install breakout box, leaving ECA disconnected. Disconnect 4WD LOW or Overdrive Cancel Switch.

4WD LOW Circuit – Measure resistance between Key Power Circuit at the fuse panel (+ probe) and test pin No. 12 (– probe) at the breakout box.

OCS–OCIL Circuit – Measure resistance between Key Power Circuit at the fuse panel (+ probe) and test pin No. 32 (– probe) at the breakout box.

If resistance is less than 5 ohms, go to next step. If resistance is 5 ohms or more, check for a faulty indicator bulb (4WD LOW LED or OCIL) or defective fuse in fuse panel. If fuse is okay, repair open circuit, remove breakout box and reconnect ECA. Rerun QUICK TEST.

CIRCUIT TEST TC (Cont.)

Fuse Panel 90JO9316

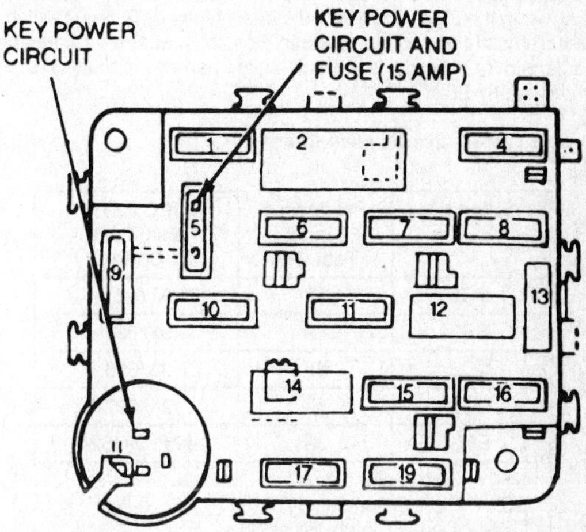

KEY POWER CIRCUIT
KEY POWER CIRCUIT AND FUSE (15 AMP)

10) Checking Continuity of the 4WD LOW or Overdrive Cancel Switch Harness – With key off, breakout box installed and ECA disconnected, disconnect appropriate switch.

4WD LOW Circuit – Measure resistance between test pin No. 12 at the breakout box and 4WD LOW circuit at the 4WD LOW switch vehicle harness.

4WD LOW Circuit 90BO9317

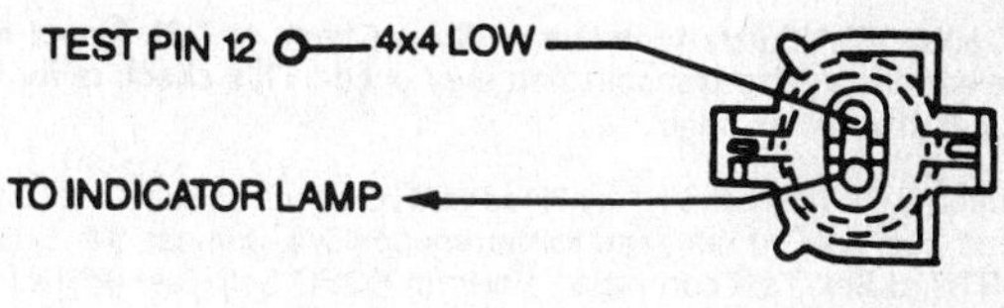

TEST PIN 12
4x4 LOW
TO INDICATOR LAMP

OCS-OCIL Circuit – Measure resistance between KEY PWR at fuse panel (ohmmeter positive lead) and power side of OCS harness connector (ohmmeter negative probe). Measure resistance between test pin No. 41 at breakout box and signal side of OCS harness connector.

OCS-OCIL Circuit 91C14268

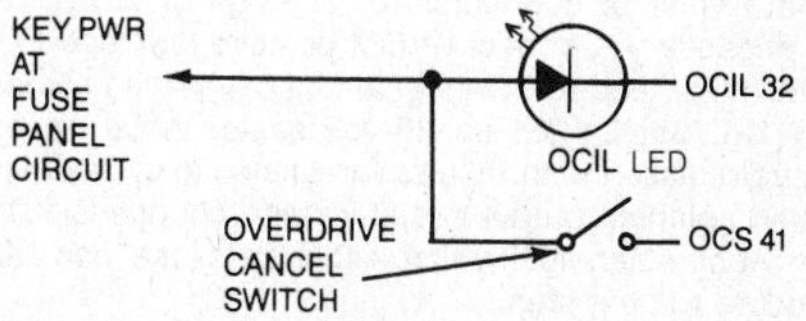

KEY PWR AT FUSE PANEL CIRCUIT
OCIL 32
OCIL LED
OVERDRIVE CANCEL SWITCH
OCS 41

If resistance is less than 5 ohms, go to next step. If resistance is 5 ohms or more, repair open circuit(s) as necessary, remove breakout box, reconnect components and rerun QUICK TEST.

11) Checking Circuit(s) for Shorts to Power – With key off, ensure breakout box is installed and ECA is disconnected. Set DVOM on 200-k/ohm scale.

4WD LOW Circuit – Disconnect 4WD LOW switch. Measure resistance between test pin No. 12 and test pins No. 37 and 57 at the breakout box.

OCS-OCIL Circuit – Disconnect OCS switch. Measure resistance between test pin No. 41 and test pins No. 37 and 57 at the breakout box. Measure resistance between test pin No. 32 and test pins No. 37 and 57 at the breakout box. If resistance(s) are 10 k/ohms or more, remove breakout box, replace appropriate switch and rerun QUICK TEST. If resistance(s) are less than 10 k/ohms, repair short circuit(s), remove breakout box, reconnect ECA and rerun QUICK TEST.

12) Service Code 91, 92, 93, 94, 98 and 99 Circuit Identification – These service codes indicate that the appropriate on/off solenoid is out of Self-Test range. This may cause harsh, early or late shifting. Reading

CIRCUIT TEST TC (Cont.)

should be 9-14.5 volts when ON and less than 1.0 volt when OFF. Code 98 indicates Electronic Pressure Control (EPC) solenoid may have a faulty driver in the ECA. Code 99 indicates a faulty EPC circuit which may cause harsh shifting and clutch wear. Possible causes for these codes are: solenoid resistance is out of limits, harness circuit is open or grounded, faulty ECA.

Solenoid & Circuit Identification Chart 91D14269

Solenoid	Processor Signal Test Pin	K.O.E.O. Self-Test Code
SS1	52	91/621
SS2	19	92/622
CCS	55	93/626
CCC	53	94/627
EPC	38	998, 99/624

SS1 - Shift Solenoid #1
SS2 - Shift Solenoid #2
CCS - Coast Clutch Solenoid
CCC - Converter Clutch Solenoid
EPC - Electronic Pressure Control

If any of the listed codes are present, go to step **15)** for 7.3L Diesel vehicles or next step for all others. If codes are not present, go to KOEO Self-Test procedures.

13) Enter Output State Check – Turn key off and wait 10 seconds, set DVOM on 20-volt scale. A VOM or DVOM MUST be used for this test.

CAUTION: DO NOT perform Output State Check on 7.3L Diesel-E4OD vehicles, damage to transmission may occur. This check is for 5.8L/7.5L E4OD vehicles only.

Connect DVOM negative (–) test lead to STO circuit at Self-Test connector and positive (+) test lead to battery positive. Jumper STI circuit to SIG RTN at Self-Test connector. Perform KOEO Self-Test until all Continuous Codes have been displayed. DVOM will indicate less than 1.0 volt when test is complete. Depress and release throttle. If voltage increases, remain in Output State Check and go to next step. If voltage does not increase, depress throttle to WOT and release. If STO voltage does not increase, go to CIRCUIT TEST QC, step **1)**, leaving test equipment hooked up.

14) Check Suspect E4OD Solenoid Electrical Operation – With KOEO, disconnect transmission solenoid bulkhead connector. Use a mirror to inspect both ends of connector for damage or corrosion. Service or repair as necessary. Connect DVOM positive test lead to VPWR circuit and negative test lead to ECA signal test pin at the bulkhead connector (see step **12)**. Set DVOM on 20-volt scale. While observing DVOM, depress and release the throttle several times to cycle output on and off. If suspected solenoid output circuit voltage change is 1.0 volt or more, service or repair solenoid. If voltage change is less than 1.0 volt, remove jumper and go to next step.

15) Checking E4OD Transmission Solenoid Resistance – Turn key off and wait 10 seconds. Disconnect ECA 60-pin connector and inspect for corroded or damaged pins. Service or repair as necessary. Install breakout box, leave ECA disconnected. Connect transmission bulkhead connector. Set DVOM on 200-ohm scale. Measure resistance between test pins No. 37 and 57 and ECA signal test pin at the breakout box (step **12)**. If resistance is within specification, go to step **17)**. See SOLENOID RESISTANCE CHART. If resistance is not as specified, go to next step.

16) Checking Continuity of E4OD Solenoid Harness – Turn key off and wait 10 seconds. Install breakout box, leaving ECA disconnected. Disconnect transmission bulkhead connector. Measure resistance between the ECA signal test pin at the breakout box and transmission bulkhead connector (see step **12)**. Measure resistance between test pins No. 37 and 57 (test pin No. 35 on 7.3L Diesel) at the breakout box and EPC PWR and VPWR pins at the E4OD transmission bulkhead connector (refer to circuit diagram at start of test). If all resistances are less than 5 ohms, go to next step. If resistance is 5 ohms or more, remove breakout box, repair open circuit and reconnect ECA and solenoids. Rerun QUICK TEST.

CIRCUIT TEST TC (Cont.)

Solenoid Resistance Chart 90HO9320

Ambient Temperature			Resistance (OHMS)	
°C	°F	Solenoid	MIN	MAX
– 40 to 0	– 40 to 32	SS, CCC, CCS	16.00	20.50
		EPC	3.25	4.25
0 to 110	32 to 230	SS, CCC, CSS	20.50	30.00
		EPC	4.25	6.50

17) Checking E4OD Solenoid Harness for Short to Ground – Turn key off and wait 10 seconds. Install breakout box, leaving ECA disconnected. Ensure transmission bulkhead connector is disconnected. Set DVOM on 200-k/ohm scale. Measure resistance between ECA signal test pin (see table in step **12)** and test pins No. 40, 46 and 60 at the breakout box. Measure resistance between the ECA signal test pin at the breakout box and chassis ground. If all resistances are 10 k/ohms or more, go to next step. If resistances are less than 10 k/ohms, repair short circuit(s), remove breakout box, reconnect ECA and solenoid(s). Rerun QUICK TEST.

18) Checking E4OD Solenoid Harness for Short to Power – Turn key off and wait 10 seconds. Install breakout box, leaving ECA disconnected. Ensure transmission bulkhead connector is disconnected. Set DVOM on 200-k/ohm scale. Measure resistance between ECA signal test pin (see table in step **12)**) and test pins No. 37 and 57 at breakout box. If all resistances are 10 k/ohms or more, go to next step. If resistances are less than 10 k/ohms, repair short circuit(s), remove breakout box, reconnect ECA and solenoid(s). Rerun QUICK TEST.

19) Checking Voltage of VPWR to E4OD Solenoids – Turn key off and wait 10 seconds. Install breakout box, ensure ECA is connected. Ensure transmission bulkhead connector is disconnected. Set DVOM on 20-volt scale. With KOEO, measure voltage between test pins No. 37 and 57 at the bulkhead connector and chassis or battery ground. If voltage is 10.5 volts or more, go to next step. If voltage is less than 10.5 volts, replace ECA, reconnect components and rerun QUICK TEST.

20) Check Solenoid Driver Signal – With key off, install breakout box and leave ECA connected. Disconnect transmission bulkhead connector. Connect a test light between test pin No. 37 or 57 and the ECA signal test pin (refer to table in step **12)**) at the breakout box. With KOEO, wait 10 seconds. Initiate KOEO Self-Test. If test light flashes momentarily and then stays off, repair transmission solenoids as necessary, driver signal is okay. If test light does not flash, replace ECA, reconnect solenoid(s) and rerun QUICK TEST. If test light is always on, solenoid driver is shorted to ground in ECA. Replace ECA, reconnect solenoid(s) and rerun QUICK TEST.

21) Code 26: Check Transmission Oil Operating Temperature – Code 26 indicates Transmission Oil Temperature (TOT) sensor is out of Self-Test range. Correct voltage is 0.21-3.50. Possible causes for this fault are: TOT resistance is out of range or ECA is faulty. Drive vehicle normally in city traffic for 20-30 minutes to bring transmission oil temperature to at least 50° F (10°C). In extremely cold weather a longer warm-up drive may be necessary. Rerun QUICK TEST. If code 26 is still present, go to next step. If code 26 is no longer present, service or repair other codes as necessary.

22) Checking for VREF at Throttle Position Sensor (TPS) – Refer to wiring circuit diagrams in CIRCUIT TESTS DH and DQ. Turn key off and wait 10 seconds. Disconnect ECA 60-pin connector and inspect for corroded or damaged pins. Service or repair as necessary. Install breakout box and connect ECA to breakout box. Disconnect TPS (FIPL on 7.3L Diesel) and set DVOM on 20-volt scale. With KOEO, measure voltage between VREF and SIG RTN at the TPS (or FIPL) vehicle harness connector. If voltage is 4.0-6.0 volts, reconnect TPS (or FIPL) and go to next step. If voltage is not as specified, go to CIRCUIT TEST C, step **1)**.

23) Checking Resistance of TOT Sensor – Ensure transmission temperature is 50° F (10°C), if transmission has cooled down, repeat test drive. Turn key off and wait 10 seconds. Ensure breakout box is installed and ECA is disconnected. Ensure bulkhead connector is connected at transmission. Set DVOM on 200-k/ohm scale. With KOEO, ensure transmission oil pan is "warm to touch" on side away from exhaust manifold.

CIRCUIT TEST TC (Cont.)

Measure resistance between test pin No. 42 (test pin No. 7 on 7.3L Diesel) and test pin No. 46 at the breakout box. If resistance is within specification, go to next step. See TOT RESISTANCE CHART. If resistance is not as specified, repair or replace TOT sensor.

TOT Resistance Chart 90JO9321

Transmission Oil Temperature		Resistance Range (ohms)
°C	°F	
0 - 20	32 - 58	100K - 37K
21 - 40	59 - 104	37K - 16K
41 - 70	105 - 158	16K - 5K
71 - 90	159 - 194	5K - 2.7K
91 - 110	195 - 230	2.7K - 1.5K
111 - 130	231 - 266	1.5K - 0.8K

24) Checking TOT Sensor Resistance in Relation to Oil Temperature Change – TOT sensor may be within specification range (.8-100 k/ohms) and not correspond to temperature. Ensure transmission fluid is at operating temperature. Measure TOT resistance again and compare to resistance recorded in step **23)**. If resistance increased or decreased due to temperature change, replace ECA. If resistance did not change, replace breakout box, reconnect ECA, and replace temperature sensor.

25) Code 56: Attempt to Generate Code 66 – Code 56 indicates TOT signal is greater than Self-Test maximum value of 4.80 volts. Possible causes for this fault are: faulty TOT sensor, open harness circuit, faulty ECA. Turn key off and wait 10 seconds. Disconnect transmission bulkhead connector from TOT sensor. Inspect for corroded or damaged pins. Service or repair as necessary. Insert a jumper wire at the bulkhead connector between TOT SIGNAL and SIG RTN. Run KOEO Self-Test. If Code 66 is present, remove jumper wire and service or replace TOT sensor. If Code 66 is not present, remove jumper wire and go to next step.

26) Check Continuity of TOT SIGNAL and SIG RTN Circuit – Turn key off and wait 10 seconds. Ensure bulkhead connector is disconnected at transmission. Disconnect ECA 60-pin connector and inspect for corroded or damaged pins. Service or repair as necessary. Install breakout box, leave ECA disconnected. Measure resistance between TOT SIGNAL at the bulkhead connector and test pin No. 42 (test pin No. 7 on 7.3L Diesel) at the breakout box. Measure the resistance between SIG RTN at the bulkhead connector and test pin 46 at the breakout box. If both resistances are less than 5 ohms, replace ECA, remove breakout box, reconnect ECA and bulkhead connector. Rerun QUICK TEST. If resistances are 5 ohms or more, repair open circuits, remove breakout box and reconnect ECA. Rerun QUICK TEST.

27) Code 66: Attempt to Generate Code 56 – Code 66 indicates that TOT signal is less than 0.15 volt (Self-Test minimum value). Possible causes for this fault are: faulty TOT sensor, grounded harness or faulty ECA. Turn key off and wait 10 seconds, disconnect transmission connector from bulkhead connector. Inspect for corroded or damaged pins. Service or repair as necessary. Run KOEO Self-Test. If Code 56 is present, service or replace TOT sensor. If Code 56 is not present, go to next step.

28) Checking VREF At TPS – Refer to wiring circuit diagrams in CIRCUIT TESTS DH and DQ. Turn key off and wait 10 seconds. Disconnect ECA 60-pin connector and inspect for corroded or damaged pins. Service or repair as necessary. Install breakout box and connect ECA to breakout box. Disconnect TPS (FIPL on 7.3L Diesel) and set DVOM on 20-volt scale. With KOEO, measure voltage between VREF and SIG RTN at the TPS (or FIPL) vehicle harness connector. If voltage is 4.0-6.0 volts, reconnect TPS (or FIPL) and go to next step. If voltage is not as specified, go to CIRCUIT TEST C, step **1)**.

29) Checking TOT Signal for Short to Ground – Turn key off and wait 10 seconds. Ensure bulkhead is disconnected at transmission. With breakout box installed and ECA disconnected, set DVOM on 200-k/ohm scale. Measure resistance between test pin No. 42 (test pin No. 7 on 7.3L Diesel) and test pins No. 40, 46 and 60 at the breakout box. If all resistances are 10 k/ohms or more, replace ECA and remove breakout box. Reconnect components and rerun QUICK TEST. If resistances are less than 10 k/ohms, repair short circuit, remove breakout box and reconnect components. Rerun QUICK TEST.

CIRCUIT TEST TC (Cont.)

30) Checking MLP, TOT Sensor and E4OD Solenoid Drive Cycle – Bring engine to operating temperature. Verify transmission fluid level and that all components are connected. Run KOEO Self-Test and record Continuous Memory Codes. If Codes 49, 59 or 69 are present, go to step **36)**. If Codes are not present, record and clear Continuous Memory Codes.

Select "D" range and enable "OD". Drive vehicle in city traffic using moderate acceleration. Hold throttle opening steady while transmission is shifting through all four gears and hold throttle steady for an additional 15 seconds.

Apply brakes on coming to a stop and remained stopped for 20 seconds. Repeat previous drive step. Rerun KOEO Self-Test and record Continuous Memory Codes. If a Code 11/111 is present, go to next step. If Code 29/452 is present, go to CIRCUIT TEST DP, step **1)**. For Codes 56, 62, 66, 67 or 99, go to step **32)**.

31) Attempt to Generate Continuous Memory Code 56, 62, 66, 67 and 99 – Before performing any procedures in this step, complete the drive cycle test. Drive vehicle approximately 15 minutes over a rough road to simulate road shock. Observe MIL LED while driving for indication of a fault. If MIL flashes ON and OFF, go to next step. If light does not flash, fault may not be duplicated at this time. Testing is complete.

32) Check Circuit Using KOEO Continuous Monitor Mode – Enter KOEO Continuous Monitor Mode. Observe VOM or STAR LED for indication of a fault while performing the following.

MLP Sensor (Code 67) – Lightly tap on MLP sensor to simulate road shock. Wiggle connector at MLP sensor.

Transmission Solenoids (Codes 62 or 99) and TOT Sensor (Codes 56 or 66) – Wiggle transmission bulkhead connector.

If a fault is indicated, isolate fault and service or repair as necessary. Clear Continuous Memory Codes and rerun QUICK TEST. If a fault is not indicated, go to step **35)**.

33) Checking EEC-IV Harness – Ensure vehicle is still in KOEO Continuous Monitor Mode. Observe VOM for an indication of a fault while performing the following: using illustration in step **34)**, grasp harness close to sensor or transmission connector and perform "Wiggle" test while working from transmission to dash panel and ECA. If a fault is indicated, isolate fault and service as necessary. Clear Continuous Memory Codes and rerun QUICK TEST. If no fault is indicated, go to step **35)**.

34) Circuit Diagram for Continuous Monitor Mode – Refer to E4OD Vehicle Harness Circuit Diagram.

E4OD Vehicle Harness Circuit 90BO9322

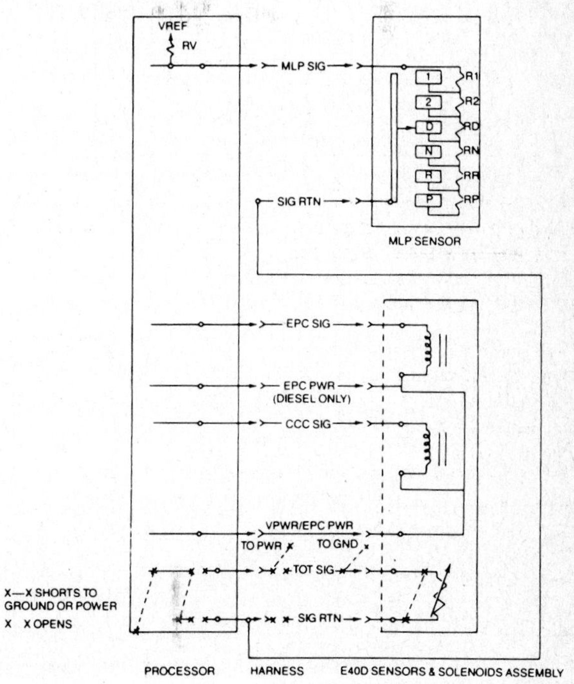
VREF
RV
MLP SIG
1
2
D
N
R
P
R1
R2
RD
RN
RR
RP
SIG RTN
MLP SENSOR
EPC SIG
EPC PWR
(DIESEL ONLY)
CCC SIG
VPWR/EPC PWR
TO PWR
TO GND
TOT SIG
SIG RTN
X—X SHORTS TO GROUND OR POWER
X X OPENS
PROCESSOR
HARNESS
E40D SENSORS & SOLENOIDS ASSEMBLY

1991 ENGINE PERFORMANCE
Self-Diagnostics – EEC-IV (Cont.)

CIRCUIT TEST TC (Cont.)

35) Checking ECA and Harness Connectors – Turn key off and wait 10 seconds. Disconnect ECA 60-pin connector. Disconnect ECA 60-pin connector and inspect for corroded or damaged pins. Service or repair as necessary. If connectors and terminals are okay, fault may not be duplicated at this time. Clear Continuous Memory Codes. If connectors or terminals are faulty, service or repair as necessary. Clear codes and rerun QUICK TEST.

36) Isolating Faults for Continuous Memory Codes 49, 59, and 69 – Codes 49, 59 and 69 indicate that the transmission went through 4 consecutive incorrect shifts in an upward or downward shift sequence. When changing a gear the SS1 or SS2 solenoid remained ON or OFF an extended amount of time. Possible causes for these faults are: intermittent harness continuity, stuck shift solenoid. Rerun KOEO Self-Test. If any other codes appear during the KOEO Self-Test in addition to Codes 49, 59 or 69, service other codes first. If other codes do not appear, go to next step.

37) Checking Circuits Using KOEO Continuous Monitor Mode – Enter KOEO Continuous Monitor Mode. Observe VOM or STAR LED for indication of a fault while performing the following: wiggle, shake or bend a small section of system harness while working from dash panel and ECA to transmission bulkhead connector. If a fault is indicated, disconnect connectors and inspect connectors and harness for damage. Clear codes and rerun QUICK TEST. If a fault is not indicated, service or replace SS1 and SS2 solenoids as necessary.

1991 ENGINE PERFORMANCE
Trouble Shooting – No Codes

Aerostar, Bronco, Explorer, Ranger, "E" & "F" Series

NOTE: Unless otherwise specified, references to "F" Series includes "F" Series Super Duty.

INTRODUCTION

Before attempting to diagnose driveability symptoms or intermittent faults that cause driveability problems, perform steps in appropriate BASIC DIAGNOSTIC PROCEDURES and SELF-DIAGNOSTICS articles. Use this article to diagnose driveability problems that exist when a hard fault code is not present.

A symptom can be defined as an indication or characteristic of a condition which causes a driveability complaint. Often a customer's complaint of a driveability symptom will be any condition which is different from when the car was purchased or new. Always understand the customer's perception of the symptom. Symptom checks are intended to direct the technician to malfunctioning component or system so that further diagnosis may be performed. A symptom should lead to further testing of specific components or systems, or verification of adjustment specifications.

An intermittent driveability problem can be defined as one that comes and goes during any particular drive cycle. This type of problem includes electrical circuits or component problems that may or may not set a soft code in the ECA memory. This means the problem may turn the CHECK ENGINE or SERVICE ENGINE SOON light on or cause it to flicker without setting a code in memory. The intermittent problem could occur in a circuit not monitored by diagnostics. The key word in this definition is INTERMITTENT. If the problem is happening all the time, treat it as a symptom, not as an intermittent.

NOTE: It is also possible that certain driveability concerns have been rectified by the manufacturer through revised calibration of the Electronic Control Assembly (ECA) computer control unit. Check with manufacturer for latest information on updated calibration information and control units.

NOTE: To verify adjustment specifications, refer to ON-VEHICLE ADJUSTMENTS or SERVICE & ADJUSTMENT SPECIFICATIONS articles.

SYMPTOMS

DRIVEABILITY SYMPTOMS

Symptom checks cannot be used properly unless the problem or driveability characteristic actually happens while the vehicle is being tested. To reduce diagnostic time, perform steps in appropriate BASIC DIAGNOSTIC PROCEDURES and SELF-DIAGNOSTICS articles have been performed before attempting to diagnose a symptom.

DIAGNOSTIC ROUTINES are used to identify systems and components that should be checked to identify a fault. Perform the check or adjustment as indicated in the chart. A reference may be given to direct the technician to another test procedure or to a CIRCUIT TEST in the appropriate SELF-DIAGNOSTICS article. This will give additional information to check a component or circuit.

On vehicles equipped with EEC-IV systems, a chart is provided to direct the technician to CIRCUIT TESTS in the appropriate SELF-DIAGNOSTICS article. This is the circuit or component most likely to be the cause of the applicable driveability symptom. This chart should only be used in conjunction with the DIAGNOSTIC ROUTINES.

Title	Routine
No Crank No Start	200
Cranks Normally But Won't Start	201
Starts Normally But Won't Run (Stalls)	202
Cranks Normally But Slow to Start	203
Rough Idle	204
Misses Under Load	205
Low Idle (Stalls on Deceleration or Quick Stop)	206
Hesitates or Stalls on Acceleration	207
Backfire (Induction or Exhaust)	208
Lack of Power	209
Surges at Steady Speed	210
High Idle (Engine Diesels)	211
Engine Noise	212
Poor Fuel Economy	213
High Oil Consumption	214
Spark Knock/Pinging	215
Engine Vibrates at Normal/High Speeds	216
Engine Runs Cold	217
Engine Runs Hot	218
Exhaust Smoke	219
Gas Smell	220
"CHECK ENGINE" /"SERVICE ENGINE SOON" Light Always On or Never On "CHECK ENGINE"/"CHECK DCL" Message On	221
State Emission Test Failure	222
Improper Shift	223
Shift Indicator Light and Audible Chimes "ON"	224

91F09244 Courtesy of Ford Motor Co.

Fig. 1: Diagnostic Routine Index

INTERMITTENTS

INTERMITTENT PROBLEM DIAGNOSIS

Use intermittent test procedures to locate intermittent driveability problems that do not occur when the vehicle is being tested. These problems may cause a noticeable driveability problem or cause the CHECK ENGINE or SERVICE ENGINE SOON warning light to illuminate on some vehicles.

Intermittent fault testing requires the duplication of circuit or component failure in order to identify the fault. These procedures may lead to the computer recording a fault code (on some systems) which may help in diagnosis.

If problem vehicle does not produce fault codes, it will be necessary to monitor voltage or resistance values using a Digital Volt-Ohmmeter (DVOM) while attempting to reproduce conditions that will create an intermittent fault. A change in status on the DVOM will indicate a fault has been located.

When using a DVOM or Scan tool to pinpoint faults, monitor voltage reading with ignition on or vehicle running. A change in status on the voltmeter while performing intermittent test procedures will indicate area of fault.

When using an ohmmeter to detect problems in the circuit, monitor circuit resistance (ohms) with ignition off or with battery disconnected. A change in ohmmeter reading while performing test procedures will indicate area of fault.

TEST PROCEDURES

Intermittent Simulation – To reproduce the conditions that create an intermittent fault so it may be identified during testing, some of the following methods may be used:

- Applying light vibration to components.
- Heating a component.
- Wiggling or bending a wiring harness.
- Applying humidity to a component.
- Removing or applying a vacuum supply source.

Monitor circuit/component voltage or resistance while attempting to simulate intermittent. If vehicle is running, monitor for self-diagnostic codes. See appropriate SELF-DIAGNOSTICS article. Use the results of these tests to identify a faulty component or an area that should be closely checked for the problem.

1991 ENGINE PERFORMANCE
Trouble Shooting – No Codes (Cont.)

NOTE: For additional information on connecting test equipment and operating Continuous Monitor Mode test procedures, see appropriate SELF-DIAGNOSTICS article.

Continuous Monitor Mode (WIGGLE TEST) – This test allows a technician to attempt to re-create an intermittent fault while monitoring the system. This mode, also called the WIGGLE TEST, may be used in both Key On Engine Off (KOEO) and Key On Engine Running (KOER) Self-Test modes. The CIRCUIT TESTS in appropriate SELF-DIAGNOSTICS article specify the use of this procedure to identify intermittent faults in specific circuits or components.

KOEO Wiggle Test Procedure – Connect test equipment. Turn ignition on and activate self-test with jumper lead or diagnostic tester. Wait 10 seconds, deactivate and then reactivate self-test. WIGGLE TEST mode has been achieved. Tap, move and wiggle the suspected sensor and/or harness area. If a fault is detected, a code may be stored in memory and indicated at the diagnostic tester or scan tool. Record or retrieve code and perform CIRCUIT TEST indicated in CONTINUOUS MEMORY CODES chart. See appropriate SELF-DIAGNOSTICS article.

KOER Wiggle Test Procedure – Connect test equipment. Turn ignition off and wait 10 seconds. Start engine. Activate self-test with jumper lead or diagnostic tester. Wait 10 seconds, deactivate and then reactivate self-test. DO NOT turn engine off. Engine running Wiggle Test mode has been achieved. Tap, move and wiggle the suspected sensor and/or harness area. If a fault is detected, a code may be stored in memory and indicated at the diagnostic tester or scan tool. Record or retrieve code and perform CIRCUIT TEST indicated in CONTINUOUS MEMORY CODES chart. See appropriate SELF-DIAGNOSTICS article.

DIAGNOSTIC ROUTINE 200
NO CRANK AND NO START

System	Component	Reference
Starting	Battery Starter Relay Starter Neutral Drive Switch/Clutch Switch/Brake Interlock Switch Ignition Switch Transmission Linkage Adjusment	Charge or replace battery Check charging and starting systems
EEC	Neutral Drive Switch/Clutch Switch	See SELF-DIAGNOSTICS article
Base Engine	Flywheel Engine Siezed	Check engine mechanical condition
Fuel Delivery	Injectors	See SYSTEM & COMPONENT TESTING article

91I09245

Courtesy of Ford Motor Co.

1991 ENGINE PERFORMANCE
Trouble Shooting – No Codes (Cont.)

DIAGNOSTIC ROUTINE 201
CRANKS NORMALLY BUT WON'T START

System	Component	Reference
EEC	Quick Test	See SELF-DIAGNOSTICS article
Ignition	Electrical Connections Secondary Ignition Wires Spark Plugs Fouled Ignition Switch DSII and TFI IV: Ignition Coil Ignition Module Rotor Alignment Distributor Cap, Adapter, Rotor & Stator DIS/EDIS: Single or Dual Hall Crankshaft Sensors Hall Camshaft Sensor DIS/EDIS Ignition Module Coil Pack(s)	**DSII and TFI IV:** See NO-START DIAGNOSIS in BASIC DIAGNOSTIC PROCEDURES article **DIS/EDIS**: See NO-START DIAGNOSIS in BASIC DIAGNOSTIC PROCEDURES article
Fuel Delivery	Filter Pump Water/Dirt/Rust Contamination in Fuel Lines Tank (Fuel Supply) Dual Tanks (Selector Switch) Sender Filter Fuel Pressure Regulator Injectors Inertia Switch	Perform a visual inspection See FUEL SYSTEM in SYSTEM & COMPONENT TESTING article
Fuel Charging Assy.	Electrical Connections Throttle Linkages	Perform a visual inspection See FUEL SYSTEM in SYSTEM & COMPONENT TESTING article
Basic Engine	Camshaft Timing Compression	Check engine mechanical condition
EGR	Valve	See SYSTEM & COMPONENT TESTING article
Exhaust	Catalyst Exhaust	Visually inspect for blockage.

91I13456

Courtesy of Ford Motor Co.

1991 ENGINE PERFORMANCE
Trouble Shooting – No Codes (Cont.)

DIAGNOSTIC ROUTINE 202
CRANKS NORMALLY BUT WON'T RUN (STALLS)

System	Component	Reference
Fuel Charging Assy	Curb or Fast Idle Speed Electrical and Vacuum Connections	Perform a visual inspection See ON-VEHICLE ADJUSTMENTS article
EEC	Quick Test	See SELF-DIAGNOSTICS article
Fuel Delivery	Filter Pump Water/Dirt/Rust Contamination in Fuel Lines Tank (Fuel Supply) Sender Filter Fuel Pressure Regulator Injectors Inertia Switch	Perform a visual inspection See FUEL SYSTEM in SYSTEM & COMPONENT TESTING article
Ignition	Electrical Connections Secondary Ignition Wires Ignition Switch DSII and TFI IV: Ignition Coil Ignition Module Rotor Alignment Distributor Cap, Adapter, Rotor & Stator Ballast Resistor DIS/EDIS: Single or Dual Hall Crankshaft Sensors Hall Camshaft Sensor DIS/EDIS Ignition Module Coil Pack(s)	**DSII and TFI IV:** See NO-START DIAGNOSIS in BASIC DIAGNOSTIC PROCEDURES article **DIS/EDIS:** See NO-START DIAGNOSIS in BASIC DIAGNOSTIC PROCEDURES article
Exhaust	Component (Restricted)	Inspect exhaust system
EGR	Valve	See SYSTEM & COMPONENT TESTING article
Basic Engine	Camshaft and Valve Train	Check engine mechanical condition

91J13457

Courtesy of Ford Motor Co.

1991 ENGINE PERFORMANCE
Trouble Shooting – No Codes (Cont.)

DIAGNOSTIC ROUTINE 203
CRANKS NORMALLY BUT SLOW TO START

System	Component	Reference
Ignition	Scope Engine for: Spark Plugs, Coil, Secondary Ignition Wires Spark Plugs Fouled DSII and TFI IV: Distributor Cap, Adapter & Rotor DIS/EDIS: Single or Dual Hall Crankshaft Sensors Hall Camshaft Sensor DIS/EDIS Ignition Module Coil Pack(s)	**DSII and TFI IV.** Perform a visual inspection See NO-START DIAGNOSIS in BASIC DIAGNOSTIC PROCEDURES article **DIS/EDIS**: See NO-START DIAGNOSIS in BASIC DIAGNOSTIC PROCEDURES article
EEC	Quick Test	See SELF-DIAGNOSTICS article
Fuel Delivery	Filter Pump Water/Dirt/Rust Contamination in Fuel Lines Fuel Pressure Regulator Sender Filter Injectors	Perform a visual inspection See FUEL SYSTEM in SYSTEM & COMPONENT TESTING and ON-VEHICLE ADJUSTMENTS article
Fuel Charging Assy	Curb or Fast Idle Speeds Electrical and Vacuum Connections	Perform a visual inspection See ON-VEHICLE ADJUSTMENTS article
Exhaust	Component (Restricted)	Check exhaust system
Induction and Vacuum Distribution	Vacuum Leaks Air Cleaner Element Restricted	Perform a visual inspection
Cooling	Electric Fan (Hot Start Only)	Check cooling system
EGR	Valve	See SYSTEM & COMPONENT TESTING article
PCV	Valve	
EVAP	Components	

91A13458

Courtesy of Ford Motor Co.

1991 ENGINE PERFORMANCE
Trouble Shooting – No Codes (Cont.)

DIAGNOSTIC ROUTINE 204
ROUGH IDLE

System	Component	Reference
Cooling	Fan or Electric Fan (Loose or Cracked)	Perform a visual inspection
Ignition	Scope Engine For: Spark Plug, Coil, Secondary Wires, Distributor Cap, Adapter and Rotor Ignition Timing	See NO-START DIAGNOSIS in BASIC DIAGNOSTIC PROCEDURES and ON-VEHICLE ADJUSTMENTS article
EEC	Quick Test	See SELF-DIAGNOSTICS article
Fuel Charging Assy	Curb or Fast Idle Speeds Electrical and Vacuum Connections	Perform a visual inspection See FUEL SYSTEM in SYSTEM & COMPONENT TESTING and ON-VEHICLE ADJUSTMENTS article
Fuel Delivery	Fuel Pressure Regulator Injectors Fuel Rail	See FUEL SYSTEM in SYSTEM & COMPONENT TESTING article
Vacuum Distribution	Vacuum Leaks	Perform a visual and audible inspection
EGR	Valve Vacuum Regulator	See SYSTEM & COMPONENT TESTING article
Cooling	Thermostat	Check cooling system
Basic Engine	Compression Valve Train Camshaft Intake Manifold Gaskets	Check engine mechanical condition
PCV	Valve	See SYSTEM & COMPONENT TESTING article
EVAP	Components	
Exhaust	Pipes, Muffler, Catalyst Resonator, Heat Control Valve	Check exhaust system

91B13459

Courtesy of Ford Motor Co.

DIAGNOSTIC ROUTINE 205
MISSES UNDER LOAD

System	Component	Reference
Ignition	Scope Engine For: Spark Plug, Coil, Secondary Wires, Distributor Cap, Adapter and Rotor Timing	See NO-START DIAGNOSIS in BASIC DIAGNOSTIC PROCEDURES and ON-VEHICLE ADJUSTMENTS article
EEC	Quick Test	See SELF-DIAGNOSTICS article
Fuel Delivery	Filter Pump Lines Fuel Pressure Regulator Sender Filter Injectors	Perform a visual inspection See FUEL SYSTEM in SYSTEM & COMPONENT TESTING article
Fuel Charging Assy	Electrical and Vacuum Connections	Perform a visual inspection See FUEL SYSTEM in SYSTEM & COMPONENT TESTING and ON-VEHICLE ADJUSTMENTS article
EGR	Valve	See SYSTEM & COMPONENT TESTING article

91E13460

Courtesy of Ford Motor Co.

1991 ENGINE PERFORMANCE
Trouble Shooting – No Codes (Cont.)

DIAGNOSTIC ROUTINE 206
LOW IDLE (STALLS ON DECELERATION OR QUICK STOP)

System	Component	Reference
Fuel Charging Assy	Curb or Fast Idle Speed Electrical and Vacuum Connections Throttle Devices	Perform a visual inspection See FUEL SYSTEM in SYSTEM & COMPONENT TESTING article
EEC	Quick Test	See SELF-DIAGNOSTICS article
EGR	Valve	See SYSTEM & COMPONENT TESTING article
Base Transmission (E4OD Only)	Transmission Oil Level Converter Clutch Control Solenoid	Check transmission

90G09329

Courtesy of Ford Motor Co.

DIAGNOSTIC ROUTINE 207
HESITATES OR STALLS ON ACCELERATION

System	Component	Reference
EEC	Quick Test	See SELF-DIAGNOSTICS article
Ignition	Scope Engine For: Spark Plug, Coil, Secondary Wires, Distributor Cap, Adapter and Rotor Ignition Timing	See NO-START DIAGNOSIS in BASIC DIAGNOSTIC PROCEDURES and ON-VEHICLE ADJUSTMENTS article
Fuel Charging Assy	Electrical & Vacuum Connections Curb or Fast Idle Speeds	Perform a visual inspection See SYSTEM & COMPONENT TESTING and ON-VEHICLE ADJUSTMENTS article
Fuel Delivery	Filter Pump Water/Dirt/Rust Contamination in Fuel Lines Fuel Pressure Regulator Sender Filter Injectors	
Vacuum Distribution	Vacuum Leaks	Perform a visual and audible inspection
Induction	Air Cleaner Duct, Stove Pipe, and Valve Inter-Cooler Tube (Air Leaks)	See SYSTEM & COMPONENT TESTING article.
EGR	Valve	
PCV	Valve	
Exhaust (Restriction)	With Backpressure EGR System	
Base Transmission (E4OD and A4LD)	Converter Clutch Control Solenoid Converter Clutch Override Converter Clutch	See SELF DIAGNOSTICS article

91F13461

Courtesy of Ford Motor Co.

1991 ENGINE PERFORMANCE
Trouble Shooting – No Codes (Cont.)

DIAGNOSTIC ROUTINE 208
BACKFIRE (INTAKE OR EXHAUST)

System	Component	Reference
Ignition	Scope Engine For: Spark Plug, Coil, Secondary Wires, Distributor Cap and Rotor, Crossed Wires Ignition Timing	See NO-START DIAGNOSIS in BASIC DIAGNOSTIC PROCEDURES and ON-VEHICLE ADJUSTMENTS article
Vacuum Distribution	Vacuum Hoses, or Connections Leak(s)	Perform a visual and audible inspection
EEC	Quick Test	See SELF-DIAGNOSTICS article
Thermactor	Thermactor System Components	See SYSTEM & COMPONENT TESTING article
Pulse Air	Pulse Air System Components	
Basic Engine	Intake Manifold Gaskets Compression Check Camshaft Valves	Check engine mechanical condition
Exhaust	Components (Restricted)	Check exhaust system
Fuel Delivery	Filter Pump Water, Dirt, Rust, Contamination in Fuel Lines Fuel Pressure Regulator Injectors Sender Filter	Perform a visual inspection See FUEL SYSTEM in SYSTEM & COMPONENT TESTING and BASIC DIAGNOSTIC PROCEDURES article

91G13462

Courtesy of Ford Motor Co.

1991 ENGINE PERFORMANCE
Trouble Shooting – No Codes (Cont.)

DIAGNOSTIC ROUTINE 209
LACK OF POWER

System	Component	Reference
Ignition	Timing	See ON-VEHICLE ADJUSTMENTS
EEC	Quick Test	See SELF-DIAGNOSTICS article
Fuel Delivery	Filter Pump Lines Fuel Pressure Regulator Sender Filter Injectors	Perform a visual inspection See FUEL SYSTEM in SYSTEM & COMPONENT TESTING article
Fuel Charging Assy	Electrical and Vacuum Connections Curb or Fast Idle Speed	See BASIC DIAGNOSTIC PROCEDURES and FUEL SYSTEM in SYSTEM & COMPONENT TESTING article
Ignition	Scope Engine For: Spark Plugs, Coil, etc.	See BASIC DIAGNOSTIC PROCEDURES article
Exhaust	Components (Restricted)	Check exhaust system
Cooling	Thermostat	Check cooling system
Vacuum Distribution	Vacuum Leaks	Perform a visual and audible inspection
Induction	Air Cleaner Duct and Valve and Element	See SYSTEM & COMPONENT TESTING article
EGR	Valve	
Basic Engine	Compression Check Camshaft Valves	See BASIC DIAGNOSTIC PROCEDURES article
Drive Train	Clutch, Automatic Transmission, Brakes	Check transmission and drive train components

90C09332

Courtesy of Ford Motor Co.

1991 ENGINE PERFORMANCE
Trouble Shooting – No Codes (Cont.)

DIAGNOSTIC ROUTINE 210
SURGES AT STEADY SPEED

System	Component	Reference
EEC	Quick Test	See SELF-DIAGNOSTICS article
Fuel Delivery	Filter Pump Lines Fuel Pressure Regulator Sender Filter	Perform a visual inspection See FUEL SYSTEM in SYSTEM & COMPONENT TESTING article
Fuel Charging Assy	Electrical & Vacuum Connections Curb or Fast Idle Speeds	Perform a visual inspection See ON-VEHICLE ADJUSTMENTS article
Ignition	Scope Engine For: Spark Plugs, Coil, Secondary Ignition Wires, etc., Timing	See BASIC DIAGNOSTIC PROCEDURES article
Vacuum Distribution	Vacuum Leaks	Perform a visual and audible inspection
EGR	Valve	See SYSTEM & COMPONENT TESTING article
Induction	Air Cleaner Duct and Element	
EVAP	Components	
Basic Engine	Valve Train and Camshaft Intake Manifold Gaskets	See BASIC DIAGNOSTIC PROCEDURES article
Thermactor	Thermactor System Components	See SYSTEM & COMPONENT TESTING article

90E09333

Courtesy of Ford Motor Co.

DIAGNOSTIC ROUTINE 211
HIGH IDLE (ENGINE "DIESELS")

System	Component	Reference
Fuel Charging Assy	Curb or Fast Idle Speeds Electrical and Vacuum Connections Throttle Positioner Throttle Plate and Linkage Speed Control Chain	Perform visual inspection See BASIC DIAGNOSTIC PROCEDURES and FUEL SYSTEMS in SYSTEM & COMPONENT TESTING article
Vacuum Distribution	Vacuum Leaks	Perform a visual and audible inspection
EEC	EEC-IV Quick Test	See SELF-DIAGNOSTICS article
Air Intake System	Vacuum Leaks	Perform visual and audible inspection
Cooling	Overheating	Check cooling system
Air Conditioning	A/C Clutch A/C Demand A/C Cycling Pressure Switch A/C Refrigerant Charge	Check Air Conditioning system

91H13463

Courtesy of Ford Motor Co.

1991 ENGINE PERFORMANCE
Trouble Shooting – No Codes (Cont.)

DIAGNOSTIC ROUTINE 212
ENGINE NOISE

System	Component	Reference
Squeal, Click, or Chirp	Oil Level (low) Valve Train Drive Belts (loose) Belt Driven Components EEC Solenoids	Perform a visual and audible inspection Check engine mechanical condition
Rumble, Grind	Belt Driven Components	
Rattle	Component (loose)	
Hiss	Thermactor System (leak) Vacuum Distribution System (leak) Induction System (leak) Spark Plug (loose)	Perform a visual and audible inspection See BASIC DIAGNOSTIC PROCEDURES article
	Cooling System (leak)	Perform a visual inspection
	EVAP System (leak)	
Snap	Secondary Ignition	Perform a visual and audible inspection
Rap, Roar	Exhaust System (leak) Pulse Air System (air cleaner)	Check exhaust system
Knock	Connecting Rod Bearing (worn) Main Bearing (worn) Piston Pin (loose) Piston to Bore Clearance (cold engine)	Check engine mechanical condition
	Mechanical Fuel Pump	
	Detonation	Go to Diagnostic Routine 215

90A13631

Courtesy of Ford Motor Co.

1991 ENGINE PERFORMANCE
Trouble Shooting – No Codes (Cont.)

DIAGNOSTIC ROUTINE 213
POOR FUEL ECONOMY

NOTE: Since fuel consumption is drastically increased for city driving, short-run operation, stop and go driving, trailer towing, extended winter warm-up periods, etc., as opposed to "trip" mileage, an attempt should be made to determine these factors when confronted with "poor mileage" conditions. However, since the operator is not always at fault, the following is appended:

System	Component	Reference
Fuel Charging Assy	Electrical & Vacuum Connections	Perform a visual inspection See ON-VEHICLE ADJUSTMENTS article
Fuel Delivery	Fuel Return Line Blocked Fuel Pressure Regulator	See BASIC DIAGNOSTIC PROCEDURES article
Induction	Air Cleaner Duct and Valve Air Cleaner Element (Restricted)	Perform a visual inspection
Ignition	Scope Engine For: Spark Plug, Coil, Secondary Wires, Distributor Cap, Adapter and Rotor Ignition Timing	See BASIC DIAGNOSTIC PROCEDURES article
EEC	Quick Test	See SELF-DIAGNOSTICS article
Cooling	Thermostat	Check cooling system
Factors External to the Engine	Tire Pressure & Type Clutch Operation Converter Clutch Override Automatic Transmission Shift Pattern and Fluid Level Brake Drag Exhaust System Speedometer/Odometer Gear Ratio Axle Ratio Vehicle Load Road & Weather Conditions Aftermarket Add-Ons	Perform a manual and visual inspection
Base Transmission (E4OD Only)	Converter Clutch Control Solenoid	See SELF-DIAGNOSTICS article

90J09335

Courtesy of Ford Motor Co.

1991 ENGINE PERFORMANCE
Trouble Shooting – No Codes (Cont.)

DIAGNOSTIC ROUTINE 214
HIGH OIL CONSUMPTION

NOTE: If the condition cannot be verified, clean engine, if necessary, change oil and filter (at customer's expense), seal and have customer drive 500 miles (804.5 Km) or enough distance to consume two quarts before returning for re-examination.

System	Component	Reference
External Leaks	Rocker Cover Gasket, Crankshaft Seals, Engine Assembly	Perform a visual inspection
Proper Dipstick	Overfilling (sometimes accomplished by the "short stick" gas station procedure).	Perform a manual and visual inspection
Induction	Air Cleaner Element (Sealing)	Perform a visual inspection
PCV	Valve	See SYSTEM & COMPONENT TESTING article
Internal Leaks (blue smoke from tailpipe)	Valve Guides Valve Stem Seals Intake Manifold and Gasket Cylinder Head Drain Passages Piston Rings	Check engine mechanical condition

90C13633

Courtesy of Ford Motor Co.

DIAGNOSTIC ROUTINE 215
SPARK KNOCK (PINGS)

NOTE: If the above fails to correct the condition, it is recommended that the owner change his source of fuel and use higher octane fuel.

System	Component	Reference
Ignition	Timing	See ON-VEHICLE ADJUSTMENTS
EEC	Quick Test	See SELF-DIAGNOSTICS article
Vacuum Distribution	Vacuum Leaks PVS	Perform a visual and audible inspection. See SYSTEM & COMPONENT TESTING article
Cooling	Overheating	Check cooling system
Basic Engine	Oil Level Compression Check Intake Manifold Gasket	See BASIC DIAGNOSTIC PROCEDURES article
Fuel Delivery	Injectors	See SYSTEM & COMPONENT TESTING article
PCV	Valve	
EGR	Verify correct application, then diagnose.	
Induction	Air Cleaner Duct and Valve Assembly	
Thermactor	Thermactor System Components	
Base Transmission (E4OD Non-Diesel Only)	Transmission Controls	See SELF-DIAGNOSTICS article

90B09336

Courtesy of Ford Motor Co.

1991 ENGINE PERFORMANCE
Trouble Shooting – No Codes (Cont.)

DIAGNOSTIC ROUTINE 216
ENGINE VIBRATES AT NORMAL OR HIGH SPEED

System	Component	Reference
Engine Accessories	Fan Belt Driven Components Engine Mounts Engine Vibration Damper	Perform a manual and visual inspection
Otherwise	Non-Engine Components: Drive Line, Tires, Wheel Balance	

90D09337 Courtesy of Ford Motor Co.

DIAGNOSTIC ROUTINE 217
ENGINE RUNS COLD

System	Component	Reference
Gauge System	Gauge, Sender	See appropriate SAFETY EQUIPMENT article
Cooling	Thermostat	Check cooling system

91I13464 Courtesy of Ford Motor Co.

DIAGNOSTIC ROUTINE 218
ENGINE RUNS HOT

System	Component	Reference
Cooling	Thermostat Coolant Level Radiator or A/C Condenser Pressure Cap and Overflow System External Leaks Belts and Belt Tension Fan and Fan Clutch Electric Fan (If So Equipped)	See BASIC DIAGNOSTIC PROCEDURES article
Gauge System	Gauge, Sender	See appropriate SAFETY EQUIPMENT article
EEC	Quick Test	See SELF-DIAGNOSTICS article
Ignition	Timing	See ON-VEHICLE ADJUSTMENTS article
Basic Engine	Oil Level Internal Leak(s) Core Sand in Head/Block Water Pump	Check engine mechanical condition
Brake	Brakes (dragging)	Check brake system

91J13465 Courtesy of Ford Motor Co.

1991 ENGINE PERFORMANCE
Trouble Shooting – No Codes (Cont.)

DIAGNOSTIC ROUTINE 219
EXHAUST SMOKE

NOTE: White Smoke is normal during warm-up.

System	Component	Reference
Black Smoke (rich mixture)	Air Cleaner Element (Restricted)	Perform a visual inspection
	Fuel Pressure Regulator Injectors	See SYSTEM & COMPONENT TESTING article
	EEC Components	See SELF-DIAGNOSTICS article
Blue Smoke (burning oil)	PCV Valve	Check engine mechanical condition See BASIC DIAGNOSTIC PROCEDURES article
	Valve Guides/Stems/Seals Oil Drain Passages in Head	
	Rings (not seated, seized, gummed up, worn) Cylinder bores (scuffed)	
White Smoke (coolant in combustion)	Thermactor Vacuum Delay Valve (restricted) EGR Cooler Intake Manifold (cracked/porous) Cylinder Head/Gasket (leaks) Block (cracked/porous)	See SYSTEM & COMPONENT TESTING article

90H09339

Courtesy of Ford Motor Co.

DIAGNOSTIC ROUTINE 220
GAS SMELL

System	Component	Reference
Fuel Delivery	Fuel Filter (leaks) Injectors (leaking) Fuel Pump (leaks) Fuel Line, Pump to Tank (leaks) Fuel Tank (leaks) Fuel Tank Filler Neck/Cap (leaks) Fuel Return Line (Blocked) Fuel Pressure Regulator	Perform a visual inspection. See FUEL SYSTEM in SYSTEM & COMPONENT TESTING article
EVAP	Carbon Canister, Solenoid, Hoses (leaks)	See SYSTEM & COMPONENT TESTING article

90L09340

Courtesy of Ford Motor Co.

DIAGNOSTIC ROUTINE 221
"CHECK ENGINE" OR "SERVICE ENGINE SOON" LIGHT ALWAYS OR NEVER ON "CHECK ENGINE"/"CHECK DCL" MESSAGE ON

System	Component	Reference
EEC	Quick Test	See SELF-DIAGNOSTICS article

90B13640

Courtesy of Ford Motor Co.

1991 ENGINE PERFORMANCE
Trouble Shooting – No Codes (Cont.)

DIAGNOSTIC ROUTINE 222
STATE EMISSION TEST FAILURE

NOTE: Canada and some states or metropolitan areas in the United States require periodic Idle Emission Tests. All Ford products have been designed to pass these tests. If a Ford product fails an Idle Emission Test, it is probable that 1) The engine temperature was not warm and stabilized prior to the test. 2) The vehicle had idled excessively long prior to the test.

Prior to starting any repairs, complaints of Idle Emission Test failure should be verified.

The following example encompasses most of the emissions measurement modes of the current state idle test procedures:

- Ensure that the engine is at normal operating temperature and that all accessories are turned off.
- Read emissions at idle.
- Run engine at 2500 ± 300 rpm.
- Read emissions within 30 seconds.
- Return engine speed to idle.
- Read emissions within 30 seconds.

If any emission components are replaced, Keep Alive Memory (KAM) should be cleared before repeating State Emission Test procedure. Refer to Quick Test Appendix.

System	Component	Reference
EEC	Quick Test	See SELF-DIAGNOSTICS article
Ignition	Scope Engine For: Spark Plug, Coil, Secondary Wires, Distributor Cap, Adapter and Rotor Timing	See BASIC DIAGNOSTIC PROCEDURES article
Vacuum Distribution	Vacuum Leaks/Blockage	Perform a visual and audible inspection
Fuel Charging Assy	Curb or Fast Idle Speeds Electrical and Vacuum Connections	Perform a visual inspection. See FUEL SYSTEM in SYSTEM & COMPONENT TESTING article and ON-VEHICLE ADJUSTMENTS article
Fuel Delivery	Injectors Fuel Rail	See SYSTEM & COMPONENT TESTING article
EGR	Valve Vacuum Regulator	
PCV	Valve	
EVAP	Carbon Canister, Purge Solenoid	
Thermactor	Thermactor Air Dump	
Exhaust	Pipes, Muffler, Catalyst Resonator, Heat Control Valve	Check exhaust system
Cooling	Unstabilized Engine Temperature	Go to Routine 218
Basic Engine	Scheduled Maintenance Compression Valve Train Camshaft Intake Manifold Gaskets	Check engine mechanical condition. See BASIC DIAGNOSTIC PROCEDURES article

90B09341

Courtesy of Ford Motor Co.

DIAGNOSTIC ROUTINE 223
IMPROPER SHIFT

System	Component	Reference
Base Transmission (E4OD, A4LD, AXODE Only)	Converter Clutch Control Solenoid Converter Clutch Electronic Pressure Control Solenoid Shift Solenoids Modulated Lock Up Solenoid 4 X 4 Low Switch	See SELF-DIAGNOSTICS article
EEC (E4OD, A4LD AXODE Only)	EEC-IV Quick Test	See SELF-DIAGNOSTICS article

91E09253

Courtesy of Ford Motor Co.

1991 ENGINE PERFORMANCE
Trouble Shooting – No Codes (Cont.)

EEC-IV SYMPTOM DIAGNOSTIC CHART
(CIRCUIT TEST REFERENCE)

Symptom	Circuit Test & Step Number								
	2.3L EFI	2.9L EFI	3.0L EFI	4.0L MA EFI	4.9L EFI	5.0L EFI	5.8L EFI	7.3L DIESEL	7.5L EFI
Engine runs rough or misses Surges Lack of power Rough idle Erratic rpm	S2	S2*	S2	S2*	S2	S2	S2	—	S2
Engine Stalls Stalls in Self-Test	S1	S1	S1	S1	S1	S1	S1	—	S1
Stall during parking maneuvers	FF3	FF3	FF3	—	—	FF3	—	—	—
A/C Compressor runs continuously	KM35	—	—	—	KM35	—	—	—	—
Surges with A/C on at idle	KM30	—	—	—	—	—	—	—	—
A/C does not cut off under WOT conditions	KM15	KM15	KM15	KM15	—	—	—	—	—
A/C not functioning	KM1	KM1	KM1	KM1	—	—	—	—	—
Low idle with A/C On	KM43	KM43	KM43	KM43	KM43	KM43	KM43	—	KM43
"CHECK ENGINE" or "SERVICE ENGINE SOON" light always on	ML1	ML1	ML1	ML1	ML1	ML1	ML1	—	ML1
"CHECK ENGINE" or "SERVICE ENGINE SOON" light never on	ML4	ML4	ML4	ML4	ML4	ML4	ML4	—	ML4
"CHECK ENGINE" or "SERVICE ENGINE SOON" light on intermittently	ML10	ML10	ML10	ML10	ML10	ML10	ML10	—	ML10
"CHECK ENGINE" or "SERVICE ENGINE SOON" light flashing with erratic idle	ML15	ML15	ML15	ML15	ML15	ML15	ML15	—	ML15
Stumble after hot restart	H21	H21	H21	H21	H21	H21	H21	—	H21
Fuel pump runs with engine off	J22	—	—	—	—	—	—	—	—
Gasoline fumes under hood	—	—	KD1	KD1	KD1	—	KD1	—	KD1
Exhaust Odor Black Smoke	H1	H1	H1	H1	H1	H1	H1	—	H1
Spark knock	KP3	—	—	KP3	DG1	DG1	—	—	—
Poor idle quality Rolling idle Shifts harshly Poor fuel economy	—	—	DP1	—	—	—	—	DJ1	—
Overdrive Cancel Indicator (OCI) light always off (E4OD only)	—	—	—	—	TC13	TC13	TC13	TC13	TC13
Hard to Start (cold)	NB25	—	—	—	—	—	—	—	—
Tachometer Inoperative (Vehicles with Tachometer)	—	—	—	—	—	—	—	DJ1	—
4 x 4 Low Indicator Light Always Off (with harsh shift) (always on with sluggish shift) — E4OD Only	—	—	—	—	TC11	TC11	TC11	TC11	TC11
Tachometer indicates a low vehicle rpm	—	—	—	—	—	—	—	DJ1	—

* Verify that MAF sensor is properly connected.

91H13455

Courtesy of Ford Motor Co.

1991 ENGINE PERFORMANCE
Trouble Shooting – No Codes (Cont.)

DIESEL TROUBLE SHOOTING

EVALUATING NORMAL DIESEL EXHAUST SMOKE

The following is a description of what is normal and expected exhaust smoke for a vehicle with a diesel engine. Diesel exhaust smoke can be classified into 2 categories according to the color of the smoke.

Blue/White Smoke – Blue/White smoke may be observed at engine start-up, whether the engine is up to operating temperature or not. This start-up smoke will be observed at all ambient temperatures and should last no longer than a minute after the vehicle is driven.

When ambient temperature is below 50°F (10°C), Blue/White smoke can return after engine warm-up due to extended idling. This is due to the combustion chambers cooling down during periods of extended idling.

Heavy Blue/White Smoke – Heavy Blue/White smoke will occur when the engine is operated at wide open throttle with the transmission in neutral or with a lightly loaded vehicle in any gear. The smoke is a normal characteristic for a diesel engine with a light minimum-maximum governor spring in the fuel injection pump. This results in the following characteristics due to the engine operating above its rated speed (3300 RPM) in a no-load or lightly loaded condition:

- Heavy Blue/White smoke.
- Fuel injection pump governor hunting resulting in high speed engine RPM surging.
- Engine sputtering or missing.

The condition can be eliminated by not operating the engine above its maximum full load rated speed of 3300 RPM.

NOTE: Chassis fuel system air leaks may also cause continuous heavy Blue/White smoke.

Black Smoke – Black smoke occurs whenever the engine is working hard. The engine works hard when it is going up a steep grade, pulling a trailer, carrying a heavy load, or during acceleration. More Black smoke will be observed when operating the vehicle at higher altitudes. If Black smoke is observed while the engine is idling (at low altitude) or under normal driving conditions, the problem should be diagnosed as soon a possible.

ENGINE CRANKS BUT WILL NOT START (ENGINE COLD)

NOTE: If ignition switch is left in the ON position for an extended period of time or the engine is not started within the 2 minute cycle time, the glow plug system must be reset by turning the ignition switch to the OFF position.

1) Check and follow correct starting procedure. Correct starting procedure is located on driver's side sun visor. If vehicle does not start using correct starting procedure, go to next step. If vehicle starts, return vehicle to customer.

2) Open hood and listen for glow plug module power relay click when ignition switch is turned to ON position. The glow plug module power relay is mounted on top of solid-state glow plug module circuit board. The complete assembly is mounted on rear of intake manifold. If relay clicks, go to next step. If relay does not click, go to GLOW PLUG TESTING.

3) Loosen one injector nozzle line nut one-half to one turn. Crank engine and observe injector line. If fuel is discharged from loosened injector line, go to GLOW PLUG TESTING. If fuel is not discharged from loosened injector line, tighten injector line nut and go to next step.

4) Crank engine and check voltage at Fuel Shutoff (FS) solenoid. FS solenoid terminal is located at front of injection pump. Voltage must be at least 9 volts. Check FS solenoid terminal for dirt, corrosion, loose or broken electrical connection and repair or replace as necessary. If solenoid terminal and electrical connection are okay and at least 9 volts are present while cranking, go to next step. If at least 9 volts is not present, check Red/Light Green wire from FS solenoid to ignition switch. Repair wire as necessary, repeat this test. *See Fig. 2.*

5) Crank engine and check voltage at Cold Advance (CA) solenoid. CA solenoid is located at left rear of injection pump. Voltage must be at least 9 volts. If at least 9 volts are not present, verify switching function of Engine Temperature Switch (ETS), located behind thermostat housing. If at least 9 volts are not present at ETS, check Red/Light Green wire from ETS to ignition switch. Repair wire as necessary and repeat this test. *See Fig. 2.*

ENGINE CRANKS BUT WILL NOT START (ENGINE WARM)

1) Check and follow correct starting procedure. Correct starting procedure is located on driver's side sun visor. If vehicle does not start using correct starting procedure, go to next step. If vehicle starts, return vehicle to customer.

2) Loosen one injector nozzle line nut one-half to one turn. Crank engine and observe injector line. If fuel is discharged from loosened injector line, go to ENGINE PERFORMANCE DIAGNOSIS. If fuel is not discharged from loosened injector line, tighten injector line nut and go to next step.

3) Crank engine and check voltage at Fuel Shutoff (FS) solenoid. FS solenoid terminal is located at front of injection pump. Voltage must be at least 9 volts. Check FS solenoid terminal for dirt, corrosion, loose or broken electrical connection and repair or replace as necessary. If solenoid terminal and electrical connection are okay and at least 9 volts are present while cranking, go to next step. If at least 9 volts are not present, check Red/Light Green wire from FS solenoid to ignition switch. Repair wire as necessary, repeat this test. *See Fig. 2.*

ENGINE QUITS, STALLS OR STUMBLES

1) Check and/or adjust dynamic injection pump timing. See DYNAMIC TIMING in ON-VEHICLE ADJUSTMENTS article. If injection pump timing and idle speed is correct, go to next step.

2) Crank engine and check voltage at Fuel Shutoff (FS) solenoid. FS solenoid terminal is located at front of injection pump. Voltage must be at least 9 volts. Check FS solenoid terminal for dirt, corrosion, loose or broken electrical connection and repair or replace as necessary. If solenoid terminal and electrical connection are okay and at least 9 volts are present while cranking, go to next step. If at least 9 volts are not present, check Red/Light Green wire from FS solenoid to ignition switch. Repair wire as necessary, repeat this test. *See Fig. 2.*

3) If engine is hot, go to next step. If engine is cold, crank engine and check voltage at Cold Advance (CA) solenoid. CA solenoid is located at left rear of injection pump. Voltage must be no less than 9 volts. If at least 9 volts are not present, verify switching function of Engine Temperature Switch (ETS), located behind thermostat housing. If at least 9 volts are not present at ETS, check Red/Light Green wire from ETS to ignition switch. Repair wire as necessary, repeat this test. *See Fig. 2.*

4) If engine is hot, check for voltage at Cold Advance (CA) solenoid. CA solenoid is located at left rear of injection pump. Voltage should not be present. If voltage is not present at CA solenoid, go to ENGINE PERFORMANCE DIAGNOSIS. If voltage is present, replace engine temperature switch and repeat this step.

ENGINE MISSES

NOTE: Engine will miss when cold if one or more glow plugs are not heating.

1) If engine misses only when cold, go to GLOW PLUG TESTING. If engine misses at normal operating temperature, go to next step.

2) Run engine at RPM which makes miss most pronounced. Momentarily loosen injector line nut on one injector one-half to one turn. Then tighten connection. Check each cylinder in the same manner. If miss is not isolated to a specific cylinder, go to ENGINE PERFORMANCE DIAGNOSIS. If miss is isolated to a specific cylinder(s), go to next step.

1991 ENGINE PERFORMANCE
Trouble Shooting – No Codes (Cont.)

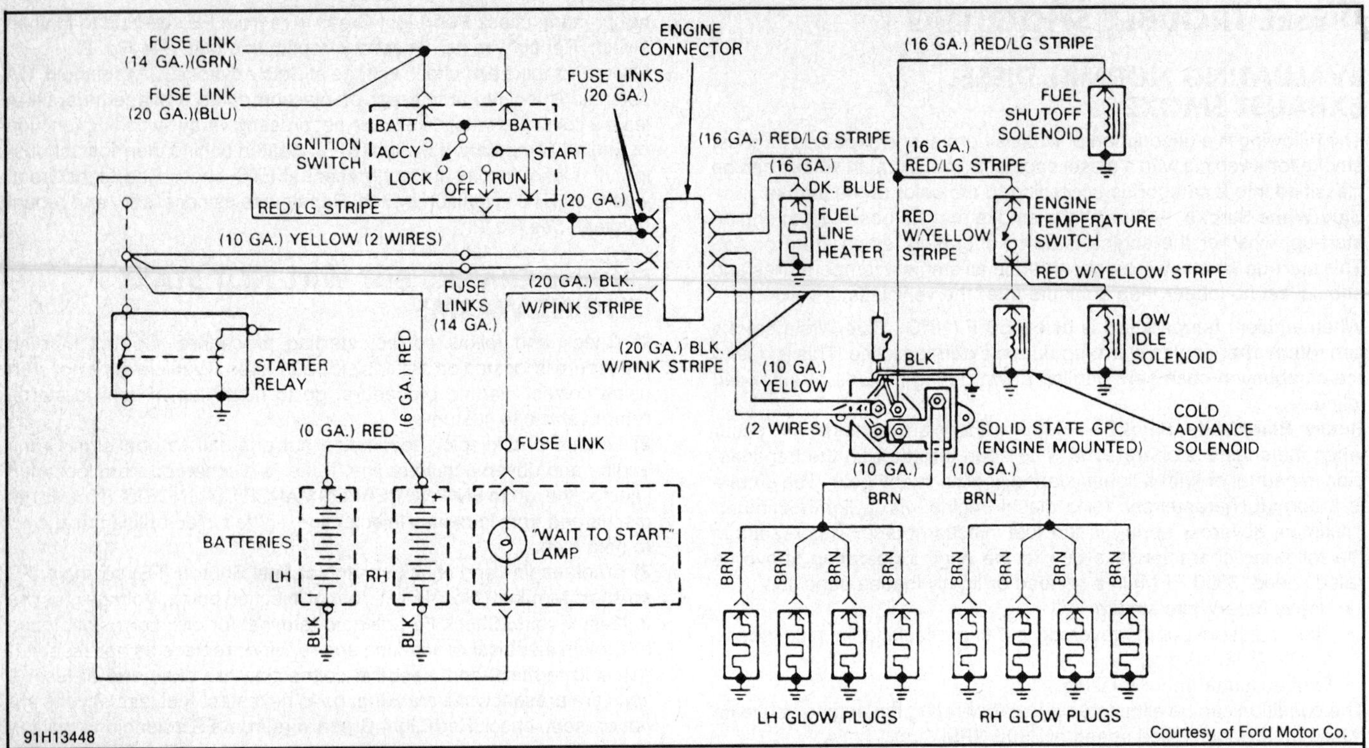
FUSE LINK
(14 GA.)(GRN)
FUSE LINK
(20 GA.)(BLU)
ENGINE
CONNECTOR
FUSE LINKS
(20 GA.)
BATT
ACCY
START
IGNITION
SWITCH
LOCK
OFF
RUN
RED LG STRIPE
(20 GA.)
(10 GA.) YELLOW (2 WIRES)
FUSE
LINKS
(14 GA.)
(20 GA.) BLK.
W/PINK STRIPE
STARTER
RELAY
(20 GA.) BLK.
W/PINK STRIPE
(6 GA.) RED
(0 GA.) RED
FUSE LINK
BATTERIES
LH
RH
"WAIT TO START"
LAMP
BLK
(16 GA.) RED/LG STRIPE
FUEL
SHUTOFF
SOLENOID
(16 GA.) RED/LG STRIPE
(16 GA.)
RED/LG STRIPE
(16 GA.)
DK. BLUE
FUEL
LINE
HEATER
RED
W/YELLOW
STRIPE
ENGINE
TEMPERATURE
SWITCH
RED W/YELLOW STRIPE
LOW
IDLE
SOLENOID
(10 GA.)
YELLOW
(2 WIRES)
SOLID STATE GPC
(ENGINE MOUNTED)
COLD
ADVANCE
SOLENOID
(10 GA.)
(10 GA.)
BRN
LH GLOW PLUGS
RH GLOW PLUGS
91H13448
Courtesy of Ford Motor Co.

Fig. 2: 7.3L Glow Plug Circuit Wiring Diagram

3) Check injection nozzle line(s) for kinks or restrictions. Replace any line that is kinked or restricted. Remove suspect nozzle(s) from engine and test. See INJECTION NOZZLE TESTING. Replace any nozzle that does not pass test. If lines and nozzles are okay, go to next step.

4) Perform cylinder compression test. See MECHANICAL CHECKS in SERVICE & ADJUSTMENT SPECIFICATIONS article. If cylinder compression is within specifications, go to ENGINE PERFORMANCE DIAGNOSIS. If cylinder compression is not within specifications, perform CRANKCASE PRESSURE TEST. See ENGINE PERFORMANCE DIAGNOSIS. If crankcase pressure is okay, repair or replace valve train as necessary. If crankcase pressure is excessive, overpower cylinder as necessary.

ENGINE KNOCKS

1) Ensure all engine driven accessories are operating properly and are not the cause of the knock. Verify that engine is not overheating. If engine is overheating, determine cause and repair as necessary. If engine is not overheating, go to next step.

2) Momentarily loosen injector line nut on one injector one-half to one turn. Then tighten connection. Check each cylinder in the same manner. If knock is not isolated to a specific cylinder, go to ENGINE PERFORMANCE DIAGNOSIS. If knock is isolated to a specific cylinder(s), go to next step.

3) Check injection nozzle line(s) for kinks or restrictions. Replace any line that is kinked or restricted. Remove suspect nozzle(s) from engine and test. See INJECTION NOZZLE TESTING. Replace any nozzle that does not pass test. If lines and nozzles are okay, go to ENGINE PERFORMANCE DIAGNOSIS.

LOW OIL PRESSURE WITH PROPER OIL

1) Using Pressure Tester Kit (014-00761) and Adapter (5633) verify accuracy of oil pressure sender. If oil pressure sender is accurate and operating normally, go to next step. If oil pressure sender is not accurate, replace sender and repeat this step.

2) Change engine oil and filter and run engine until engine reaches normal operating temperature. Check oil pressure. If oil pressure is okay, return vehicle to customer. If oil pressure is unsatisfactory, repair or replace lubrication system components as necessary.

BLUE/WHITE SMOKE (ENGINE AT NORMAL OPERATING TEMPERATURE)

1) Refer to EVALUATING NORMAL DIESEL EXHAUST SMOKE. If smoke is considered abnormal, verify engine is at normal operating temperature and go to step **3)**. If engine is not at normal operating temperature, go to next step.

2) Remove thermostat and test for proper operation and replace as necessary. If thermostat is operating normally, replace thermostat with integral air bleed check valve and repeat step **1)**.

3) Check engine oil level. If oil level is correct, go to next step. If oil level is to high, drain excess oil. If problem still exists, go to next step.

4) Perform CHECK FUEL RETURN PRESSURE test. See ENGINE PERFORMANCE DIAGNOSTICS. If fuel return pressure is okay, perform entire ENGINE PERFORMANCE DIAGNOSTICS. If fuel return pressure is high, repair or replace fuel return line(s) as necessary.

EXCESSIVE BLACK SMOKE

1) Refer to EVALUATING NORMAL DIESEL EXHAUST SMOKE. If smoke occurs under light load and/or low altitude, go to next step. If smoke occurs under heavy load, this is normal when going up steep grades, pulling a trailer, maximum load, maximum acceleration or at high altitudes.

2) Visually inspect exhaust system for dents or kinks which could cause restriction. If exhaust system is okay, go to next step. If dents, kinks or restriction is found, repair or replace exhaust as necessary. If problem still exists, go to next step.

3) Perform CHECK AIR INTAKE RESTRICTION test. See ENGINE PERFORMANCE DIAGNOSTICS. If air intake restriction check is okay go to next step. If air intake restriction is found, replace air filter element and/or repair system and repeat this test.

4) Check and/or adjust dynamic injection pump timing. See DYNAMIC TIMING in ON-VEHICLE ADJUSTMENTS article. If injection pump timing and idle speed is correct, go to next step.

5) Check injection nozzle line(s) for kinks or restrictions. Replace any line that is kinked or restricted. Remove injection nozzles from engine and test. See INJECTION NOZZLE TESTING. Replace any nozzle that does not pass test. If lines and nozzles are okay, replace injection pump.

1991 ENGINE PERFORMANCE
Trouble Shooting – No Codes (Cont.)

"WAIT-TO-START" INDICATOR TESTING

WAIT-TO-START Indicator Stays On – Disconnect WAIT-TO-START indicator connector at glow plug module. *See Fig. 3.* Turn ignition switch to ON position. If indicator is on, repair wiring to indicator. If indicator is off, disconnect batteries and replace glow plug module.

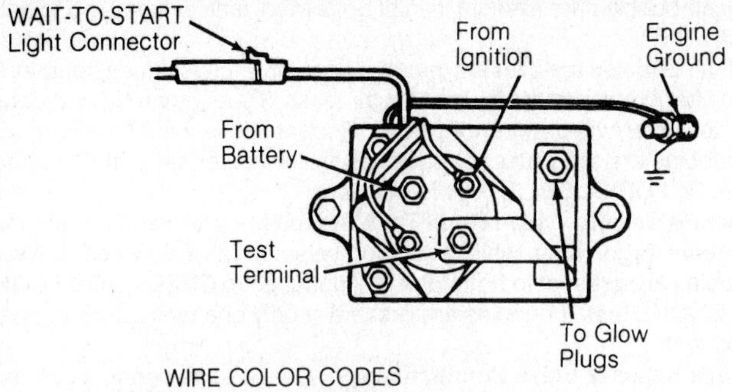
WAIT-TO-START
Light Connector
From
Ignition
Engine
Ground
From
Battery
Test
Terminal
To Glow
Plugs

WIRE COLOR CODES

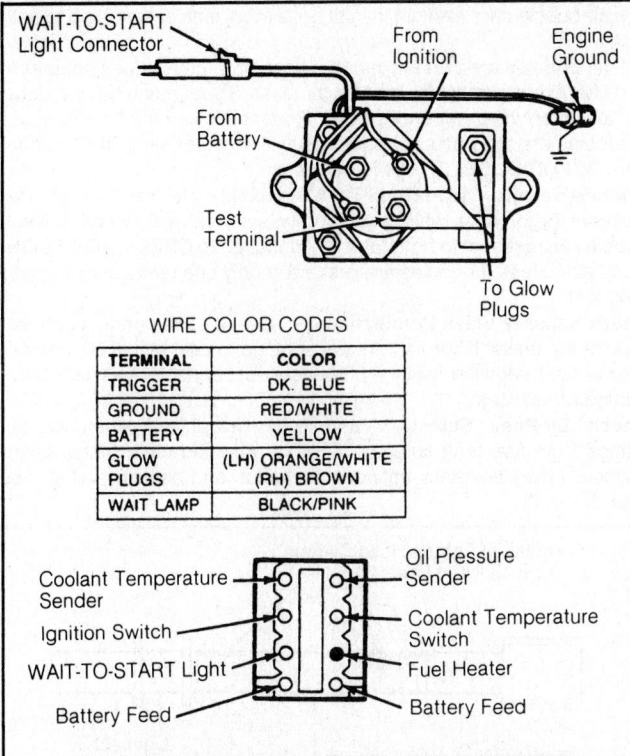

TERMINAL	COLOR
TRIGGER	DK. BLUE
GROUND	RED/WHITE
BATTERY	YELLOW
GLOW PLUGS	(LH) ORANGE/WHITE (RH) BROWN
WAIT LAMP	BLACK/PINK

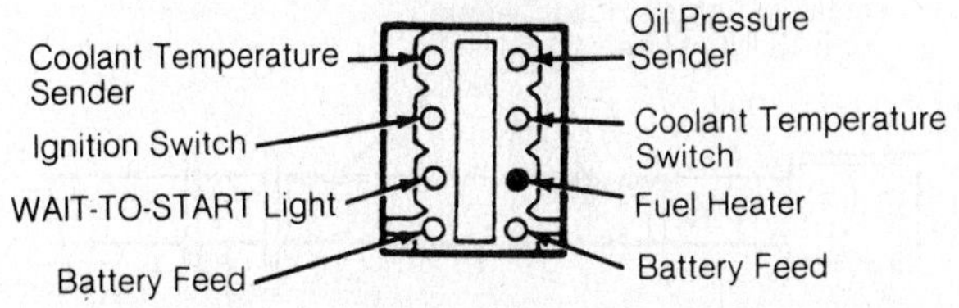
Coolant Temperature
Sender
Ignition Switch
WAIT-TO-START Light
Battery Feed
Oil Pressure
Sender
Coolant Temperature
Switch
Fuel Heater
Battery Feed

ELECTRICAL CONNECTOR, GLOW PLUG HARNESS TO CHASSIS HARNESS, CHASSIS SIDE VIEW

TERMINAL	WIRE COLOR CODES
IGNITION SWITCH	RED W/LIGHT GREEN STRIPE
"WAIT TO START" LAMP	BLACK W/PINK STRIPE
BATTERY FEED	YELLOW
BATTERY FEED	YELLOW
OIL PRESSURE SENDER	WHITE W/RED STRIPE
COOLANT TEMPERATURE SENDER	RED W/WHITE STRIPE
COOLANT TEMPERATURE SWITCH	RED W/BLACK STRIPE
IGNITION LEAD TO FUEL HEATER	DARK BLUE

91I13449 Courtesy of Ford Motor Co.

Fig. 3: 7.3L Glow Plug System Diagnostic Test Points

WAIT-TO-START Indicator Does Not Turn On – Disconnect WAIT-TO-START indicator connector at glow plug module. *See Fig. 3.* Connect a jumper wire between harness side of connector and ground. Turn ignition switch to ON position. If indicator is on, go to GLOW PLUG TESTING. If indicator is off, check light bulb and wiring and repair as necessary.

GLOW PLUG TESTING

WARNING: DO NOT by-pass the timed pulse function of the glow plug system. A constant 12-volt current to glow plugs will cause them to overheat and fail within seconds, possibly resulting in severe engine damage.

Check Glow Plugs – With ignition off, disconnect glow plug connectors at glow plugs. Connect a 12-volt test light between a convenient power source and each glow plug terminal. If test light illuminates, go to next test. If test light does not illuminate, replace glow plug and go to next test.

Check Harness – With ignition off, disconnect glow plug connectors at glow plugs. Squeeze sides of glow plug module protective cover and remove cover. Using an ohmmeter or test light, check continuity between each glow plug lead and test terminal of glow plug module. *See Fig. 3.* If all leads check okay, go to next test. If any lead has an open circuit or is shorted to ground, repair or replace lead as necessary then go to next test.

Check Control Unit – Ensure ignition switch is off. Connect an ohmmeter between glow plug module ground wire terminal eyelet and negative battery terminal of each battery. *See Fig. 3.* If less than one ohm is indicated, go to next test. If greater than one ohm is indicated, clean or repair ground connection then go to next test.

Check Supply Voltage – Ensure ignition switch is off. Connect voltmeter positive lead to glow plug module positive terminal. *See Fig. 3.* Connect voltmeter negative lead to ground. If voltage is 10 volts or more, go to next test. If voltage is less than 10 volts, repair power supply wiring or recharge battery then go to next test.

Check Voltage From Ignition Switch – Connect voltmeter positive lead to glow plug module ignition terminal. *See Fig. 3.* Connect voltmeter negative lead to ground. Turn ignition switch to ON position. If voltage is 8 volts or more, go to next test. If voltage is less than 8 volts, check fusible link, repair wiring or recharge battery as necessary. Go to next test.

Functional Test – **1)** With ignition switch off, connect a 12-volt test light between glow plug module test terminal and ground. *See Fig. 3.* Position test light so that it can be seen from driver's seat. Turn ignition switch to ON position and monitor test light. Compare test light times to chart. *See Fig. 4.* Total test light ON time includes time from the beginning of the initial ON cycle to the end of the last ON-OFF cycle measured in seconds.

Control* Unit Temp. °F	"Wait-to-Start" Indicator "ON" Time (Sec.)	Test Light Total Time (Sec.)
– 20°C	7-15	35-70
0°F	7-12	25-60
35°F	5-12	15-35
70°F	3-5	7-15
105°F	1-3	3-5
140°F	1 or Less	1-3

* Temperature of control unit, not ambient temperature.

91C13450 Courtesy of Ford Motor Co.

Fig. 4: 7.3L Glow Plug Module Functional Test Chart

NOTE: The WAIT-TO-START indicator and/or test light may not illuminate if engine temperature is at or near operating temperature.

2) If test light times are within specifications, system is functioning correctly. End of test. If test light times are not within specifications, disconnect both batteries and replace glow plug module. Repeat FUNCTIONAL TEST.

FUEL SYSTEM AIR LEAK TESTING

NOTE: Before starting this test procedure, verify that the fuel tank(s) contain at least a half tank of fuel. The fuel level compensates for the range of vehicle attitudes that may uncover the fuel sender pick-up hose or sender by-pass in the fuel tank when the fuel level is low. Visually inspect fuel system for obvious problems such as kinked hoses, damaged lines or push-connect fittings. Make necessary repairs before continuing.

1991 ENGINE PERFORMANCE
Trouble Shooting – No Codes (Cont.)

CAUTION: Use care when removing or installing hose to the plastic fitting at the fuel injection nozzle return lines. Lubricate hose with diesel fuel to ease installation.

Check For Bubbles Or Foam – 1) Remove rubber fuel return by-pass hose which connects fuel filter outlet fitting by-pass orifice to return lines at fuel injection nozzles. Install a 12" (305 mm) length of 3/16" clear polyvinyl chloride, Tygon hose in place of rubber hose just removed. Ensure hose clamps are installed and tightened.

2) Run engine at approximately 3000 RPM for 2-3 minutes to clear air from system that was introduced when hose was installed. Observe clear fuel hose for air bubbles at 3000 RPM. Any continuous stream of bubbles larger than 1/16" indicates air ingestion. A moving concentration of bubbles of any size, or foam, is unacceptable.

3) If moving concentration of bubbles of any size, or foam is not observed, problem is elsewhere in system. Remove Tygon hose and install original hose. If moving concentration of bubbles of any size, or foam is observed, go to next test.

Check Direction Of Flow – Observe direction of flow of bubbles. Bubbles should flow from fuel filter outlet fitting to fuel injection nozzle return system. If bubbles flow in direction described, go to next test for single tank systems. For vehicles with dual tank system, go to CHECK FUEL FILTER/WATER SEPARATOR FOR BUBBLES test. If bubbles do not flow in direction described, fuel system is restricted. Go to FUEL FILTER OUTLET PRESSURE test. See ENGINE PERFORMANCE DIAGNOSIS.

Check Hose Connections – Check for damage to hose connections at rubber fuel hose from chassis fuel line to mechanical fuel pump and at inlet and outlet hoses at water separator. Tighten hose clamps to 8-13 INCH Lbs. (1-1.5 N.m). After tightening hose clamps, run engine for 5 minutes at 3000 RPM and check for air bubbles in Tygon hose. If bubbles are not observed, problem is resolved. Replace Tygon hose with original hose. If bubbles are still observed, go to next test.

Check Fuel Filter/Water Separator For Bubbles – 1) Disconnect fuel filter/water separator inlet hose. Install hose adapter, and tighten hose clamps to 8-13 INCH Lbs. (1-1.5 N.m). *See Fig. 5*. Disconnect fuel filter/water separator outlet hose. Install hose adapter, and tighten hose clamps to 8-13 INCH Lbs. (1-1.5 N.m).

NOTE: Disconnect hoses and install adapters one a time to prevent hose mix-up.

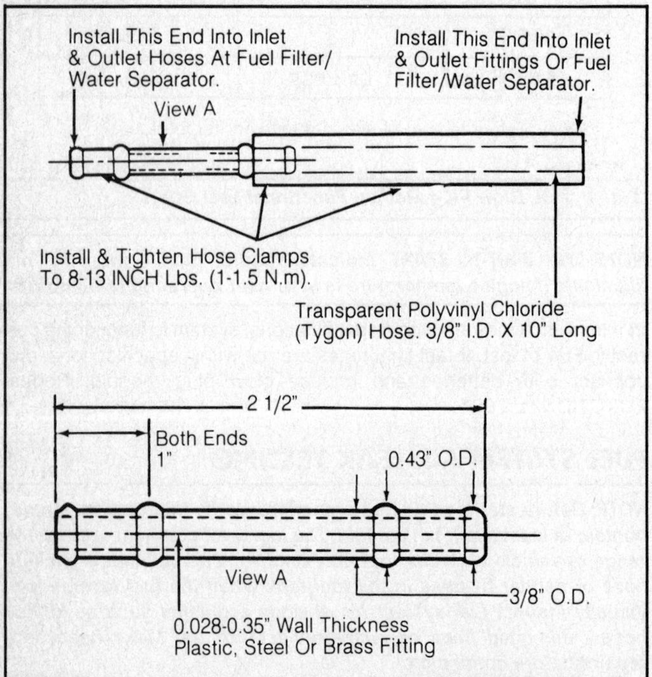
Install This End Into Inlet & Outlet Hoses At Fuel Filter/ Water Separator.
Install This End Into Inlet & Outlet Fittings Or Fuel Filter/Water Separator.
View A
Install & Tighten Hose Clamps To 8-13 INCH Lbs. (1-1.5 N.m).
Transparent Polyvinyl Chloride (Tygon) Hose. 3/8" I.D. X 10" Long
2 1/2"
Both Ends 1"
0.43" O.D.
View A
3/8" O.D.
0.028-0.35" Wall Thickness Plastic, Steel Or Brass Fitting
91D13451
Courtesy of Ford Motor Co.

Fig. 5: Fuel Filter/Water Separator Adapter (2 Required)

2) Operate engine at 1500 RPM for 5 minutes to develop steady fuel flow. Then, operate engine at 3000 RPM for an additional 2 minutes and check for bubbles in hose adapters.

3) If air bubbles are present in inlet hose (single tank system), repair hoses and connections between fuel filter/ water separator as necessary. Repeat this test to confirm repair.

4) If air bubbles are present in inlet hose (dual tank system), go to next test.

5) If air bubbles are present in outlet hose only, check hose adapter at fuel filter/water separator inlet for air leaks. Turn engine off and operate fuel filter/water separator drain. Repeat this test to confirm repair. If bubbles are still present, replace fuel filter/water separator. Repeat CHECK FOR BUBBLES OR FOAM test.

Operate Selector Valve (Dual Tank System) – Start and run engine. Observe Tygon hose while switching selector valve between tanks. If bubbles are present in both tank positions, go to CHECK HOSE CONNECTIONS test. If bubbles are present in only one tank position, go to next test.

Check Selector Valve Connections – Check push-connect connectors for tightness. If connectors are tight, go to next test. If connectors are not tight, repair or replace push-connect connectors as necessary and go to next test.

Check By-Pass Selector Valve – 1) Disconnect push-connect fittings from fuel tank selector valve for affected tank. Install push-connect fitting adapters between fuel lines and selector valve. *See Figs. 6 and 7.*

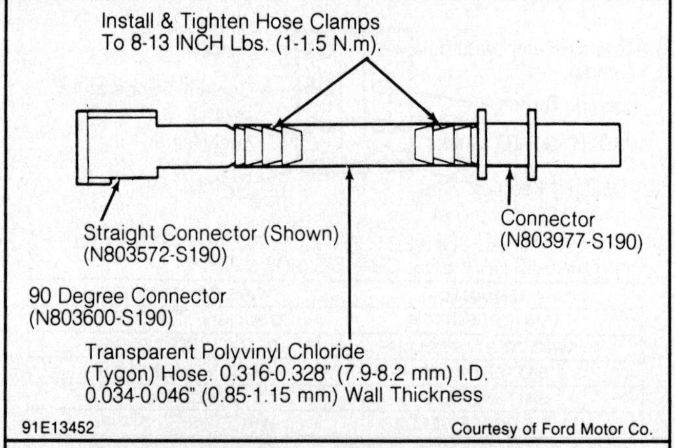
Install & Tighten Hose Clamps To 8-13 INCH Lbs. (1-1.5 N.m).
Straight Connector (Shown) (N803572-S190)
Connector (N803977-S190)
90 Degree Connector (N803600-S190)
Transparent Polyvinyl Chloride (Tygon) Hose. 0.316-0.328" (7.9-8.2 mm) I.D. 0.034-0.046" (0.85-1.15 mm) Wall Thickness
91E13452
Courtesy of Ford Motor Co.

Fig. 6: Fuel Tank/Selector Valve Adapter (2 Required)

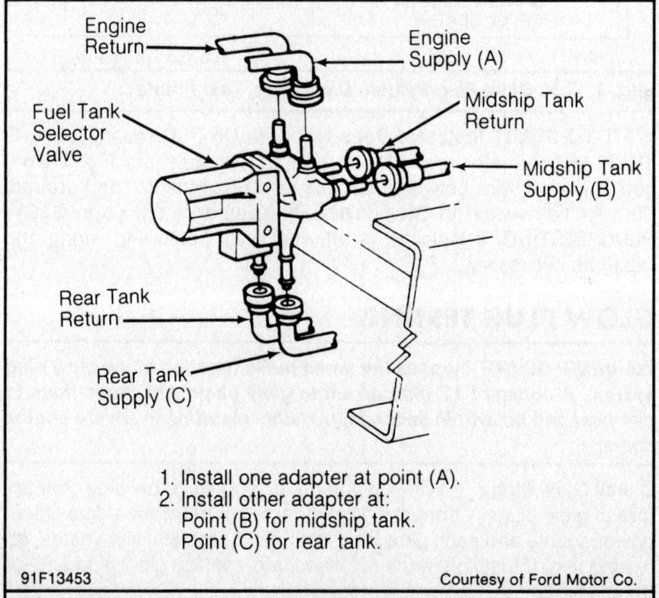
Engine Return
Engine Supply (A)
Fuel Tank Selector Valve
Midship Tank Return
Midship Tank Supply (B)
Rear Tank Return
Rear Tank Supply (C)
1. Install one adapter at point (A).
2. Install other adapter at:
Point (B) for midship tank.
Point (C) for rear tank.
91F13453
Courtesy of Ford Motor Co.

Fig. 7: Identifying Fuel Tank/Selector Valve Connector Locations

2) Run engine at 3000 RPM for 2-3 minutes to clear any air ingested during adapter installation. Run engine an additional 2 minutes and observe transparent fuel lines in adapters.
3) If bubbles are not present in either adapter, air leak is between fuel tank selector valve and fuel filter/water separator. Repair or replace lines and connectors as necessary. Repeat CHECK FOR BUBBLES OR FOAM test.
4) If bubbles are present in both adapters, air leak is between fuel tank and selector valve. Repair or replace fuel lines or connectors as necessary. Repeat CHECK FOR BUBBLES OR FOAM test.
5) If bubbles are present in selector valve outlet adapter only, replace fuel tank selector valve and repeat CHECK FOR BUBBLES OR FOAM test.

INJECTION NOZZLE TESTING

WARNING: Always wear appropriate approved safety glasses when performing injector test. Use only liquid approved for use in tester, SAE calibration No. 208629 (SAE J968D or ISO 4113). Keep hands and other body parts away from nozzle being tested. The liquid discharged leaves the nozzle tip with sufficient force to penetrate the skin and cause serious injury. Nozzle tip should be enclosed in a transparent receptacle if available.

1) Prepare Test Stand (014-003000) for making test according to manufacturers instructions. Fill test stand reservoir with clean calibration fluid. Open tester valve slightly and operate tester handle to expel air from tester and outlet pipe. Operate tester until solid fluid (without bubbles) flows from end of outlet pipe. Close tester valve.
2) Connect injection nozzle to test stand. Care should be taken to avoid cross-threading. Tighten connector nut securely. Bleed air from nozzle. Open tester valve and operate tester handle for 8-10 quick strokes to expel air (bleed) from injection nozzle. Fluid should discharge from spray hole in nozzle tip.
3) Check nozzle opening pressure. Close pump valve and operate pump handle in slow even strokes to bring system up to pressure. Record highest pressure reached before nozzle opens. Repeat operation, increasing pump handle speed if necessary to establish consistent readings. A new nozzle should open at 1800-1950 psi. (126.56-138.51 kg/cm²). A used nozzle should open at minimum 1425 psi. (100.19 kg/cm²).
4) Check for tip leakage. Blow nozzle tip dry with filtered compressed air. Operate test pump to maintain pressure at approximately 200 psi (14.06 kg/cm²) below opening pressure obtained in step **3)**. Wetting of nozzle tip is acceptable as long as a drop does not fall within 5 seconds.
5) After testing is completed, make sure to open pump valve to release built up pressure. Remove nozzle and cap tip and inlet. If nozzle passes opening and leakage test, it is suitable for further service in engine. If nozzle does not pass both tests, replace nozzle.

ENGINE PERFORMANCE DIAGNOSIS

NOTE: Repair each problem detected before going on to the next step. If repair corrects the original complaint, it will not be necessary to proceed to the next step. However, if complaint is not corrected, continue with the test until complaint is corrected.

Check For External Leakage – With engine running, visually inspect for leakage of fuel, engine oil and coolant. Ensure air cleaner is properly installed and dirt is getting past element. If no leakage is found, go to next test. If leakage is found, repair or replace faulty component(s) as necessary and go to next test.
Check Exhaust System – Visually inspect exhaust system for dents or kinks which could cause restriction. If exhaust system is okay, go to next test. If dents or kinks are found, repair or replace faulty component as necessary and go to next test.
Check For Air In Fuel – **1)** Install a length of clear PVC hose in place of rubber hose between fuel filter outlet and injection nozzle return system. Run engine at 3000 RPM and check for bubbles in clear hose. Fuel should flow from fuel filter/water separator toward fuel return system. On vehicles with dual tanks, check with tank selector valve in each position for am minimum of 2 minutes.
2) If fuel flow direction is okay and bubbles are less than 1/16" (1.58 mm) diameter, go to next test. If fuel flow direction is okay and bubbles are greater than 1/16" (1.58 mm) diameter, go to FUEL SYSTEM AIR LEAK TESTING. Repeat this test when air leaks are eliminated. If fuel flow direction is not correct, go to CHECK FUEL RETURN PRESSURE test. Repeat this test when fuel flow direction is corrected.
Check For Fuel Contamination – Obtain a fuel sample and visually examine fuel in a clear container (including bottom of container), for particles, clouding, or liquid contamination, such as water. If fuel sample is okay, go to next test. If fuel sample is contaminated, replace fuel filter. Clean and/or replace fuel system as necessary. Ensure fuel if clean and go to next test.
Check Fuel For Cetane Value – **1)** Using Cetane Tester included in Dynamic Timing Meter (078-00200), check cetane value of fuel sample taken in previous test. Temperature of fuel must be 75-95°F (24-36°C) to obtain accurate results. Fill hydrometer container with fuel until hydrometer floats. Spin container gently to break surface tension of fuel. Read number at lowest point of fuel level in hydrometer. Compare readings to DIESEL FUEL CETANE VALUES table to determine cetane value.

DIESEL FUEL CETANE VALUES

Hydrometer Reading	Cetane Value
.837	50
.846	47
.849	46
.858	43
.862	42
.876	38

2) Cetane value should be a minimum of 40. If cetane value is greater than 40, go to next test. If cetane value is less than 40, inform owner to change fuel source. DO NOT replace fuel injection pump because of low cetane problem.
Fuel Filter Outlet Pressure – Remove air bleed orifice hose from fuel filter fitting. Install Adapter (5651) and Pressure Test Kit (014-00761). *See Fig. 8*. Run engine at 3300 RPM, with no load. Record pressure reading. On dual tank vehicles, check both tanks. Pressure should be a minimum of one psi at 3300 RPM. If pressure is at least one psi at 3300 RPM, go to FUEL PUMP CAPACITY test. If pressure is less than one psi at 3300 RPM, go to next test.

Fuel Supply Pump Outlet Pressure – Remove vacuum purge valve from fuel filter adapter. Install Adapter (3019) and Pressure Test Kit (014-00761). *See Fig. 8*. Ensure hose clamp is closed on sampling hose. Leave adapter from previous test installed and cap end. Run engine at idle, no load. Record pressure reading. On dual tank vehicles, check both tanks. Pressure should be at least 2 psi at idle. If pressure is less than 2 psi at idle, replace fuel filter and repeat FUEL FILTER OUTLET PRESSURE test. If pressure is not at least 2 psi at idle, go to next test.
Fuel Pump Capacity – Position end of sample hose on Adapter (3019) in clear, one quart, graduated container. Follow procedures for FUEL SUPPLY PUMP OUTLET PRESSURE test and open clamp on sample hose, allowing fuel to flow into fuel container, for 30 seconds. Record volume. On dual tank vehicles, check both tanks. Volume should be at least one pint in 30 seconds at idle, no load. If pressure and volume are okay, go to CHECK FUEL RETURN PRESSURE test. If pressure is okay and volume is not, go to next test. If volume is okay and pressure is not, replace fuel supply pump and repeat FUEL FILTER OUTLET PRESSURE test. If pressure and volume are both inadequate, go to next test.
Check Restriction At Fuel Supply Pump – Connect fuel return line removed in FUEL FILTER OUTLET PRESSURE test. Install Adapter (5632) and Pressure Test Kit (014-00761) to fuel supply pump inlet. *See Fig. 8*. With rear wheels off the ground and transmission in neutral or park, run engine at 3300 RPM. Record vacuum reading. On dual tank vehicles, check both tanks. Vacuum reading should be less than

1991 ENGINE PERFORMANCE
Trouble Shooting – No Codes (Cont.)

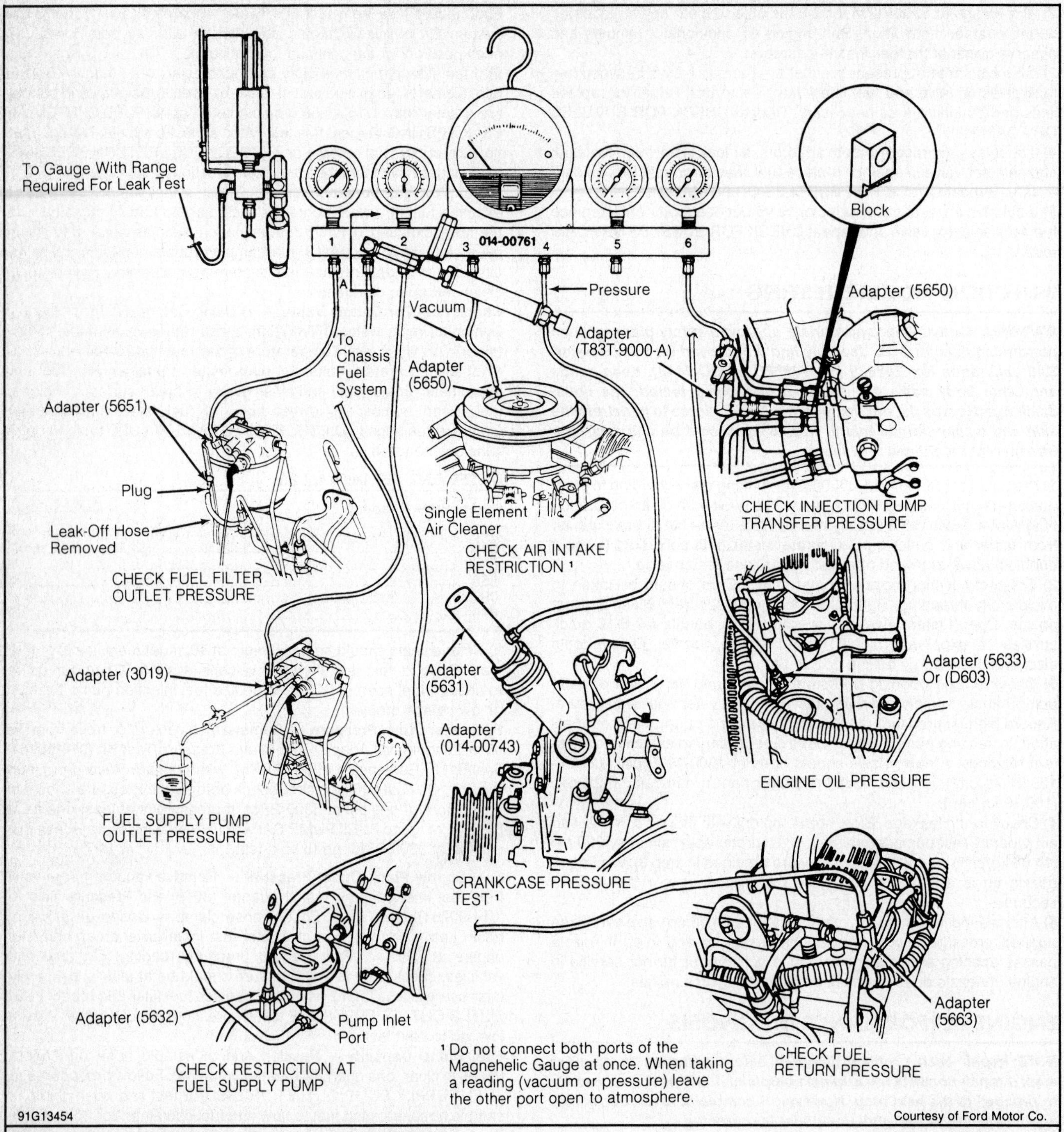
To Gauge With Range
Required For Leak Test
014-00761
1
2
3
4
5
6
Block
A
Pressure
Adapter (5650)
Vacuum
Adapter
(T83T-9000-A)
To
Chassis
Fuel
System
Adapter
(5650)
Adapter (5651)
Plug
Leak-Off Hose
Removed
Single Element
Air Cleaner
CHECK INJECTION PUMP
TRANSFER PRESSURE
CHECK AIR INTAKE
RESTRICTION ¹
CHECK FUEL FILTER
OUTLET PRESSURE
Adapter (3019)
Adapter
(5631)
Adapter (5633)
Or (D603)
Adapter
(014-00743)
ENGINE OIL PRESSURE
FUEL SUPPLY PUMP
OUTLET PRESSURE
CRANKCASE PRESSURE
TEST ¹
Adapter (5632)
Pump Inlet
Port
Adapter
(5663)
CHECK RESTRICTION AT
FUEL SUPPLY PUMP
¹ Do not connect both ports of the
Magnehelic Gauge at once. When taking
a reading (vacuum or pressure) leave
the other port open to atmosphere.
CHECK FUEL
RETURN PRESSURE
91G13454
Courtesy of Ford Motor Co.

Fig. 8: Installing Diesel Engine Pressure Test Kit (014-00761)

1991 ENGINE PERFORMANCE
Trouble Shooting – No Codes (Cont.)

6" Hg. If vacuum reading is less than 6" Hg, go to next test. If vacuum is greater than 6" Hg., repair or replace restricted chassis fuel line(s) and repeat FUEL FILTER OUTLET PRESSURE test.

Check Fuel Return Pressure – Remove fuel return line at junction fitting at left rear of engine. Install Adapter (5663) and Pressure Test Kit (014-00761) to fuel supply pump inlet. *See Fig. 8.* Connect fuel return hose removed in FUEL FILTER OUTLET PRESSURE test. Run engine at 3300 RPM, no load and transmission in neutral or park. Record pressure reading. On dual tank vehicles check both tanks. Maximum pressure should not exceed 2 psi at 3300 RPM. If pressure does not exceed 2 psi at 3300 RPM, go to next test. If pressure exceeds 2 psi at 3300 RPM, repair or replace fuel return line(s) as necessary and repeat this test.

Check Air Intake Restriction – Remove cap on air cleaner test port and install Adapter (5650) and Pressure Test Kit (014-00761) to fuel supply pump inlet. *See Fig. 8.* Run engine at 3300 RPM, no load. Record restriction reading. Restriction should not exceed 25" of H_2O. If reading is more than 2" of H_2O but less than 25" of H_2O, remove adapter. Install cap on air cleaner port and go to next test. If reading is 25" of H_2O or greater, replace air filter element and check intake system for blockage. Repeat this test. If reading is less than 2" of H_2O, correct restriction in fitting on air cleaner test port and repair this test.

Check Injection Pump Transfer Pressure – **1)** Remove screw from transfer pump pressure port cover. Install Transfer Pump Pressure Adapter (T83T-9000-A) through cover and "O" ring and into port. Install Pressure Test Kit (014-00761) *See Fig. 8.* Ensure fittings are tight and not leaking. Run engine at 3300 RPM, with no load and transmission in neutral or park. Record pressure reading. Pressure reading should be 90-110 psi.

2) If pressure reading is 90-110 psi, go to next test. If pressure reading is not as specified, replace injection pump. If performance problem still exists after installing new injection pump, check and adjust injection pump dynamic timing. See DYNAMIC INJECTION PUMP TIMING. If problem still exists after adjusting timing, go to next test.

CAUTION: Full throttle stop screw is not adjustable. Tampering may cause injection pump damage.

Accelerator Linkage Adjustment – With engine off, check that throttle lever stop screw contacts injection pump stop at full accelerator pedal depression. If adjustment is correct, go to next test. If adjustment is not correct, adjust or repair throttle linkage as necessary and go to next test.

Check Engine Idle Speed – Connect tachometer and check curb idle speed. Idle speed should be 600-700 RPM in Neutral (man. trans.) or Drive (auto. trans.). If idle speed is correct, go to next test. If idle speed is not as specified, adjust as necessary and go to next test.

NOTE: Engine must be at normal operating temperature of 192-212°F (89-100°C) when checking/setting dynamic timing.

Dynamic Injection Pump Timing – **1)** Bring engine to normal operating temperature. Stop engine and install Dynamic Timing Meter (078-00200) into timing probe hole until it almost touches vibration damper.

2) Attach clamp from Timing Meter Adapter (078-00201) or equivalent to the line pressure sensor on No. 1 injector nozzle ("F" Series) or No. 4 injector nozzle ("E" Series) and connect to dynamic timing meter. Connect dynamic timing meter to battery and dial in minus 20 degrees offset on meter.

3) Disconnect cold start advance terminal connector from solenoid terminal. With transmission in neutral and rear wheels raised, start engine. Using Throttle Control Tool (D83T-9000-E), set engine speed to 2000 RPM with no accessory load.

4) Observe injection timing on dynamic timing meter. Injection timing should be 8.5 degrees BTDC at 2000 RPM. Apply battery voltage to cold start advance solenoid. Activating cold start advance solenoid terminal can increase engine speed. Adjust throttle if necessary.

5) Timing at 2000 RPM should be advanced at least one degree before the timing obtained in first timing check. If the advance is more than one degree, and base timing is within 2 degrees of specification, go to next test. If the advance is more than one degree, and base timing is not within 2 degrees of specification, adjust timing. If problem still exists, go to next test. If the advance is less than one degree, replace injection pump and repeat this test.

NOTE: Perform this test only if engine has an obvious combustion knock or miss.

Check Injection Nozzles And Inlet Lines – Check injection nozzle inlet lines for kinks or restriction and repair or replace as necessary. Check injection nozzles. See INJECTION NOZZLE TESTING. Replace any injection nozzle that does not pass test. If performance problem still exists, go to next test.

Crankcase Pressure Test – Remove crankcase depression regulator valve and securely plug opening to prevent blow-by. Remove oil filler cap and install Adapter (5631) and install Pressure Test Kit (014-00761) *See Fig. 8.* Ensure dipstick is seated in dipstick tube. Run engine at 3000 RPM, with no load and transmission in neutral. Record pressure reading. Pressure reading should not exceed 6" of H_2O at 3300 RPM. If crankcase pressure is less than 6" of H_2O at 3300 RPM, replace injection pump and check and adjust timing. If crankcase pressure is greater than 6" of H_2O at 3300 RPM, problem is internal to engine. Repair engine as necessary.

1991 ENGINE PERFORMANCE
System & Component Testing – EEC-IV

Aerostar, Bronco, Explorer, Ranger, "E" & "F" Series

NOTE: Unless otherwise specified, references to "F" Series include "F" Series Super Duty.

INTRODUCTION

Prior to testing separate components or systems, it is recommended that all procedures listed in BASIC DIAGNOSTIC PROCEDURES article be performed. Since many computer controlled and monitored components will set a service code if they malfunction, check EEC-IV system and retrieve service codes. See Quick Test procedure in SELF-DIAGNOSTICS – EEC-IV article. If service codes are present see appropriate CIRCUIT TEST in SELF-DIAGNOSTICS – EEC-IV article.

NOTE: Testing individual components does not isolate shorts or opens. Perform all voltage tests with a Digital Volt-Ohmmeter (DVOM) that has a minimum 10-megohm input impedance, unless stated otherwise in test procedure. Use ohmmeter to isolate wiring harness shorts or opens.

NOTE: For wiring diagrams not shown in testing procedures, see WIRING DIAGRAMS article in ENGINE PERFORMANCE.

COMPUTERIZED ENGINE CONTROLS

ELECTRONIC CONTROL ASSEMBLY (ECA)

Ground Circuits – 1) Using a DVOM, check for continuity to ground on ECA terminals No. 40 and 60. *See Fig. 1*. Resistance should be zero ohms. If resistance is not zero ohms, repair open to ground.

2) Using a voltmeter, touch negative lead of voltmeter to a good ground. Touch positive lead of voltmeter to each ground terminal. With vehicle running, the voltmeter should indicate less than one volt. If voltmeter reading is greater than one volt or more, check for open, corrosion or loose connection on ground lead.

Power Circuits – Using a voltmeter, check for battery voltage between ECA terminal No. 1 (KAPWR) and ground. Check for battery voltage at terminals No. 37 and 57 (VPWR). If battery voltage is not present, power is not being supplied from EEC power relay. See CIRCUIT TEST B in SELF-DIAGNOSTICS – EEC-IV article.

ECA LOCATION

Application	Location
Aerostar	Left Firewall, Left of Master Cyl.
Bronco & "F" Series	Left Firewall, Below Brake Fluid Reservoir
Explorer & Ranger	Behind Right Kick Panel
"E" Series	Right Fender Apron, Under Blower Motor

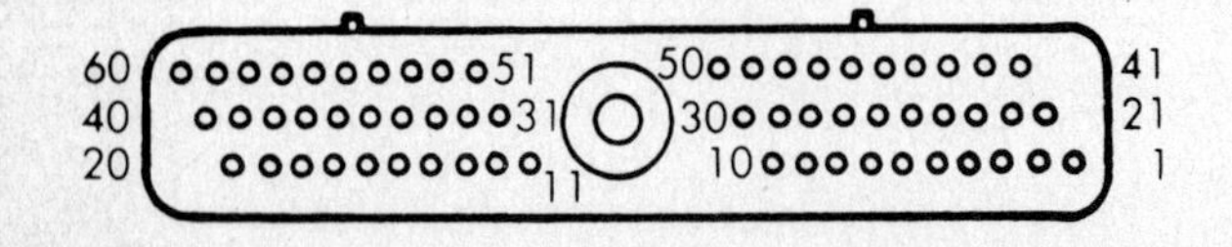
60
40
20
51
31
11
50
30
10
41
21
1
90I09354
Courtesy of Ford Motor Co.

Fig. 1: Identifying ECA 60-Pin Connector Terminals

ENGINE SENSORS & SWITCHES (ECA INPUTS)

NOTE: For additional sensor testing specifications see SENSOR OPERATING RANGE CHARTS article.

Air Charge Temperature (ACT) Sensor – 1) On 2.3L and 4.9L, sensor is located on intake runner number one. On 2.9L, sensor is located on top right side of engine above valve cover. On 3.0L and 4.0L, sensor is located on top left side of engine, behind idle air bypass valve. On 5.0L and 5.8L, sensor is located on top center of engine near intake runner number 6. On 7.5L, sensor is located behind distributor.

2) Sensor requires a 5-volt reference signal during engine operation. With sensor disconnected, sensor may be checked by measuring resistance between sensor terminals. For specifications, see SENSOR OPERATING RANGE CHARTS article. For additional testing information and circuit testing of sensor, see CIRCUIT TEST DA in SELF-DIAGNOSTICS – EEC-IV article.

Barometric Pressure Sensor (BP) – Faults in barometric pressure sensor or circuit should set a service code. See Quick Test procedure in SELF-DIAGNOSTICS – EEC-IV article. If no service code has been set, see CIRCUIT TEST DF in SELF-DIAGNOSTICS – EEC-IV article for sensor specifications.

Clutch Switch – See NEUTRAL DRIVE SWITCH (NDS) & A/C INPUT.

Cylinder Identification Sensor (CID) & Crankshaft Sensor – CID sensor is mounted at crankshaft. Disconnect sensor connector and measure resistance across sensor terminals. Resistance should be 300-750 ohms. If resistance is not as specified, replace sensor.

Engine Coolant Temperature (ECT) Sensor – Sensor is located in intake manifold cooling passage at front of most engines. On 2.3L, sensor is mounted on left side of engine above oil filter. Sensor requires a 5-volt reference signal during engine operation. With sensor disconnected, sensor may be checked by measuring resistance between sensor terminals. For specifications, see SENSOR OPERATING RANGE CHARTS article. For additional testing information and circuit testing of sensor, see CIRCUIT TEST DA in SELF-DIAGNOSTICS – EEC-IV article.

EGR Valve Position (EVP) Sensor/EGR Vacuum Regulator (EVR) Solenoid – Faults in sensor or circuit should set a service code. See Quick Test procedure in SELF-DIAGNOSTICS – EEC-IV article. If no service code has been set, see CIRCUIT TEST DN in SELF-DIAGNOSTICS – EEC-IV article for sensor specifications and circuit testing procedure.

Engine RPM Sensor (RPMS) – This sensor is used only on diesel engines. Disconnect RPMS electrical connector. Using DVOM, measure resistance across sensor terminals. Resistance should be 2400-2800 ohms. Replace sensor if not as specified. Faults in RPMS or sensor circuit should set a service code. See Quick Test procedure in SELF-DIAGNOSTICS – EEC-IV article. If no service code has been set, see CIRCUIT TEST DJ in SELF-DIAGNOSTICS – EEC-IV article for additional sensor testing and specifications.

Fuel Injection Pump Lever (FIPL) Sensor – This sensor may also be referred to as Throttle Position Sensor (TP Or TPS). Faults in FIPL sensor or circuit should set a service code. See Quick Test procedure in SELF-DIAGNOSTICS – EEC-IV article. If no service code has been set, see CIRCUIT TEST DQ in SELF-DIAGNOSTICS – EEC-IV article for additional sensor testing and specifications. Ensure none of the following conditions exist.

- Binding Throttle Or Speed Control Linkage
- Idle Speed And Throttle Stop Improperly Adjusted
- Choke/High Cam System Sticking

Heated Exhaust Gas Oxygen (HEGO) Sensor – Vehicle may be equipped with one or two HEGO sensors. They are located in the exhaust pipe upstream of the catalytic converters. Faults in sensor or circuit should set a service code. See Quick Test procedure in SELF-DIAGNOSTICS – EEC-IV article. If no service code has been set, see CIRCUIT TEST H in SELF-DIAGNOSTICS – EEC-IV article for additional sensor specifications and circuit testing procedures. Ensure that none of the following conditions exist.

- Moisture Inside Sensor/Harness Connector
- HEGO Sensor Coated With Contaminants
- Sensor Circuit Open Or Shorted To Ground

Inertia Switch – Ensure key is off. Inertia switches may be found in the following locations:

- On Aerostar & "E" Series, on right kick panel, just forward of door opening.
- On Bronco & "F" Series, on floorboard to left and above steering column.

- On Explorer, under instrument panel, to right of transmission hump.

Push down on reset button to ensure switch is closed. Measure resistance between terminals on switch. If resistance is 5 ohms or less, switch is okay. For additional circuit testing information refer to CIRCUIT TEST J in SELF-DIAGNOSTICS – EEC-IV article. If resistance is greater than 5 ohms, replace switch.

NOTE: In closed position, reset button can be depressed an additional 1/16" against spring. This is normal and does not affect switch operation.

Knock Sensor (KS) – The KS is located on cylinder block. Faults in sensor or circuit should set a service code. See Quick Test procedure in SELF-DIAGNOSTICS – EEC-IV article. If no service code has been set, see CIRCUIT TEST DG in SELF-DIAGNOSTICS – EEC-IV article for additional sensor specifications and circuit testing procedures. Sensor is tested by substitution or by manually generating a knock to ensure sensor will set a service code.

Manifold Absolute Pressure (MAP) Sensor – Sensor is located on engine or firewall and is connected to intake manifold by a vacuum supply hose. Remove vacuum supply hose to sensor. Install vacuum pump to sensor and apply 18 in. Hg vacuum. Sensor should hold vacuum. If sensor does not hold vacuum, replace sensor. Faults in MAP sensor or circuit should set a service code. See Quick Test procedure in SELF-DIAGNOSTICS – EEC-IV article. If no service code has been set, see CIRCUIT TEST DF in SELF-DIAGNOSTICS – EEC-IV article for additional sensor testing and specifications.

Mass Airflow (MAF) Sensor – Faults in MAF sensor or circuit should set a service code. See Quick Test procedure in SELF-DIAGNOSTICS – EEC-IV article. If no service code has been set, see CIRCUIT TEST DC in SELF-DIAGNOSTICS – EEC-IV article for sensor and circuit testing and specifications.

Neutral Drive Switch (NDS) A/C Input – With ignition switch in OFF position, set DVOM to 200-ohm scale. Locate NDS switch (on transmission) and clutch switch (on clutch pedal linkage). Disconnect harness at both switches. Measure resistance across NDS terminals with transmission in Neutral and across clutch switch terminals with clutch pedal fully depressed. If each resistance is greater than 5 ohms, switches are open. Replace switches. Faults in switches or switch circuits should set a service code. See Quick Test procedure in SELF-DIAGNOSTICS – EEC-IV article. If no service code has been set, see CIRCUIT TEST TA in SELF-DIAGNOSTICS – EEC-IV article for additional switch testing and specifications.

Power Steering Pressure Switch (PSPS) – **1)** Disconnect PSPS connector at steering gearbox. Set DVOM to 200-ohm scale and connect test leads to switch. With steering wheel centered, resistance should be less than 10 ohms. Start engine and turn steering wheel one-half turn and then return it to centered position.

2) Resistance should change from less than 10 ohms to infinity and return to less than 10 ohms when steering wheel is returned to centered position. Faulty PSPS or circuit should set a service code. See Quick Test procedure in SELF-DIAGNOSTICS – EEC-IV article. If no service code has been set, see CIRCUIT TEST FF in SELF-DIAGNOSTICS – EEC-IV article for additional switch testing and specifications.

Throttle Position Sensor (TP Or TPS) – Faults in TP sensor or circuit should set a service code. See Quick Test procedure in SELF-DIAGNOSTICS – EEC-IV article. If no service code has been set, see CIRCUIT TEST DH in SELF-DIAGNOSTICS – EEC-IV article for additional sensor testing and specifications. Ensure none of the following conditions exist.

- Binding Throttle Linkage
- TP Sensor Loose Or Not Seated Properly
- Throttle Plate Not Fully Closed

Vehicle Speed Sensor (VSS) – Disconnect VSS electrical connector. Using DVOM measure resistance across sensor terminals. Resistance should be 190-250 ohms. Replace sensor if not within specification. Faults in VSS sensor or circuit should set a service code. See Quick Test procedure in SELF-DIAGNOSTICS – EEC-IV article. If no service code has been set, see CIRCUIT TEST DP in SELF-DIAGNOSTICS – EEC-IV article for additional sensor testing and specifications.

MODULES, MOTORS, RELAYS & SOLENOIDS

RELAYS

Fuel Pump Relay – Remove relay from vehicle. Connect battery voltage to terminal "C". Ground terminal "D". *See Fig. 2.* Measure resistance between terminals "A" and "B". Resistance should be less than one ohm with power applied and greater than 10 k/ohms with power removed.

NOTE: For more fuel delivery system testing, see CIRCUIT TEST J in SELF-DIAGNOSTICS article.

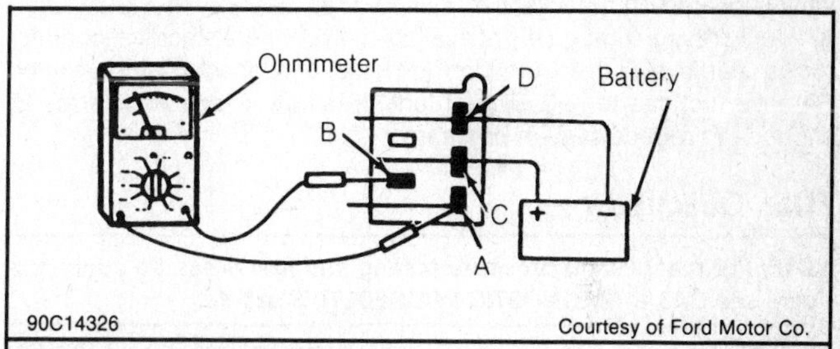
Ohmmeter
D
Battery
B
C
A
90C14326
Courtesy of Ford Motor Co.

Fig. 2: Testing Fuel Pump Relay

SOLENOIDS

Air Management Solenoids (AM1 & AM2) – Disconnect solenoid harness connectors, and measure resistance across terminals. Resistance should be 50-100 ohms. If resistance is not as specified, replace solenoid. Faults in AM1 or AM2 solenoids or circuits should set a service code. See Quick Test procedure in SELF-DIAGNOSTICS – EEC-IV article. If no service code has been set, see CIRCUIT TEST KC in SELF-DIAGNOSTICS – EEC-IV article for additional solenoid and circuit testing.

Canister Purge (CANP) Solenoid – See FUEL EVAPORATION under EMISSION SYSTEMS & SUB-SYSTEMS.

EGR Solenoid – See EXHAUST GAS RECIRCULATION under EMISSION SYSTEMS & SUB-SYSTEMS.

Idle Speed Control (ISC) Solenoid – **1)** Solenoid is by-pass air type solenoid. Ensure ignition is off. Disconnect ISC solenoid harness connector. Set DVOM to 200-ohm scale. Measure resistance between ISC solenoid terminals. *See Fig. 3.* There is a diode in solenoid, connect DVOM (+) test lead to VPWR terminal and DVOM (–) lead to ISC terminal.

2) Resistance should be 7-13 ohms. If resistance is not as specified, replace solenoid. Faults in ISC solenoid or circuit should set a service code. See Quick Test procedure in SELF-DIAGNOSTICS –EEC-IV article. If no service code has been set, see CIRCUIT TEST KE in SELF-DIAGNOSTICS – EEC-IV article for additional solenoid testing and specifications.

FUEL SYSTEM

NOTE: In testing procedures, references to KOEO refer to Key On Engine Off. References to KOER refer to Key On Engine Running.

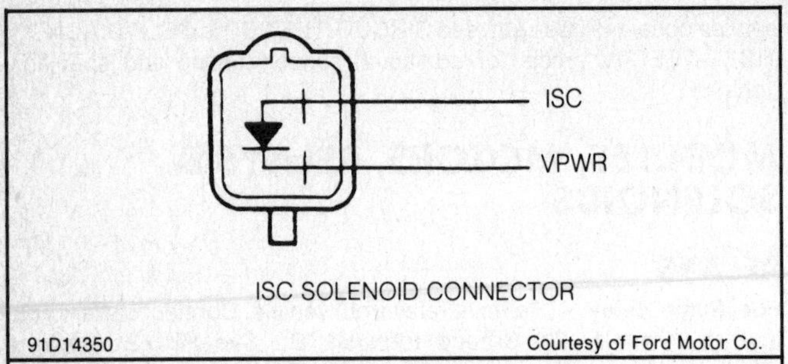
ISC
VPWR
ISC SOLENOID CONNECTOR
91D14350
Courtesy of Ford Motor Co.

Fig. 3: Identifying ISC Solenoid Connector

FUEL SYSTEM PRESSURE RELEASE

1) Remove fuel tank cap. Using Fuel Pressure Gauge (T80L-9974-B), release pressure from system at pressure relief valve (Schrader valve), located on fuel injection manifold rail.

2) If fuel pressure gauge is not available, disconnect electrical connector to inertia switch located on left side of luggage compartment. Remove fuel cap to release fuel tank pressure. Crank engine for 15 seconds to reduce system pressure.

FUEL DELIVERY

NOTE:* *For fuel system pressure testing and fuel pressure specifications, see BASIC DIAGNOSTIC PROCEDURES article.

Fuel Pump Relay – See MODULES, MOTORS, RELAYS & SOLENOIDS.

Fuel Pump Testing – **1)** Visually inspect entire fuel delivery system for leaks, damaged or kinked lines and hoses. Ensure battery is fully charged and fuses are okay. Ensure adequate fuel is available in fuel tank. Release fuel pressure. See FUEL SYSTEM PRESSURE RELEASE. Install fuel pressure gauge. With Key On Engine Off (KOEO) to activate pump, check and record fuel pressure. See appropriate FUEL PRESSURE SPECIFICATIONS table. Proceed to the appropriate step, as indicated:

- If fuel pressure is within specification, go to step **2)**.
- If fuel pressure is zero, go to step **5)**.
- If fuel pressure is low, go to step **11)**.
- If fuel pressure is high, go to step **12)**.

FUEL PRESSURE SPECIFICATIONS (GASOLINE) – psi (kg/cm²)

Engine	Pressure KOER	Pressure KOEO
4.9L	45-60 (3.16-4.22)	40-60 (3.52-4.22)
All Others	30-45 (2.11-3.16)	35-40 (2.46-2.81)

FUEL PRESSURE SPECIFICATIONS (DIESEL)

Application	psi (kg/cm²)
Filter Inlet	[1] 2 (.14)
Filter Outlet	[2] 1 (.07)
Return Line	[2] 2 (.14)

[1] – At idle.
[2] – At 3300 RPM.

2) Check fuel injectors. See FUEL INJECTORS. Crank or run vehicle. Using a mechanic's stethoscope, listen for regularly spaced operating sounds at each injector. If sound is present, check fuel injectors for flow and leakage. Clean or replace injectors as necessary.

3) If injector operating sound is not present, check fuel injector resistance. See FUEL INJECTORS. If injectors are not within specification, replace as necessary. If injectors are within specification, check injector electrical connections for continuity to ECA. If no continuity exists in circuit, check for 12 volts at each injector lead.

4) If voltage is not present at injectors, see Quick Test procedure in SELF-DIAGNOSTICS – EEC-IV article. Faults in injector circuit should set a service code. If no service code has been set, see CIRCUIT TEST H, in SELF-DIAGNOSTICS – EEC-IV article.

5) If fuel pressure is zero, ensure battery is fully charged and key is off. Ground fuel pump lead at SELF-TEST connector. Using a jumper lead, ground FP terminal. *See Fig. 4.* Ensure connection is okay at pump/sender unit. Turn key on, leaving engine off. Listen for sound of fuel pump. If pump is running, porceed to next step. If pump is not running, proceed to step **7)**.

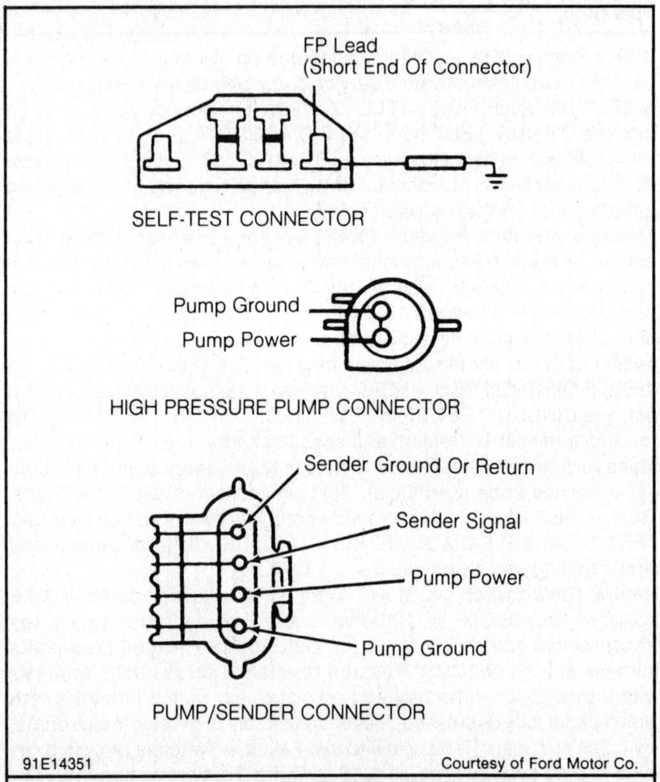
FP Lead
(Short End Of Connector)
SELF-TEST CONNECTOR
Pump Ground
Pump Power
HIGH PRESSURE PUMP CONNECTOR
Sender Ground Or Return
Sender Signal
Pump Power
Pump Ground
PUMP/SENDER CONNECTOR
91E14351
Courtesy of Ford Motor Co.

Fig. 4: Identifying Fuel Pump & Self-Test Connectors

6) Check condition of high-pressure fuel filter. If filter is free of contamination check fuel pressure regulator, go to step **12)**. If filter is contaminated, replace filter and recheck system pressure as outlined in step **1)**.

7) Turn key off and disconnect fuel pump/sender or high pressure pump connector. Set DVOM on 200-ohm scale. Measure resistance between pump ground at connector and chassis ground. If resistance is one ohm or more, repair open circuit to ground. If resistance is less than one ohm, go to next step.

8) Ensure key is off and battery is fully charged. Disconnect harness connector from pump/sender unit. Ground FP terminal at SELF-TEST connector. With KOEO and DVOM on 20-volt scale, measure voltage at Pump Power terminal of pump/sender or high pressure pump connector. If voltage is 10.5 volts or more, replace pump/sender assembly. If voltage is not as specified, go to next step.

9) With KOEO, check voltage at fuel pump inertia switch. If voltage is 10.5 volts or more at both inertia switch terminals, repair wire between inertia switch and pump. If voltage is not as specified, reset or replace inertia switch as necessary and go to next step.

10) Ensure key is off and battery is fully charged. Ground FP terminal at SELF-TEST connector. With KOEO and DVOM on 20-volt scale, measure voltage at fuel pump relay (Brown wire). If voltage is 10.5 volts or more at relay, repair Brown wire between fuel pump relay and inertia switch. If voltage is not as specified, check voltage supply to fuel pump relay and to terminal No. 1 at ECA. For additional circuit testing information see CIRCUIT TEST J in SELF-DIAGNOSTICS EEC-IV article.

11) Ground FP terminal at SELF-TEST connector. Using a DVOM, check voltage at fuel pump terminal (Pink/Black wire). If voltage at fuel pump is within .5 volt of battery voltage, go to step **6)**. If voltage is not as specified, go to step **5)**.

12) Check engine compartment for leaks and ensure engine produces normal engine vacuum. See FUEL PRESSURE REGULATOR test procedure.

CAUTION: Inspect fuel system for leaks or damage before testing fuel pump.

Fuel Pressure Regulator – 1) Ensure key is off. Connect fuel pressure gauge to Schrader valve on fuel rail. Ensure manifold vacuum supply tube is connected to fuel pressure regulator. Start and run engine for 10 seconds. Stop engine and wait 10 seconds. Start and operate engine for 10 seconds. Stop engine and remove pressure regulator vacuum hose. *See Fig. 5.* Check vacuum port for fuel.

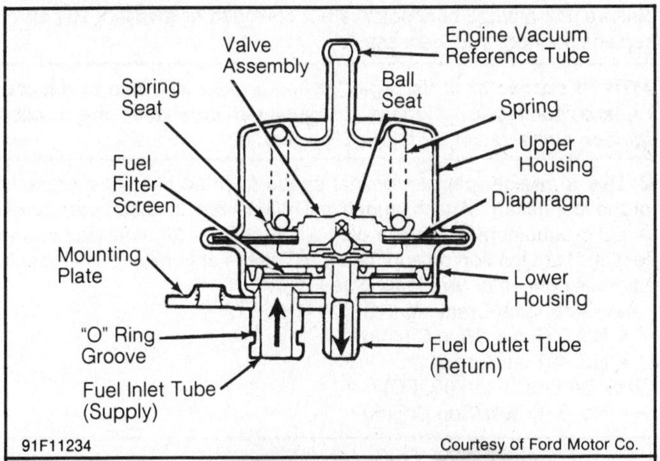
Valve Assembly
Engine Vacuum Reference Tube
Spring Seat
Ball Seat
Spring
Upper Housing
Fuel Filter Screen
Diaphragm
Mounting Plate
Lower Housing
"O" Ring Groove
Fuel Outlet Tube (Return)
Fuel Inlet Tube (Supply)
91F11234
Courtesy of Ford Motor Co.

Fig. 5: Identifying Fuel Pressure Regulator Components

2) If fuel is present, replace fuel pressure regulator and repeat test. If fuel is not present, start and run engine for 30 seconds. Stop engine and check fuel pressure gauge. If fuel pressure does not drop, go to step **4)**. If fuel pressure drops more than 5 psi (.4 kg/cm²) in 60 seconds, disconnect and plug fuel return line at engine. Cycle ignition key on and off until normal fuel pressure is obtained.

3) Turn key off and check fuel pressure gauge. If gauge drops more than 5 psi (.4 kg/cm²) in 30 seconds, replace high pressure fuel pump (dual pump system) or fuel sender/pump assembly (single pump type). If gauge does not drop more than 5 psi (.4 kg/cm²) in 30 seconds, replace fuel pressure regulator.

4) Ensure key is off. Relieve fuel pressure. Remove fuel pressure regulator. Check "O" ring, gasket and mounting surfaces for cracks, cuts or other damage. Connect vacuum pump to fuel return tube and apply 20 in. Hg. If maximum vacuum loss exceeds 10 in. Hg in 10 seconds, replace regulator. If maximum vacuum loss does not exceed 10 in. Hg in 10 seconds, recheck entire fuel delivery system for cause of fuel pressure loss.

Fuel Selector Valve (Diesel) – Remove fuel selector valve. Perform checks as indicated in fuel selector valve specification table. *See Fig. 6.* Replace selector valve if operation is not correct.

Fuel Selector Valve (Gasoline) – Fuel selector valve is mechanically operated and uses in-tank pump pressure to control fuel supply and return. Front or rear tank indication is controlled by the selector switch.

FUEL CONTROL

Fuel Injectors – 1) Connect tachometer to engine. Run engine at idle. Disconnect and reconnect injectors individually. If each injector causes a momentary drop in engine speed of at least 100 RPM, injectors are giving proper fuel delivery. RPM drop should only be momentary as ISC will attempt to re-establish correct idle RPM.

2) Replace any injectors that do not cause sufficient drop in engine speed. When test is complete and all injectors cause equal drop in speed, shut off engine. In order to check curb idle, refer to emission control specifications on decal in engine compartment.

Injector Circuit – 1) Disconnect all injector harness connectors. Using digital ohmmeter, check resistance across terminals of each injector. See appropriate injector resistance table.

2) Disconnect injector bank harness connector, and check resistance of injector bank. See INJECTOR BANK RESISTANCE table. Repair wiring or replace any injector circuit not within specification.

INDIVIDUAL INJECTOR RESISTANCE

Engine	Ohms
2.3L & 3.0L	15.0-18.0
All Others	13.0-16.0

INJECTOR BANK RESISTANCE

Engine	Ohms
2.3L	7.0-9.5
2.9L, 3.0L & 4.9L	5.0-6.5
5.0L, 5.8L & 7.5L	3.0-4.0

IDLE CONTROL SYSTEM

NOTE: See IDLE SPEED CONTROL (ISC) SOLENOID test procedures under SOLENOIDS. Curb idle and fast idle speed are controlled by ECA and are not adjustable. Some throttle bodies have a sludge-tolerant design with a special coated throttle bore. A Yellow/Black warning decal on these units warns against backing off throttle plate adjustment screw to avoid throttle plate sticking in bore. Faults in idle control system components or circuit should set a service code. See Quick Test procedure in SELF-DIAGNOSTICS – EEC-IV article.

Valve Position	Selector Valve Elec. Table					Fuel Flow		
	Apply Voltage At Pins		Measure Resistance On Pins			Check Flow of Ports		
	1	2	3	4	5	Front Port	Pump Port	Rear Port
Front	(–)	(+)	Less than 1.0 OHM		Open	Connected		Blocked
Rear	(+)	(–)	Open	Less Than 1.0 Ohm		Blocked	Connected	

90D09356 Courtesy of Ford Motor Co.

Fig. 6: Fuel Selector Valve Specification Table

IGNITION SYSTEMS

NOTE: For additional information and descriptions see IGNITION SYSTEMS in THEORY & OPERATION article. Perform spark output check in BASIC DIAGNOSTIC PROCEDURES article before entering these tests. Some ignition systems require that Quick Test procedure be performed prior to testing. This will retrieve trouble codes from the EEC-IV system. See SELF-DIAGNOSTICS - EEC-IV article.

IGNITION SYSTEM ACRONYMS [1]

Acronym	Definition
BAT+ or BAT (+)	Battery Positive
BAT- or BAT (-)	Battery Negative
BOB	Breakout Box
CBD	Closed Bowl Distributor (TFI-IV)
CCD	Computer Controlled Dwell (TFI-IV)
CID	Cylinder Identification
C1, C2, C3	Coil Drive (Coils 1, 2 & 3)
DIS	Distributorless Ignition System
ECA	Electronic Control Assembly (EEC-Processor, Computer, Processor)
EDIS	Electronic Distributorless Ignition System
DPI	Dual Plug Inhibit (High Signal - Right Plugs Fire, Low Signal - Both Sides Fire)
IDM	Ignition Diagnostic Monitor (Diagnostic Signal to ECA)
IGGND	Ignition Ground (Low Current Ground Reference)
KOEC	Key On Engine Cranking (Testing Condition)
KOEO	Key On Engine Off (Testing Condition)
KOER	Key On Engine Running (Testing Condition)
PIP	Profile Ignition Pickup (Crankshaft Sensor Signal)
PWR GND	Power Ground Circuit to DIS Module
SAW	Spark Angle Word
SPOUT	Spark Output (ECA Spark Control Signal)
TFI or TFI-IV	Thick Film Ignition (IV is 4th Generation)
VPWR or VBAT	Battery Power or Battery Voltage
VRS or VR Sensor	Variable Reluctance Sensor (Crankshaft)

[1] - Not all circuits and components are used in all systems.

IGNITION SYSTEM IDENTIFICATION

Application	System
2.3L Ranger	DIS
2.9L Ranger	TFI-IV
3.0L Aerostar & Ranger	TFI-IV
4.0L Aerostar, Explorer & Ranger	EDIS
4.9L Bronco, "E" & "F" Series	TFI-IV
5.0L Bronco, "E" & "F" Series	TFI-IV
5.8L Bronco, "E" & "F" Series	TFI-IV
7.5L "E" & "F" Series	[1] TFI-IV

[1] - Closed Bowl Distributor (CBD)

TFI-IV SYSTEM

NOTE: Before testing components and circuits of this system, ensure system is identified as to location of TFI module (distributor mounted or CBD type). Additional system and circuit testing for this system is located in appropriate CIRCUIT TESTS in SELF-DIAGNOSTICS -EEC-IV article.

Preliminary Check - Ensure the following preliminary checks have been performed:

- Visually inspect engine compartment to ensure all vacuum hoses and spark plug wires are properly routed and securely connected.
- Examine all wiring harnesses and connectors for damage.
- Ensure TFI module is securely fastened to distributor base or cowl.
- Ensure battery is fully charged.
- Turn all accessories off during diagnosis.

Test Equipment - The following test equipment should be used in TFI-IV ignition system tests.

- Spark Tester (D81P-6666-A)
- Volt-Ohmmeter
- 12-Volt Test Light
- Small Straight Pin
- Remote Starter Switch
- E-Core Ignition Coil (E73F-12029-AB)
- Ignition Coil Secondary Wire

Diagnostic Aids - The following information should be noted during testing:

- A spark plug with a broken side electrode is NOT sufficient to check for spark and may lead to incorrect results.
- When instructed to inspect a wiring harness, both a visual inspection and a continuity test should be performed.
- When making measurements on a wiring harness or connector, perform a WIGGLE test while measuring.
- References to SPOUT in-line connector apply to both in-line and shorting-bar type connectors.
- Test procedures are intended to identify faulty components or wiring while fault is present. If complaint is an intermittent condition, refer to TROUBLE SHOOTING - NO CODES article.

Primary Circuit Test (Except Closed Bowl Distributor) - 1) Disconnect terminal "S" at starter relay to allow testing of ignition primary circuit without cranking motor. Ensure ignition is off. Push down on connector tab and disconnect harness connector from TFI module. Ensure TFI module connector is not corroded or swollen. Repair or replace connector as necessary.

NOTE: If connector is damaged or has broken tabs due to misuse, replace connector. A loose or damaged connector may cause ignition signal faults during KOER operation.

2) Use a straight pin or terminal spade from an old TFI module to probe connector. Attach negative DVOM lead to distributor base. Avoid ground contact with straight pin or positive terminal lead during testing. Turn ignition on and measure voltage at following TFI module harness connector terminals: *See Fig. 7.*

Key On Engine Cranking (KOEC)

- No. 3 (Power/Run Circuit)
- No. 4 (Start Circuit)

Key On Engine Off (KOEO)

- No. 3 (Power/Run Circuit)

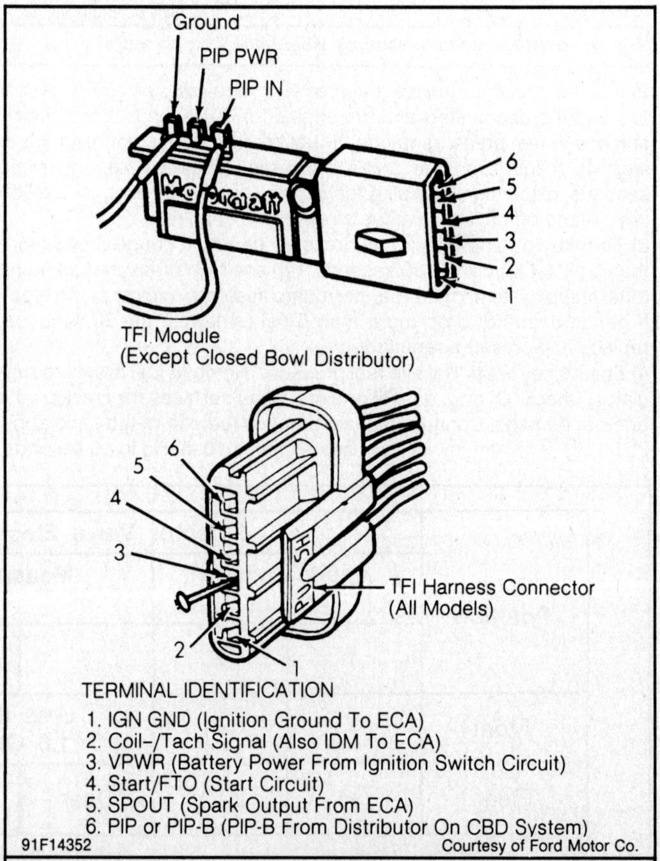
Ground
PIP PWR
PIP IN
6
5
4
3
2
1
TFI Module
(Except Closed Bowl Distributor)
6
5
4
3
2
1
TFI Harness Connector
(All Models)
TERMINAL IDENTIFICATION
1. IGN GND (Ignition Ground To ECA)
2. Coil-/Tach Signal (Also IDM To ECA)
3. VPWR (Battery Power From Ignition Switch Circuit)
4. Start/FTO (Start Circuit)
5. SPOUT (Spark Output From ECA)
6. PIP or PIP-B (PIP-B From Distributor On CBD System)
91F14352
Courtesy of Ford Motor Co.

Fig. 7: Identifying TFI-IV Ignition Module & Connector Terminals

3) Turn ignition off and remove test pin. Reconnect wire to "S" terminal on relay. If approximately 90% of Battery Voltage (VBAT) is not present at these terminals, repair open circuits in wiring harness as necessary. Check ignition switch for faults. See appropriate wiring diagram. If voltage was as specified, reconnect module and go to next step.

4) Attach a 12-volt test light between ground and coil negative (-)/tach terminal No. 2 at TFI module. Turn ignition on, and crank engine. If test light flashes brightly during cranking, go to appropriate PIP SENSOR/ STATOR TEST. If test light stays on during cranking, check for open in coil negative circuit between coil and TFI module connector. Repair circuit as necessary. If no open circuits are found, ignition module is shorted internally. Replace TFI module and retest.

5) If test light is always dim or off during cranking, check voltage to coil positive (+) terminal. If voltage is not present with key on or during cranking, repair open in primary circuit between battery and coil positive (+). If light flashes intermittently, check ignition module resistance. If voltage is available at coil, go to COIL TEST and check ignition coil.

Primary Circuit Test (Closed Bowl Distributor) – 1) Disconnect terminal "S" at starter relay to allow testing of ignition primary circuit without cranking motor. Ensure ignition is off. Push down on connector tab and disconnect harness connector from TFI module. Ensure TFI module connector is not corroded or swollen. Repair or replace connector as necessary.

NOTE: If connector is damaged or has broken tabs due to misuse, replace connector. A loose or damaged connector may cause ignition signal faults during KOER operation.

2) Use a straight pin or terminal spade from an old TFI module to probe connector. Avoid ground contact, between straight pin and ground, during testing. Using a DVOM, turn ignition on and measure voltage at following vehicle harness connector terminals of the cowl mounted TFI module: *See Fig. 7.*

Key On Engine Cranking (KOEC)
- No. 3 (Power/Run Circuit)
- No. 4 (Start Circuit)

Key On Engine Off (KOEO)
- No. 3 (Power/Run Circuit)

If approximate Battery Voltage (VBAT) is not present at these terminals, repair open circuits in wiring harness as necessary. See appropriate wiring diagram in WIRING DIAGRAMS article in ENGINE PERFORMANCE.

3) If battery voltage is as specified, check module ground circuit. With TFI module disconnected and KOEO, measure voltage at terminal No. 6. If voltage is greater than .5 volt, ground circuit has high resistance or is open. Repair as necessary.

4) Ensure ignition is off. Disconnect distributor connector. Turn ignition on. With DVOM set on DC voltage scale, connect positive (+) lead to terminal No. 8 (terminal No. 4 on 3.0L Aerostar and Ranger). Connect negative (-) lead to distributor or engine ground. *See Fig. 8.*

5) Cycle ignition switch between ON and START positions. Battery voltage should be present in both positions. If not, service or repair circuit as necessary. If okay, go to next step.

6) Use a DVOM to check ignition ground circuits continuity. Measure resistance between distributor base and terminals No. 2 and No. 6 at distributor connector (terminal No. 3 on 3.0L Aerostar and Ranger). If resistance at each terminal is less than 3 ohms, circuit is okay. If resistance is 3 ohms or more, repair ground circuit as necessary. *See Fig. 9.*

TFI Module Resistance Test – 1) Remove TFI module from distributor or disconnect cowl. Measure resistance of TFI module circuits. See TFI MODULE RESISTANCE table. *See Figs. 7-9.*

2) If resistance is as specified, suspect faulty PIP sensor/stator. If resistance is NOT as specified, replace TFI-IV module.

TFI MODULE RESISTANCE

Between Terminals	Ohms
GND & PIP IN	Greater Than 500
PIP PWR & PIP IN	Less Than 2000
PIP PWR & TFI PWR	Less Than 200
GND & IGN GND	Less Than 2
PIP IN & PIP	Less Than 200

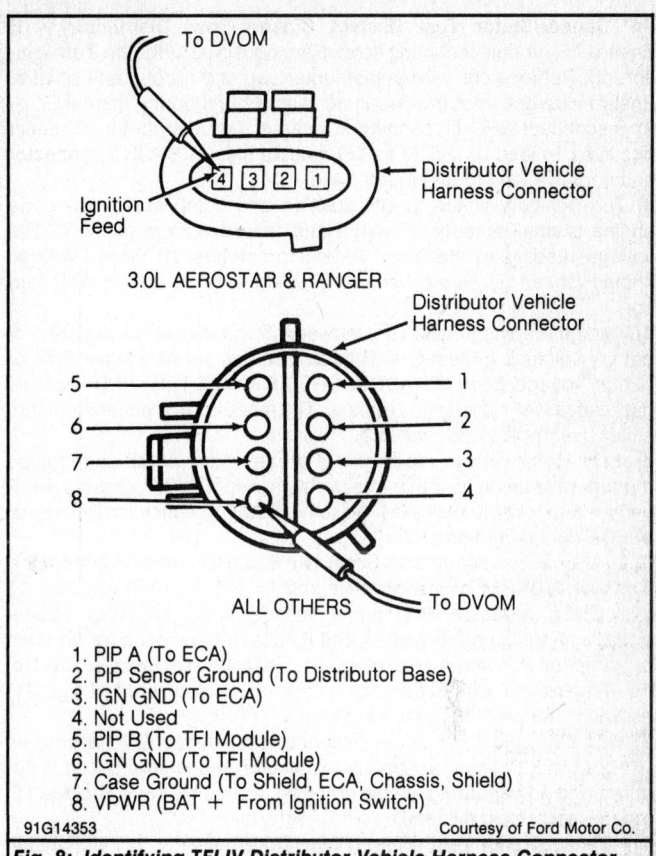

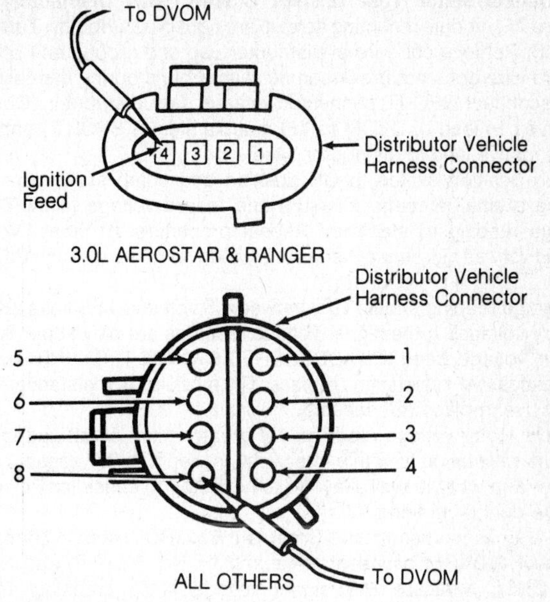

To DVOM
Ignition Feed
4 3 2 1
Distributor Vehicle Harness Connector
3.0L AEROSTAR & RANGER
Distributor Vehicle Harness Connector
5 6 7 8
1 2 3 4
ALL OTHERS
To DVOM
1. PIP A (To ECA)
2. PIP Sensor Ground (To Distributor Base)
3. IGN GND (To ECA)
4. Not Used
5. PIP B (To TFI Module)
6. IGN GND (To TFI Module)
7. Case Ground (To Shield, ECA, Chassis, Shield)
8. VPWR (BAT + From Ignition Switch)

91G14353 Courtesy of Ford Motor Co.

Fig. 8: Identifying TFI-IV Distributor Vehicle Harness Connector

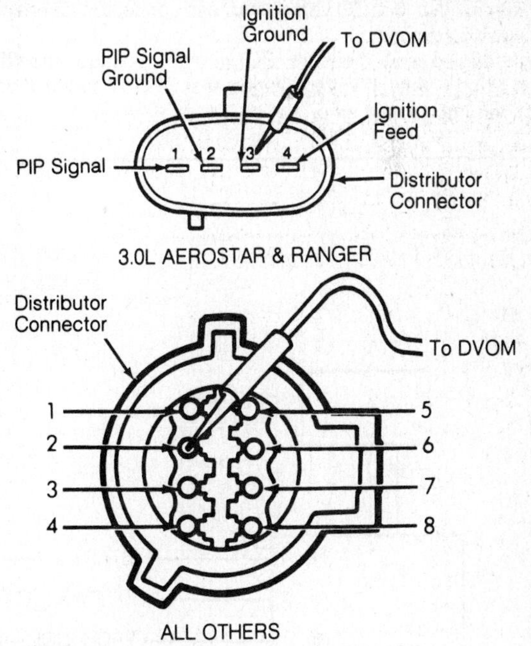

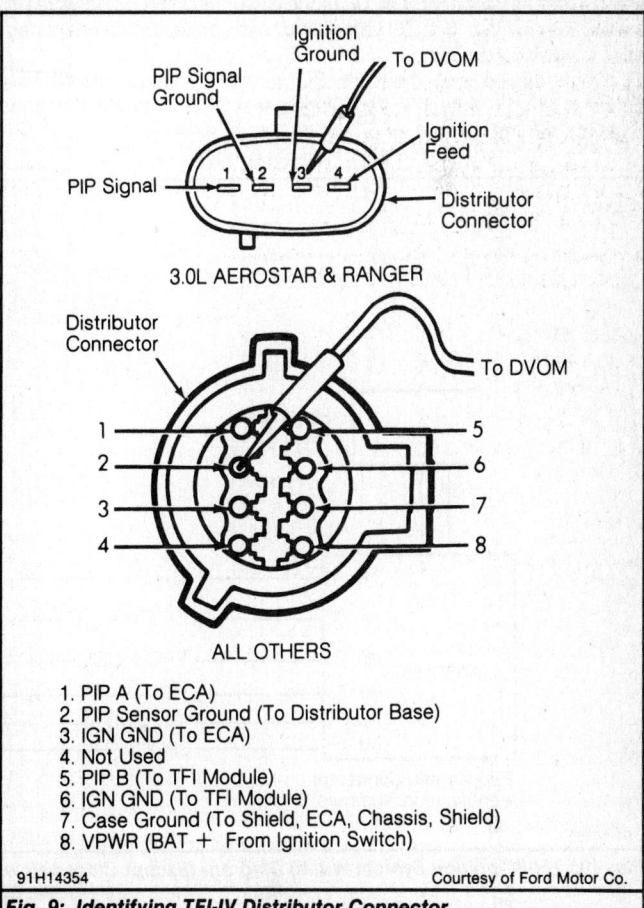

Ignition Ground
To DVOM
PIP Signal Ground
Ignition Feed
PIP Signal
1 2 3 4
Distributor Connector
3.0L AEROSTAR & RANGER
Distributor Connector
To DVOM
1 2 3 4
5 6 7 8
ALL OTHERS
1. PIP A (To ECA)
2. PIP Sensor Ground (To Distributor Base)
3. IGN GND (To ECA)
4. Not Used
5. PIP B (To TFI Module)
6. IGN GND (To TFI Module)
7. Case Ground (To Shield, ECA, Chassis, Shield)
8. VPWR (BAT + From Ignition Switch)

91H14354 Courtesy of Ford Motor Co.

Fig. 9: Identifying TFI-IV Distributor Connector

1991 ENGINE PERFORMANCE
System & Component Testing – EEC-IV (Cont.)

PIP Sensor/Stator Test (Except Closed Bowl Distributor) – 1) Ensure TFI module mounting screws are tight on distributor. Turn ignition off. Remove coil wire at distributor cap and ground end of wire. Ensure wire does not break contact with ground during this test.

2) Disconnect SPOUT connector located near distributor. Connect positive (+) lead of DVOM to TFI module side of SPOUT connector and negative lead to distributor base.

3) Turn ignition switch to ON position and bump starter to rotate engine a small amount. Measure and record voltage (allow DVOM voltage reading to stabilize). Repeat procedure 10 times. Voltage should vary as hall sensor vanes and windows rotate through PIP sensor.

4) Voltage reading should vary between .5 volt and 11.5 volts (90% of battery voltage). If the higher voltage readings are only about 70% of battery voltage, go to TFI MODULE RESISTANCE TEST. If TFI module has excessive resistance, replace TFI module. If resistance is not excessive, replace PIP sensor.

5) If the lower voltage readings are greater than .5 volt and ignition module resistance is within specification, replace PIP sensor. If PIP sensor and module test okay, go to next step to check for PIP signal at ECA during cranking.

6) Turn ignition off and install Break Out Box (BOB) at ECA connector. Connect a DVOM between test terminals No. 56 (PIP) and No. 16 (IGN GND). Measure PIP signal voltage while cranking engine. Voltage should vary between 4 and 6 volts. If not, check for an open or grounded PIP circuit or an open IGN GND circuit at test terminal No. 16. Repair circuits as necessary. If circuits are okay, but PIP signal is erratic or not present, go to next step.

7) With ECA and TFI module disconnected, connect DVOM positive (+) lead to PIP circuit at harness connector and ensure circuit is not shorted to power during engine cranking. If circuit is okay, replace TFI module and retest system.

PIP Sensor/Stator Test (Closed Bowl Distributor) – 1) With ignition off, ensure distributor is connected to vehicle harness. Disconnect vehicle harness connector at TFI module. Connect DVOM positive (+) lead to terminal No. 6 at TFI vehicle harness connector. Connect negative (-) lead to ground.

2) Crank engine and measure DC voltage. Voltage should vary between 4 and 6 volts. If voltage varies, test SPOUT circuit. If voltage does not vary go to next step.

3) With ignition off, disconnect distributor connector. Using DVOM, measure resistance between terminals No. 1 and No. 5 at distributor connector. If resistance is 200 ohms or more, replace faulty PIP sensor.

4) Disconnect vehicle harness connector at TFI module. Measure resistance between terminal No. 6 (PIP) at TFI module vehicle harness connector and terminal No. 5 (PIP to TFI Module) at distributor vehicle harness connector. If resistance is 5 ohms or more, repair open in circuit and retest. Check circuit for short to ground. Test circuit for short to power with KOEO. Service or replace wiring as necessary.

5) Disconnect ECA connector and measure resistance between terminal No. 56 (PIP) at ECA 60-pin connector and terminal No. 5 (PIP to ECA Module) at distributor vehicle harness connector. If resistance is 5 ohms or more, repair open in circuit and retest. Check circuit for short to ground. Test circuit for short to power with KOEO. Service or replace wiring as necessary.

6) Measure resistance between distributor connector terminal No. 2 (PIP SIG GND) and ground. Measure resistance between IGN GND, distributor connector terminal No. 6 (terminal No. 3 on 3.0L Aerostar or Ranger) and ground. If resistance is less than one ohm in both cases, ground circuit is okay. If resistance is one ohm or more in both cases, check PIP sensor mounting screws in distributor base for corrosion and tightness.

Coil Test – 1) Attach negative (-) VOM lead to distributor base and measure battery voltage. Turn ignition switch to RUN position. Measure voltage at coil positive (+) terminal of ignition coil and turn ignition off. Voltage should be 10.5-12 volts. If voltage is as specified, go to next step. If voltage is not as specified, repair ignition switch or wiring circuit to coil. See appropriate wiring diagram in WIRING DIAGRAMS article in ENGINE PERFORMANCE.

2) Ensure ignition is off. Disconnect coil primary connector and inspect both contacts for corrosion or damage. Service or replace as necessary. Using a DVOM, measure primary circuit resistance. If resistance is not .3-1.0 ohm at 70°F, replace coil and retest system.

3) Remove secondary coil wire from coil tower and inspect contact for signs of arcing or corrosion. Using a DVOM, measure resistance between coil tower connector and coil negative (-) terminal. If resistance is not 8000-11,500 ohms, replace coil.

Spark Timing Advance Test – 1) This procedure is applicable to all TFI-IV equipped vehicles. Spark advance is controlled by ECA. This

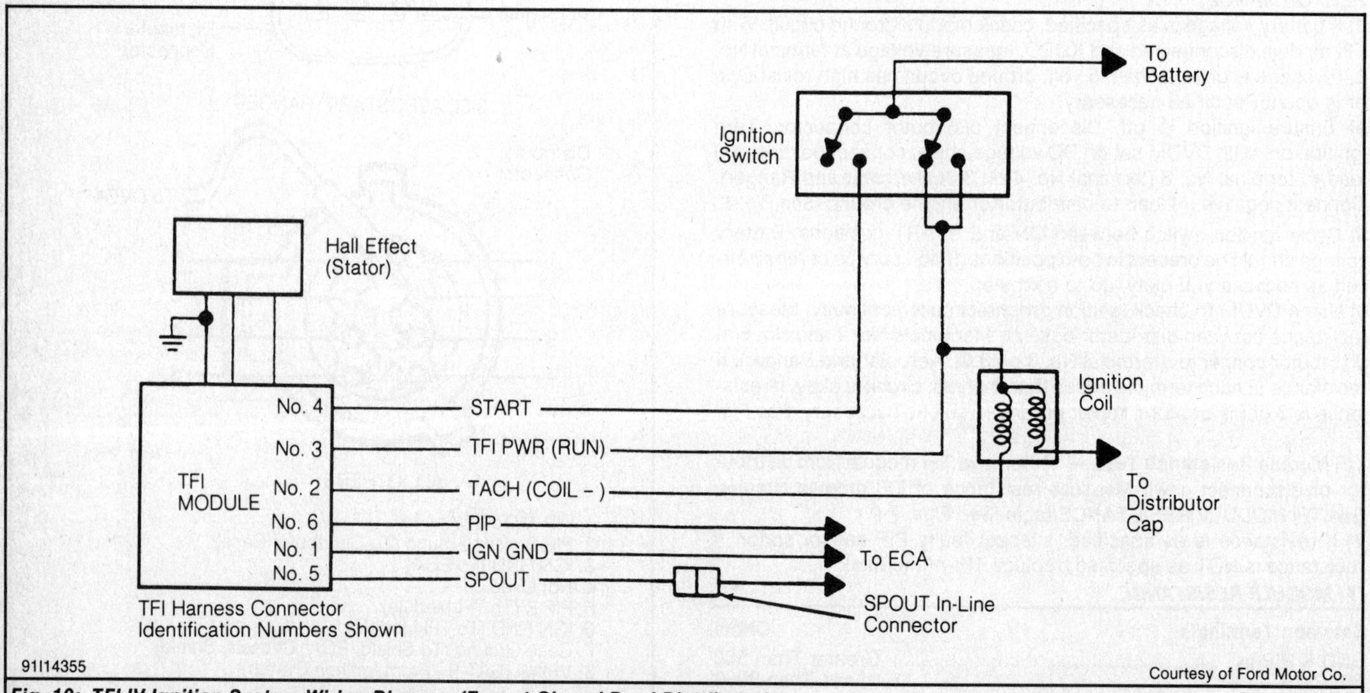
To
Battery
Ignition
Switch
Hall Effect
(Stator)
Ignition
Coil
No. 4
START
No. 3
TFI PWR (RUN)
TFI
MODULE
No. 2
TACH (COIL -)
No. 6
PIP
No. 1
IGN GND
No. 5
SPOUT
To
Distributor
Cap
To ECA
SPOUT In-Line
Connector
TFI Harness Connector
Identification Numbers Shown
91I14355
Courtesy of Ford Motor Co.

Fig. 10: TFI-IV Ignition System Wiring Diagram (Except Closed Bowl Distributor)

procedure checks the capability of ignition module to receive spark timing commands from ECA on the SPOUT circuit. A varying voltage signal is necessary on SPOUT circuit for ECA to transmit data. A KOER Code 18 or Code 213 may be set when SPOUT circuit is open or shorted. For additional information on TFI ignition systems see THEORY & OPERATION article.

2) Check SPOUT circuit voltage at TFI module. Ensure ignition switch is in OFF position. Disconnect SPOUT in-line connector near TFI module. If connector is SHORTING BAR type, remove SHORTING BAR.

3) Attach negative (-) voltmeter lead to distributor base and positive (+) lead to TFI module side of the SPOUT connector. Start engine and measure voltage at idle. Measure voltage at ECA side of SPOUT connector.

4) Voltage readings should be 4-8 volts. If voltage on TFI module side is okay, TFI module is okay. This voltage signal is necessary for TFI module to receive ECA SPOUT signal. If voltage signal from ECA to SPOUT connector is as specified, circuit from ECA to SPOUT connector is okay. If either voltage signal is not as specified, go to next test. If both voltage signals are as specified, check ignition timing advance.

5) Check SPOUT circuit continuity. Push TFI module connector tab to release connector. Separate wiring harness connector from ignition module. Inspect for dirt, corrosion and damage.

6) Using a small straight pin inserted into harness connector terminal No. 5, measure resistance between terminal and TFI module side of SPOUT connector. Resistance should be less than 5 ohms. If resistance is 5 ohms or more, repair wiring as necessary.

7) Measure resistance between ECA side of SPOUT connector and pin No. 36 at ECA connector. If resistance is less than 5 ohms, go to next step. If resistance is 5 ohms or more, repair wiring between SPOUT connector and ECA.

8) Check Ignition Timing Advance. With SPOUT connector disconnected, run engine at idle and ensure timing is at base timing adjustment. See ON-VEHICLE ADJUSTMENTS article. Stop engine.

9) Connect SPOUT connector and start engine. Timing should advance from base timing specification. Increase engine RPM and ensure timing advances. If time does not advance, check TFI module. If module is okay, replace ECA.

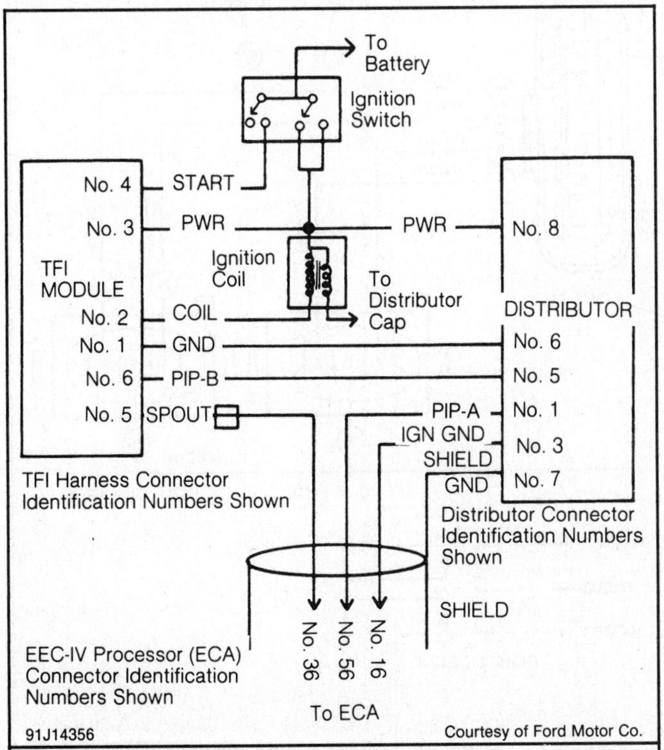

To Battery
Ignition Switch
No. 4
START
No. 3
PWR
PWR
No. 8
TFI MODULE
Ignition Coil
To Distributor Cap
No. 2
COIL
DISTRIBUTOR
No. 1
GND
No. 6
No. 6
PIP-B
No. 5
No. 5
SPOUT
PIP-A
No. 1
IGN GND
No. 3
SHIELD
GND
No. 7
TFI Harness Connector Identification Numbers Shown
Distributor Connector Identification Numbers Shown
SHIELD
No. 36
No. 56
No. 16
EEC-IV Processor (ECA) Connector Identification Numbers Shown
To ECA
91J14356
Courtesy of Ford Motor Co.

Fig. 11: TFI-IV Ignition System Wiring Diagram (Closed Bowl Distributor)

DIS SYSTEM (2.3L RANGER)

NOTE: Start all diagnostics with EEC-IV Quick Test. See SELF-DIAGNOSTICS – EEC-IV article. These tests are dependent on results and service codes received during Quick Test procedures.

CAUTION: DO NOT connect ECA to DIS diagnostic cable. The 60-pin connector on this harness may be connected to an additional Breakout Box (BOB) only. If ECA is connected to DIS diagnostic cable, it may be damaged.

Preliminary Check – Ensure the following preliminary checks have been performed:

- Visually inspect engine compartment to ensure all vacuum hoses and spark plug wires are properly and securely connected.
- Check all wiring harnesses and connectors for damaged insulation, burned, overheating, damaged pins, loose or broken conditions. Check sensor shield connector. Ensure DIS module mounting screws are tight.
- Ensure battery is fully charged.
- Turn all accessories off during diagnosis.

Test Equipment – The following test equipment is necessary to complete DIS ignition system tests.

- DIS Diagnostic Cable (Rotunda 007-00044)
- Spark Tester (Neon Bulb Type)
- Digital Volt-Ohmmeter (DVOM)
- Remote Starter Switch
- Breakout Box (BOB) With 2.3L DP DIS Overlay
- High Voltage Spark Tester (A spark plug with a broken side electrode is not sufficient to check for spark and may lead to incorrect results.)
- Tachometer
- Inductive Type Timing Light (DO NOT use "advance knob", if equipped, as it will not work correctly with DIS Ignition Systems.)
- Test Light (LED Type) Or Logic Probe (LED Type)

CAUTION: A 12-volt incandescent (high voltage) test light SHOULD NOT be used to test CID or PIP circuit signals. It will load the circuit and may cause incorrect measurements or faulty DIS/ECA operations (engine stall).

Diagnostic Aids – PINPOINT TESTS A through F are intended to diagnose hard faults. Intermittent failures may be difficult to diagnose using these procedures.

A Breakout Box (BOB) connected to DIS diagnostic cable is referred to as DIS BOB. If a second BOB is connected to the ECA vehicle harness connector it is referred to as ECA BOB. This test setup allows testing of DIS components and vehicle harness circuits.

Circuits are identified in all capitals, example: IGND = Ignition Ground. Manufacturers BOB overlay identification is in brackets, example: (J2) = IGND (J2). This indicates test terminal number or circuit identification number.

NOTE: Unless specified otherwise in a specific test step, all voltage and resistance tests of DIS ignition system are performed at the BOB connected to the DIS diagnostic cable.

NOTE: When performing PINPOINT TEST procedures for the 2.3L DIS (Ranger) system, refer to Figs. 12 and 13.

2.3L RANGER DIS PINPOINT TEST INDEX

Application	Pinpoint Test & Step
No Start & No Ignition Service Codes Present	A1
No Start & Code 211 (PIP Circuit Fault)	A1
Hard Start Or No Start With Erratic Cranking	B1
Normal Start & Code 222 (Loss Of IDM, Right Side)	B1
Code 218 (Loss Of IDM, Left Side)	C1
Code 224 (Erratic IDM)	D1
Code 223 (Loss Of Dual Plug Input)	E1
Code 213 (SPOUT Open)	F1
Lack Of Power Complaint	F1

1991 ENGINE PERFORMANCE
System & Component Testing - EEC-IV (Cont.)

PINPOINT TEST A - 1) Perform EEC-IV Quick Test - See SELF-DIAGNOSTICS - EEC-IV article. If service codes are not present, go to step **2)**. If service codes (KOEO, KOER or Continuous Memory Codes) are present, service the codes first. If vehicle still will not start, go to step **2)**.

2) Check For Spark During Cranking - Using a Neon Bulb Spark Tester (D89P6666-A), check for spark at each right side spark plug wire while cranking. If spark is consistent on all right side plug wires (one spark per crank revolution), go to step **3)**. If spark is not consistent, go to step **8)**.

3) Check PIP Circuit At DIS Module When Cranking - Connect DIS diagnostic cable to BOB (DIS BOB). Use 2.3L DP DIS overlay. Connect LED test light positive lead to BOB PIP EEC (J31) and negative lead to BOB BAT - (J60). Crank engine. If LED test light blinks continuously during cranking, go to step **4)**. If LED test light does not blink continuously during cranking, replace DIS module. There is no PIP output. Remove all test equipment. Reconnect all components. Clear Continuous Memory Codes and rerun Quick Test.

4) Check PIP Circuit To ECA Continuity With Key Off - Ensure key is off. Disconnect vehicle harness from ECA. Set DVOM on 200-ohm scale. Measure resistance between PIP EEC (J31) at DIS BOB and vehicle harness connector pin PIP (No. 56). If resistance is less than 5 ohms, go to CIRCUIT TEST A in SELF-DIAGNOSTICS article. If resistance is 5 ohms or more, PIP circuit is open, repair harness or connectors as necessary. Remove all test equipment. Reconnect all components. Clear Continuous Memory Codes and rerun Quick Test.

5) Spark Fault, Determine Missing Spark Combination - As a result of an inconsistent spark test in step No. **2)**, determine if spark is missing from cylinders No. 1 and 4 or from cylinders No. 2 and 3. If spark is missing from either pair of cylinders, go to step **7)**. If spark is not missing from a pair of cylinders, go to step **6)**.

6) Spark Fault, Check Plugs & Wires - Ensure key is off. Check plug wires for insulation damage, looseness, shorting or other damage. Remove plugs and check for damage, wear, carbon deposits and proper plug gap. If plugs and wires are okay, reinstall an go to step **7)**. If plugs and wires are not okay, service or replace defective plugs or wires as necessary. Remove all test equipment. Reconnect all components. Clear Continuous Memory Codes and rerun Quick Test.

7) Spark Fault, Check VBAT At DIS BOB - Ensure DIS diagnostic cable is connected to BOB. Select 2.3L DP DIS overlay. Connect LED test light negative lead to IGN D (J2) and positive LED test light lead to VBAT D (J5). Turn ignition on. If LED test light is on, go to step **8)**. If

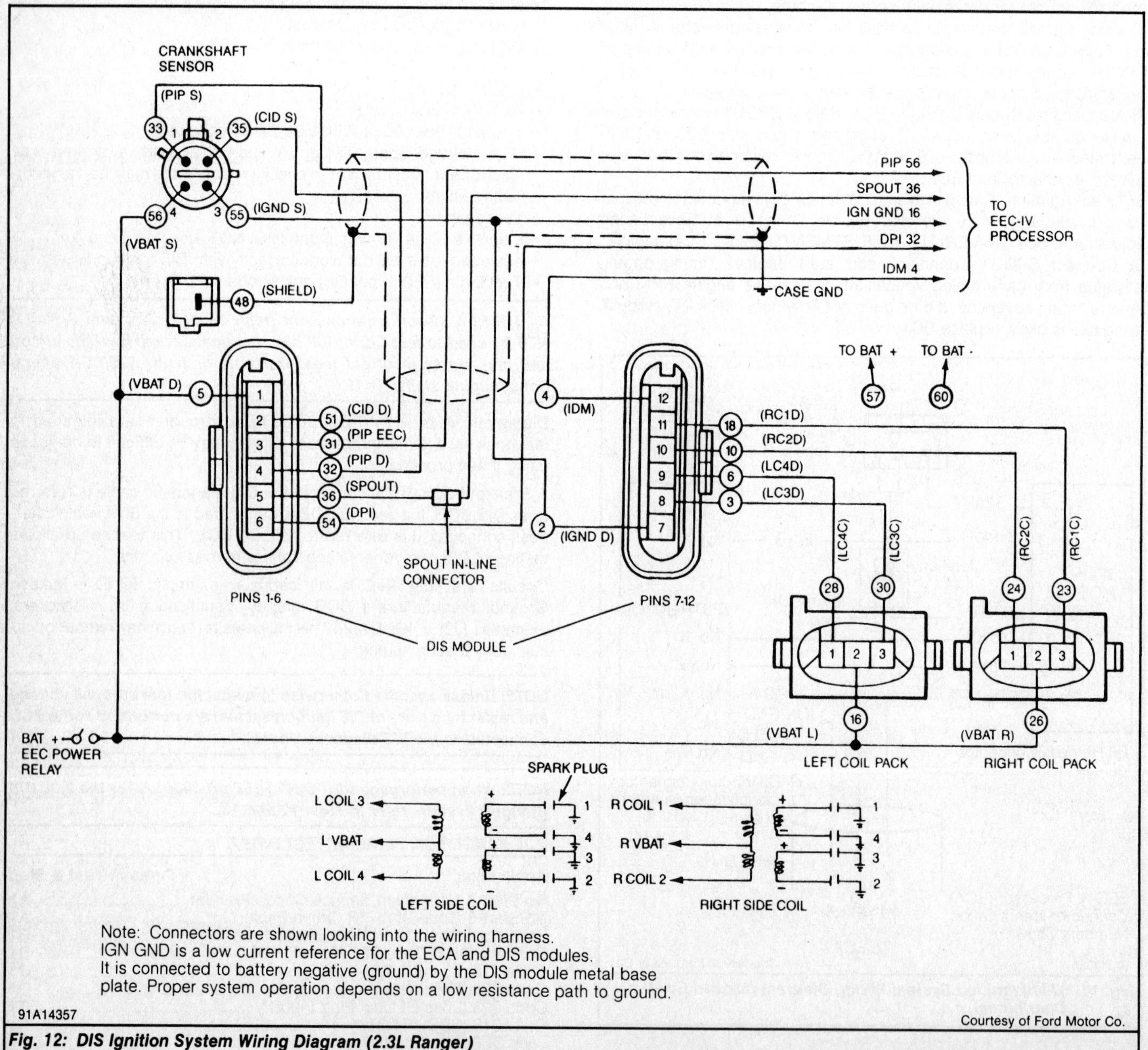
CRANKSHAFT SENSOR
(PIP S)
(CID S)
(IGND S)
(VBAT S)
(SHIELD)
PIP 56
SPOUT 36
IGN GND 16
DPI 32
IDM 4
CASE GND
TO EEC-IV PROCESSOR
TO BAT +
TO BAT -
(VBAT D)
(CID D)
(PIP EEC)
(PIP D)
(SPOUT)
(DPI)
(IDM)
(IGND D)
(RC1D)
(RC2D)
(LC4D)
(LC3D)
(LC4C)
(LC3C)
(RC2C)
(RC1C)
SPOUT IN-LINE CONNECTOR
PINS 1-6
PINS 7-12
DIS MODULE
BAT +
EEC POWER RELAY
(VBAT L)
(VBAT R)
LEFT COIL PACK
RIGHT COIL PACK
SPARK PLUG
L COIL 3
L VBAT
L COIL 4
R COIL 1
R VBAT
R COIL 2
LEFT SIDE COIL
RIGHT SIDE COIL
Note: Connectors are shown looking into the wiring harness.
IGN GND is a low current reference for the ECA and DIS modules.
It is connected to battery negative (ground) by the DIS module metal base plate. Proper system operation depends on a low resistance path to ground.
91A14357
Courtesy of Ford Motor Co.

Fig. 12: DIS Ignition System Wiring Diagram (2.3L Ranger)

LED test light is not on, service harness and connectors. Remove all test equipment and reconnect all components. Clear Continuous Memory Codes and rerun Quick Test.

8) Check Ignition Ground Circuit (IGND) At DIS Module - Ensure ignition is off. Set DVOM on 200-ohm scale. Measure resistance between IGND D (J2) at DIS BOB and ground (J60 or VBAT-). If resistance is less than 5 ohms, go to step **10)**. If resistance is 5 ohms or more, go to step **9)**.

9) IGND Circuit Fault, Check DIS Mounting Screws - Ensure key is off. If mounting surface and screws are clean and tight, fault is an open in ignition ground circuit, replace DIS module. If they are not, clean, tighten or replace mounting screws. Clean mounting surface area of DIS module. Ensure mounting surface is coated with heat sink compound. Remove all test equipment and reconnect all components. Clear Continuous Memory Codes and rerun Quick Test.

10) Spark Fault, Check Voltage At RC1D & RC2D During Engine Cranking - With key off, install right side ignition coil (C1 and C2) diagnostic cable tee. Turn key on. Connect LED test light positive lead to RC1D (J18) and connect negative lead to BAT - (J60). Then connect LED test light positive lead to RC2D (J10) and connect negative lead to BAT - (J60). If test light was on in both test positions, go to step **14)**. If test light was not on in both test positions, go to step **11)**.

11) Right Coil Fault, Isolate DIS Module - With key off, disconnect DIS diagnostic cable module tee (pin Nos. 7-12) from DIS module. Repeat procedure in step **10)**. If LED test light was on in both test positions, replace DIS module. Coil packs may be damaged as module was shorting C1 and C2 driver circuit to ground. Remove all test equipment and reconnect all components. Clear Continuous Memory Codes and rerun Quick Test. If LED test light was not on in both test positions, go to step **12)**.

12) Check VBAT, Right Coil Pack - Connect LED test light positive lead to VBAT R (J26) and negative lead to BAT - (J60). Turn key on. If LED test light is on, go to step **13)**. If LED test light is not on, locate and repair open circuit in right side coil VBAT. Remove all test equipment and reconnect all components. Clear Continuous Memory Codes and rerun Quick Test.

13) Check Right Coil Circuit - Connect LED test light positive lead to RC1C (J23) and connect negative lead to BAT - (J60). Then connect LED test light positive lead to RC2C (J24) and connect negative lead to BAT - (J60). Turn ignition on in each test position and observe test light. If test light was on in both test positions, one or both coil wires are shorted to VBAT. Repair or replace harness or connectors. Remove all test equipment and reconnect all components. Clear Continuous Memory Codes and rerun Quick Test. If test light was not on in both test positions, replace right coil pack. Remove all test equipment and reconnect all components. Clear Continuous Memory Codes and rerun Quick Test.

14) Check PIP D At DIS Module - Connect LED test light positive lead to PIP D (J32) and negative lead to BAT - (J60). Crank engine and observe test light. If test light blinks continuously during cranking, go to step **15)**. If test light does not blink continuously during cranking, go to step **19)**.

15) Check DIS Module Coil Drivers - Connect LED test light positive lead to RC1D (J18) and negative lead to BAT - (J60). Then connect LED test light positive lead to RC2D (J10) and negative lead to BAT - (J60).Crank engine and observe test light. If test light blinks continuously during cranking in both test positions, go to step **16)**. If test light does not blink continuously during cranking, replace DIS module. Remove all test equipment and reconnect all components. Clear Continuous Memory Codes and rerun Quick Test.

16) Check VBAT, Right Coil Pack - Connect LED test light positive lead to VBAT R (J26) and negative lead to BAT - (J60). Turn key on. If LED test light is on, go to step **17)**. If LED test light is not on, locate and repair open circuit in right side coil VBAT. Remove all test equipment and reconnect all components. Clear Continuous Memory Codes and rerun Quick Test.

17) Check Right Coil Circuit - Connect LED test light positive lead to RC1C (J23) and connect negative lead to BAT - (J60). Then connect LED test light positive lead to RC2C (J24) and connect negative lead to BAT - (J60). Turn ignition on in each test position and observe test

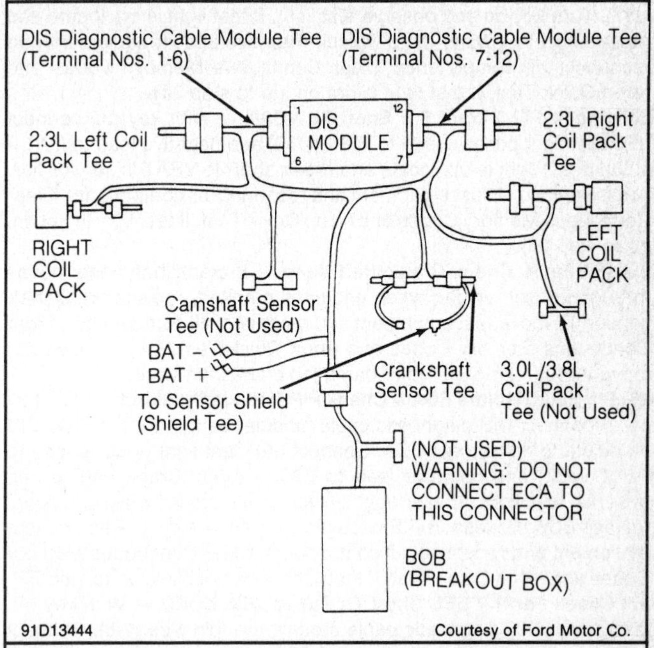
DIS Diagnostic Cable Module Tee (Terminal Nos. 1-6)
DIS Diagnostic Cable Module Tee (Terminal Nos. 7-12)
DIS MODULE
2.3L Left Coil Pack Tee
2.3L Right Coil Pack Tee
RIGHT COIL PACK
LEFT COIL PACK
Camshaft Sensor Tee (Not Used)
BAT -
BAT +
To Sensor Shield (Shield Tee)
Crankshaft Sensor Tee
3.0L/3.8L Coil Pack Tee (Not Used)
(NOT USED) WARNING: DO NOT CONNECT ECA TO THIS CONNECTOR
BOB (BREAKOUT BOX)
91D13444
Courtesy of Ford Motor Co.

Fig. 13: DIS Diagnostic Cable Diagram (2.3L Ranger)

light. If test light was on in both test positions, go to step **18)**. If test light was not on in both test positions, one or both coil wires may be shorted to ground. Repair or replace harness or connectors. Remove all test equipment and reconnect all components. Clear Continuous Memory Codes and rerun Quick Test.

18) Check Right Coil Circuit - Repeat test procedure in step **17)** and crank engine at each test position. If test light blinks continuously during cranking, replace right coil pack. Remove all test equipment and reconnect all components. Clear Continuous Memory Codes and rerun Quick Test. If test light does not blink continuously, one or both coil wires may be open. Check connections, repair or replace harness as necessary. Remove all test equipment and reconnect all components. Clear Continuous Memory Codes and rerun Quick Test.

19) Isolate DIS Module From PIP D During Cranking - With key off, disconnect DIS diagnostic cable module tee (pin Nos. 1-6) from DIS module. Connect LED test light positive lead to PIP D (J32) and negative lead to IGND S (J55). Crank engine and observe test light. If test light blinks continuously during cranking, go to step **26)**. If test light does not blink during cranking, go to step **20)**.

20) Check Crankshaft Sensor VBAT - With key on, connect LED test light positive lead to VBAT (J56) and negative lead to IGND D (J2). If test light is on, go to step **21)**. If test light is not on, locate and repair open in VBAT circuit to sensor. Remove all test equipment and reconnect all components. Clear Continuous Memory Codes and rerun Quick Test.

21) Check Crankshaft Sensor Ignition Ground - Turn key off and disconnect ECA. Disconnect diagnostic cable from crankshaft sensor. Set DVOM to 200-ohm scale. Measure resistance between IGND S (J55) and BAT - (J60). If resistance is less than 5 ohms, go to step **22)**. If resistance is 5 ohms or more, locate and repair open or high resistance in circuit. Remove all test equipment and reconnect all components. Clear Continuous Memory Codes and rerun Quick Test.

22) Check Crankshaft Sensor PIP S - Turn key off and reconnect ECA to harness. Connect diagnostic cable to crankshaft sensor. Connect LED test light positive lead to PIP S (J33) and negative lead to IGND D (J2). Crank engine and observe test light. If test light blinks continuously, locate and repair open circuit between sensor and DIS module. Remove all test equipment and reconnect all components. Clear Continuous Memory Codes and rerun Quick Test. If test light does not blink, go to step **23)**.

23) Check PIP Circuit For Short To Ground - Turn key off and disconnect diagnostic cable from DIS module (pin Nos. 1-6). Connect LED test light positive lead to PIP S (J33) and negative lead to BAT +

(J57). Turn key on and observe test light. If test light is on, locate and repair short to ground in PIP circuit. Remove all test equipment and reconnect all components. Clear Continuous Memory Codes and rerun Quick Test. If test light is not on, go to step **24)**.

24) Check PIP Circuit For Short To VBAT – With key on, connect LED test light positive lead to PIP S (J33) and negative lead to BAT – (J60). If test light is on, locate and repair short to VBAT in sensor harness. Remove all test equipment and reconnect all components. Clear Continuous Memory Codes and rerun Quick Test. If test light is not on, go to step **25)**.

25) PIP Fault, Check Crankshaft Vane – If crankshaft vane moves through sensor air gap when engine is cranked, replace crankshaft sensor. Remove test equipment and reconnect all components. Clear Continuous Memory Codes and rerun Quick Test. If vane does not move through air gap, repair damaged crankshaft vane.

26) PIP Fault, Isolate ECA & Check PIP D While Cranking – With key off, reconnect DIS diagnostic cable module tee (pin Nos. 1-6) to DIS module and disconnect ECA. Connect LED test light positive lead to PIP D (J32) and negative lead to BAT – (J60). Crank engine and observe test light. If test light blinks continuously while cranking, replace ECA processor. PIP circuit is shorted internally. Remove test equipment and reconnect all components. Clear Continuous Memory Codes and rerun Quick Test. If test light does not blink, go to step **27)**.

27) Check For PIP EEC Short To Power With KOEO – With key off, disconnect DIS diagnostic cable module tee (pin Nos. 1-6). Connect LED test light positive lead to PIP EEC (J31) and negative lead to BAT – (J60). If test light is on, repair harness and connectors for PIP short to power. Remove test equipment and reconnect all components. Clear Continuous Memory Codes and rerun Quick Test. If test light is not on, go to step **28)**.

28) Check PIP EEC For Short To Ground – With key off, connect LED test light positive lead to PIP EEC (J31) and negative lead to BAT + (J57). If test light is on, repair harness and connectors for PIP EEC short to ground. Remove test equipment and reconnect all components. Clear Continuous Memory Codes and rerun Quick Test. If test light is not on, replace DIS module. No PIP output. Remove test equipment and reconnect all components. Clear Continuous Memory Codes and rerun Quick Test.

PINPOINT TEST B – 1) Verify Hard Cranking – Attempt to start vehicle 5 times. If engine starts normally at least once out of 5 attempts, but when it fails to start cranking RPM is erratic, ignition is firing out of time due to CID signal fault. If engine fails to start at least once, go to step **2)**. If engine starts at least once, go to step **8)**.

2) CID Fault, Check CID D Circuit During KOER – With key off, install DIS diagnostic cable module tee (pin Nos. 1-6) to DIS module. Connect diagnostic cable negative lead to battery. Connect diagnostic cable to DIS BOB. Use 2.3L DP DIS overlay. Connect LED test light positive lead to CID D (J51) and negative lead to IGND D (J2). Start engine and observe test light. If test light blinks continuously, replace DIS module. Module does not respond to CID input. Remove test equipment and reconnect all components. Clear Continuous Memory Codes and rerun Quick Test. If test light does not blink, go to step **3)**.

3) Isolate DIS Module From CID Circuit – Turn key off and disconnect diagnostic cable from DIS module (pin Nos. 1-6). Crank engine and observe test light. If test light blinks continuously, replace DIS module. Remove all test equipment and reconnect all components. Clear Continuous Memory Codes and rerun Quick Test. If test light does not blink, go to step **4)**.

4) Check Crankshaft Sensor CID Signal Output – Turn key off and reconnect diagnostic cable connector to DIS module (pin Nos. 1-6). Connect LED test light positive lead to CID S (J35) and negative lead to BAT – (J60). Start engine and observe test light. If test light blinks continuously, locate and repair open in CID circuit. Remove all test equipment and reconnect all components. Clear Continuous Memory Codes and rerun Quick Test. If test light does not blink, go to step **5)**.

5) Check CID For Short To Ground – With key off, disconnect diagnostic cable CID sensor tee from CID sensor. Disconnect diagnostic cable from DIS module (pin Nos. 1-6). Connect LED test light positive lead to BAT + (J57) and negative lead to CID D (J51). Turn key on and observe test light. If test light is on, service or repair connectors or harness. CID is shorted to ground. Remove test equipment and reconnect all components. Clear Continuous Memory Codes and rerun Quick Test. If test light is not on, go to step **6)**.

6) Check For CID Short To Power – With ignition still on, connect LED test light positive lead to CID D (J51) and negative lead to BAT – (J60). If test light is on, check and repair connectors and harness as necessary. CID is shorted to power. Remove test equipment and reconnect all components. Clear Continuous Memory Codes and rerun Quick Test. If test light is not on, go to step **7)**.

7) Check CID Vane – If crankshaft vane moves through sensor air gap when engine is cranked, replace crankshaft sensor. Remove test equipment and reconnect all components. Clear Continuous Memory Codes and rerun Quick Test. If vane does not move through air gap, repair damaged crankshaft vane.

8) Check DPI Signal At DIS Module – With key off, install DIS diagnostic cable module tee (pin Nos. 1-6) to DIS module. Connect DIS diagnostic cable to ECA BOB. Use 2.3L DP DIS overlay. turn key on and connect LED test light positive lead to DPI (J54) and negative lead to BAT – (J60). If test light is on, go to step **11)**. If test light is not on, go to step **9)**.

9) Isolate DIS Module From DPI Circuit – With key off, disconnect DIS diagnostic cable module tee (pin Nos. 1-6) from DIS module and turn key on. If test light is off, replace DIS module. Remove test equipment and reconnect all components. Clear Continuous Memory Codes and rerun Quick Test. If test light is on, go to step **10)**.

10) Isolate ECA From DPI Circuit – With key off, disconnect ECA from vehicle harness. Connect LED test light positive lead to DPI (J54) and negative lead to BAT – (J60). Turn key on and observe test light. If test light is on, locate and repair short to VBAT in harness. Remove all test equipment and reconnect all components. Clear Continuous Memory Codes and rerun Quick Test. If test light is not on, replace ECA. Remove test equipment and reconnect all components. Clear Continuous Memory Codes and rerun Quick Test.

11) Check IDM Signal At DIS Module – Connect LED test light positive lead to IDM (J4) and negative lead to BAT – (J60). Start engine and observe test light. If test light blinks continuously, replace ECA. IDM is okay at DIS module. If test light does not blink, go to step **12)**.

12) Isolate ECA From IDM Circuit – Turn key off and disconnect ECA. Crank engine and observe test light. If test light blinks continuously, replace ECA as it is holding the IDM low. If test light does not blink, go to step **13)**.

13) Check IDM For Short To Ground – Turn key off and disconnect HEGO sensor. Disconnect diagnostic cable from DIS module (pin Nos. 7-12). Set DVOM to 20-k/ohm scale. Measure resistance between IDM (J4) and BAT – (J60). If resistance is less than 10 k/ohms, locate and repair short to ground in harness between DIS module and ECA. Remove all test equipment and reconnect all components. Clear Continuous Memory Codes and rerun Quick Test. If resistance is 10 k/ohms or more, replace DIS module. Remove all test equipment and reconnect all components. Clear Continuous Memory Codes and rerun Quick Test.

PINPOINT TEST C – 1) Check For Left Side Spark With KOER – Start engine and using spark tester, check for spark at each left spark plug wire. If spark is present at any left spark plug wire, go to step **2)**. If spark is not present, go to PINPOINT TEST D, Step **1)**.

2) Check IDM With KOER – With key off, install DIS diagnostic cable module tee (pin Nos. 7-12) to DIS module. Connect DIS diagnostic cable to BOB. Use 2.3L DP DIS overlay. Connect LED test light positive lead to IDM (J4) and negative lead to BAT – (J60). Start engine and observe test light. If test light blinks continuously, go to step **3)**. If test light does not blink, go to step **4)**.

3) Check IDM To ECA Continuity To ECA – With key off, disconnect ECA. Crank engine and observe test light. If test light blinks continuously, replace ECA. ECA does not respond to IDM input. Remove test equipment and reconnect all components. Clear Continuous Memory Codes and rerun Quick Test. If test light does not blink, go to step **4)**.

4) Isolate ECA & Check IDM Circuit During Cranking – With key off, disconnect ECA. Crank engine and observe test light. If test light blinks continuously, replace ECA. The ECA is shorting IDM. If test light does not blink, go to step **5)**.

5) Check IDM For Short To Power – With key off, and disconnect HEGO sensor. Disconnect DIS diagnostic cable module tee (pin Nos. 7-12) from DIS module. Set DVOM on 20-k/ohm scale. Measure resistance between IDM (J4) and VBAT D (J5). If resistance is less than 10 k/ohms, check connectors and service or replace harness. IDM is shorted to VBAT. Remove test equipment and reconnect all components. Clear Continuous Memory Codes and rerun Quick Test. If resistance is 10 k/ohms or more, go to step **6)**.

6) Check IDM For Short To Ground –With key off and disconnect diagnostic cable connector from DIS module (pin Nos. 7-12). Set DVOM on 20-k/ohm scale. Measure resistance between IDM (J4) and BAT – (J60). If resistance is 10 k/ohm or less, check connectors and service or replace harness. IDM is shorted to ground. Remove test equipment and reconnect all components. Clear Continuous Memory Codes and rerun Quick Test. If resistance is 10 k/ohm or more, replace DIS module. IDM is shorted in DIS module. Remove test equipment and reconnect all components. Clear Continuous Memory Codes and rerun Quick Test.

PINPOINT TEST D – 1) Check For Spark During Cranking – Using a spark tester, check for spark at all spark plug wires with engine running. If spark is consistent on all spark plug wires, go to PINPOINT TEST E, step **1)**. If spark us not consistent, go to step **2)**.

2) Check For Spark At Right Plug Wires During Cranking – If spark is present on all right side spark plug wires, go to step **3)**. If spark is not present on all right side spark plug wires, go to step **10)**.

3) Left Spark Fault, Isolate Plugs & Wires – If spark was missing from both cylinder Nos. 1 and 4 or both cylinder Nos. 2 and 3, go top step **5)**. If not go to step **4)**.

4) Check Left Side Spark Plugs & Wires – Check left spark plug wires for insulation damage, looseness, shorting or damage. Remove and check left spark plugs for damage, wear, carbon deposits and proper plug gap. If spark plugs and wires are okay, reinstall plugs and wires and go to step **5)**. If spark plugs or wires are defective, service or replace damaged component. Remove test equipment and reconnect all components. Clear Continuous Memory Codes and rerun Quick Test.

5) Left Spark Fault, Check Module Output – With key off, install diagnostic cable. Connect diagnostic cable to breakout box. Use 2.3L overlay. Disconnect diagnostic cable connector from DIS module vehicle harness connector (pin Nos. 7-12). Connect a jumper wire between IGND S (J55) and BAT – (J60). Connect a jumper wire between DPI (J54) and IGND S (J55). If spark was missing from cylinder Nos. 1 and 4, connect LED test light positive lead to VBAT D (J5) and negative lead to LC3D (J3). If spark was missing from cylinder Nos. 2 and 3, connect LED test light positive lead to VBAT D (J5) and negative lead to LC4D (J6). Crank engine and observe test light. If test light blinks continuously, go to step **6)**. If test light does not blink, replace DIS module. Remove all test equipment and reconnect all components. Clear Continuous Memory Codes and rerun Quick Test.

6) Left Spark Fault, Check Left Coil Pack VBAT – Turn key off and remove jumper wires. Reconnect diagnostic cable connector to DIS module harness (pin Nos. 7-12). Connect LED test light positive lead to BAT L (J15) and negative lead to BAT – (J60). Turn key on and observe test light. If test light is on, go to step **7)**. If test light is not on, locate and repair open circuit in left coil pack. Remove all test equipment and reconnect all components. Clear Continuous Memory Codes and rerun Quick Test.

7) Left Spark Fault, Isolate Left Coil Pack – Turn key off and disconnect HEGO sensor. Disconnect diagnostic cable from left coil pack. If spark was missing from cylinder Nos. 1 and 4 in step **3)**, connect LED test light positive lead to BAT + (J57) and negative lead to LC3C (J30). If spark was missing from cylinder Nos. 2 and 3 in step **3)**, connect LED test light positive lead to BAT + (J57) and negative lead to LC4C (J28). Crank engine and observe test light. If test light blink continuously. replace left coil pack. Remove all test equipment and reconnect all components. Clear Continuous Memory Codes and rerun Quick Test. If test light does not blink, go to step **8)**.

8) Check For Open – Turn key off and disconnect diagnostic cable connector from DIS module (pin Nos. 7-12). Set DVOM to 20-ohm scale. If spark was missing from cylinder Nos. 1 and 4, measure resistance between LC3D (J3) and LC3C (J30). If spark was missing from cylinder Nos. 2 and 3, measure resistance between LC4D (J6) and LC4C (J28). If resistance is less than 5 ohms, go to step **9)**. If resistance is 5 ohms or more, locate and repair open circuit between left coil pack and DIS module. Remove all test equipment and reconnect all components. Clear Continuous Memory Codes and rerun Quick Test.

9) Check For Shorts – If spark was missing from cylinder Nos. 1 and 4, measure resistance between LC3D (J3) and BAT – (J57). If spark was missing from cylinder Nos. 2 and 3, measure resistance between LC4D (J6) and BAT – (J57). If resistance is less than 10 k/ohms, locate and repair short VBAT between DIS module and coil pack. Remove all test equipment and reconnect all components. Clear Continuous Memory Codes and rerun Quick Test. If resistance is 10 k/ohms or more, locate and repair short to ground. Remove all test equipment and reconnect all components. Clear Continuous Memory Codes and rerun Quick Test.

10) Check Module Output – Turn key off and disconnect HEGO sensor. Install diagnostic cable and disconnect diagnostic cable from DIS module harness (pin Nos. 7-12). Connect diagnostic cable to breakout box and select 2.3L DIS overlay. Connect jumper wire between IGNDS (J55) and BAT – (J60) at breakout box. If spark was missing from cylinder Nos. 1 and 4, connect LED test light positive lead to RC1D (J18) and negative lead to BAT + (J57). If spark was missing from cylinder Nos. 2 and 3, connect LED test light positive lead to RC2D (J10) and negative lead to BAT + (J57). Crank engine and observe test light. If test light blinks continuously, go to step **11)**. If test light does not blink, replace DIS module. Remove all test equipment and reconnect all components. Clear Continuous Memory Codes and rerun Quick Test.

11) Isolate Right Coil Pack – Turn key off and disconnect diagnostic cable from right coil pack. If spark was missing from cylinder Nos. 1 and 4, connect LED test light positive lead to RC1C (J23) and negative lead to BAT + (J57). If spark was missing from cylinder Nos. 2 and 3, connect LED test light positive lead to RC2C (J24) and negative lead to BAT + (J57). Crank engine and observe test light. If test light blinks continuously, replace right coil pack. Remove all test equipment and reconnect all components. Clear Continuous Memory Codes and rerun Quick Test. If test light did not blink, go to step **12)**.

12) Check For Open – Turn key off and disconnect diagnostic cable connector from DIS module (pin Nos. 7-12). Set DVOM to 20-ohm scale. If spark was missing from cylinder Nos. 1 and 4, measure resistance between RC1D (J18) and RC1C (J23). If spark was missing from cylinder Nos. 2 and 3, measure resistance between RC2D (J10) and RC1C (J23). If resistance is less than 5 ohms, go to step **13)**. If resistance is 5 ohms or more, locate and repair open circuit between right coil pack and DIS module. Remove all test equipment and reconnect all components. Clear Continuous Memory Codes and rerun Quick Test.

13) Check For Shorts – Disconnect HEGO sensor. If spark was missing from cylinder Nos. 1 and 4, measure resistance between RC1D (J18) and BAT – (J60). If spark was missing from cylinder Nos. 2 and 3, measure resistance between RC2D (J10) and BAT – (J60). If resistance is less than 10 k/ohms, locate and repair short to ground between DIS module and coil pack. Remove all test equipment and reconnect all components. Clear Continuous Memory Codes and rerun Quick Test. If resistance is 10 k/ohms or more, locate and repair short to VBAT. Remove all test equipment and reconnect all components. Clear Continuous Memory Codes and rerun Quick Test.

PINPOINT TEST E – 1) Isolate SPOUT High – With key off, disconnect HEGO sensor. Install DIS diagnostic cable to DIS BOB and DIS module. Use 2.3L DP DIS overlay. Connect LED test light positive lead to SPOUT (J36) and negative lead to BAT – (J60). Start engine and observe test light. If test light blinks continuously, go to step **2)**. If test light does not blink, go step **3)** and check SPOUT.

2) Check Dual Plug Operation – Using a Neon Spark Tester, check for spark at each left side plug wire with engine running. If spark is pre-

1991 ENGINE PERFORMANCE
System & Component Testing – EEC-IV (Cont.)

sent at one or more wires, go to step **6)**. If spark was not present at one or more wires, go to step **11)**.

3) Isolate SPOUT To ECA – Turn key off and remove SPOUT harness plug from SPOUT in-line vehicle harness connector. Connect LED test light positive lead to ECA side of SPOUT vehicle harness connector and negative lead to main ground. *See Fig. 14.* If test light blinks continuously after engine is started, go to step **5)**. If test light does not blink continuously after engine is started, go to step **4)**.

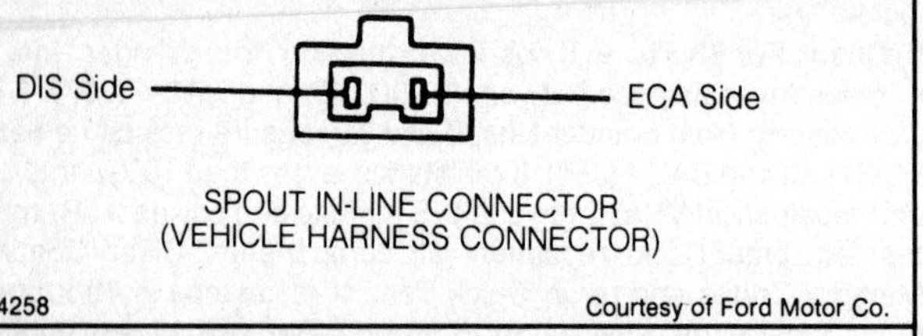
DIS Side
ECA Side
SPOUT IN-LINE CONNECTOR
(VEHICLE HARNESS CONNECTOR)
91B14258
Courtesy of Ford Motor Co.

Fig. 14: Identifying SPOUT Connector Terminals

4) Check For Short To VBAT – Turn key off and disconnect ECA. Disconnect positive battery cable. Set DVOM to 20-k/ohm scale. Measure resistance between VBAT + (J57) and ECA side of SPOUT vehicle harness connector. *See Fig. 14.* If resistance is 10 k/ohms or more, locate and repair short to VBAT in harness between SPOUT connector and ECA. Remove all test equipment and reconnect all components. Clear Continuous Memory Codes and rerun Quick Test. If resistance is 10 k/ohms or more, replace ECA. Remove all test equipment and reconnect all components. Clear Continuous Memory Codes and rerun Quick Test.

5) Check For Short To VBAT – Turn key off and disconnect diagnostic cable connector from DIS module (pins No . 1-6). Set DVOM to 20-k/ohm scale. Measure resistance between VBAT + (J57) and DIS side of SPOUT vehicle harness connector. *See Fig. 14*. If resistance is less than 10 k/ohms, locate and repair short to VBAT + in harness between SPOUT connector and DIS module. Remove all test equipment and reconnect all components. Clear Continuous Memory Codes and rerun Quick Test. If resistance is 10 k/ohms or more, replace DIS module. Remove all test equipment and reconnect all components. Clear Continuous Memory Codes and rerun Quick Test.

6) Check DIS Module IDM Output – Connect LED test light positive lead to IDM D (J4) and negative lead to BAT – (J60). Crank or start engine and observe test light. If test light blinks continuously, go to step **7)**. If test light does not blink, go to step **8)**.

7) Check IDM Circuit Continuity – Turn key off and set DVOM to 20-ohm scale. Measure resistance between test pin No. 4 (IDM) at ECA vehicle harness connector and IDM (J4) at DIS connector. If resistance is less than 5 ohms, replace ECA. Remove all test equipment and reconnect all components. Clear Continuous Memory Codes and rerun Quick Test. If resistance is 5 ohms or more, locate and repair open in IDM circuit between DIS module and ECA. Remove all test equipment and reconnect all components. Clear Continuous Memory Codes and rerun Quick Test.

8) Isolate ECA – Turn key off and disconnect ECA. Crank engine and observe test light. If test light blinks continuously, replace ECA. Remove all test equipment and reconnect all components. Clear Continuous Memory Codes and rerun Quick Test. If test light does not blink, go to step **9)**.

9) Check For Short To Ground – Turn key off and disconnect diagnostic cable connector from DIS module (pin Nos. 7-12). Remove LED test light. Set DVOM to 20-ohm scale. Measure resistance between IDM (J4) and BAT – (J60). If resistance is less than 5 ohms, locate and repair short to ground in IDM circuit. Remove all test equipment and reconnect all components. Clear Continuous Memory Codes and rerun Quick Test. If resistance is 5 ohms or more, go to step **10)**.

10) Check For Short To VBAT – Measure resistance between IDM (J4) and BAT + (J57). If resistance is less than 5 ohms, locate and repair short to VBAT between DIS module and ECA. Remove all test equipment and reconnect all components. Clear Continuous Memory Codes and rerun Quick Test. If resistance is 5 ohms or more, replace DIS module. Remove all test equipment and reconnect all components. Clear Continuous Memory Codes and rerun Quick Test.

11) Check Continuity – Turn key off and install diagnostic cable. Disconnect diagnostic cable connector from DIS module (pin Nos. 1-6). Connect diagnostic cable to breakout box. Select 2.3L overlay. Disconnect ECA. Set DVOM to 20-ohm scale. Measure resistance between DPI (pin No. 32) of ECA harness connector and DPI (J54) of breakout box. If resistance is less than 5 ohms, go to step **12)**. If resistance is 5 ohms or more, locate and repair open DPI circuit between DIS module and ECA. Remove all test equipment and reconnect all components. Clear Continuous Memory Codes and rerun Quick Test.

12) Check For Short To VBAT – Measure resistance between DPI (J54) and BAT + (J57). If resistance is 5 ohms or more, go to step **13)**. If resistance is less than 5 ohms, locate and repair to VBAT in harness between DIS module and ECA. Remove all test equipment and reconnect all components. Clear Continuous Memory Codes and rerun Quick Test.

CAUTION: In the next step, be careful not to jumper the DPI (J54) circuit to VBAT + or BAT + as this high voltage will damage the ECA.

13) Isolate ECA – Turn key off, reconnect ECA and connect a jumper wire between DPI (J54) and BAT – (J60). Start engine and check for spark at any left side spark plug or wire. If spark is present, replace ECA. Remove all test equipment and reconnect all components. Clear Continuous Memory Codes and rerun Quick Test. If spark is not present, replace DIS module. Remove all test equipment and reconnect all components. Clear Continuous Memory Codes and rerun Quick Test.

PINPOINT TEST F – 1) Check Timing At Idle – With key off, install timing light. Ensure transmission is in Park or Neutral. Check timing with engine running at normal operating temperature. If timing advance is greater than 19 degrees BTDC, timing advance is okay, check engine mechanical condition, see BASIC DIAGNOSTIC PROCEDURES article. If timing is not as specified, go to step **2)**.

2) Check SPOUT Function – Turn key off and disconnect HEGO sensor. Install diagnostic cable and connect diagnostic cable to breakout box. Use 2.3L overlay. Disconnect diagnostic cable from DIS module (pin Nos. 1-6). Connect LED test light positive lead to SPOUT (J36) and negative lead to BAT – (J60). Crank or start engine and observe test light. If test light blinks continuously, replace DIS module. Remove all test equipment and reconnect all components. Clear Continuous Memory Codes and rerun Quick Test. If problem still exists, replace ECA. Remove all test equipment and reconnect all components. Clear Continuous Memory Codes and rerun Quick Test. If test light does not blink, go to step **3)**.

3) Isolate SPOUT Fault – Turn key off and remove SPOUT harness jumper plug from SPOUT vehicle harness connector. Connect diagnostic cable to DIS module (pins. No. 1-6). Connect LED test light positive lead to EEC side of SPOUT vehicle harness connector and negative lead to BAT – (J60). Start engine and observe test light. If test light blinks continuously, reconnect diagnostic cable connector to DIS module (pin Nos. 1-6) and go to step **6)**. If test light does not blink continuously, reconnect diagnostic cable connector to DIS module (pin Nos. 1-6) and go to step **4)**.

4) Check Continuity – Turn key off and disconnect ECA. Set DVOM to 20-ohm scale. Measure resistance between SPOUT (pin No. 36) of ECA vehicle harness connector and ECA side of SPOUT vehicle harness connector. If resistance is less than 5 ohms, go to step **5)**. If resistance is 5 ohms or more, locate and repair open circuit between SPOUT connector and ECA. Remove all test equipment and reconnect all components. Clear Continuous Memory Codes and rerun Quick Test.

5) Check SPOUT For Short To Ground – Turn key off and disconnect ECA. Set DVOM to 20-k/ohm scale. Measure resistance between BAT – (J60) and ECA side of SPOUT vehicle harness connector. If resistance is less than 10 k/ohms, locate and repair short to ground between ECA and SPOUT connector. Remove all test equipment and reconnect all components. Clear Continuous Memory Codes and rerun Quick Test. If resistance is 10 k/ohms or more, replace ECA.

1991 ENGINE PERFORMANCE
System & Component Testing – EEC-IV (Cont.)

Remove all test equipment and reconnect all components. Clear Continuous Memory Codes and rerun Quick Test.

6) Check SPOUT Circuit Continuity – Turn key off and measure resistance between SPOUT (J36) and DIS side of SPOUT vehicle harness connector. If resistance is less than 5 ohms, go to step **7)**. If resistance is 5 ohms or more, locate and repair open circuit between DIS module and SPOUT vehicle harness connector. Remove all test equipment and reconnect all components. Clear Continuous Memory Codes and rerun Quick Test.

7) Check SPOUT For Short To Ground – Turn key off and disconnect diagnostic cable connector from DIS module (pin Nos. 1-6). Measure resistance between BAT – (J60) and SPOUT (J36). If resistance is less than 10 k/ohms, locate and repair short to ground in harness between DIS module and SPOUT vehicle harness connector. Remove all test equipment and reconnect all components. Clear Continuous Memory Codes and rerun Quick Test. If resistance is 10 k/ohms or more, replace DIS module. Remove all test equipment and reconnect all components. Clear Continuous Memory Codes and rerun Quick Test.

EDIS SYSTEM
(4.0L AEROSTAR, EXPLORER & RANGER)

NOTE: Start all diagnostics with charts in TROUBLE SHOOTING – NO CODES article. Perform Quick Test procedure in SELF-DIAGNOSTICS – EEC-IV article before entering this test. These tests are dependent on results of Quick Test procedure.

NOTE: The EDIS Diagnostic Cable (Rotunda 007-00059) should be used to diagnose this system. This cable is equipped with additional circuits and components used to enhance and modify signals for testing purposes. If an aftermarket test cable is used, or diagnosis is being performed using only a DVOM, ensure technician is familiar with system wiring diagram and system operation.

Preliminary Checkout – Visually inspect the engine compartment to ensure all vacuum hoses and spark plug wires are properly and securely connected. Examine all wiring harnesses and connectors for damaged insulation, burned, overheated, damaged pins, loose or broken conditions. Check sensor shield connector. Ensure EDIS module mounting screw is tight. Ensure battery is fully charged and all accessories are off during diagnosis.

Test Equipment – Following equipment should be used in these test procedures.

- EDIS Diagnostic Cable (Rotunda 007-00059)
- Spark Tester (Neon Bulb Type)
- Volt-Ohmmeter (Rotunda 007-00001)
- Remote Starter Switch
- 2 Breakout Boxes (BOB), For DIS (DIS BOB) And ECA (ECA BOB)
- Spark Tester (D81P-6666-A Or equivalent)
- Inductive Timing Light
- Test Light (LED Type) Or Logic Probe (LED Type)

Diagnostic Aids – When making measurements on a wiring harness, both a visual inspection and a continuity test should be performed.

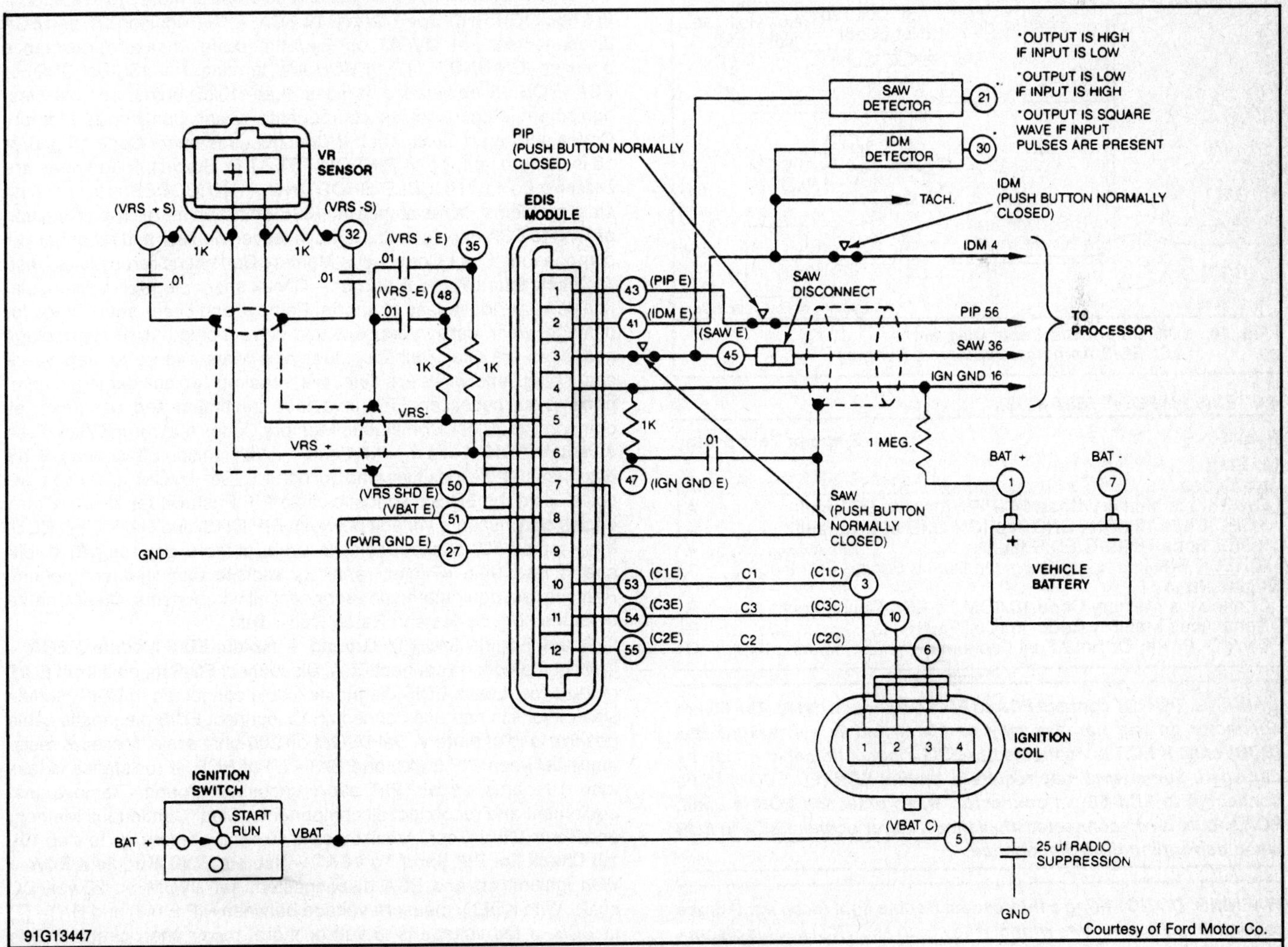
°OUTPUT IS HIGH IF INPUT IS LOW
°OUTPUT IS LOW IF INPUT IS HIGH
°OUTPUT IS SQUARE WAVE IF INPUT PULSES ARE PRESENT
SAW DETECTOR
IDM DETECTOR
21
30
VR SENSOR
PIP (PUSH BUTTON NORMALLY CLOSED)
EDIS MODULE
TACH.
IDM (PUSH BUTTON NORMALLY CLOSED)
(VRS + S)
(VRS -S)
1K
1K
.01
32
(VRS + E)
35
(VRS -E)
48
IDM 4
SAW DISCONNECT
(PIP E)
43
(IDM E)
41
(SAW E)
45
PIP 56
SAW 36
IGN GND 16
TO PROCESSOR
VRS-
VRS +
1 MEG.
47
(IGN GND E)
BAT +
BAT -
1
7
(VRS SHD E)
50
(VBAT E)
51
SAW (PUSH BUTTON NORMALLY CLOSED)
GND
(PWR GND E)
27
VEHICLE BATTERY
(C1E)
C1
(C1C)
53
3
(C3E)
C3
(C3C)
54
10
(C2E)
C2
(C2C)
55
6
IGNITION COIL
IGNITION SWITCH
START
RUN
BAT +
VBAT
(VBAT C)
5
25 uf RADIO SUPPRESSION
GND
91G13447
Courtesy of Ford Motor Co.

Fig. 15: EDIS Ignition System Wiring Diagram (4.0L EDIS Aerostar, Explorer & Ranger)

1991 ENGINE PERFORMANCE
System & Component Testing – EEC-IV (Cont.)

Inspect terminal connector pins for damage and corrosion, when directed to remove a connector.

- Spark timing adjustments are not possible. Timing is controlled by the EDIS module with input from the ECA.
- When checking voltage drop to GROUND, circuit must have a voltage drop of less than one volt.
- Battery voltage (VBAT) is any voltage reading within 2 volts of actual battery voltage.
- Spark timing will vary at idle due to feedback spark strategy used to control idle speed.
- DO NOT connect positive lead of EDIS diagnostic cable to battery or connect cable to VR sensor until directed to.
- SAW and IDM signal detectors in EDIS diagnostic cable will not work unless diagnostic cable battery leads are connected to battery.
- When using DVOM to measure DC voltage always connect positive lead to BOB terminal A (+) and negative lead to A (-).

CAUTION: DO NOT use a 12-volt incandescent (high voltage) test light to test circuit signals, as it will load the circuit and may cause incorrect measurements or faulty EDIS/ECA operations (engine stall).

NOTE: When using PINPOINT TEST procedures for the 4.0L EDIS (Aerostar, Explorer & Ranger) system, refer to Figs. 15 & 16.

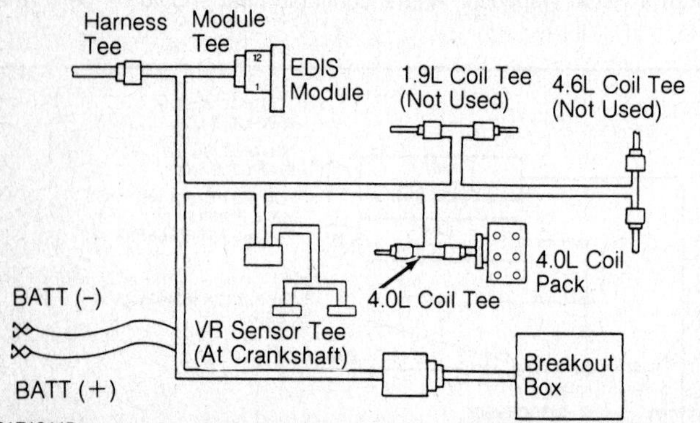
Harness Tee
Module Tee
EDIS Module
1.9L Coil Tee (Not Used)
4.6L Coil Tee (Not Used)
4.0L Coil Pack
4.0L Coil Tee
BATT (-)
BATT (+)
VR Sensor Tee (At Crankshaft)
Breakout Box

91E13445 Courtesy of Ford Motor Co.

Fig. 16: EDIS Diagnostic Cable Diagram (4.0L EDIS Aerostar, Explorer & Ranger)

4.0L EDIS PINPOINT TEST INDEX

Result	Pinpoint Test & Step
No Start	
No Codes	A1
Continuous Memory Code 14 (PIP Signal At ECA fault)	A1
KOEO Code 16 (IDM, GND and IGN GND at EAC fault)	A1
KOER Code 18 (EAC/EDIS fault)	A1
"CHECK ENGINE" Light Stays On During Engine Cranking	A1
Engine Runs	
Continuous Memory Code 18 (IDM To ECA Circuit Fault)	B1
Continuous Memory Code 45 (Coil Fault)	D1
Lack Of Power Or Poor Fuel Economy	C1

WARNING: DO NOT connect ECA to EDIS diagnostic cable. The 60-pin connector on this harness may be connected to a Breakout Box (BOB) only. If ECA is connected to EDIS diagnostic cable it may be damaged. Some tests may require a second BOB (ECA BOB) to be connected to ECA 60-pin connector. When a second BOB is used, ECA should be disconnected at all times. Never connect ECA to BOB when performing EDIS diagnostics

WARNING: DO NOT bring a fluorescent trouble light (drop light) close to vehicle ignition system wiring. If key is on and VR sensor is disconnected, light may cause EDIS module to fire ignition coil.

PINPOINT TEST A – 1) Perform EEC-IV Quick Test – If Quick Test was performed according to the procedures in SELF-DIAGNOSTICS – EEC-IV article, go to step **2)**. If Quick Test was not tested as specified, go to article and perform Quick Test procedure.

2) Check For Spark During Cranking – Using a spark tester, check for spark at all spark plug wires while cranking. If spark was present and consistent on ALL spark plug wires (one spark per crankshaft revolution), go to step **3)**. If spark was not as specified, go to step **7)**.

3) Check PIP Signal At EDIS Module – With ignition off, connect EDIS diagnostic cable to BOB, EDIS module and coil pack. DO NOT connect VR sensor tee. Use EDIS diagnostic "6" overlay on BOB (if available). Connect EDIS diagnostic cable negative lead to battery, leaving positive lead disconnected. Set EDIS diagnostic cable box switch to "4/6 Cylinder" position. Set DVOM on 20-volt AC scale. Crank engine, and measure voltage between PIP E (43) and BAT- (7) at BOB. If stabilized AC voltage reading is 4.5 volts or more, go to step **4)**. If reading was less than 4.5 volts, go to step **8)**.

4) Check For PIP Open To ECA – With ignition off, disconnect ECA. Connect ECA BOB to ECA harness connector. Set DVOM on 200-ohm scale. Measure resistance between PIP E (43) at BOB and PIP (56) at ECA BOB. If resistance is less than 5 ohms, go to step **5)**. If resistance is 5 ohms or more, repair open circuit. Remove test equipment and reconnect all components. Clear Continuous Memory Codes and rerun Quick Test.

5) Check IGN GND At EDIS Module – With ignition off and ECA disconnected, set DVOM on 2-k/ohm scale. Measure resistance between IGN GND E (47) and BAT- (7) at BOB. If resistance is less than 1025 ohms, go to step **6)**. If resistance is 1025 ohms or more, go to step **11)**.

6) Check IGN GND Open Circuit To ECA – With ignition off, and ECA disconnected, set DVOM on 2-k/ohm scale, measure resistance between IGN GND E (47) at BOB and terminal No. 16 (IGN GND) of ECA BOB. If resistance is less than 1025 ohms, remove test equipment. Reconnect all components. Clear Continuous Memory Codes and rerun Quick Test. If Continuous Memory Code 16 and/or 18 is still present, go to PINPOINT TEST B, Step **1)**. If no codes are present, go to TROUBLE SHOOTING – NO CODES article for no start problems. If resistance is 1025 ohms or more, repair ignition ground to ECA open circuit. Remove test equipment and reconnect all components. Clear Continuous Memory Codes and rerun Quick Test.

7) Check Spark Plugs & Wires – Check spark plug wires for insulation damage, looseness or shorts. Remove and check spark plugs for damage, wear, carbon deposits and correct plug gap. If spark plugs and wires are okay, reinstall plugs and wires and go to step **12)**. If spark plugs and wires are defective, repair or replace damaged components as necessary. Remove test equipment and reconnect all components. Clear Continuous Memory Codes and rerun Quick Test.

8) Isolate EDIS Module – PIP Fault – With ignition off, connect EDIS diagnostic cable positive lead to battery. Set DVOM to 20-volt AC scale. Hold the EDIS diagnostic cable PIP Push Button down. Crank engine and measure voltage between PIP E (43) and BAT- (7) at BOB. If the settled AC voltage reading is 4 volts or more, go to step **9)**. If voltage is less than 4 volts, repair or replace damaged component. Remove test equipment and reconnect all components. Clear Continuous Memory Codes and Rerun Quick Test.

9) Check For PIP Short To Ground – Isolate EDIS Module & ECA – With ignition off, disconnect ECA. Disconnect EDIS module from EDIS module tee. Leave EDIS diagnostic cable connected to EDIS module side of vehicle harness connector. Disconnect EDIS diagnostic cable positive lead at battery. Set DVOM on 200-ohm scale. Measure resistance between PIP E (43) and BAT- (7) at BOB. If resistance is less than 10 ohms, repair PIP short circuit to ground. Remove test equipment and reconnect all components. Clear Continuous Memory and Rerun Quick Test. If resistance is 10 ohms or more, go to step **10)**.

10) Check For PIP Short To VBAT – Isolate EDIS Module & ECA – With ignition off and ECA disconnected, set DVOM on 20-volt DC scale. With KOEO, measure voltage between PIP E (43) and BAT- (7) at BOB. If DC voltage is .5 volt or more, repair short circuit. PIP is shorted to power. Remove test equipment and reconnect all components. Clear Continuous Memory Codes and rerun Quick Test.

If voltage less than .5 volt, replace ECA. PIP circuit is shorted internally in ECA. Remove test equipment and reconnect all components. Clear Continuous Memory and Rerun Quick Test.

11) Check PWR GND To EDIS Module - IGN GND Fault - With ignition off, set DVOM on 2-k/ohm scale. Measure resistance between PWR GND E (27) and BAT- (7) at BOB. If resistance is less than 1050 ohms, replace EDIS module. Ground circuit is open in EDIS module. Remove test equipment and reconnect all components. Clear Continuous Memory Codes and rerun Quick Test. If resistance is 1050 ohms or more, repair open circuit. PWR GND circuit to EDIS module is open. Remove test equipment and reconnect all components. Clear Continuous Memory and Rerun Quick Test.

12) Check Vehicle Performance - If the original problem was vehicle cranks but does not start, go to step **13)**. If not, go to PINPOINT TEST D step **1)**.

13) Check PWR GND to EDIS Module - With ignition off and ECA disconnected, connect EDIS diagnostic cable to BOB, EDIS module, and coil pack. Do not connect VR sensor tee. Use EDIS "6" overlay (if available). Connect EDIS diagnostic cable negative lead to battery, leave positive lead disconnected. Set EDIS diagnostic cable box switch to "4/6 cylinder" position. Set DVOM on 2-k/ohm scale. measure resistance between PWR GND (27) and BAT- (7) at BOB. If resistance is less than 5 ohms, go to step **14)**. If resistance is 5 ohms or more, repair open circuit. Remove all test equipment and reconnect all components. Clear Continuous Memory Codes and rerun Quick Test.

14) Check For VBAT Open To EDIS Module - With ignition off and ECA disconnected, set DVOM on 20-volt DC scale. With KOEO, measure voltage between VBAT E (51) and BAT- (7) at BOB. If DC voltage is 10.5 volts or more, go to step **15)**. If voltage is less than 10.5 volts, repair open VBAT to EDIS module circuit. Remove all test equipment and reconnect all components. Clear Continuous Memory and Rerun Quick Test.

15) Check VRS (+) Bias At EDIS Module - With ignition off and ECA disconnected, set DVOM on 20-volt DC scale. With KOEO, measure voltage between VRS+ E (35) and BAT- (7) at BOB. If the DC voltage is .8-2.2 volts, proceed to step **16)**. If voltage is not as specified, proceed to step **17)**.

16) Check VRS Amplitude At EDIS Module - With ignition off, reconnect ECA. Disconnect EDIS diagnostic cable negative lead from battery. Set DVOM on 20-volt AC scale. Crank engine, and measure voltage between VRS+ E (35) and VRS- E (48) at BOB. If stabilized AC voltage reading is .4 volt or more, go to PINPOINT TEST D, step **1)**. If voltage is less than .4 volt, go to step **25)**.

17) Check VRS (+) Bias - Isolate VR Sensor - With ignition off and ECA disconnected, disconnect VR sensor from vehicle harness connector. Set DVOM on 20-volt DC scale. With KOEO, measure voltage between VRS+ E (35) and BAT- (7) at BOB. If DC voltage is .8-2.2 volts, go to step **21)**. If voltage is not .8-2.2 volts, go to step **18)**.

18) Check VRS (+) High Or Low - If bias voltage reading in step **17)** was less than .8 volt, go to step **19)**. If bias voltage reading in step **17)** was .8 volt or more, go to step **20)**.

19) Check VRS (+) For Short To Ground - Isolate EDIS Module - With ignition off and ECA disconnected, disconnect EDIS module from EDIS diagnostic cable module tee, leave diagnostic cable connected to vehicle harness connector. Set DVOM on 2-k/ohm scale. Measure resistance between VRS+ E (35) and BAT- (7) at BOB. If resistance is less than 1025 ohms, repair short circuit. VRS (+) is shorted to ground. Remove test equipment and reconnect all components. Clear Continuous Memory Codes and rerun Quick Test. If resistance is 1025 ohms or more, replace EDIS module. VRS (+) is shorted to ground. Remove test equipment and reconnect all components. Clear Continuous Memory Codes and rerun Quick Test.

20) Check VRS (+) For Short To Power - Isolate EDIS Module - With ignition off and ECA disconnected, disconnect EDIS module from EDIS diagnostic cable module tee, leave EDIS diagnostic cable connected to vehicle harness connector. Set DVOM on 20-volt DC scale. With KOEO, measure voltage between VRS+ E (35) and BAT- (7) at BOB. If DC voltage is .5 volt or more, repair short circuit. VRS (+) circuit is shorted to power. Remove test equipment and reconnect all components. Clear Continuous Memory Codes and rerun Quick Test. If voltage is less than .5 volt, replace EDIS module. VRS (+) circuit is shorted to power. Remove test equipment and reconnect all components. Clear Continuous Memory Codes and rerun Quick Test.

21) Check VRS (-) Bias - With ignition off and ECA disconnected, set DVOM on 20-volt DC scale. With KOEO, measure voltage between VRS- E (48) and BAT- (7) at BOB. If DC voltage is .8-2.2 volts, replace VR sensor. Short to ground in VR sensor. Remove test equipment and reconnect all components. Clear Continuous Memory Codes and rerun Quick Test. If voltage is not .8-2.2 volts, proceed to step **22)**.

22) Check VRS (-) Signal High Or Low - If DC bias voltage reading in step **21)** is less than .8 volt, go to step **23)**. If voltage is .8 volt or more, go to step **24)**.

23) Check VRS (-) For Short To Ground - Isolate EDIS Module - With ignition off and ECA disconnected, disconnect EDIS module from EDIS diagnostic cable module tee, leave diagnostic cable connected to vehicle harness connector. Set DVOM on 2-k/ohm scale. Measure resistance between VRS- E (48) and BAT- (7) at BOB. If resistance is less than 1025 ohms, repair short circuit. VRS circuit is shorted to ground. Remove test equipment and reconnect all components. Clear Continuous Memory Codes and rerun Quick Test. If resistance is 1025 ohms or more, replace EDIS module. VRS circuit is shorted to ground. Remove test equipment and reconnect all components. Clear Continuous Memory Codes and rerun Quick Test.

24) Check VRS (-) For Short To VBAT - Isolate EDIS Module - With ignition off and ECA disconnected, disconnect EDIS module from EDIS diagnostic cable module tee, leaving EDIS diagnostic cable connected to vehicle harness connector. Set DVOM on 20-volt DC scale. With KOEO, measure voltage between VRS- E (48) and BAT- (7) at BOB. If DC voltage is .5 volt or more, repair short circuit. VRS (-) circuit is shorted to VBAT. Remove test equipment, and reconnect all components. Clear Continuous Memory Codes, and rerun Quick Test. If voltage is less than .5 volt, replace EDIS module. VRS (-) circuit is shorted to VBAT. Remove test equipment, and reconnect all components. Clear Continuous Memory Codes, and rerun Quick Test.

25) Check VRS Amplitude At EDIS Module - Isolate EDIS Module - With ignition off and ECA disconnected, disconnect EDIS module from EDIS diagnostic cable module tee, leave diagnostic cable connected to vehicle harness connector. Set DVOM on 20-volt AC scale. Crank engine and measure voltage between VRS+ E (35) and VRS- E (48) at BOB. If stabilized AC voltage reading is .4 volt or more, replace EDIS module. VRS (+) circuit is shorted to VRS (-). Remove test equipment and reconnect all components. Clear Continuous Memory Codes and rerun Quick Test. If stabilized AC voltage reading is less than .4 volt, go to step **26)**.

26) Check VRS Resistance - With ignition off and ECA disconnected, disconnect EDIS diagnostic cable negative lead from battery. Set DVOM on 20-k/ohm scale. Measure resistance between VRS- E (48) and VRS+ E (35) at BOB. If resistance is 2580-2470 ohms, go to step **27)**. If resistance is not 2580-2700 ohms, go to step **28)**.

27) Check VRS Air Gap - With ignition off, check VRS air gap. Ensure there is an air gap between sensor and trigger wheel. Air gap is not adjustable. If air gap is okay, replace VR sensor. Remove all test equipment and reconnect all components. Clear Continuous Memory Codes and rerun Quick Test. If air gap is not okay, repair or replace components as required. Remove test equipment and reconnect all components. Clear Continuous Memory Codes and rerun Quick Test.

28) Check VRS High Or Low Resistance - With ignition off and ECA disconnected, disconnect EDIS diagnostic cable negative lead from battery. Set DVOM on 20-k/ohm scale. Measure resistance between VRS- E (48) and VRS+ E (35) at BOB. If resistance is less than 2550 ohms, go to step **29)**. If resistance is 2550 ohms or more, go to step **30)**.

29) Check VRS (+) For Short To VRS (-) (Isolate VRS) - With ignition off and ECA disconnected, disconnect VR sensor from vehicle harness connector. Set DVOM on 200-k/ohm scale. Measure resistance between VRS+ E (35) and VRS- E (48) at BOB. If resistance is 3000 ohms or more, replace VR sensor. Sensor windings are shorted. Remove test equipment and reconnect all components. Clear Continuous Memory Codes and rerun Quick Test. If resistance

1991 ENGINE PERFORMANCE
System & Component Testing – EEC-IV (Cont.)

is less than 3000 ohms, repair short circuit. VRS (+) shorted to VRS (-). Remove test equipment, and reconnect all components. Clear Continuous Memory Codes, and rerun Quick Test.

30) Check For VRS (+) Open Circuit (Resistance High Fault) – With ignition off and ECA disconnected, connect EDIS diagnostic cable VR sensor tee to VR sensor and vehicle harness connector. Set DVOM on 20-k/ohm scale. Measure resistance between VRS+ S (31) and VRS+ E (35) at BOB. If resistance is 2025 ohms or more, repair open circuit. VRS (+) circuit is open. Remove test equipment and reconnect all components. Clear Continuous Memory Codes and rerun Quick Test. If resistance is less than 2025 ohms, go to step **31)**.

31) Check For VRS (-) Open Circuit (Resistance High Fault) – With ignition off and ECA disconnected, set DVOM on 20-k/ohm scale. Measure resistance between VRS- S (32) and VRS- E (48) at BOB. If resistance is less than 2025 ohms, replace VR sensor. Resistance is high. Remove test equipment and reconnect all components. Clear Continuous Memory Codes and rerun Quick Test. If resistance is 2025 ohms or more, repair open circuit. VRS (-) circuit is open. Remove test equipment and reconnect all components. Clear Continuous Memory Codes and rerun Quick Test.

CAUTION: Never connect ECA to ECA BOB when performing EDIS diagnostics unless directed to do so.

PINPOINT TEST B – 1) Check For IDM Short High – With ignition off, connect EDIS diagnostic cable to BOB, EDIS module, and coil pack. Do not connect VR sensor tee. Use EDIS "6" overlay. Connect EDIS diagnostic cable negative and positive leads to battery. Set EDIS diagnostic cable box switch to "4/6 cylinder" position. Set DVOM on 20-volt DC scale. Start engine and measure voltage between diagnostic cable IDM DETECTOR (30) and BAT- (7) at BOB. If pulses are present, the IDM detector output will be 5-7 volts DC. If DC voltage is 5-7 volts, go to step **2)**. If DC voltage is not 5-7 volts, go to step **3)**.

2) Check For IDM Open – With ignition off, disconnect ECA. Disconnect EDIS module from EDIS module tee, leave EDIS diagnostic cable connected to vehicle harness connector. Connect ECA BOB to ECA harness connector. Set DVOM on 200-ohm scale. Measure resistance between IDM E (41) at BOB, and terminal No. 4 at ECA BOB. If resistance is less than 5 ohms, replace ECA. IDM signal at ECA is okay. Remove test equipment and reconnect all components. Clear Continuous Memory Codes and rerun Quick Test. If resistance is 5 ohms or more, repair open circuit. Remove test equipment and reconnect all components. Clear Continuous Memory Codes and rerun Quick Test.

3) Check IDM Output From EDIS Module – Isolate Harness – With ignition off, ensure ECA is connected. Set DVOM on 20-volt DC scale. Start engine and push EDIS IDM button at the EDIS diagnostic cable connector to BOB. Measure voltage between diagnostic cable IDM DETECTOR (30) and BAT- (7) at BOB. If DC voltage is 5-7 volts, go to step **4)**. If voltage is not 5-7 volts, replace EDIS module. No IDM output from module. Remove test equipment and reconnect all components. Clear Continuous Memory Codes and rerun Quick Test.

4) Check For IDM Short In ECA – Isolate ECA – With ignition off, disconnect ECA. Set DVOM on 20-volt DC scale. Crank engine and measure voltage between diagnostic cable IDM DETECTOR (30) and BAT- (7) at BOB. If DC voltage is 4.4-6.0 volts, replace ECA. IDM circuit is shorted in ECA. Remove test equipment and reconnect all components. Clear Continuous Memory Codes and rerun Quick Test. If voltage is not as specified, go to step **5)**.

5) Check For IDM Short To Ground In Harness – With ignition off, disconnect ECA. Disconnect EDIS module from diagnostic cable module tee, leave EDIS diagnostic cable connected to vehicle harness connector. Set DVOM on 20-k/ohm scale. Measure resistance between IDM E (41) and BAT- (7) at BOB. If resistance is less than 5 ohms, repair short circuit. IDM is shorted to VBAT. Remove test equipment and reconnect all components. Clear Continuous Memory Codes and rerun Quick Test. If resistance is 5 ohms or more, go to step **6)**.

6) Check For IDM Short To VBAT In Harness – With ignition off, disconnect ECA. Set DVOM on 20-volt DC scale. With KOEO, measure voltage between IDM E (41) and BAT- (7) at BOB. If DC voltage is .5 volt or more, repair short circuit. IDM is shorted to VBAT between EDIS module and ECA. Remove test equipment and reconnect all components. Clear Continuous Memory Codes and rerun Quick Test. If voltage is not as specified, repair short circuit or replace harness IDM is shorted to another wire between EDIS module and ECA. Remove test equipment and reconnect all components. Clear Continuous Memory Codes and rerun Quick Test.

CAUTION: Never connect ECA to ECA BOB when performing EDIS diagnostics unless directed to do so.

PINPOINT TEST C – 1) Check Base Ignition Timing – With ignition off, install EDIS diagnostic cable to BOB, EDIS module, and coil pack. Do not connect VR sensor tee. Use EDIS "6" overlay (if available). Connect EDIS diagnostic cable negative and positive leads to battery. Set EDIS diagnostic cable box switch to "4/6 cylinder" position. Connect timing light (must be EDIS/DIS compatible). Start engine and allow it to warm up. If timing is 10±2 degrees BTDC when EDIS diagnostic cable SAW button is pushed, go to step **2)**. If timing is not as specified, proceed to step **8)**.

2) Check For Advance Spark Angle – If engine timing is greater than 15 degrees BTDC when diagnostic cable SAW button is released, EDIS Ignition System is okay. Go to TROUBLE SHOOTING – NO-CODES article for further driveability symptom diagnosis. If timing is not as specified, go to step **3)**.

3) Check SAW At EDIS Module – With ignition off, set DVOM on 20-volt DC scale. Start engine and measure voltage between EDIS diagnostic cable SAW DETECTOR (21) and BAT- (7) at BOB. If DC voltage reading is 5-7 volts, replace EDIS module. SAW input to EDIS module is okay but no spark advance is present. Remove test equipment and reconnect all components. Clear Continuous Memory Codes and rerun Quick Test. If DC voltage is not 5-7 volts, proceed to step **4)**.

4) Check For SAW Short In EDIS Module – Isolate EDIS Module – With ignition off and ECA connected, set DVOM on 20-volt DC scale. Push EDIS diagnostic cable SAW button at EDIS diagnostic cable connector to BOB. Start engine and measure voltage between SAW DETECTOR (21) and BAT- (7) at BOB. If DC voltage reading is 5-7 volts, replace EDIS module. SAW circuit is shorted in EDIS module. Remove test equipment and reconnect all components. Clear Continuous Memory Codes and rerun Quick Test. If DC voltage is not 5-7 volts, proceed to step **5)**.

5) Check For SAW Short To Ground In Harness – With ignition off, disconnect ECA. Disconnect EDIS module from EDIS diagnostic cable module tee. Leave EDIS diagnostic cable connected to vehicle harness connector. Disconnect HEGO connector. Set DVOM on 200-ohm scale. Measure resistance between SAW E (45) and BAT- (7) at BOB. If resistance is less than 100 ohms, repair short circuit. Remove test equipment and reconnect all components. Clear Continuous Memory Codes and rerun Quick Test. If resistance is 100 ohms or more, reconnect HEGO sensor and go to step **6)**.

6) Check For SAW Short To VBAT In Harness – With ignition off, and ECA disconnected, set DVOM on 20-volt DC scale. With KOEO, measure voltage between SAW E (45) and BAT- (7) at BOB. If DC voltage reading is less than .5 volt, repair short circuit. SAW is shorted to VBAT. Remove test equipment and reconnect all components. Clear Continuous Memory Codes and rerun Quick Test. If voltage is .5 volt or more, go to step **7)**.

7) Check For SAW Open – With ignition off and ECA disconnected, connect ECA BOB to ECA harness connector. Set DVOM on 200-ohm scale. Measure resistance between SAW E (45) at BOB and terminal No. 36 at ECA BOB. If resistance is less than 5 ohms, replace ECA. SAW is not being transmitted by ECA. Remove test equipment and reconnect all components. Clear Continuous Memory Codes and rerun Quick Test. If resistance is not as specified, repair open circuit. Remove test equipment and reconnect all components. Clear Continuous Memory Codes and rerun Quick Test.

8) Inspect VR Sensor/Trigger Wheel – If VR sensor or trigger wheel is damaged, loose or misaligned, replace or repair components as required. Remove test equipment and reconnect all components. Clear Continuous Memory Codes and rerun Quick Test. If trigger wheel and VR sensor are not damaged or loose, replace EDIS module. Module cannot control timing. Remove test equipment and reconnect all components. Clear Continuous Memory Codes and rerun Quick Test.

CAUTION: Never connect ECA to ECA BOB when performing EDIS diagnostics unless directed to do so.

PINPOINT TEST D – 1) Check For VBAT Open To Coil – With ignition off and ECA connected, install EDIS diagnostic cable to BOB, EDIS module, and coil pack. Do not connect VR sensor tee. Use EDIS "6" overlay (if available). Connect EDIS diagnostic cable negative lead to battery. Set EDIS diagnostic cable box switch to "4/6 cylinder" position. Set DVOM on 20-volt DC scale. With KOEO, measure voltage between VBAT C (5) and BAT– (7) at BOB. If DC voltage is 10.5 volts or more, go to step **2)**. If voltage is less than 10.5, repair open VBAT to EDIS module circuit. Remove test equipment and reconnect all components. Clear Continuous Memory Codes and rerun Quick Test.

2) Verify Vehicle Operating Mode – If vehicle will crank and start, go to step **4)**. If vehicle will not crank and start, go to step **3)**.

3) Check C1, C2, C3 In Sequence At Coil Pack During Cranking – With ignition off and ECA connected, set DVOM on 20-volt AC scale, crank engine and measure voltage between BAT– (7) and each coil C1C (3), C2C (6), C3C (10) at BOB. If stabilized AC voltage reading is less than .2 volt, replace coil pack. Remove all test equipment and reconnect all components. Clear Continuous Memory Codes and rerun Quick Test. If voltage is .2 volt or more, go to step **5)**.

4) Check C1, C2, C3 In Sequence At Coil Pack With Engine Running – With ignition off and ECA connected, set DVOM on 20-volt AC scale, crank engine and measure voltage between BAT– (7) and each coil C1C (3), C2C (6), C3C (10) at BOB. If stabilized AC voltage reading is less than 1.0 volt, replace coil pack. Remove all test equipment, and reconnect all components. Clear Continuous Memory Codes, and rerun Quick Test. If voltage is 1.0 volt or more, go to step **5)**.

5) Check C1, C2, C3 In Sequence At Coil Pack – KOEO Coil Fault – With ignition off and ECA disconnected, set DVOM on 20-volt DC scale. With KOEO, measure voltage between BAT– (7) and each coil C1C (3), C2C (6), C3C (10) at BOB. If each DC voltage reading is 10.5 volts or more, go to step **6)**. If voltage is less than 10.5 volts, go to step **10)**.

6) Check C1, C2, C3 In Sequence At EDIS Module – KOEO Coil Fault – With ignition off and ECA disconnected, set DVOM on 20-volt DC scale. With KOEO, measure voltage between BAT– (7) and each coil C1E (53), C2E (55), C3E (54) at BOB. If each DC voltage reading is 10.5 volts or more, go to step **7)**. If voltage is less than 10.5 volts, repair open circuit. Remove all test equipment and reconnect all components. Clear Continuous Memory Codes and rerun Quick Test.

7) Check C1, C2, C3 In Sequence At Coil Pack – Isolate Coil –With ignition off and ECA disconnected, disconnect coil pack from coil tee. Leave EDIS diagnostic cable connected to vehicle harness connector. Set DVOM on 20-volt DC scale. With KOEO, measure voltage between BAT– (7) and each coil C1C (3), C2C (6), C3C (10) at BOB. If each DC voltage reading is less than .5 volt, go to step **9)**. If voltage is .5 volt or more, go to step **8)**.

8) Check C1, C2, C3 In Sequence At Coil Pack – Isolate EDIS Module – With ignition off and ECA disconnected, disconnect EDIS module from EDIS module tee. Leave EDIS diagnostic cable connected to vehicle harness connector. Set DVOM on 20-volt DC scale. With KOEO, measure voltage between BAT– (7) and each coil C1C (3), C2C (6), C3C (10) at BOB. If each DC voltage reading is less than .5 volt, replace EDIS module. Remove all test equipment and reconnect all components. Clear Continuous Memory Codes and rerun Quick Test. If voltage is .5 volt or more, repair short circuit. Remove all test equipment and reconnect all components. Clear Continuous Memory Codes and rerun Quick Test.

9) Check C1, C2, C3 Coil Primary – With ignition off and ECA disconnected, reconnect coil pack to coil tee. Set DVOM on 20-ohm scale. Measure resistance between VBAT C (5) and each coil C1C (3), C2C (6), C3C (10) at BOB. If each resistance reading is .8 ohms or more, replace EDIS module. Remove all test equipment and reconnect all components. Clear Continuous Memory Codes and rerun Quick Test. If resistance reading less than .8 ohm, replace coil pack. Remove all test equipment and reconnect all components. Clear Continuous Memory Codes and rerun Quick Test.

10) Check C1, C2, C3 Short To Ground In Coil Pack – With ignition off and ECA disconnected, set DVOM on 2-k/ohm scale. Measure resistance between BAT– (7) and each coil C1C (3), C2C (6), C3C (10) at BOB. If each resistance reading is less than 1200 ohms, go to step **11)**. If resistance reading is 1200 ohms or more, replace coil pack. Remove all test equipment, and reconnect all components. Clear Continuous Memory Codes, and rerun Quick Test.

11) Check C1, C2, C3 Short To Ground In Harness – With ignition off and ECA disconnected, disconnect EDIS coil tee from coil pack and vehicle harness connector. Disconnect EDIS module from EDIS module tee, leaving EDIS cable connected to vehicle harness connector. Set DVOM on 2-k/ohm scale. Measure resistance between BAT– (7) and each coil C1C (3), C2C (6), C3C (10) at BOB. If any resistance reading is less than 5 ohms, repair short. Remove all test equipment, and reconnect all components. Clear Continuous Memory Codes, and rerun Quick Test. If any resistance reading is 5 ohms or more, replace EDIS module. Remove all test equipment, and reconnect all components. Clear Continuous Memory Codes, and rerun Quick Test.

EMISSION SYSTEMS & SUB-SYSTEMS

AIR INJECTION

Air Supply Pump – Check belt tension and adjust to proper tension, if necessary. Disconnect air supply hose from by-pass control valve. Start engine. Pump is operating satisfactorily if airflow is felt at pump outlet and airflow increases as engine speed is increased. If this condition is not met, replace pump.

CAUTION: DO NOT pry on the air supply pump to adjust belt tension. Aluminum housing of pump may collapse.

Air Silencer/Filter (Air Pump & Pulse Air Inlet) – Inspect hoses and air silencer for leaks. Disconnect hose from air silencer outlet. Remove silencer from vehicle, and visually inspect for plugging. If no plugging or leaks are found, silencer is okay. If any plugging or leaks are found, repair or replace as required.

Air By-Pass Valve (Normally Closed) – 1) Disconnect air supply hose at valve outlet. *See Fig. 17.* Remove vacuum line from vacuum nipple and check for presence of vacuum at nipple. There must be vacuum present at nipple before proceeding.

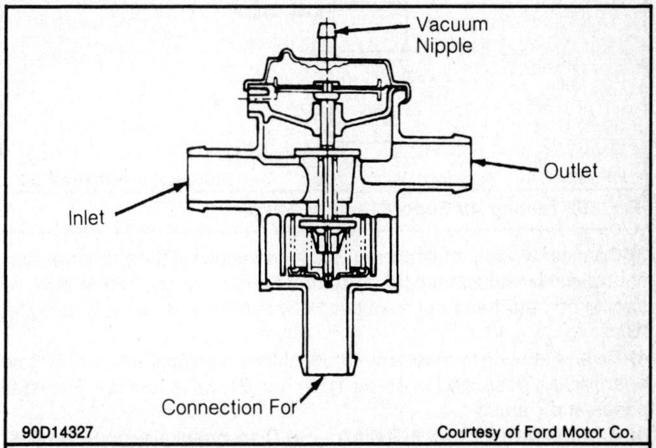
Vacuum
Nipple
Outlet
Inlet
Connection For
90D14327
Courtesy of Ford Motor Co.

Fig. 17: Testing Normally Closed Air By-Pass Valve

2) Reconnect vacuum line to vacuum nipple. With engine at 1500 RPM, air pump supply air should be heard and felt at air by-pass valve outlet.
3) With engine still at 1500 RPM, disconnect vacuum line. Air at outlet should decrease significantly or shut off. Air pump supply air should now be heard or felt at silencer ports or at dump port.

1991 ENGINE PERFORMANCE
System & Component Testing – EEC-IV (Cont.)

4) If the normally closed air by-pass valve does not perform as described in steps **2)** and **3)**, check the air pump for faults. If air pump is operating satisfactorily, replace air by-pass valve.

Air Check Valve – 1) Visually inspect thermactor hoses, tubes, control valve(s) and check valve(s) for leaks that may be due to backflow of exhaust gases. If holes are found and/or traces of exhaust gas products are evident, check valve may be suspect.

2) Valve should allow free flow of air in direction of arrow only. *See Fig. 18*. The valve(s) should check (or block) the free flow of exhaust gas air in the opposite direction.

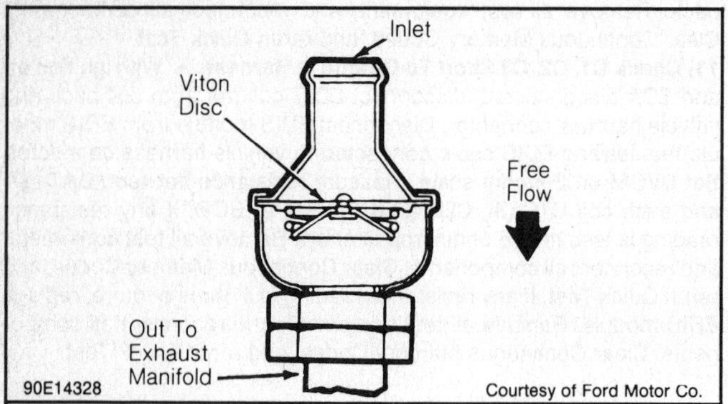
Inlet
Viton
Disc
Free
Flow
Out To
Exhaust
Manifold
90E14328
Courtesy of Ford Motor Co.

Fig. 18: Testing Air Check Valve

3) If air does not flow as indicated or if exhaust gas backflows opposite of direction of arrow in illustration, replace check valve.

Air Supply Control Valve – 1) Disconnect air supply hose at inlet. Accelerate engine to 1500 RPM and verify presence of airflow in hose. Reconnect air supply hose to valve inlet.

2) Disconnect air supply hoses at outlets "A" and "B". *See Fig. 19*. Remove vacuum line at vacuum nipple. Accelerate engine to 1500 RPM. Airflow should be heard and felt at outlet "B" with little or no airflow at outlet "A".

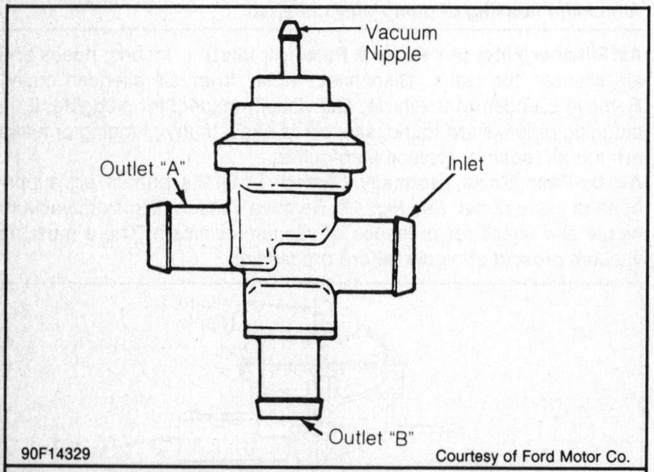
Vacuum
Nipple
Outlet "A"
Inlet
Outlet "B"
90F14329
Courtesy of Ford Motor Co.

Fig. 19: Testing Air Supply Control Valve

3) Connect a vacuum line from manifold vacuum fitting to air supply control valve vacuum nipple. Accelerate engine to 1500 RPM. Airflow should be heard and felt at outlet "A" with little or no airflow at outlet "B".

4) If valve does not meet above conditions, replace valve. If airflow operates as described in steps **1)**, **2)** and **3)**, valve is okay. Reinstall hoses and clamps.

Air Control Valve (Switch-Relief) – 1) Disconnect air supply hose at inlet. Accelerate engine to 1500 RPM and verify presence of airflow in hose. Reconnect air supply hose to valve inlet.

2) Carefully disconnect the air supply hoses at outlets "A" and "B". *See Fig. 20*. Carefully remove vacuum line at vacuum nipple. Accelerate engine to 1500 RPM. Airflow should be heard and felt at outlet "B" with little or no airflow at outlet "A".

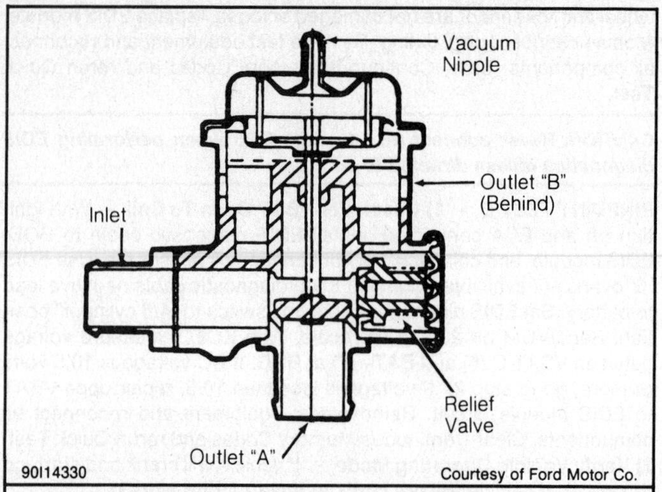
Vacuum
Nipple
Outlet "B"
(Behind)
Inlet
Relief
Valve
Outlet "A"
90I14330
Courtesy of Ford Motor Co.

Fig. 20: Testing Air Control Valve (Switch-Relief)

3) Connect a vacuum line from manifold vacuum fitting to air control valve vacuum nipple. Accelerate engine to 1500 RPM. Airflow should be heard and felt at outlet "A" with little or no airflow at outlet "B".

4) If the conditions in steps **2)** and **3)** are not met, replace the air control valve. If the valve operates satisfactorily, restore all hose and vacuum connections.

Air Pump Resonator – Visually inspect for holes. Remove hoses and check for restricted ports. Replace resonator if holes or ports are restricted. Reconnect hoses and install clamps.

Combination Air By-Pass/Air Control Valve – 1) Disconnect hoses from outlets "A" and "B". *See Fig. 21*. Disconnect and plug vacuum line to port "D". With engine operating at 1500 RPM, airflow should be noted coming out of by-pass vents.

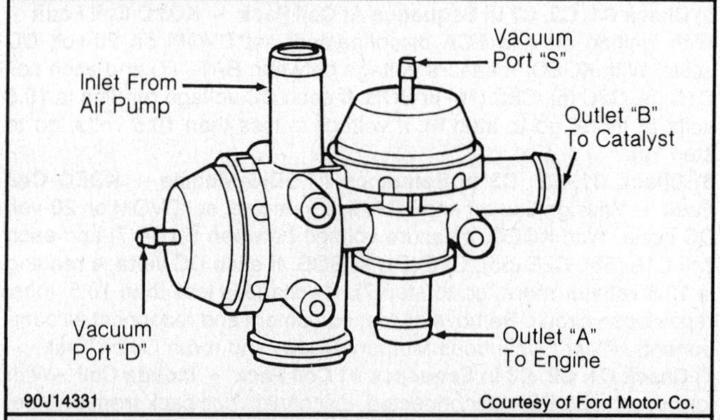
Vacuum
Port "S"
Inlet From
Air Pump
Outlet "B"
To Catalyst
Vacuum
Port "D"
Outlet "A"
To Engine
90J14331
Courtesy of Ford Motor Co.

Fig. 21: Testing Combination Air By-Pass/Air Control Valve

2) Reconnect vacuum line to port "D". Disconnect and plug vacuum line to port "S". Ensure vacuum is present in line to vacuum port "D". Accelerate engine to 1500 RPM. Airflow should be noted coming out of outlet "B". No airflow should be detected at outlet "A".

3) Apply 8-10 in. Hg vacuum to port "S". With engine operating at 1500 RPM, airflow should be noted coming out of outlet "A". If valve is bleed type, less air will flow from outlet "A" or "B", and the main discharge will change when vacuum is applied to port "S".

4) If the conditions in the above steps are not met, replace valve. If above conditions are met, valve is okay. Reconnect hoses and vacuum lines.

Dual Thermactor Air Control Solenoid Valve – The function of each valve can be determined by externally energizing the valve with vacuum lines attached. Check the resistance of each solenoid. Resistance should be 51-108 ohms when checked at the coil terminals. If the resistance is not 51-108 ohms, solenoid should be replaced.

Thermactor Idle Vacuum (TIV) Valve – 1) With engine at idle and transmission in NEUTRAL, apply vacuum to small nipple and place fingers over the TIV valve atmospheric vent holes. *See Fig. 22*. If no vacuum is sensed, the TIV is damaged and must be replaced. If vacuum is sensed, go to next step.

2) With engine still at idle, apply vacuum to TIV valve large nipple from using a vacuum pump. See TIV VALVE (LARGE NIPPLE) VACUUM SPECIFICATIONS table. If vacuum is not held, the TIV is damaged and must be replaced. If no vacuum is sensed, replace valve.

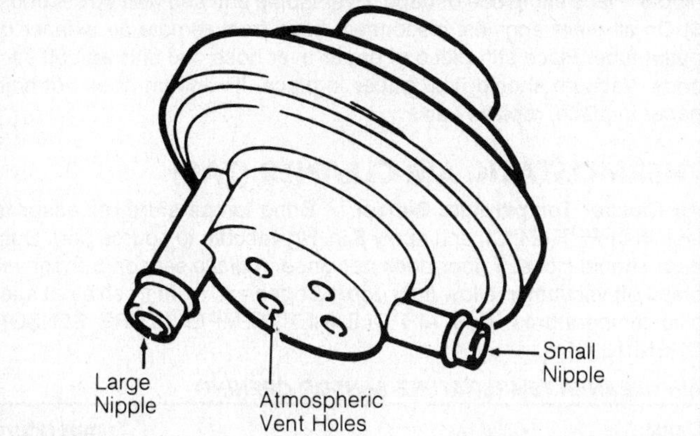

Large
Nipple
Atmospheric
Vent Holes
Small
Nipple

90A14332 Courtesy of Ford Motor Co.

Fig. 22: Locating Thermactor Idle Vacuum (TIV) Valve Vents

TIV VALVE (LARGE NIPPLE) VACUUM SPECIFICATIONS

TIV Decal Color Code	In. Hg
Ash	5.1-10
Red	11.8-15.2

Vacuum Control Valve (VCV) – 1) A 2-port valve may be in open or closed position when engine is cold, but should reverse when engine is warmed to operating temperature.

2) For 3-port valves, with a cold engine, passage "A" to "B" should be closed and passage "A" to "C" should be open. *See Fig. 23.* With engine at normal operating temperature, the VCV should be open between "A" and "B" and closed between "A" and "C".

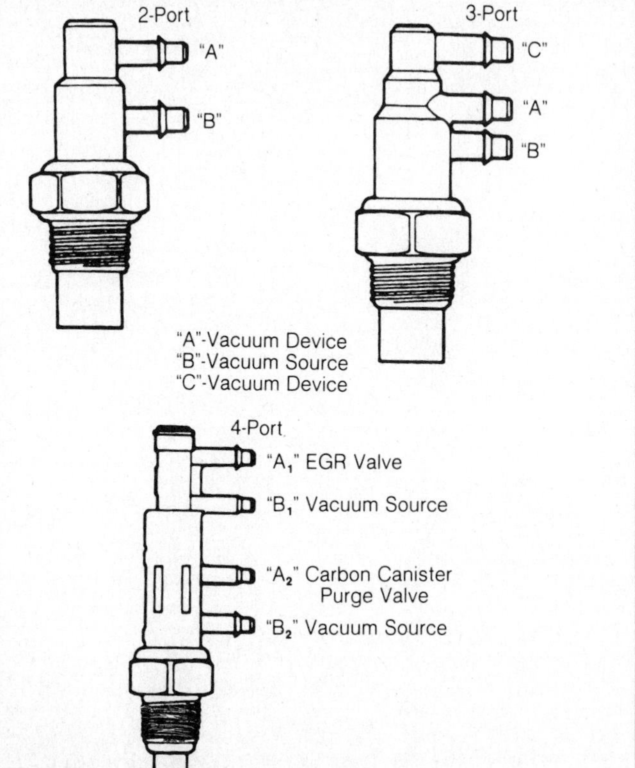

2-Port
"A"
"B"
3-Port
"C"
"A"
"B"
"A"-Vacuum Device
"B"-Vacuum Source
"C"-Vacuum Device
4-Port
"A_1," EGR Valve
"B_1," Vacuum Source
"A_2," Carbon Canister Purge Valve
"B_2," Vacuum Source

90B14333 Courtesy of Ford Motor Co.

Fig. 23: Identifying Vacuum Control Valve Ports

3) For the 4-port valve, check "A_1," to "B_1," and "A_2," to "B_2," separately. *See Fig. 23.* A 4-port valve may be in open or closed position when engine is cold, but should reverse when engine is warmed to operating temperature. If these conditions are not met, replace the valve.

Electrical Vacuum Control Valve – 1) Electrical vacuum control valve may be either open or closed at room temperature, but should reverse the position when engine is at full operating temperature. While engine is cold, measure continuity across switch terminals. *See Fig. 24.* Note if switch is open or closed.

2) Warm engine to normal operating temperature. Measure continuity across switch terminals again. Continuity should be opposite of cold condition. If switch continuity does not switch, replace valve. Check vacuum function of valve as described in VACUUM CONTROL VALVE above.

Vacuum Check Valve – Apply 16 in. Hg vacuum to check side of valve and trap. If vacuum remains greater than 15 in. Hg for 10 seconds, valve operation is normal. If vacuum drops faster, replace valve.

Vacuum Reservoir – When charged with 15-20 in. Hg vacuum, vacuum loss should not exceed .5 in. Hg in 60 seconds. If vacuum loss is faster, replace reservoir.

Pulse Air Valve – With engine at normal operating temperature and at curb idle, remove inlet hose from valve. A suction should be felt at valve inlet. If suction is not felt, replace valve.

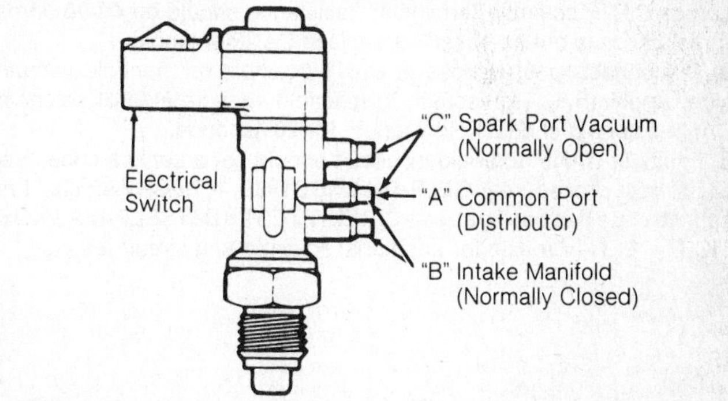

Electrical
Switch
"C" Spark Port Vacuum
(Normally Open)
"A" Common Port
(Distributor)
"B" Intake Manifold
(Normally Closed)

90C14334 Courtesy of Ford Motor Co.

Fig. 24: Identifying Electrical Vacuum Control Valve Ports

EXHAUST GAS RECIRCULATION (EGR)

Electronic EGR Valve (EEGR) & Pressure Feedback Electronic (PFE) – 1) Ensure all vacuum hoses are correctly routed and securely attached. Replace any crimped or broken hoses. Ensure there is less than 1 in. Hg vacuum to EGR valve at idle with engine at normal operating temperature.

NOTE: EVR solenoid has a constant internal leak. You will notice a small vacuum signal of less than 1 in. Hg vacuum at idle.

2) Install tachometer. Disconnect Idle Air By-Pass Valve electrical connector (if equipped). Remove and plug vacuum hose at EGR valve. Start engine and idle in neutral. Note idle speed. Using hand vacuum pump, slowly apply 5-10 in. Hg vacuum to EGR valve. When vacuum is fully applied to EGR valve, engine should do one or more of the following:

- Engine should stall.
- Idle speed should drop more than 100 RPM.
- Idle speed should return to normal when vacuum is released.

3) Repair or replace EGR valve if none of the above occurs. Reconnect idle air by-pass valve electrical connector. Unplug and reconnect vacuum hose at EGR valve.

EGR Vacuum Regulator (EVR) – Faults in EVR or circuit should set a service code. See Quick Test procedure in SELF-DIAGNOSTICS – EEC-IV article. If no service code has been set, see CIRCUIT TEST DN in SELF-DIAGNOSTICS – EEC-IV article for diagnostic procedures.

On 2.3L Ranger (1989-91), intermittent operation or failure of EVR may be caused by water in EVR or vacuum hoses connected to it. If water

1991 ENGINE PERFORMANCE
System & Component Testing – EEC-IV (Cont.)

or moisture is found in EVR or hoses connected to it, install new service part, available from manufacturer, in an inverted position. Use shop air to clear water and moisture from vacuum hoses. Clear Continuous Memory Codes if set and run Quick Test to verify repair.

EGR Solenoid – Remove EGR solenoid harness connector. Measure resistance across solenoid terminals. Resistance should be 65-110 ohms. Set DVOM to 200-k/ohm scale. Measure resistance between each solenoid terminal and ground or side of solenoid. Resistance should be 10 k/ohms or more. If resistance is not as specified in either test, replace solenoid.

Vacuum Check Valve – Apply 16 in. Hg vacuum to check side of valve and trap. If vacuum remains greater than 15 in. Hg for 10 seconds, valve operation is normal. If not, replace valve.

Vacuum Reservoir – When charged with 15-20 in. Hg vacuum, vacuum loss should not exceed .5 in. Hg in 60 seconds. If it does, replace reservoir.

FUEL EVAPORATION

Canister Purge Regulator (CPR) Valve – With CPR valve de-energized, apply 5 in. Hg vacuum to source port. Valve should not pass air. Apply 9-14 volts to one electrical terminal and ground the other. Valve should open and pass air. If valve does not operate as described, replace valve.

Canister Purge (CANP) Solenoid – 1) Disconnect CANP solenoid harness connector. Set DVOM to 200-ohm scale. Measure resistance across CANP solenoid terminals. Resistance should be 40-90 ohms. If resistance is not as specified, replace CANP solenoid.

2) Disconnect vacuum hose at CANP solenoid on manifold vacuum side. Apply 16 in. Hg vacuum to manifold vacuum side of solenoid. CANP solenoid should hold vacuum for 20 seconds.

3) Faults in CANP solenoid or circuit should set a service code. See Quick Test procedure in SELF-DIAGNOSTICS – EEC-IV article. If no service code has been set, see CIRCUIT TEST KD in SELF-DIAGNOSTICS – EEC-IV article for additional solenoid and circuit testing.

POSITIVE CRANKCASE VENTILATION (PCV)

PCV Valve – 1) Remove PCV valve from rocker cover grommet. Shake valve. Valve should rattle when shaken. If valve does not rattle, replace valve.

2) Start engine and warm to normal operating temperature. On 2.3L, 2.9L and 4.9L engines, remove corrugated hose from oil separator nipple. Place stiff piece of paper over nipple end and wait 60 seconds.

3) On all other engines, disconnect hose from remote air cleaner or outlet tube. Place stiff piece of paper over hose end and wait 60 seconds. Vacuum should hold paper in place. If vacuum does not hold paper in place, replace valve.

THERMOSTATIC AIR CLEANER (TAC)

Air Cleaner Temperature Sensor – Bring temperature of sensor to less than 75°F (24°C), and apply 8 in. Hg vacuum to source port. Duct door should close. If door does not close, replace sensor. Sensor will bleed off vacuum to allow duct door to open and let in fresh air at specific temperatures. See AIR CLEANER TEMPERATURE SENSOR OPENING table.

AIR CLEANER TEMPERATURE SENSOR OPENING

Color	Temperature
Brown	70°F (21°C)
Pink, Black or Red	90°F (32°C)
Blue, Yellow or Green	105°F (41°C)

Air Control Door – When a vacuum of 8 in. Hg or more is applied to vacuum motor, door should stay in proper position for as long as vacuum is applied. If vacuum bleeds off and door returns to rest position, replace vacuum motor.

Aerostar, Bronco, Explorer, Ranger, "E" & "F" Series

NOTE: Unless otherwise specified, references to "F" Series includes "F" Series Super Duty.

NOTE: Unless stated otherwise in testing procedures, perform all voltage tests using a Digital Volt-Ohmmeter (DVOM) with a minimum 10-megohm input impedance. Voltage readings may vary slightly due to battery condition or charging rate.

INTRODUCTION

Pin voltage charts are supplied to reduce diagnostic time. Checking pin voltages at the Electronic Control Assembly (ECA), determines whether it's receiving and transmitting proper voltage signals. Charts may also help determine if ECA harness is shorted or opened.

Diagnostic values are based on engine at normal operating temperature. Key On Engine Off (KOEO) and Hot Idle tests are recorded with transmission selector lever in Park (A/T) or Neutral (M/T) position. Vehicles with manual transmission use 3rd gear for 30 MPH values and 4th gear for 55 MPH values.

Reference values may differ due to component tolerances, driving conditions and weather. The ACT and ECT values may vary greatly with temperature. The values given were recorded at approximately 600 feet above sea level at 50-70°F (15°C).

ECA LOCATION

ECA LOCATION

Application	Location
Aerostar	Left Rear Eng. Compartment
Bronco & "F" Series	Left Rear Eng. Comp. Near Brake Fluid Reservoir
"E" Series	Right Rear Eng. Comp. Under Blower Motor
Explorer	Below Dash at Right Kick Panel
Ranger	Behind Right Cowl Panel

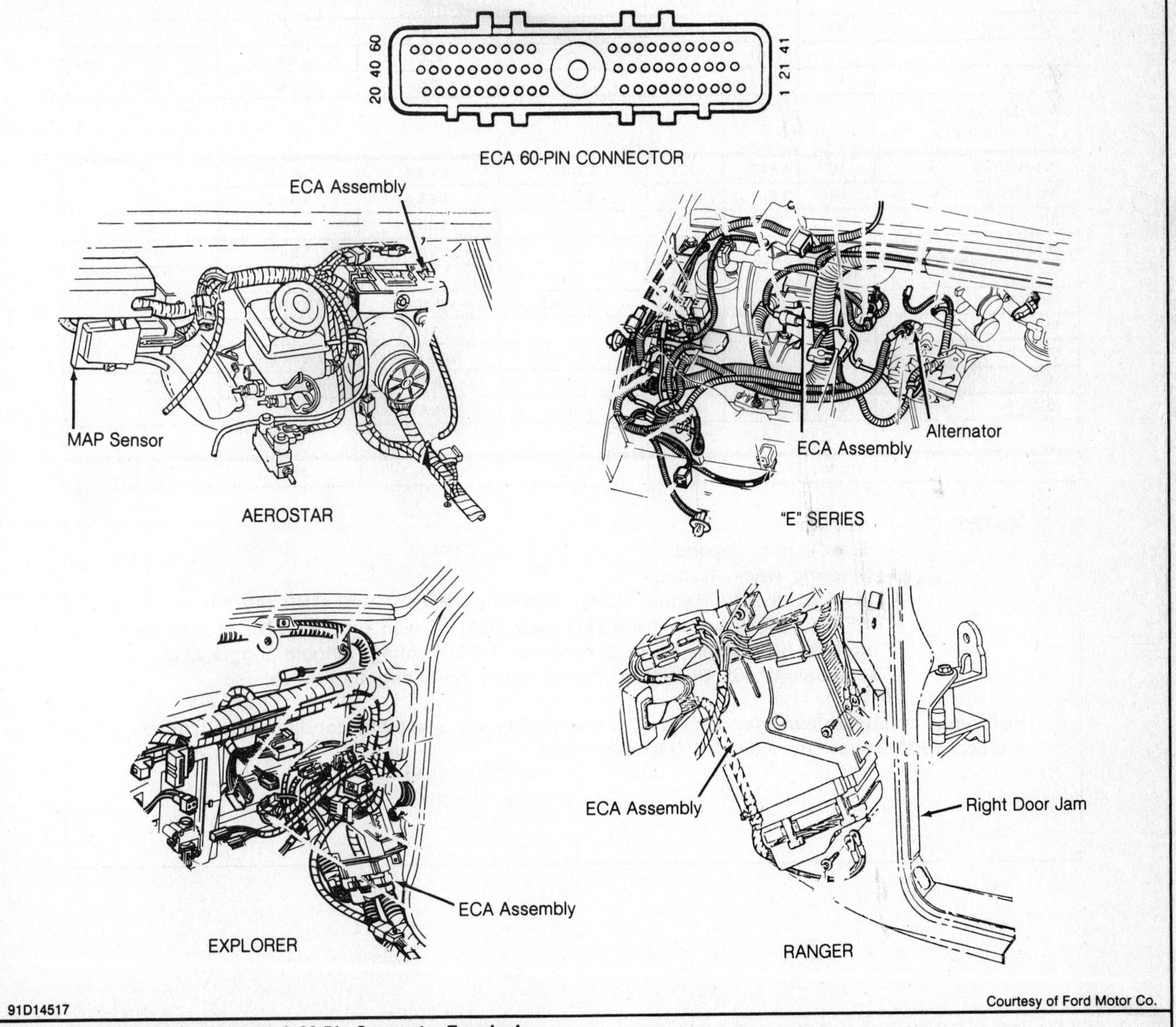
60
40
20
41
21
1
ECA 60-PIN CONNECTOR
ECA Assembly
MAP Sensor
AEROSTAR
Alternator
ECA Assembly
"E" SERIES
ECA Assembly
EXPLORER
ECA Assembly
Right Door Jam
RANGER
91D14517
Courtesy of Ford Motor Co.

Fig. 1: Identifying ECA Locations & 60-Pin Connector Terminals

1991 ENGINE PERFORMANCE
Pin Voltage Charts (Cont.)

ECA CHECKS

2.3L RANGER
AUTOMATIC TRANSMISSION

SENSORS/ INPUTS	Signal Pin #	KOEO	Units	HOT IDLE	30 MPH	55 MPH	Units
OCT ADJ	44	0	DCV	0	0	0	DCV
MAF red	14	0④	DCV	.7④	1.3-1.5④	1.9-2.3④	DCV
TP	47	.9	DCV	.9	1.0-1.1	1.4-1.6	DCV
ECT	7	.8	DCV	.8	.8	.8	DCV
ACT	25	1.2	DCV	1.4	2.1	2.3	DCV
IDM	4	10	RPM	660-740	1700-1770	2190-2250	RPM
PIP	56	10	RPM	660-740	1700-1770	2190-2250	RPM
HEGO	29	.03	DCV	switching⑤	switching⑤	switching⑤	DCV
BOO	2	0	DCV	VBAT②	0	0	DCV
FPM red	8	0	DCV	VBAT	VBAT	VBAT	DCV
ACCS	10	0	DCV	VBAT①	0	0	DCV
VSS+	3	0	MPH	0	30	55	MPH
PSPS	24	0	DCV	10.0③	0	0	DCV
ACD	43	0	DCV	VBAT①	0	0	DCV
NDS	30	0	DCV	0	5.0	5.0	DCV
STI	48	5.0	DCV	5.0	5.0	5.0	DCV
ACTUATORS/ OUTPUTS							
INJ BANK 2	59	VBAT④	DCV	3.4-3.7	4.9-5.4	6.6-7.6	mS
INJ BANK 1	58	VBAT④	DCV	3.4-3.7	4.9-5.4	6.6-7.6	mS
SS 3/4	52	VBAT	DCV	VBAT	VBAT	.2	DCV
STO/MIL	17	.1	DCV	VBAT	VBAT	VBAT	DCV
WAC	54	.1	DCV	.1	.1	.1	DCV
ISC-BPA	21	VBAT	DCV	9.5-VBAT	9.2-10.2	8.8-9.4	DCV
FP	22	VBAT	DCV	.1	.1	.1	DCV
SPOUT	36	10	RPM	660-740	1700-1770	2190-2250	RPM
DPI	32	11.0④	DCV	0④	0④	0④	DCV
CCO	53	VBAT	DCV	VBAT	VBAT	.3	DCV
OTHER							
IGN TIMING	TIMING	N/A	DEG	18-22	25-29	25-29	DEG

NOTES:
① — A/C on.
② — Brake pedal applied.
③ — Steering wheel turned.
④ — Monitor in DCV Manual Mode, Reference Pin to PWR GND (40/60).
⑤ — HEGO should switch from rich (red LED) to lean (green LED), or lean to rich, at least once every 3 seconds. HEGO voltage should toggle above and below .450 DCV, and should never be a negative value.

Reference values shown may vary ± 20% depending on operating conditions and other factors. RPM values are axle and tire dependent.

91G14270

Courtesy of Ford Motor Co.

Fig. 2: ECA Pin Voltage Checks (Ranger 2.3L with Automatic Transmission)

1991 ENGINE PERFORMANCE
Pin Voltage Charts (Cont.)

2.3L RANGER
MANUAL TRANSMISSION

SENSORS/ INPUTS	Signal Pin #	KOEO	Units	HOT IDLE	30 MPH	55 MPH	Units
OCT ADJ	44	0	DCV	0	0	0	DCV
MAF red	14	0④	DCV	.5④	1.3-1.4④	1.8-2.2④	DCV
TP	47	1.0	DCV	1.0	1.2	1.4-1.5	DCV
EVP	27	.4	DCV	.4	.5-.7	1.2-1.6	DCV
ECT	7	.7	DCV	.7	.7	.7	DCV
ACT	25	1.4	DCV	1.6	1.8-2.2	1.8-2.2	DCV
IDM	4	12	RPM	720-780	1420-1480	2120-2220	RPM
PIP	56	12	RPM	720-780	1420-1480	2120-2220	RPM
HEGO	29	.02	DCV	switching⑤	switching⑤	switching⑤	DCV
BOO	2	0	DCV	VBAT②	0	0	DCV
FPM red	8	0	DCV	VBAT	VBAT	VBAT	DCV
ACCS	10	0	DCV	VBAT①	0	0	DCV
VSS+	3	0	MPH	0	30	55	MPH
PSPS	24	0	DCV	10.0③	0	0	DCV
ACD	43	0	DCV	VBAT①	0	0	DCV
STI	48	5.0	DCV	5.0	5.0	5.0	DCV
ACTUATORS/ OUTPUTS							
INJ BANK 2	59	VBAT④	DCV	3.3-3.5	4.7-5.4	6.2-7.2	mS
INJ BANK 1	58	VBAT④	DCV	3.3-3.5	4.7-5.4	6.2-7.2	mS
EVR	33	VBAT④	DCV	0	0-40	30-50	%
STO/MIL	17	.6	DCV	VBAT	VBAT	VBAT	DCV
WAC	54	.1	DCV	.1	.1	.1	DCV
ISC-BPA	21	VBAT	DCV	11.0-VBAT	9.5-11.0	8.8-9.4	DCV
FP	22	VBAT	DCV	.9	.9	.9	DCV
SPOUT	36	12	RPM	720-780	1420-1480	2120-2220	RPM
DPI	32	11.0④	DCV	0④	0④	0④	DCV
OTHER							
IGN TIMING	TIMING	N/A	DEG	18-24	25-29	27-32	DEG

NOTES:
① — A/C on.
② — Brake pedal applied.
③ — Steering wheel turned.
④ — Monitor in DCV Manual Mode, Reference Pin to PWR GND (40/60).
⑤ — HEGO should switch from rich (red LED) to lean (green LED), or lean to rich, at least once every 3 seconds. HEGO voltage should toggle above and below .450 DCV, and should never be a negative value.

Reference values shown may vary ± 20% depending on operating conditions and other factors. RPM values are axle and tire dependent.

91H14271

Courtesy of Ford Motor Co.

Fig. 3: ECA Pin Voltage Checks (Ranger 2.3L with Manual Transmission)

1991 ENGINE PERFORMANCE
Pin Voltage Charts (Cont.)

2.9L RANGER
AUTOMATIC TRANSMISSION

SENSORS/ INPUTS	Signal Pin #	KOEO	Units	HOT IDLE	30 MPH	55 MPH	Units
TP	47	.9	DCV	.9	1.0-1.2	1.3-1.4	DCV
ECT	7	.6	DCV	.6	.6	.6	DCV
ACT	25	2.1	DCV	2.1	2.2	2.3	DCV
MAP	45	157	Hz	104-108	104-112	116-120	Hz
IDM	4	1	RPM	830-870	1400-1500	2040-2080	RPM
PIP	56	1	RPM	830-870	1400-1500	2040-2080	RPM
HEGO	29	.02	DCV	switching④	switching④	switching④	DCV
BOO	2	0	DCV	VBAT②	0	0	DCV
FPM red	8	0	DCV	VBAT	VBAT	VBAT	DCV
ACCS	10	.1	DCV	VBAT①	.1	.1	DCV
VSS+	3	0	MPH	0	30	55	MPH
NDS	30	0	DCV	0	VBAT	VBAT	DCV
STI	48	5.0	DCV	5.0	5.0	5.0	DCV
ACTUATORS/ OUTPUTS							
INJ BANK 2	59	VBAT③	DCV	3.3-3.5	4.0-5.0	5.5-6.5	mS
INJ BANK 1	58	VBAT③	DCV	3.3-3.5	4.0-5.0	5.5-6.5	mS
SS 3/4	52	VBAT	DCV	VBAT	VBAT	VBAT	DCV
STO/MIL	17	.6	DCV	VBAT	VBAT	VBAT	DCV
WAC	54	.1	DCV	.1	.1	.1	DCV
ISC-BPA	21	VBAT	DCV	10.0-11.0	8.0-9.5	6.8-8.0	DCV
FP	22	VBAT	DCV	.8	.8	.8	DCV
SPOUT	36	1	RPM	830-870	1400-1500	2040-2080	RPM
CCO	53	VBAT	DCV	VBAT	VBAT	VBAT	DCV
OTHER							
IGN TIMING	TIMING	N/A	DEG	25-27	30-36	32-36	DEG

NOTES: ① — A/C on.
② — Brake pedal applied.
③ — Monitor in DCV Manual Mode, Reference Pin to PWR GND (40/60).
④ — HEGO should switch from rich (red LED) to lean (green LED), or lean to rich, at least once every 3 seconds. HEGO voltage should toggle above and below .450 DCV, and should never be a negative value.

Reference values shown may vary ± 20% depending on operating conditions and other factors. RPM values are axle and tire dependent.

91I14272

Courtesy of Ford Motor Co.

Fig. 4: ECA Pin Voltage Checks (Ranger 2.9L with Automatic Transmission)

2.9L RANGER
MANUAL TRANSMISSION

SENSORS/ INPUTS	Signal Pin #	KOEO	Units	HOT IDLE	30 MPH	55 MPH	Units
TP	47	.9	DCV	.9	1.0-1.2	1.3-1.4	DCV
ECT	7	.6	DCV	.6	.6	.6	DCV
ACT	25	2.1	DCV	2.1	2.2	2.3	DCV
MAP	45	157	Hz	104-108	104-112	116-120	Hz
IDM	4	1	RPM	830-870	1400-1500	2040-2080	RPM
PIP	56	1	RPM	830-870	1400-1500	2040-2080	RPM
HEGO	29	.02	DCV	switching④	switching④	switching④	DCV
BOO	2	0	DCV	VBAT②	0	0	DCV
FPM red	8	0	DCV	VBAT	VBAT	VBAT	DCV
ACCS	10	.1	DCV	VBAT①	.1	.1	DCV
VSS+	3	0	MPH	0	30	55	MPH
NGS/CES	30	0	DCV	0	VBAT	VBAT	DCV
STI	48	5.0	DCV	5.0	5.0	5.0	DCV
ACTUATORS/ OUTPUTS							
INJ BANK 2	59	VBAT③	DCV	3.3-3.5	4.0-5.0	5.5-6.5	mS
INJ BANK 1	58	VBAT③	DCV	3.3-3.5	4.0-5.0	5.5-6.5	mS
STO/MIL	17	.6	DCV	VBAT	VBAT	VBAT	DCV
WAC	54	.1	DCV	.1	.1	.1	DCV
ISC-BPA	21	VBAT	DCV	10.0-11.0	8.0-9.5	6.8-8.0	DCV
FP	22	VBAT	DCV	.8	.8	.8	DCV
SPOUT	36	1	RPM	830-870	1400-1500	2040-2080	RPM
OTHER							
IGN TIMING	TIMING	N/A	DEG	25-27	30-36	32-36	DEG

NOTES: ① — A/C on.
② — Brake pedal applied.
③ — Monitor in DCV Manual Mode, Reference Pin to PWR GND (40/60).
④ — HEGO should switch from rich (red LED) to lean (green LED), or lean to rich, at least once every 3 seconds. HEGO voltage should toggle above and below .450 DCV, and should never be a negative value.

Reference values shown may vary ± 20% depending on operating conditions and other factors. RPM values are axle and tire dependent.

91J14273

Courtesy of Ford Motor Co.

Fig. 5: ECA Pin Voltage Checks (Ranger 2.9L with Manual Transmission)

1991 ENGINE PERFORMANCE
Pin Voltage Charts (Cont.)

3.0L AEROSTAR
AUTOMATIC TRANSMISSION

SENSORS/ INPUTS	Signal Pin #	KOEO	Units	HOT IDLE	30 MPH	55 MPH	Units
TP	47	.8	DCV	.8	1.0-1.1	1.1-1.5	DCV
ECT	7	.7	DCV	.7	.7	.7	DCV
ACT	25	2.4	DCV	2.1	2.4	3.2	DCV
MAP	45	157	Hz	110-112	110-115	115-120	Hz
IDM	4	7	RPM	840-870	1300-1400	2450-2520	RPM
PIP	56	7	RPM	840-870	1300-1400	2450-2520	RPM
HEGO	29	.04	DCV	switching⑤	switching⑤	switching⑤	DCV
BOO	2	0	DCV	VBAT②	0	0	DCV
FPM red	8	0④	DCV	VBAT④	VBAT④	VBAT④	DCV
ACCS	10	.1	DCV	VBAT①	.1	.1	DCV
VSS+	3	0	MPH	0	30	55	MPH
PSPS	24	0	DCV	10.0③	0	0	DCV
NDS	30	0	DCV	0	VBAT	VBAT	DCV
STI	48	5.0	DCV	5.0	5.0	5.0	DCV
ACTUATORS/ OUTPUTS							
INJ BANK 2	59	VBAT④	DCV	5.6-6.0	7.5-8.5	10.5-11.5	mS
INJ BANK 1	58	VBAT④	DCV	5.6-6.0	7.5-8.5	10.5-11.5	mS
SS 3/4	52	VBAT	DCV	VBAT	VBAT	.7	DCV
STO/MIL	17	.6	DCV	VBAT	VBAT	VBAT	DCV
CANP	31	VBAT	DCV	VBAT	4.0-9.5	.2	DCV
WAC	54	.1	DCV	.1	.1	.1	DCV
ISC-BPA	21	VBAT	DCV	10.5-11.8	9.2-10.0	7.0-9.2	DCV
FP	22	VBAT	DCV	.9	.9	.9	DCV
SPOUT	36	7	RPM	840-870	1300-1400	2450-2520	RPM
CCO	53	VBAT	DCV	VBAT	VBAT	.7	DCV
OTHER							
IGN TIMING	TIMING	N/A	DEG	13-18	32-34	36-38	DEG

NOTES: ① — A/C on.
② — Brake pedal applied.
③ — Steering wheel turned.
④ — Monitor in DCV Manual Mode, Reference Pin to PWR GND (40/60).
⑤ — HEGO should switch from rich (red LED) to lean (green LED), or lean to rich, at least once every 3 seconds. HEGO voltage should toggle above and below .450 DCV, and should never be a negative value.

Reference values shown may vary ± 20% depending on operating conditions and other factors. RPM values are axle and tire dependent.

91A14274

Courtesy of Ford Motor Co.

Fig. 6: ECA Pin Voltage Checks (Aerostar 3.0L with Automatic Transmission)

3.0L AEROSTAR
MANUAL TRANSMISSION

SENSORS/ INPUTS	Signal Pin #	KOEO	Units	HOT IDLE	30 MPH	55 MPH	Units
TP	47	.8	DCV	.8	1.0-1.1	1.1-1.5	DCV
ECT	7	.7	DCV	.7	.7	.7	DCV
ACT	25	2.4	DCV	2.1	2.4	3.2	DCV
MAP	45	157	Hz	110-112	110-115	115-120	Hz
IDM	4	7	RPM	840-870	1300-1400	2450-2520	RPM
PIP	56	7	RPM	840-870	1300-1400	2450-2520	RPM
HEGO	29	.04	DCV	switching⑤	switching⑤	switching⑤	DCV
BOO	2	0	DCV	VBAT②	0	0	DCV
FPM red	8	0④	DCV	VBAT④	VBAT④	VBAT④	DCV
ACCS	10	.1	DCV	VBAT①	.1	.1	DCV
VSS+	3	0	MPH	0	30	55	MPH
PSPS	24	0	DCV	10.0③	0	0	DCV
STI	48	5.0	DCV	5.0	5.0	5.0	DCV
ACTUATORS/ OUTPUTS							
INJ BANK 2	59	VBAT④	DCV	5.6-6.0	7.5-8.5	10.5-11.5	mS
INJ BANK 1	58	VBAT④	DCV	5.6-6.0	7.5-8.5	10.5-11.5	mS
STO/MIL	17	.6	DCV	VBAT	VBAT	VBAT	DCV
CANP	31	VBAT	DCV	VBAT	4.0-9.5	.2	DCV
WAC	54	.1	DCV	.1	.1	.1	DCV
ISC-BPA	21	VBAT	DCV	10.5-11.8	9.2-10.0	7.0-9.2	DCV
FP	22	VBAT	DCV	.9	.9	.9	DCV
SPOUT	36	7	RPM	840-870	1300-1400	2450-2520	RPM
OTHER							
IGN TIMING	TIMING	N/A	DEG	13-18	32-34	36-38	DEG

NOTES: ① — A/C on.
② — Brake pedal applied.
③ — Steering wheel turned.
④ — Monitor in DCV Manual Mode, Reference Pin to PWR GND (40/60).
⑤ — HEGO should switch from rich (red LED) to lean (green LED), or lean to rich, at least once every 3 seconds. HEGO voltage should toggle above and below .450 DCV, and should never be a negative value.

Reference values shown may vary ± 20% depending on operating conditions and other factors. RPM values are axle and tire dependent.

91B14275

Courtesy of Ford Motor Co.

Fig. 7: ECA Pin Voltage Checks (Aerostar 3.0L with Manual Transmission)

1991 ENGINE PERFORMANCE
Pin Voltage Charts (Cont.)

3.0L RANGER
AUTOMATIC TRANSMISSION

SENSORS/ INPUTS		Signal Pin #	KOEO	Units	HOT IDLE	30 MPH	55 MPH	Units
MAF	red	14	0③	DCV	.9③	1.4-1.6③	1.9-2.4③	DCV
TP		47	.7	DCV	.7	.9-1.0	1.0-1.2	DCV
ECT		7	.6	DCV	.6	.6	.6	DCV
ACT		25	1.9	DCV	2.0	2.1	2.3	DCV
BP		45	157	Hz	157	157	157	Hz
IDM		4	7	RPM	820-880	1580-1680	2780-2880	RPM
PIP		56	7	RPM	820-880	1580-1680	2780-2880	RPM
HEGO		29	.03	DCV	switching④	switching④	switching④	DCV
BOO		2	0	DCV	VBAT②	0	0	DCV
FPM	red	8	0	DCV	VBAT	VBAT	VBAT	DCV
ACCS		10	0	DCV	VBAT①	0	0	DCV
VSS+		3	0	MPH	0	30	55	MPH
NDS		30	0	DCV	0	5.0	5.0	DCV
STI		48	5.0	DCV	5.0	5.0	5.0	DCV
ACTUATORS/ OUTPUTS								
INJ BANK 2		59	VBAT③	DCV	3.7-3.9	4.4-4.6	5.0-6.0	mS
INJ BANK 1		58	VBAT③	DCV	3.7-3.9	4.4-4.6	5.0-5.0	mS
SS 3/4		52	VBAT	DCV	VBAT	VBAT	VBAT	DCV
STO/MIL		17	.2	DCV	VBAT	VBAT	VBAT	DCV
CANP		31	VBAT	DCV	VBAT	9.1-10.1	.2-8.7	DCV
WAC		54	.1	DCV	.1	.1	.1	DCV
ISC-BPA		21	VBAT	DCV	10.3-11.8	8.5-9.5	4.0-9.2	DCV
FP		22	VBAT	DCV	.1	.1	.1	DCV
SPOUT		36	7	RPM	820-880	1580-1680	2780-2880	RPM
CCO		53	VBAT	DCV	VBAT	VBAT	VBAT	DCV
OTHER								
IGN TIMING		TIMING	N/A	DEG	20-24	30-34	32-36	DEG

NOTES: ① — A/C on.
② — Brake pedal applied.
③ — Monitor in DCV Manual Mode, Reference Pin to PWR GND (40/60).
④ — HEGO should switch from rich (red LED) to lean (green LED), or lean to rich, at least once every 3 seconds. HEGO voltage should toggle above and below .450 DCV, and should never be a negative value.

Reference values shown may vary ± 20% depending on operating conditions and other factors. RPM values are axle and tire dependent.

91C14276

Courtesy of Ford Motor Co.

Fig. 8: ECA Pin Voltage Checks (Ranger 3.0L with Automatic Transmission)

3.0L RANGER
MANUAL TRANSMISSION

SENSORS/ INPUTS	Signal Pin #	KOEO	Units	HOT IDLE	30 MPH	55 MPH	Units
MAF red	14	0③	DCV	.9③	1.4-1.6③	1.9-2.4③	DCV
TP	47	.7	DCV	.7	.9-1.0	1.0-1.2	DCV
ECT	7	.6	DCV	.6	.6	.6	DCV
ACT	25	1.9	DCV	2.0	2.1	2.3	DCV
BP	45	157	Hz	157	157	157	Hz
IDM	4	7	RPM	820-880	1580-1680	2780-2880	RPM
PIP	56	7	RPM	820-880	1580-1680	2780-2880	RPM
HEGO	29	.03	DCV	switching④	switching④	switching④	DCV
BOO	2	0	DCV	VBAT②	0	0	DCV
FPM red	8	0	DCV	VBAT	VBAT	VBAT	DCV
ACCS	10	0	DCV	VBAT①	0	0	DCV
VSS+	3	0	MPH	0	30	55	MPH
STI	48	5.0	DCV	5.0	5.0	5.0	DCV
ACTUATORS/ OUTPUTS							
INJ BANK 2	59	VBAT③	DCV	3.7-3.9	4.4-4.6	5.0-6.0	mS
INJ BANK 1	58	VBAT③	DCV	3.7-3.9	4.4-4.6	5.0-6.0	mS
STO/MIL	17	.2	DCV	VBAT	VBAT	VBAT	DCV
CANP	31	VBAT	DCV	VBAT	9.1-10.1	.2-8.7	DCV
WAC	54	.1	DCV	.1	.1	.1	DCV
ISC-BPA	21	VBAT	DCV	10.3-11.8	8.5-9.5	4.0-9.2	DCV
FP	22	VBAT	DCV	.1	.1	.1	DCV
SPOUT	36	7	RPM	820-880	1580-1680	2780-2880	RPM
OTHER							
IGN TIMING	TIMING	N/A	DEG	20-24	30-34	32-36	DEG

NOTES: ① — A/C on.
② — Brake pedal applied.
③ — Monitor in DCV Manual Mode, Reference Pin to PWR GND (40/60).
④ — HEGO should switch from rich (red LED) to lean (green LED), or lean to rich, at least once every 3 seconds. HEGO voltage should toggle above and below .450 DCV, and should never be a negative value.

Reference values shown may vary ± 20% depending on operating conditions and other factors. RPM values are axle and tire dependent.

91D14277

Courtesy of Ford Motor Co.

Fig. 9: ECA Pin Voltage Checks (Ranger 3.0L with Manual Transmission)

1991 ENGINE PERFORMANCE
Pin Voltage Charts (Cont.)

4.0L AEROSTAR
AUTOMATIC TRANSMISSION

SENSORS/ INPUTS	Signal Pin #	KOEO	Units	HOT IDLE	30 MPH	55 MPH	Units
OCT ADJ	44	0	DCV	0	0	0	DCV
MAF red	14	0③	DCV	.7③	1.3-1.4③	1.7-2.0③	DCV
TP	47	.9	DCV	.9	1.2-1.3	1.4-1.6	DCV
ECT	7	.6	DCV	.6	.6	.6	DCV
ACT	25	1.7	DCV	2.0	2.8	3.0	DCV
BP	45	158	Hz	158	158	158	Hz
IDM	4	4	RPM	740-840	1330-1430	1900-2000	RPM
PIP	56	4	RPM	740-840	1330-1430	1900-2000	RPM
HEGO	29	.02	DCV	switching④	switching④	switching④	DCV
BOO	2	0	DCV	VBAT②	0	0	DCV
FPM red	8	0	DCV	VBAT	VBAT	VBAT	DCV
ACCS	10	0	DCV	VBAT①	0	0	DCV
VSS+	3	0	MPH	0	30	55	MPH
NDS	30	0	DCV	0	5.0	5.0	DCV
STI	48	5.0	DCV	5.0	5.0	5.0	DCV
ACTUATORS/ OUTPUTS							
INJ BANK 2	59	VBAT③	DCV	3.3-3.5	4.0-4.6	5.0-6.0	mS
INJ BANK 1	58	VBAT③	DCV	3.3-3.5	4.0-4.6	5.0-6.0	mS
SS 3/4	52	VBAT	DCV	VBAT	VBAT	0	DCV
STO/MIL	17	.1	DCV	VBAT	VBAT	VBAT	DCV
CANP	31	VBAT	DCV	VBAT	7.0-9.0	.2	DCV
WAC	54	.1	DCV	.1	.1	.1	DCV
ISC-BPA	21	VBAT	DCV	8.0-VBAT	8.5-9.5	5.5-9.0	DCV
FP	22	VBAT	DCV	.1	.1	.1	DCV
SAW	36	4	RPM	740-840	1330-1430	1900-2000	RPM
CCO	53	VBAT	DCV	VBAT	VBAT	0	DCV
OTHER							
IGN TIMING	TIMING	N/A	DEG	N/A	N/A	N/A	DEG

NOTES: ① — A/C on.
② — Brake pedal applied.
③ — Monitor in DCV Manual Mode, Reference Pin to PWR GND (40/60).
④ — HEGO should switch from rich (red LED) to lean (green LED), or lean to rich, at least once every 3 seconds. HEGO voltage should toggle above and below .450 DCV, and should never be a negative value.

Reference values shown may vary ± 20% depending on operating conditions and other factors. RPM values are axle and tire dependent.

91E14278

Courtesy of Ford Motor Co.

Fig. 10: ECA Pin Voltage Checks (Aerostar 4.0L with Automatic Transmission)

1991 ENGINE PERFORMANCE
Pin Voltage Charts (Cont.)

4.0L EXPLORER
AUTOMATIC TRANSMISSION

SENSORS/ INPUTS	Signal Pin #	KOEO	Units	HOT IDLE	30 MPH	55 MPH	Units
OCT ADJ	44	0	DCV	0	0	0	DCV
MAF red	14	0③	DCV	.7③	1.3-1.4③	1.7-2.0③	DCV
TP	47	.9	DCV	.9	1.2-1.3	1.4-1.6	DCV
ECT	7	.6	DCV	.6	.6	.6	DCV
ACT	25	1.7	DCV	2.0	2.8	3.0	DCV
BP	45	158	Hz	158	158	158	Hz
IDM	4	4	RPM	740-840	1330-1430	1900-2000	RPM
PIP	56	4	RPM	740-840	1330-1430	1900-2000	RPM
HEGO	29	.02	DCV	switching④	switching④	switching④	DCV
BOO	2	0	DCV	VBAT②	0	0	DCV
FPM red	8	0	DCV	VBAT	VBAT	VBAT	DCV
ACCS	10	0	DCV	VBAT①	0	0	DCV
VSS+	3	0	MPH	0	30	55	MPH
NDS	30	0	DCV	0	5.0	5.0	DCV
STI	48	5.0	DCV	5.0	5.0	5.0	DCV
ACTUATORS/ OUTPUTS							
INJ BANK 2	59	VBAT③	DCV	3.3-3.5	4.0-4.6	5.0-6.0	mS
INJ BANK 1	58	VBAT③	DCV	3.3-3.5	4.0-4.6	5.0-6.0	mS
SS 3/4	52	VBAT	DCV	VBAT	VBAT	0	DCV
STO/MIL	17	.1	DCV	VBAT	VBAT	VBAT	DCV
CANP	31	VBAT	DCV	VBAT	7.0-9.0	.2	DCV
WAC	54	.1	DCV	.1	.1	.1	DCV
ISC-BPA	21	VBAT	DCV	8.0-VBAT	8.5-9.5	5.5-9.0	DCV
FP	22	VBAT	DCV	.1	.1	.1	DCV
SAW	36	4	RPM	740-840	1330-1430	1900-2000	RPM
CCO	53	VBAT	DCV	VBAT	VBAT	0	DCV
OTHER							
IGN TIMING	TIMING	N/A	DEG	N/A	N/A	N/A	DEG

NOTES: ① — A/C on.
② — Brake pedal applied.
③ — Monitor in DCV Manual Mode, Reference Pin to PWR GND (40/60).
④ — HEGO should switch from rich (red LED) to lean (green LED), or lean to rich, at least once every 3 seconds. HEGO voltage should toggle above and below .450 DCV, and should never be a negative value.

Reference values shown may vary ± 20% depending on operating conditions and other factors. RPM values are axle and tire dependent.

91F14279

Courtesy of Ford Motor Co.

Fig. 11: ECA Pin Voltage Checks (Explorer 4.0L with Automatic Transmission)

1991 ENGINE PERFORMANCE
Pin Voltage Charts (Cont.)

4.0L EXPLORER
MANUAL TRANSMISSION

SENSORS/ INPUTS	Signal Pin #	KOEO	Units	HOT IDLE	30 MPH	55 MPH	Units
OCT ADJ	44	0	DCV	0	0	0	DCV
MAF red	14	0③	DCV	.7③	1.3-1.4③	1.7-2.0③	DCV
TP	47	.9	DCV	.9	1.2-1.3	1.4-1.6	DCV
ECT	7	.6	DCV	.6	.6	.6	DCV
ACT	25	1.7	DCV	2.0	2.8	3.0	DCV
BP	45	158	Hz	158	158	158	Hz
IDM	4	4	RPM	740-840	1330-1430	1900-2000	RPM
PIP	56	4	RPM	740-840	1330-1430	1900-2000	RPM
HEGO	29	.02	DCV	switching④	switching④	switching④	DCV
BOO	2	0	DCV	VBAT②	0	0	DCV
FPM red	8	0	DCV	VBAT	VBAT	VBAT	DCV
ACCS	10	0	DCV	VBAT①	0	0	DCV
VSS+	3	0	MPH	0	30	55	MPH
NGS/CES	30	0	DCV	0	5.0	5.0	DCV
STI	48	5.0	DCV	5.0	5.0	5.0	DCV
ACTUATORS/ OUTPUTS							
INJ BANK 2	59	VBAT③	DCV	3.3-3.5	4.0-4.6	5.0-6.0	mS
INJ BANK 1	58	VBAT③	DCV	3.3-3.5	4.0-4.6	5.0-6.0	mS
STO/MIL	17	.1	DCV	VBAT	VBAT	VBAT	DCV
CANP	31	VBAT	DCV	VBAT	7.0-9.0	.2	DCV
WAC	54	.1	DCV	.1	.1	.1	DCV
ISC-BPA	21	VBAT	DCV	8.0-VBAT	8.5-9.5	5.5-9.0	DCV
FP	22	VBAT	DCV	.1	.1	.1	DCV
SAW	36	4	RPM	740-840	1330-1430	1900-2000	RPM
OTHER							
IGN TIMING	TIMING	N/A	DEG	N/A	N/A	N/A	DEG

NOTES: ① — A/C on.
② — Brake pedal applied.
③ — Monitor in DCV Manual Mode, Reference Pin to PWR GND (40/60).
④ — HEGO should switch from rich (red LED) to lean (green LED), or lean to rich, at least once every 3 seconds. HEGO voltage should toggle above and below .450 DCV, and should never be a negative value.

Reference values shown may vary ± 20% depending on operating conditions and other factors. RPM values are axle and tire dependent.

91I14280

Courtesy of Ford Motor Co.

Fig. 12: ECA Pin Voltage Checks (Explorer 4.0L with Manual Transmission)

1991 ENGINE PERFORMANCE
Pin Voltage Charts (Cont.)

4.0L RANGER
AUTOMATIC TRANSMISSION

SENSORS/ INPUTS	Signal Pin #	KOEO	Units	HOT IDLE	30 MPH	55 MPH	Units
OCT ADJ	44	0	DCV	0	0	0	DCV
MAF red	14	0③	DCV	.7③	1.3-1.4③	1.7-2.0③	DCV
TP	47	.9	DCV	.9	1.2-1.3	1.4-1.6	DCV
ECT	7	.6	DCV	.6	.6	.6	DCV
ACT	25	1.7	DCV	2.0	2.8	3.0	DCV
BP	45	158	Hz	158	158	158	Hz
IDM	4	4	RPM	740-840	1330-1430	1900-2000	RPM
PIP	56	4	RPM	740-840	1330-1430	1900-2000	RPM
HEGO	29	.02	DCV	switching④	switching④	switching④	DCV
BOO	2	0	DCV	VBAT②	0	0	DCV
FPM red	8	0	DCV	VBAT	VBAT	VBAT	DCV
ACCS	10	0	DCV	VBAT①	0	0	DCV
VSS+	3	0	MPH	0	30	55	MPH
NDS	30	0	DCV	0	5.0	5.0	DCV
STI	48	5.0	DCV	5.0	5.0	5.0	DCV
ACTUATORS/ OUTPUTS							
INJ BANK 2	59	VBAT③	DCV	3.3-3.5	4.0-4.6	5.0-6.0	mS
INJ BANK 1	58	VBAT③	DCV	3.3-3.5	4.0-4.6	5.0-6.0	mS
SS 3/4	52	VBAT	DCV	VBAT	VBAT	0	DCV
STO/MIL	17	.1	DCV	VBAT	VBAT	VBAT	DCV
CANP	31	VBAT	DCV	VBAT	7.0-9.0	.2	DCV
WAC	54	.1	DCV	.1	.1	.1	DCV
ISC-BPA	21	VBAT	DCV	8.0-VBAT	8.5-9.5	5.5-9.0	DCV
FP	22	VBAT	DCV	.1	.1	.1	DCV
SAW	36	4	RPM	740-840	1330-1430	1900-2000	RPM
CCO	53	VBAT	DCV	VBAT	VBAT	0	DCV
OTHER							
IGN TIMING	TIMING	N/A	DEG	N/A	N/A	N/A	DEG

NOTES: ① — A/C on.
② — Brake pedal applied.
③ — Monitor in DCV Manual Mode, Reference Pin to PWR GND (40/60).
④ — HEGO should switch from rich (red LED) to lean (green LED), or lean to rich, at least once every 3 seconds. HEGO voltage should toggle above and below .450 DCV, and should never be a negative value.

Reference values shown may vary ± 20% depending on operating conditions and other factors. RPM values are axle and tire dependent.

91J14281

Courtesy of Ford Motor Co.

Fig. 13: ECA Pin Voltage Checks (Ranger 4.0L with Automatic Transmission)

1991 ENGINE PERFORMANCE
Pin Voltage Charts (Cont.)

4.0L RANGER
MANUAL TRANSMISSION

SENSORS/ INPUTS	Signal Pin #	KOEO	Units	HOT IDLE	30 MPH	55 MPH	Units
OCT ADJ	44	0	DCV	0	0	0	DCV
MAF red	14	0③	DCV	.7③	1.3-1.4③	1.7-2.0③	DCV
TP	47	.9	DCV	.9	1.2-1.3	1.4-1.6	DCV
ECT	7	.6	DCV	.6	.6	.6	DCV
ACT	25	1.7	DCV	2.0	2.8	3.0	DCV
BP	45	158	Hz	158	158	158	Hz
IDM	4	4	RPM	740-840	1330-1430	1900-2000	RPM
PIP	56	4	RPM	740-840	1330-1430	1900-2000	RPM
HEGO	29	.02	DCV	switching④	switching④	switching④	DCV
BOO	2	0	DCV	VBAT②	0	0	DCV
FPM red	8	0	DCV	VBAT	VBAT	VBAT	DCV
ACCS	10	0	DCV	VBAT①	0	0	DCV
VSS+	3	0	MPH	0	30	55	MPH
NGS/CES	30	0	DCV	0	5.0	5.0	DCV
STI	48	5.0	DCV	5.0	5.0	5.0	DCV
ACTUATORS/ OUTPUTS							
INJ BANK 2	59	VBAT③	DCV	3.3-3.5	4.0-4.6	5.0-6.0	mS
INJ BANK 1	58	VBAT③	DCV	3.3-3.5	4.0-4.6	5.0-6.0	mS
STO/MIL	17	.1	DCV	VBAT	VBAT	VBAT	DCV
CANP	31	VBAT	DCV	VBAT	7.0-9.0	.2	DCV
WAC	54	.1	DCV	.1	.1	.1	DCV
ISC-BPA	21	VBAT	DCV	8.0-VBAT	8.5-9.5	5.5-9.0	DCV
FP	22	VBAT	DCV	.1	.1	.1	DCV
SAW	36	4	RPM	740-840	1330-1430	1900-2000	RPM
OTHER							
IGN TIMING	TIMING	N/A	DEG	N/A	N/A	N/A	DEG

NOTES: ① — A/C on.
② — Brake pedal applied.
③ — Monitor in DCV Manual Mode, Reference Pin to PWR GND (40/60).
④ — HEGO should switch from rich (red LED) to lean (green LED), or lean to rich, at least once every 3 seconds. HEGO voltage should toggle above and below .450 DCV, and should never be a negative value.

Reference values shown may vary ± 20% depending on operating conditions and other factors. RPM values are axle and tire dependent.

91A14282

Courtesy of Ford Motor Co.

Fig. 14: ECA Pin Voltage Checks (Ranger 4.0L with Manual Transmission)

4.9L BRONCO, "E" & "F" SERIES
AUTOMATIC TRANSMISSION (EXCEPT E4OD)

SENSORS/ INPUTS	Signal Pin #	KOEO	Units	HOT IDLE	30 MPH	55 MPH	Units
TP	47	**1.0**	DCV	**1.0**	**1.2-1.3**	**1.5-1.6**	DCV
EVP	27	**.3**	DCV	**.3**	**1.2-2.0**	**2.5-3.5**	DCV
ECT	7	**.6**	DCV	**.6**	**.6**	**.6**	DCV
ACT	25	**1.0**	DCV	**1.0**	**1.4**	**1.6**	DCV
MAP	45	**157**	Hz	**106**	**114-120**	**120-130**	Hz
IDM	4	**4**	RPM	**600-700**	**1050-1150**	**1840-1940**	RPM
PIP	56	**4**	RPM	**600-700**	**1050-1150**	**1840-1940**	RPM
KS	23	**2.5**	DCV	**2.5**	**2.5**	**2.5**	DCV
HEGO	29	**.04**	DCV	**switching④**	**switching④**	**switching④**	DCV
FPM red	8	**0**	DCV	**VBAT**	**VBAT**	**VBAT**	DCV
ACCS	10	**0**	DCV	**VBAT①**	**0**	**0**	DCV
VSS+	3	**0**	MPH	**0**	**30**	**55**	MPH
ACD	43	**0**	DCV	**VBAT①**	**0**	**0**	DCV
NDS	30	**0**	DCV	**0**	**5.0**	**5.0**	DCV
STI	48	**5.0**	DCV	**5.0**	**5.0**	**5.0**	DCV
ACTUATORS/ OUTPUTS							
INJ BANK 2	59	**VBAT③**	DCV	**6.8-7.0**	**9.5-10.5**	**12.0-13.0**	mS
INJ BANK 1	58	**VBAT③**	DCV	**6.8-7.0**	**9.5-10.5**	**12.0-13.0**	mS
EVR	33	**VBAT③**	DCV	**0**	**0**	**0**	%
STO/MIL	17	**.1**	DCV	**VBAT**	**VBAT**	**VBAT**	DCV
CANP	31	**VBAT**	DCV	**VBAT**	**.2-5.0**	**.2**	DCV
ISC-BPA	21	**VBAT**	DCV	**8.0-11.0**	**6.5-9.0**	**5.0-6.5**	DCV
FP	22	**VBAT**	DCV	**.1**	**.1**	**.1**	DCV
SPOUT	36	**4**	RPM	**600-700**	**1050-1150**	**1840-1940**	RPM
AM1	51	**VBAT**	DCV	**VBAT**	**.1**	**.1**	DCV
AM2 ②	11	**VBAT**	DCV	**VBAT**	**VBAT**	**VBAT**	DCV
OTHER							
IGN TIMING	TIMING	**N/A**	DEG	**17-20**	**24-28**	**24-30**	DEG

NOTES: ① — A/C on.
② — If equipped (over 8500# with C6 transmission onl
③ — Monitor in DCV Manual Mode, Reference Pin to PWR GND (40/60).
④ — HEGO should switch from rich (red LED) to lean (green LED), or lean to rich, at least once every 3 seconds. HEGO voltage should toggle above and below .450 DCV, and should never be a negative value.

Reference values shown may vary ± 20% depending on operating conditions and other factors. RPM values are axle and tire dependent.

91B14283

Courtesy of Ford Motor Co.

Fig. 15: ECA Pin Voltage Checks (Bronco, "E" & "F" Series 4.9L with Automatic Transmission; Except E4OD)

1991 ENGINE PERFORMANCE
Pin Voltage Charts (Cont.)

4.9L BRONCO, "E" & "F" SERIES
AUTOMATIC TRANSMISSION (E4OD)

SENSORS/ INPUTS		Signal Pin #	KOEO	Units	HOT IDLE	30 MPH	55 MPH	Units
TP		47	1.0	DCV	1.0	1.2-1.3	1.5-1.6	DCV
EVP		27	.3	DCV	.3	1.2-2.0	2.5-3.5	DCV
ECT		7	.6	DCV	.6	.6	.6	DCV
ACT		25	1.0	DCV	1.0	1.4	1.6	DCV
MAP		45	157	Hz	106	114-120	120-130	Hz
IDM		4	4	RPM	700-800	1240-1340	1630-1730	RPM
OCS	red	41	0	DCV	0	0	0	DCV
PIP		56	4	RPM	700-800	1240-1340	1630-1730	RPM
TOT	red	42	2.0③	DCV	1.9③	1.3③	1.1③	DCV
KS		23	2.5	DCV	2.5	2.5	2.5	DCV
HEGO		29	.04	DCV	switching④	switching④	switching④	DCV
4x4L	red	12	VBAT③	DCV	VBAT③	VBAT③	VBAT③	DCV
BOO		2	0	DCV	VBAT②	0	0	DCV
FPM	red	8	0	DCV	VBAT	VBAT	VBAT	DCV
ACCS		10	0	DCV	VBAT①	0	0	DCV
VSS+		3	0	MPH	0	30	55	MPH
ACD		43	0	DCV	VBAT①	0	0	DCV
MLPS		30	4.5	DCV	4.5	2.1	2.1	DCV
STI		48	5.0	DCV	5.0	5.0	5.0	DCV
ACTUATORS/ OUTPUTS								
INJ BANK 2		59	VBAT③	DCV	7.2-7.6	8.5-9.5	13.0-14.5	mS
INJ BANK 1		58	VBAT③	DCV	7.2-7.6	8.5-9.5	13.0-14.5	mS
SS1		52	.3	DCV	.3	VBAT	VBAT	DCV
EVR		33	VBAT③	DCV	0	0	0	%
EPC		38	7.3	DCV	7.7	7.7	8.2	DCV
STO/MIL		17	.1	DCV	VBAT	VBAT	VBAT	DCV
ISC-BPA		21	VBAT	DCV	7.5-9.5	6.5-9.0	5.0-6.5	DCV
FP		22	VBAT	DCV	.1	.1	.1	DCV
SS2	blue	19	VBAT	DCV	VBAT	.4	.4	DCV
SPOUT		36	4	RPM	700-800	1240-1340	1630-1730	RPM
OCIL		32	VBAT③	DCV	VBAT③	VBAT③	0③	DCV
AM1		51	VBAT	DCV	VBAT	.1	.1	DCV
CCC		53	VBAT	DCV	VBAT	.4	.4	DCV
CCS		55	VBAT	DCV	VBAT	VBAT	.4	DCV
OTHER								
IGN TIMING		TIMING	N/A	DEG	17-20	24-28	24-30	DEG

NOTES: ① — A/C on.
② — Brake pedal applied.
③ — Monitor in DCV Manual Mode, Reference Pin to PWR GND (40/60).
④ — HEGO should switch from rich (red LED) to lean (green LED), or lean to rich, at least once every 3 seconds. HEGO voltage should toggle above and below .450 DCV, and should never be a negative value.

Reference values shown may vary ± 20% depending on operating conditions and other factors. RPM values are axle and tire dependent.

91C14284 Courtesy of Ford Motor Co.

Fig. 16: ECA Pin Voltage Checks (Bronco, "E" & "F" Series 4.9L with E4OD Automatic Transmission)

4.9L BRONCO, "E" & "F" SERIES
MANUAL TRANSMISSION

SENSORS/ INPUTS	Signal Pin #	KOEO	Units	HOT IDLE	30 MPH	55 MPH	Units
TP	47	1.0	DCV	1.0	1.2-1.3	1.5-1.6	DCV
EVP	27	.3	DCV	.3	1.2-2.0	2.5-3.5	DCV
ECT	7	.6	DCV	.6	.6	.6	DCV
ACT	25	1.0	DCV	1.0	1.4	1.6	DCV
MAP	45	157	Hz	106	114-120	120-130	Hz
IDM	4	5	RPM	700-800	1100-1200	1630-1730	RPM
PIP	56	5	RPM	700-800	1100-1200	1630-1730	RPM
KS	23	2.5	DCV	2.5	2.5	2.5	DCV
HEGO	29	.04	DCV	switching③	switching③	switching③	DCV
FPM red	8	0	DCV	VBAT	VBAT	VBAT	DCV
ACCS	10	0	DCV	VBAT①	0	0	DCV
VSS+	3	0	MPH	0	30	55	MPH
ACD	43	0	DCV	VBAT①	0	0	DCV
CES	30	0	DCV	0	5.0	5.0	DCV
STI	48	5.0	DCV	5.0	5.0	5.0	DCV
ACTUATORS/ OUTPUTS							
INJ BANK 2	59	VBAT②	DCV	6.2-6.4	8.5-9.5	12.5-13.5	mS
INJ BANK 1	58	VBAT②	DCV	6.2-6.4	8.5-9.5	12.5-13.5	mS
EVR	33	VBAT②	DCV	0	0	0	%
STO/MIL	17	.1	DCV	VBAT	VBAT	VBAT	DCV
CANP	31	VBAT	DCV	VBAT	.2-5.0	.2	DCV
ISC-BPA	21	VBAT	DCV	8.0-11.0	6.5-9.0	5.0-6.5	DCV
FP	22	VBAT	DCV	.1	.1	.1	DCV
SPOUT	36	5	RPM	700-800	1100-1200	1630-1730	RPM
AM1	51	VBAT	DCV	VBAT	.1	.1	DCV
AM2	11	VBAT	DCV	VBAT	VBAT	VBAT	DCV
OTHER							
IGN TIMING	TIMING	N/A	DEG	17-20	24-28	24-30	DEG

NOTES: ① — **A/C on.**
② — **Monitor in DCV Manual Mode, Reference Pin to PWR GND (40/60).**
③ — **HEGO should switch from rich (red LED) to lean (green LED), or lean to rich, at least once every 3 seconds. HEGO voltage should toggle above and below .450 DCV, and should never be a negative value.**

Reference values shown may vary ± 20% depending on operating conditions and other factors. RPM values are axle and tire dependent.

91D14285

Courtesy of Ford Motor Co.

Fig. 17: ECA Pin Voltage Checks (Bronco, "E" & "F" Series 4.9L with Manual Transmission)

1991 ENGINE PERFORMANCE
Pin Voltage Charts (Cont.)

5.0L BRONCO, "E" & "F" SERIES
AUTOMATIC TRANSMISSION (EXCEPT E4OD)

SENSORS/ INPUTS		Signal Pin #	KOEO	Units	HOT IDLE	30 MPH	55 MPH	Units
TP		47	.9	DCV	.9	1.0-1.1	1.2-1.3	DCV
EVP		27	.4	DCV	.4	.4-2.5	2.2-4.2	DCV
ECT		7	.6	DCV	.6	.6	.6	DCV
ACT		25	1.2	DCV	1.2	1.2	1.2	DCV
MAP		45	157	Hz	103-105	104-112	118-124	Hz
IDM		4	4	RPM	700-800	1300-1400	2200-2300	RPM
PIP		56	4	RPM	700-800	1300-1400	2200-2300	RPM
KS		23	2.5	DCV	2.5	2.5	2.5	DCV
HEGO		29	.04	DCV	switching⑤	switching⑤	switching⑤	DCV
FPM	red	8	0④	DCV	VBAT④	VBAT④	VBAT④	DCV
ACCS		10	0	DCV	VBAT①	0	0	DCV
VSS+		3	0	MPH	0	30	55	MPH
PSPS		24	0	DCV	11.0③	0	0	DCV
NDS		30	0	DCV	0	VBAT	VBAT	DCV
STI		48	5.0	DCV	5.0	5.0	5.0	DCV
ACTUATORS/ OUTPUTS								
INJ BANK 2		59	VBAT④	DCV	4.4-5.6	6.0-7.6	8.0-11.4	mS
INJ BANK 1		58	VBAT④	DCV	4.4-5.6	6.0-7.6	8.0-11.4	mS
EVR		33	VBAT④	DCV	0	0	0	%
STO/MIL		17	.6	DCV	VBAT	VBAT	VBAT	DCV
ISC-BPA		21	VBAT	DCV	7.5-9.5	6.0-9.0	5.0-7.5	DCV
FP		22	VBAT	DCV	.9	.9	.9	DCV
SPOUT		36	4	RPM	700-800	1300-1400	2200-2300	RPM
AM1		51	VBAT	DCV	VBAT	.2	.2	DCV
AM2		11	VBAT	DCV	VBAT	VBAT	VBAT	DCV
OTHER								
IGN TIMING		TIMING	N/A	DEG	14-20	28-36	30-40	DEG

NOTES:
① — A/C on.
② — Clutch pedal depressed.
③ — Steering wheel turned.
④ — Monitor in DCV Manual Mode, Reference Pin to PWR GND (40/60).
⑤ — HEGO should switch from rich (red LED) to lean (green LED), or lean to rich, at least once every 3 seconds. HEGO voltage should toggle above and below .450 DCV, and should never be a negative value.

Reference values shown may vary ± 20% depending on operating conditions and other factors. RPM values are axle and tire dependent.

91E14286

Courtesy of Ford Motor Co.

Fig. 18: ECA Pin Voltage Checks (Bronco, "E" & "F" Series 5.0L with Automatic Transmission; Except E4OD)

1991 ENGINE PERFORMANCE
Pin Voltage Charts (Cont.)

5.0L BRONCO & "F" SERIES
AUTOMATIC TRANSMISSION (E4OD)

SENSORS/ INPUTS	Signal Pin #	KOEO	Units	HOT IDLE	30 MPH	55 MPH	Units
TP	47	.9	DCV	.9	1.0-1.1	1.2-1.3	DCV
EVP	27	.4	DCV	.4	.4-2.5	3.5-4.5	DCV
ECT	7	.6	DCV	.6	.6	.6	DCV
ACT	25	1.2	DCV	1.2	1.2	1.2	DCV
MAP	45	157	Hz	103-105	112-120	122-140	Hz
IDM	4	4	RPM	680-780	1240-1340	1650-1750	RPM
OCS red	41	.1	DCV	.1	.1	.1	DCV
PIP	56	4	RPM	680-780	1240-1340	1650-1750	RPM
TOT red	42	2.3③	DCV	1.7③	1.2③	1.2③	DCV
KS	23	2.5	DCV	2.5	2.5	2.5	DCV
HEGO	29	.03	DCV	switching④	switching④	switching④	DCV
4x4L red	12	VBAT③	DCV	VBAT③	VBAT③	VBAT③	DCV
BOO	2	0	DCV	VBAT②	0	0	DCV
FPM red	8	0③	DCV	VBAT③	VBAT③	VBAT③	DCV
ACCS	10	0	DCV	VBAT①	0	0	DCV
VSS+	3	0	MPH	0	30	55	MPH
MLPS	30	4.5	DCV	4.5	2.1	2.1	DCV
STI	48	5.0	DCV	5.0	5.0	5.0	DCV
ACTUATORS/ OUTPUTS							
INJ BANK 2	59	VBAT③	DCV	4.4-5.0	6.4-7.8	9.8-12.0	mS
INJ BANK 1	58	VBAT③	DCV	4.4-5.0	6.4-7.8	9.8-12.0	mS
SS1	52	.4③	DCV	.4③	VBAT③	VBAT③	DCV
EVR	33	VBAT③	DCV	0	0	0	%
EPC	38	7.5	DCV	9.2	9.2	9.2	DCV
STO/MIL	17	.2	DCV	VBAT	VBAT	VBAT	DCV
CANP	31	VBAT	DCV	VBAT	.2-9.0	.2	DCV
ISC-BPA	21	VBAT	DCV	8.0-9.5	6.5-9.5	5.0-7.5	DCV
FP	22	VBAT	DCV	.1	.1	.1	DCV
SS2 blue	19	VBAT	DCV	VBAT	.4	VBAT	DCV
SPOUT	36	4	RPM	680-780	1240-1340	1650-1750	RPM
OCIL	32	VBAT	DCV	VBAT	VBAT	VBAT	DCV
AM1	51	VBAT	DCV	.2	VBAT	VBAT	DCV
AM2	11	VBAT	DCV	VBAT	VBAT	VBAT	DCV
CCC	53	VBAT	DCV	VBAT	.4	.4	DCV
CCS	55	VBAT	DCV	VBAT	VBAT	VBAT	DCV
OTHER							
IGN TIMING	TIMING	N/A	DEG	14-20	28-36	30-40	DEG

NOTES: ① — A/C on.
② — Brake pedal applied.
③ — Monitor in DCV Manual Mode, Reference Pin to PWR GND (40/60).
④ — HEGO should switch from rich (red LED) to lean (green LED), or lean to rich, at least once every 3 seconds. HEGO voltage should toggle above and below .450 DCV, and should never be a negative value.

Reference values shown may vary ± 20% depending on operating conditions and other factors. RPM values are axle and tire dependent.

91F14287

Courtesy of Ford Motor Co.

Fig. 19: ECA Pin Voltage Checks (Bronco & "F" Series 5.0L with E4OD Automatic Transmission)

1991 ENGINE PERFORMANCE
Pin Voltage Charts (Cont.)

5.0L BRONCO, "E" & "F" SERIES
MANUAL TRANSMISSION

SENSORS/ INPUTS	Signal Pin #	KOEO	Units	HOT IDLE	30 MPH	55 MPH	Units
TP	47	.9	DCV	.9	1.0-1.1	1.2-1.3	DCV
EVP	27	.4	DCV	.4	.4-2.5	2.2-4.2	DCV
ECT	7	.6	DCV	.6	.6	.6	DCV
ACT	25	1.2	DCV	1.2	1.2	1.2	DCV
MAP	45	157	Hz	103-105	104-112	118-124	Hz
IDM	4	4	RPM	700-800	1300-1400	2200-2300	RPM
PIP	56	4	RPM	700-800	1300-1400	2200-2300	RPM
KS	23	2.5	DCV	2.5	2.5	2.5	DCV
HEGO	29	.04	DCV	switching⑤	switching⑤	switching⑤	DCV
FPM red	8	0④	DCV	VBAT④	VBAT④	VBAT④	DCV
ACCS	10	0	DCV	VBAT①	0	0	DCV
VSS+	3	0	MPH	0	30	55	MPH
PSPS	24	0	DCV	11.0③	0	0	DCV
CES	30	0	DCV	VBAT②	0	0	DCV
STI	48	5.0	DCV	5.0	5.0	5.0	DCV
ACTUATORS/ OUTPUTS							
INJ BANK 2	59	VBAT④	DCV	4.4-5.6	6.0-7.6	8.0-11.4	mS
INJ BANK 1	58	VBAT④	DCV	4.4-5.6	6.0-7.6	8.0-11.4	mS
EVR	33	VBAT④	DCV	0	0	0	%
STO/MIL	17	.6	DCV	VBAT	VBAT	VBAT	DCV
ISC-BPA	21	VBAT	DCV	7.5-9.5	6.0-9.0	5.0-7.5	DCV
FP	22	VBAT	DCV	.9	.9	.9	DCV
SPOUT	36	4	RPM	700-800	1300-1400	2200-2300	RPM
AM1	51	VBAT	DCV	VBAT	.2	.2	DCV
AM2	11	VBAT	DCV	VBAT	VBAT	VBAT	DCV
OTHER							
IGN TIMING	TIMING	N/A	DEG	14-20	28-36	30-40	DEG

NOTES: ① — A/C on.
② — Clutch pedal depressed.
③ — Steering wheel turned.
④ — Monitor in DCV Manual Mode, Reference Pin to PWR GND (40/60).
⑤ — HEGO should switch from rich (red LED) to lean (green LED), or lean to rich, at least once every 3 seconds. HEGO voltage should toggle above and below .450 DCV, and should never be a negative value.

Reference values shown may vary ± 20% depending on operating conditions and other factors. RPM values are axle and tire dependent.

91G14288

Courtesy of Ford Motor Co.

Fig. 20: ECA Pin Voltage Checks (Bronco, "E" & "F" Series 5.0L with Manual Transmission)

1991 ENGINE PERFORMANCE
Pin Voltage Charts (Cont.)

5.8L "E" & "F" SERIES
AUTOMATIC TRANSMISSION (EXCEPT E4OD)

SENSORS/ INPUTS	Signal Pin #	KOEO	Units	HOT IDLE	30 MPH	55 MPH	Units
TP	47	.9	DCV	.9	1.0-1.1	1.1-1.2	DCV
EVP	27	.3	DCV	.3	.4	.6-3.0	DCV
ECT	7	.6	DCV	.6	.6	.6	DCV
ACT	25	1.0	DCV	1.0	1.3	1.6	DCV
MAP	45	157	Hz	108-112	110-120	130-140	Hz
IDM	4	4	RPM	750-850	1250-1350	1600-1700	RPM
PIP	56	4	RPM	750-850	1250-1350	1600-1700	RPM
HEGO	29	.04	DCV	switching③	switching③	switching③	DCV
FPM red	8	0	DCV	VBAT	VBAT	VBAT	DCV
ACCS	10	0	DCV	VBAT①	0	0	DCV
VSS+	3	0	MPH	0	30	55	MPH
NDS	30	0	DCV	0	VBAT	VBAT	DCV
STI	48	5.0	DCV	5.0	5.0	5.0	DCV
ACTUATORS/ OUTPUTS							
INJ BANK 2	59	VBAT②	DCV	5.0-5.8	6.0-6.8	6.4-7.0	mS
INJ BANK 1	58	VBAT②	DCV	5.0-5.8	6.0-6.8	6.4-7.0	mS
EVR	33	VBAT②	DCV	0	0	0	%
STO/MIL	17	.6	DCV	VBAT	VBAT	VBAT	DCV
CANP	31	VBAT	DCV	VBAT	VBAT	.2	DCV
ISC-BPA	21	VBAT	DCV	7.0-8.5	7.0-8.0	3.0-4.0	DCV
FP	22	VBAT	DCV	.9	.9	.9	DCV
SPOUT	36	4	RPM	750-850	1250-1350	1600-1700	RPM
AM1	51	VBAT	DCV	.2	VBAT	VBAT	DCV
AM2	11	VBAT	DCV	VBAT	VBAT	VBAT	DCV
OTHER							
IGN TIMING	TIMING	N/A	DEG	14-18	30-36	36-44	DEG

NOTES: ① — A/C on.
② — Monitor in DCV Manual Mode, Reference Pin to PWR GND (40/60).
③ — HEGO should switch from rich (red LED) to lean (green LED), or lean to rich, at least once every 3 seconds. HEGO voltage should toggle above and below .450 DCV, and should never be a negative value.

Reference values shown may vary ± 20% depending on operating conditions and other factors. RPM values are axle and tire dependent.

91H14289

Courtesy of Ford Motor Co.

Fig. 21: ECA Pin Voltage Checks ("E" & "F" Series 5.8L with Automatic Transmission; Except E4OD)

1991 ENGINE PERFORMANCE
Pin Voltage Charts (Cont.)

5.8L BRONCO, "E" & "F" SERIES
AUTOMATIC TRANSMISSION (E4OD)

SENSORS/ INPUTS		Signal Pin #	KOEO	Units	HOT IDLE	30 MPH	55 MPH	Units
TP		47	.9	DCV	.9	1.0-1.1	1.1-1.2	DCV
EVP		27	.3	DCV	.3	.4	.6-3.0	DCV
ECT		7	.6	DCV	.6	.6	.6	DCV
ACT		25	1.0	DCV	1.0	1.3	1.6	DCV
MAP		45	157	Hz	108-112	110-120	130-140	Hz
IDM		4	4	RPM	750-850	1250-1350	1600-1700	RPM
OCS	red	41	.1	DCV	.1	.1	.1	DCV
PIP		56	4	RPM	750-850	1250-1350	1600-1700	RPM
TOT	red	42	1.0	DCV	1.0	1.2	1.0	DCV
HEGO		29	.04	DCV	switching④	switching④	switching④	DCV
4x4L	red	12	VBAT	DCV	VBAT	VBAT	VBAT	DCV
BOO		2	0	DCV	VBAT②	0	0	DCV
FPM	red	8	0	DCV	VBAT	VBAT	VBAT	DCV
ACCS		10	0	DCV	VBAT①	0	0	DCV
VSS+		3	0	MPH	0	30	55	MPH
MLPS		30	4.5	DCV	4.5	2.1	2.1	DCV
STI		48	5.0	DCV	5.0	5.0	5.0	DCV
ACTUATORS/ OUTPUTS								
INJ BANK 2		59	VBAT③	DCV	5.0-5.8	6.0-6.8	6.4-7.0	mS
INJ BANK 1		58	VBAT③	DCV	5.0-5.8	6.0-6.8	6.4-7.0	mS
SS1		52	.3	DCV	.4	VBAT	VBAT	DCV
EVR		33	VBAT③	DCV	0	0	0	%
EPC		38	7.2	DCV	8.6	9.0	9.0	DCV
STO/MIL		17	.1	DCV	VBAT	VBAT	VBAT	DCV
CANP		31	VBAT	DCV	VBAT	VBAT	.2	DCV
ISC-BPA		21	VBAT	DCV	7.0-8.5	7.0-8.0	3.0-4.0	DCV
FP		22	VBAT	DCV	.1	.1	.1	DCV
SS2	blue	19	VBAT	DCV	VBAT	.3	VBAT	DCV
SPOUT		36	4	RPM	750-850	1250-1350	1600-1700	RPM
OCIL		32	VBAT	DCV	VBAT	VBAT	VBAT	DCV
AM1		51	VBAT	DCV	.2	VBAT	VBAT	DCV
AM2		11	VBAT	DCV	VBAT	VBAT	VBAT	DCV
CCC		53	VBAT	DCV	VBAT	.4	.4	DCV
CCS		55	VBAT	DCV	VBAT	VBAT	VBAT	DCV
OTHER								
IGN TIMING		TIMING	N/A	DEG	14-18	30-36	36-44	DEG

NOTES: ① — A/C on.
② — Brake pedal applied.
③ — Monitor in DCV Manual Mode, Reference Pin to PWR GND (40/60).
④ — HEGO should switch from rich (red LED) to lean (green LED), or lean to rich, at least once every 3 seconds. HEGO voltage should toggle above and below .450 DCV, and should never be a negative value.

Reference values shown may vary ± 20% depending on operating conditions and other factors. RPM values are axle and tire dependent.

91A14290

Courtesy of Ford Motor Co.

Fig. 22: ECA Pin Voltage Checks (Bronco, "E" & "F" Series 5.8L with E4OD Automatic Transmission)

1991 ENGINE PERFORMANCE
Pin Voltage Charts (Cont.)

5.8L "E" & "F" SERIES MANUAL TRANSMISSION

SENSORS/ INPUTS	Signal Pin #	KOEO	Units	HOT IDLE	30 MPH	55 MPH	Units
TP	47	.9	DCV	.9	1.0-1.1	1.1-1.2	DCV
EVP	27	.3	DCV	.3	.4	.6-3.0	DCV
ECT	7	.6	DCV	.6	.6	.6	DCV
ACT	25	1.0	DCV	1.0	1.3	1.6	DCV
MAP	45	157	Hz	108-112	110-120	130-140	Hz
IDM	4	4	RPM	750-850	1250-1350	1600-1700	RPM
PIP	56	4	RPM	750-850	1250-1350	1600-1700	RPM
HEGO	29	.04	DCV	switching④	switching④	switching④	DCV
FPM red	8	0	DCV	VBAT	VBAT	VBAT	DCV
ACCS	10	0	DCV	VBAT①	0	0	DCV
VSS+	3	0	MPH	0	30	55	MPH
CES	30	0	DCV	VBAT②	0	0	DCV
STI	48	5.0	DCV	5.0	5.0	5.0	DCV
ACTUATORS/ OUTPUTS							
INJ BANK 2	59	VBAT③	DCV	5.0-5.8	6.0-6.8	6.4-7.0	mS
INJ BANK 1	58	VBAT③	DCV	5.0-5.8	6.0-6.8	6.4-7.0	mS
EVR	33	VBAT③	DCV	0	0	0	%
STO/MIL	17	.6	DCV	VBAT	VBAT	VBAT	DCV
CANP	31	VBAT	DCV	VBAT	VBAT	.2	DCV
ISC-BPA	21	VBAT	DCV	7.0-8.5	7.0-8.0	3.0-4.0	DCV
FP	22	VBAT	DCV	.9	.9	.9	DCV
SPOUT	36	4	RPM	750-850	1250-1350	1600-1700	RPM
AM1	51	VBAT	DCV	.2	VBAT	VBAT	DCV
AM2	11	VBAT	DCV	VBAT	VBAT	VBAT	DCV
OTHER							
IGN TIMING	TIMING	N/A	DEG	14-18	30-36	36-44	DEG

NOTES: ① — A/C on.
② — Clutch pedal depressed.
③ — Monitor in DCV Manual Mode, Reference Pin to PWR GND (40/60).
④ — HEGO should switch from rich (red LED) to lean (green LED), or lean to rich, at least once every 3 seconds. HEGO voltage should toggle above and below .450 DCV, and should never be a negative value.

Reference values shown may vary ± 20% depending on operating conditions and other factors. RPM values are axle and tire dependent.

91B14291

Courtesy of Ford Motor Co.

Fig. 23: ECA Pin Voltage Checks ("E" & "F" Series 5.8L with Manual Transmission)

1991 ENGINE PERFORMANCE
Pin Voltage Charts (Cont.)

7.3L DIESEL "E" & "F" SERIES
AUTOMATIC TRANSMISSION (E4OD)

SENSORS/ INPUTS		Signal Pin #	KOEO	Units	HOT IDLE	30 MPH	55 MPH	Units
TP		47	1.0	DCV	1.0	1.2-1.4	1.7-2.0	DCV
TOT		7	2.9	DCV	2.8	2.1	2.1	DCV
BP		45	157	Hz	157	157	157	Hz
RPMS(+)		4	0	RPM	540-640	300-400	250-350	RPM
OCS	red	41	.1	DCV	.1	.1	.1	DCV
4x4L	red	12	VBAT	DCV	VBAT	VBAT	VBAT	DCV
BOO		2	0	DCV	VBAT②	0	0	DCV
ACCS		10	0	DCV	VBAT①	0	0	DCV
VSS(+)		3	0	MPH	0	30	55	MPH
MLPS		30	4.5	DCV	4.5	2.1	2.1	DCV
STI		48	5.0	DCV	5.0	5.0	5.0	DCV
ACTUATORS/ OUTPUTS								
SS1		52	.3	DCV	.4	0	0	DCV
EPC		38	9.0	DCV	7.6	7.6	8.0	DCV
STO		17	VBAT	DCV	VBAT	VBAT	VBAT	DCV
SS2	blue	19	VBAT	DCV	VBAT	.4	.4	DCV
TAC		36	0	RPM	540-640	300-400	250-350	RPM
OCIL/TMIL		32	VBAT	DCV	VBAT	VBAT	0	DCV
CCC		53	VBAT	DCV	VBAT	.3	.3	DCV
CCS		55	VBAT	DCV	VBAT	VBAT	.4	DCV
OTHER								
IGN TIMING		TIMING	N/A	DEG	N/A	N/A	N/A	DEG

NOTES: ① — **A/C on.**
② — **Brake pedal applies.**

Reference values shown may vary ± 20% depending on operating conditions and other factors. RPM values are axle and tire dependent.

91C14292

Courtesy of Ford Motor Co.

Fig. 24: ECA Pin Voltage Checks (Diesel "E" & "F" Series 7.3L with E4OD Automatic Transmission)

1991 ENGINE PERFORMANCE
Pin Voltage Charts (Cont.)

7.5L "E" & "F" SERIES
AUTOMATIC TRANSMISSION (EXCEPT E4OD)

SENSORS/ INPUTS	Signal Pin #	KOEO	Units	HOT IDLE	30 MPH	55 MPH	Units
TP	47	1.0	DCV	1.0	1.1-1.3	1.3-1.5	DCV
EVP	27	.4	DCV	.4	.4	.4-4.0	DCV
ECT	7	.6	DCV	.6	.6	.6	DCV
ACT	25	1.2	DCV	1.4	1.5	1.7	DCV
MAP	45	157	Hz	101-104	106-116	114-124	Hz
IDM	4	4	RPM	650-750	1350-1550	1800-2080	RPM
PIP	56	4	RPM	650-750	1350-1550	1800-2080	RPM
HEGO	29	.02	DCV	switching③	switching③	switching③	DCV
FPM red	8	0	DCV	VBAT	VBAT	VBAT	DCV
ACCS	10	0	DCV	VBAT①	0	0	DCV
NDS	30	0	DCV	0	VBAT	VBAT	DCV
STI	48	5.0	DCV	5.0	5.0	5.0	DCV
ACTUATORS/ OUTPUTS							
INJ BANK 2	59	VBAT②	DCV	5.6-6.2	6.6-8.6	9.0-11.0	mS
INJ BANK 1	58	VBAT②	DCV	5.6-6.2	6.6-8.6	9.0-11.0	mS
EVR	33	VBAT②	DCV	0	0	0	%
STO/MIL	17	.6	DCV	VBAT	VBAT	VBAT	DCV
CANP	31	VBAT	DCV	VBAT	VBAT	.2	DCV
ISC-BPA	21	VBAT	DCV	8.0-10.5	8.0-9.5	6.0-8.5	DCV
FP	22	VBAT	DCV	.8	.8	.8	DCV
SPOUT	36	4	RPM	650-750	1350-1550	1800-2080	RPM
AM1	51	VBAT	DCV	.2	.2	.2	DCV
OTHER							
IGN TIMING	TIMING	N/A	DEG	18-22	36-42	38-46	DEG

NOTES: ① — A/C on.
② — Monitor in DCV Manual Mode, Reference Pin to PWR GND (40/60).
③ — HEGO should switch from rich (red LED) to lean (green LED), or lean to rich, at least once every 3 seconds. HEGO voltage should toggle above and below .450 DCV, and should never be a negative value.

Reference values shown may vary ± 20% depending on operating conditions and other factors. RPM values are axle and tire dependent.

91D14293

Courtesy of Ford Motor Co.

Fig. 25: ECA Pin Voltage Checks ("E" & "F" Series 7.5L with Automatic Transmission; Except E4OD)

1991 ENGINE PERFORMANCE
Pin Voltage Charts (Cont.)

7.5L "E" & "F" SERIES
AUTOMATIC TRANSMISSION (E4OD)

SENSORS/ INPUTS		Signal Pin #	KOEO	Units	HOT IDLE	30 MPH	55 MPH	Units
TP		47	1.0	DCV	1.0	1.1-1.3	1.3-1.5	DCV
EVP		27	.3	DCV	.3	.4	.4-4.0	DCV
ECT		7	.6	DCV	.6	.6	.6	DCV
ACT		25	.8	DCV	1.0	2.2	2.6	DCV
MAP		45	157	Hz	101-104	106-116	114-124	Hz
IDM		4	4	RPM	650-750	1300-1400	1730-1830	RPM
OCS	red	41	0	DCV	0	0	0	DCV
PIP		56	4	RPM	650-750	1300-1400	1730-1830	RPM
TOT	red	42	1.3	DCV	1.3	1.6	1.6	DCV
HEGO		29	.02	DCV	switching④	switching④	switching④	DCV
4x4L	red	12	VBAT	DCV	VBAT	VBAT	VBAT	DCV
BOO		2	0	DCV	VBAT②	0	0	DCV
FPM	red	8	0	DCV	VBAT	VBAT	VBAT	DCV
ACCS		10	0	DCV	VBAT①	0	0	DCV
VSS+		3	0	MPH	0	30	55	MPH
MLPS		30	4.5	DCV	4.5	2.1	2.1	DCV
STI		48	5.0	DCV	5.0	5.0	5.0	DCV
ACTUATORS/ OUTPUTS								
INJ BANK 2		59	VBAT③	DCV	6.0-6.6	7.8-8.2	10.0-11.6	mS
INJ BANK 1		58	VBAT③	DCV	6.0-6.6	7.8-8.2	10.0-11.6	mS
SS1		52	.3	DCV	.3	VBAT	VBAT	DCV
EVR		33	VBAT③	DCV	0	0	0	%
EPC		38	7.3	DCV	8.8	9.2	9.2	DCV
STO/MIL		17	.1	DCV	VBAT	VBAT	VBAT	DCV
CANP		31	VBAT	DCV	VBAT	VBAT	.2	DCV
ISC-BPA		21	VBAT	DCV	8.0-10.5	7.0-8.5	4.0-6.5	DCV
FP		22	VBAT	DCV	.1	.1	.1	DCV
SS2	blue	19	VBAT	DCV	VBAT	.4	VBAT	DCV
SPOUT		36	4	RPM	650-750	1300-1400	1730-1830	RPM
OCIL		32	VBAT	DCV	VBAT	VBAT	VBAT	DCV
AM1		51	VBAT	DCV	.1	.1	.1	DCV
CCC		53	VBAT	DCV	VBAT	.4	.4	DCV
CCS		55	VBAT	DCV	VBAT	VBAT	VBAT	DCV
OTHER								
IGN TIMING		TIMING	N/A	DEG	22-28	36-42	38-46	DEG

NOTES: ① — A/C on.
② — Brake pedal applied.
③ — Monitor in DCV Manual Mode, Reference Pin to PWR GND (40/60).
④ — HEGO should switch from rich (red LED) to lean (green LED), or lean to rich, at least once every 3 seconds. HEGO voltage should toggle above and below .450 DCV, and should never be a negative value.

Reference values shown may vary ± 20% depending on operating conditions and other factors. RPM values are axle and tire dependent.

91E14294

Courtesy of Ford Motor Co.

Fig. 26: ECA Pin Voltage Checks ("E" & "F" Series 7.5L with E4OD Automatic Transmission)

7.5L "E" & "F" SERIES
MANUAL TRANSMISSION

SENSORS/ INPUTS	Signal Pin #	KOEO	Units	HOT IDLE	30 MPH	55 MPH	Units
TP	47	1.0	DCV	1.0	1.1-1.3	1.3-1.5	DCV
EVP	27	.4	DCV	.4	.4	.4-4.0	DCV
ECT	7	.6	DCV	.6	.6	.6	DCV
ACT	25	1.2	DCV	1.4	1.5	1.7	DCV
MAP	45	157	Hz	101-104	106-116	112-120	Hz
IDM	4	4	RPM	650-750	1350-1550	1800-2080	RPM
PIP	56	4	RPM	650-750	1350-1550	1800-2080	RPM
HEGO	29	.02	DCV	switching④	switching④	switching④	DCV
FPM red	8	0	DCV	VBAT	VBAT	VBAT	DCV
ACCS	10	0	DCV	VBAT①	0	0	DCV
NGS/CES	30	0	DCV	VBAT②	0	VBAT	DCV
STI	48	5.0	DCV	5.0	5.0	5.0	DCV
ACTUATORS/ OUTPUTS							
INJ BANK 2	59	VBAT③	DCV	5.6-6.2	6.6-8.6	9.0-11.0	mS
INJ BANK 1	58	VBAT③	DCV	5.6-6.2	6.6-8.6	9.0-11.0	mS
EVR	33	VBAT③	DCV	0	0	0	%
STO/MIL	17	.6	DCV	VBAT	VBAT	VBAT	DCV
CANP	31	VBAT	DCV	VBAT	VBAT	.2	DCV
ISC-BPA	21	VBAT	DCV	8.0-10.5	8.0-9.5	6.0-8.5	DCV
FP	22	VBAT	DCV	.8	.8	.8	DCV
SPOUT	36	4	RPM	650-750	1350-1550	1800-2080	RPM
AM1	51	VBAT	DCV	.2	.2	.2	DCV
OTHER							
IGN TIMING	TIMING	N/A	DEG	18-22	36-42	38-46	DEG

NOTES: ① — A/C on.
② — Clutch pedal depressed.
③ — Monitor in DCV Manual Mode, Reference Pin to PWR GND (40/60).
④ — HEGO should switch from rich (red LED) to lean (green LED), or lean to rich, at least once every 3 seconds. HEGO voltage should toggle above and below .450 DCV, and should never be a negative value.

Reference values shown may vary ± 20% depending on operating conditions and other factors. RPM values are axle and tire dependent.

91F14295

Courtesy of Ford Motor Co.

Fig. 27: ECA Pin Voltage Checks ("E" & "F" Series 7.5L with Manual Transmission)

1991 ENGINE PERFORMANCE
Sensor Operating Range Charts

Aerostar, Bronco, Explorer, Ranger, "E" & "F" Series

NOTE: Unless otherwise specified, references to "F" Series includes "F" Series Super Duty.

INTRODUCTION

Sensor operating range information can help determine if a sensor is out of calibration. An out-of-calibration sensor may not set a trouble code, but it will cause driveability problems.

NOTE: Unless stated otherwise in test procedure, perform all voltage tests using a Digital Volt-Ohmmeter (DVOM) with a minimum 10-megohm input impedance.

ACT & ECT SENSORS

ACT & ECT SENSORS SPECIFICATIONS

Temperature F (°C)	[1] Voltage	Ohms
50 (10)	3.51	58,700
68 (20)	3.07	37,300
86 (30)	2.60	24,200
104 (40)	2.13	16,150
122 (50)	1.70	10,970
140 (60)	1.33	7700
158 (70)	1.33	7700
176 (80)	.78	3840
194 (90)	.60	2800
212 (100)	.46	2007

[1] – Voltage calculations are based on a VREF of 5.0 volts. Actual values may vary up to 15% due to sensor and VREF variations.

EGR VALVE POSITION (EVP) SENSOR

EVP SENSOR VOLTAGE

EGR Valve Opening (%)	[1] Voltage
0	0.40
10	0.75
20	1.10
30	1.45
40	1.80
50	2.15
60	2.50
70	2.85
80	3.20
90	3.55
100	3.90

[1] – Voltage calculations are based on a VREF of 5.0 volts. Actual values may vary up to 15% due to sensor and VREF variations.

EXHAUST GAS OXYGEN (EGO) SENSOR

EGO SENSOR VOLTAGE

Condition	[1] Voltage
Increasing Engine Speed	Increases
Decreasing Engine Speed	Decreases
Engine At Idle	0.2-0.8

[1] – Measure between oxygen sensor and ground.

MASS AIRFLOW (MAF) SENSOR

MAF SENSOR DATA SPECIFICATIONS

Engine Condition [1]	[2] Voltage
Idle	.6
20 MPH	1.1
40 MPH	1.7
60 MPH	2.1

[1] – Engine at normal operating temperature.
[2] – Voltage may vary depending on vehicle load and temperature.

MANIFOLD ABSOLUTE PRESSURE (MAP) SENSOR

MAP SENSOR SPECIFICATIONS

Manifold Vacuum (In. Hg)	[1] Frequency (Hz)
0	159
3	150
6	141
9	133
12	125
15	117
18	109
21	102
24	95
27	88
30	80

[1] – Frequency value may vary by 15 percent.

MAP SENSOR VOLTAGE OUTPUT

Elevation (Feet)	Volts
0	1.55-1.63
1000	1.52-1.60
2000	1.49-1.57
3000	1.46-1.54
4000	1.43-1.51
5000	1.40-1.48
6000	1.37-1.45
7000	1.35-1.43

MAP/BP SENSOR SPECIFICATIONS

Barometric Pressure (In. Hg)	[1] Frequency (Hz)
17.1	122.4
18.3	125.5
19.5	128.7
20.7	131.9
21.8	135.1
23.0	138.3
24.2	141.8
25.4	145.4
26.6	148.9
27.7	152.5
28.9	156.1
30.1	159.6
31.0	162.4

[1] – Frequency value may vary by 15 percent.

MANUAL LEVER POSITION (MLP) SENSOR

MLP SENSOR SPECIFICATIONS

Position	[1] Voltage	[1] Ohms
P	4.41	4160
R	3.60	1440
N	2.83	2733
D	2.09	401
2	1.37	211
1	.68	81

[1] – Value may vary by 15 percent.

1991 ENGINE PERFORMANCE
Sensor Operating Range Charts (Cont.)

THROTTLE POSITION SENSOR (TPS)

TPS VOLTAGE

Throttle Angle	[1] Voltage
0°	0.50
10°	0.97
20°	1.44
30°	1.90
40°	2.37
50°	2.84
60°	3.31
70°	3.78
80°	4.24

[1] – Voltage may vary by 15 percent.

TRANSMISSION OIL TEMPERATURE (TOT) SENSOR

TOT SENSOR (AODE) SPECIFICATIONS

Temperature °F (°C)	[1] Voltage	[1] Ohms
32 (0)	3.88	96,255
41 (5)	3.71	75,201
50 (10)	3.53	59,175
59 (15)	3.32	46,883
68 (20)	3.10	37,387
77 (25)	2.86	30,000
86 (30)	2.62	24,215
95 (35)	2.38	19,657
104 (40)	2.15	16,043
113 (45)	1.92	13,161
122 (50)	1.71	10,050
131 (55)	1.51	8990
140 (60)	1.33	7487
149 (65)	1.17	6265
158 (70)	1.03	5260
167 (75)	.90	4450
176 (80)	.78	3775
185 (85)	.69	3215
194 (90)	.60	2750
200 (95)	.52	2361

[1] – Value may vary by 15 percent.

1991 ENGINE PERFORMANCE
Wiring Diagrams

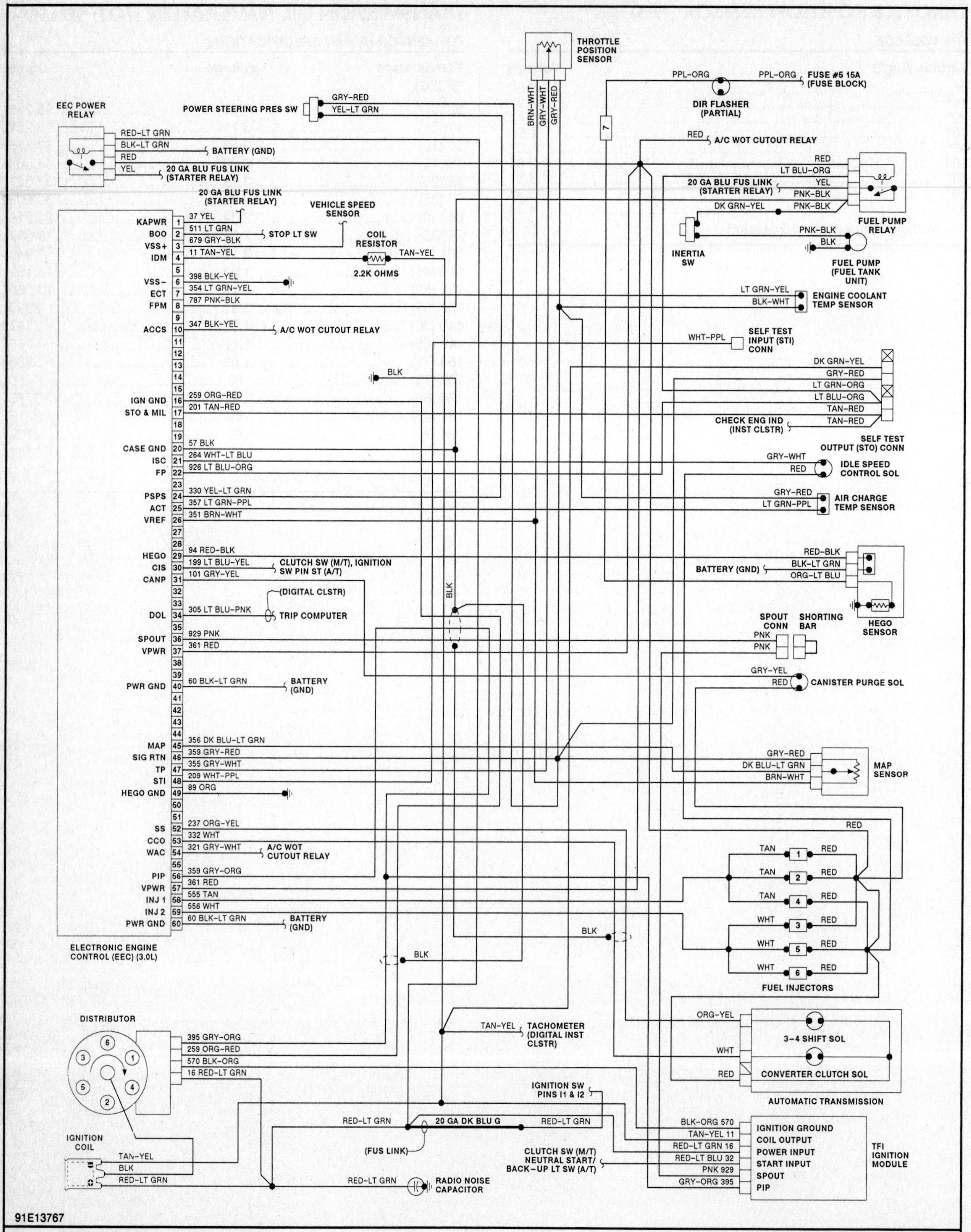
THROTTLE POSITION SENSOR
EEC POWER RELAY
POWER STEERING PRES SW
BATTERY (GND)
20 GA BLU FUS LINK (STARTER RELAY)
VEHICLE SPEED SENSOR
STOP LT SW
COIL RESISTOR
2.2K OHMS
A/C WOT CUTOUT RELAY
CLUTCH SW (M/T), IGNITION SW PIN ST (A/T)
(DIGITAL CLSTR)
TRIP COMPUTER
ELECTRONIC ENGINE CONTROL (EEC) (3.0L)
KAPWR
BOO
VSS+
IDM
VSS-
ECT
FPM
ACCS
IGN GND
STO & MIL
CASE GND
ISC
FP
PSPS
ACT
VREF
HEGO
CIS
CANP
DOL
SPOUT
VPWR
PWR GND
MAP
SIG RTN
TP
STI
HEGO GND
SS
CCO
WAC
PIP
INJ 1
INJ 2
DIR FLASHER (PARTIAL)
FUSE #5 15A (FUSE BLOCK)
FUEL PUMP RELAY
INERTIA SW
FUEL PUMP (FUEL TANK UNIT)
ENGINE COOLANT TEMP SENSOR
SELF TEST INPUT (STI) CONN
CHECK ENG IND (INST CLSTR)
SELF TEST OUTPUT (STO) CONN
IDLE SPEED CONTROL SOL
AIR CHARGE TEMP SENSOR
HEGO SENSOR
SPOUT CONN
SHORTING BAR
CANISTER PURGE SOL
MAP SENSOR
FUEL INJECTORS
3-4 SHIFT SOL
CONVERTER CLUTCH SOL
AUTOMATIC TRANSMISSION
DISTRIBUTOR
IGNITION COIL
TACHOMETER (DIGITAL INST CLSTR)
IGNITION SW PINS I1 & I2
20 GA DK BLU G
(FUS LINK)
RADIO NOISE CAPACITOR
CLUTCH SW (M/T) NEUTRAL START/ BACK-UP LT SW (A/T)
TFI IGNITION MODULE
IGNITION GROUND
COIL OUTPUT
POWER INPUT
START INPUT
SPOUT
PIP
91E13767

Fig. 1: Wiring Diagram (Aerostar 3.0L)

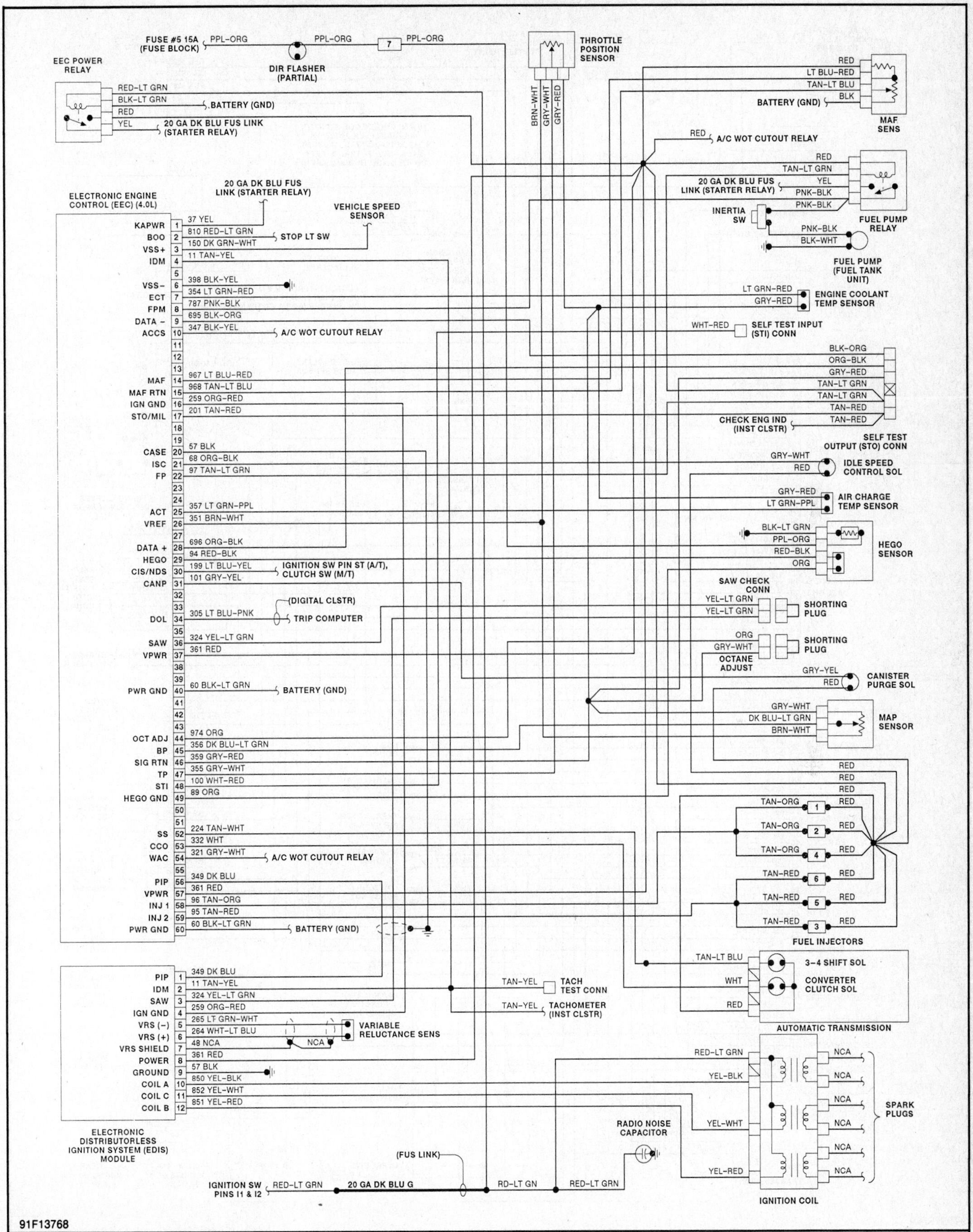
FUSE #5 15A (FUSE BLOCK)
PPL-ORG
DIR FLASHER (PARTIAL)
THROTTLE POSITION SENSOR
EEC POWER RELAY
BATTERY (GND)
20 GA DK BLU FUS LINK (STARTER RELAY)
MAF SENS
A/C WOT CUTOUT RELAY
FUEL PUMP RELAY
ELECTRONIC ENGINE CONTROL (EEC) (4.0L)
VEHICLE SPEED SENSOR
STOP LT SW
INERTIA SW
FUEL PUMP (FUEL TANK UNIT)
ENGINE COOLANT TEMP SENSOR
SELF TEST INPUT (STI) CONN
CHECK ENG IND (INST CLSTR)
SELF TEST OUTPUT (STO) CONN
IDLE SPEED CONTROL SOL
AIR CHARGE TEMP SENSOR
HEGO SENSOR
IGNITION SW PIN ST (A/T), CLUTCH SW (M/T)
SAW CHECK CONN
SHORTING PLUG
(DIGITAL CLSTR)
TRIP COMPUTER
OCTANE ADJUST
CANISTER PURGE SOL
MAP SENSOR
FUEL INJECTORS
3-4 SHIFT SOL
CONVERTER CLUTCH SOL
AUTOMATIC TRANSMISSION
TACH TEST CONN
TACHOMETER (INST CLSTR)
VARIABLE RELUCTANCE SENS
SPARK PLUGS
RADIO NOISE CAPACITOR
(FUS LINK)
IGNITION SW PINS I1 & I2
20 GA DK BLU G
IGNITION COIL
ELECTRONIC DISTRIBUTORLESS IGNITION SYSTEM (EDIS) MODULE
91F13768

Fig. 2: Wiring Diagram (Aerostar 4.0L)

1991 ENGINE PERFORMANCE
Wiring Diagrams (Cont.)

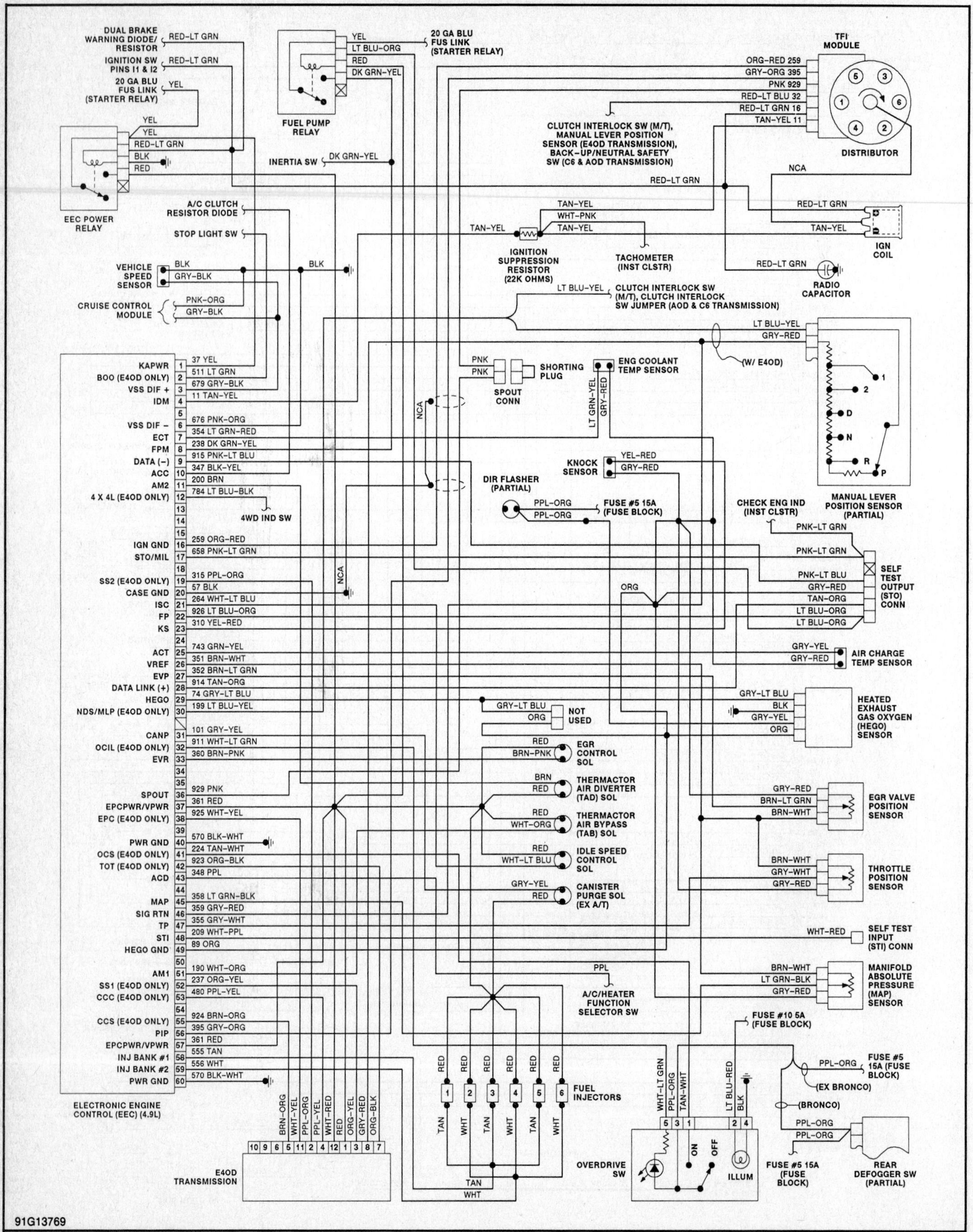
DUAL BRAKE WARNING DIODE/ RESISTOR
IGNITION SW PINS I1 & I2
20 GA BLU FUS LINK (STARTER RELAY)
EEC POWER RELAY
A/C CLUTCH RESISTOR DIODE
STOP LIGHT SW
VEHICLE SPEED SENSOR
CRUISE CONTROL MODULE
FUEL PUMP RELAY
INERTIA SW
TFI MODULE
DISTRIBUTOR
CLUTCH INTERLOCK SW (M/T), MANUAL LEVER POSITION SENSOR (E4OD TRANSMISSION), BACK-UP/NEUTRAL SAFETY SW (C6 & AOD TRANSMISSION)
IGNITION SUPPRESSION RESISTOR (22K OHMS)
TACHOMETER (INST CLSTR)
IGN COIL
RADIO CAPACITOR
CLUTCH INTERLOCK SW (M/T), CLUTCH INTERLOCK SW JUMPER (AOD & C6 TRANSMISSION)
(W/ E4OD)
SHORTING PLUG
SPOUT CONN
ENG COOLANT TEMP SENSOR
MANUAL LEVER POSITION SENSOR (PARTIAL)
KNOCK SENSOR
DIR FLASHER (PARTIAL)
FUSE #5 15A (FUSE BLOCK)
CHECK ENG IND (INST CLSTR)
4WD IND SW
SELF TEST OUTPUT (STO) CONN
AIR CHARGE TEMP SENSOR
HEATED EXHAUST GAS OXYGEN (HEGO) SENSOR
NOT USED
EGR CONTROL SOL
THERMACTOR AIR DIVERTER (TAD) SOL
THERMACTOR AIR BYPASS (TAB) SOL
IDLE SPEED CONTROL SOL
CANISTER PURGE SOL (EX A/T)
EGR VALVE POSITION SENSOR
THROTTLE POSITION SENSOR
SELF TEST INPUT (STI) CONN
MANIFOLD ABSOLUTE PRESSURE (MAP) SENSOR
A/C/HEATER FUNCTION SELECTOR SW
FUSE #10 5A (FUSE BLOCK)
FUSE #5 15A (FUSE BLOCK)
(EX BRONCO)
(BRONCO)
REAR DEFOGGER SW (PARTIAL)
FUEL INJECTORS
OVERDRIVE SW
ILLUM
E4OD TRANSMISSION
ELECTRONIC ENGINE CONTROL (EEC) (4.9L)
KAPWR 1 37 YEL
BOO (E4OD ONLY) 2 511 LT GRN
VSS DIF + 3 679 GRY-BLK
IDM 4 11 TAN-YEL
5
VSS DIF − 6 676 PNK-ORG
ECT 7 354 LT GRN-RED
FPM 8 238 DK GRN-YEL
DATA (−) 9 915 PNK-LT BLU
ACC 10 347 BLK-YEL
AM2 11 200 BRN
4 X 4L (E4OD ONLY) 12 784 LT BLU-BLK
13
14
15
IGN GND 16 259 ORG-RED
STO/MIL 17 658 PNK-LT GRN
18
SS2 (E4OD ONLY) 19 315 PPL-ORG
CASE GND 20 57 BLK
ISC 21 264 WHT-LT BLU
FP 22 926 LT BLU-ORG
KS 23 310 YEL-RED
24
ACT 25 743 GRN-YEL
VREF 26 351 BRN-WHT
EVP 27 352 BRN-LT GRN
DATA LINK (+) 28 914 TAN-ORG
HEGO 29 74 GRY-LT BLU
NDS/MLP (E4OD ONLY) 30 199 LT BLU-YEL
101 GRY-YEL
CANP 31 911 WHT-LT GRN
OCIL (E4OD ONLY) 32 360 BRN-PNK
EVR 33
34
35
SPOUT 36 929 PNK
EPCPWR/VPWR 37 361 RED
EPC (E4OD ONLY) 38 925 WHT-YEL
39
PWR GND 40 570 BLK-WHT
OCS (E4OD ONLY) 41 224 TAN-WHT
TOT (E4OD ONLY) 42 923 ORG-BLK
ACD 43 348 PPL
44
MAP 45 358 LT GRN-BLK
SIG RTN 46 359 GRY-RED
TP 47 355 GRY-WHT
STI 48 209 WHT-PPL
HEGO GND 49 89 ORG
50
AM1 51 190 WHT-ORG
SS1 (E4OD ONLY) 52 237 ORG-YEL
CCC (E4OD ONLY) 53 480 PPL-YEL
54
CCS (E4OD ONLY) 55 924 BRN-ORG
PIP 56 395 GRY-ORG
EPCPWR/VPWR 57 361 RED
INJ BANK #1 58 555 TAN
INJ BANK #2 59 556 WHT
PWR GND 60 570 BLK-WHT
ORG-RED 259
GRY-ORG 395
PNK 929
RED-LT BLU 32
RED-LT GRN 16
TAN-YEL 11
NCA
91G13769

Fig. 3: Wiring Diagram (Bronco 4.9L & "F" Series 4.9L)

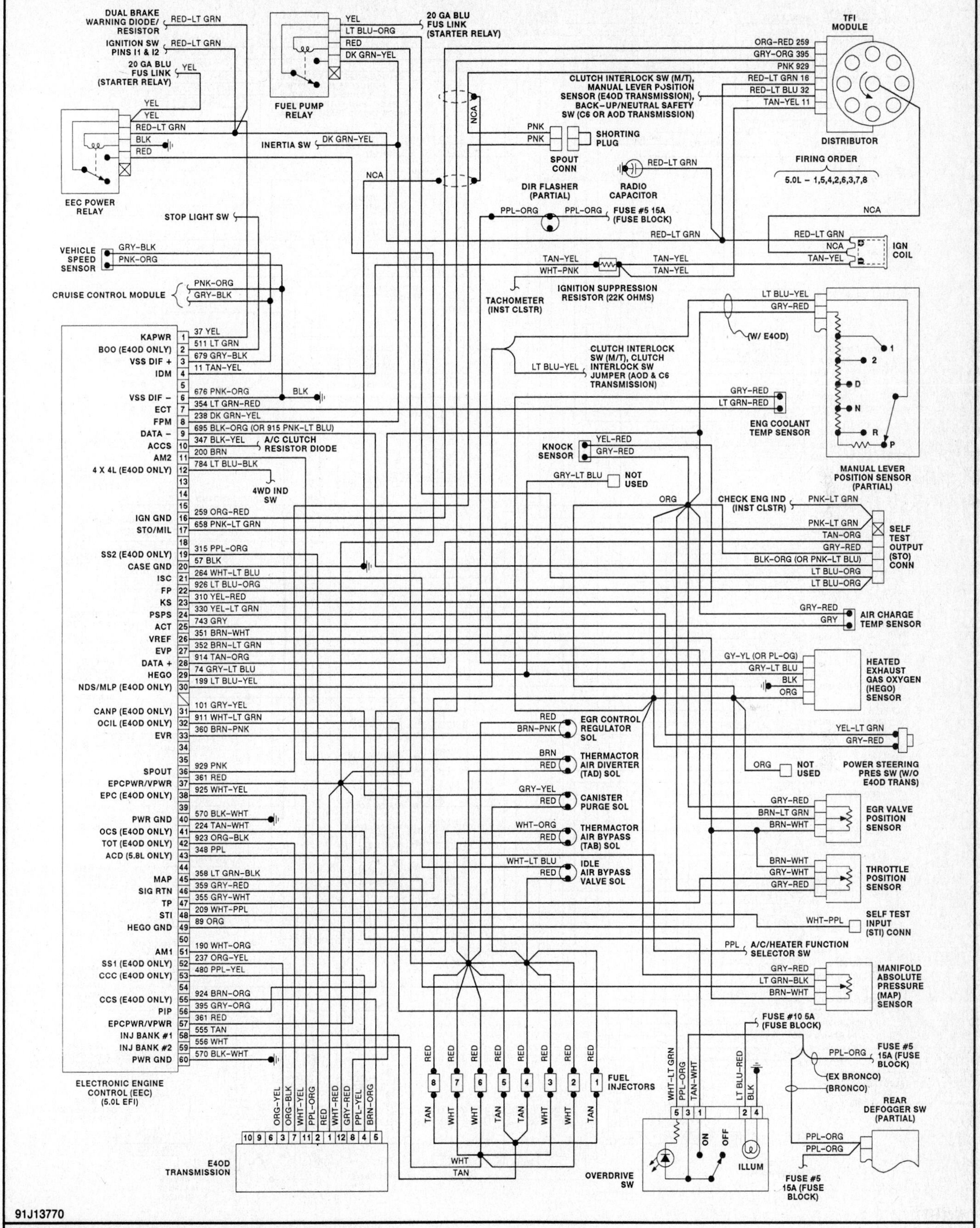

DUAL BRAKE WARNING DIODE/ RESISTOR
RED-LT GRN
IGNITION SW PINS I1 & I2
20 GA BLU FUS LINK (STARTER RELAY)
YEL
BLK
RED
EEC POWER RELAY
LT BLU-ORG
DK GRN-YEL
20 GA BLU FUS LINK (STARTER RELAY)
FUEL PUMP RELAY
INERTIA SW
NCA
STOP LIGHT SW
VEHICLE SPEED SENSOR
GRY-BLK
PNK-ORG
CRUISE CONTROL MODULE
TFI MODULE
ORG-RED 259
GRY-ORG 395
PNK 929
RED-LT GRN 16
RED-LT BLU 32
TAN-YEL 11
DISTRIBUTOR
CLUTCH INTERLOCK SW (M/T), MANUAL LEVER POSITION SENSOR (E4OD TRANSMISSION), BACK-UP/NEUTRAL SAFETY SW (C6 OR AOD TRANSMISSION)
PNK
SHORTING PLUG
SPOUT CONN
RADIO CAPACITOR
FIRING ORDER
5.0L - 1,5,4,2,6,3,7,8
DIR FLASHER (PARTIAL)
PPL-ORG
FUSE #5 15A (FUSE BLOCK)
IGN COIL
TAN-YEL
WHT-PNK
TACHOMETER (INST CLSTR)
IGNITION SUPPRESSION RESISTOR (22K OHMS)
LT BLU-YEL
GRY-RED
(W/ E4OD)
CLUTCH INTERLOCK SW (M/T), CLUTCH INTERLOCK SW JUMPER (AOD & C6 TRANSMISSION)
1
2
D
N
R
P
LT GRN-RED
ENG COOLANT TEMP SENSOR
KNOCK SENSOR
YEL-RED
MANUAL LEVER POSITION SENSOR (PARTIAL)
GRY-LT BLU
NOT USED
ORG
CHECK ENG IND (INST CLSTR)
PNK-LT GRN
TAN-ORG
BLK-ORG (OR PNK-LT BLU)
LT BLU-ORG
SELF TEST OUTPUT (STO) CONN
GRY
AIR CHARGE TEMP SENSOR
GY-YL (OR PL-OG)
HEATED EXHAUST GAS OXYGEN (HEGO) SENSOR
KAPWR 1 37 YEL
BOO (E4OD ONLY) 2 511 LT GRN
VSS DIF + 3 679 GRY-BLK
IDM 4 11 TAN-YEL
5
VSS DIF - 6 676 PNK-ORG
ECT 7 354 LT GRN-RED
FPM 8 238 DK GRN-YEL
DATA - 9 695 BLK-ORG (OR 915 PNK-LT BLU)
ACCS 10 347 BLK-YEL
A/C CLUTCH RESISTOR DIODE
AM2 11 200 BRN
4 X 4L (E4OD ONLY) 12 784 LT BLU-BLK
13
4WD IND SW
14
15
IGN GND 16 259 ORG-RED
STO/MIL 17 658 PNK-LT GRN
18
SS2 (E4OD ONLY) 19 315 PPL-ORG
CASE GND 20 57 BLK
ISC 21 264 WHT-LT BLU
FP 22 926 LT BLU-ORG
KS 23 310 YEL-RED
PSPS 24 330 YEL-LT GRN
ACT 25 743 GRY
VREF 26 351 BRN-WHT
EVP 27 352 BRN-LT GRN
DATA + 28 914 TAN-ORG
HEGO 29 74 GRY-LT BLU
NDS/MLP (E4OD ONLY) 30 199 LT BLU-YEL
CANP (E4OD ONLY) 31 101 GRY-YEL
OCIL (E4OD ONLY) 32 911 WHT-LT GRN
EVR 33 360 BRN-PNK
34
35
SPOUT 36 929 PNK
EPCPWR/VPWR 37 361 RED
EPC (E4OD ONLY) 38 925 WHT-YEL
39
PWR GND 40 570 BLK-WHT
OCS (E4OD ONLY) 41 224 TAN-WHT
TOT (E4OD ONLY) 42 923 ORG-BLK
ACD (5.8L ONLY) 43 348 PPL
44
MAP 45 358 LT GRN-BLK
SIG RTN 46 359 GRY-RED
TP 47 355 GRY-WHT
STI 48 209 WHT-PPL
HEGO GND 49 89 ORG
50
AM1 51 190 WHT-ORG
SS1 (E4OD ONLY) 52 237 ORG-YEL
CCC (E4OD ONLY) 53 480 PPL-YEL
54
CCS (E4OD ONLY) 55 924 BRN-ORG
PIP 56 395 GRY-ORG
EPCPWR/VPWR 57 361 RED
INJ BANK #1 58 555 TAN
INJ BANK #2 59 556 WHT
PWR GND 60 570 BLK-WHT
ELECTRONIC ENGINE CONTROL (EEC) (5.0L EFI)
EGR CONTROL REGULATOR SOL
BRN-PNK
THERMACTOR AIR DIVERTER (TAD) SOL
BRN
GRY-YEL
CANISTER PURGE SOL
WHT-ORG
THERMACTOR AIR BYPASS (TAB) SOL
WHT-LT BLU
IDLE AIR BYPASS VALVE SOL
YEL-LT GRN
POWER STEERING PRES SW (W/O E4OD TRANS)
EGR VALVE POSITION SENSOR
BRN-LT GRN
BRN-WHT
THROTTLE POSITION SENSOR
GRY-WHT
WHT-PPL
SELF TEST INPUT (STI) CONN
PPL
A/C/HEATER FUNCTION SELECTOR SW
LT GRN-BLK
MANIFOLD ABSOLUTE PRESSURE (MAP) SENSOR
FUSE #10 5A (FUSE BLOCK)
PPL-ORG
FUSE #5 15A (FUSE BLOCK)
(EX BRONCO)
(BRONCO)
REAR DEFOGGER SW (PARTIAL)
FUEL INJECTORS
8 7 6 5 4 3 2 1
WHT
TAN
ORG-YEL
ORG-BLK
WHT-YEL
PPL-ORG
WHT-RED
GRY-YEL
PPL-YEL
BRN-ORG
10 9 6 3 7 11 2 1 12 8 4 5
E4OD TRANSMISSION
WHT-LT GRN
TAN-WHT
LT BLU-RED
5 3 1 2 4
ON
OFF
ILLUM
OVERDRIVE SW
91J13770

Fig. 4: Wiring Diagram (Bronco 5.0L & "F" Series 5.0L)

1991 ENGINE PERFORMANCE
Wiring Diagrams (Cont.)

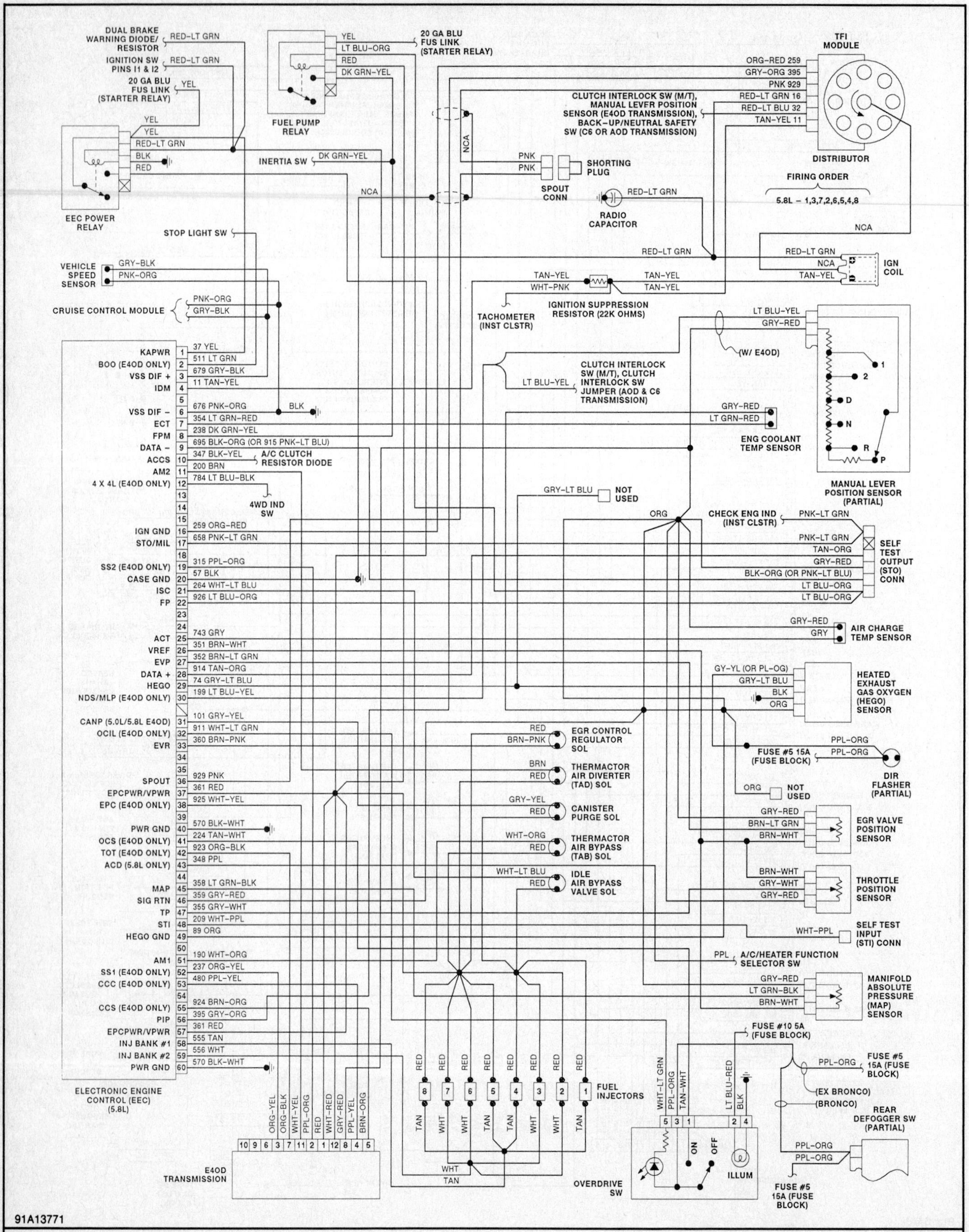
DUAL BRAKE WARNING DIODE/ RESISTOR
IGNITION SW PINS I1 & I2
20 GA BLU FUS LINK (STARTER RELAY)
EEC POWER RELAY
FUEL PUMP RELAY
20 GA BLU FUS LINK (STARTER RELAY)
INERTIA SW
STOP LIGHT SW
VEHICLE SPEED SENSOR
CRUISE CONTROL MODULE
TFI MODULE
DISTRIBUTOR
FIRING ORDER
5.8L – 1,3,7,2,6,5,4,8
CLUTCH INTERLOCK SW (M/T), MANUAL LEVER POSITION SENSOR (E4OD TRANSMISSION), BACK-UP/NEUTRAL SAFETY SW (C6 OR AOD TRANSMISSION)
SHORTING PLUG
SPOUT CONN
RADIO CAPACITOR
IGN COIL
TACHOMETER (INST CLSTR)
IGNITION SUPPRESSION RESISTOR (22K OHMS)
CLUTCH INTERLOCK SW (M/T), CLUTCH INTERLOCK SW JUMPER (AOD & C6 TRANSMISSION)
(W/ E4OD)
ENG COOLANT TEMP SENSOR
MANUAL LEVER POSITION SENSOR (PARTIAL)
A/C CLUTCH RESISTOR DIODE
4WD IND SW
NOT USED
CHECK ENG IND (INST CLSTR)
SELF TEST OUTPUT (STO) CONN
AIR CHARGE TEMP SENSOR
HEATED EXHAUST GAS OXYGEN (HEGO) SENSOR
EGR CONTROL REGULATOR SOL
THERMACTOR AIR DIVERTER (TAD) SOL
CANISTER PURGE SOL
THERMACTOR AIR BYPASS (TAB) SOL
IDLE AIR BYPASS VALVE SOL
FUSE #5 15A (FUSE BLOCK)
DIR FLASHER (PARTIAL)
EGR VALVE POSITION SENSOR
THROTTLE POSITION SENSOR
SELF TEST INPUT (STI) CONN
A/C/HEATER FUNCTION SELECTOR SW
MANIFOLD ABSOLUTE PRESSURE (MAP) SENSOR
FUSE #10 5A (FUSE BLOCK)
FUEL INJECTORS
FUSE #5 15A (FUSE BLOCK)
(EX BRONCO)
(BRONCO)
REAR DEFOGGER SW (PARTIAL)
OVERDRIVE SW
ILLUM
ON
OFF
E4OD TRANSMISSION
ELECTRONIC ENGINE CONTROL (EEC) (5.8L)
KAPWR 1 37 YEL
BOO (E4OD ONLY) 2 511 LT GRN
VSS DIF + 3 679 GRY-BLK
IDM 4 11 TAN-YEL
5
VSS DIF – 6 676 PNK-ORG
ECT 7 354 LT GRN-RED
FPM 8 238 DK GRN-YEL
DATA – 9 695 BLK-ORG (OR 915 PNK-LT BLU)
ACCS 10 347 BLK-YEL
AM2 11 200 BRN
4 X 4L (E4OD ONLY) 12 784 LT BLU-BLK
13
14
15
IGN GND 16 259 ORG-RED
STO/MIL 17 658 PNK-LT GRN
18
SS2 (E4OD ONLY) 19 315 PPL-ORG
CASE GND 20 57 BLK
ISC 21 264 WHT-LT BLU
FP 22 926 LT BLU-ORG
23
24
ACT 25 743 GRY
VREF 26 351 BRN-WHT
EVP 27 352 BRN-LT GRN
DATA + 28 914 TAN-ORG
HEGO 29 74 GRY-LT BLU
NDS/MLP (E4OD ONLY) 30 199 LT BLU-YEL
CANP (5.0L/5.8L E4OD) 31 101 GRY-YEL
OCIL (E4OD ONLY) 32 911 WHT-LT GRN
EVR 33 360 BRN-PNK
34
35
SPOUT 36 929 PNK
EPCPWR/VPWR 37 361 RED
EPC (E4OD ONLY) 38 925 WHT-YEL
39
PWR GND 40 570 BLK-WHT
OCS (E4OD ONLY) 41 224 TAN-WHT
TOT (E4OD ONLY) 42 923 ORG-BLK
ACD (5.8L ONLY) 43 348 PPL
44
MAP 45 358 LT GRN-BLK
SIG RTN 46 359 GRY-RED
TP 47 355 GRY-WHT
STI 48 209 WHT-PPL
HEGO GND 49 89 ORG
50
AM1 51 190 WHT-ORG
SS1 (E4OD ONLY) 52 237 ORG-YEL
CCC (E4OD ONLY) 53 480 PPL-YEL
54
CCS (E4OD ONLY) 55 924 BRN-ORG
PIP 56 395 GRY-ORG
EPCPWR/VPWR 57 361 RED
INJ BANK #1 58 555 TAN
INJ BANK #2 59 556 WHT
PWR GND 60 570 BLK-WHT
ORG-RED 259
GRY-ORG 395
PNK 929
RED-LT GRN 16
RED-LT BLU 32
TAN-YEL 11
91A13771

Fig. 5: Wiring Diagram (Bronco 5.8L & "F" Series 5.8L)

1991 ENGINE PERFORMANCE
Wiring Diagrams (Cont.)

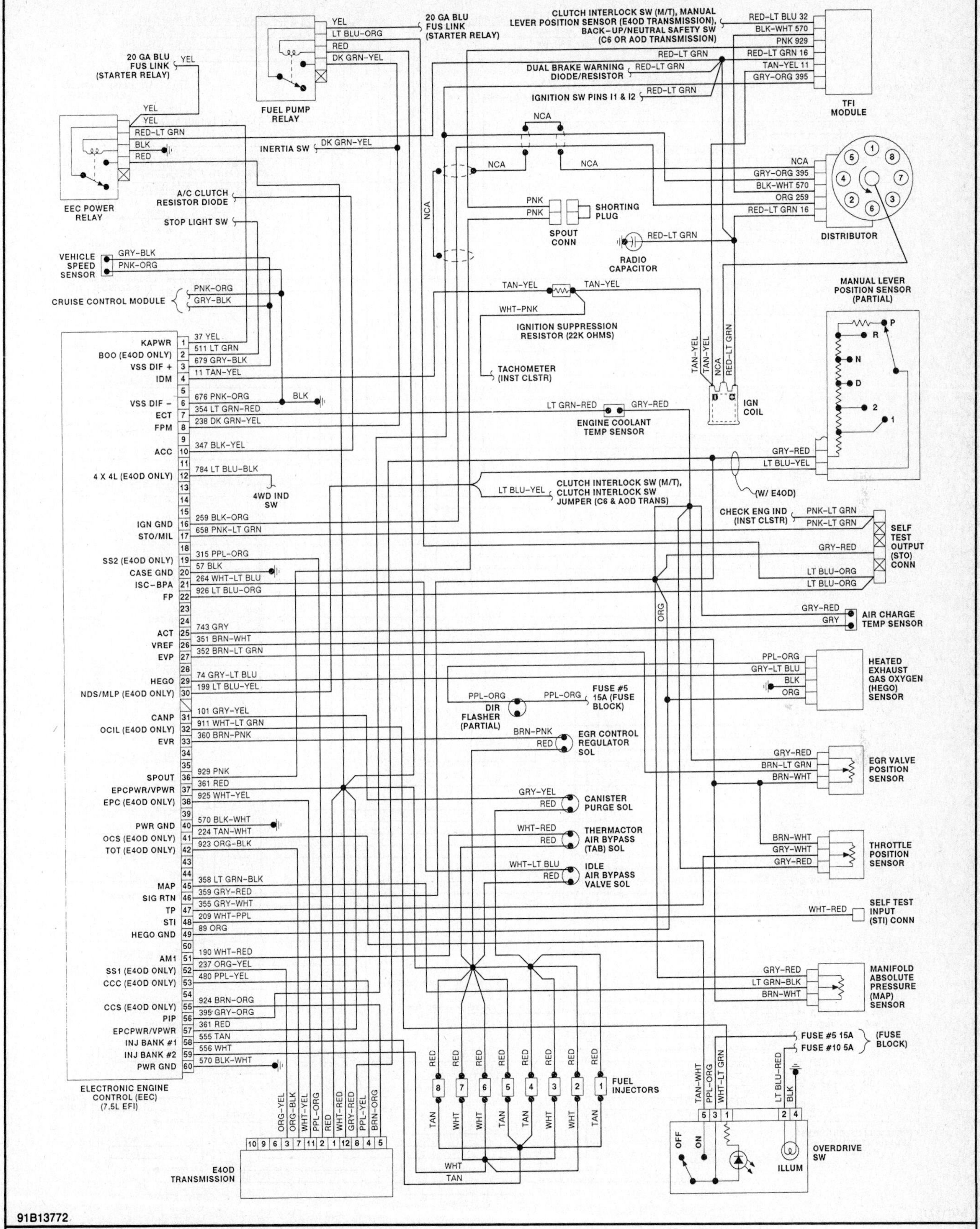
20 GA BLU FUS LINK (STARTER RELAY)
YEL
LT BLU-ORG
RED
DK GRN-YEL
FUEL PUMP RELAY
20 GA BLU FUS LINK (STARTER RELAY)
CLUTCH INTERLOCK SW (M/T), MANUAL LEVER POSITION SENSOR (E4OD TRANSMISSION), BACK-UP/NEUTRAL SAFETY SW (C6 OR AOD TRANSMISSION)
RED-LT BLU 32
BLK-WHT 570
PNK 929
RED-LT GRN 16
TAN-YEL 11
GRY-ORG 395
TFI MODULE
DUAL BRAKE WARNING DIODE/RESISTOR
IGNITION SW PINS I1 & I2
RED-LT GRN
EEC POWER RELAY
BLK
INERTIA SW
NCA
A/C CLUTCH RESISTOR DIODE
STOP LIGHT SW
PNK
SHORTING PLUG
SPOUT CONN
GRY-ORG 395
BLK-WHT 570
ORG 259
RED-LT GRN 16
DISTRIBUTOR
RADIO CAPACITOR
VEHICLE SPEED SENSOR
GRY-BLK
PNK-ORG
CRUISE CONTROL MODULE
TAN-YEL
WHT-PNK
IGNITION SUPPRESSION RESISTOR (22K OHMS)
MANUAL LEVER POSITION SENSOR (PARTIAL)
P
R
N
D
2
1
TACHOMETER (INST CLSTR)
IGN COIL
KAPWR
BOO (E4OD ONLY)
VSS DIF +
IDM
VSS DIF -
ECT
FPM
ACC
4 X 4L (E4OD ONLY)
IGN GND
STO/MIL
SS2 (E4OD ONLY)
CASE GND
ISC-BPA
FP
ACT
VREF
EVP
HEGO
NDS/MLP (E4OD ONLY)
CANP
OCIL (E4OD ONLY)
EVR
SPOUT
EPCPWR/VPWR
EPC (E4OD ONLY)
PWR GND
OCS (E4OD ONLY)
TOT (E4OD ONLY)
MAP
SIG RTN
TP
STI
HEGO GND
AM1
SS1 (E4OD ONLY)
CCC (E4OD ONLY)
CCS (E4OD ONLY)
PIP
EPCPWR/VPWR
INJ BANK #1
INJ BANK #2
PWR GND
37 YEL
511 LT GRN
679 GRY-BLK
11 TAN-YEL
676 PNK-ORG
354 LT GRN-RED
238 DK GRN-YEL
347 BLK-YEL
784 LT BLU-BLK
259 BLK-ORG
658 PNK-LT GRN
315 PPL-ORG
57 BLK
264 WHT-LT BLU
926 LT BLU-ORG
743 GRY
351 BRN-WHT
352 BRN-LT GRN
74 GRY-LT BLU
199 LT BLU-YEL
101 GRY-YEL
911 WHT-LT GRN
360 BRN-PNK
929 PNK
361 RED
925 WHT-YEL
570 BLK-WHT
224 TAN-WHT
923 ORG-BLK
358 LT GRN-BLK
359 GRY-RED
355 GRY-WHT
209 WHT-PPL
89 ORG
190 WHT-RED
237 ORG-YEL
480 PPL-YEL
924 BRN-ORG
395 GRY-ORG
361 RED
555 TAN
556 WHT
570 BLK-WHT
LT GRN-RED
GRY-RED
ENGINE COOLANT TEMP SENSOR
4WD IND SW
LT BLU-YEL
CLUTCH INTERLOCK SW (M/T), CLUTCH INTERLOCK SW JUMPER (C6 & AOD TRANS)
(W/ E4OD)
CHECK ENG IND (INST CLSTR)
PNK-LT GRN
SELF TEST OUTPUT (STO) CONN
LT BLU-ORG
ORG
AIR CHARGE TEMP SENSOR
PPL-ORG
GRY-LT BLU
HEATED EXHAUST GAS OXYGEN (HEGO) SENSOR
DIR FLASHER (PARTIAL)
FUSE #5 15A (FUSE BLOCK)
BRN-PNK
EGR CONTROL REGULATOR SOL
BRN-LT GRN
BRN-WHT
EGR VALVE POSITION SENSOR
GRY-YEL
CANISTER PURGE SOL
WHT-RED
THERMACTOR AIR BYPASS (TAB) SOL
WHT-LT BLU
IDLE AIR BYPASS VALVE SOL
GRY-WHT
THROTTLE POSITION SENSOR
SELF TEST INPUT (STI) CONN
LT GRN-BLK
MANIFOLD ABSOLUTE PRESSURE (MAP) SENSOR
FUSE #5 15A
FUSE #10 5A
(FUSE BLOCK)
ELECTRONIC ENGINE CONTROL (EEC) (7.5L EFI)
ORG-YEL
ORG-BLK
WHT-YEL
PPL-ORG
WHT-RED
GRY-RED
PPL-YEL
BRN-ORG
E4OD TRANSMISSION
FUEL INJECTORS
TAN
WHT
TAN-WHT
PPL-ORG
WHT-LT GRN
LT BLU-RED
OFF
ON
ILLUM
OVERDRIVE SW
91B13772

Fig. 6: Wiring Diagram (Bronco 7.5L & "F" Series 7.5L)

1991 ENGINE PERFORMANCE
Wiring Diagrams (Cont.)

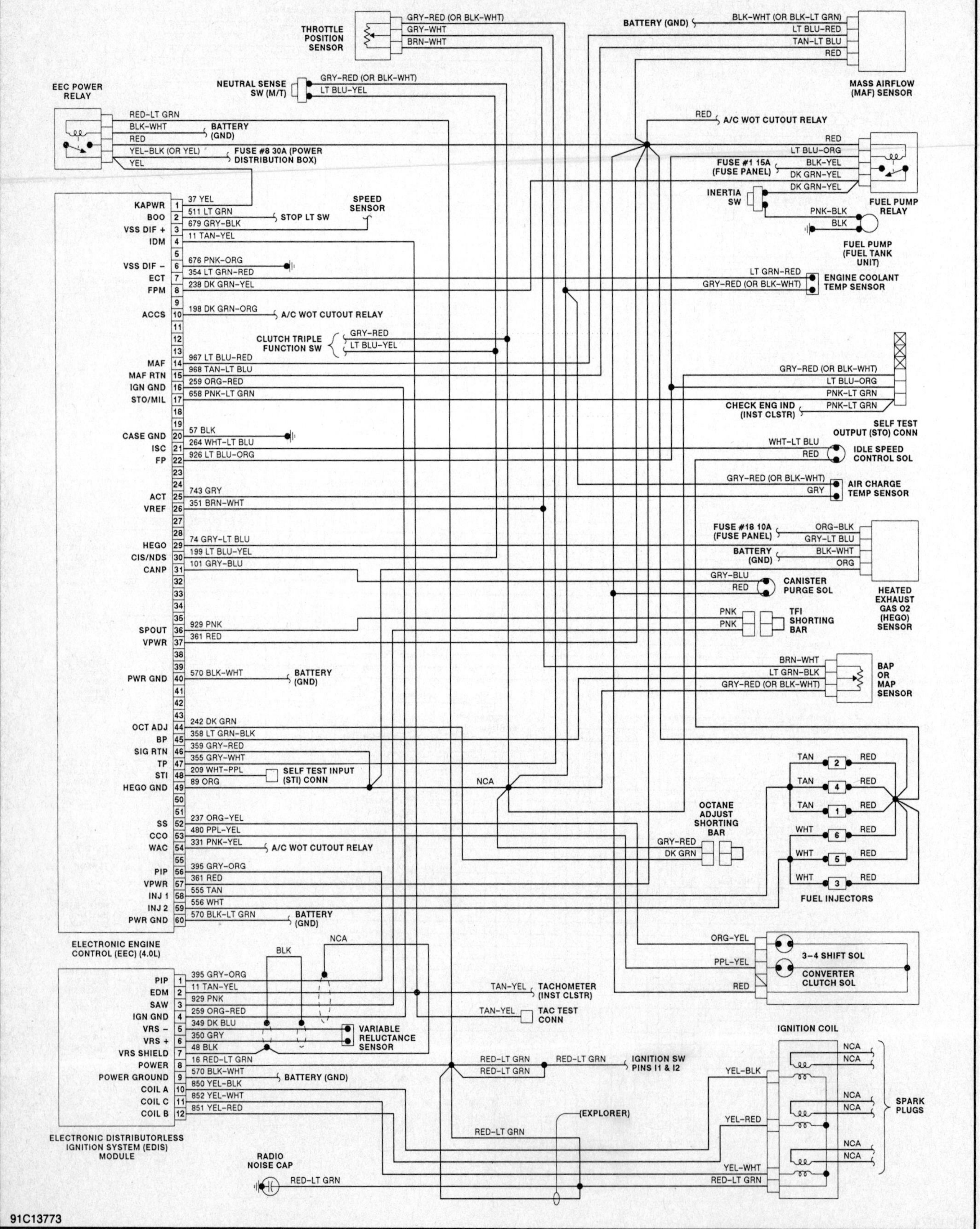
THROTTLE POSITION SENSOR
GRY-RED (OR BLK-WHT)
GRY-WHT
BRN-WHT
BATTERY (GND)
BLK-WHT (OR BLK-LT GRN)
LT BLU-RED
TAN-LT BLU
RED
MASS AIRFLOW (MAF) SENSOR
EEC POWER RELAY
NEUTRAL SENSE SW (M/T)
LT BLU-YEL
RED-LT GRN
BLK-WHT
BATTERY (GND)
RED
YEL-BLK (OR YEL)
FUSE #8 30A (POWER DISTRIBUTION BOX)
YEL
A/C WOT CUTOUT RELAY
LT BLU-ORG
FUSE #1 15A (FUSE PANEL)
BLK-YEL
DK GRN-YEL
INERTIA SW
PNK-BLK
BLK
FUEL PUMP RELAY
FUEL PUMP (FUEL TANK UNIT)
KAPWR 1 37 YEL
BOO 2 511 LT GRN
STOP LT SW
SPEED SENSOR
VSS DIF + 3 679 GRY-BLK
IDM 4 11 TAN-YEL
VSS DIF – 6 676 PNK-ORG
ECT 7 354 LT GRN-RED
FPM 8 238 DK GRN-YEL
LT GRN-RED
ENGINE COOLANT TEMP SENSOR
ACCS 10 198 DK GRN-ORG
CLUTCH TRIPLE FUNCTION SW
GRY-RED
LT BLU-YEL
MAF 14 967 LT BLU-RED
MAF RTN 15 968 TAN-LT BLU
IGN GND 16 259 ORG-RED
STO/MIL 17 658 PNK-LT GRN
PNK-LT GRN
CHECK ENG IND (INST CLSTR)
SELF TEST OUTPUT (STO) CONN
CASE GND 20 57 BLK
ISC 21 264 WHT-LT BLU
FP 22 926 LT BLU-ORG
WHT-LT BLU
IDLE SPEED CONTROL SOL
AIR CHARGE TEMP SENSOR
GRY
ACT 25 743 GRY
VREF 26 351 BRN-WHT
FUSE #18 10A (FUSE PANEL)
ORG-BLK
GRY-LT BLU
ORG
HEGO 29 74 GRY-LT BLU
CIS/NDS 30 199 LT BLU-YEL
CANP 31 101 GRY-BLU
GRY-BLU
CANISTER PURGE SOL
HEATED EXHAUST GAS O2 (HEGO) SENSOR
PNK
TFI SHORTING BAR
SPOUT 36 929 PNK
VPWR 37 361 RED
BRN-WHT
LT GRN-BLK
BAP OR MAP SENSOR
PWR GND 40 570 BLK-WHT
OCT ADJ 44 242 DK GRN
BP 45 358 LT GRN-BLK
SIG RTN 46 359 GRY-RED
TP 47 355 GRY-WHT
STI 48 209 WHT-PPL
SELF TEST INPUT (STI) CONN
HEGO GND 49 89 ORG
NCA
TAN
WHT
OCTANE ADJUST SHORTING BAR
SS 52 237 ORG-YEL
CCO 53 480 PPL-YEL
WAC 54 331 PNK-YEL
DK GRN
PIP 56 395 GRY-ORG
VPWR 57 361 RED
INJ 1 58 555 TAN
INJ 2 59 556 WHT
PWR GND 60 570 BLK-LT GRN
FUEL INJECTORS
ELECTRONIC ENGINE CONTROL (EEC) (4.0L)
ORG-YEL
3-4 SHIFT SOL
PPL-YEL
CONVERTER CLUTCH SOL
PIP 1 395 GRY-ORG
EDM 2 11 TAN-YEL
SAW 3 929 PNK
IGN GND 4 259 ORG-RED
VRS – 5 349 DK BLU
VRS + 6 350 GRY
VRS SHIELD 7 48 BLK
POWER 8 16 RED-LT GRN
POWER GROUND 9 570 BLK-WHT
COIL A 10 850 YEL-BLK
COIL C 11 852 YEL-WHT
COIL B 12 851 YEL-RED
TACHOMETER (INST CLSTR)
TAC TEST CONN
VARIABLE RELUCTANCE SENSOR
RED-LT GRN
IGNITION SW PINS I1 & I2
IGNITION COIL
SPARK PLUGS
(EXPLORER)
ELECTRONIC DISTRIBUTORLESS IGNITION SYSTEM (EDIS) MODULE
RADIO NOISE CAP
91C13773

Fig. 7: Wiring Diagram (Explorer & Ranger 4.0L)

1991 ENGINE PERFORMANCE
Wiring Diagrams (Cont.)

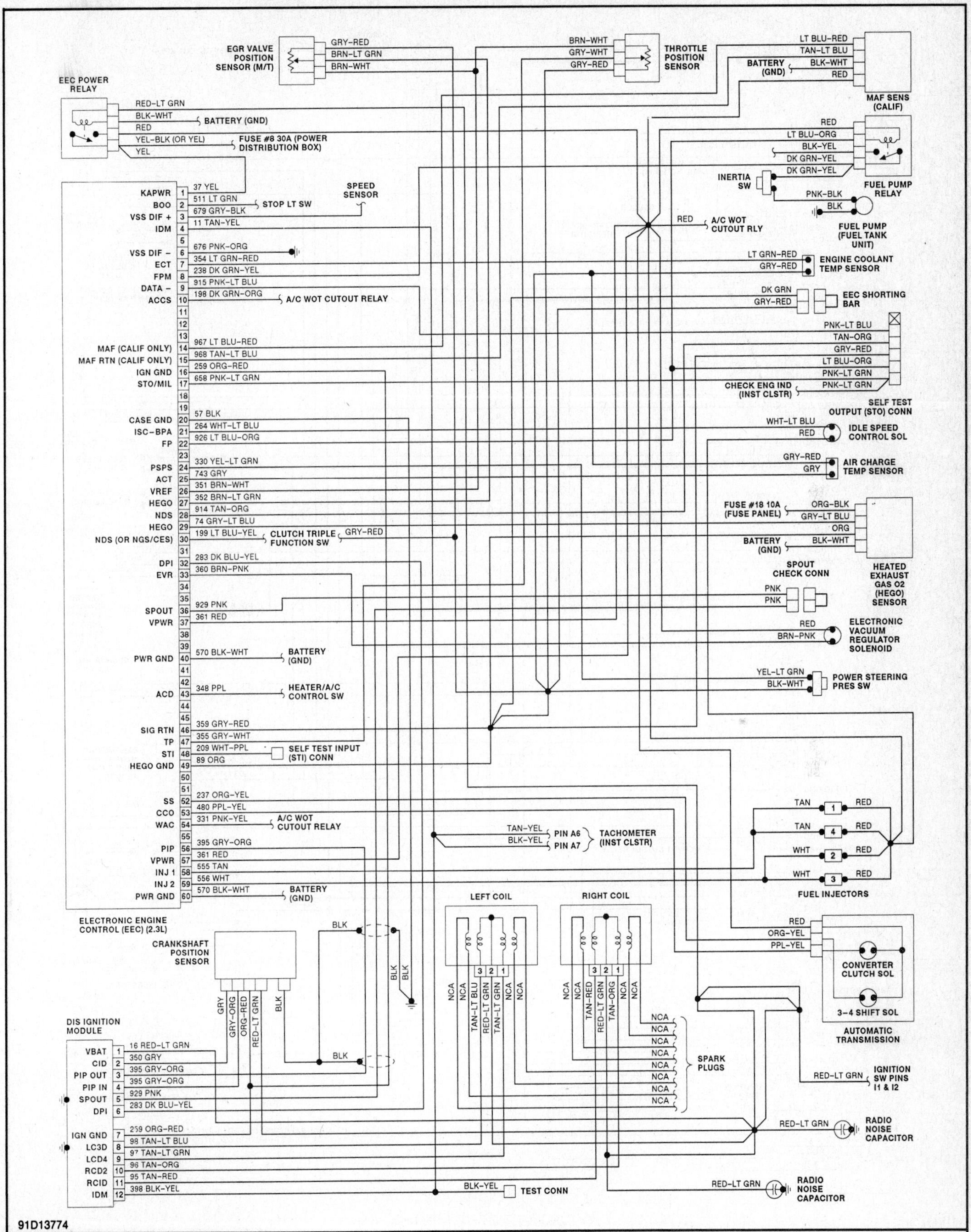
EEC POWER RELAY
RED-LT GRN
BLK-WHT
BATTERY (GND)
RED
YEL-BLK (OR YEL)
FUSE #8 30A (POWER DISTRIBUTION BOX)
YEL
EGR VALVE POSITION SENSOR (M/T)
GRY-RED
BRN-LT GRN
BRN-WHT
THROTTLE POSITION SENSOR
BRN-WHT
GRY-WHT
GRY-RED
LT BLU-RED
TAN-LT BLU
BATTERY (GND)
BLK-WHT
RED
MAF SENS (CALIF)
RED
LT BLU-ORG
BLK-YEL
DK GRN-YEL
DK GRN-YEL
FUEL PUMP RELAY
INERTIA SW
PNK-BLK
BLK
FUEL PUMP (FUEL TANK UNIT)
SPEED SENSOR
STOP LT SW
RED
A/C WOT CUTOUT RLY
LT GRN-RED
GRY-RED
ENGINE COOLANT TEMP SENSOR
DK GRN
GRY-RED
EEC SHORTING BAR
PNK-LT BLU
TAN-ORG
GRY-RED
LT BLU-ORG
PNK-LT GRN
PNK-LT GRN
CHECK ENG IND (INST CLSTR)
SELF TEST OUTPUT (STO) CONN
WHT-LT BLU
RED
IDLE SPEED CONTROL SOL
GRY-RED
GRY
AIR CHARGE TEMP SENSOR
FUSE #18 10A (FUSE PANEL)
ORG-BLK
GRY-LT BLU
ORG
BATTERY (GND)
BLK-WHT
HEATED EXHAUST GAS O2 (HEGO) SENSOR
SPOUT CHECK CONN
PNK
PNK
RED
BRN-PNK
ELECTRONIC VACUUM REGULATOR SOLENOID
YEL-LT GRN
BLK-WHT
POWER STEERING PRES SW
KAPWR 1 37 YEL
BOO 2 511 LT GRN
VSS DIF + 3 679 GRY-BLK
IDM 4 11 TAN-YEL
5
VSS DIF – 6 676 PNK-ORG
ECT 7 354 LT GRN-RED
FPM 8 238 DK GRN-YEL
DATA – 9 915 PNK-LT BLU
ACCS 10 198 DK GRN-ORG
A/C WOT CUTOUT RELAY
11
12
13 967 LT BLU-RED
MAF (CALIF ONLY) 14 968 TAN-LT BLU
MAF RTN (CALIF ONLY) 15 259 ORG-RED
IGN GND 16 658 PNK-LT GRN
STO/MIL 17
18
19
CASE GND 20 57 BLK
ISC-BPA 21 264 WHT-LT BLU
FP 22 926 LT BLU-ORG
23
PSPS 24 330 YEL-LT GRN
ACT 25 743 GRY
VREF 26 351 BRN-WHT
HEGO 27 352 BRN-LT GRN
NDS 28 914 TAN-ORG
HEGO 29 74 GRY-LT BLU
NDS (OR NGS/CES) 30 199 LT BLU-YEL
CLUTCH TRIPLE FUNCTION SW
GRY-RED
31
DPI 32 283 DK BLU-YEL
EVR 33 360 BRN-PNK
34
35
SPOUT 36 929 PNK
VPWR 37 361 RED
38
39
PWR GND 40 570 BLK-WHT
BATTERY (GND)
41
42
ACD 43 348 PPL
HEATER/A/C CONTROL SW
44
45
SIG RTN 46 359 GRY-RED
TP 47 355 GRY-WHT
STI 48 209 WHT-PPL
SELF TEST INPUT (STI) CONN
HEGO GND 49 89 ORG
50
51
SS 52 237 ORG-YEL
CCO 53 480 PPL-YEL
WAC 54 331 PNK-YEL
A/C WOT CUTOUT RELAY
55
PIP 56 395 GRY-ORG
VPWR 57 361 RED
INJ 1 58 555 TAN
INJ 2 59 556 WHT
PWR GND 60 570 BLK-WHT
BATTERY (GND)
ELECTRONIC ENGINE CONTROL (EEC) (2.3L)
TAN-YEL
BLK-YEL
PIN A6
PIN A7
TACHOMETER (INST CLSTR)
TAN
RED
TAN
RED
WHT
RED
WHT
RED
FUEL INJECTORS
CRANKSHAFT POSITION SENSOR
BLK
BLK
BLK
GRY
GRY-ORG
ORG-RED
RED-LT GRN
BLK
BLK
LEFT COIL
RIGHT COIL
3 2 1
3 2 1
NCA
NCA
TAN-LT BLU
RED-LT GRN
TAN-LT GRN
NCA
NCA
NCA
NCA
TAN-RED
RED-LT GRN
TAN-ORG
NCA
NCA
NCA
NCA
NCA
NCA
NCA
NCA
NCA
NCA
SPARK PLUGS
RED
ORG-YEL
PPL-YEL
CONVERTER CLUTCH SOL
3-4 SHIFT SOL
AUTOMATIC TRANSMISSION
RED-LT GRN
IGNITION SW PINS I1 & I2
DIS IGNITION MODULE
VBAT 1 16 RED-LT GRN
CID 2 350 GRY
PIP OUT 3 395 GRY-ORG
PIP IN 4 395 GRY-ORG
SPOUT 5 929 PNK
DPI 6 283 DK BLU-YEL
IGN GND 7 259 ORG-RED
LC3D 8 98 TAN-LT BLU
LCD4 9 97 TAN-LT GRN
RCD2 10 96 TAN-ORG
RCID 11 95 TAN-RED
IDM 12 398 BLK-YEL
RED-LT GRN
RADIO NOISE CAPACITOR
BLK-YEL
TEST CONN
RED-LT GRN
RADIO NOISE CAPACITOR
91D13774

Fig. 8: Wiring Diagram (Ranger 2.3L)

1991 ENGINE PERFORMANCE
Wiring Diagrams (Cont.)

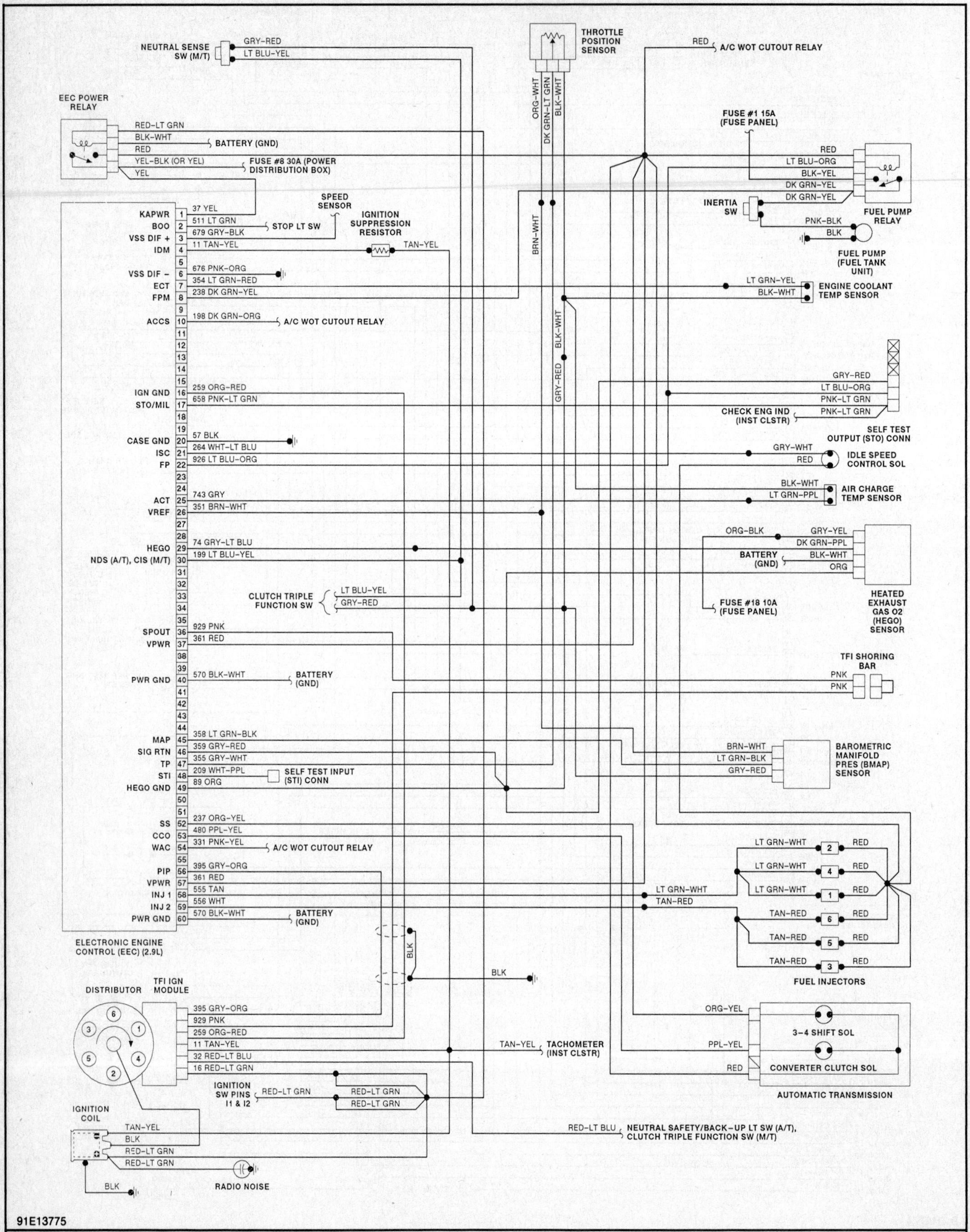
NEUTRAL SENSE SW (M/T)
GRY-RED
LT BLU-YEL
THROTTLE POSITION SENSOR
ORG-WHT
DK GRN-LT GRN
BLK-WHT
RED
A/C WOT CUTOUT RELAY
EEC POWER RELAY
RED-LT GRN
BLK-WHT
BATTERY (GND)
RED
YEL-BLK (OR YEL)
FUSE #8 30A (POWER DISTRIBUTION BOX)
YEL
FUSE #1 15A (FUSE PANEL)
LT BLU-ORG
BLK-YEL
DK GRN-YEL
DK GRN-YEL
INERTIA SW
FUEL PUMP RELAY
PNK-BLK
BLK
FUEL PUMP (FUEL TANK UNIT)
KAPWR 1 37 YEL
BOO 2 511 LT GRN
VSS DIF + 3 679 GRY-BLK
IDM 4 11 TAN-YEL
5
VSS DIF - 6 676 PNK-ORG
ECT 7 354 LT GRN-RED
FPM 8 238 DK GRN-YEL
9
ACCS 10 198 DK GRN-ORG
11
12
13
14
15
IGN GND 16 259 ORG-RED
STO/MIL 17 658 PNK-LT GRN
18
19
CASE GND 20 57 BLK
ISC 21 264 WHT-LT BLU
FP 22 926 LT BLU-ORG
23
24
ACT 25 743 GRY
VREF 26 351 BRN-WHT
27
28
HEGO 29 74 GRY-LT BLU
NDS (A/T), CIS (M/T) 30 199 LT BLU-YEL
31
32
33
34
35
SPOUT 36 929 PNK
VPWR 37 361 RED
38
39
PWR GND 40 570 BLK-WHT
41
42
43
44
MAP 45 358 LT GRN-BLK
SIG RTN 46 359 GRY-RED
TP 47 355 GRY-WHT
STI 48 209 WHT-PPL
HEGO GND 49 89 ORG
50
51
SS 52 237 ORG-YEL
CCO 53 480 PPL-YEL
WAC 54 331 PNK-YEL
55
PIP 56 395 GRY-ORG
VPWR 57 361 RED
INJ 1 58 555 TAN
INJ 2 59 556 WHT
PWR GND 60 570 BLK-WHT
SPEED SENSOR
STOP LT SW
IGNITION SUPPRESSION RESISTOR
TAN-YEL
A/C WOT CUTOUT RELAY
BRN-WHT
BLK-WHT
GRY-RED
LT GRN-YEL
BLK-WHT
ENGINE COOLANT TEMP SENSOR
GRY-RED
LT BLU-ORG
PNK-LT GRN
PNK-LT GRN
CHECK ENG IND (INST CLSTR)
SELF TEST OUTPUT (STO) CONN
GRY-WHT
RED
IDLE SPEED CONTROL SOL
BLK-WHT
LT GRN-PPL
AIR CHARGE TEMP SENSOR
ORG-BLK
GRY-YEL
DK GRN-PPL
BATTERY (GND)
BLK-WHT
ORG
HEATED EXHAUST GAS O2 (HEGO) SENSOR
FUSE #18 10A (FUSE PANEL)
CLUTCH TRIPLE FUNCTION SW
LT BLU-YEL
GRY-RED
TFI SHORING BAR
PNK
PNK
BATTERY (GND)
BRN-WHT
LT GRN-BLK
GRY-RED
BAROMETRIC MANIFOLD PRES (BMAP) SENSOR
SELF TEST INPUT (STI) CONN
A/C WOT CUTOUT RELAY
BATTERY (GND)
LT GRN-WHT
TAN-RED
LT GRN-WHT
LT GRN-WHT
LT GRN-WHT
TAN-RED
TAN-RED
TAN-RED
RED
2
4
1
6
5
3
FUEL INJECTORS
ELECTRONIC ENGINE CONTROL (EEC) (2.9L)
BLK
BLK
DISTRIBUTOR
TFI IGN MODULE
6
3
1
5
4
2
395 GRY-ORG
929 PNK
259 ORG-RED
11 TAN-YEL
32 RED-LT BLU
16 RED-LT GRN
TAN-YEL
TACHOMETER (INST CLSTR)
ORG-YEL
PPL-YEL
RED
3-4 SHIFT SOL
CONVERTER CLUTCH SOL
AUTOMATIC TRANSMISSION
IGNITION SW PINS I1 & I2
RED-LT GRN
RED-LT GRN
RED-LT GRN
IGNITION COIL
TAN-YEL
BLK
RED-LT GRN
RED-LT GRN
RED-LT BLU
NEUTRAL SAFETY/BACK-UP LT SW (A/T), CLUTCH TRIPLE FUNCTION SW (M/T)
RADIO NOISE
BLK
91E13775

Fig. 9: Wiring Diagram (Ranger 2.9L)

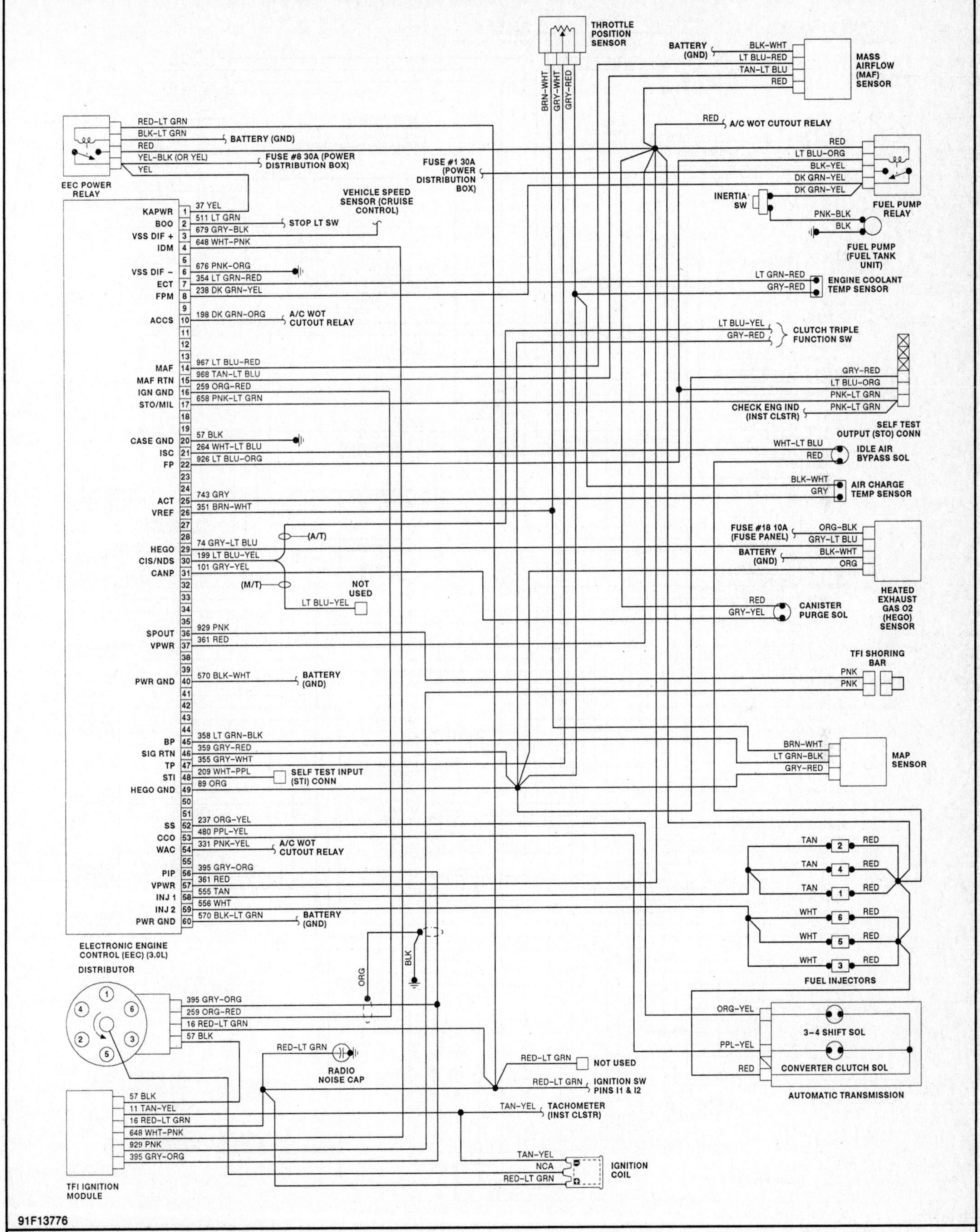
THROTTLE POSITION SENSOR
BRN-WHT
GRY-WHT
GRY-RED
BATTERY (GND)
BLK-WHT
LT BLU-RED
TAN-LT BLU
RED
MASS AIRFLOW (MAF) SENSOR
RED-LT GRN
BLK-LT GRN
BATTERY (GND)
RED
YEL-BLK (OR YEL)
FUSE #8 30A (POWER DISTRIBUTION BOX)
YEL
EEC POWER RELAY
A/C WOT CUTOUT RELAY
FUSE #1 30A (POWER DISTRIBUTION BOX)
LT BLU-ORG
BLK-YEL
DK GRN-YEL
INERTIA SW
PNK-BLK
BLK
FUEL PUMP RELAY
FUEL PUMP (FUEL TANK UNIT)
VEHICLE SPEED SENSOR (CRUISE CONTROL)
KAPWR 1 37 YEL
BOO 2 511 LT GRN
STOP LT SW
VSS DIF + 3 679 GRY-BLK
IDM 4 648 WHT-PNK
VSS DIF − 6 676 PNK-ORG
ECT 7 354 LT GRN-RED
FPM 8 238 DK GRN-YEL
ACCS 10 198 DK GRN-ORG
A/C WOT CUTOUT RELAY
LT GRN-RED
GRY-RED
ENGINE COOLANT TEMP SENSOR
LT BLU-YEL
CLUTCH TRIPLE FUNCTION SW
MAF 14 967 LT BLU-RED
MAF RTN 15 968 TAN-LT BLU
IGN GND 16 259 ORG-RED
STO/MIL 17 658 PNK-LT GRN
PNK-LT GRN
CHECK ENG IND (INST CLSTR)
SELF TEST OUTPUT (STO) CONN
CASE GND 20 57 BLK
ISC 21 264 WHT-LT BLU
FP 22 926 LT BLU-ORG
WHT-LT BLU
IDLE AIR BYPASS SOL
GRY
AIR CHARGE TEMP SENSOR
ACT 25 743 GRY
VREF 26 351 BRN-WHT
(A/T)
HEGO 29 74 GRY-LT BLU
CIS/NDS 30 199 LT BLU-YEL
CANP 31 101 GRY-YEL
(M/T)
NOT USED
LT BLU-YEL
FUSE #18 10A (FUSE PANEL)
ORG-BLK
GRY-LT BLU
ORG
HEATED EXHAUST GAS O2 (HEGO) SENSOR
GRY-YEL
CANISTER PURGE SOL
SPOUT 36 929 PNK
VPWR 37 361 RED
TFI SHORING BAR
PNK
PWR GND 40 570 BLK-WHT
BATTERY (GND)
BP 45 358 LT GRN-BLK
SIG RTN 46 359 GRY-RED
TP 47 355 GRY-WHT
STI 48 209 WHT-PPL
SELF TEST INPUT (STI) CONN
HEGO GND 49 89 ORG
LT GRN-BLK
MAP SENSOR
SS 52 237 ORG-YEL
CCO 53 480 PPL-YEL
WAC 54 331 PNK-YEL
A/C WOT CUTOUT RELAY
PIP 56 395 GRY-ORG
VPWR 57 361 RED
INJ 1 58 555 TAN
INJ 2 59 556 WHT
PWR GND 60 570 BLK-LT GRN
BATTERY (GND)
TAN
WHT
FUEL INJECTORS
ELECTRONIC ENGINE CONTROL (EEC) (3.0L)
DISTRIBUTOR
ORG
395 GRY-ORG
259 ORG-RED
16 RED-LT GRN
57 BLK
ORG-YEL
3-4 SHIFT SOL
PPL-YEL
CONVERTER CLUTCH SOL
AUTOMATIC TRANSMISSION
RADIO NOISE CAP
NOT USED
IGNITION SW PINS I1 & I2
TAN-YEL
TACHOMETER (INST CLSTR)
11 TAN-YEL
648 WHT-PNK
929 PNK
395 GRY-ORG
NCA
IGNITION COIL
TFI IGNITION MODULE
91F13776

Fig. 10: Wiring Diagram (Ranger 3.0L)

1991 ENGINE PERFORMANCE
Wiring Diagrams (Cont.)

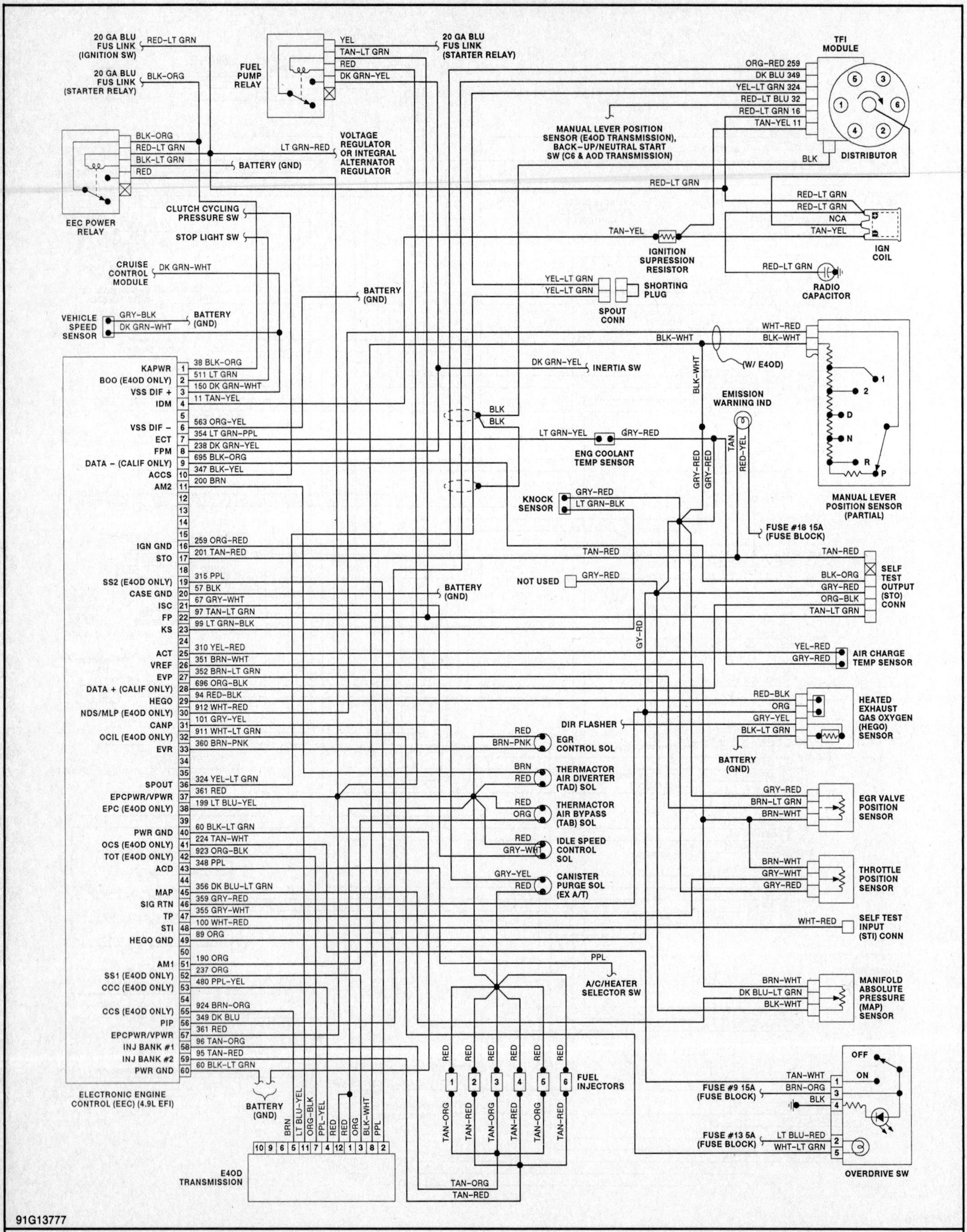
20 GA BLU FUS LINK (IGNITION SW)
RED-LT GRN
20 GA BLU FUS LINK (STARTER RELAY)
BLK-ORG
FUEL PUMP RELAY
YEL
TAN-LT GRN
RED
DK GRN-YEL
20 GA BLU FUS LINK (STARTER RELAY)
TFI MODULE
ORG-RED 259
DK BLU 349
YEL-LT GRN 324
RED-LT BLU 32
RED-LT GRN 16
TAN-YEL 11
DISTRIBUTOR
BLK
MANUAL LEVER POSITION SENSOR (E4OD TRANSMISSION), BACK-UP/NEUTRAL START SW (C6 & AOD TRANSMISSION)
BLK-ORG
RED-LT GRN
BLK-LT GRN
RED
LT GRN-RED
BATTERY (GND)
VOLTAGE REGULATOR OR INTEGRAL ALTERNATOR REGULATOR
EEC POWER RELAY
CLUTCH CYCLING PRESSURE SW
STOP LIGHT SW
CRUISE CONTROL MODULE
DK GRN-WHT
VEHICLE SPEED SENSOR
GRY-BLK
DK GRN-WHT
BATTERY (GND)
RED-LT GRN
RED-LT GRN
RED-LT GRN
NCA
TAN-YEL
TAN-YEL
IGNITION SUPRESSION RESISTOR
IGN COIL
RED-LT GRN
RADIO CAPACITOR
YEL-LT GRN
YEL-LT GRN
SHORTING PLUG
SPOUT CONN
BATTERY (GND)
WHT-RED
BLK-WHT
BLK-WHT
BLK-WHT
(W/ E4OD)
DK GRN-YEL
INERTIA SW
EMISSION WARNING IND
TAN
RED-YEL
MANUAL LEVER POSITION SENSOR (PARTIAL)
1
2
D
N
R
P
KAPWR 1 38 BLK-ORG
BOO (E4OD ONLY) 2 511 LT GRN
VSS DIF + 3 150 DK GRN-WHT
IDM 4 11 TAN-YEL
5
VSS DIF – 6 563 ORG-YEL
ECT 7 354 LT GRN-PPL
FPM 8 238 DK GRN-YEL
DATA – (CALIF ONLY) 9 695 BLK-ORG
ACCS 10 347 BLK-YEL
AM2 11 200 BRN
12
13
14
15
IGN GND 16 259 ORG-RED
STO 17 201 TAN-RED
18
SS2 (E4OD ONLY) 19 315 PPL
CASE GND 20 57 BLK
ISC 21 67 GRY-WHT
FP 22 97 TAN-LT GRN
KS 23 99 LT GRN-BLK
24
ACT 25 310 YEL-RED
VREF 26 351 BRN-WHT
EVP 27 352 BRN-LT GRN
DATA + (CALIF ONLY) 28 696 ORG-BLK
HEGO 29 94 RED-BLK
NDS/MLP (E4OD ONLY) 30 912 WHT-RED
CANP 31 101 GRY-YEL
OCIL (E4OD ONLY) 32 911 WHT-LT GRN
EVR 33 360 BRN-PNK
34
35
SPOUT 36 324 YEL-LT GRN
EPCPWR/VPWR 37 361 RED
EPC (E4OD ONLY) 38 199 LT BLU-YEL
39
PWR GND 40 60 BLK-LT GRN
OCS (E4OD ONLY) 41 224 TAN-WHT
TOT (E4OD ONLY) 42 923 ORG-BLK
ACD 43 348 PPL
44
MAP 45 356 DK BLU-LT GRN
SIG RTN 46 359 GRY-RED
TP 47 355 GRY-WHT
STI 48 100 WHT-RED
HEGO GND 49 89 ORG
50
AM1 51 190 ORG
SS1 (E4OD ONLY) 52 237 ORG
CCC (E4OD ONLY) 53 480 PPL-YEL
54
CCS (E4OD ONLY) 55 924 BRN-ORG
PIP 56 349 DK BLU
EPCPWR/VPWR 57 361 RED
INJ BANK #1 58 96 TAN-ORG
INJ BANK #2 59 95 TAN-RED
PWR GND 60 60 BLK-LT GRN
ELECTRONIC ENGINE CONTROL (EEC) (4.9L EFI)
BLK
BLK
LT GRN-YEL
GRY-RED
ENG COOLANT TEMP SENSOR
GRY-RED
GRY-RED
KNOCK SENSOR
GRY-RED
LT GRN-BLK
FUSE #18 15A (FUSE BLOCK)
TAN-RED
TAN-RED
SELF TEST OUTPUT (STO) CONN
BLK-ORG
GRY-RED
ORG-BLK
TAN-LT GRN
NOT USED
GRY-RED
BATTERY (GND)
GY-RD
YEL-RED
GRY-RED
AIR CHARGE TEMP SENSOR
RED-BLK
ORG
GRY-YEL
BLK-LT GRN
HEATED EXHAUST GAS OXYGEN (HEGO) SENSOR
BATTERY (GND)
DIR FLASHER
RED
BRN-PNK
EGR CONTROL SOL
BRN
RED
THERMACTOR AIR DIVERTER (TAD) SOL
RED
ORG
THERMACTOR AIR BYPASS (TAB) SOL
RED
GRY-WHT
IDLE SPEED CONTROL SOL
GRY-YEL
RED
CANISTER PURGE SOL (EX A/T)
GRY-RED
BRN-LT GRN
BRN-WHT
EGR VALVE POSITION SENSOR
BRN-WHT
GRY-WHT
GRY-RED
THROTTLE POSITION SENSOR
WHT-RED
SELF TEST INPUT (STI) CONN
PPL
A/C/HEATER SELECTOR SW
BRN-WHT
DK BLU-LT GRN
BLK-WHT
MANIFOLD ABSOLUTE PRESSURE (MAP) SENSOR
RED
RED
RED
RED
RED
RED
1
2
3
4
5
6
FUEL INJECTORS
TAN-ORG
TAN-RED
TAN-ORG
TAN-RED
TAN-ORG
TAN-RED
TAN-ORG
TAN-RED
OFF
ON
TAN-WHT
FUSE #9 15A (FUSE BLOCK)
BRN-ORG
BLK
FUSE #13 5A (FUSE BLOCK)
LT BLU-RED
WHT-LT GRN
OVERDRIVE SW
BATTERY (GND)
BRN
LT BLU-YEL
ORG-BLK
PPL-YEL
RED
RED
ORG
BLK-WHT
PPL
10 9 6 5 11 7 4 12 1 3 8 2
E4OD TRANSMISSION
91G13777

Fig. 11: Wiring Diagram ("E" Series 4.9L)

1991 ENGINE PERFORMANCE
Wiring Diagrams (Cont.)

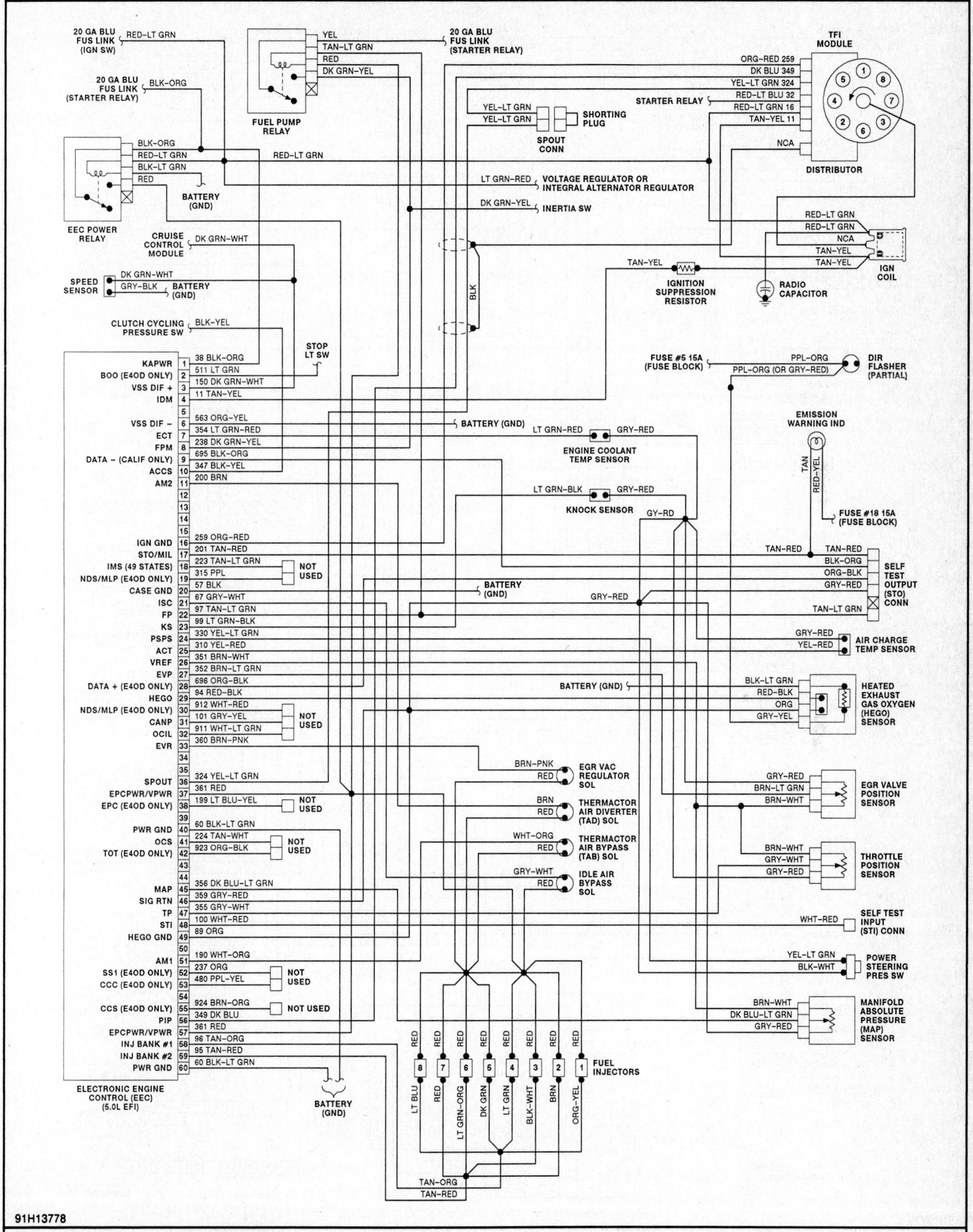
20 GA BLU FUS LINK (IGN SW)
RED-LT GRN
20 GA BLU FUS LINK (STARTER RELAY)
BLK-ORG
YEL
TAN-LT GRN
RED
DK GRN-YEL
FUEL PUMP RELAY
20 GA BLU FUS LINK (STARTER RELAY)
TFI MODULE
ORG-RED 259
DK BLU 349
YEL-LT GRN 324
RED-LT BLU 32
RED-LT GRN 16
TAN-YEL 11
NCA
STARTER RELAY
YEL-LT GRN
SHORTING PLUG
SPOUT CONN
DISTRIBUTOR
BLK-ORG
RED-LT GRN
BLK-LT GRN
RED
BATTERY (GND)
EEC POWER RELAY
LT GRN-RED
VOLTAGE REGULATOR OR INTEGRAL ALTERNATOR REGULATOR
DK GRN-YEL
INERTIA SW
CRUISE CONTROL MODULE
DK GRN-WHT
SPEED SENSOR
GRY-BLK
BLK
TAN-YEL
IGNITION SUPPRESSION RESISTOR
RADIO CAPACITOR
IGN COIL
CLUTCH CYCLING PRESSURE SW
BLK-YEL
STOP LT SW
FUSE #5 15A (FUSE BLOCK)
PPL-ORG
PPL-ORG (OR GRY-RED)
DIR FLASHER (PARTIAL)
KAPWR 1 38 BLK-ORG
BOO (E4OD ONLY) 2 511 LT GRN
VSS DIF + 3 150 DK GRN-WHT
IDM 4 11 TAN-YEL
5
VSS DIF – 6 563 ORG-YEL
ECT 7 354 LT GRN-RED
FPM 8 238 DK GRN-YEL
DATA – (CALIF ONLY) 9 695 BLK-ORG
ACCS 10 347 BLK-YEL
AM2 11 200 BRN
12
13
14
15
IGN GND 16 259 ORG-RED
STO/MIL 17 201 TAN-RED
IMS (49 STATES) 18 223 TAN-LT GRN
NDS/MLP (E4OD ONLY) 19 315 PPL
CASE GND 20 57 BLK
ISC 21 67 GRY-WHT
FP 22 97 TAN-LT GRN
KS 23 99 LT GRN-BLK
PSPS 24 330 YEL-LT GRN
ACT 25 310 YEL-RED
VREF 26 351 BRN-WHT
EVP 27 352 BRN-LT GRN
DATA + (E4OD ONLY) 28 696 ORG-BLK
HEGO 29 94 RED-BLK
NDS/MLP (E4OD ONLY) 30 912 WHT-RED
CANP 31 101 GRY-YEL
OCIL 32 911 WHT-LT GRN
EVR 33 360 BRN-PNK
34
35
SPOUT 36 324 YEL-LT GRN
EPCPWR/VPWR 37 361 RED
EPC (E4OD ONLY) 38 199 LT BLU-YEL
39
PWR GND 40 60 BLK-LT GRN
OCS 41 224 TAN-WHT
TOT (E4OD ONLY) 42 923 ORG-BLK
43
44
MAP 45 356 DK BLU-LT GRN
SIG RTN 46 359 GRY-RED
TP 47 355 GRY-WHT
STI 48 100 WHT-RED
HEGO GND 49 89 ORG
50
AM1 51 190 WHT-ORG
SS1 (E4OD ONLY) 52 237 ORG
CCC (E4OD ONLY) 53 480 PPL-YEL
54
CCS (E4OD ONLY) 55 924 BRN-ORG
PIP 56 349 DK BLU
EPCPWR/VPWR 57 361 RED
INJ BANK #1 58 96 TAN-ORG
INJ BANK #2 59 95 TAN-RED
PWR GND 60 60 BLK-LT GRN
NOT USED
ELECTRONIC ENGINE CONTROL (EEC) (5.0L EFI)
BATTERY (GND)
LT GRN-RED
GRY-RED
ENGINE COOLANT TEMP SENSOR
LT GRN-BLK
KNOCK SENSOR
GY-RD
EMISSION WARNING IND
TAN
RED-YEL
FUSE #18 15A (FUSE BLOCK)
TAN-RED
BLK-ORG
ORG-BLK
GRY-RED
TAN-LT GRN
SELF TEST OUTPUT (STO) CONN
YEL-RED
AIR CHARGE TEMP SENSOR
BLK-LT GRN
RED-BLK
ORG
GRY-YEL
HEATED EXHAUST GAS OXYGEN (HEGO) SENSOR
BRN-PNK
EGR VAC REGULATOR SOL
BRN
THERMACTOR AIR DIVERTER (TAD) SOL
WHT-ORG
THERMACTOR AIR BYPASS (TAB) SOL
GRY-WHT
IDLE AIR BYPASS SOL
BRN-LT GRN
BRN-WHT
EGR VALVE POSITION SENSOR
GRY-WHT
THROTTLE POSITION SENSOR
WHT-RED
SELF TEST INPUT (STI) CONN
YEL-LT GRN
BLK-WHT
POWER STEERING PRES SW
DK BLU-LT GRN
MANIFOLD ABSOLUTE PRESSURE (MAP) SENSOR
FUEL INJECTORS
LT BLU
LT GRN-ORG
DK GRN
LT GRN
BLK-WHT
ORG-YEL
TAN-ORG
91H13778

Fig. 12: Wiring Diagram ("E" Series 5.0L)

1991 ENGINE PERFORMANCE
Wiring Diagrams (Cont.)

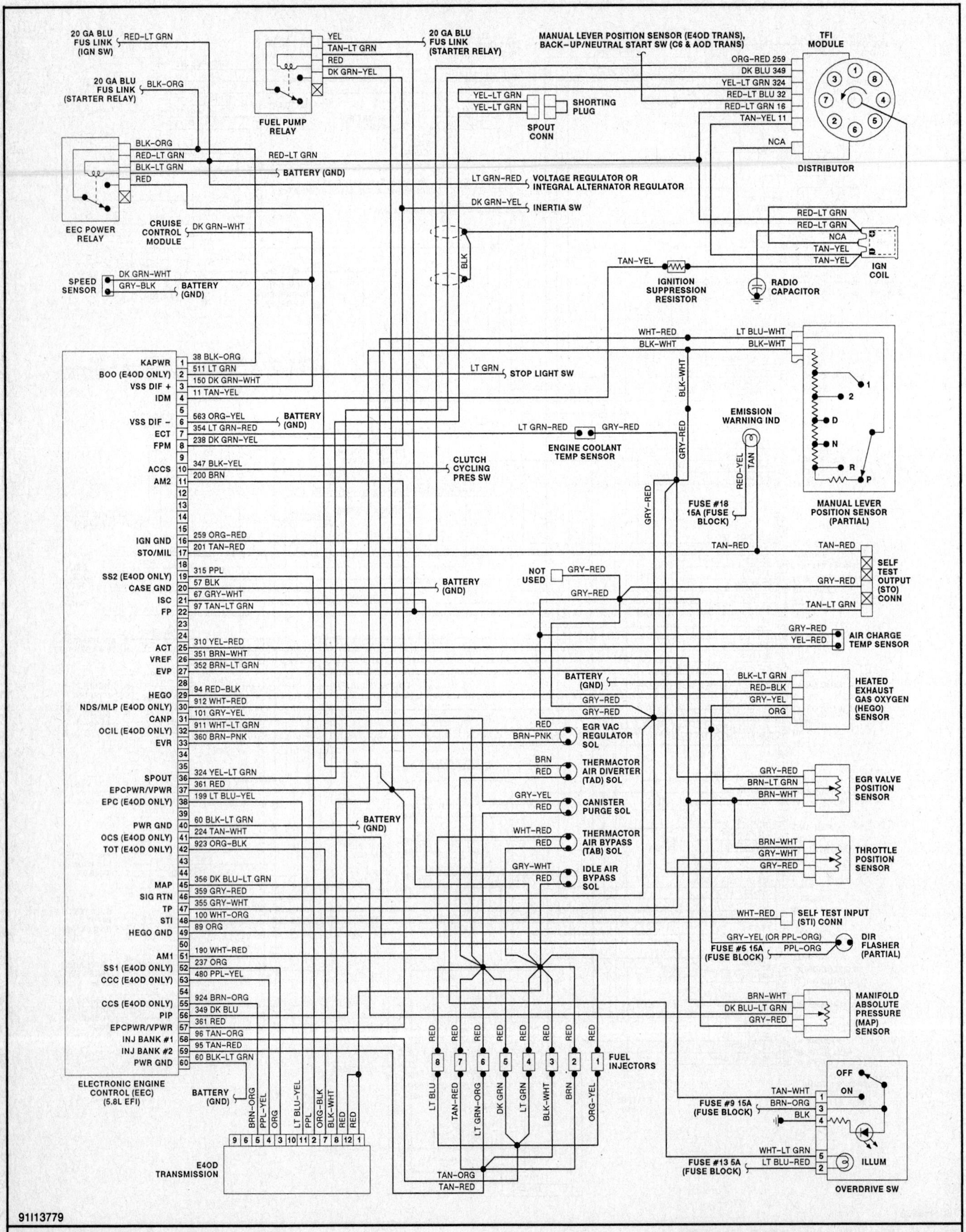
20 GA BLU FUS LINK (IGN SW)
RED-LT GRN
20 GA BLU FUS LINK (STARTER RELAY)
BLK-ORG
YEL
TAN-LT GRN
RED
DK GRN-YEL
FUEL PUMP RELAY
20 GA BLU FUS LINK (STARTER RELAY)
MANUAL LEVER POSITION SENSOR (E4OD TRANS), BACK-UP/NEUTRAL START SW (C6 & AOD TRANS)
TFI MODULE
ORG-RED 259
DK BLU 349
YEL-LT GRN 324
RED-LT BLU 32
RED-LT GRN 16
TAN-YEL 11
NCA
DISTRIBUTOR
YEL-LT GRN
YEL-LT GRN
SHORTING PLUG
SPOUT CONN
BLK-ORG
RED-LT GRN
BLK-LT GRN
RED
EEC POWER RELAY
RED-LT GRN
BATTERY (GND)
LT GRN-RED
VOLTAGE REGULATOR OR INTEGRAL ALTERNATOR REGULATOR
DK GRN-YEL
INERTIA SW
CRUISE CONTROL MODULE
DK GRN-WHT
BLK
RED-LT GRN
RED-LT GRN
NCA
TAN-YEL
TAN-YEL
IGN COIL
TAN-YEL
IGNITION SUPPRESSION RESISTOR
RADIO CAPACITOR
SPEED SENSOR
DK GRN-WHT
GRY-BLK
BATTERY (GND)
WHT-RED
BLK-WHT
LT BLU-WHT
BLK-WHT
BLK-WHT
KAPWR 1 38 BLK-ORG
BOO (E4OD ONLY) 2 511 LT GRN
VSS DIF + 3 150 DK GRN-WHT
IDM 4 11 TAN-YEL
5
VSS DIF – 6 563 ORG-YEL
ECT 7 354 LT GRN-RED
FPM 8 238 DK GRN-YEL
9
ACCS 10 347 BLK-YEL
AM2 11 200 BRN
12
13
14
15
IGN GND 16 259 ORG-RED
STO/MIL 17 201 TAN-RED
18
SS2 (E4OD ONLY) 19 315 PPL
CASE GND 20 57 BLK
ISC 21 67 GRY-WHT
FP 22 97 TAN-LT GRN
23
24
ACT 25 310 YEL-RED
VREF 26 351 BRN-WHT
EVP 27 352 BRN-LT GRN
28
HEGO 29 94 RED-BLK
NDS/MLP (E4OD ONLY) 30 912 WHT-RED
CANP 31 101 GRY-YEL
OCIL (E4OD ONLY) 32 911 WHT-LT GRN
EVR 33 360 BRN-PNK
34
35
SPOUT 36 324 YEL-LT GRN
EPCPWR/VPWR 37 361 RED
EPC (E4OD ONLY) 38 199 LT BLU-YEL
39
PWR GND 40 60 BLK-LT GRN
OCS (E4OD ONLY) 41 224 TAN-WHT
TOT (E4OD ONLY) 42 923 ORG-BLK
43
44
MAP 45 356 DK BLU-LT GRN
SIG RTN 46 359 GRY-RED
TP 47 355 GRY-WHT
STI 48 100 WHT-ORG
HEGO GND 49 89 ORG
50
AM1 51 190 WHT-RED
SS1 (E4OD ONLY) 52 237 ORG
CCC (E4OD ONLY) 53 480 PPL-YEL
54
CCS (E4OD ONLY) 55 924 BRN-ORG
PIP 56 349 DK BLU
EPCPWR/VPWR 57 361 RED
INJ BANK #1 58 96 TAN-ORG
INJ BANK #2 59 95 TAN-RED
PWR GND 60 60 BLK-LT GRN
ELECTRONIC ENGINE CONTROL (EEC) (5.8L EFI)
BATTERY (GND)
LT GRN
STOP LIGHT SW
BATTERY (GND)
LT GRN-RED
GRY-RED
ENGINE COOLANT TEMP SENSOR
CLUTCH CYCLING PRES SW
EMISSION WARNING IND
RED-YEL
TAN
GRY-RED
GRY-RED
FUSE #18 15A (FUSE BLOCK)
1
2
D
N
R
P
MANUAL LEVER POSITION SENSOR (PARTIAL)
TAN-RED
TAN-RED
BATTERY (GND)
NOT USED
GRY-RED
GRY-RED
GRY-RED
TAN-LT GRN
SELF TEST OUTPUT (STO) CONN
GRY-RED
YEL-RED
AIR CHARGE TEMP SENSOR
BATTERY (GND)
BLK-LT GRN
RED-BLK
GRY-YEL
ORG
GRY-RED
GRY-RED
HEATED EXHAUST GAS OXYGEN (HEGO) SENSOR
RED
BRN-PNK
EGR VAC REGULATOR SOL
BRN
RED
THERMACTOR AIR DIVERTER (TAD) SOL
GRY-YEL
RED
CANISTER PURGE SOL
WHT-RED
RED
THERMACTOR AIR BYPASS (TAB) SOL
GRY-WHT
RED
IDLE AIR BYPASS SOL
BATTERY (GND)
GRY-RED
BRN-LT GRN
BRN-WHT
EGR VALVE POSITION SENSOR
BRN-WHT
GRY-WHT
GRY-RED
THROTTLE POSITION SENSOR
WHT-RED
SELF TEST INPUT (STI) CONN
GRY-YEL (OR PPL-ORG)
PPL-ORG
FUSE #5 15A (FUSE BLOCK)
DIR FLASHER (PARTIAL)
BRN-WHT
DK BLU-LT GRN
GRY-RED
MANIFOLD ABSOLUTE PRESSURE (MAP) SENSOR
RED
RED
RED
RED
RED
RED
RED
RED
8
7
6
5
4
3
2
1
FUEL INJECTORS
LT BLU
TAN-RED
LT GRN-ORG
DK GRN
LT GRN
BLK-WHT
BRN
ORG-YEL
BRN-ORG
PPL-YEL
ORG
LT BLU-YEL
PPL
ORG-BLK
BLK-WHT
RED
RED
9 6 5 4 3 10 11 2 7 8 12 1
E4OD TRANSMISSION
TAN-ORG
TAN-RED
OFF
ON
TAN-WHT
BRN-ORG
BLK
FUSE #9 15A (FUSE BLOCK)
1
3
4
WHT-LT GRN
LT BLU-RED
FUSE #13 5A (FUSE BLOCK)
5
2
ILLUM
OVERDRIVE SW
91I13779

Fig. 13: Wiring Diagram ("E" Series 5.8L)

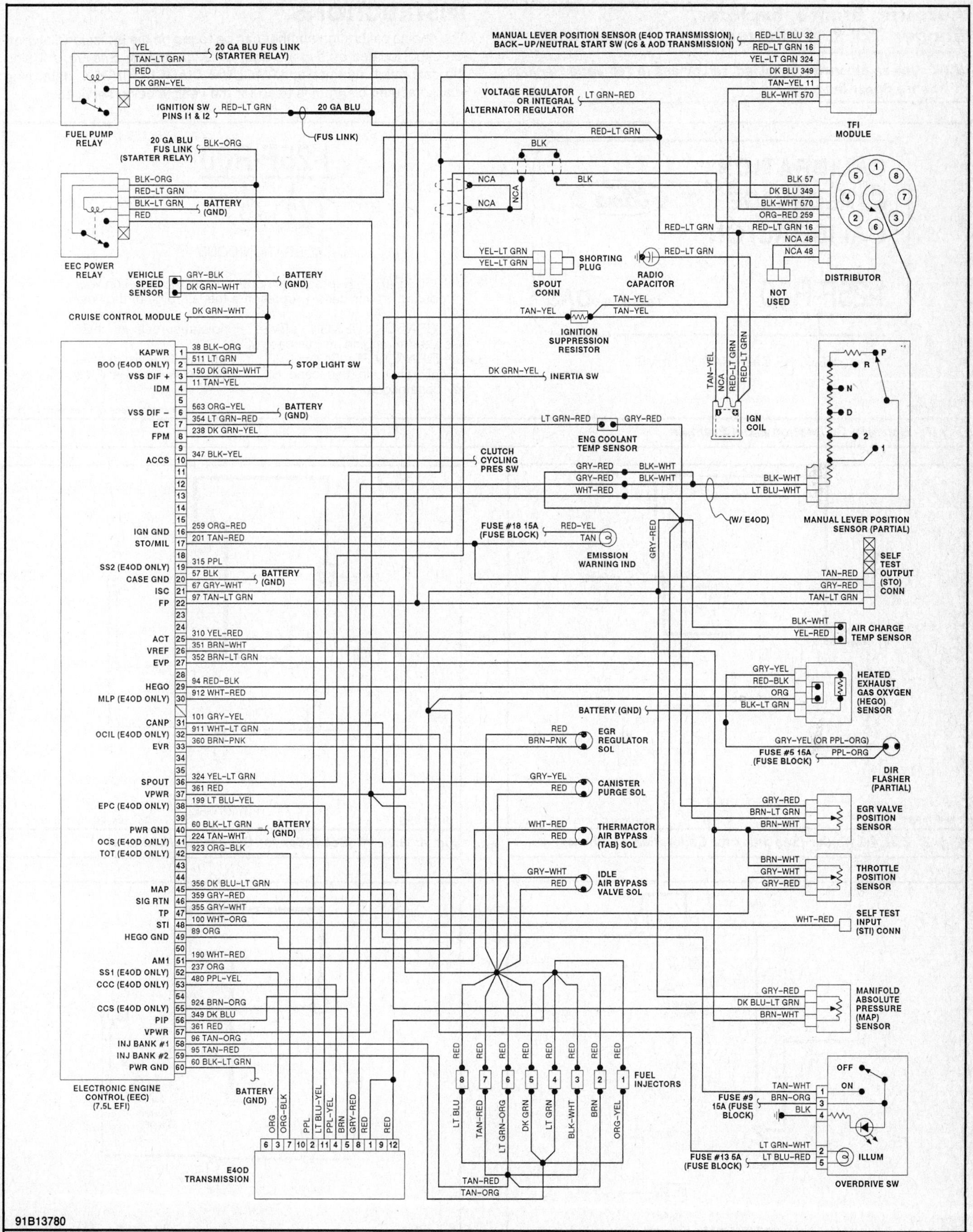

FUEL PUMP RELAY
YEL
TAN-LT GRN
RED
DK GRN-YEL
20 GA BLU FUS LINK (STARTER RELAY)
IGNITION SW PINS I1 & I2
RED-LT GRN
20 GA BLU
(FUS LINK)
20 GA BLU FUS LINK (STARTER RELAY)
BLK-ORG
EEC POWER RELAY
BLK-ORG
RED-LT GRN
BLK-LT GRN
RED
BATTERY (GND)
VEHICLE SPEED SENSOR
GRY-BLK
DK GRN-WHT
BATTERY (GND)
CRUISE CONTROL MODULE
DK GRN-WHT
MANUAL LEVER POSITION SENSOR (E4OD TRANSMISSION), BACK-UP/NEUTRAL START SW (C6 & AOD TRANSMISSION)
RED-LT BLU 32
RED-LT GRN 16
YEL-LT GRN 324
DK BLU 349
TAN-YEL 11
BLK-WHT 570
TFI MODULE
VOLTAGE REGULATOR OR INTEGRAL ALTERNATOR REGULATOR
LT GRN-RED
RED-LT GRN
BLK
NCA
NCA
NCA
BLK
BLK 57
DK BLU 349
BLK-WHT 570
ORG-RED 259
RED-LT GRN 16
NCA 48
NCA 48
RED-LT GRN
NOT USED
DISTRIBUTOR
YEL-LT GRN
YEL-LT GRN
SHORTING PLUG
SPOUT CONN
RED-LT GRN
RADIO CAPACITOR
TAN-YEL
TAN-YEL
TAN-YEL
IGNITION SUPPRESSION RESISTOR
TAN-YEL
NCA
RED-LT GRN
RED-LT GRN
IGN COIL
KAPWR 1 38 BLK-ORG
BOO (E4OD ONLY) 2 511 LT GRN
VSS DIF + 3 150 DK GRN-WHT
IDM 4 11 TAN-YEL
5
VSS DIF − 6 563 ORG-YEL
ECT 7 354 LT GRN-RED
FPM 8 238 DK GRN-YEL
9
ACCS 10 347 BLK-YEL
11
12
13
14
15
IGN GND 16 259 ORG-RED
STO/MIL 17 201 TAN-RED
18
SS2 (E4OD ONLY) 19 315 PPL
CASE GND 20 57 BLK
ISC 21 67 GRY-WHT
FP 22 97 TAN-LT GRN
23
24
ACT 25 310 YEL-RED
VREF 26 351 BRN-WHT
EVP 27 352 BRN-LT GRN
28
HEGO 29 94 RED-BLK
MLP (E4OD ONLY) 30 912 WHT-RED
CANP 31 101 GRY-YEL
OCIL (E4OD ONLY) 32 911 WHT-LT GRN
EVR 33 360 BRN-PNK
34
35
SPOUT 36 324 YEL-LT GRN
VPWR 37 361 RED
EPC (E4OD ONLY) 38 199 LT BLU-YEL
39
PWR GND 40 60 BLK-LT GRN
OCS (E4OD ONLY) 41 224 TAN-WHT
TOT (E4OD ONLY) 42 923 ORG-BLK
43
44
MAP 45 356 DK BLU-LT GRN
SIG RTN 46 359 GRY-RED
TP 47 355 GRY-WHT
STI 48 100 WHT-ORG
HEGO GND 49 89 ORG
50
AM1 51 190 WHT-RED
SS1 (E4OD ONLY) 52 237 ORG
CCC (E4OD ONLY) 53 480 PPL-YEL
54
CCS (E4OD ONLY) 55 924 BRN-ORG
PIP 56 349 DK BLU
VPWR 57 361 RED
INJ BANK #1 58 96 TAN-ORG
INJ BANK #2 59 95 TAN-RED
PWR GND 60 60 BLK-LT GRN
STOP LIGHT SW
BATTERY (GND)
BATTERY (GND)
BATTERY (GND)
ELECTRONIC ENGINE CONTROL (EEC) (7.5L EFI)
DK GRN-YEL
INERTIA SW
LT GRN-RED
GRY-RED
ENG COOLANT TEMP SENSOR
CLUTCH CYCLING PRES SW
GRY-RED
GRY-RED
WHT-RED
BLK-WHT
BLK-WHT
BLK-WHT
LT BLU-WHT
(W/ E4OD)
MANUAL LEVER POSITION SENSOR (PARTIAL)
P
R
N
D
2
1
FUSE #18 15A (FUSE BLOCK)
RED-YEL
TAN
EMISSION WARNING IND
GRY-RED
SELF TEST OUTPUT (STO) CONN
TAN-RED
GRY-RED
TAN-LT GRN
BLK-WHT
YEL-RED
AIR CHARGE TEMP SENSOR
GRY-YEL
RED-BLK
ORG
BLK-LT GRN
HEATED EXHAUST GAS OXYGEN (HEGO) SENSOR
BATTERY (GND)
RED
BRN-PNK
EGR REGULATOR SOL
GRY-YEL (OR PPL-ORG)
FUSE #5 15A (FUSE BLOCK)
PPL-ORG
DIR FLASHER (PARTIAL)
GRY-YEL
RED
CANISTER PURGE SOL
GRY-RED
BRN-LT GRN
BRN-WHT
EGR VALVE POSITION SENSOR
WHT-RED
RED
THERMACTOR AIR BYPASS (TAB) SOL
BRN-WHT
GRY-WHT
GRY-RED
THROTTLE POSITION SENSOR
GRY-WHT
RED
IDLE AIR BYPASS VALVE SOL
WHT-RED
SELF TEST INPUT (STI) CONN
GRY-RED
DK BLU-LT GRN
BRN-WHT
MANIFOLD ABSOLUTE PRESSURE (MAP) SENSOR
RED RED RED RED RED RED RED RED
8 7 6 5 4 3 2 1
FUEL INJECTORS
LT BLU
TAN-RED
LT GRN-ORG
DK GRN
LT GRN
BLK-WHT
BRN
ORG-YEL
TAN-RED
TAN-ORG
BATTERY (GND)
ORG
ORG-BLK
PPL
LT BLU-YEL
PPL-YEL
BRN
GRY-RED
RED
RED
6 3 7 10 2 11 4 5 8 1 9 12
E4OD TRANSMISSION
OFF
ON
TAN-WHT
BRN-ORG
BLK
FUSE #9 15A (FUSE BLOCK)
1
3
4
LT GRN-WHT
LT BLU-RED
2
5
FUSE #13 5A (FUSE BLOCK)
ILLUM
OVERDRIVE SW
91B13780

Fig. 14: Wiring Diagram ("E" Series 7.5L)

1991 ENGINE PERFORMANCE
Vacuum Diagrams

Aerostar, Bronco, Explorer, Ranger, "E" & "F" Series

NOTE: Unless otherwise specified, references to "F" Series include "F" Series Super Duty.

INSTRUCTIONS

The engine calibration number can be found on the Emission Calibration Label located on driver's door or "B" pillar post. *See Fig. 1*. Using the calibration number and VACUUM DIAGRAM INDEX, determine which vacuum diagram is used for the vehicle being serviced.

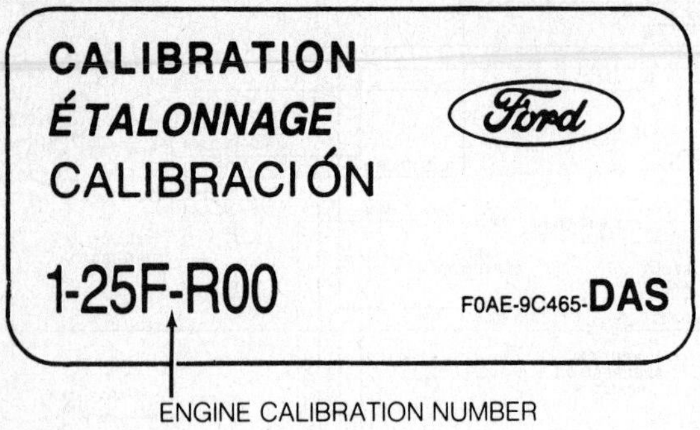
CALIBRATION
ÉTALONNAGE
CALIBRACIÓN
Ford
1-25F-R00
F0AE-9C465-DAS
ENGINE CALIBRATION NUMBER

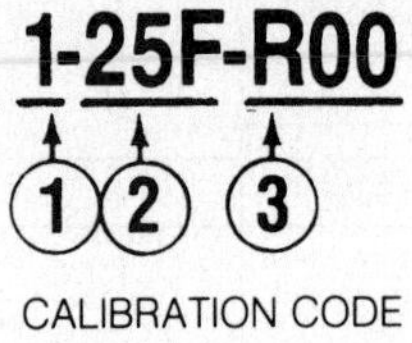
1-25F-R00
1
2
3
CALIBRATION CODE

1. MODEL YEAR – Represents model year that calibration was introduced. In this case 1 represents the last digit of the year 1991.
2. CALIBRATION DESIGN LEVEL – Indicates design level assigned to engine. In this case 25F.
3. CALIBRATION REVISION LEVEL – Represents revision level of calibration. In this case R00. Numbers will increase as revisions occur.

91F14360 Courtesy of Ford Motor Co.

Fig. 1: Emission Calibration Label Example

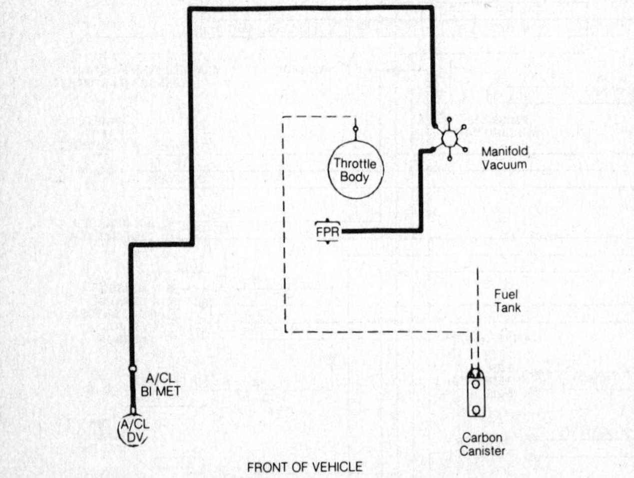
Throttle Body
Manifold Vacuum
FPR
Fuel Tank
A/CL BI MET
A/CL DV
Carbon Canister
FRONT OF VEHICLE

90F14980 Courtesy of Ford Motor Co.

Fig. 2: 2.3L 4-Cylinder (See Index for Calibration Numbers)

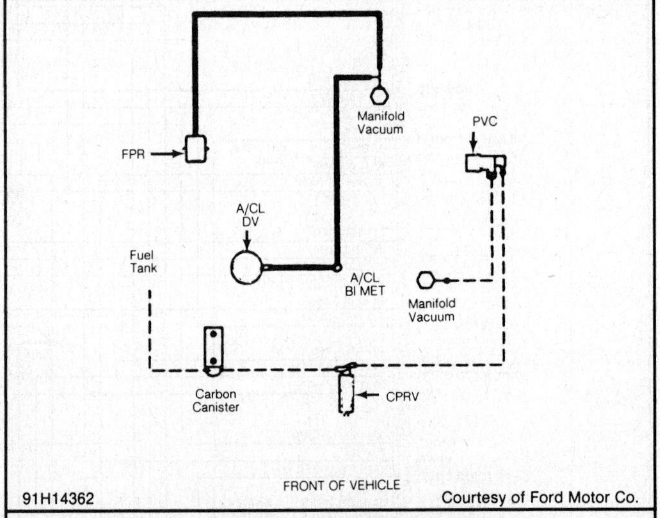
Manifold Vacuum
PVC
FPR
A/CL DV
Fuel Tank
A/CL BI MET
Manifold Vacuum
Carbon Canister
CPRV
FRONT OF VEHICLE

91H14362 Courtesy of Ford Motor Co.

Fig. 4: 3.0L V6 (See Index for Calibration Numbers)

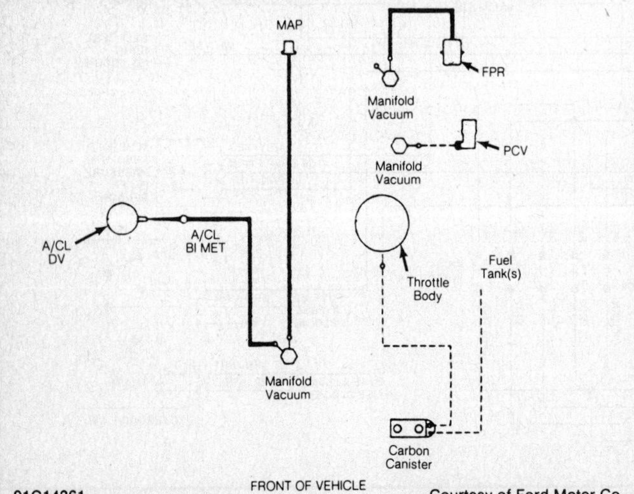
MAP
FPR
Manifold Vacuum
PCV
Manifold Vacuum
A/CL DV
A/CL BI MET
Throttle Body
Fuel Tank(s)
Manifold Vacuum
Carbon Canister
FRONT OF VEHICLE

91G14361 Courtesy of Ford Motor Co.

Fig. 3: 2.9L V6 (See Index for Calibration Numbers)

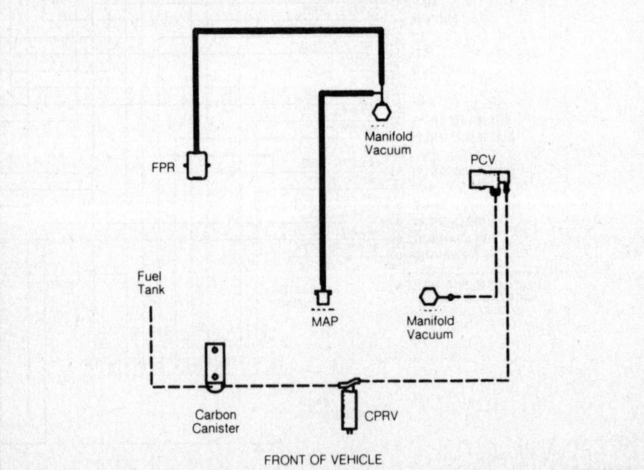
Manifold Vacuum
PCV
FPR
Fuel Tank
MAP
Manifold Vacuum
Carbon Canister
CPRV
FRONT OF VEHICLE

90A14985 Courtesy of Ford Motor Co.

Fig. 5: 3.0L V6 (See Index for Calibration Numbers)

1991 ENGINE PERFORMANCE
Vacuum Diagrams (Cont.)

VACUUM DIAGRAM INDEX

Engine & Model	Application	Transmission	A/C	Non A/C	Calibration	Fig. No.
2.3L 4-Cylinder						
Ranger [1]	Calif./Fed.	Auto./Man.	X	X	0-50T-R10	2
2.9L V6						
Ranger [1]	Calif./Fed.	Auto./Man.	X	X	0-66H-R10	3
Ranger [1]	Calif./Fed.	Auto./Man.	X	X	9-65H-R00	3
3.0L V6						
Aerostar, Ranger [1]	Calif./Fed.	[4]	X	X	1-56F-R00	4
Aerostar, Ranger	Calif./Fed.	[4]	X	X	9-55J-R11	5
Aerostar, Ranger	Calif./Fed.	[4]	X	X	9-56J-R11	5
4.0L V6						
Aerostar, Explorer, Ranger [1,2]	Fed.	[4]	X	X	0-57B-R00	6
Aerostar, Explorer, Ranger [1,2]	Calif.	[4]	X	X	0-57R-R00	6
Aerostar, Explorer, Ranger [1,2]	Fed.	[4]	X	X	0-58A-R00	6
Aerostar, Explorer, Ranger [1,2]	Fed.	[4]	X	X	0-58B-R00	6
Aerostar, Explorer, Ranger [1]	Calif.	[4]	X	X	0-58P-R00	6
Aerostar, Explorer, Ranger [1]	Calif.	[4]	X	X	0-58P-R00	6
Aerostar, Explorer, Ranger [1]	Calif.	[4]	X	X	0-58R-R00	6
Aerostar, Explorer, Ranger [1,2]	Fed.	[4]	X	X	1-58A-R10	6
Aerostar, Explorer, Ranger [1,2]	Fed.	[4]	X	X	1-58B-R10	6
Aerostar, Explorer, Ranger [2]	Fed.	[4]	X	X	1-58K-R10	7
Aerostar, Explorer, Ranger [2]	Fed.	[4]	X	X	1-58K-R11	7
Aerostar, Explorer, Ranger [1]	Calif.	[4]	X	X	1-58P-R10	6
Aerostar, Explorer, Ranger [1]	Calif.	[4]	X	X	1-58R-R10	6
4.9L 6-Cylinder, Heavy Duty						
Bronco, F150/350, E150/350 [3]	Fed.	Man.	X	X	1-71J-R00	[4]
Bronco, F150/350, E150/350 [3]	Fed.	Auto.	X	X	1-72J-R00	[4]
5.0L V8						
Bronco, F150/350, E150/350 [2]	[4]	[4]	[4]	[4]	[4]	[4]
5.8L V8						
Bronco, F150/350, E150/350	Fed.	[4]	X	X	1-64M-R10	8
Bronco, F150/350, E150/350	Calif./Fed.	[4]	X	X	1-64P-R10	9
5.8L V8, Heavy Duty						
Bronco, F150/350, E150/350 [3]	[4]	[4]	[4]	[4]	1-75A-R00	[4]
Bronco, F150/350, E150/350 [3]	[4]	[4]	[4]	[4]	1-76A-R00	[4]
Bronco, F150/350, E150/350 [3]	[4]	[4]	[4]	[4]	1-76B-R00	[4]
Bronco, F150/350, E150/350 [3]	[4]	[4]	[4]	[4]	1-76C-R00	[4]
Bronco, F150/350, E150/350 [3]	[4]	[4]	[4]	[4]	9-76C-R12	[4]
7.5L V8, Heavy Duty						
F250/350, E250/350	[4]	[4]	[4]	[4]	1-97A-R00	[4]
F250/350, E250/350	[4]	[4]	[4]	[4]	1-98A-R00	[4]
F250/350, E250/350	[4]	[4]	[4]	[4]	1-98B-R00	[4]
F250/350, E250/350	[4]	[4]	[4]	[4]	1-98C-R00	[4]
F250/350, E250/350	[4]	[4]	[4]	[4]	1-98E-R00	[4]
F250/350, E250/350	[4]	[4]	[4]	[4]	1-98F-R00	[4]

[1] – Equipped with A/CL-DV.
[2] – Over 3450 lbs. Curb Weight.
[3] – Over 6000 lbs. GVWR.
[4] – Information not available.

1991 ENGINE PERFORMANCE
Vacuum Diagrams (Cont.)

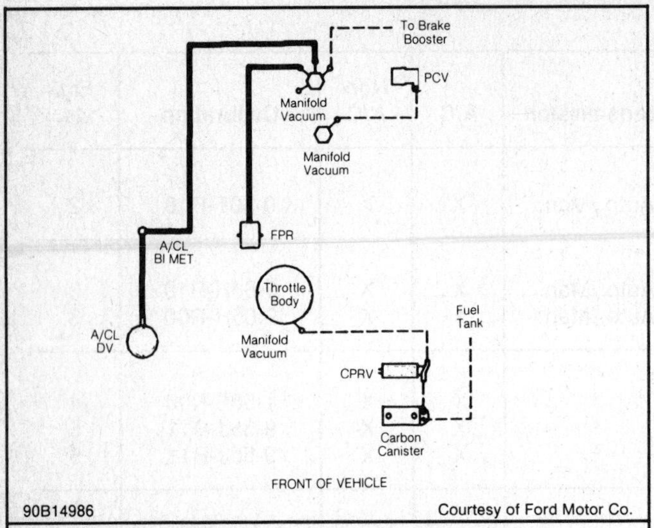
To Brake Booster
PCV
Manifold Vacuum
Manifold Vacuum
A/CL BI MET
FPR
Throttle Body
A/CL DV
Manifold Vacuum
Fuel Tank
CPRV
Carbon Canister
FRONT OF VEHICLE
90B14986
Courtesy of Ford Motor Co.

Fig. 6: 4.0L V6 (See Index for Calibration Numbers)

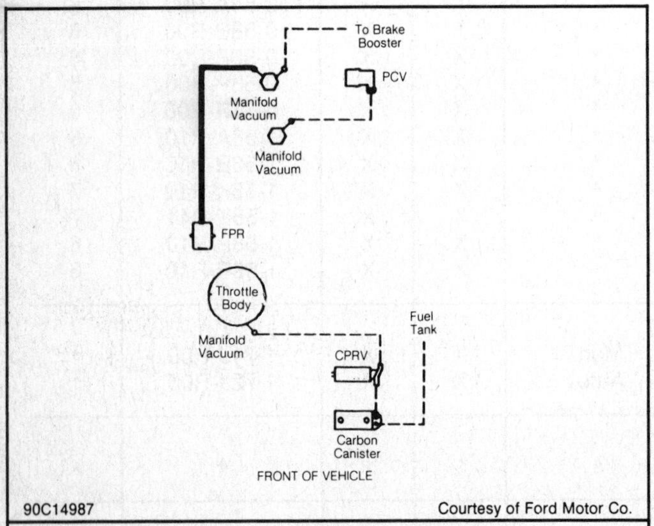
To Brake Booster
PCV
Manifold Vacuum
Manifold Vacuum
FPR
Throttle Body
Manifold Vacuum
Fuel Tank
CPRV
Carbon Canister
FRONT OF VEHICLE
90C14987
Courtesy of Ford Motor Co.

Fig. 7: 4.0L V6 (See Index for Calibration Numbers)

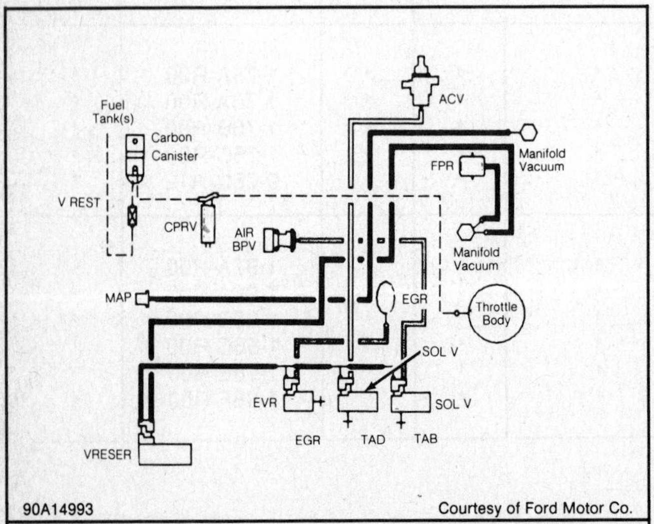
ACV
Fuel Tank(s)
Carbon Canister
Manifold Vacuum
FPR
V REST
CPRV
AIR BPV
Manifold Vacuum
MAP
EGR
Throttle Body
SOL V
EVR
SOL V
EGR
TAD
TAB
VRESER
90A14993
Courtesy of Ford Motor Co.

Fig. 8: 5.8L V8 (See Index for Calibration Numbers)

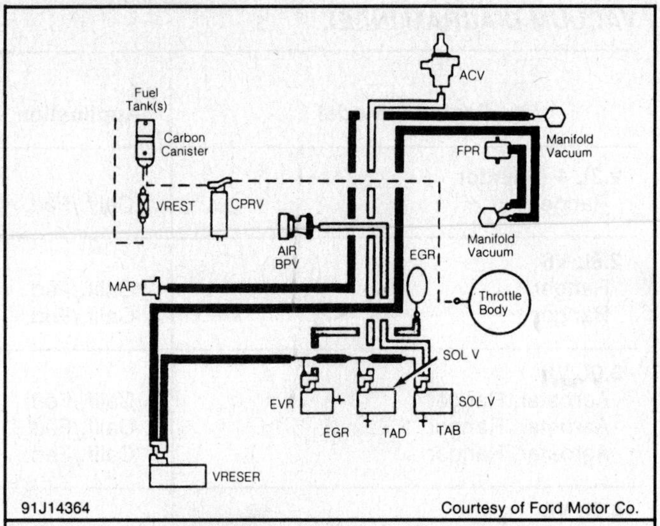
ACV
Fuel Tank(s)
Carbon Canister
Manifold Vacuum
FPR
VREST
CPRV
AIR BPV
Manifold Vacuum
EGR
MAP
Throttle Body
SOL V
EVR
SOL V
EGR
TAD
TAB
VRESER
91J14364
Courtesy of Ford Motor Co.

Fig. 9: 5.8L V8 (See Index for Calibration Numbers)

EMISSION CONTROL DEVICE ABBREVIATIONS

A/CL-BI MET – Air Cleaner Bi-Metallic Sensor
A/CL-DV – Air Cleaner Duct Valve
ACV – Air Control Valve
AIR-BPV – Air By-Pass Valve
AIS – Air Injection System
CAT – Catalytic Converter
CPRV – Canister Purge Regulator Valve
DIV – Diverter
EFCA – Electronic Fuel Control Assembly
EGR – Exhaust Gas Recirculation
EVR – Emission Vacuum Regulator
FPR – Fuel Pressure Regulator
MAP – Manifold Absolute Pressure
PCV – Positive Crankcase Ventilation
SOLV – Vacuum Solenoid Valve
SRV – AIS Solenoid Valve
TAB – Thermactor By-pass
TAD – Thermactor Diverter
TB – Throttle Body
VCK-V – Vacuum Check Valve
VRESER – Vacuum Reservoir
V-REST – Vacuum Restrictor

Aerostar, Bronco, Explorer, Ranger, "E" & "F" Series

NOTE: Unless specified otherwise, references to "F" Series include "F" Series Super Duty.

INTRODUCTION

Removal, overhaul and installation procedures are covered in this article. If component removal and installation is primarily an unbolt and bolt-on procedure, only a torque specification may be furnished.

IGNITION SYSTEM

DISTRIBUTOR

Removal & Installation - 1) Disconnect distributor from wiring harness. Mark position of No. 1 cylinder wire tower on distributor base for reference when installing distributor.

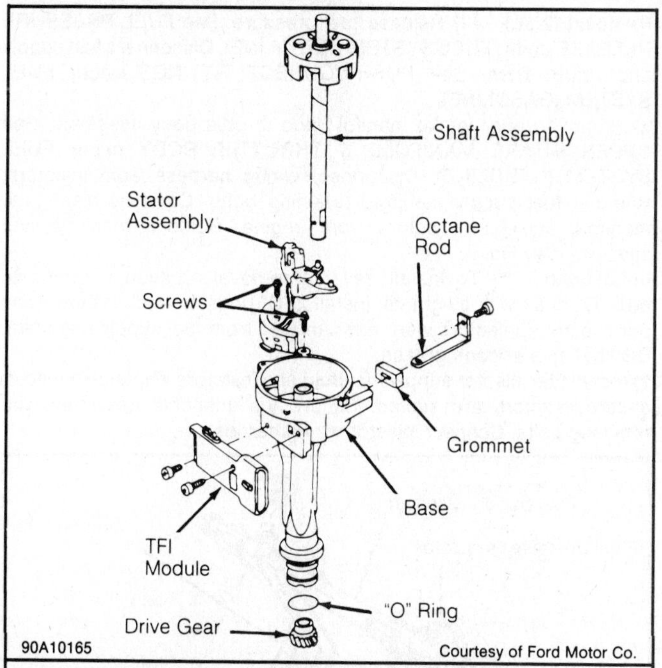
Shaft Assembly
Stator Assembly
Octane Rod
Screws
Grommet
Base
TFI Module
"O" Ring
Drive Gear
90A10165
Courtesy of Ford Motor Co.

Fig. 1: Exploded View of TFI-IV Open Bowl Distributor (2.9L, 4.9L, 5.0L & 5.8L)

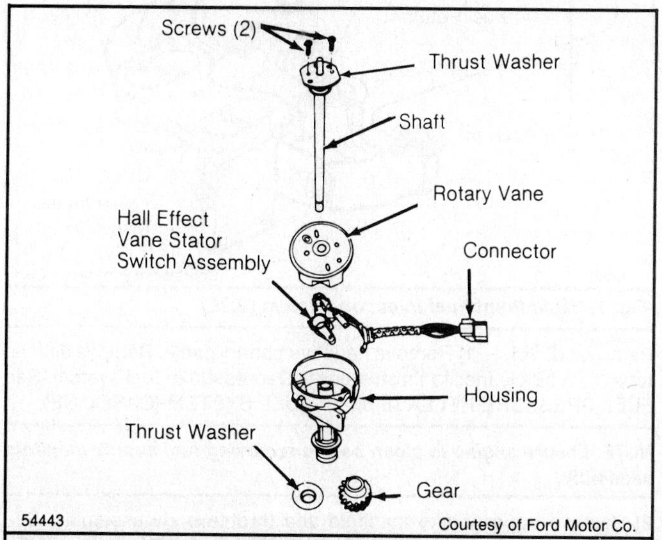
Screws (2)
Thrust Washer
Shaft
Rotary Vane
Hall Effect Vane Stator Switch Assembly
Connector
Housing
Thrust Washer
Gear
54443
Courtesy of Ford Motor Co.

Fig. 2: Exploded View of TFI-IV Open Bowl Distributor (3.0L & 7.5L)

2) Loosen distributor cap hold-down screws. Remove cap carefully to prevent damaging rotor blade and spring. Position cap and attached wires aside.

3) Remove rotor by pulling upward from the distributor shaft. Remove distributor hold-down bolt and clamp. Remove distributor. Cover distributor opening in cylinder block or head with clean shop towel. To install, reverse removal procedure.

CRANKSHAFT SENSOR

Removal (2.3L) - 1) Disconnect negative battery cable. Remove accessory belt(s). Remove crankshaft pulley, hub and belt guide. Remove timing belt outer cover retaining bolt. Release 8 cover interlocking tabs.

2) Remove timing belt cover. Disconnect crankshaft sensor wire connector from engine harness. Remove crankshaft sensor 4-wire connector by prying out on Red retaining clip. *See Fig. 3.*

CAUTION: Always turn engine in direction of normal rotation (clockwise as viewed from front of engine).

3) Rotate crankshaft and position crankshaft keyway at 10 o'clock position to place vane window of inner and outer vane cups over crankshaft timing sensor. Remove crankshaft sensor retaining bolts and plastic wire harness retainer. Remove crankshaft sensor.

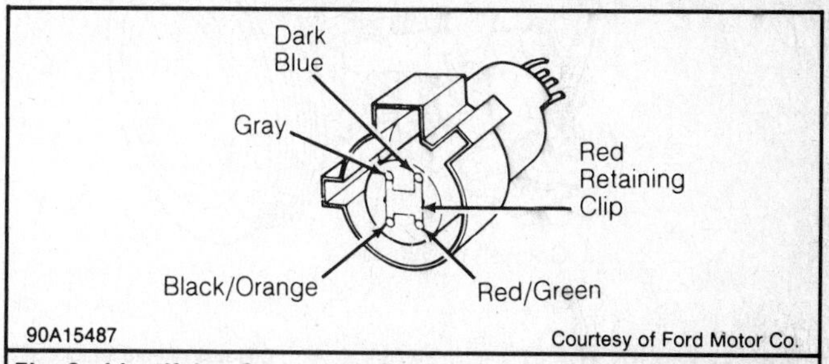
Dark Blue
Gray
Red Retaining Clip
Black/Orange
Red/Green
90A15487
Courtesy of Ford Motor Co.

Fig. 3: Identifying Crankshaft Sensor Connector Terminals

Installation - 1) Position crankshaft sensor wires behind inner timing belt cover. Hold crankshaft sensor in place and install bolts finger tight. DO NOT tighten. Reconnect wire connectors to engine harness.

2) With Crankshaft Sensor Positioner (T89P-6316-A) in place, rotate crankshaft until outer vane of crankshaft pulley hub assembly engages both sides of crankshaft sensor positioner. *See Fig. 4.* Tighten crankshaft sensor bolts.

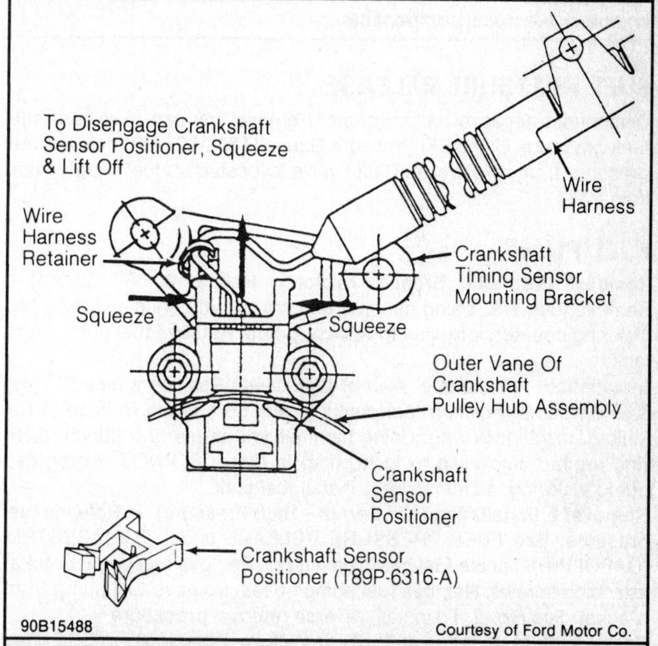
To Disengage Crankshaft Sensor Positioner, Squeeze & Lift Off
Wire Harness
Wire Harness Retainer
Crankshaft Timing Sensor Mounting Bracket
Squeeze
Squeeze
Outer Vane Of Crankshaft Pulley Hub Assembly
Crankshaft Sensor Positioner
Crankshaft Sensor Positioner (T89P-6316-A)
90B15488
Courtesy of Ford Motor Co.

Fig. 4: Positioning Crankshaft Sensor (2.3L)

1991 ENGINE PERFORMANCE
Removal, Overhaul & Installation (Cont.)

CAUTION: Always turn engine in direction of normal rotation (clockwise as viewed from front of engine).

3) Rotate crankshaft until vane on crankshaft pulley hub assembly is no longer engaged in crankshaft sensor positioner. Remove crankshaft sensor positioner. Install new plastic wire harness retainer and trim off excess.

4) Rotate crankshaft 90 degrees (1/4 turn) clockwise and measure outer vane-to-sensor air gap. Air gap must be .018-.039" (.46-1.0 mm). To complete installation, reverse removal procedure.

Removal (4.0L) – Disconnect negative battery cable. Disconnect crankshaft (variable reluctance) sensor wire connector from engine harness. Remove crankshaft sensor mounting screws. Remove crankshaft sensor. *See Fig. 5.*

Installation – Place crankshaft sensor in correct position. Install mounting screws and tighten. Reconnect crankshaft sensor wire connector.

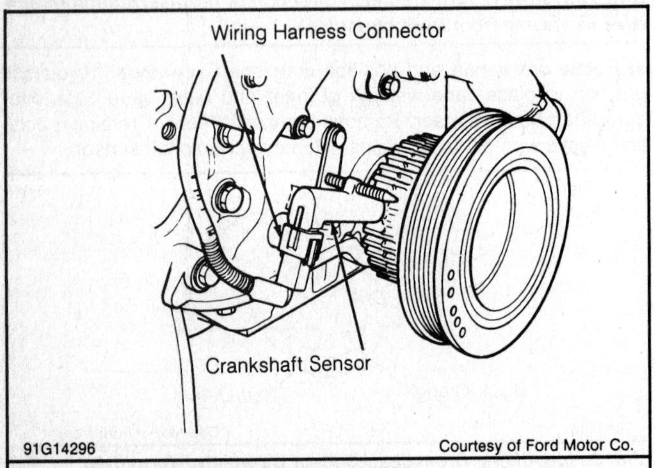
Wiring Harness Connector
Crankshaft Sensor
91G14296
Courtesy of Ford Motor Co.

Fig. 5: Locating Crankshaft Sensor (4.0L)

FUEL SYSTEM (GASOLINE)

FUEL SYSTEM PRESSURE RELEASE

WARNING: ALWAYS relieve fuel pressure before disconnecting any fuel injection-related component. DO NOT allow fuel to contact engine or electrical components.

FUEL PRESSURE RELEASE

Disconnect negative battery cable. Remove fuel cap to release fuel tank pressure. Using EFI Pressure Gauge (T80L-9974-B), release fuel pressure from relief valve. Relief valve is located on fuel supply manifold.

FUEL PUMP

Removal (Aerostar, Bronco, Explorer, Ranger & "F" Series) – Remove fuel tank. Using hammer and brass drift punch, carefully tap lock ring counterclockwise to release pump. Remove fuel pump from tank.

Installation – Wipe seal area of tank clean. Position a new "O" ring seal on pump. Position fuel pump in tank so fuel return hose is not kinked. Install lock ring. Using hammer and brass drift punch, drive ring around clockwise to lock pump in place. DO NOT overtighten pump lock ring, as it may leak. Install fuel tank.

Removal & Installation ("E" Series – High Pressure) – Release fuel pressure. See FUEL PRESSURE RELEASE under FUEL SYSTEM (GASOLINE). Locate fuel pump on left rail. Remove fuel pump bracket attaching screws. Remove fuel pump hoses. Remove fuel pump from bracket. *See Fig. 6.* To install, reverse removal procedure.

Removal & Installation ("E" Series – Low Pressure) – "E" Series low pressure (boost) fuel pump is located inside the fuel tank. Removal and installation procedures are the same as removal and installation procedures for Aerostar, Bronco, Explorer, Ranger, and "F" Series.

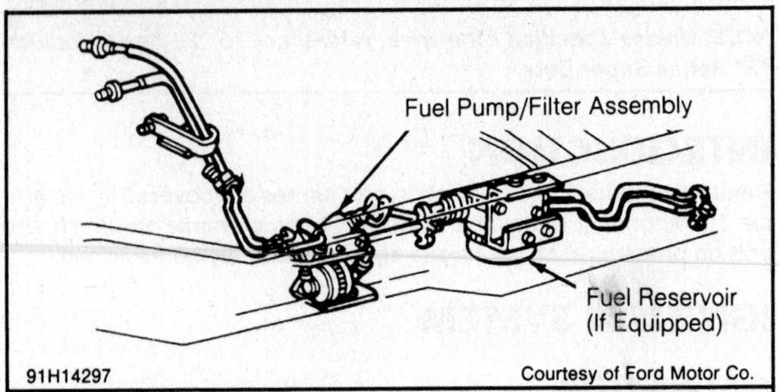
Fuel Pump/Filter Assembly
Fuel Reservoir
(If Equipped)
91H14297
Courtesy of Ford Motor Co.

Fig. 6: Locating High Pressure Fuel Pump ("E" Series)

FUEL SUPPLY MANIFOLD ASSEMBLY

Removal (2.3L) – **1)** Release fuel pressure. See FUEL PRESSURE RELEASE under FUEL SYSTEM (GASOLINE). Disconnect fuel supply and return lines. See PUSH-CONNECT FITTINGS under FUEL SYSTEM (GASOLINE).

2) Remove upper intake manifold and throttle body assembly. See UPPER INTAKE MANIFOLD & THROTTLE BODY under FUEL SYSTEM (GASOLINE). Disconnect wiring harness from injectors. Remove fuel supply manifold retaining bolts. Carefully disengage manifold and fuel injectors from engine. Remove manifold and injectors. *See Fig. 7.*

Installation – **1)** To install, reverse removal procedure. Lubricate new "O" rings with a light oil. Install 2 "O" rings on each injector (one per injector if injectors were not removed from fuel supply manifold). DO NOT use silicone grease.

2) Install fuel injector supply manifold and injectors in intake manifold; ensure injectors are seated. Secure fuel manifold assembly with retaining bolts. Connect injector wiring harness.

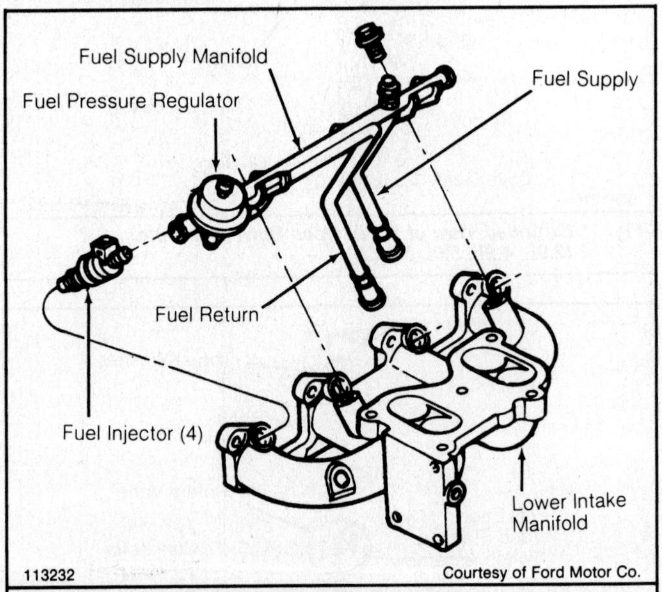
Fuel Supply Manifold
Fuel Supply
Fuel Pressure Regulator
Fuel Return
Fuel Injector (4)
Lower Intake
Manifold
113232
Courtesy of Ford Motor Co.

Fig. 7: Multi-Point Fuel Injection System (2.3L)

Removal (2.9L) – **1)** Remove negative battery cable. Remove air inlet tube from air cleaner to throttle body. Depressurize fuel system. See FUEL PRESSURE RELEASE under FUEL SYSTEM (GASOLINE).

NOTE: Ensure engine is clean before removing fuel supply manifold assembly.

2) Remove upper intake manifold and throttle body assembly. See UPPER INTAKE MANIFOLD & THROTTLE BODY under FUEL SYSTEM (GASOLINE). Disconnect crossover fuel hose, fuel supply, and fuel return line from fuel supply manifold. See PUSH-CONNECT FITTINGS under FUEL SYSTEM (GASOLINE).

3) Remove fuel supply manifold retaining bolts. Carefully remove fuel supply manifold from lower intake manifold. Remove fuel injector retainer clips, and inspect for corrosion and damage. Remove injector(s) from fuel supply manifold and wipe injector recesses clean with dry cloth.

Installation - 1) To install, clean injectors and injector recesses. Lightly grease recesses. Check "O" rings for correct seating. Install 3 injectors on right recess of intake manifold, then install 3 on left.

2) Position and press down firmly on fuel rail to ensure fuel injectors are fully seated in fuel rail and intake manifold. Install fasteners. To complete installation, reverse removal procedure. *See Fig. 8.*

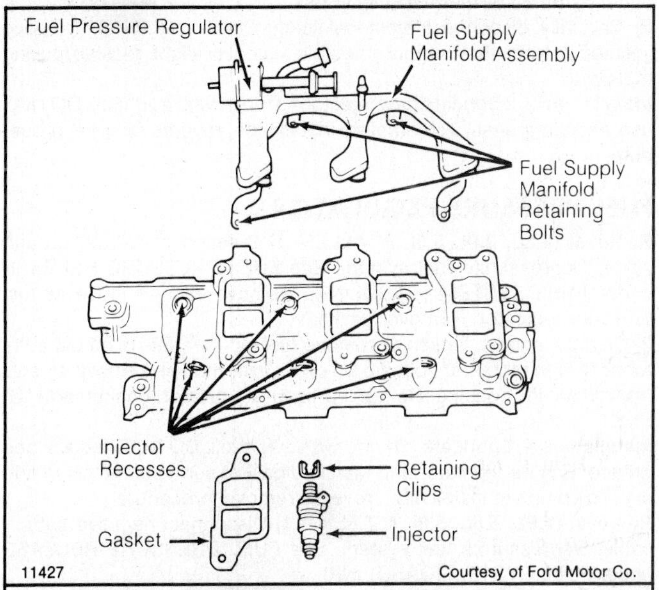
Fuel Pressure Regulator
Fuel Supply Manifold Assembly
Fuel Supply Manifold Retaining Bolts
Injector Recesses
Retaining Clips
Gasket
Injector
11427
Courtesy of Ford Motor Co.

Fig. 8: Multi-Point Fuel Injection System (2.9L)

Removal (3.0L) - 1) Depressurize fuel system. See FUEL PRESSURE RELEASE under FUEL SYSTEM (GASOLINE). Remove throttle body. Disconnect fuel supply and return lines. See PUSH-CONNECT FITTINGS under FUEL SYSTEM (GASOLINE).

2) Disconnect wiring harness at fuel injectors. *See Fig. 9.* Disconnect vacuum hose from fuel pressure regulator. Remove fuel assembly manifold bolts (2 on each side). Carefully disengage fuel supply manifold from fuel injectors by lifting and gently rocking rail.

3) Remove injectors from fuel supply manifold using a slight lifting/rocking motion. Place removed components in a clean container to avoid dirt or other contamination.

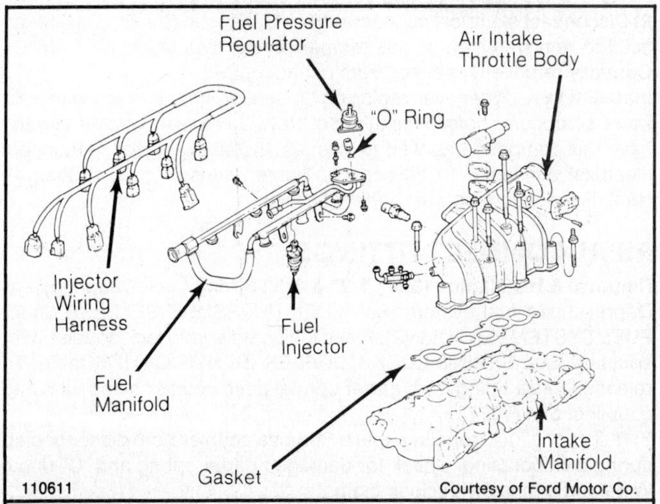
Fuel Pressure Regulator
Air Intake Throttle Body
"O" Ring
Injector Wiring Harness
Fuel Injector
Fuel Manifold
Intake Manifold
Gasket
110611
Courtesy of Ford Motor Co.

Fig. 9: Multi-Point Fuel Injection System (3.0L)

Installation - Lubricate new injector "O" rings with a light oil. DO NOT use silicone grease. Carefully install fuel supply manifold and injectors into lower manifold, one side at a time. To complete installation, reverse removal procedure.

Removal (4.0L) - 1) Disconnect battery ground cable. Remove snow/ice shield. Remove air inlet tube from air cleaner to throttle body. Depressurize fuel system. See FUEL PRESSURE RELEASE under FUEL SYSTEM (GASOLINE).

NOTE: Ensure engine is clean before removing fuel supply manifold assembly.

2) Remove upper intake manifold and throttle body assembly. See UPPER INTAKE MANIFOLD & THROTTLE BODY under FUEL SYSTEM (GASOLINE). Disconnect fuel supply line fitting at fuel manifold.

3) Disconnect fuel return line from fuel pressure regulator. See PUSH-CONNECT FITTINGS under FUEL SYSTEM (GASOLINE). Remove fuel manifold retaining bolts. Remove fuel manifold. Remove injectors from manifold.

Installation - Lubricate new injector "O" rings with a light oil. DO NOT use silicone grease. Carefully install fuel supply manifold and injectors into lower manifold, one side at a time. To complete installation, reverse removal procedure.

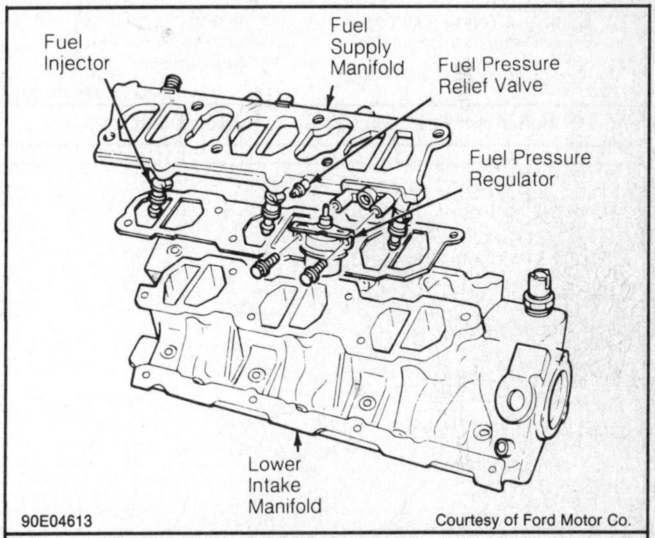
Fuel Injector
Fuel Supply Manifold
Fuel Pressure Relief Valve
Fuel Pressure Regulator
Lower Intake Manifold
90E04613
Courtesy of Ford Motor Co.

Fig. 10: Multi-Point Fuel Injection System (4.0L)

Removal & Installation (4.9L) - 1) Remove upper intake manifold assembly. See UPPER INTAKE MANIFOLD & THROTTLE BODY under FUEL SYSTEM (GASOLINE). Disconnect fuel supply and fuel return lines. See PUSH-CONNECT FITTINGS under FUEL SYSTEM (GASOLINE).

2) Disconnect vacuum hose from fuel pressure regulator. Remove strap surrounding fuel supply manifold, injector electrical harness, and main vacuum harness.

3) Remove fuel supply manifold retaining studs. Carefully disengage fuel supply manifold from fuel injectors, and remove manifold. To install, reverse removal procedure. Ensure injectors are well seated in manifold assembly.

Removal & Installation (5.0L, 5.8L & 7.5L) - 1) Disconnect battery ground cable. Depressurize fuel system. See FUEL PRESSURE RELEASE under FUEL SYSTEM (GASOLINE). Remove upper intake manifold and throttle body assembly. See UPPER INTAKE MANIFOLD & THROTTLE BODY under FUEL SYSTEM (GASOLINE).

2) Disconnect fuel supply and return line connections at fuel supply manifold. See PUSH-CONNECT FITTINGS under FUEL SYSTEM (GASOLINE). Remove fuel supply manifold retaining bolts. Carefully disengage fuel supply manifold from fuel injectors. To install, reverse removal procedure. *See Figs. 11 and 12.*

1991 ENGINE PERFORMANCE
Removal, Overhaul & Installation (Cont.)

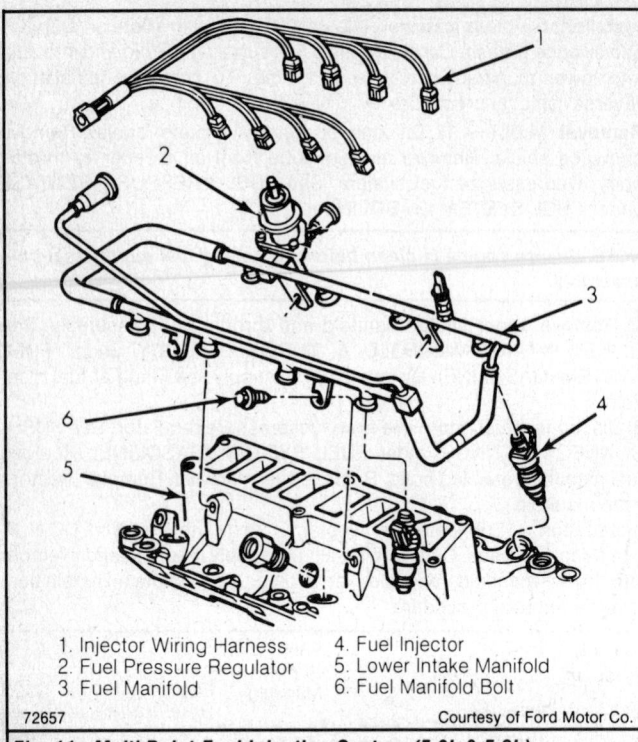

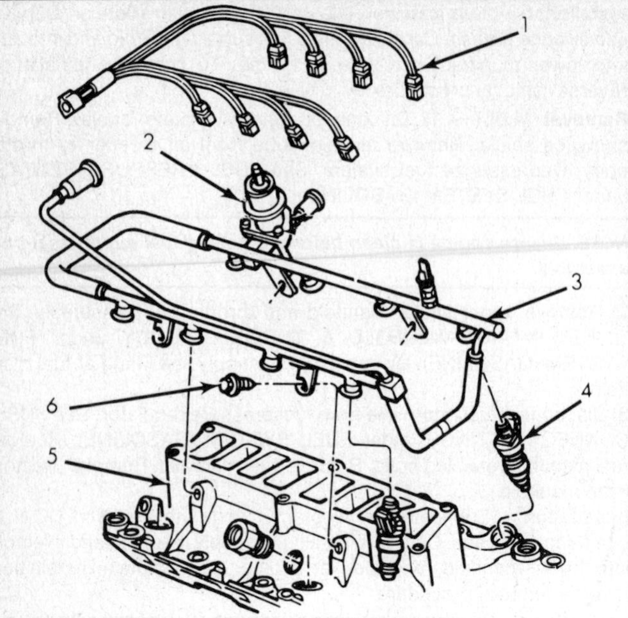
1
2
3
4
5
6
1. Injector Wiring Harness
2. Fuel Pressure Regulator
3. Fuel Manifold
4. Fuel Injector
5. Lower Intake Manifold
6. Fuel Manifold Bolt
72657
Courtesy of Ford Motor Co.

Fig. 11: Multi-Point Fuel Injection System (5.0L & 5.8L)

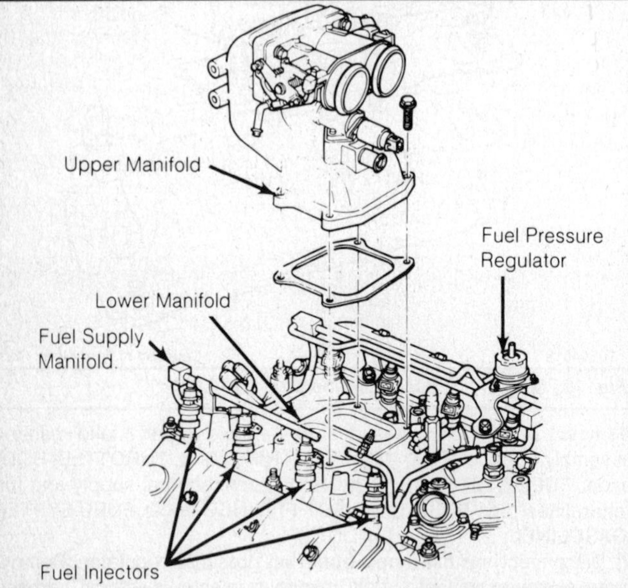
Upper Manifold
Fuel Pressure Regulator
Lower Manifold
Fuel Supply Manifold.
Fuel Injectors
72658
Courtesy of Ford Motor Co.

Fig. 12: Multi-Point Fuel Injection System (7.5L)

FUEL INJECTORS

Removal (2.3L & 3.0L) - 1) Depressurize fuel system. See FUEL PRESSURE RELEASE under FUEL SYSTEM (GASOLINE). Disconnect wiring harness from each injector.

2) Remove fuel supply manifold. See FUEL SUPPLY MANIFOLD ASSEMBLY under FUEL SYSTEM (GASOLINE). Remove injectors from fuel supply manifold using a rocking/pulling motion.

Installation - Lubricate new injector "O" rings with a light oil. DO NOT use silicone grease. To complete installation, reverse removal procedure.

Removal (2.9L & 4.0L) - 1) Depressurize fuel system. See FUEL PRESSURE RELEASE under FUEL SYSTEM (GASOLINE). Remove upper intake manifold and throttle body assembly. See UPPER INTAKE MANIFOLD & THROTTLE BODY under FUEL SYSTEM (GASOLINE).

2) Remove fuel supply manifold. See FUEL SUPPLY MANIFOLD ASSEMBLY under FUEL SYSTEM (GASOLINE). Remove wiring harness from injector(s). Remove injector retaining clips(s). Remove injectors from fuel supply manifold using a rocking/pulling motion.

Installation - Lubricate new injector "O" rings with a light oil. DO NOT use silicone grease. To complete installation, reverse removal procedure.

Removal (4.9L, 5.0L, 5.8L & 7.5L) - 1) Disconnect negative battery cable. Depressurize fuel system. See FUEL PRESSURE RELEASE under FUEL SYSTEM (GASOLINE). Remove upper intake manifold assembly. See UPPER INTAKE MANIFOLD & THROTTLE BODY under FUEL SYSTEM (GASOLINE).

2) Carefully disconnect electrical lead(s) from injector(s). Remove injector(s) from fuel supply manifold using a slight rocking/pulling motion.

Installation - Lubricate new injector "O" rings with a light oil. DO NOT use silicone grease. To complete installation, reverse removal procedure.

FUEL PRESSURE REGULATOR

Removal (2.3L, 2.9L 3.0L & 4.0L) - 1) Disconnect battery ground cable. Depressurize fuel system. See FUEL PRESSURE RELEASE under FUEL SYSTEM (GASOLINE). Remove vacuum hose at fuel pressure regulator. Remove fuel line.

2) On 3.0L models, loosen or remove fuel rail-to-intake manifold bolts for access to regulator housing screws. On all models, remove screws from regulator housing. Remove pressure regulator, gasket, and "O" ring.

Installation - Lubricate "O" ring with a light oil. DO NOT use silicone grease. Ensure regulator and manifold gasket surfaces are clean and dry. To complete installation, reverse removal procedure.

Removal (4.9L, 5.0L, 5.8L & 7.5L) - 1) Disconnect negative battery cable. Depressurize fuel system. See FUEL PRESSURE RELEASE under FUEL SYSTEM (GASOLINE).

2) Remove vacuum hose from fuel pressure regulator. Remove Allen head screws from fuel pressure regulator housing. Remove fuel pressure regulator, gasket, and "O" ring.

Installation - Lubricate "O" ring with a light oil. DO NOT use silicone grease. Ensure regulator and manifold gasket surfaces are clean and dry. To complete installation, reverse removal procedure.

HEATED EXHAUST GAS OXYGEN (HEGO) SENSOR

Removal - 1) Disconnect negative battery terminal. locate O_2 sensor mounted in the exhaust pipe below exhaust manifold or "Y" pipe junction, near catalytic converter inlet. Ensure sensor is free of contaminants. DO NOT use cleaning solvents of any type.

2) Disconnect electrical connector from O_2 sensor. Sensor may be difficult to remove when engine temperature is less than 120°F (48°C). Carefully remove O_2 sensor from exhaust pipe.

Installation - Whenever replacing O_2 sensor, coat threads with anti-seize compound before installation. New O_2 sensors should already have this compound applied to threads. Install O_2 sensor. Reconnect electrical connector to O_2 sensor. Tighten sensor to 30 ft. lbs. (41 N.m). Reconnect negative battery terminal.

PUSH-CONNECT FITTINGS

Removal & Installation (3/8", 1/2" & 5/8" Spring Lock Coupling) -1) Depressurize fuel system. See FUEL PRESSURE RELEASE under FUEL SYSTEM (GASOLINE). Place indicated spring lock coupler over coupling. See SPRING LOCK COUPLER IDENTIFICATION table. To release female fitting from garter spring, push coupler along tube into coupling. *See Fig. 13.*

2) Pull spring lock coupling apart. Remove coupler from disconnected spring lock coupling. Check for damaged garter spring and "O" rings. Wipe end of lines with clean cloth.

3) To install, place new "O" rings onto tube. Lubricate ends of lines with clean refrigerant oil. Locate White indicator ring (if equipped) which may have slipped down length of tube. Insert White indicator ring into cage of male fitting.
4) Push fitting together with a slight twisting motion. The White indicator ring should pop free of cage to indicate that male fitting is properly seated over flared end of female fitting.

SPRING LOCK COUPLER IDENTIFICATION

Application	Tool Number
3/8" Line	D87L-9280-A
1/2" Line	D87L-9280-B
5/8" Line	T83P-19623-C

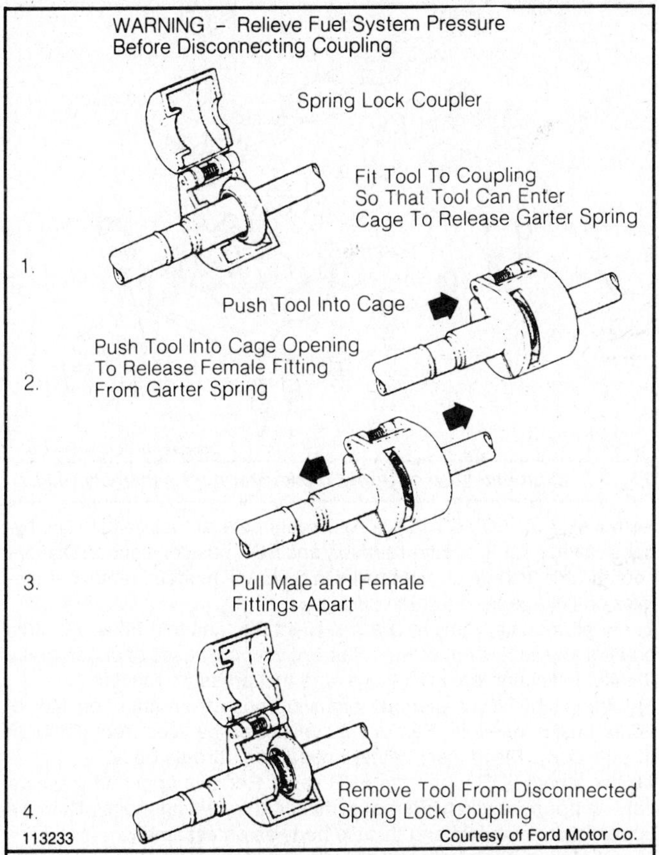
WARNING - Relieve Fuel System Pressure Before Disconnecting Coupling
Spring Lock Coupler
Fit Tool To Coupling So That Tool Can Enter Cage To Release Garter Spring
1.
Push Tool Into Cage
Push Tool Into Cage Opening To Release Female Fitting From Garter Spring
2.
3.
Pull Male and Female Fittings Apart
Remove Tool From Disconnected Spring Lock Coupling
4.
113233
Courtesy of Ford Motor Co.

Fig. 13: Disconnecting Fuel Lines with Spring Lock Coupler

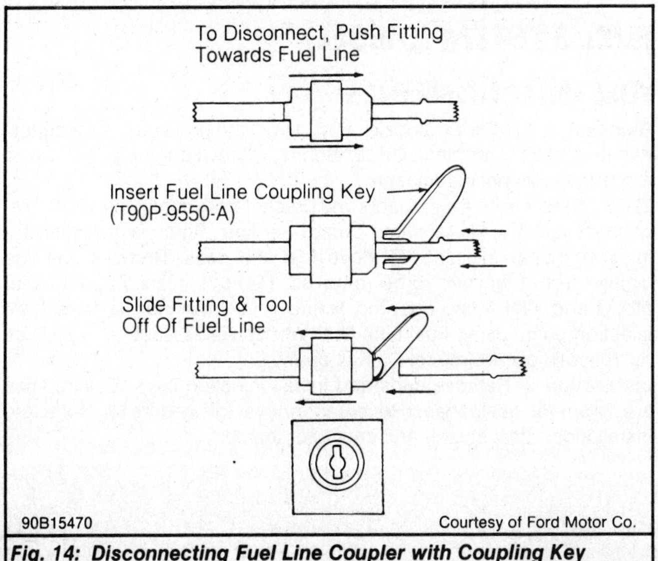
To Disconnect, Push Fitting Towards Fuel Line
Insert Fuel Line Coupling Key (T90P-9550-A)
Slide Fitting & Tool Off Of Fuel Line
90B15470
Courtesy of Ford Motor Co.

Fig. 14: Disconnecting Fuel Line Coupler with Coupling Key

Removal & Installation (Fuel Line Coupler) - Disengage locking tabs on connector retainer and separate retainer halves. Disengage fitting from regulator by pushing fitting toward regulator and inserting Fuel Line Coupling Key (T90P-9550-A). *See Fig. 14.* Remove fuel supply manifold assembly. See FUEL SUPPLY MANIFOLD ASSEMBLY under FUEL SYSTEM (GASOLINE).

UPPER INTAKE MANIFOLD & THROTTLE BODY

Removal (2.3L) - 1) Remove throttle linkage shield. Disconnect throttle linkage, cruise control and kickdown cable. Unbolt accelerator cable and position aside. Disconnect wire connectors from throttle position sensor and air by-pass valve.
2) Disconnect air intake hose from throttle body. Remove air intake and PCV hoses from throttle body. Disconnect water by-pass hose. Disconnect EGR tube by removing flange nut. Remove 5 upper intake manifold retaining bolts. Remove intake manifold and throttle body assembly.
Installation - Clean gasket surfaces. DO NOT allow gasket material to fall into intake manifold. Reverse removal procedure to complete installation.
Removal (2.9L) - 1) Disconnect electrical connectors at air by-pass valve, throttle position sensor, EGR sensor and Air Charge Temperature (ACT) sensor. Remove air cleaner-to-throttle body air inlet tube.
2) Remove snow/ice shield to expose throttle linkage. Disconnect throttle cable from ball stud. Disconnect upper intake manifold vacuum connectors, both front and rear fittings including EGR valve, and vacuum line to fuel pressure regulator.
3) Disconnect PCV closure tube from under throttle body. Disconnect PCV vacuum tube from under manifold. Remove canister purge line from fitting near power steering pump. Disconnect EGR tube from EGR valve by removing flange nut.
4) Loosen bolt retaining A/C line at upper rear of upper manifold. Disengage retainer. Remove 6 upper intake manifold retaining bolts. Remove upper intake manifold and throttle body as an assembly.
Installation - Clean and inspect mounting faces of lower and upper intake manifolds. Install the upper intake manifold and throttle body assembly to the lower manifold. To complete installation, reverse removal procedure.

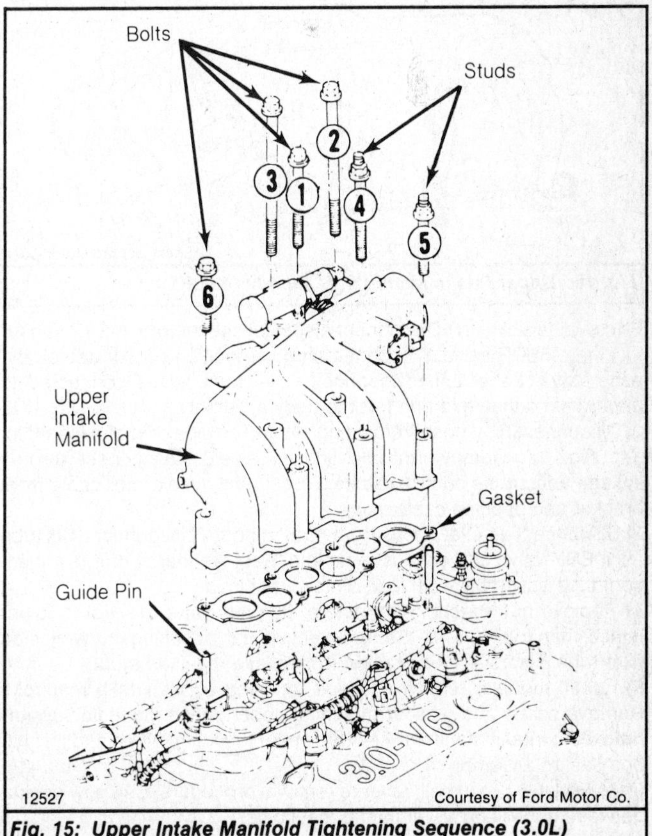
Bolts
Studs
1
2
3
4
5
6
Upper Intake Manifold
Gasket
Guide Pin
3.0-V6
12527
Courtesy of Ford Motor Co.

Fig. 15: Upper Intake Manifold Tightening Sequence (3.0L)

1991 ENGINE PERFORMANCE
Removal, Overhaul & Installation (Cont.)

Removal (3.0L) – 1) Ensure ignition switch is in OFF position. Loosen clamps and remove engine air outlet tube between air cleaner and throttle body. Remove snow/ice shield to expose throttle linkage.
2) Remove throttle cable bracket, and disconnect cable from ball stud on throttle body. Disconnect and mark vacuum hoses at vacuum fittings on intake manifold.
3) Remove accelerator and cruise control cables from accelerator mounting bracket and throttle lever. Remove alternator support brace. Disconnect wiring harness at throttle position sensor, air by-pass valve, and air charge temperature sensor.
4) Remove 4 retaining bolts and 2 stud bolts. Lift air intake throttle body assembly from guide pins on lower intake assembly. Remove and discard gasket from lower intake manifold assembly. *See Fig. 15.*
Installation – Clean and oil manifold bolt threads. Install new manifold gasket. If injectors were removed, lubricate new injector "O" rings with a light oil. DO NOT use silicone grease. To complete installation, reverse removal procedure.

Removal (4.0L) – 1) Disconnect electrical connectors at air by-pass valve, throttle position sensor and air charge temperature sensor. Remove snow/ice shield to expose throttle linkage. Remove throttle cable bracket.
2) Disconnect cable from ball stud on throttle body. Remove air cleaner-to-throttle body air inlet tube. Disconnect upper intake manifold vacuum connectors. Disconnect PCV valve from rocker cover.
3) Disconnect spark plug wires at rear of manifold. Remove canister purge line from fitting in throttle housing. On Aerostar, remove bolt retaining engine oil dipstick tube.
4) On all models, remove A/C line-to-upper upper manifold bolt. Remove 6 upper manifold retaining bolts. Remove upper intake and throttle body, as an assembly, from lower intake and fuel supply manifolds. *See Fig. 16.*
Installation – Clean and oil manifold bolt threads. Install new manifold gasket. If injectors were removed, lubricate new injector "O" rings with a light oil. DO NOT use silicone grease. To complete installation, reverse removal procedure.

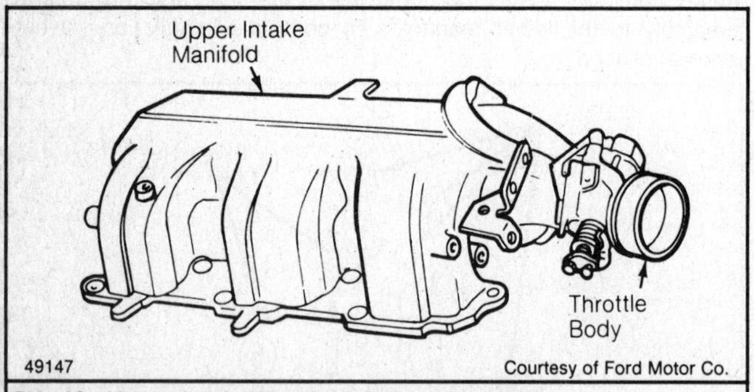
Upper Intake
Manifold
Throttle
Body
49147
Courtesy of Ford Motor Co.

Fig. 16: Upper Intake Manifold Assembly (4.0L)

Removal (4.9L) – 1) Disconnect electrical connectors at EVP sensor located on EGR valve. Disconnect throttle position sensor and air bypass valve. Label and disconnect all vacuum hoses connected to upper intake manifold and throttle body assembly.
2) Disconnect PCV hose from fitting located on side of intake manifold. *See Fig. 17.* Remove throttle linkage shield. Disconnect throttle linkage and cruise control cables. Disconnect accelerator cable from bracket and position cable aside.
3) Disconnect air inlet hoses from throttle body. Disconnect EGR tube from EGR valve and exhaust manifold. Remove thermactor (air injection) tube assembly from lower intake manifold.
4) Remove nut attaching thermactor by-pass valve bracket to lower intake manifold. On "E" Series, remove nut attaching transmission filler tube. Remove tube bracket from intake manifold stud.
5) On all models, remove 7 studs retaining upper intake manifold. Remove screw and washer attaching upper intake manifold support bracket to intake manifold. Remove upper intake manifold and throttle body as an assembly.
Installation – To install, reverse removal procedure. Use new gasket between upper and lower intake manifolds.

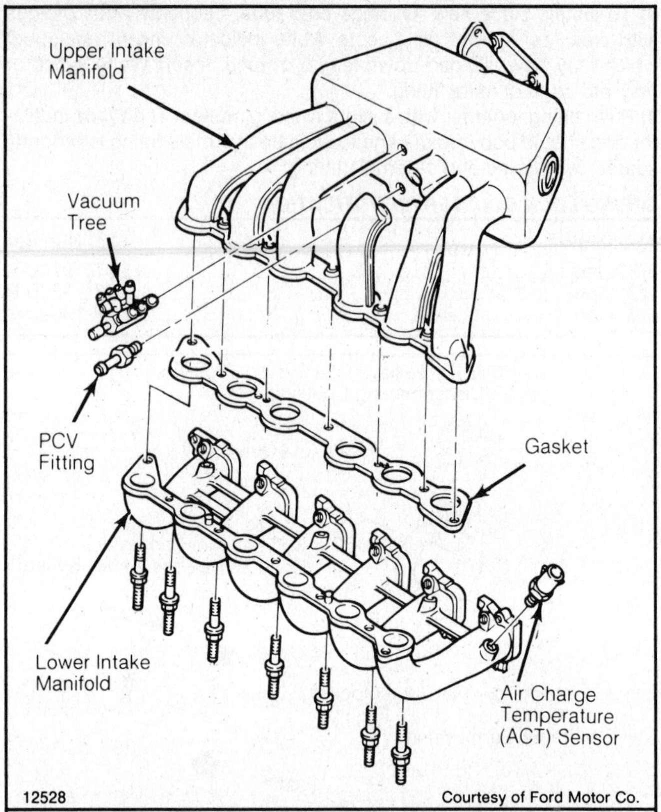
Upper Intake
Manifold
Vacuum
Tree
PCV
Fitting
Gasket
Lower Intake
Manifold
Air Charge
Temperature
(ACT) Sensor
12528
Courtesy of Ford Motor Co.

Fig. 17: Exploded View of Upper Intake Manifold Assembly (4.9L)

Removal (5.0L, 5.8L & 7.5L) – 1) Disconnect electrical leads at air bypass valve, throttle position sensor, and EGR position sensor. Disconnect throttle linkage at pivot ball. On 5.0L A/T models, remove transmission linkage from throttle body.
2) On all models, remove bracket-to-intake manifold bolts. Position bracket and cables out of way. Remove vacuum hoses at upper intake manifold vacuum tee, EGR valve, and fuel pressure regulator.
3) Disconnect PCV system by removing hose from fitting on rear of upper intake manifold. Remove 2 canister purge lines from fitting on throttle body. Disconnect heater hoses from throttle body.
4) Disconnect EGR tube from EGR valve. Remove upper intake manifold support bracket. Remove manifold retaining bolts. Remove upper intake manifold and throttle body as an assembly.
Installation – To install, reverse removal procedure. Use new gasket between upper and lower intake manifolds.

FUEL SYSTEM (DIESEL)

FUEL INJECTION LINES

Removal – 1) Clean nozzle and surrounding area. Disconnect negative battery terminal. On "E" Series, remove engine cover. On all models, disconnect air cleaner.
2) Disconnect accelerator cable and bracket from intake manifold. Disconnect fuel filter-to-injection pump fuel line. Remove fuel filter-to-injection pump fuel line. Remove fuel line caps. Remove fuel line clamps from fuel lines to be removed. Remove injection pump inlet elbow and inlet fitting adaptor. Remove injection nozzle lines from injection pump using Fuel Line Nut Wrench (T83T-9396-A). Tag lines for reassembly reference. Cap all openings.
Installation – Remove caps and install injection lines. Ensure lines are properly positioned. Reverse removal procedure to complete installation. Start engine and check for leaks.

FUEL PUMP

Removal & Installation (7.3L Diesel) - 1) Loosen but DO NOT remove fuel lines and fuel pump retaining bolts. Fuel pump should be loose. If fuel pump is not loose, apply hand pressure to break gasket seal.
2) Rotate engine until fuel pump is loose. Remove fuel lines and fuel pump retaining bolts. Remove fuel pump and gasket. To install, reverse removal procedure.

INJECTION PUMP

CAUTION: Fuel system contamination will damage finely machined parts within injection pump and injector nozzles. Clean fittings with fuel oil or solvent and blow dry with compressed air before disconnecting fuel lines. Cap all open fittings. Injection pump can be severely damaged if engine is washed or steam cleaned while engine is hot or running.

Removal - 1) Disconnect ground cables from both batteries. On "E" Series, remove engine cover. On all models, remove air cleaner. Cover intake opening in manifold. Remove injection pump drive gear cover plate. Ensure timing marks are aligned.
2) Rotate crankshaft until No. 1 piston is at TDC of compression stroke. Remove injection pump-to-drive gear bolts. Disconnect electrical connectors at injection pump. Remove fast idle solenoid bracket assembly for access to injection pump mounting nuts.
3) Disconnect accelerator cable and speed control cable from throttle lever. Remove accelerator cable bracket and cables. If necessary, remove fuel filter and bracket. Disconnect 90-degree fuel return hose elbow at governor on injection pump.

NOTE: Unless pump is being replaced or serviced, DO NOT disconnect injection lines from pump when removing pump from engine. Reference mark lines-to-pump position before disconnecting.

4) If removing injection pump with injection lines connected to pump, disconnect lines at injector nozzles. If removing injection pump without lines connected to pump, remove line retaining clips.
5) Disconnect lines from pump using Fuel Line Nut Wrench (T83T-9396-A). Remove injection lines in the following sequence: 5-6-4-8-3-1-7-2. Odd number cylinders are on right bank, with No. 1 cylinder closest to front of engine.

CAUTION: Ensure No. 1 piston is at TDC of compression stroke before removing injector pump. Pulley "Y" marks should be aligned.

6) On all applications, remove 3 injection pump-to-injection pump drive gear cover nuts using Injection Pump Mounting Wrench (T86T-9000-C). On "F" Series, lift injection pump (or pump with lines connected) out of engine compartment. On "E" Series, remove injection pump (or pump with lines attached) through passenger compartment.
Installation - 1) Install new "O" ring on injection pump drive gear end. Install pump into position, aligning dowel on pump drive shaft with hole in drive gear. If necessary, rotate pump drive shaft to align dowel with hole.
2) Install and hand tighten 3 injection pump-to-drive gear cover nuts. Align timing mark on top radius of injection pump with mark on injection pump drive gear cover. To complete installation, reverse removal procedure.

THROTTLE POSITION SENSOR (TPS)

NOTE: On 7.3L engines, a Fuel Injection Pump Lever (FIPL) sensor is used instead of a TPS. For FIPL service procedures, see ON-VEHICLE ADJUSTMENTS article.

Removal (2.3L, 2.9L, 3.0L, 4.0L & 4.9L) - Remove air by-pass valve (if necessary). Disconnect TPS wiring harness connector. Remove TPS retaining screws. Remove TPS and gasket.
Installation - Position TPS and gasket on throttle body, with tangs correctly aligned with throttle shaft blade. Reverse removal procedure to complete installation.

NOTE: Slide tangs into position over throttle shaft blade, then rotate TPS, CLOCKWISE only, to installed position. Failure to do so may cause excessive idle speeds.

Removal (5.0L, 5.8L & 7.5L) - Disconnect TPS wiring harness connector. Scribe a reference line across TPS and throttle body. Remove TPS retaining screws. Remove TPS and gasket.
Installation - Position TPS and gasket on throttle body, with wiring harness connector parallel to venturi boxes. Rotate TPS clockwise to align scribe marks. Reverse removal procedure to complete installation.

TORQUE SPECIFICATIONS

TORQUE SPECIFICATIONS

Application	Ft. Lbs. (N.m)
Fuel Supply Manifold Bolts	
2.3L	15-22 (20-30)
3.0L & 4.0L	7-10 (10-14)
4.9L & 5.0L	12-15 (16-20)
Lower Intake Manifold Bolts	
Except 2.3L & 7.5L	15-22 (20-30)
2.9L	11-15 (15-20)
3.0L	24 (32)
4.0L	15-18 (20-25)
4.9L, 5.0L & 5.8L	22-32 (30-43)
Throttle Body-To-Manifold	
2.3L	12-18 (16-24)
2.9L, 3.0L & 4.0L	6-9 (8-12)
4.9L, 5.0L, 5.8L & 7.5L	12-18 (16-24)
Upper Intake Manifold Bolts	
Except 2.3L & 3.0L	15-22 (20-30)
2.9L	11-15 (15-20)
4.0L	15-18 (20-25)
4.9L, 5.0L, 5.8L & 7.5	12-18 (16-24)
	INCH Lbs. (N.m)
Crankshaft Sensor	
2.3L	22-31 (2.5-3.5)
4.0L	75-106 (9-12)
Fuel Pressure Regulator	
Except 2.9L & 4.0L	26-40 (3-4.5)
2.9L & 4.0L	72-96 (8-11)
Fuel Supply Manifold Bolts	
2.9L & 3.0L	72-84 (8-11)
Pressure Relief Valve Cap	4-6 (.5-.7)
Thermostat Housing Bolts	72-96 (8-11)
Throttle Position Sensor Screws	
2.3L & 2.9L	25-33 (2.8-3.8)
3.0L	15 (1.5)
4.0L	11-16 (1.2-2.8)
4.9L, 5.0L & 5.8L	18-27 (2.0-3.0)

1991 ELECTRICAL
Alternators – With Internal Regulator

Aerostar, Bronco, Ranger, "E" & "F" Series, "F" Series Super Duty

NOTE: Unless otherwise specified, references to "F" Series include "F" Series Super Duty.

DESCRIPTION

The Motorcraft Integral Alternator/Regulator (IAR) uses a solid-state voltage regulator mounted to the rear housing. The charging system consists of an alternator/regulator assembly, charge indicator (light or gauge), battery and required circuitry. Charging systems are equipped with a fusible link, used to prevent system damage. Some models are equipped with indicator lights while others use voltmeters.

When the ignition is turned on, voltage is applied through the charge indicator "I" circuit to the voltage regulator. The voltage regulator is activated and allows current flow from the battery to the alternator through circuit "A". When the engine is started, the rotation of the alternator creates AC current which passes through the rectifier assembly and is converted to DC current. DC current is supplied to the vehicle's electrical system by the output terminal located on the rear housing.

ADJUSTMENTS

BELT TENSION

Inspect belt for fraying and proper routing. *See Figs. 2-9.* If fraying has occurred, ensure belt and tensioner are aligned properly. If tensioner has reached its limit of travel, belt is excessively stretched and replacement of belt is required. Check belt tension at position shown in figures. *See Figs. 2-9.* On engines with belts requiring manual adjustment, adjust tension to specification. See ALTERNATOR BELT ADJUSTMENT SPECIFICATIONS table.

ALTERNATOR BELT ADJUSTMENT SPECIFICATIONS

Application	New Belt Lbs. (kg)	[1] Used Belt Lbs. (kg)
2.3L		
Fixed	150-190 (68-86)	140-160 (64-73)
With Tensioner [2]	150-190 (68-86)	140-160 (64-73)
2.9L	120-160 (54-73)	110-130 (50-59)
3.0L		
Fixed	120-160 (54-73)	110-130 (50-59)
With Tensioner [2]	150-190 (68-86)	140-160 (64-73)
4.0L With Tensioner [2]	108-132 (49-60)	108-132 (49-60)
4.9L With Tensioner [2]	[3] [4]	[3] [4]
5.0L With Tensioner [2]	[5] [6]	[5] [6]
5.8L With Tensioner [2]	[5] [6]	[5] [6]
7.3L With 1/2" Belt	140-180 (64-82)	95-115 (43-52)
7.3L Ambulance	140-160 (64-73)	140-160 (64-73)
7.5L	160-200 (73-91)	110-130 (50-59)

[1] – Any belt operated for 10 minutes.
[2] – Tension is correct if tensioner is within indicator marks.
[3] – 90 lbs. (41 kg) minimum for vehicles with 60 and 75-amp alternators.
[4] – 117 lbs. (53 kg) minimum for vehicles with 100-amp alternators.
[5] – 77 lbs. (35 kg) minimum for vehicles with 60 and 75-amp alternators.
[6] – 111 lbs. (50 kg) minimum for vehicles with 100-amp alternators.

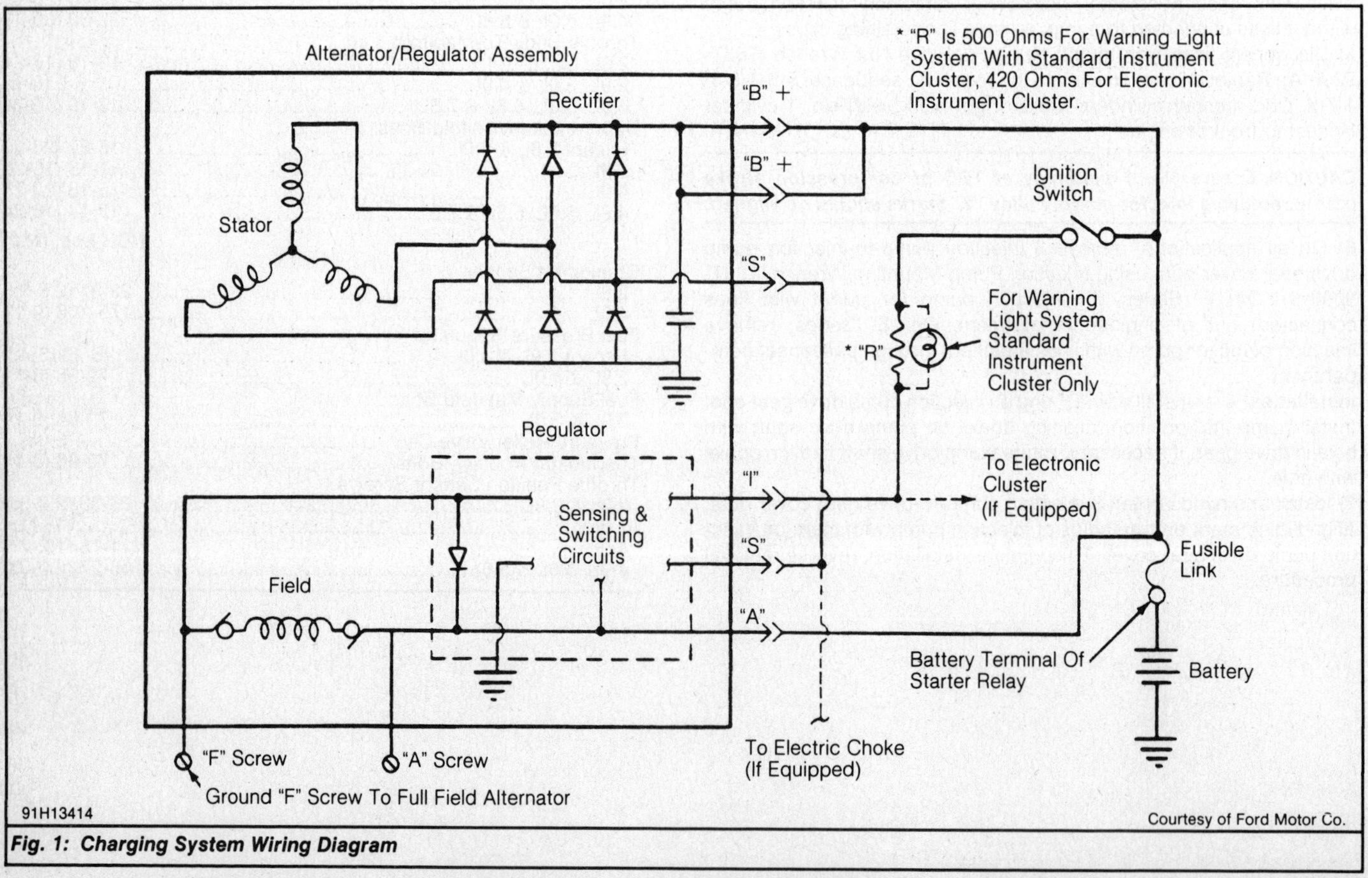
Alternator/Regulator Assembly
Rectifier
Stator
"B" +
"B" +
"S"
* "R" Is 500 Ohms For Warning Light System With Standard Instrument Cluster, 420 Ohms For Electronic Instrument Cluster.
Ignition Switch
For Warning Light System Standard Instrument Cluster Only
* "R"
Regulator
Sensing & Switching Circuits
Field
"I"
"S"
"A"
To Electronic Cluster (If Equipped)
Fusible Link
Battery Terminal Of Starter Relay
Battery
To Electric Choke (If Equipped)
"F" Screw
"A" Screw
Ground "F" Screw To Full Field Alternator
91H13414
Courtesy of Ford Motor Co.

Fig. 1: Charging System Wiring Diagram

1991 ELECTRICAL
Alternators – With Internal Regulator (Cont.)

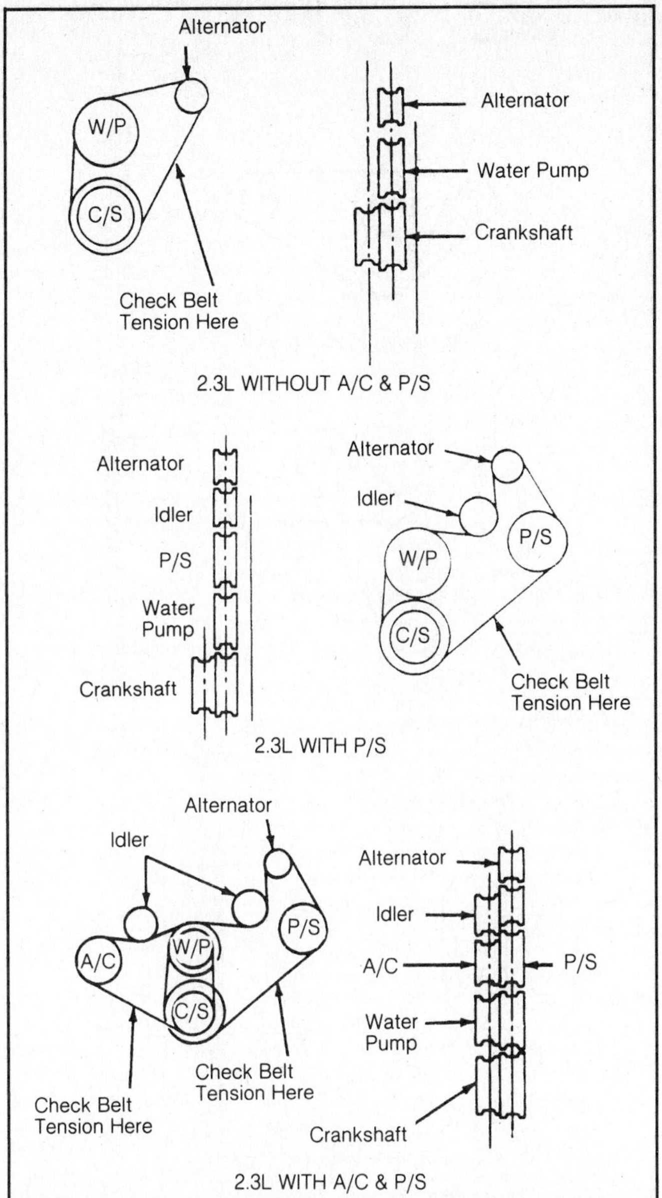
Alternator
W/P
C/S
Check Belt
Tension Here
Alternator
Water Pump
Crankshaft
2.3L WITHOUT A/C & P/S
Alternator
Idler
P/S
Water
Pump
Crankshaft
Alternator
Idler
P/S
W/P
C/S
Check Belt
Tension Here
2.3L WITH P/S
Alternator
Idler
A/C
W/P
C/S
P/S
Check Belt
Tension Here
Check Belt
Tension Here
Alternator
Idler
A/C
P/S
Water
Pump
Crankshaft
2.3L WITH A/C & P/S

91I13415 Courtesy of Ford Motor Co.

Fig. 2: Checking Belt Tension (2.3L)

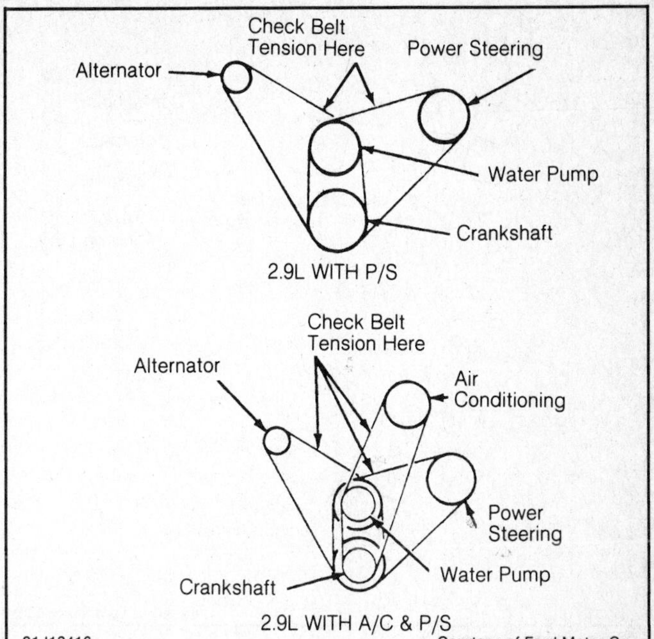
Alternator
Check Belt
Tension Here
Power Steering
Water Pump
Crankshaft
2.9L WITH P/S
Check Belt
Tension Here
Alternator
Air
Conditioning
Power
Steering
Water Pump
Crankshaft
2.9L WITH A/C & P/S

91J13416 Courtesy of Ford Motor Co.

Fig. 3: Checking Belt Tension (2.9L)

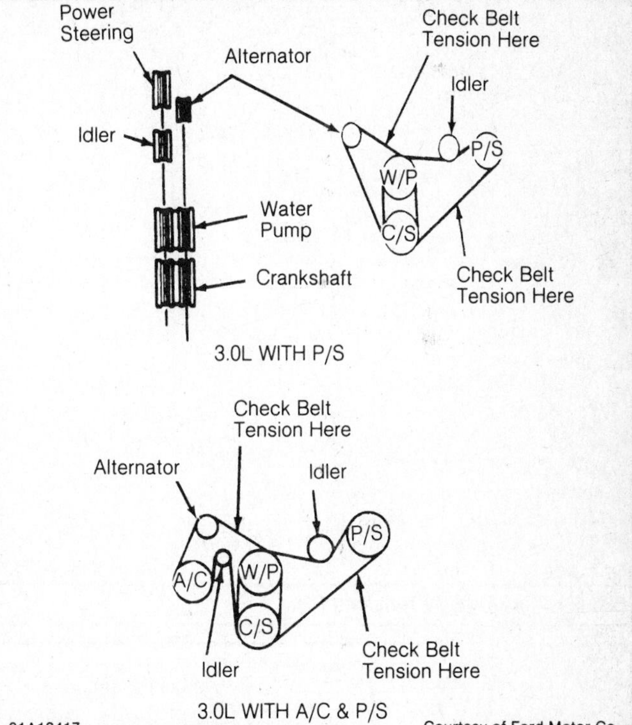
Power
Steering
Alternator
Idler
Water
Pump
Crankshaft
Check Belt
Tension Here
Idler
W/P
C/S
P/S
Check Belt
Tension Here
3.0L WITH P/S
Check Belt
Tension Here
Alternator
Idler
A/C
W/P
C/S
P/S
Idler
Check Belt
Tension Here
3.0L WITH A/C & P/S

91A13417 Courtesy of Ford Motor Co.

Fig. 4: Checking Belt Tension (3.0L)

VOLTAGE REGULATOR

Solid state regulator is used. Regulator is factory calibrated and cannot be adjusted.

TROUBLE SHOOTING

***NOTE:** See TROUBLE SHOOTING article in GENERAL INFORMATION.*

ON-VEHICLE TESTING

TESTING PRECAUTIONS

Battery – When charging battery, remove ground cable before connecting charger. If booster battery is used to start engine, negative cable of booster must be connected to vehicle frame. Disconnect negative booster cable first.

CHARGING SYSTEM TEST

***NOTE:** Ensure that battery is fully charged and battery connections are clean and secure. Check that alternator drive belt is adjusted to proper tension.*

1) Ensure that all accessories are turned off. Connect voltmeter to battery. Attach tachometer and start engine. Operate at 1500 RPM with no electrical load. Voltmeter reading should increase, but it should not exceed 2 volts more than battery voltage. Reading should be taken when voltmeter stabilizes.

1991 ELECTRICAL
Alternators – With Internal Regulator (Cont.)

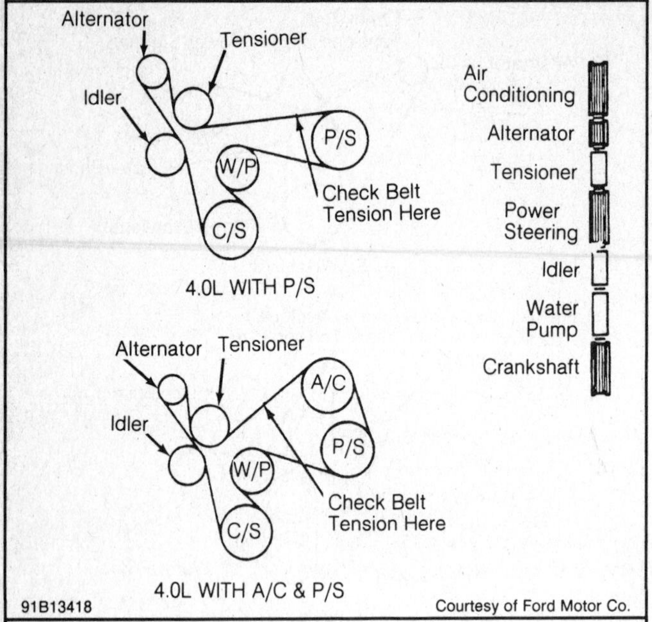
Alternator
Tensioner
Idler
P/S
W/P
Check Belt Tension Here
C/S
4.0L WITH P/S
Air Conditioning
Alternator
Tensioner
Power Steering
Idler
Water Pump
Crankshaft
Alternator
Tensioner
Idler
A/C
P/S
W/P
Check Belt Tension Here
C/S
4.0L WITH A/C & P/S
91B13418
Courtesy of Ford Motor Co.

Fig. 5: Checking Belt Tension (4.0L)

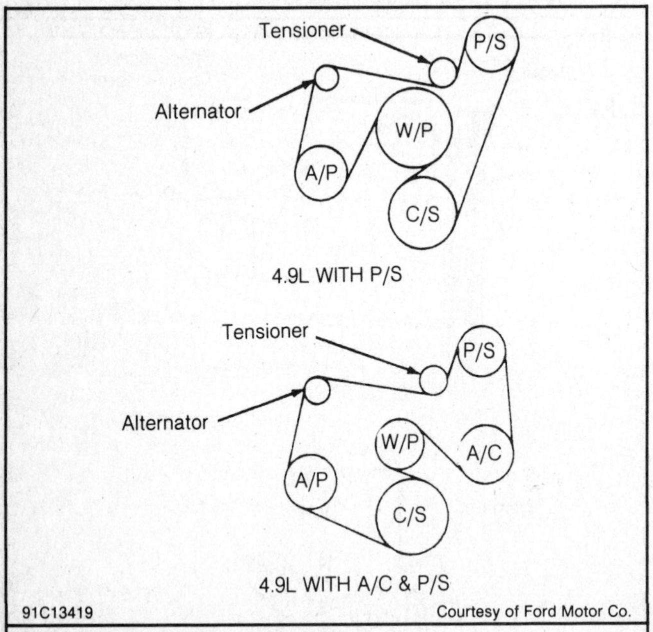
Tensioner
P/S
Alternator
W/P
A/P
C/S
4.9L WITH P/S
Tensioner
P/S
Alternator
W/P
A/C
A/P
C/S
4.9L WITH A/C & P/S
91C13419
Courtesy of Ford Motor Co.

Fig. 6: Checking Belt Tension (4.9L)

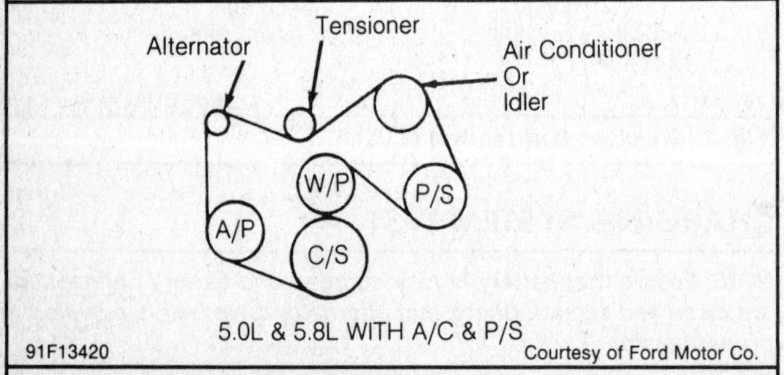
Alternator
Tensioner
Air Conditioner Or Idler
W/P
P/S
A/P
C/S
5.0L & 5.8L WITH A/C & P/S
91F13420
Courtesy of Ford Motor Co.

Fig. 7: Checking Belt Tension (5.0L & 5.8L)

2) With engine operating, turn heater or A/C blower motor to HIGH position. Turn on headlights to high beam. Increase engine speed to 2000 RPM. Voltmeter should indicate at least .5 volt above battery voltage.

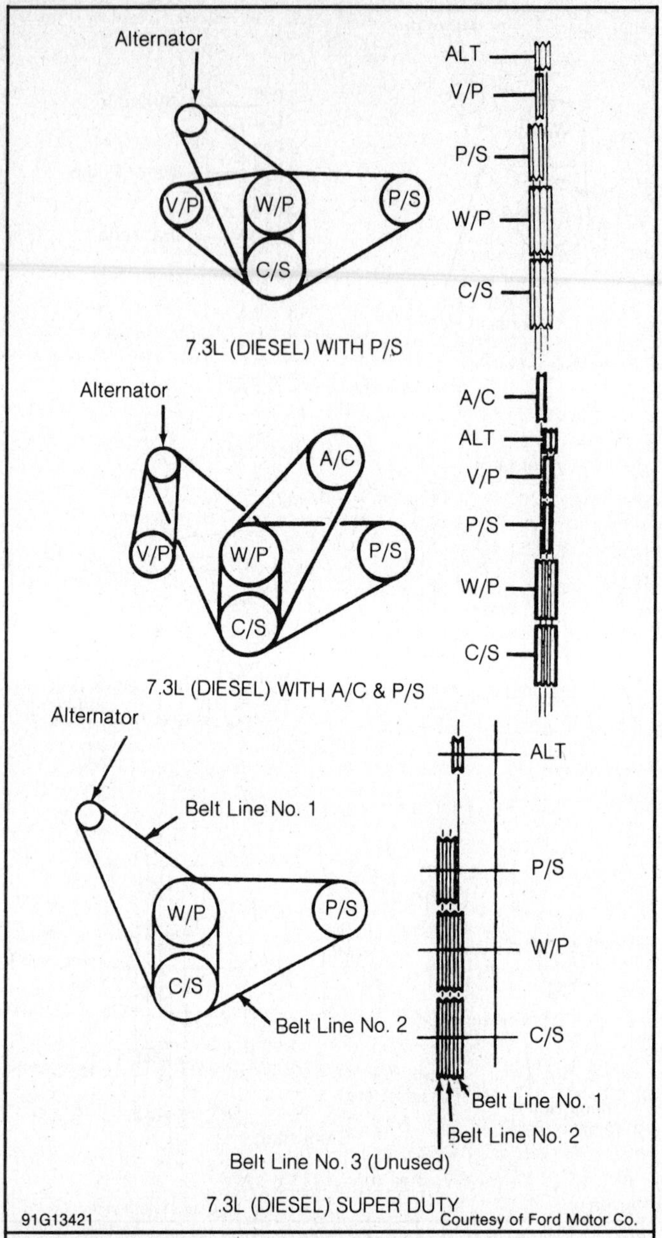
Alternator
ALT
V/P
P/S
W/P
C/S
V/P
W/P
P/S
C/S
7.3L (DIESEL) WITH P/S
Alternator
A/C
ALT
V/P
P/S
W/P
C/S
A/C
V/P
W/P
P/S
C/S
7.3L (DIESEL) WITH A/C & P/S
Alternator
ALT
Belt Line No. 1
P/S
W/P
P/S
W/P
C/S
C/S
Belt Line No. 2
Belt Line No. 1
Belt Line No. 2
Belt Line No. 3 (Unused)
7.3L (DIESEL) SUPER DUTY
91G13421
Courtesy of Ford Motor Co.

Fig. 8: Checking Belt Tension (7.3L Diesel)

TEST RESULTS

High Voltage – 1) If voltmeter reading exceeds battery voltage by 2.5 volts or more, stop engine. Turn on ignition switch. Connect voltmeter negative lead to alternator housing.

2) Connect voltmeter positive lead to alternator output post of starter solenoid. Note voltage reading. Move voltmeter positive lead to terminal "A" on rear of alternator and note reading. *See Fig. 10.*

3) Difference between voltage readings should not exceed .5 volt. If difference exceeds .5 volt, check terminal "A" wiring circuit for high resistance. Repair as necessary. If voltage reading still exceeds battery voltage by .5 volt or more, check for loose regulator-to-alternator mounting screws. Recheck voltage.

4) If excessive voltage still exists, turn ignition off. Connect positive voltmeter lead to regulator terminal "A" screw. Install remaining lead on alternator terminal "F" screw. Voltage should be the same at both locations.

5) Different voltage readings indicate a defective regulator, grounded brush lead or grounded rotor coil. If readings were the same, resistance is normal in the ground circuit. Replace the voltage regulator.

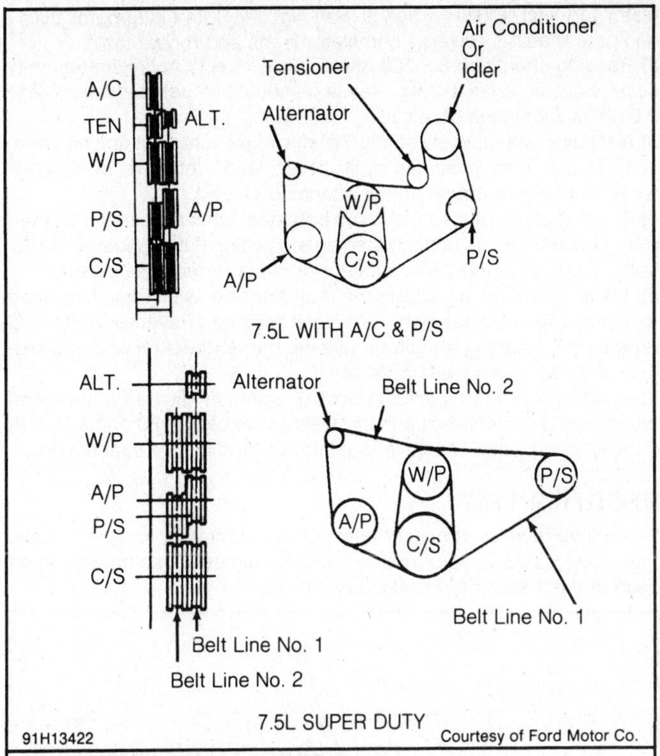
A/C
TEN
ALT.
W/P
P/S
A/P
C/S
Tensioner
Alternator
Air Conditioner
Or
Idler
W/P
C/S
P/S
A/P
7.5L WITH A/C & P/S
ALT.
Alternator
Belt Line No. 2
W/P
A/P
P/S
C/S
W/P
P/S
A/P
C/S
Belt Line No. 1
Belt Line No. 1
Belt Line No. 2
7.5L SUPER DUTY
91H13422
Courtesy of Ford Motor Co.

Fig. 9: Checking Belt Tension (7.5L)

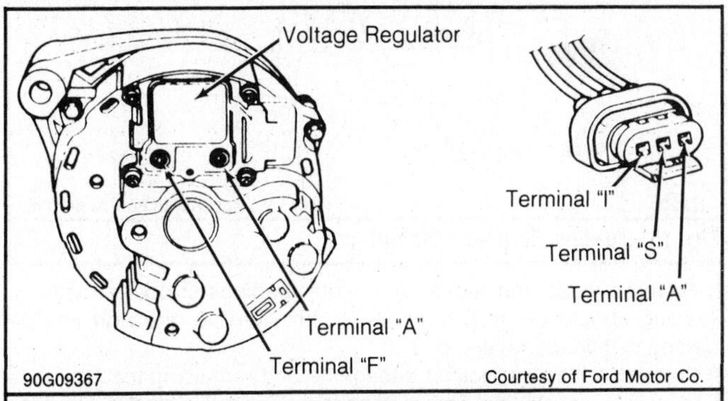
Voltage Regulator
Terminal "I"
Terminal "S"
Terminal "A"
Terminal "A"
Terminal "F"
90G09367
Courtesy of Ford Motor Co.

Fig. 10: Identifying Alternator/Regulator Terminals

Low Voltage – 1) If voltage reading exceeds battery voltage by less than .5 volt, disconnect wiring plug from regulator. Connect ohmmeter between terminals "A" and "F". *See Fig. 10.* Reading should exceed 2.4 ohms. Replace alternator if reading is less than 2.4 ohms.

2) If reading exceeds 2.4 ohms, connect wiring plug at regulator. Connect voltmeter negative lead to alternator case. Connect positive lead to regulator terminal "A" screw. Voltmeter should read battery voltage. If no voltage is present, check terminal "A" wiring circuit.

3) If reading shows battery voltage, connect voltmeter negative lead to alternator housing. Ensure ignition switch is off. Connect positive lead to regulator terminal "F" screw.

4) Battery voltage should exist. If battery voltage does not exist, replace alternator due to open circuit.

5) If battery voltage exists, connect voltmeter negative lead to alternator housing. Turn ignition on. Connect positive lead to regulator terminal "F" screw.

6) Reading should be 1.5 volts or less. If reading exceeds 1.5 volts, perform test procedure on "I" circuit. See "S" & "I" CIRCUIT under CIRCUIT TESTS in this article.

7) On readings of 1.5 volts or less, disconnect alternator wire connector. Connect 12-gauge jumper wire between alternator BAT terminal and corresponding terminal on wiring plug. *See Fig. 11.*

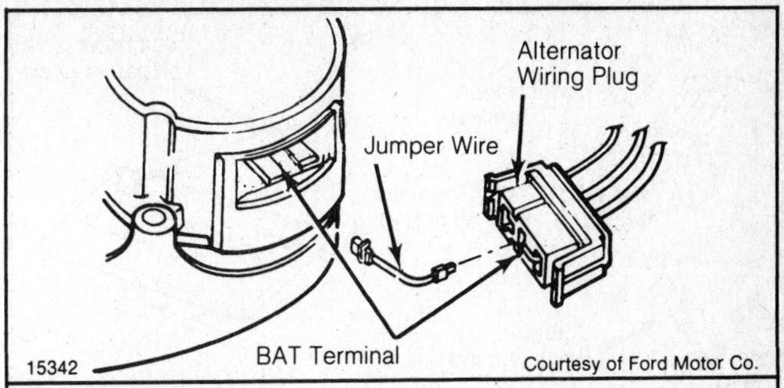
Alternator
Wiring Plug
Jumper Wire
BAT Terminal
15342
Courtesy of Ford Motor Co.

Fig. 11: Installing Jumper Wire Between Alternator & Wiring Plug

8) Connect voltmeter positive lead to jumper wire at BAT terminal. Connect remaining lead to ground. Start engine. Turn heater or A/C blower motor to HIGH position.

9) Turn on headlights (high beams). Increase engine speed to 2000 RPM. If reading exceeds battery voltage by .5 volt or more, repair alternator-to-starter wiring.

10) If reading does not exceed battery voltage by more than .5 volt, connect jumper wire from alternator housing to regulator terminal "F". Connect voltmeter positive lead to jumper wire. Connect remaining lead to ground.

11) Start engine. Turn on all accessories. Increase engine speed to 2000 RPM. If reading exceeds battery voltage by more than .5 volt, replace regulator. If reading falls short of battery voltage by .5 volt or more, replace alternator.

CIRCUIT TESTS

Current Drain Check (Without Trip Computer) – Ensure all accessories are turned off. Disconnect either battery cable. Connect a test light between the battery cable and battery post. If light does not come on, no current drain exists. If light does come on, check individual circuits to find source of current drain.

Current Drain Check (With Trip Computer) – Ensure all accessories are turned off. Disconnect either battery cable. Connect an ammeter between either battery cable and battery post. Allow one minute for system stabilization. If current drain is .05 amp or less, system is okay. If current drain is more than .05 amp, check individual circuits to find source of current drain.

Fusible Link Circuit – Ensure battery is fully charged and in good condition. Turn ignition on. Using a voltmeter and with harness connector connected, check for battery voltage at alternator BAT terminal. *See Fig. 13.* If battery voltage is present, circuit is okay. If no voltage is present, replace fusible link.

NOTE: The fusible link is a short length of insulated wire that is integral with the circuit between the starter solenoid and the alternator.

"S" & "I" Circuit – 1) Remove wiring plug from regulator. Install jumper wire from regulator terminal "A" to wiring plug terminal "A". Install jumper wire from regulator terminal "F" to rear of alternator housing.

2) Connect voltmeter negative lead to battery negative terminal. Start engine and connect voltmeter positive lead to regulator terminal "S" and then to the terminal "I". Note reading at each location. *See Fig. 12.*

3) If voltage reading of terminal "S" is approximately 1/2 of the terminal "I" voltage, replace regulator. If voltage is not present, repair wiring.

BENCH TESTING

CAUTION: Do not use digital meters to perform following tests.

RECTIFIER SHORT & STATOR GROUNDED TEST

1) Perform test before alternator disassembly. Adjust ohmmeter to lowest scale. Place ohmmeter lead on alternator BAT terminal. Place remaining lead on the STA terminal and note reading. *See Fig. 13.* Reverse ohmmeter leads and note reading.

1991 ELECTRICAL
Alternators – With Internal Regulator (Cont.)

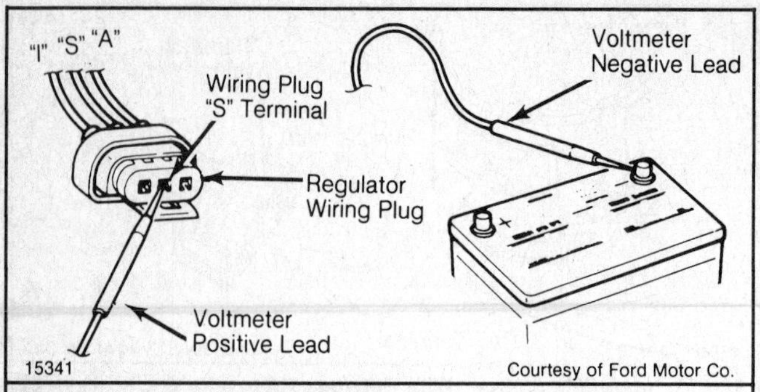
"I" "S" "A"
Wiring Plug
"S" Terminal
Voltmeter
Negative Lead
Regulator
Wiring Plug
Voltmeter
Positive Lead
15341
Courtesy of Ford Motor Co.

Fig. 12: Testing "S" & "I" Circuit

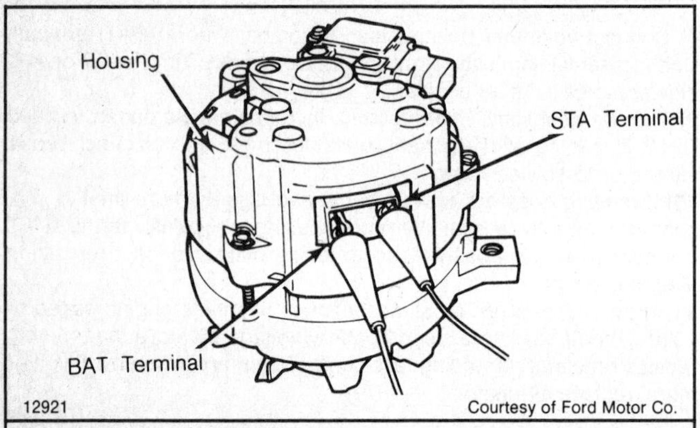
Housing
STA Terminal
BAT Terminal
12921
Courtesy of Ford Motor Co.

Fig. 13: Testing Positive Diodes

2) Reading should show movement in one direction only. This indicates rectifier diodes are being checked in reverse current direction. Low reading of approximately 6.5 ohms with leads reversed indicates that positive diodes are being checked in forward current direction.

3) Readings in both directions indicates defective positive diode or shorted radio suppression capacitor. Radio suppression capacitor is built into the rectifier assembly.

4) Place ohmmeter lead on STA terminal and remaining lead on alternator housing. Reading in both directions indicates a grounded stator winding, defective negative diode, a grounded stator lead wire or shorted radio suppression capacitor.

5) Check for bad connection in rectifier if no reading is obtained in either direction or excessive resistance is obtained.

OPEN FIELD OR SHORT CIRCUIT TEST

1) Perform test before alternator disassembly. Adjust ohmmeter to lowest scale. Place ohmmeter leads on regulator terminal "A" and regulator terminal "F" screw heads. *See Fig. 14.* Rotate alternator pulley and note reading. Reverse ohmmeter leads and repeat test.

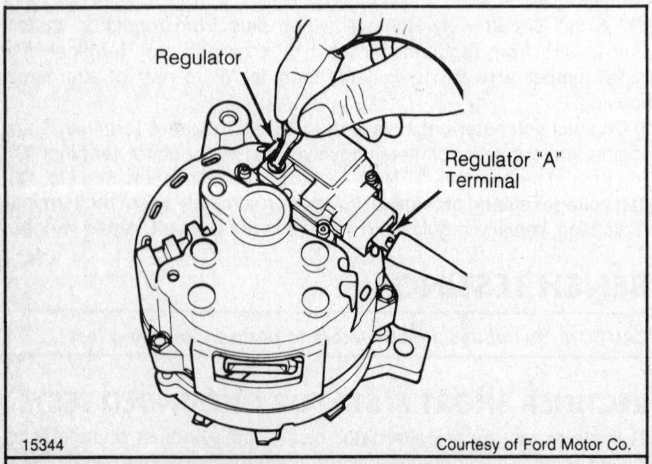
Regulator
Regulator "A"
Terminal
15344
Courtesy of Ford Motor Co.

Fig. 14: Testing Field for Open or Short Circuit

2) Reading should be 2.2-100 ohms in one direction. Fluctuation may occur while pulley is turning. Reading should fluctuate between 2.2 to 9.0 ohms with leads reversed.

3) A reading with approximately 9 ohms in one direction and no continuity in the other indicates open brush lead, defective brushes or loose regulator-to-brush holder attaching screws.

4) Reading of less than 2.2 ohms in both directions indicates a shorted rotor or defective regulator. Reading exceeding 9 ohms in both directions indicates a defective regulator or loose terminal "F" screw.

5) Place one lead on alternator rear housing with remaining lead touching regulator terminal "F". Note reading. Reverse leads and repeat test. Reading should be infinite in one direction and approximately 9 ohms with leads reversed.

6) Reading less than infinite in both directions indicates a grounded brush lead or defective regulator. Reading exceeding 9 ohms in both directions indicates defective regulator or terminal "A" connection.

RECTIFIER TEST

1) Remove rectifier from alternator. Adjust ohmmeter to lowest scale. Place one lead on one of rectifier BAT terminals. Place other lead on each of the 3 stator terminals. *See Fig. 15.*

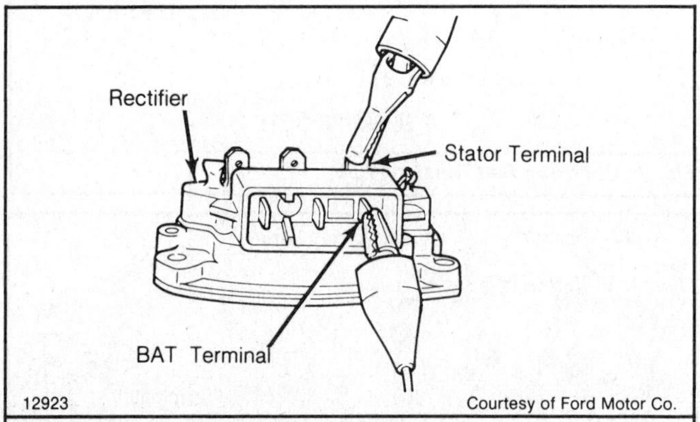
Rectifier
Stator Terminal
BAT Terminal
12923
Courtesy of Ford Motor Co.

Fig. 15:. Testing Rectifier Assembly

2) Reverse leads and repeat test. Note readings in both directions. Reading should be approximately 7 ohms in one direction and no reading with leads reversed.

3) Place one lead on rectifier base plate and remaining lead on each of the 3 stator terminals. This is done to test negative diodes. Reverse leads and repeat test.

4) Reading should be approximately 7 ohms in one direction and no continuity with leads reversed. If readings are not correct, replace rectifier.

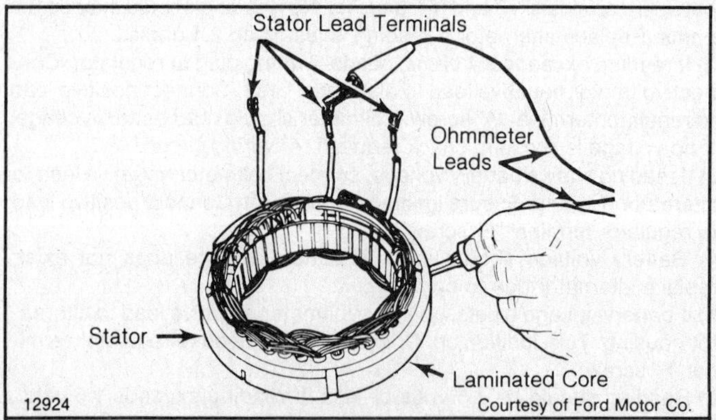
Stator Lead Terminals
Ohmmeter
Leads
Stator
Laminated Core
12924
Courtesy of Ford Motor Co.

Fig. 16: Testing Stator for Ground & Opens

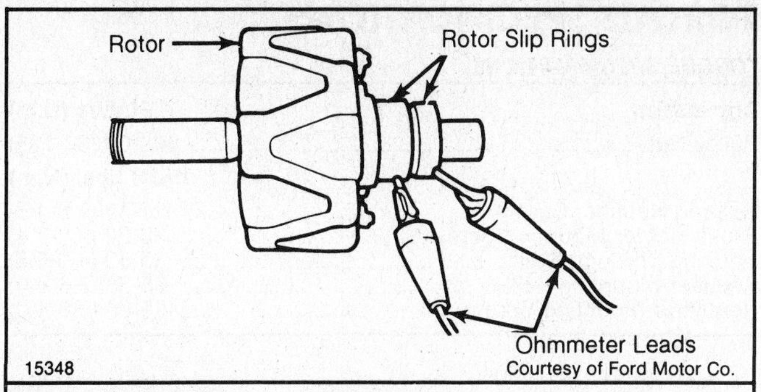
Rotor
Rotor Slip Rings
Ohmmeter Leads
15348
Courtesy of Ford Motor Co.

Fig. 17: Testing Rotor for Open Circuit

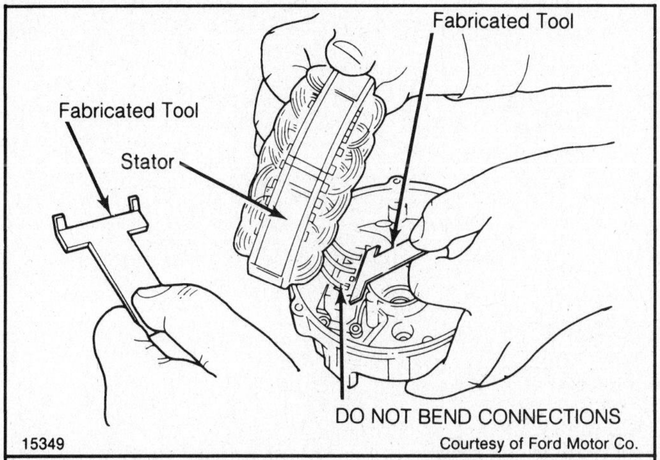
Fabricated Tool
Fabricated Tool
Stator
DO NOT BEND CONNECTIONS
15349
Courtesy of Ford Motor Co.

Fig. 18: Removing Connector Block

STATOR COIL GROUND TEST

1) Stator must be removed from the rectifier. Set ohmmeter to 1000-ohm scale. Place ohmmeter lead on the stator lead terminals and remaining lead on the stator laminated core. *See Fig. 16.*

2) Ensure lead makes good connection with stator core. Ohmmeter should show no continuity. Stator winding is grounded to the core if reading is obtained. Replace stator if grounded.

STATOR OPEN TEST

1) Separate stator from rectifier. Adjust ohmmeter to lowest scale. Place one lead to a stator terminal. Place remaining lead on another stator terminal. Note meter reading. Ohmmeter reading should be obtained.

2) Stator winding is open if reading is not obtained. Replace stator coil if open is found. Repeat test procedure on remaining stator terminals.

ROTOR OPEN OR SHORT TEST

1) Adjust ohmmeter to lowest scale. Place each ohmmeter lead on rotor slip rings. *See Fig. 17.* Note ohmmeter reading. Reading should be 2.0-3.9 ohms.

2) Reading exceeding specification indicates a damaged slip ring, welded connection or a broken wire. Low reading indicates a shorted wire or slip ring.

3) Place one ohmmeter lead to a slip ring and remaining lead on rotor shaft. No continuity should be indicated. Rotor coil is grounded to shaft if reading is obtained. Repair or replace rotor if defective.

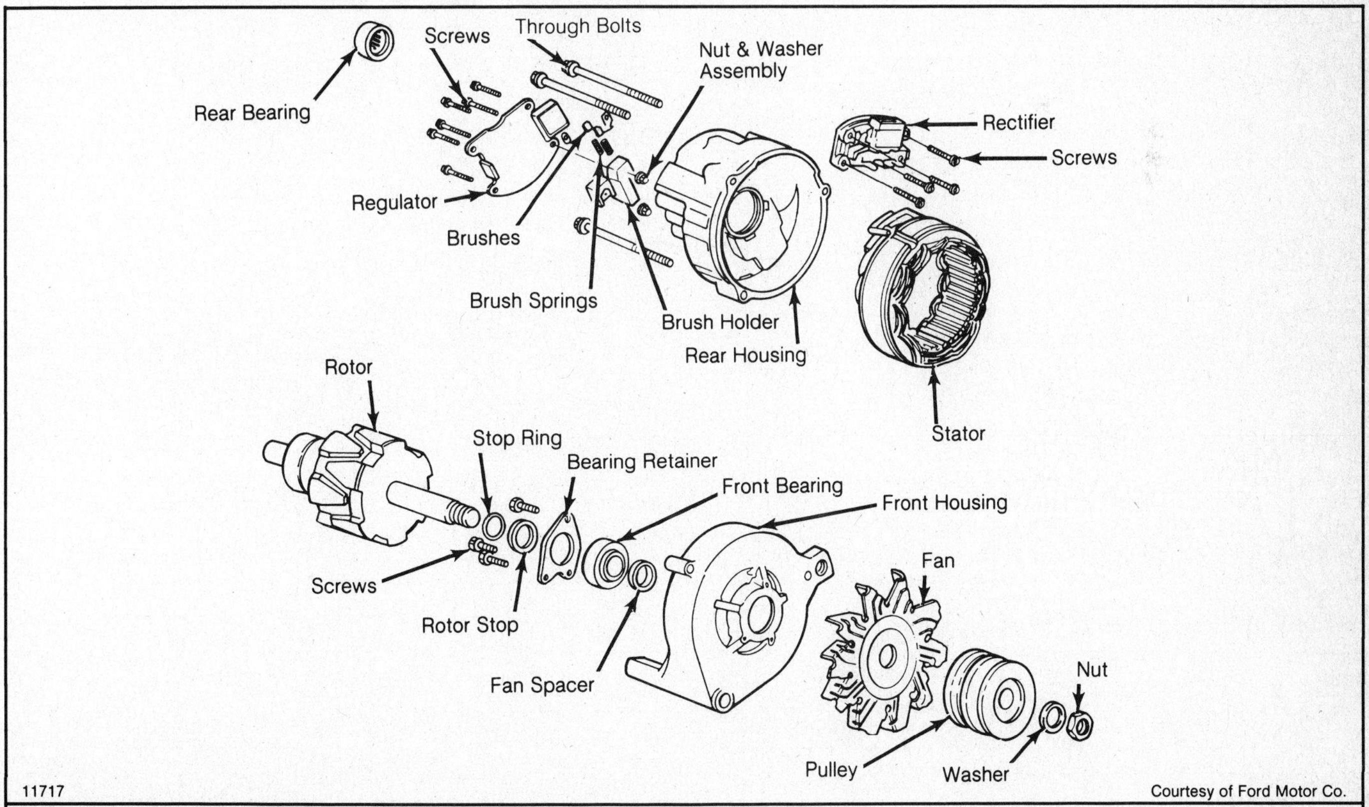
Rear Bearing
Screws
Through Bolts
Nut & Washer Assembly
Rectifier
Screws
Regulator
Brushes
Brush Springs
Brush Holder
Rear Housing
Stator
Rotor
Stop Ring
Bearing Retainer
Front Bearing
Front Housing
Fan
Screws
Rotor Stop
Fan Spacer
Nut
Pulley
Washer
11717
Courtesy of Ford Motor Co.

Fig. 19: Exploded View of Alternator With Internal Regulator

1991 ELECTRICAL
Alternators – With Internal Regulator (Cont.)

OVERHAUL

NOTES & CAUTION

- Fabricate small tool, and carefully pry connector block upward. DO NOT bend connections. Remove stator from rear housing. *See Fig. 18*.
- Check brush length. Replace brushes if worn less than .250" (6.35 mm). Replace all damaged components.
- Use only high-temperature bearings when rebuilding alternator. Standard bearings will result in alternator failure.
- Clean rectifier base plate with a clean cloth. Apply a 3/32" (2.0 mm) wide by 3/4" (20 mm) long strip of Heat Sink Compound (ESF-M99G138-A) lengthwise across rectifier base plate.
- Rectifier is cooled by conducting heat directly into alternator rear housing. Failure to apply heat sink compound may cause rectifier overheating.
- Retain brushes in place by inserting a 1 3/8" piece of stiff insulated wire into brush holder pin hole. Install nuts and washers in retaining slots of brush holder.
- Place a small amount of waterproof sealer over brush pin hole. Do not use silicone sealer. Rotate pulley to check for freedom of movement.

TORQUE SPECIFICATIONS

TORQUE SPECIFICATIONS

Application	Ft. Lbs (N.m)
Pulley Nut	60-100 (82-135)
	INCH Lbs. (N.m)
Bearing Retainer Screw	24-42 (2.8-4.5)
Brush Holder Mounting Screw	20-30 (2.3-3.4)
Housing Through Bolt	35-60 (4.0-6.8)
Rectifier Mounting Screw	25-35 (2.8-4.0)
Regulator Mounting Screw	25-35 (2.8-4.0)

1991 ELECTRICAL
Alternators – Leece/Neville 165-Amp

Bronco, "F" Series

DESCRIPTION

The Leece/Neville 165-amp alternator is a self-current limiting unit with a fully adjustable solid state regulator. Negative output terminal is internally grounded.

The alternator features sealed ball bearings, with slip rings and brushes that are in a sealed housing mounted on the slip ring end housing. Six diodes mounted in heat sinks convert AC current to DC current. A capacitor, connected between the heat sinks, assists in suppressing transient voltage spikes which could possibly damage the diodes.

The brushes and voltage regulator are located in a waterproof housing that may be removed for service or inspection without disassembling the alternator.

ADJUSTMENTS

BELT TENSION

Inspect belt for fraying and proper routing. *See Figs. 2-5.* If fraying has occurred, ensure belt and tensioner are aligned properly. If tensioner has reached its limit of travel, belt is excessively stretched and belt replacement is required. On engines with belts requiring manual adjustment, adjust tension to specification. See ALTERNATOR BELT ADJUSTMENT SPECIFICATIONS table.

ALTERNATOR BELT ADJUSTMENT SPECIFICATIONS

Application	New Belt Lbs. (kg)	[1] Used Belt Lbs. (kg)
4.9L With Tensioner [2]	[3]	[3]
5.0L With Tensioner [2]	[4]	[4]
5.8L With Tensioner [2]	[4]	[4]
7.3L With 1/2" Belt	140-180 (64-82)	95-115 (43-52)
7.3L Ambulance	140-160 (64-73)	140-160 (64-73)
7.5L	160-200 (73-91)	110-130 (50-59)

[1] – Any belt operated for 10 minutes or more.
[2] – Tension is correct if tensioner is within indicator marks.
[3] – 117 lbs. (53 kg) minimum tension.
[4] – 111 lbs. (50 kg) minimum tension.

VOLTAGE REGULATOR

See OUTPUT TEST under ON-VEHICLE TESTING for voltage regulator adjustment procedure.

TROUBLE SHOOTING

NOTE: See TROUBLE SHOOTING article in GENERAL INFORMATION.

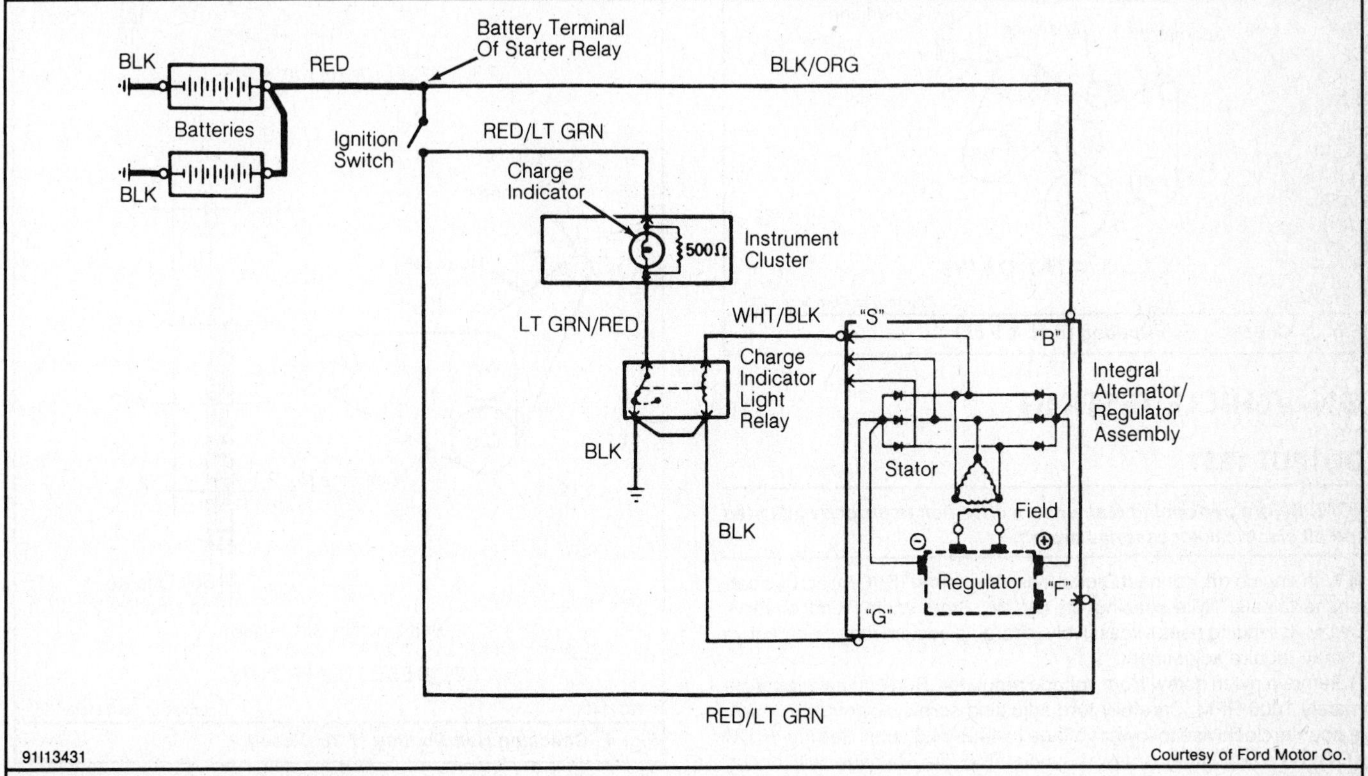
Battery Terminal
Of Starter Relay
BLK
RED
BLK/ORG
Batteries
BLK
Ignition
Switch
RED/LT GRN
Charge
Indicator
500Ω
Instrument
Cluster
LT GRN/RED
WHT/BLK
"S"
"B"
Charge
Indicator
Light
Relay
Integral
Alternator/
Regulator
Assembly
BLK
Stator
Field
BLK
Regulator
"F"
"G"
RED/LT GRN
91I13431
Courtesy of Ford Motor Co.

Fig. 1: Charging System Wiring Diagram

1991 ELECTRICAL
Alternators – Leece/Neville 165-Amp (Cont.)

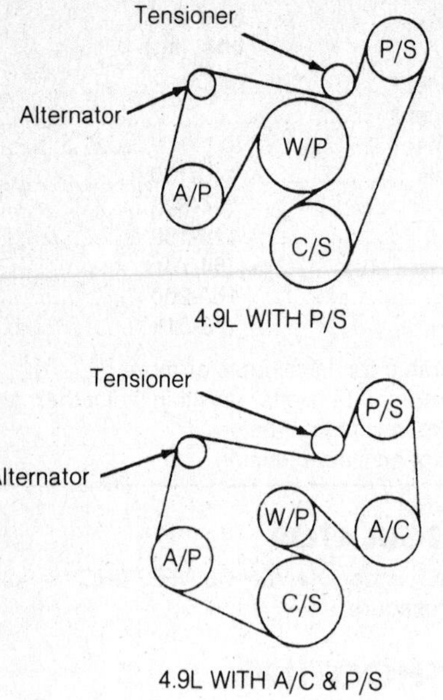
Tensioner
P/S
Alternator
W/P
A/P
C/S
4.9L WITH P/S
Tensioner
P/S
Alternator
W/P
A/C
A/P
C/S
4.9L WITH A/C & P/S

91C13419 Courtesy of Ford Motor Co.

Fig. 2: Checking Belt Routing (4.9L)

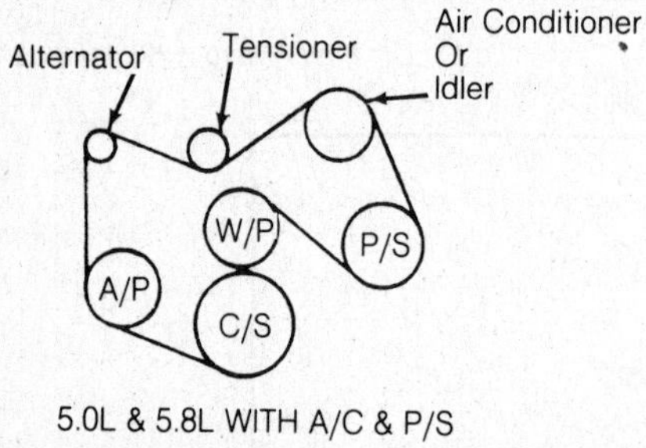
Alternator
Tensioner
Air Conditioner
Or
Idler
W/P
P/S
A/P
C/S
5.0L & 5.8L WITH A/C & P/S

91F13420 Courtesy of Ford Motor Co.

Fig. 3: Checking Belt Routing (5.0L & 5.8L)

ON-VEHICLE TESTING

OUTPUT TEST

NOTE: Before performing test, ensure drive belt is properly adjusted and all electrical accessories are off.

1) With engine off, connect Digital Volt/Ohmmeter (DVOM) across battery terminals. Note reading on DVOM. Start engine and observe DVOM. If reading rises excessively, charging system may be defective or may require adjustment.

2) Remove nylon screw from voltage regulator. Run engine at approximately 1000 RPM. Carefully turn adjusting screw clockwise to raise, or counterclockwise to lower voltage to 14.2-14.3 volts. *See Fig. 6*. DO NOT force adjusting screw beyond stop, as damage will occur. Replace nylon screw in voltage regulator adjustment hole to prevent entry of foreign material into regulator.

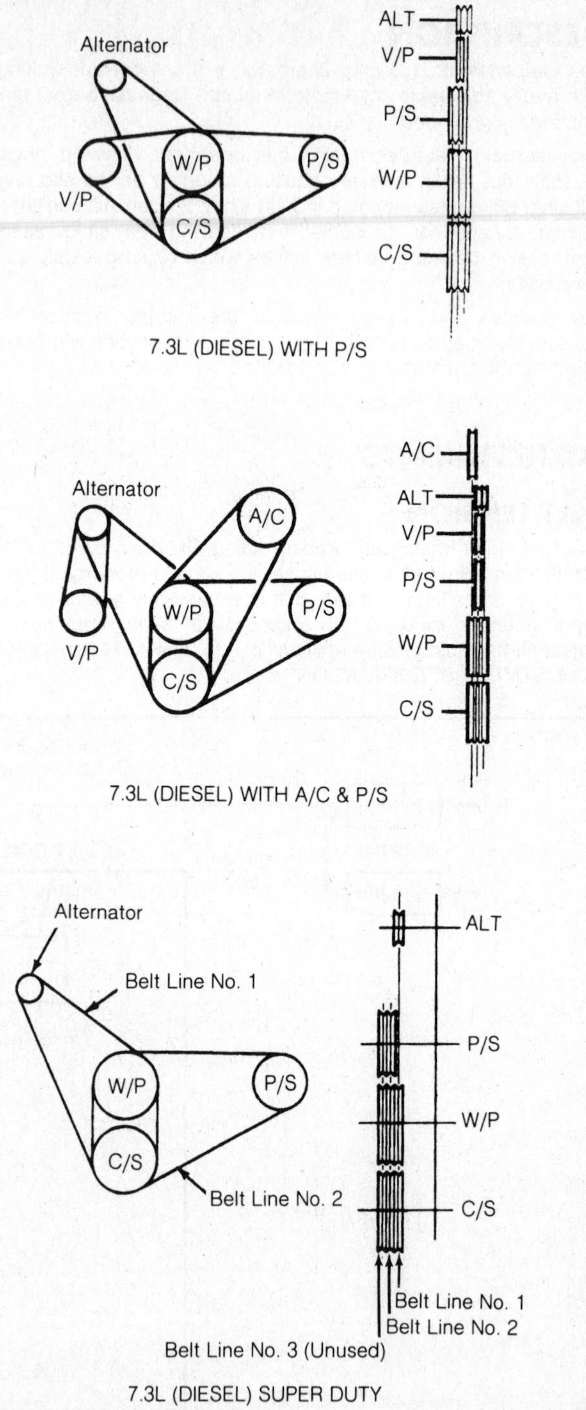
Alternator
ALT
V/P
P/S
W/P
C/S
W/P
P/S
V/P
C/S
7.3L (DIESEL) WITH P/S
A/C
ALT
V/P
P/S
W/P
C/S
Alternator
A/C
W/P
P/S
V/P
C/S
7.3L (DIESEL) WITH A/C & P/S
Alternator
ALT
Belt Line No. 1
P/S
W/P
P/S
W/P
C/S
Belt Line No. 2
C/S
Belt Line No. 1
Belt Line No. 2
Belt Line No. 3 (Unused)
7.3L (DIESEL) SUPER DUTY

91G13421 Courtesy of Ford Motor Co.

Fig. 4: Checking Belt Routing (7.3L Diesel)

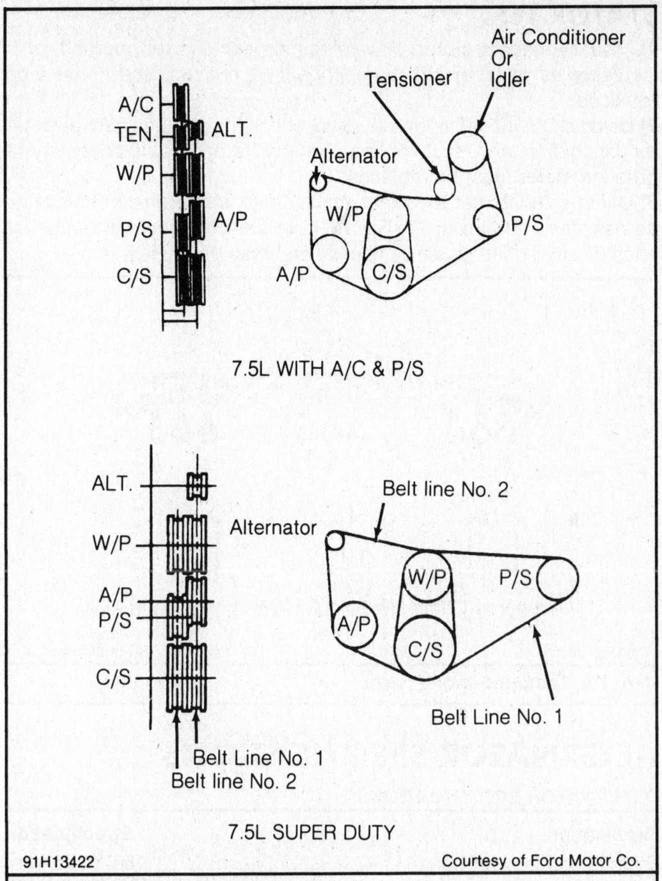

Air Conditioner
Or
Idler
Tensioner
A/C
TEN.
ALT.
W/P
Alternator
W/P
P/S
A/P
P/S
C/S
A/P
C/S
7.5L WITH A/C & P/S
ALT.
Belt line No. 2
Alternator
W/P
W/P
P/S
A/P
P/S
A/P
C/S
C/S
Belt Line No. 1
Belt Line No. 1
Belt line No. 2
7.5L SUPER DUTY
91H13422
Courtesy of Ford Motor Co.

Fig. 5: Checking Belt Routing (7.5L)

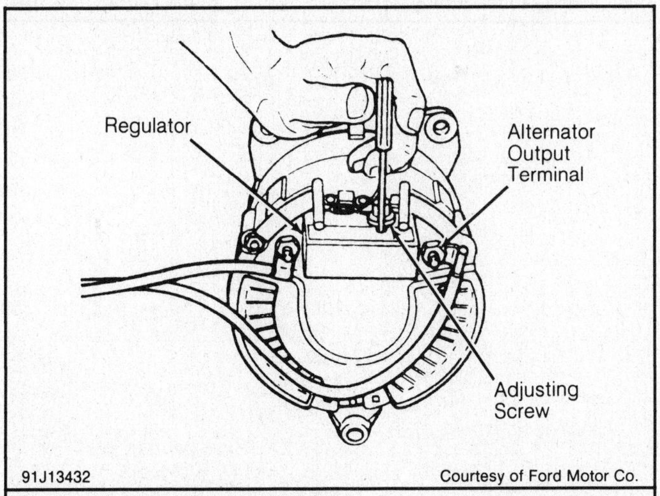

Regulator
Alternator
Output
Terminal
Adjusting
Screw
91J13432
Courtesy of Ford Motor Co.

Fig. 6: Adjusting Voltage Regulator

3) If output voltage is excessively high and cannot be lowered by adjustment, the regulator is at fault and must be replaced. If output voltage is excessively low and cannot be raised by adjustment, either the alternator or regulator may be at fault. To determine if the fault is with the alternator or the regulator, go to next step.

4) Attach one end of short jumper wire to negative rectifier terminal and other end to a stiff piece of wire at least 1 1/2" long. Insert wire with jumper wire attached into the small hole in the end of the brush holder so it firmly contacts the terminal of the outer brush. *See Fig. 7*. With engine at fast idle, observe DVOM. If output voltage rises, the alternator is okay and a faulty regulator is indicated. If output voltage does not raise, alternator is at fault and will need to be repaired.

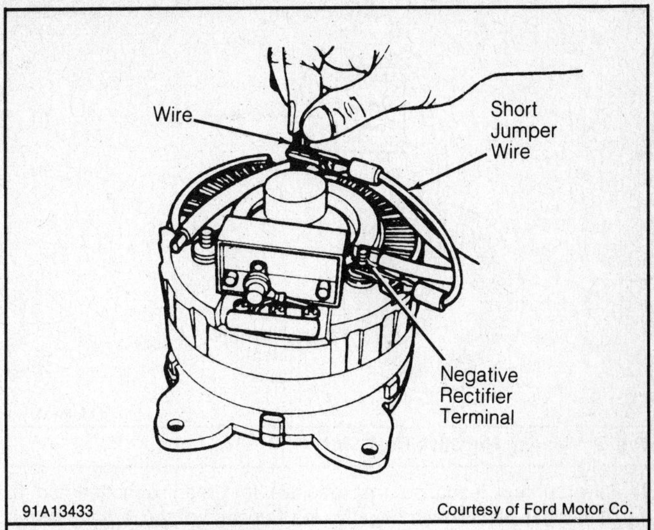

Wire
Short
Jumper
Wire
Negative
Rectifier
Terminal
91A13433
Courtesy of Ford Motor Co.

Fig. 7: Full-Fielding Alternator

BENCH TESTING

DIODE TEST

***NOTE:** These tests may be performed on heat sink assemblies without removing them from brush end housing. The stator and capacitor must be disconnected from the heat sinks. Diodes should be tested with a diode tester, but an ohmmeter or a battery powered test light may be substituted.*

Positive Heat Sink Test – 1) Connect diode tester positive lead to positive heat sink and touch negative lead to each of the 3 diode terminals. *See Fig. 8*. A high resistance should be indicated. If any of the 3 diodes shows a low resistance, diode is shorted and entire heat sink must be replaced.

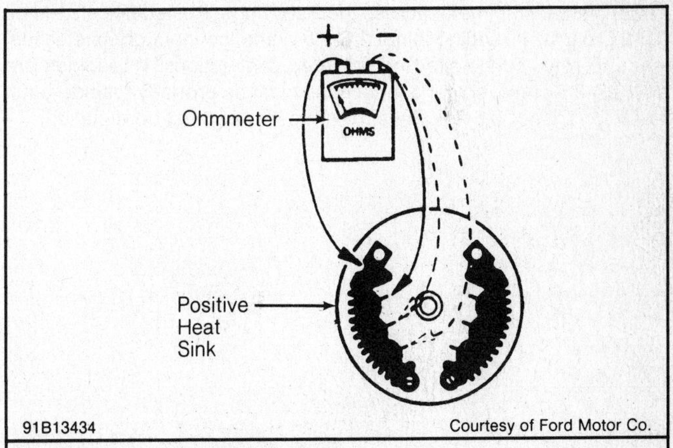

+
–
Ohmmeter
OHMS
Positive
Heat
Sink
91B13434
Courtesy of Ford Motor Co.

Fig. 8: Testing Positive Heat Sink

2) Reverse test leads so that negative test lead is connected to positive heat sink. Touch negative lead to each of the 3 diode terminals. A low resistance should be indicated. If any of the 3 diodes shows a high resistance, diode is open and entire heat sink must be replaced.

Negative Heat Sink Test – 1) Connect diode tester negative lead to negative heat sink and touch positive lead to each of the 3 diode terminals. *See Fig. 9*. A high resistance should be indicated. If any of the 3 diodes shows a low resistance, diode is shorted and entire heat sink must be replaced.

1991 ELECTRICAL
Alternators – Leece/Neville 165-Amp (Cont.)

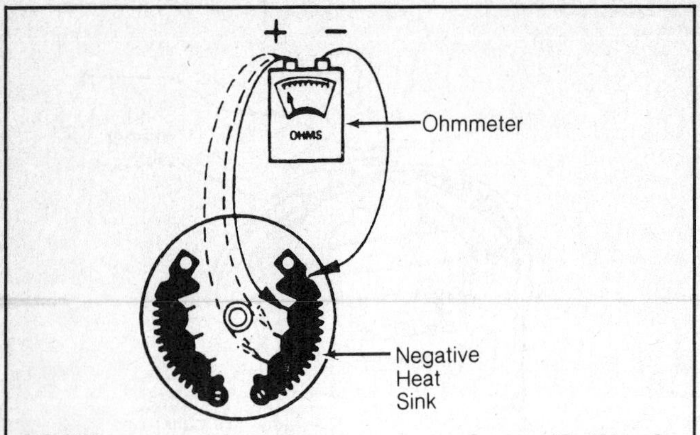
+
–
Ohmmeter
OHMS
Negative
Heat
Sink

91C13435 Courtesy of Ford Motor Co.

Fig. 9: Testing Negative Heat Sink

2) Reverse test leads so that positive test lead is connected to negative heat sink. Touch negative lead to each of the 3 diode terminals. A low resistance should be indicated. If any of the 3 diodes shows a high resistance, diode is open and entire heat sink must be replaced.

CAPACITOR TEST

1) The capacitor connected across the heat sinks may be tested with a capacitor tester if available. The capacitor value is .158 microfarad and 100 working volts DC.

2) If a capacitor tester is not available, an ohmmeter may be used to test capacitor for shorts. Connect ohmmeter across capacitor terminals. A reading under 20 m/ohms indicates a shorted or leaking capacitor which must be replaced.

ROTOR TEST

1) Connect one ohmmeter test lead to rotor shaft and the other test lead to each of the 2 slip rings. If a zero reading is observed, rotor assembly is grounded and must be replaced.

2) Connect an ohmmeter across the 2 slip rings. Resistance should be 2.6-2.9 ohms. If reading is not 2.6-2.9 ohms, connect ohmmeter test leads to rotor coil-to-slip ring soldered connections. If readings are now 2.6-2.9 ohms, solder connections must be properly resoldered. If readings are not 2.6-2.9 ohms, rotor assembly must be replaced.

STATOR TEST

1) Visually inspect stator. If windings appear charred, burned, or if insulation is missing and bare copper is noticed, stator must be replaced.

2) Using a DVOM set to lowest scale, check for grounds between stator lamination and each of the 3 stator terminals. If continuity is present, stator must be replaced.

3) Using a DVOM set to lowest scale, check stator phase resistance across stator terminals. *See Fig. 10*. If resistance is about the same for each of the 3 phases, stator is okay and may be reused.

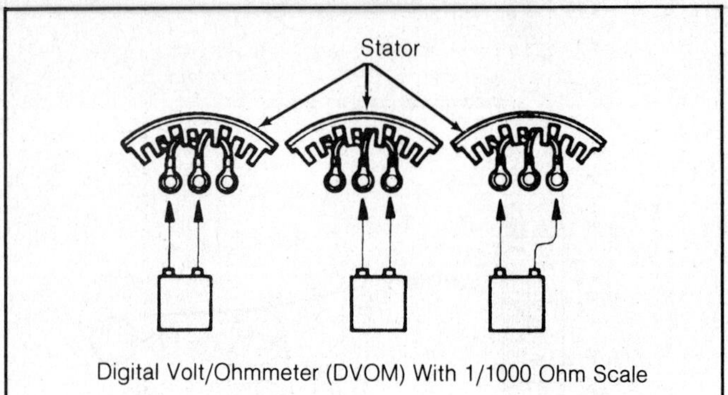
Stator
Digital Volt/Ohmmeter (DVOM) With 1/1000 Ohm Scale

91D13436 Courtesy of Ford Motor Co.

Fig. 10: Testing Stator Phases

ALTERNATOR SPECIFICATIONS

ALTERNATOR SPECIFICATIONS

Application	Specification
Brush Length Wear Limit	.188" (4.76 mm)
Capacitor Value	.158 microfarad
Rotor Resistance	2.6-2.9 ohms
Voltage Regulator Setting	14.2-14.3 volts

1991 ELECTRICAL
Alternators – Leece/Neville 165-Amp (Cont.)

OVERHAUL

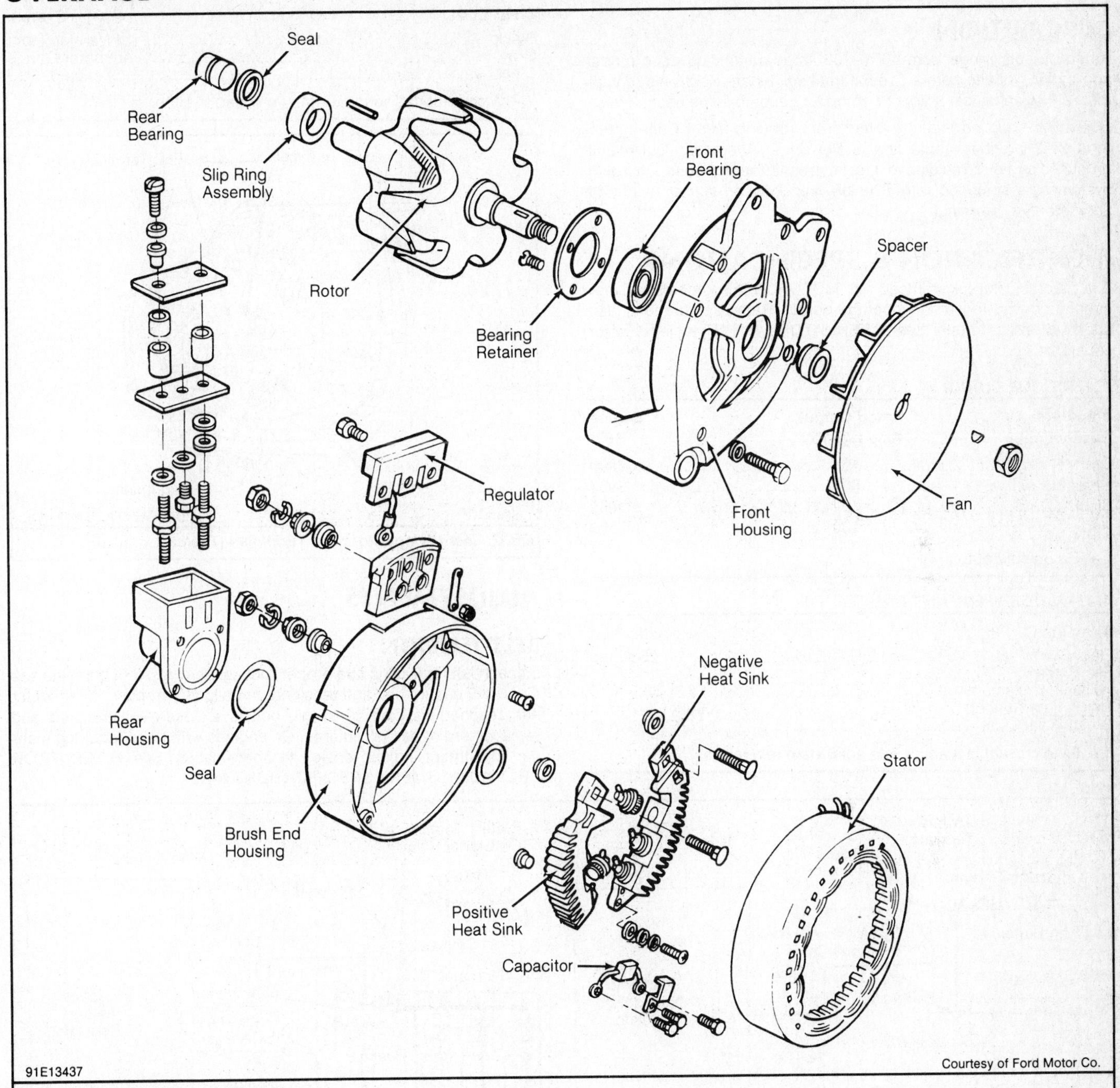
Seal
Rear Bearing
Slip Ring Assembly
Rotor
Bearing Retainer
Front Bearing
Spacer
Fan
Front Housing
Regulator
Rear Housing
Seal
Brush End Housing
Negative Heat Sink
Stator
Positive Heat Sink
Capacitor
91E13437
Courtesy of Ford Motor Co.

Fig. 11: Exploded View of Alternator

1991 ELECTRICAL
Alternators – With External Regulator

"E" & "F" Series

DESCRIPTION

Rated outputs range from 40 to 100 amps depending upon model application. All alternators use external solid-state electronic regulators. Either an indicator light or ammeter gauge may be used.

Current is supplied to the system from rotating field of alternator, through 2 brushes contacting 2 slip rings. Alternating current is produced and then rectified to direct current through diodes. Charging systems are equipped with a fusible link between starter relay and alternator BAT terminal.

IDENTIFICATION & SPECIFICATIONS

Alternator is color-ink stamped with MOTORCRAFT trademark. Color stamp is coded for rated amperage output. Rated amperage is also stamped on frame end. See ALTERNATOR OUTPUT table for color code.

ALTERNATOR OUTPUT

Amperage Application	Rated Output Amps @ 15V	Engine RPM
Orange	40	2900
Green	60	2900
Black	70	1640
Red	[1] 100	[1] 2900

[1] – Rated cold output.

ALTERNATOR SPECIFICATIONS

Alternator	Specification
Field Current at 12 Volts	[1] 4.25 Amps
Slip Rings	
Minimum Diameter	1.22" (30.9 mm)
Maximum Runout	.0005" (.127 mm)
Brush Wear Limit	.250" (6.35 mm)

[1] – Field current is 4 amps with solid state regulators.

VOLTAGE REGULATOR APPLICATION

Color Code	System
Black	Warning Light
Gray	Ammeter Gauge
Clear	[1]

[1] – A clear-coded regulator may be used in either system.

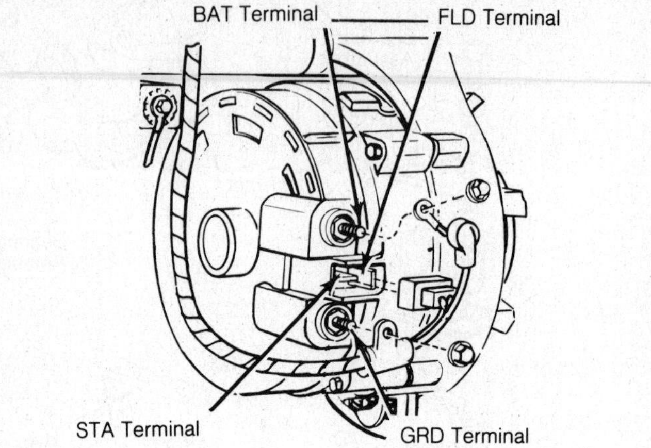
BAT Terminal
FLD Terminal
STA Terminal
GRD Terminal

15331 Courtesy of Ford Motor Co.

Fig. 2: Identifying Alternator Terminals (Typical)

ADJUSTMENTS

BELT TENSION

Inspect belt for fraying and proper routing. *See Figs. 3-6.* If fraying has occurred, ensure belt and tensioner are aligned properly. If tensioner has reached its limit of travel, belt is excessively stretched and replacement of belt is required. On engines with belts requiring manual adjustment, adjust tension to specification. See ALTERNATOR BELT ADJUSTMENT SPECIFICATIONS table.

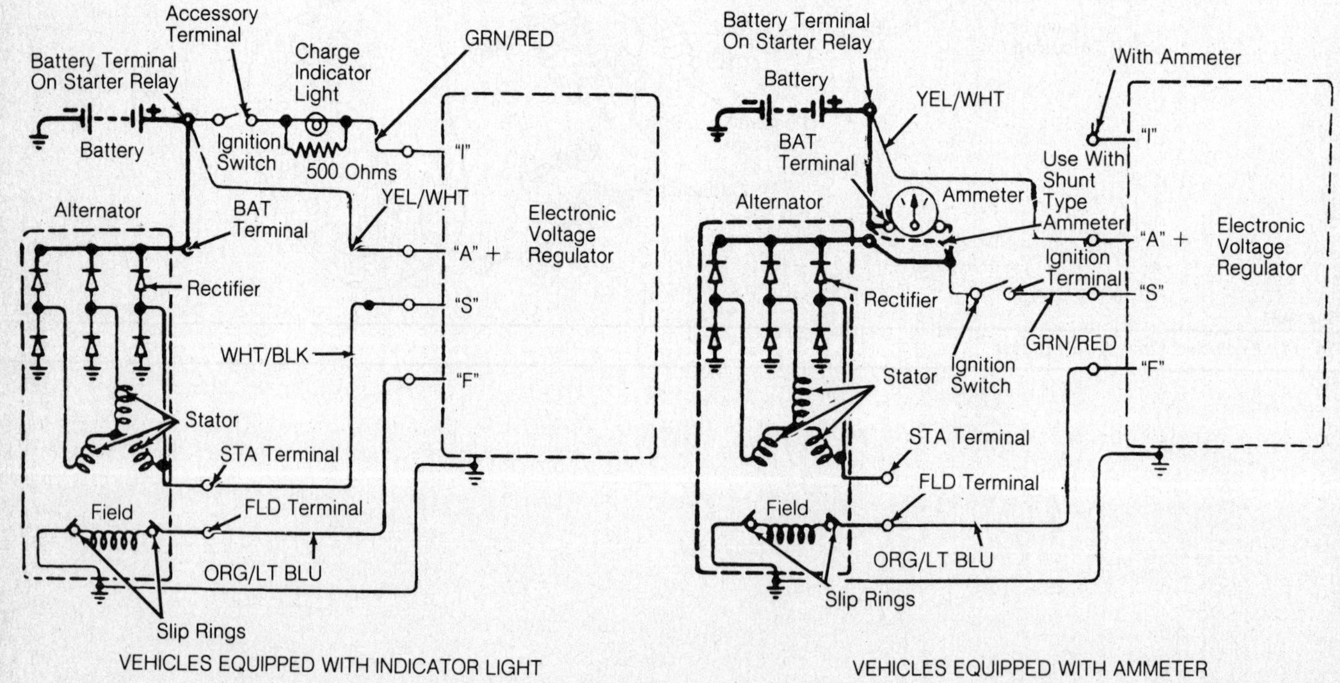
Accessory Terminal
Battery Terminal On Starter Relay
Charge Indicator Light
GRN/RED
Battery
Ignition Switch
500 Ohms
"I"
Alternator
BAT Terminal
YEL/WHT
Electronic Voltage Regulator
"A" +
Rectifier
"S"
WHT/BLK
"F"
Stator
STA Terminal
Field
FLD Terminal
ORG/LT BLU
Slip Rings
VEHICLES EQUIPPED WITH INDICATOR LIGHT
Battery Terminal On Starter Relay
Battery
YEL/WHT
With Ammeter
"I"
BAT Terminal
Use With Shunt Type Ammeter
Alternator
Ammeter
"A" +
Electronic Voltage Regulator
Ignition Terminal
"S"
Rectifier
GRN/RED
Ignition Switch
Stator
"F"
STA Terminal
FLD Terminal
Field
ORG/LT BLU
Slip Rings
VEHICLES EQUIPPED WITH AMMETER

91I13423 91J13424 Courtesy of Ford Motor Co.

Fig. 1: Charging System Wiring Diagram

1991 ELECTRICAL
Alternators – With External Regulator (Cont.)

ALTERNATOR BELT ADJUSTMENT SPECIFICATIONS

Application	New Belt Lbs. (kg)	[1] Used Belt Lbs. (kg)
4.9L With Tensioner [2]	[3] [4]	[3] [4]
5.0L With Tensioner [2]	[5] [6]	[5] [6]
5.8L With Tensioner [2]	[5] [6]	[5] [6]
7.3L With 1/2" Belt	140-180 (64-82)	95-115 (43-52)
7.3L Ambulance	140-160 (64-73)	140-160 (64-73)
7.5L	160-200 (73-91)	110-130 (50-59)

[1] – Any belt operated for 10 minutes.
[2] – Tension is correct if tensioner is within indicator marks.
[3] – 90 Lbs. (41 kg) minimum for vehicles with 60 and 75-amp alternators.
[4] – 117 Lbs. (53 kg) minimum for vehicles with 100-amp alternators.
[5] – 77 Lbs. (35 kg) minimum for vehicles with 60 and 75-amp alternators.
[6] – 111 Lbs. (50 kg) minimum for vehicles with 100-amp alternators.

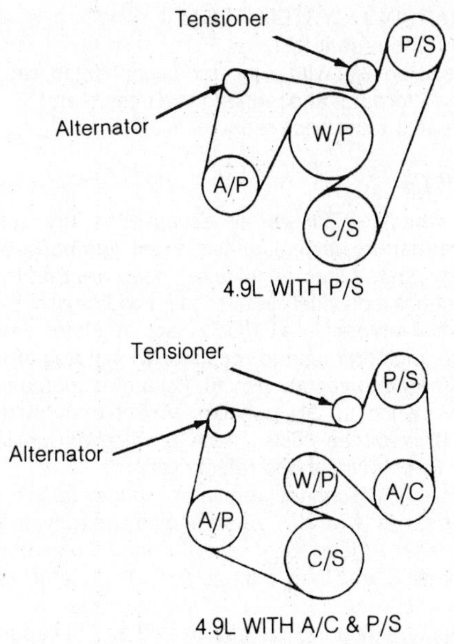
Tensioner
P/S
Alternator
W/P
A/P
C/S
4.9L WITH P/S
Tensioner
P/S
Alternator
W/P
A/C
A/P
C/S
4.9L WITH A/C & P/S

91C13419 Courtesy of Ford Motor Co.

Fig. 3: Checking Belt Tension (4.9L)

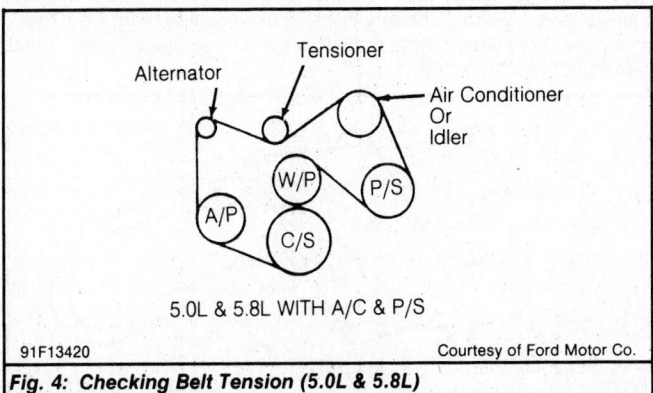

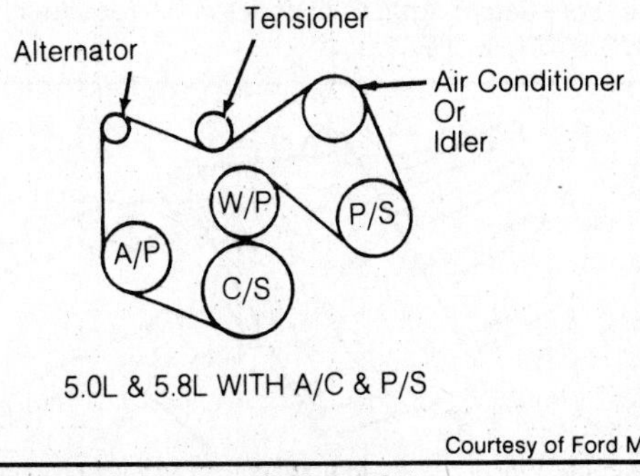
Tensioner
Alternator
Air Conditioner
Or
Idler
W/P
P/S
A/P
C/S
5.0L & 5.8L WITH A/C & P/S

91F13420 Courtesy of Ford Motor Co.

Fig. 4: Checking Belt Tension (5.0L & 5.8L)

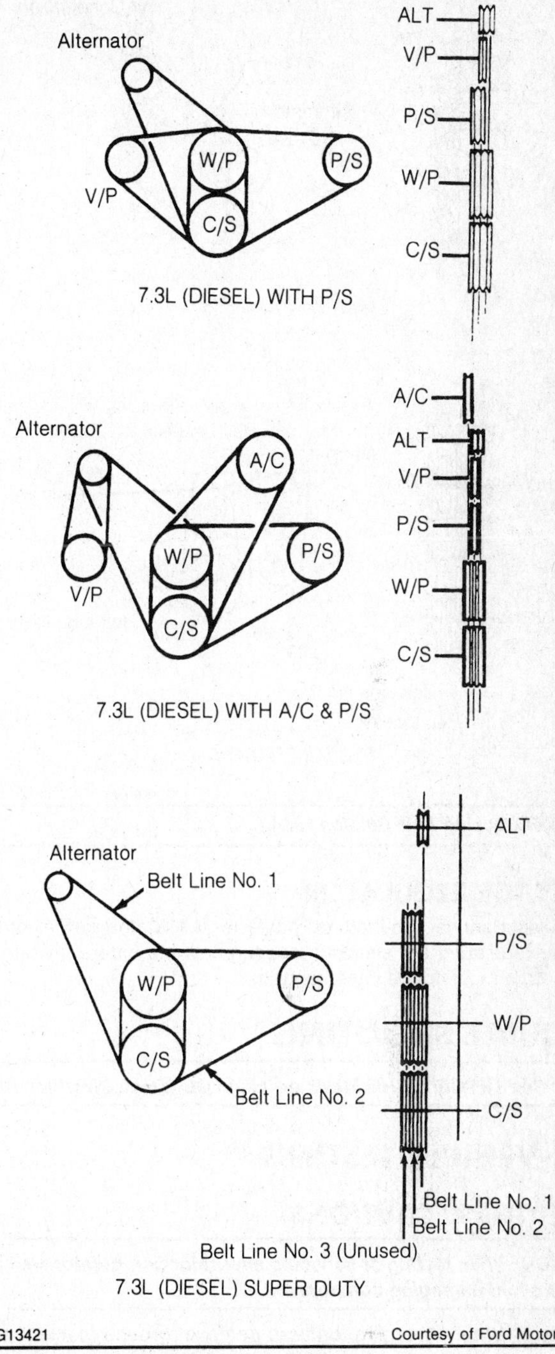
Alternator
ALT
V/P
P/S
W/P
P/S
V/P
C/S
W/P
C/S
7.3L (DIESEL) WITH P/S
A/C
Alternator
ALT
A/C
V/P
P/S
W/P
P/S
V/P
W/P
C/S
C/S
7.3L (DIESEL) WITH A/C & P/S
ALT
Alternator
Belt Line No. 1
P/S
W/P
P/S
W/P
C/S
C/S
Belt Line No. 2
Belt Line No. 1
Belt Line No. 2
Belt Line No. 3 (Unused)
7.3L (DIESEL) SUPER DUTY

91G13421 Courtesy of Ford Motor Co.

Fig. 5: Checking Belt Tension (7.3L Diesel)

1991 ELECTRICAL
Alternators – With External Regulator (Cont.)

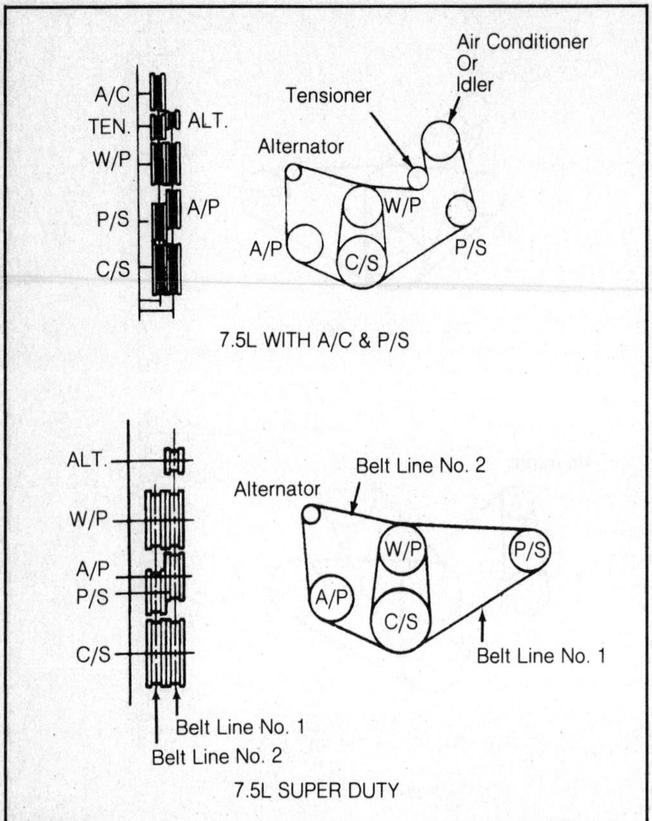
Air Conditioner
Or
Idler
A/C
TEN.
ALT.
Tensioner
W/P
Alternator
P/S
A/P
W/P
A/P
P/S
C/S
C/S
7.5L WITH A/C & P/S
ALT.
Belt Line No. 2
Alternator
W/P
P/S
A/P
P/S
A/P
C/S
C/S
Belt Line No. 1
Belt Line No. 1
Belt Line No. 2
7.5L SUPER DUTY
91H13422
Courtesy of Ford Motor Co.

Fig. 6: Checking Belt Tension (7.5L)

VOLTAGE REGULATOR

No adjustment is required or possible. All Motorcraft electronic voltage regulators are similar in appearance, but different internally. Regulators must not be interchanged.

TROUBLE SHOOTING

NOTE: See TROUBLE SHOOTING article in GENERAL INFORMATION.

ON-VEHICLE TESTING

TESTING PRECAUTIONS

CAUTION: When testing or servicing alternator or regulator, use caution to avoid damaging components.

Battery – When charging battery, remove ground cable before connecting charger. If booster battery is used to start engine, negative booster cable must be connected to vehicle frame. Disconnect negative booster cable first.

Alternator & Regulator – DO NOT ground field circuit between alternator and regulator, or operate alternator on an open circuit with field winding energized. DO NOT ground output terminal or polarize alternator. Turn ignition switch to OFF position when working on regulator.

Fuse Link – The fuse link is a short, integral with the wiring harness. It is smaller gauge than the circuit it protects, and burns out when current flow exceeds circuit rating.

A burned-out fuse link will usually have bubbled insulation. In extreme cases, bare wire may show through the insulation. Use an ohmmeter to check fusible link continuity.

CHARGING SYSTEM TEST

NOTE: Ensure battery is fully charged and connections are clean and tight. Check alternator drive belt adjustment and alignment.

1) Ensure all accessories are turned off. Connect voltmeter to battery. Attach tachometer and start engine. Operate at 1500 RPM with no electrical load. Voltmeter reading should increase, but should be no more than 2.5 volts greater than battery voltage. Reading should be taken when voltmeter stabilizes.

2) With engine operating, turn heater or A/C blower motor to HIGH position. Turn on headlights to high beam. Increase engine speed to 2000 RPM. Voltmeter should indicate at least .5 volt more than battery voltage.

TEST RESULTS

1) If voltmeter reads 2.5 volts or more greater than battery voltage, stop engine, and connect jumper wire between regulator base and alternator frame. Repeat CHARGING SYSTEM TEST.

2) If voltage is less than 2.5 volts greater than battery voltage, check ground connections on alternator and regulator. Repeat test once repair is made.

3) If overvoltage condition still exists, disconnect regulator wiring plug and repeat CHARGING SYSTEM TEST. If condition is corrected, replace regulator and repeat test.

4) If overvoltage still exists with regulator disconnected, repair wiring harness between alternator and regulator circuits "A" and "F". Connect regulator, and repeat tests once repair is made.

CIRCUIT TESTS

Current Drain Check – Ensure all accessories are turned off. Disconnect either battery cable. Connect a test light between battery cable and battery post. If light remains off, no current drain exists. If light comes on, check individual circuits to find source of current drain.

"S" Circuit With Ammeter – **1)** Disconnect regulator wiring plug. Connect positive voltmeter lead to regulator wiring plug terminal "S". Connect negative lead to secure ground. Voltmeter should read zero.

2) Turn ignition switch to ON position. Voltmeter should indicate battery voltage. If no voltage exists, check "S" wire from ignition switch for open circuit. Repair wiring and retest system.

"S" & "I" Circuit – **1)** Disconnect regulator wiring plug. Install jumper wire between terminals "A" and "F". Start engine and allow to idle. Connect voltmeter negative lead to ground. Connect voltmeter positive lead first to terminal "S" and then to terminal "I" of regulator wiring plug. *See Fig. 7.*

2) "S" circuit voltage reading should be 1/2 of "I" circuit voltage reading. Replace regulator if voltage readings are correct. Remove jumper wire from regulator wiring plug. Connect plug to regulator, and repeat CHARGING SYSTEM TEST.

3) If no voltage exists, check for damaged wiring. Connect voltmeter positive lead to positive battery post. Remove jumper wire from regulator wire connector. Attach connector to regulator, and repeat CHARGING SYSTEM TEST.

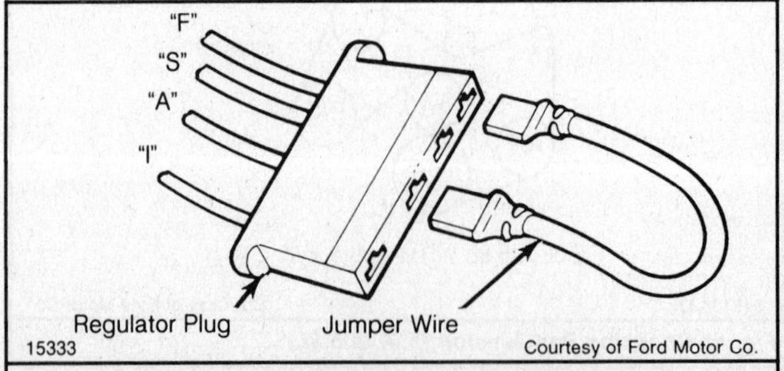
"F"
"S"
"A"
"I"
Regulator Plug
Jumper Wire
15333
Courtesy of Ford Motor Co.

Fig. 7: Identifying Regulator Connector Terminals & Installing Jumper Wire

1991 ELECTRICAL
Alternators – With External Regulator (Cont.)

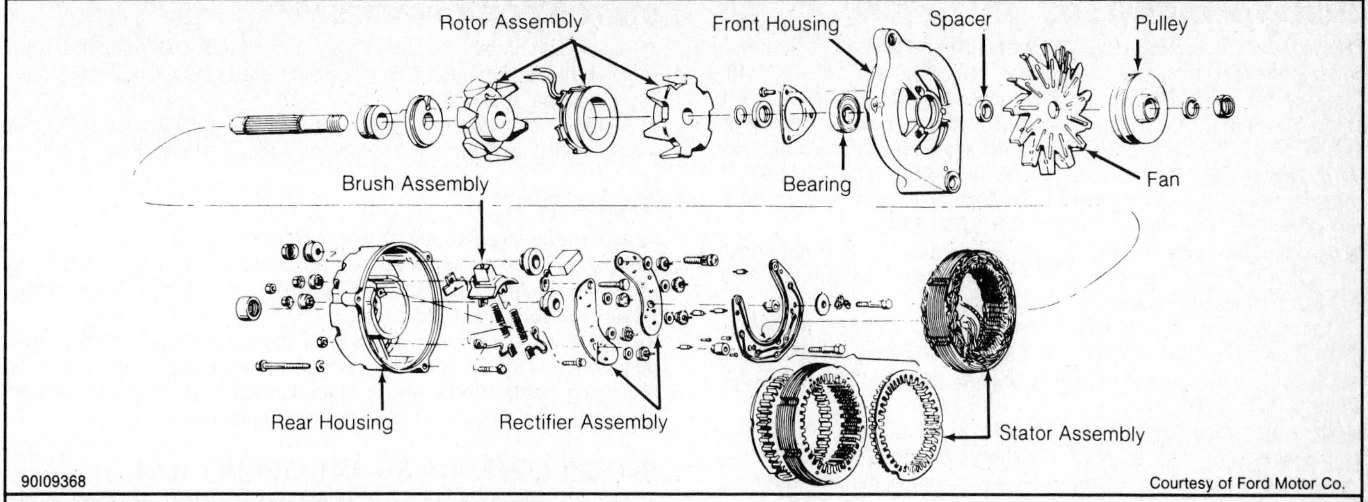
Rotor Assembly
Front Housing
Spacer
Pulley
Fan
Brush Assembly
Bearing
Rear Housing
Rectifier Assembly
Stator Assembly
90I09368
Courtesy of Ford Motor Co.

Fig. 8: Exploded View of 40, 60 & 65-Ampere Alternator

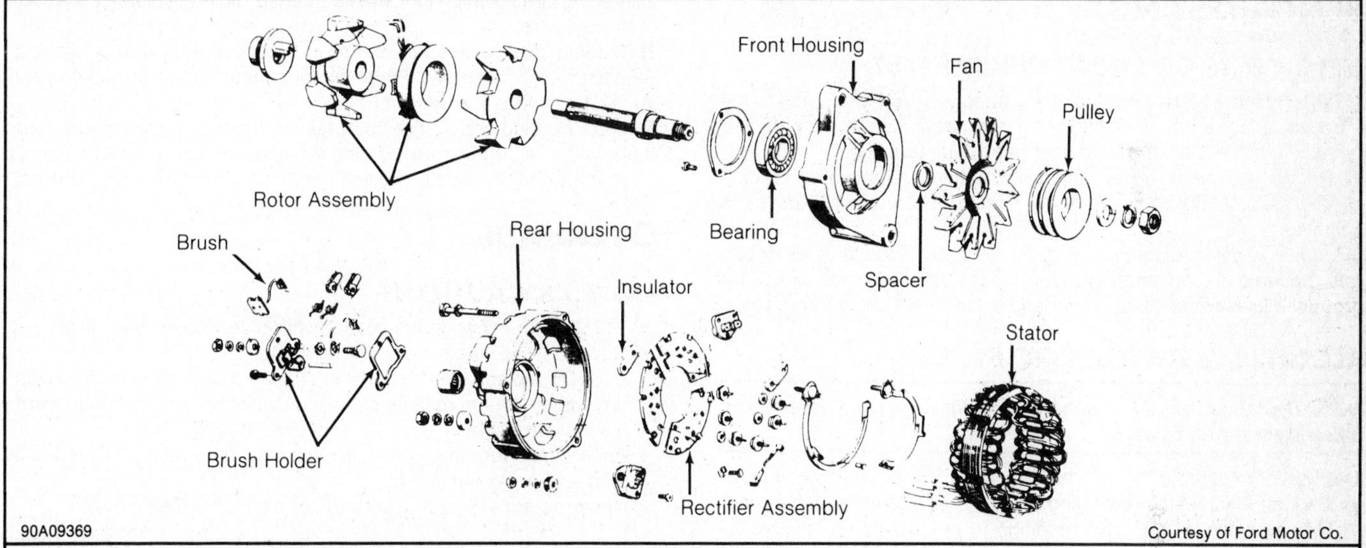
Front Housing
Fan
Pulley
Rotor Assembly
Bearing
Brush
Rear Housing
Spacer
Insulator
Stator
Brush Holder
Rectifier Assembly
90A09369
Courtesy of Ford Motor Co.

Fig. 9: Exploded View of 70-Ampere Alternator

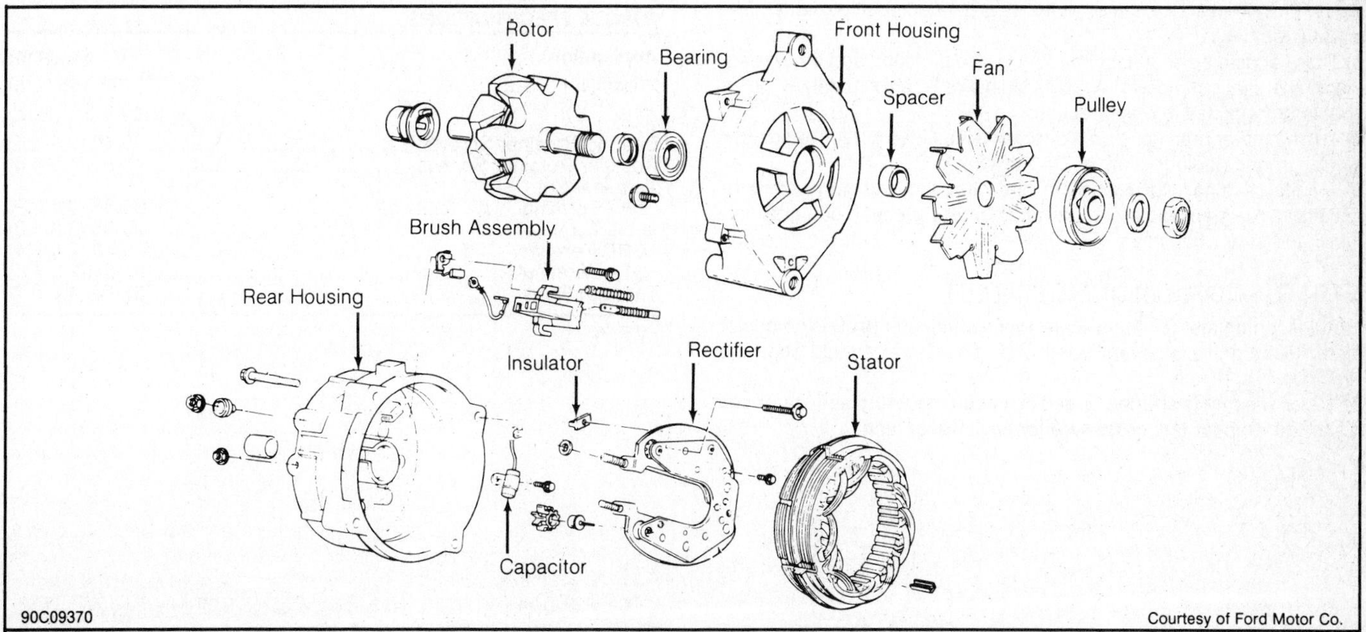
Rotor
Front Housing
Bearing
Fan
Spacer
Pulley
Brush Assembly
Rear Housing
Rectifier
Insulator
Stator
Capacitor
90C09370
Courtesy of Ford Motor Co.

Fig. 10: Exploded View of 70-Ampere Alternator

1991 ELECTRICAL
Alternators – With External Regulator (Cont.)

UNDERVOLTAGE TEST

1) Disconnect regulator wiring plug. Install ohmmeter lead on negative battery terminal. Install remaining lead on terminal "F" of the plug. Ohmmeter reading should exceed 2.4 ohms. If reading is less than 2.4 ohms, check for grounded field circuit in wiring harness or alternator.
2) If reading is 2.4 ohms or more, connect a jumper wire from terminal "A" to terminal "F". Repeat step **2)** of CHARGING SYSTEM TEST. If voltage is more than .5 volt greater than battery voltage, test regulator wiring. See "S" & "I" CIRCUIT under CIRCUIT TESTS.
3) If voltage remains low with jumper wire installed, remove jumper wire. DO NOT plug wiring connector into regulator. Disconnect FLD terminal from rear of alternator.
4) Connect jumper wire between alternator BAT and FLD terminals. Repeat step **2)** of CHARGING SYSTEM TEST. If voltage reading now indicates .5 volt greater than battery voltage, repeat "S" & "I" CIRCUIT under CIRCUIT TESTS.
5) If less than battery voltage is indicated, place voltmeter positive lead on the alternator BAT terminal. If battery voltage is now indicated, replace alternator. If no voltage is indicated, repair the alternator-to-starter relay wire or fusible link.

BENCH TESTING

FIELD OPEN OR SHORT CIRCUIT TEST

1) Perform test before alternator disassembly. Adjust ohmmeter to the x1 scale. Place ohmmeter probe on alternator FLD terminal. Place remaining ohmmeter probe on alternator GRD terminal.
2) Rotate alternator pulley and note reading. Ohmmeter reading should be 2.4–100 ohms. Reading should fluctuate while pulley is spinning.
3) Infinite reading indicates open brush lead, damaged brushes or bad rotor assembly. If ohmmeter reading is less than 2.4 ohms, check for grounded brush assembly, grounded field terminal, or defective rotor.

RECTIFIER & STATOR CIRCUIT TEST

***NOTE:** Digital ohmmeters cannot be accurately used to perform following test procedure.*

1) Adjust ohmmeter to the x1 scale. Place ohmmeter probe on alternator BAT terminal. Place remaining probe on STA terminal. Note reading. Reverse probes and note reading.
2) Perform same test procedure using STA and GRD terminals. An ohmmeter reading in both directions indicates defective negative diode, grounded stator, stator terminal, grounded positive diode plate or BAT terminal.
3) There should be an infinite reading in one direction and a low reading in the other direction. A low reading of approximately 6 ohms should be obtained in one direction.
4) An ohmmeter reading in both directions indicates defective positive diode, grounded diode plate or BAT terminal.
5) Infinite reading with probes in one direction and no reading or excessive resistance in other, indicates bad connection on stator terminal and stator bolt head.

STATOR COIL GROUNDED TEST

1) Adjust ohmmeter to x1000 scale. Place ohmmeter probes on one of stator leads and stator laminated core. Ohmmeter should show no reading.
2) Stator winding is shorted if reading is obtained. Replace stator coil if shorted. Repeat test procedure for each stator lead.

STATOR COIL OPEN TEST

1) Adjust ohmmeter to x1 scale. With stator coil removed from rectifier, place ohmmeter probes on each stator lead. Ohmmeter reading should be obtained.
2) Stator winding is open if reading is not obtained. Replace stator coil if open is found. Repeat test procedure on remaining stator leads.

DIODE TEST

1) Adjust ohmmeter to the x1 scale. Remove rectifier assembly from alternator. Place ohmmeter probe on terminal bolt. Touch remaining probe on each of 3 stator lead terminals. Note ohmmeter reading. Reverse probes and repeat test.
2) Diodes should show a reading of approximately 6 ohms in one direction, and infinite readings with probes reversed. Repeat test for remaining set of diodes using other terminal bolt. Replace rectifier assembly if readings are not within specification.

ROTOR OPEN OR SHORT CIRCUIT TEST

1) Adjust ohmmeter to x1 scale. With rotor removed, place ohmmeter probes on a rotor slip ring. Reading should be 2.0-3.5 ohms. Reading exceeding specification indicates damaged slip ring solder connection or broken wire.
2) Reading lower than specification indicates shorted wire or slip ring. Replace rotor if damaged. Place one ohmmeter probe on slip ring and remaining probe on rotor shaft.
3) Meter reading should not be obtained. If reading is obtained, rotor is shorted to shaft. Ensure slip ring terminals or solder is not touching rotor shaft. This causes a shorted condition. Replace rotor if shorted.

OVERHAUL

NOTES & CAUTIONS

- DO NOT interchange application with older model alternators.
- Never use an electromechanical voltage regulator.
- DO NOT replace 500-ohm resistor (located behind instrument cluster) with a 15-ohm resistance wire on vehicles equipped with warning indicator light.
- Ensure field terminal connector is installed on field (FLD) terminal stud and not ground stud.
- Never polarize or test alternator by grounding field circuit.

TORQUE SPECIFICATIONS

TORQUE SPECIFICATIONS

Application	Ft. Lbs. (N.m)
Pulley Nut	60-100 (82-136 N.m)
	INCH Lbs. (N.m)
Bearing Retainer Screws	25-40 (2.8-4.5)
Rectifier Retainer Screws	40-50 (4.5-5.6)
Terminal Nut	
BAT Terminal	30-55 (3.4-6.2)
FLD Terminal	25-35 (2.8-4.0)
GRD Terminal	25-30 (2.8-3.4)
STA Terminal	25-35 (2.8-4.0)
Through Bolts	35-60 (4.0-6.7)

Explorer

DESCRIPTION

The Motorcraft Integral Alternator/Regulator (IAR) with internal fan uses a solid-state voltage regulator mounted to the rear housing. The charging system consists of an alternator/regulator assembly, charge indicator (light or gauge), battery and required circuitry. Charging systems are equipped with a fusible link, used to prevent system damage. Some models are equipped with indicator lights while others use voltmeters. *See Fig. 1*.

When the ignition is turned on, voltage is applied through the charge indicator circuit "I" to the voltage regulator. The voltage regulator is activated and allows current flow from the battery to the alternator field circuit through circuit "A". When the engine is started, the rotation of the alternator creates AC current, which passes through the rectifier assembly where it is converted to DC current. DC current is supplied to the vehicle's electrical system by the output terminal located on the rear housing.

ADJUSTMENTS

BELT TENSION

Inspect belt for fraying and proper routing. *See Fig. 2*. If fraying has occurred, ensure belt and tensioner are aligned properly. If tensioner has reached its limit of travel, belt is excessively stretched and belt replacement is required. Check belt tension at position shown in figure. *See Fig. 2*. See ALTERNATOR BELT ADJUSTMENT SPECIFICATIONS table.

ALTERNATOR BELT ADJUSTMENT SPECIFICATIONS

Application	New Belt Lbs. (kg)	[1] Used Belt Lbs. (kg)
4.0L With Tensioner [2]	108-132 (49-60)	108-132 (49-60)

[1] – Any belt operated for 10 minutes or more.
[2] – Tension is correct if tensioner is within indicator marks.

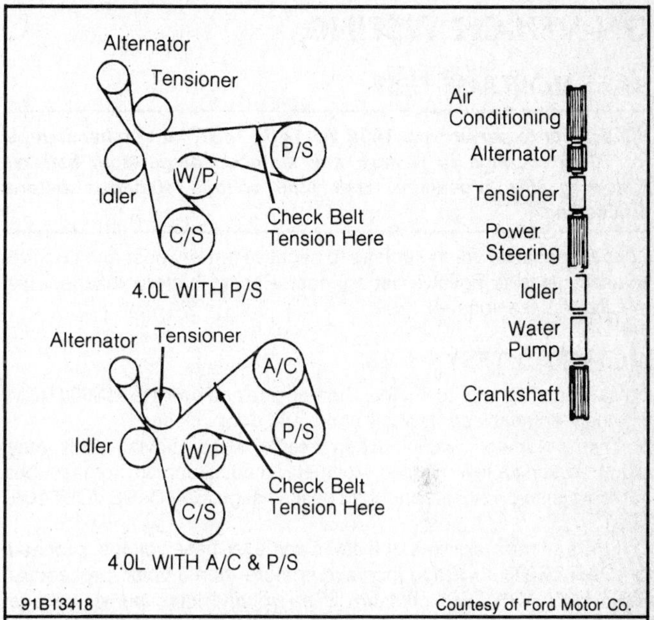
Alternator
Tensioner
P/S
W/P
Idler
Check Belt Tension Here
C/S
4.0L WITH P/S
Alternator
Tensioner
A/C
P/S
Idler
W/P
Check Belt Tension Here
C/S
4.0L WITH A/C & P/S
Air Conditioning
Alternator
Tensioner
Power Steering
Idler
Water Pump
Crankshaft
91B13418
Courtesy of Ford Motor Co.

Fig. 2: Checking Belt Tension (4.0L)

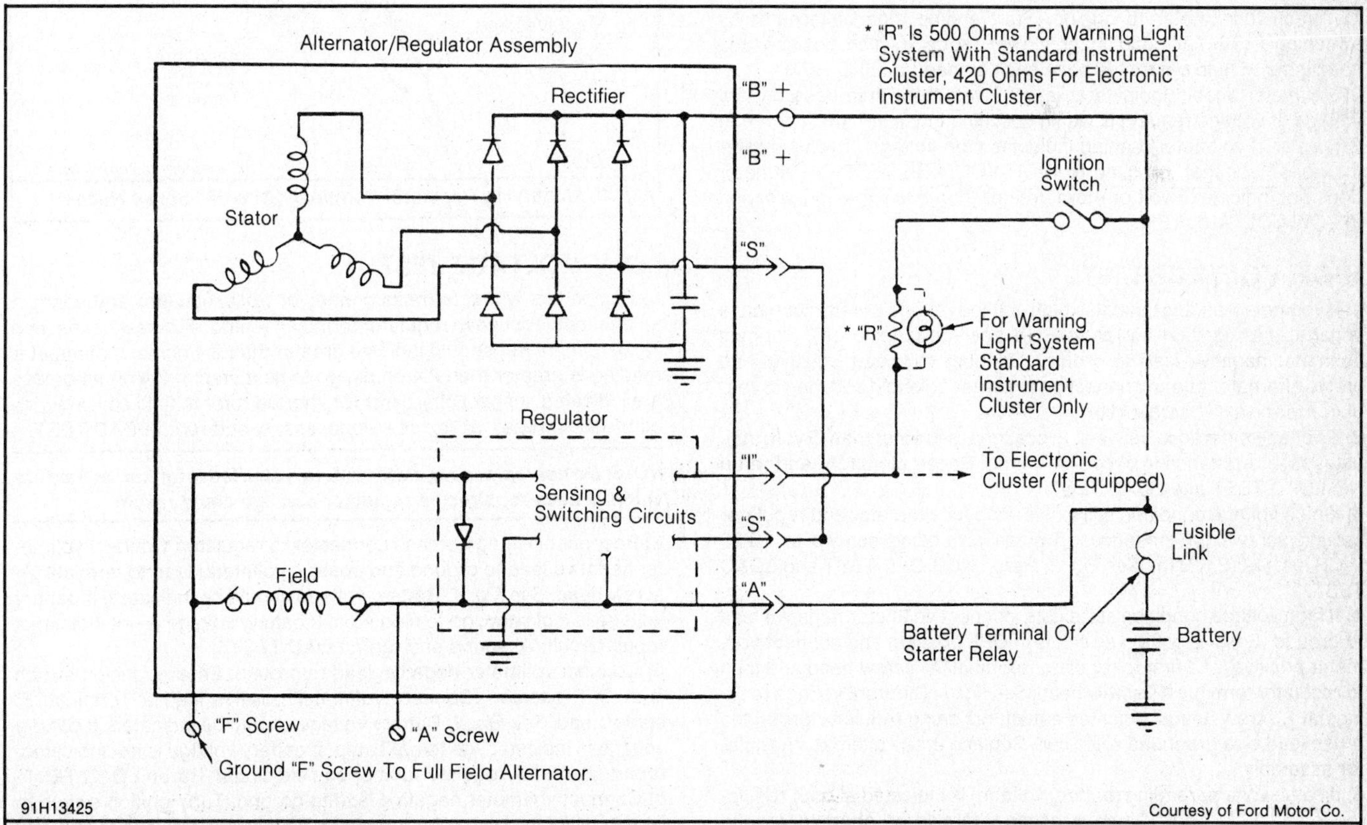
Alternator/Regulator Assembly
* "R" Is 500 Ohms For Warning Light System With Standard Instrument Cluster, 420 Ohms For Electronic Instrument Cluster.
Rectifier
"B" +
"B" +
Ignition Switch
Stator
"S"
* "R"
For Warning Light System Standard Instrument Cluster Only
Regulator
"I"
To Electronic Cluster (If Equipped)
Sensing & Switching Circuits
"S"
Fusible Link
Field
"A"
Battery Terminal Of Starter Relay
Battery
"F" Screw
"A" Screw
Ground "F" Screw To Full Field Alternator.
91H13425
Courtesy of Ford Motor Co.

Fig. 1: Charging System Wiring Diagram

Alternators – With Internal Fan & Regulator (Cont.)

VOLTAGE REGULATOR

Solid state regulator is used. Regulator is factory calibrated and cannot be adjusted.

TROUBLE SHOOTING

***NOTE:** See TROUBLE SHOOTING article in GENERAL INFORMATION.*

ON-VEHICLE TESTING

BASE VOLTAGE TEST

***NOTE:** Prior to performing BASE VOLTAGE TEST, turn on headlamps for 10-15 seconds to remove any surface charge from battery. Following this procedure, wait until voltage stabilizes before proceeding.*

Connect negative voltmeter lead to negative battery post and positive voltmeter lead to positive battery post. Record battery voltage. This reading is base voltage.

NO-LOAD TEST

1) Attach tachometer to engine. Start engine and operate at 1500 RPM with no electrical load (foot off brake and doors closed).

2) Take voltmeter reading when needle stops moving. This may require waiting a few minutes. Voltmeter reading should increase, but not more than 3 volts greater than base voltage. See BASE VOLTAGE TEST.

3) If the voltage increases at least .5 volt over base voltage, proceed to LOAD TEST. If voltage increase is more than 3 volts, proceed to HIGH VOLTAGE TEST. If there is no voltage increase, or voltage increase is less than .5 volt, proceed to LOW VOLTAGE TEST.

LOAD TEST

1) Attach tachometer to engine. Start engine. Load alternator by switching heater/air conditioner blower motor to high position and headlights to high beam. Increase engine speed to 2000 RPM.

2) Voltmeter should indicate at least .5 volt more than base battery voltage. If voltage reading is within specification, alternator operation is normal. If voltmeter reading indicates high voltage (3 volts greater than base voltage), proceed to HIGH VOLTAGE TEST. If voltmeter does not indicate .5 volt or more greater than base voltage, proceed to LOW VOLTAGE TEST.

HIGH VOLTAGE TEST

1) If voltmeter reading indicates high voltage (3 volts greater than base voltage), turn ignition switch to RUN position (engine off). Connect voltmeter negative lead to ground. Connect voltmeter positive lead first to alternator output connection at starter solenoid and then to regulator terminal "A" screw head.

2) A voltage difference between 2 locations of greater than .5 volt, indicates high resistance in circuit "A" wiring. Repair circuit "A" and rerun NO-LOAD TEST and LOAD TEST.

3) If high voltage condition still exists, inspect alternator and regulator ground screws for looseness. Tighten grounding screws to 16-25 INCH lbs. (1.8-2.8 N.m). *See Fig. 3.* Rerun NO-LOAD TEST and LOAD TEST.

4) If high voltage condition still exists, connect voltmeter negative lead to ground. Ensure ignition switch is in OFF position and connect voltmeter positive lead first to regulator terminal "A" screw head and then to regulator terminal "F" screw head. *See Fig. 4.* Different voltage readings at 2 screw heads indicates a malfunctioning regulator grounded brush lead or a grounded rotor coil. Replace entire alternator/regulator assembly.

5) If same voltage reading (battery voltage) is indicated at both regulator terminal "A" and "F" screw heads, there is no short to ground through alternator field/brushes. Replace regulator and rerun NO-LOAD TEST and LOAD TEST.

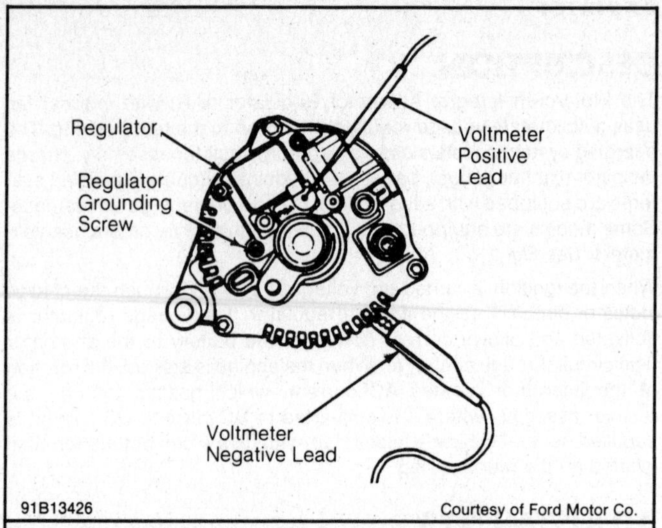
Regulator
Regulator Grounding Screw
Voltmeter Positive Lead
Voltmeter Negative Lead
91B13426
Courtesy of Ford Motor Co.

***Fig. 3:** Identifying Regulator Grounding Screw*

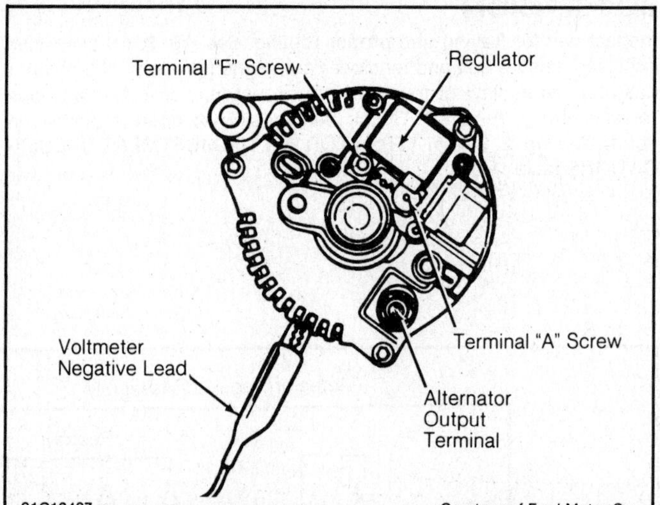
Terminal "F" Screw
Regulator
Voltmeter Negative Lead
Terminal "A" Screw
Alternator Output Terminal
91C13427
Courtesy of Ford Motor Co.

***Fig. 4:** Identifying Regulator Terminal "A" & "F" Screw Heads*

LOW VOLTAGE TEST

1) Disconnect wiring harness connector from regulator and connect an ohmmeter between regulator terminal "A" and "F" screw heads. *See Fig. 4.* Ohmmeter should indicate greater than 2.4 ohms. If ohmmeter reading is greater than 2.4 ohms, go to next step. If 2.4 ohms or less are indicated, inspect alternator for shorted rotor to field coil or shorted brushes. repair or replace as necessary and rerun LOAD TEST.

***NOTE:** Do not replace regulator before a shorted rotor coil or field circuit has been repaired as regulator damage could result.*

2) Reconnect wiring harness connector to regulator. Connect voltmeter negative lead to ground and positive voltmeter lead to terminal "A" screw head. *See Fig. 4.* Battery voltage should be indicated. If battery voltage is indicated, go to next step. If battery voltage is not indicated, repair circuit "A" wiring and rerun LOAD TEST.

3) Connect voltmeter negative lead to ground. Ensure ignition switch is in OFF position. Connect voltmeter positive lead to terminal "F" screw head. *See Fig. 4.* Battery voltage should be indicated. If battery voltage is indicated, go to next step. If battery voltage is not indicated, repair alternator/regulator unit open field circuit. Rerun LOAD TEST.

4) Connect voltmeter negative lead to ground. Turn ignition switch to RUN position (engine off). Connect voltmeter positive lead to terminal "F" screw head. *See Fig. 4.* Voltmeter should indicate 2 volts or less. If 2 volts or less is indicated, go to next step. If greater than 2 volts is indicated, go to REGULATOR CIRCUIT "S" TEST. If circuit "I" test is normal, replace regulator and rerun LOAD TEST.

5) Perform LOAD TEST, but connect voltmeter positive lead to alternator output terminal. *See Fig. 4*. If voltage rises greater than .5 volts above base voltage, repair wiring harness between alternator output terminal and starter relay battery terminal. If voltage does not rise greater than .5 volts above base voltage, go to next step.

6) Perform LOAD TEST and measure voltage drop from battery positive terminal to terminal "A" of regulator (with wiring harness connector connected). Voltage drop should not exceed .5 volt. If voltage drop does not exceed .5 volt, go to next step. If voltage drop exceeds .5 volt, repair wiring harness between alternator regulator and starter relay.

7) Connect a jumper wire from alternator rear housing to regulator terminal "F" screw. *See Fig. 5*. Rerun LOAD TEST with voltmeter positive lead connected to alternator output terminal. If voltage rises .5 volt or more greater than base voltage, replace regulator. If voltage does not exceed .5 volt greater than base voltage, repair alternator.

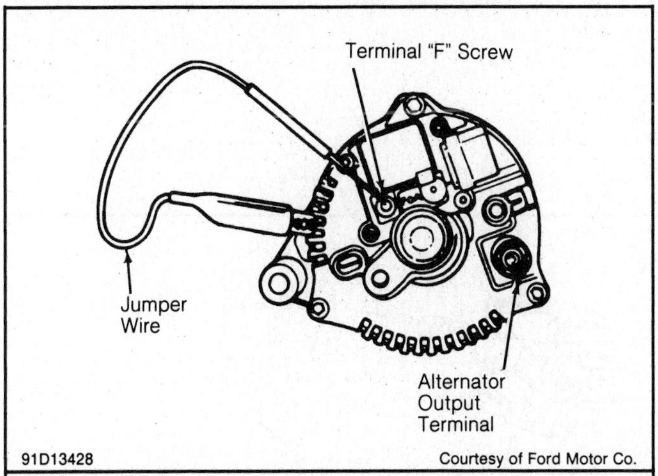
Terminal "F" Screw
Jumper Wire
Alternator Output Terminal
91D13428
Courtesy of Ford Motor Co.

Fig. 5: Connecting Jumper Wire to Regulator Terminal "F" Screw (Full Field)

REGULATOR CIRCUIT "S" TEST

1) Disconnect wiring harness connector from regulator. Connect a jumper wire between regulator terminal "A" and terminal "A" of wiring harness connector. Connect a jumper wire between regulator terminal "F" screw head and ground on alternator rear housing. *See Fig. 6*.

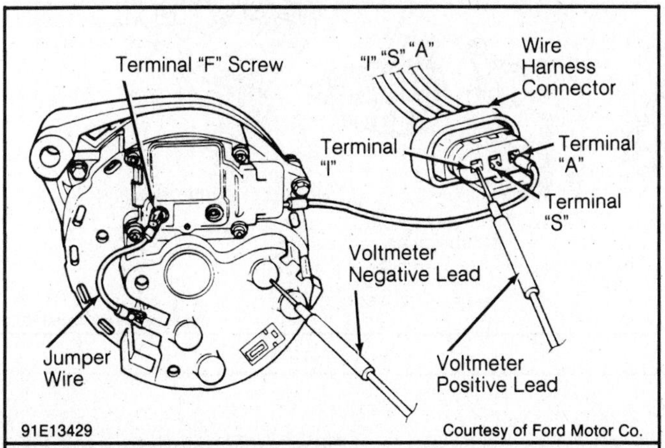
Terminal "F" Screw
"I" "S" "A"
Wire Harness Connector
Terminal "I"
Terminal "A"
Terminal "S"
Voltmeter Negative Lead
Jumper Wire
Voltmeter Positive Lead
91E13429
Courtesy of Ford Motor Co.

Fig. 6: Testing Regulator Circuit "S"

2) Start engine and allow to idle. Connect voltmeter negative lead to ground. Connect voltmeter positive lead to terminal "S" and then to terminal "I" of wiring harness connector. *See Fig. 6*. The voltage at terminal "S" should be approximately one-half the voltage at terminal "I". If voltage readings are normal, remove jumper wires and replace regulator. Rerun LOAD TEST.

3) If voltage is not present, remove jumper wires and repair faulty wiring circuit in alternator. Reconnect regulator harness connector and rerun LOAD TEST to confirm repair.

FIELD CIRCUIT DRAIN TEST

NOTE: Connect voltmeter negative lead to alternator rear housing for all the following voltage readings.

1) Turn ignition switch to OFF position. Connect voltmeter positive lead to terminal "F" screw head. *See Fig. 6*. Battery voltage should be indicated. If less than battery voltage is indicated, go to next step. If battery voltage is indicated, system is functioning properly and further testing is not needed.

2) Connect positive voltmeter lead to terminal "I" of wiring harness connector (with ignition off). *See Fig. 6*. If no voltage is indicated, go to next step. If voltage is indicated, repair circuit "I" from ignition switch to eliminate voltage source.

3) Connect positive voltmeter lead to terminal "S" of wiring harness connector (with connector connected to regulator). If voltage is indicated, go to next step. If no voltage is indicated, replace regulator.

4) Disconnect wiring harness connector from regulator. Connect voltmeter positive lead to terminal "S" of wiring harness connector. *See Fig. 6*. If voltage is indicated, repair wiring harness to eliminate voltage source. If no voltage is indicated, replace alternator rectifier assembly.

BENCH TESTING

NOTE: Digital ohmmeter CANNOT be used for bench tests.

RECTIFIER ASSEMBLY TEST

1) Remove and disassemble alternator. Set ohmmeter in x1 range. Connect one ohmmeter probe to positive diode lead and other probe to heat sink at positive side. Reverse ohmmeter probes. There should be continuity only in the direction from diode lead to heat sink and an infinite reading with probes reversed. If meter readings are not as specified, replace positive rectifier assembly.

2) Connect one ohmmeter probe to negative diode lead and other probe to heat sink at negative side. Reverse ohmmeter probes. There should be continuity only in the direction from heat sink to diode lead and an infinite reading with probes reversed. If meter readings are not as specified, replace negative rectifier assembly.

3) Check diode trio. There should be continuity in only one direction. Replace if readings are not as specified.

RADIO SUPPRESSION CAPACITOR TEST

NOTE: This is an open or shorted circuit test and does not measure capacitance value.

1) Remove and disassemble alternator. Set ohmmeter to 1000-ohm range. Connect one ohmmeter probe to terminal "B+" and other probe to rectifier base plate assembly. Reverse probes while observing ohmmeter needle.

2) One position should give an infinite reading, indicating reverse current direction through diodes. Other position should read about 1000 ohms resistance, indicating forward direction of current. The same reading in both directions indicates inoperative rectifier assembly.

3) To check capacitor, connect probes to rectifier assembly terminal "B+" and base plate. If needle jumps momentarily and then returns to previous position, capacitor is okay. If needle does not jump, replace rectifier assembly. Radio suppression capacitor must be replaced as a complete unit.

STATOR COIL GROUNDED TEST

1) Remove and disassemble alternator. This test determines if stator coil is properly insulated. Remove stator from alternator. Set ohmmeter in 1000-ohm range.

2) Connect one ohmmeter probe to one stator lead and other probe to stator laminated core. Ohmmeter reading should be infinity. If meter

Alternators – With Internal Fan & Regulator (Cont.)

needle moves, stator winding is shorted to core and stator must be replaced. Repeat test for each stator lead.

NOTE: DO NOT touch metal ohmmeter probes or stator leads during resistance test. Incorrect reading will result.

STATOR COIL OPEN TEST

Remove and disassemble alternator. Disconnect stator from rectifier. *See Fig. 7.* Place ohmmeter in x1 range. Connect one ohmmeter probe to one stator lead and touch other probe to another stator lead. If no meter movement occurs, an open exists and stator should be replaced. Repeat test for each stator lead.

ROTOR OPEN OR SHORT CIRCUIT TEST

1) Remove and disassemble alternator. *See Fig. 7.* Remove rotor. Set ohmmeter to x1 range. Contact each probe to one rotor slip ring. Meter should read 2.0-3.9 ohms. Higher reading indicates damaged slip ring solder connection or broken wire.

2) Lower reading indicates shorted wire or slip ring. Replace rotor if damaged. Contact ohmmeter probe to one slip ring and other probe to rotor shaft. Ohmmeter reading should be infinite. Readings other than infinite indicate rotor is shorted to shaft. Replace rotor if shorted.

ALTERNATOR SPECIFICATIONS

NOTE: Specification listed is only one available from manufacturer.

ALTERNATOR SPECIFICATIONS

Application	In. (mm)
Brush Length Wear Limit	.30 (8)

OVERHAUL

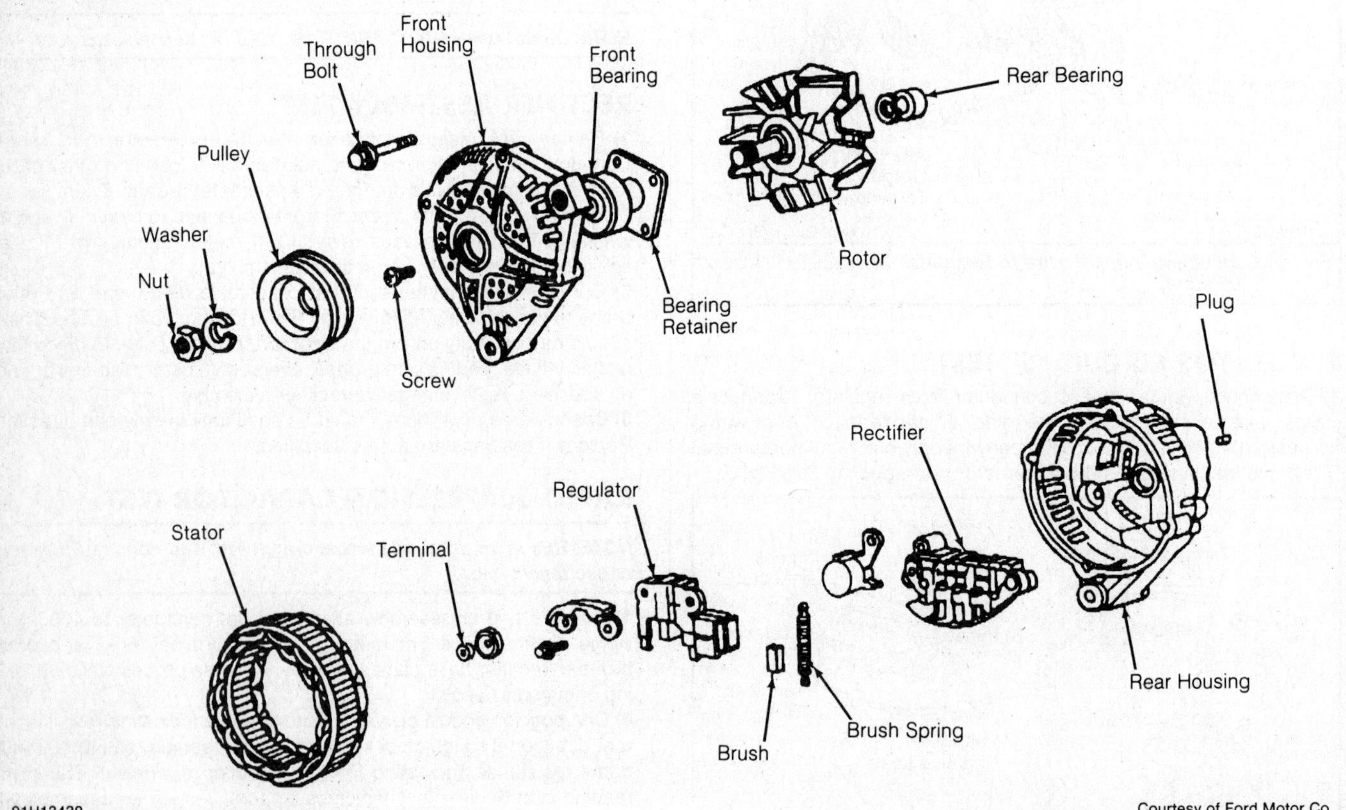
Front Housing
Through Bolt
Front Bearing
Rear Bearing
Pulley
Washer
Nut
Screw
Bearing Retainer
Rotor
Plug
Rectifier
Regulator
Stator
Terminal
Rear Housing
Brush Spring
Brush
91H13430
Courtesy of Ford Motor Co.

Fig. 7: Exploded View of Alternator

1991 ELECTRICAL
Starters – Motorcraft Gear Reduction

Aerostar, Explorer, Ranger (Except 2.9L)

DESCRIPTION

The permanent magnet, gear reduction type starter used on 2.3L, 3.0L and 4.0L engines has an externally mounted, solenoid actuated drive. The starting system consists of a starter, (ignition) switch, relay, neutral start switch (A/T) or clutch switch (M/T), battery and circuit wiring.

When the ignition switch is turned to the START position, the starter relay is actuated through the starter control circuit. This energizes the starter solenoid, creating a magnetic field around the solenoid windings.

As the magnetic field draws the iron plunger core into the solenoid coil, the plunger's contact disc closes the circuit between the battery and the motor feed terminals. Current can then flow to the starter motor, as the solenoid pull-in coil is by-passed.

The hold-in coil keeps the drive pinion gear engaged with the flywheel, until the ignition switch is released from the START position. An overrunning clutch in the drive assembly protects the starter from excessive speeds (engine RPM), during the period after the engine starts and before the operator releases the ignition switch from the START position.

ON-VEHICLE TESTING

CAUTION: Before testing starter, ensure transmission is in Park on A/T models or Neutral on M/T models.

SYSTEM FUNCTION TEST

1) If the engine cannot be started, turn heater blower motor on and turn off all other accessories. Use cables to jump-start vehicle.
2) If engine starts, check charging system. If engine does not start, clean and tighten connections at battery posts, starter relay, and battery ground at engine. Check for positive short to ground. If okay, replace starter.

STARTER RELAY TEST

1) Attach cables to jump-start vehicle (if necessary). Disconnect terminal "S" of starter relay. *See Fig. 1.* Connect remote starter switch between terminal "S" and positive battery terminal. Ensure transmission is in Park on A/T models or Neutral on M/T models.

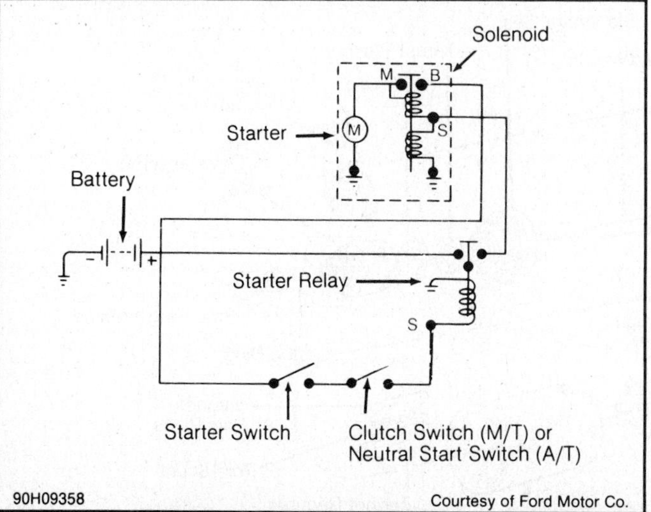
Solenoid
M
B
Starter
M
S
Battery
Starter Relay
S
Starter Switch
Clutch Switch (M/T) or
Neutral Start Switch (A/T)
90H09358
Courtesy of Ford Motor Co.

Fig. 1: Starter System Electrical Schematic

2) Crank engine with remote starter. If engine cranks, relay is okay. Check ignition switch, neutral switch or clutch switch and circuitry for open or loose connections. If engine does not crank, replace relay.

SOLENOID TEST

1) If engine does not start, ensure battery is fully charged and in good condition. Ensure all cable connections are clean and tight. Attach cables to jump-start vehicle (if necessary).
2) Connect remote starter switch between starter solenoid terminal "B" and "M". *See Figs. 1 and 2.* Ensure transmission is in Park on A/T models or Neutral on M/T models. Crank engine with remote starter switch. If engine cranks, replace solenoid. If engine does not crank, replace starter.

LOAD TEST

1) Connect starter load tester and voltmeter on battery terminals. Ensure no current is flowing through the ammeter and carbon pile of tester. Disconnect terminal "S" of starter relay.
2) Connect remote starter switch between terminal "S" and positive battery terminal. Ensure transmission is in Park on A/T models or Neutral on M/T models prior to testing starter.
3) Crank engine with ignition off and note voltmeter reading. Stop cranking engine. Turn carbon pile tester rheostat knob to match voltage obtained while cranking. Note ammeter reading. Replace or repair starter if current exceeds specification. See STARTER SPECIFICATIONS at end of article.

BENCH TESTING

NO-LOAD TEST

1) Connect voltmeter to battery terminals. Connect battery, jumper cables and starter load tester to starter. *See Fig. 2.* The starter will operate without a load. Ensure no current is flowing through the ammeter and carbon pile of tester.

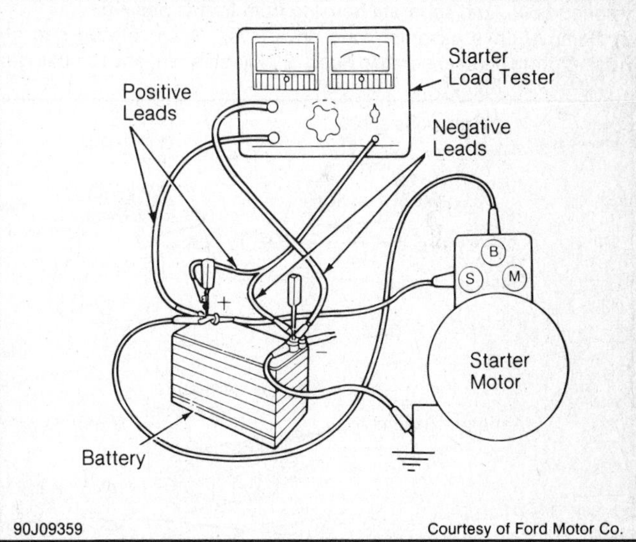
Starter
Load Tester
Positive
Leads
Negative
Leads
B
S
M
+
−
Starter
Motor
Battery
90J09359
Courtesy of Ford Motor Co.

Fig. 2: Testing Starter No-Load

2) Note voltmeter reading. Disconnect battery from starter. Turn carbon pile to achieve voltage obtained while starter was operating. Note ammeter reading. Replace or repair starter if current exceeds specification. See STARTER SPECIFICATIONS at end of article.

ARMATURE OPEN CIRCUIT TEST

An open armature circuit can be detected by inspecting the commutator for evidence of burning. If burning is present, replace armature assembly. Check for damage to other related components.

ARMATURE GROUNDED CIRCUIT TEST

Connect ohmmeter leads to the armature and commutator. *See Fig. 3.* Ohmmeter should read infinite. If ohmmeter shows any other value, replace starter.

1991 ELECTRICAL
Starters – Motorcraft Gear Reduction (Cont.)

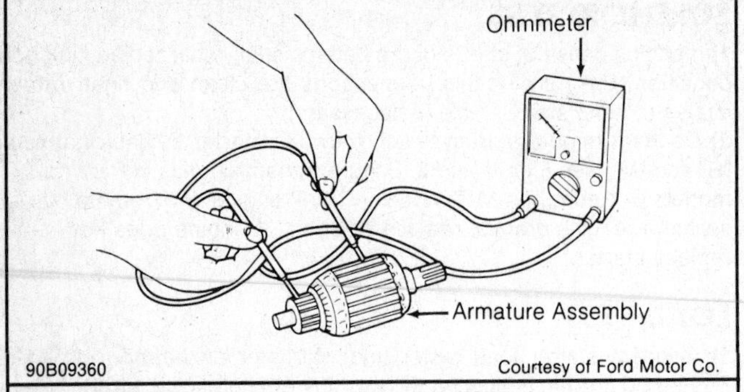
Ohmmeter
Armature Assembly
90B09360
Courtesy of Ford Motor Co.

Fig. 3: Checking Armature For Grounded Circuit

REMOVAL & INSTALLATION

Removal – Disconnect negative battery cable. Raise vehicle. Disconnect positive battery cable from starter and ground cable (if equipped). Remove starter solenoid wiring. Remove starter mounting bolts or nuts. Remove starter from vehicle.

Installation – 1) Position starter assembly to flywheel housing and start bolts. Hold starter against mounting surface, fully inserted into pilot hole. Tighten bolts or nuts to specification.

2) Connect positive battery cable and solenoid wiring to starter. Tighten to specification. Lower vehicle. Connect negative battery cable. Check starter operation.

OVERHAUL

Disassembly – 1) Remove connector from "M" terminal. Remove solenoid retaining screws and solenoid. Remove starter housing through bolts, and separate housing from frame. *See Fig. 4.*

2) Remove drive assembly and drive lever. Remove stop ring and retainer from shaft assembly. Push "E" ring off shaft, and remove gear assembly from shaft. Remove brush end plate and brush assembly. Pull armature out of frame.

Inspection – Check armature winding for separated or burned insulation. Check for open or shorted circuits. Check armature shaft and bearings for scoring or excessive wear. Check commutator for excessive runout. Machine commutator if runout exceeds .005" (.12 mm).

Reassembly – 1) Reverse disassembly procedure. Lubricate armature shaft and splines with low temperature grease. Fill drive end housing bearing bore approximately 1/4 full with grease.

2) Tighten through bolts to 55-75 INCH lbs. (6.2-8.5 N.m). Position solenoid so solenoid plunger is attached to drive lever. Perform NO-LOAD TEST to ensure current draw is within specification.

STARTER SPECIFICATIONS

STARTER SPECIFICATIONS

Application	Specifications
Brush Length Wear Limit	.66" (16.8 mm)
Current Draw	
No-Load	60-80 Amps
Under Load	140-200 Amps
Normal Cranking RPM	170-220

TORQUE SPECIFICATIONS

TORQUE SPECIFICATIONS

Application	Ft. Lbs. (N.m)
Mounting Bolts	15-20 (20-27)
	INCH Lbs. (N.m)
"B" & "M" Terminal Nut	80-120 (9.0-13.5)
Brush Plate Screws	20-30 (2.3-3.4)
Positive Cable Mounting Nut	70-130 (7.9-14.6)
Solenoid Bolts	45-54 (5.1-6.1)
Through Bolts	55-75 (6.2-8.5)

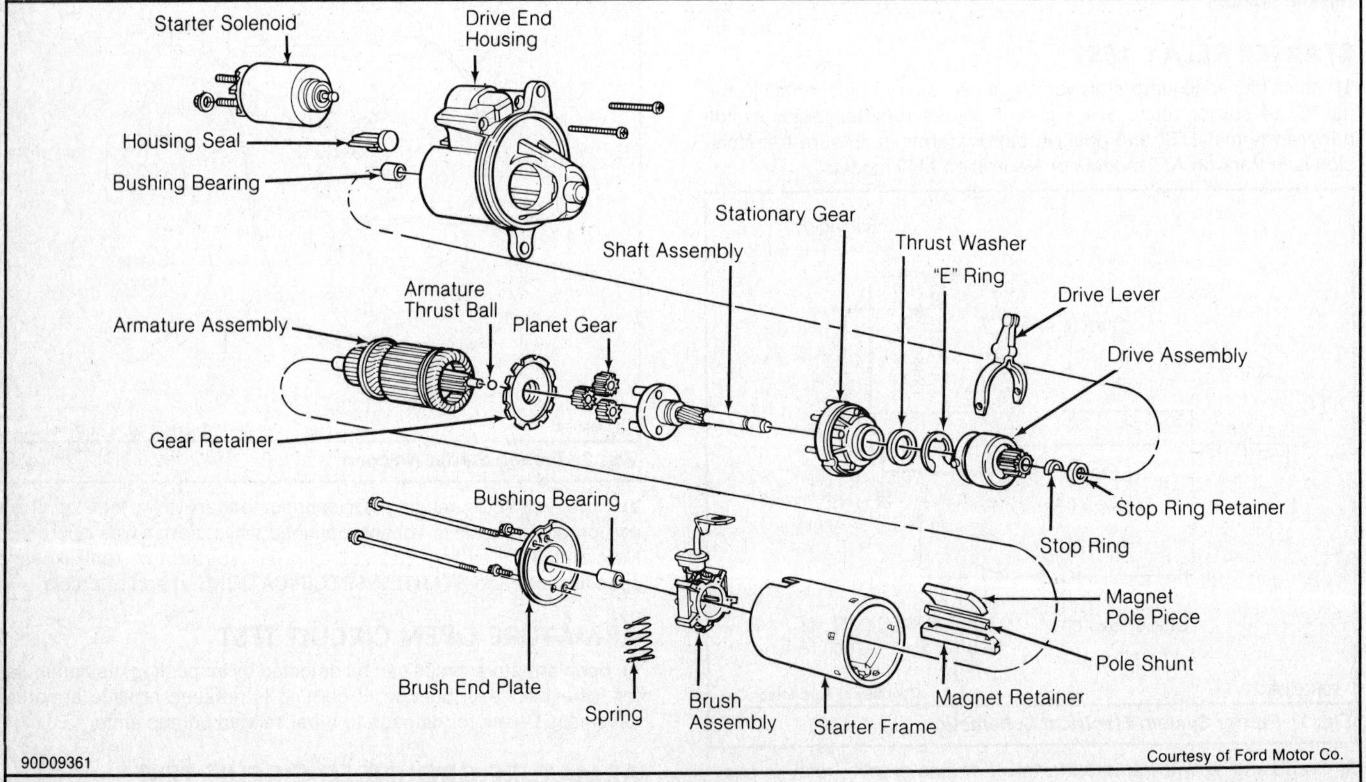
Starter Solenoid
Drive End
Housing
Housing Seal
Bushing Bearing
Stationary Gear
Shaft Assembly
Thrust Washer
"E" Ring
Drive Lever
Armature
Thrust Ball
Armature Assembly
Planet Gear
Drive Assembly
Gear Retainer
Stop Ring Retainer
Bushing Bearing
Stop Ring
Magnet
Pole Piece
Pole Shunt
Brush End Plate
Spring
Brush
Assembly
Starter Frame
Magnet Retainer
90D09361
Courtesy of Ford Motor Co.

Fig. 4: Exploded View Of 2.3L, 3.0L & 4.0L Motorcraft Gear Reduction Starter

1991 ELECTRICAL
Starters – Motorcraft Positive Engagement

Bronco, Ranger 2.9L, "E" & "F" Series, "F" Series Super Duty

NOTE: Unless otherwise specified, references to "F" Series include "F" Series Super Duty.

DESCRIPTION

The Motorcraft positive engagement starter motor is used on all gasoline engine vehicles, except Aerostar and Explorer models and Ranger 2.3L, 3.0L and 4.0L models. The starter system includes a starter (ignition) switch, starter relay, neutral start switch (A/T) or clutch interlock switch (M/T), battery and heavy circuit wiring.

When the ignition switch is turned to the START position, the starter relay is actuated through the starter control circuit. This connects the starter motor to battery, permitting current to flow through the grounded field coil, actuating a movable pole shoe. *See Fig. 1*. The pole shoe forces the starter drive plunger lever to engage the starter and flywheel gears.

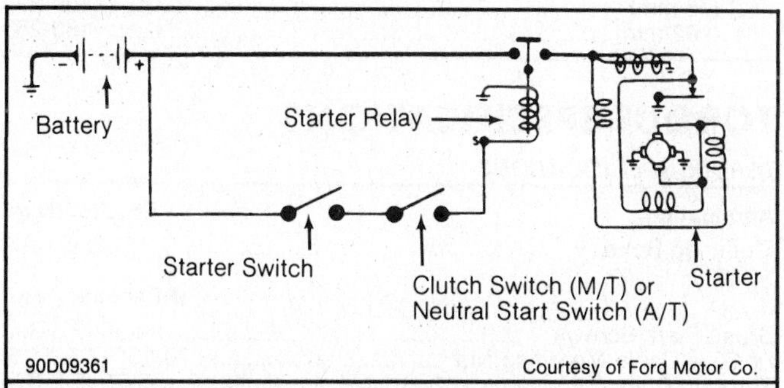
Battery
Starter Relay
Starter Switch
Clutch Switch (M/T) or
Neutral Start Switch (A/T)
Starter
90D09361
Courtesy of Ford Motor Co.

Fig. 1: Starter System Circuit Electrical Schematic

ON-VEHICLE TESTING

CAUTION: Before testing starter, ensure transmission is in Park on A/T models or Neutral on M/T models.

SYSTEM FUNCTION TEST

1) If the engine cannot be started, turn heater blower motor on and turn off all other accessories. Use cables to jump-start vehicle.

2) If engine starts, check charging system. See CHARGING SYSTEM tables in TROUBLE SHOOTING article in GENERAL INFORMATION. If engine does not start, clean and tighten connections at battery posts, starter relay, relay bracket and battery ground at engine. Check for positive short to ground. If no short is found, perform STARTER RELAY TEST.

STARTER RELAY TEST

1) If vehicle will not start and battery is fully charged, disconnect terminal "S" (Red/Blue) from starter relay terminal. Connect remote starter between terminal "S" of starter relay and positive battery terminal.

2) Crank engine with remote starter. If engine cranks, relay is okay. Check ignition, neutral safety or clutch switch operation and wiring circuits. If starter does not operate, replace relay.

3) If starter spins but does not engage engine, check armature shaft for corrosion. Repair as necessary. If armature shaft is okay, replace starter.

LOAD TEST

1) Connect starter load tester and voltmeter on battery terminals. Ensure no current is flowing through the ammeter and carbon pile of tester. Disconnect terminal "S" of starter relay.

2) Connect remote starter switch between terminal "S" and positive battery terminal. Ensure transmission is in Park on A/T models or Neutral on M/T models prior to testing starter.

3) Crank engine with ignition off and note voltmeter reading. Stop cranking engine. Turn tester carbon pile to achieve voltage obtained while cranking. Note ammeter reading. Remove carbon pile load. Replace or repair starter if current exceeds specification. See STARTER SPECIFICATIONS at end of article.

BENCH TESTING

NO-LOAD TEST

1) Connect voltmeter to battery terminals. Connect battery, jumper cables and starter tester to starter. *See Fig. 2.* The starter will operate without a load. Ensure no current is flowing through the ammeter and carbon pile of tester.

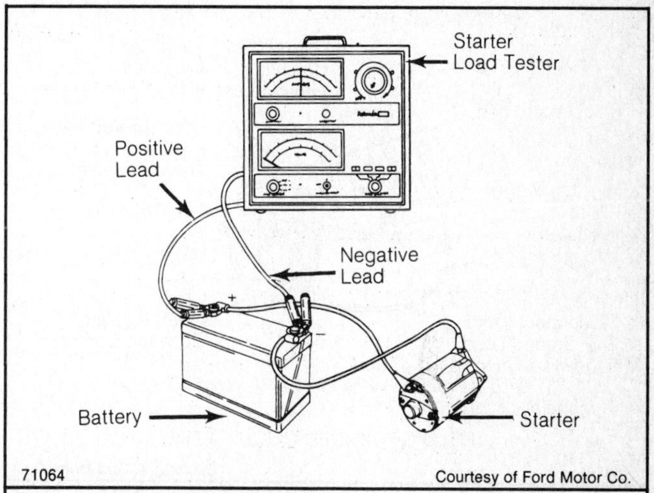
Starter
Load Tester
Positive
Lead
Negative
Lead
Battery
Starter
71064
Courtesy of Ford Motor Co.

Fig. 2: Testing Starter No-Load

2) Note voltmeter reading. Disconnect battery from starter. Turn carbon pile to achieve voltage obtained while starter was operating. Note ammeter reading. Remove carbon pile load. Repair or replace starter if current exceeds specification. See STARTER SPECIFICATIONS at end of article.

ARMATURE OPEN CIRCUIT TEST

An open armature circuit can be detected by inspecting the commutator for evidence of burning. If burning is present, replace armature assembly. Check for damage to other related components.

ARMATURE & FIELD GROUNDED CIRCUIT TEST

Connect voltmeter and battery terminals to components. *See Fig. 3.* If voltmeter shows any voltage, windings are grounded.

REMOVAL & INSTALLATION

Removal – Disconnect negative battery cable. Raise vehicle. Disconnect positive battery cable from starter and ground cable (if equipped). Remove starter mounting bolts or nuts. Remove starter from vehicle.

Installation – **1)** Position starter assembly to flywheel housing and start bolts. Hold starter against mounting surface, fully inserted into pilot hole. Tighten bolts or nuts to specification.

2) Connect positive battery cable to starter. Tighten to specification. Lower vehicle. Connect negative battery cable. Check starter operation.

1991 ELECTRICAL

Starters – Motorcraft Positive Engagement (Cont.)

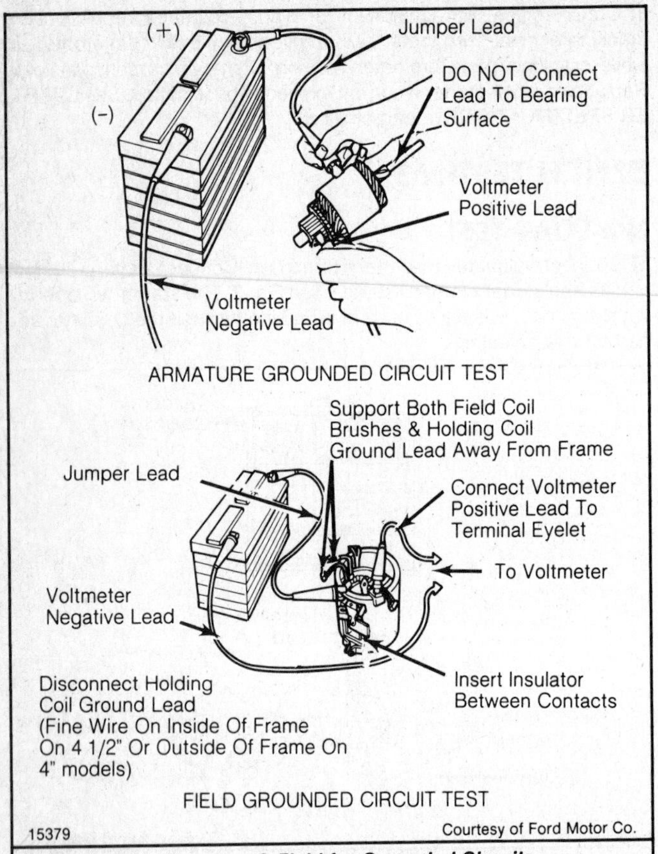
(+)
Jumper Lead
DO NOT Connect
Lead To Bearing
Surface
(-)
Voltmeter
Positive Lead
Voltmeter
Negative Lead
ARMATURE GROUNDED CIRCUIT TEST
Support Both Field Coil
Brushes & Holding Coil
Ground Lead Away From Frame
Jumper Lead
Connect Voltmeter
Positive Lead To
Terminal Eyelet
To Voltmeter
Voltmeter
Negative Lead
Insert Insulator
Between Contacts
Disconnect Holding
Coil Ground Lead
(Fine Wire On Inside Of Frame
On 4 1/2" Or Outside Of Frame On
4" models)
FIELD GROUNDED CIRCUIT TEST
15379
Courtesy of Ford Motor Co.

Fig. 3: Testing Armature & Field for Grounded Circuits

OVERHAUL

Disassembly – Note location of brush holder with respect to end terminal. *See Fig. 4*. On field coil which operates drive gear actuating lever, bend edges on field coil retaining sleeve and remove sleeve and retainers. Cut positive brush leads from field coils as close to field connection point as possible.

Reassembly – Replace brushes using a 300-watt soldering iron and rosin core solder. Lubricate armature shaft splines with Lubriplate 777. Fill drive end housing bearing bore approximately 1/4 full with Grease (ESB-M1C63-A). Tighten through bolts to 55-75 INCH lbs. (6.2-8.5 N.m).

STARTER SPECIFICATIONS

STARTER SPECIFICATIONS

Application	Specifications
Brush Length Wear Limit	.25" (6.3 mm)
Current Draw	
No-Load	
3" (78 mm)	60-80 Amps
4" (102 mm)	80 Amps
Under Load	
3" (78 mm)	130-220 Amps
4" (102 mm)	150-200 Amps
Normal Cranking RPM	
3" (78 mm)	100-230
4" (102 mm)	180-250

TORQUE SPECIFICATIONS

TORQUE SPECIFICATIONS

Application	Ft. Lbs. (N.m)
Mounting Bolts	15-20 (21-27)
	INCH Lbs. (N.m)
Brush Plate Screws	20-30 (2.3-3.4)
Positive Cable Mounting Nut	70-130 (7.9-14.6)
Through Bolts	55-75 (6.2-8.5)

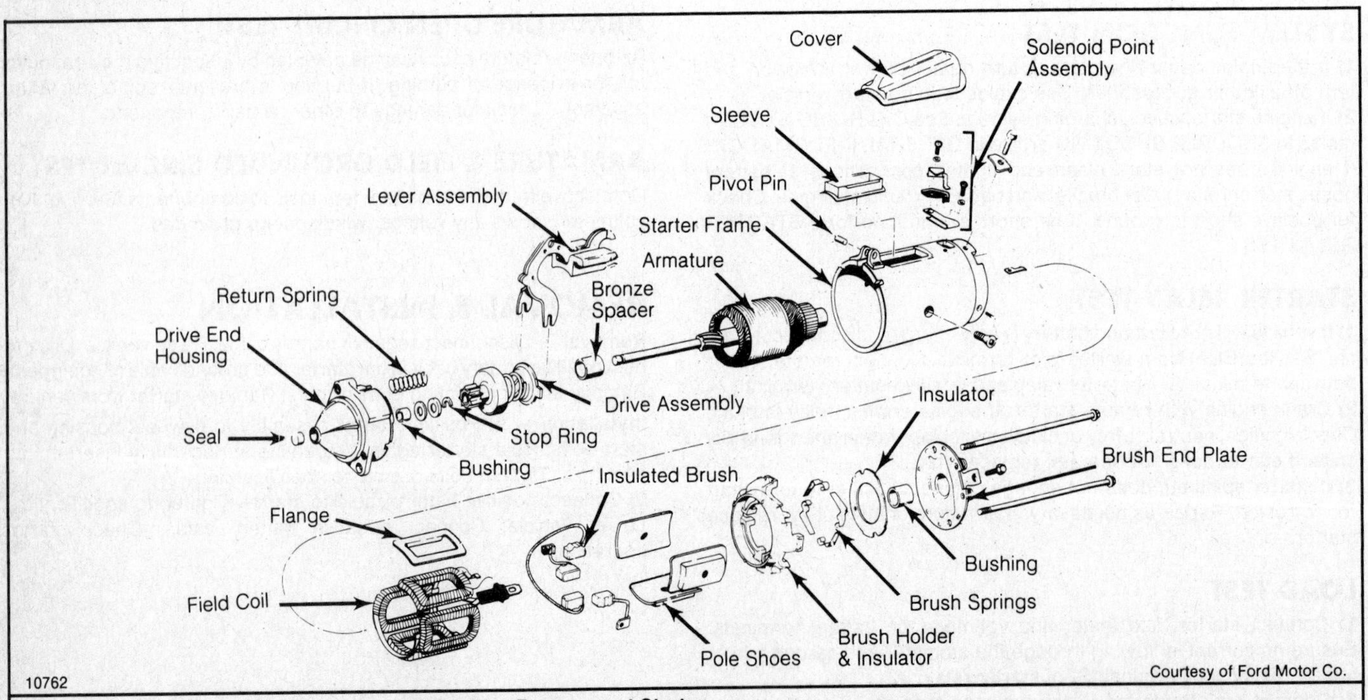
Cover
Solenoid Point
Assembly
Sleeve
Pivot Pin
Lever Assembly
Starter Frame
Armature
Return Spring
Bronze
Spacer
Drive End
Housing
Drive Assembly
Seal
Stop Ring
Bushing
Insulator
Brush End Plate
Insulated Brush
Flange
Bushing
Field Coil
Brush Springs
Brush Holder
& Insulator
Pole Shoes
10762
Courtesy of Ford Motor Co.

Fig. 4: Exploded View of Typical Motorcraft Positive Engagement Starter

Starters – Mitsubishi Gear Reduction

"E" & "F" Series With 7.3L Diesel Engine

DESCRIPTION

The starter used on the 7.3L Diesel engine is a permanent magnet, gear reduction type. It has an externally mounted, solenoid actuated drive and an auxiliary switch. The system consists of a starter (ignition) switch, safety relay, battery and circuit wiring.

When the ignition switch is turned to the START position, the contact in the auxiliary switch closes and current passes through the auxiliary switch to the safety relay contact to ground. As current passes through the auxiliary switch, its plunger closes the circuit to allow current flow to solenoid coils "P" and "H". *See Fig. 1.*

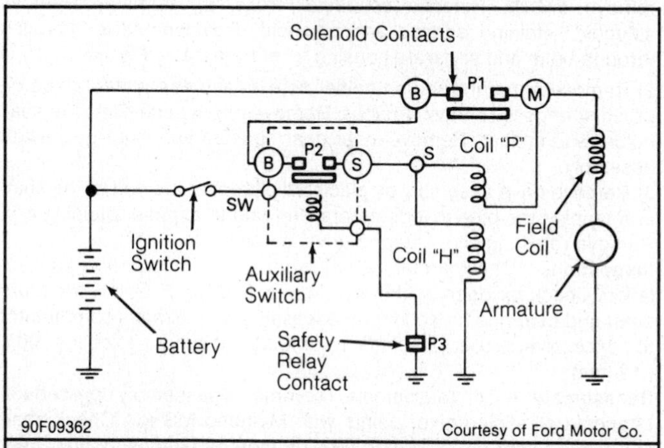
Solenoid Contacts
B
P1
M
P2
B
S
S
Coil "P"
SW
L
Ignition Switch
Auxiliary Switch
Coil "H"
Field Coil
Armature
Battery
Safety Relay Contact
P3
90F09362
Courtesy of Ford Motor Co.

Fig. 1: Starter System Electrical Schematic

When current passes through the coils, the plunger engages and causes the drive pinion to engage with the flywheel ring gear. When the pinion has engaged completely, the main solenoid P1 closes, allowing battery current to flow to the starter motor. When the P1 contact is closed, no current flows in coil "P" and the solenoid plunger is held in by coil "H".

When the ignition is released to the RUN position, contact P2 opens and causes the main contact P1 to open. The starter then disengages and stops, enabling the drive pinion to disengage from the flywheel ring gear.

ADJUSTMENTS

PINION GAP

1) Secure starter in vise. Connect a switch in series with starter solenoid and battery. Connect a switch and battery in series with auxiliary switch and starter housing. *See Fig. 2.*

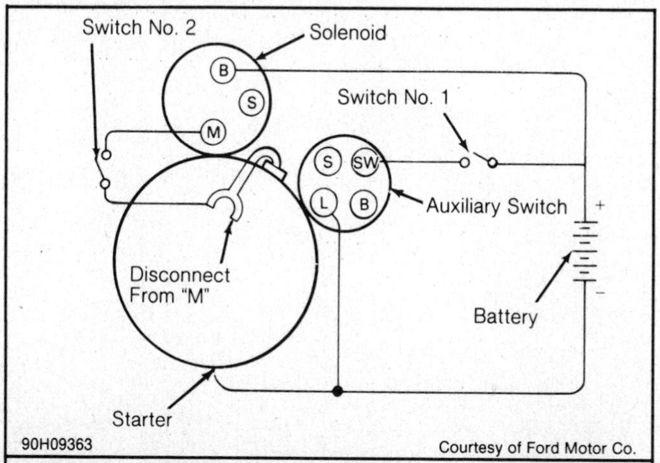
Switch No. 2
Solenoid
B
S
M
Switch No. 1
S
SW
L
B
Auxiliary Switch
+
-
Disconnect From "M"
Battery
Starter
90H09363
Courtesy of Ford Motor Co.

Fig. 2: Extending Starter Drive for Pinion Gap Measurement

2) Turn both switches on. Starter drive should extend and motor should run. Turn switch No. 2 off. The motor should stop running and the drive pinion should remain extended. With the drive pinion extended outward, measure the gap between the pinion and stop ring.

3) The pinion gap should be .004-.100" (.10-2.5 mm). If adjustment is required, change the shims between the solenoid and the drive end housing. Add shims to decrease gap and remove shims to increase gap. *See Fig. 3.*

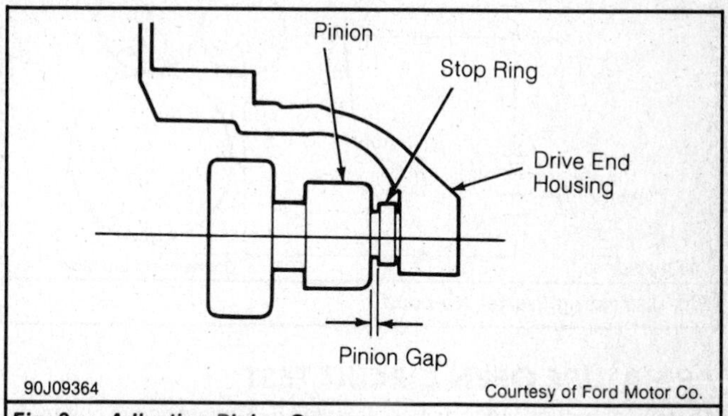
Pinion
Stop Ring
Drive End Housing
Pinion Gap
90J09364
Courtesy of Ford Motor Co.

Fig. 3: : Adjusting Pinion Gap

ON-VEHICLE TESTING

CAUTION: Before testing starter, ensure transmission is in Park on A/T models or Neutral on M/T models.

SYSTEM FUNCTION TEST

1) If the engine cannot be started, use cables to jump-start vehicle. If engine starts, check charging system.

2) If engine does not start, clean and tighten connections at battery posts and battery ground at engine. Check for positive short to ground. If no short exists, perform AUXILIARY SWITCH TEST and SOLENOID TEST.

AUXILIARY SWITCH TEST

Ensure battery is fully charged and in good condition. With all auxiliary switch wiring disconnected, check for continuity between terminals. *See Fig. 2.* See AUXILIARY SWITCH SPECIFICATIONS table. Check contact plate for excessive pitting. Repair or replace as necessary.

AUXILIARY SWITCH SPECIFICATIONS

Terminals	Ohmmeter Reading
SW & L	Continuity
SW & B	Continuity
L & S	No Continuity
B & S	No Continuity

SOLENOID TEST

If engine does not start, ensure battery is fully charged and in good condition. With all solenoid wiring disconnected, check for continuity between terminals. See SOLENOID SPECIFICATIONS table. Check contact plate for excessive pitting. Repair or replace as necessary.

SOLENOID SPECIFICATIONS

Terminals	Ohmmeter Reading
S & M	Continuity
S & Ground	Continuity
B & M	No Continuity

BENCH TESTING

NO-LOAD TEST

1) Secure starter in vise. Ensure pinion gap is correct. See ADJUSTMENTS in this article. Attach jumper lead between battery

1991 ELECTRICAL
Starters – Mitsubishi Gear Reduction (Cont.)

positive post and solenoid terminal "B". Attach remote start switch between battery positive post and auxiliary switch "SW". *See Fig. 4.*
2) Starter should rotate at a smooth, consistent speed. If not, ensure shim adjustment for armature-to-starter housing clearance is correct. If shim adjustment is okay, replace starter.

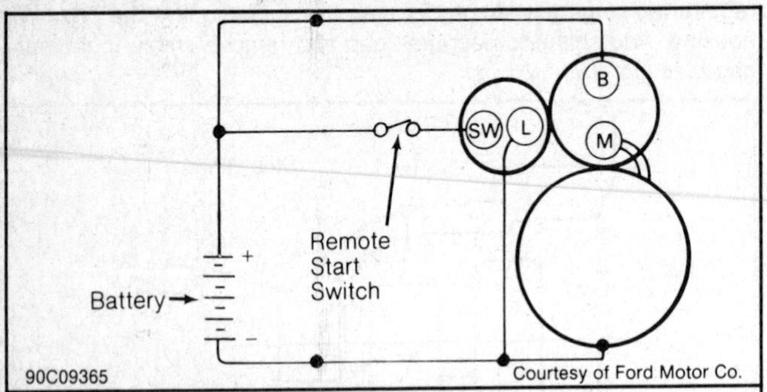
B
SW
L
M
Remote
Start
Switch
Battery
+
-
90C09365
Courtesy of Ford Motor Co.
Fig. 4: Testing Starter No-Load

ARMATURE OPEN CIRCUIT TEST

An open armature circuit can be detected by inspecting the commutator for evidence of burning. If burning is present, replace armature assembly. Check for damage to other related components.

ARMATURE & FIELD GROUNDED CIRCUIT TEST

1) Connect voltmeter leads to negative battery terminal and starter commutator. Connect jumper cable to positive battery terminals and armature. *See Fig. 5.* If voltmeter shows any voltage, windings are grounded.
2) Connect voltmeter leads to negative battery terminal and starter brush holder. Connect jumper wire to battery negative terminal and starter frame. *See Fig. 5.* If any voltage is indiccated, replace starter.

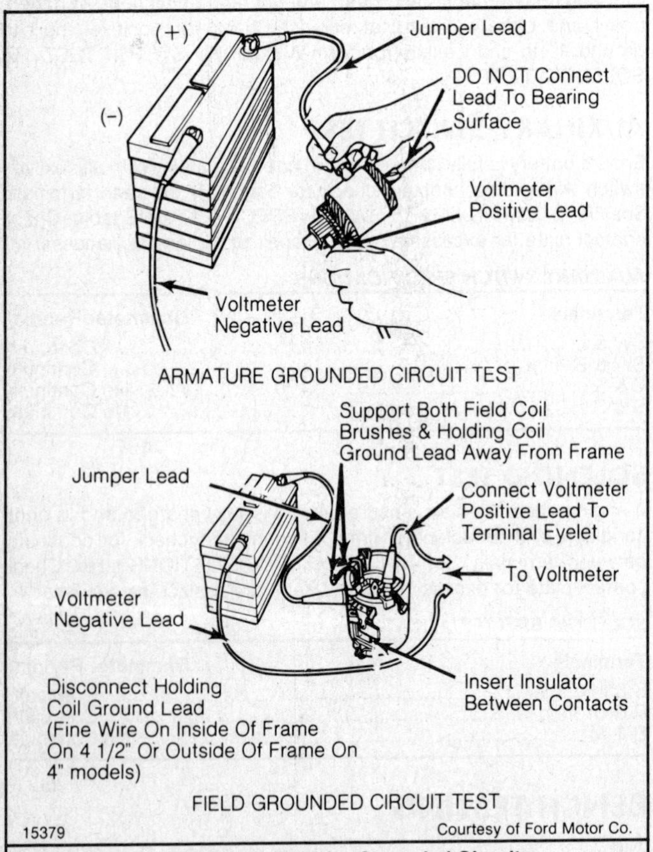
(+)
Jumper Lead
DO NOT Connect
Lead To Bearing
Surface
(-)
Voltmeter
Positive Lead
Voltmeter
Negative Lead
ARMATURE GROUNDED CIRCUIT TEST
Support Both Field Coil
Brushes & Holding Coil
Ground Lead Away From Frame
Jumper Lead
Connect Voltmeter
Positive Lead To
Terminal Eyelet
To Voltmeter
Voltmeter
Negative Lead
Disconnect Holding
Coil Ground Lead
(Fine Wire On Inside Of Frame
On 4 1/2" Or Outside Of Frame On
4" models)
Insert Insulator
Between Contacts
FIELD GROUNDED CIRCUIT TEST
15379
Courtesy of Ford Motor Co.
Fig. 5: Testing Armature & Field for Grounded Circuits

REMOVAL & INSTALLATION

Removal – Disconnect negative battery cable. Raise vehicle. Disconnect wiring from starter solenoid and auxiliary switch. Remove starter mounting bolts or nuts. Remove starter from vehicle.
Installation – **1)** Hold starter against mounting surface, fully inserted into pilot hole. Install bolts or nuts and tighten to specification. See TORQUE SPECIFICATIONS at end of article.
2) Connect all wiring to auxiliary switch and solenoid. Lower vehicle. Connect negative battery cable. Check starter operation.

OVERHAUL

Disassembly – **1)** Remove auxiliary switch retaining screws and remove switch. Remove connector from "M" terminal. Remove solenoid retaining screws and solenoid. Remove starter housing through bolts and separate housing from frame. *See Fig. 6.*
2) Remove armature , brush holder screws and end plate. Lift up on brush springs to remove brushes. Remove brush plate. Remove seal, holder and spacer. Remove inner gear housing and inner gear/shaft assembly.
3) Remove drive assembly by placing a pipe over the end of the shaft and tapping the pipe to loosen retaining ring to expose retaining clip. Remove retaining clip, ring and drive assembly.
Inspection – Check armature winding for separated or burned insulation. Check for open or shorted circuits. *See Fig. 5.* Check armature shaft and bearings for scoring or excessive wear. Check commutator for excessive runout. Machine commutator if runout exceeds .005" (.12 mm).
Reassembly – To reassemble, reverse disassembly procedure. Lubricate all sliding/pivot points with Multemp MS #2. Check shaft end play to verify a .001-.020" (.02-.05 mm) gap between inner gear housing and outer gear housing. Add or remove shim(s) as necessary.

TORQUE SPECIFICATIONS

TORQUE SPECIFICATIONS

Application	Ft. Lbs. (N.m)
Mounting Bolts	15-20 (20-27)
	INCH Lbs. (N.m)
Positive Cable Mounting Nut	70-130 (7.9-14.6)

1991 ELECTRICAL
Starters - Mitsubishi Gear Reduction (Cont.)

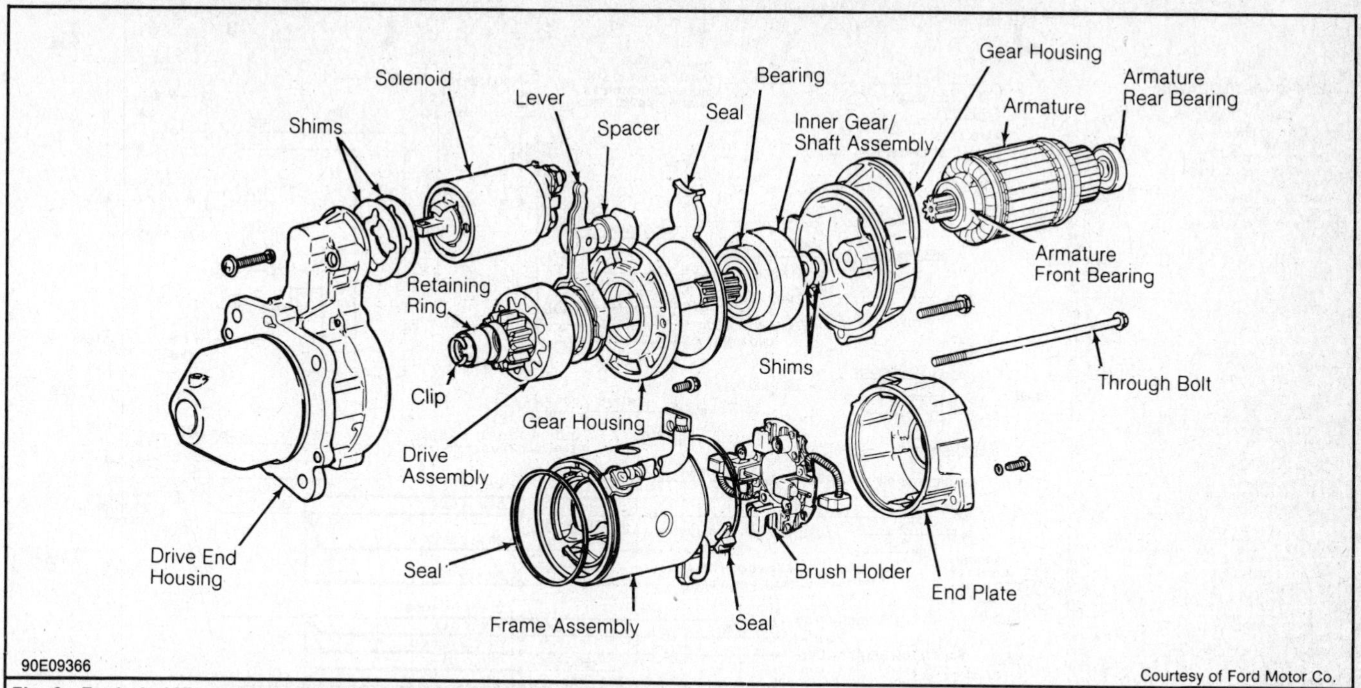
Solenoid
Lever
Shims
Spacer
Seal
Bearing
Gear Housing
Inner Gear/
Shaft Assembly
Armature
Armature
Rear Bearing
Retaining
Ring
Armature
Front Bearing
Shims
Through Bolt
Clip
Gear Housing
Drive
Assembly
Drive End
Housing
Seal
Brush Holder
End Plate
Frame Assembly
Seal
90E09366
Courtesy of Ford Motor Co.

Fig. 6: Exploded View of Mitsubishi Gear Reduction Starter (7.3L Diesel)

1991 WIRING DIAGRAMS
Aerostar

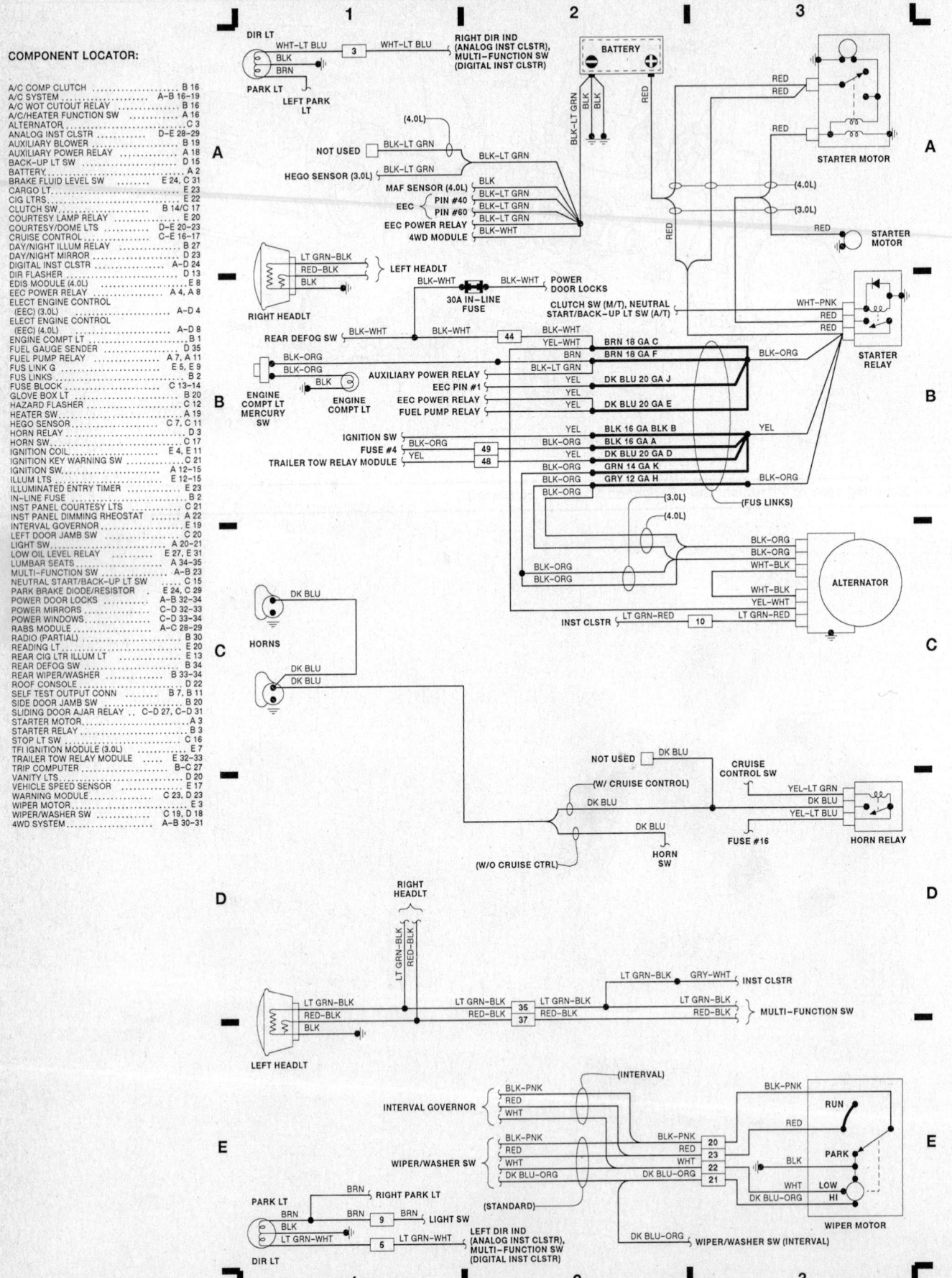

COMPONENT LOCATOR:

A/C COMP CLUTCH	B 16
A/C SYSTEM	A–B 16–19
A/C WOT CUTOUT RELAY	B 16
A/C/HEATER FUNCTION SW	A 16
ALTERNATOR	C 3
ANALOG INST CLSTR	D–E 28–29
AUXILIARY BLOWER	B 19
AUXILIARY POWER RELAY	A 18
BACK–UP LT SW	D 15
BATTERY	A 2
BRAKE FLUID LEVEL SW	E 24, C 31
CARGO LT	E 23
CIG LTRS	E 22
CLUTCH SW	B 14/C 17
COURTESY LAMP RELAY	E 20
COURTESY/DOME LTS	D–E 20–23
CRUISE CONTROL	C–E 16–17
DAY/NIGHT ILLUM RELAY	B 27
DAY/NIGHT MIRROR	D 23
DIGITAL INST CLSTR	A–D 24
DIR FLASHER	D 13
EDIS MODULE (4.0L)	E 8
EEC POWER RELAY	A 4, A 8
ELECT ENGINE CONTROL (EEC) (3.0L)	A–D 4
ELECT ENGINE CONTROL (EEC) (4.0L)	A–D 8
ENGINE COMPT LT	B 1
FUEL GAUGE SENDER	D 35
FUEL PUMP RELAY	A 7, A 11
FUS LINK G	E 5, E 9
FUS LINKS	B 2
FUSE BLOCK	C 13–14
GLOVE BOX LT	B 20
HAZARD FLASHER	C 12
HEATER SW	A 19
HEGO SENSOR	C 7, C 11
HORN RELAY	D 3
HORN SW	C 17
IGNITION COIL	E 4, E 11
IGNITION KEY WARNING SW	C 21
IGNITION SW	A 12–15
ILLUM LTS	E 12–15
ILLUMINATED ENTRY TIMER	E 23
IN–LINE FUSE	B 2
INST PANEL COURTESY LTS	C 21
INST PANEL DIMMING RHEOSTAT	A 22
INTERVAL GOVERNOR	E 19
LEFT DOOR JAMB SW	C 20
LIGHT SW	A 20–21
LOW OIL LEVEL RELAY	E 27, E 31
LUMBAR SEATS	A 34–35
MULTI–FUNCTION SW	A–B 23
NEUTRAL START/BACK–UP LT SW	C 15
PARK BRAKE DIODE/RESISTOR	E 24, C 29
POWER DOOR LOCKS	A–B 32–34
POWER MIRRORS	C–D 32–33
POWER WINDOWS	C–D 33–34
RABS MODULE	A–C 28–29
RADIO (PARTIAL)	B 30
READING LT	E 20
REAR CIG LTR ILLUM LT	E 13
REAR DEFOG SW	B 34
REAR WIPER/WASHER	B 33–34
ROOF CONSOLE	D 22
SELF TEST OUTPUT CONN	B 7, B 11
SIDE DOOR JAMB SW	B 20
SLIDING DOOR AJAR RELAY	C–D 27, C–D 31
STARTER MOTOR	A 3
STARTER RELAY	B 3
STOP LT SW	C 16
TFI IGNITION MODULE (3.0L)	E 7
TRAILER TOW RELAY MODULE	E 32–33
TRIP COMPUTER	B–C 27
VANITY LTS	D 20
VEHICLE SPEED SENSOR	E 17
WARNING MODULE	C 23, D 23
WIPER MOTOR	E 3
WIPER/WASHER SW	C 19, D 18
4WD SYSTEM	A–B 30–31

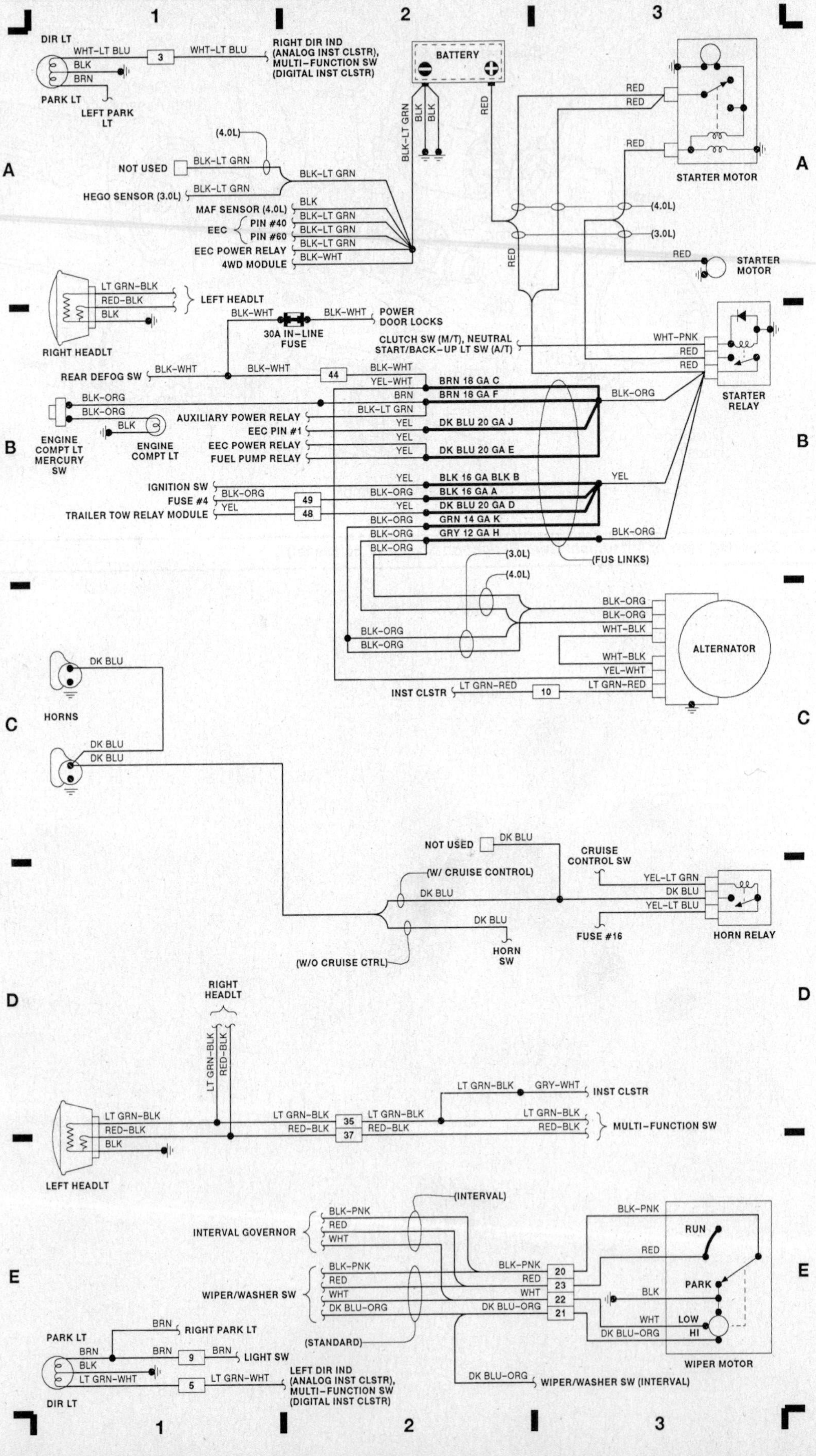
1
2
3
A
B
C
D
E
DIR LT
PARK LT
LEFT PARK LT
RIGHT DIR IND (ANALOG INST CLSTR), MULTI–FUNCTION SW (DIGITAL INST CLSTR)
BATTERY
STARTER MOTOR
NOT USED
HEGO SENSOR (3.0L)
MAF SENSOR (4.0L)
EEC PIN #40
EEC PIN #60
EEC POWER RELAY
4WD MODULE
LEFT HEADLT
RIGHT HEADLT
POWER DOOR LOCKS
30A IN–LINE FUSE
CLUTCH SW (M/T), NEUTRAL START/BACK–UP LT SW (A/T)
REAR DEFOG SW
STARTER RELAY
ENGINE COMPT LT MERCURY SW
ENGINE COMPT LT
AUXILIARY POWER RELAY
EEC PIN #1
FUEL PUMP RELAY
BRN 18 GA C
BRN 18 GA F
DK BLU 20 GA J
DK BLU 20 GA E
IGNITION SW
FUSE #4
TRAILER TOW RELAY MODULE
BLK 16 GA BLK B
BLK 16 GA A
DK BLU 20 GA D
GRN 14 GA K
GRY 12 GA H
(FUS LINKS)
ALTERNATOR
INST CLSTR
HORNS
NOT USED
CRUISE CONTROL SW
(W/ CRUISE CONTROL)
HORN RELAY
FUSE #16
HORN SW
(W/O CRUISE CTRL)
LEFT HEADLT
RIGHT HEADLT
INST CLSTR
MULTI–FUNCTION SW
INTERVAL GOVERNOR
(INTERVAL)
WIPER/WASHER SW
(STANDARD)
RUN
PARK
LOW
HI
WIPER MOTOR
WIPER/WASHER SW (INTERVAL)
PARK LT
RIGHT PARK LT
LIGHT SW
LEFT DIR IND (ANALOG INST CLSTR), MULTI–FUNCTION SW (DIGITAL INST CLSTR)
DIR LT

1991 WIRING DIAGRAMS
Aerostar (Cont.)

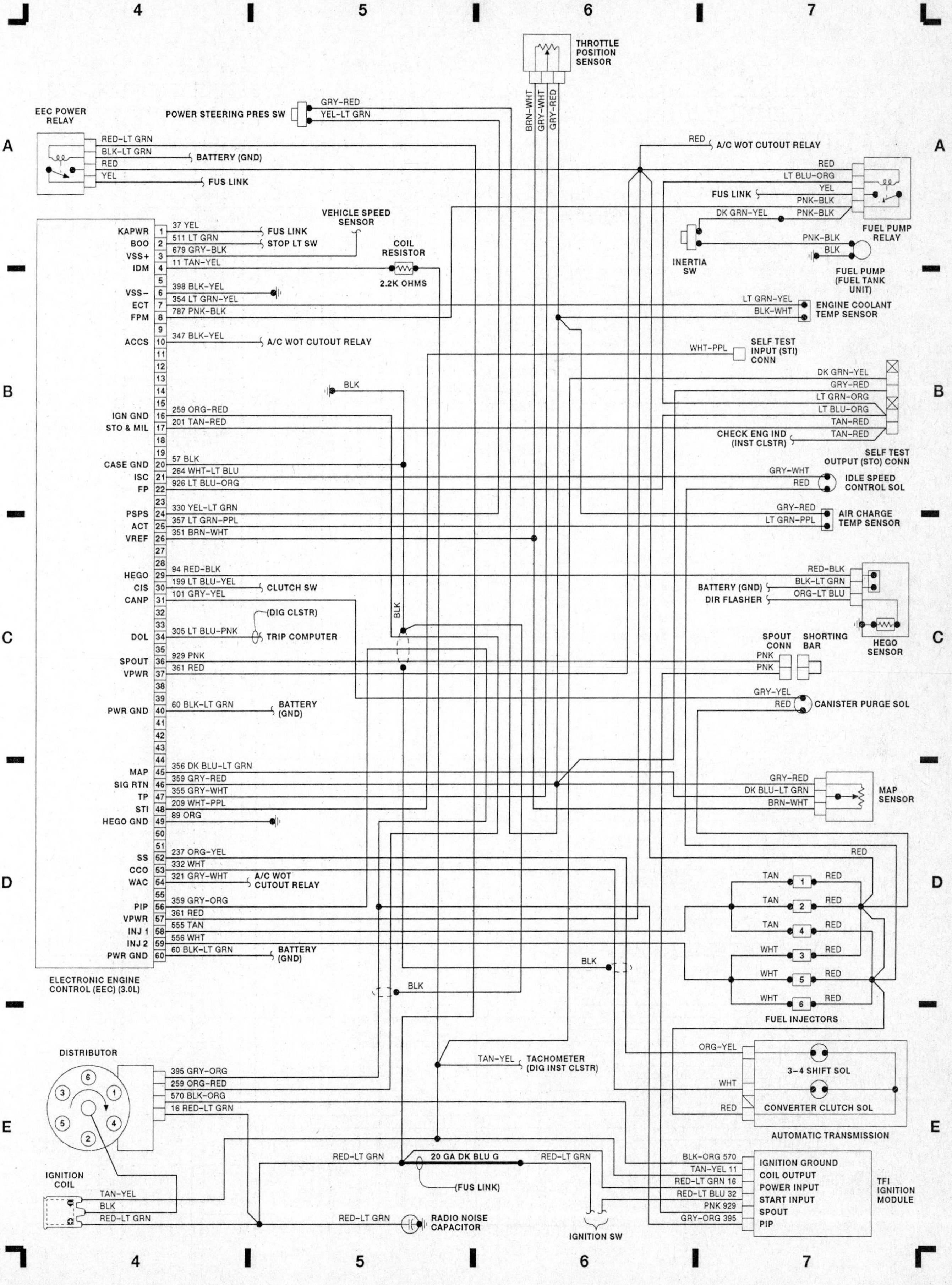

THROTTLE POSITION SENSOR
BRN-WHT
GRY-WHT
GRY-RED
EEC POWER RELAY
POWER STEERING PRES SW
GRY-RED
YEL-LT GRN
RED-LT GRN
BLK-LT GRN
BATTERY (GND)
RED
YEL
FUS LINK
RED
A/C WOT CUTOUT RELAY
LT BLU-ORG
PNK-BLK
DK GRN-YEL
FUEL PUMP RELAY
INERTIA SW
FUEL PUMP (FUEL TANK UNIT)
VEHICLE SPEED SENSOR
COIL RESISTOR
2.2K OHMS
KAPWR 1 37 YEL FUS LINK
BOO 2 511 LT GRN STOP LT SW
VSS+ 3 679 GRY-BLK
IDM 4 11 TAN-YEL
VSS- 6 398 BLK-YEL
ECT 7 354 LT GRN-YEL
FPM 8 787 PNK-BLK
ACCS 10 347 BLK-YEL A/C WOT CUTOUT RELAY
LT GRN-YEL
BLK-WHT
ENGINE COOLANT TEMP SENSOR
WHT-PPL
SELF TEST INPUT (STI) CONN
BLK
DK GRN-YEL
GRY-RED
LT GRN-ORG
LT BLU-ORG
TAN-RED
IGN GND 16 259 ORG-RED
STO & MIL 17 201 TAN-RED
CHECK ENG IND (INST CLSTR)
SELF TEST OUTPUT (STO) CONN
CASE GND 20 57 BLK
ISC 21 264 WHT-LT BLU
FP 22 926 LT BLU-ORG
GRY-WHT
IDLE SPEED CONTROL SOL
PSPS 24 330 YEL-LT GRN
ACT 25 357 LT GRN-PPL
VREF 26 351 BRN-WHT
AIR CHARGE TEMP SENSOR
HEGO 29 94 RED-BLK
CIS 30 199 LT BLU-YEL CLUTCH SW
CANP 31 101 GRY-YEL
RED-BLK
BLK-LT GRN
ORG-LT BLU
BATTERY (GND)
DIR FLASHER
HEGO SENSOR
(DIG CLSTR)
DOL 34 305 LT BLU-PNK TRIP COMPUTER
SPOUT 36 929 PNK
VPWR 37 361 RED
SPOUT CONN
SHORTING BAR
PNK
GRY-YEL
CANISTER PURGE SOL
PWR GND 40 60 BLK-LT GRN BATTERY (GND)
MAP 45 356 DK BLU-LT GRN
SIG RTN 46 359 GRY-RED
TP 47 355 GRY-WHT
STI 48 209 WHT-PPL
HEGO GND 49 89 ORG
DK BLU-LT GRN
BRN-WHT
MAP SENSOR
SS 52 237 ORG-YEL
CCO 53 332 WHT
WAC 54 321 GRY-WHT A/C WOT CUTOUT RELAY
PIP 56 359 GRY-ORG
VPWR 57 361 RED
INJ 1 58 555 TAN
INJ 2 59 556 WHT
PWR GND 60 60 BLK-LT GRN BATTERY (GND)
ELECTRONIC ENGINE CONTROL (EEC) (3.0L)
TAN
WHT
FUEL INJECTORS
BLK
DISTRIBUTOR
395 GRY-ORG
259 ORG-RED
570 BLK-ORG
16 RED-LT GRN
TAN-YEL
TACHOMETER (DIG INST CLSTR)
ORG-YEL
3-4 SHIFT SOL
CONVERTER CLUTCH SOL
AUTOMATIC TRANSMISSION
IGNITION COIL
BLK
RED-LT GRN
20 GA DK BLU G
FUS LINK
RADIO NOISE CAPACITOR
IGNITION SW
BLK-ORG 570
TAN-YEL 11
RED-LT GRN 16
RED-LT BLU 32
PNK 929
GRY-ORG 395
IGNITION GROUND
COIL OUTPUT
POWER INPUT
START INPUT
SPOUT
PIP
TFI IGNITION MODULE

1991 WIRING DIAGRAMS
Aerostar (Cont.)

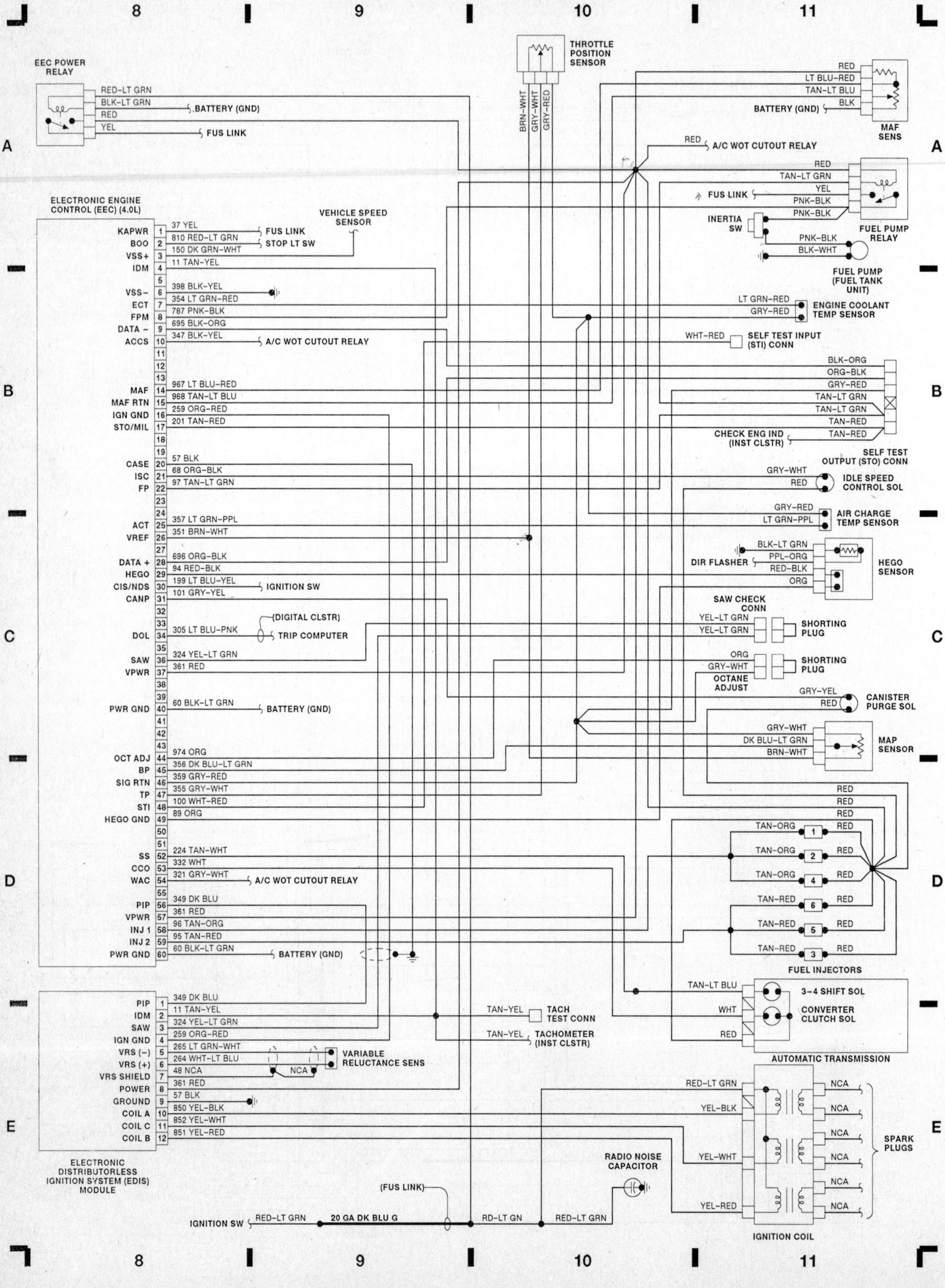
8
9
10
11
A
B
C
D
E
EEC POWER RELAY
RED-LT GRN
BLK-LT GRN
RED
YEL
BATTERY (GND)
FUS LINK
THROTTLE POSITION SENSOR
BRN-WHT
GRY-WHT
GRY-RED
RED
LT BLU-RED
TAN-LT BLU
BLK
BATTERY (GND)
MAF SENS
A/C WOT CUTOUT RELAY
TAN-LT GRN
PNK-BLK
FUEL PUMP RELAY
INERTIA SW
BLK-WHT
FUEL PUMP (FUEL TANK UNIT)
ELECTRONIC ENGINE CONTROL (EEC) (4.0L)
VEHICLE SPEED SENSOR
KAPWR 1 37 YEL
BOO 2 810 RED-LT GRN
VSS+ 3 150 DK GRN-WHT
IDM 4 11 TAN-YEL
STOP LT SW
VSS- 6 398 BLK-YEL
ECT 7 354 LT GRN-RED
FPM 8 787 PNK-BLK
DATA - 9 695 BLK-ORG
ACCS 10 347 BLK-YEL
MAF 14 967 LT BLU-RED
MAF RTN 15 968 TAN-LT BLU
IGN GND 16 259 ORG-RED
STO/MIL 17 201 TAN-RED
CASE 20 57 BLK
ISC 21 68 ORG-BLK
FP 22 97 TAN-LT GRN
ACT 25 357 LT GRN-PPL
VREF 26 351 BRN-WHT
DATA + 28 696 ORG-BLK
HEGO 29 94 RED-BLK
CIS/NDS 30 199 LT BLU-YEL
CANP 31 101 GRY-YEL
IGNITION SW
(DIGITAL CLSTR)
TRIP COMPUTER
DOL 34 305 LT BLU-PNK
SAW 36 324 YEL-LT GRN
VPWR 37 361 RED
PWR GND 40 60 BLK-LT GRN
OCT ADJ 44 974 ORG
BP 45 356 DK BLU-LT GRN
SIG RTN 46 359 GRY-RED
TP 47 355 GRY-WHT
STI 48 100 WHT-RED
HEGO GND 49 89 ORG
SS 52 224 TAN-WHT
CCO 53 332 WHT
WAC 54 321 GRY-WHT
PIP 56 349 DK BLU
VPWR 57 361 RED
INJ 1 58 96 TAN-ORG
INJ 2 59 95 TAN-RED
PWR GND 60 60 BLK-LT GRN
ENGINE COOLANT TEMP SENSOR
LT GRN-RED
GRY-RED
WHT-RED
SELF TEST INPUT (STI) CONN
BLK-ORG
ORG-BLK
CHECK ENG IND (INST CLSTR)
TAN-RED
SELF TEST OUTPUT (STO) CONN
GRY-WHT
IDLE SPEED CONTROL SOL
LT GRN-PPL
AIR CHARGE TEMP SENSOR
BLK-LT GRN
PPL-ORG
RED-BLK
ORG
DIR FLASHER
HEGO SENSOR
SAW CHECK CONN
YEL-LT GRN
SHORTING PLUG
GRY-WHT
OCTANE ADJUST
GRY-YEL
CANISTER PURGE SOL
DK BLU-LT GRN
MAP SENSOR
TAN-ORG
FUEL INJECTORS
TAN-LT BLU
WHT
3-4 SHIFT SOL
CONVERTER CLUTCH SOL
AUTOMATIC TRANSMISSION
PIP 1 349 DK BLU
IDM 2 11 TAN-YEL
SAW 3 324 YEL-LT GRN
IGN GND 4 259 ORG-RED
VRS (-) 5 265 LT GRN-WHT
VRS (+) 6 264 WHT-LT BLU
VRS SHIELD 7 48 NCA
POWER 8 361 RED
GROUND 9 57 BLK
COIL A 10 850 YEL-BLK
COIL C 11 852 YEL-WHT
COIL B 12 851 YEL-RED
TAN-YEL
TACH TEST CONN
TACHOMETER (INST CLSTR)
VARIABLE RELUCTANCE SENS
NCA
ELECTRONIC DISTRIBUTORLESS IGNITION SYSTEM (EDIS) MODULE
RED-LT GRN
YEL-BLK
YEL-WHT
YEL-RED
SPARK PLUGS
IGNITION COIL
RADIO NOISE CAPACITOR
(FUS LINK)
IGNITION SW
20 GA DK BLU G
RD-LT GN

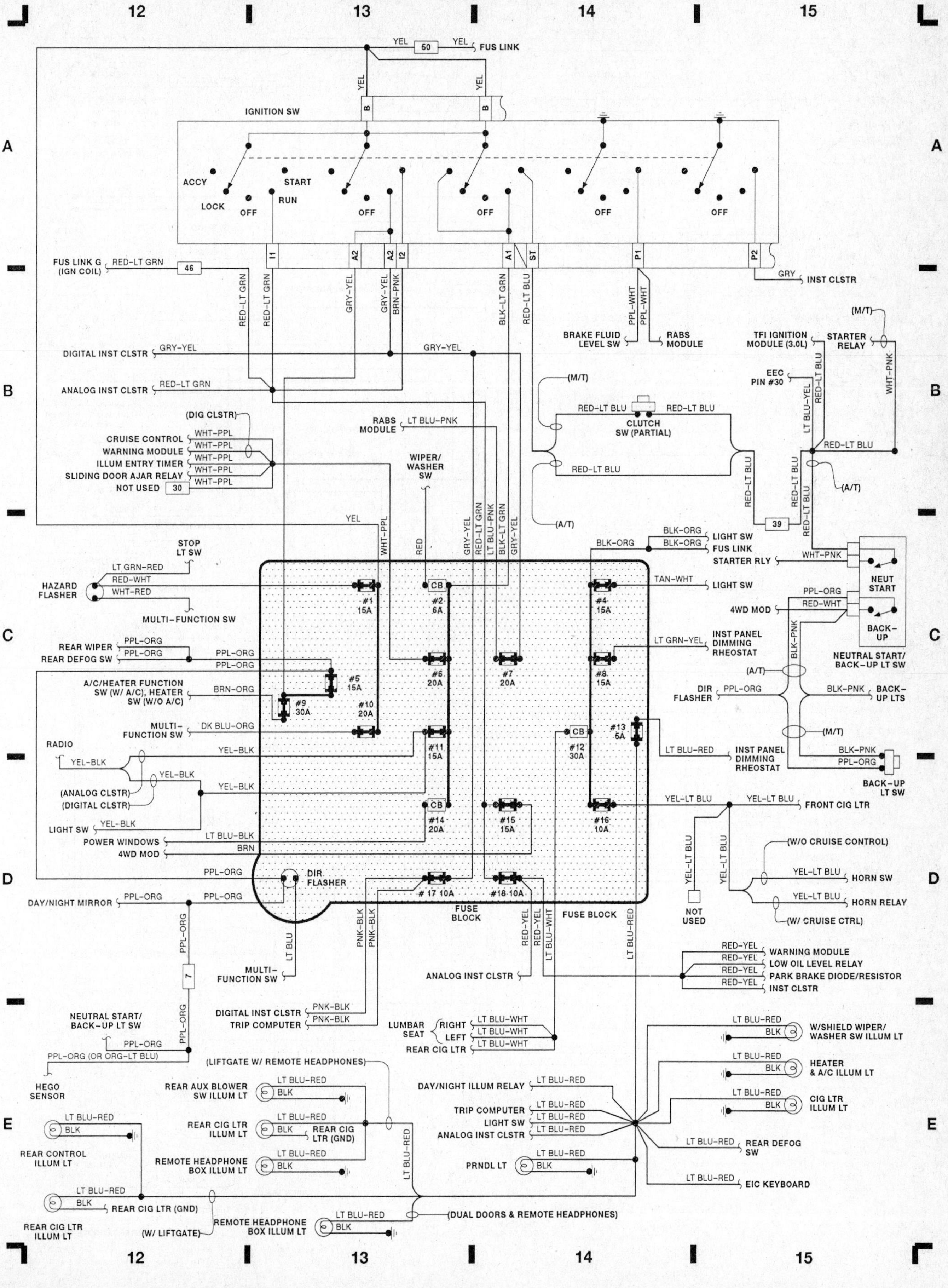

12
13
14
15
A
B
C
D
E
FUS LINK
IGNITION SW
ACCY
START
LOCK
OFF
RUN
FUS LINK G (IGN COIL)
INST CLSTR
BRAKE FLUID LEVEL SW
RABS MODULE
TFI IGNITION MODULE (3.0L)
STARTER RELAY
DIGITAL INST CLSTR
ANALOG INST CLSTR
EEC PIN #30
CLUTCH SW (PARTIAL)
(DIG CLSTR)
CRUISE CONTROL
WARNING MODULE
ILLUM ENTRY TIMER
SLIDING DOOR AJAR RELAY
NOT USED
WIPER/ WASHER SW
LIGHT SW
STARTER RLY
STOP LT SW
HAZARD FLASHER
MULTI-FUNCTION SW
NEUT START
4WD MOD
BACK-UP
REAR WIPER
REAR DEFOG SW
INST PANEL DIMMING RHEOSTAT
NEUTRAL START/ BACK-UP LT SW
A/C/HEATER FUNCTION SW (W/ A/C), HEATER SW (W/O A/C)
DIR FLASHER
BACK-UP LTS
RADIO
(ANALOG CLSTR)
(DIGITAL CLSTR)
BACK-UP LT SW
FRONT CIG LTR
POWER WINDOWS
(W/O CRUISE CONTROL)
DIR. FLASHER
HORN SW
DAY/NIGHT MIRROR
FUSE BLOCK
HORN RELAY
NOT USED
(W/ CRUISE CTRL)
WARNING MODULE
LOW OIL LEVEL RELAY
PARK BRAKE DIODE/RESISTOR
INST CLSTR
TRIP COMPUTER
LUMBAR SEAT
RIGHT
LEFT
REAR CIG LTR
W/SHIELD WIPER/ WASHER SW ILLUM LT
HEGO SENSOR
(LIFTGATE W/ REMOTE HEADPHONES)
HEATER & A/C ILLUM LT
REAR AUX BLOWER SW ILLUM LT
DAY/NIGHT ILLUM RELAY
CIG LTR ILLUM LT
REAR CIG LTR ILLUM LT
REAR CIG LTR (GND)
REAR CONTROL ILLUM LT
REMOTE HEADPHONE BOX ILLUM LT
PRNDL LT
REAR DEFOG SW
EIC KEYBOARD
(W/ LIFTGATE)
(DUAL DOORS & REMOTE HEADPHONES)

1991 WIRING DIAGRAMS
Aerostar (Cont.)

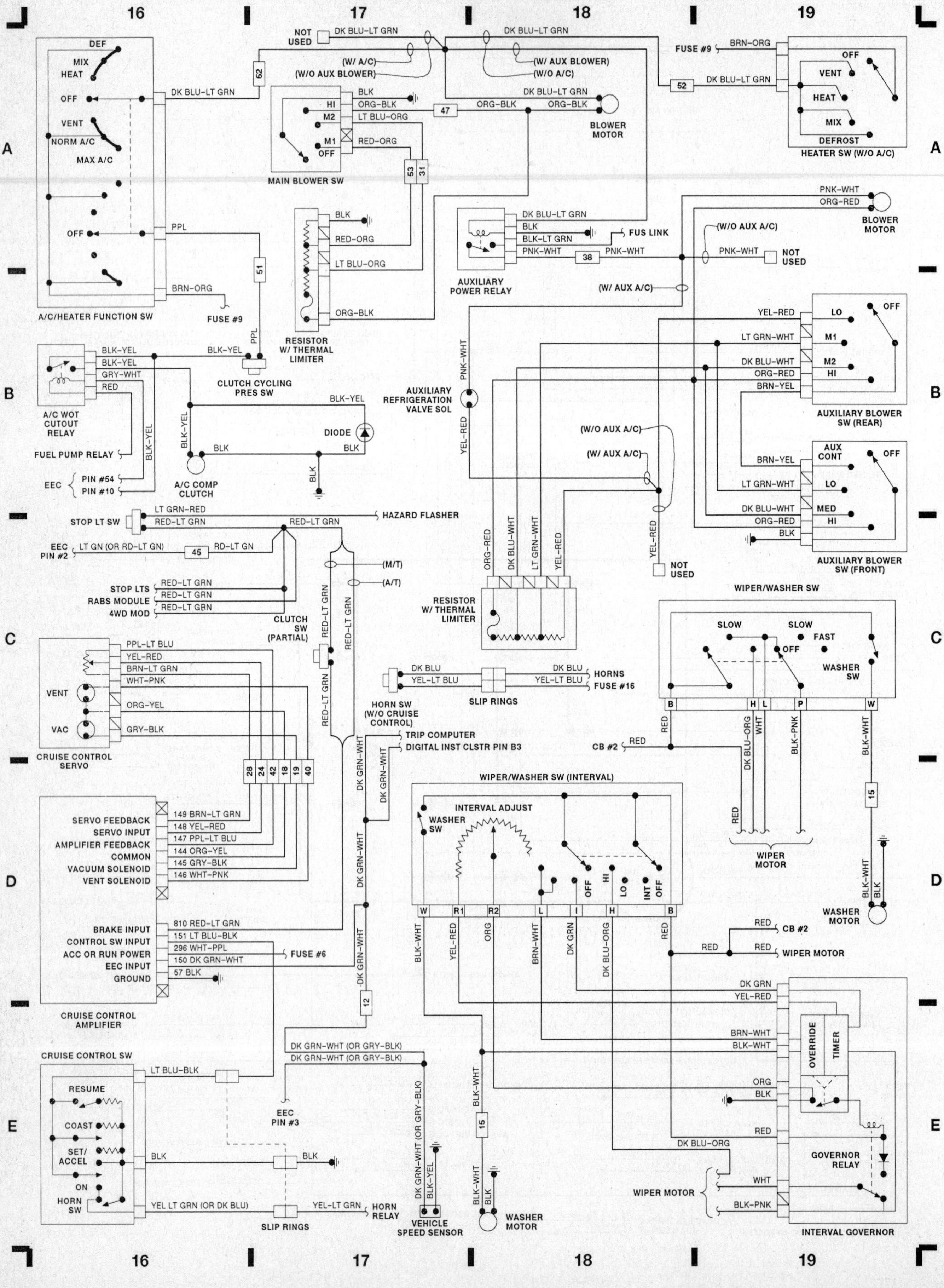
16
17
18
19
A/C/HEATER FUNCTION SW
DEF
MIX
HEAT
OFF
VENT
NORM A/C
MAX A/C
MAIN BLOWER SW
BLOWER MOTOR
HEATER SW (W/O A/C)
FUSE #9
NOT USED
(W/ A/C)
(W/O AUX BLOWER)
(W/ AUX BLOWER)
(W/O A/C)
RESISTOR W/ THERMAL LIMITER
AUXILIARY POWER RELAY
FUS LINK
(W/O AUX A/C)
(W/ AUX A/C)
CLUTCH CYCLING PRES SW
A/C WOT CUTOUT RELAY
FUEL PUMP RELAY
EEC PIN #54 PIN #10
A/C COMP CLUTCH
DIODE
AUXILIARY REFRIGERATION VALVE SOL
AUXILIARY BLOWER SW (REAR)
AUXILIARY BLOWER SW (FRONT)
STOP LT SW
HAZARD FLASHER
EEC PIN #2
STOP LTS
RABS MODULE
4WD MOD
CLUTCH SW (PARTIAL)
(M/T)
(A/T)
WIPER/WASHER SW
SLOW
FAST
WASHER SW
CRUISE CONTROL SERVO
VENT
VAC
HORN SW (W/O CRUISE CONTROL)
SLIP RINGS
HORNS
FUSE #16
TRIP COMPUTER
DIGITAL INST CLSTR PIN B3
CB #2
WIPER MOTOR
WIPER/WASHER SW (INTERVAL)
INTERVAL ADJUST
CRUISE CONTROL AMPLIFIER
SERVO FEEDBACK
SERVO INPUT
AMPLIFIER FEEDBACK
COMMON
VACUUM SOLENOID
VENT SOLENOID
BRAKE INPUT
CONTROL SW INPUT
ACC OR RUN POWER
EEC INPUT
GROUND
FUSE #6
WASHER MOTOR
CRUISE CONTROL SW
RESUME
COAST
SET/ ACCEL
ON
HORN SW
EEC PIN #3
HORN RELAY
VEHICLE SPEED SENSOR
OVERRIDE
TIMER
GOVERNOR RELAY
INTERVAL GOVERNOR
16
17
18
19

1991 WIRING DIAGRAMS
Aerostar (Cont.)

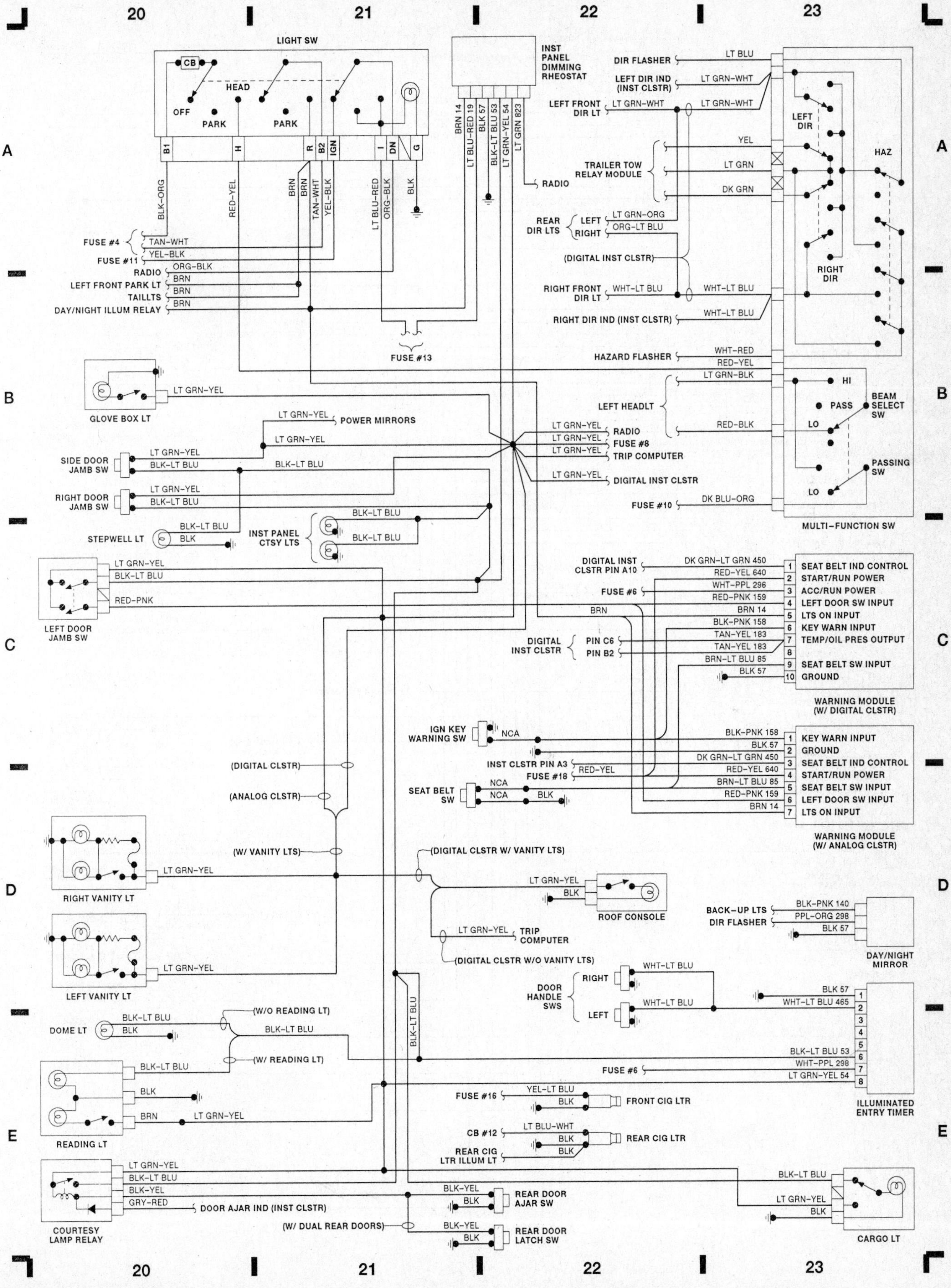

LIGHT SW
INST PANEL DIMMING RHEOSTAT
MULTI-FUNCTION SW
GLOVE BOX LT
SIDE DOOR JAMB SW
RIGHT DOOR JAMB SW
STEPWELL LT
INST PANEL CTSY LTS
LEFT DOOR JAMB SW
WARNING MODULE (W/ DIGITAL CLSTR)
WARNING MODULE (W/ ANALOG CLSTR)
IGN KEY WARNING SW
SEAT BELT SW
RIGHT VANITY LT
LEFT VANITY LT
ROOF CONSOLE
DAY/NIGHT MIRROR
DOOR HANDLE SWS
DOME LT
READING LT
ILLUMINATED ENTRY TIMER
FRONT CIG LTR
REAR CIG LTR
COURTESY LAMP RELAY
REAR DOOR AJAR SW
REAR DOOR LATCH SW
CARGO LT

1991 WIRING DIAGRAMS
Aerostar (Cont.)

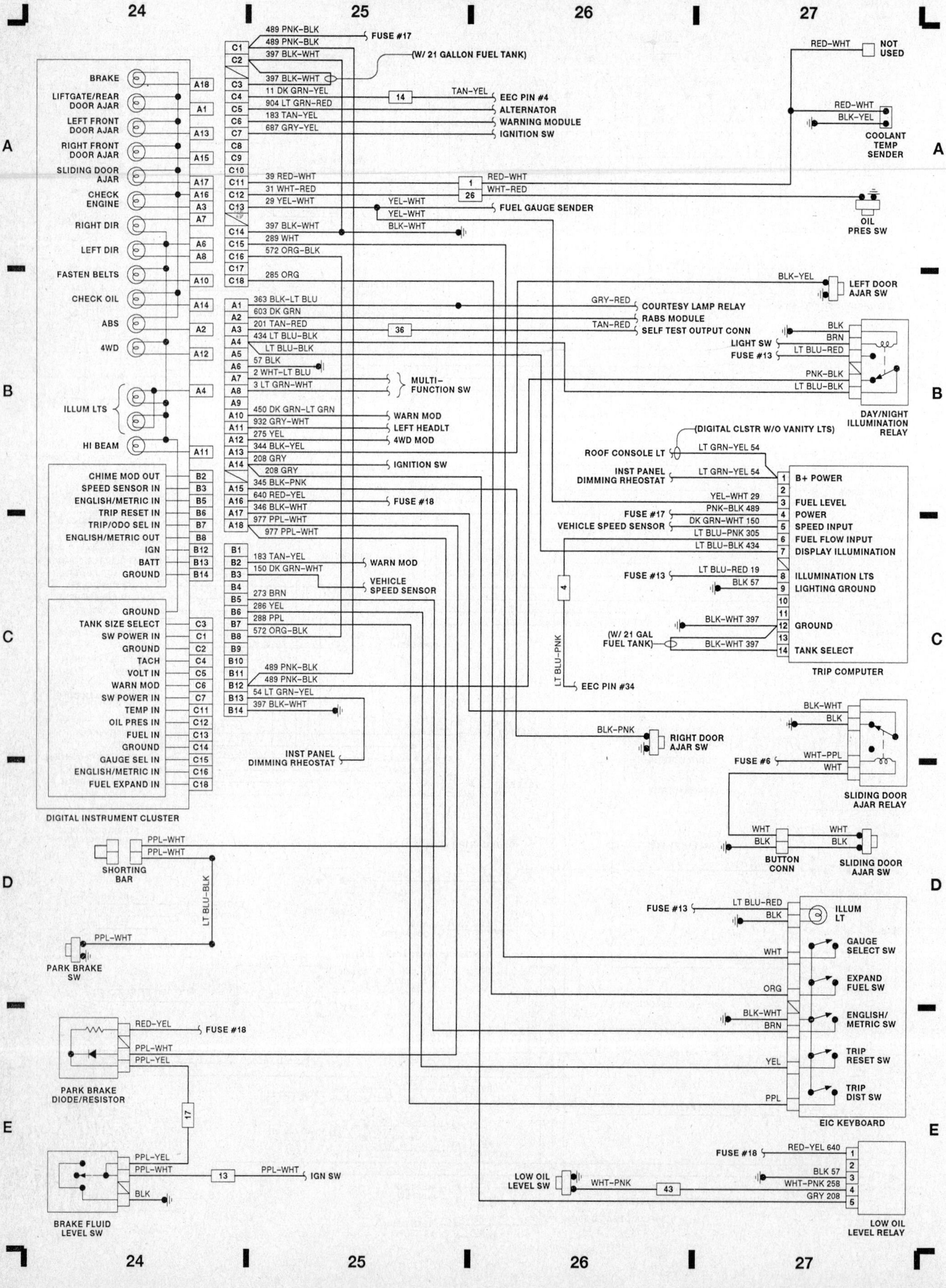
24
25
26
27
A
B
C
D
E
BRAKE
LIFTGATE/REAR DOOR AJAR
LEFT FRONT DOOR AJAR
RIGHT FRONT DOOR AJAR
SLIDING DOOR AJAR
CHECK ENGINE
RIGHT DIR
LEFT DIR
FASTEN BELTS
CHECK OIL
ABS
4WD
ILLUM LTS
HI BEAM
CHIME MOD OUT
SPEED SENSOR IN
ENGLISH/METRIC IN
TRIP RESET IN
TRIP/ODO SEL IN
ENGLISH/METRIC OUT
IGN
BATT
GROUND
GROUND
TANK SIZE SELECT
SW POWER IN
GROUND
TACH
VOLT IN
WARN MOD
SW POWER IN
TEMP IN
OIL PRES IN
FUEL IN
GROUND
GAUGE SEL IN
ENGLISH/METRIC IN
FUEL EXPAND IN
DIGITAL INSTRUMENT CLUSTER
489 PNK-BLK
489 PNK-BLK
FUSE #17
397 BLK-WHT
(W/ 21 GALLON FUEL TANK)
397 BLK-WHT
11 DK GRN-YEL
904 LT GRN-RED
183 TAN-YEL
687 GRY-YEL
TAN-YEL
EEC PIN #4
ALTERNATOR
WARNING MODULE
IGNITION SW
39 RED-WHT
31 WHT-RED
29 YEL-WHT
RED-WHT
WHT-RED
YEL-WHT
YEL-WHT
BLK-WHT
FUEL GAUGE SENDER
397 BLK-WHT
289 WHT
572 ORG-BLK
285 ORG
RED-WHT
NOT USED
RED-WHT
BLK-YEL
COOLANT TEMP SENDER
OIL PRES SW
BLK-YEL
LEFT DOOR AJAR SW
363 BLK-LT BLU
603 DK GRN
201 TAN-RED
434 LT BLU-BLK
LT BLU-BLK
57 BLK
2 WHT-LT BLU
3 LT GRN-WHT
450 DK GRN-LT GRN
932 GRY-WHT
275 YEL
344 BLK-YEL
208 GRY
208 GRY
345 BLK-PNK
640 RED-YEL
346 BLK-WHT
977 PPL-WHT
977 PPL-WHT
GRY-RED
COURTESY LAMP RELAY
RABS MODULE
TAN-RED
SELF TEST OUTPUT CONN
MULTI-FUNCTION SW
WARN MOD
LEFT HEADLT
4WD MOD
IGNITION SW
FUSE #18
BLK
BRN
LIGHT SW
FUSE #13
LT BLU-RED
PNK-BLK
LT BLU-BLK
DAY/NIGHT ILLUMINATION RELAY
(DIGITAL CLSTR W/O VANITY LTS)
ROOF CONSOLE LT
LT GRN-YEL 54
INST PANEL DIMMING RHEOSTAT
LT GRN-YEL 54
YEL-WHT 29
PNK-BLK 489
FUSE #17
DK GRN-WHT 150
VEHICLE SPEED SENSOR
LT BLU-PNK 305
LT BLU-BLK 434
FUSE #13
LT BLU-RED 19
BLK 57
BLK-WHT 397
(W/ 21 GAL FUEL TANK)
BLK-WHT 397
B+ POWER
FUEL LEVEL
POWER
SPEED INPUT
FUEL FLOW INPUT
DISPLAY ILLUMINATION
ILLUMINATION LTS
LIGHTING GROUND
GROUND
TANK SELECT
TRIP COMPUTER
183 TAN-YEL
150 DK GRN-WHT
273 BRN
286 YEL
288 PPL
572 ORG-BLK
489 PNK-BLK
489 PNK-BLK
54 LT GRN-YEL
397 BLK-WHT
WARN MOD
VEHICLE SPEED SENSOR
INST PANEL DIMMING RHEOSTAT
LT BLU-PNK
EEC PIN #34
BLK-PNK
RIGHT DOOR AJAR SW
BLK-WHT
BLK
FUSE #6
WHT-PPL
WHT
SLIDING DOOR AJAR RELAY
WHT
BLK
BUTTON CONN
WHT
BLK
SLIDING DOOR AJAR SW
PPL-WHT
PPL-WHT
SHORTING BAR
LT BLU-BLK
PPL-WHT
PARK BRAKE SW
FUSE #13
LT BLU-RED
BLK
ILLUM LT
WHT
GAUGE SELECT SW
ORG
EXPAND FUEL SW
BLK-WHT
BRN
ENGLISH/METRIC SW
YEL
TRIP RESET SW
PPL
TRIP DIST SW
EIC KEYBOARD
RED-YEL
FUSE #18
PPL-WHT
PPL-YEL
PARK BRAKE DIODE/RESISTOR
17
PPL-YEL
PPL-WHT
13
PPL-WHT
IGN SW
BLK
BRAKE FLUID LEVEL SW
LOW OIL LEVEL SW
WHT-PNK
43
FUSE #18
RED-YEL 640
BLK 57
WHT-PNK 258
GRY 208
LOW OIL LEVEL RELAY

1991 WIRING DIAGRAMS
Aerostar (Cont.)

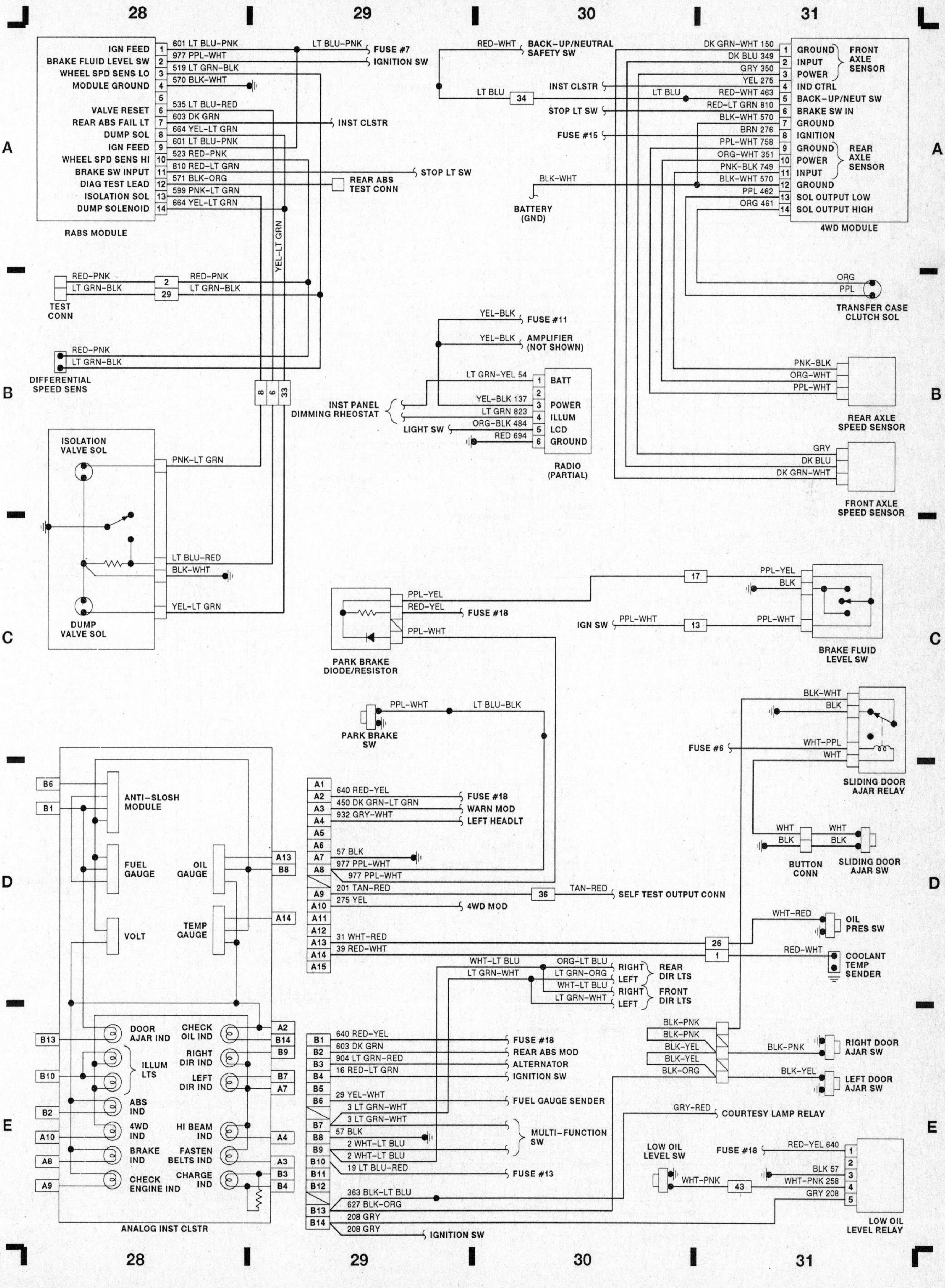
RABS MODULE
4WD MODULE
RADIO (PARTIAL)
ISOLATION VALVE SOL
DUMP VALVE SOL
TEST CONN
DIFFERENTIAL SPEED SENS
TRANSFER CASE CLUTCH SOL
REAR AXLE SPEED SENSOR
FRONT AXLE SPEED SENSOR
PARK BRAKE DIODE/RESISTOR
BRAKE FLUID LEVEL SW
PARK BRAKE SW
SLIDING DOOR AJAR RELAY
SLIDING DOOR AJAR SW
BUTTON CONN
OIL PRES SW
COOLANT TEMP SENDER
RIGHT DOOR AJAR SW
LEFT DOOR AJAR SW
LOW OIL LEVEL SW
LOW OIL LEVEL RELAY
ANALOG INST CLSTR
ANTI-SLOSH MODULE
FUEL GAUGE
OIL GAUGE
VOLT
TEMP GAUGE
SELF TEST OUTPUT CONN
COURTESY LAMP RELAY
MULTI-FUNCTION SW

1991 WIRING DIAGRAMS
Aerostar (Cont.)

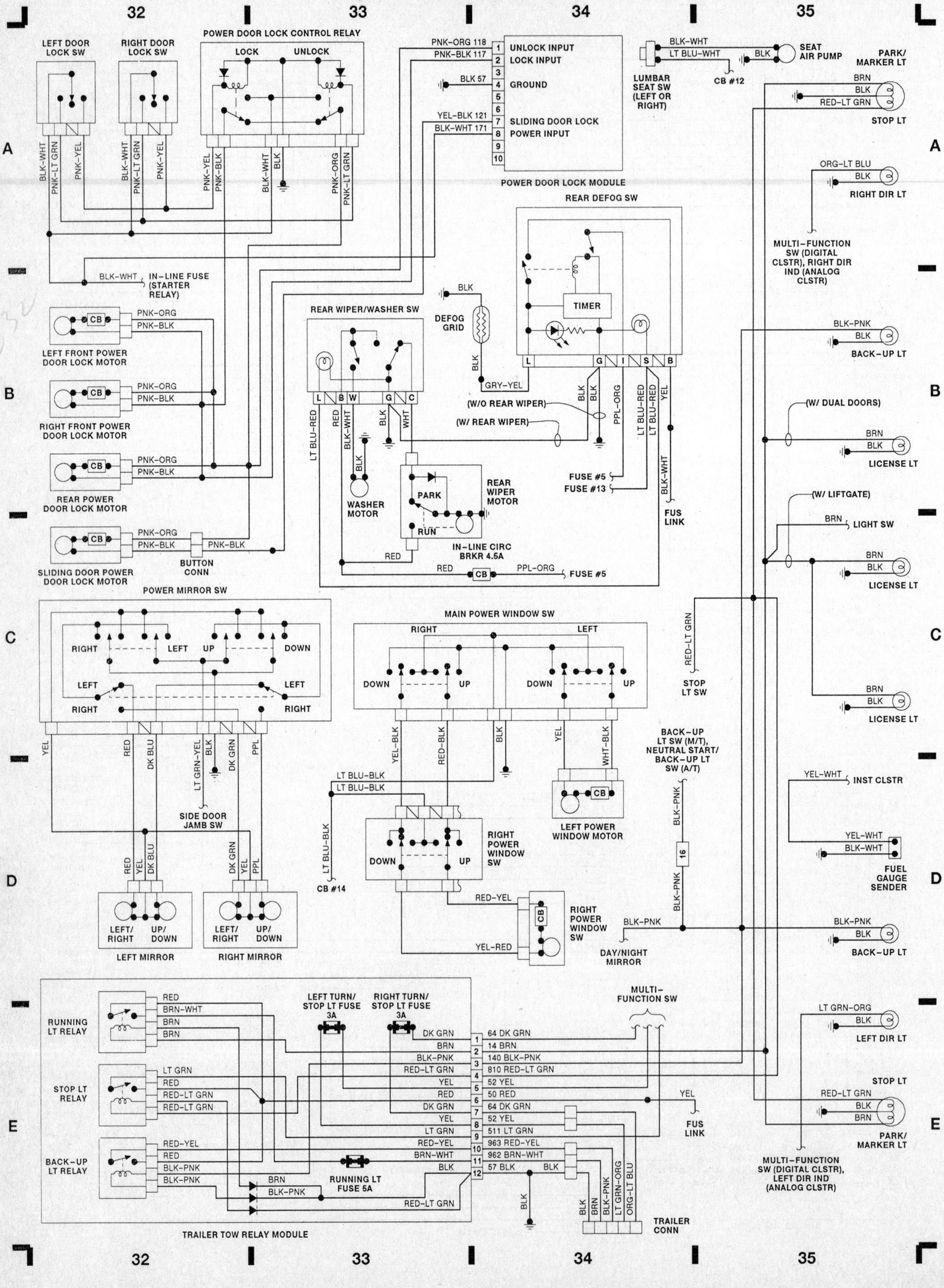
32
33
34
35
A
B
C
D
E
LEFT DOOR LOCK SW
RIGHT DOOR LOCK SW
POWER DOOR LOCK CONTROL RELAY
LOCK
UNLOCK
UNLOCK INPUT
LOCK INPUT
GROUND
SLIDING DOOR LOCK POWER INPUT
POWER DOOR LOCK MODULE
PNK-ORG 118
PNK-BLK 117
BLK 57
YEL-BLK 121
BLK-WHT 171
BLK-WHT
LT BLU-WHT
SEAT AIR PUMP
LUMBAR SEAT SW (LEFT OR RIGHT)
CB #12
PARK/ MARKER LT
STOP LT
RIGHT DIR LT
MULTI-FUNCTION SW (DIGITAL CLSTR), RIGHT DIR IND (ANALOG CLSTR)
IN-LINE FUSE (STARTER RELAY)
LEFT FRONT POWER DOOR LOCK MOTOR
RIGHT FRONT POWER DOOR LOCK MOTOR
REAR POWER DOOR LOCK MOTOR
SLIDING DOOR POWER DOOR LOCK MOTOR
BUTTON CONN
REAR DEFOG SW
TIMER
DEFOG GRID
REAR WIPER/WASHER SW
(W/O REAR WIPER)
(W/ REAR WIPER)
WASHER MOTOR
REAR WIPER MOTOR
PARK
RUN
IN-LINE CIRC BRKR 4.5A
FUSE #5
FUSE #13
FUS LINK
BACK-UP LT
LICENSE LT
(W/ DUAL DOORS)
(W/ LIFTGATE)
LIGHT SW
POWER MIRROR SW
RIGHT
LEFT
UP
DOWN
SIDE DOOR JAMB SW
LEFT MIRROR
RIGHT MIRROR
LEFT/ RIGHT
UP/ DOWN
MAIN POWER WINDOW SW
LEFT POWER WINDOW MOTOR
RIGHT POWER WINDOW SW
RIGHT POWER WINDOW SW
CB #14
STOP LT SW
BACK-UP LT SW (M/T), NEUTRAL START/ BACK-UP LT SW (A/T)
INST CLSTR
FUEL GAUGE SENDER
DAY/NIGHT MIRROR
RUNNING LT RELAY
STOP LT RELAY
BACK-UP LT RELAY
LEFT TURN/ STOP LT FUSE 3A
RIGHT TURN/ STOP LT FUSE 3A
RUNNING LT FUSE 5A
MULTI-FUNCTION SW
64 DK GRN
14 BRN
140 BLK-PNK
810 RED-LT GRN
52 YEL
50 RED
64 DK GRN
52 YEL
511 LT GRN
963 RED-YEL
962 BRN-WHT
57 BLK
TRAILER TOW RELAY MODULE
TRAILER CONN
LEFT DIR LT
MULTI-FUNCTION SW (DIGITAL CLSTR), LEFT DIR IND (ANALOG CLSTR)

1991 WIRING DIAGRAMS
Bronco & "F" Series

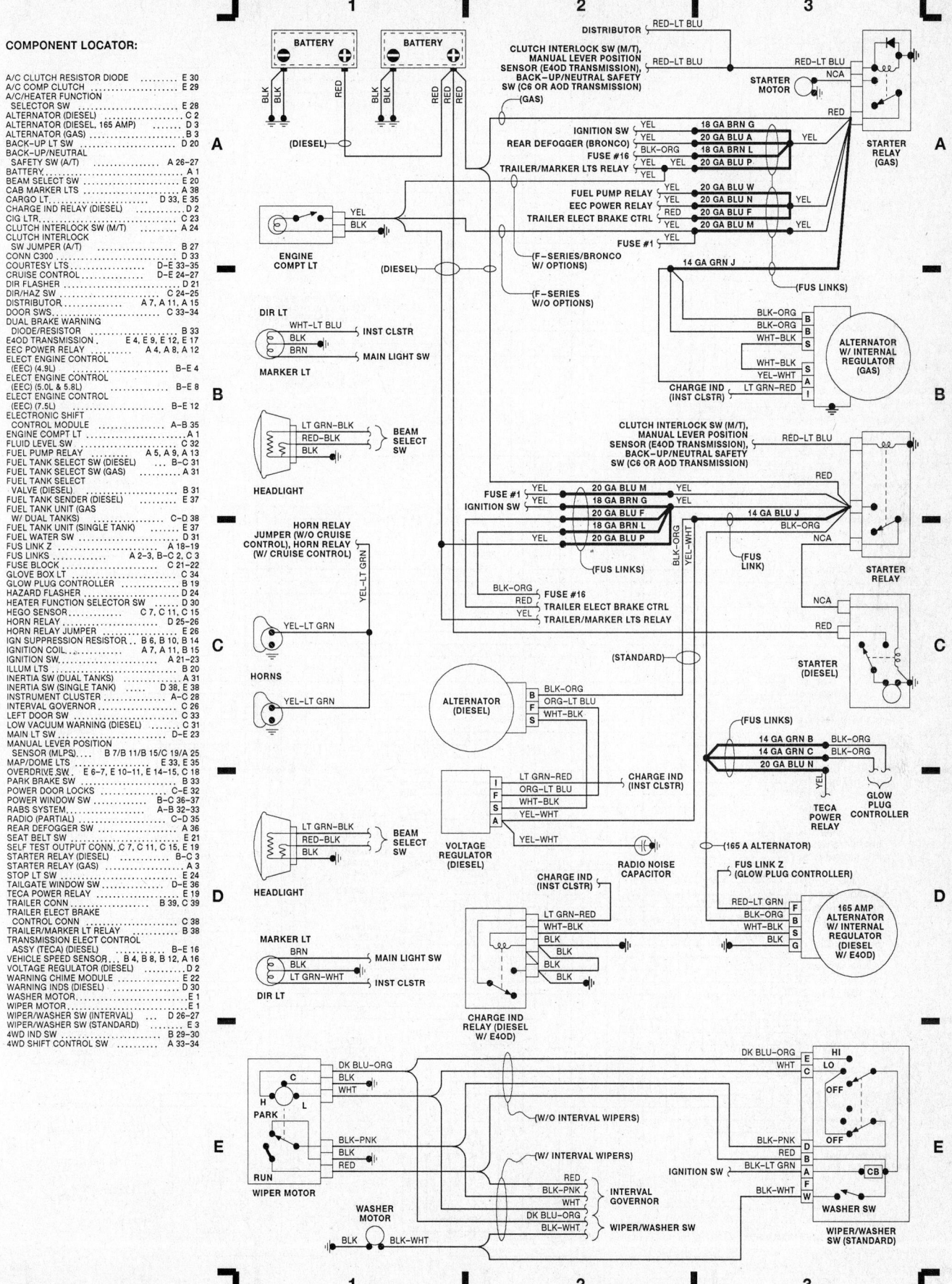

COMPONENT LOCATOR:

A/C CLUTCH RESISTOR DIODE	E 30
A/C COMP CLUTCH	E 29
A/C/HEATER FUNCTION SELECTOR SW	E 28
ALTERNATOR (DIESEL)	C 2
ALTERNATOR (DIESEL, 165 AMP)	D 3
ALTERNATOR (GAS)	B 3
BACK-UP LT SW	D 20
BACK-UP/NEUTRAL SAFETY SW (A/T)	A 26-27
BATTERY	A 1
BEAM SELECT SW	E 20
CAB MARKER LTS	A 38
CARGO LT	D 33, E 35
CHARGE IND RELAY (DIESEL)	D 2
CIG LTR	C 23
CLUTCH INTERLOCK SW (M/T)	A 24
CLUTCH INTERLOCK SW JUMPER (A/T)	B 27
CONN C300	D 33
COURTESY LTS	D-E 33-35
CRUISE CONTROL	D-E 24-27
DIR FLASHER	D 21
DIR/HAZ SW	C 24-25
DISTRIBUTOR	A 7, A 11, A 15
DOOR SWS	C 33-34
DUAL BRAKE WARNING DIODE/RESISTOR	B 33
E4OD TRANSMISSION	E 4, E 9, E 12, E 17
EEC POWER RELAY	A 4, A 8, A 12
ELECT ENGINE CONTROL (EEC) (4.9L)	B-E 4
ELECT ENGINE CONTROL (EEC) (5.0L & 5.8L)	B-E 8
ELECT ENGINE CONTROL (EEC) (7.5L)	B-E 12
ELECTRONIC SHIFT CONTROL MODULE	A-B 35
ENGINE COMPT LT	A 1
FLUID LEVEL SW	C 32
FUEL PUMP RELAY	A 5, A 9, A 13
FUEL TANK SELECT SW (DIESEL)	B-C 31
FUEL TANK SELECT SW (GAS)	A 31
FUEL TANK SELECT VALVE (DIESEL)	B 31
FUEL TANK SENDER (DIESEL)	E 37
FUEL TANK UNIT (GAS W/ DUAL TANKS)	C-D 38
FUEL TANK UNIT (SINGLE TANK)	E 37
FUEL WATER SW	D 31
FUS LINK Z	A 18-19
FUS LINKS	A 2-3, B-C 2, C 3
FUSE BLOCK	C 21-22
GLOVE BOX LT	C 34
GLOW PLUG CONTROLLER	B 19
HAZARD FLASHER	D 24
HEATER FUNCTION SELECTOR SW	D 30
HEGO SENSOR	C 7, C 11, C 15
HORN RELAY	D 25-26
HORN RELAY JUMPER	E 26
IGN SUPPRESSION RESISTOR	B 6, B 10, B 14
IGNITION COIL	A 7, A 11, B 15
IGNITION SW	A 21-23
ILLUM LTS	B 20
INERTIA SW (DUAL TANKS)	A 31
INERTIA SW (SINGLE TANK)	D 38, E 38
INSTRUMENT CLUSTER	A-C 28
INTERVAL GOVERNOR	C 26
LEFT DOOR SW	C 33
LOW VACUUM WARNING (DIESEL)	C 31
MAIN LT SW	D-E 23
MANUAL LEVER POSITION SENSOR (MLPS)	B 7/B 11/B 15/C 19/A 25
MAP/DOME LTS	E 33, E 35
OVERDRIVE SW	E 6-7, E 10-11, E 14-15, C 18
PARK BRAKE SW	B 33
POWER DOOR LOCKS	C-E 32
POWER WINDOW SW	B-C 36-37
RABS SYSTEM	A-B 32-33
RADIO (PARTIAL)	C-D 35
REAR DEFOGGER SW	A 36
SEAT BELT SW	E 21
SELF TEST OUTPUT CONN	C 7, C 11, C 15, E 19
STARTER RELAY (DIESEL)	B-C 3
STARTER RELAY (GAS)	A 3
STOP LT SW	E 24
TAILGATE WINDOW SW	D-E 36
TECA POWER RELAY	E 19
TRAILER CONN	B 39, C 39
TRAILER ELECT BRAKE CONTROL CONN	C 38
TRAILER/MARKER LT RELAY	B 38
TRANSMISSION ELECT CONTROL ASSY (TECA) (DIESEL)	B-E 16
VEHICLE SPEED SENSOR	B 4, B 8, B 12, A 16
VOLTAGE REGULATOR (DIESEL)	D 2
WARNING CHIME MODULE	E 22
WARNING INDS (DIESEL)	D 30
WASHER MOTOR	E 1
WIPER MOTOR	E 1
WIPER/WASHER SW (INTERVAL)	D 26-27
WIPER/WASHER SW (STANDARD)	E 3
4WD IND SW	B 29-30
4WD SHIFT CONTROL SW	A 33-34

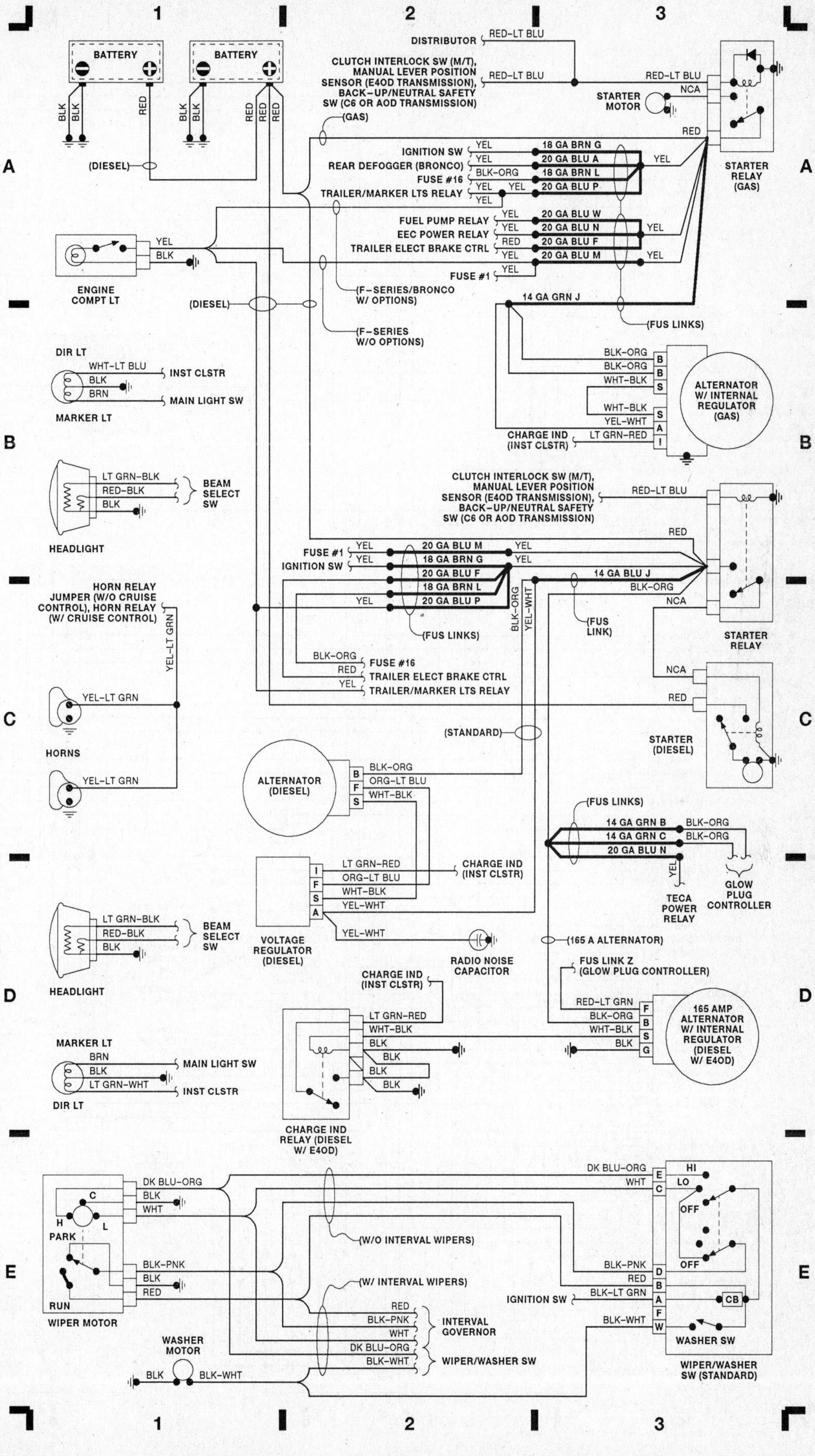

1
2
3
A
B
C
D
E
BATTERY
BATTERY
DISTRIBUTOR
CLUTCH INTERLOCK SW (M/T), MANUAL LEVER POSITION SENSOR (E4OD TRANSMISSION), BACK-UP/NEUTRAL SAFETY SW (C6 OR AOD TRANSMISSION)
STARTER MOTOR
STARTER RELAY (GAS)
IGNITION SW
REAR DEFOGGER (BRONCO)
FUSE #16
TRAILER/MARKER LTS RELAY
FUEL PUMP RELAY
EEC POWER RELAY
TRAILER ELECT BRAKE CTRL
FUSE #1
ENGINE COMPT LT
(DIESEL)
(GAS)
(F-SERIES/BRONCO W/ OPTIONS)
(F-SERIES W/O OPTIONS)
(FUS LINKS)
DIR LT
INST CLSTR
MAIN LIGHT SW
MARKER LT
ALTERNATOR W/ INTERNAL REGULATOR (GAS)
CHARGE IND (INST CLSTR)
HEADLIGHT
BEAM SELECT SW
STARTER RELAY
HORN RELAY JUMPER (W/O CRUISE CONTROL), HORN RELAY (W/ CRUISE CONTROL)
HORNS
(FUS LINK)
STARTER (DIESEL)
(STANDARD)
ALTERNATOR (DIESEL)
GLOW PLUG CONTROLLER
TECA POWER RELAY
VOLTAGE REGULATOR (DIESEL)
RADIO NOISE CAPACITOR
(165 A ALTERNATOR)
FUS LINK Z (GLOW PLUG CONTROLLER)
165 AMP ALTERNATOR W/ INTERNAL REGULATOR (DIESEL W/ E4OD)
CHARGE IND RELAY (DIESEL W/ E4OD)
WIPER MOTOR
PARK
RUN
(W/O INTERVAL WIPERS)
(W/ INTERVAL WIPERS)
INTERVAL GOVERNOR
WIPER/WASHER SW
WASHER MOTOR
WASHER SW
WIPER/WASHER SW (STANDARD)

1991 WIRING DIAGRAMS
Bronco & "F" Series (Cont.)

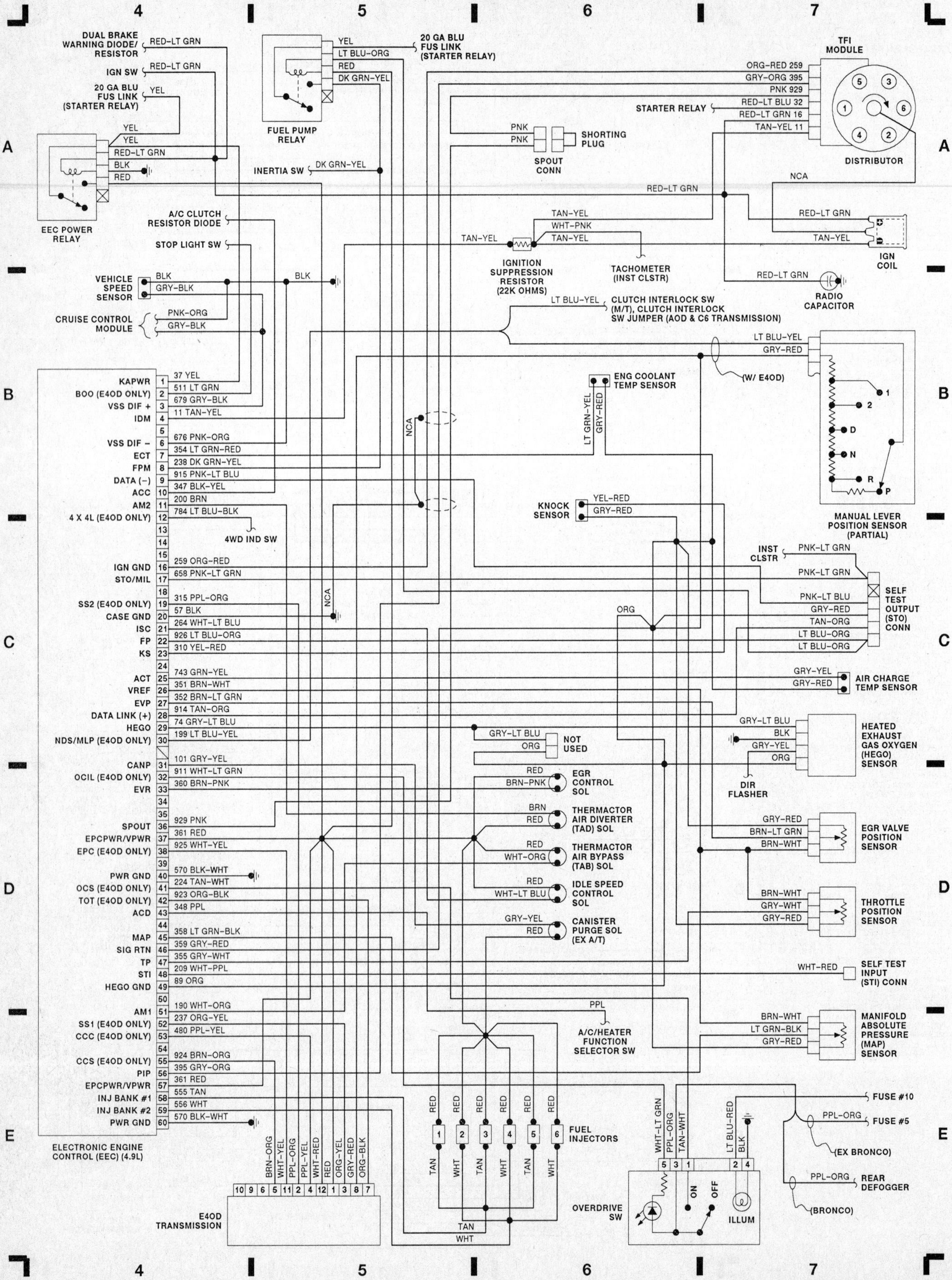
4
5
6
7
A
B
C
D
E
DUAL BRAKE WARNING DIODE/ RESISTOR
RED-LT GRN
IGN SW
RED-LT GRN
20 GA BLU FUS LINK (STARTER RELAY)
YEL
YEL
YEL
RED-LT GRN
BLK
RED
EEC POWER RELAY
YEL
LT BLU-ORG
RED
DK GRN-YEL
20 GA BLU FUS LINK (STARTER RELAY)
FUEL PUMP RELAY
INERTIA SW
DK GRN-YEL
TFI MODULE
ORG-RED 259
GRY-ORG 395
PNK 929
RED-LT BLU 32
RED-LT GRN 16
TAN-YEL 11
STARTER RELAY
DISTRIBUTOR
PNK
PNK
SHORTING PLUG
SPOUT CONN
NCA
RED-LT GRN
A/C CLUTCH RESISTOR DIODE
STOP LIGHT SW
TAN-YEL
WHT-PNK
TAN-YEL
TAN-YEL
RED-LT GRN
TAN-YEL
IGN COIL
IGNITION SUPPRESSION RESISTOR (22K OHMS)
TACHOMETER (INST CLSTR)
RED-LT GRN
RADIO CAPACITOR
VEHICLE SPEED SENSOR
BLK
GRY-BLK
BLK
CRUISE CONTROL MODULE
PNK-ORG
GRY-BLK
LT BLU-YEL
CLUTCH INTERLOCK SW (M/T), CLUTCH INTERLOCK SW JUMPER (AOD & C6 TRANSMISSION)
LT BLU-YEL
GRY-RED
(W/ E4OD)
MANUAL LEVER POSITION SENSOR (PARTIAL)
1
2
D
N
R
P
KAPWR 1 37 YEL
BOO (E4OD ONLY) 2 511 LT GRN
VSS DIF + 3 679 GRY-BLK
IDM 4 11 TAN-YEL
5 676 PNK-ORG
VSS DIF – 6 354 LT GRN-RED
ECT 7 238 DK GRN-YEL
FPM 8 915 PNK-LT BLU
DATA (–) 9 347 BLK-YEL
ACC 10 200 BRN
AM2 11 784 LT BLU-BLK
4 X 4L (E4OD ONLY) 12
13
14
15 259 ORG-RED
IGN GND 16 658 PNK-LT GRN
STO/MIL 17
18 315 PPL-ORG
SS2 (E4OD ONLY) 19 57 BLK
CASE GND 20 264 WHT-LT BLU
ISC 21 926 LT BLU-ORG
FP 22 310 YEL-RED
KS 23
24 743 GRN-YEL
ACT 25 351 BRN-WHT
VREF 26 352 BRN-LT GRN
EVP 27 914 TAN-ORG
DATA LINK (+) 28 74 GRY-LT BLU
HEGO 29 199 LT BLU-YEL
NDS/MLP (E4OD ONLY) 30
101 GRY-YEL
CANP 31 911 WHT-LT GRN
OCIL (E4OD ONLY) 32 360 BRN-PNK
EVR 33
34
35 929 PNK
SPOUT 36 361 RED
EPCPWR/VPWR 37 925 WHT-YEL
EPC (E4OD ONLY) 38
39 570 BLK-WHT
PWR GND 40 224 TAN-WHT
OCS (E4OD ONLY) 41 923 ORG-BLK
TOT (E4OD ONLY) 42 348 PPL
ACD 43
44 358 LT GRN-BLK
MAP 45 359 GRY-RED
SIG RTN 46 355 GRY-WHT
TP 47 209 WHT-PPL
STI 48 89 ORG
HEGO GND 49
50 190 WHT-ORG
AM1 51 237 ORG-YEL
SS1 (E4OD ONLY) 52 480 PPL-YEL
CCC (E4OD ONLY) 53
54 924 BRN-ORG
CCS (E4OD ONLY) 55 395 GRY-ORG
PIP 56 361 RED
EPCPWR/VPWR 57 555 TAN
INJ BANK #1 58 556 WHT
INJ BANK #2 59 570 BLK-WHT
PWR GND 60
ELECTRONIC ENGINE CONTROL (EEC) (4.9L)
4WD IND SW
NCA
NCA
ENG COOLANT TEMP SENSOR
LT GRN-YEL
GRY-RED
KNOCK SENSOR
YEL-RED
GRY-RED
INST CLSTR
PNK-LT GRN
PNK-LT GRN
PNK-LT BLU
GRY-RED
TAN-ORG
LT BLU-ORG
LT BLU-ORG
SELF TEST OUTPUT (STO) CONN
ORG
GRY-YEL
GRY-RED
AIR CHARGE TEMP SENSOR
GRY-LT BLU
ORG
NOT USED
GRY-LT BLU
BLK
GRY-YEL
ORG
HEATED EXHAUST GAS OXYGEN (HEGO) SENSOR
DIR FLASHER
RED
BRN-PNK
EGR CONTROL SOL
BRN
RED
THERMACTOR AIR DIVERTER (TAD) SOL
RED
WHT-ORG
THERMACTOR AIR BYPASS (TAB) SOL
RED
WHT-LT BLU
IDLE SPEED CONTROL SOL
GRY-YEL
RED
CANISTER PURGE SOL (EX A/T)
GRY-RED
BRN-LT GRN
BRN-WHT
EGR VALVE POSITION SENSOR
BRN-WHT
GRY-WHT
GRY-RED
THROTTLE POSITION SENSOR
WHT-RED
SELF TEST INPUT (STI) CONN
PPL
A/C/HEATER FUNCTION SELECTOR SW
BRN-WHT
LT GRN-BLK
GRY-RED
MANIFOLD ABSOLUTE PRESSURE (MAP) SENSOR
FUSE #10
PPL-ORG
FUSE #5
(EX BRONCO)
PPL-ORG
REAR DEFOGGER
(BRONCO)
RED
RED
RED
RED
RED
RED
1
2
3
4
5
6
FUEL INJECTORS
TAN
WHT
TAN
WHT
TAN
WHT
TAN
WHT
BRN-ORG
WHT-YEL
PPL-ORG
PPL-YEL
WHT-RED
RED
ORG-YEL
GRY-RED
ORG-BLK
10 9 6 5 11 2 4 12 1 3 8 7
E4OD TRANSMISSION
WHT-LT GRN
PPL-ORG
TAN-WHT
LT BLU-RED
BLK
5 3 1
2 4
ON
OFF
OVERDRIVE SW
ILLUM

1991 WIRING DIAGRAMS
Bronco & "F" Series (Cont.)

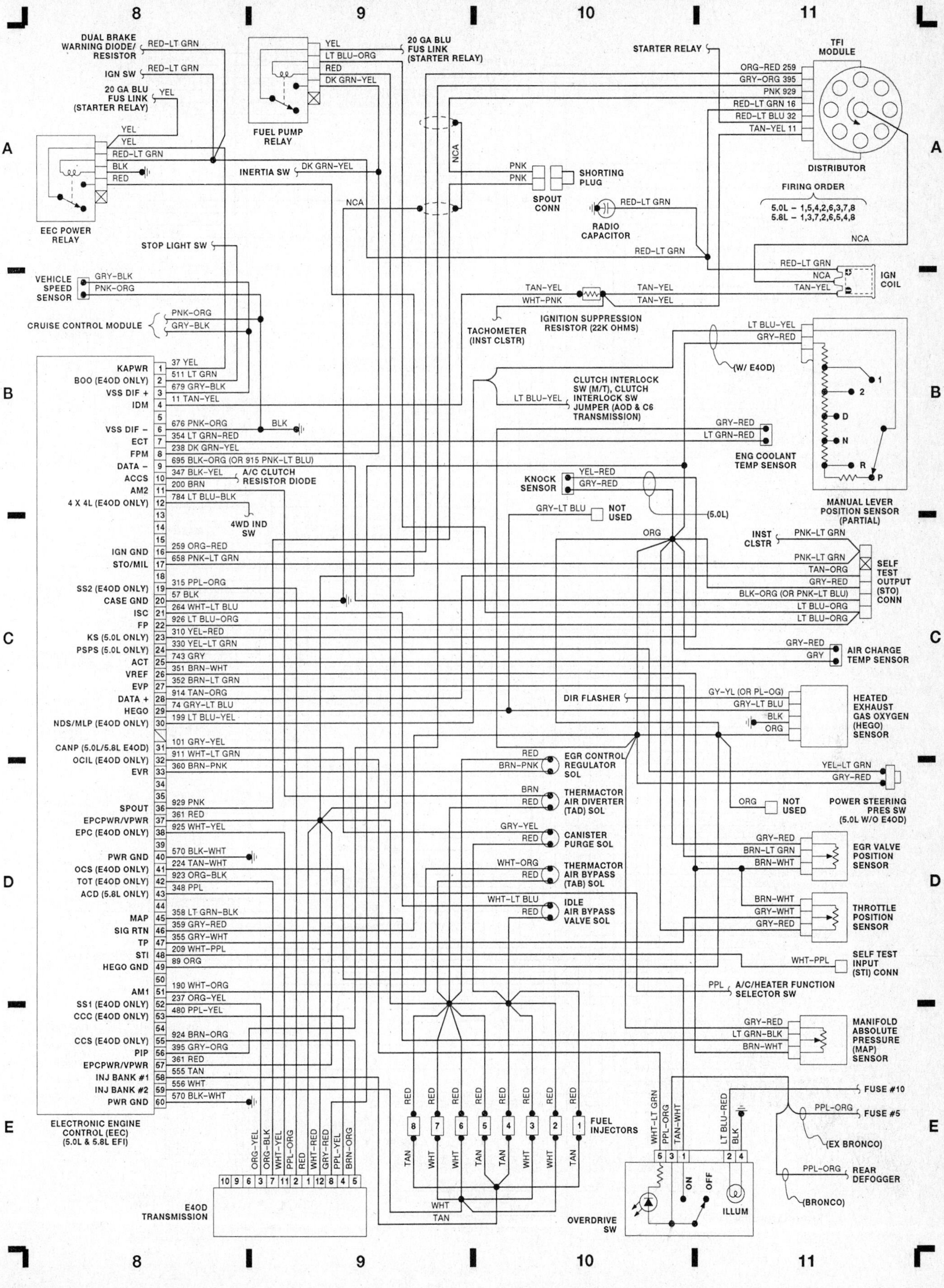
8
9
10
11
A
B
C
D
E
DUAL BRAKE WARNING DIODE/ RESISTOR
RED-LT GRN
IGN SW
20 GA BLU FUS LINK (STARTER RELAY)
YEL
RED-LT GRN
BLK
RED
EEC POWER RELAY
FUEL PUMP RELAY
LT BLU-ORG
DK GRN-YEL
20 GA BLU FUS LINK (STARTER RELAY)
INERTIA SW
NCA
STOP LIGHT SW
VEHICLE SPEED SENSOR
GRY-BLK
PNK-ORG
CRUISE CONTROL MODULE
STARTER RELAY
TFI MODULE
ORG-RED 259
GRY-ORG 395
PNK 929
RED-LT GRN 16
RED-LT BLU 32
TAN-YEL 11
DISTRIBUTOR
FIRING ORDER
5.0L – 1,5,4,2,6,3,7,8
5.8L – 1,3,7,2,6,5,4,8
PNK
SHORTING PLUG
SPOUT CONN
RADIO CAPACITOR
IGN COIL
TAN-YEL
WHT-PNK
TACHOMETER (INST CLSTR)
IGNITION SUPPRESSION RESISTOR (22K OHMS)
LT BLU-YEL
GRY-RED
(W/ E4OD)
CLUTCH INTERLOCK SW (M/T), CLUTCH INTERLOCK SW JUMPER (AOD & C6 TRANSMISSION)
MANUAL LEVER POSITION SENSOR (PARTIAL)
KAPWR 1 37 YEL
BOO (E4OD ONLY) 2 511 LT GRN
VSS DIF + 3 679 GRY-BLK
IDM 4 11 TAN-YEL
5
VSS DIF – 6 676 PNK-ORG
ECT 7 354 LT GRN-RED
FPM 8 238 DK GRN-YEL
DATA – 9 695 BLK-ORG (OR 915 PNK-LT BLU)
ACCS 10 347 BLK-YEL
AM2 11 200 BRN
4 X 4L (E4OD ONLY) 12 784 LT BLU-BLK
13
14
15
IGN GND 16 259 ORG-RED
STO/MIL 17 658 PNK-LT GRN
18
SS2 (E4OD ONLY) 19 315 PPL-ORG
CASE GND 20 57 BLK
ISC 21 264 WHT-LT BLU
FP 22 926 LT BLU-ORG
KS (5.0L ONLY) 23 310 YEL-RED
PSPS (5.0L ONLY) 24 330 YEL-LT GRN
ACT 25 743 GRY
VREF 26 351 BRN-WHT
EVP 27 352 BRN-LT GRN
DATA + 28 914 TAN-ORG
HEGO 29 74 GRY-LT BLU
NDS/MLP (E4OD ONLY) 30 199 LT BLU-YEL
CANP (5.0L/5.8L E4OD) 31 101 GRY-YEL
OCIL (E4OD ONLY) 32 911 WHT-LT GRN
EVR 33 360 BRN-PNK
34
35
SPOUT 36 929 PNK
EPCPWR/VPWR 37 361 RED
EPC (E4OD ONLY) 38 925 WHT-YEL
39
PWR GND 40 570 BLK-WHT
OCS (E4OD ONLY) 41 224 TAN-WHT
TOT (E4OD ONLY) 42 923 ORG-BLK
ACD (5.8L ONLY) 43 348 PPL
44
MAP 45 358 LT GRN-BLK
SIG RTN 46 359 GRY-RED
TP 47 355 GRY-WHT
STI 48 209 WHT-PPL
HEGO GND 49 89 ORG
50
AM1 51 190 WHT-ORG
SS1 (E4OD ONLY) 52 237 ORG-YEL
CCC (E4OD ONLY) 53 480 PPL-YEL
54
CCS (E4OD ONLY) 55 924 BRN-ORG
PIP 56 395 GRY-ORG
EPCPWR/VPWR 57 361 RED
INJ BANK #1 58 555 TAN
INJ BANK #2 59 556 WHT
PWR GND 60 570 BLK-WHT
A/C CLUTCH RESISTOR DIODE
4WD IND SW
ELECTRONIC ENGINE CONTROL (EEC) (5.0L & 5.8L EFI)
ENG COOLANT TEMP SENSOR
KNOCK SENSOR
YEL-RED
GRY-RED
GRY-LT BLU
NOT USED
(5.0L)
ORG
INST CLSTR
PNK-LT GRN
SELF TEST OUTPUT (STO) CONN
TAN-ORG
BLK-ORG (OR PNK-LT BLU)
LT BLU-ORG
AIR CHARGE TEMP SENSOR
GRY
DIR FLASHER
GY-YL (OR PL-OG)
HEATED EXHAUST GAS OXYGEN (HEGO) SENSOR
EGR CONTROL REGULATOR SOL
BRN-PNK
THERMACTOR AIR DIVERTER (TAD) SOL
BRN
YEL-LT GRN
POWER STEERING PRES SW (5.0L W/O E4OD)
CANISTER PURGE SOL
GRY-YEL
EGR VALVE POSITION SENSOR
BRN-LT GRN
BRN-WHT
THERMACTOR AIR BYPASS (TAB) SOL
WHT-ORG
IDLE AIR BYPASS VALVE SOL
WHT-LT BLU
THROTTLE POSITION SENSOR
GRY-WHT
SELF TEST INPUT (STI) CONN
WHT-PPL
A/C/HEATER FUNCTION SELECTOR SW
PPL
MANIFOLD ABSOLUTE PRESSURE (MAP) SENSOR
LT GRN-BLK
FUSE #10
FUSE #5
PPL-ORG
(EX BRONCO)
REAR DEFOGGER
(BRONCO)
FUEL INJECTORS
8 7 6 5 4 3 2 1
TAN
WHT
E4OD TRANSMISSION
10 9 6 3 7 11 2 1 12 8 4 5
ORG-YEL
GRY-BLK
WHT-YEL
PPL-ORG
WHT-RED
PPL-YEL
BRN-ORG
OVERDRIVE SW
WHT-LT GRN
PPL-ORG
TAN-WHT
LT BLU-RED
5 3 1 2 4
ON
OFF
ILLUM

1991 WIRING DIAGRAMS
Bronco & "F" Series (Cont.)

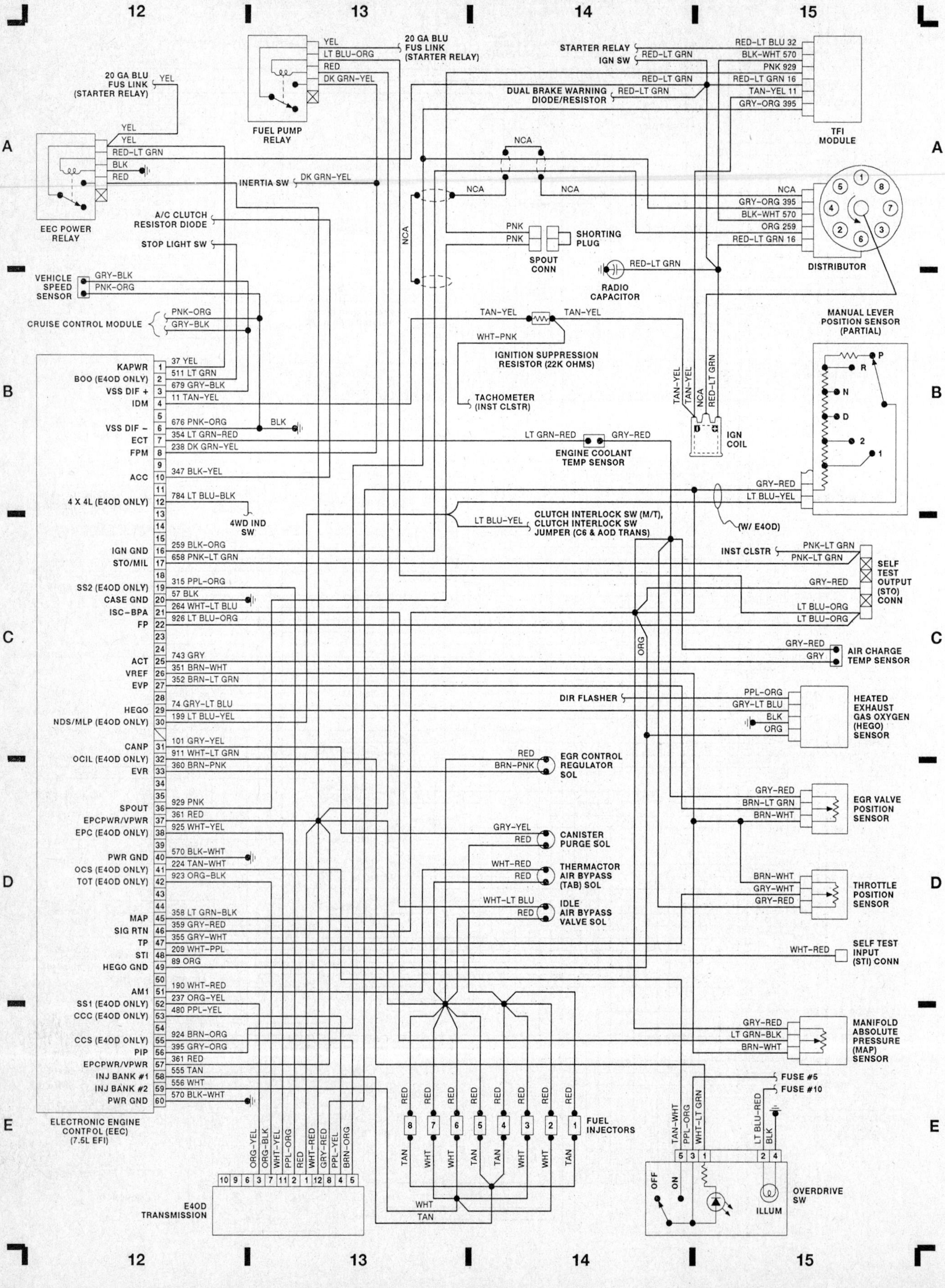
12
13
14
15
A
B
C
D
E
20 GA BLU FUS LINK (STARTER RELAY)
YEL
LT BLU-ORG
RED
DK GRN-YEL
FUEL PUMP RELAY
STARTER RELAY
IGN SW
RED-LT GRN
DUAL BRAKE WARNING DIODE/RESISTOR
RED-LT BLU 32
BLK-WHT 570
PNK 929
RED-LT GRN 16
TAN-YEL 11
GRY-ORG 395
TFI MODULE
EEC POWER RELAY
BLK
INERTIA SW
DK GRN-YEL
NCA
A/C CLUTCH RESISTOR DIODE
STOP LIGHT SW
PNK
SHORTING PLUG
SPOUT CONN
GRY-ORG 395
BLK-WHT 570
ORG 259
RED-LT GRN 16
DISTRIBUTOR
RADIO CAPACITOR
VEHICLE SPEED SENSOR
GRY-BLK
PNK-ORG
CRUISE CONTROL MODULE
TAN-YEL
WHT-PNK
IGNITION SUPPRESSION RESISTOR (22K OHMS)
TACHOMETER (INST CLSTR)
MANUAL LEVER POSITION SENSOR (PARTIAL)
P
R
N
D
2
1
IGN COIL
KAPWR
BOO (E4OD ONLY)
VSS DIF +
IDM
VSS DIF –
ECT
FPM
ACC
4 X 4L (E4OD ONLY)
IGN GND
STO/MIL
SS2 (E4OD ONLY)
CASE GND
ISC-BPA
FP
ACT
VREF
EVP
HEGO
NDS/MLP (E4OD ONLY)
CANP
OCIL (E4OD ONLY)
EVR
SPOUT
EPCPWR/VPWR
EPC (E4OD ONLY)
PWR GND
OCS (E4OD ONLY)
TOT (E4OD ONLY)
MAP
SIG RTN
TP
STI
HEGO GND
AM1
SS1 (E4OD ONLY)
CCC (E4OD ONLY)
CCS (E4OD ONLY)
PIP
EPCPWR/VPWR
INJ BANK #1
INJ BANK #2
PWR GND
37 YEL
511 LT GRN
679 GRY-BLK
11 TAN-YEL
676 PNK-ORG
354 LT GRN-RED
238 DK GRN-YEL
347 BLK-YEL
784 LT BLU-BLK
259 BLK-ORG
658 PNK-LT GRN
315 PPL-ORG
57 BLK
264 WHT-LT BLU
926 LT BLU-ORG
743 GRY
351 BRN-WHT
352 BRN-LT GRN
74 GRY-LT BLU
199 LT BLU-YEL
101 GRY-YEL
911 WHT-LT GRN
360 BRN-PNK
929 PNK
361 RED
925 WHT-YEL
570 BLK-WHT
224 TAN-WHT
923 ORG-BLK
358 LT GRN-BLK
359 GRY-RED
355 GRY-WHT
209 WHT-PPL
89 ORG
190 WHT-RED
237 ORG-YEL
480 PPL-YEL
924 BRN-ORG
395 GRY-ORG
361 RED
555 TAN
556 WHT
570 BLK-WHT
4WD IND SW
LT GRN-RED
GRY-RED
ENGINE COOLANT TEMP SENSOR
LT BLU-YEL
CLUTCH INTERLOCK SW (M/T), CLUTCH INTERLOCK SW JUMPER (C6 & AOD TRANS)
(W/ E4OD)
INST CLSTR
PNK-LT GRN
SELF TEST OUTPUT (STO) CONN
LT BLU-ORG
ORG
AIR CHARGE TEMP SENSOR
DIR FLASHER
PPL-ORG
GRY-LT BLU
HEATED EXHAUST GAS OXYGEN (HEGO) SENSOR
EGR CONTROL REGULATOR SOL
BRN-PNK
BRN-LT GRN
BRN-WHT
EGR VALVE POSITION SENSOR
GRY-YEL
CANISTER PURGE SOL
WHT-RED
THERMACTOR AIR BYPASS (TAB) SOL
GRY-WHT
THROTTLE POSITION SENSOR
WHT-LT BLU
IDLE AIR BYPASS VALVE SOL
SELF TEST INPUT (STI) CONN
LT GRN-BLK
MANIFOLD ABSOLUTE PRESSURE (MAP) SENSOR
FUSE #5
FUSE #10
FUEL INJECTORS
TAN-WHT
PPL-ORG
WHT-LT GRN
LT BLU-RED
OFF
ON
ILLUM
OVERDRIVE SW
ELECTRONIC ENGINE CONTROL (EEC) (7.5L EFI)
E4OD TRANSMISSION
ORG-YEL
ORG-BLK
WHT-YEL
PPL-ORG
WHT-RED
GRY-RED
PPL-YEL
BRN-ORG
WHT
TAN

1991 WIRING DIAGRAMS
Bronco & "F" Series (Cont.)

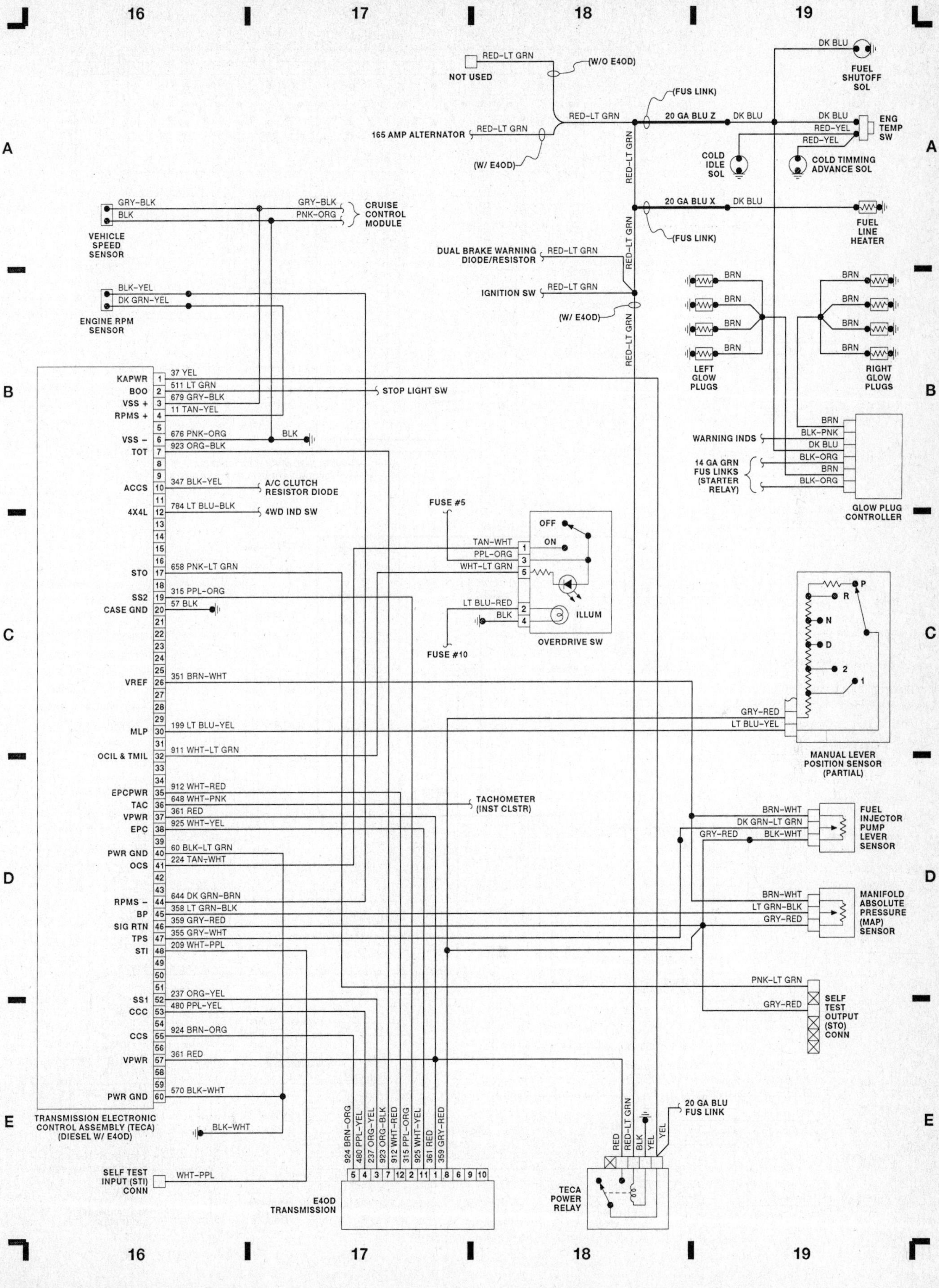
16
17
18
19
A
B
C
D
E
NOT USED
RED-LT GRN
(W/O E4OD)
165 AMP ALTERNATOR
(W/ E4OD)
(FUS LINK)
20 GA BLU Z
DK BLU
FUEL SHUTOFF SOL
ENG TEMP SW
RED-YEL
COLD IDLE SOL
COLD TIMMING ADVANCE SOL
20 GA BLU X
FUEL LINE HEATER
VEHICLE SPEED SENSOR
GRY-BLK
BLK
PNK-ORG
CRUISE CONTROL MODULE
DUAL BRAKE WARNING DIODE/RESISTOR
IGNITION SW
BRN
LEFT GLOW PLUGS
RIGHT GLOW PLUGS
ENGINE RPM SENSOR
BLK-YEL
DK GRN-YEL
KAPWR 1 37 YEL
BOO 2 511 LT GRN
STOP LIGHT SW
VSS + 3 679 GRY-BLK
RPMS + 4 11 TAN-YEL
VSS − 6 676 PNK-ORG
TOT 7 923 ORG-BLK
ACCS 10 347 BLK-YEL
A/C CLUTCH RESISTOR DIODE
4X4L 12 784 LT BLU-BLK
4WD IND SW
STO 17 658 PNK-LT GRN
SS2 19 315 PPL-ORG
CASE GND 20 57 BLK
VREF 26 351 BRN-WHT
MLP 30 199 LT BLU-YEL
OCIL & TMIL 32 911 WHT-LT GRN
EPCPWR 35 912 WHT-RED
TAC 36 648 WHT-PNK
TACHOMETER (INST CLSTR)
VPWR 37 361 RED
EPC 38 925 WHT-YEL
PWR GND 40 60 BLK-LT GRN
OCS 41 224 TAN-WHT
RPMS − 44 644 DK GRN-BRN
BP 45 358 LT GRN-BLK
SIG RTN 46 359 GRY-RED
TPS 47 355 GRY-WHT
STI 48 209 WHT-PPL
SS1 52 237 ORG-YEL
CCC 53 480 PPL-YEL
CCS 55 924 BRN-ORG
VPWR 57 361 RED
PWR GND 60 570 BLK-WHT
TRANSMISSION ELECTRONIC CONTROL ASSEMBLY (TECA) (DIESEL W/ E4OD)
BLK-WHT
SELF TEST INPUT (STI) CONN
WHT-PPL
WARNING INDS
BLK-PNK
BLK-ORG
14 GA GRN FUS LINKS (STARTER RELAY)
GLOW PLUG CONTROLLER
FUSE #5
OFF
ON
TAN-WHT
PPL-ORG
WHT-LT GRN
LT BLU-RED
ILLUM
OVERDRIVE SW
FUSE #10
P
R
N
D
2
1
GRY-RED
LT BLU-YEL
MANUAL LEVER POSITION SENSOR (PARTIAL)
BRN-WHT
DK GRN-LT GRN
BLK-WHT
FUEL INJECTOR PUMP LEVER SENSOR
LT GRN-BLK
MANIFOLD ABSOLUTE PRESSURE (MAP) SENSOR
PNK-LT GRN
SELF TEST OUTPUT (STO) CONN
924 BRN-ORG
480 PPL-YEL
237 ORG-YEL
923 ORG-BLK
912 WHT-RED
315 PPL-ORG
925 WHT-YEL
361 RED
359 GRY-RED
5 4 3 7 12 2 11 1 8 6 9 10
E4OD TRANSMISSION
20 GA BLU FUS LINK
RED
YEL
TECA POWER RELAY

1991 WIRING DIAGRAMS
Bronco & "F" Series (Cont.)

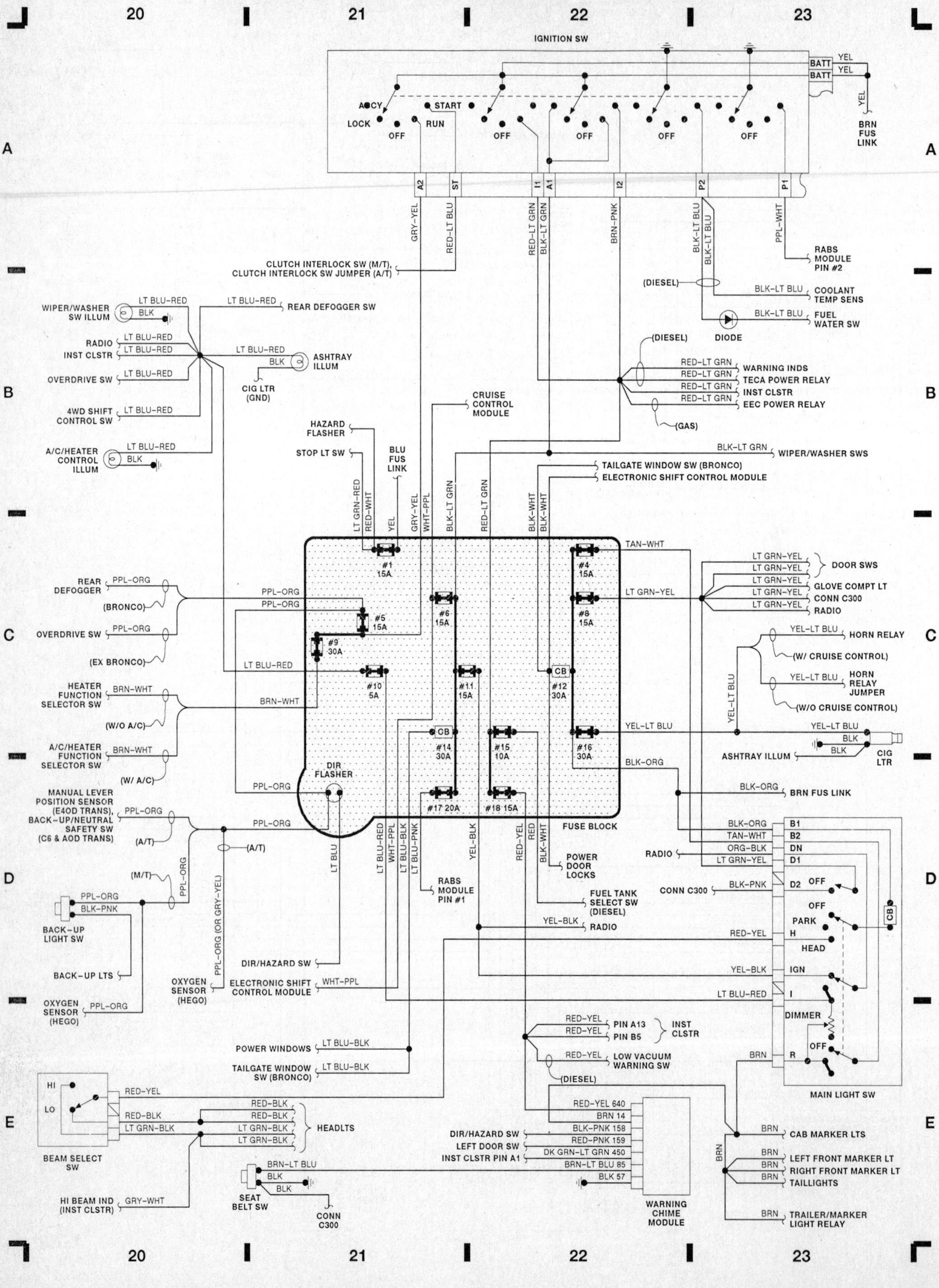
20
21
22
23
IGNITION SW
BATT
YEL
ACCY
START
LOCK
RUN
OFF
BRN FUS LINK
A2
ST
I1
A1
I2
P2
P1
GRY-YEL
RED-LT BLU
RED-LT GRN
BLK-LT GRN
BRN-PNK
BLK-LT BLU
PPL-WHT
CLUTCH INTERLOCK SW (M/T),
CLUTCH INTERLOCK SW JUMPER (A/T)
RABS MODULE PIN #2
(DIESEL)
COOLANT TEMP SENS
FUEL WATER SW
DIODE
WIPER/WASHER SW ILLUM
LT BLU-RED
BLK
REAR DEFOGGER SW
RADIO
INST CLSTR
ASHTRAY ILLUM
OVERDRIVE SW
CIG LTR (GND)
4WD SHIFT CONTROL SW
A/C/HEATER CONTROL ILLUM
WARNING INDS
TECA POWER RELAY
INST CLSTR
EEC POWER RELAY
(GAS)
CRUISE CONTROL MODULE
HAZARD FLASHER
STOP LT SW
BLU FUS LINK
WIPER/WASHER SWS
TAILGATE WINDOW SW (BRONCO)
ELECTRONIC SHIFT CONTROL MODULE
LT GRN-RED
RED-WHT
YEL
WHT-PPL
BLK-WHT
TAN-WHT
#1 15A
#4 15A
DOOR SWS
GLOVE COMPT LT
CONN C300
LT GRN-YEL
REAR DEFOGGER
PPL-ORG
(BRONCO)
#5 15A
#6 15A
#8 15A
#9 30A
OVERDRIVE SW
(EX BRONCO)
YEL-LT BLU
HORN RELAY
(W/ CRUISE CONTROL)
HORN RELAY JUMPER
(W/O CRUISE CONTROL)
#10 5A
#11 15A
CB
#12 30A
HEATER FUNCTION SELECTOR SW
BRN-WHT
(W/O A/C)
A/C/HEATER FUNCTION SELECTOR SW
(W/ A/C)
#14 30A
#15 10A
#16 30A
ASHTRAY ILLUM
CIG LTR
BLK-ORG
DIR FLASHER
MANUAL LEVER POSITION SENSOR (E4OD TRANS), BACK-UP/NEUTRAL SAFETY SW (C6 & AOD TRANS)
(A/T)
#17 20A
#18 15A
FUSE BLOCK
BRN FUS LINK
(M/T)
LT BLU
LT BLU-RED
LT BLU-BLK
LT BLU-PNK
YEL-BLK
RED-YEL
RED
POWER DOOR LOCKS
RADIO
B1
B2
DN
D1
ORG-BLK
BACK-UP LIGHT SW
BLK-PNK
RABS MODULE PIN #1
FUEL TANK SELECT SW (DIESEL)
CONN C300
D2
OFF
PARK
H
HEAD
IGN
I
DIMMER
R
PPL-ORG (OR GRY-YEL)
DIR/HAZARD SW
BACK-UP LTS
OXYGEN SENSOR (HEGO)
ELECTRONIC SHIFT CONTROL MODULE
PIN A13
PIN B5
INST CLSTR
LOW VACUUM WARNING SW
POWER WINDOWS
TAILGATE WINDOW SW (BRONCO)
(DIESEL)
BRN
MAIN LIGHT SW
HI
LO
BEAM SELECT SW
RED-BLK
LT GRN-BLK
HEADLTS
RED-YEL 640
BRN 14
BLK-PNK 158
RED-PNK 159
DK GRN-LT GRN 450
BRN-LT BLU 85
BLK 57
DIR/HAZARD SW
LEFT DOOR SW
INST CLSTR PIN A1
CAB MARKER LTS
LEFT FRONT MARKER LT
RIGHT FRONT MARKER LT
TAILLIGHTS
TRAILER/MARKER LIGHT RELAY
SEAT BELT SW
BRN-LT BLU
HI BEAM IND (INST CLSTR)
GRY-WHT
CONN C300
WARNING CHIME MODULE

1991 WIRING DIAGRAMS
Bronco & "F" Series (Cont.)

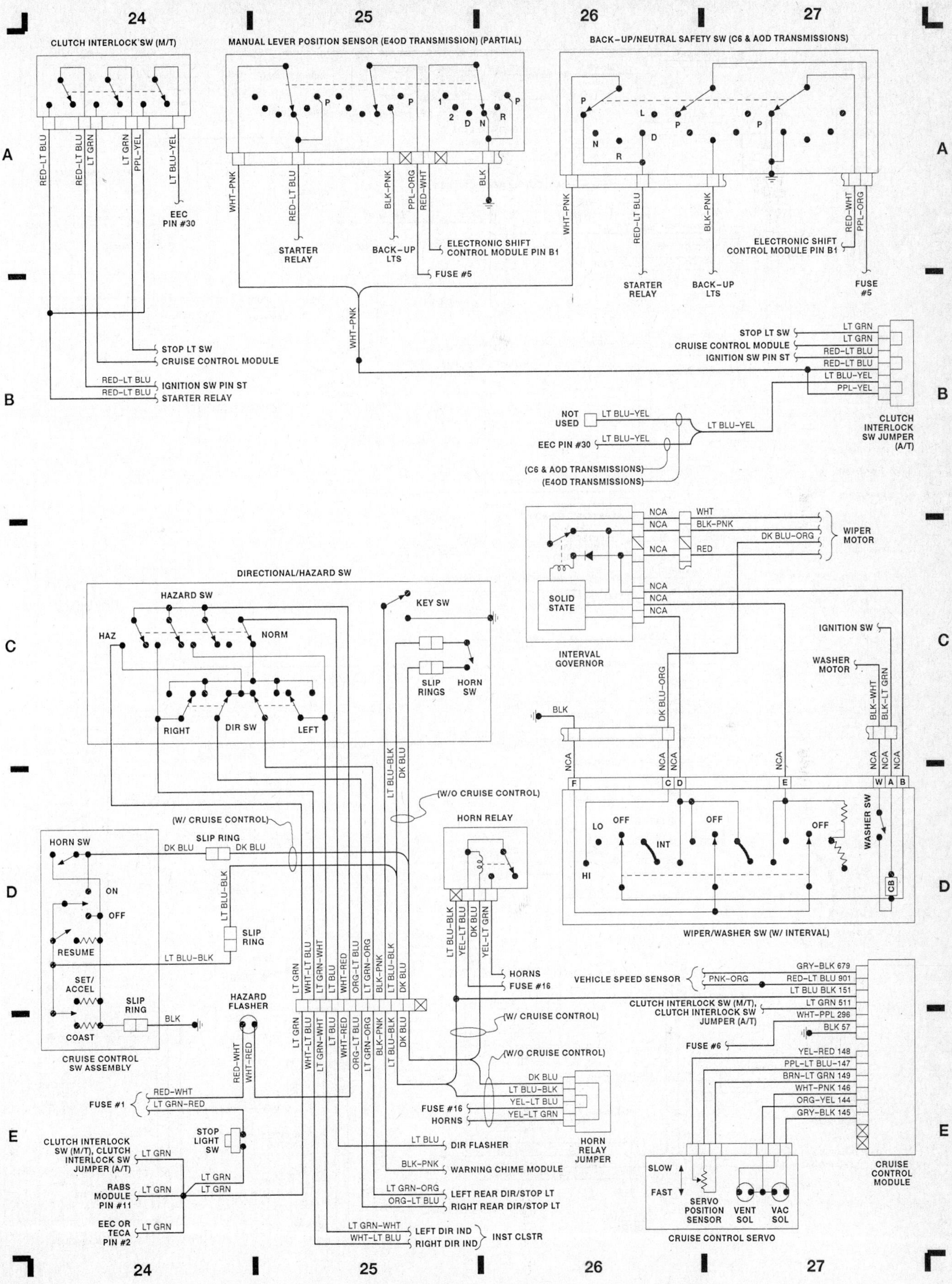
24
25
26
27
CLUTCH INTERLOCK SW (M/T)
MANUAL LEVER POSITION SENSOR (E4OD TRANSMISSION) (PARTIAL)
BACK-UP/NEUTRAL SAFETY SW (C6 & AOD TRANSMISSIONS)
EEC PIN #30
STARTER RELAY
BACK-UP LTS
ELECTRONIC SHIFT CONTROL MODULE PIN B1
FUSE #5
STOP LT SW
CRUISE CONTROL MODULE
IGNITION SW PIN ST
CLUTCH INTERLOCK SW JUMPER (A/T)
NOT USED
(C6 & AOD TRANSMISSIONS)
(E4OD TRANSMISSIONS)
WIPER MOTOR
SOLID STATE
INTERVAL GOVERNOR
IGNITION SW
WASHER MOTOR
DIRECTIONAL/HAZARD SW
HAZARD SW
HAZ
NORM
KEY SW
SLIP RINGS
HORN SW
RIGHT
DIR SW
LEFT
(W/O CRUISE CONTROL)
(W/ CRUISE CONTROL)
HORN RELAY
SLIP RING
ON
OFF
RESUME
SET/ ACCEL
COAST
CRUISE CONTROL SW ASSEMBLY
HAZARD FLASHER
LO
HI
INT
WASHER SW
CB
WIPER/WASHER SW (W/ INTERVAL)
HORNS
FUSE #16
VEHICLE SPEED SENSOR
CLUTCH INTERLOCK SW (M/T), CLUTCH INTERLOCK SW JUMPER (A/T)
FUSE #6
GRY-BLK 679
RED-LT BLU 901
LT BLU BLK 151
LT GRN 511
WHT-PPL 296
BLK 57
YEL-RED 148
PPL-LT BLU-147
BRN-LT GRN 149
WHT-PNK 146
ORG-YEL 144
GRY-BLK 145
FUSE #1
STOP LIGHT SW
RABS MODULE PIN #11
EEC OR TECA PIN #2
DIR FLASHER
WARNING CHIME MODULE
LEFT REAR DIR/STOP LT
RIGHT REAR DIR/STOP LT
LEFT DIR IND
RIGHT DIR IND
INST CLSTR
HORN RELAY JUMPER
SLOW
FAST
SERVO POSITION SENSOR
VENT SOL
VAC SOL
CRUISE CONTROL SERVO
CRUISE CONTROL MODULE

1991 WIRING DIAGRAMS
Bronco & "F" Series (Cont.)

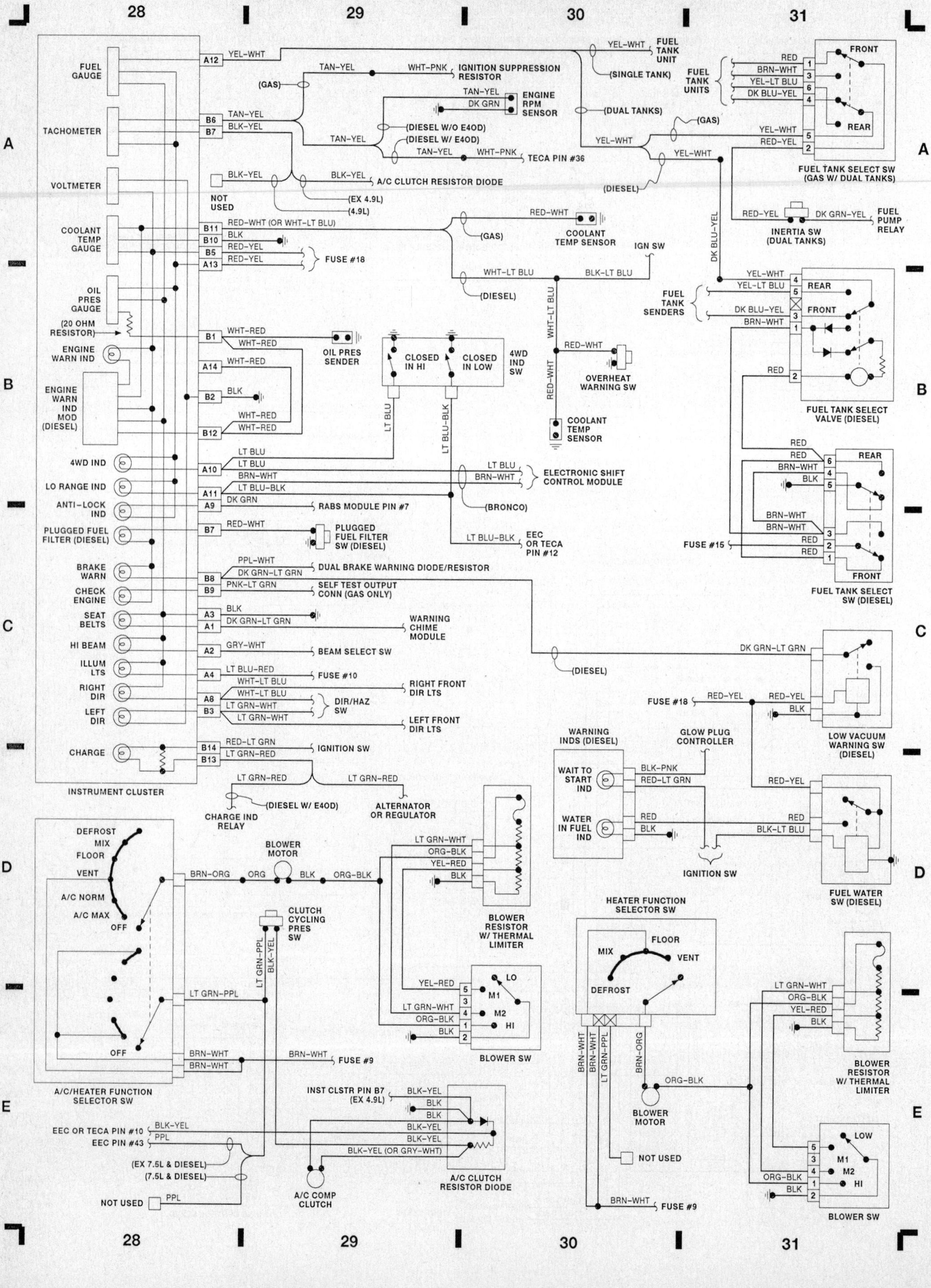
28
29
30
31
A
B
C
D
E
FUEL GAUGE
TACHOMETER
VOLTMETER
COOLANT TEMP GAUGE
OIL PRES GAUGE
(20 OHM RESISTOR)
ENGINE WARN IND
ENGINE WARN IND MOD (DIESEL)
4WD IND
LO RANGE IND
ANTI-LOCK IND
PLUGGED FUEL FILTER (DIESEL)
BRAKE WARN
CHECK ENGINE
SEAT BELTS
HI BEAM
ILLUM LTS
RIGHT DIR
LEFT DIR
CHARGE
INSTRUMENT CLUSTER
A12
YEL-WHT
TAN-YEL
WHT-PNK
IGNITION SUPPRESSION RESISTOR
(GAS)
TAN-YEL
DK GRN
ENGINE RPM SENSOR
B6
B7
TAN-YEL
BLK-YEL
(DIESEL W/O E4OD)
(DIESEL W/ E4OD)
TAN-YEL
WHT-PNK
TECA PIN #36
NOT USED
BLK-YEL
A/C CLUTCH RESISTOR DIODE
(EX 4.9L)
(4.9L)
YEL-WHT
FUEL TANK UNIT
(SINGLE TANK)
(DUAL TANKS)
(GAS)
(DIESEL)
FUEL TANK UNITS
RED
BRN-WHT
YEL-LT BLU
DK BLU-YEL
FRONT
REAR
YEL-WHT
RED-YEL
FUEL TANK SELECT SW (GAS W/ DUAL TANKS)
B11
B10
B5
A13
RED-WHT (OR WHT-LT BLU)
BLK
RED-YEL
RED-YEL
FUSE #18
RED-WHT
(GAS)
COOLANT TEMP SENSOR
IGN SW
WHT-LT BLU
BLK-LT BLU
(DIESEL)
DK BLU-YEL
RED-YEL
DK GRN-YEL
INERTIA SW (DUAL TANKS)
FUEL PUMP RELAY
FUEL TANK SENDERS
YEL-WHT
YEL-LT BLU
DK BLU-YEL
BRN-WHT
RED
REAR
FRONT
FUEL TANK SELECT VALVE (DIESEL)
B1
WHT-RED
OIL PRES SENDER
A14
B2
B12
CLOSED IN HI
CLOSED IN LOW
4WD IND SW
RED-WHT
OVERHEAT WARNING SW
COOLANT TEMP SENSOR
LT BLU
LT BLU-BLK
A10
A11
A9
B7
LT BLU
BRN-WHT
LT BLU-BLK
DK GRN
ELECTRONIC SHIFT CONTROL MODULE
(BRONCO)
RABS MODULE PIN #7
RED-WHT
PLUGGED FUEL FILTER SW (DIESEL)
EEC OR TECA PIN #12
B8
B9
PPL-WHT
DK GRN-LT GRN
PNK-LT GRN
DUAL BRAKE WARNING DIODE/RESISTOR
SELF TEST OUTPUT CONN (GAS ONLY)
A3
A1
WARNING CHIME MODULE
A2
GRY-WHT
BEAM SELECT SW
A4
LT BLU-RED
FUSE #10
A8
B3
WHT-LT BLU
LT GRN-WHT
RIGHT FRONT DIR LTS
DIR/HAZ SW
LEFT FRONT DIR LTS
B14
B13
RED-LT GRN
LT GRN-RED
IGNITION SW
(DIESEL W/ E4OD)
CHARGE IND RELAY
ALTERNATOR OR REGULATOR
FUSE #15
FUEL TANK SELECT SW (DIESEL)
(DIESEL)
DK GRN-LT GRN
LOW VACUUM WARNING SW (DIESEL)
FUSE #18
WARNING INDS (DIESEL)
WAIT TO START IND
WATER IN FUEL IND
GLOW PLUG CONTROLLER
BLK-PNK
RED-LT GRN
BLK-LT BLU
IGNITION SW
FUEL WATER SW (DIESEL)
DEFROST
MIX
FLOOR
VENT
A/C NORM
A/C MAX
OFF
BRN-ORG
ORG
BLK
ORG-BLK
BLOWER MOTOR
CLUTCH CYCLING PRES SW
LT GRN-PPL
BLK-YEL
BRN-WHT
FUSE #9
A/C/HEATER FUNCTION SELECTOR SW
LT GRN-WHT
ORG-BLK
YEL-RED
BLOWER RESISTOR W/ THERMAL LIMITER
LO
M1
M2
HI
BLOWER SW
HEATER FUNCTION SELECTOR SW
BLOWER MOTOR
NOT USED
INST CLSTR PIN B7 (EX 4.9L)
EEC OR TECA PIN #10
EEC PIN #43
PPL
(EX 7.5L & DIESEL)
(7.5L & DIESEL)
NOT USED
BLK-YEL (OR GRY-WHT)
A/C COMP CLUTCH
A/C CLUTCH RESISTOR DIODE
LOW

1991 WIRING DIAGRAMS
Bronco & "F" Series (Cont.)

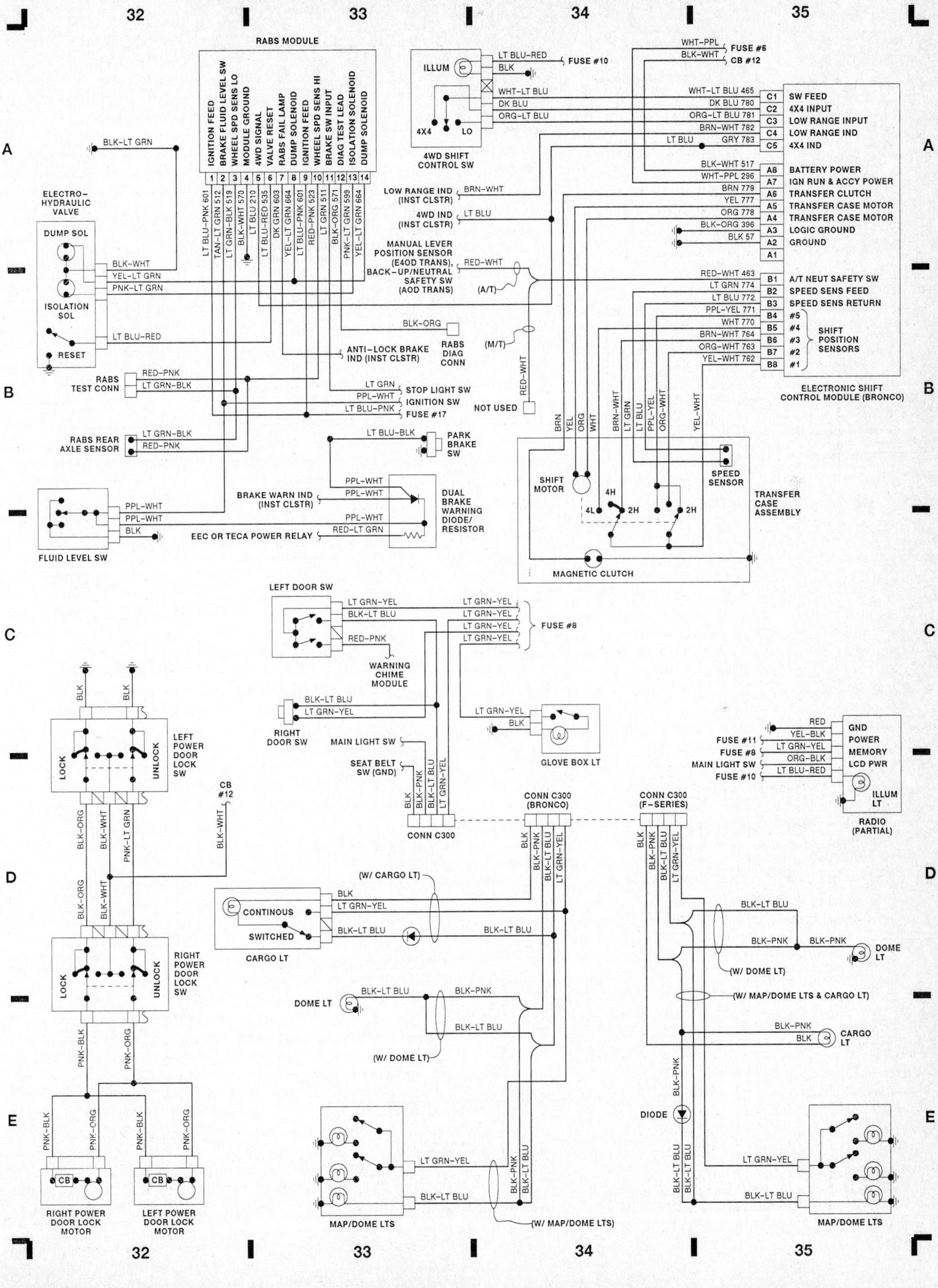
32
33
34
35
A
B
C
D
E
RABS MODULE
IGNITION FEED
BRAKE FLUID LEVEL SW
WHEEL SPD SENS LO
MODULE GROUND
4WD SIGNAL
VALVE RESET
RABS FAIL LAMP
DUMP SOLENOID
IGNITION FEED
WHEEL SPD SENS HI
BRAKE SW INPUT
DIAG TEST LEAD
ISOLATION SOLENOID
DUMP SOLENOID
LT BLU-PNK 601
TAN-LT GRN 512
LT GRN-BLK 519
BLK-WHT 570
LT BLU 210
LT BLU-RED 535
DK GRN 603
YEL-LT GRN 664
LT BLU-PNK 601
RED-PNK 523
LT GRN 511
BLK-ORG 571
PNK-LT GRN 599
PNK-LT GRN 664
BLK-LT GRN
ELECTRO-HYDRAULIC VALVE
DUMP SOL
ISOLATION SOL
RESET
BLK-WHT
YEL-LT GRN
PNK-LT GRN
LT BLU-RED
RABS TEST CONN
RED-PNK
LT GRN-BLK
RABS REAR AXLE SENSOR
FLUID LEVEL SW
PPL-WHT
BLK
ILLUM
4X4
LO
4WD SHIFT CONTROL SW
LT BLU-RED
FUSE #10
WHT-LT BLU
DK BLU
ORG-LT BLU
LOW RANGE IND (INST CLSTR)
BRN-WHT
4WD IND (INST CLSTR)
LT BLU
MANUAL LEVER POSITION SENSOR (E4OD TRANS), BACK-UP/NEUTRAL SAFETY SW (AOD TRANS)
RED-WHT
(A/T)
(M/T)
BLK-ORG
RABS DIAG CONN
ANTI-LOCK BRAKE IND (INST CLSTR)
LT GRN
STOP LIGHT SW
IGNITION SW
FUSE #17
NOT USED
LT BLU-BLK
PARK BRAKE SW
BRAKE WARN IND (INST CLSTR)
DUAL BRAKE WARNING DIODE/ RESISTOR
EEC OR TECA POWER RELAY
RED-LT GRN
WHT-PPL
FUSE #6
CB #12
WHT-LT BLU 465
DK BLU 780
ORG-LT BLU 781
BRN-WHT 782
GRY 783
BLK-WHT 517
WHT-PPL 296
BRN 779
YEL 777
ORG 778
BLK-ORG 396
BLK 57
RED-WHT 463
LT GRN 774
LT BLU 772
PPL-YEL 771
WHT 770
BRN-WHT 764
ORG-WHT 763
YEL-WHT 762
C1 SW FEED
C2 4X4 INPUT
C3 LOW RANGE INPUT
C4 LOW RANGE IND
C5 4X4 IND
A8 BATTERY POWER
A7 IGN RUN & ACCY POWER
A6 TRANSFER CLUTCH
A5 TRANSFER CASE MOTOR
A4 TRANSFER CASE MOTOR
A3 LOGIC GROUND
A2 GROUND
A1
B1 A/T NEUT SAFETY SW
B2 SPEED SENS FEED
B3 SPEED SENS RETURN
B4 #5
B5 #4
B6 #3
B7 #2
B8 #1
SHIFT POSITION SENSORS
ELECTRONIC SHIFT CONTROL MODULE (BRONCO)
SHIFT MOTOR
4H
4L
2H
SPEED SENSOR
TRANSFER CASE ASSEMBLY
MAGNETIC CLUTCH
LEFT DOOR SW
LT GRN-YEL
BLK-LT BLU
RED-PNK
FUSE #8
WARNING CHIME MODULE
RIGHT DOOR SW
MAIN LIGHT SW
SEAT BELT SW (GND)
GLOVE BOX LT
LEFT POWER DOOR LOCK SW
LOCK
UNLOCK
BLK-ORG
BLK-WHT
PNK-LT GRN
CB #12
RIGHT POWER DOOR LOCK SW
PNK-BLK
PNK-ORG
RIGHT POWER DOOR LOCK MOTOR
LEFT POWER DOOR LOCK MOTOR
CB
CONN C300
CONN C300 (BRONCO)
CONN C300 (F-SERIES)
BLK-PNK
BLK-LT BLU
LT GRN-YEL
(W/ CARGO LT)
CONTINOUS
SWITCHED
CARGO LT
DOME LT
(W/ DOME LT)
MAP/DOME LTS
(W/ MAP/DOME LTS)
(W/ MAP/DOME LTS & CARGO LT)
CARGO LT
DIODE
RED
YEL-BLK
ORG-BLK
GND
POWER
MEMORY
LCD PWR
ILLUM LT
FUSE #11
MAIN LIGHT SW
RADIO (PARTIAL)

1991 WIRING DIAGRAMS
Bronco & "F" Series (Cont.)

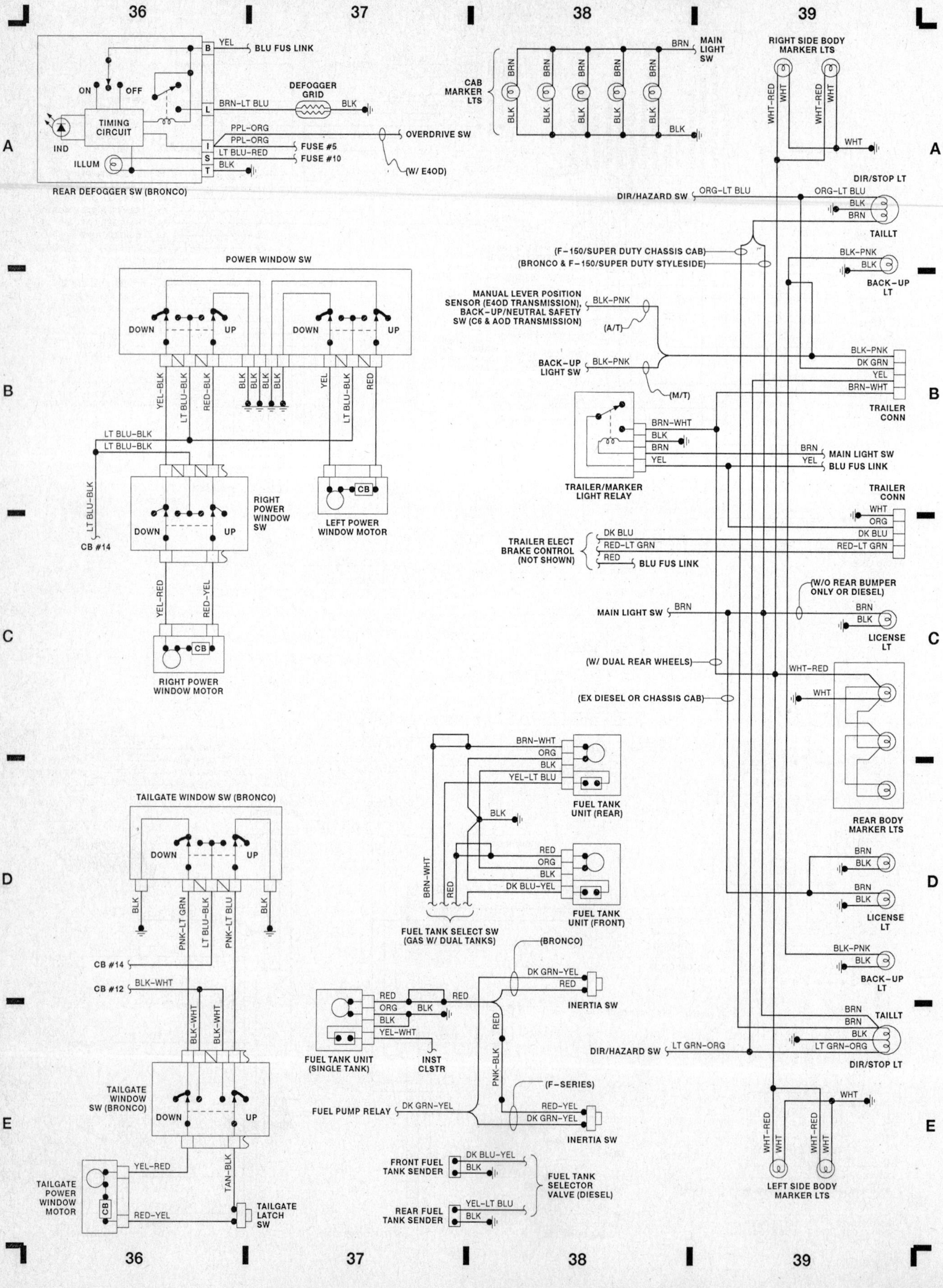
36
37
38
39
A
B
C
D
E
REAR DEFOGGER SW (BRONCO)
TIMING CIRCUIT
ON
OFF
IND
ILLUM
YEL
BLU FUS LINK
DEFOGGER GRID
BRN-LT BLU
BLK
PPL-ORG
OVERDRIVE SW
LT BLU-RED
FUSE #5
FUSE #10
(W/ E4OD)
CAB MARKER LTS
BRN
MAIN LIGHT SW
RIGHT SIDE BODY MARKER LTS
WHT-RED
WHT
DIR/STOP LT
DIR/HAZARD SW
ORG-LT BLU
TAILLT
(F-150/SUPER DUTY CHASSIS CAB)
(BRONCO & F-150/SUPER DUTY STYLESIDE)
BLK-PNK
BACK-UP LT
MANUAL LEVER POSITION SENSOR (E4OD TRANSMISSION), BACK-UP/NEUTRAL SAFETY SW (C6 & AOD TRANSMISSION)
(A/T)
BACK-UP LIGHT SW
(M/T)
DK GRN
BRN-WHT
TRAILER CONN
TRAILER/MARKER LIGHT RELAY
BLU FUS LINK
POWER WINDOW SW
DOWN
UP
YEL-BLK
LT BLU-BLK
RED-BLK
RED
LT BLU-BLK
RIGHT POWER WINDOW SW
LEFT POWER WINDOW MOTOR
CB
CB #14
YEL-RED
RED-YEL
RIGHT POWER WINDOW MOTOR
ORG
DK BLU
RED-LT GRN
TRAILER ELECT BRAKE CONTROL (NOT SHOWN)
(W/O REAR BUMPER ONLY OR DIESEL)
LICENSE LT
(W/ DUAL REAR WHEELS)
(EX DIESEL OR CHASSIS CAB)
REAR BODY MARKER LTS
YEL-LT BLU
FUEL TANK UNIT (REAR)
DK BLU-YEL
FUEL TANK UNIT (FRONT)
FUEL TANK SELECT SW (GAS W/ DUAL TANKS)
TAILGATE WINDOW SW (BRONCO)
PNK-LT GRN
LT BLU-BLK
PNK-LT BLU
CB #12
BLK-WHT
(BRONCO)
DK GRN-YEL
INERTIA SW
YEL-WHT
FUEL TANK UNIT (SINGLE TANK)
INST CLSTR
PNK-BLK
LT GRN-ORG
(F-SERIES)
RED-YEL
FUEL PUMP RELAY
TAILGATE WINDOW SW (BRONCO)
TAILGATE POWER WINDOW MOTOR
TAN-BLK
TAILGATE LATCH SW
FRONT FUEL TANK SENDER
REAR FUEL TANK SENDER
FUEL TANK SELECTOR VALVE (DIESEL)
LEFT SIDE BODY MARKER LTS

1991 WIRING DIAGRAMS
Explorer & Ranger

COMPONENT LOCATOR:

A/C COMP CLUTCH	D 25
A/C WOT CUTOUT RELAY	C 25
ALTERNATOR	B1,C1
ASHTRAY ASSEMBLY	C 39
BACK-UP LT SW	B 20
BATTERY	A 2
BLOWER MOTOR	C 24
BRAKE DIODE/RESISTOR	B 23
CARGO LT	B 42, C 41
CIG LTR	C 39
CLUTCH CYCLING SW	E 25–26
CLUTCH TRIPLE FUNCTION SW	A 20
CLUTCH TRIPLE FUNCTION SW JUMPER	A 20
COURTESY/DOME LTS	A–B 40–42, C–D 40–41
CRUISE CONTROL SYSTEM	A–C 26–27
DIR FLASHER	E 22
DIS IGNITION MODULE (2.3L)	E 4
EDIS MODULE (4.0L)	E 16
EEC POWER RELAY (2.3L)	A 4
EEC POWER RELAY (2.9L)	A 8
EEC POWER RELAY (3.0L)	A 12
EEC POWER RELAY (4.0L)	A 16
ELECT ENGINE CTRL (EEC) (2.3L)	A–D 4
ELECT ENGINE CTRL (EEC) (2.9L)	A–D 8
ELECT ENGINE CTRL (EEC) (3.0L)	A–D 12
ELECT ENGINE CTRL (EEC) (4.0L)	A–D 16
ELECTRONIC SHIFT CONTROL SYSTEM	A–C 24–25
ENGINE COMPT LT	E 1–2
FLUID LEVEL SW	B 23
FUEL PUMP RELAY (2.3L)	A 7
FUEL PUMP RELAY (2.9L)	A 11
FUEL PUMP RELAY (3.0L)	A 15
FUEL PUMP RELAY (4.0L)	A 19
FUEL TANK SENDER	B 35, D 33
FUS LINKS	A 2–3
FUSE PANEL	C–E 21–22
GLOVE BOX LT	C 28
HAZARD FLASHER	E 31
HEADLT SW	C–D 30–31
HEATER/A/C CONTROL SW	D–E 24
HEGO SENSOR (2.3L)	C 7
HEGO SENSOR (2.9L)	C 11
HEGO SENSOR (3.0L)	C 15
HEGO SENSOR (4.0L)	C 19
HORN RELAY	A 26
HORN SW	A 26
IGNITION SW	A 21–23
INSTRUMENT CLUSTER	A–E 32–35
KEY WARNING SW	B 29
LEFT FRONT DOOR SW	A 41, D 40
LOW OIL LEVEL RELAY	A 28
LUMBAR SEAT SW	D 39
MAF SENSOR (2.3L)	A 7
MAF SENSOR (3.0L)	A 15
MAP SENSOR (4.0L)	A 19
MULTI-FUNCTION SW	D 28–29
NEUTRAL SAFETY/BACK-UP LT SW	B 20
PARK BRAKE SW	B 23
POWER DISTRIBUTION BOX	D–E 3
POWER DOOR LOCKS	D–E 36–39
POWER MIRROR SW	C–D 36–37
POWER WINDOWS	A–B 36–39
RABS SYSTEM	C–E 26–27
RADIO (PARTIAL)	C 29–30
REAR DEFOGGER	E 40
REAR WIPER/WASHER	E 41–42
SELF TEST OUTPUT CONN (2.3L)	B 7
SELF TEST OUTPUT CONN (2.9L)	B 11
SELF TEST OUTPUT CONN (3.0L)	B 15
SELF TEST OUTPUT CONN (4.0L)	B 19
SPEED SENSOR	B 26
STARTER RELAY	A 3
STOP LT SW	E 31
TFI IGNITION MODULE (2.9L)	E 8
TFI IGNITION MODULE (3.0L)	E 12
TRAILER TOW RELAYS (EXPLORER)	C–D 42
VANITY MIRROR LTS	B 40
WARNING CHIMES	A–B 29
WIPER/WASHER SYSTEM	A–B 30–31
4X4 IND SW	B 35

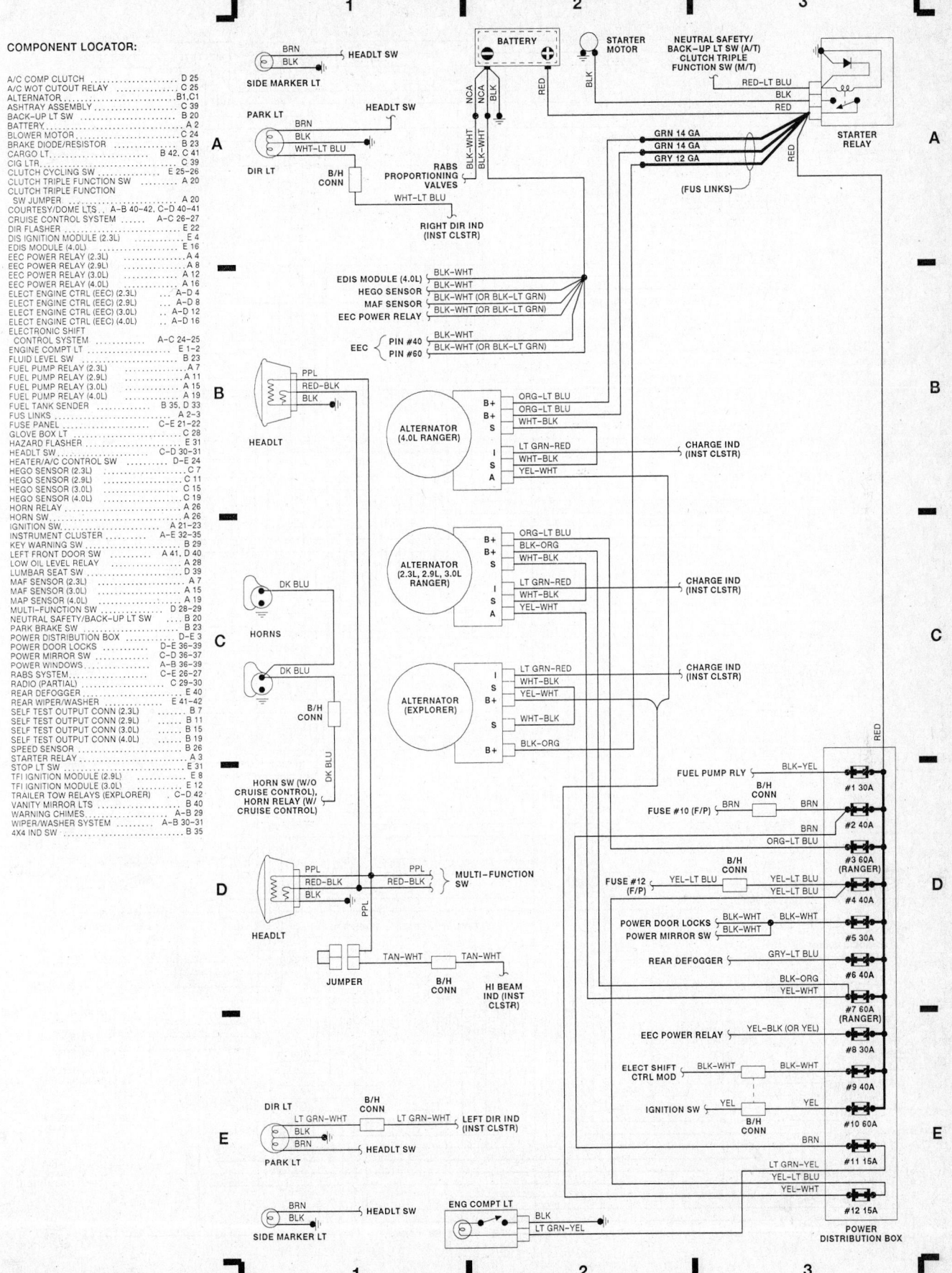

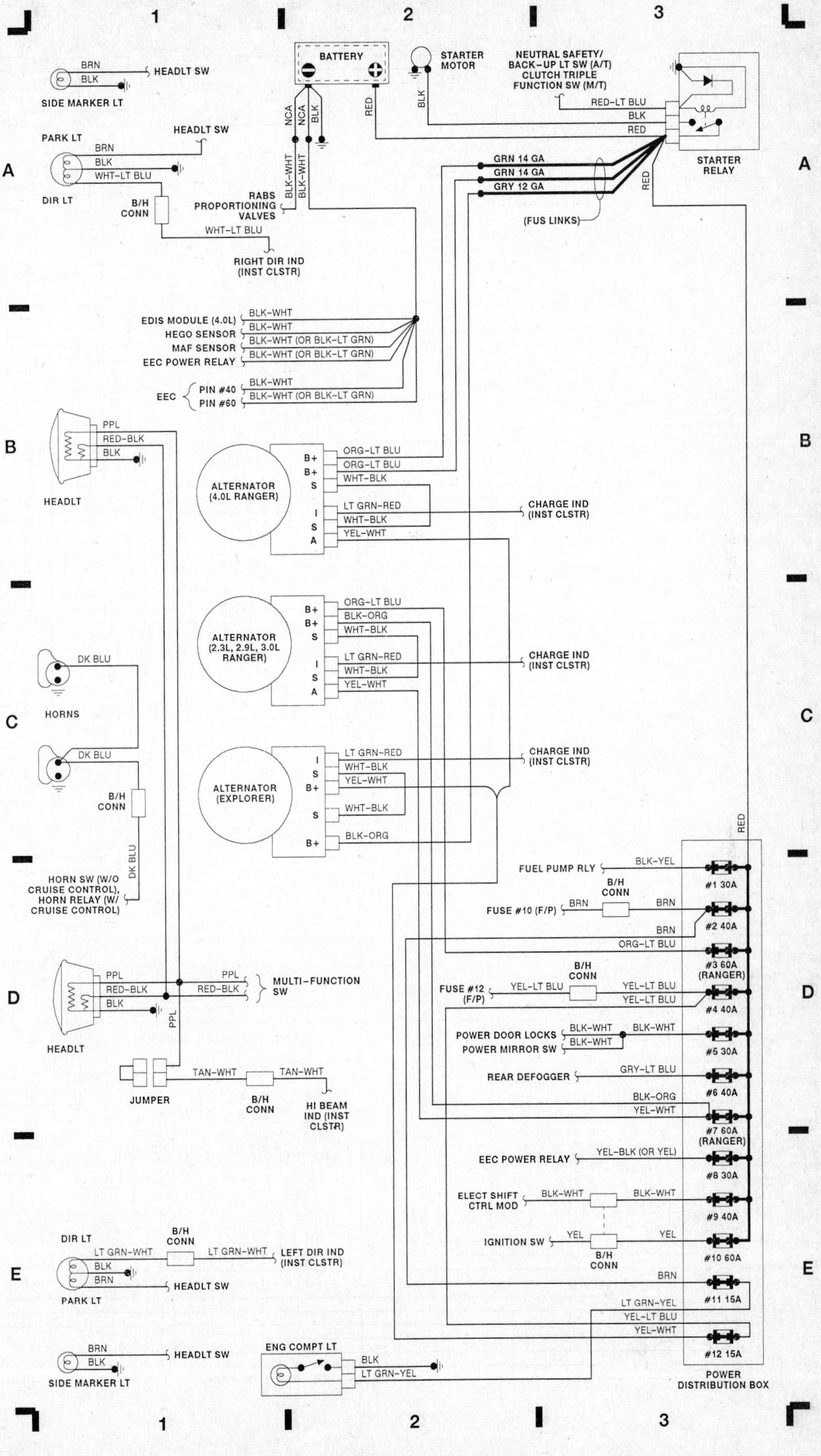
SIDE MARKER LT
HEADLT SW
PARK LT
DIR LT
B/H CONN
RIGHT DIR IND (INST CLSTR)
BATTERY
STARTER MOTOR
NEUTRAL SAFETY/ BACK-UP LT SW (A/T) CLUTCH TRIPLE FUNCTION SW (M/T)
STARTER RELAY
GRN 14 GA
GRY 12 GA
(FUS LINKS)
RABS PROPORTIONING VALVES
EDIS MODULE (4.0L)
HEGO SENSOR
MAF SENSOR
EEC POWER RELAY
EEC PIN #40 PIN #60
HEADLT
ALTERNATOR (4.0L RANGER)
CHARGE IND (INST CLSTR)
ALTERNATOR (2.3L, 2.9L, 3.0L RANGER)
ALTERNATOR (EXPLORER)
HORNS
HORN SW (W/O CRUISE CONTROL), HORN RELAY (W/ CRUISE CONTROL)
MULTI-FUNCTION SW
JUMPER
HI BEAM IND (INST CLSTR)
FUEL PUMP RLY
FUSE #10 (F/P)
FUSE #12 (F/P)
POWER DOOR LOCKS
POWER MIRROR SW
REAR DEFOGGER
EEC POWER RELAY
ELECT SHIFT CTRL MOD
IGNITION SW
#1 30A
#2 40A
#3 60A (RANGER)
#4 40A
#5 30A
#6 40A
#7 60A (RANGER)
#8 30A
#9 40A
#10 60A
#11 15A
#12 15A
POWER DISTRIBUTION BOX
LEFT DIR IND (INST CLSTR)
ENG COMPT LT

1991 WIRING DIAGRAMS
Explorer & Ranger (Cont.)

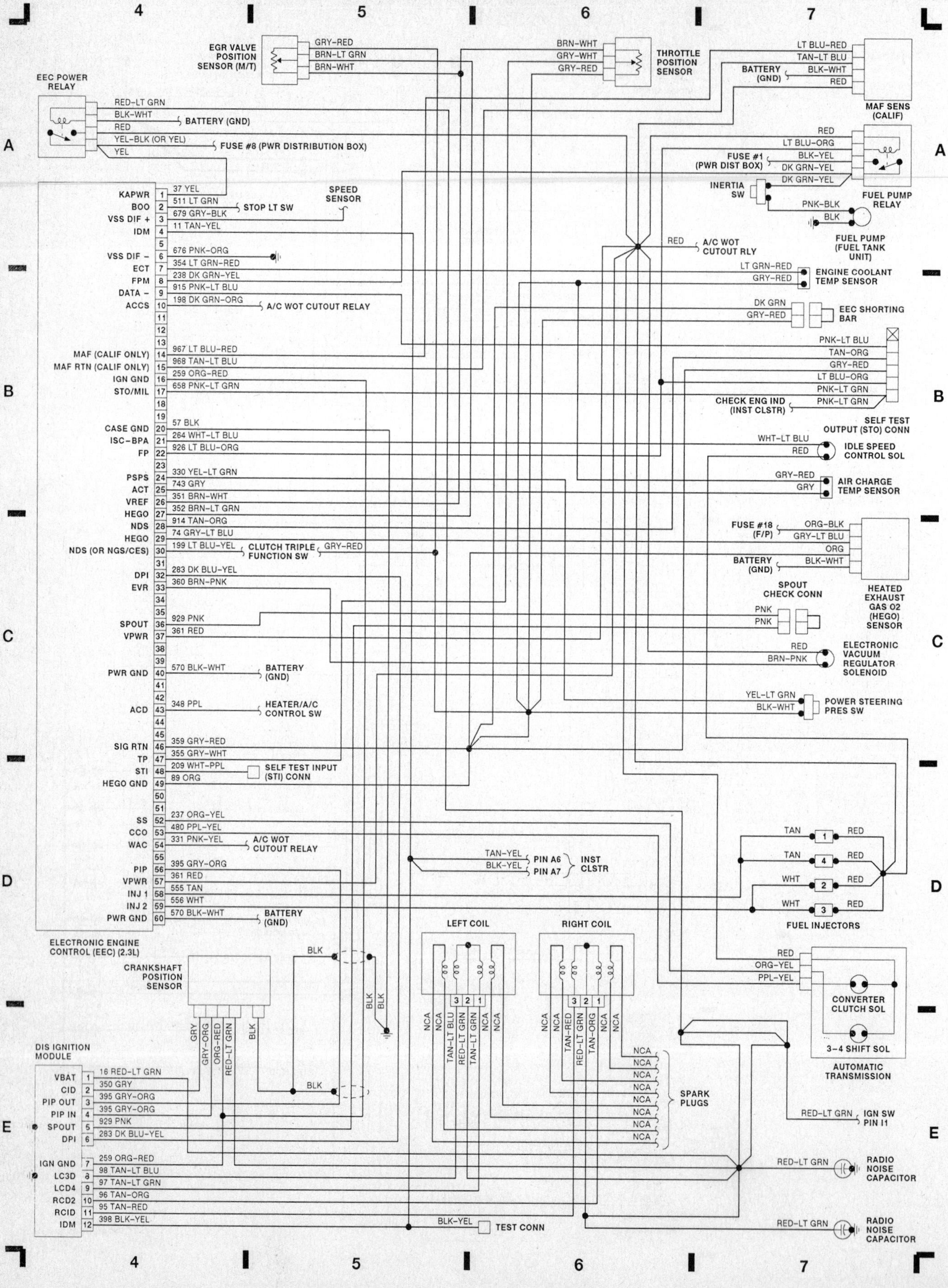
EGR VALVE POSITION SENSOR (M/T)
THROTTLE POSITION SENSOR
EEC POWER RELAY
BATTERY (GND)
FUSE #8 (PWR DISTRIBUTION BOX)
MAF SENS (CALIF)
FUSE #1 (PWR DIST BOX)
INERTIA SW
FUEL PUMP RELAY
FUEL PUMP (FUEL TANK UNIT)
SPEED SENSOR
STOP LT SW
A/C WOT CUTOUT RLY
ENGINE COOLANT TEMP SENSOR
A/C WOT CUTOUT RELAY
EEC SHORTING BAR
CHECK ENG IND (INST CLSTR)
SELF TEST OUTPUT (STO) CONN
IDLE SPEED CONTROL SOL
AIR CHARGE TEMP SENSOR
FUSE #18 (F/P)
CLUTCH TRIPLE FUNCTION SW
HEATED EXHAUST GAS O2 (HEGO) SENSOR
SPOUT CHECK CONN
ELECTRONIC VACUUM REGULATOR SOLENOID
HEATER/A/C CONTROL SW
POWER STEERING PRES SW
SELF TEST INPUT (STI) CONN
A/C WOT CUTOUT RELAY
PIN A6
PIN A7
INST CLSTR
FUEL INJECTORS
ELECTRONIC ENGINE CONTROL (EEC) (2.3L)
KAPWR 1 37 YEL
BOO 2 511 LT GRN
VSS DIF + 3 679 GRY-BLK
IDM 4 11 TAN-YEL
VSS DIF – 6 676 PNK-ORG
ECT 7 354 LT GRN-RED
FPM 8 238 DK GRN-YEL
DATA – 9 915 PNK-LT BLU
ACCS 10 198 DK GRN-ORG
MAF (CALIF ONLY) 14 967 LT BLU-RED
MAF RTN (CALIF ONLY) 15 968 TAN-LT BLU
IGN GND 16 259 ORG-RED
STO/MIL 17 658 PNK-LT GRN
CASE GND 20 57 BLK
ISC-BPA 21 264 WHT-LT BLU
FP 22 926 LT BLU-ORG
PSPS 24 330 YEL-LT GRN
ACT 25 743 GRY
VREF 26 351 BRN-WHT
HEGO 27 352 BRN-LT GRN
NDS 28 914 TAN-ORG
HEGO 29 74 GRY-LT BLU
NDS (OR NGS/CES) 30 199 LT BLU-YEL
DPI 32 283 DK BLU-YEL
EVR 33 360 BRN-PNK
SPOUT 36 929 PNK
VPWR 37 361 RED
PWR GND 40 570 BLK-WHT
ACD 43 348 PPL
SIG RTN 46 359 GRY-RED
TP 47 355 GRY-WHT
STI 48 209 WHT-PPL
HEGO GND 49 89 ORG
SS 52 237 ORG-YEL
CCO 53 480 PPL-YEL
WAC 54 331 PNK-YEL
PIP 56 395 GRY-ORG
VPWR 57 361 RED
INJ 1 58 555 TAN
INJ 2 59 556 WHT
PWR GND 60 570 BLK-WHT
CRANKSHAFT POSITION SENSOR
LEFT COIL
RIGHT COIL
SPARK PLUGS
CONVERTER CLUTCH SOL
3–4 SHIFT SOL
AUTOMATIC TRANSMISSION
IGN SW PIN I1
DIS IGNITION MODULE
VBAT 1 16 RED-LT GRN
CID 2 350 GRY
PIP OUT 3 395 GRY-ORG
PIP IN 4 395 GRY-ORG
SPOUT 5 929 PNK
DPI 6 283 DK BLU-YEL
IGN GND 7 259 ORG-RED
LC3D 8 98 TAN-LT BLU
LCD4 9 97 TAN-LT GRN
RCD2 10 96 TAN-ORG
RCID 11 95 TAN-RED
IDM 12 398 BLK-YEL
TEST CONN
RADIO NOISE CAPACITOR
RADIO NOISE CAPACITOR

1991 WIRING DIAGRAMS
Explorer & Ranger (Cont.)

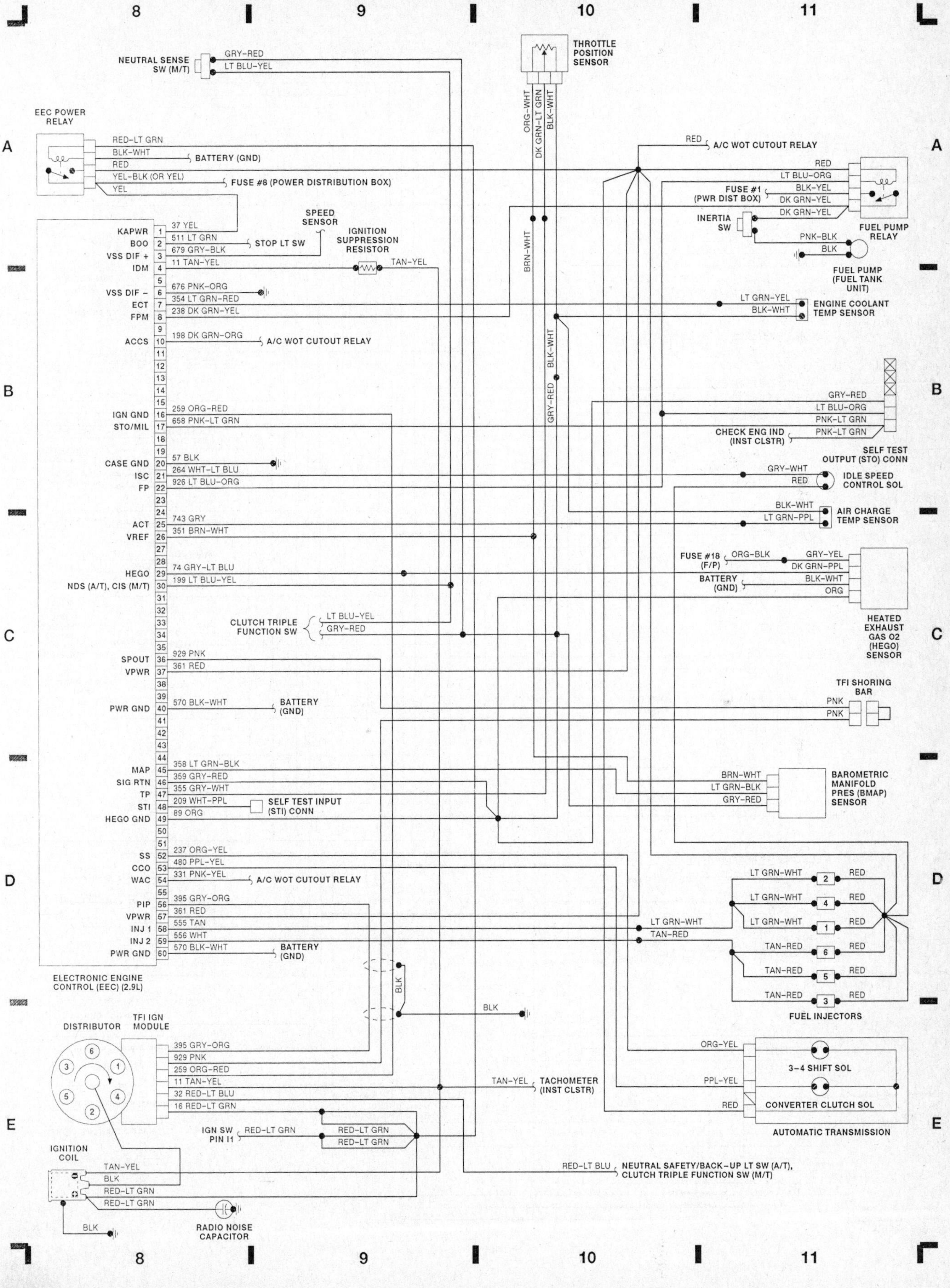
NEUTRAL SENSE SW (M/T)
THROTTLE POSITION SENSOR
EEC POWER RELAY
BATTERY (GND)
FUSE #8 (POWER DISTRIBUTION BOX)
A/C WOT CUTOUT RELAY
FUSE #1 (PWR DIST BOX)
INERTIA SW
FUEL PUMP RELAY
FUEL PUMP (FUEL TANK UNIT)
SPEED SENSOR
STOP LT SW
IGNITION SUPPRESSION RESISTOR
KAPWR
BOO
VSS DIF +
IDM
VSS DIF −
ECT
FPM
ACCS
IGN GND
STO/MIL
CASE GND
ISC
FP
ACT
VREF
HEGO
NDS (A/T), CIS (M/T)
SPOUT
VPWR
PWR GND
MAP
SIG RTN
TP
STI
HEGO GND
SS
CCO
WAC
PIP
INJ 1
INJ 2
37 YEL
511 LT GRN
679 GRY-BLK
11 TAN-YEL
676 PNK-ORG
354 LT GRN-RED
238 DK GRN-YEL
198 DK GRN-ORG
259 ORG-RED
658 PNK-LT GRN
57 BLK
264 WHT-LT BLU
926 LT BLU-ORG
743 GRY
351 BRN-WHT
74 GRY-LT BLU
199 LT BLU-YEL
929 PNK
361 RED
570 BLK-WHT
358 LT GRN-BLK
359 GRY-RED
355 GRY-WHT
209 WHT-PPL
89 ORG
237 ORG-YEL
480 PPL-YEL
331 PNK-YEL
395 GRY-ORG
555 TAN
556 WHT
ENGINE COOLANT TEMP SENSOR
CHECK ENG IND (INST CLSTR)
SELF TEST OUTPUT (STO) CONN
IDLE SPEED CONTROL SOL
AIR CHARGE TEMP SENSOR
FUSE #18 (F/P)
HEATED EXHAUST GAS O2 (HEGO) SENSOR
CLUTCH TRIPLE FUNCTION SW
TFI SHORING BAR
SELF TEST INPUT (STI) CONN
BAROMETRIC MANIFOLD PRES (BMAP) SENSOR
FUEL INJECTORS
ELECTRONIC ENGINE CONTROL (EEC) (2.9L)
DISTRIBUTOR
TFI IGN MODULE
16 RED-LT GRN
32 RED-LT BLU
TACHOMETER (INST CLSTR)
3-4 SHIFT SOL
CONVERTER CLUTCH SOL
AUTOMATIC TRANSMISSION
IGN SW PIN I1
IGNITION COIL
RADIO NOISE CAPACITOR
NEUTRAL SAFETY/BACK-UP LT SW (A/T), CLUTCH TRIPLE FUNCTION SW (M/T)

1991 WIRING DIAGRAMS
Explorer & Ranger (Cont.)

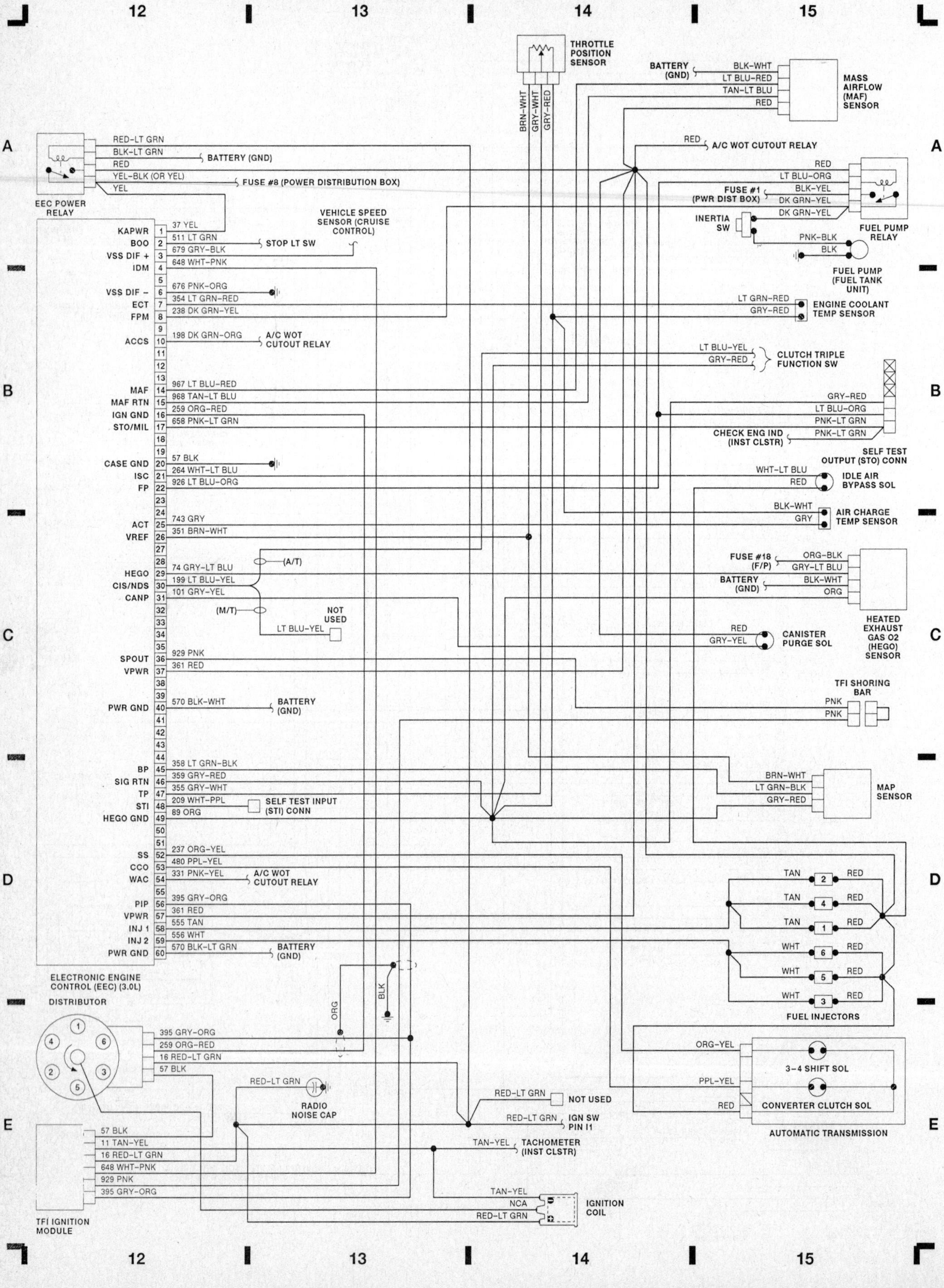
12
13
14
15
A
B
C
D
E
THROTTLE POSITION SENSOR
BRN-WHT
GRY-WHT
GRY-RED
BATTERY (GND)
BLK-WHT
LT BLU-RED
TAN-LT BLU
RED
MASS AIRFLOW (MAF) SENSOR
RED-LT GRN
BLK-LT GRN
BATTERY (GND)
RED
YEL-BLK (OR YEL)
FUSE #8 (POWER DISTRIBUTION BOX)
YEL
EEC POWER RELAY
A/C WOT CUTOUT RELAY
LT BLU-ORG
FUSE #1 (PWR DIST BOX)
BLK-YEL
DK GRN-YEL
INERTIA SW
PNK-BLK
BLK
FUEL PUMP RELAY
FUEL PUMP (FUEL TANK UNIT)
VEHICLE SPEED SENSOR (CRUISE CONTROL)
KAPWR 1 37 YEL
BOO 2 511 LT GRN
STOP LT SW
VSS DIF + 3 679 GRY-BLK
IDM 4 648 WHT-PNK
5
VSS DIF – 6 676 PNK-ORG
ECT 7 354 LT GRN-RED
FPM 8 238 DK GRN-YEL
9
ACCS 10 198 DK GRN-ORG
A/C WOT CUTOUT RELAY
11
12
13
MAF 14 967 LT BLU-RED
MAF RTN 15 968 TAN-LT BLU
IGN GND 16 259 ORG-RED
STO/MIL 17 658 PNK-LT GRN
18
19
CASE GND 20 57 BLK
ISC 21 264 WHT-LT BLU
FP 22 926 LT BLU-ORG
23
24
ACT 25 743 GRY
VREF 26 351 BRN-WHT
27
28 74 GRY-LT BLU
(A/T)
HEGO 29 199 LT BLU-YEL
CIS/NDS 30 101 GRY-YEL
CANP 31
32
(M/T)
NOT USED
33
34 LT BLU-YEL
35
SPOUT 36 929 PNK
VPWR 37 361 RED
38
39
PWR GND 40 570 BLK-WHT
BATTERY (GND)
41
42
43
44
BP 45 358 LT GRN-BLK
SIG RTN 46 359 GRY-RED
TP 47 355 GRY-WHT
STI 48 209 WHT-PPL
SELF TEST INPUT (STI) CONN
HEGO GND 49 89 ORG
50
51
SS 52 237 ORG-YEL
CCO 53 480 PPL-YEL
WAC 54 331 PNK-YEL
A/C WOT CUTOUT RELAY
55
PIP 56 395 GRY-ORG
VPWR 57 361 RED
INJ 1 58 555 TAN
INJ 2 59 556 WHT
PWR GND 60 570 BLK-LT GRN
BATTERY (GND)
ELECTRONIC ENGINE CONTROL (EEC) (3.0L)
LT GRN-RED
GRY-RED
ENGINE COOLANT TEMP SENSOR
LT BLU-YEL
GRY-RED
CLUTCH TRIPLE FUNCTION SW
GRY-RED
LT BLU-ORG
PNK-LT GRN
CHECK ENG IND (INST CLSTR)
PNK-LT GRN
SELF TEST OUTPUT (STO) CONN
WHT-LT BLU
RED
IDLE AIR BYPASS SOL
BLK-WHT
GRY
AIR CHARGE TEMP SENSOR
FUSE #18 (F/P)
ORG-BLK
GRY-LT BLU
BATTERY (GND)
BLK-WHT
ORG
HEATED EXHAUST GAS O2 (HEGO) SENSOR
RED
GRY-YEL
CANISTER PURGE SOL
TFI SHORING BAR
PNK
PNK
BRN-WHT
LT GRN-BLK
GRY-RED
MAP SENSOR
TAN 2 RED
TAN 4 RED
TAN 1 RED
WHT 6 RED
WHT 5 RED
WHT 3 RED
FUEL INJECTORS
DISTRIBUTOR
ORG
BLK
395 GRY-ORG
259 ORG-RED
16 RED-LT GRN
57 BLK
RED-LT GRN
RADIO NOISE CAP
RED-LT GRN
NOT USED
RED-LT GRN
IGN SW PIN I1
TAN-YEL
TACHOMETER (INST CLSTR)
ORG-YEL
3-4 SHIFT SOL
PPL-YEL
RED
CONVERTER CLUTCH SOL
AUTOMATIC TRANSMISSION
57 BLK
11 TAN-YEL
16 RED-LT GRN
648 WHT-PNK
929 PNK
395 GRY-ORG
TFI IGNITION MODULE
TAN-YEL
NCA
RED-LT GRN
IGNITION COIL

1991 WIRING DIAGRAMS
Explorer & Ranger (Cont.)

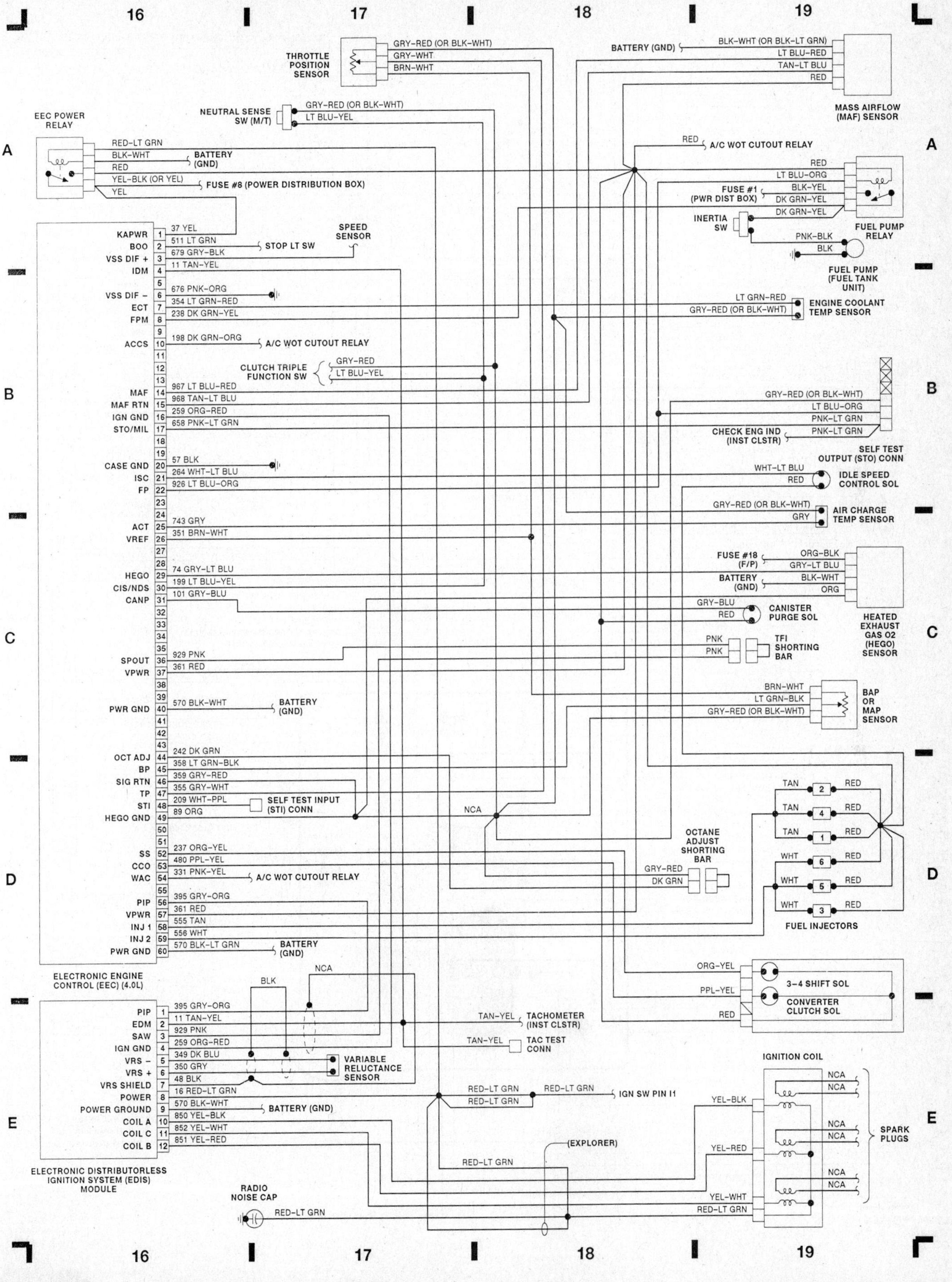
THROTTLE POSITION SENSOR
GRY-RED (OR BLK-WHT)
GRY-WHT
BRN-WHT
BATTERY (GND)
BLK-WHT (OR BLK-LT GRN)
LT BLU-RED
TAN-LT BLU
RED
MASS AIRFLOW (MAF) SENSOR
NEUTRAL SENSE SW (M/T)
LT BLU-YEL
EEC POWER RELAY
RED-LT GRN
BLK-WHT
RED
YEL-BLK (OR YEL)
YEL
FUSE #8 (POWER DISTRIBUTION BOX)
A/C WOT CUTOUT RELAY
LT BLU-ORG
BLK-YEL
DK GRN-YEL
FUSE #1 (PWR DIST BOX)
FUEL PUMP RELAY
INERTIA SW
PNK-BLK
BLK
FUEL PUMP (FUEL TANK UNIT)
KAPWR 1 37 YEL
BOO 2 511 LT GRN
VSS DIF + 3 679 GRY-BLK
IDM 4 11 TAN-YEL
STOP LT SW
SPEED SENSOR
VSS DIF – 6 676 PNK-ORG
ECT 7 354 LT GRN-RED
FPM 8 238 DK GRN-YEL
ACCS 10 198 DK GRN-ORG
ENGINE COOLANT TEMP SENSOR
LT GRN-RED
CLUTCH TRIPLE FUNCTION SW
GRY-RED
MAF 14 967 LT BLU-RED
MAF RTN 15 968 TAN-LT BLU
IGN GND 16 259 ORG-RED
STO/MIL 17 658 PNK-LT GRN
CHECK ENG IND (INST CLSTR)
PNK-LT GRN
SELF TEST OUTPUT (STO) CONN
CASE GND 20 57 BLK
ISC 21 264 WHT-LT BLU
FP 22 926 LT BLU-ORG
IDLE SPEED CONTROL SOL
WHT-LT BLU
ACT 25 743 GRY
VREF 26 351 BRN-WHT
AIR CHARGE TEMP SENSOR
GRY
HEGO 29 74 GRY-LT BLU
CIS/NDS 30 199 LT BLU-YEL
CANP 31 101 GRY-BLU
FUSE #18 (F/P)
ORG-BLK
GRY-LT BLU
BLK-WHT
ORG
HEATED EXHAUST GAS O2 (HEGO) SENSOR
CANISTER PURGE SOL
GRY-BLU
SPOUT 36 929 PNK
VPWR 37 361 RED
PNK
TFI SHORTING BAR
PWR GND 40 570 BLK-WHT
BATTERY (GND)
BAP OR MAP SENSOR
LT GRN-BLK
OCT ADJ 44 242 DK GRN
BP 45 358 LT GRN-BLK
SIG RTN 46 359 GRY-RED
TP 47 355 GRY-WHT
STI 48 209 WHT-PPL
HEGO GND 49 89 ORG
SELF TEST INPUT (STI) CONN
NCA
SS 52 237 ORG-YEL
CCO 53 480 PPL-YEL
WAC 54 331 PNK-YEL
OCTANE ADJUST SHORTING BAR
DK GRN
PIP 56 395 GRY-ORG
VPWR 57 361 RED
INJ 1 58 555 TAN
INJ 2 59 556 WHT
PWR GND 60 570 BLK-LT GRN
TAN
WHT
FUEL INJECTORS
ELECTRONIC ENGINE CONTROL (EEC) (4.0L)
BLK
ORG-YEL
PPL-YEL
3-4 SHIFT SOL
CONVERTER CLUTCH SOL
PIP 1 395 GRY-ORG
EDM 2 11 TAN-YEL
SAW 3 929 PNK
IGN GND 4 259 ORG-RED
VRS – 5 349 DK BLU
VRS + 6 350 GRY
VRS SHIELD 7 48 BLK
POWER 8 16 RED-LT GRN
POWER GROUND 9 570 BLK-WHT
COIL A 10 850 YEL-BLK
COIL C 11 852 YEL-WHT
COIL B 12 851 YEL-RED
TACHOMETER (INST CLSTR)
TAC TEST CONN
VARIABLE RELUCTANCE SENSOR
IGN SW PIN I1
IGNITION COIL
SPARK PLUGS
(EXPLORER)
ELECTRONIC DISTRIBUTORLESS IGNITION SYSTEM (EDIS) MODULE
RADIO NOISE CAP

1991 WIRING DIAGRAMS
Explorer & Ranger (Cont.)

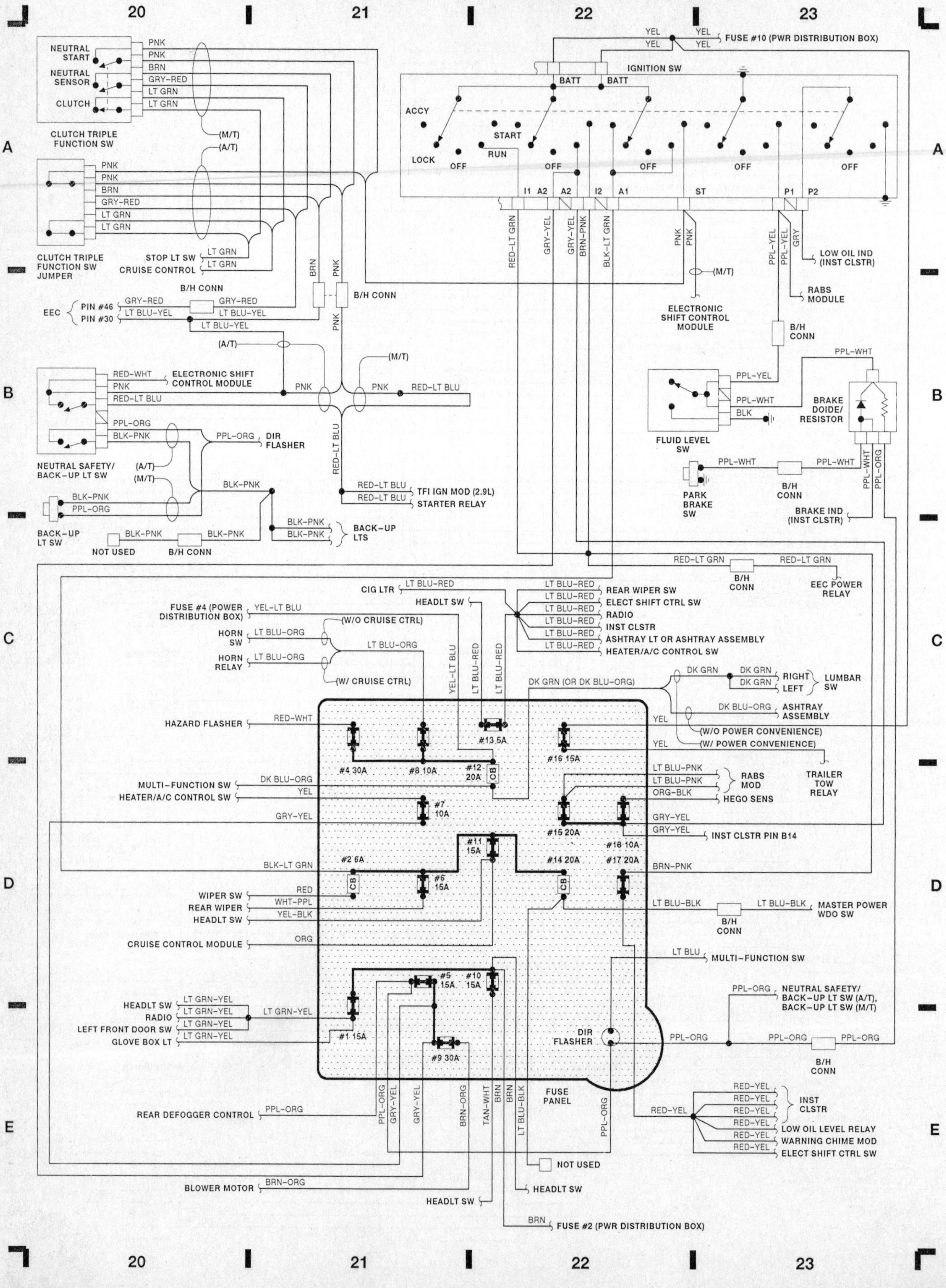
NEUTRAL START
NEUTRAL SENSOR
CLUTCH
CLUTCH TRIPLE FUNCTION SW
CLUTCH TRIPLE FUNCTION SW JUMPER
STOP LT SW
CRUISE CONTROL
B/H CONN
EEC
PIN #46
PIN #30
ELECTRONIC SHIFT CONTROL MODULE
NEUTRAL SAFETY/ BACK-UP LT SW
DIR FLASHER
BACK-UP LT SW
NOT USED
BACK-UP LTS
TFI IGN MOD (2.9L)
STARTER RELAY
FUSE #10 (PWR DISTRIBUTION BOX)
IGNITION SW
BATT
ACCY
LOCK
OFF
START
RUN
LOW OIL IND (INST CLSTR)
RABS MODULE
FLUID LEVEL SW
BRAKE DOIDE/ RESISTOR
PARK BRAKE SW
BRAKE IND (INST CLSTR)
EEC POWER RELAY
CIG LTR
HEADLT SW
FUSE #4 (POWER DISTRIBUTION BOX)
HORN SW
HORN RELAY
(W/O CRUISE CTRL)
(W/ CRUISE CTRL)
REAR WIPER SW
ELECT SHIFT CTRL SW
RADIO
INST CLSTR
ASHTRAY LT OR ASHTRAY ASSEMBLY
HEATER/A/C CONTROL SW
RIGHT
LEFT
LUMBAR SW
ASHTRAY ASSEMBLY
(W/O POWER CONVENIENCE)
(W/ POWER CONVENIENCE)
TRAILER TOW RELAY
RABS MOD
HEGO SENS
HAZARD FLASHER
MULTI-FUNCTION SW
INST CLSTR PIN B14
WIPER SW
REAR WIPER
CRUISE CONTROL MODULE
MASTER POWER WDO SW
NEUTRAL SAFETY/ BACK-UP LT SW (A/T), BACK-UP LT SW (M/T)
LEFT FRONT DOOR SW
GLOVE BOX LT
DIR FLASHER
FUSE PANEL
REAR DEFOGGER CONTROL
LOW OIL LEVEL RELAY
WARNING CHIME MOD
ELECT SHIFT CTRL SW
BLOWER MOTOR
FUSE #2 (PWR DISTRIBUTION BOX)

1991 WIRING DIAGRAMS
Explorer & Ranger (Cont.)

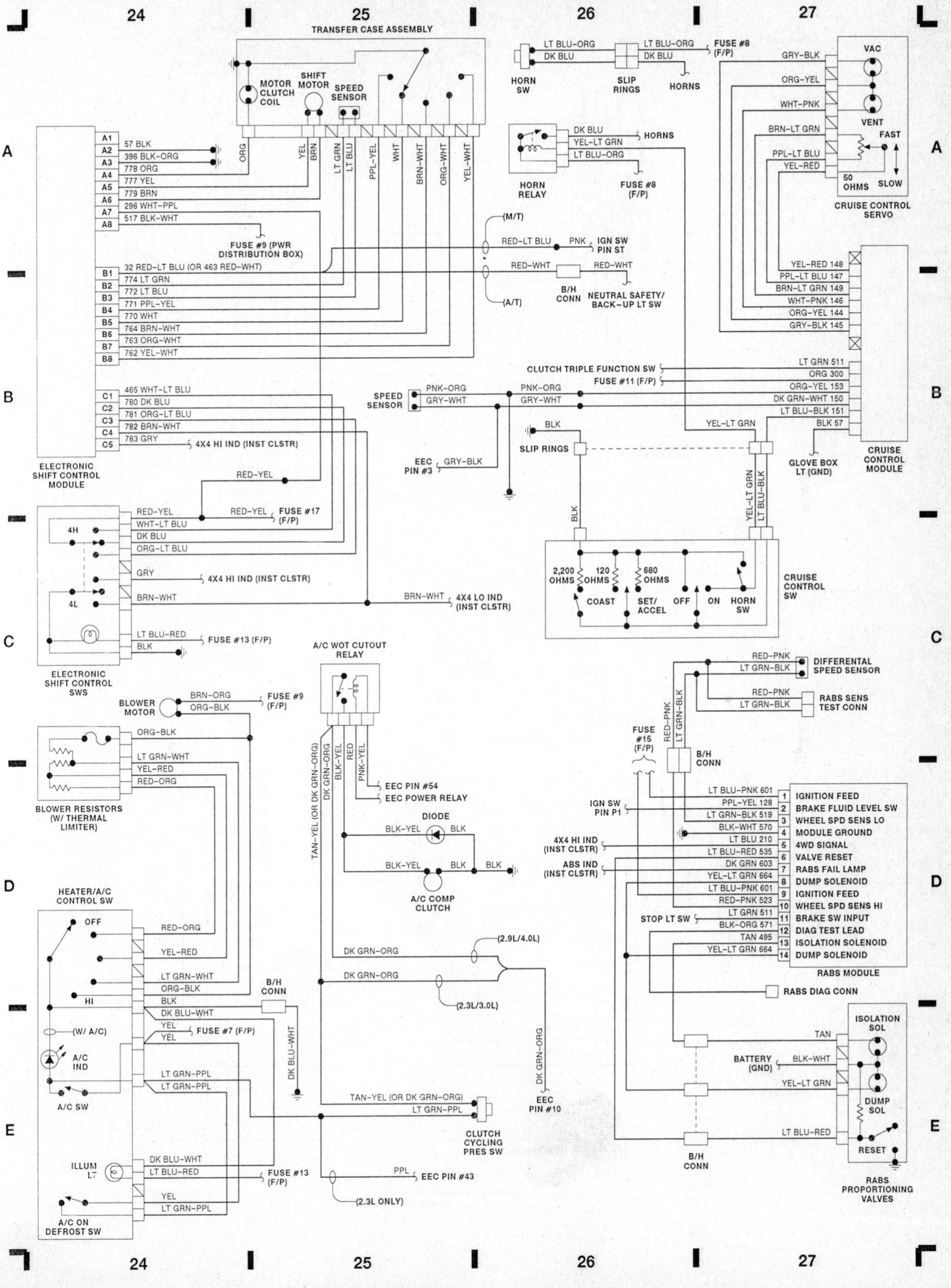
24
25
26
27
A
B
C
D
E
TRANSFER CASE ASSEMBLY
MOTOR CLUTCH COIL
SHIFT MOTOR
SPEED SENSOR
ORG
YEL
BRN
LT GRN
LT BLU
PPL-YEL
WHT
BRN-WHT
ORG-WHT
YEL-WHT
A1
A2
A3
A4
A5
A6
A7
A8
57 BLK
396 BLK-ORG
778 ORG
777 YEL
779 BRN
296 WHT-PPL
517 BLK-WHT
FUSE #9 (PWR DISTRIBUTION BOX)
B1
B2
B3
B4
B5
B6
B7
B8
32 RED-LT BLU (OR 463 RED-WHT)
774 LT GRN
772 LT BLU
771 PPL-YEL
770 WHT
764 BRN-WHT
763 ORG-WHT
762 YEL-WHT
C1
C2
C3
C4
C5
465 WHT-LT BLU
780 DK BLU
781 ORG-LT BLU
782 BRN-WHT
783 GRY
4X4 HI IND (INST CLSTR)
ELECTRONIC SHIFT CONTROL MODULE
LT BLU-ORG
DK BLU
HORN SW
SLIP RINGS
HORNS
FUSE #8 (F/P)
YEL-LT GRN
HORN RELAY
(M/T)
RED-LT BLU
PNK
IGN SW PIN ST
RED-WHT
B/H CONN
NEUTRAL SAFETY/ BACK-UP LT SW
(A/T)
GRY-BLK
ORG-YEL
WHT-PNK
BRN-LT GRN
PPL-LT BLU
YEL-RED
VAC
VENT
FAST
SLOW
50 OHMS
CRUISE CONTROL SERVO
YEL-RED 148
PPL-LT BLU 147
BRN-LT GRN 149
WHT-PNK 146
ORG-YEL 144
GRY-BLK 145
CLUTCH TRIPLE FUNCTION SW
FUSE #11 (F/P)
LT GRN 511
ORG 300
ORG-YEL 153
DK GRN-WHT 150
LT BLU-BLK 151
BLK 57
SPEED SENSOR
PNK-ORG
GRY-WHT
BLK
SLIP RINGS
EEC PIN #3
GLOVE BOX LT (GND)
CRUISE CONTROL MODULE
RED-YEL
FUSE #17 (F/P)
WHT-LT BLU
DK BLU
ORG-LT BLU
GRY
4X4 HI IND (INST CLSTR)
BRN-WHT
4X4 LO IND (INST CLSTR)
4H
4L
LT BLU-RED
FUSE #13 (F/P)
ELECTRONIC SHIFT CONTROL SWS
LT BLU-BLK
2,200 OHMS
120 OHMS
680 OHMS
COAST
SET/ ACCEL
OFF
ON
HORN SW
CRUISE CONTROL SW
A/C WOT CUTOUT RELAY
BLOWER MOTOR
BRN-ORG
ORG-BLK
FUSE #9 (F/P)
LT GRN-WHT
RED-ORG
BLOWER RESISTORS (W/ THERMAL LIMITER)
TAN-YEL (OR DK GRN-ORG)
DK GRN-ORG
BLK-YEL
RED
PNK-YEL
EEC PIN #54
EEC POWER RELAY
DIODE
A/C COMP CLUTCH
RED-PNK
LT GRN-BLK
DIFFERENTIAL SPEED SENSOR
RABS SENS TEST CONN
FUSE #15 (F/P)
IGN SW PIN P1
4X4 HI IND (INST CLSTR)
ABS IND (INST CLSTR)
STOP LT SW
LT BLU-PNK 601
PPL-YEL 128
LT GRN-BLK 519
BLK-WHT 570
LT BLU 210
LT BLU-RED 535
DK GRN 603
YEL-LT GRN 664
LT BLU-PNK 601
RED-PNK 523
LT GRN 511
BLK-ORG 571
TAN 495
YEL-LT GRN 664
1 IGNITION FEED
2 BRAKE FLUID LEVEL SW
3 WHEEL SPD SENS LO
4 MODULE GROUND
5 4WD SIGNAL
6 VALVE RESET
7 RABS FAIL LAMP
8 DUMP SOLENOID
9 IGNITION FEED
10 WHEEL SPD SENS HI
11 BRAKE SW INPUT
12 DIAG TEST LEAD
13 ISOLATION SOLENOID
14 DUMP SOLENOID
RABS MODULE
RABS DIAG CONN
HEATER/A/C CONTROL SW
OFF
HI
(W/ A/C)
A/C IND
A/C SW
DK BLU-WHT
FUSE #7 (F/P)
LT GRN-PPL
(2.9L/4.0L)
(2.3L/3.0L)
EEC PIN #10
CLUTCH CYCLING PRES SW
PPL
EEC PIN #43
(2.3L ONLY)
ILLUM LT
A/C ON DEFROST SW
ISOLATION SOL
TAN
BATTERY (GND)
BLK-WHT
DUMP SOL
RESET
RABS PROPORTIONING VALVES

1991 WIRING DIAGRAMS
Explorer & Ranger (Cont.)

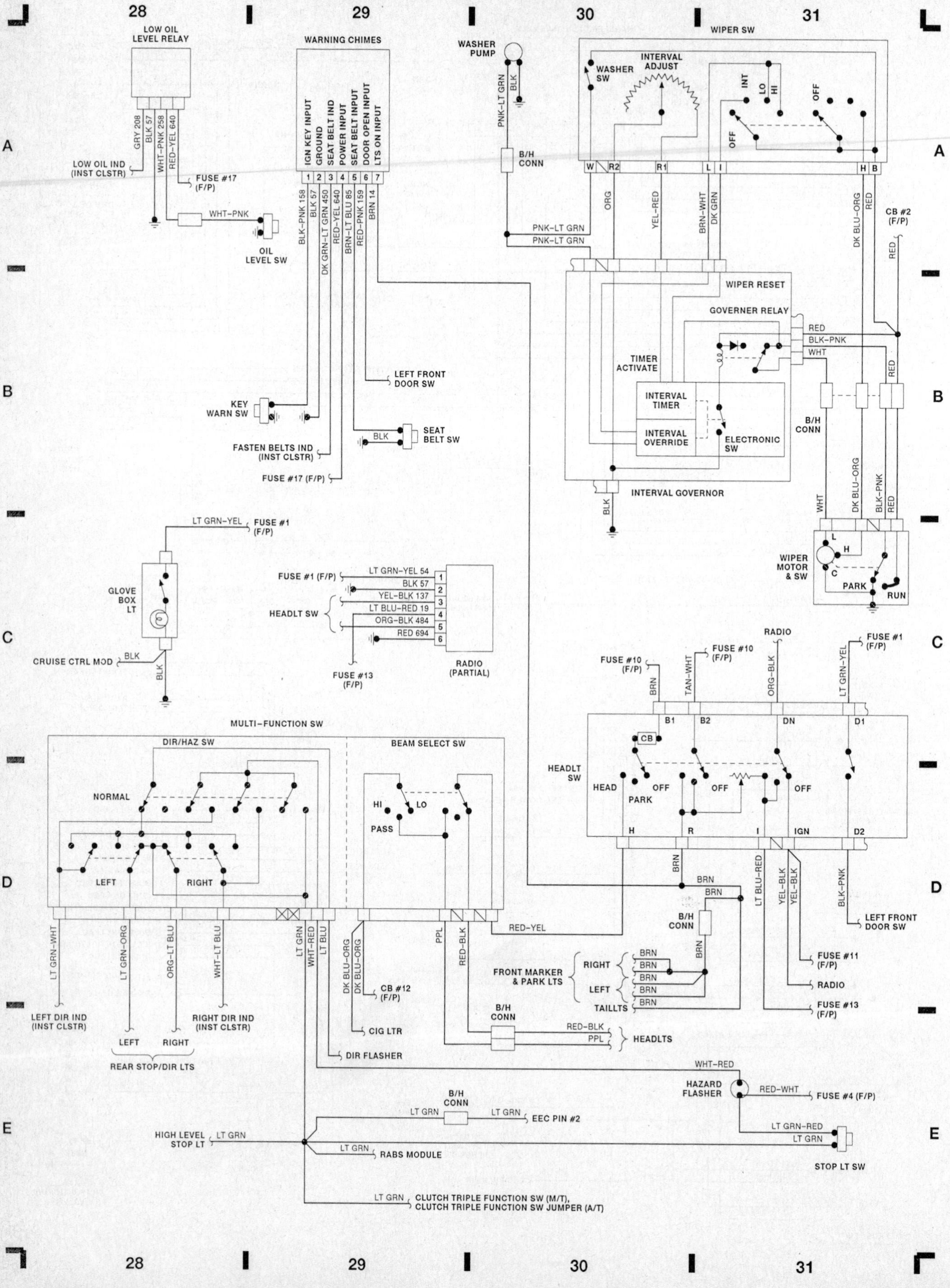
28
29
30
31
LOW OIL LEVEL RELAY
WARNING CHIMES
WASHER PUMP
WIPER SW
WASHER SW
INTERVAL ADJUST
INT
LO
HI
OFF
GRY 208
BLK 57
WHT-PNK 258
RED-YEL 640
LOW OIL IND (INST CLSTR)
FUSE #17 (F/P)
IGN KEY INPUT
GROUND
SEAT BELT IND
POWER INPUT
SEAT BELT INPUT
DOOR OPEN INPUT
LTS ON INPUT
PNK-LT GRN
BLK
B/H CONN
WHT-PNK
OIL LEVEL SW
BLK-PNK 158
BLK 57
DK GRN-LT GRN 450
RED-YEL 640
BRN-LT BLU 85
RED-PNK 159
BRN 14
ORG
YEL-RED
BRN-WHT
DK GRN
DK BLU-ORG
RED
CB #2 (F/P)
WIPER RESET
GOVERNER RELAY
BLK-PNK
WHT
TIMER ACTIVATE
INTERVAL TIMER
INTERVAL OVERRIDE
ELECTRONIC SW
INTERVAL GOVERNOR
LEFT FRONT DOOR SW
KEY WARN SW
SEAT BELT SW
FASTEN BELTS IND (INST CLSTR)
FUSE #17 (F/P)
WIPER MOTOR & SW
PARK
RUN
LT GRN-YEL
FUSE #1 (F/P)
GLOVE BOX LT
LT GRN-YEL 54
YEL-BLK 137
LT BLU-RED 19
ORG-BLK 484
RED 694
HEADLT SW
FUSE #13 (F/P)
RADIO (PARTIAL)
CRUISE CTRL MOD
RADIO
FUSE #10 (F/P)
BRN
TAN-WHT
ORG-BLK
MULTI-FUNCTION SW
DIR/HAZ SW
BEAM SELECT SW
NORMAL
HI
LO
PASS
LEFT
RIGHT
HEAD
OFF
CB
IGN
LT GRN-WHT
LT GRN-ORG
ORG-LT BLU
WHT-LT BLU
LT GRN
WHT-RED
LT BLU
DK BLU-ORG
PPL
RED-BLK
RED-YEL
LT BLU-RED
YEL-BLK
LEFT DIR IND (INST CLSTR)
RIGHT DIR IND (INST CLSTR)
REAR STOP/DIR LTS
CB #12 (F/P)
CIG LTR
DIR FLASHER
FRONT MARKER & PARK LTS
TAILLTS
HEADLTS
FUSE #11 (F/P)
HAZARD FLASHER
RED-WHT
FUSE #4 (F/P)
EEC PIN #2
HIGH LEVEL STOP LT
RABS MODULE
LT GRN-RED
STOP LT SW
CLUTCH TRIPLE FUNCTION SW (M/T),
CLUTCH TRIPLE FUNCTION SW JUMPER (A/T)

1991 WIRING DIAGRAMS
Explorer & Ranger (Cont.)

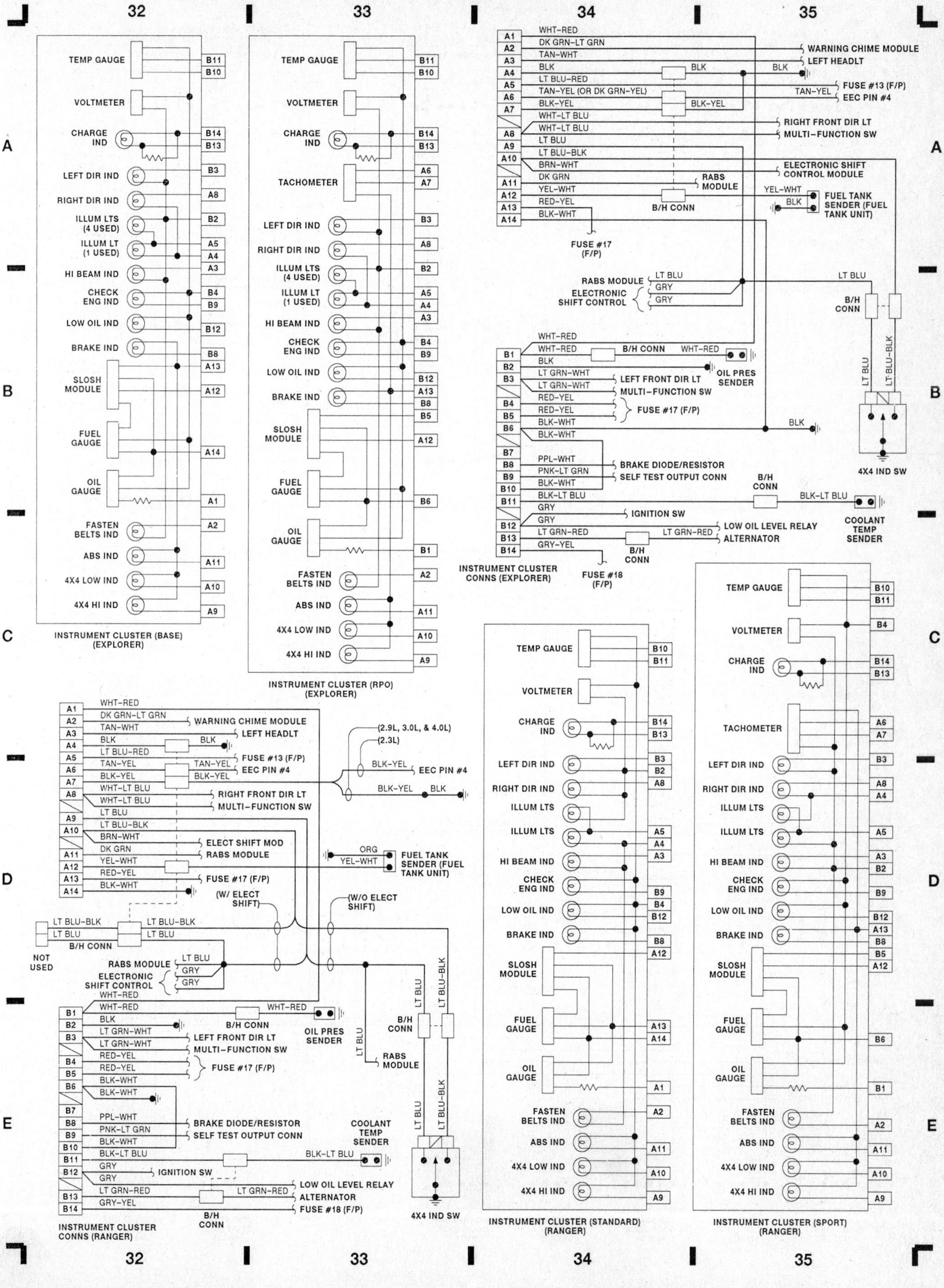
32
33
34
35
A
B
C
D
E
TEMP GAUGE
VOLTMETER
CHARGE IND
TACHOMETER
LEFT DIR IND
RIGHT DIR IND
ILLUM LTS (4 USED)
ILLUM LT (1 USED)
ILLUM LTS
HI BEAM IND
CHECK ENG IND
LOW OIL IND
BRAKE IND
SLOSH MODULE
FUEL GAUGE
OIL GAUGE
FASTEN BELTS IND
ABS IND
4X4 LOW IND
4X4 HI IND
INSTRUMENT CLUSTER (BASE) (EXPLORER)
INSTRUMENT CLUSTER (RPO) (EXPLORER)
INSTRUMENT CLUSTER CONNS (EXPLORER)
INSTRUMENT CLUSTER CONNS (RANGER)
INSTRUMENT CLUSTER (STANDARD) (RANGER)
INSTRUMENT CLUSTER (SPORT) (RANGER)
WHT-RED
DK GRN-LT GRN
TAN-WHT
BLK
LT BLU-RED
TAN-YEL (OR DK GRN-YEL)
BLK-YEL
WHT-LT BLU
LT BLU
LT BLU-BLK
BRN-WHT
DK GRN
YEL-WHT
RED-YEL
BLK-WHT
LT GRN-WHT
PPL-WHT
PNK-LT GRN
BLK-LT BLU
GRY
LT GRN-RED
GRY-YEL
ORG
WARNING CHIME MODULE
LEFT HEADLT
FUSE #13 (F/P)
EEC PIN #4
RIGHT FRONT DIR LT
MULTI-FUNCTION SW
ELECTRONIC SHIFT CONTROL MODULE
ELECT SHIFT MOD
RABS MODULE
FUEL TANK SENDER (FUEL TANK UNIT)
B/H CONN
FUSE #17 (F/P)
ELECTRONIC SHIFT CONTROL
OIL PRES SENDER
LEFT FRONT DIR LT
BRAKE DIODE/RESISTOR
SELF TEST OUTPUT CONN
IGNITION SW
LOW OIL LEVEL RELAY
ALTERNATOR
FUSE #18 (F/P)
COOLANT TEMP SENDER
4X4 IND SW
NOT USED
(2.9L, 3.0L, & 4.0L)
(2.3L)
(W/ ELECT SHIFT)
(W/O ELECT SHIFT)

1991 WIRING DIAGRAMS
Explorer & Ranger (Cont.)

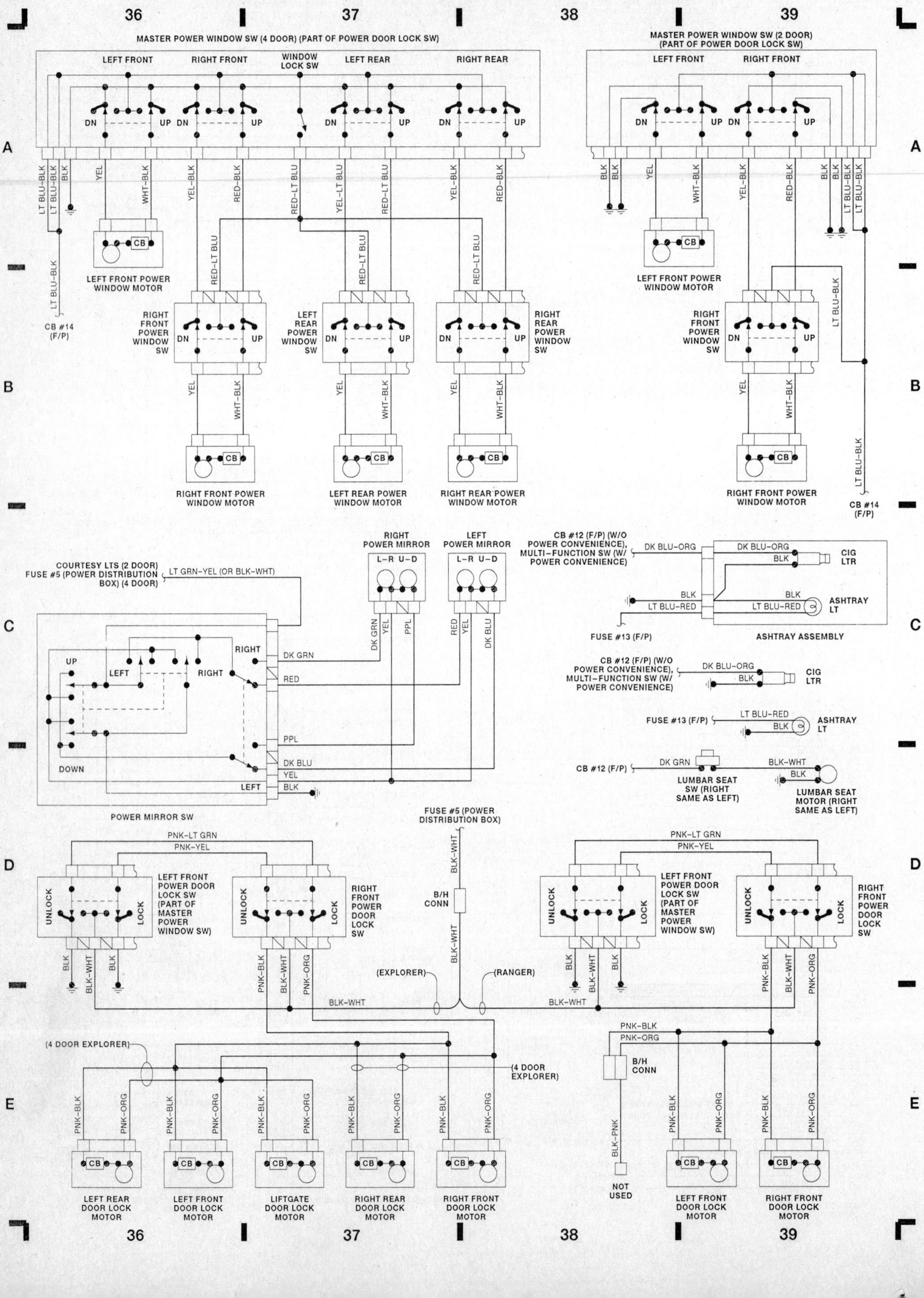
36
37
38
39
A
B
C
D
E
MASTER POWER WINDOW SW (4 DOOR) (PART OF POWER DOOR LOCK SW)
LEFT FRONT
RIGHT FRONT
WINDOW LOCK SW
LEFT REAR
RIGHT REAR
DN
UP
LT BLU-BLK
BLK
YEL
WHT-BLK
YEL-BLK
RED-BLK
RED-LT BLU
YEL-LT BLU
CB
LEFT FRONT POWER WINDOW MOTOR
CB #14 (F/P)
RIGHT FRONT POWER WINDOW SW
LEFT REAR POWER WINDOW SW
RIGHT REAR POWER WINDOW SW
RIGHT FRONT POWER WINDOW MOTOR
LEFT REAR POWER WINDOW MOTOR
RIGHT REAR POWER WINDOW MOTOR
MASTER POWER WINDOW SW (2 DOOR) (PART OF POWER DOOR LOCK SW)
RIGHT POWER MIRROR
LEFT POWER MIRROR
L-R U-D
DK GRN
PPL
RED
DK BLU
COURTESY LTS (2 DOOR) FUSE #5 (POWER DISTRIBUTION BOX) (4 DOOR)
LT GRN-YEL (OR BLK-WHT)
UP
LEFT
RIGHT
DOWN
POWER MIRROR SW
CB #12 (F/P) (W/O POWER CONVENIENCE), MULTI-FUNCTION SW (W/ POWER CONVENIENCE)
DK BLU-ORG
CIG LTR
LT BLU-RED
ASHTRAY LT
FUSE #13 (F/P)
ASHTRAY ASSEMBLY
CB #12 (F/P)
DK GRN
BLK-WHT
LUMBAR SEAT SW (RIGHT SAME AS LEFT)
LUMBAR SEAT MOTOR (RIGHT SAME AS LEFT)
FUSE #5 (POWER DISTRIBUTION BOX)
PNK-LT GRN
PNK-YEL
UNLOCK
LOCK
LEFT FRONT POWER DOOR LOCK SW (PART OF MASTER POWER WINDOW SW)
RIGHT FRONT POWER DOOR LOCK SW
B/H CONN
(EXPLORER)
(RANGER)
PNK-BLK
PNK-ORG
(4 DOOR EXPLORER)
BLK-PNK
NOT USED
LEFT REAR DOOR LOCK MOTOR
LEFT FRONT DOOR LOCK MOTOR
LIFTGATE DOOR LOCK MOTOR
RIGHT REAR DOOR LOCK MOTOR
RIGHT FRONT DOOR LOCK MOTOR

1991 WIRING DIAGRAMS
Explorer & Ranger (Cont.)

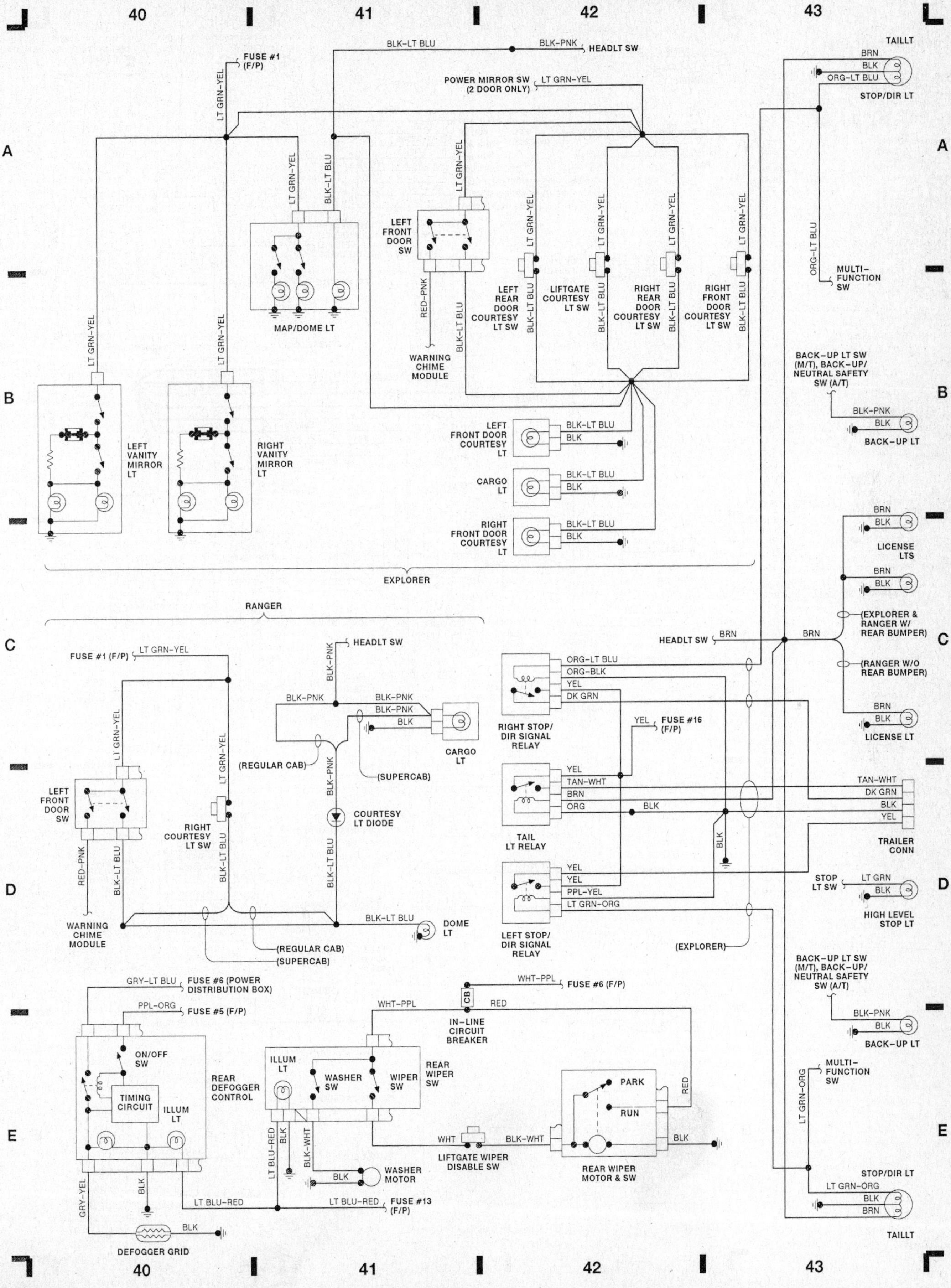
FUSE #1 (F/P)
BLK-LT BLU
BLK-PNK
HEADLT SW
POWER MIRROR SW (2 DOOR ONLY)
LT GRN-YEL
TAILLT
BRN
BLK
ORG-LT BLU
STOP/DIR LT
MAP/DOME LT
LEFT FRONT DOOR SW
RED-PNK
WARNING CHIME MODULE
LEFT REAR DOOR COURTESY LT SW
LIFTGATE COURTESY LT SW
RIGHT REAR DOOR COURTESY LT SW
RIGHT FRONT DOOR COURTESY LT SW
MULTI-FUNCTION SW
BACK-UP LT SW (M/T), BACK-UP/NEUTRAL SAFETY SW (A/T)
BACK-UP LT
LEFT VANITY MIRROR LT
RIGHT VANITY MIRROR LT
LEFT FRONT DOOR COURTESY LT
CARGO LT
RIGHT FRONT DOOR COURTESY LT
LICENSE LTS
EXPLORER
RANGER
(EXPLORER & RANGER W/ REAR BUMPER)
(RANGER W/O REAR BUMPER)
LICENSE LT
FUSE #1 (F/P)
HEADLT SW
(REGULAR CAB)
(SUPERCAB)
COURTESY LT DIODE
RIGHT COURTESY LT SW
ORG-BLK
YEL
DK GRN
RIGHT STOP/DIR SIGNAL RELAY
FUSE #16 (F/P)
TAN-WHT
ORG
TAIL LT RELAY
TRAILER CONN
STOP LT SW
LT GRN
HIGH LEVEL STOP LT
PPL-YEL
LT GRN-ORG
LEFT STOP/DIR SIGNAL RELAY
DOME LT
(EXPLORER)
GRY-LT BLU
FUSE #6 (POWER DISTRIBUTION BOX)
PPL-ORG
FUSE #5 (F/P)
ON/OFF SW
TIMING CIRCUIT
ILLUM LT
REAR DEFOGGER CONTROL
WHT-PPL
FUSE #6 (F/P)
CB
RED
IN-LINE CIRCUIT BREAKER
WASHER SW
WIPER SW
REAR WIPER SW
PARK
RUN
REAR WIPER MOTOR & SW
WHT
BLK-WHT
LIFTGATE WIPER DISABLE SW
LT BLU-RED
BLK-WHT
WASHER MOTOR
FUSE #13 (F/P)
GRY-YEL
DEFOGGER GRID
LT GRN-ORG
40
41
42
43
A
B
C
D
E

1991 WIRING DIAGRAMS
"E" Series

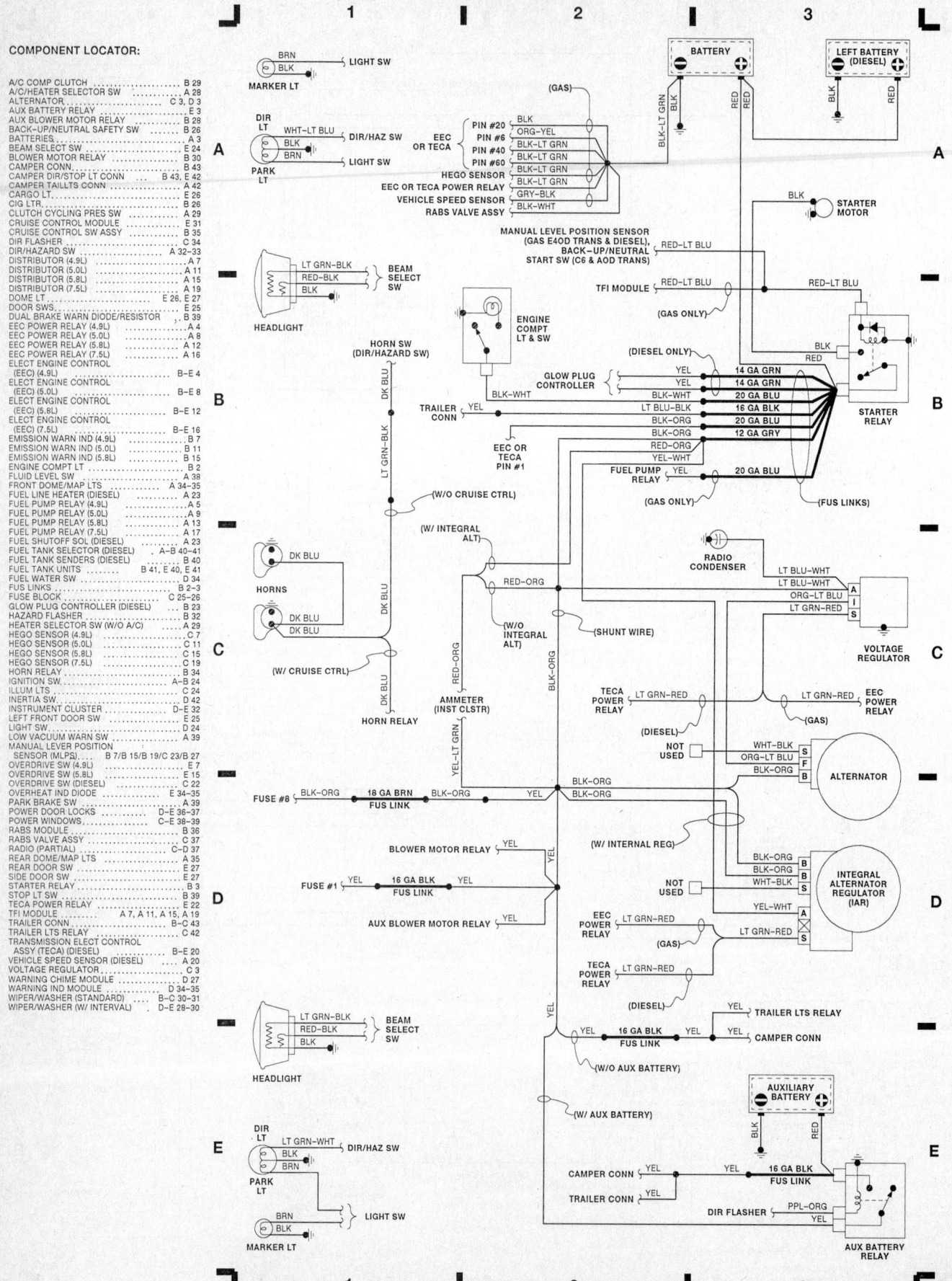

COMPONENT LOCATOR:

A/C COMP CLUTCH	B 29
A/C/HEATER SELECTOR SW	A 28
ALTERNATOR	C 3, D 3
AUX BATTERY RELAY	E 3
AUX BLOWER MOTOR RELAY	B 28
BACK-UP/NEUTRAL SAFETY SW	B 26
BATTERIES	A 3
BEAM SELECT SW	E 24
BLOWER MOTOR RELAY	B 30
CAMPER CONN	B 43
CAMPER DIR/STOP LT CONN	B 43, E 42
CAMPER TAILLTS CONN	A 42
CARGO LT	E 26
CIG LTR	B 26
CLUTCH CYCLING PRES SW	A 29
CRUISE CONTROL MODULE	E 31
CRUISE CONTROL SW ASSY	B 35
DIR FLASHER	C 34
DIR/HAZARD SW	A 32–33
DISTRIBUTOR (4.9L)	A 7
DISTRIBUTOR (5.0L)	A 11
DISTRIBUTOR (5.8L)	A 15
DISTRIBUTOR (7.5L)	A 19
DOME LT	E 26, E 27
DOOR SWS	E 25
DUAL BRAKE WARN DIODE/RESISTOR	B 39
EEC POWER RELAY (4.9L)	A 4
EEC POWER RELAY (5.0L)	A 8
EEC POWER RELAY (5.8L)	A 12
EEC POWER RELAY (7.5L)	A 16
ELECT ENGINE CONTROL (EEC) (4.9L)	B–E 4
ELECT ENGINE CONTROL (EEC) (5.0L)	B–E 8
ELECT ENGINE CONTROL (EEC) (5.8L)	B–E 12
ELECT ENGINE CONTROL (EEC) (7.5L)	B–E 16
EMISSION WARN IND (4.9L)	B 7
EMISSION WARN IND (5.0L)	B 11
EMISSION WARN IND (5.8L)	B 15
ENGINE COMPT LT	B 2
FLUID LEVEL SW	A 38
FRONT DOME/MAP LTS	A 34–35
FUEL LINE HEATER (DIESEL)	A 23
FUEL PUMP RELAY (4.9L)	A 5
FUEL PUMP RELAY (5.0L)	A 9
FUEL PUMP RELAY (5.8L)	A 13
FUEL PUMP RELAY (7.5L)	A 17
FUEL SHUTOFF SOL (DIESEL)	A 23
FUEL TANK SELECTOR (DIESEL)	A–B 40–41
FUEL TANK SENDERS (DIESEL)	B 40
FUEL TANK UNITS	B 41, E 40, E 41
FUEL WATER SW	D 34
FUS LINKS	B 2–3
FUSE BLOCK	C 25–26
GLOW PLUG CONTROLLER (DIESEL)	B 23
HAZARD FLASHER	B 32
HEATER SELECTOR SW (W/O A/C)	A 29
HEGO SENSOR (4.9L)	C 7
HEGO SENSOR (5.0L)	C 11
HEGO SENSOR (5.8L)	C 15
HEGO SENSOR (7.5L)	C 19
HORN RELAY	B 34
IGNITION SW	A–B 24
ILLUM LTS	C 24
INERTIA SW	D 42
INSTRUMENT CLUSTER	D–E 32
LEFT FRONT DOOR SW	E 25
LIGHT SW	D 24
LOW VACUUM WARN SW	A 39
MANUAL LEVER POSITION SENSOR (MLPS)	B 7/B 15/B 19/C 23/B 27
OVERDRIVE SW (4.9L)	E 7
OVERDRIVE SW (5.8L)	E 15
OVERDRIVE SW (DIESEL)	C 22
OVERHEAT IND DIODE	E 34–35
PARK BRAKE SW	A 39
POWER DOOR LOCKS	D–E 36–37
POWER WINDOWS	C–E 38–39
RABS MODULE	B 36
RABS VALVE ASSY	C 37
RADIO (PARTIAL)	C–D 37
REAR DOME/MAP LTS	A 35
REAR DOOR SW	E 27
SIDE DOOR SW	E 27
STARTER RELAY	B 3
STOP LT SW	B 39
TECA POWER RELAY	E 22
TFI MODULE	A 7, A 11, A 15, A 19
TRAILER CONN	B–C 43
TRAILER LTS RELAY	C 42
TRANSMISSION ELECT CONTROL ASSY (TECA) (DIESEL)	B–E 20
VEHICLE SPEED SENSOR (DIESEL)	A 20
VOLTAGE REGULATOR	C 3
WARNING CHIME MODULE	D 27
WARNING IND MODULE	D 34–35
WIPER/WASHER (STANDARD)	B–C 30–31
WIPER/WASHER (W/ INTERVAL)	D–E 28–30

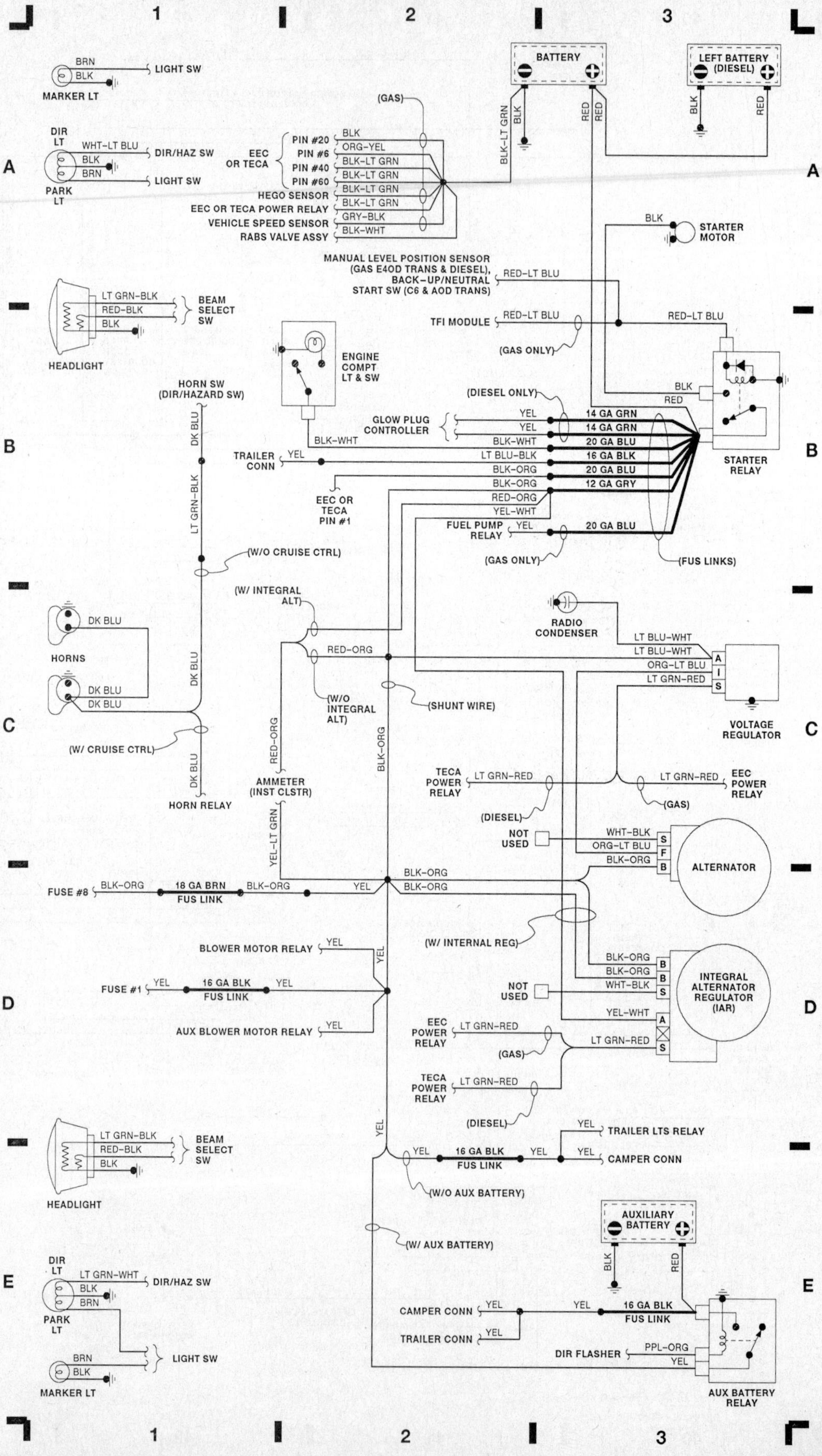
1
2
3
A
B
C
D
E
MARKER LT
LIGHT SW
DIR LT
PARK LT
DIR/HAZ SW
BATTERY
LEFT BATTERY (DIESEL)
(GAS)
EEC OR TECA
PIN #20
PIN #6
PIN #40
PIN #60
HEGO SENSOR
EEC OR TECA POWER RELAY
VEHICLE SPEED SENSOR
RABS VALVE ASSY
STARTER MOTOR
MANUAL LEVEL POSITION SENSOR (GAS E4OD TRANS & DIESEL), BACK-UP/NEUTRAL START SW (C6 & AOD TRANS)
TFI MODULE
(GAS ONLY)
HEADLIGHT
BEAM SELECT SW
ENGINE COMPT LT & SW
HORN SW (DIR/HAZARD SW)
(DIESEL ONLY)
GLOW PLUG CONTROLLER
TRAILER CONN
14 GA GRN
20 GA BLU
16 GA BLK
12 GA GRY
EEC OR TECA PIN #1
FUEL PUMP RELAY
(GAS ONLY)
(FUS LINKS)
STARTER RELAY
(W/O CRUISE CTRL)
(W/ INTEGRAL ALT)
RADIO CONDENSER
HORNS
(W/O INTEGRAL ALT)
(SHUNT WIRE)
VOLTAGE REGULATOR
(W/ CRUISE CTRL)
AMMETER (INST CLSTR)
HORN RELAY
TECA POWER RELAY
EEC POWER RELAY
(GAS)
(DIESEL)
NOT USED
ALTERNATOR
FUSE #8
18 GA BRN
FUS LINK
(W/ INTERNAL REG)
BLOWER MOTOR RELAY
FUSE #1
16 GA BLK
AUX BLOWER MOTOR RELAY
INTEGRAL ALTERNATOR REGULATOR (IAR)
TRAILER LTS RELAY
CAMPER CONN
(W/O AUX BATTERY)
AUXILIARY BATTERY
(W/ AUX BATTERY)
DIR FLASHER
AUX BATTERY RELAY

1991 WIRING DIAGRAMS
"E" Series (Cont.)

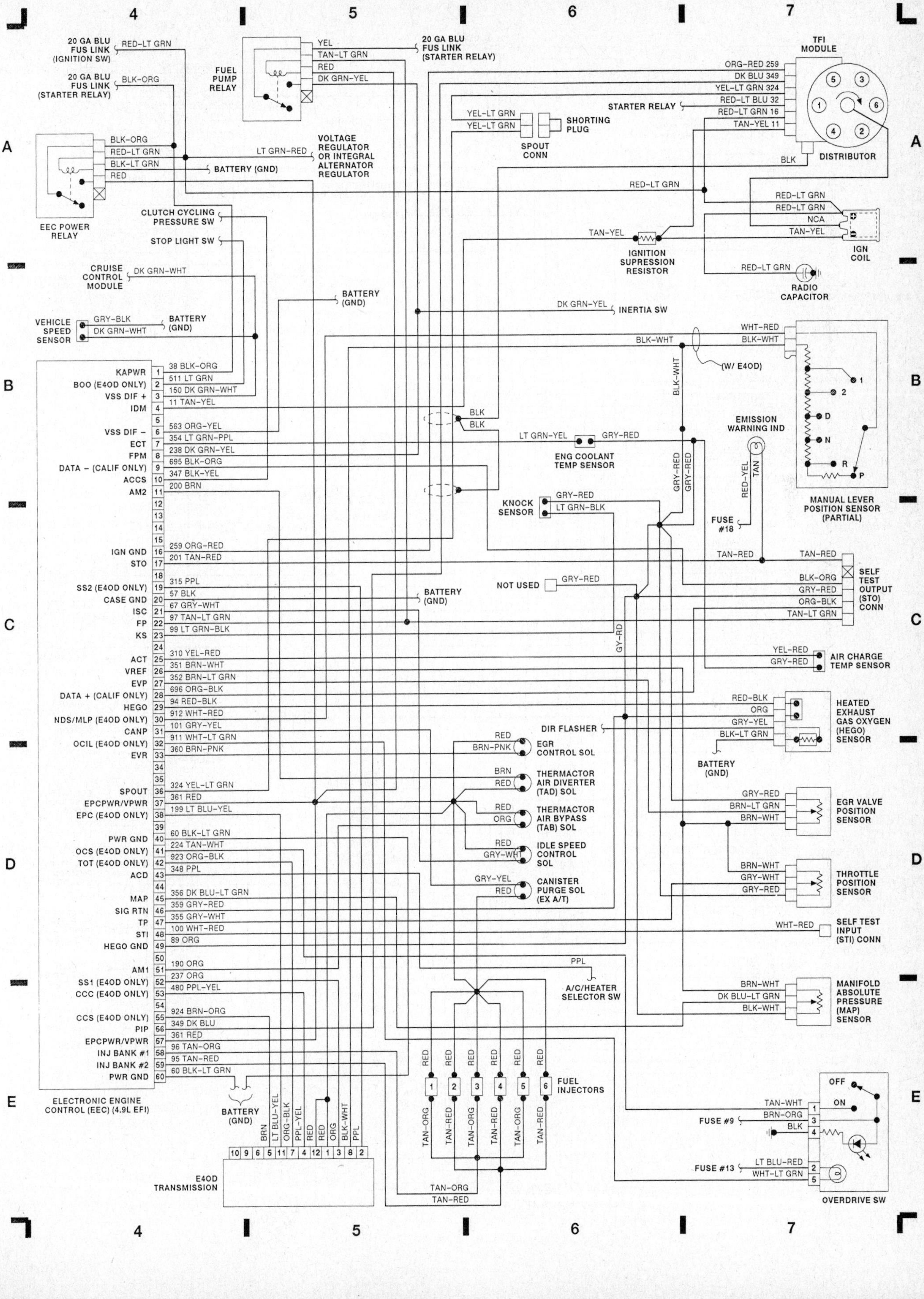

20 GA BLU FUS LINK (IGNITION SW)
RED-LT GRN
20 GA BLU FUS LINK (STARTER RELAY)
BLK-ORG
FUEL PUMP RELAY
YEL
TAN-LT GRN
RED
DK GRN-YEL
20 GA BLU FUS LINK (STARTER RELAY)
TFI MODULE
ORG-RED 259
DK BLU 349
YEL-LT GRN 324
RED-LT BLU 32
RED-LT GRN 16
TAN-YEL 11
STARTER RELAY
YEL-LT GRN
SHORTING PLUG
SPOUT CONN
DISTRIBUTOR
BLK
EEC POWER RELAY
BLK-LT GRN
LT GRN-RED
VOLTAGE REGULATOR OR INTEGRAL ALTERNATOR REGULATOR
BATTERY (GND)
CLUTCH CYCLING PRESSURE SW
STOP LIGHT SW
CRUISE CONTROL MODULE
DK GRN-WHT
VEHICLE SPEED SENSOR
GRY-BLK
IGNITION SUPRESSION RESISTOR
TAN-YEL
NCA
IGN COIL
RADIO CAPACITOR
INERTIA SW
WHT-RED
BLK-WHT
(W/ E4OD)
EMISSION WARNING IND
ENG COOLANT TEMP SENSOR
LT GRN-YEL
GRY-RED
KNOCK SENSOR
LT GRN-BLK
FUSE #18
RED-YEL
TAN
MANUAL LEVER POSITION SENSOR (PARTIAL)
TAN-RED
SELF TEST OUTPUT (STO) CONN
BLK-ORG
ORG-BLK
TAN-LT GRN
NOT USED
GY-RD
AIR CHARGE TEMP SENSOR
YEL-RED
HEATED EXHAUST GAS OXYGEN (HEGO) SENSOR
RED-BLK
ORG
GRY-YEL
BLK-LT GRN
DIR FLASHER
EGR CONTROL SOL
BRN-PNK
THERMACTOR AIR DIVERTER (TAD) SOL
BRN
THERMACTOR AIR BYPASS (TAB) SOL
IDLE SPEED CONTROL SOL
GRY-WHT
CANISTER PURGE SOL (EX A/T)
EGR VALVE POSITION SENSOR
BRN-LT GRN
BRN-WHT
THROTTLE POSITION SENSOR
SELF TEST INPUT (STI) CONN
A/C/HEATER SELECTOR SW
PPL
MANIFOLD ABSOLUTE PRESSURE (MAP) SENSOR
DK BLU-LT GRN
KAPWR 1 38 BLK-ORG
BOO (E4OD ONLY) 2 511 LT GRN
VSS DIF + 3 150 DK GRN-WHT
IDM 4 11 TAN-YEL
5 563 ORG-YEL
VSS DIF – 6 354 LT GRN-PPL
ECT 7 238 DK GRN-YEL
FPM 8 695 BLK-ORG
DATA – (CALIF ONLY) 9 347 BLK-YEL
ACCS 10 200 BRN
AM2 11
IGN GND 16 259 ORG-RED
STO 17 201 TAN-RED
18 315 PPL
SS2 (E4OD ONLY) 19 57 BLK
CASE GND 20 67 GRY-WHT
ISC 21 97 TAN-LT GRN
FP 22 99 LT GRN-BLK
KS 23
ACT 25 310 YEL-RED
VREF 26 351 BRN-WHT
EVP 27 352 BRN-LT GRN
DATA + (CALIF ONLY) 28 696 ORG-BLK
HEGO 29 94 RED-BLK
NDS/MLP (E4OD ONLY) 30 912 WHT-RED
CANP 31 101 GRY-YEL
OCIL (E4OD ONLY) 32 911 WHT-LT GRN
EVR 33 360 BRN-PNK
SPOUT 36 324 YEL-LT GRN
EPCPWR/VPWR 37 361 RED
EPC (E4OD ONLY) 38 199 LT BLU-YEL
39 60 BLK-LT GRN
PWR GND 40 224 TAN-WHT
OCS (E4OD ONLY) 41 923 ORG-BLK
TOT (E4OD ONLY) 42 348 PPL
ACD 43
MAP 45 356 DK BLU-LT GRN
SIG RTN 46 359 GRY-RED
TP 47 355 GRY-WHT
STI 48 100 WHT-RED
HEGO GND 49 89 ORG
AM1 51 190 ORG
SS1 (E4OD ONLY) 52 237 ORG
CCC (E4OD ONLY) 53 480 PPL-YEL
CCS (E4OD ONLY) 55 924 BRN-ORG
PIP 56 349 DK BLU
EPCPWR/VPWR 57 361 RED
INJ BANK #1 58 96 TAN-ORG
INJ BANK #2 59 95 TAN-RED
PWR GND 60 60 BLK-LT GRN
ELECTRONIC ENGINE CONTROL (EEC) (4.9L EFI)
BATTERY (GND)
BRN
LT BLU-YEL
ORG-BLK
PPL-YEL
BLK-WHT
10 9 6 5 11 7 4 12 1 3 8 2
E4OD TRANSMISSION
FUEL INJECTORS
1 2 3 4 5 6
TAN-ORG
TAN-RED
OVERDRIVE SW
OFF
ON
TAN-WHT
BRN-ORG
FUSE #9
FUSE #13
LT BLU-RED
WHT-LT GRN

1991 WIRING DIAGRAMS
"E" Series (Cont.)

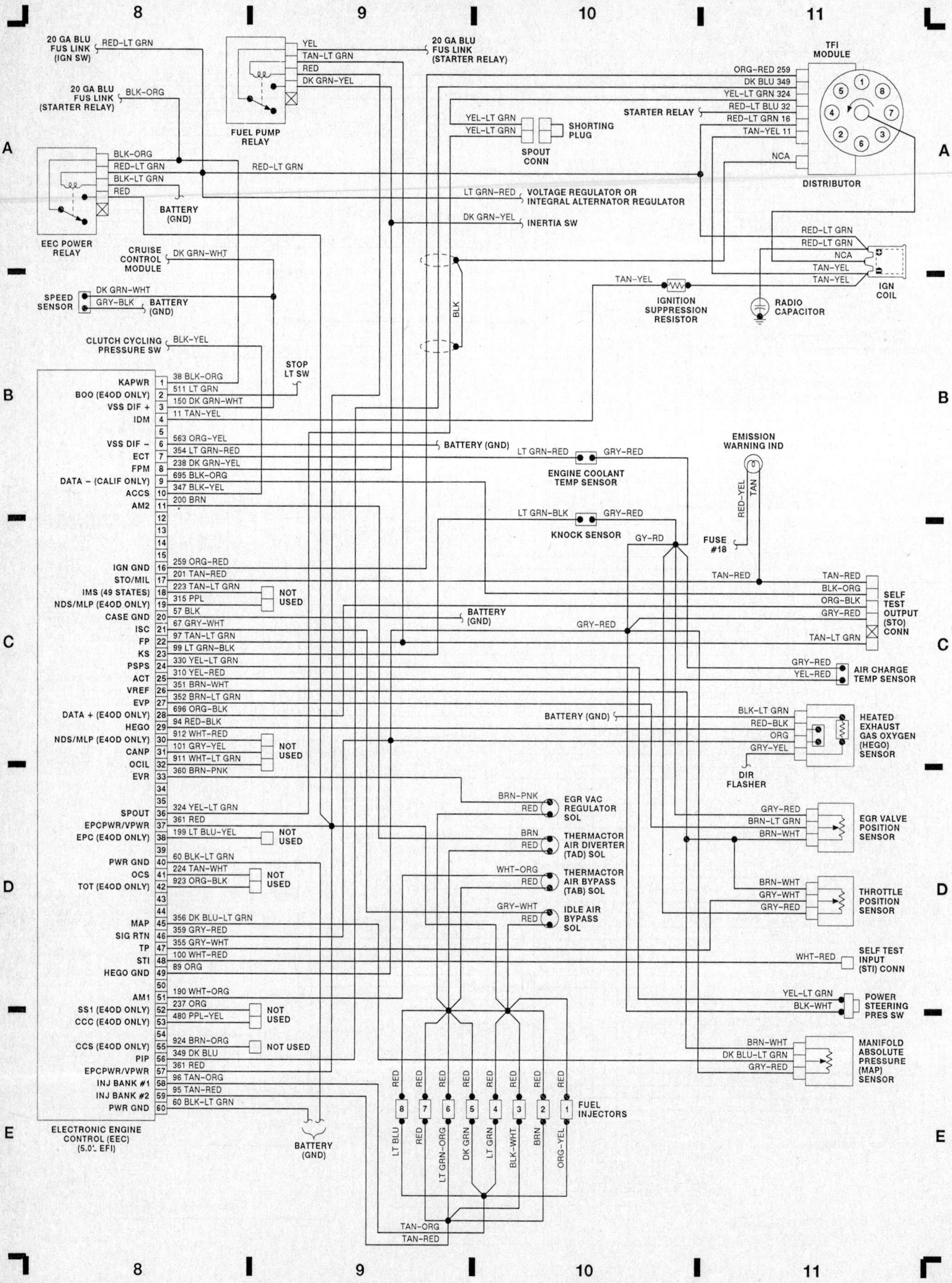

8
9
10
11
A
B
C
D
E
20 GA BLU FUS LINK (IGN SW)
RED-LT GRN
20 GA BLU FUS LINK (STARTER RELAY)
BLK-ORG
YEL
TAN-LT GRN
RED
DK GRN-YEL
FUEL PUMP RELAY
20 GA BLU FUS LINK (STARTER RELAY)
TFI MODULE
ORG-RED 259
DK BLU 349
YEL-LT GRN 324
RED-LT BLU 32
RED-LT GRN 16
TAN-YEL 11
NCA
STARTER RELAY
DISTRIBUTOR
YEL-LT GRN
SHORTING PLUG
SPOUT CONN
BLK-ORG
RED-LT GRN
BLK-LT GRN
RED
BATTERY (GND)
EEC POWER RELAY
LT GRN-RED
VOLTAGE REGULATOR OR INTEGRAL ALTERNATOR REGULATOR
DK GRN-YEL
INERTIA SW
CRUISE CONTROL MODULE
DK GRN-WHT
SPEED SENSOR
GRY-BLK
BATTERY (GND)
BLK
TAN-YEL
IGNITION SUPPRESSION RESISTOR
RADIO CAPACITOR
IGN COIL
CLUTCH CYCLING PRESSURE SW
BLK-YEL
STOP LT SW
KAPWR 1 38 BLK-ORG
BOO (E4OD ONLY) 2 511 LT GRN
VSS DIF + 3 150 DK GRN-WHT
IDM 4 11 TAN-YEL
5
VSS DIF – 6 563 ORG-YEL
ECT 7 354 LT GRN-RED
FPM 8 238 DK GRN-YEL
DATA – (CALIF ONLY) 9 695 BLK-ORG
ACCS 10 347 BLK-YEL
AM2 11 200 BRN
12
13
14
15
IGN GND 16 259 ORG-RED
STO/MIL 17 201 TAN-RED
IMS (49 STATES) 18 223 TAN-LT GRN
NDS/MLP (E4OD ONLY) 19 315 PPL
CASE GND 20 57 BLK
ISC 21 67 GRY-WHT
FP 22 97 TAN-LT GRN
KS 23 99 LT GRN-BLK
PSPS 24 330 YEL-LT GRN
ACT 25 310 YEL-RED
VREF 26 351 BRN-WHT
EVP 27 352 BRN-LT GRN
DATA + (E4OD ONLY) 28 696 ORG-BLK
HEGO 29 94 RED-BLK
NDS/MLP (E4OD ONLY) 30 912 WHT-RED
CANP 31 101 GRY-YEL
OCIL 32 911 WHT-LT GRN
EVR 33 360 BRN-PNK
34
35
SPOUT 36 324 YEL-LT GRN
EPCPWR/VPWR 37 361 RED
EPC (E4OD ONLY) 38 199 LT BLU-YEL
39
PWR GND 40 60 BLK-LT GRN
OCS 41 224 TAN-WHT
TOT (E4OD ONLY) 42 923 ORG-BLK
43
44
MAP 45 356 DK BLU-LT GRN
SIG RTN 46 359 GRY-RED
TP 47 355 GRY-WHT
STI 48 100 WHT-RED
HEGO GND 49 89 ORG
50
AM1 51 190 WHT-ORG
SS1 (E4OD ONLY) 52 237 ORG
CCC (E4OD ONLY) 53 480 PPL-YEL
54
CCS (E4OD ONLY) 55 924 BRN-ORG
PIP 56 349 DK BLU
EPCPWR/VPWR 57 361 RED
INJ BANK #1 58 96 TAN-ORG
INJ BANK #2 59 95 TAN-RED
PWR GND 60 60 BLK-LT GRN
NOT USED
ELECTRONIC ENGINE CONTROL (EEC) (5.0L EFI)
BATTERY (GND)
BATTERY (GND)
LT GRN-RED
GRY-RED
ENGINE COOLANT TEMP SENSOR
LT GRN-BLK
KNOCK SENSOR
GY-RD
EMISSION WARNING IND
RED-YEL
TAN
FUSE #18
TAN-RED
BLK-ORG
ORG-BLK
GRY-RED
TAN-LT GRN
SELF TEST OUTPUT (STO) CONN
BATTERY (GND)
YEL-RED
AIR CHARGE TEMP SENSOR
BLK-LT GRN
RED-BLK
ORG
GRY-YEL
HEATED EXHAUST GAS OXYGEN (HEGO) SENSOR
DIR FLASHER
BRN-PNK
EGR VAC REGULATOR SOL
BRN
THERMACTOR AIR DIVERTER (TAD) SOL
WHT-ORG
THERMACTOR AIR BYPASS (TAB) SOL
GRY-WHT
IDLE AIR BYPASS SOL
BRN-LT GRN
BRN-WHT
EGR VALVE POSITION SENSOR
GRY-WHT
THROTTLE POSITION SENSOR
WHT-RED
SELF TEST INPUT (STI) CONN
YEL-LT GRN
BLK-WHT
POWER STEERING PRES SW
DK BLU-LT GRN
MANIFOLD ABSOLUTE PRESSURE (MAP) SENSOR
FUEL INJECTORS
8 7 6 5 4 3 2 1
LT BLU
LT GRN-ORG
DK GRN
LT GRN
BLK-WHT
BRN
ORG-YEL
TAN-ORG
TAN-RED

1991 WIRING DIAGRAMS
"E" Series (Cont.)

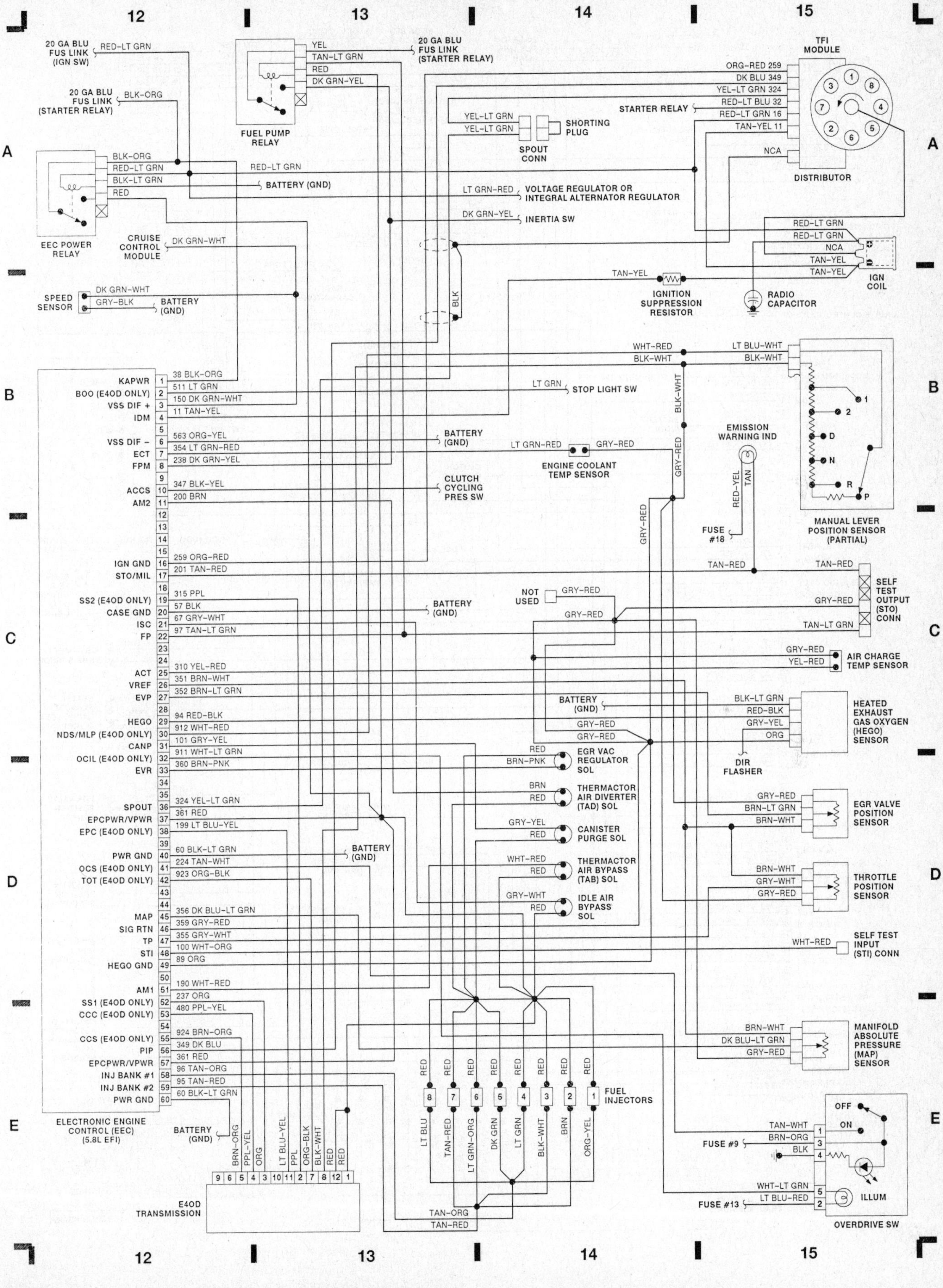
12
13
14
15
20 GA BLU FUS LINK (IGN SW)
RED-LT GRN
20 GA BLU FUS LINK (STARTER RELAY)
BLK-ORG
YEL
TAN-LT GRN
RED
DK GRN-YEL
FUEL PUMP RELAY
20 GA BLU FUS LINK (STARTER RELAY)
TFI MODULE
ORG-RED 259
DK BLU 349
YEL-LT GRN 324
RED-LT BLU 32
RED-LT GRN 16
TAN-YEL 11
NCA
STARTER RELAY
DISTRIBUTOR
YEL-LT GRN
SHORTING PLUG
SPOUT CONN
EEC POWER RELAY
BATTERY (GND)
VOLTAGE REGULATOR OR INTEGRAL ALTERNATOR REGULATOR
LT GRN-RED
DK GRN-YEL
INERTIA SW
CRUISE CONTROL MODULE
DK GRN-WHT
SPEED SENSOR
GRY-BLK
IGN COIL
TAN-YEL
IGNITION SUPPRESSION RESISTOR
RADIO CAPACITOR
BLK
KAPWR
BOO (E4OD ONLY)
VSS DIF +
IDM
VSS DIF -
ECT
FPM
ACCS
AM2
IGN GND
STO/MIL
SS2 (E4OD ONLY)
CASE GND
ISC
FP
ACT
VREF
EVP
HEGO
NDS/MLP (E4OD ONLY)
CANP
OCIL (E4OD ONLY)
EVR
SPOUT
EPCPWR/VPWR
EPC (E4OD ONLY)
PWR GND
OCS (E4OD ONLY)
TOT (E4OD ONLY)
MAP
SIG RTN
TP
STI
HEGO GND
AM1
SS1 (E4OD ONLY)
CCC (E4OD ONLY)
CCS (E4OD ONLY)
PIP
EPCPWR/VPWR
INJ BANK #1
INJ BANK #2
PWR GND
38 BLK-ORG
511 LT GRN
150 DK GRN-WHT
11 TAN-YEL
563 ORG-YEL
354 LT GRN-RED
238 DK GRN-YEL
347 BLK-YEL
200 BRN
259 ORG-RED
201 TAN-RED
315 PPL
57 BLK
67 GRY-WHT
97 TAN-LT GRN
310 YEL-RED
351 BRN-WHT
352 BRN-LT GRN
94 RED-BLK
912 WHT-RED
101 GRY-YEL
911 WHT-LT GRN
360 BRN-PNK
324 YEL-LT GRN
361 RED
199 LT BLU-YEL
60 BLK-LT GRN
224 TAN-WHT
923 ORG-BLK
356 DK BLU-LT GRN
359 GRY-RED
355 GRY-WHT
100 WHT-ORG
89 ORG
190 WHT-RED
237 ORG
480 PPL-YEL
924 BRN-ORG
349 DK BLU
361 RED
96 TAN-ORG
95 TAN-RED
60 BLK-LT GRN
ELECTRONIC ENGINE CONTROL (EEC) (5.8L EFI)
STOP LIGHT SW
LT GRN
WHT-RED
BLK-WHT
LT BLU-WHT
MANUAL LEVER POSITION SENSOR (PARTIAL)
EMISSION WARNING IND
FUSE #18
RED-YEL
TAN
ENGINE COOLANT TEMP SENSOR
GRY-RED
CLUTCH CYCLING PRES SW
TAN-RED
SELF TEST OUTPUT (STO) CONN
NOT USED
TAN-LT GRN
AIR CHARGE TEMP SENSOR
YEL-RED
HEATED EXHAUST GAS OXYGEN (HEGO) SENSOR
BLK-LT GRN
RED-BLK
GRY-YEL
ORG
DIR FLASHER
EGR VAC REGULATOR SOL
BRN-PNK
THERMACTOR AIR DIVERTER (TAD) SOL
BRN
CANISTER PURGE SOL
THERMACTOR AIR BYPASS (TAB) SOL
IDLE AIR BYPASS SOL
GRY-WHT
EGR VALVE POSITION SENSOR
BRN-LT GRN
BRN-WHT
THROTTLE POSITION SENSOR
SELF TEST INPUT (STI) CONN
WHT-RED
MANIFOLD ABSOLUTE PRESSURE (MAP) SENSOR
DK BLU-LT GRN
FUEL INJECTORS
LT BLU
TAN-RED
LT GRN-ORG
DK GRN
LT GRN
BLK-WHT
ORG-YEL
BATTERY (GND)
BRN-ORG
PPL-YEL
LT BLU-YEL
PPL
ORG-BLK
E4OD TRANSMISSION
TAN-ORG
OVERDRIVE SW
OFF
ON
TAN-WHT
FUSE #9
FUSE #13
WHT-LT GRN
LT BLU-RED
ILLUM

1991 WIRING DIAGRAMS
"E" Series (Cont.)

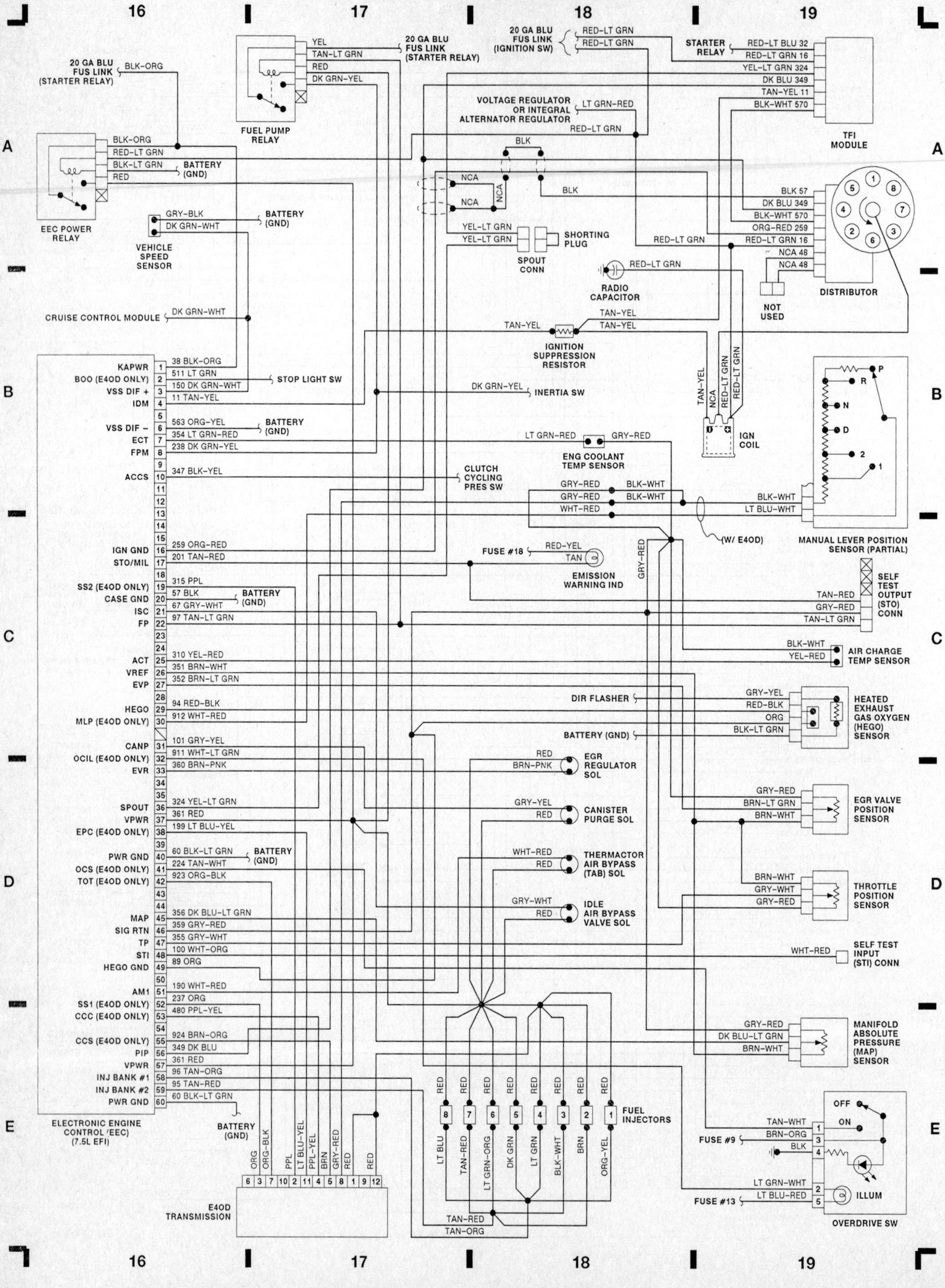
16
17
18
19
A
B
C
D
E
20 GA BLU FUS LINK (STARTER RELAY)
BLK-ORG
YEL
TAN-LT GRN
RED
DK GRN-YEL
FUEL PUMP RELAY
20 GA BLU FUS LINK (STARTER RELAY)
20 GA BLU FUS LINK (IGNITION SW)
RED-LT GRN
STARTER RELAY
RED-LT BLU 32
RED-LT GRN 16
YEL-LT GRN 324
DK BLU 349
TAN-YEL 11
BLK-WHT 570
TFI MODULE
VOLTAGE REGULATOR OR INTEGRAL ALTERNATOR REGULATOR
LT GRN-RED
RED-LT GRN
BLK-LT GRN
BATTERY (GND)
EEC POWER RELAY
GRY-BLK
DK GRN-WHT
VEHICLE SPEED SENSOR
BLK
NCA
BLK 57
DK BLU 349
BLK-WHT 570
ORG-RED 259
RED-LT GRN 16
NCA 48
DISTRIBUTOR
NOT USED
YEL-LT GRN
SHORTING PLUG
SPOUT CONN
RADIO CAPACITOR
CRUISE CONTROL MODULE
TAN-YEL
IGNITION SUPPRESSION RESISTOR
IGN COIL
KAPWR 1 38 BLK-ORG
BOO (E4OD ONLY) 2 511 LT GRN
VSS DIF + 3 150 DK GRN-WHT
IDM 4 11 TAN-YEL
5
VSS DIF – 6 563 ORG-YEL
ECT 7 354 LT GRN-RED
FPM 8 238 DK GRN-YEL
9
ACCS 10 347 BLK-YEL
11
12
13
14
15
IGN GND 16 259 ORG-RED
STO/MIL 17 201 TAN-RED
18
SS2 (E4OD ONLY) 19 315 PPL
CASE GND 20 57 BLK
ISC 21 67 GRY-WHT
FP 22 97 TAN-LT GRN
23
24
ACT 25 310 YEL-RED
VREF 26 351 BRN-WHT
EVP 27 352 BRN-LT GRN
28
HEGO 29 94 RED-BLK
MLP (E4OD ONLY) 30 912 WHT-RED
CANP 31 101 GRY-YEL
OCIL (E4OD ONLY) 32 911 WHT-LT GRN
EVR 33 360 BRN-PNK
34
SPOUT 36 324 YEL-LT GRN
VPWR 37 361 RED
EPC (E4OD ONLY) 38 199 LT BLU-YEL
39
PWR GND 40 60 BLK-LT GRN
OCS (E4OD ONLY) 41 224 TAN-WHT
TOT (E4OD ONLY) 42 923 ORG-BLK
43
44
MAP 45 356 DK BLU-LT GRN
SIG RTN 46 359 GRY-RED
TP 47 355 GRY-WHT
STI 48 100 WHT-ORG
HEGO GND 49 89 ORG
50
AM1 51 190 WHT-RED
SS1 (E4OD ONLY) 52 237 ORG
CCC (E4OD ONLY) 53 480 PPL-YEL
54
CCS (E4OD ONLY) 55 924 BRN-ORG
PIP 56 349 DK BLU
VPWR 57 361 RED
INJ BANK #1 58 96 TAN-ORG
INJ BANK #2 59 95 TAN-RED
PWR GND 60 60 BLK-LT GRN
ELECTRONIC ENGINE CONTROL (EEC) (7.5L EFI)
STOP LIGHT SW
INERTIA SW
CLUTCH CYCLING PRES SW
ENG COOLANT TEMP SENSOR
GRY-RED
BLK-WHT
WHT-RED
LT BLU-WHT
(W/ E4OD)
MANUAL LEVER POSITION SENSOR (PARTIAL)
P R N D 2 1
FUSE #18
RED-YEL
TAN
EMISSION WARNING IND
SELF TEST OUTPUT (STO) CONN
TAN-RED
AIR CHARGE TEMP SENSOR
YEL-RED
DIR FLASHER
GRY-YEL
RED-BLK
ORG
HEATED EXHAUST GAS OXYGEN (HEGO) SENSOR
BATTERY (GND)
EGR REGULATOR SOL
BRN-PNK
CANISTER PURGE SOL
EGR VALVE POSITION SENSOR
BRN-LT GRN
BRN-WHT
THERMACTOR AIR BYPASS (TAB) SOL
THROTTLE POSITION SENSOR
GRY-WHT
IDLE AIR BYPASS VALVE SOL
SELF TEST INPUT (STI) CONN
MANIFOLD ABSOLUTE PRESSURE (MAP) SENSOR
DK BLU-LT GRN
FUEL INJECTORS
8 7 6 5 4 3 2 1
LT BLU
TAN-RED
LT GRN-ORG
DK GRN
LT GRN
BLK-WHT
BRN
ORG-YEL
TAN-ORG
OVERDRIVE SW
OFF
ON
TAN-WHT
BRN-ORG
FUSE #9
LT GRN-WHT
LT BLU-RED
FUSE #13
ILLUM
E4OD TRANSMISSION
6 3 7 10 2 11 4 5 8 1 9 12
ORG-BLK
PPL
LT BLU-YEL
PPL-YEL
GRY-RED

1991 WIRING DIAGRAMS
"E" Series (Cont.)

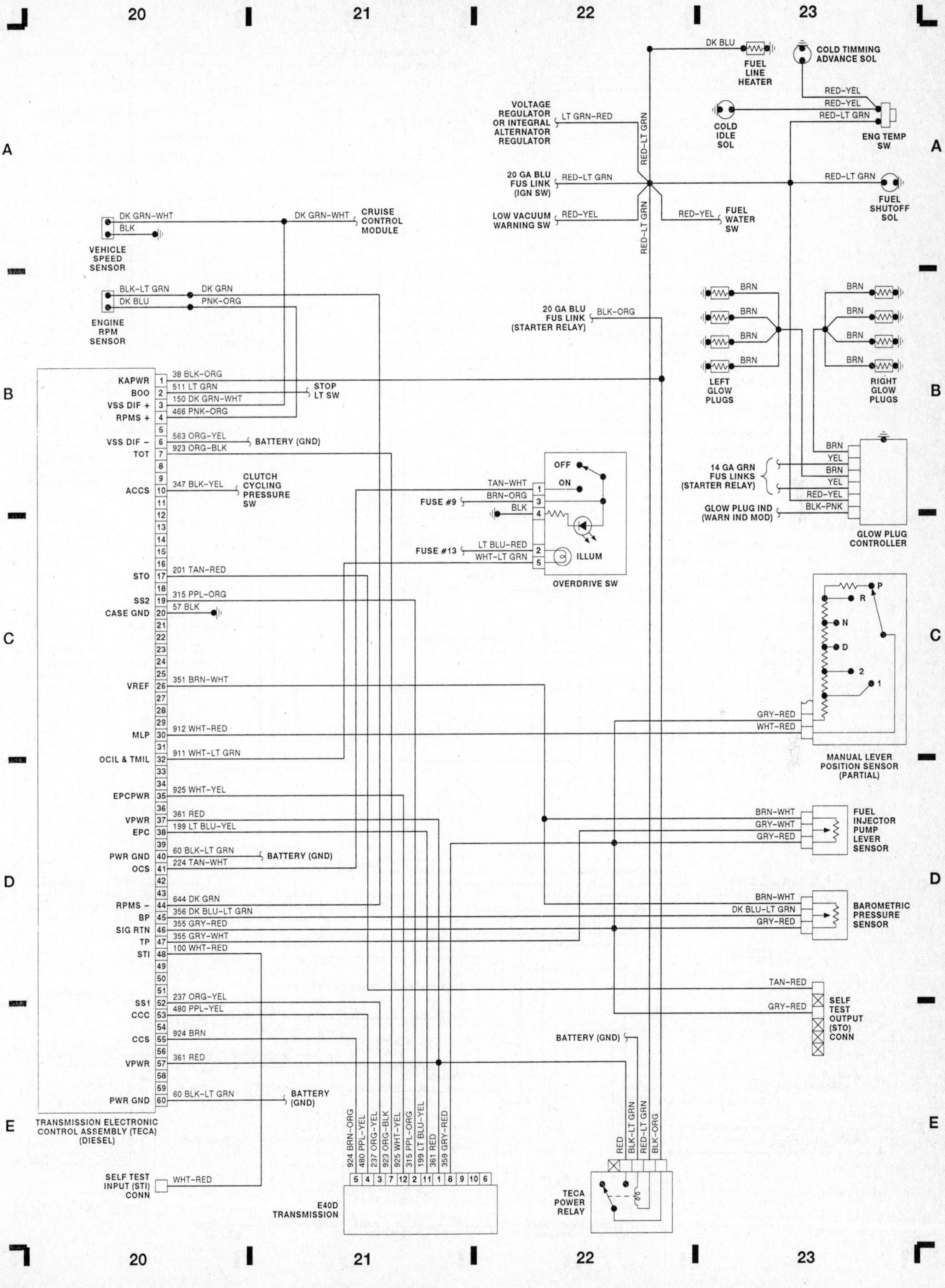

20
21
22
23
A
B
C
D
E
DK BLU
FUEL LINE HEATER
COLD TIMMING ADVANCE SOL
RED-YEL
RED-YEL
RED-LT GRN
COLD IDLE SOL
ENG TEMP SW
VOLTAGE REGULATOR OR INTEGRAL ALTERNATOR REGULATOR
LT GRN-RED
RED-LT GRN
20 GA BLU FUS LINK (IGN SW)
RED-LT GRN
RED-LT GRN
FUEL SHUTOFF SOL
LOW VACUUM WARNING SW
RED-YEL
RED-YEL
FUEL WATER SW
DK GRN-WHT
BLK
VEHICLE SPEED SENSOR
DK GRN-WHT
CRUISE CONTROL MODULE
BLK-LT GRN
DK GRN
DK BLU
PNK-ORG
ENGINE RPM SENSOR
20 GA BLU FUS LINK (STARTER RELAY)
BLK-ORG
BRN
LEFT GLOW PLUGS
RIGHT GLOW PLUGS
KAPWR 1 38 BLK-ORG
BOO 2 511 LT GRN
VSS DIF + 3 150 DK GRN-WHT
RPMS + 4 466 PNK-ORG
STOP LT SW
5
VSS DIF − 6 563 ORG-YEL
BATTERY (GND)
TOT 7 923 ORG-BLK
8
9
ACCS 10 347 BLK-YEL
CLUTCH CYCLING PRESSURE SW
OFF
ON
TAN-WHT 1
BRN-ORG 3
FUSE #9
BLK 4
FUSE #13
LT BLU-RED 2
WHT-LT GRN 5
ILLUM
OVERDRIVE SW
BRN
YEL
BRN
YEL
RED-YEL
BLK-PNK
14 GA GRN FUS LINKS (STARTER RELAY)
GLOW PLUG IND (WARN IND MOD)
GLOW PLUG CONTROLLER
STO 17 201 TAN-RED
SS2 19 315 PPL-ORG
CASE GND 20 57 BLK
P
R
N
D
2
1
VREF 26 351 BRN-WHT
GRY-RED
WHT-RED
MLP 30 912 WHT-RED
OCIL & TMIL 32 911 WHT-LT GRN
MANUAL LEVER POSITION SENSOR (PARTIAL)
EPCPWR 35 925 WHT-YEL
VPWR 37 361 RED
EPC 38 199 LT BLU-YEL
BRN-WHT
GRY-WHT
GRY-RED
FUEL INJECTOR PUMP LEVER SENSOR
PWR GND 40 60 BLK-LT GRN
BATTERY (GND)
OCS 41 224 TAN-WHT
RPMS − 44 644 DK GRN
BP 45 356 DK BLU-LT GRN
SIG RTN 46 355 GRY-RED
TP 47 355 GRY-WHT
STI 48 100 WHT-RED
BRN-WHT
DK BLU-LT GRN
GRY-RED
BAROMETRIC PRESSURE SENSOR
TAN-RED
GRY-RED
SELF TEST OUTPUT (STO) CONN
SS1 52 237 ORG-YEL
CCC 53 480 PPL-YEL
CCS 55 924 BRN
BATTERY (GND)
VPWR 57 361 RED
PWR GND 60 60 BLK-LT GRN
BATTERY (GND)
TRANSMISSION ELECTRONIC CONTROL ASSEMBLY (TECA) (DIESEL)
924 BRN-ORG
480 PPL-YEL
237 ORG-YEL
923 ORG-BLK
925 WHT-YEL
315 PPL-ORG
199 LT BLU-YEL
361 RED
359 GRY-RED
5 4 3 7 12 2 11 1 8 9 10 6
E40D TRANSMISSION
RED
BLK-LT GRN
RED-LT GRN
BLK-ORG
TECA POWER RELAY
SELF TEST INPUT (STI) CONN
WHT-RED
20
21
22
23

1991 WIRING DIAGRAMS
"E" Series (Cont.)

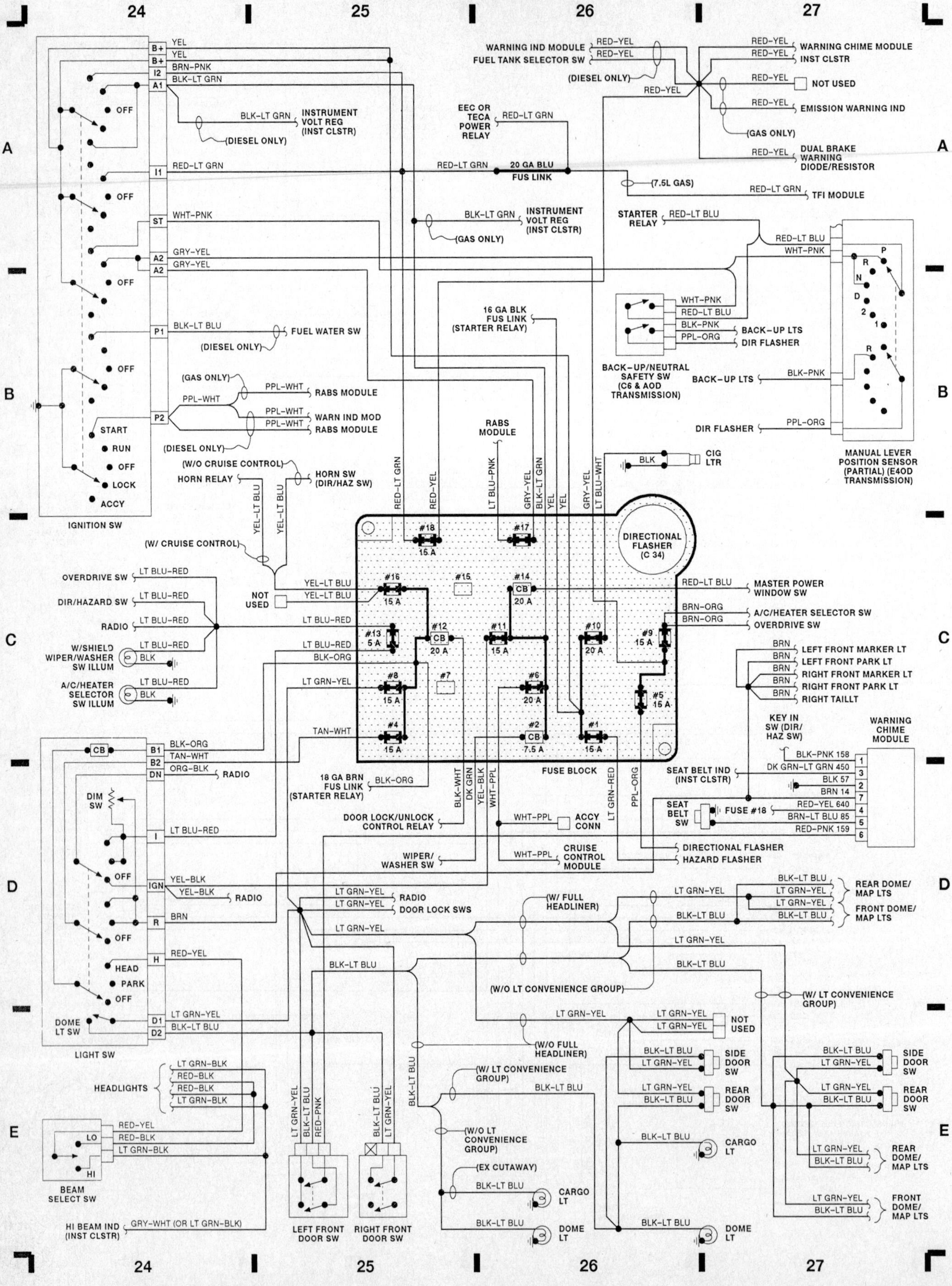
24
25
26
27
A
B
C
D
E
IGNITION SW
OFF
START
RUN
LOCK
ACCY
B+
I2
A1
I1
ST
A2
P1
P2
YEL
BRN-PNK
BLK-LT GRN
RED-LT GRN
WHT-PNK
GRY-YEL
BLK-LT BLU
PPL-WHT
INSTRUMENT VOLT REG (INST CLSTR)
(DIESEL ONLY)
(GAS ONLY)
FUEL WATER SW
RABS MODULE
WARN IND MOD
(W/O CRUISE CONTROL)
HORN RELAY
HORN SW (DIR/HAZ SW)
(W/ CRUISE CONTROL)
EEC OR TECA POWER RELAY
20 GA BLU FUS LINK
WARNING IND MODULE
FUEL TANK SELECTOR SW
RED-YEL
WARNING CHIME MODULE
INST CLSTR
NOT USED
EMISSION WARNING IND
DUAL BRAKE WARNING DIODE/RESISTOR
(7.5L GAS)
TFI MODULE
STARTER RELAY
RED-LT BLU
16 GA BLK FUS LINK (STARTER RELAY)
BACK-UP/NEUTRAL SAFETY SW (C6 & AOD TRANSMISSION)
BLK-PNK
PPL-ORG
BACK-UP LTS
DIR FLASHER
MANUAL LEVER POSITION SENSOR (PARTIAL) (E4OD TRANSMISSION)
CIG LTR
BLK
RABS MODULE
YEL-LT BLU
LT BLU-PNK
BLK-LT GRN
LT BLU-WHT
DIRECTIONAL FLASHER (C 34)
FUSE BLOCK
#18 15 A
#17
#16 15 A
#15
#14 CB 20 A
#13 5 A
#12 CB 20 A
#11 15 A
#10 20 A
#9 15 A
#8 15 A
#7
#6 20 A
#5 15 A
#4 15 A
#2 CB 7.5 A
#1 15 A
OVERDRIVE SW
DIR/HAZARD SW
RADIO
W/SHIELD WIPER/WASHER SW ILLUM
A/C/HEATER SELECTOR SW ILLUM
LT BLU-RED
BLK-ORG
LT GRN-YEL
TAN-WHT
MASTER POWER WINDOW SW
BRN-ORG
A/C/HEATER SELECTOR SW
OVERDRIVE SW
BRN
LEFT FRONT MARKER LT
LEFT FRONT PARK LT
RIGHT FRONT MARKER LT
RIGHT FRONT PARK LT
RIGHT TAILLT
KEY IN SW (DIR/HAZ SW)
WARNING CHIME MODULE
BLK-PNK 158
DK GRN-LT GRN 450
BLK 57
BRN 14
RED-YEL 640
BRN-LT BLU 85
RED-PNK 159
SEAT BELT IND (INST CLSTR)
SEAT BELT SW
FUSE #18
18 GA BRN FUS LINK (STARTER RELAY)
DOOR LOCK/UNLOCK CONTROL RELAY
WIPER/WASHER SW
WHT-PPL
ACCY CONN
CRUISE CONTROL MODULE
DIRECTIONAL FLASHER
HAZARD FLASHER
LT GRN-RED
LIGHT SW
CB
B1
B2
DN
DIM SW
IGN
R
H
D1
D2
HEAD
PARK
DOME LT SW
ORG-BLK
YEL-BLK
RED-YEL
DOOR LOCK SWS
(W/ FULL HEADLINER)
(W/O LT CONVENIENCE GROUP)
(W/ LT CONVENIENCE GROUP)
(W/O FULL HEADLINER)
REAR DOME/MAP LTS
FRONT DOME/MAP LTS
SIDE DOOR SW
REAR DOOR SW
CARGO LT
DOME LT
(EX CUTAWAY)
HEADLIGHTS
LT GRN-BLK
RED-BLK
BEAM SELECT SW
LO
HI
HI BEAM IND (INST CLSTR)
GRY-WHT (OR LT GRN-BLK)
LEFT FRONT DOOR SW
RIGHT FRONT DOOR SW

1991 WIRING DIAGRAMS
"E" Series (Cont.)

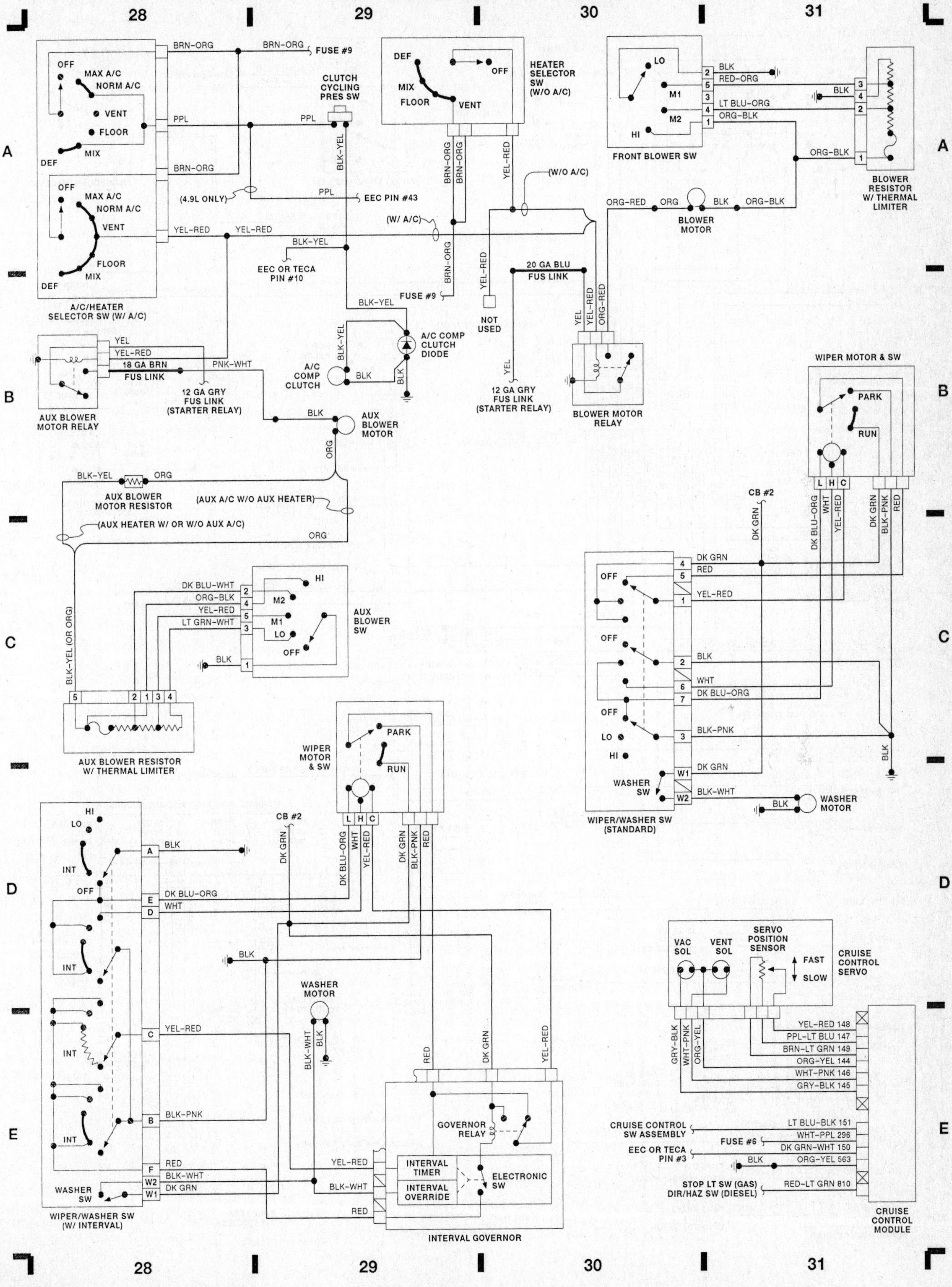
28
29
30
31
A/C/HEATER SELECTOR SW (W/ A/C)
OFF
MAX A/C
NORM A/C
VENT
FLOOR
MIX
DEF
BRN-ORG
FUSE #9
CLUTCH CYCLING PRES SW
PPL
BLK-YEL
(4.9L ONLY)
EEC PIN #43
YEL-RED
(W/ A/C)
EEC OR TECA PIN #10
HEATER SELECTOR SW (W/O A/C)
BRN-ORG
YEL-RED
(W/O A/C)
NOT USED
20 GA BLU FUS LINK
12 GA GRY FUS LINK (STARTER RELAY)
YEL
BLOWER MOTOR RELAY
FRONT BLOWER SW
LO
M1
M2
HI
BLK
RED-ORG
LT BLU-ORG
ORG-BLK
ORG-RED
ORG
BLOWER MOTOR
BLOWER RESISTOR W/ THERMAL LIMITER
AUX BLOWER MOTOR RELAY
YEL-RED
18 GA BRN FUS LINK
PNK-WHT
12 GA GRY FUS LINK (STARTER RELAY)
A/C COMP CLUTCH DIODE
A/C COMP CLUTCH
AUX BLOWER MOTOR
AUX BLOWER MOTOR RESISTOR
(AUX A/C W/O AUX HEATER)
(AUX HEATER W/ OR W/O AUX A/C)
BLK-YEL (OR ORG)
DK BLU-WHT
LT GRN-WHT
AUX BLOWER SW
AUX BLOWER RESISTOR W/ THERMAL LIMITER
WIPER MOTOR & SW
PARK
RUN
CB #2
DK GRN
DK BLU-ORG
WHT
BLK-PNK
RED
WIPER/WASHER SW (STANDARD)
WASHER SW
BLK-WHT
WASHER MOTOR
WIPER/WASHER SW (W/ INTERVAL)
INT
INTERVAL GOVERNOR
GOVERNOR RELAY
INTERVAL TIMER
INTERVAL OVERRIDE
ELECTRONIC SW
VAC SOL
VENT SOL
SERVO POSITION SENSOR
FAST
SLOW
CRUISE CONTROL SERVO
GRY-BLK
WHT-PNK
ORG-YEL
YEL-RED 148
PPL-LT BLU 147
BRN-LT GRN 149
ORG-YEL 144
WHT-PNK 146
GRY-BLK 145
CRUISE CONTROL SW ASSEMBLY
LT BLU-BLK 151
FUSE #6
WHT-PPL 296
EEC OR TECA PIN #3
DK GRN-WHT 150
ORG-YEL 563
STOP LT SW (GAS) DIR/HAZ SW (DIESEL)
RED-LT GRN 810
CRUISE CONTROL MODULE

1991 WIRING DIAGRAMS
"E" Series (Cont.)

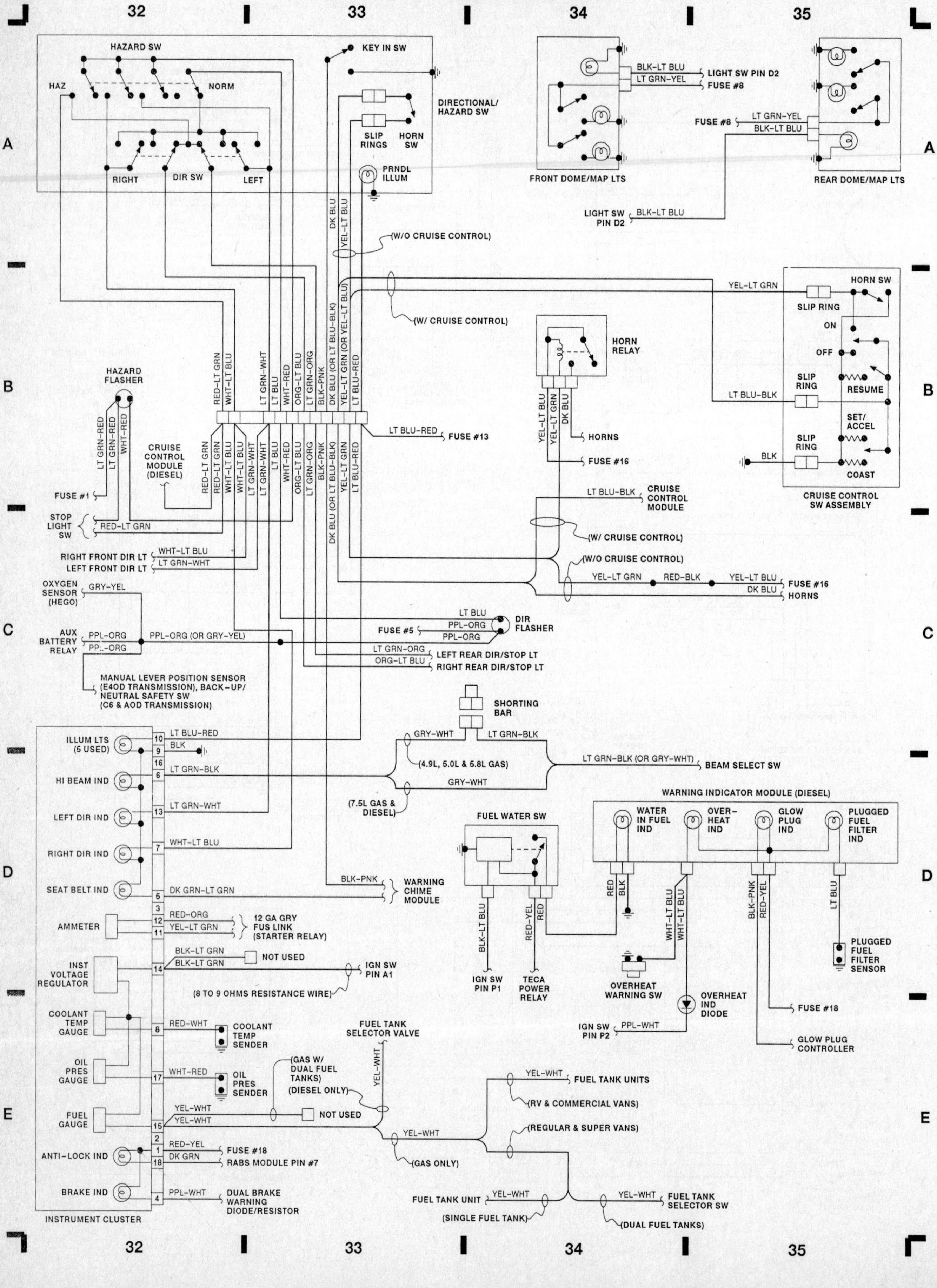
32
33
34
35
A
B
C
D
E
HAZARD SW
HAZ
NORM
RIGHT
DIR SW
LEFT
KEY IN SW
DIRECTIONAL/
HAZARD SW
SLIP RINGS
HORN SW
PRNDL ILLUM
DK BLU
YEL-LT BLU
(W/O CRUISE CONTROL)
(W/ CRUISE CONTROL)
BLK-LT BLU
LT GRN-YEL
LIGHT SW PIN D2
FUSE #8
FRONT DOME/MAP LTS
REAR DOME/MAP LTS
LIGHT SW PIN D2
YEL-LT GRN
HORN SW
SLIP RING
ON
OFF
RESUME
SET/ACCEL
COAST
BLK
LT BLU-BLK
CRUISE CONTROL SW ASSEMBLY
HORN RELAY
HAZARD FLASHER
LT GRN-RED
WHT-RED
CRUISE CONTROL MODULE (DIESEL)
RED-LT GRN
WHT-LT BLU
LT GRN-WHT
LT BLU
WHT-RED
ORG-LT BLU
LT GRN-ORG
BLK-PNK
DK BLU (OR LT BLU-BLK)
YEL-LT GRN (OR YEL-LT BLU)
LT BLU-RED
FUSE #13
YEL-LT BLU
YEL-LT GRN
DK BLU
HORNS
FUSE #16
LT BLU-BLK
CRUISE CONTROL MODULE
FUSE #1
STOP LIGHT SW
RED-LT GRN
RIGHT FRONT DIR LT
LEFT FRONT DIR LT
(W/ CRUISE CONTROL)
(W/O CRUISE CONTROL)
RED-BLK
FUSE #16
HORNS
OXYGEN SENSOR (HEGO)
GRY-YEL
AUX BATTERY RELAY
PPL-ORG
PPL-ORG (OR GRY-YEL)
FUSE #5
LT BLU
DIR FLASHER
LT GRN-ORG
ORG-LT BLU
LEFT REAR DIR/STOP LT
RIGHT REAR DIR/STOP LT
MANUAL LEVER POSITION SENSOR (E4OD TRANSMISSION), BACK-UP/NEUTRAL SAFETY SW (C6 & AOD TRANSMISSION)
SHORTING BAR
GRY-WHT
LT GRN-BLK
(4.9L, 5.0L & 5.8L GAS)
LT GRN-BLK (OR GRY-WHT)
BEAM SELECT SW
(7.5L GAS & DIESEL)
ILLUM LTS (5 USED)
HI BEAM IND
LEFT DIR IND
RIGHT DIR IND
SEAT BELT IND
AMMETER
INST VOLTAGE REGULATOR
COOLANT TEMP GAUGE
OIL PRES GAUGE
FUEL GAUGE
ANTI-LOCK IND
BRAKE IND
INSTRUMENT CLUSTER
DK GRN-LT GRN
BLK-PNK
WARNING CHIME MODULE
RED-ORG
YEL-LT GRN
12 GA GRY FUS LINK (STARTER RELAY)
BLK-LT GRN
NOT USED
IGN SW PIN A1
(8 TO 9 OHMS RESISTANCE WIRE)
RED-WHT
COOLANT TEMP SENDER
WHT-RED
OIL PRES SENDER
FUEL TANK SELECTOR VALVE
(GAS W/ DUAL FUEL TANKS)
(DIESEL ONLY)
YEL-WHT
NOT USED
(GAS ONLY)
RED-YEL
FUSE #18
DK GRN
RABS MODULE PIN #7
PPL-WHT
DUAL BRAKE WARNING DIODE/RESISTOR
FUEL TANK UNITS
(RV & COMMERCIAL VANS)
(REGULAR & SUPER VANS)
FUEL TANK UNIT
(SINGLE FUEL TANK)
FUEL TANK SELECTOR SW
(DUAL FUEL TANKS)
FUEL WATER SW
BLK-LT BLU
RED-YEL
RED
IGN SW PIN P1
TECA POWER RELAY
WARNING INDICATOR MODULE (DIESEL)
WATER IN FUEL IND
OVER-HEAT IND
GLOW PLUG IND
PLUGGED FUEL FILTER IND
WHT-LT BLU
BLK-PNK
RED-YEL
LT BLU
PLUGGED FUEL FILTER SENSOR
OVERHEAT WARNING SW
OVERHEAT IND DIODE
IGN SW PIN P2
FUSE #18
GLOW PLUG CONTROLLER

1991 WIRING DIAGRAMS
"E" Series (Cont.)

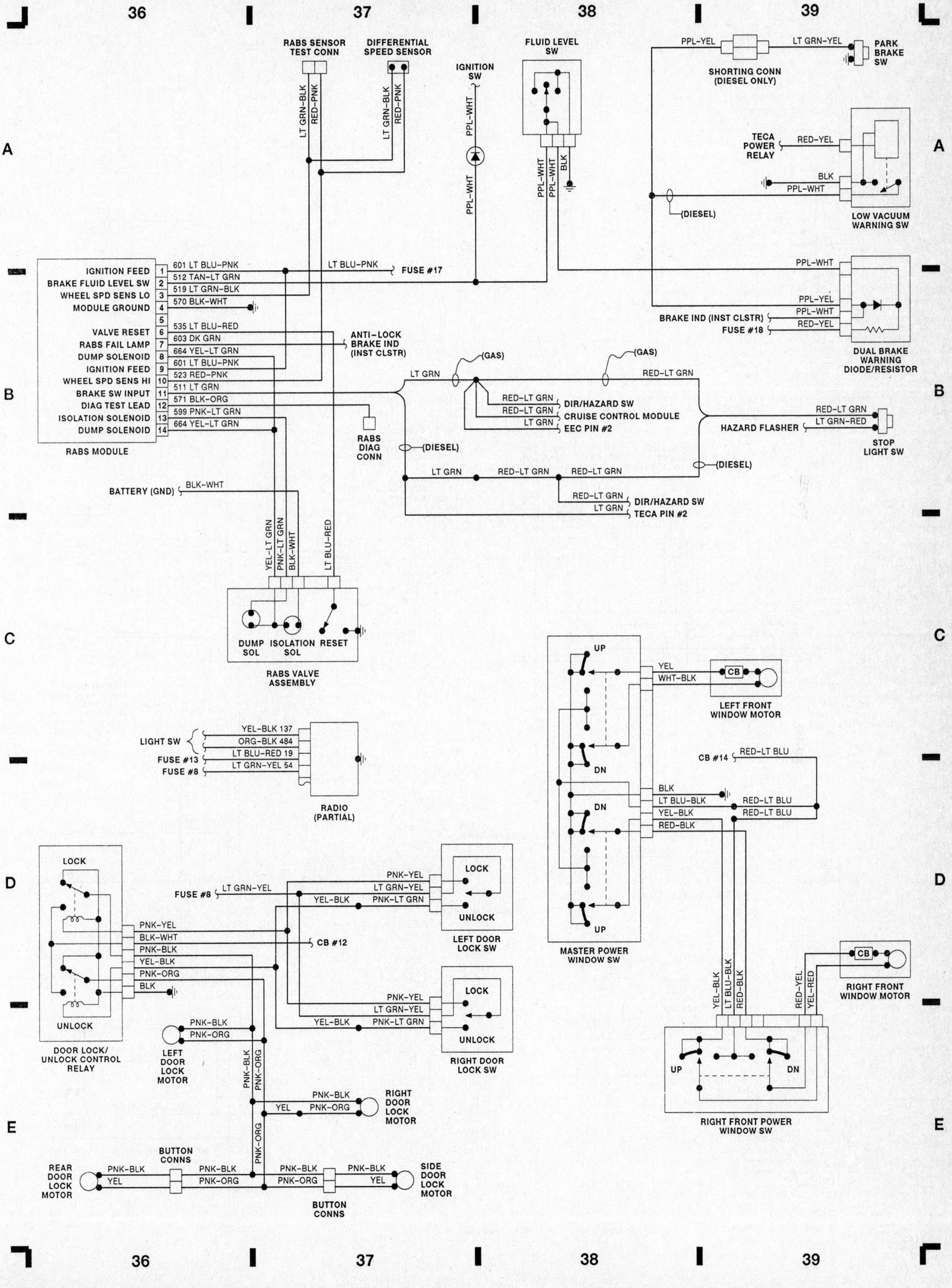
RABS SENSOR TEST CONN
DIFFERENTIAL SPEED SENSOR
IGNITION SW
FLUID LEVEL SW
PPL-YEL
LT GRN-YEL
PARK BRAKE SW
SHORTING CONN (DIESEL ONLY)
TECA POWER RELAY
RED-YEL
BLK
PPL-WHT
(DIESEL)
LOW VACUUM WARNING SW
IGNITION FEED
BRAKE FLUID LEVEL SW
WHEEL SPD SENS LO
MODULE GROUND
VALVE RESET
RABS FAIL LAMP
DUMP SOLENOID
IGNITION FEED
WHEEL SPD SENS HI
BRAKE SW INPUT
DIAG TEST LEAD
ISOLATION SOLENOID
DUMP SOLENOID
RABS MODULE
601 LT BLU-PNK
512 TAN-LT GRN
519 LT GRN-BLK
570 BLK-WHT
535 LT BLU-RED
603 DK GRN
664 YEL-LT GRN
601 LT BLU-PNK
523 RED-PNK
511 LT GRN
571 BLK-ORG
599 PNK-LT GRN
664 YEL-LT GRN
LT BLU-PNK
FUSE #17
ANTI-LOCK BRAKE IND (INST CLSTR)
BRAKE IND (INST CLSTR)
FUSE #18
DUAL BRAKE WARNING DIODE/RESISTOR
(GAS)
LT GRN
RED-LT GRN
DIR/HAZARD SW
CRUISE CONTROL MODULE
EEC PIN #2
HAZARD FLASHER
LT GRN-RED
STOP LIGHT SW
RABS DIAG CONN
TECA PIN #2
BATTERY (GND)
YEL-LT GRN
PNK-LT GRN
BLK-WHT
LT BLU-RED
DUMP SOL
ISOLATION SOL
RESET
RABS VALVE ASSEMBLY
LIGHT SW
FUSE #13
FUSE #8
YEL-BLK 137
ORG-BLK 484
LT BLU-RED 19
LT GRN-YEL 54
RADIO (PARTIAL)
UP
DN
YEL
WHT-BLK
CB
LEFT FRONT WINDOW MOTOR
CB #14
RED-LT BLU
LT BLU-BLK
YEL-BLK
RED-BLK
MASTER POWER WINDOW SW
RIGHT FRONT WINDOW MOTOR
RED-YEL
YEL-RED
RIGHT FRONT POWER WINDOW SW
LOCK
UNLOCK
DOOR LOCK/ UNLOCK CONTROL RELAY
LT GRN-YEL
PNK-YEL
PNK-BLK
PNK-ORG
CB #12
LEFT DOOR LOCK SW
RIGHT DOOR LOCK SW
LEFT DOOR LOCK MOTOR
RIGHT DOOR LOCK MOTOR
REAR DOOR LOCK MOTOR
BUTTON CONNS
SIDE DOOR LOCK MOTOR

1991 WIRING DIAGRAMS
"E" Series (Cont.)

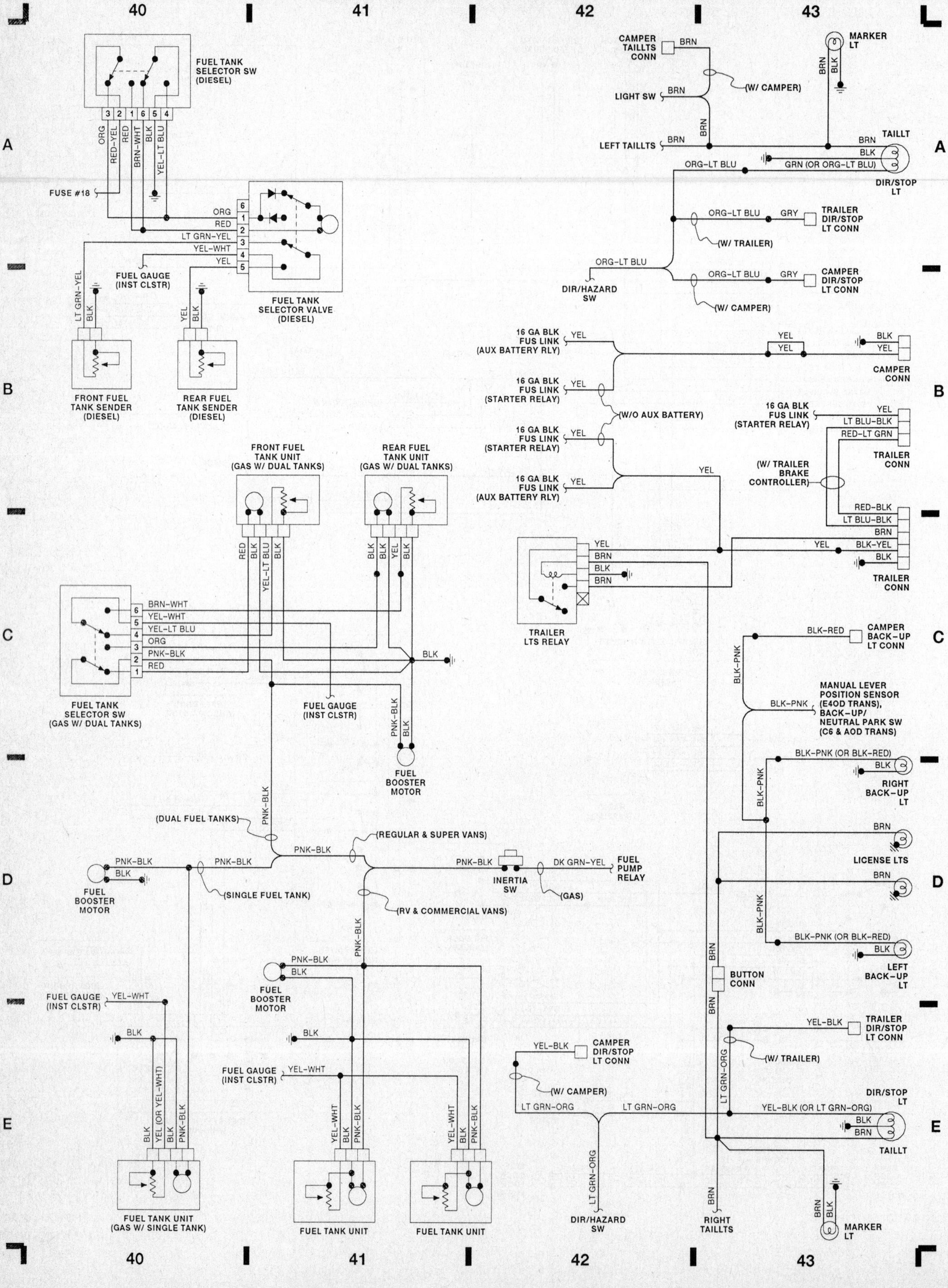
40
41
42
43
FUEL TANK SELECTOR SW (DIESEL)
FUSE #18
FUEL GAUGE (INST CLSTR)
FUEL TANK SELECTOR VALVE (DIESEL)
FRONT FUEL TANK SENDER (DIESEL)
REAR FUEL TANK SENDER (DIESEL)
FRONT FUEL TANK UNIT (GAS W/ DUAL TANKS)
REAR FUEL TANK UNIT (GAS W/ DUAL TANKS)
FUEL TANK SELECTOR SW (GAS W/ DUAL TANKS)
FUEL BOOSTER MOTOR
(DUAL FUEL TANKS)
(REGULAR & SUPER VANS)
(SINGLE FUEL TANK)
(RV & COMMERCIAL VANS)
INERTIA SW
(GAS)
FUEL PUMP RELAY
FUEL TANK UNIT (GAS W/ SINGLE TANK)
FUEL TANK UNIT
CAMPER TAILLTS CONN
(W/ CAMPER)
LIGHT SW
LEFT TAILLTS
MARKER LT
TAILLT
DIR/STOP LT
TRAILER DIR/STOP LT CONN
(W/ TRAILER)
DIR/HAZARD SW
CAMPER DIR/STOP LT CONN
16 GA BLK FUS LINK (AUX BATTERY RLY)
16 GA BLK FUS LINK (STARTER RELAY)
(W/O AUX BATTERY)
CAMPER CONN
TRAILER CONN
(W/ TRAILER BRAKE CONTROLLER)
TRAILER LTS RELAY
CAMPER BACK-UP LT CONN
MANUAL LEVER POSITION SENSOR (E4OD TRANS), BACK-UP/ NEUTRAL PARK SW (C6 & AOD TRANS)
RIGHT BACK-UP LT
LICENSE LTS
LEFT BACK-UP LT
BUTTON CONN
RIGHT TAILLTS
A
B
C
D
E

1991 SAFETY EQUIPMENT
Analog Instrument Panels

Aerostar, Bronco, Explorer, Ranger, "E" & "F" Series

***NOTE:* Unless specified otherwise, references to "F" Series include "F" Series Super Duty.**

DESCRIPTION & OPERATION

The analog instrument panel, for all models except Aerostar, is equipped with the following standard equipments: voltage/temperature gauge and oil pressure/fuel gauge. The tachometer is a available as optional equipment. Aerostar, Bronco, Explorer, Ranger and "F" Series use magnetic-type gauges to monitor fuel level, coolant temperature and oil pressure. The magnetic gauge system does not use Instrument Voltage Regulator (IVR). All "E" Series use bimetallic-type gauges that incorporate IVR.

The IVR controls and maintains an average pulsating voltage of 5 volts, which is delivered to each gauge. To prevent radio interference, a suppression choke is used in line between printed circuit and IVR.

TESTING

OIL PRESSURE INDICATOR LIGHT

1) Turn ignition on, but do not start engine. Indicator light should come on. Start engine. Warning light should go out within 3 or 4 seconds.
2) To test oil pressure switch, turn ignition on but do not start engine. If indicator light does not come on, disconnect wire at oil pressure switch terminal and ground.
3) If light comes on, oil pressure switch is defective. If light does not come on, check for bad bulb or open wiring in bulb circuit. See appropriate chassis wiring diagram in WIRING DIAGRAMS.

LOW OIL LEVEL WARNING LIGHT

1) With ignition on and engine off, light should come on. If light does not come on, check fuse in fuse panel and wiring. Start engine. Light will go out if oil level is not low.
2) If oil level is low by 1.5 qts. (1.4L) or more, the oil pan sensor will be grounded, causing light to remain on until ignition is turned off. If low oil level light does not come on, check the following:

- Circuit fuse
- Low oil level relay located on right side of steering column reinforcement
- Indicator light

3) To test oil pan sensor, disconnect wire at sensor and verify proper oil level in engine.
4) Connect a VOM to sensor terminal and ground. With oil at proper full level, reading should be greater than 100,000 ohms (sensor open). Drain 2 qts. of oil from oil pan and recheck. Reading should be less than 1000 ohms. See appropriate chassis wiring diagram in WIRING DIAGRAMS.

***NOTE:* It may take 5 minutes or more for oil to drain from sensor to get low oil level reading. Sensor must be horizontal when performing this test.**

CHARGE INDICATOR LIGHT

1) The Integral Alternator Regulator (IAR) has a circuit that will indicate a high or low battery voltage condition. The charge indicator light will come on if alternator is not charging, or is overcharging. If either of these conditions exists, see appropriate ALTERNATOR article in ELECTRICAL.
2) If charge indicator light does not come on with ignition switch in RUN position (engine off), check ignition switch-to-regulator terminal "I" circuit. Verify circuit is not open or indicator bulb is not blown. Replace bulb if necessary and recheck.
3) If indicator light still does not come on, disconnect wiring connector from regulator. Connect a jumper wire from "I" terminal to battery negative post. *See Fig. 1.* Turn ignition switch to RUN position (engine off).

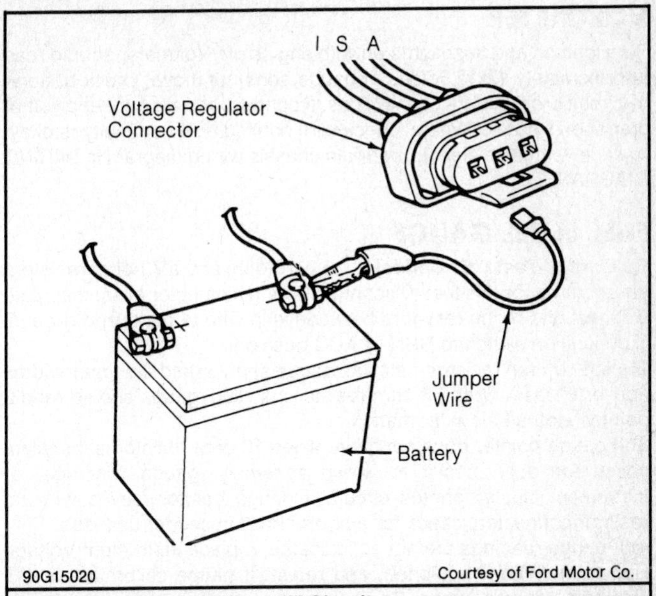
I S A
Voltage Regulator
Connector
Jumper
Wire
Battery
90G15020
Courtesy of Ford Motor Co.

Fig. 1: Checking Regulator "I" Circuit

If indicator light does not come on, check bulb for continuity and replace if necessary. If bulb is good, perform voltage regulator "I" circuit tests. See appropriate ALTERNATOR article in ELECTRICAL.
4) On Bronco, "E" and "F" Series, check 500-ohm resistor across indicator light. On all others, if indicator light comes on, remove jumper wire and reconnect regulator connector. Connect VOM negative lead to negative battery post. Connect positive lead to voltage regulator terminal "A" screw at alternator. Battery voltage should be indicated.
5) If battery voltage is not indicated, repair circuit "A" wiring. If battery voltage is present, clean and tighten ground connections of alternator and regulator. Turn ignition to RUN (engine off). If indicator light still does not come on, replace regulator. See appropriate chassis wiring diagram in WIRING DIAGRAMS.

SHIFT INDICATOR LIGHT

1) The shift indicator light is intended to help driver obtain optimum fuel economy. On EEC-IV vehicles, the system is integrated into the EEC module. System is controlled by engine speed and manifold vacuum. Light does not come on in top gear. When engine speed is greater than 900 RPM and engine vacuum is greater than 5 in. Hg at part throttle, light comes on to indicate gear should be upshifted.
2) There is a one-second delay before the light comes on. If light does not come on, check indicator bulb, printed circuit and cluster connector power and tightness. If these are okay, check circuit from cluster to transmission. See appropriate chassis wiring diagram in WIRING DIAGRAMS.

4WD INDICATOR

If the 4WD or low range indicator lights do not come on when 4WD or low range is engaged, check fuse No. 18. If the fuse is okay, check indicator bulbs. If bulbs are okay, check indicator switch continuity. See appropriate chassis wiring diagram in WIRING DIAGRAMS.

ANTI-LOCK BRAKE INDICATOR

See ANTI-LOCK – RABS article in BRAKES.

AMMETER

1) With engine off, turn headlights on. Meter pointer should move toward "D" (discharge) side of gauge. If pointer does not function as indicated, check continuity between battery and ammeter.
2) If there is continuity, replace ammeter. If ammeter pointer moves toward "C" (charge) side of gauge with lights on and engine off, reverse ammeter connections. See appropriate chassis wiring diagram in WIRING DIAGRAMS.

1991 SAFETY EQUIPMENT
Analog Instrument Panels (Cont.)

VOLTMETER

Turn ignition and headlights on with engine off. Voltmeter should read approximately 12-12.5 volts. If gauge does not move, check battery-to-circuit breaker wire connections. If connections are tight and voltmeter shows no movement, check wire continuity. If continuity is okay, replace voltmeter. See appropriate chassis wiring diagram in WIRING DIAGRAMS.

FUEL LEVEL GAUGE

Calibration Test ("E" Series) - 1) A 10-ohm and a 73-ohm resistors are required for this test. Disconnect wiring connector at sending unit. Connect one of the resistors between lead wire terminal and ground. Turn ignition switch to RUN or ACC position.

2) With 10-ohm resistor installed, gauge should read 2 pointer widths above "F" mark. With 73-ohm resistor installed, gauge should read 2 pointer widths below "E" mark.

3) If gauge pointer does not move when 10-ohm resistor is installed, check for open circuit in wiring assembly, gauge windings, or instrument cluster printed circuit. If gauge pointer moves with no resistor connected, check for a short circuit in sender unit lead.

4) If gauge readings are not as indicated, replace Instrument Voltage Regulator (IVR) if equipped, and retest. If gauge calibration is still incorrect, replace gauge. See appropriate chassis wiring diagram in WIRING DIAGRAMS.

Calibration Test (Bronco & "F" Series) - 1) Use 22-ohm and 145-ohm resistors. Install 22-ohm resistor in circuit between gauge and ground. Repeat same procedure with 145-ohm resistor.

2) The 22-ohm resistor should produce an empty reading, while the 145-ohm resistor will cause gauge to read full. See appropriate chassis wiring diagram in WIRING DIAGRAMS.

Calibration Test (Aerostar, Explorer & Ranger) - 1) Use Rotunda Gauge Tester (021-00055) to check fuel gauge. Place ignition switch in OFF position. Install rotunda gauge tester in circuit. Set tester to 22-ohm position. Turn ignition on. Wait 60 seconds, and then read fuel gauge.

2) If gauge reads "E", go to step **5)**. If gauge does not read "E", turn ignition switch off, then turn it back on. Tap on instrument panel and wait one minute. If gauge goes to "E", check for intermittent B+ connection at cluster connector, or damaged printed circuit.

3) Repair as necessary and repeat test. If after repeating test, gauge does not read "E", turn ignition off. Remove instrument cluster and inspect printed circuit for damage. Remove slosh module located on back of cluster. Connect jumper wire from gauge tester to fuel gauge terminal "S" (Yellow/White wire).

4) Turn ignition on and observe gauge. If gauge does not read "E", replace gauge. If gauge reads "E", replace slosh module.

5) Turn ignition off. Set rotunda gauge tester to 145-ohm setting. Turn ignition on, wait 60 seconds, and read fuel gauge. If gauge reads "F", check sender circuit wiring for shorts or opens with ohmmeter. If gauge does not read "F", turn ignition off and remove instrument cluster. See INSTRUMENT CLUSTER under REMOVAL & INSTALLATION.

6) Inspect printed circuit to ensure loop connecting fuel sender input to fuel gauge is cut. If loop is not cut, correctly cut printed circuit at loop. Remove slosh module from rear of cluster, and connect jumper wire from gauge tester to fuel gauge terminal "S" (Yellow/White wire). Reconnect cluster connector and recheck gauge.

7) If fuel gauge reads "F", replace slosh module. If gauge does not read "F", replace gauge. Check fuel gauge resistance using ohmmeter. Gauge should read EMPTY at 22.5 ohms and FULL at 145 ohms. See appropriate chassis wiring diagram in WIRING DIAGRAMS.

OIL PRESSURE GAUGE

Calibration Test (With Tester) - 1) Disconnect connector from oil sender and connect to Rotunda Gauge Tester No. 021-00055. Attach other tester lead to ground on vehicle. Turn ignition switch to ACC position. Turn tester switch to IVR CHECK position. A flashing light indicates IVR and wiring are functional.

2) Place tester switch in LOW (73 ohms) position. If gauge does not move, go to step **3)**. If gauge reads "L", set gauge tester to HIGH (9.7 ohms) position. If gauge reads approximately midrange on scale, replace sender. If gauge does not read approximately midrange on scale, go to step **3)**.

3) Check sender circuit wiring for shorts and opens with ohmmeter. If wiring is okay, replace gauge. If wiring is shorted or open, repair wiring as necessary. See appropriate chassis wiring diagram in WIRING DIAGRAMS.

Calibration Test (Without Tester) - 1) Test oil pressure gauge with a 10-ohm resistor for high calibration, and a 73-ohm resistor for low calibration.

2) Turn ignition on and connect a 10-ohm resistor between gauge lead and ground. The pointer should read at midrange on scale. Remove 10-ohm resistor, and connect 73-ohm resistor. Gauge reading should be around the "L" mark.

3) If gauge readings are not as indicated, replace gauge and retest. If readings are as indicated, replace oil pressure sender. See appropriate chassis wiring diagram in WIRING DIAGRAMS.

TEMPERATURE GAUGE

Calibration Test (With Tester) - 1) Disconnect connector from temperature sender and connect to Rotunda Gauge Tester (021-00055). Attach other tester lead to ground on vehicle. Turn ignition switch to ACC position. Turn tester switch to IVR CHECK position. A flashing light indicates IVR and wiring are functional.

2) Place tester switch in LOW (73 ohms) position. If gauge does not move, go to step **3)**. If gauge reads "C", set gauge tester to HIGH (9.7 ohms) position. If gauge reads "H", replace sender. If gauge does not read "H", go to step **3)**.

3) Check sender circuit wiring for shorts and opens with ohmmeter. If wiring is okay, replace gauge. If wiring is shorted or open, repair wiring as necessary. See appropriate chassis wiring diagram in WIRING DIAGRAMS.

Calibration Test (Without Tester) - 1) Test temperature gauge with a 10-ohm resistor for high calibration, and a 73-ohm resistor for low calibration.

2) Turn ignition on and connect a 10-ohm resistor between gauge lead and ground. Pointer should read within band around "H" mark. Connect 73-ohm resistor in place of 10-ohm resistor. Gauge should now read around "C" mark.

3) If gauge readings are not as indicated, replace gauge and retest. If readings are as indicated, replace temperature sender. See appropriate chassis wiring diagram in WIRING DIAGRAMS.

TACHOMETER

NOTE: Information is not available on Aerostar, Explorer and Ranger.

Bronco, "E" & "F" Series (Gasoline Engines) - 1) The tachometer on Bronco and "F" Series can be used on 6-cylinder or V8 engines. Tachometer terminals "B" (12 volts), "C" (coil negative) and "G" (ground) are connected when used on 6-cylinder engines. A fourth terminal, "8" (V8 ground), is grounded through wiring harness for V8 operation. *See Fig. 2.*

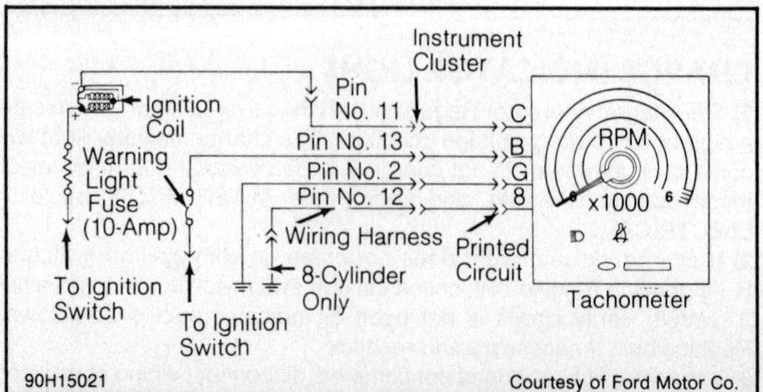
Instrument
Cluster
Pin
No. 11
Ignition
Coil
Pin No. 13
Warning
Light
Fuse
(10-Amp)
Pin No. 2
Pin No. 12
C
B
G
8
RPM
x1000
Wiring Harness
Printed
Circuit
8-Cylinder
Only
To Ignition
Switch
To Ignition
Switch
Tachometer
90H15021
Courtesy of Ford Motor Co.

Fig. 2: Tachometer Wiring Schematic (Gasoline Engines)

1991 SAFETY EQUIPMENT
Analog Instrument Panels (Cont.)

2) Check fuse and replace if blown. Check for loose wiring connections in engine compartment or at instrument cluster. Secure where necessary. Disconnect negative battery cable. Remove instrument cluster. See INSTRUMENT CLUSTER under REMOVAL & INSTALLATION. Check resistance and voltage using a Volt-Ohmmeter (VOM).

3) Check pin No. 2 of cluster harness connector "B" for resistance to ground. Reading should be one ohm or less. *See Fig. 3*. Check pin No. 7 of cluster harness connector "A" for resistance to ground (V8), or open circuit (6-cylinder). Reading should be one ohm or less.

4) Check pin No. 6 of connector "A" for resistance to negative terminal of ignition coil. Reading should be one ohm or less. Connect battery and turn ignition on. Check voltage at pin No. 13 of connector "A". Voltage should be 12 volts. Turn ignition off. Disconnect battery.

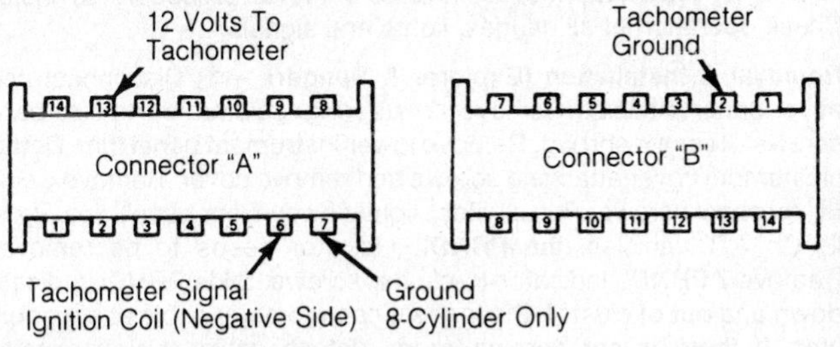
12 Volts To
Tachometer
Tachometer
Ground
14 13 12 11 10 9 8
7 6 5 4 3 2 1
Connector "A"
Connector "B"
1 2 3 4 5 6 7
8 9 10 11 12 13 14
Tachometer Signal
Ignition Coil (Negative Side)
Ground
8-Cylinder Only

90I15022 Courtesy of Ford Motor Co.

Fig. 3: Identifying Terminals of Cluster Harness Connectors "A" & "B" (Gasoline Engines)

5) If readings are not as specified, problem is not in tachometer. Service wiring. If readings are as specified, check for loose or missing cluster connection clips. Check for damaged printed circuit. Reseat or replace missing clips. Replace printed circuit as necessary. If connection clips and printed circuit are okay, replace tachometer. See appropriate chassis wiring diagram in WIRING DIAGRAMS.

E250/350 & F250/350 (7.3L Diesel – Automatic Transmission) – This tachometer circuit is run through the DCP-100 Transmission Controller. If tachometer is inoperative, start engine and let idle. At

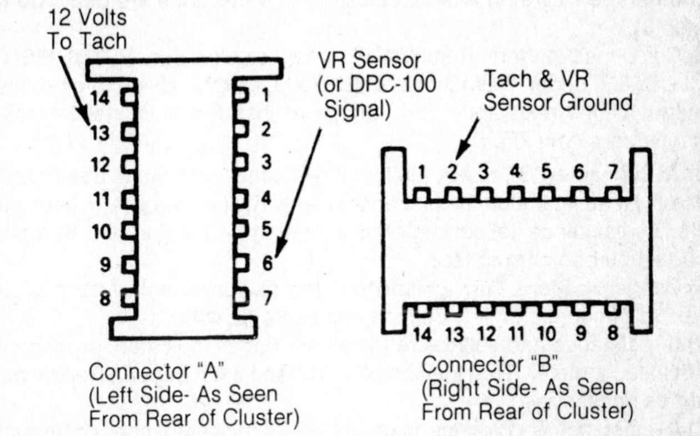
12 Volts
To Tach
VR Sensor
(or DPC-100
Signal)
Tach & VR
Sensor Ground
14 13 12 11 10 9 8
1 2 3 4 5 6 7
1 2 3 4 5 6 7
14 13 12 11 10 9 8
Connector "A"
(Left Side- As Seen
From Rear of Cluster)
Connector "B"
(Right Side- As Seen
From Rear of Cluster)

117107 Courtesy of Ford Motor Co.

Fig. 6: Identifying Instrument Cluster Harness Connectors Terminals (7.3L Diesel)

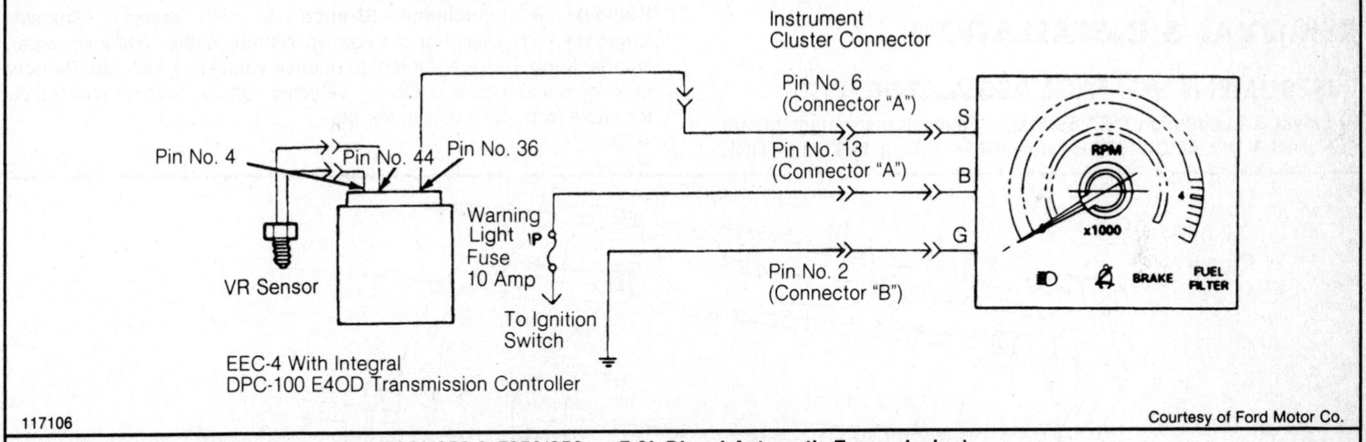
Instrument
Cluster Connector
Pin No. 6
(Connector "A")
S
Pin No. 4
Pin No. 44
Pin No. 36
Pin No. 13
(Connector "A")
B
Warning
Light
Fuse
10 Amp
G
Pin No. 2
(Connector "B")
VR Sensor
To Ignition
Switch
EEC-4 With Integral
DPC-100 E4OD Transmission Controller
RPM
x1000
BRAKE
FUEL
FILTER

117106 Courtesy of Ford Motor Co.

Fig. 4: Tachometer Wiring Schematic (E250/350 & F250/350 – 7.3L Diesel Automatic Transmission)

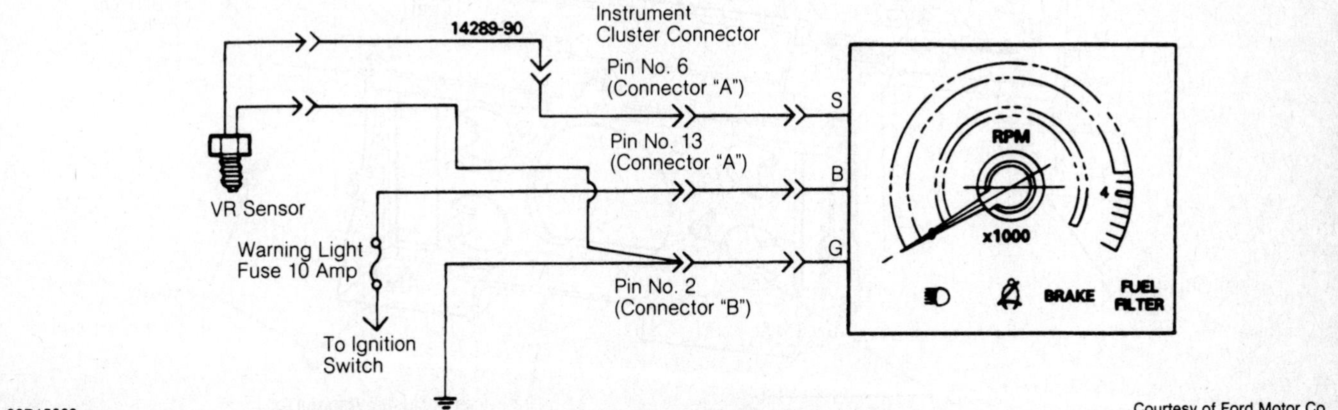
14289-90
Instrument
Cluster Connector
Pin No. 6
(Connector "A")
S
Pin No. 13
(Connector "A")
B
VR Sensor
Warning Light
Fuse 10 Amp
G
Pin No. 2
(Connector "B")
To Ignition
Switch
RPM
x1000
BRAKE
FUEL
FILTER

90B15009 Courtesy of Ford Motor Co.

Fig. 5: Tachometer Wiring Schematic (E250/350 & F250/35 – 7.3L Diesel Manual Transmission)

1991 SAFETY EQUIPMENT
Analog Instrument Panels (Cont.)

connector "A", check AC voltage output signal at Pin No. 6. *See Fig. 4.* Voltage should be at least 300 mV. If voltage is not as specified, replace tachometer.

E250/350 & F250/350 (7.3L Diesel – Manual Transmission) – 1) The electronic-operated tachometer, mounted in the instrument cluster assembly, indicates engine speed in Revolutions Per Minute (RPM). The tachometer receives its signal from the Variable Reluctance Sensor (VRS) mounted in injection pump timing gear cover.

2) If tachometer is inoperative or erratic, check fuse. If fuse is blown, check for short circuit. Check for loose wire connections in engine compartment or at instrument cluster. If connections are okay, go to step **3)**.

3) Disconnect battery. Remove instrument cluster. See INSTRUMENT CLUSTER under REMOVAL & INSTALLATION. Using digital test meter, check resistance and voltage at instrument cluster harness connectors. *See Fig. 5.*

4) At connector "B", check pin No. 2 resistance to ground. *See Figs. 5 and 6.* Reading should be one ohm or less. At connector "A", check pin No. 6 resistance to corresponding mating connector pin. Reading should be one ohm or less.

5) Connect battery. Turn ignition to RUN position. Check voltage at pin No. 13 of connector "A". Voltage should be 12 volts.

6) If resistance and voltage readings are not as indicated, problem is not in tachometer. Turn ignition off and disconnect battery. Repair wiring as necessary.

7) If resistance and voltage readings are as indicated, check for loose tachometer retention clips at rear of instrument cluster. Check for damaged printed circuit. Check VRS in injection pump timing gear cover. Repair or replace as necessary.

8) Remove sensor and check resistance across sensor terminals. If reading is not 2000-3000 ohms, replace sensor.

REMOVAL & INSTALLATION

INSTRUMENT VOLTAGE REGULATOR (IVR)

Removal & Installation ("E" Series) – Remove instrument cluster. See INSTRUMENT CLUSTER under REMOVAL & INSTALLATION. Disconnect printed circuit connector buttons from IVR. Remove retaining screw and remove IVR. To install, reverse removal procedure.

INSTRUMENT CLUSTER

NOTE: In some cases, it may be necessary to remove speedometer cable at the transmission, and pulling cable through cowl.

Removal & Installation (Aerostar) – 1) Disconnect negative battery cable. Remove 7 cluster housing-to-cluster screws. Remove cluster housing. Remove 4 cluster-to-instrument panel screws. *See Fig. 7.* Disconnect wiring harness connectors from rear of cluster. Disconnect speedometer cable.

2) Before installation, apply a 3/16" ball of silicone lubricant to drive hole of speedometer head. Reverse removal procedure to install. Check operation of all gauges, lights and signals.

Removal & Installation (Explorer & Ranger) – 1) Disconnect negative battery cable. Remove 2 steering column shroud-to-panel screws. Remove shroud. Remove lower instrument panel trim. Detach cluster trim cover attaching screws and remove cover. Remove 4 cluster-to-panel screws. Pull cluster slightly away from panel. *See Fig. 8.*

2) On A/T vehicles, the PRNDL indicator needs to be removed. Remove 2 PRNDL indicator-to-cluster screws. Slide PRNDL indicator down and out of cluster. Disconnect speedometer cable at speedometer. If there is not enough room, detach cable at transmission. Disconnect wiring harness connector from printed circuit.

3) Disconnect bulbs from sockets and remove instrument cluster. Before installation, apply a 3/16" ball of silicone lubricant to drive hole of speedometer head. Reverse removal procedure to install. Check operation of all gauges, lights and signals.

Removal & Installation (Bronco & "F" Series – Gasoline Engines) – 1) Disconnect negative battery cable. Remove wiper/washer knob. Use a hook tool to release each knob lock tab. Remove steering column shroud. On A/T vehicles, remove loop on shift indicator cable from column retainer pin.

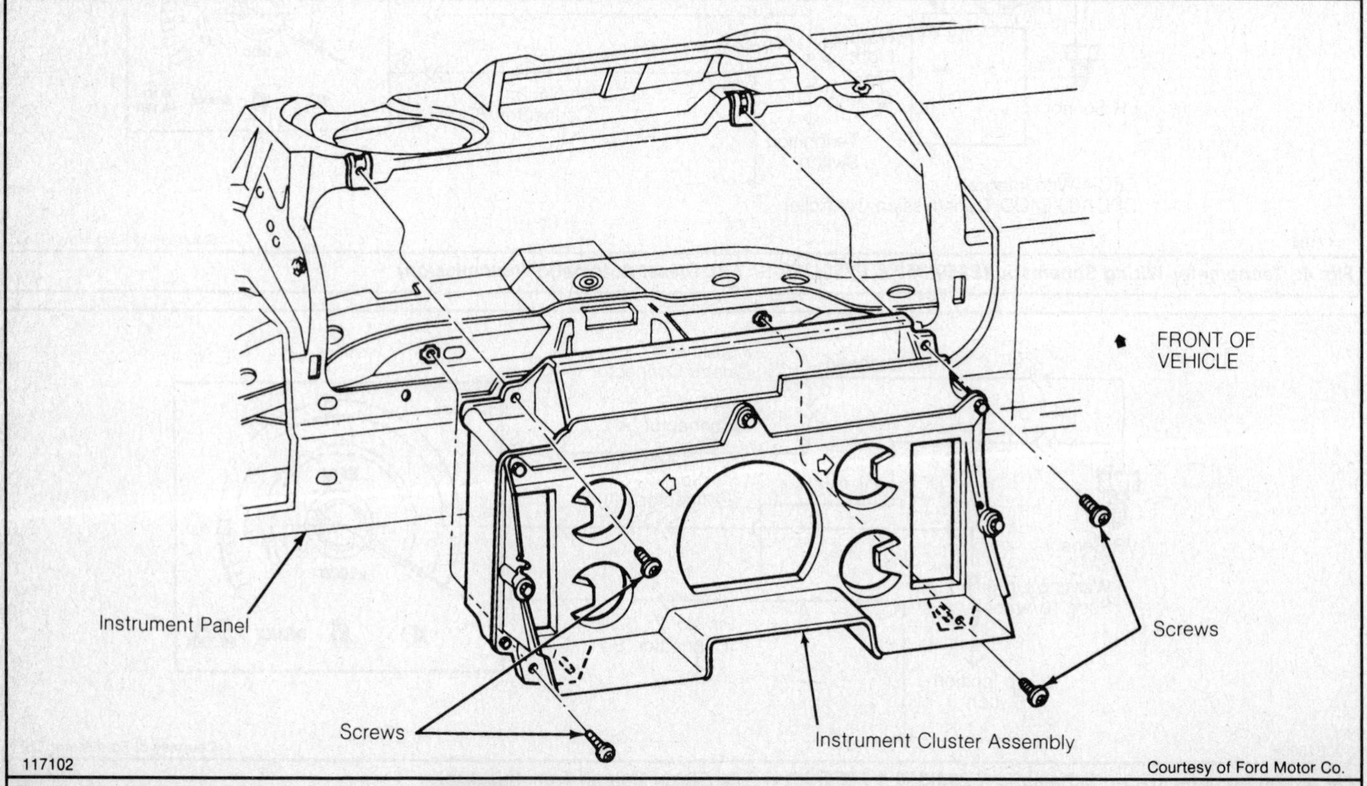
FRONT OF
VEHICLE
Instrument Panel
Screws
Screws
Instrument Cluster Assembly
117102
Courtesy of Ford Motor Co.

Fig. 7: Exploded View of Instrument Panel (Aerostar)

1991 SAFETY EQUIPMENT
Analog Instrument Panels (Cont.)

2) Remove bracket screw from cable bracket, and slide bracket out of slot in tube. Remove cluster finish panel. *See Fig. 9*. Remove 4 cluster-to-panel screws. Pull cluster away from panel to disconnect speedometer cable and electrical connectors. To install, reverse removal procedure.

Removal & Installation ("E" Series - Gasoline Engine) - Disconnect negative battery cable. Remove 7 instrument cluster attaching screws. *See Fig. 10*. Position cluster away from panel to access speedometer cable. Disconnect speedometer cable and harness connector from printed circuit. Remove cluster assembly from panel. To install, reverse removal procedure.

Removal & Installation (E250/350 & F250/350 - 7.3L Diesel) - Disconnect battery. Remove instrument cluster. Remove 6 cluster lens-to-cluster backplate screws, and remove cluster lens. Remove tachometer by prying tachometer dial away from cluster backplate (tachometer is retained to backplate by clips). To install, reverse removal procedure.

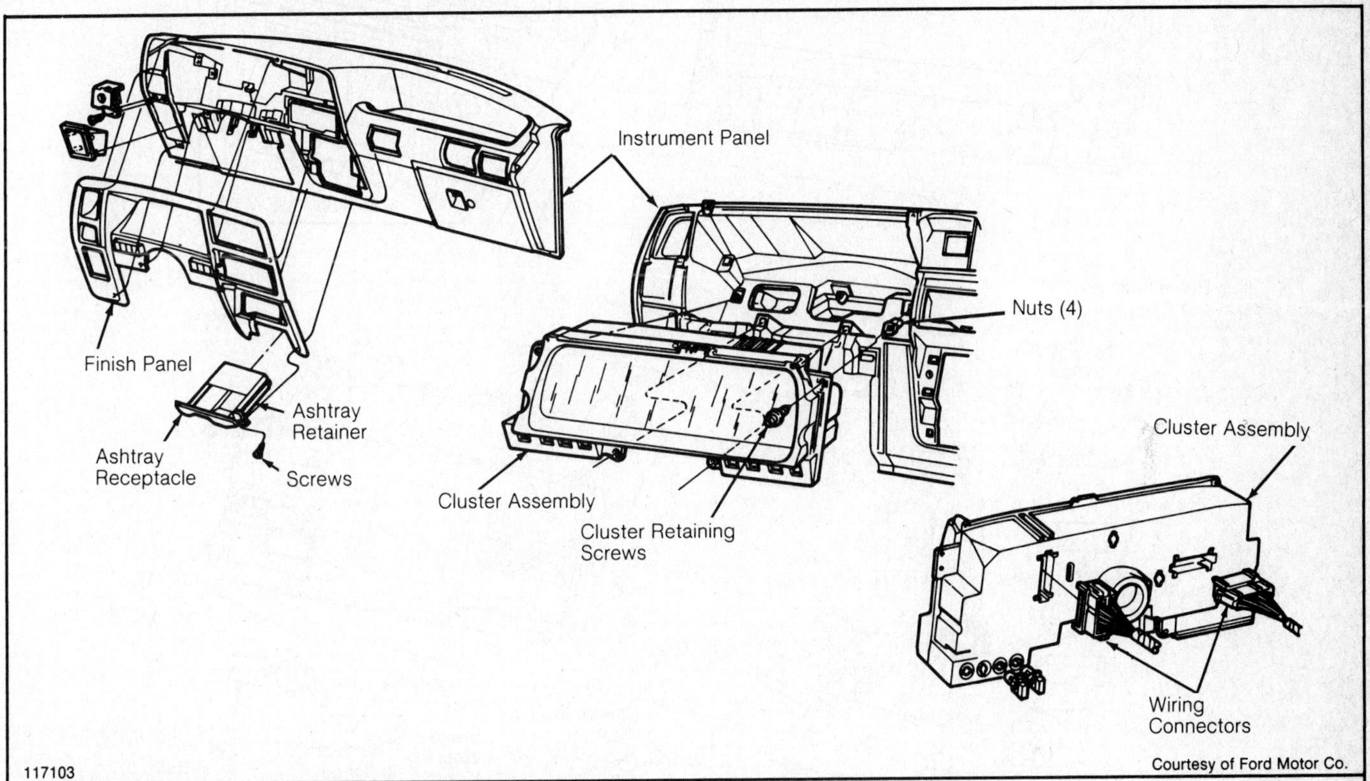
Instrument Panel
Nuts (4)
Finish Panel
Ashtray Retainer
Ashtray Receptacle
Screws
Cluster Assembly
Cluster Retaining Screws
Cluster Assembly
Wiring Connectors
117103
Courtesy of Ford Motor Co.

Fig. 8: Exploded View of Instrument Panel (Explorer & Ranger)

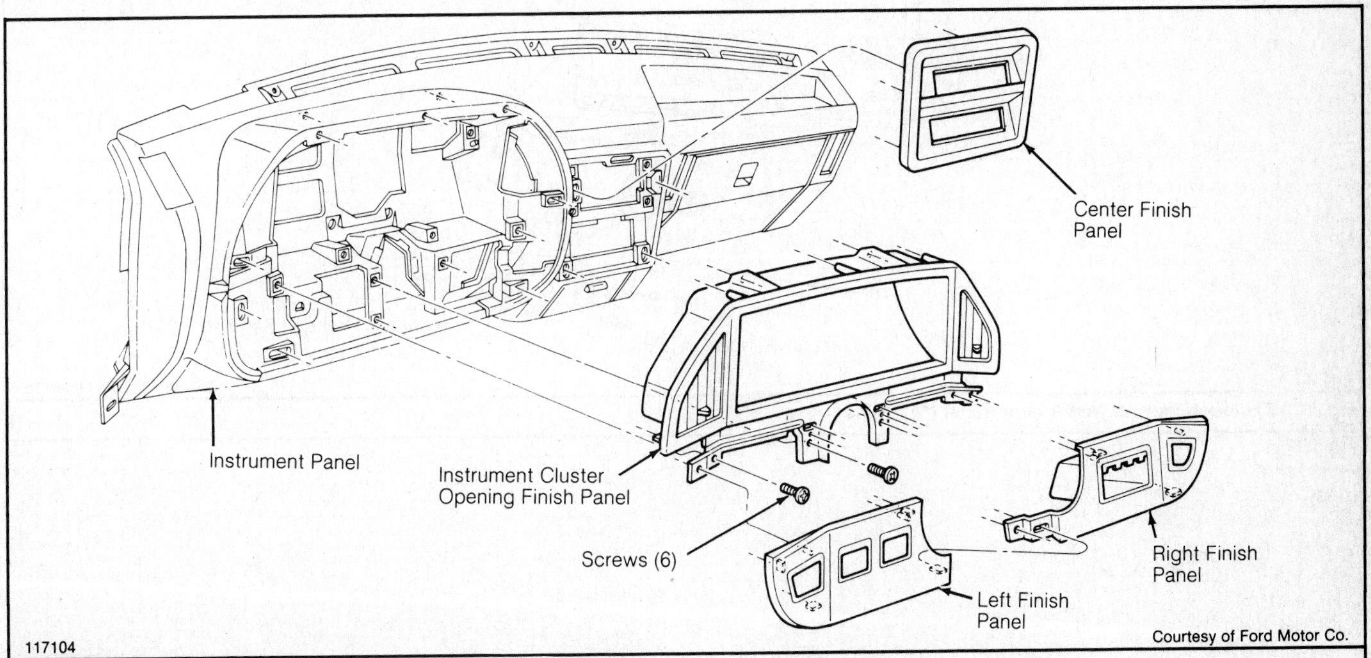
Center Finish Panel
Instrument Panel
Instrument Cluster Opening Finish Panel
Screws (6)
Right Finish Panel
Left Finish Panel
117104
Courtesy of Ford Motor Co.

Fig. 9: Exploded View of Instrument Panel (Bronco & "F" Series)

1991 SAFETY EQUIPMENT
Analog Instrument Panels (Cont.)

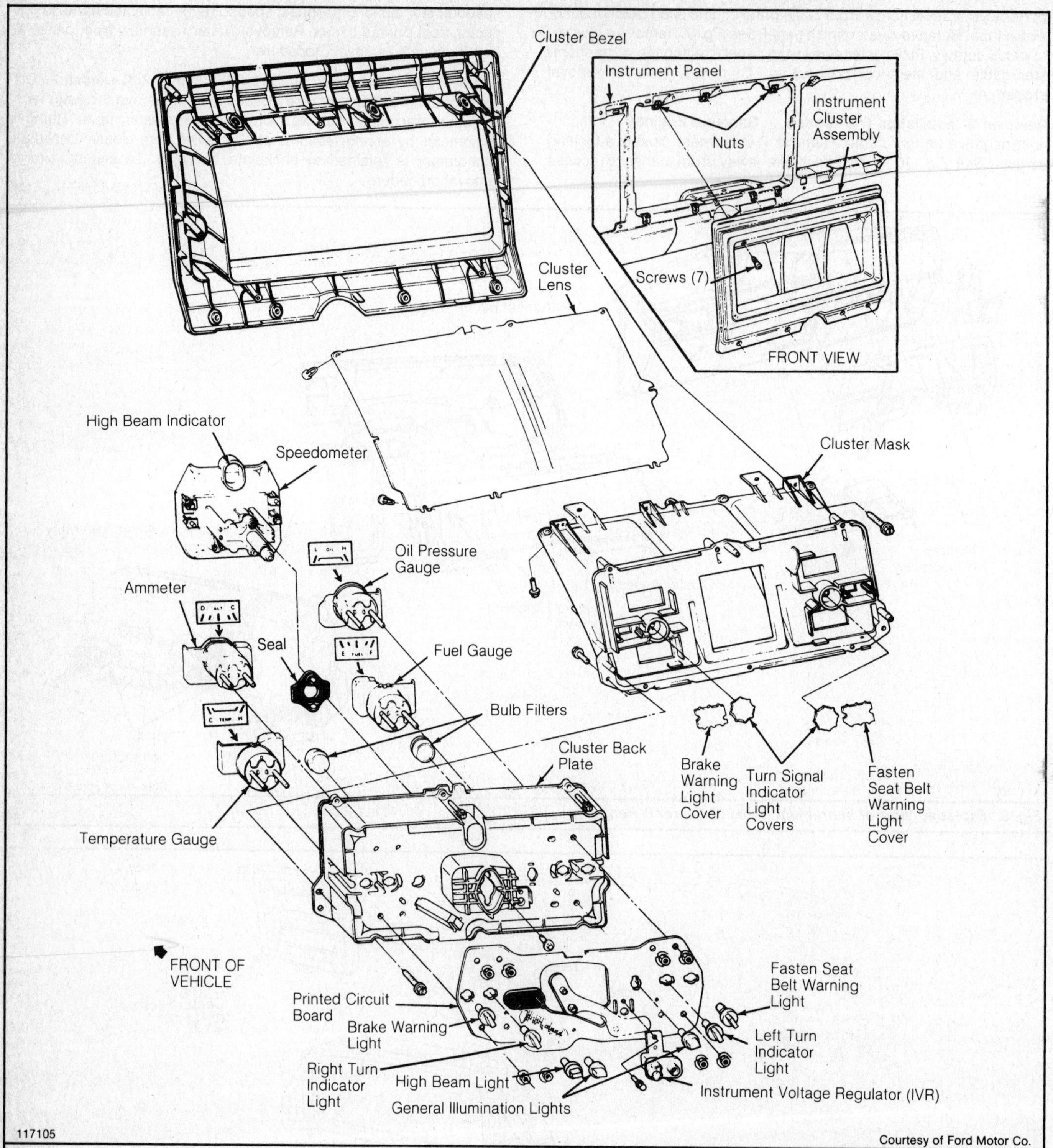
Cluster Bezel
Instrument Panel
Instrument Cluster Assembly
Nuts
Screws (7)
FRONT VIEW
Cluster Lens
High Beam Indicator
Speedometer
Cluster Mask
Oil Pressure Gauge
Ammeter
Seal
Fuel Gauge
Bulb Filters
Cluster Back Plate
Brake Warning Light Cover
Turn Signal Indicator Light Covers
Fasten Seat Belt Warning Light Cover
Temperature Gauge
FRONT OF VEHICLE
Printed Circuit Board
Brake Warning Light
Right Turn Indicator Light
High Beam Light
General Illumination Lights
Fasten Seat Belt Warning Light
Left Turn Indicator Light
Instrument Voltage Regulator (IVR)
117105

Courtesy of Ford Motor Co.

Fig. 10: Exploded View of Instrument Panel ("E" Series)

1991 SAFETY EQUIPMENT
Electronic Instrument Panels

Aerostar

DESCRIPTION & OPERATION

The optional Electronic Instrument Cluster (EIC) consists of 2 multi-colored Liquid Crystal Display (LCD) modules and a graphic warning display center. The 2 electronic modules are speedometer/odometer module, and tachometer/multigauge module. The EIC is operational with ignition switch in RUN position.

The EIC is illuminated by bulbs which are a part of the cluster, not the modules. When headlights are turned on, LCD bulbs are switched over to the dimming rheostat through a relay. The EIC communicates warnings and acknowledges commands through tones sounded through a connection to a tone generator.

It is normal for the 2 displays to be slightly out of sync with each other. Each time the ignition is turned on, the electronic display will go through a bulb check by momentarily lighting all display segments and turning them off. The left display is a tachometer/multigauge module, displaying fuel remaining, engine temperature, oil pressure, charging system voltage or engine RPM.

The center cluster display is a speedometer/odometer module, displaying vehicle speed in either MPH or km/h and trip mileage. The right display provides information on washer fluid level and warning lights, including DOOR-AJAR, HIGH-BEAMS ON, FASTEN SEAT BELT and BRAKE SYSTEM FAILURE. *See Fig. 1.*

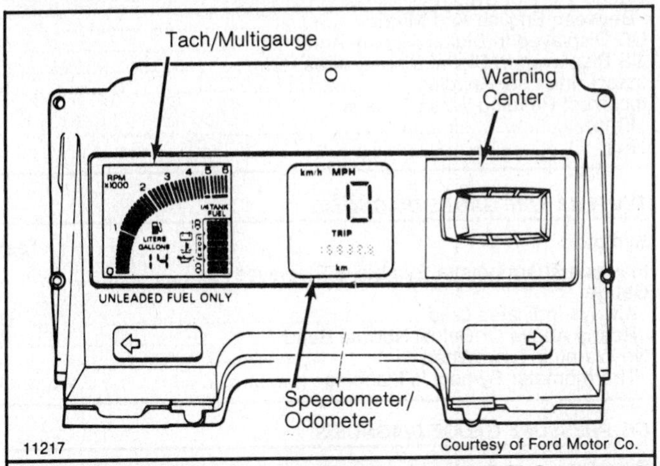
Tach/Multigauge
Warning
Center
RPM
x1000
UNLEADED FUEL ONLY
km/h MPH
TRIP
Speedometer/
Odometer
11217
Courtesy of Ford Motor Co.

Fig. 1: Identifying Electronic Instrument Cluster (EIC) Components

SWITCH CONTROL MODULE

English/Metric – Depressing ENGLISH/METRIC switch changes cluster readout between English and Metric gauge measurements.

Trip/Distance – Depressing TRIP/DISTANCE switch will display either trip or accumulated odometer mileage.

Trip Reset – Depressing TRIP RESET switch will cancel trip mileage recorded by speedometer module memory. This switch operates only when trip odometer readout has been previously selected.

Gauge Select – The GAUGE SELECT switch controls display of 4 different gauges on tach/multigauge module. The fuel tank level gauge will automatically be displayed when ignition is turned on. Depressing GAUGE SELECT switch one time will change display to temperature gauge.

Depressing switch again will display oil pressure. Depressing switch a third time will change to battery voltage. Depressing switch again will blank out display. Depressing switch again will return to fuel tank level gauge.

Expand Fuel (Below 1/4 Tank) – Depressing EXPAND FUEL switch will display, in analog form, last one-quarter fuel tank. A full scale display (8 bar segments lit) indicates 1/4 TANK FULL. Zero bar segments indicate an empty tank. After 5 seconds, readout returns to previous function.

TEMPERATURE GAUGE

The temperature gauge is accessed by depressing GAUGE SELECT switch once. Temperature is indicated by bar segments lit on display. If temperature is greater than normal, temperature display will appear in multigauge area. Thermometer warning symbol on display center will flash and a warning tone will sound.

FUEL GAUGE

Analog – The following fuel level displays are available on the analog fuel gauge: "E", 1/4, 1/2, 3/4 and "F". When ignition is turned on, fuel gauge will display full level to ensure all bar segments are operational. The bars of the analog fuel gauge represent relative percentage of fuel left. It does not necessarily agree with digital fuel gauge transition points.

"F" is displayed for fuel levels greater than 15 gals. (57L) for a 17-gal. (64L) tank, or fuel levels greater than 19 gals. (72L) for a 21-gal. (79L) tank. "E" is displayed for fuel levels less than 2 gals. (7.5L) for either tank. The gas pump symbol will flash when fuel level is at 2 gals. (7.5L) for 17-gal. (64L) tank, or 3 gals. (12L) for 21-gal. (79L) tank.

Digital – This display area indicates the number of gallons or liters of fuel remaining, depending on position of ENGLISH/METRIC switch. When ignition is turned on, complete fuel gauge readout is displayed to ensure that display segments are operational (display reads 88).

ODOMETER

Vehicle Distance – The accumulated mileage is stored in a non-volatile memory every 10 miles, and every time ignition is turned off. If speedometer module does not receive a valid odometer signal, the ERROR symbol will appear in odometer display area.

When a defective speedometer/odometer module is replaced, an "S" symbol is displayed in upper right-hand corner of display. A sticker showing previous mileage must be affixed to driver's door pillar.

Trip Distance – Depressing TRIP/DISTANCE switch will change accumulated mileage display to a 4-digit accumulated trip mileage display. If speedometer module does not receive a valid odometer signal, the ERROR symbol will appear in odometer display area.

OIL PRESSURE

The oil pressure reading can be accessed by depressing GAUGE SELECT switch 2 times. The relative oil pressure is indicated by number of bar segments lit on multigauge display.

If oil pressure drops below normal, oil pressure display will automatically appear in display area along with oil can warning symbol. A warning tone will also be heard.

SPEEDOMETER

The speedometer module receives speed and distance signals from a transmission-mounted speed sensor. The maximum speedometer reading is 85 MPH or 199 km/h. When ignition is turned on, entire speedometer readout is displayed (display reads 188) to ensure all display segments are operational.

If a defective speedometer module has been replaced, an "S" symbol is displayed in upper right-hand corner of display. A sticker showing previous mileage must be affixed to driver's door pillar.

TACHOMETER

The moving tachometer bar graph receives a signal from ignition coil. When engine speed is 0-6000 RPM, each bar segment represents 250 RPM for 3.0L engine. When engine speed is 0-5000 RPM, each bar segment represents 200 RPM for 4.0L engine. Tachometer for 3.0L engine will read 6500 RPM for all engine speeds greater than 6000 RPM. Tachometer for 4.0L engine will read 6000 RPM for all engine speeds greater 4900 RPM.

VOLTMETER

The voltmeter reading can be accessed by depressing GAUGE SELECT switch 3 times. The charging voltage is indicated by number

1991 SAFETY EQUIPMENT
Electronic Instrument Panels (Cont.)

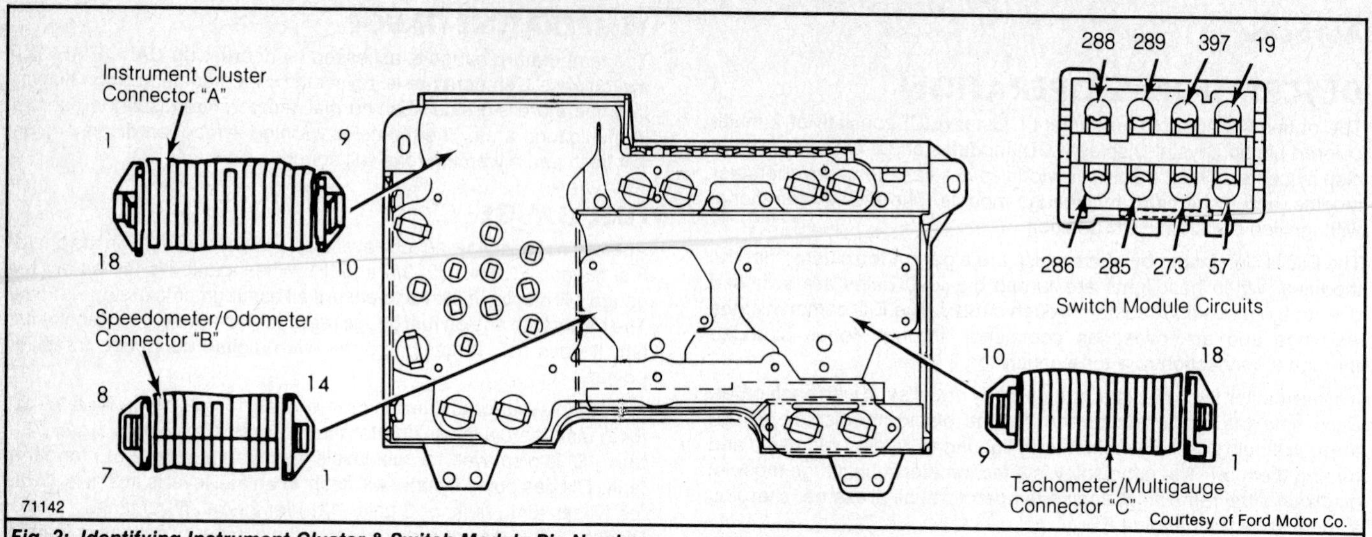
Instrument Cluster
Connector "A"
1
9
18
10
Speedometer/Odometer
Connector "B"
8
14
7
1
288
289
397
19
286
285
273
57
Switch Module Circuits
10
18
9
1
Tachometer/Multigauge
Connector "C"
71142
Courtesy of Ford Motor Co.

Fig. 2: Identifying Instrument Cluster & Switch Module Pin Numbers

of bar segments lit on display. If battery charging rate is above or below normal, voltmeter display will automatically appear along with battery warning symbol and warning tone.

TESTING & DIAGNOSIS

HOW TO USE DIAGNOSTIC TESTS

If a specific display problem exists or system malfunction occurs during self-test procedure, locate symptom in appropriate table under DIAGNOSTIC TEST DIRECTORY and proceed to the recommended test. Follow test procedures to diagnose and correct malfunction. Ensure pin numbers mentioned throughout article are correctly identified. *See Fig. 2*. After all problems have been diagnosed and repaired, repeat self-test. See SELF-TESTS.

HOW TO USE SELF-TESTS

If a general performance test of cluster operation is desired, and a specific display problem does not exist, go to SELF-TESTS. Follow self-test procedure for each module.

DIAGNOSTIC TEST DIRECTORY

Refer to the following tables for directories of tests and symptoms.

TACHOMETER/MULTIGAUGE MODULE DIAGNOSIS

Symptom	Test
All Display Segments Stuck On	C
Display Is	
Backlit But Blank	B
Dimly Lit	A
Incorrect At All Times	C
Missing Segments	C
Not Illuminated	A
Scrambled	C
Totally Black	A
Module Does Not Respond To Buttons	T
No Signal Tone	
When Buttons Are Pushed	Y
When Driver Alert Is Displayed	Y

TACHOMETER DIAGNOSIS

Symptom	Test
No Tach Reading	E
Tach Reading Always High Or Low	D
Tach Reading Erratic	E

FUEL GAUGE DIAGNOSIS

Symptom	Test
Gauge Will Not Switch Between English And Metric	F
CO Displayed In Digital Display Area	G
CS Displayed In Digital Display Area	H
Inaccurate Fuel Reading	K
Incorrect Reading When Tank Is	
Empty	J
Full	I

TEMPERATURE GAUGE DIAGNOSIS

Symptom	Test
Flashing Thermometer Symbol Is Displayed	L
Gauge	
Always Indicates Cold	N
Reads Above Or Below Normal Band	S
No Warning Tone When Thermometer Symbol Is Flashing	M

OIL PRESSURE GAUGE DIAGNOSIS

Symptom	Test
Flashing Oil Can Symbol Is Displayed	O
Gauge	
Always Indicates Low Pressure	Q
Indicates Erratic Pressure Readings	Q
No Warning Tone When Oil Can Symbol Is Flashing	P

VOLTAGE GAUGE DIAGNOSIS

Symptom	Test
Does Not Display Charge Alert Symbol	R

SPEEDOMETER/ODOMETER MODULE DIAGNOSIS

Symptom	Test
All Display Segments Stuck On	V
Display Is	
Backlit But Blank	U
Dimly Lit	A
Incorrect At All Times	V
Missing Segments	V
Not Illuminated	A
Scrambled	V
Totally Black	A
Display Will Not Switch Between English And Metric	W
Module Does Not Respond To Buttons	T
No Signal Tone	
When Buttons Are Pushed	X

1991 SAFETY EQUIPMENT
Electronic Instrument Panels (Cont.)

SPEEDOMETER DIAGNOSIS

Symptom	Test
Display	
Constantly Reads Too High Or Too Low	Z
Reads Zero MPH At All Speeds	Y
Speed Jumps Up And Down Erratically	AA

TRIP ODOMETER DIAGNOSIS

Symptom	Test
Display Will Not	
Reset	HH
Switch Between Total Mileage And Trip Mileage	GG

ODOMETER DIAGNOSIS

Symptom	Test
Display has "S" Illuminated In Upper R.H. Corner	CC
Display Reads ERROR	BB
Odometer Counts 10 Miles Then Jumps Back 10 Miles	DD
Odometer Does Not Accumulate Mileage	DD
Odometer Reading Is	
Constantly Too High Or Too Low	EE
More Or Less Mileage Than Actual	FF

SELF-TESTS

TACHOMETER/MULTIGAUGE SELF-TEST

1) Enter self-test mode by holding GAUGE SELECT button in while turning ignition on. System is now in self-test mode. Advance through tests by successively pressing GAUGE SELECT button. Exit self-test mode by completing self-test or turning ignition off.

2) A steady tone and 8 bar segments lit in tachometer bar graph display indicates a passed test. Absence of a tone, combined with 24 bar segments lit in tachometer bar graph display indicates a failed test. The test number is indicated by the number of bars lit on multigauge.

NOTE: **If test No. 1 fails, replace tachometer module.**

Tests are as follows.

- Test 1 - Microcomputer Check (RAM/ROM/Timer Test)
- Test 2 - LCD Driver Frequency
- Test 3 - Tachometer RPM Input
- Test 4 - Sensor Input - English button should be out. Walking segment on multigauge indicates sampling time. Hexadecimal number can range from 00 to FF, with the 00 appearing with zero volt or ohm, and FF appearing with high volts or high ohms. This test can be used as a wiggle test to check wiring for intermittents. Intermittents or changes in sensor values will appear as large changes in the counts number.

Reset Circuit Self-Test Patterns 90B15017

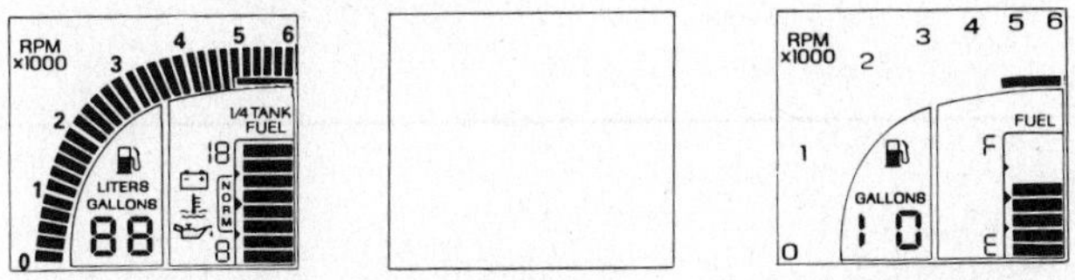

DISPLAY PROVE OUT ALL ON — DISPLAY PROVE OUT ALL OFF — NORMAL OPERATION

- Test 4A - Charging Volts
- Test 4B - Oil Pressure
- Test 4C - Fuel Level
- Test 4D - Engine Temperature
- Test 5 - Switch Input
- Test 6 - Fuel Memory Check
- Test 7 - Display Test - Nine different display patterns appear to check all segments. See SELF-TEST PATTERN DISPLAY.
- Test 8 - Reset Circuit Check (Watch Dog Test) - Test passes if all display segments are lit. See RESET CIRCUIT SELF-TEST PATTERNS

If, at any time during these tests, results in display areas are incorrect, replace tach/multigauge module. Recheck cluster operation.

Self-Test Pattern Display 117101

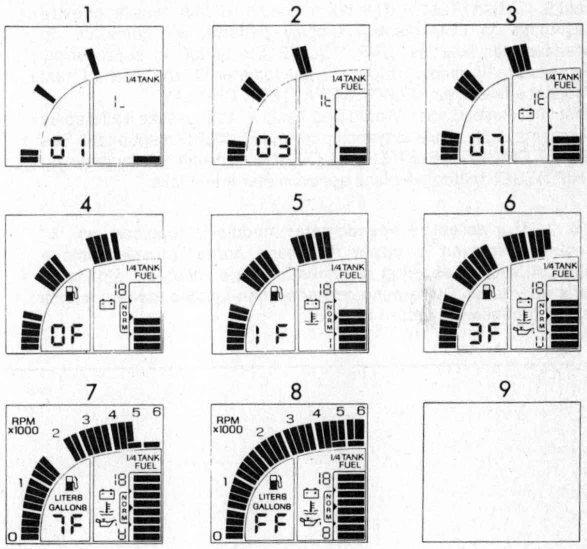
1
2
3
4
5
6
7
8
9

1991 SAFETY EQUIPMENT
Electronic Instrument Panels (Cont.)

SPEEDOMETER/ODOMETER SELF-TEST

NOTE: During self-test, the following display areas will assume new functions: the right-hand digit (zero to 9 MPH) of the speedometer display area is the pass/fail indicator, and the outer right-hand digit (10th digit) of the odometer display area is the test counter for tests 1-8.

1) Enter self-test mode by holding TRIP RESET button in and turning ignition on. Advance through tests by successively pressing TRIP RESET button. A steady tone and a "P" on speedometer display indicates passed test. No tone and an "F" on speedometer display indicates failed test.

2) The test number is shown on the 10th digit of odometer. Exit test mode by completing WATCH DOG TEST (TEST 10) or turning ignition off. If test failed, replace tachometer/multigauge module and recheck cluster operation. If test passed, go to next step.

NOTE: If tests No. 1, 2 and 7 fail, replace speedometer module.

Tests are as follows.

- Test 1 - Microcomputer Check (RAM/ROM/Timer Test)
- Test 2 - Prove Out Detect
- Test 3 - LCD Driver Frequency
- Test 4 - Speed Input
- Test 5 - Odometer Non-Volatile Memory Check - Checks for errors in odometer memory. Odometer is still functional if test does not pass. Odometer is not usable only if all memory locations are bad and ERROR is displayed on odometer.
- Test 6 - Switch Input
- Test 7 - Trip Odometer Non-Volatile Memory Check
- Test 8 - Thermistor Test
- Test 9 - Display Test - This test is used to identify missing or extra segments on LCD display. Display patterns will come up on speedometer face as TRIP ODOMETER button is successively depressed 10 times. Replace speedometer if any part of test sequence fails. See SELF-TEST PATTERN DISPLAY.
- Test 10 - Reset Circuit (Watch Dog Test) - Test passes if all display segments light while advancing through display sequence. See RESET CIRCUIT SELF-TEST PATTERNS. Activate test by pressing TRIP RESET button. Replace speedometer if test fails.

NOTE: If a defective speedometer module is replaced, an "S" symbol is displayed in upper right-hand corner of speedometer display. A sticker showing previous mileage must be affixed to driver's door pillar. Performing odometer non-volatile memory check will reset trip mileage record to zero.

Self-Test Pattern Display 17219

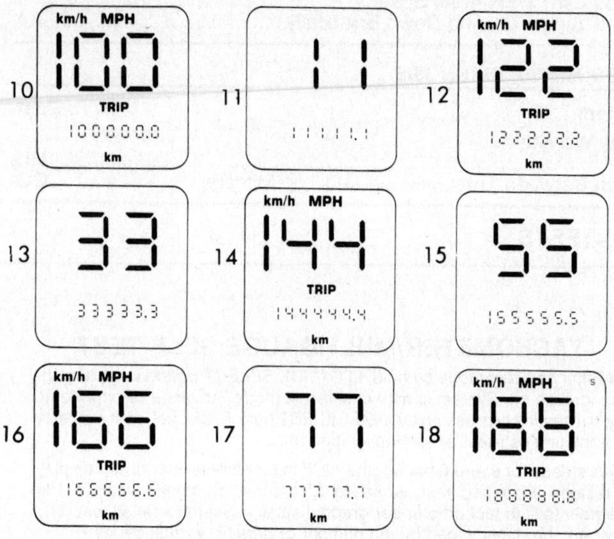
10
km/h MPH
100
TRIP
100000.0
km
11
11
111111.1
12
km/h MPH
122
TRIP
122222.2
km
13
33
333333.3
14
km/h MPH
144
TRIP
144444.4
km
15
55
555555.5
16
km/h MPH
166
TRIP
166666.6
km
17
77
777777.7
km
18
km/h MPH
188
TRIP
188888.8
km

Reset Circuit Self-Test Patterns 90C15018

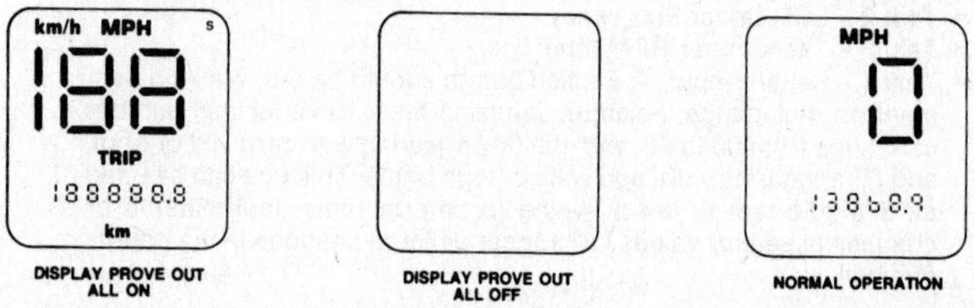
km/h MPH
188
TRIP
188888.8
km
DISPLAY PROVE OUT ALL ON
DISPLAY PROVE OUT ALL OFF
MPH
0
13868.9
NORMAL OPERATION

DIAGNOSTIC TESTS

TEST A

1) Turn ignition switch to RUN position. Check for backlighting of speedometer/odometer and tachometer/multigauge modules. If other modules are properly lit, replace bad illumination bulbs. If other modules are dim or Black, go to step **2)**.

CAUTION: Halogen illumination bulbs are pressurized and may shatter if handled incorrectly. Wear eye protection when replacing or inspecting these bulbs.

2) Turn ignition switch to RUN position. Check for display backlighting. Turn ignition off. Turn headlights on. Move dimmer control to maximum brightness. Check for display backlighting.

3) If display does not illuminate in either condition, go to step **4)**. If display only illuminates with ignition on, go to step **6)**. If display only illuminates with headlights on, go to step **4)**. If display illuminates, but very dimly, go to step **9)**.

4) Disconnect negative battery cable. Remove EIC. Reconnect harness (with cluster removed). Reconnect negative battery cable. Turn ignition switch to RUN position. Using a voltmeter, measure voltage between pins No. A4 (circuit No. 434) and A6 (circuit No. 57) of instrument cluster connector "A". *See Fig. 2.* See appropriate wiring diagram in WIRING DIAGRAMS.

5) If voltage between pins No. A4 and A6 is greater than 10 volts, correct open in ground circuit No. 57 (pin No. A6). If voltage is less than 10 volts, check power at pin No. A4, circuit No. 434, fuse and relay.

6) Disconnect negative battery cable. Remove EIC. Reconnect harness (with cluster removed). Reconnect negative battery cable. Turn headlights on and move dimmer to maximum brightness.

7) Using a voltmeter, measure voltage between pins No. A4 (circuit No. 434) and A6 (circuit No. 57). *See Fig. 2.* See appropriate chassis wiring diagram in WIRING DIAGRAMS. If voltage between pins No. A4 (circuit No. 434) and A6 (circuit No. 57) is greater than 10 volts, correct open in ground circuit No. 57 (pin No. A6). If voltage is less than 10 volts, go to next step.

8) Turn headlights on and move dimmer to maximum brightness. If instrument panel general illumination (switches, heater control panel, etc.) is not okay, check illumination relay and connecting circuits No. 434, 57 and 19. If general illumination is okay, check dimmer circuit No. 195 or dimmer fuse.

9) Disconnect negative battery cable. Remove EIC. Reconnect harness (with cluster removed). Reconnect negative battery cable. Turn ignition switch to RUN position. Check bulbs for burnt out filaments and replace bulbs if necessary.

CAUTION: Halogen illumination bulbs are pressurized and may shatter if handled incorrectly. Wear eye protection when replacing or inspecting these bulbs.

TEST B

1) Turn ignition switch to RUN position. If display is backlit but blank, check for proper operation of speedometer/odometer. If speedometer/odometer operates properly, go to step **2)**. If speedometer/odometer is not operating properly, go to step **5)**.

2) Disconnect negative battery cable. Remove EIC and prevent connector from shorting. Reconnect negative battery cable. Turn ignition switch to RUN position.

3) Using a voltmeter, check voltage at circuit No. 489 (pin No. C1). *See Fig. 2.* Refer to appropriate chassis wiring diagram in WIRING DIAGRAMS. If voltage is greater than 10 volts, go to step **4)**. If voltage is less than 10 volts, check circuit No. 489 for open between cluster pin No. C1 and splice.

4) Using an ohmmeter, check for continuity between circuit No. 397 (pin No. C2) and negative battery cable. If continuity is present, replace tachometer/multigauge module and recheck cluster operation. If no continuity exists, check for open in cluster ground circuit No. 397 (Pin No. C2).

5) Check for bad fuse in circuit No. 489. If fuse is bad, go to step **6)** before replacing fuse. If fuse is okay, go to step **2)**.

6) Before replacing fuse, turn ignition off and disconnect negative battery cable. Connect ohmmeter between circuit No. 489 and fuse ground. If continuity is present, replace fuse and recheck cluster operation. If continuity is not present, correct short in circuit No. 489. Replace fuse and recheck cluster operation.

TEST C

1) Turn ignition switch to RUN position and observe display. If all display segments light normally, then return to normal operation, go to next step. If display does not light properly, replace tachometer/multigauge assembly.

2) Ensure ENGLISH/METRIC switch is in English (released) position. Depress and hold GAUGE SELECT switch in while turning ignition switch to RUN position. Ensure display shows all zeros and note number of bar segments lit on tachometer display. Release GAUGE SELECT switch.

3) If 24 bar segments were lit on tachometer display, replace tachometer/multigauge module and recheck cluster operation. If module does not respond when GAUGE SELECT switch is depressed, go to TEST T. If normal display was shown (8 bar segments lit on tachometer and one bar lit on multigauge), go to next step.

4) Ensure ENGLISH/METRIC switch is in English (released) position. Depress and hold GAUGE SELECT switch in while turning ignition switch to RUN position. Advance to display portion of test by pushing GAUGE SELECT switch until test display appears (8 segments and a number 69). If display is correct, go to next step. If display is not correct, replace tachometer/multigauge module. See INITIAL TEST DISPLAY PATTERN.

Initial Test Display Pattern 71132

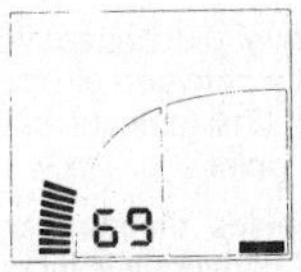
69

5) Continue advancing through each step of test display by depressing GAUGE SELECT button. Ensure the displays match the following. See TEST DISPLAY PATTERN. If all test display patterns are correct, system is okay. If display areas are incorrect, replace tachometer/multigauge module and recheck cluster operation.

Test Display Pattern 71133

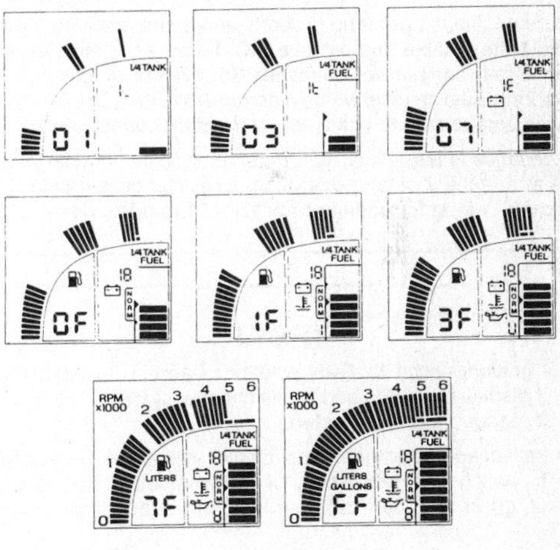
1/4 TANK
FUEL
RPM x1000
LITERS
GALLONS

TEST D

1) Ensure engine is operating properly and is not misfiring. Depress and hold GAUGE SELECT switch. After 5 seconds, a tone will be produced, and tachometer option display will appear. Display will remain as long as switch is depressed.

Typical Tach Option Display 17220

4-Cyl.

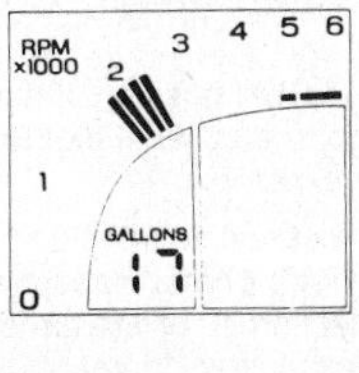
RPM x1000
0
1
2
3
4
5
6
GALLONS

V6

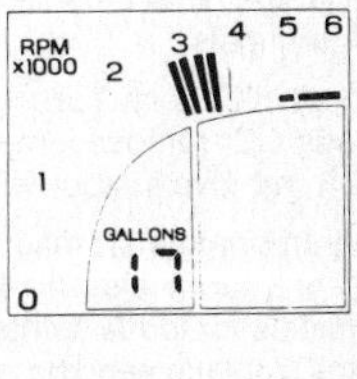
RPM x1000
0
1
2
3
4
5
6
GALLONS

1991 SAFETY EQUIPMENT
Electronic Instrument Panels (Cont.)

TEST D (Cont.)

2) If option display appears, go to step **3)**. If option display does not appear, repeat step **1)** (ensure GAUGE SELECT switch is fully depressed). Go to TEST X.

3) Note position of tachometer readout. If tachometer option readout bar segments point toward 2000 RPM, tachometer is wired for use with 4-cylinder engine. If tachometer option readout bar segments point toward 3000 RPM, tachometer is wired for use with V6 engine.

4) Ensure tachometer option display and engine match. If tachometer option and engine type match, replace tachometer and recheck cluster operation. If tachometer option and engine type do not match, tachometer wiring is incorrect. Go to step **5)** or **7)**, depending on engine type.

5) On vehicles with 4-cylinder engines, disconnect negative battery cable, and remove EIC. Check continuity between pin No. C9 (circuit No. 398) and ground. *See Fig. 2.* See appropriate chassis wiring diagram in WIRING DIAGRAMS. Continuity should exist. Check continuity between pin No. C10 (circuit No. 644) and ground. Continuity should not exist.

6) If continuity is as specified, replace tachometer/multigauge module and recheck cluster operation. If continuity is incorrect, repair as necessary to create a ground at pin No. C9 (circuit No. 398) and an open at pin No. C10 (circuit No. 644).

7) On vehicles with V6 engines, disconnect negative battery cable, and remove EIC. Check continuity between pin No. C9 (circuit No. 398) and ground, and between pin No. C10 (circuit No. 644) and ground. Continuity should not exist at either point.

8) If continuity is okay, replace tachometer/multigauge module and recheck cluster operation. If continuity is incorrect, repair as necessary to create an open at both pins No. C9 (circuit No. 398) and C10 (circuit 644) and recheck cluster operation.

TEST E

1) Ensure engine is operating properly and is not misfiring. Disconnect negative battery cable and remove EIC. Using an ohmmeter, measure resistance between pin No. C4 (circuit No. 11) and ignition coil. *See Fig. 2.* See appropriate chassis wiring diagram in WIRING DIAGRAMS. Move coil wiring side to side to check for intermittent connection.

2) If resistance is less than 100 ohms, replace tachometer/multigauge module and recheck cluster operation. If resistance is greater than 100 ohms, check wiring for open in circuit No. 11 (pin No. C4).

TEST F

1) Turn ignition switch to RUN position. Depress ENGLISH/METRIC switch. If display responds and labels change, system is okay. If display does not respond, go to next step.

2) Ensure speedometer/odometer display responds when ENGLISH/METRIC switch is depressed. If speedometer/odometer display responds, go to step **3)**. If display does not respond, go to step **3)** of TEST T.

3) Depress ENGLISH/METRIC switch several times. If fuel gauge sticks in METRIC mode, replace tachometer/multigauge module and recheck cluster operation. If fuel gauge sticks in ENGLISH mode, go to step **3)** of TEST T.

TEST G

1) Disconnect negative battery cable. Lower fuel tank to gain access to fuel sending unit connector. Unplug fuel sending unit connector, and install a jumper wire between variable resistance terminal of sender and ground terminals.

2) Reconnect battery. Turn ignition switch to RUN position. If digital display reads CO, remove jumper wire and go to step **4)**. If digital display reads CS, remove jumper wire and go to next step.

3) Using an ohmmeter, measure resistance of fuel sending unit (across sending unit terminals). If resistance is 14-163 ohms, inspect sending unit terminals for loose or intermittent connection. If resistance is not 14-163 ohms, replace sending unit and recheck cluster operation.

TEST G (Cont.)

4) Disconnect negative battery cable. Remove EIC; prevent connections from shorting. Connect jumper wire between variable resistance terminal and ground terminals of harness.

5) Check continuity between pins No. C13 (circuit No. 29) and C14 (circuit No. 397) on cluster. *See Fig. 2.* See appropriate chassis wiring diagram in WIRING DIAGRAMS. If continuity exists, replace tachometer/multigauge module and recheck cluster operation. If continuity does not exist, correct open in fuel sending unit wiring (circuit No. 29).

TEST H

1) Disconnect negative battery cable. Remove EIC and prevent connections from shorting. Using an ohmmeter, measure resistance between pins C13 and C14. *See Fig. 2.* See appropriate chassis wiring diagram in WIRING DIAGRAMS. If resistance is 14-163 ohms, replace tachometer/multigauge module and recheck cluster operation. If resistance is not 14-163 ohms, go to next step.

2) Disconnect negative battery cable. Lower fuel tank to unplug fuel sending unit connector. Unplug fuel sending unit connector. Measure resistance between pins C13 and C14 of cluster. If resistance is greater than 10,000 ohms, replace fuel sending unit and recheck cluster operation. If resistance is less than 10,000 ohms, correct short in harness.

TEST I

1) Ensure fuel tank is filled. Observe digital fuel gauge for "F" display. If a number, instead of an "F", is displayed, go to step **2)**. If "F" is displayed, system is okay.

2) Depress and hold GAUGE SELECT switch. After 5 seconds, a tone will be produced, and fuel option display will appear. Display will remain as long as switch is depressed.

Typical Fuel Option Display 17221

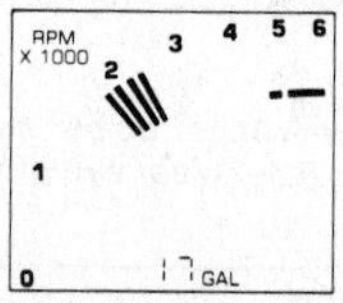
RPM
X 1000
1
2
3
4
5
6
0
GAL

3) If option display appears, go to step **4)**. If display does not appear, repeat step **2)** (ensure GAUGE SELECT switch is fully depressed). If, after repeating test, display does not appear, go to TEST S.

4) Observe fuel readout during option display mode. Fuel option readout corresponds with size of fuel tank. Ensure proper fuel option display and tank size match.

5) If fuel option and tank size match, go to step **8)**. If fuel option and tank size do not match, go to step **6)** or **7)**, depending on fuel tank size.

6) On vehicles with 17-gallon fuel tank, disconnect negative battery cable and remove EIC. Check continuity between pin No. C3 (circuit No. 396) and ground. *See Fig. 2.* See appropriate chassis wiring diagram in WIRING DIAGRAMS. Continuity should not exist. If continuity exists, repair as necessary to create an open at pin No. C3 (circuit No. 396).

7) On vehicles with 21-gallon fuel tank, disconnect negative battery cable and remove EIC. Check continuity between pin No. C3 (circuit No. 396) and ground. Continuity should exist. If continuity is not present, repair as necessary to create a closed circuit No. 396 (pin No. C3). Recheck cluster operation.

8) Ensure correct fuel tank filler neck is installed. Replace if necessary. If filler neck is okay, disconnect negative battery cable. Lower fuel tank to gain access to fuel sending unit connector, and remove fuel sending unit.

TEST I (Cont.)

9) Using an ohmmeter, measure resistance of fuel sending unit (across sending unit terminals). Resistance at EMPTY stop should be 14-17 ohms. Resistance at FULL stop should be 156-163 ohms. If resistance values are okay, go to next step. If resistance values are incorrect, replace fuel sending unit and recheck cluster operation.

10) Inspect sending unit for free movement in tank. Check tank for damage and/or distortion. If tank is okay, replace tachometer/multigauge module and recheck cluster operation. If tank is distorted or damaged, repair or replace as necessary.

TEST J

1) Disconnect negative battery cable. Lower fuel tank to gain access to fuel sending unit connector and remove fuel sending unit. Using an ohmmeter, measure resistance of fuel sending unit (across sending unit terminals). Resistance at EMPTY stop should be 14-17 ohms. Resistance at FULL stop should be 156-163 ohms.

2) If resistance values are okay at EMPTY and FULL stops, go to step **3)**. If resistance values are incorrect at either or both stops, replace fuel sending unit and recheck cluster operation.

3) Inspect sending unit for free movement in tank. Check tank for damage and/or distortion. If tank is okay, replace tachometer/multigauge module and recheck cluster operation. Replace tank if distorted or damaged.

TEST K

1) Depress and hold GAUGE SELECT switch. After 5 seconds, a tone will be produced, and fuel option display will appear. Display will remain as long as switch is depressed.

Typical Fuel Option Display 17222

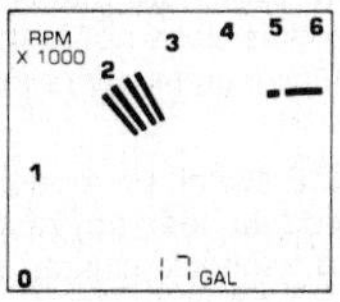

RPM
X 1000
1
2
3
4
5
6
0
GAL

2) If option display appears, go to step **3)**. If display does not appear, repeat step **1)** (ensure GAUGE SELECT switch is fully depressed). If, after repeating test, display does not appear, go to TEST T.

3) Observe fuel readout during option display mode. Digital fuel display should correspond with fuel tank size. Ensure proper fuel option display and tank size match.

4) If fuel option and tank size match, go to step **7)**. If fuel option and tank size do not match, go to step **5)** or **6)**, depending on fuel tank size.

5) On vehicles with 17-gallon fuel tank, disconnect negative battery cable, and remove EIC. Check continuity between pin No. C3 (circuit No. 396) and ground. *See Fig. 2.* See appropriate chassis wiring diagram in WIRING DIAGRAMS. If continuity exists, replace multigauge module. If continuity does not exist, repair wiring.

6) On vehicles with 21-gallon fuel tank, disconnect negative battery cable and remove EIC. Check continuity between pin No. C3 (circuit No. 396) and ground. If continuity does not exist, repair as necessary to create a closed circuit No. 396 (pin No. C3). Recheck cluster operation. If continuity exists, replace multigauge module.

7) Disconnect negative battery cable. Lower fuel tank to gain access to fuel sending unit connector. Replace fuel sending unit with a 32-34 ohm resistor. Reconnect negative battery cable.

8) Turn ignition switch to RUN position. Gauge should indicate 2-3 gallons (9-11 liters) of fuel remaining. If gauge reading is okay, go to step **9)**. If gauge reading is inaccurate, go to step **11)**.

9) Disconnect negative battery cable. Remove EIC, and prevent connections from shorting. Jump sending unit connector. Using an ohmmeter, measure resistance between pins A12 and A13 on cluster.

TEST K (Cont.)

10) If resistance is greater than one ohm, correct short in pin No. C13 (circuit No. 29). Recheck cluster operation. If resistance is zero to one ohm, disconnect negative battery cable and check fuel sending unit for binding or sticking; replace if necessary.

11) If fuel sending unit is okay, check tank for damage and/or distortion. If tank is not damaged, problem is caused by other vehicle system(s). If tank is damaged, repair or replace as necessary.

TEST L

1) Unplug wire to temperature sending unit. Turn ignition switch to RUN position. Temperature gauge should indicate cold engine (one bar segment lit). If gauge display is okay, replace temperature sending unit and recheck cluster operation. If gauge is incorrect, go to next step.

2) Disconnect negative battery cable. Unplug wire to temperature sending unit. Remove EIC. Using an ohmmeter, measure resistance between pins No. C11 and C14. *See Fig. 2.* See appropriate chassis wiring diagram in WIRING DIAGRAMS. If resistance is greater than 10,000 ohms, replace tachometer/multigauge module and recheck cluster operation. If resistance is less than 10,000 ohms, correct short in pin No. C11 (circuit No. 39).

TEST M

Before testing, note the following:

- Warning tone is not active until engine reaches 600 RPM.
- Warning tone generator will not respond if another sound is being produced.
- Warning tone is only given for temperatures above normal.

Turn ignition on. Depress GAUGE SELECT switch. If tone is produced, system is okay. If no tone is produced, go to TEST X.

TEST N

1) Unplug temperature sending unit. Jump sending unit connector wires. Turn ignition switch to RUN position. Multigauge should show blinking thermometer symbol, and light top and bottom 2 bar segments of multigauge.

2) If temperature gauge display is incorrect, go to step **3)**. If gauge display is okay, remove jumper wire and go to step **5)**.

3) Disconnect negative battery cable. Remove EIC. Ensure jumper wire is connected in place of temperature sending unit. Check continuity between pins No. C11 and C14 of cluster. *See Fig. 2.* See appropriate chassis wiring diagram in WIRING DIAGRAMS.

4) If continuity exists, replace tachometer/multigauge module and recheck cluster operation. If continuity does not exist, correct open at pin No. C11 (circuit No. 39) or temperature sending unit. Recheck cluster operation.

5) Run engine at normal operating temperature. Measure temperature sending unit resistance. If resistance is less than 8000 ohms, replace tachometer/multigauge module and recheck cluster operation. If resistance is greater than 8000 ohms, go to next step.

6) Check cooling system and thermostat for proper operation. Check coolant level. Repair or replace cooling system components as necessary. If cooling system is okay, replace temperature sending unit and recheck cluster operation.

TEST O

1) Unplug wire to oil pressure sending unit. Turn ignition switch to RUN position. Depress GAUGE SELECT switch 2 times. Oil pressure display should indicate low pressure (oil can symbol flashing), and one bar segment should be lit on multigauge.

2) If display is okay, replace oil pressure sending unit and recheck cluster operation. If display is incorrect, go to next step.

3) Disconnect negative battery cable. Unplug oil pressure sending unit connector. Remove EIC. Measure resistance between pins No. C12 (circuit No. 31) and C14 (circuit No. 397). *See Fig. 2.* See appropriate chassis wiring diagram in WIRING DIAGRAMS. If resistance is greater than 10,000 ohms, replace tachometer/multigauge module and recheck cluster operation. If resistance is less than 10,000 ohms, correct short in circuit No. 31.

1991 SAFETY EQUIPMENT
Electronic Instrument Panels (Cont.)

TEST P

Before testing, note the following:
- Warning tone is not active until engine reaches 600 RPM.
- Warning tone generator will not respond if another sound is being produced.

Turn ignition switch to RUN position. Depress GAUGE SELECT switch. If tone is heard, system is okay. If no tone is produced, go to TEST X.

TEST Q

1) Ensure engine is not low on oil, and that oil pressure is okay. Unplug wire to oil pressure sending unit. Connect a jumper wire from sending unit lead wire to ground.

2) Turn ignition switch to RUN position. Oil pressure gauge should indicate low pressure (oil can symbol flashing), and bottom and top 2 bars should be lit on multigauge. If display is okay, remove jumper wire and go to step **4)**. If display is incorrect, remove jumper wire and go to next step.

3) Disconnect negative battery cable. Remove EIC. Using an ohmmeter, check continuity between pin No. C12 (circuit No. 31) and end of oil pressure sending unit connector. *See Fig. 2.* See appropriate chassis wiring diagram in WIRING DIAGRAMS. If continuity is present, go to step **4)**. If continuity is not present, correct open in circuit No. 31.

4) Secure unplugged cluster connectors from shorting. Unplug wire from oil pressure sending unit. Reconnect negative battery cable, and start engine. Using engine as ground, measure resistance of oil pressure sending unit.

5) Slowly increase and decrease engine RPM. Resistance of oil pressure sending unit should fluctuate between 9-40 ohms. If resistance is ever less than 9 or more than 40 ohms, replace oil pressure sending unit and recheck cluster operation. If resistance is okay, go to next step.

6) Disconnect negative battery cable. Measure resistance between sending unit case and battery ground. If resistance is less than one ohm, replace tachometer/multigauge module and recheck cluster operation. If resistance is greater than one ohm, correct poor engine ground.

TEST R

1) Turn ignition switch to RUN position, but do not start engine. Depress GAUGE SELECT switch 3 times. Multigauge should indicate charging system failure (battery symbol flashing). If display is correct, system is okay. If display is incorrect, go to next step.

2) Jump terminal "I" of voltage regulator to battery ground. If display is now correct, repair or replace voltage regulator and recheck cluster operation. If display is still incorrect, turn ignition off. Unplug connector to voltage regulator, and turn ignition switch to RUN position.

3) Voltage at terminal "I" on connector should be about 12 volts. If voltage is okay, replace tachometer/multigauge module and recheck cluster operation. If voltage is not 12 volts, correct open in circuit 904.

TEST S

1) Ensure cooling cluster operation is okay. Run engine at normal operating temperature. Stop engine. Remove temperature sender wiring connector. Measure and record temperature sender resistance. If resistance is 1200-6000 ohms, go to step **2)**. If resistance is not 1200-6000 ohms, replace temperature sender and recheck cluster operation.

2) Reconnect temperature sender wiring. Turn ignition switch to RUN or ACC position. Check number of bar segments lit and engine coolant temperature. Ensure number of bar segments and engine coolant temperature correspond. See TEMPERATURE GAUGE BAR SEGMENTS table.

TEST S (Cont.)

TEMPERATURE GAUGE BAR SEGMENTS

Coolant Temp. °F (°C)	No. Of Bar Segments Lit
0-120 (-17.8-48.9)	1
120-150 (48.9-65.6)	2
150-180 (65.6-82.2)	3
180-230 (82.2-110.0)	4
230-240 (110.0-115.6)	5
240-250 (115.6-121.1)	6
250-260 (121.1-126.6)	7
260-270 (126.6-132.2)	8

3) If display is okay, system is operating properly. If number of bar segments lit does not correspond with engine temperature, remove EIC. Measure resistance between pin No. C14 (circuit No. 397) and C11 (circuit No. 39). *See Fig. 2.* See appropriate chassis wiring diagram in WIRING DIAGRAMS. Resistance should not vary more than 10 ohms from reading in step **1)**.

4) If resistance varies more than 10 ohms, check for poor connection and/or corrosion at temperature sender or in sender wiring. If resistance does not vary more than 10 ohms from reading in step **1)**, replace tachometer/multigauge module and recheck cluster operation.

TEST T

NOTE: If a defective speedometer module is replaced, an "S" symbol is displayed in upper right-hand corner of speedometer display, and a sticker showing previous mileage must be affixed to driver's door pillar.

1) Turn ignition switch to RUN position. Depress GAUGE SELECT switch. If tone is produced but tachometer/multigauge module does not respond, replace tachometer/multigauge module and recheck cluster operation. If tone is not produced, go to step **6)**.

2) Depress EXPAND FUEL switch on module. If tone is produced but tachometer/multigauge module does not respond, replace tachometer/multigauge module. Recheck cluster operation. If no tone is produced, go to step **6)**.

3) Depress TRIP DISTANCE switch on module. If tone is produced but speedometer/odometer module does not respond, replace speedometer/odometer module and recheck cluster operation. If tone is not produced, go to step **6)**.

4) Depress TRIP RESET switch on module. If tone is produced but speedometer/odometer module does not respond, replace speedometer/odometer module and recheck cluster operation. If tone is not produced, go to step **6)**.

5) Depress ENGLISH/METRIC switch on module. If tone is produced but speedometer/odometer module does not respond, replace speedometer/odometer module and recheck cluster operation. If tone is not produced, go to next step.

6) Unplug connector from affected switch module to vehicle wiring harness. Measure resistance between colored wire of affected module switch and Black wire (ground). See MODULE SWITCH WIRE COLOR table.

MODULE SWITCH WIRE COLOR

Wire Color	Module Switch
White	GAUGE SELECT
Orange	EXPAND FUEL
Purple	TRIP DISTANCE
Yellow	TRIP RESET
Brown	ENGLISH/METRIC

7) Resistance should be less than 10 ohms when switch is depressed, and greater than 10,000 ohms when switch is released. If resistance of wire is incorrect, replace switch module assembly and recheck cluster operation. If resistance of wire is okay, go to next step.

8) Disconnect negative battery cable and remove EIC. Check continuity between mating switch module connector and cluster connector. If continuity is not present, correct open in connector wiring. If continuity is present, go to next step.

TEST T (Cont.)

9) Check continuity of switch module ground between mating switch module and cluster connectors (between cluster pins No. B14 and C14, and Black/White wire at switch connector). *See Fig. 2.* See appropriate chassis wiring diagram in WIRING DIAGRAMS.

10) If continuity is not present, correct open in ground circuit No. 397. If continuity is present, replace module in circuit with affected switch and wire. Recheck cluster operation.

TEST U

NOTE: If a defective speedometer module is replaced, an "S" symbol is displayed in upper right-hand corner of speedometer display. Also, a sticker showing previous mileage must be affixed to driver's door pillar.

1) Turn ignition switch to RUN position. If display is backlit but blank, check multigauge operation. If multigauge operates properly, go to step **2)**. If multigauge does not operate properly, go to step **7)**.

2) Disconnect negative battery cable, and remove EIC. Secure unplugged cluster connectors from shorting. Reconnect negative battery cable. Turn ignition switch to RUN position.

3) Measure voltage at pins No. A14 and B17. *See Fig. 2.* See appropriate chassis wiring diagram in WIRING DIAGRAMS. If voltage is more than 10 volts at both pins, go to step **4)**. If voltage is less than 10 volts at either pin, correct open at pin No. B17 (circuit No. 54) and/or pin No. A14 (circuit No. 489) as necessary. Recheck cluster operation.

4) Disconnect negative battery cable, and remove EIC. Secure unplugged cluster connectors from shorting. Reconnect negative battery cable. Check voltage at pin No. B13 (circuit No. 54).

5) If voltage at pin No. B13 (circuit No. 54) is more than 12 volts, go to step **6)**. If voltage at pin No. B13 (circuit No. 54) is less than 12 volts, correct open in circuit No. 54.

6) Using an ohmmeter, check continuity between pin No. B14 (circuit No. 397) and negative battery cable. If continuity is present, replace speedometer/odometer module, and recheck cluster operation. If continuity is not present, correct open in circuit between cluster and ground.

7) Check for bad fuse in circuit No. 489 (pin No. B12) and/or circuit No. 54 (pin No. B13). If fuse is okay, go to step **2)**. If fuse is blown, go to next step.

8) Before replacing fuse, turn ignition off and disconnect negative battery cable. Check for short between circuit side of fuse and ground. If a short condition is present, correct short. If short condition is not present, replace fuse and recheck cluster operation.

TEST V

NOTE: If a defective speedometer module is replaced, an "S" symbol is displayed in upper right-hand corner of speedometer display. Also, a sticker showing previous mileage must be affixed to driver's door pillar.

1) Turn ignition switch to RUN position, and observe speedometer display. If all display segments light up, then go out, go to step **2)**. If display is missing segments, or segments are half-lit, replace speedometer/odometer module and recheck cluster operation.

2) Place ENGLISH/METRIC switch in ENGLISH position. Depress and hold TRIP RESET switch while turning ignition switch to RUN position. Observe display reaction. Release TRIP RESET switch.

3) If display did not enter test mode (did not respond to switch being depressed) go to step **1)** of TEST T. If all readouts are displayed as zeros, go to step **4)**. If display reads "F" on right-hand digit of speedometer, replace speedometer/odometer module and recheck cluster operation.

4) Ensure ENGLISH/METRIC switch is in ENGLISH position. Depress and hold TRIP RESET switch while turning ignition switch to RUN position. Repeatedly depress TRIP RESET switch until all zeros are displayed. See TEST DISPLAY FOR ZEROS.

TEST V (Cont.)

Test Display For Zeros 90D15019

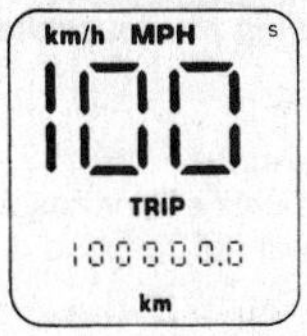
km/h MPH
S
TRIP
km

5) If any segments are half-lit, missing or scrambled, replace speedometer/odometer module and recheck cluster operation. If display is complete, depress TRIP RESET switch to advance display through test displays. When test display of "eights" is shown, all labels and symbols should be displayed, and display should read 188. See TEST DISPLAY FOR EIGHTS.

Test Display For Eights 6829

km/h MPH
S
TRIP
km

6) If any segments are half-lit or scrambled, replace speedometer/odometer module and recheck cluster operation. If all segments appear correct throughout testing, system is okay.

TEST W

NOTE: If a defective speedometer module is replaced, an "S" symbol is displayed in upper right-hand corner of speedometer display, and a sticker showing previous mileage must be affixed to driver's door pillar.

1) Turn ignition switch to RUN position. Depress ENGLISH/METRIC switch. If labels in all display areas change from English to Metric, system is okay. If display does not change when switch is depressed, go to next step.

2) Depress ENGLISH/METRIC switch several times. If display remains in ENGLISH mode, go to step **3)**. If display remains in METRIC mode, replace speedometer/odometer module and recheck cluster operation.

3) Unplug connector at push switches. Using an ohmmeter, measure resistance between Brown and Black/White wires (ground) of connector leading to switches.

4) Resistance with ENGLISH/METRIC switch depressed should be less than 10 ohms. Resistance with ENGLISH/METRIC switch released should be greater than 10,000 ohms. If resistance values are okay, go to step **5)**. If resistance values are incorrect, replace switch module and recheck cluster operation.

5) Disconnect negative battery cable and remove EIC. Check continuity between switch module connector and pin No. B5 (circuit No. 273). *See Fig. 2.* See appropriate chassis wiring diagram in WIRING DIAGRAMS.

6) If continuity is present, replace speedometer/odometer module and recheck cluster operation. If continuity is not present, correct open in circuit No. 273.

1991 SAFETY EQUIPMENT
Electronic Instrument Panels (Cont.)

TEST X

NOTE: If a defective speedometer module is replaced, an "S" symbol is displayed in upper right-hand corner of speedometer display. Also, a sticker showing previous mileage must be affixed to driver's door pillar.

Before testing, note the following:
- Warning tone is not active until engine reaches 600 RPM.
- Warning tone generator will not respond if another sound is being produced.

1) Turn ignition switch to RUN position. Depress each module switch (GAUGE SELECT, EXPAND FUEL, ENGLISH/METRIC, etc.). If tone is produced for all switches, system is okay.

2) If tone is not produced for any module switch, go to step **3)**. If tone is produced for some switches, go to step **7)**.

3) Check for FASTEN SEAT BELT and KEY IN IGNITION warning tones. If tones are produced, go to step **4)**. If tones are not produced, repair/replace tone generator module and recheck cluster operation.

4) Disconnect negative battery cable. Remove cluster and secure connectors from shorting. Reconnect negative battery cable. Turn ignition switch to RUN position. Ensure FASTEN SEAT BELT warning tone is produced.

5) After tone has stopped, connect a jumper wire between pin No. B2 and ground, and listen for tone (test 1). *See Fig. 2.* See appropriate chassis wiring diagram in WIRING DIAGRAMS. Remove jumper wire. Connect a jumper between pin No. B6 and ground, and listen for a tone (test 2).

6) If tone is produced in both tests, replace tachometer/multigauge module and recheck cluster operation. If tone is not produced in either test, correct open in circuit No. 183 (pin No. B2) and recheck cluster operation.

7) Identify which switch groups do not produce a tone when depressed. If ENGLISH/METRIC, TRIP DIST and TRIP RESET switches (speedometer/odometer wiring circuit) do not produce a tone, go to step **8)**. If GAUGE SELECT and EXPAND FUEL switches (tachometer/multigauge wiring circuit) do not produce a tone, go to step **11)**.

8) Disconnect negative battery cable. Remove cluster and secure connectors from shorting. Reconnect negative battery cable. Turn ignition switch to RUN position. Ensure FASTEN SEAT BELT warning tone is produced.

9) After tone has stopped, connect a jumper wire between pin No. B2 and ground. If tone is produced, replace speedometer/odometer module and recheck cluster operation.

10) If tone is not produced, correct open in circuit No. 183 (between pin No. B2 and tone generator) and recheck cluster operation.

11) Disconnect negative battery cable. Remove cluster and secure connectors from shorting. Reconnect negative battery cable. Turn ignition switch to RUN position. Verify FASTEN SEAT BELT warning tone is operating.

12) After warning tone has stopped, connect a jumper wire between pin No. C6 and ground. If tone is produced, replace tachometer/multigauge module and recheck cluster operation. If tone is not produced, correct open in circuit No. 183 (between pin No. C6 and tone generator) and recheck cluster operation.

TEST Y

NOTE: If a defective speedometer module is replaced, an "S" symbol is displayed in upper right-hand corner of speedometer display. Also, a sticker showing previous mileage must be affixed to driver's door pillar.

1) Turn ignition switch to RUN position and observe display. If all display segments come on and then go out, go to step **2)**. If segment display is incorrect, replace speedometer/odometer module and recheck cluster operation.

2) Check for proper advancement of speedometer reading while vehicle is moving forward. If speedometer display operates properly, go to step **3)**. If display does not advance correctly, replace speedometer/odometer module and recheck cluster operation.

3) If vehicle is not equipped with cruise control, go to step **4)**. Test drive vehicle and check cruise control system operation. If system does not operate properly, go to step **4)**. If system operates properly, go to step **8)**.

TEST Y (Cont.)

4) Disconnect speed sensor connector. Measure resistance across connector leads. If resistance is less than 500 ohms, correct short in wiring circuit No. 150, and recheck cluster operation.

5) If resistance is greater than 500 ohms, check resistance across speed sensor terminals. If resistance is not 200-230 ohms, replace sensor and recheck cluster operation. If resistance is 200-230 ohms, go to next step.

6) Disconnect speed sensor from transmission. Check driven gear for damage and ensure retainer clip is in position. Replace driven gear and/or retainer clip as necessary and recheck cluster operation. If driven gear and retainer clip are okay, go to next step.

7) Check drive gear on transmission output shaft for wear and/or damage, replace as necessary, and recheck cluster operation. If gear is okay, go to next step.

8) Reconnect speed sensor wiring. Disconnect negative battery cable and remove cluster. Check resistance between pin No. B3 and pin No. B14 of connector. *See Fig. 2.* See appropriate chassis wiring diagram in WIRING DIAGRAMS.

9) If resistance is 160-230 ohms, replace speedometer/odometer module and recheck cluster operation. If resistance is not 160-230 ohms, correct open in circuit No. 150 and recheck cluster operation.

TEST Z

NOTE: If a defective speedometer module is replaced, an "S" symbol is displayed in upper right-hand corner of speedometer display. Also, a sticker showing previous mileage must be affixed to driver's door pillar.

1) Ensure correct size tires are installed on vehicle. If tire size is correct, record odometer reading. Test drive vehicle over a known distance and record odometer reading again. If odometer reading varies from actual mileage, go to next step.

2) Remove speed sensor from transmission and ensure correct drive and driven gears are installed. If correct drive and driven gears are installed, replace speedometer/odometer module and recheck cluster operation.

TEST AA

NOTE: If a defective speedometer module is replaced, an "S" symbol is displayed in upper right-hand corner of speedometer display. Also, a sticker showing previous mileage must be affixed to driver's door pillar.

1) Remove speed sensor from transmission. Ensure gear teeth are not damaged, gear does not slip on shaft, and retainer clip is in position. Replace driven gear and/or retainer clip if necessary and recheck cluster operation. If gear and retainer clip are okay, go to next step.

2) Measure resistance across harness wires of connector. If resistance is less than 500 ohms, correct short in wiring circuit No. 150, and recheck cluster operation.

3) If resistance is greater than 500 ohms, check resistance across speed sensor terminals. If resistance is not 200-230 ohms, replace sensor and recheck cluster operation. If resistance is 200-230 ohms, go to next step.

4) Reconnect speed sensor wiring. Disconnect negative battery cable and remove cluster. Check resistance between pin No. B3 and pin No. B14 of connector. *See Fig. 2.* See appropriate chassis wiring diagram in WIRING DIAGRAMS.

5) If resistance is intermittent, replace speedometer/odometer module and recheck cluster operation. If resistance is not intermittent, service circuit No. 150 between cluster and speed sensor and recheck cluster operation.

TEST BB

NOTE: If a defective speedometer module is replaced, an "S" symbol is displayed in upper right-hand corner of speedometer display. Also, a sticker showing previous mileage must be affixed to driver's door pillar.

Turn ignition switch to RUN position. Check odometer display. If odometer display reads ERROR, replace speedometer/odometer module and recheck cluster operation.

TEST CC

NOTE: If a defective speedometer module is replaced, an "S" symbol is displayed in upper right-hand corner of speedometer display. Also, a sticker showing previous mileage must be affixed to driver's door pillar.

1) To determine if speedometer/odometer module is an original or a replacement, turn off ignition. Depress and hold TRIP RESET switch while turning ignition switch to RUN position.

2) Observe option code on odometer readout. See OPTION CODE DISPLAY illustration. Check option code against module type in OPTION CODE DISPLAY table to determine if speedometer/odometer module is an original or a replacement.

Option Code Display 17224

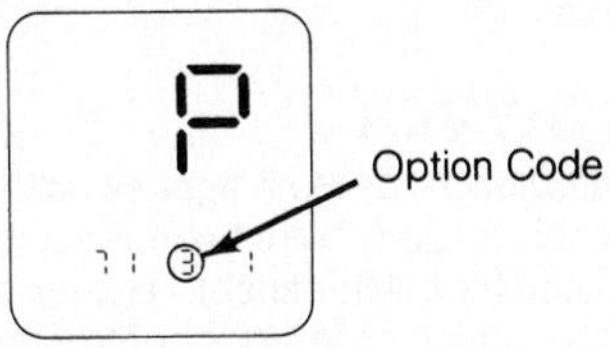
Option Code

OPTION CODE DISPLAY

Option Code	Module Type
2	Replacement
3	Replacement
6	Original
7	Original
E	Original
O	Replacement
R	Replacement

3) If an "S" symbol is displayed on an original speedometer/odometer module, replace module and recheck cluster operation. If an "S" symbol is displayed on replacement module, system is okay.

TEST DD

NOTE: If a defective speedometer module is replaced, an "S" symbol is displayed in upper right-hand corner of speedometer display. Also, a sticker showing previous mileage must be affixed to driver's door pillar.

1) Test drive vehicle at least 10 miles to check for proper odometer operation. If odometer accumulates 10 miles then jumps back 10 miles, replace speedometer/odometer module and recheck cluster operation.

2) If odometer will not accumulate mileage, check speedometer operation. If operation is not okay, go to TEST Y. If operation is okay, replace speedometer/odometer module and recheck cluster operation.

TEST EE

Odometer symptoms are diagnosed and corrected by performing the following tests in this order: Z, V and FF. If TESTS Z, V and FF are performed, and no problems exist, system is okay.

TEST FF

NOTE: If a defective speedometer module is replaced, an "S" symbol is displayed in upper right-hand corner of speedometer display. Also, a sticker showing previous mileage must be affixed to driver's door pillar.

1) Verify symptom by test driving vehicle. If symptom exists, turn ignition off. Depress and hold TRIP RESET switch while turning ignition switch to RUN position. Display should show all zeros (test 1).

2) Release TRIP RESET switch and note speedometer display. A "P" symbol should appear in place of the right-hand speedometer digit, and a "1" should appear in the odometer's tenths position (test 2). See COMPUTER SELF-TEST DISPLAY.

Computer Self-Test Display 17225

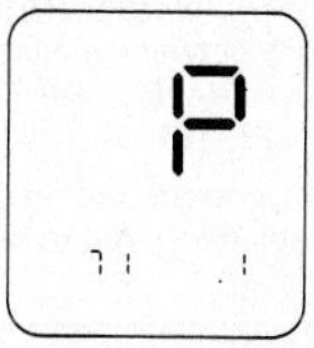

3) If either test (1 or 2) failed, replace speedometer/odometer module, and recheck cluster operation. If display passes both tests, depress TRIP RESET switch 4 times and note display.

Memory Self-Test Display 6830

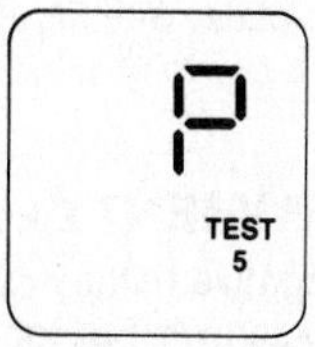
TEST
5

4) A "P" symbol should appear in place of the right-hand speedometer digit, and a "5" should appear in the odometer's tenths position. If test failed, replace speedometer/odometer module, and recheck cluster operation. If display is okay, go to next step.

5) Check operation of speedometer. If operation is okay, replace speedometer/odometer module, and recheck cluster operation. If speedometer constantly reads too high or too low, go to Test Z. If speedometer display is erratic, go to TEST AA.

TEST GG

NOTE: If a defective speedometer module is replaced, an "S" symbol is displayed in upper right-hand corner of speedometer display. Also, a sticker showing previous mileage must be affixed to driver's door pillar.

1) Turn ignition switch to RUN position. After FASTEN SEAT BELT warning tone has stopped, depress TRIP DIST switch. If tone is present, replace speedometer/odometer module and recheck cluster operation. If tone is not present, go to next step.

2) Unplug connector at push-button switches. Measure resistance between Purple and Black/White wires. Resistance should be less than 10 ohms when switch is depressed, and greater than 10,000 ohms when switch is released.

3) If resistance is incorrect, replace switch assembly and recheck cluster operation. If resistance is okay, disconnect negative battery cable, and remove EIC. Check continuity between mating switch module connector and cluster circuit No. 288 (pin No. B7). *See Fig. 2.* See appropriate chassis wiring diagram in WIRING DIAGRAMS.

4) If continuity is not present, correct open in circuit No. 288 (pin No. B7). If continuity is present, replace speedometer/odometer module, and recheck cluster operation.

1991 SAFETY EQUIPMENT
Electronic Instrument Panels (Cont.)

TEST HH

NOTE: If a defective speedometer module is replaced, an "S" symbol is displayed in upper right-hand corner of speedometer display. Also, a sticker showing previous mileage must be affixed to driver's door pillar.

1) Turn ignition switch to RUN position. After FASTEN SEAT BELT warning tone has stopped, depress TRIP RESET switch. If tone is present, replace speedometer/odometer module and recheck cluster operation. If tone is not present, go to next step.

2) Unplug connector at push-button switches. Measure resistance between Yellow wire and Black/White wire. Resistance should be less than 10 ohms when switch is depressed, and greater than 10,000 ohms when switch is released.

3) If resistance is incorrect, replace switch assembly and recheck cluster operation. If resistance is okay, disconnect negative battery cable and remove EIC. Check continuity between mating switch module connector and cluster circuit No. 286 (pin No. B6). *See Fig. 2*. See appropriate wiring diagram in WIRING DIAGRAMS.

4) If continuity is not present, correct open in circuit No. 286 (pin No. B6). If continuity is present, replace speedometer/odometer module and recheck cluster operation.

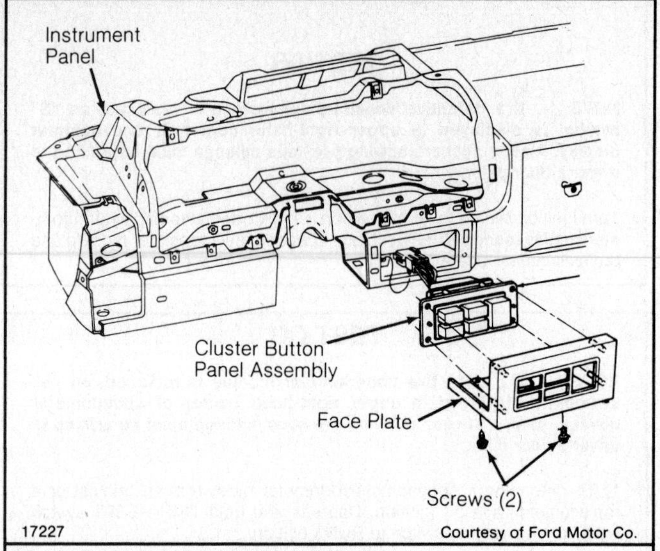
Instrument Panel
Cluster Button Panel Assembly
Face Plate
Screws (2)
17227
Courtesy of Ford Motor Co.

Fig. 3: Exploded View of EIC Button Panel

REMOVAL & INSTALLATION

CLUSTER BUTTON PANEL

Removal & Installation – Disconnect negative battery cable. Remove button panel face plate. *See Fig. 3*. Pull button panel from instrument panel. Disconnect wiring connector. To install, reverse removal procedure.

ELECTRONIC INSTRUMENT CLUSTER (EIC)

Removal – Disconnect negative battery cable. Remove cluster trim. Remove 4 cluster mounting screws. Pull top of cluster toward steering wheel. Unplug 3 connectors behind cluster. Pull bottom of cluster out.
Installation – Insert bottom of cluster into instrument panel aligning pins. To complete installation, reverse removal procedure.

ELECTRONIC MODULE

Removal – Remove EIC. Remove 5 screws attaching lens/mask assembly to cluster. Remove 3 screws from back of module. Lift flex circuit from locator pins. Remove module from cluster.
Installation – Using alcohol and a lint-free cloth, remove dust and/or fingerprints from module displays and cluster lens. To install, reverse removal procedure.

HEADLIGHT SWITCH

Removal & Installation – 1) Main light switch is located in left side instrument panel control pod. To remove, disconnect negative battery cable. Remove 5 cluster finish panel-to-cluster screws.
2) Remove 3 screws attaching left side control cluster. Disconnect wiring connector. Remove 2 light switch-to-control pod screws. To install, reverse removal procedure.

WIRING DIAGRAMS

See appropriate chassis wiring diagram in WIRING DIAGRAMS.

1991 SAFETY EQUIPMENT
Rear Window Defogger

Aerostar, Bronco, Explorer

DESCRIPTION & OPERATION

The system consists of a control assembly, an indicator light, grid lines on inside surface of window and system wiring. Each grid line consists of 2 layers. The first layer is Brown as viewed from the exterior. The second layer is Silver as viewed from interior. A 40-amp in-line circuit breaker and 15-amp fuse protect defogger circuitry on Aerostar. A fusible link and 15-amp fuse protect Bronco and Explorer defogger circuits.

The 40-amp circuit breaker is in underhood power distribution box. The fusible link is connected near the starter relay. A control switch turns system on or off. A timer-controlled relay turns system off after about 10 minutes of operation. When switch is in ON position, contacts in control assembly are mechanically closed. This provides current to grids, indicator light and control timer.

Contacts will remain closed until control timer turns system off, or ignition switch is turned off. Power to grids and indicator light is supplied directly from battery side of starter relay through a fusible link on Aerostar and Bronco. Power for control timer comes from accessory terminal of ignition switch. Power is available when ignition switch is in RUN or ACC position.

TESTING

NOTE: Rear defogger test procedure for Bronco and control switch test procedure for Aerostar are not available from manufacturer.

REAR DEFOGGER SWITCH TEST

Explorer – **1)** Ground pin No. 4, and connect a jumper wire between pins No. 3 and No. 2. *See Fig. 1.* Connect a 12 volt test light between pin No. 1 and ground. Apply power to pin No. 2. Test light and indicator light should not light. If test light and/or indicator light come on, replace switch.

2) Momentarily push right side of defogger rocker switch to on position. Test light and indicator light should come on and stay on after switch is released. Test light and indicator light should go off when defogger switch is pushed to OFF position, 10 minutes have passed or jumper wire between pins No. 2 and No. 3 is removed.

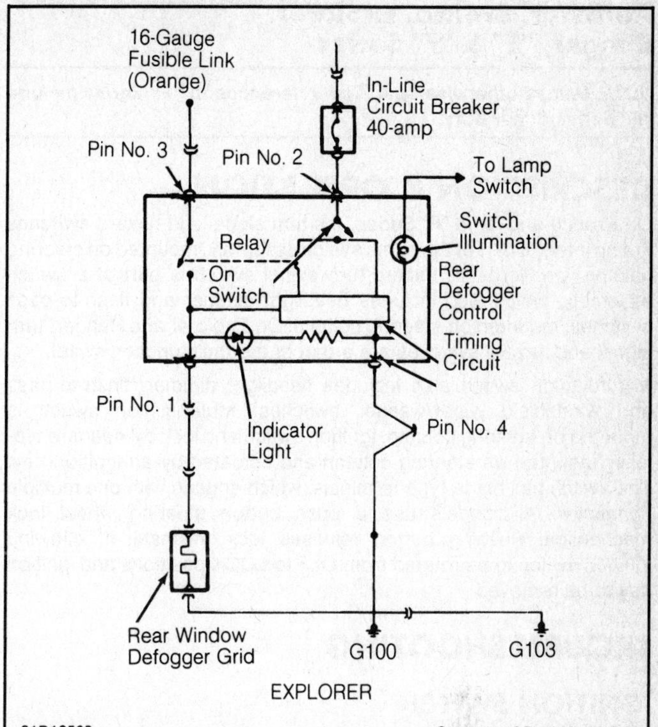
16-Gauge
Fusible Link
(Orange)
In-Line
Circuit Breaker
40-amp
Pin No. 3
Pin No. 2
To Lamp
Switch
Switch
Illumination
Relay
On
Switch
Rear
Defogger
Control
Timing
Circuit
Pin No. 1
Indicator
Light
Pin No. 4
Rear Window
Defogger Grid
G100
G103
EXPLORER
91D13568
Courtesy of Ford Motor Co.

Fig. 1: Testing Rear Defogger Switch (Explorer)

WINDOW GRID

1) Using a bright lamp inside vehicle, visually inspect wire grid from outside. A broken grid wire will appear as a brown spot. Start engine and run at idle. Put control switch to ON position. Indicator light should light.

2) Using a voltmeter, check for 10-13 volts at broad Red/Brown strips on rear window. A low voltage reading indicates a loose ground wire (pigtail) connection at ground screw. With negative voltmeter lead grounded, touch positive lead to each ground line of heated rear window at its midpoint.

3) A reading of approximately 6 volts indicates proper circuit function. If zero volts are found, circuit is broken between midpoint and hot side of grid line. A reading of 12 volts indicates circuit is broken between midpoint of grid line and ground.

WIRING DIAGRAMS

See appropriate chassis wiring diagram in WIRING DIAGRAMS.

1991 SAFETY EQUIPMENT
Steering Column Switches

Aerostar, Bronco, Explorer, Ranger, "E" & "F" Series

***NOTE:* Unless otherwise specified, references to "F" Series include "F" Series Super Duty.**

DESCRIPTION & OPERATION

On Bronco and "E" & "F" Series, the turn signal and hazard switches are an integral part of the same switch assembly, mounted on steering column. On Aerostar, hazard/turn signal switch is part of a switch assembly, which also includes headlight dimmer and flash-to-pass switches, mounted on steering column. On Explorer and Ranger, turn signal and hazard switches are a part of the multifunction switch.

Multifunction switch also includes headlight dimmer, flash-to-pass and windshield wiper/washer switches. Multifunction switch is mounted on steering column. Ignition switch and lock cylinder are typically mounted on steering column and actuated by an ignition key. The switch has blade-type terminals, which engage with one multiple connector. All models use a push button steering wheel lock mechanism. Pushing button releases lock mechanism, allowing ignition switch to be rotated from OFF to LOCK positions and ignition key to be removed.

TROUBLESHOOTING

IGNITION SWITCH

1) Before performing continuity tests on A/T vehicles, determine if an engine-won't-crank condition exists with shift lever in both Park and Neutral. If no-crank problem occurs in only one shift position, neutral start switch located on transmission is probable cause.

2) For an engine-won't-crank condition on M/T vehicles, ensure clutch/starter interlock switch is working properly. A misadjusted, rather than malfunctioning, switch may cause accessories to fail to operate with ignition switch in RUN position or to remain on when ignition is turned off. See ADJUSTMENTS.

TESTING

HAZARD SWITCH POWER TEST

1) Connect test light to ground. Touch test light probe to hazard or multifunction switch terminal (circuit No. 385, White/Red wire). *See Figs. 1 and 2*. If test light glows, power circuit to hazard switch is okay. If test light does not glow, check for open circuit between hazard switch and fuse block. Repair as necessary.

2) See HAZARD/TURN SIGNAL SWITCH CONTINUITY (AEROSTAR), MULTIFUNCTION SWITCH CONTINUITY (EXPLORER & RANGER) or HAZARD/TURN SIGNAL SWITCH OUTPUT (BRONCO, "E" & "F" SERIES) table.

TURN SIGNAL SWITCH POWER TEST

1) Place ignition switch to RUN position. Connect test light to ground. Touch test light probe to turn signal or multifunction switch feed terminal (circuit No. 44, Light Blue wire). *See Figs. 1 and 2*. If test light flashes, power circuit to turn signal switch is okay.

2) If test light does not flash, replace flasher or check for open circuit No. 44 (Light Blue wire) and repair as necessary. See HAZARD/TURN SIGNAL SWITCH CONTINUITY (AEROSTAR), MULTIFUNCTION SWITCH CONTINUITY (EXPLORER & RANGER) or HAZARD/TURN SIGNAL SWITCH OUTPUT (BRONCO, "E" & "F" SERIES) table.

MULTIFUNCTION SWITCH CONTINUITY (EXPLORER & RANGER)

Switch Position & Continuity	Between Circuits
Turn Signal Off	
Yes	511, 5 & 9
No	511, 2, 3, 44 & 385 44, 2, 3, 5, 9 & 385 385, 2 & 3
Left Turn	
Yes	511 & 5; 44, 3 & 9
No	511, 3, 9, 44 & 385 44, 2, 5 & 385 385 & 2
Right Turn	
Yes	511 & 9; 44, 2 & 5
No	511, 2, 5, 44 & 385 44, 3, 9 & 385; 385 & 2
Hazard	
Yes	385, 2, 3, 5, 9 & 511
No	385 & 44; 44, 2, 3, 5 & 9
Headlight Dimmer (High)	
Yes	15 & 12
No	15, 13 & 196; 196 & 12
Headlight Dimmer (Low)	
Yes	15 & 13
No	15, 12 & 196; 196 & 13
Flash-To-Pass	
Yes	15 & 13; 196 & 12
No	15, 12 & 196

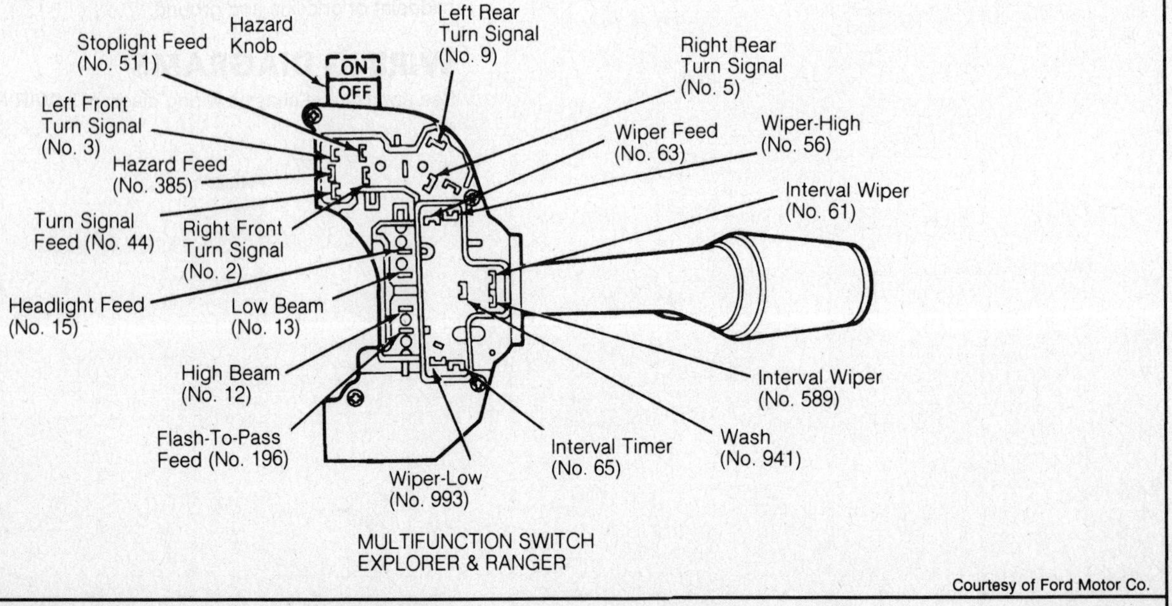
Stoplight Feed
(No. 511)
Hazard
Knob
ON
OFF
Left Rear
Turn Signal
(No. 9)
Right Rear
Turn Signal
(No. 5)
Left Front
Turn Signal
(No. 3)
Wiper Feed
(No. 63)
Wiper-High
(No. 56)
Hazard Feed
(No. 385)
Interval Wiper
(No. 61)
Turn Signal
Feed (No. 44)
Right Front
Turn Signal
(No. 2)
Headlight Feed
(No. 15)
Low Beam
(No. 13)
High Beam
(No. 12)
Interval Wiper
(No. 589)
Flash-To-Pass
Feed (No. 196)
Interval Timer
(No. 65)
Wash
(No. 941)
Wiper-Low
(No. 993)
MULTIFUNCTION SWITCH
EXPLORER & RANGER
91J13564
Courtesy of Ford Motor Co.

Fig. 1: Testing Multifunction Switch Continuity (Explorer & Ranger)

1991 SAFETY EQUIPMENT
Steering Column Switches (Cont.)

MULTIFUNCTION SWITCH CONTINUITY (EXPLORER & RANGER) (Cont.)

Windshield Washer Off	
No	63 & 941
Windshield Washer On	
Yes	63 & 941
Wiper Off	
No	63, 56, 993, 65 & 941
Low Speed	
Yes	63 & 993
No	63, 941, 56 & 65
High Speed	
Yes	63, 993 & 56
No	63, 941 & 65
Interval Wiper [1]	
Yes	[2] 63 & 65
No	63, 993 & 56

[1] - Knob turned to maximum time interval.
[2] - Resistance between circuits No. 589 and 61 should be greater than 7000 Ohms but less than 13,000 Ohms. If knob is rotated to minimum time interval position, resistance should drop to less than 880 Ohms but greater than 420 Ohms.

HAZARD/TURN SIGNAL SWITCH OUTPUT (BRONCO, "E" & "F" SERIES)

Switch Position	Battery Voltage At Circuit
Bronco	
Left Front	No. 3 (Light Green/White)
Left Rear	No. 9 (Light Green/Orange)
Right Front	No. 2 (White/Light Blue)
Right Rear	No. 5 (Orange/Light Blue)
"E" & "F" Series	
Left Front	No. 3 (Green/White)
Left Rear	No. 283 (Yellow/Black)
Right Front	No. 2 (White/Black)
Right Rear	No. 282 (Green)

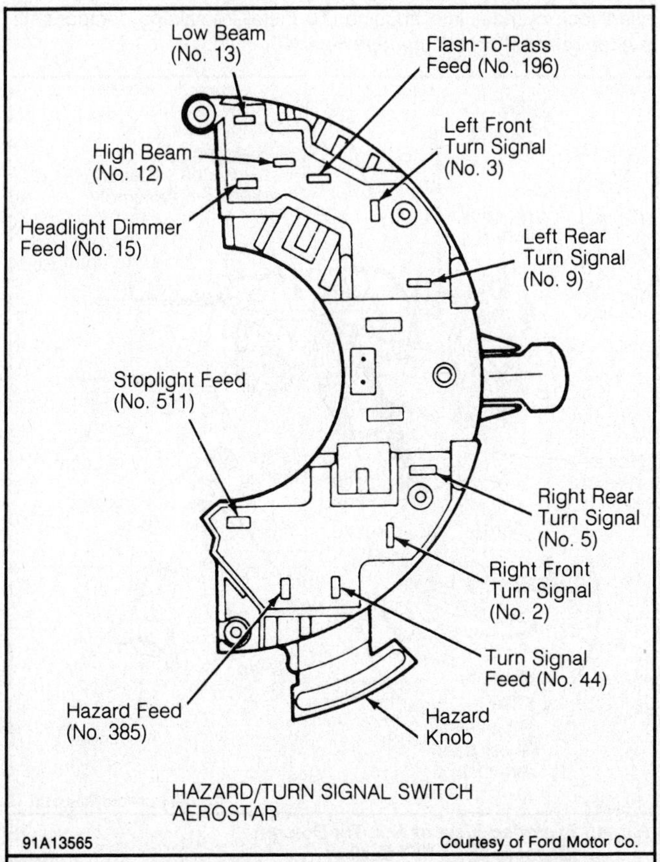
Low Beam (No. 13)
Flash-To-Pass Feed (No. 196)
High Beam (No. 12)
Left Front Turn Signal (No. 3)
Headlight Dimmer Feed (No. 15)
Left Rear Turn Signal (No. 9)
Stoplight Feed (No. 511)
Right Rear Turn Signal (No. 5)
Right Front Turn Signal (No. 2)
Turn Signal Feed (No. 44)
Hazard Feed (No. 385)
Hazard Knob
HAZARD/TURN SIGNAL SWITCH AEROSTAR
91A13565
Courtesy of Ford Motor Co.

Fig. 2: Testing Hazard & Turn Signal Switch Continuity (Aerostar)

HAZARD/TURN SIGNAL SWITCH CONTINUITY (AEROSTAR)

Switch Position & Continuity	Between Circuits
Turn Signal Off	
Yes	511, 5 & 9
No	511 & Ground; 44, 2, 3, 5 & 9
Left Turn	
Yes	44, 3 & 9; 511 & 5
No	44 & Ground; 44 & 5
Right Turn	
Yes	44, 2 & 5; 511 & 9
No	44 & Ground; 44 & 9
Hazard	
Yes	385, 2, 3, 5 & 9; 511, 2, 3, 5 & 9
No	385, 44 & Ground
Headlight Dimmer (Low)	
Yes	15 & 13
No	15 & 12
Headlight Dimmer (High)	
Yes	15 & 12
No	15 & 13
Flash-To-Pass	
Yes	196 & 12
No	196 & 13

IGNITION SWITCH

1) To check steering column ignition system for mechanical operation, rotate lock cylinder through all switch positions. Movement should not bind, and lock cylinder should return from START to RUN position without assistance.

2) If binding or incorrect modes are encountered, ignition switch should be adjusted. After adjustment, if binding or incorrect modes are still evident, lock cylinder should either be disassembled and inspected for damage or ignition switch should be replaced.

3) To check electrical function of ignition switch, lower steering column, and disconnect ignition switch connector. Test switch continuity using a self-powered test light or ohmmeter. Continuity should not exist between chassis ground and any terminal, except circuits No. 41 and 977 in START position only.

4) See IGNITION SWITCH CONTINUITY table for terminal identification. If continuity is not as specified, replace ignition switch. *See Fig. 3.*

IGNITION SWITCH CONTINUITY

Switch Position	Continuity
Accessory	37 & 297
Lock	No Continuity
Off	No Continuity
Run	37, 16, 687 & 297
Start	977, 41 & Ground; 37, 32, 262 & possibly 16

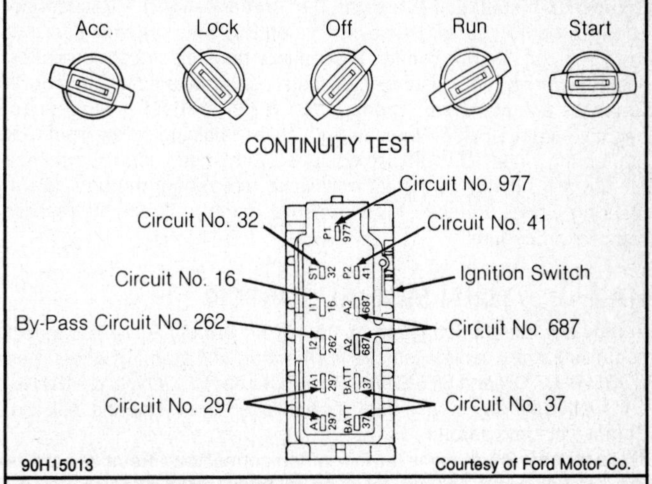
Acc.
Lock
Off
Run
Start
CONTINUITY TEST
Circuit No. 977
Circuit No. 32
Circuit No. 41
Circuit No. 16
Ignition Switch
By-Pass Circuit No. 262
Circuit No. 687
Circuit No. 297
Circuit No. 37
90H15013
Courtesy of Ford Motor Co.

Fig. 3: Testing Ignition Switch Continuity

1991 SAFETY EQUIPMENT
Steering Column Switches (Cont.)

ADJUSTMENTS

IGNITION SWITCH

NOTE: Ignition switch on Aerostar cannot be adjusted. If problem exists with ignition switch, replace switch.

Explorer & Ranger – 1) Ignition switch is properly adjusted if:
- In ACCESSORY, accessory circuit is operative and steering wheel is locked. Automatic shift lever cannot be moved.
- In LOCK, all ignition switch electrical circuits are inoperative and steering wheel is locked. Automatic shift lever cannot be moved.
- In OFF, all ignition switch electrical circuits are inoperative and steering wheel is unlocked. Automatic shift lever can be moved.
- In ON (RUN), all ignition switch circuits or accessory circuits are operative except starter circuit and warning light check circuit. Steering wheel is unlocked and automatic shift lever can be moved.
- In START, only engine ignition, warning light check and starter circuits are operative. Steering wheel is unlocked and automatic shift lever can be moved.

2) On all models, disconnect negative battery cable. Locate ignition switch on top of steering column tube. Remove ignition switch connector. Rotate ignition key back and forth to each side of LOCK position until a 5/64 inch (1.98 mm) drill bit can be inserted into ignition switch lock pin hole.
3) Loosen 2 ignition switch mounting nuts, turn switch to LOCK position (feel for detent) and remove ignition key from cylinder. Move switch up or down along column tube. Locate mid-position of rod lash. Tighten 2 mounting nuts to 40-65 INCH lbs. (4.51-7.34 N.m).
4) Remove drill bit. Plug in electrical connector. Ensure all accessories are deactivated when switch is in OFF position, and ensure all modes function correctly.

REMOVAL & INSTALLATION

STEERING WHEEL

Removal & Installation – 1) Set front wheels in straight-ahead position. Remove horn button. See HORN BUTTON under REMOVAL & INSTALLATION. Place reference marks on steering wheel and shaft for reassembly reference. Remove steering wheel nut or bolt and damper (if equipped).
2) Using Steering Wheel Puller (T67L-3600-A), remove steering wheel. To install, reverse removal procedure. Align reference marks. Install retaining nut. See TORQUE SPECIFICATIONS table at end of article. Ensure damper is aligned with holes of steering wheel.

HORN BUTTON

Removal & Installation (Aerostar, Explorer & Ranger) – Disconnect negative battery cable. Remove horn button cover retaining screws from rear of steering wheel. Disconnect horn electrical connector. Remove horn button assembly. To install, reverse removal procedure.
Removal & Installation (Bronco, "E" & "F" Series) – Disconnect negative battery cable. Remove horn cover retaining screw from rear of steering wheel. On vehicles equipped with speed control, squeeze "J" clip ground wire terminal firmly while removing it through hole in steering wheel. Remove horn button assembly. To install, reverse removal procedure.

HAZARD/TURN SIGNAL SWITCH

Removal & Installation (Bronco, "E" & "F" Series) – 1) Disconnect negative battery cable. Remove horn button and steering wheel. See HORN BUTTON and STEERING WHEEL under REMOVAL & INSTALLATION. Unscrew turn signal switch lever from steering column. Remove column shroud.
2) Disconnect 2 turn signal switch wiring connectors. Remove screws attaching switch to column. On fixed columns, remove switch assembly from vehicle by guiding switch and connector plug through opening in shaft socket.
3) On tilt columns, remove upper extension shroud by squeezing at 6 and 12 o'clock positions, and popping it free. To open trim shroud, remove 4 attaching screws and swing shroud downward. Peel back foam sight shield, remove 2 screws attaching shroud to steering column and remove ignition lock cylinder.
4) Remove turn signal lever by pulling and twisting. Remove shroud. Remove 2 self-tapping screws attaching turn signal switch to lock cylinder. Disconnect electrical connectors, and remove turn signal switch. To install, reverse removal procedure.
Removal & Installation (Aerostar) – 1) Disconnect negative battery cable. Remove steering wheel. See STEERING WHEEL under REMOVAL & INSTALLATION. On tilt column, remove upper extension shroud. Remove steering column shroud.
2) Remove lock cylinder. See LOCK CYLINDER under REMOVAL & INSTALLATION. Remove turn signal switch lever by grasping, pulling and twisting. Remove turn signal switch. To install, reverse removal procedure.

MULTIFUNCTION SWITCH

Removal & Installation (Explorer & Ranger) – Disconnect negative battery cable. Remove steering column shroud. Remove 2 screws attaching multifunction switch to steering column. Disconnect electrical connector. Remove switch. To install, reverse removal procedure.

LOCK CYLINDER

Removal & Installation (With Key) – 1) Disconnect negative battery cable. Remove trim shroud. Remove electrical connector from key buzzer switch. Turn ignition switch to RUN position. Place a 1/8" (3.17 mm) diameter pin in hole located in outer edge of lock cylinder housing.
2) Depress retaining pin, and pull out lock cylinder. To install, lube lock cylinder. Turn lock cylinder to ON position. Depress retaining pin, and insert lock cylinder into housing. To install remaining components, reverse removal procedure. *See Figs. 4-7.*

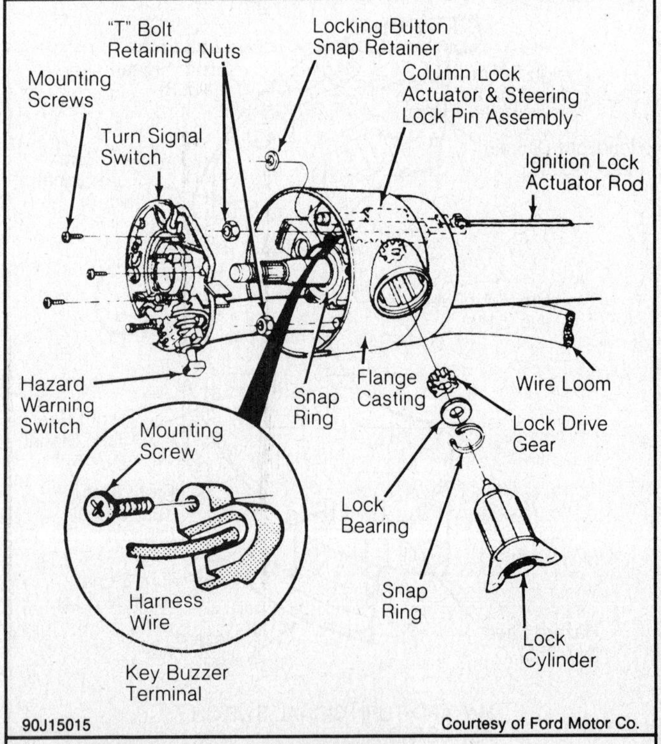
"T" Bolt
Retaining Nuts
Locking Button
Snap Retainer
Mounting
Screws
Column Lock
Actuator & Steering
Lock Pin Assembly
Turn Signal
Switch
Ignition Lock
Actuator Rod
Hazard
Warning
Switch
Snap
Ring
Flange
Casting
Wire Loom
Mounting
Screw
Lock Drive
Gear
Lock
Bearing
Harness
Wire
Snap
Ring
Lock
Cylinder
Key Buzzer
Terminal
90J15015
Courtesy of Ford Motor Co.

Fig. 4: Exploded View of Non-Tilt Column (Bronco, "E" & "F" Series)

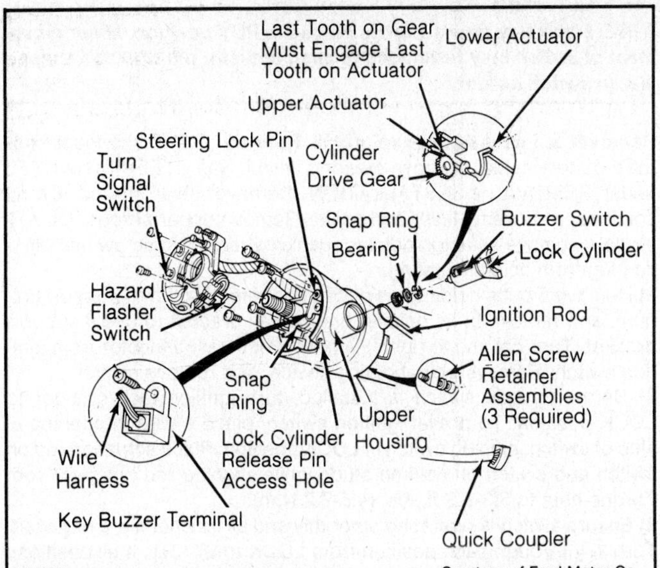

Last Tooth on Gear
Must Engage Last
Tooth on Actuator
Lower Actuator
Upper Actuator
Steering Lock Pin
Turn
Signal
Switch
Cylinder
Drive Gear
Snap Ring
Buzzer Switch
Bearing
Lock Cylinder
Hazard
Flasher
Switch
Ignition Rod
Allen Screw
Retainer
Assemblies
(3 Required)
Snap
Ring
Upper
Housing
Lock Cylinder
Release Pin
Access Hole
Wire
Harness
Key Buzzer Terminal
Quick Coupler

117374 Courtesy of Ford Motor Co.

Fig. 5: Exploded View of Tilt Column (Bronco, "E" & "F" Series)

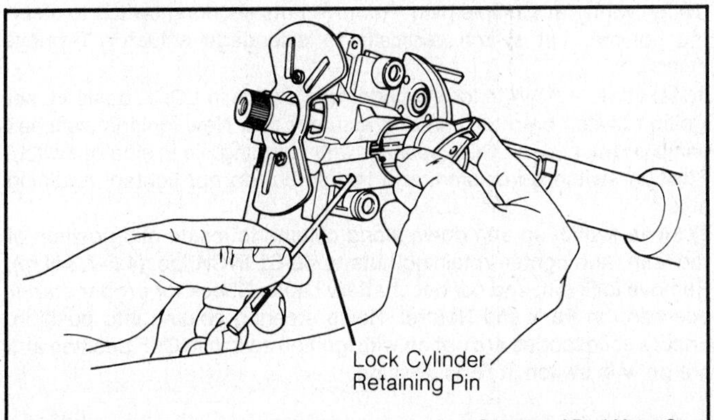

Lock Cylinder
Retaining Pin

90I15014 Courtesy of Ford Motor Co.

Fig. 6: Removing Lock Cylinder (Aerostar)

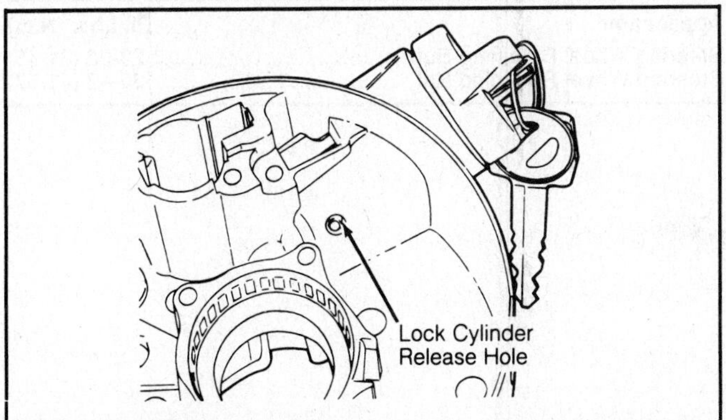

Lock Cylinder
Release Hole

15227 Courtesy of Ford Motor Co.

Fig. 7: Removing Lock Cylinder (Non-Tilt – Bronco, "E" & "F" Series)

Removal (Without Key – Aerostar, Explorer & Ranger) – 1) Use this procedure to remove ignition lock cylinder if key is missing or cylinder is frozen. Disconnect negative battery cable. Remove steering wheel. See STEERING WHEEL under REMOVAL & INSTALLATION. Remove steering column trim shrouds and connector from key buzzer switch. Use a 1/8" (3.17 mm) drill bit to drill out retaining pin. DO NOT drill deeper than 1/2" (12.7 mm).

2) Place a chisel at base of lock cylinder cap. Using a hammer, strike chisel with sharp blows to break cap away from lock cylinder. Using a 3/8" (9.52 mm) drill bit, drill out center of lock cylinder key slot. Drill down approximately 1 3/4" (44 mm) until lock cylinder breaks away from base of lock cylinder.

3) Remove metal shavings from lock cylinder housing. Remove snap ring, washer and lock cylinder drive gear. Thoroughly clean all metal shavings and other foreign materials from housing. Carefully inspect housing for damage. If damage is apparent, replace housing.

Installation – 1) Install ignition lock drive gear, washer and snap ring. Lubricate cylinder cavity with lock cylinder lubricant. Turn ignition switch to RUN position. Depress retaining pin, and insert new lock cylinder into lock cylinder housing.

2) Before turning key to OFF position, ensure cylinder is fully seated and aligned into interlocking washer (Aerostar) or drive gear (Explorer/Ranger). Use key to rotate cylinder to ensure correct mechanical operation in all positions.

3) Install electrical connector into key buzzer switch. Connect negative battery cable. Check ignition switch functions, and ensure column locks when switch is in LOCK position.

Removal (Without Key, Non-Tilt – Bronco, "E" & "F" Series) –1) Use this procedure to remove ignition lock cylinder if key is missing or cylinder is frozen. Disconnect negative battery cable. Remove steering wheel and turn signal lever. Remove column trim shrouds to gain access to ignition switch.

2) Detach and lower steering column from brake pedal support bracket. Remove ignition switch and key buzzer terminal. Pin key buzzer terminal in LOCK position. Remove turn signal switch. *See Fig. 4.* Remove upper bearing snap ring and "T" bolt retaining nuts, which secure flange casting to outer tube.

3) Remove entire flange casting, upper shaft bearing, lock cylinder assembly, ignition switch actuator and actuator rod by pulling assembly over end of steering column shaft.

4) Remove lock actuator insert and "T" bolts. Remove PRND21 insert on A/T vehicles or key release lever on M/T vehicles. Replace flange, lock cylinder assembly, lock gear assembly, lock bearing, upper bearing retainer and actuator assembly.

Installation – 1) Install key release lever assembly (M/T vehicles) or PRND21 insert (A/T vehicles). Install "T" bolts and lock actuator insert. After assembling flange casting, install a new upper bearing.

2) Set lock actuator on drive gear. Install hazard/turn signal switch and key buzzer. Install ignition switch, and check for proper operation after adjustment. Install steering column to brake pedal support bracket. Install column trim shrouds, steering wheel and pads.

3) Install turn signal lever. Using ignition key, rotate lock cylinder to ensure proper operation in all positions. Connect negative battery cable, and check for proper start in Park and Neutral. Ensure vehicle does not start in Drive or Reverse.

Removal (Without Key, Tilt – Bronco, "E" & "F" Series) – 1) Use this procedure to remove ignition lock cylinder if key is missing or cylinder is frozen. Disconnect negative battery cable. Remove steering column trim shrouds. Tape gap between steering wheel hub, and cover casting. Cover entire circumference of casting. Cover driver seat and floor area to protect upholstery.

2) Pull out hazard switch, and tape it under steering column, providing clearance for drilling out lock cylinder retaining pin. Lock cylinder retaining pin is located outside of steering column flange casting, near hazard button.

3) Tilt steering column to full-up position. If necessary, center punch retaining pin using a prick punch. Using a 1/8" (3.17 mm) drill bit and a right angle drill, drill out pin. DO NOT drill deeper than 1/2" (12.7 mm). After retaining pin is out, tilt steering column to full-down position.

4) Place a chisel at base of ignition lock cylinder cap. Using a hammer, strike chisel with sharp blows to break cap away from lock cylinder. Using a 3/8" (9.8 mm) drill bit, drill down center of lock cylinder. Drill down approximately 1 3/4" (44 mm) or until lock cylinder breaks loose from casting housing.

5) Remove lock cylinder and metal shavings from housing. Remove steering wheel. See STEERING WHEEL under REMOVAL & INSTALLATION. Remove turn signal lever and turn signal switch. Remove key

1991 SAFETY EQUIPMENT
Steering Column Switches (Cont.)

buzzer terminal. Lift turn signal switch up and over end of steering shaft, but do not disconnect.

6) Remove 4 screws from flange casting, and lift casting over steering shaft, allowing turn signal switch to pass through flange casting. Remove upper actuator. Remove drive gear, snap ring and washer from flange casting. Thoroughly clean components. Carefully inspect all components for wear and damage from drilling. Replace parts as required.

Installation – 1) Lubricate tang of lock cylinder. Attach upper actuator to lower actuator, and lubricate upper actuator. Reassemble flange casting, upper actuator, turn signal switch and lever, drive gear, lock cylinder, steering wheel, pad and steering column trim shrouds.

2) Insert ignition key, and rotate lock cylinder to ensure correct operation in all positions. Connect battery cable. Check for proper start in Park or Neutral. Ensure vehicle does not start in Drive or Reverse.

IGNITION SWITCH

Removal & Installation (Aerostar) – 1) Disconnect negative battery cable. Rotate lock cylinder to lock position. Remove steering wheel. See STEERING WHEEL under REMOVAL & INSTALLATION. On tilt columns, remove upper extension housing by squeezing at 6 and 12 o'clock positions. Remove panel on right side of steering column by removing 2 screws and pulling outward. Remove 4 screws holding trim shroud, and swing bottom panel open. Remove 2 screws attaching shroud to retaining plate.

2) Remove key lock cylinder. Remove shroud by first raising left side past turn signal lever, and then pulling right side up past lock cylinder boss until it clears lock cylinder. Shroud can now be worked past instrument panel.

3) Disconnect ignition switch electrical connector. Remove break-off bolts retaining switch to lock cylinder housing. *See Fig. 8*. Remove switch from actuator pin.

4) Install replacement switch by aligning holes on switch casting base with holes in cylinder housing. Tighten new break-off bolts until they break off, approximately 18-26 ft. lbs. (4-6 N.m). Install electrical connector to switch. Rotate key in lock cylinder to RUN position, and install lock cylinder. To install, reverse removal procedures.

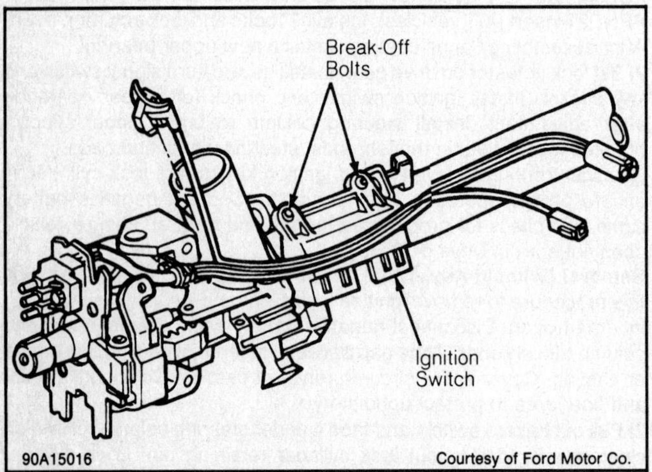
Break-Off
Bolts
Ignition
Switch
90A15016
Courtesy of Ford Motor Co.

Fig. 8: Removing Ignition Switch (Aerostar)

NOTE: Make sure new switch is placed in RUN position. Minor movement of switch may be needed to align actuator pin with "U" shaped slot in switch carrier.

Removal & Installation (Explorer & Ranger) – 1) Disconnect negative battery cable. Remove steering wheel. See STEERING WHEEL under REMOVAL & INSTALLATION. Remove lower shroud. On tilt columns, remove tilt lever and collar. Remove upper shroud. On A/T models, remove selector indicator cable by removing screw and plastic plug from column casting.

2) Remove 5 bolts holding toe plate at bottom of column. Support column, and remove bolts holding breakaway bracket to pedal support bracket. Turn column to right. Remove electrical connector from ignition switch. Remove bolts holding switch, and remove switch.

3) Before ignition switch is installed, turn ignition lock cylinder to LOCK position. To preset ignition switch, place a wire in opening in side of switch, pinning switch in LOCK position. Place actuation rod on switch and switch on column studs while aligning rod hole with rod. Torque nuts to 3.3-5.3 ft. lbs. (4.5-7.2 N.m).

4) Ensure switch is operating smoothly and all functions are engaged. Turn key through each position from LOCK to START. If all positions are not correct with key operation, see ADJUSTMENTS. To install, reverse removal procedures.

Removal (Bronco, "E" & "F" Series) – Disconnect negative battery cable. Remove steering column shroud and lower column. Disconnect switch wiring at multiple plug. Remove nuts securing switch to steering column. Lift switch vertically to disengage actuator. Remove switch.

Installation – 1) With lock cylinder and switch in LOCK position, set ignition switch onto column and actuator rod. New ignition switches come positioned in LOCK position with shipping pin in side of switch. Position switch on column, and install, but do not tighten, retaining nuts.

2) Move switch up and down along column to locate mid-position of rod lash, and tighten retaining nuts to 40-65 INCH lbs. (4.5-7.3 N.m). Remove lock pin, and connect battery cable. Check for proper starter operation in Park and Neutral. Raise steering column into position. Ensure accessories are not on with ignition switch in OFF position and are on with switch in RUN position.

TORQUE SPECIFICATIONS

TORQUE SPECIFICATIONS

Application	Ft. Lbs. (N.m)
Steering Wheel Retaining Bolt	23-33 (31-45)
Steering Wheel Retaining Nut	30-42 (41-57)

1991 SAFETY EQUIPMENT
Wiper/Washer Systems – Bronco, "E" & "F" Series

NOTE: Unless otherwise specified, references to "F" Series include "F" Series Super Duty.

DESCRIPTION & OPERATION

The 2-speed permanent magnet windshield wiper motor uses a 3-brush assembly. On Bronco and "F" Series vehicles, low speed is accomplished by using White wire brush and ground brush. High speed circuit uses Blue/Orange wire brush and grounded brush. On "E" Series, the grounded Yellow wire brush and Blue wire brush are used for low speed operation. High speed circuit uses White/Orange wire brush and grounded brush.

Interval operation is controlled by a variable resistor, mounted in wiper control switch. This variable resistor works with electronic governor to control variable pause operation. The resistor controls current going to electronic governor. Washer system consists of a control switch incorporated into wiper switch, a reservoir and motor assembly, nozzles and connecting hoses.

On Bronco and "F" Series, circuit breaker is located in wiper control switch on systems using rotary-type switch. On "E" Series, circuit breaker is fuse panel-mounted for systems using slide control switch. Amperage ratings for rotary and slide circuit breakers are 7 and 7.5 amps, respectively.

ADJUSTMENTS

WIPER ARM & BLADE ASSEMBLY

1) Remove wiper arm and blade assemblies from pivot shafts. Turn on wiper switch to allow motor to move pivots 3 or 4 cycles, and turn wiper switch Off. Wiper pivot shafts will be in Park position.

2) Install arm and blade assemblies on pivot shafts. Adjust clearance between wiper blade and cowl top. On "E" Series, clearance should be 2.75-4.25" (70-107 mm) for driver's side and 3.25-4.75" (83-120 mm) for passenger's side. On Bronco and "F" Series, clearance should be 1.9-3.1" (48-80 mm) for driver's side and 1.7-3.0" (44-76 mm) for passenger's side.

DIAGNOSIS & TESTING

STANDARD WIPER SYSTEM TESTS (BRONCO & "F" SERIES)

High Speed Test – 1) When wiper switch is in HI position, current flows from ignition switch through wiper switch to wiper motor high terminal. *See Fig. 1*. If problem exists in high speed circuit, check for voltage at wiper motor circuit No. 56 (Blue/Orange wire).

2) If voltage is not present, check voltage at circuit No. 297 (Black/Light Green wire) of wiper switch connector. If voltage is present at circuit No. 297 but not at circuit No. 56, replace wiper switch.

3) If voltage is not present at circuit No. 297, locate short or open. If voltage is present at circuit No. 56 and wiper motor does not run, connect jumper wire between wiper motor ground circuit and chassis ground. If motor runs, repair ground. If motor does not run, replace wiper motor.

Low Speed Test – 1) When wiper switch is in LO position, current flows from ignition switch through wiper switch to wiper motor low speed terminal. *See Fig. 1*. If problem exists in low speed circuit, check for voltage at circuit No. 58 (White wire) of wiper motor connector.

2) If voltage is not present, check for voltage at circuit No. 297 (Black/Light Green wire) of wiper switch connector. If voltage is present at circuit No. 297 but not at circuit No. 58, replace wiper switch. If voltage is not present at circuit No. 297, trace circuit back to source of problem.

3) If voltage is present at circuit No. 58 and wiper motor does not run, connect a jumper wire between wiper motor ground and chassis ground. If wiper motor runs, repair ground. If motor does not run, replace wiper motor.

Park Test – 1) When wipers are turned off, system will complete one cycle through wiper motor park switch. Current flows from ignition switch through wiper switch to wiper motor park switch for 9/10th of one cycle. *See Fig. 1*.

2) At last 1/10th of cycle, park switch moves from run position to park position (ground). This stops wiper motor in park position. If a problem exists in park circuit, check for voltage at circuits No. 58 (White wire), No. 28 (Black/Pink wire) and No. 63 (Red wire) of wiper motor connector.

3) If voltage is present on all 3 circuits and wiper blades are not parked, ground motor ground circuit to vehicle body. If motor parks, repair ground. If motor does not park, replace motor. If voltage is present only at circuit No. 63, replace wiper motor.

4) If voltage is present only at circuits No. 63 and No. 28, replace wiper switch. If voltage is still not present at circuit No. 58, check circuits No. 58 and No. 28 for opens or shorts.

STANDARD WIPER SYSTEM TESTS ("E" SERIES)

High Speed Test – 1) When wiper switch is in HI position, current flows from ignition switch through internal circuit breaker and wiper switch, and then through circuit No. 61 (Yellow wire) to wiper motor common brush. *See Fig. 2*.

2) From common brush, current flows across wiper motor armature through circuit No. 58 (White/Orange wire) to wiper switch to ground. Wiper motor is not grounded. If a malfunction occurs in high speed circuit, check for voltage at circuit No. 61 (Yellow wire) at wiper motor connector.

3) If voltage is present and wiper motor does not run, ground circuit No. 58 (White/Orange wire). If motor runs, repair wiper switch ground or replace switch. If motor does not run with circuit No. 58 grounded, repair motor.

4) If voltage is present at circuit No. 65 (Green wire) only, replace wiper switch. If voltage is not present at circuit No. 65 (Green wire), trace circuit to short or open.

Low Speed Test – 1) When wiper switch is in LO position, current flows from ignition switch through circuit breaker, and then through circuit No. 61 (Yellow wire) to wiper motor common brush. From common brush current flows across motor armature through circuit No. 56 (Blue wire) to wiper switch to ground. Wiper motor is not grounded. *See Fig. 2*.

2) If problem occurs in low speed circuit, check for voltage at circuit No. 61 (Yellow wire) of wiper motor connector. If voltage is present but wiper motor does not run, ground circuit No. 56 (Blue wire). If motor runs, repair wiper ground circuit or replace wiper switch.

3) If wiper motor does not run with circuit No. 56 (Blue wire) grounded, repair or replace motor. If voltage is present at circuit No. 65 (Green wire) only, replace wiper switch. If voltage is not present at circuit No. 65, trace circuit back to short or open.

Park Test – 1) A set of contacts, attached to circuit No. 63 (Red wire) inside wiper motor, oscillates between circuit No. 65 (Green wire) and ground when wipers are running. When wiper switch is turned off, motor contacts remain on circuit No. 65 (Green wire) for 9/10th of one cycle and on ground circuit for 1/10th of one cycle. *See Fig. 2*.

2) Current flows from circuit No. 65 (Green wire) through wiper motor park switch and circuit No. 63 (Red wire) to wiper switch. From wiper switch, current flows through circuit No. 61 (Yellow wire), through common brush in wiper motor. From common brush current flows through low speed brush to wiper switch and to ground.

3) If wipers do not park, check for voltage at circuits No. 63 (Red wire) and No. 61 (Yellow wire) of wiper motor connector. If both terminals show voltage, connect a jumper wire between circuit No. 56 (Blue wire) and chassis ground. If motor parks, repair ground circuit or replace wiper switch. If motor does not run, replace motor.

4) If voltage is present at circuit No. 63 (Red wire) but not at circuit No. 61 (Yellow wire), replace wiper switch. If voltage is present at circuit No. 65 (Green wire) but not at circuit No. 63 (Red wire), replace park switch. If no voltage is present at circuit No. 65, trace circuit for open or short.

1991 SAFETY EQUIPMENT
Wiper/Washer Systems – Bronco, "E" & "F" Series (Cont.)

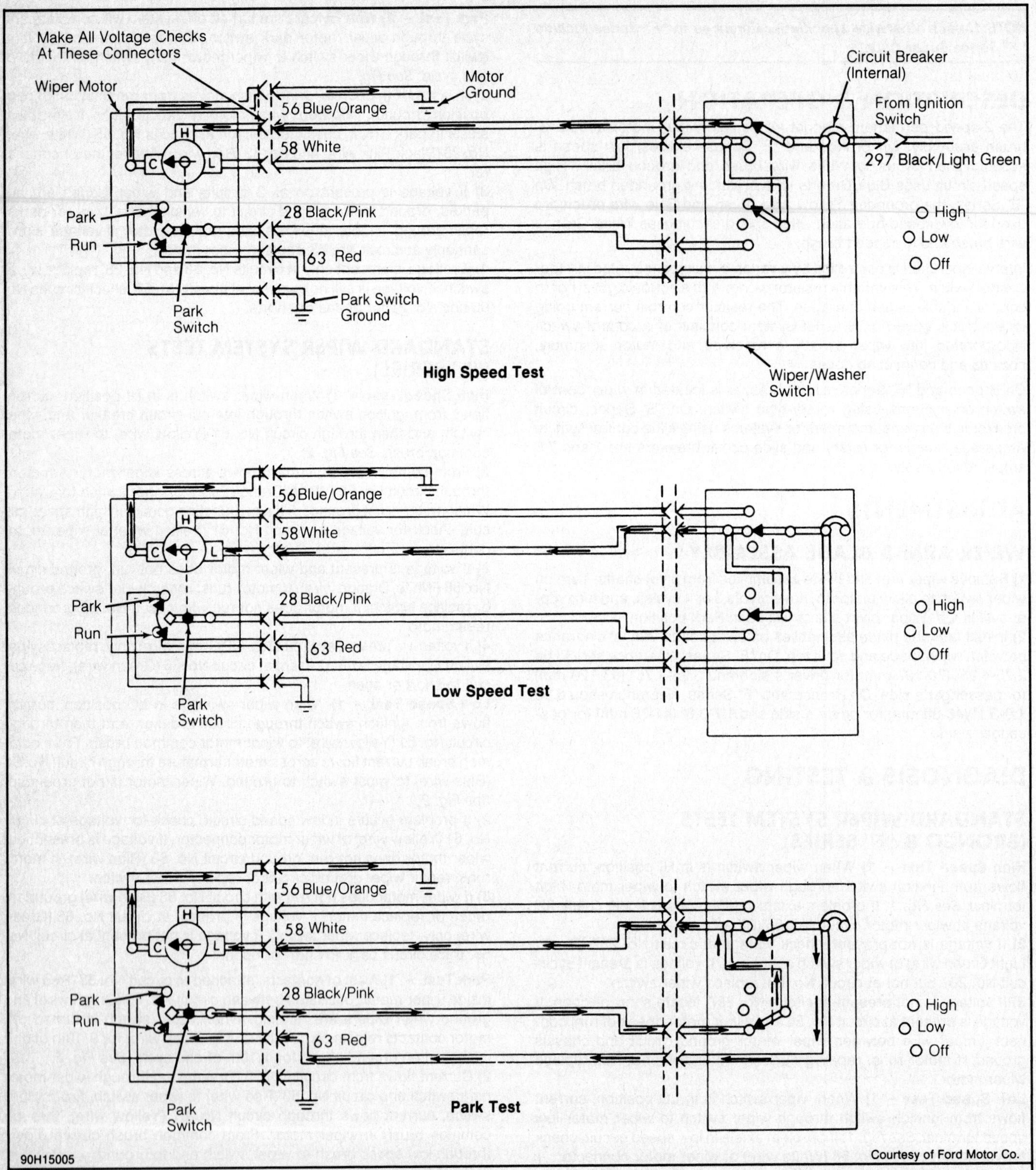
Make All Voltage Checks At These Connectors
Wiper Motor
Motor Ground
56 Blue/Orange
58 White
H
C
L
Park
Run
28 Black/Pink
63 Red
Park Switch Ground
Park Switch
Circuit Breaker (Internal)
From Ignition Switch
297 Black/Light Green
High
Low
Off
Wiper/Washer Switch
High Speed Test
Low Speed Test
Park Test
90H15005
Courtesy of Ford Motor Co.

Fig. 1: Testing Standard Wiper System (Bronco & "F" Series)

Wiper/Washer Systems – Bronco, "E" & "F" Series (Cont.)

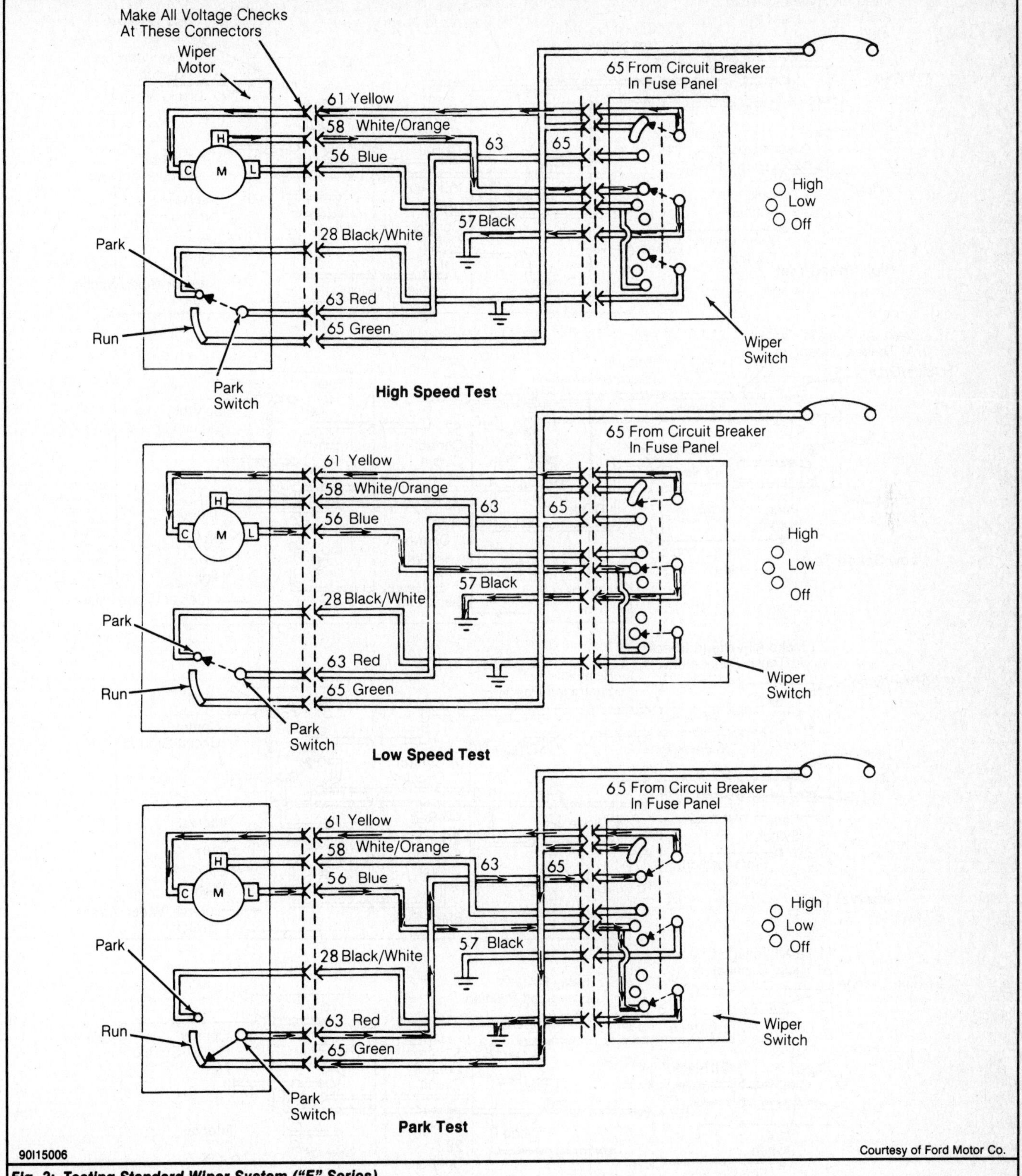
Make All Voltage Checks
At These Connectors
Wiper
Motor
65 From Circuit Breaker
In Fuse Panel
61 Yellow
58 White/Orange
63
65
56 Blue
H
C
M
L
57 Black
28 Black/White
Park
63 Red
65 Green
Run
Park
Switch
High
Low
Off
Wiper
Switch
High Speed Test
Low Speed Test
Park Test
90I15006
Courtesy of Ford Motor Co.

Fig. 2: Testing Standard Wiper System ("E" Series)

1991 SAFETY EQUIPMENT

Wiper/Washer Systems – Bronco, "E" & "F" Series (Cont.)

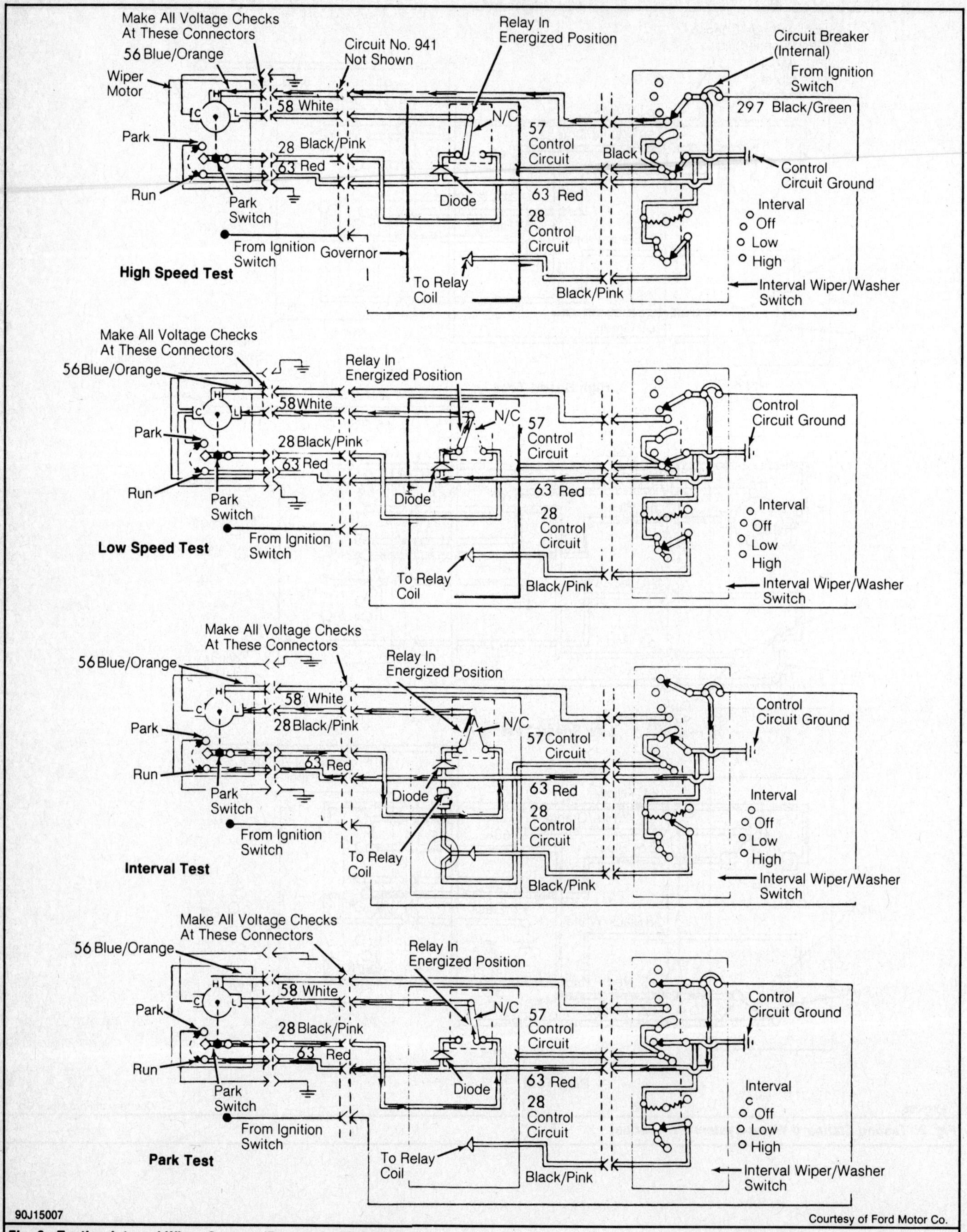
Make All Voltage Checks
At These Connectors
56 Blue/Orange
Wiper
Motor
Circuit No. 941
Not Shown
Relay In
Energized Position
Circuit Breaker
(Internal)
From Ignition
Switch
297 Black/Green
58 White
N/C
57
Control
Circuit
Park
28 Black/Pink
63 Red
Black
Control
Circuit Ground
Run
Park
Switch
Diode
63 Red
Interval
28
Control
Circuit
Off
Low
High
From Ignition
Switch
Governor
High Speed Test
To Relay
Coil
Black/Pink
Interval Wiper/Washer
Switch
Low Speed Test
Interval Test
Park Test
90J15007
Courtesy of Ford Motor Co.

Fig. 3: Testing Interval Wiper System (Bronco & "F" Series)

1991 SAFETY EQUIPMENT
Wiper/Washer Systems – Bronco, "E" & "F" Series (Cont.)

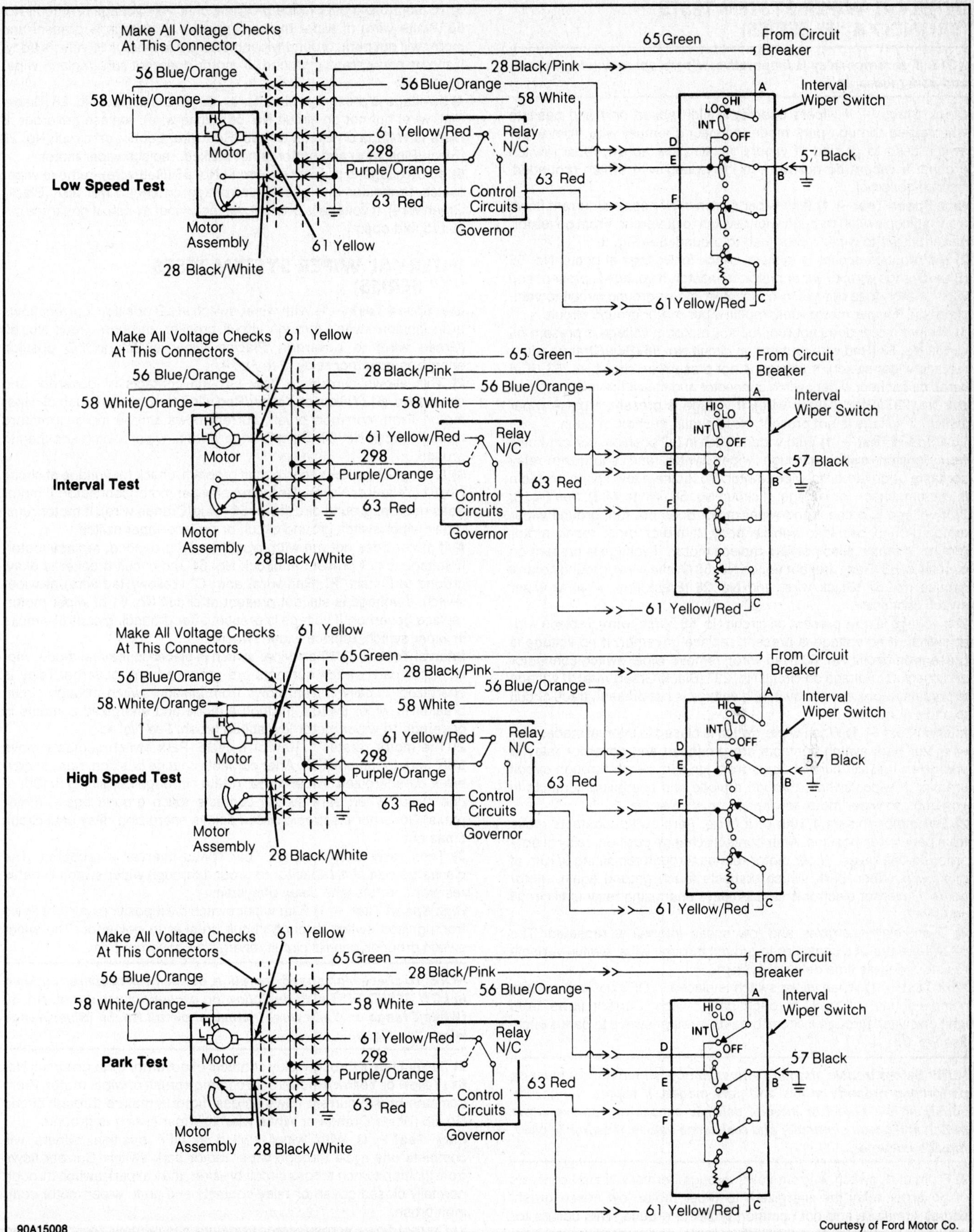
Make All Voltage Checks At This Connector
56 Blue/Orange
58 White/Orange
Motor
Low Speed Test
Motor Assembly
28 Black/White
61 Yellow
65 Green
From Circuit Breaker
28 Black/Pink
56 Blue/Orange
58 White
61 Yellow/Red
Relay N/C
298 Purple/Orange
63 Red
Control Circuits
Governor
Interval Wiper Switch
57 Black
61 Yellow/Red
Make All Voltage Checks At This Connectors
Interval Test
High Speed Test
Park Test
90A15008
Courtesy of Ford Motor Co.

Fig. 4: Testing Interval Wiper System ("E" Series)

1991 SAFETY EQUIPMENT
Wiper/Washer Systems – Bronco, "E" & "F" Series (Cont.)

INTERVAL WIPER SYSTEM TESTS (BRONCO & "F" SERIES)

NOTE: If governor relay is inoperative, wipers operate in high speed and park modes only.

Quick Check – If wipers operate in high speed only and hesitate when going through park mode, connect a jumper wire from wiper switch case to ground. If wipers work in low speed, repair switch ground. If wipers do not work in low speed with switch grounded, replace governor.

High Speed Test – 1) With wiper switch in HI position, current flows from ignition switch through wiper switch to governor. From governor, current flows to wiper motor then to ground. *See Fig. 3*.

2) If a problem occurs in system, check for voltage at circuit No. 56 (Blue/Orange wire) of wiper motor connector. If voltage is present and wiper motor does not run, ground wiper motor ground circuit to vehicle body. If wiper motor runs, repair wiper motor ground circuit.

3) If wiper motor does not run, replace motor. If voltage is present on circuit No. 63 (Red wire) but not on circuit No. 56 (Blue/Orange wire), replace wiper switch. If voltage is not present on circuit No. 63 (Red wire), disconnect wiper switch connector and check for voltage on circuit No. 297 (Black/Green wire). If voltage is present, replace wiper switch. If voltage is not present, trace circuit to short or open.

Low Speed Test – 1) With wiper switch in LO position, current flows from ignition switch through wiper switch and energized relay contacts of governor to wiper motor. To locate a low speed problem in system, check for voltage at circuit No. 58 (White wire). *See Fig. 3*.

2) If voltage is present and wiper motor does not run, ground wiper motor ground circuit to vehicle body. If motor runs, repair motor ground. If motor does not run, replace motor. If voltage is present on circuit No. 63 (Red wire) but not on No. 58 (White wire), ground control circuits No. 57 (Black wire) and No. 28 (Black/Pink wire) at wiper switch connector.

3) If voltage is now present on circuit No. 58 (White wire), replace wiper switch. If no voltage is present, replace governor. If no voltage is present on circuit No. 63 (Red wire), remove wiper switch connector and check for voltage on circuit No. 297 (Black/Green wire). If voltage is present, replace wiper switch. If voltage is not present, trace circuit to short or open.

Interval Test – 1) When wiper switch is placed in Interval mode, wiper motor park switch contacts are grounded and governor relay is energized. Initially current flows from ignition switch through circuit breaker in wiper switch, through a diode and energized contacts in governor, to wiper motor low speed brush. *See Fig. 3*.

2) The motor rotates 1/10th of a cycle. Park switch contacts move from park to run position. After contacts change position, relay in governor de-energizes. Wiper motor rotates through remaining 9/10th of one cycle. When park switch contacts touch ground again, motor parks. Governor electronic circuit delays energizing relay until circuit times out.

3) Then relay energizes and low speed interval is repeated. The discharge rate of a capacitor to ground through wiper switch variable resistor controls time delay of system.

Park Test – 1) When wiper switch is placed in OFF position, wipers complete one full cycle through park switch. Current flows from ignition switch through a circuit breaker in wiper switch to park switch. *See Fig. 3*.

NOTE: Before trouble shooting interval mode, wiper system must be performing properly in low and park modes. If wipers run continuously at low speed or interval delay is excessive, remove wiper switch and check continuity and resistance values. If switch is okay, replace governor.

2) From park switch, current flows through normally closed contacts of governor relay (de-energized) to wiper motor low speed brush, across armature and out common brush to ground. This occurs for 9/10th of one cycle. At last 1/10th of cycle, park switch moves from run to park, stopping motor in park position.

3) To diagnose a park mode problem, check for voltage on circuit No. 58 (White wire) of wiper motor connector. If voltage is present and motor will not park, ground wiper motor ground circuit to vehicle body. If motor parks, repair ground. If motor does not run, replace wiper motor.

4) If voltage is present at circuits No. 63 (Red wire) and No. 28 (Black/Pink wire) but not on circuit No. 58 (White wire), replace governor. If there is voltage on circuit No. 63 (Red wire) but not on circuit No. 28 (Black/Pink wire) and motor is not parked, replace wiper motor.

5) If no voltage is present on circuit No. 63 (Red wire), remove wiper switch connector and check for voltage on circuit No. 297 (Black/Green wire). If voltage is present, replace wiper switch. If not, trace circuit to find open.

INTERVAL WIPER SYSTEM TESTS ("E" SERIES)

Low Speed Test – 1) With wiper switch in LO position, current flows from ignition switch through circuit breaker, through circuit No. 65 (Green wire) to governor. Placing wiper switch in LO position energizes governor relay. *See Fig. 4*.

2) This allows current to flow through contacts of governor and circuits No. 61 (Yellow or Yellow/Red wire) to common brush of wiper motor. From common brush, current flows across motor armature through circuit No. 56 (Blue/Orange wire) to wiper switch and then to ground.

3) To diagnose a low speed circuit problem, check for voltage at circuit No. 61 (Yellow or Yellow/Red wire) of wiper motor connector. If motor does not run, ground circuit No. 56 (Blue/Orange wire). If motor runs, repair wiper switch ground circuit or replace wiper switch.

4) If motor does not run with circuit No. 56 grounded, replace motor. If voltage is not present at circuit No. 61 and circuit breaker is okay, ground terminals "F" (Red wire) and "C" (Yellow/Red wire) at wiper switch. If voltage is still not present at circuit No. 61 of wiper motor, replace governor. If voltage is present after grounding control circuits in wiper switch, replace wiper switch.

Interval Test – 1) When wiper switch is placed in Interval mode, wiper motor park switch contacts are grounded and governor relay is energized. Initially current flows from ignition switch through circuit breaker in wiper switch, through a diode and energized contacts in governor, to wiper motor low speed brush. *See Fig. 4*.

2) The motor rotates 1/10th of a cycle. Park switch contacts move from park to run position. After contacts change position, relay in governor de-energizes. Wiper motor rotates through remaining 9/10th of one cycle. When park switch contacts touch ground again, motor parks. Governor electronic circuit delays energizing relay until circuit times out.

3) Then relay energizes and low speed interval is repeated. The discharge rate of a capacitor to ground through wiper switch variable resistor controls time delay of system.

High Speed Test – 1) With wiper switch in HI position, current flows from ignition switch through circuit breaker to governor. The wiper switch grounds control circuit, energizing governor relay.

NOTE: To check high speed operation, use same procedures outlined in LOW SPEED TEST with the following exception: use circuit No. 58 (White/Orange or White wire) instead of circuit No. 56 (Blue/Orange wire). See Fig. 4.

2) Current flows through relay contacts of governor through circuit No. 61 (Yellow or Yellow/Red wire) to common brush of wiper motor. From common brush, current flows across motor armature through circuit No. 58 (White/Orange or White wire) to wiper switch to ground.

Park Test – 1) With wiper switch in OFF position, wipers will complete one cycle through wiper motor park switch. Current flows from ignition switch across circuit breaker, then to park switch through normally closed governor relay contacts and on to wiper motor common brush.

2) Current flows across motor armature and out low speed brush to ground. This occurs for 9/10th of one cycle. At last 1/10th of cycle,

Wiper/Washer Systems – Bronco, "E" & "F" Series (Cont.)

park switch moves from run position to park (ground). To diagnose a park mode problem, check for voltage at circuits No. 61 (Yellow/Red or Yellow wire) of wiper motor connector. *See Fig. 4*.

3) If voltage is present and motor does not park, ground circuit No. 56 (Blue/Orange wire). If motor parks, repair ground circuit or replace wiper switch. If motor does not run, replace motor. If voltage is present on circuits No. 65 (Green wire) and No. 63 (Red wire), but not on circuit No. 61, replace governor.

4) If voltage is present on circuit No. 65 (Green wire) but not on circuit No. 63 (Red wire), repair or replace park switch. If voltage is not present on circuit No. 65 (Green wire), trace circuit back to find open circuit.

WIPER MOTOR CURRENT DRAW TEST

Bronco & "F" Series – 1) Disconnect wiper linkage and harness connector from wiper motor. Connect negative lead of ammeter to battery positive post and ammeter positive lead to low speed terminal at wiper connector. *See Fig. 5*. Measure and record current draw.

2) Move ammeter positive lead to high speed terminal at electrical plug. Maximum allowable current draw for either speed is 3.5 amps.

"E" Series – 1) Disconnect wiper linkage and harness connector from wiper motor. Connect positive lead of ammeter to wiper motor connector center terminal. Connect negative ammeter lead to battery positive post. *See Fig. 5*.

2) Connect a jumper wire between negative battery post and low speed terminal on motor end plate. Check and record current draw. Move jumper wire from low speed terminal to high speed terminal. Measure and record current draw.

3) Maximum allowable current draw for either speed is 3.5 amps. If current draw exceeds maximum, check output arm for binding or damage before replacing motor.

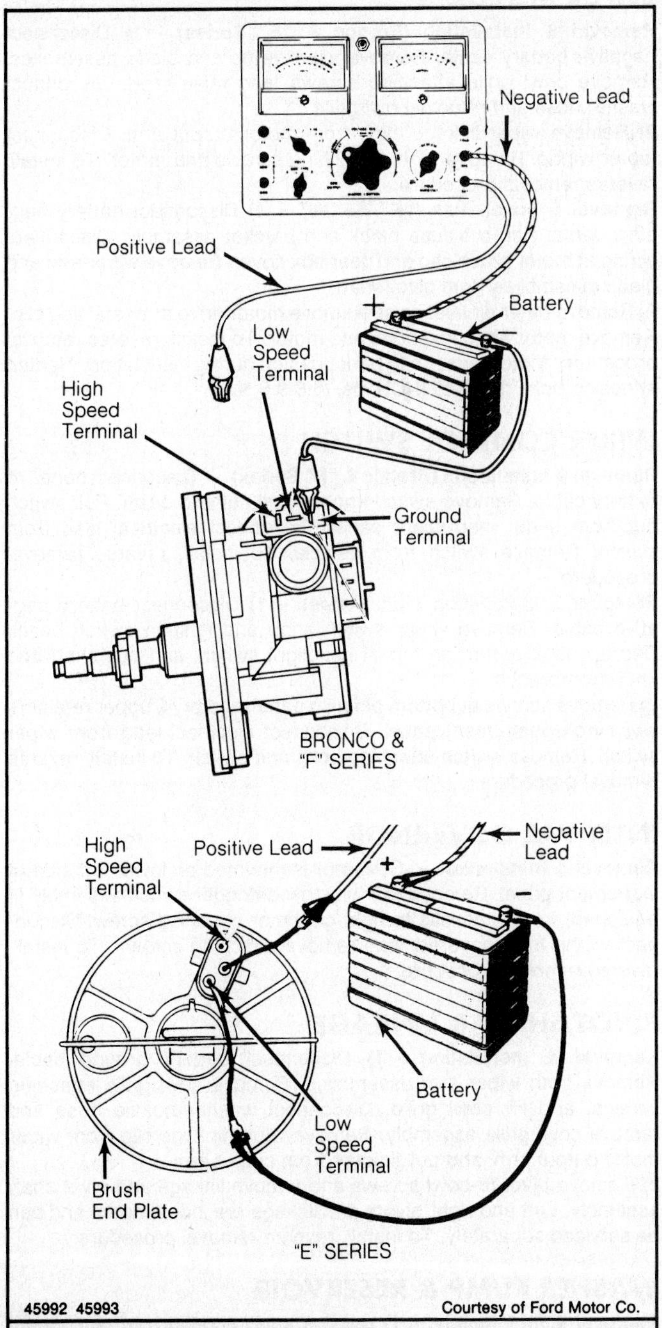
Negative Lead
Positive Lead
Battery
Low Speed Terminal
High Speed Terminal
Ground Terminal
BRONCO & "F" SERIES
High Speed Terminal
Positive Lead
Negative Lead
Battery
Low Speed Terminal
Brush End Plate
"E" SERIES
45992 45993
Courtesy of Ford Motor Co.

Fig. 5: Testing Wiper Motor Current Draw

CIRCUIT BREAKER TEST

NOTE: Some Bronco and "F" Series wiper switch connectors may have 7 terminals and others may have 6 terminals with external ground wire.

Bronco & "F" Series – 1) Two separate tests are used to check wiper switch circuit breakers. A Special Ford Digital Volt-Ohmmeter (DVOM 007-00001), 3 jumper wires and a 12-volt battery are needed to perform first test. Before connecting DVOM to wiper switch connector, short leads of meter together. Adjust current draw until it equals circuit breaker rating.

2) Connect DVOM, jumper wires and battery to wiper switch connector. *See Fig. 6*. Leave DVOM connected to wiper switch for 10 minutes, holding circuit breaker current rating on ammeter. If circuit breaker opens during the 10 minutes, replace wiper switch assembly. If circuit breaker does not open, proceed to step **3)** for next test.

3) Remove leads from switch and short tester leads together. Adjust current draw to 14 amps. Connect test leads to switch. Hold current at 14 amps; current reading on ammeter should drop to zero within 20 seconds. If current reading does not drop, replace wiper switch assembly.

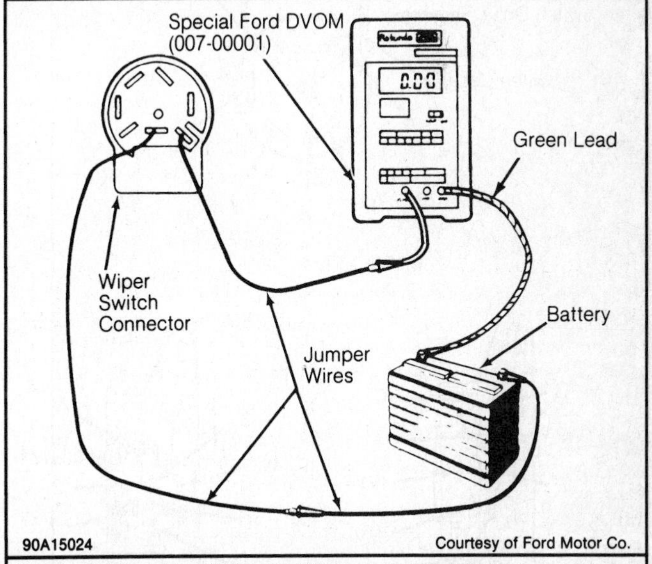
Special Ford DVOM (007-00001)
Green Lead
Wiper Switch Connector
Jumper Wires
Battery
90A15024
Courtesy of Ford Motor Co.

Fig. 6: Testing Circuit Breaker (Bronco & "F" Series)

WIPER SWITCH CONTINUITY TEST

NOTE: Some Bronco and "F" Series wiper switch connectors may have 7 terminals and others may have 6 terminals with external ground wire.

Wiper/Washer Systems – Bronco, "E" & "F" Series (Cont.)

1) To check switch continuity, see appropriate WIPER SWITCH CONTINUITY table. *See Fig. 7.* Either a self-powered test light or an ohmmeter can be used to test a standard 2-speed switch. Use an ohmmeter to test switch on interval system.
2) To detect marginal switch operation, slide switch (or rotate knob) while obtaining readings. If switch does not test as indicated or if poor continuity exists in any switch position, replace switch.

WIPER SWITCH CONTINUITY (BRONCO & "F" SERIES)

Switch Position	Standard Wiper System Terminals	[1] Interval Wiper System Terminals
OFF	C-D, A-B	A-B, D-E
LO	A-B-C	A-B, D-E-F
HI	A-B-E	D-E-F, A-B-C
Wash	A-B-W1	A-B-W1
Interval	...	A-B, E-F

[1] – Resistance between terminals "D" and "E" should be a minimum of 200-1000 ohms and a maximum of 5600-8400 ohms. *See Fig. 7.*

WIPER SWITCH CONTINUITY ("E" SERIES)

Switch Position	Standard Wiper System Terminals	[1] Interval Wiper System Terminals
OFF	1-5, 3-7	A-E
LO	1-4, 2-7	B-E-F-C
HI	1-4, 2-6	D-B-F-C
Wash	W1-W2	W1-W2
Interval	...	B-E-F

[1] – Resistance between terminals "F" and "C" will vary from 420-880 at minimum dwell to 8000-13,000 ohms at maximum dwell. In OFF position, resistance should be a maximum of 18,000 ohms. *See Fig. 7.*

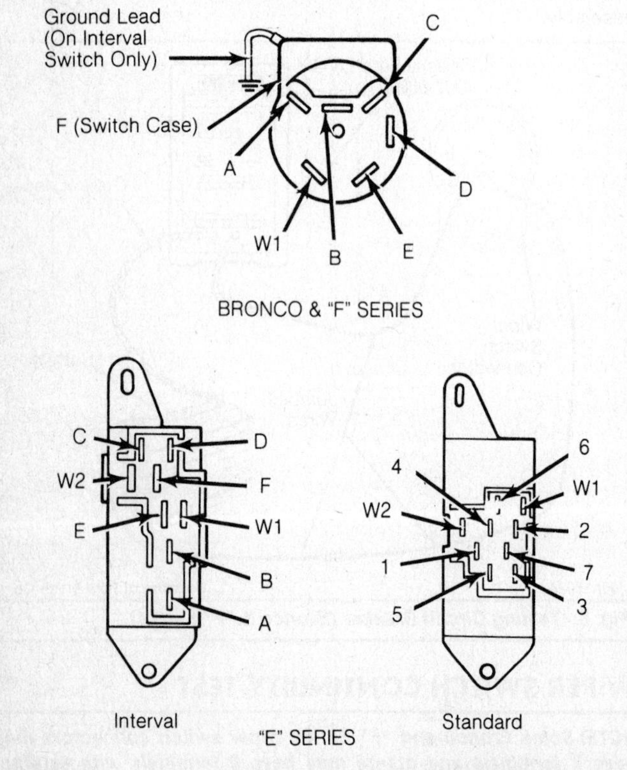
Ground Lead (On Interval Switch Only)
C
F (Switch Case)
A
D
W1
B
E
BRONCO & "F" SERIES
C
D
W2
F
E
W1
B
A
4
6
W1
W2
2
1
7
5
3
Interval
"E" SERIES
Standard
45990 45991
Courtesy of Ford Motor Co.

Fig. 7: Testing Wiper Switch Continuity

INTERVAL GOVERNOR TEST

If interval operation is unsatisfactory, check motor current draw, control switch and appropriate wiring. If motor, switch and wiring check out okay, replace interval governor assembly.

WASHER PUMP MOTOR CURRENT DRAW TEST

Connect ammeter negative lead to battery positive and positive lead to washer motor terminal. Connect jumper wire from remaining washer motor terminal to negative battery post. Operate washer pump. Acceptable current draw is 1.7-4.0 amps while washer motor is running. Replace washer motor if current draw is not within specification.

REMOVAL & INSTALLATION

WIPER MOTOR

Removal & Installation (Bronco & "F" Series) – 1) Disconnect negative battery cable. Remove wiper arms and blade assemblies. Remove cowl grille attaching screws, and raise cowl. Disconnect washer hose and remove cowl grille.
2) Remove wiper linkage clips from motor output arm. Disconnect motor wiring. Remove motor attaching screws and motor. To install, reverse removal procedure.
Removal & Installation ("E" Series) – 1) Disconnect battery negative cable. Remove fuse block and bracket assembly. Disconnect wiring at motor brush cap and gear box cover. Remove wiper arm and blade assemblies from pivot shaft.
2) Remove outer air inlet cowl. Remove motor drive arm retaining clip. Remove motor attaching bolts and motor. To install, reverse removal procedure. Motor must be in park position during installation. Tighten attaching bolts to 60-85 INCH lbs. (6.8-9.6 N.m).

WIPER CONTROL SWITCH

Removal & Installation (Bronco & "F" Series) – Disconnect negative battery cable. Remove switch knob, bezel nut and bezel. Pull switch out from under instrument panel. Disconnect electrical lead from switch. Remove switch from vehicle. To install, reverse removal procedure.
Removal & Installation ("E" Series) – 1) Disconnect battery negative cable. Remove wiper switch knob and ignition switch bezel. Depress lock button on top of headlight switch, and pull shaft and knob from switch.
2) Remove screws at bottom of finish panel, and pry 2 upper retainers away from instrument panel. Disconnect electrical lead from wiper switch. Remove switch attaching bolts and switch. To install, reverse removal procedure.

INTERVAL GOVERNOR

Removal & Installation – Governor is mounted on lower left side of instrument panel. Remove rear window defogger switch assembly (if equipped) to gain access to right governor attaching screw. Disconnect wiring from governor and remove attaching screws. To install, reverse removal procedure.

PIVOT SHAFT & LINKAGE

Removal & Installation – 1) Disconnect battery ground cable. Remove both wiper arm assemblies. Remove cowl grille attaching screws, and lift cowl grille. Disconnect washer nozzle hose and remove cowl grille assembly. Remove wiper linkage clip from wiper motor output arm, and pull linkage from output arm.
2) Remove pivot-to-cowl screws and remove linkage and pivot shaft assembly. Left and right pivots and linkage are independent and can be serviced separately. To install, reverse removal procedure.

WASHER PUMP & RESERVOIR

Removal & Installation – 1) Using a small screwdriver, disconnect lock tab wire connector. Remove hose, and drain reservoir. Remove pump retaining screws.

Wiper/Washer Systems – Bronco, "E" & "F" Series (Cont.)

2) Remove reservoir attaching screws. To install, reverse removal procedure. Fill reservoir before electrical connections are made.

WIPER ARMS

Removal & Installation – 1) Raise blade end of arm off windshield, and move slide latch away from pivot shaft to unlock wiper arm from shaft. Disconnect wiper washer hose (if equipped) and pull wiper arm off pivot shaft.

2) To install wiper arms, ensure wiper motor is in park position. Connect washer hose (if equipped), and push arm over pivot shaft. Raise blade of wiper arm and push slide latch into lock under pivot shaft head. Lower blade onto windshield. If blade does not touch windshield, slide latch is not completely in place.

OVERHAUL

COVER & SWITCH ASSEMBLY

Disassembly & Reassembly ("E" Series) – Remove 4 cover retaining screws. Remove assembly. Replace with appropriate kit. Ensure ground strap is under cover screw. Tighten screws to 15-25 INCH lbs. (1.7-2.8 N.m).

NOTE: "E" Series switch assembly is identified by letter "U" stamped on outside surface. Bronco and "F" Series wiper motor is not serviceable and must be replaced as an assembly.

BRUSH END PLATE

Disassembly & Reassembly ("E" Series) – 1) Observe and record position of bail retainer. Pry retainer off using a screwdriver. Remove end plate and plug. *See Fig. 8*. Replace with appropriate kit. When installing new kit, use a fine wire probe through hub opening to position brushes on commutator.

2) Rotate end plate until key is positioned in notch, and assemble plug. DO NOT over-bend bail retainer during installation.

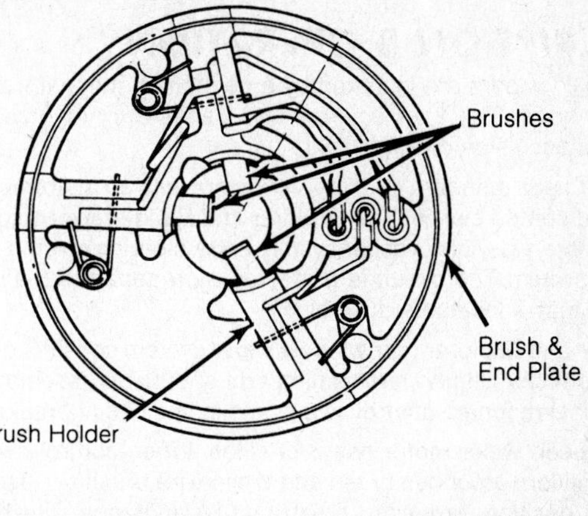
Brushes
Brush & End Plate
Brush Holder
15040
Courtesy of Ford Motor Co.

Fig. 8: Motor Brush End Plate Assembly

WASHER MOTOR, SEAL & IMPELLER

Disassembly & Reassembly – 1) Remove reservoir assembly from vehicle. Pry out retaining ring with a small screwdriver. Using pliers, grip wall surrounding electrical terminal and pull out motor, seal and impeller assembly.

2) To assemble, lubricate outside of new seal with powdered graphite. Ensure reservoir chamber is clean. Align small tab on pump end cap with slot in reservoir so seal seats tightly against bottom of pump cavity. To complete reassembly, reverse disassembly procedure.

1991 SAFETY EQUIPMENT
Wiper/Washer Systems – All Others

Aerostar, Explorer, Ranger

DESCRIPTION & OPERATION

Windshield wipers are actuated by a permanent magnet, rotary-type electric motor. The 2 wiper arms and blades are mounted on pivot shafts at each side of windshield.

Aerostar uses standard and interval wipers with an instrument panel-mounted control switch. The Explorer and Ranger are equipped only with the interval wiper/washer system and a steering column-mounted control switch. The circuit is protected by a separate 6-amp circuit breaker that is located at fuse block.

Aerostar and Explorer rear window wiper system consists of a motor mounted inside liftgate, articulating arm and blade assembly, instrument panel-mounted control switch and in-line circuit breaker.

The 2-speed wiper motor has 3 brushes. When control switch is in LOW position, grounded brush and White wire brush are used. When in HIGH position, grounded brush and Blue/Orange wire brush are used. This by-passes part of the armature winding.

When control switch is placed in park position, motor will continue through one low speed revolution until park switch center contact moves to park ground contact. This will dynamically stop the motor in the park position.

INTERVAL WIPER/WASHER

Low and high speed wiper operation is the same as standard wiper system. When wiper control switch is in Interval position, wipers make single wipes which are separated by a pause. The control wheel above wiper control switch lever sets length of pause, from about one second to about 12 seconds.

Washer functions are not the same as standard system. To operate the windshield washers, push control lever in. If control lever is off when pushed in, wipers will automatically wipe and wash windshield. After lever is released, wipers will continue to operate for one to four more cycles before returning to park position.

If control lever is in Interval position when pushed in, pause cycle will be overridden. The wipers will operate in low to give simultaneous wiper/washer action. After lever is released, wipers will continue to wash for 1-4 more cycles before returning to pause cycle.

ADJUSTMENTS

WIPER ARM ADJUSTMENT

Install arm and blade assemblies on pivot shafts. On Aerostar, distance between wiper blade and top of cowl grille is 2.4-3.5" (61-89 mm) on windshield and 2.3-3.3" (60-85 mm) on rear window. On Explorer and Ranger, measurement is 2-3.2" (50-81 mm) on driver's side and 2.2-3.4" (55-86 mm) on passenger's side.

TROUBLE SHOOTING

WIPERS INOPERATIVE IN ALL POSITIONS

Battery Voltage Test – 1) Unplug wiper motor connector and set control switch on HIGH. Check for battery voltage on circuits No. 63 (Red wire) and No. 56 (Dark Blue/Orange wire). See appropriate chassis wiring diagram in WIRING DIAGRAMS.

2) If battery voltage is present on both terminals, go to GROUND TEST. If battery voltage is present on either circuit, check for the following conditions, and service or repair as necessary.

- Malfunctioning interval governor
- Malfunctioning wiper switch
- Open connector
- Open in circuit No. 56 (Dark Blue/Orange)

3) If voltage is not present at either terminal, check for the following conditions, and service or repair as necessary.

- Open circuit breaker in fuse panel
- Open connector
- Open in circuit No. 63 (Red wire)

Ground Test – Ground wiper motor case to vehicle body ground. If wiper motor runs, repair wiper motor ground wire. If wiper motor does not run, perform wiper motor current draw test. See WIPER MOTOR CURRENT DRAW TEST under TESTING. If current draw is okay, check linkage for binding. If current draw is not okay, service or repair as required.

WIPERS INOPERATIVE OR ERRATIC IN INTERMITTENT OR LOW

1) Run wipers in HIGH position. If wipers do not hesitate, go to step **2)**. If wipers hesitate when they pass through the park position, check interval governor ground under mounting screw. If ground is okay, interval governor is defective; service as required. If ground is not secure, tighten interval governor mounting screws to improve.

2) Unplug wiper motor connector and set wiper switch to LOW position. Check circuit No. 58 (White wire) for battery voltage. If battery voltage is present, check for malfunctioning wiper motor. Perform WIPER MOTOR CURRENT DRAW TEST and service as required.

3) If voltage is not present, check for the following conditions, and service or replace as necessary.

- Open connector
- Malfunctioning wiper switch
- Malfunctioning interval governor
- Open in circuit No. 58 (White wire)

WIPERS RUN IN OFF POSITION

Unplug wiper control switch and turn ignition to run. If wipers park, wiper control switch. If wipers continue to run, check for a malfunctioning interval governor or wiper motor.

WIPERS WILL NOT PARK

Use ignition key to stop wipers so they are not in park position. Unplug wiper motor and connect jumpers to motor connector. *See Figs. 4 and 5*. If wipers park, check for the following conditions.

- Open connection
- Malfunctioning interval governor
- Open in circuits No. 58 (White wire) or 28 (Black/Pink wire)

Service or repair as required. If wipers do not park, replace wiper motor.

WIPERS DO NOT RUN WHEN WASHER IS ACTIVATED

Ensure wipers work with switch in LOW and HIGH positions. If wipers work, replace interval governor. If wipers do not work, check for malfunctioning wiper switch and interval governor. Service or replace as required.

TESTING

WIPER MOTOR CURRENT DRAW TEST

1) Disconnect negative battery cable. Disconnect linkage from motor. Disconnect wiper connector for on-vehicle testing. Connect negative lead from ammeter to battery positive post.

2) Connect positive lead to low speed connection (White wire) and then to high speed connection (Dark Blue/Orange wire) at connector plug. *See Figs. 1 and 2*. Motor current draw should not exceed 3 amps.

1991 SAFETY EQUIPMENT
Wiper/Washer Systems – All Others (Cont.)

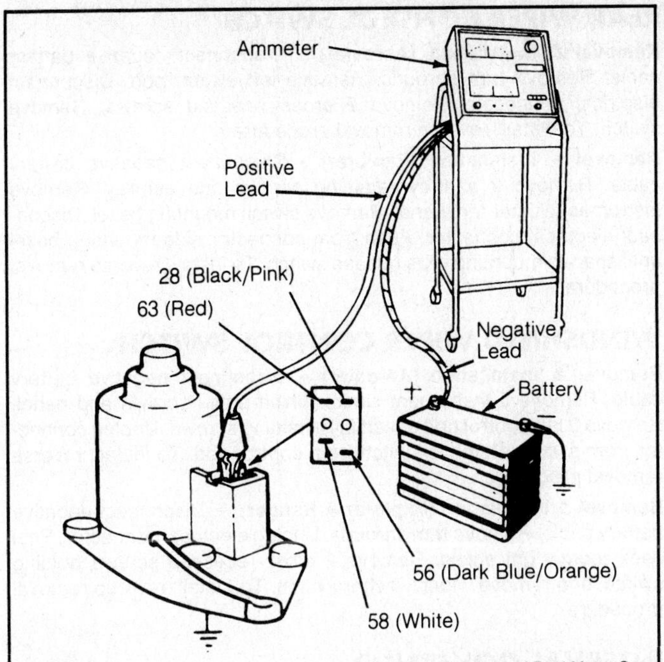
Ammeter
Positive
Lead
28 (Black/Pink)
63 (Red)
Negative
Lead
+
Battery
–
56 (Dark Blue/Orange)
58 (White)

91B13566 Courtesy of Ford Motor Co.

Fig. 1: Testing Wiper Motor Current Draw (Aerostar)

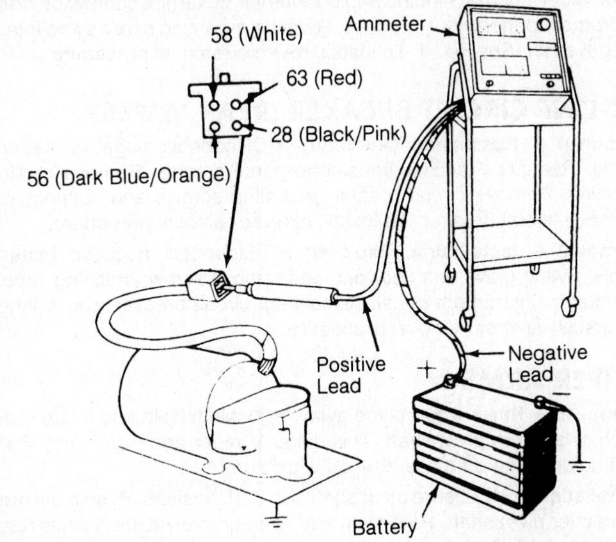
58 (White)
Ammeter
63 (Red)
28 (Black/Pink)
56 (Dark Blue/Orange)
Positive
Lead
+
Negative
Lead
–
Battery

91C13567 Courtesy of Ford Motor Co.

Fig. 2: Testing Wiper Motor Current Draw (Explorer & Ranger)

CIRCUIT BREAKER TEST

NOTE: To check for correct circuit breaker operation, perform both of the following tests.

1) Before connecting circuit breaker to volt-amp tester, short leads together, and adjust current draw until it equals circuit breaker rating. Connect breaker to ammeter. Leave breaker connected to tester for 10 minutes. Hold current reading on ammeter at rated current. If circuit breaker opens during 10 minutes, replace circuit breaker.

2) Short tester leads together and adjust current draw until it is twice rated current. Connect breaker. Hold current reading on ammeter at twice rated current. Circuit breaker should open and current should drop to zero within 30 seconds. If not, replace circuit breaker.

WIPER SWITCH CONTINUITY TEST

Aerostar – **1)** Check continuity between switch terminals. *See Fig. 3.* See WIPER SWITCH CONTINUITY table. Either a self-powered test light or an ohmmeter can be used with standard system. An ohmmeter must be used with interval wiper system.

2) To detect marginal operation of switch, move switch lever while each reading is taken. If switch does not show continuity or shows poor continuity in any position, replace switch.

WIPER SWITCH CONTINUITY

Switch Position	Standard Wiper System	Interval Wiper System
Off	[1] P-L	.....
Low	B-L	B-L
High	B-H	[2] B-H-L
Wash	B-W	B-W
Interval	.....	[3] B-I

[1] – No continuity between terminals P and L.
[2] – No continuity between terminals H and L.
[3] – Variable resistance between terminals R1 and R2 must be 420-13,000 ohms.

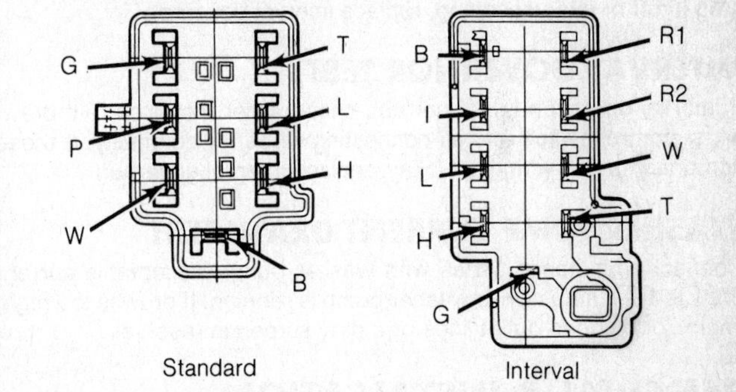
G
T
P
L
H
W
B
Standard
B
R1
R2
I
W
L
T
H
G
Interval

90J15023 Courtesy of Ford Motor Co.

Fig. 3: Identifying Wiper Switch Connector Terminals

PARK TEST

1) Use ignition switch to stop wiper blades so blades are not in park position. Connect jumper wires. *See Figs. 4 and 5.* Wiper should run one full cycle and then park. If motor will not park or will not run to park position, replace motor.

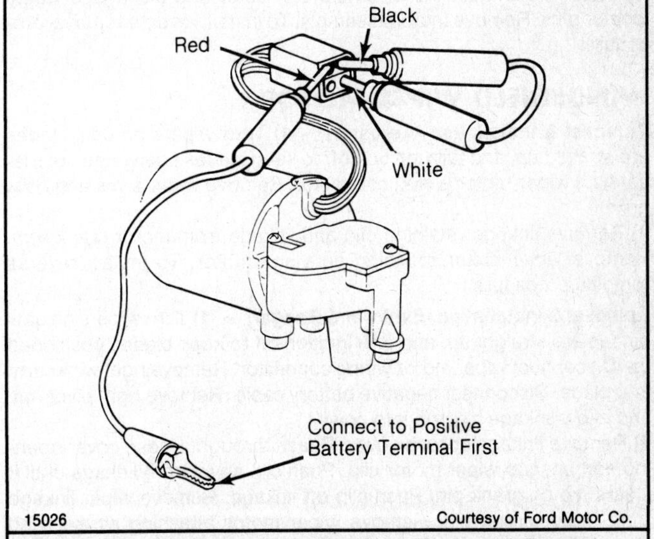
Black
Red
White
Connect to Positive
Battery Terminal First

15026 Courtesy of Ford Motor Co.

Fig. 4: Performing Wiper Motor Park Test (Explorer & Ranger)

1991 SAFETY EQUIPMENT
Wiper/Washer Systems – All Others (Cont.)

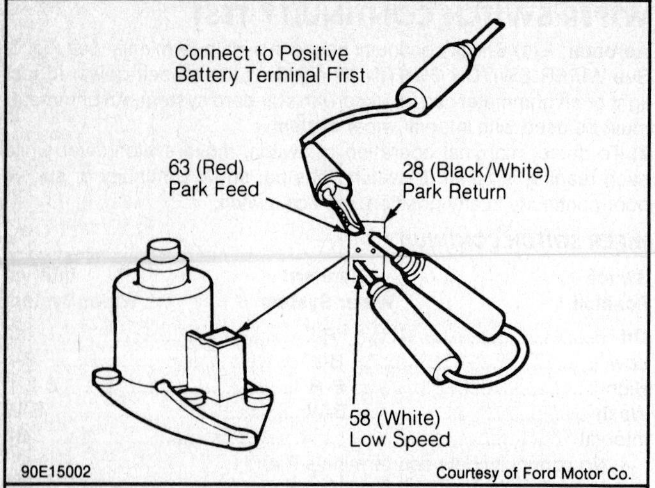
Connect to Positive
Battery Terminal First
63 (Red)
Park Feed
28 (Black/White)
Park Return
58 (White)
Low Speed
90E15002
Courtesy of Ford Motor Co.

Fig. 5: Performing Wiper Motor Park Test (Aerostar)

2) If motor stops, check windshield wiper manual control switch and wiring for continuity. If switch and wiring are okay and wiper does not stop in off or interval setting, replace interval governor.

INTERVAL GOVERNOR TEST

If interval operation is not correct, check wiper motor current draw, wiper control switch and all connecting wires for continuity. If these components and wiring are okay, replace interval governor.

WASHER PUMP CURRENT DRAW TEST

Connect ammeter in series with washer pump. Acceptable current draw is 1.7-4 amps while washer pump is running. If draw is too high, check for plugged outlet lines or a dirty screen in reservoir.

REMOVAL & INSTALLATION

REAR WIPER MOTOR

Removal & Installation (Aerostar & Explorer) – 1) Disconnect negative battery cable. Remove wiper arm and blade assembly. Remove pivot shaft attaching nut, washer and pivot block. Remove liftgate trim panel.

2) On Aerostar, unplug electrical connector and remove motor wiring pins from inner panel. Remove rear wiper motor.

3) On Explorer, remove motor bracket attaching screw and rectangular plate. Disconnect the electrical connector and disengage wiring locator pins. Remove motor assembly. To install, reverse removal procedure.

WINDSHIELD WIPER MOTOR

Removal & Installation (Aerostar) – 1) Turn wipers on until blades are straight up, and turn ignition off to keep blades positioned up. Disconnect wiper motor wiring connector. Remove wiper arms and cowl grille.

2) Remove linkage retaining clip and linkage from motor crank arm. Remove wiper motor retaining nuts and motor. To install, reverse removal procedure.

Removal & Installation (Explorer & Ranger) – 1) Turn wipers on until blades are straight up, and turn ignition off to keep blades positioned up. Disconnect wiper motor wiring connector. Remove right wiper arm and blade. Disconnect negative battery cable. Remove right pivot nut, and allow linkage to drop into cowl.

2) Remove linkage access cover. Reach through access cover opening and unsnap wiper motor clip. Push clip away from linkage until it clears nib on crank pin. Push clip off linkage. Remove wiper linkage from motor crank pin. Remove wiper motor attaching screws and motor. To install, reverse removal procedure.

REAR WIPER CONTROL SWITCH

Removal & Installation (Aerostar) – Disconnect negative battery cable. Remove trim shrouds. Remove left switch pod. Disconnect electrical connector. Remove 2 cross-recessed screws. Remove switch. To install, reverse removal procedure.

Removal & Installation (Explorer) – Disconnect negative battery cable. Remove 2 ashtray retaining screws and ashtray. Remove instrument cluster trim panel. Remove switch mounting bezel. Disconnect electrical connector. Push from connector side mounting bezel until snap-in mounting clips release switch. To install, reverse removal procedure.

WINDSHIELD WIPER CONTROL SWITCH

Removal & Installation (Aerostar) – Disconnect negative battery cable. Remove 5 instrument cluster finish panel screws and panel. Remove 3 left control pod assembly retaining screws. Unplug connector from switch. Remove switch from control pod. To install, reverse removal procedure.

Removal & Installation (Explorer & Ranger) – Disconnect negative battery cable. Remove trim shrouds. Unplug electrical connector. Peel back foam sight shield. Remove 2 cross-recessed screws holding switch, and remove wiper/washer switch. To install, reverse removal procedure.

INTERVAL GOVERNOR

Removal & Installation – Disconnect negative battery cable. Remove steering column shroud. Unplug interval governor connector from wiper control switch. Unplug interval governor connector from instrument panel wiring harness. Remove mounting screws and interval governor. *See Fig. 6.* To install, reverse removal procedure.

IN-LINE CIRCUIT BREAKER (REAR WIPER)

Removal & Installation (Aerostar) – Disconnect negative battery cable. Remove 7 cluster housing-to-panel screws. Remove cluster housing. Remove circuit breaker mounting screws and connectors. Remove circuit breaker. To install, reverse removal procedure.

Removal & Installation (Explorer) – Disconnect negative battery cable. Swing glove box door out, and remove screw attaching circuit breaker to instrument panel. Disconnect circuit breaker from wiring. To install, reverse removal procedure.

WIPER ARMS

Removal – Raise wiper blade away from windshield and move slide latch away from pivot shaft. This unlocks wiper arm from pivot shaft and holds blade off glass. Pull off wiper arm.

Installation – 1) Ensure pivot shaft is in park position. Push main arm head over pivot shaft. Hold main arm head onto pivot shaft while raising blade end of wiper arm.

2) Push slide latch into lock under pivot shaft head. Lower blade to windshield. If blade does not touch windshield, slide latch is not properly positioned.

PIVOT SHAFT & LINKAGE

Removal & Installation (Aerostar) – Remove wiper arms. Remove cowl top grille. Remove clip retaining linkage to crank arm of wiper motor. Remove 4 pivot retaining screws. Remove linkage from vehicle. To install, reverse removal procedure.

Removal (Explorer & Ranger) Remove wiper arms. Remove left or right linkage access cover (left and right linkage assemblies are serviced separately). Remove left pivot nut, lower linkage and slide linkage out through left access opening.

Installation – Install clip completely on right linkage. Ensure clip is completely on. DO NOT put linkage on motor crank pin and then attempt to install clip. Slide left pivot shaft and linkage through access opening, and position pivot shaft in place. Reinstall left wiper pivot shaft nut and linkage cover.

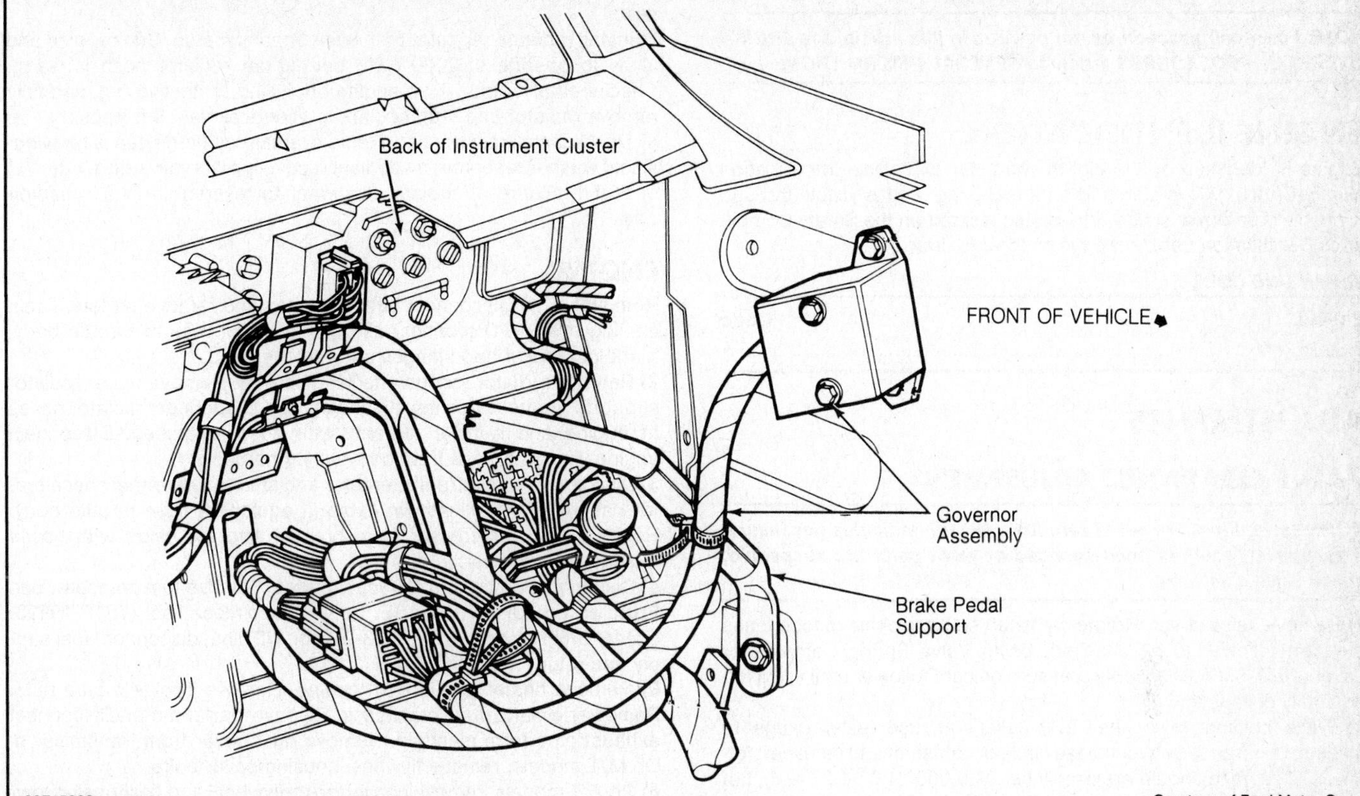

Back of Instrument Cluster
FRONT OF VEHICLE
Governor
Assembly
Brake Pedal
Support
90F15003
Courtesy of Ford Motor Co.

Fig. 6: Locating Windshield Wiper Interval Governor

WASHER PUMP & RESERVOIR (REAR WIPER)

Removal & Installation – Remove right side quarter trim panel. Disconnect filler hose. Disconnect pump electrical connector. Remove screws attaching reservoir to quarter panel, and remove reservoir. To install, reverse removal procedure.

WASHER PUMP & RESERVOIR (WINDSHIELD)

Removal & Installation – **1)** Remove reservoir assembly from vehicle. Remove pump washer retaining ring. Using pliers, grip washer pump wall and pull pump out. Remove seal and impeller assembly. Clean reservoir.

2) To install washer pump, align small projection on motor end cap with slot in reservoir. Using a one-inch, 12-point socket, hand press retaining ring against motor end plate. Install reservoir on vehicle.

WIRING DIAGRAMS

See appropriate chassis wiring diagram in WIRING DIAGRAMS.

1991 ENGINES
2.3L 4-Cylinder

Ranger

NOTE: For repair procedures not covered in this article, see ENGINE OVERHAUL PROCEDURES article in GENERAL INFORMATION.

ENGINE IDENTIFICATION

Engine is identified by the eighth character of Vehicle Identification Number (VIN). VIN is stamped on a metal tag, and is visible through windshield on driver's side. VIN is also located on the Safety Compliance Certification Label on edge of driver's door.

VIN ENGINE CODE

Engine	Code
2.3L PFI	A

ADJUSTMENTS

VALVE CLEARANCE ADJUSTMENT

NOTE: Valve lifters are set at zero lash. No adjustment is necessary. If valve seat/face has been serviced or worn parts are suspected, check valve clearance.

1) Remove valve cover. Rotate camshaft so base circle of lobe faces the cam follower to be checked. Using Valve Spring Compressor Lever (T88T-6565-BH), apply pressure on cam follower until valve lifter is fully collapsed.
2) While holding valve lifter fully collapsed, use feeler gauge to measure clearance between base circle of camshaft and camshaft follower. Clearance should preferably be .040-.050" (1.01-1.27 mm), but allowable clearance is .035-.055" (.89-1.40 mm).
3) If clearance exceeds specification, inspect camshaft follower for damage. If camshaft follower is not damaged, check for sticking valve. Ensure valve spring height and camshaft lobe lift are within specification. See VALVES & VALVE SPRINGS table and CAMSHAFT & AUXILIARY SHAFT table under ENGINE SPECIFICATIONS at end of article.
4) If components are within specification, inspect valve lifter for faulty operation. See HYDRAULIC VALVE LIFTER under REMOVAL & INSTALLATION. Replace components as necessary. Install valve cover.

REMOVAL & INSTALLATION

NOTE: For reassembly reference, label all electrical connectors, vacuum hoses and fuel lines before removal. Also place mating marks on engine hood and other major assemblies before removal.

FUEL PRESSURE RELEASE

To release fuel pressure, disconnect negative battery cable. Remove fuel cap to release fuel tank pressure. Remove relief valve cap from fuel rail. Connect fuel pressure gauge to relief valve and release fuel pressure into a suitable container.

COOLING SYSTEM BLEEDING

1) Fill cooling system with 50/50 mixture of coolant and water. Pause several minutes for circulation. Fill radiator to filler neck seat. Install radiator cap fully, then back off to first stop.

WARNING: When engine is operating, NEVER remove radiator cap under any conditions. Failure to follow instruction could cause personal injury, or damage cooling system or engine. Always wrap protective material around radiator cap to avoid injury from hot coolant.

2) Place heater controls to maximum heat. Start engine and operate at 2000 RPM for approximately 3-4 minutes. Turn engine off. Using protective rag, carefully remove radiator cap. Add coolant to filler neck seat.
3) Install radiator cap fully, then back off to first stop. Start engine and allow to operate at 2000 RPM until upper radiator hose is warm. Check heater output. Turn engine off. Using protective rag, carefully remove radiator cap. Add coolant to filler neck seat if necessary.
4) Tightly install radiator cap. Remove small cap (large cap is for windshield washer reservoir) on coolant recovery reservoir. Add 1.1 qt. (1L) of 50/50 mixture of coolant and water to reservoir. Install reservoir cap.

ENGINE

Removal – 1) Disconnect battery cables and remove battery. Drain cooling system. Disconnect air cleaner outlet tube at throttle body. Mark location of hood hinges and remove hood.
2) Remove radiator shroud attaching screws. Remove upper radiator supports. Remove cooling fan and shroud. Disconnect radiator hoses at engine and remove radiator with hoses attached. Disconnect engine wiring harness from body wiring harness.
3) Disconnect wiring from alternator and starter. Disconnect accelerator cable and A/T kickdown cable (if equipped) from throttle body. Remove A/C compressor from bracket and set aside with hoses attached (if equipped).
4) Disconnect power brake vacuum hose. Release fuel pressure. See FUEL PRESSURE RELEASE. Using Disconnect Tool (T81P-19623-G1) for 3/8" line or (T81P-19623-G2) for 1/2" line, disconnect fuel supply and return lines. *See Fig. 1.*
5) Remove heater hoses from engine. Remove engine mount nuts. Raise vehicle and drain crankcase. Remove starter motor. Disconnect exhaust pipe from manifold. Remove dust cover from transmission. On M/T models, remove flywheel housing cover bolts.
6) On A/T models, remove converter-to-flywheel and bellhousing lower bolts. On all applications, support transmission and lower vehicle. Remove upper bellhousing-to-engine bolts. Attach engine hoist and lift engine from vehicle.

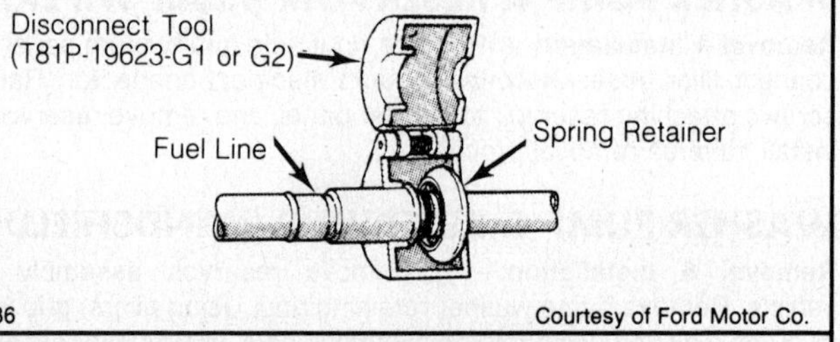
Disconnect Tool
(T81P-19623-G1 or G2)
Fuel Line
Spring Retainer
71536
Courtesy of Ford Motor Co.

Fig. 1: Disconnecting Fuel Supply & Return Lines

Installation – To install, reverse removal procedure. Tighten bolts to specification. See TORQUE SPECIFICATIONS table at end of article. Fill or top off all engine fluids. Fill and bleed air from cooling system. See COOLING SYSTEM BLEEDING under REMOVAL & INSTALLATION.

INTAKE MANIFOLDS

Removal (Upper & Lower) – 1) Disconnect negative battery cable. Drain coolant. Release fuel pressure. See FUEL PRESSURE RELEASE under REMOVAL & INSTALLATION. Mark and disconnect electrical wiring, vacuum lines and vacuum fittings from upper intake manifold. Remove throttle linkage shield. Remove throttle, cruise control and kickdown linkages.
2) Remove air intake hose and crankcase vent hose. Disconnect PCV hose from underside of upper intake manifold. Disconnect coolant bypass hose at lower intake manifold. Disconnect EGR tube from EGR valve.
3) Using Disconnect Tool (T81P-19623-G1) for 3/8" line or (T81P-19623-G2) for 1/2" line, disconnect fuel supply and return lines. *See Fig. 1.* Remove upper intake manifold bolts. Remove upper intake manifold and throttle body assembly. Remove lower intake manifold bolts. Remove manifold and gasket.

1991 ENGINES
2.3L 4-Cylinder (Cont.)

Installation - 1) Clean gasket mating surfaces. Clean and oil bolt threads. Install new gasket. Position lower intake manifold to cylinder head and install bolts finger tight.

2) Tighten bolts in sequence to specification *See Fig. 2.* See TORQUE SPECIFICATIONS table at end of article. To complete installation, reverse removal procedure. Fill and bleed air from cooling system. See COOLING SYSTEM BLEEDING under REMOVAL & INSTALLATION.

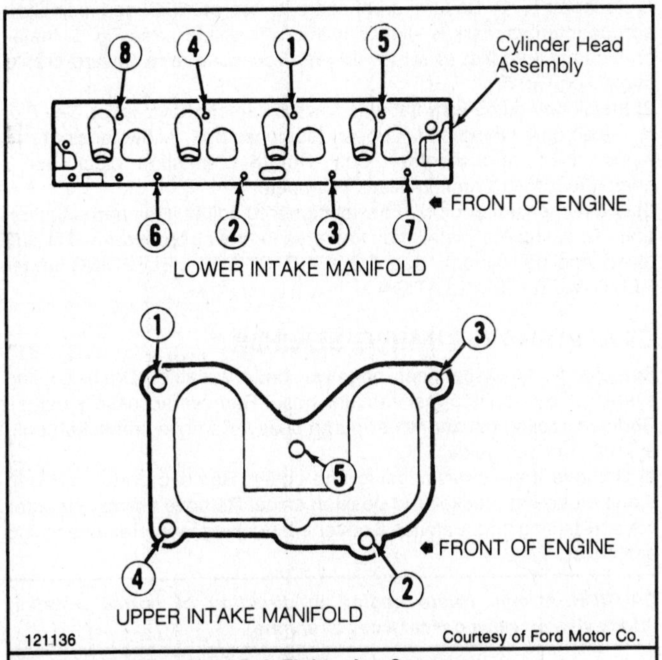
8
4
1
5
Cylinder Head Assembly
FRONT OF ENGINE
6
2
3
7
LOWER INTAKE MANIFOLD
1
3
5
FRONT OF ENGINE
4
2
UPPER INTAKE MANIFOLD
121136
Courtesy of Ford Motor Co.

Fig. 2: Intake Manifold Bolt Tightening Sequence

EXHAUST MANIFOLD

Removal & Installation - 1) Remove air cleaner and duct assembly. Remove EGR tube from exhaust manifold. Disconnect oxygen sensor. Remove heater hoses attached to valve cover. Disconnect inlet pipe from exhaust manifold.

2) Remove exhaust manifold mounting bolts and remove manifold. To install, position exhaust manifold on cylinder head; tighten bolts, in sequence, to specification in 2 steps. *See Fig. 3.* See TORQUE SPECIFICATIONS table at end of article. To complete installation, reverse removal procedure.

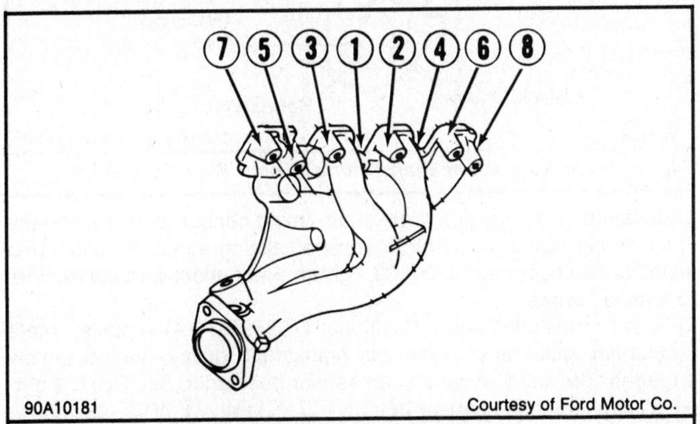
7
5
3
1
2
4
6
8
90A10181
Courtesy of Ford Motor Co.

Fig. 3: Exhaust Manifold Tightening Sequence

CYLINDER HEAD

Removal - 1) Drain cooling system. Remove air cleaner assembly and air inlet tube. Remove heater hose attached to valve cover. Remove spark plug wires. Remove spark plugs and oil dipstick. Mark and disconnect vacuum hoses. Remove valve cover.

2) Remove upper and lower intake manifolds. See INTAKE MANIFOLDS under REMOVAL & INSTALLATION. Remove accessory belt(s). Remove alternator and bracket retaining bolts. Remove power steering pump and bracket (if equipped). Remove upper radiator hose. Remove timing belt cover and remove belt. See TIMING BELT & COVER under REMOVAL & INSTALLATION.

3) Remove 4 nuts and/or stud bolts retaining heat stove to exhaust manifold. Remove exhaust manifold. Remove timing belt idler and 2 bracket bolts. Remove timing belt idler spring stop from cylinder head. Remove cylinder head bolts evenly. Lift cylinder head off engine, using care not to bend inner timing belt cover.

Inspection - Inspect cylinder head for warpage. Resurface if warpage exceeds specification. See CYLINDER HEAD table under ENGINE SPECIFICATIONS at end of article. DO NOT machine more than .010" (.25 mm) from original cylinder head thickness. Clean and tap cylinder head bolt holes in cylinder block.

CAUTION: Before installing cylinder head, ensure crankshaft is at TDC. Position camshaft so valves for No. 1 cylinder are closed. Failure to properly position camshaft and crankshaft may result in valves contacting pistons during installation. See Fig. 4.

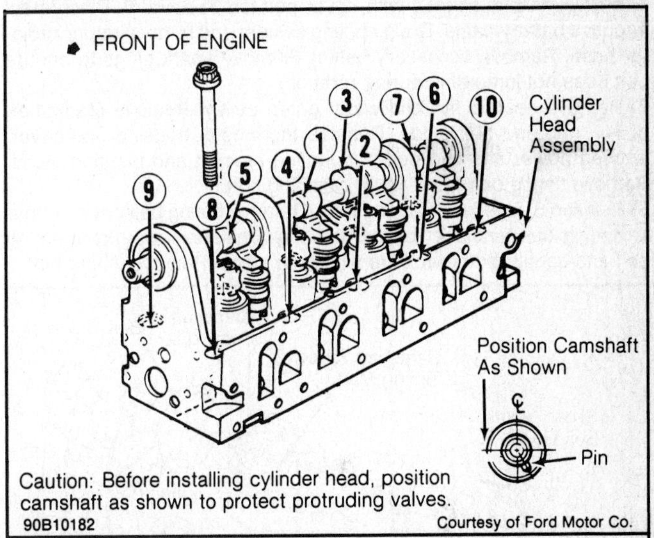
FRONT OF ENGINE
3
7
6
10
Cylinder Head Assembly
1
2
5
4
9
8
Position Camshaft As Shown
℄
Pin
Caution: Before installing cylinder head, position camshaft as shown to protect protruding valves.
90B10182
Courtesy of Ford Motor Co.

Fig. 4: Cylinder Head Bolt Tightening Sequence

Installation - Clean all gasket mating surfaces and replace all gaskets. Install new head gasket on block. Install cylinder head and tighten bolts to specification in 2 steps, and in sequence. *See Fig. 4.* See TORQUE SPECIFICATIONS table at end of article. To complete installation, reverse removal procedure. Fill and bleed cooling system. See COOLING SYSTEM BLEEDING under REMOVAL & INSTALLATION.

CAUTION: If valves/seats were serviced, check and adjust valve clearance. See VALVE CLEARANCE ADJUSTMENT under ADJUSTMENTS.

FRONT COVER OIL SEAL

Removal - Ensure crankshaft is set at TDC and camshaft sprocket timing mark is aligned with cover pointer. *See Fig. 5.* Remove timing belt. See TIMING BELT & COVER under REMOVAL & INSTALLATION. Using Crank Timing Sprocket (T74P-6306-A), remove crankshaft sprocket. Using Front Cover Seal Remover (T74P-6700-B), remove front cover oil seal.

CAUTION: Always rotate crankshaft in direction of normal rotation (clockwise as viewed from front of engine).

Installation - 1) Install new seal using Seal Installer (T74P-6150-A). Install timing belt. Release belt tensioner pulley. Remove one spark plug from each cylinder to ensure timing belt does not jump timing during crankshaft rotation.

1991 ENGINES
2.3L 4-Cylinder (Cont.)

2) Rotate crankshaft clockwise 2 complete turns to remove slack from belt. Tighten tensioner adjustment and pivot bolts. To complete installation, reverse removal procedure. Fill and bleed cooling system. See COOLING SYSTEM BLEEDING under REMOVAL & INSTALLATION.

CHECKING VALVE TIMING

CAUTION: Always rotate crankshaft in direction of normal rotation (clockwise as viewed from front of engine). Reverse rotation may cause timing belt to jump time.

1) Remove access plug from engine front cover. Rotate crankshaft clockwise and position No. 1 cylinder on TDC of compression stroke. Align crankshaft damper TDC mark with pointer on timing belt cover.
2) Looking through plug hole of outer timing belt cover, ensure camshaft sprocket timing mark is aligned with cover pointer. *See Fig. 5.* If all timing marks are not aligned, timing belt must be removed, sprockets properly positioned and timing belt reinstalled.

TIMING BELT & COVER

Removal – 1) Ensure crankshaft is set at TDC and camshaft sprocket timing mark is aligned with cover pointer. *See Fig. 5.* Disconnect negative battery cable. Drain cooling system and remove upper radiator hose. Remove accessory belt(s). Remove spark plugs to ensure belt does not jump time during rotation.
2) Remove cooling fan and water pump pulley. Remove crankshaft pulley, hub and belt guide. Remove thermostat housing and cover. Loosen power steering pump mounting bracket and position aside. Remove timing belt outer cover retaining bolt.
3) Release 8 cover interlocking tabs. Remove timing belt cover. Loosen timing belt tensioner pulley bolt. Pry tensioner away from timing belt and tighten bolt to hold tensioner in place. Remove timing belt.

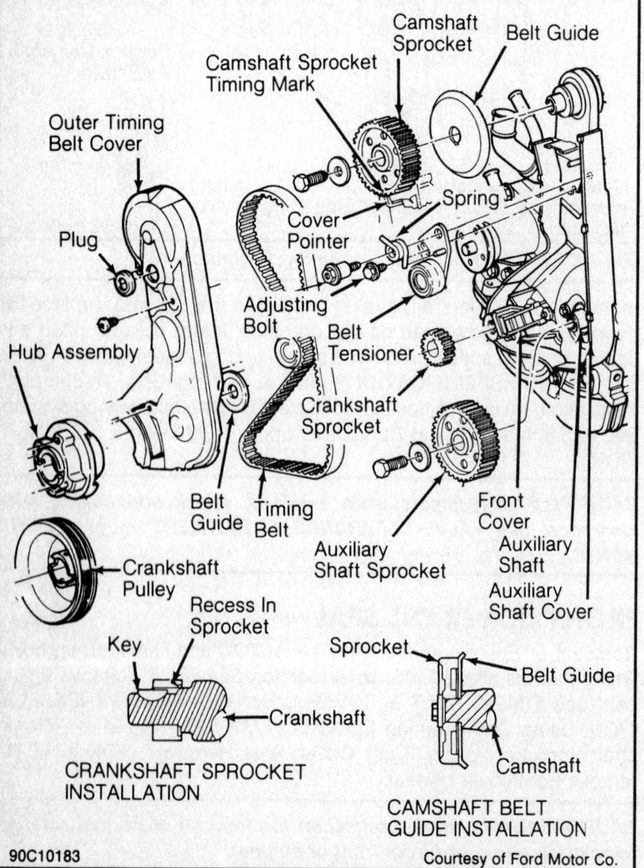
Camshaft Sprocket
Belt Guide
Camshaft Sprocket Timing Mark
Outer Timing Belt Cover
Spring
Cover Pointer
Plug
Adjusting Bolt
Belt Tensioner
Hub Assembly
Crankshaft Sprocket
Belt Guide
Timing Belt
Front Cover
Auxiliary Shaft Sprocket
Auxiliary Shaft
Auxiliary Shaft Cover
Crankshaft Pulley
Recess In Sprocket
Key
Crankshaft
Sprocket
Belt Guide
Camshaft
CRANKSHAFT SPROCKET INSTALLATION
CAMSHAFT BELT GUIDE INSTALLATION
90C10183
Courtesy of Ford Motor Co.

Fig. 5: Exploded View of Timing Belt & Components

NOTE: If crankshaft timing sensor was removed, see CRANKSHAFT TIMING SENSOR under REMOVAL & INSTALLATION for installation procedure.

CAUTION: Always rotate engine in direction of normal rotation (clockwise as viewed from front of engine).

Installation – 1) Ensure crankshaft is set at TDC and camshaft sprocket timing mark is aligned with cover pointer. *See Fig. 5.* Install crankshaft sprocket (if removed) with recessed area toward crankshaft. *See Fig. 5.*
2) Install belt guide with flat side toward camshaft sprocket. *See Fig. 5.* Install new timing belt. Loosen tensioner bolt. Allow tensioner to adjust itself, and retighten bolt. Rotate crankshaft clockwise 2 complete turns to remove slack from belt.
3) Loosen tensioner bolt. Allow tensioner to adjust itself and retighten bolt. To complete installation, reverse removal procedure. Fill and bleed cooling system. See COOLING SYSTEM BLEEDING under REMOVAL & INSTALLATION.

CRANKSHAFT TIMING SENSOR

Removal – 1) Disconnect negative battery cable. Drain cooling system and remove upper radiator hose. Remove accessory belt(s). Remove cooling fan and water pump pulley. Remove crankshaft pulley, hub and belt guide.
2) Remove thermostat housing and cover. Remove power steering pump mounting bracket and position aside. Remove timing belt outer cover retaining bolt. Release 8 cover interlocking tabs. Remove timing belt cover.

CAUTION: Always rotate engine in direction of normal rotation (clockwise as viewed from front of engine).

3) Disconnect crankshaft timing sensor wire connector from engine harness. Remove crankshaft timing sensor 4-wire connector by prying out Red retaining clip. *See Fig. 6.* Rotate crankshaft to position crankshaft keyway at 10 o'clock position.
4) This will place vane window of both inner and outer vane cups over the crankshaft timing sensor. Remove crankshaft timing sensor retaining bolts and plastic wire harness retainer. Remove crankshaft timing sensor assembly.

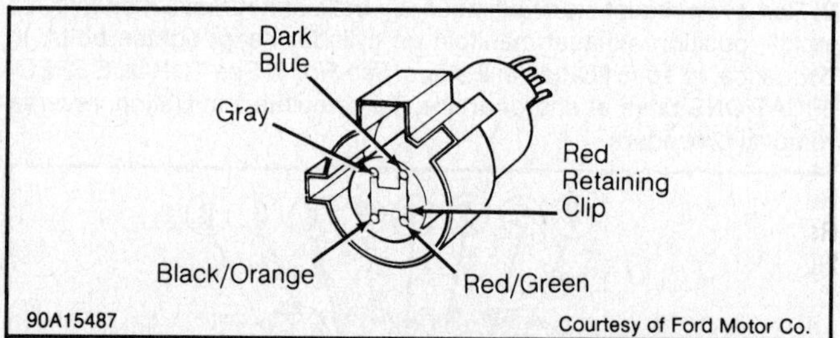
Dark Blue
Gray
Red Retaining Clip
Black/Orange
Red/Green
90A15487
Courtesy of Ford Motor Co.

Fig. 6: Identifying Crankshaft Timing Sensor Wire Connector

Installation – 1) Position crankshaft timing sensor wires behind the inner timing belt cover. Hold crankshaft timing sensor in place and install bolts finger tight. DO NOT tighten. Reconnect wire connectors to engine harness.
2) With Crankshaft Sensor Positioner (T89P-6316-A) in place, rotate crankshaft until outer vane on crankshaft pulley hub assembly engages both sides of crankshaft sensor positioner. *See Fig. 7.* Tighten crankshaft timing sensor bolts.
3) Rotate crankshaft until vane on crankshaft pulley hub assembly is no longer engaged in crankshaft sensor positioner. Remove crankshaft sensor positioner. Install new plastic wire harness retainer and trim off excess.
4) Rotate crankshaft 90 degrees (1/4 turn) clockwise and measure outer vane-to-sensor air gap. Air gap must be .018-.039" (.46-1.0 mm). To complete installation, reverse removal procedure. Fill and bleed cooling system. See COOLING SYSTEM BLEEDING under REMOVAL & INSTALLATION.

1991 ENGINES
2.3L 4-Cylinder (Cont.)

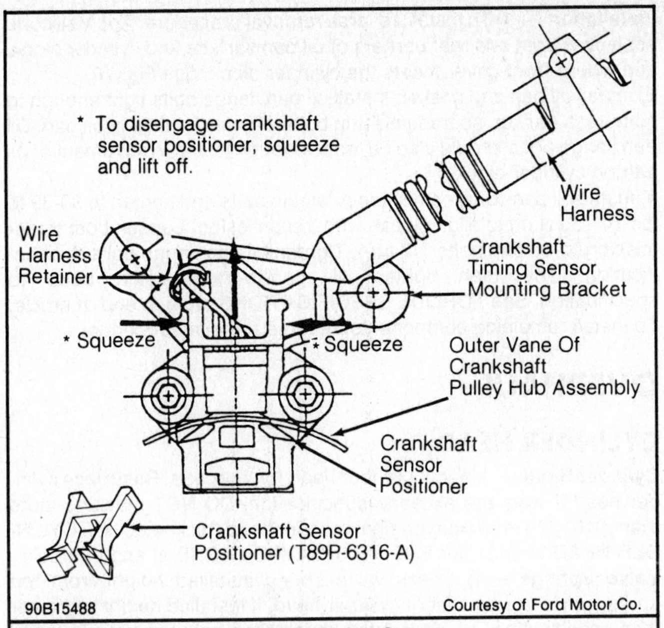
* To disengage crankshaft sensor positioner, squeeze and lift off.
Wire Harness
Wire Harness Retainer
Crankshaft Timing Sensor Mounting Bracket
* Squeeze
* Squeeze
Outer Vane Of Crankshaft Pulley Hub Assembly
Crankshaft Sensor Positioner
Crankshaft Sensor Positioner (T89P-6316-A)
90B15488
Courtesy of Ford Motor Co.

Fig. 7: Positioning Crankshaft Timing Sensor

HYDRAULIC VALVE LIFTER

Removal – Remove valve cover. Rotate camshaft so base circle of cam is facing the lifter to be removed. Using Valve Spring Compressor Lever (T88T-6565-BH), collapse valve spring and rotate cam follower to one side. Remove valve lifter.

Inspection – Replace valve lifters as complete assemblies only. Test lifters with Leak-Down Tester 6500-E. Lifters cannot be checked with engine oil in them. Use hydraulic tester fluid. Fluid can be obtained from tester manufacturer. Time required for the plunger to leak down 1/8" (3.2 mm) travel with 50-lb. load is 2-8 seconds.

Installation – To install, reverse removal procedure.

CAMSHAFT

NOTE: To ensure installation to original location, keep all components in order.

Removal – **1)** Drain cooling system. Remove air cleaner assembly. Mark and disconnect spark plug wires and vacuum hoses. Remove valve cover. Remove upper radiator hose. Remove alternator belt. Remove alternator mounting bracket bolts and position bracket aside. Remove fan shroud.

2) Using a Valve Spring Compressor Lever (T88T-6565-BH), depress and remove camshaft followers. Remove timing belt. See TIMING BELT & COVER under REMOVAL & INSTALLATION. Remove camshaft sprocket using Cam and Auxiliary Shaft Sprocket Remover (T74P-6256-B). Remove seal using Front Cover Seal Remover (T74P-6700-B).

3) Check camshaft end play. If end play is not within specification, replace thrust plate. See CAMSHAFT & AUXILIARY SHAFT table under ENGINE SPECIFICATIONS at end of article. Remove camshaft rear thrust plate. Raise vehicle and remove both left and right engine support bolts and nuts.

4) Place a block of wood between engine block and transmission jack. Raise engine as high as it will go. Place block of wood between engine mount and chassis brackets. Carefully remove camshaft to avoid damaging journals and lobes.

NOTE: When replacing camshaft, ensure threaded plug is in the rear of new camshaft. If plug is missing, remove threaded plug from old camshaft and install.

Inspection – **1)** Clean all components and gasket mating surfaces. Check lobe lift and camshaft-to-bearing clearance. To check camshaft lobe lift, measure distances "A" and "B" of each cam lobe. *See Fig. 8.*

2) Distance "A" minus distance "B" equals cam lobe lift. Check lift of each lobe and note all readings. If readings are not within specification, replace camshaft and all rocker arms. See CAMSHAFT & AUXILIARY SHAFT table under ENGINE SPECIFICATIONS at end of article.

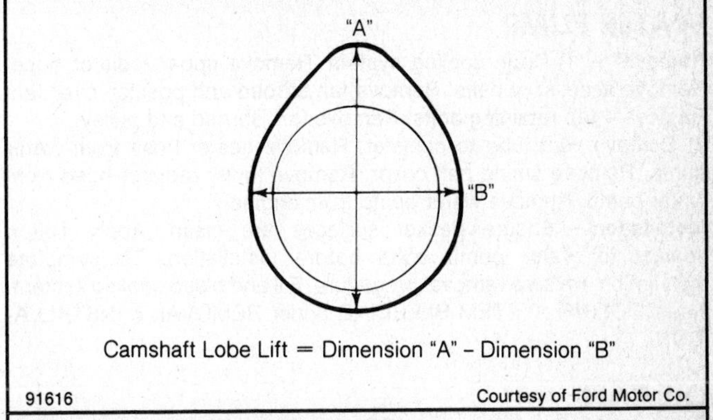
"A"
"B"
Camshaft Lobe Lift = Dimension "A" - Dimension "B"
91616
Courtesy of Ford Motor Co.

Fig. 8: Measuring Camshaft Lobe Lift

Installation – **1)** Completely dip camshaft in engine oil. Carefully slide camshaft into cylinder head. Lower engine and tighten engine mount bolts or nuts. Install camshaft rear thrust plate. Recheck camshaft end play.

2) If end play is not within specification, replace thrust plate. See CAMSHAFT & AUXILIARY SHAFT table under ENGINE SPECIFICATIONS at end of article. Lubricate camshaft seal and install using Seal Installer (T74P-6150-A). Install camshaft sprocket. To complete installation, reverse removal procedure. Fill and bleed cooling system. See COOLING SYSTEM BLEEDING under REMOVAL & INSTALLATION.

AUXILIARY SHAFT

Removal & Installation – **1)** Remove timing belt. See TIMING BELT & COVER under REMOVAL & INSTALLATION. Remove auxiliary shaft sprocket bolt and remove sprocket. Check auxiliary shaft end play. If end play is not within specification, replace thrust plate. See CAMSHAFT & AUXILIARY SHAFT table under ENGINE SPECIFICATIONS at end of article.

2) Remove thrust plate bolts and remove thrust plate. Carefully pull out auxiliary shaft. If bearings are to be replaced, use a slide hammer with Puller Attachment Tool (T58L-101-B) to remove bearings, and a driver to install bearings. Ensure oil holes in bearings align with oil holes in cylinder block.

3) To install, completely dip auxiliary shaft in engine oil. Carefully slide shaft into bore. Ensure shaft rotates freely. To complete installation, reverse removal procedure.

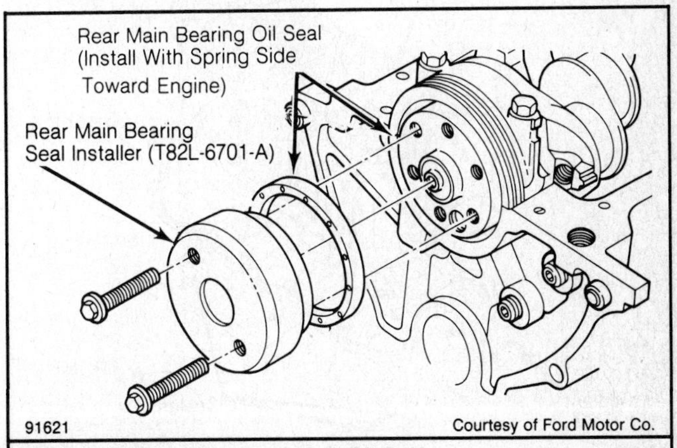
Rear Main Bearing Oil Seal (Install With Spring Side Toward Engine)
Rear Main Bearing Seal Installer (T82L-6701-A)
91621
Courtesy of Ford Motor Co.

Fig. 9: Installing Rear Crankshaft Oil Seal

1991 ENGINES
2.3L 4-Cylinder (Cont.)

REAR CRANKSHAFT OIL SEAL

Removal & Installation – Remove transmission. Remove flywheel/ flexplate. Remove rear oil seal with slide hammer. Use care not to damage crankshaft sealing surface. Coat seal surfaces with engine oil. Using Rear Main Bearing Seal Installer (T82L-6701-A), install seal until firmly seated. *See Fig. 9.* To complete installation, reverse removal procedure.

WATER PUMP

Removal – **1)** Drain cooling system. Remove upper radiator hose. Remove accessory belts. Remove fan shroud and position over fan. Remove 4 fan retaining bolts. Remove fan, shroud and pulley.

2) Remove vent tube to canister. Remove heater hose from water pump. Remove timing belt cover. Remove lower radiator hose from water pump. Remove water pump from engine.

Installation – Ensure gasket surfaces are clean. Apply Teflon sealant to water pump bolts before installation. To complete installation, reverse removal procedure. Fill and bleed cooling system. See COOLING SYSTEM BLEEDING under REMOVAL & INSTALLATION.

OIL PAN

NOTE: On A/T models, oil pan is removed from front of engine compartment. On M/T models, oil pan is removed from rear of engine compartment.

Removal – **1)** Disconnect negative battery cable. Disconnect air cleaner outlet tube at throttle body. Remove oil dipstick. Remove engine mount retaining nuts.

2) On A/T models, disconnect oil cooler lines at radiator. Drain cooling system and remove radiator and shroud.

3) On all models, raise and support vehicle. Drain engine oil. Disconnect wiring and remove starter. Disconnect exhaust manifold tube at inlet pipe bracket of thermactor check valve.

4) Disconnect catalytic converter at inlet pipe. Remove transmission mount-to-crossmember nuts.

5) On A/T models, disconnect oil cooler lines at transmission. Remove front crossmember.

6) On M/T models, disconnect right front shock absorber lower mount bolt. On all models, raise engine approximately 2 1/2" and support in this position. On A/T models, raise transmission slightly.

7) On all models, remove oil pan bolts. Remove oil level sensor assembly from oil pan. Remove oil pump, pick-up tube and oil pump drive. Remove oil pan from the front on A/T models, or from rear on M/T models.

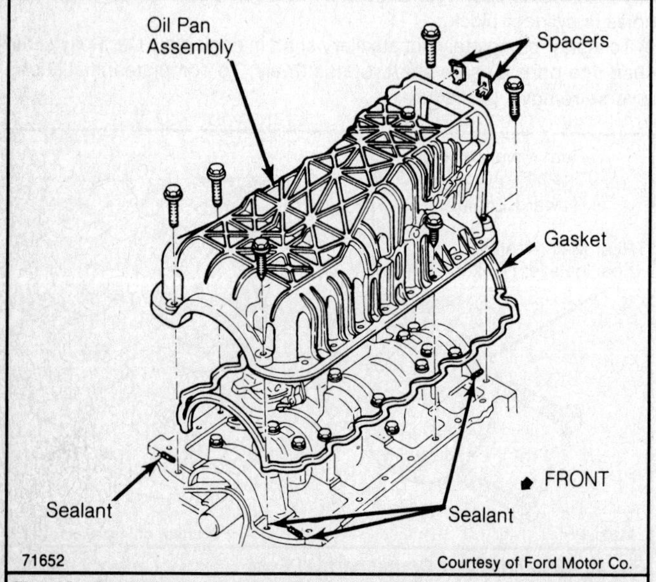
Oil Pan
Assembly
Spacers
Gasket
FRONT
Sealant
Sealant
71652
Courtesy of Ford Motor Co.

Fig. 10: Exploded View of Oil Pan Assembly

Installation – **1)** To install, reverse removal procedure. Apply silicone sealant at front and rear corners of oil pan surface and cylinder block, and where front cover meets the cylinder block. *See Fig. 10.*

2) Install oil pan and gasket. Install oil pan flange bolts tight enough to compress gasket, so transmission bolts align with holes in oil pan. Oil pan flange bolts should also be loose enough to allow movement of oil pan on cylinder block.

3) Install oil pan-to-transmission retaining bolts and tighten to 30-39 ft. lbs. (41-53 N.m) to align oil pan with transmission. Loosen both transmission-to-oil pan bolts 1/2 turn. Tighten oil pan flange bolts to specification, and then tighten oil pan-to-transmission bolts to specification. See TORQUE SPECIFICATIONS table at end of article. To install remaining components, reverse removal procedure.

OVERHAUL

CYLINDER HEAD

Cylinder Head – Inspect cylinder head for warpage. Resurface cylinder head if warpage exceeds specification. DO NOT machine more than .010" (.25 mm) from original cylinder head thickness. See CYLINDER HEAD table under ENGINE SPECIFICATIONS at end of article.

Valve Springs – **1)** Check valve spring installed height from top spring coil to spring seat of cylinder head. If installed height is greater than specification, spacer(s) may be installed between cylinder head and valve spring to obtain correct installed height. See VALVES & VALVE SPRINGS table under ENGINE SPECIFICATIONS at end of article.

CAUTION: DO NOT install spacers unless necessary. Use of excess spacers will cause premature component failure.

2) With spring(s) removed, measure spring out-of-square, free length and pressure at specified length. If measurements are not within specification, replace spring(s). See VALVES & VALVE SPRINGS table.

Valve Stem Oil Seals – Use Valve Stem Oil Seal Installer (T87L-6571-AH) to install seal. Install seal until it bottoms on valve guide. Oversize seals must be used on guides that have been reamed for oversize valves.

Valve Guides – Valve guides must be reamed for an oversized valve if valve stem oil clearance is not within specification. See CYLINDER HEAD table under ENGINE SPECIFICATIONS at end of article. Always use reamers in proper sequence (smallest first). If oversized valve or valve stem seal is not available, valve guide may be bored out to use a service bushing.

NOTE: Always grind valve seat after valve guide has been reamed or service bushing has been installed.

Valve Seat – No replacement procedure is given by manufacturer.

Valves – During valve servicing, DO NOT remove more than .010" (.25 mm) from end of valve stem.

Seat Correction Angles – Grind valve seat to a true 45-degree angle. If seat width is too wide after grinding, use a 30-degree stone to lower seat or a 60-degree stone to raise seat.

CYLINDER BLOCK ASSEMBLY

Piston & Rod Assembly – Install piston on connecting rod in correct location. *See Fig. 11.* Install piston and connecting rod in engine, with notch or arrow on top of piston pointing toward front of engine.

Fitting Pistons – **1)** Check piston-to-bore clearance. See PISTONS, PINS & RINGS table under ENGINE SPECIFICATIONS at end of article. Standard size pistons are color-coded Red, Blue or Yellow on the piston dome. See PISTON SELECTION table. Oversize pistons are also available.

2) If bore diameter is in lower one-third of specification, use a Red-coded piston. If bore diameter is in middle one-third of specification, use a Blue-coded piston. If bore diameter is in upper one-third of specification, use a Yellow-coded piston. Use proper size piston to obtain specified clearance.

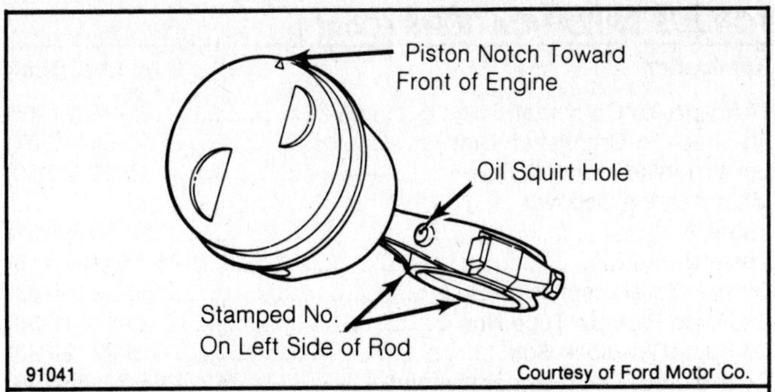

Piston Notch Toward
Front of Engine
Oil Squirt Hole
Stamped No.
On Left Side of Rod
91041
Courtesy of Ford Motor Co.

Fig. 11: Positioning Piston on Connecting Rod

PISTON SELECTION

Cylinder Bore Diameter In. (mm)	Piston Color Code
3.7795-3.7810 (95.999-96.037)	Red
3.7810-3.7825 (96.037-96.076)	Blue
3.7825-3.7840 (96.076-96.114)	Yellow

Piston Rings – **1)** Select proper ring set for bore diameter. Place ring in cylinder bore in which it will be installed. Use piston to square ring and place ring below normal ring wear area. Measure ring end gap. If ring gap is not within specification, try another ring set. See PISTONS, PINS & RINGS table under ENGINE SPECIFICATIONS at end of article.

2) Check side clearance of rings after installing on piston. Ensure clearance is within specification around entire circumference. Replace piston and/or rings if clearance is not within specification. See PISTONS, PINS & RINGS table. Ensure rings are properly spaced on piston before installing piston into cylinder. *See Fig. 12.*

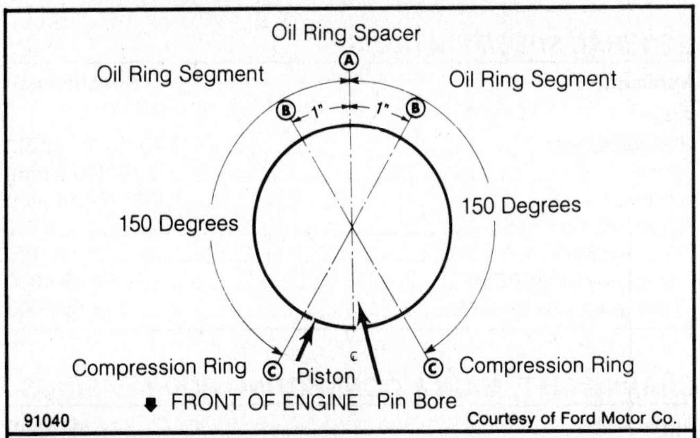

Oil Ring Spacer
Oil Ring Segment
Oil Ring Segment
1°
1°
150 Degrees
150 Degrees
Compression Ring
Piston
Compression Ring
FRONT OF ENGINE
Pin Bore
91040
Courtesy of Ford Motor Co.

Fig. 12: Positioning Rings on Piston

Rod Bearings – **1)** Ensure oil squirt hole in connecting rod is properly positioned with arrow on top of piston. *See Fig. 11.* Use Plastigage method to check rod bearing clearance.

2) If proper oil clearance cannot be obtained using standard bearings, try a combination of undersize bearings. DO NOT use any other bearing combination other than what is listed. See UNDERSIZE MAIN & ROD BEARING COMBINATIONS table.

3) If use of bearing combinations does not bring clearance within specification, machine or replace crankshaft as necessary. Always replace bearings in pairs. See CRANKSHAFT, MAIN & CONNECTING ROD BEARINGS table under ENGINE SPECIFICATIONS at end of article.

Crankshaft & Main Bearings – **1)** When checking main bearing clearance in vehicle, position a jack under adjoining bearing counterweight being checked. Remove only one main bearing cap at a time.

2) Use Plastigage method to check main bearing clearance. If clearance is not within specification, replace bearings. Machine or

UNDERSIZE MAIN & ROD BEARING COMBINATIONS [1]

Excess Bearing Clearance In. (mm)	Use Upper Bearing In. (mm)	Use Lower Bearing In. (mm)
.0-.0005 (.0-.013)	.001 (.03)	[2]
.0005-.0010 (.013-.026)	.001 (.03)	.001 (.03)
.0010-.0015 (.026-.039)	.002 (.05)	.001 (.03)
.0015-.0020 (.039-.052)	.002 (.05)	.002 (.05)

[1] – DO NOT use any other bearing combination other than what is listed. If use of bearing combinations does not bring clearance within specification, machine or replace crankshaft as necessary.

[2] – Use standard bearing.

replace crankshaft as necessary. See CRANKSHAFT, MAIN & CONNECTING ROD BEARINGS table under ENGINE SPECIFICATIONS at end of article.

3) If proper oil clearance cannot be obtained using standard bearings, try a combination of undersize bearings. DO NOT use any other bearing combination other than what is listed. See UNDERSIZE MAIN & ROD BEARING COMBINATIONS table.

4) If use of bearing combinations does not bring clearance within specification, machine or replace crankshaft as necessary. Always replace bearings in pairs. See CRANKSHAFT, MAIN & CONNECTING ROD BEARINGS table under ENGINE SPECIFICATIONS.

5) Tighten main bearing cap bolts finger tight. Pry crankshaft forward and tighten bearing caps to specification. See TORQUE SPECIFICATIONS table at end of article.

6) Check crankshaft end play. Replace thrust bearing if end play is not within specification. Thrust bearing is No. 3 (from front) main bearing in block. See CRANKSHAFT, MAIN & CONNECTING ROD BEARINGS table under ENGINE SPECIFICATIONS.

Cylinder Block – **1)** Using a feeler gauge and straightedge, check cylinder block head gasket surface for warpage. DO NOT machine more than .010" (.25 mm) from original gasket surface. Check cylinder bore for wear, taper, out-of-round and piston fit. Repair or replace as necessary. See CYLINDER BLOCK table under ENGINE SPECIFICATIONS at end of article.

2) Install all main bearing caps and tighten to specification before honing cylinder bore. See TORQUE SPECIFICATIONS table at end of article. Use ONLY a spring-loaded type cylinder hone. After honing, thoroughly clean bore with detergent and water solution. Rinse solution from bore thoroughly with clean water. Wipe bore clean with lint free cloth. Lubricate cylinder bores with engine oil.

ENGINE OILING

ENGINE LUBRICATION SYSTEM

System is pressure fed from a rotor-type oil pump. Oil flows through oil filter before entering main oil gallery. *See Fig. 13.*

Crankcase Capacity – Crankcase capacity is 4 qts. (3.79L) without oil filter and 5 qts. (4.74L) with oil filter.

Oil Pressure – Normal oil pressure at 2000 RPM should be 40-60 psi (2.8-4.2 kg/cm²) with engine at normal operating temperature.

Oil Pressure Relief Valve – Oil pressure relief valve is located in oil pump body. Valve is not adjustable.

OIL PUMP

Removal & Disassembly – **1)** Remove oil pan. See OIL PAN under REMOVAL & INSTALLATION. Disconnect pick-up tube from main bearing cap stud. Remove oil pump attaching bolts. Remove oil pump assembly with oil pump drive shaft.

2) Remove pick-up tube from pump. Disassemble oil pump. Note direction of component installation for reassembly reference.

Inspection – Inspect components for damage. Measure rotor end clearance, outer race-to-housing clearance and rotor tip clearance. Check clearance between pressure relief valve and bore. Measure relief valve tension. Replace oil pump assembly if measurements are not within specifications. See OIL PUMP SPECIFICATIONS table.

1991 ENGINES
2.3L 4-Cylinder (Cont.)

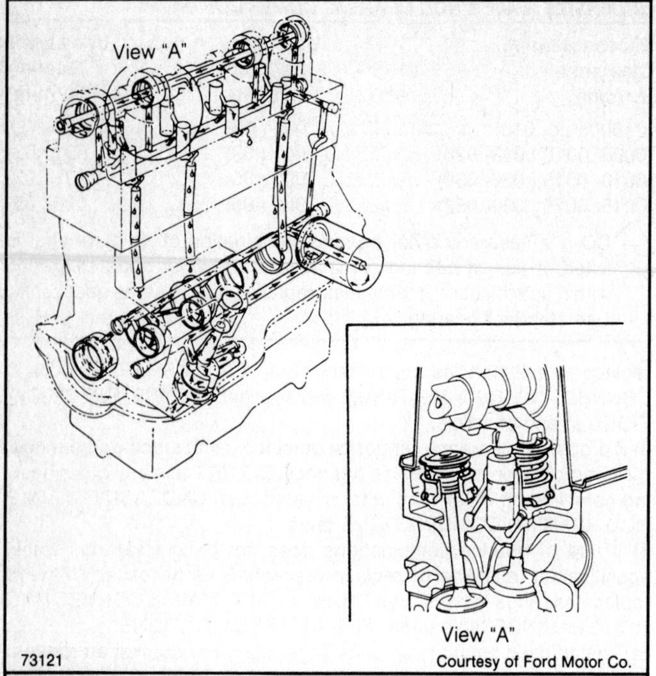
View "A"
View "A"
73121
Courtesy of Ford Motor Co.

Fig. 13: Cross-Sectional View of Engine Oiling System

OIL PUMP SPECIFICATIONS

Application	In. (mm)
Drive Shaft-To-Housing Bearing Clearance	.0015-.0030 (.038-.076)
Maximum Assembled Rotor End Clearance	.004 (.10)
Maximum Rotor Tip Clearance	.012 (.30)
Outer Race-To-Housing Clearance	.001-.013 (.03-.33)
Relief Valve-To-Bore Clearance	.0015-.0030 (.038-.076)
Relief Valve Spring Tension	[1]

[1] – Spring tension should be 12.6-14.5 lbs. @ 1.20" (5.7-6.8 kg @ 30.5 mm).

Reassembly & Installation – To reassemble, reverse disassembly procedure. Ensure rotors are installed in original location. Ensure oil pump spins freely after reassembly. To install, reverse removal procedure using new gaskets. Prime oil pump assembly before installation.

TORQUE SPECIFICATIONS

TORQUE SPECIFICATIONS

Application	Ft. Lbs. (N.m)
Auxiliary Shaft Sprocket Bolt	28-40 (38-54)
Bellhousing-To-Engine Bolt	28-38 (38-51)
Camshaft Sprocket Bolt	50-71 (68-97)
Connecting Rod Cap Nut	
Step 1	25-30 (34-41)
Step 2	30-36 (41-49)
Crankshaft Damper Bolt	103-133 (140-180)
Cylinder Head Bolt [1]	
Step 1	50-60 (68-81)
Step 2	80-90 (109-122)
Engine Mount Bracket-To-Engine Bolt	45-60 (62-81)
Engine Mount Nuts	65-85 (88-115)
Engine Mount-To- Bracket Bolt	65-85 (88-115)
Exhaust Manifold Bolt [2]	
Step 1	15-17 (20-23)
Step 2	20-30 (27-41)

TORQUE SPECIFICATIONS (Cont.)

Application	Ft. Lbs. (N.m)
Flexplate-To-Converter Bolt	20-34 (27-46)
Flywheel-To-Crankshaft Bolt	56-64 (76-87)
Lower Intake Manifold Bolt [3]	15-22 (20-30)
Main Bearing Cap Nut	
Step 1	50-60 (68-81)
Step 2	75-85 (102-115)
Oil Pan-To-Transmission Bolt	30-39 (41-53)
Oil Pump Pick-Up Tube Nut	30-41 (41-56)
Oil Pump-To-Block Bolt	15-22 (20-30)
Rear Mount-To-Crossmember Nut	65-80 (88-108)
Rear Mount-To-Transmission Bolt	60-80 (81-108)
Starter Bolt	15-20 (20-27)
Transmission Oil Cooler Lines	16-22 (22-30)
Upper Intake Manifold Bolt [3]	15-22 (20-30)
Water Pump Bolt [4]	15-22 (20-30)
	INCH Lbs. (N.m)
Auxiliary Shaft Thrust Plate Bolt	72-108 (8-12)
Camshaft Thrust Plate Bolt	72-108 (8-12)
Engine Front Cover Bolt	72-108 (8-12)
Oil Pan-To-Block Bolt	90-120 (10-14)
Spark Plug	60-120 (7-14)
Valve Cover Bolt	60-97 (7-11)

[1] – Tighten in proper sequence. *See Fig. 4.*
[2] – Tighten in proper sequence. *See Fig. 3.*
[3] – Tighten in proper sequence. *See Fig. 2.*
[4] – Apply sealant to bolt threads.

ENGINE SPECIFICATIONS

GENERAL SPECIFICATIONS

Application	Specification
2.3L	
Displacement	140 Cu. In. (2.3L)
Bore	3.78" (96.0 mm)
Stroke	3.126" (79.40 mm)
Compression Ratio	9.5:1
Fuel System	PFI
Horsepower @ RPM	90 @ 4000
Torque Ft. Lbs.@ RPM	134 @ 2000

CRANKSHAFT, MAIN & CONNECTING ROD BEARINGS

Application	In. (mm)
2.3L	
Crankshaft	
End Play	
Desired	.004-.008 (.10-.20)
Allowable	.012 (.30)
Main Bearings	
Journal Diameter	2.3982-2.3990 (60.914-60.935)
Journal Out-Of-Round	.0006 (.015)
Journal Taper [1]	.0006 (.015)
Oil Clearance	
Desired	.0008-.0015 (.020-.038)
Allowable	.0008-.0026 (.020-.066)
Connecting Rod Bearings	
Journal Diameter	2.0462-2.0472 (51.973-51.998)
Journal Out-Of-Round	.0006 (.015)
Journal Taper [1]	.0006 (.015)
Oil Clearance	
Desired	.0008-.0015 (.020-.038)
Allowable	.0008-.0026 (.020-.066)

[1] – Specification listed is per 1" (25.4 mm)

1991 ENGINES
2.3L 4-Cylinder (Cont.)

CONNECTING RODS

Application	In. (mm)
2.3L	
Bore Diameter	
Pin Bore	.9096-.9112 (23.104-23.144)
Center-To-Center Length	5.2031-5.2063 (132.159-132.240)
Maximum Bend	.012 (.30)
Maximum Twist	.024 (.61)
Side Play	
Standard	.0035-.0105 (.089-.267)
Service Limit	.014 (.36)

PISTONS, PINS & RINGS

Application	In. (mm)
2.3L	
Pistons	
Clearance	.0014-.0022 (.036-.056)
Diameter [1]	
Red	3.7768-3.7779 (95.931-95.959)
Pins	
Diameter [2]	.9119-.9124 (23.162-23.175)
Piston Fit	.0002-.0004 (.005-.010)
Rod Fit	Press Fit
Rings	
No. 1 & 2	
End Gap	.010-.020 (.25-.50)
Side Clearance	.002-.004 (.05-.10)
No. 3 (Oil)	
End Gap (Steel Rail)	.015-.049 (.38-1.24)
Side Clearance	Snug Fit

1 – Diameter of Blue and Yellow pistons are not available from manufacturer. Piston diameter is measured at .57" (14.6 mm) from bottom of skirt, at 90 degrees to piston pin. To select correct pistons, see FITTING PISTONS under CYLINDER BLOCK ASSEMBLY.

2 – Standard diameter listed. Available in .001" (.02 mm) and .002" (.05 mm) oversize.

VALVES & VALVE SPRINGS

Application	Specification
2.3L	
Intake Valves	
Face Angle	44°
Head Diameter	1.72-1.75" (43.7-44.5 mm)
Stem Diameter	.3416-.3423" (8.677-8.694 mm)
Exhaust Valves	
Face Angle	44°
Head Diameter	1.49-1.51" (37.8-38.4 mm)
Stem Diameter	.3411-.3418" (8.664-8.682 mm)
Valve Margin	.031" (.79 mm)
Valve Springs	
Free Length (Approx.)	1.877" (47.68 mm)
Installed Height	1.49-1.55" (37.8-39.4 mm)
Out-Of-Square	.078" (1.98 mm)
Pressure	Lbs. @ In. (kg @ mm)
Valve Closed	66-74 @ 1.52 (30-34 @ 38.6)
Valve Open	128-142 @ 1.12 (58-64 @ 28.4)

CYLINDER BLOCK

Application	In. (mm)
2.3L	
Cylinder Bore	
Standard Diameter	3.7795-3.7825 (95.999-96.076)
Maximum Deck Warpage [1]	.003 (.08)
Maximum Out-Of-Round	.0015 (.038)
Maximum Taper	.010 (.25)

1 – Specification listed is per 6" (152.4 mm). Maximum of .006" (.15 mm) overall. DO NOT machine more than .010" (.25 mm) from original gasket surface.

CYLINDER HEAD

Application	Specification
2.3L	
Maximum Warpage [1]	.003" (.08 mm)
Valve Seats	
Intake Valve	
Seat Angle	45°
Seat Width	.060-.080" (1.52-2.03 mm)
Maximum Seat Runout	.0016" (.041 mm)
Exhaust Valve	
Seat Angle	45°
Seat Width	.070-.090" (1.78-2.29 mm)
Maximum Seat Runout	.0016" (.041 mm)
Valve Guides	
Intake Valve	
Valve Stem-To-Guide	
Oil Clearance	
Standard	.0010-.0027" (.025-.069 mm)
Service Limit	.0055" (.140 mm)
Exhaust Valve	
Valve Stem-To-Guide	
Oil Clearance	
Standard	.0015-.0032" (.038-.081 mm)
Service Limit	.0055" (.140 mm)

1 – Specification listed is taken within a 6" (152 mm) area. Overall warpage is .006" (.15 mm). DO NOT machine more than .010" (.25 mm) from original gasket surface.

VALVE LIFTERS

Application	In. (mm)
2.3L	
Bore Diameter	.8430-.9449 (21.412-24.000)
Collapsed Lifter Clearance	
Desired	.040-.050 (1.02-1.27)
Allowable	.035-.055 (.89-1.40)
Lifter Diameter	.8422-.8427 (21.392-21.405)
Oil Clearance	.0007-.0027 (.018-.069)

CAMSHAFT & AUXILIARY SHAFT

Application	In. (mm)
2.3L	
Auxiliary Shaft	
End Play	.001-.007 (.03-.18)
Camshaft	
End Play	
Standard	.001-.007 (.03-.18)
Service Limit	.006 (.15)
Journal Diameter	1.7713-1.7720 (44.991-45.009)
Lobe Lift	.2381 (6.048)
Oil Clearance	
Standard	.001-.003 (.03-.08)
Service Limit	.006 (.15)

1991 ENGINES
2.9L V6

Ranger

NOTE: For repair procedures not covered in this article, see ENGINE OVERHAUL PROCEDURES article in GENERAL INFORMATION.

ENGINE IDENTIFICATION

Engine is identified by the eighth character of Vehicle Identification Number (VIN). The VIN is stamped on a metal plate, and is visible through windshield on left upper side of instrument panel. VIN is also located on Safety Compliance Certification Label attached to left door or left door pillar.

VIN ENGINE CODE

Engine	Code
2.9L PFI	T

ADJUSTMENTS

VALVE CLEARANCE ADJUSTMENT

1) Adjust one cylinder at a time. Rotate crankshaft and position valve being adjusted on lowest portion of camshaft lobe (valve completely closed). Loosen adjusting screw until rocker arm backlash is achieved. Turn in adjusting screw until rocker arm initially contacts valve tip.

2) To achieve nominal working position of valve lifter, turn in adjusting screw 1.5 turns, or the equivalent of .07" (1.8 mm). Repeat procedure to adjust remaining valves.

REMOVAL & INSTALLATION

NOTE: For installation reference, label all electrical connectors, vacuum hoses and fuel lines before removal. Also place mating marks on engine hood and other major assemblies before removal.

FUEL PRESSURE RELEASE

To release fuel pressure, disconnect negative battery cable. Remove fuel cap to release fuel tank pressure. Remove relief valve cap from fuel rail. Connect fuel pressure gauge to relief valve and release fuel pressure into a suitable container.

COOLING SYSTEM BLEEDING

1) Fill cooling system with 50/50 mixture of coolant and water. Pause several minutes for circulation. Fill radiator to filler neck seat. Install radiator cap fully, then back off to first stop.

WARNING: NEVER remove radiator cap with engine operating under any conditions. Failure to follow instruction may cause damage to cooling system, engine or personal injury. Always wrap protective material around radiator cap to avoid injury from hot coolant.

2) Place heater controls to maximum heat. Start engine and operate at 2000 RPM for approximately 3-4 minutes. Turn engine off. Using a protective rag, carefully remove radiator cap. Add coolant to filler neck seat.

3) Install radiator cap fully and back off to first stop. Start engine and allow to operate at 2000 RPM until upper radiator hose is warm. Check heater output. Turn engine off. Using a rag, carefully remove radiator cap. Add coolant to filler neck seat if necessary.

4) Tightly install radiator cap. Remove small cap (large cap is for windshield washer reservoir) on coolant recovery reservoir. Add 1.1 qt. (1L) of 50/50 water and coolant mixture to reservoir. Install reservoir cap.

ENGINE

Removal – 1) Disconnect negative battery cable and drain cooling system. Remove hood, air cleaner and intake duct assembly. Remove fan shroud and position over fan. Remove radiator with hoses and shroud. Remove alternator and bracket.

2) Remove A/C compressor and power steering pump with hoses attached (if equipped). Disconnect heater hoses from engine. Release fuel pressure. See FUEL PRESSURE RELEASE under REMOVAL & INSTALLATION. Disconnect fuel supply line from fuel injector rail. Using Fuel Line Coupling Key (T90P-9550-A), disconnect fuel return line from fuel pressure regulator. *See Fig. 1.*

3) Disconnect brake booster vacuum hose. Disconnect throttle cable linkage and shield at throttle body and intake manifold. Disconnect all vacuum hoses from rear vacuum fitting in upper intake manifold.

4) Disconnect wiring from coil, oil pressure sending unit and engine coolant temperature sending units. Disconnect injector harness, air charge temperature sensor and throttle position sensor.

5) Raise and support vehicle. Disconnect exhaust pipes from manifolds. Remove starter and front engine mount nuts or through bolts. Remove ground wires from engine block. On A/T vehicles, remove converter inspection cover and disconnect flywheel from converter.

6) Remove kickdown rod and bellhousing mounting bolts. Remove adapter plate-to-converter housing bolt. On M/T vehicles, remove clutch housing bolts and hydraulic clutch hose. On all models, remove engine front support-to-crossmember nuts and bolts.

7) Lower vehicle and attach engine hoist to brackets at exhaust manifolds. Ensure all wires and hoses are disconnected before raising engine. Support transmission. Raise engine slightly and carefully pull engine forward from transmission without damaging rear cover plate. Remove engine from vehicle.

Installation – To install, reverse removal procedure. Tighten bolts to specification. See TORQUE SPECIFICATIONS table at end of article. Fill or top off all engine fluids. Fill and bleed air from cooling system. See COOLING SYSTEM BLEEDING under REMOVAL & INSTALLATION.

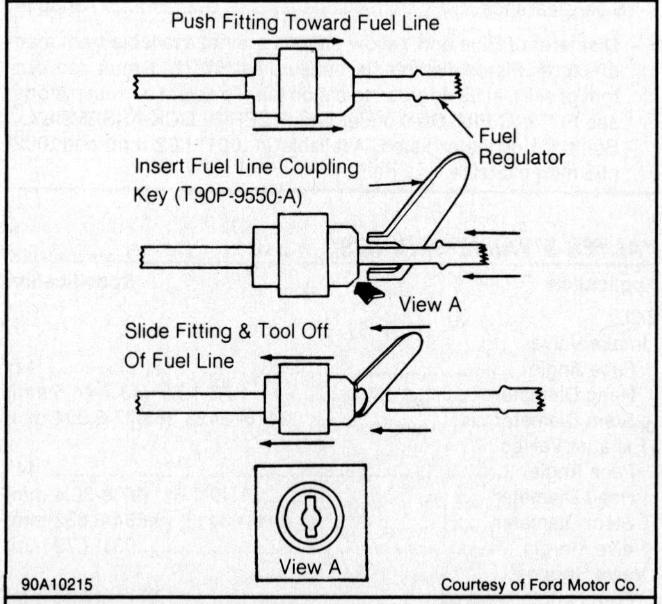
Push Fitting Toward Fuel Line
Fuel
Regulator
Insert Fuel Line Coupling
Key (T90P-9550-A)
View A
Slide Fitting & Tool Off
Of Fuel Line
View A
90A10215
Courtesy of Ford Motor Co.

Fig. 1: Disconnecting Fuel Return Line Coupling

INTAKE MANIFOLDS

Removal (Upper & Lower) – 1) Disconnect negative battery cable. Remove air intake duct. Release fuel system pressure. See FUEL PRESSURE RELEASE under REMOVAL & INSTALLATION.

2) Disconnect fuel supply line from fuel rail. Using Fuel Line Coupling Key (T90P-9550-A), disconnect fuel return line from pressure regulator. *See Fig. 1.* Disconnect throttle cable and bracket assembly.

3) Disconnect vacuum hoses from upper intake manifold. Disconnect electrical connectors at throttle body, upper and lower intake manifolds and distributor. Disconnect fuel injector wiring harness.

4) Remove upper intake manifold. Drain cooling system. Remove coolant hoses as necessary. Remove distributor cap and spark plug wires as an assembly. Rotate engine and position No. 1 cylinder on TDC of compression stroke.

5) Reference mark location of distributor rotor and housing for installation. Remove distributor hold-down and distributor. Note location of valve cover reinforcement pieces and remove valve covers.

6) Remove lower intake manifold bolts/nuts, noting length of bolts for installation to original position. Remove lower intake manifold. Remove gasket material from lower intake manifold and cylinder block.

Installation - 1) Apply sealing compound to mating surfaces. Place new lower intake manifold gasket into position. Ensure tab on right cylinder head gasket fits into cutout in lower intake manifold gasket.

2) Apply sealing compound to attaching bolt bosses on lower intake manifold and position manifold onto engine. Tighten bolts in sequence to specification. *See Fig. 2.* See TORQUE SPECIFICATIONS table at end of article.

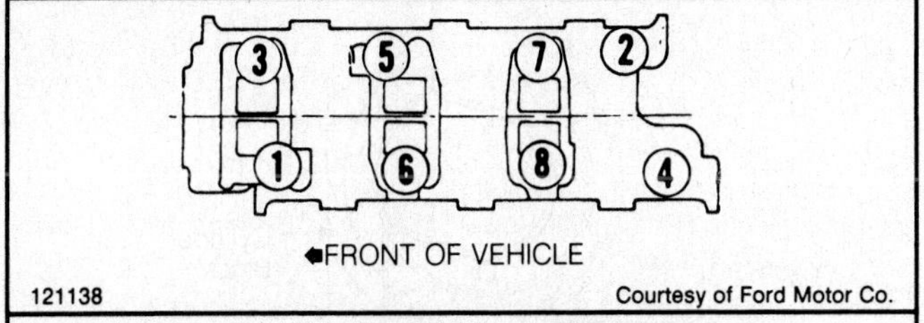
3
5
7
2
1
6
8
4
FRONT OF VEHICLE
121138
Courtesy of Ford Motor Co.

Fig. 2: Lower Intake Manifold Tightening Sequence

3) Noting reference marks made in removal procedure, install distributor. Install new valve cover gaskets and valve covers. Install valve cover retaining bolts with reinforcement pieces in original position. *See Fig. 3.*

CAUTION: Failure to properly install valve cover reinforcement pieces will cause valve cover damage and oil leakage.

4) Install distributor cap and wires. Using a small screwdriver, coat inside of each spark plug wire connector (at spark plug end) with silicone grease. Connect spark plug wires at spark plugs.

5) Apply sealing compound to mating surfaces of upper and lower intake manifolds. Install new upper intake manifold gaskets and upper intake manifold. Connect all electrical connectors at throttle body, intake manifold assembly and distributor. Connect fuel injector subharness to main Electronic Engine Control (EEC) harness.

6) Install and adjust throttle linkage bracket assembly and cover. Install coolant hoses. Connect negative battery cable. Refill and bleed cooling system. See COOLING SYSTEM BLEEDING under REMOVAL & INSTALLATION.

7) Check ignition timing and reset idle speed to specification as listed on emissions label. Run engine at fast idle and check for coolant and oil leaks.

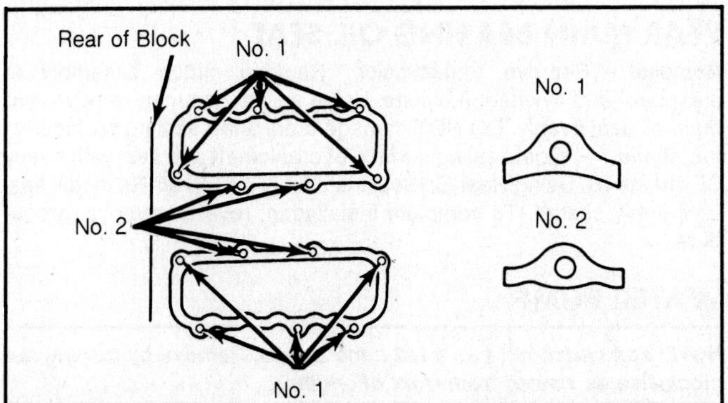
Rear of Block
No. 1
No. 1
No. 2
No. 2
No. 1
71546
Courtesy of Ford Motor Co.

Fig. 3: Locating Valve Cover Reinforcement Pieces

EXHAUST MANIFOLD

Removal & Installation - Disconnect exhaust pipe from exhaust manifold. Remove exhaust manifold-to-cylinder head bolts. Lift exhaust manifold from cylinder head and out of vehicle. To install, reverse removal procedure. Tighten all bolts to specification. See TORQUE SPECIFICATIONS table at end of article.

CYLINDER HEAD

Removal - 1) Disconnect negative battery cable. Remove upper and lower intake manifolds. See INTAKE MANIFOLDS under REMOVAL & INSTALLATION. Remove rocker shaft assembly. See VALVE COVER & ROCKER ARM SHAFT ASSEMBLY under REMOVAL & INSTALLATION. Remove push rods and keep in order for installation to original location.

2) Remove exhaust manifold from cylinder head. Loosen and remove cylinder head bolts evenly. Discard cylinder head bolts. Remove cylinder head. Remove and discard cylinder head gasket.

Inspection - Measure cylinder head and cylinder block mating surfaces for warpage. If cylinder head or cylinder block warpage exceeds specification, DO NOT remove more than .010" (.25 mm) material from original surface of cylinder head or block. See CYLINDER HEAD table under ENGINE SPECIFICATIONS at end of article.

CAUTION: Left and right head gaskets are not interchangeable. Each gasket has FRONT and TOP marks. Always use NEW cylinder head bolts.

Installation - 1) Position head gasket on cylinder block with FRONT and TOP marks in proper position. Install fabricated alignment dowels in cylinder block to keep gasket in place and assist in cylinder head alignment. Position cylinder head on block. Install NEW cylinder head bolts.

2) Tighten cylinder head bolts in sequence to specification. *See Fig. 4.* See TORQUE SPECIFICATIONS table at end of article. Apply heavy SF engine oil to both ends of push rods and install.

3) To complete installation, reverse removal procedure. Adjust valve clearance. See VALVE CLEARANCE ADJUSTMENT under ADJUSTMENTS. Fill and bleed cooling system. See COOLING SYSTEM BLEEDING under REMOVAL & INSTALLATION.

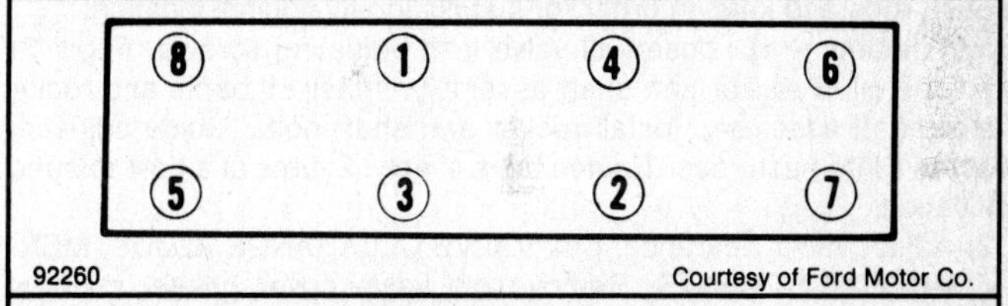
8
1
4
6
5
3
2
7
92260
Courtesy of Ford Motor Co.

Fig. 4: Cylinder Head Bolt Tightening Sequence

FRONT COVER OIL SEAL

Removal - Drain cooling system and remove radiator. Remove water pump drive belt, crankshaft pulley and vibration damper. Using a 3-finger seal puller and slide hammer, remove front cover oil seal.

Installation - Coat sealing surface of new seal with heavy SF engine oil. Slide oil seal onto crankshaft. Install seal into recess of front cover until even with surface of cover. To complete installation, reverse removal procedure. Fill and bleed cooling system. See COOLING SYSTEM BLEEDING under REMOVAL & INSTALLATION.

TIMING CHAIN & SPROCKETS

Removal - 1) Remove oil pan. See OIL PAN under REMOVAL & INSTALLATION. Position No. 1 cylinder on TDC of compression stroke. Ensure damper timing marks align properly. Drain cooling system and remove radiator. Remove heater and radiator hoses.

2) Remove accessory drive belts. Remove A/C compressor and power steering bracket (if equipped). Remove alternator and drive belt(s).

NOTE: Fan clutch nut has a left-hand thread. Remove by turning nut clockwise as viewed from front of engine.

3) Remove fan and clutch assembly using Fan Clutch Holder (T83T-6312-A) and Nut Wrench (T83T-6312-B). *See Fig. 6.* Remove water

1991 ENGINES
2.9L V6 (Cont.)

pump. Remove crankshaft damper. Remove front cover bolts and cover.

CAUTION: Note timing mark alignment of camshaft and crankshaft sprockets for installation reference.

4) Secure timing chain tensioner with clip. Remove camshaft sprocket retaining bolt. Remove camshaft sprocket and timing chain. Remove crankshaft sprocket.

Installation – 1) Ensure crankshaft and camshaft are in TDC position. Slot on camshaft should face slot on crankshaft. Align position dowel on back of crankshaft sprocket with slot on crankshaft face. Install crankshaft sprocket until it seats against crankshaft.

2) Feed timing chain around crankshaft sprocket and camshaft sprocket. Install camshaft sprocket and timing chain as an assembly. Install camshaft sprocket bolt and tighten to specification. See TORQUE SPECIFICATIONS table at end of article.

3) To complete installation, reverse removal procedure. Fill and bleed cooling system. See COOLING SYSTEM BLEEDING under REMOVAL & INSTALLATION. Operate engine at fast idle and check for coolant and oil leaks. Adjust ignition timing.

VALVE COVER & ROCKER ARM SHAFT ASSEMBLY

Removal – 1) Release pressure from fuel system. See FUEL PRESSURE RELEASE under REMOVAL & INSTALLATION. Remove spark plug wires. Remove plastic retainer from coupling at fuel pressure regulator. Disconnect fuel line coupling using Fuel Line Coupling Key (T90P-9550-A). *See Fig. 1.* Using 2 wrenches, disconnect fuel supply line.

2) On vehicles with A/C, remove dipstick tube and bracket and left engine lifting hook. On all models, remove PCV valve hose and breather. Remove valve cover bolts and reinforcement pieces, and note location for installation. Lightly tap valve cover with plastic hammer to break valve cover seal and remove valve cover.

3) Remove rocker arm shaft assembly retaining bolts evenly, 2 turns at a time. Remove rocker arm shaft assembly and oil baffle. Remove push rods and keep in order for installation to original location.

Installation – 1) Loosen all valve lash adjusting screws. Apply SF engine oil to rocker arm shaft assembly. Install oil baffle and rocker arm shaft assembly. Install rocker arm shaft bolts. Guide adjusting screws into push rods. Tighten bolts evenly, 2 turns at a time to specification.

2) Adjust valve clearance. See VALVE CLEARANCE ADJUSTMENT under ADJUSTMENTS. Remove old valve cover gasket material. Install new gaskets on valve covers. Install valve covers. Install valve cover retaining bolts with reinforcement pieces in proper position. *See Fig. 3.*

3) Tighten retaining bolts to specification. See TORQUE SPECIFICATIONS table at end of article. To complete installation, reverse removal procedure.

CAUTION: Failure to properly install reinforcement pieces will cause valve cover damage and oil leakage.

CAMSHAFT

Removal – 1) Remove upper and lower intake manifolds. See INTAKE MANIFOLDS under REMOVAL & INSTALLATION. Remove rocker arm shaft assemblies and push rods. See VALVE COVER & ROCKER ARM SHAFT ASSEMBLY under REMOVAL & INSTALLATION.

2) Remove timing chain and camshaft sprocket. See TIMING CHAIN & SPROCKETS under REMOVAL & INSTALLATION. Remove valve lifters and keep in order for installation to original location. Remove camshaft thrust plate and spacer ring. Carefully remove camshaft out of cylinder block.

Inspection – Measure camshaft bearing journals and lobes for wear. If journals and lobes are not within specification, replace camshaft and valve lifters. See CAMSHAFT table under ENGINE SPECIFICATIONS at end of article.

Installation – 1) Coat camshaft journals and lobes with heavy SF engine oil (50W). Install spacer ring with chamfered side toward camshaft. Install key into camshaft. Carefully install camshaft into cylinder block.

2) Install thrust plate and tighten bolts. Ensure thrust plate covers main oil galley hole. *See Fig. 5.* Check camshaft end play. If end play is not within specification, replace thrust plate. See CAMSHAFT table under ENGINE SPECIFICATIONS at end of article.

3) To complete installation, reverse removal procedure. Adjust valve clearance. See VALVE CLEARANCE ADJUSTMENT under ADJUSTMENTS.

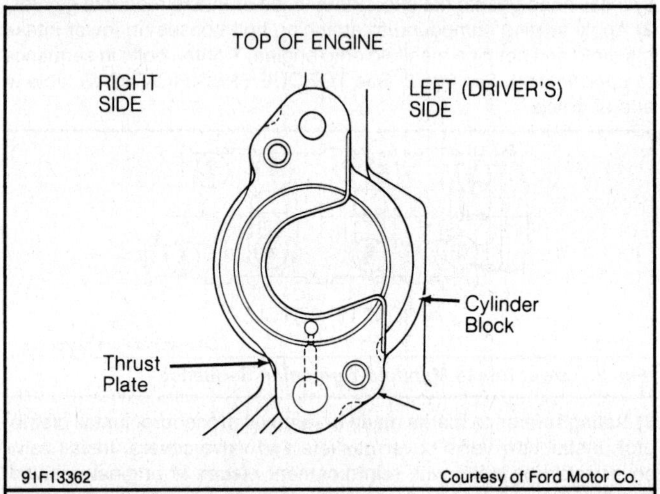
TOP OF ENGINE
RIGHT SIDE
LEFT (DRIVER'S) SIDE
Cylinder Block
Thrust Plate
91F13362
Courtesy of Ford Motor Co.

Fig. 5: Installing Camshaft Thrust Plate

CAMSHAFT BEARINGS

Removal – Remove engine. See ENGINE under REMOVAL & INSTALLATION. Remove camshaft. See CAMSHAFT under REMOVAL & INSTALLATION. Remove flywheel/flexplate and rear bearing core plug. Using Cam Bearing Replacer Kit (T71P-6250-A), remove camshaft bearings.

Installation – 1) Install camshaft bearings using Cam Bearing Replacer Kit. Ensure oil hole in bearing aligns with oil hole in cylinder block. Front bearing must be installed .040-.060" (1.02-1.52 mm) from front face of block.

2) Check oil hole alignment of No. 2 and 3 bearings by inserting a rod of smaller diameter into oil passage. Rod should pass into camshaft bore. Coat sealing edge of new rear bearing core plug with oil resistant sealer.

3) Use a proper size driver ONLY and install core plug. To complete installation, reverse removal procedure.

REAR MAIN BEARING OIL SEAL

Removal – Remove transmission. Remove clutch assembly (if equipped) and flywheel/flexplate. Using a slide hammer, remove rear main oil seal evenly. DO NOT damage crankshaft sealing surface.

Installation – Coat sealing surface of crankshaft and seal with heavy SF engine oil. Using Rear Oil Seal Installer (T72C-6165-R), install seal until firmly seated. To complete installation, reverse removal procedure.

WATER PUMP

NOTE: Fan clutch nut has a left-hand thread. Remove by turning nut clockwise as viewed from front of engine.

Removal – 1) Drain cooling system. Disconnect lower radiator hose and heater return hose from water pump. Remove fan and clutch assembly using Fan Clutch Holder (T83T-6312-A) and Nut Wrench (T83T-6312-B). *See Fig. 6.* Remove by turning nut clockwise, as nut has left-hand thread.

2) Remove alternator belt. Remove alternator and bracket (if A/C equipped). Remove water pump pulley. Remove water pump attaching bolts and note different bolt lengths for installation reference. Remove water pump assembly.

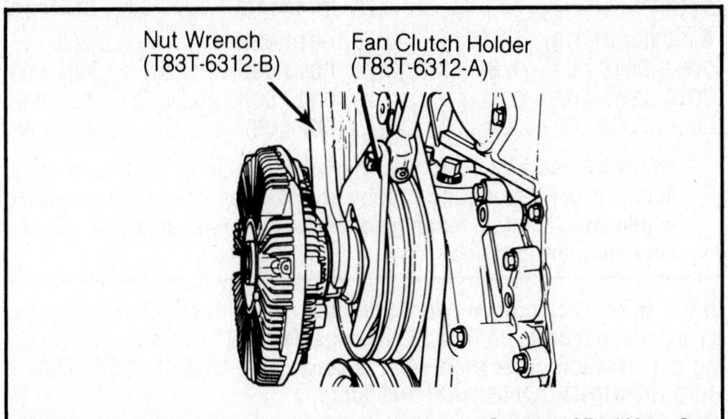
Nut Wrench
(T83T-6312-B)
Fan Clutch Holder
(T83T-6312-A)
91356
Courtesy of Ford Motor Co.

Fig. 6: Removing Fan & Clutch Assembly

Installation - 1) Remove gasket material from water pump-to-engine front cover mating surfaces. Apply sealer to both sides of new gasket. Place gasket on water pump. Position water pump and install 2 bolts finger tight.

2) Install remaining bolts to proper location and tighten to specification. See TORQUE SPECIFICATIONS table at end of article. To complete installation, reverse removal procedure. Fill and bleed cooling system. See COOLING SYSTEM BLEEDING under REMOVAL & INSTALLATION.

OIL PAN

Removal - 1) Disconnect negative battery cable. Remove air intake tube. Position No. 1 cylinder on TDC of compression stroke. Remove distributor cap. Reference mark distributor rotor and body, and remove distributor. Remove fan shroud, and position back over cooling fan.

2) Remove front engine mount-to-crossmember nuts. Raise and support vehicle. Drain engine oil and remove oil filter. On A/T vehicles, disconnect transmission filler tube and oil cooler lines.

3) On 4WD vehicles, disconnect exhaust pipes from exhaust manifolds. On all models, disconnect front stabilizer bar (if equipped). Disconnect and lower oil cooler bracket (if equipped). Remove starter motor.

4) Raise engine slightly. Place wooden blocks between front engine mounts and crossmember, and lower engine. Remove oil pan bolts. On 4WD vehicles, remove oil pump retaining bolts and lower pump into oil pan. On all models, remove oil pan and gasket.

Installation - 1) To install, reverse removal procedure. Apply silicone sealant at front and rear corners of oil pan surface and cylinder block, and where front cover meets the cylinder block.

2) Install oil pan bolts. Tighten bolts in 2 steps to specification using specified procedure. *See Fig. 7.* See TORQUE SPECIFICATIONS table at end of article. To install remaining components, reverse removal procedure. Tighten bolts to specification.

OVERHAUL

CYLINDER HEAD

Cylinder Head - 1) Clean head gasket mating surface. Clean carbon from combustion chambers. Use care not to damage surfaces. Check cylinder head for cracks, burrs, nicks and warpage.

2) DO NOT machine more than .010" (.25 mm) from original cylinder head surface to correct warpage. Replace cylinder head as necessary. See CYLINDER HEAD table under ENGINE SPECIFICATIONS at end of article.

CAUTION: DO NOT machine more than .010" (.25 mm) from cylinder head original thickness.

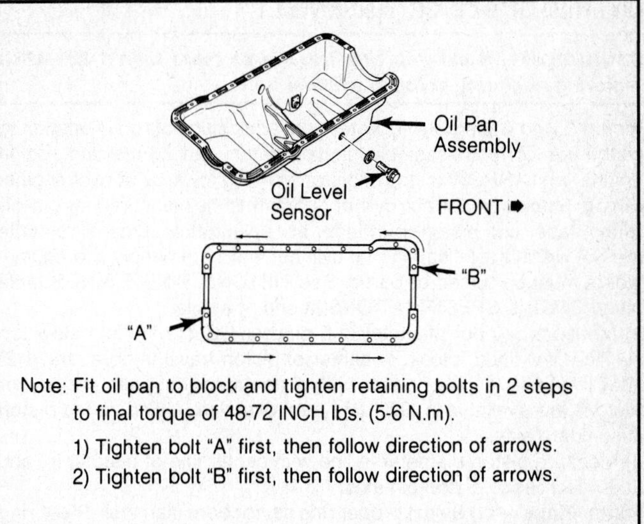
Oil Pan
Assembly
Oil Level
Sensor
FRONT
"B"
"A"
Note: Fit oil pan to block and tighten retaining bolts in 2 steps
to final torque of 48-72 INCH lbs. (5-6 N.m).
1) Tighten bolt "A" first, then follow direction of arrows.
2) Tighten bolt "B" first, then follow direction of arrows.
90B13533
Courtesy of Ford Motor Co.

Fig. 7: Oil Pan Bolt Tightening Sequence

Valve Springs - 1) Inspect valve spring free length and pressure. Replace valve spring if free length and pressure are not within specification. See VALVES & VALVE SPRINGS table under ENGINE SPECIFICATIONS at end of article.

2) Measure valve spring installed height from top of spring seat to underside of spring retainer. Ensure installed height is within specification. See VALVES & VALVE SPRINGS table under ENGINE SPECIFICATIONS at end of article.

3) If installed height is not within specification, a .03" (.8 mm) shim can be installed between cylinder head and valve spring to obtain correct height.

CAUTION: DO NOT install valve spring spacers unless necessary. Using more spacers than required can result in spring breakage or worn camshaft lobes.

Valve Stem Oil Seals - Use Valve Stem Oil Seal Installer (T73P-6571-A) for seal installation. Install seal until it bottoms on valve guide. Oversize seals must be used on guides that have been reamed for oversize valves.

Valve Guides - 1) Valve guides must be reamed for an oversized valve if valve stem oil clearance is not within specification. See CYLINDER HEAD table under ENGINE SPECIFICATIONS at end of article. Valves are available in .015" (.38 mm) and .030" (.76 mm) oversize.

2) If oversized valves or oversized valve stem oil seals are not available, valve guide may be bored out to use a service bushing. Always use reamers in proper sequence (smallest first).

NOTE: Always grind valve seat after valve guide has been reamed or service bushing has been installed.

Valve Seat - Ensure valve seat angle, seat width and seat runout are within specification. See CYLINDER HEAD table under ENGINE SPECIFICATIONS at end of article. Valve seats must be ground when valve guide is reamed or replaced. Replacement information is not available from manufacturer.

Valves - Ensure head diameter, valve face runout, stem diameter and valve margin are within specification. See VALVES & VALVE SPRINGS table under ENGINE SPECIFICATIONS at end of article.

CAUTION: DO NOT remove more than .010" (.25 mm) from end of valve stem when resurfacing tip of valve.

Seat Correction Angles - Grind valve seat to a true 45-degree angle. If seat width is too wide after grinding, use a 30-degree stone to lower seat or a 60-degree stone to raise seat.

1991 ENGINES
2.9L V6 (Cont.)

CYLINDER BLOCK ASSEMBLY

CAUTION: NEVER cut into ring travel area more than 1/32" when removing ridge ring at top of cylinder bore.

Piston & Rod Assembly - Note installed position of rod in relation to piston for correct assembly. Install piston and connecting rod in engine, with ARROW on top of piston pointing towards front of engine.

Fitting Pistons - **1)** Each cylinder bore must be measured for out-of-round, taper and piston-to-cylinder bore clearance. If measurements are not within specification or if cylinder walls are deeply scored, cylinders must be honed or bored. See PISTONS, PINS & RINGS table under ENGINE SPECIFICATIONS at end of article.

2) Measure cylinder diameter in 3 places: 1/2" (12.7 mm) below top surface of cylinder block, at center of piston travel in bore, and 1/2" (12.7 mm) above top of piston with piston at lowest point in cylinder. Pistons are available in .020" (.51 mm) oversize. A Red coded piston is standard size.

3) Measure piston diameter in line with center line of piston pin, and at 90 degrees to piston pin axis.

Piston Rings - **1)** Select proper ring set for bore diameter. Place ring in cylinder bore in which it will be installed. Use piston to square ring and place ring below normal ring wear area. Measure ring end gap. If ring gap is not within specification, try another ring set. See PISTONS, PINS & RINGS table under ENGINE SPECIFICATIONS at end of article.

2) Check side clearance of rings after installing on piston. Ensure clearance is within specification around entire circumference. Replace piston and/or rings if clearance is not within specification. See PISTONS, PINS & RINGS table under ENGINE SPECIFICATIONS at end of article. Ensure rings are properly spaced on piston before installing pistons into cylinder. *See Fig. 8.*

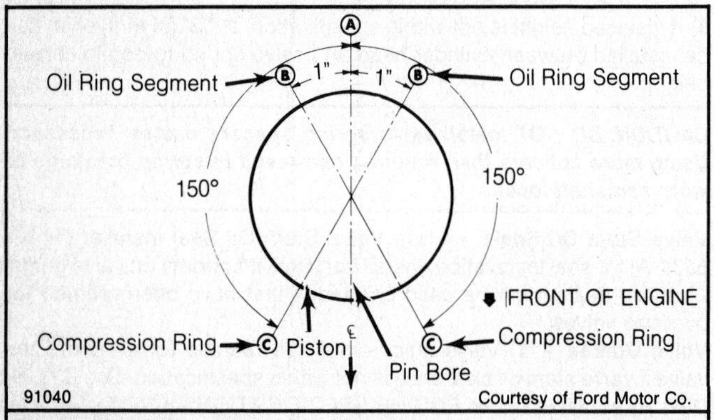
A
Oil Ring Segment
B
1"
1"
B
Oil Ring Segment
150°
150°
FRONT OF ENGINE
Compression Ring
C
Piston
C
Compression Ring
Pin Bore
91040
Courtesy of Ford Motor Co.

Fig. 8: Positioning Piston Ring Gaps

Rod Bearings - **1)** Clean crankshaft journal and rod bearing bore. Ensure oil hole on rod is not restricted. Check each crankshaft journal for out-of-round. Use Plastigage method to check rod bearing clearance.

2) If proper oil clearance cannot be obtained with standard bearings, try a combination of undersize bearings. DO NOT use any other bearing combination other than what is listed. See UNDERSIZE MAIN & ROD BEARING COMBINATIONS table.

3) If use of bearing combinations does not bring oil clearance within specification, machine or replace crankshaft as necessary. Always replace bearings in pairs. See CRANKSHAFT, MAIN & CONNECTING ROD BEARINGS table under ENGINE SPECIFICATIONS at end of article.

Crankshaft & Main Bearings - **1)** When checking main bearing clearance in vehicle, position a jack under adjoining bearing counterweight being checked. Remove only one main bearing cap at a time.

2) Use Plastigage method and check main bearing clearance. If clearance is not within specification, replace bearings. Machine or replace crankshaft as necessary. See CRANKSHAFT, MAIN & CONNECTING ROD BEARINGS table under ENGINE SPECIFICATIONS at end of article.

UNDERSIZE MAIN & ROD BEARING COMBINATIONS [1]

Excess Bearing Clearance In. (mm)	Use Upper Bearing In. (mm)	Use Lower Bearing In. (mm)
.0-.0005 (.0-.013)	.001 (.03)	[2]
.0005-.0010 (.013-.026)	.001 (.03)	.001 (.03)
.0010-.0015 (.026-.039)	.002 (.05)	.001 (.03)
.0015-.0020 (.039-.052)	.002 (.05)	.002 (.05)

[1] - DO NOT use any other bearing combination other than what is listed. If use of bearing combinations does not bring clearance within specification, machine or replace crankshaft as necessary.

[2] - Use standard bearing.

3) If proper oil clearance cannot be obtained with standard bearings, try a combination of undersize bearings. DO NOT use any other bearing combination other than what is listed. See UNDERSIZE MAIN & ROD BEARING COMBINATIONS table.

4) If use of bearing combinations does not bring clearance within specification, machine or replace crankshaft as necessary. Always replace bearings in pairs. See CRANKSHAFT, MAIN & CONNECTING ROD BEARINGS table under ENGINE SPECIFICATIONS at end of article.

5) Install main bearing caps in original location. Ensure arrow on No. 1 and No. 3 main bearing caps face towards front of engine. Tighten main bearing cap bolts finger tight. Pry crankshaft forward and tighten bearing caps to specification.

6) Check crankshaft end play. Replace thrust bearing if end play is not within specification. See CRANKSHAFT, MAIN & CONNECTING ROD BEARINGS table under ENGINE SPECIFICATIONS at end of article. Thrust bearing is No. 3 (from front) main bearing in block.

Cylinder Block - **1)** Using a feeler gauge and straightedge, check cylinder block head gasket surface for warpage. Check cylinder bore for wear, taper, out-of-round and piston fit. Repair or replace as necessary. See CYLINDER BLOCK table under ENGINE SPECIFICATIONS at end of article.

2) Install all main bearing caps and tighten to specification before honing cylinder bore. See TORQUE SPECIFICATIONS table at end of article. Use ONLY a spring-loaded type cylinder hone. After honing, thoroughly clean bore with detergent and water solution. Rinse solution from bore thoroughly with clean water. Wipe bore clean with lint free cloth. Lubricate cylinder bores with engine oil.

ENGINE OILING

ENGINE LUBRICATION SYSTEM

System is pressure fed from a rotor-type oil pump. Oil flows through oil filter before entering main oil gallery.

Crankcase Capacity - Crankcase capacity is 4 qts. (3.8L) without filter and 5 qts. (4.75L) with filter.

Oil Pressure - Normal oil pressure at 2000 RPM should be 40-60 psi (2.8-4.2 kg/cm²) with engine at normal operating temperature.

Oil Pressure Regulator Valve - Oil pressure regulator valve is located in oil pump body. Valve is nonadjustable.

OIL PUMP

Removal & Disassembly - Remove oil pan. See OIL PAN under REMOVAL & INSTALLATION. On 4WD vehicles, remove oil pump assembly from oil pan. On 2WD vehicles, disconnect pick-up tube from main bearing cap stud. Remove oil pump attaching bolts. Remove oil pump assembly with oil pump drive shaft attached. On all models, remove pick-up tube from pump. Disassemble oil pump. Note direction of component installation for reassembly reference.

Inspection - Inspect components for damage. Measure rotor end clearance, outer race-to-housing clearance and rotor tip clearance. Check clearance between pressure relief valve and bore. Measure relief valve tension. Replace oil pump assembly if measurements are not within specifications. See OIL PUMP SPECIFICATIONS table.

NOTE: Oil pump is serviced as an assembly only. Replace assembly if measurements are not within specification. See OIL PUMP SPECIFICATIONS table.

OIL PUMP SPECIFICATIONS

Application	Specification In. (mm)
Drive Shaft-To-Housing Bearing Clearance	.0015-.0030 (.038-.076)
Outer Race-To-Housing Clearance	.001-.013 (.03-.33)
Relief Valve Spring Tension	[1]
Relief Valve-To-Bore Clearance	.0015-.0030 (.038-.076)
Rotor Assembly End Play	.004 (.10)

[1] – Relief valve spring tension should be 13.6-14.7 lbs. @ 1.39" (6.2-6.7 kg @ 35.3 mm).

Reassembly & Installation – To reassemble, reverse disassembly procedure. Ensure rotors are installed in original location. Ensure oil pump spins freely after reassembly. To install, reverse removal procedure; use new gaskets. Tighten bolts to specification. See TORQUE SPECIFICATIONS table at end of article. Prime oil pump assembly before installation.

TORQUE SPECIFICATIONS

TORQUE SPECIFICATIONS

Application	Ft. Lbs. (N.m)
Bellhousing-To-Engine Bolt	28-38 (38-51)
Camshaft Sprocket Bolt	19-28 (26-38)
Camshaft Thrust Plate Bolt	13-16 (18-22)
Connecting Rod Nut	19-24 (26-33)
Crankshaft Damper Bolt	85-96 (116-131)
Cylinder Head Bolt [1]	
Step 1	22 (30)
Step 2	51-55 (69-75)
Step 3	Additional 90 degrees
Engine Mount-To-Chassis Bolt	71-94 (96-127)
Engine Mount-To-Engine Bracket Bolt	65-85 (88-115)
Exhaust Manifold Bolt	20-30 (27-41)
Fan Clutch-To-Water Pump Nut [2]	30-100 (41-137)
Flexplate-To-Converter Bolt	20-34 (27-46)
Flywheel-To-Crankshaft Bolt	47-52 (64-71)
Front Cover Bolt	13-16 (18-22)
Main Bearing Cap Bolt	65-75 (88-102)
Rear Mount-To-Crossmember Nut	65-85 (88-115)
Rear Mount-To-Transmission Bolt	60-80 (81-108)
Rocker Arm Shaft Bolt	43-50 (58-68)
Starter Bolt	15-20 (20-27)
Water Pump Pulley Bolt	14-22 (19-30)
	INCH Lbs. (N.m)
Lower Intake Manifold Bolt [3]	
Step 1	Hand Start & Snug
Step 2	36-72 (4-8)
Step 3	72-132 (8-15)
Step 4	132-180 (15-21)
Step 5 [4]	180-216 (21-25)
Oil Pan Bolt [5]	48-72 (5-8)
Oil Pump Case Bolt	80-115 (9-13)
Throttle Body-To-Intake Bolt	80-115 (9-13)
Timing Chain	
Guide Bolt	80-115 (9-13)
Tensioner Bolt	80-115 (9-13)
Upper Intake Manifold Bolt [6]	
Step 1	84 (10)
Step 2	180-216 (21-25)

TORQUE SPECIFICATIONS (Cont.)

Application	INCH Lbs. (N.m)
Valve Cover Bolt	36-60 (4-7)
Water Pump Bolt	84-108 (10-12)

[1] – Tighten in sequence. *See Fig. 4.*
[2] – Left-hand thread.
[3] – Tighten in sequence. *See Fig. 2.*
[4] – Repeat tightening procedure after engine reaches normal operating temperature.
[5] – Tighten in sequence. *See Fig. 7.*
[6] – Tightening sequence is not available from manufacturer.

ENGINE SPECIFICATIONS

GENERAL SPECIFICATIONS

Application	Specification
2.9L	
Displacement	177 Cu. In.
Bore	3.66" (92.9 mm)
Stroke	2.83" (71.9 mm)
Compression Ratio	9.0:1
Fuel System	PFI
Horsepower @ RPM	140 @ 4600
Torque Ft. Lbs. @ RPM	170 @ 2600

CRANKSHAFT, MAIN & CONNECTING ROD BEARINGS

Application	In. (mm)
2.9L	
Crankshaft End Play	
Standard	.004-.008 (.10-.20)
Wear Limit	.012 (.30)
Main Bearings	
Journal Diameter	2.2433-2.2441 (56.980-57.000)
Journal Out-Of-Round	.0006 (.015)
Journal Taper [1]	.0006 (.015)
Oil Clearance	
Desired	.0008-.0015 (.020-.038)
Allowable	.0005-.0019 (.013-.048)
Connecting Rod Bearings	
Journal Diameter	2.1252-2.1260 (53.980-54.000)
Journal Out-Of-Round	.0006 (.015)
Journal Taper [1]	.0006 (.015)
Oil Clearance	
Desired	.0006-.0016 (.015-041)
Allowable	.0005-.0022 (.013-.056)

[1] – Specification is per 1" (25.4 mm).

CONNECTING RODS

Application	In. (mm)
2.9L	
Bore Diameter	
Pin Bore	.9450-.9452 (24.003-24.008)
Crankpin Bore	2.2370-2.2378 (56.820-56.840)
Center-To-Center Length	5.139-5.141 (130.51-130.58)
Maximum Bend [1]	.002 (.05)
Maximum Twist [1]	.006 (.15)
Side Play	
Standard	.004-.011 (.10-.28)
Wear Limit	.014 (.36)

[1] – Specification listed is measured at the ends of an 8" (203 mm) bar, 4" (102 mm) on each side of rod center line.

1991 ENGINES
2.9L V6 (Cont.)

PISTONS, PINS & RINGS

Application	In. (mm)
2.9L	
Pistons	
Clearance	.0011-.0019 (.028-.048)
Diameter [1]	3.6605-3.6615 (92.976-93.002)
Pins	
Piston Fit	.0003-.0006 (.008-.015)
Rings	
No. 1 & 2	
End Gap	.015-.023 (.038-.058)
Side Clearance	.0020-.0033 (.051-.084)
No. 3 (Oil)	
End Gap	.015-.055 (.38-1.40)
Side Clearance	Snug Fit

[1] – Measured at piston pin bore center line, at 90-degree angle to piston pin.

CYLINDER BLOCK

Application	In. (mm)
2.9L	
Cylinder Bore	
Standard Diameter	3.6614-3.6630 (93.000-93.040)
Maximum Taper	.010 (.25)
Out-Of-Round	
Standard	.0015 (.038)
Wear Limit	.005 (.13)
Maximum Deck Warpage	[1]

[1] – No more than .003" (.08 mm) in any 6" (152.4 mm) section and no more than .006" (.15 mm) overall. DO NOT remove more than .010" (.25 mm) material from original deck if machining is required.

VALVES & VALVE SPRINGS

Application	Specification
2.9L	
Intake Valves	
Face Angle	44°
Head Diameter	1.78-1.81" (45.2-46.0 mm)
Minimum Margin	.031" (.79 mm)
Stem Diameter	.3159-.3167" (8.024-8.044 mm)
Exhaust Valves	
Face Angle	44°
Head Diameter	1.41-1.42" (35.8-36.1 mm)
Minimum Margin	.031" (.79 mm)
Stem Diameter	.3149-.3156" (7.998-8.016 mm)
Valve Springs	
Free Length	1.91" (49.0 mm)
Installed Height	1.58-1.61" (40.1-40.9 mm)
Out-Of-Square	.078" (1.98 mm)
Pressure	Lbs. @ In. (kg @ mm)
Valve Closed	60-68 @ 1.59 (27-31 @ 40.4)
Valve Open	138-149 @ 1.22 (63-68 @ 31.0)

CYLINDER HEAD

Application	Specification
2.9L	
Maximum Warpage	[1]
Valve Seats	
Intake Valve	
Seat Angle	45°
Seat Width	.060-.079" (1.52-2.01 mm)
Maximum Seat Runout	.0015" (.038 mm)
Exhaust Valve	
Seat Angle	45°
Seat Width	.060-.079" (1.52-2.01 mm)
Maximum Seat Runout	.0015" (.038 mm)
Valve Guides	
Valve Guide I.D.	.3174-.3184" (8.062-8.087 mm)
Intake Valve	
Valve Stem-To-Guide	
Oil Clearance	.0008-.0025" (.020-.064 mm)
Exhaust Valve	
Valve Stem-To-Guide	
Oil Clearance	.0018-.0035" (.046-.089 mm)

[1] – No more than .003" (.08 mm) in any 6" (152.4 mm) section and no more than .006" (.15 mm) overall. DO NOT remove more than .010" (.25 mm) material from original surface if machining is required.

CAMSHAFT

Application	In. (mm)
2.9L	
Journal Diameter	
Journal No. 1	1.7285-1.7293 (43.904-43.924)
Journal No. 2	1.7135-1.7143 (43.523-43.543)
Journal No. 3	1.6985-1.6992 (43.142-43.160)
Journal No. 4	1.6835-1.6842 (42.761-42.779)
Bearing I.D.	
Journal No. 1	1.7302-1.7310 (43.947-43.967)
Journal No. 2	1.7152-1.7160 (43.566-43.586)
Journal No. 3	1.7002-1.7010 (43.185-43.205)
Journal No. 4	1.6852-1.6860 (42.804-42.824)
End Play	
Standard	.0008-.0040 (.020-.101)
Wear Limit	.009 (.23)
Journal Runout	.005 (.13)
Journal Out-Of-Round	.0003 (.008)
Lobe Lift	
Intake	.3588 (9.113)
Exhaust	.3703 (9.406)
Maximum Lobe Wear	.005 (.13)
Journal-To-Bearing	
Oil Clearance	
Standard	.0010-.0026 (.025-.066)
Wear Limit	.006 (.15)

VALVE LIFTERS

Application	In. (mm)
2.9L	
Lifter Diameter	.8736-.8741 (22.189-22.202)
Oil Clearance	
Standard	.0009-.0024 (.023-.061)
Wear Limit	.005 (.13)

1991 ENGINES
3.0L V6

Aerostar, Ranger

NOTE: For repair procedures not covered in this article, see ENGINE OVERHAUL PROCEDURES article in GENERAL INFORMATION.

ENGINE IDENTIFICATION

Engine may be identified by the eighth character of the Vehicle Identification Number (VIN). VIN plate is attached to upper left corner of instrument panel, near windshield. The VIN is also found on the Safety Compliance Certification Label on left door lock pillar.

VIN ENGINE CODE

Engine	Code
3.0L PFI	U

ADJUSTMENTS

VALVE CLEARANCE ADJUSTMENT

NOTE: Valve lifters are set at zero lash. No adjustment is necessary. If valve seat/face has been serviced or worn parts are suspected, check valve clearance.

1) Following procedure is done with front cover removed. Rotate crankshaft to position "A". *See Fig. 1.* Completely collapse No. 1 intake valve lifter. While holding valve lifter fully collapsed, use feeler gauge to measure clearance of No. 1 intake valve between rocker arm and tip of valve stem.
2) Collapsed valve clearance should be .088-.189" (2.23-4.80 mm) on all valves. Repeat procedure for specified valves. See VALVE ADJUSTMENT SEQUENCE table.

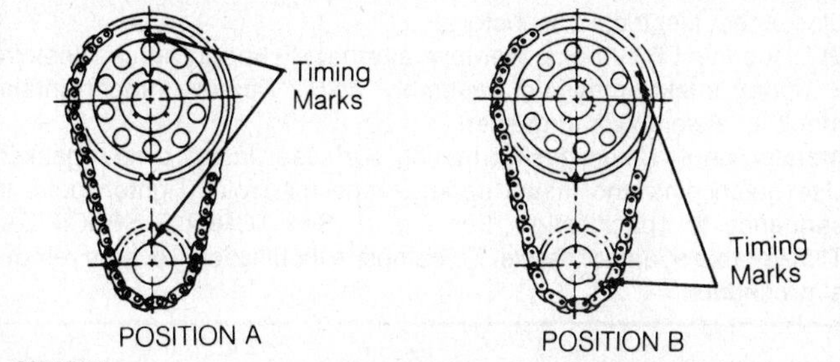
Timing Marks
Timing Marks
POSITION A
POSITION B
90E10185
Courtesy of Ford Motor Co.

Fig. 1: Identifying Valve Adjustment Positions

3) Rotate crankshaft to position "B". *See Fig. 1.* While holding valve lifter fully collapsed, use feeler gauge to measure clearance of No. 1 exhaust valve between rocker arm and tip of valve stem. Repeat procedure for specified valves. See VALVE ADJUSTMENT SEQUENCE table.
4) If valve clearance on any valve is not .088-.189" (2.23-4.80 mm), grind valve stem or replace valve as necessary. See VALVES & VALVE SPRINGS table under ENGINE SPECIFICATIONS at end of article.

NOTE: DO NOT remove more than .010" (.25) from end of valve stem when resurfacing tip of valve.

VALVE ADJUSTMENT SEQUENCE

Crankshaft Position	Adjust Exhaust Valves Of Cylinders	Adjust Intake Valves Of Cylinders
A	2 & 5	1 & 4
B	1, 3, 4 & 6	2, 3, 5 & 6

REMOVAL & INSTALLATION

NOTE: For reassembly reference, label all electrical connectors, vacuum hoses and fuel lines before removal. Also place mating marks on engine hood and other major assemblies before removal.

FUEL PRESSURE RELEASE

To release fuel pressure, disconnect negative battery cable. Remove fuel cap to release fuel tank pressure. Remove relief valve cap from fuel rail. Connect fuel pressure gauge to relief valve and release fuel pressure into a suitable container.

COOLING SYSTEM BLEEDING

1) Fill cooling system with 50/50 mixture of coolant and water. Pause several minutes for circulation. Fill radiator to filler neck seat. Install radiator cap fully, then back off to first stop.

WARNING: When engine is operating, NEVER remove radiator cap under any conditions. Failure to follow instruction could damage cooling system or engine, or cause personal injury. Always wrap protective material around radiator cap to avoid injury from hot coolant.

2) Place heater controls to maximum heat. Start engine and operate at 2000 RPM for approximately 3-4 minutes. Turn engine off. Using a protective rag, carefully remove radiator cap. Add coolant to filler neck seat.
3) Install radiator cap fully then back off to first stop. Start engine and allow to operate at 2000 RPM until upper radiator hose is warm. Check heater output. Turn engine off. Using a protective rag, carefully remove radiator cap. Add coolant to filler neck seat if necessary.
4) Tightly install radiator cap. Remove small cap (large cap is for windshield washer reservoir) on coolant recovery reservoir. Add 1.1 qt. (1L) of 50/50 mixture of coolant and water to reservoir. Install reservoir cap.

ENGINE

Removal (Aerostar) – 1) Disconnect negative battery cable. Drain cooling system. Remove air cleaner and intake duct assembly. Remove radiator hoses and fan shroud. Remove left-handed nut retaining clutch fan to pulley. Remove cooling fan. Disconnect Barometric Manifold Absolute Pressure (BMAP) sensor. Remove throttle linkage shroud.
2) Disconnect throttle linkage at throttle body. Remove accessory drive belts. Disconnect injector harness connector from main Electronic Engine Control (EEC) harness. Disconnect Engine Coolant Temperature (ECT) sensor.
3) Disconnect canister purge solenoid hoses from solenoid. Disconnect power steering pump pressure switch. Remove heater hoses. Remove breather tube from air cleaner and valve cover. Remove transmission oil cooler lines from radiator (if equipped).
4) Remove radiator retaining bolts and radiator. Remove oil fill tube-to-alternator bracket nut. Remove A/C compressor and set aside (if equipped). Remove transmission oil fill tube bolt from top of manifold (if equipped). Disconnect alternator connectors.
5) Remove brake booster vacuum line from brake booster. Remove bolt retaining steering gear at top of shaft. Remove engine cover. Disconnect radio frequency interference suppressor.
6) Disconnect Thick Film Ignition (TFI) connector at distributor. Disconnect oil pressure sender. Release fuel pressure. See FUEL PRESSURE RELEASE under REMOVAL & INSTALLATION. Using Disconnect Tool (D87L-9280-A) for 3/8" line or (D87L-9280-B) for 1/2" line, disconnect fuel supply and return lines. *See Fig. 2.*
7) On M/T models, position shifter in Neutral. Remove shift lever-to-floor retaining bolts. Remove shift lever-to-transmission retaining bolts. Remove shift lever. Raise and support vehicle.
8) Disconnect oil level sensor connector from oil pan. Mark drive shaft-to-flange position and remove drive shaft. Pull speedometer

1991 ENGINES
3.0L V6 (Cont.)

cable from rear of transmission. Remove starter connections and remove starter.

9) On M/T models, remove hydraulic hose-to-slave cylinder lock pin in clutch housing. Remove and plug hose. Disconnect back-up light switch, shift indicator and neutral switch wires. On A/T models, disconnect neutral start switch and 3-4 shift solenoid connectors. Disconnect selector and kickdown cable from transmission lever.

10) Disconnect vacuum modulator hose. Remove converter access cover and adapter plate bolts from lower end of converter housing. Remove flywheel-to-converter retaining nuts. Disconnect oxygen sensor. Disconnect transmission oil cooler lines from transmission (if equipped).

11) Place transmission jack under transmission. Place a safety chain around transmission. Raise transmission slightly. Remove transmission mount-to-crossmember nuts. Remove mount (if necessary). Remove crossmember-to-bracket bolts and nuts. Remove crossmember.

12) Remove bellhousing-to-engine fasteners. Slide transmission rearward. Lower transmission from vehicle. Disconnect exhaust pipes from manifolds. Remove exhaust pipe and converter. Remove front wheels. Remove engine ground straps. Remove stabilizer bar nuts and disconnect stabilizer bar from lower control arms.

13) Disconnect and plug brake lines at bracket on frame behind spindles. Place jack under lower control arm and raise jack until tension is applied to coil spring. Remove upper spindle-to-control arm ball joint bolt and nut. Slowly lower jack to disconnect spindle from ball joint.

14) Position Drive Train Removal Lift (109-00002) under crossmember and engine assembly. Lower vehicle until crossmember rests on lift. Place wood blocks under front crossmember and rear of engine (or transmission if assembled) to keep unit level.

15) Install safety chains around crossmember and lift. With engine and crossmember securely supported on lift, remove 3 engine and crossmember-to-frame retaining bolts from each side of vehicle.

16) Slowly lower engine assembly from vehicle. Ensure A/C compressor and wiring harnesses do not interfere with removal process. Raise body from engine and crossmember assembly. Remove motor mount nuts. Remove engine from crossmember.

Installation – To install, reverse removal procedure. Tighten bolts to specification. See TORQUE SPECIFICATIONS table at end of article. Check and fill all fluid levels. Bleed brakes. Fill and bleed air from cooling system. See COOLING SYSTEM BLEEDING under REMOVAL & INSTALLATION. Start engine and check for leaks. Check front end alignment and adjust as necessary.

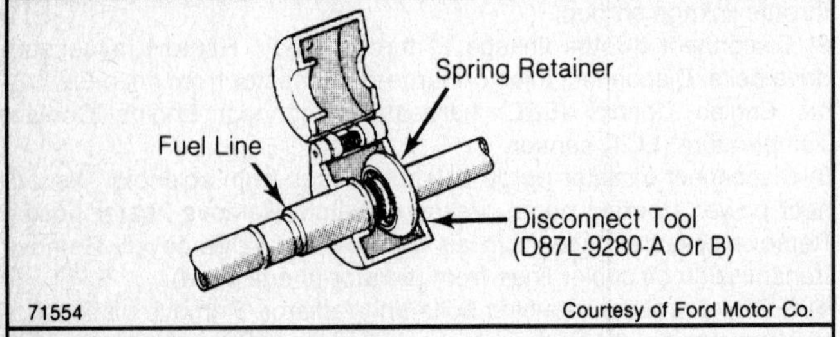
Spring Retainer
Fuel Line
Disconnect Tool
(D87L-9280-A Or B)
71554
Courtesy of Ford Motor Co.

Fig. 2: Disconnecting Fuel Lines

Removal (Ranger) – **1)** Disconnect negative battery cable and drain cooling system. Remove hood, air cleaner and intake duct assembly. Remove fan shroud and position over fan. Remove radiator with hoses and shroud. Remove alternator and bracket.

2) Remove A/C compressor and power steering pump with hoses attached (if equipped). Disconnect heater hoses from engine. Release fuel pressure. See FUEL PRESSURE RELEASE under REMOVAL & INSTALLATION. Using Disconnect Tool (D87L-9280-A) for 3/8" line or (D87L-9280-B) for 1/2" line, disconnect fuel supply and return lines. *See Fig. 2.*

3) Disconnect brake booster vacuum hose. Disconnect throttle cable linkage and shield at throttle body and intake manifold. Disconnect all vacuum hoses from rear vacuum fitting in upper intake manifold.

4) Disconnect wiring from coil, oil pressure sending unit and engine coolant temperature sending units. Disconnect injector harness, air charge temperature sensor and throttle position sensor.

5) Mark distributor rotor and body position for installation reference. Remove distributor. Raise and support vehicle. Remove 2 lower bolts from A/C compressor. Disconnect oil level sensor connector from oil pan. Disconnect oil pressure sender connector.

6) Remove transmission oil cooler line bracket from right side of engine. Disconnect exhaust pipes from manifolds. Remove starter and front engine mount nuts or through bolts. Remove ground wires from engine block. On A/T models, remove converter inspection cover and disconnect flywheel from converter.

7) Remove kickdown rod and bellhousing mounting bolts. Remove adapter plate-to-converter housing bolt. On M/T models, remove bellhousing bolts and hydraulic clutch hose. On all models, remove engine front support-to-crossmember nuts and bolts.

8) Lower vehicle and attach engine hoist to brackets at exhaust manifolds. Remove remaining A/C compressor bolts and set compressor aside. Ensure all wires and hoses are disconnected before raising engine. Support transmission. Raise engine slightly and carefully pull engine forward from transmission without damaging rear cover plate. Remove engine from vehicle.

Installation – To install, reverse removal procedure. Tighten bolts to specification. See TORQUE SPECIFICATIONS table at end of article. Fill or top off all engine fluids. Fill and bleed air from cooling system. See COOLING SYSTEM BLEEDING under REMOVAL & INSTALLATION. Bleed clutch hydraulic system (if equipped). Adjust ignition timing and idle speed.

INTAKE MANIFOLDS

NOTE: Upper and lower intake manifold service procedures are covered separately.

Removal (Upper) – **1)** Disconnect negative battery cable. Remove air cleaner duct hose. Remove throttle linkage shield and disconnect linkage. Mark and disconnect vacuum hoses from throttle body. Mark and disconnect electrical connectors.

2) Disconnect PCV hose. Remove alternator support brace. Remove 6 upper intake manifold assembly bolts. Remove upper intake manifold assembly and gasket.

Installation – Clean gasket mating surfaces. Install a new gasket. Use guide pins and install upper intake manifold. Tighten bolts in sequence to specification. *See Fig. 3.* See TORQUE SPECIFICATIONS table at end of article. To complete installation, reverse removal procedure.

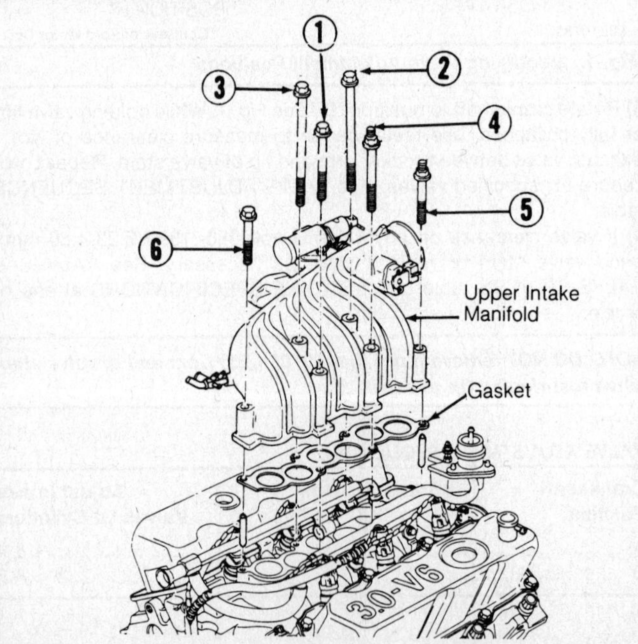
1
2
3
4
5
6
Upper Intake
Manifold
Gasket
3.0-V6
90D10184
Courtesy of Ford Motor Co.

Fig. 3: Upper Intake Manifold Tightening Sequence

1991 ENGINES
3.0L V6 (Cont.)

Removal (Lower) - 1) Remove upper intake manifold as previously described. Drain cooling system. Release fuel pressure. See FUEL PRESSURE RELEASE under REMOVAL & INSTALLATION.

2) Using Disconnect Tool (D87L-9280-A) for 3/8" line or (D87L-9280-B) for 1/2" line, disconnect fuel supply and return lines. *See Fig. 2.* Remove fuel injector wiring harness. Remove upper radiator hose and heater hoses.

3) Disconnect wiring harness connectors as necessary. Remove alternator-to-throttle body bracket. Position No. 1 piston on TDC of compression stroke. Mark and remove spark plug wires from spark plugs. Remove distributor cap with plug wires.

4) Mark distributor rotor and body position for installation reference. Remove distributor. On Aerostar, remove ignition coil from left cylinder head. On all models, remove valve covers. See VALVE COVERS under REMOVAL & INSTALLATION.

5) On No. 3 intake valve, loosen rocker arm bolt. Rotate rocker arm aside and remove push rod. Remove lower intake manifold retaining bolts. Remove lower intake manifold (with fuel rail and injectors) as an assembly. Remove and discard end seals and side gaskets.

Installation - 1) Lightly oil all retaining bolts and stud threads before installation. Apply silicone sealer to 4 intersecting corners of cylinder block and cylinder head. Install front and rear intake manifold seals. Position lower intake manifold gaskets in place with locking tabs over tabs on cylinder head gaskets.

2) Carefully install lower intake manifold. Install manifold retaining bolts and tighten in sequence to specification. *See Fig. 4.* See TORQUE SPECIFICATIONS table at end of article.

3) Install No. 3 cylinder intake valve push rod. Rotate crankshaft until No. 3 intake push rod is at its lowest point on camshaft lobe. Position rocker arm on valve and tighten rocker arm bolt to specification. See TORQUE SPECIFICATIONS table at end of article.

4) To complete installation, reverse removal procedure. Fill and bleed cooling system. See COOLING SYSTEM BLEEDING under REMOVAL & INSTALLATION.

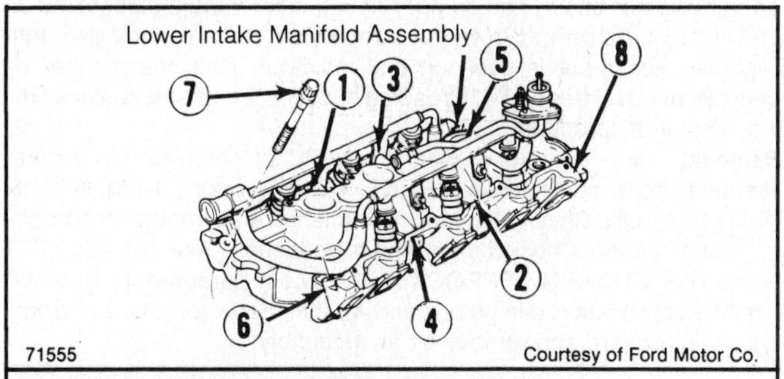
Lower Intake Manifold Assembly
7
1
3
5
8
2
6
4
71555
Courtesy of Ford Motor Co.

Fig. 4: Lower Intake Manifold Tightening Sequence

EXHAUST MANIFOLDS

Removal - Disconnect negative battery cable. Remove spark plugs. Remove oil dipstick tube retaining nut from left cylinder head, and rotate tube off of stud. Separate inlet pipe from exhaust manifold. Remove exhaust manifold bolts. Remove exhaust manifold.

Installation - Clean carbon from mating surfaces. Lightly oil threads of bolts and stud before installation. Install exhaust manifold(s) and tighten bolts to specification. See TORQUE SPECIFICATIONS table at end of article. To complete installation, reverse removal procedure.

VALVE COVERS

NOTE: Valve covers have integral (built-in) gaskets which are made to last the life of the vehicle. If necessary, replacement gaskets are available.

Removal - 1) Disconnect negative battery cable. On Aerostar, remove fresh air hose from air cleaner. On all models, mark and remove spark plug wires from spark plugs. Remove spark plug wire separators from valve cover studs. For left valve cover, remove upper intake manifold. See INTAKE MANIFOLDS under REMOVAL & INSTALLATION.

2) Remove PCV valve. Disconnect injector wiring harness bracket from left valve cover studs. For right valve cover on Aerostar, remove oil filler tube. On Ranger, disconnect engine wiring harness connectors from right valve cover.

3) On all models, disconnect injector wiring harness bracket from right valve cover studs. Disconnect breather hose. On all applications, remove valve cover retaining bolts and studs.

4) Carefully slide a thin knife between cylinder head and valve cover. Cut silicone sealer; DO NOT cut integral gasket. Remove valve cover(s).

Installation - 1) Replace valve cover gasket if necessary. Ensure gasket lies flat in valve cover channel. Lightly oil threads of bolts and studs. Ensure sealing surfaces are clean.

2) Apply a bead of silicone sealant to intake manifold-to-cylinder head joining area. Install valve cover and tighten bolts to specification. See TORQUE SPECIFICATIONS table at end of article. To complete installation, reverse removal procedure.

CYLINDER HEAD

Removal - 1) Remove upper and lower intake manifolds. See INTAKE MANIFOLDS under REMOVAL & INSTALLATION. Remove accessory drive belts and idler. When removing left cylinder head, remove power steering pump bracket retaining bolts. Remove power steering pump and bracket as an assembly (with hoses attached) .

2) On Aerostar, remove ignition coil bracket and coil. On all models, remove dipstick tube retaining nut from exhaust manifold. Rotate or remove dipstick tube. When removing right cylinder head, remove alternator bracket and adjusting arm.

3) Remove spark plugs. Remove exhaust manifolds. See EXHAUST MANIFOLDS under REMOVAL & INSTALLATION. Remove PCV valve and valve covers. See VALVE COVERS under REMOVAL & INSTALLATION.

4) Loosen rocker arm bolts and move rocker arm off push rod. Keep push rods in order for installation reference, and remove push rods. Remove and discard cylinder head retaining bolts. Remove cylinder head and gasket.

Inspection - Clean head gasket mating surfaces. Clean carbon from combustion chambers. DO NOT damage surfaces. Check cylinder head for cracks, burrs, nicks and warpage. DO NOT machine more than .010" (.25 mm) from original cylinder head surface to correct warpage. Replace cylinder head as necessary. See CYLINDER HEAD table under ENGINE SPECIFICATIONS at end of article.

Installation - 1) Replace locating dowels in cylinder block if damaged. Position new head gasket over locating dowels on cylinder block, with marked side in proper position.

NOTE: "V" notch below TRUCK marking on gasket indicates right-hand head gasket. "V" notch above TRUCK marking on gasket indicates left-hand head gasket. See Fig. 5. Ensure UP mark on gasket faces upward.

2) Install cylinder head and new cylinder head bolts. Tighten cylinder head bolts in sequence to specification. *See Fig. 5.* See TORQUE SPECIFICATIONS table at end of article. Dip each push rod end in Oil Conditioner (D9AZ-19579-CA). Install push rods in their original location.

3) For each valve, rotate crankshaft until lifter rests on heel of camshaft lobe. Position rocker arm over push rod and install fulcrum. Tighten rocker arm bolt to 96 INCH lbs. (11 N.m). After all rocker arms have been installed, tighten rocker arm bolts (camshaft may be in any position) to a final torque of 24 ft. lbs. (33 N.m).

CAUTION: Rocker arms must be fully seated in cylinder head and push rods must be seated in rocker arm sockets before final tightening. If all original components removed are reinstalled, valve clearance check is not required. If valves/seats were serviced, check and adjust valve clearance. See VALVE CLEARANCE ADJUSTMENT under ADJUSTMENTS.

1991 ENGINES
3.0L V6 (Cont.)

4) To complete installation, reverse removal procedure. Tighten all bolts/nuts to specification. See TORQUE SPECIFICATIONS table at end of article. Fill and bleed cooling system. See COOLING SYSTEM BLEEDING under REMOVAL & INSTALLATION.

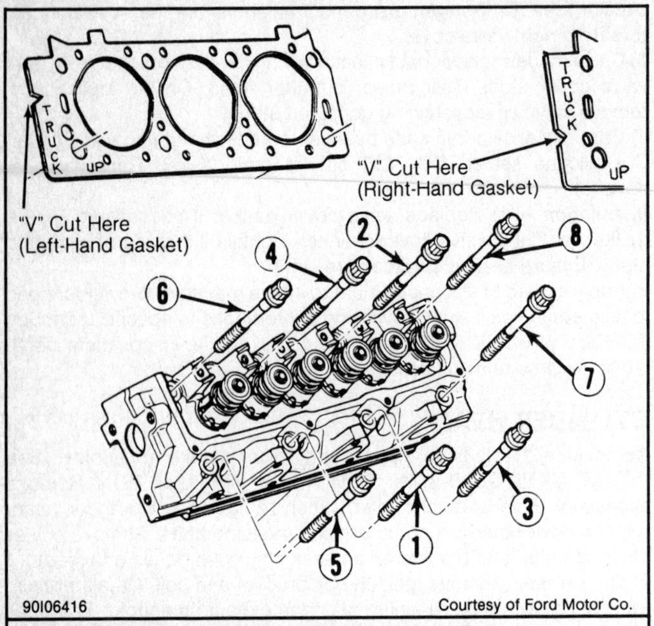
"V" Cut Here
(Right-Hand Gasket)
"V" Cut Here
(Left-Hand Gasket)
TRUCK
UP
1
2
3
4
5
6
7
8
90I06416
Courtesy of Ford Motor Co.

Fig. 5: Cylinder Head Gasket Position & Head Bolt Tightening Sequence

FRONT COVER OIL SEAL

Removal – Disconnect negative battery cable. Remove accessory drive belts. Remove crankshaft belt pulley. Remove crankshaft damper using Crankshaft Damper Remover and Adapter (T58P-6316-D and T82L-6316-B). Pry seal out carefully to avoid damaging sealing surface.

Installation – Lubricate lip of seal with clean engine oil. Using a proper size seal installer, install seal. Lubricate damper seal surface with engine oil. Apply RTV sealer to damper keyway. To complete installation, reverse removal procedure. Tighten bolts to specification. See TORQUE SPECIFICATIONS table at end of article.

FRONT COVER

Removal – **1)** Remove negative battery cable. Drain cooling system. Remove accessory drive belts. Remove left-handed nut retaining clutch fan to pulley. Remove cooling fan and water pump pulley. Remove A/C bracket, brace and compressor as an assembly (if equipped). Remove alternator adjusting arm and brace, and position alternator aside.

2) On Ranger, remove upper motor mount nuts. Position No. 1 piston on TDC of compression stroke. Remove distributor cap with plug wires. Mark distributor rotor and body position for installation reference. Remove distributor.

3) On all models, remove crankshaft belt pulley. Using Crankshaft Damper Remover and Adapter (T58P-6316-D and T82L-6316-B), remove crankshaft damper. Remove hoses from water pump.

4) Remove oil pan. See OIL PAN under REMOVAL & INSTALLATION. Remove 10 bolts retaining front cover and water pump assembly to engine. *See Fig. 6.* Remove front cover and water pump as an assembly.

Installation – **1)** Clean all gasket mating surfaces. Coat both surfaces of new front cover gasket with sealing compound. Install front cover gasket. Install front cover. Lightly oil threads of bolt and stud, except those with Teflon sealant, before installation. *See Fig. 6.*

2) Tighten bolts to specifications. See TORQUE SPECIFICATIONS table at end of article. To complete installation, reverse removal procedure. Fill and bleed cooling system. See COOLING SYSTEM BLEEDING under REMOVAL & INSTALLATION.

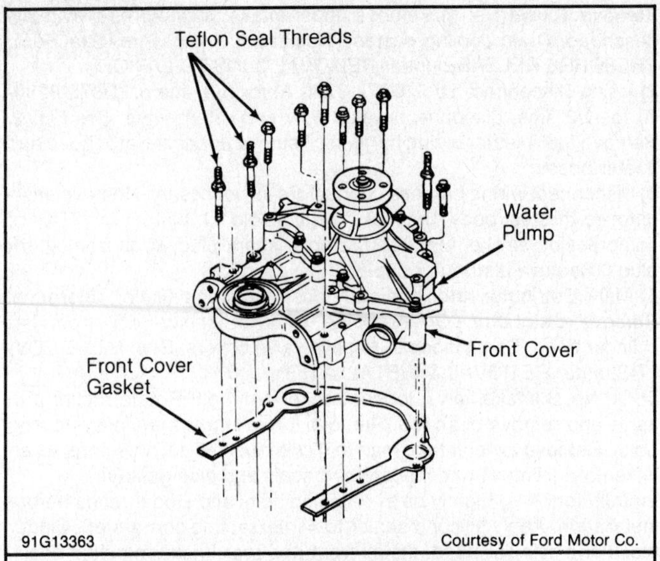
Teflon Seal Threads
Water
Pump
Front Cover
Front Cover
Gasket
91G13363
Courtesy of Ford Motor Co.

Fig. 6: Removing & Installing Water Pump & Front Cover Assembly

TIMING CHAIN & SPROCKETS

NOTE: Check timing chain deflection (stretch) before removal to determine component wear.

Inspection – **1)** Remove left-side valve cover. See VALVE COVERS under REMOVAL & INSTALLATION. Loosen No. 5 exhaust rocker arm and rotate to one side. Install a dial indicator on end of push rod. Turn crankshaft clockwise until No. 1 piston is at TDC to take up slack on right side of chain. The damper timing mark should point to TDC.

2) Zero dial indicator. Slowly turn crankshaft counterclockwise until slightest movement is seen on dial indicator. Note the number of degrees of travel from TDC. If reading exceeds 6 degrees, replace timing chain and sprockets.

Removal – Position No. 1 piston on TDC of compression stroke. Remove front cover. See FRONT COVER under REMOVAL & INSTALLATION. Check alignment of camshaft and crankshaft sprocket timing marks. Check timing chain deflection. See INSPECTION under TIMING CHAIN & SPROCKETS (previous paragraphs). Remove camshaft sprocket retaining bolt and washer. Slide sprockets and timing chain forward and remove as an assembly.

CAUTION: DO NOT replace camshaft sprocket retaining bolt with standard bolt. Original camshaft bolt has a drilled oil passage.

Installation – **1)** Ensure No. 1 piston is still at TDC of compression stroke. Assemble timing chain and sprockets so sprocket timing marks are aligned. *See Fig. 7.* Install chain and sprockets as an assembly. Lubricate timing chain and sprockets with engine oil.

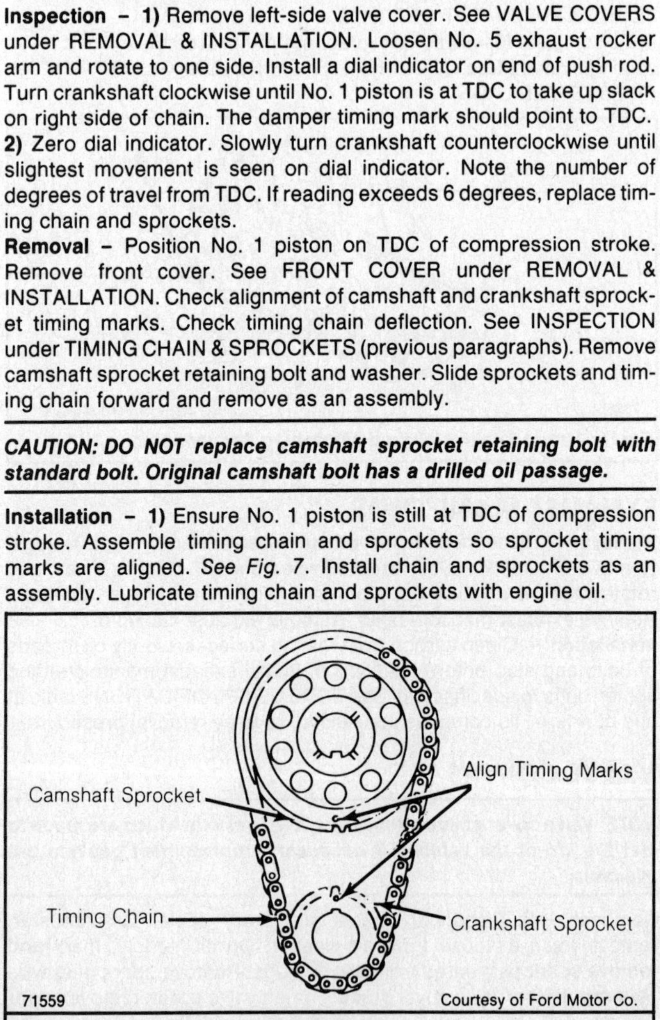
Align Timing Marks
Camshaft Sprocket
Timing Chain
Crankshaft Sprocket
71559
Courtesy of Ford Motor Co.

Fig. 7: Aligning Sprocket Timing Marks

2) Apply RTV sealer to damper keyway. To complete installation, reverse removal procedure. Tighten bolts and nuts to specifications. See TORQUE SPECIFICATIONS table at end of article.

CAMSHAFT

Removal - 1) Remove negative battery cable. Drain cooling system. Remove air cleaner hoses. Remove upper and lower radiator hose. Remove radiator, shroud and A/C condenser (if equipped). Remove left-handed nut retaining clutch fan to pulley and remove cooling fan.
2) Release fuel pressure. See FUEL PRESSURE RELEASE under REMOVAL & INSTALLATION. Using Disconnect Tool (D87L-9280-A) for 3/8" line or (D87L-9280-B) for 1/2" line, disconnect fuel supply and return lines. *See Fig. 2.*
3) Mark and disconnect vacuum hoses and electrical connectors. Remove accessory drive belts. Remove water pump pulley. Remove lower intake manifold. See INTAKE MANIFOLDS under REMOVAL & INSTALLATION.
4) Position No. 1 piston on TDC of compression stroke. Mark distributor rotor and body location for installation reference. Remove distributor. Remove valve covers. See VALVE COVERS under REMOVAL & INSTALLATION. Loosen rocker arms and rotate off push rods. Keeping in order of removal, remove push rods and valve lifters.
5) Check camshaft end play. If end play is not within specification, replace thrust plate. See CAMSHAFT table under ENGINE SPECIFICATIONS at end of article. Check timing chain deflection and remove timing chain and camshaft sprocket. See TIMING CHAIN & SPROCKETS under REMOVAL & INSTALLATION. Remove camshaft thrust plate. Remove camshaft.
Inspection - Inspect journal diameter, lobe lift, oil clearance and runout. Replace camshaft if these are not within specification. See CAMSHAFT table under ENGINE SPECIFICATIONS at end of article.
Installation - 1) Lubricate camshaft lobes and journals with heavy SAE 50W engine oil. Carefully slide camshaft through bearings in cylinder block. Install thrust plate and recheck camshaft end play. Install timing chain and sprocket as an assembly.

CAUTION: DO NOT replace camshaft sprocket retaining bolt with standard bolt. Original camshaft bolt has a drilled oil passage.

2) Ensure crankshaft and camshaft sprockets are aligned. *See Fig. 7.* Install camshaft sprocket washer and retaining bolt, and tighten to specification. See TORQUE SPECIFICATIONS table at end of article. Lubricate hydraulic valve lifters and bores with heavy SAE 50W engine oil.
3) Install lifters in their original bores. Lubricate push rods with heavy SAE 50W engine oil. Install push rods in their original location. For each valve, rotate crankshaft until lifter rests on heel of camshaft lobe. Position rocker arm over push rod and install fulcrum.
4) Tighten rocker arm bolt to 96 INCH lbs. (11 N.m). After all rocker arms have been installed, tighten rocker arm bolts (camshaft may be in any position) to a final torque of 24 ft. lbs. (33 N.m). To complete installation, reverse removal procedure.
5) Tighten bolts/nuts to specification. See TORQUE SPECIFICATIONS table at end of article. Fill or top off all fluids. Fill and bleed cooling system. See COOLING SYSTEM BLEEDING under REMOVAL & INSTALLATION. Start engine and check for leaks. Check and adjust ignition timing as necessary.

CAMSHAFT BEARINGS

Removal - 1) Remove camshaft. See CAMSHAFT under REMOVAL & INSTALLATION. Check camshaft bearing clearance. If clearance is not within specification, replace camshaft bearings. See CAMSHAFT table under ENGINE SPECIFICATIONS at end of article.
2) Standard and .015" (.38 mm) undersize camshaft bearings are available. To replace camshaft bearings, remove rear camshaft bearing bore plug. Remove camshaft bearings with Camshaft Bearing Set (T65L-6250-A).

NOTE: When installing new camshaft bearings, ensure bearing oil hole is aligned with oil hole in bearing bore.

Installation - 1) Align oil hole in bearing with oil hole in bearing bore. Using camshaft bearing set, install new camshaft bearings. Ensure front bearing is installed .020-.035" (.51-.89 mm) below front face of cylinder block.
2) Coat sealing edge of new rear camshaft bearing bore plug with oil resistant sealer and install bore plug. To complete installation, reverse removal procedure.

REAR CRANKSHAFT OIL SEAL

Removal & Installation - Remove transmission. Remove clutch assembly (if equipped). Remove flywheel/flexplate. Using a slide hammer, remove rear oil seal. Use care not to damage crankshaft sealing surface. Coat seal surfaces with heavy SF engine oil. Use proper size seal installer. Install seal until firmly seated. To complete installation, reverse removal procedure.

WATER PUMP

Removal - 1) Disconnect negative battery cable. Drain cooling system. Remove left-handed nut retaining clutch fan to pulley. Remove cooling fan. Remove accessory drive belts. Remove water pump pulley.
2) Remove alternator adjusting arm and brace from throttle body. Remove lower radiator and heater hose from water pump. Rotate belt adjuster aside. Remove 11 water pump bolts. Remove water pump. *See Fig. 6.*
Installation - Clean all gasket surfaces. Lightly oil threads of bolt and stud, except those with Teflon sealant, before installation. *See Fig. 6.* Use sealant on bolts going into water jacket. Apply contact adhesive to new gasket and position on water pump. Install water pump. To complete installation, reverse removal procedure. Fill and bleed system. See COOLING SYSTEM BLEEDING under REMOVAL & INSTALLATION.

OIL PAN

Removal (Aerostar) - Disconnect negative battery cable. Remove dipstick. Raise and support vehicle. Remove retainer clip and electrical connector at oil low level sensor (if equipped). Drain engine oil. Remove starter motor. Remove transmission inspection cover. Remove oil pan bolts, oil pan and gasket.
Installation - To install, reverse removal procedure. Apply silicone sealant at front and rear corners of oil pan surface and cylinder block, and where front cover meets cylinder block. Tighten bolts to specification. See TORQUE SPECIFICATIONS table at end of article. Start engine and check for oil leaks.
Removal (Ranger) - 1) Disconnect negative battery cable. Remove dipstick. Disconnect fan shroud and position over fan. Remove motor mount nuts from frame. Position No. 1 piston at TDC of compression stroke.
2) Mark distributor rotor and body location for installation reference. Remove distributor. Raise and support vehicle. Remove retainer clip and electrical connector at oil low level sensor. Drain engine oil.
3) Remove starter motor. Remove transmission inspection cover. On 2WD models, remove right front axle assembly. See FRONT AXLE under REMOVAL & INSTALLATION in appropriate SUSPENSION article.
4) Remove oil pan bolts. Using a suitable lifting device, raise engine approximately 2 inches. Be careful not to damage oil pump pick-up tube and carefully remove oil pan. Remove oil pan gasket.
Installation - Clean gasket mating surfaces. To install, reverse removal procedure. Apply silicone sealant at front and rear corners of oil pan surface and cylinder block, and where front cover meets cylinder block. Tighten bolts to specification. See TORQUE SPECIFICATIONS table at end of article. Start engine and check for leaks.

OVERHAUL

CYLINDER HEAD

Cylinder Head - 1) Clean head gasket mating surface. Clean carbon from combustion chambers. Use care not to damage surfaces. Check cylinder head for cracks, burrs, nicks and warpage.

1991 ENGINES
3.0L V6 (Cont.)

2) DO NOT machine more than .010" (.25 mm) from original cylinder head surface to correct warpage. Replace cylinder head as necessary. See CYLINDER HEAD table under ENGINE SPECIFICATIONS at end of article.

Valve Springs – 1) Measure valve spring installed height from top of spring seat to underside of spring retainer. Ensure installed height is within specification. See VALVES & VALVE SPRINGS table under ENGINE SPECIFICATIONS at end of article.

2) If installed height is not within specification, a .03" (.8 mm) shim can be installed between cylinder head and valve spring to obtain correct height. Inspect valve spring free length and pressure. Replace valve spring if free length and pressure are not within specification. See VALVES & VALVE SPRINGS table.

CAUTION: DO NOT install valve spring spacers unless necessary. Using more spacers than required can result in spring breakage or worn camshaft lobes.

Valve Stem Oil Seals – Intake and exhaust valve stems are not interchangeable. Use a 5/8" deep socket to install new valve stem seals.

Valve Guides – 1) Valve guides must be reamed for an oversized valve if valve stem oil clearance exceeds specification. See CYLINDER HEAD table under ENGINE SPECIFICATIONS at end of article. Valve guides are available in .015" (.38 mm) and .030" (.76 mm) oversize.

2) If oversized valves or oversized valve stem oil seals are not available, valve guide may be bored out to use a service bushing. Always use reamers in proper sequence (smallest first).

NOTE: Always grind valve seat after valve guide has been reamed or service bushing has been installed.

Valve Seat – Ensure valve seat angle, seat width and seat runout are within specification. See CYLINDER HEAD table under ENGINE SPECIFICATIONS at end of article. Valve seats must be ground when valve guide is reamed or replaced. Replacement information is not available from manufacturer.

Valves – Ensure head diameter, valve face runout, stem diameter and valve margin are within specification. See VALVES & VALVE SPRINGS table under ENGINE SPECIFICATIONS at end of article.

CAUTION: DO NOT remove more than .010" (.25 mm) from end of valve stem when resurfacing tip of valve.

Seat Correction Angles – Grind valve seat to a true 45-degree angle. If seat width is too wide after grinding, use a 30-degree stone to lower seat or a 60-degree stone to raise seat. See CYLINDER HEAD table under ENGINE SPECIFICATIONS at end of article.

CYLINDER BLOCK ASSEMBLY

Piston & Rod Assembly – Install piston on connecting rod, with piston notch on the same side as the button on connecting rod. *See Fig. 8.* Install piston and connecting rod in engine, with notch on top of piston toward front of engine.

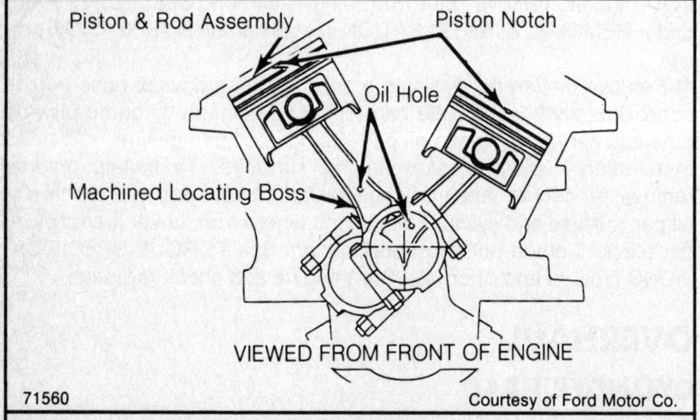
Piston & Rod Assembly
Piston Notch
Oil Hole
Machined Locating Boss
VIEWED FROM FRONT OF ENGINE
71560
Courtesy of Ford Motor Co.

Fig. 8: Positioning Piston & Connecting Rod

Fitting Pistons – 1) Check piston-to-bore clearance. See PISTONS, PINS & RINGS table under ENGINE SPECIFICATIONS at end of article. Standard size pistons are color-coded Red, Blue or Yellow on the piston dome. See PISTONS, PINS & RINGS table. Oversize pistons are also available.

2) If bore diameter is in lower one-third of specification, use a Red coded piston. If bore diameter is in middle one-third of specification, use a Blue coded piston. If bore diameter is in upper one-third of specification, use Yellow coded piston. Use proper size piston to obtain specified clearance. See PISTON SELECTION table.

PISTON SELECTION

Cylinder Bore Diameter In. (mm)	Piston Color Code
3.5043-3.5053 (89.009-89.035)	Red
3.5053-3.5063 (89.035-89.060)	Blue
3.5063-3.5073 (89.060-89.085)	Yellow

Piston Rings – 1) Select rings for bore diameter. Place ring in cylinder bore in which it will be installed. Use piston to square ring in bore and place ring below normal ring wear area. Measure ring end gap. If ring gap is not within specification, try another ring set. See PISTONS, PINS & RINGS table under ENGINE SPECIFICATIONS at end of article.

2) Check side clearance of rings after installing on piston. Ensure clearance is within specification around entire circumference. Replace piston and/or rings if clearance is not as specified. See PISTONS, PINS & RINGS table under ENGINE SPECIFICATIONS. Ensure rings are properly spaced on piston before installing pistons into cylinder. *See Fig. 9.*

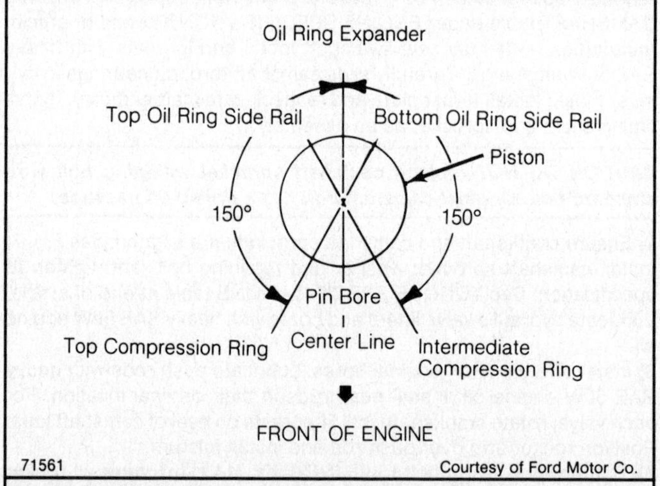
Oil Ring Expander
Top Oil Ring Side Rail
Bottom Oil Ring Side Rail
Piston
150°
150°
Pin Bore
Center Line
Top Compression Ring
Intermediate
Compression Ring
FRONT OF ENGINE
71561
Courtesy of Ford Motor Co.

Fig. 9: Positioning Piston Ring End Gaps

Rod Bearings – 1) Use Plastigage method and check rod bearing clearance. If proper oil clearance cannot be obtained with standard bearings, try a combination of undersize bearings. DO NOT use any other bearing combination other than what is listed. See UNDERSIZE MAIN & ROD BEARING COMBINATIONS table.

UNDERSIZE MAIN & ROD BEARING COMBINATIONS [1]

Excess Bearing Clearance In. (mm)	Use Upper Bearing In. (mm)	Use Lower Bearing In. (mm)
.0-.0005 (.0-.013)	.001 (.025)	[2]
.0005-0010 (.013-.026)	.001 (.025)	.001 (.025)
.0010-.0015 (.026-.039)	.002 (.050)	.001 (.025)
.0015-.0020 (.039-.052)	.002 (.050)	.002 (.050)

[1] – DO NOT use any other bearing combination other than what is listed. If use of bearing combinations does not bring clearance within specification, machine or replace crankshaft as necessary.

[2] – Use standard bearing.

2) If use of bearing combinations does not bring clearance within specification, machine or replace crankshaft. Always replace bearings in pairs. See CRANKSHAFT, MAIN & CONNECTING ROD BEARINGS table under ENGINE SPECIFICATIONS at end of article.

Crankshaft & Main Bearings - 1) When checking main bearing clearance in vehicle, position a jack under adjoining bearing counterweight being checked. Remove one main bearing cap at a time.

2) Use Plastigage method and check main bearing clearance. If proper oil clearance cannot be obtained with standard bearings, try a combination of undersize bearings. DO NOT use any other bearing combination other than what is listed. See UNDERSIZE MAIN & ROD BEARING COMBINATIONS table.

3) If use of bearing combinations does not bring clearance within specification, machine or replace crankshaft. Always replace bearings in pairs. See CRANKSHAFT, MAIN & CONNECTING ROD BEARINGS table under ENGINE SPECIFICATIONS at end of article.

4) Tighten main bearing cap bolts finger tight. Pry crankshaft forward and tighten bearing caps to specification. See TORQUE SPECIFICATIONS table at end of article.

5) Check crankshaft end play. Replace thrust bearing if end play is not within specification. Thrust bearing is No. 3 (from front) main bearing in block. See CRANKSHAFT, MAIN & CONNECTING ROD BEARINGS table under ENGINE SPECIFICATIONS.

Cylinder Block - 1) Using a feeler gauge and straightedge, check cylinder block head gasket surface for warpage. Check cylinder bore for wear, taper, out-of-round and piston fit. See CYLINDER BLOCK table under ENGINE SPECIFICATIONS at end of article.

CAUTION: DO NOT machine more than .010" (.25 mm) of material from original cylinder block head surface.

2) Install all main bearing caps and tighten to specification before honing cylinder bore. Ensure bearing caps are installed in their original location, with arrow on cap pointing toward front of engine.

3) Use ONLY a spring-loaded type cylinder hone. After honing, thoroughly clean bore with detergent and water solution. Rinse solution from bore thoroughly with clean water. Wipe bore clean with lint free cloth. Lubricate cylinder bores with engine oil.

ENGINE OILING

ENGINE LUBRICATION SYSTEM

Engine lubrication system is a force-feed type. The oil is supplied under full pressure to crankshaft, connecting rods, camshaft bearing and valve lifters. A controlled volume of oil is supplied to rocker arms and push rods. All other moving parts are lubricated by splash or gravity flow. Oil flows through oil filter before entering main oil gallery.

Crankcase Capacity - Capacity is 4.5 qts. (4.25L) with oil filter.

Oil Pressure - Normal oil pressure at 2500 RPM should be 40-60 psi (2.8-4.2 kg/cm²) with engine at normal operating temperature.

Pressure Relief Valve - Pressure relief valve is located in oil pump and is nonadjustable.

OIL PUMP

Removal & Disassembly - Remove oil pan. See OIL PAN under REMOVAL & INSTALLATION. Remove oil pump baffle. Remove oil pump retaining bolts. Remove oil pump and pick-up tube assembly. Remove oil pump drive shaft. Remove and replace gasket. Disassemble oil pump. Note direction of component installation for reassembly.

Inspection - Inspect components for damage. Measure rotor end clearance, outer race-to-housing clearance, and rotor tip clearance. Check relief valve-to-bore clearance. Measure relief valve tension. Replace oil pump assembly if measurements are not within specifications. See OIL PUMP SPECIFICATIONS table.

NOTE: Oil pump is serviced as an assembly. Replace assembly if out of specifications. See OIL PUMP SPECIFICATIONS table.

Reassembly & Installation - To reassemble, reverse disassembly procedure. Ensure components are installed in original location. To install, reverse removal procedure. Tighten bolts to specification. See TORQUE SPECIFICATIONS table. Fill crankcase.

OIL PUMP SPECIFICATIONS

Application	In. (mm)
Drive Shaft-To-Housing Clearance	.0005-.0019 (.013-.048)
Gear Backlash	.008-.012 (.20-.31)
Gear Height Clearance	.0003-.0032 (.008-.081)
Idler Shaft-To-Idler Gear	.0015-.0027 (.038-.069)
Idler-To-Driver Gear	
Radial Clearance	.002-.006 (.05-.15)
Relief Valve Spring Tension	[1]
Relief Valve-To-Bore Clearance	.0017-.0029 (.043-.074)

[1] - Tension should be 9-10 lbs. @ 1.11" (4.08-4.54 kg @ 28.2 mm).

TORQUE SPECIFICATIONS

TORQUE SPECIFICATIONS

Application	Ft. Lbs. (N.m)
Bellhousing-To-Engine Bolt	28-38 (38-51)
Camshaft Sprocket Bolt	46 (62)
Connecting Rod Cap Nut	26 (35)
Crankshaft Damper Bolt	107 (145)
Cylinder Head Bolt [1]	
Step 1	59 (80)
Step 2	Loosen One Full Turn
Step 3	37 (51)
Step 4	68 (92)
Engine Front Cover-To-Block	
6-mm Bolt	[2]
8-mm Bolt	19 (25)
Engine Mount-To-Chassis Bolt	71-94 (96-127)
Engine Mount-To-Engine Bracket Bolt	71-94 (96-127)
Exhaust Manifold Bolt	19 (25)
Fan Clutch-To-Water Pump Nut [3]	30-100 (41-137)
Flexplate-To-Converter Bolt	20-34 (27-46)
Flywheel Bolt	59 (80)
Front Crossmember-To-Frame Nut	145-195 (196-264)
Idler Pulley Bolt	30-40 (40-55)
Lower Intake Manifold Bolt [4]	
1st Step	11 (15)
2nd Step	18 (24)
Main Bearing Cap Bolt	66 (90)
Oil Pump Bolt	30-40 (40-55)
Rear Mount-To-Crossmember Nut	71-94 (96-127)
Rear Mount-To-Transmission Bolt	60-80 (81-108)
Rocker Arm Bolt	
Step 1	[5]
Step 2	24 (33)
Spark Plug	11 (15)
Starter Bolt	15-20 (20-27)
Upper Intake Manifold Bolt [6]	15-22 (20-30)
	INCH Lbs. (N.m)
Camshaft Thrust Plate Bolt	84 (10)
Fuel Rail Bolt	84 (10)
Oil Pan Bolt	84 (10)
Valve Cover Bolt	108 (12)
Water Pump Bolt [7]	84 (10)

[1] - Tighten bolts in sequence. *See Fig. 5.*
[2] - Tighten to 84 INCH lbs. (10 N.m).
[3] - Left-hand thread.
[4] - Tighten bolts in sequence. *See Fig. 4.*
[5] - Tighten to 96 INCH lbs. (11 N.m).
[6] - Tighten in sequence. *See Fig. 3.*
[7] - Apply sealant to designated bolts. *See Fig. 6.*

1991 ENGINES
3.0L V6 (Cont.)

ENGINE SPECIFICATIONS

GENERAL SPECIFICATIONS

Application	Specification
3.0L	
Displacement	182 Cu. In. (3.0L)
Bore	3.50" (89 mm)
Stroke	3.14" (80 mm)
Compression Ratio	9.3:1
Fuel System	PFI
Horsepower @ RPM	140 @ 4800
Torque Ft. Lbs. @ RPM	165 @ 3000

CRANKSHAFT, MAIN & CONNECTING ROD BEARINGS

Application	In. (mm)
3.0L	
Crankshaft End Play	.004-.008 (.10-.20)
Main Bearings	
Journal Diameter	2.5190-2.5198 (63.973-64.003)
Journal Out-Of-Round	.0003 (.008)
Journal Taper	[1] .0003 (.008)
Journal Runout	.002 (.05)
Oil Clearance	
Desired	.0010-.0014 (.025-.036)
Allowable	.0005-.0023 (.013-.058)
Connecting Rod Bearings	
Journal Diameter	2.1253-2.1261 (53.983-54.003)
Journal Out-Of-Round	.0003 (.008)
Journal Taper	[1] .0003 (.008)
Oil Clearance	
Desired	.0010-.0014 (.025-.036)
Allowable	.0009-.0027 (.023-.069)

[1] – Specification listed is per 1" (25.4 mm).

CONNECTING RODS

Application	In. (mm)
3.0L	
Bore Diameter	
Pin Bore	.9096-.9112 (23.104-23.145)
Crankpin Bore	2.250 (57.15)
Center-To-Center Length	5.53 (140.5)
Maximum Bend	[1] .0016 (.040)
Maximum Twist	[1] .003 (.08)
Side Play	.006-.014 (.15-.36)

[1] – Specification listed is per 1" (25.4 mm)

PISTONS, PINS & RINGS

Application	In. (mm)
3.0L	
Pistons [1]	
Clearance	.0012-.0023 (.030-.058)
Diameter	
Red	3.5024-3.5031 (89.962-89.978)
Blue	3.5035-3.5041 (88.988-89.004)
Yellow	3.5045-3.5051 (89.014-89.030)
Pins	
Diameter	.9119-.9124 (23.162-23.175)
Piston Fit	.0002-.0005 (.005-.013)
Rod Fit	Press Fit
Rings	
No. 1 & 2	
End Gap	.010-.020 (.25-.51)
Side Clearance	.0016-.0037 (.041-.094)
No. 3 (Oil)	
End Gap	.010-.049 (.25-1.24)
Side Clearance	Snug Fit

[1] – Pistons are color-coded on dome of pistons. For correct piston selection, see FITTING PISTONS under CYLINDER BLOCK ASSEMBLY.

CYLINDER BLOCK

Application	In. (mm)
3.0L	
Cylinder Bore	
Standard Diameter	3.50 (89.0)
Maximum Taper	.002 (.05)
Maximum Out-Of-Round	.002 (.05)
Maximum Deck Warpage	[1] .003 (.08)

[1] – Specification is within a 6" (152 mm) area. DO NOT machine more than .010" (.25 mm) from original gasket surface.

VALVES & VALVE SPRINGS

Application	Specification
3.0L	
Intake Valves	
Face Angle	44°
Head Diameter	1.57" (39.9 mm)
Minimum Margin	.0313" (.794 mm)
Stem Diameter	.3126-.3134" (7.940-7.960 mm)
Exhaust Valves	
Face Angle	44°
Head Diameter	1.30" (33.0 mm)
Minimum Margin	.0313" (.794 mm)
Stem Diameter	.3121-.3129" (7.927-7.948 mm)
Valve Springs	
Free Length	1.84" (46.7 mm)
Installed Height	1.58" (40.1 mm)
Out-Of-Square	.078" (1.98 mm)
Pressure	Lbs. @ In. (kg @ mm)
Valve Closed	65 @ 1.58 (30 @ 40.1)
Valve Open	180 @ 1.16 (82 @ 29.5)

1991 ENGINES
3.0L V6 (Cont.)

CYLINDER HEAD

Application	Specification
3.0L	
Maximum Warpage	[1] .007" (.18 mm)
Valve Seats	
Seat Angle	45°
Seat Width	.06-.08" (1.5-2.0 mm)
Maximum Seat Runout	.001" (.03 mm)
Valve Guides	
Intake Valve	
Valve Guide I.D.	.3433-.3443" (8.720-8.745 mm)
Valve Stem-To-Guide Oil Clearance	.0010-.0027 (.025-.069 mm)
Exhaust Valve	
Valve Guide I.D.	.3433-.3443" (8.720-8.745 mm)
Valve Stem-To-Guide Oil Clearance	.0015-.0032" (.038-.081 mm)

[1] - Maximum cylinder head wear limit is .010" (2.5 mm). DO NOT machine more than .010" (.25 mm) from original cylinder head thickness.

CAMSHAFT

Application	In. (mm)
3.0L	
Bearing Bore	
1 & 4	2.1531-2.1541 (54.689-54.714)
2 & 3	2.1334-2.1344 (54.188-54.214)
End Play	.001 (.03)
Journal Diameter	2.0074-2.0084 (50.988-51.013)
Journal Runout	.002 (.05)
Lobe Lift	.26 (6.60)
Lobe Wear Limit	.005 (.13)
Oil Clearance	.001-.003 (.03-.08)

VALVE LIFTERS

Application	In. (mm)
3.0L	
Bore Diameter	.8752-.8767 (22.230-22.268)
Collapsed Lifter Clearance	.088-.189 (2.24-4.80)
Lifter Diameter	.874 (22.20)
Oil Clearance	.0007-.0027 (.018-.069)

1991 ENGINES
4.0L V6

Aerostar, Explorer, Ranger

NOTE: For repair procedures not covered in this article, see ENGINE OVERHAUL PROCEDURES article in GENERAL INFORMATION.

ENGINE IDENTIFICATION

The 4.0L V6 engine may be identified by Vehicle Identification Number (VIN). The VIN is stamped on a metal tab attached to left side of instrument panel, and is visible through the windshield. The VIN is also stamped on the Safety Certification Decals mounted on driver's front door lock panel, and on the Engine Identification Label mounted on valve cover.

The eighth character of VIN identifies the engine, and tenth character, letter "M", indicates 1991 model. All label numbers are necessary for determining correct and unique parts to specific engines. DO NOT remove labels at any time.

VIN ENGINE CODE

Engine	Code
4.0L PFI	X

ADJUSTMENTS

VALVE CLEARANCE ADJUSTMENT

The 4.0L engine uses hydraulic roller lifters and nonadjustable rocker arms. Lifters are not adjustable; if lifters are found to be excessively worn or noisy, repair or replace as necessary.

REMOVAL & INSTALLATION

NOTE: For reassembly reference, label all electrical connectors, vacuum hoses and fuel lines before removal. Also place mating marks on engine hood and other major assemblies before removal.

FUEL PRESSURE RELEASE

Disconnect negative battery cable. Remove fuel tank filler cap to release tank pressure. Attach a fuel pressure gauge to pressure relief valve on fuel rail. Release fuel pressure.

COOLING SYSTEM BLEEDING

1) Fill cooling system with 50/50 mixture of coolant and water. Pause several minutes for circulation. Fill radiator to filler neck seat. Install radiator cap fully then back off to first stop.

WARNING: When engine is operating, NEVER remove radiator cap under any conditions. Failure to follow instruction could damage cooling system or engine, or cause personal injury. Always wrap protective material around radiator cap to avoid injury from hot coolant.

2) Place heater controls to maximum heat. Start engine and operate at 2000 RPM for approximately 3-4 minutes. Turn engine off. Use a protective rag, and carefully remove radiator cap. Add coolant to filler neck seat.

3) Install radiator cap fully, then back off to first stop. Start engine and allow to operate at 2000 RPM until upper radiator hose is warm. Check heater output. Turn engine off. Use protective rag, and carefully remove radiator cap. Add coolant to filler neck seat if necessary.

4) Tightly install radiator cap. Remove small cap (large cap is for windshield washer reservoir) on coolant recovery reservoir. Add 1.1 qt. (1L) of 50/50 mixture of coolant and water to reservoir. Install reservoir cap.

ENGINE

NOTE: Aerostar engine assembly can be removed through the front of the engine compartment without transmission attached.

Removal – 1) Disconnect negative battery cable. On Aerostar, remove front grille and bumper cover. On all models, remove air cleaner tube and assembly. Discharge A/C system (if equipped) and remove A/C condenser. Drain engine oil. Disconnect and remove power steering and transmission coolers.

2) Drain cooling system. Remove upper and lower radiator hoses. Disconnect radiator fan shroud and position over fan. Remove radiator. Remove accessory drive belt. On Aerostar, remove right front air diverter flap. Remove center hood latch support.

3) Remove A/C compressor (if equipped). Remove oil fill tube. Remove engine cover. Remove ice/snow shield. Remove power steering hoses, pump and bracket. Remove transmission dipstick tube. On all models, remove alternator. Disconnect exhaust system from exhaust manifolds. Disconnect wiring and remove starter.

4) On A/T models, remove converter-to-flexplate bolts. Remove bolt securing transmission oil cooler bracket. Remove both engine mount-to-frame bolts. Remove converter housing-to-engine bolts, except 2 upper bolts. Remove left motor mount from engine. Remove 2 upper converter housing bolts.

5) On M/T models, disconnect electrical connectors at transmission and transfer case. On all models, release fuel pressure. See FUEL PRESSURE RELEASE under REMOVAL & INSTALLATION. Using Fuel Line Coupling Key (T90P-9550-A), disconnect fuel supply and return lines at fuel supply manifold. *See Fig. 1.* Disconnect throttle linkage and bracket. Remove heater hoses.

6) Mark and disconnect all engine vacuum hoses. Disconnect throttle position switch connector. Remove throttle body from upper intake manifold. Disconnect engine wiring harness main connectors. Install engine lifting brackets on right-front and left-rear of engine. Remove engine.

Installation – To install, reverse removal procedure. Evacuate and recharge A/C system (if equipped). Check and top off all fluid levels. Fill and bleed air from cooling system. See COOLING SYSTEM BLEEDING under REMOVAL & INSTALLATION.

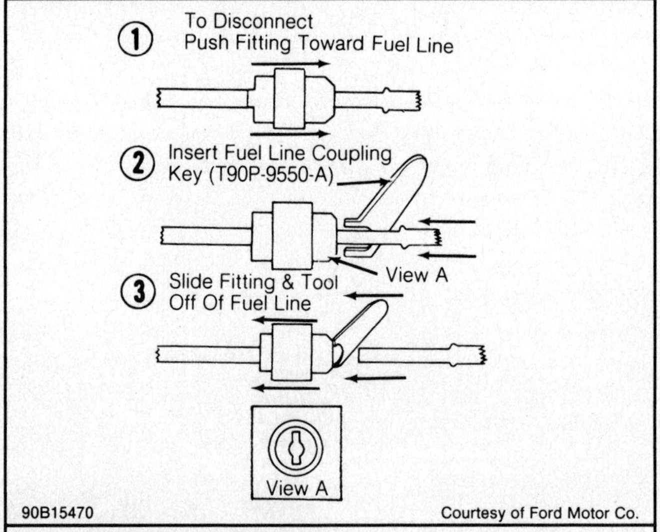
1
To Disconnect
Push Fitting Toward Fuel Line
2
Insert Fuel Line Coupling
Key (T90P-9550-A)
View A
3
Slide Fitting & Tool
Off Of Fuel Line
View A
90B15470
Courtesy of Ford Motor Co.

Fig. 1: Disconnecting Fuel Lines

INTAKE MANIFOLDS

Removal (Upper) – 1) Remove negative battery cable. Disconnect Throttle Position Sensor (TPS) and Air Charge Temperature (ACT) sensor wire connectors. Disconnect air by-pass valve. Remove snow/ice shield to expose throttle linkage. Remove throttle cable and bracket from throttle body.

2) Remove air inlet tube from air cleaner. Mark and disconnect vacuum lines from upper intake manifold. Remove PCV valve. Disconnect spark plug wires. Remove canister purge hose from throttle body. On Aerostar, remove oil dipstick tube retaining bolt.

3) On all models, remove A/C hose retaining bolt at rear of upper manifold. Remove DIS ignition coil and bracket. Remove intake manifold bolts. Remove upper intake manifold and throttle body as an assembly.

Installation – Clean and inspect mounting surfaces. Position new gasket on mounting studs. Install upper intake manifold and tighten bolts to specifications. See TORQUE SPECIFICATIONS table at end of article. To complete installation, reverse removal procedure.

Removal (Lower) – **1)** Remove upper intake manifold as previously described. Disconnect electrical connections from fuel injectors and from lower intake manifold. Release fuel pressure. See FUEL PRESSURE RELEASE under REMOVAL & INSTALLATION. Using Fuel Line Coupling Key (T90P-9550-A), disconnect fuel supply and return lines at fuel supply manifold. *See Fig. 1.*

2) Remove valve covers. See VALVE COVERS under REMOVAL & INSTALLATION. Remove lower intake manifold attaching bolts/nuts. Remove lower intake manifold assembly and gasket.

Installation – Clean gasket mating surfaces. Install intake manifold gaskets. Apply silicone sealer at 4 corners of cylinder block sealing surface. Install lower intake manifold within 15 minutes of silicone sealer application. Tighten bolts in sequence to specification. *See Fig. 2.* See TORQUE SPECIFICATIONS table at end of article.

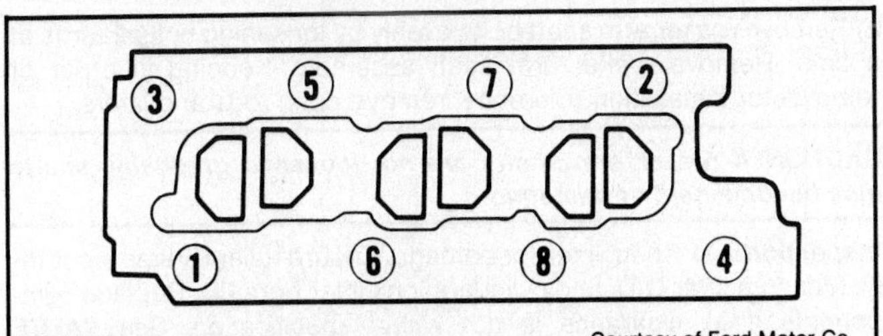
3
5
7
2
1
6
8
4

90C15471 Courtesy of Ford Motor Co.

Fig. 2: Lower Intake Manifold Tightening Sequence

EXHAUST MANIFOLDS

Removal – **1)** On left exhaust manifold, remove oil dipstick tube support bracket. It may be necessary to remove power steering pressure and return hose. If removing right exhaust manifold, drain cooling system.

2) Remove heater hose support bracket and heater hoses. On both exhaust manifolds, remove exhaust pipe-to-manifold attaching bolts. Remove exhaust manifold-to-cylinder head bolts. Remove exhaust manifolds.

Installation – Clean all mating surfaces. Lightly oil all bolt/stud threads before installation. Install exhaust manifold on cylinder head and tighten to specification. See TORQUE SPECIFICATIONS table at end of article. To complete installation, reverse removal procedure. Fill and bleed cooling system if necessary. See COOLING SYSTEM BLEEDING under REMOVAL & INSTALLATION.

VALVE COVERS

Removal – **1)** Disconnect negative battery cable. Remove spark plug wires. Release fuel pressure. See FUEL PRESSURE RELEASE under REMOVAL & INSTALLATION. Using Fuel Line Coupling Key (T90P-9550-A), disconnect fuel supply and return lines at fuel supply manifold. *See Fig. 1.*

2) If removing left valve cover, it may be necessary to remove upper intake manifold. See INTAKE MANIFOLDS under REMOVAL & INSTALLATION. On right valve cover, remove DIS ignition coil and bracket assembly.

3) Remove PCV hose and breather. Keeping in removal order, remove valve cover attaching bolts and load distribution washers. Remove valve covers.

Installation – Clean all gasket surfaces. Position new gasket in place. Install valve cover. Install valve cover load distribution washers in their original location. Install valve cover screws and tighten to specification. See TORQUE SPECIFICATIONS table at end of article. To complete installation, reverse removal procedure.

CAUTION: Failure to use new valve cover gaskets and valve cover load distribution washers will result in oil leaks.

CYLINDER HEAD

Removal – **1)** Disconnect negative battery cable. Drain cooling system. Release fuel pressure. See FUEL PRESSURE RELEASE under REMOVAL & INSTALLATION. Remove upper and lower intake manifolds. See INTAKE MANIFOLDS under REMOVAL & INSTALLATION. Remove exhaust manifold. See EXHAUST MANIFOLDS under REMOVAL & INSTALLATION.

2) Remove valve covers. See VALVE COVERS under REMOVAL & INSTALLATION. Remove spark plugs. Remove accessory drive belt. If removing left cylinder head, remove A/C compressor (if equipped). Remove power steering pump and bracket, and position aside.

3) If removing right cylinder head, remove alternator and bracket. On all cylinder heads, remove rocker arm shaft bolts evenly by loosening bolts 2 turns at a time. Remove rocker arm shaft assembly.

CAUTION: If rocker arm shafts are not loosened gradually, shafts may become bent or damaged.

4) Mark push rod location for installation reference, and remove push rods. Remove and discard cylinder head bolts. Remove cylinder head(s) and gaskets.

Inspection – Check dowels in cylinder block and replace as necessary. Check cylinder head warpage. Resurface cylinder head if warpage exceeds specification. See CYLINDER HEAD table under ENGINE SPECIFICATIONS at end of article. DO NOT machine more than .010" (.25 mm) from original cylinder head surface.

CAUTION: Always use NEW cylinder head bolts when installing cylinder heads.

Installation – **1)** Ensure all bolt holes in cylinder block are clean. Install head gasket and cylinder head. Install new cylinder head bolts. Tighten cylinder head bolts in sequence to specification. *See Fig. 3.* See TORQUE SPECIFICATIONS table at end of article.

2) Coat push rods with Oil Conditioner (D9AZ-19579-CA) and install in original position. Install rocker arm shaft assembly to cylinder head. Guide rocker arms onto push rods.

3) Tighten rocker arm bolts evenly to specification. To complete installation, reverse removal installation. Fill and bleed cooling system. See COOLING SYSTEM BLEEDING under REMOVAL & INSTALLATION.

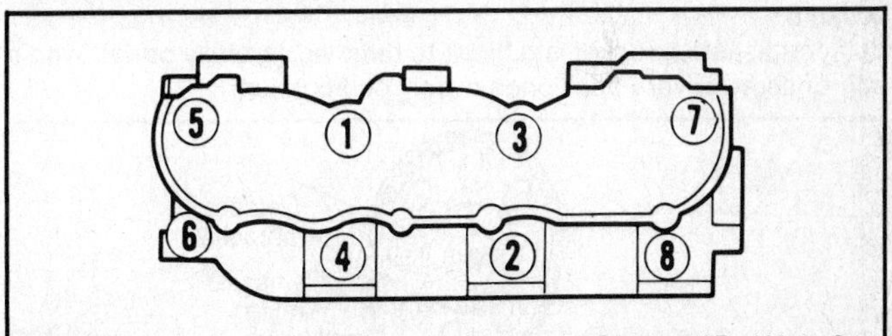
5
1
3
7
6
4
2
8

90D15472 Courtesy of Ford Motor Co.

Fig. 3: Cylinder Head Bolt Tightening Sequence

FRONT CRANKSHAFT OIL SEAL

Removal & Installation – **1)** Remove accessory drive belts. Remove crankshaft damper retaining bolt. Using Crankshaft Damper Remover (T74P-6316-A), remove crankshaft damper. Carefully pry seal from timing cover; DO NOT damage front cover or crankshaft.

2) To install, lubricate new seal lip with engine oil. Using Front Cover Aligner (T74P-6019-A) and Crankshaft Front Seal Installer (T90T-6701-A), install front crankshaft seal. Apply silicone sealer to crankshaft keyway.

3) Coat crankshaft damper sealing surface with engine oil. Install crankshaft damper. Tighten to specification. See TORQUE SPECIFICATIONS table at end of article. Install accessory drive belts.

FRONT COVER

Removal – **1)** Remove oil pan. See OIL PAN under REMOVAL & INSTALLATION. Drain cooling system. Remove upper and lower

1991 ENGINES
4.0L V6 (Cont.)

radiator hoses. Remove radiator. Remove coolant hoses from water pump. Remove A/C compressor and power steering bracket (if equipped).

2) Remove alternator and drive belt(s). Using Fan Clutch Pulley Holder (T84T-6312-C) and Fan Clutch Nut Wrench (T84T-6312-D), remove fan and clutch assembly. *See Fig.8.*

CAUTION: Fan clutch nut has left-hand threads. Remove nut by turning nut clockwise as viewed from front of engine.

3) If equipped with A/C, remove alternator and bracket. Remove water pump pulley. Remove water pump attaching bolts and remove pump. Remove gasket. Using Crankshaft Damper Remover (T74P-6316-A), remove crankshaft damper.

4) Remove crankshaft timing sensor assembly. Note bolt location for installation reference; front cover bolts have different lengths. Remove front cover bolts and remove cover. Remove gasket.

Installation – 1) Clean front cover mating surfaces. Apply sealing compound to gasket surfaces. Place new timing cover gasket into position. Position front cover on engine. Insert front cover bolts into their original location.

2) Tighten bolts to specification. See TORQUE SPECIFICATIONS table at end of article. Apply silicone sealer to crankshaft keyway. To complete installation, reverse removal procedure. Install oil pan. See OIL PAN under REMOVAL & INSTALLATION. Fill or top off all fluids. Fill and bleed air from cooling system. See COOLING SYSTEM BLEEDING under REMOVAL & INSTALLATION.

TIMING CHAIN & SPROCKETS

Removal – 1) Position No. 1 piston at TDC of compression stroke. Remove front cover. See FRONT COVER under REMOVAL & INSTALLATION. Remove oil pan. See OIL PAN under REMOVAL & INSTALLATION.

2) Ensure all timing marks are aligned. *See Fig. 4.* Check camshaft end play. If end play is not within specification, replace camshaft thrust plate. See CAMSHAFT table under ENGINE SPECIFICATIONS at end of article.

3) Remove camshaft sprocket retaining bolt and crankshaft sprocket Woodruff key. Remove tensioner and guide rail; replace as necessary. Remove crankshaft, camshaft sprockets and timing chain as an assembly.

4) If crankshaft sprocket is difficult to remove, carefully pry off with a pair of screwdrivers positioned evenly on sprocket.

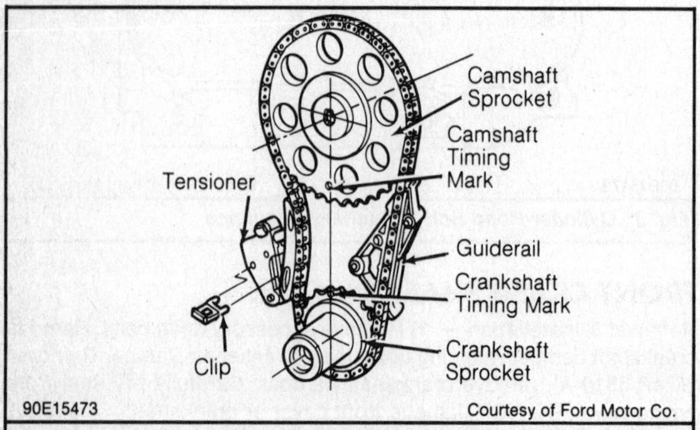
Camshaft
Sprocket
Camshaft
Timing
Mark
Tensioner
Guiderail
Crankshaft
Timing Mark
Crankshaft
Sprocket
Clip
90E15473
Courtesy of Ford Motor Co.

Fig. 4: Identifying Timing Chain & Components

Installation – 1) Install guide rail to cylinder block, with pin inserted into oil hole of block. Install 2 tensioner retaining bolts. Ensure timing marks are aligned. *See Fig. 4.* If camshaft thrust plate was removed, install thrust plate so that it covers main oil gallery. *See Fig. 5.*

2) Install crankshaft, camshaft sprocket and timing chain as an assembly. Install tensioner with clip in place to lock tensioner in retracted position. *See Fig. 4.* Install camshaft sprocket bolt and tighten to specification. See TORQUE SPECIFICATIONS table at end of article.

3) Remove clip from tensioner assembly. To complete installation, reverse removal procedure. Fill and bleed cooling system. See COOLING SYSTEM BLEEDING under REMOVAL & INSTALLATION.

NOTE: Ensure tensioner side of timing chain is held inward, and guide side is straight and tight. Ensure clip is removed from tensioner before installing front cover.

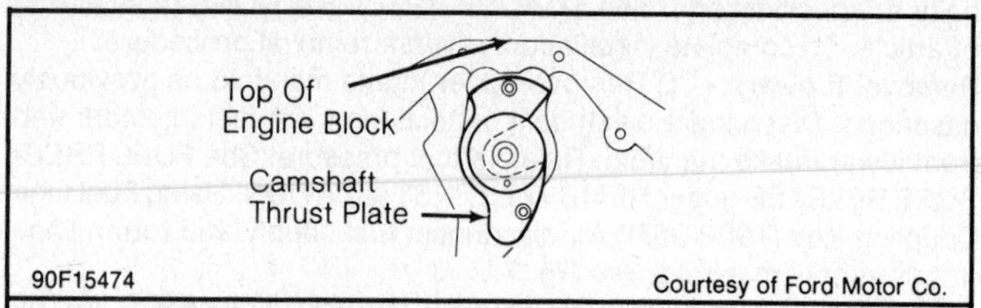
Top Of
Engine Block
Camshaft
Thrust Plate
90F15474
Courtesy of Ford Motor Co.

Fig. 5: Installing Camshaft Thrust Plate

VALVE LIFTERS

Removal – 1) Remove upper and lower intake manifolds. See INTAKE MANIFOLDS under REMOVAL & INSTALLATION. Remove valve covers. See VALVE COVERS under REMOVAL & INSTALLATION.

2) Remove rocker arm shaft bolts evenly by loosening bolts 2 turns at a time. Remove rocker arm shaft assembly. Keeping in order of removal for installation reference, remove push rods and lifters.

CAUTION: If rocker arm shafts are not loosened gradually, shafts may become bent or damaged.

Inspection – Inspect lifter for damage. Ensure roller rotates smoothly. Measure lifter O.D. and cylinder block lifter bore I.D. Replace components if oil clearance is not within specification. See VALVE LIFTERS table under ENGINE SPECIFICATIONS at end of article.

Installation – 1) Lubricate lifter and cylinder block bore with Oil Conditioner (D9AZ-19579-CA) or heavy engine oil. Install lifter in original location, with alignment tab in locating groove of bore. *See Fig. 6.* Ensure lifters slide freely in bore.

2) Coat push rods with oil conditioner and install in original position. Install rocker arm shaft assemblies and tighten shaft support bolts evenly, 2 turns at a time. Tighten to specification. See TORQUE SPECIFICATIONS table at end of article. To install remaining components, reverse removal procedure.

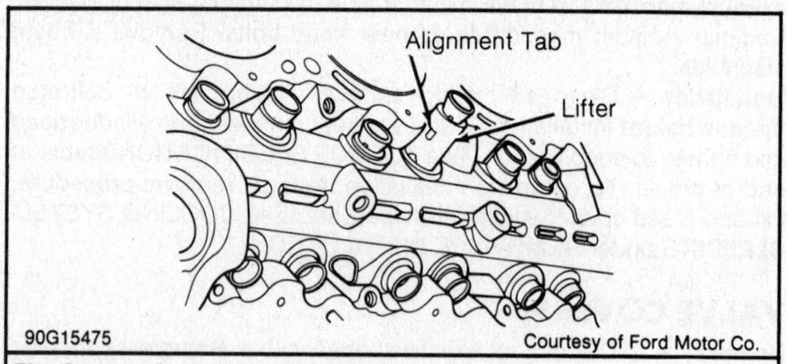
Alignment Tab
Lifter
90G15475
Courtesy of Ford Motor Co.

Fig. 6: Installing Hydraulic Lifters

CAMSHAFT

Removal – 1) Remove front cover. See FRONT COVER under REMOVAL & INSTALLATION. Remove upper and lower intake manifolds. See INTAKE MANIFOLDS under REMOVAL & INSTALLATION. Remove bolt, hold-down clamp and oil pump drive assembly from rear of engine. *See Fig. 7.*

2) Remove valve covers. See VALVE COVERS under REMOVAL & INSTALLATION. Remove valve lifters. See VALVE LIFTERS under REMOVAL & INSTALLATION. Remove timing chain and camshaft sprocket. See TIMING CHAIN & SPROCKETS under REMOVAL & INSTALLATION. Remove thrust plate attaching bolts and remove thrust plate. Slowly remove camshaft from block; DO NOT damage camshaft bearings.

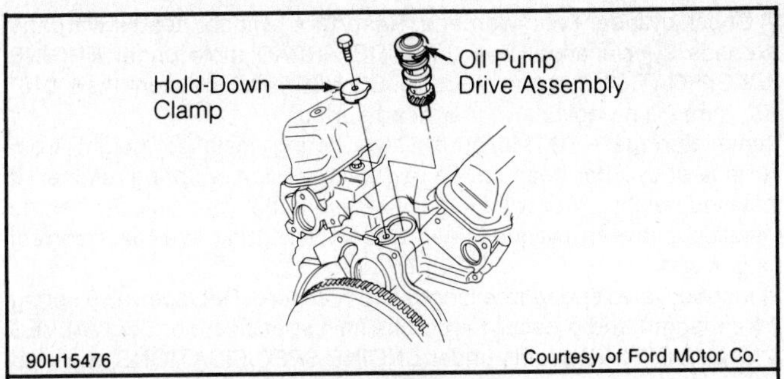
Hold-Down
Clamp
Oil Pump
Drive Assembly
90H15476
Courtesy of Ford Motor Co.

Fig. 7: Removing Oil Pump Drive Assembly

Inspection - Inspect components for damage. Check camshaft journal diameter, lobe lift and oil clearance. Replace components if damaged or not within specification. See CAMSHAFT table under ENGINE SPECIFICATIONS at end of article.

Installation - 1) Lubricate camshaft lobes and bearing surfaces with Oil Conditioner (D9AZ-19579-CA). Install camshaft; use care not to damage bearings and journal surfaces. If camshaft thrust plate was removed, install thrust plate so that it covers main oil gallery. *See Fig. 5.*

2) Ensure camshaft end play is within specification. See CAMSHAFT table under ENGINE SPECIFICATIONS at end of article. To complete installation, reverse removal procedure. Fill and bleed cooling system. See COOLING SYSTEM BLEEDING under REMOVAL & INSTALLATION.

REAR CRANKSHAFT OIL SEAL

Removal & Installation - 1) Rear main bearing oil seal is a one-piece seal. Remove transmission. On M/T models, remove clutch assembly. On all models, remove flywheel/flexplate. Punch hole in metal portion of seal with an awl. Remove seal using a slide hammer.

2) To install, lubricate seal and mating surfaces with engine oil. Install seal on crankshaft, with spring side toward crankshaft. Using Crankshaft Rear Oil Seal Replacer (T72C-6165-R), install seal into position until seal is firmly seated. To install remaining components, reverse removal procedure.

WATER PUMP

Removal - 1) Remove negative battery cable. Drain cooling system. Disconnect lower radiator hose and heater return hose from water pump. Using Fan Clutch Pulley Holder (T84T-6312-C) and Fan Clutch Nut Wrench (T84T-6312-D), remove radiator fan and clutch assembly. *See Fig. 8.*

CAUTION: Fan clutch nut has left-hand threads. Remove nut by turning nut clockwise as viewed from front of engine.

2) Remove alternator drive belt. If equipped with A/C, remove alternator and bracket. Remove water pump pulley. Remove water pump bolts and remove pump. Remove gasket.

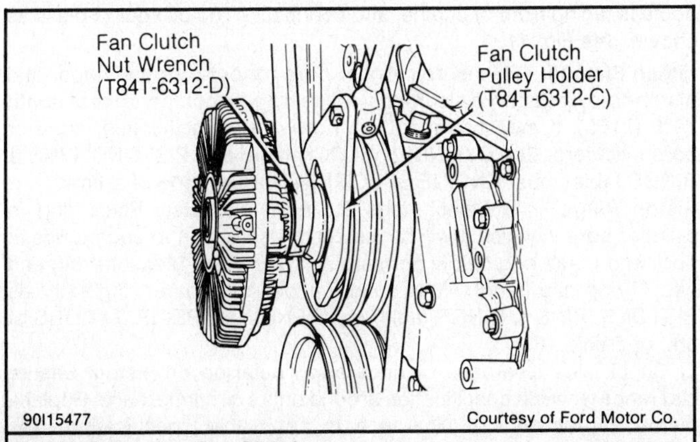
Fan Clutch
Nut Wrench
(T84T-6312-D)
Fan Clutch
Pulley Holder
(T84T-6312-C)
90I15477
Courtesy of Ford Motor Co.

Fig. 8: Removing Fan Clutch

Installation - Clean all gasket surfaces. Apply sealer to both sides of new gasket, and position gasket on water pump. Install water pump. To complete installation, reverse removal procedure. Fill and bleed cooling system. See BLEEDING COOLING SYSTEM under REMOVAL & INSTALLATION.

OIL PAN

Removal (Aerostar) - 1) Disconnect negative battery cable. Raise and support vehicle. Remove starter. On 4WD models, remove front wheels. Remove pivot bolts/nuts from both lower control arms and allow control arms to hang free.

2) Remove lower control arm rear pivot bracket from crossmember. Remove lower nuts from both motor mounts. Remove front drive axle assembly. See AXLE ASSEMBLY under REMOVAL & INSTALLATION in appropriate DRIVE AXLES article. On all models, drain engine oil and remove oil filter.

3) Disconnect low oil level sensor connector from engine oil pan. Remove 2 engine-to-transmission bolts and spacers. Remove oil pan retaining bolts/nuts. On 4WD, raise engine approximately 1" (25 mm). On all models, remove oil pan. Remove oil pan gasket and crankshaft rear main bearing cap wedge seal. *See Fig. 9.*

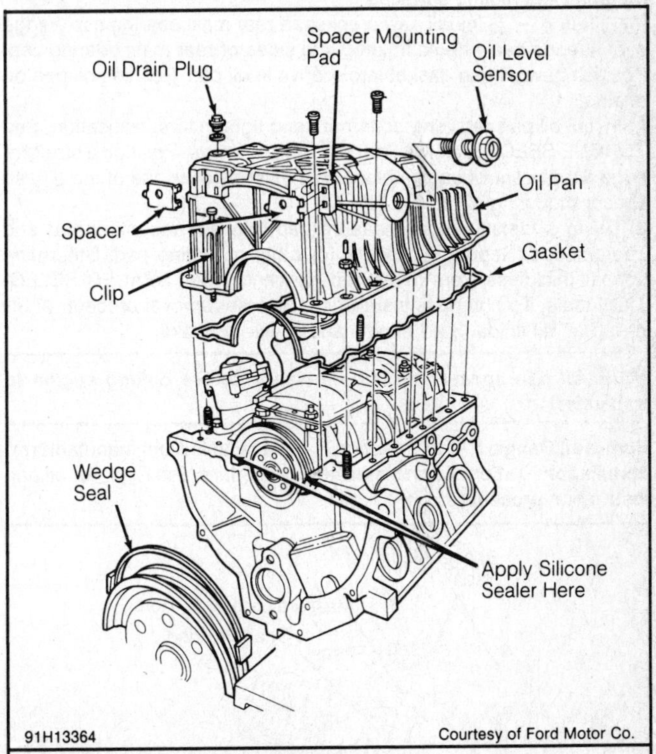
Spacer Mounting
Pad
Oil Level
Sensor
Oil Drain Plug
Oil Pan
Spacer
Gasket
Clip
Wedge
Seal
Apply Silicone
Sealer Here
91H13364
Courtesy of Ford Motor Co.

Fig. 9: Exploded View of Oil Pan Assembly

Installation - 1) Clean gasket mating surfaces. Apply small amount of silicone sealant to engine block where oil pan, rear seal and block mate. *See Fig. 9.*

2) Install new crankshaft rear main bearing cap wedge seal. Wedge seal should fit snug into sides of rear main bearing cap. Position new oil pan gasket into groove in oil pan. If installing original oil pan, go to step **4)**. If installing new oil pan go to next step.

CAUTION: If installing original oil pan, existing oil pan spacers may be used. If installing new oil pan, measure oil pan-to-transmission clearance and install correct spacers to prevent oil pan damage and/or oil leaks.

3) Position oil pan on engine without spacers. Install oil pan retaining nuts on 4 locating studs. Using a feeler gauge, measure gap between locating pads on oil pan and transmission bellhousing. Determine spacer thickness from measured clearance. See SPACER SELECTION table.

1991 ENGINES
4.0L V6 (Cont.)

SPACER SELECTION

Clearance In. (mm)	Shim Thickness In. (mm)	Shim Color Code
.011-.020 (.28-.51)	.010 (.25)	Yellow
.021-.029 (.53-.74)	.020 (.51)	Blue
.030-.039 (.76-.99)	.030 (.76)	Pink

4) Remove oil pan. Position oil pan spacers on oil pan locating pads. Install oil pan. Tighten retaining bolts/nuts tight enough to compress oil pan gasket so transmission bolts align with holes in oil pan, but loose enough to allow oil pan to move when transmission bolts are installed.

5) Install transmission-to-oil pan bolts and tighten to specification. Install and tighten all oil pan bolts to specification. See TORQUE SPECIFICATIONS table at end of article. To complete installation, reverse removal procedure. Fill or top off fluids. Start engine and check for leaks.

Removal (Explorer) – Remove engine. See ENGINE under REMOVAL & INSTALLATION. Mount engine on engine stand with oil pan facing up. Remove oil pan, gasket and rear main bearing cap wedge seal. Clean gasket mating surfaces.

Installation – 1) Install new crankshaft rear main bearing cap wedge seal. Wedge seal should fit snug into sides of rear main bearing cap. Position new oil pan gasket into groove in oil pan. Position oil pan on engine.

2) Install oil pan retaining bolts/nuts and tighten to specification. See TORQUE SPECIFICATIONS table at end of article. Position a straightedge flat on rear of engine block so it extends over one of the oil pan spacer mounting pads. *See Fig. 10.*

3) Using a feeler gauge, measure gap between mounting pad and straightedge. Repeat procedure for other mounting pad. Determine spacer thickness from measured clearance. See SPACER SELECTION table. To complete installation, reverse removal procedure. Fill or top off all fluids. Start engine and check for leaks.

NOTE: Oil pan spacers must be installed before bolting engine to transmission.

Removal (Ranger) – Information is not available from manufacturer.

Installation – For oil pan installation procedure, use Explorer oil pan installation procedure.

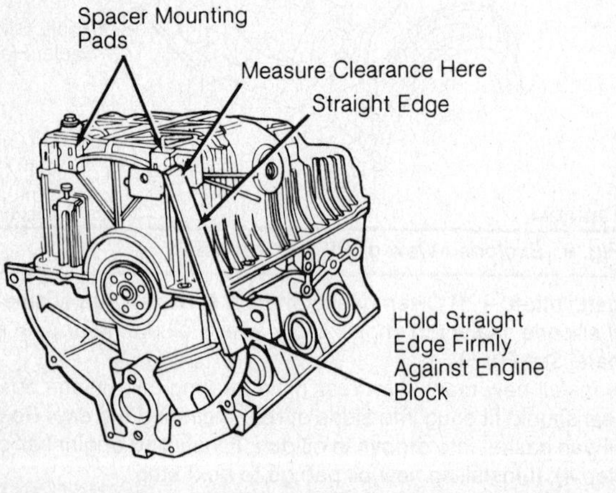
Spacer Mounting
Pads
Measure Clearance Here
Straight Edge
Hold Straight
Edge Firmly
Against Engine
Block
91I13365
Courtesy of Ford Motor Co.

Fig. 10: Measuring Oil Pan Spacer Clearance (Explorer Shown, Ranger Is Similar)

OVERHAUL

CYLINDER HEAD

Cylinder Head – 1) Clean head gasket mating surface. Clean carbon from combustion chambers. Use care not to damage surfaces. Check cylinder head for cracks, burrs, nicks and warpage.

2) Check cylinder head warpage. Resurface cylinder head if warpage exceeds specification. See CYLINDER HEAD table under ENGINE SPECIFICATIONS at end of article. DO NOT machine more than .010" (.25 mm) from original cylinder head surface.

Valve Springs – 1) Measure valve spring installed height from surface of cylinder head spring pad to underside of spring retainer. If installed height is not within specification, a .03" (.8 mm) shim can be installed between cylinder head and valve spring to obtain correct height.

2) Inspect valve spring free length and pressure. Replace valve spring if free length and pressure are not within specification. See VALVES & VALVE SPRINGS table under ENGINE SPECIFICATIONS at end of article.

CAUTION: DO NOT install valve spring spacers unless necessary. Using more spacers than required can result in spring breakage or worn camshaft lobes.

Valve Stem Oil Seals – Different types of valve stem oil seals are used on intake and exhaust valves. Use Valve Stem Installer (T90T-6571-A) to install new valve stem seals. Ensure oil seal bottoms on valve guide. Oversized oil seals must be installed when using oversized valves.

Valve Guides – 1) Valve guides must be reamed for an oversized valve if valve stem oil clearance exceeds specification. See CYLINDER HEAD table under ENGINE SPECIFICATIONS at end of article. Valves are available in .008" (.20 mm) and .016" (.41 mm) oversize.

2) If oversized valves or oversized valve stem oil seals are not available, valve guide may be bored out to use a service bushing. Always use reamers in proper sequence (smallest first).

NOTE: Always grind valve seat after valve guide has been reamed or service bushing has been installed.

Valve Seat – Ensure valve seat angle, seat width and seat runout are within specification. See CYLINDER HEAD table under ENGINE SPECIFICATIONS at end of article. Valve seats must be ground when valve guide is reamed or replaced. Replacement information is not available from manufacturer.

Valves – 1) Ensure head diameter, valve face runout, stem diameter and valve margin are within specification. See VALVES & VALVE SPRINGS table under ENGINE SPECIFICATIONS at end of article.

2) Oversize valves are available in .008" (.20 mm) and .016" (.41 mm). When servicing valve stem tip, DO NOT remove more than .010" (.25) from end of valve stem.

Seat Correction Angles – Grind valve seat to a true 45-degree angle. If seat width is too wide after grinding, use a 30-degree stone to lower seat or a 60-degree stone to raise seat. See CYLINDER HEAD table under ENGINE SPECIFICATIONS at end of article.

CYLINDER BLOCK ASSEMBLY

Piston & Rod Assembly – Ensure pistons and rods are installed in cylinder from which they were removed. Note direction of connecting rod installation on piston before removal. Ensure arrow on piston dome is facing front of engine, and connecting rod oil squirt hole is as shown. *See Fig. 11.*

Fitting Pistons – Measure cylinder bore for out-of-round, taper and piston-to-cylinder bore clearance. Measure with components at about 70°F (21°C). If measurements are not within specification, hone or bore cylinders. See CYLINDER BLOCK table and PISTONS, PINS & RINGS table under ENGINE SPECIFICATIONS at end of article.

Piston Rings – 1) Select rings for bore diameter. Place ring in cylinder bore in which it will be installed. Use piston to square ring in bore and place ring below normal ring wear area. Measure ring end gap. If ring gap is not within specification, try another ring set. See PISTONS, PINS & RINGS table under ENGINE SPECIFICATIONS at end of article.

2) Check side clearance of rings after installing on piston. Ensure clearance is within specification around entire circumference. Replace piston and/or rings if clearance is not within specification. See

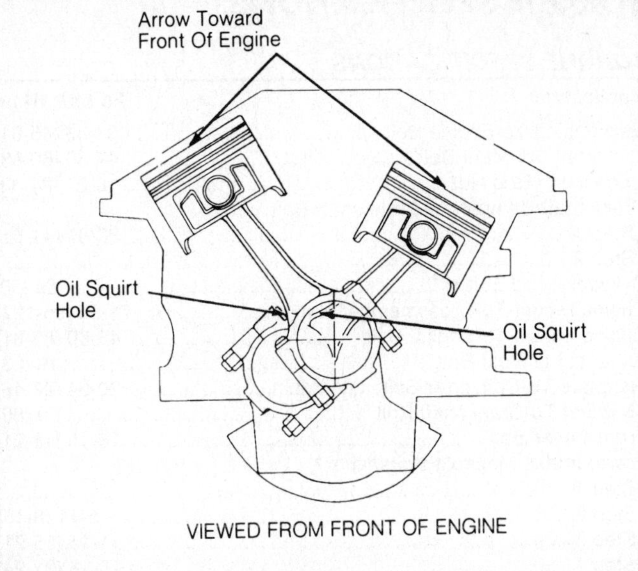

Arrow Toward
Front Of Engine
Oil Squirt
Hole
Oil Squirt
Hole
VIEWED FROM FRONT OF ENGINE

91J13366 Courtesy of Ford Motor Co.

Fig. 11: Positioning Piston & Rod Assembly

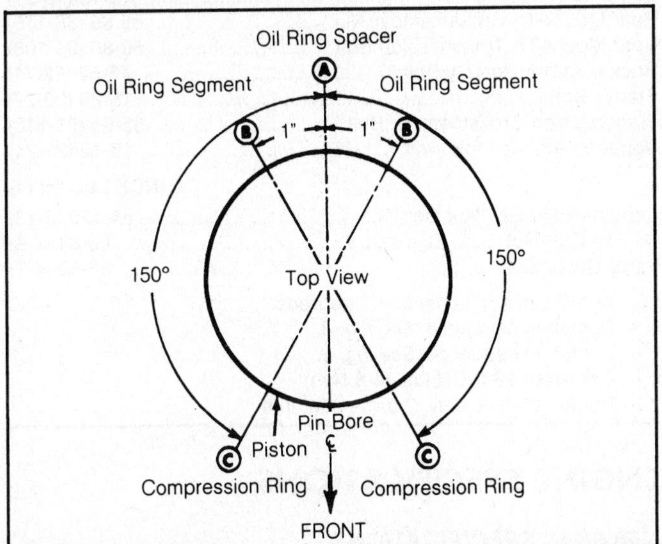

Oil Ring Spacer
Oil Ring Segment
Oil Ring Segment
A
B
B
1"
1"
150°
150°
Top View
Pin Bore
℄
Piston
C
C
Compression Ring
Compression Ring
FRONT

90A15479 Courtesy of Ford Motor Co.

Fig. 12: Positioning Piston Ring End Gaps

PISTONS, PINS & RINGS table under ENGINE SPECIFICATIONS at end of article. Ensure rings are properly spaced on piston before installing pistons into cylinder. *See Fig. 12.*

Rod Bearings – 1) Use Plastigage method and check rod bearing clearance. If proper oil clearance cannot be obtained with standard bearings, try a combination of undersize bearings. DO NOT use any other bearing combination other than what is listed. See UNDERSIZE MAIN & ROD BEARING COMBINATIONS table.

2) If use of bearing combinations does not bring clearance within specification, machine or replace crankshaft as necessary. Always replace bearings in pairs. See CRANKSHAFT, MAIN & CONNECTING ROD BEARINGS table under ENGINE SPECIFICATIONS at end of article.

Crankshaft & Main Bearings – 1) When checking main bearing clearance in vehicle, position a jack under adjoining bearing counterweight being checked. Remove one main bearing cap at a time.

2) Use Plastigage method and check main bearing clearance. If proper oil clearance cannot be obtained with standard bearings, try a combination of undersize bearings. DO NOT use any other bearing combination other than what is listed. See UNDERSIZE MAIN & ROD BEARING COMBINATIONS table.

UNDERSIZE MAIN & ROD BEARING COMBINATIONS [1]

Excess Bearing Clearance In. (mm)	Use Upper Bearing In. (mm)	Use Lower Bearing In. (mm)
.0-.0005 (.0-.013)	.001 (.025)	[2]
.0005-0010 (.013-.026)	.001 (.025)	.001 (.025)
.0010-.0015 (.026-.039)	.002 (.050)	.001 (.025)
.0015-.0020 (.039-.052)	.002 (.050)	.002 (.050)

[1] – DO NOT use any other bearing combination other than what is listed. If use of bearing combinations does not bring clearance within specification, machine or replace crankshaft as necessary.

[2] – Use standard bearing.

3) If use of bearing combinations does not bring clearance within specification, machine or replace crankshaft as necessary. Always replace bearings in pairs. See CRANKSHAFT, MAIN & CONNECTING ROD BEARINGS table under ENGINE SPECIFICATIONS at end of article.

4) Tighten main bearing cap bolts finger tight. Pry crankshaft forward and tighten bearing caps to specification. See TORQUE SPECIFICATIONS table at end of article.

5) Check crankshaft end play. Replace thrust bearing if end play is not within specification. Thrust bearing is No. 3 (from front) main bearing in block. See CRANKSHAFT, MAIN & CONNECTING ROD BEARINGS table under ENGINE SPECIFICATIONS at end of article.

Cylinder Block – 1) Using a feeler gauge and straightedge, check cylinder block head gasket surface for warpage. Check cylinder bore for wear, taper, out-of-round and piston fit. See CYLINDER BLOCK table under ENGINE SPECIFICATIONS at end of article.

CAUTION: DO NOT machine more than .010" (.25 mm) of material from original cylinder block head surface.

2) Install all main bearing caps and tighten to specification before honing cylinder bore. See TORQUE SPECIFICATIONS table at end of article. Ensure bearing caps are installed in their original location, with arrow on cap pointing towards front of engine.

3) Use ONLY a spring-loaded type cylinder hone. After honing, thoroughly clean bore with detergent and water solution. Rinse solution from bore thoroughly with clean water. Wipe bore clean with lint free cloth. Lubricate cylinder bores with engine oil.

ENGINE OILING

ENGINE LUBRICATION SYSTEM

Engine lubrication system is a force-feed type. The oil is supplied under full pressure to crankshaft, connecting rods, camshaft bearing and valve lifters. *See Fig. 13.* A controlled volume of oil is supplied to rocker arms and push rods. All other moving parts are lubricated by splash or gravity flow. Oil flows through oil filter before entering main oil gallery.

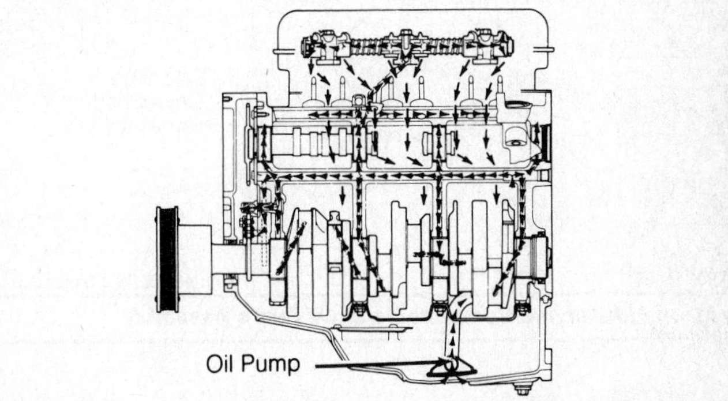

Oil Pump

90D15480 Courtesy of Ford Motor Co.

Fig. 13: Cross-Sectional View of Engine Oiling Circuit

1991 ENGINES
4.0L V6 (Cont.)

Crankcase Capacity – Crankcase capacity is 5 qts. (4.75L) with oil filter.

Oil Pressure – Oil pressure with engine at normal operating temperature is 40-60 psi (2.8-4.2 kg/cm²) at 2000 RPM.

OIL PUMP

Removal & Disassembly – Remove oil pan. See OIL PAN under REMOVAL & INSTALLATION. Remove oil pump attaching bolts. Remove oil pump and oil pump drive shaft. Disassemble oil pump. Note direction of component installation for reassembly reference.

Inspection – Inspect components for damage. Measure rotor end play and outer rotor-to-housing clearance. Measure relief valve-to-housing clearance and relief valve tension. Replace oil pump assembly if not measurements are not within specifications. See OIL PUMP SPECIFICATIONS table.

NOTE: Oil pump is serviced as an assembly only. Replace assembly if measurements are not within specifications. See OIL PUMP SPECIFICATIONS table.

OIL PUMP SPECIFICATIONS

Application	Specification In. (mm)
Outer Rotor-To-Housing Clearance	.001-.013 (.03-.33)
Rotor End Play	.004 (.10) Max.
Shaft-To-Housing Clearance	.0015-.0030 (.038-.076)
Relief Valve Spring Tension	[1]
Relief Valve-To-Housing Clearance	.0015-.0030 (.038-.076)

[1] - Spring tension is 13.6-14.7 lbs. @ 1.39" (6.2-6.7 kg @ 35 mm).

Reassembly & Installation – **1)** To reassemble, reverse disassembly procedure. Ensure components are installed in original location. To install, prime oil pump with engine oil. Rotate oil pump drive shaft to distribute oil within pump body.

2) Insert oil pump drive shaft into engine block, with pointed end of oil pump drive shaft inward. Pointed end is closest to the pressed-on retainer ring. *See Fig. 14.*

3) Position new gasket in place and install oil pump. To complete installation, reverse removal procedure. Tighten bolts to specification. See TORQUE SPECIFICATIONS table.

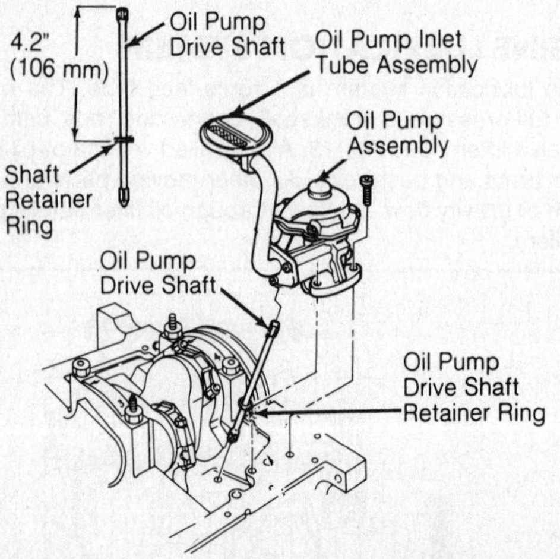
4.2"
(106 mm)
Oil Pump
Drive Shaft
Oil Pump Inlet
Tube Assembly
Oil Pump
Assembly
Shaft
Retainer
Ring
Oil Pump
Drive Shaft
Oil Pump
Drive Shaft
Retainer Ring

90C15489 Courtesy of Ford Motor Co.

Fig. 14: Identifying Components of Oil Pump Assembly

TORQUE SPECIFICATIONS

TORQUE SPECIFICATIONS

Application	Ft. Lbs. (N.m)
Bellhousing-To-Engine Bolt	33-45 (45-61)
Camshaft Sprocket Bolt	44-50 (60-68)
Connecting Rod Nut	18-24 (24-33)
Crankshaft Damper-To-Crankshaft Bolt	
Step 1	30-37 (41-51)
Step 2	[1]
Cylinder Head Bolt [2]	59 (80)
Engine Mount-To-Crossmember Nut	71-94 (96-127)
Engine Mount-To-Engine Bolt	45-60 (88-81)
Exhaust Manifold Bolt	19 (26)
Flexplate-To-Converter Bolt	20-34 (27-46)
Flywheel-To-Crankshaft Bolt	59 (80)
Front Cover Bolt	13-15 (18-21)
Lower Intake Manifold Bolts/Nuts [3]	
Step 1	[4]
Step 2	6-11 (8-15)
Step 3	11-15 (15-21)
Step 4	15-18 (21-24)
Main Bearing Cap Bolt	66-77 (90-104)
Oil Level Sensor	13-20 (18-27)
Oil Pump Retaining Bolt	13-15 (18-21)
Rear Mount-To-Crossmember Nut	65-85 (88-115)
Rear Mount-To-Transmission Bolt	60-80 (81-108)
Rocker Arm Assembly Bolt [5]	46-52 (62-71)
Starter Bolt	15-20 (20-27)
Transmission Crossmember Bolt	65-85 (88-115)
Upper Intake Manifold Bolt	15-18 (21-24)
	INCH Lbs. (N.m)
Camshaft Thrust Plate Bolt	84-120 (8-13)
Oil Pan Bolt/Nut	60-84 (7-9)
Valve Cover Bolt	36-60 (4-7)

[1] – Tighten an additional 80-90 degrees.
[2] – Tighten in sequence. *See Fig. 3.*
[3] – Tighten in sequence. *See Fig. 2.*
[4] – Tighten to 36 INCH lbs. (4-8 N.m)
[5] – Tighten bolts evenly, 2 turns at a time.

ENGINE SPECIFICATIONS

GENERAL SPECIFICATIONS

Application	Specification
4.0L	
Displacement	246 Cu. In. (4.0L)
Bore	3.95" (100.3 mm)
Stroke	3.32" (84.3 mm)
Compression Ratio	9.0:1
Fuel System	PFI

CONNECTING RODS

Application	In. (mm)
4.0L	
Bore Diameter	
Pin Bore	.9432-.9439 (23.957-23.975)
Crankpin Bore	2.2370-2.2378 (56.820-56.840)
Center-To-Center Length	5.1386-5.1413 (130.520-130.589)
Maximum Bend [1]	.002 (.05)
Maximum Twist [1]	.006 (.15)
Side Play	
Service Limit	.014 (.36)

[1] – Specification listed is measured at the ends of an 8" (203 mm) bar, 4" (102 mm) on each side of rod center line.

1991 ENGINES
4.0L V6 (Cont.)

CRANKSHAFT, MAIN & CONNECTING ROD BEARINGS

Application	In. (mm)
4.0L	
Crankshaft	
End Play	
Standard	.004-.008 (.10-.20)
Service Limit	.012 (.03)
Main Bearings	
Journal Diameter	2.2433-2.2441 (56.980-57.000)
Journal Out-Of-Round	.0006 (.015)
Journal Taper	[1] .0006 (.015)
Journal Runout	
Standard	.002 (.05)
Service Limit	.005 (.13)
Oil Clearance	
Desired	.0008-.0015 (.020-.038)
Allowable	.0005-.0019 (.013-.048)
Connecting Rod Bearings	
Journal Diameter	2.1252-2.1260 (53.980-54.000)
Journal Out-Of-Round	.0006 (.015)
Journal Taper	[1] .0006 (.015)
Oil Clearance.	
Desired	.0005-.0022 (.013-.056)
Allowable	.0003-.0024 (.008-.061)

[1] – Specification listed is per 1" (25.4 mm).

PISTONS, PINS & RINGS

Application	In. (mm)
4.0L	
Pistons	
Clearance	.0008-.0019 (.020-.048)
Diameter	[1] 3.9524-3.9531 (100.390-100.409)
Pin Bore Diameter	.9450-.9452 (24.003-24.008)
Pins	
Diameter	
Red Pin	.9446-.9448 (23.993-23.998)
Blue Pin	.9448-.9449 (23.998-24.000)
Length	2.84-2.87 (72.1-72.9)
Piston Fit	.0003-.0006 (.008-.015)
Rod Fit	Press Fit
Rings	
No. 1 & 2	
End Gap	.015-.023 (.38-.58)
Side Clearance	.0020.0033 (.051-.084)
No. 3 (Oil)	
End Gap (Steel Rail)	.015-.055 (.38-1.40)
Side Clearance	Snug Fit

[1] – Measure at piston pin bore, 90 degrees to pin.

CYLINDER BLOCK

Application	In. (mm)
4.0L	
Cylinder Bore	
Standard Diameter	3.9527-3.9543 (100.398-100.439)
Maximum Taper	.010 (.25)
Maximum Out-Of-Round	
Standard	.0015 (.038)
Service Limit	.005 (.13)
Maximum Deck Warpage [1]	
Standard Service	.003 (.08)
Service Limit	.006 (.15)

[1] – Within a 6" (152 mm) area.

VALVES & VALVE SPRINGS

Application	Specification
4.0L	
Face Angle	44°
Head Diameter	
Intake	1.71" (43.5 mm)
Exhaust	1.36" (34.5 mm)
Stem Diameter	
Intake	.3159-.3167" (8.024-8.044 mm)
Exhaust	.3149-.3156" (8.998-8.016 mm)
Valve Margin	.031" (.79 mm)
Valve Springs	
Free Length	1.91" (48.5 mm)
Installed Height	1.58-1.61" (40.1-40.9 mm)
Out-Of-Square	.078" (1.98 mm)
Pressure	Lbs. @ In. (kg @ mm)
Intake & Exhaust	
Closed	60-68 @ 1.59 (27-31 @ 37.8)
Open	138-149 @ 1.22 (63-68 @ 31.0)

CYLINDER HEAD

Application	Specification
4.0L	
Maximum Warpage [1]	.003" (.08 mm)
Valve Seats	
Seat Angle	45°
Seat Width	.060-.079" (1.52-2.00 mm)
Maximum Seat Runout	.0015" (.038 mm)
Valve Guides	
Valve Guide Bore I.D.	.3174-.3184" (8.062-8.087 mm)
Valve Stem-To-Guide	
Oil Clearance	
Intake	.0008-.0025" (.020-.064 mm)
Exhaust	.0018-.0035" (.046-.089 mm)

[1] – Specification listed is within 6" (152 mm). Overall warpage is .006" (.15 mm). DO NOT machine more than .010" (.25 mm) from original gasket surface.

CAMSHAFT

Application	In. (mm)
4.0L	
Camshaft Bearing I.D.	
No. 1	1.954-1.955 (49.64-49.66)
No. 2	1.939-1.940 (49.26-49.28)
No. 3	1.919-1.920 (48.75-48.77)
No. 4	1.924-1.925 (48.88-48.90)
End Play	
Standard	.004-.008 (.10-.20)
Service Limit	.009 (.23)
Journal Runout	.005 (.13)
Lobe Lift	.4024 (10.220)
Lobe Lift Wear Limit	.005 (.13)
Oil Clearance	
Standard	.0010-.0026 (.025-.066)
Service Limit	.006 (.15)

VALVE LIFTERS

Application	In. (mm)
4.0L	
Lifter Diameter	.8742-.8755 (22.205-22.238)
Oil Clearance	
Standard	.0005-.0022 (.013-.056)
Service Limit	.005 (.13)

1991 ENGINES
4.9L 6-Cylinder

Bronco, "E" & "F" Series

NOTE: For engine repair procedures not covered in this article, see ENGINE OVERHAUL PROCEDURES article in GENERAL INFORMATION.

ENGINE IDENTIFICATION

Engine is identified by eighth character of Vehicle Identification Number (VIN). VIN is visible through windshield on left side of instrument panel. VIN is also located on Safety Compliance Certification Label attached to left door lock pillar.

VIN ENGINE CODE

Engine	Code
4.9L (300 Cu. In.) PFI	Y

ADJUSTMENTS

VALVE CLEARANCE ADJUSTMENT

In most cases, valve clearance adjustment is not required. Positive-stop rocker arm bolts and hydraulic valve lifters automatically adjust stem-to-rocker arm clearance. However, repeated cylinder head or block surfacing will change stem-to-rocker arm clearance.

When this occurs, stem-to-rocker arm clearance will be either too excessive or too little. If clearance is excessive, it will cause valve train noise; if clearance is too little, it will prevent valve from seating. To compensate for stem-to-rocker arm clearance not within specification, a longer or shorter push rod must be installed. Push rods are available in .060" (1.52 mm) longer or shorter than original.

1) Remove rocker cover. Rotate crankshaft until No. 1 piston is at TDC of compression stroke. Slowly collapse lifter plunger using Tappet Bleed Down Wrench (T70P-6513-A) until completely bottomed.

2) While maintaining pressure on lifter, use feeler gauge to check clearance between rocker arm and valve stem tip. On all valves, desired clearance is .125-.175" (3.18-4.45 mm), and allowable range is .100-.200" (2.54-5.08 mm).

3) If clearance is less than specification, install shorter push rod. If clearance is greater than specification, install longer push rod. Rotate crankshaft 120 degrees (in direction of normal rotation) to check next set of valves in firing order sequence. Firing order is 1-5-3-6-2-4. Repeat procedure for remaining valves.

REMOVAL & INSTALLATION

FUEL PRESSURE RELEASE

Disconnect negative battery cable. Remove fuel tank filler cap to release tank pressure. Attach a fuel pressure gauge to pressure relief valve on fuel rail. Release fuel pressure.

COOLING SYSTEM BLEEDING

1) To bleed trapped air from cooling system, disconnect heater hose from water pump. Using 50/50 mixture of coolant and water, fill radiator until coolant flows from heater hose fitting at water pump. Reconnect heater hose.

2) Fill radiator until coolant is 1.5" (38 mm) below radiator cap seal. Install radiator cap. Run engine until warm. Turn off engine. CAREFULLY remove radiator cap and check level. Fill as required.

ENGINE

NOTE: Engine removal and installation procedures are for engine without transmission attached.

Removal (Bronco & "F" Series) – 1) Disconnect battery cables. Drain cooling system and crankcase. Scribe hood hinge position and remove hood. Remove throttle body inlet tubes. Remove heater hoses and air cleaner assembly. Release fuel pressure. See FUEL PRESSURE RELEASE under REMOVAL & INSTALLATION.

NOTE: Fan clutch/water pump hub has right-hand thread.

2) Using Disconnect Tool (D87L-9280-A) for 3/8" line or (D87L-9280-B) for 1/2" line, disconnect fuel supply and return lines. *See Fig. 1.* Remove radiator shroud and radiator. Using Fan Clutch Pulley Holder (T84T-6312-C) and Fan Clutch Nut Wrench (T84T-6312-D), remove fan and clutch assembly.

3) Remove water pump pulley. Disconnect accelerator cable at throttle body and remove return spring. Remove power brake vacuum hose at intake manifold. Disconnect kickdown cable at throttle body (A/T). Separate exhaust pipe from manifold.

4) Remove wiring harness from coil and all sending units. Disconnect all Electronic Engine Control (EEC) sensor connectors. Remove alternator mounting bolts and set alternator aside with wires attached. Remove power steering pump from mounting brackets and set aside with lines attached.

5) On A/C-equipped models, discharge system and disconnect pressure lines. On all models, raise and support vehicle. Remove starter and A/T filler tube bracket (if equipped). Remove upper right bolt from engine rear plate.

6) Remove all bellhousing lower retaining bolts and disconnect clutch retracting spring (if equipped). On A/T models, remove converter housing access cover and remove flex plate-to-converter nuts. Secure converter assembly in housing.

7) Remove transmission cooler lines from clip at engine. Remove converter housing lower retaining bolts. On all models, remove insulator support bracket nut from each front engine support. Lower vehicle and support transmission with floor jack.

8) Remove remaining bellhousing-to-engine bolts. Attach engine hoist to engine. Raise engine slightly to separate from transmission. Remove engine from vehicle.

Installation – To install, reverse removal procedure. Tighten bolts to specification. See TORQUE SPECIFICATIONS table at end of article. Fill or top off all fluid levels. Fill and bleed air from cooling system. See COOLING SYSTEM BLEEDING under REMOVAL & INSTALLATION.

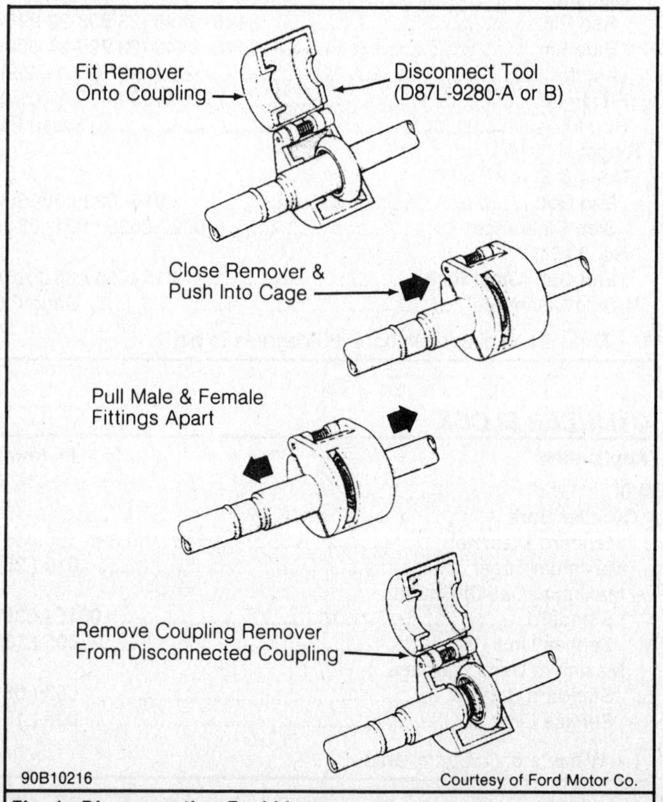
Fit Remover
Onto Coupling
Disconnect Tool
(D87L-9280-A or B)
Close Remover &
Push Into Cage
Pull Male & Female
Fittings Apart
Remove Coupling Remover
From Disconnected Coupling
90B10216
Courtesy of Ford Motor Co.

Fig. 1: Disconnecting Fuel Lines

Removal ("E" Series) – 1) Remove engine cover and air cleaner assembly. Drain cooling system. Disconnect battery. Remove front bumper, grille and lower gravel deflector. Disconnect coolant hoses and transmission oil lines from radiator (if equipped).
2) Remove radiator and shroud. Disconnect brake booster and heater hoses at intake manifold. Disconnect alternator and set aside Remove power steering pump drive belt, pump and bracket from engine.
3) Release fuel pressure. See FUEL PRESSURE RELEASE under REMOVAL & INSTALLATION. Using Disconnect Tool (D87L-9280-A) for 3/8" line or (D87L-9280-B) for 1/2" line, disconnect fuel supply and return lines. *See Fig. 1.*
4) Disconnect distributor, Electronic Engine Control (EEC) sensors and sending unit wires from engine. Disconnect accelerator cable and remove bracket from engine. Disconnect A/T kickdown cable at throttle body. Remove exhaust manifold heat deflector and exhaust pipe-to-manifold nuts.
5) Disconnect A/T vacuum line at intake manifold junction. Remove upper transmission-to-engine bolts. Remove A/T dipstick tube support at intake manifold. Raise vehicle. Drain crankcase and remove oil filter.
6) Disconnect starter wiring and remove starter. On A/T models, remove flywheel inspection cover and flexplate-to-converter nuts. On all applications, remove front engine mount nuts. Remove remaining transmission-to-engine bolts. Lower vehicle from hoist. Attach lifting device to engine. Remove engine from vehicle.
Installation – To install, reverse removal procedure. Tighten bolts to specification. See TORQUE SPECIFICATIONS table at end of article. Fill or top off all fluid levels. Fill and bleed air from cooling system. See COOLING SYSTEM BLEEDING under REMOVAL & INSTALLATION.

INTAKE MANIFOLDS & EXHAUST MANIFOLDS

Removal – 1) Disconnect negative battery cable. Disconnect electrical connectors as necessary. Disconnect PCV hose from underside of upper intake manifold. Remove throttle linkage shield.

CAUTION: When disconnecting throttle cable from ball stud, use screwdriver or similar tool to pry off. Removing by hand may damage cable.

2) Disconnect accelerator cable and speed control cable. Remove throttle body inlet hoses. Disconnect accelerator cable from bracket and set aside. Remove cable retracting spring. Disconnect and remove EGR tube.
3) Release fuel system pressure. See FUEL PRESSURE RELEASE under REMOVAL & INSTALLATION. Using Disconnect Tool (D87L-9280-A) for 3/8" line or (D87L-9280-B) for 1/2" line, disconnect fuel supply and return lines. *See Fig. 1.*
4) Remove thermactor tube assembly from lower intake manifold. Remove thermactor by-pass valve bracket retaining nut from lower intake manifold. On "E" Series, remove transmission fill tube retaining nut.
5) On all models, remove upper intake manifold retaining nuts. Remove screw and washer attaching upper intake manifold support bracket to upper intake manifold. Remove upper intake manifold and throttle body as an assembly. Remove injector heat shield.
6) Disconnect exhaust pipes from exhaust manifolds. Mark and disconnect vacuum lines for installation reference. Disconnect power brake vacuum line (if equipped). Remove lower intake manifold and exhaust manifold-to-cylinder head bolts. Remove lower intake manifold and exhaust manifolds.
Installation – 1) Clean mating surfaces of manifolds and cylinder head. Lightly coat mating surfaces with graphite grease. Install new intake/exhaust manifold gasket on cylinder head.

NOTE: If installing original exhaust manifolds, install new exhaust manifold gaskets. If installing new exhaust manifolds, install exhaust manifolds without gaskets.

2) Position lower intake/exhaust manifold assembly on cylinder head. Ensure gasket remains in position. Tighten bolts and nuts in sequence to specification. *See Fig. 2.* See TORQUE SPECIFICATIONS table at end of article. To complete installation, reverse removal procedure.

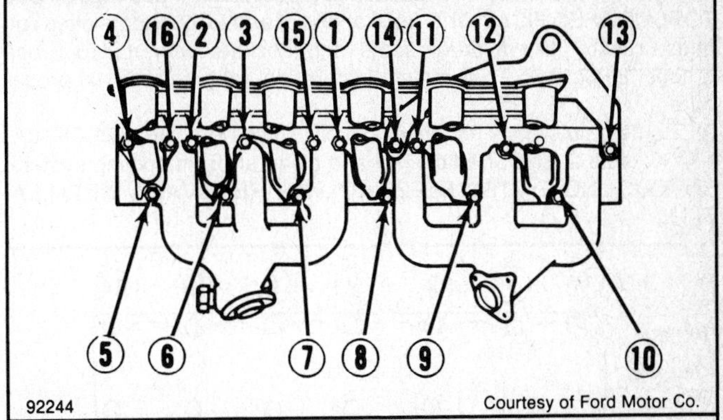
4
16
2
3
15
1
14
11
12
13
5
6
7
8
9
10
92244
Courtesy of Ford Motor Co.

Fig. 2: Lower Intake & Exhaust Manifold Tightening Sequence

CYLINDER HEAD

NOTE: Cylinder head can be removed with intake and exhaust manifolds connected.

Removal – 1) Scribe hood hinge position and remove hood. Disconnect negative battery cable. Drain cooling system and crankcase. Remove throttle body inlet tubes. Discharge A/C system. Remove the A/C compressor and condenser.
2) Disconnect heater hoses from water pump and thermostat housing. Release pressure from fuel system. See FUEL PRESSURE RELEASE under REMOVAL & INSTALLATION.

NOTE: Fan clutch/water pump hub has right-hand thread.

3) Using Disconnect Tool (D87L-9280-A) for 3/8" line or (D87L-9280-B) for 1/2" line, disconnect fuel supply and return lines. *See Fig. 1.* DO NOT bend fuel rail. Remove radiator and shroud. Using Fan Clutch Pulley Holder (T84T-6312-C) and Fan Clutch Nut Wrench (T84T-6312-D), remove fan and clutch assembly.
4) Remove water pump pulley and fan drive belt. Disconnect accelerator cable and return spring from throttle body. Disconnect power brake vacuum line from intake manifold (if equipped). Disconnect transmission kickdown cable from throttle body (if equipped).
5) Disconnect exhaust pipes from exhaust manifolds. Disconnect body ground strap and negative battery cable from engine. Disconnect Electronic Engine Control (EEC) harness and engine wiring harness from all electrical components on engine.
6) Leaving wiring attached, remove alternator and set aside. Remove air pump and alternator/air pump bracket. Remove power steering pump with hoses attached and set aside. Remove power steering pump and A/C compressor bracket.
7) Remove coil bracket and set aside. Remove rocker arm cover. Loosen rocker arm bolts and rotate rocker arms aside. Mark and remove push rods for installation reference. Disconnect spark plug wires from spark plugs.
8) Remove cylinder head bolts. Lift cylinder head and manifold assemblies from engine using appropriate lifting device. DO NOT pry between cylinder head and block, as machined surfaces may be damaged.
Inspection – 1) Clean gasket mating surfaces. Check cylinder head warpage. Resurface cylinder head if warpage exceeds specification. See CYLINDER HEAD table under ENGINE SPECIFICATIONS at end of article. Check cylinder block deck surface for warpage.
2) Resurface cylinder block if warpage exceeds specification. See CYLINDER BLOCK table under ENGINE SPECIFICATIONS at end of article. If cylinder head or cylinder block warpage exceeds specification, DO NOT remove more than .010" (.25 mm) material from original surface of cylinder head or block.
Installation – 1) Position new gasket over dowel pins on cylinder block. Using lifting device, carefully position cylinder head onto block.

1991 ENGINES
4.9L 6-Cylinder (Cont.)

Ensure dowel pins engage in head. Coat head bolt threads with engine oil and install.

2) Tighten head bolts in sequence to specification. *See Fig. 3*. See TORQUE SPECIFICATIONS table at end of article. Lubricate push rod ends, rocker arm fulcrum seats and sockets with multipurpose grease, and install. To complete installation, reverse removal procedure.

3) Tighten nuts/bolts to specification. See TORQUE SPECIFICATIONS table at end of article. Fill and bleed air from cooling system. See COOLING SYSTEM BLEEDING under REMOVAL & INSTALLATION.

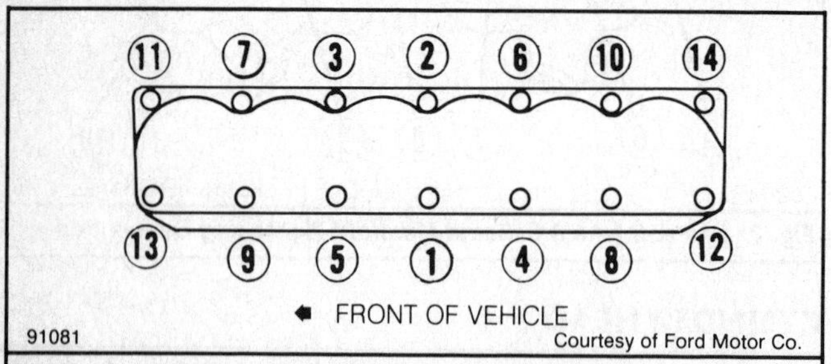
11
7
3
2
6
10
14
13
9
5
1
4
8
12
FRONT OF VEHICLE
91081
Courtesy of Ford Motor Co.

Fig. 3: Cylinder Head Bolt Tightening Sequence

FRONT COVER OIL SEAL

Removal – 1) Remove fan and shroud. Remove drive belts. Remove crankshaft pulley. Using Vibration Damper Remover (T58P-6316-D), remove vibration damper. Position Front Cover Seal Remover (T70P-6B070-B) onto seal and tighten 2 through bolts to force seal puller under the seal flange.

2) Alternately tighten 4 puller bolts 1/2 turn at a time. Remove oil seal from the front cover. Clean seal recess in front cover.

Installation – 1) Lubricate crankshaft stub, vibration damper hub I.D. and sealing surface of front cover seal with clean engine oil. DO NOT apply grease to seal. Position seal onto Front Cover Seal Installer (T70P-6B070-A).

2) Position Front Cover Seal Installer and seal onto the crankshaft end. Force seal into recess by tightening bolt. *See Fig. 4*. Remove front cover seal installer. Apply a 1/4" (6 mm) bead of silicone sealer to keyway inside vibration damper hub.

3) Using Vibration Damper Installer (T52L-6306-AEE), install vibration damper. To complete installation, reverse removal procedure. See TORQUE SPECIFICATIONS table at end of article.

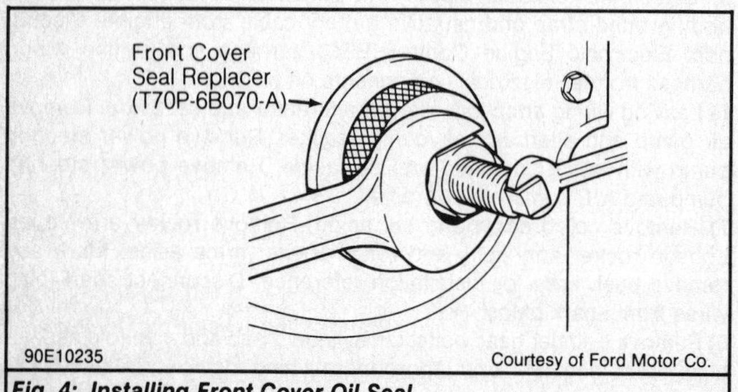
Front Cover
Seal Replacer
(T70P-6B070-A)
90E10235
Courtesy of Ford Motor Co.

Fig. 4: Installing Front Cover Oil Seal

FRONT COVER

Removal – 1) Drain cooling system and crankcase. Remove shroud and radiator. Remove drive belts. Using Fan Clutch Pulley Holder (T84T-6312-C) and Fan Clutch Nut Wrench (T84T-6312-D), remove fan and clutch assembly.

2) Remove water pump pulley. Remove power steering pump and bracket. Remove crankshaft damper retaining bolt and washer. Using Vibration Damper Remover (T58P-6316-D), remove vibration damper.

3) Remove front cover and front oil pan bolts. Loosen first 6 bolts on each side of oil pan. Lightly push down oil pan to relieve pressure on front cover. Remove front cover and gasket.

NOTE: Always replace front cover oil seal whenever front cover is removed.

Installation – 1) Clean front cover and cylinder block mating surfaces. Coat cylinder block and front cover gasket surfaces with oil resistant sealer. Install front cover gasket. Apply silicone sealer to block/pan junction and to oil pan gasket sealing surface.

2) Position front cover on cylinder block. Hand-start front cover and pan bolts. To aid front cover alignment, slide Front Cover Aligner (T61P-6019-B) over crankshaft and into seal bore.

3) Tighten front cover bolts first to obtain proper alignment, then tighten oil pan bolts. Remove front cover aligner. Install and lubricate front cover oil seal. See FRONT COVER OIL SEAL under REMOVAL & INSTALLATION.

4) Lubricate crankshaft stub, vibration damper hub I.D. and sealing surface of front cover seal with clean engine oil. DO NOT apply grease to seal. Apply a 1/4" (6 mm) bead of silicone sealer to keyway inside vibration damper hub.

5) Using Vibration Damper Replacer (T52L-6306-AEE), install vibration damper. To install remaining components, reverse removal procedure. Tighten bolts to specification. See TORQUE SPECIFICATIONS table at end of article. Fill and bleed air from cooling system. See COOLING SYSTEM BLEEDING under REMOVAL & INSTALLATION.

TIMING GEARS

CAUTION: To avoid valve train damage, NEVER rotate camshaft or crankshaft unless timing gears are installed.

Checking Timing Gear Backlash – 1) Remove engine front cover. See FRONT COVER under REMOVAL & INSTALLATION. Attach a dial indicator to engine block, with sensing stylus on camshaft gear tooth.

2) Using a dial indicator, measure gear backlash between camshaft gear and crankshaft gear at 6 equally spaced teeth. To obtain an accurate reading, hold gear firmly against block. Backlash should be .004-.010" (.10-.25 mm). If any of the 6 readings are not within specification, replace timing gears.

Removal – 1) Drain cooling system and crankcase. Remove engine front cover. See FRONT COVER under REMOVAL & INSTALLATION. Check camshaft end play. If end play is not within specification, replace camshaft thrust plate. See CAMSHAFT table under ENGINE SPECIFICATIONS at end of article.

2) Rotate engine (in direction of normal rotation) until camshaft and crankshaft gear timing marks are aligned. *See Fig. 5*. Using Camshaft Gear Puller (T82T-6256-A), remove camshaft gear. Using Vibration Damper Remover (T58P-6316-D), remove crankshaft gear. Remove Woodruff keys from camshaft and crankshaft.

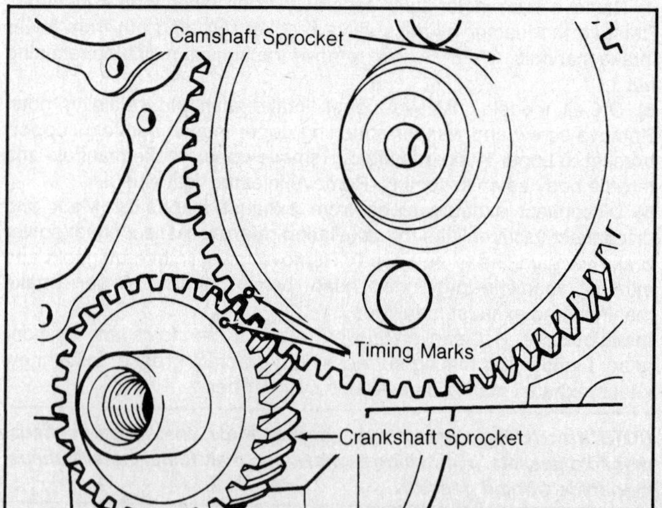
Camshaft Sprocket
Timing Marks
Crankshaft Sprocket
92251
Courtesy of Ford Motor Co.

Fig. 5: Aligning Timing Marks

Installation - 1) Ensure camshaft key spacer and thrust plate are correctly installed. Install Woodruff key into camshaft. Align camshaft gear keyway with camshaft key and install gear using Camshaft Gear Replacing Adapter (T65L-6306-A).

2) Install Woodruff key into crankshaft. Align crankshaft gear keyway with key and install crankshaft gear. Ensure timing marks on camshaft and crankshaft gears are still aligned.

3) To complete installation, reverse removal procedure. Tighten bolts to specification. See TORQUE SPECIFICATIONS table at end of article. Fill or top off all fluids. Fill and bleed air from cooling system. See COOLING SYSTEM BLEEDING under REMOVAL & INSTALLATION.

CAMSHAFT

Removal - 1) Drain cooling system and crankcase. Remove radiator and shroud. Remove rocker arm cover. Rotate engine (in direction of rotation) until No. 1 piston is at TDC. Remove distributor cap.

2) Mark distributor rotor and housing for installation reference. Remove distributor. Loosen rocker arm bolts and turn rocker arms aside. Remove push rods and mark for installation reference.

3) Remove engine side cover to expose valve lifters. Remove lifters and mark for installation reference. Remove engine front cover. See FRONT COVER under REMOVAL & INSTALLATION. Check and note camshaft end play.

4) Replace camshaft thrust plate if end play is not within specification. See CAMSHAFT table under ENGINE SPECIFICATIONS at end of article. Turn crankshaft to align gear timing marks. *See Fig. 5.*

5) Remove camshaft thrust plate bolts. Remove camshaft gear using Camshaft Gear Puller (T82T-6256-A). Remove Woodruff key, thrust plate and spacer. Carefully remove camshaft to avoid damaging lobes or bearings.

Inspection - Inspect components for damage. Check camshaft journal diameter, lobe lift, and oil clearance. Replace components if damaged or not within specification. See CAMSHAFT table under ENGINE SPECIFICATIONS at end of article.

Installation - 1) Coat camshaft lobes with multipurpose grease. Coat bearing journals with clean engine oil. Install Woodruff key, spacer and thrust plate on camshaft. Align gear keyway with key and install gear using Camshaft Gear Replacing Adapter (T65L-6306-A).

2) Install camshaft, spacer, thrust plate and gear as an assembly, ensuring timing marks are aligned. *See Fig. 5.* Tighten thrust plate bolts. Ensure camshaft end play is within specification. See CAMSHAFT table under ENGINE SPECIFICATIONS at end of article.

3) To complete installation, reverse removal procedure. Tighten bolts to specification. See TORQUE SPECIFICATIONS table at end of article. Fill and bleed air from cooling system. See COOLING SYSTEM BLEEDING under REMOVAL & INSTALLATION.

CAMSHAFT BEARINGS

NOTE: It may be necessary to remove crankshaft for access to camshaft bearings.

Removal - Remove engine. See ENGINE under REMOVAL & INSTALLATION. Install engine in engine stand. Remove flywheel/flexplate. Remove camshaft rear bearing bore plug. Remove camshaft. See CAMSHAFT under REMOVAL & INSTALLATION. Use Camshaft Bearing Remover/Installer (T65L-6250-A) to remove cam bearings.

Installation - To install cam bearings, reverse removal procedure. Ensure oil holes in bearings align with oil holes in cylinder block when installing camshaft bearings. Install front bearing so .020-.035" (.51-.89 mm) exists between front edge of bearing and face of cylinder block.

REAR MAIN BEARING OIL SEAL

Removal - 1) Remove starter and transmission. Remove clutch assembly (if equipped). Remove flexplate/flywheel. Remove engine rear cover plate. Using an awl, punch hole in oil seal metal surface between lip and block.

2) Carefully pry oil seal from recess without damaging seal surface. Clean oil seal recess in block and main bearing cap.

Installation - 1) Inspect and clean crankshaft surface. Lightly coat crankshaft and sealing surface of new oil seal with engine oil. Place seal in position with lip facing inward, and install seal using seal installer.

2) Keep installer straight in respect to center line of crankshaft. Seal is properly installed when seal installer contacts cylinder block. Coat threads of flywheel bolts with oil resistant sealer. To complete installation, reverse removal procedure. Tighten bolts to specification. See TORQUE SPECIFICATIONS table at end of article.

WATER PUMP

NOTE: Fan clutch/water pump hub has right-hand thread.

Removal - 1) Drain cooling system. Remove alternator drive belt. On A/C-equipped vehicles, remove compressor drive belt.

2) Using Fan Clutch Pulley Holder (T84T-6312-C) and Fan Clutch Nut Wrench (T84T-6312-D), remove fan and clutch assembly. Remove water pump pulley. Disconnect coolant hoses from water pump. Remove water pump.

Installation - 1) Clean all gasket mating surfaces. Coat new gasket on both sides with gasket sealer and position gasket on water pump. Install water pump and tighten attaching bolts.

2) To install remaining components, reverse removal procedure. Fill and bleed air from cooling system. See COOLING SYSTEM BLEEDING under REMOVAL & INSTALLATION.

OIL PAN

Removal (Bronco & "F" Series) - 1) Drain engine oil and cooling system. Remove upper intake manifold and throttle body. See INTAKE MANIFOLDS under REMOVAL & INSTALLATION. Disconnect negative battery cable. Raise and support vehicle. Remove starter. Remove both front engine mount-to-engine mount bracket nuts.

2) Raise engine and place 1" (25.4 mm) wood blocks between front engine mount insulators and frame brackets. Remove oil pan bolts. Lower pan and remove oil pump bolts and pick-up tube nut. Lower oil pump assembly into pan. Remove pan.

Installation - 1) To install, reverse removal procedure. Apply silicone sealant at front and rear corners of oil pan surface and cylinder block, and where front cover meets the cylinder block.

2) Install oil pan bolts and tighten using specified procedure. *See Fig. 6.* To install remaining components, reverse removal procedure. Tighten bolts to specification. See TORQUE SPECIFICATIONS table at end of article. Fill or top off fluids. Fill and bleed air from cooling system. See COOLING SYSTEM BLEEDING under REMOVAL & INSTALLATION.

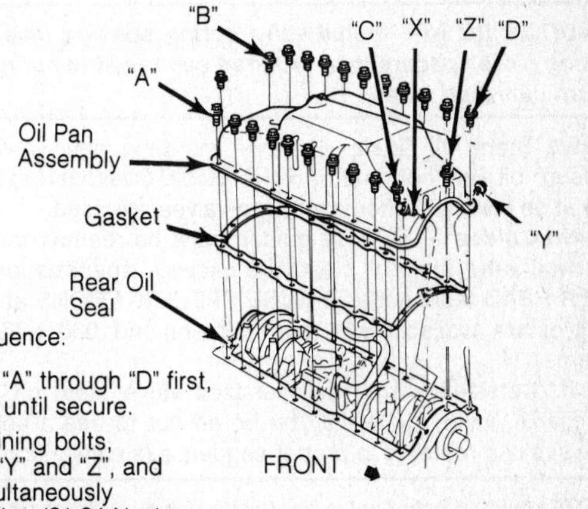

"B"
"C"
"X"
"Z"
"D"
"A"
Oil Pan Assembly
Gasket
"Y"
Rear Oil Seal
FRONT

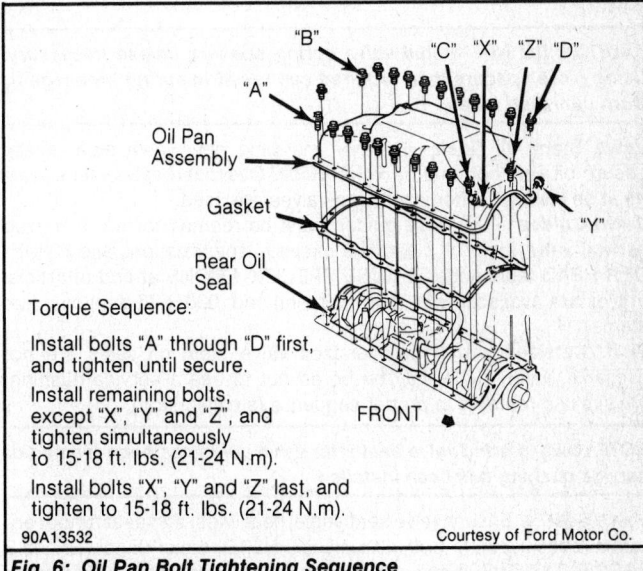

Torque Sequence:

Install bolts "A" through "D" first, and tighten until secure.

Install remaining bolts, except "X", "Y" and "Z", and tighten simultaneously to 15-18 ft. lbs. (21-24 N.m).

Install bolts "X", "Y" and "Z" last, and tighten to 15-18 ft. lbs. (21-24 N.m).

90A13532

Courtesy of Ford Motor Co.

Fig. 6: Oil Pan Bolt Tightening Sequence

1991 ENGINES
4.9L 6-Cylinder (Cont.)

Removal ("E" Series) - 1) Remove engine cover, air cleaner, air inlet tubes and EGR valve. Discharge A/C system and remove A/C compressor (if equipped).

2) Remove upper intake manifold and throttle body. See INTAKE MANIFOLDS & EXHAUST MANIFOLDS under REMOVAL & INSTALLATION. Disconnect thermactor check valve inlet hose and remove check valve. Drain engine oil and cooling system. Remove upper and lower radiator hoses. Unbolt fan shroud and reposition back on cooling fan.

3) On A/T models, disconnect oil cooler lines at radiator and remove transmission oil filler tube. On all models, disconnect exhaust pipe at exhaust manifold. Remove front engine mount nuts. Remove power steering return line clip at the front crossmember. Remove oil dipstick and starter.

4) Raise engine approximately 3" and place wooden block under engine mounts. Remove oil pan bolts. Remove oil pick-up tube from oil pump. Remove oil pan and gaskets.

Installation - 1) To install, reverse removal procedure. Apply silicone sealant at front and rear corners of oil pan surface and cylinder block, and where front cover meets the cylinder block.

2) Install oil pan bolts and tighten using specified procedure. *See Fig. 6.* To install remaining components, reverse removal procedure. Tighten bolts to specification. See TORQUE SPECIFICATIONS table at end of article.

3) Fill or top off fluids. Fill and bleed air from cooling system. See COOLING SYSTEM BLEEDING under REMOVAL & INSTALLATION.

OVERHAUL

CYLINDER HEAD

Cylinder Head - 1) Clean head gasket mating surface. Clean carbon from combustion chambers. DO NOT damage surfaces. Check cylinder head for cracks, burrs, nicks and warpage.

2) Check cylinder head warpage. Resurface cylinder head if warpage exceeds specification. See CYLINDER HEAD table under ENGINE SPECIFICATIONS at end of article. DO NOT machine more than .010" (.25 mm) from original cylinder head surface.

Valve Springs - 1) Measure valve spring installed height from surface of cylinder head spring pad to underside of spring retainer. If installed height is not within specification, a .03" (.8 mm) shim can be installed between cylinder head and valve spring to obtain correct height.

2) Inspect valve spring free length and pressure. Replace valve spring if free length and pressure are not within specification. See VALVES & VALVE SPRINGS table under ENGINE SPECIFICATIONS at end of article.

CAUTION: DO NOT install valve spring spacers unless necessary. Using more spacers than required can result in spring breakage or worn camshaft lobes.

Valve Stem Oil Seals - When installing new valve stem seals, ensure oil seal bottoms on valve guide. Oversized valve stem seals must be installed when oversized valves are used.

Valve Guides - 1) Valve guides must be reamed for an oversized valve if valve stem oil clearance exceeds specification. See CYLINDER HEAD table under ENGINE SPECIFICATIONS at end of article. Valves are available with .015" (.38 mm) and .030" (.76 mm) oversize stems.

2) If oversized valves or oversized valve stem oil seals are not available, valve guide may be bored out to use a service bushing. Always use reamers in proper sequence (smallest first).

NOTE: Always grind valve seat after valve guide has been reamed or service bushing has been installed.

Valve Seat - Ensure valve seat angle, seat width and seat runout are within specification. See CYLINDER HEAD table under ENGINE SPECIFICATIONS at end of article. Valve seats must be ground when valve guide is reamed or replaced. Seat replacement information is not available from manufacturer.

Valves - 1) Ensure head diameter, valve face runout, stem diameter and valve margin are within specification. See VALVES & VALVE SPRINGS table under ENGINE SPECIFICATIONS at end of article.

2) Oversize valves are available in .015" (.38 mm) and .030" (.76 mm). When servicing valve stem tip, DO NOT remove more than .010" (.25) from end of valve stem.

Seat Correction Angles - Grind valve seat to a true 45-degree angle. If seat width is too wide after grinding, use a 30-degree stone to lower seat or a 60-degree stone to raise seat. See CYLINDER HEAD table under ENGINE SPECIFICATIONS at end of article.

CYLINDER BLOCK ASSEMBLY

CAUTION: NEVER cut into ring travel area more than 1/32" when removing ridge ring at top of bore.

Piston & Rod Assembly - Note direction of connecting rod installation on piston before removal. Ensure pistons and rods are installed in cylinder from which they were removed. When installing piston in bore, ensure arrow on top of piston is facing front of engine and bearing tang on connecting rod is facing camshaft. *See Fig. 7.*

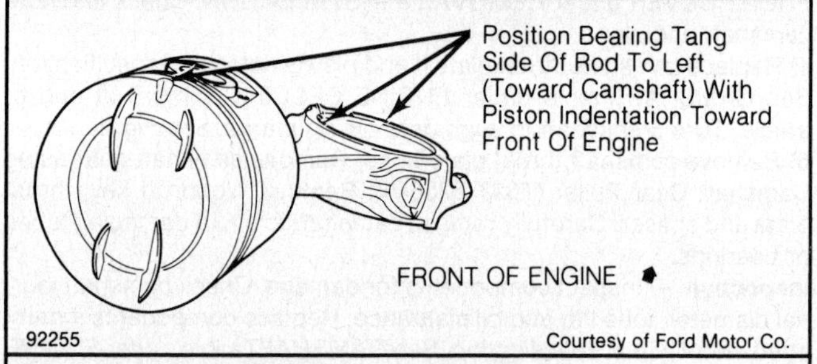
Position Bearing Tang Side Of Rod To Left (Toward Camshaft) With Piston Indentation Toward Front Of Engine
FRONT OF ENGINE
92255
Courtesy of Ford Motor Co.

Fig. 7: Positioning Piston on Connecting Rod

NOTE: Make all measurements with piston and block at normal room temperature of 70°F (21°C).

Fitting Pistons - 1) Check piston-to-bore clearance. See PISTONS, PINS & RINGS table under ENGINE SPECIFICATIONS at end of article. Standard size pistons are color-coded Red, Blue or Yellow on the piston dome. See PISTONS, PINS & RINGS table. Oversize pistons are also available.

2) If bore diameter is in lower one-third of specification, use a Red coded piston. If bore diameter is in middle one-third of specification, use a Blue coded piston. If bore diameter is in upper one-third of specification, use Yellow coded piston. Use proper size piston to obtain specified clearance. See PISTONS, PINS & RINGS table under ENGINE SPECIFICATIONS at end of article.

Piston Rings - 1) Select rings for bore diameter. Place ring in cylinder bore in which it will be installed. Use piston to square ring in bore and place ring below normal ring wear area. Measure ring end gap. If ring gap is not within specification, try another ring set. See PISTONS, PINS & RINGS table under ENGINE SPECIFICATIONS at end of article.

2) Check side clearance of rings after installing on piston. Ensure clearance is within specification around entire circumference. Replace piston and/or rings if clearance is not within specification. See PISTONS, PINS & RINGS table under ENGINE SPECIFICATIONS at end of article. Ensure rings are properly spaced on piston before installing pistons into cylinder. *See Fig. 8.*

Piston Pin Replacement - 1) Remove bearing inserts from connecting rod and cap. Mark pistons and pins to ensure assembly to original location. Remove piston rings. Using a press and Piston Pin Remover/Replacer (T68P-6135-A), press piston pin from piston and connecting rod.

2) Before assembling piston and rod, ensure connecting rod pin bore diameter and piston diameter are within specification. See PISTONS, PINS & RINGS table under ENGINE SPECIFICATIONS at end of article. Apply light coat of engine oil to parts to be assembled. When

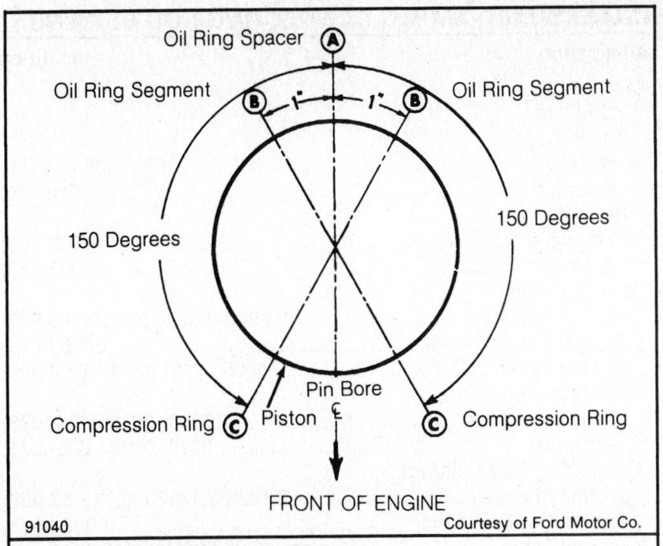

Oil Ring Spacer
A
Oil Ring Segment
B
1"
1"
B
Oil Ring Segment
150 Degrees
150 Degrees
Pin Bore
Compression Ring
C
Piston
C
Compression Ring
FRONT OF ENGINE
91040
Courtesy of Ford Motor Co.

Fig. 8: Positioning Rings on Piston

installing piston pin, ensure piston and connecting rod are assembled as shown. *See Fig. 7.*

Rod Bearings – 1) Use Plastigage method and check rod bearing clearance. If proper oil clearance cannot be obtained with standard bearings, try a combination of undersize bearings. DO NOT use any other bearing combination other than what is listed. See UNDERSIZE MAIN & ROD BEARING COMBINATIONS table.
2) If bearing combinations cannot bring clearance within specification, machine or replace crankshaft as necessary. Always replace bearings in pairs. See CRANKSHAFT, MAIN & CONNECTING ROD BEARINGS table under ENGINE SPECIFICATIONS at end of article.

UNDERSIZE MAIN & ROD BEARING COMBINATIONS [1]

Excess Bearing Clearance In. (mm)	Use Upper Bearing In. (mm)	Use Lower Bearing In. (mm)
.0-.0005 (.0-.013)	.001 (.025)	[2]
.0005-0010 (.013-.026)	.001 (.025)	.001 (.025)
.0010-.0015 (.026-.039)	.002 (.050)	.001 (.025)
.0015-.0020 (.039-.052)	.002 (.050)	.002 (.050)

[1] – DO NOT use any other bearing combination other than what is listed. If use of bearing combinations does not bring clearance within specification, machine or replace crankshaft as necessary.
[2] – Use standard bearing.

Crankshaft & Main Bearings – 1) When checking main bearing clearance in vehicle, position a jack under adjoining bearing counterweight being checked. Remove only one main bearing cap at a time.
2) Use Plastigage method and check main bearing clearance. If proper oil clearance cannot be obtained with standard bearings, try a combination of undersize bearings. DO NOT use any other bearing combination other than what is listed. See UNDERSIZE MAIN & ROD BEARING COMBINATIONS table.
3) If use of bearing combinations does not bring clearance within specification, machine or replace crankshaft as necessary. Always replace bearings in pairs. See CRANKSHAFT, MAIN & CONNECTING ROD BEARINGS table under ENGINE SPECIFICATIONS at end of article.
4) Install all bearing caps except thrust bearing cap (No. 5 from front of engine). Tighten main bearing cap bolts to 60-70 ft. lbs. (81-95 N.m). Install No. 5 bearing cap and tighten bolts finger tight. Pry crankshaft forward and pry No. 5 bearing cap to rear of engine to align thrust bearing. While retaining forward pressure on crankshaft, tighten bearing cap to 60-70 ft. lbs. (81-95 N.m).
5) Ensure crankshaft end play is within specification. Replace thrust bearing if end play is not within specification. See CRANKSHAFT, MAIN & CONNECTING ROD BEARINGS table under ENGINE SPECIFICATIONS at end of article.

Cylinder Block – 1) Using a feeler gauge and straightedge, check cylinder block head gasket surface for warpage. Check cylinder bore for wear, taper, out-of-round and piston fit. See CYLINDER BLOCK table under ENGINE SPECIFICATIONS at end of article.

CAUTION: DO NOT machine more than .010" (.25 mm) of material from original cylinder block head surface.

2) Install all main bearing caps and tighten to specification before honing cylinder bore. Ensure bearing caps are installed in their original location, with arrow on cap pointing towards front of engine.
3) Use ONLY a spring-loaded type cylinder hone. After honing, thoroughly clean bore with detergent and water solution. Rinse solution from bore thoroughly with clean water. Wipe bore clean with lint free cloth. Lubricate cylinder bores with engine oil.

ENGINE OILING

ENGINE LUBRICATION SYSTEM

Oil supply from pan is forced through lubrication system by rotor oil pump. Oil flows through full-flow oil filter, which routes oil into main oil gallery. *See Fig. 9.*

Oil gallery supplies oil to all internal engine bearings and lifters. Oil from lifters is forced through push rods to lubricate valve train. Timing gears are lubricated by splash method. Spring-loaded oil pressure relief valve is located in pump body and is nonadjustable.

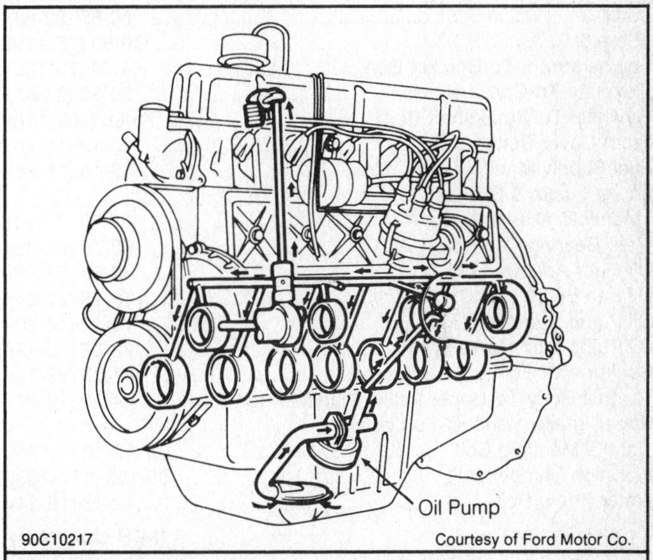

Oil Pump
90C10217
Courtesy of Ford Motor Co.

Fig. 9: Cross-Sectional View of Engine Oil Circuit

Crankcase Capacity – Crankcase capacity is 5 qts. (4.75L). Add 1 qt. (.95L) when replacing oil filter.
Oil Pressure – Normal oil pressure at 2000 RPM should be 40-60 psi (2.8-4.2 kg/cm²) with engine at normal operating temperature.

OIL PUMP

Removal & Disassembly – Remove oil pan. See OIL PAN under REMOVAL & INSTALLATION. On "F" Series, remove oil pump from oil pan. On "E" Series, remove oil pump retaining bolts and remove oil pump assembly. On all models, disassemble oil pump. Note location of component installation for reassembly reference.
Inspection – Inspect components for damage. Measure rotor end play, rotor tip clearance and outer rotor-to-housing clearance. Measure relief valve-to-bore clearance and relief valve tension. Replace oil pump assembly if measurements are not within specifications. See OIL PUMP SPECIFICATIONS table.

NOTE: Oil pump is serviced as an assembly. Replace assembly if out of specification. See OIL PUMP SPECIFICATIONS table.

1991 ENGINES
4.9L 6-Cylinder (Cont.)

OIL PUMP SPECIFICATIONS

Application	Specification In. (mm)
Outer Rotor-To-Housing Clearance	.001-.013 (.03-.33)
Relief Valve Spring Tension	[1]
Relief Valve-To-Bore Clearance	.0015-.0030 (.038-.076)
Rotor End Play	.004 (.10) Max.
Rotor Tip Clearance	.012 (.31) Max.
Shaft-To-Housing Clearance	.0015-.0030 (.038-.076)

[1] - Spring tension is 20.6-22.6 lbs.@ 2.49" (9.3-10.3 kg @ 63.2 mm).

Reassembly & Installation – 1) To reassemble, reverse disassembly procedure. Ensure components are installed in original location. To install, prime oil pump by filling inlet opening with oil and rotating pump shaft until oil emerges from outlet opening.

2) Install oil pump-to-cylinder block bolt and tighten to specification. See TORQUE SPECIFICATIONS table. To complete installation, reverse removal procedure.

TORQUE SPECIFICATIONS

TORQUE SPECIFICATIONS

Application	Ft. Lbs. (N.m)
Bellhousing-To-Engine Bolt	40-50 (54-68)
Camshaft Thrust Plate Bolt	12-18 (16-24)
Connecting Rod Cap Nut	40-45 (54-61)
Cylinder Head Bolt [1]	
Step 1	50-55 (68-75)
Step 2	60-65 (82-88)
Step 3	70-85 (95-116)
Engine Mount-To-Bracket Bolt	54-74 (73-100)
Flexplate-To-Converter Bolt	20-30 (27-41)
Flywheel-To-Crankshaft Bolt	75-85 (102-116)
Front Cover Bolt	12-18 (16-24)
Fuel Supply Manifold Bolt	12-15 (16-20)
Lower Intake & Exhaust Manifold Assembly Nut [2]	22-32 (30-44)
Main Bearing Cap Bolt	60-70 (82-95)
Oil Filter Adapter Bolt	40-50 (54-68)
Oil Pan Bolt	15-18 (21-24)
Oil Pump Attaching Bolt	10-12 (14-20)
Oil Pump Pick-Up Tube Nut	22-32 (30-43)
Rocker Arm Bolt	17-23 (23-31)
Throttle Body-To-Upper Intake Manifold Bolt	14-20 (19-27)
Upper Intake Manifold-To-Lower Intake Manifold Bolt	12-18 (16-24)
Vibration Damper Bolt	130-150 (177-203)
Water Pump Bolt	12-18 (16-24)
	INCH Lbs. (N.m)
Rocker Arm Cover Bolt [3]	70-105 (8-12)

[1] – Tighten in sequence. *See Fig. 3.*
[2] – Tighten in sequence. *See Fig. 2.*
[3] – Starting with middle bolt, tighten in a circular pattern.

ENGINE SPECIFICATIONS

GENERAL SPECIFICATIONS

Application	Specification
4.9L	
Displacement	300 Cu. In. (4.9L)
Bore	4.00" (101.6 mm)
Stroke	3.98" (101.1 mm)
Compression Ratio	8.8:1
Fuel System	PFI
Horsepower @ RPM	145 @ 3400
Torque Ft. Lbs. @ RPM	260 @ 2000

CRANKSHAFT, MAIN & CONNECTING ROD BEARINGS

Application	In. (mm)
4.9L	
Crankshaft	
End Play	
Standard	.004-.008 (.10-.20)
Wear Limit	.012 (.30)
Runout	
Standard	.002 (.05)
Wear Limit	.005 (.13)
Main Bearings	
Journal Diameter	2.3982-2.3990 (60.914-60.935)
Journal Out-Of-Round	.0006 (.015)
Journal Taper	.0005 (.013) per 1" (25.4 mm)
Oil Clearance	
Desired	.0008-.0015 (.020-.038)
Allowable	.0010-.0028 (.025-.071)
Connecting Rod Bearings	
Journal Diameter	2.1228-2.1236 (53.919-53.939)
Journal Out-Of-Round	.0006 (.015)
Journal Taper	.0006 (.015) per 1" (25.4 mm)
Oil Clearance	
Desired	.0008-.0015 (.020-038)
Allowable	.0007-.0024 (.018-.061)

CONNECTING RODS

Application	In. (mm)
4.9L	
Bore Diameter	
Pin Bore	.9734-.9742 (24.724-24.745)
Crankpin Bore	2.2750-2.2758 (57.785-57.805)
Crankpin Bearing Bore Out-Of-Round	.0006 (.015)
Center-To-Center Length	6.2082-6.2112 (157.688-157.764)
Maximum Bend [1]	.012 (.30)
Maximum Twist [1]	.024 (.61)
Side Play	
Standard	.006-.013 (.15-.33)
Wear Limit	.018 (.46)

[1] – Specification listed is measured at the ends of an 8" (203 mm) bar, 4" (102 mm) on each side of rod center line.

PISTONS, PINS & RINGS

Application	In. (mm)
4.9L	
Pistons	
Clearance	.0010-.0018 (.025-.046)
Diameter [1]	
Red Piston	3.9982-3.9988 (101.554-101.570)
Blue Piston	3.9994-4.0000 (101.585-101.600)
Yellow Piston [2]	4.0008-4.0014 (101.620-101.636)
Pins	
Diameter	
Standard	.9749-.9754 (24.762-24.775)
.001" (.03 mm) Oversize	.9760-.9763 (24.790-24.798)
.002" (.05 mm) Oversize	.9770-.9773 (24.816-24.823)
Piston Fit	[2] .0002-.0004 (.005-.010)

[1] – Measured at piston pin bore center line, at 90° angle to piston pin.
[2] – Piston fit is .0003-.0005" (.007-.013 mm) on vehicles under 8500 lbs. GVW.

1991 ENGINES
4.9L 6-Cylinder (Cont.)

PISTONS, PINS & RINGS (Cont.)

Application	In. (mm)
4.9L	
Rings	
No. 1	
End Gap	.010-.020 (.25-.51)
Side Clearance	
Standard	.0019-.0036 (.048-.091)
Wear Limit	.0056 (.142)
No. 2	
End Gap	.010-.020 (.25-.51)
Side Clearance	
Standard	.002-.004 (.05-.10)
Wear Limit	.006 (.15)
No. 3 (Oil)	
End Gap (Steel Rail)	.015-.055 (.38-1.40)
Side Clearance	Snug Fit

CYLINDER BLOCK

Application	In. (mm)
4.9L	
Cylinder Bore	
Standard Diameter	4.0000-4.0048 (101.600-101.722)
Maximum Taper	.010 (.25)
Maximum Out-Of-Round	.0015 (.038)
Maximum Deck Warpage	[1]

[1] – No more than .003" (.08 mm) within a 6" (152 mm) area, and no more than .006" (.15 mm) overall. DO NOT remove more than .010" (.25 mm) material from original deck if machining is required.

VALVES & VALVE SPRINGS

Application	Specification
4.9L	
Face Angle	44°
Head Diameter	
Intake Valve	1.769-1.793" (44.93-45.54 mm)
Exhaust Valve	1.551-1.569" (39.40-39.85 mm)
Minimum Margin	.031" (.79 mm)
Stem Diameter	
Standard	.3416-.3423" (8.677-8.694 mm)
.015 Oversize	.3566-.3573" (9.058-9.075 mm)
.030 Oversize	.3716-.3723" (9.439-9.456 mm)
Valve Springs	
Free Length	
Intake	1.96" (49.78 mm)
Exhaust	1.78" (45.21 mm)
Installed Height	
Intake	1.61-1.67" (40.89-42.42 mm)
Exhaust	1.44-1.50" (36.58-38.10 mm)
Out-Of-Square	.078" (1.98 mm)
Pressure	Lbs. @ In. (Kg @ mm)
Valve Closed	
Intake	66-74 @ 1.640 (30-34 @ 41.65)
Exhaust	66-74 @ 1.470 (30-34 @ 37.34)
Valve Open	
Intake	166-184 @ 1.240 (75-83 @ 31.50)
Exhaust	166-184 @ 1.070 (75-83 @ 27.18)

CYLINDER HEAD

Application	Specification
4.9L	
Maximum Warpage	[1]
Valve Seats	
Seat Angle	45°
Seat Width	
Intake	.060-.080" (1.52-2.03 mm)
Exhaust	.070-.090" (1.78-2.29 mm)
Maximum Seat Runout	.002" (.05 mm)
Valve Guides	
Intake	
Valve Guide I.D.	.3433-.3443" (8.720-8.745 mm)
Valve Stem-To-Guide	
Oil Clearance	
Standard	.0010-.0027" (.025-.069 mm)
Wear Limit	.0055" (.140 mm)

[1] – No more than .006" (.15 mm) within a 6" (152 mm) area, and no more than .007" (.18 mm) overall. DO NOT remove more than .010" (.25 mm) material from original surface if machining is required.

CAMSHAFT

Application	In. (mm)
4.9L	
Journal Diameter	2.017-2.018 (51.23-51.26)
Bearing I.D.	2.019-2.020 (51.28-51.31)
End Play	
Standard	.001-.007 (.03-.18)
Wear Limit	.009 (.23)
Journal Runout	.005 (.13)
Lobe Lift	[1] .249 (6.32)
Maximum Lobe Wear	.005 (.13)
Journal-To-Bearing	
Oil Clearance	
Standard	.001-.003 (.03-.08)
Wear Limit	.006 (.15)

[1] – Lobe lift is .247" (6.27 mm) on F150 (Federal emissions) with 2.47:1 or 2.75:1 axle ratio and manual transmission.

VALVE LIFTERS

Application	In. (mm)
4.9L	
Lifter Diameter	.8740-.8745 (22.200-22.212)
Oil Clearance	
Standard	.0007-.0027 (.018-.069)
Wear Limit	.005 (.13)

1991 ENGINES
5.0L & 5.8L V8

Bronco, "E" & "F" Series

NOTE: For repair procedures not covered in this article, see ENGINE OVERHAUL PROCEDURES article in GENERAL INFORMATION.

ENGINE IDENTIFICATION

Engine may be identified by the eighth character of the Vehicle Identification Number (VIN). VIN plate is attached to upper left corner of instrument panel, near windshield. The VIN is also found on the Safety Compliance Certification Label on left door or left door pillar.

VIN ENGINE CODES

Engine	Code
5.0L PFI	N
5.8L PFI	H

ADJUSTMENTS

VALVE CLEARANCE ADJUSTMENT

NOTE: The use of positive stop rocker arm bolts eliminates the need to adjust valve clearance. If valve seat/face has been serviced or worn parts are suspected, check valve clearance.

1) Using a remote starter (ignition off), rotate crankshaft until No. 1 piston is at TDC of compression stroke. Reference mark "A" indicates TDC. With No. 1 piston at TDC, mark references "B" and "C", at about 90 degrees apart. *See Fig. 1.*

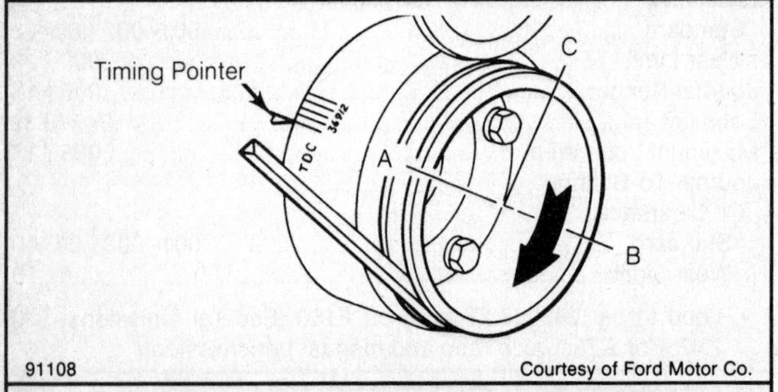
Timing Pointer
TDC
C
A
B
91108
Courtesy of Ford Motor Co.

Fig. 1: Identifying Crankshaft Positions for Valve Adjustment

2) Slowly bleed lifter down (until bottomed) using Tappet Bleed Down Wrench (T71P-6513-B) on appropriate cylinder. See VALVE CLEARANCE ADJUSTMENT table. With lifter plunger bottomed, use a feeler gauge to measure clearance between rocker arm and valve stem tip. See VALVE LIFTERS table under ENGINE SPECIFICATIONS at end of article.

3) If clearance is insufficient, install .060" (1.52 mm) undersize push rod. If clearance is excessive, install .060" (1.52 mm) oversize push rod. Check and/or adjust valve clearance on proper cylinders in relation to crankshaft position. See VALVE CLEARANCE ADJUSTMENT table.

VALVE CLEARANCE ADJUSTMENT

Crankshaft Position	Check Intake Nos.	Check Exhaust Nos.
5.0L		
"A"	1, 7, 8	1, 5, 4
"B"	5, 4	2, 6
"C"	2, 3, 6	7, 3, 8
5.8L		
"A"	1, 4, 8	1, 3, 7
"B"	3, 7	2, 6
"C"	2, 5, 6	4, 5, 8

REMOVAL & INSTALLATION

NOTE: For reassembly reference, label all electrical connectors, vacuum hoses and fuel lines before removal. Also place mating marks on engine hood and other major assemblies before removal.

FUEL PRESSURE RELEASE

Remove fuel cap to release fuel tank pressure. Remove relief valve cap. Relief valve is located on fuel rail. Connect fuel pressure gauge to relief valve. Release fuel pressure into a suitable container.

COOLING SYSTEM BLEEDING

WARNING: When engine is operating, NEVER remove radiator cap under any conditions. Failure to follow instruction could damage cooling system or engine, or cause personal injury. Always wrap protective material around radiator cap to avoid injury from hot steam or hot coolant.

1) Fill cooling system with 50/50 mixture of water and coolant. Pause several minutes for circulation. Fill radiator to filler neck seat. Disconnect heater outlet hose at water pump to bleed off trapped air. Fill radiator until coolant begins to escape.

2) Connect heater outlet hose. Fill radiator until coolant is between the cap seal in the filler neck to 1.5" (38 mm) below cap seal. Install radiator cap. Start engine and allow to warm up. Shut engine off. Allow engine to cool. Remove radiator cap and check coolant level. Top off radiator coolant as necessary.

ENGINE

Removal (Bronco & "F" Series) – 1) Drain cooling system and crankcase. Mark hood hinges and remove hood. Disconnect battery and ground cables from cylinder block. Disconnect EGR tube (if equipped). On 5.0L models, remove air intake hoses, PCV tube and carbon canister hose.

2) On 5.8L models, remove air cleaner and intake duct assembly with crankcase ventilation and carbon canister hoses attached. On all models, disconnect radiator hoses. Disconnect transmission cooler lines (if equipped). Disconnect oil cooler lines at oil filter adapter (if equipped).

3) Disconnect power steering hoses and thermactor hoses. On models with A/C, discharge A/C system. Disconnect hoses at compressor and remove A/C condenser. On all models, remove fan shroud, spacer, pulley and radiator. Remove and position alternator aside.

4) Remove brackets for thermactor pump, power steering pump, alternator and A/C compressor. Disconnect oil pressure sending unit wire. Release fuel pressure. See FUEL PRESSURE RELEASE under REMOVAL & INSTALLATION. Using Disconnect Tool (D87L-9280-A) for 3/8" line or (D87L-9280-B) for 1/2" line, disconnect fuel supply and return lines. *See Fig. 2.*

5) If hairpin-type clip is used, remove hairpin by bending tab downward so it will clear body. Using your hands, spread clip legs .125" (3 mm) and push legs into fitting. Pull hairpin clip from fitting. *See Fig. 2.* Disconnect accelerator cable, transmission shift rod and speed control linkages from throttle body.

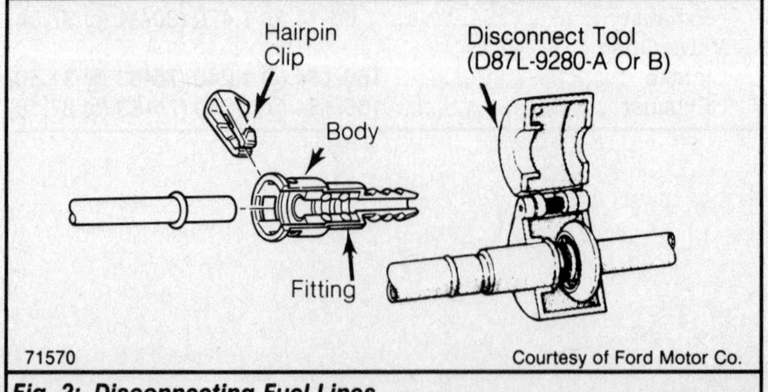
Hairpin Clip
Disconnect Tool (D87L-9280-A Or B)
Body
Fitting
71570
Courtesy of Ford Motor Co.

Fig. 2: Disconnecting Fuel Lines

6) Disconnect throttle bracket from upper intake manifold and set aside with cables attached. Disconnect vacuum lines, carbon canister hose, heater hoses and electrical wiring from engine. Disconnect primary wire at coil and brake booster hose at engine.

7) Remove bellhousing-to-engine upper bolts. Raise front of vehicle. Remove starter. Separate exhaust pipes from manifolds. Disconnect engine mounts from brackets on frame. On A/T models, remove converter inspection plate and flex plate-to-converter bolts.

8) On all models, remove remaining bellhousing-to-engine bolts. Lower vehicle and support transmission. Attach engine hoist and carefully separate engine from transmission. Carefully lift engine from vehicle without damaging rear cover plate.

Installation – To install, reverse removal procedure. Tighten bolts to specification. See TORQUE SPECIFICATIONS table at end of article. Check and top off all engine fluids. Fill and bleed air from cooling system. See COOLING SYSTEM BLEEDING under REMOVAL & INSTALLATION.

Removal ("E" Series) – 1) Remove engine cover. Disconnect battery. Drain cooling system. Remove grille assembly and gravel deflector. Remove air cleaner, air ducts and closure hose (if equipped). Remove hood lock support and condenser upper mounting brackets (if equipped).

2) Discharge A/C system. Remove A/C condenser. Disconnect lines at A/C compressor and remove compressor (if equipped). Remove accelerator cable bracket. Disconnect cruise control linkage (if equipped). Disconnect radiator hoses from radiator and heater hoses from engine.

3) Disconnect A/T lines at radiator (if equipped). Remove fan, shroud and radiator. Disconnect EGR tube (if equipped). Disconnect oil cooler lines at oil filter adapter (if equipped). Disconnect alternator wiring. Remove alternator belt.

4) Remove power steering pump, thermactor pump and alternator. Remove accessory brackets complete with accessories. Disconnect throttle linkage from throttle body and remove cable bracket.

5) On A/T models, remove shift rod. Release fuel pressure. See FUEL PRESSURE RELEASE under REMOVAL & INSTALLATION. Disconnect fuel inlet and return lines using Disconnect Tool (D87L-9280-A or B). *See Fig. 2.* Raise and support vehicle. Drain crankcase and remove oil filter.

6) Disconnect exhaust pipes from manifolds. Disconnect transmission filler tube from right cylinder head (if equipped). Remove engine mount attaching bolts and nuts. Remove starter wiring and remove starter.

7) Remove bellhousing bolts (M/T). On A/T vehicles, remove converter inspection cover bolts. Remove flex plate-to-converter nuts. Remove adapter plate-to-bellhousing bolts. Remove bellhousing lower bolts.

8) On all models, remove ground strap from engine block. Lower vehicle and support transmission. Disconnect engine wiring loom and position aside. Install Lifting Bracket (T75T-6000-A) to intake manifold. Remove upper bellhousing-to-engine bolts. Attach lifting device to engine. Carefully move engine forward and remove from vehicle.

Installation – To install, reverse removal procedure. Tighten bolts to specification. See TORQUE SPECIFICATIONS table at end of article. Check and top off all engine fluids. Fill and bleed air from cooling system. See COOLING SYSTEM BLEEDING under REMOVAL & INSTALLATION.

INTAKE MANIFOLDS

Removal (Upper) – 1) Disconnect negative battery cable. Drain cooling system. Mark and disconnect electrical connectors at upper intake components. Disconnect throttle linkage by prying with screwdriver. DO NOT pull off by hand. Disconnect kickdown linkage. Remove throttle linkage cable bracket.

2) Mark and disconnect vacuum lines at upper intake. Disconnect PCV hose from rear of upper intake. Remove 2 canister purge lines from throttle body. Disconnect heater hoses attached to throttle body. Disconnect EGR tube from EGR valve.

3) Remove upper intake support bracket. Remove 6 upper intake manifold mounting bolts. Remove upper intake manifold and throttle body as an assembly. Remove intake manifold gasket.

Installation – 1) Ensure gasket mating surfaces are clean and flat. Install new gasket on lower intake manifold. If available, install 2 guide pins in opposite corners. Install upper intake manifold and tighten bolts finger tight.

2) Evenly tighten bolts to specification. See TORQUE SPECIFICATIONS table at end of article. To complete installation, reverse removal procedure. Fill and bleed air from cooling system. See COOLING SYSTEM BLEEDING under REMOVAL & INSTALLATION.

Removal (Lower) – 1) Release fuel pressure. See FUEL PRESSURE RELEASE under REMOVAL & INSTALLATION. Disconnect negative battery cable. Using Disconnect Tool (D87L-9280-A or B), disconnect fuel supply and return line. *See Fig. 2.*

2) If hairpin-type retainer is used, remove hairpin by bending tab downward so it will clear body. Using your hands, spread clip legs .125" (3 mm) and push legs into fitting. Pull hairpin clip from fitting. *See Fig. 2.*

3) Remove upper intake manifold as previously described. Remove distributor cap and plug wires as an assembly. Position engine on No. 1 cylinder TDC of compression stroke. Align TDC marks on crankshaft damper with front cover index plate. Mark and remove distributor assembly.

4) Mark and disconnect electrical connectors and vacuum hoses from lower manifold. Remove fuel injector wiring harness. Note oxygen sensor wire-to-stud location for installation reference, and remove ground wire. Remove upper radiator hose, by-pass hose and heater outlet hose.

5) Remove air cleaner bracket. Remove ignition coil bracket and set aside. Remove lower intake manifold bolts evenly. Remove lower intake manifold and gaskets.

Installation – 1) Clean gasket mating surfaces. Apply a 1/16" (1.6 mm) bead of silicone rubber sealer on full width of each intake manifold seal (4 places). Install new lower intake manifold gaskets on cylinder block and heads.

2) Ensure gaskets are interlocked with end rubber gaskets. Install 2 guide pins in opposite corners. Install lower intake manifold and tighten bolts finger tight. Tighten bolts evenly in sequence to specification. *See Fig. 3.* See TORQUE SPECIFICATIONS table at end of article. To complete installation, reverse removal procedure. Fill and bleed air from cooling system. See COOLING SYSTEM BLEEDING under REMOVAL & INSTALLATION.

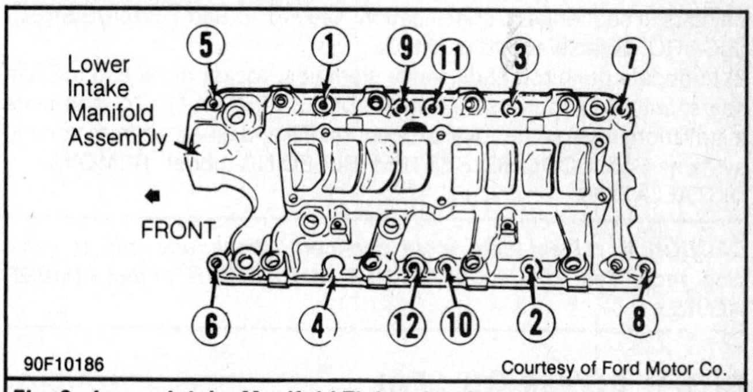
Lower
Intake
Manifold
Assembly
FRONT
5
1
9
11
3
7
6
4
12
10
2
8
90F10186
Courtesy of Ford Motor Co.

Fig. 3: Lower Intake Manifold Tightening Sequence

EXHAUST MANIFOLD

Removal – 1) Remove air cleaner, intake duct assembly and crankcase ventilation hose. Remove inlet pipe(s) from exhaust manifold. Remove exhaust manifold heat shield (if equipped).

2) On left exhaust manifold, remove dipstick tube, speed control bracket and exhaust heat control valve. On all exhaust manifolds, remove exhaust manifold bolts and remove manifold(s).

Installation – Ensure gasket mating surfaces are clean and flat. Install exhaust manifold and bolts. Tighten bolts, starting from center and moving outward, to specification. See TORQUE SPECIFICATIONS table at end of article. To complete installation, reverse removal procedure.

1991 ENGINES
5.0L & 5.8L V8 (Cont.)

CYLINDER HEAD

Removal - 1) Remove lower intake manifold. See INTAKE MANIFOLDS under REMOVAL & INSTALLATION. Remove valve cover(s). On right cylinder head, remove alternator and air pump mounting bracket complete with accessories. Swing alternator down and position aside.

2) On "E" Series, remove ignition coil. On left cylinder head, remove air cleaner inlet duct. Remove A/C compressor and power steering bracket. Remove oil dipstick tube and speed control bracket (if equipped).

3) On all applications, disconnect exhaust manifold(s) from muffler inlet pipe(s). Loosen rocker arm bolts and pivot rocker arm off push rods. Mark push rods for installation reference and remove.

4) On "E" Series, remove air supply tube assembly from rear of cylinder head. On "F" Series, disconnect thermactor air supply hoses at check valves and plug check valve. On all models, remove cylinder head bolts in reverse order of tightening sequence. *See Fig. 4.* Remove cylinder head and gasket.

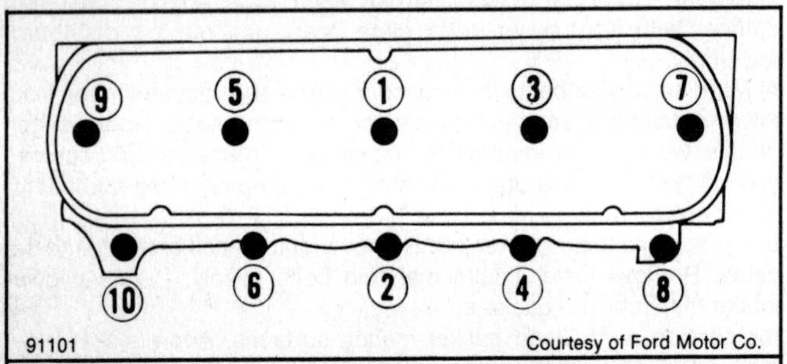
9
5
1
3
7
10
6
2
4
8
91101
Courtesy of Ford Motor Co.

Fig. 4: Cylinder Head Bolt Tightening Sequence

Inspection - Inspect cylinder head for warpage. Resurface if warpage exceeds specification. See CYLINDER HEAD table under ENGINE SPECIFICATIONS at end of article. DO NOT machine more than .010" (.25 mm) from original cylinder head thickness. Clean and tap cylinder head bolt holes in cylinder block.

Installation - 1) Ensure gasket mating surfaces are clean and flat. Properly install new cylinder head gasket as marked on gasket. DO NOT use sealer on head gasket. Install cylinder head and bolts. Tighten bolts in sequence to specification. *See Fig. 4.* See TORQUE SPECIFICATIONS table at end of article.

2) Lubricate push rod ends, valve stem tips, rocker arms and fulcrum seats with Multipurpose Grease (DOAZ-19584-AA). To complete installation, reverse removal procedure. Fill and bleed air from cooling system. See COOLING SYSTEM BLEEDING under REMOVAL & INSTALLATION.

CAUTION: If valves/seats were serviced, check and adjust valve clearance. See VALVE CLEARANCE ADJUSTMENT under ADJUSTMENTS.

FRONT COVER OIL SEAL

NOTE: Front cover seal can be replaced without removing front the cover. Use Seal Remover (T70P-6B070-B) and Seal Installer (T70P-6B070-A) to remove and install cover seal.

Removal - 1) Remove fan shroud attaching bolts. Remove fan, clutch and shroud. Remove serpentine drive belt. Remove crankshaft pulley and damper. Place Seal Remover (T70P-6B070-B) onto front cover plate over front seal.

2) Tighten 2 bolts, forcing seal remover under seal flange. Alternately tighten 2 bolts one-half turn at a time until seal is removed from engine.

Installation - Coat new seal with Lubriplate. Using Seal Installer (T70P-6B070-A), install new front cover seal. Ensure seal is fully seated and spring is properly positioned in seal. To complete installation, reverse removal procedure.

ENGINE FRONT COVER

Removal (Bronco & "F" Series) - 1) Drain cooling system. Loosen fan clutch bolts. Remove fan shroud-to-radiator bolts (if equipped), and position shroud over fan. Remove idler pulley belt. Remove all hoses and brackets attached to water pump.

2) Remove fan, clutch and pulley. Remove fan shroud (if equipped). Remove crankshaft pulley bolt. Remove crankshaft pulley and damper. Remove oil pan-to-cylinder block front cover bolts. Remove front cover and water pump as an assembly.

3) Cut oil pan gasket even with cylinder block. If replacement of front cover seal is necessary, drive out old seal with pin punch. DO NOT damage front cover seal recess.

Installation - 1) Clean all gasket surfaces. If front cover seal was removed, install new front cover oil seal. Cut and fit new oil pan gasket. Apply sealer to oil pan gasket surface and install new gasket. Coat block and front cover with gasket sealer, and position new gasket on block.

2) Place front cover on cylinder block. Install Front Cover Aligner (T61P-6019-B). It may be necessary to force cover downward slightly to compress pan gasket. Coat front cover bolts with oil-resistant sealer, and install bolts.

3) Tighten oil pan-to-front cover bolts while pushing in on front cover aligner. Tighten front cover bolts. Remove aligner. To complete installation, reverse removal procedure. Fill and bleed air from cooling system. See COOLING SYSTEM BLEEDING under REMOVAL & INSTALLATION.

Removal ("E" Series) - 1) Drain cooling system. Remove upper and lower radiator hoses. Remove radiator. Remove cooling fan and shroud. Raise vehicle on hoist. Remove A/C compressor and power steering pump bracket, and accessories. Remove crankshaft pulley.

2) Remove crankshaft damper using Crankshaft Damper Remover (T-79T-6316-A). Remove oil pan-to-front cover bolts. Remove front cover and water pump as an assembly.

3) If replacement of front cover seal is necessary, drive out old seal with pin punch, taking care not to damage front cover seal recess. Cut oil pan gasket even with cylinder block.

Installation - 1) Clean all gasket surfaces. If front cover seal was removed, install new front cover oil seal. Cut and fit new oil pan gasket. Apply sealer to oil pan gasket surface and install new gasket. Coat block and front cover with gasket sealer and position new gasket on block.

2) Place front cover on cylinder block. It may be necessary to force cover downward slightly to compress pan gasket. Coat front cover bolts with oil-resistant sealer, and install bolts.

3) Tighten oil pan-to-front cover bolts. Tighten front cover bolts to specification. See TORQUE SPECIFICATIONS table at end of article. To complete installation, reverse removal procedure. Fill and bleed air from cooling system. See COOLING SYSTEM BLEEDING under REMOVAL & INSTALLATION.

TIMING CHAIN & SPROCKET

Removal - 1) Position No. 1 piston on TDC of compression stroke. Remove front cover. See ENGINE FRONT COVER under REMOVAL & INSTALLATION. Check alignment of camshaft and crankshaft sprocket timing marks. *See Fig. 5.* Check timing chain deflection.

2) If chain deflection is not within specification, replace timing chain and sprockets. See CAMSHAFT table under ENGINE SPECIFICATIONS at end of article. Remove camshaft sprocket bolt and washer. Slide sprockets and timing chain forward and remove as an assembly.

Installation - Install crankshaft sprocket, camshaft sprocket and timing chain as an assembly. Ensure timing marks are properly aligned. *See Fig. 5.* Apply oil to timing chain and sprockets. To complete installation, reverse removal procedure. Tighten bolts and nuts to specifications. See TORQUE SPECIFICATIONS table at end of article.

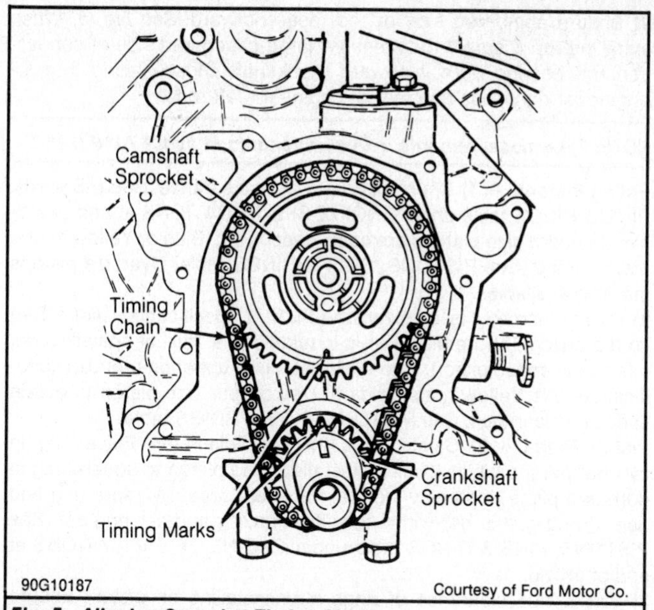
Camshaft
Sprocket
Timing
Chain
Crankshaft
Sprocket
Timing Marks
90G10187
Courtesy of Ford Motor Co.

Fig. 5: Aligning Sprocket Timing Marks

CAMSHAFT

Removal - **1)** On "E" Series, remove front grille. On all models, drain cooling system. Disconnect upper and lower radiator hoses. Disconnect transmission oil cooler lines (if equipped). Remove radiator. Remove engine front cover. See ENGINE FRONT COVER under REMOVAL & INSTALLATION.

2) Remove timing chain. See TIMING CHAIN & SPROCKET under REMOVAL & INSTALLATION. Remove upper intake manifold and throttle body as an assembly. See INTAKE MANIFOLDS under REMOVAL & INSTALLATION. Remove valve covers.

3) Loosen rocker arm fulcrum bolts, and rotate rocker arms to one side. Mark and remove push rods and valve lifters for installation reference. Check camshaft end play. If not within specification, replace camshaft thrust plate. See CAMSHAFT table under ENGINE SPECIFICATIONS.

4) Remove camshaft thrust plate and remove camshaft. Use care to avoid damage to camshaft bearings and journals.

Inspection - Clean all components and gasket mating surfaces. Check lobe lift and camshaft-to-bearing clearance. See CAMSHAFT table under ENGINE SPECIFICATIONS.

Installation - **1)** Oil camshaft journals and apply polyethylene grease to lobes. Carefully slide camshaft into position. Coat camshaft thrust plate with engine oil, and install with groove toward cylinder block.

2) Lubricate lifters with engine oil and install in the bores from which they were removed. Lubricate rocker arms, fulcrum seats, valve stem tips and push rod ends with polyethylene grease before installing.

3) To complete installation, reverse removal procedure; use new gaskets. Check and adjust valve clearance as necessary. See VALVE CLEARANCE ADJUSTMENT under ADJUSTMENTS.

REAR CRANKSHAFT OIL SEAL

Removal - **1)** Disconnect negative battery cable and remove starter. Remove transmission. Remove flywheel/flexplate and engine rear cover plate. Using a sharp awl, punch a hole into seal metal surface, between lip and block.

2) Using Jet Plug Puller (T77L-9533), screw in threaded end of puller. Remove rear oil seal.

NOTE: Use caution to prevent scratching or damaging crankshaft seal surfaces.

Installation - Coat seal surfaces with light engine oil. DO NOT use grease for seal lubrication. Using Seal Installer (T65P-6701-A), install seal until firmly seated. To install remaining components, reverse removal procedure.

WATER PUMP

Removal - **1)** Drain cooling system. Remove air cleaner and duct assembly. Remove fan shroud and position over fan. Remove A/C idler pulley and bracket (if equipped).

2) Remove all hoses and brackets attached to water pump. On "E" Series, remove radiator. On all models, remove all drive belts, fan, spacer, pulley and shroud. Remove water pump-to-front cover bolts and remove pump.

Installation - **1)** Clean all gasket mating surfaces. Coat both sides of new gasket with gasket sealer, and position on cylinder front cover.

2) Install water pump and tighten bolts. To complete installation, reverse removal procedure. Fill and bleed air from cooling system. See COOLING SYSTEM BLEEDING under REMOVAL & INSTALLATION.

OIL PAN

Removal (Bronco & "F" Series) - **1)** Remove fan shroud. Remove upper intake manifold. See INTAKE MANIFOLDS under REMOVAL & INSTALLATION. Remove front engine mount-to-frame nuts. On A/T models, disconnect oil cooler lines from radiator. On all models, disconnect exhaust pipes from exhaust manifold.

2) Drain engine oil. Support transmission and remove transmission crossmember. Remove oil pan bolts and lower oil pan. Remove oil pump bolts and pick-up tube nut. Lower oil pump assembly into pan. Remove oil pan.

Installation - To install, reverse removal procedure. Apply silicone sealant at front and rear corners of oil pan surface and cylinder block, and where front cover meets the cylinder block. To install remaining components, reverse removal procedure.

Removal ("E" Series) - **1)** Disconnect battery. Remove engine cover and air cleaner. Drain cooling system and engine oil. Remove power steering pump and A/C compressor with hoses attached and set aside (if equipped). Remove fan shroud and oil filler tube. Disconnect radiator hoses. Remove oil dipstick tube bolts and remove dipstick.

2) Raise and support vehicle. Remove splash shield from under alternator. On A/T models, disconnect transmission cooler lines at radiator. Remove transmission dipstick and tube. On all models, release fuel pressure. See FUEL PRESSURE RELEASE under REMOVAL & INSTALLATION. Disconnect fuel line at fuel rail.

3) Disconnect exhaust pipes from manifold. On M/T models, disconnect manual linkage at transmission. On all models, remove center drive shaft support and remove drive shaft from transmission. Remove engine mount nuts.

4) Place a transmission jack, with wooden support, under oil pan. Raise engine and transmission assembly. Engine and transmission assembly will pivot around rear engine mount.

5) Engine and transmission assembly must remain centered in engine compartment in order for it to be raised approximately 4" (120 mm) at front engine mounts. Use wooden blocks to support engine assembly in this position.

6) Remove oil pan bolts and lower oil pan. On 5.0L models, remove oil pump bolts and pick-up tube nut. Remove pick-up tube retaining nut from No. 3 main cap. Lower oil pump assembly into pan. On all models, remove oil pan.

Installation - **1)** To install, reverse removal procedure. Apply silicone sealant at front and rear corners of oil pan surface and cylinder block, and where front cover meets the cylinder block. Position new gasket and seals to engine block.

2) Position oil pan with pump to engine, and install oil pump. To complete installation, reverse removal procedure. Fill or top off all fluids. Fill and bleed air from cooling system. See COOLING SYSTEM BLEEDING under REMOVAL & INSTALLATION.

OVERHAUL

CYLINDER HEAD

Cylinder Head - **1)** Clean head gasket mating surface. Clean carbon from combustion chambers. Use care not to damage surfaces. Check cylinder head for cracks, burrs, nicks and warpage.

1991 ENGINES
5.0L & 5.8L V8 (Cont.)

2) DO NOT machine more than .010" (.25 mm) from original cylinder head surface to correct warpage. Replace cylinder head as necessary. See CYLINDER HEAD table under ENGINE SPECIFICATIONS at end of article.

Valve Springs – 1) Measure valve spring installed height from top of spring seat to underside of spring retainer. Ensure installed height is within specification. See VALVES & VALVE SPRINGS table under ENGINE SPECIFICATIONS at end of article.

2) If installed height is not within specification, a .03" (.8 mm) shim can be installed between cylinder head and valve spring to obtain correct height. Inspect valve spring free length and pressure. Replace valve spring if free length and pressure are not within specification. See VALVES & VALVE SPRINGS table.

CAUTION: DO NOT install valve spring spacers unless necessary. Using more spacers than required can result in spring breakage or worn camshaft lobes.

Valve Stem Oil Seals – When installing new valve stem seals, ensure oil seal bottoms on valve guide. Oversized valve stem seals must be installed when oversized valves are used.

Valve Guides – 1) Valve guides must be reamed for an oversized valve if valve stem oil clearance exceeds specification. See CYLINDER HEAD table under ENGINE SPECIFICATIONS at end of article. Valves are available in .015" (.38 mm) and .030" (.76 mm) oversize.

2) If oversized valves or oversized valve stem oil seals are not available, valve guide may be bored out to use a service bushing. Always use reamers in proper sequence (smallest first).

NOTE: Always grind valve seat after valve guide has been reamed or service bushing has been installed.

Valve Seat – Ensure valve seat angle, seat width and seat runout are within specification. See CYLINDER HEAD table under ENGINE SPECIFICATIONS at end of article. Valve seats must be ground when valve guide is reamed or replaced. Replacement information is not available from manufacturer.

Valves – Ensure head diameter, valve face runout, stem diameter and valve margin are within specification. See VALVES & VALVE SPRINGS table under ENGINE SPECIFICATIONS at end of article.

CAUTION: DO NOT remove more than .010" (.25 mm) from end of valve stem when resurfacing tip of valve.

Valve Seat Correction Angles – Grind valve seat to a true 45-degree angle. If seat width is too wide after grinding, use a 30-degree stone to lower seat or a 60-degree stone to raise seat. See CYLINDER HEAD table under ENGINE SPECIFICATIONS at end of article.

CYLINDER BLOCK ASSEMBLY

Piston & Rod Assembly – 1) Ensure pistons and rods are installed in cylinder from which they were removed. Ensure indentation on piston top is positioned as shown in illustration. *See Fig. 6.*

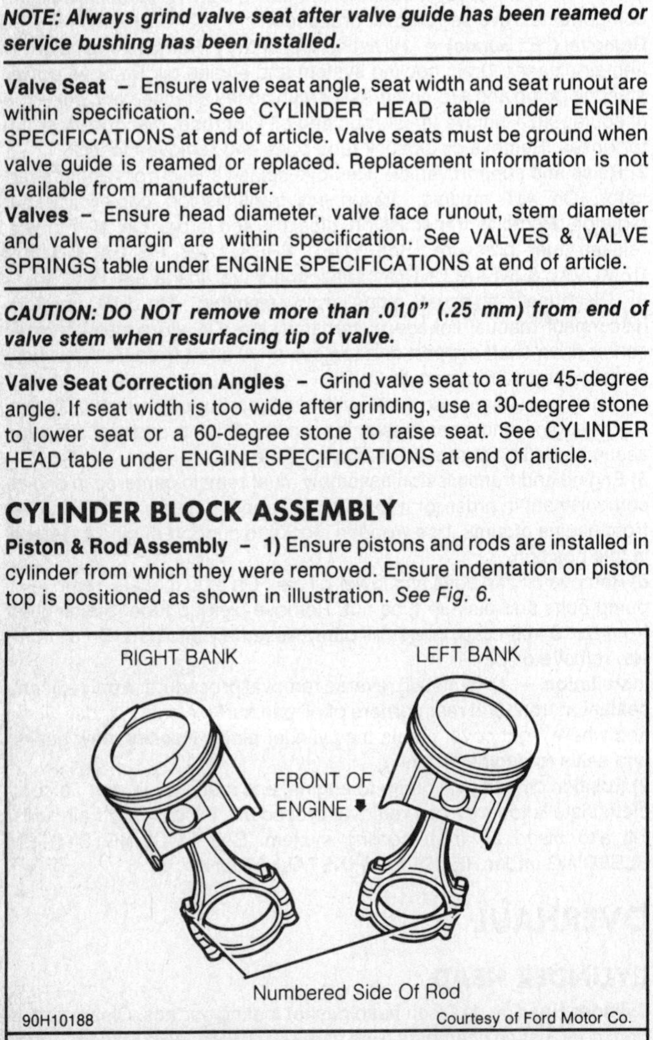
RIGHT BANK
LEFT BANK
FRONT OF ENGINE
Numbered Side Of Rod
90H10188
Courtesy of Ford Motor Co.

Fig. 6: Positioning Piston & Rod

2) Ensure numbered side of rod faces outward. *See Fig. 6.* When installing replacement rods, ensure large-chamfered side of connection rod bearing bore is toward crankshaft cheek, facing front of engine for right rods and rear of engine for left rods.

NOTE: Take measurements with components at about 70°F (21°C).

Fitting Pistons – 1) Check piston-to-bore clearance. See PISTONS, PINS & RINGS table under ENGINE SPECIFICATIONS at end of article. Standard size pistons are color-coded Red, Blue or Yellow on the piston dome. See PISTONS, PINS & RINGS table. Oversize pistons are also available.

2) If bore diameter is in lower one-third of specification, use a Red coded piston. If bore diameter is in middle one-third of specification, use a Blue coded piston. If bore diameter is in upper one-third of specification, use Yellow coded piston. Use proper size piston to obtain specified clearance. See PISTONS, PINS & RINGS table.

Piston Rings – 1) Select rings for bore diameter. Place ring in cylinder bore in which it will be installed. Use piston to square ring in bore and place ring below normal ring wear area. Measure ring end gap. If ring gap is not within specification, try another ring set. See PISTONS, PINS & RINGS table under ENGINE SPECIFICATIONS at end of article.

2) Check side clearance of rings after installing on piston. Ensure clearance is within specification around entire circumference. Replace piston and/or rings if clearance is not within specification. See PISTONS, PINS & RINGS table. Ensure rings are properly spaced on piston before installing pistons into cylinder. *See Fig. 7.*

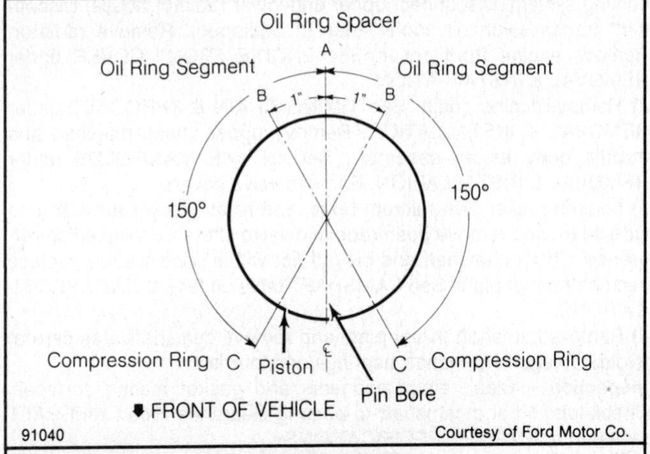
Oil Ring Spacer
A
Oil Ring Segment
Oil Ring Segment
B
1"
1"
B
150°
150°
Compression Ring
C
Piston
℄
C
Compression Ring
Pin Bore
FRONT OF VEHICLE
91040
Courtesy of Ford Motor Co.

Fig. 7: Positioning Piston Ring End Gaps

Rod Bearings – 1) Use Plastigage method and check rod bearing clearance. If proper oil clearance cannot be obtained with standard bearings, try a combination of undersize bearings. DO NOT use any other bearing combination other than what is listed. See UNDERSIZE MAIN & ROD BEARING COMBINATIONS table.

2) If use of bearing combinations does not bring clearance within specification, machine or replace crankshaft as necessary. Always replace bearings in pairs. See CRANKSHAFT, MAIN & CONNECTING ROD BEARINGS table under ENGINE SPECIFICATIONS at end of article.

UNDERSIZE MAIN & ROD BEARING COMBINATIONS [1]

Excess Bearing Clearance In. (mm)	Use Upper Bearing In. (mm)	Use Lower Bearing In. (mm)
.0-.0005 (.0-.013)	.001 (.025)	[2]
.0005-0010 (.013-.026)	.001 (.025)	.001 (.025)
.0010-.0015 (.026-.039)	.002 (.050)	.001 (.025)
.0015-.0020 (.039-.052)	.002 (.050)	.002 (.050)

[1] – DO NOT use any other bearing combination other than what is listed. If use of bearing combinations does not bring clearance within specification, machine or replace crankshaft as necessary.

[2] – Use standard bearing.

Crankshaft & Main Bearings – 1) When checking main bearing clearance in vehicle, position a jack under adjoining bearing counterweight being checked. Remove only one main bearing cap at a time.

2) Use Plastigage method and check main bearing clearance. If proper oil clearance cannot be obtained with standard bearings, try a combination of undersize bearings. DO NOT use any other bearing combination other than what is listed. See UNDERSIZE MAIN & ROD BEARING COMBINATIONS table.

3) If use of bearing combinations does not bring clearance within specification, machine or replace crankshaft as necessary. Always replace bearings in pairs. See CRANKSHAFT, MAIN & CONNECTING ROD BEARINGS table under ENGINE SPECIFICATIONS at end of article.

4) Install all bearing caps except thrust bearing cap (No. 3 from front of engine). Tighten main bearing cap bolts to specification. See TORQUE SPECIFICATIONS table at end of article. Install No. 3 bearing cap and tighten bolts finger tight.

5) Pry crankshaft forward and pry No. 3 bearing cap to rear of engine to align thrust bearing. While retaining forward pressure on crankshaft, tighten bearing cap to specification. See TORQUE SPECIFICATIONS table at end of article.

6) Ensure crankshaft end play is within specification. Replace thrust bearing if end play is not within specification. See CRANKSHAFT, MAIN & CONNECTING ROD BEARINGS table under ENGINE SPECIFICATIONS at end of article.

Cylinder Block – 1) Using a feeler gauge and straightedge, check cylinder block head gasket surface for warpage. Check cylinder bore for wear, taper, out-of-round and piston fit. See CYLINDER BLOCK table under ENGINE SPECIFICATIONS at end of article.

CAUTION: DO NOT machine more than .010" (.25 mm) of material from original cylinder block head surface.

2) Install all main bearing caps and tighten to specification before honing cylinder bore. See TORQUE SPECIFICATIONS table at end of article. Ensure bearing caps are installed in their original location, with arrow on cap pointing towards front of engine.

3) Use ONLY a spring-loaded type cylinder hone. After honing, thoroughly clean bore with detergent and water solution. Rinse solution from bore thoroughly with clean water. Wipe bore clean with lint free cloth. Lubricate cylinder bores with engine oil.

ENGINE OILING

ENGINE LUBRICATION SYSTEM

Engine lubrication system is a force-feed type. The oil is supplied under full pressure to crankshaft, connecting rods, camshaft bearing and valve lifters. A controlled volume of oil is supplied to rocker arms and push rods. All other moving parts are lubricated by splash or gravity flow. Oil flows through oil filter before entering main oil gallery. *See Fig. 8.*

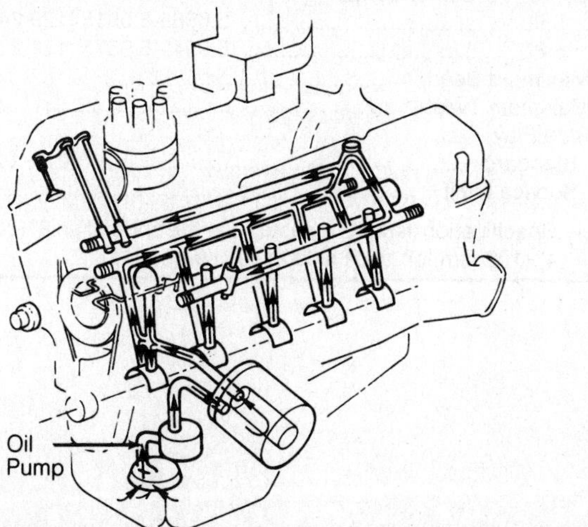
Oil
Pump

90I10189 Courtesy of Ford Motor Co.

Fig. 8: Cross-Sectional View of Engine Oil Circuit

Crankcase Capacity – Crankcase capacity is 5 qts. (4.75L). Add one additional quart (.95L) when replacing oil filter.

Oil Pressure – Normal oil pressure at 2000 RPM should be 40-60 psi (2.8-4.2 kg/cm²) with engine at normal operating temperature.

Pressure Relief Valve – Pressure relief valve is located in oil pump and is not adjustable.

OIL PUMP

Removal & Disassembly – 1) Remove oil pan. See OIL PAN under REMOVAL & INSTALLATION. Remove oil pump from oil pan. Remove oil pump drive shaft. Disassemble oil pump.

2) Note direction of component installation for reassembly reference. Drill a small hole in oil pressure relief valve cap. Install self-threading screw in drilled hole and pull on screw to remove cap.

Inspection – Inspect components for damage and wear. Measure rotor end play and outer rotor-to-housing clearance. Measure relief valve-to-bore clearance and relief valve tension. Replace oil pump assembly if measurements are not within specifications. See OIL PUMP SPECIFICATIONS table.

OIL PUMP SPECIFICATIONS

Application	Specification
Outer Rotor-To-Housing Clearance	.001-.013" (.03-.33 mm)
Relief Valve Spring Tension	
5.0L	10.6-12.2 lbs. @ 1.74" (4.8-5.5 kg @ 44.2 mm)
5.8L	18.2-20.2 lbs. @ 2.49" (8.3-9.2 kg @ 63.2 mm).
Relief Valve-To-Housing Clearance	.0015-.0030" (.038-.076 mm)
Rotor End Play	.004" (.10 mm) Max.
Shaft-To-Housing Clearance	.0015-.0030" (.038-.076 mm)

NOTE: Oil pump is serviced as an assembly only. Replace assembly if measurements are not to specifications. See OIL PUMP SPECIFICATIONS table.

Reassembly & Installation – 1) To reassemble, reverse disassembly procedure. Ensure components are installed in original location. Install new oil pressure relief valve cap. To install, prime oil pump by filling inlet opening with oil, and rotating pump shaft until oil emerges from outlet opening.

2) Install and tighten oil pump-to-cylinder block bolt to specification. See TORQUE SPECIFICATIONS table. To complete installation, reverse removal procedure.

CAUTION: If pump and drive shaft do not seat readily, DO NOT force into position. Realign drive shaft hex with distributor shaft socket and reinstall.

TORQUE SPECIFICATIONS

TORQUE SPECIFICATIONS

Application	Ft. Lbs. (N.m)
Bellhousing-To-Engine Bolt	40-50 (54-68)
Camshaft Sprocket Bolt	40-45 (54-61)
Connecting Rod Cap Nut	
5.0L	19-24 (26-33)
5.8L	40-45 (54-61)
Crankshaft Damper Bolt	70-90 (95-122)
Cylinder Head Bolt [1]	
5.0L	
Step 1	55-65 (75-88)
Step 2	65-72 (88-98)

1991 ENGINES
5.0L & 5.8L V8 (Cont.)

TORQUE SPECIFICATIONS (Cont.)

Application	Ft. Lbs. (N.m)
Cylinder Head Bolt (Cont.) [1]	
5.8L	
Step 1	85 (116)
Step 2	95 (129)
Step 3	105-112 (143-152)
Engine Front Cover Bolt	12-18 (17-24)
Exhaust Manifold Bolt	18-24 (24-33)
Flexplate-To-Converter Bolt	20-30 (27-41)
Flywheel-To-Crankshaft Bolt	75-85 (102-116)
Intake Manifold Bolts & Stud	
Lower [2]	23-25 (31-34)
Upper	12-18 (17-24)
Main Bearing Cap Bolt	
5.0L	60-70 (82-95)
5.8L	95-105 (129-143)
Oil Pan-To-Cylinder Block Bolt	11 (14)
Oil Pump Inlet Tube	10-15 (30-20)
Oil Pump-To-Cylinder Block Bolt	22-32 (30-44)
Rear Mount-To-Crossmember Nut	60-80 (81-108)
Rocker Arm Fulcrum Bolt	18-25 (24-34)
Starter Bolt	40-50 (54-68)
	INCH Lbs. (N.m)
Camshaft Thrust Plate Bolt	108-144 (12-16)
Valve Cover Bolt	36-60 (4-6)

[1] – Tighten in sequence. *See Fig. 4.*
[2] – Tighten in sequence. *See Fig. 3.*

ENGINE SPECIFICATIONS

GENERAL SPECIFICATIONS

Application	Specification
5.0L & 5.8L	
Displacement	
5.0L	302 Cu. In.
5.8L	351 Cu. In.
Bore	4.00" (101.6 mm)
Stroke	
5.0L	3.00" (76.2 mm)
5.8L	3.50" (88.9 mm)
Compression Ratio	
5.0L	9.0:1
5.8L	8.8:1
Fuel System	
5.0L	PFI
5.8L	PFI
Horsepower @ RPM	
5.0L	185 @ 3800
5.8L	210 @ 3800
Torque Ft. Lbs.@ RPM	
5.0L	270 @ 2400
5.8L	315 @ 2800

CRANKSHAFT, MAIN & CONNECTING ROD BEARINGS

Application	In. (mm)
5.0L & 5.8L	
Crankshaft	
End Play	.004-.008 (.10-.20)
Main Bearings	
Journal Diameter	
5.0L	2.2482-2.2490 (57.104-57.125)
5.8L	2.9994-3.0002 (76.185-76.205)
Journal Out-Of-Round	.0006 (.015)
Journal Taper [1]	.0005 (.013)
Journal Runout	.002 (.05)
Oil Clearance	
5.0L	
No. 1 Bearing	
Desired	.0001-.0015 (.003-.038)
Allowable	.0001-.0020 (.003-.050)
All Other Bearings	
Desired	.0008-.0015 (.020-.038)
Allowable	.0008-.0024 (.020-.061)
5.8L	
Desired	.0008-.0015 (.020-.038)
Allowable	.0008-.0026 (.020-.066)
Connecting Rod Bearings	
Journal Diameter	
5.0L	2.1228-2.1236 (53.919-53.939)
5.8L	2.3103-2.3111 (58.682-58.702)
Journal Taper [1]	.0006 (.015)
Journal Out-Of-Round	.0006 (.015)
Oil Clearance	
5.0L	
Desired	.0008-.0015 (.020-.038)
Allowable	.0007-.0024 (.018-.061)
5.8L	
Desired	.0008-.0015 (.020-.038)
Allowable	.0008-.0025 (.020-.064)

[1] – Within a 1" (25 mm) area.

CONNECTING RODS

Application	In. (mm)
5.0L & 5.8L	
Bore Diameter	
Pin Bore	.9096-.9112 (23.104-23.144)
Crankpin Bore	
5.0L	2.2390-2.2398 (56.871-56.891)
5.8L	2.4265-2.4273 (61.633-61.653)
Center-To-Center Length	
5.0L	5.0885-5.0915 (129.248-129.324)
5.8L	5.9545-5.9575 (151.244-151.321)
Maximum Bend [1]	.012 (.30)
Maximum Twist [1]	.024 (.61)
Side Play	
Standard	.010-.020 (.25-.51)
Service Limit	.023 (.58)

[1] – Specification listed is measured at the ends of an 8" (203 mm) bar, 4" (102 mm) on each side of rod center line.

1991 ENGINES
5.0L & 5.8L V8 (Cont.)

PISTONS, PINS & RINGS

Application	In. (mm)
5.0L & 5.8L	
Pistons	
Clearance	
5.0L	.0014-.0022 (.036-.056)
5.8L	.0018-.0026 (.046-.066)
Diameter (5.0L) [1]	
Red	3.9989-3.9995 (101.572-101.587)
Blue	4.0001-4.0007 (101.603-101.618)
Yellow	4.0013-4.0019 (101.633-101.648)
Diameter (5.8L) [1]	
Red	3.9978-3.9984 (101.544-101.559)
Blue	3.9990-3.9996 (101.575-101.590)
Yellow	4.0002-4.0008 (101.605-101.620)
Pins	
Diameter	.9119-.9124 (23.16-23.17)
Length	3.01-3.04 (76.45-77.21)
Piston Fit	
5.0L	.0002-.0004 (.005-.010)
5.8L	.0003-.0005 (.008-.013)
Rod Fit	Press Fit
Rings	
No. 1 & 2	
End Gap	.010-.020 (.25-.51)
Side Clearance	
No. 1	.0013-.0033 (.033-.084)
No. 2	.002-.004 (.05-.10)
No. 3 (Oil)	
End Gap (Steel Rail)	.015-.055 (.38-1.40)
Side Clearance	Snug Fit

[1] – Standard pistons are color-coded Red, Blue and Yellow on piston dome.

CYLINDER BLOCK

Application	In. (mm)
5.0 & 5.8L	
Cylinder Bore	
Standard Diameter	4.000-4.005 (101.60-101.73)
Maximum Taper	.010 (.25)
Maximum Out-Of-Round	
Standard	.0015 (.038)
Service Limit	.005 (.13)
Maximum Deck Warpage [1]	.003 (.08)

[1] – Specification is within a 6" (152 mm) area. Overall warpage is .006" (.15 mm). DO NOT machine more than .010" (.25 mm) from original gasket surface.

VALVES & VALVE SPRINGS

Application	Specification
5.0L & 5.8L	
Face Angle	44°
Head Diameter	
5.0L	
Intake	1.69" (42.9 mm)
Exhaust	1.44-1.46" (36.6-37.1 mm)
5.8L	
Intake	1.77-1.79" (45.0-45.5 mm)
Exhaust	1.45-1.47" (36.8-37.3 mm)
Stem Diameter	
Intake	.3416-.3423" (8.677-8.694 mm)
Exhaust	.3411-.3418" (8.664-8.682 mm)
Valve Margin	.031" (.79 mm)
Valve Springs	
Free Length	
Intake	2.04" (51.8 mm)
Exhaust	1.85" (47.0 mm)
Installed Height	
5.0L	
Intake	1.67-1.70 (42.4-43.2)
Exhaust	1.58-1.61 (40.1-40.9)
5.8L	
Intake	1.77-1.80 (45.0-45.7)
Exhaust	1.58-1.61 (40.1-40.9)
Out-Of-Square	.078" (1.98 mm)
Pressure	Lbs. @ In. (kg @ mm)
Intake Valve Closed	
5.0L	74-82 @ 1.50 (34-37 @ 45)
5.8L	74-82 @ 1.50 (34-37 @ 45)
Intake Valve Open	
5.0L	196-212 @ 1.36 (89-96 @ 35)
5.8L	190-210 @ 1.20 (86-95 @ 31)
Exhaust Valve Closed	
5.0L	76-84 @ 1.60 (34-38 @ 41)
5.8L	76-84 @ 1.60 (34-38 @ 41)
Exhaust Valve Open	
5.0L	190-210 @ 1.20 (86-95 @ 31)
5.8L	190-210 @ 1.20 (86-95 @ 31)

CYLINDER HEAD

Application	Specification
5.0L & 5.8L	
Maximum Warpage [1]	.003" (.08 mm)
Valve Seats	
Seat Angle	45°
Seat Width	
5.0L	.06" (1.5 mm)
5.8L	.08" (2.0 mm)
Maximum Seat Runout	.002" (.05 mm)
Valve Guides	
Intake Valve	
Valve Guide Bore I.D.	.3433-.3443" (8.720-8.745 mm)
Valve Stem-To-Guide Oil Clearance	.0010-.0027" (.025-.069 mm)
Exhaust Valve	
Valve Guide Bore I.D.	.3433-.3443" (8.720-8.745 mm)
Valve Stem-To-Guide Oil Clearance	.0015-.0032" (.038-.081 mm)

[1] – Specification listed is within 6" (152 mm). Overall warpage is .006" (.15 mm). DO NOT machine more than .010" (.25 mm) from original gasket surface.

1991 ENGINES
5.0L & 5.8L V8 (Cont.)

CAMSHAFT

Application	In. (mm)
5.0L & 5.8L	
Bearing I.D. Diameter	
No. 1	2.0825-2.0835 (52.896-52.921)
No. 2	2.0675-2.0685 (52.515-52.540)
No. 3	2.0525-2.0535 (52.134-52.159)
No. 4	2.0375-2.0385 (51.753-51.778)
No. 5	2.0225-2.0235 (51.372-51.397)
End Play	.001-.007 (.03-.18)
Journal Diameter	
No. 1	2.0805-2.0815 (52.845-52.870)
No. 2	2.0655-2.0665 (52.464-52.489)
No. 3	2.0505-2.0515 (52.083-52.108)
No. 4	2.0355-2.0365 (51.702-51.727)
No. 5	2.0205-2.0215 (51.321-51.346)
Journal Runout	.005 (.13)
Lobe Lift (5.0L)	
Intake	.2375 (6.033)
Exhaust	.2474 (6.284)
Lobe Lift (5.8L)	
Intake	.278 (7.06)
Exhaust	.283 (7.19)
Lobe Wear Limit	.005 (.13)
Oil Clearance	.001-.003 (.03-.08)
Timing Chain Deflection	.500 (12.70)

VALVE LIFTERS

Application	In. (mm)
5.0L & 5.8L	
Lifter Diameter	.8740-.8745 (22.200-22.212)
Oil Clearance	.0007-.0027 (.018-.069)
Collapsed Lifter Clearance	
5.0L	
Desired	.096-.165 (2.44-4.19)
Allowable	.071-.193 (1.80-4.90)
5.8L	
Desired	.123-.173 (3.12-4.39)
Allowable	.098-.198 (2.49-5.03)

"E" & "F" Series

NOTE: Unless specified otherwise, references to "F" Series include "F" Series Super Duty. For engine repair procedures not covered in this article, see ENGINE OVERHAUL PROCEDURES article in GENERAL INFORMATION.

ENGINE IDENTIFICATION

The eighth character of the Vehicle Identification Number (VIN) identifies the engine. The VIN is stamped on a metal tab attached to top left end of instrument panel and is visible through windshield. VIN is also located on Vehicle Safety Compliance Certification Label on left door or left door post pillar.

ENGINE IDENTIFICATION CODE

Application	Code
7.3L Diesel	M

ADJUSTMENTS

VALVE CLEARANCE ADJUSTMENT

Hydraulic valve lifters are used; no valve adjustment is required.

REMOVAL & INSTALLATION

COOLING SYSTEM BLEEDING

WARNING: When engine is operating, NEVER remove radiator cap under any conditions. Failure to follow instruction could damage cooling system or engine, or cause personal injury. Always wrap protective material around radiator cap to avoid injury from hot steam or hot coolant.

1) Fill cooling system with 50/50 mixture of water and coolant. Pause several minutes for circulation. Fill radiator to filler neck seat. Disconnect heater outlet hose at water pump to bleed off trapped air. Fill radiator until coolant begins to escape.
2) Connect heater outlet hose. Fill radiator until coolant is between the cap seal in the filler neck to 1.5" (38 mm) below cap seal. Install radiator cap. Start engine and allow to warm up. Shut engine off. Allow engine to cool. Remove radiator cap and check coolant level. Top off radiator coolant as necessary.

ENGINE

Removal ("F" Series) – 1) Disconnect negative battery cable from both batteries. Scribe hood hinge location and remove hood. Drain cooling system. Remove air cleaner and intake duct assembly. Cover intake opening.

NOTE: Fan and fan clutch assembly are secured with left-hand threads.

2) Disconnect fan shroud and place shroud over fan. Using Fan Clutch Pulley Holder (T83T-9424-A) and Fan Clutch Nut Wrench (T83T-6312-B), remove fan and clutch assembly. Remove fan shroud. Remove A/T cooler lines from radiator (if equipped).
3) Remove radiator with hoses attached. Remove A/C compressor drive belt and A/C compressor; position on upper radiator support with lines attached (if equipped). Remove power steering pump drive belt. Remove power steering pump with hoses attached and position aside.
4) Disconnect all sending unit wires and alternator wiring from engine. Disconnect accelerator and cruise control cables from injection pump. Remove accelerator cable bracket from engine and position aside. Remove transmission kickdown rod from injection pump (if equipped).
5) Disconnect main wiring harness connector from right side of engine. Disconnect engine ground strap from rear of engine. Disconnect fuel return hose from left rear of engine. Remove vacuum supply hose from pump. Remove upper transmission-to-engine bolts. Disconnect heater hoses from engine. Raise vehicle.
6) Disconnect both battery ground cables at engine. Disconnect and plug fuel supply line at fuel supply pump. Disconnect starter cables and remove starter. Disconnect exhaust pipes from manifolds. Remove engine mount-to-engine nuts. Remove flywheel inspection plate.
7) Remove flexplate-to-converter bolts (if equipped). Lower vehicle. Support transmission with floor jack. Remove 4 lower transmission-to-engine bolts. Attach lifting device to engine. Lift engine to clear No. 1 crossmember. Pull engine forward, rotate 45 degrees to left and carefully lift engine from vehicle.
Installation – To install, reverse removal procedure. Tighten bolts to specification. See TORQUE SPECIFICATIONS table at end of article. Check and top off all engine fluids. Fill and bleed air from cooling system. See COOLING SYSTEM BLEEDING under REMOVAL & INSTALLATION. Evacuate and recharge A/C system (if equipped).
Removal ("E" Series) – 1) Remove engine cover. Disconnect negative battery cable from both batteries. Remove front bumper, grille assembly and gravel deflector. Remove speed control servo bracket and set aside (if equipped). Scribe hood hinge location and remove hood.
2) Remove upper grille support. On models equipped with A/C, discharge A/C system. Disconnect hoses from condenser and remove condenser. On all models, remove transmission oil cooler and brackets. Remove radiator hoses. Disconnect fan shroud and position shroud over fan.

NOTE: Fan and fan clutch assembly are secured with left-hand threads.

3) Using Fan Clutch Pulley Holder (T83T-9424-A) and Fan Clutch Nut Wrench (T83T-6312-B), remove fan and clutch assembly. Remove fan shroud. Remove radiator. Remove vacuum pump drive belt and vacuum pump. Disconnect vacuum hose from transmission shift modulator tube.
4) Remove alternator adjusting arm and drive belt. Pivot alternator inward towards engine. Disconnect wiring from alternator. Disconnect wiring from engine sensors and switches as necessary. Remove 2 engine ground cables from bottom of engine.
5) Disconnect and plug power steering return line. Remove power steering pump with pressure hose attached and position aside. Remove power steering bracket. Remove hoses from A/C compressor (if equipped). Remove vacuum hose between vacuum regulator valve and injection pump.
6) Remove air cleaner assembly and cover air intake opening. Disconnect fuel lines at fuel filter and plug inlet hose. Remove fuel filter and bracket as an assembly. Loosen A/C compressor and rotate towards engine. Remove accelerator and speed cables from injection pump and set aside.
7) Remove cable bracket. Disconnect engine wiring harnesses from inside vehicle. Remove transmission kickdown rod. Disconnect heater hose from water pump and right cylinder head. Remove A/C hose bracket from right cylinder head (if equipped). Disconnect fuel return line from left rear of engine.
8) Remove transmission oil dipstick tube retaining bolt. Remove engine oil dipstick tube retaining bolt. Remove dipstick and dipstick tube. Remove 4 upper transmission-to-engine retaining bolts. Raise and support vehicle. Remove engine mount retaining bolts.
9) Disconnect exhaust inlet pipe from exhaust manifolds. Remove converter inspection cover. Remove 4 converter-to-flywheel nuts. Disconnect wiring from starter. Position fuel line on crossmember down and out of way. Lower vehicle. Attach engine lifting device.
10) Support transmission and remove remaining transmission-to-engine bolts. Separate engine from transmission. Raise engine high enough to clear crossmember; pull engine forward and out of vehicle.
Installation – To install, reverse removal procedure. Tighten bolts to specification. See TORQUE SPECIFICATIONS table at end of article. Check and top off all engine fluids. Fill and bleed air from cooling system. See COOLING SYSTEM BLEEDING under REMOVAL & INSTALLATION. Evacuate and recharge A/C system (if equipped).

1991 ENGINES
7.3L V8 Diesel (Cont.)

INJECTION PUMP

CAUTION: Fuel system contamination will damage finely machined parts within injection pump and injector nozzles. Clean fittings with fuel oil or solvent and blow dry with compressed air before disconnecting fuel lines. Cap all open fittings. Injection pump can be severely damaged if engine is washed or steam cleaned while engine is hot or running.

Removal – 1) Disconnect ground cables from both batteries. On "E" Series, remove engine cover. On all models, remove air cleaner. Cover intake opening in manifold.
2) Remove injection pump drive gear cover plate. Rotate crankshaft until No. 1 piston is at TDC of compression stroke. Ensure timing marks are aligned. *See Fig. 1.*
3) Remove injection pump-to-drive gear bolts. Disconnect electrical connectors at injection pump. Remove fast idle solenoid bracket assembly for access to injection pump mounting nuts.
4) Disconnect accelerator cable and speed control cable from throttle lever. Remove accelerator cable bracket and cables. If necessary, remove fuel filter and bracket. Disconnect 90-degree fuel return hose elbow at governor on injection pump.

NOTE: DO NOT disconnect injection lines from pump when removing pump from engine unless pump is being replaced or serviced. Reference mark lines-to-pump position before disconnecting.

5) If removing injection pump with injection lines connected to pump, disconnect lines at injector nozzles. If removing injection pump without lines connected to pump, remove line retaining clips.
6) Disconnect lines from pump using Fuel Line Nut Wrench (T83T-9396-A). Remove injection lines in the following sequence: 5-6-4-8-3-1-7-2. Odd number cylinders are on right bank, with No. 1 cylinder closest to front of engine.

CAUTION: Ensure No. 1 piston is at TDC of compression stroke before removing injector pump. Pulley "Y" marks should be aligned. See Fig. 1.

7) On all applications, remove 3 injection pump-to-injection pump drive gear cover nuts using Injection Pump Mounting Wrench (T86T-9000-C). On "F" Series, lift injection pump (or pump with lines connected) out of engine compartment. On "E" Series, remove injection pump (or pump with lines attached) through passenger compartment.

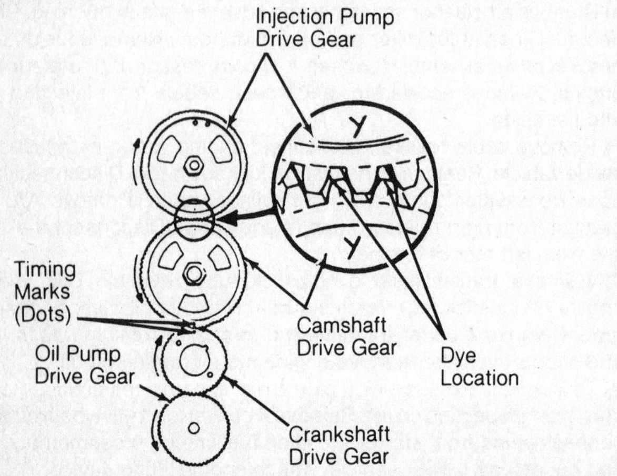
Injection Pump
Drive Gear
Y
Y
Timing
Marks
(Dots)
Oil Pump
Drive Gear
Camshaft
Drive Gear
Dye
Location
Crankshaft
Drive Gear
91687
Courtesy of Ford Motor Co.

Fig. 1: Aligning Timing Gear Marks

Installation – 1) Install new "O" ring on injection pump drive gear end. Install pump into position, aligning dowel on pump drive shaft with hole in drive gear. If necessary, rotate pump drive shaft to align dowel with hole.
2) Install and hand tighten 3 injection pump-to-drive gear cover nuts. Align timing mark on top radius of injection pump with mark on injection pump drive gear cover. *See Fig. 2.* To complete installation, reverse removal procedure.

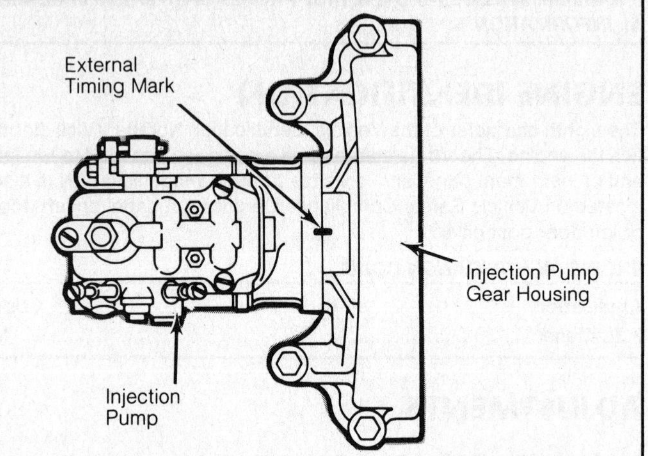
External
Timing Mark
Injection Pump
Gear Housing
Injection
Pump
91125
Courtesy of Ford Motor Co.

Fig. 2: Identifying Injection Pump-To-Pump Gear Housing Timing Marks

INJECTION PUMP DRIVE GEAR

CAUTION: To maintain injection pump drive gear-to-camshaft gear timing, CAREFULLY follow removal and installation procedures.

Removal – 1) Disconnect negative cable from both batteries. On "E" Series, remove engine cover. On all models, remove air cleaner. Cover opening in intake manifold. Remove injection pump. See INJECTION PUMP under REMOVAL & INSTALLATION. Remove injection pump drive gear cover. DO NOT remove drive gear.
2) Rotate crankshaft until No. 1 piston is at TDC of compression stroke. If injection pump drive gear dowel is at 4 o'clock position as viewed from front of engine, No. 1 cylinder is on compression stroke.
3) Ensure timing mark on vibration damper is set at TDC. Ensure "Y" timing mark on injection pump drive gear is aligned with "Y" timing mark on camshaft gear. *See Fig. 1.*
4) Without removing injection pump drive gear, slide gear back enough to expose top of camshaft gear. Note permanently dyed camshaft gear teeth adjacent to "Y" mark on camshaft gear. Remove injection pump drive gear.
Installation – 1) Clean gasket and sealing surfaces. Ensure No. 1 piston is at TDC of compression stroke. See steps **2)** and **3)** of removal procedure. Install drive gear, ensuring "Y" timing marks are properly aligned.
2) Apply a 1/8" (3.2 mm) bead of silicone sealer along bottom surface of drive gear cover. Apply thread sealing compound to drive gear cover bolt threads. Install drive gear cover and tighten to specification. See TORQUE SPECIFICATIONS table at end of article.

NOTE: With drive gear cover installed, gear remains stationary and cannot jump timing.

3) Install injection pump. Install air cleaner. Reconnect negative cables to both batteries. Run engine and check for oil, fuel and coolant leaks.

INTAKE MANIFOLD

Removal – 1) Disconnect battery ground cable from both batteries. Remove air cleaner. Cover intake opening in manifold. On "E" Series, disconnect fuel inlet and return lines from fuel filter. Remove fuel filter and bracket as an assembly.

2) On all models, remove injection pump. See INJECTION PUMP under REMOVAL & INSTALLATION. On "F" Series, disconnect fuel return hoses from No. 7 and No. 8 (rear) injector nozzles. Disconnect return hose to fuel tank. On all models, remove glow plug harness and controller. Remove engine wiring harness from engine.
3) Remove engine harness ground cable from rear of left cylinder head. Remove intake manifold-to-cylinder head bolts. Remove intake manifold. Remove valley cover (if necessary) by removing drain plug and Crankcase Depression Regulator (CDR) valve tube. Remove valley cover.
Installation - 1) Clean gasket mating surfaces. If valley cover was removed, install new valley cover with 1/8 (3.2 mm) bead of silicone sealer at ends of cylinder block.
2) Install new gaskets with intake manifold. Tighten bolts to specification in sequence. See TORQUE SPECIFICATIONS table at end of article. *See Fig. 3.* To install remaining components, reverse removal procedure.

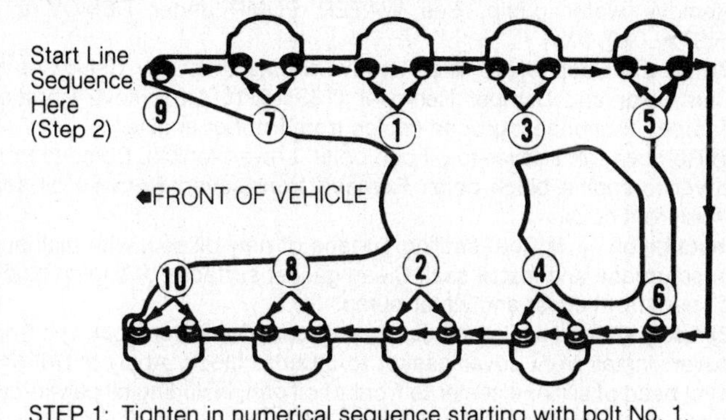

Start Line Sequence Here (Step 2)
9
7
1
3
5
FRONT OF VEHICLE
10
8
2
4
6

STEP 1: Tighten in numerical sequence starting with bolt No. 1.
STEP 2: Tighten in line sequence. Start with bolt No. 9, then follow arrows.
91983 Courtesy of Ford Motor Co.

Fig. 3: Intake Manifold Bolt Tightening Sequence

EXHAUST MANIFOLDS

Removal - Disconnect negative battery cable from both batteries. Raise and support vehicle. Disconnect exhaust pipes from manifolds. If removing right manifold, lower vehicle. If removing left manifold, leave vehicle in raised position. Remove bolts and remove exhaust manifold(s).
Installation - To install, reverse removal procedure. Apply anti-seize to manifold bolts. Install and tighten exhaust manifold bolts to specification in sequence. See TORQUE SPECIFICATIONS table at end of article. *See Fig. 4* .

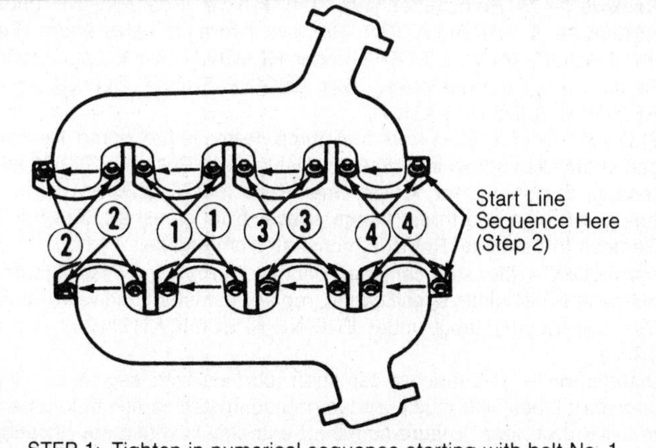

Start Line Sequence Here (Step 2)
2
2
1
1
3
3
4
4

STEP 1: Tighten in numerical sequence starting with bolt No. 1.
STEP 2: Tighten in line sequence. Start with bolt No. 4, then follow arrows.
90F10236 Courtesy of Ford Motor Co.

Fig. 4: Exhaust Manifold Tightening Sequence

CYLINDER HEADS

NOTE: The following cylinder head removal and installation procedures are for right cylinder head. Procedures for left cylinder head are similar. New cylinder heads and gaskets are interchangeable. Used cylinder heads should be installed in their original positions.

Removal - 1) Disconnect battery ground cable from both batteries. Drain cooling system. Disconnect fan shroud and position shroud over fan. Using Fan Clutch Pulley Holder (T83T-9424-A) and Fan Clutch Nut Wrench (T83T-6312-B), remove fan and clutch assembly. Remove fan shroud.

NOTE: Fan and fan clutch assembly are secured with left-hand threads.

2) Disconnect wiring harness electrical connector from top of fuel filter. Remove alternator. Remove vacuum pump. On "F" Series, remove fuel filter inlet, outlet and return lines. Cap lines and fittings to prevent fuel system contamination.
3) Remove fuel filter and bracket. On all models, remove alternator and vacuum pump mounting bracket. Remove heater hose from cylinder head. On all models, remove injection pump. See INJECTION PUMP under REMOVAL & INSTALLATION.
4) Remove intake manifold and valley cover. See INTAKE MANIFOLD under REMOVAL & INSTALLATION. Raise vehicle. Disconnect exhaust pipe from exhaust manifolds. Remove transmission dipstick tube-to-cylinder head bolt (if equipped). Lower vehicle.

CAUTION: Pre-combustion chamber inserts may fall out of cylinder head when cylinder head is removed. Ensure pre-combustion chambers DO NOT fall into combustion chamber when installing cylinder head.

5) Remove engine oil dipstick tube bolts. Remove exhaust manifold. Remove engine oil dipstick, dipstick tube and "O" ring. Remove valve cover. Keeping in order of removal, remove rocker arms and push rods. Remove injector nozzles and glow plugs. Remove and discard cylinder head bolts. Remove cylinder head.
Inspection - 1) Clean all carbon from cylinder head combustion chambers. Remove all gasket material from cylinder head and cylinder block. DO NOT scratch mating surfaces.

CAUTION: NEVER machine cylinder head or cylinder block mating surfaces. This reduces valve-to-piston clearance, causing engine damage. If cylinder head or cylinder block surface warpage exceeds specification, replace with new unit.

2) To obtain correct warpage measurement, remove pre-combustion chambers from cylinder head before measuring surface. Drive out pre-combustion chambers using a 1/4 x 8" (6.35 x 203 mm) brass drift.
3) Measure cylinder head warpage. If warpage exceeds specification, replace cylinder head. See CYLINDER HEAD table under ENGINE SPECIFICATIONS at end of article.
4) Measure warpage of cylinder block deck surface. If warpage exceeds specification, replace cylinder block. See CYLINDER BLOCK table under ENGINE SPECIFICATIONS at end of article.
Installation - 1) Lubricate and install pre-combustion chambers into cylinder head. Seat pre-combustion chamber within its bore by tapping with plastic mallet. Install cylinder head(s). DO NOT use sealer on head gaskets.
2) Install and tighten new head bolts to specification in sequence. See TORQUE SPECIFICATIONS table at end of article. *See Fig. 5.* To complete installation, reverse removal procedure. Fill and bleed air from cooling system. See COOLING SYSTEM BLEEDING under REMOVAL & INSTALLATION.

HYDRAULIC VALVE LIFTERS

Removal - Remove intake manifold and valley cover. See INTAKE MANIFOLD under REMOVAL & INSTALLATION. Remove valve covers, rocker arms and push rods, marking all components for instal-

1991 ENGINES
7.3L V8 Diesel (Cont.)

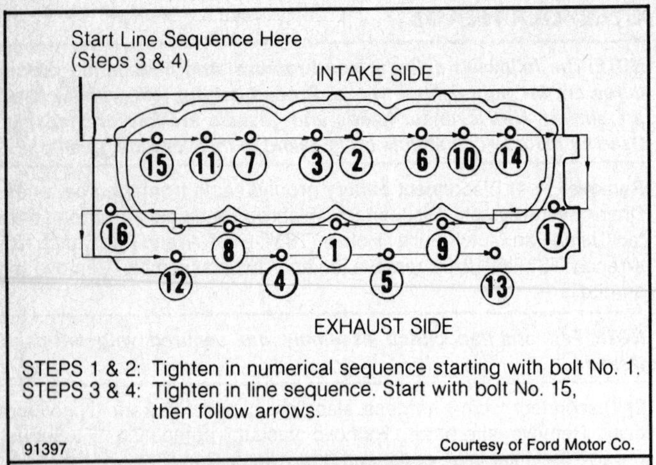
Start Line Sequence Here
(Steps 3 & 4)
INTAKE SIDE
15 11 7 3 2 6 10 14
16 8 1 9 17
12 4 5 13
EXHAUST SIDE
STEPS 1 & 2: Tighten in numerical sequence starting with bolt No. 1.
STEPS 3 & 4: Tighten in line sequence. Start with bolt No. 15, then follow arrows.
91397
Courtesy of Ford Motor Co.

Fig. 5: Cylinder Head Tightening Sequence

lation to original location. Remove lifter guide retainers. Remove valve lifters, marking each one for installation to original location.

Inspection – 1) Clean valve lifters in solvent or diesel fuel. Check valve lifter-to-bore oil clearance. If oil clearance is not within specification, replace valve lifter. See VALVE LIFTERS table under ENGINE SPECIFICATIONS at end of article.

2) Replace lifter if any part shows pitting, scoring, galling or evidence of non-rotation. Ensure lifter roller operates smoothly and without excessive play.

Installation – 1) Lubricate valve lifters and bores with clean engine oil. Install valve lifters in original positions in block. Install valve lifter guide retainers.

2) Install push rods with copper-colored end toward rocker arm. To complete installation, reverse removal procedure. Tighten bolts to specification. See TORQUE SPECIFICATIONS table at end of article.

FRONT COVER OIL SEAL

NOTE: Fan and fan clutch assembly are secured with left-hand threads.

Removal – 1) Front over oil seal can be replaced without removing front cover. Disconnect battery cables from both batteries. Disconnect fan shroud and place shroud over fan. Using Fan Clutch Pulley Holder (T83T-9424-A) and Fan Clutch Nut Wrench (T83T-6312-B), remove fan and clutch assembly. Remove fan shroud.

2) Remove accessory drive belts. Raise and support vehicle. Remove crankshaft pulley. Remove vibration damper-to-crankshaft bolt. Install Crank/Cam Gear and Damper Remover (T83T-6316-A), and remove vibration damper. Using universal seal puller, remove oil seal.

NOTE: On some engine front covers, 3 nuts are welded to front surface of cover around the outer circumference of oil seal. Seal Installer (T83T-6700-A) consists of 3 pieces: seal installer, large square washer and bridge assembly. Bridge assembly is used to install seal only if engine front cover is equipped with welded nuts.

Installation – 1) Coat sealing surface of new seal with multipurpose grease. Install oil seal using Seal Installer (T83T-6700-A). Place seal into seal installer. If necessary, rotate crankshaft to align damper key with seal installer. Install seal and seal installer over end of crankshaft.

2) If engine front cover is equipped with welded nuts, attach bridge to welded nuts. Draw seal into front cover by rotating center screw clockwise. Seal installer should bottom on front cover.

3) If engine front cover is not equipped with welded nuts, install Crank/Cam Gear Installer (T83T-6316-B) onto crankshaft end. Draw seal into front cover by rotating center screw clockwise. Seal installer should bottom on front cover.

4) On all engines, apply a 1/8" (3.2 mm) bead of silicone sealer around outside diameter of oil seal where it contacts engine front cover. Lubricate sealing surface of damper with engine oil. Install vibration damper using Crank/Cam Gear and Damper Installer (T83T-6316-B).

5) To prevent oil leakage past vibration damper keyway, apply silicone sealer to engine side of damper washer in area of keyway. Install and tighten vibration damper bolt and crankshaft pulley to specification. See TORQUE SPECIFICATIONS table at end of article. To complete installation, reverse removal procedure.

ENGINE FRONT COVER

NOTE: Fan and fan clutch assembly are secured with left-hand threads.

Removal – 1) Disconnect negative battery cables from both batteries. Drain cooling system. Remove air cleaner. Cover intake opening in manifold. Disconnect fan shroud and place shroud over fan. Using Fan Clutch Pulley Holder (T83T-9424-A) and Fan Clutch Nut Wrench (T83T-6312-B), remove fan and clutch assembly. Remove fan shroud.

2) Remove injection pump and injection pump drive gear cover. See INJECTION PUMP DRIVE GEAR under REMOVAL & INSTALLATION. Remove water pump. See WATER PUMP under REMOVAL & INSTALLATION.

3) Raise and support vehicle. Remove crankshaft pulley. Using Crank/Cam Gear and Damper Remover (T83T-6316-A), remove vibration damper. Disconnect ground cables from front of engine.

4) Remove front cover-to-oil pan bolts. Lower vehicle. Remove front cover-to-engine block bolts. Remove front cover. Remove oil seal from front cover.

Installation – 1) Coat sealing surface of new oil seal with multipurpose grease and install seal. Clean gasket surfaces of engine block, oil pan, front cover and water pump.

2) Apply silicone sealer to sealing surfaces of cylinder block and front cover. Install front cover gasket to cylinder block. Apply a 1/8" (3.2 mm) bead of silicone sealer to front of oil pan, including oil pan-to-cylinder block junction.

3) Place front cover into position, aligning holes in front cover with fabricated oil pan dowel pins (if necessary) and fabricated cylinder block dowel pins (if necessary). Install 2 bolts at top of front cover and one bolt at bottom left of cover.

4) Remove fabricated dowels (if used). Install remaining front cover bolts and oil pan bolts. Tighten to specification. See TORQUE SPECIFICATIONS table at end of article.

5) When installing water pump, apply silicone sealant to bolts as shown. *See Fig. 8* To prevent oil leakage past keyway, apply silicone sealer to engine side of vibration damper washer (in area of keyway).

6) To complete installation, reverse removal procedure. Tighten bolts to specification. See TORQUE SPECIFICATIONS table at end of article. Fill and bleed air from cooling system. See COOLING SYSTEM BLEEDING under REMOVAL & INSTALLATION.

CAMSHAFT

Removal – 1) Remove engine from vehicle. See ENGINE under REMOVAL & INSTALLATION. Remove hydraulic valve lifters. See HYDRAULIC VALVE LIFTERS under REMOVAL & INSTALLATION. Remove engine front cover. See ENGINE FRONT COVER under REMOVAL & INSTALLATION.

2) Disconnect fuel lines from fuel pump. Remove fuel pump. Remove camshaft Allen screw and washer. Using Gear Puller (T83T-6316-A), remove camshaft gear. Using Gear Puller (T77F-4220-B1), remove fuel pump cam and thrust flange spacer from camshaft. *See Fig. 6.* Remove thrust plate. Remove camshaft from engine.

Inspection – Measure camshaft bearing journals for wear. If journal diameter is not within specification, replace camshaft and valve lifters. See CAMSHAFT table under ENGINE SPECIFICATIONS at end of article.

Installation – 1) Lubricate camshaft journals with engine oil. Coat camshaft lobes with multipurpose grease. Install camshaft into bore. Install thrust plate. Ensure camshaft end play is within specification. See CAMSHAFT table under ENGINE SPECIFICATIONS at end of article.

2) Install thrust flange spacer and fuel pump cam using Crank/Cam Gear and Damper Installer (T83T-6316-B). Position camshaft to align timing marks on gears. *See Fig. 1.*

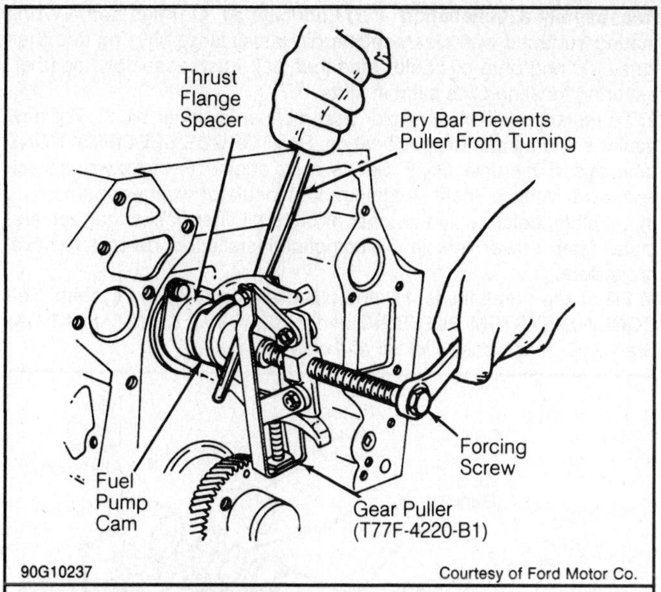

Thrust
Flange
Spacer
Pry Bar Prevents
Puller From Turning
Forcing
Screw
Fuel
Pump
Cam
Gear Puller
(T77F-4220-B1)
90G10237
Courtesy of Ford Motor Co.

Fig. 6: Removing Fuel Supply Pump Cam & Thrust Flange Spacer

3) Install camshaft gear using crank/cam gear and damper installer. Tighten camshaft gear Allen screw to specification. See TORQUE SPECIFICATIONS table at end of article. To complete installation, reverse removal procedure.

CAMSHAFT BEARINGS

NOTE: All camshaft bearings are interchangeable except front bearing, which is wider than others.

Removal - 1) Remove engine from vehicle. See ENGINE under REMOVAL & INSTALLATION. Remove camshaft. See CAMSHAFT under REMOVAL & INSTALLATION. Remove flywheel, crankshaft and rear cylinder block camshaft core plug.
2) DO NOT damage piston cooling jets at bottom of cylinder wall. Push pistons to top of cylinders. Using Camshaft Bearing Remover/Installer (T65L-6250-A), remove camshaft bearings.
Installation - 1) Install camshaft bearings using Camshaft Bearing Remover/Installer (T65L-6250-A). Ensure bearing oil holes are properly aligned with oil holes in cylinder block.
2) Install front bearing .020-.050" (.51-1.27 mm) below front face of cylinder block. Check bearing installation with straightedge and feeler gauge. Install new cylinder block camshaft core plug. To complete installation, reverse removal procedure.

REAR CRANKSHAFT OIL SEAL

Removal - Remove transmission. Remove clutch assembly (if equipped). Remove flywheel/flexplate. Remove rear engine cover-to-engine bolts and remove rear cover. Position rear cover on arbor press as shown. *See Fig. 7.* Using arbor press and 4 1/8" (105 mm) diameter spacer, remove rear oil seal from cover.
Installation - 1) Clean rear cover and engine block gasket surfaces. Remove old silicone sealer from oil pan sealing surface. Clean surface with solvent and dry thoroughly.

CAUTION: Install new oil seal, from engine block side of rear cover, even with seal bore inner surface.

2) Apply thin coat of gasket adhesive to seal bore I.D. in rear cover. Using an arbor press and Rear Crankshaft Seal Installer (T83T-6701-A), install new rear crankshaft oil seal.
3) Apply a 1/8" (3.2 mm) bead of silicone sealer around O.D. of rear seal and edge of rear cover. Apply gasket adhesive to engine block and rear cover gasket surfaces. Install rear cover gasket to engine block.

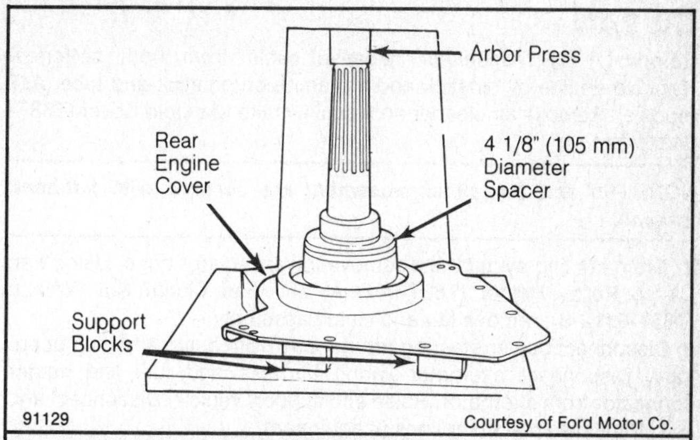

Arbor Press
Rear
Engine
Cover
4 1/8" (105 mm)
Diameter
Spacer
Support
Blocks
91129
Courtesy of Ford Motor Co.

Fig. 7: Removing Rear Crankshaft Oil Seal

4) To aid rear cover alignment, install Rear Seal Pilot (T83T-6701-B) on crankshaft. Immediately before installing rear cover, apply 1/4" (6.35 mm) bead of silicone sealer to oil pan sealing surface, including corner of cylinder block-to-pan junction.
5) Position rear cover on engine block. Install bolts and tighten to specification. See TORQUE SPECIFICATIONS table at end of article. Remove rear seal pilot from crankshaft. To complete installation, reverse removal procedure.

WATER PUMP

NOTE: Fan and fan clutch assembly are secured with left-hand threads.

Removal - 1) Disconnect ground cables from both batteries. Drain cooling system. Disconnect fan shroud and place shroud over fan. Using Fan Clutch Pulley Holder (T83T-9424-A) and Fan Clutch Nut Wrench (T83T-6312-B), remove fan and clutch assembly. Remove fan shroud.
2) Remove accessory drive belts. Disconnect heater hose from water pump. Remove heater hose fitting from water pump. Remove alternator adjusting arm and adjusting arm bracket.
3) Remove A/C compressor with hoses attached and set aside. Remove A/C brackets. Remove power steering pump with hoses attached and set aside. Remove power steering bracket. Note bolt location and remove water pump bolts. Remove water pump.
Installation - 1) Clean gasket surfaces and bolt threads. Coat 2 top bolts and 2 bottom bolts with silicone sealer. *See Fig. 8.* Install water pump and tighten to specification. See TORQUE SPECIFICATIONS table at end of article.
2) To complete installation, reverse removal procedure. Fill and bleed air from cooling system. See COOLING SYSTEM BLEEDING under REMOVAL & INSTALLATION. Start engine and check for coolant leaks.

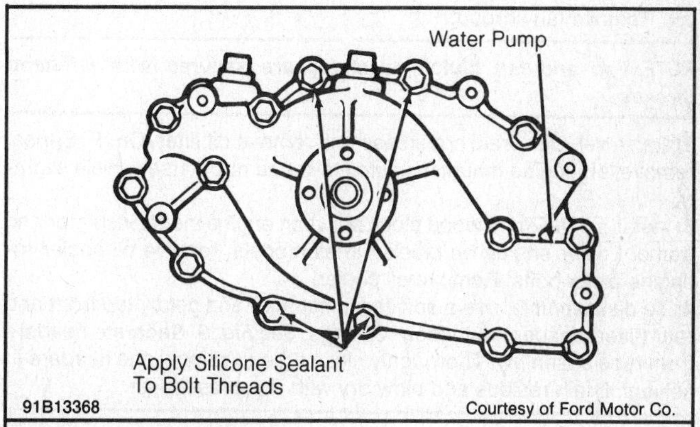

Water Pump
Apply Silicone Sealant
To Bolt Threads
91B13368
Courtesy of Ford Motor Co.

Fig. 8: Installing Water Pump

1991 ENGINES
7.3L V8 Diesel (Cont.)

OIL PAN

Removal – 1) Disconnect negative cable from both batteries. Remove engine oil dipstick and transmission dipstick and tube (A/T models). Remove air cleaner and install Intake Manifold Cover (T83T-9424-A).

NOTE: Fan and fan clutch assembly are secured with left-hand threads.

2) Drain cooling system and remove lower radiator hose. Using Fan Clutch Pulley Holder (T83T-9424-A) and Fan Clutch Nut Wrench (T83T-6312-B), remove fan and clutch assembly.
3) Disconnect power steering return hose from pump and plug openings. Disconnect alternator wiring harness and fuel line heater connector from alternator. Raise and support vehicle. Disconnect and plug transmission cooler lines (if equipped).
4) Disconnect and plug fuel pump inlet line. Drain engine oil and remove oil filter. Disconnect exhaust pipe at manifolds. Remove muffler inlet pipe from muffler flange. Remove upper inlet pipe mounting stud on right-side exhaust manifold.
5) Remove front engine mount nuts from crossmember. On A/T models, remove 2 bolts securing shift linkage bell crank to transmission. Allow linkage to hang freely. On all models, lower vehicle. On "E" Series, install Rotunda Engine Lifting Brackets (014-00312) to front of engine.
6) Connect Rotunda Engine Lifting Brackets (T70P-6000) to lift sling and raise engine until transmission contacts body. On "F" Series, install lifting sling to lifting eyes on intake manifold and raise engine until transmission contacts body.
7) Use wooden blocks to support engine; block right side up 2" (51 mm) and left side up 2.75" (69.9 mm). Remove flywheel inspection plate. Move fuel pump inlet line to rear crossmember. Remove oil pan bolts.
8) Remove transmission mount nuts. Using a transmission jack, raise transmission approximately 1" (.25 mm). Lower oil pan. It may be necessary to release oil pan from cylinder block by prying on oil pan at front and rear of pan, on left side of cylinder block in dowel holes.
9) On "F" Series, remove oil pump bolts and pick-up tube nut. Lower oil pump assembly into oil pan. On all models, remove oil pan. It may be necessary to rotate crankshaft to remove oil pan.
Installation – 1) To install, reverse removal procedure. Apply a 1/8" (3.2 mm) bead of silicone sealant on pan rails and a 1/4" (6.4 mm) bead of sealant on oil pan sealing surfaces of front and rear covers.
2) To install remaining components, reverse removal procedure. Fill or top off all fluids. Fill and bleed air from cooling system. See COOLING SYSTEM BLEEDING under REMOVAL & INSTALLATION.

OIL COOLER ASSEMBLY

Removal & Disassembly – 1) Disconnect negative cable from both batteries. Drain cooling system. Disconnect fan shroud and position shroud over fan. Using Fan Clutch Pulley Holder (T83T-9424-A) and Fan Clutch Nut Wrench (T83T-6312-B), remove fan and clutch assembly. Remove fan shroud.

NOTE: Fan and fan clutch assembly are secured with left-hand threads.

2) Raise vehicle. Drain crankcase and remove oil filter. On "F" Series, remove left engine mount insulator-to-frame nut. Raise vehicle slightly.
3) Install a 1" (25 mm) wood block between engine mount insulator and frame. Lower engine on block. On all models, remove oil cooler-to-engine block bolts. Remove oil cooler.
4) To disassemble, use a soft-faced hammer and gently tap front and rear (filter) headers to loosen "O" rings. *See Fig. 9.* Separate headers from tube assembly. Thoroughly clean tube assembly and headers in solvent. Drain residue and blow dry with compressed air.

CAUTION: To prevent leakage, use new "O" rings when assembling oil cooler assembly.

Reassembly & Installation – 1) Lubricate all "O" rings and "O" ring mating surfaces with clean engine oil. Install large "O" ring and then small "O" ring onto oil cooler tube (bundle). Push assembly together, ensuring locating clips align in slots.
2) To install, position oil cooler assembly on cylinder block with new gaskets and tighten to specification. See TORQUE SPECIFICATIONS table at end of article. On "F" Series, raise engine. Remove wood block and lower vehicle. Install engine mount insulator washer and nut.
3) On all models, apply thin coat of oil to oil filter gasket surface and install filter. Lower vehicle. To complete installation, reverse removal procedure.
4) Fill or top off all fluids. Fill and bleed air from cooling system. See COOLING SYSTEM BLEEDING under REMOVAL & INSTALLATION. Start engine and check for oil and coolant leaks.

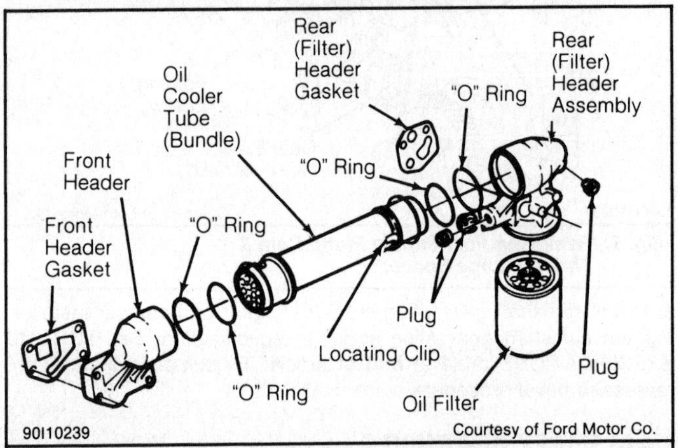
Rear
(Filter)
Header
Gasket
Rear
(Filter)
Header
Assembly
Oil
Cooler
Tube
(Bundle)
"O" Ring
Front
Header
"O" Ring
Front
Header
Gasket
"O" Ring
Plug
Locating Clip
Plug
"O" Ring
Oil Filter
90I10239
Courtesy of Ford Motor Co.

Fig. 9: Exploded View of Oil Cooler & Filter Assembly

OVERHAUL

CYLINDER HEAD

Cylinder Head – 1) Clean head gasket mating surface. Clean carbon from combustion chambers. DO NOT damage surfaces. Check cylinder head for cracks, burrs, nicks and warpage.
2) If cylinder head warpage exceeds specification, replace cylinder head. DO NOT machine cylinder head to correct warpage. See CYLINDER HEAD table under ENGINE SPECIFICATIONS at end of article.
3) Check pre-combustion chambers for cracks. Pre-combustion chamber cracks are acceptable if cracking is within the fire ring. *See Fig. 10.* If cracking extends past fire ring, replace pre-combustion chamber insert.

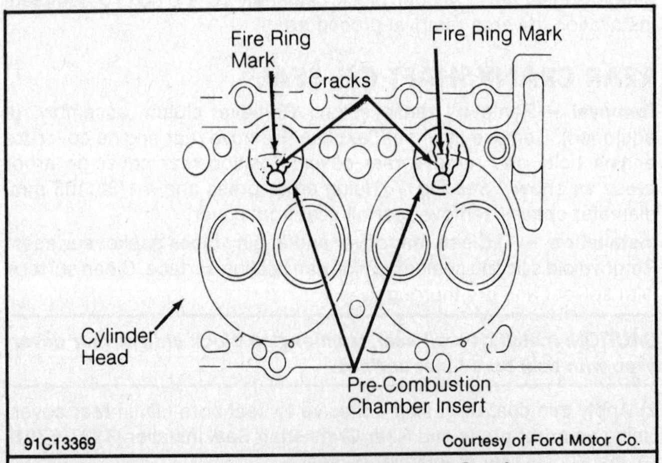
Fire Ring
Mark
Fire Ring Mark
Cracks
Cylinder
Head
Pre-Combustion
Chamber Insert
91C13369
Courtesy of Ford Motor Co.

Fig. 10: Identifying Pre-Combustion Chamber Cracks

Valve Springs – Inspect valve spring free length and pressure. Replace valve spring if free length and pressure are not within specification. See VALVES & VALVE SPRINGS table under ENGINE SPECIFICATIONS at end of article.

Valve Stem Oil Seals - Valve stem seals are used on intake valves only. Lubricate and install a new valve stem oil seal using Valve Stem Seal Replacer (T83T-6571-A).

Valve Stem Oil Shields - Both intake and exhaust valves use valve stem oil shields. Intake and exhaust oil shields are not interchangeable. Intake oil shield is smaller than exhaust oil shield. Using hand pressure, install new oil shield into underside of spring retainer until shield snaps into place.

CAUTION: If oil shield is not properly installed, oil shield will float up and down, causing excessive oil consumption.

Valve Guides - **1)** Check valve stem-to-guide clearance. If clearance is not within specification, replace valve guide insert. See CYLINDER HEAD table under ENGINE SPECIFICATION at end of article. To replace valve guide insert, drill out old valve guide insert. Ream drilled insert bore for replacement guide.

2) Carefully install replacement valve guide insert into bore using press. If necessary, chill replacement insert to ease installation. Finish reaming replacement valve guide stem bore with recommended reamer size. Always reface valve seat after valve guide has been reamed.

Valve Seat - **1)** Ensure valve seat angle, seat width and seat runout are within specification. See CYLINDER HEAD table under ENGINE SPECIFICATIONS at end of article. Valve seats must be ground when valve guide is reamed or replaced.

2) Use Exhaust Valve Seat Remover/Replacer (D83T-6084-A) to remove and install exhaust valve seats. Intake valve seat replacement information is not available from manufacturer.

Valves - Ensure head diameter, valve face runout, stem diameter and valve margin are within specification. See VALVES & VALVE SPRINGS table under ENGINE SPECIFICATIONS at end of article.

CAUTION: DO NOT remove more than .010" (.25 mm) from end of valve stem when resurfacing tip of valve.

Valve Seat Correction Angles - If seat width is too wide after grinding, use a 15-degree stone to lower seat or a 60-degree stone to raise seat. See CYLINDER HEAD table under ENGINE SPECIFICATIONS at end of article.

CYLINDER BLOCK ASSEMBLY

Piston & Rod Assembly - Ensure weight pad on connecting rod is facing away from valve indentations on top of piston. *See Fig. 11.* Ensure pistons and rods are installed in same cylinders from which they were removed. Ensure valve indentations on top of piston face center of cylinder block when installed. *See Fig. 12.*

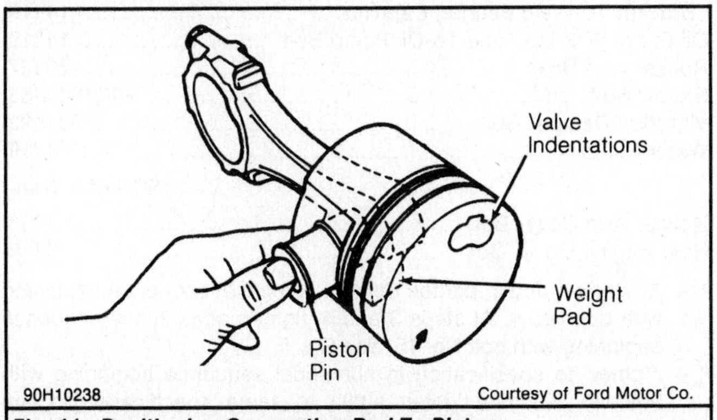
Valve
Indentations
Weight
Pad
Piston
Pin
90H10238
Courtesy of Ford Motor Co.

Fig. 11: Positioning Connecting Rod To Piston

Fitting Pistons - **1)** Measure piston diameter 1.23" (31.2 mm) below lower land of oil ring. Measure at piston pin center line, at 90-degree angle to piston pin. Measure cylinder bore for out-of-round, taper and piston-to-cylinder bore clearance.

2) If measurements are not within specification, hone or bore cylinders. See CYLINDER BLOCK table and PISTONS, PINS & RINGS table under ENGINE SPECIFICATIONS at end of article. If cylinder block needs to be bored, pistons are available in .010" (.25 mm), .020" (.51 mm) and .030" (.76 mm) oversize.

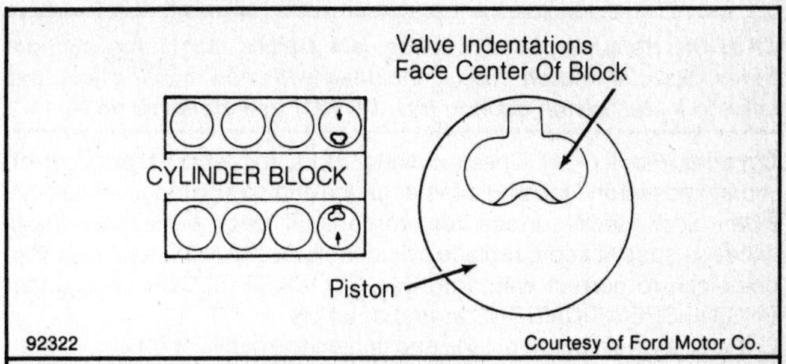
Valve Indentations
Face Center Of Block
CYLINDER BLOCK
Piston
92322
Courtesy of Ford Motor Co.

Fig. 12: Installing Piston In Cylinder Block

Piston Rings - **1)** Select rings for bore diameter. Place ring in cylinder bore in which it will be installed. Use piston to square ring in bore and place ring below normal ring wear area. Measure ring end gap. If ring gap is not within specification, try another ring set. See PISTONS, PINS & RINGS table under ENGINE SPECIFICATIONS at end of article.

2) Check side clearance of rings after installing on piston. Ensure clearance is within specification around entire circumference. Replace piston and/or rings if clearance is not within specification. See PISTONS, PINS & RINGS table under ENGINE SPECIFICATIONS.

3) Top and intermediate rings are identified by one dot (top ring) and 2 dots (intermediate ring) stamped on surface of ring, near end gap. Ensure rings are properly spaced on piston before installing pistons into cylinder. *See Fig. 13.*

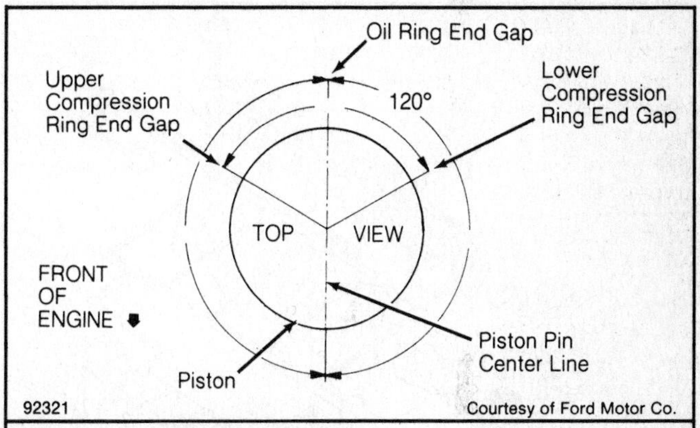
Oil Ring End Gap
Upper
Compression
Ring End Gap
120°
Lower
Compression
Ring End Gap
TOP
VIEW
FRONT
OF
ENGINE
Piston Pin
Center Line
Piston
92321
Courtesy of Ford Motor Co.

Fig. 13: Positioning Rings on Piston

Rod Bearings - Use Plastigage method and check rod bearing clearance. If clearance is not within specification, machine or replace crankshaft as necessary. Always replace bearings in pairs. See CRANKSHAFT, MAIN & CONNECTING ROD BEARINGS table under ENGINE SPECIFICATIONS at end of article.

Crankshaft & Main Bearings - **1)** When checking main bearing clearance in vehicle, position a jack under adjoining bearing counterweight being checked. Remove only one main bearing cap at a time.

2) Use Plastigage method and check main bearing clearance. If clearance is not within specification, machine or replace crankshaft as necessary. Always replace bearings in pairs. See CRANKSHAFT, MAIN & CONNECTING ROD BEARINGS table under ENGINE SPECIFICATIONS at end of article.

3) Install all bearing caps except thrust bearing cap (No. 3 from front of engine). Ensure bearing caps are installed in their original location. Tighten main bearing cap bolts to specification. See TORQUE SPECIFICATIONS table at end of article. Install No. 3 bearing cap and tighten bolts finger tight.

4) Pry crankshaft forward and pry No. 3 bearing cap to rear of engine to align thrust bearing. While retaining forward pressure on crankshaft, tighten bearing cap to specification. See TORQUE SPECIFICATIONS table at end of article.

5) Ensure crankshaft end play is within specification. Replace thrust bearing if end play is not within specification. See CRANKSHAFT, MAIN & CONNECTING ROD BEARINGS table.

1991 ENGINES
7.3L V8 Diesel (Cont.)

CAUTION: Remove piston cooling jets before machining cylinder bores. Special "patch" bolts, included with new cooling jets, are used to install piston cooling jets. DO NOT use standard bolts.

Cylinder Block – 1) Check cylinder bore for wear, taper, out-of-round and piston fit. Using a feeler gauge and straightedge, check cylinder block deck surface for warpage. If deck surface warpage exceeds specification, replace cylinder block. DO NOT machine cylinder block to correct warpage. See CYLINDER BLOCK table under ENGINE SPECIFICATIONS at end of article.

2) Install all main bearing caps and tighten to specification before honing cylinder bore. See TORQUE SPECIFICATIONS table. Ensure bearing caps are installed in their original location, with arrow on cap pointing toward front of engine.

3) Use ONLY a spring-loaded type cylinder hone. After honing, thoroughly clean bore with detergent and water solution. Rinse solution from bore thoroughly with clean water. Wipe bore clean with lint free cloth. Lubricate cylinder bores with engine oil.

ENGINE OILING

ENGINE LUBRICATION SYSTEM

Full pressure lubrication through a full flow oil filter and oil cooler is supplied by a gear-driven oil pump. Main oil gallery feeds oil through passages to camshaft and crankshaft. Valve lifter gallery feeds valve lifters. Rocker arms are fed through hollow push rods.

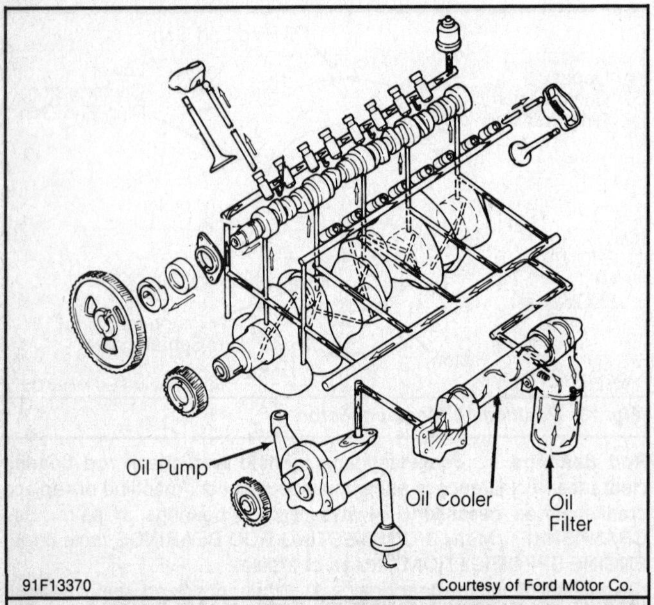
Oil Pump
Oil Cooler
Oil Filter
91F13370
Courtesy of Ford Motor Co.

Fig. 14: Cross-Sectional View of Engine Oil Circuit

Oil Cooler Assembly – Oil flows from pump to oil cooler located on left side of engine block. *See Figs. 9 and 14.* Oil flows around the outside of heat exchanger tubes inside oil cooler. Coolant flows through heat exchanger tubes where heat is transferred to coolant.

If oil is found in coolant or coolant is found in oil, check oil cooler for leakage. Areas of possible leakage include "O" rings, heat exchanger tubes inside cooler, front header and rear header.

Crankcase Capacity – Crankcase capacity is 10 qts. (9.5L) including filter change.

Oil Pressure – Normal oil pressure at 3300 RPM should be 40-70 psi (2.81-4.92 kg/cm²).

OIL PUMP

Removal & Disassembly – Remove oil pan. See OIL PAN under REMOVAL & INSTALLATION. On "F" Series, remove oil pump from oil pan. On "E" Series, remove oil pump retaining bolts. Remove oil pump and pick-up tube assembly. Disassemble oil pump. Note direction of component installation for reassembly reference.

Inspection – Inspect components for damage and wear. Check oil pump drive gear backlash. If backlash is not .006-.010" (.15-.25 mm), replace oil pump. Oil pump is serviced as an assembly.

Reassembly & Installation – 1) To reassemble, reverse disassembly procedure. Ensure components are installed in original location. To install, prime oil pump by filling inlet opening with oil and rotating pump shaft until oil emerges from outlet opening.

2) Install and tighten oil pump-to-cylinder block bolt to specification. See TORQUE SPECIFICATIONS table. To complete installation, reverse removal procedure.

TORQUE SPECIFICATIONS

TORQUE SPECIFICATIONS

Application	Ft. Lbs. (N.m)
Bellhousing-To-Engine Bolt	50-65 (68-88)
Camshaft Gear Allen Screw	15 (21)
Connecting Rod Nut	
Step 1	38 (52)
Step 2	51 (69)
Cylinder Head Bolt [1]	
Step 1	65 (88)
Step 2	90 (122)
Step 3	100 (136)
Step 4	100 (136)
Engine Mount Bracket-To-Engine Bolt	65-85 (88-115)
Exhaust Manifold Bolt [2]	35 (47)
Flexplate-To-Converter Bolt	20-30 (27-41)
Flywheel-To-Crankshaft [3]	47 (64)
Glow Plug	12 (16)
Injector Nozzle	22 (30)
Injection Pump Gear Bolt	25 (34)
Injection Pump Gear Cover Bolt [3]	14 (19)
Intake Manifold Bolt [4]	24 (33)
Main Bearing Cap Bolt	
Step 1	75 (102)
Step 2	95 (129)
Oil Cooler-To-Cylinder Block Bolt	
Front Header	24 (33)
Rear (Filter) Header	14 (19)
Oil Pan-To-Cylinder Block Bolt	
1/4" Bolt	[5]
5/16" Bolt	14 (19)
Oil Pump Pick-Up Tube	
Bracket-To-Main Bearing Cap Nut	14 (19)
Oil Pump Pick-Up Tube-To-Oil Pump Bolt	14 (19)
Rocker Arm Bolt	20 (27)
Starter Bolt	40-50 (54-68)
Vibration Damper Bolt	90 (122)
Water Pump [6]	14 (19)
	INCH Lbs. (N.m)
Rocker Arm Cover Bolt	72 (8)
Rear Engine Cover Bolt	84 (9)

[1] – At steps 1 and 2, tighten bolts in numerical sequence beginning with bolt No. 1. At steps 3 and 4, tighten bolts in line sequence beginning with bolt No. 15. *See Fig. 5.*

[2] – Tighten to specification in numerical sequence beginning with bolt No. 1, then tighten again to same specification in line sequence beginning with bolt No. 4. *See Fig. 4.*

[3] – Coat threads with thread sealing compound.

[4] – Tighten to specification in numerical sequence beginning with bolt No. 1, then tighten again to same specification in line sequence beginning with bolt No. 9. *See Fig. 3.*

[5] – Tighten to 84 INCH lbs. (9 N.m).

[6] – Apply sealant to specified bolts. *See Fig. 8.*

1991 ENGINES
7.3L V8 Diesel (Cont.)

ENGINE SPECIFICATIONS

GENERAL SPECIFICATIONS

Application	Specification
7.3L	
Displacement	444 Cu. In. (7.3L)
Bore	4.1095" (104.381 mm)
Stroke	4.1120" (104.445 mm)
Compression Ratio	21.5:1
Fuel System	Mechanical Fuel Injection
Horsepower @ RPM	180 @ 3300
Torque Ft. Lbs. @ RPM	345 @ 1400

CRANKSHAFT, MAIN & CONNECTING ROD BEARINGS

Application	In. (mm)
7.3L	
Crankshaft	
End Play	
Standard	.0025-.0085 (.064-.216)
Wear Limit	.012 (.30)
Main Bearings	
Journal Diameter	3.1228-3.1236 (79.319-79.339)
Journal Out-Of-Round	.0002 (.005)
Journal Taper [1]	.0005 (.013)
Runout	
Standard	.002 (.05)
Wear Limit	.005 (.13)
Oil Clearance	
Desired	.0018-.0036 (.046-.091)
Allowable	.0018-.0046 (.046-.117)
Connecting Rod Bearings	
Journal Diameter	2.4980-2.4990 (63.450-63.475)
Journal Out-Of-Round	.0003 (.008)
Journal Taper [1]	.0005 (.013)
Oil Clearance	.0011-.0036 (.028-.091)

[1] – Specification is within a 1" (25 mm) area.

CONNECTING RODS

Application	In. (mm)
7.3L	
Bore Diameter	
Pin Bore	1.1105-1.1108 (28.207-28.214)
Crankpin Bore	2.5001-2.5016 (63.503-63.541)
Crankpin Bearing Bore	
Maximum Out-Of-Round	.0005 (.013)
Maximum Taper	.0005 (.013)
Center-To-Center Length	7.128-7.132 (181.05-181.15)
Maximum Bend	[1] .002 (.05)
Maximum Twist	[1] .002 (.05)
Side Play	.012-.024 (.30-.61)

[1] – Specification listed is measured at the ends of an 8" (203 mm) bar, 4" (102 mm) on each side of rod center line.

PISTONS, PINS & RINGS

Application	In. (mm)
7.3L	
Pistons	
Diameter	[1] 4.1035-4.1040 (104.229-104.242)
Clearance	
Bores 1-6	.0055-.0085 (.140-.216)
Bores 7 & 8	.0060-.0085 (.152-.216)
Piston Height Above Crankcase	.010-.031 (.25-.79)
Pins	
Diameter	1.1099-1.1101 (28.191-28.197)
Piston Fit	.0003-.0007 (.007-.018)
Rod Fit	.0004-.0009 (.010-.023)
Rings	
No. 1	
End Gap	.013-.045 (.33-1.14)
Side Clearance	
Standard	.002-.004 (.05-.10)
Wear Limit	.006 (.15)
No. 2	
End Gap	.060-.085 (1.52-2.16)
Side Clearance	
Standard	.002-.004 (.05-.10)
Wear Limit	.006 (.15)
No. 3 (Oil)	
Side Clearance	
Standard	.001-.003 (.03-.08)
Wear Limit	.005 (.13)

[1] – Measure 1.23" (31.2 mm) below lower land of oil ring. Measure at piston pin bore center line, at 90-degree angle to piston pin.

CYLINDER BLOCK

Application	In. (mm)
7.3L	
Cylinder Bore	
Standard Diameter	
Bores 1-6	4.1095-4.1115 (104.381-104.432)
Bores 7 & 8	4.1100-4.1120 (104.394-104.445)
Maximum Out-Of-Round	.002 (.05)
Maximum Taper	.002 (.05)
Maximum Deck Warpage [1]	.003 (.08)

[1] – Specification is within a 6" (152.4 mm) area. Overall warpage is .006" (.15 mm). DO NOT machine cylinder block deck surface. If deck warpage exceeds specification, replace cylinder block.

VALVES & VALVE SPRINGS

Application	Specification
7.3L	
Intake Valves	
Face Angle	30°
Minimum Margin	.112" (2.84 mm)
Stem Diameter	.37165-.37235" (9.4399-9.4577 mm)
Exhaust Valves	
Face Angle	37.5°
Minimum Margin	.053" (1.35 mm)
Stem Diameter	.37165-.37235" (9.4399-9.4577 mm)
Valve Springs	
Free Length	
Intake & Exhaust	1.925-2.225" (48.90-56.52 mm)
Installed Height	
Intake	1.767" (44.88 mm)
Exhaust	1.833" (46.56 mm)
Out-Of-Square	.078" (1.98 mm)
Pressure	Lbs. @ In. (kg @ mm)
Valve Closed	
Intake & Exhaust	80 @ 1.833 (36 @ 46.56)

1991 ENGINES
7.3L V8 Diesel (Cont.)

CYLINDER HEAD

Application	Specification
7.3L	
Maximum Warpage [1]	.003" (.08 mm)
Prechamber Protrusion	[2]
Valve Seats	
Intake Valve	
Seat Angle	30°
Seat Width	.065-.095" (1.65-2.41 mm)
Maximum Seat Runout	.002" (.05 mm)
Exhaust Valve	
Seat Angle	37.5°
Seat Width	.065-.095" (1.65-2.41 mm)
Maximum Seat Runout	.002" (.05 mm)
Valve Guides	
Intake & Exhaust	
Valve Guide I.D.	.3736-.3746" (9.489-9.515 mm)
Valve Stem-To-Guide	
Maximum Oil Clearance	.0055" (.140 mm)

[1] – Specification is within a 6" (152.4 mm) area. Overall warpage is .006" (.15 mm). DO NOT machine cylinder head surface. If head warpage exceeds specification, replace cylinder head.

[2] – Within .0025" (.064 mm) above or below face of prechamber bore.

CAMSHAFT

Application	In. (mm)
7.3L	
End Play	.002-.009 (.05-.23)
Journal Diameter	2.0990-2.1000 (53.315-53.340)
Bearing I.D.	2.1015-2.1025 (53.378-53.404)
Oil Clearance	.0015-.0035 (.038-.089)
Front Bearing Installed Depth [1]	.020-.050 (.51-1.27)

[1] – Specification listed is distance from face of cylinder block to bearing.

VALVE LIFTERS

Application	In. (mm)
7.3L	
Lifter Diameter	.9209-.9217 (23.391-23.411)
Oil Clearance	.0011-.0034 (.028-.086)
Collapsed Lifter Clearance	.185 (4.70)

"E" & "F" Series

***NOTE:** Unless specified otherwise, references to "F" Series include "F" Series Super Duty. For engine repair procedures not covered in this article, see ENGINE OVERHAUL PROCEDURES article in GENERAL INFORMATION.*

ENGINE IDENTIFICATION

The eighth character of the Vehicle Identification Number (VIN) identifies engine. VIN is located near windshield on left side of instrument panel. The VIN number is also on the Safety Compliance Certification Label attached to left door lock pillar.

VIN ENGINE CODE

Engine	Code
7.5L PFI	G

ADJUSTMENTS

VALVE CLEARANCE ADJUSTMENT

1) Rotate crankshaft and position No. 1 piston on TDC of compression stroke. Make chalk mark at points "A" and "B" on crankshaft pulley at TDC. *See Fig. 1*. Rotate crankshaft 360 degrees for mark "B".

2) Using Lifter Bleed-Down Wrench (T71B-6513-B), apply pressure to push rod end of rocker arm. Slowly bleed down lifter until lifter plunger is completely bottomed. See VALVE CLEARANCE ADJUSTMENT table.

3) While holding lifter in this position, check clearance between rocker arm and valve stem tip using feeler gauge. If clearance is less than specified, install a .060" (1.52 mm) shorter push rod. If clearance is greater that specified, install a .060" (1.52 mm) longer push rod. See CAMSHAFT table under ENGINE SPECIFICATIONS at end of article.

VALVE CLEARANCE ADJUSTMENT [1]

Crankshaft Position	Check Intake Valve Nos.	Check Exhaust Valve Nos.
"A"	1, 3, 7 & 8	1, 4, 5 & 8
"B"	2, 4, 5 & 6	2, 3, 6 & 7

[1] – *See Fig. 1* for crankshaft positions.

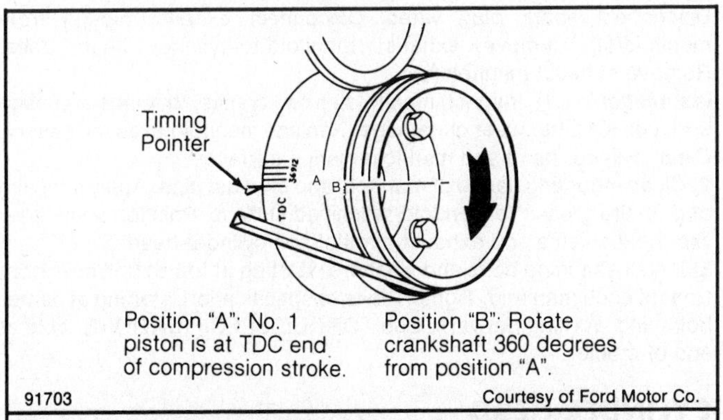
Timing
Pointer
TDC
A
B
Position "A": No. 1 piston is at TDC end of compression stroke.
Position "B": Rotate crankshaft 360 degrees from position "A".
91703
Courtesy of Ford Motor Co.

***Fig. 1:** Marking Crankshaft Position for Valve Adjustment*

REMOVAL & INSTALLATION

***NOTE:** For reassembly reference, label all electrical connectors, vacuum hoses and fuel lines before removal. Also place mating marks on engine hood and other major assemblies before removal.*

FUEL PRESSURE RELEASE

Remove fuel cap to release fuel tank pressure. Remove relief valve cap. Relief valve is located on fuel rail. Connect fuel pressure gauge to relief valve. Release fuel pressure into a suitable container.

COOLING SYSTEM BLEEDING

***WARNING:** When engine is operating, NEVER remove radiator cap under any conditions. Failure to follow instruction could damage cooling system or engine, or cause personal injury. Always wrap protective material around radiator cap to avoid injury from hot steam or hot coolant.*

1) Fill cooling system with 50/50 mixture of water and coolant. Pause several minutes for circulation. Fill radiator to filler neck seat. Disconnect heater outlet hose at water pump to bleed off trapped air. Fill radiator until coolant begins to escape.

2) Connect heater outlet hose. Fill radiator until coolant is between cap seal in filler neck to 1.5" (38 mm) below cap seal. Install radiator cap. Start engine and allow to warm up. Shut engine off. Allow engine to cool. Remove radiator cap and check coolant level. Top off radiator coolant as necessary.

ENGINE

Removal ("F" Series) – 1) Drain cooling system and crankcase. Mark hood hinges and remove hood. Disconnect battery and ground cables from cylinder block. Remove air cleaner and intake duct assembly with crankcase ventilation and carbon canister hoses attached.

2) Disconnect radiator hoses. Disconnect transmission cooler lines (if equipped). Disconnect oil cooler lines at oil filter adapter (if equipped).

***CAUTION:** DO NOT attempt to disconnect engine oil cooler lines at quick-disconnect fittings behind or at oil cooler, or damage to fittings will occur.*

3) Disconnect thermactor hoses. On models with A/C, discharge A/C system. Remove condenser and disconnect hoses at compressor. On all models, remove fan shroud, spacer, pulley and radiator. Remove and position alternator aside.

4) Disconnect oil pressure sending unit wire. Release fuel pressure. See FUEL PRESSURE RELEASE under REMOVAL & INSTALLATION. Disconnect fuel supply and return lines; use Disconnect Tool (D87L-9280-A) for 3/8" line or (D87L-9280-B) for 1/2" line. *See Fig. 2.*

5) If hairpin-type clip is used, remove hairpin by bending tab downward so it will clear body. Using your hands, spread clip legs .125" (3 mm) and push legs into fitting. Pull hairpin clip from fitting. *See Fig. 2.*

6) Disconnect accelerator cable, transmission shift rod and speed control linkages from throttle body. Disconnect throttle bracket from upper intake manifold and set aside with cables attached. Disconnect EGR tube. Disconnect vacuum lines, carbon canister hose, heater hoses and electrical wiring from engine.

7) Disconnect brake booster hose. Remove bellhousing-to-engine upper bolts. Remove oil fill dipstick and tube. Raise and support vehicle. Remove starter. Separate exhaust pipes from manifolds. Disconnect engine mounts from frame brackets. On A/T models, remove converter inspection plate and flex plate-to-converter bolts.

8) On all models, remove remaining bellhousing-to-engine bolts. Lower vehicle and support transmission. Attach engine hoist and carefully separate engine from transmission. Carefully lift engine from vehicle without damaging rear cover plate.

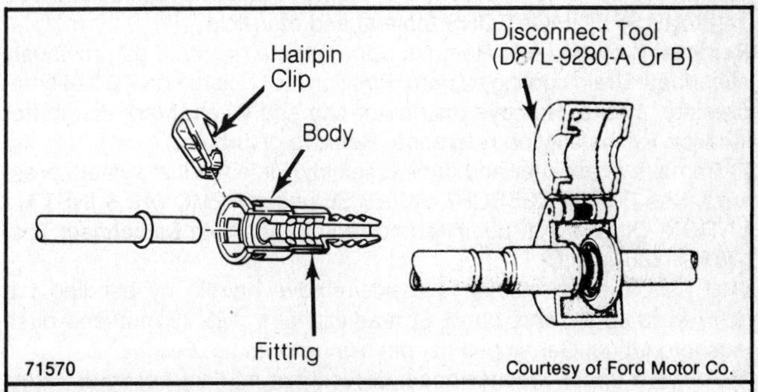
Hairpin
Clip
Body
Disconnect Tool
(D87L-9280-A Or B)
Fitting
71570
Courtesy of Ford Motor Co.

***Fig. 2:** Disconnecting Fuel Lines*

1991 ENGINES
7.5L V8 (Cont.)

Installation - To install, reverse removal procedure. Tighten bolts to specification. See TORQUE SPECIFICATIONS table at end of article. Check and top off all engine fluids. Fill and bleed air from cooling system. See COOLING SYSTEM BLEEDING under REMOVAL & INSTALLATION. Evacuate and recharge A/C system (if equipped).

Removal ("E" Series) - 1) Remove engine cover. Disconnect battery. Drain cooling system. Remove grille assembly and gravel deflector. Remove air cleaner and air ducts. Remove upper grille support, hood lock support and condenser upper mounting brackets (if equipped).

2) On models with A/C, discharge A/C system. Remove condenser and disconnect lines at A/C compressor. On all models, remove radiator hoses and heater hoses from engine. Disconnect power steering hoses. Remove power steering pump and bracket from front of engine.

3) Disconnect A/T lines at radiator. Remove fan, shroud and radiator. Disconnect EGR tube. Disconnect thermactor air pump hoses. Remove air cleaner assembly. Disconnect accelerator cable, transmission shift rod and speed control linkages from throttle body.

4) Disconnect throttle bracket from upper intake manifold and set aside with cables attached. Release fuel pressure. See FUEL PRESSURE RELEASE under REMOVAL & INSTALLATION. Disconnect fuel inlet and return lines using Disconnect Tool (D87L-9280-A or B). *See Fig. 2.*

5) Raise and support vehicle. Drain crankcase and remove oil filter. Disconnect exhaust pipes from manifolds. Disconnect transmission filler tube from right cylinder head. Remove engine mount attaching bolts and nuts. Remove starter wiring and remove starter.

NOTE: Right engine mount through bolt is installed from front of vehicle. Left engine mount through bolt is installed from rear.

6) Remove converter inspection cover bolts and remove cover. Remove flex plate-to-converter nuts. Remove bellhousing lower bolts. Remove ground strap from engine block. Lower vehicle and support transmission.

7) Disconnect engine wiring loom and position aside. Attach lifting device to engine. Remove upper bellhousing-to-engine bolts. Carefully remove engine from vehicle.

Installation - To install, reverse removal procedure. Tighten bolts to specification. See TORQUE SPECIFICATIONS table at end of article. Check and top off all engine fluids. Fill and bleed air from cooling system. See COOLING SYSTEM BLEEDING under REMOVAL & INSTALLATION. Evacuate and recharge A/C system (if equipped).

INTAKE MANIFOLDS

Removal (Upper) - 1) Disconnect negative battery cable. Disconnect throttle and A/T linkage (if equipped) from throttle body. Remove 2 bracket-to-intake manifold bolts. Set bracket and cables aside.

2) Disconnect electrical connectors and upper manifold vacuum hose connections as necessary. Disconnect EGR and PCV systems. Disconnect clean air supply hose of idle by-pass valve. Remove 4 upper intake manifold bolts. Remove upper intake manifold and throttle body as an assembly.

Installation - Clean all gasket surfaces. Position new gasket on lower intake manifold. Ensure new gasket is aligned. To complete installation, reverse removal procedure. Tighten bolts to specification. See TORQUE SPECIFICATIONS table at end of article.

Removal (Lower) - 1) Remove upper intake manifold as previously described. Drain cooling system. Position No. 1 piston on TDC of compression stroke. Remove distributor cap and wires. Mark distributor location for installation reference. Remove distributor.

2) Remove air cleaner and duct assembly. Release fuel system pressure. See FUEL PRESSURE RELEASE under REMOVAL & INSTALLATION. Disconnect fuel inlet and return lines with Disconnect Tool (D87L-9280-A or B).

3) If hairpin-type retainer is used, remove hairpin by bending tab downward so it clears body. Spread clip legs .125" (3 mm) and push legs into fitting. Gently pull hairpin clip from fitting. *See Fig. 2.*

4) Remove upper radiator hose. Disconnect coolant hoses at intake manifold and water pump. Label and disconnect vacuum hoses as necessary. Remove both thermactor exhaust air supply tubes. Remove ignition coil and mounting bracket.

5) Disconnect wiring harness from main wiring. Remove wiring harness and lower intake manifold as an assembly. Label and disconnect all other electrical wiring from intake manifold. Remove attaching bolts, and lift lower intake manifold and throttle body as an assembly.

Installation - 1) Clean all gasket surfaces. Apply 1/8" bead silicone sealer to 4 corners of cylinder block seal mounting surface. Install manifold gasket, front seal and rear seal. Apply 1/16" bead silicone sealer along full width of front and rear seal ends.

2) Install intake manifold within 15 minutes of applying sealer. Position intake manifold over 4 studs in cylinder heads. Check gasket and seal alignment before tightening.

3) Install manifold attaching bolts, studs and nuts. Tighten bolts in sequence to specification. *See Fig. 3.* See TORQUE SPECIFICATIONS table at end of article. Install fuel lines, electrical connectors and vacuum hoses. To install remaining components, reverse removal procedure.

4) Fill and bleed air from cooling system. See COOLING SYSTEM BLEEDING under REMOVAL & INSTALLATION. Check and adjust ignition timing as necessary. Start engine and allow it to reach operating temperature. Turn off engine. Retorque bolts and nuts sequentially to 22-35 ft. lbs. (30-47 N.m) to complete installation.

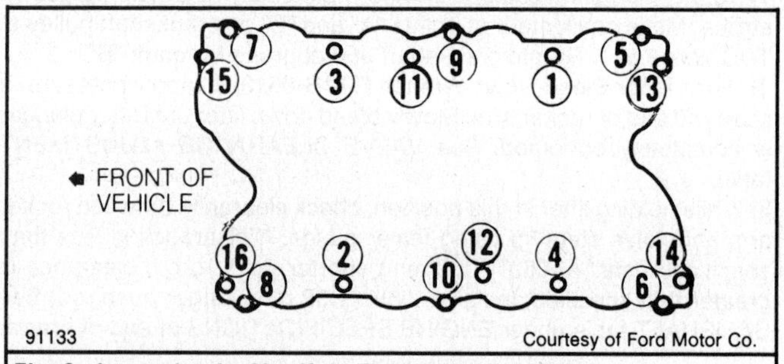
7
15
3
11
9
1
5
13
FRONT OF
VEHICLE
16
8
2
12
10
4
14
6
91133
Courtesy of Ford Motor Co.

Fig. 3: Lower Intake Manifold Tightening Sequence

EXHAUST MANIFOLD

Removal - 1) If removing right exhaust manifold, remove spark plug heat shield. If removing left exhaust manifold, disconnect EGR tube. On "E" Series, remove power steering pump support bracket.

2) On all models, remove oil dipstick tube from left exhaust manifold. Disconnect spark plug wires. Disconnect exhaust pipe(s) from manifold(s). Remove exhaust manifold-to-cylinder head bolts. Remove exhaust manifold(s).

Installation - 1) Inspect manifold(s) for cracks, damaged sealing surfaces, or other wear or damage. Replace manifold(s) as necessary. Clean cylinder head and manifold mating surfaces.

2) Clean mounting flange of manifold and exhaust pipe. Apply light film of graphite grease to manifold-machined surface. Position spark plug wire heat shields and exhaust manifold on cylinder head.

3) Install attaching bolts and washers, starting at fourth bolt hole from front of each manifold. Tighten bolts to specification, starting at center bolts and working outward. See TORQUE SPECIFICATIONS table at end of article.

CYLINDER HEAD

Removal - 1) Drain cooling system. Remove upper and lower intake manifolds. See INTAKE MANIFOLDS under REMOVAL & INSTALLATION. Disconnect exhaust pipes at manifolds. Remove drive belts. Remove thermactor air pump and bracket from right cylinder head. Remove alternator.

2) On models with A/C, discharge A/C system. Remove valves and hoses from compressor. Remove A/C compressor support bracket nuts from water pump. Remove and position compressor aside. Remove compressor mounting bracket from cylinder head.

3) On models without A/C, remove power steering pump bracket-to-left cylinder head bolts. Position pump and bracket aside. On "E" Series, disconnect oil filler tube. On all models, remove valve covers.

1991 ENGINES
7.5L V8 (Cont.)

4) Mark location for installation reference, and remove rocker arm assemblies and push rods. Remove cylinder head and exhaust manifold assemblies. Discard cylinder head gasket. Remove exhaust manifolds.

Inspection – Measure cylinder head and cylinder block mating surfaces for warpage. If cylinder head or cylinder block warpage exceeds specification, DO NOT remove more than .010" (.25 mm) material from original surface of cylinder head or block to correct warpage. See CYLINDER HEAD table under ENGINE SPECIFICATIONS at end of article.

Installation – 1) Clean gasket mating surfaces. Check flatness of cylinder head and block mating surfaces. If exhaust manifolds were removed, coat cylinder head and manifold port areas with a thin film of graphite grease, and install manifold on cylinder head.

2) Place 2 long head bolts in 2 rear lower bolt holes of left cylinder head. Place one long head bolt in rear lower bolt hole of right cylinder head. Keep bolts in position until heads are installed.

3) Position new head gaskets on block. DO NOT apply sealer to head gasket surfaces. Install cylinder head bolts. Tighten bolts in sequence to specification. *See Fig. 4.* See TORQUE SPECIFICATIONS table at end of article.

4) To complete installation, reverse removal procedure. Fill and bleed air from cooling system. See COOLING SYSTEM BLEEDING under REMOVAL & INSTALLATION. Evacuate and recharge A/C system (if equipped).

CAUTION: If valves/seats were serviced, check and adjust valve clearance. See VALVE CLEARANCE ADJUSTMENT under ADJUSTMENTS.

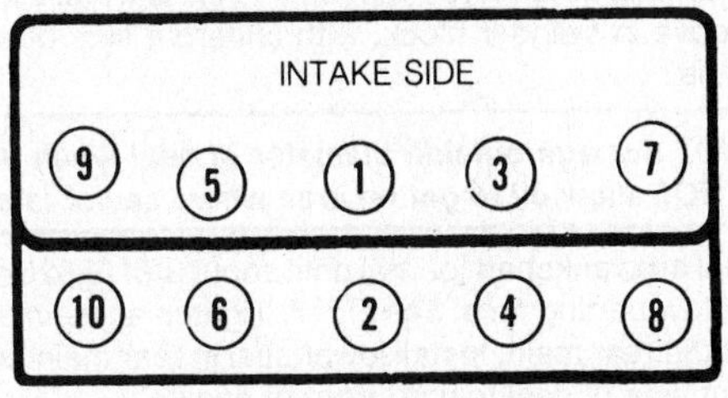
INTAKE SIDE
9
5
1
3
7
10
6
2
4
8

91410 Courtesy of Ford Motor Co.

Fig. 4: Cylinder Head Tightening Sequence

HYDRAULIC VALVE LIFTERS

NOTE: Before replacing a noisy hydraulic valve lifter, ensure valve clearance is correct. See VALVE CLEARANCE ADJUSTMENT under ADJUSTMENTS.

Removal – 1) Remove upper and lower intake manifolds. See INTAKE MANIFOLDS under REMOVAL & INSTALLATION. Remove valve covers. Loosen rocker arm fulcrum bolts and turn to one side.

2) Mark location for installation reference and remove push rods. Mark lifter location for installation reference. Remove valve lifters with a magnet. If lifters are stuck in bores, use Hydraulic Lifter Puller (T70L-6500-A).

Inspection – 1) Service lifters as an assembly only. Disassemble and clean lifters before testing. Test lifters with hydraulic lifter test fluid. DO NOT interchange parts between lifters.

2) Leak-down rate on hydraulic lifters is 10-50 seconds with 1/16" (1.6 mm) plunger travel under 50-lb. (23 kg) load. Replace lifter if it fails leak-down test, or if it is worn or damaged.

Installation – Clean outside of valve lifters. Lubricate lifters and bores with engine oil before installation. Install lifters in their original bores. If any new lifters are installed, ensure lifter moves freely in bore. To complete installation, reverse removal procedure. Fill and bleed air from cooling system. See COOLING SYSTEM BLEEDING under REMOVAL & INSTALLATION.

FRONT COVER OIL SEAL

NOTE: Front cover seal can be replaced without removing front cover.

Removal – Remove radiator fan, spacer and shroud. Remove drive belts. Remove crankshaft pulley and vibration damper. Place Seal Remover (T70P-6B070-B) onto front cover plate over front seal. Tighten 2 bolts, forcing seal remover under seal flange. Alternately tighten 2 bolts, one-half turn at a time, until seal is removed from engine.

Installation – Coat new seal with polyethylene grease and install seal using Seal Installer (T70P-6B070-A). Ensure seal is fully seated. To install remaining components, reverse removal procedure.

ENGINE FRONT COVER

Removal – 1) Disconnect negative battery cable. Drain cooling system and crankcase. Remove fan and radiator shroud. Disconnect radiator hoses at engine. Disconnect oil cooler lines (if equipped) at radiator. Remove upper radiator support and remove radiator.

2) Remove all drive belts and water pump pulley. Remove alternator and air pump assemblies with brackets. Remove A/C compressor and support bracket (if equipped). Disconnect heater hose from water pump, and loosen by-pass hose clamp at pump.

3) Remove crankshaft pulley. Using Vibration Damper Remover (T58P-6316-D), remove vibration damper and Woodruff key from crankshaft. Remove front cover-to-cylinder block bolts. Remove front cover and water pump as an assembly.

4) Cut oil pan gasket even with cylinder block face. Discard front cover gasket and pan gasket. Carefully remove old seal using a pin punch; DO NOT damage front cover seal recess.

Installation – 1) Install new front cover oil seal. Coat gasket surface of oil pan with gasket sealer. Cut and position new gasket on oil pan. Apply silicone sealer at block-to-oil pan junction. Apply gasket sealer to front cover and cylinder block gasket surfaces. Position new front cover gasket in place.

2) Position front cover on cylinder block. Install Front Cover Aligner (T68P-6019-A) on crankshaft. *See Fig. 5.* Coat threads of cover bolts with oil-resistant sealer and install bolts. It may be necessary to push cover downward to compress pan gasket.

3) While pushing in on Front Cover Aligner (T68P-6019-A), tighten oil pan-to-cover bolts. Remove front cover aligner and tighten front cover-to-cylinder block bolts. To complete installation, reverse removal procedure. Fill engine crankcase with proper grade oil. Fill and bleed air from cooling system. See COOLING SYSTEM BLEEDING under REMOVAL & INSTALLATION.

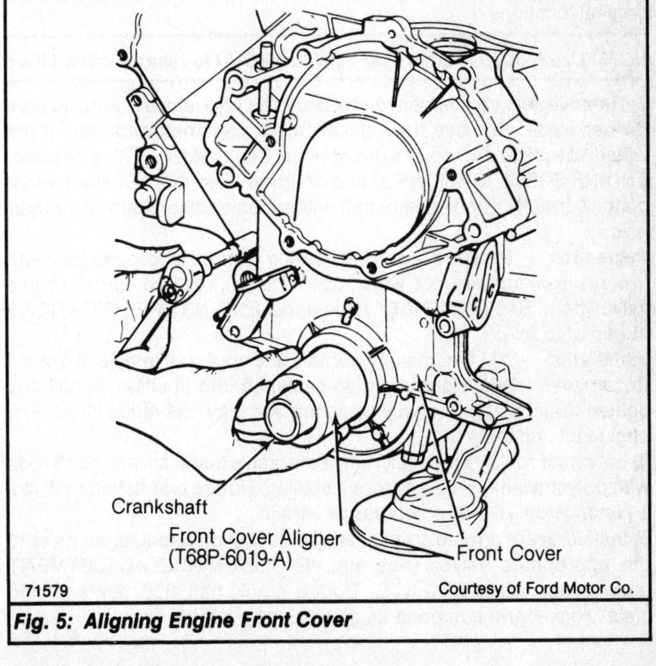
Crankshaft
Front Cover Aligner
(T68P-6019-A)
Front Cover

71579 Courtesy of Ford Motor Co.

Fig. 5: Aligning Engine Front Cover

1991 ENGINES
7.5L V8 (Cont.)

TIMING CHAIN & SPROCKET

Removal - 1) Position No. 1 piston on TDC of compression stroke. Remove front cover. See ENGINE FRONT COVER under REMOVAL & INSTALLATION. Check alignment of camshaft gear and crankshaft gear timing marks. *See Fig. 6.*

2) Check timing chain defection (stretch) for excessive wear. See CAMSHAFT table under ENGINE SPECIFICATIONS at end of article. Remove camshaft sprocket bolt and washer. Slide timing chain and sprockets forward and remove as an assembly.

Installation - Assemble and align timing chain and sprockets. *See Fig. 6.* Install chain and sprockets as an assembly. Lubricate timing chain with engine oil. Tighten bolts to specification. See TORQUE SPECIFICATIONS table at end of article. To complete installation, reverse removal procedure.

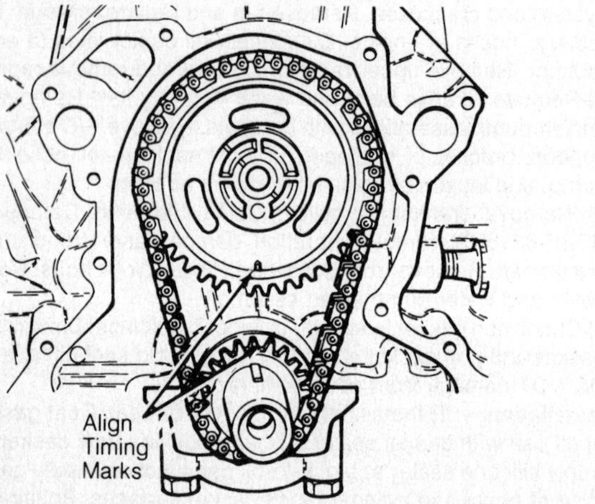
Align
Timing
Marks
90B10190
Courtesy of Ford Motor Co.

Fig. 6: Aligning Timing Marks

CAMSHAFT

Removal - 1) Remove engine front cover, timing chain and sprockets. See ENGINE FRONT COVER and TIMING CHAIN & SPROCKET under REMOVAL & INSTALLATION. Remove intake manifolds. See INTAKE MANIFOLDS under REMOVAL & INSTALLATION. Remove valve covers.

2) Loosen all rocker arm bolts and rotate rocker arms aside. Remove push rods and valve lifters, keeping them in order for installation in original locations.

NOTE: Use Hydraulic Lifter Puller (T70L-6500-A) to remove stuck lifters.

3) Remove A/C condenser-to-chassis bolts (if equipped) and set condenser aside. Remove front grille. Check camshaft end play. If not within specification, replace thrust plate. See CAMSHAFT table under ENGINE SPECIFICATIONS at end of article. Remove camshaft thrust plate. Carefully remove camshaft without damaging bearings or journals.

Inspection - Measure camshaft bearing journals and lobes for wear. If measurements are not within specification, replace camshaft and valve lifters. See CAMSHAFT table under ENGINE SPECIFICATIONS at end of article.

Installation - 1) Oil camshaft journals and apply polyethylene grease to camshaft lobes. Carefully slide camshaft into position. Install and tighten thrust plate. Recheck camshaft end play. Lubricate lifters with engine oil and install.

2) Lubricate rocker arms, fulcrum seats, valve stem tips and push rods with polyethylene grease before installing. Rotate crankshaft until No. 1 piston is on TDC of compression stroke.

3) Install rocker arm, fulcrum seats, oil deflection and fulcrum bolts to the appropriate valves. See VALVE CLEARANCE ADJUSTMENT table under ADJUSTMENTS. Rotate crankshaft 360 degrees and install rocker arm components on remaining valves.

4) Ensure fulcrum seat base is inserted into slot on cylinder head before tightening fulcrum bolts. To complete installation, reverse removal procedure. Use new gaskets where required.

CAMSHAFT BEARINGS

NOTE: It may be necessary to remove crankshaft for access to camshaft bearings.

Removal - Remove engine from vehicle. See ENGINE under REMOVAL & INSTALLATION. Remove camshaft. See CAMSHAFT under REMOVAL & INSTALLATION. Remove flywheel. Push pistons to top of cylinders. Remove camshaft rear bearing bore plug. Using Camshaft Bearing Remover/Installer Set (T65L-6250-A), remove camshaft bearings.

Installation - Using camshaft bearing remover/installer, install bearings into place. Ensure oil holes in bearings and cylinder block are aligned. Install front bearing .040-.060" (1.02-1.52 mm) behind front face of cylinder block. Coat new rear bore plug with sealer and install. To complete installation, reverse removal procedure.

REAR CRANKSHAFT OIL SEAL

Removal - 1) Remove oil pan and oil pump. Loosen all main bearing cap bolts to slightly lower crankshaft. DO NOT lower more than 1/32" (.794 mm). Remove rear main bearing cap and remove lower oil seal half. Use seal remover to remove upper seal.

2) If seal remover is not available, install a small metal screw in one end of seal. Carefully pull on screw to remove seal without damaging sealing surface.

Installation - 1) Carefully clean oil seal grooves in bearing cap and block. Coat split-lip seal halves with engine oil. Carefully install upper seal into groove in cylinder block, with undercut side of seal toward front of engine.

NOTE: DO NOT damage outside diameter of seal when installing in groove. DO NOT allow oil to get on area where sealer is applied.

2) Rotate seal on crankshaft journal until about 3/8" (9.525 mm) of seal protrudes below parting face. *See Fig. 7.* Tighten all main bearing cap bolts except the rear main. Install lower seal in rear main bearing cap, with undercut side of seal toward front of engine.

3) Allow seal to protrude about 3/8" (9.5 mm) above parting surface to mate with upper seal when cap is installed. Apply 1/16" (1.5 mm) bead of silicone sealer to both sides of cylinder block-to-cap mating surface and both sides of bearing cap. *See Fig. 8.*

4) Install and tighten rear main bearing cap before sealer sets (about 15 minutes). To complete installation, reverse removal procedure.

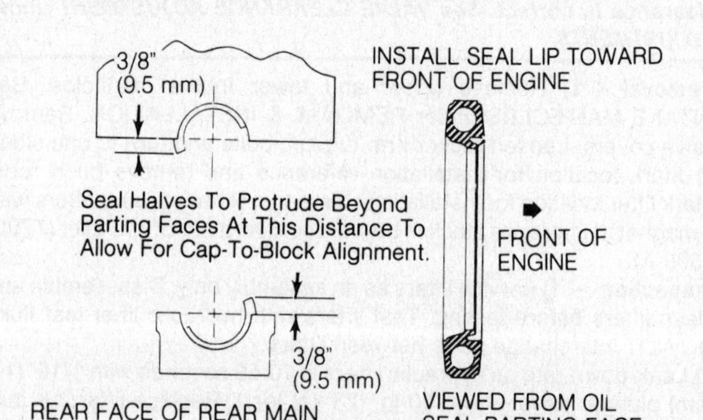
3/8"
(9.5 mm)
INSTALL SEAL LIP TOWARD
FRONT OF ENGINE
Seal Halves To Protrude Beyond
Parting Faces At This Distance To
Allow For Cap-To-Block Alignment.
FRONT OF
ENGINE
3/8"
(9.5 mm)
REAR FACE OF REAR MAIN
BEARING CAP & CYLINDER BLOCK
VIEWED FROM OIL
SEAL PARTING FACE
91076
Courtesy of Ford Motor Co.

Fig. 7: Installing Rear Crankshaft Oil Seal

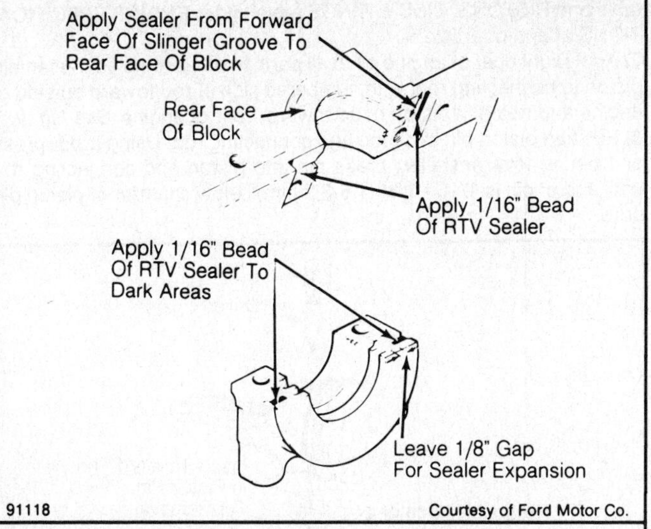
Apply Sealer From Forward Face Of Slinger Groove To Rear Face Of Block
Rear Face Of Block
Apply 1/16" Bead Of RTV Sealer
Apply 1/16" Bead Of RTV Sealer To Dark Areas
Leave 1/8" Gap For Sealer Expansion
91118
Courtesy of Ford Motor Co.

Fig. 8: Identifying Silicone Sealer Application Points

WATER PUMP

Removal - 1) Remove negative battery cable. Drain cooling system. Remove fan shroud and fan. Loosen power steering pump attaching bolts. Remove A/C compressor (if equipped). Remove A/C compressor and power steering bracket.

2) Remove all drive belts. Remove air pump, alternator and bracket. Disconnect all hoses from water pump and loosen by-pass hose clamp at pump. Remove remaining bolts and remove water pump. Remove separator plate from water pump and discard gaskets.

Installation - Clean all gasket surfaces. To install, reverse removal procedure. Use new gaskets coated on both sides with water-resistant sealer. Fill and bleed air from cooling system. See COOLING SYSTEM BLEEDING under REMOVAL & INSTALLATION.

OIL PAN

Removal - 1) Remove engine cover (if equipped) and disconnect battery. Drain cooling system. Disconnect upper and lower radiator hoses. Disconnect and remove air cleaner assembly. Disconnect throttle and transmission linkage at throttle body. Release fuel pressure. See FUEL PRESSURE RELEASE under REMOVAL & INSTALLATION.

2) Using Disconnect Tool (D87L-9280-A) for 3/8" line or (D87L-9280-B) for 1/2" line, disconnect fuel supply and return lines. *See Fig. 2.* On A/T models, disconnect transmission cooler lines at radiator.

3) On all models, disconnect engine cooler lines at oil filter adapter (if equipped). Remove fan assembly and shroud. Remove radiator. Remove power steering pump. Remove front engine mount through bolts.

CAUTION: On "E" Series, right engine through bolt is installed from front of vehicle. Left engine mount through bolt is installed from rear of vehicle.

4) Remove dipstick tube retaining nuts, and remove dipstick and tube. Remove oil filler tube and bracket (if equipped). On models with A/C, rotate or remove A/C lines at rear of compressor to clear dash. On all models, remove upper intake manifold and throttle body assembly. See INTAKE MANIFOLDS under REMOVAL & INSTALLATION.

5) Raise and support vehicle. Drain engine oil and remove oil filter. Disconnect and remove muffler inlet pipe assembly. Disconnect control linkage at transmission. On A/T models, remove transmission dipstick assembly. On all models, remove drive shaft assembly.

6) Raise engine. Engine and transmission assembly will pivot around rear engine mount. Engine and transmission assembly must be raised approximately 4" (measure at front engine mounts), and remain centered in engine compartment. Support engine with wooden blocks.

7) Remove oil pan bolts and lower oil pan. Remove oil pump bolts and pick-up tube nut. Lower oil pump assembly into pan. Remove oil pan.

Installation - To install, reverse removal procedure. Tighten bolts to specification. See TORQUE SPECIFICATIONS table at end of article. Fill or top off all fluids. Fill and bleed air from cooling system. See COOLING SYSTEM BLEEDING under REMOVAL & INSTALLATION. Start engine and check for leaks.

OVERHAUL

CYLINDER HEAD

Cylinder Head - 1) Clean head gasket mating surface. Clean carbon from combustion chambers. Use care not to damage surfaces. Check cylinder head for cracks, burrs, nicks and warpage.

2) DO NOT machine more than .010" (.25 mm) from original cylinder head surface to correct warpage. Replace cylinder head as necessary. See CYLINDER HEAD table under ENGINE SPECIFICATIONS at end of article.

Valve Springs - 1) Measure valve spring installed height from top of spring seat to underside of spring retainer. Ensure installed height is within specification. See VALVES & VALVE SPRINGS table under ENGINE SPECIFICATIONS at end of article.

2) If installed height is not within specification, a .03" (.8 mm) shim can be installed between cylinder head and valve spring to obtain correct height. Inspect valve spring free length and pressure. Replace valve spring if free length and pressure are not within specification. See VALVES & VALVE SPRINGS table under ENGINE SPECIFICATIONS.

CAUTION: DO NOT install valve spring spacers unless necessary. Using more spacers than required can result in spring breakage or worn camshaft lobes.

Valve Stem Oil Seals - Umbrella-type oil seals are used on all valves. Intake and exhaust valve stem seals are not interchangeable. Seals are identified with IN for intake and EX for exhaust. Lubricate valve stem with engine oil and install new seal with cup side down over valve guide.

Valve Guides - 1) Valve guides must be reamed for an oversized valve if valve stem oil clearance exceeds specification. See CYLINDER HEAD table under ENGINE SPECIFICATIONS at end of article. Valves are available with .015" (.38 mm) and .030" (.76 mm) oversize stems.

2) If oversized valves or oversized valve stem oil seals are not available, valve guide may be bored out to use a service bushing. Always use reamers in proper sequence (smallest first).

NOTE: Always grind valve seat after valve guide has been reamed or service bushing has been installed.

Valve Seat - Ensure valve seat angle, seat width and seat runout are within specification. See CYLINDER HEAD table under ENGINE SPECIFICATIONS at end of article. Valve seats must be ground when valve guide is reamed or replaced. Replacement information is not available from manufacturer.

Valves - Ensure head diameter, valve face runout, stem diameter and valve margin are within specification. See VALVES & VALVE SPRINGS table under ENGINE SPECIFICATIONS at end of article.

CAUTION: DO NOT remove more than .010" (.25 mm) from end of valve stem when resurfacing tip of valve.

Valve Seat Correction Angles - Grind valve seat to a true 45-degree angle. If seat width is too wide after grinding, use a 30-degree stone to lower seat or a 60-degree stone to raise seat. See CYLINDER HEAD table under ENGINE SPECIFICATIONS at end of article.

CYLINDER BLOCK ASSEMBLY

Pistons & Rod Assembly - Ensure pistons and rods are installed in their original cylinder. Ensure notch on piston top faces forward, and numbered side of rod faces outward. *See Fig. 9.* Check side play of connecting rod. See CONNECTING RODS table under ENGINE SPECIFICATIONS at end of article.

1991 ENGINES
7.5L V8 (Cont.)

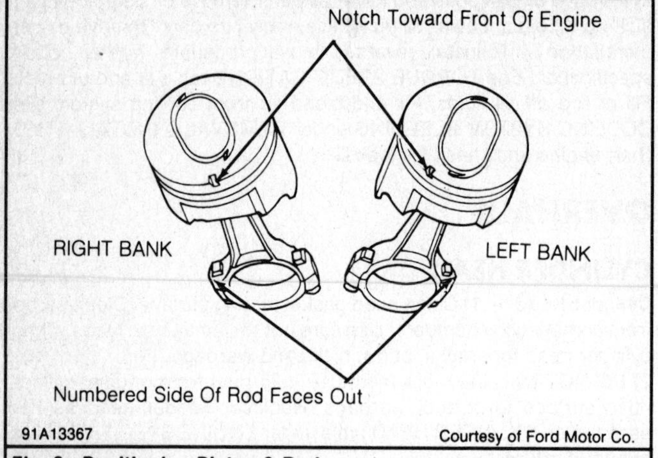
Notch Toward Front Of Engine
RIGHT BANK
LEFT BANK
Numbered Side Of Rod Faces Out
91A13367
Courtesy of Ford Motor Co.

Fig. 9: Positioning Piston & Rod

Fitting Pistons – 1) Check piston-to-bore clearance. See PISTONS, PINS & RINGS table under ENGINE SPECIFICATIONS at end of article. Standard size pistons are color-coded Red, Blue or Yellow on the piston dome. See PISTONS, PINS & RINGS table. Oversize pistons are also available.

2) If bore diameter is in lower one-third of specification, use a Red coded piston. If bore diameter is in middle one-third of specification, use a Blue coded piston. If bore diameter is in upper one-third of specification, use Yellow coded piston. Use proper size piston to obtain specified clearance. See PISTONS, PINS & RINGS table under ENGINE SPECIFICATIONS.

Piston Rings – 1) Select rings for bore diameter. Place ring in cylinder bore in which it will be installed. Use piston to square ring in bore and place ring below normal ring wear area. Measure ring end gap. If ring gap is not within specification, try another ring set. See PISTONS, PINS & RINGS table under ENGINE SPECIFICATIONS at end of article.

2) Check side clearance of rings after installing on piston. Ensure clearance is within specification around entire circumference. Replace piston and/or rings if clearance is not within specification. See PISTONS, PINS & RINGS table under ENGINE SPECIFICATIONS. Ensure rings are properly spaced on piston before installing pistons into cylinder. *See Fig. 10.*

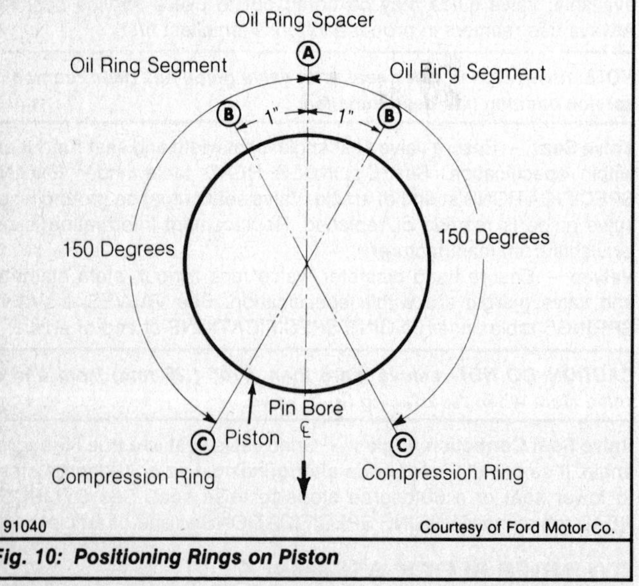
Oil Ring Spacer
A
Oil Ring Segment
Oil Ring Segment
B
1"
1"
B
150 Degrees
150 Degrees
Pin Bore
℄
C
Piston
C
Compression Ring
Compression Ring
91040
Courtesy of Ford Motor Co.

Fig. 10: Positioning Rings on Piston

Piston Pin Replacement – 1) Using an arbor press and Piston Pin Remover/Installer (T68P-6135-A), press piston pin from piston and connecting rod. *See Fig. 11.* Ensure connecting rod piston pin bore and piston pin are within specification. See CONNECTING RODS table and PISTONS, PINS & RINGS table under ENGINE SPECIFICATIONS at end of article.

2) Apply light coat of engine oil to all parts to be assembled. Assemble piston to connecting rod, with numbered side of rod toward outside of engine and notch in piston head toward front of engine. *See Fig. 9.*

3) Position piston pin in piston and connecting rod. Using arbor press and pin remover/installer, press pin into piston and connecting rod until end of pin is 1/16 - 1/8" (1.6-3.2 mm) below chamfer of piston pin bore.

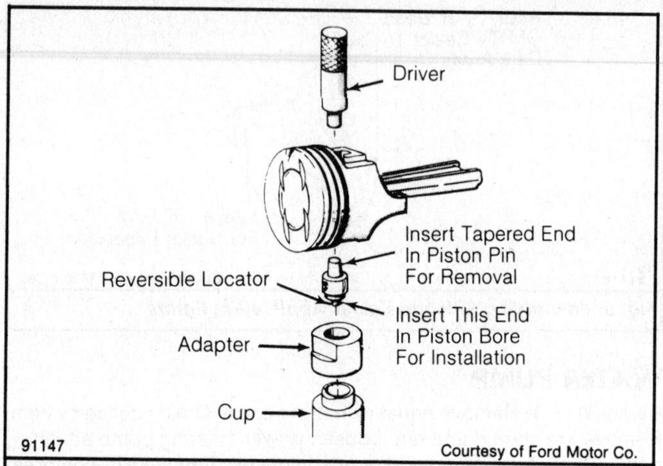
Driver
Insert Tapered End
In Piston Pin
For Removal
Reversible Locator
Insert This End
In Piston Bore
For Installation
Adapter
Cup
91147
Courtesy of Ford Motor Co.

Fig. 11: Removing & Installing Piston Pin

Rod Bearings – 1) Use Plastigage method and check rod bearing clearance. If proper oil clearance cannot be obtained with standard bearings, try a combination of undersize bearings. DO NOT use any other bearing combination other than what is listed. See UNDERSIZE MAIN & ROD BEARING COMBINATIONS table.

2) If use of bearing combinations does not bring clearance within specification, machine or replace crankshaft as necessary. Always replace bearings in pairs. See CRANKSHAFT, MAIN & CONNECTING ROD BEARINGS table under ENGINE SPECIFICATIONS at end of article.

UNDERSIZE MAIN & ROD BEARING COMBINATIONS [1]

Excess Bearing Clearance In. (mm)	Use Upper Bearing In. (mm)	Use Lower Bearing In. (mm)
.0-.0005 (.0-.013)	.001 (.025)	[2]
.0005-0010 (.013-.026)	.001 (.025)	.001 (.025)
.0010-.0015 (.026-.039)	.002 (.050)	.001 (.025)
.0015-.0020 (.039-.052)	.002 (.050)	.002 (.050)

[1] – DO NOT use any other bearing combination other than what is listed. If use of bearing combinations does not bring clearance within specification, machine or replace crankshaft as necessary.

[2] – Use standard bearing.

Crankshaft & Main Bearings – 1) When checking main bearing clearance in vehicle, position a jack under adjoining bearing counterweight being checked. Remove only one main bearing cap at a time.

2) Use Plastigage method and check main bearing clearance. If proper oil clearance cannot be obtained with standard bearings, try a combination of undersize bearings. DO NOT use any other bearing combination other than what is listed. See UNDERSIZE MAIN & ROD BEARING COMBINATIONS table.

3) If use of bearing combinations does not bring clearance within specification, machine or replace crankshaft as necessary. Always replace bearings in pairs. See CRANKSHAFT, MAIN & CONNECTING ROD BEARINGS table under ENGINE SPECIFICATIONS at end of article.

NOTE: Ensure main bearing oil holes are aligned with cylinder block oil holes.

4) Install all bearing caps except thrust bearing cap (No. 3 from front of engine). Tighten main bearing cap bolts to specification. See TORQUE SPECIFICATIONS table at end of article. Install No. 3 bearing cap and tighten bolts finger tight.
5) Pry crankshaft forward and pry No. 3 bearing cap to rear of engine to align thrust bearing. While retaining forward pressure on crankshaft, tighten bearing cap to specification. See TORQUE SPECIFICATIONS table at end of article.
6) Ensure crankshaft end play is within specification. Replace thrust bearing if end play is not within specification. See CRANKSHAFT, MAIN & CONNECTING ROD BEARINGS table under ENGINE SPECIFICATIONS at end of article.
Cylinder Block - 1) Using a feeler gauge and straightedge, check cylinder block head gasket surface for warpage. Check cylinder bore for wear, taper, out-of-round and piston fit. See CYLINDER BLOCK table under ENGINE SPECIFICATIONS at end of article.

CAUTION: DO NOT machine more than .010" (.25 mm) of material from original cylinder block head surface.

2) Install all main bearing caps and tighten to specification before honing cylinder bore. Ensure bearing caps are installed in their original location, with arrow on cap pointing toward front of engine.
3) Use ONLY a spring-loaded type cylinder hone. After honing, thoroughly clean bore with detergent and water solution. Rinse solution from bore thoroughly with clean water. Wipe bore clean with lint free cloth. Lubricate cylinder bores with engine oil.

ENGINE OILING

ENGINE LUBRICATION SYSTEM

Engine lubrication is a force-feed system. The oil is supplied under full pressure to crankshaft, connecting rods, camshaft bearing and valve lifters. A controlled volume of oil is supplied to rocker arms and push rods. All other moving parts are lubricated by splash or gravity flow. Oil flows through oil filter before entering main oil gallery. *See Fig. 12.*

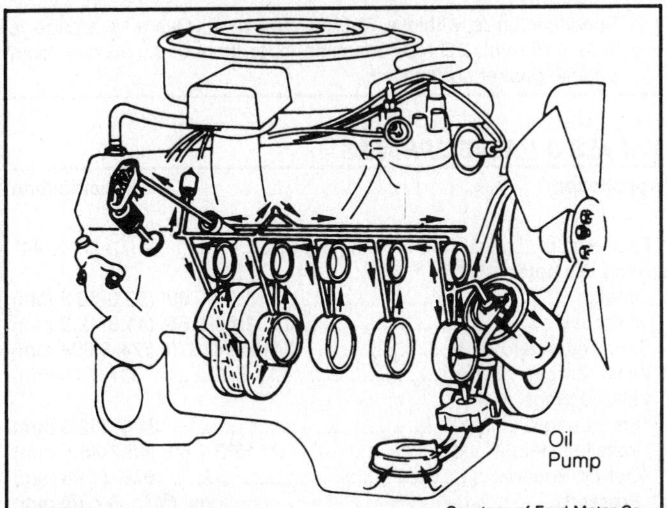
Oil
Pump
90C10191
Courtesy of Ford Motor Co.

Fig. 12: Cross-Sectional View of Engine Oil Circuit

Crankcase Capacity - Crankcase capacity is 5 qts. (4.75L). Add one additional quart (.95L) when replacing oil filter.
Oil Pressure - Normal oil pressure at 2000 RPM should be 40-65 psi (2.8-4.6 kg/cm²) with engine at operating temperature.
Oil Pressure Relief Valve - Nonadjustable oil pressure regulator valve is located in pump body.

OIL PUMP

Removal & Disassembly - Oil pump and oil pan must be removed together. See OIL PAN under REMOVAL & INSTALLATION. Disassemble oil pump. Note direction of component installation for reassembly reference.

Inspection - 1) Clean all parts thoroughly. Check pump housing, outer rotor, inner rotor, shaft and pump cover for damage, scoring or excessive wear. See OIL PUMP SPECIFICATIONS table. Remove rotor assembly from pump housing. Using feeler gauge, measure inner-to-outer rotor tip clearance.
2) Install rotor assembly in pump housing. Place a straightedge over rotor assembly and housing. Insert feeler gauge between straightedge and housing to measure rotor end play. Using a feeler gauge, measure clearance between outer rotor and pump housing.

OIL PUMP SPECIFICATIONS

Application	In. (mm)
Inner-To-Outer Rotor Tip Clearance	.012 (.30)
Outer Rotor-To-Housing Clearance	.001-.013 (.03-.33)
Relief Valve-To-Bore Clearance	.0015-.0030 (.038-.076)
Rotor End Play	.004 (.10) Max.
Shaft-To-Housing Clearance	.0015-.0030 (.038-.076)

Reassembly & Installation - 1) To reassemble, reverse disassembly procedure. Ensure components are installed in original location. Ensure oil pump spins freely after reassembly. To install, prime oil pump by filling inlet opening with oil and rotating pump shaft until oil emerges from outlet opening.
2) Install oil pump assembly and pan. To complete installation, reverse removal procedure. Tighten bolts to specification. See TORQUE SPECIFICATIONS table.

TORQUE SPECIFICATIONS

TORQUE SPECIFICATIONS

Application	Ft. Lbs. (N.m)
Bellhousing-To-Engine Bolt	40-50 (54-68)
Camshaft Sprocket Bolt	40-50 (54-68)
Connecting Rod Nut	41-45 (56-61)
Cylinder Head Bolt [1]	
Step 1	70-80 (95-109)
Step 2	100-110 (136-149)
Step 3	130-140 (176-190)
Front Engine Mount Nut	60-85 (81-115)
Front Engine Mount Through Bolt	40-58 (54-79)
Engine Front Cover	12-18 (16-24)
Engine Mount-To-Engine Bolt	50-70 (68-95)
Exhaust Manifold Bolt	22-30 (30-41)
Flexplate-To-Converter Bolt	20-30 (27-41)
Flywheel-To-Crankshaft Bolt	75-85 (102-115)
Lower Intake Manifold Bolts/Nuts [2]	
Step 1	10-12 (14-16)
Step 2	12-22 (16-30)
Step 3	22-35 (30-47)
Step 4	[3]
Main Bearing Cap Bolt	95-105 (129-142)
Oil Pump Attaching Bolt	22-32 (30-44)
Oil Pan-To-Engine Block Bolt	[4]
Rear Mount-To-Crossmember Bolt/Nut	60-80 (81-109)
Rocker Arm Fulcrum Bolt	18-25 (24-34)
Starter Bolt	40-50 (54-68)
Upper Intake Manifold Bolt	12-18 (16-24)
Vibration Damper-To-Crankshaft Bolt	70-90 (95-122)
Water Pump Bolt	12-18 (16-24)
	INCH Lbs. (N.m)
Camshaft Thrust Plate Bolt	71-108 (8-12)
Valve Cover Bolt [5]	108-132 (12-15)

[1] - Tighten in sequence. *See Fig. 4.*
[2] - Tighten in sequence. *See Fig. 3.*
[3] - Allow engine to reach normal operating temperature. Retorque lower exhaust manifold bolts/nuts to 22-35 ft. lbs. (30-47 N.m)
[4] - Tighten 1/4" bolt to 84-108 INCH lbs. (10-12 N.m). Tighten 5/16" bolt to 96-132 INCH lbs. (11-15 N.m)
[5] - Tighten in sequence, from rear to front on left side of engine and front to rear on right side of engine.

1991 ENGINES
7.5L V8 (Cont.)

ENGINE SPECIFICATIONS

GENERAL SPECIFICATIONS

Application	Specification
7.5L	
Displacement	460 Cu. In. (7.5L)
Bore	4.36" (110.7 mm)
Stroke	3.85" (97.8 mm)
Compression Ratio	8.5:1
Fuel System	PFI
Horsepower @ RPM	230 @ 3600
Torque Ft. Lbs. @ RPM	390 @ 2200

CRANKSHAFT, MAIN & CONNECTING ROD BEARINGS

Application	In. (mm)
7.5L	
Crankshaft	
End Play	
Standard	.004-.008 (.10-.20)
Service Limit	.012 (.30)
Main Bearings	
Journal Diameter	2.9994-3.0002 (76.185-76.205)
Journal Taper	.0005 (.013)
Journal Runout	
Standard	.002 (.05)
Service Limit	.005 (.13)
Maximum Journal Out-Of-Round	.0006 (.02)
Oil Clearance	
Desired	.0008-.0015 (.020-.038)
Allowable	.0008-.0026 (.020-.066)
Connecting Rod Bearings	
Journal Diameter	2.4992-2.5000 (63.480-63.500)
Journal Taper	.0006 (.015)
Maximum Journal Out-Of-Round	.0006 (.02)
Oil Clearance	
Desired	.0008-.0015 (.020-.038)
Allowable	.0008-.0025 (.020-.064)

CONNECTING RODS

Application	In. (mm)
7.5L	
Bore Diameter	
Pin Bore	1.0386-1.0393 (26.380-26.398)
Crankpin Bore	2.6522-2.6530 (67.366-67.386)
Center-To-Center Length	6.6035-6.6065 (167.729-167.805)
Maximum Bend [1]	.012 (.30)
Maximum Twist [1]	.024 (.61)
Side Play	
Standard	.010-.020 (.25-.51)
Service Limit	.023 (.058)

[1] – Specification listed is measured at the ends of an 8" (203 mm) bar, 4" (102 mm) on each side of rod center line.

PISTONS, PINS & RINGS

Application	In. (mm)
7.5L	
Pistons	
Clearance	.0022-.0030 (.056-.076)
Diameter [1]	
Red Piston	4.3577-4.3583 (110.686-110.701)
Blue Piston	4.3589-4.3595 (110.716-110.731)
Yellow Piston	4.3601-4.3607 (110.747-110.762)
Pins	
Diameter	1.0398-1.0403 (26.411-26.424)
Length	3.29-3.32 (83.6-84.3)
Piston Fit	.0002-.0005 (.005-.013)
Rod Fit	Press Fit
Rings	
No. 1 & 2	
End Gap	.010-.020 (.25-.51)
Side Clearance	.0025-.0045 (.064-.114)
No. 3 (Oil)	
End Gap (Steel Rail)	.010-.035 (.25-.89)
Side Clearance	Snug Fit

[1] – Standard pistons are color-coded Red, Blue and Yellow on piston dome.

CYLINDER BLOCK

Application	In. (mm)
7.5L	
Cylinder Bore	
Standard Diameter	4.3600-4.3636 (110.744-110.835)
Maximum Deck Warpage [1]	.003 (.08)
Maximum Out-Of-Round	
Standard	.0015 (.038)
Service Limit	.005 (.13)
Maximum Taper	.010 (.25)

[1] – Specification is within a 6" (152 mm) area. Overall warpage is .006" (.15 mm). DO NOT machine more than .010" (.25 mm) from original gasket surface.

VALVES & VALVE SPRINGS

Application	Specification
7.5L	
Face Angle	44°
Head Diameter	
Intake	1.97-1.99" (50.0-50.5 mm)
Exhaust	1.65-1.66" (41.9-42.2 mm)
Stem Diameter	.3415-.3423" (8.674-8.694 mm)
Valve Margin	.031" (.79 mm)
Valve Springs	
Free Length	2.06" (52.3 mm)
Installed Height	1.80-1.83" (45.7-46.5 mm)
Out-Of-Square	.078" (1.98 mm)
Pressure	Lbs. @ In. (kg @ mm)
Intake & Exhaust	
Closed	74-84 @ 1.81 (35-38 @ 46)
Open	218-240 @ 1.33 (99-109 @ 34)

1991 ENGINES
7.5L V8 (Cont.)

CYLINDER HEAD

Application	Specification
7.5L	
Maximum Warpage [1]	.003" (.08 mm)
Valve Seats	
Seat Angle	45°
Seat Width	.060-.080" (1.52-2.03 mm)
Maximum Seat Runout	.002" (.05 mm)
Valve Guides	
Valve Guide Bore I.D.	.3433-.3443" (8.720-8.745 mm)
Valve Stem-To-Guide	
Oil Clearance	.0010-.0027" (.025-.069 mm)

[1] - Specification is taken within a 6" (152 mm) area. Overall warpage is .006" (.15 mm). DO NOT machine more than .010" (.25 mm) from original cylinder head thickness.

CAMSHAFT

Application	In. (mm)
7.5L	
Camshaft Bearing I.D.	2.1258-2.1268 (53.995-54.021)
Journal Diameter	2.1238-2.1248 (53.945-53.970)
End Play	
Standard	.001-.006 (.03-.15)
Service Limit	.006 (.15)
Lobe Lift	
Intake	.252 (6.40)
Exhaust	.278 (7.06)
Lobe Wear	.005 (.13)
Maximum Journal Runout	.005 (.13)
Oil Clearance	
Standard	.001-.003 (.03-.08)
Service Limit	.006 (.15)
Timing Chain Deflection	.500 (12.7)

VALVE LIFTERS

Application	In. (mm)
7.5L	
Lifter Diameter	.8740-.8745 (22.200-22.212)
Oil Clearance	.0007-.0027 (.018-.069)
Collapsed Lifter Clearance	
Desired	.100-.150 (2.54-3.81)
Allowable	.075-.175 (1.91-4.45)

1991 ENGINE COOLING
Specifications

Aerostar, Bronco, Explorer, Ranger, "E" & "F" Series

NOTE: Unless specified otherwise, references to "F" Series include "F" Series Super Duty.

SPECIFICATIONS

BELT ADJUSTMENT

Inspect belt for fraying. If fraying has occurred, ensure belt and tensioner are aligned properly. *See Fig. 1.* If tensioner has reached its limit of travel, belt is excessively stretched and replacement of belt is required. If excessive noise is noticed from tensioner or idler, check for possible bearing failure. DO NOT apply belt dressing or any other additive to belt(s). Ensure belts are properly installed. *See Figs. 2-9.* See BELT TENSION ADJUSTMENT SPECIFICATIONS table.

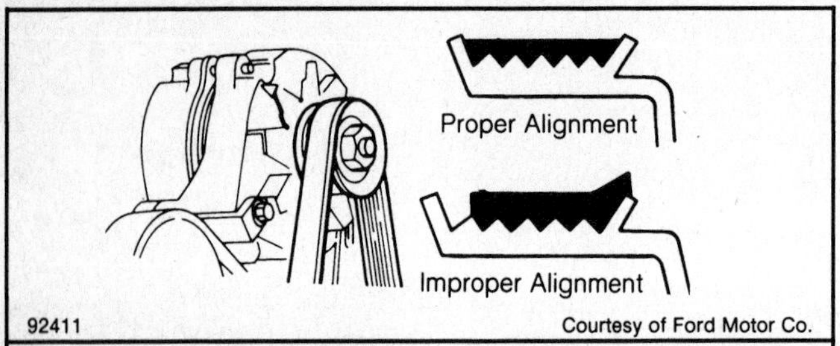
Proper Alignment
Improper Alignment
92411
Courtesy of Ford Motor Co.

Fig. 1: Aligning Serpentine Belt

BELT TENSION ADJUSTMENT SPECIFICATIONS

Application	New Belt Lbs. (kg)	[1] Used Belt Lbs. (kg)
2.3L		
Fixed	150-190 (68-86)	140-160 (64-73)
With Tensioner [2]	150-190 (68-86)	140-160 (64-73)
2.9L	120-160 (54-73)	110-130 (50-59)
3.0L		
Fixed	120-160 (54-73)	110-130 (50-59)
With Tensioner [2]	150-190 (68-86)	140-160 (64-73)
4.0L With Tensioner [2]	108-132 (49-60)	108-132 (49-60)
4.9L With Tensioner [2]	[3] [4]	[3] [4]
5.0L With Tensioner [2]	[5] [6]	[5] [6]
5.8L With Tensioner [2]	[5] [6]	[5] [6]
7.3L Except Ambulance		
Vac. Pump W/ 3/8" Belt	90-130 (41-59)	65-85 (30-39)
Vac. Pump W/ 1/2" Belt	110-150 (50-68)	75-95 (34-43)
All Other W/ 1/2" Belt	140-180 (64-82)	95-115 (43-52)
7.3L Ambulance		
Alternator	140-160 (64-73)	140-160 (64-73)
Vac. Pump	90-130 (41-59)	65-85 (30-39)
A/C & P/S	140-180 (64-82)	95-115 (43-52)
7.5L		
With Tensioner [2]	[7]	[7]
Alt. & Air Pump	160-200 (73-91)	110-130 (50-59)

[1] - Any belt that has been in operation for 10 minutes.
[2] - Tension is correct if tensioner is within indicator marks.
[3] - 90 lbs. (41 kg) minimum for vehicles with 60 and 75-amp alternators.
[4] - 117 lbs. (53 kg) minimum for vehicles with 100-amp alternators.
[5] - 77 lbs. (35 kg) minimum for vehicles with 60 and 75-amp alternators.
[6] - 111 lbs. (50 kg) minimum for vehicles with 100-amp alternators.
[7] - 94 lbs. (43 kg) minimum tension.

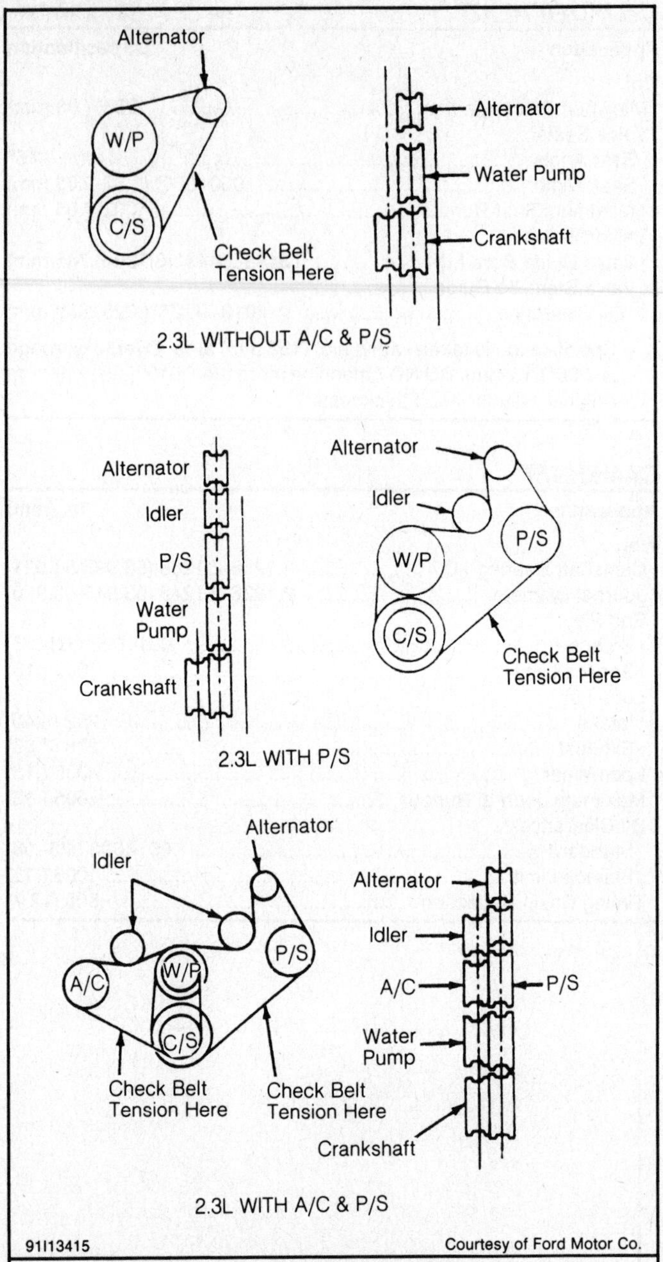
Alternator
W/P
C/S
Check Belt
Tension Here
Alternator
Water Pump
Crankshaft
2.3L WITHOUT A/C & P/S
Alternator
Idler
P/S
Water
Pump
Crankshaft
Alternator
Idler
P/S
W/P
C/S
Check Belt
Tension Here
2.3L WITH P/S
Alternator
Idler
A/C
W/P
C/S
P/S
Check Belt
Tension Here
Check Belt
Tension Here
Alternator
Idler
A/C
P/S
Water
Pump
Crankshaft
2.3L WITH A/C & P/S
91I13415
Courtesy of Ford Motor Co.

Fig. 2: Checking Belt Routing & Tension (2.3L)

1991 ENGINE COOLING
Specifications (Cont.)

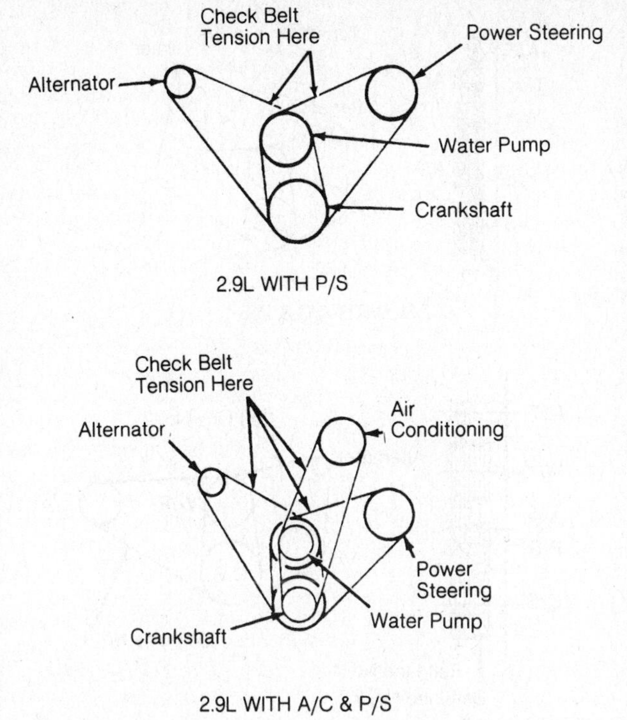
Check Belt
Tension Here
Power Steering
Alternator
Water Pump
Crankshaft
2.9L WITH P/S
Check Belt
Tension Here
Alternator
Air
Conditioning
Power
Steering
Water Pump
Crankshaft
2.9L WITH A/C & P/S

91J13416 Courtesy of Ford Motor Co.

Fig. 3: Checking Belt Routing & Tension (2.9L)

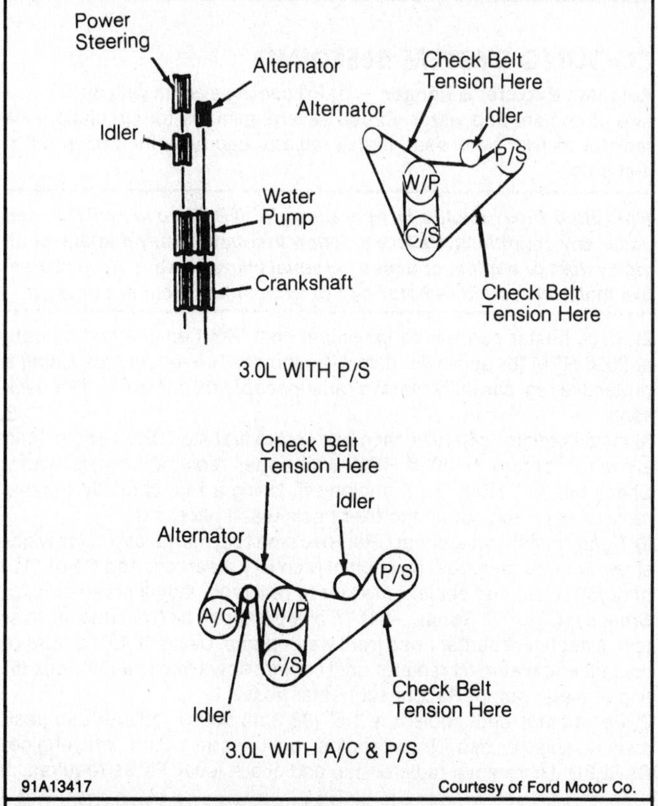
Power
Steering
Alternator
Idler
Water
Pump
Crankshaft
Check Belt
Tension Here
Alternator
Idler
P/S
W/P
C/S
Check Belt
Tension Here
3.0L WITH P/S
Check Belt
Tension Here
Idler
Alternator
P/S
A/C
W/P
C/S
Idler
Check Belt
Tension Here
3.0L WITH A/C & P/S

91A13417 Courtesy of Ford Motor Co.

Fig. 4: Checking Belt Routing & Tension (3.0L)

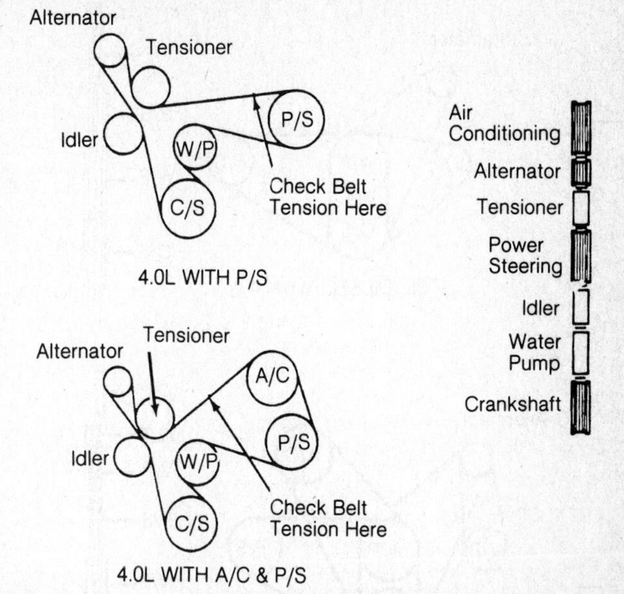
Alternator
Tensioner
P/S
Idler
W/P
C/S
Check Belt
Tension Here
4.0L WITH P/S
Air
Conditioning
Alternator
Tensioner
Power
Steering
Idler
Water
Pump
Crankshaft
Tensioner
Alternator
A/C
P/S
Idler
W/P
C/S
Check Belt
Tension Here
4.0L WITH A/C & P/S

91B13418 Courtesy of Ford Motor Co.

Fig. 5: Checking Belt Routing & Tension (4.0L)

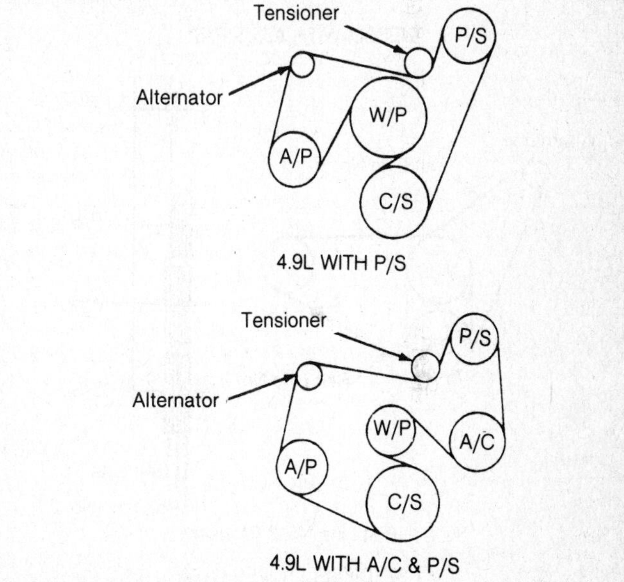
Tensioner
P/S
Alternator
W/P
A/P
C/S
4.9L WITH P/S
Tensioner
P/S
Alternator
W/P
A/C
A/P
C/S
4.9L WITH A/C & P/S

91C13419 Courtesy of Ford Motor Co.

Fig. 6: Checking Belt Routing (4.9L)

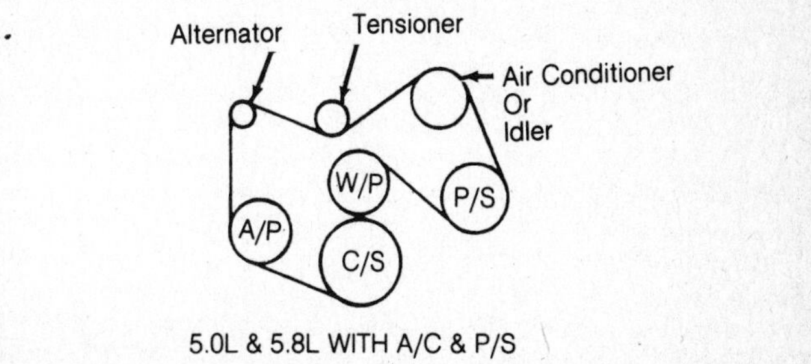
Alternator
Tensioner
Air Conditioner
Or
Idler
W/P
P/S
A/P
C/S
5.0L & 5.8L WITH A/C & P/S

91F13420 Courtesy of Ford Motor Co.

Fig. 7: Checking Belt Routing (5.0L & 5.8L)

1991 ENGINE COOLING
Specifications (Cont.)

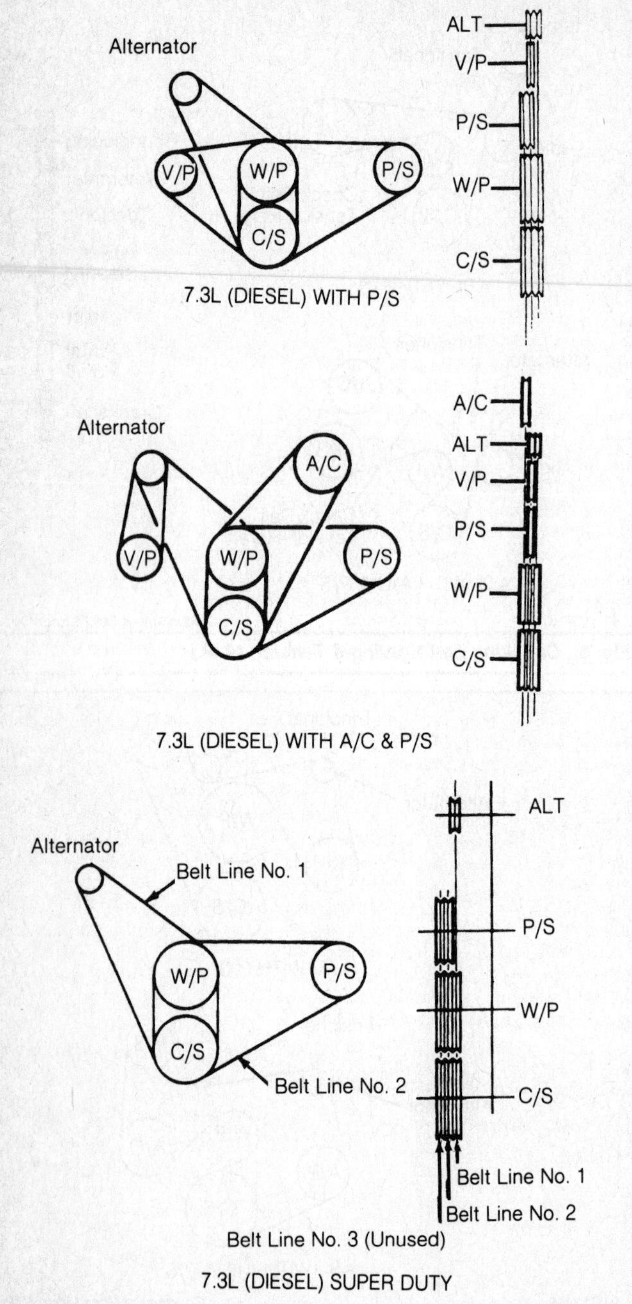
Alternator
ALT
V/P
P/S
W/P
C/S
7.3L (DIESEL) WITH P/S
Alternator
A/C
ALT
V/P
P/S
W/P
C/S
7.3L (DIESEL) WITH A/C & P/S
Alternator
Belt Line No. 1
W/P
P/S
C/S
Belt Line No. 2
ALT
P/S
W/P
C/S
Belt Line No. 1
Belt Line No. 2
Belt Line No. 3 (Unused)
7.3L (DIESEL) SUPER DUTY

91G13421 Courtesy of Ford Motor Co.

Fig. 8: Checking Belt Routing (7.3L Diesel)

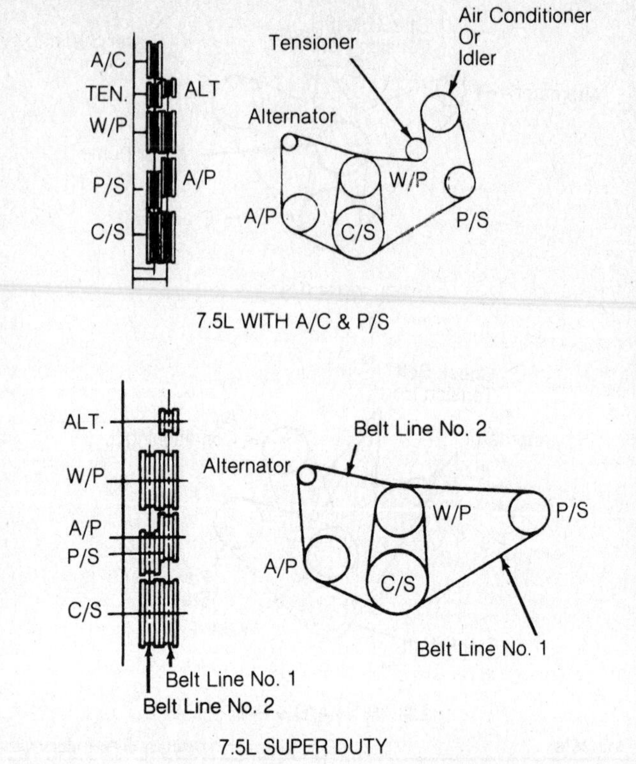
A/C
TEN.
ALT
W/P
P/S
A/P
C/S
Tensioner
Air Conditioner
Or
Idler
Alternator
W/P
A/P
C/S
P/S
7.5L WITH A/C & P/S
ALT.
W/P
A/P
P/S
C/S
Belt Line No. 1
Belt Line No. 2
Belt Line No. 2
Alternator
W/P
P/S
A/P
C/S
Belt Line No. 1
7.5L SUPER DUTY

91H13422 Courtesy of Ford Motor Co.

Fig. 9: Checking Belt Routing (7.5L)

COOLING SYSTEM BLEEDING

Aerostar, Explorer & Ranger – 1) Fill cooling system with 50/50 mixture of coolant and water. Pause several minutes for circulation. Fill radiator to filler neck seat. Install radiator cap fully, then back off to first stop.

WARNING: When engine is operating, NEVER remove radiator cap under any conditions. Failure to follow instruction may damage cooling system or engine, or cause personal injury. Always wrap protective material around radiator cap to avoid injury from hot coolant.

2) Place heater controls to maximum heat. Start engine and operate at 2000 RPM for approximately 3-4 minutes. Turn engine off. Using a protective rag, carefully remove radiator cap. Add coolant to filler neck seat.

3) Install radiator cap fully, then back off to first stop. Start engine and allow to operate at 2000 RPM until upper radiator hose is warm. Check heater output. Turn engine off. Using a rag, carefully remove radiator cap. Add coolant to filler neck seat if necessary.

4) Tightly install radiator cap. Remove small cap (large cap is for windshield washer reservoir) on coolant recovery reservoir. Add 1.1 qt. (1L) of 50/50 water and coolant mixture to reservoir. Install reservoir cap.

Bronco, "E" & "F" Series – 1) To bleed trapped air from cooling system, disconnect heater hose from water pump. Using 50/50 mixture of coolant and water, fill radiator until coolant flows from heater hose fitting at water pump. Reconnect heater hose.

2) Fill radiator until coolant is 1.5" (38 mm) below radiator cap seal. Install radiator cap. Run engine until warm. Turn off engine. CAREFULLY remove radiator cap and check level. Fill as required.

1991 ENGINE COOLING
Specifications (Cont.)

COOLING SYSTEM CAPACITIES

Application	Specification
Coolant Replacement Interval	30,000 Miles or 36 Months
Coolant Capacity	
Aerostar	
3.0L	11.8 qts. (11.2L)
4.0L	
Manual or Automatic Transmission [1]	8.1 qts. (7.6L)
Automatic Transmission [2]	8.5 qts. (8.0L)
Bronco & "F" Series	
4.9L	
Manual or Automatic Transmission [1]	13 qts. (12L)
Manual Transmission [2]	14 qts. (13L)
Automatic Transmission [3] [4]	15 qts. (14L)
Automatic Transmission [4]	14 qts. (13L)
5.0L	
Manual Transmission [1]	13 qts. (12L)
Automatic Transmission [1]	14 qts. (13L)
Manual or Automatic Transmission [3]	14 qts. (13L)
Manual or Automatic Transmission [5]	15 qts. (14L)
5.8L	
Manual Transmission [1]	15 qts. (14L)
Automatic Transmission [1]	16 qts. (15L)
Manual or Automatic Transmission [3]	16 qts. (15L)
Manual or Automatic Transmission [5]	17 qts. (16L)
7.3L	[6] 29 qts. (27L)
7.5L	18 qts. (17L)
Explorer	
4.0L	
Manual or Automatic Transmission [1]	8.1 qts. (7.6L)
Automatic Transmission [2]	8.5 qts. (8.0L)

COOLING SYSTEM CAPACITIES (Cont.)

Application	Specification
Coolant Capacity (Cont.)	
"E" Series	
4.9L	
Manual or Automatic Transmission [1]	15 qts. (14L)
Manual or Automatic Transmission [2]	18 qts. (17L)
5.0L	
Manual or Automatic Transmission [1] [3]	17.5 qts. (16.6L)
Manual or Automatic Transmission [5]	18.5 qts. (17.5L)
5.8L	
Manual or Automatic Transmission [1]	20 qts. (19L)
Manual or Automatic Transmission [2]	21 qts. (20L)
7.3L	[6] 31 qts. (29L)
7.5L	28 qts. (26L)
Ranger	
2.3L	
Manual or Automatic Transmission	7.2 qts. (6.8L)
2.9L	
Manual or Automatic Transmission [1]	7.2 qts. (6.8L)
Manual or Automatic Transmission [3]	7.8 qts. (7.4L)
3.0L	
Manual or Automatic Transmission	11.8 qts. (11.2L)
4.0L	
Manual or Automatic Transmission [1]	8.1 qts. (7.6L)
Automatic Transmission [2]	8.5 qts. (8.0L)
Pressure Cap	
All Models	13 PSI
Thermostat Opens	
7.3L Diesel	
Starts	180-192°F (82-89°C)
Fully Open	200-212°F (93-100°C)
Gasoline Engines	[7]

[1] – With standard cooling.
[2] – With A/C or super cooling.
[3] – With A/C.
[4] – With standard or super cooling.
[5] – With super cooling.
[6] – Include 5 qts. (4.7L) in reservoir bottle.
[7] – Information is not available from manufacturer.

1991 CLUTCHES
Hydraulic

Aerostar, Bronco, Explorer, Ranger, "E" & "F" Series

NOTE: Unless otherwise specified, references to "F" Series include "F" Series Super Duty.

DESCRIPTION

The hydraulic clutch control consists of the hydraulic master cylinder, slave cylinder, reservoir, and connecting hydraulic lines. The clutch disc and pressure plate are single-disc type. The clutch release bearing or bearing arm is activated by hydraulic pressure.

The pilot bearing is mounted inside the bellhousing and requires no lubrication unless the clutch assembly is serviced. The clutch linkage or pedal position requires no adjustments.

TRANSMISSION & TRANSFER CASE APPLICATION

Vehicle Model	Transmission Model
Aerostar & Explorer	Mazda M50D 5-Speed O/D
Bronco	Borg-Warner T-18 4-Speed Ford S5-42 ZF 5-Speed Mazda M50D 5-Speed O/D
Ranger	
2WD	Mazda M50D 5-Speed O/D
4WD	Mitsubishi FM146 5-Speed O/D
"E" Series	
E350	Ford S5-42 ZF 5-Speed
"F" Series	Borg-Warner T-18 4-Speed Ford S5-42 ZF 5-Speed Mazda M50D 5-Speed O/D
	Transfer Case Model
Aerostar	Spicer TC-28
Bronco	Borg-Warner 1356
Explorer & Ranger	Borg-Warner 1354
"F" Series	Borg-Warner 1356 Borg-Warner 1345

ADJUSTMENTS

CLUTCH MASTER CYLINDER PUSH ROD LENGTH ADJUSTMENT

Bronco & "F" Series – 1) Ensure attaching nut on left side of clutch pedal is tight. Remove clutch master cylinder push rod from the cross shaft lever pin. If push rod is in alignment with the cross shaft lever pin, adjustment is okay.

2) If push rod is not in alignment with the cross shaft lever pin, reinstall push rod to the cross shaft lever pin. Pump clutch pedal several times to reset position of shaft to the pedal slot.

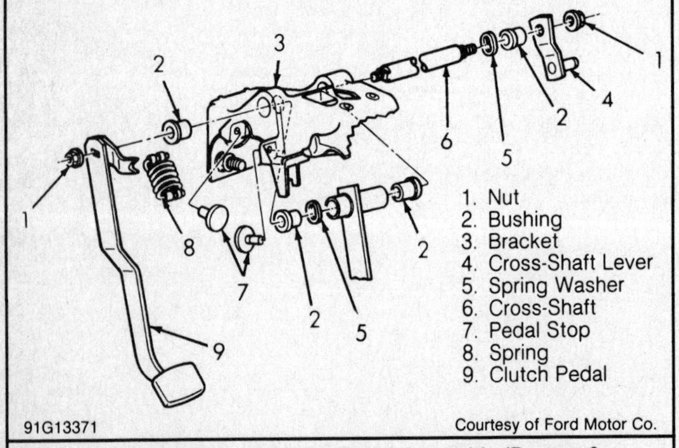
1
2
3
4
5
6
7
8
9
1. Nut
2. Bushing
3. Bracket
4. Cross-Shaft Lever
5. Spring Washer
6. Cross-Shaft
7. Pedal Stop
8. Spring
9. Clutch Pedal
91G13371
Courtesy of Ford Motor Co.

Fig. 1: Exploded View of Clutch Pedal Assembly (Bronco & "F" Series)

3) Remove clutch master cylinder push rod from lever pin and evaluate alignment. If push rod is aligned with pin, adjustment is okay. If the 2 components are still not in alignment, replace cross shaft lever. *See Fig. 1.*

CLUTCH RELEASE BEARING TRAVEL MEASUREMENT

Externally Mounted Slave Cylinder – 1) Remove slave cylinder dust shield. With clutch pedal fully depressed, measure external slave cylinder push rod travel.

2) Push rod should travel a minimum of 0.43" (10.9 mm). DO NOT replace clutch hydraulic system if measurement exceeds specification. If slave cylinder travel is less than specification, check hydraulic reservoir fluid level.

Internally Mounted Slave Cylinder – 1) Remove rubber plug from inspection port in transmission bellhousing. Position Bearing Travel Measurement Tool (D87T-4201A) through the opening and against slave cylinder. *See Fig. 2.*

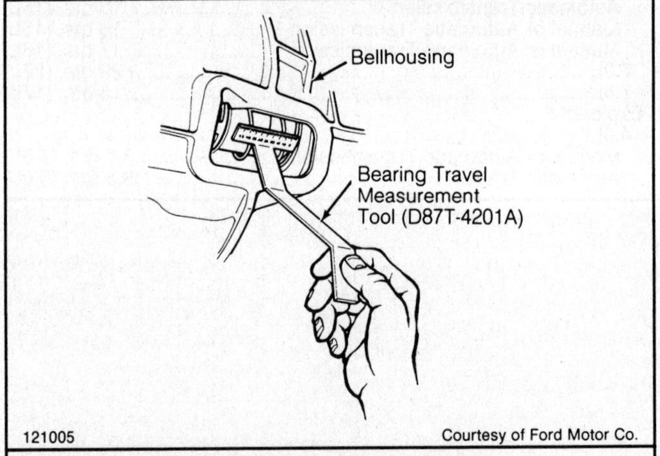
Bellhousing
Bearing Travel
Measurement
Tool (D87T-4201A)
121005
Courtesy of Ford Motor Co.

Fig. 2: Measuring Clutch Release Bearing Travel

2) Using rear edge of Black plastic bearing retainer as an indicator, take a reading with clutch pedal fully up. With clutch pedal fully depressed, take another measurement.

3) Difference between the 2 readings is total bearing travel. If bearing travel is greater than .295" (7.49 mm), replace pressure plate and or clutch disc.

4) If bearing travel is .295" (7.49 mm) or less, inspect hydraulic system for leaks. Repair leak. If no leak is found, bleed system. See HYDRAULIC SYSTEM BLEEDING under IN-VEHICLE SERVICE. Recheck bearing travel after repairs have been completed.

IN-VEHICLE SERVICE

CLUTCH/STARTER INTERLOCK SWITCH

1) Disconnect wiring connector at switch by flexing retaining tab. Test electrical continuity of switch using an ohmmeter. Switch should be open (infinity) when pedal is up and clutch is engaged. Switch should be closed (zero ohms) when clutch pedal is pressed to floor. On all models except "E" Series, if switch does not function as specified, replace switch.

2) On "E" Series models, if switch does not operate properly, check position of self-adjusting clip. Adjust switch by removing both halves of clip and positioning clip closer to switch body. Reset switch by depressing clutch pedal to floor. If switch still does not operate properly, replace switch. *See Fig. 3 or 4.*

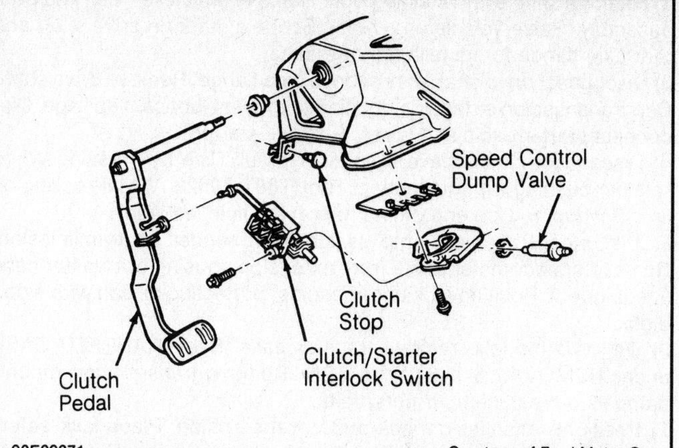
Speed Control
Dump Valve
Clutch
Stop
Clutch/Starter
Interlock Switch
Clutch
Pedal
90E09371
Courtesy of Ford Motor Co.

Fig. 3: Identifying Clutch/Starter Interlock Switch & Components ("E" Series)

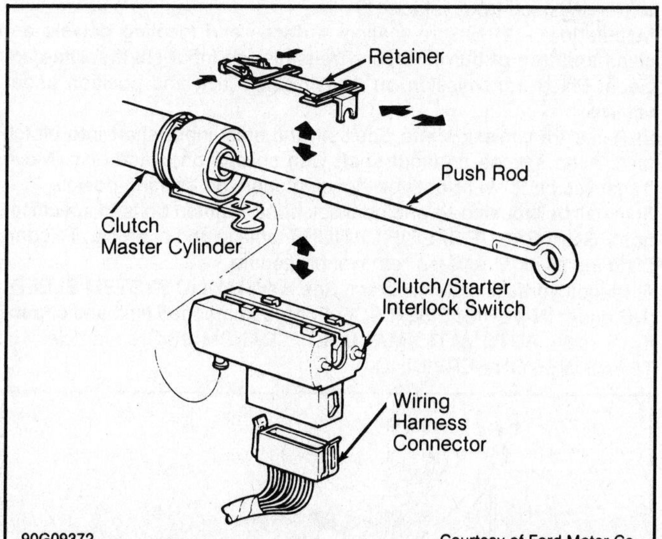
Retainer
Push Rod
Clutch
Master Cylinder
Clutch/Starter
Interlock Switch
Wiring
Harness
Connector
90G09372
Courtesy of Ford Motor Co.

Fig. 4: Identifying Clutch/Starter Interlock Switch & Components (Except "E" Series)

HYDRAULIC SYSTEM BLEEDING

Externally Mounted Slave Cylinder - 1) Remove slave cylinder from transmission bellhousing. Using a 3/32" diameter punch, remove pin that holds hydraulic line in slave cylinder. Remove hydraulic line from slave cylinder.

2) Place hydraulic line into container for waste fluid. Hold slave cylinder so hydraulic line port is at highest point. Fill slave cylinder, through hydraulic line port with DOT 3 brake fluid. Gently push on slave cylinder push rod to expel all air.

3) When all air has been expelled, install slave cylinder. Remove clutch master cylinder reservoir cap. While maintaining fluid level in reservoir, observe hydraulic line until all air has been expelled and a steady stream of fluid is flowing.

4) Install reservoir cap. Install hydraulic line and retaining pin. Top off brake fluid. With transmission in Neutral and parking brake set, start vehicle. Shift vehicle into Reverse. If gears grind, check for air in system. Repeat bleeding procedure if necessary. If no air is found and gears grind, clutch components may be defective or worn out.

Internally Mounted Slave Cylinder - 1) Clean area around reservoir cap. Fill reservoir with DOT 3 brake fluid. Place hose on bleeder screw to prevent brake fluid entering bellhousing. Loosen bleeder screw and maintain fluid level in reservoir.

2) Fluid and bubbles will flow from hose attached to slave cylinder bleeder screw. Close bleeder screw when fluid stream is free of air bubbles. Ensure proper fluid level and install reservoir cap.

3) Place light pressure on clutch pedal and open bleeder screw. Maintain pressure until pedal contacts the floor. Close bleeder screw while pedal is fully depressed. DO NOT allow pedal to return before bleeder screw is fully closed. Recheck fluid level.

4) Test system operation by starting vehicle, depressing clutch and placing gearshift in Reverse. No grinding should be heard or felt with clutch pedal within 1/2" (13 mm) of floor. If noise is heard, check for air in system. Repeat bleeding procedure if necessary.

REMOVAL & INSTALLATION

TRANSFER CASE

Removal (Spicer TC-28 - Aerostar) - 1) Raise vehicle. Remove drain plug and drain fluid from transfer case. Install plug. Disconnect electrical connector from rear of transfer case.

2) Disconnect front and rear drive shafts from transfer case output shaft yokes. Disconnect speedometer drive gear from transfer case rear cover. Remove cylinder block-to-transfer case strut.

3) Support transfer case with jack and remove bolts attaching transfer case to transmission extension housing. Slide transfer case off transmission output shaft. Lower transfer case from vehicle. Remove gasket between transfer case and transmission extension housing.

Installation - 1) Install new transfer case-to-extension housing gasket. To complete installation, reverse removal procedure. Tighten transfer case-to-extension housing bolts in sequence. *See Fig. 5.*

2) Tighten bolts to specification. See TORQUE SPECIFICATIONS table at end of article. Fill transfer case with 2.3 qts. (2.2L) of Mercon ATF (XT-2-QDX or E4AZ-19582-B).

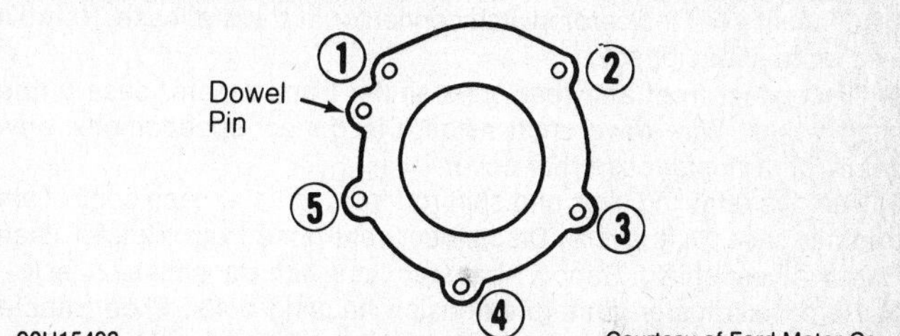
1
2
3
4
5
Dowel
Pin
90H15492
Courtesy of Ford Motor Co.

Fig. 5: Transfer Case-To-Extension Housing Tightening Sequence (Spicer TC-28 & Borg-Warner 1354)

Removal (Borg-Warner 1356 - Bronco & "F" Series) - 1) Raise vehicle. Remove skid plate (if equipped). Remove drain plug and drain fluid from transfer case. Install plug. Disconnect 4WD indicator switch at transfer case.

2) Disconnect front and rear drive shafts from transfer case output shaft yokes. Disconnect speedometer drive gear from transfer case rear cover. Disconnect vent hose from mounting bracket. Disconnect shift rod between transfer case shift lever and control lever assembly.

3) Support transfer case with jack and remove bolts attaching transfer case to transmission extension housing. Slide transfer case off transmission output shaft. Lower transfer case from vehicle. Remove gasket between transfer case and transmission extension housing.

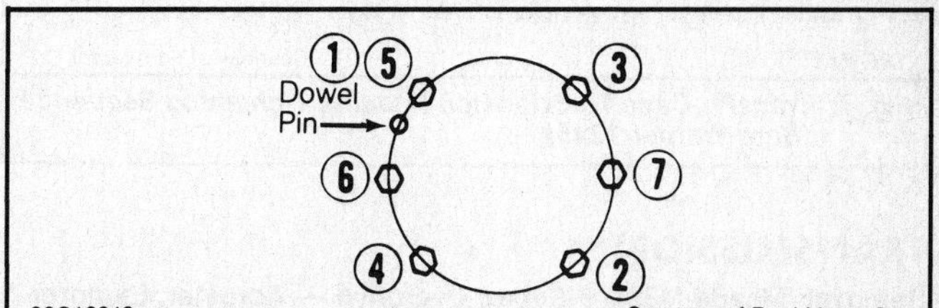
1
5
3
Dowel
Pin
6
7
4
2
90C18848
Courtesy of Ford Motor Co.

Fig. 6: Transfer Case-To-Extension Housing Tightening Sequence (Borg-Warner 1356)

1991 CLUTCHES
Hydraulic (Cont.)

Installation - 1) Install new transfer case-to-extension housing gasket. To complete installation, reverse removal procedure. Tighten transfer case-to-extension housing bolts in sequence. *See Fig. 6.*
2) Tighten bolts to specification. See TORQUE SPECIFICATIONS table at end of article. Fill transfer case with 2.0 qts. (1.9L) of Mercon ATF (XT-2-QDX or E4AZ-19582-B).

Removal (Borg-Warner 1354 - Explorer & Ranger) - 1) Raise vehicle. Remove skid plate (if equipped). Remove damper from transfer case (if equipped). Remove drain plug and drain fluid from transfer case. Install plug. Disconnect 4WD indicator switch at transfer case.
2) Disconnect front and rear drive shafts from transfer case output shaft yokes. Disconnect speedometer drive gear from transfer case rear cover. Disconnect vent hose from control lever. Remove shift lever retaining nut and lever.
3) Loosen or remove large and small bolts (one each) retaining shifter to extension housing. Remove lever assembly and bushing. Support transfer case with jack and remove bolts attaching transfer case to transmission extension housing.
4) Slide transfer case rearward off transmission output shaft. Lower transfer case from vehicle. Remove gasket from transfer case and transmission extension housing.
Installation - 1) Install new transfer case-to-extension housing gasket. To complete installation, reverse removal procedure. Tighten transfer case-to-extension housing bolts in sequence. *See Fig. 5.*

NOTE: When installing shift lever assembly, ALWAYS tighten large bolt first, then small bolt.

2) Tighten bolts to specifications. See TORQUE SPECIFICATIONS table at end of article. Fill transfer case with 1.3 qts. (1.2L) of Mercon ATF (XT-2-QDX or E4AZ-19582-B).

Removal (Borg-Warner 1345 - F150/250 4WD) - 1) Raise vehicle. Remove drain plug and drain fluid from transfer case. Replace plug. Disconnect 4WD indicator switch connector at transfer case. Remove skid plate (if equipped).
2) Disconnect front and rear drive shafts from transfer case output shaft yokes. Wire drive shaft aside. Disconnect speedometer drive gear from transfer case rear cover.
3) Remove retaining clips and shift rod from transfer case control and transfer case shift levers. Disconnect vent hose from transfer case. Remove heat shield. Support transfer case with transmission jack.
4) Remove transfer case-to-extension housing bolts. Slide transfer case off transmission output shaft. Lower transfer case from vehicle. Remove transfer case-to-extension housing gasket.
Installation - Install new transfer case-to-extension housing gasket. To complete installation, reverse removal procedure. Tighten transfer case-to-extension housing bolts in sequence. *See Fig. 7.* Tighten bolts to specifications. See TORQUE SPECIFICATIONS table at end of article. Fill transfer case with 3.3 qts. (3.0L) of Mercon ATF (XT-2-QDX or E4AZ-19582-B).

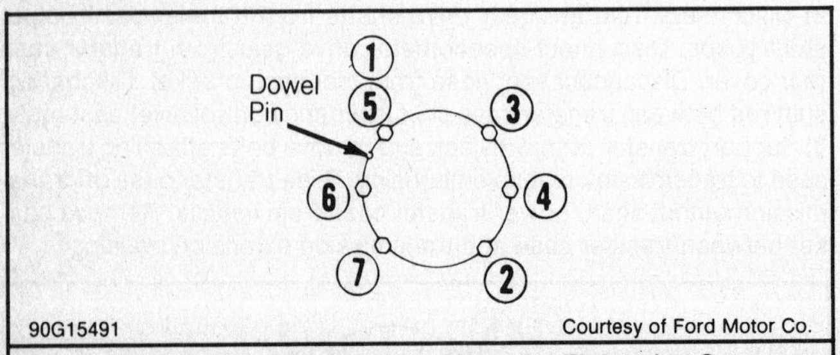
Dowel
Pin
1
5
3
6
4
7
2
90G15491
Courtesy of Ford Motor Co.

Fig. 7: Transfer Case-To-Extension Housing Tightening Sequence (Borg-Warner 1345)

TRANSMISSION

Removal (Mazda M50D 5-Speed Overdrive - Aerostar, Explorer & Ranger) - 1) Disconnect negative battery cable from battery. Shift transmission into Neutral. Remove boot assembly-to-floor bolts. Remove boot from shift lever assembly.
2) Remove shift lever retaining bolt. Remove shift lever, ball and boot assembly. Raise vehicle on a hoist. Scribe a mark on drive shaft and rear axle flange for installation reference.
3) Disconnect drive shaft at rear drive axle flange. Remove drive shaft. Cap transmission extension housing to prevent lubricant spillage. Disconnect starter cable and wires. Remove starter.
4) Disconnect clutch slave cylinder hydraulic line by pressing White retainer bushing with Disconnect Tool (T88T-70522-A) while pulling on line. *See Fig. 8.* Cap end of line to prevent fluid leakage.
5) Disconnect back-up lamp switch from sender on transmission. Remove speedometer cable from extension housing or transfer case (if equipped). Position jack under engine, protecting oil pan with wood block.
6) On 4WD models, remove transfer case. See TRANSFER CASE under REMOVAL & INSTALLATION. Remove transmission mount/damper-to-crossmember nuts/bolts.
7) Position transmission jack under transmission. Place jack safety chain around transmission. Slightly raise transmission. Remove nuts and bolts retaining crossmember to frame. Remove crossmember.
8) Remove bellhousing-to-engine bolts. Slide transmission rearward to separate bellhousing from dowel pins on rear of engine block. Lower transmission from vehicle.
Installation - 1) Ensure mating surfaces and locating dowels are clean and free of burrs. Ensure transmission input shaft splines are clean. Place transmission on transmission jack and position under vehicle.
2) Raise transmission into position and start input shaft into clutch disc. Align splines on input shaft with splines on clutch disc. Move transmission forward until bellhousing seats on locating dowels.
3) Install bellhousing-to-engine block bolts. Tighten bolts to specifications. See TORQUE SPECIFICATIONS table at end of article. To complete installation, reverse removal procedure.
4) Bleed hydraulic clutch system. See HYDRAULIC SYSTEM BLEEDING under IN-VEHICLE SERVICE. For recommended fluid and capacity, see AUTOMATIC/MANUAL TRANSMISSION article in TRANSMISSION SERVICING.

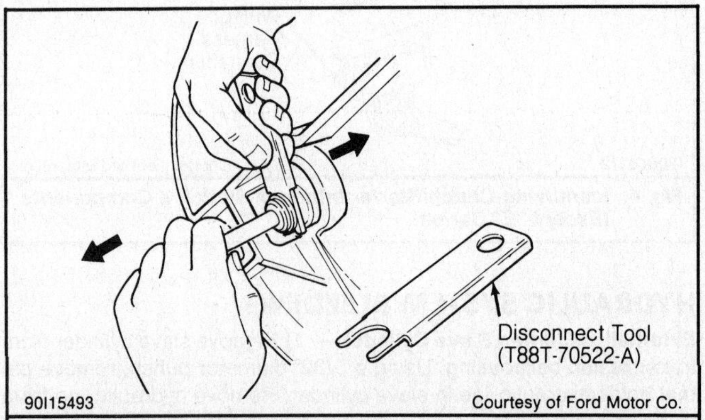
Disconnect Tool
(T88T-70522-A)
90I15493
Courtesy of Ford Motor Co.

Fig. 8: Removing Clutch Hydraulic Line (Except 7.3L Diesel)

Removal (Mazda M50D 5-Speed Overdrive - "F" Series 2WD) - 1) Shift transmission into Neutral. Remove carpet or floor mat for access. Remove shifter boot retainer screws. Slide boot up shift lever shaft. Remove shift lever retainer bolt and shift lever.
2) Raise vehicle on hoist. Disconnect speedometer cable. Disconnect back-up light switch, located on top left of transmission. Remove drain plug and drain gear oil. Install drain plug. Position transmission jack under transmission.
3) Disconnect drive shaft from extension housing and wire to one side. On models with 7.3L engine, disconnect clutch slave cylinder hydraulic line. On all others, remove clutch slave cylinder hydraulic line by pressing White retainer bushing with Disconnect Tool (T88T-70522-A) while pulling on line. *See Fig. 8.*
4) Remove transmission rear mount and lower retainer. Remove skid plate (if equipped). Remove catalytic converter heat shield. Remove 2 upper gusset-to-frame nuts from both sides. Remove transmission-to-transmission support plate bolts on crossmember. Raise transmission with transmission jack.

5) Remove nut and bolt connecting support plate to crossmember. Remove support plate. Remove right gusset. Remove nuts and bolts holding crossmember to frame. Remove crossmember.

6) Remove transmission-to-engine block bolts. Move transmission rearward until input shaft clears flywheel. Lower transmission from vehicle.

Installation - 1) Ensure transmission input shaft splines are clean and free of rust. Place transmission on transmission jack. Install guide studs in engine block. Raise transmission until input shaft splines are aligned with clutch disc splines.

2) Slide transmission forward into position on guide studs. Remove guide studs and install bell housing-to-engine bolts. Tighten to specification. See TORQUE SPECIFICATIONS table at end of article.

3) To complete installation, reverse removal procedure. Bleed hydraulic clutch system. See HYDRAULIC SYSTEM BLEEDING under IN-VEHICLE SERVICE. For recommended fluid and capacity, see AUTOMATIC/MANUAL TRANSMISSION article in TRANSMISSION SERVICING.

Removal (Mazda M50D 5-Speed Overdrive - Bronco & "F" Series 4WD) - 1) Shift transmission into Neutral. Remove carpet or floor mat for access. Remove shifter boot retainer screws. Slide boot up shift lever shaft. Remove shift lever retainer bolt and shift lever.

2) Raise vehicle on hoist. Remove drain plugs and drain gear oil from transmission and transfer case. Install drain plugs. Disconnect front and rear drive shafts from transfer case.

3) Remove clutch slave cylinder hydraulic line by pressing White retainer bushing with Disconnect Tool (T88T-70522-A) while pulling on line. *See Fig. 8.* Disconnect back-up light switch. Disconnect speedometer cable from transfer case.

4) Remove skid plate (if equipped). Position transmission jack under transfer case. Remove transfer case-to-transmission bolts. Lower transfer case. Ensure transfer case shift lever clears opening in floor pan. Remove transmission rear mount and lower retainer.

5) Remove catalytic converter heat shield. Remove 2 upper gusset-to-frame nuts from both sides. Remove transmission-to-transmission support plate bolts on crossmember. Raise transmission with transmission jack. Remove nut and bolt connecting support plate to crossmember.

6) Remove support plate. Remove right gusset. Remove crossmember-to-frame nuts and bolts. Remove crossmember. Remove bellhousing-to-engine block bolts. Move transmission rearward until input shaft clears flywheel. Lower transmission from vehicle.

Installation - 1) Ensure transmission input shaft splines are clean and free of rust. Place transmission on transmission jack. Install guide studs in engine block. Raise transmission until input shaft splines are aligned with clutch disc splines.

2) Slide transmission forward into position on guide studs. Remove guide studs and install bell housing-to-engine bolts. Tighten to specification. See TORQUE SPECIFICATIONS table at end of article.

3) To complete installation, reverse removal procedure. Bleed hydraulic clutch system. See HYDRAULIC SYSTEM BLEEDING under IN-VEHICLE SERVICE. For recommended fluid and capacity, see AUTOMATIC/MANUAL TRANSMISSION article in TRANSMISSION SERVICING.

Removal (Borg-Warner T-18 4-Speed - F150/250 2WD) - 1) Remove floor mat and body floor pan cover. Remove gearshift lever shift ball and boot. Remove insulator pad. Raise vehicle on hoist.

2) Remove drain plug and drain transmission. Install drain plug. Remove clutch slave cylinder hydraulic line by pressing White retainer bushing with Disconnect Tool (T88T-70522-A) while pulling on line. *See Fig. 8.*

3) Position transmission jack under transmission. Disconnect speedometer cable. Disconnect back-up light switch connector from rear of gearshift housing cover. Disconnect drive shaft or coupling shaft.

4) Disconnect clutch linkage from transmission and wire it aside. Remove skid plate (if equipped). Remove nuts connecting upper gusset to frame on both sides of frame. Remove nut/bolt connecting gusset to crossmember.

5) Remove left side gusset. Remove transmission mount-to-transmission bolts. Raise transmission with transmission jack. Remove nuts attaching transmission mount-to-crossmember. Remove right side gusset. Remove nuts/bolts connecting crossmember-to-frame.

6) Remove crossmember. Remove transmission-to-bellhousing bolts. Move transmission to rear until input shaft clears bellhousing. Lower and remove transmission.

Installation - 1) Ensure transmission input shaft splines are clean and free of rust. Place transmission on transmission jack. Install guide studs in engine block. Raise transmission until input shaft splines are aligned with clutch disc splines.

2) Slide transmission forward into position on guide studs. Remove guide studs and install bell housing-to-engine bolts. Tighten to specification. See TORQUE SPECIFICATIONS table at end of article.

3) To complete installation, reverse removal procedure. Bleed hydraulic clutch system. See HYDRAULIC SYSTEM BLEEDING under IN-VEHICLE SERVICE. For recommended fluid and capacity, see AUTOMATIC/MANUAL TRANSMISSION article in TRANSMISSION SERVICING.

Removal (Borg-Warner T-18 4-Speed - Bronco & F150/250 4WD) - 1) Remove floor mat and body floor pan cover. Place shift lever in REVERSE position. Remove gearshift cover. Remove insulator and dust cover. Remove transfer case shift lever, shift ball and boot as an assembly.

2) Remove transmission shift lever, shift ball and boot as an assembly. Raise vehicle on hoist. Remove drain plug and drain transmission and transfer case. Install drain plug.

3) Disconnect rear and front drive shafts and wire them aside. Remove shift linkage from transmission. Remove speedometer cable. Position transmission jack under transfer case.

4) Remove transfer case-to-transmission bolts. remove clutch slave cylinder hydraulic line by pressing White retainer bushing with Disconnect Tool (T88T-70522-A) while pulling on line. *See Fig. 8.*

5) Remove transfer case. Remove rear support bracket-to-transmission bolts. Position transmission jack under transmission. Remove rear support bracket brace. Remove transmission-to-bellhousing bolts. Remove transmission.

Installation - 1) Ensure transmission input shaft splines are clean and free of rust. Place transmission on transmission jack. Install guide studs in engine block. Raise transmission until input shaft splines are aligned with clutch disc splines.

2) Slide transmission forward onto guide studs. Remove guide studs and install bellhousing-to-engine bolts. Tighten to specification. See TORQUE SPECIFICATIONS table at end of article.

3) To complete installation, reverse removal procedure. Bleed hydraulic clutch system. See HYDRAULIC SYSTEM BLEEDING under IN-VEHICLE SERVICE. For recommended fluid and capacity, see AUTOMATIC/MANUAL TRANSMISSION article in TRANSMISSION SERVICING.

Removal (Ford S5-42 ZF 5-Speed - E350 & "F" Series 2WD) - 1) Shift transmission into Neutral. Remove carpet or floor mat. Remove ball from upper shift lever. Remove 4 screws and remove boot and bezel assembly from transmission opening cover. Remove upper shift lever attaching bolts. Remove upper shift lever from lower shift lever.

2) Raise vehicle on hoist. Disconnect speedometer cable. Disconnect back-up lamp switch, located at top left side of transmission. Remove drain plug and drain oil from transmission. Install drain plug. Position transmission jack under transmission.

3) Disconnect drive shaft and clutch linkage from transmission and wire it to one side. On "F" Series Super Duty vehicles, remove transmission parking brake from transmission. On all models, remove transmission rear mount and lower retainer.

4) On models with 7.3L engine, disconnect clutch slave cylinder hydraulic line. On all other models, remove clutch slave cylinder hydraulic line by pressing White retainer bushing with Disconnect Tool (T88T-70522-A) while pulling on line. *See Fig. 8.*

5) Remove skid plate (if equipped). Remove 2 upper gusset-to-frame nuts from both sides. Remove transmission-to-transmission support plate bolts on crossmember. Raise transmission with transmission jack. Remove nut and bolt connecting support plate to crossmember.

6) Remove support plate. Remove right gusset. Remove crossmember-to-frame nuts and bolts. Remove crossmember. Remove bellhousing-to-engine bolts. Move transmission to rear until input shaft clears engine flywheel. Lower transmission from vehicle.

Installation - 1) Ensure transmission input shaft splines are clean and free of rust. Place transmission on transmission jack. Install guide studs in engine block. Raise transmission until input shaft splines are aligned with clutch disc splines.

2) Slide transmission forward onto guide studs. Remove guide studs and install bellhousing-to-engine bolts. Tighten to specification. See TORQUE SPECIFICATIONS table at end of article.

3) To complete installation, reverse removal procedure. Bleed hydraulic clutch system. See HYDRAULIC SYSTEM BLEEDING under IN-VEHICLE SERVICE. For recommended fluid and capacity, see AUTOMATIC/MANUAL TRANSMISSION article in TRANSMISSION SERVICING.

Removal (Ford S5-42 ZF 5-Speed – Bronco & "F" Series 4WD) – 1) Shift transmission into Neutral. Remove carpet or floor mat. Remove 4 screws and remove boot and bezel assembly from transmission opening cover. Remove 2 bolts and upper shift lever from lower shift lever.

2) Raise vehicle on hoist. Remove drain plugs and drain transmission and transfer case. Install drain plug. Disconnect rear drive shaft from transfer case and wire it out of the way. Disconnect front drive shaft from transfer case and wire out of way.

3) Disconnect back-up lamp switch. Remove speedometer cable from transfer case. Remove skid plate (if equipped). Position transmission jack under transfer case.

4) On models with 7.3L engine, disconnect clutch slave cylinder hydraulic line. On all others, remove clutch slave cylinder hydraulic line by pressing White retainer bushing with Disconnect Tool (T88T-70522-A) while pulling on line. *See Fig. 8.*

5) Remove transfer case-to-transmission bolts. Carer case-to-transmission bolts. Carefully lower transfer case from vehicle, ensuring shift lever clears opening in floor pan. Remove transmission rear mount and lower retainer.

6) Remove 2 upper gusset-to-frame nuts from both sides. Remove transmission-to-transmission support plate bolts on crossmember. Raise transmission with transmission jack. Remove nut and bolt connecting support plate to crossmember.

7) Remove support plate. Remove right gusset. Remove crossmember-to-frame nuts and bolts. Remove crossmember. Remove bellhousing-to-engine bolts. Move transmission to rear until input shaft clears engine flywheel housing. Lower transmission from vehicle.

Installation – 1) Ensure transmission input shaft splines are clean and free of rust. Place transmission on transmission jack. Install guide studs in engine block. Raise transmission until input shaft splines are aligned with clutch disc splines.

2) Slide transmission forward into position on guide studs. Remove guide studs. Install bell housing-to-engine bolts and tighten to specification. See TORQUE SPECIFICATIONS table at end of article.

3) Bleed hydraulic clutch system. See HYDRAULIC SYSTEM BLEEDING under IN-VEHICLE SERVICE. To complete installation, reverse removal procedure. For recommended fluid and capacity, see AUTOMATIC/MANUAL TRANSMISSION article in TRANSMISSION SERVICING.

Removal (Mitsubishi FM146 5-Speed Overdrive – Ranger 4WD) – 1) Disconnect negative battery cable. Place gearshift selector in Neutral. Remove shift boot retainer bolts. Remove bolts attaching retainer cover to gearshift lever retainer.

2) Pull gearshift lever assembly out of control housing. Cover opening in control housing to prevent dirt from falling into transmission. Raise vehicle. Index rear drive shaft axle flange and front transfer case flange.

3) Disconnect drive shaft at both rear axle flange and transfer case. Remove front drive shaft. Install plug in transfer case adapter to prevent lubricant leakage.

4) Pull rear drive shaft rearward and disconnect drive shaft from transmission. Remove bellhousing dust shield. Disconnect clutch slave cylinder hydraulic line by pressing White retainer bushing with Disconnect Tool (T88T-70522-A) while pulling on line. *See Fig. 8.* Plug line to prevent leakage.

5) Disconnect speedometer cable. Disconnect starter motor cable, back-up lamp switch wire and neutral position switch wire. Place jack under engine block, protecting oil pan with wood block. Remove transfer case. See TRANSFER CASE under REMOVAL & INSTALLATION.

6) Remove starter. Place a transmission jack under transmission. Remove bolts attaching bellhousing-to-engine. Remove nuts/bolts attaching transmission mount and damper to crossmember.

7) Remove nuts attaching crossmember to frame side rails and remove crossmember. Lower engine jack. Work bellhousing off locating dowels and slide transmission rearward until input shaft clears clutch disc. Remove transmission from vehicle.

Installation – 1) Ensure mating surfaces and locating dowels are free of burrs. Ensure transmission input shaft splines are clean. Place transmission on transmission jack and position under vehicle. Raise transmission into position and start input shaft into clutch disc.

2) Align splines on input shaft with splines on clutch disc. Move transmission forward until bellhousing seats on locating dowels. Install bolts retaining bellhousing-to-engine block.

3) Tighten bolts to specifications. See TORQUE SPECIFICATIONS table at end of article. To complete installation, reverse removal procedure. Bleed hydraulic clutch system. See HYDRAULIC SYSTEM BLEEDING under IN-VEHICLE SERVICE. For recommended fluid and capacity, see AUTOMATIC/MANUAL TRANSMISSION article in TRANSMISSION SERVICING.

CLUTCH DISC & PRESSURE PLATE

Removal – 1) Disconnect negative battery cable. Disconnect clutch master cylinder push rod. Raise vehicle and remove starter. Disconnect clutch slave cylinder hydraulic line by pressing White retainer bushing with Disconnect Tool (T88T-70522-A) while pulling on line. *See Fig. 8.*

2) Remove transmission. See TRANSMISSION under REMOVAL & INSTALLATION. Place reference mark on pressure plate and flywheel for reassembly reference. Loosen pressure plate-to-flywheel bolts evenly until springs are expanded. Remove pressure plate and clutch disc.

Installation – 1) Clean pressure plate and flywheel surface with alcohol base solvent. Place clutch disc on flywheel. Align disc center with pilot bearing using old input shaft or clutch pilot shaft.

2) Place pressure plate on flywheel and align reference mark. Tighten bolts evenly in a crisscross sequence. Remove clutch pilot shaft. Reverse removal procedure to complete installation.

CLUTCH RELEASE BEARING

Removal (Internally Mounted Slave Cylinder) – With transmission removed, twist release bearing and carrier assembly until resistance is felt. Turning assembly further will allow the preload spring to push bearing assembly from the slave cylinder. *See Fig. 9.*

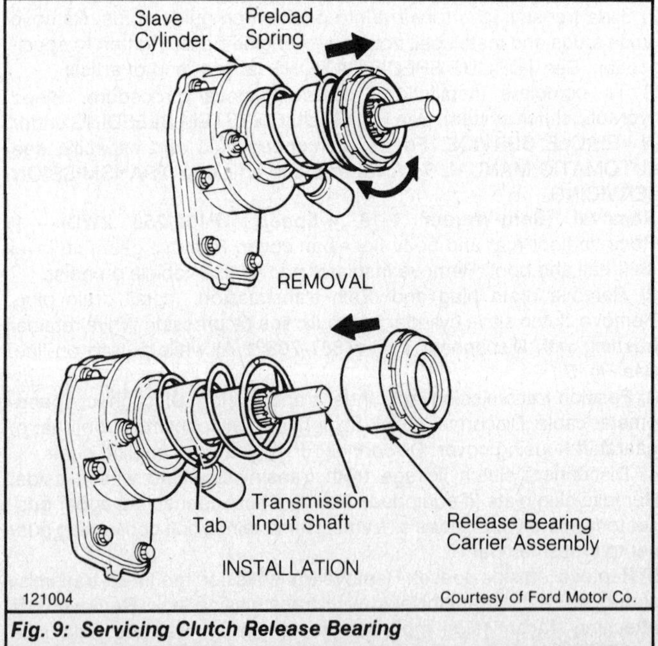
Slave Cylinder
Preload Spring
REMOVAL
Tab
Transmission Input Shaft
Release Bearing Carrier Assembly
INSTALLATION
121004
Courtesy of Ford Motor Co.

Fig. 9: Servicing Clutch Release Bearing

Installation - Prior to installation, lubricate bearing bore and bearing carrier with multipurpose grease. Install release bearing assembly to clutch slave cylinder by pushing into place.

CLUTCH PILOT BEARING

Removal - Remove transmission. See TRANSMISSION under REMOVAL & INSTALLATION. Remove pressure plate and clutch disc. See CLUTCH DISC & PRESSURE PLATE under REMOVAL & INSTALLATION. Use Impact Slide Hammer Puller (T58L-101-B) to remove pilot bearing.

Installation - Lightly coat crankshaft bore with lithium-based grease. Using Bearing Driver (T71P-7137-H) and Adapter (T74P-7137-A), install pilot bearing with seal toward transmission. Install clutch disc, pressure plate and transmission.

NOTE: Use Adapter (T74P-7137-C) on 3.0L engine.

CLUTCH HYDRAULIC SYSTEM

CAUTION: On all models, disconnect master cylinder push rod if slave cylinder is to be disconnected from release lever or bearing. Permanent damage to master cylinder will occur if master cylinder is activated with slave cylinder disconnected.

Removal - 1) Note position of clutch pedal push rod. Disconnect master cylinder push rod from clutch pedal by prying retainer bushing and push rod off shaft. Disconnect clutch/starter interlock switch connector.

2) Remove 2 nuts and support bracket retaining clutch reservoir and master cylinder assembly to firewall. On models with 7.3L engine, disconnect clutch slave cylinder hydraulic line. On all other models, disconnect clutch slave cylinder hydraulic line by pressing White retainer bushing with Disconnect Tool (T88T-70522-A) while pulling on line. *See Fig. 8.* Plug line to prevent leakage.

3) On Bronco and "F" Series, when master cylinder studs are free of dash panel, rotate cylinder 105 degrees counterclockwise to permit interlock switch to clear dash panel.

4) On all models, remove master cylinder, reservoir and hydraulic line. Plug lines. If removing slave cylinder, on vehicles with externally mounted slave cylinder, remove slave cylinder from bellhousing.

5) On vehicles with internally mounted slave cylinder, remove transmission and bellhousing. See TRANSMISSION under REMOVAL & INSTALLATION. Note position of slave cylinder and remove from bellhousing.

Installation - 1) Install slave cylinder (if removed). On models with internally mounted slave cylinders, ensure slave cylinder is properly

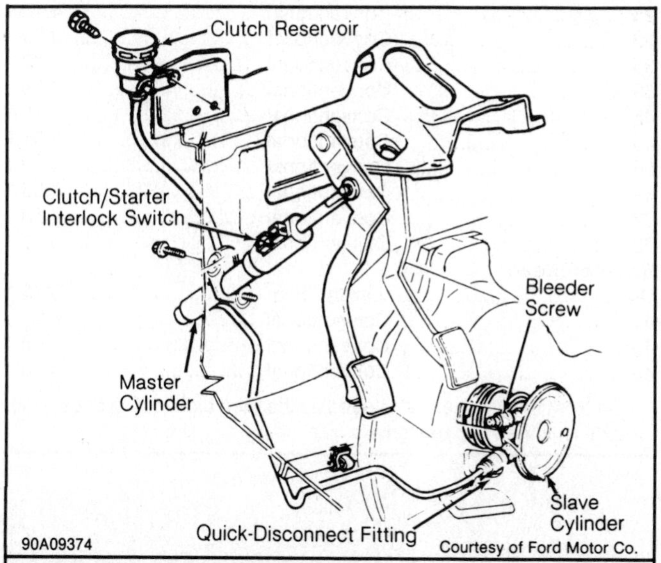

Clutch Reservoir
Clutch/Starter
Interlock Switch
Bleeder
Screw
Master
Cylinder
Slave
Cylinder
Quick-Disconnect Fitting
90A09374
Courtesy of Ford Motor Co.

Fig. 10: Schematic of Internal Slave Cylinder Hydraulic Clutch System (Typical)

engaged in notches of bellhousing. Install transmission and bellhousing. On all models, insert master cylinder push rod through opening in firewall.

2) Ensure push rod is located on correct side of clutch pedal. Attach master cylinder to firewall. Insert hydraulic line and fitting in clutch slave cylinder. Install fluid reservoir on access cover.

3) Install push rod on clutch pedal. Bleed hydraulic system. See HYDRAULIC SYSTEM BLEEDING under IN-VEHICLE SERVICE. Depress clutch pedal at least 10 times to check for proper release and smooth operation.

CLUTCH PEDAL

Removal (Aerostar, Explorer & Ranger) - 1) Disconnect push rod from clutch pedal. Disconnect clutch/starter interlock switch from pedal. Remove retainer clip from pedal shaft.

2) On Explorer and Ranger, remove left kick panel. Remove parking brake assembly and secure away from work area. On all models, remove pedal and shaft assembly from bracket.

3) Remove bushings from bracket. Remove retainer clip from end of clutch pedal shaft. Remove clutch pedal and shaft from mounting bracket.

NOTE: When clutch pedal shaft is removed from bracket, the brake pedal, bushings and spring washer will fall.

Installation - To install, reverse removal procedure. Inspect and lubricate bushings with a light film of SAE 30 engine oil. Replace bushings if worn.

Removal (Bronco, "E" & "F" Series) - 1) On Bronco and "F" Series models, disconnect clutch pedal retracting spring from clutch pedal and bracket. On "E" Series models, disconnect barbed retainer bushing on the clutch/starter interlock switch rod from clutch pedal.

2) On all models, remove retainer clip from end of clutch pedal shaft. Remove clutch pedal and shaft from mounting bracket.

Installation - To install, reverse removal procedure. Compress retracting spring in a vise and secure with a wire until it is in place. Inspect and lubricate bushings with a light film of SAE 30 engine oil or replace bushings.

TORQUE SPECIFICATIONS

TORQUE SPECIFICATIONS (TRANSMISSION)

Application	Ft. Lbs. (N.m)
Aerostar, Explorer & Ranger	
Bellhousing-To-Engine Bolt	28-38 (38-52)
Drive Shaft U-Bolt	10-15 (14-21)
Starter Bolt	15-20 (21-27)
Transfer Case-To-Extension Housing	
Aerostar (Spicer TC-28) [1]	23-35 (31-47)
Explorer & Ranger (Borg-Warner 1354) [1]	25-35 (34-47)
Transmission Mount-To-Crossmember Nut	60-80 (81-109)
Transmission-To-Bellhousing Bolt	30-40 (41-54)
Crossmember-To-Right Frame Nut	110-140 (149-190)
Crossmember-To-Left Frame Nut	
Except Ranger 2.3L 4WD	110-140 (149-190)
Ranger 2.3L 4WD	75-95 (102-129)
Pressure Plate Bolts [2]	15-24 (21-33)
Bronco, "E" & "F" Series	
Bellhousing-To-Engine Bolt	40-50 (54-68)
Front Drive Shaft-To-Front Output Yoke Nut	10-15 (14-21)
Starter Bolt	15-20 (21-27)
Transfer Case-To-Extension Housing	
Bronco & "F" Series (Borg-Warner 1356) [3]	25-43 (34-58)
F150/250 4WD (Borg-Warner 1345) [4]	25-43 (34-58)
Transmission Mount-To-Crossmember Nut	60-80 (81-109)
Pressure Plate-To-Flywheel Bolt [2]	
4.9L, 5.0L & 5.8L	
10" Clutch	15-20 (21-27)
11" Clutch	20-29 (27-39)
7.3L & 7.5L	15-20 (21-27)
All Other Models	20-29 (27-39)

[1] - Tighten in sequence. *See Fig. 5.*
[2] - Tighten in a crisscross pattern.
[3] - Tighten in sequence. *See Fig. 6.*
[4] - Tighten in sequence. *See Fig. 7.*

1991 DRIVE AXLES
Axle Ratio Identification

Aerostar, Bronco, Explorer, Ranger, "E" & "F" Series

IDENTIFICATION

Front axle identification tag is located under cover-to-carrier bolt. Rear axle identification tag is located under cover-to-carrier bolt or on front side of differential carrier. See appropriate differential article for identification tag interpretation. Vehicle axle application can also be determined through axle code on the Safety Certification Label located on left door pillar.

NOTE: All differential codes listed in AXLE RATIO IDENTIFICATION table are Ford Motor Co. production number codes.

AXLE RATIO IDENTIFICATION

Application	Ratio
Front Axles (4WD)	
Aerostar	
Dana 28-2	[1]
Bronco & F150	
Dana 44 IFS	
E9TA-KA [2], E9TA-RA [2]	3.07:1
E8TA-TC [2], E9TA-LA [2], E9TA-MA [4], E9TA-SA	3.54:1
E8T1-UC [2], E9TA-NA [2]	4.09:1
Explorer & Ranger	
Dana 35 IFS	
F17A-KB [2], F17A-UA [2], F07A-GB [2], F07A-GC [2], F07A-HB [2], F07A-HC [2], F17A-JA [2]	3.55:1
F07A-BB [2], F07A-BC [2], F07A-EB [2], F07A-EC [2], F17A-GA [2], F17A-HA [2], F17A-HB [2], F17A-VA	3.73:1
F07A-LA [2], F07A-LB [2], F07A-MA [2], F07A-MB [2], F17A-XA [2]	4.10:1
F250	
Dana 44 IFS-HD	
E9TA-KA [2], E9TA-RA [2]	3.07:1
E8TA-TC [2], E9TA-LA [2], E9TA-MA [4], E9TA-SA	3.54:1
E8T1-UC [2], E9TA-NA [2]	4.09:1
F250 Heavy Duty	
Dana 50 IFS	
E8TA-ZC [2]	3.54:1
E8TA-YC	4.10:1
F350	
Dana 60 Monobeam	
E8TA-VB [2]	3.54:1
E8TA-XB [2], E8TA-AAA [2]	4.10:1
Rear Axles	
Aerostar	
7 1/8" Ring Gear	
D448A	3.45:1
7 1/2" Ring Gear	
664A [2]	3.45:1
665A [3], 666A [2]	3.73:1
667A [3]	4.10:1
8 3/4" Ring Gear	[1]
Bronco, E150 & F150	
8 3/4" Ring Gear	
812D [2]	2.73:1
720C [2], 804S [2], 806D [2]	3.08:1
724S [2], 730D [2], 731P [4], 733D [4], 807D [4], 808D [2], 809S [4], 810S [2], 811T [4], 816T [2]	3.55:1
815D [4], 819D [4]	4.10:1
Explorer	
8 3/4" Ring Gear	[1]
E250/350	
Dana 60	[1]
E350 (Dual Rear Wheel)	
Dana 70	[1]
"F" Series Super Duty, Stripped & Motorhome Chassis	
Dana 80	[1]

AXLE RATIO IDENTIFICATION (Cont.)

Application	Ratio
"F" Series (With Full Floating Axle)	
10 1/4" Ring Gear	
125C [2], 126C [2], 166C [2], 183C [2], 186C [2]	3.55:1
129C [2], 130C [2], 131C [2], 132C [2], 168C [2], 169C [4], 170C [2], 171C [4], 189C [2], 190C [2], 191C [4], 192C [4]	4.10:1
"F" Series (With Semi-Floating Axle)	
10 1/4" Ring Gear	
106C [2], 107C [2]	3.55:1
110C [2], 111C [2]	4.10:1
Ranger	
7 1/2" Ring Gear	
302B [2], 304B [2], 396D [2], 398D [2]	3.45:1
307B [3], 310B [2], 308D [2], 309D [3], 390D [2], 392D [2]	3.73:1
311B [3], 313B [3]	4.10:1
8 3/4" Ring Gear	[1]

[1] – Information not available from manufacturer.
[2] – Conventional differential with 2 pinion gears.
[3] – Traction-Lok differential.
[4] – Limited slip differential.

SAFETY CERTIFICATION LABEL AXLE CODE

Code	Type	Ratio
Aerostar		
B2	Limited Slip	4.10:1
B4	Limited Slip	3.73:1
B9	Limited Slip	3.55:1
15 & 25	Conventional	3.27:1
23	Conventional	3.45:1
24 & 34	Conventional	3.73:1
35	Conventional	3.27:1
29	Conventional	3.55:1
Bronco & "F" Series [1]		
B5	Limited Slip	4.10:1
B9	Limited Slip	3.55:1
C5	Limited Slip	4.10:1
D5	Limited Slip	4.10:1
F5	Limited Slip	4.10:1
H5	Limited Slip	4.10:1
H8	Limited Slip	3.08:1
H9	Limited Slip	3.55:1
W5	Limited Slip	4.00:1
12	Conventional	2.73:1
18	Conventional	3.08:1
19	Conventional	3.55:1
25	Conventional	4.10:1
29	Conventional	3.55:1
35	Conventional	4.10:1
39	Conventional	3.55:1
45	Conventional	4.10:1
49	Conventional	3.55:1
65	Conventional	4.10:1
69	Conventional	3.55:1
72	Conventional	4.63:1
73	Conventional	5.13:1
Explorer (Rear)		
D4	Limited Slip	3.73:1
41	Conventional	3.27:1
43	Conventional	3.08:1
45	Conventional	3.55:1

[1] – On front axles, when "2" is used as the third digit in axle code, front axle is limited slip design.

1991 DRIVE AXLES
Axle Ratio Identification (Cont.)

SAFETY CERTIFICATION LABEL AXLE CODE (Cont.)

Code	Type	Ratio
"E" Series (Rear)		
B4	Limited Slip	3.73:1
C2	Limited Slip	4.10:1
C3	Limited Slip	3.54:1
E2	Limited Slip	4.10:1
H9	Limited Slip	3.08:1
18	Conventional	3.08:1
19	Conventional	3.55:1
23	Conventional	3.54:1
24	Conventional	3.73:1
32	Conventional	4.10:1
33	Conventional	3.54:1
52	Conventional	4.10:1
53	Conventional	3.54:1
62	Conventional	4.10:1
Ranger (Rear)		
F5	Limited Slip	3.55:1
F6	Limited Slip	3.73:1
F7	Limited Slip	4.10:1
82	Conventional	3.08:1
84	Conventional	3.45:1
85	Conventional	3.55:1
86	Conventional	3.73:1
87	Conventional	4.10:1

1991 DRIVE AXLES
7 1/2" Ring Gear Differentials

Aerostar, Ranger

***NOTE:** The 7 1/2" ring gear differential is used in Ford integral rear axle housing only. For Aerostar front differential, see DANA 28-2 FRONT AXLE article. For Ranger front differential, see DANA IFS FRONT AXLE article.*

DESCRIPTION

The rear axle is a hypoid design ring and pinion gear encased in an integral cast iron axle housing. The hypoid gear set contains an overhung drive pinion supported by 2 opposed tapered roller bearings. Pinion bearing preload is maintained by a collapsible spacer on the pinion shaft and adjusted by the pinion nut. Semi-floating axle shafts are retained by "C" locks at splined end of shafts.

On models equipped with Rear Anti-Lock Braking System (RABS), a multi-tooth excitor ring is pressed on the differential case behind the ring gear. An electronic speed sensor is retained in a bore at the top of the axle housing.

AXLE RATIO & IDENTIFICATION

A metal tag stamped with axle model, date of manufacture, ratio, ring gear diameter and assembly plant is attached to rear cover. *See Fig. 1.* Use information on tag to order replacement parts. Vehicle axle application can also be determined through axle code on Safety Certification Label located on left door pillar. See AXLE RATIO IDENTIFICATION article.

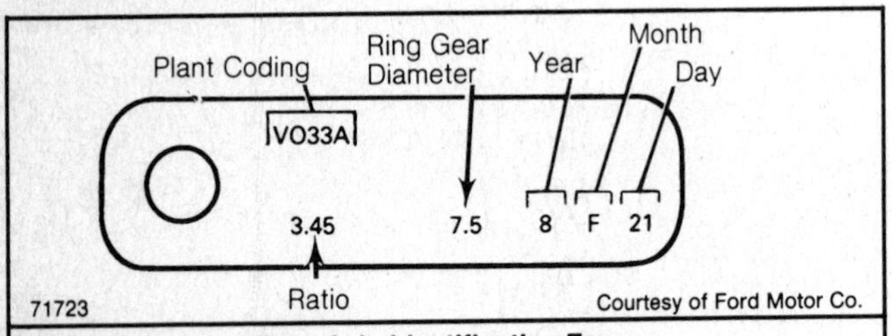
Plant Coding
Ring Gear Diameter
Year
Month
Day
VO33A
3.45
7.5
8
F
21
Ratio
71723
Courtesy of Ford Motor Co.

***Fig. 1:** Examining Rear Axle Identification Tag*

REMOVAL & INSTALLATION

AXLE SHAFT & BEARING

Removal – 1) Raise and support vehicle. Remove rear wheel assemblies and brake drums. Drain lubricant, and remove housing cover.

2) For all ratio axles except 3.73:1 and 4.10:1, remove differential pinion shaft lock bolt and pinion shaft. Push axle toward center, and remove "C" locks from button end of axle shaft.

***NOTE:** Pinion gears may be left in place. When axle shafts are removed, reinstall pinion shaft and lock bolt.*

3) On 3.73:1 and 4.10:1 ratio axles, remove pinion shaft lock bolt. Place hand behind differential case and push out pinion shaft until step on shaft contacts ring gear. Remove "C" locks from shafts.

4) On all ratio axles, carefully remove axles. DO NOT cut axle seal. Using a slide hammer and puller, remove bearing and seal as a unit.

Installation – 1) Lubricate bearing with rear axle lubricant, and install bearings using a driver. Install seal. If seal becomes cocked during installation, replace it with a new one.

***NOTE:** On 3.73:1 and 4.10:1 ratio axles, ensure pinion shaft step contacts ring gear before inserting axle into housing.*

2) Carefully insert axle into housing. DO NOT damage oil seal. Start splines into side gear, and push axle firmly until button end of axle shaft can be seen in case.

3) Install "C" locks, and then pull shafts outward to seat locks in counterbore of differential side gears. Position pinion shaft through case and pinion gears, aligning shaft hole with lock bolt hole. Install and tighten lock bolt to specification. See TORQUE SPECIFICATIONS table at end of article.

4) Clean gasket mounting surfaces, and apply silicone sealant in a 1/8-3/16" wide bead on face of axle housing. Install housing cover, and add lubricant until lubricant level reaches bottom of filler hole. Install filler plug.

***NOTE:** Always install a NEW plastic housing cover with NEW bolts on axle assemblies equipped with plastic housing cover.*

REAR AXLE HOUSING ASSEMBLY

Removal – 1) Raise vehicle, and support with safety stands under rear crossmember.

2) On Aerostar models, release parking brake cable tension. From underneath vehicle, pull front cable rearward about 2". Carefully clamp cable behind crossmember, ensuring cable coating is not damaged. Remove parking brake cables from equalizer. Compress tabs on retainers and pull cables through rear crossmember.

3) On all models, remove housing cover, and drain lubricant. Remove axle shafts. See AXLE SHAFT & BEARING under REMOVAL & INSTALLATION. Remove brake backing plates, and secure to frame. Mark and disconnect drive shaft at companion flange or end yoke.

4) Disconnect axle vent from housing (at brake junction block on some models). Disconnect brake line from housing clips. Disconnect upper control arms and shock absorbers from housing.

5) Lower housing on jack until coil springs can be removed. Disconnect lower control arms from housing, and remove housing.

Installation – To install, reverse removal procedure. Apply locking compound to threads holding axle vent and brake block (if used) to axle housing.

PINION FLANGE & OIL SEAL

***NOTE:** Pinion flange and oil seal replacement affects bearing preload. Reset preload during reassembly.*

Removal – 1) Raise and support vehicle. Remove rear wheel assemblies and brake drums. Mark companion flange and drive shaft end yoke for installation reference. Remove drive shaft.

2) Install plug in transmission extension housing to prevent oil leakage. Using an INCH lb. torque wrench, measure and record torque required to rotate pinion through several revolutions.

3) Mark companion flange or end yoke in relation to pinion shaft for installation reference. Hold companion flange or end yoke, and remove pinion nut. Using Puller (T77F-4220-B), remove companion flange. Using a screwdriver, remove pinion seal.

Installation – 1) Ensure pinion shaft splines are free of burrs. If necessary, remove burrs using fine crocus cloth. Lubricate area between seal lips. Using Drive Pinion Oil Seal Replacer (T79P-4676-A), install seal into axle housing.

***NOTE:** If seal becomes cocked during installation, replace it with a new one.*

2) Align marks on flange and pinion. Apply a small amount of lubricant to companion flange splines. Install flange and new integral nut and washer. Hold companion flange or end yoke, and gradually tighten nut.

3) While checking pinion bearing preload, rotate pinion until obtaining original preload. DO NOT back off pinion nut to reduce preload. See DIFFERENTIAL ASSEMBLY SPECIFICATIONS table under DIFFERENTIAL SPECIFICATIONS.

***NOTE:** If desired preload is exceeded, install a new collapsible spacer, and retighten nut until obtaining proper preload.*

4) Install drive shaft, ensuring marks align. Apply locking compound to bolt threads, and tighten bolts to specification. See TORQUE SPECIFICATIONS table at end of article. Fill axle with lubricant. Install and tighten filler plug.

REAR ANTI-LOCK BRAKE SENSOR ASSEMBLY

Removal – Remove sensor hold-down bolt. Carefully remove sensor. DO NOT let any dirt fall into axle housing.

Installation – If using old sensor, replace sensor "O" ring. On all applications, lubricate sensor "O" ring with motor oil. Hold sensor on sides and push into axle housing. Install hold-down bolt, and tighten to 25-30 ft. lbs. (34-41 N.m).

DIFFERENTIAL ASSEMBLY

Removal & Installation – Removal and installation of differential assembly is covered in overhaul procedure. See DIFFERENTIAL ASSEMBLY under OVERHAUL.

DIAGNOSIS & TESTING

RING GEAR RUNOUT TEST

1) Install Dial Indicator (4201-C) on axle housing with tip of indicator contacting back face of ring gear. A space is provided between excitor ring and ring gear for measuring ring gear runout. Set dial indicator to zero. Rotate ring gear, and record reading.

2) Maximum runout is .004" (.10 mm). If reading exceeds .004" (.10 mm), check for improper tightening on ring gear bolts or for dirt between ring gear and case.

3) If runout still exceeds .004" (.10 mm), check for warped ring gear, worn differential bearings or warped differential case. Proceed to DIFFERENTIAL RUNOUT DIAGNOSIS.

DIFFERENTIAL RUNOUT DIAGNOSIS

1) Check ring gear runout before disassembly. If ring gear runout exceeds .004" (.10 mm), warped ring gear, damaged case, excessively worn differential bearings or foreign material between mating surfaces could cause condition.

2) Remove differential case from axle housing, and remove ring gear-to-case bolts. Remove ring gear. Install differential assembly with bearing races and shims into axle housing.

3) Tighten bearing cap bolts to 70-85 ft. lbs. (95-115 N.m). Rotate differential to ensure bearings are seated properly. Using a dial indicator, check runout of differential case flange.

4) If runout is within .003" (.08 mm), install a new ring and pinion gear. If runout exceeds specification, ring gear is true. Check for either a damaged case or worn bearings.

5) Remove differential case (carrier) and bearings from axle housing. Install new differential bearings on case hubs, and install differential assembly in axle housing without ring gear.

6) Check case runout with new bearings. If runout is now within .003" (.08 mm), use new bearings for assembly. If runout is still excessive, axle housing is damaged and should be replaced.

OVERHAUL

DIFFERENTIAL ASSEMBLY

NOTE: Differential case and drive pinion may be serviced in vehicle.

Disassembly – **1)** Raise vehicle, and support with safety stands under rear crossmember. Mark drive shaft-to-companion flange, and remove drive shaft. Remove axle shafts (if not already removed). See AXLE SHAFT & BEARING under REMOVAL & INSTALLATION.

2) Check and record ring gear runout. See RING GEAR RUNOUT TEST under DIAGNOSIS & TESTING. Mark differential bearing caps and note arrow position for reassembly reference. Loosen bearing cap bolts. Attach Differential Housing Spreader (4000-E) on case.

3) Attach dial indicator to housing, and spread case .015" (.38 mm). Pry differential case, bearing races and shims out until loose in bearing caps. *See Fig. 2.* Remove bearing caps, differential and differential housing spreader.

NOTE: Bearing races and caps must be installed in original positions.

4) Using puller, remove differential side bearings. Mark differential case and ring gear for reassembly reference. Remove and discard ring gear mounting bolts.

5) Press or tap off ring gear. Using a soft face hammer, tap excitor ring to remove. Replace excitor ring if removed. Drive out pinion shaft lock pin and shaft using a punch. Remove pinion gears, side gears and thrust washers.

NOTE: DO NOT remove pinion bearing races unless damaged. Replace bearings if races are replaced.

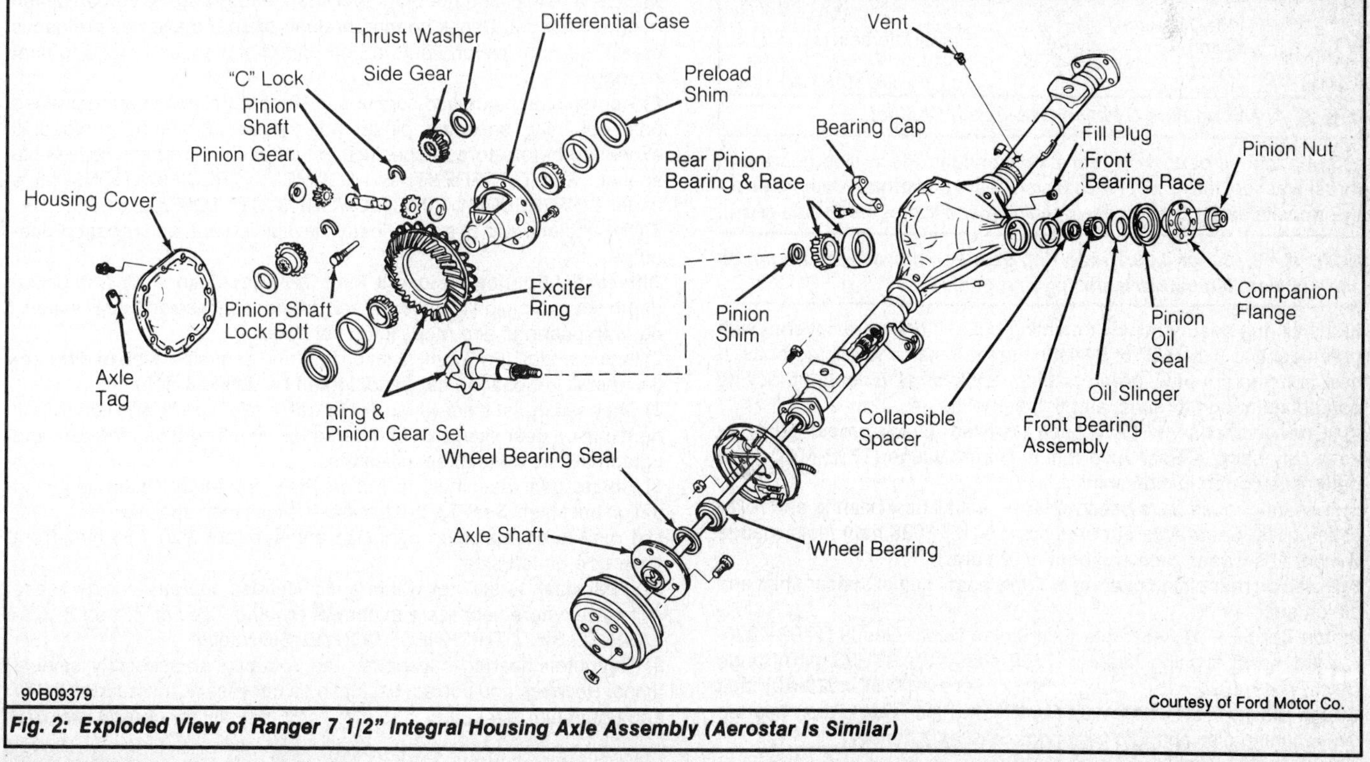
Differential Case
Thrust Washer
Side Gear
"C" Lock
Pinion Shaft
Pinion Gear
Housing Cover
Axle Tag
Pinion Shaft Lock Bolt
Ring & Pinion Gear Set
Exciter Ring
Preload Shim
Vent
Bearing Cap
Rear Pinion Bearing & Race
Pinion Shim
Fill Plug
Front Bearing Race
Pinion Nut
Companion Flange
Pinion Oil Seal
Oil Slinger
Front Bearing Assembly
Collapsible Spacer
Wheel Bearing Seal
Axle Shaft
Wheel Bearing
90B09379
Courtesy of Ford Motor Co.

Fig. 2: Exploded View of Ranger 7 1/2" Integral Housing Axle Assembly (Aerostar Is Similar)

1991 DRIVE AXLES
7 1/2" Ring Gear Differentials (Cont.)

6) Remove pinion nut and companion flange. Drive pinion out of front bearing using a soft face hammer. Remove pinion from rear of housing. Using Seal Remover (1175-AC and T50T-100A), remove pinion seal.
7) Using Pinion Bearing Replacer (T71P-4621-B), remove front pinion bearing. Measure and record thickness of shim located behind bearing.

Cleaning & Inspection – Clean all parts thoroughly in cleaning solvent. Examine pinion and ring gear teeth for scoring, excessive wear and chipping. Check bearing races for deep scores or galling. Check carrier bearings for pitting and scoring. Check roller ends for stepping. Replace any components showing damage or wear.

NOTE: Replace ring and pinion gear set in matched sets. DO NOT reuse ring gear bolts.

Reassembly & Adjustments – **1)** If replacing ring gear and pinion, note original factory shim thickness to adjust for variations in axle housing casting and original gear set dimension. *See Fig. 3.* Variations are marked on pinion gear head and ring gear.

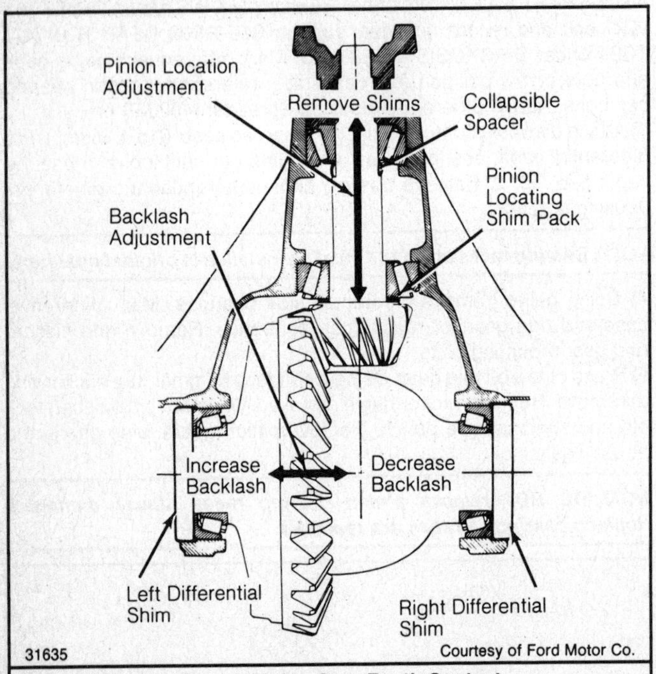
Pinion Location
Adjustment
Remove Shims
Collapsible
Spacer
Pinion
Locating
Shim Pack
Backlash
Adjustment
Increase
Backlash
Decrease
Backlash
Left Differential
Shim
Right Differential
Shim
31635
Courtesy of Ford Motor Co.

Fig. 3: Adjusting Ring & Pinion Gear Tooth Contact

2) Lubricate all parts with rear axle lubricant. Place side gears and thrust washers into case. Place pinion gears and thrust washers exactly opposite each other in case openings, and in mesh with side gears.

NOTE: If a 3.73:1 or 4.10:1 ratio ring gear is removed, ensure pinion shaft is installed before installing ring gear.

3) Install ring gear with new mounting bolts. If bolts are covered with green coating over 1/2" of threaded area, install and tighten bolts. If new bolts do not have green coating, apply small amount of locking compound to bolt threads, and tighten bolts.
4) If new components have been installed, check proper gear set assembly using a Rear Axle Pinion Depth Gauge (T79P-4020-A) to determine correct pinion shim.
5) If bearing races have been replaced, install new bearing and roller assemblies. Seat races in bores so a .0015" (.038 mm) feeler gauge will not fit between race and bottom of bore.
6) Press on rear pinion bearing to firmly seat against spacer shim and pinion gear.

Pinion Depth – **1)** Assemble Axle Pinion Depth Gauge (T79P-4020-A), and install Aligning Adapter (T76P-4020-A3), .89" (23 mm) Gauge Disc (T78P-4020-A15), Gauge Block Screw (T76P-4020-A9) and Gauge Block (T76P-4020-A10). *See Fig. 4.* Place rear pinion bearing over aligning disc and into bearing race of axle housing.

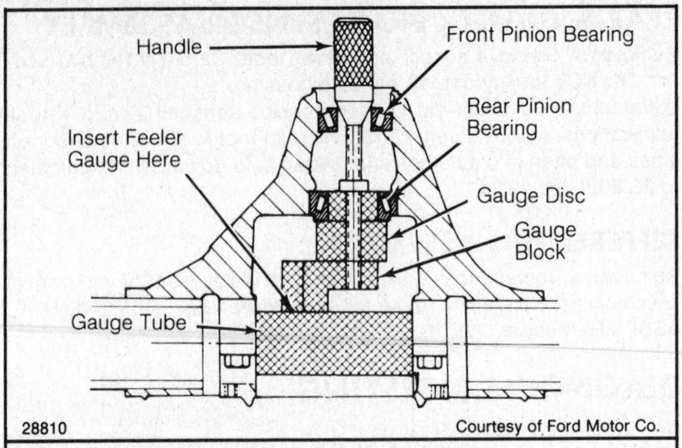
Handle
Front Pinion Bearing
Rear Pinion
Bearing
Insert Feeler
Gauge Here
Gauge Disc
Gauge
Block
Gauge Tube
28810
Courtesy of Ford Motor Co.

Fig. 4: Installing Pinion Depth Measuring Tools

2) Install front pinion bearing into front bearing race. Place tool handle onto screw, and hand tighten. Ensure pinion depth measuring tool is properly installed and tightened.
3) Apply a light film of oil to pinion bearings. Rotate gauge block several times to seat bearings. Rotational torque on gauge block assembly with new bearings should be 20 INCH lbs. (2.25 N.m).
4) Final position of gauge block should be 45 degrees above axle shaft centerline. Clean differential bearing bores thoroughly, and install gauge tube. Tighten bearing cap bolts.
5) Using flat pinion shims as a gauge for shim selection, hold gauge block in proper position and measure clearance between gauge block and tube. If pinion has a plus (+) marking, subtract this amount from measured clearance.
6) If pinion has a minus (-) marking, add this amount to measured clearance. Correct shim selection is accomplished when a slight drag is felt as shim is drawn between gauge block and tube.

Pinion Bearing Preload – **1)** Place pre-selected shim on pinion shaft. Press bearing onto shaft until bearing and shim are firmly seated against shoulder of shaft. Install new collapsible spacer on pinion shaft. Lubricate bearings with axle lubricant.
2) Install front pinion bearing in housing. Install new pinion oil seal. Insert companion flange into seal, and hold firmly in place. From rear of axle housing, insert pinion shaft into flange.
3) Start a new pinion nut on pinion shaft, and gradually tighten pinion nut (hold flange). Check bearing preload often. As soon as preload is measured, turn pinion shaft in both directions several times to seat bearings.
4) Tighten pinion nut, and continue to measure pinion bearing preload until obtaining specified pinion nut torque. If bearing preload is exceeded before torque specification is reached, replace collapsible spacer. See DIFFERENTIAL ASSEMBLY SPECIFICATIONS table under DIFFERENTIAL SPECIFICATIONS. See TORQUE SPECIFICATIONS table at end of article. Install new pinion nut, and repeat procedures.

Differential Bearing Preload & Ring Gear Backlash – **1)** With pinion depth set and pinion installed, place differential case and gear assembly with bearings and races into axle housing.
2) Install a .265" (6.73 mm) shim on left (ring gear side) side of differential. Install left bearing cap, and tighten bolts finger tight.
3) Choose largest shim which will fit with a slight drag, and install it on right (pinion gear side) side of differential. Install right bearing cap, and tighten all cap bolts to specification.
4) Rotate gear assembly to ensure free operation. Check ring and pinion backlash. *See Fig. 5.* If backlash is less than specified, add .020" (.51 mm) to shim size on right side and subtract .020" (.51 mm) from shim size on left side.
5) If backlash is still not within specifications, increase or decrease shim size where necessary to correct reading. *See Fig. 6.* See BACKLASH-TO-SHIM THICKNESS CONVERSION table.
6) Retighten bearing cap bolts, and rotate gear assembly several times. Recheck and correct backlash as necessary. Increase both left and right shim sizes .006" (.15 mm), and reinstall for correct preload.

1991 DRIVE AXLES
7 1/2" Ring Gear Differentials (Cont.)

NOTE: After adjustments are made, ensure ring gear runout is within specifications.

7) Ensure shims are seated and gear assembly turns freely. Using white marking compound, check gear tooth contact pattern. See GEAR TOOTH CONTACT PATTERNS article in GENERAL INFORMATION.

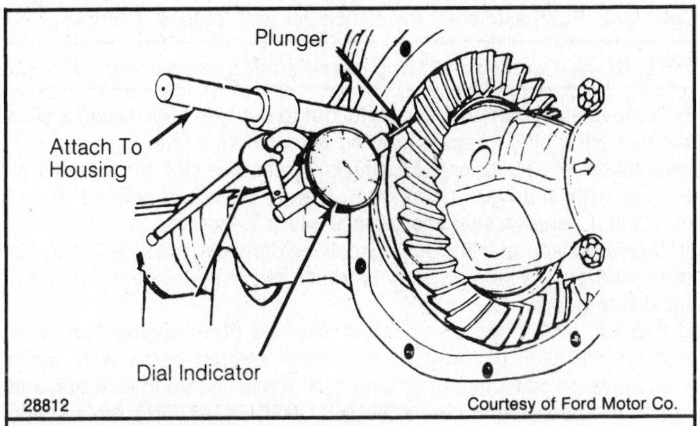
Plunger
Attach To Housing
Dial Indicator
28812
Courtesy of Ford Motor Co.

Fig. 5: Measuring Ring Gear Backlash

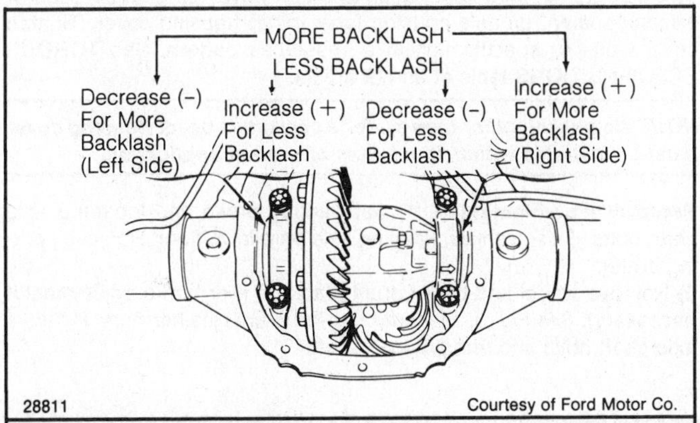
MORE BACKLASH
LESS BACKLASH
Decrease (−) For More Backlash (Left Side)
Increase (+) For Less Backlash
Decrease (−) For Less Backlash
Increase (+) For More Backlash (Right Side)
28811
Courtesy of Ford Motor Co.

Fig. 6: Adjusting Backlash

BACKLASH-TO-SHIM THICKNESS CONVERSION

Required Change In Backlash In. (mm)	Change In Shim Thickness In. (mm)
.001 (.03)	.002 (.05)
.002 (.05)	.002 (.05)
.003 (.08)	.004 (.10)
.004 (.10)	.006 (.15)
.005 (.13)	.006 (.15)
.006 (.15)	.008 (.20)
.007 (.18)	.010 (.25)
.008 (.20)	.010 (.25)
.009 (.23)	.012 (.30)
.010 (.25)	.014 (.35)
.011 (.28)	.014 (.35)
.012 (.30)	.016 (.41)
.013 (.33)	.018 (.46)
.014 (.35)	.018 (.46)
.015 (.38)	.020 (.51)

Final Assembly – **1)** Clean differential case housing lip, and apply a continuous bead of silicone sealant. If housing cover is plastic, install new cover and bolts. If housing cover is steel, ensure mating surface is clean, and install cover.

2) Install backing plates and drive shaft, and tighten bolts. Install wheel bearings, seals, brake drums and wheel assemblies. Fill axle housing with lubricant. Adjust brakes if necessary.

DIFFERENTIAL SPECIFICATIONS

DIFFERENTIAL ASSEMBLY SPECIFICATIONS

Application	Specifications
Capacity	
Aerostar	3.5 Pts. (1.7L)
Ranger	5.0 Pts. (2.5L)
Companion Flange Runout	.010" (.25 mm)
Differential Case Flange Runout	.003" (.08 mm)
Maximum Backlash Variation Between Teeth	.004" (.10 mm)
Maximum Ring Gear Runout	.004" (.10 mm)
Nominal Left Shim Thickness (For Diagnosis)	.027" (6.7 mm)
Pinion Gear Thrust Washer Thickness	.030-.032" (.76-.81 mm)
Ring Gear Backlash	.008-.015" (.20-.38 mm)
Ring Gear Back Face Runout	.004" (.10 mm)
Side Gear Thrust Washer Thickness	.030-.032" (.76-.81 mm)
	INCH Lbs. (N.m)
Pinion Bearing Preload	
New Bearings	16-29 (1.8-3.2)
Original Bearings	8-14 (.9-1.6)

TORQUE SPECIFICATIONS

TORQUE SPECIFICATIONS

Application	Ft. Lbs. (N.m)
Anti-Lock Sensor Bolt	25-30 (34-41)
Bearing Cap Bolt	70-85 (95-115)
Drive Shaft-To-Flange Nut	70-95 (95-129)
Leaf Spring U-Bolt Nuts	55-75 (75-102)
Pinion Shaft Lock Bolt	15-30 (21-41)
Pinion Nut	170 (230)
Ring Gear Bolt	70-85 (95-115)
Rear Anti-Lock Sensor Bolt	25-30 (34-41)
Rear Cover Bolt	15-20 (21-27)
Wheel Lug Nut	100 (136)

1991 DRIVE AXLES
8 3/4" & 10 1/4" Ring Gear Differentials

Aerostar, Bronco, Explorer, Ranger, E150, "F" Series

DESCRIPTION

Rear axle is a hypoid-design ring and pinion gear encased in an integral cast iron axle housing. A one-piece differential case contains a conventional 2-pinion differential assembly.

To signal rear anti-lock brake system operation, rear axles use an exciter ring pressed on the differential case behind the ring gear, and a sensor mounted in axle housing. A space is provided between ring gear and exciter ring for measuring ring gear runout.

The F250 Heavy Duty (HD) and F350 with full-floating axles, and the F250 with semi-floating axles are equipped with 10 3/4 ring gear differential. Aerostar, Bronco, Explorer, Ranger, E150 and F150 are equipped with 8 3/4 ring gear differential. On all models except Aerostar, rear axle housing is equipped with leaf springs. On Aerostar, rear axle housing is equipped with coil springs.

AXLE RATIO & IDENTIFICATION

A metal tag stamped with axle model, date of manufacture, ratio, ring gear diameter and assembly plant is attached to rear cover. Use information on tag to order replacement parts. *See Fig. 1.* Vehicle axle application can also be determined by the axle code on the Safety Certification Label located on left door pillar. See AXLE RATIO IDENTIFICATION article.

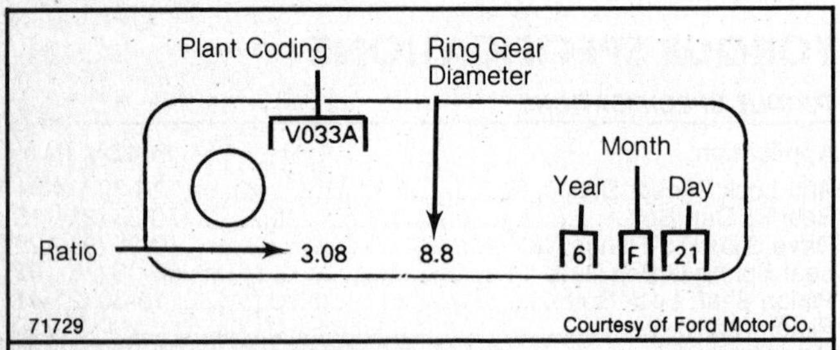
Plant Coding
Ring Gear Diameter
V033A
Month
Year
Day
Ratio
3.08
8.8
6
F
21
71729
Courtesy of Ford Motor Co.

Fig. 1: Rear Axle Identification Tag

REMOVAL & INSTALLATION

AXLE SHAFTS & BEARINGS

Removal (Semi-Floating) – 1) Raise vehicle and support with safety stands. Remove wheel assemblies and brake drums. Remove housing cover, and drain lubricant.

2) Remove differential pinion shaft lock bolt and remove pinion shaft. *See Fig. 2.* Push axle shaft toward center and remove "C" locks.

NOTE: DO NOT damage "O" ring in axle shaft groove under "C" lock.

3) Remove axle shaft, being careful not to cut axle seal. Using a slide hammer and puller, remove bearing and seal as a unit.

Installation – 1) Lubricate bearing with rear axle lubricant and install bearing with a driver. Install seal. If seal becomes cocked during installation, remove seal and replace with a new one.

2) Carefully insert axle in housing to avoid damaging oil seal. Install "C" locks, and push shafts outward to seat locks in counterbore of differential side gears.

3) Replace pinion gears and thrust washers (if removed). Turn gear assembly to align pinion gear and thrust washer bores with pinion shaft holes on case. Install pinion shaft. Apply Loctite to lock bolt and tighten to specification. See TORQUE SPECIFICATIONS table at end of article.

4) Clean gasket mating surfaces and apply 1/8 - 3/16" wide bead of silicone sealant on axle housing face. Install housing cover. Tighten cover bolts to specification in a crisscross pattern. See TORQUE SPECIFICATIONS table at end of article.

NOTE: No gasket, other than silicone sealant, is used. Housing cover must be installed within 15 minutes of sealant application.

Removal (Full-Floating) – 1) Set parking brake and loosen 8 axle shaft bolts. Raise vehicle, keeping axle parallel to floor. Release parking brake.

2) Remove wheel and brake drum (back off rear brake adjustment if necessary). *See Fig. 3.* Discard push-on drum retainer nuts. Remove axle shaft bolts and remove axle shaft.

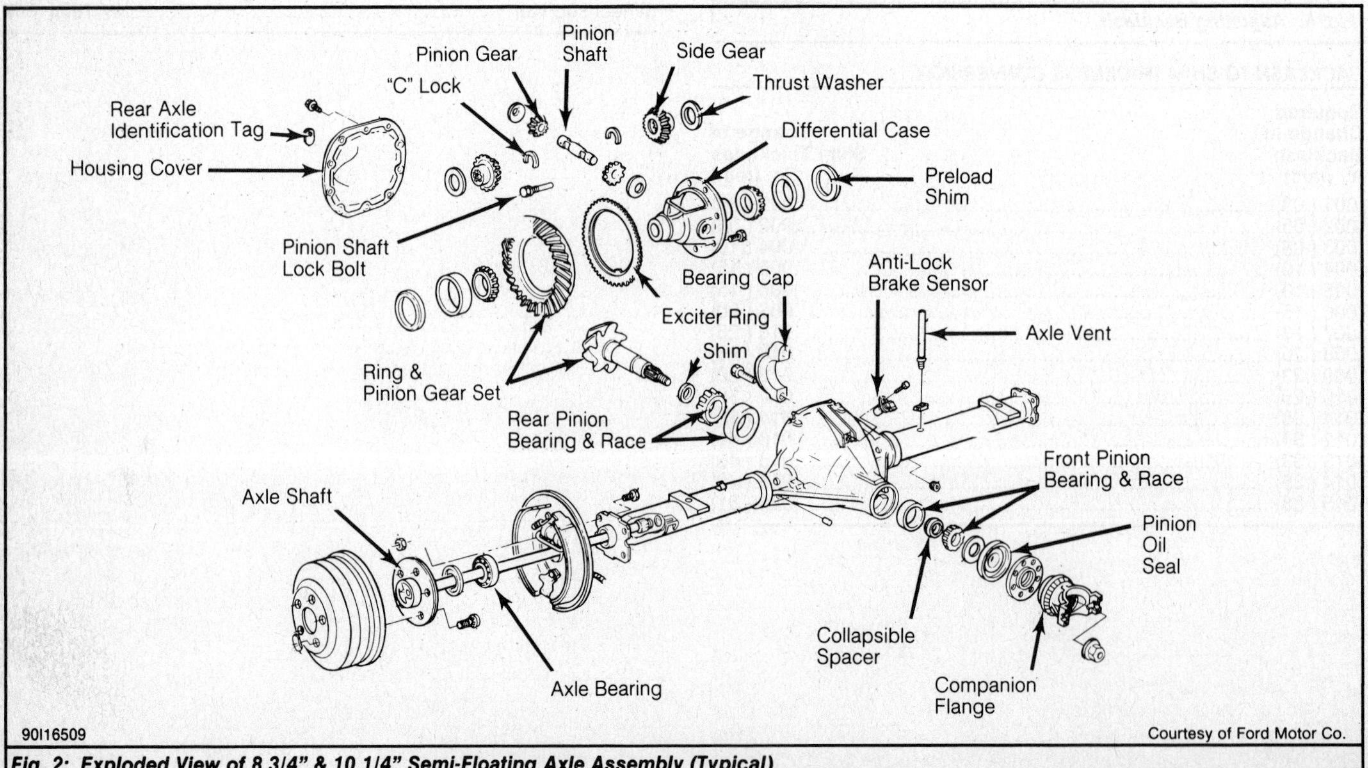
Pinion Gear
Pinion Shaft
Side Gear
"C" Lock
Thrust Washer
Rear Axle Identification Tag
Differential Case
Housing Cover
Preload Shim
Pinion Shaft Lock Bolt
Anti-Lock Brake Sensor
Bearing Cap
Exciter Ring
Axle Vent
Shim
Ring & Pinion Gear Set
Rear Pinion Bearing & Race
Front Pinion Bearing & Race
Axle Shaft
Pinion Oil Seal
Collapsible Spacer
Axle Bearing
Companion Flange
90I16509
Courtesy of Ford Motor Co.

Fig. 2: Exploded View of 8 3/4" & 10 1/4" Semi-Floating Axle Assembly (Typical)

1991 DRIVE AXLES
8 3/4" & 10 1/4" Ring Gear Differentials (Cont.)

NOTE: Left-side hub nut has left-hand threads. Right-side hub has right-hand threads. Hub nut is stamped with RH for right side, or LH for left side.

3) Install Hub Wrench (T85T-4252-AH) so drive tangs engage 4 slots in hub nut. Remove hub nut. Hub nut will ratchet during removal.
4) Install Step Plate Adapter (D80L-630-7) and Hub Puller (D80L-1002-L); loosen hub to point of removal. Remove puller and step plate. Remove hub assembly.
5) Place hub in soft-jawed vise. Remove hub seal and inner bearing. Reposition hub in vise and remove inner and outer bearing race with brass drift.

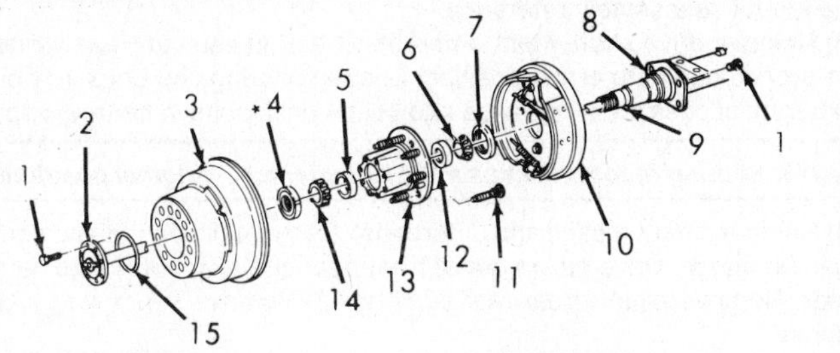
1
2
3
*4
5
6
7
8
9
1
10
11
12
13
14
15

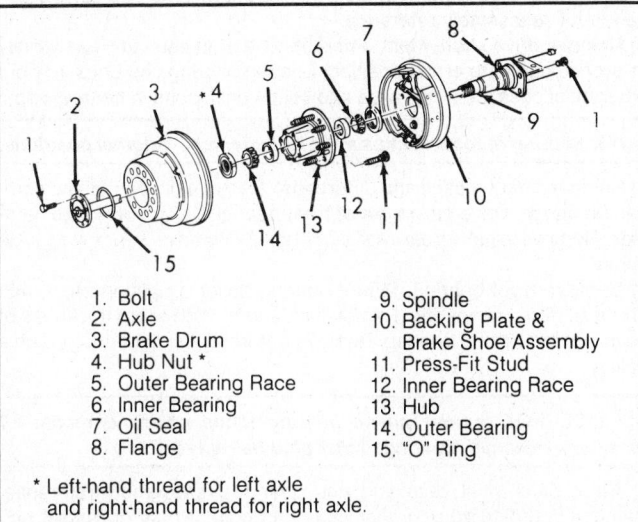

1. Bolt
2. Axle
3. Brake Drum
4. Hub Nut *
5. Outer Bearing Race
6. Inner Bearing
7. Oil Seal
8. Flange
9. Spindle
10. Backing Plate & Brake Shoe Assembly
11. Press-Fit Stud
12. Inner Bearing Race
13. Hub
14. Outer Bearing
15. "O" Ring

* Left-hand thread for left axle and right-hand thread for right axle.

91H13372 Courtesy of Ford Motor Co.

Fig. 3: Exploded View of Full Floating Axle Assembly

Installation - 1) While holding Driver Handle (T80T-4000-W) and Bearing Race Replacer (T75T-1225-A) straight, install outer and inner bearing races. Place hub inner bearing in race.
2) Install oil seal using Hub Oil Seal Installer (T85T-1175-AH), ensuring Ford logo on seal faces up. Strike tool handle until hub seal seats fully.
3) Clean spindle and coat with axle lubricant. Pack hub bearings, bearing and roller assembly using lithium-base lubricant. Push hub and outer bearing onto spindle. Install hub nut on spindle.

CAUTION: Ensure hub nut tab is located in keyway before thread engagement.

4) Install Hub Wrench (T85T-4252-AH) on spindle. Tighten hub nut to 55-65 ft. lbs. (75-88 N.m). After tightening to specification, ratchet back 5 clicks on hub nut. Clicking will be heard if procedure is performed correctly.
5) Check axle shaft "O" ring and replace if necessary. Install axle shaft. Coat axle shaft bolt threads with Loctite. Install but DO NOT tighten axle shaft bolts.
6) Install brake drum and wheel. Check lubricant level and add if necessary. Tighten wheel lug nuts and adjust brakes (if necessary). Lower vehicle and tighten axle shaft bolts to 60-80 ft. lbs. (81-109 N.m).

REAR AXLE HOUSING ASSEMBLY

Removal (Except Aerostar) - 1) Loosen wheel lug nuts and axle shaft retaining bolts. Remove shock absorbers and stabilizer bar mounts. Raise vehicle until weight is off the rear springs.
2) Remove parking brake cable from cable support and brackets. Disconnect brake line from housing clips and wheel cylinders. Disconnect rear "U" joint. Mark drive shaft for installation reference. Remove drive shaft. Disconnect axle housing vent house.
3) Support axle housing assembly with floor jack. Remove spring "U" bolt nuts and remove "U" bolt. Carefully lower axle housing assembly from vehicle. Roll axle housing out from vehicle. Drain lubricant. Remove wheels and mount axle housing in workbench.

Installation - To install, reverse removal procedure. Apply locking compound to threads holding the axle vent and brake block (if used) to axle housing.
Removal (Aerostar) - 1) Raise and support vehicle. Disconnect parking brake cables. Remove anti-lock brake sensor from axle housing. Mark drive shaft for installation reference. Remove drive shaft and plug transmission extension housing to prevent fluid leakage.
2) Disconnect hydraulic brake lines. Support axle housing with floor jack. Disconnect shock absorbers from lower control arms. Lower axle housing until coil springs are no longer under compression. Remove lower coil spring retainer first, then remove upper retainer. Remove coil springs and spring seats.
3) Raise axle housing to normal load position. Note axle housing-to-lower control arm bolt position for installation reference. Remove lower control arms. Remove upper control arm-to-axle housing bolt.
4) Remove upper control arm from axle housing. Mark cam adjuster-to-axle housing bushing position for installation reference. *See Fig. 4.* Lower axle housing and remove from vehicle.

CAUTION: Upper control arm bushing is an eccentric-type bushing which, depending on its position, controls drive pinion angle. When removing upper control arm, ALWAYS mark cam adjuster-to-axle housing bushing position for installation reference. Nominal position (zero degree) of drive pinion angle is with axle housing bushing notch at 6 o'clock position. See Fig. 4.

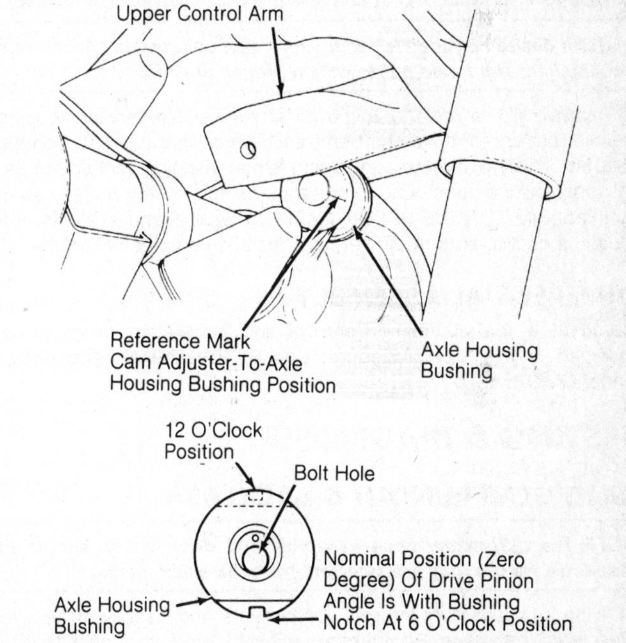
Upper Control Arm
Reference Mark
Cam Adjuster-To-Axle
Housing Bushing Position
Axle Housing
Bushing
12 O'Clock
Position
Bolt Hole
Axle Housing
Bushing
Nominal Position (Zero
Degree) Of Drive Pinion
Angle Is With Bushing
Notch At 6 O'Clock Position

91A13375 Courtesy of Ford Motor Co.

Fig. 4: Referencing Cam Adjuster To Axle Housing Bushing

Installation - 1) Raise axle housing into position. Position upper control arm over cam adjuster and axle housing bushing. Ensure cam adjuster-to-axle housing bushing position is correct according to reference mark made previously. Lower axle housing to spring-unloaded position.
2) Place lower control arms in position. Install control arm-to-axle housing bolts in their original position and tighten bolts 95-130 ft. lbs. (129-176 N.m). Position spring seats on coil spring and install coil spring. Ensure tapered coil (White) of coil spring faces upward. To complete installation, reverse removal procedure. Bleed brakes.

PINION FLANGE & OIL SEAL

NOTE: Pinion flange and oil seal replacement affects bearing preload. Preload must be carefully reset during reassembly.

1991 DRIVE AXLES
8 3/4" & 10 1/4" Ring Gear Differentials (Cont.)

Removal – **1)** Raise vehicle and support with safety stands. Remove wheel assemblies and brake drums. Scribe alignment marks on companion flange and drive shaft end yoke for installation reference. Remove drive shaft.
2) Install oil seal replacer tool in transmission extension housing to prevent oil leakage. Using an INCH lb. torque wrench, measure and record torque required to rotate pinion through several revolutions.
3) Mark companion flange or end yoke in relation to pinion shaft for installation reference. Hold companion flange or end yoke and remove pinion nut. Using Puller (T70P-4221-A), remove companion flange. Using screwdriver, remove pinion seal.
Installation – **1)** Ensure pinion shaft splines are free of burrs. Remove burrs with fine crocus cloth if necessary. Lubricate area between seal lips, and install seal into axle housing using Pinion Oil Seal Replacer (T83T-4676-A).
2) Align marks on flange and pinion. Apply a small amount of lubricant to companion flange splines. Install flange and new integral nut and washer. Hold companion flange or end yoke, and gradually tighten nut while rotating pinion.

NOTE: If seal becomes cocked during installation, remove seal and install a new seal.

3) Check pinion bearing preload often, until correct preload is obtained. DO NOT back off pinion nut to reduce preload. See DIFFERENTIAL ASSEMBLY SPECIFICATIONS table under DIFFERENTIAL SPECIFICATIONS at end of article.

NOTE: If desired preload is exceeded, a new collapsible spacer must be installed. Tightened nut to obtain proper preload.

4) Remove oil seal replacer tool from transmission extension housing. Install front end of drive shaft on transmission output shaft. Connect rear end of drive shaft to companion flange, aligning scribed marks.
5) Apply locking compound to bolt threads and tighten bolts to specification. See TORQUE SPECIFICATIONS table at end of article. Add axle lubricant to bottom of filler hole. Install and tighten filler plug.

DIFFERENTIAL ASSEMBLY

Removal & Installation – Removal and installation procedure is included in overhaul procedure. See DIFFERENTIAL ASSEMBLY under OVERHAUL.

TESTING & DIAGNOSIS

RING GEAR RUNOUT & BACKLASH

NOTE: The differential case assembly and drive pinion should be inspected before they are removed from the axle housing.

1) Wipe lubricant from internal components and visually inspect for wear and/or damage. Rotate gears to check for any roughness, indicating damaged bearings or gears.
2) Check ring gear teeth for scoring, abnormal wear, or nicks. Install dial indicator on axle housing, with tip of indicator contacting back face of ring gear. Check ring gear backlash and back face runout. *See Fig. 7.*
3) Backlash should be .008-.015" (.20-.38 mm), and back face runout should not exceed .004" (.10 mm). If specification is exceeded, remove differential case from axle housing. Remove ring gear. Reinstall differential assembly. Tighten bearing cap bolts to specification.
4) Mount dial indicator so stem rides on differential case flange. Rotate differential assembly and record runout. If runout exceeds .004" (.10 mm), ring gear is okay. Case or bearings are damaged.
5) Visually inspect bearings. If bearings are okay, replace case and bearings. Recheck runout with new parts. Check gear set assembly, using rear axle Pinion Depth Gauge Set (T79P-4020-A), to determine required shim thickness.

OVERHAUL

DIFFERENTIAL ASSEMBLY

NOTE: Differential case and drive pinion may be serviced in vehicle.

Disassembly – **1)** Raise vehicle and support under rear frame crossmember with safety stands. Drain lubricant and remove housing cover. Mount dial indicator for pre-disassembly measurements. *See Fig. 7.*
2) Measure and record ring gear backlash and runout. Remove axle shafts. See AXLE SHAFTS & BEARINGS under REMOVAL & INSTALLATION. Place alignment marks on drive shaft, yoke and companion flange for reassembly reference.
3) Remove drive shaft. Mark differential bearing caps for reassembly reference and note arrow position. Loosen bearing cap bolts. Pry out differential case, bearing races and shims until loose in bearing caps.

NOTE: Bearing races and caps must be installed in original positions.

4) Remove bearing caps and differential. Remove pinion nut and companion flange. Drive pinion out of front bearing using soft-faced hammer. Remove pinion from rear of housing. Remove seal using slide hammer.
5) Remove front bearing. Mount bearing puller on pinion shaft, and press shaft out of bearing. Remove, measure, and record thickness of shim located behind bearing. Remove differential side bearings with a puller.

NOTE: DO NOT remove pinion bearing races unless damaged. If races are replaced, bearings must also be replaced.

6) Mark differential case and ring gear for reassembly reference. Remove and discard ring gear mounting bolts. Press or tap off ring gear. Remove pinion shaft lock bolt and remove shaft. Remove pinion gears, side gears and thrust washers.
Cleaning & Inspection – Clean all parts thoroughly in solvent. Examine pinion and ring gear teeth for scoring, excessive wear, nicks and chipping. Check bearing races for deep scores or galling. Check carrier bearings for wear or damage. Replace components if necessary.
Anti-Lock Brake Sensor – Check sensor pole piece for loose metal particles; clean if necessary.
Exciter Ring – Ensure exciter ring is properly pressed onto differential case. Examine ring for chips or missing teeth.
Bearing Races – Check bearing races for scores or galling. If a .0015" (.038 mm) feeler gauge can be inserted between a race and bottom of its bore at any point around the race, race must be reseated.
Bearing & Roller Assemblies – When operated in races, bearing rollers must turn without roughness. Examine roller ends for step wear. If damaged, both parts should be replaced.
Companion Flange – Ensure flange half-rounds and lugs have not been damaged. End of flange contacting bearing, counterbore and seal surface must be smooth and free of damage.
Gears – Examine pinion and ring gear teeth for scoring, excessive wear, and excessive chipping. Worn or damaged gears CANNOT be rebuilt to correct noisy condition.
Axle Housing – Ensure differential and pinion bearing bores are smooth. Remove any nicks or burrs from mounting surfaces.
Differential Case – Ensure hubs where bearings mount are smooth. Check differential case bearing shoulders for damage. Bearing assemblies will fail if they do not seat firmly against shoulders. Ensure differential side gears rotate freely in counterbores.

NOTE: Ring and pinion gear set must be replaced in matched sets.

Reassembly & Adjustments – **1)** Lubricate all parts with rear axle lubricant. Place side gears and thrust washers into case. Place pinion gears and thrust washers opposite each other in case openings, and in mesh with side gears.
2) Install ring gear with new mounting bolts. If bolts are covered with Green coating over 1/2" of threaded area, install and tighten bolts. If

1991 DRIVE AXLES
8 3/4" & 10 1/4" Ring Gear Differentials (Cont.)

new bolts do not have Green coating, apply small amount of locking compound to bolt threads then tighten bolts.

3) If bearing races have been replaced, new bearing and roller assemblies should be installed. Races must be seated in bores so a .0015" (.038 mm) feeler gauge will not fit between race and bottom of bore.

Pinion Depth - 1) Assemble Axle Pinion Depth Gauge Set (T79P-4020-A) and install aligning adapter, gauge disc, gauge block screw and gauge block.

2) Place rear pinion bearing over aligning disc and into bearing race of axle housing. Install front pinion bearing into front bearing race. Place tool handle onto screw and finger tighten. *See Fig. 5.*

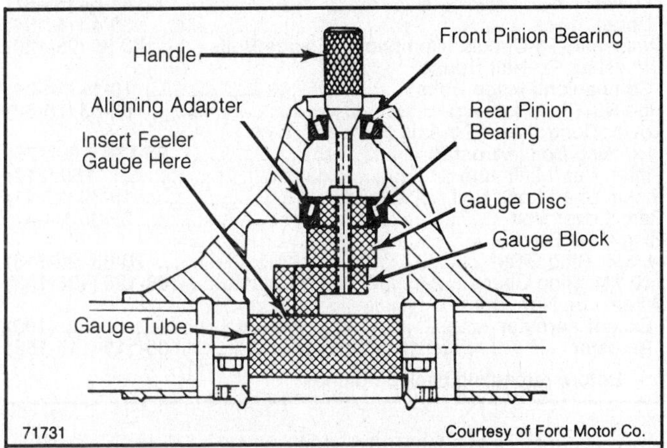
Handle
Front Pinion Bearing
Aligning Adapter
Rear Pinion Bearing
Insert Feeler Gauge Here
Gauge Disc
Gauge Block
Gauge Tube
71731
Courtesy of Ford Motor Co.

Fig. 5: Installing Pinion Depth Measuring Tools (Tools Are Included in Axle Pinion Depth Gauge Set)

3) Ensure pinion depth measuring tools are properly installed and tightened. Apply a light film of oil to pinion bearings. Rotate gauge block several times to seat bearings.

4) Rotational torque on gauge block assembly should be 20 INCH lbs. (2.25 N.m) with new bearings. Final position of gauge block should be 45 degrees above axle shaft centerline. Clean differential bearing bores thoroughly and install gauge tube.

5) Tighten bearing cap bolts to specification. See TORQUE SPECIFICATIONS table at end of article. Using flat pinion shims as a gauge for shim selection, hold gauge block in proper position and measure clearance between gauge block and tube.

6) Correct shim selection is accomplished when a slight drag is felt as shim is drawn between gauge block and tube.

Pinion Bearing Preload - 1) Place pre-selected shim on pinion shaft. Press bearing onto shaft until bearing and shim are firmly seated against shoulder of shaft. Install new collapsible spacer on pinion shaft.

2) Lubricate bearings with axle lubricant. Install front pinion bearing in housing. Install new pinion oil seal. Insert companion flange into seal and hold firmly in place.

3) From rear of axle housing, insert pinion shaft into flange. Install a new pinion nut on pinion shaft and gradually tighten pinion nut (hold flange).

NOTE: If installing a new companion flange, disregard scribed mark on pinion shaft.

4) Check bearing preload often. As soon as preload is measured, turn pinion shaft in both directions several times to seat bearings. Hold companion flange with Companion Flange Holder (T57T-4851-B) while tightening nut.

5) Tighten pinion nut and continue to measure pinion bearing preload until specified pinion torque is obtained. See DIFFERENTIAL ASSEMBLY SPECIFICATIONS table under DIFFERENTIAL SPECIFICATIONS at end of article. If bearing preload is exceeded before torque specification is reached, replace collapsible spacer.

6) Install new pinion nut and repeat procedures. DO NOT loosen pinion nut to reduce pinion bearing preload.

Differential Bearing Preload & Ring Gear Backlash - 1) With pinion depth set and pinion installed, place differential case and gear assembly with bearings and races into axle housing.

2) Install a .265" (6.73 mm) shim on left (ring gear side) side of differential. Install left bearing cap finger tight.

3) Choose largest shim that will fit with a slight drag and install it on pinion gear side (right side) of differential. Install right bearing cap and tighten all cap bolts to specification. See TORQUE SPECIFICATIONS table at end of article.

4) Rotate gear assembly to ensure free operation. Check ring and pinion backlash. *See Fig. 7.* If backlash is .008-.015" (.20-.38 mm), proceed to step **6)**. If backlash is zero, add .020" (.51 mm) to shim size on right side, and subtract .020" (.51 mm) from shim size on left side.

5) If backlash is less than .008" (.20 mm) or more than .015" (.38 mm), increase or decrease shim size where necessary to correct reading. *See Fig. 6.*

6) Retighten bearing cap bolts and rotate gear assembly several times. Recheck backlash and correct if necessary. Increase both left and right shim sizes .006" (.15 mm), and reinstall for correct preload.

7) Ensure shims are seated and gear assembly turns freely. Using marking compound, check gear tooth contact pattern. See GEAR TOOTH CONTACT PATTERNS article in GENERAL INFORMATION.

Final Assembly - 1) Clean axle housing lip and apply a continuous bead of silicone sealant. Install cover and tighten bolts.

2) Install backing plates and drive shaft. Reverse disassembly procedure to complete assembly. Fill axle with lubricant. Adjust brakes if required.

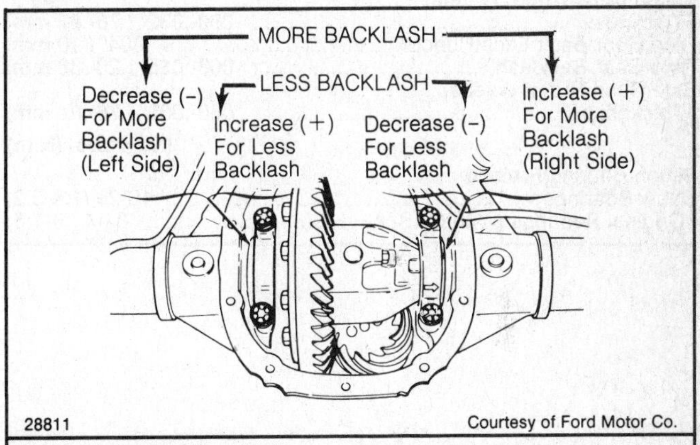
MORE BACKLASH
LESS BACKLASH
Decrease (-) For More Backlash (Left Side)
Increase (+) For Less Backlash
Decrease (-) For Less Backlash
Increase (+) For More Backlash (Right Side)
28811
Courtesy of Ford Motor Co.

Fig. 6: Adjusting Backlash

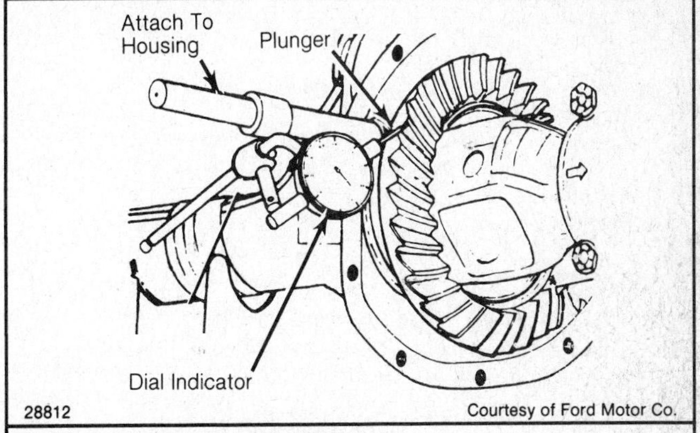
Attach To Housing
Plunger
Dial Indicator
28812
Courtesy of Ford Motor Co.

Fig. 7: Measuring Ring Gear Backlash

1991 DRIVE AXLES
8 3/4" & 10 1/4" Ring Gear Differentials (Cont.)

BACKLASH-TO-SHIM THICKNESS CONVERSION

Required Change In Backlash In. (mm)	Change In Shim Thickness In. (mm)
.001 (.03)	.002 (.05)
.002 (.05)	.002 (.05)
.003 (.08)	.004 (.10)
.004 (.10)	.006 (.15)
.005 (.13)	.006 (.15)
.006 (.15)	.008 (.20)
.007 (.18)	.010 (.25)
.008 (.20)	.010 (.25)
.009 (.23)	.012 (.30)
.010 (.25)	.014 (.35)
.011 (.28)	.014 (.35)
.012 (.30)	.016 (.41)
.013 (.33)	.018 (.46)
.014 (.35)	.018 (.46)
.015 (.38)	.020 (.51)

DIFFERENTIAL SPECIFICATIONS

DIFFERENTIAL ASSEMBLY SPECIFICATIONS

Application	Specifications
Capacity	
8 3/4" Ring Gear	5.5 pts. (2.6L)
10 1/4" Ring Gear	6.5 pts. (3.1L)
Differential Case Flange Runout	.003" (.08 mm)
Maximum Backlash Variation Between Teeth	.004" (.10 mm)
Nominal Pinion Shim Thickness	.030" (.76 mm)
Pinion Gear Thrust Washer Thickness	.030-.032" (.76-.81 mm)
Ring Gear Back Face Runout	.004" (.10 mm)
Ring Gear Backlash	.008-.015" (.20-.38 mm)
Side Gear Thrust Washer Thickness	.030-.032" (.76-.81 mm)
	INCH Lbs. (N.m)
Pinion Bearing Preload	
New Bearings	16-29 (1.8-3.2)
Original Bearings (With Oil Seal)	8-14 (.9-1.6)

TORQUE SPECIFICATIONS

TORQUE SPECIFICATIONS

Application	Ft. Lbs. (N.m)
ABS Sensor Bolt	26-30 (35-41)
Axle Shaft Bolt (Full-Floating)	60-80 (81-109)
Axle Vent Bolt	15-25 (21-34)
Backing Plate Nuts	20-40 (27-54)
Bearing Cap Bolt	
8 3/4" Ring Gear	70-85 (95-115)
10 1/4" Ring Gear	80-95 (109-129)
Coil Spring Nut (Aerostar)	
Lower	41-64 (56-87)
Upper	30-40 (41-54)
Driveshaft-To-Circular Companion Flange Bolts	70-95 (95-129)
Driveshaft-To-Half Round Companion Flange Bolts	10-15 (14-21)
Hub Nut (Full-Floating)	[1] 55-65 (75-88)
Lower Control Arm-To-Axle Housing Bolt (Aerostar)	95-130 (129-176)
Pinion Nut (Minimum)	160 (217)
Pinion Shaft Lock Bolt	15-30 (21-41)
Rear Cover Bolt	25-35 (34-47)
Ring Gear Bolt	
8 3/4" Ring Gear	70-85 (95-115)
10 1/4" Ring Gear	100-120 (136-163)
Wheel Lug Nut	
Except Aerostar	140 (190)
Aerostar	85-115 (115-156)

[1] – Before ratcheting back 5 notches.

1991 DRIVE AXLES
Dana 60, 70 & 80 Differentials

Front Axle: F350
Rear Axle: E250, E250 HD, E350, "F" Series Super Duty

DESCRIPTION

The Dana 60 (monobeam) front axle, with full-floating axles, is used on F350 4WD. Other than parts required for front-wheel drive, axle is identical to Dana 60 rear axle. The Dana 60 rear axle, with semi-floating axles, is used on light duty (less than 8500 GVW) E250 models.

The Dana 60 rear axle, with full-floating axles, is used on E250 Heavy Duty (HD), and E350 with single rear wheels. The Dana 70 rear axle, with full-floating axles, is used on E350 with dual rear wheels. The Dana 80 rear axle, with full-floating axles, is used on "F" Series Super Duty.

All Dana axle assemblies are an integral-type housing with hypoid gear ring and pinion. Stamped steel cover is removable for inspection and repair of differential. Drive pinion depth, pinion bearing preload and differential side bearing preload are all set by shims.

On Dana axle assemblies with full-floating axle shafts, vehicle loads are supported by axle housings. Axle shafts of full-floating rear assemblies may be removed without disturbing wheel bearings. Full-floating axle shafts are held in place by bolts attached to hub.

On Dana axle assemblies with semi-floating axle shafts, the axle shaft rides on axle bearing, which is pressed into outer end of axle housing tube. Semi-floating axles are retained in the axle by "C" clips positioned in a slot at end of splined axle shaft.

NOTE: For removal and installation procedures for E350 4WD front drive axle component parts not covered in this article, see appropriate LOCKING HUBS and 4WD STEERING KNUCKLES articles.

AXLE RATIO & IDENTIFICATION

Axle identification can be determined by the axle code on the Safety Certification Label on left door pillar. In addition, a metal identification tag stamped with gear ratio and diameter is secured to axle housing by 2 bolts. *See Fig. 1.* If axle is equipped with limited-slip differential, the gear ratio will have the letter "L" in the number. See AXLE RATIO IDENTIFICATION article.

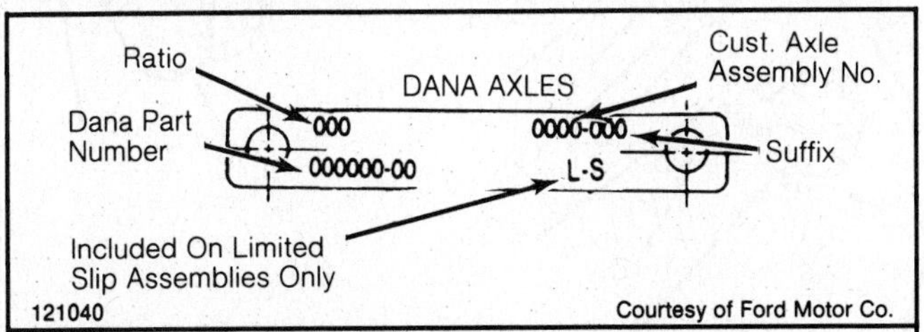
Ratio
DANA AXLES
Cust. Axle Assembly No.
Dana Part Number
000
0000-000
000000-00
L-S
Suffix
Included On Limited Slip Assemblies Only
121040
Courtesy of Ford Motor Co.

Fig. 1: Rear Axle Identification Tag

REMOVAL & INSTALLATION

HUB, BEARING & AXLE SHAFT (FULL-FLOATING)

Removal (F350 – Front) – 1) Raise and support vehicle. Remove tire and wheel assembly. Remove disc brake caliper and support out of way. Remove caliper and secure to frame. Remove locking hub screws and remove hub cover.

2) Remove snap ring from end of axle. Remove outer hub retaining ring from hub housing. Remove locking hub from housing by installing 2 cap screws in locking hub outer ring and pull out of hub.

3) Using Spanner Lock Nut Wrench (D85T-1197-A), remove spindle lock nut, retaining washer, and bearing adjusting nut. Pull hub and rotor assembly off spindle. Remove inner grease seal and inner bearing.

4) Inspect bearings and bearing races for wear and pitting. If replacement is necessary, drive outer race from bearing hub using a punch and hammer. Install new race; be careful not to chip or dent race. Ensure new race is fully seated in hub.

5) Match mark spindle and knuckle, and remove bolts or nuts. Tap spindle with soft-faced hammer, and remove spindle and splash shield. Pull axle shaft through knuckle. Remove spacer from axle shaft if necessary.

6) Inspect needle bearing and seal in spindle or axle housing. Inspect axle shaft "U" joint and shaft splines for wear. Replace as necessary. Lettering on spindle needle bearing must face rear of spindle.

Installation – 1) Install axle shaft through knuckle, and engage in axle gear splines. Install spacer (if removed) with chamfered side inboard against axle shaft. Align match marks and install spindle. Clean bearings and hub. Pack bearings with multipurpose grease and apply grease to hub races.

2) Install inner bearing, and install new grease seal. Wipe spindle clean, and lightly coat spindle with grease. Install hub on spindle; be careful not to damage seal. Install outer bearing adjusting nut.

3) Using spanner socket, tighten bearing adjusting nut in 3 steps. See FRONT HUB BEARING ADJUSTING SPECIFICATIONS table. Install retaining ring, making sure adjusting nut lock pin engages hole in ring. Install spindle lock nut and tighten to specification. See FRONT HUB BEARING ADJUSTING SPECIFICATIONS table.

4) Lightly grease locking hub assembly and install in hub. Install outer retaining ring and axle snap ring. Install locking hub cover and tighten retaining screws. See TORQUE SPECIFICATIONS table at end of article. To complete installation, reverse removal procedure. Check hub for proper operation.

FRONT HUB BEARING ADJUSTING SPECIFICATIONS

Application	Ft. Lbs. (N.m)
Adjusting Nut [1]	
Step 1	50 (68)
Step 2 [2]	31-39 (42-53)
Step 3	Back Off 90 Degrees
Lock Nut	160-205 (217-278)

[1] – Maximum hub end play should be .004" (.10 mm).
[2] – Loosen and retorque.

CAUTION: The hub nuts have right-hand thread for right spindle, and left-hand thread for left spindle. DO NOT use power impact tools on hub nuts.

Removal (E250 HD, E350 & "F" Series Super Duty) – 1) Set parking brake. Loosen axle flange bolts. Release parking brake. Raise and support vehicle. Remove tire and wheel assembly.

2) Remove axle shaft bolts and lock washers. *See Fig. 2.* Discard bolts and washers. Remove axle shaft, and discard gasket. Remove brake drums. Using Hub Wrench (T85T-4252-AH), remove bearing adjusting nut(s). Remove hub assembly. Remove inner hub seal and bearing. Inspect bearings and races for wear.

Installation – 1) To replace bearing race, drive race from bearing hub using a brass drift and hammer. Install new bearing race; be careful not to chip or dent race. Ensure new race is fully seated in hub.

2) Pack bearings with lithium-base grease. Install new seal. Carefully install hub on axle spindle to avoid damaging seal lip and spindle threads. Install outer bearing and adjusting nut.

3) Install adjusting nut, ensuring hub nut tab aligns with keyway in axle. Using Hub Wrench Tool (T85T-4252-AH), tighten bearing adjusting nut in 3 steps. See REAR HUB BEARING ADJUSTING SPECIFICATIONS table. Hub will ratchet as torque is applied.

4) To complete installation, reverse removal procedure. Install new axle shaft bolts, lock washers and gasket. Tighten lug nuts to specification. See TORQUE SPECIFICATIONS table at end of article.

NOTE: DO NOT interchange 2-piece, swiveling lug nuts with 1-piece, cone-shaped lug nuts.

1991 DRIVE AXLES
Dana 60, 70 & 80 Differentials (Cont.)

REAR HUB BEARING ADJUSTING SPECIFICATIONS

Application	Ft. Lbs. (N.m)
Adjusting Nut	
Step 1	65-75 (88-102)
Step 2	Back Off 90 Degrees
Step 3	15-20 (20-27)

AXLE SHAFTS & BEARINGS (SEMI-FLOATING)

Removal (E250) – **1)** Raise and support vehicle. Remove wheels and brake drums. Remove housing cover to drain lubricant. Remove lock bolt from pinion shaft in ring gear case. *See Fig. 3.*

2) Remove differential pinion shaft from ring gear case. Push flanged end of axle shaft toward center of vehicle. Remove "C" clip from inner end of axle shaft. Pull axle shaft out of housing tube.

NOTE: DO NOT rotate differential side gears when removing axle shafts. Turning idle gears may cause gear and thrust washers to fall out of opening in ring gear case.

3) Pry oil seal out of axle tube and discard seal. Using Push-Puller (T81P-1104-C), Adapters (T81P-1104-B) for coarse threads or (D81T-1104-A) for fine threads, and Rear Wheel Bearing Remover (T81T-1225-A), remove bearing from axle housing.

WARNING: Wear safety glasses when removing bearing from housing, as bearing could shatter under pressure.

4) Ensure bearing bore has no burrs or excessive wear. Clean bore with metal cleaning solvent. Contamination in bore could cause premature failure of new bearing.

Installation – **1)** Coat bearing with axle lubricant when installing in axle bore. Using push-puller, adapters, Step Plate (D80L-630-1) and Rear Axle Bearing Installer (T80T-4000-X), install bearing in axle bore. Ensure bearing does not cock in bore while installing.

2) Install NEW oil seal in bore using push-puller, adapters, step plate, and Rear Oil Seal Installer (T80T-4000-Y). Ensure seal does not cock in bore. Fill space between seal and bearing with No. 2 E.P. lithium grease.

3) Carefully slide axle shaft through seal and bearing. Engage side gear with splines on axle shaft. Push axle shaft toward center and install "C" clip. Install differential pinion shaft. Ensure pinion gear thrust washers are in place.

CAUTION: Unit is equipped with 2 types of pinion shaft lock bolts. One type has threads that are coated with locking compound, and has 5/32" hexagram (6-point star) socket head. DO NOT reuse lock bolts coated with locking compound. The other type uses off-set threads, and has 12-point drive head. Lock bolts with off-set threads may be used through 4 removal and installation procedures.

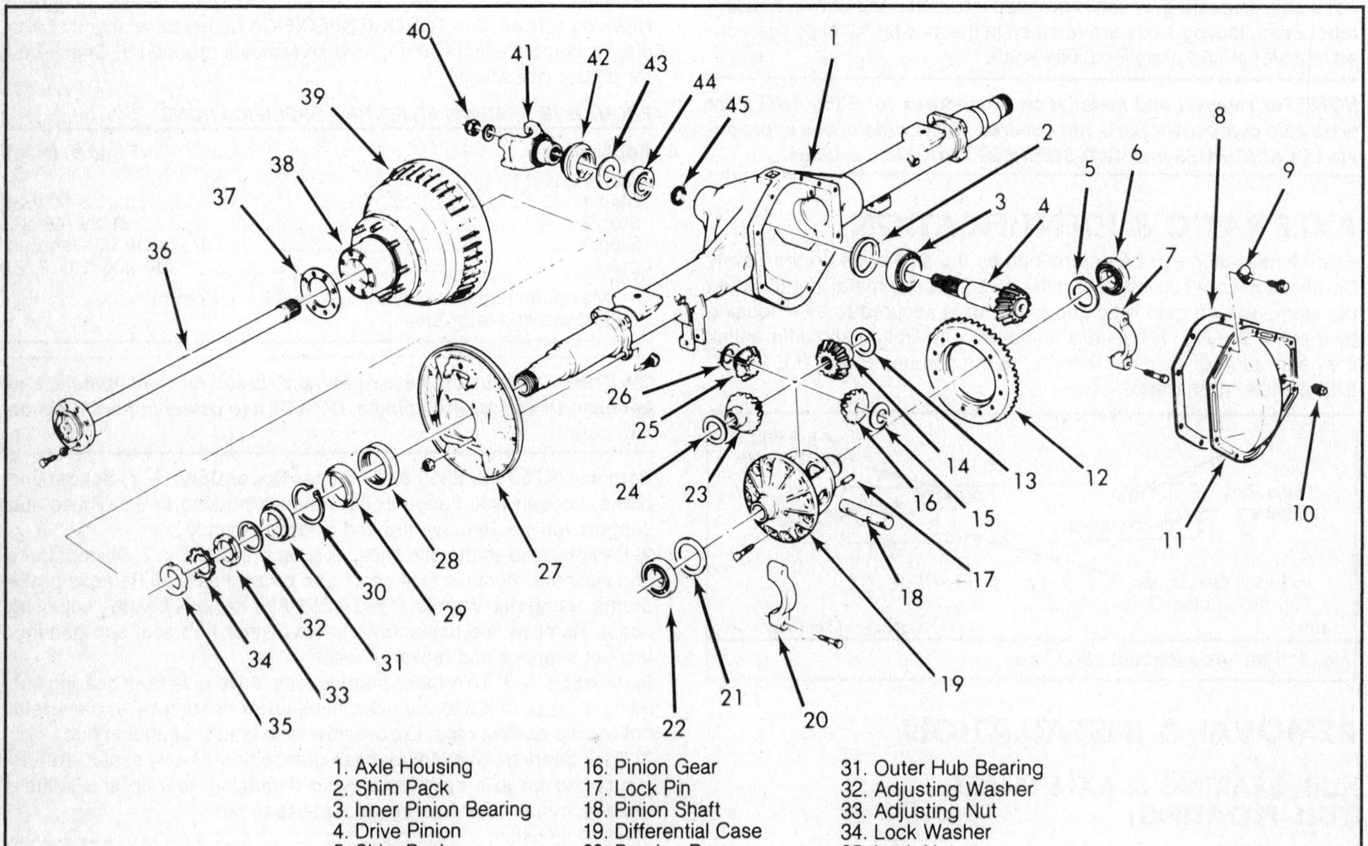
1
2
3
4
5
6
7
8
9
10
11
12
13
14
15
16
17
18
19
20
21
22
23
24
25
26
27
28
29
30
31
32
33
34
35
36
37
38
39
40
41
42
43
44
45

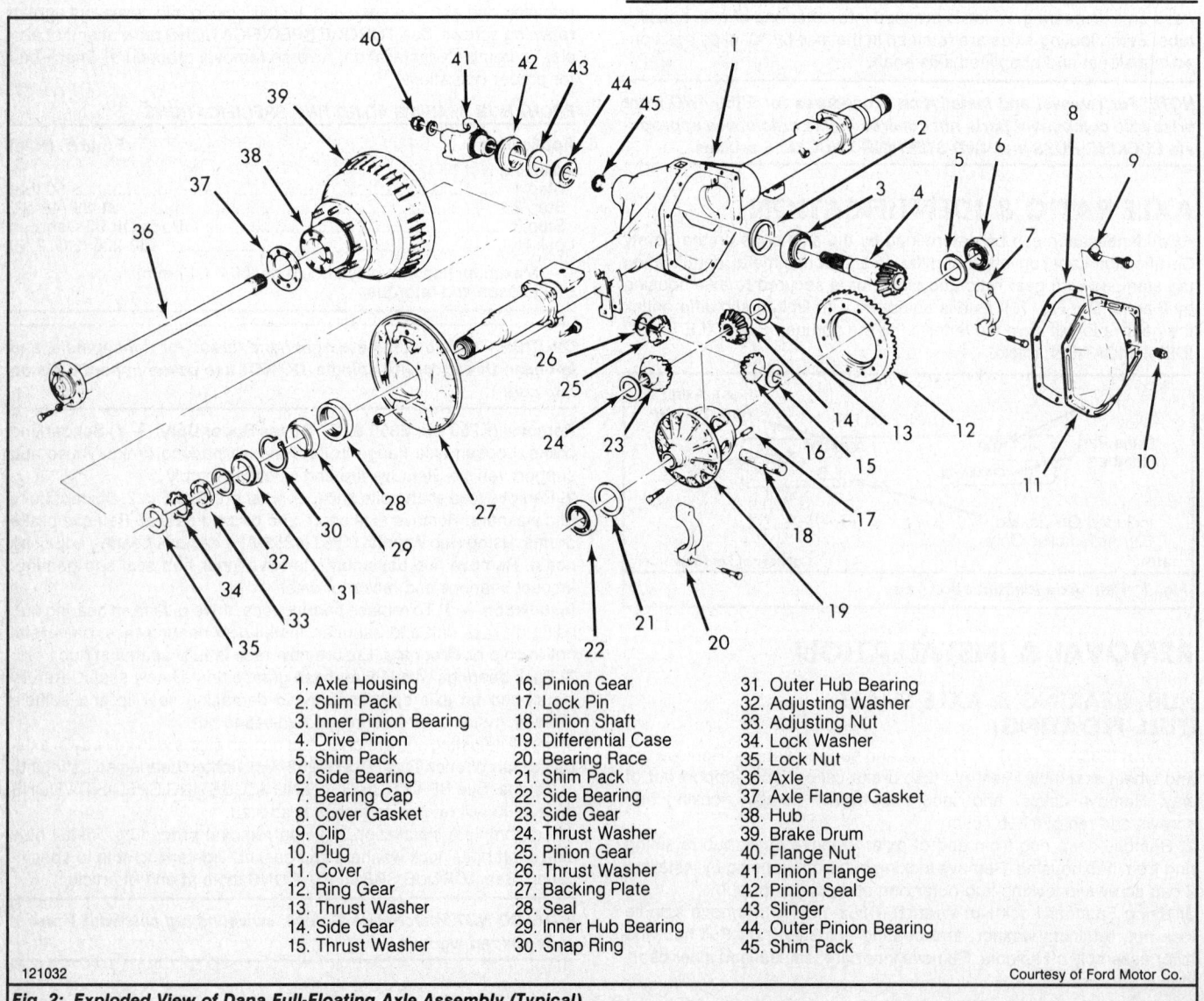

1. Axle Housing
2. Shim Pack
3. Inner Pinion Bearing
4. Drive Pinion
5. Shim Pack
6. Side Bearing
7. Bearing Cap
8. Cover Gasket
9. Clip
10. Plug
11. Cover
12. Ring Gear
13. Thrust Washer
14. Side Gear
15. Thrust Washer
16. Pinion Gear
17. Lock Pin
18. Pinion Shaft
19. Differential Case
20. Bearing Race
21. Shim Pack
22. Side Bearing
23. Side Gear
24. Thrust Washer
25. Pinion Gear
26. Thrust Washer
27. Backing Plate
28. Seal
29. Inner Hub Bearing
30. Snap Ring
31. Outer Hub Bearing
32. Adjusting Washer
33. Adjusting Nut
34. Lock Washer
35. Lock Nut
36. Axle
37. Axle Flange Gasket
38. Hub
39. Brake Drum
40. Flange Nut
41. Pinion Flange
42. Pinion Seal
43. Slinger
44. Outer Pinion Bearing
45. Shim Pack

121032 Courtesy of Ford Motor Co.

Fig. 2: Exploded View of Dana Full-Floating Axle Assembly (Typical)

1991 DRIVE AXLES
Dana 60, 70 & 80 Differentials (Cont.)

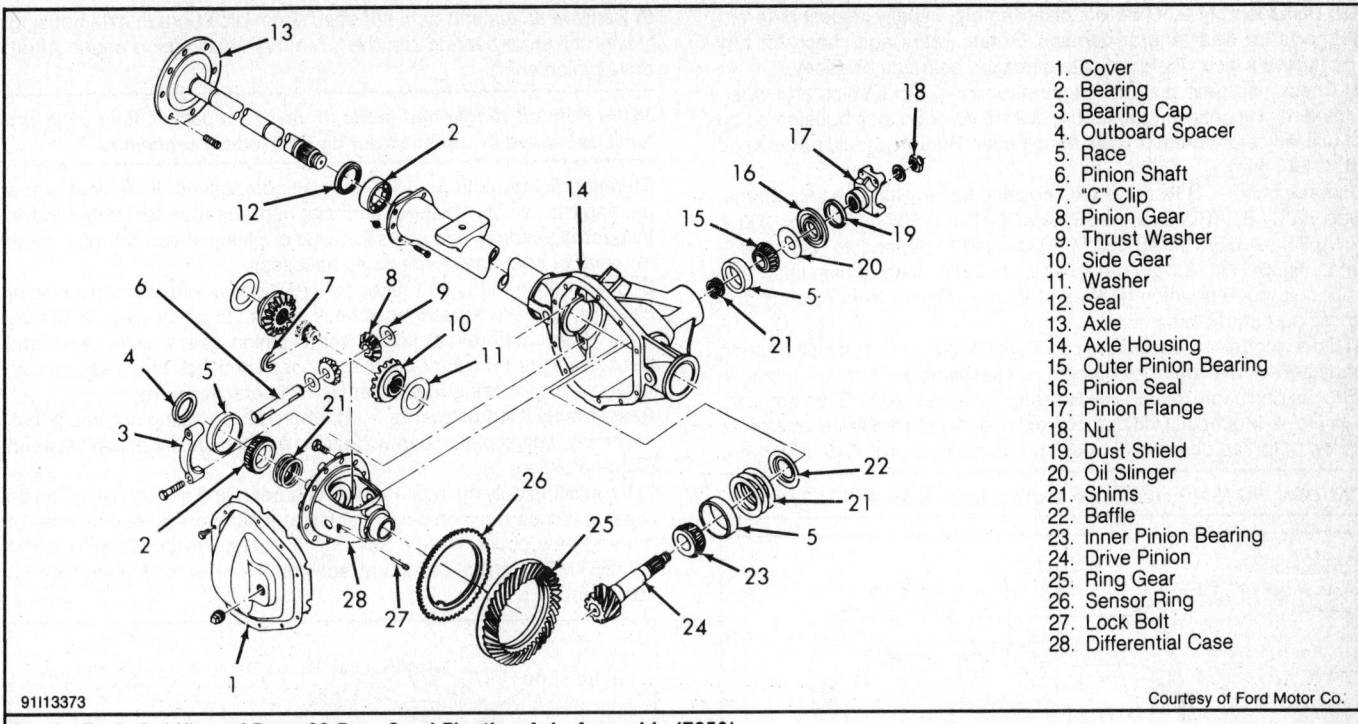

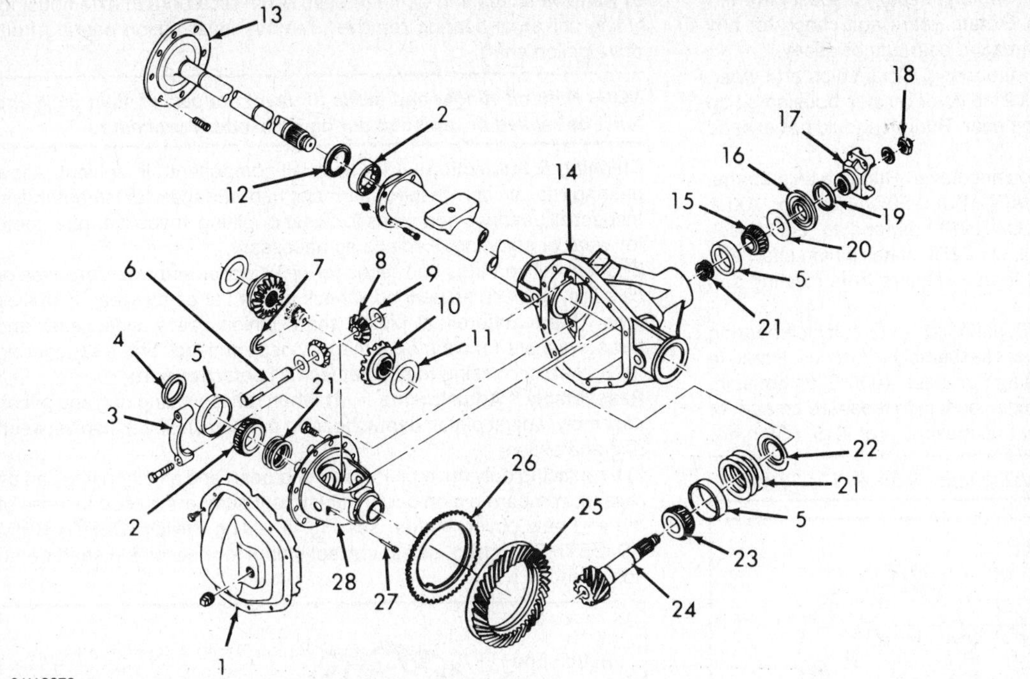
1. Cover
2. Bearing
3. Bearing Cap
4. Outboard Spacer
5. Race
6. Pinion Shaft
7. "C" Clip
8. Pinion Gear
9. Thrust Washer
10. Side Gear
11. Washer
12. Seal
13. Axle
14. Axle Housing
15. Outer Pinion Bearing
16. Pinion Seal
17. Pinion Flange
18. Nut
19. Dust Shield
20. Oil Slinger
21. Shims
22. Baffle
23. Inner Pinion Bearing
24. Drive Pinion
25. Ring Gear
26. Sensor Ring
27. Lock Bolt
28. Differential Case
91I13373
Courtesy of Ford Motor Co.

Fig. 3: Exploded View of Dana 60 Rear Semi-Floating Axle Assembly (E250)

4) Line up hole in pinion shaft with hole in ring gear case. Install lock bolt and tighten to 20-25 ft. lbs. (27-34 N.m). Clean any oil film off cover and housing surface. Apply bead of silicone rubber sealer 1/8 - 1/4" high and wide on cover plate in place of gasket. Bead must go inside bolt holes, not outside or over holes.
5) Install 2 bolts in cover to use as guides for mounting cover on axle housing. Install remaining bolts and tighten evenly to 30-40 ft. lbs. (41-54 N.m). Allow one-hour drying time before filling axle housing and operating vehicle. To complete installation, reverse removal procedure.

AXLE HOUSING ASSEMBLY

Removal (F350 – Front) – 1) Raise and support vehicle. Remove tire and wheel assembly. Remove hubs, spindles and axles. See HUB, BEARING & AXLE SHAFT (FULL-FLOATING) under REMOVAL & INSTALLATION.
2) Remove left and right tie rod ends. Remove stabilizer bar links, lower shock mounts and track bar bolt. Mark drive shaft position for installation reference. Disconnect front drive shaft at front pinion yoke, and wire shaft to frame. Disconnect axle housing vent tube, and plug opening.
3) Support axle housing with floor jack. Remove spring "U" bolt nuts, and remove "U" bolt. Carefully lower axle housing assembly from vehicle and remove.
Installation – 1) Check all bushings and mounting hardware for wear or damage. Place axle housing assembly on floor jack. Position assembly under vehicle and raise until assembly contacts springs. Ensure leaf spring center bolt is recessed with hole in axle housing spring plate.
2) To complete installation, reverse removal procedure. Tighten all bolts and nuts to specification. See FRONT HUB BEARING ADJUSTING SPECIFICATION table under HUB, BEARING & AXLE SHAFT (FULL-FLOATING), and TORQUE SPECIFICATIONS table at end of article. Fill axle housing assembly with gear oil. Check wheel alignment.
Removal & Installation (E250, E250 HD, E350 & "F" Super Duty – Rear) – 1) Loosen wheel lug nuts and axle shaft retaining bolts. Remove shock absorbers and stabilizer bar mounts. Raise vehicle until weight is off the rear springs.
2) Disconnect brake hose from frame and parking brake cable at equalizer. Remove parking brake cable from cable support and brackets. Disconnect rear "U" joint. Disconnect anti-lock wiring from axle sensor and height sensing linkage (if equipped).
3) Support axle assembly with floor jack. Remove spring "U" bolt nuts, and remove "U" bolt. Carefully lower axle housing assembly from vehicle. Roll axle housing assembly out from vehicle. Drain lubricant. Remove wheels and mount assembly in workbench. To install, reverse removal procedure.

PINION FLANGE & SEAL

Removal – 1) Raise and support vehicle. Mark drive shaft position for installation reference. Disconnect drive shaft and wire shaft to frame. Using Companion Flange Holding Tool (T57T-4851-B), remove pinion nut.

CAUTION: Hammering on companion flange could result in damage to ring and pinion gear.

2) Using Puller (T65L-4851-B), remove companion flange. Carefully remove pinion oil seal to prevent damage to housing seal surface.
Installation – 1) Lubricate seal lip with gear lubricant. Using Oil Seal Replacer (T83T-4676-A), install pinion seal in axle housing.
2) Install companion flange on pinion shaft. Install pinion washer and nut. Using companion flange holder, tighten pinion nut to specification. See TORQUE SPECIFICATIONS table at end of article. To complete installation, reverse removal procedure.

DIFFERENTIAL ASSEMBLY

Removal & Installation – Removal and installation procedure is included in overhaul procedure. See DIFFERENTIAL ASSEMBLY under OVERHAUL.

OVERHAUL

DIFFERENTIAL ASSEMBLY

NOTE: It is recommended, but not necessary, that axle housing be removed for overhaul. See Fig. 2 or 3 to identify differential components throughout overhaul procedure.

1991 DRIVE AXLES
Dana 60, 70 & 80 Differentials (Cont.)

Pre-Disassembly – 1) Before disassembly, visually inspect differential parts for wear and/or damage. Rotate gears and check for any roughness which would indicate damaged bearings or gears.
2) Check ring gear teeth for signs of scoring, nicks/chips and wear. Measure ring gear runout. Mount dial indicator on axle housing so tip of dial indicator contacts back of ring gear. Runout should not exceed .004" (.10 mm).
Disassembly – 1) Remove axle housing cover. Remove axle shafts. See HUB, BEARING & AXLE SHAFT (FULL-FLOATING) or AXLE SHAFTS & BEARINGS (SEMI-FLOATING), depending on model, under REMOVAL & INSTALLATION. On E250, install pinion shaft and lock bolt to keep pinion gears and thrust washers from rotating and dropping out of case.
2) On all models, note bearing cap identification letters. If side bearing caps are not identified, mark them for reassembly reference. Remove side bearing caps. Install Axle Housing Spreader (4000-E) on housing. *See Fig. 4*. Mount dial indicator on axle housing to measure amount of spread. Spread differential housing to a maximum of .015" (.38 mm).

CAUTION: DO NOT spread axle housing more than .015" (.38 mm).

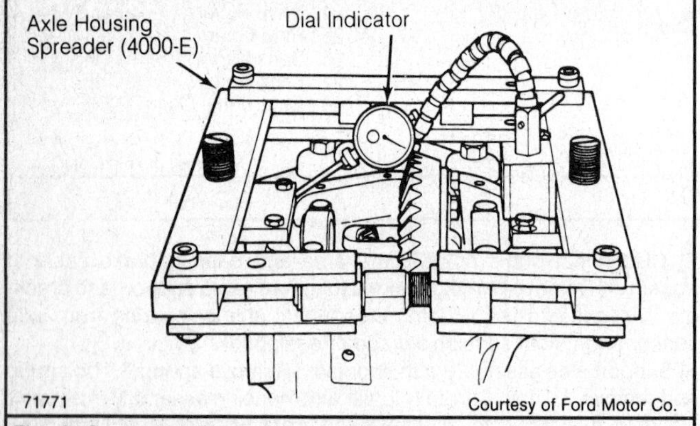
Axle Housing
Spreader (4000-E)
Dial Indicator
71771
Courtesy of Ford Motor Co.

Fig. 4: Spreading Dana Axle Housing

3) Remove dial indicator after housing has been spread. Carefully pry differential assembly out of housing. Remove spreader tool immediately to avoid housing distortion. Mark bearing races to identify which side they were removed from. Record size and position of side bearing shims between axle housing and side bearings outer races.
4) Place Universal Bearing Remover (D81L-4220-A) in vise while removing differential side bearings. Keep bearings, bearing races and shims in sets, marked with bearings' location on axle housing. Place differential case in vise with rags underneath to protect ring gear.

CAUTION: If anti-lock brake sensor ring is removed from axle housing, a new sensor ring must be installed.

5) Remove and discard ring gear bolts. Remove ring gear by tapping with soft-faced mallet. On E250, remove pinion shaft lock bolt. On all other models, remove pinion shaft lock pin. On all models, remove pinion shaft. Rotate side gears until pinion gears align with case opening. Remove pinion gears and thrust washers.
6) Remove side gears with thrust washers. Rotate nose of axle housing to horizontal position. Hold pinion flange with Pinion Flange Holder (T57T-4851-B). Remove pinion nut and washer. Using Flange Puller (D80L-1002-L), remove pinion flange. Using soft-faced hammer, tap drive pinion out of housing.

NOTE: Pinion bearing adjusting shims may remain on pinion shaft, stick to bearing, or fall loose. Collect and save shims for reassembly.

7) Remove pinion seal with Bearing Race Puller (T77F-1102-A) and slide hammer. Discard seal. Remove bearing cone and outer oil slinger. Turn nose of axle housing downward.
8) Remove outer pinion bearing race, then inner bearing race using appropriate Bearing Race Driver (D81T-4628-A/B or D) and Driver Handle (D81L-4000-A).
9) Remove shims and baffle (if used) from race bore in axle housing. Using universal bearing remover, remove inner pinion bearing from drive pinion shaft.

NOTE: Both oil slinger and baffle (if used) are part of shim pack and must be reused or replaced during reassembly procedure.

Cleaning & Inspection – 1) Clean all components in solvent. Allow bearings to air dry. Inspect all machined surfaces for smoothness. Inspect all bearings and races for wear or pitting. Inspect all gear teeth for wear or chipping. Replace as necessary.
2) Check all bearings and races for nicks, roller end wear, grooves or damage. Replace as needed. Check pinion flange for wear in sealing area. Check differential pinion shaft, pinion gears, side gears and thrust washers for wear or damage. Check anti-lock brake sensor ring for broken or missing teeth. Replace all defective parts.
Reassembly & Adjustments – 1) When reassembling ring and pinion assembly, adjust pinion depth, bearing preload and backlash between ring and pinion.
2) If replacing only drive pinion and ring gear, and axle housing can be reused, compare pinion depth adjustment numbers etched in faces of old and new pinion heads. *See Fig. 5.* Using PINION DEPTH SHIM ADJUSTMENT chart, select correct shims for new pinion shaft depth adjustment.

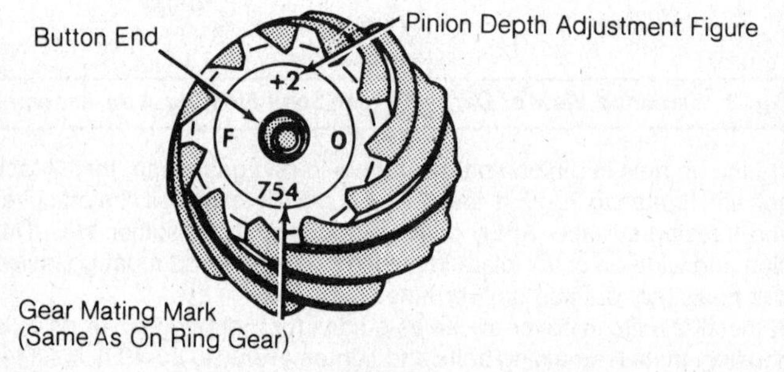
Button End
Pinion Depth Adjustment Figure
+2
F
O
754
Gear Mating Mark
(Same As On Ring Gear)
71772
Courtesy of Ford Motor Co.

Fig. 5: Locating Pinion Gear Markings

NOTE: To use PINION DEPTH SHIM ADJUSTMENT chart, dimension of old pinion shaft shim pack MUST be measured accurately. If dimension of original pinion shaft shim pack cannot be determined, Pinion Depth Gauge Set (T80T-4020-A) must be used to determine pinion depth setting. Depth gauge set must also be used if using new axle housing.

3) The pinion depth adjustment number is determined by manufacturer at time of assembly. Number represents distance that pinion shaft deviates from distance between back-face of pinion gear to center line of ring gear. *See Fig. 6* for specified distances.
4) Ring gear and pinion gear are supplied in matched sets only. Matching numbers are etched on ring and pinion gears. If using new gear set, verify matching gear mating marks. *See Fig. 5.*
5) Pinion Depth Gauge Set (T80T-4020-A) allows shim pack adjustments to be made without having to remove and replace differential bearings when setting up shim packs. *See Fig. 7.*
6) The end of the pinion gear (button end with the etched figures) on original equipment gear sets are no longer precision ground. On aftermarket gear sets, pinion gear may or may not be precision ground. The letter "B" will follow the gear set mating mark if the pinion gear is NOT precision ground.
7) Use FINAL DEPTH CHECK procedure and Gear Block (T80T-4020-F42) of Pinion Depth Gauge Set (T80T-4020-A) only when pinion gear button end is precision ground. Gear tooth contact pattern is valid verification of final pinion position for both precision ground and non-precision ground pinion gears. See GEAR TOOTH CONTACT PATTERNS article in GENERAL INFORMATION.

1991 DRIVE AXLES
Dana 60, 70 & 80 Differentials (Cont.)

PINION DEPTH SHIM ADJUSTMENT CHART (INCHES)

Old Pinion Marking	New Pinion Marking								
	-4	-3	-2	-1	0	+1	+2	+3	+4
+4	+0.008	+0.007	+0.006	+0.005	+0.004	+0.003	+0.002	+0.001	0
+3	+0.007	+0.006	+0.005	+0.004	+0.003	+0.002	+0.001	0	-0.001
+2	+0.006	+0.005	+0.004	+0.003	+0.002	+0.001	0	-0.001	-0.002
+1	+0.005	+0.004	+0.003	+0.002	+0.001	0	-0.001	-0.002	-0.003
0	+0.004	+0.003	+0.002	+0.001	0	-0.001	-0.002	-0.003	-0.004
-1	+0.003	+0.002	+0.001	0	-0.001	-0.002	-0.003	-0.004	-0.005
-2	+0.002	+0.001	0	-0.001	-0.002	-0.003	-0.004	-0.005	-0.006
-3	+0.001	0	-0.001	-0.002	-0.003	-0.004	-0.005	-0.006	-0.007
-4	0	-0.001	-0.002	-0.003	-0.004	-0.005	-0.006	-0.007	-0.008

PINION DEPTH SHIM ADJUSTMENT CHART (MILLIMETERS)

Old Pinion Marking	New Pinion Marking								
	-10	-8	-5	-3	0	+3	+5	+8	+10
+10	+0.20	+0.18	+0.15	+0.13	+0.10	+0.08	+0.05	+0.03	0
+8	+0.18	+0.15	+0.13	+0.10	+0.08	+0.05	+0.03	0	-0.03
+5	+0.15	+0.13	+0.10	+0.08	+0.05	+0.03	0	-0.03	-0.05
+3	+0.13	+0.10	+0.08	+0.05	+0.03	0	-0.03	-0.05	-0.08
0	+0.10	+0.08	+0.05	+0.03	0	-0.03	-0.05	-0.08	-0.10
-3	+0.08	+0.05	+0.03	0	-0.03	-0.05	-0.08	-0.10	-0.13
-5	+0.05	+0.03	0	-0.03	-0.05	-0.08	-0.10	-0.13	-0.15
-8	+0.03	0	-0.03	-0.05	-0.08	-0.10	-0.13	-0.15	-0.18
-10	0	-0.03	-0.05	-0.08	-0.10	-0.13	-0.15	-0.18	-0.20

Differential Case – 1) Place differential case in vise. Use multipurpose grease to lubricate side gears, pinion gears and all thrust washers. Install in case. Rotate side gears until holes in pinion gears and washers line up with holes in case.

2) Install differential pinion shaft. On E250, install new lock bolt, but DO NOT tighten at this time. On all other models, install lock pin. Using a punch and hammer, peen metal of differential case over lock pin at following 2 locations: 90 degrees to the left and right of lock pin slot.

NOTE: Tab on anti-lock sensor ring must be aligned with slot in differential case.

3) Align tab in anti-lock sensor ring with slot in differential case. Install 2 ring gear bolts, but DO NOT tighten. Using an arbor press, press sensor ring and ring gear onto differential case.

4) Apply Thread Lock Sealer (EOAZ-19554-AA) to new ring gear bolts. Install ring gear bolts and tighten evenly to specification. See TORQUE SPECIFICATIONS table at end of article.

5) On Dana 60 and 70 axles, install Master Differential Bearings (D81T-4222) on differential case. On Dana 80 axle, install Master Differential Bearings (D81T-4222-D). On all axles, install case in housing without shims.

6) Mount dial indicator with indicator tip against back of ring gear, at 90 degrees to gear. Measure and record total end play of differential case by moving it back and forth with screwdriver. *See Fig. 8.*

7) This measurement will be used later to determine proper shim pack dimension. Remove case from housing. Leave master bearings on case at this time.

1991 DRIVE AXLES
Dana 60, 70 & 80 Differentials (Cont.)

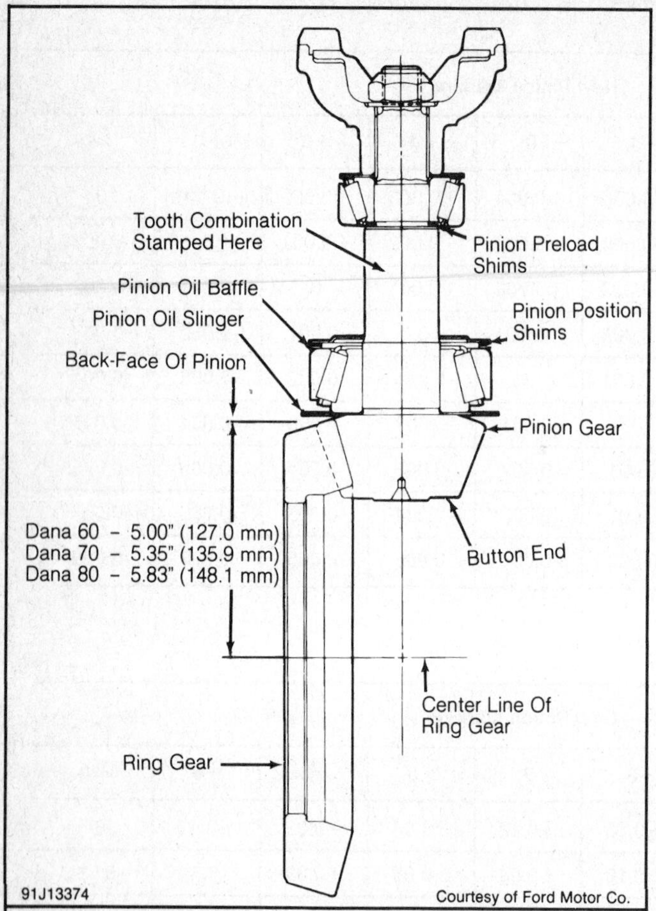
Tooth Combination
Stamped Here
Pinion Preload
Shims
Pinion Oil Baffle
Pinion Oil Slinger
Pinion Position
Shims
Back-Face Of Pinion
Pinion Gear
Dana 60 - 5.00" (127.0 mm)
Dana 70 - 5.35" (135.9 mm)
Dana 80 - 5.83" (148.1 mm)
Button End
Center Line Of
Ring Gear
Ring Gear
91J13374
Courtesy of Ford Motor Co.

Fig. 6: Identifying Drive Pinion-To-Ring Gear Position

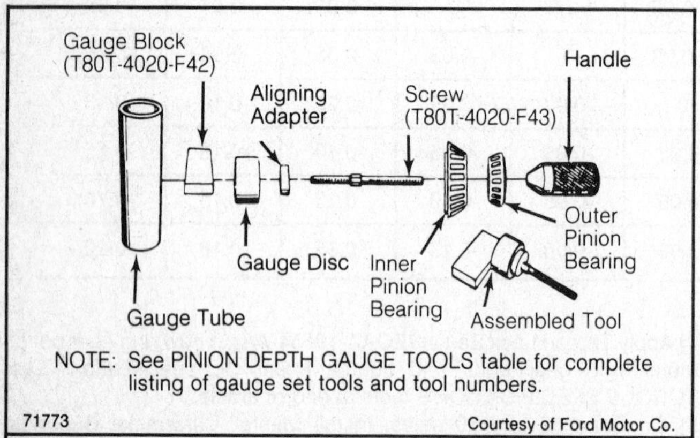
Gauge Block
(T80T-4020-F42)
Aligning
Adapter
Screw
(T80T-4020-F43)
Handle
Outer
Pinion
Bearing
Gauge Disc
Inner
Pinion
Bearing
Gauge Tube
Assembled Tool
NOTE: See PINION DEPTH GAUGE TOOLS table for complete listing of gauge set tools and tool numbers.
71773
Courtesy of Ford Motor Co.

Fig. 7: Identifying Pinion Depth Gauge Set (T80T-4020-A)

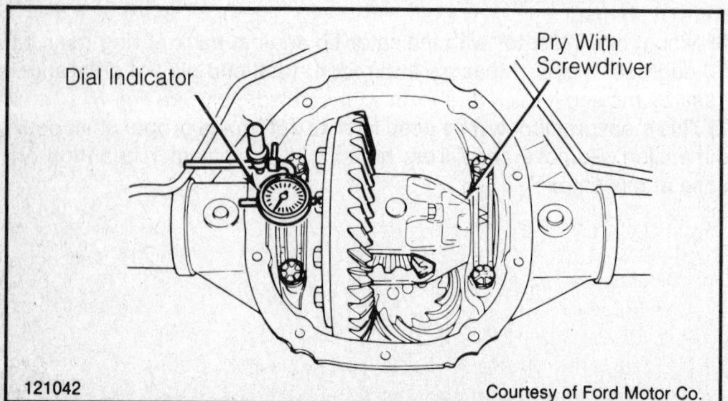
Dial Indicator
Pry With
Screwdriver
121042
Courtesy of Ford Motor Co.

Fig. 8: Measuring Differential Case End Play

Drive Pinion Bearing Race Installation – 1) Place inner and outer pinion bearing races in bores of axle housing. Place appropriate inner race installer on inner bearing race, and appropriate outer race installer on outer bearing race. See PINION BEARING INSTALLER table.
2) Install Threaded Drawbar (T75T-1176-A) through bearings. *See Fig. 9*. Tighten drawbar until bearing races are seated in axle housing bore. Install both pinion bearing races, at the same time, in axle housing.

PINION BEARING RACE INSTALLER

Application	Tool No.
Inner Bearing Race	
Dana 60 & 70	T56T-4616-B2
Dana 80	D81T-4616-A
Outer Bearing Race	
Dana 60 & 70	T56T-4616-B1
Dana 80	D67P-4616-A

NOTE: Check pinion depth gauge tools before each use. Any nicks or damage MUST be removed to ensure accurate readings.

Drive Pinion Depth – 1) Install new inner drive pinion bearing on appropriate aligning adapter and gauge disc. See PINION DEPTH GAUGE TOOLS table. *See Fig. 7*. Install outer pinion bearing (new or good used) into race. Place gauge assembly into housing, with Screw (T80T-4020-F43) extending through outer bearing.

PINION DEPTH GAUGE TOOLS [1]

Application	Tool No.
Aligning Adapter	
Dana 60	T76P-4020-A3
Dana 70	T80T-4020-F48
Dana 80	D80T-4020-R60
Gauge Block	T80T-4020-F42
Final Check Gauge Block	
Dana 60	D81T-4020-F54
Dana 70	D81T-4020-F55
Dana 80	D81T-4020-F56
Gauge Disc	
Dana 60	T78P-4020-A15
Dana 70	D80T-4020-F45
Dana 80	T88T-4020-A
Gauge Tube	
Dana 60 & 70	D80T-4020-F48
Dana 80	D81T-4020-F51
Handle	
Dana 60 & 70	T76P-4020-A11
Dana 80	T88T-4020-B
Screw	T80T-4020-F43

[1] – Complete tool set is Pinion Depth Gauge Set (T80T-4020-A).

2) Thread appropriate handle onto screw finger tight. Using 3/8" torque wrench in square drive on handle, tighten handle until preload on bearings is 20-40 INCH lbs. (2.26-4.52 N.m). Center appropriate gauge tube in side bearing bore. Install side bearing caps and tighten bolts to 80-90 ft. lbs. (108-122 N.m).
3) Place Gauge Block (T80T-4020-F42) on top of the drive pinion face underneath gauge tube. Using feeler gauge, determine clearance between gauge block and gauge tube. Correct feeler gauge will give slight drag feeling as gauge strip passes between tube and block.
4) Thickness of correct feeler gauge is thickness of shim pack to be installed under inner bearing race, when drive pinion has no number marked on face. If drive pinion has a plus (+) number marked on face, subtract that number from thickness dimension. If drive pinion has a minus (-) number marked on face, add that number to thickness dimension.

NOTE: New inner pinion bearing used during depth measurement procedure MUST be used during final assembly in order for drive pinion depth to be correct. New oil slinger and/or baffle (if used) are measured as part of shim pack.

5) Remove inner drive pinion bearing race. Install shim pack with baffle (if used) in housing bearing bore. Reinstall inner bearing race in axle housing. Using Axle Bearing/Seal Plate (T75-1165-B), arbor

1991 DRIVE AXLES
Dana 60, 70 & 80 Differentials (Cont.)

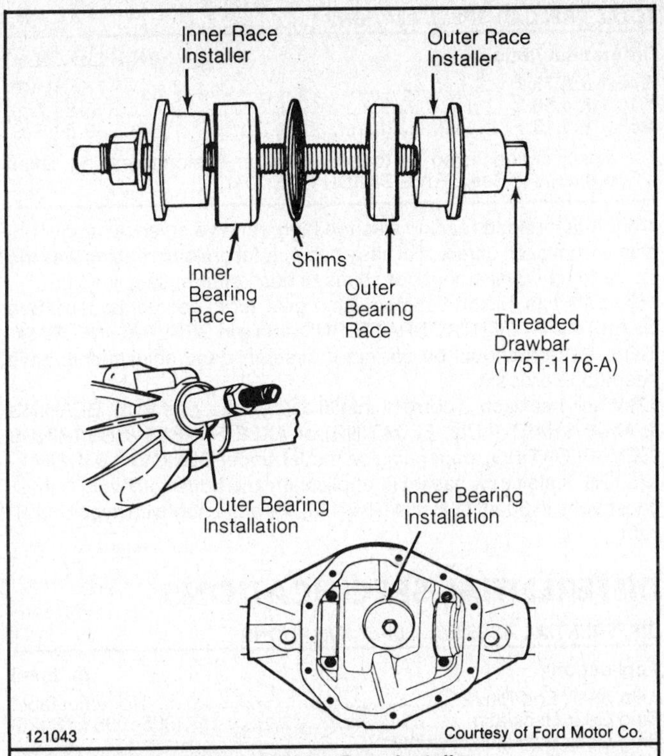
Inner Race
Installer
Outer Race
Installer
Shims
Inner
Bearing
Race
Outer
Bearing
Race
Threaded
Drawbar
(T75T-1176-A)
Outer Bearing
Installation
Inner Bearing
Installation
121043
Courtesy of Ford Motor Co.

Fig. 9: Identifying Pinion Bearing Race Installer

press and appropriate axle bearing/seal replacer, press inner drive pinion bearing and oil slinger (if used) on drive pinion. See AXLE BEARING/SEAL REPLACER table.

AXLE BEARING/SEAL REPLACER

Application	Tool No.
Dana 60	T75L-1165-DA
Dana 70	T53T-4621-C
Dana 80	D80T-4200-B

Drive Pinion Bearing Preload - 1) Install preload shims and slinger (if used) on drive pinion. Install drive pinion in housing. Install outer drive pinion bearing using press, axle bearing/seal plate and axle bearing/seal installer. Install drive pinion flange with washer and NEW nut. Tighten nut to specification. See TORQUE SPECIFICATIONS table at end of article.

2) Using INCH lb. torque wrench, measure drive pinion preload required to rotate pinion. Pinion preload should be 20-40 INCH lbs. (2-5 N.m). If preload reading is too low, remove preload shims from drive pinion. If preload reading is too high, add preload shims to drive pinion. *See Fig. 10.*

CAUTION: Use the following FINAL DEPTH CHECK procedure only if pinion gear button end is precision ground. See steps 6) and 7) of REASSEMBLY & ADJUSTMENTS procedure under DIFFERENTIAL ASSEMBLY under OVERHAUL before using procedure. If button end of pinion gear is not precision ground, go to RING & PINION GEAR BACKLASH.

Final Depth Check - 1) Install appropriate gauge tube. See PINION DEPTH GAUGE TOOLS table. Install side bearing caps and tighten bolts to 80-90 ft. lbs. (108-122 N.m).

2) Place appropriate final check gauge block on top of the drive pinion face under gauge tube. *See Fig. 11.* Hold gauge block with thumb to keep it level. Measure distance between gauge tube and gauge block with feeler gauge.

3) Check size of feeler gauge when slight drag is felt as gauge is pulled between gauge tube and gauge block. Correct reading should be .020" (.51 mm) greater than pinion depth adjustment figure etched on face of drive pinion, with tolerance of ±.002" (.05 mm).

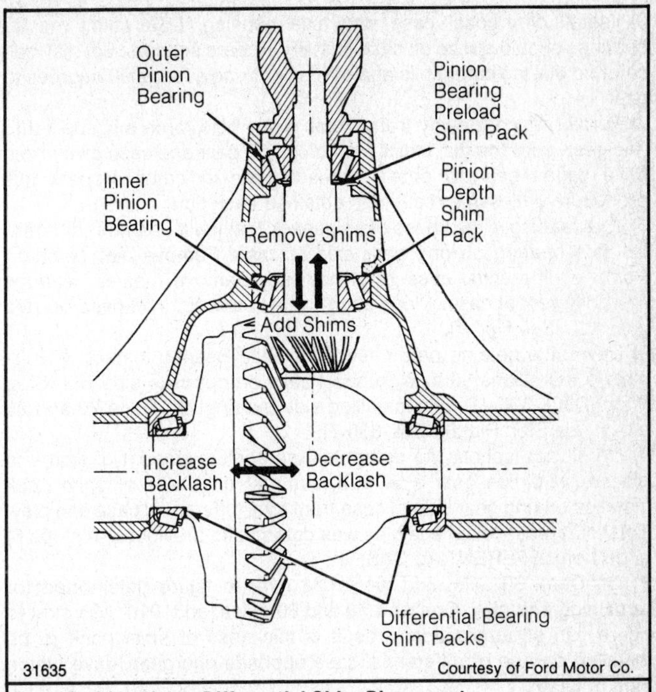
Outer
Pinion
Bearing
Pinion
Bearing
Preload
Shim Pack
Inner
Pinion
Bearing
Pinion
Depth
Shim
Pack
Remove Shims
Add Shims
Increase
Backlash
Decrease
Backlash
Differential Bearing
Shim Packs
31635
Courtesy of Ford Motor Co.

Fig. 10: Identifying Differential Shim Placement

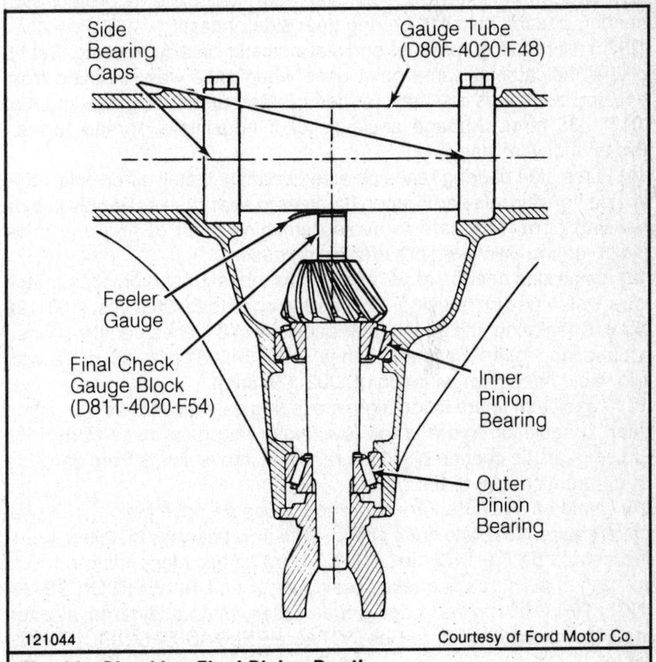
Side
Bearing
Caps
Gauge Tube
(D80F-4020-F48)
Feeler
Gauge
Final Check
Gauge Block
(D81T-4020-F54)
Inner
Pinion
Bearing
Outer
Pinion
Bearing
121044
Courtesy of Ford Motor Co.

Fig. 11: Checking Final Pinion Depth (Pinion Gear with Precision Ground Button End)

4) Drive pinion with "-2" etching should give reading of .018" (.46 mm), with tolerance of .002" (.05 mm). Acceptable range is .016-.020" (.41-.51 mm). If reading is too low, remove shims from underneath inner drive pinion bearing race. If reading is too high, add shims underneath inner drive pinion bearing race.

Ring & Pinion Gear Backlash - 1) With drive pinion depth and preload adjustments correct, remove pinion flange with holder and flange remover. Coat pinion oil seal with multipurpose grease. Install pinion oil seal.

2) Ensure spring behind lip of seal does not jump out while seal is being installed. If spring jumps out, remove and replace seal. Install pinion flange and tighten nut to specification. See TORQUE SPECIFICATIONS table at end of article.

1991 DRIVE AXLES
Dana 60, 70 & 80 Differentials (Cont.)

3) Install differential case into axle housing. Differential master bearings should still be on case. Install outboard spacers. Set dial indicator so dial indicator tip is against back of ring gear, at 90 degrees to gear.

4) Force ring gear away from pinion gear. With force still applied to ring gear, zero the dial indicator. Force ring gear and case away from drive pinion gear to obtain a reading on indicator. Repeat this procedure until same reading is obtained each time.

5) This reading is thickness of shim pack that must go under differential side bearing on ring gear side of case. Remove dial indicator. Remove differential case from housing. Remove master bearings from differential case. Place shim pack of correct thickness on ring gear hub. *See Fig. 10.*

6) Drive side bearing onto case using Side Bearing Installer (D81T-4221-A). On Dana 60 axle, support case on opposite side with Step Plate (D80L-630-7) while installing side bearing. On Dana 70 and 80 axles, use Step Plate (D80L-630-7).

7) On all applications, to determine the correct amount of shims to placed on pinion gear side hub, subtract thickness of shim pack installed on ring gear side of case from total differential case end play. Total differential case end play was determined previously in steps **6)** and **7)** of DIFFERENTIAL CASE.

8) On Dana 60 axle, add .015" (.38 mm) to figure determined for remaining end play. On Dana 70 and 80 axles, add .010" (.25 mm) to figure. On all applications, result is thickness of shim pack to be installed on hub of differential case opposite ring gear (drive pinion side of case).

9) Place shim pack on case hub and drive side bearing onto case using side bearing installer. Support case with step plate to protect side bearing already installed on ring gear side of case.

10) Install housing spreader and dial indicator on axle housing. Set tip of dial indicator at same point used when case was removed from housing during disassembly procedure. Spread housing maximum of .015" (.38 mm). Damage could occur if housing is spread further. Remove dial indicator.

11) Place side bearing races on side bearings. Install differential case in axle housing. Use soft-faced hammer to seat case assembly in axle housing bore. Use care to avoid damaging teeth of ring and drive pinion gears. Remove spreader from housing.

12) Install side bearing caps, ensuring letters stamped on caps match letters stamped on housing. Tighten cap bolts to 80-90 ft. lbs. (108-122 N.m). Check ring and pinion gear backlash in 3 places equally spaced around ring gear. Backlash range is .005-.008" (.13-.20 mm), with allowable maximum variation of .002" (.05 mm).

13) If backlash figure is too high, move ring gear closer to drive pinion gear. If backlash figure is too low, move ring gear away from drive pinion gear. To change backlash readings, move shims from one side of differential case to the other.

14) Using an INCH lb. torque wrench, measure drive pinion total preload required to rotate drive pinion. With new bearings installed, reading should be 6-9 INCH lbs. (.7-1.0 N.m) higher (depending on axle ratio) than initial reading taken previously. See DRIVE PINION BEARING PRELOAD. Initial reading was taken without differential case installed in axle housing. See TOTAL PRELOAD SPECIFICATIONS table.

TOTAL PRELOAD SPECIFICATIONS

Differential Ratio	[1] INCH Lbs. (N.m)
3.45:1 & 3.73:1	7-9 (.8-1.0)
4.10:1 & 4.56:1	6-8 (.7-.9)
4.63:1 & 5.13:1	6-8 (.7-.9)

[1] – Specification listed is to be added to preload reading taken previously. See DRIVE PINION PRELOAD.

15) If total preload reading was too high, remove an equal amount of shims from each differential case hub. If total preload reading was too low, add an equal amount of shims to each differential case hub.

16) Verify final pinion position using gear tooth contact pattern. See GEAR TOOTH CONTACT PATTERNS article in GENERAL INFORMATION. Pattern should be correct if assembly and adjustments have been done properly.

17) When backlash is correct, install axle shafts. See HUB, BEARING & AXLE SHAFT (FULL-FLOATING) or AXLE SHAFTS & BEARINGS (SEMI-FLOATING), depending on model, under REMOVAL & INSTALLATION. Install new gasket (if applicable) and housing cover. Tighten cover bolts to 30-40 ft. lbs. (41-54 N.m). Fill assembly with hypoid lubricant.

DIFFERENTIAL SPECIFICATIONS

DIFFERENTIAL ASSEMBLY SPECIFICATIONS

Application	In. (mm)
Axle Shaft End Play	Nonadjustable
Ring Gear Backlash	.005-.008 (.13-.20)
Ring Gear Backlash Maximum Variation Between Teeth	.002 (.05)
	INCH Lbs. (N.m)
Pinion Bearing Preload	
New Bearings	20-40 (2-5)
Used Bearings	10-20 (1-2)

TORQUE SPECIFICATIONS

TORQUE SPECIFICATIONS

Application	Ft. Lbs. (N.m)
Housing Cover Bolts	30-40 (41-54)
Pinion Nut	
Dana 60 & 70	250-270 (339-366)
Dana 80	440-500 (596-677)
Pinion Shaft Lock Bolt	20-25 (27-34)
"U" Joint Bolts	15-20 (21-27)
Ring Gear Bolts	
Dana 60 & 70	100-120 (136-163)
Dana 80	200-240 (272-330)
Side Bearing Cap Bolts	80-90 (108-122)
Wheel Lug Nuts	140 (190)

1991 DRIVE AXLES
Dana 28-2 Front Axle – Aerostar

DESCRIPTION

Dana model 28-2 front axle is an integral carrier housing. Center line of drive pinion is mounted on center line of ring gear. Axle housing is made of aluminum and is mounted to sub-frame assembly. Axle shafts are retained in axle housing by "C" clips in differential case. *See Fig. 1.* Drive pinion depth and differential side bearing preload are set by use of shims. Pinion bearing preload is set by use of collapsible pinion spacer.

AXLE RATIO & IDENTIFICATION

Axle application can be determined through the axle code on the Safety Certification Label on left door pillar. Additionally, a metal identification tag stamped with gear ratio and diameter is secured to housing cover. See AXLE RATIO IDENTIFICATION article.

REMOVAL & INSTALLATION

AXLE SHAFT, BEARING & OIL SEAL

NOTE: To remove axle shafts, remove axle housing assembly from vehicle. See AXLE HOUSING ASSEMBLY under REMOVAL & INSTALLATION.

Removal – 1) Remove axle housing assembly. Remove axle housing cover and drain differential fluid. Mount axle housing in Holding Fixture (T57L-500-B) using Adapters (T90T-4000-A) and Spacer (T80T-4000-B2).

2) Rotate shafts until open side of "C" clip on inner end of axle shaft can be reached. Remove "C" clip. Remove axle shaft. Remove axle housing oil seal and needle bearings using slide hammer, Collet (D80L-100-A) and Actuator Pin (D80L-100-H).

Installation – 1) Ensure bearing bore is clean and has no nicks. Place new caged needle bearing on Needle Bearing Installer (T83T-1244-A). Ensure bearing manufacturer's name and part number is facing toward tool when installed in housing bore.

2) Drive needle bearing in until bearing is fully seated in housing bore. Coat lip of seal with multipurpose grease. Drive seal into carrier using Seal Installer (T90T-3110-A). Install axle shaft so groove on shaft is visible inside differential case.

3) Install "C" clip. DO NOT tap on center of "C" clip, as clip will be damaged. Clean all sealant, oil and dirt from housing-to-cover mating surfaces. Apply continuous bead of RTV sealant 1/4-3/8" wide on housing.

NOTE: Install housing cover within 5 minutes after applying RTV sealant.

4) Sealant bead should not pass over or outside holes. Install housing cover. To complete installation, reverse removal procedure. Allow one hour cure time before filling differential.

AXLE HOUSING ASSEMBLY

Removal – 1) Raise vehicle and install safety stands under front lifting points. Mark position of drive shaft and axle flanges for installation reference. Disconnect front drive shaft from front axle companion flange.

2) Remove inboard half-shaft flange-to-axle shaft bolts (both sides). Wire half-shafts to body, maintaining level position. Remove vent hose from axle housing and cap vent fitting to prevent fluid leakage.

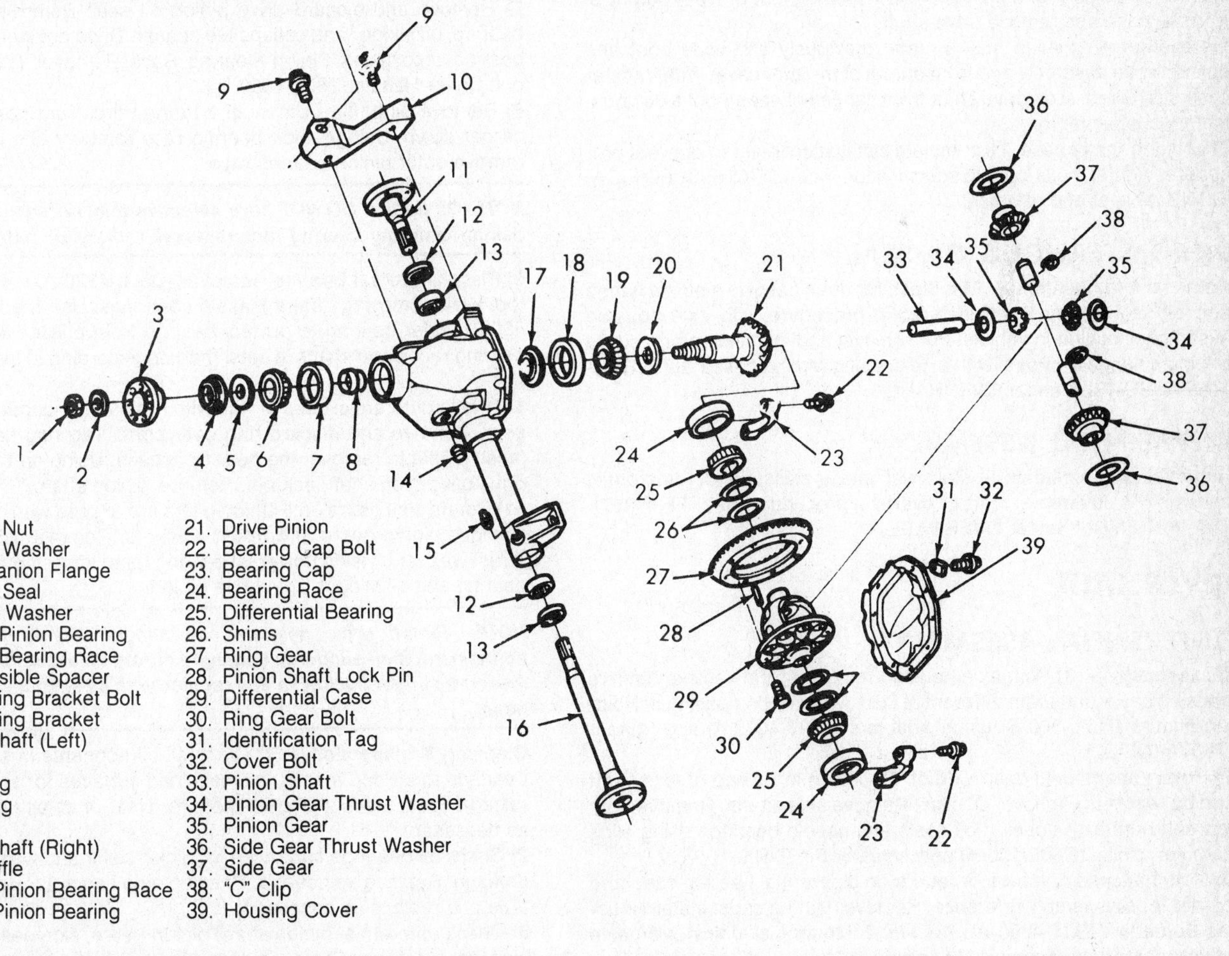

1. Pinion Nut
2. Pinion Washer
3. Companion Flange
4. Pinion Seal
5. Thrust Washer
6. Outer Pinion Bearing
7. Outer Bearing Race
8. Collapsible Spacer
9. Mounting Bracket Bolt
10. Mounting Bracket
11. Axle Shaft (Left)
12. Seal
13. Bearing
14. Fill Plug
15. Vent
16. Axle Shaft (Right)
17. Oil Baffle
18. Inner Pinion Bearing Race
19. Inner Pinion Bearing
20. Shim
21. Drive Pinion
22. Bearing Cap Bolt
23. Bearing Cap
24. Bearing Race
25. Differential Bearing
26. Shims
27. Ring Gear
28. Pinion Shaft Lock Pin
29. Differential Case
30. Ring Gear Bolt
31. Identification Tag
32. Cover Bolt
33. Pinion Shaft
34. Pinion Gear Thrust Washer
35. Pinion Gear
36. Side Gear Thrust Washer
37. Side Gear
38. "C" Clip
39. Housing Cover

91B13376

Courtesy of Ford Motor Co.

Fig. 1: Exploded View of Front Axle Housing Assembly

1991 DRIVE AXLES
Dana 28-2 Front Axle – Aerostar (Cont.)

3) Remove snubber from rear support crossmember, located below drive pinion. Support axle housing assembly with floor jack. Remove axle mounting bracket-to-crossmember lock nuts (4 places). Lower floor jack and remove axle housing assembly. Remove axle mounting bracket from axle housing, if necessary.

Installation – 1) Install axle mounting bracket to axle housing, if removed. Install mounting bracket bolts using Loctite and tighten to specification. See TORQUE SPECIFICATIONS table at end of article.

NOTE: If using new axle housing mounting bushings, tighten each lock nut to full torque in one step.

2) Insert axle housing bushing studs (4) through axle mounting brackets. Install axle housing mounting bushing stud lock nuts using Loctite, and tighten in sequence to specification.

3) Tightening sequence is as follows: left front, right front, pinion and rear. See TORQUE SPECIFICATIONS table at end of article. To complete installation, reverse removal procedure.

DRIVE SHAFT

Removal – 1) Raise and support vehicle. Mark position of drive shaft, companion flanges and splined yoke assembly-to-transfer case for installation reference. Release clamp on drive shaft dust boot using Clamp Remover (D87P-1090-A), and pull boot from transfer case.

2) Remove snubber from rear support crossmember, located below drive pinion. Remove front drive shaft-to-companion flange bolts. Remove transmission mount-to-crossmember nuts.

3) Using a floor jack, raise transfer case until transmission mount studs are almost out of crossmember. Slide drive shaft front flange between front axle housing and starter motor. When front flange has cleared, slide boot and splined yoke assembly out of front output of transfer case and remove drive shaft.

Installation – 1) Align marks made previously and slide boot and splined yoke assembly into front output of transfer case. With transfer case still raised, slide drive shaft front flange between front axle housing and starter motor.

2) Lower transfer case. To complete installation, reverse removal procedure. Tighten bolts/nuts to specification. See TORQUE SPECIFICATIONS table at end of article.

PINION FLANGE & OIL SEAL

Removal & Installation – Manufacturer does not give a pinion flange and oil seal removal and installation procedure with axle housing assembly installed in vehicle. For removal and installation procedure of pinion flange & oil seal with axle housing removed, see DIFFERENTIAL ASSEMBLY under OVERHAUL.

DIFFERENTIAL ASSEMBLY

Removal & Installation – Removal and installation of differential assembly is covered as part of overhaul procedure. See DIFFERENTIAL ASSEMBLY under OVERHAUL.

OVERHAUL

DIFFERENTIAL ASSEMBLY

Disassembly – 1) With axle housing removed from vehicle, remove housing cover and drain differential fluid. Mount axle housing in Holding Fixture (T57L-500-B) using Adapters (T90T-4000-A) and Spacer (T80T-4000-B2).

2) Rotate shafts until open side of "C" clip on inner end of axle shaft can be reached. Remove "C" clips. Remove axle shafts. Remove both left and right axle housing oil seals and needle bearings using slide hammer, Collet (D80L-100-A) and Actuator Pin (D80L-100-H).

3) Note matched numbers or letters on differential bearing caps and carrier for reassembly reference. Remove bearing caps. Install Housing Spreader (T90T-4000-A). *See Fig. 2.* Mount dial indicator on axle housing to measure amount of spread.

CAUTION: DO NOT spread carrier housing more than .015" (.38 mm). Permanent damage to housing could result.

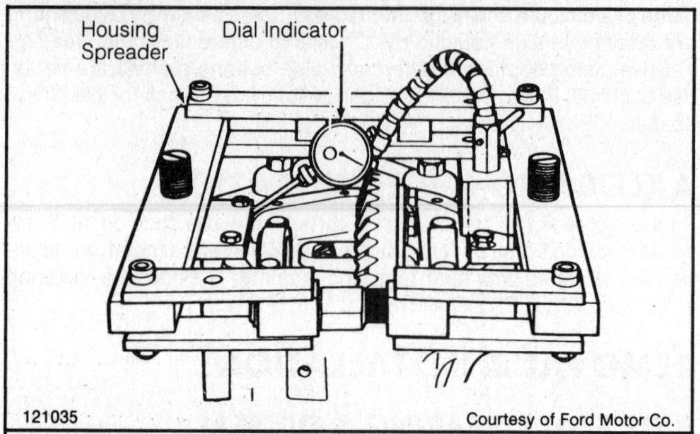
Housing Spreader
Dial Indicator
121035
Courtesy of Ford Motor Co.

Fig. 2: Spreading Axle Housing

4) Spread axle housing to a maximum of .015" (.38 mm). Remove dial indicator. Carefully pry differential assembly out of housing. Remove spreader immediately so housing does not permanently distort.

5) Remove and tag side bearing races to indicate from which side of carrier they were removed. Turn nose of axle housing up. Mark pinion companion flange-to-drive pinion position for installation reference.

6) Using Companion Flange Holder (T78P-4851-A), hold companion flange while removing drive pinion nut and washer. Remove companion flange. If flange shows wear in sealing area, replace flange. Remove drive pinion by tapping with soft-faced mallet.

7) Remove and discard drive pinion oil seal. Remove outer pinion bearing, oil slinger and collapsible spacer. Drive out inner drive pinion bearing race using Pinion Bearing Race Remover (T86T-4628-BH) and Driver Handle (T80T-4000-W).

8) Remove oil baffle from inner bearing bore. Turn nose of housing carrier down. Using pinion bearing race remover and driver handle, remove outer pinion bearing race.

NOTE: Oil baffles DO NOT have selective thicknesses. If oil baffle is damaged during bearing race removal, replace oil baffle.

9) Place Universal Bearing Remover (D81L-4220-A) in vise to secure tool while removing differential side bearings. Use Step Plate (D80L-630-3) under bearing to protect bearing from puller. Keep bearings, bearing races and shims in sets, marked according to location on carrier.

10) Place differential case in vise with rags underneath to protect ring gear. Remove and discard ring gear bolts. Tap ring gear with soft-faced mallet to remove ring gear from case. Using drift and hammer, drive out pinion shaft lock pin. Remove pinion shaft.

11) Rotate side gears until pinion gears are aligned with case opening. Remove pinion gears and thrust washers. Remove side gears with thrust washers. Using universal bearing remover, remove inner pinion bearing and oil slinger from drive pinion.

NOTE: Pinion drive selective oil slinger affects pinion depth adjustment. If oil slinger is damaged during disassembly procedure, measure slinger thickness and replace with oil slinger of equal thickness.

Cleaning & Inspection – 1) Clean all components in solvent. Allow bearings to air dry. Inspect all machined surfaces for smoothness or raised edges. Inspect all gear teeth for wear or chipping and replace as necessary.

2) Check all bearings and races for nicks, roller end wear, grooves or damage. Replace as needed. Check pinion flange for wear in sealing area and replace as necessary.

3) Check differential pinion shaft, pinion gears, side gears and thrust washers for wear or damage. Replace all defective parts. Pinion gear and ring gear must be replaced as set.

1991 DRIVE AXLES
Dana 28-2 Front Axle – Aerostar (Cont.)

Reassembly & Adjustments – 1) When reassembling ring and pinion assembly, pinion depth, pinion bearing preload, side bearing preload and backlash between ring and pinion must be adjusted.
2) If only replacing pinion shaft and ring gear and carrier housing can be reused, compare pinion depth adjustment numbers etched in faces of old and new pinion heads. *See Fig. 3.*

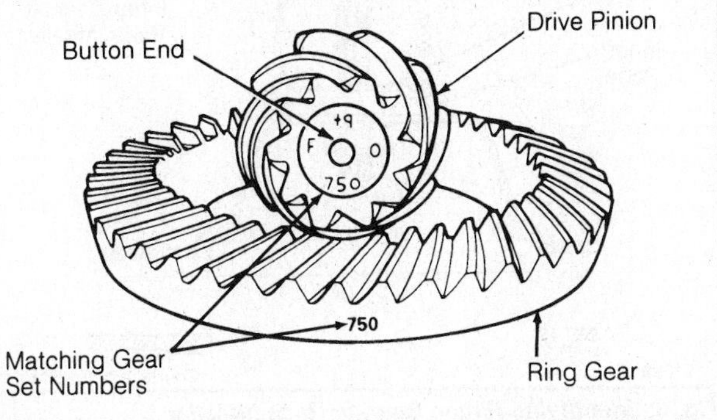
Drive Pinion
Button End
+9
F
0
750
750
Matching Gear
Set Numbers
Ring Gear

91C13377 Courtesy of Ford Motor Co.

Fig. 3: Identifying Drive Pinion & Ring Gear Markings

3) On end of drive pinion is a plus (+) figure, minus figure (-) or a zero (0) figure. Figure is determined by manufacturer at time of assembly. Number represents nominal distance that pinion shaft deviates from distance between pinion gear face and centerline of axle.
4) Nominal distance is measured from center line of ring gear to face of gear on drive pinion shaft. Using PINION DEPTH SHIM ADJUSTMENT CHART, correct shims can be selected for new pinion shaft depth adjustment.
5) For example, if original drive pinion is etched +4 (+10 mm) and new drive pinion is etched zero (0), then new selective oil slinger would be .004" (.10 mm) thicker than original selective oil slinger. See PINION DEPTH SHIM ADJUSTMENT CHART.
6) Ring gear and pinion gear are supplied in matched sets only. Matching numbers are etched on ring and pinion gears. If using new gear set, verify matching gear set numbers. *See Fig. 3.*
7) Pinion depth gauge set allows oil slinger adjustments to be made without having to remove and replace differential bearings when figuring correct pinion depth. *See Fig. 4.*

NOTE: To use PINION DEPTH SHIM ADJUSTMENT CHART procedure, old drive pinion oil slinger dimension MUST be determined accurately. If original drive pinion oil slinger dimension cannot be determined accurately, use pinion depth gauge set to determine correct pinion depth setting. Use depth gauge set if using new carrier housing.

PINION DEPTH SHIM ADJUSTMENT CHART (INCHES)

Old Pinion Marking	New Pinion Marking								
	-4	-3	-2	-1	0	+1	+2	+3	+4
+4	+0.008	+0.007	+0.006	+0.005	+0.004	+0.003	+0.002	+0.001	0
+3	+0.007	+0.006	+0.005	+0.004	+0.003	+0.002	+0.001	0	-0.001
+2	+0.006	+0.005	+0.004	+0.003	+0.002	+0.001	0	-0.001	-0.002
+1	+0.005	+0.004	+0.003	+0.002	+0.001	0	-0.001	-0.002	-0.003
0	+0.004	+0.003	+0.002	+0.001	0	-0.001	-0.002	-0.003	-0.004
-1	+0.003	+0.002	+0.001	0	-0.001	-0.002	-0.003	-0.004	-0.005
-2	+0.002	+0.001	0	-0.001	-0.002	-0.003	-0.004	-0.005	-0.006
-3	+0.001	0	-0.001	-0.002	-0.003	-0.004	-0.005	-0.006	-0.007
-4	0	-0.001	-0.002	-0.003	-0.004	-0.005	-0.006	-0.007	-0.008

PINION DEPTH SHIM ADJUSTMENT CHART (MILLIMETERS)

Old Pinion Marking	New Pinion Marking								
	-10	-8	-5	-3	0	+3	+5	+8	+10
+10	+0.20	+0.18	+0.15	+0.13	+0.10	+0.08	+0.05	+0.03	0
+8	+0.18	+0.15	+0.13	+0.10	+0.08	+0.05	+0.03	0	-0.03
+5	+0.15	+0.13	+0.10	+0.08	+0.05	+0.03	0	-0.03	-0.05
+3	+0.13	+0.10	+0.08	+0.05	+0.03	0	-0.03	-0.05	-0.08
0	+0.10	+0.08	+0.05	+0.03	0	-0.03	-0.05	-0.08	-0.10
-3	+0.08	+0.05	+0.03	0	-0.03	-0.05	-0.08	-0.10	-0.13
-5	+0.05	+0.03	0	-0.03	-0.05	-0.08	-0.10	-0.13	-0.15
-8	+0.03	0	-0.03	-0.05	-0.08	-0.10	-0.13	-0.15	-0.18
-10	0	-0.03	-0.05	-0.08	-0.10	-0.13	-0.15	-0.18	-0.20

1991 DRIVE AXLES
Dana 28-2 Front Axle – Aerostar (Cont.)

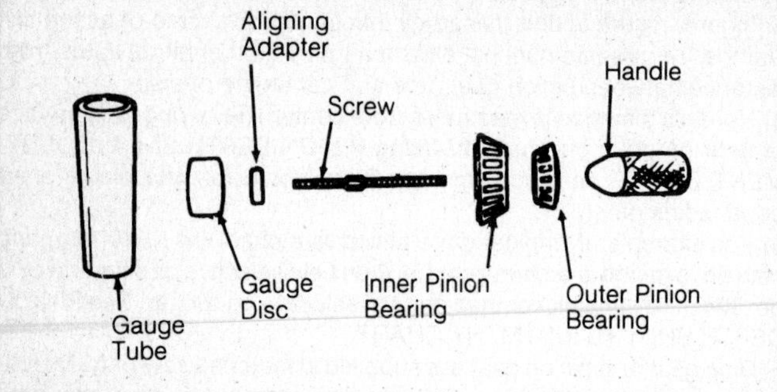
Aligning
Adapter
Handle
Screw
Gauge
Disc
Inner Pinion
Bearing
Outer Pinion
Bearing
Gauge
Tube

91D13378 Courtesy of Ford Motor Co.

Fig. 4: Identifying Pinion Depth Gauge Set

Differential Case Reassembly – 1) Position ring gear to differential case. Install new ring gear bolts and tighten to specification in a circular pattern. Place differential case into position in axle housing. Install Master Differential Bearings (T83T-4222-A) on differential case.

2) Remove all burrs and nicks from hubs so master bearings rotate freely. Install differential case in housing without shims. Mount dial indicator with indicator tip at 90 degrees to flat surface on head of ring gear bolt or flat machined surface of ring gear.

3) Using screwdriver, force differential case toward dial indicator as far as possible. Zero dial indicator with force still applied. Force differential case away from dial indicator as far as possible. Read gauge. Repeat this procedure until same reading is obtained. *See Fig. 5.*

4) This measurement is total differential case end play and will be used later to determine proper shim pack dimension. Use multipurpose grease to lubricate side gears, pinion gears and all thrust washers, and install components in differential case. Rotate side gears until holes in pinion gears and washers line up with holes in case.

5) Install differential pinion shaft. Install lock pin. Using a punch and hammer, peen metal of differential case over lock pin at 2 locations, 90 degrees to the left and right of lock pin slot. Remove differential case from housing. Leave master bearings on case at this time.

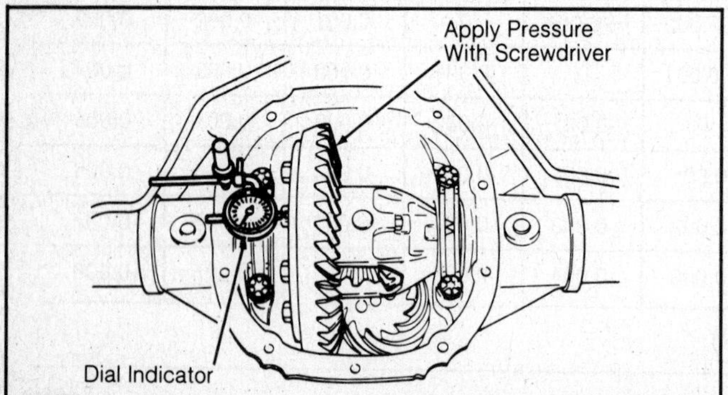
Apply Pressure
With Screwdriver
Dial Indicator

121037 Courtesy of Ford Motor Co.

Fig. 5: Measuring Differential Case End Play

Drive Pinion Bearing Race Installation – 1) Install oil baffle in inner bearing race bore of housing. Place inner and outer pinion bearing races in bores of axle housing.

2) Place inner and outer Race Installers (T71P-4616-A) on bearing races. *See Fig. 6.* Install Forcing Screw (T75T-1176-A) through bearing races. Tighten forcing screw until both bearing races are seated in axle housing.

NOTE: Tools in pinion depth gauge set must be checked for nicks or damage before each use. Any high spots on tools must be removed to ensure accurate readings.

Drive Pinion Depth – 1) Put new inner drive pinion bearing on Aligning Adapter (T76P-4020-A1) and assemble using Gauge Disc Block (T90T-4020-A). *See Fig. 4.* Put outer pinion bearing (new or good used) into race. Place depth gauge assembly into housing with Screw (T76P-4020-A9), extending through outer bearing.

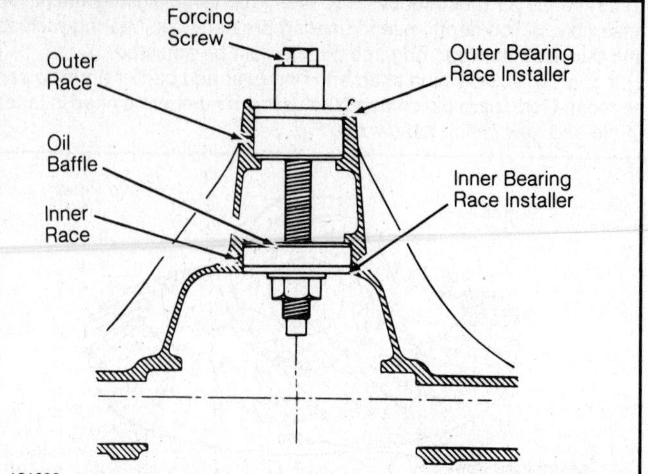
Forcing
Screw
Outer
Race
Outer Bearing
Race Installer
Oil
Baffle
Inner Bearing
Race Installer
Inner
Race

121038 Courtesy of Ford Motor Co.

Fig. 6: Identifying Pinion Bearing Race Installer

2) Thread Handle (T76P-4020-A11) onto screw finger tight. Install and center Gauge Tube (T76P-4020-A7) into differential bearing bore. Install bearing caps and tighten to specification. See TORQUE SPECIFICATIONS table at end of article. Using 3/8" drive torque wrench in square drive on handle, tighten handle until preload on bearings is 20-40 INCH lbs. (2.3-4.5 N.m).

3) Determine clearance between gauge block and gauge tube using feeler gauge. Correct feeler gauge will give feeling of slight drag as gauge passes between tube and block. *See Fig. 7.*

4) Thickness of correct feeler gauge is thickness of selective oil slinger to be installed between drive pinion head and inner pinion bearing, if drive pinion has zero marking. If drive pinion has plus (+) marking on face, subtract that number from thickness dimension. If drive pinion has minus (–) marking on face, add that number to thickness dimension.

NOTE: Inner bearing used for depth measurement must be bearing used for final assembly.

5) Using a micrometer, measure oil slinger to verify size. Place oil slinger on drive pinion. Press inner drive pinion bearing and oil slinger on drive pinion, using Axle Bearing/Seal Plate (T75L-1165-B), Pinion Bearing Replacer (T57L-4621-B) and arbor press.

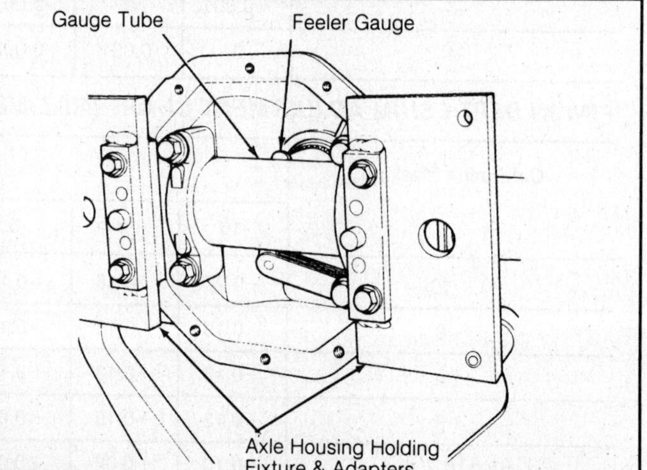
Gauge Tube
Feeler Gauge
Axle Housing Holding
Fixture & Adapters

91E13379 Courtesy of Ford Motor Co.

Fig. 7: Checking Drive Pinion Depth

Drive Pinion Bearing Preload – 1) Install drive pinion in axle housing. Install new collapsible spacer. Install outer pinion bearing and thrust washer. Lubricate and install drive pinion oil seal. Noting alignment marks made previously, install pinion companion flange, washer and

Dana 28-2 Front Axle – Aerostar (Cont.)

NEW nut on pinion shaft. Tighten pinion nut to specification. See TORQUE SPECIFICATIONS table at end of article.

2) Using an INCH-pound torque wrench, check rotational torque necessary to turn pinion. Rotational torque should be 15-35 INCH lbs. (1.7-4.0 N.m). If rotational torque is less than 15 INCH lbs. (1.7 N.m), tighten pinion nut in small increments until rotational torque of 15-35 INCH lbs. (1.7-4.0 N.m) is reached. If reading exceeds 35 INCH lbs (4.0 N.m), collapsible washer must be replaced.

CAUTION: Always use NEW collapsible spacer when reassembling drive pinion. NEVER tighten pinion flange nut more than 275 ft. lbs. (373 N.m) as collapsible spacer will be compressed too far.

Ring & Pinion Gear Backlash – 1) With drive pinion depth and preload adjustments properly made, install differential case into housing. Differential master bearings should still be on case. Force differential case away from drive pinion gear so case is fully seated in cross bores of housing.

2) Set dial indicator so tip is against head of ring gear bolt at 90 degrees to bolt. Rock ring gear so teeth of ring gear mesh fully with drive pinion gear teeth. Force ring gear teeth against drive pinion gear teeth and zero dial indicator. Force ring gear and case away from drive pinion gear. Read gauge. Repeat this procedure until same reading is obtained each time.

3) This reading, less .005" (.13 mm), is thickness of shim pack that must go under differential side bearing on ring gear side of case. Remove case from axle housing. Remove master bearings from case. Place correct shim pack on ring gear hub of case. Place side bearing on hub of case. Drive bearing onto case using Step plate (D80L-630-3), Side Bearing Replacer (T83T-4221-A) and Handle (T80T-4000-W).

4) To determine correct amount of shims to place on pinion gear side hub, subtract thickness of shim pack installed on ring gear side of case from total of differential case end play. Total differential case end play was previously determined in steps **1)** to **4)** of DIFFERENTIAL CASE REASSEMBLY. Add .010" (.25 mm) to figure determined for shim pack thickness on side opposite ring gear.

5) Place required thickness shim pack on hub of case opposite ring gear. Place step plate on ring gear side bearing to protect bearing. Drive remaining side bearing onto case with side bearing replacer. Install side bearing races on side bearings.

6) Install housing spreader and dial indicator on carrier. Spread housing to maximum of .015" (.37 mm). Install differential case in housing. Use soft-faced hammer to ensure that case seats fully in housing bore. Use care to avoid damaging teeth of ring and pinion gears.

7) Remove housing spreader and dial indicator. Install side bearing caps, ensuring letters stamped on caps match letters stamped on housing. Tighten bearing cap bolts to specification. See TORQUE SPECIFICATIONS table at end of article.

8) Check ring and pinion gear backlash in 3 places equally spaced around ring gear. Backlash range is .005-.008" (.13-20 mm) with allowable maximum variation of .003" (.08 mm). If backlash figure is too high, ring gear must be moved closer to drive pinion gear.

9) If backlash figure is too low, ring gear must be moved away from drive pinion gear. To change backlash readings, move shims from one side of differential case to other. Total thickness of end play shim packs must not change.

10) When backlash adjustment is completed, check tooth contact pattern. See GEAR TOOTH CONTACT PATTERNS article in GENERAL INFORMATION. Pattern will be correct if assembly and adjustments have been done properly. When backlash is correct, apply continuous bead of RTV sealant 1/4-3/8" wide on housing.

11) Sealant bead should not pass over or outside holes. Install housing cover. To complete installation, reverse removal procedure. Allow one hour cure time before filling differential.

ASSEMBLY SPECIFICATIONS

AXLE ASSEMBLY SPECIFICATIONS

Application	In. (mm)
Axle Shaft End Play	Non-Adjustable
Ring Gear-To-Pinion Backlash [1]	.005-.008 (.13-.20)
	INCH Lbs. (N.m)
Drive Pinion Bearing Preload	
New Bearings	15-35 (1.7-4.0)

[1] – Maximum backlash between 3 equally spaced check points is .003" (.08 mm).

TORQUE SPECIFICATIONS

TORQUE SPECIFICATIONS

Application	Ft. Lbs. (N.m)
Axle Mounting Bracket-To-Axle Housing Bolt	70-80 (95-108)
Axle Snubber Bolt	17-24 (23-33)
Axle-To-Crossmember Mounting Bushing Nut	65-85 (88-115)
Flange Bolt	22-29 (30-39)
Housing Cover Bolt	20-25 (27-34)
Pinion Flange Nut	[1] 140-275 (190-373)
Ring Gear-To-Case Bolt	45-65 (61-86)
Side Bearing Cap Bolt	30-45 (41-61)
Wheel Lug Nuts	100 (136)

[1] – Collapsible pinion spacer used. Torque pinion nut until rotational torque of pinion is 15-35 (1.7-4.0 N.m)

1991 DRIVE AXLES
Dana IFS Front Axle

Bronco, Explorer, Ranger, F150/250,

DESCRIPTION

Independent Front Suspension (IFS) front axle is of integral carrier housing, hypoid gear type. Centerline of drive pinion is mounted above centerline of ring gear. Drive pinion and ring gear bearing settings are all adjusted by shims.

Dana 35 IFS axle is used on 4WD Explorer and 4WD Ranger models. Dana 44 IFS axle is used on Bronco and F150 4WD. Dana 44 IFS-HD axle is used on F250 4WD. Dana 50 IFS axle is used on F250 HD 4WD. Dana 35 IFS and 44 IFS axles are equipped with coil springs. Dana 44 IFS-HD and 50 IFS axles are equipped with leaf springs.

AXLE RATIO & IDENTIFICATION

Axle application can be determined through the axle code on the Safety Certification Label on left door pillar. Additionally, a metal identification tag stamped with gear ratio and diameter, is secured to housing by 2 carrier bolts. If axle is equipped with limited slip differential, gear ratio will have letter "L" in the number. See AXLE RATIO IDENTIFICATION article.

REMOVAL & INSTALLATION

NOTE: For removal and installation procedures of front drive axle component parts not covered in this article, see appropriate LOCKING HUBS and 4WD STEERING KNUCKLES articles.

HUBS & BEARINGS

Removal (Explorer & Ranger With Dana 35 IFS) - 1) Raise and support vehicle. Remove wheels and tires. Remove retainer washers from wheel lug nut studs. Remove caliper with brake line attached and secure to frame with wire. DO NOT hang caliper with any tension on brake hose. Remove manual or automatic locking hub assemblies.

2) On models with manual locking hubs, remove snap ring and axle shaft spacer from spindle. Remove outer bearing lock nut with Spanner Lock Nut Wrench (T86T-1197-A). Remove lock nut washer and inner bearing adjusting nut.

3) On models with automatic locking hubs, remove snap ring and axle shaft spacer. Carefully pull plastic cam assembly from bearing adjusting nut. Remove 2 plastic thrust washers from adjusting nut.

CAUTION: Before removing adjusting nut, remove locking key from spindle keyway. Failure to clear keyway will result in thread damage on spindle.

4) Using magnet, remove locking key from spindle keyway. It may be necessary to rotate adjusting nut slightly to relieve pressure for locking key removal. Remove adjusting nut with 2 3/8" Hex Socket (T70T-4252-B).

5) On all models, remove hub and rotor. Remove outer bearing. Using Seal Remover (1175-AC), remove grease seal from rotor. Remove inner bearing. If bearings require replacement, remove races from hub using Internal Puller (D80L-943-A) and attached slide hammer.

Installation & Adjustment (With Manual Locking Hubs) - 1) If bearings are replaced, drive new races into hub. Lubricate bearings with lithium base multipurpose wheel bearing grease. Install inner bearing and seal into hub. Install hub and rotor assembly on spindle. Install outer bearing and adjusting nut. Tighten adjusting nut to 35 ft. lbs. (47 N.m) while turning hub back and forth to seat bearings.

2) Spin hub and back off adjusting nut 1/4 turn (90 degrees). Install lock washer on spindle. Mount lock washer over pin on adjusting nut, turning nut slightly if necessary to align pin. Install and tighten outer lock nut to 150 ft. lbs. (203 N.m) using spanner lock nut wrench.

3) Install axle shaft spacer. Install snap ring on end of spindle. Install manual hub assembly. Install retaining washers, wheel and tire. Check hub and rotor assembly end play. End play should be 0-.003" (0-.08 mm). To complete installation, reverse removal procedure.

Installation & Adjustment (With Automatic Locking Hubs) - 1) If bearings are replaced, drive new races into hub. Lubricate bearings with lithium base multipurpose wheel bearing grease. Install inner bearing and seal into hub. Install hub on spindle.

2) Install outer bearing and adjusting nut. Tighten adjusting nut to 35 ft. lbs. (47 N.m) while turning hub back and forth to seat bearings. Spin hub and back off adjusting nut 1/4 turn (90 degrees). Retighten adjusting nut to 16 INCH lbs. (1.8 N.m).

3) Align nearest hole in adjusting nut with center of spindle keyway slot. Advance nut to next lug, if necessary. Install locking key in spindle keyway under adjusting nut. Install 2 thrust washers. Press plastic cam assembly onto adjusting nut while lining up key in fixed cam with spindle keyway.

4) Install axle shaft spacer. Clip snap ring onto end of spindle. Install automatic locking hub assembly with 3 legs of hub assembly inserted into 3 pockets of cam assembly. Install retaining washers, wheel and tire. Check hub and rotor assembly end play. End play should be 0-.003" (0-.08 mm). To complete installation, reverse removal procedure.

Removal (Bronco & F150/250 With Manual Locking Hubs) - 1) Raise and support front of vehicle. Remove front wheels. Remove locking hubs. See LOCKING HUBS article. Remove caliper with brake line attached and secure to frame with wire. Do not hang caliper with any tension on brake hose.

2) Remove hub bearing lock nut, lock ring and adjusting nut. Using Spanner Lock Nut Wrench (T86T-1197-A), remove nuts. Remove hub and rotor. Outer bearing will slide off with hub. Remove grease seal and inner bearing. If bearings require replacement, remove races from hub with Internal Puller (T77F-1102-A) and attached slide hammer.

Installation & Adjustment - 1) If bearings are replaced, drive new races into hub. Lubricate bearings with lithium base multipurpose wheel bearing grease. Install inner bearing and seal into hub.

2) Install hub and rotor assemble on spindle. Install outer bearing and adjusting nut. Using torque wrench and Spanner Lock Nut Wrench (T86T-1197-A) tighten adjusting nut to 50-60 ft. lbs. (68-81 N.m) while turning wheel back and forth.

3) Applying inward pressure to spanner lock nut wrench to disengage locking splines, back off adjusting nut approximately 1/2 turn (180 degrees). Retighten adjusting nut to 15 ft. lbs. (20 N.m). Check hub and rotor assembly end play. End play should be 0-.004" (0-.10 mm). To complete installation, reverse removal procedure.

Removal (Bronco & F150 With Dana 44 IFS & Automatic Locking Hubs & F250 HD With Dana 50 IFS - 1) Raise and support front of vehicle. Remove wheels. Remove locking hub assembly. See LOCKING HUBS article. Remove caliper with brake line attached and secure to frame with wire. DO NOT hang caliper with any tension on brake hose.

2) Remove hub bearing lock nut, lock ring and adjusting nut. Using Spanner Lock Nut Wrench (T85T-1197-A), remove nuts. Remove hub and rotor. Outer bearing will slide off with hub. Remove grease seal and inner bearing. If bearings require replacement, remove races from hub using Internal Puller (T77F-1102-A) and attached slide hammer.

Installation & Adjustment - 1) If bearings are replaced, drive new races into hub. Install inner bearing and seal into hub. Install hub on spindle. Install outer bearing and adjusting nut.

2) Using spanner lock nut wrench, tighten inner lock nut to 50 ft. lbs. (68 N.m). Back off inner lock nut and retighten to 30-40 ft. lbs. (41-54 N.m). While rotating hub, back off inner lock nut 1/4 turn (90 degrees).

3) Install lock washer so key is positioned in spindle groove. Rotate inner lock nut so pin is aligned in nearest lock washer hole. Install and tighten outer lock nut to 160-205 ft. lbs. (217-278 N.m). Check hub and rotor assembly end play. End play should be 0-.004" (0-.10 mm). To complete installation, reverse removal procedure.

SPINDLES & AXLE SHAFTS

Removal - 1) Raise and support vehicle. Remove locking hub assemblies. See appropriate LOCKING HUBS article. Remove wheel and tire. Remove brake caliper assembly and tie to frame without any tension on brake hose. Remove hub and rotor. See HUBS & BEARINGS under REMOVAL & INSTALLATION. Unbolt spindle from

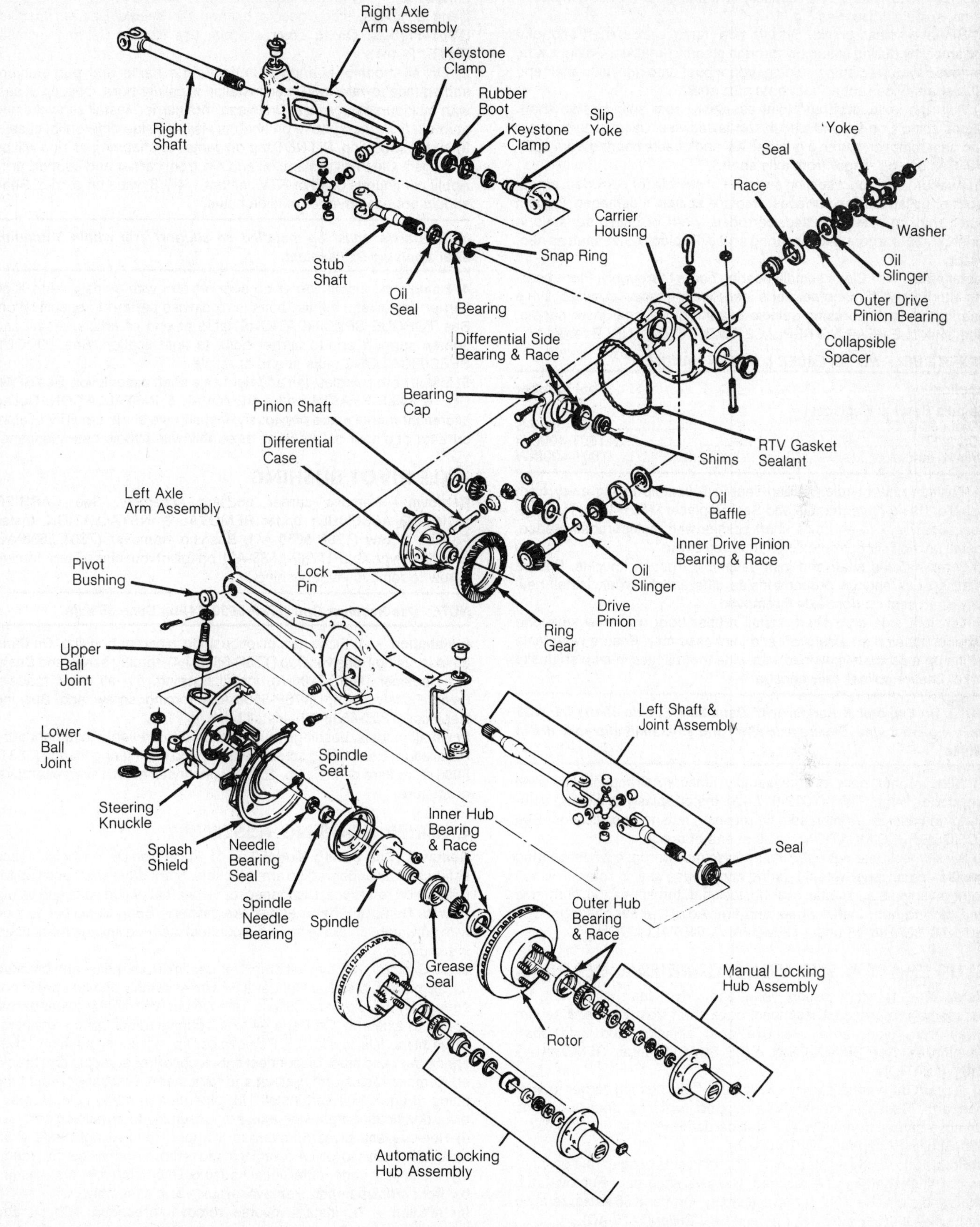

Right Axle Arm Assembly
Keystone Clamp
Rubber Boot
Keystone Clamp
Slip Yoke
Yoke
Seal
Race
Washer
Right Shaft
Carrier Housing
Snap Ring
Oil Slinger
Stub Shaft
Oil Seal
Bearing
Outer Drive Pinion Bearing
Collapsible Spacer
Differential Side Bearing & Race
Bearing Cap
Pinion Shaft
Differential Case
RTV Gasket Sealant
Shims
Oil Baffle
Left Axle Arm Assembly
Inner Drive Pinion Bearing & Race
Pivot Bushing
Lock Pin
Oil Slinger
Drive Pinion
Ring Gear
Upper Ball Joint
Left Shaft & Joint Assembly
Lower Ball Joint
Spindle Seat
Inner Hub Bearing & Race
Steering Knuckle
Seal
Splash Shield
Needle Bearing Seal
Spindle Needle Bearing
Spindle
Outer Hub Bearing & Race
Grease Seal
Manual Locking Hub Assembly
Rotor
Automatic Locking Hub Assembly
121034
Courtesy of Ford Motor Co.

Fig. 1: Exploded View of Dana Model 35 IFS Front Drive Axle Assembly (Other Models Are Similar)

1991 DRIVE AXLES
Dana IFS Front Axle (Cont.)

knuckle studs. It may be necessary to tap spindle with soft mallet to break spindle loose. *See Fig. 1*

2) Remove splash shield. On left side, remove axle shaft and joint assembly by pulling assembly through steering knuckle. On right side, remove keystone clamps holding rubber boot onto right axle shaft and stub shaft. Slide rubber boot onto stub shaft.

3) Pull right axle shaft and joint assembly from splined stub shaft. Clamp spindle on second step in soft-jawed vise. Using slide hammer and seal remover, remove grease seal and needle bearing from spindle. Remove oil slinger from axle shaft.

Inspection – Inspect sealing surfaces of spindle for corroded, pitted, worn or galled sealing surfaces. Replace spindle if damaged. Inspect outer shaft of axle for pitted, corroded, worn or galled surfaces in inner oil seal and/or needle bearing areas. Replace outer shaft as necessary.

Installation – **1)** Clean spindle bearing bores thoroughly. Place bearing into bore with manufacturer's identification facing outward. Drive bearing into spindle using spindle bearing driver and driver handle. See SPINDLE BEARING REPLACER & DRIVER HANDLE table.

SPINDLE BEARING REPLACER & DRIVER HANDLE

Application	Tool Number
Spindle Bearing Replacer	
Dana 35 & 44	T80T-4000-S
Dana 50	T80T-4000-R
Driver Handle	T80T-4000-W

2) Position new needle bearing seal with seal lip facing away from spindle. Using driver handle and Seal Replacer (T80T-4000-T), install seal. Coat seal lip and axle shaft splines with multipurpose grease. Install new oil slinger on axle shaft, if removed.

3) Slide left axle shaft and joint assembly through knuckle. Ensure shaft splines engage properly inside differential carrier. Install new axle shaft seal on right axle if removed.

4) On right side stub shaft, install rubber boot with new keystone clamps. Install right axle shaft and joint assembly. Ensure wide male spline on axle shaft is aligned with wide tooth space in stub shaft slip yoke. Ensure splines fully engage.

NOTE: On Explorer & Ranger with Dana 35 IFS, axle shafts DO NOT have a blind spline. Ensure axle shaft and stub shaft slip yoke are in phase.

5) Slide rubber boot over assembly junction. Crimp clamps with Keystone Clamp Pliers (T63P-9171-A). Install splash shield and spindle onto knuckle. Tighten spindle retaining nuts to specification. See TORQUE SPECIFICATIONS table at end of article.

6) Pack wheel bearings with lithium base multipurpose wheel bearing grease. Install inner wheel bearing and grease seal in rotor. Position rotor on spindle and install bearing, lock nut, thrust bearing, snap ring and locking hub. Install wheel and tire. Adjust wheel bearings. See HUBS & BEARINGS under REMOVAL & INSTALLATION.

STUB SHAFT & SLIP YOKE, CARRIER & BEARING

Removal – **1)** Mark pinion yoke and drive shaft alignment for reassembly reference. Disconnect drive shaft from yoke and secure away from work area. Remove both spindles and axle shaft assemblies. See SPINDLES & AXLE SHAFTS under REMOVAL & INSTALLATION.

2) Support differential carrier and remove bolts holding carrier to support arm. Separate carrier from support arm and drain lubricant. Remove carrier from vehicle. Install carrier in Holding Fixture (T57L-500-B) using Adapters (T80T-4000-B).

3) Rotate slip yoke and stub shaft until open side of snap ring on inner end of stub shaft can be reached. Remove snap ring. Remove stub shaft and slip yoke from carrier assembly. On Dana 35 axles, remove right oil seal using slide hammer and Seal Puller (1175-AC).

4) Remove left oil seal using slide hammer and Seal Puller (T74P-77248-A). Remove caged needle bearings using slide hammer and Axle Bearing Remover (T90T-1225-A). On all other axles, remove oil seal and caged needle bearings together, using slide hammer and Collet (D80L-100-A).

Installation – **1)** Ensure bearing bore is clean and has no nicks. On Dana 35 axles, place needle bearing on Needle Bearing Installer (T90T-1175-A). On all other models, use Needle Bearing Installer (T83T-1244-A).

2) On all models, bearing manufacturer's name and part number should face toward tool when installed in carrier bore. Coat lip of seal with multipurpose grease. Drive seal into carrier. Install slip yoke and stub shaft so that groove on shaft is visible inside differential case.

3) Install snap ring. DO NOT tap on center of snap ring as ring will be damaged. Clean all sealant, oil and dirt from carrier and support arm. Apply continuous bead of RTV sealant 1/4-3/8" wide on carrier. Bead should not pass over or outside holes.

NOTE: Carrier must be installed on support arm within 5 minutes after applying RTV sealant.

4) Using jack, install carrier on support arm with guide pins to align carrier. Install and tighten bolts in clockwise pattern to specification. See TORQUE SPECIFICATIONS table at end of article. Install and tighten support arm-to carrier bolts to specification. See TORQUE SPECIFICATIONS table at end of article.

5) Install both spindles, left and right axle shaft assemblies. See SPINDLE & AXLE SHAFTS under REMOVAL & INSTALLATION. Noting alignment marks made previously, install drive shaft. Let RTV sealant cure for one hour before filling assembly with hypoid gear lubricant.

AXLE PIVOT BUSHING

Removal – Remove carrier housing assembly. See CARRIER HOUSING ASSEMBLY under REMOVAL & INSTALLATION. Install Forcing Screw (T78P-5638-A1), Bushing Remover (T80T-5638-A2) and Receiver Cup (T78P-5638-A3) on pivot bushing. Turn forcing screw to remove pivot bushing.

NOTE: Use Receiver Cup (T78P-5638-A4) on Dana 35 axle.

Installation – **1)** Place new pivot bushing in carrier housing. On Dana 35 axle, using Receiver Cup (T78P-5638-A4), forcing screw and Bushing Replacer (T82T-3006-A), install bushing. On all other models, using Receiver Cup (T78P-5638-A2), forcing screw and Bushing Replacer (T80T-6538-A2), install bushing.

2) On all models, bushings must be flared to prevent movement after installation. Use forcing screw, receiver cup and Flaring Flange (T83T-3006-A) to flare bushing lip. To complete installation, reverse removal procedure.

CARRIER HOUSING ASSEMBLY

Removal (Coil Spring Models) – **1)** Raise vehicle on hoist. Place safety stands under radius arm brackets. Mark drive shaft position for installation reference. Disconnect drive shaft at pinion yoke and tie out of way. Remove wheels and brake calipers. Support caliper to side with no weight on brake hose. Disconnect steering linkage from steering knuckles.

2) On Explorer, remove left stabilizer bar link from radius arm bracket. On all models, place jack under axle arm assembly and compress coil spring slightly. On Dana 35 axle, remove nut which holds lower part of spring to axle arm. On Dana 44 axle, remove upper spring retainers.

3) On all models, lower jack. Remove coil spring, spring cushion, lower spring seat and stud. Disconnect shock absorber at radius arm bracket. Remove radius arm bracket and radius arm. Disconnect vent tube fitting (if equipped) and install 1/8" pipe plug in fitting hole. Remove pivot bolt holding right side axle arm assembly to crossmember.

4) Remove and discard keystone clamps. Remove right axle shaft assembly from slip joint. Lower jack and remove right axle arm assembly. Place jack under differential housing. Unbolt left axle arm assembly from crossmember. Remove left axle arm assembly.

Installation – To install, reverse removal procedure. Check and adjust alignment, if necessary.

Removal (Leaf Spring Models) – **1)** Raise and support vehicle. Remove tires and wheels. Remove brake calipers. Support caliper to side with no tension on brake hose. Place jack under right axle arm

assembly. Remove 2 "U" bolts holding shock absorber mounting plate and leaf springs to tube and yoke assembly.
2) Disconnect vent tube. Remove vent fitting and install 1/8" pipe plug. Remove pivot bolt holding right axle arm to crossmember. Remove keystone clamps from rubber boot. Move rubber boot off axle shaft assembly onto slip joint. Remove right axle arm assembly.
3) Pull right axle shaft out of slip joint. Place jack under left axle arm assembly. Remove 2 "U" bolts holding shock absorber mounting plate and leaf springs to tube and yoke assembly. Place jack under differential housing. Remove pivot bolt holding left axle arm assembly to crossmember. Remove left axle arm assembly.
Installation – To install, reverse removal procedure. Check and adjust alignment if necessary.

OVERHAUL

DIFFERENTIAL ASSEMBLY

Disassembly – 1) With carrier housing removed from vehicle, remove differential carrier from axle arm. Note matched numbers or letters on differential bearing caps for reassembly reference. Remove bearing caps. Install Housing Spreader (4000-E) and Spreader Adapter (T80T-4000-B). *See Fig. 2.*

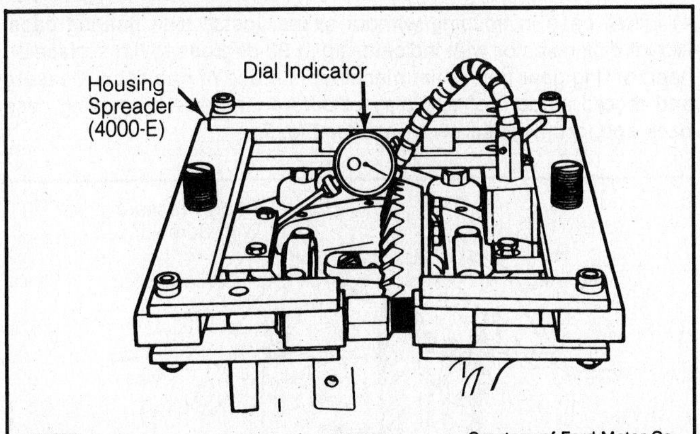
Housing
Spreader
(4000-E)
Dial Indicator
121035
Courtesy of Ford Motor Co.

Fig. 2: Spreading Dana Carrier Housing

2) Rotate slip yoke and shaft assembly so open side of snap ring on shaft is exposed. Remove snap ring from shaft. Remove slip yoke and shaft assembly from carrier. Mount dial indicator on carrier housing to measure amount of spread.

CAUTION: DO NOT spread carrier housing more than .010" (.25 mm). Permanent damage to housing could result.

3) Spread carrier housing to a maximum of .010" .25 mm. Remove dial indicator. Carefully pry differential assembly out of housing. Remove spreader immediately so that housing does not distort permanently.
4) Place carrier assembly in holding device. Using Yoke Holder (T78P-4851-A), hold yoke while removing drive pinion nut and washer. Using Yoke Remover (T65L-4851-B), remove yoke from drive pinion. If yoke shows wear in sealing area, replace yoke. Remove drive pinion by tapping with soft-faced mallet.

NOTE: Pinion bearing adjusting shims may remain on pinion shaft, stick to bearing or fall loose. Collect shims and save for reassembly.

5) Remove and discard drive pinion oil seal. Remove outer pinion bearing and oil slinger. On Dana 35 axle, remove collapsible spacer. On all models, drive out inner drive pinion bearing race using pinion bearing race remover and driver handle. See Pinion Bearing Race Remover & Driver Handle table.
6) Remove shims and oil baffle from bearing bore. Mark and keep shims and baffle together. Turn carrier over and drive out outer pinion bearing race using bearing race remover and driver handle. See Pinion Bearing Race Remover & Driver Handle table.

PINION BEARING RACE REMOVER & DRIVER HANDLE

Application	Tool Number
Driver Handle	
Dana 35	T80T-4000-W
Dana 44 & 50	D81L-4000-W
Pinion Bearing Race Remover	
Inner Bearing Race	
Dana 35	T86T-4628-AH
Dana 44	D81T-4000-W
Dana 50	D81T-4628-D
Outer Bearing Race	
Dana 35	T86T-4628-A
Dana 44 & 50	D81T-4628-D

NOTE: If oil baffle or slinger are damaged during disassembly procedure, measure them and replace with new units during reassembly. Baffle and slinger affect pinion depth and preload adjustments and are included in shim pack thickness.

7) Place Universal Bearing Remover (D81L-4220-A) in vise to secure tool while removing differential side bearings. On Dana 35 axle, use Step Plate (D80L-630-4) under bearing to protect bearing from puller. On all other models, use Step Plate (D80L-630-5). On all models, keep bearings, bearing races and shims in sets, marked as to location on carrier.
8) Place differential case in vise with rags underneath to protect ring gear. Remove and discard ring gear bolts. Tap ring gear with soft-faced mallet to remove ring gear from case. Using drift and hammer, drive out pinion shaft lock pin. Remove pinion shaft.
9) Rotate side gears until pinion gears are aligned with case opening. Remove pinion gears and spherical washers. Remove side gears with thrust washers.
Cleaning & Inspection – 1) Clean all components in solvent. Allow bearings to air dry. Inspect all machined surfaces for smoothness or raised edges. Inspect all gear teeth for wear or chipping and replace as necessary.
2) Check all bearings and races for nicks, roller end wear, grooves or any damage. Replace as needed. Check pinion yoke for wear in sealing area and replace as necessary.
3) Check differential pinion shaft, pinion gears, side gears and thrust washers for wear or damage. Replace all defective parts. Pinion gears must be replaced as sets.
Reassembly & Adjustments – 1) When reassembling ring and pinion assembly, pinion depth, pinion bearing preload, side bearing preload and backlash between ring and pinion must be adjusted.
2) If only pinion shaft and ring gear are to be replaced and carrier housing can be reused, compare pinion depth adjustment numbers etched in faces of old and new pinion heads. *See Fig. 3.* Using appropriate PINION DEPTH SHIM ADJUSTMENT chart, select correct shims for new pinion shaft depth adjustment.
3) The pinion depth adjustment number is determined by manufacturer at time of assembly. Number represents nominal distance that pinion shaft deviates from distance between pinion gear face and centerline of axle. Nominal distance is measured from centerline of ring gear to face of gear on drive pinion shaft.

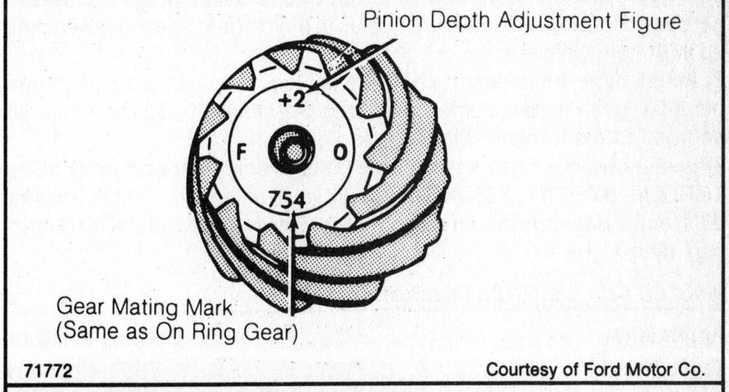
Pinion Depth Adjustment Figure
+2
F
O
754
Gear Mating Mark
(Same as On Ring Gear)
71772
Courtesy of Ford Motor Co.

Fig. 3: Locating Pinion Gear Markings

1991 DRIVE AXLES
Dana IFS Front Axle (Cont.)

PINION DEPTH SHIM ADJUSTMENT CHART (INCHES)

Old Pinion Marking	New Pinion Marking								
	-4	-3	-2	-1	0	+1	+2	+3	+4
+4	+0.008	+0.007	+0.006	+0.005	+0.004	+0.003	+0.002	+0.001	0
+3	+0.007	+0.006	+0.005	+0.004	+0.003	+0.002	+0.001	0	-0.001
+2	+0.006	+0.005	+0.004	+0.003	+0.002	+0.001	0	-0.001	-0.002
+1	+0.005	+0.004	+0.003	+0.002	+0.001	0	-0.001	-0.002	-0.003
0	+0.004	+0.003	+0.002	+0.001	0	-0.001	-0.002	-0.003	-0.004
-1	+0.003	+0.002	+0.001	0	-0.001	-0.002	-0.003	-0.004	-0.005
-2	+0.002	+0.001	0	-0.001	-0.002	-0.003	-0.004	-0.005	-0.006
-3	+0.001	0	-0.001	-0.002	-0.003	-0.004	-0.005	-0.006	-0.007
-4	0	-0.001	-0.002	-0.003	-0.004	-0.005	-0.006	-0.007	-0.008

***NOTE:* To use *PINION DEPTH SHIM ADJUSTMENT* chart procedure, old pinion shaft shim pack dimensions *MUST* be determined accurately. If original pinion shaft shim pack dimension cannot be determined accurately, Pinion Depth Gauge Set (T80T-4020-A) must be used to determine correct pinion depth setting. Depth gauge set must also be used if new carrier housing is to be used.**

4) Ring gear and pinion gear are supplied in matched sets only. Matching numbers are etched on ring and pinion gears. If new gearset is being used, verify matching gearset numbers. *See Fig. 3.*

5) Pinion Depth Gauge Set (T80T-4020-A) allows shim pack adjustment without having to remove and replace differential bearings when setting up shim packs. *See Fig. 4.*

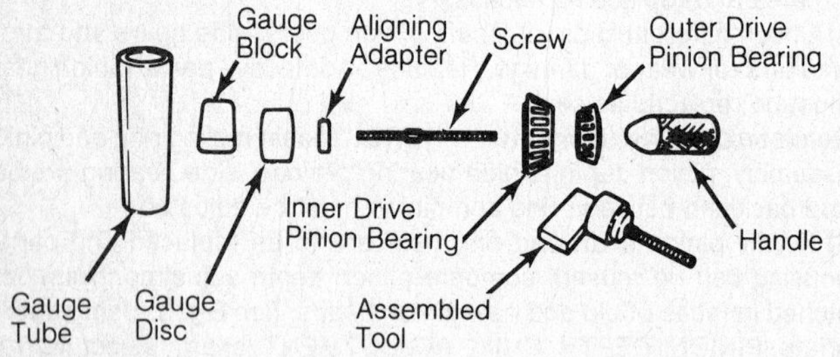
Gauge Block
Aligning Adapter
Screw
Outer Drive Pinion Bearing
Inner Drive Pinion Bearing
Handle
Gauge Tube
Gauge Disc
Assembled Tool

121036 Courtesy of Ford Motor Co.

Fig. 4: Identifying Pinion Depth Gauge Set (T80T-4020-A)

DIFFERENTIAL CASE

1) Place differential case in vise. Use multipurpose grease to lubricate side gears, pinion gears and all thrust washers and install in differential case. Rotate side gears until holes in pinion gears and washers line up with holes in case.

2) Install differential pinion shaft. Install lock pin. Using a punch and hammer, peen metal of differential case over lock pin at 2 locations, 90 degrees to the left and right of lock pin slot.

3) Install ring gear and tighten new bolts evenly to specification. See TORQUE SPECIFICATIONS table at end of article. Install master differential bearings on differential case. See Master Differential Bearings table.

MASTER DIFFERENTIAL BEARINGS

Application	Bearing Number
Dana 35	T86T-4222-AH
Dana 44	D81T-4222-B
Dana 50	D81T-4222-C

4) Install case in housing without shims. Install side bearing caps. Mount dial indicator with indicator tip at 90 degrees to flat surface on head of ring gear bolt or flat machined surface of ring gear. Measure and record amount of end play of differential case by moving case back and forth with screwdriver. *See Fig. 5.*

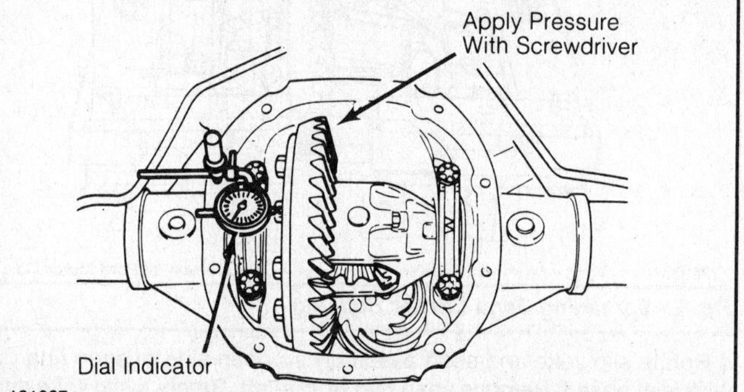
Apply Pressure With Screwdriver
Dial Indicator

121037 Courtesy of Ford Motor Co.

Fig. 5: Measuring Differential Case End Play

5) This measurement is total differential case end play and will be used later to determine proper shim pack dimension. Remove case from housing. Leave master bearings on case at this time.

DRIVE PINION BEARING RACE INSTALLATION

1) Place inner and outer pinion bearing races in bores of carrier. Place inner race installer on inner bearing race. *See Fig. 6.* See Pinion Bearing Race Installer & Forcing Screw table.

2) Place outer race installer on outer bearing race. Install forcing screw through bearings. Tighten screw until both bearing races are seated in carrier bore.

PINION BEARING RACE INSTALLER & FORCING SCREW

Application	Tool Number
Forcing Screw	T75T-1176-A
Pinion Bearing Race Installer	
Inner Bearing Race	
Dana 35	T60K-4616-A
Dana 44 & 50	T80T-4000-D
Outer Bearing Race	
Dana 35	T71P-4616-B1
Dana 44 & 50	T80T-4000-E

1991 DRIVE AXLES
Dana IFS Front Axle (Cont.)

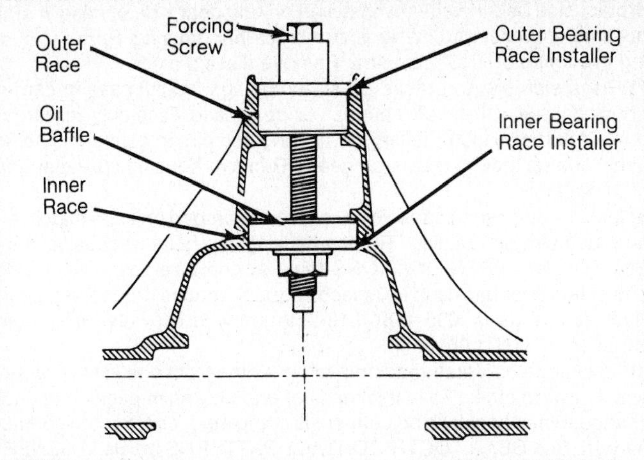
Forcing Screw
Outer Race
Outer Bearing Race Installer
Oil Baffle
Inner Bearing Race Installer
Inner Race
121038
Courtesy of Ford Motor Co.

Fig. 6: Identifying Pinion Bearing Race Installer

DRIVE PINION DEPTH

1) Put new inner drive pinion bearing on aligning adapter and assemble using gauge disc. *See Fig. 4.* See PINION DEPTH GAUGE table. Put outer pinion bearing (new or good used) into race. Place depth gauge assembly into housing with screw extending through outer bearing.

NOTE: Tools in Pinion Depth Gauge Set (T80T-4020-A) must be checked before each use for nicks or damage. Any high spots on tools must be removed to ensure accurate readings.

PINION DEPTH GAUGE

Application	Tool Number
Aligning Adapter	T76P-4020-A2
Gauge Block	
Dana 35	T76P-4020-A10
Dana 44 & 50	T80T-4020-F42
Gauge Disc	
Dana 35	PS88B878-1
Dana 44	T80T-4020-F44
Dana 50	T80T-4020-F40
Gauge Tube	
Dana 35	D80T-4020-F49
Dana 44	D80T-4020-F47
Dana 50	T80T-4020-F41
Handle	T76P-4020-A11
Screw	
Dana 35	T76P-4020-A9
Dana 44 & 50	T80T-4020-F43

2) Thread handle onto screw finger tight. Using 3/8" drive torque wrench in square drive on handle, tighten handle until preload on bearings is 15-25 INCH lbs. (1.7-2.8 N.m) on Dana 35 axle or 20-40 INCH lbs. (2.3-4.5 N.m) on Dana 44 and 50 axles. Center gauge tube in side bearing bore. Install side bearing caps and tighten bolts to specification. See TORQUE SPECIFICATIONS table at end of article.
3) Place gauge block on top of face of drive pinion underneath gauge tube. Determine clearance between gauge block and gauge tube using feeler gauge. Correct feeler gauge will give feeling of slight drag as gauge passes between tube and block.
4) On Dana 35 axles, thickness of correct feeler gauge is thickness of selective oil slinger that is to be installed between drive pinion head and inner pinion bearing, if drive pinion has zero marking.
5) On Dana 44 and 50 axles, thickness of correct feeler gauge is thickness of shim pack that is to be installed under inner bearing race, if drive pinion has zero marking.
6) On all models, if drive pinion has plus (+) marking on face, subtract that number from thickness dimension. If drive pinion has minus (-) marking on face, add that number to thickness dimension.

NOTE: Inner pinion bearing used during depth measurement procedure MUST be used for final assembly. Oil slinger and/or baffle (if equipped) are to be measured as part of shim pack.

7) On Dana 35, using a micrometer, measure oil slinger to verify size. Place oil slinger on drive pinion. Press inner drive pinion bearing and oil slinger on drive pinion, using Axle Bearing/Seal Plate (T75L-1165-B), appropriate Pinion Bearing Replacer and arbor press. See Pinion Bearing Replacer table.
8) On Dana 44 and 50 axles, remove inner pinion bearing race and install shim pack with oil baffle (if equipped) in carrier bearing bore. Reinstall inner bearing race in carrier.
9) Press inner drive pinion bearing and oil slinger (if equipped) on drive pinion, using Axle Bearing/Seal Plate (T75-1165-B), appropriate Pinion Bearing Replacer and arbor press. See Pinion Bearing Replacer table.

PINION BEARING REPLACER

Application	Tool Number
Dana 35	T85M-4621-B
Dana 44	T53T-4621-B
Dana 50	T70P-4625

DRIVE PINION BEARING PRELOAD & FINAL DEPTH CHECK

Dana 35 Axle - 1) Install drive pinion in carrier. Install new collapsible spacer. Install outer pinion bearing and thrust washer. Lubricate and install drive pinion oil seal. Install pinion yoke, washer and new nut on pinion shaft.
2) Using Yoke Installer (T85T-4851-AH), install pinion yoke. Tighten pinion yoke nut until rotational torque necessary to turn pinion is 15-25 INCH lbs. (1.7-2.8 N.m). If reading exceeds 25 INCH lbs (2.8 N.m), collapsible washer must be replaced.

CAUTION: Always use NEW collapsible spacer when reassembling drive pinion. NEVER tighten pinion yoke nut more than 350 ft. lbs. (475 N.m) as collapsible spacer will be compressed too far.

Dana 44 & 50 -1) Measure original preload shim pack and replace with new shims of equal thickness. Install drive pinion in carrier. Install new preload shim pack on pinion shaft. Install outer bearing and oil slinger. Install drive pinion yoke with washer, deflector, slinger and new nut, using Yoke Installer (T78T-4851-A).
2) Tighten pinion yoke nut to 200-220 ft. lbs. (271-298 N.m). Using torque wrench, check rotational torque necessary to turn drive pinion. Torque reading should be 20-40 INCH lbs. (2.3-4.5 N.m) if preload is correct. If preload reading is too low, remove preload shims from drive pinion. If preload reading is too high, add preload shims to drive pinion.
3) Install appropriate gauge tube. Install side bearing caps and tighten bolts to specification. See TORQUE SPECIFICATIONS table at end of article. With drive pinion at correct depth, remove pinion yoke with holder and yoke remover. Coat pinion yoke oil seal with hypoid gear oil. Install seal using Oil Seal Replacer (T80T-4000-C).
4) Ensure spring behind lip of seal does not jump out while seal is being installed. If spring does jump out, remove and replace seal. Install drive pinion yoke and tighten nut.

RING & PINION GEAR BACKLASH

Dana 35 Axle - 1) With drive pinion depth and preload adjustments properly made, install differential case into housing. Differential master bearings should still be on case. Force differential case away from drive pinion gear so that case is fully seated in cross bores of carrier.
2) Set dial indicator so that tip is against head of ring gear bolt at 90 degrees to bolt. Rock ring gear so that teeth of ring gear mesh fully with drive pinion gear teeth. Force ring gear teeth against drive pinion gear teeth and zero dial indicator. Force ring gear and case away from drive pinion gear. Repeat this procedure until same reading is obtained each time.

1991 DRIVE AXLES
Dana IFS Front Axle (Cont.)

3) This reading, less .008" (.20 mm), is thickness of shim pack that must go under differential side bearing on ring gear side of case. Remove case from carrier. Remove master bearings from case. Place correct shim pack on ring gear hub of case. Place side bearing on hub of case. Drive bearing onto case using Step plate (D80L-630-4), Side Bearing Replacer (T85M-4221-A) and Handle (T80T-4000-W).
4) To determine the correct amount of shims to placed on pinion gear side hub, subtract thickness of shim pack installed on ring gear side of case from total of differential case end play. Total differential case end play was previously determined in steps **3)** and **4)** under DIFFERENTIAL CASE. Add .002" (.08 mm) to figure determined for shim pack thickness on side opposite ring gear.
5) Place required thickness shim pack on hub of case opposite ring gear. Place step plate on ring gear side bearing to protect bearing. Drive remaining side bearing onto case with side bearing replacer. Install side bearing races on side bearings.
6) Install housing spreader and dial indicator on carrier. Spread case to maximum of .015" (.37 mm). Install differential case in carrier. Use soft-faced hammer to ensure that case seats fully in carrier bore. Use care to avoid damaging teeth of ring and pinion gears.
7) If partial or non-hunting/partial ring and pinion gear set is being used, line up mating marks on gears. Remove spreader and dial indicator. Install side bearing caps, making sure that letters stamped on caps match letters stamped on housing.
8) Tighten bearing cap bolts to specification. See TORQUE SPECIFICATIONS table at end of article. Check ring and pinion gear backlash in 3 places equally spaced around ring gear. Backlash range is .005-.008" (.13-20 mm) with allowable maximum variation of .003" (.08 mm).
9) If backlash figure is too high, ring gear must be moved closer to drive pinion gear. If backlash figure is too low, ring gear must be moved away from drive pinion gear. To change backlash readings, move shims from one side of differential case to other. Total thickness of end play shim packs must not change.
10) When backlash adjustment is completed, check tooth contact pattern. See GEAR TOOTH CONTACT PATTERNS article in GENERAL INFORMATION. Pattern will be correct if assembly and adjustments have been done properly.
11) When backlash is correct, apply bead of sealant to mating surfaces of carrier mounting face support arm. Bead should be 1/8" to 1/4" high and 1/4" to 1/2" wide. Install carrier on left axle arm assembly, using 2 carrier bolts as guide pins and being careful not to smear sealant.
12) Install remaining carrier bolts and tighten to specification in clockwise pattern. See TORQUE SPECIFICATIONS table at end of article. Install and tighten carrier shear bolt and nut. Allow one hour curing time for sealant. Fill assembly with hypoid lubricant.
Dana 44 & 50 Axles – 1) With drive pinion depth and preload adjustments properly made, install differential case into housing. Differential master bearings should still be on case. Ensure differential case is fully seated in carrier bores. Set dial indicator so that tip is against head of ring gear mounting bolt at 90 degrees to bolt.
2) Rock ring gear so that teeth of ring gear mesh fully with drive pinion gear teeth. Force ring gear teeth against drive pinion gear teeth and zero dial indicator. Force ring gear and case away from drive pinion gear. Repeat this procedure until same reading is obtained each time.
3) This reading is thickness of shim pack that must go under differential side bearing on ring gear side of case. Place shim pack of correct thickness on ring gear hub.
4) Drive side bearing onto case using Side Bearing Installer (T80T-4000-J). Subtract thickness of shim pack installed on ring gear side of case from total differential case end play. determined earlier. Total differential case end play was previously determined in steps **6)** and **7)** under DIFFERENTIAL CASE.
5) Add .010" (.25 mm) for preload to figure determined for remaining end play. Result is thickness of shim pack that is to be installed on hub of differential case opposite ring gear (drive pinion side of case).
6) Place shim pack on case hub and drive side bearing onto case using side bearing installer. Support case with Step Plate (D80L-630-5) to protect side bearing already installed on ring gear side of case. Install housing spreader and dial indicator on carrier housing. Spread housing maximum of .010" (.25 mm). Remove dial indicator.
7) Place side bearing races on side bearings. Install case in carrier housing. Use soft-faced hammer to seat case assembly in carrier bore. If partial or non-hunting/partial ring and pinion gear set is being used, line up mating marks on gears. Remove housing spreader and dial indicator.
8) Install side bearing caps. Ensure letters stamped on caps match letters stamped on housing. Tighten bearing cap bolts to specification. See TORQUE SPECIFICATIONS table at end of article. Check ring and pinion gear backlash in 3 places equally spaced around ring gear. Backlash range is .005-.009" (.13-.23 mm) with allowable maximum variation of .003" (.08 mm).
9) To change backlash readings, move shims from one side of differential case to other. Total thickness of end play shim packs must not change. When backlash adjustment is completed, check tooth contact pattern. See GEAR TOOTH CONTACT PATTERNS article in GENERAL INFORMATION.
10) When backlash is correct, apply bead of sealant to mating surfaces of carrier mounting face support arm. Bead should be 1/8" to 1/4" high and 1/4" to 1/2" wide. Using 2 guide pins, install carrier on left axle arm assembly.
11) Use new carrier bolts with adhesive-treated threads or clean old bolts and apply locking compound. Tighten carrier bolts. Install and tighten support arm tab bolts on side of carrier. Allow one hour curing time for sealant. Fill assembly with hypoid lubricant.

ASSEMBLY SPECIFICATIONS

AXLE ASSEMBLY SPECIFICATIONS

Application	In. (mm)
Axle Shaft End Play	Non-Adjustable
Ring Gear-To-Pinion Backlash	
Dana 35	.005-.008 (.13-.20)
Dana 44 & 50	.005-.009 (.13-.23)
	INCH Lbs. (N.m)
Drive Pinion Bearing Preload	
Dana 35	15-25 (1.7-2.8)
Dana 44 & 50	20-40 (2.3-4.5)

TORQUE SPECIFICATIONS

TORQUE SPECIFICATIONS

Application	Ft. Lbs. (N.m)
Axle Pivot Bolt	120-150 (163-203)
Axle Pivot Bracket-To-Frame Bolt	70-92 (95-125)
Differential Carrier-To-Carrier Housing Bolt	
Dana 35	40-50 (54-68)
Dana 44 & 50	30-40 (41-54)
Pinion Shaft Yoke Nut	
Dana 35	200-350 (271-475)
Dana 44 & 50	200-220 (271-298)
Ring Gear-To-Case Bolt	
Dana 35	70-90 (95-122)
Dana 44 & 50	50-60 (68-81)
Side Bearing Cap Bolt	
Dana 35	47-67 (64-91)
Dana 44 & 50	80-90 (108-122)
Spindle Nut	
Dana 35	40-50 (54-68)
Dana 44 & 50	50-60 (68-81)
Support Arm-To-Carrier Housing Bolt	
Dana 35	75-95 (102-129)
Dana 44 & 50	85-100 (115-136)
Wheel Lug Nuts	
All Except Bronco, Ranger & F150	140 (190)
Bronco, Ranger & F150	100 (136)

1991 DRIVE AXLES
Dana Limited Slip Differential

Bronco Front Axle,
E250/350 Rear Axle,
"F" Series Front Axle

DESCRIPTION & OPERATION

Limited slip Dana Trac-Lok models 44 IFS, 44 IFS-HD and 60-1U 2-pinion differentials, and Dana Power-Lok model 70 4-pinion differential have the same power flow as the conventional differential.

The limited slip differential adds a more direct power flow. This more direct power flow takes place automatically as driving conditions demand. The more direct power flow is transmitted to axles through clutch packs.

Clutch packs permit regular differential action for turning corners and transmit equal torque to both wheels when driving straight ahead. When one wheel tries to spin because of reduced traction, clutch packs automatically provide more torque to wheel with greater traction.

AXLE RATIO & IDENTIFICATION

Axle application is identified by axle code on Safety Certification Label on left door pillar. Additionally, a metal identification tag, stamped with gear ratio and diameter, is secured to housing. *See Fig. 1*. If axle is equipped with limited slip differential, the gear ratio will include an "L" in the code. See AXLE RATIO IDENTIFICATION article.

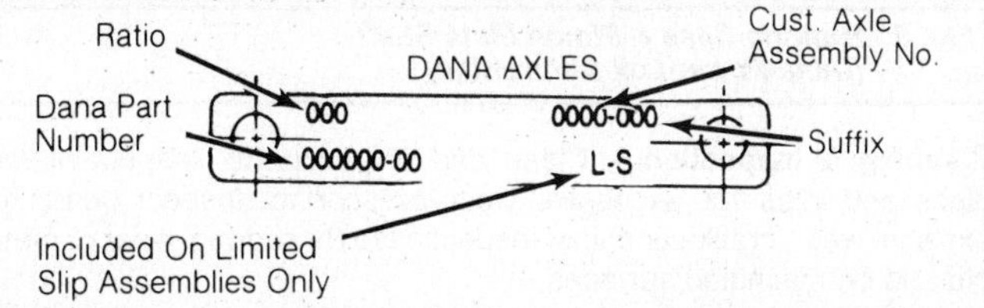
Ratio
DANA AXLES
Cust. Axle Assembly No.
Dana Part Number
000
0000-000
Suffix
000000-00
L-S
Included On Limited Slip Assemblies Only

121040 Courtesy of Ford Motor Co.

Fig. 1: Rear Axle Identification Tag

LUBRICATION

NOTE: If noise or roughness occurs, ensure differential fluid level is correct and fluid is not contaminated.

1) Check lubricant level every 5000 miles or 5 months. Use only Ford Hypoid Gear Lubricant (C6AZ-19580-E or ESW-M2C105-A). Add 2 ounces of Friction Modifier (C8AZ-19B546-A or EST-M2C118-A) for front axles and 8 ounces for rear axles.
2) If noise or roughness is present, operate vehicle to warm lubricant. Drain lubricant while warm. Fill differential with specified lubricant and operate vehicle for 10 miles, making 10 or more figure-8 turns.
3) If slight noise or roughness remains, allow additional 90 miles to flush old lubricant from clutch packs. If noise or roughness remains, disassemble and repair differential.

REMOVAL & INSTALLATION

See DANA 60, 70 & 80 DIFFERENTIALS or DANA IFS FRONT AXLE article.

OVERHAUL

DIFFERENTIAL CASE ASSEMBLY

NOTE: Differential bearings DO NOT have to be removed to overhaul limited slip differential. An axle shaft secured in a vise, with the splines extending about 3" above the jaws, makes an excellent holding fixture for differential case.

Disassembly (Models 44 IFS, 44 IFS-HD & 60-1U) – 1) On models 44 IFS and 60-1U, use a small drift punch to remove roll pin retaining cross shaft. On model 60-1U, remove lock screw retaining cross shaft. Cross shaft is slip fit and may be lifted out without tools.
2) On all models, position Step Plate (T83T-4205-A4) into position on bottom side gear. *See Fig. 2.* Apply grease to centering hole of step plate. Install Forcing Nut (T83T-4205-A2) and Forcing Screw (T83T-4205-A3) into differential case. *See Fig. 3.*
3) Guide forcing screw into step plate. Tighten forcing screw lightly. This will move side gears away from pinion gears and relieve the normal loaded condition. Using a shim or piece of gauge stock of .030" (.762 mm) thickness, push out spherical thrust washers. *See Fig. 4.*

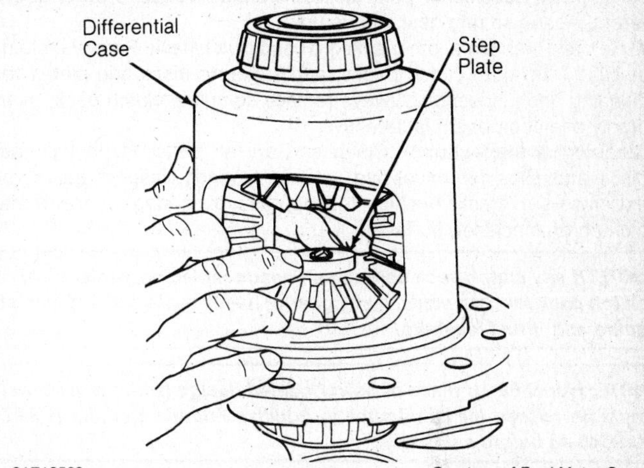
Differential Case
Step Plate

91E13569 Courtesy of Ford Motor Co.

Fig. 2: Installing Step Plate (Dana Trac-Lok Differential)

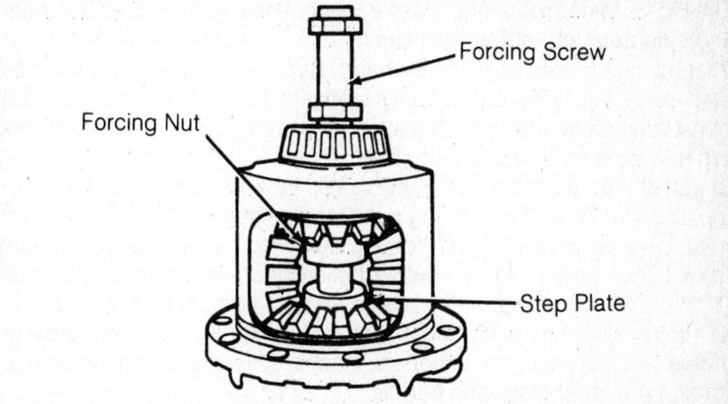
Forcing Screw
Forcing Nut
Step Plate

91G13389 Courtesy of Ford Motor Co.

Fig. 3: Installing Forcing Nut & Forcing Screw (Dana Trac-Lok Differential)

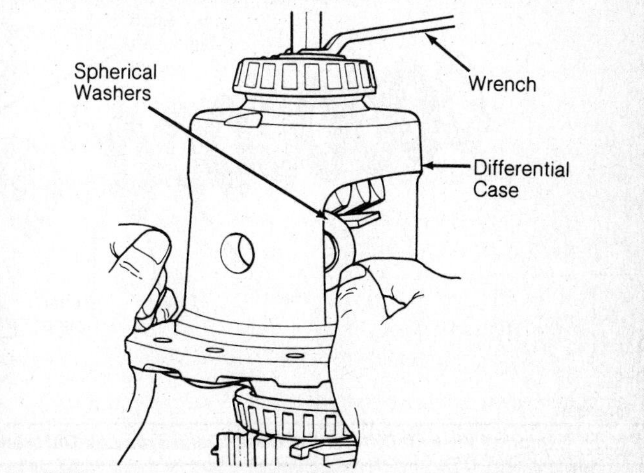
Spherical Washers
Wrench
Differential Case

91J13390 Courtesy of Ford Motor Co.

Fig. 4: Removing Thrust Washers (Dana Trac-Lok Differential)

1991 DRIVE AXLES
Dana Limited Slip Differential (Cont.)

4) Momentarily loosen forcing screw. This is very important to relieve pressure on clutch pack. Retighten forcing screw until a very slight movement of pinion gears is seen. Insert Handle (T83T-4205-A1) into pinion mate shaft bore, and rotate differential case.

5) Rotate differential case until pinion gears can be removed through large opening of differential case. When attempting to rotate side gear, some tightening or loosening of forcing screw may be necessary to permit gear movement.

6) Hold top side gear and clutch pack in case by hand and remove forcing screw and gear rotating tool. Then remove top side gear and clutch pack. Keep clutch pack discs and plates in exact order. Flip differential case so ring gear side is up.

7) Remove step plate, other side gear and clutch pack. Remove retainer clips from both clutch packs, and separate discs and plates for cleaning and inspection. Always replace complete clutch pack, even if only one component is defective.

Cleaning & Inspection - Clean and dry all parts. Inspect plates, discs and clips for excessive wear or scoring. Inspect gears for extreme wear, cracks or chips. Inspect case for scoring, wear or metal pick-up on machined surfaces.

NOTE: If any clutch pack component needs replacing, replace entire clutch pack for both sides. If any gear(s) needs replacing, replace all gears and thrust washers.

NOTE: Model 60-1U discs of newer coated design (without grooves), must be soaked for 20 minutes in Additive Friction Modifier (C8AZ-19B546-A) before assembly.

Reassembly (Model 44 IFS, 44 IFS-HD & 60-1U) - 1) Lubricate thrust face of side gear, discs and plates with Hypoid Gear Lubricant (C6AZ-19580-E). Assemble discs and plates onto side gear splines. *See Fig. 5*. Install retainer clips to ears of plates. Assemble clutch pack and side gear into differential case.

2) Hold clutch pack in place by hand. Reposition case and assemble step plate into side gear. Apply lubricant to centering hole of step plate. Assemble other clutch pack and side gear. Ensure retainer clips are fully seated in pockets of case.

3) Install step plate on top of side gear. Insert forcing screw through top of case. Thread on forcing nut. Position pinion gears in place and hold there by hand. Tighten forcing screw to move side gears away from pinion gears. While holding pinion gears in place, use Handle (T83T-4205-A1) inserted into pinion mate shaft hole to rotate case.

4) Pinion gears should rotate into case. Tighten forcing screw to increase clearance for spherical washers. Remove forcing screw, forcing nut, step plate and handle.

Disassembly (Model 70) - 1) Mark ring half and cover half of differential case. Mark pinion mate shafts and ramps. *See Fig. 6*. Clamp differential in a soft-jawed vise and loosen, but do not remove, bolts holding case halves together. Place case assembly on bench with ring gear side down.

2) Remove case attaching bolts and cover half of case. Remove pinion mate gear, side gear ring and clutch pack. Keep these parts in cover half of case so they will be installed in their original positions. Remove other parts from drive gear half of case.

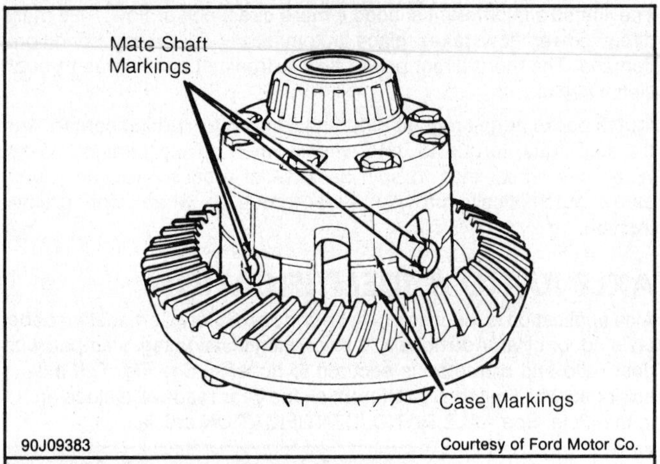
Mate Shaft
Markings
Case Markings
90J09383
Courtesy of Ford Motor Co.

Fig. 6: Marking Case & Pinion Mate Shaft (Dana Power-Lok Differential)

Cleaning & Inspection - Clean and dry all parts. Inspect plates, discs and clips for excessive wear or scoring. Inspect gears for extreme wear, cracks or chips. Inspect case for scoring, wear or metal pick-up on machined surfaces.

NOTE: If any clutch pack component needs replacing, replace entire clutch pack for both sides. If any gear(s) needs replacing, replace all gears and thrust washers.

Reassembly (Model 70) - 1) Position side gear ring from drive gear half of case on pinion flange. Coat clutch plates with Hypoid Gear Lubricant (C6AZ-19580-E or ESW-M2C105-A). Assemble parts in correct order. *See Fig. 7*.

2) Install ring gear half of case over clutch pack and side gear ring. Ensure clutch pack lugs enter slots in case and case bottoms on clutch pack. Hold assembly together and turn case half upside down.

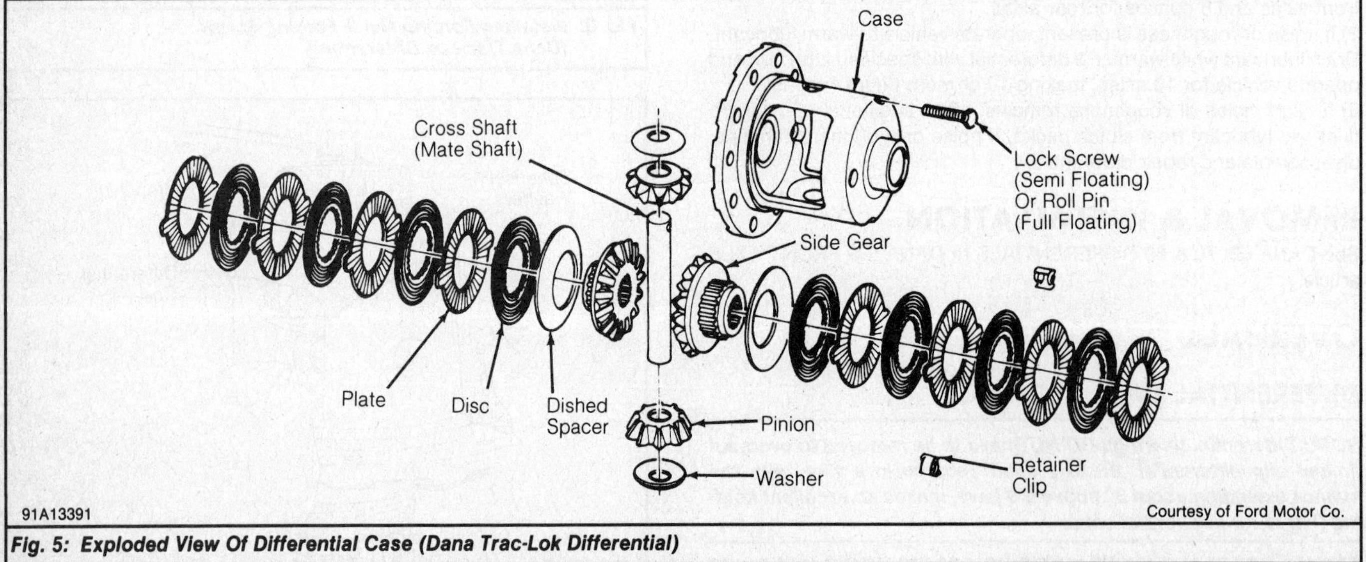
Case
Cross Shaft
(Mate Shaft)
Lock Screw
(Semi Floating)
Or Roll Pin
(Full Floating)
Side Gear
Plate
Disc
Dished
Spacer
Pinion
Washer
Retainer
Clip
91A13391
Courtesy of Ford Motor Co.

Fig. 5: Exploded View Of Differential Case (Dana Trac-Lok Differential)

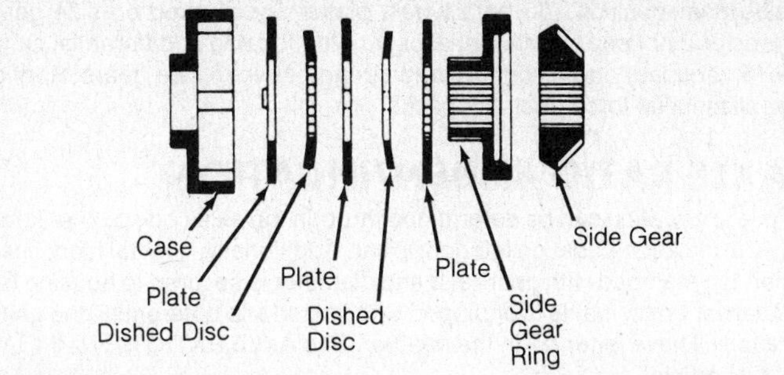

Case
Plate
Dished Disc
Plate
Dished
Disc
Plate
Side
Gear
Ring
Side Gear
91B13392
Courtesy of Ford Motor Co.

Fig. 7: Exploded View Of Clutch Pack (Dana Power-Lok Differential)

3) Install gear in side gear ring. Install mate shaft and pinions on side gear ring. Align mate shaft and case markings. Install cover half mate shaft and pinions. Align case markings. *See Fig. 6.*

4) Install side gear on pinions. Position side gear ring on side gear and pinions. Assemble clutch pack on side gear. Align clutch plate lugs, and install all parts in case. Position cover half of case over assembly.

5) Align case marks made during disassembly. Lubricate bolt threads with axle lube, and install case bolts. *See Fig. 8.* Using both axle shafts, align side gear and side gear ring splines. Tighten case bolts to 65-70 ft. lbs. (89-94 N.m).

6) If bolt heads are marked "180" or have 7 radial lines, tighten case bolts to 90-100 ft. lbs. (122-136 N.m). Remove axle shafts. If properly assembled, each pinion mate cross shaft should be tight on its ramp. If clearance is present, it should not exceed .010" (.254 mm).

TORQUE SPECIFICATIONS

TORQUE SPECIFICATIONS

Application	Ft. Lbs. (N.m)
Case Bolt	[1] 65-70 (89-94)

[1] – If bolt heads are marked "180" or have 7 radial lines, tighten case bolts to 90-100 ft. lbs. (122-136 N.m).

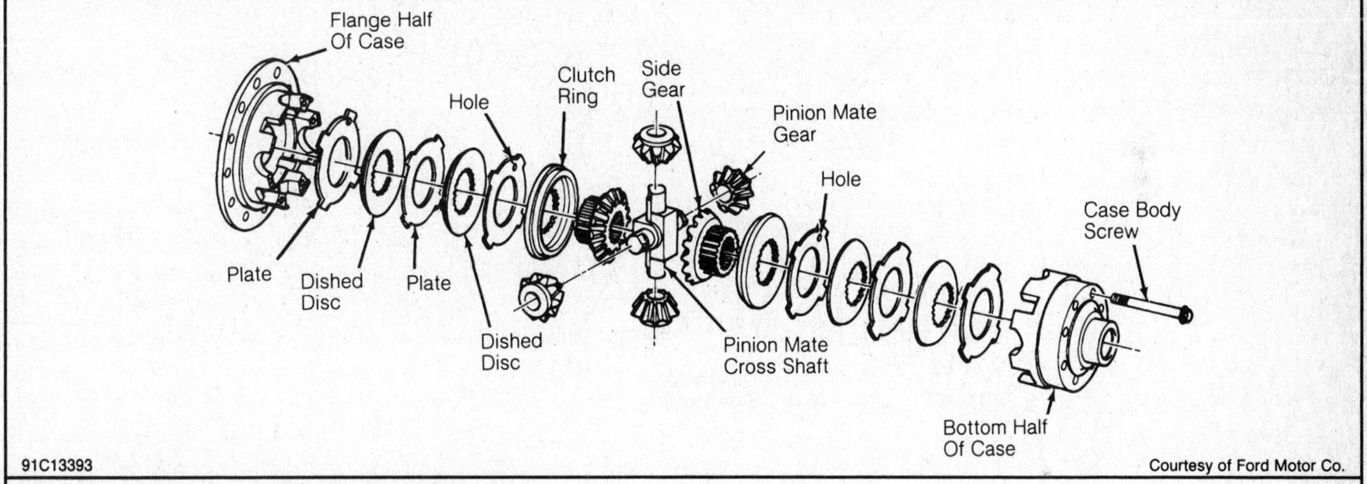

Flange Half
Of Case
Hole
Clutch
Ring
Side
Gear
Pinion Mate
Gear
Hole
Case Body
Screw
Plate
Dished
Disc
Plate
Dished
Disc
Pinion Mate
Cross Shaft
Bottom Half
Of Case
91C13393
Courtesy of Ford Motor Co.

Fig. 8: Exploded View Of Differential (Dana Power-Lok)

1991 DRIVE AXLES
Traction-Lok 7 1/2" & 8 3/4" Differential

Aerostar, Bronco, Explorer, E150, F150, Ranger

DESCRIPTION

The positive traction 7 1/2" and 8 3/4" limited slip differentials employ 2 sets of multiple disc clutches to control differential action. A differential with 7 1/2" or 8 3/4" ring gear is available on Aerostar, Explorer and Ranger models. The differential with 8 3/4" ring gear is available on Bronco, E150 and F150. The 7 1/2" side gear mounting distance is controlled by 7 plates on each side: 3 steel, 4 friction and maximum of 2 steel shims selectively fit to control side gear position.

The 8 3/4" side gear mounting distance is controlled by 7 plates on each side: 4 steel, 3 friction and one steel shim selectively fit to control side gear position. On both types, plates are stacked on side gear hubs and housed in differential case. Also located in differential case is "S" shaped, one-piece, preload spring between side gears. Spring applies initial force to clutch packs.

AXLE RATIO & IDENTIFICATION

Axle application can be determined through the axle code on the Safety Certification Label on left door pillar. Additionally, a metal identification tag stamped with gear ratio and diameter is secured to housing by 2 carrier bolts. If axle is equipped with limited slip differential, the gear ratio will have letter "L" in the number. See AXLE RATIO IDENTIFICATION article.

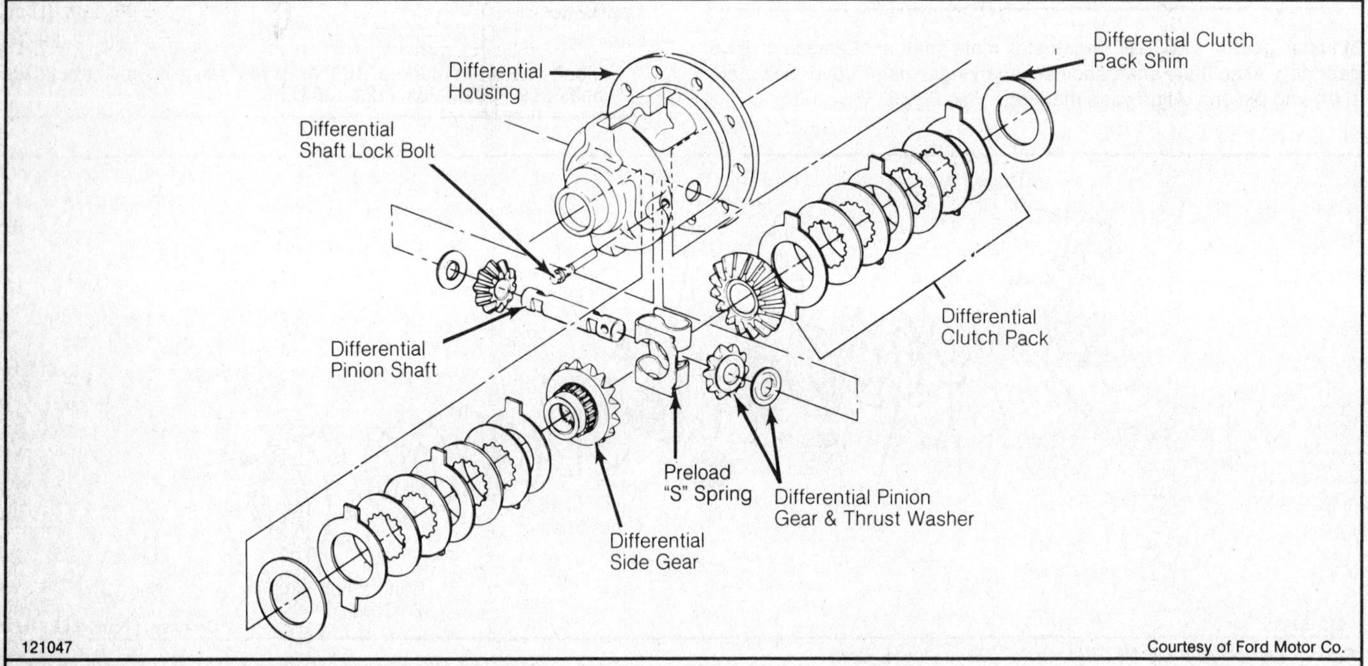
Differential Housing
Differential Clutch Pack Shim
Differential Shaft Lock Bolt
Differential Clutch Pack
Differential Pinion Shaft
Preload "S" Spring
Differential Pinion Gear & Thrust Washer
Differential Side Gear
121047
Courtesy of Ford Motor Co.

Fig. 1: Exploded View of 7 1/2" Traction-Lok Differential

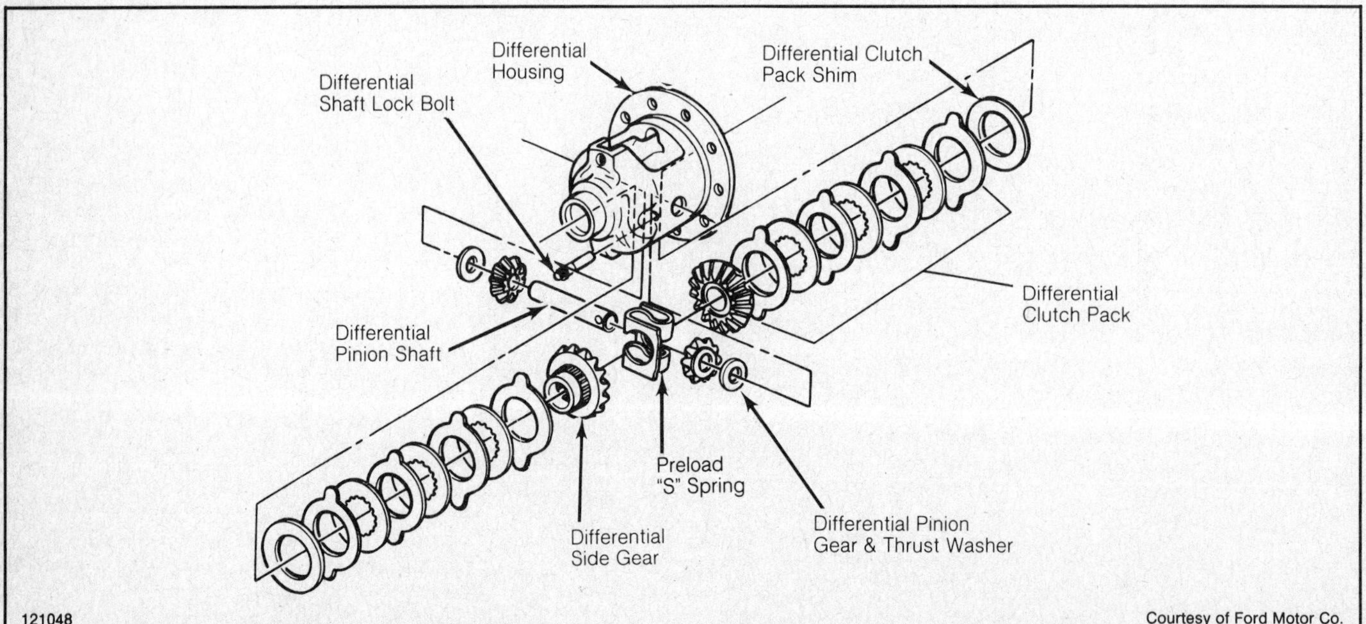
Differential Housing
Differential Clutch Pack Shim
Differential Shaft Lock Bolt
Differential Clutch Pack
Differential Pinion Shaft
Preload "S" Spring
Differential Side Gear
Differential Pinion Gear & Thrust Washer
121048
Courtesy of Ford Motor Co.

Fig. 2: Exploded View of 8 3/4" Traction-Lok Differential

1991 DRIVE AXLES
Traction-Lok 7 1/2" & 8 3/4" Differential (Cont.)

LUBRICATION

Check lubricant level every 5000 miles or 5 months. Use only Ford Hypoid Gear Lubricant (E0AZ-19580-A or ESP-M2C154-A) and Friction Modifier (C8AZ-19B546-A or EST-M2C118-A).

ON-VEHICLE TESTING

NOTE: A slight noise in differential on tight turns after extended highway driving is considered acceptable and has no detrimental effect.

1) Raise one wheel and leave opposite wheel firmly on ground. Install Traction-Lok Torque Adapter (T59L-4204-A) on wheel mounting studs. Place transmission in "N".
2) Using a torque wrench, note torque required to keep wheel rotating through several revolutions. Break-away torque should be 20 ft. lbs. (27 N.m). Torque may decrease while turning wheel. Wheel should turn smoothly without slipping.

REMOVAL & INSTALLATION

DIFFERENTIAL

NOTE: In-vehicle adjustments are possible without removing differential case from axle housing. On Aerostar with plastic axle housing cover, replace old cover with new one whenever it is removed.

Removal & Installation – Differentials are removed and installed using same procedures as conventional differentials. See 7 1/2" RING GEAR DIFFERENTIALS and 8 3/4" & 10 1/4" RING GEAR DIFFERENTIALS articles.

CLUTCH PACKS

Removal – 1) Raise vehicle. Remove rear wheels and brake drums. Remove cover from axle housing and drain lubricant. Working through cover opening, remove pinion shaft lock bolt and pinion shaft.
2) Push axle shafts inward until "C" locks at button end of shafts are clear of side gear recess. Remove "C" locks. Pull axle shafts out of housing.

NOTE: Carefully remove drive shafts to avoid damaging axle seals. Shafts must be completely removed from axle housing.

3) Using drift, drive "S" shaped preload spring half-way out of differential housing. Rotate differential housing 180 degrees. Hold "S" shaped preload spring with pliers and tap spring until it is removed from differential. *See Fig. 3.*

NOTE: Because of spring tension, remove preload spring carefully.

4) Using Pinion Rotator (T84P-4205-A for 7 1/2" or T80P-4205-A for 8 3/4") with a 12" extension, rotate pinion gears until gears can be removed from differential. Remove side gears and clutch pack with shim. Tag gears and clutch packs as left and right side. DO NOT use cleaning solvent on clutch plate surfaces.

NOTE: DO NOT interchange clutches or shims.

5) Inspect clutch plates for uneven or extreme wear. Steel plates must be free from burrs, nicks and scratches. Internally splined clutch plates should be inspected for condition of material. Replace plates if internal teeth are worn or thickness is less than .058" (1.5 mm).
6) Install Differential Clutch Gauge (T84P-4946-A for 7 1/2" or T80P-4946-A for 8 3/4") on side gear clutch pack without shim. Tighten to 60 INCH lbs. (6.7 N.m). Using feeler gauge, select thickest blade that will enter between clutch gauge and clutch pack. *See Fig. 4.* This reading will be thickness of new shim for that clutch pack. Repeat procedure for opposite clutch pack.
Installation – 1) Lubricate friction plates with Friction Modifier (C8AZ-19B546-A or EST-M2C118-A) before reassembly. Install left side gear, clutch pack and new shim into cavity of differential housing. Repeat on right side.

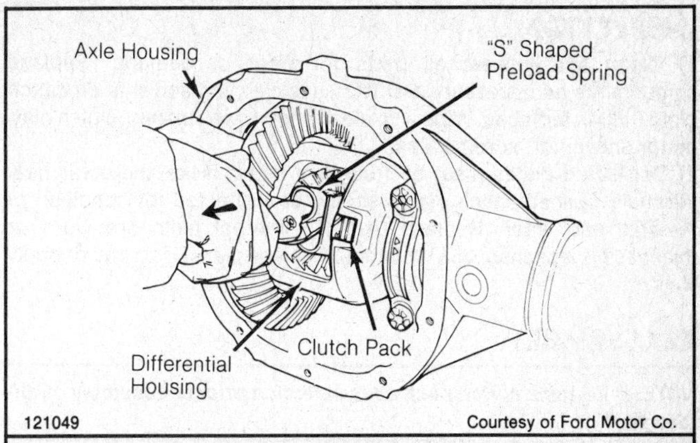
Axle Housing
"S" Shaped
Preload Spring
Differential
Housing
Clutch Pack
121049
Courtesy of Ford Motor Co.

Fig. 3: Removing Clutch Pack Preload Spring

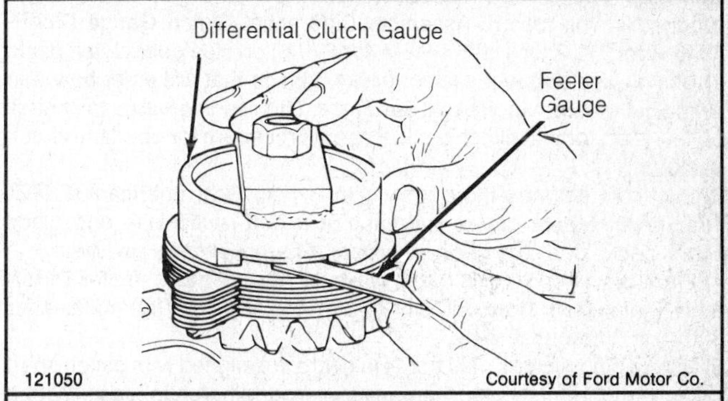
Differential Clutch Gauge
Feeler
Gauge
121050
Courtesy of Ford Motor Co.

Fig. 4: Measuring Clutch Pack Shim Size

2) Place pinion gears and thrust washers 180 degrees apart on side gears. Install pinion gear rotator with 12" extension. Rotate tool until pinion gears are aligned with pinion shaft hole. Remove tool from differential housing.
3) Using soft-faced hammer, drive "S" shaped preload spring into position. Ensure spring is undamaged. Install axle shafts and "C" locks. Push axle shaft as far outboard as possible. Install pinion shaft and lock bolt. Apply Threadlock and Sealer (E0AZ-19554-B) to lock bolt.
4) Install rear drums and wheels. See ON-VEHICLE TESTING to ensure unit is set up correctly. Using Silicone Sealant (D6AZ-19562-B), install rear cover assembly and tighten bolts to specification. Fill axle assembly with lubricant to bottom of filler hole and install oil filler plug.

OVERHAUL

DISASSEMBLY

1) Remove carrier assembly from vehicle. See 7 1/2" RING GEAR DIFFERENTIALS and 8 3/4" & 10 1/4" RING GEAR DIFFERENTIALS articles. Remove and discard bolts securing ring gear to differential case assembly.
2) Tap ring gear with a soft-faced hammer to remove. Remove differential pinion shaft lock bolt and pinion shaft. Using a drift, drive out "S" shaped preload spring.

NOTE: Because of spring tension, remove preload spring carefully.

3) Using Pinion Gear Rotator (T84P-4205-A for 7 1/2" or T80P-4205-A for 8 3/4"), rotate pinion gears until gears and thrust washers can be removed. Remove side gears, thrust washers, clutch plates and shims from right and left cavities and tag them accordingly.

NOTE: DO NOT interchange clutches or shims.

1991 DRIVE AXLES
Traction-Lok 7 1/2" & 8 3/4" Differential (Cont.)

INSPECTION

1) Clean and inspect all parts for wear or damage. Replace components as necessary. DO NOT use cleaning solvents on clutch plate friction surfaces. Wipe with clean shop towel. Inspect clutch plates for uneven or extreme wear.

2) Dog-eared plates must be free from burrs, nicks and scratches. Internally splined clutch plates should be inspected for condition of material and wear. Replace plates if internal teeth are worn or thickness is less than .058" (1.5 mm). Replace plates if scored or badly worn.

REASSEMBLY

NOTE: Determine clutch pack shim selection prior to assembly of differential.

1) Lubricate clutch plates with Friction Modifier (C8AZ-19B546-A or EST-M2C118-A). Assemble clutch pack on side gear (no shim is required at this point). Assemble Differential Clutch Gauge (T84P-4946-A for 7 1/2" or T80P-4946-A for 8 3/4") on side gear clutch pack.

2) Using a feeler gauge, select thickest blade that will enter between clutch gauge and clutch pack. *See Fig. 4*. This reading will be thickness of new shim for that clutch pack. Repeat procedure for opposite clutch pack.

3) Lubricate all parts thoroughly with Hypoid Gear Lubricant (E0AZ-19580-AA). Mount differential case in a soft-jawed vise and place clutch packs and side gears in proper differential case cavities.

4) Place pinion gears and thrust washers on side gears. Install Differential Pinion Gear Rotator (T84P-4205-A for 7 1/2" or T80P-4205-A for 8 3/4") in differential case.

5) Rotate pinion gears until bores in gears are aligned with pinion shaft holes in differential case. Remove tool from differential case. With a soft-faced hammer, install "S" shaped preload spring in differential case.

6) Install pinion shaft and lock bolt. DO NOT tighten lock bolt yet. Before installing differential in vehicle, check bench torque.

7) Using Traction-Lok Torque Adapter (T59L-4204-A), check torque required to rotate one side gear while other is held stationary. *See Fig. 5*. Initial break-away torque should be 20 ft. lbs. (27 N.m). Rotating torque required to keep side gear turning may fluctuate.

8) Lightly coat pinion shaft lock bolt threads with Threadlock and Sealer (E0AZ-19554-B). Install in case and tighten. Clean tapped holes in ring gear with solvent.

9) If new bolts have a green coating over approximately 1/2" of threaded area, use as is. If not coated, apply a small amount of threadlock and sealer. Tighten to 70-85 ft. lbs. (95-115 N.m).

10) Install differential case and ring gear. Using Silicone Sealant (D6AZ-19562-B), install rear cover assembly and tighten bolts. Fill axle assembly with lubricant to bottom of filler hole and install oil filler plug.

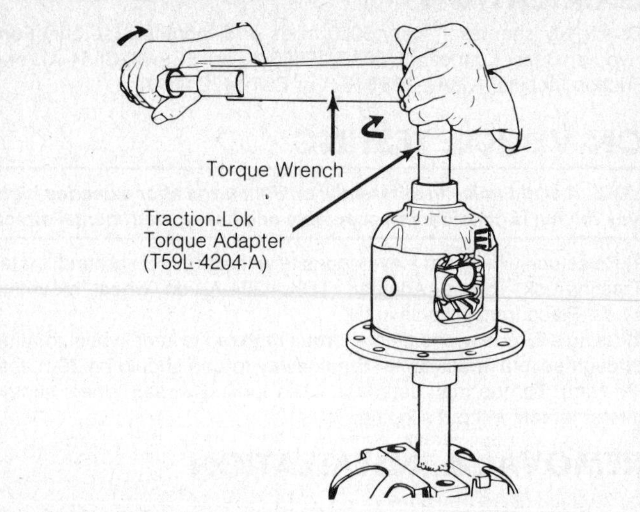
Torque Wrench
Traction-Lok
Torque Adapter
(T59L-4204-A)
121051
Courtesy of Ford Motor Co.

Fig. 5: Checking Operation of Traction-Lok Differential

ASSEMBLY SPECIFICATIONS

AXLE ASSEMBLY SPECIFICATIONS

Application	In. (mm)
7 1/2" Differential	
Ring Gear Runout	.004 (.102)
Ring Gear-To-Pinion Backlash	.008-.15 (.20-.38)
8 3/4" Differential	
Ring Gear Runout	.008 (.203)
Ring Gear-To-Pinion Backlash	.008-.18 (.20-.46)

TORQUE SPECIFICATIONS

TORQUE SPECIFICATIONS

Application	Ft. Lbs. (N.m)
Axle Pivot Bolt	120-150 (163-203)
Axle Pivot Bracket-To-Frame Bolt	70-92 (95-124)
Axle Stud	190-230 (258-311)
Oil Filler Plug	15-30 (20-41)
Pinion Shaft Lock Bolt	15-30 (20-41)
Pinion Shaft Yoke Nut	160-170 (217-230)
Rear Cover Assembly Bolt	25-35 (34-47)
Ring Gear-To-Case Bolt	70-90 (95-115)
Side Bearing Cap Bolt	75-85 (102-115)
	INCH Lbs. (N.m)
Drive Pinion Bearing Preload	
7 1/2" Differential	
New Bearings	16-29 (1.8-3.2)
Used Bearings	8-14 (.9-1.6)
8 3/4" Differential	
New Bearings	17-27 (2.0-3.0)
Used Bearings	8-14 (.9-1.6)

1991 DRIVE AXLES
Traction-Lok 10 1/4" Ring Gear Differential

F250/350

DESCRIPTION

The traction-lok axle assembly is identical to conventional axle assembly except for differential case. The traction-lok differential case employs 2 sets of multiple disc clutches to control differential action. Side gear mounting distance is controlled by 10 plates on each side: 5 splined plates, 5 stationary plates and one Belleville spring plate. Plates are stacked on side gear hubs and housed in differential case.

AXLE RATIO & IDENTIFICATION

Axle application can be determined through the axle code on the Safety Certification Label on left door pillar. Additionally, a metal identification tag, stamped with gear ratio and diameter, is secured to housing by 2 carrier bolts. If axle is equipped with limited slip differential, the gear ratio will have letter "L" in the number. See AXLE MODEL IDENTIFICATION table in AXLE RATIO IDENTIFICATION article.

LUBRICATION

Check lubricant level every 5000 miles or 5 months. Use Ford Hypoid Gear Lubricant (E0AZ-19580-A or ESP-M2C154-A) and Friction Modifier (C8AZ-19B546-A or EST-M2C118-A).

ON-VEHICLE TESTING

NOTE: A slight noise in differential on tight turns after extended highway driving is considered acceptable and has no detrimental effect.

1) Raise one wheel and leave opposite wheel firmly on ground. Install Traction-Lok Torque Adapter (T59L-4204-A) on wheel mounting studs. Place transmission in Neutral.
2) Using a torque wrench, note torque required to keep wheel rotating through several revolutions. Break-away torque should be 30 ft. lbs. (41 N.m). Torque may decrease while turning wheel. Wheel should turn smoothly without slipping.

REMOVAL & INSTALLATION

Differential is removed and installed using same procedure as conventional differential. See REMOVAL & INSTALLATION procedure in 8 3/4" & 10 1/4" RING GEAR DIFFERENTIALS article.

OVERHAUL

DISASSEMBLY

1) With carrier assembly removed from vehicle, remove and discard bolts securing ring gear to differential case assembly. Remove ring gear by tapping gear with a soft-faced hammer, or press gear from case.
2) Remove differential pinion shaft lock bolt. Install Differential Holder (D83T-4205-A) in a vise. Install differential assembly onto holder with ring gear side facing up. Using a drift, drive pinion shaft from case.
3) Install Step Plate (D83T-4205-C2) in bottom side gear bore. *See Fig. 2.* Apply a small amount of grease to step plate centering hole. Install Nut (part of D83T-4205-C) in upper side gear. Hold nut in position while installing Hex Head Screw (part of D83T-4205-C). *See Fig. 3.*

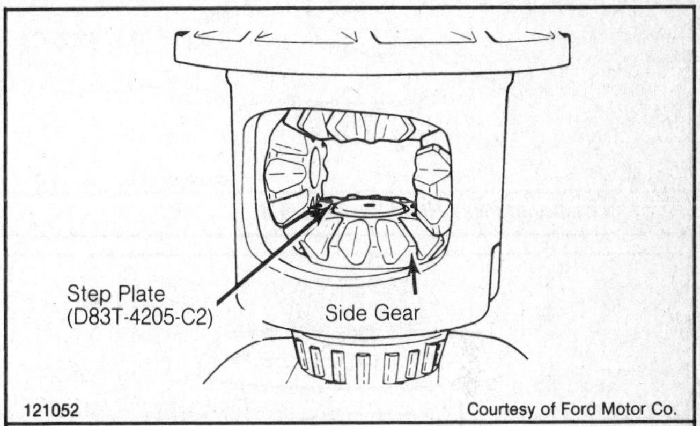
Step Plate
(D83T-4205-C2)
Side Gear
121052
Courtesy of Ford Motor Co.

Fig. 2: Installing Step Plate in Side Gear Bore

4) Install a bar in hole of nut to keep nut from turning, and tighten hex head screw to force side gears away from pinion mating gears. Using a proper size feeler gauge, push pinion gear thrust washers out from between pinion gears and case.
5) Remove thrust washers and back off hex head screw until loose (about one turn). Ensure vise is tightened securely. Using Differential Rotating Handle (T86T-4205-A) installed in pinion shaft bore, turn case to remove pinion gears.

NOTE: When separating clutch plates, note disassembly sequence. Clutch plates must be reassembled in the same sequence.

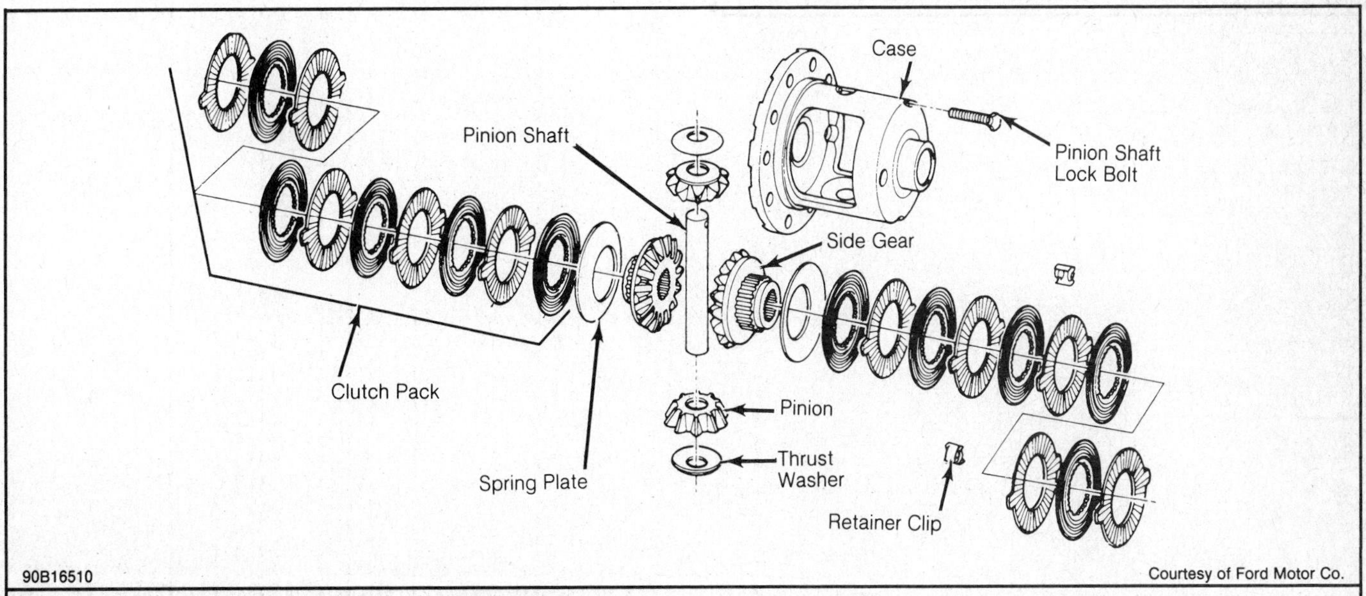
Case
Pinion Shaft
Pinion Shaft
Lock Bolt
Side Gear
Clutch Pack
Pinion
Thrust
Washer
Spring Plate
Retainer Clip
90B16510
Courtesy of Ford Motor Co.

Fig. 1: Exploded View of 10 1/4" Traction-Lok Differential

Traction-Lok 10 1/4" Ring Gear Differential (Cont.)

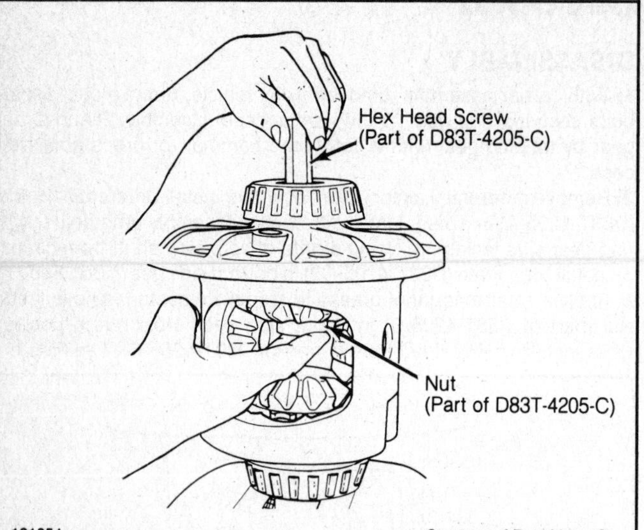
Hex Head Screw
(Part of D83T-4205-C)
Nut
(Part of D83T-4205-C)
121054
Courtesy of Ford Motor Co.

Fig. 3: Positioning Hex Head Screw & Nut

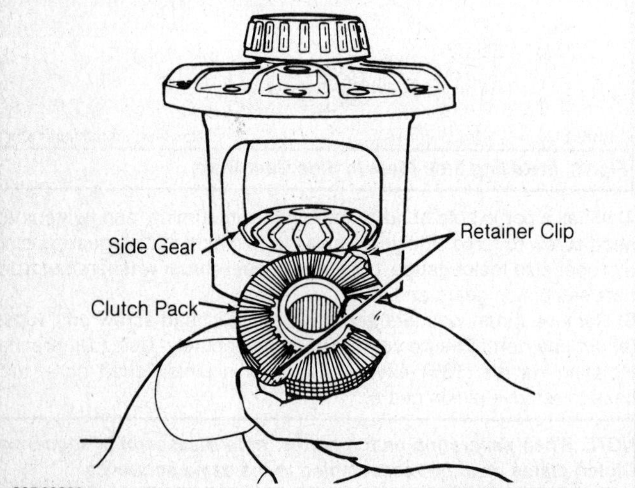
Side Gear
Retainer Clip
Clutch Pack
90D09380
Courtesy of Ford Motor Co.

Fig. 4: Removing Side Gear, Retainer Clip & Clutch Pack

6) Remove hex head screw and step plate. Remove side gears, retainer clips and clutch pack assemblies. *See Fig. 4*. Remove retainer clips from both clutch packs. Separate, clean and inspect clutch plates.

NOTE: DO NOT clean clutch components with solvent. Clutch components should be cleaned with a lint-free shop towel only.

INSPECTION

Inspect clutch plates for uneven or extreme wear. Steel plates must be free from burrs, nicks and scratches. Internally splined clutch plates should be inspected for condition of material. Replace plates if internal teeth are worn. Replace plates if scored or thickness is less than .058" (1.5 mm).

REASSEMBLY

1) To reassemble, reverse disassembly procedures. Lubricate clutch plates with Friction Modifier (C8AZ-19B546-A or EST-M2C118-A). Lubricate side gear thrust face and thrust washers with Hypoid Gear Lubricant (E0AZ-19580-A or ESP-M2C154-A).

2) Ensure thrust washers are installed with concave side facing inward. Ensure clutch plate retainer clips are completely assembled and seated into clutch plates ears. *See Fig. 1*.

3) Apply Threadlock and Sealer (E0AZ-19554-B) to ring gear bolts and tighten to 100-120 ft. lbs. (135-162 N.m). Tighten pinion shaft lock bolt to 15-30 ft. lbs. (20-40 N.m).

TORQUE SPECIFICATIONS

TORQUE SPECIFICATIONS

Application	Ft. Lbs. (N.m)
Bearing Cap Bolt	80-95 (108-129)
Pinion Nut	160 (217)
Pinion Shaft Lock Bolt	15-30 (20-40)
Rear Cover Bolt	25-35 (34-47)
Ring Gear Bolt	100-120 (135-163)
Wheel Lug Nut	140 (190)

1991 DRIVE AXLES
4WD Steering Knuckles

Aerostar, Bronco, Explorer, Ranger, "F" Series

NOTE: Unless specified otherwise, references to "F" Series include "F" Series Super Duty.

DESCRIPTION

Open steering knuckles, used on all models, provide a sharper turning angle, decreasing vehicle's turning radius. On Aerostar, steering knuckles are attached to upper and lower control arms by ball joints. On all models except F350, steering knuckles are attached to axle by ball joints. On F350, steering knuckles are attached to axle by king pins.

REMOVAL & INSTALLATION

BALL JOINT TYPE

Removal (Except Aerostar & F350) - 1) Raise and support vehicle. Remove wheel and tire. Remove locking hub, spindle and caliper. See REMOVAL & INSTALLATION in appropriate BRAKES article. See REMOVAL & INSTALLATION in LOCKING HUBS article. Disconnect steering linkage if necessary.

2) Disconnect tie-rod from knuckle. Remove upper ball joint snap ring. Loosen upper and lower ball joint mount nuts. Remove camber adjuster. Break ball joints loose from axle housing and separate components. Remove knuckle.

3) To remove ball joints, place steering knuckle in vise and remove snap ring from bottom ball joint socket (if equipped). Remove lower ball joint first, and then upper ball joint.

NOTE: Lower ball joint must always be installed first.

Installation - Install lower and upper ball joints in steering knuckle (if removed). Put new nut on lower ball joint. Place knuckle onto axle arm. Install camber adjuster in same position as when removed. Install nuts and snap rings onto ball joints. To complete installation, reverse removal procedure.

CAUTION: If proper tightening sequence is not followed, excessive steering knuckle turning effort may result. See TORQUE SPECIFICATIONS table at end of article. When aligning ball joint nut to install cotter pin, always tighten nut to align. Never loosen nut to align hole.

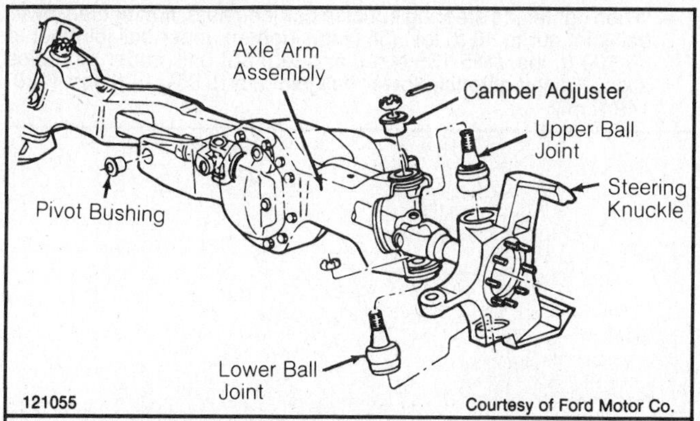
Axle Arm
Assembly
Camber Adjuster
Upper Ball
Joint
Steering
Knuckle
Pivot Bushing
Lower Ball
Joint
121055
Courtesy of Ford Motor Co.

Fig. 1: Exploded View of Ball Joint-Type Steering Knuckle (Except Aerostar & F350)

Removal (Aerostar) - 1) Position front wheels in straight-ahead position. Raise vehicle with weight resting on lower control arms to keep chassis springs compressed. Remove wheel and tire. Remove brake caliper and rotor. See REMOVAL & INSTALLATION in appropriate BRAKES article.

WARNING: DO NOT remove nut from lower control arm ball joint unless chassis spring is compressed by weight of vehicle resting on lower control arm.

2) Remove cotter pin and nut from tie rod end. *See Fig. 2.* Disconnect tie rod end from steering knuckle. Remove cotter pin and nut from lower control arm ball joint at steering knuckle. Separate lower control arm from steering knuckle.

3) Remove nut and washer from outer axle shaft. Using Hub Remover/ Installer (T81P-1104-A and C) with Hub Knuckle Adapters (T83P-1104-BH1 and T88P-1104-A1) or equivalent, free the outer axle shaft from splines in center of hub and bearing assembly.

4) Remove bolt and nut retaining steering knuckle to upper control arm ball joint. Separate and remove steering knuckle from upper control arm ball joint. Wire axle shaft to body to maintain in level position.

Installation - 1) With hub attached to steering knuckle, position hub over outer axle shaft. Ensure outer axle shaft splines are aligned in center of hub. Position steering knuckle over lower ball joint stud on lower control arm. Install lower ball joint nut and tighten to specification. See TORQUE SPECIFICATIONS table at end of article. Install cotter pin.

2) Install washer and hub nut. Lightly tighten hub nut to seat CV joint on back side of steering knuckle. DO NOT tighten to specification at this time.

3) Position steering knuckle to upper control arm ball joint stud. Install bolt and nut and tighten to specification. See TORQUE SPECIFICATIONS table at end of article. Connect tie rod end to steering knuckle. Tighten nut and install cotter pin.

4) Tighten hub nut to 170-210 ft. lbs. (230-285 N.m). Install rotor and caliper. Install wheel and tire. Install wheel nuts and tighten to specification. Lower vehicle.

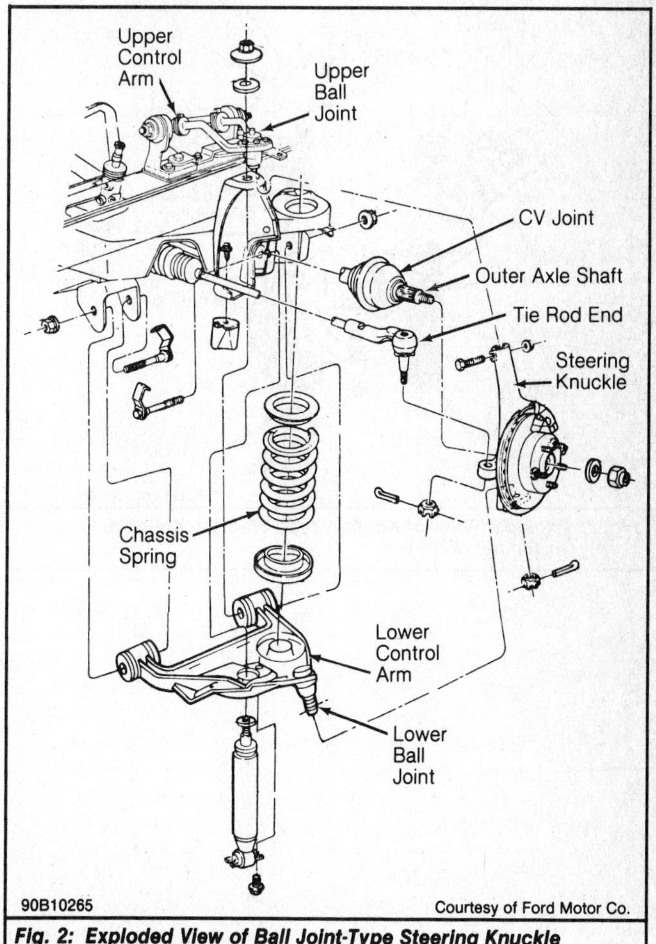
Upper
Control
Arm
Upper
Ball
Joint
CV Joint
Outer Axle Shaft
Tie Rod End
Steering
Knuckle
Chassis
Spring
Lower
Control
Arm
Lower
Ball
Joint
90B10265
Courtesy of Ford Motor Co.

Fig. 2: Exploded View of Ball Joint-Type Steering Knuckle Assembly (Aerostar)

1991 DRIVE AXLES
4WD Steering Knuckles (Cont.)

KINGPIN TYPE

Removal (F350) – 1) Raise and support vehicle. Remove wheel and tire. Remove brake caliper. Remove locking hub. See appropriate LOCKING HUBS article.

2) Remove hub and rotor assembly. See ROTOR under REMOVAL & INSTALLATION in appropriate BRAKES article. Remove spindle, splash shield and caliper support from steering knuckle. Carefully pull axle shaft assembly through hole in steering knuckle.

3) Disconnect steering linkage at steering knuckle. Evenly remove bolts from spindle cap. *See Fig. 3.* Spring pressure will force cap upward. Remove spindle cap, compression spring and gasket.

4) Remove lower kingpin and retainer. Remove tapered bushing. Remove steering knuckle from axle housing. Using 7/8" hex stock, remove upper kingpin from axle housing. Using 2-jaw puller and Step Plate (D80L-630-7), remove grease seal, bearing, bearing cup and grease retainer.

Installation – 1) Coat grease retainer-to-lower kingpin contact surface with RTV sealant. Install grease retainer in axle housing with concave portion toward upper kingpin.

2) Install bearing cup until it bottoms on grease retainer. Pack bearing and axle housing area with grease and install bearing. Using Seal Installer (T86T-3110-AH), install new grease seal.

3) Install upper kingpin and tighten to specification. Install steering knuckle and tapered bushing. Install lower kingpin and retainer. Evenly tighten retainer bolts to specification. See TORQUE SPECIFICATIONS table.

4) Install retainer, compression spring and spindle cap. Tighten spindle cap bolts to specification. Lubricate upper and lower kingpins through grease fittings.

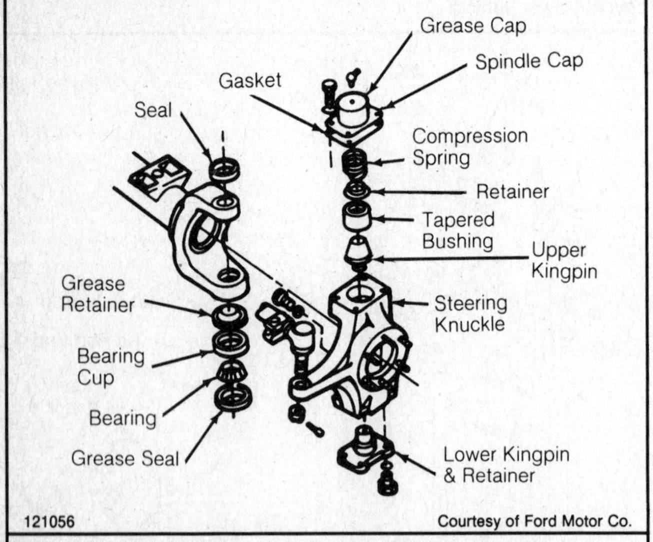
Grease Cap
Spindle Cap
Gasket
Seal
Compression Spring
Retainer
Tapered Bushing
Upper Kingpin
Grease Retainer
Steering Knuckle
Bearing Cup
Bearing
Grease Seal
Lower Kingpin & Retainer
121056
Courtesy of Ford Motor Co.

Fig. 3: Exploded View of Kingpin Type Steering Knuckle Assembly (F350)

ADJUSTMENTS

TURNING ANGLE

NOTE: Turning angle is nonadjustable. If turning angle is not within specification, replace worn or damaged parts. See TURNING ANGLE SPECIFICATIONS table.

TURNING ANGLE SPECIFICATIONS

Application	Turning Angle In Degrees
Aerostar, Explorer & Ranger	[1]
Bronco	[2] 36.0
"F" Series	
F150	[2] 36.0
F250 w/Model 44 Front Axle	33.4
F250 w/Model 50 Front Axle	30.3
F350	30.3

[1] – Information not available from manufacturer.
[2] – Turning angle should be 34 degrees on models with 10 X 15 tires.

TORQUE SPECIFICATIONS

TORQUE SPECIFICATIONS

Application	Ft. Lbs. (N.m)
Ball Joint Type	
Ball Joint Nut	
Aerostar	
Lower	80-120 (108-163)
Upper	27-37 (37-50)
Bronco & F150/250	
Lower	90-110 (122-149)
Upper	100 (136)
Explorer & Ranger	
Upper & Lower	[1]
Spindle-To-Steering Knuckle Bolt	
Bronco & F150/250	50-60 (68-81)
Explorer & Ranger	35-45 (47-61)
Kingpin Type	
Lower Kingpin Bolt	70-90 (95-122)
Spindle Cap Bolt	70-90 (95-122)
Upper Kingpin	500-600 (678-813)
Wheel Lug Nut	
Aerostar, Explorer & Ranger	85-115 (115-156)
Bronco & F150	100 (136)
F250/350	140 (190)

[1] – When tightening steering knuckle ball joint nuts, first tighten lower ball joint nut to 40 ft. lbs. (54 N.m). Tighten upper ball joint nut to 85-100 ft. lbs. (115-136 N.m), and turn nut until cotter pin holes align. Finish tightening lower ball joint nut to 95-110 ft. lbs. (129-149 N.m).

1991 DRIVE AXLES
Locking Hubs

Bronco, Explorer, Ranger, "F" Series

DESCRIPTION

The front driving axle hub locks are either automatically or manually actuated. When actuated, hub lock body assembly locks hub and wheel and tire assembly to front drive axle shaft.

When released, front drive axle shaft is disengaged from hub body assembly and hub and tire and wheel assembly rotate freely on spindle. Two opposed tapered roller bearings allow hub and wheel and tire assembly to rotate on spindle. A hub seal is installed behind inner bearing to prevent wheel bearing lubricant from contaminating brake pad and rotor surfaces.

OPERATION

AUTOMATIC LOCKING HUBS

When using 2WD, shift transfer case in 2H position by pushing selector LOW RANGE and/or 4 X 4 push buttons until both Amber indicator lights are off. To disengage automatic locking hubs, move vehicle in opposite direction (forward or reverse) and drive a minimum of 10 feet in a straight line. Always disengage hub locks before driving vehicle on dry, hard pavement.

Shifting Between 2H & 4H – Transfer case can be shifted between 2H and 4H with vehicle stopped or at normal road speed by depressing selector 4 X 4 button. The Amber indicator light will illuminate when vehicle is in 4WD.

Shifting Between High/Low Ranges – Stop vehicle and shift transmission to Neutral. On manual transmission models, disengage the clutch before depressing LOW RANGE button. On all models, LOW RANGE light should illuminate. DO NOT attempt to shift from or to low range with vehicle in motion.

MANUAL LOCKING HUBS

When using 2WD, shift transfer case to 2H position and manually turn hub lock selector knob counterclockwise to FREE position. When using 4WD, lock both hubs by turning selector knob clockwise to LOCK position. If hub teeth do not engage with knob in this position, a slight movement of wheel in either direction will complete locking procedure.

If vehicle is stopped, place transmission in Neutral and select transfer case shift position. If vehicle is moving, transfer case may be shifted between 2H and 4H only, providing hub locks are in LOCK position. Shifting to or from 4L position requires vehicle be fully stopped and transmission in Neutral.

Both hubs must be set in same function to avoid excess front differential wear on non-traction-lock front axles or steering pull on traction-lock front axles.

CAUTION: DO NOT shift to or from 4L when vehicle is in motion or gear clash will damage transfer case. Also, transfer case will be damaged if shifted from 2H to 4H with hub locks in the FREE position when vehicle is in motion.

ADJUSTMENTS

FRONT WHEEL BEARINGS

Bronco, F150/250 W/Dana 44 IFS and Manual Locking Hubs – 1) Raise and support front of vehicle. Remove front wheels. Remove locking hubs. See MANUAL LOCKING HUBS under REMOVAL & INSTALLATION.

2) Using a torque wrench and Spanner Lock Nut Wrench (T86T-1197-A), unlock wheel bearing adjusting nut locking splines by applying inward pressure. Tighten adjusting nut to 50-60 ft. lbs. (68-81 N.m) while turning wheel back and forth. *See Fig. 1.*

NOTE: Adjusting nut will not tighten past 70 ft. lbs. (95 N.m). Threaded portion of nut will ratchet in the assembly.

3) Applying inward pressure to spanner lock nut wrench to disengage locking splines, back off adjusting nut approximately 1/2 turn (180 degrees). Retighten adjusting nut to 15 ft. lbs. (20 N.m).

4) Final end play of hub and rotor assembly should be 0-.004" (0-.10 mm). Install locking hub and wheels. Install wheels and tighten wheel lug nuts to specification. See TORQUE SPECIFICATIONS table at end of article.

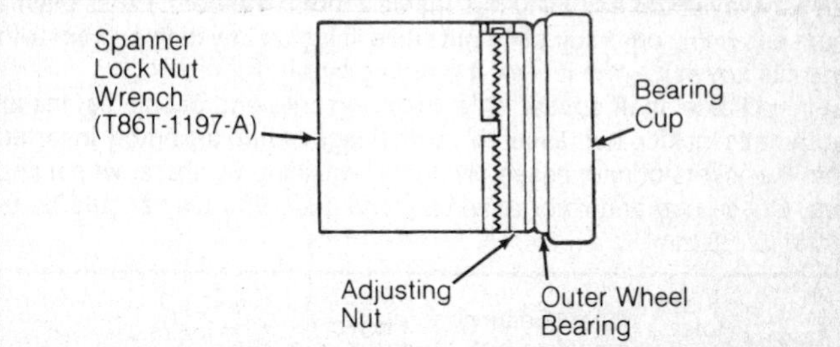
Spanner
Lock Nut
Wrench
(T86T-1197-A)
Bearing
Cup
Adjusting
Nut
Outer Wheel
Bearing
117357
Courtesy of Ford Motor Co.

Fig. 1: Adjusting Wheel Bearings (Bronco & F150/250 with Dana 44 IFS & Manual Locking Hubs)

Bronco & F150 With Automatic Locking Hubs, F250 HD (Dana 50 IFS Axle) & F350 (Dana 60 Monobeam Axle) – 1) Raise and support front of vehicle. Remove wheels. Remove locking hub assembly. See AUTOMATIC LOCKING HUB or MANUAL LOCKING HUB under REMOVAL & INSTALLATION.

2) Remove outer lock nut with Spanner Lock Nut Wrench (D85T-1197-A). *See Fig. 2.* Remove lock washer. Tighten inner lock nut to 50 ft. lbs. (68 N.m). Back off inner lock nut and retighten to 50 ft. lbs. (68 N.m). While rotating hub, back off inner lock nut 90 degrees.

3) Install lock washer so key is positioned in spindle groove. Rotate inner lock nut so pin is aligned in nearest lock washer hole. Install and tighten outer lock nut to 160-205 ft. lbs. (217-278 N.m). Final end play of hub and rotor assembly should be 0-.004" (0-.10 mm).

4) If end play is beyond specification remove hub and bearing assembly and inspect components for excessive wear or damage. Replace hub and/or bearing assemblies as necessary, then reinstall components. Install hub locks. Install wheels and tighten wheel hug nuts to specification. See TORQUE SPECIFICATIONS table at end of article.

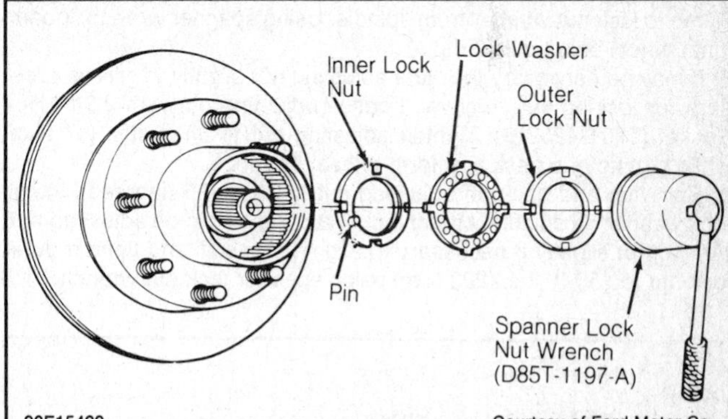
Inner Lock
Nut
Lock Washer
Outer
Lock Nut
Pin
Spanner Lock
Nut Wrench
(D85T-1197-A)
90E15499
Courtesy of Ford Motor Co.

Fig. 2: Adjusting Wheel Bearings (Bronco & F150 with Auto. Hubs, F250 HD Dana 50 IFS & F350 Dana 60 Monobeam Axles)

Explorer & Ranger With Dana 35 IFS and Automatic Locking Hubs – 1) Raise and support vehicle. Remove wheels and tires. Remove retaining washers from wheel lug nut studs. See Fig. 3.

2) Remove automatic locking hub assemblies. Remove snap ring and axle shaft spacer. Carefully pull plastic cam assembly from bearing adjusting nut. Remove 2 plastic thrust washers from adjusting nut.

CAUTION: Before removing adjusting nut, remove locking key from spindle keyway. Failure to clear keyway will result in thread damage on spindle.

3) Using magnet, remove locking key from spindle keyway. It may be necessary to rotate adjusting nut slightly to relieve pressure for lock-

1991 DRIVE AXLES
Locking Hubs (Cont.)

ing key removal. Loosen adjusting nut with 2 3/8" Hex Socket (T70T-4252-B).

4) Tighten adjusting nut to 35 ft. lbs. (47 N.m) while turning hub back and forth to seat bearings. Spin hub and back off adjusting nut 1/4 turn (90 degrees). Retighten adjusting nut to 16 INCH lbs. (1.8 N.m).

5) Align nearest hole in adjusting nut with center of spindle keyway slot. Advance nut to next lug, if necessary. Install locking key in spindle keyway under adjusting nut. Install 2 thrust washers. Press plastic cam assembly onto adjusting nut while lining up key in fixed cam with spindle keyway.

6) Install axle shaft spacer. Clip snap ring onto end of spindle. Install automatic locking hub assembly with 3 legs of hub assembly inserted into 3 pockets of cam assembly. Install retaining washers, wheel and tire. Check hub and rotor assembly end play. End play should be 0-.003" (0-.08 mm).

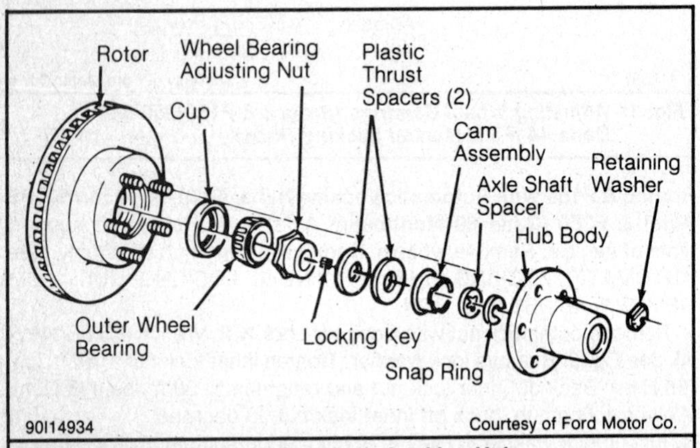
Rotor
Wheel Bearing Adjusting Nut
Plastic Thrust Spacers (2)
Cup
Cam Assembly
Retaining Washer
Axle Shaft Spacer
Hub Body
Outer Wheel Bearing
Locking Key
Snap Ring
90I14934
Courtesy of Ford Motor Co.

Fig. 3: Exploded View of Automatic Locking Hub (Explorer & Ranger)

Explorer & Ranger With Dana 35 IFS and Manual Locking Hubs – 1) Raise and support vehicle. Remove wheels and tires. Remove retaining washers from wheel lug nut studs. *See Fig. 4*. Remove manual locking hub assemblies.

2) Remove snap ring and axle shaft spacer from spindle. Remove outer bearing lock nut using Spanner Lock Nut Wrench (T86T-1197-A). Remove lock nut washer from spindle. Using spanner wrench, loosen inner wheel bearing lock nut.

3) It may be necessary to rotate adjusting nut slightly to relieve pressure for locking key removal. Loosen adjusting nut with 2 3/8" Hex Socket (T70T-4252-B). Tighten adjusting nut to 35 ft. lbs. (47 N.m) while turning hub back and forth to seat bearings.

4) Spin hub and back off adjusting nut 1/4 turn (90 degrees). Install lock washer on spindle. Mount lock washer over pin on adjusting nut, turning nut slightly if necessary to align pin. Install and tighten outer lock nut to 150 ft. lbs. (203 N.m) using spanner lock nut wrench.

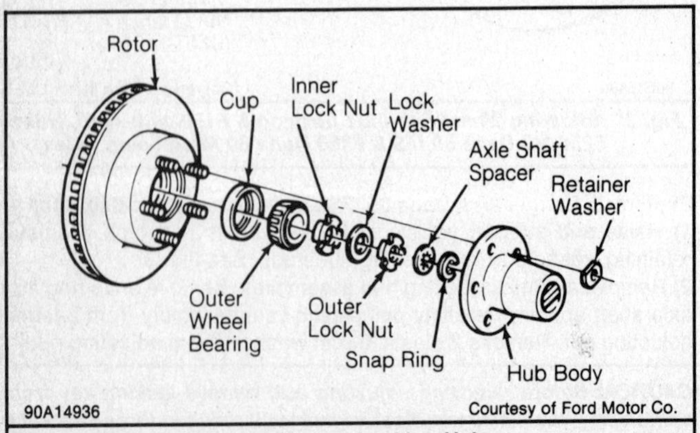
Rotor
Cup
Inner Lock Nut
Lock Washer
Axle Shaft Spacer
Retainer Washer
Outer Wheel Bearing
Outer Lock Nut
Snap Ring
Hub Body
90A14936
Courtesy of Ford Motor Co.

Fig. 4: Exploded View of Manual Locking Hubs (Explorer & Ranger)

5) Install axle shaft spacer. Install snap ring on end of spindle. Install manual hub assembly. Install retaining washers, wheel and tire. Check hub and rotor assembly end play. End play should be 0-.003" (0-.08 mm).

REMOVAL & INSTALLATION

AUTOMATIC LOCKING HUBS

Removal (Bronco & F150) – 1) Raise vehicle and install safety stands. Using Torx bit (T25), remove locking hub cap assembly-to-body assembly screws. Remove cap assembly and bearing components. *See Fig. 5.*

NOTE: DO NOT drop ball bearing, race, spring retainer or spring during disassembly.

2) Remove rubber seal. Remove seal bridge retainer (small metal stamping) from spring retainer ring space. Remove retainer ring by closing ends with needle-nose pliers while pulling hub lock from wheel hub.

3) If wheel hub and spindle are to be removed, remove "C" washer from stub shaft groove. Remove splined spacer from shaft.

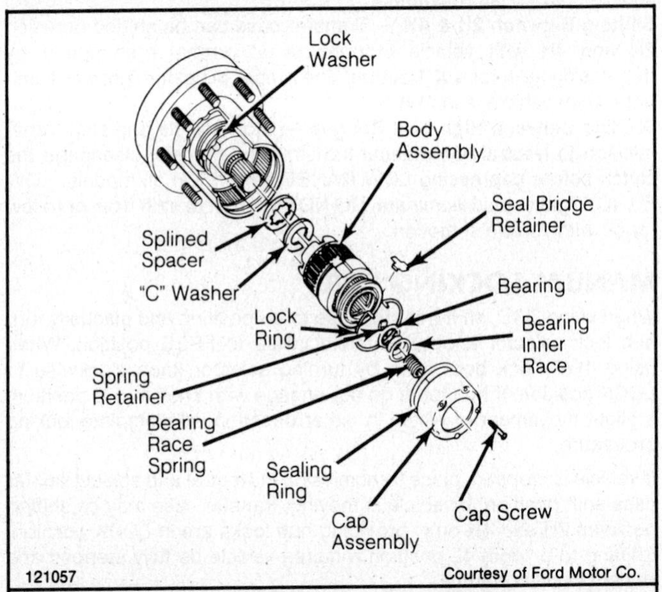
Lock Washer
Body Assembly
Seal Bridge Retainer
Splined Spacer
"C" Washer
Bearing
Lock Ring
Bearing Inner Race
Spring Retainer
Bearing Race Spring
Sealing Ring
Cap Assembly
Cap Screw
121057
Courtesy of Ford Motor Co.

Fig. 5: Exploded View of Automatic Locking Hub (Bronco & F150)

Inspection – Wash locking hub cap bearing, race and retainer in clean solvent. Inspect for excessive wear or damage. Replace components as needed. Thoroughly blow dry parts with compressed air. Repack bearing with lithium grease, position bearing assembly in race.

Installation – 1) Install splined spacer and "C" washer onto axle shaft. Remove excess grease from hub lock and hub splines before installation.

2) Start locking hub assembly into hub. Ensure large tangs are lined up with lock washer and outside diameter and inside diameter splines are in line with hub and axle shaft splines.

3) Install retainer ring by closing ring ends with needle-nose pliers and, at the same time, push locking hub assembly into hub. Install seal bridge retainer (narrow end first).

4) Install rubber seal over locking hub. Install locking hub cap assembly. Ensure ball bearing, race, spring and retainer are in proper position. Tighten Torx screws to specification. See TORQUE SPECIFICATIONS table at end of article.

Removal & Installation – To remove and install automatic locking hub assembly, see EXPLORER & RANGER WITH DANA 35 IFS AND AUTOMATIC LOCKING HUBS under ADJUSTMENTS.

1991 DRIVE AXLES
Locking Hubs (Cont.)

MANUAL LOCKING HUBS

Removal (Bronco & "F" Series) – 1) Remove Allen screws securing locking hub cap assembly. Remove cap assembly and bearing components. Remove snap ring (retainer ring) from end of axle shaft. **2)** Remove lock ring (seated in groove of wheel hub). Slide hub body assembly out of wheel hub. If necessary, install 2 cap screws and pull body from out of hub.

NOTE: DO NOT pack grease into cap assembly. Excess grease can cause an increase in dialing effort.

Installation – To install locking hub assembly components, reverse removal procedure. Install locking hub cap assembly and tighten cap screws to specification. See TORQUE SPECIFICATIONS table at end of article.

Removal (Explorer & Ranger) – 1) Raise and support vehicle. Remove wheel assembly. Remove retainer washers from lug nut studs and remove locking hub body assembly.

2) To remove internal hub lock assembly from locking hub body assembly, remove outer lock ring seated in hub body groove. Internal assembly, spring and clutch gear will now slide out of hub body. DO NOT remove screw from plastic dial. Reassemble hub assembly in reverse order of disassembly.

Installation – Install reassembled manual locking hub body assembly on spindle. Install retainer washers and wheel. Torque wheel lug nuts to specification. See TORQUE SPECIFICATIONS table.

TORQUE SPECIFICATIONS

TORQUE SPECIFICATIONS

Application	Ft. Lbs. (N.m)
Wheel Lug Nuts	
Except F250/350	100 (136)
F250/350	140 (190)
	INCH Lbs. (N.m)
Locking Cap Assembly Screws [1]	
Bronco & "F" Series	
Automatic Locking Hub	40-50 (4.5-5.6 N.m)
Manual Locking Hub	40-60 (4.5-6.8)

[1] – Tighten in a circular pattern.

1991 DRIVE AXLES
FWD Axle Shafts – Aerostar

DESCRIPTION

Aerostar 4WD front axle assembly consists of a half-shaft, axle shaft, constant velocity (CV) joint, single "U" joint and 2 dust boots. CV joint is located at outboard end and single "U" joint at inboard end of half-shaft. CV joint cannot be repaired and must be replaced as an assembly. Half-shaft flange is bolted to axle shaft flange. *See Fig. 1.* Half-shaft is retained in outer CV joint by circlips. Axle shafts are retained in axle housing by "C" clips in differential case. CV joint is enclosed in a CV joint boot. Boot maintains lubrication in the joint and prevents contamination of CV lubricant. CV boot must be replaced when signs of leakage or cracks are present.

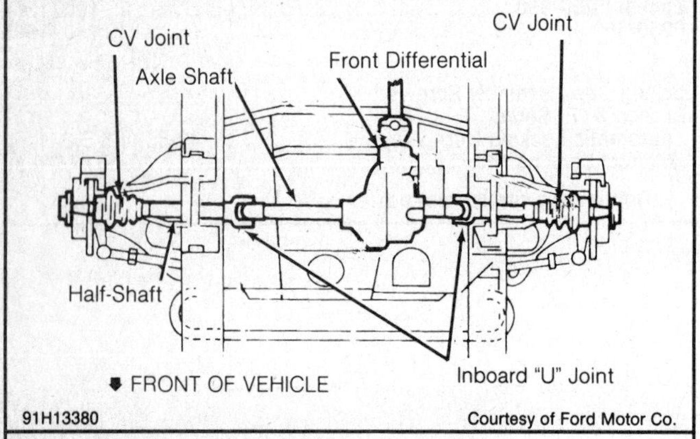
CV Joint
Axle Shaft
Front Differential
CV Joint
Half-Shaft
FRONT OF VEHICLE
Inboard "U" Joint
91H13380
Courtesy of Ford Motor Co.

Fig. 1: Identifying Front Axle Shaft Assemblies

TROUBLE SHOOTING

NOTE: See TROUBLE SHOOTING article in GENERAL INFORMATION.

REMOVAL, DISASSEMBLY, REASSEMBLY & INSTALLATION

FRONT AXLE SHAFTS

NOTE: To remove axle shafts, axle housing assembly must be removed from vehicle.

Removal – 1) Remove axle housing assembly. See DANA 28-2 FRONT AXLE article. Remove axle housing cover and drain differential fluid. Mount axle housing in Holding Fixture (T57L-500-B) using Adapters (T90T-4000-A) and Spacer (T80T-4000-B2).

2) Rotate shafts until open side of "C" clip on inner end of axle shaft can be reached. Remove "C" clip. Remove axle shaft. Remove axle housing oil seal and needle bearings using slide hammer, Collet (D80L-100-A) and Actuator Pin (D80L-100-H).

Installation – 1) Ensure bearing bore is clean and has no nicks. Place new caged needle bearing on Needle Bearing Installer (T83T-1244-A). Ensure bearing manufacturer's name and part number is facing toward tool when installed in housing bore.

2) Drive needle bearing until bearing is fully seated in housing bore. Coat lip of seal with multipurpose grease. Drive seal into carrier using Seal Installer (T90T-3110-A). Install axle shaft so that groove on shaft is visible inside differential case.

3) Install "C" clip. DO NOT tap on center of "C" clip, as clip will be damaged. Clean all sealant, oil and dirt from housing-to-cover mating surfaces. Apply continuous bead of RTV sealant 1/4-3/8" wide on housing.

NOTE: Housing cover must be installed within 5 minutes after applying RTV sealant.

4) Sealant bead should not pass over or outside holes. Install housing cover. To complete installation, reverse removal procedure. Allow one hour cure time before filling differential.

HALF-SHAFT ASSEMBLY

Removal – 1) Raise and support vehicle. Remove front wheels. Remove and hub nut and washer. Discard hub nut. Mark differential axle shaft flange-to-half-shaft flange position for installation reference. Disconnect half-shaft from axle shaft flange. Wire end of half-shaft to underbody of vehicle.

CAUTION: DO NOT allow half-shaft to hang unsupported. Damage to outboard CV joint may occur.

2) Remove lower shock absorber bolts, and position shock out of way. Remove rubber jounce bumper. Using Front Hub Remover/Installer (T81P-1104-C and T81P-1104-A) and Hub Adapters (T83P-1104-BH1 and T86P-1104-A1), separate CV joint stub axle shaft from hub and rotor assembly. Remove half-shaft assembly from vehicle.

CAUTION: Once half-shaft(s) has been removed, DO NOT allow vehicle height to be supported by hub bearing.

Disassembly – 1) Secure half-shaft in soft-jawed vise. Remove slip yoke boot clamps. *See Fig. 2.* Separate outboard shaft from slip yoke assembly. Remove and discard slip yoke boot.

2) Cut and remove large boot clamp. Roll back boot over shaft and remove boot. Clean all parts in cleaning solvent. Inspect CV joint and slip yoke assembly for excessive wear, pitting, rust and broken parts. If CV joint is faulty, complete outer shaft assembly must be replaced.

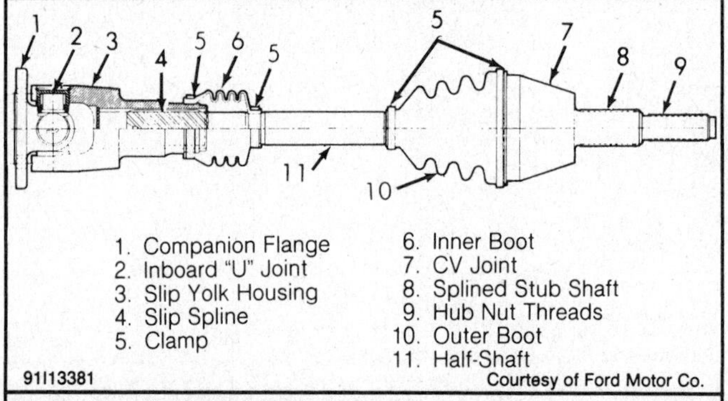
1
2
3
4
5
6
5
5
7
8
9
11
10
1. Companion Flange
2. Inboard "U" Joint
3. Slip Yolk Housing
4. Slip Spline
5. Clamp
6. Inner Boot
7. CV Joint
8. Splined Stub Shaft
9. Hub Nut Threads
10. Outer Boot
11. Half-Shaft
91I13381
Courtesy of Ford Motor Co.

Fig. 2: Identifying Half-Shaft Assembly

Reassembly – 1) Fill CV joint area around balls with approximately 2.8 ounces of CV Joint Grease (E2FZ-19590-B). Spread approximately 40 ounces of CV JOINT grease evenly inside large boot. Assemble large boot onto outboard shaft and joint assembly.

2) Ensure boot is seated in grooves. Tighten clamp using crimping pliers. Assemble small boot and clamps onto outboard shaft and joint assembly. DO NOT tighten clamps at this time. Coat spline end of outboard shaft and joint assembly using Long-Life Lubricant (C1AZ-19590-BA).

3) Insert outboard shaft spline end into inner slip yoke assembly. Slip boot into place, and ensure boot is seated in grooves. Tighten clamps using Octiker Crimper (D87P-1090-A).

Installation – 1) With splines aligned, install outboard CV stub shaft into hub and rotor assembly. Install washer and new hub nut. To prevent rotor from turning, insert steel rod into rotor diameter and rotate clockwise until rod contacts steering knuckle.

2) Tighten hub nut to 170-210 ft. lbs. (230-285 N.m). Noting alignment marks made previously, install half-shaft flange to differential axle shaft flange. Install and tighten flange bolts to specification. See TORQUE SPECIFICATIONS table. To complete installation, reverse removal procedure.

TORQUE SPECIFICATIONS

TORQUE SPECIFICATIONS

Application	Ft. Lbs. (N.m)
Axle Hub Nut	170-210 (230-285)
Flange Bolts	22-29 (30-39)
Wheel Lug Nuts	100 (136)

1991 DRIVE AXLES
Drive Shaft

Aerostar, Bronco, Explorer Ranger, "E" & "F" Series

NOTE: Unless otherwise specified, references to "F" Series include "F" Series Super Duty.

DESCRIPTION

Drive shafts may have one shaft, 2 shafts with a center bearing or 3 shafts with slip joints. Three shafts are used on 4WD vehicles. Location of slip joints vary with model application. *See Fig. 1.*

Front Drive Shaft – Power flow is transferred to front axle from transfer case by the front drive shaft. The shaft has a splined stub shaft end, encased in a rubber boot, a slip yoke (attached to the transfer case) and a universal joint at each end.

Rear Drive Shaft – Steel or aluminum shafts use a slip yoke, splined into the transmission output shaft. Yoke is connected to the drive shaft by a universal joint. A second universal joint is used where the drive shaft connects to the rear axle companion flange. Two-piece rear drive shafts are equipped with center support bearings (used in conjunction with a coupling shaft).

INSPECTION

If abnormal vibration or driveline noise is present, check the following as possible sources:

Drive Shaft – Check drive shaft for damage or dents that could affect balance. Check for undercoating adhering to shafts. If present, clean shafts thoroughly.

Check shaft-to-pinion yoke or companion flange index marks. If marks are not aligned, disconnect shaft and index marks so they are as close as possible.

Check for missing balance weight(s) or improperly seated or defective universal joint(s).

Center Bearing – Check for loose drive shaft center bearing mounting bolts. Replace bearing insulator if deteriorated or oil-soaked.

Universal Joints – Check for foreign material stuck in joints. Ensure joint is lubricated and there is no play between the bearing and cross shaft. Check for loose bolts and worn or seized bearings.

Engine & Transmission Mountings – Tighten mounting bolts. If mountings are deteriorated, replace them.

Tires & Wheels – Check tire inflation and wheel balance. Check for foreign objects in tread, damaged tread, mismatched tread patterns or incorrect tire size.

MAINTENANCE

Whenever drive shaft is removed from vehicle, clean yoke with solvent. Lubricate inside diameter of seal with hydraulic seal lubricant, and outside diameter of seal with transmission fluid.

ADJUSTMENTS

DRIVE SHAFT PHASING

1-Piece Shafts (Except "F" Series Super Duty) – Ensure flange on each end of drive shaft is in same plane. Check for arrows on slip joint and drive shaft to aid in alignment. If flanges are not in same plane, disassemble universal joint and align.

2-Piece Shafts ("F" Series Super Duty) – Rotate transmission until yoke ears are on a horizontal plane. If 2-piece shaft is correctly installed, center line of yoke ears at each end of individual shafts will be parallel. *See Fig. 2.* If flanges are not in same plane, remove drive shaft. Install drive shaft with yokes aligned to a horizontal plane.

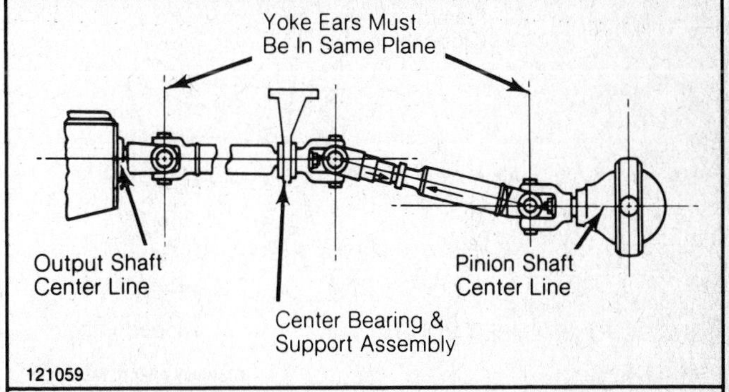
Yoke Ears Must
Be In Same Plane
Output Shaft
Center Line
Center Bearing &
Support Assembly
Pinion Shaft
Center Line
121059

Fig. 2: Illustrating Phase Alignment of 2-Piece Drive Shafts

3-Piece Shafts ("F" Series Super Duty) – **1)** An adjustable support plate is used to allow for different applications. The correct position is determined by attaching the support plate to the holes provided in the frame side rail. *See Fig. 3.*

2) On models with main spring only, use No. 3 hole to mount support plate to crossmember. On models with main spring and auxiliary spring, use No. 1 hole to mount support plate to crossmember. Ensure universal joint alignment is on the same plane.

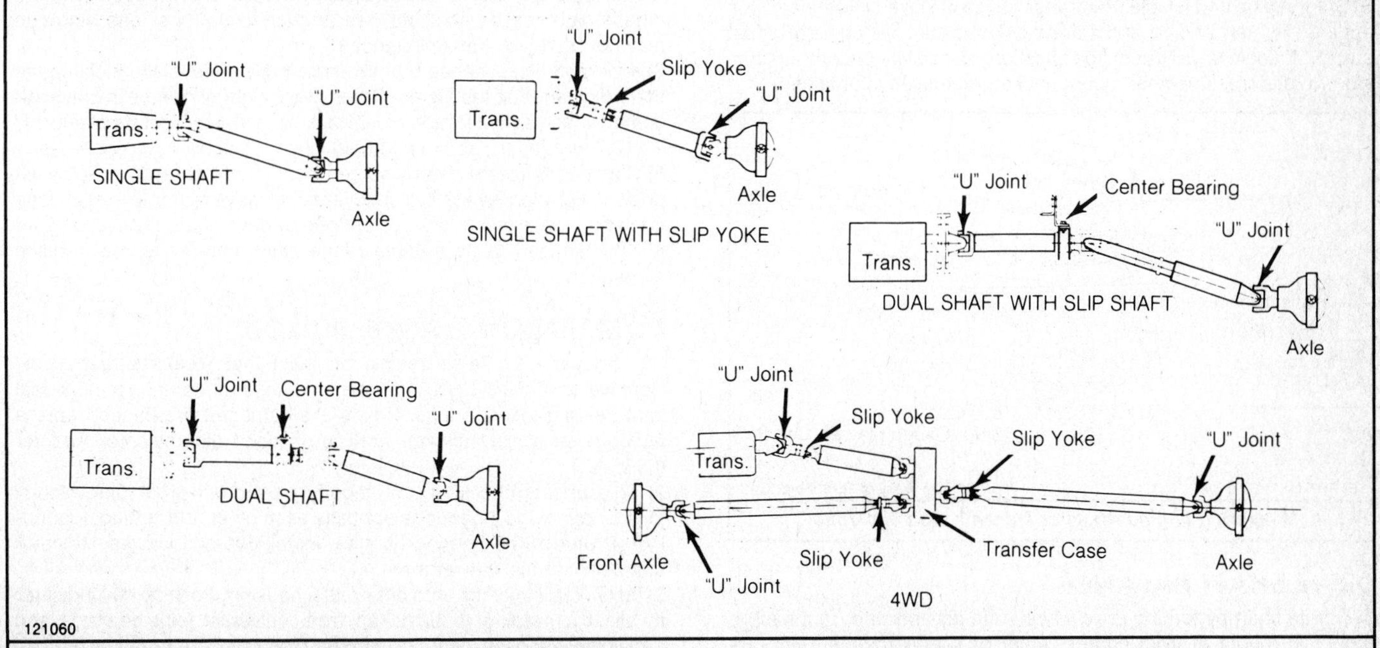
"U" Joint
"U" Joint
Trans.
SINGLE SHAFT
Axle
"U" Joint
Slip Yoke
"U" Joint
Trans.
Axle
SINGLE SHAFT WITH SLIP YOKE
"U" Joint
Center Bearing
"U" Joint
Trans.
DUAL SHAFT WITH SLIP SHAFT
Axle
"U" Joint
Center Bearing
"U" Joint
Trans.
DUAL SHAFT
Axle
"U" Joint
Slip Yoke
Trans.
Slip Yoke
"U" Joint
Front Axle
"U" Joint
Slip Yoke
Transfer Case
Axle
4WD
121060

Fig. 1: Identifying 5 Commonly Used Drive Shaft Combinations

1991 DRIVE AXLES
Drive Shaft (Cont.)

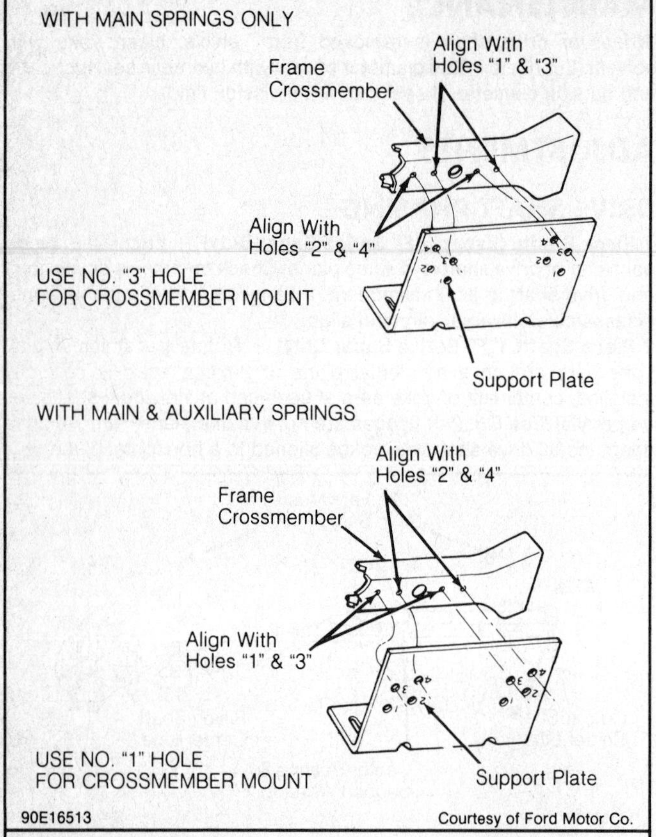
WITH MAIN SPRINGS ONLY
Frame
Crossmember
Align With
Holes "1" & "3"
Align With
Holes "2" & "4"
USE NO. "3" HOLE
FOR CROSSMEMBER MOUNT
Support Plate
WITH MAIN & AUXILIARY SPRINGS
Align With
Holes "2" & "4"
Frame
Crossmember
Align With
Holes "1" & "3"
USE NO. "1" HOLE
FOR CROSSMEMBER MOUNT
Support Plate
90E16513
Courtesy of Ford Motor Co.

Fig. 3: Illustrating Alignment Of 3-Piece Drive Shafts Support Plates ("F" Series Super Duty)

ENGINE ANGLE

1) Rotate drive shaft until transmission slip yoke ear is parallel to floor. Place spirit gauge or protractor flush against yoke ear. *See Fig. 4.* Record the angle reading.

2) If angle is one degree or more beyond specification, start engine and warm to normal operating temperature. See ENGINE ANGLE SPECIFICATION table. Turn engine off. Loosen but DO NOT remove engine and transmission mount fasteners.

3) Start engine and let idle. Put transmission in Drive or 1st gear. Stop engine. Tighten engine and transmission mount fasteners. Repeat step **1)**. If angle is still out of specification, place shim under transmission to rear crossmember mount until correct angle is obtained.

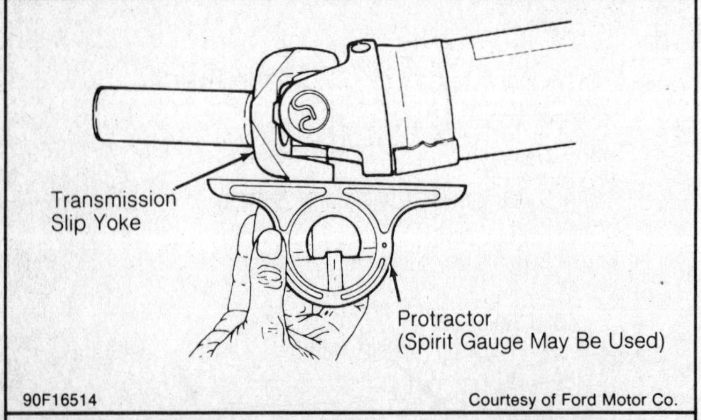
Transmission
Slip Yoke
Protractor
(Spirit Gauge May Be Used)
90F16514
Courtesy of Ford Motor Co.

Fig. 4: Measuring Engine Angle at Transmission Slip Yoke

DRIVE SHAFT BALANCE

1) Rotate shaft by turning drive wheel. Use dial indicator to measure runout. If runout at front and/or center of shaft exceeds .035" (.89 mm), replace drive shaft.

ENGINE ANGLE SPECIFICATION

Application	[1] Angle
Aerostar & "E" Series	4.0
Bronco, Explorer, Ranger & "F" Series	5.5

[1] – Angle expressed in degrees to horizontal.

2) If runout at front and/or center is okay but rear runout exceeds .035" (.89 mm), rotate the shaft and mark the high spot on shaft. Scribe index mark on drive shaft. Disconnect drive shaft at rear flange.

3) Rotate shaft 180 degrees and connect shaft. Repeat runout check. If runout is now less than .035" (.89 mm), but shaft still vibrates, proceed to step **4)**. If runout still exceeds .035" (.89 mm), rotate shaft and scribe another mark on the high spot of shaft.

4) If the 2 marks made are approximately 1" (25 mm) apart, replace drive shaft. If the 2 marks made are approximately 180 degrees apart, replace the flange. *See Fig. 5.* If drive shaft is within specification, but still vibrates, mark shaft in 4 positions, 90 degrees apart.

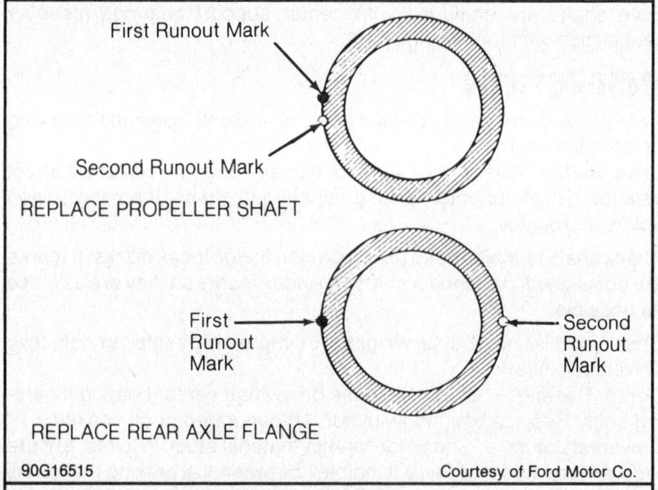
First Runout Mark
Second Runout Mark
REPLACE PROPELLER SHAFT
First
Runout
Mark
Second
Runout
Mark
REPLACE REAR AXLE FLANGE
90G16515
Courtesy of Ford Motor Co.

Fig. 5: Reading Drive Shaft Runout Marks

5) Place marks approximately 6" (152 mm) forward of weld, at rear end of shaft. Number marks 1, 2, 3 and 4. Place screw-type hose clamp so clamp head is in No. 1 position, and rotate shaft with engine.

6) If there is little or no change, move clamp head to No. 2 position, and repeat test. Continue procedure until vibration is at lowest level. If no difference is noted with clamp head moved to all 4 positions, vibration may not be drive shaft imbalance.

7) If vibration is lessened but not completely gone, place 2 clamps at that point, and run test again. Combined weight of clamps in one position may increase vibration. If vibration is increased, rotate clamps 1/2" (12.7 mm) apart, above and below best position, and repeat test.

8) Continue to rotate clamps as necessary, until vibration is at lowest point. If vibration level is still unacceptable, leave rear clamp(s) in position and repeat procedure at front end of drive shaft. If vibration cannot be reduced to acceptable range using this procedure, replace drive shaft.

COMPANION FLANGE RUNOUT

"F" Series – 1) Raise vehicle on hoist that supports rear axles. Remove driveshaft. Check companion flange for damage to universal joint bearing locating lugs. If lugs are damaged or shaved, replace flange. Use a dial indicator and cup-shaped dial indicator Adapter (6565-AC).

2) To fabricate checking tool, modify a used universal joint. Modify joint by removing 2 bearings opposite each other and cutting or grinding off one of the bearing flanges. Install cup-shaped dial indicator adapter onto dial indicator stem.

3) Install dial indicator onto differential housing. Position dial indicator to allow a reading to be taken from universal joint bearings and remaining exposed bearing journal. Turn companion flange so dial indicator cup-shaped adapter rests on machined surface of bearing.

Flange Bearing Cup Runout	Driveshaft Universal Cross-Shaft Runout — Inch												
	0.000	0.001	0.002	0.003	0.004	0.005	0.006	0.007	0.008	0.009	0.010	0.011	0.012
0.000	0.000	0.001	0.002	0.003	0.004	0.005	0.006	0.007	0.008	0.009	0.010	0.011	0.012
0.001	0.001	0.0013	0.0022	0.0032	0.0042	0.0051	0.0061	0.0071	0.0081	0.0091	0.0010	0.011	0.012
0.002	0.002	0.0022	0.0027	0.0037	0.0045	0.0053	0.0062	0.0072	0.0082	0.0092	0.0101	0.0111	0.0121
0.003	0.003	0.0032	0.0036	0.0042	0.005	0.0058	0.0067	0.0077	0.0085	0.0094	0.0104	0.0113	0.0123
0.004	0.004	0.0042	0.0045	0.005	0.0057	0.0064	0.0072	0.0081	0.009	0.0097	0.0107	0.0116	0.0126
0.005	0.005	0.0051	0.0053	0.0058	0.0063	0.0071	0.0078	0.0087	0.0094	0.0102	0.0111	0.012	0.013
0.006	0.006	0.0061	0.0062	0.0068	0.0072	0.0078	0.0085	0.0092	0.010	0.0108	0.0116	0.124	0.0134
0.007	0.007	0.0071	0.0073	0.0075	0.0081	0.0087	0.0093	0.0099	0.0103	0.0114	0.0122	0.013	0.0138
0.008	0.008	0.0081	0.0082	0.0087	0.009	0.0094	0.010	0.0104	0.011	0.012	0.0128	0.0135	0.0144
0.009	0.009	0.0091	0.0092	0.0094	0.0097	0.102	0.108	0.0114	0.012	0.0127	0.0134	0.0141	0.015
0.010	0.010	0.010	0.0101	0.0104	0.0107	0.0111	0.0116	0.0122	0.0128	0.0134	0.0141	0.0148	0.0156
0.011	0.011	0.011	0.0111	0.0113	0.0116	0.012	0.0124	0.013	0.0135	0.0141	0.0148	0.0154	0.0162
0.012	0.012	0.012	0.0121	0.0123	0.0126	0.013	0.0134	0.0138	0.0144	0.015	0.0156	0.0162	0.0169

The total (combined) companion flange runout is located in the square where the columns containing the flange bearing cup runout and universal cross shaft runout readings intersect.

91E13395 Courtesy of Ford Motor Co.

Fig. 6: Checking Combined Companion Flange Runout

4) Rotate companion flange side-to-side slightly. This will be the point at which dial indicator adapter is closest to center of flange rotation. Carefully pull dial indicator stem back. Rotate companion flange 180 degrees. Slightly rotate flange side-to-side. Record reading.

5) Rotate flange 90 degrees and position dial indicator adapter on machined end of exposed bearing journal. Zero dial indicator and rotate flange side-to-side. With dial indicator at zero, pull dial indicator stem back. Rotate flange 180 degrees.

6) Rotate modified checking tool on bearing flange, 180 degrees. Position exposed bearing flange on dial indicator adapter. Rock universal joint back and forth. Rotate flange side-to-side to establish point where dial indicator hand will reverse direction.

7) This will determine the universal joint cross shaft runout. Repeat steps **3-6)** at least 3 times and average the readings. To determine combined companion flange runout, see Fig. 6. If readings exceed specifications, reposition companion flange 180 degrees on pinion shaft. Repeat steps **3-6)**.

CAUTION: BEFORE removing companion flange, check and record pinion nut torque. Also check and record pinion bearing preload. Original settings must be repeated after flange is repositioned.

CAUTION: NEVER back off pinion nut to reduce preload. If a decrease in preload is necessary, a new collapsible pinion spacer and pinion nut must be installed.

8) If repeat measurements still exceed specification, reposition flange another 90 degrees and repeat steps **3-6)**. If runout is still too much, replace companion flange and recheck runout. If necessary rotate new flange on pinion shaft to obtain proper runout.

9) If runout is still too much after replacement of flange, replace ring gear and pinion. Repeat steps **3-6)** until proper runout is obtained. Install drive shaft and road test vehicle. If drive shaft vibrations are present, rotate drive shaft on companion flange, and road test vehicle.

DRIVE SHAFT ANGLE

Protractor Method – Measure ride height. Vehicle must be in curb weight (unloaded) condition. Specified pinion angles correspond to measured ride height. See appropriate DRIVE SHAFT ANGLES or PINION ANGLES table. Place protractor any place along bottom of drive shaft. Record reading. Adjust drive shaft angle by installing tapered shims between rear springs and spring seats.

Pinion Angle Level Gauge Method – Rotate drive shaft so one drive shaft yoke ear is facing down. Remove universal joint snap ring. Place pinion angle level gauge under flange ear. *See Fig. 7*. Record reading. See appropriate DRIVE SHAFT ANGLES or PINION ANGLES table. Adjust pinion angle by installing tapered shims between rear springs and spring seats.

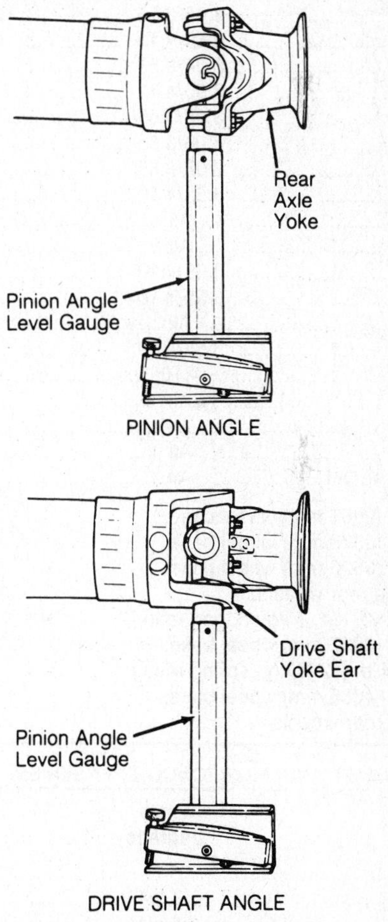

Rear
Axle
Yoke
Pinion Angle
Level Gauge
PINION ANGLE
Drive Shaft
Yoke Ear
Pinion Angle
Level Gauge
DRIVE SHAFT ANGLE

91D13394 Courtesy of Ford Motor Co.

Fig. 7: Checking Drive Shaft & Pinion Angles

PINION ANGLE

NOTE: Pinion angle adjustment procedure for Aerostar not available from manufacturer.

Protractor Method – **1)** Place protractor in vertical position, flush against 2 differential cover retaining bolts. Rotate protractor bubble indicator so the 90 degree marks align with indexing marks.

1991 DRIVE AXLES
Drive Shaft (Cont.)

2) Calibrate bubble to the level mark and read angle. For example, if protractor reads 85 degrees, pinion angle reading is 5 degrees. Adjust pinion angle by installing tapered shims between rear springs and spring seats. See appropriate DRIVE SHAFT ANGLES or PINION ANGLES table.

Pinion Angle Level Gauge Method – Rotate drive shaft so one ear of pinion flange is facing down. *See Fig. 7.* Remove universal joint snap ring. Place pinion angle level gauge under flange ear. Record reading. See appropriate DRIVE SHAFT ANGLES or PINION ANGLES table. Adjust pinion angle by installing tapered shims between rear springs and spring seats.

FRONT AXLE PINION ANGLES (BRONCO & "F" SERIES)

Application	Axle Type	Pinion Angle Degrees
Bronco & F150 4WD	Dana 44 IFS	2 3/4
F250 LD 4WD	Dana 44 IFSHD	6 3/4
F250 HD 4WD	Dana 50 IFS	6 3/4
F350 4WD	Dana 60	4 1/2

REAR AXLE PINION ANGLES (BRONCO & "F" SERIES)

Application	Axle Ratio	Pinion Angle Degrees
Bronco 4WD	3.08/3.55	10
Bronco 4WD	3.50/4.11	10 3/4
F150	3.08/3.55	5
4WD	3.50/4.11	5 1/2
2WD [1]	3.08/3.55	6
2WD [2]	3.08/3.55	6
2WD [2 3 4]	3.08/3.55	7 1/4
F250 LD	3.55/4.10	7 1/4
2WD	All	7 1/4
2WD [5]	All	7 1/2
F250 HD [2]	3.55/4.10	6 1/4
4WD [7]	3.55/4.10	6
2WD [2 7 6]	All	6 1/4
F350 4WD [4]	3.55/4.10	6
F350 [9]	4.10	4 1/2
2WD [4]	All	6 1/4
2WD [9]	All	4 1/4
2WD [8 9]	All	4 1/4
"F" Series Super Duty	All	7

[1] – With 117" (2967 mm) wheel base.
[2] – With 133" (3378 mm) wheel base.
[3] – With 139" (3526 mm) wheel base.
[4] – With single rear wheels.
[5] – With 2450 lb. (1111 kg.) spring rating.
[6] – With 155" (3937 mm) wheel base.
[7] – With 2811 lb. (1275 kg.) spring rating.
[8] – With 161" (4085 mm) wheel base.
[9] – With dual rear wheels.

REAR DRIVE SHAFT ANGLES (BRONCO & "F" SERIES)

Application	Angle Degrees	Ride Height In. (mm)
Bronco		
4.9L	11	6.31 (160)
5.0/5.8L	12 1/4	6.31 (160)
5.0L [1]	11 1/4	6.31 (160)
5.0L [2]	12 1/2	6.31 (160)
F150 4WD [3]		
4.9L	13	10.80 (274)
5.0/5.8L	14	10.80 (274)
5.0L [1]	13 1/4	10.80 (274)
5.0L [4]	14 1/4	10.80 (274)
F150 4WD [5]		
4.9L	9 1/4	10.80 (274)
5.0/5.8L	9 3/4	10.80 (274)
5.0L [1]	9 1/4	10.80 (274)
5.0L [2]	10	10.80 (274)

REAR DRIVE SHAFT ANGLES (BRONCO & "F" SERIES) (Cont.)

Application	Angle Degrees	Ride Height In. (mm)
F150 4WD [6]		
4.9L	8 1/4	10.80 (274)
5.0/5.8L	9 1/4	10.80 (274)
5.0L [1]	8 1/4	10.80 (274)
5.0L [2]	9 1/4	10.80 (274)
F150 2WD		
All Trans. [10]	7 1/4	8.87 (225)
All Trans. [11]	8	8.26 (210)
All Trans. Exc. [5]	5 1/2	8.87 (225)
All Exc. M4	6 1/2	8.80 (223)
All Exc. C5 & C6 [7]	6	8.87 (225)
All Exc. C5 & C6 [7 12]	7 3/4	8.80 (223)
AOD & C6 [7 13]	7 1/2	8.80 (223)
AOD & C6 [7 6]	6 1/2	8.80 (223)
M4 Trans.	7	8.80 (223)
M4 Trans.	6	8.87 (225)
F250 LD 4WD	9 3/4	10.62 (270)
F250 LD 2WD [16]		
AOD, C6 & M4 Trans. [14]	7	8.58 (218)
AOD, C6 & M4 Trans. [15]	7 3/4	9.44 (240)
F250 LD 2WD [7]		
C6 Trans. [14]	8 3/4	8.58 (218)
C6 Trans. [15]	10	9.44 (240)
F250 HD 4WD		
All	10	11.12 (282)
All	10	10.94 (278)
F250 HD 4WD [6]		
All	10 1/4	11.12 (282)
All	10	10.94 (278)
F250 HD 2WD [7]		
C6 & M4 Trans.	9 3/4	9.17 (233)
C6 & M4 Trans.	9 1/2	8.54 (217)
C6 Trans. [6]	7 1/2	9.17 (233)
C6 Trans. [6]	7 1/2	8.54 (217)
F250 HD 2WD		
C6 Trans.	7 3/4	9.17 (233)
C6 Trans.	7 3/4	8.54 (217)
F350 (SRW) 2WD		
C6 Trans.	7 3/4	8.54 (216)
C6 Trans. [7]	9 3/4	8.54 (216)
M5HD Trans. [7]	9 1/2	8.54 (216)
C6 Trans. [8]	7 1/4	8.58 (217)
C6 Trans. [7 9]	6 1/2	8.58 (217)
M5HD Trans. [7 9]	6 1/2	8.58 (217)
F350 (SRW) 4WD	12	10.94 (278)
F350 (DRW)	11 1/4	N/A
"F Series Super Duty		
M5HD Trans. [7 8]	9	10.24" (260)
M5HD Trans. [7 9]	6 3/4	10.24" (260)

[1] – AOD transmission with 3.55 axle ratio.
[2] – AOD transmission with 4.11 axle ratio.
[3] – With 117" (2967 mm) wheel base.
[4] – With AOD4 transmission.
[5] – With 133" (3378 mm) wheel base.
[6] – With 155" (3937 mm) wheel base.
[7] – With 2-piece drive shaft.
[8] – With 137" (3475 mm) wheel base.
[9] – With 161" (4085 mm) wheel base.
[10] – With 1235 lb. (560 kg.) spring rating.
[11] – With 1375 lb. (623 kg.) spring rating.
[12] – With 1660 lb. (752 kg.) spring rating.
[13] – With 139" (3526 mm) spring rating.
[14] – With 1700 lb. (771 kg.) spring rating.
[15] – With 2450 lb. (1111 kg.) spring rating.
[16] – Except 2-piece drive shaft.

1991 DRIVE AXLES
Drive Shaft (Cont.)

REAR DRIVE SHAFT ANGLES ("E" SERIES)

Application	Angle Degrees	Ride Height In. (mm)
E150		
C6 & M4 Trans. [1,5]	6	5.08 (129)
C6 & M4 Trans. [2,5]	6 1/2	5.60 (142)
C6 & M4 Trans. [3,5]	6 1/2	6.72 (171)
C6 & M4 Trans. [4,5]	7	5.74 (146)
AOD Trans. [1,5]	4 3/4	5.08 (129)
AOD Trans. [2,5]	5 1/4	5.60 (142)
AOD Trans. [3,5]	5 1/2	6.72 (171)
AOD Trans. [4,5]	5 3/4	5.74 (146)
AOD Trans. [1,6]	3 1/2	5.08 (129)
AOD Trans. [2,6]	3 3/4	5.60 (142)
AOD Trans. [3,6]	4 1/4	6.72 (171)
AOD Trans. [4,6]	4	5.74 (146)
AOD Trans. [1,6,7]	2 1/2	5.08 (129)
AOD Trans. [2,6,7]	2 3/4	5.60 (142)
AOD Trans. [3,6,7]	3 1/2	6.72 (171)
AOD Trans. [4,6,7]	3 1/4	5.74 (146)
C6 & M4 Trans. [1,6]	4 1/2	5.08 (129)
C6 & M4 Trans. [2,6]	4 3/4	5.60 (142)
C6 & M4 Trans. [3,6]	5 1/4	6.72 (171)
C6 & M4 Trans. [4,6]	5	5.74 (146)
C6 & M4 Trans. [1,6,7]	4	5.08 (129)
C6 & M4 Trans. [2,6,7]	4 1/4	5.60 (142)
C6 & M4 Trans. [3,6,7]	5	6.72 (171)
C6 & M4 Trans. [4,6,7]	4 3/4	5.74 (146)
E250		
AOD & C6 Trans. [6]	6	7.52 (191)
AOD & C6 Trans. [6]	6 1/4	8.22 (209)
AOD & C6 Trans. [6]	5 1/2	7.20 (183)
AOD & C6 Trans. [6]	6	8.12 (206)
AOD Trans. [6,7]	6	7.52 (191)
AOD Trans. [6,7]	6 1/2	8.22 (209)
AOD Trans. [6,7]	5 1/4	7.20 (183)
AOD Trans. [6,7]	6	8.12 (206)
E350		
C6 Trans.	6	9.54 (242)
C6 Trans.	7 1/2	8.12 (206)
C6 Trans.	6 1/2	7.50 (190)
C6 Trans. [7]	6 1/4	7.50 (146)
C6 Trans. [7]	4 1/2	7.50 (146)

[1] – With 1250 lb. (567 kg.) spring rating.
[2] – With 1450 lb. (657 kg.) spring rating.
[3] – With 1685 lb. (764 kg.) spring rating.
[4] – With 1750 lb. (793 kg.) spring rating.
[5] – With 124" (3150 mm) wheel base.
[6] – With 138" (3505 mm) wheel base.
[7] – With 2-piece drive shaft.

REAR AXLE PINION ANGLES ("E" SERIES)

Application	Axle Ratio	Pinion Angle Degrees
E150 [16]		
[1,2,3]	3.55	5
[4]	3.55	5 1/4
E150 [5]		
[1,2,4]	3.55	6 1/2
[3]	3.55	7
E250		
[6,7,9]	3.54/3.73	5
[8]	3.07/3.54/4.10	4
[10]	3.07/3.54/4.10	5
E350		
[11]	3.07/3.54/4.10	4 1/2
[12]	3.07/3.54/4.10	4 3/4
[13,14]	3.07/3.54/4.10	5
[15]	3.54/4.10	5

[1] – With 1250 lb. (566 kg.) spring rating.
[2] – With 1450 lb. (658 kg.) spring rating.
[3] – With 1685 lb. (764 kg.) spring rating.
[4] – With 1750 lb. (794 kg.) spring rating.
[5] – With 138" (3505 mm) wheel base.
[6] – With 1825 lb. (828 kg.) spring rating.
[7] – With 2100 lb. (952 kg.) spring rating.
[8] – With 2365 lb. (1072 kg.) spring ratio.
[9] – With 2450 lb. (1111 kg.) spring rating.
[10] – With 2700 lb. (1224 kg.) spring rating.
[11] – With 2850 lb. (1292 kg.) spring rating.
[12] – With 2950 lb. (1338 kg.) spring rating.
[13] – With 3300 lb. (1496 kg.) spring rating.
[14] – With 158" (4013 mm) wheel base.
[15] – With 176" (4470 mm) wheel base.
[16] – With 124" (3150 mm) wheel base.

REAR DRIVE SHAFT & PINION ANGLES (AEROSTAR)

Drive Shaft Angle Degrees	Ride Height In. (mm)	Pinion Angle Degrees
1.0	1.4 (36)	0.1
1.3	1.8 (46)	0.5
1.6	2.2 (56)	0.9
1.9	2.6 (66)	1.2
2.3	3.0 (76)	1.6
2.6	3.4 (86)	1.8
3.0	3.8 (96)	2.1
3.3	4.2 (106)	2.3
3.7	4.6 (116)	2.5
4.1	5.0 (126)	2.7
4.4	5.4 (136)	2.8
4.8	5.7 (146)	2.9
5.2	6.1 (156)	3.0
5.6	6.5 (166)	3.0

1991 DRIVE AXLES
Drive Shaft (Cont.)

REAR DRIVE SHAFT ANGLES (EXPLORER & RANGER)

Application	Angle Degrees	Ride Height In. (mm)
Explorer 2WD & 4WD	13.7	6.3 (161)
Ranger Reg. Cab		
2WD		
A4LD Trans. [1]	7.3	7.4 (190)
M5 Trans. [1]	7.2	7.4 (190)
A4LD & M5 Trans. [2]	6.4	8.0 (205)
4WD (Exc. STX)		
All Trans. [1]	10.7	10.6 (270)
All Trans. [2]	10.2	10.6 (270)
4WD (Inc. STX)		
All Trans. [1]	11.2	11.0 (280)
All Trans. [2]	10.3	11.0 (280)
Ranger Super Cab 2WD		
All Trans.	5.2	7.8 (200)
Ranger Super Cab 4WD		
All Trans.	8.6	10.6 (270)

[1] - With 107" (2743 mm) wheel base.
[2] - With 113" (2895 mm) wheel base.

PINION ANGLES (EXPLORER & RANGER)

Application	Angle (Degrees)
Explorer 2WD & 4WD	
All Trans.	10.2
Ranger Reg. Cab 2WD	
A4LD & M5 Trans.	6.9
Ranger Reg. Cab 4WD (Exc. STX)	
All Trans. [1]	9.2
All Trans. [2]	6.0
Ranger Reg. Cab 4WD (Inc. STX)	
All Trans. [1]	9.0
All Trans. [2]	6.0
Ranger Super Cab 2WD	
All Trans.	6.7
Ranger Super Cab 4WD	
All Trans.	5.7

[1] - With 107" (2743 mm) wheel base.
[2] - With 113" (2895 mm) wheel base.

OVERHAUL

NOTE: Universal joints should not be disassembled unless external leakage or damage has occurred.

SINGLE CARDAN UNIVERSAL JOINTS

Removal & Disassembly - 1) Scribe alignment marks on yoke and shaft to allow reassembly in original position. If joints are rusted or corroded, apply penetrating oil before pressing out bearing cups or trunnion pin. Disconnect yoke or flange attaching bolts, and remove drive shaft from vehicle.

NOTE: DO NOT use a pry bar to hold drive shaft while loosening bolts. Damage to bearing seals may result.

2) Remove retaining strap (if equipped). Remove bushing retainers from yoke. Press out rollers and bearings. Remove last roller and bushing assembly by pressing on end of universal joint cross shaft.
3) Remove universal joint cross shaft assembly from yoke. DO NOT remove seal retainers from cross shaft. Cross shaft and retainers are serviced as an assembly.

Reassembly & Installation - 1) Coat roller and bearing assemblies with lubricant, and fill reservoirs in ends of cross shaft. Place cross shaft assembly in drive shaft yoke, and place roller and bushing assemblies into position.
2) Press both bushing assemblies into yoke until retainers can be installed, carefully keeping cross shaft aligned in center of bushings. Install retainers, and then repeat procedure for remaining bushings. Install strap (if equipped). Install drive shaft in vehicle, aligning scribe marks.

DOUBLE CARDAN UNIVERSAL JOINTS

NOTE: When handling drive shaft after removal, support shafts on both sides when moved horizontally. DO NOT allow shaft to hang freely or bend at sharp angle.

Removal & Disassembly - 1) Scribe alignment marks on yoke and shaft to allow reassembly in original position. If joints are rusted or corroded, apply penetrating oil before pressing out bearing cups or cross shaft. Disconnect yoke attaching bolts and flange attaching bolts.

NOTE: To obtain correct clearance, cross shafts must be installed on bosses in original positions.

2) Remove drive shaft from vehicle and position assembly in vise. Mark position of cross shafts, center yoke and center yoke socket in relationship with drive shaft yoke to drive shaft tube. *See Fig. 8.*
3) Remove snap rings in front of center yoke. Using "C" clamp, tighten screw until bearing protrudes 3/8" (10 mm). Remove drive shaft from vise. Tighten protruding part of bearing in vise. Tap against center yoke with hammer until bearing is free of yoke.
4) Using this method, remove all bearings from cross shaft. Remove cross shaft from center yoke. Remove center yoke socket from stud. Remove rubber seal from centering ball stud. Remove snap rings from center and drive shaft yokes. Install "C" clamp on bearing.

NOTE: Centering ball is located inside center yoke socket. If centering ball replacement is required, replace center yoke socket.

5) Tighten clamp until bearing is pressing outward and center yoke is pressed as far as possible. Clamp exposed end of bearing in vise, and hammer on center yoke until bearing is free.
6) Press against cross shaft with "C" clamp to remove remaining bearing. Remove center yoke from cross shaft. Remove cross shaft from drive shaft using same procedure.

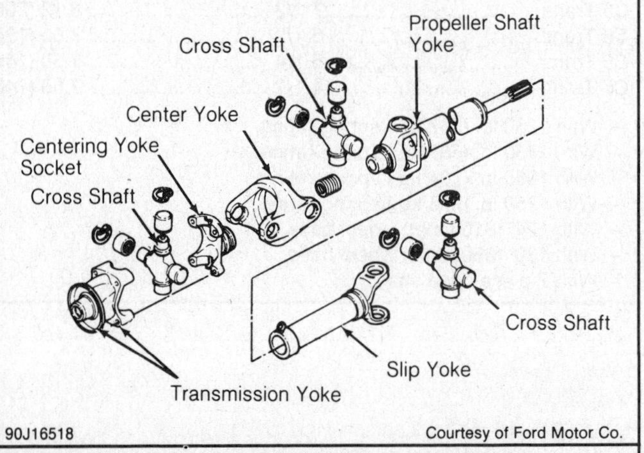
Cross Shaft
Propeller Shaft Yoke
Center Yoke
Centering Yoke Socket
Cross Shaft
Cross Shaft
Slip Yoke
Transmission Yoke
90J16518
Courtesy of Ford Motor Co.

Fig. 8: Exploded View of Double Cardan Universal Joint

Reassembly - 1) Place cross shaft in drive shaft yoke. Ensure cross shaft bosses are installed in original position. Using "C" clamp, press in bearings, and install snap rings. Fill center socket and coat centering ball with grease.
2) Position center yoke over cross shaft. Press in bearings and install snap rings. Install new seal on centering ball stud. Place centering socket over stud. Place front cross shaft in yoke. Ensure cross shaft bosses (or lubrication plugs) are installed in original position.
3) Place cross shaft loosely on center stop. Press first set of bearings into center yoke, then install second set. Install snap rings. Apply pressure to center yoke socket and install remaining bearing cup. If

replacement kit is used, remove plugs, lubricate "U" joints and reinstall plugs.

NOTE: When installed, the drive shaft assembly must have yoke ears at each end of the shaft on same plane.

Installation (1-Piece Shaft – Front) – 1) Clean yoke and inspect machined surface for scratches, nicks or burrs. Check for arrows on slip joint and drive shaft to aid in alignment.
2) Connect single end of drive shaft to front axle. Install "U" bolts and tighten nuts. Connect double cardan joint to transfer case. Install "U" bolts and tighten nuts.
Installation (1-Piece Shaft – Rear) – 1) Clean yoke and inspect machined surface for scratches, nicks or burrs. Check for arrows on slip joint and drive shaft to aid in alignment. Lubricate yoke spline and install into transmission output shaft.
2) Connect drive shaft to rear companion flange. On all except E350 models, install "U" bolts and tighten to 15 ft. lbs. (20 N.m). On E350 models, connect drive shaft flange to rear axle flange and tighten bolts to 70-95 ft. lbs. (95-129 N.m).
Installation (2-Piece & 3-Piece Shafts) – 1) Rotate transmission until yoke ears are on a horizontal plane. Clean yoke and inspect machined surface for scratches, nicks or burrs. Ensure all spines are lubricated.
2) Provide support for drive shaft during installation to prevent damage to universal joints. Align marks noted during removal. Connect front joint coupling shaft to transmission yoke and tighten bolts.
3) Ensure center bearing does not twist in support plate. Connect front and rear coupling shaft (if equipped). Attach universal joint to rear axle flange and tighten nuts to specification.

TORQUE SPECIFICATIONS

TORQUE SPECIFICATIONS

Application	Ft. Lbs. (N.m)
Coupling Shaft-To-Yoke Bolt	
5/8"	148-164 (201-222)
3/4"	175-240 (238-325)
7/8"	250-300 (339-406)
Center Bearing Bracket Support Bolts	37-54 (51-73)
Circular Flange-To-Rear Axle Flange Bolts	70-95 (95-129)
Universal Joint Adapter-To-Rear Axle Bolts	60-70 (82-95)
Universal Joint-To-Rear Yoke Bolts	90-110 (123-149)
Universal Joint-To-Transfer Case Bolts	25 (33)
Universal Joint "U" Bolts	
5/16"	15 (20)
3/8"	26 (35)
7/16"	40 (54)

1991 BRAKES
Anti-Lock – RABS

Aerostar, Bronco, Explorer, Ranger, "E" & "F" Series

DESCRIPTION & OPERATION

The Rear Anti-Lock Brake System (RABS) is designed to prevent rear brake lock-up. This is done by controlling the amount of hydraulic fluid pressure to the rear wheel cylinders. The system consists of 2 warning lights (Red BRAKE and Yellow REAR ANTILOCK), a computer module, an electro-hydraulic valve, speed sensor and exciter ring. *See Figs. 1-4*.

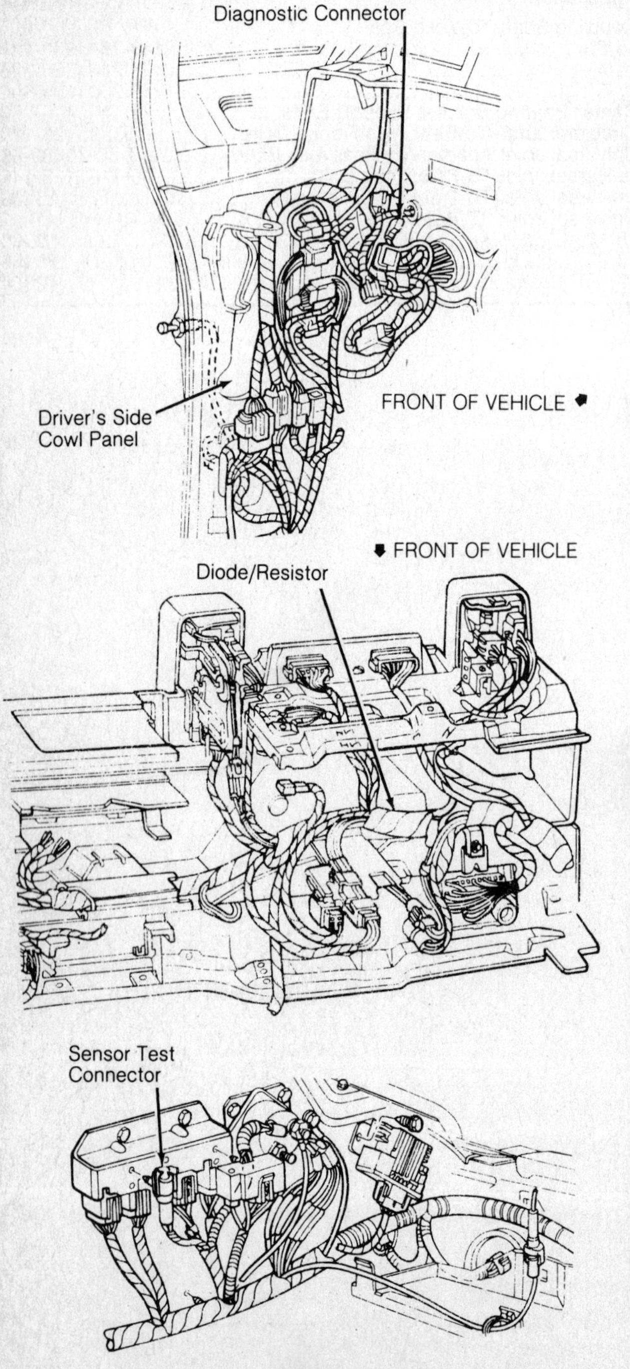
Diagnostic Connector
Driver's Side Cowl Panel
FRONT OF VEHICLE
FRONT OF VEHICLE
Diode/Resistor
Sensor Test Connector

NOTE: Control module is located on driver's side of engine cover, under instrument panel.

90G06137 Courtesy of Ford Motor Co.

Fig. 1: Locating Control Module, Diode/Resistor & Diagnostic Connector (Aerostar)

The control module continually monitors rear wheel speed. Wheel speed is sensed by speed sensor mounted on rear axle. As vehicle moves, teeth on exciter ring, located on ring gear inside the differential case, pass by the speed sensor probe. This induces an AC voltage signal in sensor circuit.

When brakes are applied, control module senses reduced wheel speed. If rate of deceleration is too great, indicating lock-up is occurring, the control module activates the electro-hydraulic valve. The valve, located on frame rail, then closes an internal isolation valve, isolating rear wheel cylinders from master cylinder. This stops rear brake pressure from increasing further.

If rate of deceleration is still too great, control module will activate dump solenoid with a series of rapid pulses, bleeding rear wheel cylinder fluid into the electro-hydraulic valve accumulator. This allows rear wheels to spin back up to vehicle speed. Dump and isolation valves will continue to be pulsed in a way that allows rear wheels to rotate, while maintaining maximum deceleration during braking.

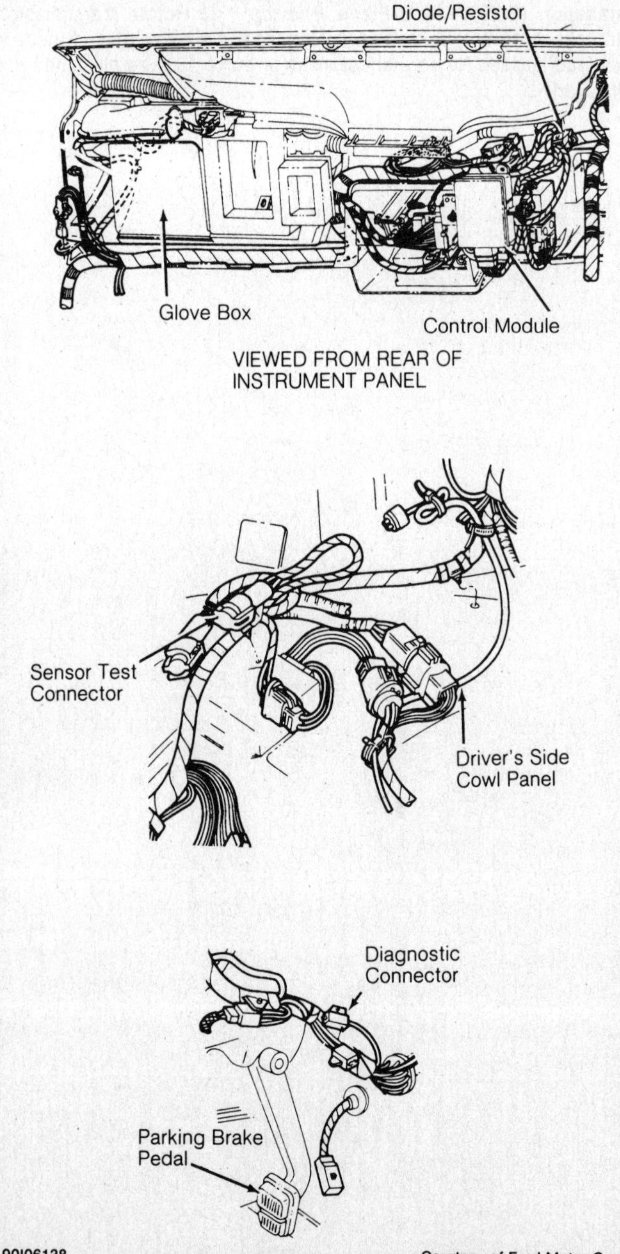
Diode/Resistor
Glove Box
Control Module
VIEWED FROM REAR OF INSTRUMENT PANEL
Sensor Test Connector
Driver's Side Cowl Panel
Diagnostic Connector
Parking Brake Pedal

90I06138 Courtesy of Ford Motor Co.

Fig. 2: Locating Control Module, Diode/Resistor & Diagnostic Connector (Bronco & "F" Series)

1991 BRAKES
Anti-Lock – RABS (Cont.)

When vehicle comes to a complete stop and brake pedal has been released, control module de-energizes isolation valve. Any fluid in accumulator is returned to master cylinder and braking is returned to normal.

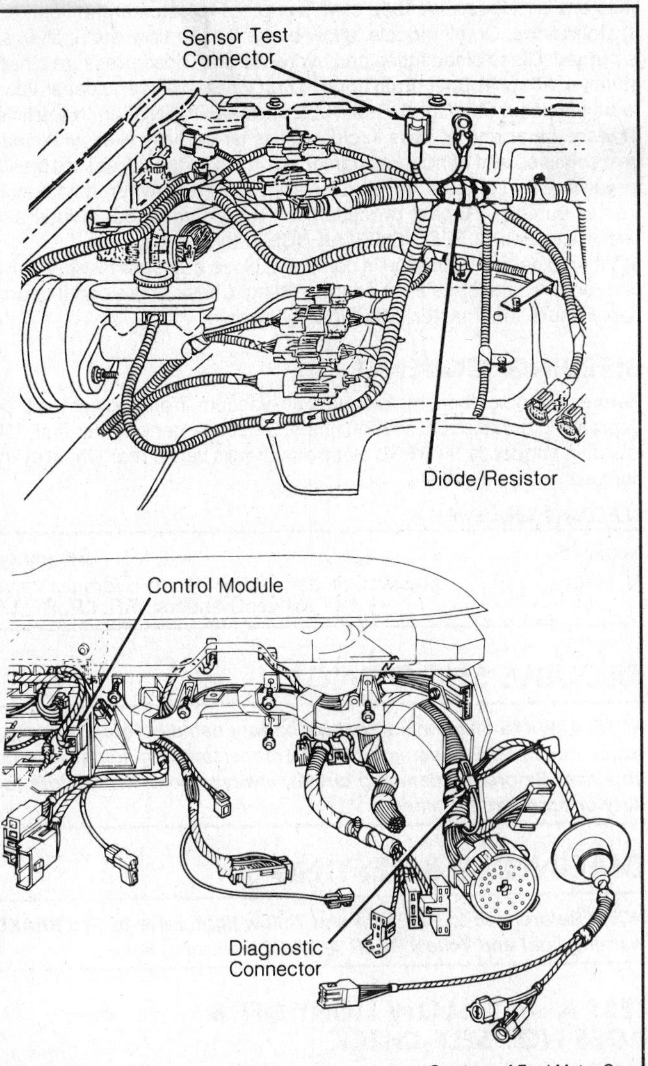
Sensor Test Connector
Diode/Resistor
Control Module
Diagnostic Connector

90A06139 Courtesy of Ford Motor Co.

Fig. 3:* *Locating Control Module, Diode/Resistor & Diagnostic Connector (Explorer & Ranger)

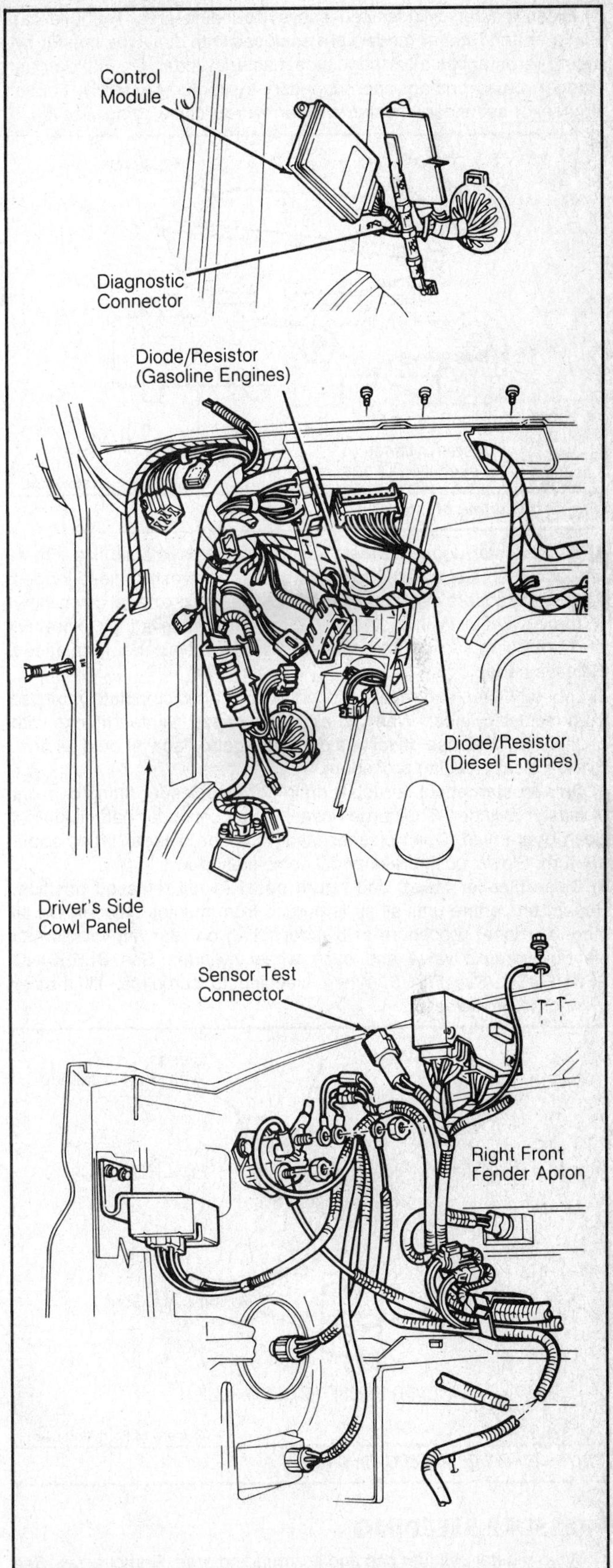
Control Module
Diagnostic Connector
Diode/Resistor (Gasoline Engines)
Diode/Resistor (Diesel Engines)
Driver's Side Cowl Panel
Sensor Test Connector
Right Front Fender Apron

90C06140 Courtesy of Ford Motor Co.

Fig. 4:* *Locating Control Module, Diode/Resistor & Diagnostic Connector ("E" Series)

BLEEDING BRAKE SYSTEM

Hydraulic system bleeding is necessary whenever air enters the system. If master cylinder lines have been disconnected or master cylinder has run dry, bleed master cylinder and brakes at all 4 wheels. Bleed brakes with pressure bleeding equipment or by manually pumping brake pedal while using bleeder tubes. Always bleed brake lines in sequence. See BLEEDING SEQUENCE in this article.

MANUAL BLEEDING

CAUTION: DO NOT allow reservoir to run dry during bleeding operation. If brake fluid is spilled on vehicle paint, immediately rinse off with water.

NOTE: Manual bleeding procedure for Bronco and "E" and "F" Series vehicles is not available from manufacturer. Procedure is similar to other models.

1991 BRAKES
Anti-Lock – RABS (Cont.)

1) Clean master cylinder cap and surrounding area. Remove cap. Explorer and Ranger models are equipped with dual type master cylinder. Aerostar has a cartridge type master cylinder. On Explorer and Ranger, bleed primary and secondary systems separately. Loosen primary or secondary master cylinder hydraulic line fitting. *See Fig. 5.*

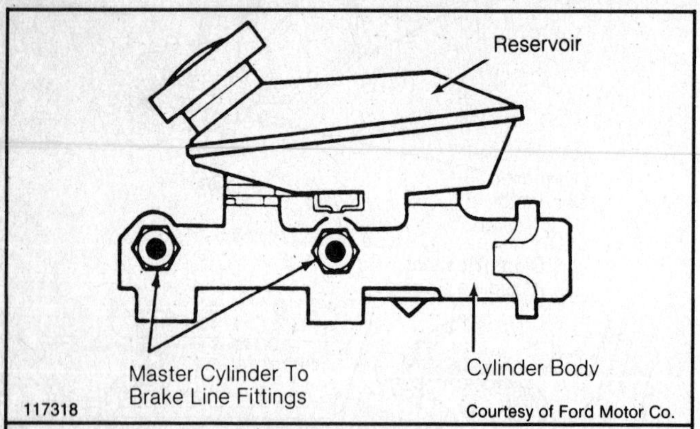
Reservoir
Master Cylinder To Brake Line Fittings
Cylinder Body
117318
Courtesy of Ford Motor Co.

Fig. 5: Bleeding Master Cylinder (Typical)

2) On Aerostar, loosen either master cylinder hydraulic line. On all models, wrap a cloth around brake lines (on Aerostar, bleed longest line first) to absorb escaping brake fluid. Push brake pedal down slowly, forcing air out. With pedal fully depressed, tighten fittings to prevent air from being sucked into master cylinder when pedal is released. Release pedal.

3) Loosen fitting, and repeat procedure until air is completely purged from master cylinder. When all air has escaped, tighten fittings with pedal down. Release pedal and depress again. Pedal should be firm. If not, repeat bleeding procedure.

4) On Aerostar, attach a rubber drain hose to bleeder fitting on front of master cylinder. Submerge hose in small container half filled with clean brake fluid. Open bleeder fitting. Loosen bleeder fitting about 3/4 turn. Slowly push brake pedal completely down.

5) Close bleeder fitting, and return pedal to full released position. Repeat procedure until all air is purged from master cylinder. On all models, repeat procedure at bleeder fitting on rear anti-lock brake electro-hydraulic valve and each wheel cylinder. See BLEEDING SEQUENCE. *See Fig. 6.* When bleeding is complete, fill master cylinder to proper lever.

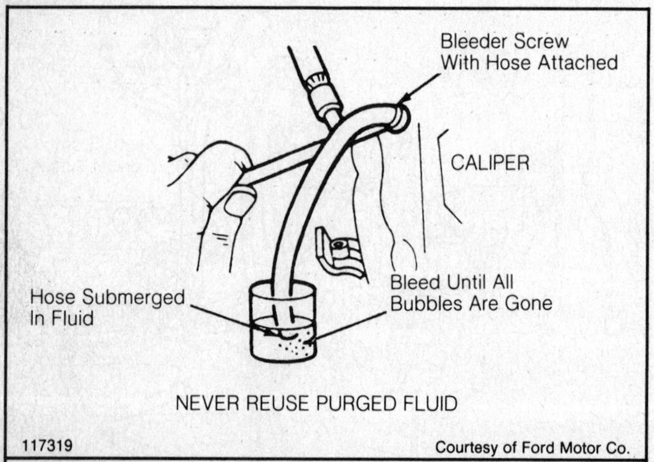
Bleeder Screw With Hose Attached
CALIPER
Bleed Until All Bubbles Are Gone
Hose Submerged In Fluid
NEVER REUSE PURGED FLUID
117319
Courtesy of Ford Motor Co.

Fig. 6: Bleeding Wheel Cylinders

PRESSURE BLEEDING

1) Clean master cylinder cap and surrounding area. Remove cap. *See Fig. 5.* With pressure tank at least 1/2 full of specified fluid and charged between 10-30 psi (.7-2.0 kg/cm²), connect tank to master cylinder using adapters. Follow equipment manufacturer's pressure instructions.

CAUTION: NEVER exceed 50 psi (3.5 kg/cm²) during bleeding.

2) Open pressure bleeder valve. On Aerostar, attach one end of rubber drain tube to master cylinder bleeder fitting. Open bleed fitting. On all others, bleed master cylinder primary and secondary hydraulic lines one at a time. Put shop towels in place to catch brake fluid.

3) Open lines. On all models, allow brake fluid to flow out until all air is purged. Close bleed fitting and hydraulic line. Close pressure bleeder valve. Attach rubber drain hose to first wheel cylinder bleeder valve to be serviced. *See Fig. 6.* See BLEEDING SEQUENCE in this article.

4) Place other end of hose in clean glass jar partially filled with clean brake fluid so end of hose is submerged in fluid. Open pressure bleeder valve. Open bleeder fitting. Close bleeder fitting when fluid flow is free of bubbles. Repeat procedure on remaining wheel cylinders in sequence. See BLEEDING SEQUENCE in this article.

5) When bleeding operation is complete, close pressure bleeder valve and remove tank hose from adapter fitting. Check brake pedal operation. Ensure that master cylinder is full of fluid.

BLEEDING SEQUENCE

Before bleeding system, exhaust all vacuum from power unit by depressing brake pedal several times. Bleed master cylinder first, followed in sequence by RABS electro-hydraulic valve, rear wheel cylinders and front calipers.

BLEEDING SEQUENCE

Application	Sequence
All Models	Master Cylinder, RABS Electro-Hydraulic Valve Wheel Cylinders: RR, LR, RF, LF

TROUBLE SHOOTING

NOTE: ALWAYS disconnect positive battery cable before measuring resistance on RABS system or incorrect resistance readings may be obtained. Before condemning circuit, always check connectors for dirty or corroded terminals.

DIAGNOSIS & TESTING

NOTE: References to Red light and Yellow light, refer to Red BRAKE warning light and Yellow REAR ANTILOCK warning light.

TEST A – YELLOW LIGHT OFF & DOES NOT SELF-CHECK

1) Ensure control module connector is fully engaged. If not, engage connector, and retest system. If connector is engaged, disconnect battery. Unplug control module connector. Measure resistance between connector pin No. 4 and ground. *See Fig. 7.*

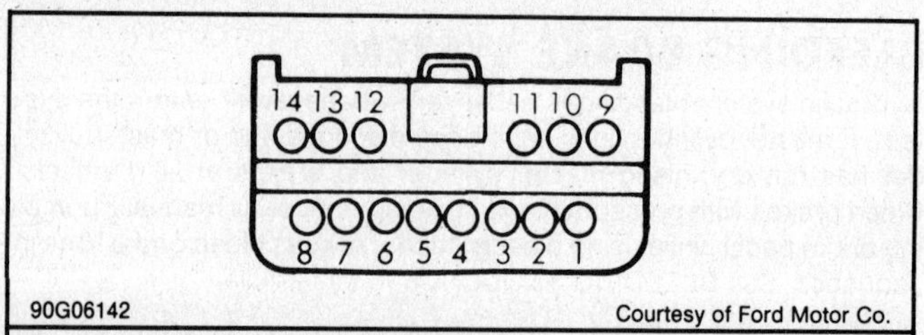
14 13 12
11 10 9
8 7 6 5 4 3 2 1
90G06142
Courtesy of Ford Motor Co.

Fig. 7: Identifying Control Module Pins

2) If resistance is one ohm or more, check for open circuit between pin No. 4 and ground. If resistance is less than one ohm, reconnect battery. Turn ignition on. Check voltage at connector pin No. 7. If voltage is 9 volts or more, replace control module.

3) If voltage is less than 9 volts, check Yellow ABS light 15-amp fuse. If fuse is bad, check for short between fuse and warning lights. Replace fuse and retest system. If fuse is okay, check voltage at fuse. If voltage is less than 9 volts, check fuse panel or vehicle electrical system.

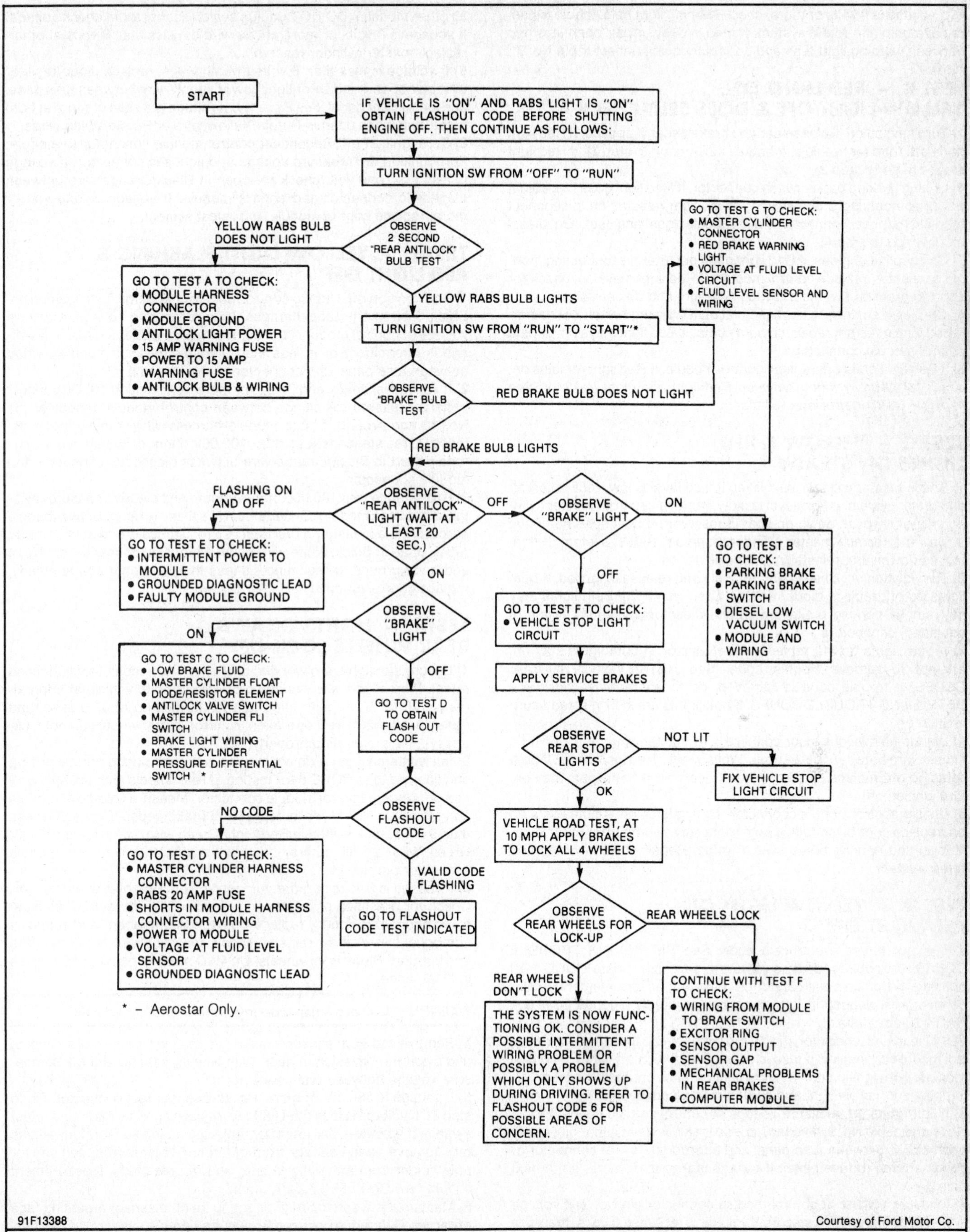

START
IF VEHICLE IS "ON" AND RABS LIGHT IS "ON" OBTAIN FLASHOUT CODE BEFORE SHUTTING ENGINE OFF. THEN CONTINUE AS FOLLOWS:
TURN IGNITION SW FROM "OFF" TO "RUN"
YELLOW RABS BULB DOES NOT LIGHT
OBSERVE 2 SECOND "REAR ANTILOCK" BULB TEST
GO TO TEST A TO CHECK: • MODULE HARNESS CONNECTOR • MODULE GROUND • ANTILOCK LIGHT POWER • 15 AMP WARNING FUSE • POWER TO 15 AMP WARNING FUSE • ANTILOCK BULB & WIRING
GO TO TEST G TO CHECK: • MASTER CYLINDER CONNECTOR • RED BRAKE WARNING LIGHT • VOLTAGE AT FLUID LEVEL CIRCUIT • FLUID LEVEL SENSOR AND WIRING
YELLOW RABS BULB LIGHTS
TURN IGNITION SW FROM "RUN" TO "START"*
OBSERVE "BRAKE" BULB TEST
RED BRAKE BULB DOES NOT LIGHT
RED BRAKE BULB LIGHTS
FLASHING ON AND OFF
OBSERVE "REAR ANTILOCK" LIGHT (WAIT AT LEAST 20 SEC.)
OFF
OBSERVE "BRAKE" LIGHT
ON
GO TO TEST E TO CHECK: • INTERMITTENT POWER TO MODULE • GROUNDED DIAGNOSTIC LEAD • FAULTY MODULE GROUND
GO TO TEST B TO CHECK: • PARKING BRAKE • PARKING BRAKE SWITCH • DIESEL LOW VACUUM SWITCH • MODULE AND WIRING
ON
OFF
OBSERVE "BRAKE" LIGHT
GO TO TEST F TO CHECK: • VEHICLE STOP LIGHT CIRCUIT
ON
GO TO TEST C TO CHECK: • LOW BRAKE FLUID • MASTER CYLINDER FLOAT • DIODE/RESISTOR ELEMENT • ANTILOCK VALVE SWITCH • MASTER CYLINDER FLI SWITCH • BRAKE LIGHT WIRING • MASTER CYLINDER PRESSURE DIFFERENTIAL SWITCH *
OFF
APPLY SERVICE BRAKES
GO TO TEST D TO OBTAIN FLASH OUT CODE
OBSERVE REAR STOP LIGHTS
NOT LIT
FIX VEHICLE STOP LIGHT CIRCUIT
OK
VEHICLE ROAD TEST, AT 10 MPH APPLY BRAKES TO LOCK ALL 4 WHEELS
NO CODE
OBSERVE FLASHOUT CODE
GO TO TEST D TO CHECK: • MASTER CYLINDER HARNESS CONNECTOR • RABS 20 AMP FUSE • SHORTS IN MODULE HARNESS CONNECTOR WIRING • POWER TO MODULE • VOLTAGE AT FLUID LEVEL SENSOR • GROUNDED DIAGNOSTIC LEAD
VALID CODE FLASHING
GO TO FLASHOUT CODE TEST INDICATED
OBSERVE REAR WHEELS FOR LOCK-UP
REAR WHEELS LOCK
REAR WHEELS DON'T LOCK
CONTINUE WITH TEST F TO CHECK: • WIRING FROM MODULE TO BRAKE SWITCH • EXCITOR RING • SENSOR OUTPUT • SENSOR GAP • MECHANICAL PROBLEMS IN REAR BRAKES • COMPUTER MODULE
THE SYSTEM IS NOW FUNCTIONING OK. CONSIDER A POSSIBLE INTERMITTENT WIRING PROBLEM OR POSSIBLY A PROBLEM WHICH ONLY SHOWS UP DURING DRIVING. REFER TO FLASHOUT CODE 6 FOR POSSIBLE AREAS OF CONCERN.
* – Aerostar Only.
91F13388
Courtesy of Ford Motor Co.

Fig. 8: RABS Trouble Shooting Chart

1991 BRAKES
Anti-Lock – RABS (Cont.)

4) If voltage is 9 volts or more, check warning light bulb. If bulb is bad, replace bulb and retest system. If bulb is okay, repair open in wiring between warning light fuse and control module connector pin No. 7.

TEST B – RED LIGHT ON, YELLOW LIGHT OFF & DOES SELF-CHECK

1) Turn ignition on. Release parking brake pedal, if applied. If Red light goes off, road test vehicle. If brakes lock-up, go to step **2)**. If Red light stays on, go to step **2)**.
2) Unplug parking brake switch connector. If Red light goes out, adjust or replace parking brake switch. If Red light remains on, disconnect module harness connector from module (gas engines). On diesel engines, go to step **4)**.
3) On gasoline engines, if Red light goes out after disconnecting module connector, replace control module. If Red light stays on, check for short to ground in wiring between Red light and diode/resistor.
4) On diesel engines, disconnect vacuum warning switch connector. If Red light goes off, repair vacuum pump. If Red light stays on, unplug control module connector.
5) If Red light goes off, replace control module. If Red light remains on, check for shorted wiring between Red light and diode/resistor. *See Figs. 1-4* for diode/resistor locations.

TEST C – YELLOW & RED LIGHTS ON STEADY

1) Check master cylinder fluid level. If fluid level is low, refill reservoir and retest system. If fluid level is okay, remove cap from master cylinder. Carefully push down on float in reservoir. If float does not move downward, replace master cylinder reservoir. Retest system. If float moves downward, reinstall master cylinder cap.
2) Turn ignition on. Check parking brake and release if applied. If both lights go off, replace diode/resistor. *See Figs. 1-4*. If both lights stay on, remove parking brake switch and diesel low vacuum switch (if equipped) connectors.
3) If both lights go off, replace diode/resistor. If both lights stay on, attempt to retrieve trouble code. See RETRIEVING TROUBLE CODES. If trouble code is retrieved, go to appropriate code. See RETRIEVING TROUBLE CODES. If both lights are still on steady, turn ignition off.
4) Unplug fluid level sensor connector, at master cylinder. Connect a jumper wire between the 2 Purple/White wires. Turn ignition on. If both lights go off, replace master cylinder reservoir. If both lights stay on, turn ignition off.
5) Unplug control module connector. Turn ignition on. If both lights go off, replace control module. If both lights stay on, check for short in fluid level and parking brake switch wiring. Repair short in wiring and retest system.

TEST D – YELLOW LIGHT ON, RED LIGHT OFF

1) Attempt to retrieve trouble code. See RETRIEVING TROUBLE CODES. If trouble code was retrieved, see appropriate CODE 1-16 heading. If trouble code cannot be retrieved, ensure master cylinder connector is plugged in fully. If connector is fully plugged in, check RABS 20-amp fuse.
2) If fuse is bad, check for short in wiring between fuse panel and control module connector. If fuse is okay, turn ignition off. Unplug control module. Turn ignition on. If Yellow light remains on, repair short in wiring between Yellow light and control module connector.
3) If light goes off, measure voltage at control module connector pin No. 1 and at pin No. 9. If voltage is less than 9 volts at either pin, repair open circuit between fuse panel and appropriate pin at connector or power source to fuse panel. If voltage is 9 volts or more, go to next step.
4) Measure voltage at control module connector pin No. 2. If voltage is 8 volts or more, go to step **6)**. If voltage is less than 8 volts, measure voltage at each of 2 Purple/White wires at fluid level switch on Bronco and "E" and "F" Series (Purple/White wire and Purple/Yellow wire on all other models). DO NOT unplug switch connector to check voltage. If voltage is 8 volts or more at one wire but less than 8 volts at other, replace master cylinder reservoir.
5) If voltage is less than 8 volts at both wires, replace diode/resistor or repair open in indicator light power supply wire between fuse panel and instrument panel. *See Figs. 1-4.* If voltage is 8 volts or more at both wires, check for open in Purple/Yellow wire or Purple/White wires.
6) Turn ignition off. Reconnect control module connector to module. Turn ignition on. Measure voltage at diagnostic connector. If voltage is less than one volt, check for open in Black/Orange wire between diagnostic connector and control module. If voltage is one volt or more, replace control module and retest system.

TEST E – YELLOW LIGHT FLASHING & RED LIGHT OFF

1) Turn ignition off. Unplug control module connector. Turn ignition on. Shake instrument panel harness while measuring voltage. Measure voltage at control module connector pin No. 1 and at pin No. 9. If voltage is intermittent or is less than 9 volts, check for open in wiring between fuse panel and connector pin No. 1 and pin No. 9.
2) If voltage is steady and 9 volts or more, turn ignition off. Disconnect battery. Measure resistance between control module connector pin No. 12 and ground. Shake module harness while measuring resistance. If resistance is less than 100,000 ohms or resistance varies, repair short in Black/Orange wire between diagnostic connector and module connector.
3) If resistance was 100,000 ohms or more and steady, measure resistance between module connector pin No. 4 and ground. Shake module harness while measuring resistance. If resistance is one ohm or more, repair open in Black/White wire between module connector pin No. 4 and body ground. If resistance is less than one ohm and is steady, replace control module.

TEST F – LIGHTS OKAY & REAR WHEELS LOCK-UP

1) Ensure stoplights are working properly. If not, repair stoplights and retest. If stoplights are working properly, operate vehicle at approximately 10 MPH. Apply brakes to attempt lock-up of all brakes, and observe left rear wheel operation in mirror. If rear wheels do not lock-up, system is operating properly.
2) Intermittent wiring problem may be occurring during normal driving conditions. Go to CODE 6 for testing. If rear wheels lock up, turn ignition off. Unplug control module connector. Measure voltage at module connector pin No. 11 while depressing brake pedal. If voltage is less than 9 volts, repair open in Red/Light Green wire on Aerostar or Light Green wire on all others, between stoplight switch and module connector pin No. 11.
3) If voltage is 9 volts or more, turn ignition off. Remove speed sensor. Check for presence of exciter ring and condition of teeth. If damage to component is found, replace damaged component and retest. If components are okay, reinstall speed sensor. Raise rear of vehicle and support. Block front wheels. On 4WD models, place transfer case in 2WD mode.

WARNING: Use care when working around rotating wheels.

---

4) Remove cap from sensor test connector. *See Figs. 1-4*. Start engine and place transmission in gear. With wheels rotating at 5 MPH, measure voltage between test connector pins.
5) If voltage is 650 mV or more, reinstall sensor test connector. Go to step **7)**. If voltage is less than 650 mV, replace speed sensor and retest system. If voltage is still low after replacing speed sensor, turn engine off. Remove speed sensor from differential. Measure speed sensor pole height from mounting face to end of pole piece. Measurement should be 1.07-1.08" (27.2-27.4 mm).
6) Measure between top of exciter ring teeth to sensor mounting face of carrier. Difference between 2 measurements is sensor gap. If difference is more than .050" (1.27 mm), check for defective sensor or carrier housing. If difference is less than .050" (1.27 mm), go to step **7)**.

7) Check rear brakes for mechanical problems such as grabbing, locking and pulling. Repair brakes as necessary. If rear brakes are okay, replace control module and retest.

TEST G – YELLOW LIGHT SELF-CHECKS, RED LIGHT DOES NOT SELF-CHECK

Ensure connector on brake fluid level switch, at the master cylinder, is plugged in fully. If not, reconnect and retest. If connector is okay, apply parking brake and check Red warning light. If Red warning light does not come on, check bulb or an open in light circuit. If light comes on, go to TEST D – YELLOW LIGHT ON, RED LIGHT OFF, step **4)**.

RETRIEVING TROUBLE CODES

Rear Anti-Lock Brake System (RABS) has a self-test capability. There are 2 warning lights, located on instrument panel, to inform driver of malfunction. Red BRAKE warning light indicates low fluid level, parking brake on or low vacuum (diesel models). Yellow REAR ANTILOCK warning light comes on when control module detects a malfunction and/or anti-lock brake system is inoperative. Both lights should come on for approximately 2 seconds when ignition is turned on or when cranking engine. *See Fig. 8.*

When Yellow REAR ANTILOCK warning light comes on during normal operation, a trouble code can be received from control module. Code will be lost if vehicle is shut off before code is retrieved. In some cases, code may reappear when vehicle is restarted. In other cases, vehicle may have to be driven to reproduce problem.

WARNING: Block front and rear wheels to prevent vehicle from moving while trouble codes are being retrieved.

NOTE: If multiple system faults exist, only first detected fault code can be received.

If Red BRAKE warning light is on because of low brake fluid level, together with Yellow REAR ANTILOCK warning light, Yellow warning light will not flash trouble code but will glow steadily. System faults concerning brake fluid level switch and power loss to control module, will cause anti-lock brake system to deactivate. Yellow warning light will come on but control module will not generate a trouble code.

Before retrieving trouble code, ensure vehicle is on a level area. Transmission should be in Park or Neutral. Note if Red BRAKE warning light is on. Apply parking brake. Keep ignition on so code will not be lost. Locate rear anti-lock brake diagnostic connector and attach jumper wire. *See Figs. 1-4.* Momentarily ground other end of jumper wire. When ground is contacted then broken, Yellow REAR ANTILOCK warning light will flash trouble code. A code consists of a number of short flashes and one long flash. Count each flash, short and long to obtain code number.

NO CODES

Some system faults light REAR ANTILOCK warning light, but do not set a trouble code. See RETRIEVING TROUBLE CODES. If trouble code should be set but cannot be retrieved, refer to RABS TROUBLE SHOOTING CHART. *See Fig. 8.* Ensure a good momentary ground is made at diagnostic connector.

CODE 1

Code 1 is not a valid code. Perform RETRIEVING TROUBLE CODES again. If Code 1 appears again, go to TEST E – YELLOW LIGHT FLASHING & RED LIGHT OFF under DIAGNOSIS & TESTING.

CODE 2 (OPEN ISOLATE CIRCUIT)

1) Turn ignition off. Disconnect battery. Unplug control module harness connector. Measure resistance between module connector pin No. 13 and ground. If resistance is 6 ohms or less, replace control module and retest system.

2) If resistance is greater than 6 ohms, reconnect module connector. On Bronco, "E" and "F" Series, disconnect electro-hydraulic valve connector. On all others, go to step **4)**. On Bronco, "E" and "F" Series, measure resistance between ground pin (harness side) and ground. *See Fig. 9.*

3) If resistance is one ohm or more, repair open in ground circuit wire. If resistance is less than one ohm, measure resistance between isolation solenoid pin and ground pin on valve side. *See Fig. 9.* If resistance is 6 ohms or less, repair open between isolation solenoid valve and control module.

4) On all others, disconnect electro-hydraulic valve connector. *See Fig. 9.* Measure resistance between isolation solenoid pin and ground pin on valve side. If resistance is greater than 6 ohms, replace electro-hydraulic valve and retest. If resistance is 6 ohms or less, repair open between isolation solenoid valve and control module.

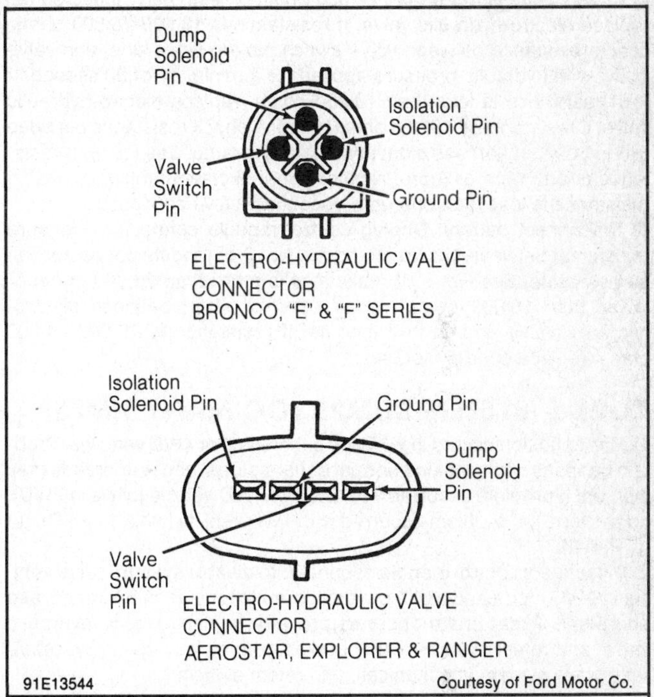
Dump
Solenoid
Pin
Isolation
Solenoid Pin
Valve
Switch
Pin
Ground Pin
ELECTRO-HYDRAULIC VALVE
CONNECTOR
BRONCO, "E" & "F" SERIES
Isolation
Solenoid Pin
Ground Pin
Dump
Solenoid
Pin
Valve
Switch
Pin
ELECTRO-HYDRAULIC VALVE
CONNECTOR
AEROSTAR, EXPLORER & RANGER
91E13544
Courtesy of Ford Motor Co.

Fig. 9: Identifying Electro-Hydraulic Valve Connector Pins

CODE 3 (OPEN DUMP CIRCUIT)

1) Turn ignition off. Disconnect battery. Unplug control module connector. Measure resistance between pin No. 8 or 14 and ground on valve side. *See Fig. 9.* If resistance is less than 3 ohms, replace control module. If resistance is 3 ohms or more, reconnect module connector.

2) Unplug electro-hydraulic valve connector. Measure resistance between dump solenoid pin and ground pin on valve side. If resistance is less than 3 ohms, repair open between dump valve connector and control module. If resistance is 3 ohms or more, replace electro-hydraulic valve.

CODE 4 (CLOSED VALVE SWITCH OR OPEN DUMP VALVE)

Bronco, "E" & "E" Series – 1) When this occurs, Red BRAKE warning light will be on. Unplug electro-hydraulic valve connector. Measure resistance between valve switch pin (on valve side) and valve body. *See Fig. 9.* If resistance is less than 10,000 ohms, replace electro-hydraulic valve.

2) If resistance is 10,000 ohms or more, measure resistance between valve switch pin and ground pin on valve side. *See Fig. 9.* If resistance is 10,000 ohms or less, replace electro-hydraulic valve. If resistance is more than 10,000 ohms, disconnect battery.

3) Unplug control module connector. Measure resistance between module connector pin No. 6 (on harness side) and ground. *See Fig. 7.*

If resistance is 100,000 ohms or more, replace control module. If resistance is less than 100,000 ohms, repair short between valve and control module.

CODE 4 (CLOSED VALVE SWITCH OR OPEN DUMP VALVE)

Explorer & Ranger – 1) When this occurs, Red BRAKE warning light will be on. Unplug electro-hydraulic valve connector. Measure resistance between valve switch pin (on valve side) and valve body. *See Fig. 9*. If resistance is less than 10,000 ohms, replace electro-hydraulic valve. If resistance is 10,000 ohms or more, check resistance between valve switch pin (on valve side) and solenoid ground pin. *See Fig. 9*.

2) If resistance is more than 26,000 ohms or less than 18,000 ohms, replace electro-hydraulic valve. If resistance is 18,000-26,000 ohms, check resistance between valve switch pin (on valve side) and valve body, with hydraulic pressure applied for a minimum of 30 seconds.

3) If resistance is less than 10,000 ohms, replace electro-hydraulic valve. If resistance is 10,000 ohms or more, check resistance between ground pin (on harness side) and chassis ground. *See Fig. 9*. If resistance is one ohm or more, repair open in isolation solenoid wire. If resistance is less than one ohm, reconnect valve connector.

4) Disconnect battery. Unplug control module connector. Measure resistance between pin No. 4 and pin No. 6 at module connector, on harness side. *See Fig. 7*. If resistance is more than 26,000 ohms or lower than 18,000 ohms, repair open or short between electro-hydraulic valve and control module. If resistance is 18,000-26,000 ohms, replace control module.

CODE 5 (SYSTEM DUMPS TOO MANY TIMES)

1) This condition occurs in 2WD, on either 2WD or 4WD vehicles. Problem happens when making normal or hard stops, and rear brakes may lock up. If problem occurred with 2WD or 4WD vehicle (while in 2WD), go to step **2)**. If problem occurred with 4WD vehicle (while in 4WD), go to step **3)**.

2) Disconnect control module connector to disable system. Drive vehicle in 2WD mode and make several normal stops to check rear brake operation. If rear brake operates properly, replace electro-hydraulic valve, and retest system. If rear brakes grab or lock up easily, repair rear brake system (mechanical), and retest system.

3) Unplug control module connector. Turn ignition on. Shift transfer case into 4WD mode. Measure voltage between pin No. 5 and chassis ground. *See Fig. 7*. If voltage is less than one volt, replace electro-hydraulic valve. If voltage is one volt or more, repair or replace 4WD indicator switch, located on transfer case.

CODE 6 (SPEED SENSOR SIGNAL RAPIDLY CUTS IN AND OUT)

1) This condition only happens while driving. Turn ignition off. Disconnect battery. Measure resistance between module connector pins No. 3 and 10, while shaking wiring harness between speed sensor and module connector. *See Fig. 7*. If reading is erratic, repair loose connection in sensor leads.

2) If resistance is 1000-2000 ohms and steady, remove speed sensor. Check for build up of metal chips on sensor pole. If metal chips are present, drain and clean differential. Check exciter ring for broken or chipped teeth. If no metal chips are present, remove sensor from carrier.

3) Inspect exciter ring for damaged teeth. If teeth are okay and no visible lateral runout is seen, reinstall speed sensor. If teeth are damaged and lateral runout is visible, repair differential.

4) To check for low or erratic sensor output, raise vehicle to allow rear wheels to spin freely. Start engine. With rear wheels rotating at 5 MPH, measure voltage between test connector pins. If voltage is 650 mV or more and steady, replace control module. If voltage is less than 650 mV and/or is erratic, replace speed sensor and test connector cap. Retest system.

CODE 7 (NO ISOLATE VALVE SELF-TEST)

1) Turn ignition off. Unplug electro-hydraulic valve connector. Measure resistance between isolation solenoid pin and ground pin at valve. *See Fig. 9*. If resistance is less than 3 ohms, replace valve. If resistance is 3 ohms or more, turn ignition off, and disconnect battery.

2) With electro-hydraulic valve connector still apart, unplug control module connector. Measure resistance between module pin No. 13 and chassis ground. *See Fig. 7*. If resistance is 20,000 ohms or more, replace control module. If resistance is less than 20,000 ohms, repair short between electro-hydraulic valve and control module.

CODE 8 (NO DUMP VALVE SELF-TEST)

1) Turn ignition off. Unplug electro-hydraulic valve connector. Measure resistance between dump solenoid pin and ground pin at valve. *See Fig. 9*. If resistance is less than one ohm, replace electro-hydraulic valve. If resistance is one ohm or more, turn ignition off, and disconnect battery.

2) With electro-hydraulic valve connector still apart, unplug control module connector. Measure resistance between module connector pins No. 8 or 14 and ground. *See Fig. 7*. If resistance is 20,000 ohms or more, replace control module. If resistance is less than 20,000 ohms, repair short between electro-hydraulic valve and control module.

CODE 9 (HIGH SENSOR RESISTANCE)

1) Turn ignition off. Unplug speed sensor connector at sensor. Measure resistance between sensor pins. If resistance is 2500 ohms or more, replace sensor. If resistance is less than 2500 ohms, disconnect battery. Reconnect speed sensor connector. Unplug control module connector.

2) Measure resistance between module connector pins No. 3 and 10. *See Fig. 7*. If resistance is less than 2500 ohms, replace control module. If resistance is 2500 ohms or more, repair open between speed sensor and control module. If jumper harness between speed sensor and frame rail is defective, replace ONLY with original equipment High Flex Wire. Splice Connector (E6EB-14488-AA) MUST be used.

CODE 10 (LOW SENSOR RESISTANCE)

1) Turn ignition off. Unplug speed sensor connector at sensor. Measure resistance between sensor pins. If resistance is 1000 ohms or less, replace sensor. If resistance is more than 1000 ohms, disconnect battery. With speed sensor connector apart from sensor, unplug control module connector.

2) Measure resistance between module pin No. 10 and chassis ground. *See Fig. 7*. If resistance is less than 20,000 ohms, repair short to ground between speed sensor and control module. If jumper harness between speed sensor and frame rail is defective, replace ONLY with original equipment High Flex Wire. Splice Connector (E6EB-14488-AA) MUST be used.

3) If resistance is 20,000 ohms or more, measure resistance between module connector pins No. 3 and 10. If resistance is 20,000 ohms or more, replace control module. If resistance is less than 20,000 ohms, repair short between speed sensor wires. If jumper harness between speed sensor and frame rail is defective, replace ONLY with original equipment High Flex Wire. Splice Connector (E6EB-14488-AA) MUST be used.

CODE 11 (STOPLIGHT SWITCH CIRCUIT)

1) This condition occurs only when driving above 35 MPH. Depress brake pedal and check stoplight operation. If stoplights do not operate, repair stoplight circuit, and retest system. If stoplights operate properly, turn ignition off. Unplug control module connector. Measure voltage at module connector pin No. 11 while depressing brake pedal. *See Fig. 7*.

2) If voltage is less than 9 volts, repair open between stoplight switch and control module. If voltage is 9 volts or more, check 4-way flasher and wiring. A problem with 4-way flasher or wiring could cause feedback through stoplight circuit.

1991 BRAKES
Anti-Lock – RABS (Cont.)

CODE 12 (FLUID LEVEL SWITCH CLOSED DURING A STOP)

Bronco, "E" & "F" Series – When this occurs, Red BRAKE warning light will be on. For test procedure, see TEST C under DIAGNOSIS & TESTING. Skip step **3)**.

CODE 12 (LOSS OF BRAKE FLUID FOR ONE SECOND DURING STOP)

Explorer & Ranger – When this occurs, Red BRAKE warning light will be on. Check brake fluid level. If low, check complete system for leaks, and repair as necessary. Refill master cylinder. If fluid level is okay, replace control module.

CODE 13 (SPEED SENSOR CHECK)

This code indicates control module speed circuit phase lock loop failure, detected during module self-test. Replace control module.

CODE 14 (PROGRAM CHECK)

This code indicates control module program check sum failure detected during self-test. Replace control module.

CODE 15 (MEMORY FAILURE)

This code indicates control module RAM failure detected during self-test. Replace control module.

CODE 16

This code should not occur. Recheck flashing sequence. If codes continue to occur, replace control module.

REMOVAL & INSTALLATION

ELECTRO-HYDRAULIC VALVE

Removal & Installation – Disconnect and plug brake lines connected to electro-hydraulic valve. Unplug electrical connector. Remove mounting bolts retaining valve to frame. Remove valve. To install, reverse removal procedure.

SPEED SENSOR

Removal & Installation – Unplug speed sensor connector. Remove hold-down bolt and sensor. To install, ensure "O" ring is positioned on sensor and sensor tip is clean of all metal particles. Lightly lubricate "O" ring with engine oil. Install sensor. DO NOT use force to install sensor. Install hold-down bolt.

CONTROL MODULE

Removal & Installation – On "E" Series, remove parking brake actuator assembly. Remove screws attaching control module behind kick panel. Remove control module. On all other models, remove screws attaching control module to dash panel bracket. Remove control panel. To install, reverse removal procedure.

EXCITER RING

Removal & Installation – Remove differential case from axle housing. See appropriate article in DRIVE AXLES. Exciter ring must be pressed off differential case, and discarded. To install, reverse removal procedure.

TORQUE SPECIFICATIONS

TORQUE SPECIFICATIONS

Application	Ft. Lbs. (N.m)
Brake Lines	
1/2"-20	10-17 (14-23)
7/16"-24	10-15 (14-20)
3/8"-24	10-15 (14-20)
Electro-Hydraulic Valve Mounting Bolts	
Bronco & "F" Series	12-17 (16-23)
Explorer & Ranger	11-14 (15-19)
"E" Series	19-24 (26-32)
Speed Sensor Hold-Down Bolt	25-30 (34-41)
	INCH Lbs. (N.m)
Electro-Hydraulic Valve Mounting Bolts	
Aerostar	30-40 (3.4-4.5)

1991 BRAKES
Anti-Lock – RABS (Cont.)

WIRING DIAGRAMS

For anti-lock brake system wiring diagrams, see Figs. 10-13. Also refer to appropriate chassis wiring diagram in WIRING DIAGRAMS.

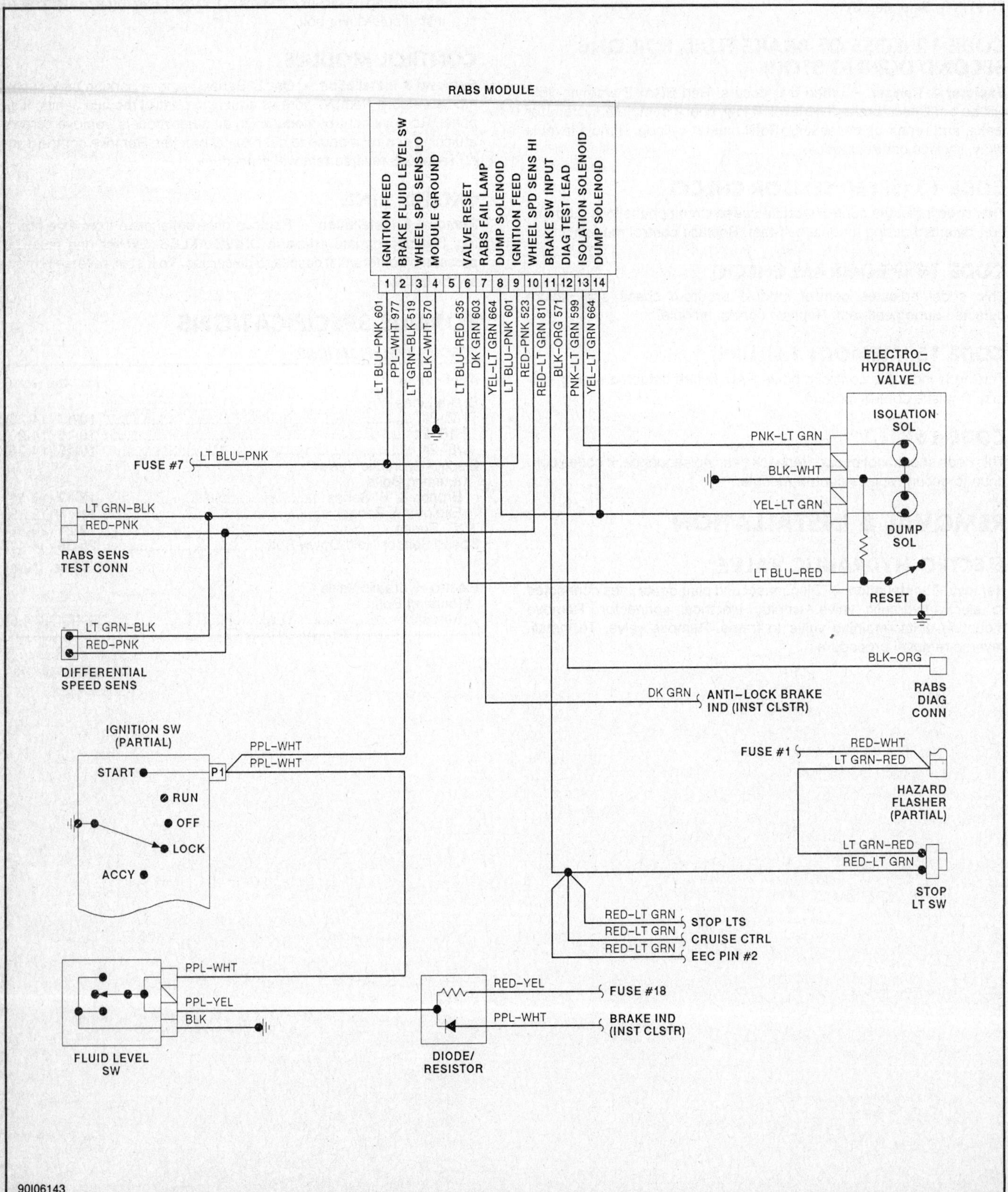
RABS MODULE
IGNITION FEED
BRAKE FLUID LEVEL SW
WHEEL SPD SENS LO
MODULE GROUND
VALVE RESET
RABS FAIL LAMP
DUMP SOLENOID
IGNITION FEED
WHEEL SPD SENS HI
BRAKE SW INPUT
DIAG TEST LEAD
ISOLATION SOLENOID
DUMP SOLENOID
1 2 3 4 5 6 7 8 9 10 11 12 13 14
LT BLU–PNK 601
PPL–WHT 977
LT GRN–BLK 519
BLK–WHT 570
LT BLU–RED 535
DK GRN 603
YEL–LT GRN 664
LT BLU–PNK 601
RED–PNK 523
RED–LT GRN 810
BLK–ORG 571
PNK–LT GRN 599
YEL–LT GRN 664
ELECTRO-HYDRAULIC VALVE
ISOLATION SOL
PNK–LT GRN
BLK–WHT
YEL–LT GRN
DUMP SOL
LT BLU–RED
RESET
FUSE #7
LT BLU–PNK
LT GRN–BLK
RED–PNK
RABS SENS TEST CONN
LT GRN–BLK
RED–PNK
DIFFERENTIAL SPEED SENS
BLK–ORG
RABS DIAG CONN
DK GRN
ANTI–LOCK BRAKE IND (INST CLSTR)
IGNITION SW (PARTIAL)
PPL–WHT
PPL–WHT
START
P1
RUN
OFF
LOCK
ACCY
FUSE #1
RED–WHT
LT GRN–RED
HAZARD FLASHER (PARTIAL)
LT GRN–RED
RED–LT GRN
STOP LT SW
RED–LT GRN
STOP LTS
RED–LT GRN
CRUISE CTRL
RED–LT GRN
EEC PIN #2
PPL–WHT
PPL–YEL
BLK
FLUID LEVEL SW
RED–YEL
FUSE #18
PPL–WHT
BRAKE IND (INST CLSTR)
DIODE/ RESISTOR
90I06143

Fig. 10: Rear Anti-Lock Brake System (RABS) Wiring Diagram (Aerostar)

1991 BRAKES
Anti-Lock – RABS (Cont.)

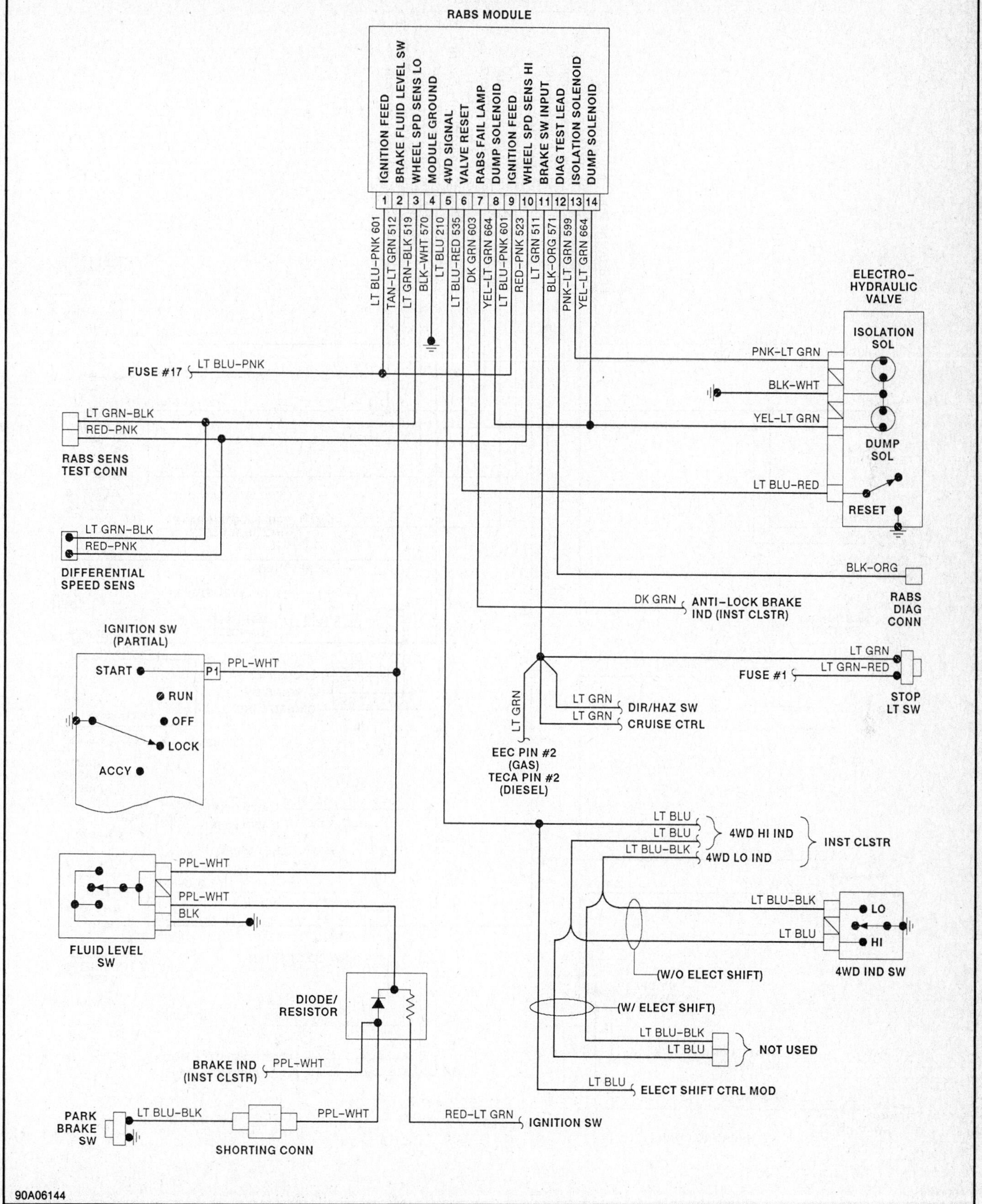
RABS MODULE
IGNITION FEED
BRAKE FLUID LEVEL SW
WHEEL SPD SENS LO
MODULE GROUND
4WD SIGNAL
VALVE RESET
RABS FAIL LAMP
DUMP SOLENOID
IGNITION FEED
WHEEL SPD SENS HI
BRAKE SW INPUT
DIAG TEST LEAD
ISOLATION SOLENOID
DUMP SOLENOID
1 2 3 4 5 6 7 8 9 10 11 12 13 14
LT BLU-PNK 601
TAN-LT GRN 512
LT GRN-BLK 519
BLK-WHT 570
LT BLU 210
LT BLU-RED 535
DK GRN 603
YEL-LT GRN 664
LT BLU-PNK 601
RED-PNK 523
LT GRN 511
BLK-ORG 571
PNK-LT GRN 599
YEL-LT GRN 664
ELECTRO-HYDRAULIC VALVE
ISOLATION SOL
PNK-LT GRN
BLK-WHT
YEL-LT GRN
DUMP SOL
LT BLU-RED
RESET
FUSE #17
LT BLU-PNK
LT GRN-BLK
RED-PNK
RABS SENS TEST CONN
LT GRN-BLK
RED-PNK
DIFFERENTIAL SPEED SENS
BLK-ORG
RABS DIAG CONN
DK GRN
ANTI-LOCK BRAKE IND (INST CLSTR)
IGNITION SW (PARTIAL)
START
P1
PPL-WHT
RUN
OFF
LOCK
ACCY
LT GRN
LT GRN-RED
FUSE #1
STOP LT SW
LT GRN
LT GRN
DIR/HAZ SW
LT GRN
CRUISE CTRL
EEC PIN #2 (GAS)
TECA PIN #2 (DIESEL)
LT BLU
LT BLU
4WD HI IND
LT BLU-BLK
4WD LO IND
INST CLSTR
PPL-WHT
PPL-WHT
BLK
FLUID LEVEL SW
LT BLU-BLK
LO
LT BLU
HI
4WD IND SW
(W/O ELECT SHIFT)
(W/ ELECT SHIFT)
DIODE/ RESISTOR
LT BLU-BLK
LT BLU
NOT USED
BRAKE IND (INST CLSTR)
PPL-WHT
LT BLU
ELECT SHIFT CTRL MOD
PARK BRAKE SW
LT BLU-BLK
PPL-WHT
RED-LT GRN
IGNITION SW
SHORTING CONN
90A06144

Fig. 11: Rear Anti-Lock Brake System (RABS) Wiring Diagram (Bronco & "F" Series)

1991 BRAKES
Anti-Lock – RABS (Cont.)

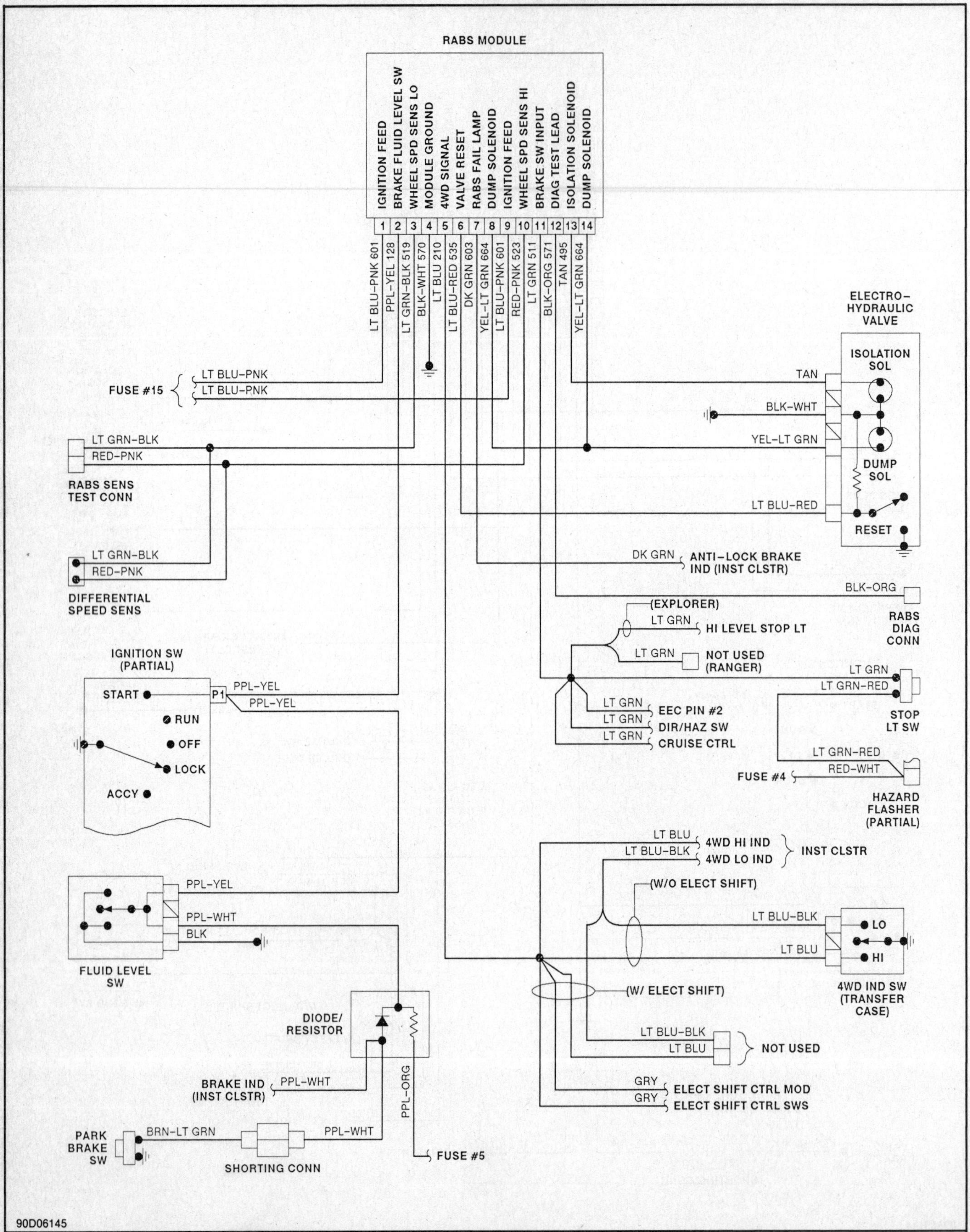
RABS MODULE
1 IGNITION FEED
2 BRAKE FLUID LEVEL SW
3 WHEEL SPD SENS LO
4 MODULE GROUND
5 4WD SIGNAL
6 VALVE RESET
7 RABS FAIL LAMP
8 DUMP SOLENOID
9 IGNITION FEED
10 WHEEL SPD SENS HI
11 BRAKE SW INPUT
12 DIAG TEST LEAD
13 ISOLATION SOLENOID
14 DUMP SOLENOID
LT BLU-PNK 601
PPL-YEL 128
LT GRN-BLK 519
BLK-WHT 570
LT BLU 210
LT BLU-RED 535
DK GRN 603
YEL-LT GRN 664
LT BLU-PNK 601
RED-PNK 523
LT GRN 511
BLK-ORG 571
TAN 495
YEL-LT GRN 664
ELECTRO-HYDRAULIC VALVE
ISOLATION SOL
DUMP SOL
RESET
TAN
BLK-WHT
YEL-LT GRN
LT BLU-RED
FUSE #15
LT BLU-PNK
LT BLU-PNK
LT GRN-BLK
RED-PNK
RABS SENS TEST CONN
LT GRN-BLK
RED-PNK
DIFFERENTIAL SPEED SENS
DK GRN
ANTI-LOCK BRAKE IND (INST CLSTR)
BLK-ORG
RABS DIAG CONN
(EXPLORER)
LT GRN
HI LEVEL STOP LT
LT GRN
NOT USED (RANGER)
LT GRN
LT GRN-RED
STOP LT SW
LT GRN
EEC PIN #2
LT GRN
DIR/HAZ SW
LT GRN
CRUISE CTRL
LT GRN-RED
RED-WHT
FUSE #4
HAZARD FLASHER (PARTIAL)
IGNITION SW (PARTIAL)
START
RUN
OFF
LOCK
ACCY
P1
PPL-YEL
PPL-YEL
LT BLU
4WD HI IND
LT BLU-BLK
4WD LO IND
INST CLSTR
(W/O ELECT SHIFT)
LT BLU-BLK
LT BLU
LO
HI
4WD IND SW (TRANSFER CASE)
(W/ ELECT SHIFT)
LT BLU-BLK
LT BLU
NOT USED
GRY
ELECT SHIFT CTRL MOD
GRY
ELECT SHIFT CTRL SWS
PPL-YEL
PPL-WHT
BLK
FLUID LEVEL SW
DIODE/ RESISTOR
BRAKE IND (INST CLSTR)
PPL-WHT
PPL-ORG
FUSE #5
PARK BRAKE SW
BRN-LT GRN
SHORTING CONN
PPL-WHT
90D06145

Fig. 12: Rear Anti-Lock Brake System (RABS) Wiring Diagram (Explorer & Ranger)

1991 BRAKES
Anti-Lock – RABS (Cont.)

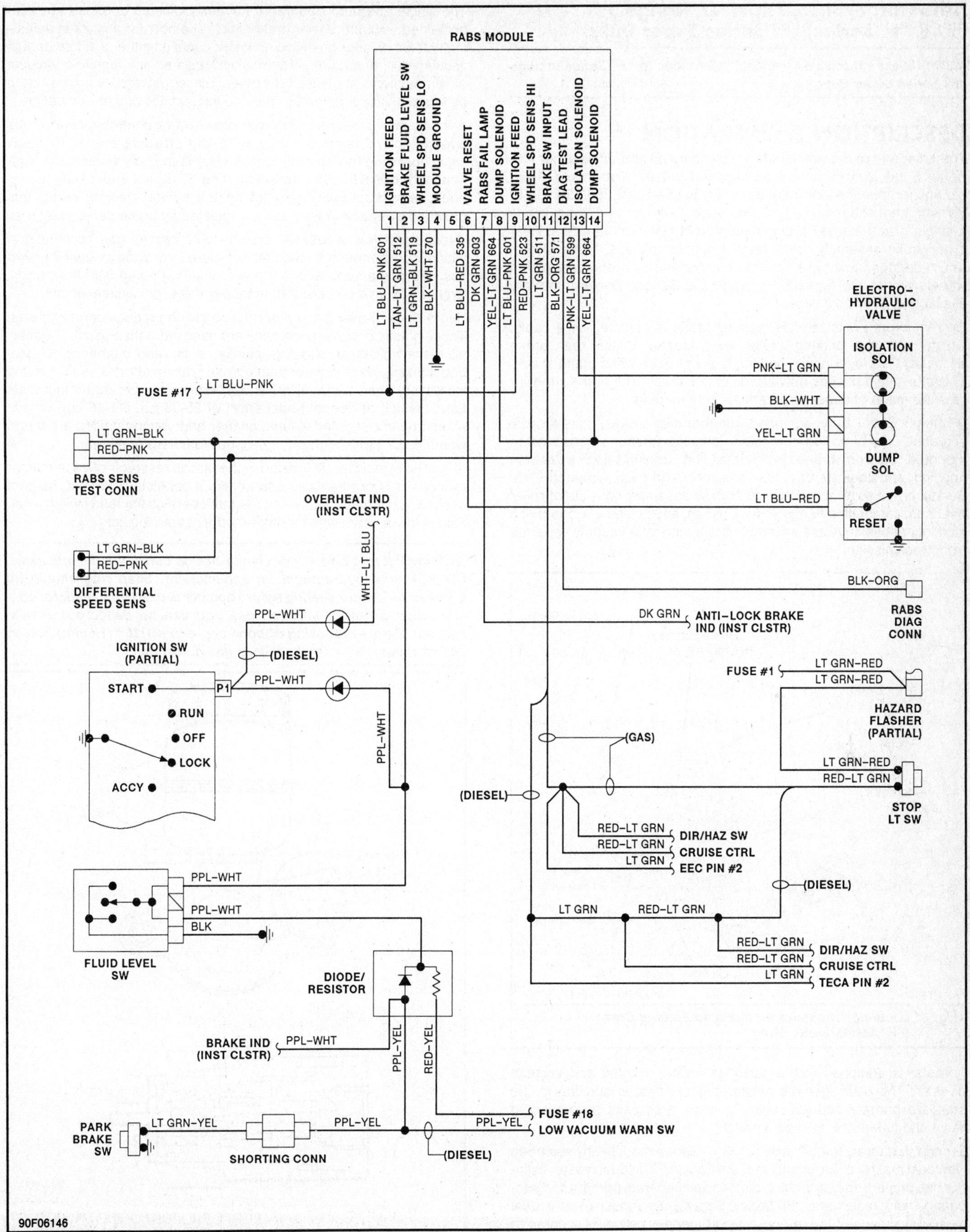
RABS MODULE
IGNITION FEED
BRAKE FLUID LEVEL SW
WHEEL SPD SENS LO
MODULE GROUND
VALVE RESET
RABS FAIL LAMP
DUMP SOLENOID
IGNITION FEED
WHEEL SPD SENS HI
BRAKE SW INPUT
DIAG TEST LEAD
ISOLATION SOLENOID
DUMP SOLENOID
1 2 3 4 5 6 7 8 9 10 11 12 13 14
LT BLU–PNK 601
TAN–LT GRN 512
LT GRN–BLK 519
BLK–WHT 570
LT BLU–RED 535
DK GRN 603
YEL–LT GRN 664
LT BLU–PNK 601
RED–PNK 523
LT GRN 511
BLK–ORG 571
PNK–LT GRN 599
YEL–LT GRN 664
ELECTRO–HYDRAULIC VALVE
ISOLATION SOL
PNK–LT GRN
BLK–WHT
YEL–LT GRN
DUMP SOL
LT BLU–RED
RESET
FUSE #17
LT BLU–PNK
LT GRN–BLK
RED–PNK
RABS SENS TEST CONN
OVERHEAT IND (INST CLSTR)
WHT–LT BLU
LT GRN–BLK
RED–PNK
DIFFERENTIAL SPEED SENS
BLK–ORG
RABS DIAG CONN
PPL–WHT
DK GRN
ANTI–LOCK BRAKE IND (INST CLSTR)
IGNITION SW (PARTIAL)
(DIESEL)
START
P1
PPL–WHT
FUSE #1
LT GRN–RED
LT GRN–RED
HAZARD FLASHER (PARTIAL)
RUN
OFF
LOCK
ACCY
PPL–WHT
(GAS)
LT GRN–RED
RED–LT GRN
(DIESEL)
STOP LT SW
RED–LT GRN
DIR/HAZ SW
RED–LT GRN
CRUISE CTRL
LT GRN
EEC PIN #2
PPL–WHT
(DIESEL)
PPL–WHT
LT GRN
RED–LT GRN
BLK
FLUID LEVEL SW
RED–LT GRN
DIR/HAZ SW
RED–LT GRN
CRUISE CTRL
LT GRN
TECA PIN #2
DIODE/ RESISTOR
BRAKE IND (INST CLSTR)
PPL–WHT
PPL–YEL
RED–YEL
FUSE #18
PPL–YEL
LOW VACUUM WARN SW
PARK BRAKE SW
LT GRN–YEL
PPL–YEL
SHORTING CONN
(DIESEL)
90F06146

Fig. 13: Rear Anti-Lock Brake System (RABS) Wiring Diagram ("E" Series)

1991 BRAKES
Disc & Drum

Aerostar, Bronco, Explorer, Ranger, "E" & "F" Series, "F" Series Super Duty

***NOTE:** Unless otherwise specified, references to "F" Series include "F" Series Super Duty.*

DESCRIPTION & OPERATION

Front disc and rear drum brakes are standard on all models except "F" Series Super Duty, which comes with front and rear disc brakes. A single anchor, dual piston brake assembly is used on E250/350, F250/350 and front and rear on "F" Series Super Duty. All other models use a single piston, pin rail sliding caliper front disc brake system. Rear drum brake assembly consists of a support plate, 2 brake shoes, return springs, automatic adjuster components and one dual piston wheel cylinder. On Aerostar, Explorer and Ranger, brake drums are available in 9" and 10" sizes.

On rear drum brake models, parking brake is actuated by a cable, which pulls the parking brake lever located inside rear brake assembly. The lever pivots parking brake strut between brake shoes. This movement pushes outward on brake shoes. The brake shoe linings are made of asbestos-free fiberglass material.

"F" Series Super Duty, equipped with rear disc brakes, uses a cable actuated, transmission mounted parking brake. Transmission mounted parking brake is situated on transmission extension housing, and consists of a case assembly and cable actuated 9"x3" Bendix brake assembly. *See Fig. 1.* Case assembly consists of roller bearings, companion flange and mainshaft, assembled in a one-piece aluminum housing. Case assembly has a lubrication supply separate from transmission.

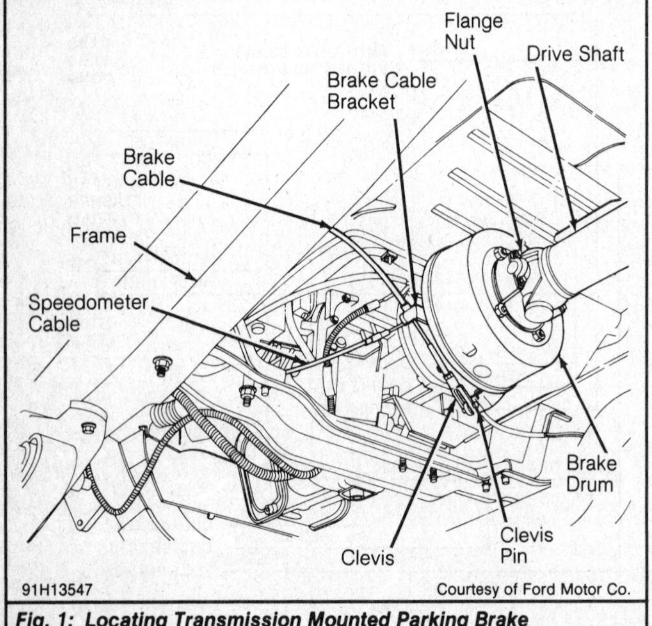
Flange
Nut
Drive Shaft
Brake Cable
Bracket
Brake
Cable
Frame
Speedometer
Cable
Brake
Drum
Clevis
Pin
Clevis
91H13547
Courtesy of Ford Motor Co.

***Fig. 1:** Locating Transmission Mounted Parking Brake ("F" Series Super Duty)*

Aerostar is equipped with a cartridge master cylinder and vacuum booster. The cartridge-type master cylinder has, in addition to the standard primary and secondary pistons, a by-pass proportioning valve and differential pressure switch.

Bronco, Explorer, Ranger and "E" & "F" Series models are equipped with dual master cylinder and vacuum booster. The dual master cylinder has primary and secondary pistons and separate primary and secondary fluid reservoirs. "F" Series Super Duty model uses a dual master cylinder and hydro-boost. On all models, caliper is secured to steering knuckle by 2 caliper retaining pins. Aerostar, Explorer and Ranger use a dual-diaphragm vacuum booster; all others use single or dual-diaphragm vacuum booster.

The single and dual-diaphragm (tandem) vacuum boosters are self-contained, vacuum power brake units. The booster assists in actuating master cylinder push rod. Booster contains either a single or dual vacuum-suspended diaphragm which uses engine manifold vacuum or atmospheric pressure for power. Diesel powered vehicles use a belt-driven vacuum pump to provide vacuum for booster actuation.

A mechanically operated booster check valve controls power brake application and release in relation to foot pressure applied to check valve operating rod. Booster check valve is the only serviceable component of brake booster assembly. The "F" Series Super Duty hydro-boost is hydraulically operated by the power steering pump and provides a variable power assist regulated by brake pedal pressure.

Hydro-boost has a reserve system (compressed gas accumulator) which stores enough fluid under pressure to provide at least 2 power assisted brake applications if power steering pump fluid flow stops. Brakes can also be operated manually if reserve system is lost.

Hydro-boost power units in normal condition produce certain noises. These noises occur when brakes are used more than usual. In general, these noises are hissing, clunks, clicks and chattering. Hydro-boost hisses when greater than normal braking effort is used. Hissing increases when pedal effort and operating temperatures increase. Loud hissing at normal pedal effort of 25-35 lbs. (11-16 kg.) or less should be investigated. Clunk, chatter and clicking noises are heard when brake pedal is quickly released from hard braking.

A fluid level indicator is located in the plastic reservoir of each master cylinder. It is not serviced separately. It consists of a float, magnet assembly and reed switch. The magnet operates the reed switch when fluid is low and activates a dash-mounted warning light.

***WARNING:** Hydro-boost unit should not be carried by accumulator. DO NOT drop hydro-boost on accumulator. Snap ring should be checked for proper seating before booster is used. Accumulator contains high pressure nitrogen gas and can be dangerous if mishandled. Before disposing of boosters, drill a 1/16" (1.6mm) hole in end of accumulator can to relieve gas pressure.*

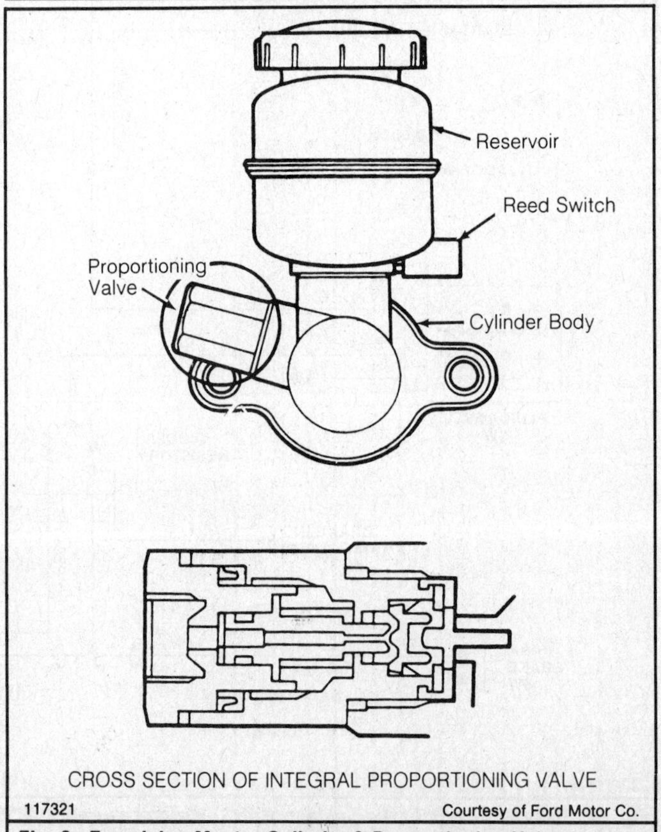
Reservoir
Reed Switch
Proportioning
Valve
Cylinder Body
CROSS SECTION OF INTEGRAL PROPORTIONING VALVE
117321
Courtesy of Ford Motor Co.

***Fig. 2:** Examining Master Cylinder & Proportioning Valve (Bronco, "E" & "F" Series)*

The cartridge-type master cylinder on Aerostar uses a pressure differential warning switch. This switch lights brake warning light on dash if pressure in either front or rear brake system becomes too low.

Aerostar and some Bronco and "E" & "F" Series vehicles use a proportioning valve integral with master cylinder. *See Fig. 2*. This proportioning valve has a by-pass feature. The proportioning valve restricts hydraulic pressure to the rear brakes to prevent lock-up. The by-pass feature allows full hydraulic pressure to the rear brakes in case of front brake system failure.

"F" Series Super Duty vehicles are equipped with a height sensing proportioning valve. *See Fig. 3*. The height sensing proportioning valve monitors changes in vehicle height. This valve automatically provides optimum front-to-rear brake balance, regardless of vehicle load. The valve controls pressure to rear brakes by sensing vehicle load conditions through movement between rear axle and body. As vehicle load increases (resulting in decreased vehicle height), higher brake line pressure to rear brakes is allowed. The valve is located on No. 5 crossmember.

CAUTION: If height sensing proportioning valve linkage is disconnected, proper indexing will be lost. A new sensing valve must be installed. The new sensing valve will have the shaft pre-set and secured internally. If shaft turns freely, DO NOT USE.

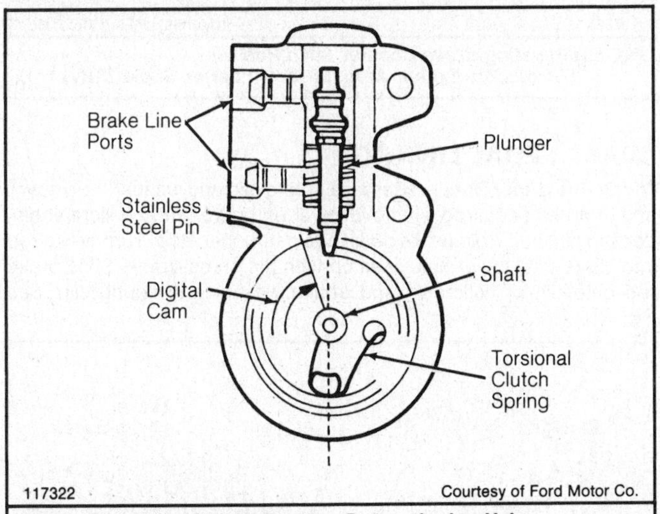
Brake Line
Ports
Plunger
Stainless
Steel Pin
Shaft
Digital
Cam
Torsional
Clutch
Spring
117322
Courtesy of Ford Motor Co.

Fig. 3: Examining Height Sensing Proportioning Valve ("F" Series Super Duty)

CAUTION: Aftermarket load leveling kits, air shocks or modifications which change curb ride height and/or spring deflection rate provide false readings to height sensing proportioning valve. These modifications may result in unsatisfactory brake performance, which in turn could result in an accident.

BLEEDING BRAKE SYSTEM

Bleed hydraulic system whenever air has been introduced into system. Bleed master cylinder and brakes at all 4 wheels if master cylinder lines have been disconnected or master cylinder has run dry. Bleed brakes with pressure bleeding equipment or by manually pumping brake pedal while using bleeder tubes. Always bleed brake lines in sequence. See BLEEDING SEQUENCE.

NOTE: Do not allow reservoir to run dry during bleeding operation.

MANUAL BLEEDING

NOTE: Manual bleeding procedures for Bronco and "E" & "F" Series vehicles are not available from manufacturer, but should be similar to other manual bleeding procedures.

1) Clean master cylinder cap and surrounding area. Remove cap. Explorer and Ranger models are equipped with dual-type master cylinder. Aerostar has a cartridge-type master cylinder. On Explorer and Ranger, bleed primary and secondary systems separately. On Explorer and Ranger, loosen primary or secondary master cylinder hydraulic line fitting. *See Fig. 4*.

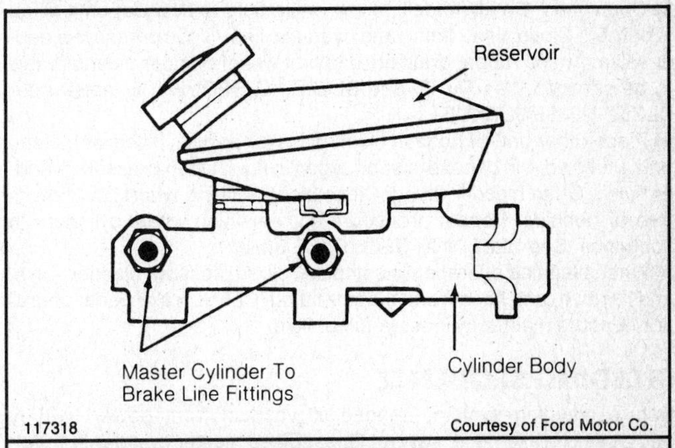
Reservoir
Master Cylinder To
Brake Line Fittings
Cylinder Body
117318
Courtesy of Ford Motor Co.

Fig. 4: Bleeding Master Cylinder (Typical)

2) On Aerostar, loosen either master cylinder hydraulic line. On all models, wrap a cloth around brake lines to absorb escaping brake fluid (on Aerostar, bleed longest line first). Slowly push brake pedal down to force out air. With pedal fully depressed, tighten fittings to prevent air from being sucked into master cylinder when pedal is released. Release pedal.

3) Repeat procedure until air is completely purged from master cylinder. When all air has escaped, tighten fittings with pedal down. Release pedal, and depress again. If pedal is not firm, repeat bleeding procedure.

4) On Aerostar, attach a rubber drain hose to bleeder fitting on front of master cylinder. Submerge hose in small container half-filled with clean brake fluid. Open bleeder fitting. Loosen bleeder fitting about 3/4 turn. Slowly push down brake pedal completely.

5) Close bleeder fitting, and return pedal to fully released position. Repeat procedure until all air is purged from master cylinder. On all models, repeat procedure at bleeder fitting on Rear Anti-Lock Brake Electro-Hydraulic Valve and each wheel cylinder. *See Fig. 5*. See BLEEDING SEQUENCE table under BLEEDING SEQUENCE. When bleeding is complete, fill master cylinder to proper level.

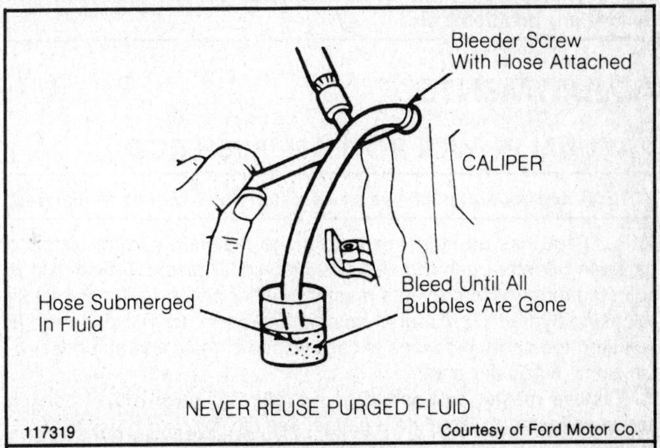
Bleeder Screw
With Hose Attached
CALIPER
Bleed Until All
Bubbles Are Gone
Hose Submerged
In Fluid
NEVER REUSE PURGED FLUID
117319
Courtesy of Ford Motor Co.

Fig. 5: Bleeding Wheel Cylinders (Typical)

PRESSURE BLEEDING

1) Clean master cylinder cap and surrounding area. Remove cap. With pressure tank at least 1/2 full of specified fluid and charged between 10-30 psi (.7-2.0 kg/cm²), use adapters to connect tank to master cylinder. Follow equipment manufacturer's pressure instructions.

1991 BRAKES
Disc & Drum (Cont.)

CAUTION: NEVER exceed 50 psi (3.5 kg/cm²) during bleeding.

2) Open pressure bleeder valve. On Aerostar, attach one end of rubber drain tube to master cylinder bleeder fitting. Open bleed fitting. On all others, bleed master cylinder primary and secondary hydraulic lines individually. Put shop towels in place to catch brake fluid.
3) Open lines. On all models, allow brake fluid to flow out until all air is purged. Close bleed fitting and hydraulic line. Close pressure bleeder valve. Attach rubber drain hose to first wheel cylinder bleeder valve to be serviced. *See Fig. 5.* See BLEEDING SEQUENCE table under BLEEDING SEQUENCE.
4) Place other end of hose in clean glass jar partially filled with clean brake fluid so end of hose is submerged in fluid. Open pressure bleeder valve. Open bleeder fitting. Close bleeder fitting when fluid flow is free of bubbles. Repeat procedure on remaining wheel cylinders in sequence. See BLEEDING SEQUENCE table.
5) When bleeding operation is complete, close pressure bleeder valve, and remove tank hose from adapter fitting. Check brake pedal operation. Ensure master cylinder is full of fluid.

BLEEDING SEQUENCE

Before bleeding system, remove all vacuum from power unit by depressing brake pedal several times. Bleed master cylinder first, followed in sequence by rear wheel cylinders, anti-lock system components (if equipped) and calipers. See BLEEDING SEQUENCE table.

BLEEDING SEQUENCE

Application	Sequence
All Models	RR, LR, ABS Valve (if equipped), RF, LF

BLEEDING HYDRO-BOOST UNIT

"F" Series Super Duty - 1) Fill power steering pump reservoir with Motorcraft MERCON multipurpose automatic transmission fluid. Crank engine several seconds with coil wire disconnected. Check and add fluid if necessary. Start engine. Turn wheels from lock-to-lock twice.
2) Turn engine off. Depress brake pedal several times to discharge accumulator. Start engine, and turn wheels from lock-to-lock twice. If foaming occurs, stop engine, and allow foam to dissipate. Repeat lock-to-lock procedure until all air is removed from system.

NOTE: Hydro-boost is generally self-bleeding. Listed procedure will normally bleed air from system. Normal vehicle operation will remove any additional air.

ADJUSTMENTS

VACUUM POWER BOOSTER PUSH ROD

NOTE: Brake booster push rod on Aerostar should not be readjusted.

1) Push rod has an adjustment screw to maintain correct distance between booster push rod and master cylinder piston. If push rod is adjusted too long, it prevents master cylinder piston from completely releasing hydraulic pressure, causing brakes to drag. If push rod is adjusted too short, it causes excessive pedal travel and an undesirable clunk in booster area.
2) Remove master cylinder to gain access to push rod. To check screw adjustment, fabricate a gauge. *See Fig. 6.*
3) Place gauge against master cylinder mounting surface of booster. Adjust push rod screw by turning it until end of screw just touches inner edge of gauge slot.

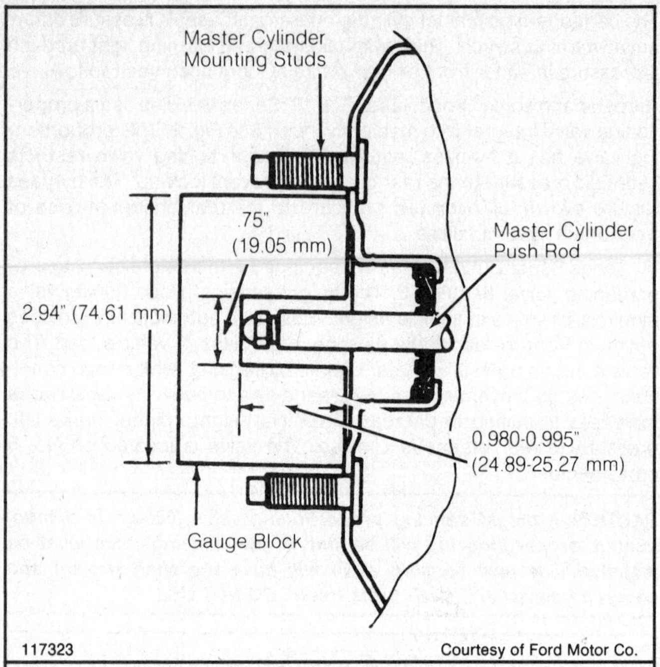
Master Cylinder
Mounting Studs
.75"
(19.05 mm)
Master Cylinder
Push Rod
2.94" (74.61 mm)
0.980-0.995"
(24.89-25.27 mm)
Gauge Block
117323
Courtesy of Ford Motor Co.

Fig. 6: Adjusting Brake Booster Push Rod (All Models Except Aerostar & "F" Series Super Duty)

BRAKE PEDAL LINKAGE

"F" Series Super Duty - Remove spring clip and washer from lower end of brake pedal rod. Remove lower end of rod from bellcrank pin. Loosen jam nut. Hold brake pedal against rubber stop. Turn brake rod into clevis until lower hole lines up with pin on bellcrank. Slide brake rod onto pin of bellcrank, and attach washer and spring clip. *See Fig. 7.*

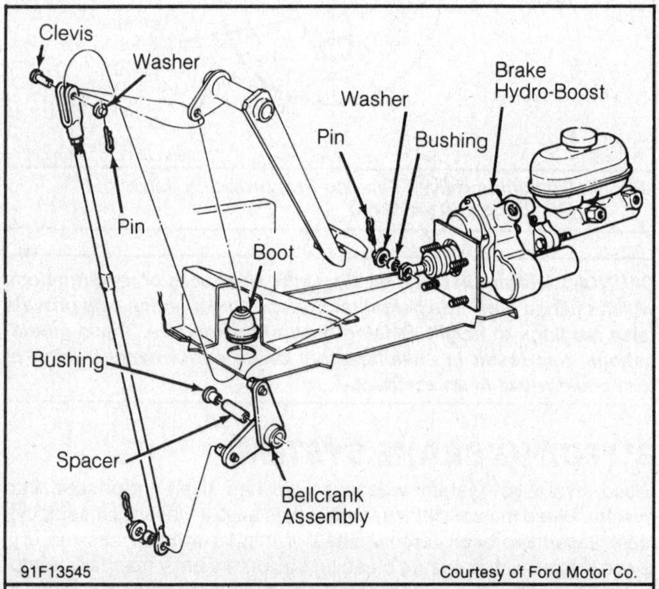
Clevis
Washer
Brake
Hydro-Boost
Washer
Pin
Bushing
Pin
Boot
Bushing
Spacer
Bellcrank
Assembly
91F13545
Courtesy of Ford Motor Co.

Fig. 7: Adjusting Brake Pedal Linkage ("F" Series Super Duty)

HEIGHT SENSING PROPORTIONING VALVE

"F" Series Super Duty - 1) Raise rear of vehicle using body jacks to gain a clearance of 6 5/8" (168 mm) between bottom surface of each rubber jounce bumper and rear axle housing. *See Fig. 8.* Remove nut from valve shaft, and remove leading arm.

1991 BRAKES
Disc & Drum (Cont.)

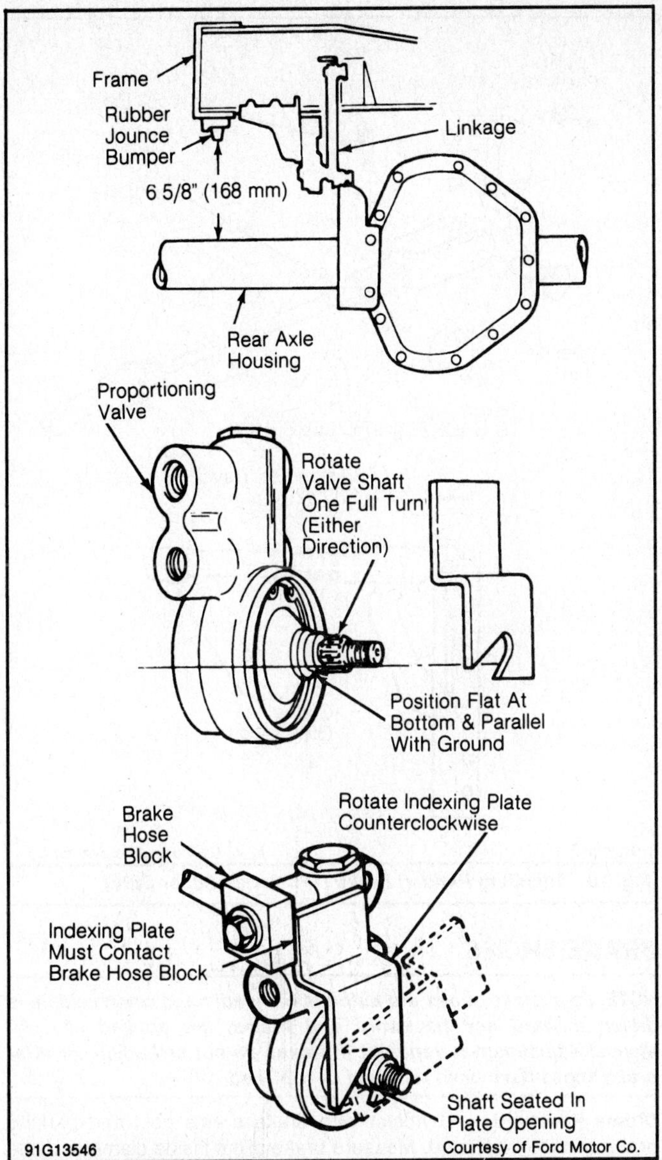
Frame
Rubber
Jounce
Bumper
Linkage
6 5/8" (168 mm)
Rear Axle
Housing
Proportioning
Valve
Rotate
Valve Shaft
One Full Turn
(Either
Direction)
Position Flat At
Bottom & Parallel
With Ground
Brake
Hose
Block
Rotate Indexing Plate
Counterclockwise
Indexing Plate
Must Contact
Brake Hose Block
Shaft Seated In
Plate Opening
91G13546
Courtesy of Ford Motor Co.

Fig. 8: Adjusting Height Sensing Proportioning Valve ("F" Series Super Duty)

2) Remove bushing and clip from leading arm. Install new bushing and clip from linkage kit (E8TZ-2L 193-A). Rotate valve shaft one full turn in either direction. Position valve shaft with flat at bottom and parallel with ground. *See Fig. 8*.

3) Install Indexing Plate (T90T-2588-A) on valve shaft. Install so flat on indexing plate is aligned with flat on valve shaft. Indexing plate slot must be fully seated on valve shaft. Upper surface of indexing plate must rest on valve body.

4) Rotate indexing plate counterclockwise until edge of indexing plate touches brake hose block. *See Fig. 8*. While holding indexing plate in position, install leading arm of linkage over splined part of valve shaft. Fully seat leading arm onto splines. Reinstall valve shaft nut. Remove indexing plate.

PARKING BRAKE

NOTE: Aerostar parking brake system is self-adjusting and requires no adjustment. On all other models except "F" Series Super Duty, initial adjustment procedure must be performed if tension limiter is replaced. If tensioner limiter has not been replaced, use field adjustment to remove cable slack.

Initial Adjustment (Explorer & Ranger) – Adjust rear brakes before adjusting parking brake cable. Ensure rear brakes are cold. Apply parking brake to fully depressed position. Secure threaded rod end of right hand brake cable to prevent it from spinning. Turn equalizer nut 2 1/2" up rod. Ensure cinch strap has slipped so less than 1 3/8" of strap remains exposed. *See Fig. 9*.

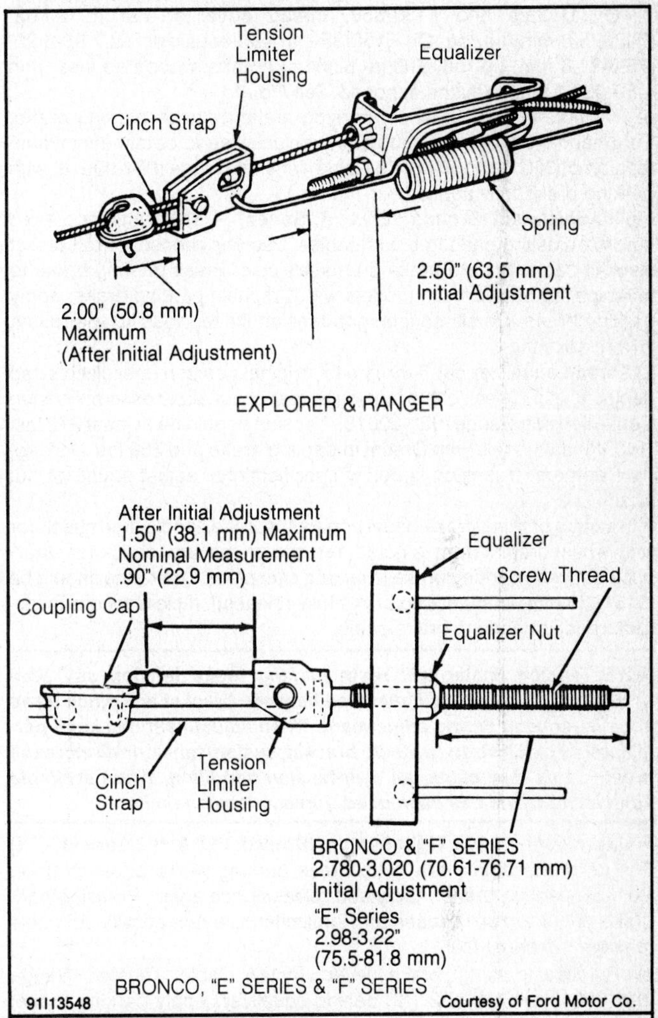
Tension
Limiter
Housing
Equalizer
Cinch Strap
Spring
2.50" (63.5 mm)
Initial Adjustment
2.00" (50.8 mm)
Maximum
(After Initial Adjustment)
EXPLORER & RANGER
After Initial Adjustment
1.50" (38.1 mm) Maximum
Nominal Measurement
.90" (22.9 mm)
Equalizer
Screw Thread
Coupling Cap
Equalizer Nut
Cinch
Strap
Tension
Limiter
Housing
BRONCO & "F" SERIES
2.780-3.020 (70.61-76.71 mm)
Initial Adjustment
"E" Series
2.98-3.22"
(75.5-81.8 mm)
BRONCO, "E" SERIES & "F" SERIES
91I13548
Courtesy of Ford Motor Co.

Fig. 9: Adjusting Parking Brake (Except Aerostar & "F" Series Super Duty)

Field Adjustment (Explorer & Ranger) – **1)** Adjust service brakes before adjusting parking brake cable. Ensure brake drums are cold. Apply parking brake to fully depressed position. Grip threaded rod to prevent it from spinning.

2) Thread equalizer nut 6 full turns past its original position on threaded rod. Check cable tension at rear of equalizer assembly using Cable Tension Gauge (021-00018). If tension is not 400-600 lbs. (182-272 kg), repeat step **2)**.

3) Release pedal, and check rear wheel drag. If drag is noted, remove drums, and check for clearance between parking brake lever and cam plate. Cables should be tight enough to allow full application of rear brakes and loose enough to allow full release of rear brakes.

NOTE: Tension limiter will reset parking brake tension any time system is disconnected if distance between bracket and cinch strap hook is reduced during adjustment. When adjustment has been performed so cinch strap contacts bracket, system tension will increase greatly. This may cause an over-tension condition. When available adjustment travel has been used, replace tension limiter.

NOTE: If rear brake shoes are removed for any reason, parking brake cable tension should be checked and adjusted.

1991 BRAKES
Disc & Drum (Cont.)

Initial Adjustment (Bronco, "E" & "F" Series) – 1) Adjust rear brakes before adjusting parking brake cables. Press parking brake lever to last detent position. On models with hand operated (Orschein) parking brake, turn handle adjustment knob clockwise to end of travel. Apply parking brake. On all models, grip tension limiter housing to prevent it from spinning.

2) On Bronco and F150/350, thread equalizer nut 2.78-3.02" (70.5-76.8 mm) up rod. On E150/350, thread equalizer nut 2.98-3.22" (75.6-81.8 mm) up rod. Ensure cinch strap has slipped so less than 1.50" (38.1 mm) remains exposed. *See Fig. 9*.

3) On models with Orschein parking brake, release parking brake. Turn handle adjustment knob counterclockwise to obtain a minimum tension of 350 lbs. (159 kg) on Cable Tension Gauge (021-00018) with parking brake fully applied.

Field Adjustment (Bronco, "E" & "F" Series) – 1) Adjust rear brakes before adjusting parking brake cables. Use this procedure to correct slack in cable. Ensure brake drums are cold. Press parking brake to fully applied position. On models with Orschein parking brake, apply parking brake. On all models, grip tension limiter housing to prevent it from spinning.

2) Thread equalizer nut 6 turns past original position until cinch strap begins to slip. Check cable tension at rear of equalizer assembly using Cable Tension Gauge (021-00018). Tension should be at least 310 lbs. (140 kg) on models with Orschein parking brake and 350 lbs. (159 kg) on all others. If tension is below specifications, adjust equalizer nut again.

3) Release parking brake pedal or parking brake handle, and check for rear wheel drag. If drag is noted, remove drums, and check for clearance between parking brake lever and cam plate. Clearance should be .015" (.38 mm) with parking brake fully released. If clearance is incorrect, readjust parking brake cable.

NOTE: Tension limiter will reset parking brake tension any time system is disconnected if distance between bracket and cinch strap hook is reduced during adjustment. When adjustment has been performed so cinch strap contacts bracket, system tension will increase greatly. This may cause an over-tension condition. When available adjustment travel has been used, replace tension limiter.

Field Adjustment For Tight System (Bronco, "E" & "F" Series) – 1) Ensure brake drums are cold. Press parking brake pedal to floor. Release parking brake. Apply and release once again. Pressing park brake pedal to floor causes tension limiter to automatically set cable tension and pedal feel.

2) Release parking brake lever. Install Cable Tension Gauge (021-00018) on cable, 2 1/2" behind equalizer. Apply parking brake. Cable tension should be a minimum of 350 lbs. (159 kg). If tension is below specification, repeat procedure.

Transmission Mounted Parking Brake Field Adjustment ("F" Series Super Duty) – 1) Use this procedure to correct excess parking brake actuation lever travel. On foot actuated lever, raise vehicle and set on jack stands. Shift transmission to Neutral, and release parking brake. Loosen parking brake clevis adjusting jam nut several turns.

2) Remove lock pin and clevis pin from clevis. *See Fig. 10*. Hold lever and cable, removing slack. Screw adjusting clevis onto threaded end of cable until parking brake lever hole and clevis hole meet. Rotate clevis about 10 turns. Tighten jam nut. Rotate driveshaft to ensure rear brakes are not dragging. Lower vehicle to ground. Check parking brake for proper operation.

3) On vehicles with Orschein hand actuated parking brake lever, turn handle adjustment knob to obtain one inch of travel. *See Fig. 10*. Release parking brake. Loosen parking brake clevis adjusting jam nut several times. Install parking brake cable into parking brake mounting bracket.

4) Hold parking brake actuation lever in applied position. Screw adjusting clevis onto threaded end of cable until parking brake lever hole and clevis hole meet. Rotate clevis about 10 turns. Tighten jam nut. Assemble clevis to parking brake actuation lever. Check parking brake for proper operation. Turn adjustment knob on parking brake actuation lever for additional adjustment.

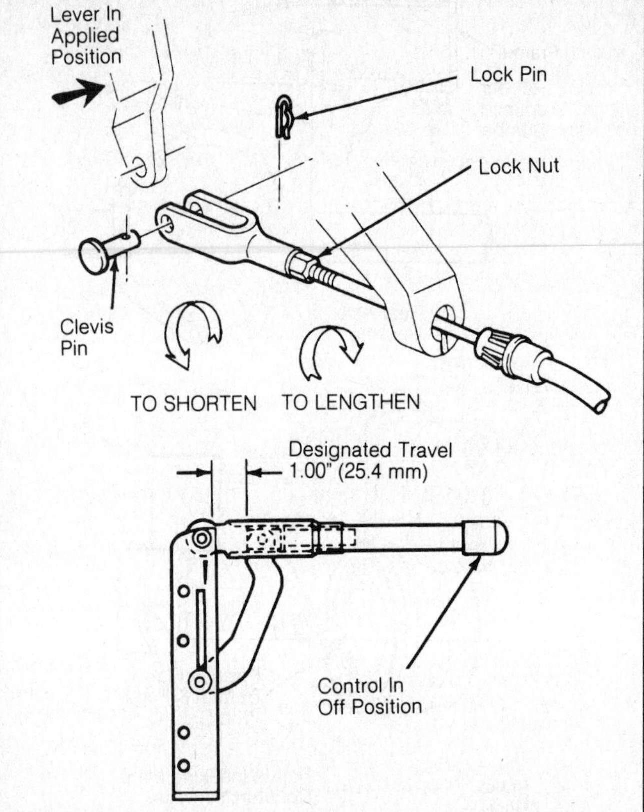
Lever In
Applied
Position
Lock Pin
Lock Nut
Clevis
Pin
TO SHORTEN
TO LENGTHEN
Designated Travel
1.00" (25.4 mm)
Control In
Off Position
91J13549
Courtesy of Ford Motor Co.

Fig. 10: Adjusting Parking Brake ("F" Series Super Duty)

BRAKE SHOES

NOTE: Rear brake shoes are automatically adjusted when vehicle is driven forward and backward and brakes are applied sharply. Manual adjustment is required if brakes do not self-adjust or after brake shoes have been removed or replaced.

Drums Removed – 1) Adjust with brake drums cold and parking brake correctly adjusted. Measure brake drum inside diameter using brake shoe adjustment gauge. *See Fig. 11*.

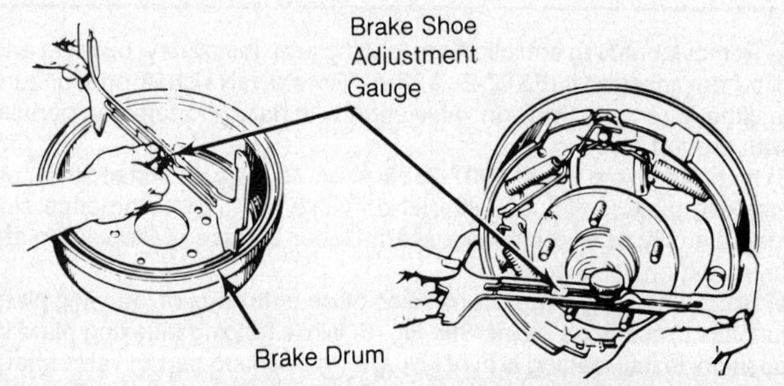
Brake Shoe
Adjustment
Gauge
Brake Drum
117331
Courtesy of Ford Motor Co.

Fig. 11: Measuring Brake Drum & Shoe Diameter

2) Reverse adjustment gauge. Apply gauge to brake shoes on a line parallel to ground and through center of axle. Hold adjusting lever away from adjusting screw. Turn screw until outside diameter of shoes contacts gauge. *See Fig. 11*.

3) Install brake drum and wheel assembly. Complete adjustment by applying brakes quickly several times while driving vehicle alternately forward and backward. Check brake operation by stopping often while driving forward.

1991 BRAKES
Disc & Drum (Cont.)

Drums Installed - **1)** Raise vehicle, and support with safety stands. Remove adjusting hole cover rubber plug. Turn adjusting screw and expand brake shoes until drag is felt against brake drum.
2) Loosen adjusting screw 10-12 notches. Drum should rotate freely without drag. If drum does not rotate freely, remove wheel and drum. Lubricate brake shoe contact areas on backing plate.
3) Reinstall wheel and drum. Install adjusting hole cover. Apply brakes. If brake pedal travels more than halfway to floor, clearance between brake shoes and drums is too great. Additional adjustment is required.

DISC PADS

As brake pads wear, caliper piston remains in constant contact with brake pad, eliminating need for adjustment.

TROUBLE SHOOTING

MASTER CYLINDER

Changes in brake pedal feel or travel signal something could be wrong in brake system. When diagnosing brake system problems, use brake warning light, pedal feel/travel and fluid level as indicators. Following symptoms indicate brake trouble:

Pedal goes down fast.
- This could be caused by leaks or air in system.

Pedal goes down slowly.
- This could be caused by external or internal leaks.

Pedal is low and/or feels spongy.
- This may be caused by empty master cylinder reservoir, reservoir cap vent holes clogged, rear brakes out of adjustment or air in system.

Pedal effort too high.
- Check for binding or obstruction in pedal linkage. Check for poor booster assist.

Brake warning light is on.
- Check for low fluid level, ignition wires too close to fluid level indicator assembly, damaged indicator float, low vacuum (diesel) or applied parking brake.

HYDRO-BOOST UNIT

Use following list of symptoms to aid in diagnosing hydro-boost problems:

Brake pedal returns slowly.
- Check for restriction in return line between hydro-boost and power steering reservoir.
- Check for incorrectly connected return line.
- Reposition brake pedal or add return spring.
- Replace hydro-boost.

Brakes grab.
- Tighten power steering belt.
- Flush steering system while pumping brake pedal.
- Replace hydro-boost.

Hydro-boost chatter/Pedal vibration.
- Tighten power steering belt.
- Check for low fluid level.

Accumulator leaks down/No reserve brake application.
- Replace hydro-boost.

High brake pedal effort.
- Tighten or replace power steering belt.
- Low fluid level.
- Replace hydro-boost.

Brakes apply by themselves.
- Restriction in return line.
- Return line not connected correctly.
- Replace hydro-boost.

TESTING

POWER BRAKE FUNCTION TEST

1) With engine stopped, remove all vacuum in system by pumping brake pedal several times. Push pedal down as far as it will go. If pedal moves downward slowly, hydraulic system is leaking. Check hydraulic system for leaks.
2) With pedal pushed down as far as it will go, start engine. If pedal moves downward, vacuum system is okay. If pedal does not change position, a problem exists in vacuum system. Check vacuum system for leaks.

MASTER CYLINDER

Bronco, "E" & "F" Series - **1)** To check master cylinder for internal leak, fill reservoir as necessary. If fluid level remains constant after several brake applications, measure wheel turning torque necessary to rotate wheels with brakes applied.
2) To measure, shift transmission into Neutral, and raise front wheels. Apply brakes with a minimum force of 100 lbs. (45 kg), and hold about 15 seconds. With brakes applied, attempt to rotate front wheels with 75 ft. lbs. (102 N.m) of torque. If either wheel rotates, check front chamber of master cylinder, and replace parts as necessary. Repeat test for rear wheels.

BRAKE WARNING LIGHT

1) Brake warning light should only come on when ignition is in start position or when ignition is on with parking brake applied or fluid level low. On diesel vehicles, brake warning light should also come on when vacuum is low.
2) If brake warning light does not come on when brake fluid is low, manually push reservoir float to bottom of reservoir. If light still does not come on, check circuit fuse, wiring and bulb. Repair as necessary. If bulb and related circuitry are okay, replace reservoir assembly.
3) If brake warning light does not come on when parking brake is applied, check parking brake switch, circuit wiring and bulb. Repair as necessary. With parking brake released and master cylinder reservoir full, turn ignition on. If warning light is on, check for shorted, grounded or defective warning switches or wiring. Repair as necessary. Turn ignition to start position. If brake warning light does not come on as a bulb check function, check fuse, bulb and wiring. Repair as necessary.

BRAKE PEDAL RESERVE

1) If complaint is low or bottoming out brake pedal, run engine at idle with transmission in Park or Neutral. Lightly depress brake pedal 3 or 4 times. Wait 15 seconds for vacuum to build in booster. Depress brake pedal until it stops moving downward.
2) While holding pedal down, raise engine speed to about 2000 RPM. Release accelerator pedal. Brake pedal should move downward as engine speed returns to idle. If results are correct, system has proper pedal reserve. If results are not correct, check for adequate vacuum. If vacuum is okay, replace vacuum booster.

HYDRO-BOOST RESERVE

Charge system with pressure by holding steering wheel on steering stop or by holding brake pedal down with 100 lbs. (45 kg) of force for 5 seconds with engine idling. Turn engine off. After 8-12 hours, depress brake pedal with engine off. If power reserve is not present, replace hydro-boost unit.

CAUTION: DO NOT hold brake pedal with 100 lbs. (45 kg) of force for longer than 5 seconds at a time.

VACUUM POWER BOOSTER

1) With a "T" fitting, connect vacuum gauge into vacuum line between engine and power brake booster. With engine at operating temperature, gauge should read 15-19 in. Hg (51-64 kPa) at idle with transmis-

1991 BRAKES
Disc & Drum (Cont.)

sion in Neutral. If reading is below specifications, stop engine, disconnect vacuum hose at power brake booster and cap open end of hose and open port of vacuum "T".

2) Start engine, and allow it to idle. If vacuum reading is still less than 15-19 in. Hg (51-64 kPa), engine is producing low vacuum and problem must be corrected. If vacuum is to specification, check plastic check valve, rubber grommet and vacuum hose connection at power brake booster.

3) With low engine vacuum corrected and/or leaking components replaced, start engine, and allow it to idle. Stop engine, and depress brake pedal, holding down a few seconds. If vacuum drops to zero, booster is leaking and requires replacement.

REMOVAL & INSTALLATION

DISC BRAKE CALIPERS & PADS

Removal - 1) To prevent master cylinder overflow when caliper piston is depressed, remove and discard some brake fluid from master cylinder. Raise vehicle, and support with safety stands.

2) Remove front wheel assembly. Place a large "C" clamp on caliper. Tighten clamp to bottom piston in cylinder bore. Remove clamp.

3) Remove dirt around caliper pin tabs. Tap upper caliper pin toward inboard side of vehicle until pin tabs touch spindle face.

4) Insert screwdriver into slot provided behind pin tabs on inboard side of pin. Using pliers, compress end of pin while using screwdriver to pry until tabs slip into spindle groove.

5) Place a 7/16" diameter punch on end of pin, and drive caliper pin out of caliper slide groove. Repeat procedure for lower pin. Remove caliper from rotor. Remove outer brake pad. Compress anti-rattle spring clip, and remove inner brake pad. Support caliper aside.

6) On Aerostar, Explorer and Ranger, replace pads if lining is less than .12" (3.0 mm) thick at any point. On Bronco, E150 and F150, replace pads if lining is less than .06" (1.5 mm) above backing plate at any point. On E250/350, F250/350 and "F" Series Super Duty, replace pads if lining is less than .03" (.8 mm) above backing plate at any point.

CAUTION: During installation, DO NOT tap caliper pin too far into spindle groove. If this happens, tap pin in other direction until tabs snap back into place. Tabs on each end of caliper pin must be free to catch on spindle flanks.

Installation - Use "C" clamp to push caliper piston into piston bore until it bottoms out. To install, reverse removal procedure. Bleed air from brake system.

BRAKE SHOES

Removal (Except E250/350 & F250/350) - 1) Remove wheel assembly and drum. Place a wheel cylinder clamp over ends of wheel cylinder. Disengage adjusting lever from adjusting screw by pulling backwards on lever cable. *See Fig. 12.*

2) Move outboard side of adjusting screw upward, and back off pivot nut as far as possible. Pull adjusting lever, cable and adjusting spring down and toward rear to unhook pivot hook from large hole in secondary shoe. DO NOT pry pivot hook from hole.

3) Remove adjusting spring and adjusting lever. Remove secondary shoe-to-anchor spring. Remove primary shoe-to-anchor spring. Unhook cable anchor, and remove anchor pin plate.

4) Remove cable guide, shoe hold-down springs, brake shoes, adjusting screw, pivot nut and socket. Remove parking brake link spring and link. Note color and position of springs for reassembly.

5) Disconnect parking brake cable from lever. Remove secondary shoe. Disassemble parking brake lever from shoe by removing retaining clip and spring washer.

Installation - Clean and sand brake shoe contact points on backing plate. Apply a light coating of lithium base grease to contact points. Lubricate adjusting cable eye and anchor pin area. Lubricate adjusting screw, pivot and socket. To install, reverse removal procedure.

Removal (E250/350 & F250/350) - 1) Remove wheel assembly and brake drum. Remove parking brake lever assembly retaining nut from backing plate. Remove parking brake lever assembly. *See Fig. 13.* Remove adjusting cable assembly from anchor pin, cable guide and adjusting lever.

2) Remove brake shoe return springs, hold-down springs and brake shoes. Remove and disassemble adjusting screw assembly.

Installation - Clean and sand brake shoe contact points on backing plate. Apply a light coating of lithium base grease to contact points. Lubricate adjusting cable eye and anchor pin area. Lubricate adjusting screw, pivot and socket. To install, reverse removal procedure.

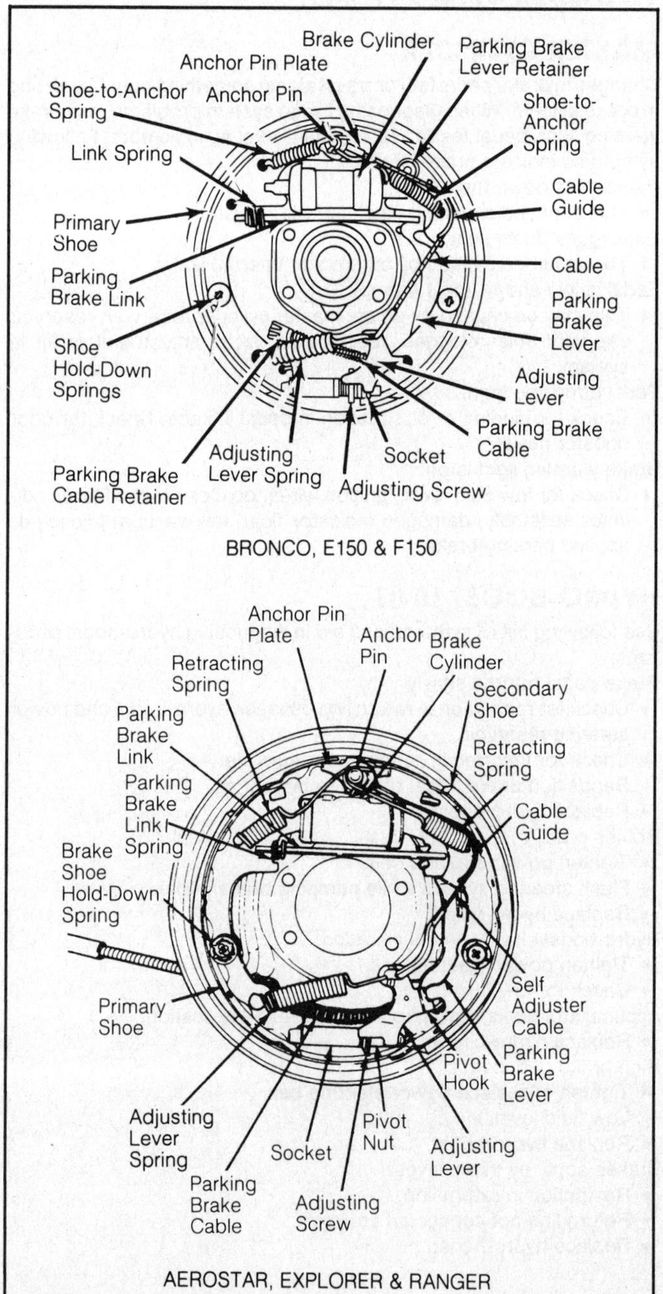
Brake Cylinder
Parking Brake Lever Retainer
Anchor Pin Plate
Shoe-to-Anchor Spring
Anchor Pin
Shoe-to-Anchor Spring
Link Spring
Cable Guide
Primary Shoe
Cable
Parking Brake Link
Parking Brake Lever
Shoe Hold-Down Springs
Adjusting Lever
Parking Brake Cable
Adjusting Lever Spring
Socket
Parking Brake Cable Retainer
Adjusting Screw
BRONCO, E150 & F150
Anchor Pin Plate
Anchor Pin
Brake Cylinder
Retracting Spring
Secondary Shoe
Parking Brake Link
Retracting Spring
Parking Brake Link Spring
Cable Guide
Brake Shoe Hold-Down Spring
Self Adjuster Cable
Primary Shoe
Parking Brake Lever
Pivot Hook
Adjusting Lever Spring
Pivot Nut
Socket
Adjusting Lever
Parking Brake Cable
Adjusting Screw
AEROSTAR, EXPLORER & RANGER
117333
Courtesty of Ford Motor Co.

Fig. 12: Examining Rear Brake Assemblies (Except E250/350 & F250/350)

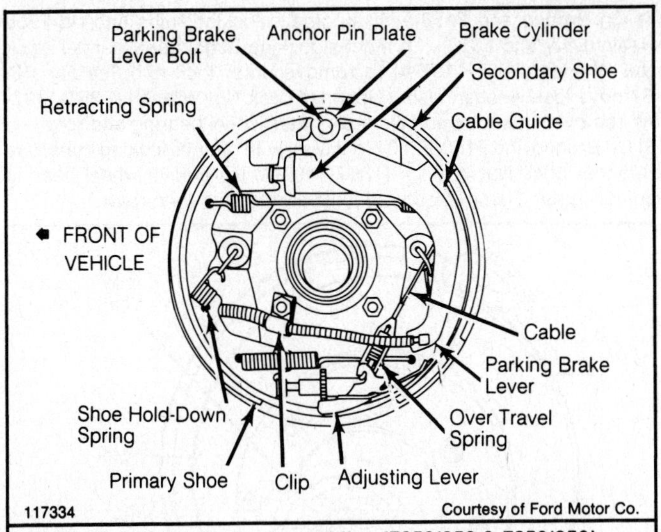
Parking Brake Lever Bolt
Anchor Pin Plate
Brake Cylinder
Secondary Shoe
Retracting Spring
Cable Guide
FRONT OF VEHICLE
Cable
Parking Brake Lever
Shoe Hold-Down Spring
Over Travel Spring
Primary Shoe
Clip
Adjusting Lever
117334
Courtesy of Ford Motor Co.

Fig. 13: Examining Brake Assemblies (E250/350 & F250/350)

BRAKE ROTOR

Removal & Installation (2WD Models) – 1) Raise vehicle, and support with safety stands. Remove wheel and caliper assemblies. Remove dust cap, cotter pin, nut, washer and outer bearing. Carefully remove hub and rotor assembly. Remove inner bearing and seal.
2) To install, reverse removal procedure. Adjust front wheel bearings. While rotating rotor, tighten adjusting nut to 17-25 ft. lbs. (23-34 N.m). Back off adjusting nut 120-180 degrees. Install bearing retainer and new cotter pin.
Removal & Installation (Aerostar 4WD) – Raise vehicle, and support with safety stands. Remove wheel and caliper assemblies. See DISC BRAKE CALIPERS & PADS under REMOVAL & INSTALLATION. Remove rotor retainer clips. Remove rotor. To install, reverse removal procedure.

NOTE: Information for rotor removal on vehicles with Dana 28 Series front axle is not available from manufacturer.

Removal (Explorer & Ranger 4WD W/Automatic Locking Hubs) – 1) Raise vehicle, and support with safety stands. Remove wheel assembly and caliper. See DISC BRAKE CALIPER & PADS under REMOVAL & INSTALLATION. Remove retainer washers from lug nut studs. Remove automatic locking hub housing from spindle.
2) Remove snap ring from end of spindle shaft. Remove axle spacer. *See Fig. 14*. Carefully pull plastic moving cam off wheel bearing adjusting nut. Remove 2 plastic thrust spacers from adjusting nut. Using a magnet, remove locking key.

CAUTION: DO NOT pry on plastic cam or spacers during removal as damage may result. To prevent damaging spindle threads, remove locking key before removing adjusting nut.

3) If necessary, rotate adjusting nut slightly to relieve pressure on locking key. Using Hex Lock Nut Wrench (T70T-4252-B), remove wheel bearing adjusting nut. Remove outer wheel bearing, and then remove rotor.

Installation – When installing rotor, outer bearing and adjusting nut, tighten adjusting nut to 35 ft. lbs (47 N.m) to seat bearings. Spin rotor, and back off adjusting nut 1/4 turn. Tighten adjusting nut to 16 INCH lbs. (1.8 N.m). To install remaining components, reverse removal procedure. *See Fig. 14*. After assembly is complete, wheel to spindle end play should be .001-.003" (.02-.08 mm).

CAUTION: Extreme caution must be used when aligning adjusting nut lug with spindle locking key slot to prevent damage to locking key. Extreme caution must be used when aligning fixed cam key with spindle key slot to prevent damage to fixed cam.

Removal (Explorer & Ranger 4WD W/Manual Locking Hubs) – 1) Raise vehicle, and support with safety stands. Remove wheel assembly and caliper. See DISC BRAKE CALIPER & PADS under REMOVAL & INSTALLATION. Remove retainer washers from lug nut studs. Remove manual locking hub housing from spindle.
2) Remove snap ring from end of spindle shaft. Remove axle spacer. *See Fig. 15*. Using Lock Nut Wrench (T86T-1197-A), remove outer wheel bearing lock-nut. Remove lock washer. Using Lock Nut Wrench (T86T-1197-A), remove inner wheel bearing lock nut, outer wheel bearing and rotor.

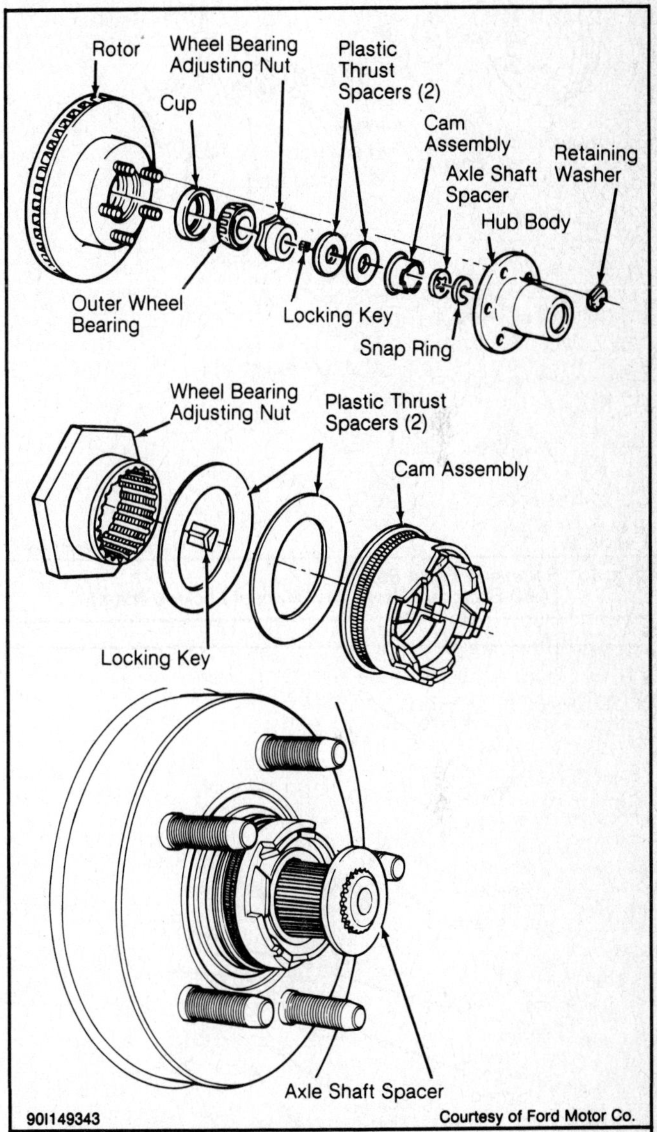
Rotor
Wheel Bearing Adjusting Nut
Plastic Thrust Spacers (2)
Cup
Cam Assembly
Retaining Washer
Axle Shaft Spacer
Hub Body
Outer Wheel Bearing
Locking Key
Snap Ring
Wheel Bearing Adjusting Nut
Plastic Thrust Spacers (2)
Cam Assembly
Locking Key
Axle Shaft Spacer
90I149343
Courtesy of Ford Motor Co.

Fig. 14: Removing Front Rotor (4WD Explorer & Ranger w/Automatic Locking Hubs)

Installation – When installing rotor, outer bearing and inner lock nut, tighten inner lock nut to 35 ft. lbs (47 N.m) to seat bearings. Spin rotor, and back off inner lock nut 1/4 turn. Tighten inner lock nut to 16 INCH lbs. (1.8 N.m). To install remaining components, reverse removal procedure. *See Fig. 15*. After assembly is complete, wheel to spindle end play should be .001-.003" (.02-.08 mm).
Removal (Bronco & F150 4WD W/Automatic & Manual Locking Hubs, F250, F250 H.D. & F350 4WD W/Manual Locking Hubs) – 1) Raise vehicle, and support with safety stands. Remove wheel assembly and caliper. On Bronco and F150 Series with automatic locking hubs, separate hub cap from hub body assembly by removing 5 Torx (TX25) head cap screws. *See Fig. 16*. Remove cap. DO NOT drop spring, ball bearing, bearing race or retainer.

1991 BRAKES
Disc & Drum (Cont.)

NOTE: Information for rotor removal on F250/F350 with automatic locking hubs is not available from manufacturer. Procedure should be similar to other locking hub procedures.

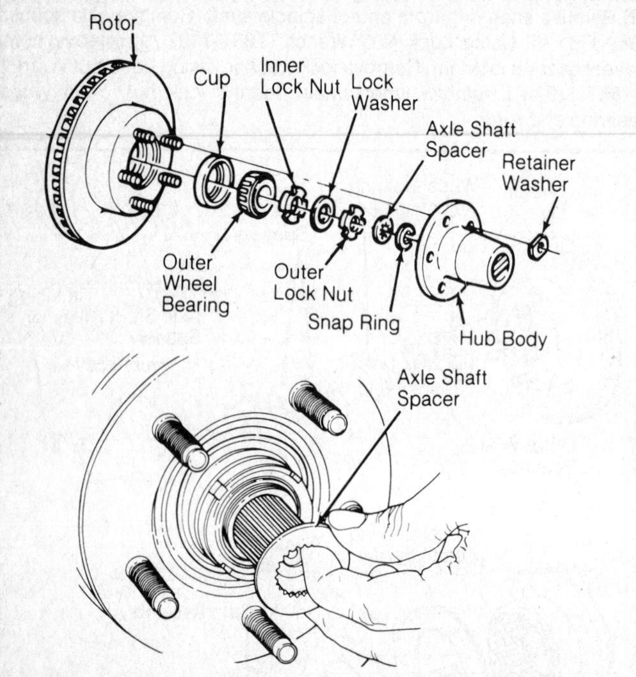
Rotor
Cup
Inner
Lock Nut
Lock
Washer
Axle Shaft
Spacer
Retainer
Washer
Outer
Wheel
Bearing
Outer
Lock Nut
Snap Ring
Hub Body
Axle Shaft
Spacer
90A14936
Courtesy of Ford Motor Co.

Fig. 15: Removing Front Rotor (4WD Explorer & Ranger w/Manual Locking Hubs)

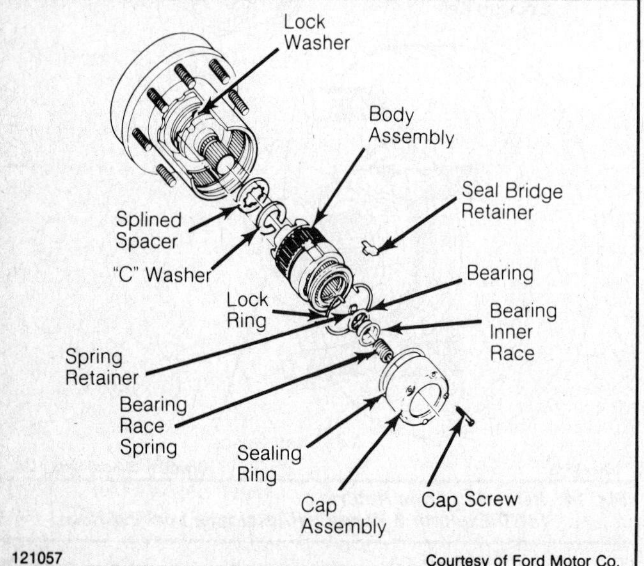
Lock
Washer
Body
Assembly
Seal Bridge
Retainer
Splined
Spacer
"C" Washer
Bearing
Lock
Ring
Bearing
Inner
Race
Spring
Retainer
Bearing
Race
Spring
Sealing
Ring
Cap
Assembly
Cap Screw
121057
Courtesy of Ford Motor Co.

Fig. 16: Removing Front Rotor (4WD Bronco & "F" Series)

2) Remove rubber seal and seal bridge from retainer ring space. Remove retainer ring by squeezing ends together. Remove hub body assembly. Remove "C" washer and splined spacer from spindle. On Bronco and "F" Series with manual locking hubs, separate hub cap from hub body assembly by removing 6 Allen head screws.

3) Remove snap ring attaching hub body assembly to spindle. Remove lock ring seated in groove of hub. *See Fig. 17.* Remove hub body assembly. If hub body does not come out easily, install 2 hub cap screws into hub body, and pull hub body out of hub.

4) On Bronco and F150 with automatic locking hubs and on F250 Heavy Duty and F350 with manual locking hubs, use Spanner Lock Nut Wrench (D85T-1197-A) to remove outer lock nut. *See Fig. 18.* Remove lock washer. Using Spanner Lock Nut Wrench (D85T-1197-A), remove inner lock nut. Remove outer wheel bearing and rotor.

5) On Bronco and F150/F250 Light Duty with manual locking hubs, use Spanner Lock Nut Wrench (T86T-1197-A) to remove wheel bearing adjusting nut. Remove outer wheel bearing, and then rotor.

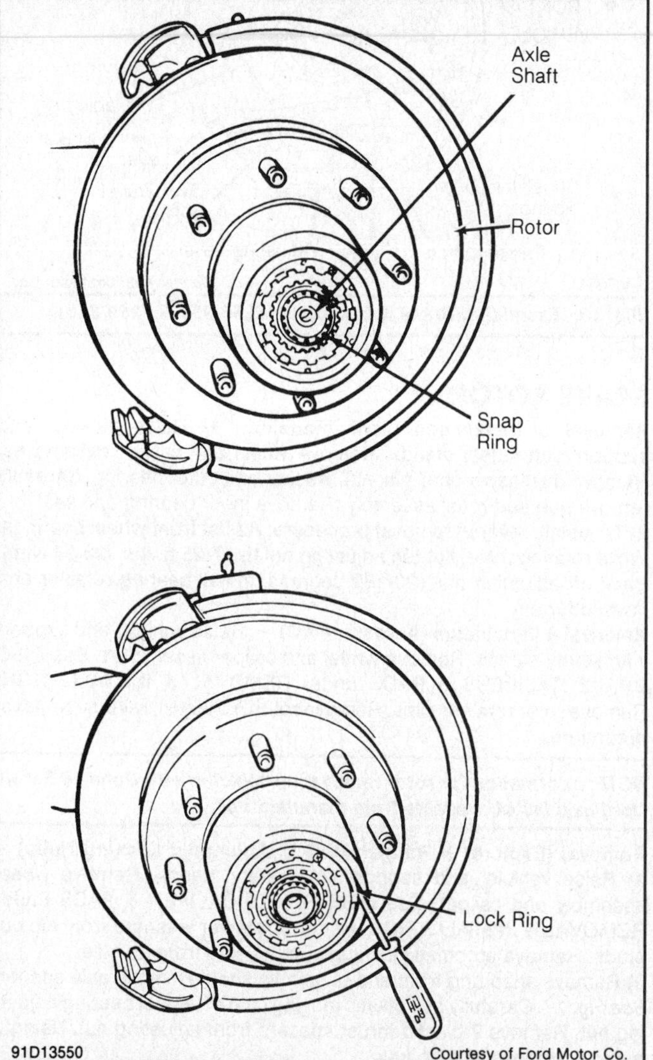
Axle
Shaft
Rotor
Snap
Ring
Lock Ring
91D13550
Courtesy of Ford Motor Co.

Fig. 17: Removing Front Hub (4WD Bronco & "F" Series)

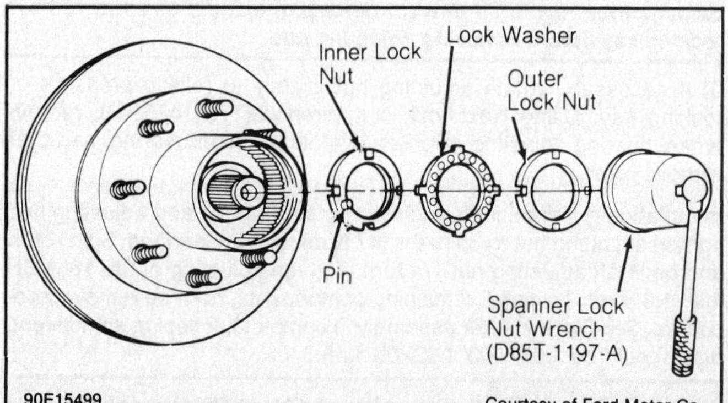
Lock Washer
Inner Lock
Nut
Outer
Lock Nut
Pin
Spanner Lock
Nut Wrench
(D85T-1197-A)
90E15499
Courtesy of Ford Motor Co.

Fig. 18: Removing Outer Lock Nut (Bronco & F150 w/Automatic Locking Hubs, F250 H.D. & F350 w/Manual Locking Hubs)

1991 BRAKES
Disc & Drum (Cont.)

Installation - 1) On Bronco and F150 with automatic locking hubs and on F250 Heavy Duty and F350 with manual locking hubs, install rotor and outer wheel bearing. Install inner lock nut. While rotating disc back and forth, seat bearing by using Spanner Lock Nut Wrench (D85T-1197-A) to tighten inner lock nut to 50 ft. lbs. (68 N.m). Back off inner lock nut, and retighten to 30-40 ft. lbs. (41-54 N.m).

2) Install lock washer so key is in spindle groove. Tighten inner lock nut to engage lock nut pin in nearest lock washer hole. Install outer lock nut, and tighten to 160-205 ft. lbs. (217-278 N.m). Spindle end play should be less than .004" (.10 mm).

3) On Bronco and F150/250 Light Duty with manual locking hubs, install rotor and outer wheel bearing. Install adjusting nut. While rotating disc back and forth, seat bearing by using Spanner Lock Nut Wrench (T86T-1197-A) to tighten adjusting nut to 70 ft. lbs. (95 N.m).

4) Back off adjusting nut 90 degrees, and retighten to 15-20 ft. lbs. (20-27 N.m). Spindle end play should be zero. To install remaining hub body components, reverse removal procedure. *See Fig. 16*.

Removal ("F" Series Super Duty) - 1) Set parking brake, and loosen axle shaft bolts. Raise rear of vehicle, and place on jack stands. Release parking brake. Remove and discard axle shaft attaching bolts and washers. Use heavy duty wheel dolly to lift wheel, taking weight off wheel bearings.

2) If dolly is not available, remove wheel assembly. Remove axle shaft, and discard gasket. Remove disc brake caliper. See DISC BRAKE CALIPERS & PADS under REMOVAL & INSTALLATION. Using Hub Wrench (T88T-4252-A), remove wheel bearing hub nut. *See Fig. 19*. Remove outer bearing. Remove hub and rotor assembly. To remove rotor from hub, remove 10 External Torx (E-18) head machine screws.

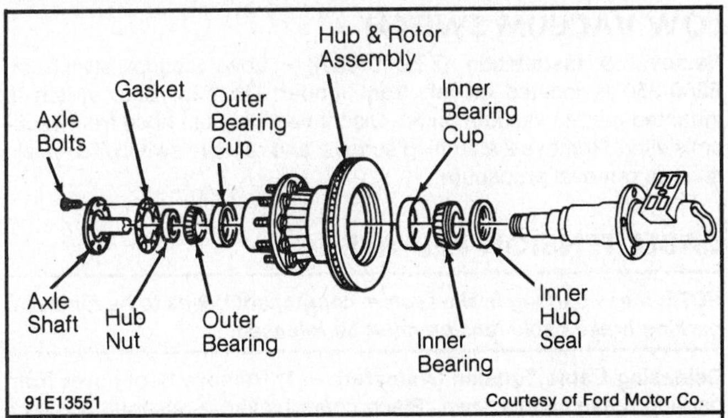
Hub & Rotor Assembly
Gasket
Outer Bearing Cup
Inner Bearing Cup
Axle Bolts
Axle Shaft
Hub Nut
Outer Bearing
Inner Bearing
Inner Hub Seal
91E13551
Courtesy of Ford Motor Co.

Fig. 19: Removing Hub & Rotor Assembly ("F" Series Super Duty)

Installation - 1) Put electrical wiring over axle housing spindle to prevent damage. Apply sealant to hub-to-rotor screws. Place hub and rotor assembly onto axle housing spindle. Remove electrical tape. Install outer wheel bearing race and bearing. Install hub nut, ensuring hub nut tab is in hub tab slot before starting threads.

2) Use Hub Wrench (T88T-4252-A) to tighten hub nut. Push inward on socket to prevent ratcheting action of hub nut. Rotate hub while tightening hub nut to 65-75 ft. lbs. (88-102 N.m). Back off hub nut 90 degrees, and retighten to 15-20 ft. lbs (20-27 N.m). End play of hub and rotor should be zero.

NOTE: Hub nuts are right-hand thread on both sides. Each hub is stamped RH to show thread direction. DO NOT use power impact tools to remove or install hub nuts. Hub nuts will ratchet unless Hub Wrench (T88T-4252-A) is used for removal and installation.

WHEEL CYLINDERS

Removal & Installation - Remove wheel assembly, drum and brake shoes. Remove wheel cylinder connecting links. Disconnect hydraulic brake line from cylinder. Remove wheel cylinder retaining bolts and lock washers. Remove wheel cylinder from backing plate. To install, reverse removal procedure. Adjust brakes, and bleed hydraulic system. See BLEEDING BRAKE SYSTEM.

MASTER CYLINDER

Removal & Installation - 1) On "F" Series Super Duty, with engine off, pump brake pedal several times to discharge hydro-boost accumulator. On all others, disconnect brake warning light indicator wire from indicator switch. With engine off, depress brake pedal to bleed vacuum from brake booster.

2) On all models, disconnect brake lines at master cylinder. Remove nuts retaining master cylinder to brake booster. Remove master cylinder. To install, reverse removal procedure. Bleed brake system. See BLEEDING BRAKE SYSTEM.

VACUUM POWER BOOSTER

Removal & Installation (All Except "F" Series Super Duty) - 1) Disconnect stoplight switch to prevent battery discharge. Support master cylinder. Remove vacuum hose from booster check valve. Remove master cylinder mount nuts. Pull master cylinder away from booster to allow booster removal.

2) From inside cab, remove cotter pin holding stoplight switch to brake pedal arm. *See Fig. 20*. Remove bushing and spacers. Remove booster mount nuts, and then remove booster. To install, reverse removal procedure.

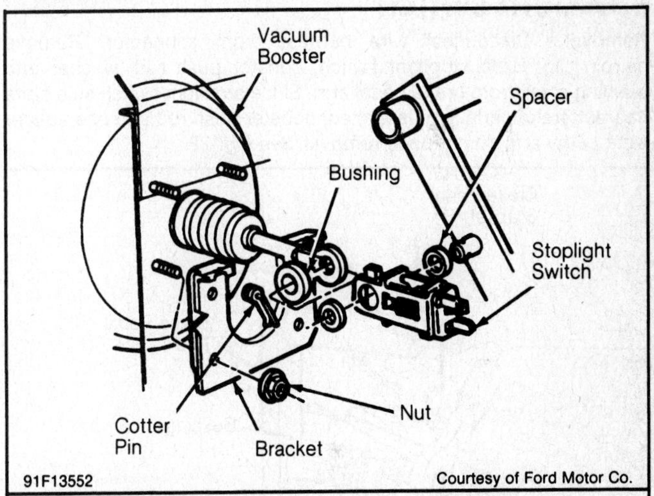
Vacuum Booster
Spacer
Bushing
Stoplight Switch
Nut
Cotter Pin
Bracket
91F13552
Courtesy of Ford Motor Co.

Fig. 20: Removing Vacuum Power Booster (Typical)

HYDRO-BOOST

Removal & Installation ("F" Series Super Duty) - 1) With engine off, pump brake pedal several times to discharge accumulator. Remove master cylinder from hydro-boost, and prop aside.

2) Disconnect 3 hydraulic lines from hydro-boost. Disconnect input push rod from brake pedal. Remove 4 hydro-boost mount nuts, and then remove hydro-boost. To install, reverse removal procedure. Bleed power steering system.

TRANSMISSION MOUNTED PARKING BRAKE

Removal ("F" Series Super Duty) - 1) Shift transmission into gear, and disconnect parking brake cable. Pedal or lever must be in fully released position. Set vehicle on jack stands. Disconnect speedometer cable. Remove bolts attaching driveshaft to parking brake assembly output flange.

2) Remove driveshaft, and secure aside. Remove bolts attaching parking brake assembly to transmission extension housing. *See Fig. 21*. Remove assembly from transmission.

Installation - Using 6 new bolts, attach parking brake assembly to transmission extension housing. Fill parking brake assembly to bottom of fill hole with Motorcraft MERCON multipurpose automatic transmission fluid. To complete installation, reverse removal procedure.

1991 BRAKES
Disc & Drum (Cont.)

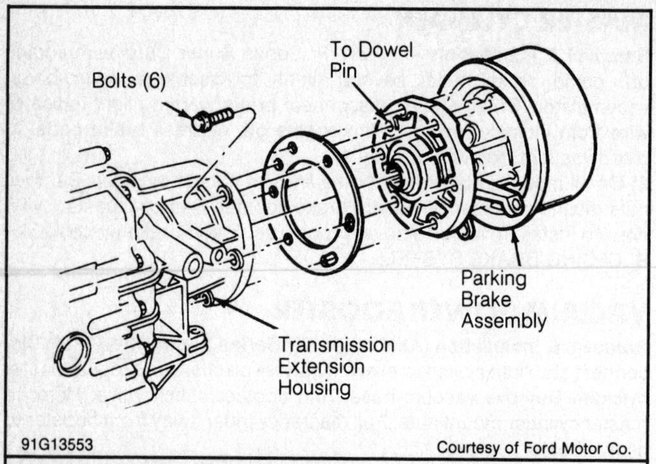
To Dowel
Pin
Bolts (6)
Parking
Brake
Assembly
Transmission
Extension
Housing
91G13553
Courtesy of Ford Motor Co.

Fig. 21: Removing Transmission Mounted Parking Brake ("F" Series Super Duty)

STOPLIGHT SWITCH

Removal – Disconnect wire harness from connector. Remove hairpin clip. Slide stoplight switch, booster push rod, washer and bushing away from brake pedal arm. Since stoplight switch side plate nearest brake pedal arm is slotted, booster push rod and one spacer from pedal arm do not need removal. *See Fig. 22.*

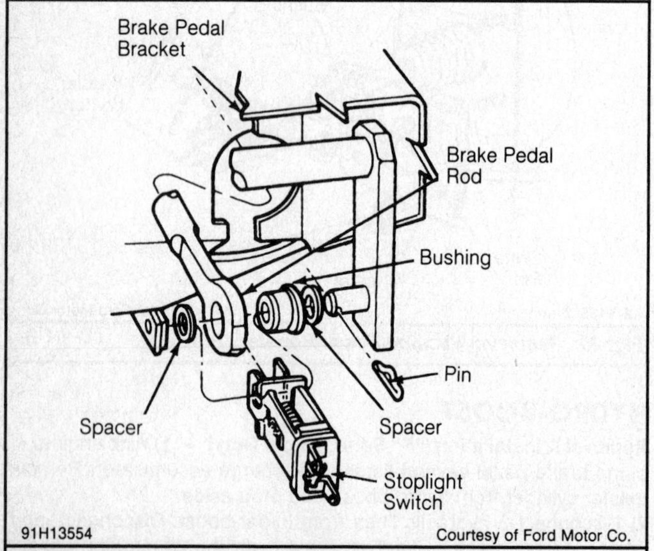
Brake Pedal
Bracket
Brake Pedal
Rod
Bushing
Pin
Spacer
Spacer
Stoplight
Switch
91H13554
Courtesy of Ford Motor Co.

Fig. 22: Removing Stoplight Switch

Installation – Position switch so slotted side is facing pedal arm. Swing switch up and down, trapping booster push rod between switch side plates. Push switch and push rod firmly against pedal arm. Install remaining parts, and check stoplight operation.

HEIGHT SENSING PROPORTIONING VALVE

CAUTION: If height sensing proportioning valve linkage is disconnected, proper indexing will be lost. A new sensing valve must be installed. New sensing valve will have shaft pre-set and secured internally. If shaft turns freely, DO NOT USE.

Removal & Installation ("F" Series Super Duty) – 1) With rear wheels on ground, lift frame to obtain 6 5/8" of clearance between bottom edge of rubber jounce bumper and top axle housing on both sides. *See Fig. 8.* Use this position to install pre-indexed height sensing proportioning valve.

CAUTION: Aftermarket load leveling kits, air shocks or modifications which change curb ride height and/or spring deflection rate provide false readings to height sensing proportioning valve. These modifications may result in unsatisfactory brake performance, which in turn could result in an accident.

2) Remove linkage arm mount nut, and remove linkage arm. Disconnect brake line from valve. Remove height sensing proportioning valve mount bolts. Remove height sensing proportioning valve. To install, reverse removal procedure. Bleed system. See BLEEDING BRAKE SYSTEM.

NOTE: When servicing other rear suspension components, remove 2 nuts attaching height sensing proportioning valve linkage to rear axle cover plate, thus eliminating need to replace height sensing proportioning valve.

BRAKE BOOSTER VACUUM PUMP

Removal & Installation (7.3L Diesel) – Remove hose from vacuum pump outlet. Remove vacuum pump belt. Remove pivot and adjustment bolts. Remove vacuum pump. To install, reverse removal procedure. Brake warning light comes on until vacuum builds up to normal level.

NOTE: Vacuum pump is serviced only as a unit. Vacuum pump pulley can be replaced separately.

LOW VACUUM SWITCH

Removal & Installation (7.3L Diesel) – Low vacuum switch on E250/350 is located on left front fender. On F250/350, switch is mounted next to vacuum pump. Disconnect vacuum hose from vacuum switch. Remove 2 attaching screws, and remove switch. To install, reverse removal procedure.

CABLE TENSION RELEASE

NOTE: If any parking brake system component needs to be removed, parking brake cable tension must be released.

Releasing Cable Tension (Aerostar) – 1) Remove boot cover from parking brake control lever. Place control lever in released position. Insert a steel pin through pawl lock-out pin hole. *See Fig. 23.*

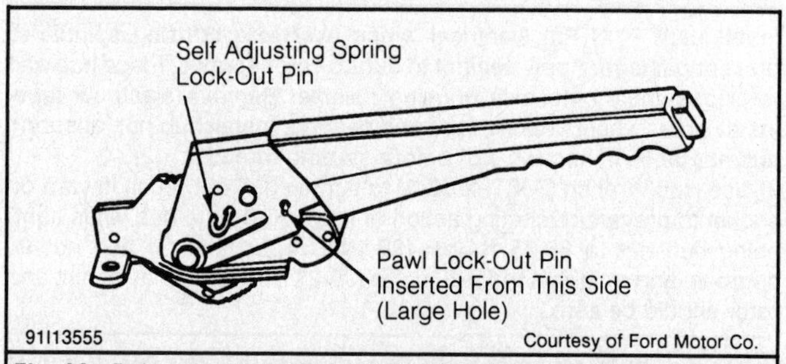
Self Adjusting Spring
Lock-Out Pin
Pawl Lock-Out Pin
Inserted From This Side
(Large Hole)
91I13555
Courtesy of Ford Motor Co.

Fig. 23: Releasing Park Brake Cable Tension (Aerostar)

2) Insert pin from inboard side at a slightly upward and forward angle and sweep downward and rearward to move self-adjusting pawl. This procedure locks out self-adjusting pawl.
3) Raise vehicle with helper inside on hoist. Pull rearward on equalizer about 1-2 1/2" (25.4-57.1 mm), rotating self-adjuster reel backward.
4) With equalizer pulled rearward, have helper inside vehicle insert a steel pin through self-adjusting spring lock-out holes in lever arm and lever body, locking ratchet wheel in cable released position.

CAUTION: DO NOT remove steel pin until cables are connected to equalizer. If pin is removed too soon, ratchet wheel spring will unwind, releasing tension. Entire assembly must be removed to reset tension.

Resetting Cable Tension (Aerostar) - Connect parking brake cables to equalizer. Remove steel pin from spring lock-out hole, keeping fingers clear. Remove steel pin from pawl lock-out hole, restoring tension to parking brake cable. Apply and release parking brake several times to set cable tension.

Resetting Control Assembly Spring Tension (Aerostar) - **1)** Parking brake control assembly spring tension is lost when coil spring unwinds and disengages from tab on wheel. This occurs when a cable breaks, when servicing system without inserting lock pin or if lock pin is removed before brake cables are connected.

2) Remove parking brake control lever assembly. Hook end of coil spring on wheel tab. *See Fig. 24*. Insert a steel pin through pawl lock-out pin holes. Insert pin from inboard side at a slightly upward and forward angle and sweep downward and rearward to move self-adjusting pawl. This procedure locks out self-adjusting pawl.

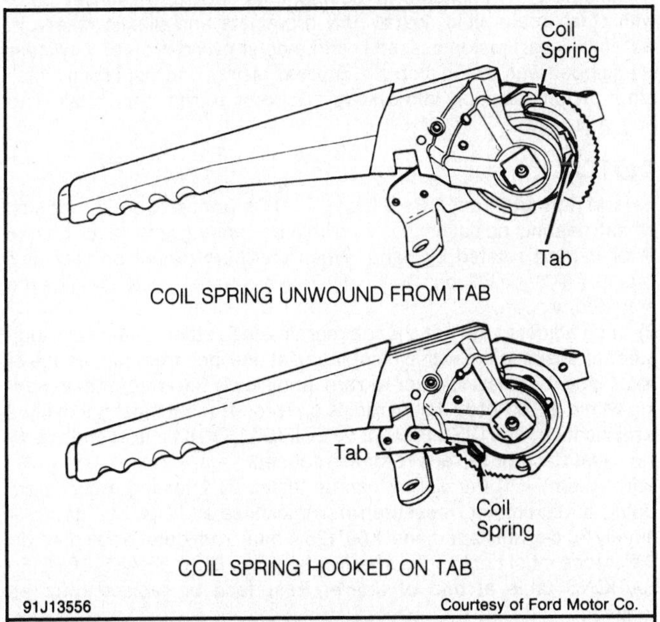
Coil Spring
Tab
COIL SPRING UNWOUND FROM TAB
Tab
Coil Spring
COIL SPRING HOOKED ON TAB
91J13556
Courtesy of Ford Motor Co.

Fig. 24: Resetting Spring Tension (Aerostar)

3) Slip a spare front cable around pulley. Insert cable anchor pin into pivot hole in ratchet plate assembly. With cable on floor, place foot on cable, or clamp end of cable in a vise.

4) Pull on brake control assembly, holding mounting bracket tightly against body of control assembly. Pull until cable tension rotates cable track in order to fully insert lock pin. Insert lock pin so control assembly is in released position. Install parking brake control lever assembly.

OVERHAUL

DISC BRAKE CALIPER

NOTE: Use same disassembly procedures for single and dual piston calipers.

Disassembly - **1)** Remove caliper. See DISC BRAKE CALIPERS & PADS under REMOVAL & INSTALLATION. Drain fluid from caliper. Secure caliper in a vise. Place a block of wood between caliper and piston(s). *See Fig. 25*. Apply low air pressure to brake hose inlet. Air pressure forces piston(s) outward.

CAUTION: DO NOT place fingers between wood and piston as piston leaves caliper.

2) If piston is jammed or seized and does not come out easily, use a brass hammer to lightly tap caliper while applying air pressure. DO NOT pry piston from bore. After piston comes out, remove seal and dust boot. Discard seals and boots.

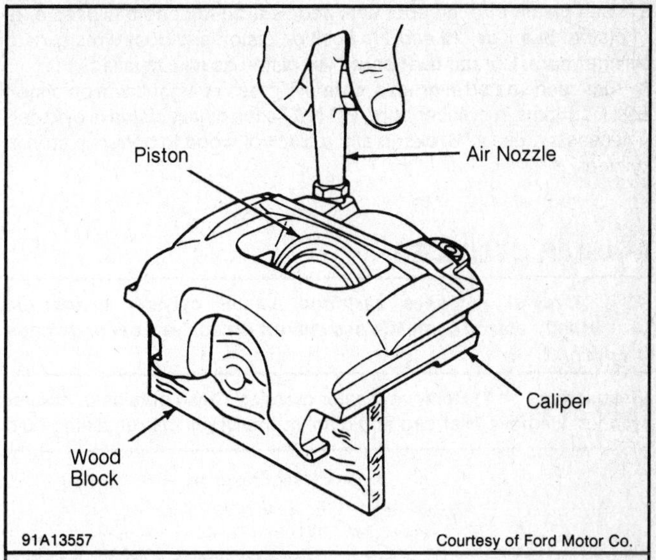
Piston
Air Nozzle
Caliper
Wood Block
91A13557
Courtesy of Ford Motor Co.

Fig. 25: Removing Caliper Piston

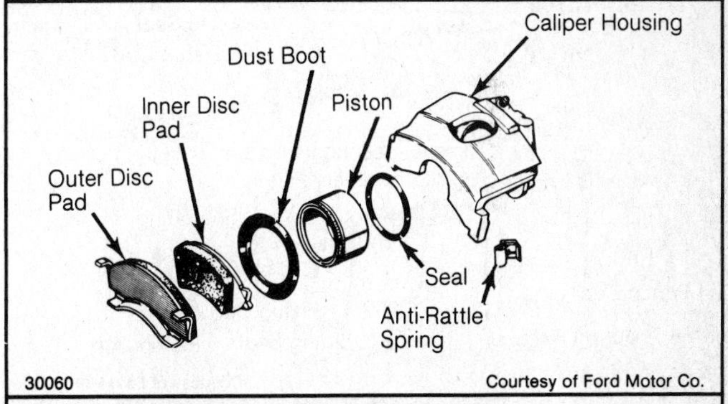
Caliper Housing
Dust Boot
Inner Disc Pad
Piston
Outer Disc Pad
Seal
Anti-Rattle Spring
30060
Courtesy of Ford Motor Co.

Fig. 26: Exploded View of Single Piston Caliper (Bronco, E150 & F150; Others Similar)

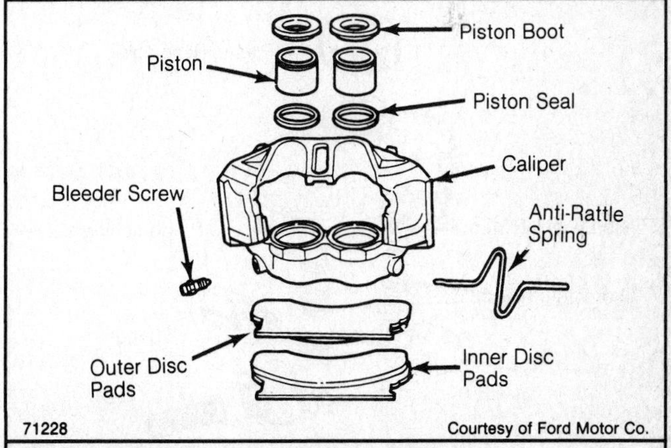
Piston Boot
Piston
Piston Seal
Caliper
Bleeder Screw
Anti-Rattle Spring
Outer Disc Pads
Inner Disc Pads
71228
Courtesy of Ford Motor Co.

Fig. 27: Exploded View of Dual Piston Caliper (E250/350 & F250/350; "F" Series Super Duty Similar)

Cleaning & Inspection - **1)** Carefully clean rust and corrosion from caliper machined surfaces using a wire brush. DO NOT get wire brush in cylinder bores. Clean all components with isopropyl alcohol, and dry with compressed air.

2) Inspect cylinder bore, seal grooves and boot grooves for wear or damage. If bores are scored, corroded or worn, replace caliper. Replace anti-rattle clip, caliper support spring and key.

Reassembly - **1)** Lubricate piston seal with clean brake fluid, and install in cylinder bore groove. Lubricate cylinder with clean brake fluid. Coat piston and outside beads of dust boot with clean brake fluid.

1991 BRAKES
Disc & Drum (Cont.)

2) Push piston through boot until boot is around bottom (closed end) of piston. *See Figs. 26 and 27*. Position piston and boot directly over cylinder bore. Spread dust boot over piston as it is installed.
3) With bead seated in groove, carefully press straight down on piston until it bottoms in cylinder bore. DO NOT cock or jam piston in cylinder. If necessary, use a "C" clamp and a block of wood to bottom piston in cylinder.

MASTER CYLINDER

NOTE: Aerostar recessed cartridge master cylinder cannot be overhauled; replace complete assembly if excessive wear or damage is apparent.

Disassembly - 1) Remove master cylinder. Clean outside of master cylinder. Remove filler cap and diaphragm. Drain any remaining fluid from cylinder. On dual master cylinder used on Bronco and "E" & "F" Series vehicles, remove stop bolt from bottom of master cylinder.
2) On all models, remove proportioning valve (if equipped). Depress piston, and remove snap ring from end of master cylinder bore. *See Figs. 28 and 29*. Remove piston assembly from cylinder bore. Carefully apply air pressure in outlet port of cylinder to remove remaining piston assembly from bore.

NOTE: Manufacturer does not recommend honing of cylinder bore.

Inspection - Clean all parts with isopropyl alcohol, and blow dry with compressed air. Ensure all ports and vents are open and free of foreign matter. Inspect master cylinder bore and all parts for excessive wear or damage. If bore is damaged, replace master cylinder.
Reassembly - Lubricate all components, including cylinder bore, with clean brake fluid. Install new grommets and plastic reservoir. Carefully insert piston assembly into master cylinder bore. If cylinder is equipped with piston stop pin, depress piston, and install pin. Install other piston assembly into cylinder. Depress piston, and install snap ring in groove.

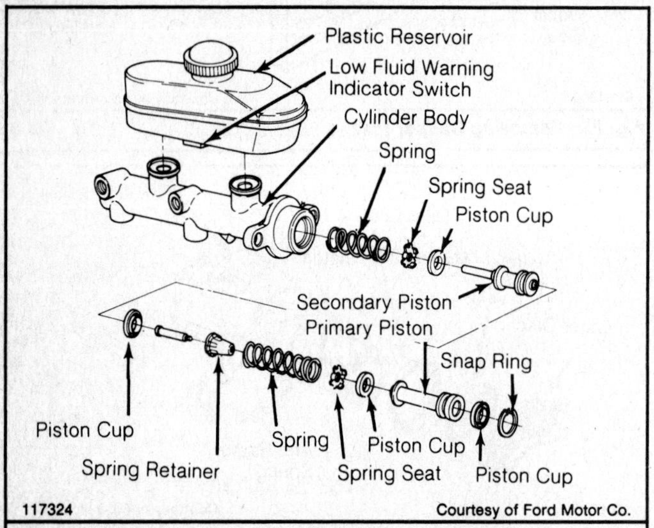
Plastic Reservoir
Low Fluid Warning Indicator Switch
Cylinder Body
Spring
Spring Seat
Piston Cup
Secondary Piston
Primary Piston
Snap Ring
Piston Cup
Spring
Piston Cup
Spring Retainer
Spring Seat
Piston Cup
117324
Courtesy of Ford Motor Co.

Fig. 28: Exploded View of Master Cylinder Assembly (Aerostar, Explorer & Ranger)

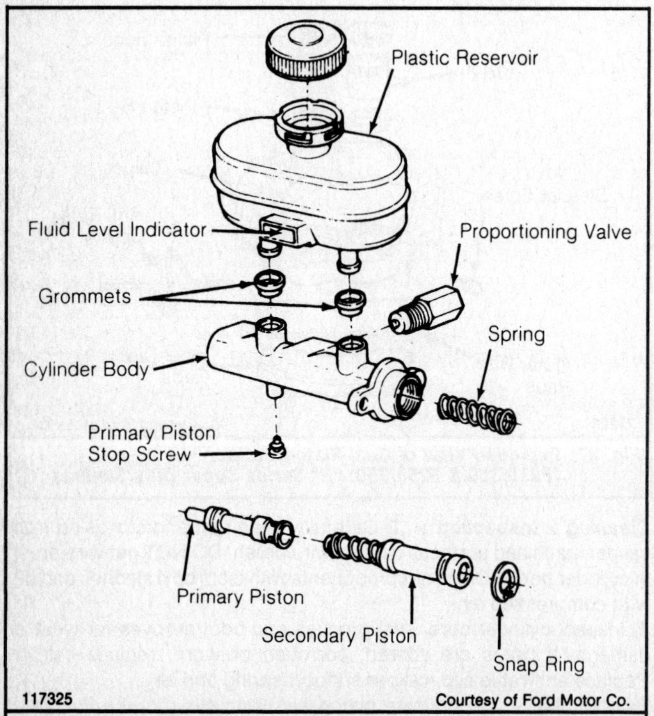
Plastic Reservoir
Fluid Level Indicator
Proportioning Valve
Grommets
Spring
Cylinder Body
Primary Piston Stop Screw
Primary Piston
Secondary Piston
Snap Ring
117325
Courtesy of Ford Motor Co.

Fig. 29: Exploded View of Master Cylinder Assembly (Bronco, "E" & "F" Series)

ROTOR

Lateral Runout (Front & Rear Disc) - 1) On front disc brakes, tighten wheel bearing adjusting nut to eliminate bearing end play. Ensure rotor can be rotated by hand. When checking runout on rear disc brakes ("F" Series Super Duty only), make sure rear axle bearings are adjusted properly.
2) Once adjusted, do not change rear bearing setting. Attach dial indicator to suspension, with indicator tip set one inch from outer edge of rotor face. Set dial indicator to zero, and slowly turn rotor. Take reading within a 6.00" (152.4 mm) radius on rotor. Runout must not exceed specification. See DISC BRAKE SPECIFICATIONS table at end of article. Resurface or replace rotor as required.
Parallelism - 1) Parallelism can be tested by 2 testing procedures. Using a micrometer, measure rotor thickness at 12 points, approximately 30 degrees apart and 1.00" (25.4 mm) from outer edge of rotor. Difference must not exceed specification. See DISC BRAKE SPECIFICATIONS table at end of article. Resurface or replace rotor as required.
2) Mount rotor on a brake lathe. Attach 2 dial indicators, one on each side of rotor, with tip of indicators contacting rubbing surface of rotor directly opposite each other and 1.00" (25.4 mm) from outer edge of rotor. Zero both indicators, and rotate rotor. Note indicator reading. If reading exceeds specification, resurface or replace as required. See DISC BRAKE SPECIFICATIONS table at end of article.
Discard Thickness - Using micrometer, measure thickness of rotor. Disc brake rotors have a minimum wear thickness. Minimum wear thickness is not refinishing dimension. See DISC BRAKE SPECIFICATIONS table at end of article.

CAUTION: Never refinish a rotor down to minimum wear or discard thickness.

Maximum Allowable Stock Removal - 1) To measure maximum allowable stock remaining for refinishing on inner rotor face, use Disc Rotor Surface Gauge And Ball (T71P-1102-A). *See Fig. 30*. Remove inner grease seal and bearing from rotor. Wipe inner and outer bearing cups clean.
2) Carefully place gauge ball in inner bearing cup. DO NOT drop. Set micrometer at base line setting number. Using a 2 1/8" (54 mm) gauge ball, base line setting is .256" (6.50 mm). Position micrometer gauge bar on inner rotor face with micrometer centered over gauge ball.
3) To measure distance between micrometer base line setting and gauge ball, turn micrometer down to touch top of ball. Calculate difference between reading and base line setting; difference is maximum allowable stock which can be removed from inner rotor face.
4) When micrometer is set at base line setting and micrometer end touches top of ball, no additional material may be removed from rotor. If micrometer must be retracted from base line setting to allow gauge bar legs to rest on rotor face, rotor has been refinished beyond allowable limit. Replace rotor.

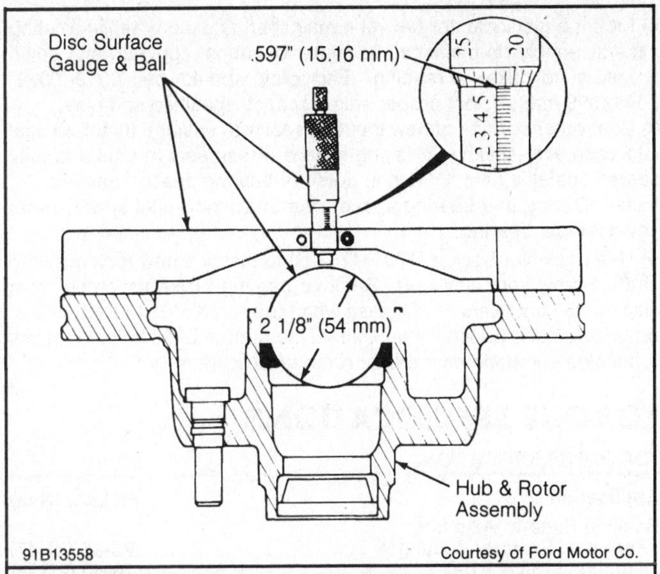
Disc Surface
Gauge & Ball
.597" (15.16 mm)
2 1/8" (54 mm)
Hub & Rotor
Assembly
91B13558
Courtesy of Ford Motor Co.

Fig. 30: Measuring Maximum Allowable Refinishing Stock

WHEEL CYLINDERS

Disassembly – With wheel cylinder removed from vehicle, remove rubber boots from ends of cylinders. Remove pistons, piston cups, return spring and piston expander from cylinder. Remove bleeder screw. Inspect cylinder bore for damage.

Reassembly – If cylinder bore is lightly pitted or scratched, hone or replace as necessary. Coat all parts with clean brake fluid. To assemble, reverse disassembly procedures. Clamp brake cylinder pistons against ends of cylinder.

TRANSMISSION MOUNTED PARKING BRAKE

Disassembly ("F" Series Super Duty) – 1) Remove parking brake assembly. See TRANSMISSION MOUNTED PARKING BRAKE under REMOVAL & INSTALLATION. Mount parking brake assembly in vise using brass jaw protectors. Using Lock Nut Socket (T70T-4252-D), remove lock nut from mainshaft. Using a 3-jaw puller or a press with Adapter (D880L-1013-A), remove mainshaft, brake drum and output flange. *See Fig. 31.*

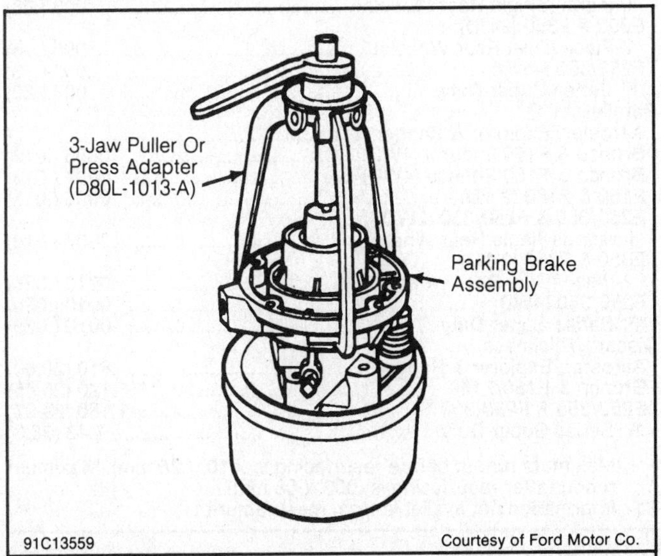
3-Jaw Puller Or
Press Adapter
(D80L-1013-A)
Parking Brake
Assembly
91C13559
Courtesy of Ford Motor Co.

Fig. 31: Removing Lock Nut, Mainshaft, Brake Drum & Output Flange ("F" Series Super Duty)

2) Remove snap ring holding speedometer drive gear onto shaft, and then remove speedometer drive gear. Using Puller (D80L-1002-L) with Bearing Cone Remover (D79L-4621-A) and Step Plate (D80L-630-6), remove inner bearing cone from mainshaft.

3) Remove parking brake assembly from vise. Turn brake assembly over, and mount threaded end of mainshaft in vise using brass jaw protectors. Remove 4 nuts attaching output flange and brake drum to output shaft. Remove brake drum and flange from output shaft.

NOTE: Drum, flange and mainshaft are balanced as a unit. They must be marked to ensure parts are assembled in same position.

4) Using Bearing Cup Puller (T77F-1102-A), remove output shaft oil seal, spacer, "O" ring, bearing and bearing cup from input shaft end of case. Remove splash shield and brake assembly from case. *See Fig. 32.* Remove brake actuating lever and lever spring from case.

5) Using Bearing Cup Puller (T77F-1102-A), remove outer bearing cup. Unscrew and remove vent from case.

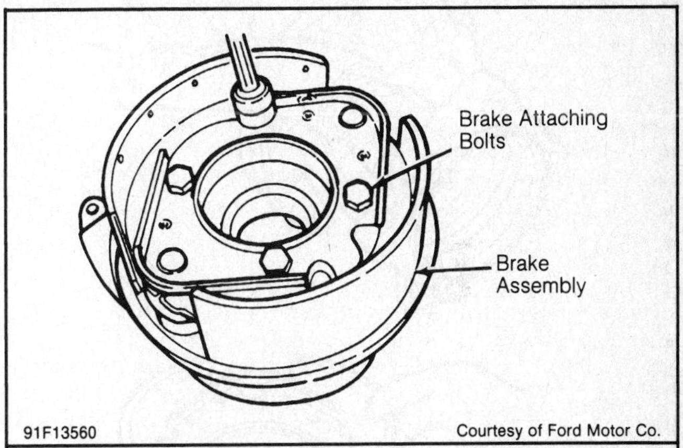
Brake Attaching
Bolts
Brake
Assembly
91F13560
Courtesy of Ford Motor Co.

Fig. 32: Removing Splash Shield & Brake Assembly ("F" Series Super Duty)

Reassembly – 1) Using Bearing Cup Installer (T88T-2598-E), install bearing cup into case. Install inner bearing. Apply a light coat of sealer to outer edge of oil seal. Place oil seal in case with sealing lip facing inward. Press seal into case flush with bore surface using Seal Installer (T88T-2598-C).

2) Install actuating lever spring on boss in case. *See Fig. 33.* Apply a light coat of lithium base grease to actuating lever ball. Install ball end of lever into hole in boss through coiled end of spring. Position backing plate and brake assembly onto case.

3) Insert actuating lever (cam end) into position in brake assembly. Install and tighten brake assembly mount bolts. Attach return spring to actuating lever, and bend long end of spring to snap over lever. Place mainshaft with flanged end up in vise using brass jaw protectors.

4) Install brake drum and output flange onto flanged end of mainshaft. Install output flange onto brake drum, aligning marks made during disassembly. Proper installation maintains proper component balance. Install and tighten output flange mount nuts. Remove mainshaft and drum assembly from vise. Turn assembly over, and clamp in vise again.

5) Install case onto mainshaft, guiding shaft through oil seal and bearing. Using Bearing Installer (T88T-2598-F), seat output bearing onto mainshaft. Install speedometer drive gear and snap ring onto mainshaft. Using Bearing Cup Installer (T88T-2598-D), install input bearing cup into housing.

NOTE: Mainshaft shim determines end play. Shims are available in thicknesses of .0019" (.048 mm).

6) Install shim on mainshaft. Install inner bearing onto mainshaft. To measure end play, install bearing spacer, without "O" ring, onto mainshaft. Clamp case assembly and mainshaft in vise. Use Lock Nut Socket (T70T-4252-D) to screw hex nut onto mainshaft.

1991 BRAKES
Disc & Drum (Cont.)

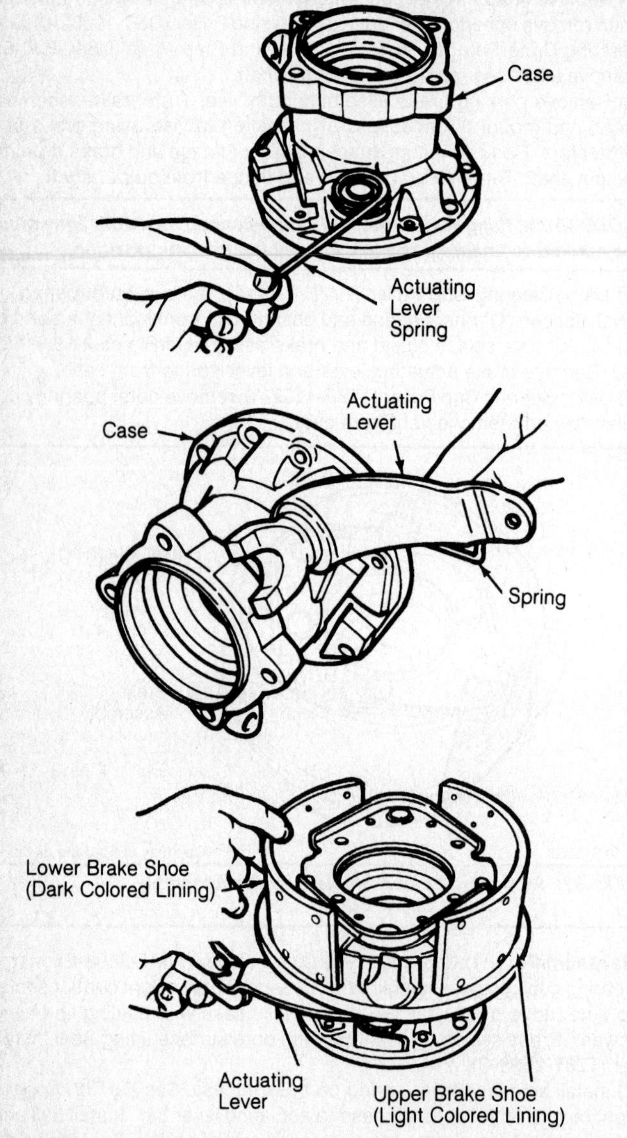
Case
Actuating
Lever
Spring
Case
Actuating
Lever
Spring
Lower Brake Shoe
(Dark Colored Lining)
Actuating
Lever
Upper Brake Shoe
(Light Colored Lining)

91G13561 Courtesy of Ford Motor Co.

Fig. 33: Installing Lever Spring, Actuating Lever, Backing Plate & Brake Assembly ("F" Series Super Duty)

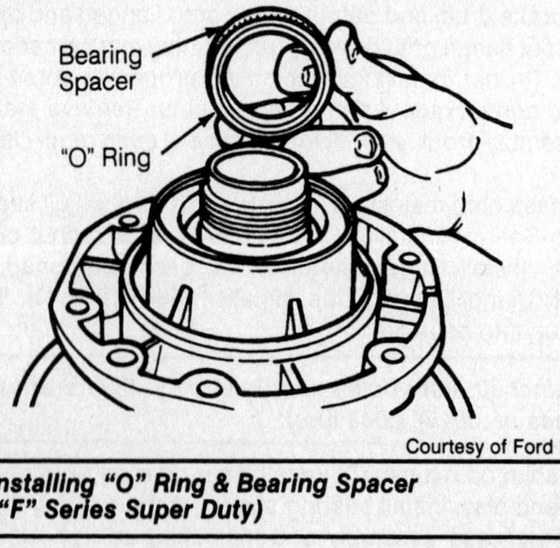
Bearing
Spacer
"O" Ring

91H13562 Courtesy of Ford Motor Co.

Fig. 34: Installing "O" Ring & Bearing Spacer ("F" Series Super Duty)

7) Mount a dial indicator between mainshaft and case. While rotating case assembly on mainshaft to center bearings, apply up and down pressure to take a reading. End play should be .0019-.0039" (.048-.099 mm). Select proper shim to reach specified end play.

8) Coat outer surface of new input oil seal with sealant. Install oil seal into case with sealing lip facing inward. Press seal in until it is fully seated. Install a new "O" ring in notch of bearing spacer. *See Fig. 34.* Install "O" ring and bearing spacer onto mainshaft until spacer butts against input bearing.

9) Use Lock Nut Socket (T70T-4252-D) to install a new lock nut onto shaft. Screw vent into case. Remove parking brake assembly from vise. Install onto vehicle. Fill case with Motorcraft MERCON multipurpose automatic transmission fluid. Fill to bottom of fill hole. To install remaining components, reverse removal procedure.

TORQUE SPECIFICATIONS

TORQUE SPECIFICATIONS

Application	Ft. Lbs. (N.m)
Backing Plate-to-Axle Bolt	
Aerostar, Explorer & Ranger	25-35 (34-47)
Bronco, E150 & F150	20-40 (27-54)
F250/350	50-70 (68-95)
Booster-To-Dash	13-25 (18-34)
Height Sensing Proportioning Valve	
Flex Hose Bolt	28-34 (38-46)
Linkage Arm	8-10 (11-14)
Mounting Bolts	12-18 (16-24)
Hydraulic Tube Nuts	
3/8" & 7/16"	10-15 (14-20)
1/2" & 9/16"	10-17 (14-23)
Master Cylinder-To-Booster	13-25 (18-34)
Pressure Differential Valve [1]	13-16 (18-22)

[1] – On Ranger only.

DISC BRAKE SPECIFICATIONS

DISC BRAKE SPECIFICATIONS

Application	In. (mm)
Lateral Runout [1]	
Aerostar, Explorer & Ranger	.003 (.08)
Bronco & F150 Integral (4WD)	.003 (.08)
Bronco & F150 2-Piece (4WD)	.005 (.13)
E150 & F150 (2WD)	.003 (.08)
E250/350 & F250/350 (2WD)	
Integral (Single Rear Wheels)	.003 (.08)
E350 & F350 (2WD)	
2-Piece (Dual Rear Wheels)	.005 (.13)
F250/350 (4WD)	.005 (.13)
"F" Series Super Duty	.008 (.20)
Parallelism	
Aerostar, Explorer & Ranger	[2]
Bronco & F150 Integral (4WD)	.0005 (.013)
Bronco & F150 2-Piece (4WD)	.0007 (.018)
E150 & F150 (2WD)	.0005 (.013)
E250/350 & F250/350 (2WD)	
Integral (Single Rear Wheels)	.0007 (.018)
E350 & F350 (2WD)	
2-Piece (Dual Rear Wheels)	.0010 (.025)
F250/350 (4WD)	.0010 (.025)
"F" Series Super Duty	.0010 (.025)
Discard Thickness	
Aerostar, Explorer & Ranger	.810 (20.60)
Bronco & E150/F150	1.120 (28.45)
E250/350 & F250/350	1.180 (29.97)
"F" Series Super Duty	1.43 (36.3)

[1] – Maximum runout before resurfacing is .010" (.25 mm). Maximum runout after resurfacing is .003" (.08 mm).
[2] – Information not available from manufacturer.

1991 BRAKES
Disc & Drum (Cont.)

DRUM BRAKE SPECIFICATIONS

DRUM BRAKE SPECIFICATIONS

Application	In. (mm)
Drum Diameter	
Aerostar, Explorer & Ranger (9")	9.00 (228.6)
Aerostar, Explorer & Ranger (10")	10.00 (254.0)
Bronco, E150 & F150	11.00 (279.4)
E250/350 [1] & F250 [1]/350 [2]	12.00 (304.8)
Maximum Drum Refinish Diameter	
Aerostar, Explorer & Ranger (9")	9.060 (230.10)
Aerostar, Explorer & Ranger (10")	10.060 (255.50)
Bronco, E150 & F150	11.060 (280.92)
E250/350 [1] & F250 [1]/350 [2]	12.060 (306.32)
Discard Thickness	
Aerostar, Explorer & Ranger (9")	9.090 (230.89)
Aerostar, Explorer & Ranger (10")	10.090 (256.29)
Bronco, E150 & F150	11.090 (281.69)
E250/350 [1] & F250 [1]/350 [2]	12.090 (307.09)

[1] – Includes Heavy Duty.
[2] – Includes "F" Series Super Duty.

1991 WHEEL ALIGNMENT
Specifications & Procedures

Aerostar, Bronco, Explorer, Ranger, "E" & "F" Series

NOTE: Unless specified otherwise, references to "F" Series include "F" Series Super Duty.

NOTE: Before performing wheel alignment, perform visual and mechanical inspection of wheels, tires and suspension components. See PRE-ALIGNMENT INSTRUCTIONS in WHEEL ALIGNMENT THEORY & OPERATION article in GENERAL INFORMATION.

RIDING HEIGHT ADJUSTMENT

PRE-MEASUREMENT PROCEDURE

Check tire pressure for correct inflation. Specifications can be found on door pillar, side wall of tire, sun visor or glove box. Ensure trunk is empty (except for spare tire and jack). Normalize springs by bouncing vehicle several times.

Measure riding height as shown. *See Figs. 1 and 2.* Refer to RIDING HEIGHT SPECIFICATIONS table. If riding height is not within specification, check suspension parts and repair as necessary before proceeding with wheel alignment. For lean correction, use front shim (389117-S2) or rear shim (E37A-5742-AA) for adjustment of 1/4" (6 mm) or less.

RIDING HEIGHT SPECIFICATIONS

Application	Front	[1] Lean
Aerostar	[2]	[3] 0.75"
Bronco (2WD)	3.3-5.5"	[3] 0.75"
Bronco (4WD)	3.3-4.8"	[3] 0.75"
Explorer	[2]	[2]
Ranger (2WD)	3.3-4.8"	[3] 0.75"
Ranger (4WD)	2.5-4.5"	[3] 0.75"
"E" Series		
E150	4.0-6.0"	[3] 0.75"
E250/350	4.0-5.5"	[3] 0.75"
"F" Series (2WD)		
F150	3.3-5.5"	[3] 0.75"
F250	3.3-5.5"	[3] .75"
Super-Duty	3.1-5.5"	[3] 0.75"
"F" Series (4WD)		
F150	3.3-4.8"	[3] 0.75"
F250	5.0-6.8"	[3] 0.75"
F350	[2]	[3] 0.75"

[1] - Maximum side-to-side height difference with vehicle empty.
[2] - Information is not available from manufacturer.
[3] - Specification is measured at center of front wheel house opening. Maximum side-to-side height difference at center of rear wheel house opening is 0.63".

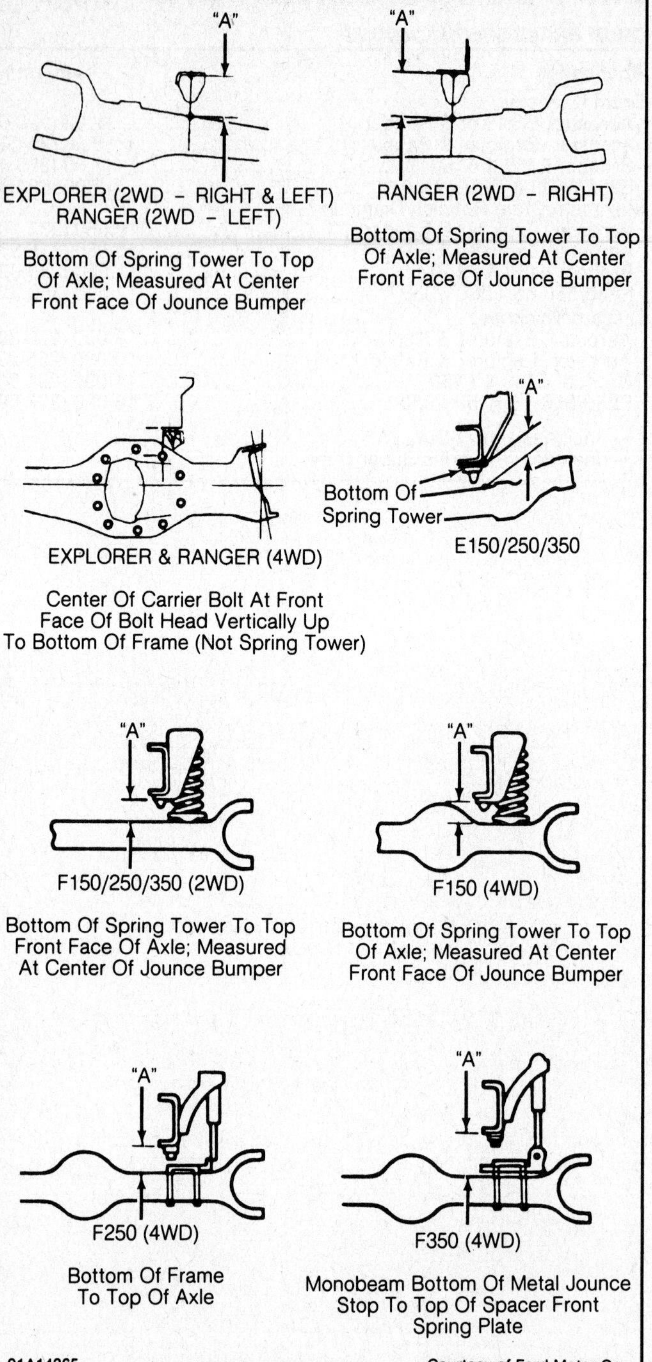
"A"
EXPLORER (2WD - RIGHT & LEFT)
RANGER (2WD - LEFT)
Bottom Of Spring Tower To Top Of Axle; Measured At Center Front Face Of Jounce Bumper
"A"
RANGER (2WD - RIGHT)
Bottom Of Spring Tower To Top Of Axle; Measured At Center Front Face Of Jounce Bumper
EXPLORER & RANGER (4WD)
Center Of Carrier Bolt At Front Face Of Bolt Head Vertically Up To Bottom Of Frame (Not Spring Tower)
"A"
Bottom Of Spring Tower
E150/250/350
"A"
F150/250/350 (2WD)
Bottom Of Spring Tower To Top Front Face Of Axle; Measured At Center Of Jounce Bumper
"A"
F150 (4WD)
Bottom Of Spring Tower To Top Of Axle; Measured At Center Front Face Of Jounce Bumper
"A"
F250 (4WD)
Bottom Of Frame To Top Of Axle
"A"
F350 (4WD)
Monobeam Bottom Of Metal Jounce Stop To Top Of Spacer Front Spring Plate
91A14365
Courtesy of Ford Motor Co.

Fig. 1: Measuring Front Axle Gap

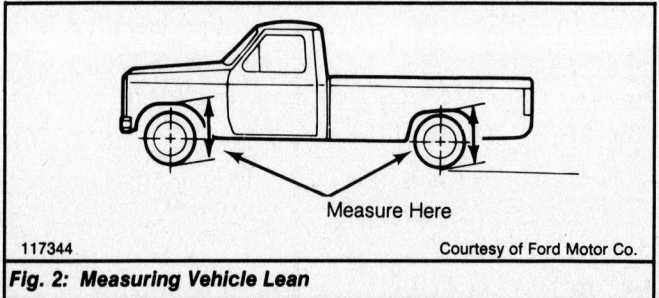

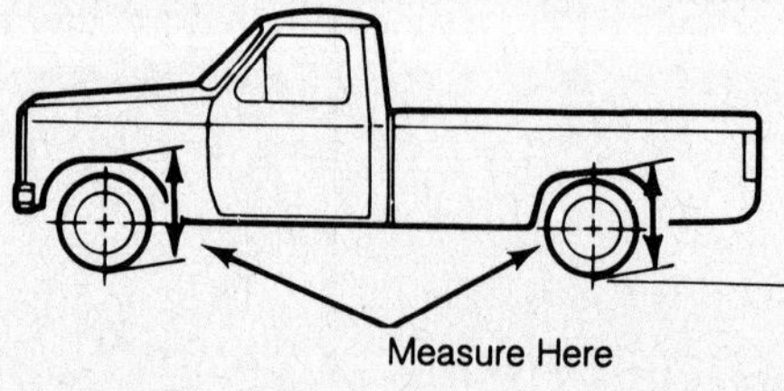
Measure Here
117344
Courtesy of Ford Motor Co.

Fig. 2: Measuring Vehicle Lean

JACKING & HOISTING

FLOOR JACK

Aerostar - To raise front of vehicle, position floor jack under horizontal portion of underbody frame member, behind front wheel of side to be lifted. *See Fig. 3.* To raise rear of vehicle, position floor jack under horizontal portion of underbody frame member, ahead of wheel on side to be lifted.

All Other Models - Floor jack may be used under rear axle, or front suspension lower control arms while observing following precautions:

- Never use jack on any part of underbody.
- DO NOT raise entire vehicle at side rail, with jack midway between front and rear wheels, or permanent body damage may result.
- DO NOT allow lifting plate fingers to contact axle cover plate when lifting at rear axle housing.
- If vehicle is equipped with a stabilizer bar, DO NOT lift at rear axle housing. *See Figs. 4-10.*

1991 WHEEL ALIGNMENT
Specifications & Procedures (Cont.)

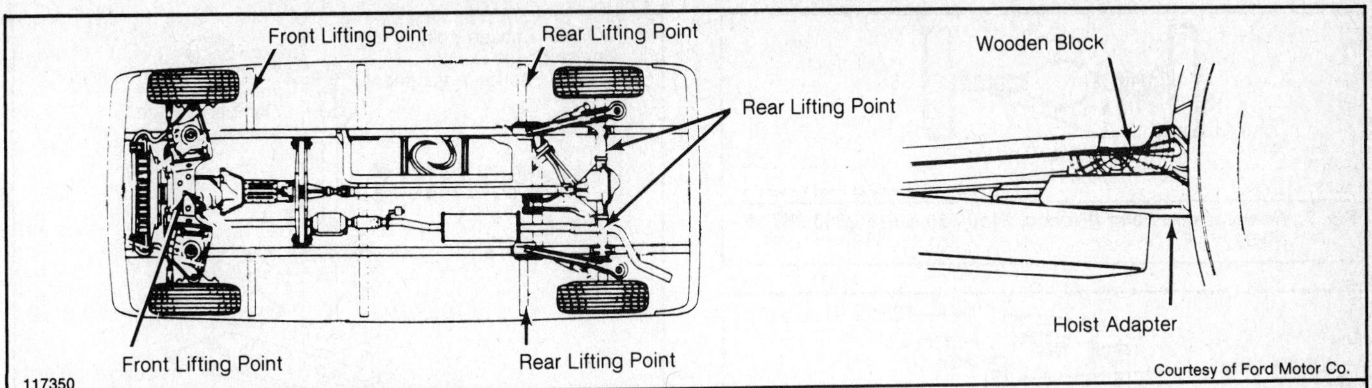
Front Lifting Point
Rear Lifting Point
Rear Lifting Point
Wooden Block
Hoist Adapter
Front Lifting Point
Rear Lifting Point
117350
Courtesy of Ford Motor Co.

Fig. 3: Hoisting & Jacking Contact Points (Aerostar)

BUMPER JACK

Use bumper jack, if supplied as original equipment with vehicle, to change flat tire only. If vehicle is not supplied with a bumper-type jack, DO NOT lift vehicle with by at any time.

NOTE: Always follow hoist manufacturer's instructions. DO NOT allow hoist or adapters to contact exhaust or steering components. Frame contact must be made. Use adapters if necessary.

AXLE CONTACT HOIST

Ensure hoist contacts lower control arms or front crossmember, and rear axle.

FRAME CONTACT HOIST

Aerostar – Vehicle may be raised on single-post or twin-post swiveling arm, or ramp-type drive hoist. If using single-post hoist, ensure lifting arms, pads or ramps are positioned at proper lifting points, and adequate underbody clearance is maintained. To ensure underbody clearance, place wooden blocks between lifting pads and frame at lift points. *See Fig. 3.*

If vehicle is raised on a twin-post hoist, use caution not to damage suspension, rear axle cover and/or steering linkage components. The front end adapters should be carefully positioned, as near wheels as possible, to ensure maximum contact under center of lower suspension arms or spring supports.

Rear suspension hoist adapters (forks) should be placed under rear axle tubes. These adapters must not interfere with lower control arm mounting brackets or hydraulic brake tubes. To avoid damage, DO NOT allow hoisting forks to contact axle housing rear cover, stabilizer bar or brackets.

All Other Models – Vehicle may be raised on single-post or twin-post swiveling arm, or ramp-type drive hoist as long as wide hoist adapters are used. If using single-post hoist, ensure lifting arms, pads or ramps are positioned at proper lifting points, and adequate underbody clearance is maintained.

If vehicle is to be raised on a twin-post hoist, use caution not to damage suspension, rear axle cover and/or steering linkage components. DO NOT allow lift pads to contact exhaust system components. *See Figs. 4-10.*

CAUTION: If removing rear axle, fuel tank, spare tire or liftgate, and single-post hoist is used, anchor vehicle to hoist. Place jack stands under vehicle, or add weight on rear end of vehicle to prevent tipping when center of gravity changes.

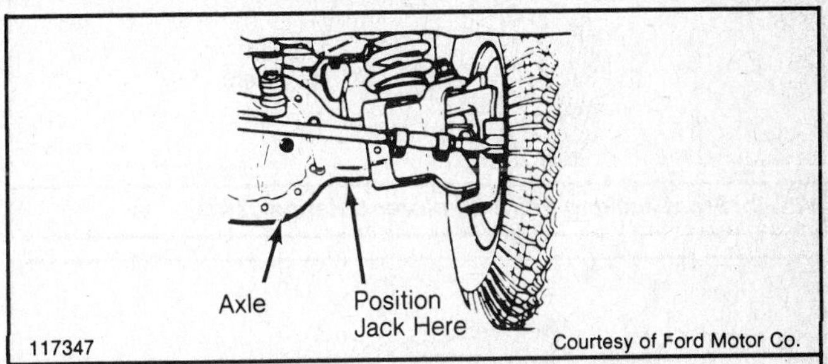
Axle
Position
Jack Here
117347
Courtesy of Ford Motor Co.

Fig. 4: Front Jacking Point (Bronco & F150/350 4WD)

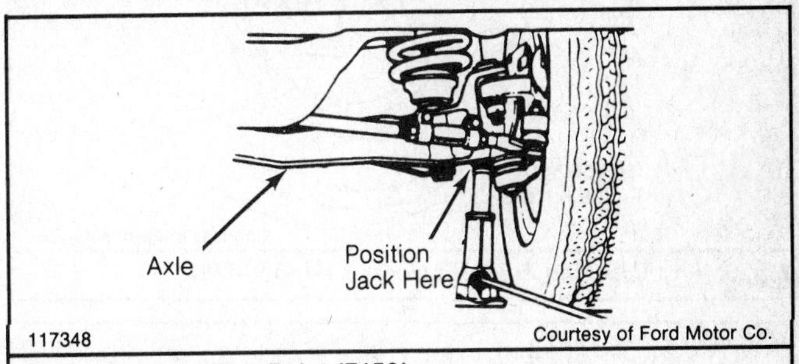
Axle
Position
Jack Here
117348
Courtesy of Ford Motor Co.

Fig. 5: Front Jacking Point (E150)

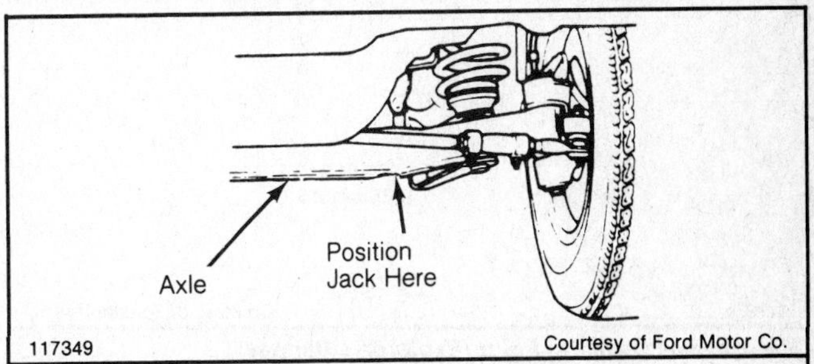
Axle
Position
Jack Here
117349
Courtesy of Ford Motor Co.

Fig. 6: Front Jacking Point (E250/350 & F250/350 2WD)

ALIGNMENT PROCEDURES

CAMBER & CASTER ADJUSTMENT

Aerostar – To adjust front camber, loosen 2 upper control arm nuts. Add or remove equal amount of shims from shim pack. Adding or removing an unequal amount of shims from shim pack will change caster. *See Fig. 11.* Tighten upper control arm nuts to 70-100 ft. lbs. (95-135 N.m) when adjustment is complete.

Explorer & Ranger (Dana 28 Axle) – 1) Measure camber to determine if adjustment is required. If camber adjustment is required, raise vehicle. Remove front wheel and caliper assembly.

1991 WHEEL ALIGNMENT
Specifications & Procedures (Cont.)

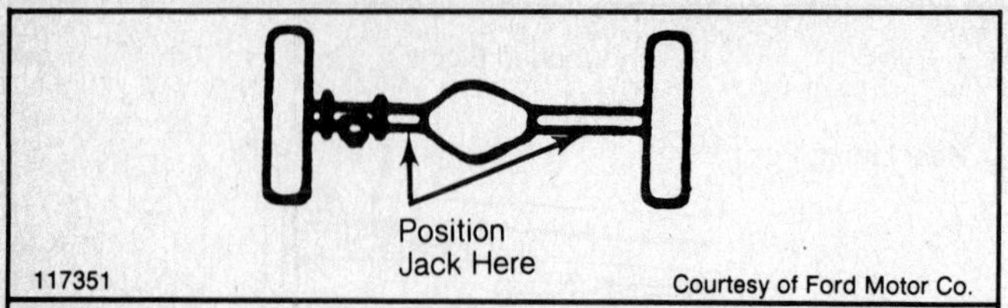
Position
Jack Here
117351
Courtesy of Ford Motor Co.

Fig. 7: Rear Jacking Point (Bronco, E150/350 & F150/350 2WD & 4WD)

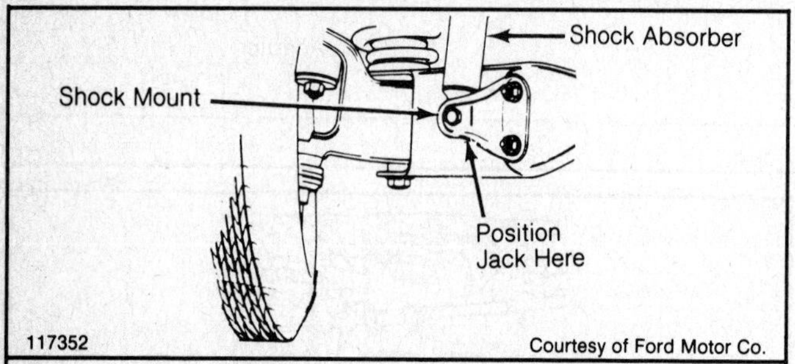
Shock Absorber
Shock Mount
Position
Jack Here
117352
Courtesy of Ford Motor Co.

Fig. 8: Front Jacking Point (Explorer & Ranger 2WD)

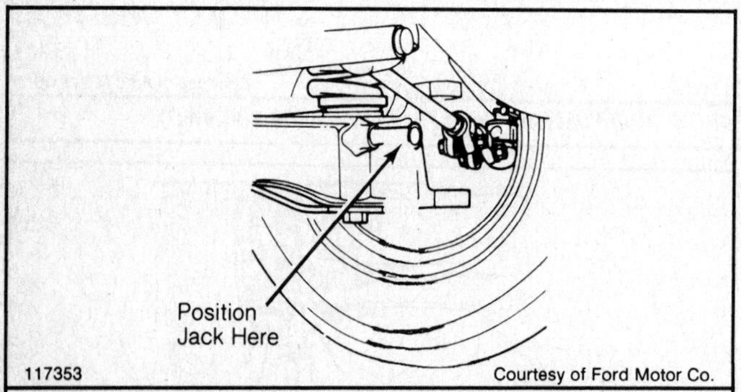
Position
Jack Here
117353
Courtesy of Ford Motor Co.

Fig. 9: Front Jacking Point (Explorer & Ranger 4WD)

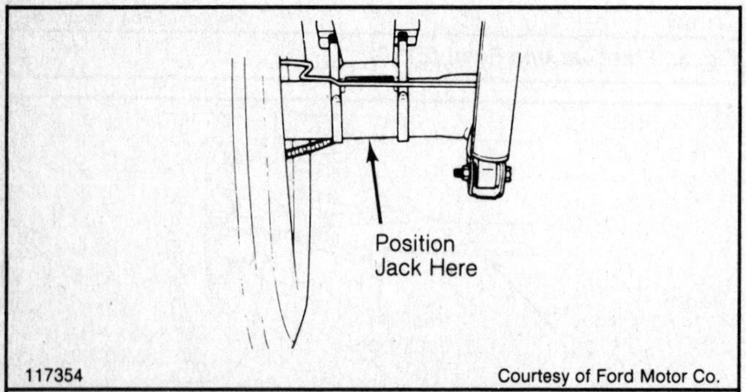
Position
Jack Here
117354
Courtesy of Ford Motor Co.

Fig. 10: Rear Jacking Point (Explorer & Ranger)

2) Remove upper ball joint castle nut and discard. Remove camber adjuster and rotate 180 degrees. *See Fig. 12.* Install new upper ball joint castle nut and tighten to 104 ft. lbs. (104 N.m). Install caliper and wheel assembly. Check alignment to verify correct adjustment.

NOTE: DO NOT bend axles or radius arms to change alignment.

Explorer & Ranger (Dana 35 Axle) – 1) Measure camber and caster to determine if adjustment is required. Record specifications for use in selection of camber/caster adjusters. To adjust, raise vehicle and remove front wheel assembly. Remove caliper and steering knuckle assembly.

2) Remove pinch bolt and camber/caster adjuster from axle. *See Fig. 12.* Install appropriate camber/caster adjuster and rotate to desired adjustment. See CAMBER/CASTER ADJUSTER SPECIFICATION

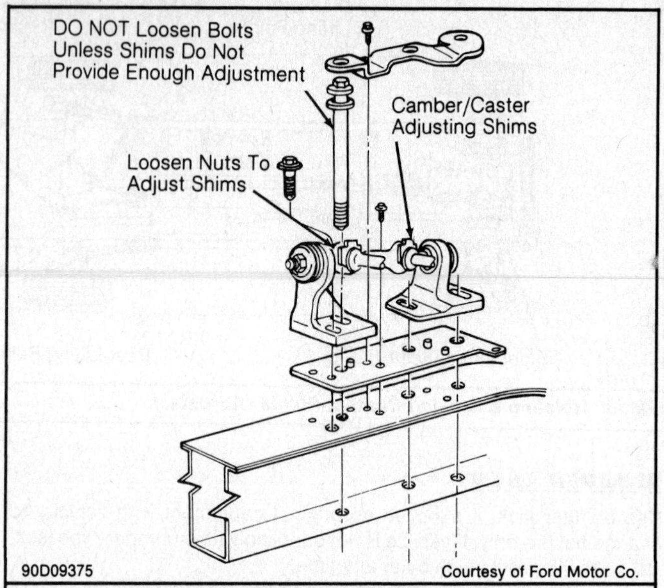
DO NOT Loosen Bolts
Unless Shims Do Not
Provide Enough Adjustment
Camber/Caster
Adjusting Shims
Loosen Nuts To
Adjust Shims
90D09375
Courtesy of Ford Motor Co.

Fig. 11: Adjusting Front Camber/Caster (Aerostar)

table. Install caliper, steering knuckle and wheel assembly. Check alignment to verify correct adjustment.

CAMBER/CASTER ADJUSTER SPECIFICATION

Adjuster Type	Degree Range
0.5	0.75
1.0	2.0
1.5	3.0

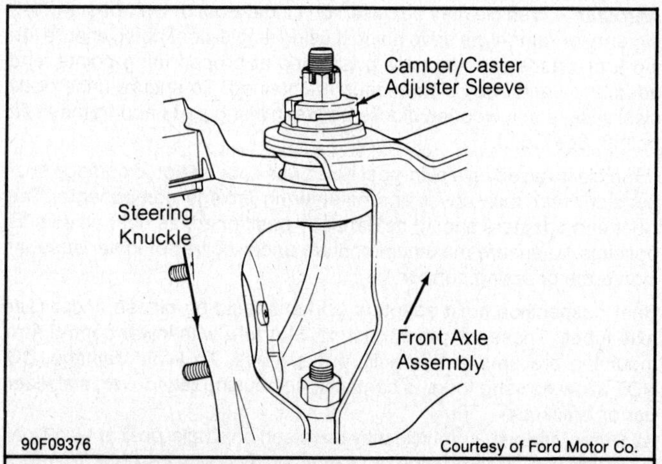
Camber/Caster
Adjuster Sleeve
Steering
Knuckle
Front Axle
Assembly
90F09376
Courtesy of Ford Motor Co.

Fig. 12: Adjusting Camber/Caster (Bronco, Ranger & "F" Series Shown; Others Similar)

"E" Series – There is no manufacturer-approved method of camber adjustment. If caster adjustment is necessary, install Caster Service Kit (E5TZ-3KO64-A) on radius arm to correct excessive caster split.

"F" Series (2WD) – 1) Measure camber and caster to determine if adjustment is required. Record specifications for use in selection of camber/caster adjusters. To adjust, raise vehicle and remove front wheel assembly. Remove caliper and steering knuckle assembly.

2) Remove upper ball joint castle nut and discard. Install appropriate camber/caster adjuster and rotate to desired adjustment. See CAMBER/CASTER ADJUSTER SPECIFICATION table. Install new upper ball joint castle nut and tighten to 104 ft. lbs. (104 N.m). Install caliper and wheel assembly. Check alignment to verify correct adjustment.

F150/250 (4WD) – 1) Camber can be adjusted by changing the upper ball joint mounting sleeve. If camber adjustment is required, raise vehicle and remove front wheel assembly.

2) Remove caliper and steering knuckle assembly. Remove ball joint mounting sleeve using pitman arm puller (if necessary). Install replacement ball joint mounting sleeve.
3) If increased camber is required, point arrow on mounting sleeve outward. If decreased camber is required, point arrow on mounting sleeve inward. Install caliper and steering knuckle/ball joint assembly. Apply Loctite and partially tighten lower ball joint to 40 ft. lbs. (54 N.m).
4) Install new upper ball joint and tighten to 85-100 ft. lbs. (115-135 N.m). Tighten lower ball joint to 95-110 ft. lbs. (54 N.m). Install wheel assembly and check alignment to verify correct adjustment.
F350 (4WD) - Camber and caster are not adjustable on 4WD and "F" Series Super Duty monobeam-design vehicles.

TOE-IN ADJUSTMENT

Aerostar - Start engine. Center steering wheel. Secure steering wheel with holder and turn engine off. Loosen tie rod end lock nut. Loosen steering gear dust boot clamp(s) at tie rod end. Turn tie rod end to obtain correct toe-in. Tighten lock nut to 43-50 ft. lbs. (58-67 N.m). Ensure steering gear dust boot is straight after adjustment. Tighten dust boot clamp.
All Other Models - 1) Measure toe-in with front wheels straight ahead, and steering wheel locked in a centered position. Adjust toe-in by loosening clamps, and adjusting sleeve to obtain correct specification and maintain steering wheel in centered position.
2) If steering wheel is not centered to begin with, determine which tire assembly is out of adjustment, and compensate that side to center the steering wheel. Multiple attempts may be necessary to properly center steering wheel.
3) When tightening clamps, ensure clamp bolts are positioned so there will be no interference with other parts throughout entire travel of steering linkage.

WHEEL ALIGNMENT SPECIFICATIONS [1]

Application	Fraction	Decimal
Aerostar		
Camber (Degrees)	7/32 ± 1/2	(.22 ± .50)
Caster (Degrees)	4 ± 1	(4 ± 1)
Toe-in (Inches)	1/32 ± 1/8	(.03 ± .13)
Toe-in (Degrees)	1/16 ± 1/4	(.06 ± .25)
Explorer (2WD)		
Camber (Degrees)	- 1/4 ± 1/2	(- .25 ± .50)
Caster (Degrees)	5 ± 1	(5 ± 1)
Toe-in (Inches)	0 ± 1/8	(0 ± .13)
Toe-in (Degrees)	0 ± 1/4	(0 ± .25)
Explorer (4WD)		
Camber (Degrees)	- 1/4 ± 1/2	(- .25 ± .50)
Caster (Degrees)	4 1/4 ± 1 3/4	(4.25 ± 1.75)
Toe-in (Inches)	0 ± 1/8	(0 ± .13)
Toe-in (Degrees)	0 ± 1/4	(0 ± .25)
Ranger (2WD)		
Camber (Degrees)	[2]	[2]
Caster (Degrees)	[2]	[2]
Toe-in (Inches)	1/32 ± 1/8	(.03 ± .13)
Toe-in (Degrees)	1/16 ± 1/4	(0 ± .25)
Ranger (4WD)		
Camber (Degrees)	[2]	[2]
Caster (Degrees)	[2]	[2]
Toe-in (Inches)	1/32 ± 1/8	(.03 ± .13)
Toe-in (Degrees)	1/16 ± 1/4	(0 ± .25)
Bronco & F150 (2WD)		
Camber (Degrees)	[2]	[2]
Caster (Degrees)	[2]	[2]
Toe-in (Inches)	1/32 ± 1/8	(.03 ± .13)
Toe-in (Degrees)	1/16 ± 1/4	(0 ± .25)
F250/350 (2WD)		
Camber (Degrees)	[2]	[2]
Caster (Degrees)	[2]	[2]
Toe-in (Inches)	1/32 ± 1/8	(.03 ± .13)
Toe-in (Degrees)	1/16 ± 1/4	(0 ± .25)
Bronco & F150 (4WD)		
Camber (Degrees)	[2]	[2]
Caster (Degrees)	[2]	[2]
Toe-in (Inches)	1/32 ± 1/8	(.03 ± .13)
Toe-in (Degrees)	1/16 ± 1/4	(0 ± .25)
F250/350 (4WD)		
Camber (Degrees)	[2]	[2]
Caster (Degrees)	[2]	[2]
Toe-in (Inches)	1/32 ± 1/8	(.03 ± .13)
Toe-in (Degrees)	1/16 ± 1/4	(0 ± .25)

[1] - Specifications are for vehicles without aftermarket modifications. For vehicles with aftermarket modifications, *see Figs. 13 and 14.*
[2] - Standard specification is not available. Use charts and tables to determine correct camber and caster. *See Figs. 13 and 14.*

1991 WHEEL ALIGNMENT
Specifications & Procedures (Cont.)

***NOTE:** All graphs show the preferred specification. The tolerance from any specification is one degree (1°).*

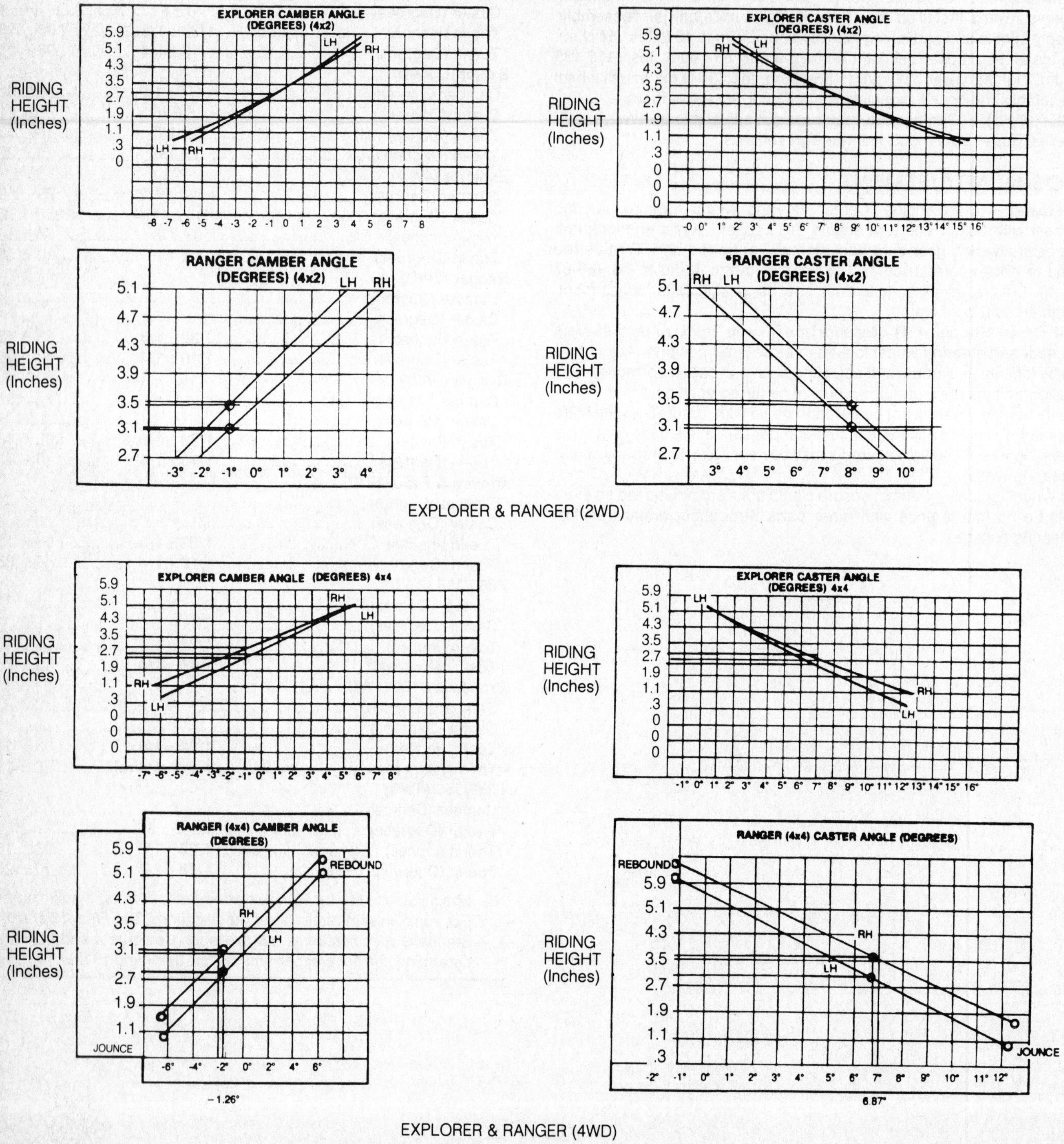
EXPLORER CAMBER ANGLE (DEGREES) (4x2)
RIDING HEIGHT (Inches)
EXPLORER CASTER ANGLE (DEGREES) (4x2)
RANGER CAMBER ANGLE (DEGREES) (4x2)
*RANGER CASTER ANGLE (DEGREES) (4x2)
EXPLORER & RANGER (2WD)
EXPLORER CAMBER ANGLE (DEGREES) 4x4
EXPLORER CASTER ANGLE (DEGREES) 4x4
RANGER (4x4) CAMBER ANGLE (DEGREES)
RANGER (4x4) CASTER ANGLE (DEGREES)
REBOUND
JOUNCE
LH
RH
– 1.26°
6.87°
EXPLORER & RANGER (4WD)

91B14366

Courtesy of Ford Motor Co.

***Fig. 13:** Camber/Caster Specification Graphs (Explorer & Ranger with Aftermarket Modifications)*

1991 WHEEL ALIGNMENT
Specifications & Procedures (Cont.)

CASTER (DEGREES)

"A" RIDE HEIGHT INCHES (MM)	F-150 2WD		F-250/350 2WD		F-250 4WD		BRONCO F-150 4WD		E-150		E-250/350	
	Min.	Max.	Min.	Max.	Min.	Max.	Min.	Max.	Min.	Max.	Min.	Max.
2½ (63.5)	—	—	—	—	—	—	—	—	—	—	—	—
2¾ (69.9)	—	—	—	—	—	—	—	—	—	—	—	—
3⅛ (79.4)	—	—	—	—	—	—	—	—	—	—	—	—
3¼ (82.6)	6	8	8½	10½	—	—	5¾	7¾	—	—	—	—
3⅜ (85.7)	5⅝	7⅝	—	—	—	—	5½	7½	—	—	—	—
3½ (88.9)	5¼	7¼	7¾	9¾	—	—	5⅛	7⅛	—	—	—	—
4 (101.6)	4 3/16	6 3/16	6½	8½	—	—	4	6	7½	9½	6⅞	8⅞
4¼ (108.0)	3½	5½	5¾	7¾	—	—	3	5	6⅞	8⅞	6¼	8¼
4½ (114.3)	3	5	5¼	7¼	—	—	2½	4½	6¼	8¼	5⅝	7⅝
4¾ (120.7)	2⅜	4⅜	4¾	6¾	—	—	2	4	5⅝	7⅝	5	7
5 (127.0)	1¾	3¾	4	6	3⅛	5⅛	—	—	5	7	4⅜	6⅜
5½ (139.7)	⅝	2⅝	2¾	4¾	3 3/16	5 3/16	—	—	3¾	5¾	3⅛	5⅛
6 (152.4)	—	—	—	—	3¼	5¼	—	—	3¼	5¼	—	—
6¼ (158.8)	—	—	—	—	3⅜	5⅜	—	—	—	—	—	—
6¾ (171.5)	—	—	—	—	3½	5½	—	—	—	—	—	—

CAMBER (DEGREES)

"A" RIDE HEIGHT INCHES (MM)	F-150 2WD		F-250/350 2WD		F-250 4WD		BRONCO F-150 4WD		E-150		E-250/350	
	Min.	Max.	Min.	Max.	Min.	Max.	Min.	Max.	Min.	Max.	Min.	Max.
2½ (63.5)	—	—	—	—	—	—	—	—	—	—	—	—
2¾ (69.9)	—	—	—	—	—	—	—	—	—	—	—	—
3⅛ (79.4)	—	—	—	—	—	—	-1¾	-¼	—	—	—	—
3¼ (82.6)	-1⅛	⅜	-2¾	-1¼	—	—	-1¼	0	—	—	—	—
3⅜ (85.7)	-¾	¾	-2¼	-1	—	—	-1⅛	⅛	—	—	—	—
3½ (88.9)	-¼	1¼	-1⅛	-⅜	—	—	-¾	¾	—	—	—	—
4 (101.6)	⅝	2	-¾	¾	—	—	¼	1¾	—	—	-½	⅞
4¼ (108.0)	1⅜	2⅞	0	1½	—	—	1	2½	-⅝	⅝	⅛	1⅜
4½ (114.3)	2	3⅜	½	2	—	—	1⅝	3⅛	0	1¼	½	1¾
4¾ (120.7)	2⅝	3⅞	1¼	2¾	—	—	2	3½	⅜	1⅝	⅞	1½
5 (127.0)	3¼	4½	2	3½	-2	-½	—	—	⅞	2⅛	1⅜	2⅝
5½ (139.7)	4¼	5½	3¼	4¾	-⅝	⅝	—	—	1⅞	3⅛	2⅜	3⅝
6 (152.4)	—	—	—	—	¾	2¼	—	—	2⅞	4⅛	—	—
6¼ (158.8)	—	—	—	—	1¼	2¾	—	—	—	—	—	—
6¾ (171.5)	—	—	—	—	2⅝	4⅛	—	—	—	—	—	—

91C14367

Fig. 14: Camber/Caster Specification Tables (Bronco, "E" & "F" Series with Aftermarket Modifications)

TORQUE SPECIFICATIONS

TORQUE SPECIFICATIONS

Application	Ft. Lbs. (N.m)
Ball Joint Nut	104 (141)
Camber Adjuster Pinch Nut	48-65 (65-88)
Control Arm Nuts	70-100 (95-135)
Tie Rod End Clamp Bolt	14 (19)
Tie Rod Lock Nut	46 (62)

1991 SUSPENSION
Front – Aerostar 2WD

DESCRIPTION

Front suspension is an unequal length control arm system. System consists of spindles, upper and lower control arms, ball joints, bushings, adjustment shims, coil springs, shock absorbers and a stabilizer bar. *See Fig. 1*.

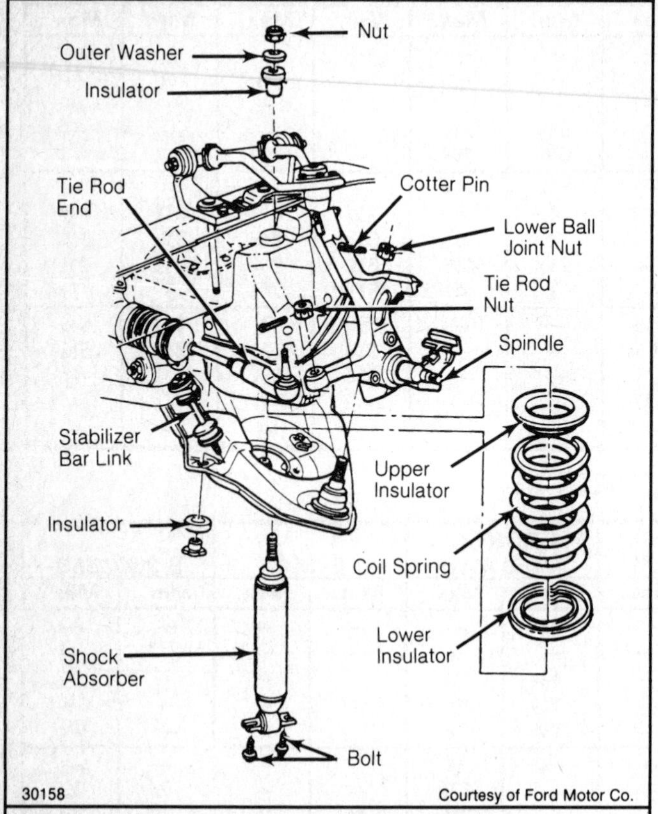
Nut
Outer Washer
Insulator
Tie Rod End
Cotter Pin
Lower Ball Joint Nut
Tie Rod Nut
Spindle
Stabilizer Bar Link
Upper Insulator
Insulator
Coil Spring
Lower Insulator
Shock Absorber
Bolt
30158
Courtesy of Ford Motor Co.

Fig. 1: Exploded View of Front Suspension (Aerostar)

ADJUSTMENTS & INSPECTION

WHEEL ALIGNMENT SPECIFICATIONS & PROCEDURES

NOTE: See SPECIFICATIONS & PROCEDURES article in WHEEL ALIGNMENT.

WHEEL BEARING ADJUSTMENT

1) Raise and support vehicle. Remove wheel cover and grease cap. Remove cotter pin and retainer. Loosen adjusting nut 3 turns. Back off disc brake pads to obtain running clearance between rotor and pads.
2) While rotating wheel assembly, tighten adjusting nut to 17-25 ft. lbs. (23-34 N.m) to seat bearing. Loosen adjusting nut 1/2 turn (180 degrees). Retighten to 18-20 INCH lbs. (2.0-2.3 N.m).
3) Align retainer with cotter pin hole and place on adjusting nut. Install cotter pin. Install grease cap and wheel cover. Before driving vehicle, pump brake pedal several times to restore normal pedal position.

BALL JOINT CHECKING

Lower & Upper Ball Joint – Raise and support vehicle under axle. Move lower edge of tire in and out while watching lower spindle arm and lower part of axle jaw. If movement exceeds 1/32" (.794 mm), replace lower ball joint. To check upper ball joint, move upper edge of tire in and out. If movement between upper spindle arm and upper axle exceeds 1/32" (.794 mm), replace upper ball joint.

REMOVAL & INSTALLATION

NOTE: Any time the steering linkage is disconnected from the spindle, the steering system must be placed in the centered position.

COIL SPRING

Removal – **1)** Place steering wheel and steering system in the centered position. Raise vehicle on hoist. Remove tire and wheel assembly. Disconnect stabilizer bar link bolt from lower control arm.
2) Remove shock 2 absorber-to-lower control arm bolts. Remove upper nut and washer retaining shock absorber. Remove shock absorber.
3) Support vehicle with safety stands under vehicle jacking pads. Using Spring Compressor (D78P-5310-A), compress coil spring.
4) Loosen 2 lower control arm pivot bolts. Remove cotter pin. Loosen but DO NOT remove nut attaching lower ball joint to spindle.
5) Using Pitman Arm Puller (T64P-3590-F), loosen lower ball joint. Remove puller. Support lower control arm with a jack and remove ball joint nut. Lower control arm and remove spring.

Installation – Compress coil spring. Position coil spring assembly into lower control arm. To complete installation, reverse removal procedure.

LOWER CONTROL ARM

Removal – **1)** Place steering wheel and steering system in centered position. Raise and support vehicle with safety stands under frame.
2) Remove coil spring. See COIL SPRING under REMOVAL & INSTALLATION in this article. Remove lower control bolts. Remove lower control arm. Replace entire lower control arm assembly to service bushings.

Installation – **1)** Position lower control arm in crossmember. Ensure bolts are installed in proper direction. *See Fig. 2.* Install nut and tighten until snug. DO NOT tighten nut to specified torque at this time.
2) Inspect lower ball joint boot seal for damage and replace if required. Install coil spring. With vehicle in normal ride height position, tighten lower control arm-to-crossmember bolts to 100-140 ft. lbs. (136-190 N.m).

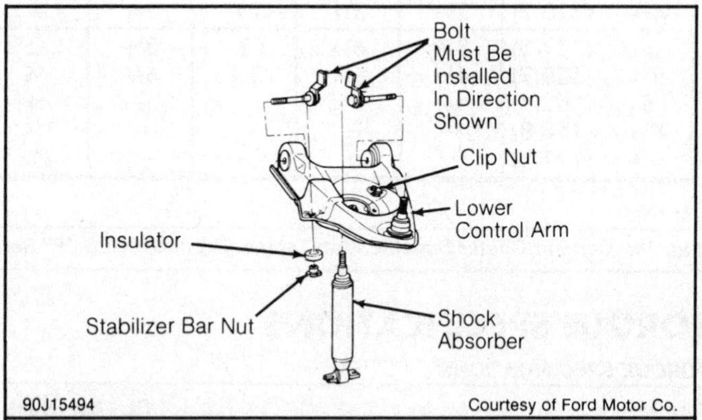
Bolt Must Be Installed In Direction Shown
Clip Nut
Lower Control Arm
Insulator
Stabilizer Bar Nut
Shock Absorber
90J15494
Courtesy of Ford Motor Co.

Fig. 2: Exploded View of Lower Control Arm Assembly

UPPER CONTROL ARM, BALL JOINT & MOUNTING BRACKETS

WARNING: When servicing upper control arm and ball joint assemblies, service one side of vehicle at a time. NEVER service both sides at the same time.

Removal – **1)** Place steering wheel and steering system in centered position. Raise and support vehicle with safety stands under body rail.
2) Remove spindle. See SPINDLE under REMOVAL & INSTALLATION in this article. Remove bolt retaining bolt retainer plate and remove plate. Mark position of control arm mounting brackets on the flat plate. *See Fig. 3*.

1991 SUSPENSION
Front – Aerostar 2WD (Cont.)

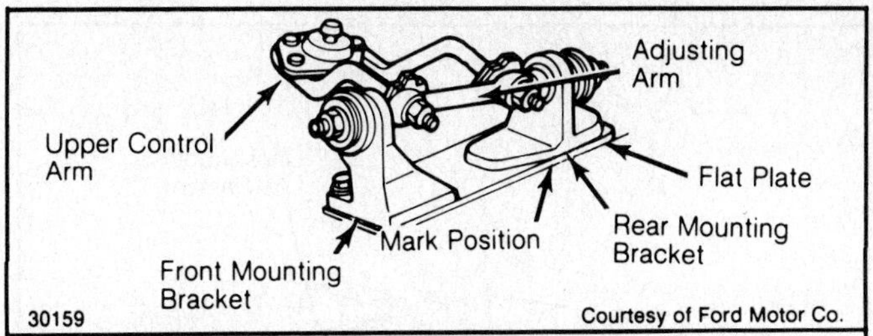
Adjusting Arm
Upper Control Arm
Flat Plate
Rear Mounting Bracket
Mark Position
Front Mounting Bracket
30159
Courtesy of Ford Motor Co.

Fig. 3: Positioning Upper Control Arm Bracket

3) Remove bolt and washer retaining front mounting bracket to flat plate. From beneath frame rail, remove 3 nuts from bolts retaining 2 upper control arm mounting brackets to body rail.
4) Remove mounting 3 long bracket-to-body rail bolts by rotating upper control arm out of position. Remove upper control arm, adjusting arm, mounting bracket and flat plate from vehicle.
5) If servicing upper control arm/upper ball joint assembly or mounting bracket/adjusting arm assembly, remove nuts retaining upper control arm to adjusting arm.
6) Note exact position and number of shims on each control arm stud. Remove upper control arm from adjusting arm. Adjusting arm and mounting brackets are serviced as an assembly. Upper control arm and ball joint are serviced as an assembly.

Installation – 1) Install adjusting arm to control arm. Install shims, as removed, on control arm studs. Install and tighten nuts retaining shims to control arm.
2) Install boot seal on upper and/or lower ball joint. Place flat plate for mounting brackets in position on body rail. Install and tighten bolt to 10-14 ft. lbs. (14-18 N.m).
3) Place mounting brackets and upper control arm assembly in position on flat plate. Install 3 long mounting bracket-to-body rail bolts.
4) Rotate or rock upper control arm and mounting bracket assembly until bolt heads rest against mounting bracket. Ensure studs extend through body rail.
5) Place mounting brackets in position marked on flat plate during removal. Install and tighten nuts and washers retaining mounting bracket bolts to body rail to 145-195 ft. lbs. (197-264 N.m).
6) To minimize alignment corrections, ensure mounting brackets DO NOT move from marked position on flat plate. Install and tighten the front mounting bracket-to-flat plate bolt to 35-47 ft. lbs. (47-64 N.m).

CAUTION: Torque required for mounting bracket to body rail nuts and bolts is critical. Tighten to specification.

7) Install bolt retaining plate in position on mounting bracket and flat plate assembly. Tighten bolt to 10-14 ft. lbs. (14-19 N.m).
8) Install spindle. See SPINDLE under REMOVAL & INSTALLATION in this article. Check caster, camber and toe-in, and adjust if necessary. Use service adjustment shims, as required, for caster and camber revisions.

SPINDLE

NOTE: When disconnecting steering linkage from spindle, place steering wheel in centered position.

Removal – 1) Raise and support vehicle with safety stands under the frame. Remove wheel and tire assembly. Remove caliper, rotor and dust shield from spindle. Remove cotter pin and tie rod end-to-spindle lower arm nut.
2) Using Pitman Arm Puller (T64P-3590-F), disconnect tie rod end. Ensure floor jack is supporting lower control arm. Remove cotter pin and loosen spindle-to-lower control arm joint nut.

WARNING: Use extreme caution in step 3) when lowering control arm. Coil spring may quickly expand with dangerous force.

3) Using Pitman Arm Puller (T64P-3590-F), loosen lower ball joint. Remove puller and ball joint retaining nut. With vehicle body supported on safety stands, slowly lower control arm until lower ball joint is disengaged from spindle.
4) Remove bolt and nut retaining spindle to upper control arm ball joint. Remove spindle from vehicle.

Installation – 1) Position spindle on upper ball joint. Install and tighten spindle nut and bolt to 27-37 ft. lbs. (37-50 N.m). Inspect upper and lower ball joint boot seals for damage and replace (if necessary).
2) Install and tighten lower ball joint nut to 80-120 ft. lbs. (109-163 N.m). Install cotter pin. Install and tighten tie rod end nut to 52-74 ft. lbs. (71-100 N.m).
3) Install cotter pin. Install dust shield, rotor and caliper. Install wheel and tire assembly.

STABILIZER BAR (FRONT)

Removal – 1) Remove stabilizer bar-to-lower-control arm link assembly. *See Fig. 4.* Remove insulators and disconnect bar from links. If required, remove nuts retaining links to lower control arm. Remove insulators and links.

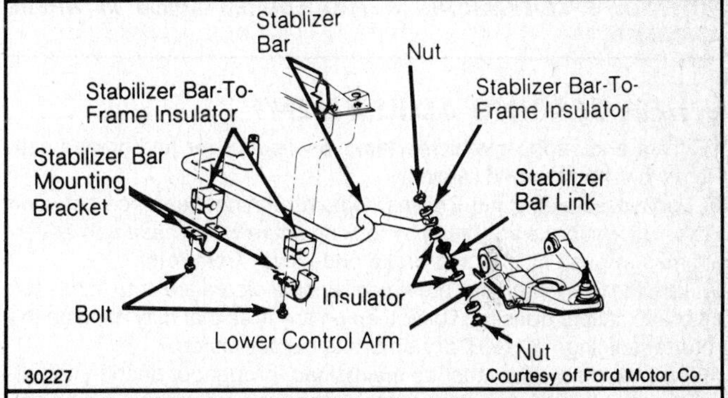
Stablizer Bar
Nut
Stabilizer Bar-To-Frame Insulator
Stablizer Bar-To-Frame Insulator
Stabilizer Bar Mounting Bracket
Stabilizer Bar Link
Insulator
Bolt
Lower Control Arm
Nut
30227
Courtesy of Ford Motor Co.

Fig. 4: Exploded View of Stabilizer Bar & Components

2) Remove stabilizer bar mounting brackets-to-frame bolts. Remove stabilizer bar. If required, remove insulators from stabilizer bar.

Installation – 1) If removed, install insulators on stabilizer bar. Place bar, insulators and mounting bracket on frame. Install and tighten bolts to 16-24 ft. lbs. (22-33 N.m).
2) Connect link and insulators to lower control arm. Connect links and insulators to stabilizer bar. Install and tighten nuts to 108-143 INCH lbs. (12-16 N.m).

TORQUE SPECIFICATIONS

TORQUE SPECIFICATIONS

Application	Ft. Lbs. (N.m)
Bolt Retainer-To-Frame Bolt	10-14 (14-19)
Jounce Bumper-To-Frame Bolt	24-33 (33-45)
Lower Control Arm-To-No. 1 Crossmember Bolt	[1] 100-140 (136-190)
Mounting Bracket-To-Frame Rail Bolt	145-195 (197-264)
Rebound Bumper-To-Frame Bolt	15-21 (20-27)
Shock Absorber	
To Lower Control Arm Bolt	16-24 (22-33)
To Upper Spring Seat Stud Nut	25-35 (34-47)
Spindle-To-Lower Ball Joint Nut	[2] 80-120 (109-163)
Spindle-To-Upper Ball Joint Nut	27-37 (37-50)
Stabilizer Bar Mounting Bracket-To-Frame Bolt	16-24 (22-33)
Tie Rod End-To-Spindle Arm Nut	[2] 52-74 (71-100)
Upper Control Arm-To-Adjusting Arm Nut	70-100 (95-136)
Wheel Lug Nut	100 (136)
	INCH Lbs. (N.m)
Stabilizer Bar-To-Lower Control Arm Nut	108-143 (12-16)
Stabilizer Bar-To-Stabilizer Link Nut	108-143 (12-16)

[1] – Tighten to specification with vehicle in normal ride height position and all other fasteners tightened to specification.
[2] – Tighten to specification and, if required, advance to next castellation to install cotter pin.

1991 SUSPENSION
Front – Explorer & Ranger 2WD

DESCRIPTION

Front suspension is coil spring, twin "I" beam-type. Suspension consists of coil spring, "I" beam axle arms, radius arm, upper and lower ball joint, spindle, tie rod, shock absorber and optional stabilizer bar. One end of each axle is attached to spindle and radius arm assembly. Other end is attached to a frame pivot bracket.

Spindle is connected to axle by upper and lower ball joints. Ball joints are sealed and do not require lubrication. Spindle movement is controlled by tie rods and steering linkage.

ADJUSTMENTS & INSPECTION

WHEEL ALIGNMENT SPECIFICATIONS & PROCEDURES

NOTE: See SPECIFICATIONS & PROCEDURES article in WHEEL ALIGNMENT.

WHEEL BEARING ADJUSTMENT

1) Raise and support vehicle. Remove wheel cover and grease cap. Remove cotter pin and retainer.
2) Loosen adjusting nut 3 turns. Obtain running clearance between brake rotor surface and lining by rocking entire wheel assembly several times to push caliper and brake pads away from rotor.
3) An alternate method of obtaining running clearance is to lightly tap on brake caliper housing. Do not tap on any area that may damage the rotor and lining. DO NOT pry on brake caliper piston.
4) Running clearance must be maintained throughout bearing adjustment procedure. If proper clearance cannot be maintained, brake caliper must be removed.
5) While rotating wheel, tighten adjusting nut to 17-25 ft. lbs. (23-34 N.m). Back off adjusting nut 1/2 turn (180 degrees). Tighten adjusting nut to 18-20 INCH lbs. (2.0-2.3 N.m). Install lock cap and new cotter pin.
6) Place retainer on adjusting nut. Align nut with cotter pin hole in spindle. If retainer will not align, remove retainer and reposition on adjusting nut. DO NOT turn adjusting nut to align cotter pin holes.
7) Install cotter pin. Check front wheel rotation. If wheel rotates properly, install grease cap and wheel cover.
8) If rotation is noisy or rough, remove, inspect and lubricate bearings. Before driving vehicle, pump brake pedal several times to restore normal pedal position.

BALL JOINT CHECKING

Lower & Upper Ball Joint – Raise and support vehicle under axle. Move lower edge of tire in and out while watching lower spindle arm and lower part of axle jaw. If movement exceeds 1/32" (.8 mm), replace lower ball joint. To check upper ball joint, move upper edge of tire in and out. If movement between upper spindle arm and upper axle exceeds 1/32" (.8 mm), replace upper ball joint.

REMOVAL & INSTALLATION

AXLE

Removal – 1) Remove spindle, coil spring and stabilizer bar (if equipped). See SPINDLE, COIL SPRING and STABILIZER BAR.
2) Remove spring lower seat from radius arm. Remove stabilizer bar bracket and radius arm-to-front axle bolt. Remove axle-to-frame pivot bolt and remove axle.
Installation – 1) Install axle and axle-to-frame pivot bolt finger tight. *See Fig. 1.* Install opposite end of axle on radius arm. Install axle-to-radius arm bolt from underneath bracket and tighten to specification.
2) Install lower spring seat on radius arm. Ensure spring seat hole indexes over radius arm-to-axle bolt. Install remaining components. Tighten axle-to-frame pivot bolt to specification with vehicle at normal operating height. See TORQUE SPECIFICATIONS table at end of article.

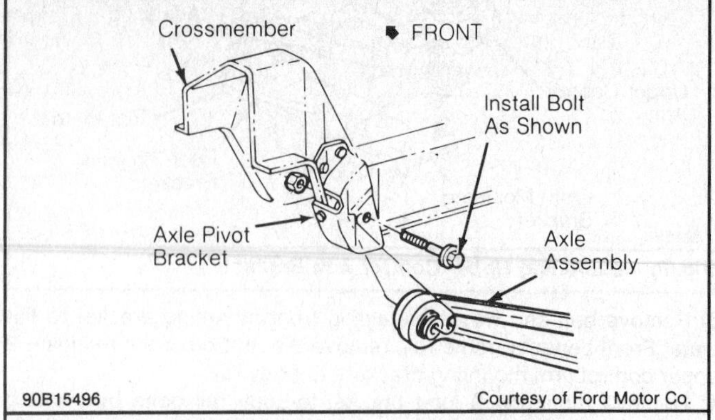
Crossmember
FRONT
Install Bolt
As Shown
Axle Pivot
Bracket
Axle
Assembly
90B15496
Courtesy of Ford Motor Co.

Fig. 1: Exploded View of Axle Pivot Bracket Assembly

AXLE PIVOT BRACKET

Removal – Remove spindle and front axle. See SPINDLE and AXLE. Remove axle pivot bracket bolts and bracket.
Installation – 1) Install axle pivot bracket on the frame. Install front and rear mounting bolts and retainers from inside of pivot bracket out through crossmember. *See Fig. 1.*
2) Loosely install nuts on outside of crossmember. Tighten nuts to specification. To complete installation, reverse removal procedure.

NOTE: Special nuts are used for this application to provide proper clearance. Use proper nuts or install a 0.20" (5.1 mm) thick hardened washer under each nut if standard nuts are used.

AXLE PIVOT BUSHING

Removal – 1) Remove coil spring. See COIL SPRING. If left axle bushing is to be replaced, remove axle pivot bolt. Pull pivot end of axle downward until bushing is exposed.
2) If pivot bushing in right axle is to be removed, axle must be removed to gain access to pivot bushing. Remove axle. See AXLE under REMOVAL & INSTALLATION.
3) Install Forcing Screw (T78P-5638-A1), Bushing Remover (T80T-5638-A2) and Receiver Cup (T78P-5638-A3) onto pivot bushing. Turn forcing screw and remove pivot bushing. *See Fig. 2.*

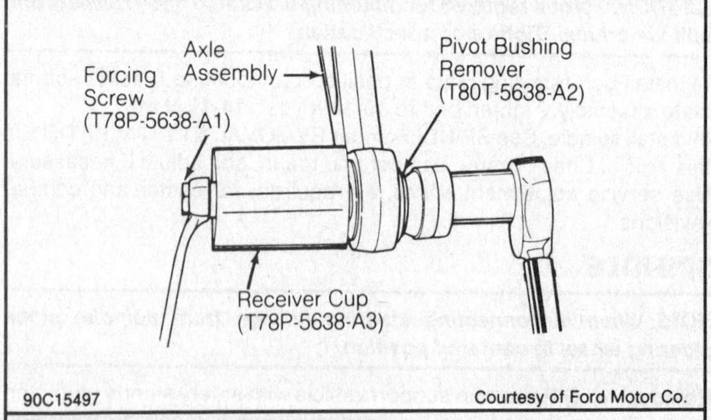
Forcing
Screw
(T78P-5638-A1)
Axle
Assembly
Pivot Bushing
Remover
(T80T-5638-A2)
Receiver Cup
(T78P-5638-A3)
90C15497
Courtesy of Ford Motor Co.

Fig. 2: Replacing Axle Pivot Bushing

Installation – Install bushing in axle using receiver cup, forcing screw, and installation cup. To complete installation, reverse removal procedure. Lower vehicle. With weight on suspension, tighten pivot bushing nut to specification.

BALL JOINT (UPPER & LOWER)

NOTE: Always remove lower ball joint prior to removing upper ball joint. Install lower ball joint prior to installing upper ball joint. DO NOT heat ball joint or spindle during ball joint replacement procedure.

Removal – 1) Remove spindle. See SPINDLE. Install spindle assembly in vise and remove snap ring from ball joint. Assemble "C" Frame (T74P-4635-C), and installation cup on lower ball joint. *See Fig. 3.*

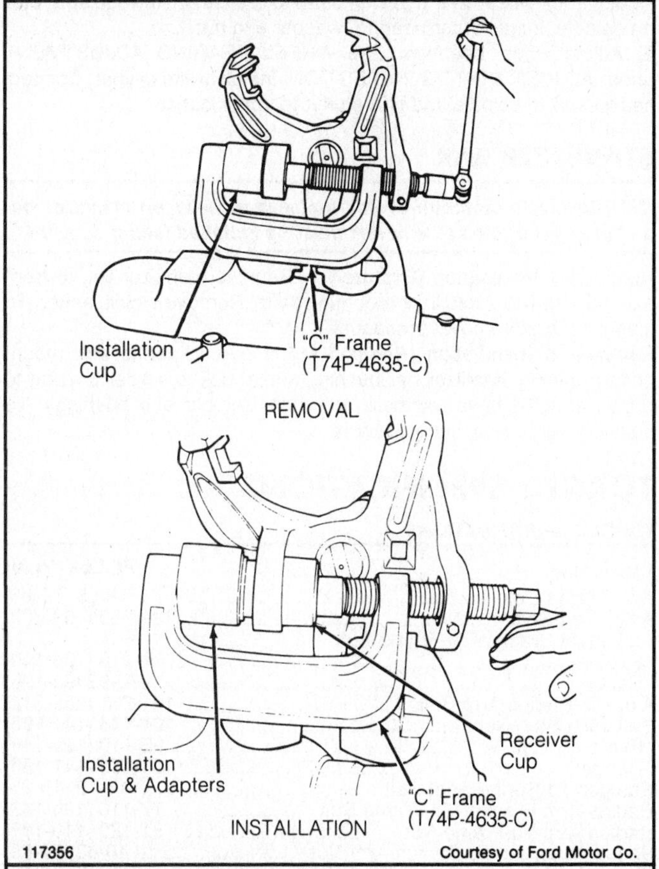
Installation Cup
"C" Frame (T74P-4635-C)
REMOVAL
Receiver Cup
Installation Cup & Adapters
"C" Frame (T74P-4635-C)
INSTALLATION
117356
Courtesy of Ford Motor Co.

Fig. 3: Removing & Installing Ball Joint

2) Turn forcing screw clockwise until lower ball joint is removed from spindle. Assemble "C" frame and installation cup on upper ball joint. Turn forcing screw clockwise until upper ball joint is removed from spindle.

Installation – To install, reverse removal procedure using installation cup, adapters and receiver cup. *See Fig. 3.* Install lower ball joint prior to installing upper ball joint. Install spindle.

CAMBER ADJUSTER

Removal – Remove cotter pin and loosen lower ball joint nut to the end of stud ONLY. Remove upper ball joint camber adjuster clamp bolt from top of axle. Using Ball Joint Remover (D81T-3010-B), remove camber adjuster from upper ball joint stud. *See Fig. 4.*

Installation – Install camber adjuster into axle. Ensure slot of adjuster aligns with axle. Install adjuster on upper ball joint stud. Install clamp bolt in axle and tighten to specification. Tighten lower ball joint nut to specification. See TORQUE SPECIFICATIONS table at end of article.

COIL SPRING

Removal & Installation – 1) Raise and support front of vehicle with safety stands under frame and place a jack under axle. Disconnect shock absorber from lower bracket. Remove nut holding lower retainer to spring seat. Remove lower retainer.

NOTE: Axle must be supported by jack during removal and installation procedure. If brake hose length does not permit adequate clearance, remove brake caliper or compress spring with Spring Compressor (T81P-5310-A).

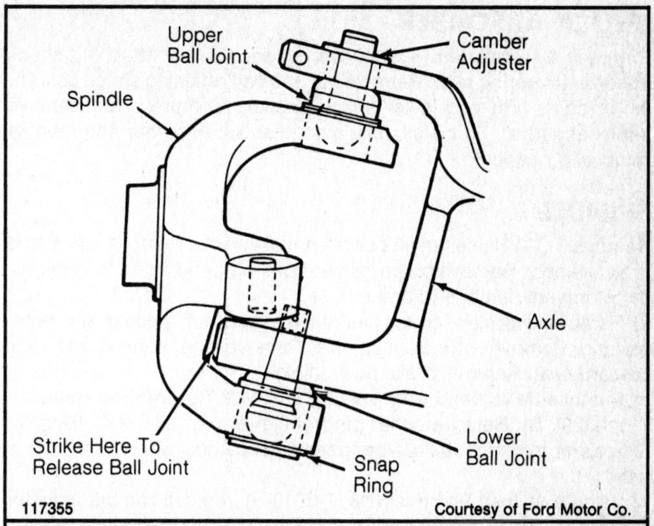
Upper Ball Joint
Camber Adjuster
Spindle
Axle
Strike Here To Release Ball Joint
Snap Ring
Lower Ball Joint
117355
Courtesy of Ford Motor Co.

Fig. 4: Removing Spindle

2) Lower axle as far as possible without stretching brake hose. Using pry bar, lift coil spring over bolt that passes through lower spring seat. Rotate spring so retainer on upper spring seat is cleared and remove spring. To install, reverse removal procedure.

RADIUS ARM

Removal & Installation – 1) Remove coil spring. See COIL SPRING under REMOVAL & INSTALLATION. Loosen axle pivot bolt. Remove lower spring seat from radius arm. Remove radius arm-to-axle bolt. *See Fig. 5.*

2) Remove nut and radius arm bushing from rear of radius arm. Remove inner bushing and retainer from radius arm stud. *See Fig. 5.* To install, reverse removal procedure.

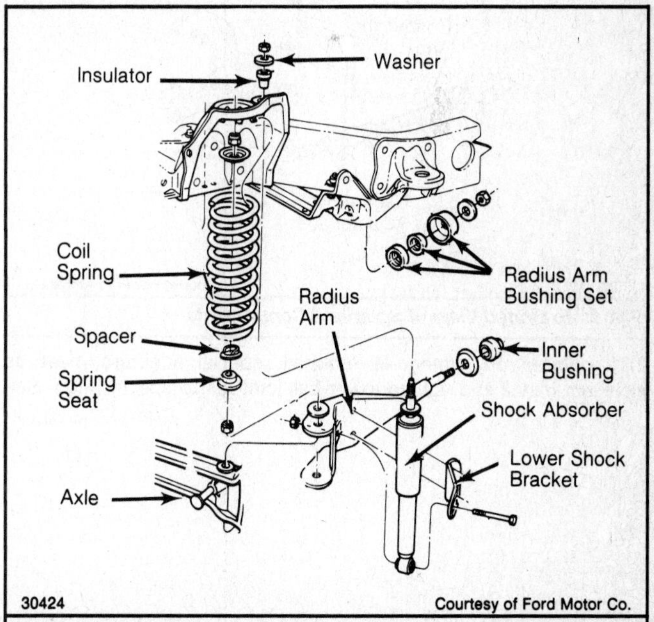
Insulator
Washer
Coil Spring
Radius Arm Bushing Set
Radius Arm
Spacer
Inner Bushing
Spring Seat
Shock Absorber
Lower Shock Bracket
Axle
30424
Courtesy of Ford Motor Co.

Fig. 5: Exploded View of Coil Spring & Radius Arm Components

RADIUS ARM BUSHING

Removal & Installation – 1) Loosen radius arm-to-axle pivot bolt. Loosen upper shock absorber bolt and compress shock. Remove nut and washer attaching radius arm to radius arm bracket.

2) Remove bushing and components from rear of radius arm. Move radius arm and axle assembly forward, out of radius arm bracket. Remove inner bushing and retainer. To install, reverse removal procedure.

1991 SUSPENSION
Front – Explorer & Ranger 2WD (Cont.)

SHOCK ABSORBER

Removal & Installation – Remove nut and washer attaching shock absorber to spring seat. Remove nut and bolt retaining shock absorber to radius arm and lower shock bracket. Compress and remove shock absorber. To install, fully extend shock absorber and reverse removal procedure.

SPINDLE

Removal – **1)** Raise and support front of vehicle. Remove wheel and tire assembly. Remove brake caliper from rotor and wire it to underbody to prevent damage to brake hose.

2) Remove dust cap, cotter pin, nut retainer, nut, washer and outer bearing. Remove rotor from spindle. Remove inner bearing and seal. Discard seal. Remove brake dust shield.

3) Remove tie rod end from spindle arm with Tie Rod End Remover (Tool-3290-D). Remove cotter pin from lower ball joint stud. Remove axle clamp bolt from axle. Note position of camber adjuster on top of axle.

4) Using Ball Joint Remover (D81T-3010-B), remove camber adjuster from upper ball joint stud and axle. Strike inside area of axle to release lower ball joint. *See Fig. 4.* Remove spindle and ball joint assembly from axle.

CAUTION: DO NOT use pickle fork to separate ball joint. This will damage the seal and ball joint socket.

Installation – **1)** Ensure upper and lower ball joint seals are in place. Install spindle and ball joints in axle. Install camber adjuster in upper spindle over upper ball joint stud. Ensure slot of adjuster aligns with axle. *See Fig. 6.*

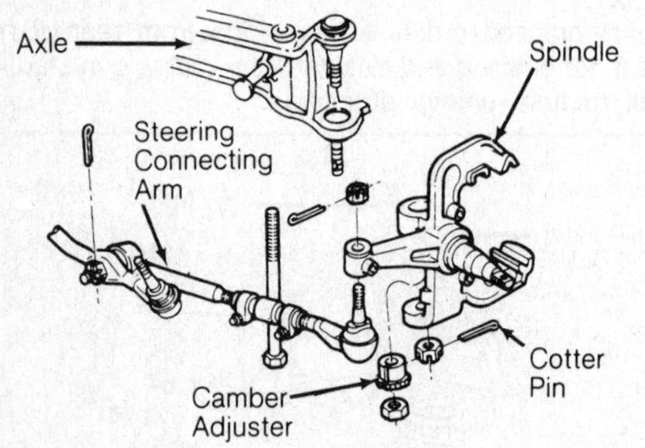
Axle
Spindle
Steering
Connecting
Arm
Cotter
Pin
Camber
Adjuster

90A15495 Courtesy of Ford Motor Co.

Fig. 6: Exploded View of Spindle & Components

2) If camber adjustment is required, special adapters must be installed. Install and tighten lower ball joint nut to specification. See TORQUE SPECIFICATIONS table at end of article. Continue tightening castellated nut until it lines up with hole in stud. Install cotter pin.

3) Install axle clamp bolt and tighten to specification. Install dust shield. Pack wheel bearings with bearing grease. Install hub and rotor on spindle. Install outer bearing, washer and nut.

4) Adjust wheel bearings. See WHEEL BEARING ADJUSTMENT under ADJUSTMENTS & INSPECTION. Install brake caliper. Connect tie rod end to spindle and tighten nut to specification.

STABILIZER BAR

CAUTION: Note direction of link installation between stabilizer bar and axle. Protrusion side of link must be installed facing outward.

Removal & Installation (Explorer) – Remove stabilizer link-to-front axle nut. Remove stabilizer mounting bolts. Remove stabilizer bar. To install, reverse removal procedure.

Removal & Installation (Ranger) – Remove "U" bolts and mount bolts retaining stabilizer bar bushing and shock absorber bracket to radius arm. Remove retainers and stabilizer bar and bushings. To install, reverse removal procedure.

TORQUE SPECIFICATIONS

TORQUE SPECIFICATIONS

Application	Ft. Lbs. (N.m)
Axle Clamp Bolt	48-65 (65-88)
Axle Pivot Bolt [1]	120-150 (163-203)
Axle Pivot Bracket-To-Frame Bolt	
Explorer	77-110 (104-149)
Ranger	70-92 (95-125)
Axle-To-Radius Arm Bolt	191-231 (258-312)
Ball Joint Stud Nut [2]	104-146 (141-198)
Explorer	95-110 (129-149)
Ranger	104-146 (141-198)
Bumper-To-Spring Seat Bolt	11-19 (15-26)
Radius Arm Bracket-To-Frame Bolt	77-110 (104-149)
Radius Arm-To-Frame Nut	81-120 (110-163)
Shock Absorber-To-Radius Arm Nut	40-63 (54-85)
Shock Absorber-To-Spring Seat Nut	25-35 (34-47)
Stabilizer Bar	
Explorer	
Mount Bolt	35-50 (47-68)
Stabilizer Link-To-Axle Bracket Bolt	29-44 (39-60)
Stabilizer Link-To-Stabilizer Bar Nut	40-60 (54-81)
Ranger	
Mount Bolt	35-50 (47-68)
Stabilizer Bar "U" Bolt	35-50 (47-68)
Stabilizer Link-To-Stabilizer Bar Nut	30-44 (41-60)
Tie Rod Nut [2]	51-75 (69-102)

[1] – Tighten to specification with vehicle in normal ride height position and all other fasteners tightened to specification.

[2] – Tighten to specification and, if required, advance to next castellation to install cotter pin.

1991 SUSPENSION
Front – "E" & "F" Series 2WD

NOTE: Unless otherwise specified, references to "F" Series include "F" Series Super Duty.

DESCRIPTION

On all models except "F" Series Super Duty model, front suspension consists of a coil spring, twin "I" beam-type front axle assembly. "I" beams are mounted to a frame pivot bracket at one end, and to spindle and a radius arm at the other. Springs are mounted between frame spring pocket and axle.

"F" Series Super Duty models use leaf springs with a solid "I" beam axle. Springs are attached to fixed bracket on the rear and movable shackle on the front.

ADJUSTMENTS & INSPECTION

WHEEL ALIGNMENT SPECIFICATIONS & PROCEDURES

NOTE: See SPECIFICATIONS & PROCEDURES article in WHEEL ALIGNMENT.

WHEEL BEARING ADJUSTMENT

"E" Series & "F" Series Except Super Duty Stripped Chassis – 1) Raise and support vehicle. Remove wheel cover and grease cap. Remove cotter pin and retainer. Loosen adjusting nut 3 turns.

2) Obtain running clearance between brake rotor surface and lining by rocking entire wheel assembly several times to push caliper and brake pads away from rotor.

3) An alternate method of obtaining running clearance is to lightly tap on brake caliper housing. DO NOT tap on any area which may damage rotor and lining. DO NOT pry on brake caliper piston.

4) Running clearance must be maintained throughout bearing adjustment procedure. If proper clearance cannot be maintained, caliper must be removed.

5) Tighten adjusting nut to 17-25 ft. lbs. (23-34 N.m) while rotating brake rotor in opposite direction. Back off adjusting nut 120-180 degrees. Install retainer and new cotter pin without loosening retaining nut. Bearing end play should be .00025-.005" (.006-.127 mm). Bend ends of cotter pin around castellated flange of lock nut.

"F" Series Super Duty Stripped Chassis – 1) Raise and support vehicle. Remove wheel cover and grease cap. Remove cotter pin and retainer. Loosen adjusting nut 3 turns.

2) Obtain running clearance between brake rotor surface and lining by rocking entire wheel assembly several times to push caliper and brake pads away from rotor.

3) An alternate method of obtaining running clearance is to lightly tap on brake caliper housing. DO NOT tap on any area which may damage rotor and lining. DO NOT pry on brake caliper piston.

4) Running clearance must be maintained throughout bearing adjustment procedure. If proper clearance cannot be maintained, caliper must be removed.

5) Tighten adjusting nut to 17-25 ft. lbs. (23-34 N.m) while rotating brake rotor in opposite direction. Back off adjusting nut 120-180 degrees. Tighten adjusting nut to 18-20 INCH lbs. (2.03-2.26 N.m) while rotating brake rotor. Install retainer and new cotter pin without loosening retaining nut. Bearing end play should be .00025-.005" (.006-.127 mm). Torque required to turn hub should be 10-25 INCH lbs. (1.13-2.82 N.m). Bend ends of cotter pin around castellated flange of lock nut.

BALL JOINT & SPINDLE PIN CHECKING

Raise and support vehicle. Ensure wheel bearings are properly adjusted. Grasp lower edge of tire and move wheel in and out while watching for spindle movement. Spindle movement must not exceed 1/32" (.794 mm) at upper or lower arms, relative to axle. If movement exceeds limit, replace ball joints or install new spindle pins and bushings.

REMOVAL & INSTALLATION

FRONT WHEEL BEARINGS

Removal & Installation – 1) Raise front of vehicle, and remove wheels. Remove brake caliper, and wire it to underbody to prevent damage to brake hose.

2) Remove grease cap from hub. Remove cotter pin, lock nut, adjusting nut and flat washer from spindle. Remove outer wheel bearing. Pull hub and rotor from spindle. Remove grease seal and inner wheel bearing.

3) Clean bearings, inspect for damage and replace as necessary. To install, fill inside of hub, flush with inside diameter of beading cones, with Lithium-base grease. To complete in installation, reverse removal procedure. Adjust wheel bearings. See WHEEL BEARING ADJUSTMENT under ADJUSTMENTS & INSPECTION.

SHOCK ABSORBER

Removal & Installation ("E" Series) – Remove upper shock retaining nut. Disconnect shock absorber from lower bracket. Remove shock absorber, washers and rubber insulators. To install, reverse removal procedure using new rubber bushings. See TORQUE SPECIFICATIONS tables at end of article.

Removal ("F" Series Except Super Duty) – Hold upper shock retaining nut. Loosen stud by turning hex on exposed lower part of stud. Disconnect shock absorber from lower bracket. Compress shock absorber and remove shock absorber. Cut bushing from upper spring seat. See TORQUE SPECIFICATIONS tables at end of article.

Installation – To install, reverse removal procedure. Coat upper spring seat with soap solution and install new insulator.

Removal & Installation ("F" Series Super Duty) – 1) Remove shock absorber-to-upper bracket nut. Remove shock absorber-to-spring spacer nut and remove shock absorber.

2) To install, reverse removal procedure. Coat upper spring seat with soap solution and install new bushing.

SPINDLE

Removal ("E" Series & "F" Series Super Duty) – 1) Raise vehicle and support under front axle. Remove wheel assembly. Remove brake caliper and wire it to underbody to prevent damage to brake hose. Remove grease cap, cotter pin, lock nut, adjusting nut, flat washer and outer wheel bearing.

2) Remove brake rotor and brake dust shield. Remove inner wheel bearing and seal. Remove tie rod cotter pin and nut. Using Tie Rod Remover (TOOL-3290-D), separate tie rod end from spindle arm.

3) Remove nut and lock washer from spindle pin lock bolt. *See Fig. 1.* Tap out spindle pin lock bolt. Remove upper and lower spindle pin plugs. Drive spindle pin out from top of axle. Remove spindle, thrust bearing, shims and seals. *See Fig. 1.*

NOTE: On "F" Series Super Duty models, a seal is used at top and bottom of spindle pin.

Installation – 1) Ensure spindle pin bore is free of nicks, burrs and corrosion. Lightly coat bore surface with a lithium-based grease. Install spindle pin seal with metal backing facing toward the bushing.

2) Press seal into position. Use care not to bend seal casing. Install NEW thrust bearing with lip flange facing toward lower bushing. Install thrust bearing until firmly seated against spindle surface.

3) Lightly coat bushing surface with lithium-based grease and place spindle in position on axle. Hold spindle and thrust bearing tightly against axle and measure distance between spindle and top of axle. Select proper thickness shim(s) and install.

4) Install spindle pin with "T" marking toward top, and notch in pin aligned with spindle pin lock bolt hole in axle. Drive spindle pin through bushings from top of axle until spindle pin notch aligns with spindle pin lock bolt hole. Install spindle pin lock bolt with threads pointing forward and groove facing spindle pin notch.

5) Firmly drive spindle pin lock bolt into position and install lock washer and nut. Tighten nut to specification. Install upper and lower plugs and tighten to specification.

1991 SUSPENSION
Front – "E" & "F" Series 2WD (Cont.)

6) Lubricate spindle pin and bushings through grease fittings until grease seeps past upper seal at top and from thrust bearing slip joint at bottom. If grease fails to appear, recheck installation procedure.
7) To complete installation, reverse removal procedure. Adjust wheel bearings. See WHEEL BEARING ADJUSTMENT under ADJUSTMENTS & INSPECTION. Check and adjust toe-in.

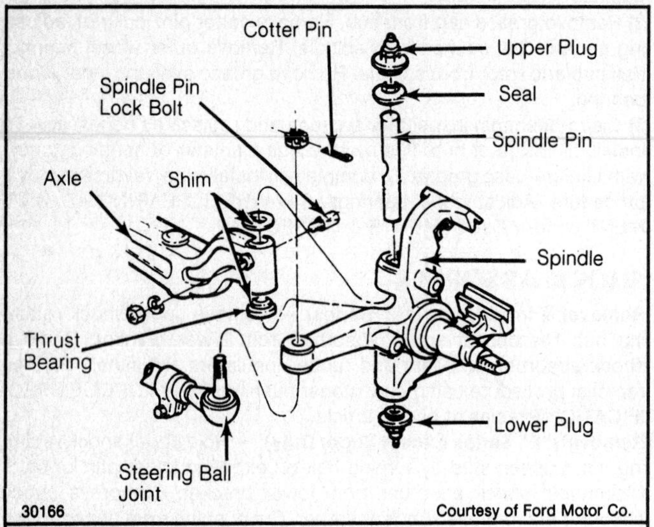
Cotter Pin
Upper Plug
Seal
Spindle Pin
Lock Bolt
Spindle Pin
Axle
Shim
Spindle
Thrust
Bearing
Lower Plug
Steering Ball
Joint
30166
Courtesy of Ford Motor Co.

Fig. 1: Exploded View of Spindle with Spindle Pin Assembly (Typical)

Removal ("F" Series Except Super Duty) – 1) Raise vehicle and support under front axle. Remove wheel assembly. Remove brake caliper and wire it to underbody to prevent damage to brake hose. Remove grease cap, cotter pin, lock nut, adjusting nut, flat washer and outer wheel bearing.
2) Remove brake rotor and brake dust shield. Remove inner bearing and seal. Remove cotter pin and nut from tie rod end. Using Tie Rod Remover (TOOL-3290-D), remove tie rod end from spindle arm.
3) Remove cotter pin and nut from lower ball joint. Remove nut from axle clamp bolt and remove bolt. Note position of camber adjuster on top of axle. *See Fig. 2.* Remove camber adjuster from upper ball joint.
4) Strike axle to break lower ball joint loose from axle. *See Fig. 2.* Remove spindle assembly.

CAUTION: DO NOT use pickle fork to separate ball joint from spindle, as seal and ball joint socket will be damaged.

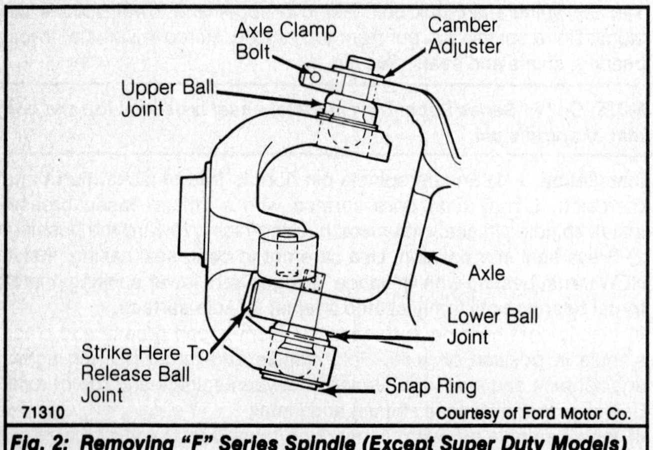
Axle Clamp
Bolt
Camber
Adjuster
Upper Ball
Joint
Axle
Lower Ball
Joint
Strike Here To
Release Ball
Joint
Snap Ring
71310
Courtesy of Ford Motor Co.

Fig. 2: Removing "F" Series Spindle (Except Super Duty Models)

Installation – 1) Ensure ball joint seals are in position. Place spindle and ball joints into axle. Install lower ball joint nut and tighten to specification. See TORQUE SPECIFICATIONS tables at end of article.
2) Install camber adjuster over upper ball joint stud. Ensure camber adjuster is properly aligned. If camber adjustment is required, special camber adjusters must be installed. Tap camber adjuster into spindle. Tighten upper ball joint nut to specification.
3) Install cotter pin. Install axle clamp bolt and tighten to specification. To complete installation, reverse removal procedure. Adjust wheel bearings. See WHEEL BEARING ADJUSTMENT under ADJUSTMENTS & INSPECTION. Check and adjust toe-in. See SPECIFICATIONS & PROCEDURES article in WHEEL ALIGNMENT.

SPINDLE PIN BUSHINGS

Removal & Installation ("E" Series & "F" Series Super Duty) – 1) Remove spindle. See SPINDLE under REMOVAL & INSTALLATION. Install spindle in a vise.
2) On E150 models, use Reamer (T53T-3110-DA), Bushing Remover/Installer Driver (D82T-3110-G) and Driver Handle (D82T-3110-C) for bushing service.
3) On E250/350 models, use Reamer (D82T-3110-A), Bushing Remover/Installer Driver (D82T-3110-B) and Driver Handle (D82T-3110-C) for bushing service.
4) On "F" Series Super Duty models, use Reamer (D88T-3110-BH), Bushing Remover/Installer Driver (D88T-3110-AH) and Driver Handle (T80T-4000-W) for bushing service.
5) On all applications, each side of bushing remover/installer driver is marked with "T" or "B". Use "T" side to install top spindle bushing and "B" side for bottom spindle bushing. Remove seal from bottom of upper bushing bore. Top spindle bushing should be removed first. Install driver handle through bottom bore.
6) Position new bushing on "T" side of bushing remover/installer driver so bushing open end grooves will face outward when installed. Position new bushing and remover/installer driver over old bushing. Drive old bushing out, while installing new bushing. Install bushing until remover/installer driver is seated.
7) Bushing must be installed minimum distance of .080" (2.03 mm) from bottom of upper spindle boss. Using "B" side, repeat procedure and install bottom bushing. Proper minimum depth of bottom bushing is 0.130" (3.30 mm) from top of lower spindle boss. Using reamer, ream bushings I.D. to be .001-.003" (.03-.08 mm) larger than diameter of new spindle pin. Ream top bushing first.
8) Install smaller diameter of reamer through top bore and into bottom bore until cutting blades are positioned in top bushing. Rotate reamer until cutting blades clear top bushing.
9) Ream bottom bushing. Larger diameter portion of reamer acts as a pilot in top bushing to properly ream bottom bushing. Remove all metal shavings and lubricate bushings and spindle pins.
10) Install a new seal on bushing remover/installer driver on side marked with "T" stamping. Using handle and remover/installer driver, install seal in bottom of top bushing bore. To complete installation, reverse removal procedure.

BALL JOINTS

Removal ("F" Series Except Super Duty) – 1) Remove spindle. See SPINDLE under REMOVAL & INSTALLATION. Install spindle in a vise. Remove snap ring from lower ball joint.
2) Using "C" Frame (T74P-4635-C) and Receiver Cup (D81T-3010-A4), rotate forcing screw clockwise until ball joint is removed from spindle. Repeat procedure to remove upper ball joint. *See Fig. 3.*

CAUTION: DO NOT heat ball joint or spindle when replacing ball joint.

Installation – 1) Lower ball joint must be installed first. Install lower ball joint squarely in spindle. Using "C" Frame, Receiver Cup, Installation Cup and Adapters (D81T-3010-A1 and D81T-3010-A3), install ball joint until firmly seated.
2) Repeat procedure for upper ball joint installation. Install snap rings. To complete installation, reverse removal procedure. Tighten bolts/nuts to specifications. See TORQUE SPECIFICATIONS tables at end of article.

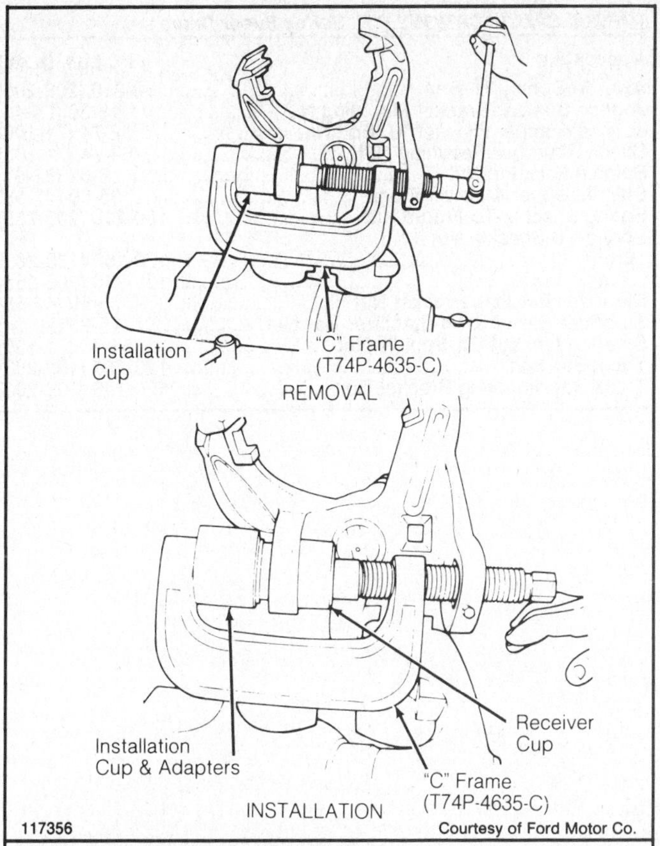
Installation Cup
"C" Frame (T74P-4635-C)
REMOVAL
Receiver Cup
Installation Cup & Adapters
"C" Frame (T74P-4635-C)
INSTALLATION
117356
Courtesy of Ford Motor Co.

Fig. 3: Removing & Installing Ball Joint ("F" Series Except Super Duty)

COIL SPRING

NOTE: Support axle with a floor jack during coil spring removal and installation procedures. If brake hose length does not permit adequate clearance, remove brake caliper.

Removal ("E" Series & "F" Series Except Super Duty) – Raise front of vehicle with jack stands under frame and floor jack under axle. Disconnect shock absorber from lower bracket. Remove upper spring retainer bolts and remove retainer. Remove lower spring retainer-to-spring seat and axle. Lower floor jack and remove spring.

Installation – Place spring in position and slowly raise front axle. Position spring lower retainer over stud, lower insulator (if equipped), and lower seat. Position upper retainer over spring coil and against spring upper seat. Tighten bolts/nuts to specification. See TORQUE SPECIFICATIONS tables at end of article. To complete installation, reverse removal procedure.

LEAF SPRING

Removal ("F" Series Super Duty) – 1) Raise front of vehicle so weight is off front springs and tires are touching the floor. Support axle with jack to release weight from spring "U" bolts.

2) Disconnect shock absorber from spring spacer. Spacer is located below "U" bolts. Remove front and rear spring shackle bolts and stabilizer bar bracket. Remove "U" bolts and leaf spring.

Installation – To install, reverse removal procedure. Apply Lubricant (C1AZ-19590-BA) to spring bushings prior to shackle bolt installation. Ensure spring is aligned with spring seat and axle. Tighten bolts to specification. See TORQUE SPECIFICATIONS tables at end of article.

FRONT AXLE

Removal ("E" Series & "F" Series Except Super Duty) – Remove spindle. See SPINDLE under REMOVAL & INSTALLATION. Remove coil spring and stabilizer bar (if equipped). Remove lower spring seat from radius arm. Remove radius arm-to-front axle bolt. Remove axle-to-frame pivot bolt and remove axle.

Installation – 1) Install axle with frame pivot bolt finger tight. Connect radius arm to front axle. Install lower spring seat, ensuring it aligns over radius arm bolt. Ensure spring seat pin engages with slot in radius arm.

2) Install remaining components. Tighten axle-to-frame pivot bolt to specification with vehicle at normal operating height.

Removal & Installation ("F" Series Super Duty) – 1) Raise front of vehicle so weight is off front springs and tires are touching the floor. Raise axle slightly and remove both wheels. Remove brake caliper and secure out of the way.

2) Temporarily install both wheels. Disconnect stabilizer bar links at stabilizer bar. Disconnect steering linkage from spindle. Disconnect track bar from axle (if equipped). Remove "U" bolts and stabilizer bar bracket. Raise vehicle and roll axle out from under vehicle. To install, reverse removal procedure. Tighten bolts to specification. See TORQUE SPECIFICATIONS tables at end of article.

RADIUS ARM

NOTE: Support axle with a floor jack during coil spring removal and installation procedures. If brake hose length does not permit adequate clearance, remove brake caliper.

Removal ("E" Series & "F" Series Except Super Duty) – 1) Raise and support vehicle with safety stands under frame and jack under axle. Remove wheels. Disconnect link from stabilizer bar (if equipped).

2) Disconnect shock absorber from lower bracket. Remove coil spring. See COIL SPRING under REMOVAL & INSTALLATION. Remove lower spring seat from radius arm.

3) Remove radius arm-to-axle bolt. Remove nut, washer, insulator and spacer from rear radius arm mount. Remove radius arm.

Installation – To install, reverse removal procedure. Tighten bolts to specification

STABILIZER BAR

Removal & Installation ("E" Series & "F" Series Except Super Duty) – Disconnect stabilizer bar from link assembly. Remove retaining bolts and stabilizer bar. Remove link assembly from axle brackets. To install, reverse removal procedure. Tighten bolts to specification. See TORQUE SPECIFICATIONS tables at end of article.

CAUTION: Ensure link assembly is installed on axle bracket with bend area toward front of vehicle.

Removal & Installation ("F" Series Super Duty) – Disconnect stabilizer bar from link assembly. Remove retaining bolts and stabilizer bar from front axle. Remove link assembly from frame rail. Loosely install stabilizer bar assembly. Ensure stabilizer bar is centered on front axle and insulators are properly positioned. Tighten bolts to specification. See TORQUE SPECIFICATIONS tables at end of article.

TRACK BAR

Removal & Installation ("F" Series Super Duty) – Remove track bar-to-crossmember bolt. Remove track bar-to-axle bracket bolt and remove track bar. To install, reverse removal procedure.

1991 SUSPENSION
Front – "E" & "F" Series 2WD (Cont.)

TORQUE SPECIFICATIONS

TORQUE SPECIFICATIONS ("E" Series)

Application	Ft. Lbs. (N.m.)
Axle Pivot Bracket-To-Frame Bolt	50-70 (68-95)
Axle-To-Pivot Bracket Bolt	120-150 (163-203)
Axle-To-Radius Arm Bolt	240-320 (326-433)
Coil Spring-To-Lower Retainer Nut	70-100 (95-136)
Coil Spring Upper Retainer-To-Spring Seat Bolt	20-30 (27-41)
Jounce Bumper-To-Frame Bolt	20-30 (27-41)
Radius Arm-To-Rear Bracket Nut	80-120 (109-163)
Radius Arm Rear Bracket-To-Frame Bolt	75-105 (102-142)
Shock Absorber Bracket-To-Radius Arm Bolt	70-95 (95-129)
Shock Absorber-To-Lower Bracket Bolt	40-60 (54-81)
Shock Absorber-To-Upper Spring Seat Nut	18-28 (24-38)
Spindle Lock Pin Nut	35-50 (47-68)
Spindle Upper & Lower Plugs	35-50 (47-68)
Stabilizer Bar Link-To-Bracket Bolt	40-60 (54-81)
Stabilizer Bar Link-To-Stabilizer Bar	18-28 (24-38)
Stabilizer Bar Retainer Mount Bolt	15-25 (20-34)
Tie Rod End-To-Spindle Nut	70-100 (95-136)

TORQUE SPECIFICATIONS ("F" Series Except Super Duty)

Application	Ft. Lbs. (N.m.)
Axle Clamp Bolt	48-65 (65-88)
Axle Pivot Bracket-To-Frame Bolt	77-109 (104-148)
Axle-To-Pivot Bracket Bolt	120-150 (163-203)
Axle-To-Radius Arm Bolt	269-329 (364-446)
Ball Joint-To-Spindle Nut	95-110 (129-149)
Coil Spring-To-Lower Retainer Nut	70-100 (95-136)
Coil Spring Upper Retainer-To-Spring Seat Nut	13-18 (18-24)
Jounce Bumper-To-Frame Bolt	14-22 (19-30)
Radius Arm-To-Rear Bracket Nut	80-120 (109-163)
Radius Arm Rear Bracket-To-Frame Bolt	77-100 (104-136)
Shock Absorber Bracket-To-Radius Arm Bolt	27-37 (37-50)
Shock Absorber-To-Lower Bracket Bolt	52-74 (71-100)
Shock Absorber-To-Upper Spring Seat Nut	25-35 (34-47)
Stabilizer Bar Link-To-Bracket	52-74 (71-100)
Stabilizer Bar Link-To-Stabilizer Bar	52-74 (71-100)
Stabilizer Bar Retainer-To-Frame Crossmember	
Mounting Bracket Bolt	27-37 (37-50)
Tie Rod End-To-Spindle Nut	70-100 (95-136)

TORQUE SPECIFICATIONS ("F" Series Super Duty)

Application	Ft. Lbs. (N.m.)
Axle-To-Spring "U" Bolt	150-210 (203-285)
Jounce Bumper Bracket Mounting Nut	18-30 (24-41)
Jounce Bumper Bracket "U" Bolt Nut	52-74 (71-100)
Shock Absorber Retaining Nut	52-74 (71-100)
Spindle Lock Pin Nut	38-62 (52-84)
Spindle Upper & Lower Plugs	35-50 (47-68)
Spring Shackle-To-Frame Nut	150-210 (203-285)
Spring-To-Shackle Nut	
Front	120-150 (163-203)
Rear	150-210 (203-285)
Stabilizer Bar Link Bracket Nut	35-50 (47-68)
Stabilizer Bar Link-To-Stabilizer Bar Nut	15-25 (20-34)
Steering Linkage-To-Spindle Nut	52-74 (71-100)
Track Bar Bolt	120-150 (163-203)
Track Bar Mounting Bracket Bolt	120-150 (163-203)

1991 SUSPENSION
Front - 4WD Coil Spring - Except Aerostar

Bronco, Explorer, Ranger, F150

DESCRIPTION

Independent Front Suspension (IFS) consists of a 2-piece axle assembly, 2 coil springs and 2 radius arms. Front driving axle consists of 2 independent axle arm assemblies. One end of each axle arm assembly is anchored to the frame. The other end of each axle arm assembly is supported by coil spring and radius arm.

NOTE: For additional information on 4WD drive axles, see appropriate article in DRIVE AXLES.

ADJUSTMENTS & INSPECTION

WHEEL ALIGNMENT SPECIFICATIONS & PROCEDURES

NOTE: See SPECIFICATIONS & PROCEDURES article in WHEEL ALIGNMENT.

WHEEL BEARING ADJUSTMENT

Bronco & F150 (Automatic Locking Hub) - 1) Raise and support front of vehicle. Remove wheels. Remove locking hub assembly. See AUTOMATIC LOCKING HUBS under REMOVAL & INSTALLATION. Remove outer lock nut with Spanner Lock Nut Wrench (D85T-1197-A). *See Fig. 1.*

2) Remove lock washer. Tighten inner lock nut to 50 ft. lbs. (68 N.m). Back off inner lock nut and retighten to 30-40 ft. lbs. (41-54 N.m). While rotating hub, back off lock nut 90 degrees. Install lock washer so key is positioned in spindle groove.

3) Rotate inner lock nut so pin is aligned in nearest lock washer hole. Install and tighten outer lock nut to 160-205 ft. lbs. (217-278 N.m). Final end play of hub should be .00-.004" (.00-.11 mm). Torque required to rotate hub and rotor should not exceed 20 INCH lbs. (2.3 N.m). Install hub locks and wheels.

Bronco & F150 (Manual Locking Hub) - 1) Raise and support front of vehicle. Remove front wheels. Remove locking hubs. See MANUAL LOCKING HUBS under REMOVAL & INSTALLATION.

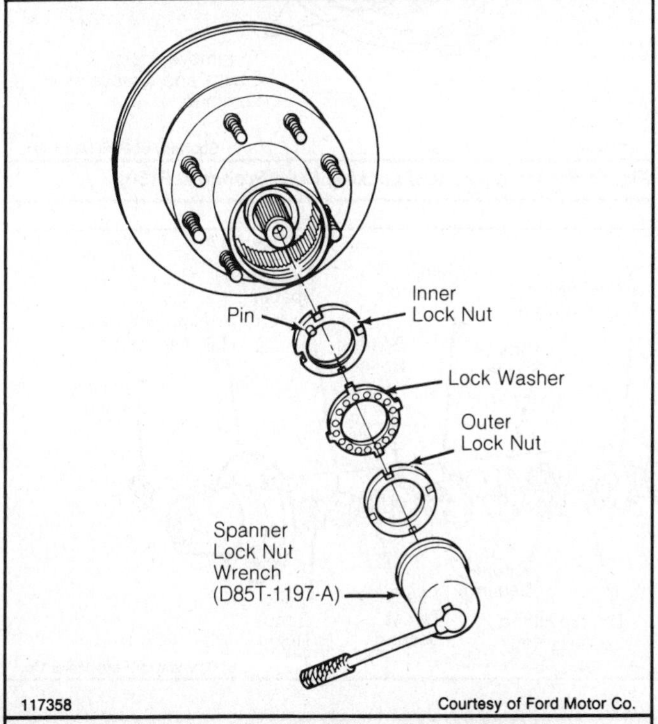
Pin
Inner
Lock Nut
Lock Washer
Outer
Lock Nut
Spanner
Lock Nut
Wrench
(D85T-1197-A)
117358
Courtesy of Ford Motor Co.

Fig. 1: Adjusting Wheel Bearing (Automatic Locking Hub)

2) Use a torque wrench and Spanner Lock Nut Wrench (T86T-1197-A) to unlock wheel bearing adjusting nut locking splines by applying inward pressure. *See Fig. 2.* Tighten adjusting nut to 70 ft. lbs. (95 N.m) while turning wheel back and forth to seat bearing.

3) Apply inward pressure to spanner lock nut wrench to disengage locking splines, and back off adjusting nut approximately 1/4 turn (90 degrees). Retighten adjusting nut to 15-20 ft. lbs. (20-27 N.m). Final end play of hub on spindle should be 0.00" (0.00 mm). Torque required to turn hub and rotor assembly should not exceed 20 INCH lbs. (2.3 N.m). Install locking hub and wheels.

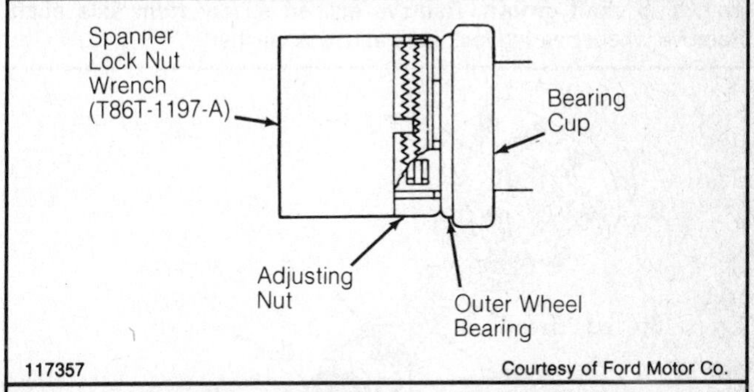
Spanner
Lock Nut
Wrench
(T86T-1197-A)
Bearing
Cup
Adjusting
Nut
Outer Wheel
Bearing
117357
Courtesy of Ford Motor Co.

Fig. 2: Adjusting Wheel Bearing (Manual Locking Hub)

Explorer & Ranger (Automatic Locking Hubs) - 1) Raise and support vehicle. Remove front wheels. Remove retainer washers from lug nut studs and remove automatic locking hub assembly from spindle. See AUTOMATIC LOCKING HUBS under REMOVAL & INSTALLATION.

2) Using Lock Nut Wrench (T70T-4252-B) or 2 3/8" Hex Lock Nut Wrench, loosen wheel bearing adjusting nut. While rotating hub and rotor assembly, tighten adjusting nut to 35 ft. lbs. (47 N.m) to seat bearings. Spin rotor and back off nut 1/4 turn (90 degrees). Retighten adjusting nut to 16 INCH lbs. (1.8 N.m).

3) Align closest lug in wheel bearing adjusting nut with center of spindle keyway slot. Advance nut to next lug if necessary. Install double-hump locking key in keyway under adjusting nut. Install locking hub assembly. Final end play of hub on spindle should be .00-.003" (.00-.08 mm). Torque required to turn hub and rotor assembly should not exceed 25 INCH lbs. (2.8 N.m). Install locking hub assembly and wheels.

Explorer & Ranger (Manual Locking Hub) - 1) Raise and support vehicle. Remove wheels. Remove manual locking hub assembly. See MANUAL LOCKING HUB under REMOVAL & INSTALLATION. Remove outer wheel bearing lock nut from spindle using 4-Prong Lock Nut Wrench (T86T-1197-A).

2) Remove lock nut washer from spindle. Loosen inner wheel bearing lock nut using 4-Prong Lock Nut Wrench (T86T-1197-A). Ensure tabs on wrench engage slots in inner lock nut, and lock nut pin fits in slot on spanner wrench.

3) Tighten inner lock nut to 35 ft. lbs. (47 N.m) while spinning rotor. Spin rotor and loosen lock nut 1/4 turn (90 degrees). Retighten inner lock nut to 16 INCH lbs. (1.8 N.m). Install lock washer on spindle. If necessary, turn inner lock nut slightly to engage lock nut pin with nearest lock washer hole.

4) Install and tighten outer wheel bearing lock nut to 150 ft. lbs. (203 N.m). Install axle shaft spacer. Install manual locking hub assembly. Final end play of hub on spindle should be .00-.003" (.00-.08 mm). Torque required to turn hub and rotor assembly should not exceed 25 INCH lbs. (2.8 N.m). Install locking hub and wheels.

BALL JOINT CHECKING

Raise and support vehicle. Ensure wheel bearings are properly adjusted. See WHEEL BEARING ADJUSTMENT under ADJUSTMENTS & INSPECTION. Hold wheel and move in and out while watching front spindle. Spindle movement must not exceed 1/32" (.794 mm) at upper or lower arms, relative to the axle. Replace ball joints if worn beyond limit.

1991 SUSPENSION
Front – 4WD Coil Spring – Except Aerostar (Cont.)

REMOVAL & INSTALLATION

AUTOMATIC LOCKING HUBS

Removal (Bronco & F150) – 1) Using Torx Bit (T-25), remove 5 bolts from cap assembly. Remove cap assembly. *See Fig. 3*. DO NOT drop spring, ball bearing, bearing race or spring retainer.

2) Remove rubber sealing ring and seal bridge retainer. Remove retainer ring by closing ends with needle nose pliers while pulling hub lock from wheel hub.

3) If wheel hub and spindle are to be removed, remove "C" washer from stub shaft groove. Remove splined spacer from axle shaft. Remove wheel bearing lock nuts and lock washer.

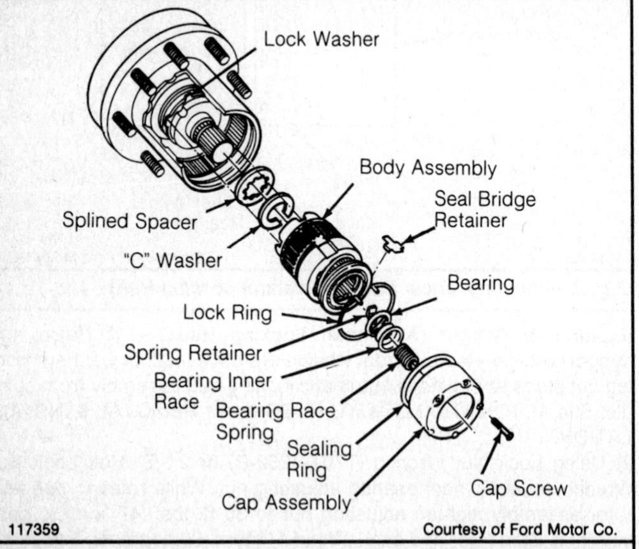
Lock Washer
Body Assembly
Seal Bridge Retainer
Splined Spacer
"C" Washer
Bearing
Lock Ring
Spring Retainer
Bearing Inner Race
Bearing Race Spring
Sealing Ring
Cap Screw
Cap Assembly
117359
Courtesy of Ford Motor Co.

Fig. 3: Exploded View of Automatic Locking Hub (Bronco & F150)

Installation – 1) Install splined spacer and "C" washer on axle shaft. *See Fig. 3*. Remove excessive grease from hub lock and splines. Align all splines, and install body assembly into wheel. Ensure large tangs line up with wheel bearing lock washer cutouts. Install lock ring.

2) Install seal bridge retainer with narrow end first. Install rubber sealing ring over hub lock. Install cap assembly, ensuring ball bearing, spring, race and retainer are in place. Tighten cap assembly bolts to 40-50 INCH lbs. (4.5-5.6 N.m) as follows: tighten one, skip one, tighten one, etc.

Removal (Explorer & Ranger) – 1) Raise and support vehicle. Remove front wheels. Remove retainer washers from lug nut studs and remove automatic locking hub assembly from spindle. *See Fig. 4*. Remove snap ring from end of spindle shaft. Remove axle shaft spacer. Being careful not to damage plastic moving cam or thrust spacers, pull cam assembly off wheel bearing adjusting nut, and remove 2 plastic thrust spacers from adjusting nut.

CAUTION: DO NOT pry on cam or spacers during removal, as it may damage cam or spacers.

2) Using a magnet, remove double-hump locking key. It may be necessary to rotate adjusting nut slightly to relieve pressure against locking key before key can be removed.

CAUTION: To prevent damage to spindle threads, look into spindle keyway under adjusting nut and remove separate locking key before removing adjusting nut (if necessary).

Installation – To install, reverse removal procedure. Ensure cam assembly key is aligned with spindle keyway. Ensure automatic locking hub assembly legs are aligned with 3 cam assembly pockets. Final end play of hub on spindle should be .00-.003" (.00-.08 mm). Torque required to turn hub and rotor assembly should not exceed 25 INCH lbs. (2.8 N.m).

MANUAL LOCKING HUBS

Removal & Installation (Bronco & F150) – 1) Remove Allen head bolts and remove manual locking hub cover. Remove snap ring retaining axle shaft in hub body assembly. Remove locking hub body-to-wheel hub lock ring.

2) Install 2 bolts to remove locking hub body. *See Fig. 5*. To install locking hub, reverse removal procedure. Tighten Allen head bolts to 40-60 INCH lbs. (4-6 N.m). DO NOT pack locking hub cover with grease.

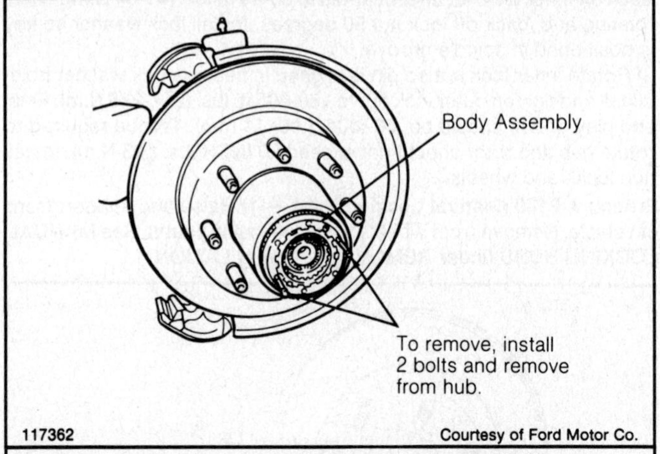
Body Assembly
To remove, install 2 bolts and remove from hub.
117362
Courtesy of Ford Motor Co.

Fig. 5: Removing Manual Locking Hub (Bronco & F150)

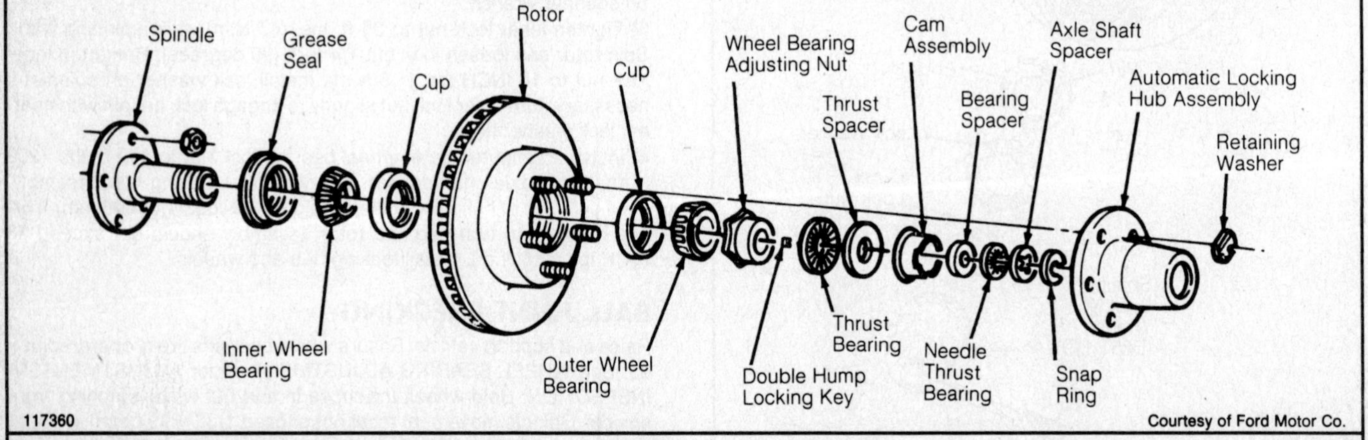
Spindle
Grease Seal
Rotor
Cup
Cup
Wheel Bearing Adjusting Nut
Cam Assembly
Axle Shaft Spacer
Automatic Locking Hub Assembly
Thrust Spacer
Bearing Spacer
Retaining Washer
Thrust Bearing
Inner Wheel Bearing
Outer Wheel Bearing
Double Hump Locking Key
Needle Thrust Bearing
Snap Ring
117360
Courtesy of Ford Motor Co.

Fig. 4: Exploded View of Automatic Locking Hub (Explorer & Ranger)

1991 SUSPENSION
Front – 4WD Coil Spring – Except Aerostar (Cont.)

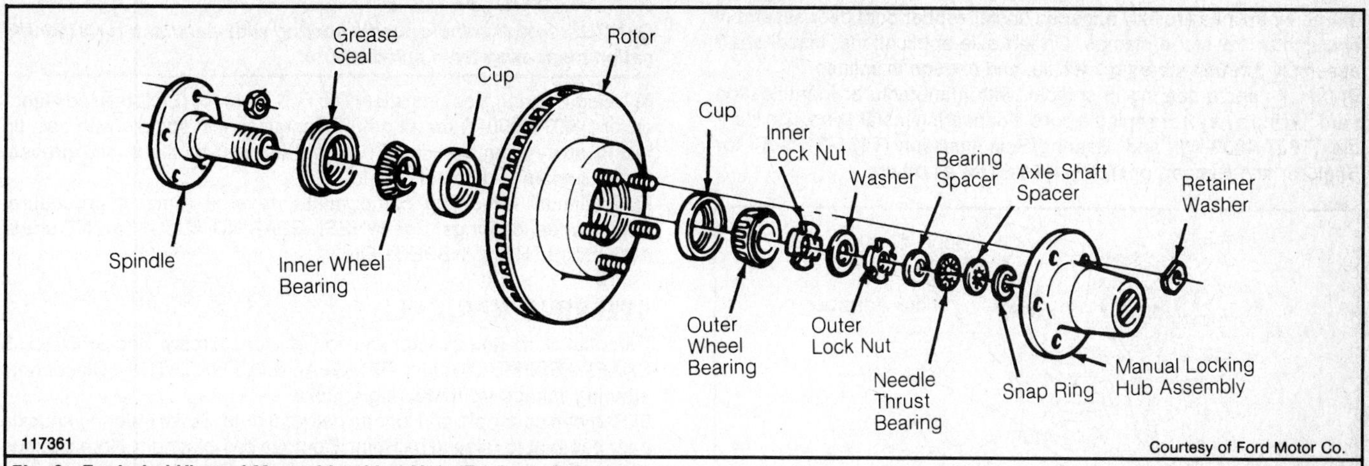
Grease Seal
Rotor
Cup
Cup
Inner Lock Nut
Washer
Bearing Spacer
Axle Shaft Spacer
Retainer Washer
Spindle
Inner Wheel Bearing
Outer Wheel Bearing
Outer Lock Nut
Needle Thrust Bearing
Snap Ring
Manual Locking Hub Assembly
117361
Courtesy of Ford Motor Co.

Fig. 6: Exploded View of Manual Locking Hub (Explorer & Ranger)

Removal (Explorer & Ranger) – 1) Raise and support vehicle. Remove front wheels. Remove retainer washers from lug nut studs. Remove manual locking hub assembly from spindle. *See Fig. 6.*
2) Remove snap ring from end of spindle. Remove axle shaft spacer, needle thrust bearing and bearing spacer from spindle.
Installation – To install hub assembly, reverse removal procedure. Final end play of hub on spindle should be .00-.003" (.00-.08 mm). Torque required to turn hub and rotor assembly should not exceed 25 INCH lbs. (2.8 N.m).

SHOCK ABSORBER

Removal & Installation – Remove nut and washer holding shock absorber to upper spring seat. Remove lower shock absorber-to-radius arm retaining bolts. Remove shock absorber from lower bracket. Compress shock absorber and remove. To install, reverse removal procedure.

QUAD SHOCK ABSORBERS

Removal & Installation (Bronco & F150) – Remove nut, washer and rubber bushings from upper end of shock absorbers. Remove nut from lower end of shock absorber, and remove shock absorber. Replace rubber bushings when replacing shock absorbers. To install, reverse removal procedure.

SPINDLE & SHAFT ASSEMBLY

Removal – 1) Raise and support vehicle. Remove wheel assembly. Remove caliper from rotor. Remove locking hub. See AUTOMATIC LOCKING HUBS or MANUAL LOCKING HUBS under REMOVAL & INSTALLATION.
2) Remove wheel bearings, lock nuts, hub and rotor. Remove spindle-to-steering knuckle nuts. Tap spindle with plastic hammer to free spindle from steering knuckle. *See Fig. 7.* Remove spindle, spindle seat (if equipped) and splash shield.
3) On right side applications, remove and discard keystone clamp from shaft assembly and stub shaft. Slide rubber boot onto stub shaft. Remove shaft assembly from right axle. *See Fig. 7.*
4) Remove left shaft assembly (if required). On all applications, wrap spindle in protective cloth and place second step of spindle in soft-jawed vise.
5) Remove oil seal using slide hammer and Seal Remover (TOOL-1175-AC) for Explorer and Ranger, or Cup Puller (T77F-1102-A) for all others. Remove needle bearing from spindle. Press seal (Explorer and Ranger) or "V" seal and slinger (all others) from shaft assembly. *See Fig. 7.*
Installation – 1) Clean all dirt and grease from spindle bearing bore. Ensure bearing bore is free of nicks and burrs. On Explorer and Ranger, install seal on shaft assembly using press and Seal Installer (T83T-3132-A).
2) On all other models, press slinger on shaft assembly. Install "V" seal on shaft assembly, with seal lip toward spindle. Install plastic spacer (located against "V" seal) on shaft assembly, with chamfered edge against shaft assembly.
3) On right side applications, install rubber boot and NEW keystone clamps on stub shaft. Install right shaft assembly into stub shaft, with stub shaft missing spline aligned with shaft assembly.

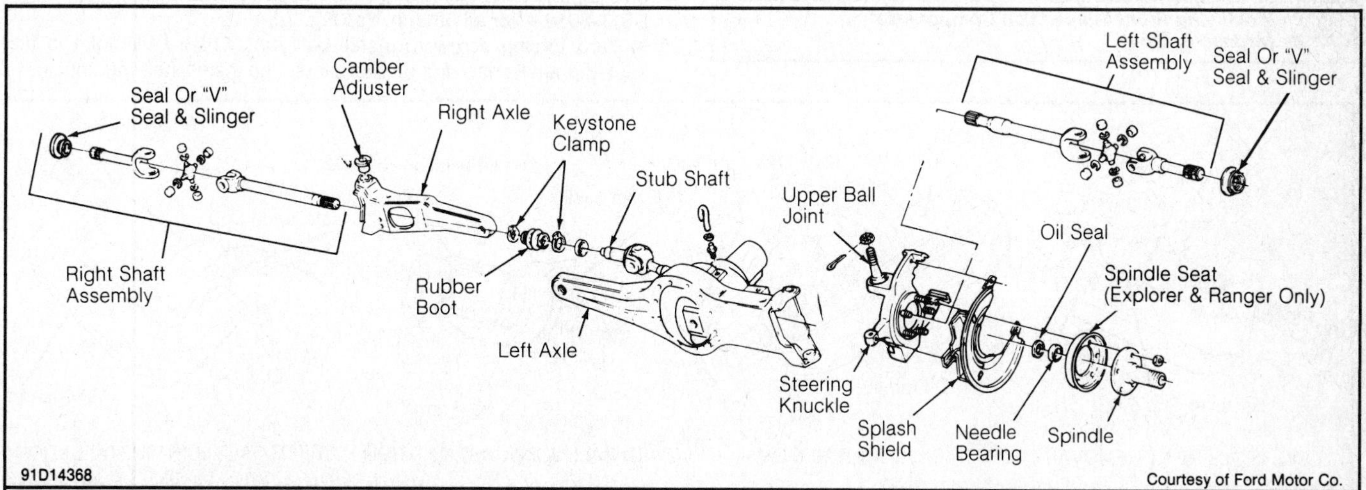
Seal Or "V" Seal & Slinger
Camber Adjuster
Right Axle
Keystone Clamp
Stub Shaft
Upper Ball Joint
Left Shaft Assembly
Seal Or "V" Seal & Slinger
Oil Seal
Spindle Seat (Explorer & Ranger Only)
Right Shaft Assembly
Rubber Boot
Left Axle
Steering Knuckle
Splash Shield
Needle Bearing
Spindle
91D14368
Courtesy of Ford Motor Co.

Fig. 7: Exploded View of Spindle & Components

4) Ensure splines are fully engaged. Install rubber boot over assembly and tighten keystone clamps. On left axle applications, install shaft assembly through steering knuckle, and engage in splines.
5) Install needle bearing in spindle, with manufacturer identification mark facing away from spindle bore. For bearing installation, use Handle (T80T-4000-W), and Bearing/Seal Installer (T83T-3123-A) for Explorer and Ranger, or (T80T-4000-S) for all others.

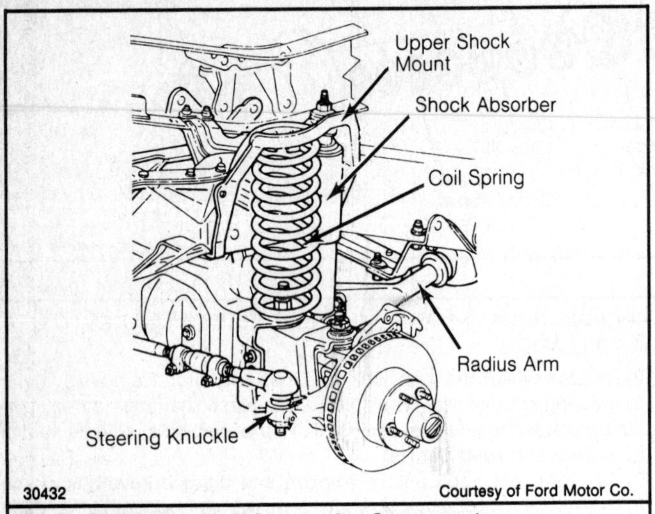
Upper Shock Mount
Shock Absorber
Coil Spring
Radius Arm
Steering Knuckle
30432
Courtesy of Ford Motor Co.

Fig. 8: Identifying Front Suspension Components (Explorer & Ranger)

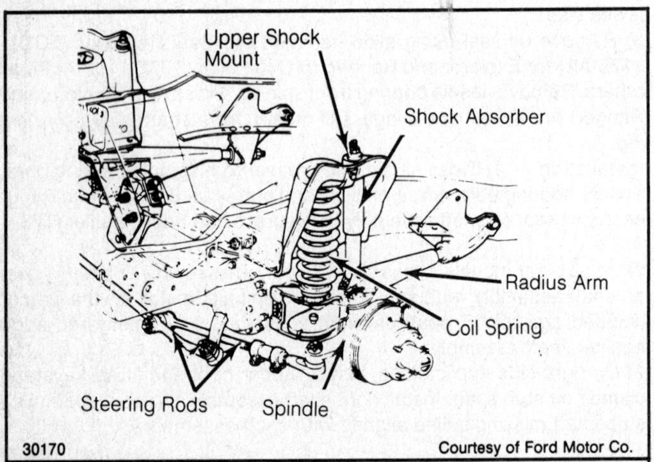
Upper Shock Mount
Shock Absorber
Radius Arm
Coil Spring
Steering Rods
Spindle
30170
Courtesy of Ford Motor Co.

Fig. 9: Identifying Front Suspension Components (Bronco & F150)

CAUTION: Install spindle needle bearing with manufacturer's identification mark away from spindle bore.

6) Using Bearing/Seal Installer (T83T-3123-A) for Explorer and Ranger, or (T80T-4000-T) for all others, install seal in spindle with seal lip facing away from spindle. Coat seal lip with multipurpose grease. Install spindle and splash shield.
7) To install remaining components, reverse removal procedure. Adjust wheel bearings. See WHEEL BEARING ADJUSTMENT under ADJUSTMENTS & INSPECTION.

STEERING KNUCKLE

Removal – 1) Remove spindle and shaft assembly. See SPINDLE & SHAFT ASSEMBLY under REMOVAL & INSTALLATION. Disconnect steering linkage from steering knuckle.
2) Remove cotter pin and loosen ball joint nuts. Strike steering knuckle near ball joint to release ball joint. Remove ball joint nuts. Note position of camber adjuster on top of axle. *See Fig. 7.* Remove camber adjuster and steering knuckle.

CAUTION: Camber adjuster must be installed in original location to maintain proper wheel alignment.

Installation – To install, reverse removal procedure. Ensure camber adjuster is installed in original position. Install NEW nuts on ball joints. Install remaining components.

BALL JOINT

NOTE: Always remove lower ball joint before removing upper ball joint. Install lower ball joint before installing upper ball joint. DO NOT heat ball joint or axle to aid in installation.

Removal – 1) Remove steering knuckle. See STEERING KNUCKLE under REMOVAL & INSTALLATION. Remove snap ring from bottom ball joint socket.
2) Assemble "C" Frame (T74P-4635-C) and Receiver Cup (T83T-3050-A for Explorer and Ranger, or D81T-3010-A4 for all others) on the lower ball joint. *Fig. 10.*
3) Turn forcing screw clockwise until lower ball joint is removed from spindle. Repeat procedure to remove upper ball joint. *See Fig. 10.*
Installation – 1) Lower ball joint must be installed first. Assemble "C" Frame, Receiver Cup (T80T-3010-A for Explorer and Ranger, or T80T-3010-A3 for all others), and Installation Cup (T83T-3050-A for Explorer and Ranger, or D81T-3010-A for all others). *See Fig. 10.*
2) Turn forcing screw to install ball joint. Ensure ball joint is fully seated. To install upper ball joint, assemble "C" Frame, Receiver Cup (T80T-3050-A for Explorer and Ranger, or T80T-3010-A3 for all others), and Installation Cup (T83T-3050-A for Explorer and Ranger, D81T-3010-A for all others). *See Fig. 10.*
3) Turn forcing screw to install ball joint. Ensure ball joint is fully seated. Install snap ring on ball joints, and install steering knuckle.

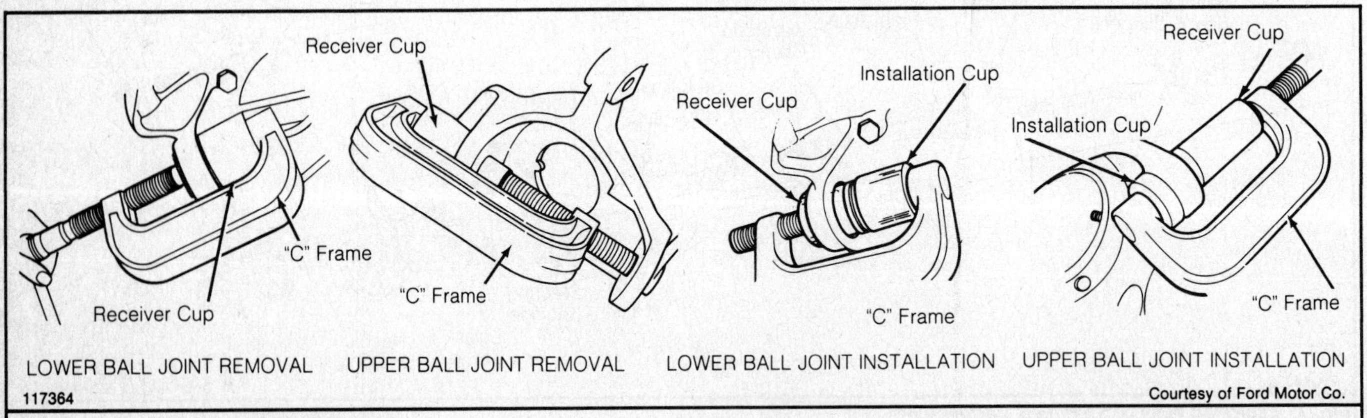
Receiver Cup
"C" Frame
Receiver Cup
"C" Frame
Installation Cup
Receiver Cup
"C" Frame
Receiver Cup
Installation Cup
"C" Frame
LOWER BALL JOINT REMOVAL
UPPER BALL JOINT REMOVAL
LOWER BALL JOINT INSTALLATION
UPPER BALL JOINT INSTALLATION
117364
Courtesy of Ford Motor Co.

Fig. 10: Removing & Installing Ball Joint

1991 SUSPENSION
Front – 4WD Coil Spring – Except Aerostar (Cont.)

COIL SPRING

NOTE: Axle must be supported by jack during removal and installation procedure. If brake hose length does not permit adequate clearance, remove brake caliper.

Removal (Bronco & F150) – Raise and support vehicle under frame rails and support axle with jack. Remove shock absorber-to-lower shock mount bolt. Remove lower spring retainer nut. Remove spring upper retainer. *See Fig. 11.* Lower axle to relieve spring tension. Remove coil spring and lower spring mount.

Installation – Place spring into position. Ensure top of coil is correctly seated in upper spring seat. To complete installation, reverse removal procedure.

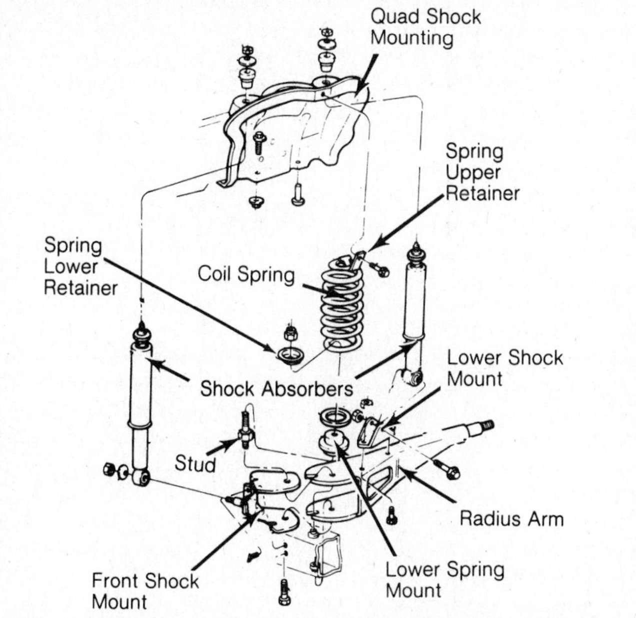
Quad Shock Mounting
Spring Upper Retainer
Spring Lower Retainer
Coil Spring
Lower Shock Mount
Shock Absorbers
Stud
Radius Arm
Front Shock Mount
Lower Spring Mount
30172
Courtesy of Ford Motor Co.

Fig. 11: Exploded View of Coil Spring (Bronco & F150)

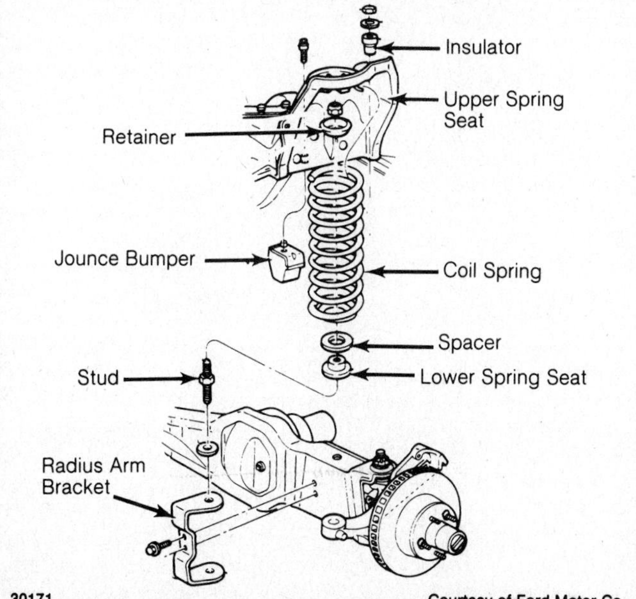
Insulator
Upper Spring Seat
Retainer
Jounce Bumper
Coil Spring
Spacer
Stud
Lower Spring Seat
Radius Arm Bracket
30171
Courtesy of Ford Motor Co.

Fig. 12: Exploded View of Coil Spring (Explorer & Ranger)

Removal (Explorer & Ranger) – **1)** Raise and support vehicle. Support axle with jack. Disconnect shock absorber from radius arm.

2) Remove coil spring-to-axle nut and remove retainer. *See Fig. 12.* Lower axle until spring tension is removed and adequate clearance exists for spring removal.

3) Remove spring by rotating upper coil out of tabs in upper spring seat. Remove spacer and lower seat. Stud in axle may need to be removed to provide clearance.

Installation – Install stud in axle (if removed). Install lower seat and spacer over stud bolt. Position upper end of spring coil in spring stop area of upper spring seat. To complete installation, reverse removal procedure.

RADIUS ARM

Removal (Explorer & Ranger) – **1)** Remove coil spring. See COIL SPRING under REMOVAL & INSTALLATION. Loosen axle pivot bolt. Remove spring lower seat and stud from radius arm.

2) Remove radius arm-to-axle and radius arm bracket bolts. *See Fig. 12.* Remove nut, washer and bushing from rear of radius arm at frame bracket. Remove radius arm.

Installation – To install, reverse removal procedure. DO NOT tighten stud until rear nut on radius arm has been tightened to specification. See appropriate TORQUE SPECIFICATIONS table at end of article.

Removal (Bronco & F150) – **1)** Remove coil spring. See COIL SPRING under REMOVAL & INSTALLATION. Loosen axle pivot bolt. Remove spring lower seat and stud from radius arm.

2) Remove radius arm-to-axle and radius arm bracket bolts. Remove nut, washer and bushing from rear of radius arm at frame bracket. Move axle forward and remove radius arm.

Installation – To install, reverse removal procedure. Clean and apply Loctite to radius arm-to-axle bolt and stud before installation. To install remaining components, reverse removal procedure.

FRONT AXLE ASSEMBLY

Removal & Installation – For removal and installation procedure, see appropriate article in DRIVE AXLES.

STABILIZER BAR

Removal & Installation (Explorer & Ranger) – Remove bolts and retainers from center and right end of stabilizer bar. Remove stabilizer bar-to-stabilizer bar link bolt. Remove stabilizer bar and bushings. To install, reverse removal procedure.

Removal & Installation (Bronco & F150) – Remove stabilizer bar-to-stabilizer link bolts. Remove stabilizer bar retainer bolts. Remove stabilizer bar and bushings. To install, reverse removal procedure.

TORQUE SPECIFICATIONS

TORQUE SPECIFICATIONS (BRONCO & F150)

Application	Ft. Lbs. (N.m)
Axle Pivot Bracket-To-Frame Bolt	77-110 (104-149)
Ball Joint Nut	
Lower	90-110 (122-149)
Upper	100 (136)
Lower Spring Retainer Nut	70-100 (95-136)
Radius Arm Bracket-To-Frame Bolt	77-110 (104-149)
Radius Arm-To-Axle Lower Bolt	320-340 (434-461)
Radius Arm-To-Axle Upper Stud	240-260 (325-353)
Rear Radius Arm Nut	80-120 (109-163)
Shock Absorber Mounting Bolt	
Lower	52-74 (71-100)
Upper	25-35 (34-47)
Spindle-To-Steering Knuckle Bolt	50-60 (68-81)
Stabilizer Bar	
To Stabilizer Link	52-74 (71-100)
Retaining Nut	27-37 (37-50)
Stabilizer Bar Link-To-Bracket Bolt	52-74 (71-100)
Upper Spring Retainer Bolt	13-18 (18-24)
Wheel Lug Nut	100 (136)

1991 SUSPENSION
Front – 4WD Coil Spring – Except Aerostar (Cont.)

TORQUE SPECIFICATIONS (EXPLORER & RANGER)

Application	Ft. Lbs. (N.m)
Axle Pivot Bolt	120-150 (163-203)
Ball Joint Nut	
Lower	95-110 (129-149)
Upper	85-100 (115-136)
Radius Arm Bracket	
Front Bolt	27-37 (37-50)
Lower Bolt	160-220 (217-298)
Upper Stud	190-230 (258-312)
Radius Arm-To-Frame Bracket Nut	80-120 (109-163)
Shock Absorber-To-Radius Arm Bolt	41-63 (56-85)
Shock Absorber-To-Upper Seat Bolt	25-35 (34-47)
Spindle-To-Steering Knuckle Bolt	40-50 (54-68)
Spring Retainer Nut	70-100 (95-136)
Stabilizer Bar Retainer Bolt	35-50 (47-68)
Stabilizer Bar "U" Bolt Nut	35-50 (47-68)
Wheel Lug Nut	100 (136)

1991 SUSPENSION
Front – 4WD Coil Spring – Aerostar

DESCRIPTION

The independent front suspension consists of steering knuckles, upper and lower control arms, coil springs, shock absorbers and stabilizer bar. Integral ball joints and bushings are mounted in the control arms. Movement of upper control arm provides for adjustment of caster and camber. Individual axle shafts are splined into the hub assembly. The 4WD hubs are constantly engaged and cannot be disengaged.

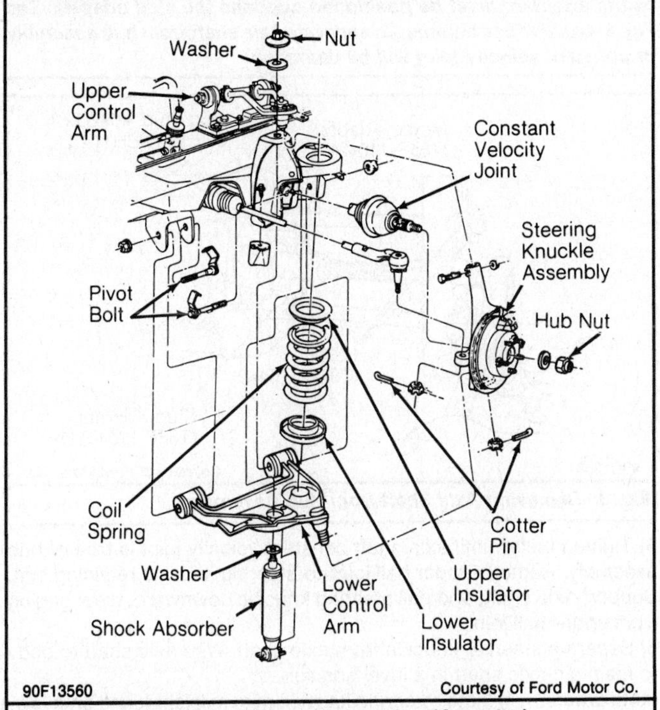
Washer
Nut
Upper
Control
Arm
Constant
Velocity
Joint
Steering
Knuckle
Assembly
Pivot
Bolt
Hub Nut
Coil
Spring
Cotter
Pin
Washer
Lower
Control
Arm
Upper
Insulator
Shock Absorber
Lower
Insulator
90F13560
Courtesy of Ford Motor Co.

Fig. 1: Exploded View of Front Suspension (Aerostar)

ADJUSTMENTS & INSPECTION

WHEEL ALIGNMENT SPECIFICATIONS & PROCEDURES

NOTE: See SPECIFICATIONS & PROCEDURES article in WHEEL ALIGNMENT.

WHEEL BEARING ADJUSTMENT

Front wheel bearings are not adjustable. If service is required, bearings and hub assembly are replaced as a unit.

BALL JOINT CHECKING

Lower & Upper Ball Joint – Raise and support vehicle under lower control arm. Move lower edge of tire in and out while watching lower steering knuckle arm and lower part of lower control arm. If movement exceeds 1/32" (.794 mm), replace lower control arm. To check upper ball joint, move upper edge of tire in and out. If movement between upper steering knuckle arm and upper control arm exceeds 1/32" (.794 mm), replace upper control arm.

REMOVAL & INSTALLATION

NOTE: Any time the steering linkage is disconnected from the steering knuckle, the steering system must be placed in the centered position.

AXLE SHAFT

Removal – 1) Place wheels in straight-ahead position. Raise and support vehicle. Remove wheel assembly. Install steel rod through hole in brake rotor. Rotate rotor until steel rod contacts steering knuckle, preventing rotor and hub from moving. Remove hub nut and washer from axle shaft.

2) Place reference mark on axle shaft flange and drive axle flange for reassembly reference. Remove axle shaft flange-to-drive axle flange bolts. Separate axle shaft from drive axle flange.

CAUTION: Support axle shaft when disconnected from drive axle flange. DO NOT allow axle shaft to hang unsupported or constant velocity joint on axle shaft will be damaged.

3) Remove shock absorber-to-lower control arm bolts. *See Fig. 1.* Move shock absorber aside. Remove bumper from front drive axle crossmember. Install Puller (T81P-1104-C), Metric Stud Adapter (T83P-1104-BH1), Stud Adapter (T86P-1104-A1) and Metric Adapter (T81P-1104-A) on hub. *See Fig. 3.*

CAUTION: Ensure metric adapters are fully threaded on wheel stud. Metric adapters must be positioned opposite stud adapter. See Fig. 3. DO NOT use hammer to separate axle shaft from hub assembly or constant velocity joint will be damaged.

4) Tighten puller until axle shaft constant velocity joint is free of hub assembly. Remove axle shaft assembly.

Installation – 1) Install axle shaft in hub assembly. Push axle shaft in hub assembly as far as possible. Install rotor on hub (if removed) with 2 wheel lug nuts. Install steel rod through rotor. Rotate rotor until steel rod contacts steering knuckle.

CAUTION: Always install NEW hub nut. DO NOT reuse old hub nut.

2) Install NEW hub nut and tighten to specification. DO NOT use impact to tighten hub nut. To install remaining components, reverse removal procedure. Ensure reference marks are aligned on axle shaft flange and drive axle flange. Tighten bolts to specification.

BALL JOINT

Ball joint is not serviced separately. If ball joint is defective, control arm must be replaced as a unit.

COIL SPRING

Removal – 1) Place wheels in centered position. Raise and support vehicle. Remove wheels. Disconnect stabilizer bar link-to-lower control arm bolt. *See Fig. 2.* Remove shock absorber.

2) Using Spring Compressor (D78P-5310-A), compress coil spring. Loosen lower control arm pivot bolts. *See Fig. 1.* Remove cotter pin from lower ball joint-to-steering knuckle nut and loosen nut. DO NOT remove nut.

3) Using Pitman Arm Puller (T64P-3590-F), loosen lower ball joint from steering knuckle. Remove puller. Support lower control arm with floor jack. Remove nut from ball joint.

CAUTION: Ensure lower control arm is supported with floor jack before removing nut from lower ball joint.

4) Separate lower ball joint from lower control arm. Release floor jack and allow lower control arm to move downward. Remove coil spring with upper and lower insulators. *See Fig. 1.*

NOTE: If new coil spring is to be installed, measure compressed length of coil spring removed. Adjust new coil spring compressed length to that of coil spring removed for installation purposes.

Installation – 1) To install, reverse removal procedure. Install lower ball joint nut and tighten to specification. Install cotter pin. It may be necessary to advance ball joint nut for cotter pin installation. DO NOT back nut off.

2) Tighten pivot bolts to specification with vehicle on the ground at normal operating height.

1991 SUSPENSION
Front – 4WD Coil Spring – Aerostar (Cont.)

HUB & BEARING ASSEMBLY

NOTE: Wheel bearings and hub assembly are not individually serviceable. If wheel bearings are defective, replace wheel bearings and hub assembly as a unit.

Removal & Installation – 1) Remove steering knuckle. See STEERING KNUCKLE under REMOVAL & INSTALLATION.
2) Remove 3 hub-to-steering knuckle bolts. Remove hub assembly and dust shield. To install, reverse removal procedure.

LOWER CONTROL ARM

CAUTION: Before removing lower control arm, vehicle should be supported under the front crossmember.

Removal – Remove coil spring. See COIL SPRING under REMOVAL & INSTALLATION in this article. Note direction of pivot bolt installation. *See Fig. 1.* Remove pivot bolts and lower control arm. Lower control arm assembly must be replaced if ball joint or bushings are defective.
Installation – To install, reverse removal procedure. Ensure pivot bolts are installed in proper direction. *See Fig. 1.*

CAUTION: Pivot bolts must be tightened to specification with vehicle on the ground and at normal operating height.

SHOCK ABSORBER

Removal & Installation – Remove nut and washer from top of shock absorber. Remove shock absorber-to-lower control arm bolts. Remove shock absorber. To install, reverse removal procedure. Tighten bolts/nuts to specification.

STABILIZER BAR

Removal & Installation – Remove stabilizer bar-to-link assembly at lower control arms. *See Fig. 2.* Remove link assembly from lower control arm if necessary. Remove mounting bracket bolts and mounting brackets. Remove stabilizer bar with frame insulators. To install, reverse removal procedure. Tighten bolts to specification.

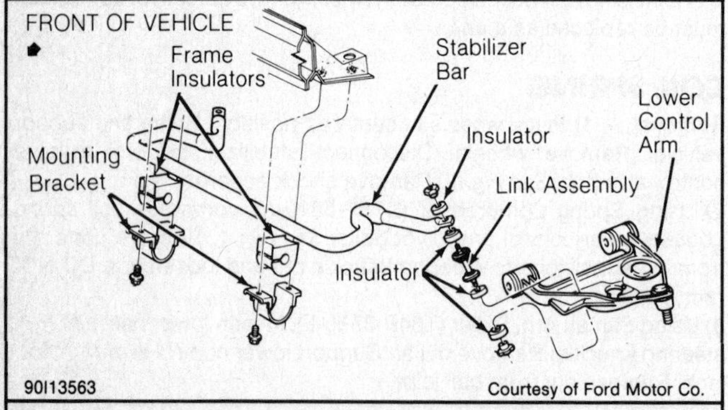
FRONT OF VEHICLE
Frame Insulators
Stabilizer Bar
Lower Control Arm
Insulator
Mounting Bracket
Link Assembly
Insulator
90I13563
Courtesy of Ford Motor Co.
Fig. 2: Exploded View of Stabilizer Bar Assembly

STEERING KNUCKLE

Removal – 1) Place wheels in straight-ahead position. Remove hub nut and washer from axle shaft. *See Fig. 1.* Raise vehicle on twin post hoist. Place jack stands under the frame. Twin post hoist is used to maintain pressure on the coil spring.
2) Remove wheel assembly. Remove brake caliper retaining pins and brake caliper. Support brake caliper out of the way. Remove rotor. Remove cotter pin from tie rod-to-steering knuckle nut and remove nut. Using Puller (T64P-3590-F), separate tie rod from steering knuckle.

CAUTION: Ensure twin post hoist is supporting lower control arm to maintain pressure on the coil spring.

3) Remove cotter pin from lower ball joint-to-steering knuckle nut and loosen nut. DO NOT remove nut. Using puller, loosen lower ball joint from steering knuckle. Remove puller and nut.
4) Pull downward on lower control arm. Disengage lower ball joint from steering knuckle. Install Puller (T81P-1104-C), Metric Stud Adapter (T83P-1104-BH1), Stud Adapter (T86P-1104-A1) and Metric Adapter (T81P-1104-A) on the hub. *See Fig. 3.*

CAUTION: Ensure metric adapters are fully threaded on wheel stud. Metric adapters must be positioned opposite the stud adapter. See Fig. 3. DO NOT use hammer to separate axle shaft from hub assembly or constant velocity joint will be damaged.

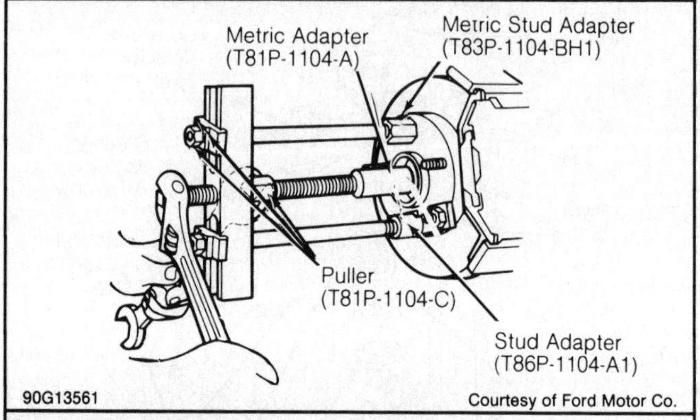
Metric Adapter
(T81P-1104-A)
Metric Stud Adapter
(T83P-1104-BH1)
Puller
(T81P-1104-C)
Stud Adapter
(T86P-1104-A1)
90G13561
Courtesy of Ford Motor Co.
Fig. 3: Removing Axle Shaft from Hub Assembly

5) Tighten puller until axle shaft constant velocity joint is free of hub assembly. Remove upper ball joint-to-steering knuckle retaining bolt. Support axle shaft, and pull steering knuckle downward, disengaging from upper ball joint.
6) Separate steering knuckle from axle shaft. Wire axle shaft to body to maintain axle shaft in a level position.
Installation – 1) Install steering knuckle over axle shaft and onto lower ball joint. Ensure axle shaft splines are engaged with hub assembly. Install lower ball joint nut, and tighten to specification.
2) Install cotter pin. If necessary, advance ball joint nut for cotter pin installation. DO NOT back nut off. Install rotor on hub (if removed) with 2 wheel lug nuts. Install steel rod through rotor. Rotate rotor until steel rod contacts steering knuckle.

CAUTION: Always install NEW hub nut. DO NOT reuse hub nut.

3) Install NEW hub nut and tighten nut just enough to seat constant velocity joint of the axle shaft. DO NOT tighten hub nut to specification at this time. Install upper ball joint in steering knuckle. Install and tighten retaining bolt to specification. See TORQUE SPECIFICATIONS table at end of article.
4) Install tie rod on steering knuckle. Tighten tie rod nut to specification. It may be necessary to advance tie rod nut for cotter pin installation. DO NOT back nut off.
5) Tighten hub nut to specification. DO NOT use impact to tighten hub nut. It will be necessary to use steel rod installed in step **2)** to hold hub from turning. To install remaining components, reverse removal procedure.

UPPER CONTROL ARM

CAUTION: When servicing upper control arm components, service ONLY one side at a time. DO NOT service both sides at the same time. Manufacturer recommends that steering knuckle be removed during service procedure.

Removal – 1) Place wheels in straight-ahead position. Raise vehicle on twin post hoist. Place jack stands under body rail. Twin post hoist is used to maintain pressure on the coil spring.
2) Remove steering knuckle. See STEERING KNUCKLE under REMOVAL & INSTALLATION. Remove bolt retainer bracket. *See Fig. 4.*

1991 SUSPENSION
Front – 4WD Coil Spring – Aerostar (Cont.)

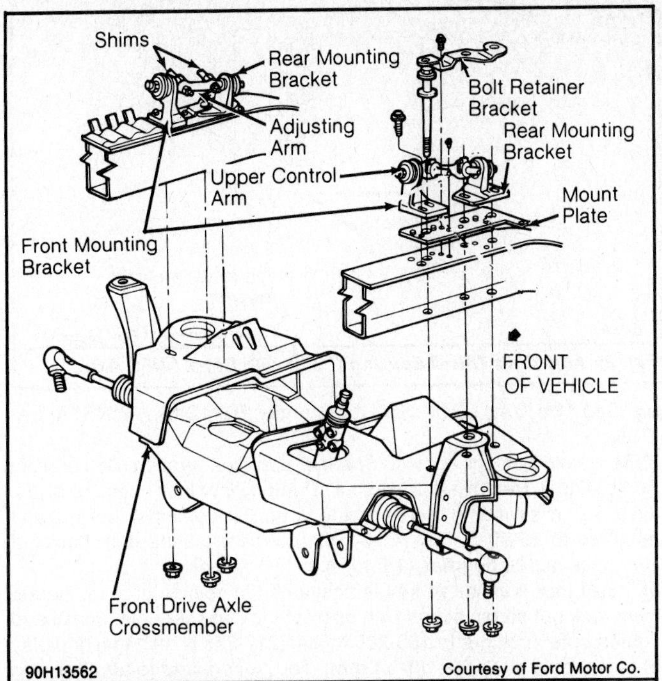
Shims
Rear Mounting Bracket
Bolt Retainer Bracket
Rear Mounting Bracket
Adjusting Arm
Upper Control Arm
Mount Plate
Front Mounting Bracket
FRONT OF VEHICLE
Front Drive Axle Crossmember
90H13562
Courtesy of Ford Motor Co.

Fig. 4: Exploded View of Upper Control Arm & Components

CAUTION: Front and rear mounting bracket position on mounting plate must be marked before removing upper control arm.

3) Mark position of front and rear mounting brackets on mounting plate. *See Fig. 4.* Remove front and rear mounting bracket bolts. Remove upper control arm assembly and mounting plate.

4) If upper control arm is to be removed from adjusting arm, note location and number of shims. *See Fig. 4.* Remove upper control arm-to-adjusting arm nuts. Separate upper control arm from adjusting arm. Mounting brackets and adjusting arm are serviced as a complete unit.

CAUTION: Before removing upper control arm from adjusting arm, note location and number of shim installed at adjusting arm. See Fig. 4. Shims must be installed in original location to maintain wheel alignment.

Installation – To install, reverse removal procedure. Install mounting brackets in original position. Ensure mounting brackets do not move when bolts are tightened to specification. Check and adjust wheel alignment. See SPECIFICATIONS & PROCEDURES article in WHEEL ALIGNMENT.

TORQUE SPECIFICATIONS

TORQUE SPECIFICATIONS

Application	Ft. Lbs. (N.m)
Axle Shaft-To-Drive Axle Flange Bolt	19-26 (26-35)
Bolt Retainer Bracket Bolt	10-14 (14-19)
Bumper-To-Crossmember Bolt	24-33 (33-45)
Control Arm Front Mount Bracket-To-Mount Plate Bolt	35-47 (47-64)
Control Arm Mount Bracket-To-Frame Rail Bolt	145-195 (197-264)
Hub Nut [1]	170-210 (230-285)
Link Assembly Bolt	10-12 (14-16)
Lower Ball Joint Nut	80-120 (109-163)
Mount Plate-To-Frame Rail Bolt	10-14 (14-19)
Pivot Bolt [2]	100-140 (136-190)
Shock Absorber	
Lower Bolt	16-24 (22-33)
Upper Nut	25-35 (34-47)
Stabilizer Bar Mount Bracket Bolt	16-24 (22-33)
Tie Rod-To-Steering Knuckle Nut	52-74 (71-100)
Upper Ball Joint Bolt	27-37 (37-51)
Upper Control Arm-To-Adjusting Arm Nut	70-100 (95-136)
Wheel Lug Nut	100 (136)

1 – Use NEW nut. DO NOT tighten with impact.
2 – Tighten to specification with vehicle on ground and at normal operating height.

1991 SUSPENSION
Front – 4WD Leaf Spring

F250/350

NOTE: ***Unless specified otherwise, references to "F" Series include "F" Series Super Duty.***

DESCRIPTION

The standard F250 uses a Dana 44IFS (Independent Front Suspension) axle and F250 Heavy Duty (HD) uses a Dana 50IFS axle. System consist of a 2-piece drive axle with ball joint-supported steering knuckle. F350 uses a Dana 60 Monobeam axle system, consisting of a solid drive axle with kingpin-supported steering knuckles. All drive axles are suspended by semi-elliptic leaf-type springs.

FRONT AXLE IDENTIFICATION

Application	Axle
F250	[1] Dana 44IFS
F250 HD	[1] Dana 50IFS
F350	Dana 60 Monobeam

[1] – IFS is Independent Front Suspension.

NOTE: ***For additional information on 4WD drive axles, see appropriate article in DRIVE AXLES.***

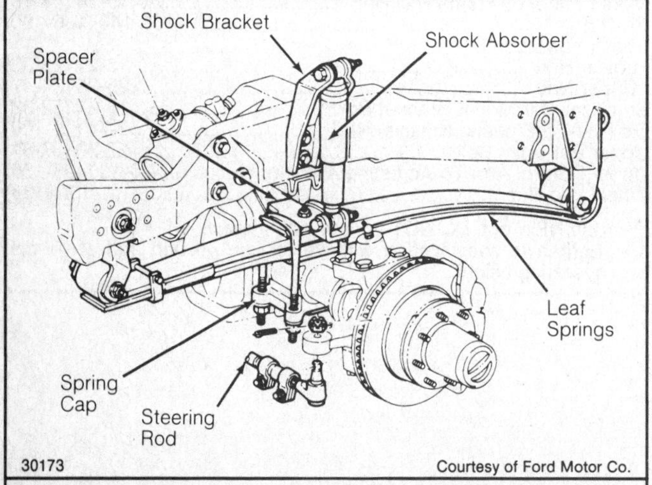
Shock Bracket
Shock Absorber
Spacer Plate
Leaf Springs
Spring Cap
Steering Rod
30173
Courtesy of Ford Motor Co.

Fig. 1: Identifying Leaf Spring Suspension Components (Typical)

ADJUSTMENTS & INSPECTION

WHEEL ALIGNMENT SPECIFICATIONS & PROCEDURES

See SPECIFICATIONS & PROCEDURES article in WHEEL ALIGNMENT.

WHEEL BEARING ADJUSTMENT

F250 (Dana 44IFS Axle) – 1) Raise and support front of vehicle. Remove front wheels. Remove locking hubs. See MANUAL LOCKING HUBS under REMOVAL & INSTALLATION.

2) Use a torque wrench and Spanner Lock Nut Wrench (T86T-1197-A) to unlock locking splines of wheel bearing adjusting nut by applying inward pressure. *See Fig. 2.* Tighten adjusting nut to 70 ft. lbs. (95 N.m) while turning hub and rotor back and forth to seat bearing.

3) Apply inward pressure to spanner lock nut wrench to disengage locking splines, and back off adjusting nut approximately 1/4 turn (90 degrees). Retighten adjusting nut to 15-20 ft. lbs. (20-27 N.m). Final end play of hub on spindle should be 0.00" (0.00 mm). Torque required to turn hub and rotor assembly should not exceed 20 INCH lbs. (2.3 N.m). Install locking hub and wheels.

F250 HD & F350 (Dana 50IFS Or 60 Monobeam Axle) – 1) Raise and support front of vehicle. Remove wheels. Remove locking hub assembly. See MANUAL LOCKING HUBS under REMOVAL & INSTALLATION.

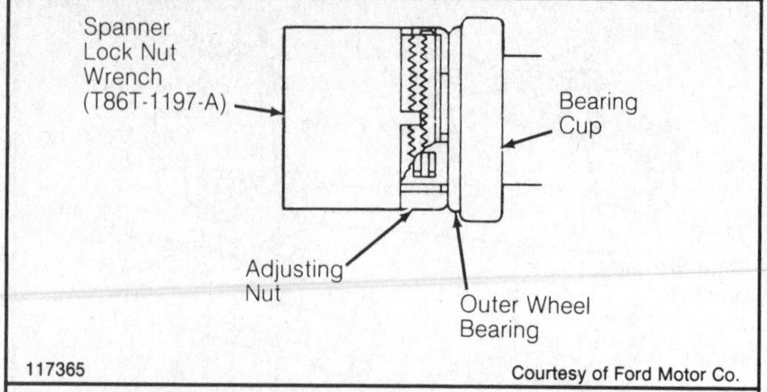
Spanner Lock Nut Wrench (T86T-1197-A)
Bearing Cup
Adjusting Nut
Outer Wheel Bearing
117365
Courtesy of Ford Motor Co.

Fig. 2: Adjusting Wheel Bearing (F250 with Dana 44IFS Axle)

2) Remove outer lock nut with Spanner Lock Nut Wrench (D85T-1197-A). *See Fig. 3.* Remove lock washer. Tighten inner lock nut to 50 ft. lbs. (68 N.m) while rotating hub back and forth. Back off inner lock nut and retighten to 30-40 ft. lbs. (41-54 N.m). While rotating hub, back off inner lock nut 90 degrees (1/4 turn).

3) Install lock washer so key is positioned in spindle groove. Rotate inner lock nut so pin aligns with nearest lock washer hole. Install and tighten outer lock nut to 160-205 ft. lbs. (217-278 N.m). Final end play of hub should be 0-.004" (0-.11 mm). Torque required to turn hub and rotor assembly should not exceed 20 INCH lbs. (2.3 N.m). Install locking hub and wheels.

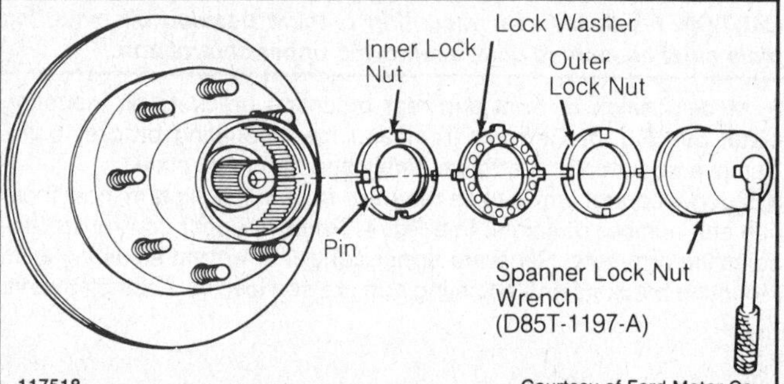
Lock Washer
Inner Lock Nut
Outer Lock Nut
Pin
Spanner Lock Nut Wrench (D85T-1197-A)
117518
Courtesy of Ford Motor Co.

Fig. 3: Adjusting Wheel Bearing (F250 HD & F350)

BALL JOINT CHECKING

F250 – 1) Raise and support vehicle. Ensure wheel bearings are properly adjusted. See WHEEL BEARING ADJUSTMENT under ADJUSTMENTS & INSPECTION. Hold tire at top and bottom. Move wheel and watch for movement of spindle assembly.

2) If spindle assembly moves more than 1/32" (.794 mm) at upper or lower arms (relative to axle), replace upper and/or lower ball joint as necessary.

KINGPIN CHECKING

F350 – Information is not available from manufacturer.

REMOVAL & INSTALLATION

MANUAL LOCKING HUBS

Removal – Remove 6 Allen head bolts and remove manual locking hub cover. Remove snap ring retaining axle shaft in hub body assembly. Remove locking hub body-to-wheel hub lock ring. Install 2 bolts to remove locking hub body. *See Fig. 4.*

Installation – To install locking hub, reverse removal procedure. Tighten Allen head bolts to 35-53 INCH lbs. (4-6 N.m). DO NOT pack locking hub cover with grease.

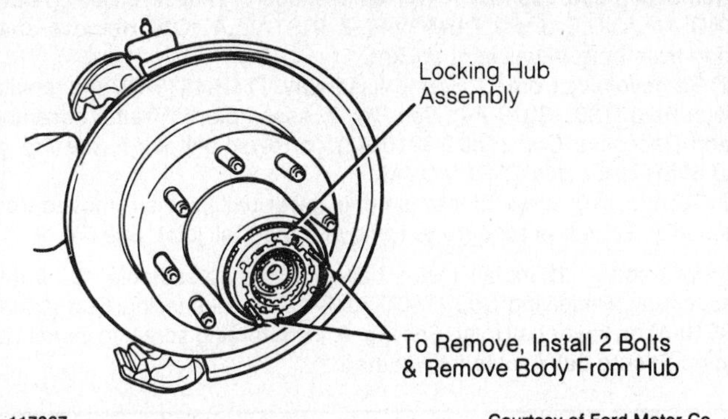
Locking Hub
Assembly
To Remove, Install 2 Bolts
& Remove Body From Hub
117367
Courtesy of Ford Motor Co.

Fig. 4: Removing Manual Locking Hub

SHOCK ABSORBERS

WARNING: Shock absorbers are gas filled. DO NOT puncture or apply heat to shock absorber.

Removal & Installation – Remove upper and lower shock absorber bolts. Compress shock absorber and remove. Remove upper shock bushing. To install, reverse removal procedure.

SPINDLE & SHAFT ASSEMBLY

Removal (F250/250 HD) – 1) Raise and support vehicle. Remove wheel and tire assembly. Remove locking hub. See MANUAL LOCKING HUBS under REMOVAL & INSTALLATION. Using Spanner Lock Nut Wrench (D85T-1197-A), remove outer lock nut, lock ring and adjusting nut. *See Figs. 3 and 5.*

2) Remove brake caliper and support aside. DO NOT hang by flexible brake hose. Wire caliper to frame. Remove hub and rotor assembly. Remove spindle-to-steering knuckle nuts. Tap spindle with plastic hammer to free spindle from steering knuckle. *See Fig. 5.* Remove spindle and splash shield.

3) On right side applications, remove and discard keystone clamp from stub shaft assembly and stub shaft. Slide rubber boot onto stub shaft. Remove shaft assembly from right axle.

4) Remove left shaft assembly (if required). Wrap spindle in protective cloth and place second step of spindle in soft-jawed vise. Using slide hammer and Cup Puller (T77F-1102-A), remove oil seal and needle bearing from spindle. Press "V" seal and slinger from shaft assembly. *See Fig. 5.*

Installation – 1) Clean dirt and grease from spindle bearing bore. Press slinger on shaft assembly. Install "V" seal on shaft assembly with seal lip toward spindle. Install plastic spacer (located against "V" seal) on shaft assembly, with chamfered edge against shaft assembly.

2) On right side applications, install rubber boot and NEW keystone clamps on stub shaft. Align right shaft assembly into stub shaft, so stub shaft missing spline is aligned with gapless male shaft assembly. Install shaft assembly.

3) Ensure splines are fully engaged. Install rubber boot over assembly and tighten keystone clamps. On left axle applications, install shaft assembly through steering knuckle and engage in splines.

CAUTION: Install spindle needle bearing so manufacturer's identification mark is away from spindle bore.

4) Using Bearing/Seal Installer (T80T-4000-S) and Handle (T80T-4000-W) for Dana 44IFS axles, or Bearing/Seal Installer (T80T-4000-R) for Dana 50IFS axles, install needle bearing in spindle, with manufacturer identification mark facing away from spindle bore.

5) Using Bearing/Seal Installer (T80T-4000-T), install oil seal in spindle, with seal lip facing away from spindle. Coat seal lip with multipurpose grease. Install spindle and splash shield. To install remaining components, reverse removal procedure.

6) Tighten bolts/nuts to specification. See appropriate TORQUE SPECIFICATIONS table at end of article. Adjust wheel bearings. See WHEEL BEARING ADJUSTMENT under ADJUSTMENTS & INSPECTION.

Removal (F350) – 1) Raise and support vehicle. Remove front wheels. Remove locking hub. See MANUAL LOCKING HUBS under REMOVAL & INSTALLATION. Using Spanner Lock Nut Wrench (D85T-1197-A), remove wheel bearing outer lock nut, lock washer and adjusting nut. *See Fig. 6.*

2) Remove brake caliper and support aside. DO NOT hang by flexible brake hose. Remove hub and rotor assembly. Remove spindle-to-steering knuckle nuts. Tap spindle with plastic hammer to free spindle from steering knuckle. *See Fig. 6.*

3) Remove spindle and splash shield. Remove seal from spindle. Using puller, remove needle bearing from spindle. Pull shaft assembly from axle housing. Remove bronze spacer from axle shaft (if required).

Installation – 1) Clean dirt and grease from spindle bearing bore. Install shield and "V" seal on shaft assembly. *See Fig. 6.* Coat seal lip and "V" seal on shaft assembly with multipurpose grease. Install shaft assembly.

CAUTION: Install spindle needle bearing so manufacturer's identification mark is away from spindle bore.

2) Ensure shaft splines are fully engaged. Install bronze spacer on shaft assembly, with chamfered side against shaft assembly. Using Bearing/Seal Installer (T80T-4000-R) and Handle (T80T-4000-W), install needle bearing in spindle, with manufacturer identification mark facing away from spindle bore.

3) Pack bearing with grease. Install seal in spindle. Install spindle and splash shield. To complete installation, reverse removal procedure. Adjust wheel bearings. See WHEEL BEARING ADJUSTMENT under ADJUSTMENTS & INSPECTION.

STEERING KNUCKLE

Removal (F250/250 HD) – 1) Remove spindle and shaft assembly. See SPINDLE & SHAFT ASSEMBLY under REMOVAL & INSTALLATION. Disconnect steering linkage from steering knuckle.

2) Remove cotter pin and loosen ball joint nuts. Strike steering knuckle near ball joint to release ball joint. Remove nuts from ball joint studs. Note position of camber adjuster on top of axle. *See Fig. 5.* Remove camber adjuster and steering knuckle.

CAUTION: Camber adjuster must be installed in original location to maintain proper wheel alignment.

Installation – Ensure camber adjuster is installed in original position. Install NEW nuts on ball joints, and tighten to specifications. See appropriate TORQUE SPECIFICATIONS table at end of article. To complete installation, reverse removal procedure.

Removal (F350) – 1) Remove spindle and shaft assembly. See SPINDLE & SHAFT ASSEMBLY under REMOVAL & INSTALLATION. Alternately remove spindle cap bolts. *See Fig. 6.*

CAUTION: Use care when removing spindle cap, as cap is under spring pressure.

2) Remove spindle cap, compression spring, retainer, and gasket. Remove lower kingpin and retainer. Remove tapered bushing from top of upper kingpin. Remove steering knuckle from axle housing.

3) Using a 7/8" hex bar stock, remove upper kingpin from axle housing. *See Fig. 7.* Using 2-jaw puller and Step Plate (D80L-630-7), remove grease seal, bearing, bearing cup, and grease retainer. *See Fig. 6.*

Installation – 1) Coat grease retainer-to-lower kingpin contact surface with silicon-type sealant. Install grease retainer in axle housing, with concave portion toward upper kingpin.

2) Install bearing cup until it bottoms on grease retainer. Pack bearing and axle housing area with grease and install bearing. Using Seal Installer (T86T-3110-AH), install new grease seal.

3) Install upper kingpin and tighten to specification. See appropriate TORQUE SPECIFICATIONS table at end of article. Install steering

1991 SUSPENSION
Front – 4WD Leaf Spring (Cont.)

knuckle and tapered bushing. Install lower kingpin and retainer. Alternately tighten bolts to specification.

4) Install retainer, compression spring, and spindle cap. Tighten spindle cap bolts to 70-90 ft. lbs. (95-122 N.m). To complete installation, reverse removal procedure. Lubricate upper kingpin through grease fitting. Lubricate lower kingpin through flush-type fitting on bottom of kingpin.

BALL JOINT

NOTE: Always remove lower ball joint before removing upper ball joint. Install lower ball joint before installing upper ball joint. DO NOT heat ball joint or axle to aid in installation.

Removal (F250/250 HD) – 1) Remove steering knuckle. See STEERING KNUCKLE under REMOVAL & INSTALLATION. Remove snap ring from bottom ball joint socket.

2) Remove plug from "C" Frame Assembly (T74P-4635-C), and replace with Plug (T80T-3010-A4). *See Fig. 8.* Assemble "C" frame assembly and Receiving Cup (T80T-3010-A2) on lower ball joint. *See Fig. 9,* LOWER BALL JOINT REMOVAL.

3) Turn forcing screw clockwise until lower ball joint is removed from spindle. Repeat procedure to remove upper ball joint. *See Fig. 9.*

Installation – 1) Install lower ball joint first. Assemble "C" frame assembly, Receiving Cup (T80T-3010-A3) and Installing Cup (D81T-3010-A) on lower ball joint. *See Fig. 9.* Turn forcing screw to install ball joint. Ensure ball joint is fully seated.

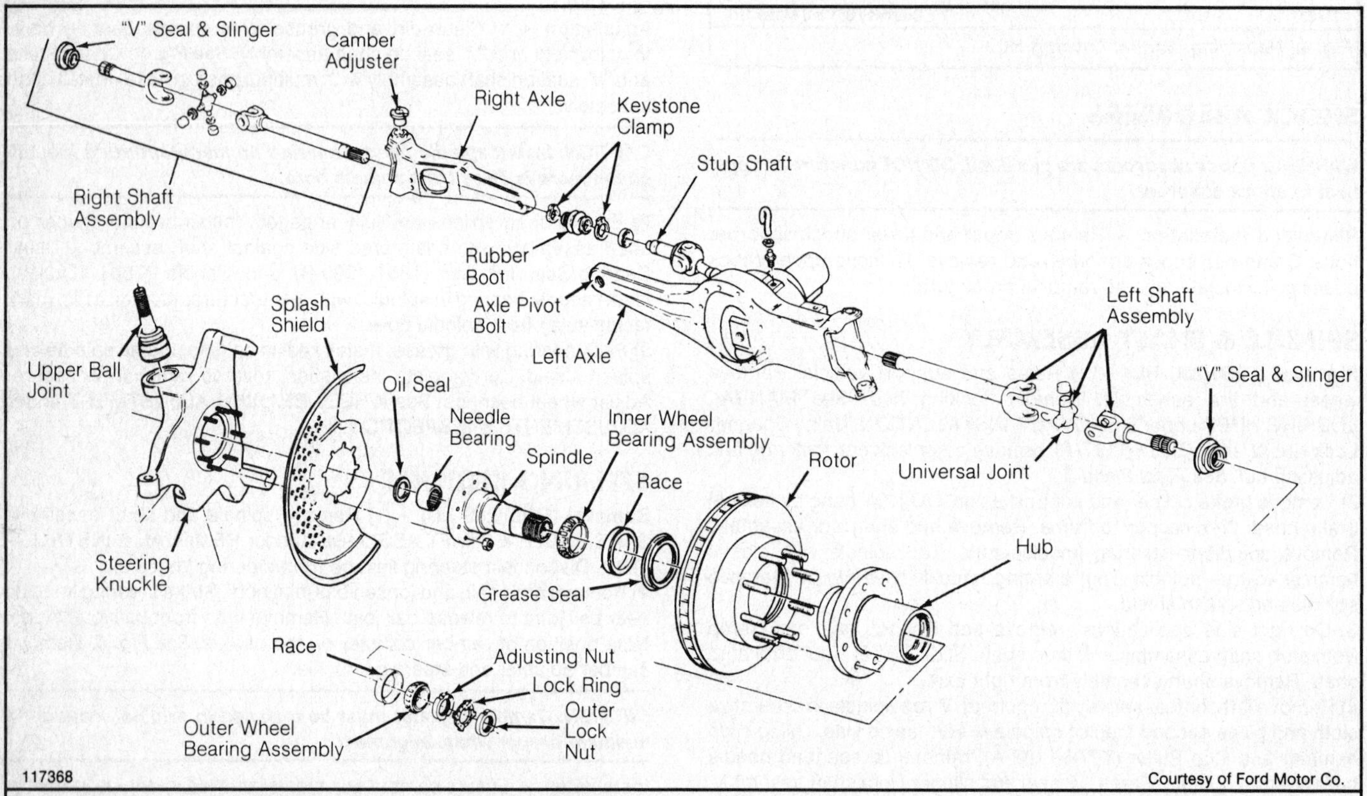
"V" Seal & Slinger
Camber Adjuster
Right Axle
Keystone Clamp
Stub Shaft
Right Shaft Assembly
Rubber Boot
Axle Pivot Bolt
Left Axle
Left Shaft Assembly
"V" Seal & Slinger
Splash Shield
Upper Ball Joint
Oil Seal
Needle Bearing
Inner Wheel Bearing Assembly
Spindle
Race
Rotor
Universal Joint
Steering Knuckle
Grease Seal
Hub
Race
Adjusting Nut
Lock Ring
Outer Lock Nut
Outer Wheel Bearing Assembly
117368
Courtesy of Ford Motor Co.

Fig. 5: Exploded View of Spindle & Components (F250/250 HD)

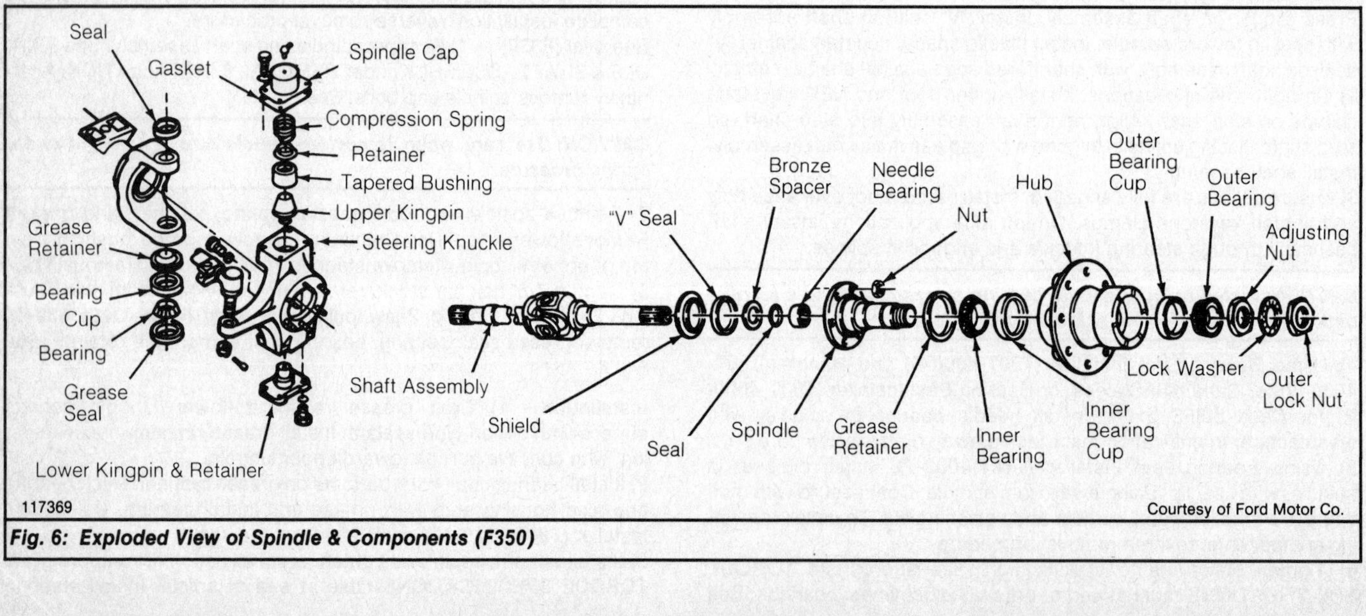
Seal
Gasket
Spindle Cap
Compression Spring
Retainer
Tapered Bushing
Upper Kingpin
Steering Knuckle
Grease Retainer
Bearing Cup
Bearing
Grease Seal
Shaft Assembly
Lower Kingpin & Retainer
"V" Seal
Bronze Spacer
Needle Bearing
Nut
Hub
Outer Bearing Cup
Outer Bearing
Adjusting Nut
Lock Washer
Outer Lock Nut
Shield
Seal
Spindle
Grease Retainer
Inner Bearing
Inner Bearing Cup
117369
Courtesy of Ford Motor Co.

Fig. 6: Exploded View of Spindle & Components (F350)

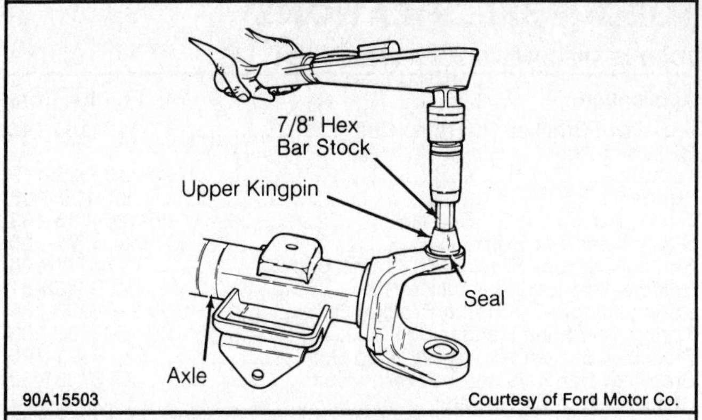
7/8" Hex
Bar Stock
Upper Kingpin
Seal
Axle
90A15503
Courtesy of Ford Motor Co.

Fig. 7: Removing Upper Kingpin (F350)

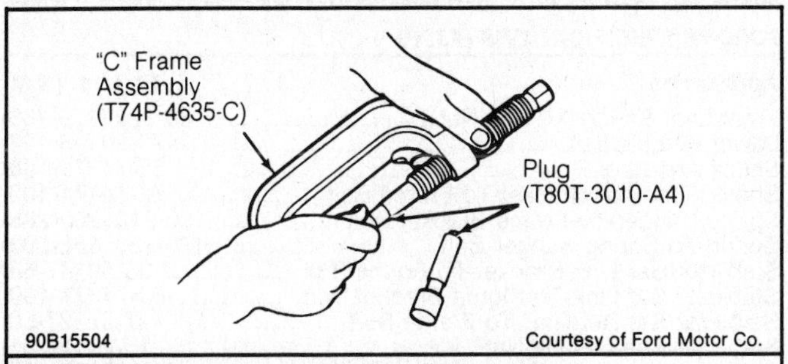
"C" Frame
Assembly
(T74P-4635-C)
Plug
(T80T-3010-A4)
90B15504
Courtesy of Ford Motor Co.

Fig. 8: Replacing Plug on "C" Frame Assembly

2) To install upper ball joint, assemble "C" frame, Receiving Cup (T80T-3010-A3) and Replacer (T80T-3010-A1). Turn forcing screw to install ball joint. Ensure ball joint is fully seated. Install snap ring on lower ball joints and install steering knuckle. See STEERING KNUCKLE under REMOVAL & INSTALLATION.

LEAF SPRING ASSEMBLY

Removal – 1) Raise and support vehicle frame, with weight off front springs and wheels touching ground. Support drive axle to prevent axle rotation. Remove lower shock absorber bolts.
2) On F350, remove track bar bolts from spring cap and track bar mounting bracket. On all models, remove "U" bolts, spring cap, and spacer plate. *See Fig. 1.* Remove spring-to-hanger bolts and remove spring.
Installation – To install, reverse removal procedure. On F350, track bar must be installed with vehicle at normal operating height.

AXLE PIVOT BUSHING

Removal (F250/250 HD) – 1) Front axle must be removed. Raise and support vehicle. Remove front wheels and brake calipers. DO NOT let brake caliper hang by flex hose. Disconnect steering linkage at steering knuckles. Support right axle with jack.
2) Remove leaf spring "U" bolts. Disconnect axle vent tube and plug opening. Remove right axle pivot bolt. Remove keystone clamps and rubber boot from shaft assembly. *See Fig. 5.* Remove right axle assembly while pulling shaft assembly from stub shaft.
3) For left axle applications, disconnect drive shaft from differential. Place jack under left axle and differential. Remove leaf spring "U" bolts. Remove left axle pivot bolt. Lower jack and remove axle.
4) Install Forcing Screw (T78P-5638-A1), Bushing Remover (T80T-5638-A1) and Receiving Cup (T78P-5638-A3) onto pivot bushing. *See Fig. 10.* Turn forcing screw and remove pivot bushing.
Installation – 1) Place new pivot bushing in axle housing bore. Install Receiving Cup (T78P-5638-A2), Forcing Screw (T78P-5638-A1) and Pivot Bushing Replacer (T80T-5638-A2) onto axle housing. *See Fig. 10.* Turn forcing screw to press bushing into bore.

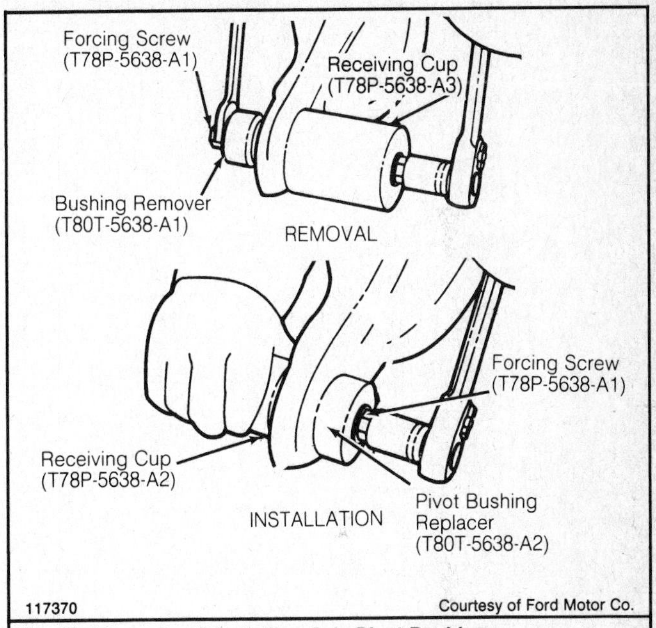
Forcing Screw
(T78P-5638-A1)
Receiving Cup
(T78P-5638-A3)
Bushing Remover
(T80T-5638-A1)
REMOVAL
Forcing Screw
(T78P-5638-A1)
Receiving Cup
(T78P-5638-A2)
INSTALLATION
Pivot Bushing
Replacer
(T80T-5638-A2)
117370
Courtesy of Ford Motor Co.

Fig. 10: Removing & Installing Axle Pivot Bushing

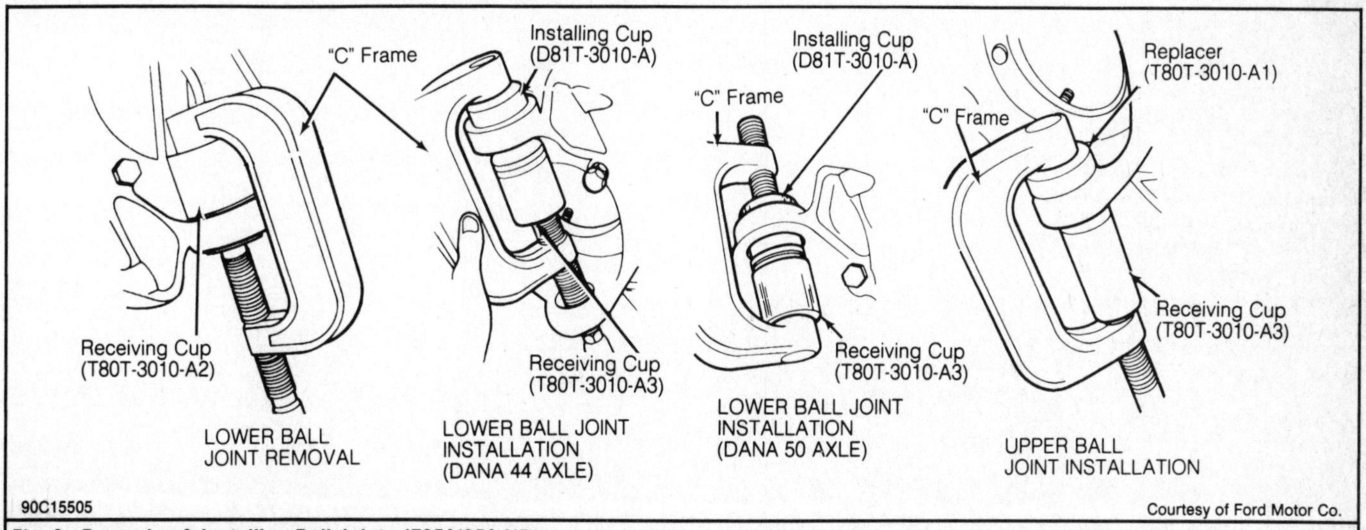
"C" Frame
Installing Cup
(D81T-3010-A)
Installing Cup
(D81T-3010-A)
"C" Frame
Replacer
(T80T-3010-A1)
"C" Frame
Receiving Cup
(T80T-3010-A3)
Receiving Cup
(T80T-3010-A2)
Receiving Cup
(T80T-3010-A3)
Receiving Cup
(T80T-3010-A3)
LOWER BALL
JOINT REMOVAL
LOWER BALL JOINT
INSTALLATION
(DANA 44 AXLE)
LOWER BALL JOINT
INSTALLATION
(DANA 50 AXLE)
UPPER BALL
JOINT INSTALLATION
90C15505
Courtesy of Ford Motor Co.

Fig. 9: Removing & Installing Ball Joints (F250/250 HD)

1991 SUSPENSION
Front – 4WD Leaf Spring (Cont.)

2) To install axle, reverse removal procedure. On right side applications, install rubber boot and NEW keystone clamps on stub shaft. Install right shaft assembly into stub shaft, so stub shaft missing spline is aligned with shaft assembly.

3) Ensure splines are fully engaged. Install rubber boot over assembly and tighten keystone clamps. To complete installation, reverse removal procedure. Check wheel alignment.

STABILIZER BAR

Removal – On F250/250 HD, remove stabilizer bar links from stabilizer bar and spring cap. On F350, remove stabilizer bar links from mount brackets. On all models, remove stabilizer bar mounts and remove stabilizer bar.

Installation – Loosely assemble entire stabilizer bar assembly. Ensure stabilizer bar bushings are seated in retainers. To complete installation, reverse removal procedure. Tighten to specifications. See appropriate TORQUE SPECIFICATIONS table.

TORQUE SPECIFICATIONS

TORQUE SPECIFICATIONS (F250/250 HD)

Application	Ft. Lbs. (N.m)
Axle Pivot Bracket-To-Frame Bolt	77-110 (104-149)
Ball Joint Nut	
Lower	90-110 (122-149)
Upper	100 (136)
Front Leaf Spring "U" Bolt Nut	85-120 (115-163)
Shock Absorber Bolt	52-74 (71-100)
Shock Absorber Bracket-To-Frame Bolt	52-74 (71-100)
Spindle-To-Steering Knuckle Nut	50-60 (68-81)
Spring Hanger-To-Frame Bracket Bolt	150-210 (203-285)
Spring-To-Spring Hanger Bolt	120-150 (163-203)
Stabilizer Bar Link-To-Spring Cap Bolt	52-74 (71-100)
Stabilizer Bar Retainer-To-Frame Bolt	27-37 (37-50)
Stabilizer Bar-To-Link Nut	15-25 (20-34)
Tie Rod End-To-Spindle Nut	52-74 (71-100)
Wheel Lug Nut	140 (190)

TORQUE SPECIFICATIONS (F350)

Application	Ft. Lbs. (N.m)
Front Leaf Spring "U" Bolt Nut	85-120 (115-163)
Lower Kingpin Bolt	70-90 (95-122)
Shock Absorber Bolt	52-74 (71-100)
Shock Absorber Bracket-To-Frame Bolt	52-74 (71-100)
Spring Hanger-To-Frame Bracket Bolt	150-210 (203-285)
Spring-To-Spring Hanger Bolt	120-150 (163-203)
Stabilizer Bar Link Bracket-To-Frame Bolt	35-50 (47-68)
Stabilizer Bar Link-To-Mount Bracket Bolt	52-74 (71-100)
Stabilizer Bar Retainer-To-Frame Bolt	27-37 (37-50)
Stabilizer Bar-To-Link Nut	15-25 (20-34)
Steering Linkage-To-Steering Knuckle Nut	70-100 (95-136)
Tie Rod End-To-Spindle Nut	52-74 (71-100)
Track Bar Mount Bracket-To-Frame Bolt	77-110 (104-149)
Track Bar-To-Mount Bolt	120-150 (163-203)
Upper Kingpin To Spindle	500-600 (678-813)
Wheel Lug Nut	140 (190)

1991 STEERING
Steering Columns – Aerostar, Explorer & Ranger

DESCRIPTION

Steering columns are available in standard and tilt column models. Both models are of modular design. Wiper/washer, turn signal/hazard, horn/dimmer and ignition switches are mounted on column. Switches can be serviced by removing upper column shroud and steering wheel.

The energy-absorbing steering column collapses upon frontal impact. A cylindrical impact bumper is used on upper bracket to absorb impact loads. Key release button prevents inadvertent locking of steering wheel. Ignition switch is operated by a pin, mounted on lock actuator rack. It is pinion-driven by rotating ignition key.

ADJUSTMENTS

IGNITION SWITCH

NOTE: Ignition switch on Aerostar cannot be adjusted. If problem exists with ignition switch, replace switch.

Explorer & Ranger – 1) Ignition switch is properly adjusted if:
- In ACCESSORY, accessory circuit is operative and steering wheel is locked. Automatic shift lever cannot be moved.
- In LOCK, all ignition switch electrical circuits are inoperative and steering wheel is locked. Automatic shift lever cannot be moved.
- In OFF, all ignition switch electrical circuits are inoperative and steering wheel is unlocked. Automatic shift lever can be moved.
- In ON (RUN), all ignition switch circuits or accessory circuits are operative except starter circuit and warning light check circuit. Steering wheel is unlocked and automatic shift lever can be moved.
- In START, only engine ignition, warning light check and starter circuits are operative. Steering wheel is unlocked and automatic shift lever can be moved.

2) On all models, disconnect negative battery cable. Locate ignition switch on top of steering column tube. Remove ignition switch connector. Rotate ignition key back and forth to each side of LOCK position until a 5/64 inch (1.98 mm) drill bit can be inserted into ignition switch lock pin hole.
3) Loosen 2 ignition switch mounting nuts, turn key to LOCK position (feel for detent) and remove ignition key from cylinder. Move switch up or down along column tube. Locate mid-position of rod lash. Tighten 2 mounting nuts to 40-65 INCH lbs. (4.51-7.34 N.m).
4) Remove drill bit. Plug in electrical connector. Confirm all accessories are deactivated when switch is in OFF position. Ensure all modes function correctly.

REMOVAL & INSTALLATION

STEERING WHEEL & HORN PAD

Removal & Installation – 1) Disconnect negative battery cable. Remove horn cover retaining screws. Disconnect horn switch and speed control electrical connectors. Remove horn cover.
2) Set front wheels in straight-ahead position. Mark steering wheel and shaft for installation reference. Remove steering wheel retaining bolt. Using Steering Wheel Remover (T67L-3600-A), remove steering wheel.
3) To install, reverse removal procedure. Tighten steering wheel retaining bolt to specification. See TORQUE SPECIFICATIONS table at end of article.

TURN SIGNAL & HAZARD FLASHER SWITCH

Removal & Installation (Aerostar) – 1) Disconnect negative battery cable. Remove steering wheel. See STEERING WHEEL & HORN PAD under REMOVAL & INSTALLATION. On tilt columns, remove upper extension shroud. Remove steering column shroud.
2) Remove lock cylinder. See LOCK CYLINDER under REMOVAL & INSTALLATION. Remove turn signal switch lever by grasping, pulling and twisting. Remove turn signal switch. To install, reverse removal procedure.

MULTIFUNCTION SWITCH

Removal & Installation (Explorer & Ranger) – Disconnect negative battery cable. Remove steering column shroud. Remove 2 screws attaching multifunction switch to steering column. Disconnect electrical connector. Remove switch. To install, reverse removal procedure.

LOCK CYLINDER

Removal & Installation (With Key) – 1) Disconnect negative battery cable. Remove trim shroud. Remove electrical connector from key warning switch. Turn ignition switch to ON position. On Ranger and Explorer A/T models, shift selector must be in Park. On all models, place a 1/8" (3.17 mm) diameter pin in hole located in outer edge of lock cylinder housing.
2) Depress retaining pin and pull out lock cylinder. *See Fig. 1.* To install, lube lock cylinder. Turn lock cylinder to ON position. Depress retaining pin. Insert lock cylinder into housing. To install remaining components, reverse removal procedure.

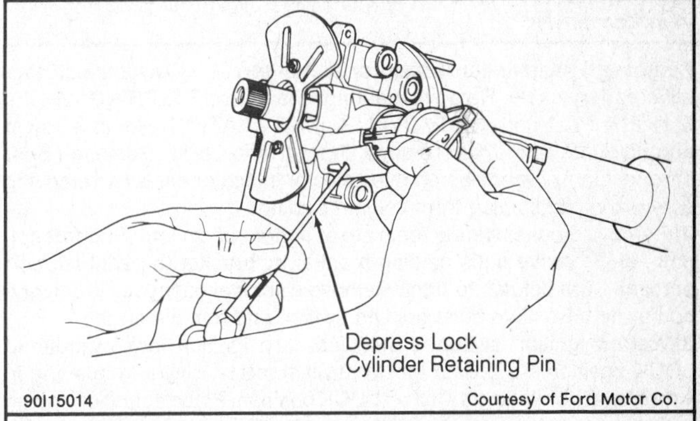
Depress Lock
Cylinder Retaining Pin
90I15014
Courtesy of Ford Motor Co.

Fig. 1: Removing Ignition Lock Cylinder (Typical)

Removal (Without Key) – 1) Use this procedure to remove ignition lock cylinder if key is missing or cylinder is frozen. Disconnect negative battery cable. Remove steering wheel. See STEERING WHEEL & HORN PAD under REMOVAL & INSTALLATION. Remove steering column trim shrouds and connector from key warning switch. Use a 1/8" (3.17 mm) drill bit to drill out retaining pin. DO NOT drill deeper than 1/2" (12.7 mm).
2) Place a chisel at base of lock cylinder cap. Using a hammer, strike chisel with sharp blows to break cap away from lock cylinder. Using a 3/8" (9.52 mm) drill bit, drill out center of lock cylinder key slot. Drill down approximately 1 3/4" (44 mm) until lock cylinder breaks away from base of lock cylinder.
3) Remove metal shavings from lock cylinder housing. Remove snap ring, washer and lock cylinder drive gear. Thoroughly clean all metal shavings and other foreign materials from housing. Carefully inspect housing for damage. If damage is apparent, replace housing.
Installation – 1) Install ignition lock drive gear, washer and snap ring. Lubricate cylinder cavity with lock cylinder lubricant. Turn ignition switch to RUN position. Depress retaining pin and insert new lock cylinder into lock cylinder housing.
2) Ensure cylinder is fully seated and aligned into interlocking washer (Aerostar) or drive gear (Explorer/Ranger) before turning key to OFF position. Use key to rotate cylinder, ensuring correct mechanical operation in all positions.
3) Install electrical connector into key warning switch. Connect negative battery cable. Check ignition switch functions, and ensure column locks when switch is in LOCK position.

1991 STEERING
Steering Columns – Aerostar, Explorer & Ranger (Cont.)

IGNITION SWITCH

Removal & Installation (Aerostar) – 1) Disconnect negative battery cable. Rotate lock cylinder to LOCK position. Remove steering wheel. See STEERING WHEEL & HORN PAD under REMOVAL INSTALLATION. On tilt columns, remove upper extension housing by squeezing at 6 and 12 o'clock positions. Remove panel on right side of steering column by removing 2 screws and pulling outward. Remove 4 screws holding trim shroud, and swing bottom panel open. Remove 2 screws attaching shroud to retaining plate.

2) Remove key lock cylinder. Remove shroud by first raising left side past turn signal lever, and then pulling right side up past lock cylinder boss until it clears lock cylinder. Shroud can now be worked past instrument panel.

3) Disconnect ignition switch electrical connector. Remove break-off head bolts retaining switch to lock cylinder housing. Remove switch from actuator pin. Install replacement switch by aligning holes on switch casting base with holes in cylinder housing.

4) Tighten new break-off head bolts until they break off, approximately 18-26 ft. lbs. (4-6 N.m). Install electrical connector to switch. Rotate key in lock cylinder to RUN position, and install lock cylinder. To install, reverse removal procedures.

NOTE: Ensure new switch is placed in RUN position. Minor movement of switch may be needed to align actuator pin with "U" shaped slot in switch carrier.

Removal & Installation (Explorer & Ranger) – 1) Disconnect negative battery cable. Remove steering wheel. See STEERING WHEEL & HORN PAD under REMOVAL & INSTALLATION. Remove lower shroud. On tilt columns, remove tilt lever and collar. Remove upper shroud. On A/T models, remove selector indicator cable by removing screw and plastic plug from column casting.

2) Remove 5 bolts holding toe plate at bottom of column. Support column, and remove bolts holding breakaway bracket to pedal support bracket. Turn column to right. Remove electrical connector from ignition switch. Remove bolts holding switch, and remove switch.

3) Before ignition switch is installed, turn ignition lock cylinder to LOCK position. To preset ignition switch, place a wire in opening in side of switch, pinning switch in LOCK position. Place actuation rod on switch and switch on column studs while aligning rod hole with rod. Tighten nuts to 3.3-5.3 ft. lbs. (4.5-7.2 N.m).

4) Ensure switch is operating smoothly and all functions are engaged. Turn key through each position from LOCK to START. If all positions are not correct with key operation, see ADJUSTMENTS. To install, reverse removal procedures.

STEERING COLUMN

Removal & Installation (Aerostar) – 1) Disconnect negative battery cable. Remove bolt attaching intermediate shaft to steering column shaft. Compress intermediate shaft until clear of steering column shaft.

2) Remove steering wheel. See STEERING WHEEL & HORN PAD under REMOVAL & INSTALLATION. Remove steering column trim shrouds. On tilt columns, remove upper extension shroud by squeezing it at 6 and 12 o'clock positions.

3) On all models, remove steering column cover on instrument panel. Disconnect all electrical connections to steering column switches. Loosen steering column-to-lower instrument panel bracket bolts. DO NOT remove bolts.

4) Remove screws attaching steering column toe plate to dash. Support steering column. Remove steering column-to-lower instrument panel bracket bolts. Lower steering column, and remove from vehicle.

5) To install steering column, reverse removal procedure. Tighten all nuts and bolts to specifications. See TORQUE SPECIFICATIONS table at end of article.

Removal & Installation (Explorer & Ranger) – 1) Disconnect negative battery cable. On A/T models, place transmission in Neutral. On all models, remove bolt attaching intermediate shaft-to-steering column shaft. Compress intermediate shaft until clear of steering column shaft.

2) On A/T models, remove nuts attaching shift cable bracket to steering column bracket. Disconnect shift cable from column lever. On tilt columns, ensure steering wheel is in full-up position before removing steering wheel.

3) On all models, remove steering wheel. See STEERING WHEEL & HORN PAD under REMOVAL & INSTALLATION. On tilt columns, remove tilt lever. Remove steering column collar by squeezing it at 6 and 12 o'clock positions.

4) On all models, remove screws attaching panel trim cover. Remove trim cover. Remove screws from bottom of steering panel shroud. Remove bottom half of shroud by pulling shroud down and toward rear of vehicle. Lift top half of shroud from column.

5) On A/T models, disconnect selector indicator actuation cable by removing screw from column casting and plastic plug at end of cable. To remove plastic plug from shift lever socket casting, push on nose of plug until head clears casting, and then pull plug from casting.

6) On all models, remove plastic clip holding multifunction switch wiring to steering column bracket. Remove screws attaching multifunction switch. Remove multifunction switch from column, leaving wiring connected to switch. Position switch and wiring aside.

7) Disconnect key warning buzzer electrical connector from horn brush. Remove screw holding horn brush electrical connector to column. Remove horn brush electrical connector. Remove screws attaching toe plate-to-dash panel. Loosen toe plate clamp bolt.

8) Support steering column, and remove bolts holding steering column to instrument panel bracket. Disconnect ignition switch wiring connector. Carefully remove column from vehicle.

9) To install steering column, reverse removal procedure. Tighten all nuts and bolts to specifications. See TORQUE SPECIFICATIONS table at end of article.

OVERHAUL

When overhauling steering columns, refer to exploded view illustrations. *See Figs. 2-7.*

1991 STEERING
Steering Columns – Aerostar, Explorer & Ranger (Cont.)

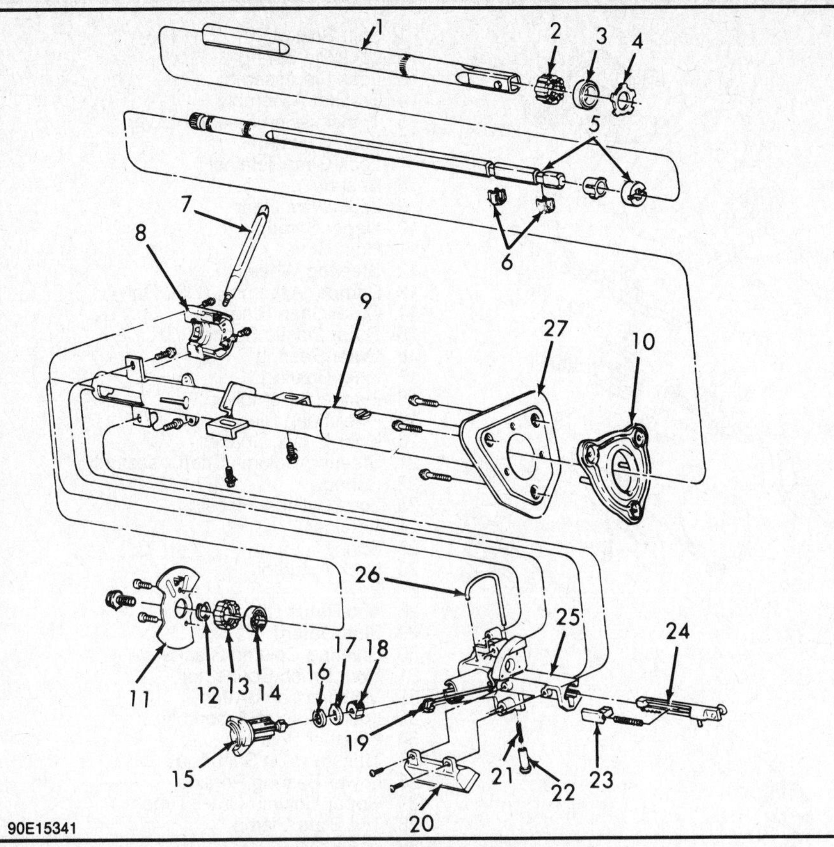

1. Lower Steering Shaft
2. Lower Bearing Sleeve
3. Lower Bearing
4. Lower Bearing Retainer
5. Upper Steering Shaft Assembly
6. Anti-Rattle Clip
7. Turn Signal Switch Handle
8. Turn Signal & Emergency Flasher Switch
9. Column Outer Tube Assembly
10. Steering Column Lower Seal
11. Steering Column Retainer Plate
12. Upper Bearing Retainer
13. Upper Bearing Sleeve
14. Upper Steering Column Bearing
15. Lock Cylinder
16. Snap Ring
17. Lock Cylinder Bearing
18. Lock Cylinder Gear
19. Ignition Key Warning Switch
20. Ignition Switch Assembly
21. Lock Actuator Knob Spring
22. Lock Actuator Knob
23. Lock Pawl
24. Steering Column Lock Actuator
25. Steering Column Lock Housing
26. Steering Column Lock Actuator Lever
27. Steering Column Toe Plate

90E15341

Courtesy of Ford Motor Co.

Fig. 2: Exploded View of Standard Steering Column (Aerostar)

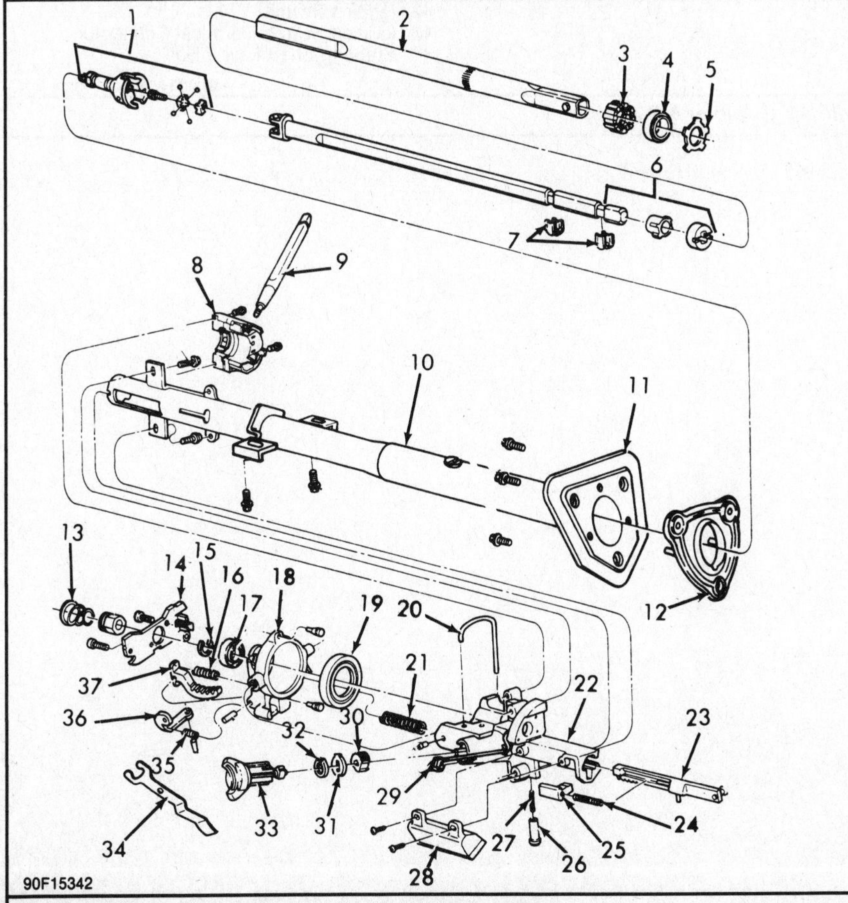

1. Upper Steering Shaft Coupling
2. Lower Steering Shaft
3. Lower Bearing Sleeve
4. Lower Bearing
5. Lower Bearing Retainer
6. Upper Steering Shaft Assembly
7. Anti-Rattle Clip
8. Turn Signal & Emergency Flasher Switch
9. Turn Signal Switch Handle
10. Column Outer Tube Assembly
11. Steering Column Toe Plate
12. Steering Column Lower Seal
13. Upper Bearing Spring
14. Steering Column Retainer Plate
15. Upper Bearing Snap Ring
16. Column Locking Lever Spring
17. Steering Column Upper Bearing
18. Upper Tube Flange
19. Upper Bearing Assembly
20. Lock Actuator Lever
21. Column Position Spring
22. Column Lock Cylinder Housing
23. Column Lock Actuator Assembly
24. Steering Column Lock Spring
25. Steering Column Lock Pawl
26. Column Lock Actuator Knob
27. Column Lock Actuator Spring
28. Ignition Switch Assembly
29. Ignition Key Warning Switch
30. Lock Cylinder Gear
31. Lock Cylinder Bearing
32. Lock Cylinder Bearing Snap Ring
33. Lock Cylinder
34. Lock Actuator Cover
35. Column Release Lever Spring
36. Column Release Lever
37. Column Locking Lever

90F15342

Courtesy of Ford Motor Co.

Fig. 3: Exploded View of Tilt Steering Column (Aerostar)

Steering Columns – Aerostar, Explorer & Ranger (Cont.)

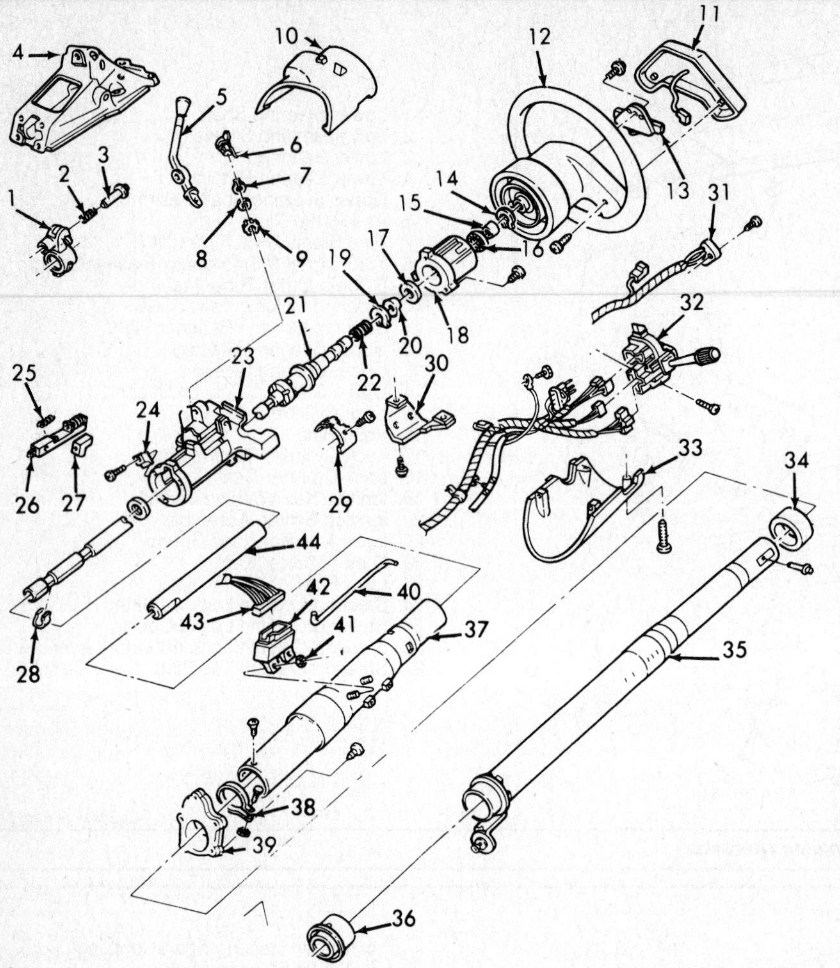

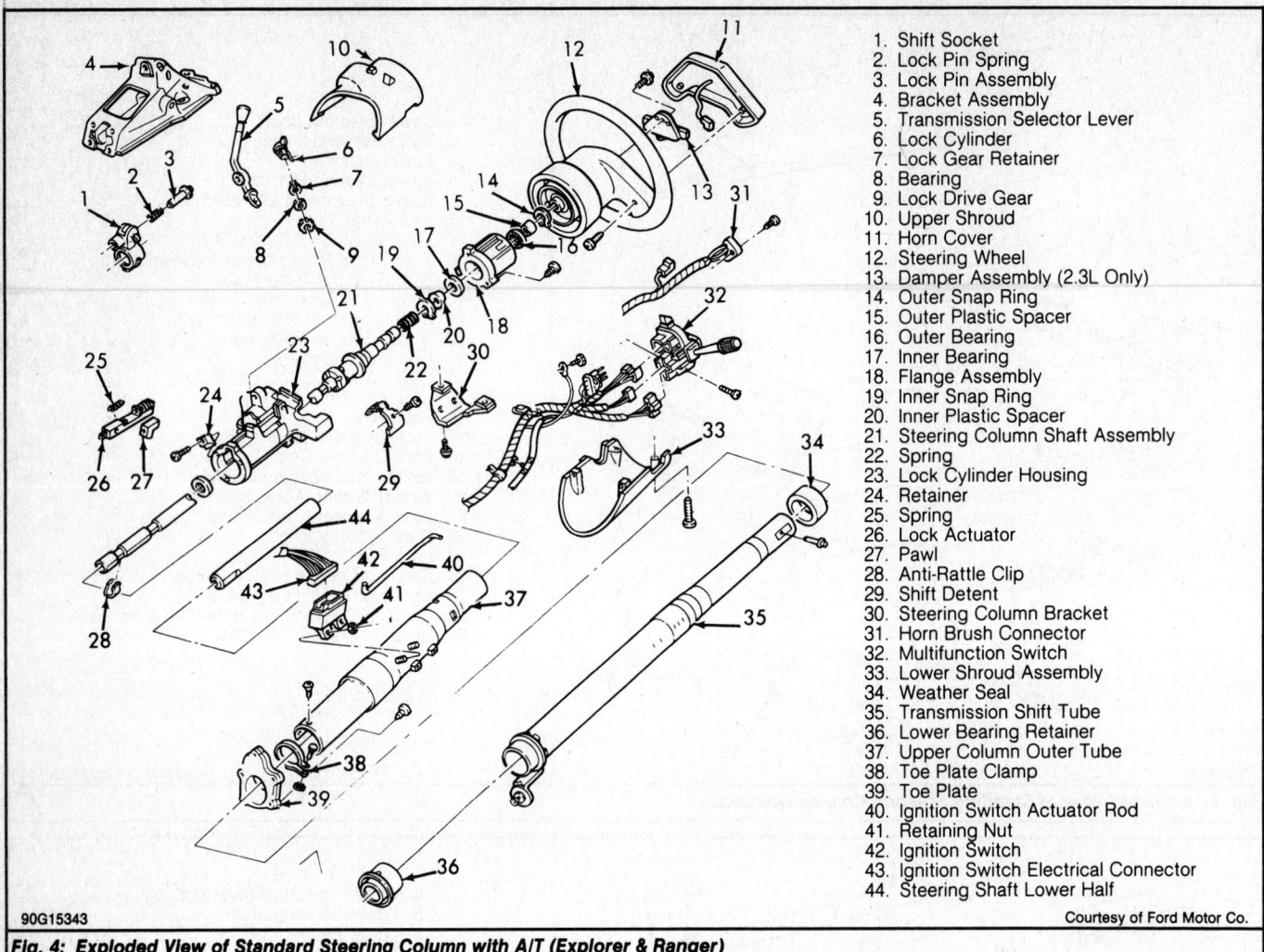

1. Shift Socket
2. Lock Pin Spring
3. Lock Pin Assembly
4. Bracket Assembly
5. Transmission Selector Lever
6. Lock Cylinder
7. Lock Gear Retainer
8. Bearing
9. Lock Drive Gear
10. Upper Shroud
11. Horn Cover
12. Steering Wheel
13. Damper Assembly (2.3L Only)
14. Outer Snap Ring
15. Outer Plastic Spacer
16. Outer Bearing
17. Inner Bearing
18. Flange Assembly
19. Inner Snap Ring
20. Inner Plastic Spacer
21. Steering Column Shaft Assembly
22. Spring
23. Lock Cylinder Housing
24. Retainer
25. Spring
26. Lock Actuator
27. Pawl
28. Anti-Rattle Clip
29. Shift Detent
30. Steering Column Bracket
31. Horn Brush Connector
32. Multifunction Switch
33. Lower Shroud Assembly
34. Weather Seal
35. Transmission Shift Tube
36. Lower Bearing Retainer
37. Upper Column Outer Tube
38. Toe Plate Clamp
39. Toe Plate
40. Ignition Switch Actuator Rod
41. Retaining Nut
42. Ignition Switch
43. Ignition Switch Electrical Connector
44. Steering Shaft Lower Half

90G15343

Courtesy of Ford Motor Co.

Fig. 4: Exploded View of Standard Steering Column with A/T (Explorer & Ranger)

1991 STEERING
Steering Columns – Aerostar, Explorer & Ranger (Cont.)

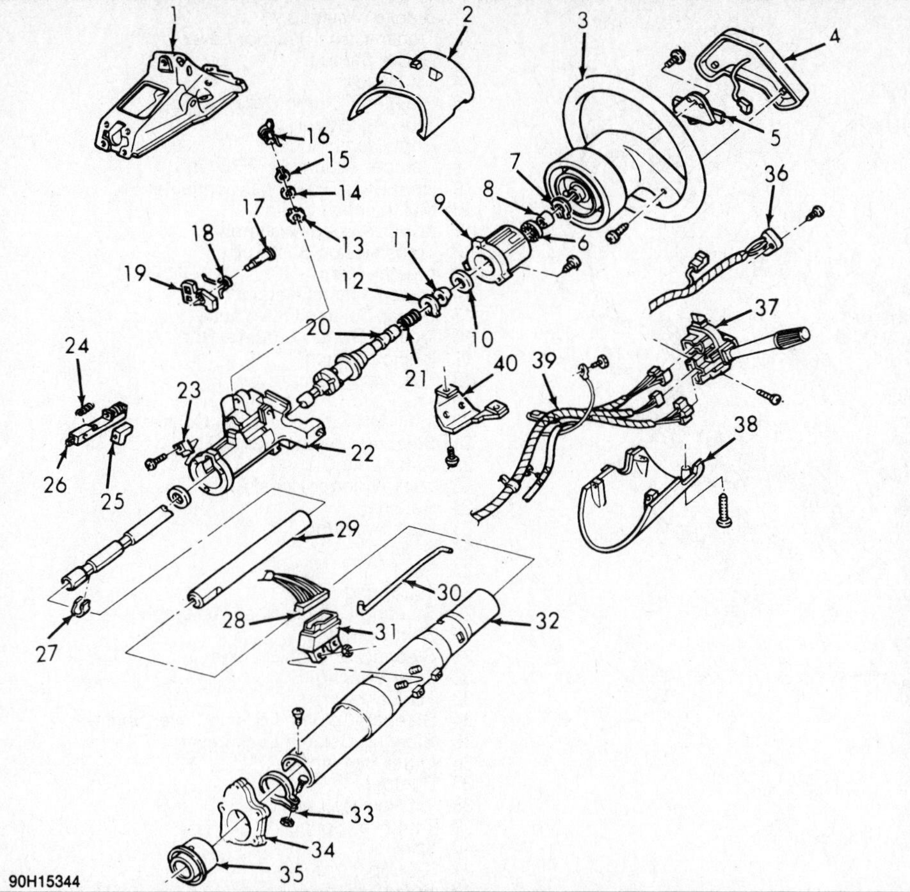
90H15344

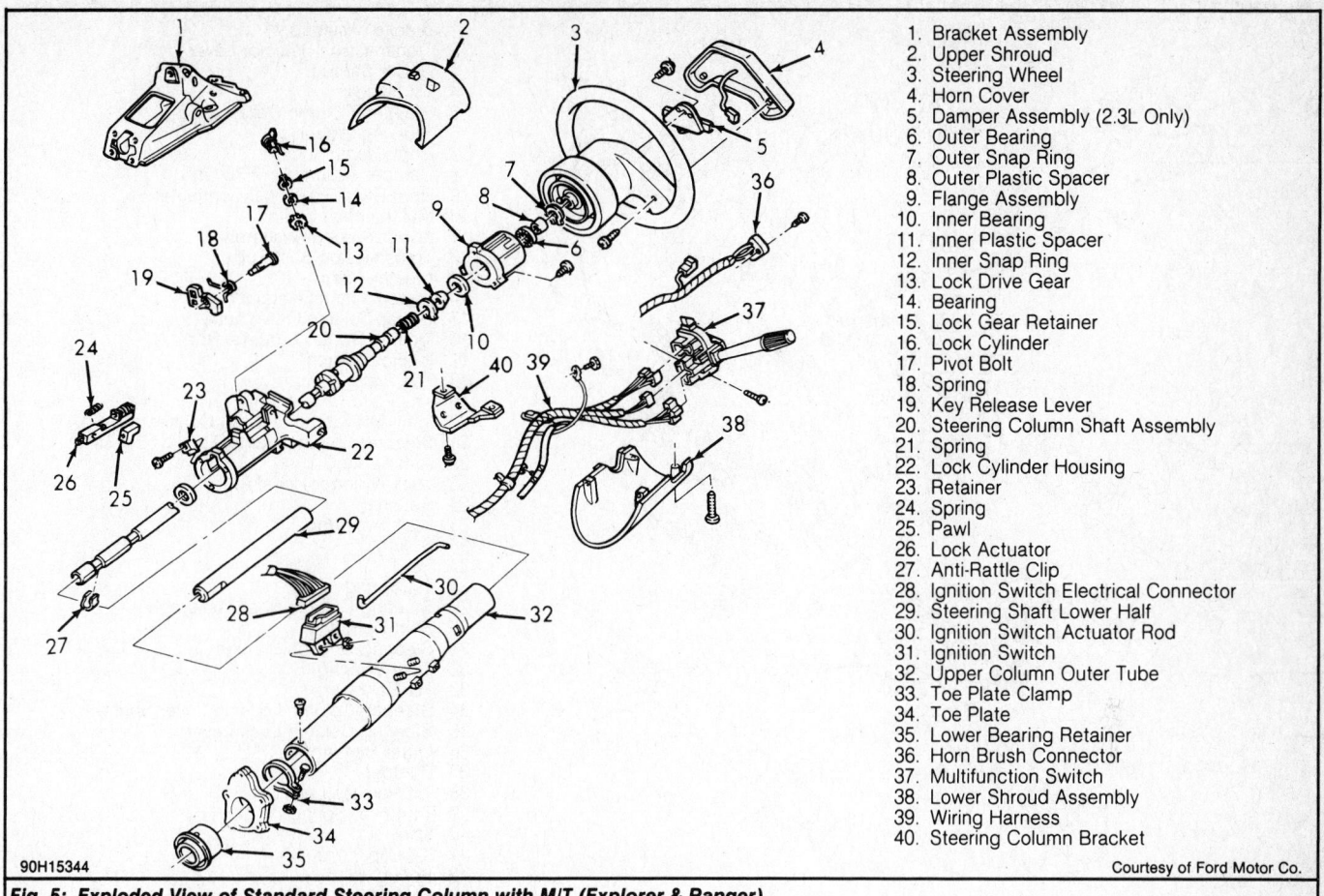

1. Bracket Assembly
2. Upper Shroud
3. Steering Wheel
4. Horn Cover
5. Damper Assembly (2.3L Only)
6. Outer Bearing
7. Outer Snap Ring
8. Outer Plastic Spacer
9. Flange Assembly
10. Inner Bearing
11. Inner Plastic Spacer
12. Inner Snap Ring
13. Lock Drive Gear
14. Bearing
15. Lock Gear Retainer
16. Lock Cylinder
17. Pivot Bolt
18. Spring
19. Key Release Lever
20. Steering Column Shaft Assembly
21. Spring
22. Lock Cylinder Housing
23. Retainer
24. Spring
25. Pawl
26. Lock Actuator
27. Anti-Rattle Clip
28. Ignition Switch Electrical Connector
29. Steering Shaft Lower Half
30. Ignition Switch Actuator Rod
31. Ignition Switch
32. Upper Column Outer Tube
33. Toe Plate Clamp
34. Toe Plate
35. Lower Bearing Retainer
36. Horn Brush Connector
37. Multifunction Switch
38. Lower Shroud Assembly
39. Wiring Harness
40. Steering Column Bracket

Courtesy of Ford Motor Co.

Fig. 5: Exploded View of Standard Steering Column with M/T (Explorer & Ranger)

Steering Columns – Aerostar, Explorer & Ranger (Cont.)

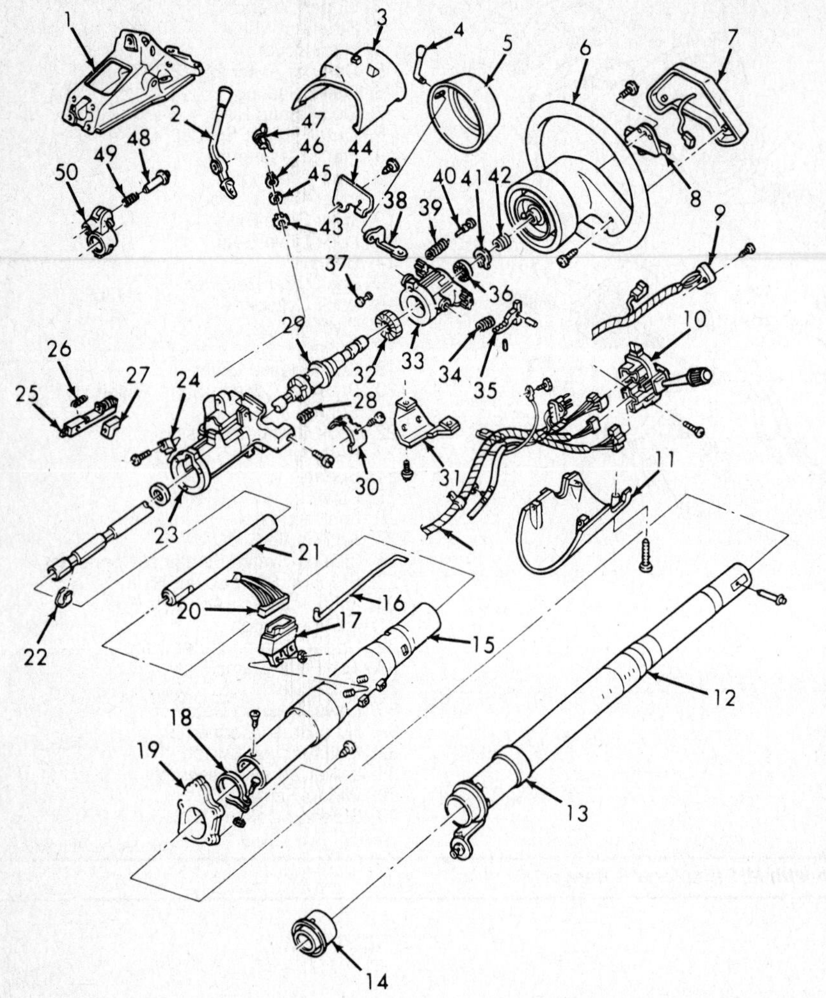

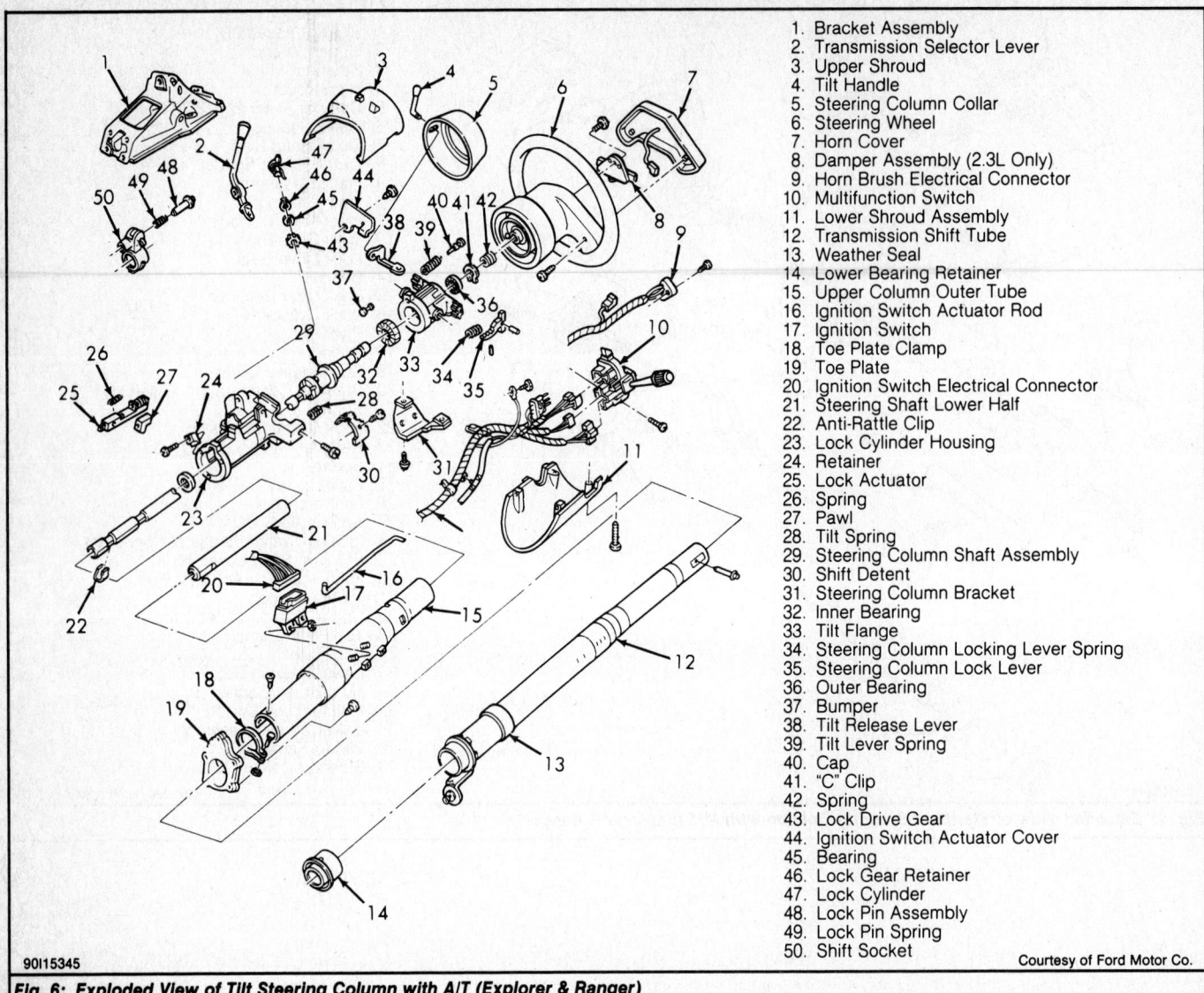

1. Bracket Assembly
2. Transmission Selector Lever
3. Upper Shroud
4. Tilt Handle
5. Steering Column Collar
6. Steering Wheel
7. Horn Cover
8. Damper Assembly (2.3L Only)
9. Horn Brush Electrical Connector
10. Multifunction Switch
11. Lower Shroud Assembly
12. Transmission Shift Tube
13. Weather Seal
14. Lower Bearing Retainer
15. Upper Column Outer Tube
16. Ignition Switch Actuator Rod
17. Ignition Switch
18. Toe Plate Clamp
19. Toe Plate
20. Ignition Switch Electrical Connector
21. Steering Shaft Lower Half
22. Anti-Rattle Clip
23. Lock Cylinder Housing
24. Retainer
25. Lock Actuator
26. Spring
27. Pawl
28. Tilt Spring
29. Steering Column Shaft Assembly
30. Shift Detent
31. Steering Column Bracket
32. Inner Bearing
33. Tilt Flange
34. Steering Column Locking Lever Spring
35. Steering Column Lock Lever
36. Outer Bearing
37. Bumper
38. Tilt Release Lever
39. Tilt Lever Spring
40. Cap
41. "C" Clip
42. Spring
43. Lock Drive Gear
44. Ignition Switch Actuator Cover
45. Bearing
46. Lock Gear Retainer
47. Lock Cylinder
48. Lock Pin Assembly
49. Lock Pin Spring
50. Shift Socket

90I15345

Courtesy of Ford Motor Co.

Fig. 6: Exploded View of Tilt Steering Column with A/T (Explorer & Ranger)

1991 STEERING

Steering Columns – Aerostar, Explorer & Ranger (Cont.)

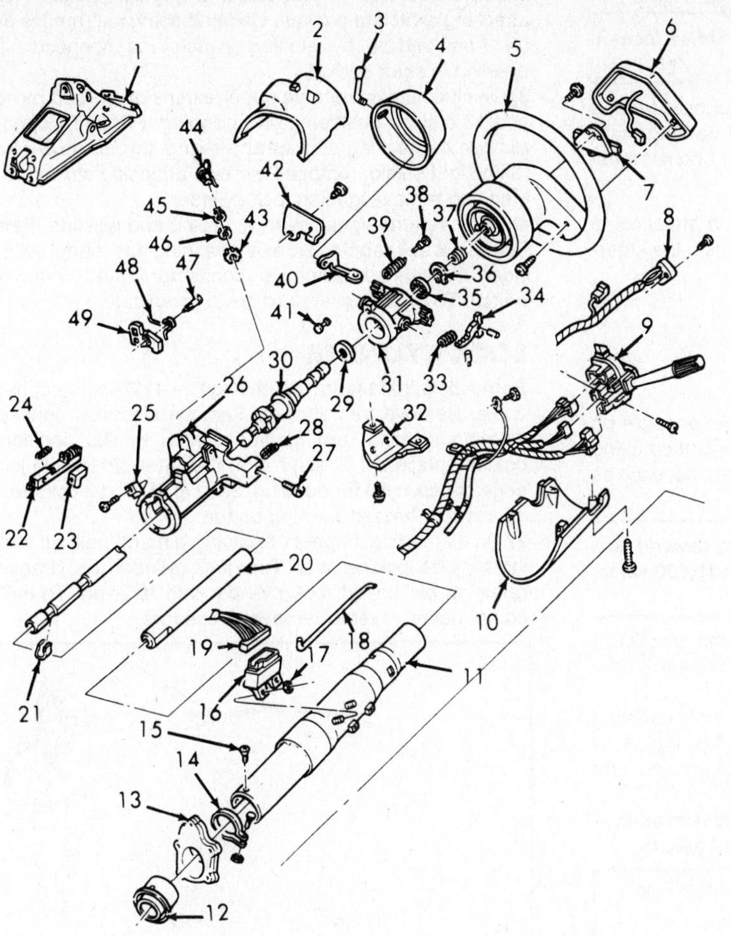

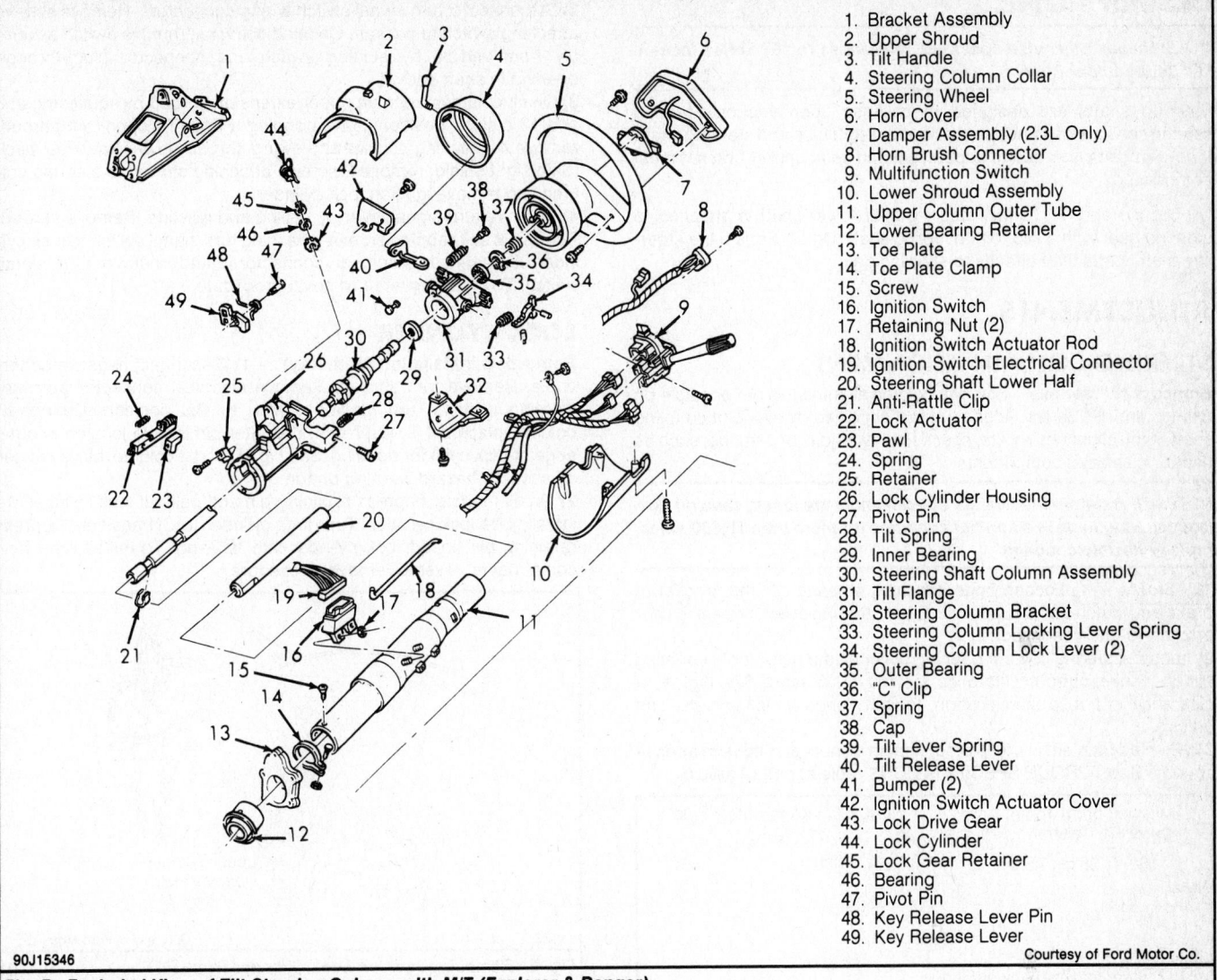

1. Bracket Assembly
2. Upper Shroud
3. Tilt Handle
4. Steering Column Collar
5. Steering Wheel
6. Horn Cover
7. Damper Assembly (2.3L Only)
8. Horn Brush Connector
9. Multifunction Switch
10. Lower Shroud Assembly
11. Upper Column Outer Tube
12. Lower Bearing Retainer
13. Toe Plate
14. Toe Plate Clamp
15. Screw
16. Ignition Switch
17. Retaining Nut (2)
18. Ignition Switch Actuator Rod
19. Ignition Switch Electrical Connector
20. Steering Shaft Lower Half
21. Anti-Rattle Clip
22. Lock Actuator
23. Pawl
24. Spring
25. Retainer
26. Lock Cylinder Housing
27. Pivot Pin
28. Tilt Spring
29. Inner Bearing
30. Steering Shaft Column Assembly
31. Tilt Flange
32. Steering Column Bracket
33. Steering Column Locking Lever Spring
34. Steering Column Lock Lever (2)
35. Outer Bearing
36. "C" Clip
37. Spring
38. Cap
39. Tilt Lever Spring
40. Tilt Release Lever
41. Bumper (2)
42. Ignition Switch Actuator Cover
43. Lock Drive Gear
44. Lock Cylinder
45. Lock Gear Retainer
46. Bearing
47. Pivot Pin
48. Key Release Lever Pin
49. Key Release Lever

90J15346

Courtesy of Ford Motor Co.

Fig. 7: Exploded View of Tilt Steering Column with M/T (Explorer & Ranger)

TORQUE SPECIFICATIONS

TORQUE SPECIFICATIONS

Application	Ft. Lbs. (N.m)
Column-To-Instrument Panel Bracket Bolts	
Aerostar	11-17 (15-23)
Explorer & Ranger	19-27 (25-36)
Column Toe Plate-To-Dash Screws	
Aerostar	11-17 (15-23)
Cylinder Housing-To-Bracket Bolts	13-20 (17-28)
Intermediate Shaft-To-Steering Column Shaft	
Aerostar	30-42 (41-57)
Explorer & Ranger	25-35 (34-47)
Shift Cable Bracket Bolt	
Explorer & Ranger	13-22 (18-30)
Steering Wheel Retaining Bolt	23-33 (31-45)
	INCH Lbs. (N.m)
Column Toe Plate-To-Dash Screws	
Explorer & Ranger	60-96 (7-11)
Multifunction Switch Screws	
Explorer & Ranger	18-26 (2-3)
Toe Plate Clamp	
Explorer & Ranger	72-156 (25-36)

1991 STEERING
Steering Columns – Bronco, "E" & "F" Series

DESCRIPTION

NOTE: Unless otherwise specified, references to "F" Series include "F" Series Super Duty.

Steering shafts are designed to collapse upon impact. Steering column consists of an outer tube, internal shift tube and steering shaft. If column collapses due to impact, column and support bracket must be replaced.

On Bronco and "F" Series, steering gear lower shaft is attached to steering gear with a slip-joint coupling shaft. On "E" Series, the steering shaft is attached directly to steering gear.

ADJUSTMENTS

STEERING COLUMN ALIGNMENT

Bronco & "F" Series – Steering column alignment is not possible on Bronco and "F" Series. Alignment is maintained by slip-joint coupling shaft. If misalignment exists, check for indications of damage, such as bent or displaced components.

NOTE: If it is determined flange coupling nuts are loose, causing flexible coupling to be in a non-flat condition for more than 12,000 miles, replace flexible coupling.

"E" Series – 1) Loosen bolts attaching steering column bracket to brake and clutch pedal support. Loosen steering column opening cover plate-to-dash panel bolts.
2) Loosen steering column opening cover clamp bolt. Verify coupling pin to flange cut-out clearance is .160 (4.06 mm). *See Fig. 1.* If clearance is not to specification, loosen flange coupling nuts, and adjust.
3) When adjustment is completed, tighten all nuts and bolts to specifications. See TORQUE SPECIFICATIONS table at end of article.

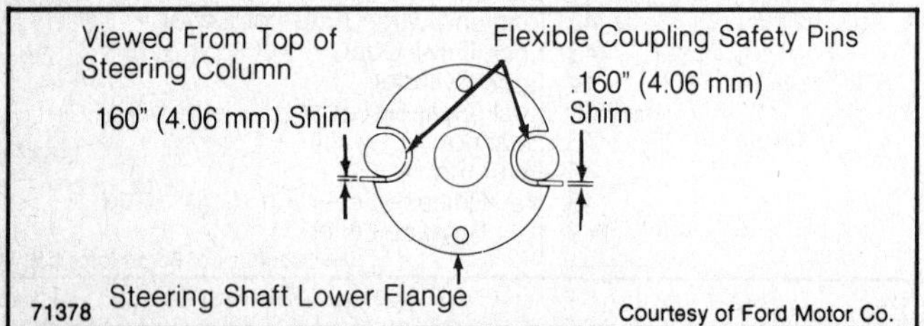
Viewed From Top of
Steering Column
Flexible Coupling Safety Pins
160" (4.06 mm) Shim
.160" (4.06 mm)
Shim
Steering Shaft Lower Flange
71378
Courtesy of Ford Motor Co.

Fig. 1: Aligning Steering Column ("E" Series)

REMOVAL & INSTALLATION

STEERING WHEEL & HORN PAD

Removal & Installation – 1) Disconnect negative battery cable. Remove horn cover retaining screws. Disconnect horn switch and speed control electrical connectors (if equipped). Remove horn cover.
2) Set front wheels in straight-ahead position. Place reference marks on steering wheel and shaft for installation reference. Remove steering wheel retaining bolt. Remove steering wheel using Steering Wheel Remover (T67L-3600-A).
3) To install, reverse removal procedure. Tighten steering wheel retaining bolt to specification. See TORQUE SPECIFICATIONS table at end of article.

TURN SIGNAL & HAZARD FLASHER SWITCH

Removal & Installation – 1) Disconnect negative battery cable. Remove horn pad switch and steering wheel. See STEERING WHEEL & HORN PAD under REMOVAL & INSTALLATION. Unscrew turn signal switch lever from steering column. Remove column shroud.
2) Disconnect 2 turn signal switch wiring connectors. Remove screws attaching switch to column. On fixed columns, remove switch assembly from vehicle by guiding switch and connector plug through opening in shaft socket.
3) On tilt columns, remove upper extension shroud by squeezing at 6 and 12 o'clock positions, and popping it free. To open trim shroud, remove 4 attaching screws and swing shroud downward. Peel back foam sight shield, remove 2 screws attaching shroud to steering column and remove ignition lock cylinder.
4) Remove turn signal lever by pulling and twisting. Remove shroud. Remove 2 self-tapping screws attaching turn signal switch to lock cylinder. Disconnect electrical connectors, and remove turn signal switch. To install, reverse removal procedure.

LOCK CYLINDER

Removal & Installation (With Key) – 1) Disconnect negative battery cable. Remove trim shroud. Remove electrical connector from key warning switch. Turn ignition switch to ON position. On non-tilt column, place a 1/8" (3.17 mm) diameter pin in hole located in outer edge of lock cylinder housing. *See Fig. 2.* On tilt column, pin is located adjacent to hazard warning button.
2) On all models, depress retaining pin and pull out lock cylinder. To install, lube lock cylinder. Turn lock cylinder to ON position. Depress retaining pin. Insert lock cylinder into housing. To install remaining components, reverse removal procedure.

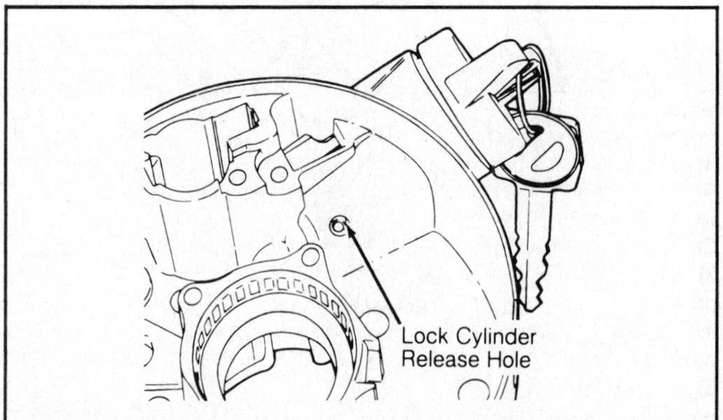
Lock Cylinder
Release Hole
15227
Courtesy of Ford Motor Co.

Fig. 2: Removing Ignition Lock Cylinder (Non-Tilt)

Removal (Without Key, Non-Tilt) – 1) Use this procedure to remove ignition lock cylinder if key is missing or cylinder is frozen. Disconnect negative battery cable. Remove steering wheel and turn signal lever. Remove column trim shrouds to gain access to ignition switch.
2) Detach and lower steering column from brake pedal support bracket. Remove ignition switch and key buzzer terminal. Pin key buzzer terminal in LOCK position. Remove turn signal switch. *See Fig. 3.* Remove upper bearing snap ring and "T" bolt retaining nuts securing flange casting to outer tube.
3) Remove entire flange casting, upper shaft bearing, lock cylinder assembly, ignition switch actuator and actuator rod by pulling assembly over end of steering column shaft.
4) Remove lock actuator insert, "T" bolts and PRND21 insert (A/T vehicles) or key release lever (M/T vehicles). Replace flange, lock cylinder assembly, lock gear assembly, lock bearing, upper bearing retainer and actuator assembly.
Installation – 1) Install key release lever assembly (M/T vehicles) or PRND21 insert (A/T vehicles). Install "T" bolts and lock actuator insert. After assembling flange casting, install a new upper bearing.
2) Set lock actuator on drive gear. Install turn signal/hazard switch and key warning. Install ignition switch, and check for proper operation after adjustment. Install steering column to brake pedal support bracket. Install column trim shrouds, steering wheel and pads.
3) Install turn signal lever. Using ignition key, rotate lock cylinder to ensure proper operation in all positions. Connect negative battery cable, and check for proper start in Park and Neutral. Ensure vehicle does not start in Drive or Reverse.

1991 STEERING
Steering Columns – Bronco, "E" & "F" Series (Cont.)

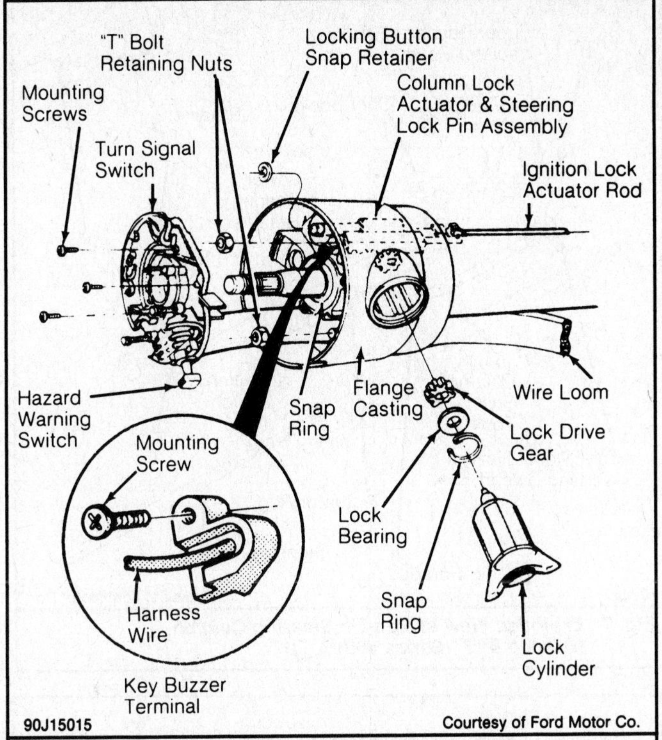
"T" Bolt
Retaining Nuts
Locking Button
Snap Retainer
Column Lock
Actuator & Steering
Lock Pin Assembly
Mounting
Screws
Turn Signal
Switch
Ignition Lock
Actuator Rod
Hazard
Warning
Switch
Mounting
Screw
Snap
Ring
Flange
Casting
Wire Loom
Lock Drive
Gear
Lock
Bearing
Harness
Wire
Snap
Ring
Lock
Cylinder
Key Buzzer
Terminal
90J15015
Courtesy of Ford Motor Co.

Fig. 3: Exploded View of Non-Tilt Column Mechanism

Removal (Without Key, Tilt) – **1)** Disconnect negative battery cable. Remove steering column trim shrouds. Tape gap between steering wheel hub and cover casting. Cover entire circumference of casting. Cover driver seat and floor area to protect upholstery.

2) Pull out hazard flasher switch, and tape it under steering column, providing clearance for drilling out lock cylinder retaining pin. Lock cylinder retaining pin is located outside steering column flange casting, near hazard flasher button.

3) Tilt steering column to full-up position. If necessary, center punch retaining pin using a prick punch. Using a 1/8" (3.17 mm) drill bit and a right angle drill, drill out pin. DO NOT drill deeper than 1/2" (12.7 mm). After retaining pin is out, tilt steering column to full-down position.

4) Place a chisel at base of ignition lock cylinder cap. Using a hammer, strike chisel with sharp blows to break cap away from lock cylinder. Using a 3/8" (9.8 mm) drill bit, drill down center of lock cylinder. Drill down approximately 1 3/4" (44 mm) until lock cylinder breaks loose from casting housing.

5) Remove lock cylinder and metal shavings from housing. Remove steering wheel. See STEERING WHEEL & HORN PAD under REMOVAL & INSTALLATION. Remove turn signal lever and turn signal switch. Remove key buzzer terminal. Lift turn signal switch up and over end of steering shaft, but do not disconnect.

6) Remove 4 screws from flange casting, and lift casting over steering shaft, allowing turn signal switch to pass through flange casting. Remove upper actuator. *See Fig. 4.* Remove drive gear, snap ring and washer from flange casting. Thoroughly clean components. Carefully inspect all components for wear and damage from drilling. Replace parts as required.

Installation – **1)** Lubricate tang of lock cylinder. Attach upper actuator to lower actuator, and lubricate upper actuator. Reassemble flange casting, upper actuator, turn signal switch and lever, drive gear, lock cylinder, steering wheel, pad and steering column trim shrouds.

2) Insert ignition key and rotate lock cylinder to verify correct operation in all positions. Connect battery cable. Check for proper start in Park or Neutral. Ensure vehicle does not start in Drive or Reverse.

IGNITION SWITCH

Removal – Disconnect negative battery cable. Remove steering column shroud and lower column. Disconnect switch wiring at multiple plug. Remove nuts securing switch to steering column. Lift switch vertically to disengage actuator. Remove switch.

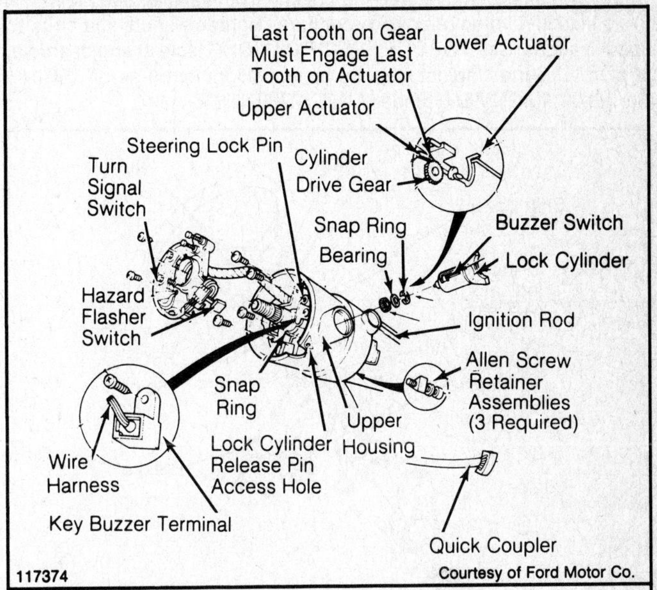
Last Tooth on Gear
Must Engage Last
Tooth on Actuator
Lower Actuator
Upper Actuator
Steering Lock Pin
Turn
Signal
Switch
Cylinder
Drive Gear
Snap Ring
Bearing
Buzzer Switch
Lock Cylinder
Hazard
Flasher
Switch
Ignition Rod
Allen Screw
Retainer
Assemblies
(3 Required)
Snap
Ring
Upper
Housing
Wire
Harness
Lock Cylinder
Release Pin
Access Hole
Key Buzzer Terminal
Quick Coupler
117374
Courtesy of Ford Motor Co.

Fig. 4: Exploded View of Tilt Column Mechanism

Installation – **1)** With lock cylinder and switch in LOCK position, set ignition switch onto column and actuator rod. New ignition switches come positioned in LOCK position with shipping pin in side of switch. Position switch on column, and install, but do not tighten, retaining nuts.

2) Move switch up and down along column to locate mid-position of rod lash, and tighten retaining nuts to 40-65 INCH lbs. (4.5-7.3 N.m). Remove lock pin, and connect battery cable. Check for proper starter operation in Park and Neutral. Raise steering column into position. Verify accessories are not on with ignition switch in OFF position and are on with switch in RUN position.

STEERING COLUMN

Removal & Installation – **1)** Set parking brake. Disconnect negative battery cable.

2) On Bronco and "F" Series, remove bolt and nut attaching intermediate shaft to steering column. *See Fig. 5.*

3) On "E" Series, remove nuts attaching flexible coupling to steering shaft flange.

NOTE: On tilt columns, ensure steering wheel is in UP position before removing steering wheel.

4) On all models, disconnect shift linkage rod(s) from steering column. Remove steering wheel. See STEERING WHEEL & HORN PAD under REMOVAL & INSTALLATION.

5) Remove steering column floor opening cover plate screws. Remove shroud by loosening screw at bottom, selecting transmission gear position "1" (A/T models) and spreading shroud open.

6) Pull shroud out of instrument panel opening while pulling up and away from column.

Steering Columns – Bronco, "E" & "F" Series (Cont.)

7) On Bronco and "F" Series A/T models, remove transmission indicator cable.

8) On all models, remove instrument panel column opening cover. Remove bolts attaching column support bracket to pedal support bracket. Disconnect turn signal/hazard warning and ignition switch wiring harness. Remove steering column from vehicle. *See Fig. 6.*

9) To install, reverse removal procedure. Tighten all nuts and bolts to specifications. See TORQUE SPECIFICATIONS table at end of article.

10) On "E" Series, adjust steering column alignment. See STEERING COLUMN ALIGNMENT under ADJUSTMENTS.

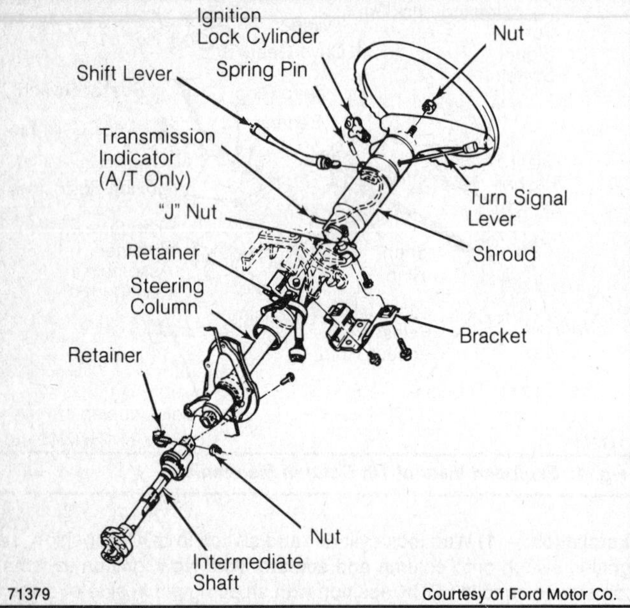
Ignition Lock Cylinder
Nut
Shift Lever
Spring Pin
Transmission Indicator (A/T Only)
Turn Signal Lever
"J" Nut
Shroud
Retainer
Steering Column
Bracket
Retainer
Nut
Intermediate Shaft

71379 Courtesy of Ford Motor Co.

Fig. 5: Removing Steering Column (Bronco & "F" Series)

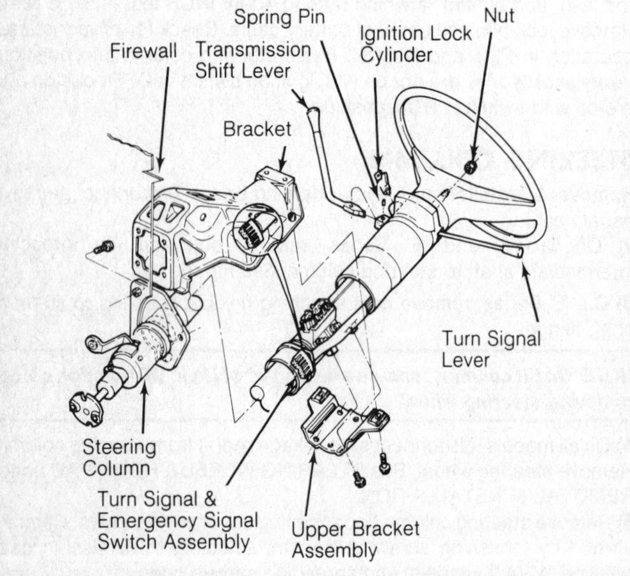
Spring Pin
Nut
Firewall
Transmission Shift Lever
Ignition Lock Cylinder
Bracket
Turn Signal Lever
Steering Column
Turn Signal & Emergency Signal Switch Assembly
Upper Bracket Assembly

71380 Courtesy of Ford Motor Co.

Fig. 5: Removing Steering Column ("E" Series)

OVERHAUL

Refer to appropriate illustration when overhauling steering columns. *See Figs. 7-11.*

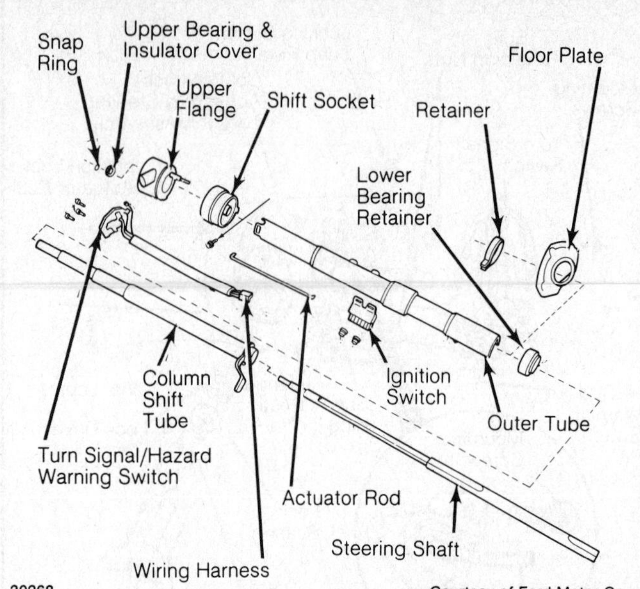
Snap Ring
Upper Bearing & Insulator Cover
Upper Flange
Shift Socket
Floor Plate
Retainer
Lower Bearing Retainer
Column Shift Tube
Ignition Switch
Outer Tube
Turn Signal/Hazard Warning Switch
Actuator Rod
Steering Shaft
Wiring Harness

30268 Courtesy of Ford Motor Co.

Fig. 7: Exploded View of Non-Tilt Steering Column (Bronco & "F" Series with A/T)

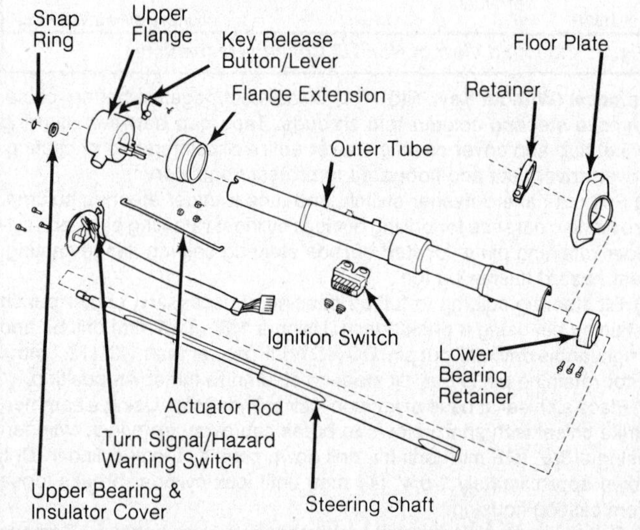
Snap Ring
Upper Flange
Key Release Button/Lever
Floor Plate
Flange Extension
Retainer
Outer Tube
Ignition Switch
Lower Bearing Retainer
Actuator Rod
Turn Signal/Hazard Warning Switch
Upper Bearing & Insulator Cover
Steering Shaft

30270 Courtesy of Ford Motor Co.

Fig. 8: Exploded View of Non-Tilt Steering Column (Bronco & "F" Series with M/T)

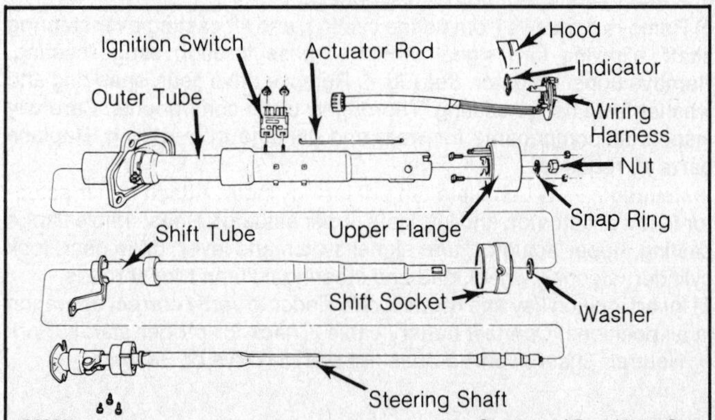
Hood
Ignition Switch
Actuator Rod
Indicator
Outer Tube
Wiring Harness
Nut
Snap Ring
Shift Tube
Upper Flange
Shift Socket
Washer
Steering Shaft

30269 Courtesy of Ford Motor Co.

Fig. 9: Exploded View of Non-Tilt Steering Column ("E" Series with A/T)

1991 STEERING
Steering Columns – Bronco, "E" & "F" Series (Cont.)

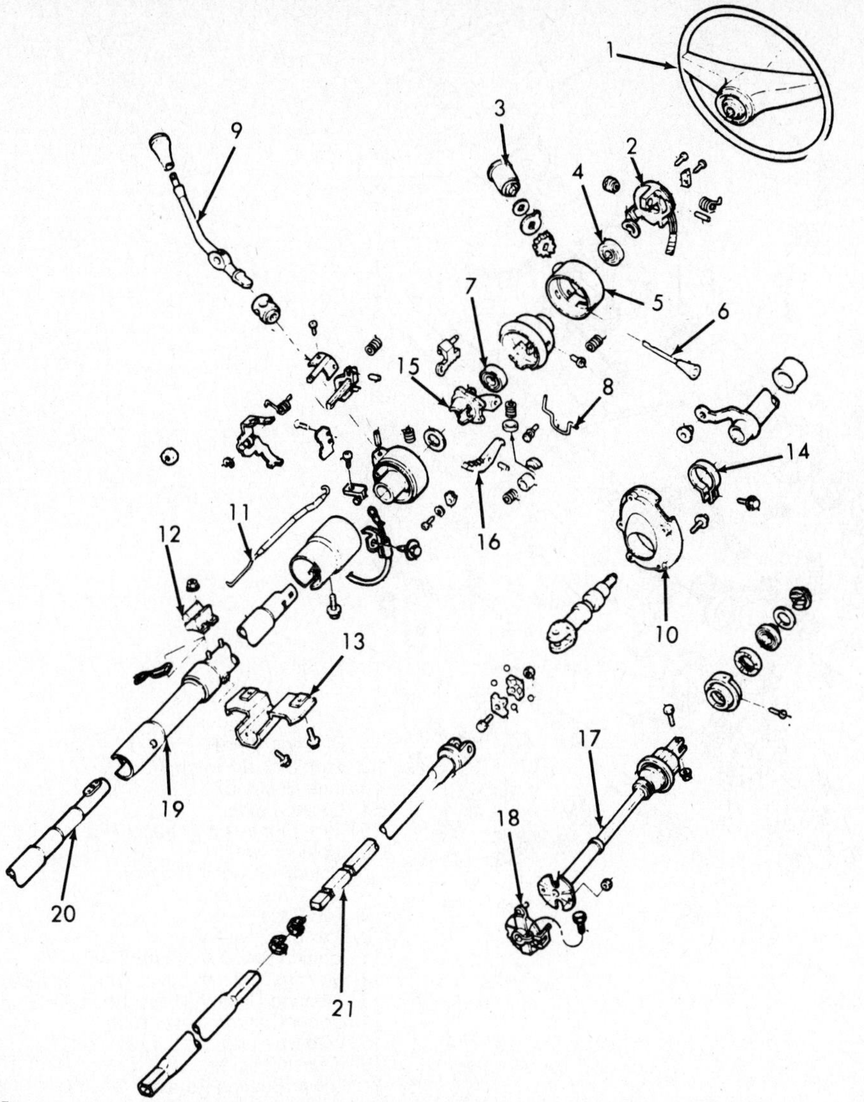
1
2
3
4
5
6
7
8
9
10
11
12
13
14
15
16
17
18
19
20
21
90A15347

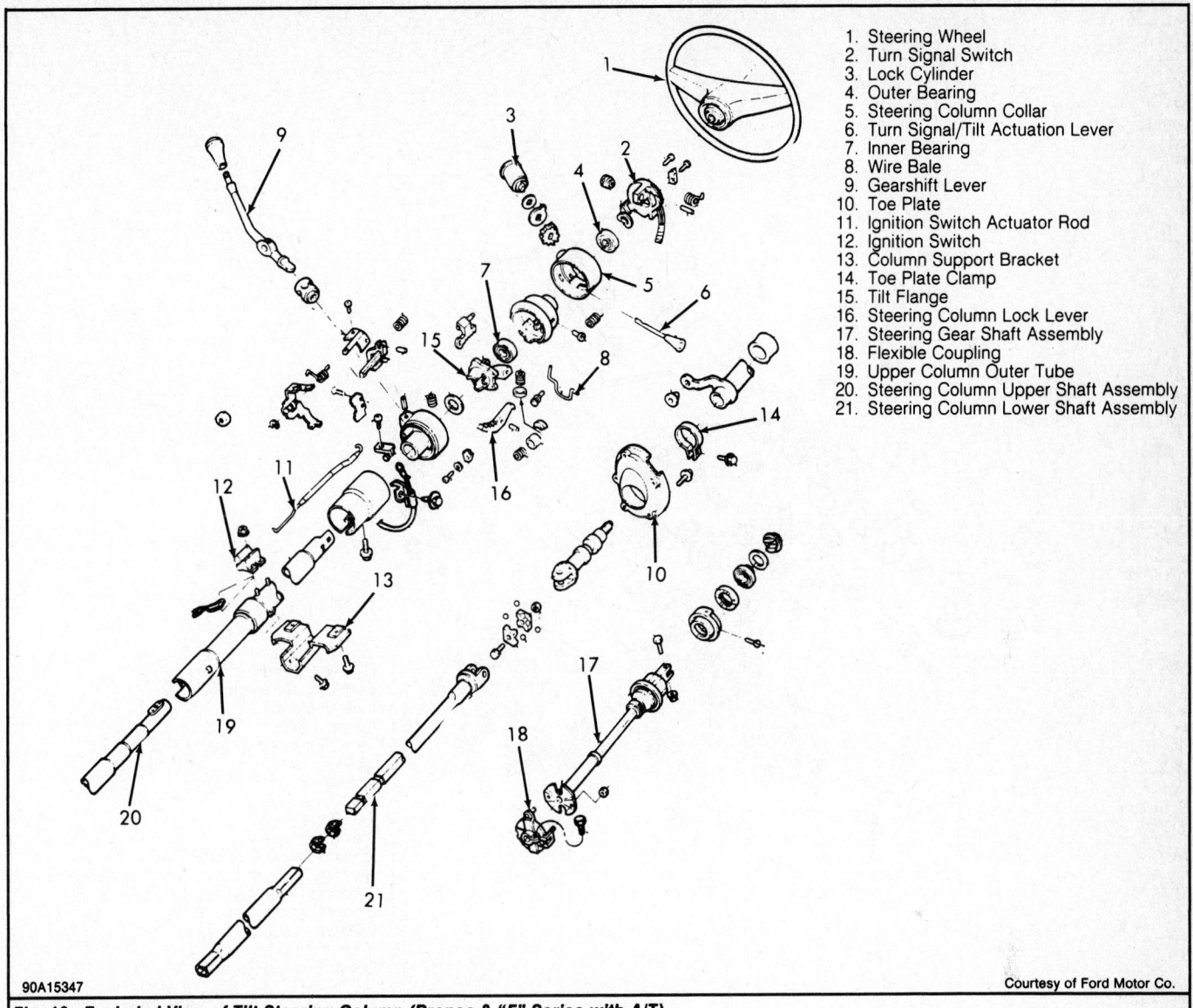

1. Steering Wheel
2. Turn Signal Switch
3. Lock Cylinder
4. Outer Bearing
5. Steering Column Collar
6. Turn Signal/Tilt Actuation Lever
7. Inner Bearing
8. Wire Bale
9. Gearshift Lever
10. Toe Plate
11. Ignition Switch Actuator Rod
12. Ignition Switch
13. Column Support Bracket
14. Toe Plate Clamp
15. Tilt Flange
16. Steering Column Lock Lever
17. Steering Gear Shaft Assembly
18. Flexible Coupling
19. Upper Column Outer Tube
20. Steering Column Upper Shaft Assembly
21. Steering Column Lower Shaft Assembly

Courtesy of Ford Motor Co.

Fig. 10: Exploded View of Tilt Steering Column (Bronco & "F" Series with A/T)

1991 STEERING

Steering Columns – Bronco, "E" & "F" Series (Cont.)

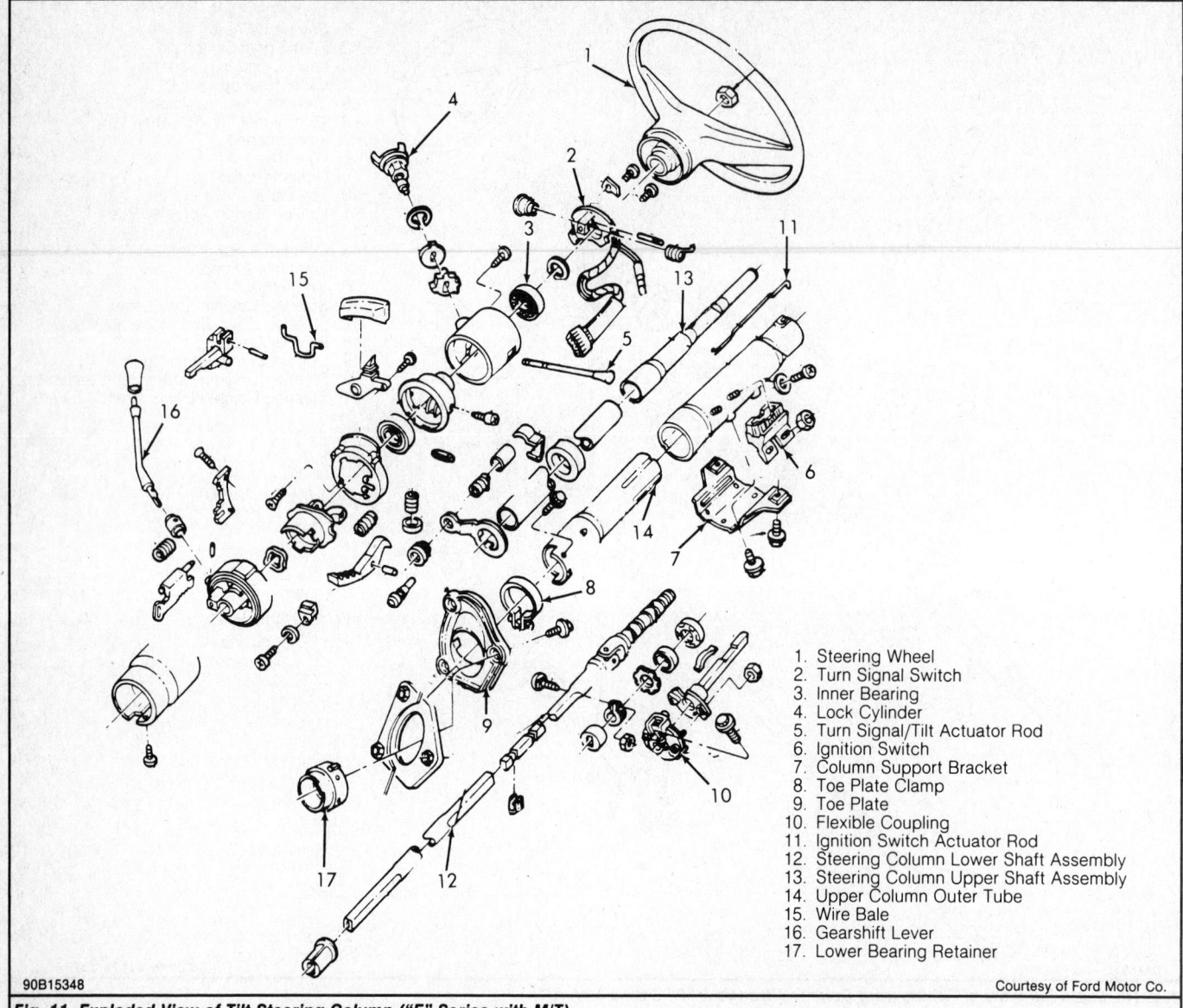

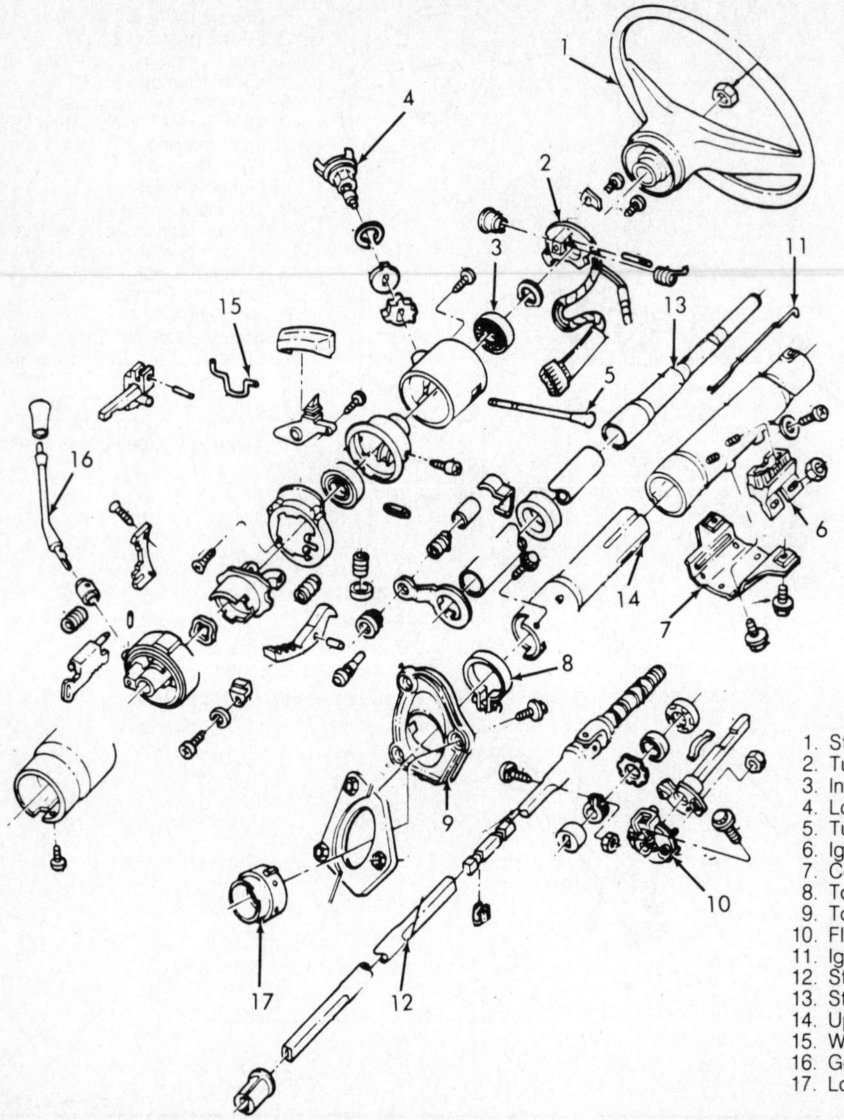
1
2
3
4
5
6
7
8
9
10
11
12
13
14
15
16
17
1. Steering Wheel
2. Turn Signal Switch
3. Inner Bearing
4. Lock Cylinder
5. Turn Signal/Tilt Actuator Rod
6. Ignition Switch
7. Column Support Bracket
8. Toe Plate Clamp
9. Toe Plate
10. Flexible Coupling
11. Ignition Switch Actuator Rod
12. Steering Column Lower Shaft Assembly
13. Steering Column Upper Shaft Assembly
14. Upper Column Outer Tube
15. Wire Bale
16. Gearshift Lever
17. Lower Bearing Retainer
90B15348
Courtesy of Ford Motor Co.

Fig. 11 Exploded View of Tilt Steering Column ("E" Series with M/T)

TORQUE SPECIFICATIONS

TORQUE SPECIFICATIONS

Application	Ft. Lbs. (N.m)
Bronco & "F" Series	
Floor Opening Cover Plate	6-10 (8-14)
Intermediate Shaft Flex Coupling-To-Steering	
Gear Bolt	24-34 (33-46)
Intermediate Shaft-To-Steering Column Nut	24-34 (34-46)
Pedal Support Bracket Bolts	19-27 (26-37)
Steering Column	
Cover Plate Clamp Bolt	8-18 (11-24)
Support Bracket Nuts	13-38 (18-51)
Steering Wheel-To-Steering Shaft Nut	30-42 (41-57)
"E" Series	
Lower Bearing Retainer Clamp Nut	9-18 (12-24)
Steering Column	
Coupling Flange Nuts	14-21 (19-28)
Floor Opening	
Plate-To-Dash Panel Bolts	12-18 (16-24)
Opening Cover Clamp Bolt	12-18 (16-24)
Support Bracket Bolts	19-27 (26-37)
Steering Wheel-To-Steering Shaft Nut	30-42 (41-57)

TORQUE SPECIFICATIONS (Cont.)

Application	INCH Lbs. (N.m)
Bronco , "E" & "F" Series	
Bearing Retainer	
Lower	12-20 (1.4-2.3)
Upper [1]	12-20 (1.4-2.3)
Column Cover (Tilt)	40-50 (4.5-5.6)
Flange Retainer Allen Screw (Tilt)	50-68 (5.6-7.7)
Flange To Outer Tube	60-75 (6.8-8.5)
Ignition Switch Retaining Nut	40-65 (4.5-7.3)
Lock Actuator Insert	15-25 (1.7-2.8)
Selector Indicator Cable Bracket Screw [1]	20 (2.3)
Shift Tube Retaining Nut	35-50 (4.0-5.6)
Steering Column Flange Extension Screws	
Non-Tilt	15-22 (1.7-2.5)
Tilt	10-20 (1.1-2.3)
Steering Column Shroud Screw [1]	10-15 (1.1-1.7)
Steering Wheel Horn Cover Screws	7-11 (.8-1.2)
Turn Signal Lever Screw	30-45 (3.4-5.1)
Turn Signal Switch Screws	
Non-Tilt	15-25 (1.7-2.8)
Tilt	20-30 (2.3-3.4)

[1] – Bronco and "F" Series only.

1991 STEERING
Manual Recirculating Ball

Ranger

DESCRIPTION

The steering gear is a worm and recirculating ball type. Needle bearing and bushing support the sector shaft in the housing. The worm shaft spiral groove floats on 2 continuous rows of ball bearings recirculating thorough the ball nut via return guide tubes. Teeth on the ball nut mate with the sector shaft.

NOTE: There are 2 types of manual ball nut gears: constant manual ball nut and variable ratio manual nut ball. Except for sector shaft, housing and sector cover, these gears use common parts. Use manufacturer's gear model number to identify gear.

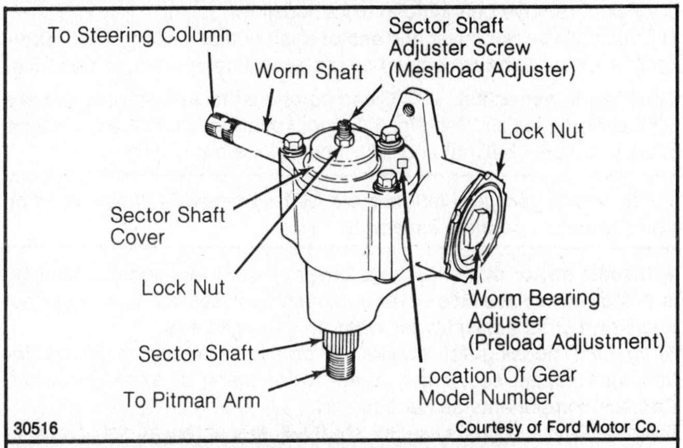
To Steering Column
Worm Shaft
Sector Shaft
Adjuster Screw
(Meshload Adjuster)
Lock Nut
Sector Shaft
Cover
Lock Nut
Worm Bearing
Adjuster
(Preload Adjustment)
Sector Shaft
Location Of Gear
Model Number
To Pitman Arm
30516
Courtesy of Ford Motor Co.

Fig. 1: Identifying Recirculating Ball Steering Gear

INSPECTION & ADJUSTMENTS

PRELOAD & MESHLOAD IN-VEHICLE CHECK

NOTE: Before checking preload or meshload, ensure steering column is properly aligned and intermediate shaft flex coupling is not distorted.

1) Place reference mark on pitman arm and sector shaft for reassembly. Remove pitman arm retaining nut. Remove pitman arm from sector shaft with Pitman Arm Puller (T64P-3590-F).
2) Lubricate worm shaft seal with a drop of ATF. Remove horn pad from steering wheel. Turn steering wheel slowly against one stop. Place INCH lb. torque wrench on steering wheel nut.
3) Measure torque (preload) required to rotate steering wheel at a constant speed, approximately 1 1/2 turns. If preload is not 2-6 INCH lbs. (.22-.68 N.m), readjust preload. See MESHLOAD & WORM PRELOAD ADJUSTMENT. If preload is within specifications, check meshload.
4) Rotate steering wheel from stop-to-stop, noting total number of revolutions. Turn steering wheel back half way, to center position. Using an INCH lb. torque wrench, measure highest torque required to rotate steering wheel back and forth 90 degrees through center position.
5) Meshload must be within 4-10 INCH lbs. (.45-1.13 N.m) over the measured preload reading. Meshload can be set while steering gear is on vehicle.

NOTE: Adjust worm preload with steering gear off vehicle.

MESHLOAD & WORM PRELOAD ADJUSTMENT

1) Remove steering gear from vehicle. See STEERING GEAR under REMOVAL & INSTALLATION. Ensure sector cover bolts are tight. See TORQUE SPECIFICATIONS table at end of article. Loosen worm bearing adjuster lock nut. Tighten worm bearing adjuster nut until all end play is removed.
2) Lubricate worm shaft seal with a drop of ATF. Carefully turn worm shaft to right stop. Using and INCH lb. torque wrench, measure torque (preload) required to rotate wormshaft to left, in a constant motion, for approximately 1 1/2 turns. Tighten or loosen adjuster nut until preload of 5-6 INCH lbs. (.56-.68 N.m) is reached.
3) Tighten adjuster lock nut to specification. To adjust meshload, rotate worm shaft from stop-to-stop, counting total number of turns. Then turn back halfway from center. Using and INCH lb. torque wrench, observe highest reading while worm shaft is turned approximately 90 degrees either way across center. If highest reading (meshload) is not within 9-11 INCH lbs. (102-124 N.m), turn sector shaft adjusting screw as required.
4) Meshload must be at least 4 INCH lbs. over preload. Tighten lock nut to specification while holding adjusting screw. Reverse removal procedures to install remaining components. Ensure reference mark is aligned on pitman arm and sector shaft. Torque pitman arm retaining nut to specification.

REMOVAL & INSTALLATION

STEERING GEAR

Removal – Slide flex coupling shield up intermediate shaft. Remove flex coupling-to-steering gear pinch bolt. Remove pitman arm retaining nut and lock washer. Using Pitman Arm Puller (T64P-3590-F), remove pitman arm. Remove steering gear-to-frame bolts. Remove steering gear.

Installation – Center worm shaft in steering gear. Ensure flat on worm gear shaft faces straight up and aligns with flat on flex coupling. Install steering gear on frame. Tighten bolts to specification. See TORQUE SPECIFICATIONS table at end of article. To install remaining components, reverse removal procedure. Align 2 blocked teeth on pitman arm with 4 missing teeth on sector shaft. Tighten pitman arm nut to specification.

SECTOR SHAFT SEAL

Removal – 1) Place steering wheel in center of travel. Remove pitman arm nut. Mark pitman arm-to-sector shaft relation for installation reference. Using Pitman Arm Puller (T64P-3590-F), remove pitman arm.
2) Remove sector shaft cover retaining bolts. Lift sector shaft and cover from housing. *See Fig. 2.* Using a screwdriver, pry sector shaft seal from housing. Use care not to damage housing area. Note direction of seal for installation.
3) Loosen sector shaft adjuster screw lock nut. Rotate adjuster screw clockwise and remove cover from sector shaft. Inspect gear lubricant for contamination. Steering gear must be overhauled if contamination exists.

Installation – 1) Lubricate new sector shaft seal with steering gear lubricant. Position seal in housing bore. Using proper size socket, tap seal into housing until it bottoms.
2) Install sector shaft so center tooth of sector shaft enters center tooth of ball nut. Fill housing with Steering Gear Grease (C3AZ-19578-A). Install new sector shaft cover gasket on gear housing. Apply a thin bead of sealant to sector shaft cover.
3) Using a screwdriver through the center hole, align adjuster screw and install cover on sector shaft. *See Fig. 2.* Turn adjuster screw counterclockwise until sector cover is flush with housing.
4) Coat cover bolts with non-hardening sealant. Install cover retaining bolts. Tighten only if there is a lash between sector shaft and worm shaft. The lash can be obtained by turning adjusting screw clockwise. Tighten cover bolts to specification. Install sector shaft lock nut. Perform adjustments on steering box. See INSPECTION & ADJUSTMENTS.

OVERHAUL

STEERING GEAR

Disassembly – 1) Remove steering gear. See STEERING GEAR under REMOVAL & INSTALLATION. Place steering gear in a holding fixture. Worm shaft should be centered in steering gear. Remove sector shaft cover bolts. Remove sector shaft and cover from housing.

1991 STEERING
Manual Recirculating Ball (Cont.)

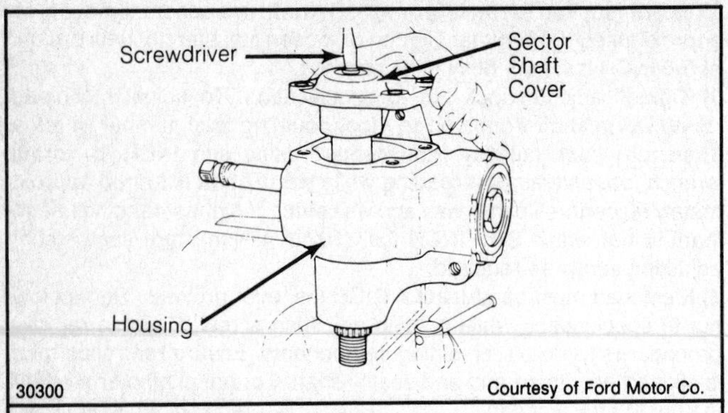
Screwdriver
Sector Shaft Cover
Housing
30300
Courtesy of Ford Motor Co.

Fig. 2: Installing Sector Shaft Cover

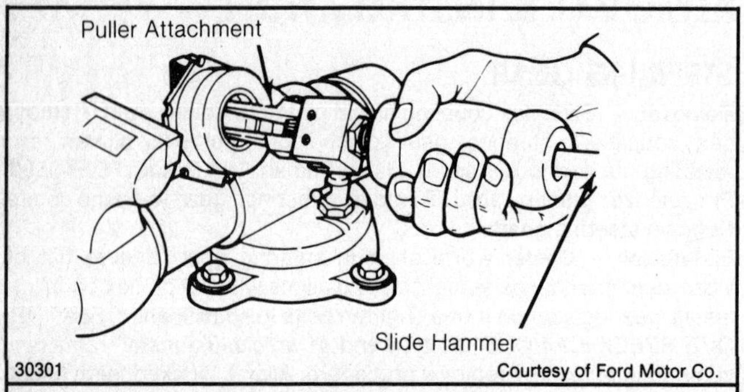
Puller Attachment
Slide Hammer
30301
Courtesy of Ford Motor Co.

Fig. 3: Removing Worm Adjuster Bearing Cup

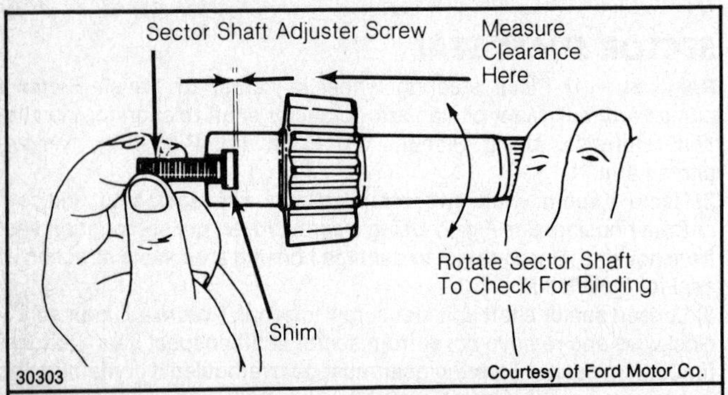
Sector Shaft Adjuster Screw
Measure Clearance Here
Rotate Sector Shaft To Check For Binding
Shim
30303
Courtesy of Ford Motor Co.

Fig. 4: Checking Sector Shaft "T" Slot Clearance

Loosen lock nut. Rotate adjuster screw clockwise to remove cover from shaft. DO NOT lose shim located on adjuster screw.

NOTE: Worm gear and ball nut are NOT serviceable. If damaged or worn, replace complete assembly.

2) Loosen worm bearing adjuster lock nut. Remove worm bearing adjuster and worm shaft thrust bearing. Remove worm shaft and ball nut assembly from housing. Remove upper thrust bearing.

CAUTION: DO NOT allow ball nut to rotate down worm shaft, as ball guides may be damaged.

3) Use slide hammer and Puller Attachment (T58L-101-B) to remove worm bearing adjuster bearing cup. *See Fig. 3.* Using a bearing driver or socket, remove bearing cup from housing.

4) Bushing in sector cover and sector shaft needle bearing is not serviceable. Cover or housing must be replaced if component is defective.

Cleaning & Inspection – 1) Clean components with solvent and dry with compressed air. See Fig. 5. Inspect bearings and races for signs of wear. Inspect ball nut and worm shaft for wear or pitting.

NOTE: Worm gear and ball nut are NOT serviceable. If damaged or worn, replace complete assembly.

2) Inspect sector shaft fit at side cover bushing assembly. If bushing is defective, replace side cover and bushing assembly. Check ball nut and worm shaft assembly for wear and straightness.

3) Inspect housing for cracks or damage. Inspect bearings for damage. Inspect sector gear teeth for chipping or excessive wear. Replace components as needed.

Reassembly – 1) Install sector shaft adjuster screw and shim in sector shaft. Using feeler gauge, measure clearance between adjuster screw and bottom of sector shaft "T" slot. *See Fig. 4.*

2) The adjuster screw clearance should be .004" (.10 mm). Check shim clearance by sliding feeler gauge between sector shaft adjuster screw recess and adjuster screw face.

3) Once correct shim is determined, install shim and adjuster screw. Hold sector shaft adjuster screw while turning sector shaft. If sector shaft does not turn freely, recheck shim clearance. Install ball nut and wormshaft.

4) Lubricate all seals, bearings and sector shaft before installation. Coat worm bearing adjuster, sector shaft adjuster screw and sector shaft cover bolts with Silicone sealant prior to installation.

5) Screw worm bearing adjuster down until nearly all end play has been removed. Lubricate steering gear by rotating worm shaft until ball nut is at end of its travel. Pack grease into steering gear housing.

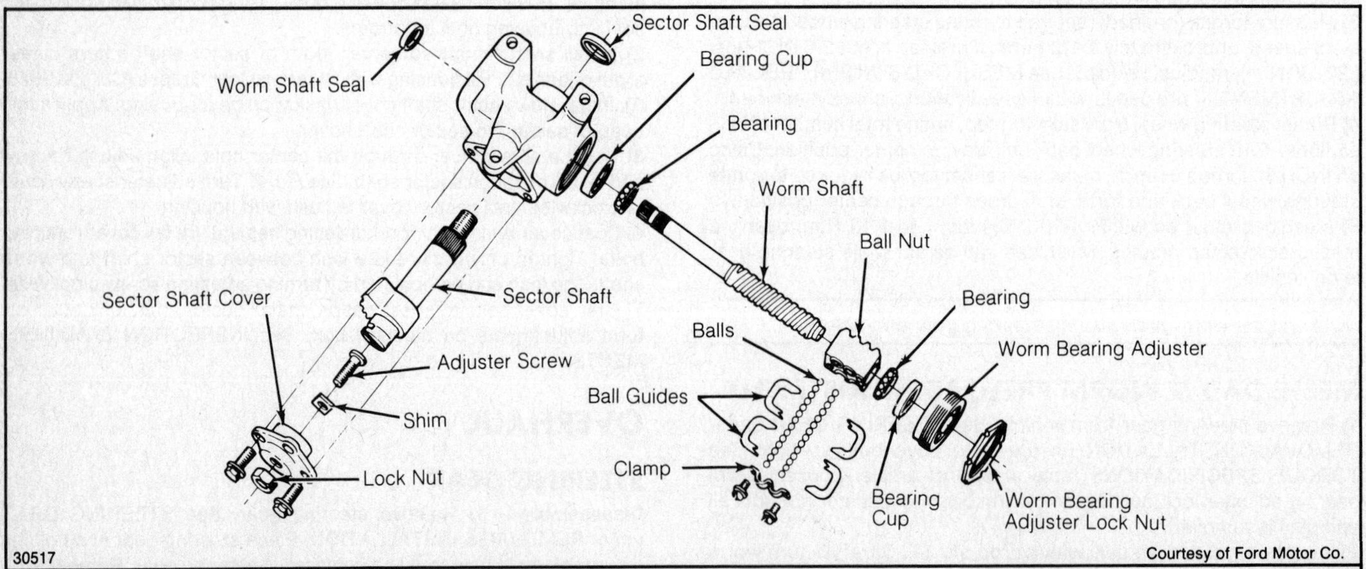
Sector Shaft Seal
Bearing Cup
Worm Shaft Seal
Bearing
Worm Shaft
Ball Nut
Sector Shaft Cover
Sector Shaft
Bearing
Balls
Worm Bearing Adjuster
Adjuster Screw
Ball Guides
Shim
Clamp
Lock Nut
Bearing Cup
Worm Bearing Adjuster Lock Nut
30517
Courtesy of Ford Motor Co.

Fig. 5: Exploded View of Recirculating Ball Steering Gear

1991 STEERING
Manual Recirculating Ball (Cont.)

Rotate ball nut to other end of its travel and pack more grease into housing.

6) Place ball nut in center of its travel. Insert sector shaft assembly, containing adjuster screw and shim, into housing. Center tooth of sector gear must engage center rack tooth space in ball nut.

7) Apply a thin bead of sealant to sector shaft cover. Using a screwdriver through the center hole, align adjuster screw and install cover on sector shaft. *See Fig. 2.* Turn adjuster screw counterclockwise until sector cover is flush with housing.

8) Coat cover bolts with non-hardening sealant. Install cover retaining bolts. Tighten only if there is a lash between sector shaft and worm shaft. The lash can be obtained by turning adjusting screw clockwise. Tighten cover bolts to specification. Install sector shaft lock nut. Perform adjustments on steering box. See INSPECTION & ADJUSTMENTS.

TORQUE SPECIFICATIONS

TORQUE SPECIFICATIONS

Application	Ft. Lbs. (N.m)
Adjuster Screw Lock Nut	14-25 (19-34)
Flex Coupling Pinch Bolt	25-35 (34-47)
Pitman Arm Nut	170-230 (230-312)
Sector Shaft Cover Bolt	32-40 (43-54)
Steering Gear-To-Frame Bolt	54-66 (74-89)
Worm Bearing Adjuster Lock Nut	166-187 (225-254)

1991 STEERING
Integral Power Steering

Bronco, Explorer, Ranger, "E" & "F" Series

NOTE: Unless otherwise specified, references to "F" Series include "F" Series Super Duty.

DESCRIPTION

Integral power steering unit consists of a worm and 1-piece rack piston, meshed to sector shaft teeth. System includes a rotary hydraulic valve, input shaft, control valve sleeve and torsion bar. Hydraulic action is generated by relative rotary motion between input shaft and worm/sleeve assembly. *See Fig. 1.*

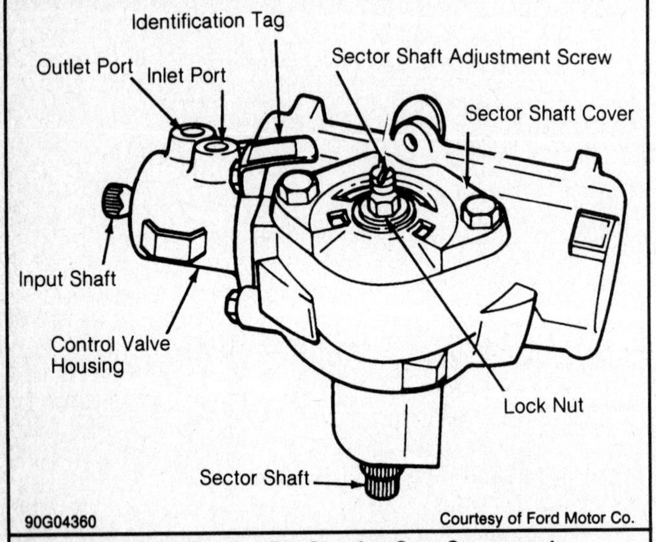
Identification Tag
Outlet Port
Inlet Port
Sector Shaft Adjustment Screw
Sector Shaft Cover
Input Shaft
Control Valve Housing
Lock Nut
Sector Shaft
90G04360
Courtesy of Ford Motor Co.

Fig. 1: Identifying Torsion Bar Steering Gear Components

The C-II power steering pump is used on Bronco, Explorer, Ranger, F150-350 and "F" series super duty vehicles. Pump is a belt-driven, slipper-type integral pump with a fiberglass/nylon reservoir. Reservoir is attached to rear of pump housing plate. Pump body is encased within housing and reservoir.

Hoses are attached with quick disconnect fittings, located below filler neck at outboard side of reservoir. An identification tag with basic model number is attached to reservoir. *See Fig. 2.*

The Saginaw power steering pump is used on E150-350 vehicles. Pump is a vane-type pump. The reservoir is sealed against the pump housing, all parts are integral and submerged in oil. The filler neck is on the reservoir.

Rectangular pumping vanes driven by a shaft, move fluid from intake to pressure cavities of cam ring. Oil is picked up and forced into cavities of thrust plate, to holes in cam ring and pressure plate. The flow control valve, regulates supplied oil to the steering gear unit. *See Fig. 3.*

LUBRICATION

CAPACITY

Information not provided by manufacturer.

FLUID TYPE

Use Ford Premium Power Steering Fluid (E6AZ-19582-AA) or Type F ATF fluid.

FLUID LEVEL CHECK

Fluid level may be checked when fluid is either hot or cold. If fluid is cold, approximately 75°F (24°C), check fluid level using the cold full mark on dipstick. If fluid is hot, approximately 177°F (77°C), check fluid level using the hot full mark on dipstick. Add fluid through dipstick opening if needed and recheck. DO NOT overfill.

HYDRAULIC SYSTEM BLEEDING

Raise and support vehicle. Fill reservoir to specified level. Run engine until power steering fluid reaches normal operating temperature, approximately 165-175°F (74-79°C). Turn steering wheel from lock-to-lock until fluid level no longer decreases and no bubbles exist. DO NOT hold steering wheel in far left or right position. Check fluid level in reservoir and top off as necessary.

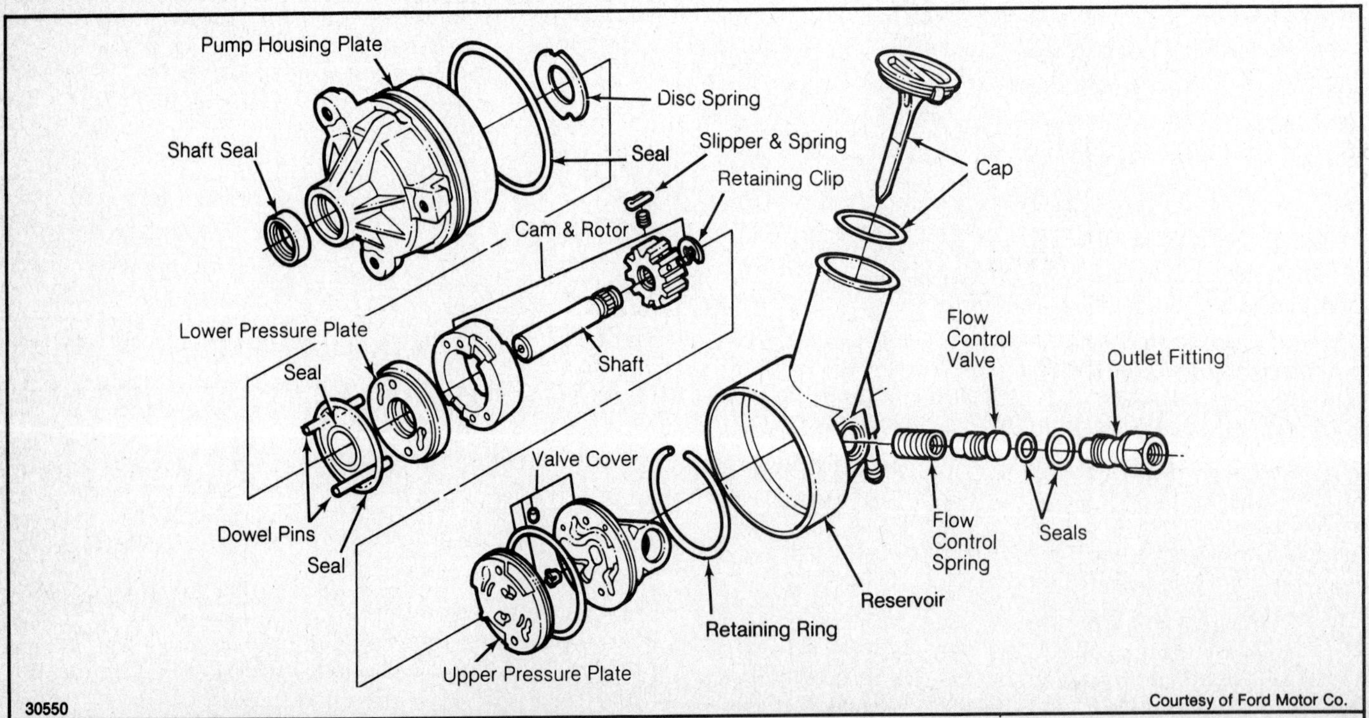
Pump Housing Plate
Disc Spring
Shaft Seal
Seal
Slipper & Spring
Retaining Clip
Cap
Cam & Rotor
Lower Pressure Plate
Seal
Shaft
Flow Control Valve
Outlet Fitting
Valve Cover
Dowel Pins
Seal
Flow Control Spring
Seals
Reservoir
Retaining Ring
Upper Pressure Plate
30550
Courtesy of Ford Motor Co.

Fig. 2: Exploded View of C-II Power Steering Pump (Bronco, Explorer, Ranger & "F" Series)

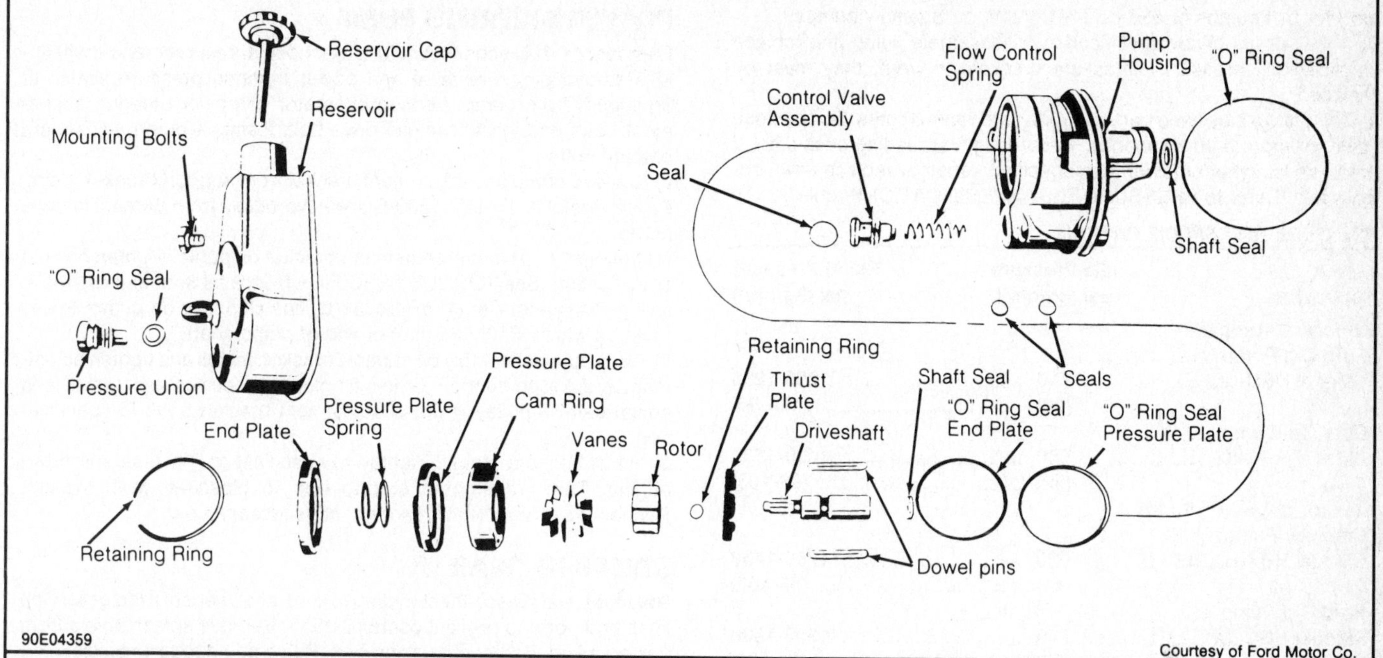
Reservoir Cap
Reservoir
Mounting Bolts
"O" Ring Seal
Pressure Union
Flow Control Spring
Pump Housing
"O" Ring Seal
Control Valve Assembly
Seal
Shaft Seal
Retaining Ring
Thrust Plate
Shaft Seal
Seals
"O" Ring Seal End Plate
"O" Ring Seal Pressure Plate
Driveshaft
Pressure Plate
Cam Ring
Pressure Plate Spring
End Plate
Vanes
Rotor
Retaining Ring
Dowel pins
90E04359
Courtesy of Ford Motor Co.

Fig. 3: Exploded View of Saginaw Pump ("E" Series)

ADJUSTMENTS

POWER STEERING PUMP BELT

BELT ADJUSTMENT

Application	New Belt Lbs. (kg)	[1] Used Belt Lbs. (kg)
2.3L		
Fixed	150-190 (68-86)	140-160 (64-73)
With Tensioner [2]	150-190 (68-86)	140-160 (64-73)
2.9L	120-160 (54-73)	110-130 (50-59)
3.0L		
Fixed	120-160 (54-73)	110-130 (50-59)
With Tensioner [2]	150-190 (68-86)	140-160 (64-73)
4.0L With Tensioner [2]	108-132 (49-60)	108-132 (49-60)
4.9L With Tensioner [2]	[3]	[3]
5.0L With Tensioner [2]	[4]	[4]
5.8L With Tensioner [2]	[4]	[4]
7.3L Except Ambulance		
1/2" Belt	140-180 (64-82)	95-115 (43-52)
7.3L Ambulance		
A/C & P/S	140-180 (64-82)	95-115 (43-52)
7.5L		
With Tensioner [2]	[5]	[5]

[1] – Any belt operated for 10 minutes.
[2] – Tension is correct if tensioner is within indicator marks.
[3] – 90 Lbs. (41 kg) minimum for vehicles with 60 & 75 amp alternators. 117 Lbs. (53 kg) minimum for vehicles with 100 amp alternators.
[4] – 77 Lbs. (35 kg) minimum for vehicles with 60 & 75 amp alternators. 111 Lbs. (50 kg) minimum for vehicles with 100 amp alternators.
[5] – 94 Lbs. (43 kg) minimum tension.

STEERING GEAR MESHLOAD

1) Reference mark pitman arm and sector shaft. Using Pitman Arm Puller (T64P-3590-F), remove pitman arm from sector shaft. Disconnect fluid return line at pump reservoir. Cap reservoir return line pipe. Place end of return line in clean container.

2) Turn steering wheel in both directions several times to drain fluid. Remove horn button from steering wheel. Turn steering wheel until positioned 45 degrees from left or right steering stop.

3) Using an INCH lb. torque wrench on steering wheel nut, record torque required to turn steering shaft 1/8 turn toward center at 45 degrees from stop position. Turn steering wheel to center position. Record torque required to move steering shaft back and forth across center position. compare the two readings. If new vehicle (less than 5000 miles) center reading should be 12-24 INCH lbs. (1.3-2.7 N.m) If NOT, adjust. If vehicle has more than 5000 miles or sector shaft has been replaced, Compare over center torque with torque recorded at 45 degrees from stop. If centering torque is greater than or less than 45 degrees recorded torque by 10 INCH lbs. (1.13 N.m) adjust to 9-13 INCH lbs. (1.0-1.4 N.m).

4) To adjust, loosen lock nut, turn adjusting screw until reading across center position is obtained, Refer to Step 3). Tighten lock nut while holding adjusting screw in place. Attach pitman arm. Reconnect hoses. Attach horn button.

TESTING

PRESSURE TEST

NOTE: For testing, use Power Steering Analyzer (D79L-33610-A) with flow meter.

Preparation – 1) With belt tension correct, disconnect power steering pump pressure hose. Keep hose end raised to prevent fluid loss. Connect pressure hose of gauge to power steering pump fitting. Connect other hose from valve side of tester to steering gear inlet.

2) Open valve. Run engine until fluid reaches normal operating temperature of 165-175°F (74-79°C). Check fluid level. Add fluid as required.

Pressure Test – 1) Start engine and let idle for approximately 2 minutes. Record flow. If flow is less than 1.6 gallons per minutes (6.1 L per minutes) on Explorer and Ranger or 2 gallons per minute (7.6L per minute) on Bronco, "E" and "F" Series, pump may require repair. Continue test.

1991 STEERING
Integral Power Steering (Cont.)

2) If pressure is greater than 150 psi (11 kg/cm²), check hoses for restrictions. Partially close valve to build up pressure to 740 psi (52 kg/cm²) for C-II pumps or 620 psi (44 kg/cm²) on Saginaw pumps.
3) If flow drops below specification, disassemble pump and replace cam pack. If pressure plates are cracked or worn, they must be replaced.
4) Completely close and partially open gate valve 3 times. Do not close valve for more than 5 seconds. Record highest reading each time. If pressure is higher or lower than specified, repair or replace flow control valve. Refer to PRESSURE TEST SPECIFICATIONS table.

PRESSURE TEST SPECIFICATIONS

Application	Idle Pressure psi (kg/cm²)	Relief Pressure psi (kg/cm²)
Explorer & Ranger		
Ford C-II Pump		
Model HBC-KC	740 (52)	1050-1230 (74-86)
Ford C-II Pump		
Model HBC-KE	740 (52)	1400-1530 (98-108)
Bronco, "E" & "F" Series		
Saginaw Pump		
Model HBA-HA/HB	620 (44)	1250-1450 (88-102)
Ford C-II Pump		
Model HBC-JX	740 (52)	1300-1530 (91-108)
Ford C-II Pump		
Model HBC-JY	740 (52)	1350-1530 (95-108)

5) Set engine speed at 1500 RPM. Record flow. If flow varies more than 1 gallon (3.8L) per minute from pressure measured in step **1)**, flow control valve in pump must be repaired or replaced.
6) Turn steering wheel to left and right stops. Pressure should be nearly the same as maximum relief pressure. Flow should drop below .5 gallon (1.9L) per minute.
7) If pressure and flow are not as specified, steering gear is leaking internally. Remove steering gear. Remove flow control valve. Repair or replace damaged parts. Check rack piston and valve seals for damage.
8) If pressure and flow are good, turn steering wheel slightly in both directions and release quickly while watching pressure gauge. Needle should move from normal backpressure reading and snap back as wheel is released.
9) If gauge reacts slowly, or sticks, rotary valve in steering gear is sticking. Repair or replace rotary valve.
10) If system is severely contaminated, both hoses, control valve, and pump must be disassembled and cleaned. If problem still exists, check ball joints, linkage and other front suspension members.

VALVE SPOOL CENTERING

1) Install a 0-2000 psi pressure gauge and valve assembly between power steering pump and high pressure line. ENSURE gauge valve is completely OPEN. Remove horn button from steering wheel. Attach an INCH lb. torque wrench to steering wheel nut. Center steering wheel. Set engine idle to 1000 RPM. Using torque wrench, rotate steering shaft to either side of center to obtain reading of 250 psi (17.5 kg/cm²) in each direction.

NOTE: Power steering fluid must be at normal operating temperature and at correct level.

2) Torque reading should be equal in both directions at 250 psi (17.5 kg/cm²) If difference between readings exceeds 6 INCH lbs. (.68 N.m), Remove steering gear, replace shaft and control assembly.

NOTE: Only control valve housing and valve seal "O" rings are serviceable.

REMOVAL & INSTALLATION

POWER STEERING PUMP

Removal – 1) Disconnect fluid return hose at reservoir and drain fluid. Remove pressure hose and power steering pressure switch (if equipped) from pump. Loosen alternator or power steering adjustment bolts enough to remove drive belt. Remove pump adjustment bracket bolts.
2) Remove pump and adjustment bracket from support bracket. Using Pulley Remover (T69L-10300-B), remove pulley from pump. Remove pump.
Installation – 1) Install adjustment bracket on pump. Tighten bolts to specification. See TORQUE SPECIFICATIONS table at end of article. Using Pulley Installer (T65P-3A733-C), install pulley on pump. Pulley must be within .010" (.25 mm) of end of pump shaft.
2) Place pump assembly on support bracket. Install and tighten adjustment bracket-to-support bracket bolts to specification. Install and adjust belt on pulley. Tighten adjustment bracket bolts to specification.
3) Install hoses to pump. Tighten to specification. Fill reservoir. Start engine. Turn wheel from stop-to-stop to bleed air from system. Recheck reservoir. Refill reservoir (if necessary).

STEERING GEAR

Removal – 1) Disconnect hydraulic lines at power steering gear. Cap lines and ports to prevent contamination. Remove splash shield from flex coupling. Remove coupling bolt. Raise and support vehicle.
2) Remove pitman arm nut and washer. Using Pitman Arm Puller (T64P-3590-F), remove pitman arm from sector shaft. Remove steering gear-to-frame attaching bolts. Work steering gear free of flex coupling, remove steering gear from vehicle.
Installation – 1) Center steering wheel. Center steering gear input shaft with indexing flat facing down. Slide flex coupling into position on steering shaft assembly. Install coupling bolt and torque to 26-34 ft. lbs. (34-47 N.m). Install steering gear-to-frame bolts and torque to 50-62 ft. lbs. (68-84 N.m).
2) With wheels in straight-ahead position, install pitman arm on sector shaft. Install washer and nut on pitman arm. Torque to 170-228 ft. lbs. (170-228 N.m). Install splash shield. Connect and tighten hydraulic lines to steering gear. Torque to 20-30 ft. lbs. (27-40 N.m).
3) Fill reservoir to proper level. Disconnect primary and secondary coil wires and isolate them from ground. Crank engine while turning steering wheel left to right to distribute fluid. Recheck fluid level, add if needed. Check for fluid leaks.

OVERHAUL

POWER STEERING PUMP

Disassembly (C-II) – 1) Remove adjustment bracket and pulley removed from pump. Remove outlet fitting, flow control valve, spring and reservoir. *See Fig. 2.*
2) Place a "C" clamp in vise. Install Lower Support Plate (T78P-3733-A2) over pump rotor shaft. *See Fig. 4.* Install Upper Compressor Plate (T78P-3733-A1) into "C" clamp. Place pump assembly into "C" clamp with rotor shaft facing down.
3) Tighten "C" clamp until slight bottoming of valve cover is felt. Insert small drift through hole in side of pump housing plate. Push valve cover retaining ring inward and remove ring. *See Fig. 5.*
4) Remove pump from "C" clamp. Remove valve cover and "O" ring seal. Push on rotor shaft. Remove rotor shaft, cam, rotor and slippers and upper plate. Remove cam insert and 2 dowel pins.
5) By tapping housing on flat surface, remove lower plate and disc spring. Remove "O" ring. Using a screwdriver, remove rotor shaft seal and seal retainer.
Reassembly – 1) Place rotor on rotor shaft splines, with large rotor counterbore facing upward. Install retaining ring in groove in end of rotor shaft. Place insert cam over rotor with recessed flat facing toward reservoir.

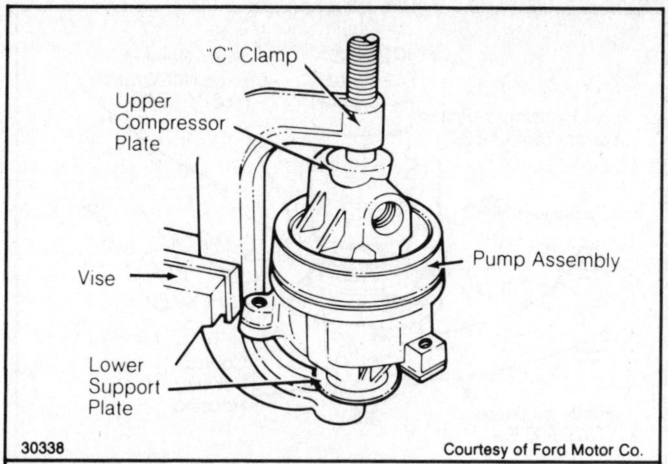
"C" Clamp
Upper Compressor Plate
Vise
Pump Assembly
Lower Support Plate
30338
Courtesy of Ford Motor Co.

Fig. 4: Mounting Pump For Disassembly

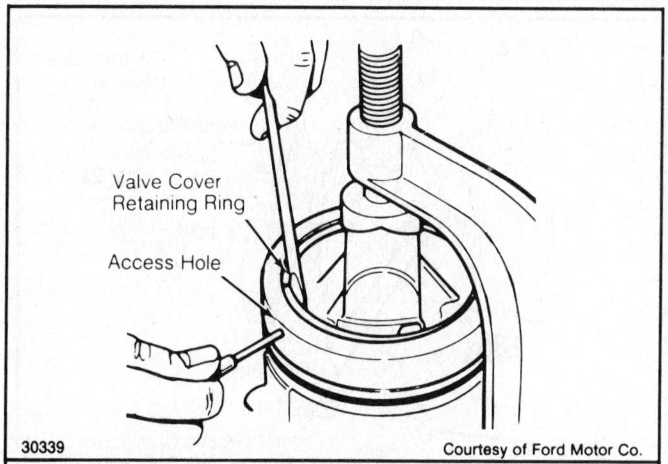
Valve Cover Retaining Ring
Access Hole
30339
Courtesy of Ford Motor Co.

Fig. 5: Removing Retaining Ring

2) With rotor extended half way out of cam, insert spring into rotor spring pocket. Work it into rotor cavity directly below recessed flat on cam. Use a slipper to compress spring. Install slipper with groove facing upward.
3) Hold cam stationary. Turn rotor either direction, one space at a time. Install another spring and slipper until all 10 rotor cavities are filled. Ensure springs and slippers do not fall out when turning rotor.
4) Using Seal Driver (T78P-3733-A3), install a new rotor shaft seal. Using a plastic mallet, drive seal and then seal retainer into bore until bottomed. Place pump housing plate on a flat surface with pulley side down.
5) Insert 2 dowel pins and disc spring (dished surface upward) into housing plate. Lubricate "O" ring seals with power steering fluid. Install seals on lower pressure plate.
6) Insert pressure plate with seals toward front of pump into pump housing plate and over dowel pins. Install disc spring (dished side up).
7) Place assembly into "C" clamp. Using Driver (T78P-3733-A3) in rotor shaft hole, press lower plate lightly until bottomed in pump plate housing, seating "O" ring. Install cam, rotor and slippers and rotor shaft assembly into pump housing plate over dowel pins.

NOTE: When installing assembly, stepped holes must be used for dowel pins. Recessed notch in cam insert must face reservoir and be approximately opposite square pump mounting boss.

8) Place upper pressure plate over dowel pins. Side of plate with square recessed notch must face reservoir and be positioned opposite square pump mounting boss. Place new "O" ring seal on valve cover. Lubricate with power steering fluid.

NOTE: Ensure plastic baffle is securely in place in valve cover. If not, apply petroleum jelly to baffle. Install baffle.

9) Place valve cover over dowel pins. Ensure valve cover outlet fitting hole is in line with square mounting boss of pump housing plate.
10) Place entire assembly in "C" clamp. Compress valve cover into pump housing plate, until retaining ring groove is exposed in pump housing plate.
11) Install valve cover retaining ring with ends near access hole in pump housing plate. Remove pump assembly from "C" clamp. Place new "O" ring seal on pump housing plate. Lubricate seal with power steering fluid. Install power steering reservoir.
12) Install flow control spring and flow control valve in valve cover. Place new "O" ring seals on outlet fitting. Lubricate seals with power steering fluid.
13) Install pump outlet fitting into valve cover. Tighten to specification. Install adjustment bracket on pump. Tighten bolts to specification. Using Pulley Installer (T65P-3A733-C), install pulley.

CAUTION: When clamping pump in vise, be careful not to exert excessive force on front hub or pump. Hammering on ANY pump components during assembly/disassembly may cause damage.

Disassembly (Saginaw) – 1) Drain pump reservoir. Clean exterior of unit. Remove mounting bracket(s). Using a puller, withdraw pulley from shaft.
2) Turn pulley shaft down. Clamp pump in a soft jawed vise at square boss on shaft housing. Remove pressure line union and "O" ring. Remove reservoir retaining studs.
3) Tap against filler tube with plastic hammer to loosen reservoir on pump body. Remove reservoir from body. Remove and discard "O" rings.
4) Using 1/8" punch, tap end plate retaining ring around until end of ring is near hole in pump body. Inserting punch in hole, disengage ring from groove in pump bore. Using a screwdriver, pry ring from body.
5) Tap end plate with a soft-faced hammer to loosen. Spring tension should push plate up. Remove spring. Remove pump from vise.
6) Invert pump and place on flat surface. Using soft-faced hammer, tap end of drive shaft to loosen pressure plate, rotor, and thrust plate assembly from body.
7) Lift pump body off rotor assembly. Flow control valve and spring should slide out of bore. Remove and discard end plate and pressure plate "O" rings.
8) Using a screwdriver, pry drive shaft oil seal from body. Lift pressure plate and cam ring from rotor. Remove rotor vanes.
9) Clamp drive shaft in soft-jawed vise, with rotor and thrust plate facing up. Remove rotor lock ring from shaft. Use care not to nick shaft or rotor. Slide rotor and thrust plate off shaft. Remove shaft from vise.
Cleaning & Inspection – 1) Clean all pump components (except drive shaft seal) in clean solvent. Blow dry. Inspect flow control valve assembly for wear, scoring, burrs or other damage. Inspect seal bore for burrs, nicks, or score marks that would allow oil to by-pass outer seal surface.
2) Check all machined surfaces of body for scratches or burrs which might allow leaks. Check "O" ring mating surfaces. Inspect pump body drive shaft bushing for excessive wear.
3) If replacement is required, replace pump body and bushing as an assembly. Inspect end cover "O" ring mating surface for nicks and burrs. Polish with oil stone (if necessary).
4) Inspect rotor ring for roughness or irregularities. Use oil stone to correct minor irregularities. Replace ring if outside cam surface is worn or scored. Check thrust plate and pressure plate for scoring and wear.
5) To remove light scoring, lap with crocus cloth until surface is smooth and flat. Clean thoroughly. Check that vanes slide freely but fit snugly into slots.
6) If vanes are loose in slots, replace rotor and/or vanes. Scoring on rotor may be removed with crocus cloth. Clean thoroughly.
Reassembly – 1) Lubricate all "O" rings, seals and seal surfaces with power steering fluid, or petroleum jelly. With pump on flat surface, drive new shaft seal in until it bottoms on bore shoulder.

1991 STEERING
Integral Power Steering (Cont.)

2) Clamp body in vise with shaft pointing down. Install end plate and pressure plate "O" rings on body. Install body to reservoir "O" rings. Install on pump body.
3) Place shaft, splined end up, in soft-jawed vise. Install thrust plate on shaft with smooth, ported side up. Slide rotor, counter bore down, over splines.
4) Install new rotor lock ring. Ensure ring is seated in groove. Install 2 dowel pins into holes in pump cavity. Insert drive shaft, rotor, and thrust plate assembly into pump cavity. Align locating holes with dowel pins.
5) Slide cam ring over rotor and onto dowel pins, with arrow on ring facing toward rear of housing. Install vanes in rotor slots with radius edge facing out towards cam ring inner surface. Position pressure plate on dowel pins with circular spring depression facing rear of housing.
6) Using a 1 1/4" socket in groove of pressure plate, press down on socket with both thumbs to seat assembly on "O" ring in pump cavity. Place spring in groove in pressure plate. Place end cover lip edge over spring.
7) Using thumb or arbor press, press end cover down below retaining ring groove. Seat retaining ring in groove. Take care to prevent cocking end plate in bore or distorting assembly.
8) Using a punch, tap retaining ring ends around in groove until opening is opposite flow control valve bore. This ensures maximum retention of retaining ring.
9) Install new "O" rings to reservoir, mounting studs, and flow control valve. Place reservoir on pump body. Align mounting stud holes. Install studs.
10) Using a soft-faced hammer, tap reservoir down on pump. Install flow control valve spring and valve assembly slotted end up. Install new "O" ring on pressure hose fitting uppermost groove.

CAUTION: DO NOT install pressure hose "O" ring in lower groove. This will restrict relief outlet orifice.

11) Install pressure hose fitting. Tighten mounting studs. Tighten hose fitting. Remove pump from vise. Install mounting bracket and pulley.

STEERING GEAR

Disassembly – 1) Remove steering gear, See STEERING GEAR under REMOVAL & INSTALLATION. Drain steering gear. Mount gear in a soft-jawed vise. Remove lock nut from adjusting screw. Center steering gear, (turn input shaft lock-to-lock, count turns, divide by two). If centered, flat surface on input shaft should be facing down.
2) Remove sector shaft cover bolts. Tap lower end of sector shaft with a soft faced hammer to loosen shaft in bore. Lift shaft and cover assembly from housing. Discard cover "O" ring. Remove sector shaft adjusting screw from cover.
3) Remove valve housing attaching bolts and identification tag. Remove valve housing, valve, piston assembly and gasket, discard gasket. Hold piston assembly over a clean container. Remove ball guide clamp screws, let guide tubes and balls fall into container. Rotate input shaft lock to lock until all balls fall from piston into container. Remove valve assembly from piston. Ensure that all balls have been removed.
4) Install valve body assembly in bench mounted Holding Fixture (T57L-500-B) or soft jawed vise. Lift valve body and loosen Allen head race nut screw from valve housing. Remove worm bearing race nut using Wrench (T66P-3553-B) and Valve Housing-to-Piston Spacer (T66P-3553-C). *See Fig. 6.* Carefully slide input shaft, worm and valve assembly out of valve housing.
Reassembly – 1) Mount valve housing in Holding Fixture (T57L-500-B) or vise with flanged end up. Lightly lubricate Teflon rings on valve sleeve. Carefully install worm and valve in housing.
2) Install worm bearing race nut in housing. Torque nut to 55-90 ft.lbs. (75-122 N.m). Install Allen head race nut set screw through housing, torque to 15-25 INCH lbs (1.7- 2.8 N.m).
3) Place piston on bench with ball guide holes facing up. *See Fig. 7.* Insert worm shaft into piston so first part of worm groove lines up with first hole in center of piston. Place ball guide in piston. Place 29 ball bearings in ball guide while turning worm counterclockwise as viewed from input end of shaft.
4) If all balls have not been fed into guide upon reaching left stop, rotate input shaft in one direction and then other while inserting remaining balls. DO NOT rotate input shaft more than 3 turns from left stop or balls will fall out of circuit.
5) Secure guides in ball nut with guide clamp. Torque ball guide clamp screw to 42-70 INCH lbs. (4.8-7.9 N.m). Apply petroleum jelly to Teflon seal on piston. Place new "O" ring on valve housing. Ensure piston ring is not damaged. Slide piston and valve into gear housing.
6) Align oil passage in valve housing with passage in gear housing. Place new "O" ring in oil passage hole of gear housing. Loosely install housing attaching bolts and identification tag. Rotate ball nut so teeth are in same plane as sector teeth. Torque valve housing-to-gear housing bolts to 30-45 ft. lbs. (41-62 N.m).
7) Place sector shaft cover "O" ring in gear housing. Turn input shaft to center piston. Apply petroleum jelly to sector shaft journal. Place sector shaft and cover into gear housing. Install and torque sector shaft cover bolts to 55-70 ft.lbs. (75-94 N.m). Perform over-center adjustment. See STEERING GEAR MESHLOAD under ADJUSTMENT in this article.

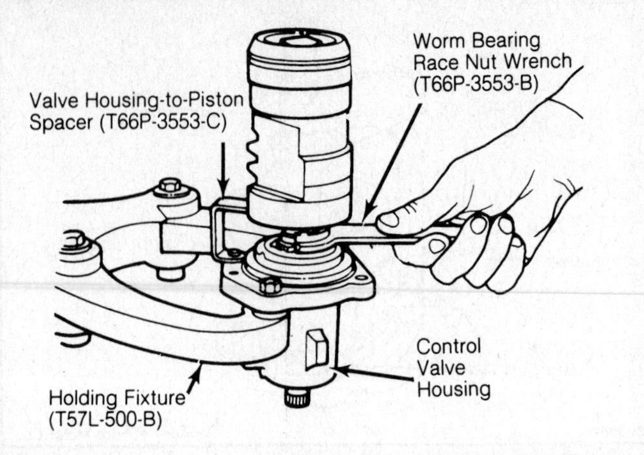
Worm Bearing
Race Nut Wrench
(T66P-3553-B)
Valve Housing-to-Piston
Spacer (T66P-3553-C)
Control
Valve
Housing
Holding Fixture
(T57L-500-B)
71422
Courtesy of Ford Motor Co.

Fig. 6: Removing Worm Bearing Race Nut

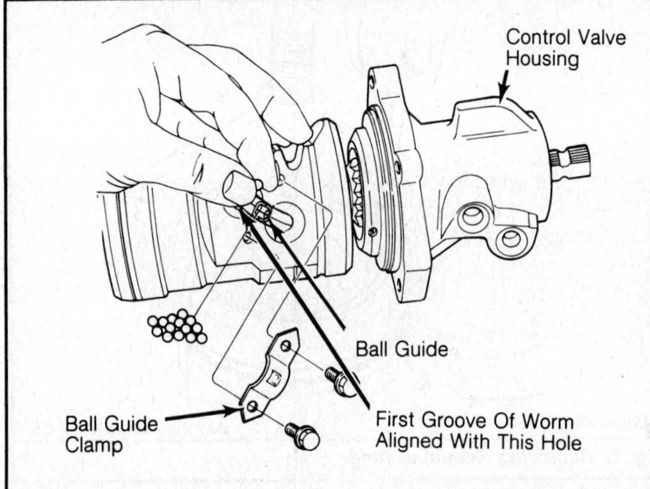
Control Valve
Housing
Ball Guide
Ball Guide
Clamp
First Groove Of Worm
Aligned With This Hole
71423
Courtesy of Ford Motor Co.

Fig. 7: Installing Ball Bearings Into Piston

STEERING GEAR HOUSING

Disassembly – Remove snap ring from lower end of gear housing. Using Puller Attachment (T58L-101-B) and Slide Hammer (T59L-100-B), remove dust seal and pressure seal from housing. Discard seals.

Reassembly – **1)** Lubricate new seals and seal bore with multi-grease. Place dust seal on Seal Installer (T77L-3576-A) so raised lip of seal faces installer. Place pressure seal on installer so lip faces away from installer. *See Fig. 8.*

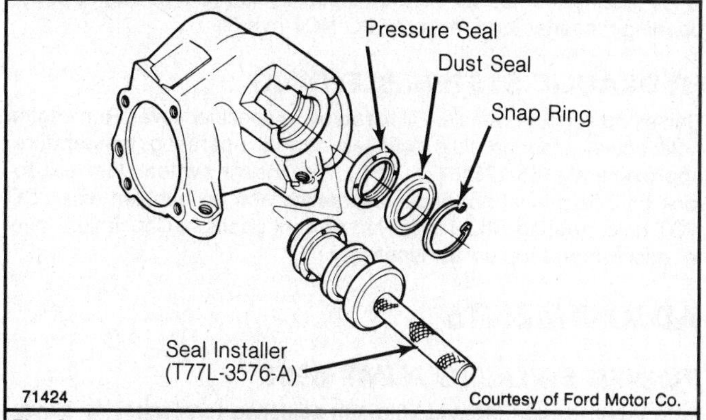
Pressure Seal
Dust Seal
Snap Ring
Seal Installer
(T77L-3576-A)
71424
Courtesy of Ford Motor Co.

Fig. 8: Installing Steering Gear Sector Shaft Seal

2) Insert installer into sector shaft bore. Drive in until seals just clear snap ring groove. DO NOT bottom seals against bearing, install snap ring. Apply grease to area between seal lips.

CONTROL VALVE HOUSING

Disassembly – **1)** Using Puller Attachment (T58L-101-B) and Slide Hammer (T59L-100-B), remove dust seal from rear of valve housing. Discard seal. Remove snap ring from valve housing. *See Fig. 9.*

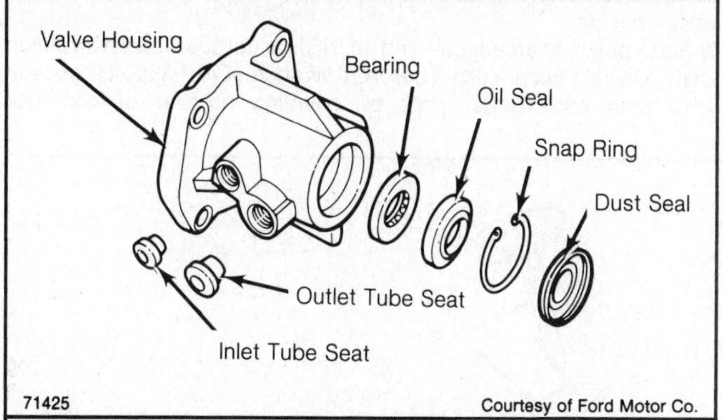
Valve Housing
Bearing
Oil Seal
Snap Ring
Dust Seal
Outlet Tube Seat
Inlet Tube Seat
71425
Courtesy of Ford Motor Co.

Fig. 9: Exploded View of Control Valve Housing

2) Turn valve housing over. Insert Driver Handle (T65P-3524-A2) and Bearing/Seal Remover (T65-3524-A3). Tap bearing and seal out of housing. Discard seal. If damaged, remove inlet tube seats using Tube Seat Remover (T74P-3504-L).

Reassembly – **1)** If tube seats were removed, coat with petroleum jelly and install with Tube Seat Installer (T74P-3504-M). Coat bearing and seal surface with petroleum jelly. Press bearing into housing using Installer (T65P-3524-A1) with metal covering rollers facing out. Bearing should rotate freely after installation.

2) Coat new oil seal in power steering fluid. Drive seal, using Installer (T65P-3524-A1), metal side out into housing. DO NOT fully seat seal. Remove Installer, place snap ring on seal and finish driving seal in until snap ring seats.

3) Place dust seal in housing with dished rubber side out. Using Installer (T65P-3524-A1), press until seal is located behind undercut in input shaft. Apply generous amount of multi-purpose grease to area between seal lips.

WORM & VALVE SLEEVE

Disassembly & Reassembly – **1)** Remove "O" rings from sleeve. *See Fig. 10.* DO NOT scratch sleeve. Mount worm end of assembly in soft-jawed vise. Place Mandrel (T75L-3517-A1) on sleeve. Install one valve sleeve ring over mandrel.

2) Using Driver (T75L-3517-A2), install rings one at a time. Rapidly push down on driver, force ring down ramp and into fourth groove of valve sleeve. Repeat 3 more times, adding Spacers (T75L-3517-A3), one additionally for each ring, under mandrel to line up next groove.

3) After all sleeve rings are installed, remove installation tools and apply a light coat of gear lubricant (SAE-80W) to sleeve and rings. Reinstall one spacer on input shaft as a pilot for Sizing Tube (T75L-3517-A4). Slide sizing tube carefully over valve sleeve rings. Ensure rings are not deformed when tube is installed.

4) Allow sizing tube to sit over rings for 5 minutes. Remove sizing tube. Check that rings turn freely in grooves.

PISTON & BALL NUT

Disassembly & Reassembly – Remove Teflon ring and "O" ring from piston and ball nut assembly. *See Fig. 10.* Dip new "O" ring in power steering fluid. Place it on piston and ball nut. Install new Teflon ring on piston and ball nut, using care not to over-stretch ring.

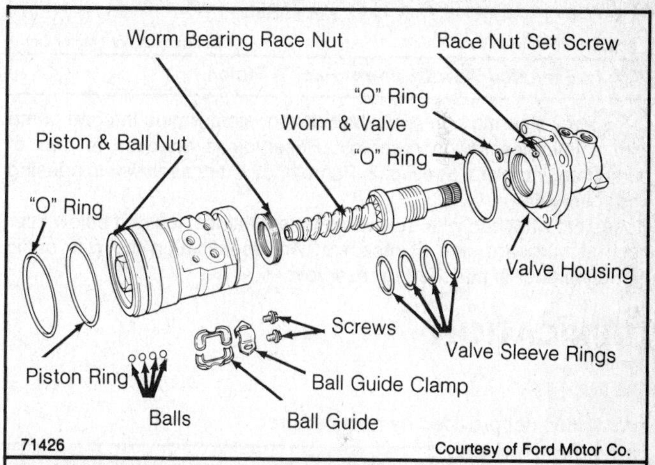
Worm Bearing Race Nut
Race Nut Set Screw
"O" Ring
Worm & Valve
Piston & Ball Nut
"O" Ring
"O" Ring
Valve Housing
Screws
Valve Sleeve Rings
Piston Ring
Ball Guide Clamp
Balls
Ball Guide
71426
Courtesy of Ford Motor Co.

Fig. 10: Exploded View of Ball Nut & Valve Housing

TORQUE SPECIFICATIONS

TORQUE SPECIFICATIONS

Application	Ft. Lbs. (N.m)
Flex Coupling Bolt	25-34 (34-46)
Mesh Load Adjusting Screw Lock Nut	35-45 (48-61)
Piston End Cap	70-110 (95-150)
Pitman Arm Nut	190-230 (230-310)
Pressure Hose-to-Gear Fitting	16-25 (22-34)
Pump Bracket Brace nuts	13-17 (18-23)
Pump Outlet Fitting	25-40 (34-54)
Pump Mounting Bracket Bolts	23-30 (30-40)
Pump Quick Connect Fitting	30-40 (41-54)
Pump-To-Bracket Bolts	30-40 (40-55)
Rack Retaining Nut	55-90 (75-122)
Return Hose-to-Gear Fitting	25-34 (34-46)
Sector Shaft Cover Bolts	55-70 (75-95)
Steering Gear-to-Frame Bolts	50-62 (68-84)
Valve Housing-to-Gear Housing Bolts	35-50 (48-68)
Worm Bearing Race Nut	55-90 (75-122)
	INCH Lbs. (N.m)
Allen Head Race Nut Set Screw	15-25 (1.6-2.8)
Ball Guide Clamp Screw	42-70 (4.7-7.9)

1991 STEERING
Power Rack & Pinion

Aerostar

DESCRIPTION

Power rack and pinion has gear and valve housings cast into a 1-piece aluminum unit. Steering gear, which is hydraulic and mechanical-type, uses internal valving to direct hydraulic fluid flow and pressure. Gear contains a rotary hydraulic fluid control valve integrated to input shaft and a boost cylinder integrated with rack. *See Fig. 1.*

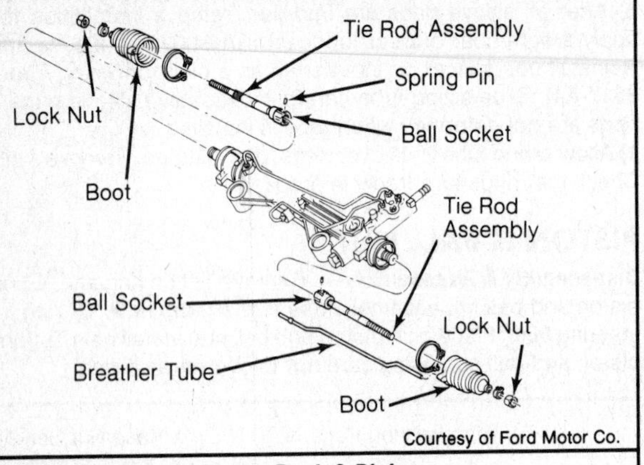
Tie Rod Assembly
Spring Pin
Lock Nut
Ball Socket
Boot
Tie Rod Assembly
Ball Socket
Lock Nut
Breather Tube
Boot
30312
Courtesy of Ford Motor Co.

Fig. 1: Exploded View Of Power Rack & Pinion

C-II power steering pump is a belt-driven, slipper-type integral pump with a fiberglass/nylon reservoir. Reservoir is attached to rear of pump housing plate. *See Fig. 2.* Pump body is encased within housing and reservoir.

Hoses are attached with quick disconnect fittings, located below filler neck at outboard side of reservoir. An identification tag with basic model number is attached to reservoir.

LUBRICATION

CAPACITY

Information not provided by manufacturer.

FLUID TYPE

Use Ford Premium Power Steering Fluid (E6AZ-19582-AA) or Type F ATF fluid.

FLUID LEVEL CHECK

Fluid level may be checked when fluid is either hot or cold. If fluid is cold, approximately 75°F (24°C), check fluid level using the cold full mark on dipstick. If fluid is hot, approximately 177°F (77°C), check fluid level using the hot full mark on dipstick. Add fluid through dipstick opening if needed and recheck. DO NOT overfill.

HYDRAULIC SYSTEM BLEEDING

Raise and support vehicle. Fill reservoir to specified level. Run engine until power steering fluid reaches normal operating temperature, approximately 165-175°F (74-79°C). Turn steering wheel from lock-to-lock until fluid level no longer decreases and no bubbles exist. DO NOT hold steering wheel in far left or right position. Check fluid level in reservoir and top up as necessary.

ADJUSTMENTS

POWER STEERING PUMP BELT

Poly V-belt design is used with self-adjusting tensioner. No adjustment is required.

RACK YOKE PLUG PRELOAD

NOTE: Steering gear and housing must be removed to perform adjustment.

1) Remove steering gear and housing. See POWER RACK & PINION STEERING GEAR under REMOVAL & INSTALLATION in this article. Drain power steering fluid by rotating input shaft lock-to-lock twice, using Pinion Shaft Torque Adapter (T74P-3504-R). Cover ports on valve housing.

2) Place pinion shaft adapter and an INCH lb. torque wrench on pinion shaft. Using Pinion Yoke Lock Nut Wrench (T78P-3504-H), loosen yoke plug nut. Center rack by counting number of complete

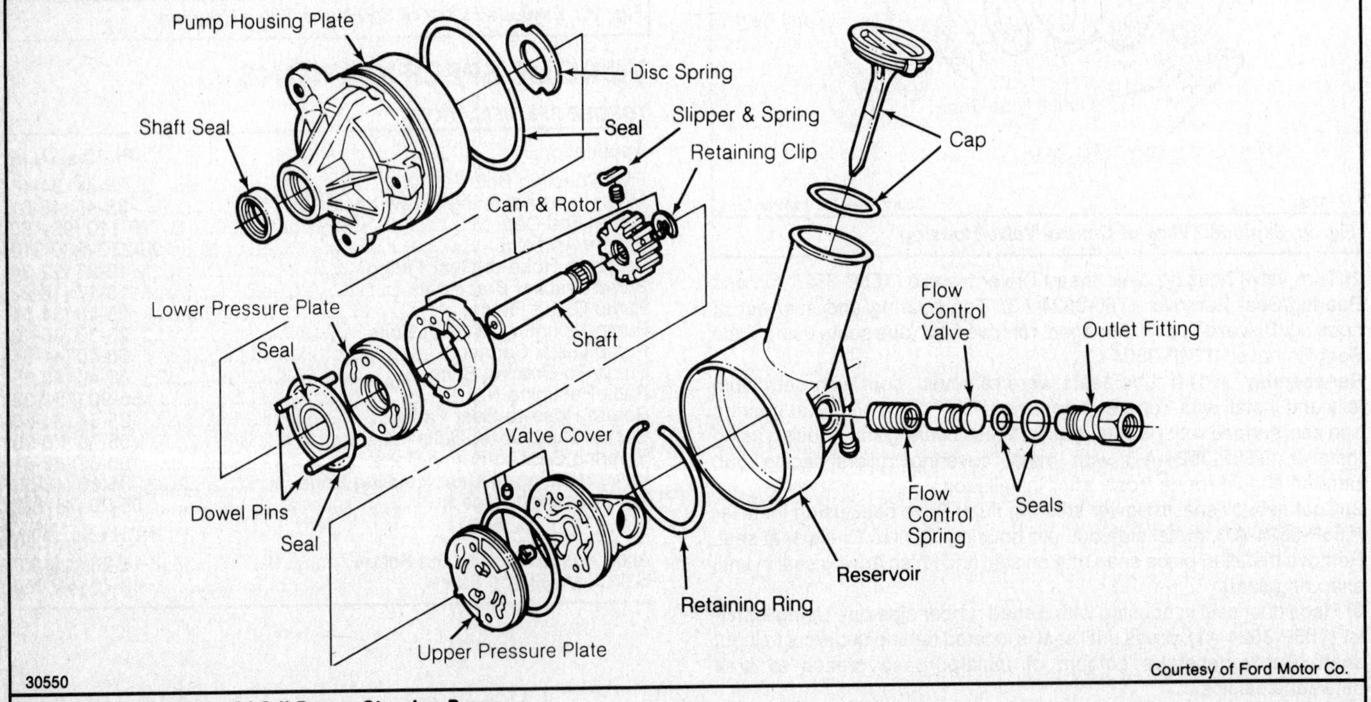
Pump Housing Plate
Disc Spring
Shaft Seal
Seal
Slipper & Spring
Retaining Clip
Cap
Cam & Rotor
Lower Pressure Plate
Seal
Shaft
Flow Control Valve
Outlet Fitting
Valve Cover
Dowel Pins
Seal
Flow Control Spring
Seals
Reservoir
Retaining Ring
Upper Pressure Plate
30550
Courtesy of Ford Motor Co.

Fig. 2: Exploded View Of C-II Power Steering Pump

revolutions of input shaft and dividing number by 2. Tighten yoke plug nut to 45-50 INCH lbs. (5.0-5.6 N.m).

3) Back off yoke plug nut 1/8 turn (44 degrees minimum and 54 degrees maximum) until torque required to turn input shaft is 7-18 INCH lbs. (.78-2.03 N.m). Hold yoke plug and tighten lock nut to 44-66 ft lbs. (60-89 N.m). Do not allow yoke plug to move while tightening. Recheck input shaft torque after tightening lock nut.

TESTING

PRESSURE TEST

NOTE: For testing, use Power Steering Analyzer (D79L-33610-A) with flow meter.

Pre-Test Preparation – 1) With belt tension correct, disconnect power steering pump pressure hose. Keep hose end raised to prevent fluid loss. Connect pressure hose of gauge to power steering pump fitting. Connect other hose from valve side of tester to steering gear inlet.

2) Open valve. Run engine until fluid reaches normal operating temperature of 165-175°F (74-79°C). Check fluid level. Add fluid as required.

Pressure Test – 1) Start engine and let idle for approximately 2 minutes. Record flow. If flow is less than 1.6 gallons per minute (6.1L per minute), pump may require repair. Continue test.

2) If pressure is greater than 150 psi (10.5 kg/cm²), check hoses for restrictions. Partially close valve to build up pressure to 740 psi (52 kg/cm²).

3) If flow drops below specification, disassemble pump and replace cam pack. If pressure plates are cracked or worn, they must be replaced.

4) Completely close and partially open gate valve 3 times. Do not close valve for more than 5 seconds. Record highest reading each time. If pressure is higher or lower than specified, repair or replace flow control valve. Refer to PRESSURE TEST SPECIFICATIONS table.

PRESSURE TEST SPECIFICATIONS

Application	Idle Pressure psi (kg/cm²)	[1] Relief Pressure psi (kg/cm²)
Aerostar		
Ford C-II Pump		
Model HBC-KC	740	1050-1230
	(52)	(74-86)
Ford C-II Pump		
Model HBC-KE	740	1400-1530
	(52)	(98-108)

[1] – Measure with steering wheel turned to extreme right or left position.

5) Set engine speed at 1500 RPM. Record flow. If flow varies more than 1 gallon (3.8L) per minute from pressure measured in step **1)**, flow control valve in pump must be repaired or replaced.

6) Turn steering wheel to left and right stops. Pressure should be nearly the same as maximum relief pressure. Flow should drop below .5 gallon (1.9L) per minute

7) If pressure and flow are not as specified, steering gear is leaking internally. Remove steering gear. Remove flow control valve. Repair or replace damaged parts. Check rack piston and valve seals for damage.

8) If pressure and flow are good, turn steering wheel slightly in both directions and release quickly while watching pressure gauge. Needle should move from normal backpressure reading and snap back as wheel is released.

9) If gauge reacts slowly, or sticks, rotary valve in steering gear is sticking. Repair or replace rotary valve.

10) If system is severely contaminated, both hoses, control valve, and pump must be disassembled and cleaned. If problem still exists, check ball joints, linkage and other front suspension members.

TURNING EFFORT CHECK

NOTE: Ensure front wheels are properly aligned and the tire pressures are correct before checking turning effort.

1) Park vehicle on a dry, concrete surface and set parking brake. Run engine at idle for 2-3 minutes. Turn steering wheel to the far left and right positions several times to warm fluid to 110-120°F (43-48°C). DO NOT hold steering wheel in far left or right position.

2) With engine running, attach a pull scale to steering wheel rim. Measure pull required to turn steering wheel one complete revolution in each direction. Effort required to turn steering wheel one complete revolution in each direction should be 29-39 INCH lbs. (3.3-4.4 N.m). If turning effort is not within specifications repair or replace power steering gear or pump as necessary.

REMOVAL & INSTALLATION

POWER STEERING PUMP & PULLEY

Removal – 1) Disconnect fluid return hose at reservoir and drain fluid. Remove pressure hose and power steering pressure switch (if equipped) from pump. Loosen alternator or power steering adjustment bolts enough to remove drive belt. Remove pump adjustment bracket bolts.

2) Remove pump and adjustment bracket from support bracket. Using Pulley Remover (T69L-10300-B), remove pulley from pump. Remove pump.

Installation – 1) Install adjustment bracket on pump. Tighten bolts to specification. See TORQUE SPECIFICATIONS table at end of article. Using Pulley Installer (T65P-3A733-C), install pulley on pump. Pulley must be within .010" (.25 mm) of end of pump shaft.

2) Place pump assembly on support bracket. Install and tighten adjustment bracket-to-support bracket bolts to specification. Install and adjust belt on pulley. Tighten adjustment bracket bolts to specification.

3) Install hoses to pump. Tighten to specification. Fill reservoir. Start engine. Turn wheel from stop-to-stop to bleed air from system. Recheck reservoir. Refill reservoir (if necessary).

POWER RACK & PINION STEERING GEAR

Removal – 1) Place front wheels in straight-ahead position. Disconnect battery ground cable. Turn ignition on. Raise and support vehicle.

2) Remove lower intermediate steering column shaft bolt. Disconnect shaft from gear. Disconnect and plug pressure and return lines at gear valve housing only. *See Fig. 3.*

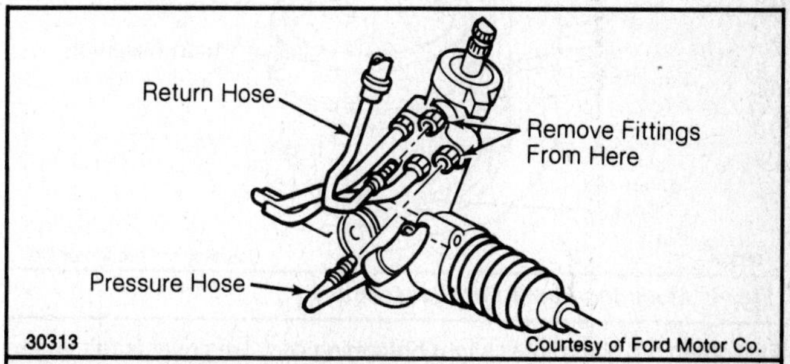
Return Hose
Remove Fittings From Here
Pressure Hose
30313
Courtesy of Ford Motor Co.

Fig. 3: Locating Pressure & Return Line

3) Remove tie rod ends from spindle arms. Remove nuts, bolts and washers retaining steering gear to crossmember, remove steering gear. Remove front and rear insulators from steering gear housing (if necessary).

Installation – Install insulators (if removed). Position steering gear on crossmember. Place steering gear, steering wheel and front wheels in straight-ahead position. To complete installation, reverse removal procedure.

1991 STEERING
Power Rack & Pinion (Cont.)

OUTER TIE ROD ENDS

Removal - 1) Place front wheels in straight-ahead position. Remove and discard cotter pin. Remove castle nut. Using Tie Rod End Remover (T64P-3590-F), separate tie rod end from spindle arm.

2) Loosen jam nut to expose threads at tie rod end. Index mark exact position of tie rod end at exposed threads for assembly reference. Remove tie rod end.

Installation - Screw tie rod end onto tie rod, to reference mark tighten jam nut to 35-50 ft. lbs. (48-68 N.m). Ensure wheels are in straight-ahead position. Connect tie rod stud to spindle arm. Install and tighten castle nut to 52-73 ft. lbs. (70-100 N.m). If necessary, advance nut to next castellation and install new cotter pin. Check and adjust toe as necessary.

NOTE: Ensure tie rod studs are seated properly in taper of spindle arm.

BOOT

Removal - Clean exterior gear housing and tie rod threads. See REMOVAL under OUTER TIE ROD ENDS. Remove tie rod outer end(s), remove boot retaining clamps and boot.

Installation - Apply silicone gasket sealer to boot inner contact area. Slide boot over tie rod assembly. Install new boot clamps. See INSTALLATION under OUTER TIE ROD ENDS. Install outer tie rod ends.

OVERHAUL

POWER STEERING PUMP

Disassembly - 1) Remove adjustment bracket and pulley removed from pump. Remove outlet fitting, flow control valve, spring and reservoir. *See Fig. 2.*

2) Place a "C" clamp in vise. Install Lower Support Plate (T78P-3733-A2) over pump rotor shaft. *See Fig. 4.* Install Upper Compressor Plate (T78P-3733-A1) into "C" clamp. Place pump assembly into "C" clamp with rotor shaft facing down.

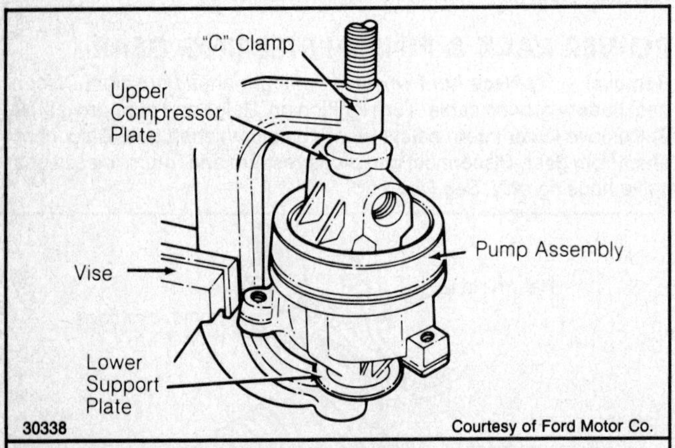
"C" Clamp
Upper Compressor Plate
Pump Assembly
Vise
Lower Support Plate
30338
Courtesy of Ford Motor Co.

Fig. 4: Mounting Pump For Disassembly

3) Tighten "C" clamp until slight bottoming of valve cover is felt. Insert small drift through hole in side of pump housing plate. Push valve cover retaining ring inward and remove ring. *See Fig. 5.*

4) Remove pump from "C" clamp. Remove valve cover and "O" ring seal. Push on rotor shaft. Remove rotor shaft, cam, rotor and slippers and upper plate. Remove cam insert and 2 dowel pins.

5) By tapping housing on flat surface, remove lower plate and disc spring. Remove "O" ring. Using a screwdriver, remove rotor shaft seal and seal retainer.

Reassembly - 1) Place rotor on rotor shaft splines, with large rotor counterbore facing upward. Install retaining ring in groove in end of rotor shaft. Place insert cam over rotor with recessed flat facing toward reservoir.

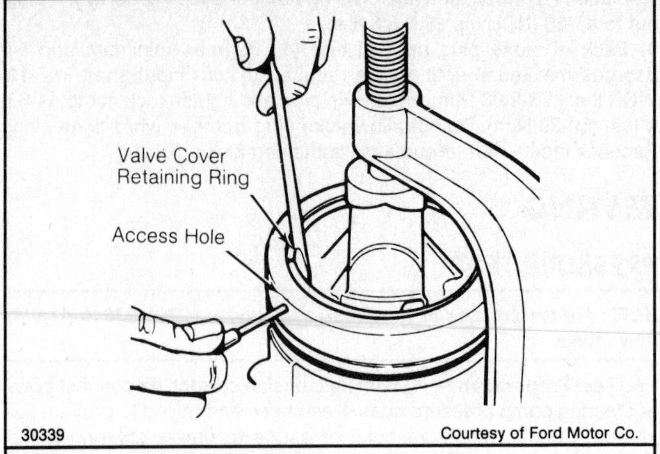
Valve Cover Retaining Ring
Access Hole
30339
Courtesy of Ford Motor Co.

Fig. 5: Removing Retaining Ring

2) With rotor extended half way out of cam, insert spring into rotor spring pocket. Work it into rotor cavity directly below recessed flat on cam. Use a slipper to compress spring. Install slipper with groove facing upward.

3) Hold cam stationary. Turn rotor either direction, one space at a time. Install another spring and slipper until all 10 rotor cavities are filled. Ensure springs and slippers do not fall out when turning rotor.

4) Using Seal Driver (T78P-3733-A3), install a new rotor shaft seal. Using a plastic mallet, drive seal and then seal retainer into bore until bottomed. Place pump housing plate on a flat surface with pulley side down.

5) Insert 2 dowel pins and disc spring (dished surface upward) into housing plate. Lubricate "O" ring seals with power steering fluid. Install seals on lower pressure plate.

6) Insert pressure plate with seals toward front of pump into pump housing plate and over dowel pins. Install disc spring (dished side up).

7) Place assembly into "C" clamp. Using Driver (T78P-3733-A3) in rotor shaft hole, press lower plate lightly until bottomed in pump plate housing, seating "O" ring. Install cam, rotor and slippers and rotor shaft assembly into pump housing plate over dowel pins.

NOTE: When installing assembly, stepped holes must be used for dowel pins. Recessed notch in cam insert must face reservoir and be approximately opposite square pump mounting boss.

8) Place upper pressure plate over dowel pins. Side of plate with square recessed notch must face reservoir and be positioned opposite square pump mounting boss. Place new "O" ring seal on valve cover. Lubricate with power steering fluid.

NOTE: Ensure plastic baffle is securely in place in valve cover. If not, apply petroleum jelly to baffle. Install baffle.

9) Place valve cover over dowel pins. Ensure valve cover outlet fitting hole is in line with square mounting boss of pump housing plate.

10) Place entire assembly in "C" clamp. Compress valve cover into pump housing plate, until retaining ring groove is exposed in pump housing plate.

11) Install valve cover retaining ring with ends near access hole in pump housing plate. Remove pump assembly from "C" clamp. Place new "O" ring seal on pump housing plate. Lubricate seal with power steering fluid. Install power steering reservoir.

12) Install flow control spring and flow control valve in valve cover. Place new "O" ring seals on outlet fitting. Lubricate seals with power steering fluid.

13) Install pump outlet fitting into valve cover. Tighten to specification. Install adjustment bracket on pump. Tighten bolts to specification. Using Pulley Installer (T65P-3A733-C), install pulley.

POWER RACK & PINION STEERING GEAR

Disassembly – 1) Remove steering gear from vehicle. See POWER RACK & PINION STEERING GEAR under REMOVAL & INSTALLATION. Clean exterior of steering gear. Loosen tie rod jam nut, mark position of tie rod ends for assembly reference. Mount gear in Holding Fixture (T57L-500-B) or soft jawed vise.

2) Remove boot retaining clamps, boots, jam nuts and breather tube. Using Lock Nut Wrench (T78P-3504-H), loosen yoke plug lock nut. Loosen yoke plug. Remove pinion bearing bottom plug. To remove pinion bearing lock nut, install Torque Adapter (T74P-3504-R) over input shaft. *See Fig. 6.*

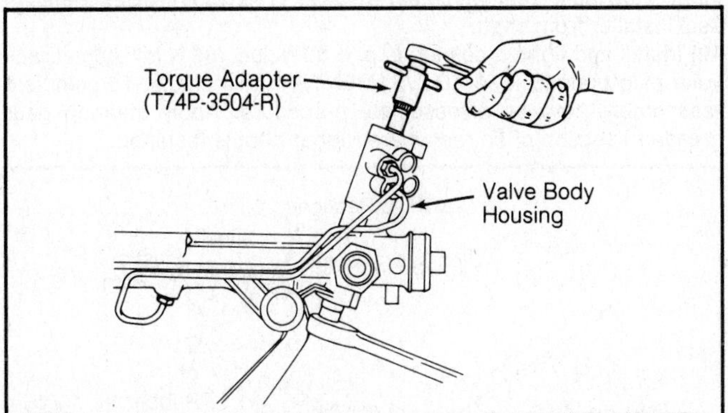

Torque Adapter
(T74P-3504-R)
Valve Body
Housing

30314 Courtesy of Ford Motor Co.

Fig. 6: Removing Pinion Bearing Lock Nut

3) Using an awl, pry pinion bearing dust seal from housing. DO NOT scratch housing inner surface. Remove pinion bearing snap ring. Using Valve Body Puller (T78P-3504-B) remove input shaft and valve body. *See Fig. 7.*

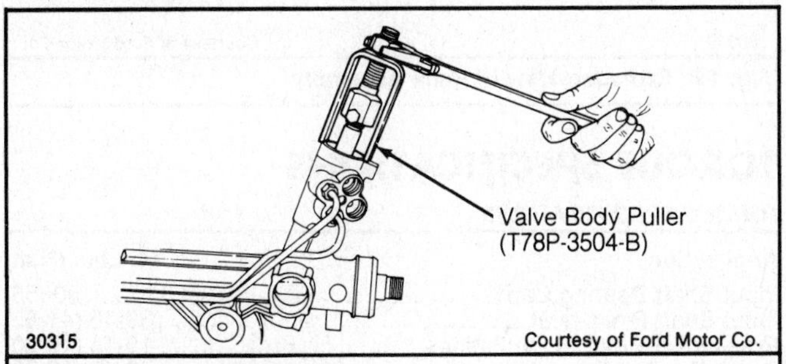

Valve Body Puller
(T78P-3504-B)

30315 Courtesy of Ford Motor Co.

Fig. 7: Removing Valve Body

4) To remove lower pinion shaft seal, insert Seal Remover (T78P-3504-E2) and Spacer Collet (D82P-3504-E1) until spacer and remover bottom. Hold large nut while tightening small nut, until expander tightens. *See Fig. 8.*

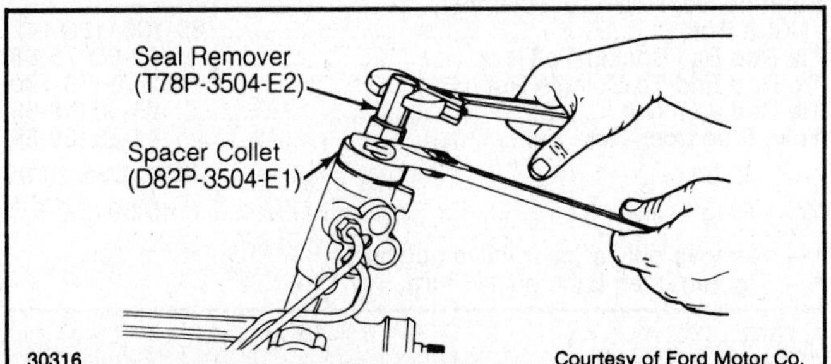

Seal Remover
(T78P-3504-E2)
Spacer Collet
(D82P-3504-E1)

30316 Courtesy of Ford Motor Co.

Fig. 8: Removing Lower Pinion Shaft Seal

5) Insert slide hammer into rear of seal remover. Pull seal from housing. Inspect lower pinion bearing. Use slide hammer and Puller Attachment (T58L-101-A) to pull bearing from valve housing.

6) Thread point of Lock Nut Pin Remover (D81P-3504-N) into spring pin in ball socket. Finger tighten lock nut pin remover. Tighten nut on lock nut pin remover. Remove and discard spring pin. *See Fig. 9.*

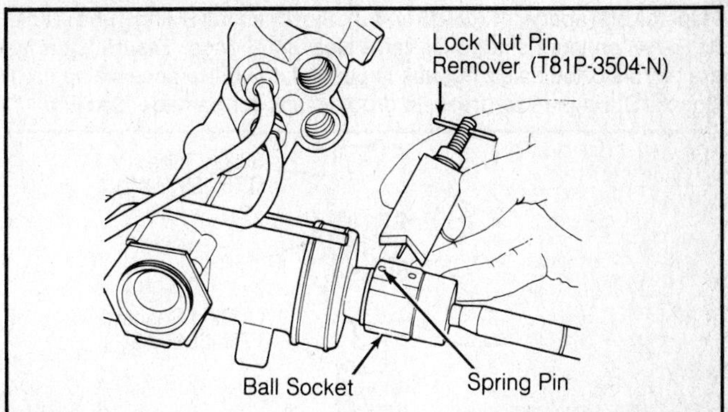

Lock Nut Pin
Remover (T81P-3504-N)
Ball Socket
Spring Pin

30317 Courtesy of Ford Motor Co.

Fig. 9: Removing Spring Pin

7) Pull rack out to expose several teeth. Hold rack with adjustable wrench and Socket Wrench (T74P-3504-U). Remove both tie rod ball joint sockets. Remove steering rack.

Cleaning & Inspection – Examine parts for wear and contamination. Replace as needed. Inspect yoke to ensure that insert is seated flush with yoke body. If pinion teeth are pitted or worn, or if upper bearing is damaged or binding, replace entire steering gear assembly as a unit.

Reassembly – 1) Using Socket Wrench (T74P-3504-U) and holding rack with adjustable pliers, install both tie rod ball joint sockets. Rest ball joint socket on wooden block. To install new spring pin, hold spring pin with needle-nose pliers while tapping spring pin in lightly with plastic hammer.

2) Using Pinion Bearing Driver (T78P-3504-G), install new bearing (if removed). Ensure bearing is seated against shoulder in bore. Coat lower pinion oil seal with steering gear grease.

3) Place seal on Seal Installer (T78P-3504-F), with lip of seal facing toward installer. Support housing on clean surface. Drive seal in until seated against shoulder.

4) If valve "O" rings were not removed, go to step **9**). If "O" rings were removed, mount pinion end of valve assembly in soft-jawed vise. Lubricate Mandrel (T75L-3517-A1) with Type F transmission fluid. Install mandrel over valve assembly.

5) Slide one valve "O" ring over mandrel. Place Slide Ring Pusher (T75L-3517-A2) on mandrel, push down rapidly on ring pusher, forcing "O" ring down into fourth groove of valve sleeve. Install one "O" Ring Spacer (T75L-3517-A3) on input shaft, keeping next "O" ring from passing third groove of valve sleeve. Repeat this step until all "O" rings and spacers are on shaft. *See Fig. 10.*

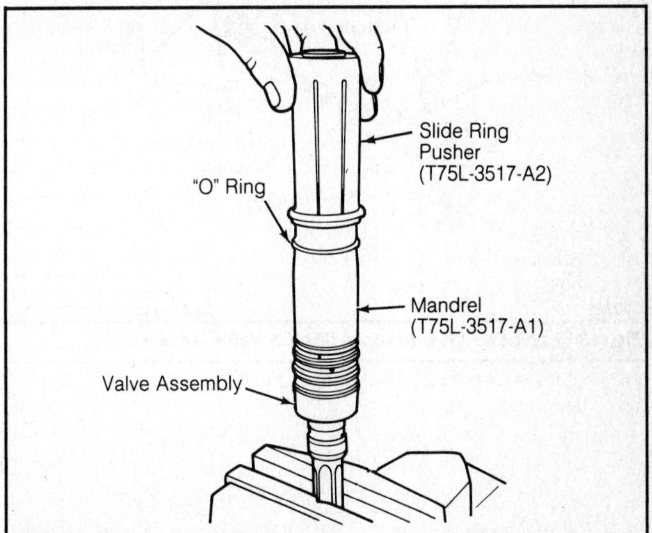

Slide Ring
Pusher
(T75L-3517-A2)
"O" Ring
Mandrel
(T75L-3517-A1)
Valve Assembly

30318 Courtesy of Ford Motor Co.

Fig. 10: Installing Valve "O" Rings

1991 STEERING
Power Rack & Pinion (Cont.)

6) Install one spacer (T75L-3517-A3). Slowly install Sizing Tube (T75L-3517-A4) on input shaft over valve sleeve "O" rings. Ensure "O" rings are not distorted as sizing tube is pushed down. Remove sizing tube. Check "O" rings move freely in grooves and for damage. *See Fig. 11.*

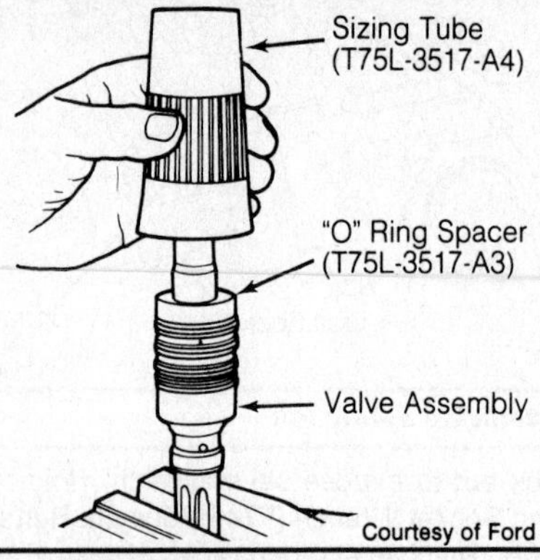
Sizing Tube
(T75L-3517-A4)
"O" Ring Spacer
(T75L-3517-A3)
Valve Assembly

30319 Courtesy of Ford Motor Co.

Fig. 11: Installing "O" Ring Sizing Tube

7) Position rack in housing so that right end of rack protrudes 9/16" (14 mm) from socket to housing. *See Fig. 12.* Place Valve Body Inserter (T78P-3504-C) into top of valve housing. Lubricate valve shaft, and install into housing. Align flat spot "D" shape of shaft facing backward (180° from yoke nut). Ensure shaft teeth mesh with rack teeth. Push valve assembly in by hand until fully seated.

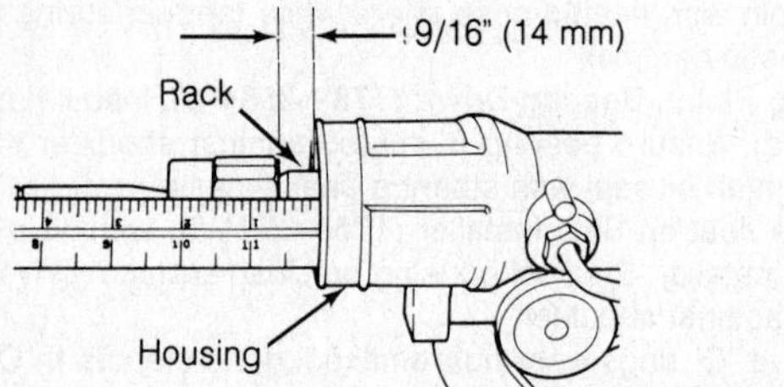
9/16" (14 mm)
Rack
Housing

30320 Courtesy of Ford Motor Co.

Fig. 12: Aligning Rack With Rack Housing

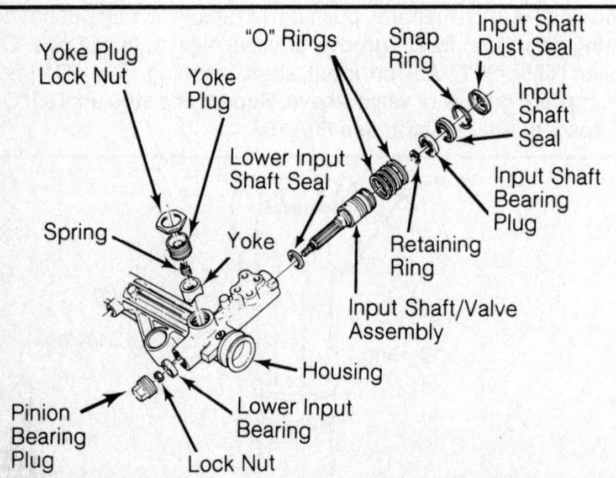
Yoke Plug
Lock Nut
"O" Rings
Snap
Ring
Input Shaft
Dust Seal
Yoke
Plug
Input
Shaft
Seal
Lower Input
Shaft Seal
Input Shaft
Bearing
Plug
Spring
Yoke
Retaining
Ring
Input Shaft/Valve
Assembly
Housing
Pinion
Bearing
Plug
Lower Input
Bearing
Lock Nut

30321 Courtesy of Ford Motor Co.

Fig. 13: Exploded View of Input Shaft & Valve Assembly

8) Install Pinion Shaft Torque Adapter (T74P-3504-R) onto input shaft. Install nut onto pinion end of valve assembly. Hold pinion shaft with torque adapter. Tighten nut to 30-44 ft. lbs. (40-55 N.m). Ensure pinion is centered, counting the input shaft turns from center to stops. If unequal remove shaft, move rack one tooth, reinstall pinion shaft. Repeat until centered.

9) Slide pinion shaft bearing over shaft and into valve bore. Using Bearing Installer (T78P-3504-D), firmly seat bearing into bore. Lightly coat input shaft seal with steering gear grease. Install with lip facing gear housing. Drive seal in until fully seated. Install snap ring. Slide Input Shaft Seal Installer (T85T-3504-CH1) over input shaft. Install input shaft dust seal with Seal Installer (T85T-3504-CH2). Remove seal installer from shaft.

10) Install and tighten bearing cap to 50 ft. lbs. (67 N.m). Adjust rack yoke plug preload. See ADJUSTMENTS in this article. To complete reassembly, reverse disassembly procedure. Apply steering gear grease to section of tie rod where rubber boot is fastened.

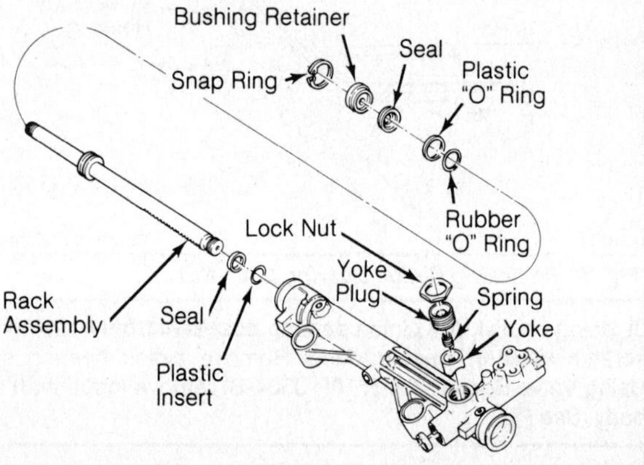
Bushing Retainer
Seal
Snap Ring
Plastic
"O" Ring
Rubber
"O" Ring
Lock Nut
Yoke
Plug
Rack
Assembly
Seal
Spring
Yoke
Plastic
Insert

30322 Courtesy of Ford Motor Co.

Fig. 14: Exploded View of Rack Assembly

TORQUE SPECIFICATIONS

TORQUE SPECIFICATIONS

Application	Ft. Lbs. (N.m)
Input Shaft Bearing Cap	50 (68)
Input Shaft Pinion Nut	30-40 (41-55)
Pressure & Return Line Fittings [1]	10-15 (15-20)
Pump Bracket Brace Nuts	13-17 (18-23)
Pump Outlet Fitting	25-40 (34-54)
Pump Mounting Bracket	23-30 (30-40)
Pump Quick Connect Fitting	30-40 (41-54)
Pump-To-Bracket	30-40 (41-55)
Steering Column Lower Intermediate Shaft-To-Gear Bolt	30-42 (41-56)
Steering Gear-To-Crossmember Nut & Bolt	80-105 (108-142)
Tie Rod Ball Socket-To-Rack	55-65 (75-88)
Tie Rod End-To-Spindle Nut	52-73 (70-100)
Tie Rod Jam Nut	35-50 (48-68)
Yoke Plug Lock Nut	44-66 (60-89)
	INCH Lbs. (N.m)
Yoke Plug [2]	45-50 (5.0-5.6)

[1] – Remove only at gear valve housing.
[2] – Tighten, then back off 1/8 turn.

1991 STEERING
Bendix Power Steering

"F" Series Super Duty, Commercial Stripped Chassis, Motor Home Chassis

DESCRIPTION

The Bendix 300N or C-300N power steering gear is designed for medium duty vehicles with front axle weight ratings of 6000-9000 lbs. Steering gear incorporates mechanical and hydraulic components in a single housing, which also serves as the power cylinder. A separate ZF power steering pump supplies pressurized power steering fluid to power steering and brake hydro-boost units.

LUBRICATION

CAPACITY

Information is not provided by manufacturer.

FLUID TYPE

Use MERCON-II automatic transmission fluid or equivalent.

FLUID LEVEL CHECK

If fluid is cold, approximately 75°F (24°C), check fluid level using the cold full mark on dipstick. If fluid is hot, approximately 177°F (81°C), check fluid level using the hot full mark on dipstick. Fluid level must be maintained between ADD and FULL marks. Add fluid through dipstick opening, if needed, and recheck. DO NOT overfill.

HYDRAULIC SYSTEM BLEEDING

Diesel Engines – Fill reservoir. Start engine. Turn steering wheel from stop to stop several times. Stop engine. Check fluid level and refill reservoir as necessary.

Gasoline Engines – **1)** Disconnect coil wire. Fill reservoir. Crank engine with starter until fluid level remains constant. Avoid overheating starter. Refill reservoir.

2) Reconnect coil wire. Start engine and allow it to run several minutes. Turn steering from stop to stop. Stop engine. Check fluid level and add fluid as necessary.

ADJUSTMENTS

POWER STEERING PUMP BELT

BELT ADJUSTMENT

Application	New Belt Lbs. (kg)	[1] Used Belt Lbs. (kg)
5.8L With Tensioner [2]	[3]	[3]
7.3L With 1/2" Belt	140-180 (64-82)	95-115 (43-52)
7.5L With Tensioner [2]	[4]	[4]

[1] – Any belt operated for 10 minutes or longer.
[2] – Tension is correct if tensioner is within indicator marks.
[3] – 77 lbs. (35 kg) minimum for vehicles with 60 & 75-amp alternators. 111 lbs. (50 kg) minimum for vehicles with 100-amp alternators.
[4] – 94 lbs. (43 kg) minimum tension.

OUTPUT SHAFT BACKLASH

Backlash is correct when 4-18 INCH lbs. (0.50-2.0 N.m) increase in torque occurs as input shaft is rotated and piston passes through the midpoint of its travel. This torque increase will occur only as the piston travels through the midpoint of its travel, and should disappear as piston moves past the midpoint.

1) Ensure adjusting screw is turned counterclockwise as far as it will go. Rotate input shaft as far as possible in each direction. Count total turns in either direction and at same time measure average torque required to rotate shaft.

2) Rotate input shaft 180 degrees in both directions past midpoint of piston travel. The midpoint of piston travel is approximately one half the number of input shaft revolutions possible in a single direction.

3) Each time direction of input shaft rotation is changed, turn output shaft adjustment screw clockwise 1/8 - 1/4 turn. Continue this procedure until a 4-18 INCH lbs. (0.50-2.0 N.m) increase in torque is required to rotate input shaft.

4) When adjustment is correct, install lock nut and tighten to 74-88 ft. lbs. (100-119 N.m) while holding adjustment screw. Check that power steering unit turns smoothly through its entire range.

STEERING LIMITING STEM

This feature relieves most of the power assist just before steering gear piston reaches the end of its full travel, to ensure system does not contact axle stops with full hydraulic assist when wheels are turned against stops. The steering gear has 2 adjustable steering limiting stems: one internally adjustable and one externally adjustable. The internal stem must be preset during assembly.

1) Ensure axle stops are not damaged and are properly adjusted. Install Power Steering Analyzer (014-00230) in pressure line between power steering pump and steering gear.

2) Start engine and gently turn steering wheel to axle stop in each direction. Observe pressure gauge while turning wheels. This procedure should reveal which turning direction the externally adjustable steering limiting stem controls.

- In one turning direction, fluid pressure will drop substantially just before steering mechanism contacts stop. In other direction, gauge should indicate pump relief valve pressure as steering mechanism contacts axle stop. The turning direction that indicates pump relief valve pressure is the one controlled by externally adjustable steering limiting stem.
- If gauge pressure does not drop before axle stop contact in either direction, the internally adjustable steering limiting stem or valve is not functioning properly.
- If gauge pressure drops prior to axle stop contact in both directions, turn externally adjustable steering limiting stem counterclockwise and repeat test until system operates properly.

3) Return steering to straight-ahead position. Turn externally adjustable steering limiting stem clockwise to its full travel. Gently turn steering wheel in direction controlled by internally adjustable stem until steering contacts axle stop. Pressure indication on gauge should be relatively low.

4) With steering wheel held to maintain axle stop contact, turn steering limiting stem counterclockwise until gauge pressure just begins to increase. After adjustment, install plug in stem bore in housing.

TESTING

PREPARATION

1) Ensure drive belt is in good condition and tension is properly adjusted. Repair any external leaks before continuing with pressure test. Disconnect pressure line from connector at pump. Connect Power Steering Analyzer (014-00230). *See Fig. 1*.

2) Open shutoff valve fully. Start engine and purge air from system by turning steering wheel fully left and right several times. Turn engine off and check connections for leaks.

3) Check for proper fluid level at reservoir and add or remove fluid as necessary. Start engine. Partially close shutoff valve and observe pressure gauge. If pressure gauge needle vibration is excessive, repeat step **2)** to bleed air. Place thermometer into reservoir and connect tachometer to engine.

4) Ensure shutoff valve is fully open. Place front wheels in straight-ahead position, and place transmission in Neutral position. Ensure parking brake is applied.

5) Start engine and partially close shutoff valve until gauge indicates 800-1000 psi (56-70 kg/cm²). When temperature of power steering fluid reaches 120°F (49°C), open shutoff valve fully and turn engine off.

1991 STEERING
Bendix Power Steering (Cont.)

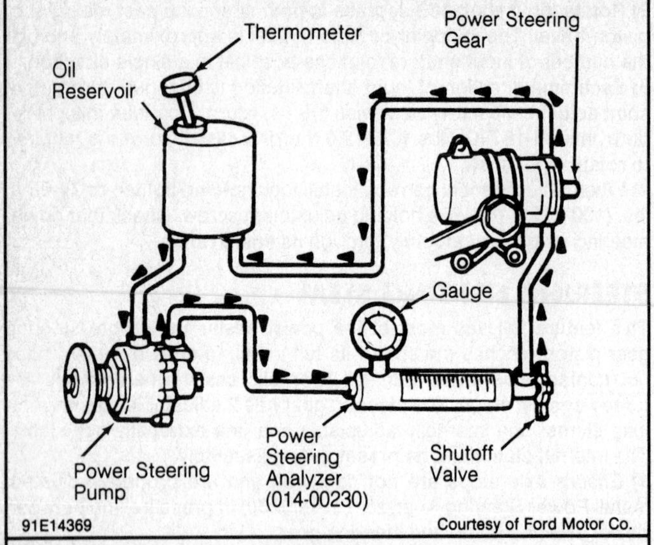
Thermometer
Power Steering
Gear
Oil
Reservoir
Gauge
Power Steering
Pump
Power
Steering
Analyzer
(014-00230)
Shutoff
Valve
91E14369
Courtesy of Ford Motor Co.

Fig. 1: Connecting Power Steering Analyzer

SYSTEM BACKPRESSURE CHECK

1) Ensure shutoff valve is fully open. Start engine and increase speed to 2200 RPM. When fluid temperature reaches 130°F (55°C), record flow rate and pressure.

2) If flow is less than 3.5 gallons (13.2L) per minute, verify correct pump is installed. If correct pump is installed, continue test.

3) If pressure exceeds 80 psi (5.6 kg/cm²), check lines for kinks or obstructions. If none are found and pressure remains high, proceed to MINIMUM PUMP FLOW TEST.

MINIMUM PUMP FLOW TEST

1) Decrease engine speed to 600 RPM. Slowly chose shutoff valve to increase pressure to 1200 psi (84.4 kg/cm²). Record flow rate at 130°F (54°C).

2) If flow rate is less than 2.2 gallons (8.3L) per minute, pump may need service, especially if flow rate at 2200 RPM is less than specification.

PUMP RELIEF PRESSURE TEST

CAUTION: DO NOT close shutoff valve for longer than 5 seconds or damage to pump may result.

1) With engine speed at 600 RPM, close shutoff valve and observe pressure gauge. Flow rate should be zero. Open shutoff valve quickly after reading gauge and note flow rate return to normal. If pressure is not between 203 psi (14.3 kg/cm²) and 255 psi (18 kg/cm²), repair or replace relief valve.

2) Allow power steering fluid to cool to 130°F (55°C). With engine at full governed RPM, close shutoff valve. Flow should read zero. Quickly open shutoff valve; flow rate should immediately return to normal. Repeat this test once, but DO NOT allow fluid temperature to exceed 200°F (93°C).

3) If flow rate does not immediately return to normal, repair or replace pump.

STEERING GEAR RELIEF PRESSURE & INTERNAL LEAKAGE TEST

WARNING: Failure to follow these procedures carefully can result in serious injury or damage to equipment.

1) Place a steel block between the axle stop and adjusting screw. The block should be a minimum of 1" (25.4 mm) thick and long enough to be inserted without danger of pinching fingers. Ensure block is square to contact points. *See Fig. 2.*

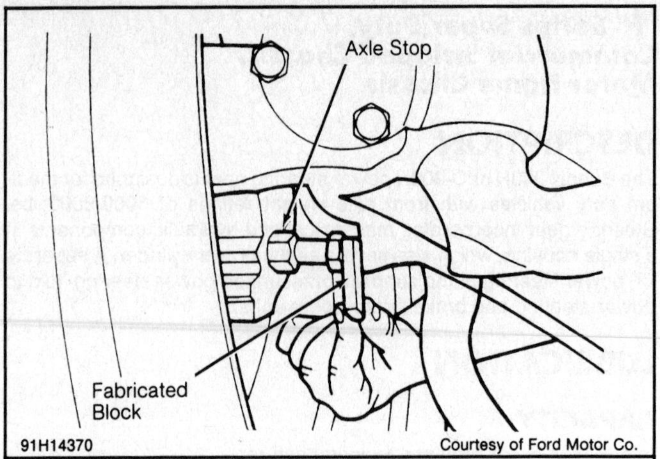
Axle Stop
Fabricated
Block
91H14370
Courtesy of Ford Motor Co.

Fig. 2: Inserting Block at Axle Stop

2) Check fluid temperature in reservoir. Temperature should be approximately 130°F (55°C) at start of test. Shutoff valve must be fully open.

3) Run engine at idle. Turn steering wheel until axle stop contacts spacer block. *See Fig. 2.* Apply sufficient torque to steering wheel to ensure power steering gear control valve is completely open. Pressure gauge should indicate pressure relief setting. If pressure is not 1900-2100 psi (134-148 kg/cm²) adjust or repair relief valve as necessary.

CAUTION: When performing this test, DO NOT hold torque on steering wheel for more than 5 seconds beyond time pressure relief setting of steering gear has been measured.

4) Temporarily set steering gear by-pass valve setting higher than setting of power steering pump relief valve. Turn engine off. Remove plug from steering gear valve body. *See Fig. 3.* Insert 3/8" O.D. washer into socket portion of plug to increase by-pass valve setting. Generally, 1/8-1/4" (3-6 mm) of additional shim thickness is sufficient.

5) Run engine at idle. Turn steering wheel until axle stop contacts spacer block. *See Fig. 2.* Apply sufficient torque to steering wheel to ensure power steering gear control valve is completely open.

6) Pressure gauge indication should be the same as power steering pump relief pressure. See PUMP RELIEF PRESSURE TEST. With system pressure at pump relief, read flow meter. If flow is greater than 3.5 quarts (3.3L) per minute, internal leakage is excessive and steering gear requires repair.

7) Repeat steps **5)** and **6)**, turning steering in opposite direction. Remove shims installed in step **4)** and reinstall plug.

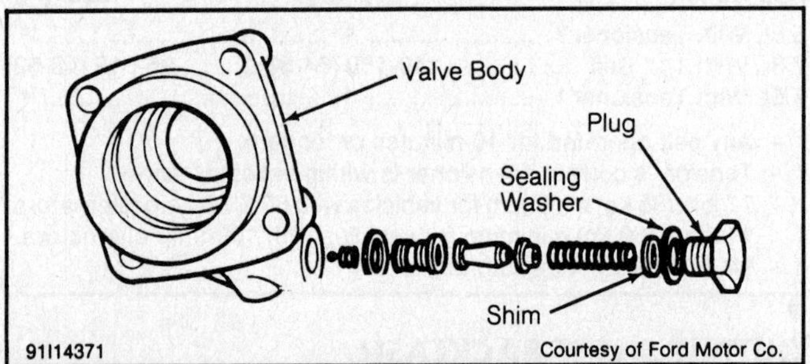
Valve Body
Plug
Sealing
Washer
Shim
91I14371
Courtesy of Ford Motor Co.

Fig. 3: Shimming Steering Gear Relief Valve

REMOVAL & INSTALLATION

POWER STEERING PUMP

Removal – 1) Using a suction gun, remove as much fluid a possible from reservoir through filler opening, or remove return hose to drain reservoir.

2) Disconnect both hoses from power steering pump. Raise both hoses, or plug disconnected hose ends to prevent fluid from draining.
3) Loosen power steering pump pivot and adjusting bolts. Remove drive belt. Remove mounting bolts. Remove pump and bracket as an assembly.
Installation – Install pump and bracket assembly. Tighten pump mounting bolts to 30-45 ft. lbs. (41-61 N.m). Install drive belt and adjust tension. Connect all lines to the correct ports. Fill reservoir and bleed system. See HYDRAULIC SYSTEM BLEEDING under LUBRICATION.

POWER STEERING GEAR

Precautions – Drain steering assembly. Remove all outside dirt, especially around fittings. Plug all ports immediately after removing hoses, before removing gear from vehicle. Tag inlet and return lines for reinstallation.

CAUTION: DO NOT strike steering gear input shaft or steering column coupling with any object during removal or installation. Severe internal damage to the steering gear may result.

Removal – **1)** Disconnect hoses from steering gear. Mark relationship of pitman arm and shaft. Remove pitman arm retaining bolt. Using Pitman Arm Puller (T64P-3590-F), remove pitman arm.
2) Remove bolt and nut securing flange and insulator to steering gear input shaft. Remove retaining bolts and steering gear.
Installation – **1)** Install steering gear. Tighten bolts to 150-205 ft. lbs. (203-278 N.m). Install intermediate shaft "U" joint and tighten to 50-70 ft. lbs. (68-95 N.m).
2) Place pitman arm on steering gear sector shaft, ensuring sure marks are aligned. Spread pitman arm with a chisel while sliding it onto sector shaft. Install bolt and nut into pitman arm and tighten to 220-300 ft. lbs. (298-407 N.m).

CAUTION: DO NOT use hammer to force pitman arm onto sector shaft. Damage to sector shaft bearings and loss of gear preload may result.

3) Connect power steering pressure and return lines to steering gear. Fill reservoir, bleed system and check for leaks.

OVERHAUL

POWER STEERING PUMP

Disassembly – **1)** Clean pump exterior. Tip pump to drain fluid from intake tube. Rotate shaft to remove fluid from internal cavities.
2) Clamp pump mounting bracket in vise. DO NOT clamp pump or pulley. Using Pulley Remover (T69L-10300-B), remove pump pulley. Push in on pump rear cover to compress internal spring. Using pliers, remove hook spring from groove in housing. *See Fig. 4.*
3) Remove cover and pressure spring. Remove internal "O" ring and back-up ring from rear cover. Remove front bearing circlip from front of housing.
4) Turn housing over and remove rear face plate. Remove "O" ring and back-up ring for rear face plate from housing. Remove rotor assembly and front face plate from housing. Check direction of rotation (arrow on cam ring) and location of set pin.
5) Clamp drive shaft in soft-jawed vise. Using a soft mallet, tap housing to remove drive shaft. Remove retaining ring and press drive shaft bearing from drive shaft. Pry drive shaft seal and needle bearing from housing.
Reassembly – **1)** Press new needle bearing into housing. Install new drive shaft seal into housing. Press new bearing onto drive shaft and install retaining ring. Install drive shaft and bearing into housing and install circlip.
2) Install "O" ring and back-up ring onto rear face plate. Install set pin, front face plate and rotor assembly into housing. Rotor cam ring must be installed with arrow pointed in direction of rotation.
3) Install "O" ring and back-up ring into rear cover housing. Place rear pressure spring into rear face plate. Position rear cover into housing. Press rear cover downward and install hook spring into housing groove. Using Pulley Installer (T65P-3A733-C), install pulley.

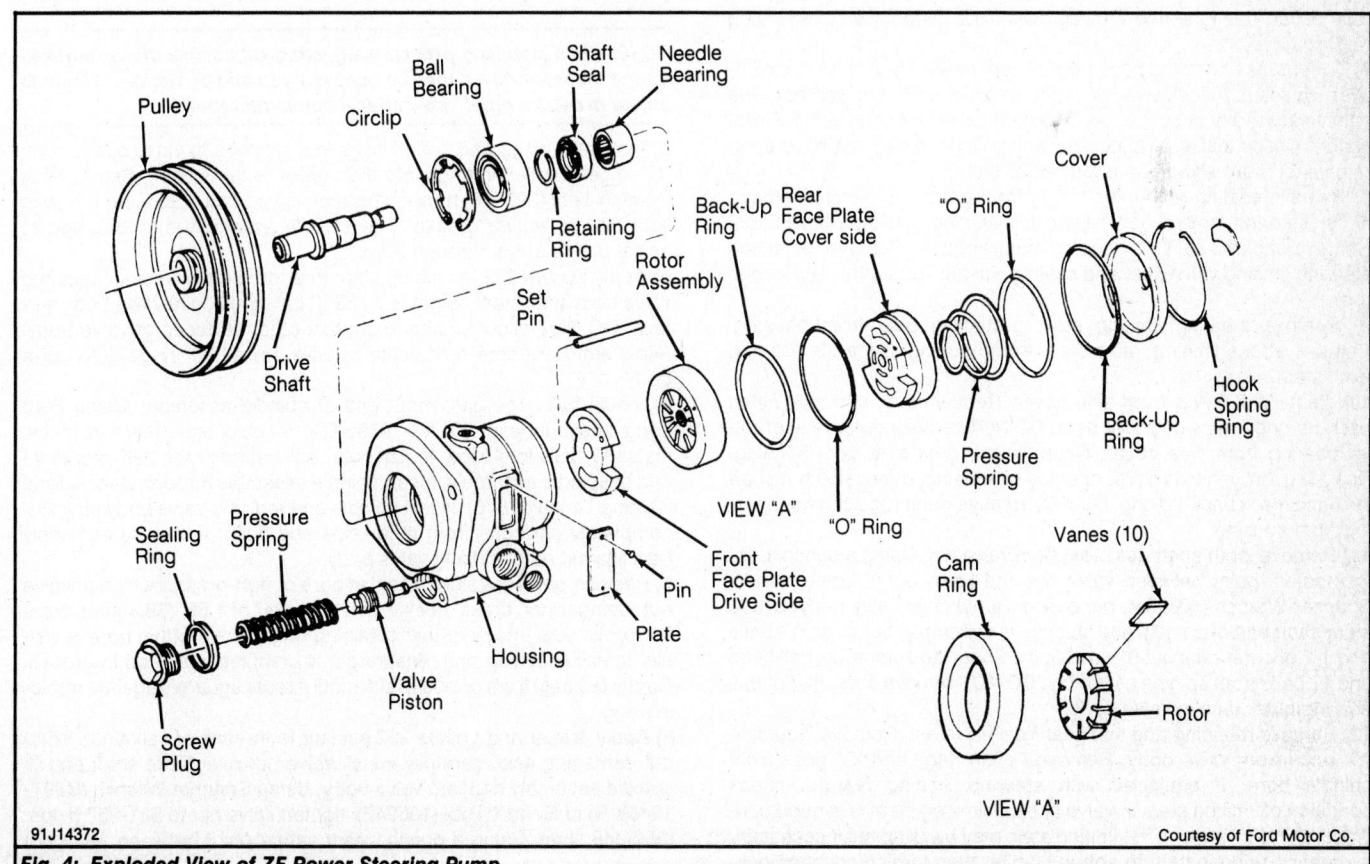

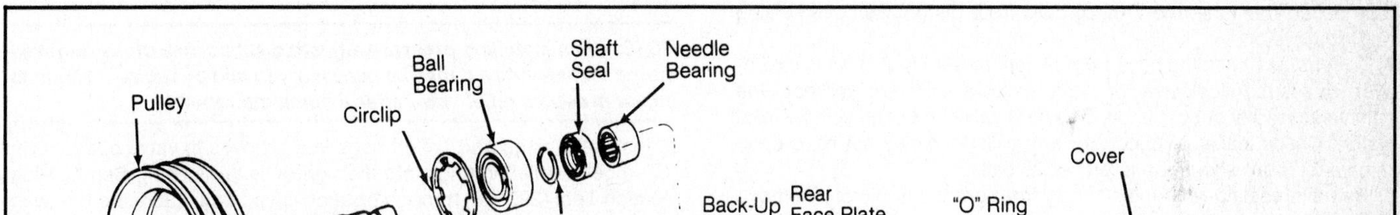
Pulley
Circlip
Ball Bearing
Shaft Seal
Needle Bearing
Retaining Ring
Drive Shaft
Set Pin
Rotor Assembly
Back-Up Ring
Rear Face Plate Cover side
"O" Ring
Cover
Hook Spring Ring
Back-Up Ring
Pressure Spring
"O" Ring
VIEW "A"
Sealing Ring
Pressure Spring
Screw Plug
Valve Piston
Housing
Plate
Pin
Front Face Plate Drive Side
Cam Ring
Vanes (10)
Rotor
VIEW "A"
91J14372
Courtesy of Ford Motor Co.

Fig. 4: Exploded View of ZF Power Steering Pump

1991 STEERING
Bendix Power Steering (Cont.)

POWER STEERING GEAR

NOTE: Several maintenance kits are available that do not require full disassembly of the steering gear. If installing one of these kits, follow the instructions provided with the kit.

Disassembly - 1) Clamp steering gear across mounting bolt bosses in soft-jawed vise. Remove dust boot from spindle assembly. Mark relationship of valve body to housing. Remove valve body retaining bolts.

2) While holding or rotating input shaft, rotate output shaft with pitman arm to separate valve body from housing. Continue to separate valve body from housing until both "O" rings on valve body can be seen. Mark relationship of pitman arm to output shaft. Remove pitman arm.

3) Remove output shaft dust boot. Remove dirt and corrosion from exposed portion of output shaft to facilitate removal. Remove lock nut from adjusting screw on side cover. Mark relationship of side cover to housing. Remove side cover bolts.

4) Separate side cover from housing by turning adjusting screw clockwise. When side cover is removed, 17 rollers in side cover bearing will fall out. These rollers MUST NOT be interchanged with rollers in housing bearing. *See Fig. 5.*

CAUTION: DO NOT attempt to remove outer race of roller bearing from side cover.

5) Loosely install pitman arm and use it to center piston and output shaft gear teeth inside side cover opening. Remove pitman arm. Remove output shaft by tapping gently on splined end with soft mallet. When output shaft is removed from housing, 17 rollers in housing bearing will fall out. These rollers MUST NOT be interchanged with rollers in side cover bearing.

CAUTION: DO NOT attempt to remove outer race of roller bearing from housing.

6) While preventing rotation of input shaft end of spindle assembly, pull valve body and piston from housing. Remove retaining ring, ball tube cover, ball tube and 7 of 26 balls from piston. Remove sealing ring from piston.

7) To remove remaining balls from piston, rotate input shaft in whichever direction (clockwise or counterclockwise) that threads the spindle assembly out of piston. Separate valve body and spindle from piston. Check inside of piston for any balls that may not have been removed. There should be a total of 26 balls.

8) Remove sealing ring and "O" ring from groove in piston. Remove either steering limiting valve seat and sealing washer from piston. Remove one of 2 balls, spring and remaining ball. Remove remaining steering limiting valve seat and sealing washer from other end of piston.

9) Remove steering limiting stem protective plug from housing. Remove stroke limiting valve stem from housing. Separate "O" ring from stem.

10) Remove "O" ring from side cover. Remove seal and split nylon back-up ring from side cover bore. DO NOT remove outer race of roller bearing from side cover. Carefully pry dust seal from housing. Reaching through side cover opening of housing, remove output shaft seal and nylon back-up ring. DO NOT remove outer race of roller bearing from housing.

11) Remove input shaft dust seal from valve nut. Using a punch, unblock safety point between valve nut and valve body. Using Bendix Spanner Wrench (106234), remove valve nut from valve body. Grasp input shaft end of spindle and lift spindle assembly, ball cage, 17 balls and 1/2 of outer race out of valve body. Separate outer race, ball cage and 17 balls from spindle assembly. DO NOT remove outer half of ball bearing outer race in valve body.

12) Remove retaining ring and seal from valve nut. Remove 2 outside "O" rings from valve body. Remove Teflon rings and "O" rings from spindle bore. If equipped with steering limiting feature, check condition of limiting stem in valve body. If limiting stem is in good condition, DO NOT remove it. Limiting stem may be removed if necessary by heating poppet stem to soften Loctite, then turning counterclockwise.

13) Remove retaining ring, adjusting screw spacer and adjusting screw from output shaft. Begin disassembly of pressure relief valve by removing plug and sealing washer from valve body. Remove spring, spring seat adjusting shim and valve piston. Remove valve seat and sealing washer.

CAUTION: DO NOT attempt disassembly of spindle assembly. Individual replacement parts are NOT available. Spindle assembly must be replaced as a single component.

Inspection - 1) Wash all parts individually in clean solvent and dry thoroughly. Discard all non-metallic parts. Broken, cracked, distorted, excessively pitted or scored parts must be replaced. Cause for replacement of any part must be corrected.

2) Inspect all parts, paying particular attention to:

- Hardness, pitting, flaking or cracks in bearing surfaces. If outer races of the roller bearings in housing or side cover are not serviceable, replace housing or side cover. If outer bearing races in valve body are not serviceable, replace entire valve body.
- Gear teeth in output shaft and piston may show signs of polishing and slight wear; however, pitting, flaking or cracks should not be present.
- Output and input shaft splines.
- Ball rolling surfaces on exterior of spindle and interior of piston for cracks, pitting, flaking or brinelling.
- Exterior of piston and interior of housing bore. Minor scuffing of piston exterior and housing bore is normal, but those parts must be replaced if there is deep scoring. DO NOT attempt to hone or bore these parts.
- Pitman arm.
- Exterior of housing and mounting lugs.
- Valve body and porting.

Reassembly - 1) Install sealing washer around pressure relief valve seat. Install seat into valve body. Tighten valve seat to 15-18 ft. lbs. (20-24 N.m). Install pressure relief valve piston spring seat and spring into valve body. Install pressure adjusting shims and seal washer onto plug. Install plug into valve body and tighten to 66-73 ft. lbs. (89-99 N.m).

NOTE: When installing pressure adjusting shims, use those removed during disassembly. It may be necessary to add or subtract shims to adjust pressure relief valve after a complete rebuild.

2) Install "O" rings and Teflon rings into grooves in valve body. Form "O" rings and Teflon rings into their grooves by pushing Bendix Ring Seating Tool (297676) through bore of valve body. Lubricate tool with light film of lithium grease. The spindle assembly may be used to assist pushing tool through bore.

3) Apply Loctite 222 to limiting stem threads. Screw limiting stem into valve body until stem height is 0.735" (18.7 mm) above valve body surface. DO NOT allow Loctite to contact other surfaces of valve body. Allow sufficient time for Loctite to cure. Install "O" rings onto valve body.

4) Install ball cage onto input end of spindle assembly. Using Ford Long Life Lubricant (C1AZ-19590-BA) to hold balls them in place, install 17 balls into cage. Install outer ball bearing race half over input end of spindle assembly. Insert spindle assembly through Bendix Ring Seating Tool (297676). Insert spindle and tool into valve body until tool completely emerges from other side and balls of bearing assembly rest against outer race in valve body.

5) Position pressure side of seal in bore of non-pressure side of valve nut. Using round brass stock with a diameter of 1.55" (39.4 mm), carefully drive seal into bore until retaining ring groove within bore is visible. Install retaining ring, ensuring it is completely seated in groove. Gently tap seal from opposite side until it rests squarely against retaining ring.

6) Apply primer and Loctite 222 sealant to threads of valve nut. Without damaging seal, carefully install valve nut over input shaft end of spindle assembly and into valve body. Using Spanner Wrench (D89T-12458-R) or Bendix Tool (106243), tighten valve nut to 221-257 ft. lbs. (300-348 N.m). Using a punch, reset safety point between valve nut

1991 STEERING
Bendix Power Steering (Cont.)

and valve body. Carefully install dust seal into valve nut. DO NOT damage seal.

7) Install one steering limiting valve seat and sealing washer into piston. Insert one ball and valve seat into piston from opposite end. Install remaining ball, sealing washer and remaining valve seat into piston. Carefully tighten each valve seat to 88-132 INCH lbs. (10-15 N.m).

8) Install "O" ring into groove in piston. Use a heat lamp or similar device to heat sealing ring to 285-320°F (140-160°C). DO NOT use an open flame. Install heated sealing ring over "O" ring in piston groove. DO NOT distort sealing ring more than necessary during installation. Using a piston ring compressor or a smooth piece of sheet metal and a large hose clamp, reshape sealing ring into piston groove. Allow approximately 10 minutes cooling time before removing compressor tool from piston.

9) Install "O" ring into groove in ball return opening of piston. Insert valve body and spindle assembly completely into piston. Ensure stroke limiting stem is not damaged and that it mates with valve seat in piston. Insert 19 balls individually into one recirculating tube hole in ball return opening in piston. Rotate input shaft end of spindle slightly after each ball is inserted. Rotate spindle in one direction only.

NOTE: When this procedure is performed correctly, spindle and valve body should screw out of piston, and balls inserted in one recirculating tube hole should appear at opposite hole. Before proceeding, ensure balls are at equal depth in both holes of piston.

10) Insert remaining 7 balls into recirculating tube halves, using lithium-base grease to hold balls in tube. Seat assembled tube halves into recirculating tube holes in piston. Lightly grease sealing surfaces of tube cover, and install tube into piston. Install retaining ring into piston to secure tube cover. After assembly, check for smooth rotation of spindle assembly in both directions.

11) Reaching through side cover opening of housing, install seal with its pressure side toward interior of housing. DO NOT distort seal more than necessary for installation. Install split nylon back-up ring into groove formed by back side of seal and housing. Ensure split surfaces of ring mate properly. Install dust seal into housing with sealing lip toward outside of housing.

12) Install "O" ring into groove around steering limiting stem. Screw stem into housing 5-6 full turns. Install 17 rollers into outer bearing race in housing, using a heavy coating of Ford Long Life Lubricant (C1AZ-19590-BA) to hold rollers in place. Rollers must be same rollers removed from this bearing during disassembly.

13) Align steering limiting stem into valve body with steering limiting valve seat in piston. Insert piston into housing so rack teeth of piston are visible through side cover opening of housing. Ensure valve body is oriented so reference marks align. Carefully slide piston and valve body assembly into housing. DO NOT damage piston guide ring and valve body "O" rings. Mount valve body to housing, and tighten bolts to 81-88 ft. lbs. (110-119 N.m). Rotate input shaft of spindle until rack teeth of piston are centered in side cover opening.

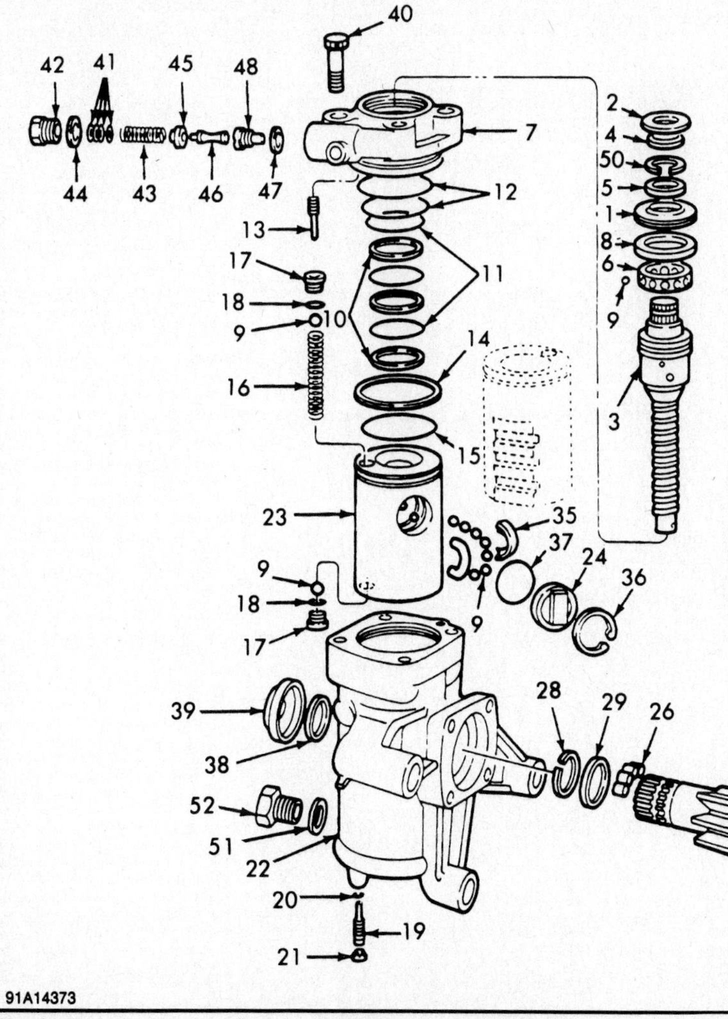
40
42
41
45
48
44
43
46
47
2
4
50
5
1
8
6
9
3
7
12
13
17
18
9
10
11
16
14
15
23
35
37
24
36
9
18
17
39
38
52
51
22
20
19
21
28
29
26
25
29
34
27
31
49
26
33
30
32
91A14373
Courtesy of Ford Motor Co.

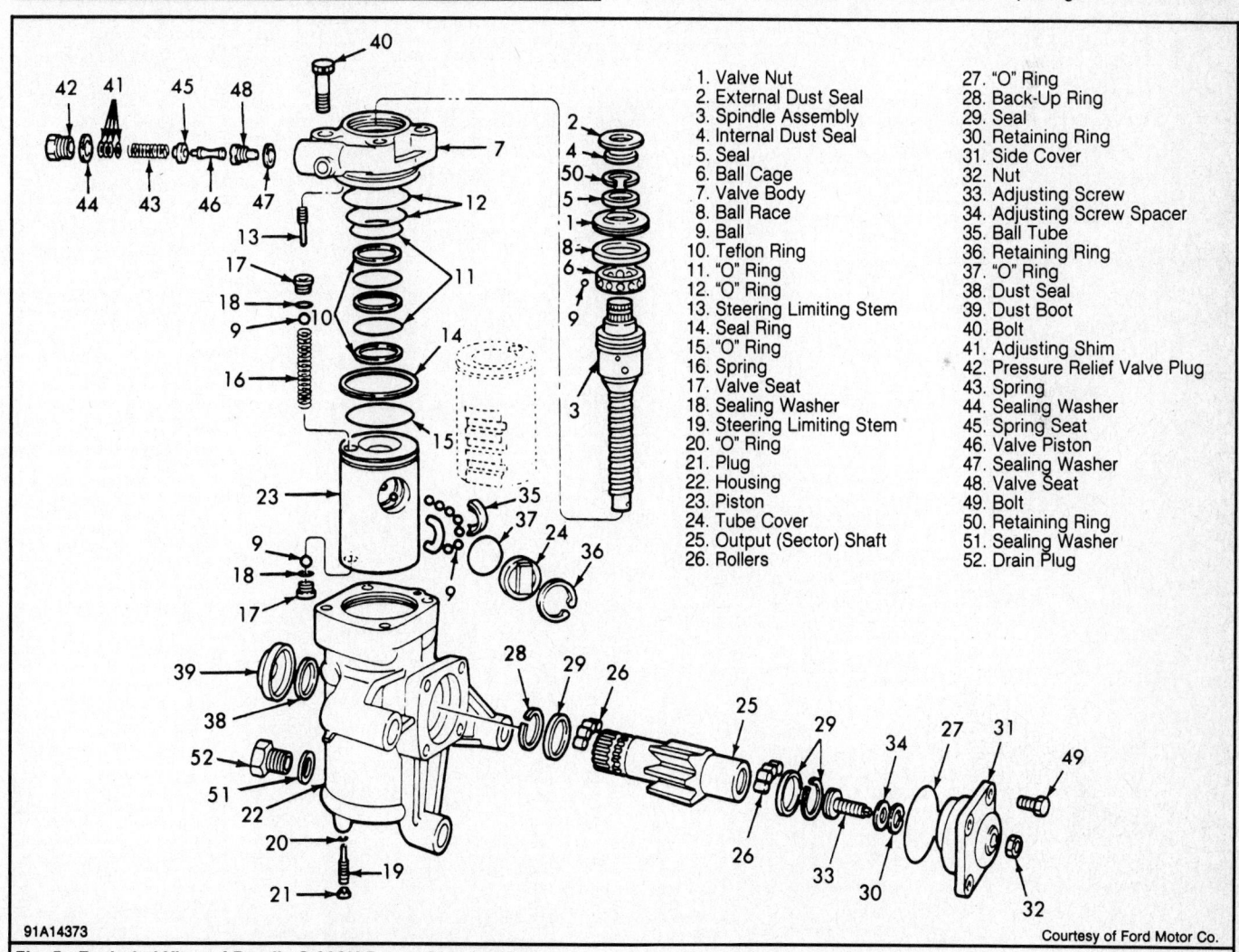

1. Valve Nut
2. External Dust Seal
3. Spindle Assembly
4. Internal Dust Seal
5. Seal
6. Ball Cage
7. Valve Body
8. Ball Race
9. Ball
10. Teflon Ring
11. "O" Ring
12. "O" Ring
13. Steering Limiting Stem
14. Seal Ring
15. "O" Ring
16. Spring
17. Valve Seat
18. Sealing Washer
19. Steering Limiting Stem
20. "O" Ring
21. Plug
22. Housing
23. Piston
24. Tube Cover
25. Output (Sector) Shaft
26. Rollers
27. "O" Ring
28. Back-Up Ring
29. Seal
30. Retaining Ring
31. Side Cover
32. Nut
33. Adjusting Screw
34. Adjusting Screw Spacer
35. Ball Tube
36. Retaining Ring
37. "O" Ring
38. Dust Seal
39. Dust Boot
40. Bolt
41. Adjusting Shim
42. Pressure Relief Valve Plug
43. Spring
44. Sealing Washer
45. Spring Seat
46. Valve Piston
47. Sealing Washer
48. Valve Seat
49. Bolt
50. Retaining Ring
51. Sealing Washer
52. Drain Plug

Fig. 5: Exploded View of Bendix C-300N Power Steering Gear

1991 STEERING
Bendix Power Steering (Cont.)

14) Install adjusting spacer over adjusting screw and secure both into output shaft with retaining ring. Maximum end play permitted for these parts is 0.002" (0.05 mm). If end play is excessive, install a different adjusting spacer. Adjusting spacers are available in 8 different thicknesses. Install seal into side cover with pressure side toward outer race of side cover roller bearing. DO NOT distort seal more than necessary for installation.

15) Install split nylon back-up ring by winding it into groove formed by side cover and back side of seal. Ensure split ring is completely seated and that diagonal split surfaces mate properly. Install "O" ring into groove in side cover.

16) Install 17 rollers into side cover outer race. Use lithium grease to hold rollers in place. The rollers must be those removed from this bearing during disassembly. Lightly lubricate seals in housing and side cover with lithium grease. Lubricate sealing surface of output shaft adjusting screw end only. Install side cover assembly onto output shaft adjuster screw, and screw assembly on as far as it will go, then back it off 1/8 turn.

17) Wrap a single layer of masking tape around splines of output shaft to protect housing seal. Lubricate exterior of tape with lithium-base grease and insert shaft and side cover assembly into housing with a twisting motion. Remove tape from output shaft.

18) Ensure side cover is positioned so reference marks align. Install side cover and tighten bolts to 81-88 ft. lbs. (110-119 N.m). Pack input and output cavities with lithium-base grease. Install dust boot onto output shaft and dust seal onto input shaft.

TORQUE SPECIFICATIONS

TORQUE SPECIFICATIONS

Application	Ft. Lbs. (N.m)
Input Shaft Valve Nut	221-257 (300-348)
Intermediate Shaft-To-Input Shaft Bolt	50-70 (68-95)
Output Shaft Adjustment Screw Lock Nut	74-88 (100-119)
Pitman Arm-To-Gear Output Shaft Nut	220-300 (298-407)
Pressure Relief Valve Plug	66-73 (89-99)
Pressure Relief Valve Seat	15-18 (20-24)
Pump Mounting Bolts	30-45 (41-61)
Side Cover Bolts	81-88 (110-119)
Steering Gear-To-Frame Rail Bolts	150-205 (203-278)
Valve Body-To-Housing Bolts	81-88 (110-119)
	INCH Lbs. (N.m)
Steering Limiting Valve Seats	88-132 (10-15)

1991 TRANSMISSION SERVICING
Automatic/Manual Transmission

Aerostar, Bronco, Explorer, Ranger, "E" & "F" Series

***NOTE:** Unless specified otherwise, references to "F" Series include "F" Series Super Duty.*

IDENTIFICATION

Use the following tables for transmission application. For oil pan gasket identification, *See Figs. 1-4.*

AUTOMATIC TRANSMISSION (A/T) APPLICATION

Model	Transmission
Aerostar, Explorer & Ranger	A4LD
Bronco, E150/250 & F150	AOD
Bronco, "E" & "F" Series	C-6
E250/350 & F250/350	E4OD

MANUAL TRANSMISSION (M/T) APPLICATION

Model	Transmission
Bronco & F150/250	Borg-Warner T-18 4-Speed
Aerostar, Bronco, Explorer, Ranger & "F" Series	Mazda M5OD 5-Speed
Ranger	Mitsubishi FM146 5-Speed OD
Bronco, E350 & "F" Series	S5-42 ZF 5 Speed

121165

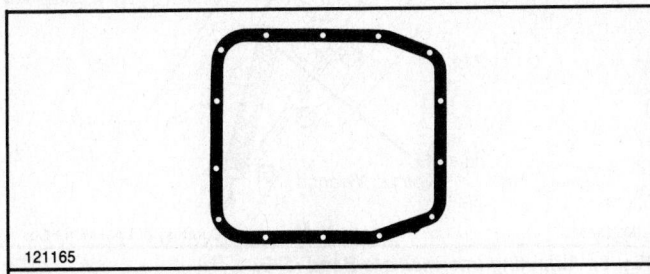

Fig. 1: Identifying Oil Pan Gasket (AOD)

121166

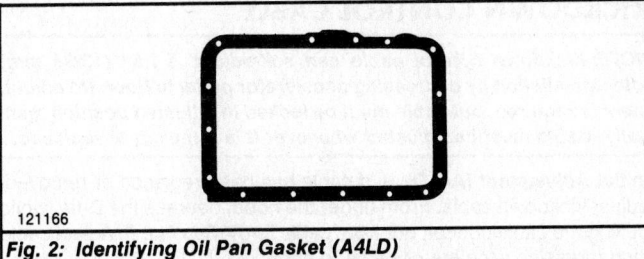

Fig. 2: Identifying Oil Pan Gasket (A4LD)

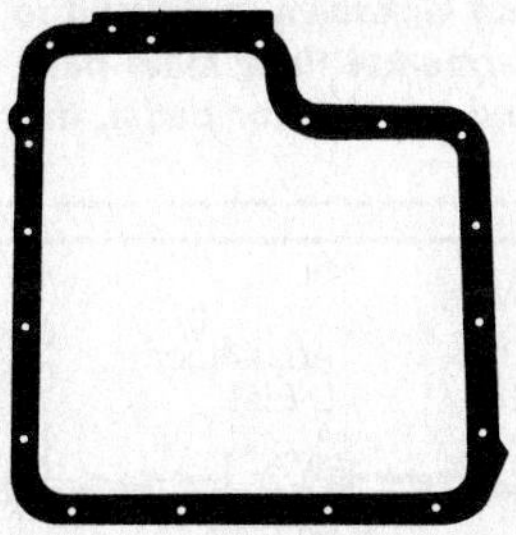
121167

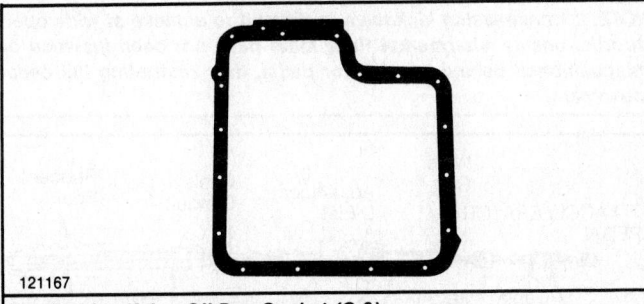

Fig. 3: Identifying Oil Pan Gasket (C-6)

LUBRICATION

SERVICE INTERVALS

Automatic Transmission – Vehicles used in normal service do not require regularly scheduled maintenance. Fluid level should be checked whenever underhood maintenance is performed or if leakage is detected. Adjust clutch bands on A4LD and C-6 when quality of shifts deteriorates, or there's indication improper band adjustment.

121168

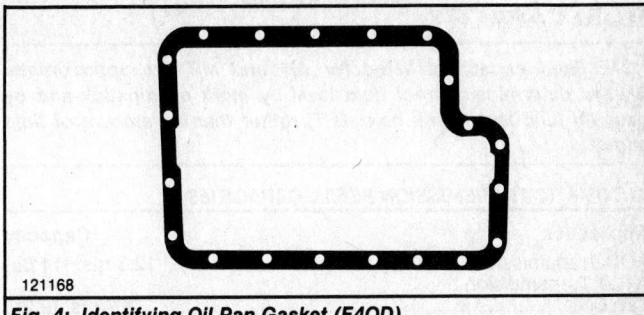

Fig. 4: Identifying Oil Pan Gasket (E4OD)

On vehicles used for fleet service or those operated under severe conditions (such as police, taxi or towing), regular transmission fluid change is required every 30,000 miles or when fluid appears discolored.

Manual Transmission – Under normal driving conditions, replace transmission fluid every 60,000 miles. Perform service every 30,000 miles if vehicle is operated under the following severe driving conditions:

- In hot weather greater than 90°F (32°C)
- Heavy loads in hilly terrain
- Maximum loads
- Towing trailer or carrying a slide-in camper
- Operating a transmission-mounted PTO

Transfer Case – Under normal driving conditions, replace transfer case fluid every 60,000 miles. Under heavy 4WD driving conditions, replace fluid more frequently.

CHECKING FLUID LEVEL

Automatic Transmission – **1)** Check fluid level with vehicle parked on level surface, engine and transmission at normal operating temperatures, and engine idling. Apply parking brake and move transmission selector lever through all ranges, ending in "P".

2) Fluid level should be between the ADD and DON'T ADD marks on dipstick (in crosshatched area). Add fluid through filler tube as needed. DO NOT overfill.

***CAUTION:** Vehicle should NOT be driven if fluid level is below the bottom hole on dipstick and outside temperature is greater than 50°F (10°C).*

Manual Transmission – Check lubricant level at filler plug hole on side of transmission. It should be level with bottom of filler hole. Add lubricant as needed.

***NOTE:** To check fluid level on vehicles with 4WD, the 4WD shift selector must NOT be in the Neutral position.*

Transfer Case – Remove filler plug. Transfer case is full if fluid drains out, or is level with opening. Add lubricant as needed.

RECOMMENDED FLUID

Automatic & Manual Transmissions – Use only proper lubricant. Except for transmission models listed in TRANSMISSION RECOMMENDED FLUID table, use Motorcraft Mercon automatic transmission fluid XT-2-QDX or DDX E4AZ-19582 in all other A/T, M/T and transfer cases.

TRANSMISSION RECOMMENDED FLUID

Application	Fluid Type
Borg-Warner T-18 4-Speed	SAE 80W
Mitsubishi FM146 5-Speed Overdrive	SAE 80W

1991 TRANSMISSION SERVICING
Automatic/Manual Transmission (Cont.)

FLUID CAPACITY

NOTE: Fluid capacities listed for A/T and M/T are approximate. Always determine correct fluid level by mark on dipstick and by gauging fluid level at fill hole (M/T) rather than by amount of fluid added.

AUTOMATIC TRANSMISSION REFILL CAPACITIES [1]

Application	Capacity
AOD Transmission	12.3 qts. (11.6L)
A4LD Transmission	
2WD	9.7 qts. (9.2L)
4WD	10 qts. (9.5L)
C-6 Transmission	
2WD Models	12.0 qts. (11.4L)
4WD Models	13.5 qts. (12.7L)
E4OD Transmission	
2WD Models	15.5 qts. (16.4L)
4WD Models	16.0 qts. (16.9L)

[1] - Includes torque converter, cooler and lines.

MANUAL TRANSMISSION REFILL CAPACITIES

Application	Capacity
Borg-Warner T-18 4-Speed	3.5 qts. (3.3L)
S5-42 ZF 5-Speed	3.4 qts. (3.2L)
Mazda M5OD 5-Speed Overdrive	3.8 qts. (3.6L)
Mitsubishi FM146 5-Speed Overdrive	2.4 qts. (2.3L)

TRANSFER CASE REFILL CAPACITIES

Application	Capacity
Borg-Warner 1345	3.3 qts. (3.0L)
Borg-Warner 1354	1.3 qts. (1.2L)
Borg-Warner 1356	1.2 qts. (1.1L)
Spicer TC28	2.2 qts. (2.1L)

DRAINING & REFILLING

Automatic Transmission - 1) Raise vehicle on hoist or jackstands. Loosen oil pan bolts and tap pan to break gasket seal. Allow fluid to drain. Remove oil pan bolts and remove oil pan. Discard used filter and gasket. Install new filter and filter gasket. Clean pan and mounting surface. Install new gasket. Install pan.

2) On all transmissions, add 3 quarts of transmission fluid. Check fluid level. See CHECKING FLUID LEVEL under LUBRICATION. When filling a dry transmission and converter, refer to AUTOMATIC TRANSMISSION REFILL CAPACITIES table. Recheck fluid level when transmission is at normal operating temperature. Do not overfill.

Manual Transmission - Raise vehicle on hoist or jackstands. Remove fill plug for easier draining, then remove drain plug. Drain fluid. Install drain plug. Refill transmission with fluid. See MANUAL TRANSMISSION REFILL CAPACITIES table. Fill transmission up to the bottom of fill hole. Install fill plug.

Transfer Case - Remove drain plug from transfer case. Remove fill plug for easier draining. With fluid fully drained, reinstall drain plug. Fill transfer case to fill plug opening with Mercon automatic transmission fluid. Install fill plug.

ADJUSTMENTS

INTERMEDIATE (FRONT) & OVERDRIVE BAND

A4LD & C-6 - 1) Clean dirt from band adjusting screw area. Remove and discard adjusting screw lock nut. Install new lock nut. Tighten adjusting screw to 120 INCH lbs. (14 N.m). *See Fig. 5 or 6.*

2) On C-6, back off adjusting screw 1 1/2 turns. On A4LD, back off adjusting screw 2 turns. Hold adjusting screw in position and tighten NEW lock nut to 35-40 ft. lbs. (48-54 N.m).

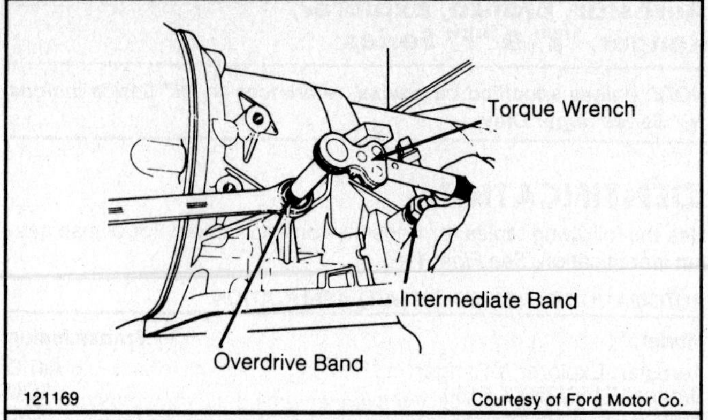
Torque Wrench
Intermediate Band
Overdrive Band
121169
Courtesy of Ford Motor Co.

Fig. 5: Adjusting Intermediate or Overdrive Band (A4LD)

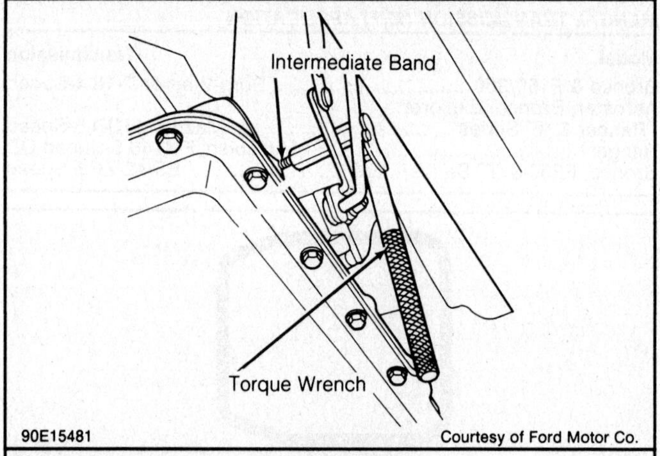
Intermediate Band
Torque Wrench
90E15481
Courtesy of Ford Motor Co.

Fig. 6: Adjusting Intermediate Band (C-6)

KICKDOWN CONTROL CABLE

NOTE: Kickdown control cable can self-adjust .5-1.5" (13-38 mm) after installation by depressing accelerator pedal to floor. No adjustment is required, but cable must be locked in adjusted position manually. Cable must be adjusted whenever it is removed or replaced.

Initial Adjustment (A4LD) - If cable has been replaced or removed, adjust kickdown cable. From under the hood, depress the D-flat while pulling the cable conduit out from cable body. *See Fig. 7.* Adjust cable by depressing accelerator pedal to floor.

NOTE: If transmission kickdown is difficult to achieve at wide open throttle, ensure aftermarket floor mats have not been installed or mispositioned behind accelerator pedal, thus restricting full pedal movement.

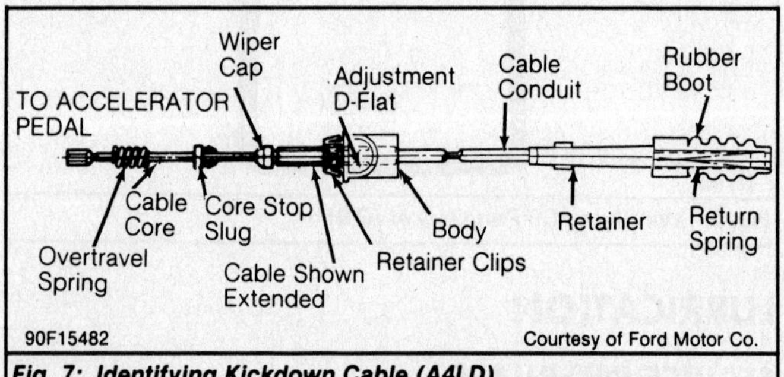
TO ACCELERATOR PEDAL
Wiper Cap
Adjustment D-Flat
Cable Conduit
Rubber Boot
Cable Core
Core Stop Slug
Body
Retainer
Return Spring
Overtravel Spring
Cable Shown Extended
Retainer Clips
90F15482
Courtesy of Ford Motor Co.

Fig. 7: Identifying Kickdown Cable (A4LD)

1991 TRANSMISSION SERVICING
Automatic/Manual Transmission (Cont.)

THROTTLE VALVE (T.V.) CONTROL CABLE

Cable Adjustment With Engine Off (AOD) – 1) T.V. control cable is set and locked to its proper length during initial assembly by pushing in locking tab at throttle body end of cable assembly. When tab is unlocked, cable is released for adjustment. Under normal circumstances, it should not be necessary to alter or readjust initial setting of T.V. control cable.

2) Set parking brake and put selector in "N". DO NOT put selector in "P". On F150/250 and Bronco with 5.0L engine, remove cable linkage protective cover. On all vehicles, ensure throttle lever is resting against idle stop. DO NOT adjust idle stop.

3) Verify cable routing is free of sharp bends or pressure points, and cable operates freely. Unlock locking tab at throttle body end by pushing up from below, and prying up the rest of the way to free cable.

4) Install a retention spring with about a 10-lb. (4.5 kg) force to hold T.V. control lever in idle position (to rear of travel). Attach spring(s) to transmission T.V. lever, and hook rear of spring to transmission case. If necessary, use 2 V8 throttle return springs to hold T.V. lever back.

5) With T.V. cable locking tab unlocked and retention spring in place, rotate transmission outer T.V. lever 10-30 degrees and return slowly. Push down locking tab until flush. Remove retention spring(s) from transmission lever.

T.V. Pressure Check & Adjustment With Engine On (AOD) – 1) Attach T.V. Pressure Gauge (T86L-70002-A) to T.V. port on transmission. Remove cover from T.V. cable linkage. Insert tapered end of T.V. Cable Control Pressure Gauge Adjuster (T86L-70332-A) between crimped slug on end of cable and plastic cable fitting attached to throttle lever. *See Fig. 8.*

2) Ensure adjuster is pushed in as far as it will go. Run engine until normal operating temperature is reached. Transmission fluids temperature should be 100-150°F (37-65°C). DO NOT perform T.V. pressure check if transmission fluid is too cold or too hot to touch.

3) Set park brake, and shift transmission to Neutral. T.V. pressure should be 26-36 psi (1.75-2.53 kg/cm²). For best transmission function, set T.V. pressure as close as possible to mean pressure. If T.V. pressure is out of range, unlock T.V. cable locking tab at throttle body. *See Fig. 8.*

4) The adjuster preload spring should cause adjusting slider to move away from throttle body, causing T.V. pressure to increase. Push on the slider from behind bracket until T.V. pressure reaches 31 psi (2.1 kg/cm²). While still holding slider, push locking tab down as far as it will go to lock slider into position.

5) Remove gauge adjuster, allowing cable to return to normal idle position. With engine still idling in Neutral, T.V. pressure should be at or near zero. If pressure is not as specified, readjust.

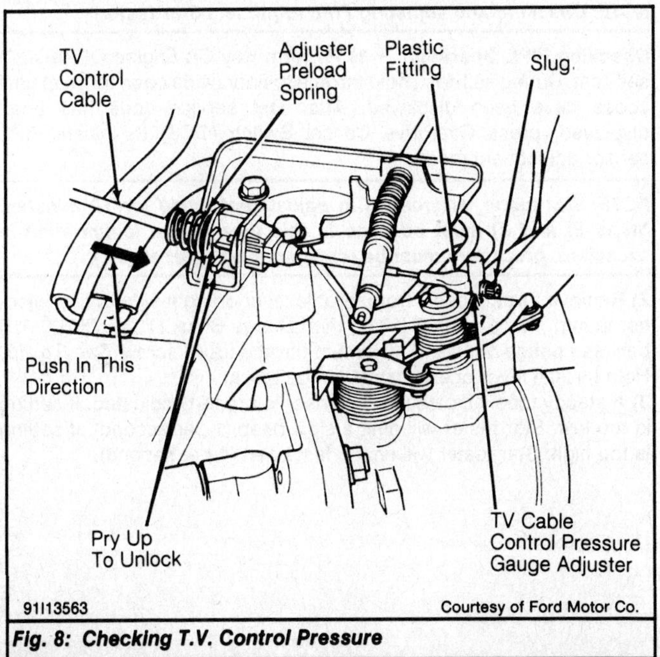
TV
Control
Cable
Adjuster
Preload
Spring
Plastic
Fitting
Slug
Push In This
Direction
Pry Up
To Unlock
TV Cable
Control Pressure
Gauge Adjuster
91I13563
Courtesy of Ford Motor Co.

Fig. 8: Checking T.V. Control Pressure

VACUUM REGULATOR VALVE (VRV)

All 7.3L V8 diesel A/T vehicles have a VRV. VRV is mounted on the left side of fuel injection pump and provides transmission with vacuum signal to control shift points. Signal strength is determined by VRV.

Checking VRV Operation – 1) With engine off, disconnect the 2-port vacuum connector from VRV. Remove throttle cable from injection pump throttle lever (on right side of pump). Disconnect throttle return spring.

2) Attach one end of return spring over throttle lever ball stud. Install other end of spring over throttle cable support bracket. Insert .515" (13 mm) Gauge Block (T83T-7B200-AH) between pump boss and wide open throttle stop screw.

3) Spring will hold throttle lever against gauge block during vacuum check and VRV adjustment. Attach vacuum pump to VAC (upper) port of VRV, and attach vacuum gauge to TRANS (lower) port. Apply and maintain 20 in. Hg vacuum. Vacuum gauge should indicate 6-8 in. Hg vacuum. If reading is not as specified, adjust VRV.

Adjusting VRV – 1) Loosen 2 VRV adjustment screws. *See Fig. 9.* With vacuum pump, gauge, gauge block and return spring in position (as during checking procedure), maintain 20 in. Hg vacuum with pump. Rotate VRV until vacuum gauge reads 6.5-7.5 in. Hg vacuum. Tighten mounting screws.

2) If correct vacuum reading cannot be obtained by adjusting VRV, replace VRV. If correct reading is obtained, remove gauge block, and connect throttle return spring. Ensure pump lever returns to idle position. Apply 20 in. Hg vacuum with vacuum pump.

3) While maintaining vacuum, cycle throttle lever from idle to wide open throttle 5 times. Vacuum gauge must indicate a minimum of 13 in. Hg vacuum at idle position. If vacuum gauge reads less than 13 in. Hg vacuum, replace VRV. Remove vacuum pump and gauge and reconnect vacuum connector to VRV. Connect throttle cable.

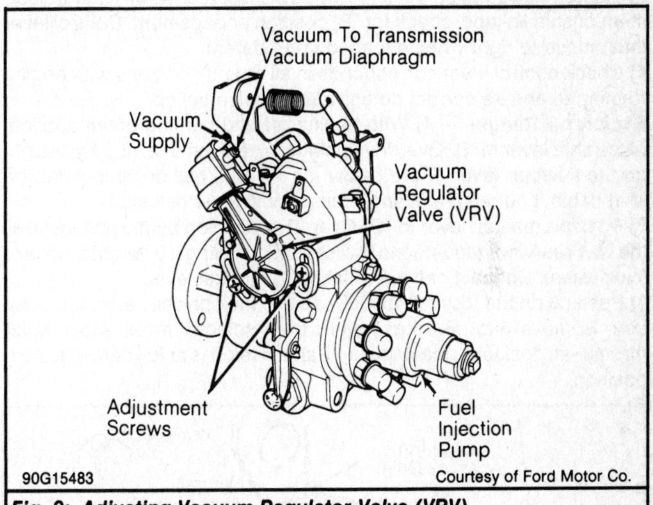
Vacuum To Transmission
Vacuum Diaphragm
Vacuum
Supply
Vacuum
Regulator
Valve (VRV)
Adjustment
Screws
Fuel
Injection
Pump
90G15483
Courtesy of Ford Motor Co.

Fig. 9: Adjusting Vacuum Regulator Valve (VRV)

GEARSHIFT LINKAGE

Bronco, "E" & "F" Series – 1) On vehicles with C-6 transmissions, move selector lever rearward against stop in "D" position. On models with AOD or E4OD transmissions, move selector lever rearward against stop in "D" Overdrive position. Hold shift lever against stop by hanging an 8-lb. (3.6 kg) weight on the selector lever.

2) Loosen bellcrank lever-to-shift rod retaining nut. *See Fig. 10.* Move transmission manual lever to "D" (C-6) or "D" Overdrive (AOD and E4OD) position by moving lever all the way rearward, then forward 2 detents.

3) With selector lever and transmission manual lever in "D" or "D" Overdrive position, tighten retaining nut to 12-18 ft. lbs. (17-24 N.m). Remove 8-lb. (3.6 kg) weight from selector lever. Check for normal operation in all selected positions.

1991 TRANSMISSION SERVICING
Automatic/Manual Transmission (Cont.)

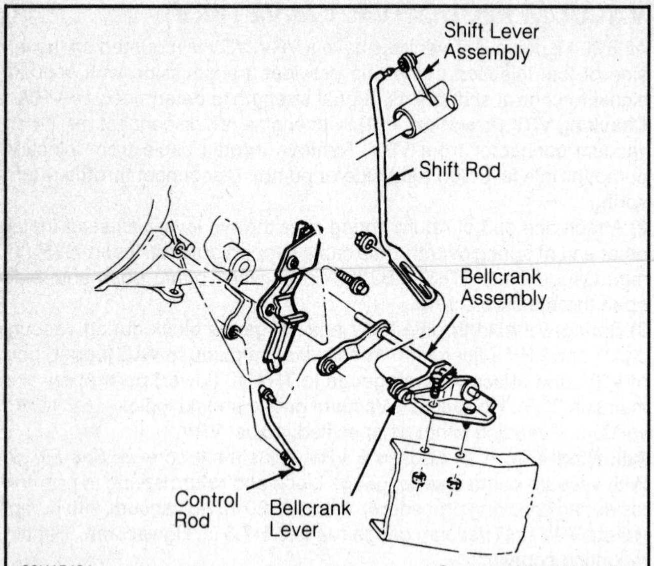
Shift Lever
Assembly
Shift Rod
Bellcrank
Assembly
Control
Rod
Bellcrank
Lever

90H15484 Courtesy of Ford Motor Co.

Fig. 10: Exploded View of Typical Shift Linkage

Aerostar – 1) From inside vehicle, place gearshift lever in "D" Overdrive position. From under vehicle, loosen adjustment screw on shift cable and remove end fitting from manual lever ball stud.

2) Position manual lever in "D" Overdrive position by moving lever all the way rearward (counterclockwise), then moving it 3 detents forward (clockwise). Connect cable end fitting to manual lever.

3) Tighten adjusting screw to 45-60 INCH lbs. (5-7 N.m). After adjustment of shift linkage, check for "P" position engagement. Control lever must move to right when engaged in "P" detent.

4) Check control lever corresponds in all detent positions with engine running to ensure correct detent/transmission action.

Explorer & Ranger – 1) With engine off and parking brake applied, place shift lever in "D" Overdrive position. Hang an 8-lb. (3.6 kg) weight on the selector lever. From below the vehicle, pull down lock tab on shift cable, and remove fitting from manual lever ball stud.

2) Position manual lever in "D" Overdrive position by moving lever all the way rearward (counterclockwise), then moving it 3 detents forward (clockwise). Connect cable end fitting to manual lever.

3) Push up on the lock tab to lock cable in the correctly adjusted position. Remove 8-lb. (3.6 kg) weight from selector lever. Move lever through all positions, making sure transmission is at full detent in each position.

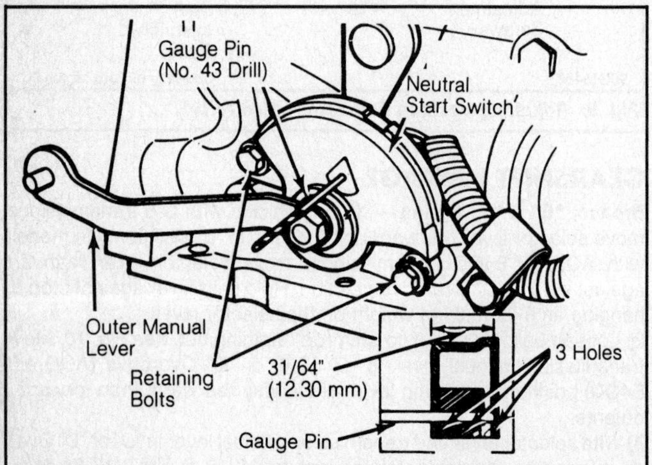
Gauge Pin
(No. 43 Drill)
Neutral
Start Switch
Outer Manual
Lever
Retaining
Bolts
31/64"
(12.30 mm)
3 Holes
Gauge Pin

121171 Courtesy of Ford Motor Co.

Fig. 11: Locating Neutral Safety Switch

NEUTRAL SAFETY SWITCH

NOTE: AOD and A4LD switches are not adjustable. Use Neutral Start Switch Socket (T74P-77247-A) to replace switch. If any other socket is used, damage to switch may occur. Information for neutral safety switch on E4OD transmission is not available from manufacturer.

C-6 – 1) With transmission shift linkage properly adjusted, loosen 2 switch attaching bolts. *See Fig. 11.* Place transmission manual lever in Neutral position. Rotate switch and insert a gauge pin (No. 43 drill bit) into gauge pin hole of switch.

2) Gauge pin must be inserted completely through all 3 holes of switch. Tighten switch attaching bolts and remove gauge pin. Check operation of switch. Engine should start in "N" or "P" positions only.

MANUAL LEVER POSITION SENSOR

E4OD Only – Remove shift linkage from transmission. Loosen manual lever position attaching bolts. Using Gear Position Sensor Adjuster (T89T-70010-J), align manual lever position sensor for Neutral gear. *See Fig. 12.* Tighten bolts to 53-70 INCH lbs. (6-8 N.m)

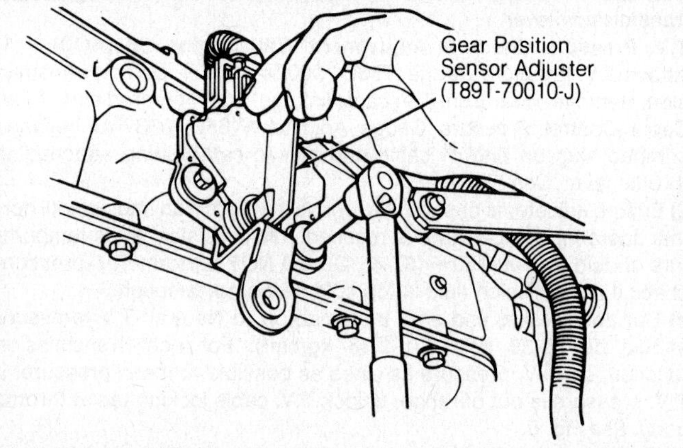
Gear Position
Sensor Adjuster
(T89T-70010-J)

90I15485 Courtesy of Ford Motor Co.

Fig. 12: Aligning Manual Lever Position Sensor for Neutral Gear (E4OD)

FUEL INJECTION PUMP LEVER (FIPL) SENSOR

NOTE: Checking and adjusting FIPL requires a Star tester.

Checking FIPL Operation – 1) Perform Key On Engine Off (KOEO) self-test. During self-test, hold throttle to floor (wide open throttle) until codes have been displayed. After last service code has been displayed, press Overdrive Cancel Switch (OCS) to initiate FIPL sensor adjustment mode.

NOTE: Star tester will remain in adjustment mode for 10 minutes. Steps 2) and 3) must be done in this time frame. If time limit is exceeded, procedure must be repeated starting at step 1).

2) Remove throttle cable from throttle lever on right side of fuel injection pump. Place a .515" (13.08 mm) Gauge Block (T83T-7B200-AH) between gauge boss and maximum throttle travel screw. *See Fig. 13.* Hold throttle lever open against gauge block.

3) A steady tone indicates FIPL sensor is properly adjusted. If setting is too low, Star tester will emit a slow beep (1 per second). If setting is too high, Star tester will emit a fast beep (4 per second).

1991 TRANSMISSION SERVICING
Automatic/Manual Transmission (Cont.)

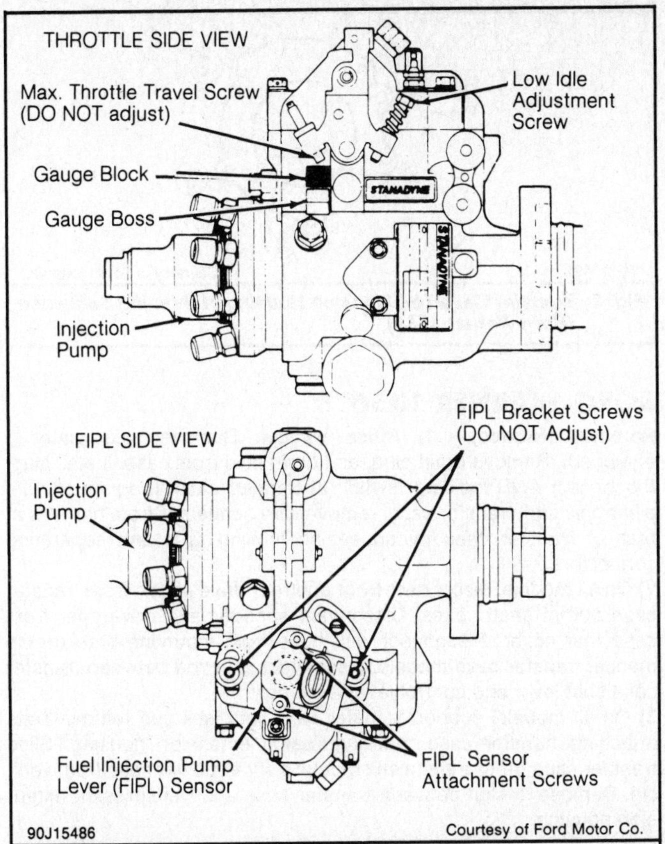
THROTTLE SIDE VIEW
Max. Throttle Travel Screw (DO NOT adjust)
Low Idle Adjustment Screw
Gauge Block
Gauge Boss
Injection Pump
FIPL SIDE VIEW
FIPL Bracket Screws (DO NOT Adjust)
Injection Pump
Fuel Injection Pump Lever (FIPL) Sensor
FIPL Sensor Attachment Screws
90J15486
Courtesy of Ford Motor Co.

Fig. 13: Identifying Fuel Injection Pump Lever (FIPL) Components

Adjusting FIPL – 1) After checking FIPL sensor operation, loosen 2 FIPL sensor-to-mounting bracket screws. Rotate FIPL sensor until a steady tone is heard from Star tester. A constant tone indicates sensor is within range.

CAUTION: FIPL sensor bracket is permanently attached to injection pump with tamper-proof screws. Movement of bracket is NOT intended as means of adjustment.

2) If FIPL sensor cannot be adjusted to obtain a steady tone, replace sensor and repeat adjustment procedure. Remove gauge block. Attach throttle cable. Start engine. Check throttle and transmission shift operation.

CAUTION: DO NOT turn maximum throttle travel screw. This screw has been preset and should not be adjusted.

1991 TRANSMISSION SERVICING
Transmission Removal & Installation

Aerostar, Bronco, Explorer, Ranger, "E" & "F" Series

NOTE: Unless otherwise specified, references to "F" Series includes "F" Series Super Duty.

MANUAL TRANSMISSION

NOTE: For manual transmission replacement procedures, see appropriate CLUTCHES article.

TRANSFER CASE (A/T)

BORG-WARNER 1345

Removal (F150/250 Series) - 1) Raise vehicle. Remove drain plug, and drain fluid from transfer case. Replace plug. Disconnect 4WD indicator switch connector at transfer case. Remove skid plate (if equipped).

2) Disconnect front and rear drive shafts from transfer case output shaft yokes. Wire drive shaft aside. Disconnect speedometer drive gear from transfer case rear cover.

3) Remove retaining clips and shift rod from transfer case control and transfer case shift levers. Disconnect vent hose from transfer case. Remove heat shield. Support transfer case with transmission jack.

4) Remove transfer case-to-extension housing bolts. Slide transfer case off transmission output shaft. Lower transfer case from vehicle. Remove transfer case-to-extension housing gasket.

Installation - 1) Install new transfer case-to-extension housing gasket. To complete installation, reverse removal procedure. Tighten transfer case-to-extension housing bolts in sequence. *See Fig. 1.*

2) Tighten bolts to specifications. See TORQUE SPECIFICATIONS tables at end of article. Fill transfer case with 3.3 qts. (3.0L) of Mercon ATF (XT-2-QDX or EAZ-19582-B).

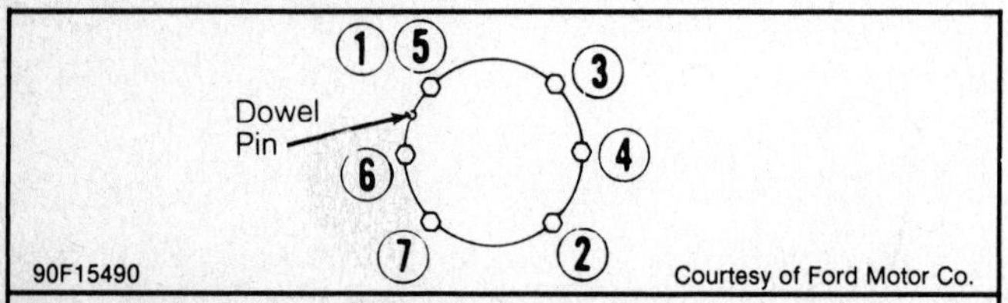
1
5
3
Dowel
Pin
4
6
7
2
90F15490
Courtesy of Ford Motor Co.

Fig. 1: Transfer Case-To-Extension Housing Tightening Sequence (Borg-Warner 1345)

BORG-WARNER 1354

Removal (Explorer & Ranger) - 1) Raise vehicle. Remove skid plate (if equipped). Remove damper from transfer case (if equipped). Remove drain plug, and drain fluid from case. Install plug. Disconnect 4WD indicator switch at transfer case.

2) Disconnect front and rear drive shafts from transfer case output shaft yokes. Disconnect speedometer drive gear from case rear cover. Disconnect vent hose from control lever. Remove shift lever retaining nut and lever.

3) Loosen or remove large and small bolts (one each) retaining shifter to extension housing. Remove lever assembly and bushing. Support transfer case with jack and remove bolts attaching transfer case to transmission extension housing.

4) Slide transfer case rearward off transmission output shaft. Lower case from vehicle. Remove gasket from transfer case and transmission extension housing.

Installation - 1) Install new transfer case-to-extension housing gasket. To complete installation, reverse removal procedure. Tighten transfer case-to-extension housing bolts in sequence. *See Fig. 2*

NOTE: When installing shift lever assembly, ALWAYS tighten large bolt first, then small bolt.

2) Tighten bolts to specifications. See TORQUE SPECIFICATIONS tables at end of article. Fill transfer case to bottom of fill hole with Mercon ATF (XT-2-QDX or EAZ-19582-B).

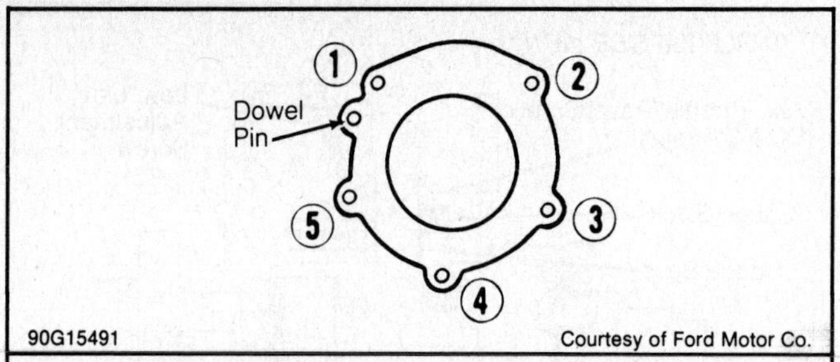
1
2
Dowel
Pin
5
3
4
90G15491
Courtesy of Ford Motor Co.

Fig. 2: Transfer Case-To-Extension Housing Tightening Sequence (Borg-Warner 1354)

BORG-WARNER 1356

Removal (Bronco) - 1) Raise vehicle. Remove skid plate (if equipped). Remove drain plug, and drain fluid from case. Install plug. Disconnect 4WD indicator switch at transfer case. If equipped with electronic shift transfer case, remove wire connector from harness at rear of transfer case by squeezing locking tabs and separating connectors.

2) On all models, disconnect front and rear drive shafts from transfer case output shaft yokes. Disconnect speedometer drive gear from case rear cover. Disconnect vent hose from mounting bracket. On manual transfer case models, disconnect shift rod between transfer case shift lever and control lever assembly.

3) On all models, support transfer case with jack and remove bolts attaching transfer case to transmission extension housing. Slide transfer case off of transmission output shaft. Lower case from vehicle. Remove gasket between transfer case and transmission extension housing.

Installation - Install new transfer case-to-extension housing gasket. To complete installation, reverse removal procedure. Tighten transfer case-to-extension housing bolts to specifications in sequence. *See Fig. 3.* See TORQUE SPECIFICATIONS tables at end of article. Fill transfer case with 2.0 qts. (1.9L) of Mercon ATF (XT-2-QDX or EAZ-19582-B).

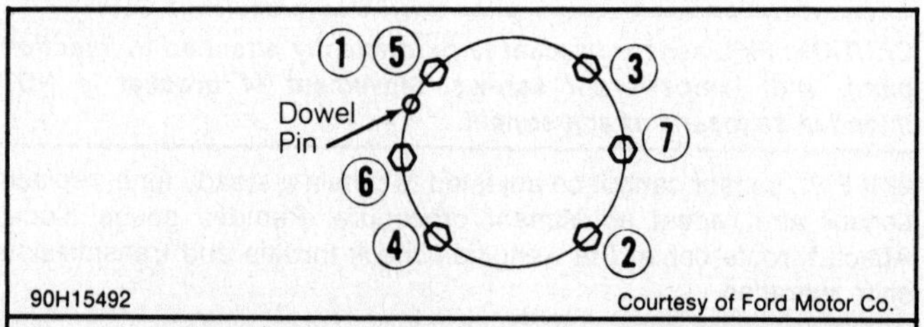
1
5
3
Dowel
Pin
7
6
4
2
90H15492
Courtesy of Ford Motor Co.

Fig. 3: Transfer Case-To-Extension Housing Tightening Sequence (Borg-Warner 1356)

SPICER TC-28

Removal (Aerostar) - 1) Raise vehicle. Remove drain plug, and drain fluid from case. Install plug. If equipped with electronic shift transfer case, remove wire connector from harness at rear of transfer case by squeezing locking tabs and separating connectors.

2) Mark drive shaft location for installation reference. Disconnect front and rear drive shafts from transfer case output shaft yokes. Disconnect speedometer drive gear from case rear cover. Remove transfer case strut from engine block and transfer case.

3) Support transfer case with jack and remove bolts attaching transfer case to transmission extension housing. Slide transfer case off transmission output shaft. Lower case from vehicle. Remove gasket from transfer case and transmission extension housing.

Installation - 1) Install new transfer case-to-extension housing gasket. To complete installation, reverse removal procedure. Tighten transfer case-to-extension housing bolts in sequence. *See Fig. 2.*

2) Tighten bolts to specifications. See TORQUE SPECIFICATIONS tables at end of article. Fill transfer case to fill plug opening with Mercon ATF (XT-2-QDX or EAZ-19582-B).

AUTOMATIC TRANSMISSION

A4LD AUTOMATIC OVERDRIVE

Removal (Aerostar, Explorer & Ranger) – 1) Disconnect negative battery cable. Raise vehicle on hoist and drain transmission fluid. Remove converter access cover. Remove converter-to-flex plate attaching nuts.

CAUTION: On 2.3L models, ALWAYS turn engine in direction of normal rotation (clockwise as viewed from front of engine).

2) Scribe a mark indexing drive shaft to rear axle flange. Disconnect drive shaft from rear axle and remove shaft from transmission. Disconnect starter cable and remove starter. Disconnect neutral start switch wires and converter clutch solenoid connector.
3) Disconnect shift rod at transmission manual lever. Remove kickdown cable from transmission. Remove vacuum line from vacuum modulator. Raise transmission with jack and remove crossmember. Lower transmission jack and allow transmission to hang.
4) On Explorer and Ranger models, place a block of wood on jack and position jack under front of engine. Raise engine and remove upper converter-to-engine bolts. On all vehicles, disconnect oil cooler lines at transmission.
5) On Aerostar models, remove upper converter-to-engine attaching bolts. On all models, disconnect speedometer cable from extension housing. Remove bolt securing filler tube to engine and remove filler tube. Secure transmission to jack with safety chain. Remove lower converter-to-engine bolts. Move transmission rearward and lower from vehicle.

NOTE: If transmission is to be removed for a long period of time, use a wooden block and a safety stand to support engine.

Installation – To install, reverse removal procedure. Ensure converter is fully engaged with pump gear during installation. Tighten bolts to specifications. See TORQUE SPECIFICATIONS tables at end of article. Fill transmission with Mercon ATF (XT-2-QDX or EAZ-19582-B). For fluid capacity, see TRANSMISSION REFILL CAPACITIES table in MANUAL/AUTOMATIC TRANSMISSION article.

AOD AUTOMATIC OVERDRIVE

Removal (Bronco, E150/250 & F150) – 1) Disconnect negative battery cable. Raise vehicle and drain transmission fluid. Remove converter drain plug access cover. Remove converter-to-flex plate attaching nuts and torque converter drain plug. Drain torque converter and reinstall drain plug.
2) Scribe a mark indexing drive shaft to rear axle flange. Disconnect drive shaft from rear axle and remove shaft from transmission. Disconnect starter cable and remove starter. Disconnect neutral start switch wires at connector.
3) Remove rear mount-to-crossmember bolts and crossmember-to-frame bolts. Remove bolts securing engine rear support to extension housing. Disconnect linkage and manual rods from transmission levers.
4) Remove bellcrank bracket-to-converter housing bolts. On 4WD models, remove transfer case. See TRANSFER CASE in this article. Raise transmission with jack and remove crossmember. Lower transmission enough to remove oil cooler lines.
5) Disconnect speedometer cable from extension housing. Remove bolt securing filler tube to engine and remove filler tube. Secure transmission to jack with safety chain. Remove converter housing-to-engine bolts. Move transmission rearward and lower from vehicle.

Installation – 1) To install, reverse removal procedure. Ensure torque converter is fully seated in transmission before and during installation procedure. Install new "O" ring on fluid filler tube end.
2) Tighten bolts to specifications. See TORQUE SPECIFICATIONS tables at end of article. Fill transmission with Mercon ATF (XT-2-QDX or EAZ-19582-B). For fluid capacity, see TRANSMISSION REFILL CAPACITIES table in AUTOMATIC/MANUAL TRANSMISSION article.

C-6

Removal (Bronco & "F" Series) – 1) Disconnect negative cable from battery. Remove upper converter housing-to-engine bolts. Raise vehicle, drain transmission pan and remove converter drain plug access cover.
2) Remove converter-to-flex plate attaching nuts and converter drain plug. Allow fluid to drain, then reinstall and tighten converter drain plug. On 2WD models, scribe a mark indexing drive shaft to rear axle flange. Disconnect drive shaft at rear axle and remove from transmission.
3) On all models, disconnect speedometer cable. Disconnect downshift and manual linkage rods from levers at transmission. Disconnect oil cooler lines from transmission. Remove vacuum line from vacuum unit. Remove retaining clip from vacuum line.
4) Disconnect starter cable from starter and remove starter. On 4WD models, remove transfer case. See TRANSFER CASE in this article. On all models, remove bolts and nuts securing rear mount to crossmember and bolts retaining crossmember to side rails.
5) Raise transmission with a transmission jack and remove both crossmembers. Secure transmission to the jack with safety chain. Remove remaining converter housing-to-engine attaching bolts. Pull transmission rearward and lower from vehicle.

Installation – 1) To install, reverse removal procedure. Ensure torque converter is fully engaged in transmission before and during installation. Install new "O" ring on fluid filler tube end. Tighten bolts to specifications. See TORQUE SPECIFICATIONS tables at end of article.
2) Fill transmission with Mercon ATF (XT-2-QDX or EAZ-19582-B). For fluid capacity, see TRANSMISSION REFILL CAPACITIES table in AUTOMATIC/MANUAL TRANSMISSION article.

Removal ("E" Series) – 1) Disconnect negative battery cable. Remove engine compartment cover and disconnect neutral start switch at plug connector. Remove flex hose from air cleaner heat tube (V8 models). On all models, remove upper converter-to-engine attaching bolts. Remove fluid filler tube-to-engine bolt.
2) Raise vehicle, drain transmission pan and remove converter drain plug access cover. Remove converter-to-flex plate attaching nuts and converter drain plug. Drain fluid and replace drain plug.
3) Scribe a mark indexing drive shaft to rear axle flange. Disconnect drive shaft. Remove filler tube. Disconnect starter cable and remove starter. Position an engine support bar to side rail and engine oil pan flanges. Disconnect oil cooler lines and vacuum lines from transmission.
4) Remove speedometer drive gear from extension housing. Remove manual and downshift linkage rods or cable controls from transmission control levers. Support transmission with transmission jack and secure with safety chain.
5) Remove bolts and nuts securing rear mount to crossmember and bolts retaining crossmember to side rails. Remove 2 support inserts and raise transmission with jack. Remove transmission crossmember. Remove remaining converter-to-engine bolts. Lower transmission out of vehicle.

Installation – 1) To install, reverse removal procedure. Ensure converter is fully engaged with pump gear during installation. Always use a new "O" ring on fluid filler tube end. Tighten bolts to specifications. See TORQUE SPECIFICATIONS tables at end of article.
2) Fill transmission with Mercon ATF (XT-2-QDX or EAZ-19582-B). For fluid capacity, see TRANSMISSION REFILL CAPACITIES table in AUTOMATIC/MANUAL TRANSMISSION article.

E4OD ELECTRONIC 4-SPEED

Removal (Bronco, "E" & "F" Series) – 1) Disconnect negative battery cable. Remove transmission dipstick. Place transmission in Neutral. Raise vehicle on hoist.
2) On 4WD models, remove front drive shaft. On all models, remove rear drive shaft. On Super Duty models, remove transmission-mounted parking brake. On all models, disconnect shift linkage.

1991 TRANSMISSION SERVICING
Transmission Removal & Installation (Cont.)

3) On 4WD models, remove transfer case shift lever linkage. On all models, disconnect manual lever position sensor connector by squeezing connector tabs and pulling on connector. Remove solenoid body connector heat shield. Remove solenoid body connector by pushing on center tab and pulling on wiring harness.

4) On 4WD models, remove 4WD switch connector from transfer case. DO NOT overextend connector tabs. Pry wiring harness locators from extension housing bracket and left side of crossmember.

5) On all models, disconnect speedometer cable. Remove torque converter lower cover and rear engine cover bolts. Remove starter. Rotate crankshaft with 15/16" socket for access to torque converter nuts. Remove torque converter-to-flexplate nuts.

6) Remove transmission filler tube. Place transmission jack under transmission. Secure transmission to jack with a safety strap. Loosen rear transmission mount nuts. Remove retaining bolts and crossmember. Disconnect cooling lines from transmission case. Cap lines and plug fittings.

7) On 4WD models, remove transfer case vent hose from detent bracket. Remove transfer case from transmission. See TRANSFER CASE in this article. On all models, remove converter housing-to-engine bolts. Pull transmission rearward and lower transmission.

Installation – 1) Before installing transmission, inspect wiring harness for damage and check connector condition. Repair or replace as required. Ensure torque converter is fully seated in transmission before and during installation procedure. Install new "O" ring on fluid filler tube end. Reverse removal procedure to complete installation.

NOTE: Check torque converter seating by placing a straightedge across the converter housing. There must be a gap between the converter pilot face and straightedge.

2) Tighten bolts to specifications. See TORQUE SPECIFICATIONS tables at end of article. Fill transmission with Mercon ATF (XT-2-QDX or EAZ-19582-B). For fluid capacity, see TRANSMISSION REFILL CAPACITIES table in AUTOMATIC/MANUAL TRANSMISSION article.

TORQUE SPECIFICATIONS

TORQUE SPECIFICATIONS (TRANSFER CASE)

Application	Ft. Lbs. (N.m)
Borg-Warner 1345	
Control Lever-To-Transfer Case Bolt	71-90 (96-122)
Drain Plug	10-14 (14-19)
Fill Plug	10-14 (14-19)
Extension Housing-To-Transfer Case Bolt [1]	25-43 (34-58)
Front Drive Shaft-To-Yoke Bolt/Nut	10-15 (14-21)
Rear Drive Shaft-To-Yoke Nut	10-15 (14-21)
Skid Plate Bolt	15-20 (21-27)
Borg-Warner 1356	
Drain Plug	9-23 (7-17)
Extension Housing-To-Transfer Case Bolt [2]	25-43 (34-58)
Front Drive Shaft-To-Yoke Bolt/Nut	10-15 (14-21)
Rear Drive Shaft-To-Yoke Nut	
Bronco	20-28 (27-34)
"F" Series	10-15 (14-21)
Skid Plate Bolt	15-20 (21-27)
Except 1345 & 1356	
Control Lever-To-Transfer Case Bolt (Explorer & Ranger)	
Large Bolt	70-90 (95-122)
Small Bolt	31-42 (42-57)
Drain Plug	14-22 (19-30)
Rear Drive Shaft-To-Transfer Case Output Flange Bolt	61-87 (83-118)
Extension Housing-To-Transfer Case Bolt [3]	25-35 (34-47)
Front Drive Shaft-to-Yoke Bolt/Nut	12-16 (16-22)
Skid Plate Bolt	15-20 (21-27)
Transfer Case Strut (Aerostar)	
Strut-To-Engine Bolt	45-60 (61-81)
Strut-To-Transfer Case Nut	55-65 (75-88)

[1] – Tighten in sequence. See Fig. 1.
[2] – Tighten in sequence. *See Fig. 3.*
[3] – Tighten in sequence. *See Fig. 2.*

TORQUE SPECIFICATIONS (TRANSMISSIONS)

Application	Ft. Lbs. (N.m)
A4LD Automatic Overdrive	
Converter Access Bolt	12-16 (16-22)
Converter-To-Flex Plate Nut	20-34 (27-46)
Converter Housing-To-Engine Bolts	28-38 (38-52)
Crossmember Bolt	60-80 (81-109)
Drive Shaft "U" Bolt Nut	70-95 (95-129)
Fill Tube Bolt	28-38 (38-52)
Rear Mount-To-Crossmember	20-30 (27-41)
Starter Bolt	15-20 (21-27)
AOD Automatic Overdrive	
Converter Access Bolt	12-16 (16-22)
Converter-To-Flex Plate Nut	20-30 (27-41)
Converter Housing-To-Engine Bolts	40-50 (54-68)
Crossmember Bolt	52-74 (71-100)
Fill Tube Bolt	28-38 (38-52)
Rear Mount-To-Crossmember	20-30 (27-41)
Starter Bolt	15-20 (21-27)
C-6	
Converter Access Bolt	12-16 (16-22)
Converter Drain Plug	18-28 (24-38)
Converter-To-Flex Plate Nut	20-30 (27-41)
Converter Housing-To-Engine Bolts	
Diesel Engine	67-87 (91-118)
Gasoline Engine	55-67 (75-91)
Crossmember Bolt	43-57 (58-77)
Rear Mount-To-Crossmember	60-80 (81-109)
Starter Bolt	
Diesel Engine	50-65 (68-88)
Gasoline Engine	40-50 (54-68)
E4OD Electronic 4-Speed	
Converter Access Bolt	12-16 (16-22)
Converter-To-Flex Plate Nut	20-30 (27-41)
Converter Housing-To-Engine Bolts	40-50 (54-68)
Crossmember Bolt	55-75 (75-102)
Fill Tube Bolt	28-38 (38-52)
Rear Mount-To-Crossmember	20-30 (27-41)
Starter Bolt	15-20 (21-27)
Transmission Cooling Line Fitting	18-23 (24-31)

GENERAL MOTORS

1991 GENERAL MOTORS CONTENTS

GENERAL INFORMATION [1]

[1] – For all GENERAL INFORMATION, see front of this manual.

ENGINE PERFORMANCE

ENGINE PERFORMANCE (Cont.)

ENGINE PERFORMANCE (Cont.)

ENGINE PERFORMANCE (Cont.)

ELECTRICAL

1991 GENERAL MOTORS CONTENTS (Cont.)

WIRING DIAGRAMS

SAFETY EQUIPMENT

SAFETY EQUIPMENT (Cont.)

ENGINES

ENGINE COOLING

CLUTCHES

1991 GENERAL MOTORS CONTENTS (Cont.)

DRIVE AXLES

DRIVE AXLES (Cont.)

BRAKES

ANTI-LOCK - RWAL

ANTI-LOCK - 4WAL

DISC & DRUM

POWER BRAKE BOOSTER - BENDIX HYDRO-BOOST

WHEEL ALIGNMENT

SPECIFICATIONS & PROCEDURES

SUSPENSION

FRONT - FWD

FRONT - 2WD COIL SPRING

FRONT - LEAF SPRING

FRONT - 4WD TORSION BAR

REAR - ELECTRONIC LEVEL CONTROL

1991 GENERAL MOTORS CONTENTS (Cont.)

STEERING

STEERING (Cont.)

TRANSMISSION SERVICING

1991 ENGINE PERFORMANCE
General Motors Introduction

1991 MODEL COVERAGE

MODEL	BODY CODE	ENGINE [1]	ENGINE ID	FUEL SYSTEM	IGNITION SYSTEM
Astro & Safari	M, L	4.3L (LB4)	Z	TBI	Magnetic
		4.3L (LU2) [2]	B	TBI	Magnetic
Blazer & Jimmy	V	5.7L (LO5)	K	TBI	Magnetic
		6.2L (LH6) [3]	C	Diesel	.....
		6.2L (LL4) [4]	J	Diesel	.....
Lumina APV, Silhouette & Trans Sport	U	3.1L (LG6)	D	TBI	Magnetic
Parcel Delivery Van (P20/35)	P	4.3L (LB4)	Z	TBI	Magnetic
		5.7L (LO5)	K	TBI	Magnetic
		6.2L (LH6) [3]	J	Diesel	.....
		6.2L (LL4) [4]	J	Diesel	.....
		7.4L (L19)	N	TBI	Magnetic
Pickup (C/K 10/35) & Sierra	C, K	4.3L (LB4)	Z	TBI	Magnetic
		5.0L (LO3)	H	TBI	Magnetic
		5.7L (LO5)	K	TBI	Magnetic
		6.2L (LH6) [3]	C	Diesel	.....
		6.2L (LL4) [4]	J	Diesel	.....
		7.4L (L19)	N	TBI	Magnetic
(R/V 35)	R, V	5.7L (LO5)	K	TBI	Magnetic
		6.2L (LH6) [3]	J	Diesel	.....
		6.2L (LL4) [4]	J	Diesel	.....
		7.4L (L19)	N	TBI	Magnetic
Suburban (R/V 15/25)	R, V	5.7L (LO5)	K	TBI	Magnetic
		6.2L (LH6) [3]	C	Diesel	.....
		6.2L (LL4) [4]	J	Diesel	.....
		7.4L (L19)	N	TBI	Magnetic
S/T Series Blazer, Bravada, Jimmy, Pickup, Sonoma & Syclone	S, T	2.5L (L38) [2]	A	TBI	Magnetic
		2.5L (LN8) [5]	E	TBI	Magnetic
		2.8L (LL2)	R	TBI	Magnetic
		4.3L (LB4)	Z	[6] TBI	Magnetic
Van (G10/35), Rally Van & Vandura	G	4.3L (LB4)	Z	TBI	Magnetic
		5.7L (LO5)	K	TBI	Magnetic
		6.2L (LH6) [3]	C	Diesel	.....
		6.2L (LL4) [4]	J	Diesel	.....
		7.4L (L19)	N	TBI	Magnetic

1 – Engine code is stamped on engine block. See ENGINE CODE LOCATION.
2 – High Output
3 – Light Duty emissions.
4 – Heavy Duty emissions.
5 – 2WD only.
6 – Port fuel injection on Syclone.

1991 ENGINE PERFORMANCE
General Motors Introduction (Cont.)

VIN DEFINITION

2GCDC14K1MR100001
① ② ③ ④ ⑤ ⑥ ⑦ ⑧ ⑨ ⑩ ⑪ ⑫ ⑬ ⑭ ⑮ ⑯ ⑰

①Indicates Nation of Origin.
②Indicates Manufacturer.
③Indicates Vehicle Division.
④Indicates Carline Code.
⑤Indicates Carline/Series.
⑥Indicates Body Type.
⑦Indicates Restraint System.
⑧Indicates Engine Code.
⑨Indicates Check Digit.
⑩Indicates Model Year.
⑪Indicates Assembly Plant.
⑫-⑰Indicates Plant Sequential Number.

MODEL YEAR VIN CODE APPLICATION

VIN Code	Model Year
K	1989
L	1990
M	1991

ENGINE CODE LOCATION [1]

LU2, LB4, LO3, LO5 & L19 – On front of engine block, on right side above timing gear cover **OR** on left side of engine block, on engine-to-transmission mating flange.

LN8 & L38 – On left side of engine block, at rear below cylinder head **OR** on left side of engine block, on engine-to-transmission mating flange.

LL2 – On front of engine block, on left side above timing gear cover **OR** on right side of engine block above engine mount.

LH6 & LL4 – On front of engine block, right side of timing gear housing casting **OR** on top of engine block, near left cylinder head-to-engine block mating surface, at front **OR** on left side of engine block, on engine-to-transmission mating flange.

LG6 – On left side of engine block, on engine-to-transmission mating flange.

[1] – See ENGINE in 1991 MODEL COVERAGE table for engine code location prefix.

1991 ENGINE PERFORMANCE
Emission Applications

1991 GENERAL MOTORS EMISSION SYSTEMS

Model, Engine & Fuel System	Emission Control Systems & Devices	Remarks
Light Duty Emissions [1]		
2.5L (151") 4-Cyl. TBI	**PCV, TAC, EVAP, TWC, EGR, SPK, O_2, CEC, CE,** EVAP-VC, EGR-SOL	[1] - Vehicles up to 8500 GVW.
2.8L (170") V6 TBI	**PCV, TAC, EVAP, TWC, EGR** [2]**, SPK, AP, O_2, CEC, CE,** EGR-SOL, AP-ACV	[2] - Ported type.
3.1L (190") V6 TBI	**PCV, TAC, EVAP, TWC, EGR, SPK, O_2, CEC, CE,** EVAP-VC, EVAP-CPTVS, EGR-SOL	[3] - Except "S" & "T" Series.
4.3L (262") V6 PFI Turbo	**PCV, EVAP, TWC, EGR, SPK, O_2, CEC, CE,** EVAP-VC, EGR-EVRV	[4] - M/T only.
4.3L (262") V6 TBI	**PCV, TAC, EVAP, TWC, EGR, SPK, AP** [3]**, O_2, CEC, CE,** EVAP-VC, EGR-SOL, AP-ACV	[5] - Vehicles over 8500 GVW.
5.0L (305") V8 TBI	**PCV, TAC, EVAP, TWC, EGR, SPK, AP** [4]**, O_2, CEC, CE,** EVAP-VC, EGR-SOL, AP-ACV	
5.7L (350") V8 TBI	**PCV, TAC, EVAP, TWC, EGR, SPK, AP** [4]**, O_2, CEC, CE,** EVAP-VC, EGR-SOL, AP-ACV	
6.2L (378") V8 Diesel	**EGR,** CD-REGVLV, EGR-SOL, EGR-EPR, HPCA, TPS, VRV	
7.4L (454") V8 TBI	**PCV, TAC, EVAP, TWC, EGR, SPK, AP, O_2, CEC, CE,** EVAP-VC, EGR-SOL, AP-ACV	
Heavy Duty Emissions [5]		
4.3L (262") V6 TBI	**PCV, TAC, EVAP, OC, EGR, SPK, O_2, CEC, CE,** EVAP-VC, EGR-SOL	
5.7L (350") V8 TBI	**PCV, TAC, EVAP, OC, EGR, SPK, O_2, CEC, CE,** EVAP-VC, EGR-SOL	
6.2L (378") V8 Diesel	**EGR,** CD-REGVLV, EGR-EPR	
7.4L (454") V8 TBI	**PCV, TAC, EVAP, OC, EGR, SPK, O_2, CEC, CE,** EVAP-VC, EGR-SOL	

NOTE: Major emission control systems are listed in bold type; components are listed in light type.

AP - Air Injection Pump System
AP-ACV - AP Air Control Valve
CD-REGVLV - Crankcase Depression Regulator Valve
CE - Check Engine Light
CEC - Computerized Engine Controls
EGR - Exhaust Gas Recirculation
EGR-SOL - EGR Solenoid
EGR-EPR - EGR Exhaust Pressure Regulator Valve
EGR-EVRV - EGR Vacuum Regulator Valve Solenoid
EPR-VLV - Exhaust Pressure Regulator Valve
EVAP - Evaporative Emission Controls
EVAP-CPTVS - EVAP Canister Purge Thermal Vacuum Switch
EVAP-VC - EVAP Vapor Canister
HPCA - Housing Pressure Cold Advance
OC - Oxidation Catalyst
O_2 - Oxygen Sensor
PCV - Positive Crankcase Ventilation
PFI - Port Fuel Injection
SPK - Spark Controls
TAC - Thermostatic Air Cleaner
TBI - Throttle Body Injection
TPS - Throttle Position Sensor
TWC - Three-Way Catalyst
VRV - Vacuum Regulator Valve

1991 ENGINE PERFORMANCE
Service & Adjustment Specifications

Astro, Blazer, Bravada, Jimmy, Lumina APV, Safari, Sierra, Silhouette, Sonoma, Syclone, Trans Sport, "C" & "K" Series, "G" Series, "P" Series, "R" & "V" Series, "S" & "T" Series

INTRODUCTION

Use this article to quickly find specifications related to servicing and on-vehicle adjustments. This article may be used for quick reference when you are familiar with proper adjustment procedures and only need a specification.

CAPACITIES

BATTERY SPECIFICATIONS

Application	Cold Crank Amps @ 0°F (-18°C)	Reserve Capacity Minutes
2.5L (VIN E)	525	90
2.8L (VIN R)	525	90
3.1L (VIN D)	525	90
4.3L (VIN Z)		
Standard	525	90
Heavy Duty	630	115
5.0L (VIN H)		
Standard	430	90
Heavy Duty	525	90
5.7L (VIN K)		
Standard	525	90
Heavy Duty	630	115
6.2L (VIN C & J)	570	90
7.4L (VIN N)	630	115

FLUID CAPACITIES

Application	[1] Quantity Qts. (L)
Crankcase	
2.5L (VIN E)	[2] 3.0 (2.8)
2.8L (VIN R)	[2] 4.0 (3.8)
3.1L (VIN D)	[2] 4.0 (3.8)
4.3L (VIN Z) [3]	[2] 4.0 (3.8)
5.0L (VIN H)	[2] 4.0 (3.8)
5.7L (VIN K)	[2] 4.0 (3.8)
6.2L (VIN C & J)	7.0 (6.6)
7.4L (VIN N)	[2] 6.0 (5.7)
Cooling System (Includes Heater) [4]	
2.5L (VIN E)	11.5 (11.0)
2.8L (VIN R)	10.5 (10.0)
3.1L (VIN D)	13.0 (12.3)
4.3L (VIN Z)	
"C" & "K" Series	10.9 (10.3)
Other Models	13.5 (12.8)
5.0L (VIN H)	17.0 (16.0)
5.7L (VIN K)	17.0 (16.0)
6.2L (VIN C & J)	25.0 (23.5)
7.4L (VIN N)	23.0 (22.0)
Automatic Transaxle (Dexron-II) [5]	
3.1L (VIN D)	4.0 (3.8)
Automatic Transmission (Dexron-II) [5]	
2.5L (VIN E)	5.0 (4.7)
2.8L (VIN R)	5.0 (4.7)
4.3L (VIN Z)	5.0 (4.7)
V8 Engines	
THM 400	4.2 (4.0)
THM 700	5.0 (4.7)

FLUID CAPACITIES (Cont.)

Application	[1] Quantity Qts. (L)
Manual Transmission	
2.5L (VIN E)	[6] 2.2 (2.0)
2.8L (VIN R)	[6] 2.2 (2.0)
4.3L (VIN Z)	[6] 2.2 (2.0)
V8 Engines	
4-Speed (117 mm)	[7] 4.2 (4.0)
5-Speed (85 mm)	[8] 1.8 (1.7)
5-Speed (109 mm)	[7] 4.2 (4.0)

[1] – Fluid capacities listed are approximate. Always fill to FULL mark.
[2] – Does not include oil filter capacity.
[3] – Use of synthetic 10W-30 motor oil is required on Turbo models.
[4] – Add 3 qts. (2.8L) coolant for models equipped with rear heater.
[5] – Drain and refill capacity only. Does not include torque converter.
[6] – Dexron-II.
[7] – SAE 80W-90.
[8] – Manual Transmission Fluid (12345349 or 1052931).

QUICK-SERVICE

SERVICE INTERVALS & SPECIFICATIONS

REPLACEMENT INTERVALS

Component	Interval (Miles)
Air Filter	30,000
Coolant	30,000
Fuel Filter	[1] 60,000
Oil & Filter	[2] 7500
Spark Plugs	30,000

[1] – On diesel engines, replace every 30,000 miles.
[2] – On diesel engines, replace every 5000 miles.

BELT TENSION

BELT ADJUSTMENT

Application	[1] Tension Lbs. (kg)
2.5L, 2.8L & 3.1L	[1]
4.3L, 5.0L & 5.7L	
New Belt	135 (61.2)
Used Belt	90 (40.8)
6.2L Diesel	
New Belt	146 (66.2)
Used Belt	67 (30.4)
7.4L	
New Belt	129.4-140.6 (58.7-63.8)
Used Belt	84.4-95.6 (38.3-43.4)

[1] – Serpentine belt tension is maintained automatically by a spring-tensioned idler pulley. No adjustment is necessary.

MECHANICAL CHECKS

ENGINE COMPRESSION

COMPRESSION SPECIFICATIONS

Application	Compression Ratio
2.5L (VIN E)	8.3:1
2.8L (VIN R)	8.9:1
3.1L (VIN D)	8.9:1
4.3L (VIN Z)	[1] 9.3:1
5.0L (VIN H)	9.3:1
5.7L (VIN K)	[2] 9.1:1
6.2L Diesel (VIN C & J)	21.3:1
7.4L (VIN N)	7.9:1

[1] – 8.6:1 – Turbo & heavy duty.
[2] – 8.3:1 – Over 8500 lbs. GVW.

1991 ENGINE PERFORMANCE
Service & Adjustment Specifications (Cont.)

VALVE CLEARANCE

***NOTE:** All models are equipped with hydraulic lifters. No adjustments are required.*

IGNITION SYSTEM

IGNITION COIL

PICK-UP COIL RESISTANCE

Application	Ohms
All Models	500-1500

HIGH TENSION WIRE RESISTANCE

HIGH TENSION WIRE RESISTANCE

Application	Ohms
All Models	30,000 Maximum

SPARK PLUGS

SPARK PLUG TYPE

Application	AC
2.5L (VIN E)	R43TS6
2.8L (VIN R)	R43TSK
3.1L (VIN D)	R43TS
4.3L (VIN Z)	
Non-Turbo	CR43TS
Turbo	CR42TS
5.0L (VIN H)	CR43TS
5.7L (VIN K)	CR43TS
7.4L (VIN N)	CR43TS

SPARK PLUG SPECIFICATIONS

Application	Gap In. (mm)	Torque Ft. Lbs. (N.m)
2.5L (VIN E)	.060 (1.52)	17 (23)
2.8L (VIN R)	.045 (1.14)	22 (30)
3.1L (VIN D)	.045 (1.14)	18 (24)
4.3L (VIN Z)		
Non-Turbo	.035 (0.89)	22 (30)
Turbo	.045 (1.14)	11 (15)
5.0L (VIN H)	.035 (0.89)	22 (30)
5.7L (VIN K)	.035 (0.89)	22 (30)
7.4L (VIN N)	.035 (0.89)	22 (30)

FIRING ORDER & TIMING MARKS

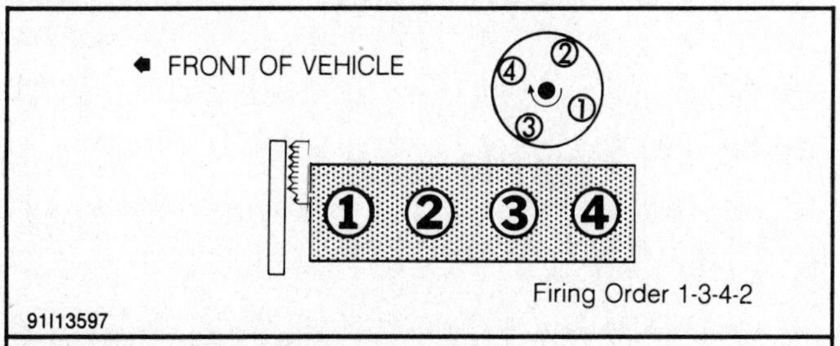
FRONT OF VEHICLE
Firing Order 1-3-4-2
91I13597

Fig. 1: Firing Order & Timing Marks (2.5L)

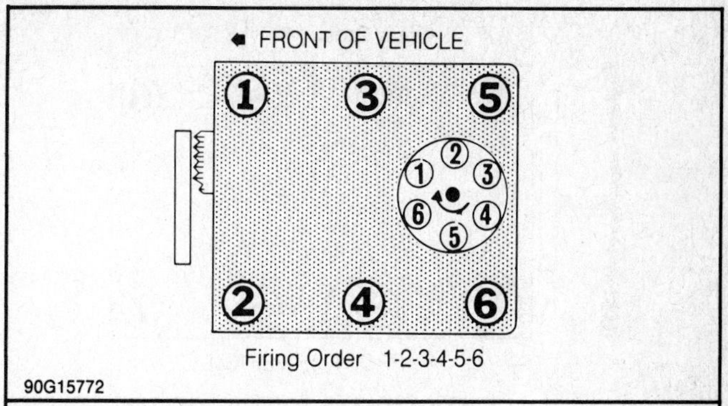
FRONT OF VEHICLE
Firing Order 1-2-3-4-5-6
90G15772

Fig. 2: Firing Order & Timing Marks (2.8L)

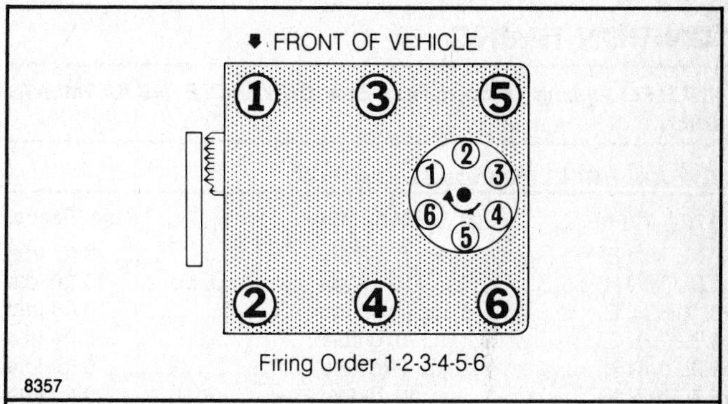
FRONT OF VEHICLE
Firing Order 1-2-3-4-5-6
8357

Fig. 3: Firing Order & Timing Marks (3.1L)

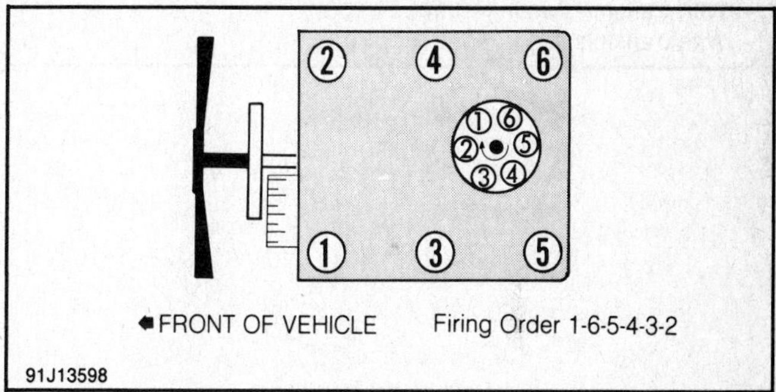
FRONT OF VEHICLE
Firing Order 1-6-5-4-3-2
91J13598

Fig. 4: Firing Order & Timing Marks (4.3L)

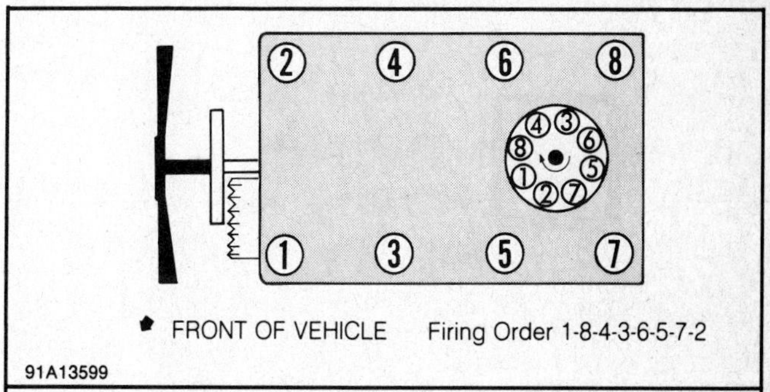
FRONT OF VEHICLE
Firing Order 1-8-4-3-6-5-7-2
91A13599

Fig. 5: Firing Order & Timing Marks (5.0L, 5.7L & 7.4L)

1991 ENGINE PERFORMANCE
Service & Adjustment Specifications (Cont.)

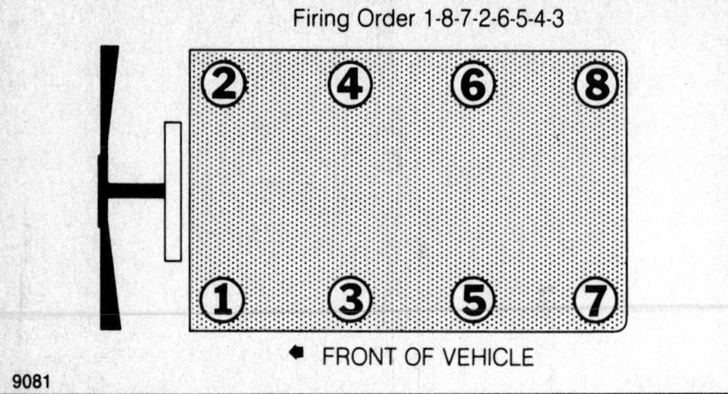
Firing Order 1-8-7-2-6-5-4-3
2
4
6
8
1
3
5
7
FRONT OF VEHICLE
9081

Fig. 6: Firing Order (6.2L Diesel)

IGNITION TIMING

***NOTE:** For timing procedures, see ON-VEHICLE ADJUSTMENTS article.*

IGNITION TIMING (Degrees BTDC @ RPM)

Application	[1] Man. Trans.	[2] Auto. Trans.
2.5L (VIN E)	8 @ Idle	8 @ Idle
2.8L (VIN R)	10 @ Idle	10 @ Idle
3.1L (VIN D)	10 @ Idle	10 @ Idle
4.3L (VIN Z)	0 @ Idle	0 @ Idle
5.0L (VIN H)	0 @ Idle	0 @ Idle
5.7L (VIN K)	0 @ Idle	0 @ Idle
7.4L (VIN N)	4 @ Idle	4 @ Idle

[1] – With transmission in Neutral.
[2] – With transmission in Neutral or Park.

FUEL SYSTEM

FUEL PUMP

***NOTE:** Fuel pump performance is a measurement of fuel pressure and volume availability, not regulated fuel pressure.*

FUEL PUMP PERFORMANCE

Application	psi (kg/cm²)
4.3L Turbo (VIN Z)	35-38 (2.5-2.7)
6.2L Diesel (VIN C & J)	6-9 (.42-.63)
All Others	9-13 (.63-.91)

INJECTOR RESISTANCE

INJECTOR RESISTANCE SPECIFICATIONS

Application	[1] Resistance (Ohms)
3.1L (VIN D)	1.2
4.3L Turbo (VIN Z)	2.0
All Others	1.3

[1] – Injector resistance specification is at 140°F (60°C).

IDLE SPEED & MIXTURE

***NOTE:** Idle mixture on fuel injected models is controlled by the Electronic Control Module (ECM) and is not adjustable.*

THROTTLE POSITION SENSOR (TPS)

***NOTE:** TPS is adjustable only on 2.8L (VIN R) and 6.2L Diesel engines. For further testing, see appropriate SELF-DIAGNOSTICS article.*

TPS ADJUSTMENT VOLTAGE

Application	[1] Voltage
2.8L (VIN R)	.42-.45
6.2L Diesel (VIN C & J)	[2] .63

[1] – At idle RPM or closed throttle.
[2] – This is TPS voltage ratio. For adjustment procedure, see ON-VEHICLE ADJUSTMENTS article.

1991 ENGINE PERFORMANCE
On-Vehicle Adjustments

Astro, Blazer, Bravada, Jimmy, Lumina APV, Safari, Sierra, Silhouette, Sonoma, Syclone, Trans Sport, "C" & "K" Series, "G" Series, "P" Series, "R" & "V" Series, "S" & "T" Series

ENGINE COMPRESSION

CAUTION: On diesel engines, DO NOT add oil to cylinders during compression check, as extensive engine damage will result.

Check engine compression pressure with engine at normal operating temperature.

On gasoline engines, remove all spark plugs. Ensure throttle plates are wide open and battery is fully charged. Remove fuel pump or ECM fuse. Disconnect primary lead to distributor or ignition coil. Crank engine through at least 4 compression strokes. The lowest cylinder reading should NOT be less than 70 percent of the highest cylinder reading. No cylinder reading should be less than 100 psi (7 kg/cm²).

On diesel engines, remove air cleaner. Install Intake Manifold Cover (J-29664-2 or J-26996-1) over intake manifold opening. Disconnect Pink wire from injection pump shutoff solenoid. Disconnect glow plug wiring and remove all glow plugs. Use Compression Gauge (J-26999) to test individual cylinders. Crank engine through at least 6 compression strokes. The lowest cylinder reading should NOT be less than 80 percent of the highest cylinder reading. No cylinder reading should be less than 380 psi (27 kg/cm²).

COMPRESSION SPECIFICATIONS

Application	Compression Ratio
2.5L (VIN E)	8.3:1
2.8L (VIN R)	8.9:1
3.1L (VIN D)	8.9:1
4.3L (VIN Z)	
Non-Turbo	[1] 9.3:1
Turbo	8.35:1
5.0L (VIN H)	9.3:1
5.7L (VIN K)	[2] 9.1:1
6.2L Diesel (VIN C & J)	21.3:1
7.4L (VIN N)	7.9:1
Gasoline Engines	
Min. Compression Pressure	100 psi (7 kg/cm²)
Max. Variation Between Cylinders	Less Than 30%
Diesel Engines	
Compression Pressure	380-400 psi (27-28 kg/cm²)
Max. Variation Between Cylinders	20%

[1] – Heavy duty: 8.6:1.
[2] – Over 8500 lbs. GVW: 8.3:1.

VALVE CLEARANCE

NOTE: All models use hydraulic lifters. No adjustments are required.

IGNITION TIMING (GASOLINE)

4-CYLINDER IGNITION TIMING

2.5L (VIN E) – 1) Set parking brake, block drive wheels and place transmission in Neutral or Park. Warm engine to normal operating temperature. Turn A/C off (if equipped). Ensure SERVICE ENGINE SOON light is off.

2) Connect jumper between ALDL connector terminals "A" and "B". SERVICE ENGINE SOON light should begin flashing. Connect timing light.

3) Note average timing of cylinders No. 1 and 4 and adjust to specification if necessary. See 4-CYLINDER IGNITION TIMING table. Remove jumper from ALDL connector. Ensure SERVICE ENGINE SOON light is off.

4-CYLINDER IGNITION TIMING (Degrees BTDC @ RPM)

Application	Man. Trans.	Auto. Trans.
2.5L (VIN E)	8 @ Idle	8 @ Idle

V6 IGNITION TIMING

2.8L (VIN R) – 1) Set parking brake, block drive wheels and place transmission in Neutral or Park. Warm engine to normal operating temperature. Turn A/C off (if equipped). Ensure SERVICE ENGINE SOON light is off.

2) Disconnect Tan/Black Electronic Spark Timing (EST) by-pass connector wire located near heater housing in passenger compartment. DO NOT disconnect 4-wire connector at distributor.

3) Connect timing light to No. 1 spark plug wire. Check timing and adjust if necessary. See V6 IGNITION TIMING table. Reconnect EST by-pass connector, and clear ECM trouble code.

3.1L (VIN D) – 1) Set parking brake, block drive wheels and place transmission in Neutral or Park. Warm engine to normal operating temperature. Turn A/C off (if equipped). Ensure SERVICE ENGINE SOON light is off.

2) Ground Tan/Black Electronic Spark Timing (EST) by-pass connector wire located in front of right strut tower. Connect timing light to No. 1 spark plug wire. Check timing and adjust if necessary. See V6 IGNITION TIMING table.

3) Disconnect ground from EST by-pass circuit, and reconnect connector. Clear ECM trouble code.

4.3L (VIN Z) – 1) Set parking brake, block drive wheels and place transmission in Neutral or Park. Warm engine to normal operating temperature. Turn A/C off (if equipped). Ensure SERVICE ENGINE SOON light is off.

2) Disconnect Tan/Black Electronic Spark Timing (EST) by-pass connector wire located near heater housing in engine compartment or near distributor or near electrical junction box cover. DO NOT disconnect 4-wire connector at distributor.

3) Connect timing light to No. 1 spark plug wire. Check timing and adjust if necessary. See V6 IGNITION TIMING table. Reconnect EST by-pass connector, and clear ECM trouble code.

V6 IGNITION TIMING (Degrees BTDC @ RPM)

Application	Man. Trans.	Auto. Trans.
2.8L (VIN R)	10 @ Idle	10 @ Idle
3.1L (VIN D)	10 @ Idle	10 @ Idle
4.3L (VIN Z)		
Non-Turbo	0 @ Idle	0 @ Idle
Turbo	[1]	[1]

[1] – Information not available from manufacturer.

V8 IGNITION TIMING

All Models (Except Diesel) – 1) Set parking brake, block drive wheels and place transmission in Neutral or Park. Warm engine to normal operating temperature. Turn A/C off (if equipped). Ensure SERVICE ENGINE SOON light is off.

2) Disconnect Tan/Black Electronic Spark Timing (EST) by-pass connector wire located behind electrical junction box cover or near distributor. DO NOT disconnect 4-wire connector at distributor.

3) Connect timing light to No. 1 spark plug wire. Check timing and adjust if necessary. See V8 IGNITION TIMING table. Reconnect EST by-pass connector, and clear ECM trouble code.

V8 IGNITION TIMING (Degrees BTDC @ RPM)

Application	Man. Trans.	Auto. Trans.
5.0L (VIN H)	0 @ Idle	0 @ Idle
5.7L (VIN K)	0 @ Idle	0 @ Idle
7.4L (VIN N)	4 @ Idle	4 @ Idle

INJECTION PUMP TIMING (DIESEL)

6.2L (VIN C & J)

1) Original factory injection pump timing is marked with a static timing mark (straight line scribed across both the pump flange and front housing). Injection pump timing is dynamically checked and marked with a dynamic timing mark (a circle scribed across both the pump flange and the front housing).

1991 ENGINE PERFORMANCE
On-Vehicle Adjustments (Cont.)

2) To properly set timing, 2 halves of dynamic timing mark (circle between pump flange and front housing) must be aligned. Engine must not be running while injection timing is set. A service/replacement pump will not be marked with dynamic timing mark (circle) and should be timed using static timing mark.
3) Check alignment of injection pump timing marks on top of engine front cover and injection pump flange. If timing marks are not aligned, loosen 3 retaining nuts and align mark on injection pump with mark on front cover. Tighten nuts to 30 ft. lbs. (41 N.m). Adjust throttle linkage.

IDLE SPEED & MIXTURE

IDLE SPEED & MIXTURE (GASOLINE)

NOTE: DO NOT attempt to adjust idle mixture and idle speed, which are controlled by the Electronic Control Module (ECM). Incorrect idle speeds are normally caused by dirty throttle plate or vacuum leaks. Ensure all vacuum components are functioning properly.

IDLE SPEED (DIESEL)

Curb Idle – Set parking brake and block drive wheels. Warm engine to operating temperature. Install Tachometer (J-26925). Air cleaner must be in place and accessories turned off. Adjust curb idle speed to specifications by turning curb idle speed screw on fuel injection pump. *See Fig. 1*. See IDLE SPEED (RPM) specifications table.
Fast Idle – 1) Set parking brake and block drive wheels. Warm engine to operating temperature. Install Tachometer (J-26925). Air cleaner must be in place and all accessories turned off.
2) Remove connector from fast idle solenoid. *See Fig. 1*. To energize solenoid, connect jumper wire from battery positive terminal to fast idle solenoid terminal. Open throttle momentarily to energize and fully extend the fast idle solenoid plunger.
3) Adjust the extended fast idle solenoid plunger by turning plunger hex head to obtain the fast idle speed. See IDLE SPEED (RPM) specifications table. Turn off engine. Remove jumper wire and test equipment. Install fast idle solenoid connector.

IDLE SPEED (RPM)

Application	Curb Idle	Fast Idle
6.2L	650	800

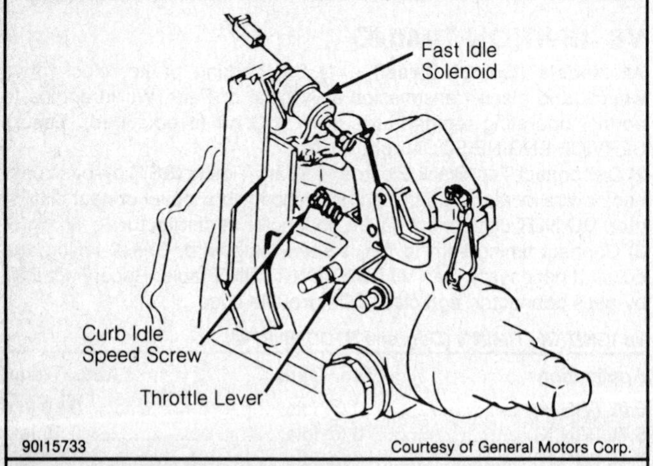
Fast Idle
Solenoid
Curb Idle
Speed Screw
Throttle Lever
90I15733
Courtesy of General Motors Corp.

Fig. 1: Adjusting Idle Speed (Diesel)

PURGING FUEL SYSTEM (DIESEL)

NOTE: If vehicle is equipped with dual tanks, perform purging procedure on each tank.

1) Park vehicle on a level surface. Place drain pan under drain hose. Open drain valve 3-4 turns. With fuel tank cap installed and using air nozzle, apply 3-5 psi (.21-.35 kg/cm²) through fuel return hose at injection pump.
2) Contaminated fuel will be forced out of tank via filter drain hose. Continue to drain fuel until clear fuel is observed flowing through drain hose. Entire fuel tank may need to be drained. Close drain valve. Install fuel return hose.

THROTTLE POSITION SENSOR (TPS)

TPS ADJUSTMENT (GASOLINE)

NOTE: On all models except 2.8L engine (VIN R), Throttle Position Sensor (TPS) is NOT adjustable. Resistance values given in TPS OUTPUT VOLTAGE table are for reference only. If resistance value is not as specified, replace TPS. For testing procedures, refer to appropriate SELF-DIAGNOSTICS or SYSTEM & COMPONENT TESTING article.

2.8L (VIN R) – Throttle Position Sensor (TPS) can also be adjusted using a Scan tester. Perform this check only when throttle body parts have been replaced or after minimum airflow has been adjusted.
1) Install 3 jumper wires between TPS and TPS wiring harness connector. Jumpers can be made using the following General Motors parts: Terminals No. 1214836 and 12014837.
2) Turn ignition to ON position. DO NOT start engine. Using a DVOM, connect test leads to Dark Blue and Black wire terminals. With throttle at closed position, TPS voltage should be .42-.45 volt.
3) If voltage reading is not as specified, rotate TPS until specified voltage is obtained. See TPS OUTPUT VOLTAGE table. If specified voltage cannot be obtained, replace TPS.
4) Tighten screws and recheck readings. Turn ignition off. Remove jumper wires and reconnect harness connector to TPS.

TPS OUTPUT VOLTAGE (Gasoline)

Application	[1] Voltage
2.5L (VIN E) [2]	1.25 or less
2.8L (VIN R)	.42-.45
3.1L (VIN D) [2]	1.25 Or Less
4.3L (VIN Z) [2]	1.25 Or Less
5.0L (VIN H) [2]	1.25 Or Less
5.7L (VIN K) [2]	1.25 Or Less
7.4L (VIN N) [2]	1.25 Or Less

[1] – At idle RPM or closed throttle.
[2] – Not adjustable.

TPS ADJUSTMENT (DIESEL)

6.2L Light Duty (VIN C) – 1) Using a DVOM, measure and record resistance of power supply voltage. This is the reference voltage. Perform the following calculations:

- Reference voltage x 0.63 = Desired signal voltage.
- Reference voltage x 0.01 = Signal voltage tolerance.

Record the desired signal voltage and signal voltage tolerance.
2) With throttle lever in the closed position, loosen throttle position sensor to injector pump screws.
3) Connect power supply across TPS ground wire (Black) and reference wire (Gray). Connect DVOM across ground wire (Black) and signal wire (Blue). *See Fig. 2*.
4) Insert a .646" Gauge Block (J-33043-A) between gauge boss on pump and WOT stop screw on throttle lever. *See Fig. 2*. Rotate TPS clockwise until DVOM reads the desired signal voltage as determined in step **1)**. Tighten TPS mounting screws to 53 INCH lbs. (6 N.m).
5) Release throttle lever and allow it to return to idle position. At idle, DVOM should read a voltage ratio of .15-.30 volts. If voltage ratio is not .15-.30 volts, check for a faulty sensor.
6) Rotate throttle lever against gauge block, and recheck desired signal voltage tolerance, determined in step **1)**. Repeat step **2)**, if readjustment is required.

1991 ENGINE PERFORMANCE
On-Vehicle Adjustments (Cont.)

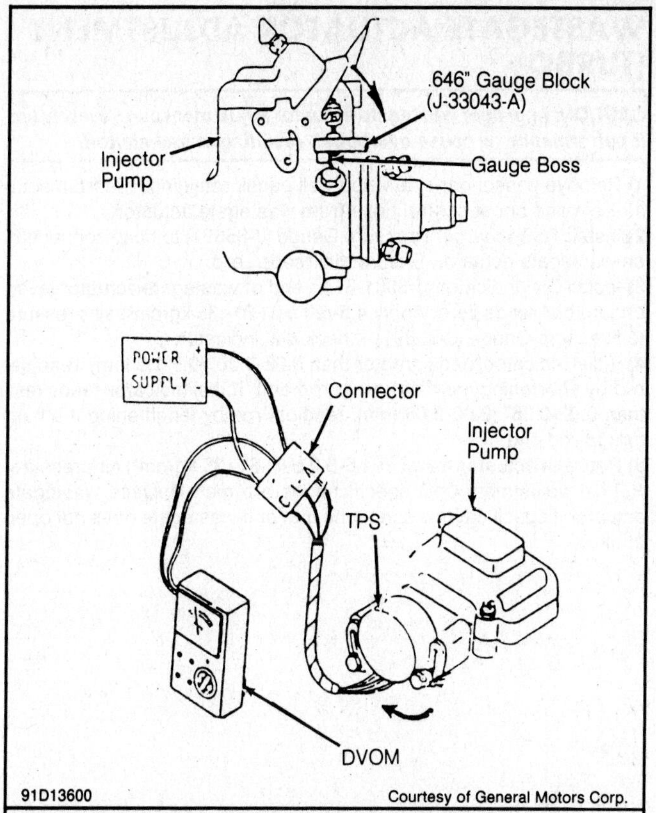
.646" Gauge Block
(J-33043-A)
Injector
Pump
Gauge Boss
POWER
SUPPLY
Connector
Injector
Pump
TPS
DVOM
91D13600
Courtesy of General Motors Corp.

Fig. 2: Adjusting TPS (6.2L Light Duty - VIN C)

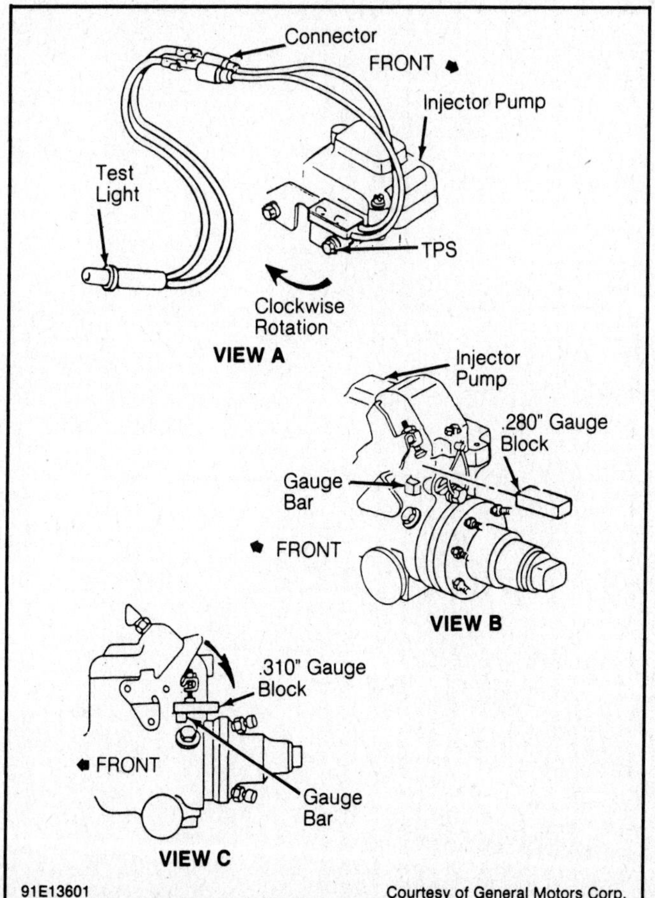
Connector
FRONT
Injector Pump
Test
Light
TPS
Clockwise
Rotation
VIEW A
Injector
Pump
.280" Gauge
Block
Gauge
Bar
FRONT
VIEW B
.310" Gauge
Block
FRONT
Gauge
Bar
VIEW C
91E13601
Courtesy of General Motors Corp.

Fig. 3: Adjusting TPS (6.2L Heavy Duty - VIN J)

6.2L Heavy Duty (VIN J) - 1) Disconnect TPS electrical connector. With throttle closed, loosen TPS mounting screws. Connect test light across TPS connector. Insert .280" Gauge Block (J-33043-A) between gauge boss and WOT stop screw on throttle shaft. *See Fig. 3.*
2) Rotate and hold throttle lever against gauge block. Rotate TPS clockwise until test light illuminates. Tighten TPS mounting screws.

NOTE: Switch point must be set only while rotating TPS body in clockwise direction.

3) Release throttle lever and allow to return to idle position. Remove .280" Gauge Block (J-33043-A). Insert a .310" Gauge Block (J-33043-A) between throttle lever and fast idle screw. *See Fig. 3.* Test light should not illuminate. If test light illuminates, TPS is not adjusted properly. Repeat step **1)**.

TPS ADJUSTMENT SPECIFICATIONS (Diesel)

Application	TPS Voltage Ratio
6.2L	
Light Duty (VIN C)	.15-.30
Heavy Duty (VIN J)	[1]

[1] - Test light is used to check TPS adjustment.

VACUUM REGULATOR VALVE/ DETENT SWITCH ADJUSTMENT (DIESEL)

1) Loosen vacuum regulator valve so it is free to rotate on pump. Attach a hand-held vacuum pump and apply 20 in. Hg to bottom port of valve. Attach vacuum gauge to top port of valve.
2) Insert 0.646" Gauge Block (J-33043) between gauge boss on injection pump and wide open stop screw on throttle lever (switch on position). *See Fig. 4*.

NOTE: Always refer to underhood Emission Control Label for correct gauge block size.

3) Rotate and hold throttle shaft against gauge block. Slowly rotate vacuum regulator valve body clockwise (facing valve) until vacuum gauge reads 10.9-12.1 in. Hg. Hold valve body at this position and tighten mounting screws.
4) Check adjustment by allowing throttle shaft to return to idle stop position, then rotate throttle shaft back against gauge block. Vacuum gauge reading must be 10.9-12.1 in. Hg. If vacuum is not within limits, reset valve.
5) With vacuum valve set, confirm detent switch point by reading resistance between ignition (Pink/Black wire) and detent terminal (Orange wire). Insert Switch Gauge (J-36142) between wide open stop pin and wide open stop screw on throttle lever. *See Fig. 4*.
6) Rotate throttle lever against switch gauge. Continuity should NOT be present. Release throttle lever and remove gauge. Rotate throttle lever to wide open throttle (lever stop screw touching pump stop pin).
7) Check switch for continuity. Switch must have less than one ohm resistance before throttle reaches wide open position. If switch does not meet specification, reset assembly by returning to step **1)** and repeating entire procedure.

1991 ENGINE PERFORMANCE
On-Vehicle Adjustments (Cont.)

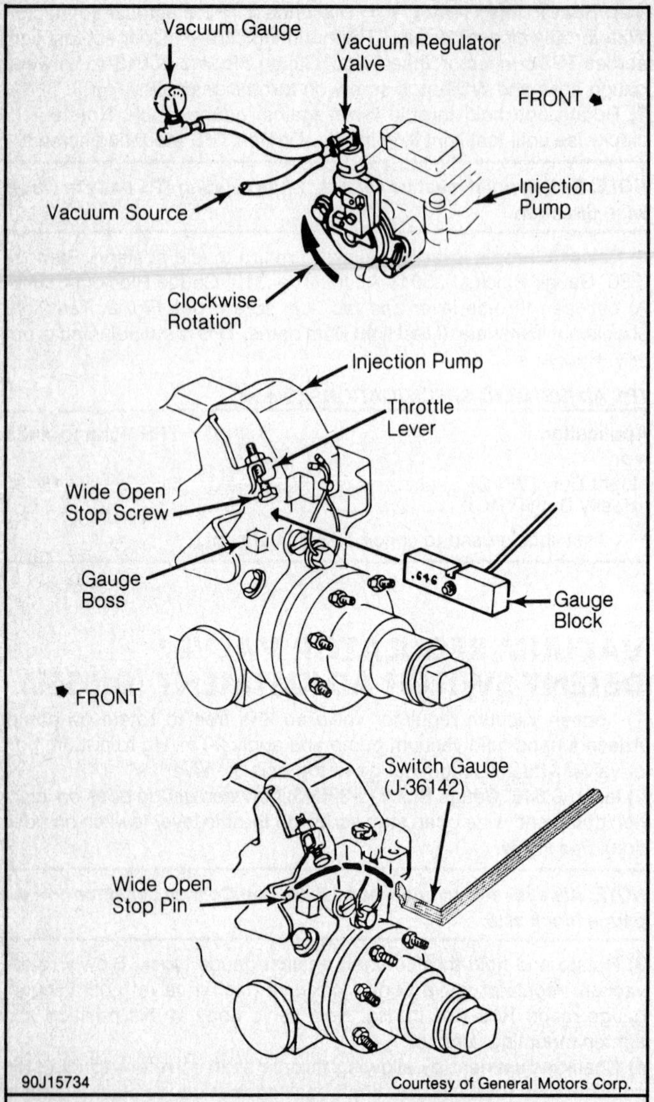
Vacuum Gauge
Vacuum Regulator Valve
FRONT
Injection Pump
Vacuum Source
Clockwise Rotation
Injection Pump
Throttle Lever
Wide Open Stop Screw
Gauge Boss
Gauge Block
FRONT
Switch Gauge (J-36142)
Wide Open Stop Pin
90J15734
Courtesy of General Motors Corp.

Fig. 4: Adjusting Vacuum Regulator Valve & Detent Switch

WASTEGATE ACTUATOR ADJUSTMENT (TURBO)

CAUTION: Improper wastegate actuator adjustment can severely limit performance or cause overboost, resulting in fuel shutoff.

1) Remove passenger side wheelwell panel, retaining wire from actuator pin and boost control hose from wastegate actuator.
2) Install Turbocharger Pressure Gauge (J-35691) to hose connection on wastegate actuator. Ensure dial reads zero.
3) Install Dial Indicator (J-8001-3) on end of wastegate actuator lever. Ensure dial reads zero. Apply 4.5-5.0 psi (.31-.35 kg/cm²) air pressure to Pressure Gauge (J-35691). Check dial indicator.
4) If dial indicator reads greater than 0.02-0.06" (0.5-1.5 mm), readjust rod by shortening it a half-turn at rod end. If dial indicator reads less than 0.02-0.06" (0.02-0.06 mm), readjust rod by lengthening it a half-turn at rod end.
5) Recheck actuator travel at 4.5-5.0 psi (.31-.35 kg/cm²) air pressure. Repeat adjustment until specifications are met. Replace wastegate actuator if specifications cannot be met or if wastegate does not open at all.

1991 ENGINE PERFORMANCE
Theory & Operation

Astro, Blazer, Bravada, Jimmy, Lumina APV, Safari, Sierra, Silhouette, Sonoma, Syclone, Trans Sport, "C" & "K" Series, "G" Series, "P" Series, "R" & "V" Series, "S" & "T" Series

INTRODUCTION

This article covers basic description and operation of engine performance-related systems and components. Read this article before diagnosing vehicles or systems with which you are not completely familiar.

AIR INDUCTION SYSTEM

TURBOCHARGER (4.3L)

The turbocharger is basically an air compressor or air pump. Its major parts include a turbine wheel, shaft, compressor wheel, turbine housing, compressor housing and center housing. The center housing contains a turbine seal, compressor seal and bearings.

The internal combustion engine is an air-breathing machine. The amount of power produced by the engine is determined not by the amount of fuel it uses, but by the amount of air it breathes in a certain period of time. Air must mix with fuel to complete the combustion cycle. When the air/fuel ratio reaches a certain point, additional fuel produces only black smoke, not more power; the denser the smoke, the more the engine is being overfueled.

The turbocharger increases the quantity and density of air in the engine combustion chambers. The increased volume of air allows more fuel to be used while maintaining the proper air/fuel ratio. The increased air and fuel allows the engine to produce more horsepower than a non-turbocharged engine.

The turbocharger uses the normally wasted energy in the engine exhaust gas. As load on the engine is increased and the throttle is opened wider, more air/fuel mixture flows into the combustion chambers. The increased flow is burned and produces a larger volume of exhaust gas. The gas enters the exhaust manifolds, flows through the turbocharger turbine housing and turns the turbine wheel and shaft. The shaft is coupled to the compressor wheel. The compressor wheel compresses the air it receives and sends it to the intake manifold. The higher pressure in the intake manifold allows a denser charge to enter the combustion chambers.

Intake manifold pressure, or "boost", is controlled by an exhaust by-pass valve, or wastegate. The wastegate is operated by a spring-loaded diaphragm-type actuator which responds to boost pressure. The actuator, which is controlled by the wastegate solenoid, opens the wastegate to allow exhaust gases to by-pass the turbine wheel, thereby maintaining the correct boost level. The wastegate solenoid is controlled by the ECM through a turbo boost relay.

CAUTION: On a turbocharged engine, any alteration to the air intake or exhaust system which upsets the air flow balance may result in serious damage to the engine.

The rotating assembly in the turbocharger can reach speeds of 130,000-140,000 RPM. An adequate supply of clean engine oil is essential for cooling and lubrication. Whenever a basic engine bearing has been damaged or the turbocharger is replaced, the oil and oil filter should be changed and the turbocharger flushed with clean engine oil.

CAUTION: Interruption or contamination of the oil supply to the turbocharger bearings can result in major turbocharger damage.

Charge Air Cooler – Before entering the combustion chambers, the air from the turbocharger is routed through an air-to-water charge air cooler. As the turbocharger compresses air, the air's temperature rises. The heated, compressed air then flows through the charge air cooler core, where it is cooled by coolant passing through the charge air cooler. The cooler, denser air allows a denser air/fuel charge to enter the combustion chambers, producing significantly more power.

The hot coolant is then routed through the charge air cooler radiator, where it releases the heat it absorbed at the charge air cooler. An electric pump mounted to the charge air cooler radiator circulates coolant through the system. Pump is controlled by the ECM through a charge air cooler air pump relay.

AIRFLOW SENSING

Speed Density – All gasoline vehicles are equipped with a MAP sensor, and use the speed density method to compute the airflow rate. ECM uses manifold pressure to calculate the airflow rate. The MAP sensor responds to manifold vacuum changes due to engine load and speed changes. The ECM sends a voltage signal to the MAP sensor. Manifold pressure changes result in resistance changes in the MAP sensor. By monitoring MAP sensor signal voltage, the ECM determines manifold pressure. If MAP sensor fails, the ECM supplies a fixed MAP value, and uses the TPS to control fuel.

2.5L and 4.3L turbo models also use a Manifold Air Temperature (MAT) sensor. Sensor allows ECM to determine intake air temperature. ECM uses signal to delay EGR until intake air temperature reaches about 40°F (5°C). If intake air temperature becomes excessively high, ECM compensates by slightly retarding timing.

COMPUTERIZED ENGINE CONTROLS (GASOLINE)

The computerized engine control system monitors and controls a variety of engine/vehicle functions. The computerized engine control system is primarily an emission control system designed to maintain a 14.7:1 air/fuel ratio under most operating conditions. When the ideal air/fuel ratio is maintained, the 3-way catalytic converter can control oxides of nitrogen (NOx), hydrocarbon (HC) and carbon monoxide (CO) emissions.

The computerized engine control system consists of Electronic Control Module (ECM), input devices (sensor and switch input signals) and output signals.

ELECTRONIC CONTROL MODULE (ECM)

NOTE: Some models use a Powertrain Control Module (PCM). The difference between an ECM and PCM is the PCM also controls electronic transmission internals and cruise control system. Unless stated otherwise, references to ECM also apply to PCM-equipped vehicles.

ECM is located in passenger compartment. For exact location of ECM, see ECM LOCATION in appropriate SELF-DIAGNOSTICS article or under COMPONENT LOCATIONS in SYSTEM & COMPONENT TESTING article. The ECM consists of the Arithmetic Logic Unit (ALU), Central Processing Unit (CPU), power supply and system memories.

The ECM has a "learning" ability which allows it to make minor corrections for fuel system variations. If battery power is interrupted, a vehicle performance change may be noticed. ECM corrects itself, and normal performance returns if vehicle is allowed to "relearn" optimum control conditions. "Relearning" occurs when vehicle is driven at normal operating temperature under part throttle, moderate acceleration and idle conditions.

Arithmetic Logic Unit (ALU) – This internal component of the ECM converts electrical signals received from various engine sensors into digital signals for use by the CPU.

Central Processing Unit (CPU) – CPU uses digital signals to perform all mathematical computations and logic functions necessary to deliver proper air/fuel mixture. CPU also calculates spark timing and idle speed. The CPU controls operation of emission control, "closed loop" fuel control and diagnostic system.

Power Supply – Power for ECM reference output signals (5 volts) and control devices (12 volts) is received from the battery through ignition circuit when ignition switch is in ON position. Keep-alive memory power is received directly from the battery.

1991 ENGINE PERFORMANCE
Theory & Operation (Cont.)

Memories - ECM uses 5 types of memory:

- **Read Only Memory (ROM)** - ROM is programmed information which only ECM can read. The ROM program cannot be changed. If battery voltage is removed, ROM information is retained.
- **Random Access Memory (RAM)** - RAM is the scratch pad for the CPU. Data input, diagnostic codes and results of calculations are constantly updated and temporarily stored in RAM. If battery voltage is removed from ECM, all information stored in RAM is lost.
- **Programmable Read Only Memory (PROM)** - PROM is factory programmed engine calibration data which "tailors" ECM for specific transmission, engine, emission, vehicle weight and rear axle ratio application. The PROM can be removed from ECM. If battery voltage is removed, PROM information is retained.
- **Calibration Package (CALPAC)** - Some models use a PROM and a CALPAC. CALPAC provides fuel delivery back-up so engine runs in case of PROM or ECM failure. Any time ECM is replaced, PROM and CALPAC must both be installed into replacement ECM. If battery voltage is removed, CALPAC information is retained.
- **Memory Calibration (MEM-CAL)** - Some vehicles may use a ECM containing a MEM-CAL unit. This assembly contains functions of PROM and CALPAC. If power to ECM is removed, MEM-CAL information is retained.

NOTE: Components are grouped into 2 categories. The first category is INPUT DEVICES, consisting of components which control or produce voltage signals monitored by the control unit. The second category is OUTPUT SIGNALS, consisting of components controlled by the control unit.

INPUT DEVICES

Vehicles are equipped with different combinations of input devices. Not all devices are used on all models. To determine the input device usage on a specific model, see appropriate wiring diagram in WIRING DIAGRAMS article in ENGINE PERFORMANCE. The available input signals include:

A/C On (A/C Request) Signal - The air conditioner "on" switch is mounted in instrument panel. This switch provides a simple "on" ("A/C request") signal, which is monitored by the ECM. The ECM uses this signal to determine control of the A/C clutch relay (if equipped) and to adjust idle speed when air conditioner compressor clutch is engaged. On some models, ECM may also activate radiator cooling fan when this signal is present. If this signal is not present on A/C equipped vehicles, vehicle may idle rough when A/C compressor cycles. To check function of the A/C switch, perform functional check of switch. See SYSTEM & COMPONENT TESTING article.

Battery Voltage - Battery voltage is monitored by ECM. If battery voltage swings low, a weak spark or improper fuel control may result. To compensate for low battery voltage, ECM may increase idle speed, advance ignition timing, increase ignition dwell or enrichen the air/fuel mixture. If voltage swings high, ECM may set a charging system fault code and turn on SERVICE ENGINE SOON light. If voltage signal swings excessively low (less than 9 volts) or excessively high (16 volts, most models), ECM shuts down for as long as condition exists. If condition is short-term, SERVICE ENGINE SOON light flickers and vehicle may stumble. Vehicle stalls if condition lasts long enough.

Brake Switch Feedback - On models equipped with cruise control systems, ECM may monitor the brake switch circuit to determine when to engage and disengage cruise control. On vehicles equipped with a Torque Converter Clutch (TCC), one circuit of brake switch is in series with the power supply for the TCC solenoid located in automatic transmission.

Coolant Temperature Sensor (CTS) - The CTS is a thermistor (temperature sensitive resistor) located in an engine coolant passage. The ECM supplies and monitors a 5-volt signal to CTS. This monitored 5-volt signal is then modified by resistance of the CTS. When coolant temperatures are low, CTS resistance is high and the ECM sees a high monitored voltage signal. When coolant temperatures are high, CTS resistance is low and the ECM sees a low monitored voltage. When fully warmed, CTS should reflect a temperature of at least 185°F (85°C).

Coolant temperature input is used in the control of fuel delivery, ignition timing, idle speed, emission control devices and converter clutch application. A CTS which is out of calibration will not set a trouble code, but can cause fuel delivery and driveability problems. A coolant sensor circuit problem should set a related trouble code.

Crank Signal - Crank signal is a 12-volt signal monitored by the ECM. Signal is present when ignition switch is in the START position. The ECM uses signal to determine the need for starting enrichment. ECM also cancels diagnostics until engine is running and 12-volt signal is no longer present.

Digital Ratio Adapter Controller (DRAC) - DRAC compensates for various axle and tire ratios by monitoring the Vehicle Speed Sensor (VSS) signal and modifying it before passing it on to the ECM and speedometer unit.

Fuel Pump Feedback - ECM monitors fuel pump circuit between fuel pump relay/oil pressure switch and fuel pump. This enables the ECM to determine if fuel pump is being energized by fuel pump relay or back-up oil pressure switch. A failure in this monitored circuit results in the setting of a related trouble code in ECM memory.

Gear Switches - Gear switches are located inside automatic transmission. Switches may be normally open or closed and change status depending upon internal hydraulic pressures. ECM uses high gear switch information in controlling emission components and engagement of Torque Converter Clutch (TCC).

Knock Sensor - The knock sensor is a piezoelectric device which detects abnormal engine vibrations (spark knock) in the engine. This vibration results in the production of a very low AC signal, which is sent from the knock sensor to the ESC controller or the MEM-CAL portion of the ECM (on models equipped with 4L80-E transmission). The ECM then retards ignition timing until the engine knock ceases.

For additional information on knock sensor operation, see ESC DETONATION RETARD OPERATION under IGNITION TIMING CONTROL SYSTEMS (GASOLINE).

A fault in the ESC circuit may set a related trouble code. When a related trouble code is not present and the ESC system is the suspected cause of a driveability problem, perform functional check of ESC system. See SYSTEM & COMPONENT TESTING article.

Manifold Absolute Pressure (MAP) Sensor - The MAP sensor measures changes in manifold pressure. Changes in manifold pressure result from engine load and speed changes. The MAP sensor converts these changes in manifold pressure into a voltage output signal to ECM (1.5 volts at idle to 4.5 volts at WOT). The ECM can monitor these signals and adjust air/fuel ratio and ignition timing under various operating conditions.

If MAP sensor fails, the ECM substitutes a fixed MAP value, and uses the TPS to control fuel delivery. A fault in the MAP circuit should set a related trouble code. If a related trouble code is not present and MAP sensor is suspected of causing a driveability problem, perform functional check of MAP sensor. See SYSTEM & COMPONENT TESTING article.

Manifold Air Temperature (MAT) Sensor (2.5L & 4.3L Turbo) - MAT sensor is a thermistor (temperature sensitive resistor) mounted in the intake manifold. Low intake air temperature produces high internal sensor resistance, while high temperature causes low internal sensor resistance. The ECM supplies and monitors a 5-volt signal to sensor through a pull-down resistor in ECM.

MAT sensor, also known as an intake air temperature sensor, allows ECM to determine intake air temperature. ECM uses signal to delay EGR until intake air temperature reaches about 40°F (5°C). If intake air temperature becomes excessively high, ECM compensates by slightly retarding timing. After a vehicle has sat overnight, MAT and CTS signals (resistance and temperature) should be close to same reading. Failure in MAT sensor circuit should set a related trouble code.

CAUTION: Measure O_2 sensor voltage with a Digital Volt-Ohmmeter (10-megohm impedance) only. Current drain of a conventional voltmeter could damage sensor.

Oxygen (O_2) Sensor - The O_2 sensor is mounted in the exhaust system and monitors oxygen content of exhaust gases. The oxygen content causes the Zirconia/Platinum-tipped O_2 sensor to produce a voltage signal which is proportional to exhaust gas oxygen concentration (0-3%) compared to outside oxygen (20-21%). This voltage signal is low (about .1 volt) when a lean mixture is present and high (about 1.0 volt) when a rich mixture is present. As ECM compensates for a lean or rich condition, this voltage signal constantly fluctuates between high and low, crossing a .45-volt reference voltage supplied by ECM on the O_2 sensor signal line. This is referred to as "cross counts".

The O_2 sensor does not function properly (produce voltage) until its temperature reaches 600°F (316°C). At temperatures less than the normal operating range of the sensor, vehicle functions in "open loop" mode, and ECM does not make air/fuel adjustments based upon O_2 sensor signals, but uses TPS and MAP or MAF values to determine air/fuel ratio from a table built into memory. When ECM reads a voltage signal greater than .45 volt from the O_2 sensor, ECM begins to alter commands to injector to produce either a leaner or richer mixture.

Once vehicle has entered "closed loop", a fault in the O_2 circuit (cooled-down sensor or open or shorted O_2 sensor circuit) is the only thing which can return vehicle to open loop. A problem in the O_2 sensor circuit should set a related trouble code.

On the 4.3L turbocharged engine, O_2 sensor uses an internal heating element. Heating element allows O_2 sensor to warm more quickly, allowing fuel system to enter closed loop operation sooner. Heating element also prevents fuel system from re-entering open loop operation, which would be a normal response to prolonged idling.

Park/Neutral (P/N) Switch - This switch is connected to transmission gear selector and signals ECM when transmission is in Park or Neutral. ECM uses this information for determining control of ignition timing, converter clutch and idle speed. To check function of P/N switch, perform functional check of switch. See SYSTEM & COMPONENT TESTING article.

Power Steering (P/S) Switch (2.5L) - This switch informs ECM of engine load conditions which exist when steering wheel is turned from center to full lock position. ECM uses this information to help control idle speed. To check function of P/S switch, perform functional check of switch. See SYSTEM & COMPONENT TESTING article.

Pressure Switch Manifold (PSM) (4L80-E Transmission) - The PSM is actually 5 pressure switches combined into a single unit mounted on the transmission valve body. The PCM supplies battery voltage on 3 separate wires to PSM. By grounding one or more of the switches in various combinations, PCM detects what gear range the vehicle operator has selected.

RPM Reference Signal - ECM monitors RPM through ignition module tach/pulse signals (on circuit No. 430) produced by the HEI module (RPM reference line of 4-wire EST connector) or camshaft position sensor signal (Hall Effect signal on 2.5L). ECM uses signal to determine control of timing, fuel delivery, EGR function and idle speed. ECM also uses signal to trigger fuel injectors.

Throttle Position Sensor (TPS) - The TPS is a variable mechanical resistor connected directly to the throttle shaft linkage. The TPS has 3 wires connected to it. One is connected to a 5-volt reference voltage supply from ECM, another is connected to ECM ground and the third is the signal return which is monitored by ECM. The voltage signal from the TPS varies from closed throttle (.5-1.0 volt) to wide open throttle (4.5-5 volts). ECM uses this signal to determine control of fuel, idle speed, spark timing and converter clutch. A problem in the TPS circuit may set a related trouble code.

Transmission Temperature Sensor (TTS) (4L80-E Transmission) - TTS is a thermistor (temperature sensitive resistor) mounted to the transmission valve body. The PCM supplies and monitors a 5-volt signal to TTS. This monitored 5-volt signal is then modified by resistance of TTS. When transmission fluid temperatures are low, TTS resistance is high and PCM sees a high monitored voltage signal. When transmission fluid temperatures are high, TTS resistance is low and PCM sees a low monitored voltage. PCM uses transmission fluid temperature input in control of converter clutch application and shift quality. Sensor circuit problem should set a related trouble code.

Vehicle Speed Sensor (VSS) - VSS is a Permanent Magnet (PM) generator mounted in transmission or transfer case. The VSS sends a pulsing signal to either the ECM or Digital Ratio Adapter Controller (DRAC), which passes the signal on to the ECM. ECM then converts this signal into Miles Per Hour (MPH) by monitoring the time interval between pulses. ECM uses this sensor input in controlling converter clutch engagement.

OUTPUT SIGNALS

NOTE: Vehicles are equipped with different combinations of computer-controlled components. Not all components listed below are used on every vehicle. For theory and operation of components, refer to indicated system.

A/C Clutch Relay - MISCELLANEOUS ECM CONTROLS.
Air Injection Control Solenoid - EMISSION SYSTEMS.
Charge Air Cooler Pump Relay (4.3L Turbo) - TURBOCHARGER.
Cooling Fan Relay (3.1L) - MISCELLANEOUS ECM CONTROLS.
SERVICE ENGINE SOON Light - SELF-DIAGNOSTIC SYSTEM.
EGR Control Solenoid Valve - EMISSION SYSTEMS.
ESC Timing Retard - IGNITION SYSTEM.
EVRV Solenoid - EMISSION SYSTEMS.
Fuel Injectors - FUEL CONTROL.
Fuel Module - FUEL DELIVERY.
Fuel Pump & Fuel Pump Relay - FUEL DELIVERY.
HEI-EST Ignition - IGNITION SYSTEM.
Idle Air Control (IAC) Valve - IDLE SPEED.
Self-Diagnostics - SELF-DIAGNOSTIC SYSTEM.
Serial Data - SELF-DIAGNOSTIC SYSTEM.
Shift Solenoids (4L80-E Transmission) - MISCELLANEOUS ECM CONTROLS.
Torque Converter Clutch - MISCELLANEOUS ECM CONTROLS.
Transmission Shift Light (Manual Transmission) - MISCELLANEOUS ECM CONTROLS.
Turbo Boost Relay (4.3L Turbo) - TURBOCHARGER.
Wastegate Solenoid (4.3L Turbo) - TURBOCHARGER.

COMPUTERIZED ENGINE CONTROLS (DIESEL)

6.2L Diesel engine with light duty emissions uses Diesel Electronic Control (DEC) system. DEC system consists of Electronic Control Module (ECM), input devices and output signals. DEC system electronically controls EGR system operation, Torque Converter Clutch (TCC) engagement, cold advance and glow plug system.

ELECTRONIC CONTROL MODULE (ECM)

Electronic Control Module (ECM) is located in passenger compartment, behind glove box. It constantly monitors information from various sensors to control EGR, TCC, cold advance and glow plug systems. ECM processes input signals from sensors and then sends necessary electrical responses to control these systems.

The ECM performs the diagnostic function of the DEC system. It can recognize operational problems, alert driver through the SERVICE ENGINE SOON light and store codes which identify problem areas to technicians making system repairs.

Memories - ECM uses 3 types of memory:

- **Read Only Memory (ROM)** - ROM is programmed information which only ECM can read. ROM program cannot be changed. If battery voltage is removed, ROM information is retained.
- **Random Access Memory (RAM)** - RAM is the scratch pad for the CPU. Data input, diagnostic codes and results of calculations are constantly updated and temporarily stored in RAM. If battery voltage is removed from ECM, all information stored in RAM is lost.

1991 ENGINE PERFORMANCE
Theory & Operation (Cont.)

- **Programmable Read Only Memory (PROM)** – PROM is factory programmed engine calibration data which "tailors" ECM for specific transmission, engine, emission, vehicle weight and rear axle ratio application. PROM can be removed from ECM. If battery voltage is removed, PROM information is retained.

INPUT DEVICES

Each sensor or switch furnishes electronic (voltage) signals to ECM. The ECM uses these input signals to control EGR, TCC, cold advance and glow plug systems. Various models are equipped with different combinations of input devices. Not all devices are used on all models. To determine the input usage on a specific model, see appropriate wiring diagram in WIRING DIAGRAMS article in ENGINE PERFORMANCE. The available input signals include:

Coolant Temperature Sensor (CTS) – CTS is a thermistor (temperature sensitive resistor). A coolant temperature of -40°F (-40°C) produces a high resistance (100,000 ohms), while a coolant temperature of 266°F (130°C) produces a low resistance (70 ohms).

ECM supplies a 5-volt reference signal through an internal resistor to CTS and measures return voltage. Voltage is high when coolant temperature is low, and low when coolant temperature is hot. By measuring voltage, ECM knows engine coolant temperature. Engine coolant temperature affects cold advance and glow plug systems.

Manifold Absolute Pressure (MAP) Sensor – MAP sensor, mounted on left side of cowl, monitors vacuum in the EGR system. It senses the actual vacuum in the EGR vacuum line and sends a signal to the ECM.

The signal is compared to the EGR duty cycle calculated by the ECM. If there is a minor difference in the vacuum value sensed and the ECM command, the ECM corrects. When a major difference is sensed, the ECM recognizes a fault and sends a full EGR signal.

Throttle Position Sensor (TPS) – TPS, mounted on the injection pump, is a variable resistor monitoring throttle opening angle for the ECM. The sensor is connected to a 5-volt reference signal and has a high resistance value when throttle is closed. At wide open throttle, the TPS resistance value is low, and output to the ECM will be near 5 volts.

Engine Speed Sensor – The engine speed sensor is a camshaft driven pick-up and is mounted at center rear of engine. The sensor receives a 5-volt reference signal and allows the ECM to measure engine RPM by the number of times reference voltage is pulsed. The engine speed sensor pulses 4 times per revolution.

Vehicle Speed Sensor (VSS) – Mounted on the transmission, VSS sends a pulsing signal to ECM for vehicle speed calculation. This calculation is used to control TCC engagement.

OUTPUT SIGNALS

NOTE: Output signals are regulated by the ECM to maintain correct driveability and exhaust emissions. For theory and operation of components, refer to indicated system.

Electronic Controller/Glow Plug Relay – FUEL CONTROL.
Cold Advance Control – FUEL CONTROL.
Torque Converter Clutch – MISCELLANEOUS ECM CONTROLS.
Exhaust Gas Recirculation System – EMISSION SYSTEMS (DIESEL).

FUEL SYSTEM (GASOLINE)

FUEL DELIVERY

Fuel Module (7.4L, 5.7L G Van & 5.7L Over 8500 GVWR) – Fuel module overrides the ECM 2-second timer and fuel pump runs 20 seconds before shutting off when vehicle is not started. This added circuit corrects hot restart problems which could cause vapor lock during high ambient temperatures.

Fuel Pump – An in-tank electric fuel pump delivers fuel to injector(s) through an in-line fuel filter. The pump is designed to supply fuel pressure in excess of vehicle requirements. The pressure relief valve in the fuel pump controls maximum fuel pump pressure.

On TBI fuel systems, pressure regulator is mounted on throttle body. On Port Fuel Injection (PFI) systems, pressure regulator is mounted on the fuel rail. Regulator keeps fuel available to injector(s) at a constant pressure. Excess fuel is returned to fuel tank through pressure regulator return line.

When ignition switch is turned to ON position, ECM turns on electric fuel pump by energizing fuel pump relay. ECM keeps pump on if engine is running or cranking (ECM is receiving reference pulses from ignition module). If there are no reference pulses and vehicle is not equipped with a fuel module, ECM turns pump off within 2 seconds after key is turned on. For additional information, see FUEL PUMP RELAY and FUEL MODULE under FUEL DELIVERY.

Fuel Pressure Regulator (TBI) – A constant fuel pressure of 9-13 psi (.6-9 kg/cm²) is maintained by a factory preset, nonadjustable, spring loaded diaphragm contained within throttle body. Spring tension maintains a constant fuel pressure to injector regardless of engine load.

Fuel Pressure Regulator (4.3L Turbo PFI) – Fuel pressure regulator is a diaphragm-operated relief valve with injector pressure on one side and manifold pressure (vacuum) on the other. Pressure regulator compensates for engine load by increasing fuel pressure when low manifold vacuum is experienced.

During periods of high manifold vacuum, regulator-to-fuel tank return orifice is fully open, keeping fuel pressure on the low side of its regulated range. As throttle valve opens, vacuum to regulator diaphragm decreases, allowing spring tension to gradually close off return passage. At wide open throttle (when vacuum is at its lowest), return orifice is restricted, providing maximum fuel volume and maintaining constant fuel pressure to injectors.

Fuel Pump Relay – When ignition switch is turned to ON position, ECM turns electric fuel pump on by energizing fuel pump relay. ECM keeps relay energized if engine is running or cranking (ECM is receiving reference pulses from ignition module). If there are no reference pulses, ECM turns pump off within 2 seconds after key on. See FUEL MODULE under FUEL DELIVERY.

As a back-up system to fuel pump relay, the oil pressure switch also activates fuel pump. The oil pressure switch is normally open until oil pressure reaches approximately 4 psi (.28 kg/cm²). If fuel pump relay fails, the oil pressure switch closes when oil pressure is obtained, and operates the fuel pump. An inoperative fuel pump relay may result in extended cranking times due to the time required to build up oil pressure. Oil pressure switch may be combined into a single unit with an oil pressure gauge sending unit or sensor.

ECM monitors fuel pump circuit between fuel pump relay/oil pressure switch and fuel pump, enabling ECM to determine if fuel pump is being energized by fuel pump relay or oil pressure switch. A failure in this monitored circuit results in the setting of a related trouble code in ECM memory.

For additional information on fuel pump activation, see BASIC DIAGNOSTIC PROCEDURES and SYSTEM & COMPONENT TESTING articles.

FUEL CONTROL

The ECM, using input signals, determines adjustments to the air/fuel mixture to provide the optimum ratio for proper combustion under all operating conditions. Throttle Body Injection (TBI) systems can operate in the "open loop" or "closed loop" mode.

Open Loop – When engine is cold and engine speed is greater than 400 RPM, ECM operates in open loop mode. In open loop, ECM calculates air/fuel ratio based upon coolant temperature and Manifold Absolute Pressure (MAP) sensor readings. Engine remains in open loop operation until O_2 sensor reaches operating temperature, coolant temperature reaches preset temperature and a specific period of time has elapsed after engine starts.

Closed Loop – When O_2 sensor reaches operating temperature, coolant temperature reaches a preset temperature and a specific period of time has passed since engine start-up, ECM operates in closed loop. In closed loop, ECM controls air/fuel ratio based upon O_2 sensor signals (in addition to other input parameters) to maintain as close to a 14.7:1 air/fuel ratio as possible. If O_2 sensor cools off (due to excessive idling) or a fault occurs in the O_2 sensor circuit, vehicle once again enters open loop mode.

Battery Voltage Correction – ECM compensates for low battery voltage by increasing injector pulse width and increasing idle RPM. ECM is able to perform these commands because of a built-in memory/learning function.

Fuel Cut-Off – When ignition is turned off, injectors are de-energized to prevent dieseling. Injectors are not energized if RPM reference pulses are not received by the ECM, even with ignition on. This prevents flooding before starting. Fuel cut-off also occurs at high engine RPM to prevent internal damage to engine. Some models may also cut off fuel injector signals during periods of sudden, closed throttle deceleration (when fuel is not needed).

Throttle Body Injection – Injectors are located in throttle body unit. All models except 2.5L use 220 Series dual injector throttle body. 2.5L models use 700 Series single injector throttle body. Battery voltage is supplied to injector when ignition is on. ECM energizes injector solenoid by providing a ground path through its internal circuitry. By regulating injector ground circuit, ECM controls injector "on" time (pulse width) to provide proper amount of fuel to engine.

Pressure regulator maintains pressure to injector at 9-13 psi (.6-.9 kg/cm²). Excess fuel passes through pressure regulator and returns to fuel tank.

In the "run" mode, ECM uses tach (RPM) signal to determine when to pulse injector. Fuel injectors are pulsed once for each engine revolution; each spray provides 1/2 the fuel required for the combustion process. Thus, 2 injections of fuel (2 rotations of crankshaft) are mixed with incoming air to produce the fuel charge for each combustion cycle. On models equipped with dual injectors in the throttle body, injectors are pulsed alternately.

Internal ECM calibration controls fuel delivery during starting, clear flood mode, deceleration and heavy acceleration.

- **Starting** – During engine starts, ECM delivers one injector pulse for each distributor reference pulse received (synchronized mode). Injector pulse width is based upon coolant temperature and throttle position. ECM determines air/fuel ratio when throttle position is less than 80 percent open. Engine starting air/fuel ratio ranges from 1.5:1 at -33°F (-36°C) to 14.7:1 at 201°F (94°C). At lower coolant temperatures, injector pulse width is wider (richer air/fuel mixture ratio). When coolant temperature is high, injector pulse width becomes narrower (leaner air/fuel ratio).
- **Clear Flood** – If engine is flooded, driver must depress accelerator pedal to Wide Open Throttle (WOT) position. At this position, ECM adjusts injector pulse width equal to an air/fuel ratio of 20:1. This air/fuel ratio is maintained as long as throttle remains in wide open position and engine speed is less than 600 RPM. If throttle position becomes less than 80 percent open and/or engine speed exceeds 600 RPM, ECM changes injector pulse width to that used during engine starting (based upon coolant temperature and manifold vacuum).
- **Heavy Acceleration** – ECM provides fuel enrichment during heavy acceleration. Sudden opening of throttle valve causes rapid increase in MAP signal. Pulse width is directly related to MAP, throttle position and coolant temperature. Higher MAP and wider throttle angles give wider injector pulse width (richer mixture). During enrichment, injector pulses are not in proportion to distributor reference signals (non-synchronized). Any reduction in throttle angle cancels fuel enrichment.
- **Deceleration** – During normal deceleration, fuel output is reduced. This reduction in available fuel serves to remove residual fuel from intake manifold. During sudden deceleration, when MAP, throttle position and engine speed are reduced to preset levels, fuel flow is cut off completely. This deceleration fuel cut-off overrides normal deceleration mode. During either deceleration mode, injector pulses are not in proportion to distributor reference signals.

Port Fuel Injection (PFI) – Individual, electrically pulsed injectors (one per cylinder) are located in intake manifold fuel rails. These injectors are next to intake valves in cylinder head.

PFI system features simultaneous double-fire injection. Fuel injectors are pulsed once for each engine revolution; each spray provides 1/2 the fuel required for the combustion process. Thus, 2 injections of fuel (2 rotations of crankshaft) are mixed with incoming air to produce the fuel charge for each combustion cycle.

Constant fuel pressure to the injectors is maintained by the fuel pressure regulator. Air/fuel mixture is regulated by the length of time injector stays open (pulse width). The ECM controls pulse width using information provided by various sensors.

IDLE SPEED (GASOLINE)

ECM controls engine idle speed depending upon engine operating conditions. The ECM senses engine operating conditions and determines the best idle speed.

Idle Air Control (IAC) Valve – The IAC valve controls engine idle speed to prevent stalling during engine load changes. The IAC valve is mounted on throttle body and controls the amount of air by-passed around the throttle plate. The IAC valve controls engine idle speed by moving its pintle in and out in steps referred to as "counts" (0 counts, fully seated; 255 counts, fully retracted). Counts can be measured by plugging a Scan tester into the Assembly Line Data Link (ALDL).

If engine RPM is too low, pintle is retracted and more air is by-passed around the throttle plate to increase engine RPM. If engine RPM is too high, pintle is extended and less air is by-passed around the throttle plate to decrease engine RPM. Normal counts on an idling engine should be 4-60. When engine is idling, ECM determines proper positioning of IAC valve based on battery voltage, coolant temperature, engine load and engine RPM.

If IAC valve is disconnected or reconnected with engine running, IAC loses its reference point and must be reset. On some models, IAC is reset by turning ignition on and off. Other models require driving vehicle at normal operating temperature over 35 MPH with circuit properly connected. Problems in IAC circuit should set a related code.

The IAC valve affects only the idle system. If valve is stuck fully open, excessive airflow into the manifold creates a high idle speed. Valve stuck closed allows insufficient airflow, resulting in low idle speed. For calibration purposes, several different IAC valves are used. Ensure replacement valve is proper design.

FUEL SYSTEM (DIESEL)

FUEL DELIVERY

A mechanical pump is mounted on the right side of engine block. Camshaft eccentric drives pump. Pump pulls fuel from the fuel tank through a primary filter. The fuel is then pumped through a secondary filter, mounted on firewall (pickups) or rear of air cleaner (vans), and to the injection pump.

The 6.2L diesel engine uses a mechanical, high pressure rotary diesel injection pump, which is gear-driven by camshaft at camshaft speed. Pump injects a precisely metered amount of fuel to each cylinder at the proper time.

High pressure fuel lines carry the fuel to an injection nozzle in each cylinder. All fuel lines are the same length to ensure no variance in timing. A rotary fuel metering valve controls engine RPM. As the accelerator pedal is depressed, throttle linkage opens fuel metering valve to allow increased fuel delivery.

Diesel Injection Pump – The high pressure diesel injection pump is mounted at top of engine, below intake manifold. The pump is gear-driven by camshaft. Pump precisely governs time and amount of fuel injection.

A built-in fuel pressure regulator and transfer pump picks up fuel at pump inlet, pushing it through a passage to the pump head. The pump head distributes fuel at transfer pump pressure 8-12 psi (.5-.8 kg/cm²) to metering valve, governor and automatic advance mechanisms. Fuel then passes to rotary fuel metering valve and into a charging passage. As pump shaft rotates, fuel is directed at high pressure through each delivery pipe to an injector.

1991 ENGINE PERFORMANCE
Theory & Operation (Cont.)

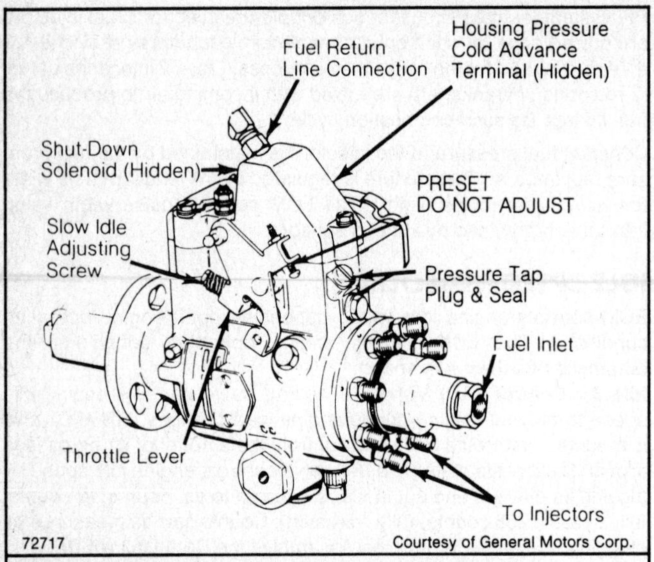
Housing Pressure
Cold Advance
Terminal (Hidden)
Fuel Return
Line Connection
Shut-Down
Solenoid (Hidden)
PRESET
DO NOT ADJUST
Slow Idle
Adjusting
Screw
Pressure Tap
Plug & Seal
Fuel Inlet
Throttle Lever
To Injectors
72717
Courtesy of General Motors Corp.

Fig. 1: Identifying Diesel Injection Pump Components

Fuel Injection Lines - Eight high pressure fuel injection lines are routed from the injection pump to an injector in each cylinder. The lines are of equal length to prevent a difference in timing between cylinders. Lines are not interchangeable and are pre-bent by the manufacturer.

FUEL CONTROL

Electronic Controller/Glow Plug Relay - The electronic controller/ glow plug relay is mounted at rear of left cylinder head. It monitors and controls glow plug operation. Controller uses four pins to determine glow plug operating requirements. Pin "B" senses voltage at starter motor solenoid. Pin "C" senses glow plug voltage. Pin "D" supplies 12 volts, through cold advance relay, to operate controller when coolant temperature is less than 80°F (27°C). Pin "E" is controller ground.

A normally operating system works as follows: at room temperature and with ignition on and engine off, the glow plugs come on for 4-6 seconds and then go off for about 4.5 seconds. The glow plugs then cycle on for about 1.5 seconds and off for about 4.5 seconds, for a total start sequence of about 20 seconds. If the engine is cranked during or after start sequence, the glow plugs will cycle on and off for a total of 25 seconds after the ignition switch is returned from the crank position, whether engine starts or not.

Glow Plugs - Glow plugs are small 6-volt heaters, powered by 12 volts to give rapid heating. Electronic controller operates glow plugs, which cycle on when ignition switch is turned to the RUN position (prior to starting the engine). The glow plugs remain pulsing a short time after engine starting, then automatically turn off.

The glow system for the LH6 (light duty emissions version) is different than the system for the LL4 (heavy duty emissions version). The LH6 system has the same glow plugs, glow plug controller and WAIT light. However, there is no temperature inhibit switch. Instead, the ECM, which receives temperature information from the coolant temperature sensor located in the water crossover of the engine, controls glow plug temperature inhibit.

The computer transposes this temperature information into a voltage signal, which it sends to the cold advance relay, ignition circuit and glow plug controller. The cold advance relay is located at the junction block in the engine compartment on the right side of the cowl. For diagnostic information on computer controlled system, see SELF-DIAGNOSTICS - DIESEL article.

CAUTION: Using a jumper wire on by-pass relay causes glow plug failure.

Glow Plug Inhibit Switch - The LL4 (heavy duty emissions version of 6.2L engine) is equipped with a glow plug inhibit switch. The inhibit switch is calibrated to open above 125°F (51.5°C) to prevent glow plug operation above this temperature.

Two types of inhibit switches are used. Switches can be identified by their cap color. A switch with a Black cap is a temperature-controlled switch. The other switch (with a non-Black cap) is an optional switch which is always closed to allow for more frequent cycling of glow plugs.

Glow Plug After-Start - Glow plug controller provides glow plug operation after starting a cold engine. This after-start operation is initiated when ignition switch is returned to RUN from START position.

Injection Nozzles - Each of the 8 combustion chambers is equipped with an injection nozzle. The injection nozzle has a single fuel inlet fitting and 2 fuel return fittings (one on each side of fuel inlet fitting). The nozzle is threaded into the cylinder head. Injection nozzles are spring loaded and calibrated to open at a specified fuel line pressure. The combustion chamber end of the nozzle has a replaceable compression seal and carbon stop seal.

Housing Pressure Cold Advance (HPCA) - The HPCA circuit is used to improve cold starting and aid in emission control. On light duty emissions (LH6 models), an ECM signal activates the HPCA circuit. On heavy duty emissions (LL4 models), a coolant temperature switch located on rear of right cylinder head controls the HPCA circuit. The circuit advances injection timing about 4 degrees when engine is cold.

When engine temperature is below 80°F (27°C), the circuit decreases housing pressure from 10 psi (.7 kg/cm²) to zero. Meanwhile, the fast idle solenoid is activated. When the temperature switch opens, the HPCA circuit is de-energized and housing pressure rises, retarding pump timing. The temperature switch closes again when engine temperature falls below 85°F (30°C).

Cold Advance Control - The cold advance control circuit is designed to advance injection pump timing about 4 degrees during cold engine operation. ECM activates this circuit through the cold advance relay to energize the cold advance solenoid. The ECM opens the circuit when coolant temperature is above 95°F (35°C).

When coolant temperature is below the switching point and with ignition on, the cold advance solenoid is continuously energized without the engine running. When coolant temperature is below the switching point and with the engine running, injection pump housing pressure is decreased from 10 psi (.7 kg/cm²) to zero, which advances injection pump timing by about 4 degrees. As engine warms, the cold advance solenoid is de-energized and the injection pump housing pressure is returned to 10 psi (.70 kg/cm²).

IDLE SPEED (DIESEL)

Curb Idle Speed - Curb idle is controlled by mechanical adjustment of the low idle speed screw. For idle speed adjustment procedure, see CURB IDLE under IDLE SPEED (DIESEL) in ON-VEHICLE ADJUSTMENTS article.

Fast Idle Speed - Fast idle solenoid controls fast idle. For adjustment of fast idle speed, see FAST IDLE under IDLE SPEED (DIESEL) in ON-VEHICLE ADJUSTMENTS article.

IGNITION SYSTEM (GASOLINE)

WARNING: High Energy Ignition Electronic Spark Timing (HEI-EST) system can produce more than 50,000 volts.

High Energy Ignition Electronic Spark Timing (HEI-EST) Distributor - The Delco-Remy HEI-EST system consists of distributor housing, rotor, cap, 7 or 8-terminal ignition module, magnetic pick-up, pole piece, pick-up coil, connecting harness and the EST portion of the ECM. The distributor is connected to the EST system by a 4-wire connector leading to Electronic Control Module (ECM).

No vacuum or centrifugal advance mechanisms are used. Based upon monitored input signals, ECM controls all spark timing changes. Some models use an additional Electronic Spark Control (ESC) system, which retards timing in case of engine detonation (knock). Most models are equipped with sealed ignition coil and ignition module connectors.

When the external teeth on the timing core approach, align with and pass the pick-up coil windings, an alternating current is produced in the pick-up coil windings. In the cranking mode, this alternating current signals switching transistors in the HEI module to make or break the ignition coil primary ground circuit. Once the engine starts, ECM takes control of primary ground circuit (EST mode).

When the primary ground circuit is removed, the magnetic field created by the flow of current in the primary windings collapses across the primary and secondary windings of the coil. This induces a high-voltage surge in the secondary windings of the coil. Secondary voltage is then discharged to the rotor, which distributes voltage to the appropriate spark plug terminal. Depending on application, the distributor module may have either a 7-terminal or an 8-terminal (sealed connector) ignition module.

The 2.5L HEI-EST system is also equipped with a Hall Effect switch located inside of the distributor. The Hall Effect switch produces a camshaft signal which is used by the ECM to trigger injectors. Loss of the camshaft signal results in a no-start condition.

IGNITION TIMING CONTROL SYSTEMS (GASOLINE)

Ignition Timing Advance – At engine speeds less than 400 RPM, ignition module controls spark advance by triggering coil(s) at a predetermined interval based on engine speed only. At engine speeds greater than 400 RPM (EST mode), ECM controls ignition timing.

ECM controls ignition timing based upon input signals from engine RPM reference line (ignition module), coolant temperature sensor, manifold air temperature sensor, throttle position sensor, knock sensor, vehicle speed sensor, gear position switch and MAP sensor.

The PROM portion of the ECM has a programmed spark advance curve based on engine speed. ECM calculates spark timing whenever an ignition pulse is present. Spark advance is controlled only when engine is running (not during cranking). ECM uses input signal values to modify PROM information, increasing or decreasing spark advance to achieve maximum performance with minimum emissions. To check ignition system operation, see BASIC DIAGNOSTIC PROCEDURES or SYSTEM & COMPONENT TESTING article.

- **Reference (RPM)** – Ignition module converts alternating current signals from pick-up coil to digital signals which are used to trigger ignition coil. On models without Hall Effect sensor, the ignition module passes signal to the ECM. On 2.5L models equipped with Hall Effect sensor, the Hall Effect switch produces a separate signal for use by the ECM. The ignition module or Hall Effect signal supplies RPM data and crankshaft position reference to the ECM. Since the signal on this circuit is used as an injector trigger reference on fuel injected vehicles, engine will not run if circuit is open or grounded.
- **By-Pass** – When the ECM receives an engine speed signal of approximately 400 RPM, it considers engine to be running and applies 5 volts to the ignition module on the by-pass wire. This causes ignition module to switch timing control over to the variable timing control circuit in the ECM. On some models, this by-pass wire contains a connector located between the 4-wire connector and the ECM. This is disconnected when adjusting base timing. On all models, an open or grounded by-pass circuit sets a related trouble code in ECM memory. The engine runs at base timing plus a small amount of advance built into the HEI module.
- **EST** – When 5 volts is present on by-pass circuit and ignition module has turned control of engine timing over to ECM, ECM advances or retards spark on this circuit based on calculations involving reference signal and other sensor input signals. If base timing is incorrectly set, entire advance curve will be incorrect.
- **Ground** – This is the reference ground circuit. It is grounded at distributor and ECM, ensuring there is no voltage drop in the EST circuit which could affect ignition operation.

ESC Detonation Retard Operation – Some models use an Electronic Spark Control (ESC) retard system along with the HEI-EST system. System consists of a knock (detonation) sensor, a high energy ignition system, an ESC controller (some models) and the ECM. On some models, the function of the ESC controller is built into the Memory Calibration (MEM-CAL) unit of the ECM.

When engine knock (detonation) occurs, knock sensor produces a low voltage AC signal. This signal goes to the ESC controller or directly to the MEM-CAL unit inside the ECM, depending upon application.

On models using an ESC controller, controller supplies the ECM with a 12-volt signal. When detonation occurs, controller grounds the 12-volt signal to the ECM, pulling the signal down to near zero volts. The ECM interprets this as a signal to retard timing. The ECM then retards spark timing until the ESC controller returns the 12-volt signal. If signal wire becomes open or grounded on models using ESC controller, ECM continuously provides full ignition timing retard.

On vehicles using ECMs containing MEM-CAL units, the ECM supplies a 5-volt DC reference signal on the knock sensor signal line. Internal circuitry of the knock sensor pulls this voltage down to about 2.5 volts. When knock occurs, the knock sensor produces an AC voltage signal which rides on the 2.5-volt DC signal to the ECM. The voltage and frequency of this signal depend upon knock signals received by the sensor. The ECM retards spark timing until signals from detonation sensor cease.

A malfunction in the ESC circuit should set a related trouble code. If a code is not present and ESC system is suspected cause of driveability problems, perform functional check of ESC system. See SYSTEM & COMPONENT TESTING article.

EMISSION SYSTEMS (GASOLINE)

AIR INJECTION SYSTEM

Air Injection Reaction (AIR) system is used to reduce carbon monoxide (CO) and hydrocarbon (HC) emissions. The AIR system provides additional oxygen to continue combustion process after exhaust gases leave the combustion chamber. This added air also brings catalytic converter up to operating temperature more quickly when engine is cold. The AIR system diverts air either to the exhaust manifold ports or to the air cleaner.

The system consists of an air pump, an Electric Air Control (EAC) valve (2.8L engine) or an electric air control valve with relief tube (4.3L and V8 engines), solenoid, check valve(s) and plumbing.

NOTE: On EAC valve, divert and signal tube locations are reversed from previous model year.

Electric Air Control (EAC) Valves With Relief Tube - When engine is cold or at wide open throttle, ECM energizes solenoid on valve, and air is directed to exhaust manifold ports. When coolant temperature increases, solenoid is de-energized and air goes into air cleaner.

At higher engine speeds, air is directed to air cleaner through pressure relief valve (if equipped), even though solenoid may be energized. Air should not be entering exhaust manifold during closed loop mode.

During deceleration, the increased manifold vacuum signal directs air to air cleaner. Check valve on air injection pipe prevents exhaust gases from entering air pump. Solenoid is de-energized under rich mixture condition or if SERVICE ENGINE SOON light is on.

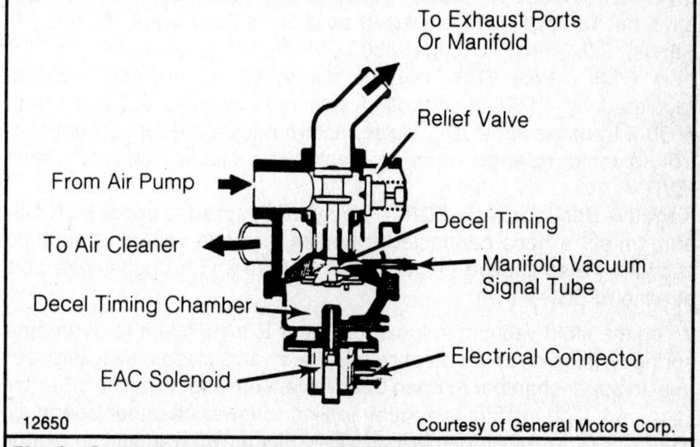
To Exhaust Ports
Or Manifold
Relief Valve
From Air Pump
Decel Timing
To Air Cleaner
Manifold Vacuum
Signal Tube
Decel Timing Chamber
Electrical Connector
EAC Solenoid
12650
Courtesy of General Motors Corp.

Fig. 2: Cross-Sectional View of EAC Valve

1991 ENGINE PERFORMANCE
Theory & Operation (Cont.)

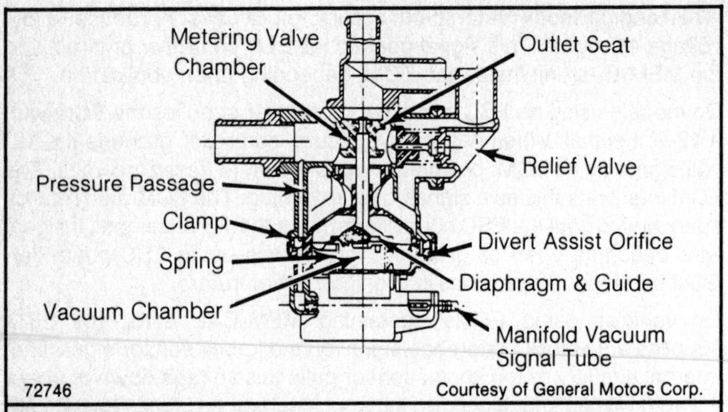
Metering Valve
Chamber
Outlet Seat
Relief Valve
Pressure Passage
Clamp
Divert Assist Orifice
Spring
Diaphragm & Guide
Vacuum Chamber
Manifold Vacuum
Signal Tube
72746
Courtesy of General Motors Corp.

Fig. 3: Cross-Sectional View of EAC Valve With Relief Tube

Air Pump - The air pump is a belt-driven, positive displacement vane-type pump. A centrifugal filter mounted behind the pulley purges air drawn into pump of dirt and contaminants. The air pump is permanently lubricated and requires no periodic service.

CAUTION: To prevent liquid from entering air pump, always cover centrifugal filter fan before cleaning engine. DO NOT oil air pump.

Check Valves - Check valves prevent the backflow of exhaust gases into the air injection system. Check valves close when exhaust gas pressure in exhaust manifold exceeds pressure delivered by pump. This occurs when air pump by-passes at high speeds, when air delivery is switched to catalytic converter, when air is diverted to either atmosphere or air cleaner or when air pump malfunctions.

Air Management System - When ECM energizes electronic air control solenoid on a cold vehicle, air is allowed to flow through control valve to exhaust manifold. As coolant temperature increases or system enters closed loop, ECM opens solenoid ground circuit, de-energizing control solenoid. Air is then routed to air cleaner.

CATALYTIC CONVERTER

A 3-way catalytic converter with dual bed is used to reduce exhaust emissions. This type of converter can reduce hydrocarbons (HC), carbon monoxide (CO) and oxides of nitrogen (NOx).

The upstream section of the converter contains a reducing/oxidizing bed to reduce NOx while oxidizing HC and CO. An air supply pipe from the AIR system injects air between the beds of the converter. Thus, the second converter bed oxidizes any remaining HC and CO to efficiently reduce exhaust emissions.

EXHAUST GAS RECIRCULATION (EGR)

The Exhaust Gas Recirculation (EGR) system is designed to reduce oxides of nitrogen (NOx) emissions by lowering combustion temperatures. A metered amount of exhaust gas is recirculated into the intake manifold and mixed with the air/fuel mixture.

There are 2 types of EGR systems used. Port EGR is used on 2.8L, 3.1L, 4.3L ("S" and "T" Series), 7.4L and 5.7L (over 8500 GVWR). Negative backpressure EGR is used on 2.5L, 4.3L (except "S" and "T" Series), 5.0L and 5.7L (under 8500 GVWR).

Port EGR - Port EGR valve is controlled by manifold vacuum regulated by an ECM-controlled solenoid. Vehicles equipped with 4L80-E transmissions use a pulse width-modulated EGR vacuum control solenoid, referred to as an Electronic Vacuum Regulator Valve (EVRV).

Negative Backpressure EGR - Vacuum is applied to upper EGR diaphragm via a hose connected to intake manifold vacuum. Manifold vacuum is also applied to lower EGR diaphragm (through intake port at base of EGR valve).

When manifold vacuum in lower chamber is insufficient to overcome spring tension on lower diaphragm, bleed valve closes, allowing vacuum in upper chamber to open EGR valve. With engine at idle or under light load, high manifold vacuum applied to lower chamber opens air bleed valve in lower diaphragm. This bleeds off vacuum in upper chamber, keeping the EGR valve closed.

EVAPORATIVE EMISSION CONTROL

All vehicles use carbon canister storage for evaporative fuel control. Evaporative emission control system stores gasoline fumes from fuel tank in a carbon canister until fumes can be drawn into engine for burning during combustion process.

The 4 basic components which may be used in evaporative emission system are activated carbon canister (all models, open at top or bottom for fresh air intake), vacuum operated canister control valve (4.3L and V8 high altitude, mounted remotely), thermostatic vacuum switch (2.8L and 3.1L, mounted in coolant passage in intake manifold) and tank pressure control valve (4.3L and V8 high altitude, mounted in hose between canister and fuel tank). For specific component application and vacuum hose routing, see VACUUM DIAGRAMS article.

Carbon Canister - Evaporative fumes from fuel tank are vented through hose(s) into a canister containing activated carbon. Activated carbon absorbs and holds fuel vapors when engine is not operating. When engine is started and engine speed is greater than idle (purge at idle would cause too rich a mixture), engine vacuum draws fuel vapors from canister into engine. A vacuum canister purge valve or thermostatic vacuum switch regulates vapors through this purge line.

Carbon canisters are open in design. When the engine is started, engine vacuum draws outside air into canister either through the top or bottom, and then through a filter in bottom of canister. This helps to purge vapors from the activated carbon.

Canister Control Valve (CCV) (High Altitude - 4.3L Except "S" & "T" Series & V8) - CCV is vacuum operated. When the engine is not running, vapor from the fuel tank is stored in the carbon canister. When the vehicle is started, vacuum to the upper port draws in the internal vacuum diaphragm, opening the port between the canister and purge valve. When engine is off, internal spring pressure closes valve diaphragm, preventing vapor from venting to atmosphere.

The canister control valve acts as both vapor vent valve and purge valve. When engine is running, manifold vacuum from PCV system pulls lower diaphragm upward. When engine is operating above idle speed, control vacuum pulls upper diaphragm upward. This allows purging of canister through PCV system.

Thermostatic Vacuum Switch (2.8L & 3.1L) - A wax pellet-type thermostatic vacuum switch is installed in the engine coolant passage in the intake manifold. Two vacuum fittings on switch connect to charcoal canister and the TBI unit. When coolant temperature is less than 115°F (46°C), switch closes, preventing purging of canister. When coolant temperature increases to greater than 115°F (46°C), switch opens, allowing purging of canister.

Fuel Tank Pressure Control Valve (High Altitude - 4.3L Except "S" & "T" Series & V8) - Fuel tank pressure control valve allows vapors to flow from the fuel tank into the EEC system. When fuel tank pressure exceeds the spring pressure on the valve diaphragm, the valve opens and allows vapors to either enter canister or, when purge is enabled, go directly to the engine.

The tank pressure control valve is located inside the gas cap on the 3.1L, in the engine compartment on "C" and "K" Series and near the fuel tank on other models.

POSITIVE CRANKCASE VENTILATION (PCV)

The PCV system provides more effective elimination of crankcase vapors. Fresh air from the air filter housing is supplied to the crankcase, where it is mixed with blow-by gases and passed through a PCV valve into the intake manifold. This mixture is then passed into the combustion chamber and burned.

The PCV valve provides primary control in this system by metering the flow (according to manifold vacuum) of the blow-by vapors. When manifold vacuum is high (at idle), the PCV restricts the flow to maintain a smooth idle condition.

Under conditions in which abnormal amounts of blow-by gases are produced (such as worn cylinders or rings), system is designed to allow excess gases to flow back through crankcase vent hose into air inlet.

Spring pressure holds PCV valve closed when engine is not running. This prevents hydrocarbon fumes from collecting in the intake manifold, a condition which could result in hard starting.

During engine operation, manifold vacuum pulls the valve open against spring pressure, permitting crankcase fumes to enter the intake manifold. Should the engine backfire, the PCV valve closes to prevent ignition of fumes in crankcase.

THERMOSTATIC AIR CLEANER (TAC)

Many models are equipped with a system for preheating the air entering the throttle body during cold engine operation.

This system maintains incoming air temperature to a point where fuel injection system can maintain lean air/fuel ratios to reduce hydrocarbon (HC) and carbon monoxide (CO) emissions. TAC systems are either vacuum motor controlled or wax pellet controlled.

Vacuum Motor Controlled (2.8L & 3.1L) –This system consists of an air cleaner assembly with integral air control door, vacuum control temperature sensor, vacuum motor, heat shroud (on exhaust manifold), heated air tube and vacuum hoses.

- **Vacuum Control Temperature Sensor** – The vacuum control temperature sensor controls the operation of the air control door. During initial start-up situations, this valve directs engine vacuum to the air control vacuum motor. The motor closes the air intake door, allowing the intake of heated manifold air. When the intake air temperature reaches a pre-calibrated value, this valve opens, allowing the intake of cooler outside air.
- **Air Control Door** – The air control door temperature sensor closes when the temperature of air entering the air cleaner is less than the calibrated temperature of the temperature sensor. This allows engine vacuum to operate the air control door vacuum motor, and warm manifold air to be routed to the throttle body.
- **Vacuum Motor** – When engine vacuum is applied to the vacuum motor, the air control door stops the intake of outside air. The air cleaner then draws in air from around the exhaust manifold.

  As air inside the air cleaner warms, the temperature sensor begins to open, bleeding off vacuum to the vacuum motor. As vacuum to vacuum motor decreases, the air control door begins to open.

  As air control door opens, outside air is allowed to enter air cleaner assembly. When air entering air cleaner reaches a predetermined temperature, the air control door opens completely and stops the intake of heated air.

Wax Pellet Controlled (Except 2.8L & 3.1L) –A self-contained, wax pellet actuated assembly mounted in the air cleaner controls the air regulator damper (hot/cold air delivery door). When incoming air is cold, wax material sealed in the actuator is in a solid contracted state. As incoming air warms, wax material expands by changing to a liquid state. This forces piston outward, repositioning air regulator damper and allowing air (either a mix of hot and cold or all cold) to enter engine.

EMISSION SYSTEMS (DIESEL)

EXHAUST GAS RECIRCULATION (EGR)

NOTE: For additional information on 6.2L light duty emission EGR system, see SELF-DIAGNOSTICS – DIESEL article.

The Exhaust Gas Recirculation (EGR) system limits formation of oxides of nitrogen (NOx) emissions by reducing peak combustion chamber temperatures in which NOx is formed. EGR system consists of EGR valve, Exhaust Pressure Regulator (EPR) valve, EPR and EGR vent solenoids and EGR fault detection. A vacuum pump is required to provide a vacuum source to operate the EGR system.

EGR Valve – EGR valve reintroduces a small amount of exhaust gas into combustion chamber, diluting air/fuel mixture and reducing combustion chamber peak temperatures, thereby reducing NOx formation.

EPR Valve – The EPR valve is mounted between the exhaust manifold and the exhaust pipe. Valve increases exhaust backpressure during idle, which increases exhaust flow through EGR system. EPR valve resembles the EFE or heat riser type valves of earlier, carbureted vehicles. A vacuum diaphragm-type actuator opens and closes valve. An ECM-controlled EGR/EPR solenoid regulates actuator.

EGR/EPR Solenoids – EGR/EPR solenoids are mounted at rear of engine as a single assembly. Using input from engine speed sensor and TPS, ECM controls EGR by controlling amount of "on" and "off" time of EGR solenoid. When EGR is not needed, ECM energizes EGR vent solenoid to vent vacuum. Vacuum which controls EGR valve controls EPR valve. ECM energizes EPR solenoid to close EPR valve at idle to increase exhaust backpressure.

EGR Fault Detection – The ECM uses input from the MAP sensor to measure amount of absolute pressure in EGR vacuum line. If a minor variation between calculated EGR and actual EGR is monitored by ECM, the ECM corrects. If variation is too great for ECM to correct, an error is detected. The ECM then enters default mode and sets a related trouble code in memory.

Vacuum Pump – A vacuum pump is mounted on the engine and provides vacuum for operating emission controls (light duty emissions), transmission modulator (heavy duty emissions with M40 automatic transmission), cruise control and heater and A/C servos. The vacuum pump is either belt- or gear-driven.

The belt-driven vacuum pump, used on "G" and "P" Series, is bracket mounted to the right front of the engine. Except for the pulley, the vacuum pump is replaced as an assembly.

The gear-driven pump, used on "R" and "V" Series, is mounted at the top rear of the engine and contains a permanently-mounted speed sensor. Pump is driven by a cam inside the drive assembly to which it mounts. On the lower end of the drive housing assembly is a drive gear which meshes with the camshaft gear in the engine. The drive gear causes the cam in the drive housing to rotate.

CAUTION: The vacuum pump drives the engine oil pump. DO NOT run engine with gear-driven vacuum pump removed.

CRANKCASE DEPRESSION REGULATOR (CDR)

The CDR valve, located on the right valve cover, is used on both light and heavy duty diesel engines. Valve prevents crankcase pressure from accumulating during idle by regulating (metering) crankcase pressure back into the engine. Intake manifold vacuum acts against a spring-loaded diaphragm to control flow of crankcase gases. Higher intake manifold vacuum levels pull diaphragm closer to the top of the outlet tube, reducing amount of gases drawn from crankcase. As intake manifold vacuum drops, spring pressure pushes diaphragm away from top of outlet, allowing more gases to flow from crankcase into intake manifold.

Optimum pressure in crankcase is one inch of water (as measured with a manometer) at idle to 3-4 inches at full load. Too little vacuum causes oil leaks; too much vacuum pulls oil into the air crossover.

SELF-DIAGNOSTIC SYSTEM

The ECM is equipped with a self-diagnostic system which detects system failures or abnormalities. When a malfunction occurs, ECM illuminates the SERVICE ENGINE SOON light located on instrument panel. When malfunction is detected and light is turned on, a corresponding trouble code is stored in ECM memory. Malfunctions are designated as either "hard failures" or "intermittent failures". For procedures on retrieving stored codes, see appropriate SELF-DIAGNOSTICS article.

"Hard Failures" – Hard failures cause SERVICE ENGINE SOON light to glow and remain on until malfunction is repaired. If light comes on and remains on during vehicle operation, cause of malfunction must be determined using diagnostic charts located in SELF-DIAGNOSTICS article. If a sensor fails, ECM uses a substitute value in its calculations to continue engine operation. Although vehicle is functional in this condition, driveability will probably be adversely affected.

"Intermittent Failures" – Intermittent failures cause SERVICE ENGINE SOON light to flicker or illuminate and go out about 10 seconds after intermittent fault goes away. However, ECM retains cor-

1991 ENGINE PERFORMANCE
Theory & Operation (Cont.)

responding trouble code in memory. If related fault does not reoccur within 50 engine restarts, related trouble code is erased from ECM memory. Sensor, connector or wiring related problems may cause intermittent failures. See TROUBLE SHOOTING - NO CODES article.

SERVICE ENGINE SOON LIGHT

As a bulb and system check, SERVICE ENGINE SOON light glows when ignition switch is turned to ON position and engine is not running. When engine is started, light should go out. If not, a malfunction has been detected in computerized engine control system or SERVICE ENGINE SOON light circuit is faulty. To verify proper operation of SERVICE ENGINE SOON light on gasoline vehicles, see DIAGNOSTIC CIRCUIT CHECK in BASIC DIAGNOSTIC PROCEDURES article. To verify proper operation of SERVICE ENGINE SOON light and retrieve trouble codes on diesel vehicles, see DIAGNOSTIC CIRCUIT CHECK chart in SELF-DIAGNOSTICS - DIESEL article.

SERIAL DATA

ECM is equipped with a serial data line. Serial date is a stream of electrical impulses which can be interpreted by special testers of other control modules. Serial data must be accessed by connecting special Scan testers to the Assembly Line Data Link (ALDL) connector. Update intervals and information contained within the data stream vary with model application.

MISCELLANEOUS ECM CONTROLS

NOTE: Although not considered true Engine Performance-related systems, some controlled devices may affect driveability if they malfunction.

A/C CLUTCH

On many models, ECM regulates operation of the A/C clutch through an ECM-controlled relay. The ECM disengages the A/C compressor when compressor load on engine may cause driveability problems (i.e. during hot restart, idle, low speed steering maneuvers and wide open throttle operation) or if A/C freon pressure drops below or rises above normal operating levels.

Freon pressure is sensed through the monitoring of high and low pressure switches or a pressure sensor which registers either high or low pressure levels. Power steering load is monitored through a power steering pressure switch. Hot restart is monitored through the coolant temperature sensor. For component application and related wiring, see wiring schematics under MISCELLANEOUS ECM CONTROLS in SYSTEM & COMPONENT TESTING article.

A/C Pressure Switches - A/C high and low pressure switches may be used in the A/C compressor clutch or compressor clutch relay circuit. Switches are normally closed, completing the circuit which energizes the compressor clutch. When system freon pressure increases beyond a certain point, high side switch opens, causing compressor clutch to disengage.

If system freon level decreases (causing freon pressure to drop), low side pressure switch opens, preventing compressor damage by causing compressor clutch to disengage.

COOLING FAN (3.1L ONLY)

ECM regulates operation of the electric cooling fan through an ECM controlled relay which controls the ground or power circuit for the cooling fan. ECM operates the cooling fan based upon engine temperature. Most systems engage electric cooling fan whenever the A/C clutch is engaged, regardless of engine temperature. As a back-up system, many models use a coolant override switch, which engages the cooling fan in case the ECM fails to energize the cooling fan relay or if the cooling fan relay malfunctions. A malfunction of the cooling fan causes engine overheating and possible detonation.

For component application and related wiring, see wiring schematics under MISCELLANEOUS ECM CONTROLS in SYSTEM & COMPONENT TESTING article.

TRANSMISSION

Converter Clutch - The transmission/transaxle converter clutch eliminates power loss of torque converter stage when vehicle is in a cruise condition, allowing driver convenience of automatic transmission and fuel economy of a manual transmission. Fused battery ignition is supplied to converter solenoid through a brake switch.

On some models, 2nd, 3rd and 4th gear hydraulic apply switches (located within transmission) may also be in series with solenoid power or ground circuit. On other models, switch status may only be monitored by ECM, without sharing power or ground with converter solenoid. For wiring reference, see wiring schematics under MISCELLANEOUS ECM CONTROLS in SYSTEM & COMPONENT TESTING article.

Converter clutch engages when vehicle is moving faster than a precalibrated speed, engine is at normal operating temperature, throttle position sensor output is not changing (indicating a steady road speed) and transmission 3rd gear or high gear switch (if equipped) and brake switch are closed.

When vehicle speed is great enough (about 20-45 MPH as indicated by the vehicle speed sensor), ECM energizes converter clutch solenoid mounted in transmission, allowing torque converter to directly connect engine to the transmission. When operating conditions indicate transmission should operate as normal, converter clutch solenoid is de-energized, allowing transmission to return to normal automatic operation. Since power for the converter solenoid is delivered through the brake switch, transmission also returns to normal automatic operation when brake pedal is depressed. To check function of converter clutch system, perform functional check of system. See MISCELLANEOUS ECM CONTROLS in SYSTEM & COMPONENT TESTING article.

Electronic Transmission (4L80-E) - On gasoline vehicles equipped with 4L80-E transmission, Powertrain Control Module (PCM) controls transmission and other vehicle functions. On diesel vehicles, Transmission Control Module (TCM) controls electronic transmission, but no other components. PCM/TCM monitors a number of engine/vehicle functions and uses data to control shift solenoid "A", shift solenoid "B", TCC and the force motor and regulate TCC engagement, upshift pattern, downshift pattern and line pressure (shift quality).

- **Shift Solenoid "A"** - Shift solenoid "A" is attached to the valve body and is a normally open exhaust valve. PCM/TCM activates solenoid by grounding it through an internal quad-driver. Solenoid "A" is on in 1st and 4th gears, but off in 2nd and 3rd. When on, solenoid redirects fluid to act on the shift valves. Solenoid "A" is Blue. Code 82 is associated with solenoid "A".
- **Shift Solenoid "B"** - Shift solenoid "B" is attached to the valve body and is a normally open exhaust valve. PCM/TCM activates solenoid by grounding it through an internal quad-driver. Solenoid "B" is on in 3rd and 4th gears, but off in 1st and 2nd. When on, solenoid redirects fluid to act on the shift valves. Solenoid "B" is Red. Codes 81, 86 and 87 are associated with solenoid "B".
- **Force Motor** - Force motor is attached to the valve body and controls line pressure by moving a pressure regulator valve against spring pressure. Force motor replaces the throttle valve or vacuum modulator used on past transmissions. PCM/TCM varies line pressure based upon engine load. Engine load is calculated from various inputs, especially the TPS.

  Line pressure is actually varied by changing the amperage applied to the force motor from zero (high pressure) to 1.1 amps (low pressure). The force motor is periodically pulsed to prevent fluid contamination from causing pressure regulator valve to stick.

Shift Light - Shift light is used on vehicles equipped with manual transmission. Light indicates best transmission shift point for maximum fuel economy. Power for light is supplied through GAUGES fuse. Light illuminates when ECM supplies a ground circuit for bulb. For wiring reference, see wiring schematics under MISCELLANEOUS ECM CONTROLS in SYSTEM & COMPONENT TESTING article.

1991 ENGINE PERFORMANCE
Basic Diagnostic Procedures

Astro, Blazer, Bravada, Jimmy, Lumina APV, Safari, Sierra, Silhouette, Sonoma, Syclone, Trans Sport, "C" & "K" Series, "G" Series, "P" Series, "R" & "V" Series, "S" & "T" Series

INTRODUCTION

The following diagnostic steps help prevent overlooking simple problems and begin diagnosis for no-start conditions.

The first step in diagnosing any driveability problem is verifying the customer's complaint by test driving vehicle under the conditions in which the problem reportedly occurred.

Before entering self-diagnostics, perform a careful and complete visual inspection. Most engine control problems result from mechanical breakdowns, poor electrical connections or damaged/misrouted vacuum hoses. Before condemning the computerized system, perform each test listed in this article.

NOTE: Perform all voltage tests with a Digital Volt-Ohmmeter (DVOM) with a minimum 10-megohm input impedance, unless stated otherwise in test procedure.

PRELIMINARY INSPECTION & ADJUSTMENTS

VISUAL INSPECTION

Visually inspect all electrical wiring. Look for chafed, stretched, cut or pinched wiring. Ensure electrical connectors fit tightly and are not corroded. Ensure vacuum hoses are properly routed and not pinched or cut. If necessary, see VACUUM DIAGRAMS article to verify routing and connections. Inspect air induction system for possible vacuum leaks.

MECHANICAL INSPECTION

Compression – Check engine mechanical condition using a compression gauge, vacuum gauge or engine analyzer capable of performing a relative compression test. If using engine analyzer, see engine analyzer instruction manual for availability and description of relative compression feature.

WARNING: DO NOT use ignition switch during compression tests on fuel injected vehicles. Use a remote starter to crank engine. Fuel injectors on many models are triggered by ignition switch during cranking mode, which can create a fire hazard or contaminate the engine's oiling system.

Exhaust System Backpressure – Before replacing any components, check exhaust system for restrictions. Use a vacuum gauge or a low pressure (1-5 psi) pressure gauge to check exhaust system.

If using a vacuum gauge, connect gauge to intake manifold vacuum, and start engine. Observe gauge while holding throttle steady at 2000-2500 RPM. If vacuum gauge reading slowly drops after stabilizing, exhaust system may be restricted.

- **Check at AIR Pipe** – Remove rubber hose at exhaust manifold AIR pipe check valve, and remove check valve. Install pressure gauge to hose and nipple via Propane Enrichment Device (J26911). Nipple should be inserted into exhaust manifold AIR pipe.
- **Check at O_2 Sensor** – Remove O_2 sensor. Install backpressure tester in place of O_2 sensor. After test is completed, coat O_2 sensor threads with anti-seize compound.
- **Diagnosis** – **1)** Start engine, and bring to operating temperature. Increase engine speed to 2000-2500 RPM. Note gauge. Exhaust system is restricted if reading exceeds 1.25 psi (.09 kg/cm²).
  2) Check exhaust system for collapsed pipe, heat distress and possible internal muffler failure. If none of these conditions exists, check for restricted catalytic converter. Replace as required.

IMPORTANT: The following table provides the location of commonly used diagnostic information. These former "A" and "C" charts are now written in text and inserted into the appropriate location in the new Engine Performance workflow. To familiarize yourself with the Engine Performance workflow, see HOW TO USE THE ENGINE PERFORMANCE SECTION in GENERAL INFORMATION.

GENERAL MOTORS A & C CHART REFERENCE TABLE

System or Component	Diagnostic Information Location
DIAGNOSTIC CIRCUIT CHECK	See DIAGNOSTIC CIRCUIT CHECK in BASIC DIAGNOSTIC PROCEDURES
A-1 & A-2, SERVICE ENGINE SOON Light	See DIAGNOSTIC CIRCUIT CHECK in BASIC DIAGNOSTIC PROCEDURES
A-3, No-Start	See NO-START DIAGNOSIS in BASIC DIAGNOSTIC PROCEDURES
A-5, Fuel Pump Relay	See RELAYS, SOLENOIDS & MOTORS in SYSTEM & COMPONENT TESTING
A-7, Fuel System Diagnosis	See BASIC FUEL SYSTEM CHECKS in BASIC DIAGNOSTIC PROCEDURES
C-1, MAP Sensor	See ENGINE SENSORS & SWITCHES in SYSTEM & COMPONENT TESTING
C-1, Power Steering Pressure Switch	See ENGINE SENSORS & SWITCHES in SYSTEM & COMPONENT TESTING
C-1, Park/Neutral Switch	See ENGINE SENSORS & SWITCHES in SYSTEM & COMPONENT TESTING
C-2, Injector Balance Test (4.3L)	See FUEL CONTROL in SYSTEM & COMPONENT TESTING
C-2, IAC Motor	See IDLE CONTROL SYSTEM in SYSTEM & COMPONENT TESTING
C-3, Canister Purge System	See EMISSION SYSTEMS & SUB-SYSTEMS in SYSTEM & COMPONENT TESTING
C-4, EST Ignition Check	See BASIC IGNITION SYSTEM CHECKS in BASIC DIAGNOSTIC PROCEDURES
C-5, ESC Ignition Check	See IGNITION SYSTEM in SYSTEM & COMPONENT TESTING
C-6, Air Injection System	See EMISSION SYSTEMS & SUB-SYSTEMS in SYSTEM & COMPONENT TESTING
C-7, EGR System	See EMISSION SYSTEMS & SUB-SYSTEMS in SYSTEM & COMPONENT TESTING
C-8, Torque Converter Clutch	[1] See MISCELLANEOUS ECM CONTROLS in SYSTEM & COMPONENT TESTING
C-8, Manual Transmission Shift Lights	[1] See MISCELLANEOUS ECM CONTROLS in SYSTEM & COMPONENT TESTING
C-10, A/C Clutch Control	[2] See MISCELLANEOUS ECM CONTROLS in SYSTEM & COMPONENT TESTING
C-12, Electric Cooling Fan Control	[3] See MISCELLANEOUS ECM CONTROLS in SYSTEM & COMPONENT TESTING

[1] – Covered in entirety in Mitchell's 1991-92 TRANSMISSION SERVICE & REPAIR manual for domestic vehicles.
[2] – Covered in entirety in Mitchell's 1991 AIR CONDITIONING & HEATING SERVICE & REPAIR supplement for domestic vehicles.
[3] – Covered in entirety in ENGINE COOLING in Mitchell's 1991 DOMESTIC LIGHT TRUCKS & VANS SERVICE & REPAIR manual, 1991 ENGINE, CLUTCH & DRIVE AXLE supplement and 1991 AIR CONDITIONING & HEATING SERVICE & REPAIR supplement for domestic vehicles.

1991 ENGINE PERFORMANCE
Basic Diagnostic Procedures (Cont.)

A-3, NO-START DIAGNOSIS

***NOTE:* For diesel information, see SELF-DIAGNOSTICS - DIESEL and TROUBLE SHOOTING - NO CODES articles.**

Definition - No-start is defined as engine cranks okay, but does not start. Engine may fire a few times.

***NOTE:* Before performing following tests, check battery condition, engine cranking speed and fuel supply.**

General Inspection - **1)** Ensure proper starting procedure is being used.

2) Visually check vacuum hoses for splits, kinks and improper connections. See underhood emission control information label. Check ignition wires for cracking, hardness and improper connections at both distributor cap and spark plugs.

3) Remove spark plugs. Check and replace as necessary.

4) Remove distributor cap and check for moisture, dust, cracks, burns and arcing to ground through coil mounting screws or rotor.

5) Try to turn distributor shaft by hand. Drive gear pin may be broken.

6) If vehicle has been exposed to very cold temperatures, ensure oil is proper viscosity and not contaminated with gasoline.

Ignition System - **1)** Disconnect tachometer wire at distributor TACH terminal (if equipped). A shorted tachometer or tachometer circuit prevents vehicle from starting.

2) Check for battery voltage at BAT terminal at distributor with ignition on. *See Figs. 2-6.* Repair as necessary.

3) Connect ST-125 spark tester to one end of plug wire, and crank engine. If spark is present, check fuel delivery.

4) If spark does not occur, disconnect 4-wire EST connector at distributor. If spark now occurs, replace pick-up coil in distributor.

5) If spark does not occur, reconnect EST connector, and check voltage at TACH terminal at distributor with ignition on.

6) If voltage is less than one volt, repair faulty coil connection or replace faulty coil. If voltage is 1-10 volts, replace ignition module, and recheck for spark. If spark still does not occur, replace ignition coil.

7) If voltage reading at TACH terminal of distributor is greater than 10 volts, remove and invert distributor cap, keeping wires connected. Fabricate an HEI coil spark tester by trimming a spark plug boot and connecting trimmed boot to ST-125 spark tester. *See Fig. 1.* Crank engine.

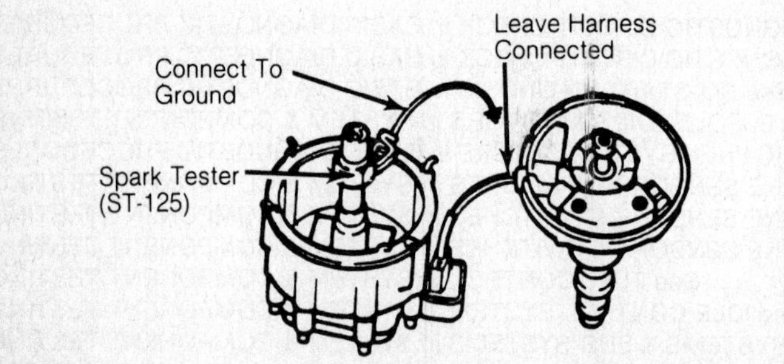
Leave Harness Connected
Connect To Ground
Spark Tester (ST-125)

90B15777 Courtesy of General Motors Corp.

***Fig. 1:* Connecting Integral Coil Spark Tester (ST-125)**

8) If spark occurs, check cap for cracks, water or other defects. Check pick-up coil connector and ignition coil lead wire colors. Ignition coil with Yellow and Red wires should be used with a Yellow pick-up coil connector. Ignition coil with White and Red wires should be used with a Clear or Black pick-up coil connector.

9) If spark does not occur, turn ignition off, and disconnect pick-up coil leads from module. Turn ignition on. With voltmeter connected to distributor TACH terminal and fabricated coil spark tester connected, momentarily touch test light, connected to a remote voltage source (1.5-8.0 volts), to ignition module terminal "P".

10) If voltage at TACH terminal does not drop, check ignition module ground, and check for open in wires from ignition coil to module. If all is okay, replace ignition module.

11) If voltage at TACH terminal drops, check for spark at spark tester as test light is removed from terminal "P". If spark occurs, check pick-up coil connections and check for 500-1500 ohms resistance at pick-up coil leads. *See Fig. 9.* Repair as necessary.

12) If spark does not occur, test ignition module with module tester. If module tests okay, check ignition coil wire. If module tester is not available, replace ignition coil, and touch terminal "P" again. If spark occurs, system is okay. If spark does not occur, reinstall original ignition coil, and replace ignition module.

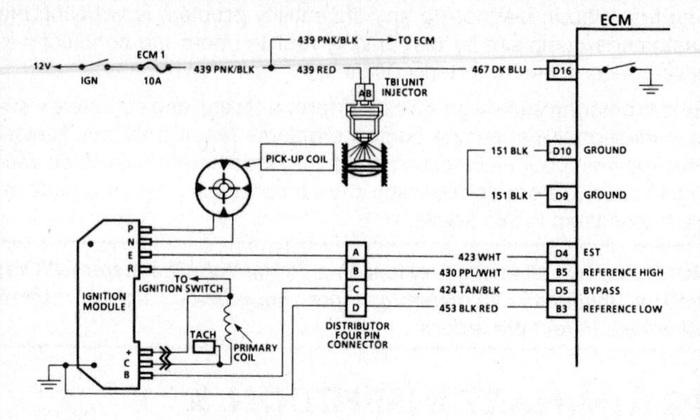
ECM
439 PNK/BLK
TO ECM
12V
ECM 1
IGN
10A
439 PNK/BLK
439 RED
TBI UNIT INJECTOR
467 DK BLU
D16
PICK-UP COIL
151 BLK
D10
GROUND
151 BLK
D9
GROUND
P N E R
IGNITION MODULE
TO IGNITION SWITCH
TACH
PRIMARY COIL
A B C D
DISTRIBUTOR FOUR PIN CONNECTOR
423 WHT
D4
EST
430 PPL/WHT
B5
REFERENCE HIGH
424 TAN/BLK
D5
BYPASS
453 BLK RED
B3
REFERENCE LOW

91F13602 Courtesy of General Motors Corp.

***Fig. 2:* HEI Ignition & Injector Circuits (2.5L)**

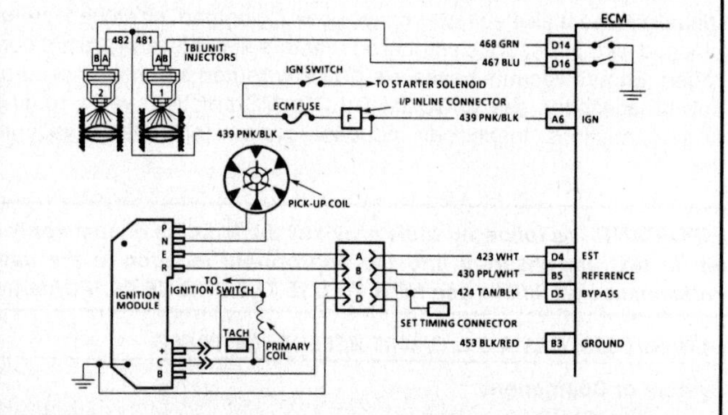
ECM
482
481
TBI UNIT INJECTORS
468 GRN
D14
467 BLU
D16
IGN SWITCH
TO STARTER SOLENOID
ECM FUSE
I/P INLINE CONNECTOR
439 PNK/BLK
A6
IGN
439 PNK/BLK
PICK-UP COIL
IGNITION MODULE
TO IGNITION SWITCH
TACH
PRIMARY COIL
423 WHT
D4
EST
430 PPL/WHT
B5
REFERENCE
424 TAN/BLK
D5
BYPASS
SET TIMING CONNECTOR
453 BLK/RED
B3
GROUND

91G13603 Courtesy of General Motors Corp.

***Fig. 3:* HEI Ignition & Injector Circuits (3.1L)**

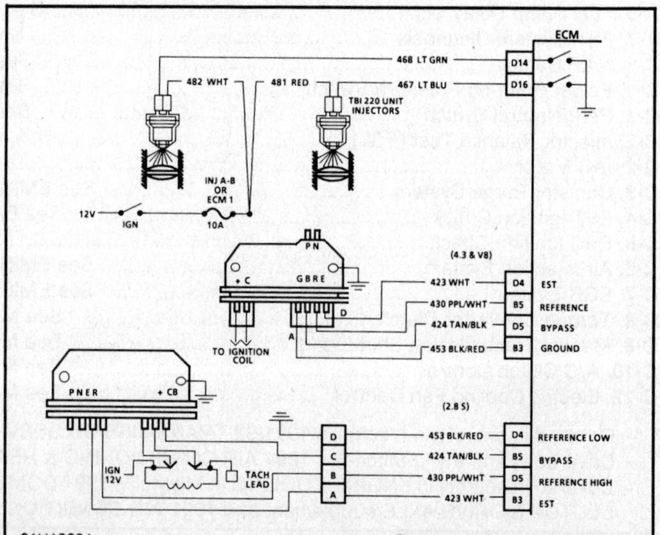
ECM
468 LT GRN
D14
482 WHT
481 RED
467 LT BLU
D16
TBI 220 UNIT INJECTORS
INJ A-B OR ECM 1
12V
IGN
10A
(4.3 & V8)
423 WHT
D4
EST
430 PPL/WHT
B5
REFERENCE
424 TAN/BLK
D5
BYPASS
453 BLK/RED
B3
GROUND
TO IGNITION COIL
(2.8 S)
P N E R
+ C B
453 BLK/RED
D4
REFERENCE LOW
424 TAN/BLK
B5
BYPASS
430 PPL/WHT
D5
REFERENCE HIGH
423 WHT
B3
EST
IGN 12V
TACH LEAD

91H13604 Courtesy of General Motors Corp.

***Fig. 4:* HEI Ignition & Injector Circuits (2.8L, 4.3L, 5.0L, 5.7L & 7.4L Without 4L80-E Transmission)**

Fuel System (TBI) – 1) Before checking fuel system for a no-start condition, check ignition for adequate spark. Check for proper fuel pump pressure (9-13 psi) and capacity (one pint in 30 seconds). See A-7, BASIC FUEL SYSTEM CHECKS (GASOLINE).

2) Crank engine, and watch for injector spray. If injector spray occurs, go to step **5)**. If no spray occurs, disconnect injector harness, and check for battery voltage at harness. Battery voltage should be present on one injector terminal. If battery voltage is not present, check for blown injector power fuse. If battery voltage is present on both terminals, check for wires shorted to one another.

3) If battery voltage is present on only one terminal, connect injector test light (also called a "node" light) to injector harness. Crank engine, and note light. If light flashes, check for stored ECM codes. See DIAGNOSTIC CIRCUIT CHECK. If no codes are present, refer to HARD START symptom in TROUBLE SHOOTING – NO CODES article. If light does not flash, momentarily touch test light from battery voltage to ECM RPM reference terminal (circuit No. 430).

4) Each time test light is removed from ECM RPM reference terminal, injector test light should flash. If test light does not flash, check for open in RPM reference wire or injector drive (ground) circuit. If wiring is okay, replace faulty ECM. Prior to replacing ECM, check ECM power and ground circuits.

5) If injector spray occurred while cranking engine, disconnect injector harness, and crank engine. If injector spray or leakage occurs, a no-start condition could be caused by excessive fuel being delivered during cranking. Repair faulty injector or injector seal. If no spray or leakage occurs, refer to HARD START symptom in TROUBLE SHOOTING – NO CODES article.

Fuel System (4.3L Turbo PFI) – 1) Before checking fuel system for a no-start condition, check ignition for adequate spark. Check for proper fuel pump pressure and capacity. See A-7, BASIC FUEL SYSTEM CHECKS (GASOLINE).

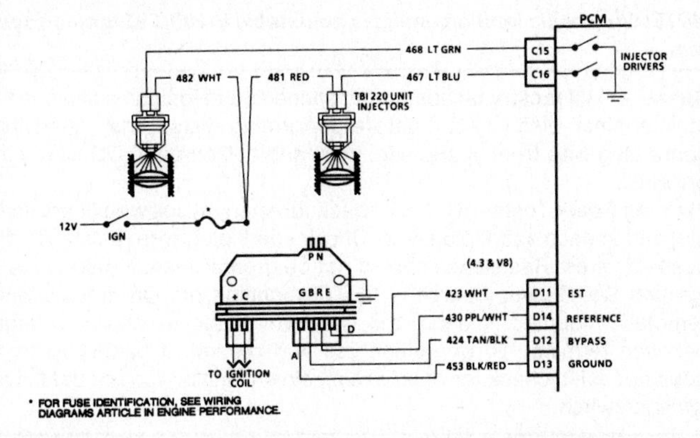
PCM
468 LT GRN
467 LT BLU
C15
C16
INJECTOR DRIVERS
482 WHT
481 RED
TBI 220 UNIT INJECTORS
12V
IGN
(4.3 & V8)
423 WHT
430 PPL/WHT
424 TAN/BLK
453 BLK/RED
D11
D14
D12
D13
EST
REFERENCE
BYPASS
GROUND
TO IGNITION COIL
* FOR FUSE IDENTIFICATION, SEE WIRING DIAGRAMS ARTICLE IN ENGINE PERFORMANCE.

91I13605 Courtesy of General Motors Corp.

Fig. 5: HEI Ignition & Injector Circuits (2.8L, 4.3L, 5.0L, 5.7L & 7.4L With 4L80-E Transmission)

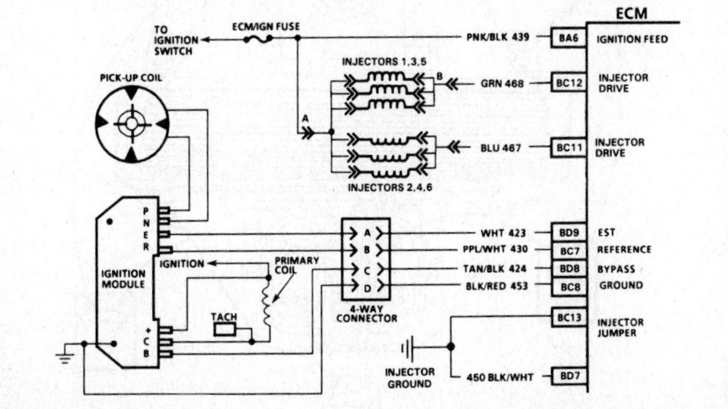
ECM
TO IGNITION SWITCH
ECM/IGN FUSE
PNK/BLK 439
BA6
IGNITION FEED
PICK-UP COIL
INJECTORS 1,3,5
GRN 468
BC12
INJECTOR DRIVE
BLU 467
BC11
INJECTOR DRIVE
INJECTORS 2,4,6
WHT 423
PPL/WHT 430
TAN/BLK 424
BLK/RED 453
BD9
BC7
BD8
BC8
EST
REFERENCE
BYPASS
GROUND
IGNITION MODULE
IGNITION
PRIMARY COIL
4-WAY CONNECTOR
TACH
BC13
INJECTOR JUMPER
INJECTOR GROUND
450 BLK/WHT
BD7

91C13609 Courtesy of General Motors Corp.

Fig. 6: HEI Ignition & Injector Circuits (4.3L Turbo PFI)

2) Disconnect injector harness. Turn ignition on, and check for battery voltage at each injector harness. Battery voltage should be present on one side of each injector. If battery voltage is not present, check for blown injector power fuse. If battery voltage is present on both injector terminals, check for wires shorted together.

3) If battery voltage is present on only one terminal, connect injector test light to injector harness. Crank engine, and note light. Repeat on other injector connectors. If light flashes, check for stored ECM codes. If no codes are present, refer to HARD START symptom in TROUBLE SHOOTING – NO CODES article.

4) If light does not flash, disconnect distributor 4-wire HEI-EST connector. Momentarily touch test light from battery voltage to ECM RPM reference wire (circuit No. 430) of 4-wire connector. Each time test light is removed from ECM RPM reference terminal, injector test light should flash. If test light does not flash, check for open in RPM reference wire or injector drive (ground) circuit. If wiring is okay, replace faulty ECM.

A-7, BASIC FUEL SYSTEM CHECKS (GASOLINE)

FUEL SYSTEM PRESSURE RELIEF

Model 700 TBI Unit (2.5L) – Place transmission gear selector in Park (Neutral on manual transmissions). Set parking brake, and block drive wheels. Loosen fuel filler cap to relieve tank pressure. Disconnect 3-terminal electrical connector at fuel tank. Start engine, and allow to run until engine stalls due to lack of fuel. Crank engine 3 seconds to remove any fuel pressure left in fuel lines. Fuel lines are now safe for servicing.

Model 220 TBI Unit (Except 2.5L) – Fuel pressure is relieved and drops to zero when ignition is turned off. To minimize risk of fire and personal injury, cover area to be disconnected with a shop rag.

Port Fuel Injection (4.3L Turbo) – Fuel system is under pressure. Pressure must be relieved prior to servicing fuel system. Fuel pressure may be relieved by one of following methods.

- Disconnect fuel pump at rear body connector. Start engine, and run it until it stalls. Crank starter 3 seconds to remove remaining fuel from fuel lines. Reconnect rear body connector.
- Install Fuel Pressure Gauge (J-34730-1) on fuel pressure connector of fuel rail. Wrap shop towel around pressure connection when installing fuel pressure gauge to absorb fuel leakage. Install gauge bleed hose in container. Open bleed valve to bleed fuel pressure.

FUEL SYSTEM PRESSURE TEST

WARNING: Begin fuel system trouble shooting and diagnosis with fuel system pressure test. Relieve fuel system pressure before disconnecting any components or installing fuel pressure gauge.

TBI – 1) Turn ignition off for 10 seconds. Turn ignition on, and listen at fuel tank for fuel pump operation. Pump should run 2 seconds (20 seconds on models equipped with fuel module). If fuel pump runs, go to next step. If fuel pump does not run, go to step **7)**.

2) If fuel pump runs, turn ignition off. Verify fuel tank has fuel. Relieve fuel pressure. See FUEL SYSTEM PRESSURE RELIEF. Remove air cleaner, and plug air cleaner vacuum ports (if equipped). Disconnect fuel line between throttle body and fuel filter. Install Fuel Pressure Gauge (J-29658A) and Adapter (J-2968A-85) between steel fuel line and flexible hose, ahead of in-line fuel filter.

3) Turn ignition on, and note reading on pressure gauge. If fuel pressure is 9-13 psi (.63-.91 kg/cm²), no problems are present. If pressure is less than 9 psi (.63 kg/cm²), go to step **5)**. If pressure is greater than 13 psi (.91 kg/cm²), turn ignition off, and bleed fuel pressure. Disconnect fuel return line downstream of pressure gauge. Insert return line into a gasoline container.

4) Turn ignition on. If pressure is now 9-13 psi (.63-.91 kg/cm²), correct restriction in fuel return line between disconnected point and fuel tank. If fuel pressure is greater than 13 psi (.91 kg/cm²), check for restricted return line (including fuel filter) downstream of pressure gauge. If no

1991 ENGINE PERFORMANCE
Basic Diagnostic Procedures (Cont.)

restrictions are present, replace fuel pressure regulator (TBI 700) or fuel meter cover/pressure regulator (TBI 220).
5) If fuel pressure was less than 9 psi (.63 kg/cm²), check for restricted line between in-tank fuel pump and pressure regulator. If fuel line is okay, disconnect injector connector. Turn ignition on. Gradually pinch fuel pressure gauge outlet hose. Note pressure.

CAUTION: DO NOT pinch off fuel return line completely. DO NOT allow fuel pressure build-up to exceed specification, as damage to fuel pressure regulator may occur.

6) If pressure is greater than 13 psi (.91 kg/cm²), replace fuel pressure regulator (TBI 700) or fuel meter cover/pressure regulator (TBI 220). If pressure is less than 9 psi (.63 kg/cm²), check for faulty fuel pump or incorrect part. Check fuel pump coupling hose and pump inlet filter in fuel tank. On models with dual fuel tanks, check for faulty fuel tank selector valve and meter switch.
7) If fuel pump did not run in step **1)**, apply 12 volts to fuel pump test connector. For fuel pump test connector location, see underhood engine component views under COMPONENT LOCATIONS in SYSTEM & COMPONENT TESTING article. If fuel pump now runs, repair open in fuel pump relay drive or power circuit or repair faulty fuel pump relay. To test relay, see FUEL PUMP RELAY in SYSTEM & COMPONENT TESTING article.
8) If fuel pump does not run with 12 volts applied to fuel pump test connector, repair open in fuel pump power or ground circuit or repair faulty fuel pump.
PFI (4.3L Turbo) – 1) Relieve fuel pressure. See FUEL PRESSURE RELIEF. Connect Fuel Pressure Gauge (J-34730-1) to fuel pressure connector on fuel rail. Turn ignition on. With ignition on and engine off, pressure should be 35-38 psi (2.46-2.67 kg/cm²). If no fuel pressure is present, go to step **5)**.
2) Start engine. Pressure should drop 3-10 psi (.21-.70 kg/cm²). Turn ignition off. Pressure should hold. If pressure does not hold, check for leaking injectors or fittings. If injectors or fittings are not leaking, replace pressure regulator.
3) If pressure is present but less than specification, check for restricted delivery line or fuel filter. Repair as necessary. If no restriction is evident, apply battery voltage to fuel pump test connector using a 10-amp fused jumper wire. For location of fuel pump test connector, see COMPONENT LOCATIONS in SYSTEM & COMPONENT TESTING article.
4) Gradually pinch off fuel delivery line between gauge and fuel rail. If fuel pressure increases to within specifications, replace fuel pressure regulator. If fuel pressure does not increase with line pinched, check for faulty in-tank fuel pump or partial blocked fuel strainer.
5) Use a 10-amp fused jumper wire to apply battery voltage to fuel pump test connector. For location of fuel pump test connector, see COMPONENT LOCATIONS in SYSTEM & COMPONENT TESTING article. Observe fuel pressure reading. If fuel pressure is still not present, check wiring between test connector and fuel pump. If wiring is okay, replace fuel pump.
6) If fuel pressure is present with voltage applied to test connector, test fuel pump relay and voltage supply to relay. See SYSTEM & COMPONENT TESTING article.

FIELD SERVICE MODE CHECK

NOTE: O_2 sensor may cool off while engine idles, causing system to enter open loop. To restore closed loop mode, run engine at part throttle several minutes and accelerate from idle to part throttle several times.

This test confirms proper fuel system operation and verifies closed loop operation. Clear codes and perform this test after any repair is completed. When performing this test, always engage parking brake and block DRIVE wheels. Parking brake on FWD models does NOT hold drive wheels.
1) Start engine. With engine running, ground diagnostic test terminal "B" of ALDL. *See Figs. 10-12.* In closed loop mode, SERVICE ENGINE SOON light flashes once per second.
2) In open loop, light flashes 2.5 times per second. A lean exhaust is indicated if light is usually off. A rich exhaust is indicated if light is usually on.

BASIC FUEL SYSTEM CHECKS (DIESEL)

FUEL PUMP FLOW TEST

1) Disconnect fuel line at fuel filter inlet. Disconnect fuel injection pump electric shut-off solenoid wire (Pink).
2) Crank engine 15 seconds. If fuel pump does not supply approximately 1/2 pint of fuel in 15 seconds, go to FUEL SYSTEM PRESSURE TEST.

FUEL SYSTEM PRESSURE TEST

CAUTION: Begin fuel system trouble shooting and diagnosis with fuel system pressure test. Relieve fuel system pressure before disconnecting any components or installing fuel pressure gauge.

1) Turn engine off. Disconnect fuel line at inlet to fuel filter assembly. Install low pressure fuel gauge to fuel line.
2) Crank or run engine 10-15 seconds. If fuel pressure is not 5.8-8.7 psi (.41-.61 kg/cm²), check fuel lines and fuel tank sending unit for restriction. If fuel lines and sending unit are okay, replace fuel pump.

C-4, BASIC IGNITION SYSTEM CHECKS (GASOLINE)

HEI-EST DISTRIBUTOR

NOTE: Only basic ignition timing is adjustable in HEI/EST ignition system.

Spark – 1) If factory tachometer is connected to ignition coil tachometer terminal, disconnect it before performing tests. When removing spark plug wire from spark plug, twist and pull on boot. DO NOT pull on wire.
2) Using Spark Tester (ST-125), check for spark at coil wire (if applicable) and at each spark plug wire. Check spark plug wire resistance on suspect wires. Resistance should not be greater than 30,000 ohms.
Ignition Coil Power Source – 1) Turn ignition on. On models with remotely mounted ignition coil, use voltmeter to check voltage between terminal "B" of ignition coil and ground. If battery voltage does not exist, check for open circuit, blown ignition fuse or defective ignition switch.

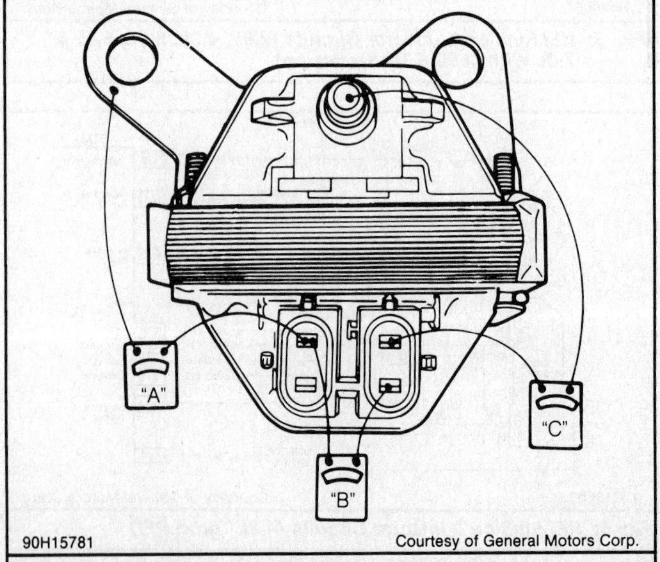
"A"
"C"
"B"
90H15781
Courtesy of General Motors Corp.

Fig. 7: Testing Ignition Coil Resistance (External Coil)

2) On models equipped with integrally mounted ignition coil, check voltage between BAT terminal and ground at distributor. If battery voltage does not exist, check for open circuit, blown ignition fuse or defective ignition switch.

Ignition Coil Resistance (Externally Mounted) – 1) Remove coil connectors and secondary coil wire. In test "A", use high ohmmeter scale. Resistance value should be very high (infinite). *See Fig. 7*. If reading is not infinite, replace coil.

2) In test "B", use low ohmmeter scale. Reading should be very low (near zero ohms). If reading is not near zero ohms, replace coil. In test "C", use high ohmmeter scale. If no continuity exists, replace coil.

Ignition Coil Resistance (Internally Mounted) – 1) Turn ignition off. Remove distributor cap and coil assembly. Invert cap. Set ohmmeter to low scale. Connect leads to coil BAT and TACH terminals. *See Fig. 8*. If resistance exceeds approximately zero, replace ignition coil.

2) Set ohmmeter on high scale. Connect one lead to coil secondary terminal and other lead first to TACH terminal and then to ground terminal. If resistance reading in BOTH instances is infinite, replace ignition coil.

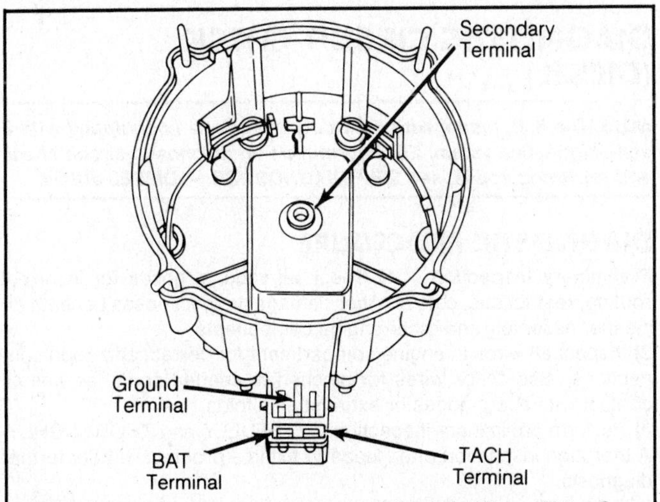

Secondary Terminal
Ground Terminal
BAT Terminal
TACH Terminal

90I16782 Courtesy of General Motors Corp.

Fig. 8: Testing Ignition Coil Resistance (Internal Coil)

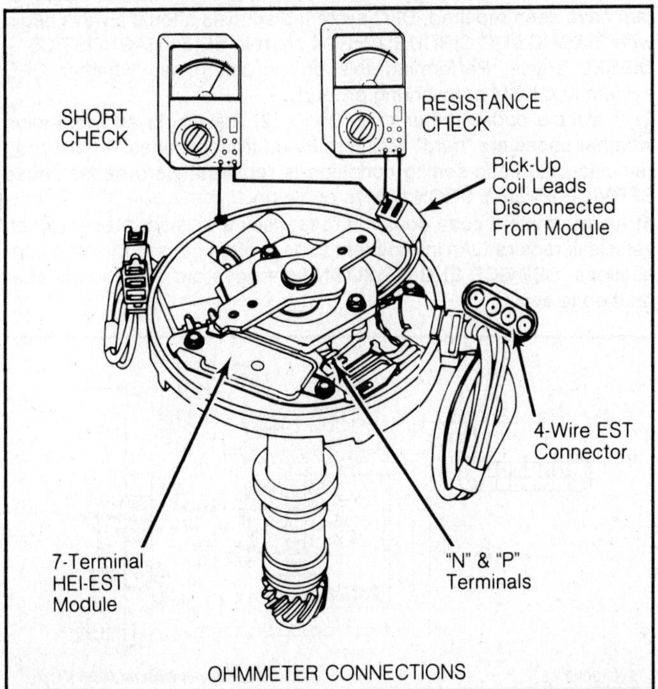

SHORT CHECK
RESISTANCE CHECK
Pick-Up Coil Leads Disconnected From Module
4-Wire EST Connector
7-Terminal HEI-EST Module
"N" & "P" Terminals
OHMMETER CONNECTIONS

90J15783 Courtesy of General Motors Corp.

Fig. 9: Checking Distributor Pick-Up Coil

Distributor Pick-Up Coil Short & Resistance Checks – 1) Disconnect pick-up coil leads from HEI-EST module terminals "N" and "P". Set ohmmeter to middle scale, and connect one lead to either pick-up coil lead and other lead to distributor housing. *See Fig. 9*. Flex pick-up coil leads by hand to check for intermittent shorts to ground. If reading is not always infinite, replace pick-up coil.

2) Connect ohmmeter between both pick-up coil leads. Check for intermittent opens by flexing wires and connectors. If resistance is not 500-1500 ohms, replace pick-up coil.

Tach Pulse (RPM) Signal – Use a Scan tester connected to ALDL connector of vehicle to check for a tach pulse signal. RPM should be indicated on tester when engine is being cranked or is running. Tach pulse (RPM reference) is indicated as a voltage signal when a DVOM (minimum 10-megohm input impedance) is touched to circuit No. 430 ECM terminal. *See Figs. 2-6*.

IDLE SPEED & IGNITION TIMING (GASOLINE)

Ensure idle speed and ignition timing are set to specifications. For adjustment procedures, see ON-VEHICLE ADJUSTMENTS article.

DIAGNOSTIC CIRCUIT CHECK (GASOLINE)

Diagnostic Circuit Check determines:

- If SERVICE ENGINE SOON light works.
- If ECM is operating and can recognize a fault.
- If any codes are stored.

After performing basic diagnostic procedures listed under PRELIMINARY INSPECTION & ADJUSTMENTS, A-7, BASIC FUEL SYSTEM CHECKS and C-4, BASIC IGNITION SYSTEM CHECKS, use self-diagnostic system for determining computer-related problems. *See Fig. 14*.

After performing necessary tests in diagnostic circuit check and if no codes are indicated and driveability problems still exist, see TROUBLE SHOOTING – NO CODES article and SCAN TESTER USAGE in SELF-DIAGNOSTICS – GASOLINE article.

1) Check SERVICE ENGINE SOON light operation. Turn ignition on with Scan tester not connected, ALDL test terminal not grounded and engine not running. SERVICE ENGINE SOON light should be on steady. If light illuminates and stays on steady, go to next step. If light does not illuminate, go to A-1, SERVICE ENGINE SOON LIGHT INOPERATIVE. If light flashes, go to step **3)**.

2) Grounding ALDL diagnostic test terminal "B" now should cause SERVICE ENGINE SOON light to flash a Code 12, followed by any codes stored in ECM memory. If light goes from bright to dim or if light remains on and does not flash Code 12, see A-2, SERVICE ENGINE SOON LIGHT ALWAYS ON OR WON'T FLASH CODE 12.

3) If light begins to flash as soon as ignition is turned on, check for a short to ground on diagnostic test terminal wire between ALDL diagnostic terminal "B" and ECM terminal. If circuit is okay, replace ECM. *See Figs. 10-12*.

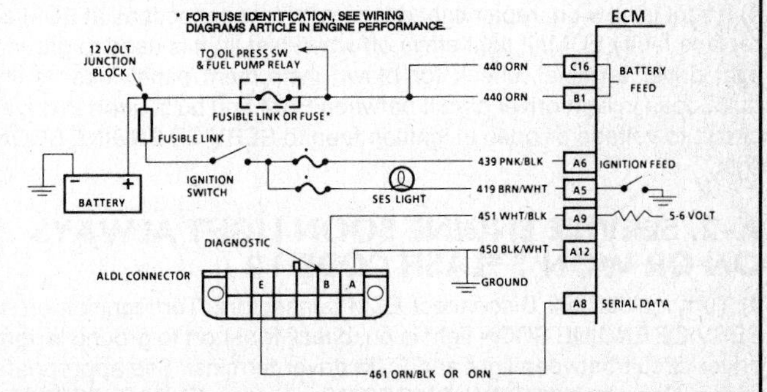

* FOR FUSE IDENTIFICATION, SEE WIRING DIAGRAMS ARTICLE IN ENGINE PERFORMANCE.
ECM
12 VOLT JUNCTION BLOCK
TO OIL PRESS SW & FUEL PUMP RELAY
440 ORN
C16
BATTERY FEED
440 ORN
B1
FUSIBLE LINK OR FUSE*
FUSIBLE LINK
439 PNK/BLK
A6
IGNITION FEED
IGNITION SWITCH
419 BRN/WHT
A5
BATTERY
SES LIGHT
451 WHT/BLK
A9
5-6 VOLT
DIAGNOSTIC
450 BLK/WHT
A12
ALDL CONNECTOR
E
B
A
GROUND
A8
SERIAL DATA
461 ORN/BLK OR ORN

91J13606 Courtesy of General Motors Corp.

Fig. 10: Fuel Injection Diagnostic Circuit Schematic (Except 4.3L Turbo & Models with 4L80-E Transmission)

1991 ENGINE PERFORMANCE
Basic Diagnostic Procedures (Cont.)

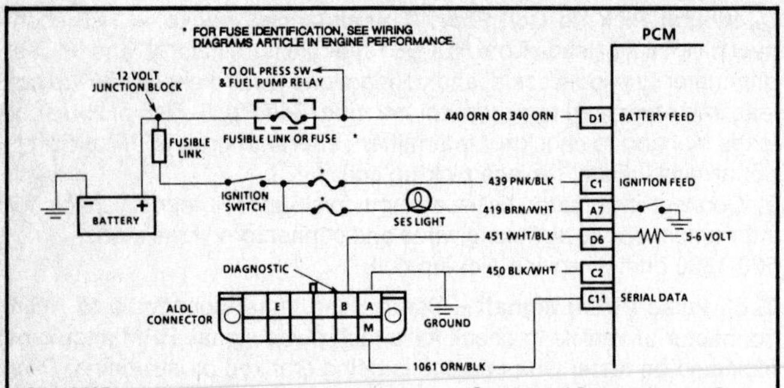
* FOR FUSE IDENTIFICATION, SEE WIRING DIAGRAMS ARTICLE IN ENGINE PERFORMANCE.
PCM
12 VOLT JUNCTION BLOCK
TO OIL PRESS SW & FUEL PUMP RELAY
440 ORN OR 340 ORN
D1
BATTERY FEED
FUSIBLE LINK
FUSIBLE LINK OR FUSE *
BATTERY
IGNITION SWITCH
439 PNK/BLK
C1
IGNITION FEED
SES LIGHT
419 BRN/WHT
A7
451 WHT/BLK
D6
5-6 VOLT
DIAGNOSTIC
450 BLK/WHT
C2
ALDL CONNECTOR
C11
SERIAL DATA
GROUND
1061 ORN/BLK

91A13607 Courtesy of General Motors Corp.

Fig. 11: Fuel Injection Diagnostic Circuit Schematic (Models with 4L80-E Transmission)

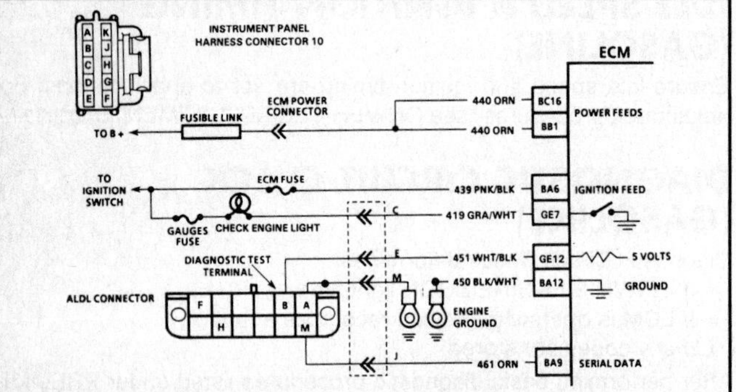
INSTRUMENT PANEL HARNESS CONNECTOR 10
ECM
ECM POWER CONNECTOR
FUSIBLE LINK
TO B+
440 ORN
BC16
440 ORN
BB1
POWER FEEDS
TO IGNITION SWITCH
ECM FUSE
439 PNK/BLK
BA6
IGNITION FEED
419 GRA/WHT
GE7
GAUGES FUSE
CHECK ENGINE LIGHT
DIAGNOSTIC TEST TERMINAL
451 WHT/BLK
GE12
5 VOLTS
450 BLK/WHT
BA12
GROUND
ALDL CONNECTOR
ENGINE GROUND
461 ORN
BA9
SERIAL DATA

91F13610 Courtesy of General Motors Corp.

Fig. 12: Fuel Injection Diagnostic Circuit Schematic (4.3L Turbo PFI)

A-1, SERVICE ENGINE SOON LIGHT INOPERATIVE

1) If SERVICE ENGINE SOON light does not illuminate with ignition on and engine off, attempt to start engine. If engine starts, go to step **3)**. If engine does not start, check fusible links at battery. Also check ECM fuse. If fusible links or ECM fuse are blown, repair short to ground.

2) If fusible links and ECM fuse are okay, turn ignition on, and check power circuits to ECM, including keep-alive memory and ignition feed. See appropriate wiring diagram in WIRING DIAGRAMS article in ENGINE PERFORMANCE for power terminal identification. If power is not available to power terminals of ECM, check for opens in power circuits. If power is available to ECM power terminals, check for poor ECM ground circuits. If circuits are okay, replace faulty ECM.

3) If engine starts and SERVICE ENGINE SOON light does not illuminate, turn ignition off. Disconnect ECM connectors. Turn ignition on, and jumper ECM SERVICE ENGINE SOON light driver terminal to ground using a test light. See appropriate wiring diagram in WIRING DIAGRAMS article in ENGINE PERFORMANCE for power terminal identification.

4) If light is now on, repair light driver terminal connections at ECM or replace faulty ECM. If light stays off when test light is used to ground light driver terminal, check for blown instrument panel fuse, faulty bulb, open in light driver circuit between ECM and bulb, short in driver circuit to voltage or open in ignition feed to SERVICE ENGINE SOON light.

A-2, SERVICE ENGINE SOON LIGHT ALWAYS ON OR WON'T FLASH CODE 12

1) Turn ignition off. Disconnect ECM connectors. Turn ignition on. If SERVICE ENGINE SOON light is on, check for short to ground in light driver circuit between light and ECM driver terminal. See appropriate wiring diagram in WIRING DIAGRAMS article in ENGINE PERFORMANCE for terminal identification.

2) If light is off with ECM connectors disconnected, turn ignition off. Reconnect ECM connectors. Turn ignition on with engine off. Using a DVOM, check voltage at ALDL diagnostic "test" terminal "B". *See Figs. 10-12.* If voltage is greater than 9 volts, check for a short to voltage on ALDL terminal "B" wire between ECM and ALDL connector.

3) If voltage is less than 5 volts, use DVOM to backprobe appropriate ECM terminal. See appropriate wiring diagram in WIRING DIAGRAMS article in ENGINE PERFORMANCE for terminal identification. If 5-6 volts is now present, repair open or short in wire between ECM and ALDL terminal "B". If voltage is 5-6 volts, go to step **4)**.

4) If voltage at terminal "B" of ALDL connector is 5-6 volts, jumper wire terminal at ECM to ground. If SERVICE ENGINE SOON light now flashes a Code 12 and ALDL terminal "A" was used when previously grounding terminal "B", check terminal "A" for open circuit.

5) If SERVICE ENGINE SOON light does not flash when ECM end of terminal "B" wire is jumpered to ground, check PROM/MEM-CAL for proper installation. If PROM/MEM-CAL is installed correctly, replace ECM. Install original PROM/MEM-CAL into replacement ECM. Repeat diagnostic circuit check. If Code 12 still does not flash, replace PROM/MEM-CAL. Replace PROM/MEM-CAL only after replacing ECM, as PROM/MEM-CAL is probably not at fault.

DIAGNOSTIC CIRCUIT CHECK (DIESEL)

NOTE: The 6.2L model with light duty emissions is equipped with a self-diagnostic system. For information on diagnostic circuit check and retrieving codes, see SELF-DIAGNOSTICS – DIESEL article.

DIAGNOSTIC PROCEDURE

Preliminary Inspection – 1) Check all vacuum hoses for incorrect routing, restrictions, cuts or other damage. Inspect hoses beneath air cleaner assembly and other engine components.

2) Inspect all wires in engine compartment for correct and good connections. Also check wires for pinched or chaffed spots, as well as contact with sharp edges or exhaust manifolds.

3) Perform preliminary inspection CAREFULLY and THOROUGHLY. A thorough inspection often leads to fixing a problem without further diagnosis.

Diagnostic Procedure – 1) Ensure all engine systems not related to Diesel Electronic Control (DEC) system are operating properly. DO NOT proceed with testing unless all problems not related to DEC system have been repaired. DEC system diagnosis should always begin with DIAGNOSTIC CIRCUIT CHECK chart in SELF-DIAGNOSTICS – DIESEL article. Performing this check determines whether DEC system and ECM are working properly.

2) If trouble codes (other than Code 12) are displayed, determine whether codes are "hard" or "intermittent" trouble codes. A hard code remains until code-setting condition is repaired. Hard codes cause SERVICE ENGINE SOON light to come on.

3) An intermittent code does not reset itself and is not present when vehicle is repaired. An intermittent code is often caused by loose connections. SERVICE ENGINE SOON light goes out 10 seconds after fault goes away.

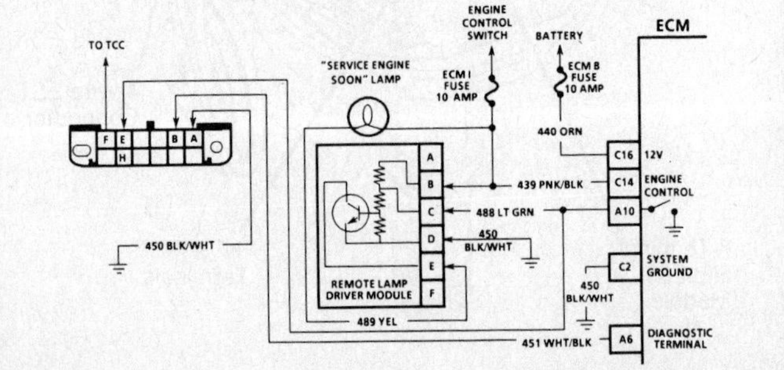
ENGINE CONTROL SWITCH
BATTERY
ECM
TO TCC
"SERVICE ENGINE SOON" LAMP
ECM I FUSE 10 AMP
ECM B FUSE 10 AMP
440 ORN
C16
12V
439 PNK/BLK
C14
ENGINE CONTROL
488 LT GRN
A10
450 BLK/WHT
450 BLK/WHT
C2
SYSTEM GROUND
REMOTE LAMP DRIVER MODULE
450 BLK/WHT
489 YEL
451 WHT/BLK
A6
DIAGNOSTIC TERMINAL

91B13608 Courtesy of General Motors Corp.

Fig. 13: Typical Diesel Fuel Injection Diagnostic Circuit Schematic

SUMMARY

If no faults were found while performing BASIC DIAGNOSTIC PROCEDURES, proceed to SELF-DIAGNOSTICS article. If no hard codes are found in self-diagnostics, or vehicle does not have a self-diagnostic system, proceed to TROUBLE SHOOTING - NO CODES article for diagnosis by symptom (i.e., ROUGH IDLE, NO START, etc.) or intermittent diagnostic procedures.

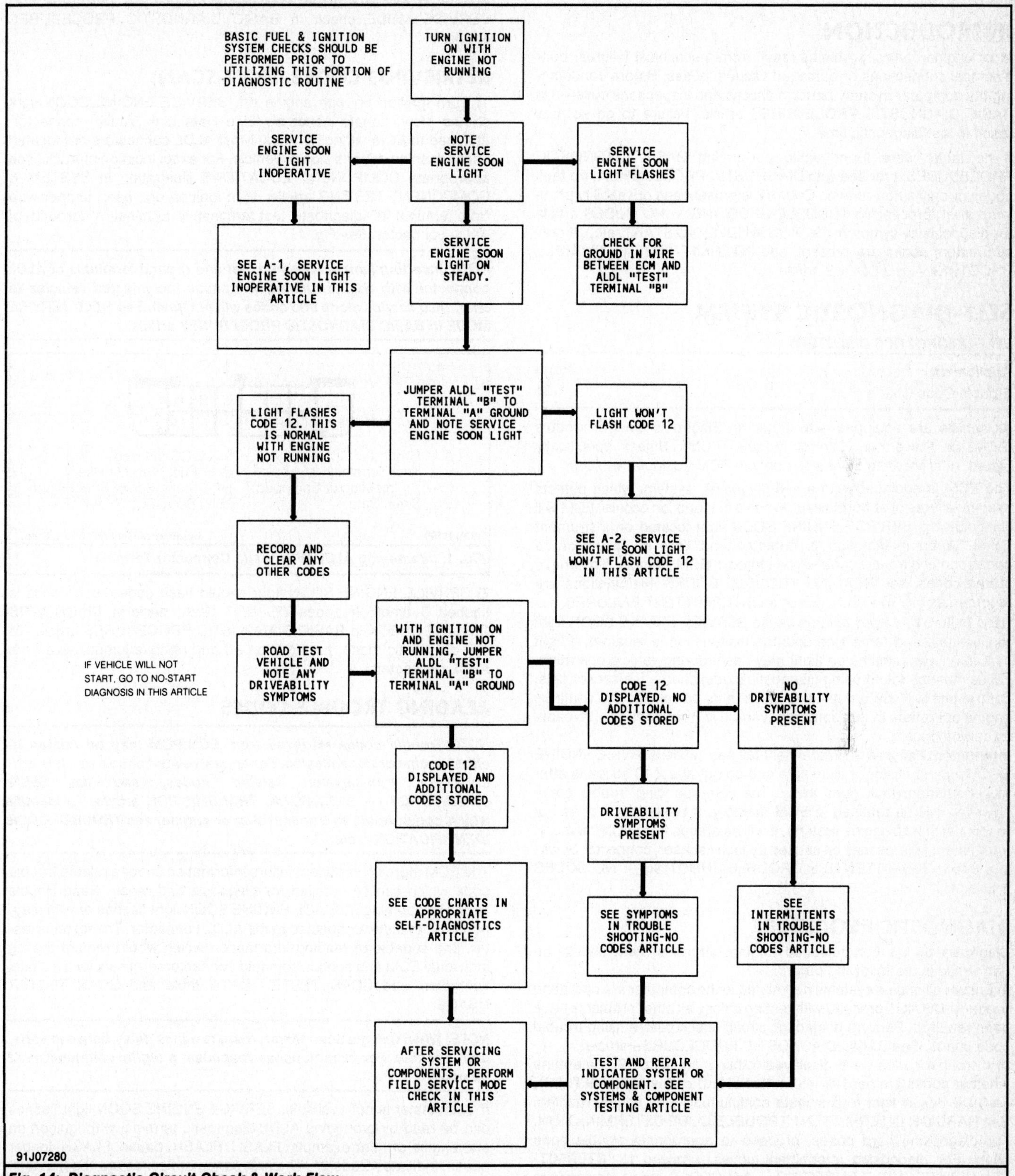
BASIC FUEL & IGNITION SYSTEM CHECKS SHOULD BE PERFORMED PRIOR TO UTILIZING THIS PORTION OF DIAGNOSTIC ROUTINE
TURN IGNITION ON WITH ENGINE NOT RUNNING
SERVICE ENGINE SOON LIGHT INOPERATIVE
NOTE SERVICE ENGINE SOON LIGHT
SERVICE ENGINE SOON LIGHT FLASHES
SEE A-1, SERVICE ENGINE SOON LIGHT INOPERATIVE IN THIS ARTICLE
SERVICE ENGINE SOON LIGHT ON STEADY.
CHECK FOR GROUND IN WIRE BETWEEN ECM AND ALDL "TEST" TERMINAL "B"
LIGHT FLASHES CODE 12. THIS IS NORMAL WITH ENGINE NOT RUNNING
JUMPER ALDL "TEST" TERMINAL "B" TO TERMINAL "A" GROUND AND NOTE SERVICE ENGINE SOON LIGHT
LIGHT WON'T FLASH CODE 12
SEE A-2, SERVICE ENGINE SOON LIGHT WON'T FLASH CODE 12 IN THIS ARTICLE
RECORD AND CLEAR ANY OTHER CODES
IF VEHICLE WILL NOT START, GO TO NO-START DIAGNOSIS IN THIS ARTICLE
ROAD TEST VEHICLE AND NOTE ANY DRIVEABILITY SYMPTOMS
WITH IGNITION ON AND ENGINE NOT RUNNING, JUMPER ALDL "TEST" TERMINAL "B" TO TERMINAL "A" GROUND
CODE 12 DISPLAYED. NO ADDITIONAL CODES STORED
NO DRIVEABILITY SYMPTOMS PRESENT
CODE 12 DISPLAYED AND ADDITIONAL CODES STORED
DRIVEABILITY SYMPTOMS PRESENT
SEE CODE CHARTS IN APPROPRIATE SELF-DIAGNOSTICS ARTICLE
SEE SYMPTOMS IN TROUBLE SHOOTING-NO CODES ARTICLE
SEE INTERMITTENTS IN TROUBLE SHOOTING-NO CODES ARTICLE
AFTER SERVICING SYSTEM OR COMPONENTS, PERFORM FIELD SERVICE MODE CHECK IN THIS ARTICLE
TEST AND REPAIR INDICATED SYSTEM OR COMPONENT. SEE SYSTEMS & COMPONENT TESTING ARTICLE
91J07280

Fig. 14: Diagnostic Circuit Check & Work Flow

1991 ENGINE PERFORMANCE
Self-Diagnostics – Gasoline

Astro, Blazer, Bravada, Jimmy, Lumina APV, Safari, Sierra, Silhouette, Sonoma, Syclone, Trans Sport, "C" & "K" Series, "G" Series, "P" Series, "R" & "V" Series, "S" & "T" Series

INTRODUCTION

Most engine control problems result from mechanical failures, poor electrical connections or damaged vacuum hoses. Before condemning the computer system, perform checks and inspections covered in BASIC DIAGNOSTIC PROCEDURES article. Failure to do so may result in lost diagnostic time.

If no faults were found while performing BASIC DIAGNOSTIC PROCEDURES, proceed with DIAGNOSTIC PROCEDURE. If no fault codes or only a non-running Code 12 is present and driveability problems exist, proceed to TROUBLE SHOOTING - NO CODES article for diagnosis by symptom (i.e. ROUGH IDLE, NO START, etc.). If only intermittent codes are present, see INTERMITTENTS in TROUBLE SHOOTING - NO CODES article.

SELF-DIAGNOSTIC SYSTEM

SELF-DIAGNOSTICS DIRECTORY

All vehicle are equipped with either an Electronic Control Module (ECM) or Powertrain Control Module (PCM). Unless specifically stated, references to ECM also apply to PCM equipped vehicles.

The ECM is equipped with a self-diagnostic system, which detects system failures or abnormalities. When a malfunction occurs, ECM will illuminate the SERVICE ENGINE SOON light located on instrument panel. When malfunction is detected and light is turned on, a corresponding trouble code will be stored in ECM memory. To retrieve stored codes, see READING TROUBLE CODES. Malfunctions are recorded as HARD FAILURES or as INTERMITTENT FAILURES.

Hard Failures - Hard failures cause SERVICE ENGINE SOON light to illuminate and remain on until the malfunction is repaired. If light comes on and remains on (light may flash) during vehicle operation, cause must be found using diagnostic (code) charts. If a sensor fails, control unit will use a substitute value in its calculations to continue engine operation. In this condition, vehicle is functional, but driveability can be poor.

Intermittent Failures - Intermittent failures cause SERVICE ENGINE SOON light to flicker or illuminate and go out about 10 seconds after the intermittent fault goes away. The corresponding trouble code; however, will be retained in ECM memory. If related fault does not reoccur within 50 engine restarts, it will be erased from ECM memory. Intermittent failures may be caused by faulty sensor, connector or wiring. See INTERMITTENTS in TROUBLE SHOOTING - NO CODES article.

DIAGNOSTIC PROCEDURE

Diagnosis of the computerized engine control system should be performed in the following order:

1) Ensure all engine systems not related to the computer are operating properly. DO NOT proceed with testing unless all other problems have been repaired. Perform diagnostic circuit check before using trouble code charts. See BASIC DIAGNOSTIC PROCEDURES article.

2) If trouble codes were displayed (other than Code 12), determine whether codes are hard or intermittent. Hard codes cause SERVICE ENGINE SOON light to illuminate continuously with engine running. See HARD OR INTERMITTENT TROUBLE CODE DETERMINATION. For diagnosing hard codes, proceed to appropriate trouble code chart. For diagnosing intermittent codes, proceed to INTERMITTENTS in TROUBLE SHOOTING - NO CODES article. Exceptions are Code 13, 15, 24, 44 and 45 charts, which can help diagnose intermittent codes.

3) If trouble codes were not displayed and a driveability problem exists, refer to SYMPTOMS in TROUBLE SHOOTING - NO CODES article. From there you will be sent to the appropriate area in SYSTEM & COMPONENT TESTING article.

4) After repairs are made, clear trouble codes and perform FIELD SERVICE MODE check in BASIC DIAGNOSTIC PROCEDURES article.

RETRIEVING CODES (NON-SCAN)

1) Turn ignition on with engine off. SERVICE ENGINE SOON light should glow. Locate Assembly Line Data Link (ALDL) connector, attached to ECM wiring harness. Most ALDL connectors are located under dash on driver's side of vehicle. For exact location of ALDL, see appropriate COMPONENT LOCATIONS illustration in SYSTEM & COMPONENT TESTING article. Turn ignition on. Insert jumper wire from terminal "B" (diagnostic test terminal) to terminal "A" (ground) of ALDL connector. *See Fig. 1.*

NOTE: Inserting jumper wire into test and ground terminals of ALDL connector with engine running will cause fuel-injected vehicles to enter field service mode and codes will not flash. See FIELD SERVICE MODE in BASIC DIAGNOSTIC PROCEDURES article.

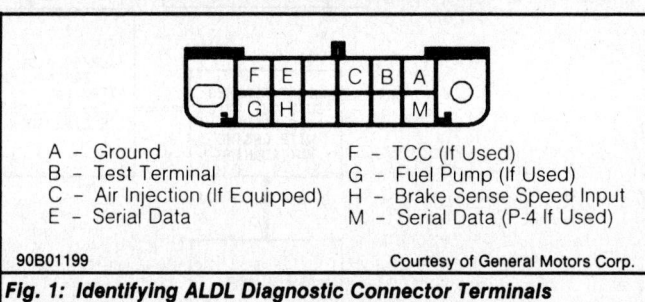

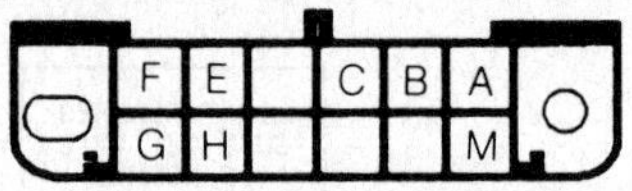
F
E
C
B
A
G
H
M
A - Ground
B - Test Terminal
C - Air Injection (If Equipped)
E - Serial Data
F - TCC (If Used)
G - Fuel Pump (If Used)
H - Brake Sense Speed Input
M - Serial Data (P-4 If Used)
90B01199
Courtesy of General Motors Corp.

Fig. 1: Identifying ALDL Diagnostic Connector Terminals

2) SERVICE ENGINE SOON light should flash codes. Each code is flashed 3 times. If codes DO NOT flash, perform DIAGNOSTIC CIRCUIT CHECK in BASIC DIAGNOSTIC PROCEDURES article. To exit diagnostic mode, turn ignition off and remove jumper wire from ALDL connector.

READING TROUBLE CODES

NOTE: Trouble codes retrieved from ECM/PCM may be related to either engine or transmission. For engine related codes, use this article. For transmission related codes, see the SELF-DIAGNOSTICS — ELECTRONIC TRANSMISSION article. To identify which codes relate to transmission or engine, see TROUBLE CODE IDENTIFICATION table.

The ECM stores component failure information under a related trouble code which can be recalled for diagnosis and repair. Read trouble codes by counting SERVICE ENGINE SOON light flashes or with diagnostic Scan tester connected to the ALDL connector. The tester is faster, and capable of reading information which would require testing individual ECM and sensor/solenoid connector terminals with a digital voltmeter. See SCAN TESTER DATA table and SCAN TESTER USAGE.

NOTE: When using a Scan tester, there is a time delay between serial data updates. For instantaneous response, a digital voltmeter must be used.

If Scan tester is not available, SERVICE ENGINE SOON light flashes can be read by grounding ALDL diagnostic terminal with ignition on and engine off. For example, FLASH, FLASH, pause, FLASH, longer pause, indicates Code 21. The first series of flashes are the first digit of trouble code. The second series of flashes are the second digit of trouble code. Trouble codes are displayed starting with the lowest code. Each code is displayed 3 times and will continue as long as ALDL is grounded.

NOTE: Trouble codes will be recorded at various operating times. Some codes require sensor or switch operation for 5 seconds and others may require longer under certain conditions. Some codes may not set in a service bay operational mode.

TROUBLE CODE IDENTIFICATION

Code	Probable Cause
12 [1]	No Engine Speed Sensor Reference Pulse To PCM/TCM
13 [1]	Open Oxygen Sensor Circuit
14 [1]	CTS Voltage Low (Sensor Or Signal Line Grounded)
15 [1]	CTS Voltage High (Sensor, Connections, Or Wires Open)
21 [1]	TPS Voltage High (Open Circuit Or Misadjusted TPS)
22 [1]	TPS Voltage Low (Circuit Grounded)
23 [1]	Intake Air Temperature Sensor Voltage High
24 [1]	Vehicle Speed Sensor Circuit Open Or Grounded
25 [1]	Intake Air Temperature Sensor Voltage Low
28	Pressure Switch Manifold Range Circuit Open Or Shorted
31 [1]	Turbocharger Wastegate Overboost
32 [1]	EGR Error (Improper Vacuum Signal)
33 [1]	MAP Voltage High (Circuit Open Or Short To Voltage)
34 [1]	MAP Voltage Low (Circuit Open Or Short To Ground)
35 [1]	IAC System Fault
39	TCC Stuck Off (Faulty TCC Solenoid)
42 [1]	EST Circuit Fault
43 [1]	ESC Fault
44 [1]	Lean Exhaust Indicated
45 [1]	Rich Exhaust Indicated
51 [1]	Improperly Installed/Faulty PROM/MEM-CAL
52 [1]	Fuel CAL-PAC Missing
53 [1]	System Voltage High (Charging System Problem)
54 [1]	Fuel Pump Circuit Voltage Low
55 [1]	Faulty ECM
58	TTS High Temperature (Sensor Or Signal Line Grounded)
59	TTS Low Temperature (Sensor, Connections, Or Wires Open)
68	Overdrive Ratio Error (Engine Rpm Greater Than Input Speed)
73	Force Motor Commanded Amperage Differs From Return
75	System Voltage Low (Charging System Problem)
81	QDM Solenoid "B" Monitored Voltage Differs From Commanded
82	QDM Solenoid "A" Monitored Voltage Differs From Commanded
83	QDM TCC Monitored Voltage Differs From Commanded
85	Undefined Gear Ratio (Input Or Output Sensor Failure)
86	Shift Solenoid "B" Stuck On (Commanded Gear Not Engaged)
87	Shift Solenoid "B" Stuck Off (Commanded Gear Not Engaged)

[1] — Engine code. For transmission code diagnosis, see SELF-DIAGNOSTICS — ELECTRONIC TRANSMISSION article.

NOTE: Trouble code charts should only be used if SERVICE ENGINE SOON light is illuminated (indicating a current problem exists). Exceptions are Code 13, 15, 24, 44 and 45 charts, which may be used to help diagnose intermittent codes. Anytime Codes 51, 52 or 55 are displayed with another code, start with 50-series code first and proceed to low profile numbered codes.

HARD OR INTERMITTENT TROUBLE CODE DETERMINATION

During any diagnostic procedure, determine if codes are due to hard or intermittent failure. Diagnostic charts will not usually help diagnose intermittent codes. To determine hard codes and intermittent codes, proceed as follows:

1) MANUALLY enter diagnostic mode. Read and record all stored trouble codes. Exit diagnostic mode and clear trouble codes. See CLEARING TROUBLE CODES.

2) Apply parking brake and place transmission in Neutral or Park. Block drive wheels and start engine. SERVICE ENGINE SOON light should go out. Run warm engine at specified curb idle for 2 minutes and note SERVICE ENGINE SOON light.

3) If SERVICE ENGINE SOON light comes on, manually enter diagnostic mode. Read and record trouble codes. This reveals hard failure codes. Codes 13, 15, 24, 44, 45 and 55 may require a road test to reset hard failure after trouble codes were cleared.

4) If SERVICE ENGINE SOON light does not come on, all stored trouble codes were intermittent failures. Exceptions are noted under DIAGNOSTIC PROCEDURE.

CLEARING TROUBLE CODES

Turn ignition switch to ON position and ground diagnostic test terminal "B" at ALDL connector. Turn ignition switch to OFF position and remove ECM fuse from fuse block for 10 seconds. Replace fuse. Remove diagnostic terminal ground lead.

ECM LOCATION

For ECM locations, see appropriate COMPONENT LOCATIONS illustration in SYSTEM & COMPONENT TESTING article.

DIAGNOSTIC MATERIALS

Diagnostic Aids – Diagnostic aids (located in many trouble code charts) are provided as additional tips to help with diagnosis when inspected circuit is okay.

Field Service Mode Check – SERVICE ENGINE SOON light indicates operational mode of engine if ALDL is grounded while engine is running. Light response confirms proper fuel system operation and verifies closed loop operation. Clear codes and perform this test after any repair is completed. Field service mode check can be found by proceeding to FIELD SERVICE MODE CHECK in BASIC DIAGNOSTIC PROCEDURES article.

SPECIAL TOOLS (DIAGNOSTIC)

NOTE: A special Scan tester, plugged into the ALDL, can read trouble codes, check system voltages on the serial data line and save a great deal of time. For additional information, see tester owner's manual. Also, see SCAN TESTER USAGE and SCAN DATA.

The computerized engine control system is most easily diagnosed using a Scan tester. However, other tools may aid in diagnosing problems if a Scan tester is unavailable. These tools are a tachometer, test light, ohmmeter, digital voltmeter with 10-megohm input impedance (minimum), vacuum pump, vacuum gauge, fuel injector test lights and 6 jumper wires 6" long (one wire with female connectors at both ends, one wire with male connector at both ends and 4 wires with male and female connectors at opposite ends). A test light, rather than a voltmeter, must be used when indicated by a diagnostic chart.

SCAN TESTER USAGE

NOTE: Before connecting Scan tester, check diagnostic system and ensure accurate information is received by Scan tester. Perform DIAGNOSTIC CIRCUIT CHECK in BASIC DIAGNOSTIC PROCEDURES article. If vehicle does not pass diagnostic circuit check, information received by Scan tester may be invalid.

The Scan tester is a specialized tester which can diagnose on-board computer control systems by providing almost instant access to circuit voltage information without crawling under dash or hood to back-probe sensors and connectors. Scan testers reduce diagnostic time by furnishing input data (voltage signals) which can be compared to specification parameters. See SCAN TESTER DATA table.

Scan testers also furnish information on output device (solenoids and motors) status. However, status parameters are only an indication output signals have been sent to devices by the ECM. They do not indicate whether devices respond properly to that signal. This must be verified at output device using a voltmeter or test light.

NOTE: Code 12 should always exist when ALDL is grounded with key on and engine off, but it may not be indicated by all makes of Scan tester.

1991 ENGINE PERFORMANCE
Self-Diagnostics – Gasoline (Cont.)

If trouble codes are not present, a problem may still exist. Driveability-related problems with codes displayed occur about 20 percent of the time, while driveability problems without codes occur about 80 percent of the time. Out-of-calibration sensors WILL NOT set a trouble code, but WILL cause driveability problems. A Scan tester is the easiest method of checking sensor specifications and other data parameters. Tester is also useful in finding intermittent wiring problems by wiggling wiring harnesses and connections (key on, engine off) while observing data parameters. See SCAN TESTER DATA table.

NOTE: Information obtained by Scan tester is only as accurate as the tester itself. If erroneous voltage signals are suspected, verify tester information using a digital voltmeter and wiring schematic. If non-existent codes are displayed, turn ignition off and remove tester. Turn ignition on and ground ALDL test terminal. If same codes are not flashed by SERVICE ENGINE SOON light as were indicated by Scan tester, tester cannot be used on vehicle and information obtained by it will not be guaranteed accurate.

SCAN DATA

NOTE: Information contained in the following table is typical of readings taken on vehicle with engine idling, upper radiator hose hot, throttle closed, transmission in Park or Neutral, closed loop status achieved and all accessories off (except as noted in tables). Data parameters are updated every 1 1/2 seconds. Not all devices and systems are used on all models. For additional information, see tester owner's manual.

SCAN TESTER DATA

Tester Position	Units Measured	Nominal Data Value
A/C Clutch	On/Off	Off (On With A/C)
A/C Request	Yes/No	No/Yes (With Request)
Battery Voltage	Volts	13.5-14.5
Block Learn	Counts	118-138 (128 Normal)
Clear Flood	On/Off	***See Tester Manual***
Coolant Temp.	°C	85-105° (Norm. Temperature)
Crank RPM	RPM	100-900
Cross Counts	Counts	0-255

SCAN TESTER DATA (Cont.)

Tester Position	Units Measured	Nominal Data Value
Desired RPM	RPM	ECM Desired RPM
EGR Duty Cycle	0-100%	0/Closed-100/Fully Open
IAC	Counts	0-50
Injector Pulse Width	Mil./Sec	.8-3.0
INT (Integrator)	Counts	110-145 (128 Normal)
Knock Retard (ESC)	Counts	0-255
Knock Signal	Yes/No	Yes When Knock Exists
MAT	°C	10-90°
MAP	Volts	1 (idle) To 4.5 (WOT)
Open/Closed Loop Status	Ol/Cl	Closed/Open During Extended Idle
O_2 Sensor	Millivolts	100 (Lean) To 999 (Rich)
P/N Switch	P/N/RDL	Park/Neutral
P/S Switch	Norm/Hi	Normal
PROM I.D.	PROM #	Original Factory Number
RPM	RPM	Spec. ±25 RPM Drive (A/T) Spec. ±50 RPM Neut. (M/T)
TCC	On/Off	Off (On With Command)
TPS	Volts	1.25 (Idle) To 5.0 (WOT)
Throttle Angle	0-100%	0 (Idle) To 100 (WOT)
Trouble Codes	Code #	No codes
Upshift Light (Man. Trans.)	On/Off	Off
VSS Or MPH	MPH	0-Actual
4th Gear Switch	On/Off	On/4th Gear

SUMMARY

If hard fault codes are not present and driveability symptoms or intermittent codes exist, proceed to TROUBLE SHOOTING – NO CODES article for diagnosis by symptom (i.e. ROUGH IDLE, NO START, etc.), or intermittent diagnostic procedures.

NOTE: The following diagnostic flow charts and mini-schematics are supplied courtesy of General Motors Corp.

TROUBLE CODE CHARTS

CODE 13, OPEN OXYGEN SENSOR CIRCUIT (EXCEPT 4.3L TURBO)

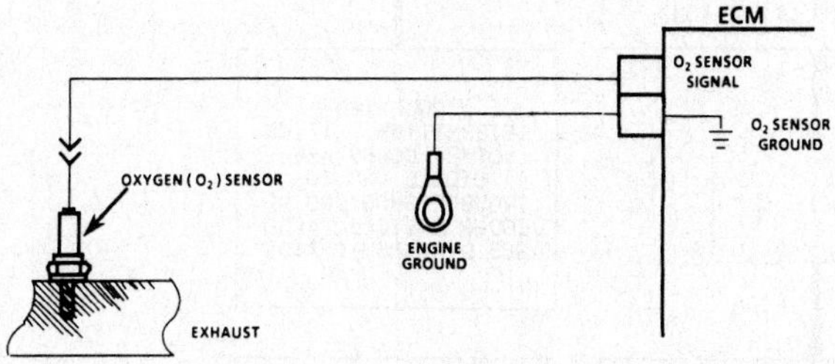

ECM
O_2 SENSOR SIGNAL
O_2 SENSOR GROUND
OXYGEN (O_2) SENSOR
ENGINE GROUND
EXHAUST

CODE 13 ECM TERMINAL & CIRCUIT WIRING IDENTIFICATION

Application	ECM Terminal	Wire Color
All With 4L80-E Transmission		
Oxygen Sensor Signal	C14	Purple
Oxygen Sensor Ground	C13	Tan
All Others		
Oxygen Sensor Signal	D7	Purple
Oxygen Sensor Ground	D6	Tan

When exhaust temperature is less than 600°F (316°C), the O_2 sensor is open and produces no voltage. An open sensor circuit or cold sensor will not all system to entire closed loop.

NOTE: Test numbers refer to test numbers on diagnostic chart.

1) Code 13 will set at normal operating temperature if at least 2 minutes have passed since engine start, Code 21 or 22 is not present, O_2 signal voltage is steady at .35-.55 volt and throttle position sensor signal is greater than idle. All conditions must be met for at least 1 minute.
2) This determines if fault is in O_2 sensor, ECM or wiring.
3) Use only a high-impedance Digital Volt-Ohmmeter (DVOM) while checking for continuity in signal and ground circuits. If ground circuit is open, voltage on signal circuit will be greater than .6 volt.

DIAGNOSTIC AIDS

Verify a clean, tight connection for ground circuit No. 413. An open circuit at sensor signal terminal or ground terminal will result in a Code 13.

1 RUN ENGINE TO OPERATING TEMPERATURE. INCREASE RPM AND HOLD FOR 2 MINUTES. VERIFY CLOSED LOOP OPERATION WHILE IN FIELD SERVICE MODE. CLOSED LOOP OPERATION?

- YES → CODE IS INTERMITTENT. IF NO OTHER CODES ARE STORED, GO TO TROUBLE SHOOTING-NO CODES ARTICLE. ALSO SEE DIAGNOSTIC AIDS
- NO ↓

2 DISCONNECT OXYGEN SENSOR AND JUMPER ECM SIDE OF HARNESS CONNECTOR TO GROUND. SCAN TESTER SHOULD DISPLAY LESS THAN .3 VOLT. DOES IT? SEE NOTE.

NOTE: IF SCAN TESTER IS NOT AVAILABLE, BACKPROBE OXYGEN SENSOR SIGNAL TERMINAL AT ECM WITH A 10-MEGOHM DVOM

- YES → FAULTY OXYGEN SENSOR OR SENSOR CONNECTION
- NO ↓

3 TURN IGNITION OFF. DISCONNECT JUMPER. TURN IGNITION ON WITH ENGINE OFF. USING A DVOM, CHECK VOLTAGE ON OXYGEN SENSOR HARNESS CONNECTOR FROM ECM.

- LESS THAN .3 VOLT → OPEN SENSOR SIGNAL LINE OR FAULTY ECM CONNECTION OR FAULTY ECM
- GREATER THAN .6 VOLT → OPEN SENSOR GROUND OR FAULTY ECM CONNECTION OR FAULTY ECM
- .3-.6 VOLT → FAULTY ECM

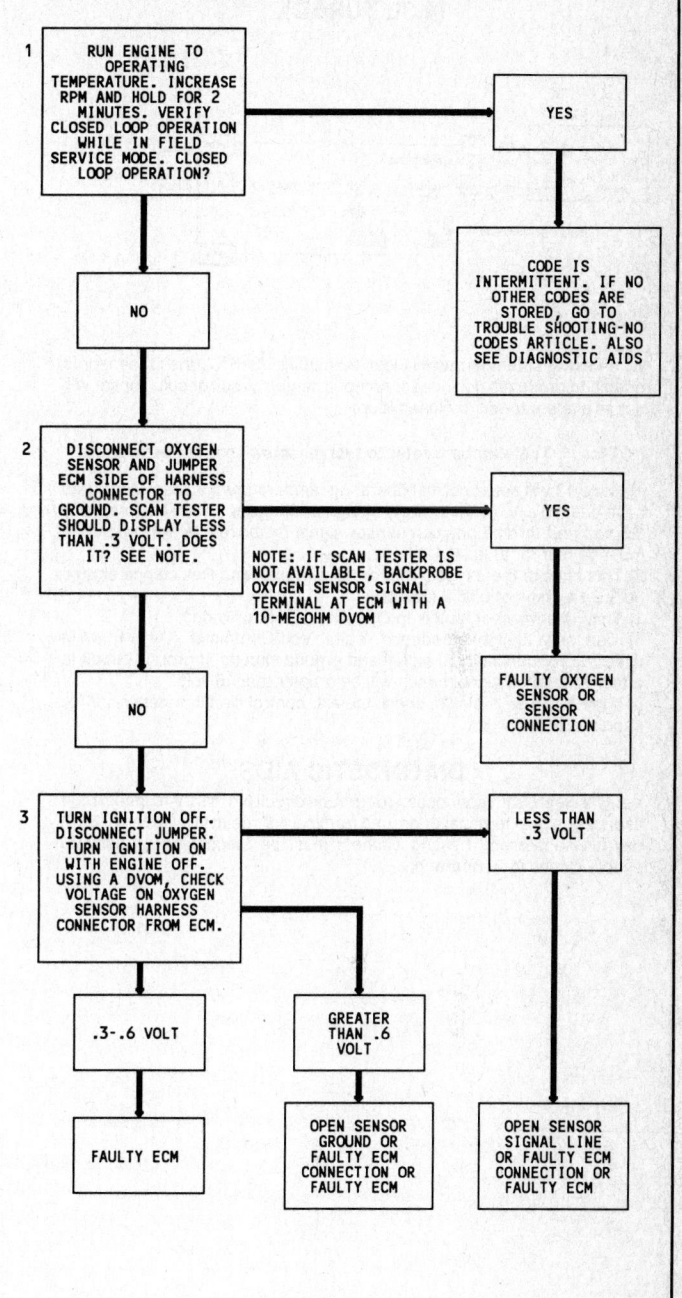

91H07378 91B07281

1991 ENGINE PERFORMANCE
Self-Diagnostics – Gasoline (Cont.)

CODE 13, OPEN OXYGEN SENSOR CIRCUIT (4.3L TURBO)

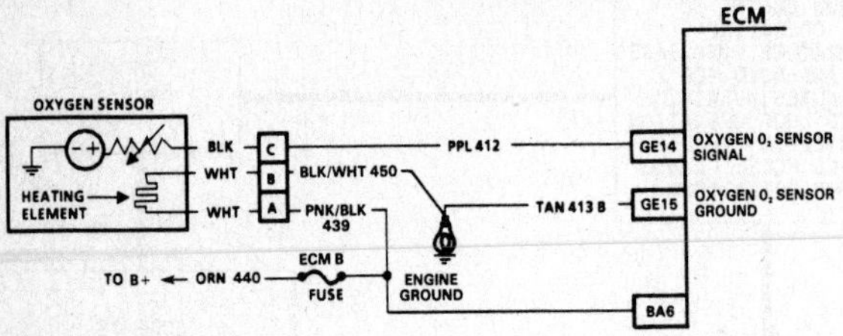
ECM
OXYGEN SENSOR
HEATING ELEMENT
BLK
WHT
WHT
C
B
A
PPL 412
BLK/WHT 450
PNK/BLK 439
TAN 413 B
GE14
OXYGEN O₂ SENSOR SIGNAL
GE15
OXYGEN O₂ SENSOR GROUND
ECM B
FUSE
TO B+
ORN 440
ENGINE GROUND
BA6

When exhaust temperature is less than 600°F (316°C), the O_2 sensor is open and produces no voltage. An open sensor circuit or cold sensor will not all system to entire closed loop.

NOTE: Test numbers refer to test numbers on diagnostic chart.

1) Code 13 will set at normal operating temperature if at least 2 minutes have passed since engine start, O_2 signal voltage is steady between .35-.55 volt and throttle position sensor signal is above idle. All conditions must be met for at least 1 minute.
2) This checks the oxygen sensor heating element. Resistance should be 3.5-14 ohms at 662°F (350°C).
3) This determines if fault is in O_2 sensor, ECM or wiring.
4) Use only a high-impedance Digital Volt-Ohmmeter (DVOM) while checking for continuity in signal and ground circuits. If ground circuit is open, voltage on signal circuit will be greater than .6 volt.
5) If the A/C fuse is blown, check the A/C control circuit or generator for short circuits.

DIAGNOSTIC AIDS

Verify a clean, tight connection for ground circuit No. 413. An open circuit at sensor signal terminal or ground terminal will result in a Code 13. Both oxygen sensor and heating element must be functioning properly to enable closed loop operation.

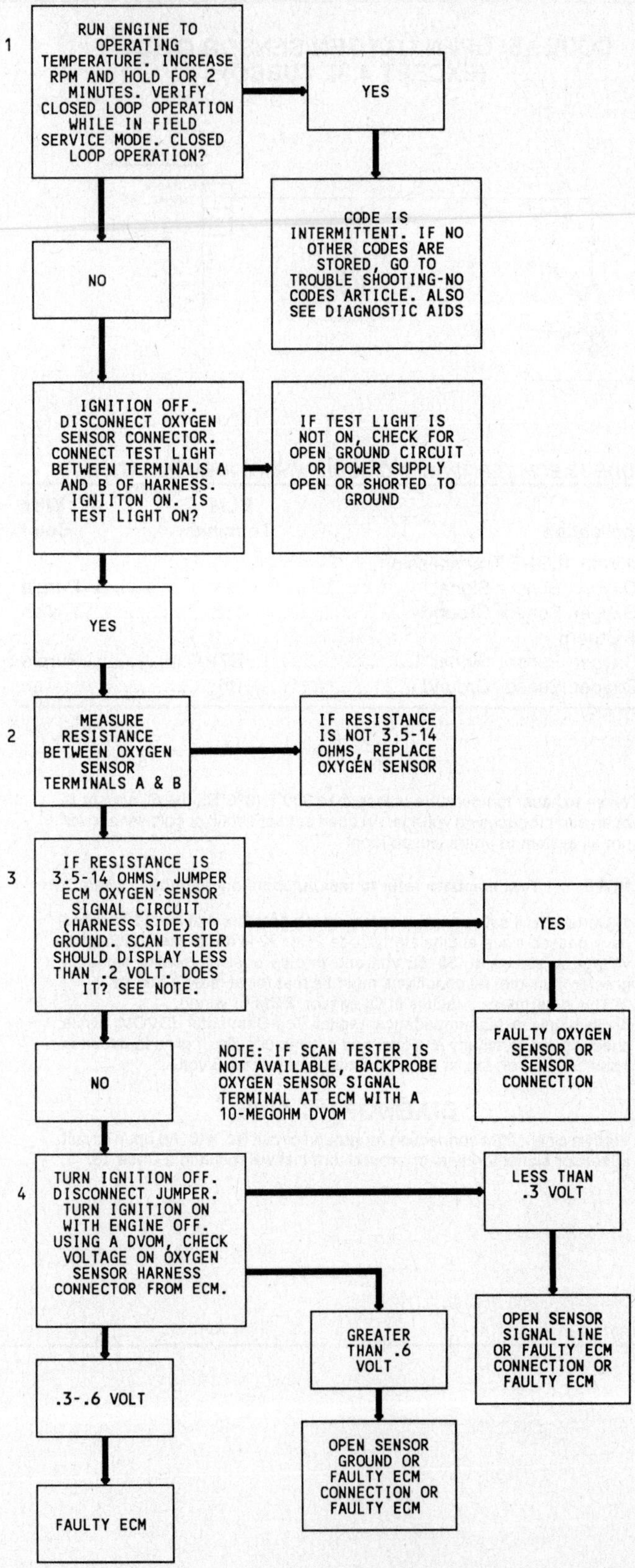
1
RUN ENGINE TO OPERATING TEMPERATURE. INCREASE RPM AND HOLD FOR 2 MINUTES. VERIFY CLOSED LOOP OPERATION WHILE IN FIELD SERVICE MODE. CLOSED LOOP OPERATION?
YES
CODE IS INTERMITTENT. IF NO OTHER CODES ARE STORED, GO TO TROUBLE SHOOTING-NO CODES ARTICLE. ALSO SEE DIAGNOSTIC AIDS
NO
IGNITION OFF. DISCONNECT OXYGEN SENSOR CONNECTOR. CONNECT TEST LIGHT BETWEEN TERMINALS A AND B OF HARNESS. IGNIITON ON. IS TEST LIGHT ON?
IF TEST LIGHT IS NOT ON, CHECK FOR OPEN GROUND CIRCUIT OR POWER SUPPLY OPEN OR SHORTED TO GROUND
YES
2
MEASURE RESISTANCE BETWEEN OXYGEN SENSOR TERMINALS A & B
IF RESISTANCE IS NOT 3.5-14 OHMS, REPLACE OXYGEN SENSOR
3
IF RESISTANCE IS 3.5-14 OHMS, JUMPER ECM OXYGEN SENSOR SIGNAL CIRCUIT (HARNESS SIDE) TO GROUND. SCAN TESTER SHOULD DISPLAY LESS THAN .2 VOLT. DOES IT? SEE NOTE.
YES
FAULTY OXYGEN SENSOR OR SENSOR CONNECTION
NO
NOTE: IF SCAN TESTER IS NOT AVAILABLE, BACKPROBE OXYGEN SENSOR SIGNAL TERMINAL AT ECM WITH A 10-MEGOHM DVOM
4
TURN IGNITION OFF. DISCONNECT JUMPER. TURN IGNITION ON WITH ENGINE OFF. USING A DVOM, CHECK VOLTAGE ON OXYGEN SENSOR HARNESS CONNECTOR FROM ECM.
LESS THAN .3 VOLT
OPEN SENSOR SIGNAL LINE OR FAULTY ECM CONNECTION OR FAULTY ECM
GREATER THAN .6 VOLT
OPEN SENSOR GROUND OR FAULTY ECM CONNECTION OR FAULTY ECM
.3-.6 VOLT
FAULTY ECM

91E13734 91G13710

CODE 14, COOLANT SENSOR SIGNAL VOLTAGE LOW

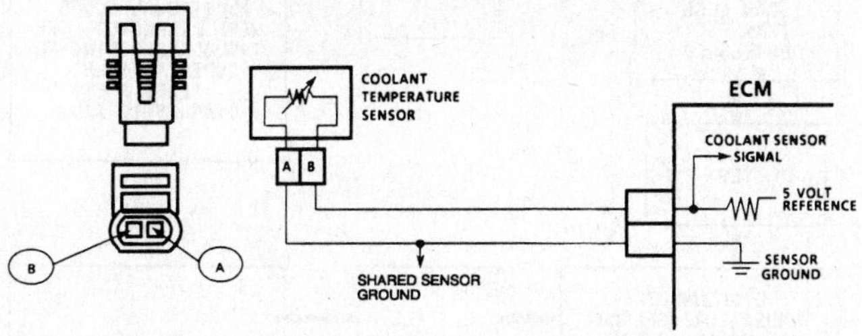

COOLANT TEMPERATURE SENSOR
A
B
ECM
COOLANT SENSOR SIGNAL
5 VOLT REFERENCE
SENSOR GROUND
SHARED SENSOR GROUND

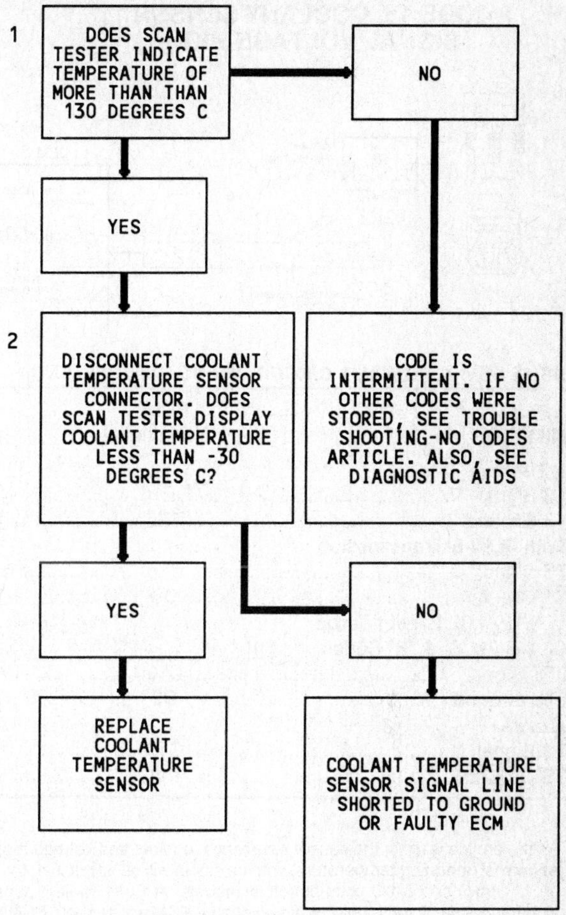

1
DOES SCAN TESTER INDICATE TEMPERATURE OF MORE THAN THAN 130 DEGREES C
NO
YES
2
DISCONNECT COOLANT TEMPERATURE SENSOR CONNECTOR. DOES SCAN TESTER DISPLAY COOLANT TEMPERATURE LESS THAN -30 DEGREES C?
CODE IS INTERMITTENT. IF NO OTHER CODES WERE STORED, SEE TROUBLE SHOOTING-NO CODES ARTICLE. ALSO, SEE DIAGNOSTIC AIDS
YES
NO
REPLACE COOLANT TEMPERATURE SENSOR
COOLANT TEMPERATURE SENSOR SIGNAL LINE SHORTED TO GROUND OR FAULTY ECM

CODE 14 ECM TERMINAL & CIRCUIT WIRING IDENTIFICATION

Application	ECM Terminal	Wire Color
4.3L Turbo		
CTS Signal	GE16	Yellow
CTS Ground	BB6	Black
All With 4L80-E Transmission		
CTS Signal	D16	Yellow
CTS Ground	D3	Black
2.8L, 3.1L, 4.3L Except Turbo, 5.0L & 5.7L "C" & "K" Series		
CTS Signal	C10	Yellow
CTS Ground	D2	Black
All Others		
CTS Signal	C10	Yellow
CTS Ground	A11	Black

The ECM uses coolant temperature sensor inputs in determining control of fuel delivery, engine timing (EST), idle (IAC) and converter clutch (TCC). As the engine warms, the sensor resistance reduces. At normal operating temperature, voltage signal will be about .5-1.1 volts (4.3L Turbo) or 1.5-2.0 volts (all other models) at ECM coolant sensor signal terminal.

NOTE: Test numbers refer to test numbers on diagnostic chart.

1) This tests if code was set because of a hard failure or intermittent condition. Code 14 sets if signal voltage indicates a coolant temperature greater than 275°F (135°C) for more than 3 seconds on 4.3L Turbo or 6 seconds on all other models.

2) This simulates conditions for a Code 15. If the ECM recognizes the open circuit by displaying a low temperature, the ECM and wiring are not at fault.

DIAGNOSTIC AIDS

After the engine is started, the temperature should rise steadily to about 194°F (90°C), then stabilize when thermostat opens. If the engine is allowed to cool overnight, the coolant temperature sensor and MAT sensor (if equipped) should read close to each other, when measured with a Scan tester.

TEMPERATURE-TO-RESISTANCE VALUES [1] [2]

°F (°C)	Ohms
210 (100)	185
160 (70)	450
100 (38)	1800
70 (20)	3400
40 (4)	7500
20 (–7)	13,500
0 (–18)	25,000
–40 (–40)	100,700

[1] – Measure resistance across sensor terminals.
[2] – Temperatures are approximates.

91J07379 91D07282

1991 ENGINE PERFORMANCE
Self-Diagnostics – Gasoline (Cont.)

CODE 15, COOLANT SENSOR SIGNAL VOLTAGE HIGH

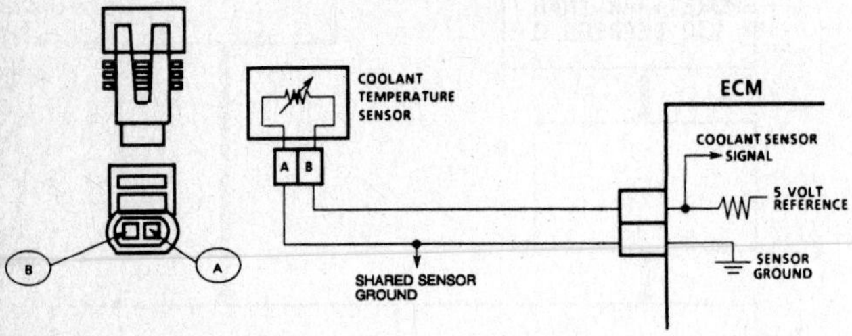
COOLANT TEMPERATURE SENSOR
A
B
ECM
COOLANT SENSOR SIGNAL
5 VOLT REFERENCE
SENSOR GROUND
SHARED SENSOR GROUND
B
A

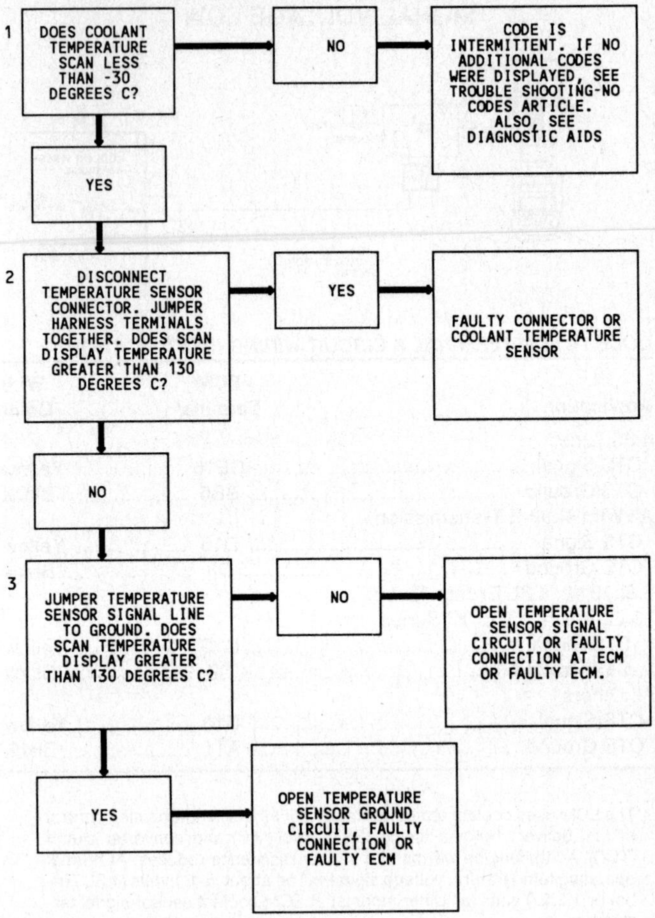
1
DOES COOLANT TEMPERATURE SCAN LESS THAN -30 DEGREES C?
NO
CODE IS INTERMITTENT. IF NO ADDITIONAL CODES WERE DISPLAYED, SEE TROUBLE SHOOTING-NO CODES ARTICLE. ALSO, SEE DIAGNOSTIC AIDS
YES
2
DISCONNECT TEMPERATURE SENSOR CONNECTOR. JUMPER HARNESS TERMINALS TOGETHER. DOES SCAN DISPLAY TEMPERATURE GREATER THAN 130 DEGREES C?
YES
FAULTY CONNECTOR OR COOLANT TEMPERATURE SENSOR
NO
3
JUMPER TEMPERATURE SENSOR SIGNAL LINE TO GROUND. DOES SCAN TEMPERATURE DISPLAY GREATER THAN 130 DEGREES C?
NO
OPEN TEMPERATURE SENSOR SIGNAL CIRCUIT OR FAULTY CONNECTION AT ECM OR FAULTY ECM.
YES
OPEN TEMPERATURE SENSOR GROUND CIRCUIT, FAULTY CONNECTION OR FAULTY ECM

CODE 15 ECM TERMINAL & CIRCUIT WIRING IDENTIFICATION

Application	ECM Terminal	Wire Color
4.3L Turbo		
CTS Signal	GE16	Yellow
CTS Ground	BB6	Black
All With 4L80-E Transmission		
CTS Signal	D16	Yellow
CTS Ground	D3	Black
2.8L, 3.1L, 4.3L Except Turbo, 5.0L & 5.7L "C" & "K" Series		
CTS Signal	C10	Yellow
CTS Ground	D2	Black
All Others		
CTS Signal	C10	Yellow
CTS Ground	A11	Black

As the engine warms, the sensor resistance reduces and voltage drops. At normal operating temperature, voltage signal will be about .5-1.1 volts (4.3L Turbo) or 1.5-2.0 volts (all other models) at ECM coolant sensor signal terminal. If sensor signal circuit opens, ECM will see -40°F (-40°C) and deliver fuel for this temperature.

NOTE: Test numbers refer to test numbers on diagnostic chart.

1) This checks if code was set as a result of a hard failure or intermittent condition. Code 15 will set if engine is running for more 50 seconds and signal voltage indicates a coolant temperature less than -22°F (-30°C) for more than 30 seconds.
2) This simulates conditions for a Code 14. If the ECM recognizes the grounded circuit and displays a high temperature, the ECM and wiring are okay.
3) This determines if problem is ECM or wiring. There should be 5 volts present at sensor when measured with a DVOM.

DIAGNOSTIC AIDS

After engine starts, temperature should rise steadily to about 194°F (90°C) and stabilize when thermostat opens. If the engine is allowed to cool overnight, the coolant temperature sensor and MAT sensor (if equipped) should read close to each other when measured with a Scan tester. Code 15 will also set if sensor signal or ground circuit is open.

TEMPERATURE-TO-RESISTANCE VALUES [1] [2]

°F (°C)	Ohms
210 (100)	185
160 (70)	450
100 (38)	1800
70 (20)	3400
40 (4)	7500
20 (–7)	13,500
0 (–18)	25,000
–40 (–40)	100,700

1 – Measure resistance across sensor terminals.
2 – Temperatures are approximates.

91J07379 91F07283

CODE 21, TPS SIGNAL VOLTAGE HIGH

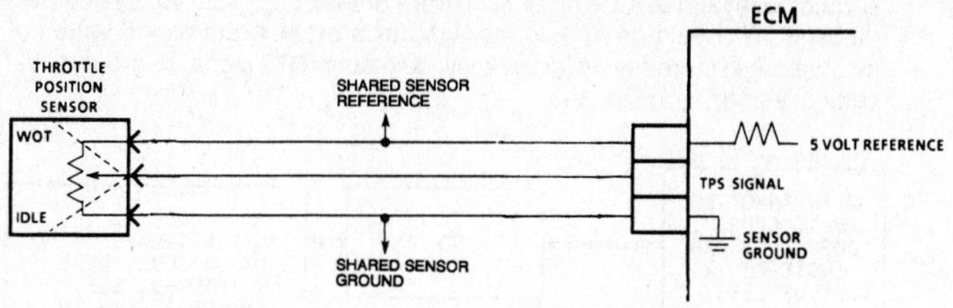
ECM
THROTTLE
POSITION
SENSOR
SHARED SENSOR
REFERENCE
WOT
IDLE
5 VOLT REFERENCE
TPS SIGNAL
SENSOR
GROUND
SHARED SENSOR
GROUND

CODE 21 ECM TERMINAL & CIRCUIT WIRING IDENTIFICATION

Application	ECM Terminal	Wire Color
4.3L Turbo		
TPS Signal	GF13	Dark Blue
TPS Ground	BB5	Black
TPS Reference	BA5	Gray
All With 4L80-E Transmission		
TPS Signal	C5	Dark Blue
TPS Ground	D3	Black
TPS Reference	C4	Gray
2.8L, 3.1L, 4.3L Except Turbo, 5.0L & 5.7L "C" & "K" Series		
TPS Signal	C13	Dark Blue
TPS Ground	D2	Black
TPS Reference	C14	Gray
All Others		
TPS Signal	C13	Dark Blue
TPS Ground	A11	Black
TPS Reference	C14	Gray

The Throttle Position Sensor (TPS) provides a varying voltage signal depending on throttle valve angle. Signal voltage varies from about .50 volt at idle to 4.5 volts at wide open throttle. On models with non-adjustable TPS, each time TPS voltage drops to less than 1.25 volts and stops, ECM assumes this is zero degrees throttle angle and measures throttle percentage angle from this point.

NOTE: **Test numbers refer to test numbers on diagnostic chart.**

1) This test confirms Code 21 and checks if fault is a hard failure or an intermittent condition. Code 21 will set if TPS voltage is greater than 2.5 volts 2-10 seconds with engine running. On 2.8L, Code 21 may set if MAP sensor signal less than 2 volts.

2) This test simulates conditions for Code 22. If the ECM recognizes the low voltage signal and sets Code 22, the ECM and power and signal circuits are not at fault.

3) This step isolates a faulty sensor, ECM or an open ground circuit.

DIAGNOSTIC AIDS

A Scan tester displays throttle position in volts. Closed throttle voltage should be less than 1.0 volt (4.3L Turbo) or less than 1.25 volts (all other models). TPS voltage should increase at a steady rate to 4.5 volts as throttle angle increases. Code 21 will also result if ground circuit is open or TPS signal circuit is shorted to voltage.

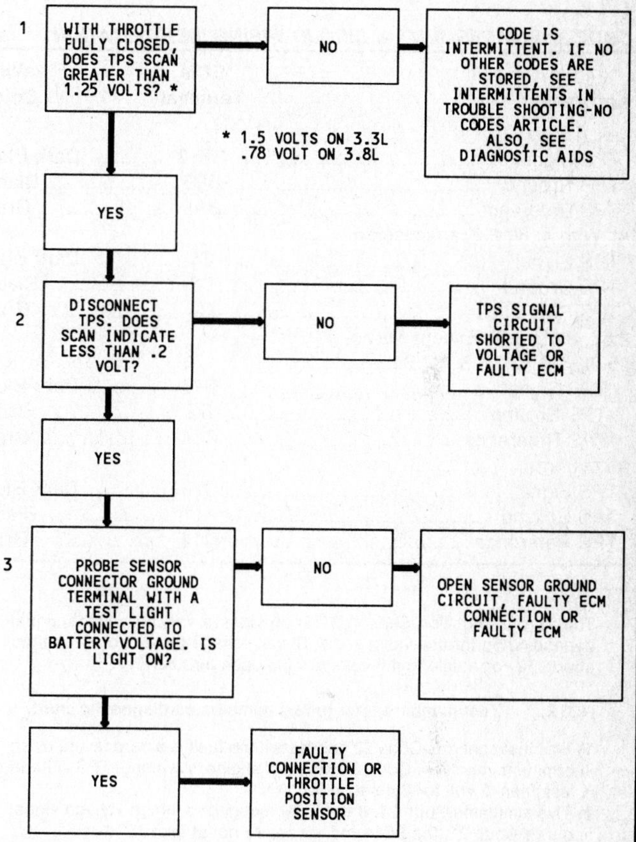
1
WITH THROTTLE FULLY CLOSED, DOES TPS SCAN GREATER THAN 1.25 VOLTS? *
NO
CODE IS INTERMITTENT. IF NO OTHER CODES ARE STORED, SEE INTERMITTENTS IN TROUBLE SHOOTING-NO CODES ARTICLE. ALSO, SEE DIAGNOSTIC AIDS
* 1.5 VOLTS ON 3.3L .78 VOLT ON 3.8L
YES
2
DISCONNECT TPS. DOES SCAN INDICATE LESS THAN .2 VOLT?
NO
TPS SIGNAL CIRCUIT SHORTED TO VOLTAGE OR FAULTY ECM
YES
3
PROBE SENSOR CONNECTOR GROUND TERMINAL WITH A TEST LIGHT CONNECTED TO BATTERY VOLTAGE. IS LIGHT ON?
NO
OPEN SENSOR GROUND CIRCUIT, FAULTY ECM CONNECTION OR FAULTY ECM
YES
FAULTY CONNECTION OR THROTTLE POSITION SENSOR

91C07385 91E07287

1991 ENGINE PERFORMANCE
Self-Diagnostics – Gasoline (Cont.)

CODE 22, TPS SIGNAL VOLTAGE LOW

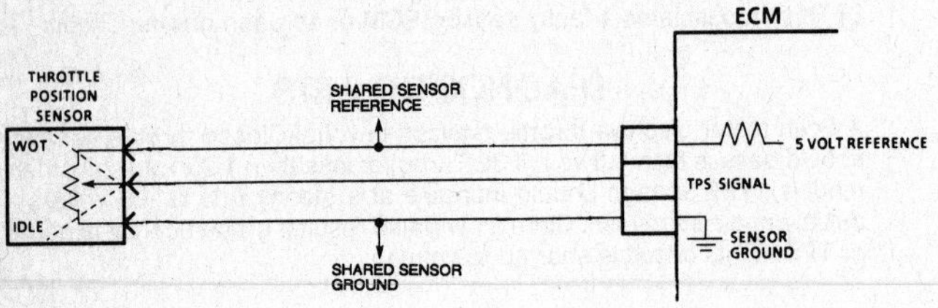
ECM
THROTTLE POSITION SENSOR
SHARED SENSOR REFERENCE
WOT
IDLE
5 VOLT REFERENCE
TPS SIGNAL
SENSOR GROUND
SHARED SENSOR GROUND

CODE 22 ECM TERMINAL & CIRCUIT WIRING IDENTIFICATION

Application	ECM Terminal	Wire Color
4.3L Turbo		
TPS Signal	GF13	Dark Blue
TPS Ground	BB5	Black
TPS Reference	BA5	Gray
All With 4L80-E Transmission		
TPS Signal	C5	Dark Blue
TPS Ground	D3	Black
TPS Reference	C4	Gray
2.8L, 3.1L, 4.3L Except Turbo, 5.0L & 5.7L "C" & "K" Series		
TPS Signal	C13	Dark Blue
TPS Ground	D2	Black
TPS Reference	C14	Gray
All Others		
TPS Signal	C13	Dark Blue
TPS Ground	A11	Black
TPS Reference	C14	Gray

The Throttle Position Sensor (TPS) provides a varying voltage signal depending on throttle valve angle. Signal voltage varies from less than about .50 volt at idle to 4.5 volts at wide open throttle.

NOTE: Test numbers refer to test numbers on diagnostic chart.

1) This test confirms Code 22 and tests if the fault is a hard failure or an intermittent condition. Code 22 will set if engine is running, TPS voltage is less than .2 volt for 2-4 seconds.
2) This simulates Code 21. If the ECM recognizes a high voltage signal and sets Code 21, the ECM and wiring are not at fault.
3) On 2.8L, check and adjust TPS. On all others, replace TPS.
4) This simulates a high voltage signal to check for on open TPS signal circuit.

DIAGNOSTIC AIDS

A Scan tester displays throttle position in volts. Closed throttle voltage should be less than 1.0 volt (4.3L Turbo) or less than 1.25 volts (all other models). TPS voltage should increase at a steady rate to 4.5 volts as throttle angle increases. Code 22 will also set if TPS signal or ground circuits are open or grounded.

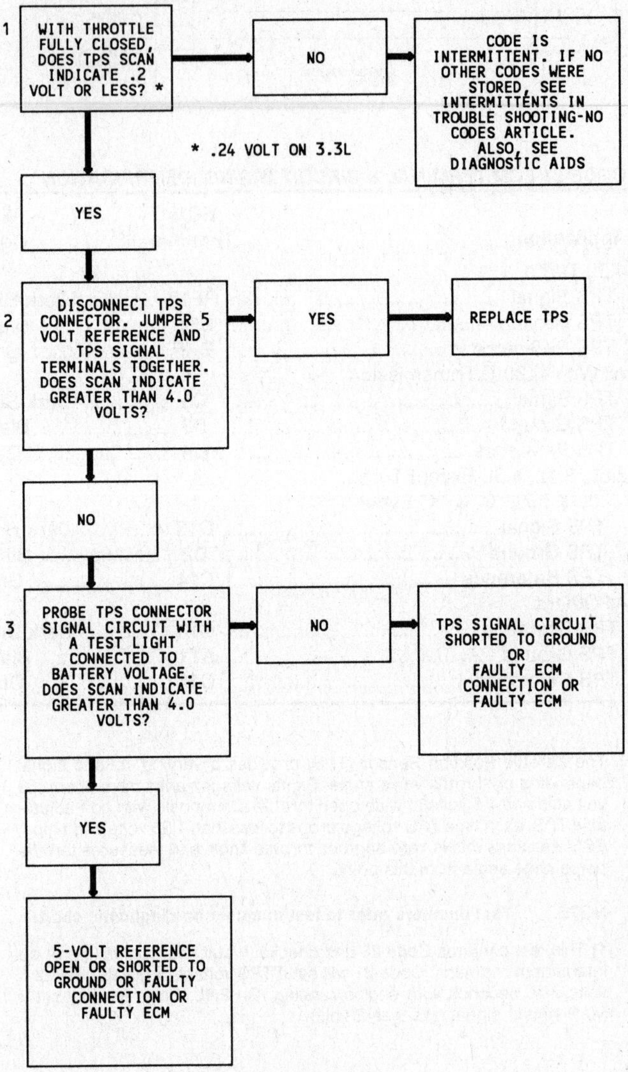
1
WITH THROTTLE FULLY CLOSED, DOES TPS SCAN INDICATE .2 VOLT OR LESS? *
NO
CODE IS INTERMITTENT. IF NO OTHER CODES WERE STORED, SEE INTERMITTENTS IN TROUBLE SHOOTING-NO CODES ARTICLE. ALSO, SEE DIAGNOSTIC AIDS
* .24 VOLT ON 3.3L
YES
2
DISCONNECT TPS CONNECTOR. JUMPER 5 VOLT REFERENCE AND TPS SIGNAL TERMINALS TOGETHER. DOES SCAN INDICATE GREATER THAN 4.0 VOLTS?
YES
REPLACE TPS
NO
3
PROBE TPS CONNECTOR SIGNAL CIRCUIT WITH A TEST LIGHT CONNECTED TO BATTERY VOLTAGE. DOES SCAN INDICATE GREATER THAN 4.0 VOLTS?
NO
TPS SIGNAL CIRCUIT SHORTED TO GROUND OR FAULTY ECM CONNECTION OR FAULTY ECM
YES
5-VOLT REFERENCE OPEN OR SHORTED TO GROUND OR FAULTY CONNECTION OR FAULTY ECM

91C07385 91G07288

CODE 23, MAT SENSOR TEMP. LOW (2.5L & 4.3L TURBO)

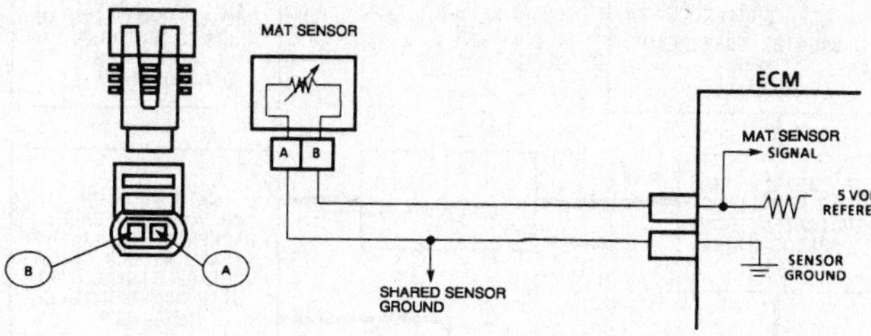

MAT SENSOR
A
B
ECM
MAT SENSOR SIGNAL
5 VOLT REFERENCE
SENSOR GROUND
SHARED SENSOR GROUND
B
A

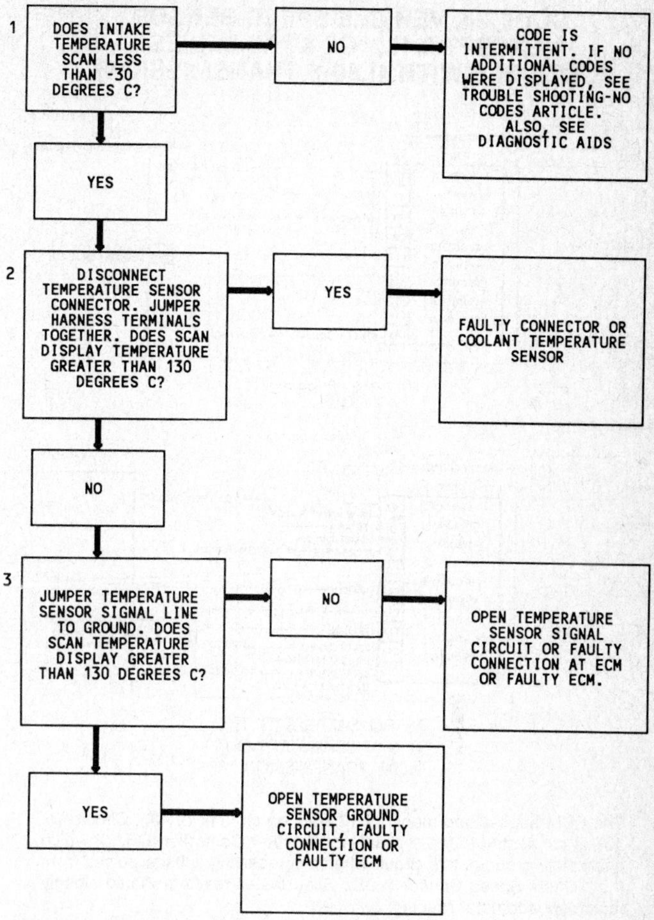

1
DOES INTAKE TEMPERATURE SCAN LESS THAN -30 DEGREES C?
NO
CODE IS INTERMITTENT. IF NO ADDITIONAL CODES WERE DISPLAYED, SEE TROUBLE SHOOTING-NO CODES ARTICLE. ALSO, SEE DIAGNOSTIC AIDS
YES
2
DISCONNECT TEMPERATURE SENSOR CONNECTOR. JUMPER HARNESS TERMINALS TOGETHER. DOES SCAN DISPLAY TEMPERATURE GREATER THAN 130 DEGREES C?
YES
FAULTY CONNECTOR OR COOLANT TEMPERATURE SENSOR
NO
3
JUMPER TEMPERATURE SENSOR SIGNAL LINE TO GROUND. DOES SCAN TEMPERATURE DISPLAY GREATER THAN 130 DEGREES C?
NO
OPEN TEMPERATURE SENSOR SIGNAL CIRCUIT OR FAULTY CONNECTION AT ECM OR FAULTY ECM.
YES
OPEN TEMPERATURE SENSOR GROUND CIRCUIT, FAULTY CONNECTION OR FAULTY ECM

CODE 23 ECM TERMINAL & CIRCUIT WIRING IDENTIFICATION

Application	ECM Terminal	Wire Color
2.5L		
Signal	C12	Tan
MAT Ground	D2	Black/Red
4.3L Turbo		
Signal	GF16	Tan
MAT Ground	BB5	Black

The ECM supplies and monitors a voltage signal (4-6 volts) to the sensor. When temperatures are low, sensor resistance is high and the ECM will see a high-monitored voltage signal. As temperature increases, sensor resistance decreases and voltage sensed by the ECM drops.

NOTE: Test numbers refer to test numbers on diagnostic chart.

1) This checks if Code 23 is a hard failure or an intermittent condition. Code 23 will set if engine is running for one minute, MAT sensor temperature is less than -22°F (-30°C) for 12 seconds and speed sensor signal is not present.
2) This simulates conditions for a Code 25. If the Scan tester displays a high temperature, the ECM and wiring are not at fault.
3) This checks for continuity of sensor signal and ground circuits.

DIAGNOSTIC AIDS

If the engine is allowed to cool overnight, the coolant and MAT sensors should read close to each other, when measured with a Scan tester. A Code 23 will also result if signal and ground circuits become open.

TEMPERATURE-TO-RESISTANCE VALUES [1] [2]

°F (°C)	Ohms
210 (100)	185
160 (70)	450
100 (38)	1800
70 (20)	3400
40 (4)	7500
20 (–7)	13,500
0 (–18)	25,000
–40 (–40)	100,700

[1] – Measure resistance across sensor terminals.
[2] – Temperatures are approximates.

91E07386 91I07289

1991 ENGINE PERFORMANCE
Self-Diagnostics – Gasoline (Cont.)

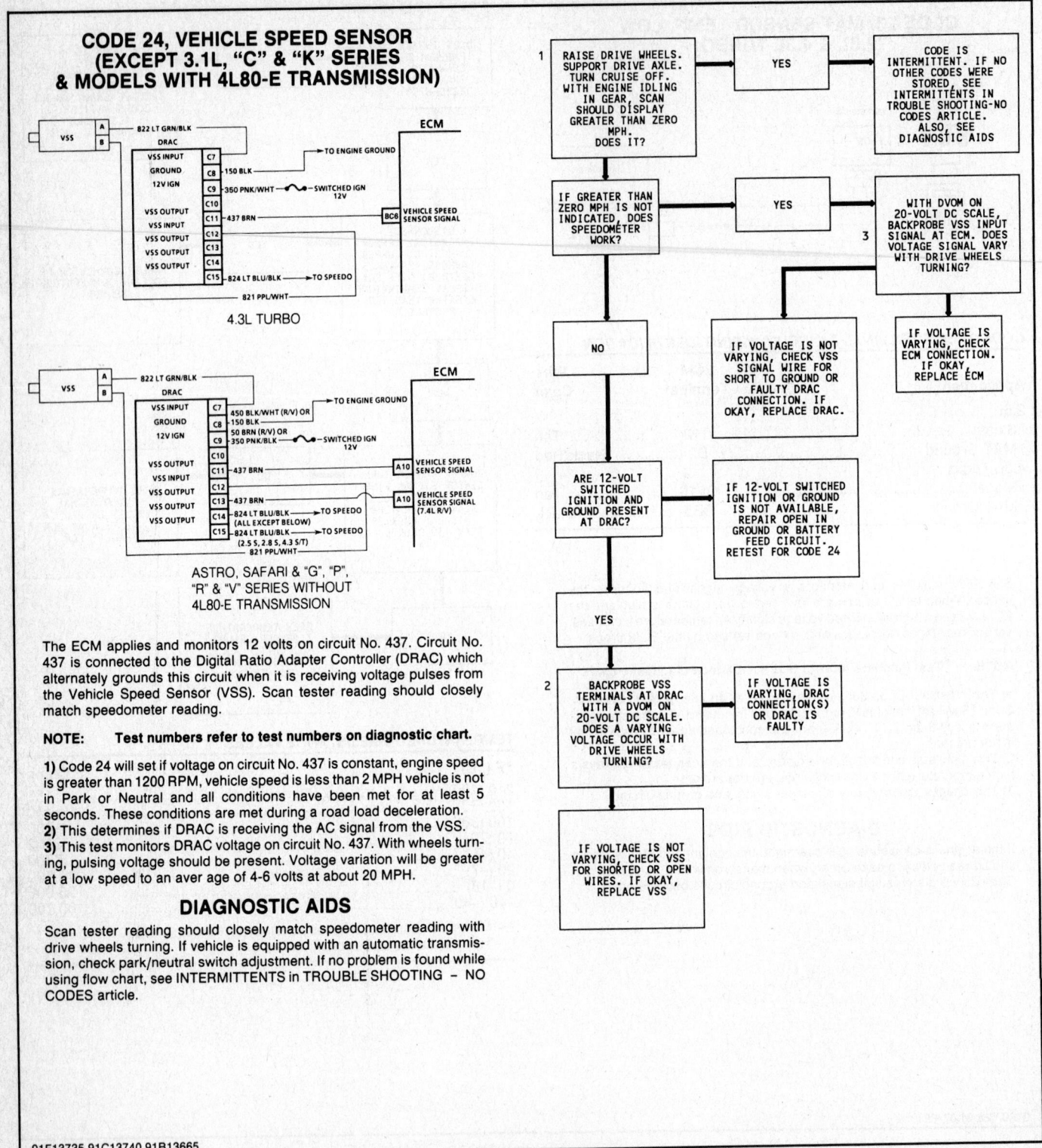

CODE 24, VEHICLE SPEED SENSOR (EXCEPT 3.1L, "C" & "K" SERIES & MODELS WITH 4L80-E TRANSMISSION)

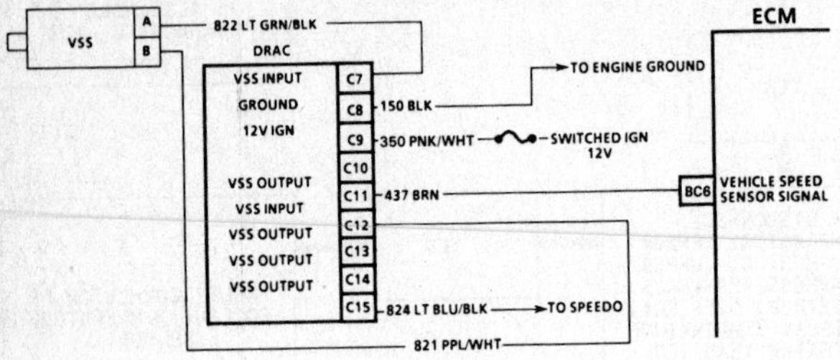
VSS
A
B
822 LT GRN/BLK
DRAC
VSS INPUT
GROUND
12V IGN
VSS OUTPUT
VSS INPUT
VSS OUTPUT
VSS OUTPUT
VSS OUTPUT
C7
C8
C9
C10
C11
C12
C13
C14
C15
150 BLK
350 PNK/WHT
SWITCHED IGN 12V
TO ENGINE GROUND
437 BRN
824 LT BLU/BLK
TO SPEEDO
821 PPL/WHT
ECM
BC6
VEHICLE SPEED SENSOR SIGNAL

4.3L TURBO

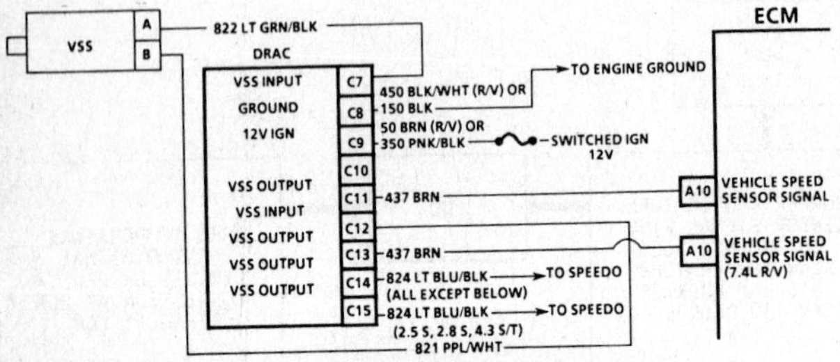
VSS
A
B
822 LT GRN/BLK
DRAC
VSS INPUT
GROUND
12V IGN
VSS OUTPUT
VSS INPUT
VSS OUTPUT
VSS OUTPUT
VSS OUTPUT
C7
C8
C9
C10
C11
C12
C13
C14
C15
450 BLK/WHT (R/V) OR
150 BLK
50 BRN (R/V) OR
350 PNK/BLK
SWITCHED IGN 12V
TO ENGINE GROUND
437 BRN
437 BRN
824 LT BLU/BLK
TO SPEEDO
(ALL EXCEPT BELOW)
824 LT BLU/BLK
TO SPEEDO
(2.5 S, 2.8 S, 4.3 S/T)
821 PPL/WHT
ECM
A10
VEHICLE SPEED SENSOR SIGNAL
A10
VEHICLE SPEED SENSOR SIGNAL (7.4L R/V)

ASTRO, SAFARI & "G", "P", "R" & "V" SERIES WITHOUT 4L80-E TRANSMISSION

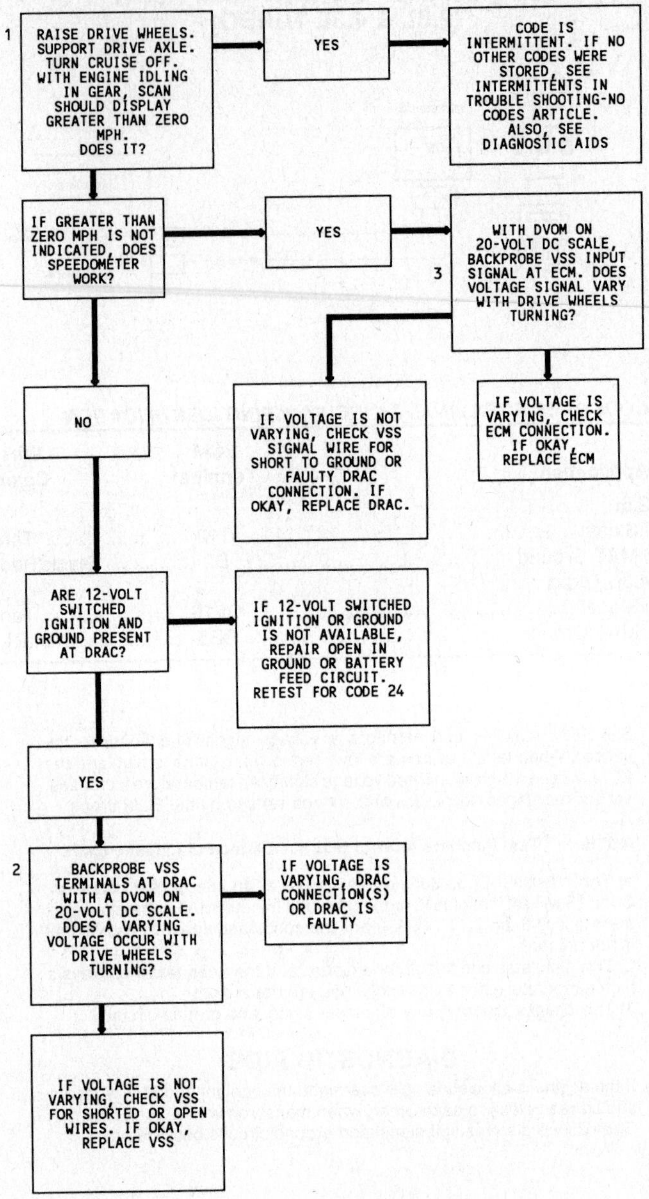
1
RAISE DRIVE WHEELS. SUPPORT DRIVE AXLE. TURN CRUISE OFF. WITH ENGINE IDLING IN GEAR, SCAN SHOULD DISPLAY GREATER THAN ZERO MPH. DOES IT?
YES
CODE IS INTERMITTENT. IF NO OTHER CODES WERE STORED, SEE INTERMITTENTS IN TROUBLE SHOOTING-NO CODES ARTICLE. ALSO, SEE DIAGNOSTIC AIDS
IF GREATER THAN ZERO MPH IS NOT INDICATED, DOES SPEEDOMETER WORK?
YES
3
WITH DVOM ON 20-VOLT DC SCALE, BACKPROBE VSS INPUT SIGNAL AT ECM. DOES VOLTAGE SIGNAL VARY WITH DRIVE WHEELS TURNING?
NO
IF VOLTAGE IS NOT VARYING, CHECK VSS SIGNAL WIRE FOR SHORT TO GROUND OR FAULTY DRAC CONNECTION. IF OKAY, REPLACE DRAC.
IF VOLTAGE IS VARYING, CHECK ECM CONNECTION. IF OKAY, REPLACE ECM
ARE 12-VOLT SWITCHED IGNITION AND GROUND PRESENT AT DRAC?
IF 12-VOLT SWITCHED IGNITION OR GROUND IS NOT AVAILABLE, REPAIR OPEN IN GROUND OR BATTERY FEED CIRCUIT. RETEST FOR CODE 24
YES
2
BACKPROBE VSS TERMINALS AT DRAC WITH A DVOM ON 20-VOLT DC SCALE. DOES A VARYING VOLTAGE OCCUR WITH DRIVE WHEELS TURNING?
IF VOLTAGE IS VARYING, DRAC CONNECTION(S) OR DRAC IS FAULTY
IF VOLTAGE IS NOT VARYING, CHECK VSS FOR SHORTED OR OPEN WIRES. IF OKAY, REPLACE VSS

The ECM applies and monitors 12 volts on circuit No. 437. Circuit No. 437 is connected to the Digital Ratio Adapter Controller (DRAC) which alternately grounds this circuit when it is receiving voltage pulses from the Vehicle Speed Sensor (VSS). Scan tester reading should closely match speedometer reading.

NOTE: Test numbers refer to test numbers on diagnostic chart.

1) Code 24 will set if voltage on circuit No. 437 is constant, engine speed is greater than 1200 RPM, vehicle speed is less than 2 MPH vehicle is not in Park or Neutral and all conditions have been met for at least 5 seconds. These conditions are met during a road load deceleration.
2) This determines if DRAC is receiving the AC signal from the VSS.
3) This test monitors DRAC voltage on circuit No. 437. With wheels turning, pulsing voltage should be present. Voltage variation will be greater at a low speed to an aver age of 4-6 volts at about 20 MPH.

DIAGNOSTIC AIDS

Scan tester reading should closely match speedometer reading with drive wheels turning. If vehicle is equipped with an automatic transmission, check park/neutral switch adjustment. If no problem is found while using flow chart, see INTERMITTENTS in TROUBLE SHOOTING – NO CODES article.

91F13735 91C13740 91B13665

CODE 24, VEHICLE SPEED SENSOR ("C" & "K" SERIES EXCEPT WITH 4L80-E TRANSMISSION)

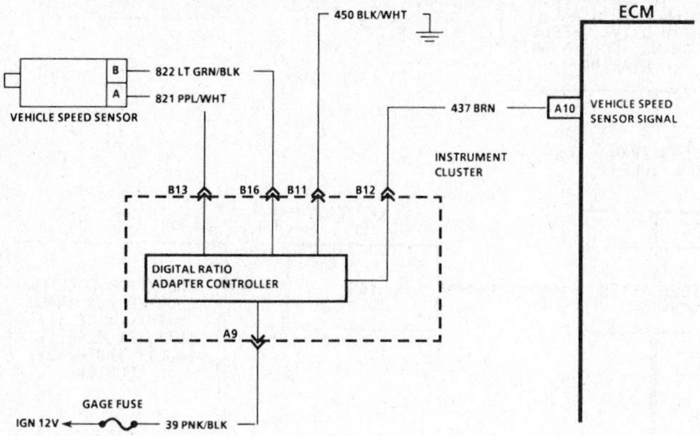

450 BLK/WHT
ECM
B
A
822 LT GRN/BLK
821 PPL/WHT
VEHICLE SPEED SENSOR
437 BRN
A10
VEHICLE SPEED SENSOR SIGNAL
INSTRUMENT CLUSTER
B13
B16
B11
B12
DIGITAL RATIO ADAPTER CONTROLLER
A9
GAGE FUSE
IGN 12V
39 PNK/BLK

The ECM applies and monitors 12 volts on circuit No. 437. Circuit No. 437 is connected to the Digital Ratio Adapter Controller (DRAC) which alternately grounds this circuit when it is receiving voltage pulses from the Vehicle Speed Sensor (VSS). Scan tester reading should closely match speedometer reading.

NOTE: **Test numbers refer to test numbers on diagnostic chart.**

1) Code 24 will set if voltage on circuit No. 437 is constant, engine speed is greater than 1200 RPM, vehicle speed is less than 2 MPH vehicle is not in Park or Neutral and all conditions have been met for at least 10 seconds. These conditions are met during a road load deceleration.
2) This test monitors DRAC voltage on circuit No. 437. With wheels turning, pulsing voltage should be present. Voltage variation will be greater at a low speed to an aver age of 4-6 volts at about 20 MPH.

DIAGNOSTIC AIDS

Scan tester reading should closely match speedometer reading with drive wheels turning. If vehicle is equipped with an automatic transmission, check park/neutral switch adjustment. If no problem is found while using flow chart, see INTERMITTENTS in TROUBLE SHOOTING – NO CODES article.

DISREGARD CODE 24 IF SET WHILE WHEELS ARE NOT TURNING.

CHART ASSUMES SPEEDOMETER IS WORKING.

1 RAISE AND SUPPORT DRIVE WHEELS. TURN CRUISE OFF. WITH GEAR SELECTOR IN DRIVE, ROTATE DRIVE WHEEL BY HAND. SCAN SHOULD INDICATE VEHICLE SPEED GREATER THAN ZERO MPH. DOES IT?

- YES → CODE IS INTERMITTENT. IF NO OTHER CODES WERE STORED, SEE INTERMITTENTS IN TROUBLE SHOOTING-NO CODES ARTICLE. ALSO, SEE DIAGNOSTIC AIDS
- NO

2 WITH DRIVE WHEELS TURNING, CHECK FOR VOLTAGE VARIATION AT ECM VSS INPUT TERMINAL WITH A DVOM ON THE 20-VOLT DC SCALE. DOES VOLTAGE VARY?

- YES → FAULTY ECM CONNECTIONS OR FAULTY ECM
- NO → REMOVE INSTRUMENT CLUSTER. CHECK FOR FAULTY CONNECTIONS, IF OKAY, REPLACE INSTRUMENT CLUSTER

91J13739 91C13666

1991 ENGINE PERFORMANCE
Self-Diagnostics – Gasoline (Cont.)

CODE 24, VEHICLE SPEED SENSOR ("C" & "K" SERIES 2WD WITH 4L80-E TRANSMISSION)

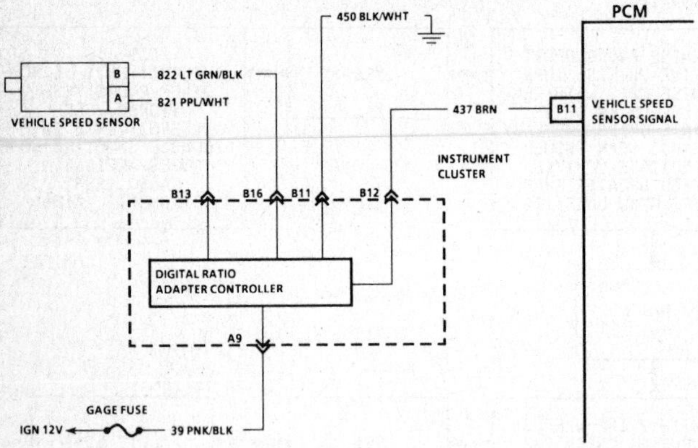
450 BLK/WHT
PCM
B
A
822 LT GRN/BLK
821 PPL/WHT
VEHICLE SPEED SENSOR
437 BRN
B11
VEHICLE SPEED SENSOR SIGNAL
INSTRUMENT CLUSTER
B13
B16
B11
B12
DIGITAL RATIO ADAPTER CONTROLLER
A9
GAGE FUSE
IGN 12V
39 PNK/BLK

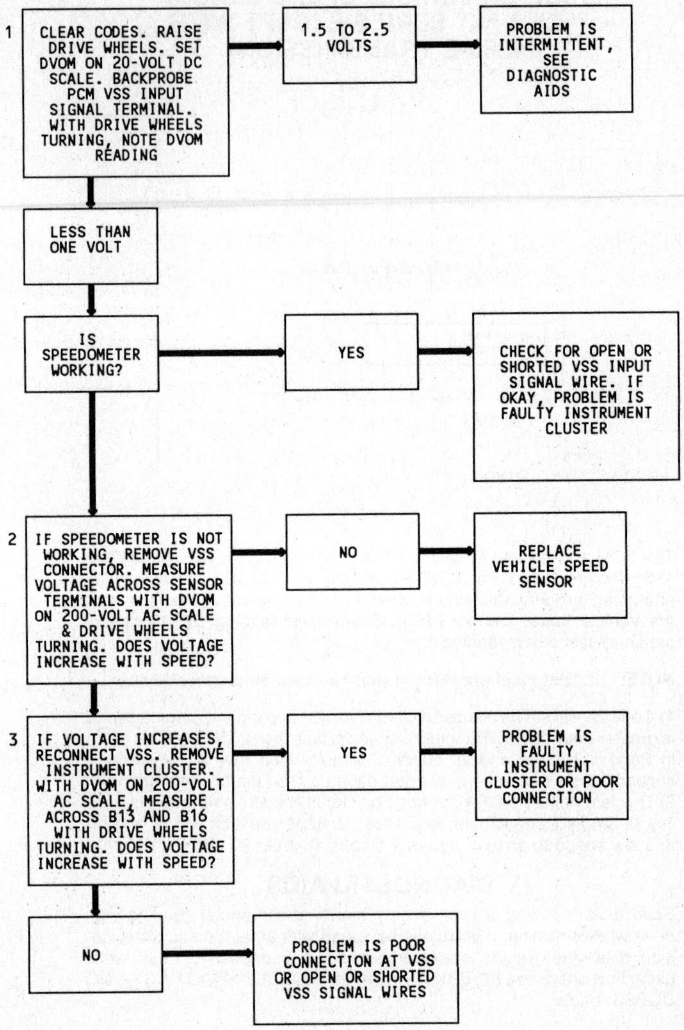
1
CLEAR CODES. RAISE DRIVE WHEELS. SET DVOM ON 20-VOLT DC SCALE. BACKPROBE PCM VSS INPUT SIGNAL TERMINAL. WITH DRIVE WHEELS TURNING, NOTE DVOM READING
1.5 TO 2.5 VOLTS
PROBLEM IS INTERMITTENT, SEE DIAGNOSTIC AIDS
LESS THAN ONE VOLT
IS SPEEDOMETER WORKING?
YES
CHECK FOR OPEN OR SHORTED VSS INPUT SIGNAL WIRE. IF OKAY, PROBLEM IS FAULTY INSTRUMENT CLUSTER
2
IF SPEEDOMETER IS NOT WORKING, REMOVE VSS CONNECTOR. MEASURE VOLTAGE ACROSS SENSOR TERMINALS WITH DVOM ON 200-VOLT AC SCALE & DRIVE WHEELS TURNING. DOES VOLTAGE INCREASE WITH SPEED?
NO
REPLACE VEHICLE SPEED SENSOR
3
IF VOLTAGE INCREASES, RECONNECT VSS. REMOVE INSTRUMENT CLUSTER. WITH DVOM ON 200-VOLT AC SCALE, MEASURE ACROSS B13 AND B16 WITH DRIVE WHEELS TURNING. DOES VOLTAGE INCREASE WITH SPEED?
YES
PROBLEM IS FAULTY INSTRUMENT CLUSTER OR POOR CONNECTION
NO
PROBLEM IS POOR CONNECTION AT VSS OR OPEN OR SHORTED VSS SIGNAL WIRES

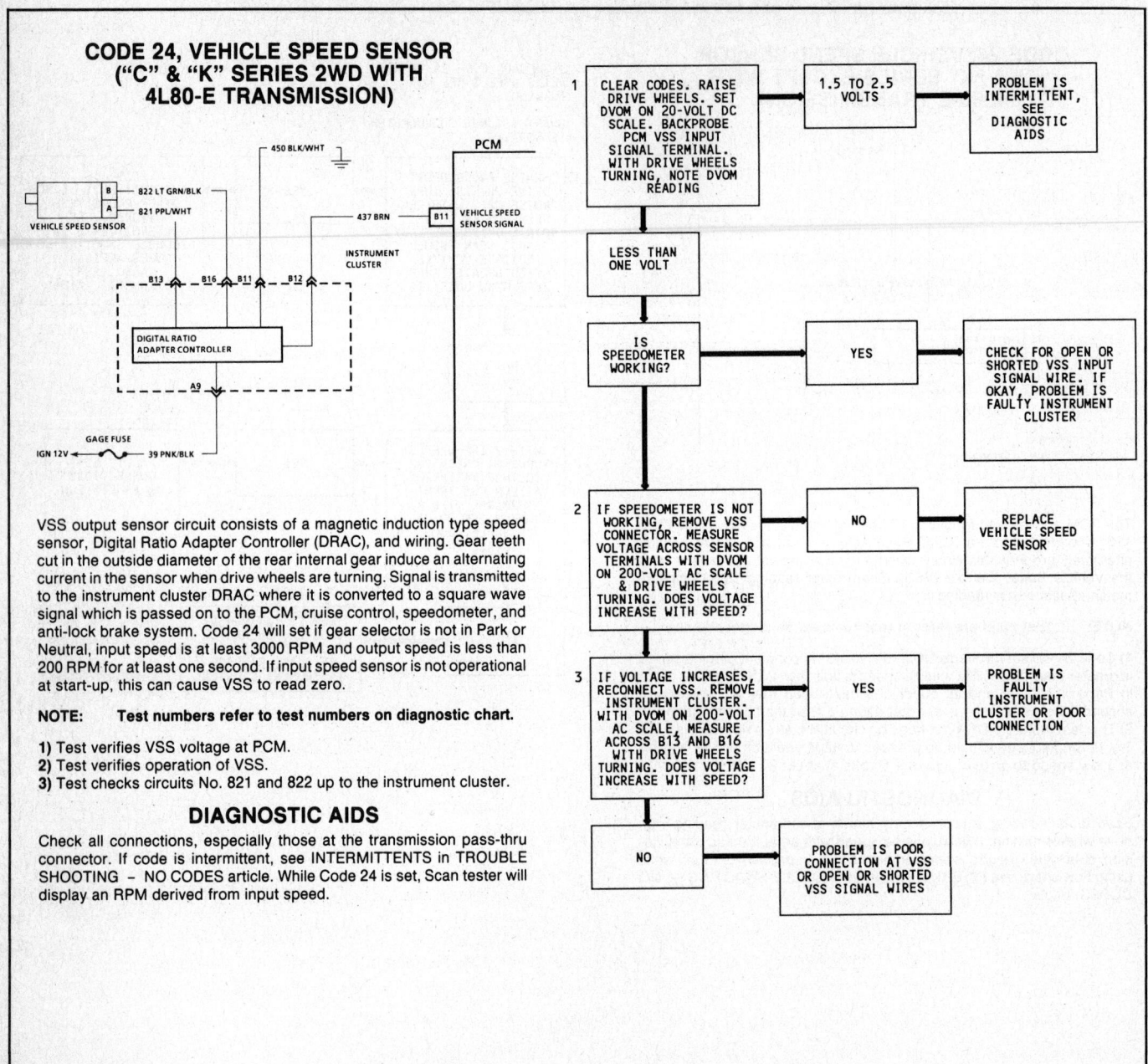

VSS output sensor circuit consists of a magnetic induction type speed sensor, Digital Ratio Adapter Controller (DRAC), and wiring. Gear teeth cut in the outside diameter of the rear internal gear induce an alternating current in the sensor when drive wheels are turning. Signal is transmitted to the instrument cluster DRAC where it is converted to a square wave signal which is passed on to the PCM, cruise control, speedometer, and anti-lock brake system. Code 24 will set if gear selector is not in Park or Neutral, input speed is at least 3000 RPM and output speed is less than 200 RPM for at least one second. If input speed sensor is not operational at start-up, this can cause VSS to read zero.

NOTE: Test numbers refer to test numbers on diagnostic chart.

1) Test verifies VSS voltage at PCM.
2) Test verifies operation of VSS.
3) Test checks circuits No. 821 and 822 up to the instrument cluster.

DIAGNOSTIC AIDS

Check all connections, especially those at the transmission pass-thru connector. If code is intermittent, see INTERMITTENTS in TROUBLE SHOOTING - NO CODES article. While Code 24 is set, Scan tester will display an RPM derived from input speed.

91I13738 91D13667

CODE 24, VEHICLE SPEED SENSOR ("2WD WITH 4L80-E TRANSMISSION EXCEPT "C" & "K" SERIES)

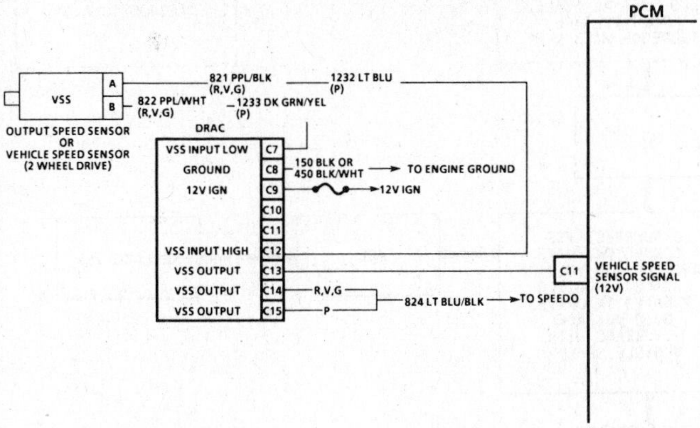

PCM
VSS
A
B
821 PPL/BLK (R,V,G)
1232 LT BLU (P)
822 PPL/WHT (R,V,G)
1233 DK GRN/YEL (P)
OUTPUT SPEED SENSOR OR VEHICLE SPEED SENSOR (2 WHEEL DRIVE)
DRAC
VSS INPUT LOW C7
GROUND C8
12V IGN C9
C10
C11
VSS INPUT HIGH C12
VSS OUTPUT C13
VSS OUTPUT C14
VSS OUTPUT C15
150 BLK OR 450 BLK/WHT
TO ENGINE GROUND
12V IGN
R,V,G
P
824 LT BLU/BLK
TO SPEEDO
C11
VEHICLE SPEED SENSOR SIGNAL (12V)

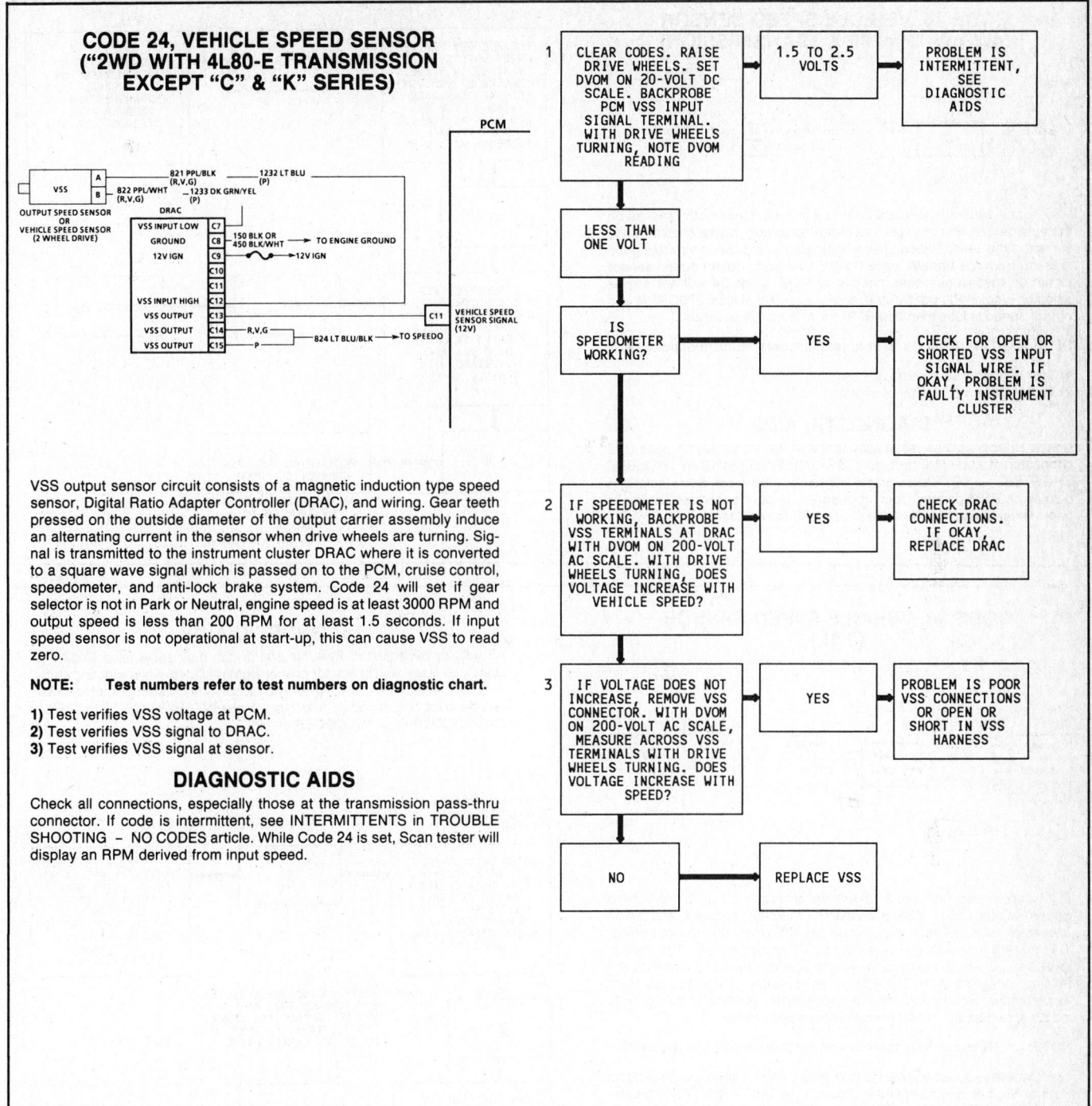

VSS output sensor circuit consists of a magnetic induction type speed sensor, Digital Ratio Adapter Controller (DRAC), and wiring. Gear teeth pressed on the outside diameter of the output carrier assembly induce an alternating current in the sensor when drive wheels are turning. Signal is transmitted to the instrument cluster DRAC where it is converted to a square wave signal which is passed on to the PCM, cruise control, speedometer, and anti-lock brake system. Code 24 will set if gear selector is not in Park or Neutral, engine speed is at least 3000 RPM and output speed is less than 200 RPM for at least 1.5 seconds. If input speed sensor is not operational at start-up, this can cause VSS to read zero.

NOTE: **Test numbers refer to test numbers on diagnostic chart.**

1) Test verifies VSS voltage at PCM.
2) Test verifies VSS signal to DRAC.
3) Test verifies VSS signal at sensor.

DIAGNOSTIC AIDS

Check all connections, especially those at the transmission pass-thru connector. If code is intermittent, see INTERMITTENTS in TROUBLE SHOOTING - NO CODES article. While Code 24 is set, Scan tester will display an RPM derived from input speed.

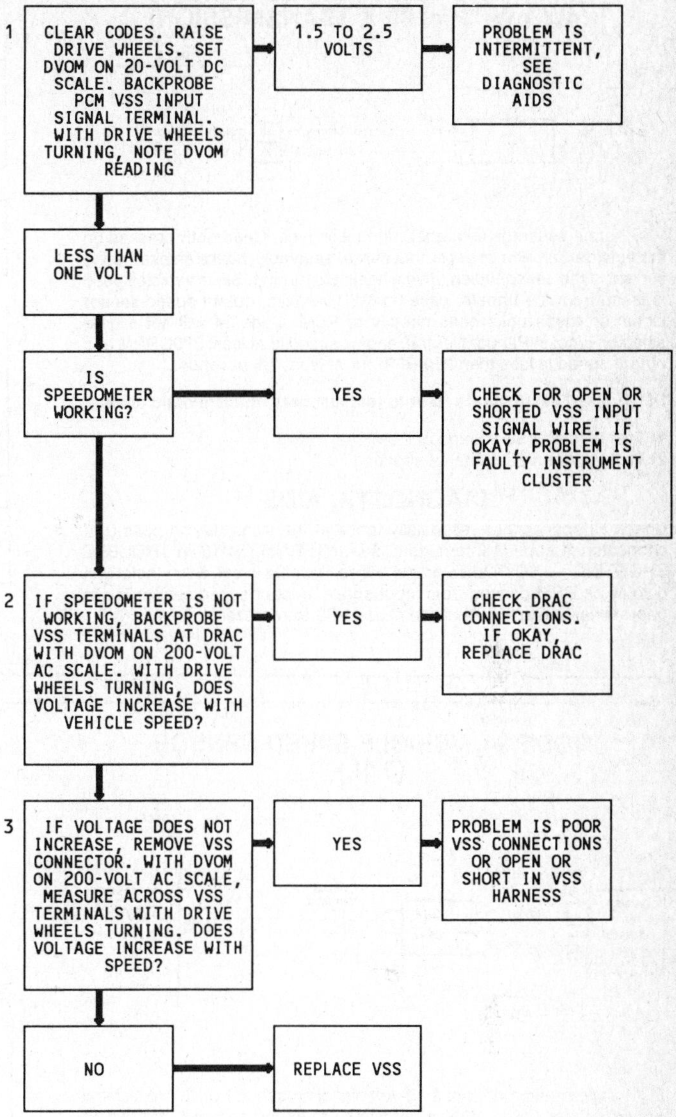

1
CLEAR CODES. RAISE DRIVE WHEELS. SET DVOM ON 20-VOLT DC SCALE. BACKPROBE PCM VSS INPUT SIGNAL TERMINAL. WITH DRIVE WHEELS TURNING, NOTE DVOM READING
1.5 TO 2.5 VOLTS
PROBLEM IS INTERMITTENT, SEE DIAGNOSTIC AIDS
LESS THAN ONE VOLT
IS SPEEDOMETER WORKING?
YES
CHECK FOR OPEN OR SHORTED VSS INPUT SIGNAL WIRE. IF OKAY, PROBLEM IS FAULTY INSTRUMENT CLUSTER
2
IF SPEEDOMETER IS NOT WORKING, BACKPROBE VSS TERMINALS AT DRAC WITH DVOM ON 200-VOLT AC SCALE. WITH DRIVE WHEELS TURNING, DOES VOLTAGE INCREASE WITH VEHICLE SPEED?
YES
CHECK DRAC CONNECTIONS. IF OKAY, REPLACE DRAC
3
IF VOLTAGE DOES NOT INCREASE, REMOVE VSS CONNECTOR. WITH DVOM ON 200-VOLT AC SCALE, MEASURE ACROSS VSS TERMINALS WITH DRIVE WHEELS TURNING. DOES VOLTAGE INCREASE WITH SPEED?
YES
PROBLEM IS POOR VSS CONNECTIONS OR OPEN OR SHORT IN VSS HARNESS
NO
REPLACE VSS

91H13737 91E13668

1991 ENGINE PERFORMANCE
Self-Diagnostics – Gasoline (Cont.)

CODE 24, VEHICLE SPEED SENSOR (4WD WITH 4L80-E TRANSMISSION)

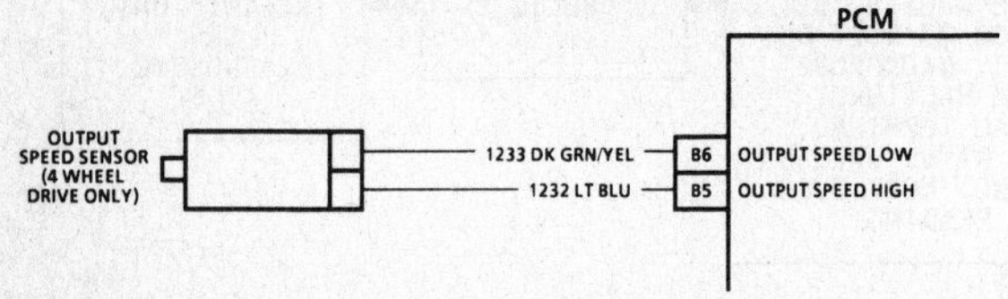
PCM
OUTPUT SPEED SENSOR (4 WHEEL DRIVE ONLY)
1233 DK GRN/YEL
1232 LT BLU
B6
B5
OUTPUT SPEED LOW
OUTPUT SPEED HIGH

VSS output sensor is a magnetic induction type. Gear teeth pressed on the outside diameter of the output carrier assembly induce an alternating current in the sensor when drive wheels are turning. Since vehicle speed is taken from the transfer case on 4WD vehicles, output speed sensor signal on these units goes directly to PCM. Code 24 will set if gear selector is not in Park or Neutral, engine speed is at least 3000 RPM and output speed is less than 200 RPM for at least 1.5 seconds.

NOTE: Test numbers refer to test numbers on diagnostic chart.

1) Test verifies VSS voltage at PCM.
2) Test verifies VSS signal at sensor.

DIAGNOSTIC AIDS

Check all connections, especially those at the transmission pass-thru connector. If code is intermittent, see INTERMITTENTS in TROUBLE SHOOTING – NO CODES article. While Code 24 is set, Scan tester will display an RPM derived from input speed. If input speed sensor is not operational at start-up, this can cause VSS to read zero.

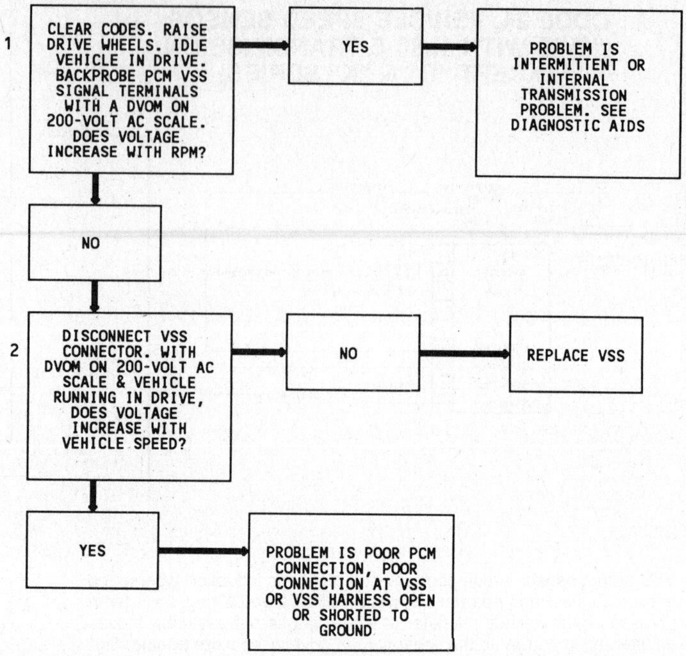
1
CLEAR CODES. RAISE DRIVE WHEELS. IDLE VEHICLE IN DRIVE. BACKPROBE PCM VSS SIGNAL TERMINALS WITH A DVOM ON 200-VOLT AC SCALE. DOES VOLTAGE INCREASE WITH RPM?
YES
PROBLEM IS INTERMITTENT OR INTERNAL TRANSMISSION PROBLEM. SEE DIAGNOSTIC AIDS
NO
2
DISCONNECT VSS CONNECTOR. WITH DVOM ON 200-VOLT AC SCALE & VEHICLE RUNNING IN DRIVE, DOES VOLTAGE INCREASE WITH VEHICLE SPEED?
NO
REPLACE VSS
YES
PROBLEM IS POOR PCM CONNECTION, POOR CONNECTION AT VSS OR VSS HARNESS OPEN OR SHORTED TO GROUND

91G13736 91F13669

CODE 24, VEHICLE SPEED SENSOR (3.1L)

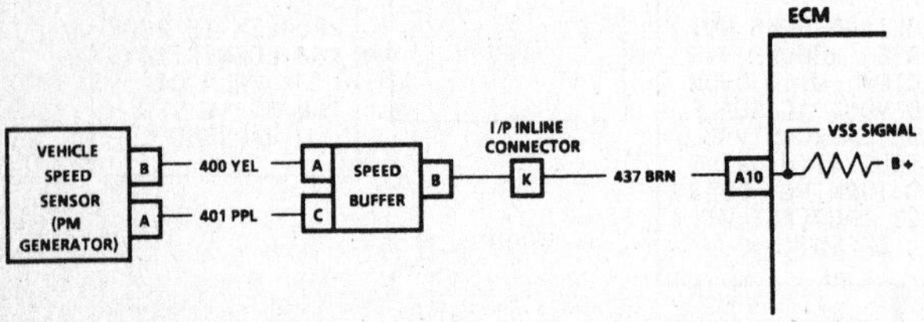
ECM
VEHICLE SPEED SENSOR (PM GENERATOR)
B
A
400 YEL
401 PPL
A
C
SPEED BUFFER
B
I/P INLINE CONNECTOR
K
437 BRN
A10
VSS SIGNAL
B+

ECM applies and monitors a 12-volt signal on circuit No. 437 to Vehicle Speed Sensor (VSS). VSS is connected to speed sensor buffer which alternately grounds and opens circuit No. 437 when wheels are turning. This pulsing action takes place about 2000 times per mile. The voltage level and pulses increase with vehicle speed. The ECM converts the pulsing voltage to MPH. The ECM uses VSS information in calculations to determine vehicle adjustments. Scan tester reading should closely match speedometer reading when wheels are turning.

NOTE: Test numbers refer to test numbers on diagnostic chart.

1) A Code 24 sets when MPH is less than 2 MPH, transmission is not in Park or Neutral, engine speed is greater than 1400 RPM, TPS is greater than 5 percent, circuit No. 437 voltage is constant and all of these conditions are met for 30 seconds. These conditions are met during a road load deceleration.
2) A steady 8-12 volts at ECM connector indicates VSS circuit is open or speed sensor is faulty. A voltage of less than one volt at IP connector indicates circuit No. 437 wire is shorted to ground. Disconnect vehicle speed sensor connector. If voltage is now greater than 10 volts, vehicle speed sensor buffer is faulty. If voltage remains less than 8 volts, circuit is grounded. If circuit is not grounded, check for faulty ECM connector or ECM. Before replacing the ECM, PROM should be checked for correct application.

DIAGNOSTIC AIDS

A faulty or misadjusted Park/Neutral switch may set a false Code 24. Use Scan tester and check for proper signal in Drive, while wiggling shifter. Scan tester MPH reading should closely match speedometer when vehicle is moving. If code is intermittent, see INTERMITTENTS in TROUBLE SHOOTING – NO CODES article.

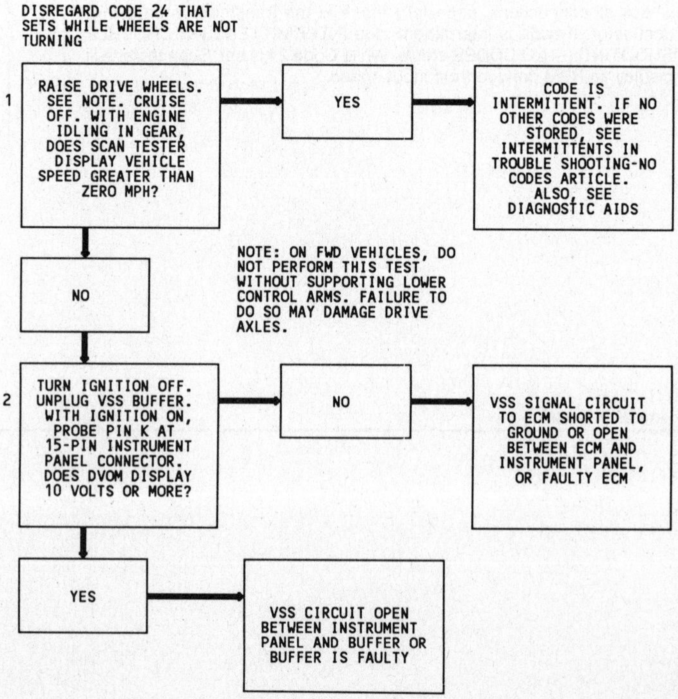
DISREGARD CODE 24 THAT SETS WHILE WHEELS ARE NOT TURNING
1
RAISE DRIVE WHEELS. SEE NOTE. CRUISE OFF. WITH ENGINE IDLING IN GEAR, DOES SCAN TESTER DISPLAY VEHICLE SPEED GREATER THAN ZERO MPH?
YES
CODE IS INTERMITTENT. IF NO OTHER CODES WERE STORED, SEE INTERMITTENTS IN TROUBLE SHOOTING-NO CODES ARTICLE. ALSO, SEE DIAGNOSTIC AIDS
NO
NOTE: ON FWD VEHICLES, DO NOT PERFORM THIS TEST WITHOUT SUPPORTING LOWER CONTROL ARMS. FAILURE TO DO SO MAY DAMAGE DRIVE AXLES.
2
TURN IGNITION OFF. UNPLUG VSS BUFFER. WITH IGNITION ON, PROBE PIN K AT 15-PIN INSTRUMENT PANEL CONNECTOR. DOES DVOM DISPLAY 10 VOLTS OR MORE?
NO
VSS SIGNAL CIRCUIT TO ECM SHORTED TO GROUND OR OPEN BETWEEN ECM AND INSTRUMENT PANEL, OR FAULTY ECM
YES
VSS CIRCUIT OPEN BETWEEN INSTRUMENT PANEL AND BUFFER OR BUFFER IS FAULTY

91D13741 91I13670

1991 ENGINE PERFORMANCE
Self-Diagnostics – Gasoline (Cont.)

CODE 25, MAT SENSOR TEMP. HIGH (2.5L & 4.3L TURBO)

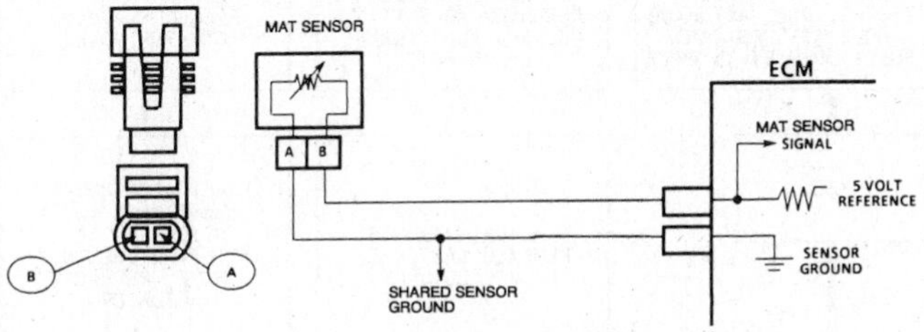
MAT SENSOR
A
B
ECM
MAT SENSOR SIGNAL
5 VOLT REFERENCE
SENSOR GROUND
SHARED SENSOR GROUND
B
A

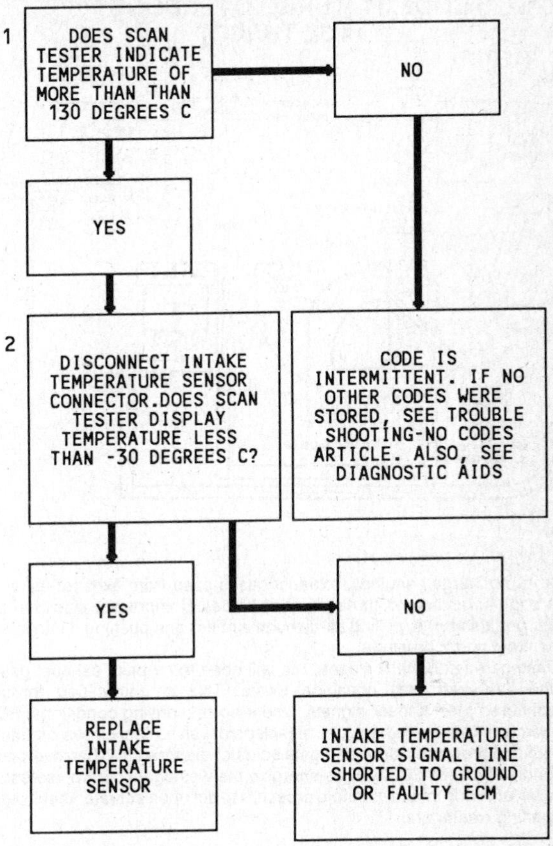
1
DOES SCAN TESTER INDICATE TEMPERATURE OF MORE THAN THAN 130 DEGREES C
NO
YES
2
DISCONNECT INTAKE TEMPERATURE SENSOR CONNECTOR.DOES SCAN TESTER DISPLAY TEMPERATURE LESS THAN -30 DEGREES C?
CODE IS INTERMITTENT. IF NO OTHER CODES WERE STORED, SEE TROUBLE SHOOTING-NO CODES ARTICLE. ALSO, SEE DIAGNOSTIC AIDS
YES
NO
REPLACE INTAKE TEMPERATURE SENSOR
INTAKE TEMPERATURE SENSOR SIGNAL LINE SHORTED TO GROUND OR FAULTY ECM

CODE 25 ECM TERMINAL & CIRCUIT WIRING IDENTIFICATION

Application	ECM Terminal	Wire Color
2.5L		
Signal	C12	Tan
MAT Ground	D2	Black/Red
4.3L Turbo		
Signal	GF16	Tan
MAT Ground	BB5	Black

The ECM applies and monitors a voltage signal (4-6 volts) to MAT sensor. When manifold air is cold, the sensor resistance is high and ECM sees a high signal voltage. As air warms, resistance decreases and voltage sensed by the ECM drops. Sensor resistance can be measured at sensor terminals with harness disconnected.

NOTE: Test numbers refer to test numbers on diagnostic chart.

1) This checks if the code is a hard failure or an intermittent condition. Code 25 will set if a VSS signal is present (2.5L) and monitored MAT sensor temperature is greater than 302°F (150°C) for 2.5L or 275°F (135°C) for 4.3L Turbo.

DIAGNOSTIC AIDS

If the engine is allowed to cool overnight, the coolant temperature sensor and MAT sensor should read close to each other, when measured with a Scan tester. A Code 25 will also result if sensor signal circuit is shorted to ground.

TEMPERATURE-TO-RESISTANCE VALUES [1] [2]

°F (°C)	Ohms
210 (100)	185
160 (70)	450
100 (38)	1800
70 (20)	3400
40 (4)	7500
20 (–7)	13,500
0 (–18)	25,000
–40 (–40)	100,700

1 – Measure resistance across sensor terminals.
2 – Temperatures are approximates.

91E07386 91I07294

1991 ENGINE PERFORMANCE
Self-Diagnostics – Gasoline (Cont.)

CODE 31, TURBO OVERBOOST (4.3L TURBO)

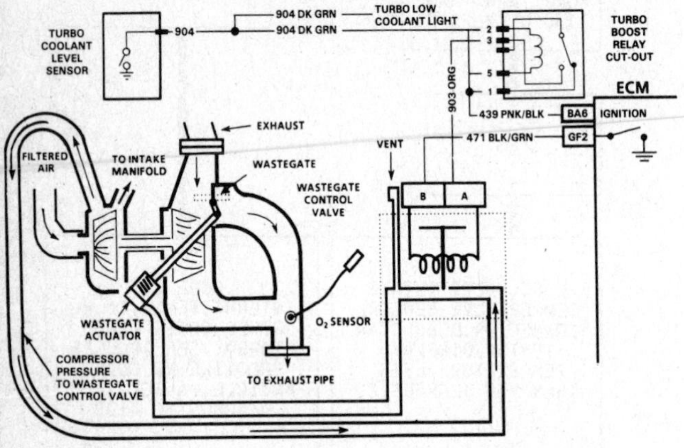
TURBO COOLANT LEVEL SENSOR
904
904 DK GRN
904 DK GRN
TURBO LOW COOLANT LIGHT
TURBO BOOST RELAY CUT-OUT
903 ORG
ECM
439 PNK/BLK
BA6
IGNITION
471 BLK/GRN
GF2
EXHAUST
FILTERED AIR
TO INTAKE MANIFOLD
WASTEGATE
VENT
WASTEGATE CONTROL VALVE
B
A
WASTEGATE ACTUATOR
O_2 SENSOR
COMPRESSOR PRESSURE TO WASTEGATE CONTROL VALVE
TO EXHAUST PIPE

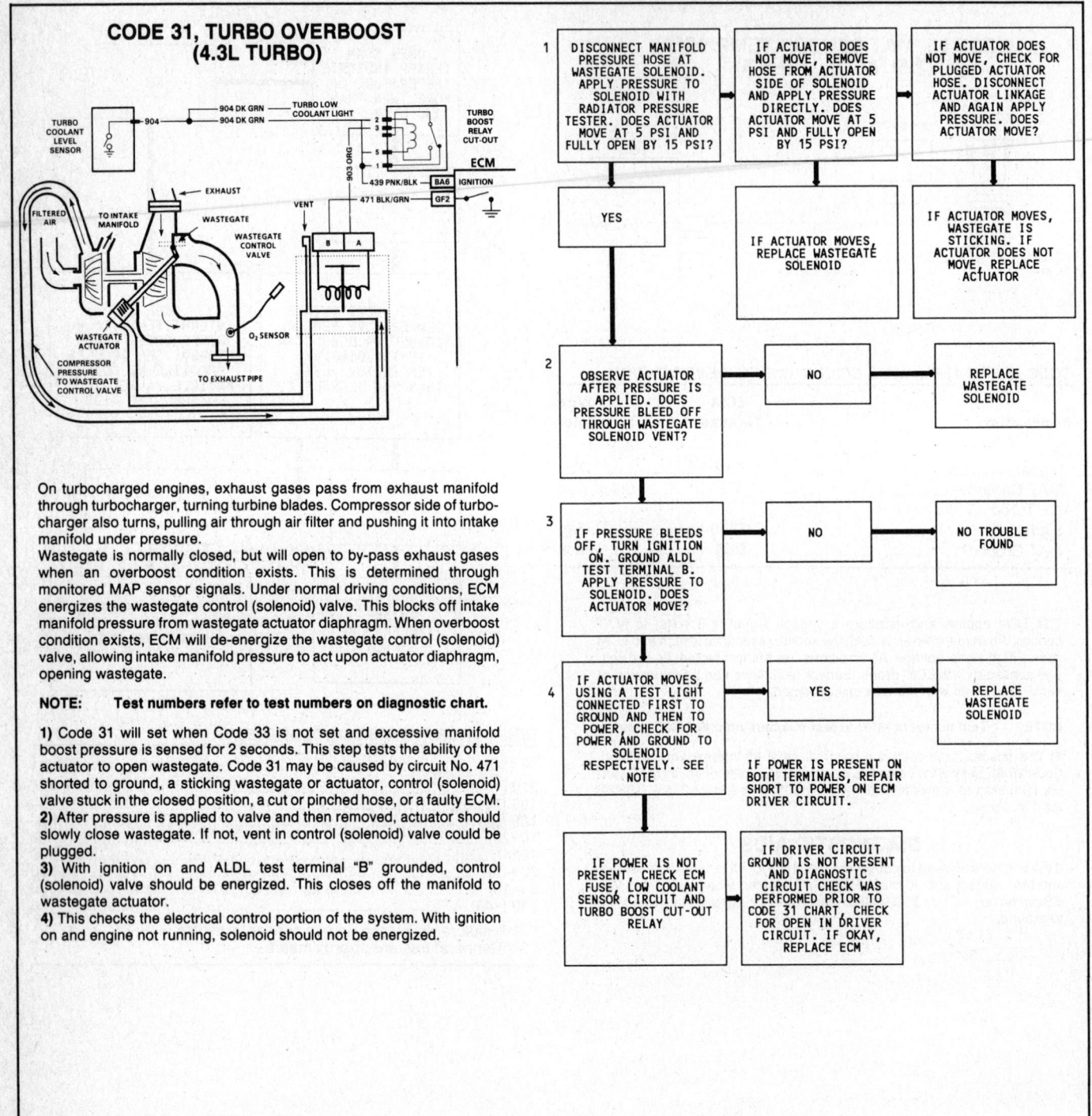

On turbocharged engines, exhaust gases pass from exhaust manifold through turbocharger, turning turbine blades. Compressor side of turbocharger also turns, pulling air through air filter and pushing it into intake manifold under pressure.

Wastegate is normally closed, but will open to by-pass exhaust gases when an overboost condition exists. This is determined through monitored MAP sensor signals. Under normal driving conditions, ECM energizes the wastegate control (solenoid) valve. This blocks off intake manifold pressure from wastegate actuator diaphragm. When overboost condition exists, ECM will de-energize the wastegate control (solenoid) valve, allowing intake manifold pressure to act upon actuator diaphragm, opening wastegate.

NOTE: Test numbers refer to test numbers on diagnostic chart.

1) Code 31 will set when Code 33 is not set and excessive manifold boost pressure is sensed for 2 seconds. This step tests the ability of the actuator to open wastegate. Code 31 may be caused by circuit No. 471 shorted to ground, a sticking wastegate or actuator, control (solenoid) valve stuck in the closed position, a cut or pinched hose, or a faulty ECM.
2) After pressure is applied to valve and then removed, actuator should slowly close wastegate. If not, vent in control (solenoid) valve could be plugged.
3) With ignition on and ALDL test terminal "B" grounded, control (solenoid) valve should be energized. This closes off the manifold to wastegate actuator.
4) This checks the electrical control portion of the system. With ignition on and engine not running, solenoid should not be energized.

1 DISCONNECT MANIFOLD PRESSURE HOSE AT WASTEGATE SOLENOID. APPLY PRESSURE TO SOLENOID WITH RADIATOR PRESSURE TESTER. DOES ACTUATOR MOVE AT 5 PSI AND FULLY OPEN BY 15 PSI?

- → IF ACTUATOR DOES NOT MOVE, REMOVE HOSE FROM ACTUATOR SIDE OF SOLENOID AND APPLY PRESSURE DIRECTLY. DOES ACTUATOR MOVE AT 5 PSI AND FULLY OPEN BY 15 PSI?
  - IF ACTUATOR MOVES, REPLACE WASTEGATE SOLENOID
  - → IF ACTUATOR DOES NOT MOVE, CHECK FOR PLUGGED ACTUATOR HOSE. DISCONNECT ACTUATOR LINKAGE AND AGAIN APPLY PRESSURE. DOES ACTUATOR MOVE?
    - IF ACTUATOR MOVES, WASTEGATE IS STICKING. IF ACTUATOR DOES NOT MOVE, REPLACE ACTUATOR
- YES

2 OBSERVE ACTUATOR AFTER PRESSURE IS APPLIED. DOES PRESSURE BLEED OFF THROUGH WASTEGATE SOLENOID VENT?

- NO → REPLACE WASTEGATE SOLENOID

3 IF PRESSURE BLEEDS OFF, TURN IGNITION ON. GROUND ALDL TEST TERMINAL B. APPLY PRESSURE TO SOLENOID. DOES ACTUATOR MOVE?

- NO → NO TROUBLE FOUND

4 IF ACTUATOR MOVES, USING A TEST LIGHT CONNECTED FIRST TO GROUND AND THEN TO POWER, CHECK FOR POWER AND GROUND TO SOLENOID RESPECTIVELY. SEE NOTE

- YES → REPLACE WASTEGATE SOLENOID
- IF POWER IS PRESENT ON BOTH TERMINALS, REPAIR SHORT TO POWER ON ECM DRIVER CIRCUIT.
- IF POWER IS NOT PRESENT, CHECK ECM FUSE, LOW COOLANT SENSOR CIRCUIT AND TURBO BOOST CUT-OUT RELAY
  - → IF DRIVER CIRCUIT GROUND IS NOT PRESENT AND DIAGNOSTIC CIRCUIT CHECK WAS PERFORMED PRIOR TO CODE 31 CHART, CHECK FOR OPEN IN DRIVER CIRCUIT. IF OKAY, REPLACE ECM

91E13742 91H13711

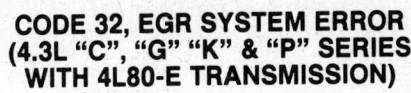

CODE 32, EGR SYSTEM ERROR (4.3L "C", "G" "K" & "P" SERIES WITH 4L80-E TRANSMISSION)

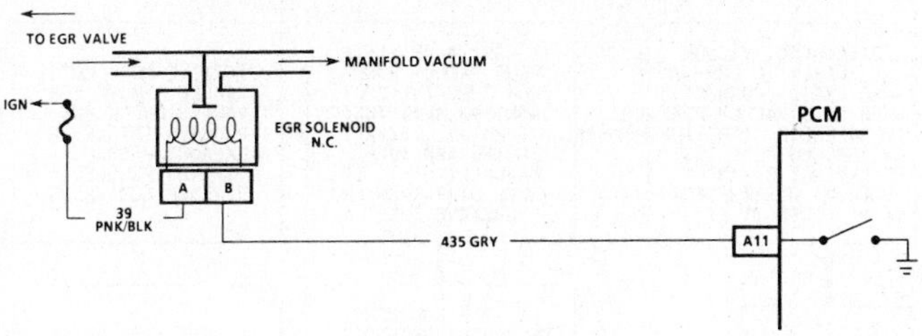
TO EGR VALVE
MANIFOLD VACUUM
IGN
EGR SOLENOID N.C.
A
B
39 PNK/BLK
PCM
435 GRY
A11

PCM controls a solenoid regulating vacuum to the EGR valve. The normally closed solenoid prevents vacuum from passing until it is energized by PCM. A properly operating EGR will directly affect fuel integrator counts. With EGR valve open, integrator counts will be less than without EGR operation. If monitored integrator counts do not change with EGR commanded, Code 32 will set.

NOTE: **Test numbers refer to test numbers on diagnostic chart.**

1) When test terminal "B" of the ALDL connector is grounded, EGR solenoid should be energized, allowing vacuum to the EGR valve. Vacuum should hold.
2) When jumper wire is removed from terminal "B", vacuum to the EGR valve should bleed through a vent in the solenoid and EGR valve should close. Vacuum gauge may or may not bleed off vacuum, however, this does not indicate a problem.
3) Determines if fault lies in electrical control part of the system, connector or solenoid.
4) This system uses a negative backpressure EGR valve. Valve should hold vacuum with engine off.
5) When engine is started, backpressure should cause vacuum to bleed off and valve should fully close.

DIAGNOSTIC AIDS

Prior to replacing PCM, check resistance of all PCM-controlled solenoids and relays. Replace any with a resistance value less than 20 ohms.

PRIOR TO USING THIS CHART, ENSURE THAT VACUUM HOSES ARE FREE OF LEAKS AND RESTRICTIONS AND THAT AT LEAST 7 IN. OF VACUUM IS BEING SUPPLIED TO SOLENOID FROM VACUUM SOURCE AT 2000 RPM.

1 IGNITION ON, ENGINE OFF. DISCONNECT EGR SOLENOID VACUUM HARNESS. GROUND ALDL TEST TERMINAL B. APPLY 10 IN. VACUUM TO MANIFOLD SIDE OF SOLENOID. VACUUM SHOULD HOLD

3 IF VACUUM HOLDS, PLUG EGR VACUUM SIDE OF SOLENOID. UNGROUND ALDL. DOES VACUUM BLEED OFF?

IF VACUUM DOES NOT BLEED OFF. DISCONNECT SOLENOID ELECTRICAL CONNECTOR. IF VACUUM DROPS, REPAIR SHORT TO GROUND IN CIRCUIT NO. 435. IF VACUUM DOES NOT BLEED OFF, REPLACE SOLENOID

2 IF 10 IN. VACUUM WILL NOT HOLD, DISCONNECT SOLENOID ELECTRICAL HARNESS. CONNECT TEST LIGHT ACROSS HARNESS TERMINALS. IS LIGHT ON?

4 IF VACUUM BLEEDS OFF, CONNECT VACUUM PUMP TO EGR VALVE. APPLY VACUUM. DIAPHRAGM SHOULD LIFT AND VACUUM SHOULD HOLD FOR AT LEAST 20 SECONDS. DOES IT?

IF DIAPHRAGM DOES NOT LIFT OR VACUUM DOES NOT HOLD FOR AT LEAST 20 SECONDS, REPLACE EGR VALVE

IF LIGHT IS ON, SOLENOID OR SOLENOID CONNECTIONS ARE FAULTY.

5 IF VACUUM HOLDS, START ENGINE. THIS IS A NEGATIVE BACKPRESSURE VALVE. VACUUM SHOULD IMMEDIATELY DROP AND EGR VALVE SHOULD SEAT. DOES IT?

IF VALVE DOES NOT SEAT AND VACUUM DOES NOT DROP, REMOVE VALVE AND CHECK FOR CARBON BUILD-UP. IF VALVE IS NOT PLUGGED, REPLACE VALVE.

IF LIGHT IS OFF, PROBE EACH HARNESS TERMINAL WITH TEST LIGHT CONNECTED TO GROUND

IF VACUUM DROPS AND VALVE SEATS, NO PROBLEM IS FOUND

LIGHT ON ONE TERMINAL. GROUND CIRCUIT BETWEEN SOLENOID AND ECM IS OPEN OR ECM IS FAULTY

LIGHT OFF ON BOTH. REPAIR OPEN IN IGNITION FEED CIRCUIT TO SOLENOID

LIGHT ON ON BOTH TERMINALS. REPAIR SHORT TO VOLTAGE ON GROUND CIRCUIT BETWEEN SOLENOID AND ECM

91J13747 91B07323

1991 ENGINE PERFORMANCE
Self-Diagnostics – Gasoline (Cont.)

CODE 32, EGR SYSTEM ERROR (ALL ENGINES WITH 4L80-E TRANSMISSION EXCEPT 4.3L)

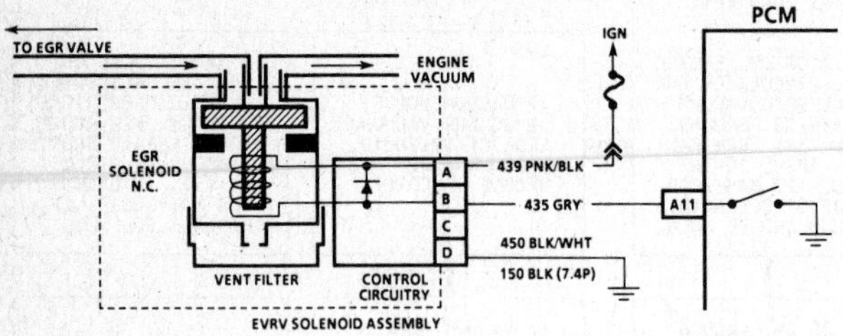
TO EGR VALVE
ENGINE VACUUM
IGN
PCM
EGR SOLENOID N.C.
A
B
C
D
439 PNK/BLK
435 GRY
A11
450 BLK/WHT
150 BLK (7.4P)
VENT FILTER
CONTROL CIRCUITRY
EVRV SOLENOID ASSEMBLY

PCM controls a solenoid that regulates vacuum to the EGR valve. The normally closed solenoid prevents vacuum from passing until it is energized by PCM. A properly operating EGR will directly affect fuel integrator counts. With EGR valve open, integrator counts will be less than without EGR operation. If monitored integrator counts do not change with EGR commanded, Code 32 will set.

ECM checks EGR operation when engine speed is greater than 1600 RPM, MAP sensor signal indicates cruise condition and throttle position are constant.

NOTE: Test numbers refer to test numbers on diagnostic chart.

1) With ignition on and engine off, solenoid should not be energized or allow vacuum to pass to EGR valve. When test terminal "B" of the ALDL connector is grounded, EGR solenoid should be energized, allowing vacuum to the EGR valve. Vacuum should hold.

2) Checks for plugged EGR passages. If passages are plugged, engine may have severe detonation on acceleration.

3) Vehicle must be driven during this test to produce sufficient load to operate EGR. Lightly accelerating (approximately 1/4 throttle) will produce a large and stable enough reading to determine if ECM is commanding system on.

DIAGNOSTIC AIDS

Prior to replacing PCM, check resistance of all PCM-controlled solenoids and relays. Replace any with a resistance value less than 20 ohms.

PRIOR TO USING CHART, VERIFY PROPER VACUUM SUPPLY AND CHECK VACUUM HOSE FOR BLOCKAGE. IF ANY OTHER CODES EXIST, DIAGNOSE THEM FIRST AND REPAIR ANY ROUGH IDLE COMPLAINT.

1 DISCONNECT VACUUM SUPPLY TO EGR SOLENOID. CONNECT HAND-HELD VACUUM PUMP TO SOLENOID. IGNITION ON. GROUND ALDL TEST TERMINAL B. APPLY VACUUM. OBSERVE EGR VALVE. DOES IT LIFT?

2 IF EGR VALVE LIFTS, PLUG VACUUM HOSE FROM THROTTLE BODY. UNGROUND ALDL TEST TERMINAL. START ENGINE AND IDLE. MANUALLY LIFT EGR VALVE DIAPHRAGM AND OBSERVE IDLE

IF IDLE DOES NOT CHANGE, REMOVE EGR VALVE. CHECK FOR PLUGGED INTAKE OR EXHAUST PASSAGES. IF NOT PLUGGED, REPLACE EGR VALVE

3 IF IDLE ROUGHENS, RECONNECT SOLENOID. CONNECT VACUUM GAUGE TO VACUUM HOSE AT EGR VALVE. PLACE TRANS. IN GEAR AND LIGHTLY ACCELERATE FROM A STOP. IS LESS THAN 10 IN. HG INDICATED?

IF LESS THAN 10 IN. HG IS INDICATED, PROBLEM IS INTERMITTENT. SEE TROUBLE SHOOTING-NO CODES ARTICLE

IF VACUUM READING IS GREATER THAN 10 IN. HG, REPLACE EGR FILTER

NO

IF EGR VALVE DOES NOT LIFT, CHECK FOR VACUUM TO EGR VALVE WHILE REPEATING STEP 1. IS VACUUM PRESENT?

IF VACUUM IS PRESENT, REPLACE EGR VALVE

IF VACUUM IS NOT PRESENT, DISCONNECT EGR SOLENOID CONNECTOR. CHECK POWER SUPPLY TO SOLENOID. IS BATTERY VOLTAGE PRESENT?

IF POWER IS NOT PRESENT AT SOLENOID CONNECTOR, REPAIR OPEN IN POWER SUPPLY

IF BATTERY VOLTAGE IS PRESENT, CONNECT TEST LIGHT ACROSS SOLENOID CONNECTOR TERMINALS WITH IGNITION ON AND ALDL TEST TERMINAL GROUNDED. IS TEST LIGHT ON?

IF TEST LIGHT IS ON, REPLACE EGR SOLENOID

IF TEST LIGHT IS NOT ON, CHECK FOR OPEN IN SOLENOID DRIVER CIRCUIT BETWEEN PCM AND SOLENOID. IF OKAY, PCM OR CONNECTIONS ARE BAD. SEE DIAGNOSTIC AIDS

91D13782 91C13781

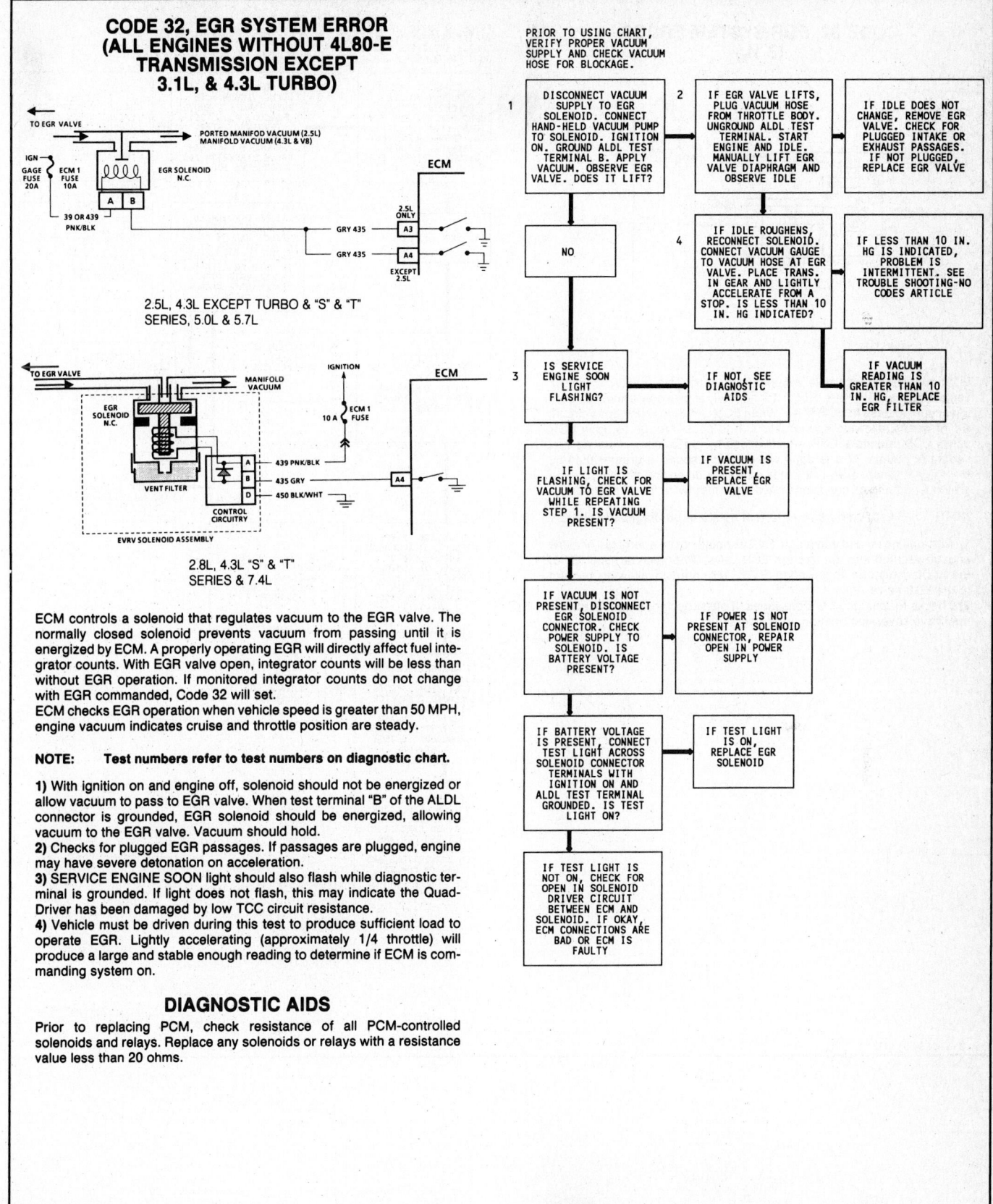

CODE 32, EGR SYSTEM ERROR (ALL ENGINES WITHOUT 4L80-E TRANSMISSION EXCEPT 3.1L, & 4.3L TURBO)

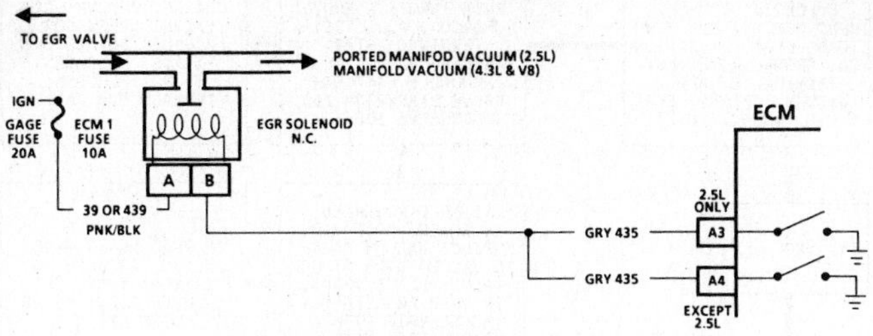
TO EGR VALVE
PORTED MANIFOD VACUUM (2.5L)
MANIFOLD VACUUM (4.3L & V8)
IGN
GAGE FUSE 20A
ECM 1 FUSE 10A
EGR SOLENOID N.C.
A
B
39 OR 439 PNK/BLK
ECM
2.5L ONLY
GRY 435
A3
GRY 435
A4
EXCEPT 2.5L

2.5L, 4.3L EXCEPT TURBO & "S" & "T" SERIES, 5.0L & 5.7L

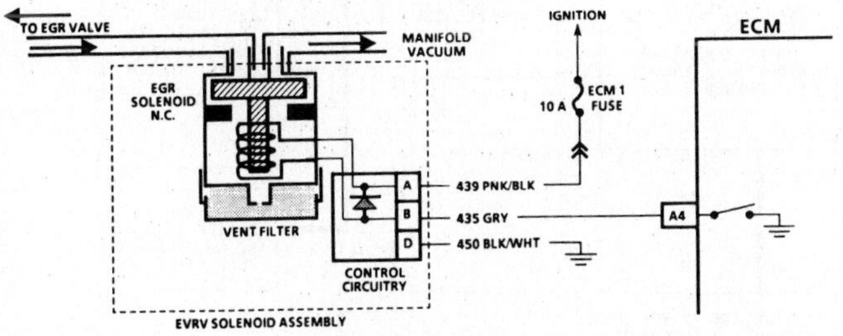
TO EGR VALVE
MANIFOLD VACUUM
IGNITION
ECM
EGR SOLENOID N.C.
10 A
ECM 1 FUSE
VENT FILTER
A
B
D
439 PNK/BLK
435 GRY
450 BLK/WHT
A4
CONTROL CIRCUITRY
EVRV SOLENOID ASSEMBLY

2.8L, 4.3L "S" & "T" SERIES & 7.4L

ECM controls a solenoid that regulates vacuum to the EGR valve. The normally closed solenoid prevents vacuum from passing until it is energized by ECM. A properly operating EGR will directly affect fuel integrator counts. With EGR valve open, integrator counts will be less than without EGR operation. If monitored integrator counts do not change with EGR commanded, Code 32 will set.
ECM checks EGR operation when vehicle speed is greater than 50 MPH, engine vacuum indicates cruise and throttle position are steady.

NOTE: Test numbers refer to test numbers on diagnostic chart.

1) With ignition on and engine off, solenoid should not be energized or allow vacuum to pass to EGR valve. When test terminal "B" of the ALDL connector is grounded, EGR solenoid should be energized, allowing vacuum to the EGR valve. Vacuum should hold.
2) Checks for plugged EGR passages. If passages are plugged, engine may have severe detonation on acceleration.
3) SERVICE ENGINE SOON light should also flash while diagnostic terminal is grounded. If light does not flash, this may indicate the Quad-Driver has been damaged by low TCC circuit resistance.
4) Vehicle must be driven during this test to produce sufficient load to operate EGR. Lightly accelerating (approximately 1/4 throttle) will produce a large and stable enough reading to determine if ECM is commanding system on.

DIAGNOSTIC AIDS

Prior to replacing PCM, check resistance of all PCM-controlled solenoids and relays. Replace any solenoids or relays with a resistance value less than 20 ohms.

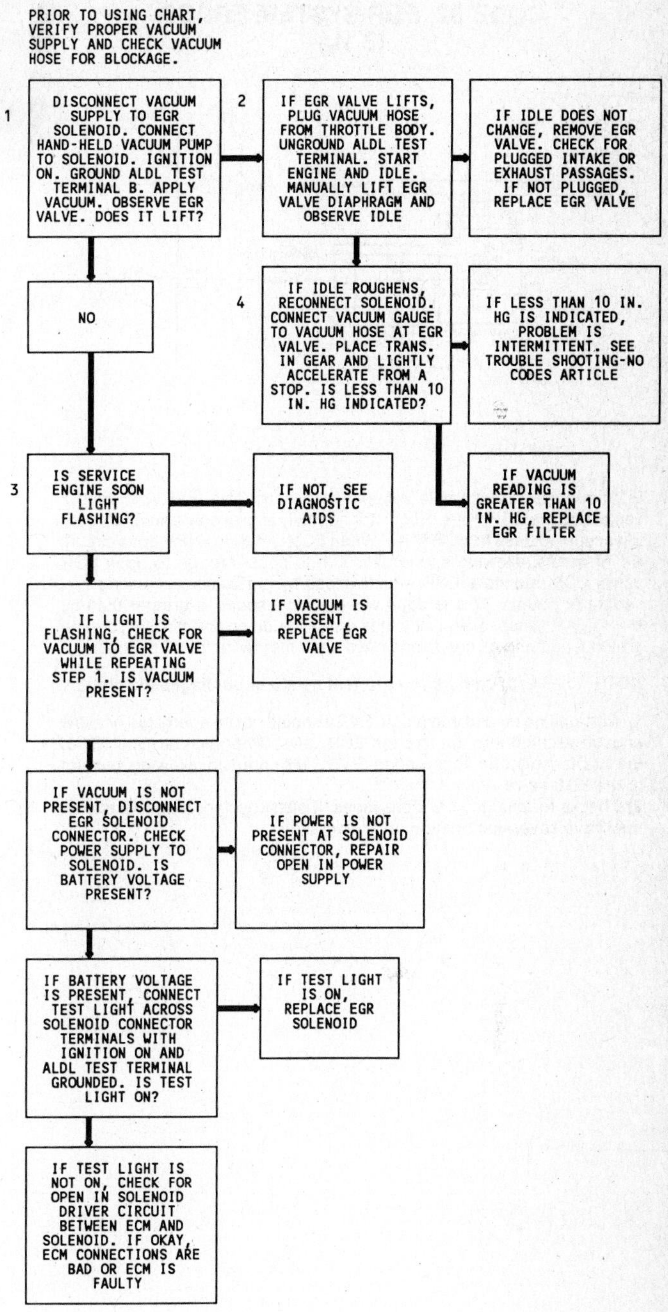
PRIOR TO USING CHART, VERIFY PROPER VACUUM SUPPLY AND CHECK VACUUM HOSE FOR BLOCKAGE.
1
DISCONNECT VACUUM SUPPLY TO EGR SOLENOID. CONNECT HAND-HELD VACUUM PUMP TO SOLENOID. IGNITION ON. GROUND ALDL TEST TERMINAL B. APPLY VACUUM. OBSERVE EGR VALVE. DOES IT LIFT?
2
IF EGR VALVE LIFTS, PLUG VACUUM HOSE FROM THROTTLE BODY. UNGROUND ALDL TEST TERMINAL. START ENGINE AND IDLE. MANUALLY LIFT EGR VALVE DIAPHRAGM AND OBSERVE IDLE
IF IDLE DOES NOT CHANGE, REMOVE EGR VALVE. CHECK FOR PLUGGED INTAKE OR EXHAUST PASSAGES. IF NOT PLUGGED, REPLACE EGR VALVE
NO
4
IF IDLE ROUGHENS, RECONNECT SOLENOID. CONNECT VACUUM GAUGE TO VACUUM HOSE AT EGR VALVE. PLACE TRANS. IN GEAR AND LIGHTLY ACCELERATE FROM A STOP. IS LESS THAN 10 IN. HG INDICATED?
IF LESS THAN 10 IN. HG IS INDICATED, PROBLEM IS INTERMITTENT. SEE TROUBLE SHOOTING-NO CODES ARTICLE
3
IS SERVICE ENGINE SOON LIGHT FLASHING?
IF NOT, SEE DIAGNOSTIC AIDS
IF VACUUM READING IS GREATER THAN 10 IN. HG, REPLACE EGR FILTER
IF LIGHT IS FLASHING, CHECK FOR VACUUM TO EGR VALVE WHILE REPEATING STEP 1. IS VACUUM PRESENT?
IF VACUUM IS PRESENT, REPLACE EGR VALVE
IF VACUUM IS NOT PRESENT, DISCONNECT EGR SOLENOID CONNECTOR. CHECK POWER SUPPLY TO SOLENOID. IS BATTERY VOLTAGE PRESENT?
IF POWER IS NOT PRESENT AT SOLENOID CONNECTOR, REPAIR OPEN IN POWER SUPPLY
IF BATTERY VOLTAGE IS PRESENT, CONNECT TEST LIGHT ACROSS SOLENOID CONNECTOR TERMINALS WITH IGNITION ON AND ALDL TEST TERMINAL GROUNDED. IS TEST LIGHT ON?
IF TEST LIGHT IS ON, REPLACE EGR SOLENOID
IF TEST LIGHT IS NOT ON, CHECK FOR OPEN IN SOLENOID DRIVER CIRCUIT BETWEEN ECM AND SOLENOID. IF OKAY, ECM CONNECTIONS ARE BAD OR ECM IS FAULTY

91I13746 91H13745 91J13671

1991 ENGINE PERFORMANCE
Self-Diagnostics – Gasoline (Cont.)

CODE 32, EGR SYSTEM ERROR
(3.1L)

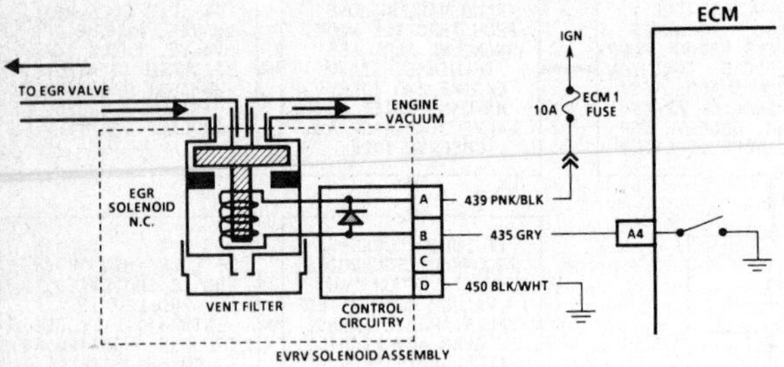
ECM
IGN
10A
ECM 1
FUSE
TO EGR VALVE
ENGINE
VACUUM
EGR
SOLENOID
N.C.
A
B
C
D
439 PNK/BLK
435 GRY
450 BLK/WHT
A4
VENT FILTER
CONTROL
CIRCUITRY
EVRV SOLENOID ASSEMBLY

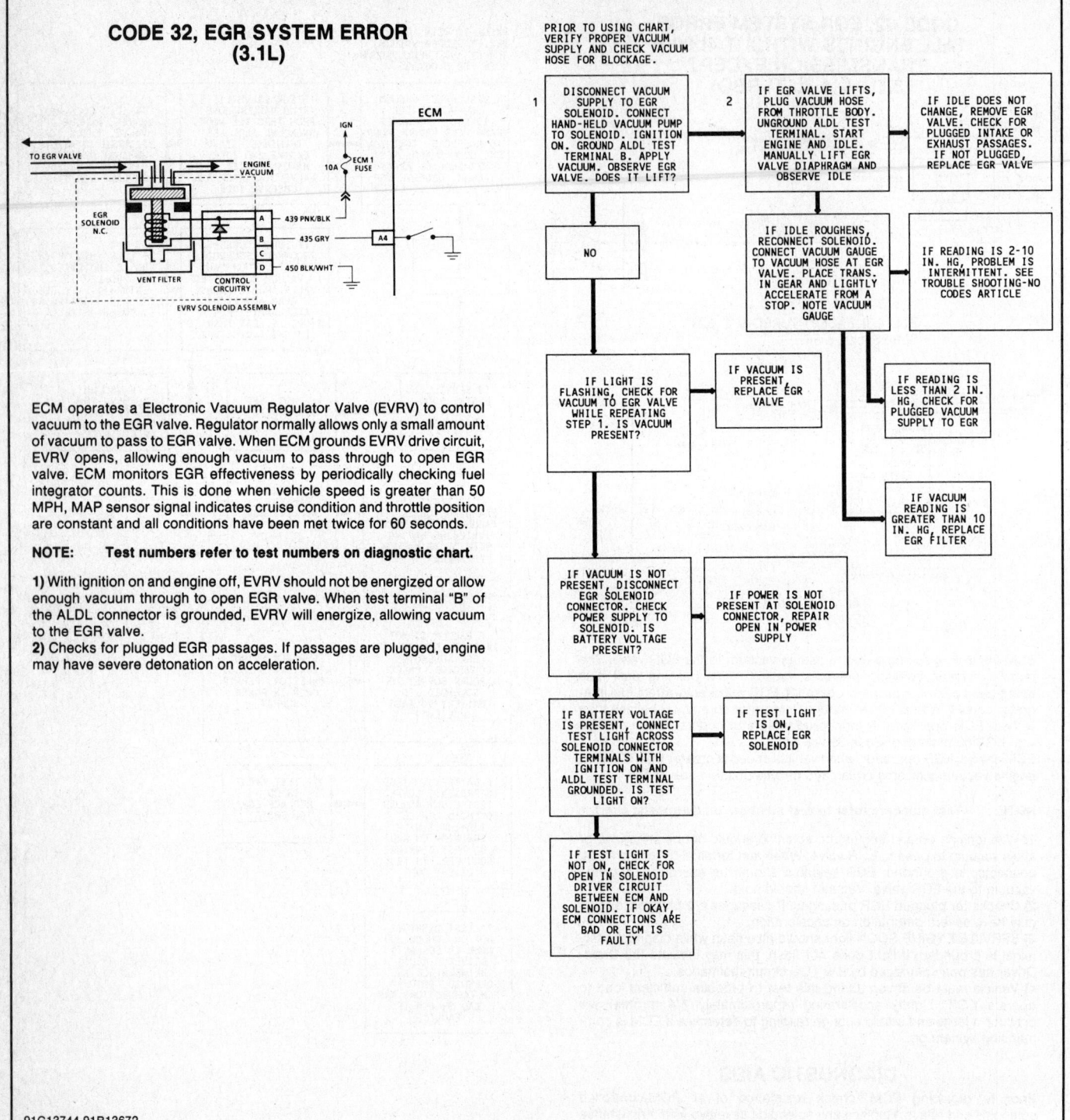

ECM operates a Electronic Vacuum Regulator Valve (EVRV) to control vacuum to the EGR valve. Regulator normally allows only a small amount of vacuum to pass to EGR valve. When ECM grounds EVRV drive circuit, EVRV opens, allowing enough vacuum to pass through to open EGR valve. ECM monitors EGR effectiveness by periodically checking fuel integrator counts. This is done when vehicle speed is greater than 50 MPH, MAP sensor signal indicates cruise condition and throttle position are constant and all conditions have been met twice for 60 seconds.

NOTE: **Test numbers refer to test numbers on diagnostic chart.**

1) With ignition on and engine off, EVRV should not be energized or allow enough vacuum through to open EGR valve. When test terminal "B" of the ALDL connector is grounded, EVRV will energize, allowing vacuum to the EGR valve.
2) Checks for plugged EGR passages. If passages are plugged, engine may have severe detonation on acceleration.

PRIOR TO USING CHART, VERIFY PROPER VACUUM SUPPLY AND CHECK VACUUM HOSE FOR BLOCKAGE.

1 DISCONNECT VACUUM SUPPLY TO EGR SOLENOID. CONNECT HAND-HELD VACUUM PUMP TO SOLENOID. IGNITION ON. GROUND ALDL TEST TERMINAL B. APPLY VACUUM. OBSERVE EGR VALVE. DOES IT LIFT?

2 IF EGR VALVE LIFTS, PLUG VACUUM HOSE FROM THROTTLE BODY. UNGROUND ALDL TEST TERMINAL. START ENGINE AND IDLE. MANUALLY LIFT EGR VALVE DIAPHRAGM AND OBSERVE IDLE

IF IDLE DOES NOT CHANGE, REMOVE EGR VALVE. CHECK FOR PLUGGED INTAKE OR EXHAUST PASSAGES. IF NOT PLUGGED, REPLACE EGR VALVE

IF IDLE ROUGHENS, RECONNECT SOLENOID. CONNECT VACUUM GAUGE TO VACUUM HOSE AT EGR VALVE. PLACE TRANS. IN GEAR AND LIGHTLY ACCELERATE FROM A STOP. NOTE VACUUM GAUGE

IF READING IS 2-10 IN. HG, PROBLEM IS INTERMITTENT. SEE TROUBLE SHOOTING-NO CODES ARTICLE

IF READING IS LESS THAN 2 IN. HG, CHECK FOR PLUGGED VACUUM SUPPLY TO EGR

IF VACUUM READING IS GREATER THAN 10 IN. HG, REPLACE EGR FILTER

NO

IF LIGHT IS FLASHING, CHECK FOR VACUUM TO EGR VALVE WHILE REPEATING STEP 1. IS VACUUM PRESENT?

IF VACUUM IS PRESENT, REPLACE EGR VALVE

IF VACUUM IS NOT PRESENT, DISCONNECT EGR SOLENOID CONNECTOR. CHECK POWER SUPPLY TO SOLENOID. IS BATTERY VOLTAGE PRESENT?

IF POWER IS NOT PRESENT AT SOLENOID CONNECTOR, REPAIR OPEN IN POWER SUPPLY

IF BATTERY VOLTAGE IS PRESENT, CONNECT TEST LIGHT ACROSS SOLENOID CONNECTOR TERMINALS WITH IGNITION ON AND ALDL TEST TERMINAL GROUNDED. IS TEST LIGHT ON?

IF TEST LIGHT IS ON, REPLACE EGR SOLENOID

IF TEST LIGHT IS NOT ON, CHECK FOR OPEN IN SOLENOID DRIVER CIRCUIT BETWEEN ECM AND SOLENOID. IF OKAY, ECM CONNECTIONS ARE BAD OR ECM IS FAULTY

91G13744 91B13672

CODE 32, EGR SYSTEM ERROR (4.3L TURBO)

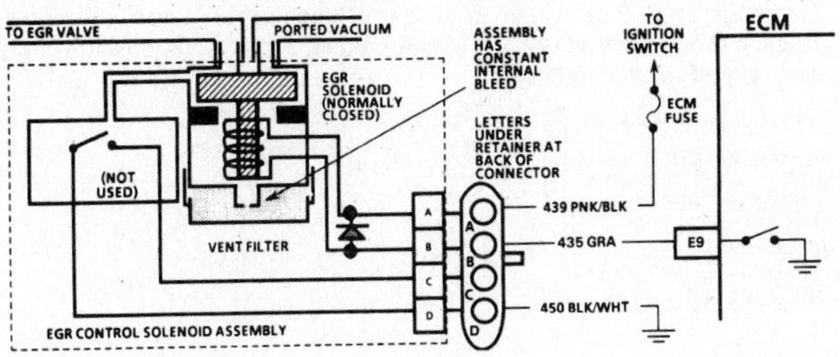

TO EGR VALVE
PORTED VACUUM
ASSEMBLY HAS CONSTANT INTERNAL BLEED
TO IGNITION SWITCH
ECM
EGR SOLENOID (NORMALLY CLOSED)
ECM FUSE
LETTERS UNDER RETAINER AT BACK OF CONNECTOR
(NOT USED)
439 PNK/BLK
VENT FILTER
435 GRA
E9
450 BLK/WHT
EGR CONTROL SOLENOID ASSEMBLY
A
B
C
D

ECM controls a solenoid that regulates vacuum to the EGR valve. The normally closed solenoid prevents vacuum from passing until it is energized by ECM. A properly operating EGR will directly affect fuel integrator counts. With EGR valve open, integrator counts will be less than without EGR operation. If monitored integrator counts do not change with EGR commanded, Code 32 will set.

NOTE: **Test numbers refer to test numbers on diagnostic chart.**

Diagnostic chart covers checks for the entire EGR system. If no trouble is found while performing chart routine, fault is an intermittent electrical problem or a sticky EGR valve.

DIAGNOSTIC AIDS

Vacuum switch in the EGR solenoid is not used. If EGR valve sticks open, a rough idle will result. If EGR solenoid vent filter becomes plugged, EGR valve will remain open or close slowly. An inoperative check valve in the ported vacuum supply line will result in faulty EGR system operation.

PRIOR TO USING CHART, VERIFY AT LEAST 20 IN. HG TO EGR SOLENOID AT 2000 RPM. IF VACUUM IS NOT ADEQUATE, CHECK HOSE AND VACUUM PORT FOR BLOCKAGE.

DISCONNECT VACUUM HOSE FROM EGR VALVE. START ENGINE. APPLY VACUUM TO EGR VALVE. DOES EGR VALVE HOLD VACUUM?

- NO → REPLACE EGR VALVE

IF EGR VALVE HOLDS VACUUM, DID APPLICATION OF VACUUM CAUSE ROUGH IDLE OR STALLING?

- IF VACUUM APPLICATION DID NOT CAUSE ROUGH IDLE OR STALLING, STOP ENGINE. TOUCH UNDERSIDE OF EGR VALVE. APPLY AND RELEASE VACUUM TO VALVE. DOES VALVE DIAPHRAGM MOVE?
  - IF VACUUM CAUSES VALVE DIAPHRAGM TO MOVE, REMOVE EGR VALVE AND CHECK FOR BLOCKED EGR VALVE PASSAGES
  - IF VACUUM DID NOT CAUSE DIAPHRAGM TO MOVE, REPLACE EGR VALVE
- YES

STOP ENGINE. DISCONNECT EGR VACUUM HOSE AT THROTTLE BODY. CONNECT VACUUM PUMP TO VACUUM HOSE TO EGR SOLENOID. TURN IGNITION ON. APPLY VACUUM. DOES EGR DIAPHRAGM MOVE?

- IF DIAPHRAGM MOVES, DISCONNECT EGR SOLENOID CONNECTOR. CONNECT TEST LIGHT ACROSS TERMINALS A & B. IS TEST LIGHT ON?
  - IF TEST LIGHT IS ON, EGR SOLENOID DRIVE CIRCUIT IS SHORTED TO GROUND BETWEEN ECM AND EGR SOLENOID
  - IF TEST LIGHT IS OFF, REPLACE EGR SOLENOID

IF DIAPHRAGM DOES NOT MOVE, GROUND ALDL TEST TERMINAL B AND APPLY AND RELEASE VACUUM. DOES DIAPHRAGM MOVE?

- IF DIAPHRAGM MOVES, NO FAULT IS CURRENTLY PRESENT. CHECK FOR INTERMITTENT ELECTRICAL CONNECTIONS

IF DIAPHRAGM DOES NOT MOVE, VERIFY POWER AND GROUND SUPPLY TO EGR SOLENOID CONNECTOR. IS POWER AND GROUND PRESENT?

- YES → CHECK FOR VACUUM LEAKS BETWEEN THROTTLE BODY AND EGR VALVE. CHECK SOLENOID ELECTRICAL CONNECTIONS. CHECK FOR PLUGGED EGR FILTER. IF OKAY, REPLACE EGR SOLENOID

IF POWER OR GROUND IS NOT PRESENT, REPAIR OPEN IN POWER OR GROUND CIRCUIT TO SOLENOID

91F13743 91I13712

1991 ENGINE PERFORMANCE
Self-Diagnostics – Gasoline (Cont.)

CODE 33, MAP SENSOR SIGNAL VOLTAGE HIGH

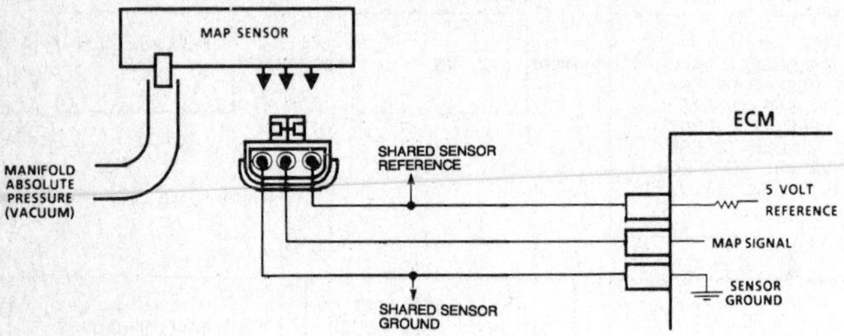
MAP SENSOR
MANIFOLD ABSOLUTE PRESSURE (VACUUM)
SHARED SENSOR REFERENCE
ECM
5 VOLT REFERENCE
MAP SIGNAL
SENSOR GROUND
SHARED SENSOR GROUND

CODE 33 ECM TERMINAL & CIRCUIT WIRING IDENTIFICATION

Application	ECM Terminal	Wire Color
Astro & Safari 4.3L & 2.5L "S" Series		
MAP Signal	C11	[1] Light Green
MAP Ground	D2	Black/Red
MAP Reference	C14	Gray
All With 4L80-E Transmission		
MAP Signal	C10	Light Green
MAP Ground	D2	Purple
MAP Reference	D4	Green
2.8L, 3.1L & V8 "C" & "K" Series		
MAP Signal	C11	[1] Light Green
MAP Ground	A11	Purple
MAP Reference	C14	Gray
4.3L Turbo		
MAP Signal	GF15	Light Green
MAP Ground	BB6	Black
MAP Reference	BA4	Gray
4.3L Except Turbo, & V8 Except "C" & "K" Series		
MAP Signal	C11	[1] Light Green
MAP Ground	D2	Purple
MAP Reference	C14	Gray

[1] — May have a Black trace.

The Manifold Absolute Pressure (MAP) sensor responds to changes in manifold pressure (vacuum). If MAP sensor fails, ECM will substitute a fixed MAP value and use the TPS input to control fuel delivery.

NOTE: Test numbers refer to test numbers on diagnostic chart.

1) This test confirms Code 33 and determines if it is a hard failure or an intermittent condition. Code 33 will set when voltage signal reading is too high and TPS voltage indicates throttle is closed.
2) This step simulates conditions for a Code 34. If the ECM recognizes and indicates low MAP signal, the ECM and 5-volt reference and MAP signal circuits are not at fault.

DIAGNOSTIC AIDS

With the ignition switch in the ON position and engine off, manifold pressure is equal to atmospheric pressure and signal voltage is high. Comparing BARO readings from a known good vehicle using the same sensor is a good way to check the accuracy of the suspected sensor. Readings should be within ± .4 volt of each other. Code 33 will also result if ground circuit is open or MAP signal circuit is shorted to voltage or to 5-volt reference circuit.

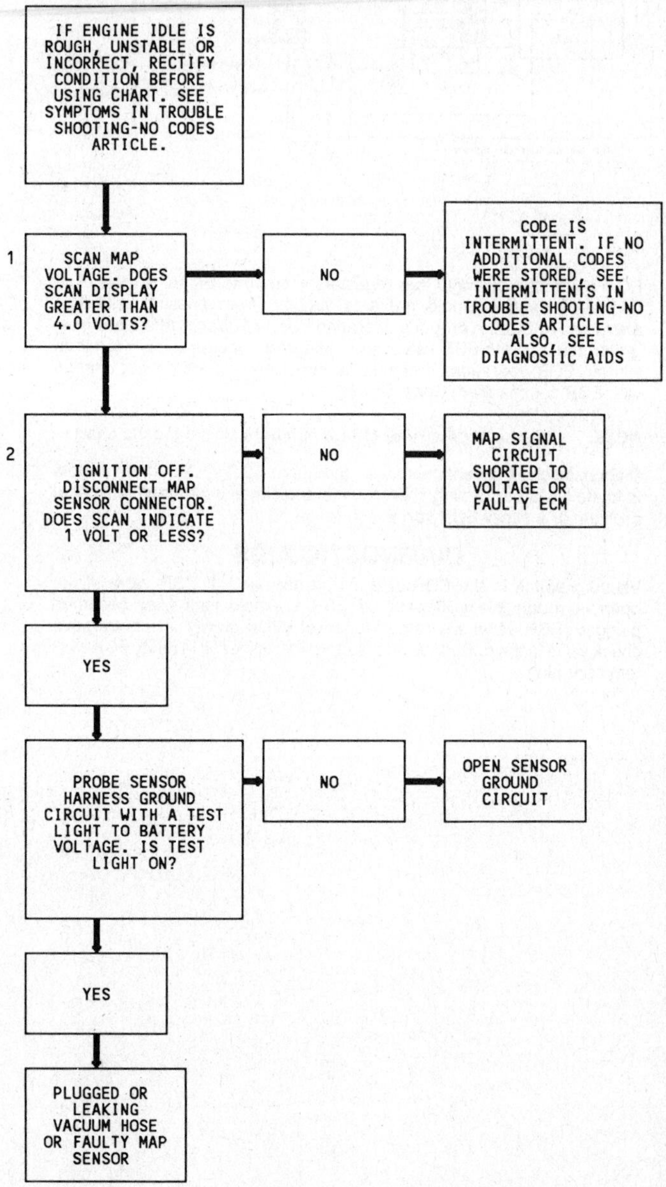
IF ENGINE IDLE IS ROUGH, UNSTABLE OR INCORRECT, RECTIFY CONDITION BEFORE USING CHART. SEE SYMPTOMS IN TROUBLE SHOOTING-NO CODES ARTICLE.
1
SCAN MAP VOLTAGE. DOES SCAN DISPLAY GREATER THAN 4.0 VOLTS?
NO
CODE IS INTERMITTENT. IF NO ADDITIONAL CODES WERE STORED, SEE INTERMITTENTS IN TROUBLE SHOOTING-NO CODES ARTICLE. ALSO, SEE DIAGNOSTIC AIDS
2
IGNITION OFF. DISCONNECT MAP SENSOR CONNECTOR. DOES SCAN INDICATE 1 VOLT OR LESS?
NO
MAP SIGNAL CIRCUIT SHORTED TO VOLTAGE OR FAULTY ECM
YES
PROBE SENSOR HARNESS GROUND CIRCUIT WITH A TEST LIGHT TO BATTERY VOLTAGE. IS TEST LIGHT ON?
NO
OPEN SENSOR GROUND CIRCUIT
YES
PLUGGED OR LEAKING VACUUM HOSE OR FAULTY MAP SENSOR

91D07423 91G07330

CODE 34, MAP SENSOR SIGNAL VOLTAGE LOW

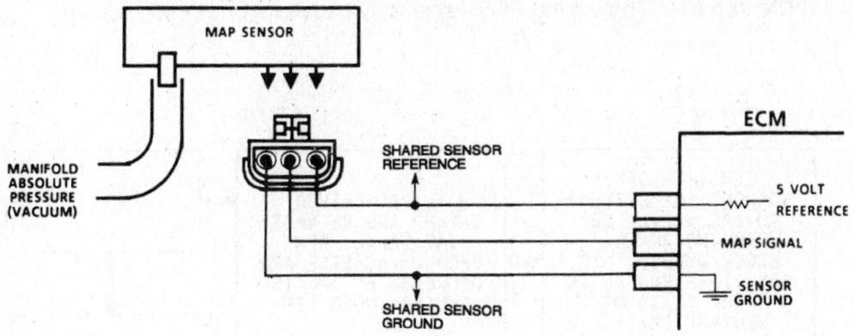
MAP SENSOR
MANIFOLD ABSOLUTE PRESSURE (VACUUM)
ECM
SHARED SENSOR REFERENCE
5 VOLT REFERENCE
MAP SIGNAL
SENSOR GROUND
SHARED SENSOR GROUND

CODE 34 ECM TERMINAL & CIRCUIT WIRING IDENTIFICATION

Application	ECM Terminal	Wire Color
Astro & Safari 4.3L & 2.5L "S" Series		
MAP Signal	C11	[1] Light Green
MAP Ground	D2	Black/Red
MAP Reference	C14	Gray
All With 4L80-E Transmission		
MAP Signal	C10	Light Green
MAP Ground	D2	Purple
MAP Reference	D4	Green
2.8L, 3.1L & V8 "C" & "K" Series		
MAP Signal	C11	[1] Light Green
MAP Ground	A11	Purple
MAP Reference	C14	Gray
4.3L Turbo		
MAP Signal	GF15	Light Green
MAP Ground	BB6	Black
MAP Reference	BA4	Gray
4.3L Except Turbo, & V8 Except "C" & "K" Series		
MAP Signal	C11	[1] Light Green
MAP Ground	D2	Purple
MAP Reference	C14	Gray

[1] — May have a Black trace.

The Manifold Absolute Pressure (MAP) sensor responds to changes in manifold pressure (vacuum). If the MAP sensor fails, the ECM will substitute a fixed MAP value and use TPS input to control fuel delivery.

NOTE: Test numbers refer to test numbers on diagnostic chart.

1) This confirms Code 34 and determines if code was a hard failure or an intermittent condition. Code 34 will set when ignition is on and MAP signal voltage is low. On some systems, engine must be running to set code.
2) Jumpering harness terminals "B" to "C" will determine if problem is sensor, ECM or wiring. If ECM recognizes and indicates high MAP signal, ECM and wiring are okay.
3) Scan tester may not display 12 volts. The important thing is the ECM recognizes the voltage as greater than 4 volts (high MAP voltage signal), indicating the ECM and MAP signal circuit are not at fault.

DIAGNOSTIC AIDS

With the ignition switch in the ON position and engine off, manifold pressure is equal to atmospheric pressure and the signal voltage will be high. Comparing BARO readings with a known good vehicle using the same sensor is a good way to check the accuracy of the suspected sensor. Readings should be within ± .4 volt of each other. A Code 34 will also result if 5-volt reference and MAP signal circuits are open or shorted to ground. If 5-volt reference circuit is not shorted to ground and a Code 22 is stored, check MAP signal circuit for short to ground.

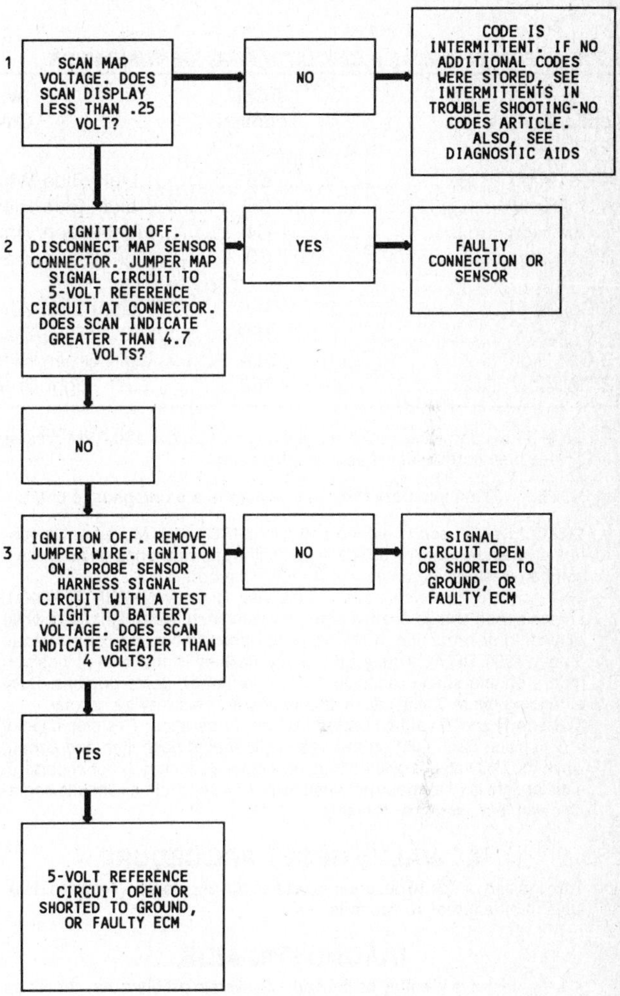
1
SCAN MAP VOLTAGE. DOES SCAN DISPLAY LESS THAN .25 VOLT?
NO
CODE IS INTERMITTENT. IF NO ADDITIONAL CODES WERE STORED, SEE INTERMITTENTS IN TROUBLE SHOOTING-NO CODES ARTICLE. ALSO, SEE DIAGNOSTIC AIDS
2
IGNITION OFF. DISCONNECT MAP SENSOR CONNECTOR. JUMPER MAP SIGNAL CIRCUIT TO 5-VOLT REFERENCE CIRCUIT AT CONNECTOR. DOES SCAN INDICATE GREATER THAN 4.7 VOLTS?
YES
FAULTY CONNECTION OR SENSOR
NO
3
IGNITION OFF. REMOVE JUMPER WIRE. IGNITION ON. PROBE SENSOR HARNESS SIGNAL CIRCUIT WITH A TEST LIGHT TO BATTERY VOLTAGE. DOES SCAN INDICATE GREATER THAN 4 VOLTS?
NO
SIGNAL CIRCUIT OPEN OR SHORTED TO GROUND, OR FAULTY ECM
YES
5-VOLT REFERENCE CIRCUIT OPEN OR SHORTED TO GROUND, OR FAULTY ECM

91D07423 91I07331

1991 ENGINE PERFORMANCE
Self-Diagnostics – Gasoline (Cont.)

CODE 35, IDLE SPEED ERROR (2.5L & 4.3L TURBO)

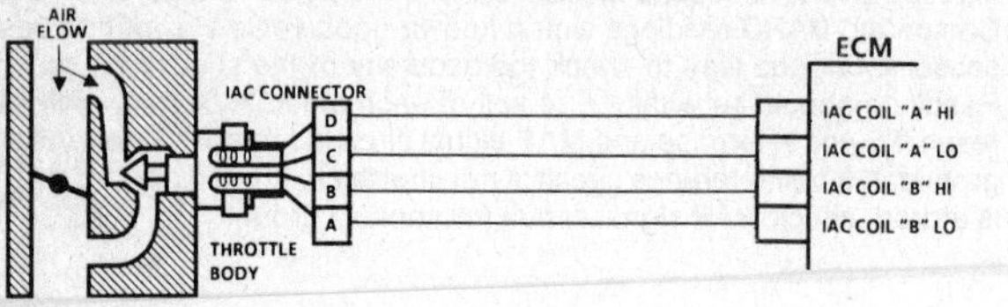
AIR FLOW
ECM
IAC CONNECTOR
D
C
B
A
IAC COIL "A" HI
IAC COIL "A" LO
IAC COIL "B" HI
IAC COIL "B" LO
THROTTLE BODY

CODE 35 ECM TERMINAL & CIRCUIT WIRING IDENTIFICATION

Application	ECM Terminal	Wire Color
2.5L		
A Coil High	C5	Light Blue/White
A Coil Low	C6	Light Blue/Black
B Coil High	C4	Light Green/White
B Coil Low	C3	Light Green/Black
4.3L Turbo		
A Coil High	GE6	Light Blue/White
A Coil Low	GE5	Blue/Black
B Coil High	GE4	Light Green/Black
B Coil Low	GE3	Light Green

Code 35 will set when closed throttle engine speed is 150 RPM greater or less than correct idle speed for 20 seconds.

NOTE: Test numbers refer to test numbers on diagnostic chart.

1) IAC driver is used to extend and retract IAC valve. Movement is verified by changing engine speed. If no engine speed change occurs, valve can be retested when removed from throttle body.
2) Checks IAC movement quality from step **1)**. Between 700-1500 RPM, engine speed should change smoothly with each tester light flash while extending or retracting. If IAC valve is retracted beyond control range (about 1500 RPM), it may take many flashes in the extend position before engine speed reduces. This is normal on some engines. Fully extending the IAC may cause engine to stall. This may be normal.
3) Steps **1)** and **2)** verified proper IAC valve operation. This step checks IAC circuits. Each light on the node light should flash Red and Green, while the IAC valve is cycled. While the color sequence is not important, if either light is off or does not flash Red and Green, check circuits beginning with poor terminal contacts.

IAC VALVE RESET PROCEDURE

Turn ignition off for 10 seconds. Start and run engine for 5 seconds. Turn ignition off another 10 seconds.

DIAGNOSTIC AIDS

A slow, unstable idle may be caused by a system problem that cannot be overcome by IAC. Scan counts will be greater than 60 if too low, and zero counts if too high. If idle is too high, stop engine. With ignition on, ground ALDL test terminal "B". Wait 45 seconds for IAC to seat, then disconnect IAC. Start engine. If idle speed is greater than 800 RPM, inspect vehicle for vacuum leaks.
System Too Lean – If air/fuel ratio is too lean, the idle speed may be either too high (check for vacuum leaks) or too low. Engine speed may vary and disconnecting the IAC may not help. Scan tester and/or digital voltmeter (10 megohm) will read an oxygen sensor output less than 300 mv (.3 volt). Check for low fuel pressure or water in the fuel.
System Too Rich – If air/fuel ratio is too rich, idle speed will be too low and Scan tester counts will usually be greater than 80. The system may be obviously rich with Black smoke from tailpipe. Scan tester and/or voltmeter will read an oxygen sensor voltage signal fixed greater than 800 mv (.8 volt). Look for high fuel pressure or leaking/sticky injectors. Remove IAC and inspect bore for foreign material or evidence of IAC valve dragging the bore. A silicone-contaminated oxygen sensor will produce lean air/fuel mixture. Oxygen sensor output would be fixed greater than 800 mv (.8 volt). This may also set Code 45.

Throttle Body – Remove IAC and inspect bore for evidence of IAC valve dragging.
IAC Valve Connections – Carefully inspect connections for looseness or corrosion.
PCV Valve – The wrong PCV valve may cause incorrect idle speed.

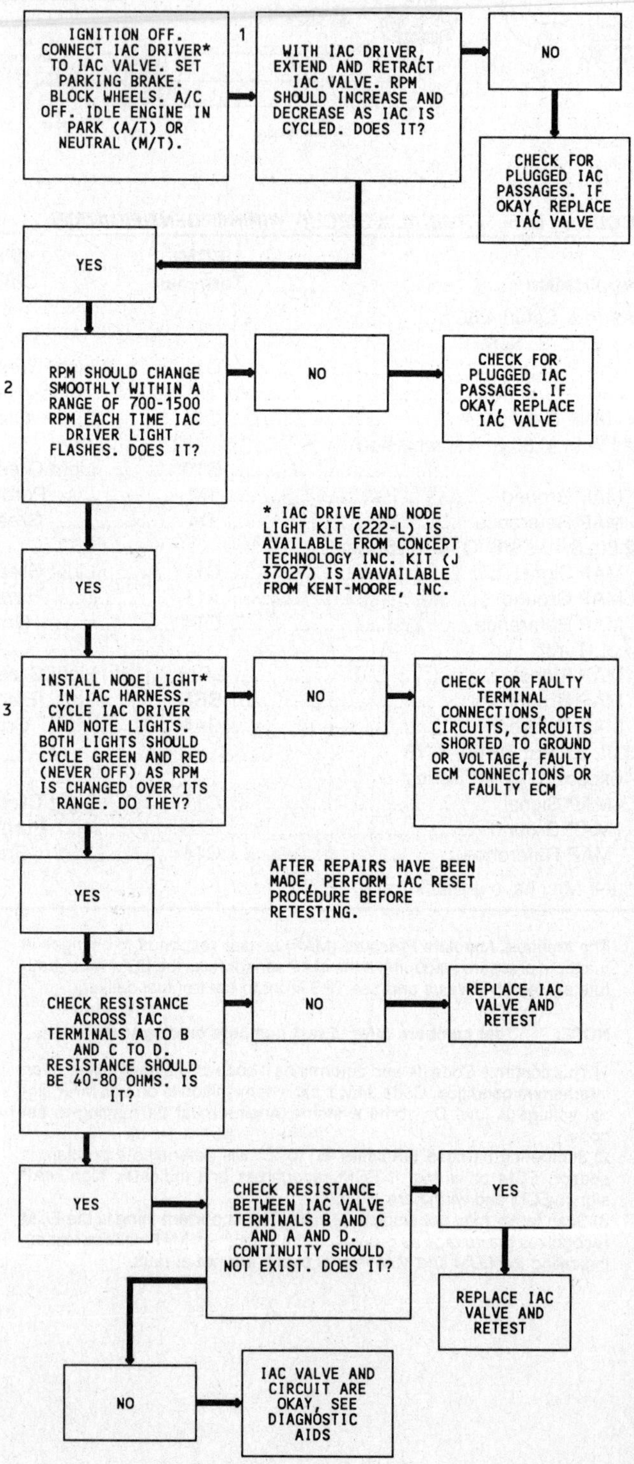
IGNITION OFF. CONNECT IAC DRIVER* TO IAC VALVE. SET PARKING BRAKE. BLOCK WHEELS. A/C OFF. IDLE ENGINE IN PARK (A/T) OR NEUTRAL (M/T).
1
WITH IAC DRIVER, EXTEND AND RETRACT IAC VALVE. RPM SHOULD INCREASE AND DECREASE AS IAC IS CYCLED. DOES IT?
NO
CHECK FOR PLUGGED IAC PASSAGES. IF OKAY, REPLACE IAC VALVE
YES
2
RPM SHOULD CHANGE SMOOTHLY WITHIN A RANGE OF 700-1500 RPM EACH TIME IAC DRIVER LIGHT FLASHES. DOES IT?
NO
CHECK FOR PLUGGED IAC PASSAGES. IF OKAY, REPLACE IAC VALVE
* IAC DRIVE AND NODE LIGHT KIT (222-L) IS AVAILABLE FROM CONCEPT TECHNOLOGY INC. KIT (J 37027) IS AVAVAILABLE FROM KENT-MOORE, INC.
YES
3
INSTALL NODE LIGHT* IN IAC HARNESS. CYCLE IAC DRIVER AND NOTE LIGHTS. BOTH LIGHTS SHOULD CYCLE GREEN AND RED (NEVER OFF) AS RPM IS CHANGED OVER ITS RANGE. DO THEY?
NO
CHECK FOR FAULTY TERMINAL CONNECTIONS, OPEN CIRCUITS, CIRCUITS SHORTED TO GROUND OR VOLTAGE, FAULTY ECM CONNECTIONS OR FAULTY ECM
YES
AFTER REPAIRS HAVE BEEN MADE, PERFORM IAC RESET PROCEDURE BEFORE RETESTING.
CHECK RESISTANCE ACROSS IAC TERMINALS A TO B AND C TO D. RESISTANCE SHOULD BE 40-80 OHMS. IS IT?
NO
REPLACE IAC VALVE AND RETEST
YES
CHECK RESISTANCE BETWEEN IAC VALVE TERMINALS B AND C AND A AND D. CONTINUITY SHOULD NOT EXIST. DOES IT?
YES
REPLACE IAC VALVE AND RETEST
NO
IAC VALVE AND CIRCUIT ARE OKAY, SEE DIAGNOSTIC AIDS

91E07428 91C07333

CODE 42, ELECTRONIC SPARK TIMING (1 OF 2)

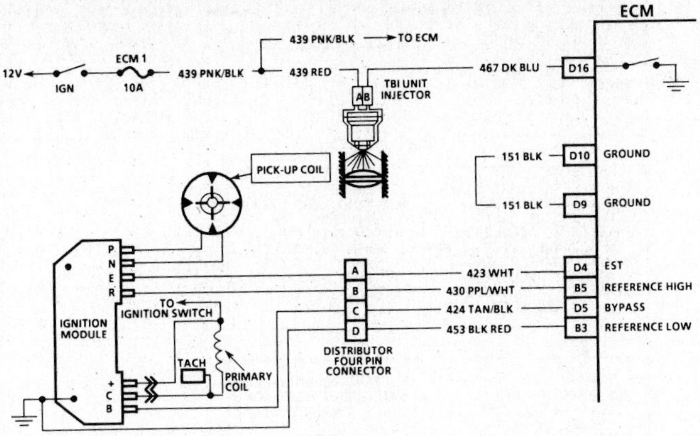
ECM
439 PNK/BLK
TO ECM
12V
IGN
ECM 1
10A
439 PNK/BLK
439 RED
467 DK BLU
D16
TBI UNIT INJECTOR
PICK-UP COIL
151 BLK
D10
GROUND
151 BLK
D9
GROUND
P
N
E
R
IGNITION MODULE
TO IGNITION SWITCH
TACH
PRIMARY COIL
A
B
C
D
DISTRIBUTOR FOUR PIN CONNECTOR
423 WHT
D4
EST
430 PPL/WHT
B5
REFERENCE HIGH
424 TAN/BLK
D5
BYPASS
453 BLK RED
B3
REFERENCE LOW

2.5L

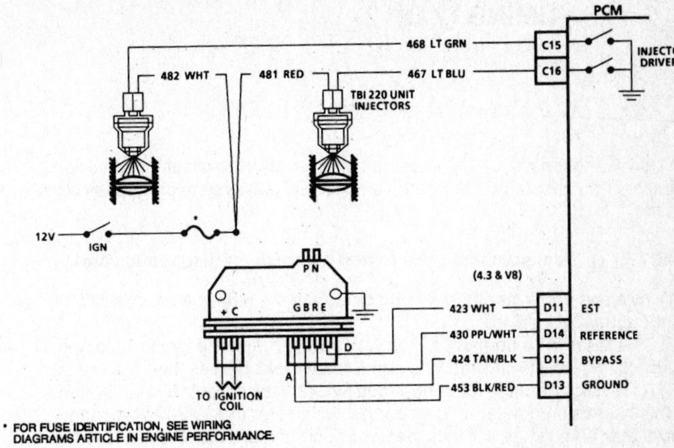
PCM
468 LT GRN
C15
467 LT BLU
C16
INJECTOR DRIVERS
482 WHT
481 RED
TBI 220 UNIT INJECTORS
12V
IGN
(4.3 & V8)
423 WHT
D11
EST
430 PPL/WHT
D14
REFERENCE
424 TAN/BLK
D12
BYPASS
453 BLK/RED
D13
GROUND
TO IGNITION COIL
* FOR FUSE IDENTIFICATION, SEE WIRING DIAGRAMS ARTICLE IN ENGINE PERFORMANCE.

ALL ENGINES WITH 4L80-E TRANSMISSION

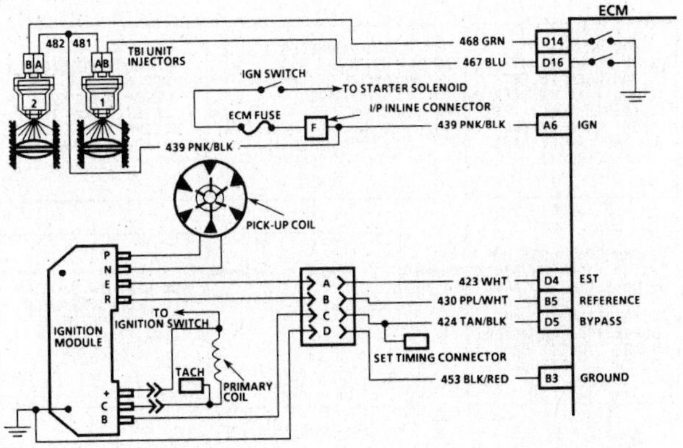
ECM
482
481
TBI UNIT INJECTORS
468 GRN
D14
467 BLU
D16
IGN SWITCH
TO STARTER SOLENOID
ECM FUSE
I/P INLINE CONNECTOR
439 PNK/BLK
A6
IGN
439 PNK/BLK
PICK-UP COIL
IGNITION MODULE
TO IGNITION SWITCH
TACH
PRIMARY COIL
423 WHT
D4
EST
430 PPL/WHT
B5
REFERENCE
424 TAN/BLK
D5
BYPASS
SET TIMING CONNECTOR
453 BLK/RED
B3
GROUND

3 1

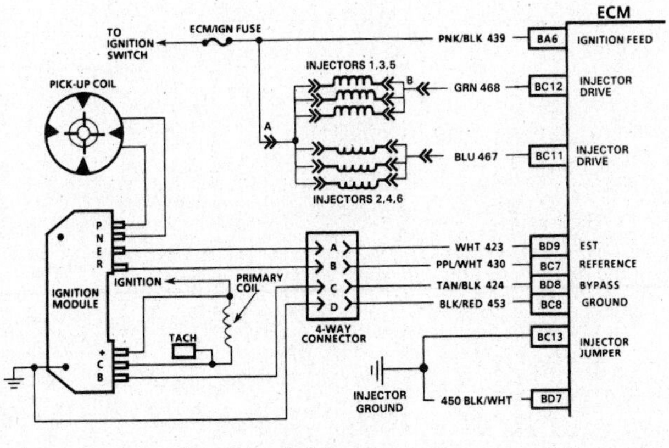
ECM
TO IGNITION SWITCH
ECM/IGN FUSE
PNK/BLK 439
BA6
IGNITION FEED
INJECTORS 1,3,5
GRN 468
BC12
INJECTOR DRIVE
BLU 467
BC11
INJECTOR DRIVE
INJECTORS 2,4,6
PICK-UP COIL
IGNITION MODULE
IGNITION
PRIMARY COIL
TACH
4-WAY CONNECTOR
WHT 423
BD9
EST
PPL/WHT 430
BC7
REFERENCE
TAN/BLK 424
BD8
BYPASS
BLK/RED 453
BC8
GROUND
BC13
INJECTOR JUMPER
INJECTOR GROUND
450 BLK/WHT
BD7

4.3L TURBO

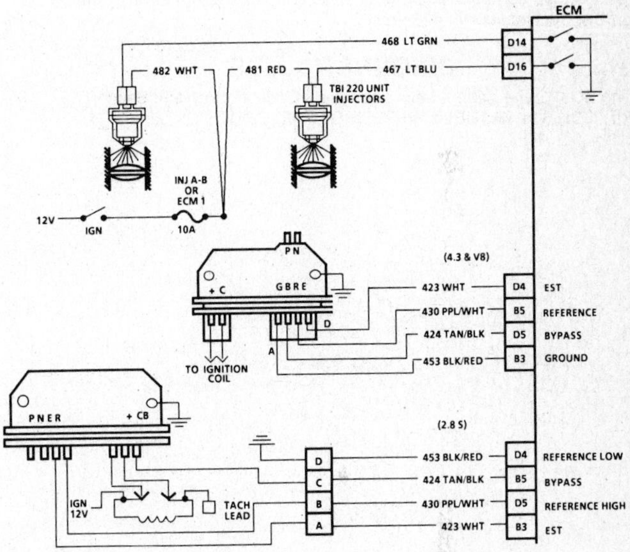
ECM
468 LT GRN
D14
482 WHT
481 RED
467 LT BLU
D16
TBI 220 UNIT INJECTORS
INJ A-B OR ECM 1
12V
IGN
10A
(4.3 & V8)
423 WHT
D4
EST
430 PPL/WHT
B5
REFERENCE
424 TAN/BLK
D5
BYPASS
453 BLK/RED
B3
GROUND
TO IGNITION COIL
(2.8 S)
453 BLK/RED
D4
REFERENCE LOW
424 TAN/BLK
B5
BYPASS
430 PPL/WHT
D5
REFERENCE HIGH
423 WHT
B3
EST
IGN 12V
TACH LEAD

ALL ENGINE WITHOUT 4L80-E TRANSMISSION
EXCEPT 2.5L, 3.1L & 4.3L TURBO

91F13602 91G13603 91C13609 91I13605 91A13604

1991 ENGINE PERFORMANCE
Self-Diagnostics – Gasoline (Cont.)

CODE 42, ELECTRONIC SPARK TIMING (2 OF 2)

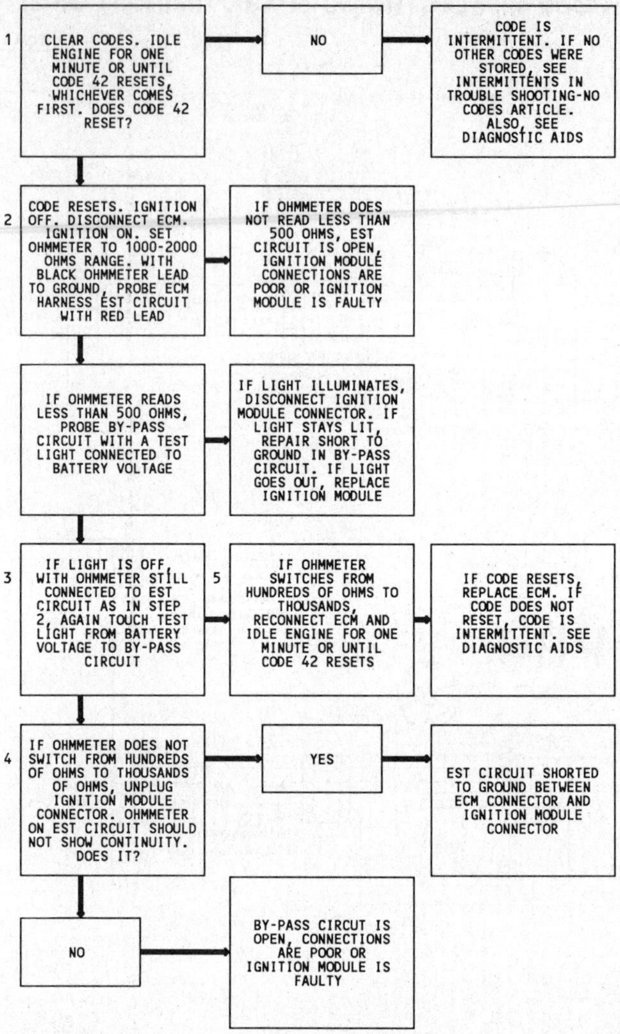
1
CLEAR CODES. IDLE ENGINE FOR ONE MINUTE OR UNTIL CODE 42 RESETS, WHICHEVER COMES FIRST. DOES CODE 42 RESET?
NO
CODE IS INTERMITTENT. IF NO OTHER CODES WERE STORED, SEE INTERMITTENTS IN TROUBLE SHOOTING-NO CODES ARTICLE. ALSO, SEE DIAGNOSTIC AIDS
2
CODE RESETS. IGNITION OFF. DISCONNECT ECM. IGNITION ON. SET OHMMETER TO 1000-2000 OHMS RANGE. WITH BLACK OHMMETER LEAD TO GROUND, PROBE ECM HARNESS EST CIRCUIT WITH RED LEAD
IF OHMMETER DOES NOT READ LESS THAN 500 OHMS, EST CIRCUIT IS OPEN, IGNITION MODULE CONNECTIONS ARE POOR OR IGNITION MODULE IS FAULTY
IF OHMMETER READS LESS THAN 500 OHMS, PROBE BY-PASS CIRCUIT WITH A TEST LIGHT CONNECTED TO BATTERY VOLTAGE
IF LIGHT ILLUMINATES, DISCONNECT IGNITION MODULE CONNECTOR. IF LIGHT STAYS LIT, REPAIR SHORT TO GROUND IN BY-PASS CIRCUIT. IF LIGHT GOES OUT, REPLACE IGNITION MODULE
3
IF LIGHT IS OFF, WITH OHMMETER STILL CONNECTED TO EST CIRCUIT AS IN STEP 2, AGAIN TOUCH TEST LIGHT FROM BATTERY VOLTAGE TO BY-PASS CIRCUIT
5
IF OHMMETER SWITCHES FROM HUNDREDS OF OHMS TO THOUSANDS, RECONNECT ECM AND IDLE ENGINE FOR ONE MINUTE OR UNTIL CODE 42 RESETS
IF CODE RESETS, REPLACE ECM. IF CODE DOES NOT RESET, CODE IS INTERMITTENT. SEE DIAGNOSTIC AIDS
4
IF OHMMETER DOES NOT SWITCH FROM HUNDREDS OF OHMS TO THOUSANDS OF OHMS, UNPLUG IGNITION MODULE CONNECTOR. OHMMETER ON EST CIRCUIT SHOULD NOT SHOW CONTINUITY. DOES IT?
YES
EST CIRCUIT SHORTED TO GROUND BETWEEN ECM CONNECTOR AND IGNITION MODULE CONNECTOR
NO
BY-PASS CIRCUT IS OPEN, CONNECTIONS ARE POOR OR IGNITION MODULE IS FAULTY

Code 42 indicates ECM has seen an open or short to ground in the High Energy Ignition Electronic Spark Timing (HEI EST) system or by-pass circuits.

NOTE: **Test numbers refer to test numbers on diagnostic chart.**

1) This test confirms Code 42 and determines if fault is a hard failure or intermittent condition.
2) This tests for a normal EST ground path through the ignition module. If circuit No. 423 is shorted to ground, reading will be less than 500 ohms.
3) As test light voltage touches circuit No. 424, the module should switch. This causes ohmmeter to "over-range" with meter in 100-200 ohm range. A higher ohm range will indicate over 5000 ohms. This test assures the module switched.
4) If module did not switch, this step tests for a short in circuit No. 423, an open in circuit No. 424 and a faulty ignition module connection or module.
5) This step confirms Code 42 is a faulty ECM and not an intermittent problem in circuits No. 423 and 424.

DIAGNOSTIC AIDS

The Scan tester cannot help diagnose a Code 42 problem. See INTERMITTENTS in TROUBLE SHOOTING – NO CODES article.

91I07345

CODE 43, ELECTRONIC SPARK CONTROL (ALL ENGINES EXCEPT 4.3L TURBO & MODELS WITH 4L80-E TRANSMISSION)

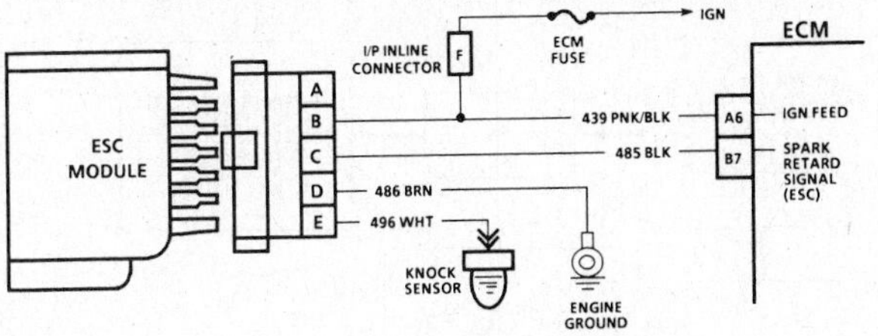

IGN
ECM
I/P INLINE CONNECTOR
F
ECM FUSE
A
B
C
D
E
ESC MODULE
439 PNK/BLK
485 BLK
486 BRN
496 WHT
A6
B7
IGN FEED
SPARK RETARD SIGNAL (ESC)
KNOCK SENSOR
ENGINE GROUND

3.1L

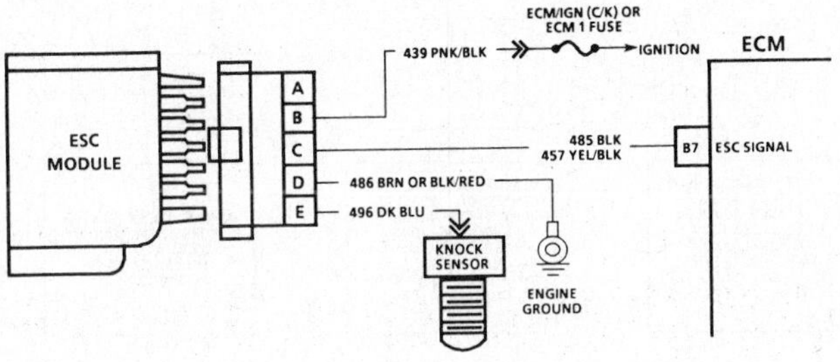

ECM/IGN (C/K) OR ECM 1 FUSE
439 PNK/BLK
IGNITION
ECM
ESC MODULE
A
B
C
D
E
485 BLK
457 YEL/BLK
B7
ESC SIGNAL
486 BRN OR BLK/RED
496 DK BLU
KNOCK SENSOR
ENGINE GROUND

EXCEPT 3.1L

DIAGNOSTIC AIDS

Code 43 can be caused by a faulty knock sensor connection at the ESC module or ECM. Also, check the controller-to-ECM signal line for an open or short to ground.

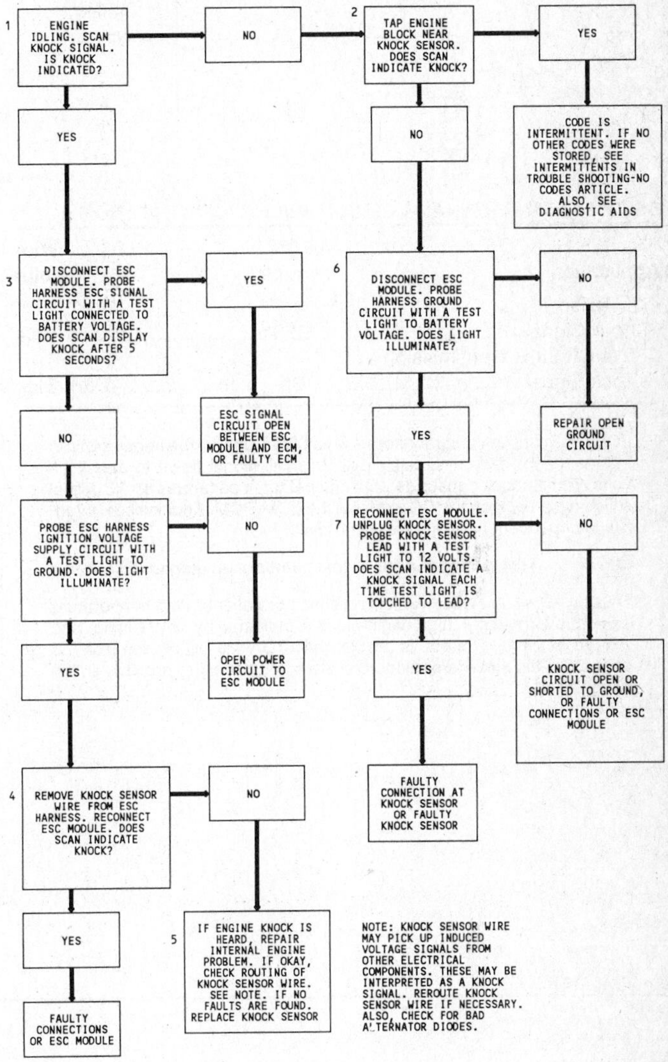

1
ENGINE IDLING. SCAN KNOCK SIGNAL. IS KNOCK INDICATED?
NO
YES
2
TAP ENGINE BLOCK NEAR KNOCK SENSOR. DOES SCAN INDICATE KNOCK?
YES
NO
CODE IS INTERMITTENT. IF NO OTHER CODES WERE STORED, SEE INTERMITTENTS IN TROUBLE SHOOTING-NO CODES ARTICLE. ALSO, SEE DIAGNOSTIC AIDS
3
DISCONNECT ESC MODULE. PROBE HARNESS ESC SIGNAL CIRCUIT WITH A TEST LIGHT CONNECTED TO BATTERY VOLTAGE. DOES SCAN DISPLAY KNOCK AFTER 5 SECONDS?
YES
ESC SIGNAL CIRCUIT OPEN BETWEEN ESC MODULE AND ECM, OR FAULTY ECM
NO
PROBE ESC HARNESS IGNITION VOLTAGE SUPPLY CIRCUIT WITH A TEST LIGHT TO GROUND. DOES LIGHT ILLUMINATE?
NO
OPEN POWER CIRCUIT TO ESC MODULE
YES
4
REMOVE KNOCK SENSOR WIRE FROM ESC HARNESS. RECONNECT ESC MODULE. DOES SCAN INDICATE KNOCK?
NO
5
IF ENGINE KNOCK IS HEARD, REPAIR INTERNAL ENGINE PROBLEM. IF OKAY, CHECK ROUTING OF KNOCK SENSOR WIRE. SEE NOTE. IF NO FAULTS ARE FOUND. REPLACE KNOCK SENSOR
YES
FAULTY CONNECTIONS OR ESC MODULE
6
DISCONNECT ESC MODULE. PROBE HARNESS GROUND CIRCUIT WITH A TEST LIGHT TO BATTERY VOLTAGE. DOES LIGHT ILLUMINATE?
NO
REPAIR OPEN GROUND CIRCUIT
YES
7
RECONNECT ESC MODULE. UNPLUG KNOCK SENSOR. PROBE KNOCK SENSOR LEAD WITH A TEST LIGHT TO 12 VOLTS. DOES SCAN INDICATE A KNOCK SIGNAL EACH TIME TEST LIGHT IS TOUCHED TO LEAD?
NO
KNOCK SENSOR CIRCUIT OPEN OR SHORTED TO GROUND, OR FAULTY CONNECTIONS OR ESC MODULE
YES
FAULTY CONNECTION AT KNOCK SENSOR OR FAULTY KNOCK SENSOR
NOTE: KNOCK SENSOR WIRE MAY PICK UP INDUCED VOLTAGE SIGNALS FROM OTHER ELECTRICAL COMPONENTS. THESE MAY BE INTERPRETED AS A KNOCK SIGNAL. REROUTE KNOCK SENSOR WIRE IF NECESSARY. ALSO, CHECK FOR BAD ALTERNATOR DIODES.

NOTE: Test numbers refer to test numbers on diagnostic chart.

1) If conditions for a Code 43 exist, Scan tester will display YES. A knock signal should exist at idle unless an internal or system problem exists.

2) Determines if system is functioning. Usually, a knock signal can be made by tapping on the exhaust manifold. If knock signal is not made, try tapping on engine block near sensor. On models with automatic transmission, it may be necessary to place gear selector lever in Drive.

3) Because Code 43 sets when the signal voltage on the spark retard line remains low, this test should cause the signal on that line to go high. The 12-volt signal should be seen by the ECM as a *no knock* signal if the ECM and wiring are okay.

4) This test determines if the knock signal is detected on the sensor-to-controller line or if the ESC module is at fault.

5) If sensor line is routed too close to secondary ignition wires, the ESC module may see the interference as a knock signal.

6) This checks ground circuit to module. An open ground will cause the voltage on the monitored line to remain constant at about 12 volts. This would cause the Code 43 functional test to fail.

7) This should generate a knock signal to the controller. This determines if the ESC controller is operating correctly.

91A13748 91B13749 91G07349

1991 ENGINE PERFORMANCE
Self-Diagnostics – Gasoline (Cont.)

CODE 43, ELECTRONIC SPARK CONTROL (4.3L TURBO & MODELS WITH 4L80-E TRANSMISSION)

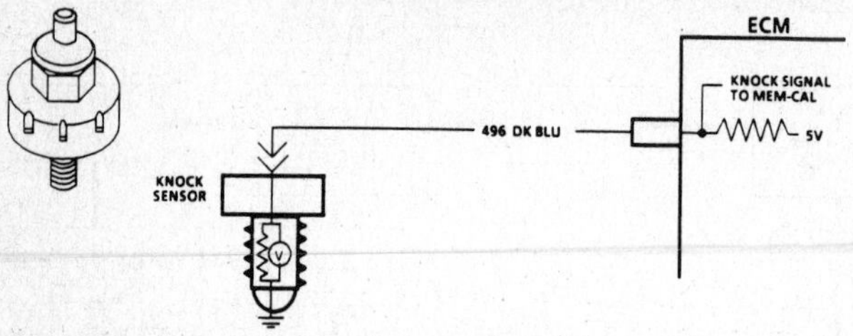
ECM
KNOCK SIGNAL TO MEM-CAL
496 DK BLU
5V
KNOCK SENSOR

CODE 43 ECM TERMINAL & CIRCUIT WIRING IDENTIFICATION

Application	ECM Terminal	Wire Color
4.3L Turbo		
Knock Signal	GF9	Dark Blue
All With 4L80-E Transmission		
Knock Signal	D5	Dark Blue

ECM/PCM applies and monitors a 5-volt DC signal to the knock sensor. Internal knock sensor circuitry pulls this DC signal down to about 2.5 volts. When knock sensor detects detonation, it generates an AC signal which rides back on the DC signal to the ECM/PCM. Knock signal intensity is dependent upon knock signal level.

NOTE: **Test numbers refer to test numbers on diagnostic chart.**

1) Code 43 will set when vehicle reaches normal operating temperature (but not overheating), high engine load is indicated by MAP sensor and voltage on circuit No. 496 is greater than 3.5 volts DC or less than 1.5 volts DC. This step determines if system is functioning properly at the current time.

2) This step determines the state of the 5-volt reference signal applied to the sensor.

3) Checks knock sensor internal resistance.

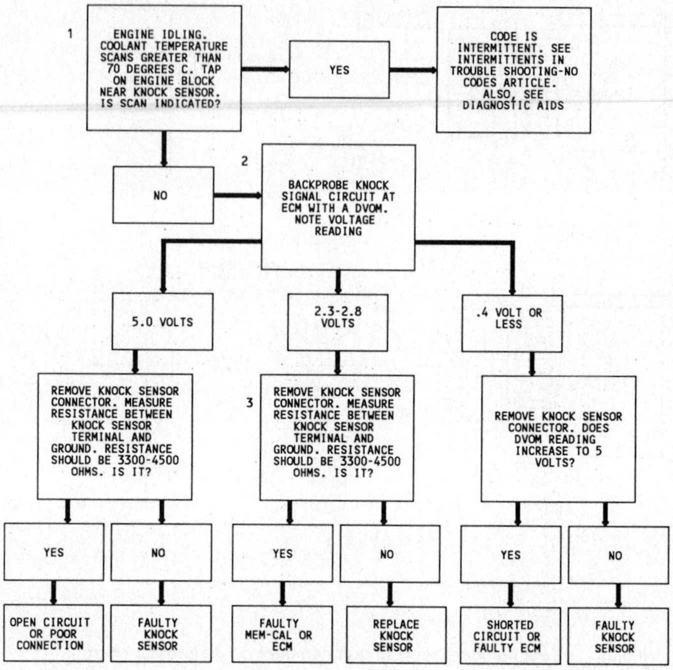
1
ENGINE IDLING. COOLANT TEMPERATURE SCANS GREATER THAN 70 DEGREES C. TAP ON ENGINE BLOCK NEAR KNOCK SENSOR. IS SCAN INDICATED?
YES
CODE IS INTERMITTENT. SEE INTERMITTENTS IN TROUBLE SHOOTING-NO CODES ARTICLE. ALSO, SEE DIAGNOSTIC AIDS
NO
2
BACKPROBE KNOCK SIGNAL CIRCUIT AT ECM WITH A DVOM. NOTE VOLTAGE READING
5.0 VOLTS
2.3-2.8 VOLTS
.4 VOLT OR LESS
REMOVE KNOCK SENSOR CONNECTOR. MEASURE RESISTANCE BETWEEN KNOCK SENSOR TERMINAL AND GROUND. RESISTANCE SHOULD BE 3300-4500 OHMS. IS IT?
3
REMOVE KNOCK SENSOR CONNECTOR. MEASURE RESISTANCE BETWEEN KNOCK SENSOR TERMINAL AND GROUND. RESISTANCE SHOULD BE 3300-4500 OHMS. IS IT?
REMOVE KNOCK SENSOR CONNECTOR. DOES DVOM READING INCREASE TO 5 VOLTS?
YES
NO
YES
NO
YES
NO
OPEN CIRCUIT OR POOR CONNECTION
FAULTY KNOCK SENSOR
FAULTY MEM-CAL OR ECM
REPLACE KNOCK SENSOR
SHORTED CIRCUIT OR FAULTY ECM
FAULTY KNOCK SENSOR

91A07445 91E07348

CODE 44, LEAN EXHAUST INDICATION (EXCEPT 4.3L TURBO)

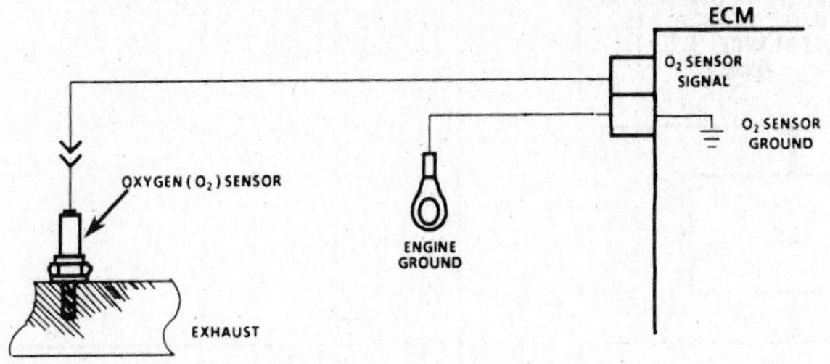

ECM
O_2 SENSOR SIGNAL
O_2 SENSOR GROUND
OXYGEN (O_2) SENSOR
ENGINE GROUND
EXHAUST

CODE 44 ECM TERMINAL & CIRCUIT WIRING IDENTIFICATION

Application	ECM Terminal	Wire Color
All With 4L80-E Transmission		
Oxygen Sensor Signal	C14	Purple
Oxygen Sensor Ground	C13	Tan
All Others		
Oxygen Sensor Signal	D7	Purple
Oxygen Sensor Ground	D6	Tan

Sensor acts like an open sensor circuit and produces no voltage when exhaust temperature is less than 600°F (316°C). An open sensor circuit or cold sensor causes "open loop" operation.

NOTE: **Test numbers refer to test numbers on diagnostic chart.**

1) Code 44 sets when O_2 sensor signal remains low for a precalibrated period and system is operating in "closed loop".

DIAGNOSTIC AIDS

Using the Scan tester, observe the Block Learn Memory (BLM) value at different RPMs. If Code 44 conditions exist, the block learn value will be around 150-172.

O² Sensor Wire – O_2 sensor wire may be mispositioned and touching exhaust manifold. Check for ground between sensor and wire connector.

Fuel Contamination – Water, even small amounts, near the in-tank fuel pump inlet can reach fuel injector, causing a lean exhaust and setting Code 44.

Fuel Pressure – System will be lean if fuel pressure is low. It may be necessary to monitor fuel pressure while driving vehicle. For fuel pressure checking procedure, see BASIC DIAGNOSTIC PROCEDURES article.

Exhaust Leaks – If the exhaust system has large leaks, exhaust system negative pressure pulses can cause outside air to be drawn into the system and past the O_2 sensor. Vacuum or crankcase leaks can also cause a lean condition.

If Code 44 is intermittent, see INTERMITTENTS in TROUBLE SHOOTING – NO CODES article.

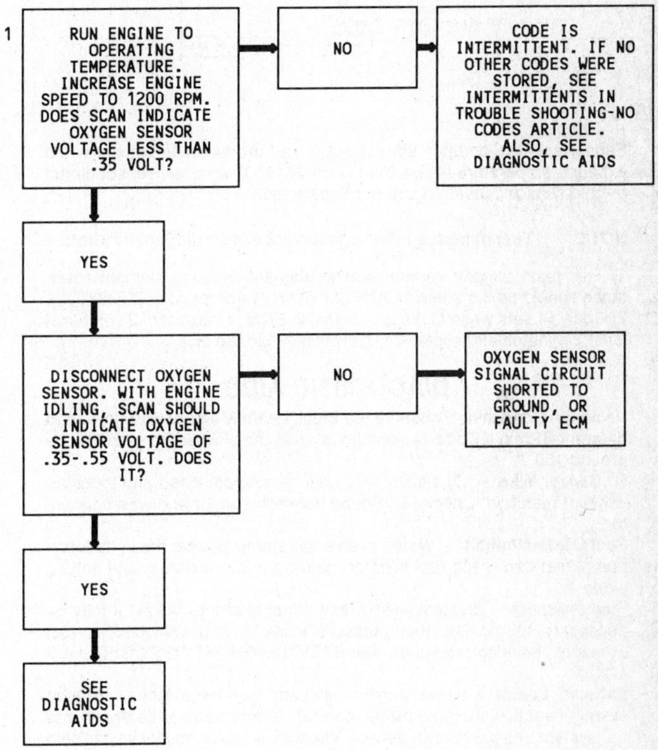

1
RUN ENGINE TO OPERATING TEMPERATURE. INCREASE ENGINE SPEED TO 1200 RPM. DOES SCAN INDICATE OXYGEN SENSOR VOLTAGE LESS THAN .35 VOLT?
NO
CODE IS INTERMITTENT. IF NO OTHER CODES WERE STORED, SEE INTERMITTENTS IN TROUBLE SHOOTING-NO CODES ARTICLE. ALSO, SEE DIAGNOSTIC AIDS
YES
DISCONNECT OXYGEN SENSOR. WITH ENGINE IDLING, SCAN SHOULD INDICATE OXYGEN SENSOR VOLTAGE OF .35-.55 VOLT. DOES IT?
NO
OXYGEN SENSOR SIGNAL CIRCUIT SHORTED TO GROUND, OR FAULTY ECM
YES
SEE DIAGNOSTIC AIDS

91H07378 91I07350

1991 ENGINE PERFORMANCE
Self-Diagnostics – Gasoline (Cont.)

CODE 44, LEAN EXHAUST INDICATION (4.3L TURBO)

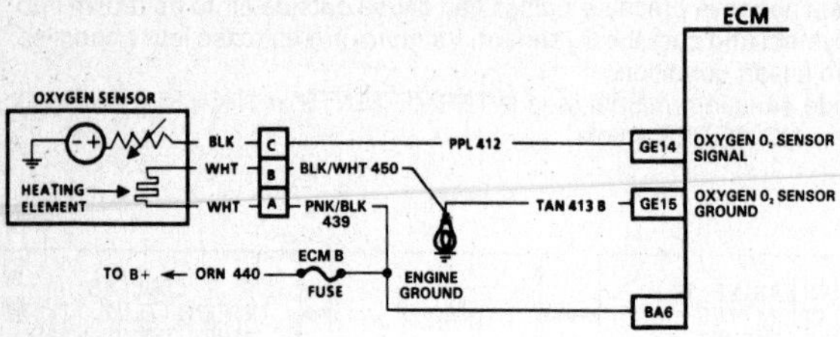
ECM
OXYGEN SENSOR
HEATING ELEMENT
BLK
WHT
WHT
C
B
A
PPL 412
BLK/WHT 450
PNK/BLK 439
TAN 413 B
GE14
OXYGEN O2 SENSOR SIGNAL
GE15
OXYGEN O2 SENSOR GROUND
ECM B
FUSE
TO B+
ORN 440
ENGINE GROUND
BA6

Sensor acts like an open sensor circuit and produces no voltage when exhaust temperature is less than 600°F (316°C). An open sensor circuit or cold sensor causes "open loop" operation.

NOTE: **Test numbers refer to test numbers on diagnostic chart.**

1) This tests oxygen sensor heating element. Heating element resistance should be 3.5 ohms at 68°F (20°C) and 14 ohms at 562°F (350°C).
2) Code 44 sets when O_2 sensor signal at ECM is less than .2 volt for at least 2 minutes and system is operating in "closed loop".

DIAGNOSTIC AIDS

Using the Scan tester, observe the Block Learn Memory (BLM) value at different RPMs. If Code 44 conditions exist, the block learn value will be around 150.

O² Sensor Wire – O_2 sensor wire may be mispositioned and touching exhaust manifold. Check for ground between sensor and wire connector.

Fuel Contamination – Water, even small amounts, near the in-tank fuel pump inlet can reach fuel injector, causing a lean exhaust and setting Code 44.

Fuel Pressure – System will be lean if fuel pressure is low. It may be necessary to monitor fuel pressure while driving vehicle. For fuel pressure checking procedure, see BASIC DIAGNOSTIC PROCEDURES article.

Exhaust Leaks – If the exhaust system has large leaks, exhaust system negative pressure pulses can cause outside air to be drawn into the system and past the O_2 sensor. Vacuum or crankcase leaks can also cause a lean condition.

If Code 44 is intermittent, see INTERMITTENTS in TROUBLE SHOOTING – NO CODES article.

1 DISCONNECT OXYGEN SENSOR CONNECTOR. MEASURE RESISTANCE BETWEEN TERMINALS A & B OF SENSOR. IS RESISTANCE 3.5-14 OHMS?
- NO → REPLACE OXYGEN SENSOR
- YES ↓

2 RUN ENGINE TO OPERATING TEMPERATURE. INCREASE ENGINE SPEED TO 1200 RPM. DOES SCAN INDICATE OXYGEN SENSOR VOLTAGE LESS THAN .35 VOLT?
- NO → CODE IS INTERMITTENT. IF NO OTHER CODES WERE STORED, SEE INTERMITTENTS IN TROUBLE SHOOTING-NO CODES ARTICLE. ALSO, SEE DIAGNOSTIC AIDS
- YES ↓

DISCONNECT OXYGEN SENSOR. WITH ENGINE IDLING, SCAN SHOULD INDICATE OXYGEN SENSOR VOLTAGE OF .35-.55 VOLT. DOES IT?
- NO → OXYGEN SENSOR SIGNAL CIRCUIT SHORTED TO GROUND, OR FAULTY ECM
- YES ↓

SEE DIAGNOSTIC AIDS

91E13734 91J13713

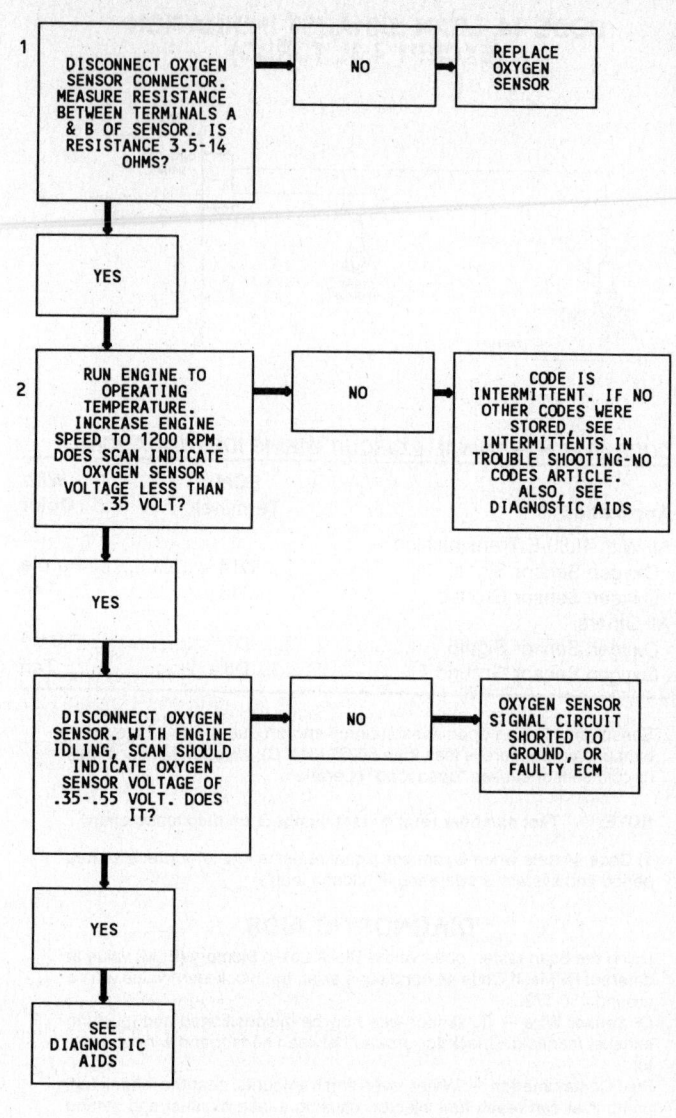

CODE 45, RICH EXHAUST INDICATION (EXCEPT 4.3L TURBO)

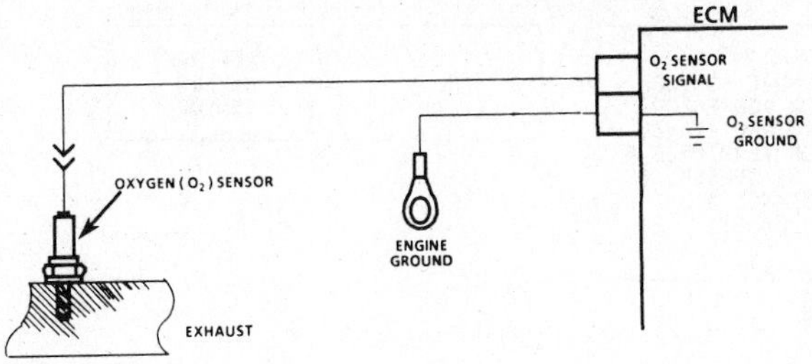
ECM
O_2 SENSOR SIGNAL
O_2 SENSOR GROUND
OXYGEN (O_2) SENSOR
ENGINE GROUND
EXHAUST

CODE 45 ECM TERMINAL & CIRCUIT WIRING IDENTIFICATION

Application	ECM Terminal	Wire Color
All With 4L80-E Transmission		
Oxygen Sensor Signal	C14	Purple
Oxygen Sensor Ground	C13	Tan
All Others		
Oxygen Sensor Signal	D7	Purple
Oxygen Sensor Ground	D6	Tan

Sensor acts like an open sensor circuit and produces no voltage when exhaust temperature is less than 600°F (316°C). An open sensor circuit or cold sensor causes "open loop" operation. Code 45 indicates a rich exhaust and diagnosis should begin with: fuel pressure, leaking injector, HEI shielding, canister purge saturation, coolant sensor, MAP sensor, O_2 sensor contamination and TPS intermittent output.

NOTE: Test numbers refer to test numbers on diagnostic chart.

1) Tests if O_2 sensor is registering a rich condition. Code 45 is set when vehicle is at operating temperature (in "closed loop"), throttle angle is greater than 5 percent, O_2 sensor signal at ECM is greater than .75 volt for 60 seconds or more.

DIAGNOSTIC AIDS

Code 45, rich exhaust, is most likely caused by one of the following:

Fuel Pressure High – If fuel pressure is too high, air/fuel ratio will be rich. For fuel pressure checking procedure, see BASIC DIAGNOSTIC PROCEDURES article. The ECM can compensate for slight increases but if air/fuel ratio becomes too rich a Code 45 will be set.

Ignition Ground – If an open occurs at circuit No. 453, HEI induced electrical "noise" may result, causing simulated reference pulses picked up by ECM on EST harness reference line. Additional pulses result in a higher than actual engine speed signal. The ECM will increase injector pulse width ("on" time) to match the increased RPM signal. Scan tester will show higher than actual RPM, which can help diagnose problem.

Fuel Canister – Charcoal canister fuel saturation will cause a rich air/fuel ratio. If full of fuel, check canister control and hoses.

MAP Sensor – If ECM senses higher than normal manifold pressure (low vacuum) the system can go rich. Disconnecting the MAP sensor allows ECM to substitute a fixed value for the MAP sensor. If rich condition disappears, replace MAP sensor and continue testing.

TPS – An intermittent TPS output will cause the system to operate rich due to a false indication of engine acceleration.

O_2 Sensor Contamination – O_2 sensor contamination, caused by silicone in certain fuels or use of improper RTV sealant, may cause a White-powdery coating to cover O_2 sensor. The false high signal voltage produced (or low oxygen content sensed) is interpreted by the ECM as a rich mixture, causing the ECM to set Code 45.

EGR Problem – EGR valve sticking open at idle is usually accompanied by a rough idle and/or stalling. If Code 45 is intermittent, see INTERMITTENTS in TROUBLE SHOOTING – NO CODES article.

1 RUN ENGINE TO OPERATING TEMPERATURE. INCREASE ENGINE SPEED TO 1200 RPM. DOES SCAN INDICATE OXYGEN SENSOR VOLTAGE GREATER THAN .75 VOLT?

- NO → CODE IS INTERMITTENT. IF NO OTHER CODES WERE STORED, SEE INTERMITTENTS IN TROUBLE SHOOTING-NO CODES ARTICLE. ALSO, SEE DIAGNOSTIC AIDS
- YES → DISCONNECT OXYGEN SENSOR. JUMPER ECM SIDE OF SENSOR HARNESS TO GROUND. WITH ENGINE IDLING, SCAN SHOULD INDICATE OXYGEN SENSOR VOLTAGE OF LESS THAN .35 VOLT. DOES IT?
  - NO → REPLACE ECM
  - YES → SEE DIAGNOSTIC AIDS

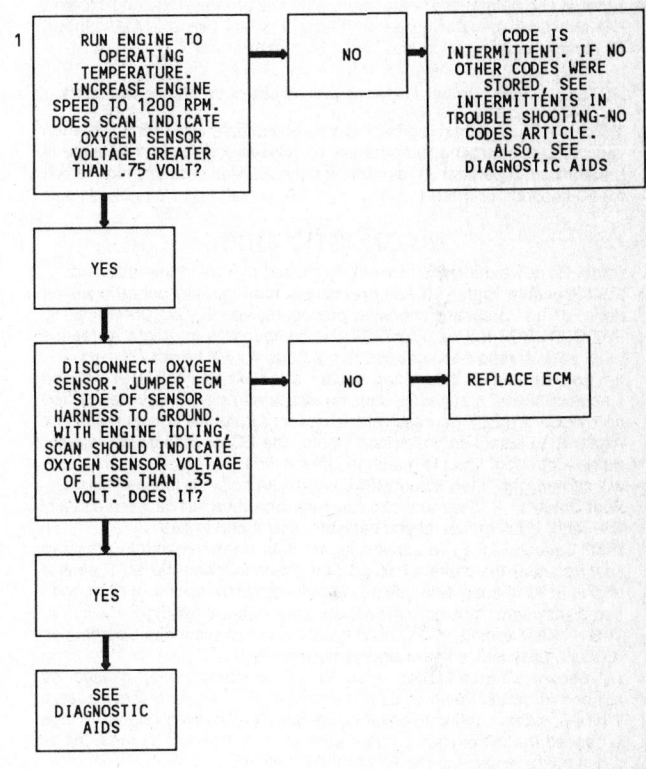

91H07378 91A07351

1991 ENGINE PERFORMANCE
Self-Diagnostics – Gasoline (Cont.)

CODE 45, RICH EXHAUST INDICATION (4.3L TURBO)

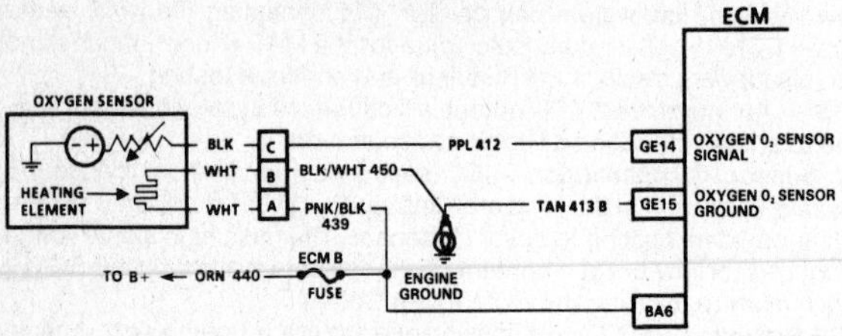
ECM
OXYGEN SENSOR
HEATING ELEMENT
BLK
WHT
WHT
C
B
A
PPL 412
BLK/WHT 450
PNK/BLK 439
TAN 413 B
GE14
OXYGEN O_2 SENSOR SIGNAL
GE15
OXYGEN O_2 SENSOR GROUND
TO B+
ORN 440
ECM B
FUSE
ENGINE GROUND
BA6

Sensor acts like an open sensor circuit and produces no voltage when exhaust temperature is less than 600°F (316°C). An open sensor circuit or cold sensor causes "open loop" operation. Code 45 indicates a rich exhaust and diagnosis should begin with: fuel pressure, leaking injector, HEI shielding, canister purge saturation, coolant sensor, MAP sensor, O_2 sensor contamination and TPS intermittent output.

NOTE: Test numbers refer to test numbers on diagnostic chart.

1) Tests if O_2 sensor is registering a rich condition. Code 45 is set when vehicle is at operating temperature (in "closed loop"), throttle angle is greater than 5 percent, O_2 sensor signal at ECM is greater than .75 volt for 50 seconds or more.

DIAGNOSTIC AIDS

Code 45, rich exhaust, is most likely caused by one of the following:
Fuel Pressure High – If fuel pressure is too high, air/fuel ratio will be rich. For fuel pressure checking procedure, see BASIC DIAGNOSTIC PROCEDURES article. The ECM can compensate for slight increases but if air/fuel ratio becomes too rich a Code 45 will be set.
Ignition Ground – If an open occurs at circuit No. 453, HEI induced electrical "noise" may result, causing simulated reference pulses picked up by ECM on EST harness reference line. Additional pulses result in a higher than actual engine speed signal. The ECM will increase injector pulse width ("on" time) to match the increased RPM signal. "Scan" tester will show higher than actual RPM, which can help diagnose problem.
Fuel Canister – Charcoal canister fuel saturation will cause a rich air/fuel ratio. If full of fuel, check canister control and hoses.
MAP Sensor – If ECM senses higher than normal manifold pressure (low vacuum) the system can go rich. Disconnecting the MAP sensor allows ECM to substitute a fixed value for the MAP sensor. If rich condition disappears, replace MAP sensor and continue testing.
TPS – An intermittent TPS output will cause the system to operate rich due to a false indication of engine acceleration.
O_2 Sensor Contamination – O_2 sensor contamination, caused by silicone in certain fuels or use of improper RTV sealant, may cause a White-powdery coating to cover O_2 sensor. The false high signal voltage produced (or low oxygen content sensed) is interpreted by the ECM as a rich mixture, causing the ECM to set Code 45.

EGR Problem – EGR valve sticking open at idle is usually accompanied by a rough idle and/or stalling. If Code 45 is intermittent, see INTERMITTENTS in TROUBLE SHOOTING – NO CODES article.

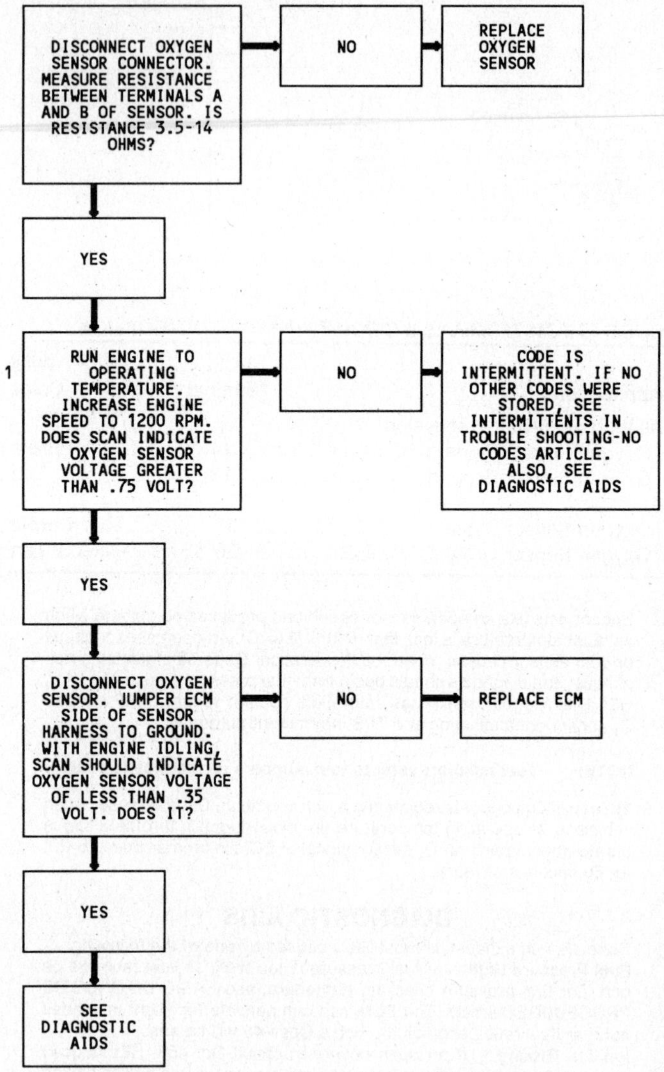
DISCONNECT OXYGEN SENSOR CONNECTOR. MEASURE RESISTANCE BETWEEN TERMINALS A AND B OF SENSOR. IS RESISTANCE 3.5-14 OHMS?
NO
REPLACE OXYGEN SENSOR
YES
1
RUN ENGINE TO OPERATING TEMPERATURE. INCREASE ENGINE SPEED TO 1200 RPM. DOES SCAN INDICATE OXYGEN SENSOR VOLTAGE GREATER THAN .75 VOLT?
NO
CODE IS INTERMITTENT. IF NO OTHER CODES WERE STORED, SEE INTERMITTENTS IN TROUBLE SHOOTING-NO CODES ARTICLE. ALSO, SEE DIAGNOSTIC AIDS
YES
DISCONNECT OXYGEN SENSOR. JUMPER ECM SIDE OF SENSOR HARNESS TO GROUND. WITH ENGINE IDLING, SCAN SHOULD INDICATE OXYGEN SENSOR VOLTAGE OF LESS THAN .35 VOLT. DOES IT?
NO
REPLACE ECM
YES
SEE DIAGNOSTIC AIDS

91E13734 91A13714

CODE 51, FAULTY PROM/MEM-CAL

Ensure all pins are fully inserted in socket. If okay, replace PROM/MEM-CAL, clear memory and recheck. If Code 51 reappears, replace ECM.

CODE 52, FAULTY CALPAK (EXCEPT 2.5L)

Ensure all pins are fully inserted in socket. If okay, replace CALPAK, clear memory and recheck. If Code 51 reappears, replace ECM.

CODE 53, SYSTEM OVERVOLTAGE (2.5L)

This code indicates a basic charging system problem. Code 53 will set when voltage at ECM terminal is greater than 17.1 volts for 2 seconds. Check and repair charging system.

CODE 55, ECM/PCM ERROR (EXCEPT 2.5L)

Ensure ECM grounds are good and MEM-CAL is properly latched. If okay, replace ECM/PCM. Clear codes and confirm closed loop operation. Check operation of SERVICE ENGINE SOON light.

CODE 54, FUEL PUMP CIRCUIT

Code 54 will set if the ECM does not see 12 volts on the fuel pump signal voltage monitor during the first 2 seconds after ignition is turned on.

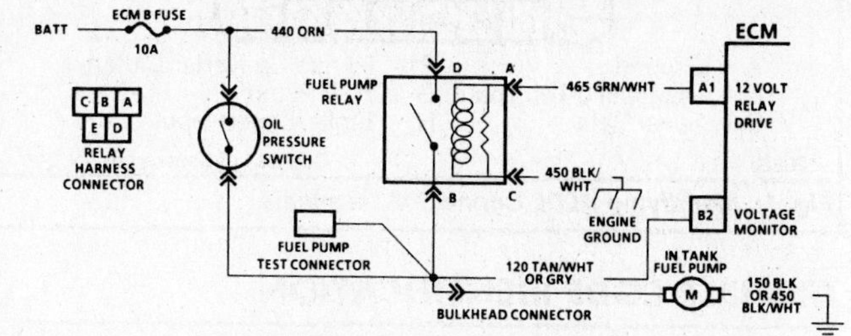
BATT
ECM B FUSE
10A
440 ORN
ECM
FUEL PUMP RELAY
D
A
465 GRN/WHT
A1
12 VOLT RELAY DRIVE
C B A
E D
RELAY HARNESS CONNECTOR
OIL PRESSURE SWITCH
450 BLK/WHT
ENGINE GROUND
B
C
B2
VOLTAGE MONITOR
FUEL PUMP TEST CONNECTOR
120 TAN/WHT OR GRY
IN TANK FUEL PUMP
M
150 BLK OR 450 BLK/WHT
BULKHEAD CONNECTOR

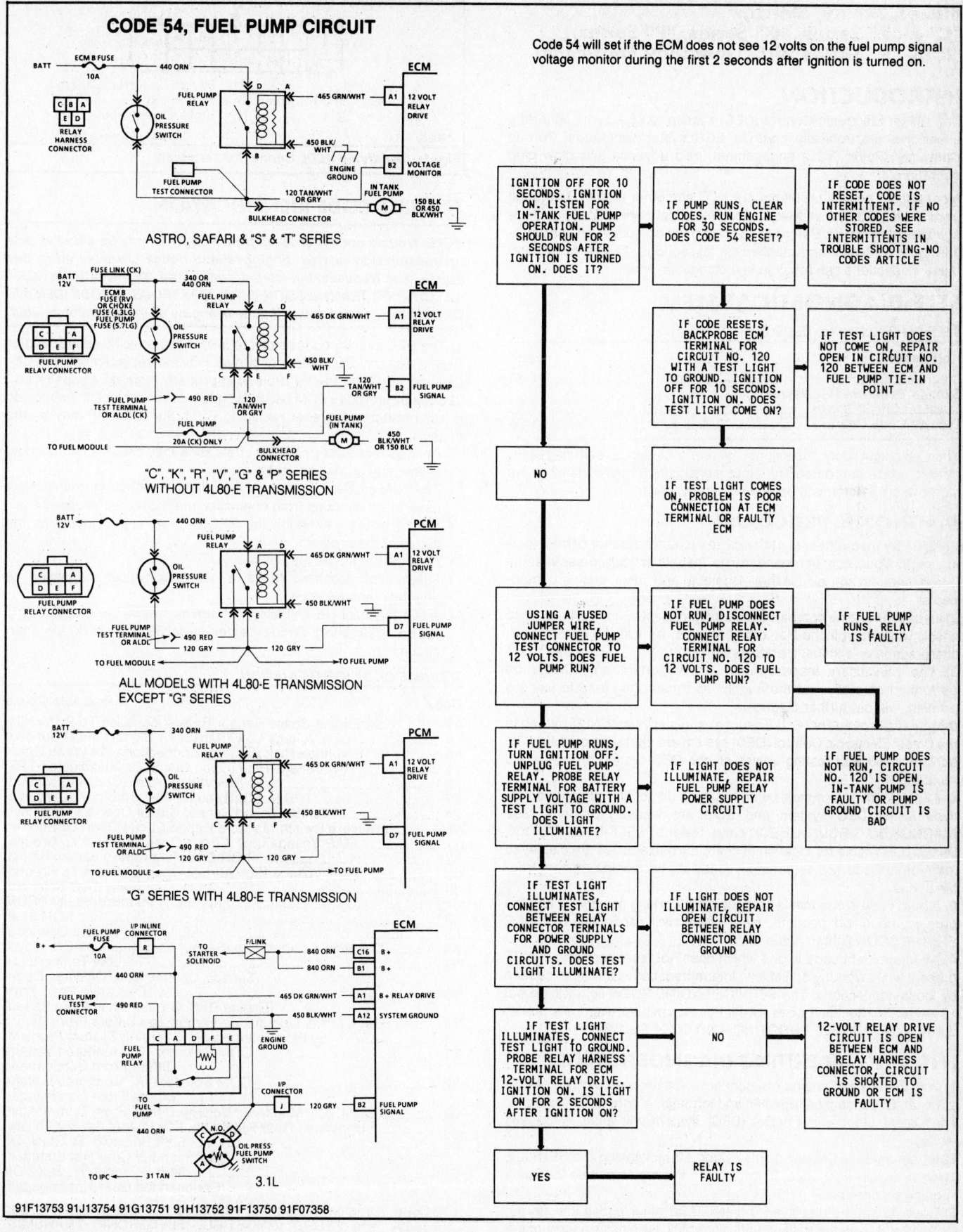

ASTRO, SAFARI & "S" & "T" SERIES

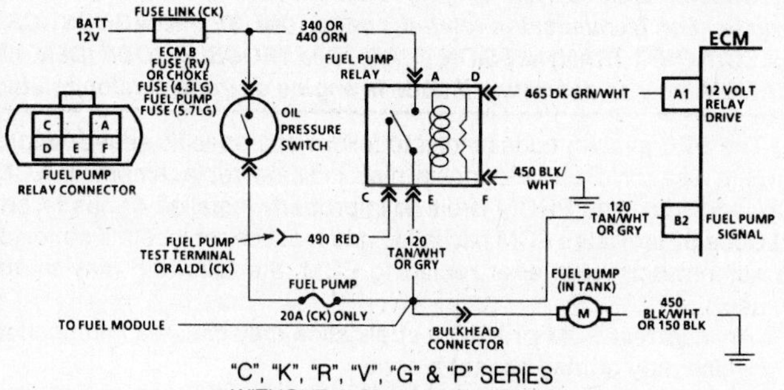
BATT 12V
FUSE LINK (CK)
ECM B FUSE (RV) OR CHOKE FUSE (4.3LG) FUEL PUMP FUSE (5.7LG)
340 OR 440 ORN
ECM
FUEL PUMP RELAY
A
D
465 DK GRN/WHT
A1
12 VOLT RELAY DRIVE
C A
D E F
FUEL PUMP RELAY CONNECTOR
OIL PRESSURE SWITCH
450 BLK/WHT
C
E
B
120 TAN/WHT OR GRY
B2
FUEL PUMP SIGNAL
FUEL PUMP TEST TERMINAL OR ALDL (CK)
490 RED
120 TAN/WHT OR GRY
FUEL PUMP
20A (CK) ONLY
FUEL PUMP (IN TANK)
M
450 BLK/WHT OR 150 BLK
TO FUEL MODULE
BULKHEAD CONNECTOR

"C", "K", "R", "V", "G" & "P" SERIES WITHOUT 4L80-E TRANSMISSION

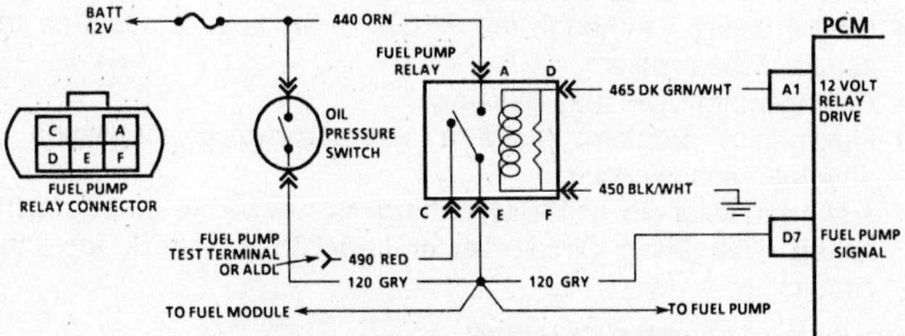
BATT 12V
440 ORN
PCM
FUEL PUMP RELAY
A
D
465 DK GRN/WHT
A1
12 VOLT RELAY DRIVE
C A
D E F
FUEL PUMP RELAY CONNECTOR
OIL PRESSURE SWITCH
450 BLK/WHT
C
E
F
D7
FUEL PUMP SIGNAL
FUEL PUMP TEST TERMINAL OR ALDL
490 RED
120 GRY
120 GRY
TO FUEL MODULE
TO FUEL PUMP

ALL MODELS WITH 4L80-E TRANSMISSION EXCEPT "G" SERIES

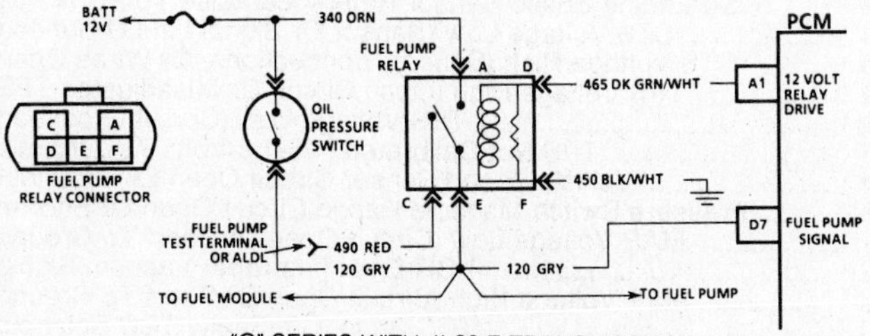
BATT 12V
340 ORN
PCM
FUEL PUMP RELAY
A
D
465 DK GRN/WHT
A1
12 VOLT RELAY DRIVE
C A
D E F
FUEL PUMP RELAY CONNECTOR
OIL PRESSURE SWITCH
450 BLK/WHT
C
E
F
D7
FUEL PUMP SIGNAL
FUEL PUMP TEST TERMINAL OR ALDL
490 RED
120 GRY
120 GRY
TO FUEL MODULE
TO FUEL PUMP

"G" SERIES WITH 4L80-E TRANSMISSION

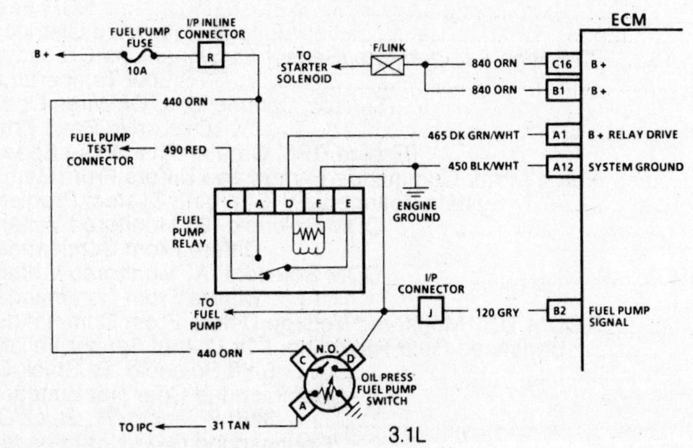
ECM
FUEL PUMP FUSE
10A
I/P INLINE CONNECTOR
R
B+
TO STARTER SOLENOID
F/LINK
840 ORN
C16
B+
840 ORN
B1
B+
440 ORN
FUEL PUMP TEST CONNECTOR
490 RED
465 DK GRN/WHT
A1
B+ RELAY DRIVE
450 BLK/WHT
A12
SYSTEM GROUND
C A D F E
FUEL PUMP RELAY
ENGINE GROUND
I/P CONNECTOR
J
120 GRY
B2
FUEL PUMP SIGNAL
TO FUEL PUMP
440 ORN
N.O.
C
B
D
A
OIL PRESS FUEL PUMP SWITCH
TO IPC
31 TAN

3.1L

91F13753 91J13754 91G13751 91H13752 91F13750 91F07358

IGNITION OFF FOR 10 SECONDS. IGNITION ON. LISTEN FOR IN-TANK FUEL PUMP OPERATION. PUMP SHOULD RUN FOR 2 SECONDS AFTER IGNITION IS TURNED ON. DOES IT?

→ IF PUMP RUNS, CLEAR CODES. RUN ENGINE FOR 30 SECONDS. DOES CODE 54 RESET?

→ IF CODE DOES NOT RESET, CODE IS INTERMITTENT. IF NO OTHER CODES WERE STORED, SEE INTERMITTENTS IN TROUBLE SHOOTING-NO CODES ARTICLE

IF CODE RESETS, BACKPROBE ECM TERMINAL FOR CIRCUIT NO. 120 WITH A TEST LIGHT TO GROUND. IGNITION OFF FOR 10 SECONDS. IGNITION ON. DOES TEST LIGHT COME ON?

→ IF TEST LIGHT DOES NOT COME ON, REPAIR OPEN IN CIRCUIT NO. 120 BETWEEN ECM AND FUEL PUMP TIE-IN POINT

IF TEST LIGHT COMES ON, PROBLEM IS POOR CONNECTION AT ECM TERMINAL OR FAULTY ECM

NO

USING A FUSED JUMPER WIRE, CONNECT FUEL PUMP TEST CONNECTOR TO 12 VOLTS. DOES FUEL PUMP RUN?

→ IF FUEL PUMP DOES NOT RUN, DISCONNECT FUEL PUMP RELAY. CONNECT RELAY TERMINAL FOR CIRCUIT NO. 120 TO 12 VOLTS. DOES FUEL PUMP RUN?

→ IF FUEL PUMP RUNS, RELAY IS FAULTY

IF FUEL PUMP DOES NOT RUN, CIRCUIT NO. 120 IS OPEN, IN-TANK PUMP IS FAULTY OR PUMP GROUND CIRCUIT IS BAD

IF FUEL PUMP RUNS, TURN IGNITION OFF. UNPLUG FUEL PUMP RELAY. PROBE RELAY TERMINAL FOR BATTERY SUPPLY VOLTAGE WITH A TEST LIGHT TO GROUND. DOES LIGHT ILLUMINATE?

→ IF LIGHT DOES NOT ILLUMINATE, REPAIR FUEL PUMP RELAY POWER SUPPLY CIRCUIT

IF TEST LIGHT ILLUMINATES, CONNECT TEST LIGHT BETWEEN RELAY CONNECTOR TERMINALS FOR POWER SUPPLY AND GROUND CIRCUITS. DOES TEST LIGHT ILLUMINATE?

→ IF LIGHT DOES NOT ILLUMINATE, REPAIR OPEN CIRCUIT BETWEEN RELAY CONNECTOR AND GROUND

IF TEST LIGHT ILLUMINATES, CONNECT TEST LIGHT TO GROUND. PROBE RELAY HARNESS TERMINAL FOR ECM 12-VOLT RELAY DRIVE. IGNITION ON. IS LIGHT ON FOR 2 SECONDS AFTER IGNITION ON?

→ NO → 12-VOLT RELAY DRIVE CIRCUIT IS OPEN BETWEEN ECM AND RELAY HARNESS CONNECTOR, CIRCUIT IS SHORTED TO GROUND OR ECM IS FAULTY

YES → RELAY IS FAULTY

1991 ENGINE PERFORMANCE
Self-Diagnostics – Diesel

Blazer, Jimmy, Sierra,
"C" & "K" Series, "G" Series, "P" Series,
"R" & "V" Series With Light Duty Emissions

INTRODUCTION

The Diesel Electronic Control (DEC) system, on 6.2L with light duty emissions, electronically controls EGR system operation, Torque Converter Clutch (TCC) engagement, cold advance and glow plug operation.

Most engine control problems are NOT computer related, but result from mechanical breakdowns, poor electrical connections, or damaged vacuum hoses. Before condemning the computer system, carefully perform visual and mechanical inspections. Failure to perform these inspections can result in lost diagnostic time.

SELF-DIAGNOSTIC SYSTEM

SELF-DIAGNOSTICS DIRECTORY

The 6.2L light duty emissions system includes a self-diagnostic system which can determine input signal circuit malfunctions. Input signal circuits determine engine function control.

DIAGNOSTIC PROCEDURE

Preliminary Inspection – 1) Check all vacuum hoses for correct routing, restrictions, cuts or other damage. Inspect difficult-to-see vacuum hoses beneath the air cleaner assembly and other engine components.

2) Inspect all engine compartment wiring for proper connections. Also check wires for pinched or chaffed spots, as well as contact with sharp edges or exhaust manifolds.

3) The preliminary inspection is very important and should be performed carefully and thoroughly, as it can often lead to fixing a problem without further diagnosis.

Diagnostic Procedure – 1) Ensure all engine systems NOT related to the Diesel Electronic Control (DEC) system are operating properly. DO NOT proceed with testing unless all non-DEC system problems are repaired.

2) ALWAYS begin diagnosis with checking diagnostic circuit to determine if the DEC system and ECM are working properly. See DIAGNOSTIC CIRCUIT CHECK chart. Refer to SELF-DIAGNOSTICS DIRECTORY table for location of chart. If trouble codes are displayed (other than Code 12), determine if codes are hard or intermittent trouble codes.

3) A hard code is one that is present while working on vehicle, and the problem condition persists. Hard codes will cause the SERVICE ENGINE SOON light to come on.

4) An intermittent code is one which does not reset itself and is NOT present while working on vehicle. Intermittent codes are often caused by loose connections. The SERVICE ENGINE SOON light will go out 10 seconds after fault goes away. For intermittent diagnosis procedures, see TROUBLE SHOOTING – NO CODES article.

ENTERING OR EXITING DIAGNOSTIC MODE

1) With key on and engine off, connect a jumper wire between ALDL terminal "B" (diagnostic terminal) and terminal "A" (ground). *See Fig. 1.* The Diesel Electronic Control (DEC) system will enter diagnostic mode.

2) In this mode, ECM will display Code 12 by flashing the SERVICE ENGINE SOON light once, followed by a short pause, then 2 flashes in quick succession.

3) Code 12 will be displayed 3 times. If no other codes are stored, Code 12 will continue to flash until diagnostic terminal is ungrounded. To exit diagnostic mode, turn ignition off and remove jumper from ALDL connector.

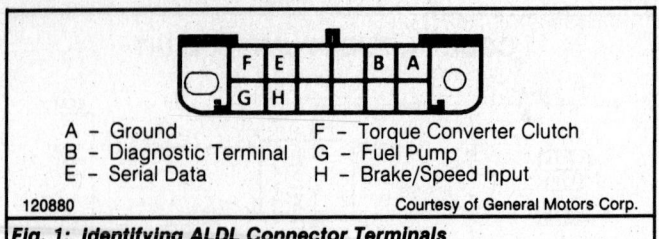

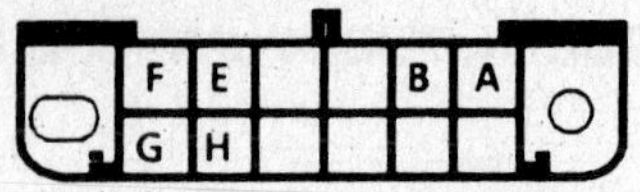
F
E
B
A
G
H

A – Ground
B – Diagnostic Terminal
E – Serial Data
F – Torque Converter Clutch
G – Fuel Pump
H – Brake/Speed Input

120880 Courtesy of General Motors Corp.

Fig. 1: Identifying ALDL Connector Terminals

TROUBLE CODE IDENTIFICATION

NOTE: Trouble codes retrieved from PCM/TCM may be either engine or transmission related. Engine-related codes are covered in this article. For transmission-related codes, see SELF-DIAGNOSTICS – ELECTRONIC TRANSMISSION article. See TROUBLE CODE IDENTIFICATION table to determine if code is engine or transmission related.

1) The DEC system codes indicate failure of a specific sensor and/or circuit. Sensor/circuit diagnosis may indicate replacement of ECM. Code 51 indicates PROM is either improperly installed or has failed.

2) Code 52 indicates ECM has failed and must be replaced. If condition is still not corrected after replacing ECM, the following may be the cause.

- An incorrect ECM or PROM application may cause a malfunction, which may or may not set a code.
- The ECM connector may be the problem. Connector terminals may have to be removed from connector to be checked properly.
- PROM failure – Although the PROM rarely fails, it could be the cause of the problem.
- Replacement ECM may be faulty.
- Intermittent problem. Make a careful physical inspection of affected sensor/circuit.
- A shorted solenoid, coil relay, or harness may be the cause of ECM failure. Use Short Circuit Tester (J-34636) to check for short circuits.

TROUBLE CODE IDENTIFICATION

Code	Probable Cause
12 [1]	No Engine Speed Sensor Reference Pulse To PCM/TCM
14 [1]	CTS Voltage Low (Sensor Or Signal Line Grounded)
15 [1]	CTS Voltage High (Sensor, Connections, Or Wires Open)
21 [1]	TPS Voltage High (Open Circuit Or Misadjusted TPS)
22 [1]	TPS Voltage Low (Circuit Grounded)
23 [1]	TPS Not Calibrated (.25-1.3 Volts At Curb Idle)
24 [1]	Vehicle Speed Sensor Circuit Open Or Grounded
28	Pressure Switch Manifold Range Circuit Open Or Shorted
31 [1]	MAP Voltage Low (Circuit Open Or Short To Ground)
32 [1]	EGR Error (Improper Vacuum Signal)
33 [1]	MAP Voltage High (Circuit Open Or Short To Ground)
39	TCC Stuck Off (Faulty TCC Solenoid)
51 [1]	Improperly Installed/Faulty PROM
52 [1]	ECM Fault
53 [1]	Voltage Reference Overload.
58	TTS High Temperature (Sensor Or Signal Line Grounded)
59	TTS Low Temperature (Sensor, Connections, Or Wires Open)
68	Overdrive Ratio Error (Engine RPM Greater Than Input Speed)
73	Force Motor Commanded Amperage Differs From Return
75	System Voltage Low (Charging System Problem)
81	QDM Solenoid "B" Monitored Voltage Differs From Commanded
82	QDM Solenoid "A" Monitored Voltage Differs From Commanded
83	QDM TCC Monitored Voltage Differs From Commanded
85	Undefined Gear Ratio (Input Or Output Sensor Failure)
86	Shift Solenoid "B" Stuck On (Commanded Gear Not Engaged)
87	Shift Solenoid "B" Stuck Off (Commanded Gear Not Engaged)

[1] – Code is engine related. For information on transmission-related codes, see SELF-DIAGNOSTICS – ELECTRONIC TRANSMISSION article.

1991 ENGINE PERFORMANCE
Self-Diagnostics – Diesel (Cont.)

CLEARING TROUBLE CODES

***NOTE:** To prevent ECM damage, ensure ignition is in OFF position when disconnecting or reconnecting power to ECM.*

Trouble codes should be cleared after repairs have been completed. Also, some diagnostic charts require codes to be cleared before using diagnostic chart. To clear codes, remove power to ECM for 30 seconds by either disconnecting battery cable and ECM pigtail to battery, or removing ECM "B" fuse.

If no hard fault codes are present (only intermittent codes exist), proceed to TROUBLE SHOOTING – NO CODES article for intermittent diagnostic procedures.

ECM LOCATION

The ECM is located under the passenger's seat riser ("G" Series), or behind right side of dash (all other models).

SPECIAL TOOLS (DIAGNOSTIC)

Special Scan testers are plugged into the ALDL connector may be used to read trouble codes, and check voltages in system on serial data line. These testers can save a great deal of time. For additional information, see owner's manual included with tester.

TEST EQUIPMENT

A tachometer, test light, Digital Volt-Ohmmeter (DVOM) with a minimum 10-megohm input impedance, a vacuum gauge, and jumper wires are required to test and diagnose the Diesel Electronic Control (DEC) system. A Scan tester may also be used to access data parameters. Tester will supply a visual reading of most inputs, and some outputs, to the ECM.

DIAGNOSTIC CHARTS

DIAGNOSTIC CIRCUIT CHECK

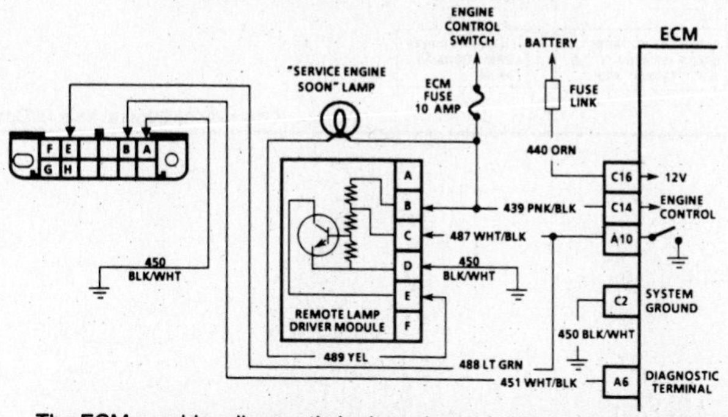
ENGINE CONTROL SWITCH
BATTERY
ECM
"SERVICE ENGINE SOON" LAMP
ECM FUSE 10 AMP
FUSE LINK
440 ORN
F E B A
G H
A
B
C
D
E
F
C16
12V
439 PNK/BLK
C14
ENGINE CONTROL
487 WHT/BLK
A10
450 BLK/WHT
450 BLK/WHT
REMOTE LAMP DRIVER MODULE
C2
SYSTEM GROUND
450 BLK/WHT
489 YEL
488 LT GRN
451 WHT/BLK
A6
DIAGNOSTIC TERMINAL

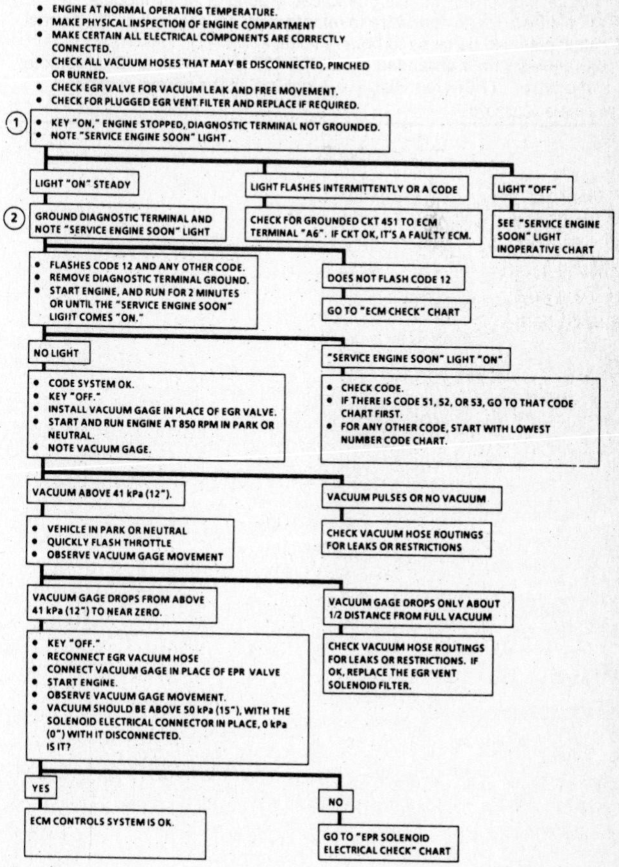
• ENGINE AT NORMAL OPERATING TEMPERATURE.
• MAKE PHYSICAL INSPECTION OF ENGINE COMPARTMENT
• MAKE CERTAIN ALL ELECTRICAL COMPONENTS ARE CORRECTLY CONNECTED.
• CHECK ALL VACUUM HOSES THAT MAY BE DISCONNECTED, PINCHED OR BURNED.
• CHECK EGR VALVE FOR VACUUM LEAK AND FREE MOVEMENT.
• CHECK FOR PLUGGED EGR VENT FILTER AND REPLACE IF REQUIRED.
1
• KEY "ON," ENGINE STOPPED, DIAGNOSTIC TERMINAL NOT GROUNDED.
• NOTE "SERVICE ENGINE SOON" LIGHT .
LIGHT "ON" STEADY
LIGHT FLASHES INTERMITTENTLY OR A CODE
LIGHT "OFF"
2
GROUND DIAGNOSTIC TERMINAL AND NOTE "SERVICE ENGINE SOON" LIGHT
CHECK FOR GROUNDED CKT 451 TO ECM TERMINAL "A6". IF CKT OK, IT'S A FAULTY ECM.
SEE "SERVICE ENGINE SOON" LIGHT INOPERATIVE CHART
• FLASHES CODE 12 AND ANY OTHER CODE.
• REMOVE DIAGNOSTIC TERMINAL GROUND.
• START ENGINE, AND RUN FOR 2 MINUTES OR UNTIL THE "SERVICE ENGINE SOON" LIGHT COMES "ON."
DOES NOT FLASH CODE 12
GO TO "ECM CHECK" CHART
NO LIGHT
"SERVICE ENGINE SOON" LIGHT "ON"
• CODE SYSTEM OK.
• KEY "OFF."
• INSTALL VACUUM GAGE IN PLACE OF EGR VALVE.
• START AND RUN ENGINE AT 850 RPM IN PARK OR NEUTRAL.
• NOTE VACUUM GAGE.
• CHECK CODE.
• IF THERE IS CODE 51, 52, OR 53, GO TO THAT CODE CHART FIRST.
• FOR ANY OTHER CODE, START WITH LOWEST NUMBER CODE CHART.
VACUUM ABOVE 41 kPa (12").
VACUUM PULSES OR NO VACUUM
• VEHICLE IN PARK OR NEUTRAL
• QUICKLY FLASH THROTTLE
• OBSERVE VACUUM GAGE MOVEMENT
CHECK VACUUM HOSE ROUTINGS FOR LEAKS OR RESTRICTIONS
VACUUM GAGE DROPS FROM ABOVE 41 kPa (12") TO NEAR ZERO.
VACUUM GAGE DROPS ONLY ABOUT 1/2 DISTANCE FROM FULL VACUUM
• KEY "OFF."
• RECONNECT EGR VACUUM HOSE
• CONNECT VACUUM GAGE IN PLACE OF EPR VALVE
• START ENGINE.
• OBSERVE VACUUM GAGE MOVEMENT.
• VACUUM SHOULD BE ABOVE 50 kPa (15"), WITH THE SOLENOID ELECTRICAL CONNECTOR IN PLACE, 0 kPa (0") WITH IT DISCONNECTED. IS IT?
CHECK VACUUM HOSE ROUTINGS FOR LEAKS OR RESTRICTIONS. IF OK, REPLACE THE EGR VENT SOLENOID FILTER.
YES
NO
ECM CONTROLS SYSTEM IS OK.
GO TO "EPR SOLENOID ELECTRICAL CHECK" CHART

The ECM provides diagnostic logic to detect faults in the Diesel Electronic Control (DEC) system. When ECM recognizes a fault, it turns on the SERVICE ENGINE SOON light and stores codes. If condition is corrected, the SERVICE ENGINE SOON light will go off. ECM recognizes errors in engine speed and EGR vacuum, as well as electrical faults involving the 5-volt reference circuit. ECM controls the following:

- Exhaust Gas Recirculation (EGR)
- Exhaust Pressure Regulation (EPR)
- Torque Converter Clutch (TCC)
- System Diagnosis
- Cold Advance & Glow Plugs

To allow proper engine control, the ECM monitors the following inputs:

- Engine RPM
- Manifold Absolute Pressure (MAP)
- Throttle Position Sensor (TPS)
- Vehicle Speed Sensor (VSS)
- Coolant Temperature Sensor (CTS)

Begin all diagnosis with diagnostic circuit check. After any DEC system repair, repeat diagnostic circuit check.

NOTE: Test numbers refer to test numbers on diagnostic chart.

1) This tests SERVICE ENGINE SOON light operation. With ignition on and engine off, light should be on.
2) Grounding ALDL diagnostic terminal "B" allows ECM to flash Code 12 and any stored codes. Light must flash on and off to be considered a proper code. If light just goes from bright to dim, it is not considered a code.

90H18843 90I13969

Courtesy of General Motors Corp.

1991 ENGINE PERFORMANCE
Self-Diagnostics – Diesel (Cont.)

SERVICE ENGINE SOON LIGHT INOPERATIVE

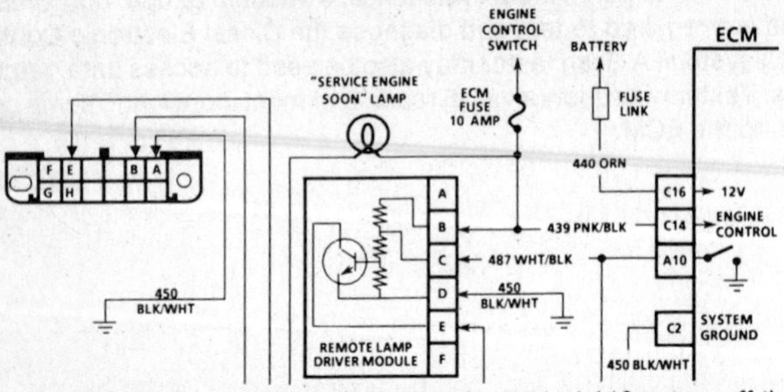
ENGINE CONTROL SWITCH
BATTERY
ECM
"SERVICE ENGINE SOON" LAMP
ECM FUSE 10 AMP
FUSE LINK
440 ORN
C16
12V
C14
ENGINE CONTROL
439 PNK/BLK
487 WHT/BLK
A10
450 BLK/WHT
SYSTEM GROUND
C2
450 BLK/WHT
REMOTE LAMP DRIVER MODULE
A
B
C
D
E
F
G
H

When engine is started, the ECM grounds terminal A10 to turn off the SERVICE ENGINE SOON light. When ALDL terminal "B" is grounded, ECM alternately grounds and opens terminal A10 to flash a code.

NOTE: **Test numbers refer to test numbers on diagnostic chart.**

1) This tests for an open ECM fuse or an open in the SERVICE ENGINE SOON light circuit, including instrument panel connector and printed circuit board. Light "on" is the normal response.
2) This tests for a shorted ECM. A grounded ECM terminal A10 will cause the SERVICE ENGINE SOON light to go off. If light comes on after disconnecting ECM, ECM is shorted. Light "on" is the normal response.
3) This tests for a grounded circuit No. 487 from terminal "C" of remote lamp driver to ECM terminal A10. It also checks for an open circuit No. 439 to terminal "B" of remote lamp driver module, a bad ground, or a faulty remote lamp driver. Because of the voltage drop through the remote lamp driver upper resistor, a normal voltage reading should be 6-11 volts. If voltage is greater than 11 volts, there is no voltage drop in the remote lamp driver module due to bad ground or faulty module.
4) This tests for an open wire to remote lamp driver terminal "B". Normal reading should be close to battery voltage.
5) This tests for a grounded circuit No. 487 from terminal "C" of remote lamp driver to ECM terminal A10. Light "on" is the normal response.

90H18843 90B13970

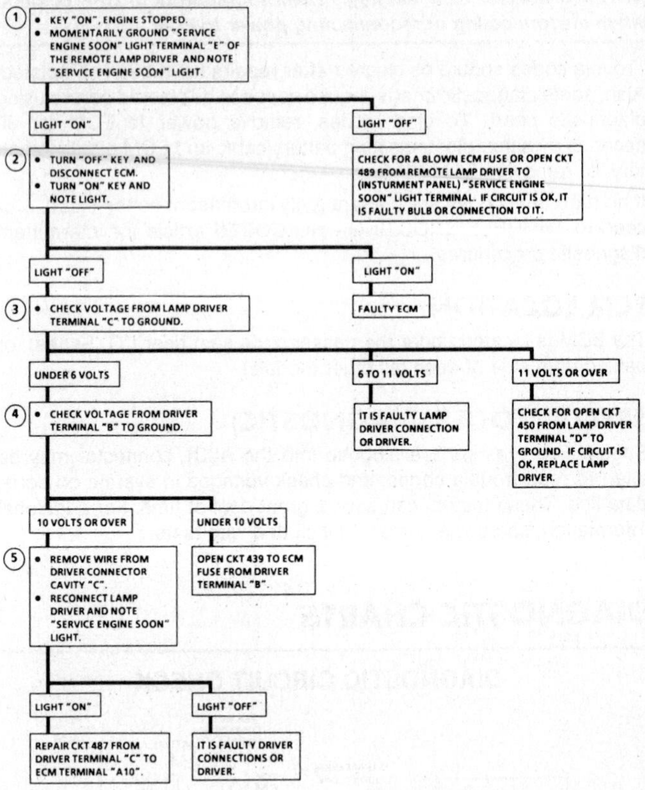
1
KEY "ON", ENGINE STOPPED.
MOMENTARILY GROUND "SERVICE ENGINE SOON" LIGHT TERMINAL "E" OF THE REMOTE LAMP DRIVER AND NOTE "SERVICE ENGINE SOON" LIGHT.
LIGHT "ON"
LIGHT "OFF"
CHECK FOR A BLOWN ECM FUSE OR OPEN CKT 489 FROM REMOTE LAMP DRIVER TO (INSTRUMENT PANEL) "SERVICE ENGINE SOON" LIGHT TERMINAL. IF CIRCUIT IS OK, IT IS FAULTY BULB OR CONNECTION TO IT.
2
TURN "OFF" KEY AND DISCONNECT ECM.
TURN "ON" KEY AND NOTE LIGHT.
LIGHT "OFF"
LIGHT "ON"
FAULTY ECM
3
CHECK VOLTAGE FROM LAMP DRIVER TERMINAL "C" TO GROUND.
UNDER 6 VOLTS
6 TO 11 VOLTS
11 VOLTS OR OVER
IT IS FAULTY LAMP DRIVER CONNECTION OR DRIVER.
CHECK FOR OPEN CKT 450 FROM LAMP DRIVER TERMINAL "D" TO GROUND. IF CIRCUIT IS OK, REPLACE LAMP DRIVER.
4
CHECK VOLTAGE FROM DRIVER TERMINAL "B" TO GROUND.
10 VOLTS OR OVER
UNDER 10 VOLTS
OPEN CKT 439 TO ECM FUSE FROM DRIVER TERMINAL "B".
5
REMOVE WIRE FROM DRIVER CONNECTOR CAVITY "C".
RECONNECT LAMP DRIVER AND NOTE "SERVICE ENGINE SOON" LIGHT.
LIGHT "ON"
LIGHT "OFF"
REPAIR CKT 487 FROM DRIVER TERMINAL "C" TO ECM TERMINAL "A10".
IT IS FAULTY DRIVER CONNECTIONS OR DRIVER.

Courtesy of General Motors Corp.

ECM CHECK, SERVICE ENGINE SOON LIGHT ON AT ALL TIMES OR WON'T FLASH CODE 12

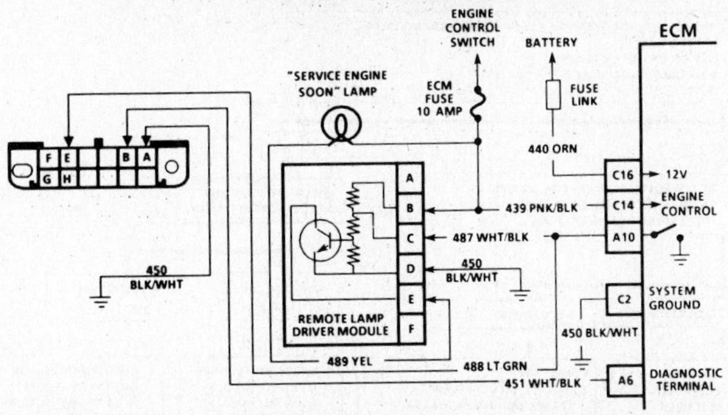

ENGINE CONTROL SWITCH
BATTERY
ECM
"SERVICE ENGINE SOON" LAMP
ECM FUSE 10 AMP
FUSE LINK
440 ORN
C16
12V
439 PNK/BLK
C14
ENGINE CONTROL
487 WHT/BLK
A10
450 BLK/WHT
450 BLK/WHT
C2
SYSTEM GROUND
REMOTE LAMP DRIVER MODULE
450 BLK/WHT
489 YEL
488 LT GRN
451 WHT/BLK
A6
DIAGNOSTIC TERMINAL

The ECM check determines why the SERVICE ENGINE SOON light remains on, or does not flash Code 12. Normally, ECM will not recognize a fault for at least 10 seconds after engine start-up. If SERVICE ENGINE SOON light remains on, ECM has lost battery power, ground, or the signal that turns the SERVICE ENGINE SOON light off. When engine is started, ECM grounds terminal A10 to turn off SERVICE ENGINE SOON light. ECM alternately grounds and opens terminal A10 to flash trouble code.

NOTE: Test numbers refer to test numbers on diagnostic chart.

1) This tests for a short to battery voltage in wire to remote lamp driver terminal "C", or a faulty remote lamp driver. Normal reading is 9-11 volts.
2) This tests if problem is related to the ECM, or the remote lamp driver. Normally, grounding remote lamp driver terminal "C" should turn light off. If light goes out when terminal "C" is grounded, problem is related to ECM and its wiring. If light does not go out, problem is related to remote lamp driver and its wiring.
3) Normally, grounding ECM terminal A10 should turn light off. If light stays on, there is an open in circuit No. 487 to remote lamp driver terminal "C".
4) This tests for open ECM circuit No. 451 to diagnostic terminal "B" in ALDL connector. The light should flash Code 12 when ECM terminal A6 is grounded.
5) This tests for proper voltage supply to ECM. Both readings should be more than 9 volts. Voltage to ECM terminal C14 comes from ignition switch. Terminal C16 has constant battery voltage for long term memory.
6) This tests for a bad ground to ECM. Terminal C2 is connected in the ECM.
7) This test distinguishes between a faulty ECM and PROM. Normal response is for Code 51 to flash even though the PROM is not installed in the ECM. If Code 51 is not flashed, ECM is faulty.

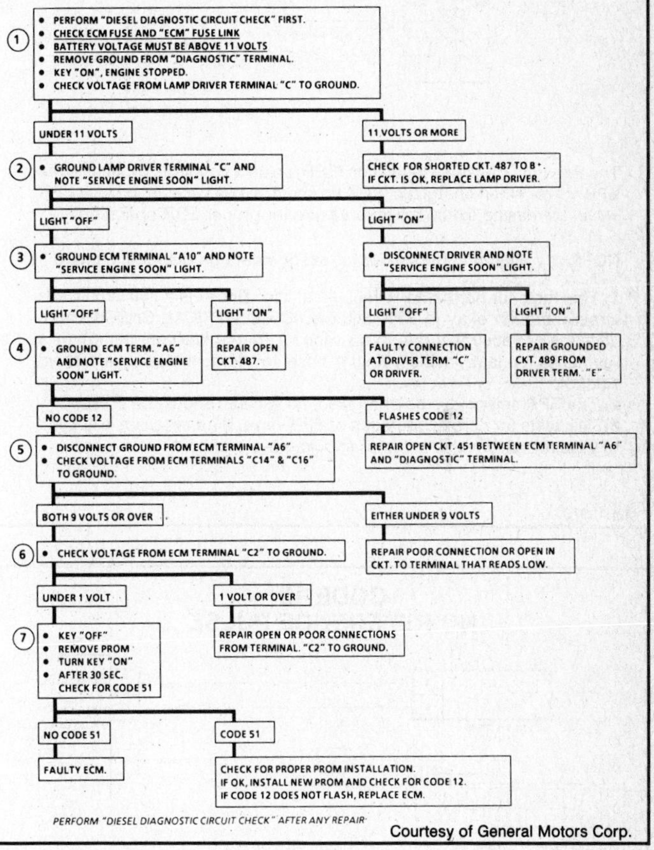

1
• PERFORM "DIESEL DIAGNOSTIC CIRCUIT CHECK" FIRST.
• CHECK ECM FUSE AND "ECM" FUSE LINK
• BATTERY VOLTAGE MUST BE ABOVE 11 VOLTS
• REMOVE GROUND FROM "DIAGNOSTIC" TERMINAL.
• KEY "ON", ENGINE STOPPED.
• CHECK VOLTAGE FROM LAMP DRIVER TERMINAL "C" TO GROUND.
UNDER 11 VOLTS
11 VOLTS OR MORE
2
• GROUND LAMP DRIVER TERMINAL "C" AND NOTE "SERVICE ENGINE SOON" LIGHT.
CHECK FOR SHORTED CKT. 487 TO B+. IF CKT. IS OK, REPLACE LAMP DRIVER.
LIGHT "OFF"
LIGHT "ON"
3
• GROUND ECM TERMINAL "A10" AND NOTE "SERVICE ENGINE SOON" LIGHT.
• DISCONNECT DRIVER AND NOTE "SERVICE ENGINE SOON" LIGHT.
LIGHT "OFF"
LIGHT "ON"
LIGHT "OFF"
LIGHT "ON"
4
• GROUND ECM TERM. "A6" AND NOTE "SERVICE ENGINE SOON" LIGHT.
REPAIR OPEN CKT. 487.
FAULTY CONNECTION AT DRIVER TERM. "C" OR DRIVER.
REPAIR GROUNDED CKT. 489 FROM DRIVER TERM. "E".
NO CODE 12
FLASHES CODE 12
5
• DISCONNECT GROUND FROM ECM TERMINAL "A6"
• CHECK VOLTAGE FROM ECM TERMINALS "C14" & "C16" TO GROUND.
REPAIR OPEN CKT. 451 BETWEEN ECM TERMINAL "A6" AND "DIAGNOSTIC" TERMINAL.
BOTH 9 VOLTS OR OVER
EITHER UNDER 9 VOLTS
6
• CHECK VOLTAGE FROM ECM TERMINAL "C2" TO GROUND.
REPAIR POOR CONNECTION OR OPEN IN CKT. TO TERMINAL THAT READS LOW.
UNDER 1 VOLT
1 VOLT OR OVER
7
• KEY "OFF"
• REMOVE PROM
• TURN KEY "ON"
• AFTER 30 SEC. CHECK FOR CODE 51
REPAIR OPEN OR POOR CONNECTIONS FROM TERMINAL. "C2" TO GROUND.
NO CODE 51
CODE 51
FAULTY ECM.
CHECK FOR PROPER PROM INSTALLATION. IF OK, INSTALL NEW PROM AND CHECK FOR CODE 12. IF CODE 12 DOES NOT FLASH, REPLACE ECM.
PERFORM "DIESEL DIAGNOSTIC CIRCUIT CHECK" AFTER ANY REPAIR

90H18843 90C13971

Courtesy of General Motors Corp.

EPR SOLENOID ELECTRICAL CHECK

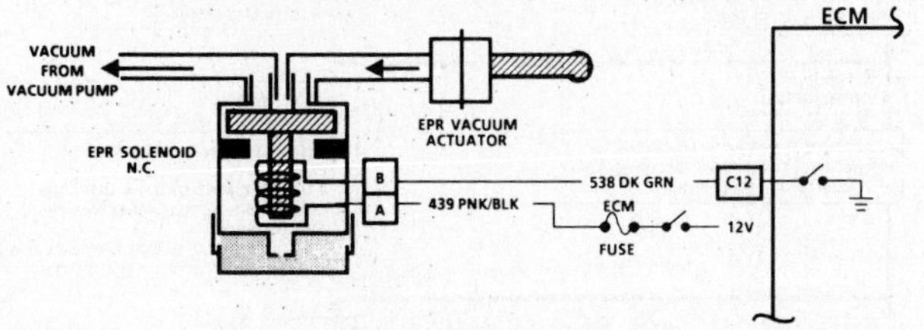

ECM
VACUUM FROM VACUUM PUMP
EPR VACUUM ACTUATOR
EPR SOLENOID N.C.
B
A
538 DK GRN
C12
439 PNK/BLK
ECM FUSE
12V

The Exhaust Pressure Regulation (EPR) solenoid controls vacuum to the EPR valve. When energized, EPR solenoid allows vacuum to close the EPR valve, increasing exhaust backpressure for proper EGR operation. The solenoid is supplied with 12 volts by ignition switch. The ECM completes ground circuit to energize the solenoid, and turn EPR on when needed (EGR operation command).

NOTE: Test numbers refer to test numbers on diagnostic chart.

1) This tests for short to ground, or a faulty ECM signal to EPR solenoid. Test light should normally be off.
2) This tests for signal to energize EPR solenoid with engine at idle. If test light is on, electrical circuits to the solenoid are okay.
3) This tests for voltage, or open circuit from terminal "B" of EPR solenoid to ECM terminal C12.

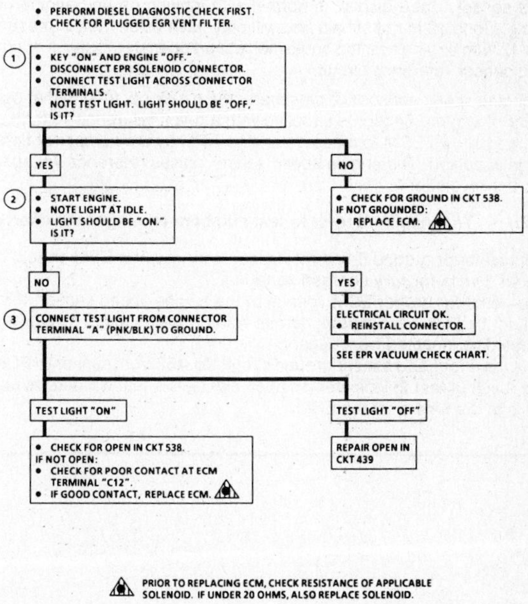

• PERFORM DIESEL DIAGNOSTIC CHECK FIRST.
• CHECK FOR PLUGGED EGR VENT FILTER.
1
• KEY "ON" AND ENGINE "OFF."
• DISCONNECT EPR SOLENOID CONNECTOR.
• CONNECT TEST LIGHT ACROSS CONNECTOR TERMINALS.
• NOTE TEST LIGHT. LIGHT SHOULD BE "OFF," IS IT?
YES
NO
2
• START ENGINE.
• NOTE LIGHT AT IDLE.
• LIGHT SHOULD BE "ON." IS IT?
• CHECK FOR GROUND IN CKT 538. IF NOT GROUNDED:
• REPLACE ECM.
NO
YES
3
CONNECT TEST LIGHT FROM CONNECTOR TERMINAL "A" (PNK/BLK) TO GROUND.
ELECTRICAL CIRCUIT OK.
• REINSTALL CONNECTOR.
SEE EPR VACUUM CHECK CHART.
TEST LIGHT "ON"
TEST LIGHT "OFF"
• CHECK FOR OPEN IN CKT 538. IF NOT OPEN:
• CHECK FOR POOR CONTACT AT ECM TERMINAL "C12".
• IF GOOD CONTACT, REPLACE ECM.
REPAIR OPEN IN CKT 439
PRIOR TO REPLACING ECM, CHECK RESISTANCE OF APPLICABLE SOLENOID. IF UNDER 20 OHMS, ALSO REPLACE SOLENOID.

90D13972

Courtesy of General Motors Corp.

1991 ENGINE PERFORMANCE
Self-Diagnostics – Diesel (Cont.)

EPR VACUUM CIRCUIT CHECK

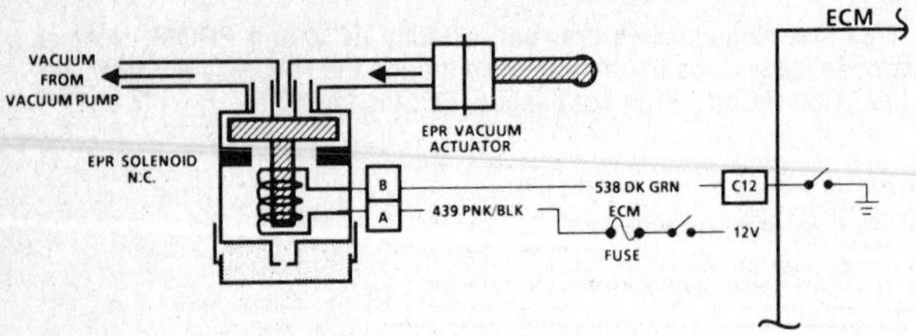
ECM
VACUUM FROM VACUUM PUMP
EPR VACUUM ACTUATOR
EPR SOLENOID N.C.
B
A
538 DK GRN
C12
439 PNK/BLK
ECM FUSE
12V

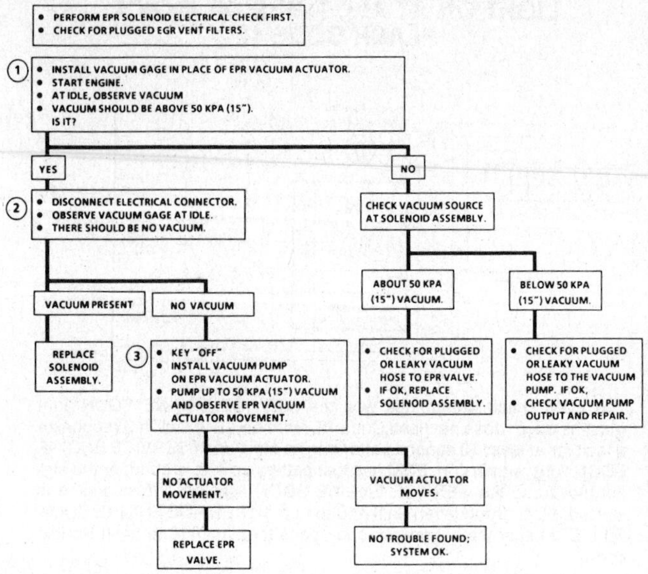
• PERFORM EPR SOLENOID ELECTRICAL CHECK FIRST.
• CHECK FOR PLUGGED EGR VENT FILTERS.
1
• INSTALL VACUUM GAGE IN PLACE OF EPR VACUUM ACTUATOR.
• START ENGINE.
• AT IDLE, OBSERVE VACUUM
• VACUUM SHOULD BE ABOVE 50 KPA (15"). IS IT?
YES
NO
2
• DISCONNECT ELECTRICAL CONNECTOR.
• OBSERVE VACUUM GAGE AT IDLE.
• THERE SHOULD BE NO VACUUM.
CHECK VACUUM SOURCE AT SOLENOID ASSEMBLY.
VACUUM PRESENT
NO VACUUM
ABOUT 50 KPA (15") VACUUM.
BELOW 50 KPA (15") VACUUM.
REPLACE SOLENOID ASSEMBLY.
3
• KEY "OFF"
• INSTALL VACUUM PUMP ON EPR VACUUM ACTUATOR.
• PUMP UP TO 50 KPA (15") VACUUM AND OBSERVE EPR VACUUM ACTUATOR MOVEMENT.
• CHECK FOR PLUGGED OR LEAKY VACUUM HOSE TO EPR VALVE.
• IF OK, REPLACE SOLENOID ASSEMBLY.
• CHECK FOR PLUGGED OR LEAKY VACUUM HOSE TO THE VACUUM PUMP. IF OK,
• CHECK VACUUM PUMP OUTPUT AND REPAIR.
NO ACTUATOR MOVEMENT.
VACUUM ACTUATOR MOVES.
REPLACE EPR VALVE.
NO TROUBLE FOUND; SYSTEM OK.

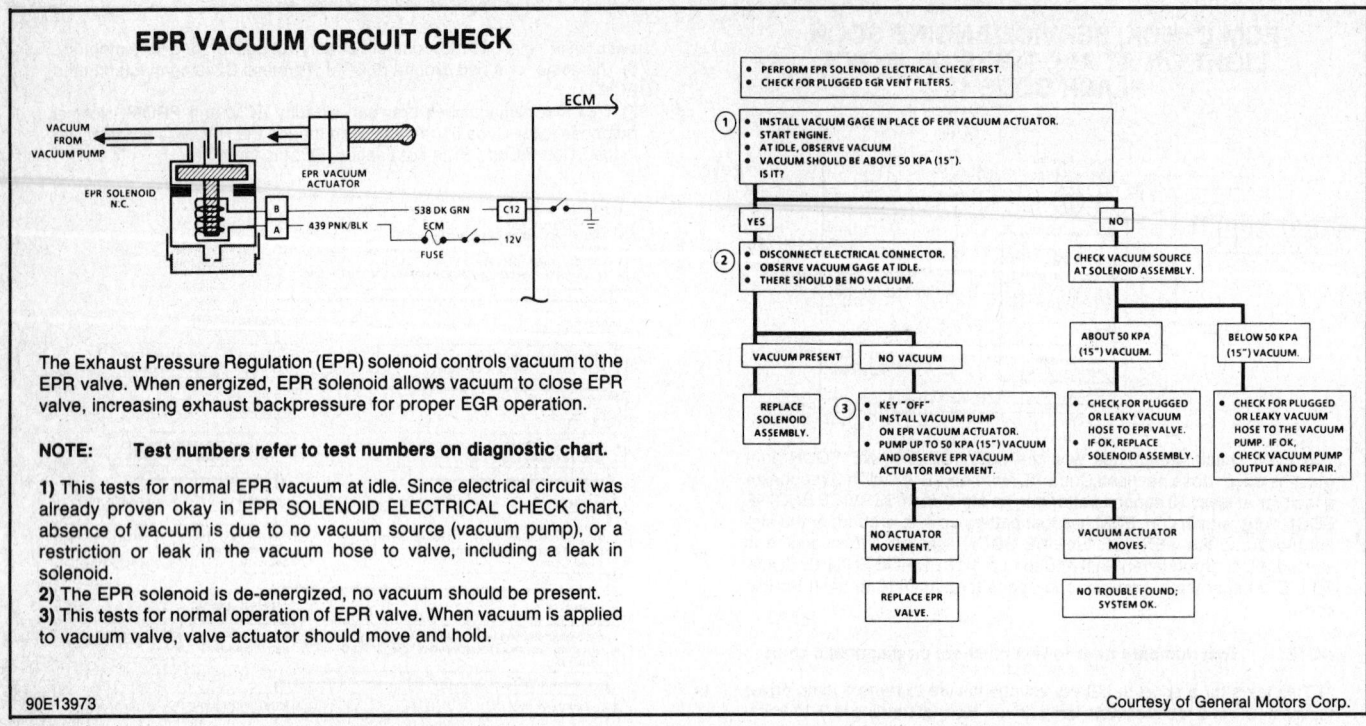

The Exhaust Pressure Regulation (EPR) solenoid controls vacuum to the EPR valve. When energized, EPR solenoid allows vacuum to close EPR valve, increasing exhaust backpressure for proper EGR operation.

NOTE: Test numbers refer to test numbers on diagnostic chart.

1) This tests for normal EPR vacuum at idle. Since electrical circuit was already proven okay in EPR SOLENOID ELECTRICAL CHECK chart, absence of vacuum is due to no vacuum source (vacuum pump), or a restriction or leak in the vacuum hose to valve, including a leak in solenoid.
2) The EPR solenoid is de-energized, no vacuum should be present.
3) This tests for normal operation of EPR valve. When vacuum is applied to vacuum valve, valve actuator should move and hold.

90E13973

Courtesy of General Motors Corp.

CODE 12
NO REFERENCE PULSE

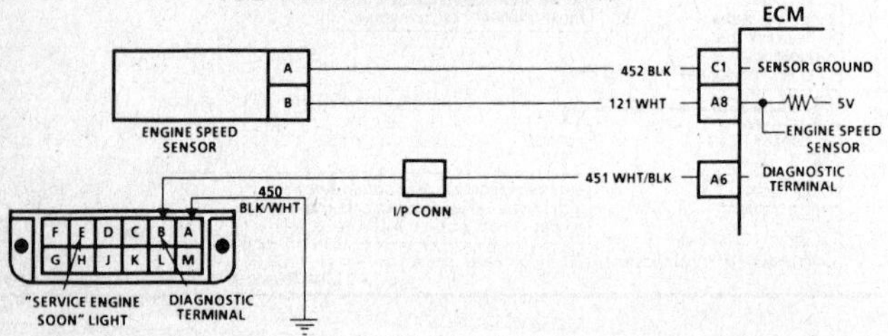
ECM
A
B
ENGINE SPEED SENSOR
452 BLK
C1
SENSOR GROUND
121 WHT
A8
5V
ENGINE SPEED SENSOR
450 BLK/WHT
I/P CONN
451 WHT/BLK
A6
DIAGNOSTIC TERMINAL
F E D C B A
G H J K L M
"SERVICE ENGINE SOON" LIGHT
DIAGNOSTIC TERMINAL

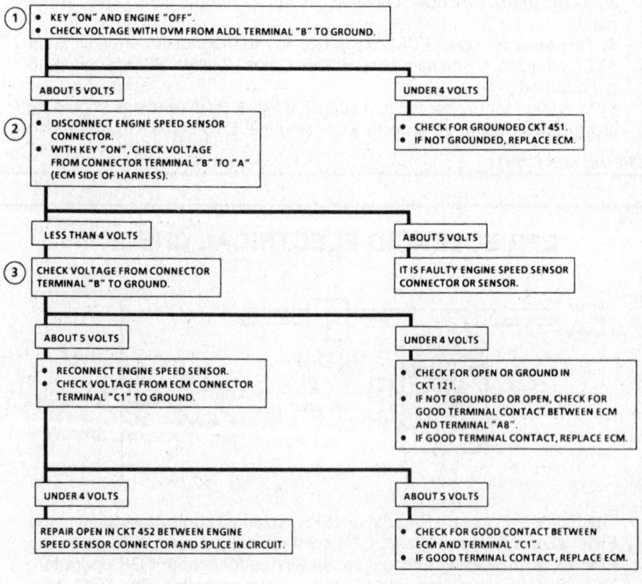
1
• KEY "ON" AND ENGINE "OFF".
• CHECK VOLTAGE WITH DVM FROM ALDL TERMINAL "B" TO GROUND.
ABOUT 5 VOLTS
UNDER 4 VOLTS
2
• DISCONNECT ENGINE SPEED SENSOR CONNECTOR.
• WITH KEY "ON", CHECK VOLTAGE FROM CONNECTOR TERMINAL "B" TO "A" (ECM SIDE OF HARNESS).
• CHECK FOR GROUNDED CKT 451.
• IF NOT GROUNDED, REPLACE ECM.
LESS THAN 4 VOLTS
ABOUT 5 VOLTS
3
CHECK VOLTAGE FROM CONNECTOR TERMINAL "B" TO GROUND.
IT IS FAULTY ENGINE SPEED SENSOR CONNECTOR OR SENSOR.
ABOUT 5 VOLTS
UNDER 4 VOLTS
• RECONNECT ENGINE SPEED SENSOR.
• CHECK VOLTAGE FROM ECM CONNECTOR TERMINAL "C1" TO GROUND.
• CHECK FOR OPEN OR GROUND IN CKT 121.
• IF NOT GROUNDED OR OPEN, CHECK FOR GOOD TERMINAL CONTACT BETWEEN ECM AND TERMINAL "A8".
• IF GOOD TERMINAL CONTACT, REPLACE ECM.
UNDER 4 VOLTS
ABOUT 5 VOLTS
REPAIR OPEN IN CKT 452 BETWEEN ENGINE SPEED SENSOR CONNECTOR AND SPLICE IN CIRCUIT.
• CHECK FOR GOOD CONTACT BETWEEN ECM AND TERMINAL "C1".
• IF GOOD TERMINAL CONTACT, REPLACE ECM.

Code 12 indicates ECM is on, and sees no reference pulse from engine speed sensor. Code display is normal with ignition on and engine not running. Code 12 is not stored and will only flash when fault is present. Code 12 with engine running could indicate an open or ground in engine speed sensor reference circuit.

The engine speed sensor is a camshaft-driven pick-up, mounted at center rear of engine. Sensor is supplied with a 5-volt reference voltage by ECM, and allows ECM to measure engine RPM by the number of times voltage is pulsed. The engine speed sensor pulses reference voltage 4 times per revolution.

NOTE: Test numbers refer to test numbers on diagnostic chart.

1) This tests for a good 5-volt reference. Normally, the ECM should be at about 5 volts for fully charged batteries.
2) This tests for proper ECM voltage to the engine speed sensor. If the circuit to the ECM is complete, normal voltage will be about 5 volts with harness disconnected from sensor.
3) This tests for good sensor ground circuit No. 452 from sensor to ECM. Since result of test **2)** indicates an open exists, this test will determine if open is in the wire or at the ECM.

90F13974

Courtesy of General Motors Corp.

CODE 14
COOLANT TEMPERATURE SENSOR SIGNAL VOLTAGE LOW

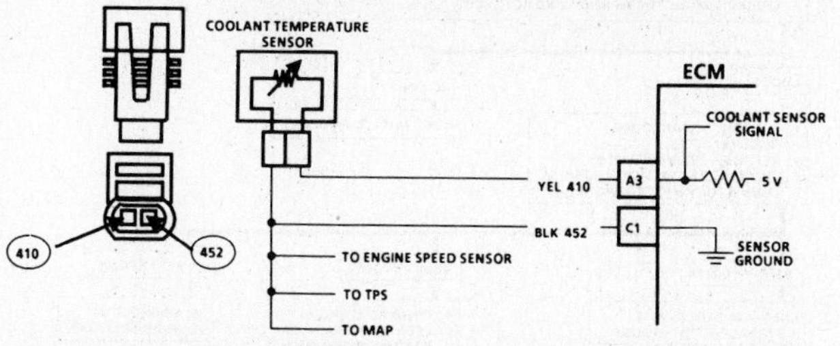

COOLANT TEMPERATURE SENSOR
ECM
COOLANT SENSOR SIGNAL
YEL 410
A3
5 V
BLK 452
C1
SENSOR GROUND
410
452
TO ENGINE SPEED SENSOR
TO TPS
TO MAP

The coolant temperature sensor uses a thermistor to control signal voltage to the ECM. The ECM applies and monitors voltage over circuit No. 410 to the sensor. When engine is cold, sensor resistance is high. The ECM will sense a high signal voltage. As the engine warms, sensor resistance becomes less and the voltage drops. At normal engine operating temperature, voltage will be about 1.5-2.0 volts.

NOTE: Test numbers refer to test numbers on diagnostic chart.

1) Code 14 will set if signal voltage indicates a coolant temperature greater than 275°F (135°C) for 3 minutes.
2) This test determines if circuit No. 410 is shorted to ground, causing conditions for Code 14.

DIAGNOSTIC AIDS

Check circuit No. 410 routing for a potential short to circuit No. 452, or ground. Scan tester displays engine temperature in degrees Celsius. After starting engine, temperature should rise to about 90°C and stabilize when thermostat opens. Test coolant sensor at various temperature levels. See COOLANT SENSOR TEMPERATURE TO RESISTANCE VALUES chart. An out-of-calibration sensor can cause poor driveability.

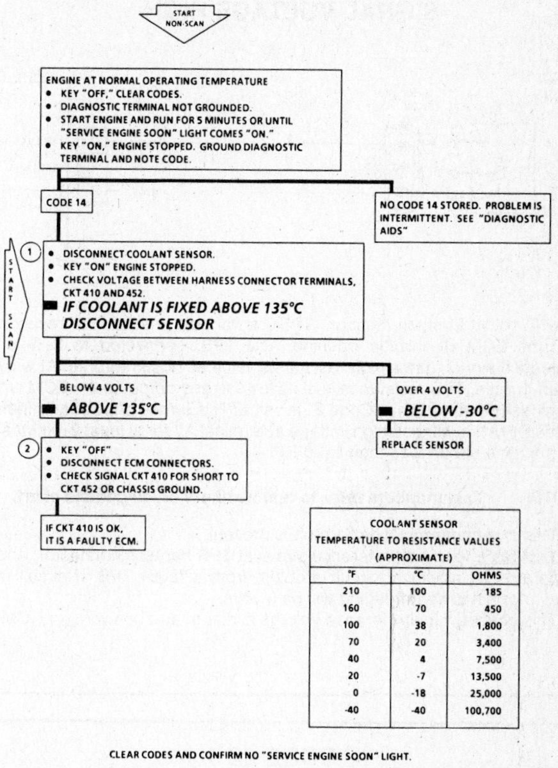

START NON-SCAN
ENGINE AT NORMAL OPERATING TEMPERATURE
• KEY "OFF," CLEAR CODES.
• DIAGNOSTIC TERMINAL NOT GROUNDED.
• START ENGINE AND RUN FOR 5 MINUTES OR UNTIL "SERVICE ENGINE SOON" LIGHT COMES "ON."
• KEY "ON," ENGINE STOPPED. GROUND DIAGNOSTIC TERMINAL AND NOTE CODE.
CODE 14
NO CODE 14 STORED. PROBLEM IS INTERMITTENT. SEE "DIAGNOSTIC AIDS"
START SCAN
1
• DISCONNECT COOLANT SENSOR.
• KEY "ON" ENGINE STOPPED.
• CHECK VOLTAGE BETWEEN HARNESS CONNECTOR TERMINALS, CKT 410 AND 452.
IF COOLANT IS FIXED ABOVE 135°C DISCONNECT SENSOR
BELOW 4 VOLTS
ABOVE 135°C
OVER 4 VOLTS
BELOW -30°C
REPLACE SENSOR
2
• KEY "OFF"
• DISCONNECT ECM CONNECTORS.
• CHECK SIGNAL CKT 410 FOR SHORT TO CKT 452 OR CHASSIS GROUND.
IF CKT 410 IS OK, IT IS A FAULTY ECM.
CLEAR CODES AND CONFIRM NO "SERVICE ENGINE SOON" LIGHT.

COOLANT SENSOR TEMPERATURE TO RESISTANCE VALUES (APPROXIMATE)

°F	°C	OHMS
210	100	185
160	70	450
100	38	1,800
70	20	3,400
40	4	7,500
20	-7	13,500
0	-18	25,000
-40	-40	100,700

90I18844 90G13975

Courtesy of General Motors Corp.

CODE 15
COOLANT TEMPERATURE SENSOR SIGNAL VOLTAGE HIGH

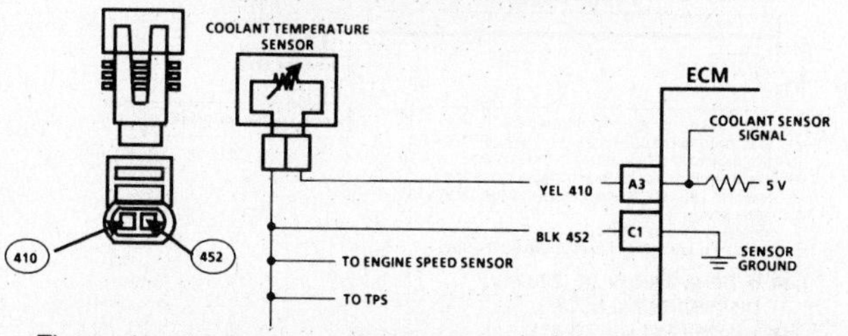

COOLANT TEMPERATURE SENSOR
ECM
COOLANT SENSOR SIGNAL
YEL 410
A3
5 V
BLK 452
C1
SENSOR GROUND
410
452
TO ENGINE SPEED SENSOR
TO TPS

The coolant temperature sensor is a thermistor which controls signal voltage to the ECM. The ECM applies and monitors voltage over circuit No. 410 to the sensor. When engine is cold, sensor resistance is high. The ECM will sense a high signal voltage. As the engine warms, sensor resistance reduces and voltage drops. At normal engine operating temperature, voltage should be 1.5-2.0 volts.

NOTE: Test numbers refer to test numbers on diagnostic chart.

1) Code 15 will set if engine has run for more than 5 minutes and coolant temperature is less than -22°F (-30°C).
2) This test simulates Code 14. If ECM recognizes the low signal voltage (high temperature), and the Scan tester reads 130°C or greater, the ECM and wiring are okay.
3) This test determines if circuit No. 410 is open. Voltage at sensor connector should be 5 volts when measured with a DVOM.

DIAGNOSTIC AIDS

Scan tester displays engine temperature in degrees Celsius. After starting engine, temperature should rise to about 90°C and stabilize when thermostat opens. If Code 12 or 21 is also set, check circuit No. 452 for faulty wiring or connections. Check terminals at sensor connector.

Test coolant sensor at various temperature levels. See COOLANT SENSOR TEMPERATURE TO RESISTANCE VALUES chart. An out-of-calibration sensor can cause poor driveability.

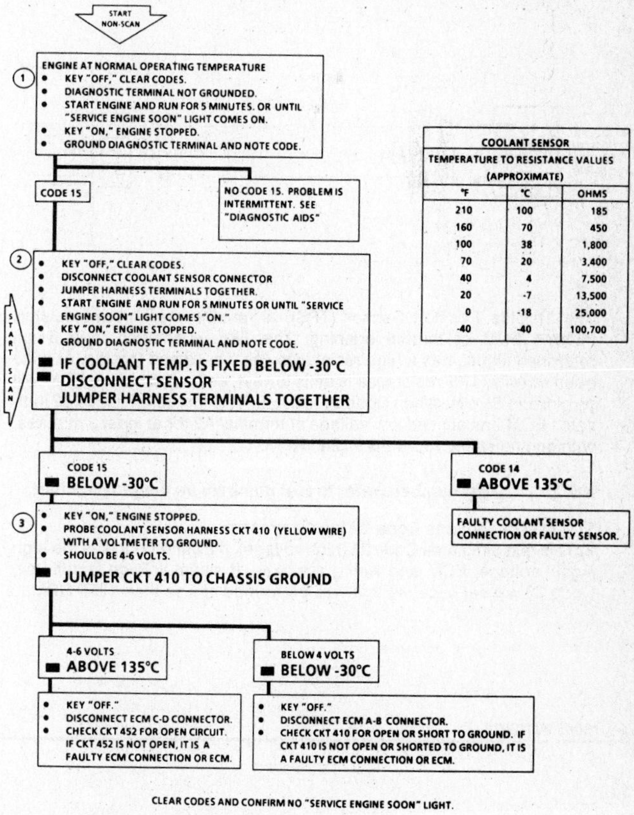

START NON-SCAN
1
ENGINE AT NORMAL OPERATING TEMPERATURE
• KEY "OFF," CLEAR CODES.
• DIAGNOSTIC TERMINAL NOT GROUNDED.
• START ENGINE AND RUN FOR 5 MINUTES. OR UNTIL "SERVICE ENGINE SOON" LIGHT COMES ON.
• KEY "ON," ENGINE STOPPED.
• GROUND DIAGNOSTIC TERMINAL AND NOTE CODE.
CODE 15
NO CODE 15. PROBLEM IS INTERMITTENT. SEE "DIAGNOSTIC AIDS"
2
• KEY "OFF," CLEAR CODES.
• DISCONNECT COOLANT SENSOR CONNECTOR
• JUMPER HARNESS TERMINALS TOGETHER.
• START ENGINE AND RUN FOR 5 MINUTES OR UNTIL "SERVICE ENGINE SOON" LIGHT COMES "ON."
• KEY "ON," ENGINE STOPPED.
• GROUND DIAGNOSTIC TERMINAL AND NOTE CODE.
START SCAN
IF COOLANT TEMP. IS FIXED BELOW -30°C
DISCONNECT SENSOR
JUMPER HARNESS TERMINALS TOGETHER
CODE 15
BELOW -30°C
CODE 14
ABOVE 135°C
FAULTY COOLANT SENSOR CONNECTION OR FAULTY SENSOR.
3
• KEY "ON," ENGINE STOPPED.
• PROBE COOLANT SENSOR HARNESS CKT 410 (YELLOW WIRE) WITH A VOLTMETER TO GROUND.
• SHOULD BE 4-6 VOLTS.
JUMPER CKT 410 TO CHASSIS GROUND
4-6 VOLTS
ABOVE 135°C
BELOW 4 VOLTS
BELOW -30°C
• KEY "OFF."
• DISCONNECT ECM C-D CONNECTOR.
• CHECK CKT 452 FOR OPEN CIRCUIT. IF CKT 452 IS NOT OPEN, IT IS A FAULTY ECM CONNECTION OR ECM.
• KEY "OFF."
• DISCONNECT ECM A-B CONNECTOR.
• CHECK CKT 410 FOR OPEN OR SHORT TO GROUND. IF CKT 410 IS NOT OPEN OR SHORTED TO GROUND, IT IS A FAULTY ECM CONNECTION OR ECM.
CLEAR CODES AND CONFIRM NO "SERVICE ENGINE SOON" LIGHT.

COOLANT SENSOR TEMPERATURE TO RESISTANCE VALUES (APPROXIMATE)

°F	°C	OHMS
210	100	185
160	70	450
100	38	1,800
70	20	3,400
40	4	7,500
20	-7	13,500
0	-18	25,000
-40	-40	100,700

90I18844 90H13976

Courtesy of General Motors Corp.

1991 ENGINE PERFORMANCE
Self-Diagnostics – Diesel (Cont.)

CODE 21
THROTTLE POSITION SENSOR SIGNAL VOLTAGE HIGH

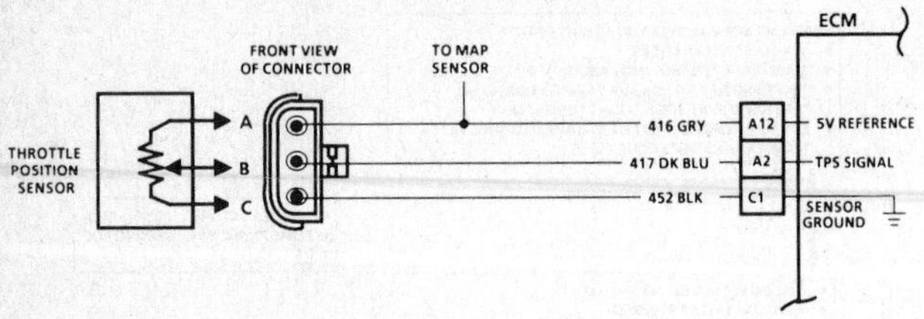
ECM
FRONT VIEW OF CONNECTOR
TO MAP SENSOR
THROTTLE POSITION SENSOR
A
B
C
416 GRY
417 DK BLU
452 BLK
A12
A2
C1
5V REFERENCE
TPS SIGNAL
SENSOR GROUND

The Throttle Position Sensor (TPS), a variable mechanical resistor, informs ECM of throttle opening. The TPS, connected to a 5-volt reference signal, has a high resistance value at closed throttle. At wide open throttle, TPS resistance is at its lowest, and output to the ECM will be close to 5 volts. When Code 21 is set, EPR is turned off. Code 21 indicates ECM has sensed high voltage at terminal A2 for at least 2 minutes, with engine speed less than 1120 RPM.

NOTE: Test numbers refer to test numbers on diagnostic chart.

1) This test confirms Code 21 fault is present.
2) This tests for 5-volt reference signal at TPS harness connector, and separates an electrical circuit problem from a faulty TPS. If circuit is okay, normal voltage reading will be 5 volts.
3) This checks if low reference voltage is due to an open wire, or ECM.

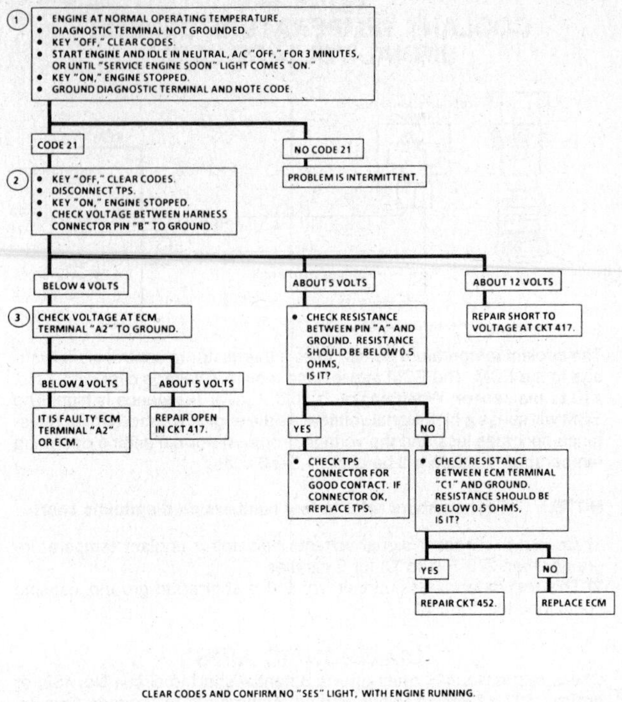
1
• ENGINE AT NORMAL OPERATING TEMPERATURE.
• DIAGNOSTIC TERMINAL NOT GROUNDED.
• KEY "OFF," CLEAR CODES.
• START ENGINE AND IDLE IN NEUTRAL, A/C "OFF," FOR 3 MINUTES, OR UNTIL "SERVICE ENGINE SOON" LIGHT COMES "ON."
• KEY "ON," ENGINE STOPPED.
• GROUND DIAGNOSTIC TERMINAL AND NOTE CODE.
CODE 21
NO CODE 21
PROBLEM IS INTERMITTENT.
2
• KEY "OFF," CLEAR CODES.
• DISCONNECT TPS.
• KEY "ON," ENGINE STOPPED.
• CHECK VOLTAGE BETWEEN HARNESS CONNECTOR PIN "B" TO GROUND.
BELOW 4 VOLTS
ABOUT 5 VOLTS
ABOUT 12 VOLTS
3
CHECK VOLTAGE AT ECM TERMINAL "A2" TO GROUND.
• CHECK RESISTANCE BETWEEN PIN "A" AND GROUND. RESISTANCE SHOULD BE BELOW 0.5 OHMS. IS IT?
REPAIR SHORT TO VOLTAGE AT CKT 417.
BELOW 4 VOLTS
ABOUT 5 VOLTS
IT IS FAULTY ECM TERMINAL "A2" OR ECM.
REPAIR OPEN IN CKT 417.
YES
NO
• CHECK TPS CONNECTOR FOR GOOD CONTACT. IF CONNECTOR OK, REPLACE TPS.
• CHECK RESISTANCE BETWEEN ECM TERMINAL "C1" AND GROUND. RESISTANCE SHOULD BE BELOW 0.5 OHMS, IS IT?
YES
NO
REPAIR CKT 452.
REPLACE ECM
CLEAR CODES AND CONFIRM NO "SES" LIGHT, WITH ENGINE RUNNING.

90I13977

Courtesy of General Motors Corp.

CODE 22
THROTTLE POSITION SENSOR SIGNAL VOLTAGE LOW

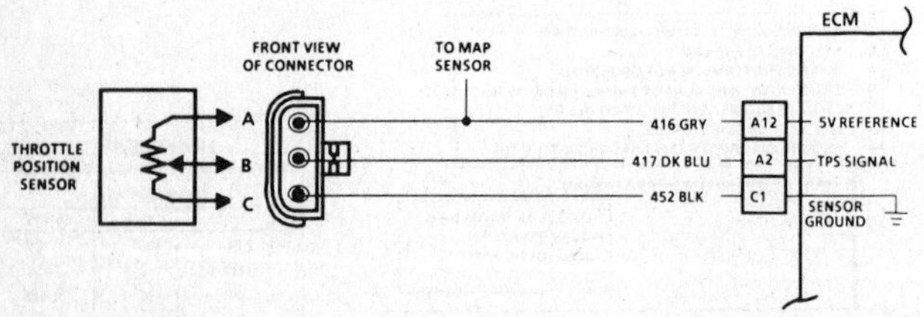
ECM
FRONT VIEW OF CONNECTOR
TO MAP SENSOR
THROTTLE POSITION SENSOR
A
B
C
416 GRY
417 DK BLU
452 BLK
A12
A2
C1
5V REFERENCE
TPS SIGNAL
SENSOR GROUND

The Throttle Position Sensor (TPS), a variable mechanical resistor, informs ECM of throttle opening. The TPS, connected to a 5-volt reference signal, has a high resistance value at closed throttle. At wide open throttle, TPS resistance is at its lowest, and output to the ECM will be close to 5 volts. When Code 21 is set, EPR is turned off. Code 22 indicates ECM has sensed low voltage at terminal A2 for at least 2 minutes, with engine speed more than 1250 RPM.

NOTE: Test numbers refer to test numbers on diagnostic chart.

1) This test confirms Code 22 fault is present.
2) This test simulates Code 21 (high voltage). If ECM recognizes the high signal voltage, ECM and wiring are okay. If signal voltage is still low, Code 23 will set because test was performed at less than 1250 RPM.

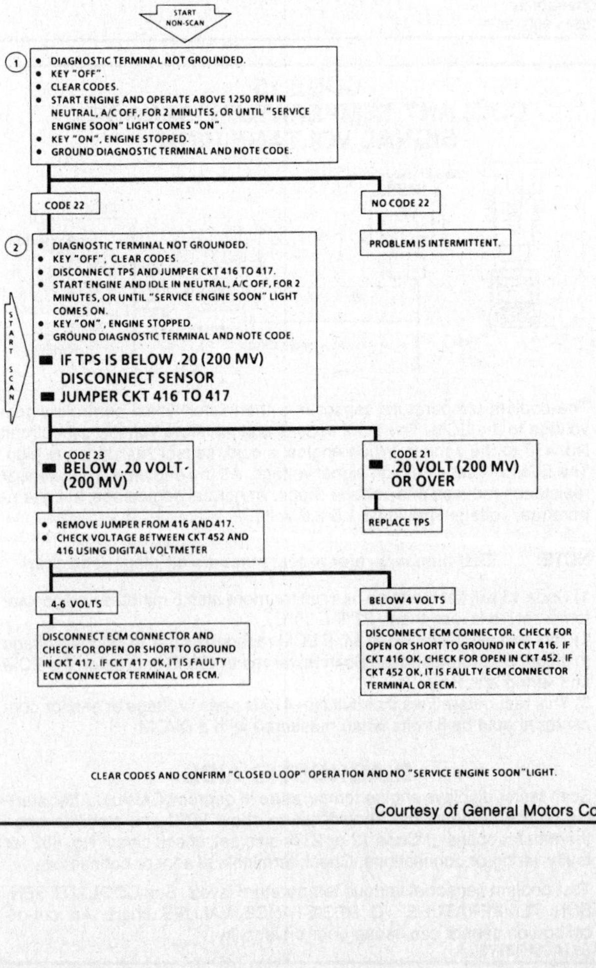
START NON-SCAN
1
• DIAGNOSTIC TERMINAL NOT GROUNDED.
• KEY "OFF".
• CLEAR CODES.
• START ENGINE AND OPERATE ABOVE 1250 RPM IN NEUTRAL, A/C OFF, FOR 2 MINUTES, OR UNTIL "SERVICE ENGINE SOON" LIGHT COMES "ON".
• KEY "ON", ENGINE STOPPED.
• GROUND DIAGNOSTIC TERMINAL AND NOTE CODE.
CODE 22
NO CODE 22
PROBLEM IS INTERMITTENT.
2
• DIAGNOSTIC TERMINAL NOT GROUNDED.
• KEY "OFF", CLEAR CODES.
• DISCONNECT TPS AND JUMPER CKT 416 TO 417.
• START ENGINE AND IDLE IN NEUTRAL, A/C OFF, FOR 2 MINUTES, OR UNTIL "SERVICE ENGINE SOON" LIGHT COMES ON.
• KEY "ON", ENGINE STOPPED.
• GROUND DIAGNOSTIC TERMINAL AND NOTE CODE.
START SCAN
IF TPS IS BELOW .20 (200 MV)
DISCONNECT SENSOR
JUMPER CKT 416 TO 417
CODE 23
BELOW .20 VOLT (200 MV)
CODE 21
.20 VOLT (200 MV) OR OVER
REPLACE TPS
• REMOVE JUMPER FROM 416 AND 417.
• CHECK VOLTAGE BETWEEN CKT 452 AND 416 USING DIGITAL VOLTMETER
4-6 VOLTS
BELOW 4 VOLTS
DISCONNECT ECM CONNECTOR AND CHECK FOR OPEN OR SHORT TO GROUND IN CKT 417. IF CKT 417 OK, IT IS FAULTY ECM CONNECTOR TERMINAL OR ECM.
DISCONNECT ECM CONNECTOR. CHECK FOR OPEN OR SHORT TO GROUND IN CKT 416. IF CKT 416 OK, CHECK FOR OPEN IN CKT 452. IF CKT 452 OK, IT IS FAULTY ECM CONNECTOR TERMINAL OR ECM.
CLEAR CODES AND CONFIRM "CLOSED LOOP" OPERATION AND NO "SERVICE ENGINE SOON" LIGHT.

90J18845 90J13978

Courtesy of General Motors Corp.

CODE 23
THROTTLE POSITION SENSOR MISADJUSTED

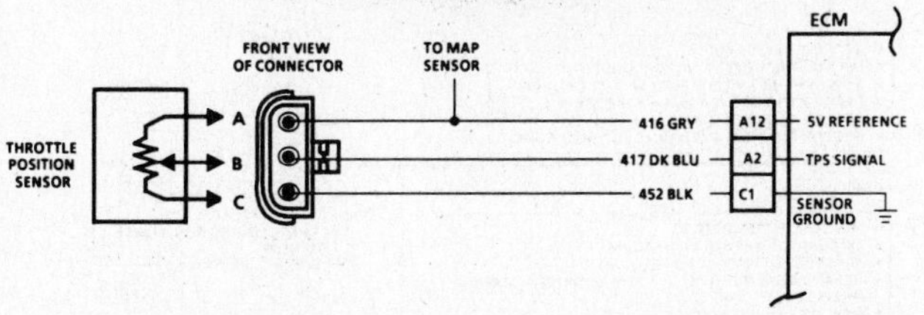
FRONT VIEW OF CONNECTOR
TO MAP SENSOR
ECM
THROTTLE POSITION SENSOR
A
B
C
416 GRY
417 DK BLU
452 BLK
A12
A2
C1
5V REFERENCE
TPS SIGNAL
SENSOR GROUND

The Throttle Position Sensor (TPS), a variable mechanical resistor, informs ECM of throttle opening. The TPS, connected to a 5-volt reference signal, has a high resistance value at closed throttle. At wide open throttle, TPS resistance is at its lowest, and output to the ECM will be close to 5 volts. Code 23 indicates ECM has noted that voltage, at terminal A2, is not .25-1.35 volts for at least 30 seconds, with engine speed at 550-650 RPM.

NOTE: **Test numbers refer to test numbers on diagnostic chart.**

1) This confirms Code 23 fault is present.
2) This test determines if sensor signal line is shorted to ground.
3) See THROTTLE POSITION SENSOR in REMOVAL, OVERHAUL & INSTALLATION article.

DIAGNOSTIC AIDS

Disregard Code 23 if SERVICE ENGINE SOON light goes out when throttle is returned to idle.

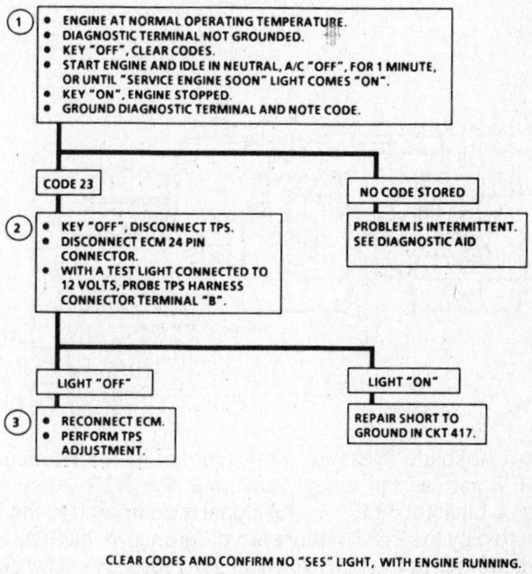
1
• ENGINE AT NORMAL OPERATING TEMPERATURE.
• DIAGNOSTIC TERMINAL NOT GROUNDED.
• KEY "OFF", CLEAR CODES.
• START ENGINE AND IDLE IN NEUTRAL, A/C "OFF", FOR 1 MINUTE, OR UNTIL "SERVICE ENGINE SOON" LIGHT COMES "ON".
• KEY "ON", ENGINE STOPPED.
• GROUND DIAGNOSTIC TERMINAL AND NOTE CODE.
CODE 23
NO CODE STORED
2
• KEY "OFF", DISCONNECT TPS.
• DISCONNECT ECM 24 PIN CONNECTOR.
• WITH A TEST LIGHT CONNECTED TO 12 VOLTS, PROBE TPS HARNESS CONNECTOR TERMINAL "B".
PROBLEM IS INTERMITTENT. SEE DIAGNOSTIC AID
LIGHT "OFF"
LIGHT "ON"
3
• RECONNECT ECM.
• PERFORM TPS ADJUSTMENT.
REPAIR SHORT TO GROUND IN CKT 417.
CLEAR CODES AND CONFIRM NO "SES" LIGHT, WITH ENGINE RUNNING.

90A13979

Courtesy of General Motors Corp.

CODE 24
VEHICLE SPEED SENSOR CIRCUIT

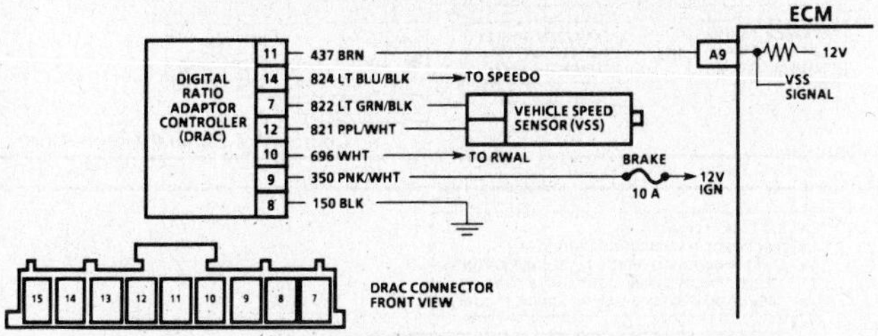
ECM
DIGITAL RATIO ADAPTOR CONTROLLER (DRAC)
11
14
7
12
10
9
8
437 BRN
824 LT BLU/BLK
822 LT GRN/BLK
821 PPL/WHT
696 WHT
350 PNK/WHT
150 BLK
TO SPEEDO
VEHICLE SPEED SENSOR (VSS)
TO RWAL
BRAKE
10 A
12V IGN
A9
12V
VSS SIGNAL
15 14 13 12 11 10 9 8 7
DRAC CONNECTOR FRONT VIEW

The ECM applies and monitors 12 volts on circuit No. 437. Circuit No. 437 connects to the Digital Ratio Adapter Controller (DRAC), which alternately grounds and opens circuit No. 437 when drive wheels are turning. The circuit is opened and closed at approximately 2000 times per mile when drive wheels are turning. The ECM calculates vehicle speed based on the time between pulses. Scan tester reading should closely match speedometer reading with drive wheels turning.

Code 24 will set under the following conditions are met for at least 10 seconds: circuit No. 437 is constant, engine speed is more than 2000 RPM, vehicle speed signal at ECM terminal A9 is less than 5 MPH (8 KM/H).

NOTE: **Test numbers refer to test numbers on diagnostic chart.**

1) This test monitors the ECM voltage on circuit No. 437. With wheels turning, the pulsating action causes varying voltage. The voltage variation will be greater at low wheel speeds, and an average of 4-6 volts at about 20 MPH (32 KM/H).
2) Less than one volt at ECM connector indicates circuit No. 437 wire is shorted to ground. Disconnect circuit No. 437 at DRAC. If voltage now reads more than 10 volts, the DRAC is faulty. If voltage remains less than 10 volts, then circuit No. 437 wire is grounded. If circuit No. 437 is not grounded, check for a faulty ECM connector or ECM.
3) A steady 8-12 volts reading at the ECM connector indicates that circuit No. 437 is open or DRAC is faulty.
4) Normal voltage indicates a possible intermittent condition.

DIAGNOSTIC AIDS

With drive wheels turning, Scan tester and speedometer reading should closely match.

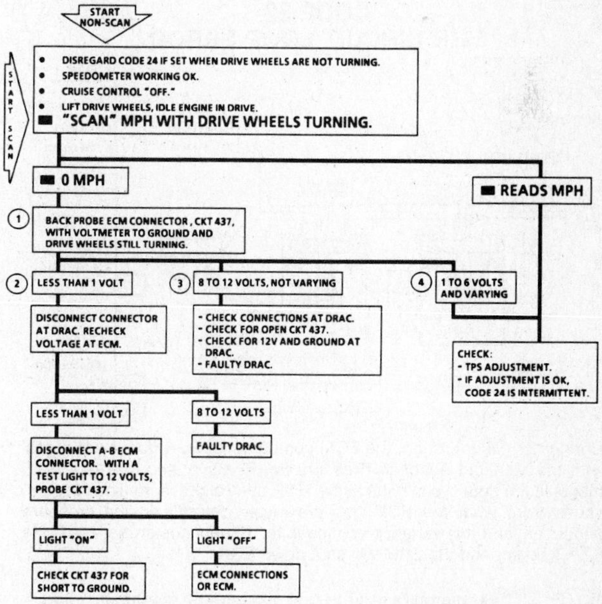
START NON-SCAN
START SCAN
• DISREGARD CODE 24 IF SET WHEN DRIVE WHEELS ARE NOT TURNING.
• SPEEDOMETER WORKING OK.
• CRUISE CONTROL "OFF."
• LIFT DRIVE WHEELS, IDLE ENGINE IN DRIVE.
"SCAN" MPH WITH DRIVE WHEELS TURNING.
0 MPH
READS MPH
1
BACK PROBE ECM CONNECTOR, CKT 437, WITH VOLTMETER TO GROUND AND DRIVE WHEELS STILL TURNING.
2
LESS THAN 1 VOLT
3
8 TO 12 VOLTS, NOT VARYING
4
1 TO 6 VOLTS AND VARYING
DISCONNECT CONNECTOR AT DRAC. RECHECK VOLTAGE AT ECM.
- CHECK CONNECTIONS AT DRAC.
- CHECK FOR OPEN CKT 437.
- CHECK FOR 12V AND GROUND AT DRAC.
- FAULTY DRAC.
CHECK:
- TPS ADJUSTMENT.
- IF ADJUSTMENT IS OK, CODE 24 IS INTERMITTENT.
LESS THAN 1 VOLT
8 TO 12 VOLTS
FAULTY DRAC.
DISCONNECT A-B ECM CONNECTOR. WITH A TEST LIGHT TO 12 VOLTS, PROBE CKT 437.
LIGHT "ON"
LIGHT "OFF"
CHECK CKT 437 FOR SHORT TO GROUND.
ECM CONNECTIONS OR ECM.

91B13632 91C13633

Courtesy of General Motors Corp.

1991 ENGINE PERFORMANCE
Self-Diagnostics – Diesel (Cont.)

CODE 31
MANIFOLD ABSOLUTE PRESSURE SENSOR SIGNAL VOLTAGE LOW

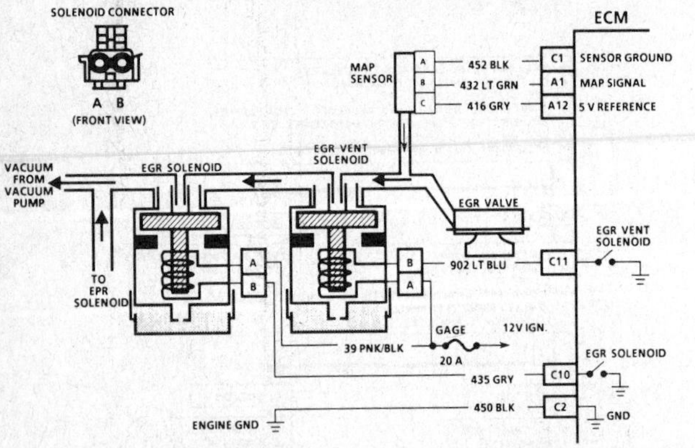
SOLENOID CONNECTOR
A B
(FRONT VIEW)
ECM
MAP SENSOR
A
B
C
452 BLK
432 LT GRN
416 GRY
C1
A1
A12
SENSOR GROUND
MAP SIGNAL
5 V REFERENCE
VACUUM FROM VACUUM PUMP
EGR SOLENOID
EGR VENT SOLENOID
EGR VALVE
TO EPR SOLENOID
902 LT BLU
C11
GAGE
12V IGN.
39 PNK/BLK
20 A
EGR SOLENOID
435 GRY
C10
450 BLK
C2
GND
ENGINE GND

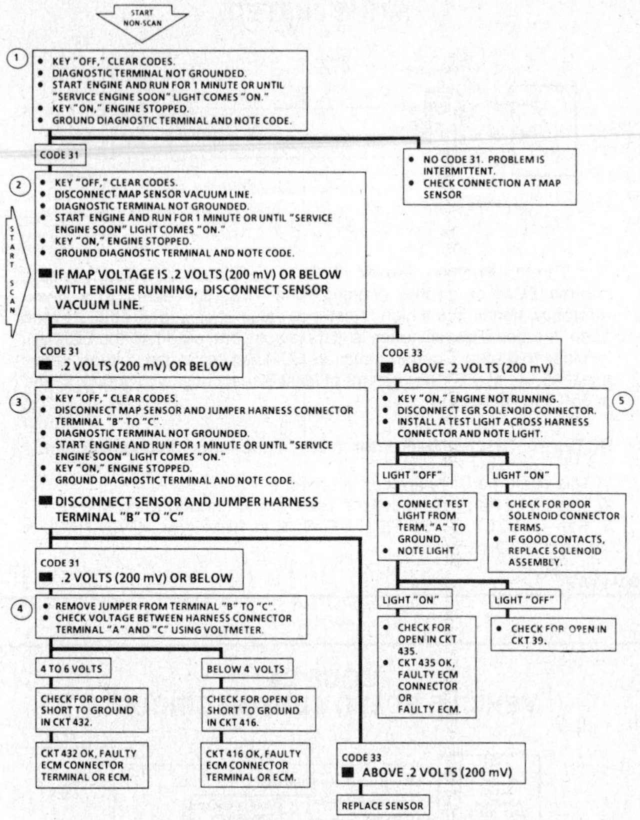
START NON-SCAN
1
KEY "OFF," CLEAR CODES.
DIAGNOSTIC TERMINAL NOT GROUNDED.
START ENGINE AND RUN FOR 1 MINUTE OR UNTIL "SERVICE ENGINE SOON" LIGHT COMES "ON."
KEY "ON," ENGINE STOPPED.
GROUND DIAGNOSTIC TERMINAL AND NOTE CODE.
CODE 31
NO CODE 31. PROBLEM IS INTERMITTENT.
CHECK CONNECTION AT MAP SENSOR
START SCAN
2
KEY "OFF," CLEAR CODES.
DISCONNECT MAP SENSOR VACUUM LINE.
DIAGNOSTIC TERMINAL NOT GROUNDED.
START ENGINE AND RUN FOR 1 MINUTE OR UNTIL "SERVICE ENGINE SOON" LIGHT COMES "ON."
KEY "ON," ENGINE STOPPED.
GROUND DIAGNOSTIC TERMINAL AND NOTE CODE.
IF MAP VOLTAGE IS .2 VOLTS (200 mV) OR BELOW WITH ENGINE RUNNING, DISCONNECT SENSOR VACUUM LINE.
CODE 31
.2 VOLTS (200 mV) OR BELOW
CODE 33
ABOVE .2 VOLTS (200 mV)
3
KEY "OFF," CLEAR CODES.
DISCONNECT MAP SENSOR AND JUMPER HARNESS CONNECTOR TERMINAL "B" TO "C".
DIAGNOSTIC TERMINAL NOT GROUNDED.
START ENGINE AND RUN FOR 1 MINUTE OR UNTIL "SERVICE ENGINE SOON" LIGHT COMES "ON."
KEY "ON," ENGINE STOPPED.
GROUND DIAGNOSTIC TERMINAL AND NOTE CODE.
DISCONNECT SENSOR AND JUMPER HARNESS TERMINAL "B" TO "C"
KEY "ON," ENGINE NOT RUNNING.
DISCONNECT EGR SOLENOID CONNECTOR.
INSTALL A TEST LIGHT ACROSS HARNESS CONNECTOR AND NOTE LIGHT.
5
LIGHT "OFF"
LIGHT "ON"
CONNECT TEST LIGHT FROM TERM. "A" TO GROUND.
NOTE LIGHT
CHECK FOR POOR SOLENOID CONNECTOR TERMS.
IF GOOD CONTACTS, REPLACE SOLENOID ASSEMBLY.
CODE 31
.2 VOLTS (200 mV) OR BELOW
4
REMOVE JUMPER FROM TERMINAL "B" TO "C".
CHECK VOLTAGE BETWEEN HARNESS CONNECTOR TERMINAL "A" AND "C" USING VOLTMETER.
LIGHT "ON"
LIGHT "OFF"
CHECK FOR OPEN IN CKT 435.
CKT 435 OK, FAULTY ECM CONNECTOR OR FAULTY ECM.
CHECK FOR OPEN IN CKT 39.
4 TO 6 VOLTS
BELOW 4 VOLTS
CHECK FOR OPEN OR SHORT TO GROUND IN CKT 432.
CHECK FOR OPEN OR SHORT TO GROUND IN CKT 416.
CKT 432 OK, FAULTY ECM CONNECTOR TERMINAL OR ECM.
CKT 416 OK, FAULTY ECM CONNECTOR TERMINAL OR ECM.
CODE 33
ABOVE .2 VOLTS (200 mV)
REPLACE SENSOR

The Manifold Absolute Pressure (MAP) sensor monitors vacuum in the EGR circuit. It senses the actual vacuum in the EGR vacuum line and sends a signal back to the ECM. The signal is compared to the EGR duty cycle calculated by the ECM. If there is a difference in the ECM command and what vacuum is at the EGR valve as sensed by the MAP sensor, the ECM makes minor adjustments. When a major difference is sensed, the ECM recognizes a fault and sends a full EGR signal.

NOTE: Test numbers refer to test numbers on diagnostic chart.

1) This confirms Code 31 fault is present.
2) If ECM recognizes and sets Code 33 (high MAP signal), the ECM, MAP sensor and wiring are okay.
3) If ECM recognizes and sets Code 33 (high MAP signal), the ECM and wiring are okay.
4) This tests for 5-volt reference signal to MAP sensor. Normally, about 5 volts should be present at MAP sensor terminal "C" with ignition on.
5) This tests for an open in the EGR solenoid circuit.

91D13634 91E13635

Courtesy of General Motors Corp.

CODE 32
EGR CIRCUIT LOOP ERROR

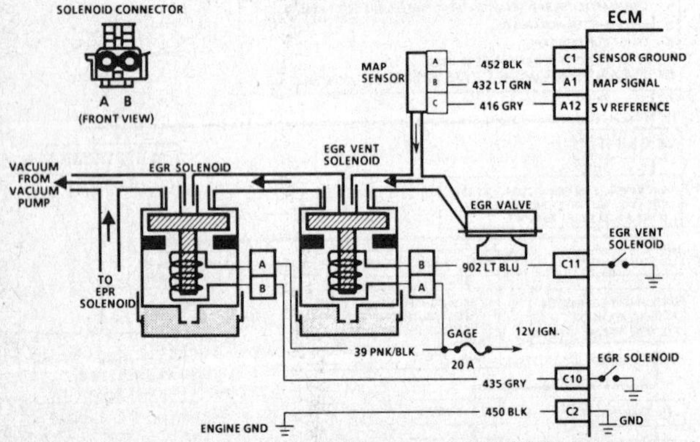
SOLENOID CONNECTOR
A B
(FRONT VIEW)
ECM
MAP SENSOR
A
B
C
452 BLK
432 LT GRN
416 GRY
C1
A1
A12
SENSOR GROUND
MAP SIGNAL
5 V REFERENCE
VACUUM FROM VACUUM PUMP
EGR SOLENOID
EGR VENT SOLENOID
EGR VALVE
TO EPR SOLENOID
902 LT BLU
C11
GAGE
12V IGN.
39 PNK/BLK
20 A
EGR SOLENOID
435 GRY
C10
450 BLK
C2
GND
ENGINE GND

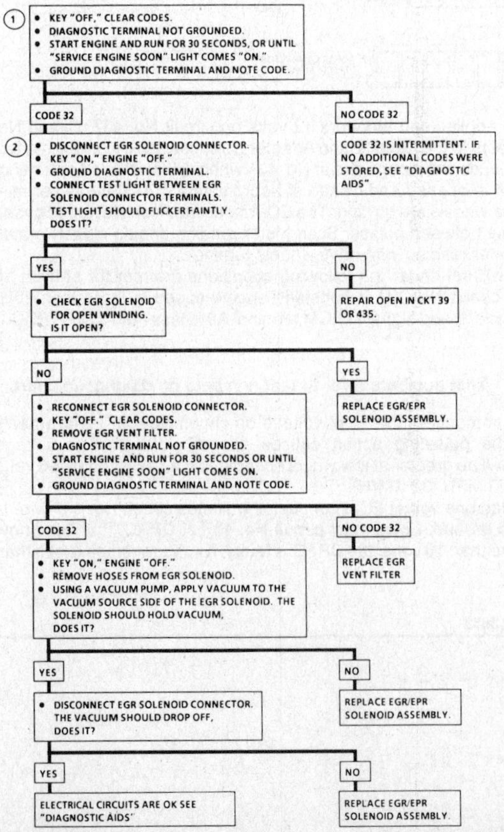
1
KEY "OFF," CLEAR CODES.
DIAGNOSTIC TERMINAL NOT GROUNDED.
START ENGINE AND RUN FOR 30 SECONDS, OR UNTIL "SERVICE ENGINE SOON" LIGHT COMES "ON."
GROUND DIAGNOSTIC TERMINAL AND NOTE CODE.
CODE 32
NO CODE 32
2
DISCONNECT EGR SOLENOID CONNECTOR.
KEY "ON," ENGINE "OFF."
GROUND DIAGNOSTIC TERMINAL.
CONNECT TEST LIGHT BETWEEN EGR SOLENOID CONNECTOR TERMINALS. TEST LIGHT SHOULD FLICKER FAINTLY. DOES IT?
CODE 32 IS INTERMITTENT. IF NO ADDITIONAL CODES WERE STORED, SEE "DIAGNOSTIC AIDS"
YES
NO
CHECK EGR SOLENOID FOR OPEN WINDING. IS IT OPEN?
REPAIR OPEN IN CKT 39 OR 435.
NO
YES
RECONNECT EGR SOLENOID CONNECTOR.
KEY "OFF." CLEAR CODES.
REMOVE EGR VENT FILTER.
DIAGNOSTIC TERMINAL NOT GROUNDED.
START ENGINE AND RUN FOR 30 SECONDS OR UNTIL "SERVICE ENGINE SOON" LIGHT COMES ON.
GROUND DIAGNOSTIC TERMINAL AND NOTE CODE.
REPLACE EGR/EPR SOLENOID ASSEMBLY.
CODE 32
NO CODE 32
KEY "ON," ENGINE "OFF."
REMOVE HOSES FROM EGR SOLENOID.
USING A VACUUM PUMP, APPLY VACUUM TO THE VACUUM SOURCE SIDE OF THE EGR SOLENOID. THE SOLENOID SHOULD HOLD VACUUM. DOES IT?
REPLACE EGR VENT FILTER
YES
NO
DISCONNECT EGR SOLENOID CONNECTOR. THE VACUUM SHOULD DROP OFF. DOES IT?
REPLACE EGR/EPR SOLENOID ASSEMBLY.
YES
NO
ELECTRICAL CIRCUITS ARE OK SEE "DIAGNOSTIC AIDS"
REPLACE EGR/EPR SOLENOID ASSEMBLY.

During normal operation, the ECM compares its EGR duty cycle signal with the Manifold Absolute Pressure (MAP) signal and makes adjustments in the duty cycle. If the actual EGR control pressure (line vacuum) varies from what the ECM has previously determined the pressure should be, and this variance continues for 10 seconds or more, a Code 32 will be set and the ECM will shut down EGR.

NOTE: Test numbers refer to test numbers on diagnostic chart.

1) This determines if Code 32 can reset.
2) This tests EGR solenoid electrical control circuit. Test light should flicker faintly if the ECM harness and connections are okay. A faintly flickering light is a slightly pulsating glow as opposed to a bright steady glow from a continuous ground path.

DIAGNOSTIC AIDS

A vacuum leak may cause a Code 32. Check all vacuum hoses and components connected to vacuum hoses for leaks. Also check cruise control and A/C systems vacuum hoses and components.

91D13634 91F13636

Courtesy of General Motors Corp.

CODE 33
MANIFOLD ABSOLUTE PRESSURE SENSOR SIGNAL VOLTAGE HIGH

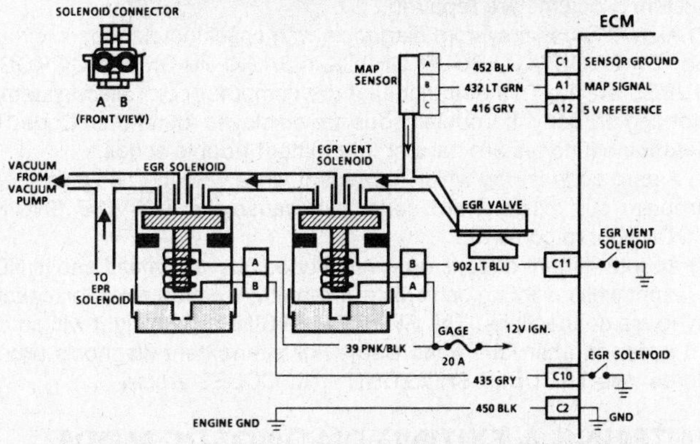

SOLENOID CONNECTOR
A B
(FRONT VIEW)
ECM
MAP SENSOR
A
B
C
452 BLK
432 LT GRN
416 GRY
C1
A1
A12
SENSOR GROUND
MAP SIGNAL
5 V REFERENCE
VACUUM FROM VACUUM PUMP
EGR SOLENOID
EGR VENT SOLENOID
EGR VALVE
TO EPR SOLENOID
902 LT BLU
C11
EGR VENT SOLENOID
GAGE
12V IGN.
39 PNK/BLK
20 A
EGR SOLENOID
435 GRY
C10
450 BLK
C2
ENGINE GND
GND

The Manifold Absolute Pressure (MAP) sensor monitors vacuum in the EGR circuit. It senses the actual vacuum in the EGR vacuum line and sends a signal back to the ECM. The signal is compared to EGR duty cycle calculated by the ECM. If there is a difference in the ECM command and what vacuum is at the EGR valve as sensed by the MAP sensor, the ECM makes minor adjustments. When a major difference is sensed, the ECM recognizes a fault and sends a full EGR signal.

NOTE: Test numbers refer to test numbers on diagnostic chart.

1) This step confirms Code 33 fault is present.
2) If the ECM recognizes and sets Code 33 (low MAP signal), the ECM and wiring are okay.
3) This determines if solenoids are stuck closed.
4) This determines whether a short circuit to ground exists in solenoid circuit, or ECM is faulty.

CHECK FOR POOR CONNECTION, PLUGGED, DISCONNECTED, OR LEAKING MAP SENSOR VACUUM HOSE. REPAIR AS REQUIRED.

START NON-SCAN

(1)
- KEY "OFF", CLEAR CODES.
- DIAGNOSTIC TERMINAL NOT GROUNDED.
- START ENGINE AND RUN FOR 1 MINUTE OR UNTIL "SERVICE ENGINE SOON" LIGHT COMES ON.
- KEY "ON", ENGINE STOPPED. GROUND DIAGNOSTIC TERMINAL AND NOTE CODE.

CODE 33 → (2)

NO CODE 33. PROBLEM IS INTERMITTENT. CHECK FOR POOR CONNECTION AT MAP SENSOR.

START SCAN

(2)
- KEY "OFF", CLEAR CODES.
- DISCONNECT MAP SENSOR ELECTRICAL CONNECTOR.
- DIAGNOSTIC TERMINAL NOT GROUNDED.
- START ENGINE AND RUN FOR 1 MINUTE OR UNTIL "SERVICE ENGINE SOON" LIGHT COMES ON.
- KEY "ON", ENGINE STOPPED.
- GROUND DIAGNOSTIC TERMINAL AND NOTE CODE.
- ■ IF MAP VOLTAGE IS ABOVE 2.5 VOLTS WITH ENGINE RUNNING, DISCONNECT SENSOR.

CODE 31 ■ BELOW 2.5 VOLTS → (3)

CODE 33 ■ 2.5 VOLTS OR OVER → CHECK FOR SHORT TO VOLTAGE IN CKT 432. IF CKT 432 IS OK, REPLACE ECM.

(3)
- DISCONNECT EGR SOLENOID CONNECTOR AND EGR VENT SOLENOID CONNECTOR.
- INSTALL VACUUM GAGE IN PLACE OF EGR VALVE.
- START ENGINE AND NOTE VACUUM.

VACUUM → (4)

NO VACUUM →
- CHECK FOR POOR OR LOW VACUUM SOURCE.
- EGR SOLENOID VALVE OR EGR VENT SOLENOID VALVE CLOSED.
- REPLACE SOLENOID IF REQUIRED.

(4)
- CONNECT 12 V TEST LIGHT ACROSS EGR SOLENOID TERMINALS "A" AND "B", THEN EGR VENT SOLENOID TERMINALS "A" AND "B".

LIGHT "ON" EITHER SOLENOID → CHECK FOR SHORT TO GROUND IN CKT 435, OR SHORT TO GROUND IN CKT 902. IF OK, REPLACE ECM.

LIGHT "OFF" BOTH SOLENOIDS → CHECK FOR OPEN IN GROUND CKT 452. IF CKT 452 IS OK, REPLACE SENSOR.

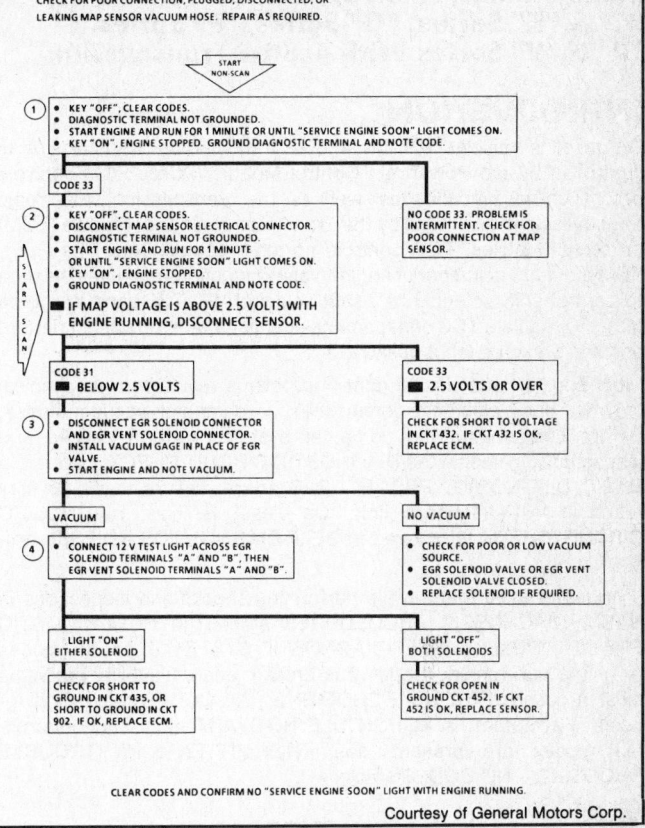

CLEAR CODES AND CONFIRM NO "SERVICE ENGINE SOON" LIGHT WITH ENGINE RUNNING.

91D13634 90G13983

Courtesy of General Motors Corp.

CODE 51
PROM PROBLEM

Ensure all pins are fully inserted in socket. If pins are fully inserted, replace PROM and recheck. If problem is not corrected, replace ECM.

- CHECK THAT ALL PINS ARE FULLY INSERTED IN THE SOCKET.
- IF OK, REPLACE PROM AND RECHECK.
- IF PROBLEM NOT CORRECTED, REPLACE ECM.

CODE 52
ECM FAULT

Ensure ECM connectors are fully inserted. Clear ECM memory. Start engine and check for SERVICE ENGINE SOON light. If light and Code 52 reappear, replace ECM. After repairs, clear ECM memory to confirm no SERVICE ENGINE SOON light.

- CHECK THAT ECM CONNECTORS ARE FULLY INSERTED.
- CLEAR MEMORY.
- START ENGINE AND CHECK FOR "SERVICE ENGINE SOON" LIGHT.
- IF LIGHT REAPPEARS, AND CODE 52, REPLACE ECM.

CODE 53
VOLTAGE REFERENCE OVERLOAD

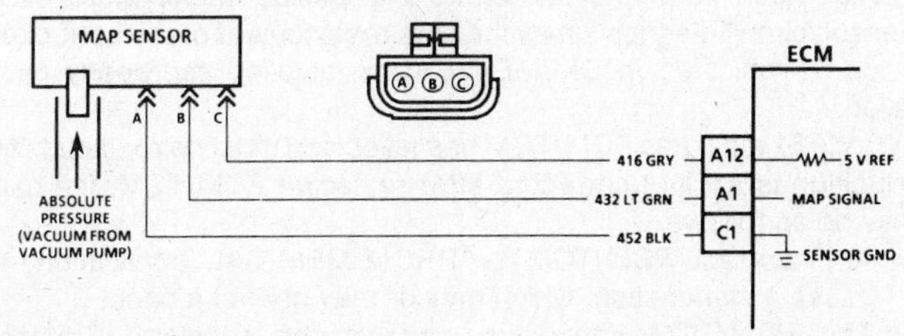

MAP SENSOR
A B C
ABSOLUTE PRESSURE (VACUUM FROM VACUUM PUMP)
ECM
416 GRY
432 LT GRN
452 BLK
A12
A1
C1
5 V REF
MAP SIGNAL
SENSOR GND

The 5-volt reference circuit is overloaded (grounded circuit). It takes 10 seconds before Code 53 will set.

NOTE: Test numbers refer to test numbers on diagnostic chart.

1) This confirms Code 53 is still present.
2) This confirms 5-volt reference signal from the ECM.
3) This tests if a short circuit to ground exists in circuit No. 416 or ECM.

(1)
- KEY "OFF," CLEAR CODES.
- START ENGINE AND RUN FOR 1 MINUTE, OR UNTIL "SES" COMES ON.
- GROUND DIAGNOSTIC TERMINAL AND NOTE CODE.

CODE 53 → (2)

NO CODE 53 → CODE 53 IS INTERMITTENT. IF ANY OTHER CODES ARE NOTED, SEE APPLICABLE CHART.

(2)
- DIAGNOSTIC TERMINAL NOT GROUNDED.
- KEY "ON" AND ENGINE NOT RUNNING.
- DISCONNECT MAP SENSOR AND CHECK VOLTAGE BETWEEN HARNESS CONNECTOR PIN "C" AND GROUND, USING DVM.

BELOW 4 VOLTS → (3)

ABOVE 4 VOLTS → REPLACE MAP SENSOR.

(3)
- DISCONNECT ECM 24 PIN CONNECTOR ONLY. CHECK FOR VOLTAGE AT ECM TERMINAL A12 TO GROUND, USING A DVM.

ABOUT 5 VOLTS → REPAIR SHORT TO GROUND IN CKT A12.

BELOW 4 VOLTS → REPLACE ECM.

90H13984

Courtesy of General Motors Corp.

1991 ENGINE PERFORMANCE
Self-Diagnostics – Electronic Transmission

**Blazer, Jimmy, Sierra,
"C" & "K" Series, "G" Series, "P" Series,
"R" & "V" Series With 4L80-E Transmission**

INTRODUCTION

On gasoline vehicles with the 4L80-E transmission, transmission is controlled by the Powertrain Control Module (PCM). PCM controls other vehicle functions as well as the transmission. Electronic transmission is controlled by the Transmission Control Module (TCM) on diesel vehicles. TCM controls no other components. The PCM/TCM monitors a number of engine/vehicle functions and uses the data to control shift solenoid "A", shift solenoid "B", TCC, and the force motor to regulate TCC engagement, upshift pattern, downshift pattern and line pressure (shift quality).

Most engine/transmission control problems result from mechanical failures, poor electrical connections or damaged vacuum hoses. Before condemning the computer system, perform checks and inspections, including the DIAGNOSTIC CIRCUIT CHECK, covered in BASIC DIAGNOSTIC PROCEDURES article. Failure to do so may result in lost diagnostic time. On diesel vehicles, DIAGNOSTIC CIRCUIT CHECK is covered in SELF-DIAGNOSTICS - DIESEL article.

If no faults were found while performing checks and inspections in BASIC DIAGNOSTIC PROCEDURES article, go to DIAGNOSTIC PROCEDURE under SELF-DIAGNOSTIC SYSTEM. If no fault codes or only a non-running Code 12 is present and driveability problems exist, proceed to TROUBLE SHOOTING - NO CODES article for diagnosis by symptom (i.e. ROUGH IDLE, NO START, etc.). If only intermittent codes are present, see INTERMITTENTS in TROUBLE SHOOTING - NO CODES article.

SELF-DIAGNOSTIC SYSTEM

Gasoline vehicles are equipped with a Powertrain Control Module (PCM). The PCM controls engine/emission functions, and electronic-controlled transmission functions. For additional information on self-diagnostic system for gasoline vehicles, see THEORY & OPERATION and SELF-DIAGNOSTICS - GASOLINE articles.

Diesel vehicles are equipped with a Transmission Control Module (TCM). TCM controls only the electronic transmission. Unless specifically stated otherwise, references to PCM also apply to TCM-equipped vehicles.

Control module is equipped with a self-diagnostic system, which detects system failures or abnormalities. When a malfunction occurs, control module will illuminate the SERVICE ENGINE SOON light located on instrument panel. When malfunction is detected and light is turned on, a corresponding trouble code will be stored in control module memory. To retrieve stored codes, see ENTERING & EXITING DIAGNOSTIC MODE in this article. Malfunctions are recorded as either HARD FAILURES or INTERMITTENT FAILURES.

SELF-DIAGNOSTICS DIRECTORY

DIAGNOSTIC PROCEDURE

Preliminary Inspection – 1) Check all vacuum hoses for correct routing, restrictions, cuts or other damage. Inspect difficult-to-see vacuum hoses beneath the air cleaner assembly and other engine components.

2) Inspect all engine compartment wiring for proper connections. Also check wires for pinched or chaffed spots, as well as contact with sharp edges or exhaust manifolds.

3) The preliminary inspection is very important and should be performed carefully and thoroughly, as it can often lead to fixing a problem without further diagnosis.

Diagnostic Procedure – 1) Ensure all non-controlled systems not related to engine or transmission control system are operating properly. DO NOT proceed with testing unless all other non-controlled system problems are repaired.

2) ALWAYS begin system diagnosis with checking diagnostic circuit. See DIAGNOSTIC CIRCUIT CHECK in BASIC DIAGNOSTIC PROCEDURES article. This determines if the computer-controlled system is working properly. If trouble codes are displayed (other than Code 12), determine if codes are hard or intermittent trouble codes.

3) A hard code is one which is present while working on vehicle, and problem still exists. Hard codes will cause the SERVICE ENGINE SOON light to come on.

4) An intermittent code is one which does not reset itself and is NOT present while working on vehicle. Intermittent codes are often caused by loose connections. The SERVICE ENGINE SOON light will go out 10 seconds after fault goes away. For intermittent diagnosis procedures, see TROUBLE SHOOTING - NO CODES article.

ENTERING & EXITING DIAGNOSTIC MODE

1) With key on and engine off, connect a jumper wire between ALDL terminal "B" (diagnostic terminal) and terminal "A" (ground). *See Fig. 1.* This places the control unit into diagnostic mode.

2) In this mode, the control unit will display Code 12 by flashing the SERVICE ENGINE SOON (SES) light. Code 12 is identified by the SES light flashing once, followed by a short pause, then 2 flashes in quick succession.

3) Code 12 will be displayed 3 times. If no other codes are stored, Code 12 will continue to flash until the diagnostic terminal is ungrounded. To exit diagnostic mode, turn ignition off and remove jumper wire from ALDL connector.

F
E
B
A
G
H

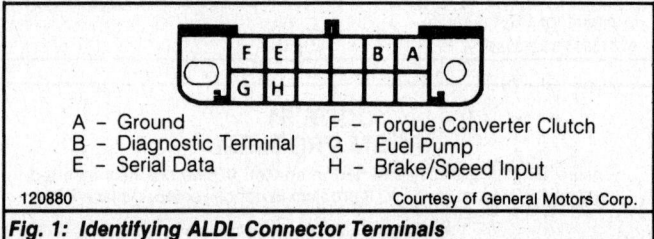

A - Ground
B - Diagnostic Terminal
E - Serial Data
F - Torque Converter Clutch
G - Fuel Pump
H - Brake/Speed Input

120880 Courtesy of General Motors Corp.

Fig. 1: Identifying ALDL Connector Terminals

TROUBLE CODE IDENTIFICATION

NOTE: Trouble codes retrieved from PCM/TCM may be related to either engine or transmission. Transmission-related codes are covered in this article. For engine-related codes, see appropriate SELF-DIAGNOSTICS article. See TROUBLE CODE IDENTIFICATION table to determine if code is transmission or engine related.

1) The system codes indicate failure of a specific sensor and/or circuit. Sensor/circuit diagnosis may indicate replacement of the control unit. Code 51 indicates PROM/MEM-CAL is installed improperly or has failed.

2) Code 52 indicates PCM/TCM has failed and must be replaced. If the condition is still not corrected after replacing PCM/TCM, the cause may be as follows.

- An incorrect PCM/TCM or PROM/MEM-CAL application may cause a malfunction, which may or may not set a code.
- The PCM/TCM connector may be the problem. Connector terminals may have to be removed from the connector to be properly checked.
- PROM/MEM-CAL failure. Although the PROM/MEM-CAL rarely fails, it could be the cause of the problem.
- Replacement PCM/TCM may be faulty.
- Intermittent problem. Make a careful physical inspection of affected sensor/circuit.
- A shorted solenoid, coil relay, or harness may be the cause of PCM/TCM failure. Use Short Circuit Tester (J-34636) to check for short circuits.

TROUBLE CODE IDENTIFICATION

Code	Probable Cause
12 [1]	No Engine Speed Sensor Reference Pulse To PCM/TCM
13 [1]	Open Oxygen Sensor Circuit (Gasoline)
14 [1]	CTS Voltage Low (Sensor Or Signal Line Grounded)
15 [1]	CTS Voltage High (Sensor, Connections, Or Wires Open)
21 [1]	TPS Voltage High (Open Circuit Or Misadjusted TPS)
22 [1]	TPS Voltage Low (Circuit Grounded)
23 [1]	TPS Not Calibrated (Diesel – .25-1.3 Volts At Curb Idle) Intake Air Temperature Sensor Voltage High (Gasoline)
24 [1]	Vehicle Speed Sensor Circuit Open Or Grounded
25 [1]	Intake Air Temperature Sensor Voltage Low (Gasoline)
28	Pressure Switch Manifold Range Circuit Open Or Shorted
31 [1]	MAP Voltage Low (Diesel) Turbocharger Wastegate Overboost (Gasoline)
32 [1]	EGR Error (Improper Vacuum Signal)
33 [1]	MAP Voltage High
34 [1]	MAP Voltage Low (Gasoline)
35 [1]	IAC System Fault (Gasoline)
39	TCC Stuck Off (Faulty TCC Solenoid)
42 [1]	EST Circuit Fault (Gasoline)
43 [1]	ESC Fault (Gasoline)
44 [1]	Lean Exhaust Indicated (Gasoline)
45 [1]	Rich Exhaust Indicated (Gasoline)
51 [1]	Improperly Installed/Faulty PROM/MEM-CAL
52 [1]	PCM/TCM Fault
53 [1]	System Voltage High (Gasoline – Charging Problem) Voltage Reference Overload (Diesel)
54 [1]	Fuel Pump Circuit Voltage Low (Gasoline)
55 [1]	Faulty ECM (Gasoline)
58	TTS High Temperature (Sensor Or Signal Line Grounded)
59	TTS Low Temperature (Sensor, Connections, Or Wires Open)
68	Overdrive Ratio Error (Engine RPM Greater Than Input Speed)
73	Force Motor Commanded Amperage Differs From Return
75	System Voltage Low (Charging System Problem)
81	QDM Solenoid "B" Monitored Voltage Differs From Commanded
82	QDM Solenoid "A" Monitored Voltage Differs From Commanded
83	QDM TCC Monitored Voltage Differs From Commanded
85	Undefined Gear Ratio (Input Or Output Sensor Failure)
86	Shift Solenoid "B" Stuck On (Commanded Gear Not Engaged)
87	Shift Solenoid "B" Stuck Off (Commanded Gear Not Engaged)

[1] – Code is engine related. For information on engine-related trouble codes, see appropriate SELF-DIAGNOSTICS article.

CLEARING TROUBLE CODES

Trouble codes should be cleared after repairs have been completed. Also, some diagnostic charts require that codes be cleared before using diagnostic chart. To clear codes, remove PCM/TCM memory battery voltage for 30 seconds.

If no hard fault codes are present (only intermittent codes exist), proceed to TROUBLE SHOOTING – NO CODES article for intermittent diagnostic procedures.

PCM/TCM LOCATION

The ECM is located under the passenger's seat riser ("G" Series), or behind right side of dash (all other models).

SPECIAL TOOLS (DIAGNOSTIC)

Special Scan testers are plugged into the ALDL may be used to read trouble codes, and check voltages in system on serial data line. These testers can save a great deal of time. For additional information, see manual included with tester.

TEST EQUIPMENT

A tachometer, test light, Digital Volt-Ohmmeter (DVOM) with a minimum 10-megohm input impedance, vacuum gauge, and jumper wires are required to test and diagnose electronic transmission control system. A Scan tester may also be used to access data parameters. Tester will supply a visual reading of most inputs, and some outputs, to the PCM/TCM. Some diagnostic flow charts require the use of a bidirectional (Tech 1) Scan tester.

TROUBLE CODE CHARTS

The following diagnostic flow charts and circuit schematics are provided courtesy of General Motors Corp.

NOTE: Some charts require the use of a bidirectional (Tech 1) Scan tester. If a bidirectional Scan tester is not available, the PCM/TCM-controlled relays and solenoids may be energized by grounding ALDL test terminal "B" with ignition on and engine off.

CODE 28, PRESSURE SWITCH MANIFOLD FAULT

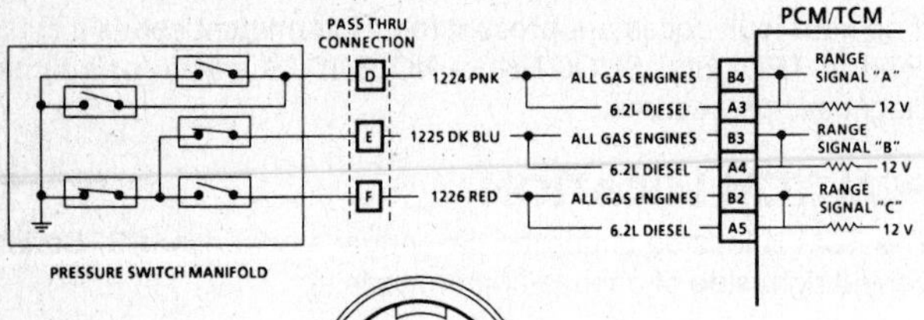
PASS THRU CONNECTION
PCM/TCM
D
1224 PNK
ALL GAS ENGINES
B4
RANGE SIGNAL "A"
6.2L DIESEL
A3
12 V
E
1225 DK BLU
ALL GAS ENGINES
B3
RANGE SIGNAL "B"
6.2L DIESEL
A4
12 V
F
1226 RED
ALL GAS ENGINES
B2
RANGE SIGNAL "C"
6.2L DIESEL
A5
12 V
PRESSURE SWITCH MANIFOLD

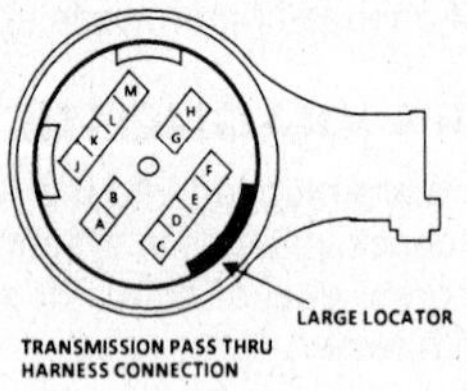
LARGE LOCATOR
TRANSMISSION PASS THRU HARNESS CONNECTION

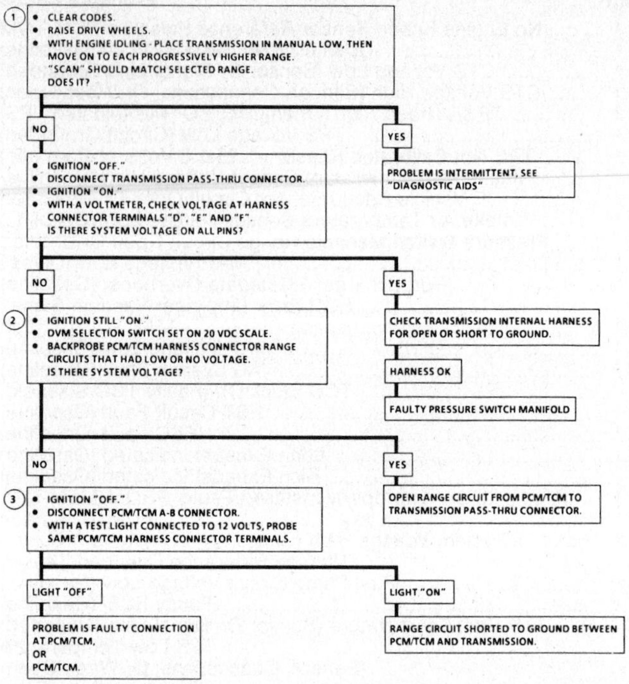
1
CLEAR CODES.
RAISE DRIVE WHEELS.
WITH ENGINE IDLING - PLACE TRANSMISSION IN MANUAL LOW, THEN MOVE ON TO EACH PROGRESSIVELY HIGHER RANGE. "SCAN" SHOULD MATCH SELECTED RANGE. DOES IT?
NO
YES
PROBLEM IS INTERMITTENT, SEE "DIAGNOSTIC AIDS"
IGNITION "OFF."
DISCONNECT TRANSMISSION PASS-THRU CONNECTOR.
IGNITION "ON."
WITH A VOLTMETER, CHECK VOLTAGE AT HARNESS CONNECTOR TERMINALS "D", "E" AND "F". IS THERE SYSTEM VOLTAGE ON ALL PINS?
NO
YES
CHECK TRANSMISSION INTERNAL HARNESS FOR OPEN OR SHORT TO GROUND.
HARNESS OK
FAULTY PRESSURE SWITCH MANIFOLD
2
IGNITION STILL "ON."
DVM SELECTION SWITCH SET ON 20 VDC SCALE.
BACKPROBE PCM/TCM HARNESS CONNECTOR RANGE CIRCUITS THAT HAD LOW OR NO VOLTAGE. IS THERE SYSTEM VOLTAGE?
NO
YES
OPEN RANGE CIRCUIT FROM PCM/TCM TO TRANSMISSION PASS-THRU CONNECTOR.
3
IGNITION "OFF."
DISCONNECT PCM/TCM A-B CONNECTOR.
WITH A TEST LIGHT CONNECTED TO 12 VOLTS, PROBE SAME PCM/TCM HARNESS CONNECTOR TERMINALS.
LIGHT "OFF"
LIGHT "ON"
PROBLEM IS FAULTY CONNECTION AT PCM/TCM, OR PCM/TCM.
RANGE CIRCUIT SHORTED TO GROUND BETWEEN PCM/TCM AND TRANSMISSION.

The Pressure Switch Manifold (PSM) is actually 5 pressure switches combined into one unit and mounted on the transmission valve body. The PCM/TCM supplies battery voltage to the PSM on 3 separate wires. By grounding one or more of these circuits through various combinations of the pressure switches inside the pressure switch manifold, the PCM/TCM detects what gear range has been selected by the vehicle operator.

NOTE: Test numbers refer to test numbers on diagnostic chart.

1) This test compares the indicated range to the range actually selected.
2) This test checks for correct voltage from the PCM/TCM to the transmission pass-thru connector.
3) This test will detect a short to ground in any one of the 3 PSM range circuits.

DIAGNOSTIC AIDS

Code 28 will set if PCM/TCM detects one of 2 "illegal" PSM combinations. See VALID PSM COMBINATION table for various combinations. Check pass-thru connector for good contact.

VALID PSM COMBINATION CHART

	A	B	C
Park	12	0	12
Reverse	0	0	12
Neutral	12	0	12
4th	12	0	0
3rd	12	12	0
2nd	12	12	12
1st	0	12	12
Illegal	0	12	0
Illegal	0	0	0

91B13673 91C13674

1991 ENGINE PERFORMANCE
Self-Diagnostics – Electronic Transmission (Cont.)

CODE 39, TORQUE CONVERTER CLUTCH STUCK "OFF" POSITION

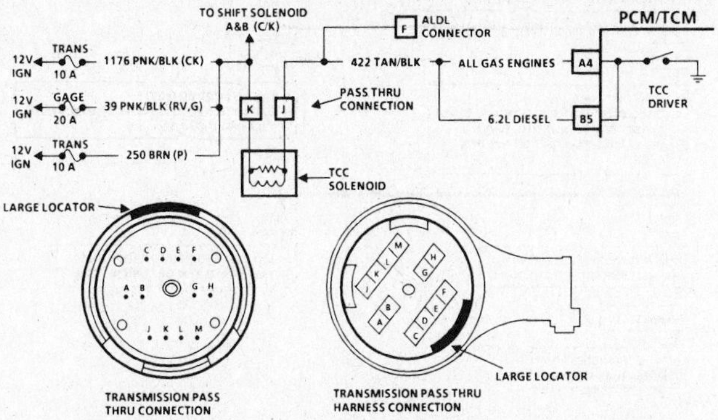
TO SHIFT SOLENOID A&B (C/K)
ALDL CONNECTOR
F
PCM/TCM
12V IGN
TRANS 10 A
1176 PNK/BLK (CK)
422 TAN/BLK
ALL GAS ENGINES
A4
12V IGN
GAGE 20 A
39 PNK/BLK (RV,G)
K
J
PASS THRU CONNECTION
TCC DRIVER
6.2L DIESEL
B5
12V IGN
TRANS 10 A
250 BRN (P)
TCC SOLENOID
LARGE LOCATOR
LARGE LOCATOR
TRANSMISSION PASS THRU CONNECTION
TRANSMISSION PASS THRU HARNESS CONNECTION

The purpose of the automatic transmission Torque Converter Clutch (TCC) feature is to eliminate power loss of the torque converter stage when vehicle is in a cruise condition. This allows the convenience of the automatic transmission, and fuel economy of a manual transmission.

Fused battery ignition voltage is supplied to the TCC solenoid, which is used inside the valve body to shift a spool valve to modulate pressure to the TCC. This modulated pressure normally allows some slight slippage of TCC.

The PCM/TCM will engage TCC by grounding circuit No. 422, energizing the solenoid.

Code 39 will set under the following conditions.

- TCC is engaged.
- TCC "slip" is greater than 65 RPM for 2 seconds.
- 2nd or 3rd gear is selected or indicated.

NOTE: **Test numbers refer to test numbers on diagnostic chart.**

1) This test determines if transmission is receiving a TCC command from the pass-thru connector. If bidirectional Scan tester is not available, TCC may be activated by grounding ALDL test terminal "B" with ignition on and engine off.
2) This test checks for power to transmission.
3) This test determines if PCM/TCM is commanding TCC to be on.

DIAGNOSTIC AIDS

Clear codes and re-check for Code 39. If code resets, problem could be internal to the transmission. Code 39 will only set in 3rd gear. TCC slip in 4th gear will set Code 68.

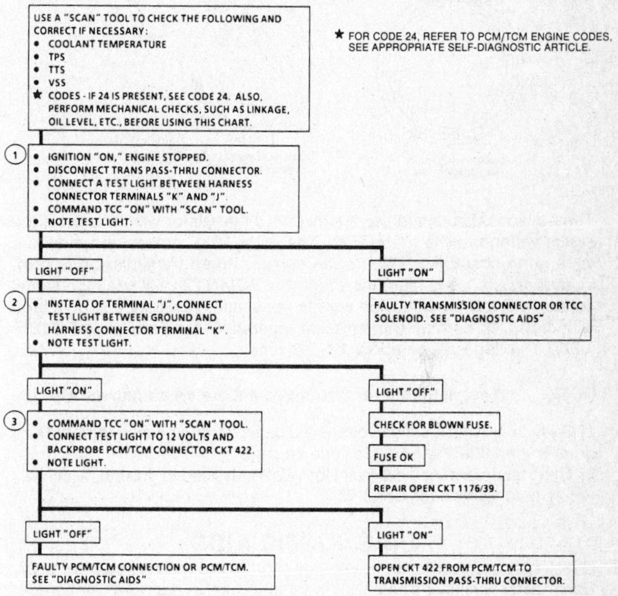
USE A "SCAN" TOOL TO CHECK THE FOLLOWING AND CORRECT IF NECESSARY:
• COOLANT TEMPERATURE
• TPS
• TTS
• VSS
★ CODES - IF 24 IS PRESENT, SEE CODE 24. ALSO, PERFORM MECHANICAL CHECKS, SUCH AS LINKAGE, OIL LEVEL, ETC., BEFORE USING THIS CHART.
★ FOR CODE 24, REFER TO PCM/TCM ENGINE CODES, SEE APPROPRIATE SELF-DIAGNOSTIC ARTICLE.
1
• IGNITION "ON," ENGINE STOPPED.
• DISCONNECT TRANS PASS-THRU CONNECTOR.
• CONNECT A TEST LIGHT BETWEEN HARNESS CONNECTOR TERMINALS "K" AND "J".
• COMMAND TCC "ON" WITH "SCAN" TOOL.
• NOTE TEST LIGHT.
LIGHT "OFF"
LIGHT "ON"
2
• INSTEAD OF TERMINAL "J", CONNECT TEST LIGHT BETWEEN GROUND AND HARNESS CONNECTOR TERMINAL "K".
• NOTE TEST LIGHT.
FAULTY TRANSMISSION CONNECTOR OR TCC SOLENOID. SEE "DIAGNOSTIC AIDS"
LIGHT "ON"
LIGHT "OFF"
3
• COMMAND TCC "ON" WITH "SCAN" TOOL.
• CONNECT TEST LIGHT TO 12 VOLTS AND BACKPROBE PCM/TCM CONNECTOR CKT 422.
• NOTE LIGHT.
CHECK FOR BLOWN FUSE.
FUSE OK
REPAIR OPEN CKT 1176/39.
LIGHT "OFF"
LIGHT "ON"
FAULTY PCM/TCM CONNECTION OR PCM/TCM. SEE "DIAGNOSTIC AIDS"
OPEN CKT 422 FROM PCM/TCM TO TRANSMISSION PASS-THRU CONNECTOR.

91D13675 91E13676

Courtesy of General Motors Corp.

CODE 53, SYSTEM VOLTAGE HIGH

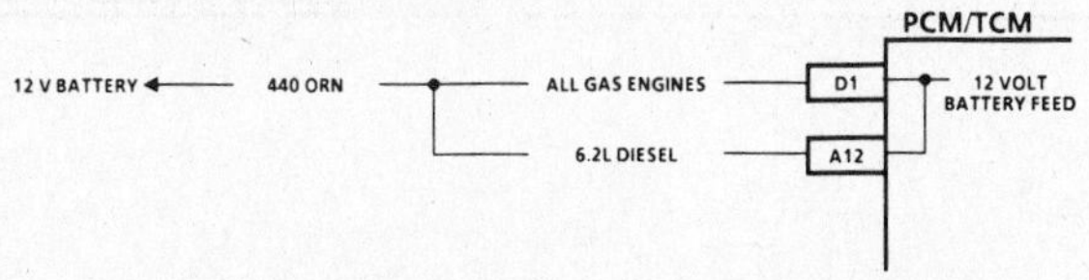
PCM/TCM
12 V BATTERY
440 ORN
ALL GAS ENGINES
D1
12 VOLT BATTERY FEED
6.2L DIESEL
A12

Code 53 will set when ignition is on and PCM terminal D1 voltage is greater than 19.5 volts for about 2 seconds. During the time the failure is present, the force motor is turned off, transmission immediately shifts to 2nd gear, and TCC operation is inhibited. The setting of additional codes may result.

NOTE: **Test numbers refer to test numbers on diagnostic chart.**

1) Normal battery voltage is 10-17.0 volts.
2) This test checks if high voltage reading is due to the alternator, circuit No. 440 or PCM. With engine running, check voltage at battery. If voltage is greater than 19.5 volts, the PCM is okay.
3) This test checks if alternator is faulty under load condition. If voltage is greater than 19.5 volts, check alternator.

NOTES ON INTERMITTENTS

Jump-starting engine, and charging battery with a battery charger may set Code 53. If code is set when an accessory is operated, check for poor connections or excessive current draw. Also, check for poor connections at starter solenoid or fusible link.

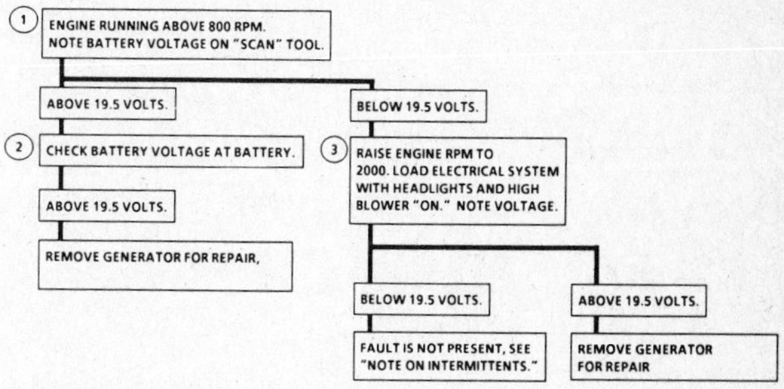
1
ENGINE RUNNING ABOVE 800 RPM. NOTE BATTERY VOLTAGE ON "SCAN" TOOL.
ABOVE 19.5 VOLTS.
BELOW 19.5 VOLTS.
2
CHECK BATTERY VOLTAGE AT BATTERY.
3
RAISE ENGINE RPM TO 2000. LOAD ELECTRICAL SYSTEM WITH HEADLIGHTS AND HIGH BLOWER "ON." NOTE VOLTAGE.
ABOVE 19.5 VOLTS.
REMOVE GENERATOR FOR REPAIR.
BELOW 19.5 VOLTS.
ABOVE 19.5 VOLTS.
FAULT IS NOT PRESENT, SEE "NOTE ON INTERMITTENTS."
REMOVE GENERATOR FOR REPAIR

91F13677 91G13678

Courtesy of General Motors Corp.

CODE 58, TRANSMISSION TEMPERATURE SENSOR CIRCUIT (HIGH TEMPERATURE INDICATED)

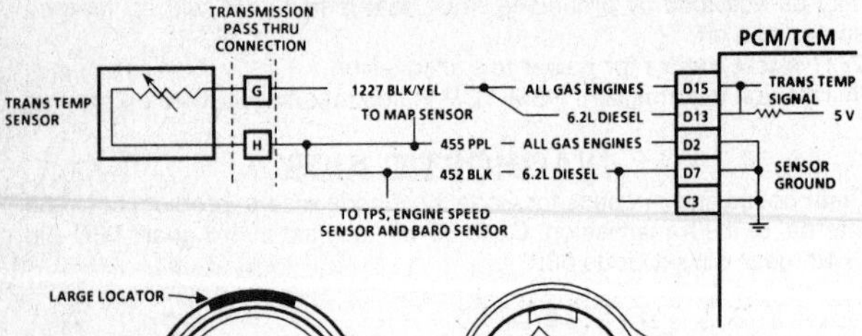
TRANSMISSION
PASS THRU
CONNECTION
PCM/TCM
TRANS TEMP
SENSOR
G
H
1227 BLK/YEL
ALL GAS ENGINES
D15
TRANS TEMP
SIGNAL
TO MAP SENSOR
6.2L DIESEL
D13
5 V
455 PPL
ALL GAS ENGINES
D2
452 BLK
6.2L DIESEL
D7
SENSOR
GROUND
C3
TO TPS, ENGINE SPEED
SENSOR AND BARO SENSOR

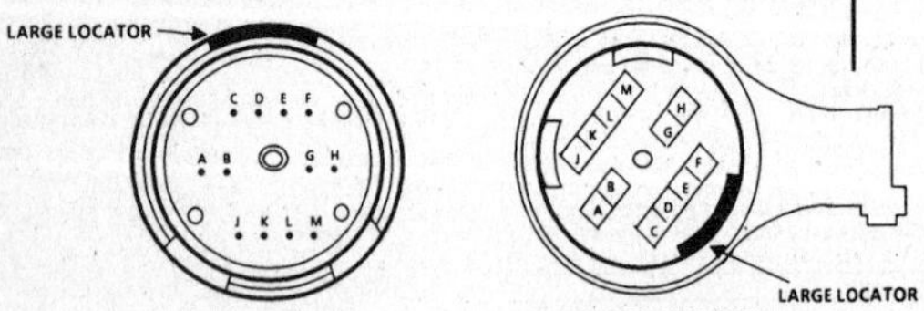
LARGE LOCATOR
C D E F
A B G H
J K L M
LARGE LOCATOR

TRANSMISSION PASS THRU CONNECTION

TRANSMISSION PASS THRU HARNESS CONNECTION

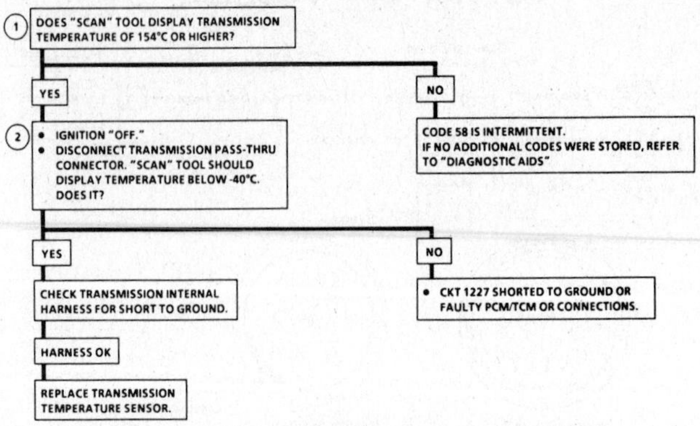
1
DOES "SCAN" TOOL DISPLAY TRANSMISSION TEMPERATURE OF 154°C OR HIGHER?
YES
NO
2
• IGNITION "OFF."
• DISCONNECT TRANSMISSION PASS-THRU CONNECTOR. "SCAN" TOOL SHOULD DISPLAY TEMPERATURE BELOW -40°C. DOES IT?
CODE 58 IS INTERMITTENT. IF NO ADDITIONAL CODES WERE STORED, REFER TO "DIAGNOSTIC AIDS"
YES
NO
CHECK TRANSMISSION INTERNAL HARNESS FOR SHORT TO GROUND.
• CKT 1227 SHORTED TO GROUND OR FAULTY PCM/TCM OR CONNECTIONS.
HARNESS OK
REPLACE TRANSMISSION TEMPERATURE SENSOR.

TRANSMISSION SENSOR – TEMPERATURE TO RESISTANCE (APPROX.)

°C	°F	MINIMUM RESISTANCE	NOMINAL RESISTANCE	MAXIMUM RESISTANCE
-40°C	-40°F	80965	100544	120123
-30°C	-20°F	42701	52426	62151
-20°C	-4°F	23458	28491	33524
-10°C	14°F	13366	16068	18770
0°C	32°F	7871	9370	10869
10°C	50°F	4771	5640	6508
20°C	68°F	2981	3500	4018
30°C	86°F	1915	2232	2550
40°C	104°F	1260	1460	1660
50°C	122°F	848.8	977.1	1105
60°C	140°F	584.1	668.7	753.4
70°C	158°F	410.3	467.2	524.2
80°C	176°F	293.7	332.7	371.7
90°C	194°F	213.9	241.0	268.2
100°C	212°F	158.1	177.4	196.8
110°C	?	118.8	132.6	146.5
120°C	?	90.40	100.6	110.8
130°C	?	69.48	77.29	85.11
140°C	?	53.96	60.13	66.29
150°C	?	42.43	47.31	52.20

The transmission temperature sensor is a thermistor which controls the signal voltage to the PCM/TCM. The PCM/TCM applies and monitors voltage on circuit No. 1227 to the sensor. When transmission is cold, sensor resistance is high; therefore, the PCM/TCM will see high signal voltage. As the transmission warms up, sensor resistance and voltage will drop. At normal transmission operating temperature of 212°F (100°C), voltage will be about 1.5-2.0 volts.

NOTE: Test numbers refer to test numbers on diagnostic chart.

1) Code 58 will set if signal voltage indicates a transmission temperature greater than 309°F (154°C) for one second.
2) This test determines if circuit No. 1227 is shorted to ground, which will result in conditions for Code 58.

DIAGNOSTIC AIDS

Check harness routing for a potential short to ground in circuit No. 1227. Scan tester displays transmission temperature in degrees Centigrade. After transmission is running, the temperature display should rise steadily to about 100°C then stabilize. Test the transmission sensor at various temperature levels to determine if sensor is out of calibration. See TRANSMISSION SENSOR – TEMPERATURE TO RESISTANCE chart. An out-of-calibration sensor could result in delayed shifts, or TCC enabled complaint.

91H13679 91A13680

CODE 59, TRANSMISSION TEMPERATURE SENSOR CIRCUIT (LOW TEMPERATURE INDICATED)

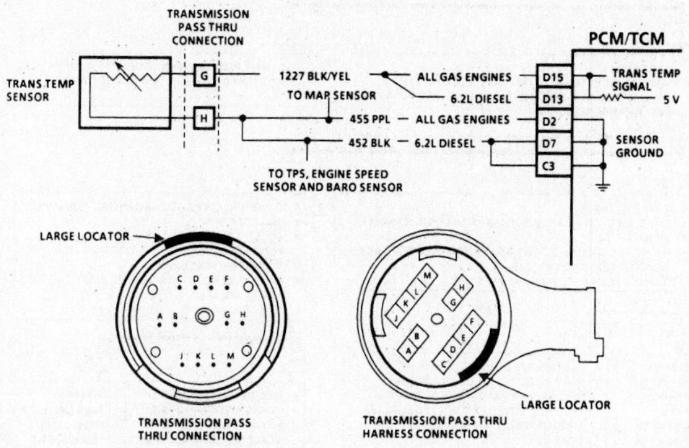

TRANSMISSION PASS THRU CONNECTION
PCM/TCM
TRANS TEMP SENSOR
G
H
1227 BLK/YEL
TO MAP SENSOR
ALL GAS ENGINES
6.2L DIESEL
455 PPL
ALL GAS ENGINES
452 BLK
6.2L DIESEL
D15
D13
D2
D7
C3
TRANS TEMP SIGNAL
5 V
SENSOR GROUND
TO TPS, ENGINE SPEED SENSOR AND BARO SENSOR
LARGE LOCATOR
LARGE LOCATOR
TRANSMISSION PASS THRU CONNECTION
TRANSMISSION PASS THRU HARNESS CONNECTION

The transmission temperature sensor is a thermistor which controls signal voltage to PCM/TCM. The PCM/TCM applies and monitors 5 volts to the sensor on circuit No. 1227. When transmission is cold, sensor resistance is high; therefore, the PCM/TCM will see high signal voltage. As transmission temperature warms up, sensor resistance and voltage drop. At normal transmission operating temperature of 212°F (100°C), voltage will be about 1.5-2.0 volts.

NOTE: Test numbers refer to test numbers on diagnostic chart.

1) Code 59 will set if signal voltage indicates a transmission temperature less than –54°F (–48°C) for one second.
2) This test simulates Code 58. If PCM/TCM recognizes the low signal voltage (high temperature) and Scan tester reads 304°F (151°C) or greater, the PCM/TCM and wiring are okay.
3) This test determines if circuit No. 1227 is open. There should be 5 volts present at the sensor connector if measuring with a DVOM.

DIAGNOSTIC AIDS

Scan tester displays transmission temperature in degrees Centigrade. After transmission is running, the displayed temperature should rise steadily to about 212°F (100°C) then stabilize. A faulty connection or an open in circuit No. 455 or circuit No. 1227 will result in a Code 59. Test the coolant sensor at various temperature levels to determine if sensor is out of calibration. See TRANSMISSION SENSOR - TEMPERATURE TO RESISTANCE chart. An out-of-calibration sensor could result in firm shifts, or TCC enabled complaint.

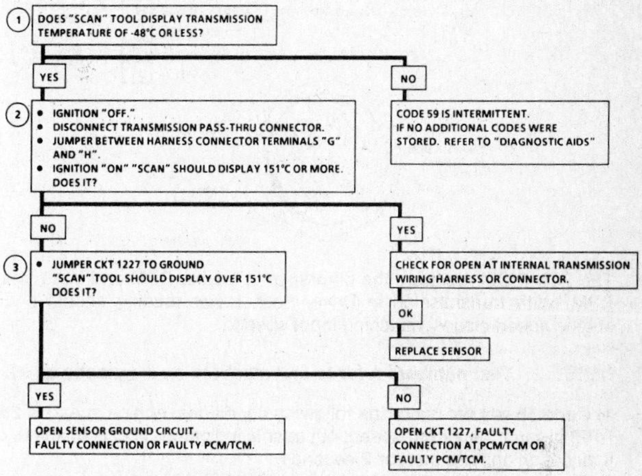

1 DOES "SCAN" TOOL DISPLAY TRANSMISSION TEMPERATURE OF -48°C OR LESS?
YES
NO
2 • IGNITION "OFF." • DISCONNECT TRANSMISSION PASS-THRU CONNECTOR. • JUMPER BETWEEN HARNESS CONNECTOR TERMINALS "G" AND "H". • IGNITION "ON" "SCAN" SHOULD DISPLAY 151°C OR MORE. DOES IT?
CODE 59 IS INTERMITTENT. IF NO ADDITIONAL CODES WERE STORED. REFER TO "DIAGNOSTIC AIDS"
NO
YES
3 • JUMPER CKT 1227 TO GROUND "SCAN" TOOL SHOULD DISPLAY OVER 151°C DOES IT?
CHECK FOR OPEN AT INTERNAL TRANSMISSION WIRING HARNESS OR CONNECTOR.
OK
REPLACE SENSOR
YES
NO
OPEN SENSOR GROUND CIRCUIT, FAULTY CONNECTION OR FAULTY PCM/TCM.
OPEN CKT 1227, FAULTY CONNECTION AT PCM/TCM OR FAULTY PCM/TCM.

TRANSMISSION SENSOR - TEMPERATURE TO RESISTANCE (APPROX.)

°C	°F	MINIMUM RESISTANCE	NOMINAL RESISTANCE	MAXIMUM RESISTANCE
-40°C	-40°F	80965	100544	120123
-30°C	-20°F	42701	52426	62151
-20°C	-4°F	23458	28491	33524
-10°C	14°F	13366	16068	18770
0°C	32°F	7871	9370	10869
10°C	50°F	4771	5640	6508
20°C	68°F	2981	3500	4018
30°C	86°F	1915	2232	2550
40°C	104°F	1260	1460	1660
50°C	122°F	848.8	977.1	1105
60°C	140°F	584.1	668.7	753.4
70°C	158°F	410.3	467.2	524.2
80°C	176°F	293.7	332.7	371.7
90°C	194°F	213.9	241.0	268.2
100°C	212°F	158.1	177.4	196.8
110°C	?	118.8	132.6	146.5
120°C	?	90.40	100.6	110.8
130°C	?	69.48	77.29	85.11
140°C	?	53.96	60.13	66.29
150°C	?	42.43	47.31	52.20

91H13679 91B13681

Courtesy of General Motors Corp.

Self-Diagnostics – Electronic Transmission (Cont.)

CODE 68, OVERDRIVE RATIO ERROR

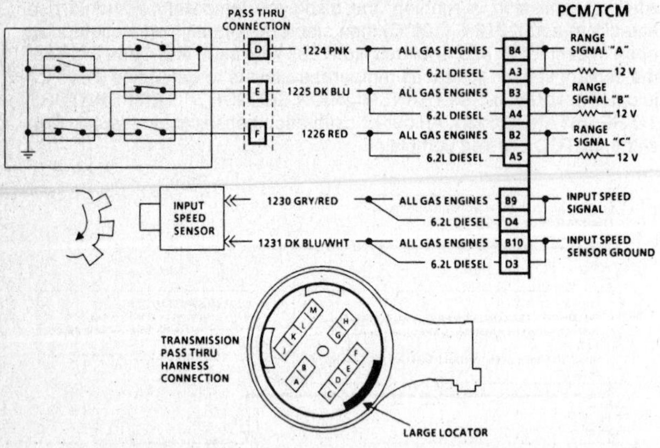
PASS THRU CONNECTION
PCM/TCM
D
1224 PNK
ALL GAS ENGINES
B4
RANGE SIGNAL "A"
6.2L DIESEL
A3
12 V
E
1225 DK BLU
ALL GAS ENGINES
B3
RANGE SIGNAL "B"
6.2L DIESEL
A4
12 V
F
1226 RED
ALL GAS ENGINES
B2
RANGE SIGNAL "C"
6.2L DIESEL
A5
12 V
INPUT SPEED SENSOR
1230 GRY/RED
ALL GAS ENGINES
B9
INPUT SPEED SIGNAL
6.2L DIESEL
D4
1231 DK BLU/WHT
ALL GAS ENGINES
B10
INPUT SPEED SENSOR GROUND
6.2L DIESEL
D3
TRANSMISSION PASS THRU HARNESS CONNECTION
M
L
K
J
H
G
F
E
D
C
B
A
LARGE LOCATOR

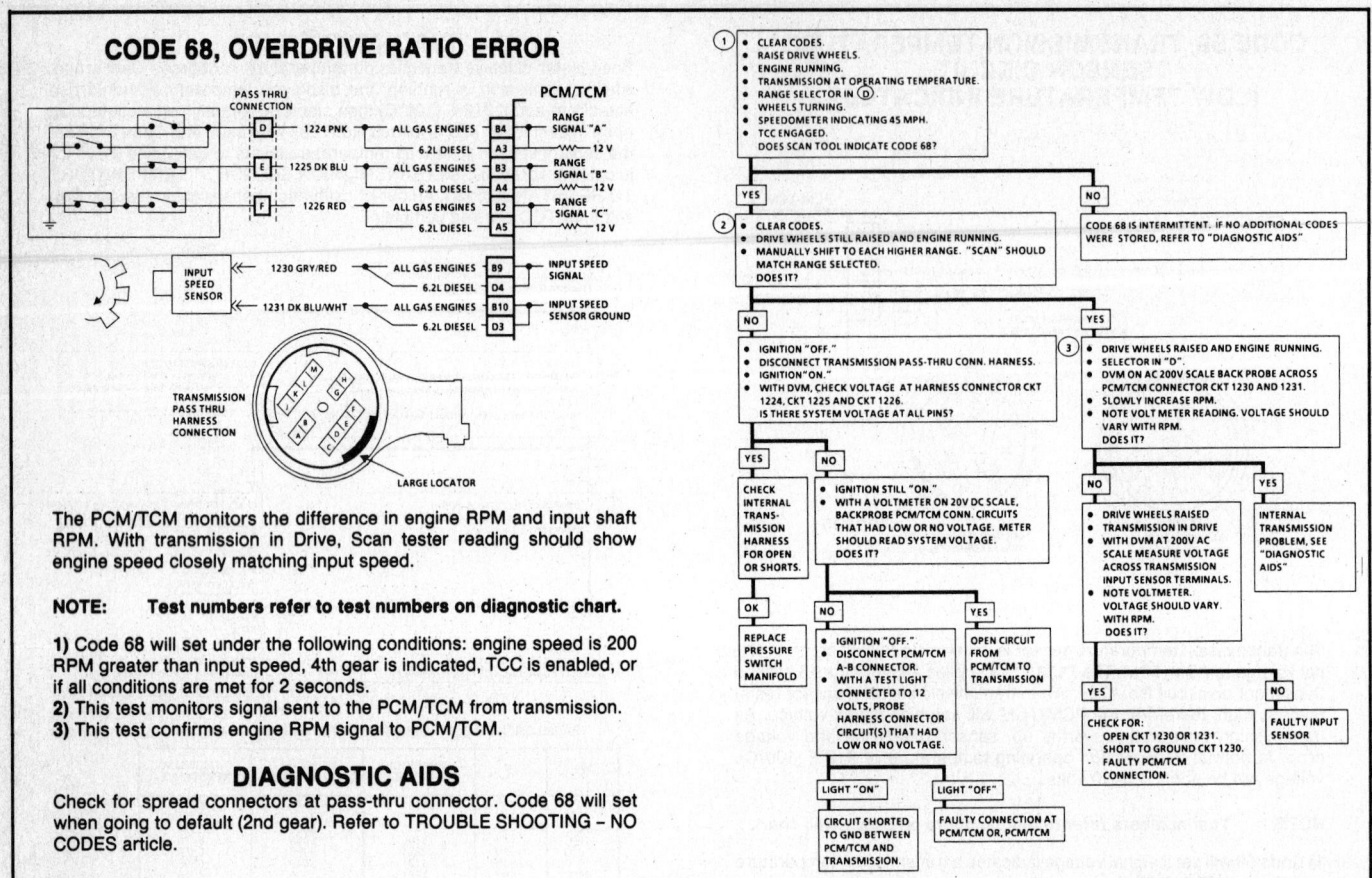

The PCM/TCM monitors the difference in engine RPM and input shaft RPM. With transmission in Drive, Scan tester reading should show engine speed closely matching input speed.

NOTE: **Test numbers refer to test numbers on diagnostic chart.**

1) Code 68 will set under the following conditions: engine speed is 200 RPM greater than input speed, 4th gear is indicated, TCC is enabled, or if all conditions are met for 2 seconds.
2) This test monitors signal sent to the PCM/TCM from transmission.
3) This test confirms engine RPM signal to PCM/TCM.

DIAGNOSTIC AIDS

Check for spread connectors at pass-thru connector. Code 68 will set when going to default (2nd gear). Refer to TROUBLE SHOOTING – NO CODES article.

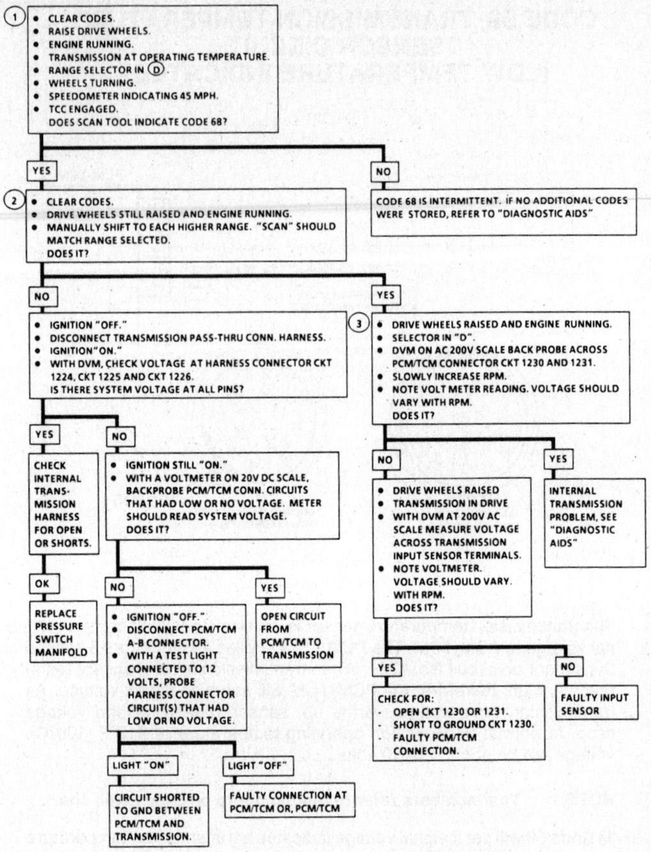
1
• CLEAR CODES.
• RAISE DRIVE WHEELS.
• ENGINE RUNNING.
• TRANSMISSION AT OPERATING TEMPERATURE.
• RANGE SELECTOR IN (D).
• WHEELS TURNING.
• SPEEDOMETER INDICATING 45 MPH.
• TCC ENGAGED.
DOES SCAN TOOL INDICATE CODE 68?
YES
NO
CODE 68 IS INTERMITTENT. IF NO ADDITIONAL CODES WERE STORED, REFER TO "DIAGNOSTIC AIDS"
2
• CLEAR CODES.
• DRIVE WHEELS STILL RAISED AND ENGINE RUNNING.
• MANUALLY SHIFT TO EACH HIGHER RANGE. "SCAN" SHOULD MATCH RANGE SELECTED.
DOES IT?
NO
YES
• IGNITION "OFF."
• DISCONNECT TRANSMISSION PASS-THRU CONN. HARNESS.
• IGNITION "ON."
• WITH DVM, CHECK VOLTAGE AT HARNESS CONNECTOR CKT 1224, CKT 1225 AND CKT 1226.
IS THERE SYSTEM VOLTAGE AT ALL PINS?
3
• DRIVE WHEELS RAISED AND ENGINE RUNNING.
• SELECTOR IN "D".
• DVM ON AC 200V SCALE BACK PROBE ACROSS PCM/TCM CONNECTOR CKT 1230 AND 1231.
• SLOWLY INCREASE RPM.
• NOTE VOLT METER READING. VOLTAGE SHOULD VARY WITH RPM.
DOES IT?
YES
NO
CHECK INTERNAL TRANS-MISSION HARNESS FOR OPEN OR SHORTS.
• IGNITION STILL "ON."
• WITH A VOLTMETER ON 20V DC SCALE, BACKPROBE PCM/TCM CONN. CIRCUITS THAT HAD LOW OR NO VOLTAGE. METER SHOULD READ SYSTEM VOLTAGE.
DOES IT?
NO
YES
• DRIVE WHEELS RAISED
• TRANSMISSION IN DRIVE
• WITH DVM AT 200V AC SCALE MEASURE VOLTAGE ACROSS TRANSMISSION INPUT SENSOR TERMINALS.
• NOTE VOLTMETER. VOLTAGE SHOULD VARY. WITH RPM.
DOES IT?
INTERNAL TRANSMISSION PROBLEM, SEE "DIAGNOSTIC AIDS"
OK
REPLACE PRESSURE SWITCH MANIFOLD
NO
YES
• IGNITION "OFF."
• DISCONNECT PCM/TCM A-B CONNECTOR.
• WITH A TEST LIGHT CONNECTED TO 12 VOLTS, PROBE HARNESS CONNECTOR CIRCUIT(S) THAT HAD LOW OR NO VOLTAGE.
OPEN CIRCUIT FROM PCM/TCM TO TRANSMISSION
YES
NO
CHECK FOR:
- OPEN CKT 1230 OR 1231.
- SHORT TO GROUND CKT 1230.
- FAULTY PCM/TCM CONNECTION.
FAULTY INPUT SENSOR
LIGHT "ON"
LIGHT "OFF"
CIRCUIT SHORTED TO GND BETWEEN PCM/TCM AND TRANSMISSION.
FAULTY CONNECTION AT PCM/TCM OR, PCM/TCM

91C13682 91D13683

Courtesy of General Motors Corp.

CODE 73, FORCE MOTOR CURRENT (CURRENT ERROR)

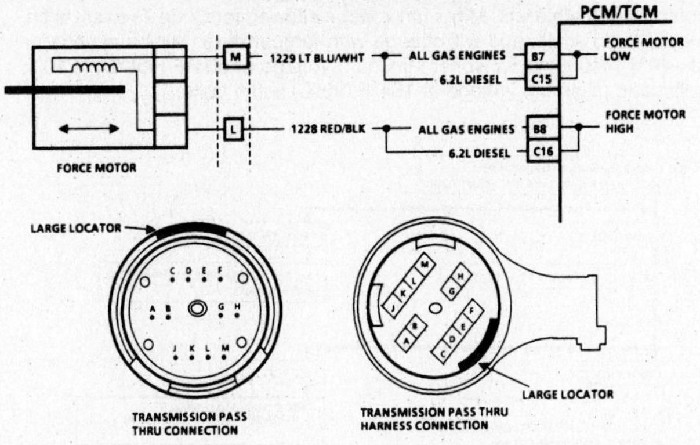
PCM/TCM
FORCE MOTOR LOW
FORCE MOTOR HIGH
M
1229 LT BLU/WHT
ALL GAS ENGINES
B7
6.2L DIESEL
C15
L
1228 RED/BLK
ALL GAS ENGINES
B8
6.2L DIESEL
C16
FORCE MOTOR
LARGE LOCATOR
TRANSMISSION PASS THRU CONNECTION
LARGE LOCATOR
TRANSMISSION PASS THRU HARNESS CONNECTION

NOTE: This flow chart requires the use of a bidirectional (Tech 1) Scan tester.

The force motor is a PCM/TCM-controlled device used to regulate transmission line pressure. The PCM/TCM looks at TPS voltage, engine RPM and other inputs to determine appropriate line pressure for a given load, then regulates the pressure by applying a varying amperage. The applied amperage can vary from 1-1.1 amps.

The PCM/TCM then monitors amperage at the return line. If the return amperage varies more than .16 amp from the commanded amperage for the duration of at least one second, Code 73 will set. Once Code 73 is set, the force motor is disabled and full line pressure will be applied until the next time the ignition switch is cycled. Code 73 will remain stored, but the force motor will resume normal function until the conditions for Code 73 re-occur.

NOTE: Test numbers refer to test numbers on diagnostic chart.

1) This procedure verifies an amperage difference of .16 amp or more, and tests the PCM/TCM's ability to control amperage to the force motor.
2) This test checks the force motor for internal shorts.

DIAGNOSTIC AIDS

Check for poor connections at PCM/TCM and transmission pass-thru connector.

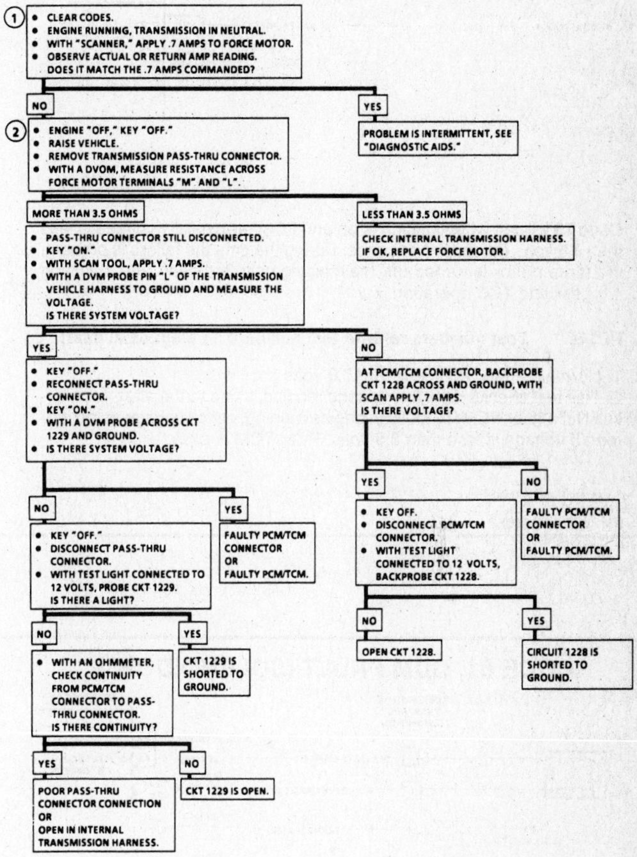
1
• CLEAR CODES.
• ENGINE RUNNING, TRANSMISSION IN NEUTRAL.
• WITH "SCANNER," APPLY .7 AMPS TO FORCE MOTOR.
• OBSERVE ACTUAL OR RETURN AMP READING.
DOES IT MATCH THE .7 AMPS COMMANDED?
NO
YES
PROBLEM IS INTERMITTENT, SEE "DIAGNOSTIC AIDS."
2
• ENGINE "OFF," KEY "OFF."
• RAISE VEHICLE.
• REMOVE TRANSMISSION PASS-THRU CONNECTOR.
• WITH A DVOM, MEASURE RESISTANCE ACROSS FORCE MOTOR TERMINALS "M" AND "L".
MORE THAN 3.5 OHMS
LESS THAN 3.5 OHMS
CHECK INTERNAL TRANSMISSION HARNESS. IF OK, REPLACE FORCE MOTOR.
• PASS-THRU CONNECTOR STILL DISCONNECTED.
• KEY "ON."
• WITH SCAN TOOL, APPLY .7 AMPS.
• WITH A DVM PROBE PIN "L" OF THE TRANSMISSION VEHICLE HARNESS TO GROUND AND MEASURE THE VOLTAGE.
IS THERE SYSTEM VOLTAGE?
YES
NO
• KEY "OFF."
• RECONNECT PASS-THRU CONNECTOR.
• KEY "ON."
• WITH A DVM PROBE ACROSS CKT 1229 AND GROUND.
• IS THERE SYSTEM VOLTAGE?
AT PCM/TCM CONNECTOR, BACKPROBE CKT 1228 ACROSS AND GROUND, WITH SCAN APPLY .7 AMPS.
IS THERE VOLTAGE?
NO
YES
FAULTY PCM/TCM CONNECTOR OR FAULTY PCM/TCM.
• KEY "OFF."
• DISCONNECT PASS-THRU CONNECTOR.
• WITH TEST LIGHT CONNECTED TO 12 VOLTS, PROBE CKT 1229.
IS THERE A LIGHT?
YES
NO
• KEY OFF.
• DISCONNECT PCM/TCM CONNECTOR.
• WITH TEST LIGHT CONNECTED TO 12 VOLTS, BACKPROBE CKT 1228.
FAULTY PCM/TCM CONNECTOR OR FAULTY PCM/TCM.
NO
YES
CKT 1229 IS SHORTED TO GROUND.
NO
YES
OPEN CKT 1228.
CIRCUIT 1228 IS SHORTED TO GROUND.
• WITH AN OHMMETER, CHECK CONTINUITY FROM PCM/TCM CONNECTOR TO PASS-THRU CONNECTOR.
IS THERE CONTINUITY?
YES
NO
POOR PASS-THRU CONNECTOR CONNECTION OR OPEN IN INTERNAL TRANSMISSION HARNESS.
CKT 1229 IS OPEN.

91E13684 91F13685

Courtesy of General Motors Corp.

1991 ENGINE PERFORMANCE
Self-Diagnostics – Electronic Transmission (Cont.)

CODE 75, SYSTEM VOLTAGE LOW

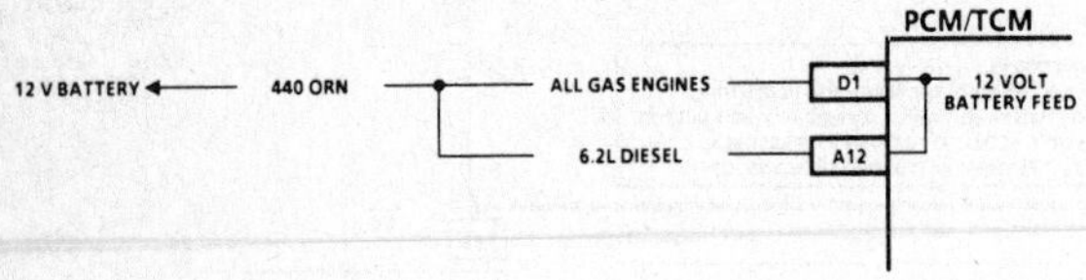
PCM/TCM
12 V BATTERY
440 ORN
ALL GAS ENGINES
D1
12 VOLT
BATTERY FEED
6.2L DIESEL
A12

Code 75 will set when ignition is on and PCM terminal D1 voltage is less than 8.6 volts for about 4 seconds. During the time the failure is present, the force motor is turned off, maintaining only 2nd gear, and inhibiting 4th gear and TCC operation.

NOTE: **Test numbers refer to test numbers on diagnostic chart.**

1) Normal battery voltage is 10-17.0 volts.
2) This test checks if the low voltage reading is due to the alternator, circuit No. 440 or PCM/TCM. With engine running, check voltage at the battery. If voltage is less than 8.6 volts, PCM/TCM is okay.

NOTE ON INTERMITTENTS

If Code sets when an accessory is operated, check for poor connections or excessive current draw. Also, check for poor connections at starter solenoid or fusible link. Minimum voltage allowed for Code 75 to set is on a graduated scale, and will change with temperature. Minimum voltage at -40°F (-40°C) is 6.7 volts. Minimum voltage at 304°F (150°C) is 10.5 volts, and minimum voltage at 194°F (90°C) is 8.6 volts.

(1) ENGINE RUNNING ABOVE 800 RPM. NOTE BATTERY VOLTAGE ON "SCAN" TOOL.

- ABOVE 9 VOLTS: FAULT IS NOT PRESENT. SEE "NOTE ON INTERMITTENTS"
- BELOW 9 VOLTS: (2) CHECK BATTERY VOLTAGE AT BATTERY.
  - BELOW 9 VOLTS: CHECK CHARGING SYSTEM. SERVICE OR REPLACE ALTERNATOR.
  - ABOVE 9 VOLTS:
    - KEY "OFF."
    - DISCONNECT PCM/TCM CONNECTORS.
    - WITH DVOM, PROBE CKT 440.
      - BELOW 9 VOLTS: OPEN OR FAULTY CKT 440.
      - ABOVE 9 VOLTS: FAULTY PCM/TCM CONNECTOR OR FAULTY PCM/TCM.

91F13677 91G13686

Courtesy of General Motors Corp.

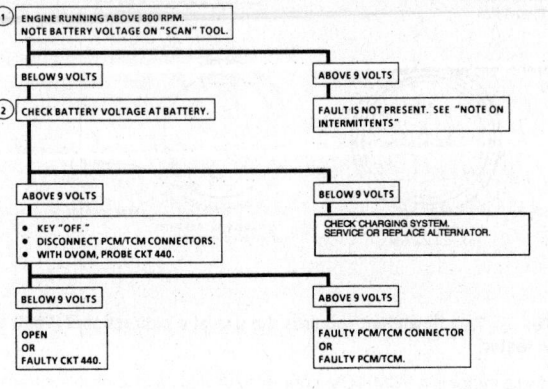

CODE 81, QDM FAULT (SOLENOID "B")

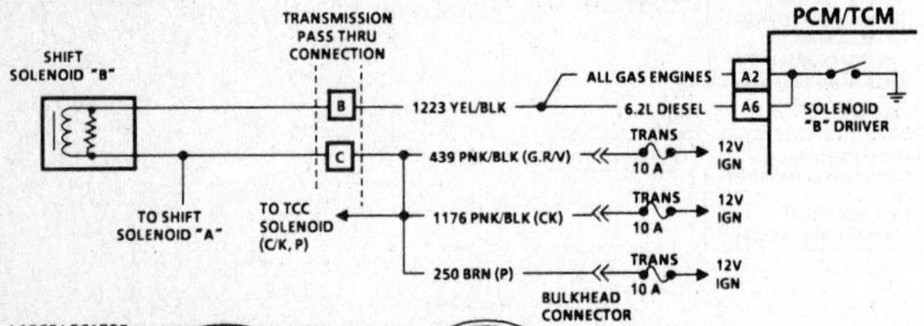
SHIFT
SOLENOID "B"
TRANSMISSION
PASS THRU
CONNECTION
PCM/TCM
B
C
1223 YEL/BLK
ALL GAS ENGINES
6.2L DIESEL
A2
A6
SOLENOID
"B" DRIVER
439 PNK/BLK (G.R/V)
TRANS
10 A
12V
IGN
TO SHIFT
SOLENOID "A"
TO TCC
SOLENOID
(C/K, P)
1176 PNK/BLK (CK)
250 BRN (P)
BULKHEAD
CONNECTOR

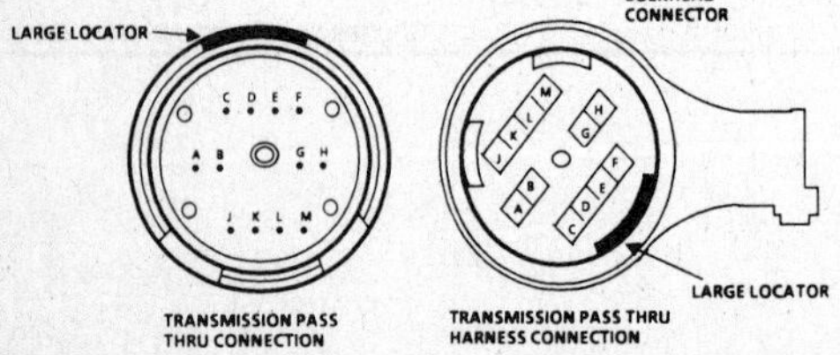
LARGE LOCATOR
TRANSMISSION PASS
THRU CONNECTION
TRANSMISSION PASS THRU
HARNESS CONNECTION

The PCM/TCM continually monitors voltage on each circuit connected to the quad driver, looking for either low or high voltage, depending on the commanded state of the devices connected to it. Code 81 will set if a fault has been detected on the shift solenoid "B" circuit. For example, if shift solenoid "B" is commanded on by the PCM/TCM, voltage on that circuit should drop when solenoid is grounded. If voltage stays up for at least .5 second, Code 81 will set. The opposite is also true. If shift solenoid "B" is off, voltage on the circuit should remain high. If voltage drops for more than .5 second, Code 81 will set.

NOTE: **Test numbers refer to test numbers on diagnostic chart.**

1) This procedure checks shift solenoid "B" and internal transmission wiring for shorts.
2) This test checks for power, from the ignition through transmission fuse, to the shift solenoid "B".
3) This test ensures circuit No. 1223 is not shorted to ground.
4) This test checks PCM/TCM's ability to ground or control shift solenoid "B". If bidirectional Scan tester is not available, solenoid may be activated by grounding ALDL test terminal "B" with ignition on and engine off.
5) This test ensures circuit No. 1223 is not shorted to ground.

DIAGNOSTIC AIDS

Check all connections, especially those at the transmission pass-thru connector. If code is intermittent, see INTERMITTENTS in TROUBLE SHOOTING – NO CODES article.

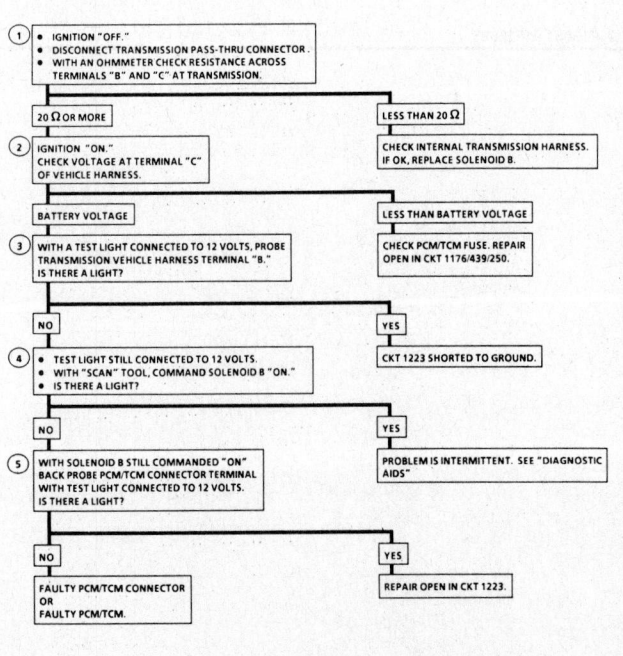

(1)
- IGNITION "OFF."
- DISCONNECT TRANSMISSION PASS-THRU CONNECTOR.
- WITH AN OHMMETER CHECK RESISTANCE ACROSS TERMINALS "B" AND "C" AT TRANSMISSION.

- LESS THAN 20 Ω: CHECK INTERNAL TRANSMISSION HARNESS. IF OK, REPLACE SOLENOID B.
- 20 Ω OR MORE: (2) IGNITION "ON." CHECK VOLTAGE AT TERMINAL "C" OF VEHICLE HARNESS.
  - LESS THAN BATTERY VOLTAGE: CHECK PCM/TCM FUSE. REPAIR OPEN IN CKT 1176/439/250.
  - BATTERY VOLTAGE: (3) WITH A TEST LIGHT CONNECTED TO 12 VOLTS, PROBE TRANSMISSION VEHICLE HARNESS TERMINAL "B." IS THERE A LIGHT?
    - YES: CKT 1223 SHORTED TO GROUND.
    - NO: (4)
      - TEST LIGHT STILL CONNECTED TO 12 VOLTS.
      - WITH "SCAN" TOOL, COMMAND SOLENOID B "ON."
      - IS THERE A LIGHT?
      - YES: PROBLEM IS INTERMITTENT. SEE "DIAGNOSTIC AIDS"
      - NO: (5) WITH SOLENOID B STILL COMMANDED "ON" BACK PROBE PCM/TCM CONNECTOR TERMINAL WITH TEST LIGHT CONNECTED TO 12 VOLTS. IS THERE A LIGHT?
        - YES: REPAIR OPEN IN CKT 1223.
        - NO: FAULTY PCM/TCM CONNECTOR OR FAULTY PCM/TCM.

91I13688 91J13689

Courtesy of General Motors Corp.

1991 ENGINE PERFORMANCE
Self-Diagnostics – Electronic Transmission (Cont.)

CODE 82, QDM FAULT (SOLENOID "A")

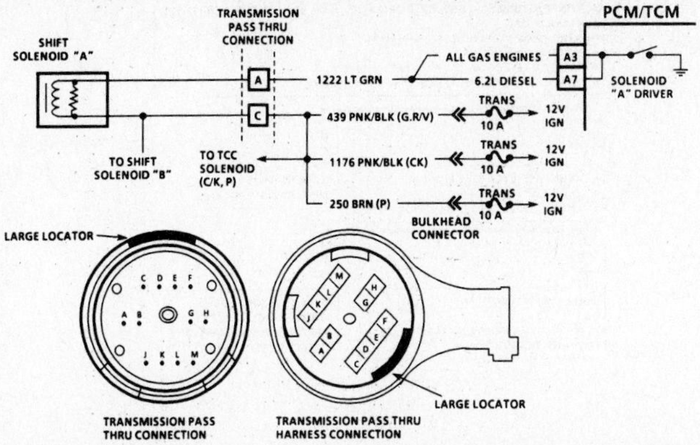
TRANSMISSION PASS THRU CONNECTION
PCM/TCM
SHIFT SOLENOID "A"
ALL GAS ENGINES
A3
1222 LT GRN
6.2L DIESEL
A7
SOLENOID "A" DRIVER
A
C
439 PNK/BLK (G,R/V)
TRANS 10 A
12V IGN
TO SHIFT SOLENOID "B"
TO TCC SOLENOID (C/K, P)
1176 PNK/BLK (CK)
250 BRN (P)
BULKHEAD CONNECTOR
LARGE LOCATOR
TRANSMISSION PASS THRU CONNECTION
TRANSMISSION PASS THRU HARNESS CONNECTION

The PCM/TCM continually monitors each circuit connected to the quad driver for either low or high voltage, depending on the commanded state of the device connected to it. Code 82 will set if there is a fault detected on the shift solenoid "A" circuit. For example, if shift solenoid "A" is commanded on by the PCM/TCM, then voltage on circuit should drop as soon as solenoid is grounded.

However, if voltage remains high for 2 seconds after the "on" command is given, Code 82 will set. The opposite is also true. If shift solenoid "A" is off, voltage on the circuit should be high. If voltage drops for .5 second or longer, Code 82 will set.

NOTE: **Test numbers refer to test numbers on diagnostic chart.**

1) This procedure checks shift solenoid "A" and internal transmission wiring harness for shorts.
2) This test checks for power, from the ignition through the fuse, to the shift solenoid.
3) This test checks circuit No. 1222 for short to ground.
4) This test checks PCM/TCM's ability to ground or control shift solenoid "A". If bidirectional Scan tester is not available, solenoid may be activated by grounding ALDL test terminal "B" with ignition on and engine off.

DIAGNOSTIC AIDS

Check all connections, especially at the transmission pass-thru connector. If code is intermittent, see INTERMITTENTS in TROUBLE SHOOTING - NO CODES article.

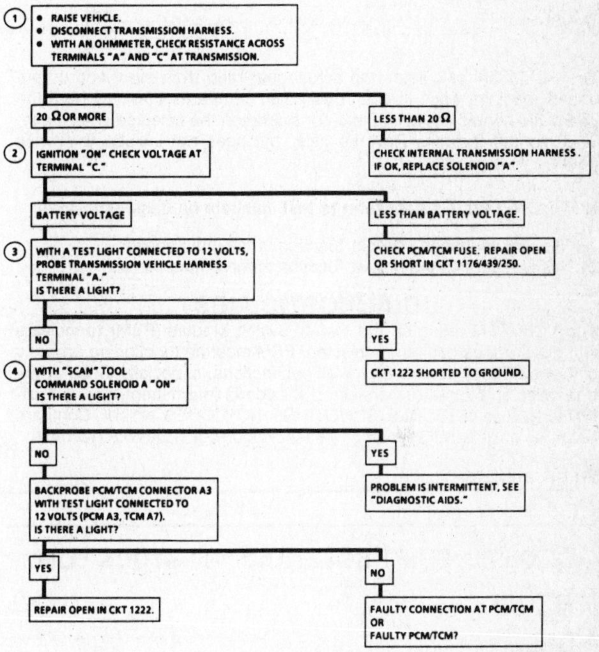
1
• RAISE VEHICLE.
• DISCONNECT TRANSMISSION HARNESS.
• WITH AN OHMMETER, CHECK RESISTANCE ACROSS TERMINALS "A" AND "C" AT TRANSMISSION.
20 Ω OR MORE
LESS THAN 20 Ω
2
IGNITION "ON" CHECK VOLTAGE AT TERMINAL "C."
CHECK INTERNAL TRANSMISSION HARNESS. IF OK, REPLACE SOLENOID "A".
BATTERY VOLTAGE
LESS THAN BATTERY VOLTAGE.
3
WITH A TEST LIGHT CONNECTED TO 12 VOLTS, PROBE TRANSMISSION VEHICLE HARNESS TERMINAL "A." IS THERE A LIGHT?
CHECK PCM/TCM FUSE. REPAIR OPEN OR SHORT IN CKT 1176/439/250.
NO
YES
4
WITH "SCAN" TOOL COMMAND SOLENOID A "ON" IS THERE A LIGHT?
CKT 1222 SHORTED TO GROUND.
NO
YES
BACKPROBE PCM/TCM CONNECTOR A3 WITH TEST LIGHT CONNECTED TO 12 VOLTS (PCM A3, TCM A7). IS THERE A LIGHT?
PROBLEM IS INTERMITTENT, SEE "DIAGNOSTIC AIDS."
YES
NO
REPAIR OPEN IN CKT 1222.
FAULTY CONNECTION AT PCM/TCM OR FAULTY PCM/TCM?

91I13688 91C13690

Courtesy of General Motors Corp.

CODE 83, TCC QDM FAULT

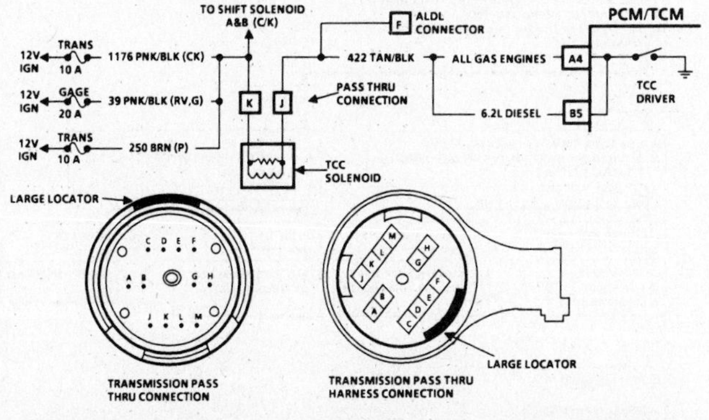
TO SHIFT SOLENOID A&B (C/K)
ALDL CONNECTOR
F
PCM/TCM
12V IGN
TRANS 10 A
1176 PNK/BLK (CK)
422 TAN/BLK
ALL GAS ENGINES
A4
GAGE 20 A
39 PNK/BLK (RV,G)
K
J
PASS THRU CONNECTION
TCC DRIVER
6.2L DIESEL
B5
250 BRN (P)
TCC SOLENOID
LARGE LOCATOR
TRANSMISSION PASS THRU CONNECTION
TRANSMISSION PASS THRU HARNESS CONNECTION

The PCM/TCM continually monitors voltage on each circuit connected to the quad driver for either low or high voltage, depending on the commanded state of the device connected to it. Code 83 will set if PCM/TCM detects an inappropriate reading on the TCC circuit. For example, if the TCC duty cycle is zero, but voltage on the TCC circuit drops as if the solenoid were on, then Code 83 will set. The TCC solenoid, because of its large current draw, is connected to 2 terminals of a single quad driver.

NOTE: **Test numbers refer to test numbers on diagnostic chart.**

1) This test checks for low resistance in the solenoid or internal transmission harness. This test also determines which circuit triggered the fault. If bidirectional Scan tester is not available, TCC may be activated by grounding ALDL test terminal "B" with ignition on and engine off.

DIAGNOSTIC AIDS

Ensure to check all connections, especially those at the transmission pass-thru connector. If code is intermittent, see INTERMITTENTS in TROUBLE SHOOTING - NO CODES article.

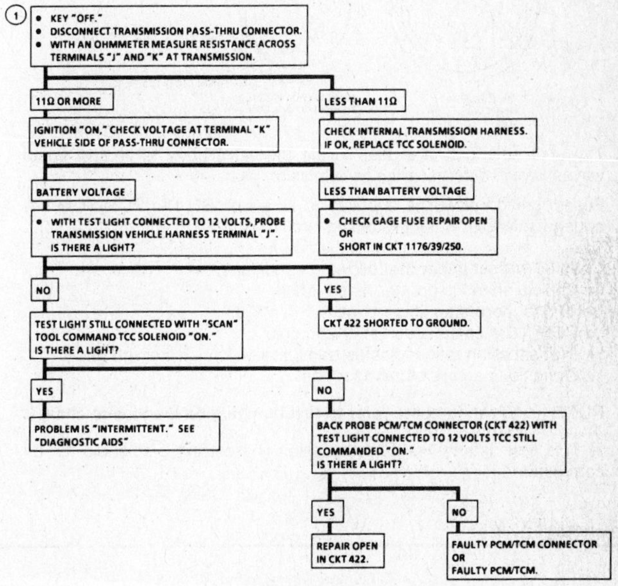
1
• KEY "OFF."
• DISCONNECT TRANSMISSION PASS-THRU CONNECTOR.
• WITH AN OHMMETER MEASURE RESISTANCE ACROSS TERMINALS "J" AND "K" AT TRANSMISSION.
11Ω OR MORE
LESS THAN 11Ω
IGNITION "ON," CHECK VOLTAGE AT TERMINAL "K" VEHICLE SIDE OF PASS-THRU CONNECTOR.
CHECK INTERNAL TRANSMISSION HARNESS. IF OK, REPLACE TCC SOLENOID.
BATTERY VOLTAGE
LESS THAN BATTERY VOLTAGE
• WITH TEST LIGHT CONNECTED TO 12 VOLTS, PROBE TRANSMISSION VEHICLE HARNESS TERMINAL "J". IS THERE A LIGHT?
• CHECK GAGE FUSE REPAIR OPEN OR SHORT IN CKT 1176/39/250.
NO
YES
TEST LIGHT STILL CONNECTED WITH "SCAN" TOOL COMMAND TCC SOLENOID "ON." IS THERE A LIGHT?
CKT 422 SHORTED TO GROUND.
YES
NO
PROBLEM IS "INTERMITTENT." SEE "DIAGNOSTIC AIDS"
BACK PROBE PCM/TCM CONNECTOR (CKT 422) WITH TEST LIGHT CONNECTED TO 12 VOLTS TCC STILL COMMANDED "ON." IS THERE A LIGHT?
YES
NO
REPAIR OPEN IN CKT 422.
FAULTY PCM/TCM CONNECTOR OR FAULTY PCM/TCM.

91D13675 91D13691

Courtesy of General Motors Corp.

1991 ENGINE PERFORMANCE
Self-Diagnostics – Electronic Transmission (Cont.)

CODE 85, UNDEFINED RATIO

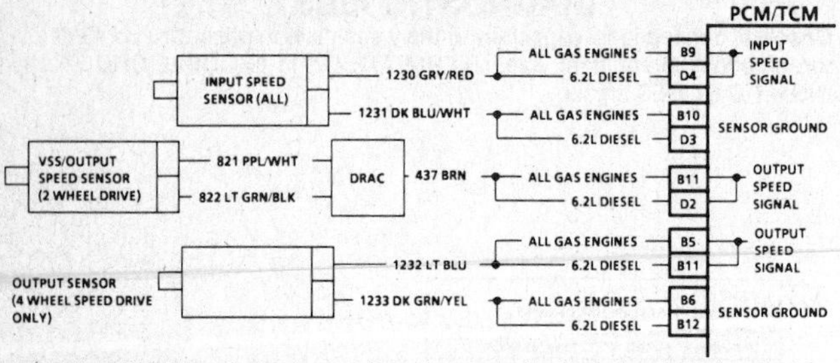
PCM/TCM
INPUT SPEED SENSOR (ALL)
1230 GRY/RED
1231 DK BLU/WHT
ALL GAS ENGINES
6.2L DIESEL
B9
D4
INPUT SPEED SIGNAL
B10
D3
SENSOR GROUND
VSS/OUTPUT SPEED SENSOR (2 WHEEL DRIVE)
821 PPL/WHT
822 LT GRN/BLK
DRAC
437 BRN
B11
D2
OUTPUT SPEED SIGNAL
OUTPUT SENSOR (4 WHEEL SPEED DRIVE ONLY)
1232 LT BLU
1233 DK GRN/YEL
B5
B11
OUTPUT SPEED SIGNAL
B6
B12
SENSOR GROUND

The PCM/TCM calculates the actual gear ratio from input and output speed readings while in each gear, then compares these to what the gear ratio should be, taking into consideration the selected gear range. This monitor includes Reverse gear, but does not include Overdrive gear.

NOTE: **Test numbers refer to test numbers on diagnostic chart.**

1) This test verifies the proper function of the input sensor.
2) This test verifies the proper function of the output sensor.

DIAGNOSTIC AIDS

The PCM/TCM relies on the Power Switch Module (PSM) to indicate what gear range has been selected. PSM must be functioning properly or Code 85 may be set. Check all connections, especially those at the transmission pass-thru connector. If code is intermittent, see INTERMITTENTS in TROUBLE SHOOTING - NO CODES article. Compare Scan tester gear ratio reading to specifications in GEAR RATIO table.

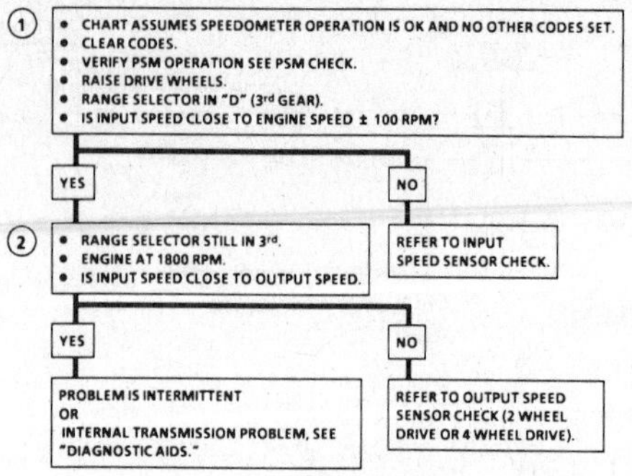
1
CHART ASSUMES SPEEDOMETER OPERATION IS OK AND NO OTHER CODES SET.
CLEAR CODES.
VERIFY PSM OPERATION SEE PSM CHECK.
RAISE DRIVE WHEELS.
RANGE SELECTOR IN "D" (3rd GEAR).
IS INPUT SPEED CLOSE TO ENGINE SPEED ± 100 RPM?
YES
NO
2
RANGE SELECTOR STILL IN 3rd.
ENGINE AT 1800 RPM.
IS INPUT SPEED CLOSE TO OUTPUT SPEED.
REFER TO INPUT SPEED SENSOR CHECK.
YES
NO
PROBLEM IS INTERMITTENT OR INTERNAL TRANSMISSION PROBLEM, SEE "DIAGNOSTIC AIDS."
REFER TO OUTPUT SPEED SENSOR CHECK (2 WHEEL DRIVE OR 4 WHEEL DRIVE).

GEAR RATIO

Gear	Less Than	More Than
1st	2.38	2.63
2nd	1.43	1.58
3rd	.95	1.05
Reverse	1.97	2.17

91E13692 91F13693 Courtesy of General Motors Corp.

CODE 86, SHIFT SOLENOID "B" STUCK "ON"

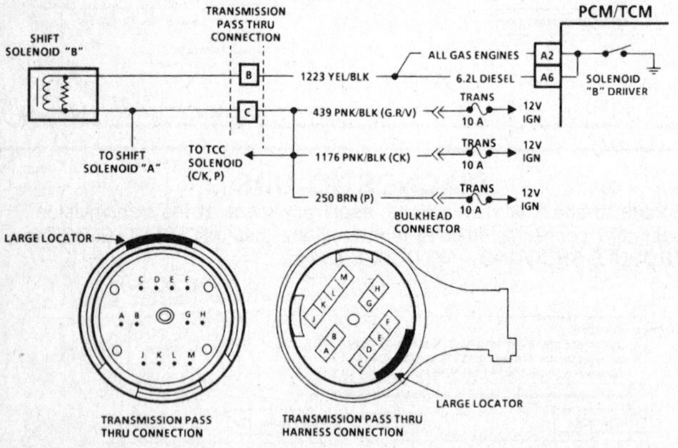
SHIFT SOLENOID "B"
TRANSMISSION PASS THRU CONNECTION
PCM/TCM
B
C
1223 YEL/BLK
ALL GAS ENGINES
6.2L DIESEL
A2
A6
SOLENOID "B" DRIIVER
439 PNK/BLK (G.R/V)
TRANS
10 A
12V IGN
TO SHIFT SOLENOID "A"
TO TCC SOLENOID (C/K, P)
1176 PNK/BLK (CK)
250 BRN (P)
BULKHEAD CONNECTOR
LARGE LOCATOR
C D E F
A B G H
J K L M
LARGE LOCATOR
TRANSMISSION PASS THRU CONNECTION
TRANSMISSION PASS THRU HARNESS CONNECTION

The shift solenoids are used inside the valve body to control spool valves, which determine the transmission gear.

Fused ignition power is supplied to solenoid "B". The PCM/TCM will engage solenoid "B" by grounding circuit No. 1223 to energize the solenoid.

Code 86 will set under the following conditions.

- Vehicle speed is greater than 7 MPH.
- TPS is more than 25 percent.
- PCM/TCM commands 1st or 2nd gear.
- Transmission ratio indicates transmission is in 3rd or 4th gear.
- Conditions are met for 6 seconds.

NOTE: **Test numbers refer to test numbers on diagnostic chart.**

1) This test determines if transmission is receiving a solenoid "B" on command.

DIAGNOSTIC AIDS

If code is intermittent, see INTERMITTENTS in TROUBLE SHOOTING - NO CODES article.

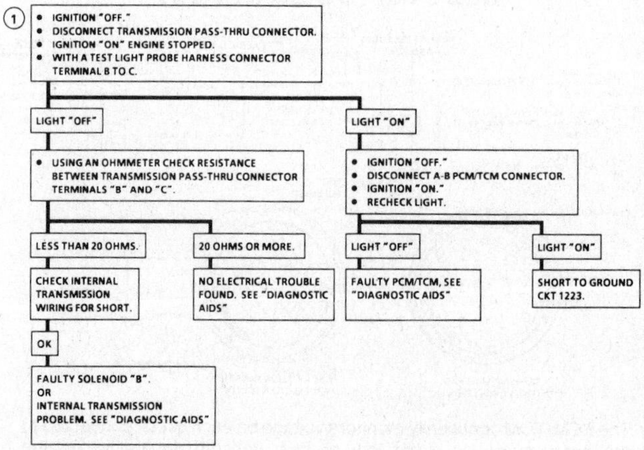
1
IGNITION "OFF."
DISCONNECT TRANSMISSION PASS-THRU CONNECTOR.
IGNITION "ON" ENGINE STOPPED.
WITH A TEST LIGHT PROBE HARNESS CONNECTOR TERMINAL B TO C.
LIGHT "OFF"
LIGHT "ON"
USING AN OHMMETER CHECK RESISTANCE BETWEEN TRANSMISSION PASS-THRU CONNECTOR TERMINALS "B" AND "C".
IGNITION "OFF."
DISCONNECT A-B PCM/TCM CONNECTOR.
IGNITION "ON."
RECHECK LIGHT.
LESS THAN 20 OHMS.
20 OHMS OR MORE.
LIGHT "OFF"
LIGHT "ON"
CHECK INTERNAL TRANSMISSION WIRING FOR SHORT.
NO ELECTRICAL TROUBLE FOUND. SEE "DIAGNOSTIC AIDS"
FAULTY PCM/TCM, SEE "DIAGNOSTIC AIDS"
SHORT TO GROUND CKT 1223.
OK
FAULTY SOLENOID "B". OR INTERNAL TRANSMISSION PROBLEM. SEE "DIAGNOSTIC AIDS"

91H13687 91G13694 Courtesy of General Motors Corp.

1991 ENGINE PERFORMANCE
Self-Diagnostics – Electronic Transmission (Cont.)

CODE 87, SHIFT SOLENOID "B" STUCK "OFF"

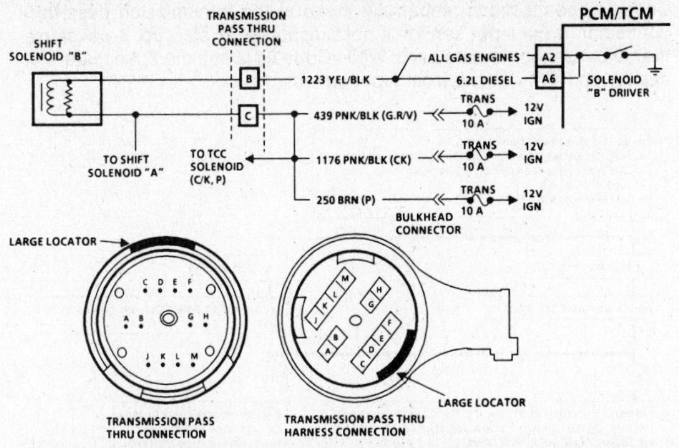

TRANSMISSION PASS THRU CONNECTION
PCM/TCM
SHIFT SOLENOID "B"
ALL GAS ENGINES
A2
1223 YEL/BLK
6.2L DIESEL
A6
SOLENOID "B" DRIIVER
439 PNK/BLK (G.R/V)
TRANS 10 A
12V IGN
TO SHIFT SOLENOID "A"
TO TCC SOLENOID (C/K, P)
1176 PNK/BLK (CK)
250 BRN (P)
BULKHEAD CONNECTOR
LARGE LOCATOR
TRANSMISSION PASS THRU CONNECTION
TRANSMISSION PASS THRU HARNESS CONNECTION

The shift solenoids are used inside the valve body to control spool valve position, which determines the transmission gear.

Fused ignition power is supplied to solenoid "B." The PCM/TCM will engage solenoid "B" by grounding circuit No. 1223 to energize the solenoid.

Code 87 will set under the following conditions.

- Vehicle speed is greater than 7 MPH.
- TPS is more than 25 percent.
- PCM/TCM commands 3rd or 4th gear.
- Transmission ratio indicates transmission is in 1st or 2nd gear.
- Conditions are met for 6 seconds.

NOTE: Test numbers refer to test numbers on diagnostic chart.

1) This test checks PCM/TCM's ability to ground or control solenoid "B". If bidirectional Scan tester is not available, solenoid may be activated by grounding ALDL test terminal "B" with ignition on and engine off.
2) This test checks the power supply and circuit No. 1223.
3) This test checks the internal transmission harness and solenoid "B".

DIAGNOSTIC AIDS

Check all connections, especially those at the transmission pass-thru connector. Fault may be an internal transmission problem.

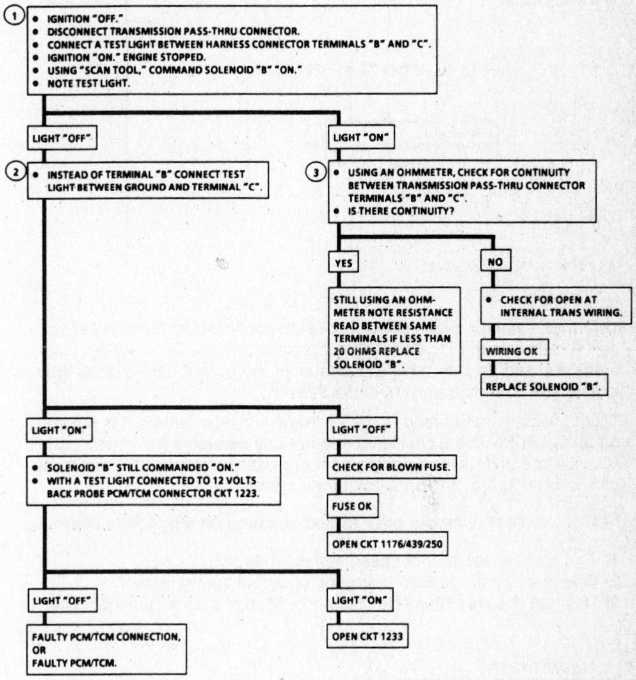

1
• IGNITION "OFF."
• DISCONNECT TRANSMISSION PASS-THRU CONNECTOR.
• CONNECT A TEST LIGHT BETWEEN HARNESS CONNECTOR TERMINALS "B" AND "C".
• IGNITION "ON." ENGINE STOPPED.
• USING "SCAN TOOL," COMMAND SOLENOID "B" "ON."
• NOTE TEST LIGHT.
LIGHT "OFF"
LIGHT "ON"
2
• INSTEAD OF TERMINAL "B" CONNECT TEST LIGHT BETWEEN GROUND AND TERMINAL "C".
3
• USING AN OHMMETER, CHECK FOR CONTINUITY BETWEEN TRANSMISSION PASS-THRU CONNECTOR TERMINALS "B" AND "C".
• IS THERE CONTINUITY?
YES
NO
STILL USING AN OHMMETER NOTE RESISTANCE READ BETWEEN SAME TERMINALS IF LESS THAN 20 OHMS REPLACE SOLENOID "B".
• CHECK FOR OPEN AT INTERNAL TRANS WIRING.
WIRING OK
REPLACE SOLENOID "B".
LIGHT "ON"
LIGHT "OFF"
• SOLENOID "B" STILL COMMANDED "ON."
• WITH A TEST LIGHT CONNECTED TO 12 VOLTS BACK PROBE PCM/TCM CONNECTOR CKT 1223.
CHECK FOR BLOWN FUSE.
FUSE OK
OPEN CKT 1176/439/250
LIGHT "OFF"
LIGHT "ON"
FAULTY PCM/TCM CONNECTION, OR FAULTY PCM/TCM.
OPEN CKT 1233

91H13687 91H13695

Courtesy of General Motors Corp.

COMPONENT CHECK CHARTS

OUTPUT SPEED SENSOR CIRCUIT CHECK (2WD – EXCEPT "C" & "K" SERIES)

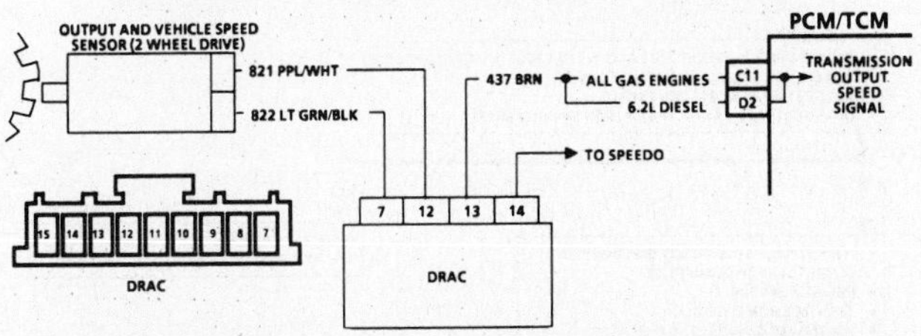

OUTPUT AND VEHICLE SPEED SENSOR (2 WHEEL DRIVE)
PCM/TCM
821 PPL/WHT
437 BRN
ALL GAS ENGINES
C11
6.2L DIESEL
D2
TRANSMISSION OUTPUT SPEED SIGNAL
822 LT GRN/BLK
TO SPEEDO
15 14 13 12 11 10 9 8 7
DRAC
7 12 13 14
DRAC

The output sensor circuit consists of a magnetic induction-type sensor, digital ratio adapter, and wiring. Gear teeth pressed on the outside diameter of the output carrier assembly induce an alternating current in the sensor.

This current is transmitted to a digital ratio adapter, where it is passed on to the PCM/TCM. The digital ratio adapter compensates for various axle ratios, and converts the signal to a square wave for use by the speedometer, cruise control and anti-lock brake system.

If the input sensor is not operational at start up, it can cause the output sensor to read zero.

NOTE: Test numbers refer to test numbers on diagnostic chart.

1) This test checks the speed signal on circuit No. 437 at the PCM/TCM from the digital ratio adapter.
2) This test checks for a speed signal from the output speed sensor to the digital ratio adapter.
3) This test checks the output speed sensor.

DIAGNOSTIC AIDS

Check all connections, especially at the transmission pass-thru connector. If code is intermittent, see INTERMITTENTS in TROUBLE SHOOTING – NO CODES article.

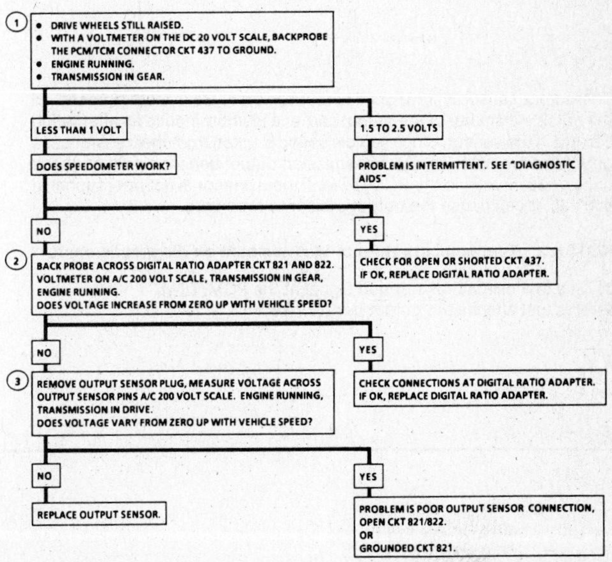

1
• DRIVE WHEELS STILL RAISED.
• WITH A VOLTMETER ON THE DC 20 VOLT SCALE, BACKPROBE THE PCM/TCM CONNECTOR CKT 437 TO GROUND.
• ENGINE RUNNING.
• TRANSMISSION IN GEAR.
LESS THAN 1 VOLT
1.5 TO 2.5 VOLTS
DOES SPEEDOMETER WORK?
PROBLEM IS INTERMITTENT. SEE "DIAGNOSTIC AIDS"
NO
YES
2
BACK PROBE ACROSS DIGITAL RATIO ADAPTER CKT 821 AND 822. VOLTMETER ON A/C 200 VOLT SCALE, TRANSMISSION IN GEAR, ENGINE RUNNING.
DOES VOLTAGE INCREASE FROM ZERO UP WITH VEHICLE SPEED?
CHECK FOR OPEN OR SHORTED CKT 437. IF OK, REPLACE DIGITAL RATIO ADAPTER.
NO
YES
3
REMOVE OUTPUT SENSOR PLUG, MEASURE VOLTAGE ACROSS OUTPUT SENSOR PINS A/C 200 VOLT SCALE. ENGINE RUNNING, TRANSMISSION IN DRIVE.
DOES VOLTAGE VARY FROM ZERO UP WITH VEHICLE SPEED?
CHECK CONNECTIONS AT DIGITAL RATIO ADAPTER. IF OK, REPLACE DIGITAL RATIO ADAPTER.
NO
YES
REPLACE OUTPUT SENSOR.
PROBLEM IS POOR OUTPUT SENSOR CONNECTION, OPEN CKT 821/822. OR GROUNDED CKT 821.

91I13696 91J13697

Courtesy of General Motors Corp.

1991 ENGINE PERFORMANCE
Self-Diagnostics – Electronic Transmission (Cont.)

OUTPUT SPEED SENSOR CIRCUIT CHECK (2WD – "C" & "K" SERIES)

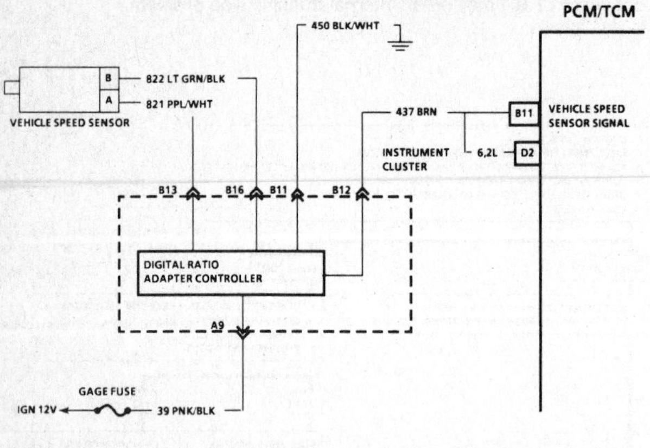
PCM/TCM
450 BLK/WHT
B
A
822 LT GRN/BLK
821 PPL/WHT
VEHICLE SPEED SENSOR
437 BRN
B11
VEHICLE SPEED SENSOR SIGNAL
INSTRUMENT CLUSTER
6.2L
D2
B13
B16
B11
B12
DIGITAL RATIO ADAPTER CONTROLLER
A9
GAGE FUSE
IGN 12V
39 PNK/BLK

The output sensor circuit consists of a magnetic induction-type sensor, digital ratio adapter located in the instrument cluster, and wiring. Gear teeth pressed on the outside diameter of the output carrier assembly induce an alternating current in the sensor.

This current is transmitted to the instrument cluster, where it is passed on to the PCM. The digital ratio adapter compensates for various axle ratios, and converts the signal to a square wave for use by the speedometer, cruise control and anti-lock brake system.

NOTE: **Test numbers refer to test numbers on diagnostic chart.**

1) This test verifies output speed sensor voltage at PCM.
2) This test directly verifies operation of output speed sensor.
3) This test checks circuits No. 821 and 822 up to the instrument cluster.

DIAGNOSTIC AIDS

Check all connections, especially those at the transmission pass-thru connector. If the input sensor is not functioning at start up, it will cause the output sensor to read zero. While Code 24 is set, the Scan tester will display an RPM derived from input speed.

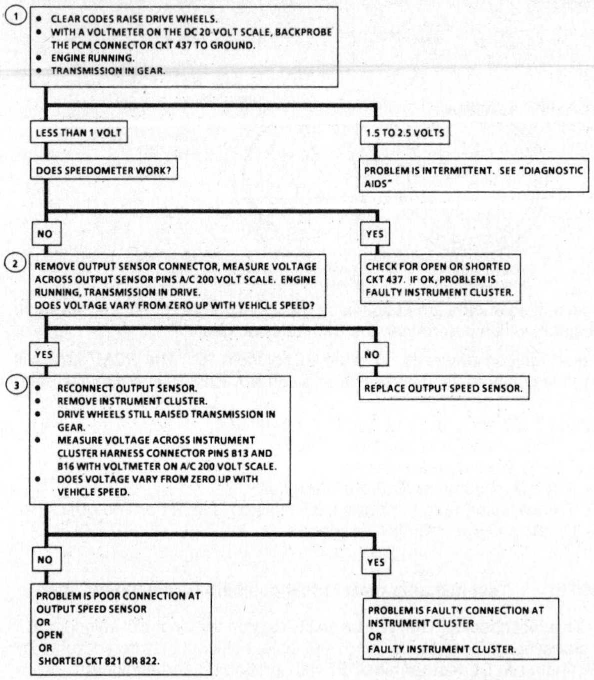
1
CLEAR CODES RAISE DRIVE WHEELS.
WITH A VOLTMETER ON THE DC 20 VOLT SCALE, BACKPROBE THE PCM CONNECTOR CKT 437 TO GROUND.
ENGINE RUNNING.
TRANSMISSION IN GEAR.
LESS THAN 1 VOLT
1.5 TO 2.5 VOLTS
DOES SPEEDOMETER WORK?
PROBLEM IS INTERMITTENT. SEE "DIAGNOSTIC AIDS"
NO
YES
2
REMOVE OUTPUT SENSOR CONNECTOR, MEASURE VOLTAGE ACROSS OUTPUT SENSOR PINS A/C 200 VOLT SCALE. ENGINE RUNNING, TRANSMISSION IN DRIVE.
DOES VOLTAGE VARY FROM ZERO UP WITH VEHICLE SPEED?
CHECK FOR OPEN OR SHORTED CKT 437. IF OK, PROBLEM IS FAULTY INSTRUMENT CLUSTER.
YES
NO
3
RECONNECT OUTPUT SENSOR.
REMOVE INSTRUMENT CLUSTER.
DRIVE WHEELS STILL RAISED TRANSMISSION IN GEAR.
MEASURE VOLTAGE ACROSS INSTRUMENT CLUSTER HARNESS CONNECTOR PINS B13 AND B16 WITH VOLTMETER ON A/C 200 VOLT SCALE.
DOES VOLTAGE VARY FROM ZERO UP WITH VEHICLE SPEED.
REPLACE OUTPUT SPEED SENSOR.
NO
YES
PROBLEM IS POOR CONNECTION AT OUTPUT SPEED SENSOR OR OPEN OR SHORTED CKT 821 OR 822.
PROBLEM IS FAULTY CONNECTION AT INSTRUMENT CLUSTER OR FAULTY INSTRUMENT CLUSTER.

91A13698 91B13699

Courtesy of General Motors Corp.

OUTPUT SPEED SENSOR CIRCUIT CHECK (4WD VEHICLES)

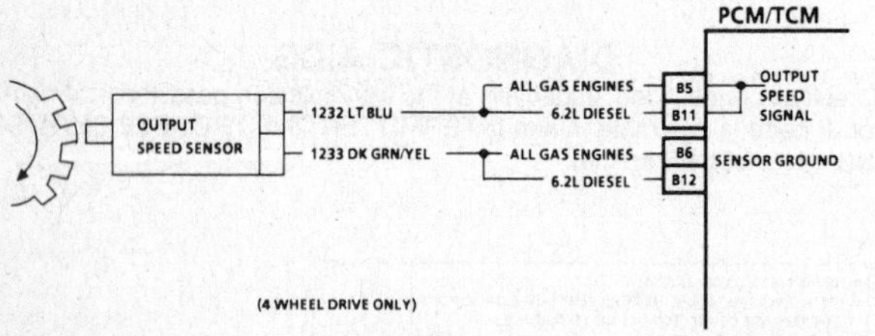
PCM/TCM
OUTPUT SPEED SENSOR
1232 LT BLU
1233 DK GRN/YEL
ALL GAS ENGINES
6.2L DIESEL
ALL GAS ENGINES
6.2L DIESEL
B5
B11
B6
B12
OUTPUT SPEED SIGNAL
SENSOR GROUND
(4 WHEEL DRIVE ONLY)

The output sensor is a magnetic induction type. Gear teeth pressed on the outside diameter of the output carrier assembly induce an alternating current in the sensor. Since vehicle speed is taken from the transfer case on 4WD drive vehicles, the transmission output sensor signal on these units goes directly to the PCM/TCM. If input sensor is not operational at start up, it can cause the output sensor to read zero.

NOTE: **Test numbers refer to test numbers on diagnostic chart.**

1) This test checks for a speed signal at the PCM/TCM.
2) This test checks the output sensor directly.

DIAGNOSTIC AIDS

Check all connections, especially at the transmission pass-thru connector. If code is intermittent, see INTERMITTENTS in TROUBLE SHOOTING – NO CODES article.

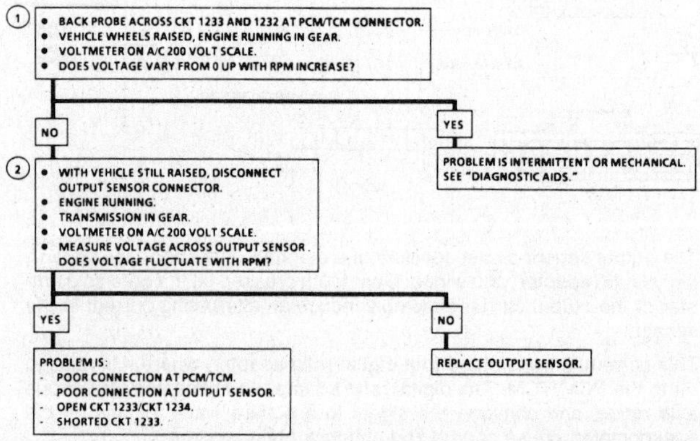
1
BACK PROBE ACROSS CKT 1233 AND 1232 AT PCM/TCM CONNECTOR.
VEHICLE WHEELS RAISED, ENGINE RUNNING IN GEAR.
VOLTMETER ON A/C 200 VOLT SCALE.
DOES VOLTAGE VARY FROM 0 UP WITH RPM INCREASE?
NO
YES
PROBLEM IS INTERMITTENT OR MECHANICAL. SEE "DIAGNOSTIC AIDS."
2
WITH VEHICLE STILL RAISED, DISCONNECT OUTPUT SENSOR CONNECTOR.
ENGINE RUNNING.
TRANSMISSION IN GEAR.
VOLTMETER ON A/C 200 VOLT SCALE.
MEASURE VOLTAGE ACROSS OUTPUT SENSOR.
DOES VOLTAGE FLUCTUATE WITH RPM?
YES
NO
PROBLEM IS:
- POOR CONNECTION AT PCM/TCM.
- POOR CONNECTION AT OUTPUT SENSOR.
- OPEN CKT 1233/CKT 1234.
- SHORTED CKT 1233.
REPLACE OUTPUT SENSOR.

91E13700 91F13701

Courtesy of General Motors Corp.

INPUT SPEED SENSOR CIRCUIT CHECK

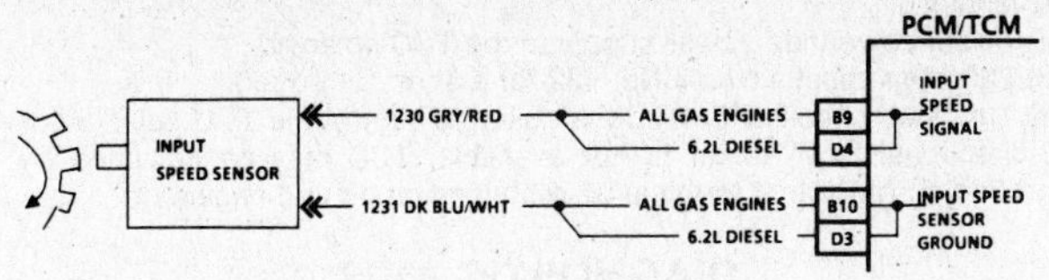

PCM/TCM
INPUT SPEED SENSOR
1230 GRY/RED
ALL GAS ENGINES
6.2L DIESEL
B9
D4
INPUT SPEED SIGNAL
1231 DK BLU/WHT
ALL GAS ENGINES
6.2L DIESEL
B10
D3
INPUT SPEED SENSOR GROUND

The input sensor is of the magnetic induction type and is located on the left side of the transmission, forward of center. Serrations in the forward clutch housing induce a small A/C current as they pass by the input sensor. While there is no specific code for an input sensor problem, the PCM/TCM uses input sensor readings to calculate gear ratio, turbine speed, TCC slip, and determine if the engine is running.

NOTE: **Test numbers refer to test numbers on diagnostic chart.**

1) This test checks the input sensor circuit up to the PCM/TCM.
2) This test checks the sensor output.

DIAGNOSTIC AIDS

Check all connectors. If code is intermittent, see INTERMITTENTS in TROUBLE SHOOTING – NO CODES article.

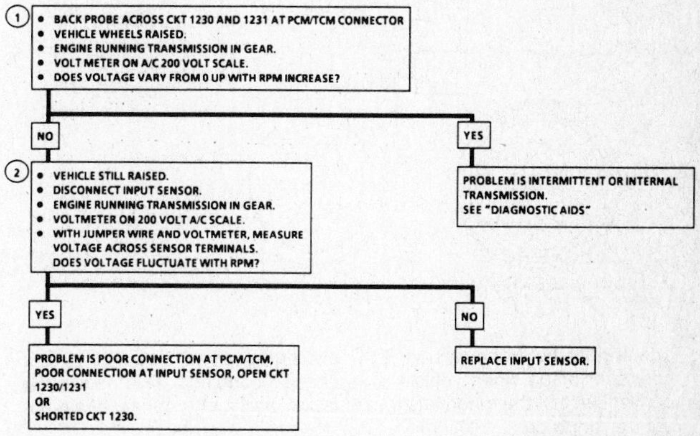

1
• BACK PROBE ACROSS CKT 1230 AND 1231 AT PCM/TCM CONNECTOR
• VEHICLE WHEELS RAISED.
• ENGINE RUNNING TRANSMISSION IN GEAR.
• VOLT METER ON A/C 200 VOLT SCALE.
• DOES VOLTAGE VARY FROM 0 UP WITH RPM INCREASE?
NO
YES
PROBLEM IS INTERMITTENT OR INTERNAL TRANSMISSION. SEE "DIAGNOSTIC AIDS"
2
• VEHICLE STILL RAISED.
• DISCONNECT INPUT SENSOR.
• ENGINE RUNNING TRANSMISSION IN GEAR.
• VOLTMETER ON 200 VOLT A/C SCALE.
• WITH JUMPER WIRE AND VOLTMETER, MEASURE VOLTAGE ACROSS SENSOR TERMINALS. DOES VOLTAGE FLUCTUATE WITH RPM?
YES
NO
PROBLEM IS POOR CONNECTION AT PCM/TCM, POOR CONNECTION AT INPUT SENSOR, OPEN CKT 1230/1231 OR SHORTED CKT 1230.
REPLACE INPUT SENSOR.

91G13702 91H13703

Courtesy of General Motors Corp.

BRAKE SIGNAL CIRCUIT CHECK (ALL ENGINES)

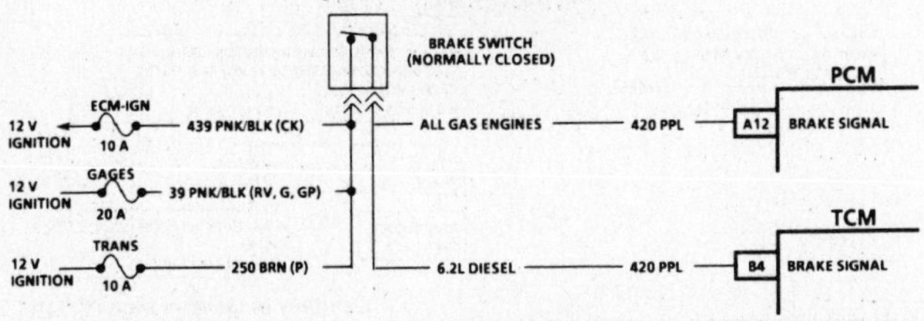

BRAKE SWITCH (NORMALLY CLOSED)
PCM
TCM
12 V IGNITION
ECM-IGN
10 A
439 PNK/BLK (CK)
ALL GAS ENGINES
420 PPL
A12
BRAKE SIGNAL
12 V IGNITION
GAGES
20 A
39 PNK/BLK (RV, G, GP)
12 V IGNITION
TRANS
10 A
250 BRN (P)
6.2L DIESEL
420 PPL
B4
BRAKE SIGNAL

The normally closed brake switch supplies a 12-volt signal on circuit No. 420 to the PCM/TCM. The signal voltage is removed when brakes are applied. An incorrect brake signal may affect TCC operation.

NOTE: **Test numbers refer to test numbers on diagnostic chart.**

1) This test checks for voltage at brake switch.
2) This test simulates closed brake switch (brakes off).
3) This test checks circuit No. 420 from brake switch to PCM/TCM.
4) This test opens circuit No. 420 and simulates condition of brakes being applied.

DIAGNOSTIC AIDS

If code is intermittent, see INTERMITTENTS in TROUBLE SHOOTING – NO CODES article. Check customer driving habits and/or unusual traffic conditions (i.e. stop and go expressway traffic).

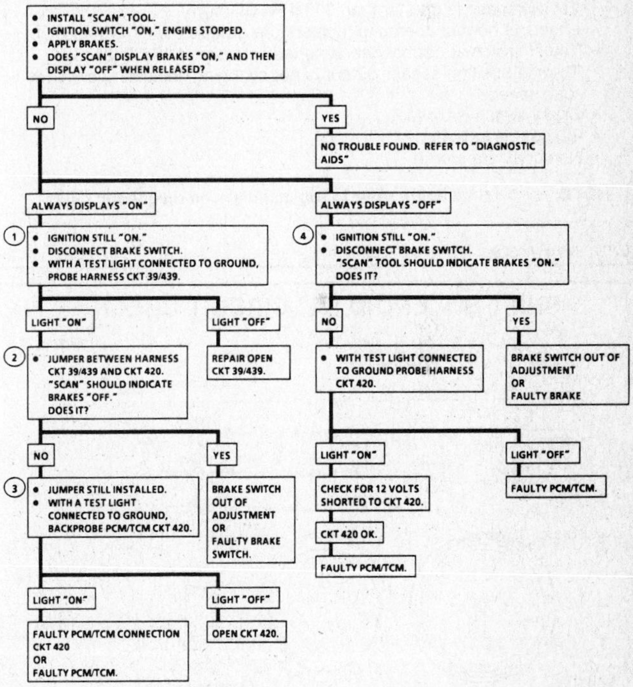

• INSTALL "SCAN" TOOL.
• IGNITION SWITCH "ON," ENGINE STOPPED.
• APPLY BRAKES.
• DOES "SCAN" DISPLAY BRAKES "ON," AND THEN DISPLAY "OFF" WHEN RELEASED?
NO
YES
NO TROUBLE FOUND. REFER TO "DIAGNOSTIC AIDS"
ALWAYS DISPLAYS "ON"
ALWAYS DISPLAYS "OFF"
1
• IGNITION STILL "ON."
• DISCONNECT BRAKE SWITCH.
• WITH A TEST LIGHT CONNECTED TO GROUND, PROBE HARNESS CKT 39/439.
4
• IGNITION STILL "ON."
• DISCONNECT BRAKE SWITCH. "SCAN" TOOL SHOULD INDICATE BRAKES "ON." DOES IT?
LIGHT "ON"
LIGHT "OFF"
NO
YES
2
• JUMPER BETWEEN HARNESS CKT 39/439 AND CKT 420. "SCAN" SHOULD INDICATE BRAKES "OFF." DOES IT?
REPAIR OPEN CKT 39/439.
• WITH TEST LIGHT CONNECTED TO GROUND PROBE HARNESS CKT 420.
BRAKE SWITCH OUT OF ADJUSTMENT OR FAULTY BRAKE
NO
YES
LIGHT "ON"
LIGHT "OFF"
3
• JUMPER STILL INSTALLED.
• WITH A TEST LIGHT CONNECTED TO GROUND, BACKPROBE PCM/TCM CKT 420.
BRAKE SWITCH OUT OF ADJUSTMENT OR FAULTY BRAKE SWITCH.
CHECK FOR 12 VOLTS SHORTED TO CKT 420.
FAULTY PCM/TCM.
CKT 420 OK.
FAULTY PCM/TCM.
LIGHT "ON"
LIGHT "OFF"
FAULTY PCM/TCM CONNECTION CKT 420 OR FAULTY PCM/TCM.
OPEN CKT 420.

91I13704 91J13705

Courtesy of General Motors Corp.

1991 ENGINE PERFORMANCE
Self-Diagnostics – Electronic Transmission (Cont.)

TORQUE CONVERTER CLUTCH (TCC) CIRCUIT CHECK

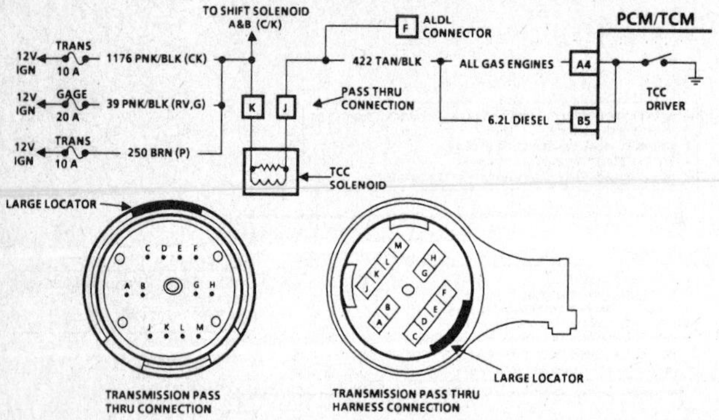
TO SHIFT SOLENOID A&B (C/K)
ALDL CONNECTOR
PCM/TCM
TRANS
12V IGN
10 A
1176 PNK/BLK (CK)
422 TAN/BLK
ALL GAS ENGINES
A4
GAGE
12V IGN
20 A
39 PNK/BLK (RV,G)
PASS THRU CONNECTION
TCC DRIVER
6.2L DIESEL
B5
TRANS
12V IGN
10 A
250 BRN (P)
TCC SOLENOID
LARGE LOCATOR
LARGE LOCATOR
TRANSMISSION PASS THRU CONNECTION
TRANSMISSION PASS THRU HARNESS CONNECTION

The automatic transmission TCC eliminates power loss of torque converter stage when vehicle is in a cruise condition. This allows the convenience of the automatic transmission, and fuel economy of a manual transmission.

Fused battery ignition is supplied to the TCC solenoid, located inside valve body, to shift a spool valve in order to modulate pressure to the TCC.
The PCM/TCM will engage TCC by grounding circuit No. 422 to energize the solenoid.
TCC will engage under the following conditions.
- Vehicle speed is greater than 30 MPH (48 km/h).
- Engine at normal operating temperature greater than 149°F (65°C).
- Transmission at normal operating temperature of 195°F (91°C).
- Throttle position sensor output is not changing, indicating a steady road speed.
- Brake switch is closed.
- 4th gear is indicated.
- No codes are stored.

NOTE: Test numbers refer to test numbers on diagnostic chart.

1) This step checks for a shorted internal transmission harness or TCC solenoid.
2) This step verifies power supply to the TCC solenoid.
3) This step checks circuit No. 422 for a short to ground.
4) This step checks PCM/TCM's ability to control the TCC solenoid. If bidirectional Scan tester is not available, TCC may be activated by grounding ALDL test terminal "B" with ignition on and engine off.

DIAGNOSTIC AIDS

Check all connections, especially those at the transmission pass-thru connector. If code is intermittent, see INTERMITTENTS in TROUBLE SHOOTING – NO CODES article. The TCC solenoid is pulse width modulated, and is designed to keep the TCC right at the point of engagement. Therefore, some slight slippage is normal.

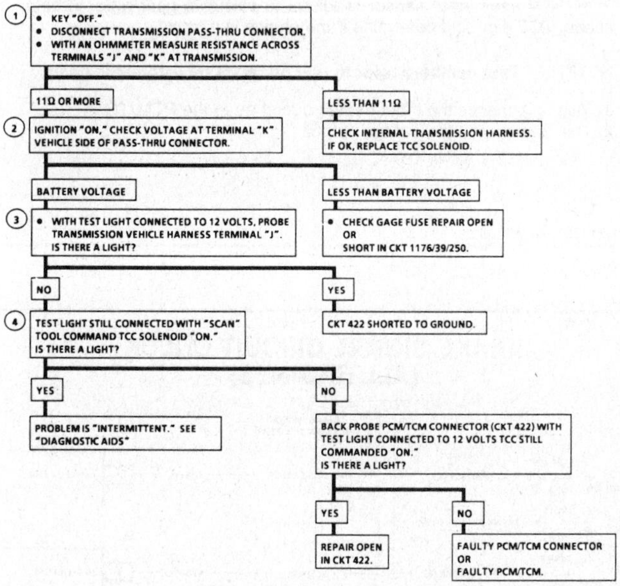
1
• KEY "OFF."
• DISCONNECT TRANSMISSION PASS-THRU CONNECTOR.
• WITH AN OHMMETER MEASURE RESISTANCE ACROSS TERMINALS "J" AND "K" AT TRANSMISSION.
11Ω OR MORE
LESS THAN 11Ω
2
IGNITION "ON," CHECK VOLTAGE AT TERMINAL "K" VEHICLE SIDE OF PASS-THRU CONNECTOR.
CHECK INTERNAL TRANSMISSION HARNESS. IF OK, REPLACE TCC SOLENOID.
BATTERY VOLTAGE
LESS THAN BATTERY VOLTAGE
3
• WITH TEST LIGHT CONNECTED TO 12 VOLTS, PROBE TRANSMISSION VEHICLE HARNESS TERMINAL "J". IS THERE A LIGHT?
• CHECK GAGE FUSE REPAIR OPEN OR SHORT IN CKT 1176/39/250.
NO
YES
4
TEST LIGHT STILL CONNECTED WITH "SCAN" TOOL COMMAND TCC SOLENOID "ON." IS THERE A LIGHT?
CKT 422 SHORTED TO GROUND.
YES
NO
PROBLEM IS "INTERMITTENT." SEE "DIAGNOSTIC AIDS"
BACK PROBE PCM/TCM CONNECTOR (CKT 422) WITH TEST LIGHT CONNECTED TO 12 VOLTS TCC STILL COMMANDED "ON." IS THERE A LIGHT?
YES
NO
REPAIR OPEN IN CKT 422.
FAULTY PCM/TCM CONNECTOR OR FAULTY PCM/TCM.

91D13675 91A13706

Courtesy of General Motors Corp.

SHIFT SOLENOID "A" CIRCUIT CHECK

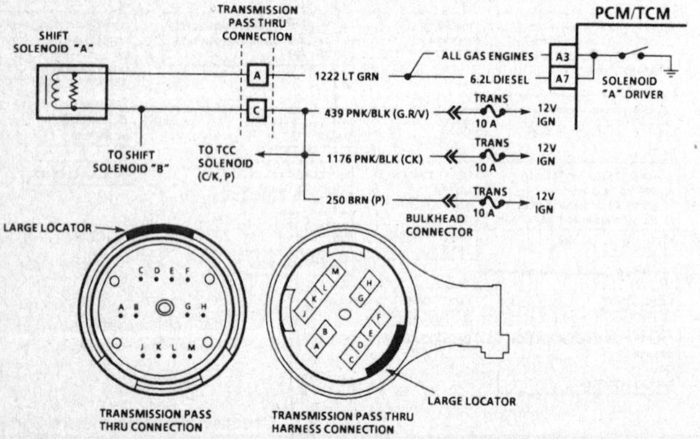
TRANSMISSION PASS THRU CONNECTION
PCM/TCM
SHIFT SOLENOID "A"
ALL GAS ENGINES
A3
A
1222 LT GRN
6.2L DIESEL
A7
SOLENOID "A" DRIVER
C
TRANS
439 PNK/BLK (G.R/V)
10 A
12V IGN
TO SHIFT SOLENOID "B"
TO TCC SOLENOID (C/K, P)
1176 PNK/BLK (CK)
250 BRN (P)
BULKHEAD CONNECTOR
LARGE LOCATOR
LARGE LOCATOR
TRANSMISSION PASS THRU CONNECTION
TRANSMISSION PASS THRU HARNESS CONNECTION

Shift solenoid "A" is attached to the valve body and is a normally open exhaust valve. The PCM/TCM activates the solenoid by grounding it through an internal quad driver. Solenoid "A" (Blue) is on in 1st and 4th gears, but is off in 2nd and 3rd gears. When solenoid is on, it redirects fluid to act on the shift valves.

NOTE: Test numbers refer to test numbers on diagnostic chart.

1) This test checks shift solenoid "A" and the internal transmission wiring harness for shorts.
2) This test checks for power, from the ignition switch through the fuse, to the shift solenoid.
3) This test checks circuit No. 1222 for a short to ground.
4) This test checks PCM/TCM's ability to ground or control the shift solenoid "A". If bidirectional Scan tester is not available, TCC may be activated by grounding ALDL test terminal "B" with ignition on and engine

DIAGNOSTIC AIDS

Check all connections, especially those at the transmission pass-thru connector. If code is intermittent, see INTERMITTENTS in TROUBLE SHOOTING – NO CODES article.

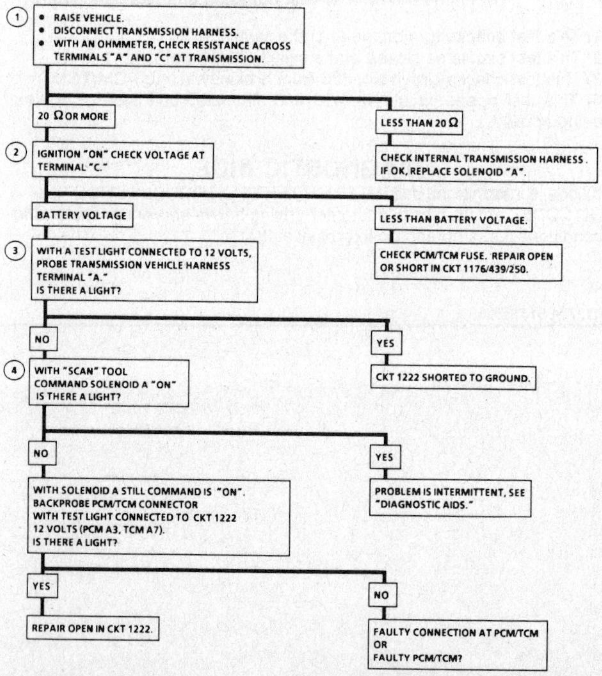
1
• RAISE VEHICLE.
• DISCONNECT TRANSMISSION HARNESS.
• WITH AN OHMMETER, CHECK RESISTANCE ACROSS TERMINALS "A" AND "C" AT TRANSMISSION.
20 Ω OR MORE
LESS THAN 20 Ω
2
IGNITION "ON" CHECK VOLTAGE AT TERMINAL "C."
CHECK INTERNAL TRANSMISSION HARNESS. IF OK, REPLACE SOLENOID "A".
BATTERY VOLTAGE
LESS THAN BATTERY VOLTAGE.
3
WITH A TEST LIGHT CONNECTED TO 12 VOLTS, PROBE TRANSMISSION VEHICLE HARNESS TERMINAL "A." IS THERE A LIGHT?
CHECK PCM/TCM FUSE. REPAIR OPEN OR SHORT IN CKT 1176/439/250.
NO
YES
4
WITH "SCAN" TOOL COMMAND SOLENOID A "ON" IS THERE A LIGHT?
CKT 1222 SHORTED TO GROUND.
NO
YES
WITH SOLENOID A STILL COMMAND IS "ON". BACKPROBE PCM/TCM CONNECTOR WITH TEST LIGHT CONNECTED TO CKT 1222 12 VOLTS (PCM A3, TCM A7). IS THERE A LIGHT?
PROBLEM IS INTERMITTENT, SEE "DIAGNOSTIC AIDS."
YES
NO
REPAIR OPEN IN CKT 1222.
FAULTY CONNECTION AT PCM/TCM OR FAULTY PCM/TCM?

91I13688 91B13707

Courtesy of General Motors Corp.

1991 ENGINE PERFORMANCE
Self-Diagnostics – Electronic Transmission (Cont.)

SHIFT SOLENOID "B" CIRCUIT CHECK

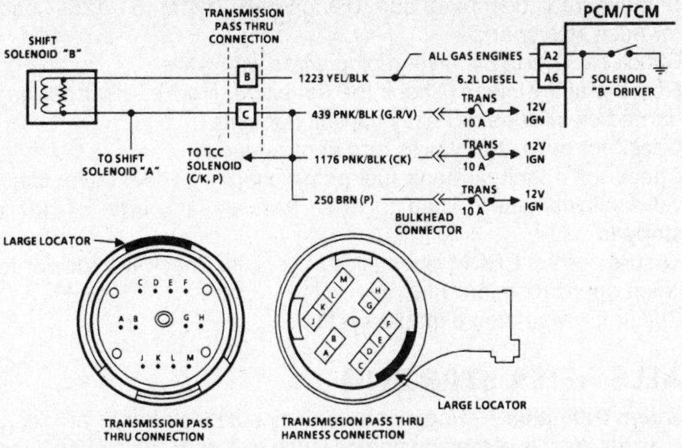

PCM/TCM
TRANSMISSION PASS THRU CONNECTION
SHIFT SOLENOID "B"
1223 YEL/BLK
ALL GAS ENGINES
6.2L DIESEL
A2
A6
SOLENOID "B" DRIVER
439 PNK/BLK (G.R/V)
TRANS 10 A
12V IGN
TO SHIFT SOLENOID "A"
TO TCC SOLENOID (C/K, P)
1176 PNK/BLK (CK)
250 BRN (P)
BULKHEAD CONNECTOR
LARGE LOCATOR
TRANSMISSION PASS THRU CONNECTION
TRANSMISSION PASS THRU HARNESS CONNECTION

The shift solenoids are used inside the valve body to control the spool valves, which determine the transmission gear. Fused ignition is supplied to solenoid "B". The PCM/TCM will engage solenoid "B" by grounding circuit No. 1223 to energize the solenoid.

NOTE: Test numbers refer to test numbers on diagnostic chart.

1) This test checks shift solenoid "B" and the internal transmission wiring for shorts.
2) This test checks for power, from the ignition through the transmission fuse, to the shift solenoid "B".
3) This test checks PCM/TCM's ability to ground or control the shift solenoid "B".
3) This test ensures circuit No. 1223 is not shorted to ground.
4) This test checks PCM/TCM's ability to ground or control the shift solenoid "B". If bidirectional Scan tester is not available, TCC may be activated by grounding ALDL test terminal "B" with ignition on and engine off.
5) This test ensures circuit No. 1223 is not shorted to ground.

DIAGNOSTIC AIDS

Check all connections, especially those at the transmission pass-thru connector. If code is intermittent, see INTERMITTENTS in TROUBLE SHOOTING – NO CODES article.

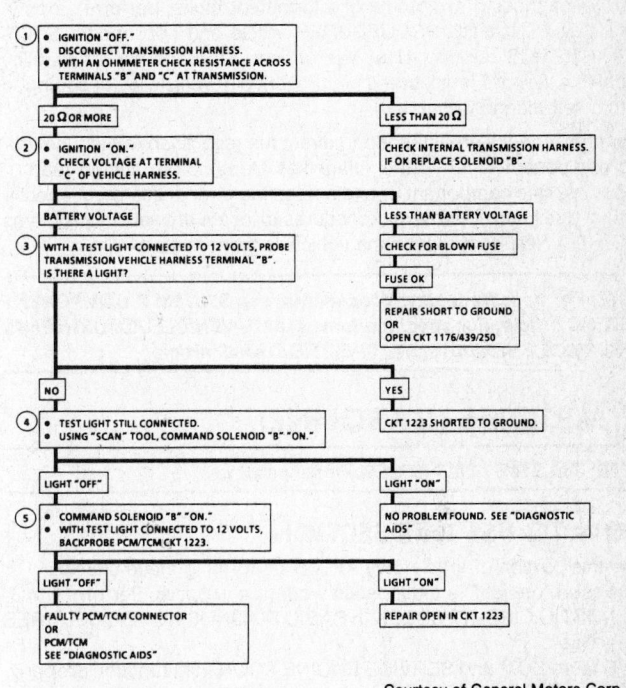

1. • IGNITION "OFF." • DISCONNECT TRANSMISSION HARNESS. • WITH AN OHMMETER CHECK RESISTANCE ACROSS TERMINALS "B" AND "C" AT TRANSMISSION.
   - LESS THAN 20 Ω: CHECK INTERNAL TRANSMISSION HARNESS. IF OK REPLACE SOLENOID "B".
   - 20 Ω OR MORE: go to 2.
2. • IGNITION "ON." • CHECK VOLTAGE AT TERMINAL "C" OF VEHICLE HARNESS.
   - LESS THAN BATTERY VOLTAGE: CHECK FOR BLOWN FUSE → FUSE OK → REPAIR SHORT TO GROUND OR OPEN CKT 1176/439/250
   - BATTERY VOLTAGE: go to 3.
3. WITH A TEST LIGHT CONNECTED TO 12 VOLTS, PROBE TRANSMISSION VEHICLE HARNESS TERMINAL "B". IS THERE A LIGHT?
   - YES: CKT 1223 SHORTED TO GROUND.
   - NO: go to 4.
4. • TEST LIGHT STILL CONNECTED. • USING "SCAN" TOOL, COMMAND SOLENOID "B" "ON."
   - LIGHT "ON": NO PROBLEM FOUND. SEE "DIAGNOSTIC AIDS"
   - LIGHT "OFF": go to 5.
5. • COMMAND SOLENOID "B" "ON." • WITH TEST LIGHT CONNECTED TO 12 VOLTS, BACKPROBE PCM/TCM CKT 1223.
   - LIGHT "OFF": FAULTY PCM/TCM CONNECTOR OR PCM/TCM SEE "DIAGNOSTIC AIDS"
   - LIGHT "ON": REPAIR OPEN IN CKT 1223

91H13687 91C13708

Courtesy of General Motors Corp.

FORCE MOTOR CIRCUIT CHECK

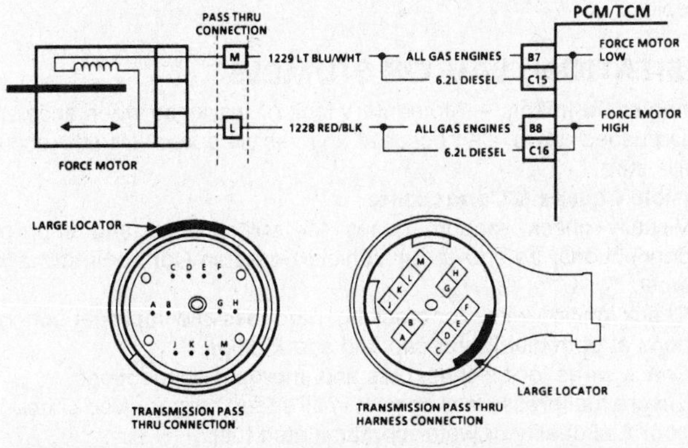

PASS THRU CONNECTION
PCM/TCM
1229 LT BLU/WHT
ALL GAS ENGINES
6.2L DIESEL
B7
C15
FORCE MOTOR LOW
1228 RED/BLK
B8
C16
FORCE MOTOR HIGH
FORCE MOTOR
LARGE LOCATOR
TRANSMISSION PASS THRU CONNECTION
TRANSMISSION PASS THRU HARNESS CONNECTION

NOTE: This flow chart requires the use of a bidirectional (Tech 1) Scan tester.

The force motor is a PCM/TCM-controlled device used to regulate transmission line pressure. The PCM/TCM looks at TPS voltage, engine RPM, and other inputs to determine the appropriate line pressure for a given load, then regulates the pressure by applying a variable amperage to the force motor. The applied amperage varies from .1-1.1 amps.

NOTE: Test numbers refer to test numbers on diagnostic chart.

1) This test verifies an amperage difference of .16 amp or more, and tests the PCM/TCM's ability to control amperage to the force motor.
2) This test checks the force motor for internal shorts.

DIAGNOSTIC AIDS

Check for poor connections at PCM/TCM, especially at transmission pass-thru connector.

1. • CLEAR CODES. • ENGINE RUNNING, TRANSMISSION IN NEUTRAL. • WITH "SCANNER," APPLY .7 AMPS TO FORCE MOTOR. • OBSERVE ACTUAL OR RETURN AMP READING. DOES IT MATCH THE .7 AMPS COMMANDED?
   - YES: PROBLEM IS INTERMITTENT, SEE "DIAGNOSTIC AIDS."
   - NO: go to 2.
2. • ENGINE "OFF," KEY "OFF." • RAISE VEHICLE. • REMOVE TRANSMISSION PASS-THRU CONNECTOR. • WITH A DVOM, MEASURE RESISTANCE ACROSS FORCE MOTOR TERMINALS "M" AND "L".
   - LESS THAN 3.5 OHMS: CHECK INTERNAL TRANSMISSION HARNESS. IF OK, REPLACE FORCE MOTOR.
   - MORE THAN 3.5 OHMS: • PASS-THRU CONNECTOR STILL DISCONNECTED. • KEY "ON." • WITH SCAN TOOL, APPLY .7 AMPS. • WITH A DVM PROBE PIN "L" OF THE TRANSMISSION VEHICLE HARNESS TO GROUND AND MEASURE THE VOLTAGE. IS THERE SYSTEM VOLTAGE?
     - YES: • KEY "OFF." • RECONNECT PASS-THRU CONNECTOR. • KEY "ON." • WITH A DVM PROBE ACROSS CKT 1229 AND GROUND. • IS THERE SYSTEM VOLTAGE?
       - YES: FAULTY PCM/TCM CONNECTOR OR FAULTY PCM/TCM.
       - NO: • KEY "OFF." • DISCONNECT PASS-THRU CONNECTOR. • WITH TEST LIGHT CONNECTED TO 12 VOLTS, PROBE CKT 1229. IS THERE A LIGHT?
         - YES: CKT 1229 IS SHORTED TO GROUND.
         - NO: • WITH AN OHMMETER, CHECK CONTINUITY FROM PCM/TCM CONNECTOR TO PASS-THRU CONNECTOR. IS THERE CONTINUITY?
           - YES: POOR PASS-THRU CONNECTOR CONNECTION OR OPEN IN INTERNAL TRANSMISSION HARNESS.
           - NO: CKT 1229 IS OPEN.
     - NO: AT PCM/TCM CONNECTOR, BACKPROBE CKT 1228 ACROSS AND GROUND, WITH SCAN APPLY .7 AMPS. IS THERE VOLTAGE?
       - NO: FAULTY PCM/TCM CONNECTOR OR FAULTY PCM/TCM.
       - YES: • KEY OFF. • DISCONNECT PCM/TCM CONNECTOR. • WITH TEST LIGHT CONNECTED TO 12 VOLTS, BACKPROBE CKT 1228.
         - NO: OPEN CKT 1228.
         - YES: CIRCUIT 1228 IS SHORTED TO GROUND.

91E13684 91D13709

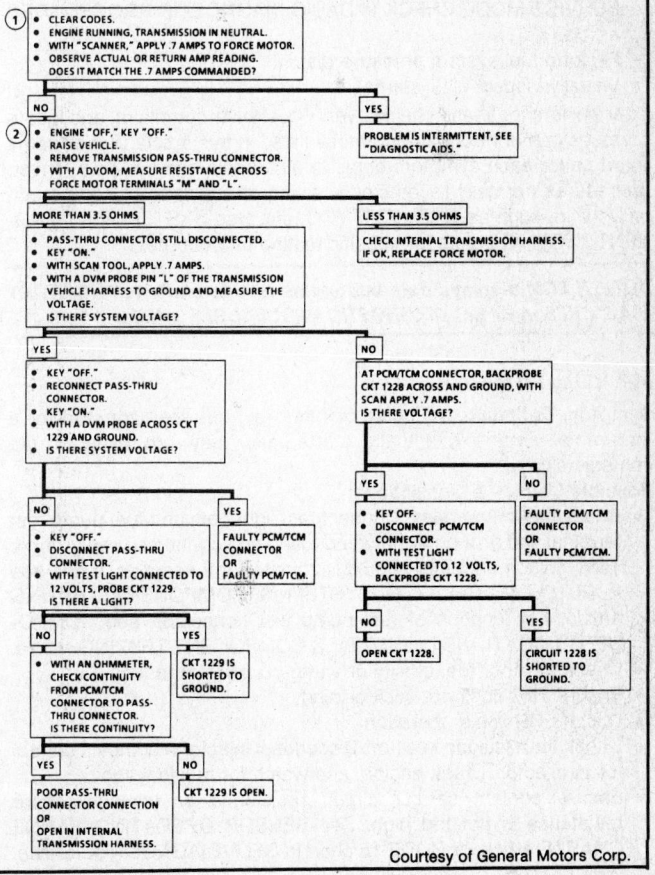

Courtesy of General Motors Corp.

1991 ENGINE PERFORMANCE
Trouble Shooting – No Codes

Astro, Blazer, Bravada, Jimmy, Lumina APV, Safari, Sierra, Silhouette, Sonoma, Syclone, Trans Sport, "C" & "K" Series, "G" Series, "P" Series, "R" & "V" Series, "S" & "T" Series

INTRODUCTION

Before diagnosing symptoms or intermittent faults, perform steps in BASIC DIAGNOSTIC PROCEDURES article and appropriate SELF-DIAGNOSTICS article. Use this article to diagnose driveability problems if a hard fault code is not present or if vehicle is not equipped with a self-diagnostic system.

Symptom checks are intended to direct the technician to malfunctioning component(s) for further diagnosis. A symptom should lead to either specific component or system testing or an adjustment specification. Use intermittent test procedures to locate driveability problems which DO NOT occur when the vehicle is being tested.

NOTE: For specific testing procedures, see SYSTEM & COMPONENT TESTING article. For specifications, see ON-VEHICLE ADJUSTMENTS or SERVICE & ADJUSTMENT SPECIFICATIONS article.

SYMPTOMS (GASOLINE)

NOTE: See SYMPTOMS (DIESEL) if necessary.

HOW TO USE THIS SECTION

Use this portion of article only AFTER performing these checks:

- Ensure on-vehicle diagnostics work (if equipped). Perform DIAGNOSTIC CIRCUIT CHECK in BASIC DIAGNOSTIC PROCEDURES article.
- Ensure ECM and SERVICE ENGINE SOON light function properly.
- Ensure no trouble codes, except intermittent ones, are stored.
- Ensure fuel control system operates properly. Perform FIELD SERVICE MODE CHECK in BASIC DIAGNOSTIC PROCEDURES article.
- Perform fuel system pressure test.
- Visually inspect all systems.

After performing these checks, verify customer complaint, and locate correct symptom from among those listed in this article. Not all items listed under each symptom apply to all models and systems. These procedures normally recommend testing of a system or component on vehicle, such as EGR, EST, TCC, etc. See SYSTEM & COMPONENT TESTING article for specific testing procedures.

NOTE: If ECM displays data but engine fails to start, see NO-START DIAGNOSIS in BASIC DIAGNOSTIC PROCEDURES article.

HARD START

Symptom Definition – Engine cranks okay, but does not start for a long time. Engine eventually starts, and may run okay or die immediately.

Possible Causes & Corrections:

- Check fuel pump relay. Connect test light between fuel pump test terminal and ground or between fuel pump connector and ground. Turn ignition on. Light should illuminate for 2 seconds. If not, see FUEL PUMP RELAY in SYSTEM & COMPONENT TESTING article. For location of fuel pump test connector, see COMPONENT LOCATIONS in SYSTEM & COMPONENT TESTING article.
- Check for poor fuel quality or water-contaminated fuel.
- Ensure TPS does not stick or bind.
- Check EGR valve operation.
- Check for a leaking injector. Disconnect injector electrical connector at injector. Crank engine, and watch for fuel leakage.
- Ensure coolant sensor circuit resistance or coolant sensor resistance is not too high. See SENSOR OPERATING RANGE CHARTS article or CODE 15 chart in SELF-DIAGNOSTICS article.
- Check ignition system for a worn distributor shaft, bare or shorted wires, incorrect pick-up coil resistance, loose ignition coil ground or moisture in distributor cap. Using Spark Tester (ST-125), check for adequate spark.
- Check for shorts by misting plug wires with water.
- Remove spark plugs. Check for wet plugs, cracks, improper gap, burned electrodes or heavy carbon deposits.
- Check for correct fuel pressure at all speeds.
- Check for a faulty in-tank fuel pump check valve. A faulty check valve allows fuel in lines to drain back to tank after engine is stopped.
- Ensure correct PROM is installed in vehicle. Check with dealer for latest application information.
- Check for restricted exhaust system.

STALLS AFTER STARTING

Symptom Definition – Engine starts okay but dies after brief idle, as soon as any load is placed on engine (such as turning on air conditioner or engaging transmission) or on initial drive-away.

Possible Causes & Corrections:

- Ensure hot air tube is connected to air cleaner.
- Check thermostatic air cleaner for proper operation.
- Check Idle Air Control (IAC) system for proper operation.
- Check PCV valve for proper operation.
- Unplug MAP sensor. ECM substitutes a default value for sensor signal. If stall condition is eliminated, replace sensor.
- Check EGR system for proper operation.
- If stall occurs when air conditioner is turned on, check for air conditioner clutch signal to ECM terminal. Voltage at A/C terminal of ECM should be battery voltage when air conditioner compressor clutch is engaged. A high voltage surge due to a shorted compressor clutch diode could cause ECM shutdown.
- Check for an overcharged A/C system.
- Check for plugged or restricted fuel lines.
- If engine starts but then immediately stalls, open distributor bypass circuit. If engine now starts and runs okay, replace distributor pick-up coil.
- Using Spark Tester (ST-125), check for a weak spark from ignition coil.

HESITATION, SAG OR STUMBLE

Symptom Definition – Momentary lack of response when accelerator is pushed down. Can occur at any vehicle speed. Usually occurs after a stop.

Possible Causes & Corrections:

- Visually check vacuum hoses for splits, kinks and improper connections, as shown on Vehicle Emission Control Information label.
- Check ignition wires for cracking, hardness and improper connections at both distributor cap and spark plugs.
- Check wires for pinches, cuts and improper connections.
- Ensure fuel pressure is correct in all speed ranges. Also check for poor fuel quality or water-contaminated fuel.
- Check for fouled spark plugs.
- Ensure correct PROM is installed in vehicle. Check with dealer for latest application information.
- Ensure TPS does not bind or stick.
- Ensure initial ignition timing is properly set.
- Ensure ECM-controlled idle speed is correct.
- Check EGR system for proper operation.
- Disconnect fuel injector electrical connectors. Crank engine, and check for injector leaks.
- Check for an open in HEI ground circuit.
- Check canister purge system for proper operation.
- Check charging system output. Repair charging system if voltage is less than 9 volts or more than 16 volts.

1991 ENGINE PERFORMANCE
Trouble Shooting – No Codes (Cont.)

VEHICLE SURGES

Symptom Definition – Engine power varies under steady throttle or cruise. Feels like vehicle speeds up and slows down even though accelerator pedal position remains constant.

Possible Causes & Corrections:

- Check thermostatic air cleaner damper door for proper operation.
- Ensure park/neutral switch is properly adjusted.
- Check for intermittent open or short to ground in Torque Converter Clutch (TCC) or HEI by-pass circuits.
- Check canister purge system for proper operation.
- Check ESC system for proper operation.
- Check EGR system for proper operation.
- Ensure initial ignition timing is properly set.
- Using Spark Tester (ST-125), check for adequate spark output.
- Check O_2 sensor for lead or RTV sealant contamination. Such contamination causes a false high voltage signal to ECM, which responds by leaning air/fuel ratio.
- Check in-line fuel filter. Replace if dirty or clogged.
- Check fuel for water contamination. Ensure fuel system pressure is correct at all engine speeds.
- Remove spark plugs, and check for wet plugs, cracks, improper gap, burned electrodes or heavy carbon deposits. Also check condition of distributor cap, rotor and spark plug wires.
- Check A/C for excessive charge.
- Check for restricted exhaust system.

LACK OF POWER OR SLUGGISH

Symptom Definition – Engine delivers less power than expected. Little or no increase in speed when accelerator is pushed down.

Possible Causes & Corrections:

- Check air filter and fuel filter. Replace if necessary. Check for incorrect fuel pressure.
- Check injector wires for short to ground at air cleaner.
- Check thermostatic air cleaner damper door for proper operation.
- Ensure initial ignition timing is properly set.
- Check TCC system for proper operation.
- Check ECM grounds.
- Check ESC system for excessive retard.
- Check EST system for proper operation.
- Ensure EGR valve is not always open.
- Check exhaust system for restrictions, such as a damaged or collapsed pipe, muffler or catalytic converter. See EXHAUST SYSTEM BACKPRESSURE under MECHANICAL INSPECTION in BASIC DIAGNOSTIC PROCEDURES article.
- Check charging system output. Repair charging system if voltage is less than 9 volts or more than 16 volts.
- Check MAP sensor output.
- Using Spark Tester (ST-125), check for available secondary voltage.
- Check engine valve timing and compression.
- Check engine for a worn camshaft.

ENGINE BACKFIRES

Symptom Definition – Fuel ignites in intake manifold or in exhaust system, making a loud popping noise.

Possible Causes & Corrections:

- Ensure EGR valve is not always open.
- Check for proper valve timing.
- Check for engine vacuum leaks. Ensure engine is tuned to specifications.
- Check for faulty air injection diverter valve or check valve.
- Check engine for sticking or leaking valves.
- Check for fuel or water in vacuum hose to MAP sensor. Also check for restricted hose.
- Using Spark Tester (ST-125), check available output voltage of ignition coil.
- Check for crossfire between spark plugs, distributor cap and spark plug wires.
- Check for an intermittent ignition system problem.
- Check for erratic spark timing or distributor reference (RPM) signal.
- Ensure initial ignition timing is properly set.

CUTS OUT, MISSES

Symptom Definition – Cuts out, misses is defined as a steady pulsation or jerking following engine speed, usually more pronounced as engine load increases. Exhaust may have a steady spitting sound at idle or low speed. Perform careful visual inspection as described in BASIC DIAGNOSTIC PROCEDURES article.

Possible Causes & Corrections:

- Check ignition wires for short or faulty insulation.
- Check distributor cap for moisture, dust or cracks. Finely mist spark plug wires with water to check for shorts.
- Connect Spark Tester (ST-125) to spark plug, and check for adequate spark.
- Check ignition system for faulty grounds.
- Ensure EST wiring harness is not routed too close to wiring. EST wiring harness routed too close to wiring may cause induced voltage signals.
- Check ignition coil connections.
- Remove spark plugs, and check for incorrect heat range, wear, cracks, wetness, improper gap or heavy deposits.
- Check for poor or contaminated fuel.
- Check for improper fuel pressure.
- Ensure EGR valve does not stick open.
- Check ECM for proper ground circuits.
- Ensure TPS does not stick or bind. TPS voltage should be less than 1.25 volts at idle.
- Check for proper pick-up coil (HEI distributor) resistance.
- Check for restricted exhaust system. See EXHAUST SYSTEM BACKPRESSURE under MECHANICAL INSPECTION in BASIC DIAGNOSTIC PROCEDURES article.
- Check for bent push rods, broken valve springs or worn camshaft lobes.

CAUTION: Grounding spark plug wire for extended periods may cause catalytic converter overheating.

Misfire Isolation – **1)** Start engine. Disconnect IAC motor. Using insulated pliers, remove one spark plug wire from a spark plug, and ground it against engine.

2) Note engine RPM as wire is grounded. Reconnect spark plug wire. Repeat procedure for all cylinders. Stop engine, and reconnect IAC motor.

3) If engine speed dropped equally (within 50 RPM) on all cylinders, refer to ROUGH, UNSTABLE OR INCORRECT IDLE symptom. If there was no engine RPM drop or no excessive variation on one or more cylinders, check spark on respective cylinder(s).

ROUGH, UNSTABLE OR INCORRECT IDLE

Symptom Definition – Engine runs unevenly at idle. If bad enough, vehicle will shake. Idle RPM may vary. Engine idles at incorrect RPM.

Possible Causes & Corrections:

- Ensure throttle linkage and/or TPS do not stick or bind.
- Ensure initial ignition timing is properly set.
- Check engine idle speed (both base and ECM idle).
- Check Idle Air Control (IAC) system. Check for foreign material in IAC bore. See DIAGNOSTIC AIDS in CODE 35 chart in appropriate SELF-DIAGNOSTICS article.
- Check EGR system for proper operation.
- Check park/neutral switch circuit. Ensure park/neutral switch is properly adjusted.
- Check power steering pressure switch circuit.
- Check exhaust system for restrictions, such as a damaged or collapsed pipe, muffler or catalytic converter. See EXHAUST SYSTEM BACKPRESSURE under MECHANICAL INSPECTION in BASIC DIAGNOSTIC PROCEDURES article.
- If rough idle occurs only when engine is hot, check PCV valve for proper operation. Check evaporative emission control system. Check for proper spark plug gap and engine compression.

1991 ENGINE PERFORMANCE
Trouble Shooting – No Codes (Cont.)

ENGINE WILL NOT IDLE

Symptom Definition – Engine starts but will not run at idle. Engine runs if accelerator is held at part throttle.

Possible Causes & Corrections:

- Problem is most likely in Idle Air Control (IAC) system. See DIAGNOSTIC AIDS in CODE 35 chart in appropriate SELF-DIAGNOSTICS article.
- Check EGR system.
- Check park/neutral switch.
- Disconnect MAP sensor. If condition is corrected, replace sensor.

POOR FUEL ECONOMY

Symptom Definition – Fuel economy, as measured by an actual road test, is noticeably lower than expected. Current fuel economy is noticeably lower than previous fuel economy.

Possible Causes & Corrections:

- Check thermostatic air cleaner damper door for proper operation. Also check for a clogged air filter.
- Check cooling system thermostat for proper heat range and operation.
- Check coolant sensor for shift in calibration. See COOLANT TEMPERATURE RESISTANCE VALUES table in SENSOR OPERATING RANGE CHARTS article.
- Ensure speedometer is properly calibrated.
- Check engine compression.
- Check for dragging brakes.
- Ensure A/C is not always on.
- Ensure initial ignition timing is properly set. Check EST and ESC for proper operation.
- Check TCC for proper operation.
- Ensure air pump output shifts to catalytic converter upon signal from TVS. Check for faulty electrical and/or vacuum circuits.
- Check exhaust system for restrictions, such as a damaged or collapsed pipe, muffler or catalytic converter. See EXHAUST SYSTEM BACKPRESSURE under MECHANICAL INSPECTION in BASIC DIAGNOSTIC PROCEDURES article.
- Check O_2 sensor for silicone or lead contamination.
- Remove spark plugs, and check for wet plugs, cracks, improper gap, burned electrodes or heavy carbon deposits.

ENGINE DIESELING/RUN-ON

Symptom Definition – Engine continues to run (but very rough) after ignition is turned off. If engine runs smoothly, check ignition switch.

Possible Causes & Corrections:

- Check for binding throttle linkage.
- Check for leaking injectors.
- Check IAC system. See DIAGNOSTIC AIDS in CODE 35 chart in appropriate SELF-DIAGNOSTICS article.
- Check engine for overheating.

DETONATION/SPARK KNOCK

Symptom Definition – A mild to severe ping, usually worse during acceleration. Engine makes sharp metallic knocks which change with degree of acceleration.

Possible Causes & Corrections:

- Check for obvious overheating problems.
- Ensure initial timing is correct.
- Check TPS adjustment and operation.
- Check fuel system for low pressure or volume. Also check for induction air leaks.
- Ensure ESC system is operating properly.
- Ensure EGR valve is not always open.
- Ensure TCC system is operating properly.
- Remove carbon from engine with top engine cleaner.
- If excessive carbon exists in combustion chamber, check for excessive oil burning due to leaking valve guide seals.
- Check for incorrect basic engine parts such as camshaft, cylinder heads and pistons.
- Ensure correct PROM is installed in vehicle. Check with dealer for latest application information.

EXCESSIVE EXHAUST EMISSION (ODORS)

Symptom Definition – Vehicle fails emission test. Vehicle may also emit "rotten egg" smell (hydrogen sulfide) from exhaust pipe.

Possible Causes & Corrections:

- Check for lead contamination of catalytic converter. Check for removal/tampering at restrictor in fuel filler neck.
- Ensure air is not being diverted to exhaust manifold and is being diverted to catalytic converter during normal engine operation.
- If emission test shows excessive carbon monoxide (CO) and hydrocarbons (HC) emissions and vehicle emits odor, check all systems and components which could cause engine to run rich. See DIAGNOSTIC AIDS in CODE 45 chart in appropriate SELF-DIAGNOSTICS article.
- If emission test shows excessive oxides of nitrogen (NOx) emissions, check all systems and components which could cause engine to run lean or too hot. See DIAGNOSTIC AIDS in CODE 44 chart in appropriate SELF-DIAGNOSTICS article.

SYMPTOMS (DIESEL)

ENGINE WILL NOT START

Possible Cause – No voltage to fuel solenoid.
Correction – Check electrical connections.
Possible Cause – Restricted air filter.
Correction – Check and/or replace air filter.
Possible Cause – Faulty glow plugs or glow plug controls.
Correction – Check and/or replace glow plugs or controls.
Possible Cause – Plugged fuel return system.
Correction – Remove restrictions.
Possible Cause – No fuel to nozzles.
Correction – Inspect fuel delivery system.
Possible Cause – No fuel to injection pump.
Correction – Inspect fuel delivery system.
Possible Cause – Clogged fuel tank filter.
Correction – Replace filter. See SYSTEM & COMPONENT TESTING article.
Possible Cause – Incorrect or contaminated fuel.
Correction – Remove and replace fuel.
Possible Cause – Incorrect pump timing.
Correction – Reset pump timing. See SYSTEM & COMPONENT TESTING article.

ENGINE STALLS AT IDLE

Possible Cause – Incorrect slow idle adjustment.
Correction – Reset idle adjustment. See ON-VEHICLE ADJUSTMENTS article.
Possible Cause – Faulty fast idle solenoid.
Correction – Replace solenoid. See SYSTEM & COMPONENT TESTING article.
Possible Cause – Plugged fuel return system.
Correction – Remove restrictions.
Possible Cause – Glow plugs turn off too soon.
Correction – Check glow plug system. See SYSTEM & COMPONENT TESTING article.
Possible Cause – Incorrect pump timing.
Correction – Check and reset timing. See ON-VEHICLE ADJUSTMENTS article.
Possible Cause – Limited fuel to injection pump.
Correction – Check fuel delivery system.
Possible Cause – Air in injection lines to nozzles.
Correction – Check line fittings.
Possible Cause – Incorrect or contaminated fuel.
Correction – Remove and replace fuel.
Possible Cause – Faulty injection pump.
Correction – Replace pump. See REMOVAL, OVERHAUL & INSTALLATION article.
Possible Cause – Fuel solenoid closes in RUN position.
Correction – Check solenoid operation. See SYSTEM & COMPONENT TESTING article.

1991 ENGINE PERFORMANCE
Trouble Shooting – No Codes (Cont.)

ENGINE STARTS, IDLES ROUGH WITHOUT UNUSUAL NOISE OR SMOKE

Possible Cause – Incorrect slow idle adjustment.
Correction – Reset slow idle adjustment. See ON-VEHICLE ADJUSTMENTS article.
Possible Cause – Leaking injection line.
Correction – Check fittings and/or replace line.
Possible Cause – Plugged fuel return line.
Correction – Remove restrictions.
Possible Cause – Air in lines to nozzles.
Correction – Check line fittings.
Possible Cause – Air in injection pump.
Correction – Check pump fittings and pump operation.
Possible Cause – Faulty nozzle.
Correction – Replace nozzle. See SYSTEM & COMPONENT TESTING article.
Possible Cause – Improper or contaminated fuel.
Correction – Remove and replace fuel.
Possible Cause – Uneven fuel distribution.
Correction – Check fuel delivery system.

ENGINE STARTS AND IDLES WITH EXCESSIVE NOISE AND/OR SMOKE

Possible Cause – Incorrect pump timing.
Correction – Adjust pump timing. See ON-VEHICLE ADJUSTMENTS article.
Possible Cause – Restricted air filter.
Correction – Check and/or replace air filter.
Possible Cause – Air in injection lines to nozzles.
Correction – Check fittings on lines.
Possible Cause – Faulty nozzle.
Correction – Replace nozzle. See SYSTEM & COMPONENT TESTING article.
Possible Cause – Improperly installed high pressure lines.
Correction – Remove lines, and reinstall properly.

ENGINE IDLES BUT MISFIRES ABOVE IDLE

Possible Cause – Plugged fuel filter.
Correction – Remove restrictions and/or replace filter.
Possible Cause – Incorrect pump timing.
Correction – Adjust pump timing. See ON-VEHICLE ADJUSTMENTS article.
Possible Cause – Incorrect or contaminated fuel.
Correction – Remove and replace fuel.

ENGINE WILL NOT IDLE

Possible Cause – Linkage binding or misadjusted.
Correction – Remove binding and readjust linkage.
Possible Cause – Restricted air filter.
Correction – Check and/or replace air filter.
Possible Cause – Defective injection pump.
Correction – Replace injection pump. See SYSTEM & COMPONENT TESTING article.

FUEL LEAKS WITH NO OTHER ENGINE MALFUNCTION

Possible Cause – Loose or broken fuel line or connection.
Correction – Check all fuel line fittings, and correct as necessary.
Possible Cause – Internal seal leak in injection pump.
Correction – Remove and replace injection pump.

LOW ENGINE POWER

Possible Cause – Restricted air intake.
Correction – Remove restrictions.
Possible Cause – Plugged fuel filter.
Correction – Remove restriction and/or replace filter.
Possible Cause – Improper throttle linkage adjustment.
Correction – Adjust linkage.
Possible Cause – Improper fuel return system.
Correction – Check fuel return system.
Possible Cause – Restricted tank-to-pump fuel supply.
Correction – Check fuel delivery system.
Possible Cause – Incorrect or contaminated fuel.
Correction – Remove and replace fuel.
Possible Cause – Restricted fuel tank filter.
Correction – Replace filter.
Possible Cause – Nozzle or glow plug compression leaks.
Correction – Check fittings, and replace as required.
Possible Cause – Plugged nozzle.
Correction – Remove restriction and/or replace nozzle.

"RAPPING" NOISE FROM CYLINDERS

Possible Cause – Air in fuel system.
Correction – Check fuel delivery system for leaks.
Possible Cause – Air in high pressure lines.
Correction – Check fittings for leaks.
Possible Cause – Nozzle sticking in open position.
Correction – Inspect and/or replace nozzle.
Possible Cause – Low nozzle opening pressure.
Correction – Check nozzle operation. See SYSTEM & COMPONENT TESTING article.

EXCESSIVE NOISE WITH BLACK SMOKE

Possible Cause – Incorrect pump timing.
Correction – Adjust pump timing. See ON-VEHICLE ADJUSTMENTS article.
Possible Cause – Incorrect pump housing pressure.
Correction – Check pump for internal leaks.
Possible Cause – Defective injection pump.
Correction – Replace injection pump. See SYSTEM & COMPONENT TESTING article.

ENGINE WILL NOT SHUT OFF WITH KEY

Possible Cause – Injection pump fuel solenoid does not return to off position.
Correction – Check solenoid operation. See SYSTEM & COMPONENT TESTING article.

TURBOCHARGER TROUBLE SHOOTING

SYMPTOMS

To trouble shoot following symptoms, refer to appropriate number under PROBABLE CAUSES.

Engine Lacks Power – Check probable causes No. 1, 3, 4, 6-11 and 16-20.
Black Smoke – Check probable causes No. 2-4, 6-11 and 16-20.
Blue Smoke – Check probable causes No. 2, 6-8, 13-15 and 17-20.
Excessive Oil Consumption – Check probable causes No. 2, 6-8, 13-15 and 17-20.
Noisy Operation – Check probable causes No. 1-8, 11-12 and 19-20.
Cyclic Sound From Turbocharger – Check probable causes No. 2, 19 and 20.
Oil Leak At Turbine Seal – Check probable causes No. 13-15 and 17-20.
Oil Leak At Compressor Seal – Check probable causes No. 2, 8-11, 13-15 and 17-20.

PROBABLE CAUSES

1) Clogged air filter element.
2) Obstructed air intake duct to turbo compressor.
3) Obstructed air outlet duct from compressor to intake manifold.
4) Obstructed intake manifold.
5) Air leak in duct from air cleaner to compressor.
6) Air leak in duct from compressor to intake manifold.
7) Air leak at intake manifold-to-engine joint.
8) Obstruction in exhaust manifold.
9) Obstruction in exhaust system.

1991 ENGINE PERFORMANCE
Trouble Shooting – No Codes (Cont.)

10) Gas leak in exhaust manifold-to-engine joint.
11) Gas leak in turbine inlet-to-exhaust manifold joint.
12) Gas leak in ducts after turbine outlet.
13) Obstructed turbocharger oil drain line.
14) Obstructed engine crankcase ventilation.
15) Turbocharger center housing sludged or coked.
16) Engine camshaft timing incorrect.
17) Worn engine piston rings or liners (blow-by).
18) Internal engine problems (valves, pistons).
19) Dirt caked on compressor wheel and/or diffused vanes.
20) Damaged turbocharger.

INTERMITTENTS

INTERMITTENT PROBLEM DIAGNOSIS

Intermittent fault testing requires duplication of circuit or component failure in order to identify fault. These procedures may lead to computer recording a fault code which may help diagnosis.

If problem vehicle does not produce fault codes, use a DVOM to monitor voltage or resistance values while attempting to reproduce conditions which will create an intermittent fault. A change in status on DVOM indicates a fault has been located.

When using a voltmeter to pinpoint faults, monitor voltage reading with ignition on or vehicle running. A change in status on voltmeter while performing test procedure indicates area of fault. See TEST PROCEDURES under INTERMITTENTS.

When using an ohmmeter to detect problems in circuit, monitor circuit resistance (ohms) with ignition switch in OFF position or with battery disconnected. A change in ohmmeter reading while performing test procedure indicates area of fault. See TEST PROCEDURES under INTERMITTENTS.

TEST PROCEDURES

Intermittent Simulation – Following methods may reproduce conditions which create an intermittent fault so fault may be identified during testing:

- Applying light vibration to components.
- Heating a component.
- Wiggling or bending a wiring harness.
- Applying humidity to a component.
- Removing or applying a vacuum supply source.

Monitor circuit/component voltage or resistance while attempting to simulate intermittent. If vehicle is running, monitor for self-diagnostic codes. Use results of these tests to identify a faulty component or an area which should be closely checked for problem.

INTERMITTENT TROUBLE SHOOTING

Symptom Definition – SERVICE ENGINE SOON light comes on but does not stay on. A stored code may or may not exist.

Possible Causes & Corrections – To determine possible causes of an intermittent SERVICE ENGINE SOON light operation:

- Check for poor mating of one connector to another. Terminals may not be fully seated. Check for improperly formed or damaged terminals. Check wire-to-terminal connections.
- Check for poor connection from ignition coil to ground or arcing at spark plug wires or plugs.
- Check wire from SERVICE ENGINE SOON light to ECM for short to ground.
- Check wire from ALDL "test" terminal for intermittent short to ground.
- Check for poor connections in ECM ground terminals.
- Check for loss of trouble code memory. To check code, disconnect TPS, and run engine at idle until SERVICE ENGINE SOON light comes on. Code 22 should be stored and retained in memory when ignition is turned off. If not, ECM is faulty.
- Check for electrical system interference caused by a defective relay or an ECM-driven solenoid or switch which may cause a sharp electrical surge. This type of problem will normally occur when faulty component is operated.
- Check for aftermarket parts which may not have been produced to manufacturers' specifications. Solenoids without original-equipment diodes for circuit protection and HEI-EST module or voltage regulator using transistors instead of silicone-chip circuitry may possibly cause voltage surges (up to 300 volts) in ECM wiring, causing temporary ECM shutdown. ECM shutdown is a normal response to system overvoltage (over 16 volts on most models). ECM repowers when condition ceases to exist. A rapid shutdown and repower could cause a flickering SERVICE ENGINE SOON light with no codes set in memory.
- Check for improper installation of electrical accessories such as auxiliary lights or 2-way radios.
- Ensure EST wires are kept away from spark plug wires, distributor wires, distributor housing, ignition coil and generator. Ensure ground wire from ECM to distributor or ignition module is connected to a good ground.
- Check for intermittent short to ground on terminal "B" (diagnostic enable) of ALDL or in SERVICE ENGINE SOON light circuit.
- On vehicles not equipped with a driver information center, use Scan tester to check for intermittent wiring problem. See SCAN TESTER USAGE in appropriate SELF-DIAGNOSTICS article.

1991 ENGINE PERFORMANCE
System & Component Testing

Astro, Blazer, Bravada, Jimmy, Lumina APV, Safari, Sierra, Silhouette, Sonoma, Syclone, Trans Sport, "C" & "K" Series, "G" Series, "P" Series, "R" & "V" Series, "S" & "T" Series

INTRODUCTION

Before testing separate components or systems, perform procedures in BASIC DIAGNOSTIC PROCEDURES article. Since many computer-controlled and monitored components set a trouble code if they malfunction, also perform procedures in appropriate SELF-DIAGNOSTICS article.

NOTE: Testing individual components does not isolate shorts or opens. Perform all voltage tests with a Digital Volt-Ohmmeter (DVOM) with a minimum 10-megohm input impedance, unless stated otherwise in test procedure. Use ohmmeter and refer to WIRING DIAGRAMS to isolate wiring harness shorts or opens.

AIR INDUCTION SYSTEMS

TURBOCHARGER (4.3L)

NOTE: No turbocharger testing information is available from manufacturer. For symptom diagnosis see TROUBLE SHOOTING - NO CODES article.

Charge Air Cooler Pump - Remove charge air cooler radiator and charge air cooler pump. See REMOVAL & INSTALLATION article. Apply battery voltage and ground to charge air cooler pump electrical terminals. If pump does not activate, replace pump.

Wastegate Diaphragm - Disconnect hose from wastegate diaphragm (actuator). Connect a radiator pressure tester to wastegate diaphragm fitting. Actuator should start to move when approximately 5 lbs. of pressure have been applied to diaphragm. Internal diaphragm return spring should return diaphragm when pressure bleeds off.

Wastegate Solenoid - Disconnect electrical connector from solenoid. Apply battery voltage and ground to solenoid electrical terminals. With solenoid energized, apply vacuum to one solenoid vacuum fitting with a hand-held vacuum pump. Vacuum should hold only while solenoid is energized.

COMPUTERIZED ENGINE CONTROLS

CONTROL UNIT

NOTE: To perform the following ground and power tests, use appropriate wiring diagram in WIRING DIAGRAMS article in ENGINE PERFORMANCE.

Ground Circuits - 1) Using an ohmmeter, check for continuity to ground on ECM ground terminals. Resistance should be zero ohms. If not, repair open to ground.

2) Using a DVOM, touch negative lead of voltmeter to a good ground. Touch positive lead of voltmeter to each ground terminal. With vehicle running, voltmeter should indicate less than one volt. If voltmeter reading is greater than one volt, check for open, corrosion or loose connection on ground circuit.

Power Circuits - 1) Using a voltmeter, check for battery voltage between ECM continuous power terminal(s) and ground. If battery voltage is not present, check for blown fuse or open fusible link. If okay, check for open in wire between ECM terminal and power source.

2) Turn ignition switch to the ON position. Using a voltmeter, check for battery voltage between ECM ignition power terminals and ground. If battery voltage is not present, check IGN fuse. If fuse is okay, check for an open in wire between battery and ignition switch, and between ignition switch and ECM terminal. If okay, check for a defective ignition switch.

3) Connect voltmeter between ground and ECM starter (crank) signal terminal. On vehicles with manual transmission/transaxle, depress clutch pedal. Turn ignition switch to the START position. Battery voltage should be present ONLY when ignition switch is in the START position.

4) If voltage is not present, check CRANK fuse or fusible link between ignition switch and ECM terminal. If fuse or fusible link is okay, check for an open in wire between ignition switch and ECM terminal, or check for a defective ignition switch.

Quad-Driver Check (Except 3.1L) -1) Remove ECM from vehicle. Using DVOM on 100/200 k/ohm scale, measure resistance between ECM case and each ECM quad-driver terminal. Touch negative DVOM lead to case and positive lead to ECM terminal. See ECM QUAD-DRIVER TERMINAL IDENTIFICATION table.

IMPORTANT: The following table provides the location of commonly used diagnostic information. These former "A" and "C" charts are now written in text and inserted into the appropriate location in the new Engine Performance workflow. To familiarize yourself with the Engine Performance workflow, see HOW TO USE THE ENGINE PERFORMANCE SECTION in GENERAL INFORMATION.

GENERAL MOTORS "A" & "C" CHART REFERENCE TABLE

System or Component	Diagnostic Information Location
DIAGNOSTIC CIRCUIT CHECK	See DIAGNOSTIC CIRCUIT CHECK in BASIC DIAGNOSTIC PROCEDURES
A-1 & A-2, SERVICE ENGINE SOON Light	See DIAGNOSTIC CIRCUIT CHECK in BASIC DIAGNOSTIC PROCEDURES
A-3, No-Start	See NO-START DIAGNOSIS in BASIC DIAGNOSTIC PROCEDURES
A-5, Fuel Pump Relay	See RELAYS, SOLENOIDS, MOTORS & MODULES in SYSTEM & COMPONENT TESTING
A-7, Fuel System Diagnosis	See BASIC FUEL SYSTEM CHECKS in BASIC DIAGNOSTIC PROCEDURES
C-1, MAP Sensor	See ENGINE SENSORS & SWITCHES in SYSTEM & COMPONENT TESTING
C-1, Power Steering Pressure Switch	See ENGINE SENSORS & SWITCHES in SYSTEM & COMPONENT TESTING
C-1, Park/Neutral Switch	See ENGINE SENSORS & SWITCHES in SYSTEM & COMPONENT TESTING
C-2, Injector Balance Test (4.3L)	See FUEL CONTROL in SYSTEM & COMPONENT TESTING
C-2, IAC Motor	See IDLE CONTROL SYSTEM in SYSTEM & COMPONENT TESTING
C-3, Canister Purge System	See EMISSION SYSTEMS & SUB-SYSTEMS in SYSTEM & COMPONENT TESTING
C-4, EST Ignition Check	See BASIC IGNITION SYSTEM CHECKS in BASIC DIAGNOSTIC PROCEDURES
C-5, ESC Ignition Check	See IGNITION SYSTEM in SYSTEM & COMPONENT TESTING
C-6, Air Injection System	See EMISSION SYSTEMS & SUB-SYSTEMS in SYSTEM & COMPONENT TESTING
C-7, EGR System	See EMISSION SYSTEMS & SUB-SYSTEMS in SYSTEM & COMPONENT TESTING
C-8, Torque Converter Clutch	[1] See MISCELLANEOUS ECM CONTROLS in SYSTEM & COMPONENT TESTING
C-8, Manual Transmission Shift Lights	[1] See MISCELLANEOUS ECM CONTROLS in SYSTEM & COMPONENT TESTING
C-10, A/C Clutch Control	[2] See MISCELLANEOUS ECM CONTROLS in SYSTEM & COMPONENT TESTING
C-12, Electric Cooling Fan Control	[3] See MISCELLANEOUS ECM CONTROLS in SYSTEM & COMPONENT TESTING

[1] - Covered in entirety in Mitchell's 1991-92 TRANSMISSION SERVICE & REPAIR manual for domestic vehicles.
[2] - Covered in entirety in Mitchell's 1991 AIR CONDITIONING & HEATING SERVICE & REPAIR supplement for domestic vehicles.
[3] - Covered in entirety in ENGINE COOLING in Mitchell's 1991 DOMESTIC LIGHT TRUCKS & VANS SERVICE & REPAIR manual, 1991 ENGINE, CLUTCH & DRIVE AXLE supplement and 1991 AIR CONDITIONING & HEATING SERVICE & REPAIR supplement for domestic vehicles.

1991 ENGINE PERFORMANCE
System & Component Testing (Cont.)

2) Each terminal should have at least 50 k/ohms resistance. If all quad-driver terminals have greater than 50 k/ohms resistance, go to step **4)**. If any terminal has less than 50 k/ohms resistance, locate driven component(s) for the quad-driver with the lowest resistance. Disconnect component from circuit and check circuit for short to voltage.
3) If circuit is not shorted to voltage, replace component before replacing ECM to prevent recurring ECM failure. See appropriate ECM QUAD-DRIVER TERMINAL IDENTIFICATION table.
4) Using a fused ammeter capable of measuring at least 2 amps, turn ignition on with engine off. Connect one lead of ohmmeter to chassis ground. Connect remaining lead to each ECM harness quad-driver circuit. Measure each circuit for sustained current flow for at least 2 minutes.

NOTE: TCC solenoid cannot be easily tested for current draw, since completed circuit depends upon internal transmission oil pressure switches.

5) If no circuit has more than .75 amp sustained current flow, replace ECM. If any circuit has more than .75 amp sustained current flow, check for short to voltage in that circuit. If short to voltage is not present, replace related solenoid or relay.

ECM QUAD-DRIVER TERMINAL IDENTIFICATION (2.5L)

QDR No.	ECM Terminal	Component
1	A5	SES Light
	A4	A/C Relay
	A2	TCC Solenoid (A/T) Shift Light (M/T)
	C1	Not Used
2	A3	EGR Solenoid
	D12	Not Used
	C2	Not Used
	A7	Not Used

ECM QUAD-DRIVER TERMINAL IDENTIFICATION (2.8L, 4.3L & V8 WITHOUT 4L80-E TRANSMISSION)

QDR No.	ECM Terminal	Component
1	A2	A/C Relay
	A3	Not Used
	C1	Not Used
	C2	EAC Solenoid
2	A4	EGR Or EVRV Solenoid
	A5	SES Light
	A7	TCC Solenoid (A/T) Shift Light (M/T)

ECM QUAD-DRIVER TERMINAL IDENTIFICATION (4.3L & V8 WITH 4L80-E TRANSMISSION)

QDR No.	ECM Terminal	Component
1	A2	Shift Solenoid B
	A3	Shift Solenoid A
	A4	TCC Solenoid
2	A7	SES Light
3	A11	EGR Or EVRV Solenoid

ENGINE SENSORS & SWITCHES

A/C ON Switch System Test – 1) Turn ignition switch to RUN position. Move mode selector switch to OFF position. With A/C control assembly connector connected, measure voltage between mode selector switch Dark Green wire (Light Green/Black on Astro and Safari) and ground. For wiring schematics, see mini-schematics in A/C CLUTCH under MISCELLANEOUS ECM CONTROLS.
2) Battery voltage should be present. If battery voltage is present, mode selector switch is operating normally. If battery voltage is not present, check wire from selector switch to fuse for an open circuit. Also check A/C high and low pressure switches for open.
3) Check voltage between mode selector Dark Green or Light Green/Black wire and ground. Voltage should not be present. If voltage was present, replace mode selector switch.
Brake Switch – Disconnect brake switch harness connector. Using an ohmmeter, check continuity between brake switch terminals. Continuity should be present. Depress brake pedal or activate brake switch, continuity should not be present.
Coolant Temperature Sensor (CTS) – If a coolant sensor-related code is present, see appropriate SELF-DIAGNOSTICS article. An out-of-calibration sensor may not set a trouble code. Use following procedure to test sensor calibration. Disconnect coolant temperature sensor connector. Measure resistance between sensor terminals. Resistance should be high when engine is cold and drop as engine warms up. See CTS RESISTANCE VALUES table.

CTS RESISTANCE VALUES

Temperature °F (°C)	Ohms
210 (100)	185
160 (70)	450
100 (38)	1800
70 (20)	3400
20 (-7)	13,500
0 (-18)	25,000
-40 (-40)	100,700

Knock Sensor – 1) Disconnect knock sensor harness connector. Using an ohmmeter, measure knock sensor resistance between sensor terminal and engine block. Resistance should be 3300-4500 ohms. Connect voltmeter between sensor terminal and ground. Set voltmeter to 2-volt AC scale.
2) Start and idle engine. Tap on engine block near sensor. A signal should be indicated on voltmeter. If no signal is indicated, replace knock sensor. Also see TIMING CONTROL SYSTEMS in this article and appropriate SELF-DIAGNOSTICS article.
Manifold Absolute Pressure (MAP) Sensor – 1) A malfunction in the MAP sensor circuit should set a related code in ECM memory. If a code is present, see appropriate SELF-DIAGNOSTICS article. An out-of-calibration sensor may not set a trouble code. Use following procedure to test sensor calibration. If driveability problems exist, MAP sensor failure is suspected and no MAP code is present, disconnect MAP sensor connector. If driveability condition improves, replace MAP sensor. Before replacing MAP sensor, check MAP vacuum hose for splits, kinks, proper routing and blockage.
2) With ignition on and engine off, check MAP sensor parameter using a Scan tester connected to the ALDL connector. Voltage should be as specified in MAP SENSOR VOLTAGE RANGE table. If MAP sensor voltage is as specified, go to next step. If voltage is not as specified, check for 5-volt reference supplied to sensor. Check harness integrity. If no problems are evident, replace MAP sensor.
3) Using a hand-held vacuum pump, apply 10 in. Hg to MAP sensor and note voltage change. Voltage should drop to about 1.0-1.5 volts less than specified in table. If voltage is not as specified or voltage reading does not immediately follow vacuum change, MAP sensor is faulty.

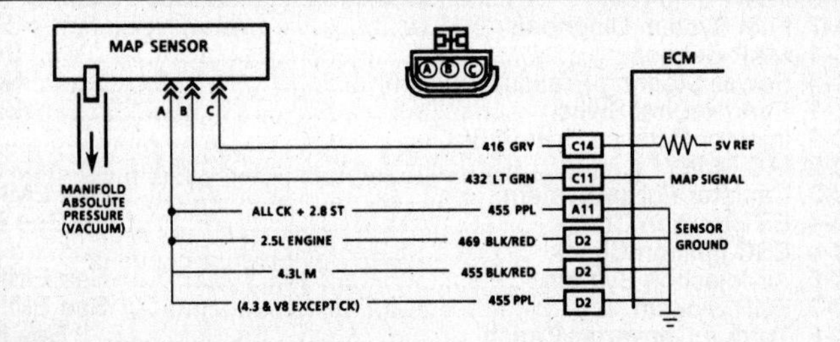
MAP SENSOR
A
B
C
ECM
MANIFOLD ABSOLUTE PRESSURE (VACUUM)
416 GRY
C14
5V REF
432 LT GRN
C11
MAP SIGNAL
ALL CK + 2.8 ST
455 PPL
A11
2.5L ENGINE
469 BLK/RED
D2
4.3L M
455 BLK/RED
D2
(4.3 & V8 EXCEPT CK)
455 PPL
D2
SENSOR GROUND

90A15735 Courtesy of General Motors Corp.

Fig. 1: Typical MAP Sensor Circuit

MAP SENSOR VOLTAGE RANGE

Altitude (Ft.)	Volts
Below 1000	3.8-5.5
1000-2000	3.6-5.3
2000-3000	3.5-5.1
3000-4000	3.3-5.0
4000-5000	3.2-4.8
5000-6000	3.0-4.6
6000-7000	2.9-4.5
7000-8000	2.8-4.3
8000-9000	2.6-4.2
9000-10,000	2.5-4.0

Manifold Air Temperature (MAT) Sensor – If a MAT sensor-related code is present, see appropriate SELF-DIAGNOSTICS article. An out-of-calibration sensor may not set a trouble code. Use following procedure to test calibration. Disconnect MAT sensor harness connector. Connect ohmmeter between sensor terminals. Sensor resistance should be as specified. See MAT SENSOR RESISTANCE table. With vehicle sitting overnight, MAT sensor and coolant sensor should have close to the same resistance reading.

MAT SENSOR RESISTANCE

Temperature °F (°C)	Ohms
210 (100)	185
160 (70)	450
100 (38)	1800
70 (20)	3400
40 (4)	7500
20 (-7)	13,500
0 (-18)	25,000
-40 (-40)	100,700

Oxygen (O_2) Sensor – 1) Start engine and warm to operating temperature. Disconnect oxygen sensor. Connect a DVOM between Purple lead of oxygen sensor and ground. Place meter on the 2-volt scale.
2) Using another DVOM on the 20-volt scale, connect voltmeter in series between Purple wire from the ECM and the positive post of battery. This will simulate a rich condition, causing ECM to respond by leaning mixture. Reading on voltmeter connected to oxygen sensor should decrease to a low voltage (less than .3 volt).
3) Move voltmeter lead from positive battery post to negative battery post. This will simulate a lean condition, causing ECM to respond by richening mixture. Reading on voltmeter connected to oxygen sensor should increase (greater than .8 volt). If reading does not change as specified, replace O_2 sensor.
4) If a second DVOM is not available, install short jumper in Purple wire from the ECM. Hold jumper in one hand and touch positive post of battery with other hand to simulate a rich condition. Touch negative post of battery to simulate a lean condition. For additional testing procedures, see appropriate SELF-DIAGNOSTICS article.
Oxygen Sensor Heating Element (4.3L Turbo PFI) – Disconnect 3-wire connector at oxygen sensor. Measure resistance between White wire terminals on sensor side of connector. Resistance should be 3.5-14 ohms. If resistance is not 3.5-14 ohms, replace oxygen sensor.
Park/Neutral (P/N) Switch – Disconnect P/N switch (located on transmission) harness connector. Connect ohmmeter between the P/N switch terminals. *See Fig. 2.* Continuity should be present only when gear shift selector is in Park or Neutral. If continuity is not present, check P/N switch adjustment or replace defective P/N switch.

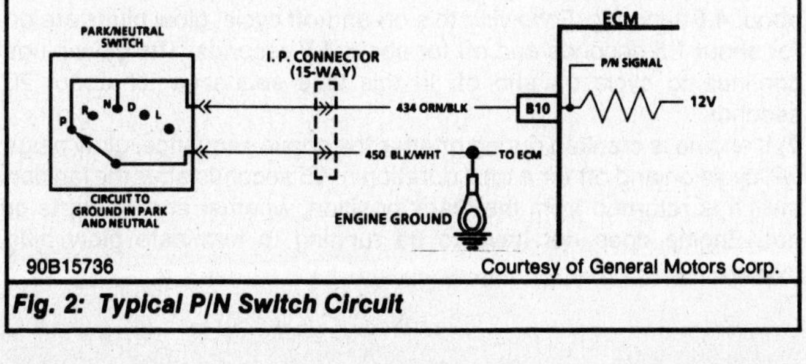

PARK/NEUTRAL SWITCH
I. P. CONNECTOR (15-WAY)
ECM
P/N SIGNAL
P
R
N
D
L
434 ORN/BLK
B10
12V
450 BLK/WHT
TO ECM
CIRCUIT TO GROUND IN PARK AND NEUTRAL
ENGINE GROUND

90B15736 Courtesy of General Motors Corp.

Fig. 2: Typical P/N Switch Circuit

Power Steering Pressure Switch (2.5L) – Disconnect P/S pressure switch harness connector. Connect ohmmeter between P/S pressure switch terminals. Start engine. With no load on power steering, continuity should not be present. Turn steering wheel to full stop, continuity should now be present. If readings are not as specified, replace defective P/S pressure switch.
Throttle Position Sensor (TPS) – 1) Install jumper wires to enable connection of a DVOM in parallel between TPS harness connectors. Connect DVOM positive lead to Dark Blue wire terminal. Connect negative lead to Black wire terminal. *See Fig. 3.*
2) Turn ignition on, engine off. Signal voltage should gradually change from less than one volt at closed throttle to about 5.0 volts at wide open throttle position. If reading is not as specified, adjust or replace TPS. See ON-VEHICLE ADJUSTMENTS article.
3) A malfunction in the TPS circuit should set a related trouble code. For further information, see appropriate SELF-DIAGNOSTICS article. Also see TPS adjustment procedure in ON-VEHICLE ADJUSTMENTS article.

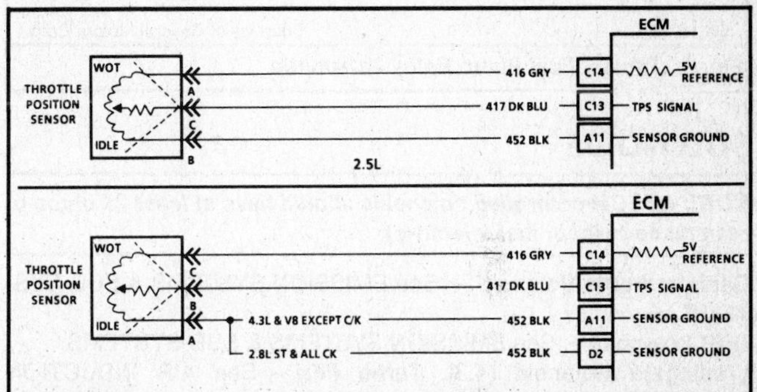

ECM
THROTTLE POSITION SENSOR
WOT
IDLE
A
C
B
416 GRY
417 DK BLU
452 BLK
C14
C13
A11
5V REFERENCE
TPS SIGNAL
SENSOR GROUND
2.5L
ECM
THROTTLE POSITION SENSOR
WOT
IDLE
C
B
A
416 GRY
417 DK BLU
4.3L & V8 EXCEPT C/K
452 BLK
2.8L ST & ALL CK
452 BLK
C14
C13
A11
D2
5V REFERENCE
TPS SIGNAL
SENSOR GROUND
SENSOR GROUND

90C15737 Courtesy of General Motors Corp.

Fig. 3: Typical Throttle Position Sensor Circuit

Vehicle Speed Sensor (PM Generator Type) – Disconnect vehicle speed sensor harness connector (located in transmission/transaxle). Place gear selector in Neutral. Raise vehicle drive wheels off the ground. Turn drive wheels by hand (greater than 3 MPH). Measure AC signal voltage between sensor terminals. Voltage reading should be varying from 0.1-0.5 volt AC as the wheel is turned. If reading is not as specified, replace vehicle speed sensor. If a code is set, refer to appropriate SELF-DIAGNOSTICS article for diagnosis.

RELAYS, SOLENOIDS, MOTORS & MODULES

RELAYS

A/C Relays – See MISCELLANEOUS ECM CONTROLS.
Cold Advance Relay (6.2L Diesel) – See DIESEL COLD ADVANCE SYSTEM CHECK under FUEL SYSTEM (DIESEL).
Fuel Pump Relay – 1) If a prolonged crank is required to start vehicle, fuel pump relay may be faulty. To verify this, start engine. With engine running, disconnect oil pressure switch (fuel pump back-up circuit). If engine stalls, fuel pump relay is faulty. If vehicle continues to run, relay is okay. Check for other causes of prolonged crank.
2) To test fuel pump relay, disconnect fuel pump relay. Refer to COMPONENT LOCATIONS at end of article. Apply battery voltage and ground to fuel pump relay winding terminals. To identify fuel pump relay terminals, see appropriate wiring diagram in WIRING DIAGRAMS article.
3) Using an ohmmeter, check continuity between fuel pump relay power and fuel pump relay drive terminals. Continuity should exist. If continuity does not exist, fuel pump relay is defective.
4) To by-pass fuel pump relay on vehicle (fuel pump not operating), turn ignition off. Disconnect fuel pump relay connector. Using a fused jumper wire, connect fuel pump test connector to positive side of battery. Fuel pump should run.

1991 ENGINE PERFORMANCE
System & Component Testing (Cont.)

5) If fuel pump runs, check for faulty connections to relay or replace defective relay. To locate fuel pump test connector, refer to COMPONENT LOCATIONS at the end of this article.

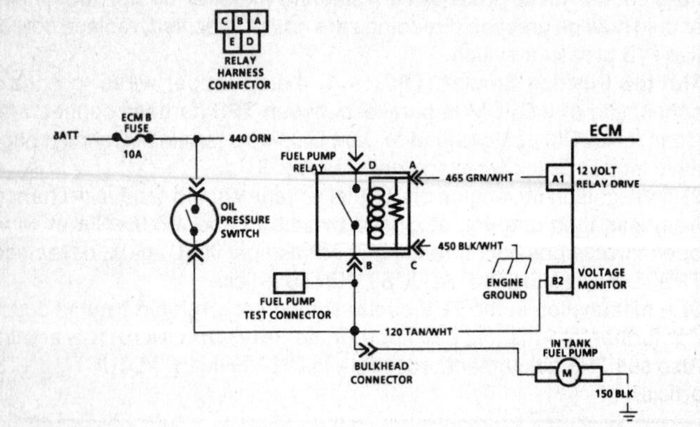
C B A
E D
RELAY HARNESS CONNECTOR
BATT
ECM B FUSE
10A
440 ORN
ECM
FUEL PUMP RELAY
D
A
465 GRN/WHT
A1
12 VOLT RELAY DRIVE
OIL PRESSURE SWITCH
450 BLK/WHT
B
C
ENGINE GROUND
B2
VOLTAGE MONITOR
FUEL PUMP TEST CONNECTOR
120 TAN/WHT
IN TANK FUEL PUMP
M
BULKHEAD CONNECTOR
150 BLK

90E15739 Courtesy of General Motors Corp.

Fig. 4: Typical Fuel Pump Relay Schematic

SOLENOIDS

NOTE: All ECM-controlled solenoids should have at least 20 ohms of resistance (except fuel injectors).

Canister Purge Solenoid – See EMISSION SYSTEMS & SUB-SYSTEMS.
EGR Solenoid – See EMISSION SYSTEMS & SUB-SYSTEMS.
Wastegate Solenoid (4.3L Turbo PFI) – See AIR INDUCTION SYSTEMS at beginning of this article.

MOTORS

Idle Air Control (IAC) Motor – See IDLE CONTROL SYSTEM.

FUEL SYSTEM (GASOLINE)

FUEL DELIVERY

NOTE: For fuel system pressure testing, see BASIC DIAGNOSTIC PROCEDURES article.

Fuel Pressure Regulator (TBI) – Fuel pressure regulator is mechanically controlled by internal spring pressure. Regulator is adjusted at factory and is not serviceable. If fuel pressure is too low, check for restricted delivery line. Also, check fuel pump pressure and volume. If fuel pressure is too high, check for restricted fuel tank return line or fuel filter. If no faults are found and pressure is too high or too low, replace fuel pressure regulator.
Fuel Pressure Regulator (PFI) – Fuel pressure regulator is a vacuum-controlled diaphragm type, which uses manifold vacuum to modify fuel pressure to compensate for engine load fuel requirements. Connect fuel pressure gauge to fuel pressure service port. Start engine and note fuel pressure. Disconnect vacuum hose from fuel pressure regulator. Fuel pressure should increase 4-10 psi (.15 kg/cm²). If pressure does not increase 4-10 psi (.15 kg/cm²), check for presence of manifold vacuum at signal line. If vacuum is not present, check for kinked, cut or split vacuum hose or plugged throttle body vacuum port. If vacuum is present and no pressure change occurred, replace fuel pressure regulator.
Fuel Pump Oil Pressure Switch (Back-Up Circuit) – To test fuel pump oil pressure switch back-up circuit, start engine. With engine running, disconnect fuel pump relay. If engine stalls, fuel pump oil pressure switch is faulty. If vehicle continues to run, switch is okay.
Fuel Pump Relay – See RELAYS, SOLENOIDS, MOTORS & MODULES.
Fuel Pump Relay By-Pass Procedure – If fuel pump will not energize, relay may be by-passed to test fuel pump. Turn ignition off. Using a fused jumper wire, apply battery voltage to fuel pump test connector. Fuel pump should turn on. For fuel pump test connector location, refer to COMPONENT LOCATIONS at end of article.

FUEL CONTROL

Fuel Injector(s) – Disconnect fuel injector harness connector. Measure resistance across injector terminals. Resistance should be as specified. See FUEL INJECTOR RESISTANCE table.
Oxygen Sensor – See ENGINE SENSORS & SWITCHES.

FUEL INJECTOR RESISTANCE

Application	[1] Ohms
TBI Except 3.1L (VIN D)	1.3
3.1L (VIN D)	1.2
4.3L Turbo PFI	[2] 2.0

[1] – Injector resistance specification is at 140°F (60°C).
[2] – Minimum reading.

IDLE CONTROL SYSTEM

Idle Air Control (IAC) Motor – **1)** Disconnect harness connector to motor. Check resistance across IAC coil terminals "A" to "B" and "C" to "D". *See Fig. 5*. Resistance should be 40-80 ohms. If okay, go to next step. If resistance is not as specified, replace IAC motor.
2) Check resistance between IAC terminals "B" to "C" and "A" to "D". Resistance should be infinite. If resistance is not as specified, replace IAC motor.

NOTE: Functional testing of Idle Air Control (IAC) motor requires a Scan tester capable of cycling ECM output devices (bidirectional) or a special IAC Driver and Node Light Set (222L or J-37027). Flow charts in the SELF-DIAGNOSTICS articles may refer to the Tech 1 tester, General Motors' bidirectional tester.

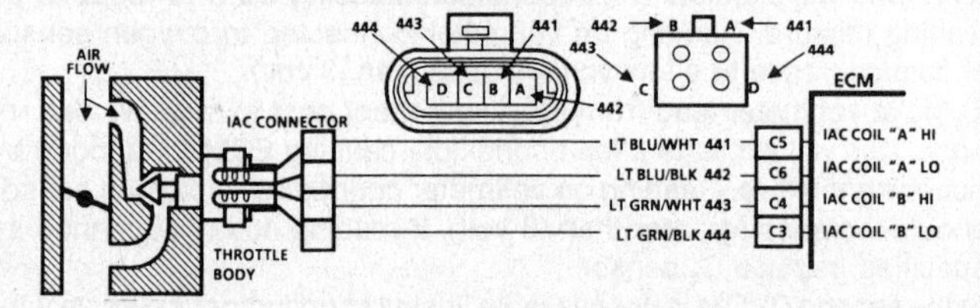
444
443
441
442
B
A
441
443
444
AIR FLOW
D C B A
442
C
D
ECM
IAC CONNECTOR
LT BLU/WHT 441
C5
IAC COIL "A" HI
LT BLU/BLK 442
C6
IAC COIL "A" LO
LT GRN/WHT 443
C4
IAC COIL "B" HI
LT GRN/BLK 444
C3
IAC COIL "B" LO
THROTTLE BODY

90H15740 Courtesy of General Motors Corp.

Fig. 5: Identifying IAC Motor Circuits (Typical)

FUEL SYSTEM (DIESEL)

NOTE: The 6.2L light duty emissions engine (LH6) uses the Diesel Electronic Control (DEC) system. For complete system testing and diagnosis of DEC system, see SELF-DIAGNOSTICS – DIESEL article.

NORMAL GLOW PLUG CIRCUIT OPERATION

A normal functioning system should operate as follows:
1) With ignition switch in the ON position, engine not running and at room temperature, glow plugs are on for 4-to-6 seconds, then off for about 4.5 seconds. Following this on-and-off cycle, glow plugs are on for about 1.5 seconds and off for about 4.5 seconds. The glow plugs continue to cycle on and off in this time sequence for about 20 seconds
2) If engine is cranked during or after the above sequence, glow plugs will cycle on and off for a total duration of 25 seconds after the ignition switch is returned from the crank position, whether engine starts or not. Engine does not have to be running to terminate glow plug cycling.

NOTE: Glow plug on-and-off times vary with engine temperature, system voltage and/or ambient temperature. Lower temperatures cause longer duration of cycling.

PRELIMINARY GLOW PLUG DIAGNOSIS

1) If system does not operate as described in NORMAL GLOW PLUG CIRCUIT OPERATION, ensure glow plug system is correctly installed. Ensure all connectors are properly attached, clean and tight. Inspect engine harness ground connection. Ensure nut securing 4-wire connector at controller is tightened to 96 INCH lbs. (11 N.m), with connector fully seated and latched.

2) Ensure controller copper stud upper nuts are tightened to 96 INCH lbs (11 N.m). DO NOT tighten lower nuts. Ensure temperature switch connector in water crossover near front of engine is tightened to 48 INCH lbs. (5.4 N.m). Inspect WAIT light on instrument panel for tight connection and operation.

INHIBIT SWITCH (BLACK CAP)

1) Remove connector from inhibit switch when engine temperature is less than 100°F (38°C). Inhibit switch is located in water crossover near front of engine. Set ohmmeter on low range. Test continuity across switch terminals. Switch should be closed (a reading of less than 1.0 ohm on meter.)

2) Test terminals for continuity to ground with a test light or ohmmeter on high scale. Light should be off. Meter should show greater than 1.0 megohm. Replace switch if results are not as specified.

3) Disconnect plug from switch terminals when engine temperature is greater than 125°F (52°C). Change ohmmeter setting to highest scale or use a self-powered test light. Test continuity across switch terminals. Test continuity from each terminal to ground. Switch should be open (test light off or high ohm reading of greater than 1.0 megohm on meter). Replace switch if it is closed. When installing replacement switch, tighten to 17 ft. lbs. (23 N.m).

GLOW PLUG SYSTEM DIAGNOSIS

Electrical Check - Turn ignition off. Disconnect all glow plug connectors. Using an ohmmeter, check resistance between each glow plug terminal and ground. Glow plug resistance should be greater than 2 ohms. Replace glow plug if resistance is not as specified.

NO START - COLD

Perform these diagnostic procedures if engine does not start when cold; GLOW PLUG light may or may not come on. Before proceeding, check fuel system to ensure it is okay. Ensure battery voltage is 12.4 volts or more with turned ignition off. Ensure cranking speed is at least 100 RPM.

1) With ignition off, measure voltage at battery stud (single wire) on glow plug. *See Fig. 6.* If no voltage is present, repair battery-to-glow plug controller circuit.

2) If no voltage is present in step **1)**, disconnect harness from all glow plugs. Using an ohmmeter, measure resistance between glow plug terminals and engine block. Replace glow plug if resistance is greater than 2 ohms. Reconnect all glow plugs before continuing with diagnosis.

3) If voltage was present in step **1)**, turn ignition off and measure voltage at glow plug feed stud (twin lead) on glow plug controller. If battery voltage is now present, relay contacts are shorted. Replace controller and all glow plugs.

4) With all glow plugs reconnected, place ignition switch in RUN position. Remove controller connector and check voltage at harness connector terminal "D". *See Fig. 6.*

5) If no voltage is present, repair open in ignition feed circuit to controller. If voltage is present, measure resistance between terminal "E" of connector and engine block (ground). If measurement is greater than one ohm, repair ground circuit to controller.

6) With ground circuit working properly in step **4)**, measure resistance between terminals "C" and "E" of connector. If reading is greater than 2 ohms, go to next step. If reading is less than 2 ohms, go to step **8)**.

7) If reading in step **5)** is greater than 2 ohms, remove connector from temperature inhibit switch and measure continuity between the 2 terminals on switch. Switch is open above 125°F (51.5°C). If reading is less than one ohm, repair glow plug circuit to controller. If reading is greater than one ohm, replace temperature inhibit switch and return to step **6)**.

8) If reading in step **5)** was less than 2 ohms, reconnect controller harness connector and ensure complete engagement. Connector locking latch should click over controller locking tab. With controller connector harness correctly connected, measure voltage at glow plug feed stud (twin lead) on glow plug controller, while turning ignition switch from OFF position to RUN position.

9) If no voltage is present, replace glow plug controller. If battery voltage is present, measure voltage at any one glow plug harness connector when turning ignition switch from OFF to RUN position. Test both right and left banks.

10) If no voltage was present in step **8)**, repair glow plug feed circuit to glow plugs. If battery voltage is present and instrument panel GLOW PLUG light does not come on, locate and repair bulb or circuit.

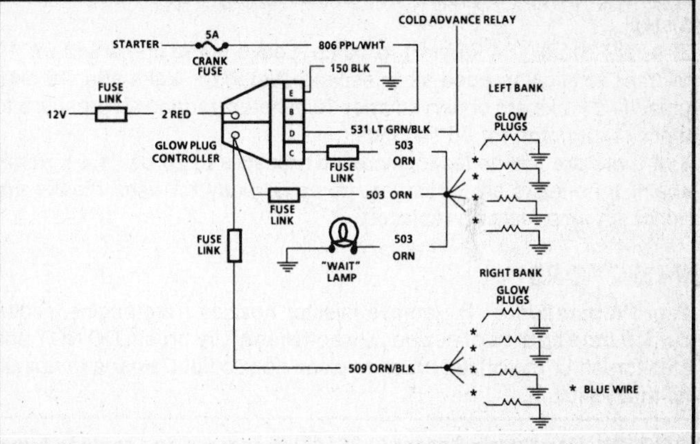

COLD ADVANCE RELAY
STARTER
5A
CRANK FUSE
806 PPL/WHT
150 BLK
FUSE LINK
12V
2 RED
E
B
D
C
531 LT GRN/BLK
GLOW PLUG CONTROLLER
LEFT BANK
GLOW PLUGS
503 ORN
FUSE LINK
503 ORN
FUSE LINK
FUSE LINK
503 ORN
"WAIT" LAMP
RIGHT BANK
GLOW PLUGS
509 ORN/BLK
* BLUE WIRE

90I15741 Courtesy of General Motors Corp.

Fig. 6: Diesel Glow Plug Circuit

DIESEL COLD ADVANCE SYSTEM CHECK

With ignition on and coolant temperature less than 80°F (27°C), the ECM grounds circuit No. 905 to the cold advance relay. Grounding circuit No. 905 turns on cold advance relay to supply 12 volts to the cold advance solenoid (in the injection pump), and glow plug controller. The cold advance solenoid is now energized, causing injection pump timing to be advanced about 4 degrees.

Cold Advance Relay - 1) Disconnect harness connector to cold advance relay. Using an ohmmeter, check resistance between relay terminals "D" and "F". *See Fig. 7.* Continuity should be present or a resistance of 20 ohms. If not, replace cold advance relay.

2) Using an ohmmeter, check continuity between relay terminals "A" and "E". Continuity should not be present. If continuity is present, replace grounded cold advance relay.

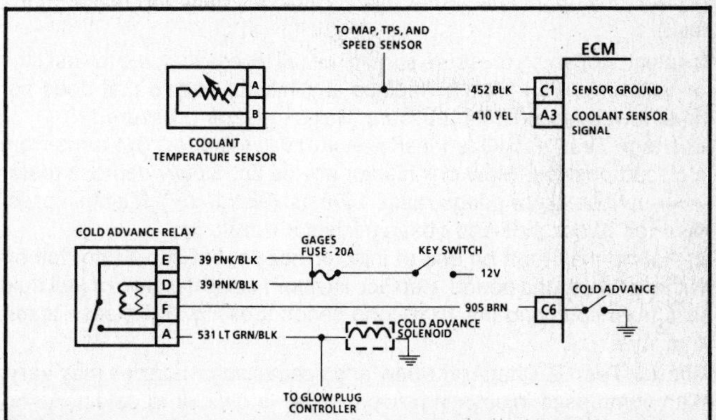

TO MAP, TPS, AND SPEED SENSOR
ECM
A
B
452 BLK
C1
SENSOR GROUND
410 YEL
A3
COOLANT SENSOR SIGNAL
COOLANT TEMPERATURE SENSOR
COLD ADVANCE RELAY
GAGES FUSE - 20A
KEY SWITCH
E
39 PNK/BLK
D
39 PNK/BLK
12V
F
905 BRN
C6
COLD ADVANCE
A
531 LT GRN/BLK
COLD ADVANCE SOLENOID
TO GLOW PLUG CONTROLLER

90J15742 Courtesy of General Motors Corp.

Fig. 7: Cold Start Advance System Schematic

1991 ENGINE PERFORMANCE
System & Component Testing (Cont.)

GLOW PLUG CONTROLLER

1) Ensure coolant temperature is less than 80°F (27°C) before beginning test. Place ignition switch in RUN position and allow glow plugs to cycle. After 2 minutes, crank engine for one second. It is NOT important that the engine starts. Return ignition switch to RUN position. Glow plugs should cycle on at least once.
2) If glow plugs do not cycle, disconnect controller connector (controller is located on top, rear of valve cover). Connect a 12-volt test light between Purple/White wire terminal of harness connector (terminal "B") and ground. With ignition switch in RUN position, test light should be off. Test light should glow when engine is cranked. *See Fig. 6.*
3) If test light does not glow as specified, repair short or open in engine harness Purple/White wire. If test light operates properly but glow plugs did not cycle, replace controller.

INJECTION PUMP HOUSING LEAKAGE TEST

1) Remove injection pump and drain all fuel. Connect an air supply line to fuel inlet fitting. Ensure air supply is clean and dry. Seal off return line fitting. Completely immerse pump assembly in a container of clean test oil.
2) Apply 20 psi (1.4 kg/cm²) to pump. Leave pump immersed for 10 minutes to allow trapped air to escape. Watch for leaks after 10 minutes. If no leaks are observed after 10 minutes, reduce air pressure to 2 psi (.14 kg/cm²) for 30 seconds.
3) If there are still no leaks, increase pressure to 20 psi (1.4 kg/cm²) again. If no leaks are observed, pump is ready for use. If leaks are noticed, pump must be replaced.

INJECTORS

Test Preparation – 1) Remove injector nozzles from engine. Clean carbon from tip area of nozzle with soft brass wire brush. DO NOT use steel brush or motorized brush to clean nozzle tip. Damage to nozzle tip may result.

CAUTION: Use Nozzle Socket (J-36142) to remove and replace injection nozzle. Attach socket to 30mm hex portion of nozzle. Failure to do so will result in damage to the injector nozzle.

2) Connect injector nozzle to injection nozzle tester. Place clear plastic tubing on both fuel return fittings to prevent bleed-off from being confused with leaks. Close tester shutoff valve to pressure gauge.
3) Fill tester with test fluid. Fill and flush nozzle assembly with test fluid by operating tester lever briskly and repeatedly. This purges air from injector nozzle and coats all parts with test fluid.

WARNING: When testing injectors, keep spray contained to avoid serious injury. DO NOT allow injector to release line pressure on hands, arms or any part of body. Pressure of atomized test spray has sufficient penetrating power to puncture flesh.

Opening Pressure Test – 1) Open tester shutoff valve 1/4 turn from closed position. Slowly depress tester lever and observe gauge. Note pressure at which needle of pressure gauge stops. Some injector nozzles may pop while other injector nozzles may drip (this is not a leak).
2) Injector opening pressure should not fall to less than the lowest limit of 1500 psi (105 kg/cm²). Replace any injector nozzle that does not meet lowest acceptable pressure. Release tester pressure.
Leakage Test – 1) Open tester shutoff valve 3/4 to 1 3/4 turns from a closed position. Blow dry injector nozzle tip. Slowly depress tester lever until pressure gauge reads 1400 psi (98 kg/cm²). Maintain pressure for 10 seconds and observe injector nozzle tip.
2) A drop may form on end of injector nozzle, but should not fall off within a 10 second period. Replace injector nozzle if a drop of test fluid falls from tip during the 10 second period. *See Fig. 8.* Release tester pressure.
Chatter Test – Chatter for new and used injector nozzles may vary. With some used injector nozzles, chatter is difficult to detect during slow actuation of tester lever. Some injector nozzles may chatter louder than others. As long as there is chatter, the injector nozzle is acceptable.

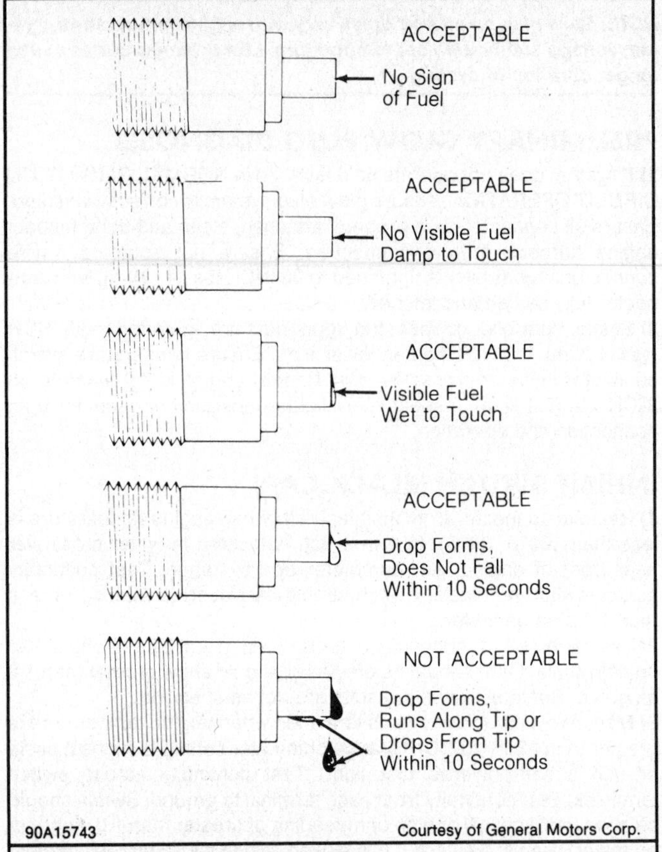
ACCEPTABLE
No Sign of Fuel
ACCEPTABLE
No Visible Fuel Damp to Touch
ACCEPTABLE
Visible Fuel Wet to Touch
ACCEPTABLE
Drop Forms, Does Not Fall Within 10 Seconds
NOT ACCEPTABLE
Drop Forms, Runs Along Tip or Drops From Tip Within 10 Seconds
90A15743
Courtesy of General Motors Corp.

Fig. 8: Injection Nozzle Leakage Test

1) Close tester shutoff lever at pressure gauge. Slowly depress lever and note whether chatter can be heard. If no chatter is heard, increase speed of lever movement until it reaches a point at which injector nozzle chatters.
2) At fast lever movement, injector nozzle may emit a "hissing" or "squealing" sound rather than normal chatter. This is acceptable. These sounds indicate that injector nozzle needle moves freely and injector nozzle seat, guide and pintle have no mechanical defects. Replace any injector nozzle assembly that does not chatter.
Spray Pattern Test – The injector nozzles used with this system have several features that make pattern testing difficult. These features include longer nozzle overlap, greater pintle-to-body clearances and an internal wave washer between injector nozzle nut and injector. Typical injector nozzle tester cannot deliver fuel with sufficient velocity to obtain proper spray patterns. DO NOT replace injector nozzle(s) based on spray pattern.

IGNITION SYSTEM

NOTE: For basic ignition system checks, see BASIC DIAGNOSTIC PROCEDURES article.

TIMING CONTROL SYSTEMS

Electronic Spark Timing (All Engines) – An open or short to ground in the Electronic Spark Timing (EST) or by-pass circuits will cause ECM to turn on SERVICE ENGINE SOON light and confirm fault causing Code 42 is present. Refer to SELF-DIAGNOSTICS — GASOLINE article.
C-5, Electronic Spark Control (ESC) Circuit (Except 2.5L, 4.3L Turbo & Vehicles With 4L80-E Transmission) – 1) An open or short circuit on ESC wire to ECM will cause a loss of 12-volt ESC controller signal. This will cause ECM to fully retard ignition timing.

2) If a Scan tester is available, connect it to the ALDL connector. Using a metal object, tap on engine next to knock sensor and note knock parameter. Knock should be indicated on Scan tester.
3) If a Scan tester is not available, backprobe ECM ESC signal terminal with a DVOM. With engine idling, 812 volts should be present at this terminal. Using a metal object, tap on engine close to knock sensor. Voltage signal at ECM terminal should drop to zero volts, and return when knock signal ceases.
4) If signal does not respond as described, check knock sensor signal to controller signal. On vehicles equipped with automatic transmission, it may be necessary to place transmission in Drive for timing change to occur. Also, see KNOCK SENSOR under ENGINE SENSORS & SWITCHES.
Electronic Spark Control (ESC) Circuit (4.3L Turbo & Vehicles With 4L80-E Transmission) - 1) An open or short circuit on the ESC wire to the ECM will set a related trouble code. A false detonation signal will not cause ECM to set a code.
2) If a Scan tester is available, connect it to the ALDL connector. Tap on engine next to knock sensor and note "knock" parameter. Knock should be indicated on Scan tester.
3) If a Scan tester is not available, connect tachometer to engine. Start engine and hold RPM above idle. Using a metal object, tap on engine close to knock sensor. A noticeable decrease in engine RPM should occur. If no RPM decrease occurred, check knock sensor to ECM circuit.
4) On vehicles equipped with automatic transmission, it may be necessary to place transmission in Drive for timing change to occur. Also, see KNOCK SENSOR under ENGINE SENSORS & SWITCHES.

EMISSION SYSTEMS & SUB-SYSTEMS (GASOLINE)

C-6, AIR INJECTION

Air Pump - Accelerate engine to approximately 1500 RPM and observe airflow from hoses. If airflow increases as engine is accelerated, pump is working properly. If airflow does not increase, check system for plugged or restricted hoses, proper pump belt tension, leaky valves or defective air injection pump.
Check Valve - Allow engine to cool. Remove check valve from engine and blow through valve in direction of check valve flow (to cylinder head). Attempt to suck back. Replace valve if airflow is allowed against the direction of flow.
Electronic Air Control (EAC) Solenoid - 1) Turn ignition on, engine off. Disconnect EAC solenoid connector. Connect test light between solenoid connector terminals. *See Fig. 9*. If test light comes on, check for grounded wire from solenoid to ECM. If wire is not grounded, replace ECM. If test light does not turn on, go to next step.
2) Ground ALDL diagnostic connector. If test light comes on, check for faulty EAC solenoid connector. If connector is okay, replace EAC valve. If test light does not turn on, connect test light between harness terminal "A" and ground. *See Fig. 9*. If test light still did not turn on, check for open in fuse or wire to ignition.

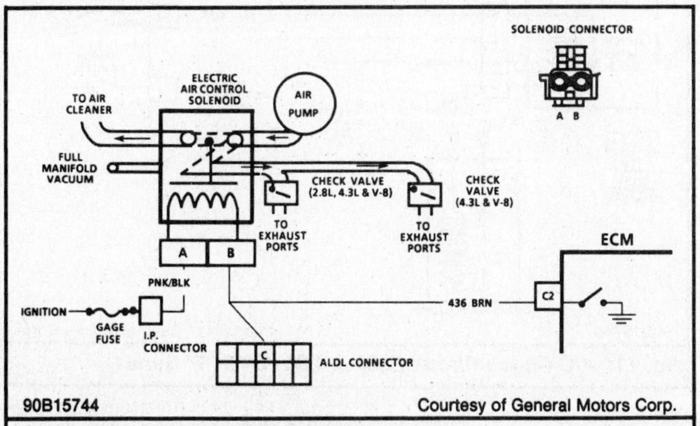

SOLENOID CONNECTOR
A B
ELECTRIC AIR CONTROL SOLENOID
TO AIR CLEANER
AIR PUMP
FULL MANIFOLD VACUUM
CHECK VALVE (2.8L, 4.3L & V-8)
CHECK VALVE (4.3L & V-8)
TO EXHAUST PORTS
TO EXHAUST PORTS
ECM
A
B
PNK/BLK
436 BRN
C2
IGNITION
GAGE FUSE
I.P. CONNECTOR
C
ALDL CONNECTOR

90B15744 Courtesy of General Motors Corp.

Fig. 9: Electronic Air Control (EAC) Circuit

3) If test light comes on, check for open in wire from solenoid to ECM. If wire is okay, check EAC solenoid resistance. If resistance is less than 20 ohms, replace EAC solenoid and perform ECM quad-driver check. If EAC solenoid resistance is greater than 20 ohms, replace ECM only.

C-7, EXHAUST GAS RECIRCULATION (EGR)

System Test - Start and run engine to normal operating temperature. With engine at idle, RPM should drop as EGR valve is opened by pushing up on underside of EGR diaphragm.

CAUTION: Wear gloves when handling hot EGR valve.

EGR Control Solenoid - 1) Disconnect EGR solenoid electrical harness connector and vacuum hoses. Connect a hand-held vacuum pump to solenoid vacuum source port. Connect vacuum gauge to solenoid EGR port. Pump up vacuum pump. Vacuum should not be present at port to EGR valve.
2) Activate EGR solenoid with a remote ground and 12-volt power supply. Vacuum should now be present at vacuum gauge. Solenoid should have at least 20 ohms of resistance.
Negative Backpressure EGR Valve - With engine off, disconnect vacuum hose to EGR valve. Connect vacuum pump to EGR and apply 10 in. Hg. If EGR diaphragm does not move up and stay up for 20 seconds, replace EGR valve.

C-3, FUEL EVAPORATION CONTROL

Vapor Canister Purge Valve (V8 High Altitude & 4.3L Except "S" & "T" Series) - 1) Install a short length of hose to lower port of purge valve. Blow into hose. Little or no air should pass into canister (a small amount of air will pass if the canister has a constant purge hole).
2) Using a hand-held vacuum pump, apply 15 in. Hg to vacuum control (upper) port. If vacuum does not hold for 20 seconds, replace canister.
3) With vacuum still applied, again try to blow through hose connected lower port. An increased flow of air should be observed. If airflow does not increase, replace canister.
Fuel Tank Pressure Control Valve (V8 High Altitude & 4.3L Except "S" & "T" Series) - 1) Install a short piece of hose on valve inlet tube (fuel tank side) and blow into hose. Diaphragm should pop open and air should pass through valve. If valve does not open, replace fuel tank pressure control valve.
2) Connect hand-held vacuum pump to upper port (small nipple) of tank pressure control valve. Apply vacuum. Vacuum should hold. If vacuum does not hold, replace tank pressure control valve.
Thermostatic Vacuum Switch (2.8L & 3.1L) - 1) With engine coolant temperature less than 115°F (46°C), air blown through one vacuum port should not exit through other port.
2) With engine coolant temperature greater than 115°F (46°C), air blown through one port should exit through of other port. If valve does not respond as indicated, replace valve.

PCV

Required Service - The PCV system may require service for obstructions if any of the following conditions exist:
- Rough Idle
- Stalling or Slow Idle Speed
- Oil Leaks
- Oil in Air Cleaner
- Sludge in Engine

A PCV leaking valve or hose could cause:
- Rough Idle
- Stalling
- High Idle Speed

If engine idles roughly, check for clogged PCV valve and for plugged or broken hoses BEFORE adjusting idle. Check correct PCV valve application to ensure the correct valve is fitted. Replace PCV valve if required.

1991 ENGINE PERFORMANCE
System & Component Testing (Cont.)

Checking PCV Valve Function (Except 2.5L) - 1) Remove PCV valve from rocker cover. Run engine at idle. Place thumb over open end of valve to check for vacuum. If there is no vacuum at valve, check for obstruction in manifold port, hoses or PCV valve. Repair or replace as necessary.
2) Turn engine off. Remove PCV valve. Shake valve and listen for rattle of check valve inside. If a clear rattle is not heard, replace PCV valve.
3) Visually inspect valve for varnish or deposits that may make PCV valve operation sticky, restricted or incompletely seated. Replace if necessary.
4) An engine must be sealed for the PCV system to function as designed. If leakage, sludging or dilution of oil is noted and the PCV system is functioning properly, check engine for cause, and repair as required to ensure PCV system will continue to function properly.
5) Since an engine operating without any crankcase ventilation can be damaged, it is important to replace PCV valve and air cleaner breather at regular intervals (at least every 30,000 miles). Check all hoses and clamps for failure or deterioration.

NOTE: The 2.5L engine does not use a conventional PCV valve. Valve consists of a fixed restricted orifice. To test valve, simply check for presence of vacuum with valve removed from rocker cover and engine running.

THERMOSTATIC AIR CLEANER

Temperature Sensor - Vacuum Motor Type (2.8L) - 1) Air cleaner temperature should be less than 86°F (30°C). Place thermometer as close as possible to sensor inside air cleaner. Start and idle engine. Damper door should close off outside air immediately.
2) When damper door starts to open snorkel passage, remove air cleaner cover and read thermometer temperature. Thermometer should read about 131°F (55°C).
3) If damper door does not open to outside air at the specified temperature, check vacuum motor diaphragm. If okay, replace defective thermostatic air cleaner temperature sensor.
Vacuum Motor Diaphragm (2.8L) - 1) Turn engine off. Disconnect vacuum hose to vacuum motor. Apply 7 in. Hg to vacuum motor. Damper door should close. If not, check if linkage is properly connected.
2) With vacuum still applied, trap vacuum in vacuum diaphragm motor by bending hose. Damper door should remain closed. If damper door does not remain closed, replace vacuum diaphragm motor assembly.
Damper Door - Wax Pellet Check (Except 2.8L) - 1) Remove air cleaner assembly from vehicle and allow to cool to less than 40° F (4° C). Damper door should be closed to outside (cold) air.
2) Reinstall air cleaner assembly. Start engine and observe damper door. As air cleaner assembly warms up, wax pellet should expand, closing off hot air delivery and opening cold air delivery.
3) If door does not respond as indicated, ensure door is not binding and calibrated damper spring is installed properly.

EMISSION SYSTEMS & SUB-SYSTEMS (DIESEL)

POSITIVE CRANKCASE VENTILATION

Crankcase Depression Regulator (CDR) - To test CDR valve, connect one hose of a water manometer to the engine oil dipstick tube. Leave other hose of manometer open to atmosphere. Install air cleaner and run engine. CDR valve specification is one inch of water pressure at idle to 3-4 inches at full load. Add amount of distance water travels down one side of gauge to distance water travels up other side of gauge to obtain reading.

EXHAUST GAS RECIRCULATION (EGR)

EGR Valve Check - With engine off, disconnect vacuum hose to EGR valve. Connect vacuum pump to EGR and apply 10 in. Hg. EGR diaphragm should move up and stay up for 20 seconds. If not, replace EGR valve.

EXHAUST PRESSURE REGULATION (EPR) SYSTEM

NOTE: For testing of the EPR system, see appropriate chart in SELF-DIAGNOSTICS - DIESEL article.

VACUUM PUMP

Connect vacuum gauge to vacuum pump inlet (small fitting). DO NOT plug or disconnect outlet fitting. With engine idling, vacuum should be 18 in. Hg one minute after start. If not, check for belt slippage, vacuum leaks or other obvious defects. If no defects are present, replace pump.

MISCELLANEOUS ECM CONTROLS

NOTE: Although not considered true engine performance-related systems, some controlled devices may affect driveability if they malfunction.

C-10, A/C CLUTCH

A/C Clutch Relay - 1) Disconnect A/C clutch relay harness connector. Using proper mini-schematic and an ohmmeter, check continuity between A/C clutch relay winding terminals. *See Figs. 10-15.* Continuity should exist. Check continuity between clutch drive circuit terminals of relay. Continuity should not exist.
2) Using jumper wires, apply ground and battery voltage to relay winding. Continuity should now exist between clutch drive circuit terminals of relay. Replace A/C clutch relay if readings are not as specified.

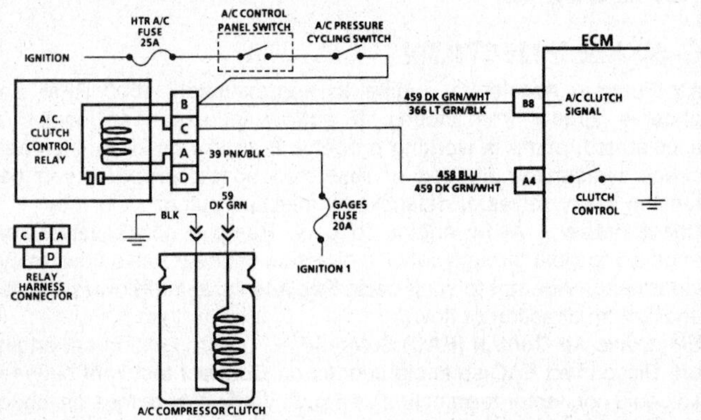
HTR A/C
FUSE
25A
A/C CONTROL
PANEL SWITCH
A/C PRESSURE
CYCLING SWITCH
IGNITION
ECM
A. C.
CLUTCH
CONTROL
RELAY
B
C
A
D
459 DK GRN/WHT
366 LT GRN/BLK
B8
A/C CLUTCH
SIGNAL
39 PNK/BLK
458 BLU
459 DK GRN/WHT
A4
CLUTCH
CONTROL
59
DK GRN
BLK
GAGES
FUSE
20A
IGNITION 1
RELAY
HARNESS
CONNECTOR
A/C COMPRESSOR CLUTCH

90C15745 Courtesy of General Motors Corp.

Fig. 10: A/C Clutch Circuit (2.5L)

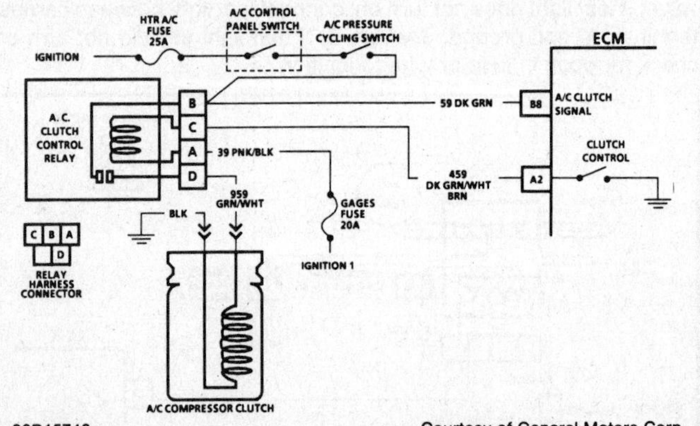
HTR A/C
FUSE
25A
A/C CONTROL
PANEL SWITCH
A/C PRESSURE
CYCLING SWITCH
IGNITION
ECM
A. C.
CLUTCH
CONTROL
RELAY
B
C
A
D
59 DK GRN
B8
A/C CLUTCH
SIGNAL
CLUTCH
CONTROL
39 PNK/BLK
459
DK GRN/WHT
BRN
A2
959
GRN/WHT
BLK
GAGES
FUSE
20A
IGNITION 1
RELAY
HARNESS
CONNECTOR
A/C COMPRESSOR CLUTCH

90D15746 Courtesy of General Motors Corp.

Fig. 11: A/C Clutch Circuit (2.8L & 4.3L "S" & "T" Series)

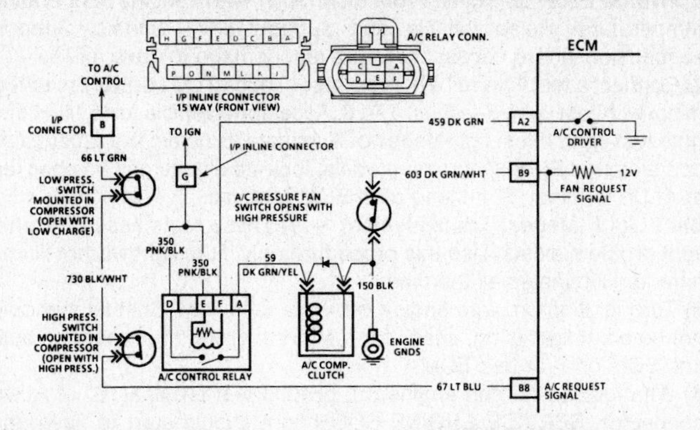

A/C RELAY CONN.
ECM
TO A/C CONTROL
I/P INLINE CONNECTOR 15 WAY (FRONT VIEW)
I/P CONNECTOR
TO IGN
I/P INLINE CONNECTOR
459 DK GRN
A2
A/C CONTROL DRIVER
66 LT GRN
603 DK GRN/WHT
B9
12V
FAN REQUEST SIGNAL
LOW PRESS. SWITCH MOUNTED IN COMPRESSOR (OPEN WITH LOW CHARGE)
A/C PRESSURE FAN SWITCH OPENS WITH HIGH PRESSURE
350 PNK/BLK
59 DK GRN/YEL
730 BLK/WHT
150 BLK
HIGH PRESS. SWITCH MOUNTED IN COMPRESSOR (OPEN WITH HIGH PRESS.)
ENGINE GNDS
A/C CONTROL RELAY
A/C COMP. CLUTCH
67 LT BLU
B8
A/C REQUEST SIGNAL

91C13724 Courtesy of General Motors Corp.

Fig. 12: A/C Clutch Circuit (3.1L)

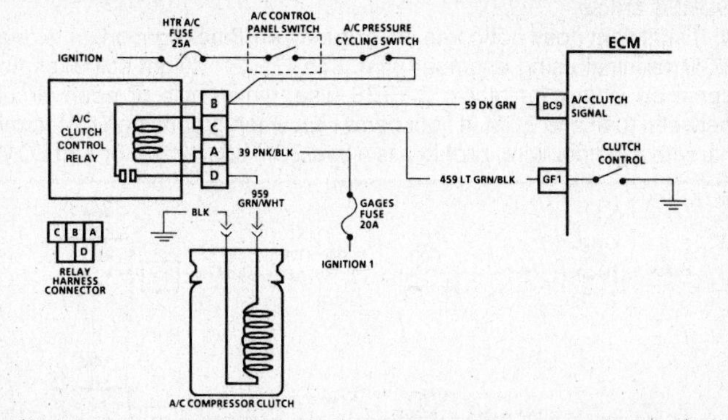

HTR A/C FUSE 25A
A/C CONTROL PANEL SWITCH
A/C PRESSURE CYCLING SWITCH
IGNITION
ECM
A/C CLUTCH CONTROL RELAY
59 DK GRN
BC9
A/C CLUTCH SIGNAL
39 PNK/BLK
CLUTCH CONTROL
459 LT GRN/BLK
GF1
BLK
959 GRN/WHT
GAGES FUSE 20A
RELAY HARNESS CONNECTOR
IGNITION 1
A/C COMPRESSOR CLUTCH

91D13725 Courtesy of General Motors Corp.

Fig. 13: A/C Clutch Circuit (4.3L Turbo PFI)

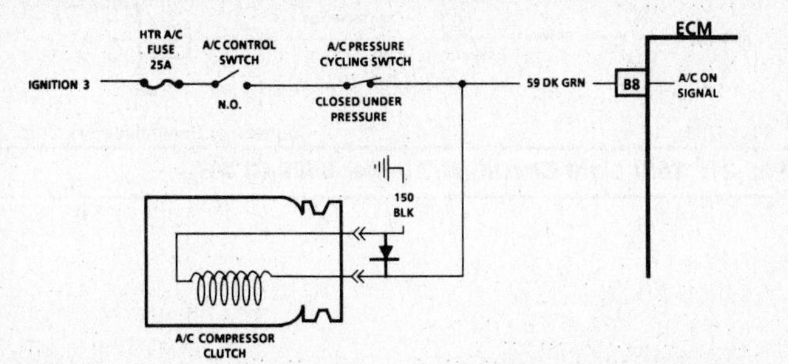

ECM
HTR A/C FUSE 25A
A/C CONTROL SWITCH
A/C PRESSURE CYCLING SWTCH
IGNITION 3
N.O.
CLOSED UNDER PRESSURE
59 DK GRN
B8
A/C ON SIGNAL
150 BLK
A/C COMPRESSOR CLUTCH

90F15748 Courtesy of General Motors Corp.

Fig. 14: A/C Clutch Circuit (4.3L M/T & 4.3L & V8 without 4L80-E Transmission)

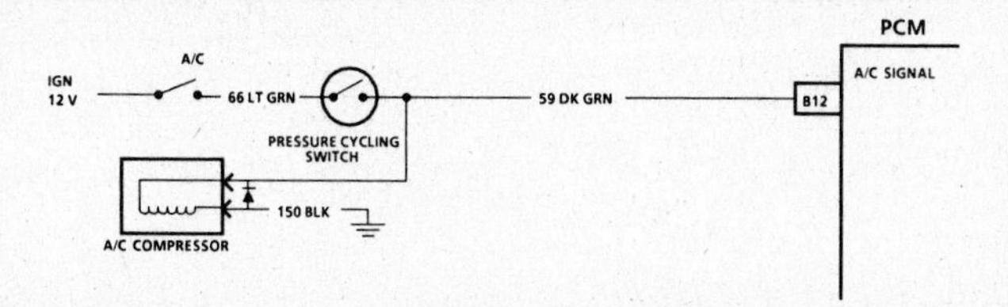

PCM
A/C
IGN 12 V
66 LT GRN
59 DK GRN
A/C SIGNAL
B12
PRESSURE CYCLING SWITCH
150 BLK
A/C COMPRESSOR

91E13726 Courtesy of General Motors Corp.

Fig. 15: A/C Clutch Circuit (4.3L & V8 with 4L80-E Transmission)

C-12, COOLING FAN (3.1L ONLY)

NOTE: For additional information on electric cooling fans, see ELECTRIC COOLING FANS article in ENGINE COOLING.

Cooling Fan Relay - 1) Disconnect cooling fan relay harness connector. Using an ohmmeter, check continuity of relay winding. *See Fig. 16.* Continuity should exist. Check continuity across power delivery terminals of relay. With relay not energized, no continuity should exist.

2) With ohmmeter still attached to power delivery terminals of relay, apply battery voltage and ground to energize relay winding. Continuity should now be present between cooling fan relay power delivery terminals. Replace cooling fan relay if readings are not as specified.

Cooling Fan Motor - Disconnect cooling fan motor harness connector. Apply battery voltage to one of the fan motor terminals and jumper the other terminal to ground. Fan motor should activate. If fan motor does not activate, replace faulty fan motor.

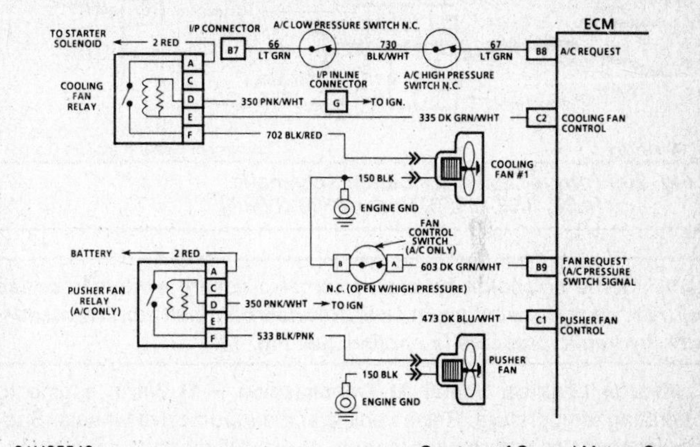

TO STARTER SOLENOID
2 RED
I/P CONNECTOR
A/C LOW PRESSURE SWITCH N.C.
ECM
B7
66 LT GRN
730 BLK/WHT
67 LT GRN
B8
A/C REQUEST
COOLING FAN RELAY
I/P INLINE CONNECTOR
A/C HIGH PRESSURE SWITCH N.C.
350 PNK/WHT
TO IGN.
335 DK GRN/WHT
C2
COOLING FAN CONTROL
702 BLK/RED
COOLING FAN #1
150 BLK
ENGINE GND
FAN CONTROL SWITCH (A/C ONLY)
BATTERY
2 RED
603 DK GRN/WHT
B9
FAN REQUEST (A/C PRESSURE SWITCH SIGNAL
PUSHER FAN RELAY (A/C ONLY)
N.C. (OPEN W/HIGH PRESSURE)
350 PNK/WHT
TO IGN
473 DK BLU/WHT
C1
PUSHER FAN CONTROL
533 BLK/PNK
PUSHER FAN
150 BLK
ENGINE GND

91H05548 Courtesy of General Motors Corp.

Fig. 16: Cooling Fan Schematic (3.1L)

C-8, TRANSMISSION

Torque Converter Clutch (TCC) Solenoid - Disconnect harness connector to TCC solenoid. Measure resistance between TCC solenoid terminals "A" and "D". *See Figs. 17-20.* Solenoid resistance should be greater than 20 ohms.

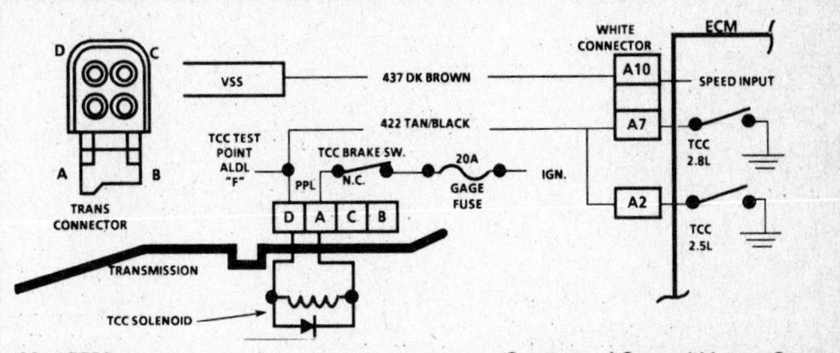

WHITE CONNECTOR
ECM
VSS
437 DK BROWN
A10
SPEED INPUT
422 TAN/BLACK
A7
TCC TEST POINT ALDL "F"
TCC BRAKE SW.
N.C.
20A GAGE FUSE
IGN.
TCC 2.8L
PPL
A2
TCC 2.5L
TRANS CONNECTOR
TRANSMISSION
TCC SOLENOID

90A15750 Courtesy of General Motors Corp.

Fig. 17: Torque Converter Clutch Schematic (2.5L)

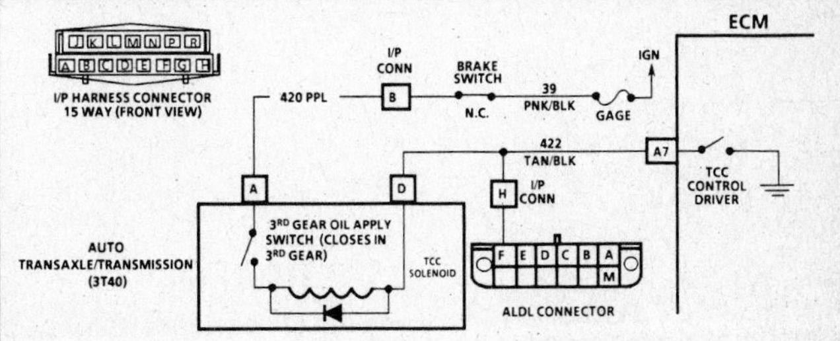

ECM
I/P HARNESS CONNECTOR 15 WAY (FRONT VIEW)
I/P CONN
BRAKE SWITCH
IGN
420 PPL
N.C.
39 PNK/BLK
GAGE
422 TAN/BLK
A7
TCC CONTROL DRIVER
I/P CONN
AUTO TRANSAXLE/TRANSMISSION (3T40)
3RD GEAR OIL APPLY SWITCH (CLOSES IN 3RD GEAR)
TCC SOLENOID
ALDL CONNECTOR

90C15752 Courtesy of General Motors Corp.

Fig. 18: Torque Converter Clutch Schematic (3.1L)

1991 ENGINE PERFORMANCE
System & Component Testing (Cont.)

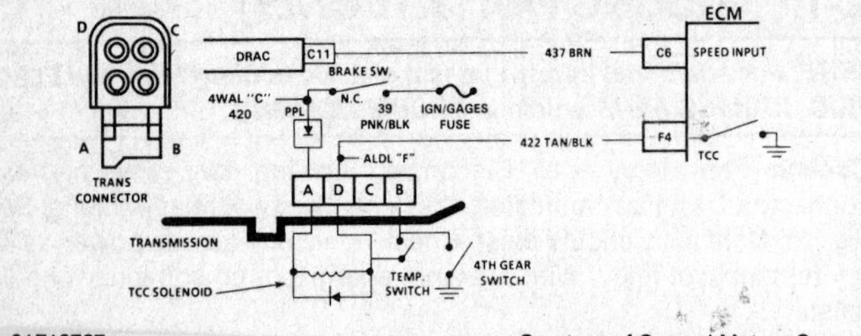
D
C
A
B
TRANS
CONNECTOR
DRAC
C11
BRAKE SW.
4WAL "C"
420
PPL
N.C.
39
PNK/BLK
IGN/GAGES
FUSE
437 BRN
C6
SPEED INPUT
ECM
422 TAN/BLK
F4
TCC
ALDL "F"
A
D
C
B
TRANSMISSION
TCC SOLENOID
TEMP.
SWITCH
4TH GEAR
SWITCH
91F13727
Courtesy of General Motors Corp.

Fig. 19: Torque Converter Clutch Schematic (4.3L Turbo PFI)

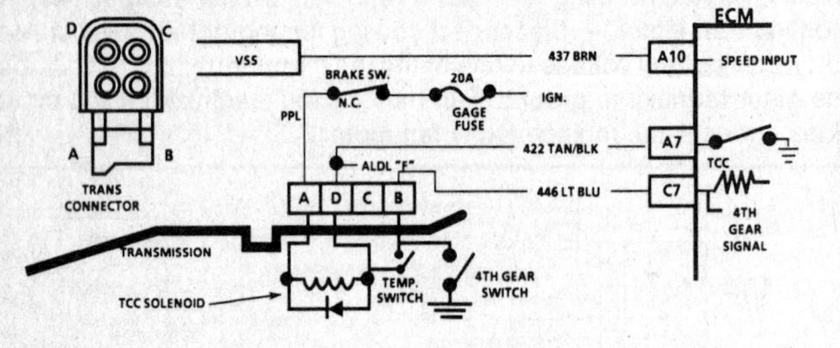
D
C
A
B
TRANS
CONNECTOR
VSS
BRAKE SW.
N.C.
PPL
20A
GAGE
FUSE
IGN.
437 BRN
A10
SPEED INPUT
ECM
422 TAN/BLK
A7
TCC
ALDL "F"
446 LT BLU
C7
4TH
GEAR
SIGNAL
A
D
C
B
TRANSMISSION
TCC SOLENOID
TEMP.
SWITCH
4TH GEAR
SWITCH
90B15751
Courtesy of General Motors Corp.

Fig. 20: Torque Converter Clutch Schematic (4.3L, 5.0L & 5.7L Under 8500 GVWR)

***NOTE:** Some solenoids have an internal pressure switch in series with the solenoid winding and will not show continuity until transmission hydraulic pressure is applied. See Fig. 18.*

Converter Lock-Up Signal At Transmission – 1) Warm engine to operating temperature. Raise vehicle and support drive wheels. Support suspension where necessary to prevent damage to drive axles.

2) Disconnect converter clutch connector at transmission. Connect a test light across terminals "A" and "D" of converter clutch harness. *See Figs. 17-20*. Start engine and place transmission in Drive. Accelerate vehicle to 45 MPH and note test light.

3) If test light is not on, check solenoid power supply wire of harness for open or short to ground. Check ground circuit for open between harness connector and ECM. If harness is okay, see CONVERTER LOCK-UP SIGNAL FROM ECM.

Converter Lock-Up Signal From ECM – 1) Warm engine to operating temperature. Raise vehicle and support drive wheels. Support suspension where necessary to prevent damage to drive axles.

2) Connect a test light to battery voltage. Touch TCC control driver terminal with test light. *See Figs. 17-20*. Accelerate vehicle to 45 MPH and note test light. If test light does not illuminate, problem is a faulty ECM connector or ECM. On some models, lock-up signal may be checked at ALDL terminal "F" instead of at ECM terminal.

Shift Light (Manual Transmission) – 1) These tests assume a shift light problem exists. Use this procedure only if the light will not illuminate, or illuminates all the time.

2) Turn ignition on, with engine off. Note shift light. Shift light should not be on. If light is on, check for a short to ground between the bulb and ECM or a for bad ECM.

3) With ignition on and engine off, ground test terminal "B" of ALDL connector. SERVICE ENGINE SOON light should start to flash and shift light should come on. If light comes on, go to next step. If SERVICE ENGINE SOON light does not flash, perform DIAGNOSTIC CIRCUIT CHECK as described in BASIC DIAGNOSTIC PROCEDURES article.

4) If shift light does not come on, ground Tan/Black light driver wire at ECM terminal using a jumper wire. *See Fig. 21*. If light still does not come on, check for blown GAGES fuse, blown bulb or open circuit between fuse and ECM. If light comes on when grounding ECM terminal with a jumper wire, problem is a bad ECM connection or bad ECM.

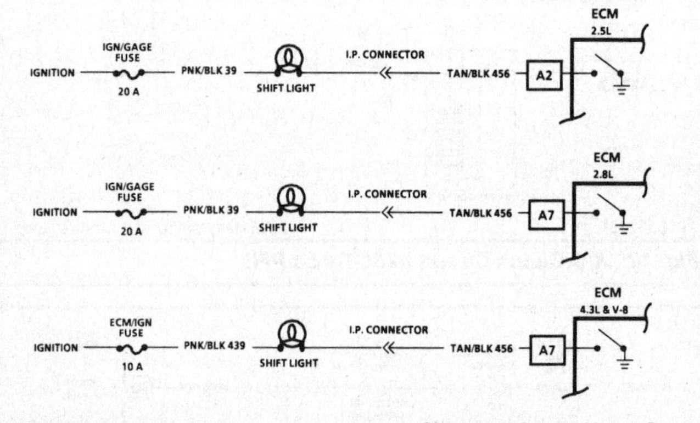
ECM
2.5L
IGNITION
IGN/GAGE
FUSE
20 A
PNK/BLK 39
SHIFT LIGHT
I.P. CONNECTOR
TAN/BLK 456
A2
ECM
2.8L
IGNITION
IGN/GAGE
FUSE
20 A
PNK/BLK 39
SHIFT LIGHT
I.P. CONNECTOR
TAN/BLK 456
A7
ECM
4.3L & V-8
IGNITION
ECM/IGN
FUSE
10 A
PNK/BLK 439
SHIFT LIGHT
I.P. CONNECTOR
TAN/BLK 456
A7
90D15753
Courtesy of General Motors Corp.

Fig. 21: Shift Light Circuit (M/T under 8500 GVWR)

COMPONENT LOCATIONS

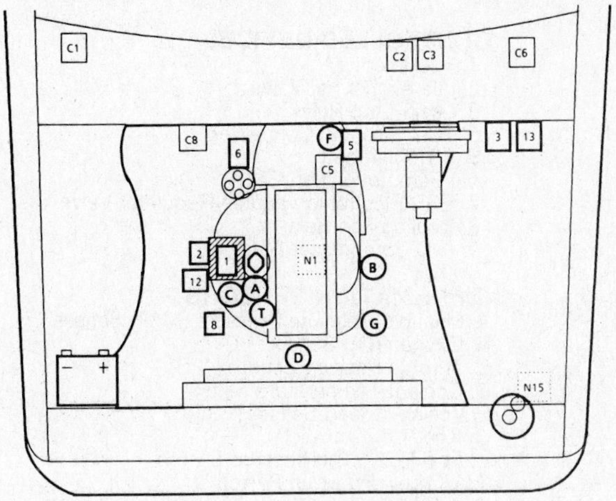

C1
C2
C3
C6
C8
6
F
5
C5
3
13
2
1
12
A
C
T
8
N1
B
G
D
N15

2.5L (VIN E) "S" SERIES

COMPUTER HARNESS
C1. Electronic Control Module (ECM)
C2. ALDL Diagnostic Connector
C3. SERVICE ENGINE SOON Light
C5. ECM Harness Ground
C6. Fuse Panel
C8. Fuel Pump Test Connector

CONTROLLED DEVICES
1. Fuel Injector
2. Idle Air Control Valve
3. Fuel Pump Relay
5. TCC Solenoid Connector
6. EST Distributor
8. Oil Pressure Switch
12. EGR Solenoid
13. A/C Compressor Relay

INFORMATION SENSORS
A. Manifold Absolute Pressure (MAP) Sensor
B. Oxygen (O_2) Sensor
C. Throttle Position Sensor (TPS)
D. Coolant Temperature Sensor
F. Vehicle Speed Sensor (VSS)
G. Power Steering Pressure Switch (PSPS)
T. Manifold Air Temperature (MAT) Sensor

EMISSIONS SYSTEMS (Not ECM Controlled)
N1. PCV Valve
N15. Fuel Vapor Canister

91J12186

Courtesy of General Motors Corp.

Fig. 22: Component Location for 2.5L (VIN E) "S" Series

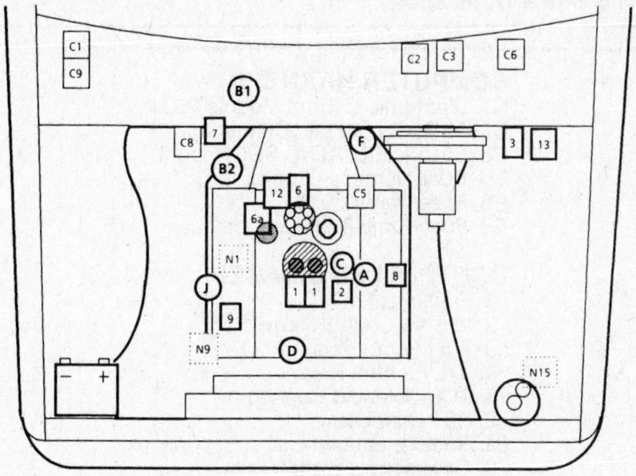

C1
C9
C2
C3
C6
B1
C8
7
F
3
13
B2
12
6
C5
6a
N1
C
A
8
1
1
2
J
9
N9
D
N15

2.8L (VIN R) "S" SERIES

COMPUTER HARNESS
C1. Electronic Control Module (ECM)
C2. ALDL Diagnostic Connector
C3. SERVICE ENGINE SOON Light
C5. ECM Harness Ground
C6. Fuse Panel
C8. Fuel Pump Test Connector
C9. Elapsed Timer Module

CONTROLLED DEVICES
1. Fuel Injector
2. Idle Air Control Valve
3. Fuel Pump Relay
6. EST Distributor
6a. Remote Ignition Coil
7. ESC Module
8. Oil Pressure Switch
9. ECA Solenoid
12. EGR Solenoid
13. A/C Compressor Relay

INFORMATION SENSORS
A. Manifold Absolute Pressure (MAP) Sensor
B1. Oxygen (O_2) Sensor (Federal)
B2. Oxygen (O_2) Sensor (California)
C. Throttle Position Sensor (TPS)
D. Coolant Temperature Sensor
F. Vehicle Speed Sensor (VSS)
J. Knock Sensor

EMISSIONS SYSTEMS (Not ECM Controlled)
N1. PCV Valve
N9. Air Pump
N15. Fuel Vapor Canister

91A12187

Courtesy of General Motors Corp.

Fig. 23: Component Location for 2.8L (VIN R) "S" Series

1991 ENGINE PERFORMANCE
System & Component Testing (Cont.)

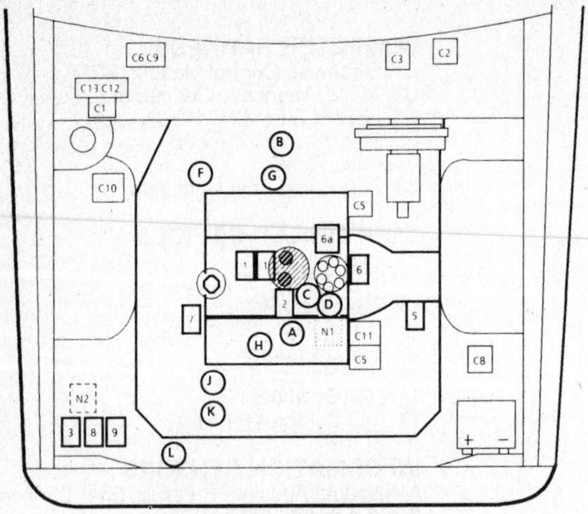

3.1L (VIN D) "U" SERIES

COMPUTER HARNESS
C1. Electronic Control Module (ECM)
C2. ALDL Diagnostic Connector
C3. SERVICE ENGINE SOON Light
C5. ECM Harness Ground
C6. Fuse Panel
C8. Fuel Pump Test Connector
C9. ECM/Fuel Pump Power Fuse
C10. Set Timing Connector
C11. Engine Grounds
C12. ESC Module
C13. VSS Buffer

CONTROLLED DEVICES
1. Fuel Injector
2. Idle Air Control Valve
3. Fuel Pump Relay
5. TCC Solenoid Connector
6. EST Distributor
6a. Remote Ignition Coil
7. EGR Electronic Vacuum Regulator Valve
8. Cooling Fan Relay
9. A/C Compressor Relay

INFORMATION SENSORS
A. Manifold Absolute Pressure (MAP) Sensor
B. Oxygen (O_2) Sensor
C. Throttle Position Sensor (TPS)
D. Coolant Temperature Sensor
F. Vehicle Speed Sensor (VSS)
G. Knock Sensor
H. Fuel Pump/Oil Pressure Switch
J. A/C Low Pressure Switch
K. A/C High Pressure Switch
L. Intermediate Pressure A/C Fan Switch

EMISSIONS SYSTEMS
(Not ECM Controlled)
N1. PCV Valve
N2. Fuel Vapor Canister

90H15757 Courtesy of General Motors Corp.

Fig. 24: Component Location for 3.1L (VIN D) "U" Series (Lumina APV, Silhouette & Trans Sport)

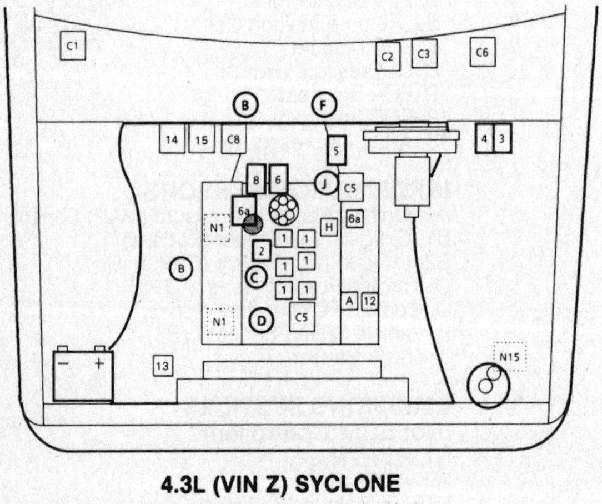

4.3L (VIN Z) SYCLONE

COMPUTER HARNESS
C1. Electronic Control Module (ECM)
C2. ALDL Diagnostic Connector
C3. SERVICE ENGINE SOON Light
C5. ECM Harness Ground
C6. Fuse Panel
C8. Fuel Pump Test Connector

CONTROLLED DEVICES
1. Fuel Injector
2. Idle Air Control Valve
3. Fuel Pump Relay
4. A/C Control Relay
5. TCC Solenoid Connector
6. EST Distributor
6a. Remote Ignition Coil
8. Oil Pressure Switch
12. EGR Solenoid or EVRV
13. Wastegate Solenoid
14. Turbo Boost Cut-Out Relay
15. Charge Air Cooler Pump Control Relay

INFORMATION SENSORS
A. Manifold Absolute Pressure (MAP) Sensor
B. Oxygen (O_2) Sensor
C. Throttle Position Sensor (TPS)
D. Coolant Temperature Sensor
F. Vehicle Speed Sensor (VSS)
H. Manifold Air Temperature (MAT) Sensor
J. Knock Sensor

EMISSIONS SYSTEMS
(Not ECM Controlled)
N1. PCV Valve
N15. Fuel Vapor Canister

91I13720 Courtesy of General Motors Corp.

Fig. 25: Component Location for 4.3L (VIN Z) Syclone

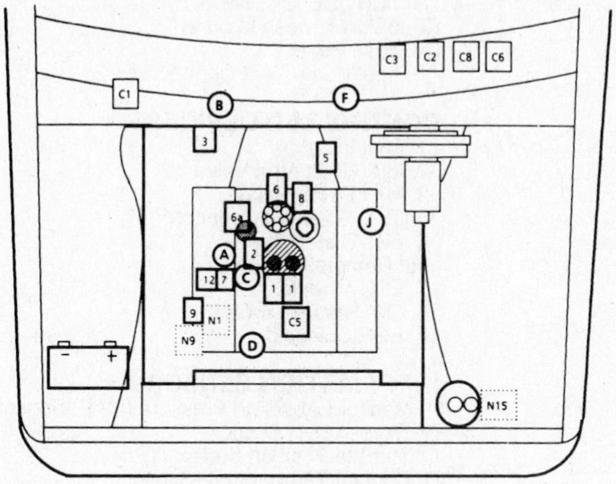

C1
C2
C3
C5
C6
C8
N1
N9
N15

4.3L (VIN Z) "C" & "K" SERIES

COMPUTER HARNESS
C1. Electronic Control Module (ECM)
C2. ALDL Diagnostic Connector
C3. SERVICE ENGINE SOON Light
C5. ECM Harness Ground
C6. Fuse Panel
C8. Fuel Pump Test Connector

CONTROLLED DEVICES
1. Fuel Injector
2. Idle Air Control Valve
3. Fuel Pump Relay
5. TCC Solenoid Connector
6. EST Distributor
6a. Remote Ignition Coil
7. ESC Module
8. Oil Pressure Switch
9. Electric Air Control (EAC) Solenoid
12. EGR Solenoid

INFORMATION SENSORS
A. Manifold Absolute Pressure (MAP) Sensor
B. Oxygen (O_2) Sensor
C. Throttle Position Sensor (TPS)
D. Coolant Temperature Sensor
F. Vehicle Speed Sensor (VSS)
J. Knock Sensor

EMISSIONS SYSTEMS
(Not ECM Controlled)
N1. PCV Valve
N9. Air Pump
N15. Fuel Vapor Canister

90I15758

Courtesy of General Motors Corp.

Fig. 26: Component Location for 4.3L (VIN Z) "C" & "K" Series

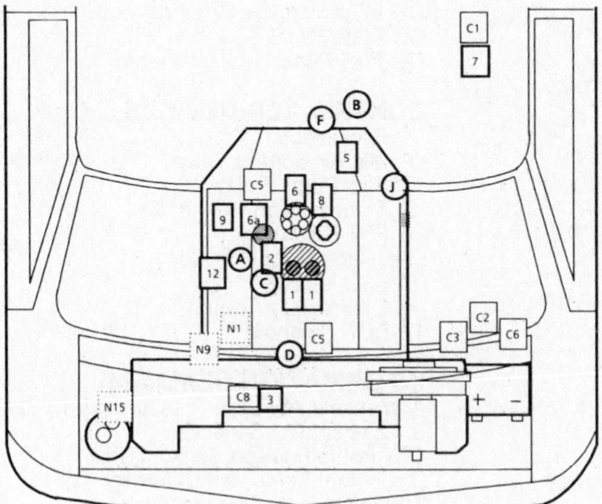

C1
C2
C3
C5
C6
C8
N1
N9
N15

4.3L (VIN Z) "G" SERIES

COMPUTER HARNESS
C1. Electronic Control Module (ECM)
C2. ALDL Diagnostic Connector
C3. SERVICE ENGINE SOON Light
C5. ECM Harness Ground
C6. Fuse Panel
C8. Fuel Pump Test Connector

CONTROLLED DEVICES
1. Fuel Injector
2. Idle Air Control Valve
3. Fuel Pump Relay
5. TCC Solenoid Connector
6. EST Distributor
6a. Remote Ignition Coil
7. ESC Module
8. Oil Pressure Switch
9. Electric Air Control (EAC) Solenoid
12. EGR Solenoid

INFORMATION SENSORS
A. Manifold Absolute Pressure (MAP) Sensor
B. Oxygen (O_2) Sensor
C. Throttle Position Sensor (TPS)
D. Coolant Temperature Sensor
F. Vehicle Speed Sensor (VSS)
J. Knock Sensor

EMISSIONS SYSTEMS
(Not ECM Controlled)
N1. PCV Valve
N9. Air Pump
N15. Fuel Vapor Canister

91E12132

Courtesy of General Motors Corp.

Fig. 27: Component Location for 4.3L (VIN Z) "G" Series

1991 ENGINE PERFORMANCE
System & Component Testing (Cont.)

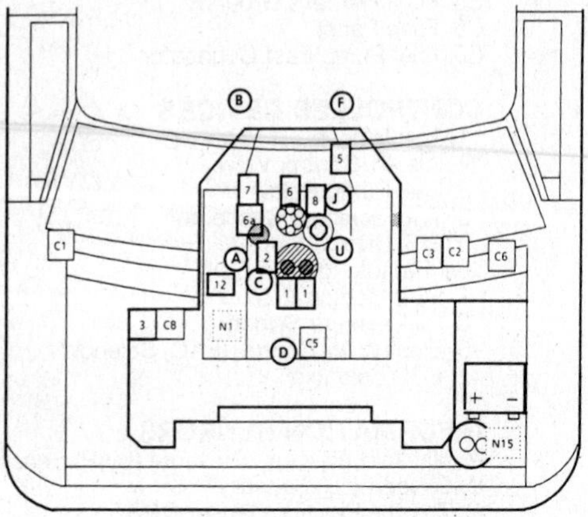
B
F
5
7
6
8
J
6a
2
A
U
C
12
1
1
C1
C3
C2
C6
3
C8
N1
D
C5
+
−
N15

4.3L (VIN Z) "L" & "M" SERIES

COMPUTER HARNESS
C1. Electronic Control Module (ECM)
C2. ALDL Diagnostic Connector
C3. SERVICE ENGINE SOON Light
C5. ECM Harness Ground
C6. Fuse Panel
C8. Fuel Pump Test Connector

CONTROLLED DEVICES
1. Fuel Injector
2. Idle Air Control Valve
3. Fuel Pump Relay
5. TCC Solenoid Connector
6. EST Distributor
6a. Remote Ignition Coil
7. ESC Module
8. Oil Pressure Switch
12. EGR Solenoid

INFORMATION SENSORS
A. Manifold Absolute Pressure (MAP) Sensor
B. Oxygen (O_2) Sensor
C. Throttle Position Sensor (TPS)
D. Coolant Temperature Sensor
F. Vehicle Speed Sensor (VSS)
J. Knock Sensor

EMISSIONS SYSTEMS
(Not ECM Controlled)
N1. PCV Valve
N15. Fuel Vapor Canister

91D12099

Courtesy of General Motors Corp.

Fig. 28: Component Location for 4.3L (VIN Z) "L" & "M" Series (Astro & Safari)

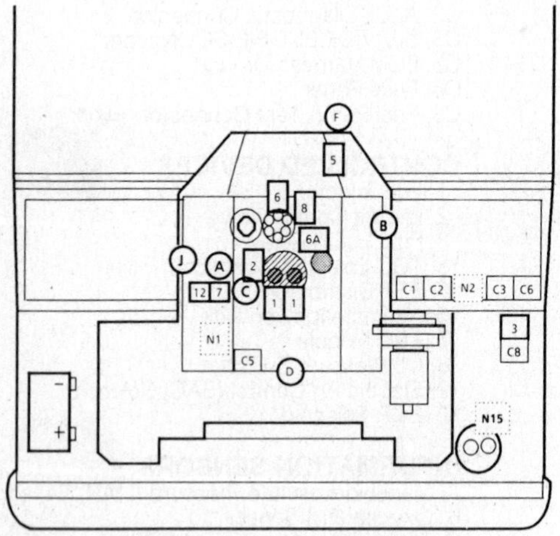
F
5
6
8
6A
B
J
A
2
C
12
7
1
1
C1
C2
N2
C3
C6
N1
C5
D
3
C8
N15
−
+

4.3L (VIN Z) "P" SERIES

COMPUTER HARNESS
C1. Electronic Control Module (ECM)
C2. ALDL Diagnostic Connector
C3. SERVICE ENGINE SOON Light
C5. ECM Harness Ground
C6. Fuse Panel
C8. Fuel Pump Test Connector

CONTROLLED DEVICES
1. Fuel Injector
2. Idle Air Control Valve
3. Fuel Pump Relay
5. Transmission Connector
6. EST Distributor
6a. Remote Ignition Coil
7. ESC Module
8. Oil Pressure Switch
12. EGR Solenoid

INFORMATION SENSORS
A. Manifold Absolute Pressure (MAP) Sensor
B. Oxygen (O_2) Sensor
C. Throttle Position Sensor (TPS)
D. Coolant Temperature Sensor
F. Vehicle Speed Sensor (VSS)
J. Knock Sensor

EMISSIONS SYSTEMS
(Not ECM Controlled)
N1. PCV Valve
N2. Fuel Module
N15. Fuel Vapor Canister

91B13723

Courtesy of General Motors Corp.

Fig. 29: Component Location for 4.3L (VIN Z) "P" Series

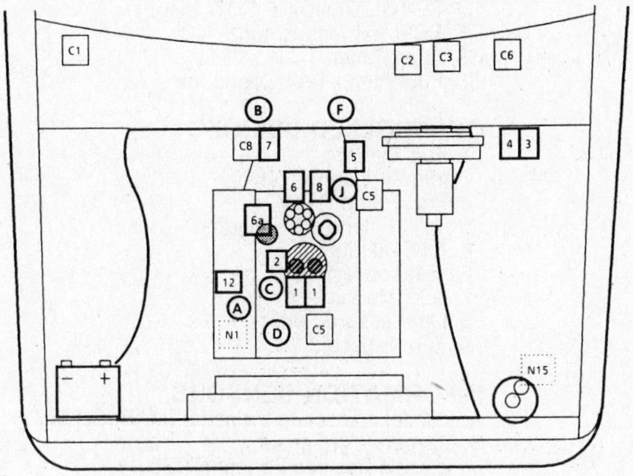

C1
C2
C3
C6
B
F
C8
7
5
4
3
6
8
J
C5
6a
2
12
C
1
1
A
N1
D
C5
N15

4.3L (VIN Z) "S" & "T" SERIES

COMPUTER HARNESS
C1. Electronic Control Module (ECM)
C2. ALDL Diagnostic Connector
C3. SERVICE ENGINE SOON Light
C5. ECM Harness Ground
C6. Fuse Panel
C8. Fuel Pump Test Connector

CONTROLLED DEVICES
1. Fuel Injector
2. Idle Air Control Valve
3. Fuel Pump Relay
4. A/C Compressor Relay
5. TCC Solenoid Connector
6. EST Distributor
6a. Remote Ignition Coil
7. ESC Module
8. Oil Pressure Switch
12. EGR Solenoid Or EVRV

INFORMATION SENSORS
A. Manifold Absolute Pressure (MAP) Sensor
B. Oxygen (O_2) Sensor
C. Throttle Position Sensor (TPS)
D. Coolant Temperature Sensor
F. Vehicle Speed Sensor (VSS)
J. Knock Sensor

EMISSIONS SYSTEMS
(Not ECM Controlled)
N1. PCV Valve
N15. Fuel Vapor Canister

91B12188

Courtesy of General Motors Corp.

Fig. 30: Component Location for 4.3L (VIN Z) "S" & "T" Series

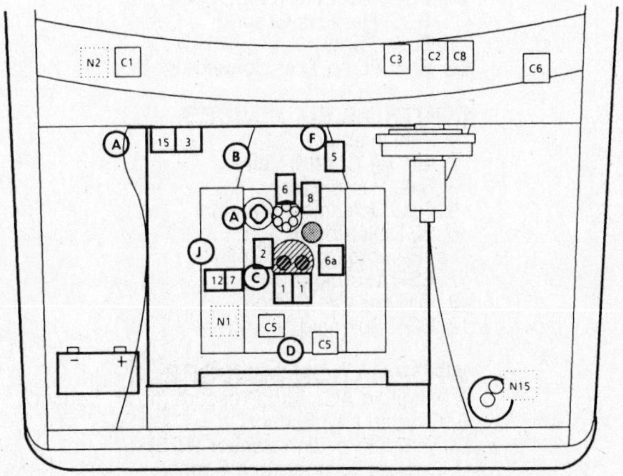

N2
C1
C3
C2
C8
C6
A
15
3
B
F
5
6
8
A
J
2
6a
12
7
C
1
1
N1
C5
D
C5
N15

5.0L (VIN H) & 5.7L (VIN K) "C" & "K" SERIES

COMPUTER HARNESS
C1. Electronic Control Module (ECM)
C2. ALDL Diagnostic Connector
C3. SERVICE ENGINE SOON Light
C5. ECM Harness Ground
C6. Fuse Panel
C8. Fuel Pump Test Connector

CONTROLLED DEVICES
1. Fuel Injector
2. Idle Air Control Valve
3. Fuel Pump Relay
5. TCC Solenoid Connector
6. EST Distributor
6a. Remote Ignition Coil
8. Oil Pressure Switch
12. EGR Solenoid
15. Fuel Pump Fuse

INFORMATION SENSORS
A. Manifold Absolute Pressure (MAP) Sensor
B. Oxygen (O_2) Sensor
C. Throttle Position Sensor (TPS)
D. Coolant Temperature Sensor
F. Vehicle Speed Sensor (VSS)
J. Knock Sensor

EMISSIONS SYSTEMS
(Not ECM Controlled)
N1. PCV Valve
N2. Fuel Module (5.7L HD only)
N15. Fuel Vapor Canister

91G12100

Courtesy of General Motors Corp.

Fig. 31: Component Location for 5.0L (VIN H) & 5.7L (VIN K) "C" & "K" Series

1991 ENGINE PERFORMANCE
System & Component Testing (Cont.)

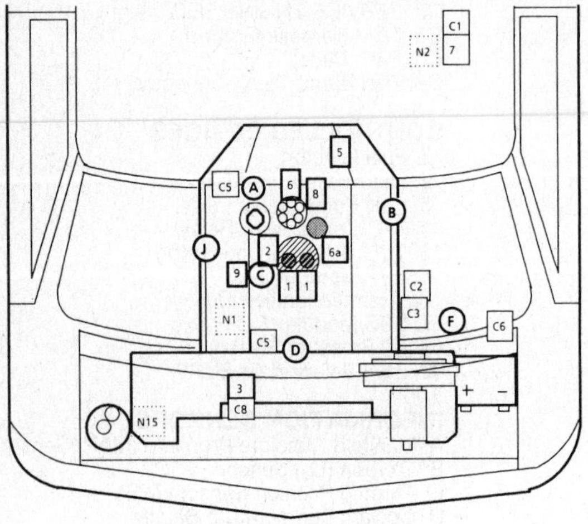
C1
N2
7
5
C5
A
6
8
B
J
2
6a
9
C
1
1
C2
C3
F
C6
N1
C5
D
3
C8
+
–
N15

5.7L (VIN K) "G" SERIES

COMPUTER HARNESS
C1. Electronic Control Module (ECM)
C2. ALDL Diagnostic Connector
C3. SERVICE ENGINE SOON Light
C5. ECM Harness Ground
C6. Fuse Panel
C8. Fuel Pump Test Connector

CONTROLLED DEVICES
1. Fuel Injector
2. Idle Air Control Valve
3. Fuel Pump Relay
5. TCC Solenoid Connector
6. EST Distributor
6a. Remote Ignition Coil
7. ESC Module
8. Oil Pressure Sensor
9. EGR Solenoid

INFORMATION SENSORS
A. Manifold Absolute Pressure (MAP) Sensor
B. Oxygen (O_2) Sensor
C. Throttle Position Sensor (TPS)
D. Coolant Temperature Sensor
F. Vehicle Speed Sensor (VSS)
J. Knock Sensor

EMISSIONS SYSTEMS
(Not ECM Controlled)
N1. PCV Valve
N2. Fuel Module

91F12133

Courtesy of General Motors Corp.

Fig. 32: Component Location for 5.7L (VIN K) "G" Series

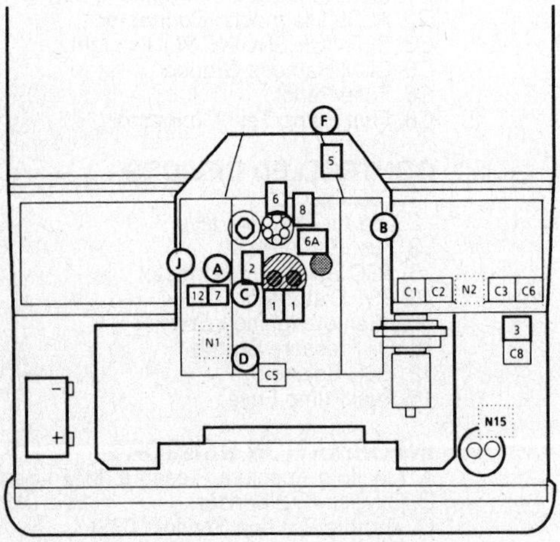
F
5
6
8
B
6A
J
A
2
12
7
C
C1
C2
N2
C3
C6
1
1
3
C8
N1
D
C5
–
+
N15

5.7L (VIN K) "P" SERIES

COMPUTER HARNESS
C1. Electronic Control Module (ECM)
C2. ALDL Diagnostic Connector
C3. SERVICE ENGINE SOON Light
C5. ECM Harness Ground
C6. Fuse Panel
C8. Fuel Pump Test Connector

CONTROLLED DEVICES
1. Fuel Injector
2. Idle Air Control Valve
3. Fuel Pump Relay
5. TCC Solenoid Connector
6. EST Distributor
6a. Remote Ignition Coil
7. ESC Module
8. Oil Pressure Switch
12. EGR Solenoid

INFORMATION SENSORS
A. Manifold Absolute Pressure (MAP) Sensor
B. Oxygen (O_2) Sensor
C. Throttle Position Sensor (TPS)
D. Coolant Temperature Sensor
F. Vehicle Speed Sensor (VSS)
J. Knock Sensor

EMISSIONS SYSTEMS
(Not ECM Controlled)
N1. PCV Valve
N2. Fuel Module
N15. Fuel Vapor Canister

91J13721

Courtesy of General Motors Corp.

Fig. 33: Component Location for 5.7L (VIN K) "P" Series

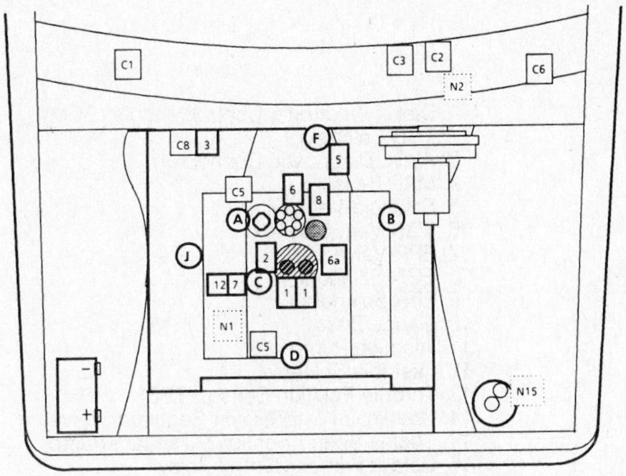

C1
C3
C2
C6
N2
C8
3
F
5
C5
6
8
A
B
J
2
6a
12
7
C
1
1
N1
C5
D
N15

5.7L (VIN K) "R" & "V" SERIES

COMPUTER HARNESS
C1. Electronic Control Module (ECM)
C2. ALDL Diagnostic Connector
C3. SERVICE ENGINE SOON Light
C5. ECM Harness Ground
C6. Fuse Panel
C8. Fuel Pump Test Connector

CONTROLLED DEVICES
1. Fuel Injector
2. Idle Air Control Valve
3. Fuel Pump Relay
5. TCC Solenoid Connector
6. EST Distributor
6a. Remote Ignition Coil
7. ESC Module
8. Oil Pressure Switch
12. EGR Solenoid

INFORMATION SENSORS
A. Manifold Absolute Pressure (MAP) Sensor
B. Oxygen (O_2) Sensor
C. Throttle Position Sensor (TPS)
D. Coolant Temperature Sensor
F. Vehicle Speed Sensor (VSS)
J. Knock Sensor

EMISSIONS SYSTEMS
(Not ECM Controlled)
N1. PCV Valve
N2. Fuel Module (5.7L HD only)
N15. Fuel Vapor Canister

91E12181

Courtesy of General Motors Corp.

Fig. 34: Component Location for 5.7L (VIN K) "R" & "V" Series

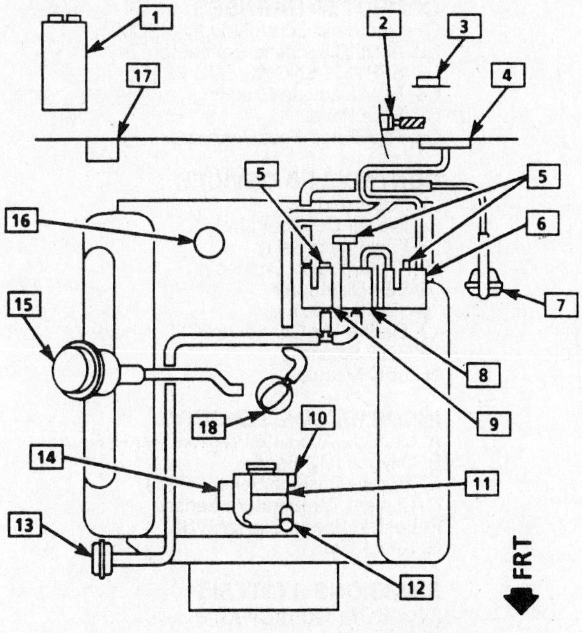

1
2
3
17
4
5
5
16
6
15
7
8
18
10
9
14
11
13
12
FRT

6.2L (VIN C) DIESEL "C" & "K" SERIES

1. Diesel Electronic Control Module (DCM)
2. TCC Solenoid
3. ALDL Diagnostic Connector
4. MAP Sensor
5. Solenoid Vent/Filter
6. EGR Vent Solenoid
7. EPR Valve
8. EGR Solenoid
9. EPR Solenoid
10. Gauge Boss
11. Injection Pump
12. Fast Idle Solenoid
13. Vacuum Pump
14. Throttle Position Sensor (TPS)
15. Crankcase Depression Regulator Valve
16. Engine Speed Sensor
17. Cold Advance Control Relay
18. EGR Valve

91I12102

Courtesy of General Motors Corp.

Fig. 35: Component Location for 6.2L (VIN C) DIESEL "C" & "K" Series

1991 ENGINE PERFORMANCE
System & Component Testing (Cont.)

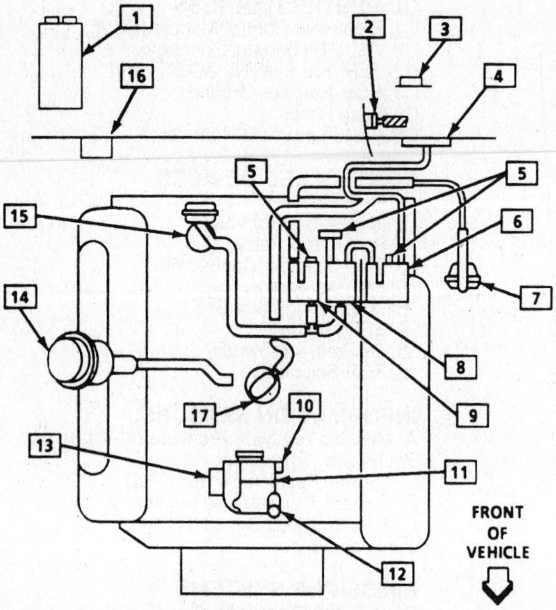
1
2
3
4
16
5
5
15
6
7
14
8
17
10
9
13
11
12
FRONT OF VEHICLE

6.2L (VIN C) DIESEL "R" & "V" SERIES

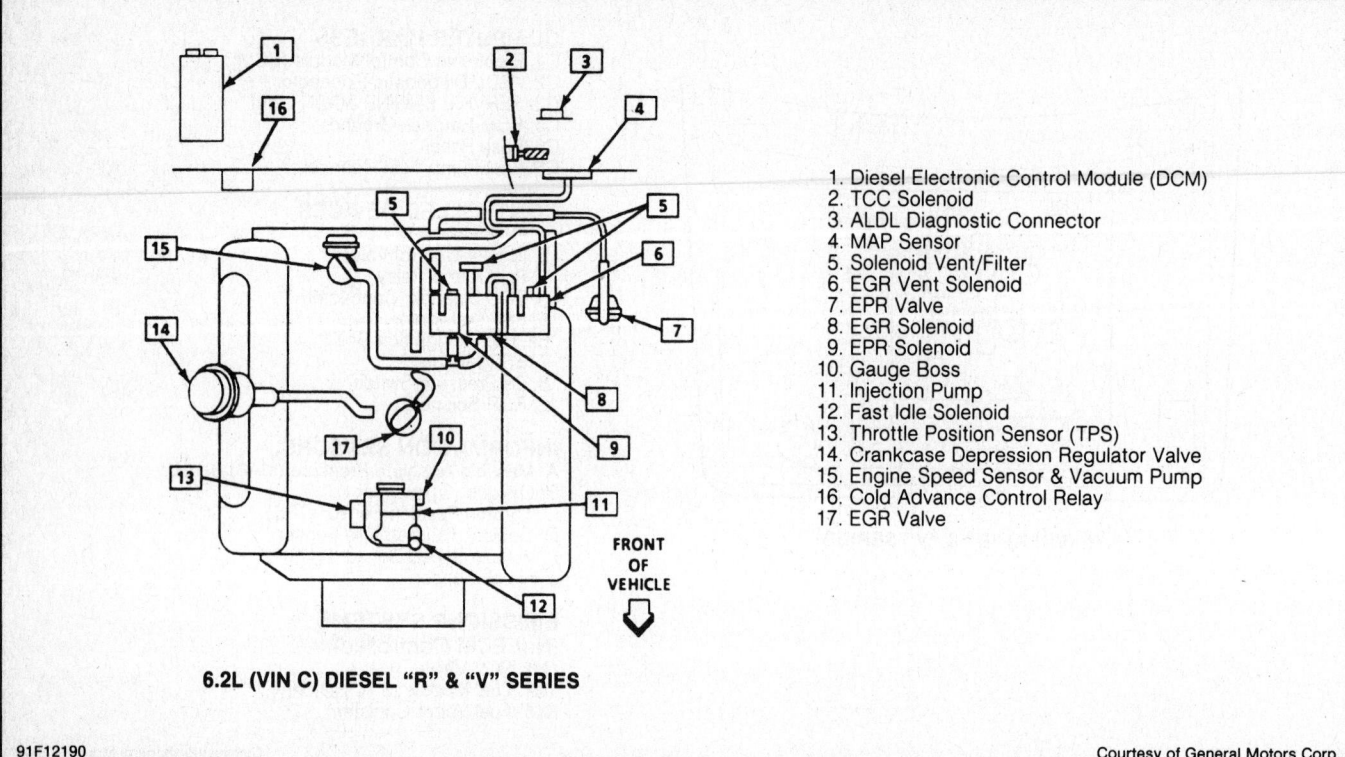

1. Diesel Electronic Control Module (DCM)
2. TCC Solenoid
3. ALDL Diagnostic Connector
4. MAP Sensor
5. Solenoid Vent/Filter
6. EGR Vent Solenoid
7. EPR Valve
8. EGR Solenoid
9. EPR Solenoid
10. Gauge Boss
11. Injection Pump
12. Fast Idle Solenoid
13. Throttle Position Sensor (TPS)
14. Crankcase Depression Regulator Valve
15. Engine Speed Sensor & Vacuum Pump
16. Cold Advance Control Relay
17. EGR Valve

91F12190

Courtesy of General Motors Corp.

Fig. 36: Component Location for 6.2L (VIN C) DIESEL "R" & "V" Series

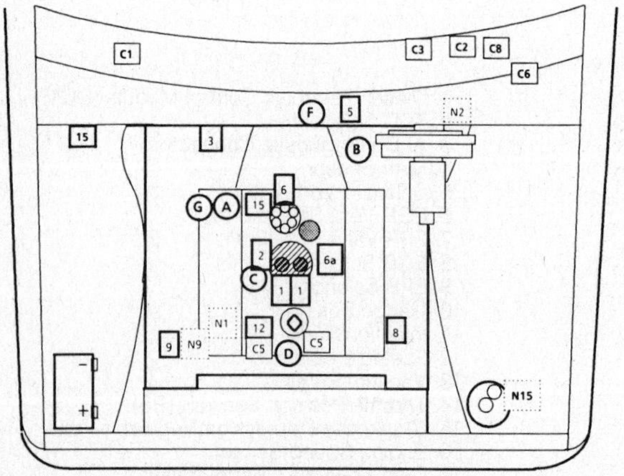
C1
C3
C2
C8
C6
F
5
N2
15
3
B
6
G
A
15
2
6a
C
1
1
N1
12
C5
8
9
N9
C5
D
N15

7.4L (VIN N) "C/K" SERIES

COMPUTER HARNESS
C1. Electronic Control Module (ECM)
C2. ALDL Diagnostic Connector
C3. SERVICE ENGINE SOON Light
C5. ECM Harness Ground
C6. Fuse Panel
C8. Fuel Pump Test Connector

CONTROLLED DEVICES
1. Fuel Injector
2. Idle Air Control Valve
3. Fuel Pump Relay
5. Transmission Connector
6. EST Distributor
6a. Ignition Coil
9. Electric Air Control (EAC) Solenoid
12. EGR Solenoid
15. ESC Module

INFORMATION SENSORS
A. Manifold Absolute Pressure (MAP) Sensor
B. Oxygen (O_2) Sensor
C. Throttle Position Sensor (TPS)
D. Coolant Temperature Sensor
F. Vehicle Speed Sensor (VSS)
G. Knock Sensor

EMISSIONS SYSTEMS
(Not ECM Controlled)
N1. PCV Valve
N2. Fuel Module
N9. Air Pump
N15. Fuel Vapor Canister

91H12101

Courtesy of General Motors Corp.

Fig. 37: Component Location for 7.4L (VIN N) "C/K" Series

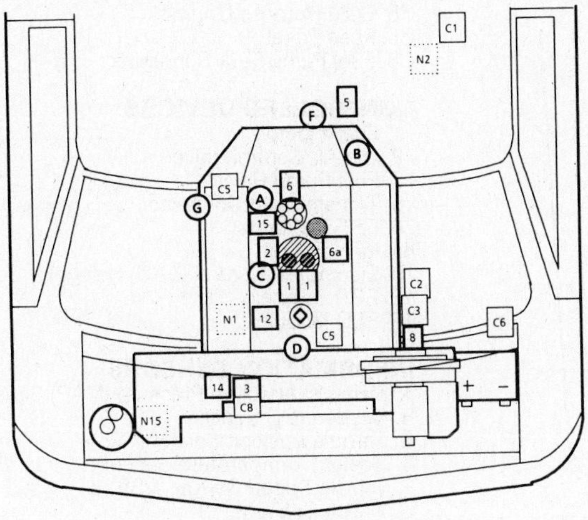
C1
N2
5
F
B
C5
6
G
A
15
2
6a
C
1
1
C2
C3
C6
N1
12
D
C5
8
14
3
C8
N15
+
−

7.4L (VIN N) "G" SERIES

COMPUTER HARNESS
C1. Electronic Control Module (ECM)
C2. ALDL Diagnostic Connector
C3. SERVICE ENGINE SOON Light
C5. ECM Harness Ground
C6. Fuse Panel
C8. Fuel Pump Test Connector

CONTROLLED DEVICES
1. Fuel Injector
2. Idle Air Control Valve
3. Fuel Pump Relay
5. Transmission Connector
6. EST Distributor
6a. Remote Ignition Coil
8. Oil Pressure Switch
12. EGR Solenoid
15. ESC Module

INFORMATION SENSORS
A. Manifold Absolute Pressure (MAP) Sensor
B. Oxygen (O_2) Sensor
C. Throttle Position Sensor (TPS)
D. Coolant Temperature Sensor
F. Vehicle Speed Sensor (VSS)
G. Knock Sensor

EMISSIONS SYSTEMS
(Not ECM Controlled)
N1. PCV Valve
N2. Fuel Module
N15. Fuel Vapor Canister

91G12134

Courtesy of General Motors Corp.

Fig. 38: Component Location for 7.4L (VIN N) "G" Series

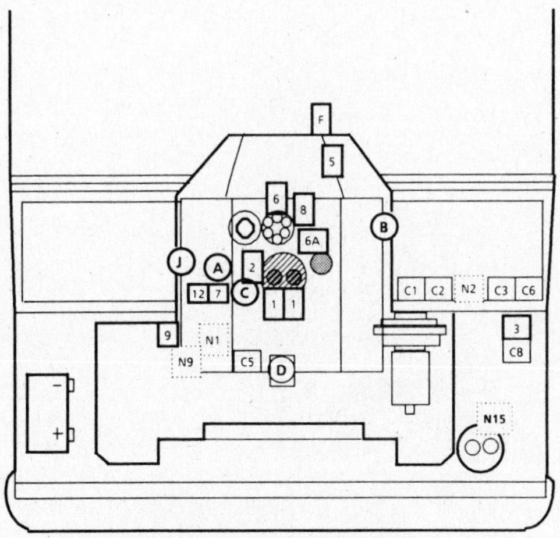
F
5
6
8
B
6A
J
A
2
12
7
C
1
1
C1
C2
N2
C3
C6
9
N1
3
C8
N9
C5
D
N15
−
+

7.4L (VIN N) "P" SERIES

COMPUTER HARNESS
C1. Electronic Control Module (ECM)
C2. ALDL Diagnostic Connector
C3. SERVICE ENGINE SOON Light
C5. ECM Harness Ground
C6. Fuse Panel
C8. Fuel Pump Test Connector

CONTROLLED DEVICES
1. Fuel Injector
2. Idle Air Control Valve
3. Fuel Pump Relay
5. Transmission Connector
6. EST Distributor
6a. Remote Ignition Coil
7. ESC Module
8. Oil Pressure Switch
9. Electric Air Control (EAC) Solenoid
12. EGR Solenoid

INFORMATION SENSORS
A. Manifold Absolute Pressure (MAP) Sensor
B. Oxygen (O_2) Sensor
C. Throttle Position Sensor (TPS)
D. Coolant Temperature Sensor
F. Vehicle Speed Sensor (VSS)
J. Knock Sensor

EMISSIONS SYSTEMS
(Not ECM Controlled)
N1. PCV Valve
N2. Fuel Module
N9. Air Pump
N15. Fuel Vapor Canister

91A13722

Courtesy of General Motors Corp.

Fig. 39: Component Location for 7.4L (VIN N) "P" Series

1991 ENGINE PERFORMANCE
System & Component Testing (Cont.)

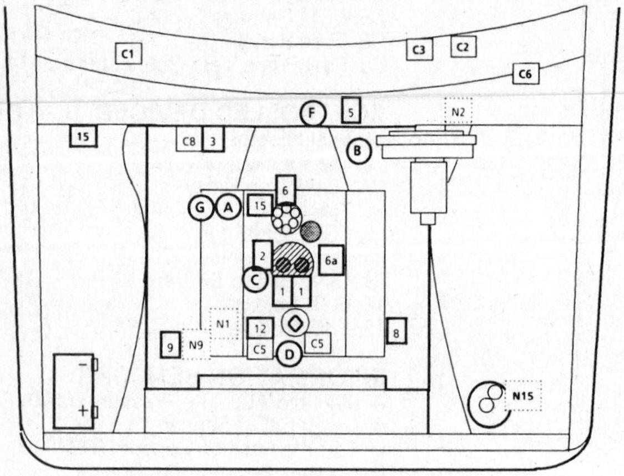
C1
C3
C2
C6
F
5
N2
15
C8
3
B
6
G
A
15
2
6a
C
1
1
N1
12
9
N9
C5
D
C5
8
N15

7.4L (VIN N) "R" & "V" SERIES

COMPUTER HARNESS
C1. Electronic Control Module (ECM)
C2. ALDL Diagnostic Connector
C3. SERVICE ENGINE SOON Light
C5. ECM Harness Ground
C6. Fuse Panel
C8. Fuel Pump Test Connector

CONTROLLED DEVICES
1. Fuel Injector
2. Idle Air Control Valve
3. Fuel Pump Relay
5. Transmission Connector
6. EST Distributor
6a. Ignition Coil
9. Electric Air Control (EAC) Solenoid
12. EGR Solenoid
15. ESC Module

INFORMATION SENSORS
A. Manifold Absolute Pressure (MAP) Sensor
B. Oxygen (O_2) Sensor
C. Throttle Position Sensor (TPS)
D. Coolant Temperature Sensor
F. Vehicle Speed Sensor (VSS)
G. Knock Sensor

EMISSIONS SYSTEMS
(Not ECM Controlled)
8. Oil Pressure Sending Unit/Switch
N1. PCV Valve
N2. Fuel Module
N9. Air Pump
N15. Fuel Vapor Canister

91C12189

Courtesy of General Motors Corp.

Fig. 40: Component Location for 7.4L (VIN N) "R" & "V" Series

1991 ENGINE PERFORMANCE
Pin Voltage Charts

Astro, Blazer, Bravada, Jimmy, Lumina APV, Safari, Sierra, Silhouette, Sonoma, Syclone, Trans Sport, "C" & "K" Series, "G" Series, "P" Series, "R" & "V" Series, "S" & "T" Series

NOTE: All voltage tests should be performed with a Digital Volt-Ohmmeter (DVOM) with a minimum 10-megohm input impedance, unless stated otherwise in testing procedures.

INTRODUCTION

PIN VOLTAGE CHARTS are supplied (when available) to reduce diagnostic time. Checking pin voltages at the electronic control unit determines if it is receiving and transmitting proper signals. Charts may also help determine if control unit harness is shorted or open.

NOTE:
This ECM voltage chart along with digital voltmeter can help save diagnosis time. Voltage readings may vary slightly depending on battery voltage and alternator output.

The following conditions must be met before testing:

- Engine at operating temperature.
- Engine in closed loop operation.
- Engine idling (Engine Run column).
- ALDL "test" terminal NOT grounded.
- Scan tester NOT installed.

PIN	PIN FUNCTION	CKT #	WIRE COLOR	NORMAL VOLTAGE	
				KEY "ON"	ENG RUN
A1	FUEL PUMP RELAY DRIVE	465	DK GRN/WHT	(1)	14
A2	SHIFT LIGHT (MT) TCC CONTROL (AT)	456 422	TAN/BLK	12	14
A3	EGR SOLENOID CONTROL	435	GRY	12	0
A4	A/C RELAY CONTROL	458 459	DK BLU BLU/WHT	(8)	(8)
A5	"SERVICE ENGINE SOON" LIGHT CONTROL	419	BRN/WHT	0	14
A6	IGN-ECM FUSE	439	PNK/BLK	12	14
A7	NOT USED				
A8	SERIAL DATA	461	ORN	(2)	(2)
A9	DIAGNOSTIC TEST TERMINAL	451	WHT/BLK	5	5
A10	SPEED SENSOR SIGNAL	437	BRN	(3)	(3)
A11	CTS & TPS SENSOR GROUND	452	BLK	0	0
A12	SYSTEM GROUND	450	BLK/WHT	0	0

PIN	PIN FUNCTION	CKT #	WIRE COLOR	NORMAL VOLTAGE	
				KEY "ON"	ENG RUN
B1	BATTERY 12 VOLTS	440	ORN	12	14
B2	FUEL PUMP SIGNAL	120	GRY TAN/WHT	(1)	14
B3	EST REFERENCE LOW	453	BLK/RED	0	0
B4	NOT USED				
B5	EST REFERENCE HIGH	430	PPL/WHT	0	1.6
B6	NOT USED				
B7	NOT USED				
B8	A/C SIGNAL	366 459	GRN/BLK GRN/WHT	(4)	(4)
B9	NOT USED				
B10	PARK/NEUTRAL SWITCH SIGNAL	434	ORN/BLK	(5)	(5)
B11	NOT USED				
B12	NOT USED				

(1) Battery voltage first two seconds
(2) Varies from 2 volts to 5 volts
(3) Varies from 0 to battery voltage depending on position of drive wheels.
(4) 0 volts A/C "OFF" battery voltage A/C "ON."
(5) 0 volts in neutral, battery voltage in gear
(6) Varies with temperature
(7) Varies
(8) 0 volts A/C "ON," battery voltage A/C "OFF"

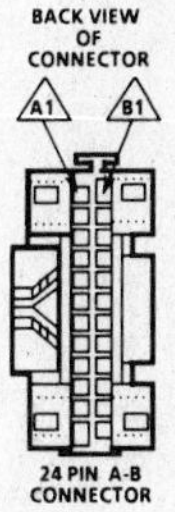
BACK VIEW OF CONNECTOR
A1
B1
24 PIN A-B CONNECTOR

PIN	PIN FUNCTION	CKT #	WIRE COLOR	NORMAL VOLTAGE	
				KEY "ON"	ENG RUN
C1	NOT USED				
C2	NOT USED				
C3	IAC "B" LOW	444	LT GRN/BLK	NOT	USABLE
C4	IAC "B" HIGH	443	LT GRN/WHT	NOT	USABLE
C5	IAC "A" HIGH	441	LT BLU/WHT	NOT	USABLE
C6	IAC "A" LOW	442	LT BLU/BLK	NOT	USABLE
C7	NOT USED				
C8	P/S SWITCH	495	BLU/ORN LT BLU	12.3	14.0
C9	CRANK SIGNAL	806	PPL PPL/WHT	(1)	0
C10	COOLANT TEMP SIGNAL	410	YEL	(2)	(2)
C11	MAP SIGNAL	432	LT GRN	4.7	1.0
C12	MAT SIGNAL	472	TAN	(2)	(2)
C13	TPS SIGNAL	417	DK BLU	(3)	6
C14	5 VOLT REF MAP & TPS	416	GRY	5	5
C15	NOT USED				
C16	BATTERY 12 VOLTS	440	ORN	12	14

PIN	PIN FUNCTION	CKT #	WIRE COLOR	NORMAL VOLTAGE	
				KEY "ON"	ENG RUN
D1	SYSTEM GROUND	450 551	BLK/WHT TAN/WHT	0	0
D2	MAP,MAT SENSOR GROUND	469	BLK/RED	0	0
D3	NOT USED				
D4	EST CONTROL	423	WHT	*	1.0
D5	EST BYPASS	424	TAN/BLK	*	4.75
D6	OXYGEN SENSOR GROUND	413	TAN	*	*
D7	OXYGEN SENSOR SIGNAL	412	PPL	(4)	(5)
D8	NOT USED				
D9	GROUND	151	BLK	0	0
D10	GROUND	151	BLK	0	0
D11	NOT USED				
D12	NOT USED				
D13	NOT USED				
D14	NOT USED				
D15	NOT USED				
D16	INJECTOR A	467	DK BLU	12	14

(1) Battery voltage when cranking
(2) About 1.0 volt, varies with temperature
(3) .6 volt to about 4.8 volts at Wide Open Throttle (WOT)
(4) .26 to .46 volts
(5) Varies from .1 volt to .9 volt
* Less than .5 volt

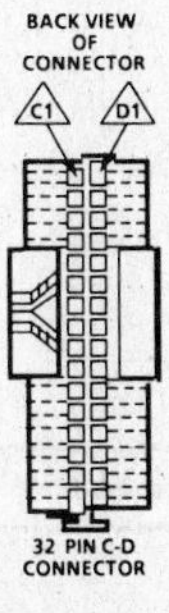
BACK VIEW OF CONNECTOR
C1
D1
32 PIN C-D CONNECTOR

91G13611 91H13612

Courtesy of General Motors Corp.

Fig. 1: ECM Terminal Identification & Pin Voltages ("S" Series Truck 2.5L)

1991 ENGINE PERFORMANCE
Pin Voltage Charts (Cont.)

NOTE:
This ECM voltage chart along with digital voltmeter can help save diagnosis time. Voltage readings may vary slightly depending on battery voltage and alternator output.

The following conditions must be met before testing:

- Engine at operating temperature.
- Engine in closed loop operation.
- Engine idling (Engine Run column).
- ALDL "test" terminal NOT grounded.
- Scan tester NOT installed.

PIN	PIN FUNCTION	CKT #	WIRE COLOR	NORMAL VOLTAGE	
				KEY "ON"	ENG RUN
A1	FUEL PUMP RELAY DRIVE	465	BLK/WHT TAN/WHT	(1)	14
A2	A/C RELAY CONTROL	459	BRN	(8)	(8)
A3	NOT USED				
A4	EGR CONTROL	435	GRY	12	14
A5	"SERVICE ENGINE SOON" LIGHT CONTROL	419	BRN/WHT	0	14
A6	IGN-ECM FUSE	439	PNK/BLK	12	14
A7	MANUAL TRANS SHIFT LAMP	456	TAN/BLK	12	14
A8	SERIAL DATA	461	ORN	(2)	(2)
A9	DIAGNOSTIC TEST TERMINAL	451	WHT/BLK	5	5
A10	VEHICLE SPEED SENSOR SIGNAL	437	BRN	(3)	(3)
A11	MAP SENSOR GROUND	455	PPL	0	0
A12	SYSTEM GROUND	450	BLK/WHT	0	0

PIN	PIN FUNCTION	CKT #	WIRE COLOR	NORMAL VOLTAGE	
				KEY "ON"	ENG RUN
B1	BATTERY 12 VOLTS	440	ORN	12	14
B2	FUEL PUMP SIGNAL	120	TAN/WHT	(1)	14
B3	EST REFERENCE "LOW"	453	BLK/RED	0	0
B4	NOT USED				
B5	EST REFERENCE "HIGH"	430	PPL/WHT	0	1.6
B6	NOT USED				
B7	ESC SIGNAL	485	BLK	9	9
B8	A/C SIGNAL	59	DK GRN	(4)	(4)
B9	NOT USED				
B10	NOT USED				
B11	NOT USED				
B12	NOT USED				

(1) Battery voltage first two seconds
(2) Varies from 2 volts to 5 volts
(3) Varies from 0 to battery voltage depending on position of drive wheels.
(4) 0 volts A/C "OFF" battery voltage A/C "ON."
(5) 0 volts in neutral, battery voltage in gear
(6) Varies with temperature
(7) Varies
(8) 0 volts A/C "ON," battery voltage A/C "OFF"

BACK VIEW OF CONNECTOR

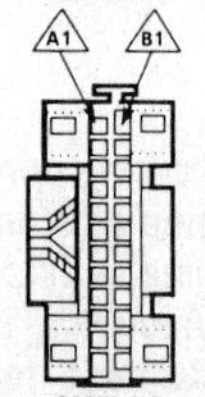
A1
B1

24 PIN A-B CONNECTOR

PIN	PIN FUNCTION	CKT #	WIRE COLOR	NORMAL VOLTAGE	
				KEY "ON"	ENG RUN
C1	NOT USED				
C2	ELECTRONIC AIR CONTROL SOLENOID	436	BRN	12	14
C3	IAC "B" LOW	444	LT GRN/ BLK	NOT	USABLE
C4	IAC "B" HIGH	443	LT GRN/ WHT	NOT	USABLE
C5	IAC "A" HIGH	441	LT BLU/ WHT	NOT	USABLE
C6	IAC "A" LOW	442	LT BLU/ BLK	NOT	USABLE
C7	NOT USED				
C8	NOT USED				
C9	CRANK SIGNAL	806	PPL/WHT	(1)	0
C10	COOLANT TEMP SIGNAL	410	YEL	(2)	(2)
C11	MAP SIGNAL	432	LT GRN	4.8	1.0
C12	NOT USED				
C13	TPS SIGNAL	417	DK BLU	(3)	6
C14	5 VOLT REF MAP & TPS	416	GRY	5	5
C15	NOT USED				
C16	BATTERY 12 VOLTS	440	ORN	12	14

PIN	PIN FUNCTION	CKT #	WIRE COLOR	NORMAL VOLTAGE	
				KEY "ON"	ENG RUN
D1	SYSTEM GROUND	551	TAN/WHT	0	0
D2	TPS, CTS SENSOR GROUND	452	BLK	0	0
D3	NOT USED				
D4	EST CONTROL	423	WHT	*	1.0
D5	EST BYPASS	424	TAN/BLK	*	4.75
D6	OXYGEN SENSOR GROUND	413	TAN	*	*
D7	OXYGEN SENSOR SIGNAL	412	PPL	(4)	(5)
D8	NOT USED				
D9	NOT USED				
D10	NOT USED				
D11	NOT USED				
D12	NOT USED				
D13	NOT USED				
D14	INJECTOR B	468	DK GRN	12	14
D15	NOT USED				
D16	INJECTOR A	467	DK BLU	12	14

(1) Battery voltage when cranking
(2) About 1.0 volt, varies with temperature
(3) .6 volt to about 4.8 volts at Wide Open Throttle (WOT)
(4) .26 to .46 volts
(5) Varies from .1 volt to .9 volt
* Less than .5 volt

BACK VIEW OF CONNECTOR

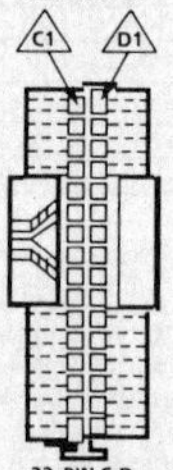
C1
D1

32 PIN C-D CONNECTOR

91I13613 91J13614

Courtesy of General Motors Corp.

Fig. 2: ECM Terminal Identification & Pin Voltages ("S" Series Truck 2.8L)

1991 ENGINE PERFORMANCE
Pin Voltage Charts (Cont.)

***NOTE:* This ECM voltage chart along with digital voltmeter can help save diagnosis time. Voltage readings may vary slightly depending on battery voltage and alternator output.**

The following conditions must be met before testing:

- Engine at operating temperature.
- Engine in closed loop operation.
- Engine idling (Engine Run column).
- ALDL "test" terminal NOT grounded.
- Scan tester NOT installed.

Note	VOLTAGE KEY "ON"	VOLTAGE ENG. RUN	CIRCUIT	PIN	WIRE COLOR
(2)	0	B+	FUEL PUMP RELAY DRIVE	A1	DK GRN/ WHT
	B+	B+	A/C CONTROL RELAY	A2	DK GRN/ WHT
			NOT USED	A3	
	B+	B+	EVRV	A4	GRY
	0	B+	"SERVICE ENGINE SOON" CONTROL	A5	BRN/ WHT
	B+	B+	IGN (ECM)	A6	PNK/ BLK
	B+	B+	TCC SOLENOID	A7	TAN/ BLK
	2-5	2-5	SERIAL DATA	A8	ORN
	5	5	DIAGNOSTIC TERMINAL	A9	WHT/ BLK
(1)	0 OR 12	0 OR 12	SPEED SENSOR SIGNAL	A10	BRN
	0	0	SENSOR GROUND	A11	PPL
	0	0	SYSTEM GROUND	A12	BLK/ WHT
	0	0	PUSHER FAN CONTROL	C1	DK BLU WHT
	B+	B+	COOLING FAN RELAY	C2	DK GRN/ WHT
	NOT USEABLE		IAC "B" LO	C3	LT GRN/ BLK
	NOT USEABLE		IAC "B" HI	C4	LT GRN/ WHT
	NOT USEABLE		IAC "A" HI	C5	LT BLU/ WHT
	NOT USEABLE		IAC "A" LO	C6	LT BLU BLK
			NOT USED	C7	
			NOT USED	C8	
(7)	0	0	CRANK DISCRETE	C9	PPL/WHT
(5)	1.6	1.6	COOLANT TEMP. SIGNAL	C10	YEL
(3)	4.75	1.1	MAP SIGNAL	C11	LT GRN
			NOT USED	C12	
	.7	.7	TPS SIGNAL	C13	DK BLU
	5	5	TPS 5 VOLT REFERENCE	C14	GRY
			NOT USED	C15	
	B+	B+	BATTERY	C16	ORN

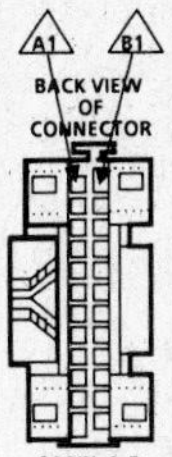
A1
B1
BACK VIEW OF CONNECTOR

24 PIN A-B CONNECTOR

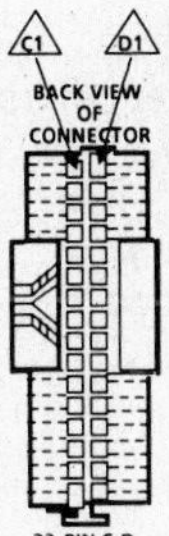
C1
D1
BACK VIEW OF CONNECTOR

32 PIN C-D CONNECTOR

WIRE COLOR	PIN	CIRCUIT	VOLTAGE KEY "ON"	VOLTAGE ENG. RUN	Note
ORN	B1	BATT 12 VOLTS	B+	B+	
GRY	B2	FUEL PUMP SIGNAL	0	B+	(4)
BLK/ RED	B3	IGNITION GROUND	0	0	
	B4	NOT USED			
PPL/ WHT	B5	DISTRIBUTOR REFERENCE HIGH	0	1.3	
	B6	NOT USED			
BLK	B7	ESC SIGNAL	9.2	9.3	
LT BLU	B8	A/C SIGNAL "OFF" "ON"	0 B+	0 B+	
DK GRN/ WHT	B9	INTER HD PRESS SW			
ORN/ BLK	B10	PARK/NEUTRAL SW. SIGNAL (A/T)	0	0	(6)
	B11	NOT USED			
	B12	NOT USED			
TAN/ WHT	D1	SYSTEM GROUND	0	0	
BLK	D2	SENSOR GROUND	0	0	
	D3	NOT USED			
WHT	D4	EST CONTROL	0	1.3	
TAN/ BLK	D5	BYPASS	0	4.75	
TAN	D6	GROUND (O_2)	0	0	
PPL	D7	O_2 SENSOR SIGNAL	3.5	1.9	(3)
	D8	NOT USED			
	D9	NOT USED			
	D10	NOT USED			
	D11	NOT USED			
	D12	NOT USED			
	D13	NOT USED			
DK GRN	D14	INJECTOR #2	B+	B+	
	D15	NOT USED			
DK BLU	D16	INJECTOR #1	B+	B+	

(1) Varies from .60 to battery voltage, depending on position of drive wheels.
(2) 12 volts for first two seconds.
(3) Varies.
(4) 12 volts when fuel pump is running.
(5) Varies with temperature.
(6) Reads battery voltage in gear.
(7) 12 volts, when engine is cranking.

91A13615

Courtesy of General Motors Corp.

Fig. 3: ECM Terminal Identification & Pin Voltages (Lumina APV, Silhouette & Trans Sport 3.1L)

1991 ENGINE PERFORMANCE
Pin Voltage Charts (Cont.)

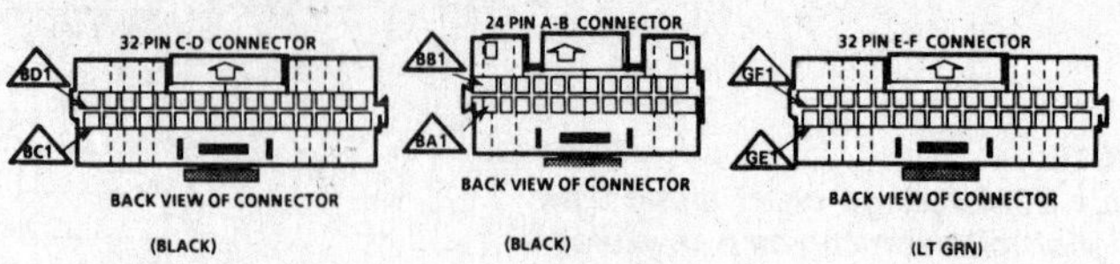
32 PIN C-D CONNECTOR
BD1
BC1
BACK VIEW OF CONNECTOR
(BLACK)
24 PIN A-B CONNECTOR
BB1
BA1
BACK VIEW OF CONNECTOR
(BLACK)
32 PIN E-F CONNECTOR
GF1
GE1
BACK VIEW OF CONNECTOR
(LT GRN)

NOTE:
This ECM voltage chart along with digital voltmeter can help save diagnosis time. Voltage readings may vary slightly depending on battery voltage and alternator output.

The following conditions must be met before testing:
- Engine at operating temperature.
- Engine in closed loop operation.
- Engine idling (Engine Run column).
- ALDL "test" terminal NOT grounded.
- Scan tester NOT installed.

BLACK 24 PIN A-B CONNECTOR

VOLTAGE KEY "ON"	VOLTAGE ENG. RUN	CIRCUIT	PIN	WIRE COLOR	WIRE COLOR	PIN	CIRCUIT	VOLTAGE KEY "ON"	VOLTAGE ENG RUN
		NOT USED	BA1		ORN	BB1	BATTERY	B+	B+
		NOT USED	BA2			BB2	NOT USED		
		NOT USED	BA3			BB3	NOT USED		∇
5.0	5.0	5 VOLTS REFERENCE	BA4	GRA		BB4	NOT USED		
5.0	5.0	5 VOLTS REFERENCE	BA5	GRA	BLK	BB5	MAT & TPS GROUND	0	0
B+	B+	IGN POWER	BA6	PNK/BLK	BLK	BB6	MAP & COOLANT GROUND	0	0
		NOT USED	BA7			BB7	NOT USED		
		NOT USED	BA8			BB8	NOT USED		
4.8	4.8	SERIAL DATA	BA9	ORN		BB9	NOT USED		
		NOT USED	BA10			BB10	NOT USED		
B+ 2 sec.	B+	FUEL PUMP RELAY	BA11	DK GRN/WHT		BB11	NOT USED		
0	0	ECM GROUND	BA12	BLK/WHT		BB12	NOT USED		

* Less than .5 Volt.
∇ Less than 1 Volt.
① A/C, Fan "OFF."

BLACK 32 PIN C-D CONNECTOR

VOLTAGE KEY "ON"	VOLTAGE ENG. RUN	CIRCUIT	PIN	WIRE COLOR	WIRE COLOR	PIN	CIRCUIT	VOLTAGE KEY "ON"	VOLTAGE ENG RUN
		NOT USED	BC1		TAN/WHT	BD1	ECM GROUND	0	0
		NOT USED	BC2			BD2	NOT USED		
		NOT USED	BC3			BD3	NOT USED		
		NOT USED	BC4			BD4	NOT USED		
		NOT USED	BC5			BD5	NOT USED		
0	0	DRAC SIGNAL	BC6	BRN		BD6	NOT USED		
0*	4.7	BYPASS	BC7	TAN/BLK	BLK/WHT	BD7	INJECTOR GROUND	0	0
0*	varies 1.2	EST	BC8	WHT	PPL/WHT	BD8	DIST. REFERENCE HI	0*	varies 1.0
① 0	0	A/C REQUEST	BC9	DK GRN	BLK/RED	BD9	DIST. REFERENCE LO	0*	0*
		NOT USED	BC10			BD10	NOT USED		
B+	B+	INJECTOR DRIVER	BC11	BLU		BD11	NOT USED		
B+	B+	INJECTOR DRIVER	BC12	GRN		BD12	NOT USED		
0*	0*	INJECTOR GROUND	BC13	BLK/WHT		BD13	NOT USED		
		NOT USED	BC14			BD14	NOT USED		
		NOT USED	BC15			BD15	NOT USED		
B+	B+	BATTERY	BC16	ORN	ORN/BLK	BD16	PARK/NEUTRAL	0*	0*

LIGHT GREEN 32 PIN E-F CONNECTOR

VOLTAGE KEY "ON"	VOLTAGE ENG. RUN	CIRCUIT	PIN	WIRE COLOR	WIRE COLOR	PIN	CIRCUIT	VOLTAGE KEY "ON"	VOLTAGE ENG RUN
		NOT USED	GE1		DK GRN/WHT	GF1	A/C CONTROL RELAY	B+	B+ ①
		NOT USED	GE2		BLK/GRN	GF2	WASTEGATE SOL.	B+	.5
NOT	USEABLE	IAC "B" LOW	GE3	LT GRN/WHT		GF3	NOT USED		
NOT	USEABLE	IAC "B" HIGH	GE4	LT GRN/BLK	TAN/BLK	GF4	TCC SOLENOID	0*	0*
NOT	USEABLE	IAC "A" LOW	GE5	BLU/BLK		GF5	NOT USED		
NOT	USEABLE	IAC "A" HIGH	GE6	LT BLU/WHT		GF6	NOT USED		
.1	B+	CHECK ENGINE LAMP	GE7	GRA/WHT		GF7	NOT USED		
B+	B+	CAC PUMP CONTROL	GE8	YEL		GF8	NOT USED		
B+	B+	EVRV CONTROL	GE9	GRA	DK BLU	GF9	ESC SIGNAL	2.4	2.4
		NOT USED	GE10			GF10	NOT USED		
		NOT USED	GE11			GF11	NOT USED		
5.0	5.0	ALDL DIAG. ENABLE	GE12	WHT/BLK		GF12	NOT USED		
		NOT USED	GE13		DK BLU	GF13	TPS SIGNAL	.84	.84
.1-.3	varies .1-.9	O^2 SENSOR SIGNAL	GE14	PPL		GF14	NOT USED		
0*	0*	O^2 SENSOR GROUND	GE15	TAN	LT GRN	GF15	MAP SIGNAL	2.2	varies .8
varies 1.5	varies 1.5	COOLANT SIGNAL	GE16	YEL	TAN	GF16	MAT SIGNAL	varies 2.4	varies 2.2

* LESS THAN .5 VOLT ∇ LESS THAN 1 VOLT ① A/C, FAN OFF

91B13616 91C13617

Courtesy of General Motors Corp.

Fig. 4: ECM Terminal Identification & Pin Voltages ("S" & "T" Series 4.3L Turbo PFI)

1991 ENGINE PERFORMANCE
Pin Voltage Charts (Cont.)

NOTE:
This ECM voltage chart along with digital voltmeter can help save diagnosis time. Voltage readings may vary slightly depending on battery voltage and alternator output.

The following conditions must be met before testing:

- Engine at operating temperature.
- Engine in closed loop operation.
- Engine idling (Engine Run column).
- ALDL "test" terminal NOT grounded.
- Scan tester NOT installed.

PIN	PIN FUNCTION	CKT #	WIRE COLOR	NORMAL VOLTAGES	
				KEY "ON"	ENG RUN
A1	FUEL PUMP RELAY DRIVE	465	DK GRN/ WHT	①	14
A2	A/C CLUTCH CONTROL	459	DK GRN/ WHT	⑦	⑦
A3	NOT USED	-	-	-	-
A4	EGR CONTROL	435	GRY	12	14
A5	"SERVICE ENGINE SOON" LIGHT CONTROL	419	BRN/WHT	0	14
A6	IGN-ECM FUSED	439	PNK/BLK	12	14
A7	TCC CONTROL	422	TAN/BLK	12	14
A8	SERIAL DATA	461	ORN/BLK ORN	②	②
A9	DIAGNOSTIC TEST TERMINAL	451	WHT/BLK	5	5
A10	VEHICLE SPEED SENSOR SIGNAL	437	BRN	③	③
A11	TPS, CTS SENSOR GROUND	452	BLK	0	0
A12	SYSTEM GROUND	450	BLK/WHT	0	0

PIN	PIN FUNCTION	CKT #	WIRE COLOR	NORMAL VOLTAGES	
				KEY "ON"	ENG RUN
B1	BATTERY 12 VOLT	440	ORN	12	14
B2	FUEL PUMP SIGNAL	120	GRY TAN/WHT	①	14
B3	EST REFERENCE LOW	453	BLK/RED	0	0
B4	NOT USED	-	-	-	-
B5	EST REFERENCE HIGH	430	PPL/WHT	0	1.6
B6	NOT USED	-	-	-	-
B7	ESC SIGNAL	485	BLK	9	9
B8	A/C SIGNAL	59	DK GRN	④	④
B9	NOT USED	-	-	-	-
B10	PARK/NUETRAL SWITCH SIGNAL	434	ORN/BLK	⑤	⑤
B11	NOT USED	-	-	-	-
B12	NOT USED	-	-	-	-

① Battery voltage first 2 seconds.
② Varies
③ Varies from .01 to battery voltage depending on position of drive wheels.
④ 0 volts A/C "OFF" battery voltage A/C "ON."
⑤ 0 volts in neutral, battery voltage in gear.
⑥ Varies with temperature
⑦ 0 Volts A/C "ON."
Battery voltage A/C "OFF."

BACK VIEW OF CONNECTOR

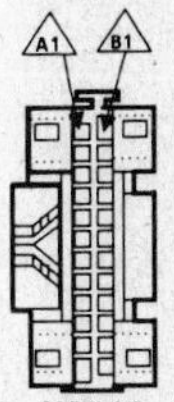
A1
B1

24 PIN A-B CONNECTOR

PIN	PIN FUNCTION	CKT #	WIRE COLOR	NORMAL VOLTAGES	
				KEY "ON"	ENG RUN
C1	NOT USED	-	-	-	-
C2	NOT USED	-	-	-	-
C3	IAC "B" LOW	444	LT GRN/ BLK	NOT	USABLE
C4	IAC "B" HIGH	443	LT GRN/ WHT	NOT	USABLE
C5	IAC "A" HIGH	441	LT BLU/ WHT	NOT	USABLE
C6	IAC "A" LOW	442	LT BLU/ BLK	NOT	USABLE
C7	HIGH GEAR SWITCH SIGNAL	446	LT BLU	12	14
C8	NOT USED	-	-	-	-
C9	CRANK SIGNAL	806	PPL PPL/WHT	①	0
C10	CTS SIGNAL	410	YEL	②	②
C11	MAP SENSOR SIGNAL	432	LT GRN LT GRN/BLK	4.8	1.0
C12	NOT USED	-	-	-	-
C13	TPS SIGNAL	417	DK BLU	③	.6
C14	MAP, TPS 5 VOLT REF.	416	GRY	5	5
C15	NOT USED	-	-	-	-
C16	BATTERY 12 VOLT	440	ORN	12	14

PIN	PIN FUNCTION	CKT #	WIRE COLOR	NORMAL VOLTAGES	
				KEY "ON"	ENG RUN
D1	SYSTEM GROUND	450 551	BLK/WHT	0	0
D2	MAP SENSOR GROUND	455	PPL BLK/RED	0	0
D3	NOT USED	-	-	-	-
D4	EST	423	WHT	*	1.0
D5	EST BYPASS	424	TAN/BLK	*	4.75
D6	OXYGEN SENSOR GROUND	413	TAN	*	*
D7	OXYGEN SENSOR SIGNAL	412	PPL	④	⑤
D8	NOT USED	-	-	-	-
D9	NOT USED	-	-	-	-
D10	NOT USED	-	-	-	-
D11	NOT USED	-	-	-	-
D12	NOT USED	-	-	-	-
D13	NOT USED	-	-	-	-
D14	INJECTOR 2 DRIVER CONTROL	468	GRN	12	14
D15	NOT USED	-	-	-	-
D16	INJECTOR 1 DRIVER CONTROL	467	BLU	12	14

① Battery voltage when cranking
② About 1.0 volt, varies with temperature
③ .6 Volt to about 4.8 volt at Wide Open Throttle (WOT)
④ .26 to .46 volt
⑤ Varies from .1 volt to .9 volt
* Less then .5 volt

BACK VIEW OF CONNECTOR

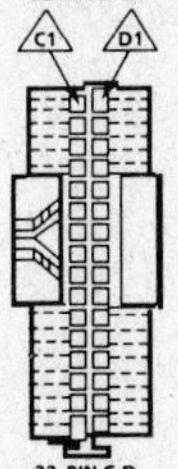
C1
D1

32 PIN C-D CONNECTOR

91D13618 91E13619

Courtesy of General Motors Corp.

Fig. 5: ECM Terminal Identification & Pin Voltages (Astro, Safari, & "S" & "T" Series 4.3L)

1991 ENGINE PERFORMANCE
Pin Voltage Charts (Cont.)

NOTE:
This ECM voltage chart along with digital voltmeter can help save diagnosis time. Voltage readings may vary slightly depending on battery voltage and alternator output.

The following conditions must be met before testing:
- Engine at operating temperature.
- Engine in closed loop operation.
- Engine idling (Engine Run column).
- ALDL "test" terminal NOT grounded.
- Scan tester NOT installed.

PIN	PIN FUNCTION	CKT #	WIRE COLOR	NORMAL VOLTAGE	
				KEY "ON"	ENG RUN
A1	FUEL PUMP RELAY DRIVE	465	DK GRN/ WHT	(1)	14
A2	NOT USED				
A3	NOT USED				
A4	EGR CONTROL	435	GRY	12	14
A5	"SERVICE ENGINE SOON" LIGHT CONTROL	419	BRN	0	14
A6	IGN-ECM FUSED	439	PNK/BLK	12	14
A7	TCC CONTROL	422	TAN/BLK	12	14
A8	SERIAL DATA	461	ORN	(2)	(2)
A9	DIAGNOSTIC TEST TERMINAL	451	BLK/WHT	5	5
A10	VEHICLE SPEED SENSOR SIGNAL	437	BRN	(3)	(3)
A11	CTS & TPS SENSOR GROUND	452	BLK	0	0
A12	SYSTEM GROUND	450	BLK/WHT	0	0

PIN	PIN FUNCTION	CKT #	WIRE COLOR	NORMAL VOLTAGE	
				KEY "ON"	ENG RUN
B1	BATTERY 12 VOLTS	440	ORN	12	14
B2	FUEL PUMP SIGNAL	120	TAN/WHT	(1)	14
B3	EST REFERENCE "LOW"	453	BLK/RED	0	0
B4	NOT USED				
B5	EST REFERENCE "HIGH"	430	PPL/WHT	0	1.6
B6	NOT USED				
B7	ESC SIGNAL	485	BLK	9	9
B8	A/C SIGNAL	59	DK GRN	(4)	(4)
B9	NOT USED				
B10	PARK/NEUTRAL SWITCH SIGNAL	434	ORN/BLK	(5)	(5)
B11	NOT USED				
B12	NOT USED				

(1) Battery voltage first two seconds
(2) Varies
(3) Varies from 0 to battery voltage depending on position of drive wheels.
(4) 0 volts A/C "OFF" battery voltage A/C "ON."
(5) 0 volts in neutral, battery voltage in gear
(6) Varies with temperature

BACK VIEW OF CONNECTOR

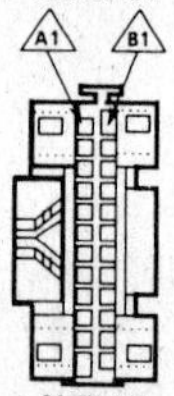
A1
B1

24 PIN A-B CONNECTOR

PIN	PIN FUNCTION	CKT #	WIRE COLOR	NORMAL VOLTAGE	
				KEY "ON"	ENG RUN
C1	NOT USED				
C2	ELECTRONIC AIR CONTROL SOLENOID	436	BRN	12	14
C3	IAC "B" LOW	444	LT GRN/ BLK	NOT	USABLE
C4	IAC "B" HIGH	443	LT GRN/ WHT	NOT	USABLE
C5	IAC "A" HIGH	441	LT BLU/ WHT	NOT	USABLE
C6	IAC "A" LOW	442	LT BLU/ BLK	NOT	USABLE
C7	HIGH GEAR SWITCH SIGNAL	446	LT BLU	12	14
C8	NOT USED				
C9	CRANK SIGNAL	806	PPL	(1)	0
C10	COOLANT TEMP SIGNAL	410	YEL	(2)	(2)
C11	MAP SIGNAL	432	LT GRN	4.8	1.0
C12	NOT USED				
C13	TPS SIGNAL	417	DK BLU	(3)	6
C14	5 VOLT REF MAP & TPS	416	GRY	5	5
C15	NOT USED				
C16	BATTERY 12 VOLT	440	ORN	12	14

PIN	PIN FUNCTION	CKT #	WIRE COLOR	NORMAL VOLTAGE	
				KEY "ON"	ENG RUN
D1	SYSTEM GROUND	450	BLK/WHT	0	0
D2	MAP SENSOR GROUND	455	PPL	0	0
D3	NOT USED				
D4	EST CONTROL	423	WHT	*	1.0
D5	EST BYPASS	424	TAN/BLK	*	4.75
D6	OXYGEN SENSOR GROUND	413	TAN	*	*
D7	OXYGEN SENSOR SIGNAL	412	PPL	(4)	(5)
D8	NOT USED				
D9	NOT USED				
D10	NOT USED				
D11	NOT USED				
D12	NOT USED				
D13	NOT USED				
D14	INJECTOR 2 DRIVER	468	GRN	12	14
D15	NOT USED				
D16	INJECTOR 1 DRIVER	467	BLU	12	14

(1) Battery voltage when cranking
(2) About 1.0 volt, varies with temperature
(3) .6 volt to about 4.8 volts at Wide Open Throttle (WOT)
(4) .26 to .46 volts
(5) Varies from .1 volt to .9 volt
* Less than .5 volt

BACK VIEW OF CONNECTOR

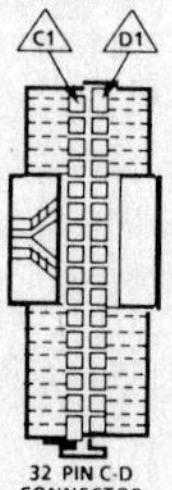
C1
D1

32 PIN C-D CONNECTOR

91H13620 91I13621

Courtesy of General Motors Corp.

Fig. 6: ECM Terminal Identification & Pin Voltages ("G" Series Van 4.3L & 5.7L)

1991 ENGINE PERFORMANCE
Pin Voltage Charts (Cont.)

NOTE:
This ECM voltage chart along with digital voltmeter can help save diagnosis time. Voltage readings may vary slightly depending on battery voltage and alternator output.

The following conditions must be met before testing:

- Engine at operating temperature.
- Engine in closed loop operation.
- Engine idling (Engine Run column).
- ALDL "test" terminal NOT grounded.
- Scan tester NOT installed.

PIN	PIN FUNCTION	CKT #	WIRE COLOR	NORMAL VOLTAGES	
				KEY "ON"	ENG RUN
A1	FUEL PUMP RELAY DRIVE	465	DK GRN/ WHT	①	14
A2	NOT USED	–	–	–	–
A3	NOT USED	–	–	–	–
A4	EGR CONTROL	435	GRY	12	14
A5	"SERVICE ENGINE SOON" LIGHT CONTROL	419	BRN	0	14
A6	IGN ECM FUSED	439	PNK/BLK	12	14
A7	TCC CONTROL	422	TAN/BLK	12	14
A8	SERIAL DATA	461	ORN	②	②
A9	DIAGNOSTIC TEST TERMINAL	451	WHT/BLK	5	5
A10	VEHICLE SPEED SENSOR SIGNAL	437	BRN	③	③
A11	MAP SENSOR GROUND	455	PPL	0	0
A12	SYSTEM GROUND	450	BLK/WHT	0	0

PIN	PIN FUNCTION	CKT #	WIRE COLOR	NORMAL VOLTAGES	
				KEY "ON"	ENG RUN
B1	BATTERY 12 VOLT	440	ORN	12	14
B2	FUEL PUMP SIGNAL	120	GRY	①	14
B3	EST REFERENCE LOW	453	BLK/RED	0	0
B4	NOT USED	–	–	–	–
B5	EST REFERENCE HIGH	430	PPL/WHT	0	1.6
B6	NOT USED	–	–	–	–
B7	ESC SIGNAL	457	YEL/BLK	9	9
B8	A/C SIGNAL	59	DK GRN	④	④
B9	NOT USED	–	–	–	–
B10	PARK/NEUTRAL SWITCH SIGNAL	434	ORN/BLK	⑤	⑤
B11	NOT USED	–	–	–	–
B12	NOT USED	–	–	–	–

① Battery voltage first 2 seconds.
② Varies
③ Varies from .01 to battery voltage depending on position of drive wheels.
④ 0 volts A/C "OFF" battery voltage A/C "ON."
⑤ 0 volts in neutral, battery voltage in gear
⑥ Varies with temperature.

BACK VIEW OF CONNECTOR

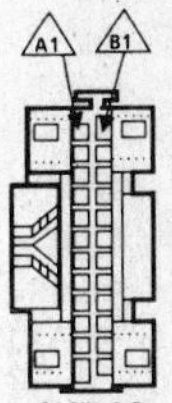
A1
B1

24 PIN A-B CONNECTOR

PIN	PIN FUNCTION	CKT #	WIRE COLOR	NORMAL VOLTAGES	
				KEY "ON"	ENG RUN
C1	NOT USED	–	–	–	–
C2	NOT USED	–	–	–	–
C3	IAC "B" LOW	444	LT GRN/ BLK	NOT	USABLE
C4	IAC "B" HIGH	443	LT GRN/ WHT	NOT	USABLE
C5	IAC "A" HIGH	441	LT BLU/ WHT	NOT	USABLE
C6	IAC "A" LOW	442	LT BLU/ BLK	NOT	USABLE
C7	HIGH GEAR SWITCH SIGNAL	446	LT BLU	12	14
C8	NOT USED	–	–	–	–
C9	CRANK SIGNAL	806	PPL/WHT	①	0
C10	CTS SIGNAL	410	YEL	②	②
C11	MAP SIGNAL	432	LT GRN	4.8	1.0
C12	NOT USED	–	–	–	–
C13	TPS SIGNAL	417	DK BLU	③	.6
C14	MAP & TPS 5 VOLT REF.	416	GRY	5	5
C15	NOT USED	–	–	–	–
C16	BATTERY 12 VOLT	440	ORN	12	14

PIN	PIN FUNCTION	CKT #	WIRE COLOR	NORMAL VOLTAGES	
				KEY "ON"	ENG RUN
D1	SYSTEM GROUND	450	BLK/WHT	0	0
D2	TPS & CTS SENSOR GROUND	452	BLK	0	0
D3	NOT USED	–	–	–	–
D4	EST	423	WHT	*	1.0
D5	EST BYPASS	424	TAN/BLK	*	4.75
D6	OXYGEN SENSOR GROUND	413	TAN	*	*
D7	OXYGEN SENSOR SIGNAL	412	PPL	④	⑤
D8	NOT USED	–	–	–	–
D9	NOT USED	–	–	–	–
D10	NOT USED	–	–	–	–
D11	NOT USED	–	–	–	–
D12	NOT USED	–	–	–	–
D13	NOT USED	–	–	–	–
D14	INJECTOR 2 DRIVER	468	GRN	12	14
D15	NOT USED	–	–	–	–
D16	INJECTOR 1 DRIVER	467	BLU	12	14

① Battery voltage when cranking
② About 1.0 volt, varies with temperature
③ .6 Volt to about 4.8 volt at Wide Open Throttle (WOT)
④ .26 to .46 volt
⑤ Varies from .1 volt to .9 volt
* Less than .5 volt

BACK VIEW OF CONNECTOR

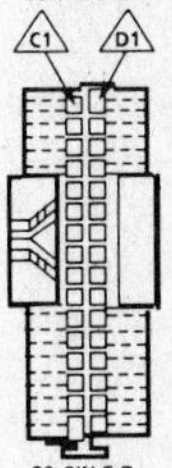
C1
D1

32 PIN C-D CONNECTOR

91J13622 91A13623

Fig. 7: ECM Terminal Identification & Pin Voltages ("C" & "K" Series 4.3L, 5.0L & 5.7L under 8600 GVWR w/o 4L80-E Transmission)

1991 ENGINE PERFORMANCE
Pin Voltage Charts (Cont.)

NOTE:
This ECM voltage chart along with digital voltmeter can help save diagnosis time. Voltage readings may vary slightly depending on battery voltage and alternator output.

The following conditions must be met before testing:
- Engine at operating temperature.
- Engine in closed loop operation.
- Engine idling (Engine Run column).
- ALDL "test" terminal NOT grounded.
- Scan tester NOT installed.

PIN	PIN FUNCTION	CKT #	WIRE COLOR	NORMAL VOLTAGES	
				KEY "ON"	ENG RUN
A1	FUEL PUMP RELAY DRIVE	465	DR GRN/ WHT	①	14
A2	NOT USED	–	–	–	–
A3	NOT USED	–	–	–	–
A4	EGR CONTROL	435	GRY	12	14
A5	"SERVICE ENGINE SOON" LIGHT CONTROL	419	BRN/WHT	0	14
A6	IGNITION - ECM FUSED	439	PNK/BLK	12	14
A7	TCC CONTROL	422	TAN/BLK	12	14
A8	SERIAL DATA	461	ORN	②	②
A9	DIAGNOSTIC TEST TERMINAL	451	WHT/BLK	5	5
A10	VEHICLE SPEED SENSOR SIGNAL	437	BRN	③	③
A11	TPS AND CTS SENSOR GROUND	452	BLK	0	0
A12	SYSTEM GROUND	450	BLK/WHT	0	0

PIN	PIN FUNCTION	CKT #	WIRE COLOR	NORMAL VOLTAGES	
				KEY "ON"	ENG RUN
B1	BATTERY 12 VOLT	440	ORN	12	14
B2	FUEL PUMP SIGNAL	120	GRY	①	14
B3	EST REFERENCE LOW	453	BLK/RED	0	0
B4	NOT USED	–	–	–	–
B5	EST REFERENCE HIGH	430	PPL/WHT	0	1.6
B6	NOT USED	–	–	–	–
B7	ESC SIGNAL	485	BLK	9	9
B8	A/C SIGNAL	59	DK GRN	④	④
B9	NOT USED	–	–	–	–
B10	NOT USED	–	–	–	–
B11	NOT USED	–	–	–	–
B12	NOT USED	–	–	–	–

① Battery voltage first 2 seconds.
② Varies
③ Varies from 0 to battery voltage depending on position of drive wheels.
④ 0 volts A/C "OFF" battery voltage A/C "ON".
⑤ 0 volts in neutral, battery voltage in gear.
⑥ Varies with temperature.

BACK VIEW OF CONNECTOR

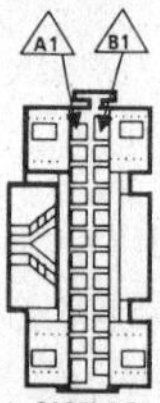
A1
B1

24 PIN A-B CONNECTOR

PIN	PIN FUNCTION	CKT #	WIRE COLOR	NORMAL VOLTAGES	
				KEY "ON"	ENG RUN
C1	NOT USED	–	–	–	–
C2	NOT USED	–	–	–	–
C3	IAC "B" LOW	444	LT GRN/ BLK	NOT	USABLE
C4	IAC "B" HIGH	443	LT GRN/ WHT	NOT	USABLE
C5	IAC "A" HIGH	441	LT BLU/ WHT	NOT	USABLE
C6	IAC "A" LOW	442	LT BLU/ BLK	NOT	USABLE
C7	HIGH GEAR SWITCH SIGNAL	446	LT BLU	12	14
C8	NOT USED	–	–	–	–
C9	CRANK SIGNAL	806	PPL/WHT	①	0
C10	CTS SIGNAL	410	YEL	②	②
C11	MAP SIGNAL	432	LT GRN	4.8	1.0
C12	NOT USED	–	–	–	–
C13	TPS SIGNAL	417	DK BLU	③	.6
C14	MAP & TPS 5 VOLT REF.	416	GRY	5	5
C15	NOT USED	–	–	–	–
C16	BATTERY 12 VOLT	440	ORN	12	14

PIN	PIN FUNCTION	CKT #	WIRE COLOR	NORMAL VOLTAGES	
				KEY "ON"	ENG RUN
D1	SYSTEM GROUND	551	TAN/WHT	0	0
D2	MAP GROUND	455	PPL	0	0
D3	NOT USED	–	–	–	–
D4	EST SIGNAL	423	WHT	*	1.0
D5	EST BYPASS	424	TAN/BLK	*	4.75
D6	OXYGEN SENSOR GROUND	413	TAN	*	*
D7	OXYGEN SENSOR SIGNAL	412	PPL	④	⑤
D8	NOT USED	–	–	–	–
D9	NOT USED	–	–	–	–
D10	NOT USED	–	–	–	–
D11	NOT USED	–	–	–	–
D12	NOT USED	–	–	–	–
D13	NOT USED	–	–	–	–
D14	INJECTOR 2 DRIVER	468	GRN	12	14
D15	NOT USED	–	–	–	–
D16	INJECTOR 1 DRIVER	467	BLU	12	14

① Battery voltage when cranking
② About 1.0 volt, varies with temperature
③ .6 Volt to about 4.8 volt at Wide Open Throttle (WOT)
④ .26 to .46 volt
⑤ Varies from .1 volt to .9 volt
* Less than .5 volt

BACK VIEW OF CONNECTOR

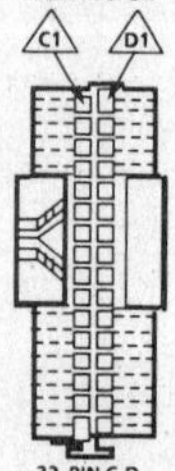
C1
D1

32 PIN C-D CONNECTOR

91B13624 91C13625

Courtesy of General Motors Corp.

Fig. 8: ECM Terminal Identification & Pin Voltages ("R" & "V" Series 5.7L & 7.4L under 8600 GVWR w/o 4L80-E Transmission)

1991 ENGINE PERFORMANCE
Pin Voltage Charts (Cont.)

NOTE:
This ECM voltage chart along with digital voltmeter can help save diagnosis time. Voltage readings may vary slightly depending on battery voltage and alternator output.

The following conditions must be met before testing:
- Engine at operating temperature.
- Engine in closed loop operation.
- Engine idling (Engine Run column).
- ALDL "test" terminal NOT grounded.
- Scan tester NOT installed.

PIN	PIN FUNCTION	CKT #	WIRE COLOR	NORMAL VOLTAGES	
				KEY "ON"	ENG RUN
A1	FUEL PUMP RELAY CONTROL	465	DK GRN/WHT	(1)	14
A2	SHIFT SOLENOID "B" CONTROL	1223	YEL/BLK	12	14
A3	SHIFT SOLENOID "A" CONTROL	1222	LT GRN	*	*
A4	TCC SOLENOID CONTROL	422	TAN/BLK	12	14
A5	NOT USED	–	–	–	–
A6	EAC CONTROL (7.4L UNDER 8500 GVW)	436	BRN	12	14
A7	"SERVICE ENGINE SOON" LAMP CONTROL	419	BRN/WHT	0	14
A8	NOT USED	–	–	–	–
A9	NOT USED	–	–	–	–
A10	NOT USED	–	–	–	–
A11	EVRV (EGR) CONTROL	435	GRY	11	12
A12	BRAKE SIGNAL	420	PPL	(2)	(2)

PIN	PIN FUNCTION	CKT #	WIRE COLOR	NORMAL VOLTAGES	
				KEY "ON"	ENG RUN
B1	NOT USED	–	–	–	–
B2	RANGE "C" SIGNAL	1226	RED	12	14
B3	RANGE "B" SIGNAL	1225	DK BLU	0	*
B4	RANGE "A" SIGNAL	1224	PNK	12	14
B5	TRANSMISSION OUTPUT SPEED SIGNAL (4WD)	1232	LT BLU	5	5
B6	TRANSMISSION OUTPUT SPEED SENSOR GROUND	1233	DK GRN/YEL	0	0
B7	FORCE MOTOR LOW	1229	LT BLU/WHT	0	.85
B8	FORCE MOTOR HIGH	1228	RED/BLK	0	4.50
B9	TRANSMISSION INPUT SPEED SIGNAL	1230	GRY/RED	0	*
B10	TRANSMISSION INPUT SPEED SENSOR GROUND	1231	DK BLU/WHT	0	0
B11	VEHICLE SPEED AND TRANSMISSION OUTPUT SPEED SIGNAL (2WD)	437	BRN	0	0
B12	A/C SIGNAL	59	DK GRN	(3)	(3)

(1) Battery voltage first 20 seconds
(2) Battery voltage brakes "OFF."
0 volts brakes "ON."
(3) 0 volts A/C "OFF" battery voltage A/C "ON."
* Less than .50 volt.

BACK VIEW OF CONNECTOR

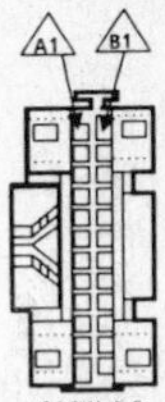
A1
B1

24 PIN A-B CONNECTOR

PIN	PIN FUNCTION	CKT #	WIRE COLOR	NORMAL VOLTAGES	
				KEY "ON"	ENG RUN
C1	FUSED IGNITION FEED	439	PNK/BLK	12	14
C2	SYSTEM GROUND	450	BLK/WHT	*	*
C3	SYSTEM GROUND	551	TAN/WHT	*	*
C4	TPS REFERENCE VOLTAGE	416	GRY	5	5
C5	TPS SIGNAL	417	DK BLU	.60	(2)
C6	IAC COIL "A" HIGH	441	LT BLU/WHT	NOT	USE-ABLE
C7	IAC COIL "A" LOW	442	LT BLU/BLK	NOT	USE-ABLE
C8	IAC COIL "B" LOW	444	LT GRY/BLK	NOT	USE-ABLE
C9	IAC COIL "B" HIGH	443	LT GRN/WHT	NOT	USE-ABLE
C10	MAP SIGNAL	432	LT GRN	4.77	1.45
C11	SERIAL DATA	(1)	(1)	(1)	(1)
C12	NOT USED	–	–	–	–
C13	O_2 SENSOR GROUND	413	TAN	0	*
C14	O_2 SIGNAL	412	PPL	(3)	(4)
C15	INJECTOR #2 CONTROL	468	DK GRN	12	14
C16	INJECTOR #1 CONTROL	467	DK BLU	12	14

PIN	PIN FUNCTION	CKT #	WIRE COLOR	NORMAL VOLTAGES	
				KEY "ON"	ENG RUN
D1	BATTERY VOLTAGE FEED	440	ORN	12	14
D2	MAP/TTS SENSOR GROUND	455	PPL	0	0
D3	TPS/CTS SENSOR GROUND	452	BLK	0	0
D4	MAP REFERENCE VOLTAGE	474	GRY	5.0	5.0
D5	ESC (KNOCK) SIGNAL	496	DK BLU	4.7	4.7
D6	DIAGNOSTIC TEST TERMINAL	451	WHT/BLK	5	5
D7	FUEL PUMP SIGNAL	120	GRY		
D8	NOT USED	–	–	–	–
D9	NOT USED	–	–	–	–
D10	NOT USED	–	–	–	–
D11	EST CONTROL	423	WHT	0	1.0
D12	EST BYPASS	424	TAN/BLK	0	4.64
D13	EST REFERENCE LOW	453	BLK/RED	0	0
D14	EST REFERENCE HIGH	430	PPL/WHT	0	1.5
D15	TRANSMISSION TEMPERATURE SIGNAL	1227	BLK/YEL	2.24	2.0
D16	COOLANT TEMPERATURE SIGNAL	410	YEL	1.5	1.69

(1) 1061 ORN/BLK or 461 ORN or 488 from 2 volts to 5 volts.
(2) .70 volts measured between terminals "C5" and "D2" 4.26v W.O.T.
(3) .26 volt to .46 volt
(4) Varies (toggles) .1 volt to .9 volt.
(5) 12 volts first 20 seconds.
* Less than .50 volt.

BACK VIEW OF CONNECTOR

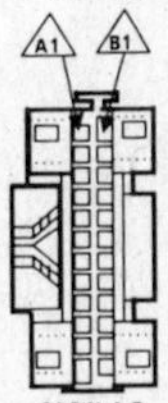
A1
B1

24 PIN A-B CONNECTOR

91D13626 91E13627

Courtesy of General Motors Corp.

Fig. 9: ECM Terminal Identification & Pin Voltages ("C", "K", "R" & "V" Series 4.3L, 5.7L & 7.4L w/ 4L80-E Transmission)

1991 ENGINE PERFORMANCE
Pin Voltage Charts (Cont.)

NOTE:
This ECM voltage chart along with digital voltmeter can help save diagnosis time. Voltage readings may vary slightly depending on battery voltage and alternator output.

The following conditions must be met before testing:
- Engine at operating temperature.
- Engine in closed loop operation.
- Engine idling (Engine Run column).
- ALDL "test" terminal NOT grounded.
- Scan tester NOT installed.

	VOLTAGE				
	KEY "ON"	ENG. RUN	CIRCUIT	PIN	WIRE COLOR
	4.76	1.66	MAP SIGNAL	A1	LT GRN
	.2 - 2.2	.2 - 2.2	TPS SIGNAL	A2	DK BLU
(2)	1.9	1.7	COOLANT SENSOR	A3	YEL
			NOT USED	A4	
			NOT USED	A5	
	5.0	5.0	DIAGNOSTIC TERMINAL	A6	WHT/ BLK
			NOT USED	A7	
	0 *	0 *	ENGINE SPEED SENSOR	A8	DK BLU/ WHT
(1)	10.72	12.32	VEHICLE SPEED SENSOR	A9	BRN
	B +	.46	ECM TO LAMP DRIVER	A10	WHT/ BLK
			NOT USED	A11	
	5.0	5.0	5 VOLT REFERENCE	A12	GRY

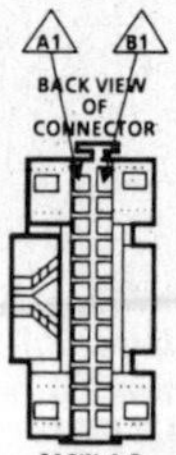
A1
B1
BACK VIEW OF CONNECTOR
24 PIN A-B CONNECTOR

WIRE COLOR	PIN	CIRCUIT	ENG. RUN	KEY "ON"
			VOLTAGE	
	B1	NOT USED		
	B2	NOT USED		
	B3	NOT USED		
	B4	NOT USED		
	B5	NOT USED		
	B6	NOT USED		
	B7	NOT USED		
	B8	NOT USED		
	B9	NOT USED		
	B10	NOT USED		
	B11	NOT USED		
	B12	NOT USED		

	KEY "ON"	ENG. RUN	CIRCUIT	PIN	WIRE COLOR
	0 *	0 *	SENSOR GROUND	C1	BLK
	0 *	0*	GROUND	C2	BLK/ WHT
			NOT USED	C3	
			NOT USED	C4	
	B +	B +	TCC SOLENOID	C5	TAN/BLK
	10.8	7.7	COLD ADVANCE	C6	DK BLU/ WHT
			NOT USED	C7	
			NOT USED	C8	
			NOT USED	C9	
(2)	.90	B +	EGR SOLENOID	C10	GRY
	.89	B +	EGR VENT SOLENOID	C11	LT BLU
	B +	.87	EPR SOLENOID	C12	DK GRN
			NOT USED	C13	
	B +	B +	ECM FUSE KEY/SWITCH	C14	PNK/BLK
			NOT USED	C15	
	B +	B +	BATTERY/ 12 VOLTS	C16	ORN

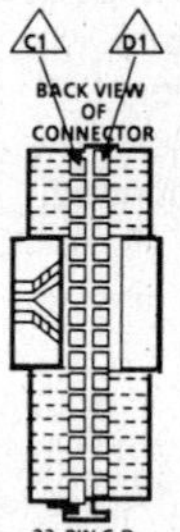
C1
D1
BACK VIEW OF CONNECTOR
32 PIN C-D CONNECTOR

WIRE COLOR	PIN	CIRCUIT	ENG. RUN	KEY "ON"
	D1	NOT USED		
	D2	NOT USED		
	D3	NOT USED		
	D4	NOT USED		
	D5	NOT USED		
	D6	NOT USED		
	D7	NOT USED		
	D8	NOT USED		
	D9	NOT USED		
	D10	NOT USED		
	D11	NOT USED		
	D12	NOT USED		
	D13	NOT USED		
	D14	NOT USED		
	D15	NOT USED		
	D16	NOT USED		

1 Varies from .60 to battery voltage depending on position of drive wheels.
2 Varies with temperature.
* Less than .5 volts,

91F13628

Courtesy of General Motors Corp.

Fig. 10: ECM Terminal Identification & Pin Voltages ("C" & "K" Series 6.2L Diesel)

1991 ENGINE PERFORMANCE
Pin Voltage Charts (Cont.)

NOTE:
This ECM voltage chart along with digital voltmeter can help save diagnosis time. Voltage readings may vary slightly depending on battery voltage and alternator output.

The following conditions must be met before testing:
- Engine at operating temperature.
- Engine in closed loop operation.
- Engine idling (Engine Run column).
- ALDL "test" terminal NOT grounded.
- Scan tester NOT installed.

PIN	PIN FUNCTION	CKT #	WIRE COLOR	NORMAL VOLTAGES	
				KEY "ON"	ENG RUN
A1	NOT USED	–	–	–	–
A2	NOT USED	–	–	–	–
A3	RANGE "A" SIGNAL	1224	PNK	12	14
A4	RANGE "B" SIGNAL	1225	DK BLU	*	*
A5	RANGE "C" SIGNAL	1226	RED	12	14
A6	SHIFT SOLENOID "B" CONTROL	1223	YEL/BLK	12	14
A7	SHIFT SOLENOID "A" CONTROL	1222	LT BRN	12	*
A8	DIAGNOSTIC TEST TERMINAL "B"	451	WHT/BLK	5	5
A9	NOT USED	–	–	–	–
A10	NOT USED	–	–	–	–
A11	NOT USED	–	–	–	–
A12	BATTERY VOLTAGE FEED	440	ORN	12	14

PIN	PIN FUNCTION	CKT #	WIRE COLOR	NORMAL VOLTAGES	
				KEY "ON"	ENG RUN
B1	NOT USED	–	–	–	–
B2	NOT USED	–	–	–	–
B3	A/C SIGNAL	59	DK GRN	(1)	(1)
B4	BRAKE SIGNAL	420	PPL	(2)	(2)
B5	TCC CONTROL	422	TAN/BLK	12	14
B6	NOT USED	–	–	–	–
B7	NOT USED	–	–	–	–
B8	NOT USED	–	–	–	–
B9	"TRANS" LAMP CONTROL	(3)	(3)	0	14
B10	SERIAL DATA	(4)	(4)	(5)	(5)
B11	NOT USED	–	–	–	–
B12	NOT USED	–	–	–	–

(1) 0 volts A/C "OFF."
Battery voltage A/C "ON."
(2) Battery voltage brakes "OFF."
0 volts brakes "ON."
(3) 419 BRN/WHT or 1234 GRY/RED.
(4) 1061 ORN/BLK or 461 ORN or 488 LT GRN.
(5) Varies 2 to 5 volts.
* Less than .50 volt.

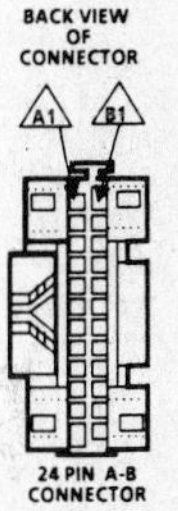
BACK VIEW OF CONNECTOR
A1
B1
24 PIN A-B CONNECTOR

PIN	PIN FUNCTION	CKT #	WIRE COLOR	NORMAL VOLTAGES	
				KEY "ON"	ENG RUN
C1	SYSTEM GROUND	450	BLK/WHT	0	0
C2	SYSTEM GROUND	551	TAN/WHT	0	0
C3	SENSOR GROUND	452	BLK	0	0
C4	TPS REFERENCE	416	GRY	5	5
C5	NOT USED	–	–	–	–
C6	NOT USED	–	–	–	–
C7	NOT USED	–	–	–	–
C8	NOT USED	–	–	–	–
C9	NOT USED	–	–	–	–
C10	NOT USED	–	–	–	–
C11	NOT USED	–	–	–	–
C12	NOT USED	–	–	–	–
C13	NOT USED	–	–	–	–
C14	NOT USED	–	–	–	–
C15	FORCE MOTOR LOW	1229	BLU/WHT	0	.85
C16	IGNITION FEED	439	PNK/BLK	12	14

PIN	PIN FUNCTION	CKT #	WIRE COLOR	NORMAL VOLTAGES	
				KEY "ON"	ENG RUN
D1	NOT USED	–	–	–	–
D2	TRANSMISSION OUTPUT SPEED SIGNAL (2WD)	437	BRN	(1)	(1)
D3	TRANSMISSION INPUT SPEED SENSOR GROUND	1230	GRY/RED	0	0
D4	TRANSMISSION INPUT SPEED SIGNAL	1230	GRY/ERD	0	(2)
D5	NOT USED	–	–	–	–
D6	ENGINE SPEED SIGNAL	(3)	(3)	0	(4)
D7	SENSOR GROUND	452	BLK	0	0
D8	TPS SIGNAL	417	DK BLU	.67	(5)
D9	NOT USED	–	–	–	–
D10	NOT USED	–	–	–	–
D11	NOT USED	–	–	–	–
D12	NOT USED	–	–	–	–
D13	TRANSMISSION TEMPERATURE SIGNAL	1227	BLK/YEL	(6)	(6)
D14	NOT USED	–	–	–	–
D15	NOT USED	–	–	–	–
D16	FORCE MOTOR HIGH	1228	RED/BLK	.11	4.43

(1) Varies from .06 to battery voltage depending on position of drive wheels.
(2) 10.5 volts AC, varies with rpm.
(3) 643 DK BLU/WHT (CK).
121 WHT (R/V, P, G).
(4) .40 volt AC, varies with rpm.
(5) .67 volt to 4.8 volts W.O.T.
(6) About 2 volts varies with temperature.

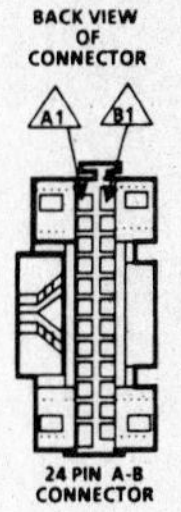
BACK VIEW OF CONNECTOR
A1
B1
24 PIN A-B CONNECTOR

91G13629 91J13630

Courtesy of General Motors Corp.

Fig. 11: ECM Terminal Identification & Pin Voltages ("R" & "V" Series 6.2L Diesel w/ 4L80-E Transmission)

1991 ENGINE PERFORMANCE
Pin Voltage Charts (Cont.)

NOTE:
This ECM voltage chart along with digital voltmeter can help save diagnosis time. Voltage readings may vary slightly depending on battery voltage and alternator output.

The following conditions must be met before testing:

- Engine at operating temperature.
- Engine in closed loop operation.
- Engine idling (Engine Run column).
- ALDL "test" terminal NOT grounded.
- Scan tester NOT installed.

Note	VOLTAGE KEY "ON"	VOLTAGE ENG. RUN	CIRCUIT	PIN	WIRE COLOR
	4.76	1.66	MAP SIGNAL	A1	LT GRN
	.2 - 2.2	.2 - 2.2	TPS SIGNAL	A2	DK BLU
(2)	1.9	1.7	COOLANT SENSOR	A3	YEL
			NOT USED	A4	
			NOT USED	A5	
	5.0	5.0	DIAGNOSTIC TERMINAL	A6	WHT/BLK
			NOT USED	A7	
	0 *	0 *	ENGINE SPEED SENSOR	A8	WHT
(1)	10.72	12.32	VEHICLE SPEED SENSOR	A9	BRN
	B +	.46	ECM TO LAMP DRIVER	A10	LT GRN
			NOT USED	A11	
	5.0	5.0	5 VOLT REFERENCE	A12	GRY
	0 *	0 *	SENSOR GROUND	C1	BLK
	0 *	0 *	GROUND	C2	BLK/WHT
			NOT USED	C3	
			NOT USED	C4	
	B +	B +	TCC SOLENOID	C5	TAN/BLK
	10.8	7.7	COLD ADVANCE	C6	BRN
			NOT USED	C7	
			NOT USED	C8	
			NOT USED	C9	
(2)	.90	B +	EGR SOLENOID	C10	GRY
(2)	.89	B +	EGR VENT SOLENOID	C11	LT BLU
	B +	.87	EPR SOLENOID	C12	DK GRN
	B +	B +	NOT USED	C13	
			ECM FUSE KEY/ SWITCH	C14	PNK/BLK
			NOT USED	C15	
	B +	B +	BATTERY/12 VOLTS	C16	ORN

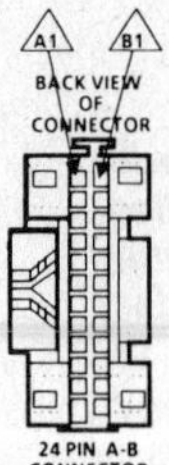
A1
B1
BACK VIEW OF CONNECTOR
24 PIN A-B CONNECTOR

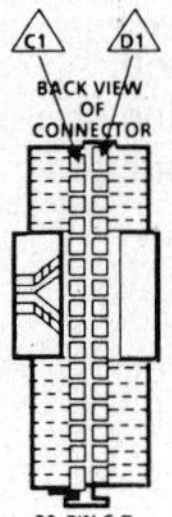
C1
D1
BACK VIEW OF CONNECTOR
32 PIN C-D CONNECTOR

WIRE COLOR	PIN	CIRCUIT	VOLTAGE KEY "ON"	VOLTAGE ENG. RUN
	B1	NOT USED		
	B2	NOT USED		
	B1	NOT USED		
	B1	NOT USED		
	B1	NOT USED		
	B1	NOT USED		
	B1	NOT USED		
	B1	NOT USED		
	B1	NOT USED		
	B1	NOT USED		
	B1	NOT USED		
	B1	NOT USED		
	D1	NOT USED		
	D2	NOT USED		
	D3	NOT USED		
	D4	NOT USED		
	D5	NOT USED		
	D6	NOT USED		
	D7	NOT USED		
	D8	NOT USED		
	D9	NOT USED		
	D10	NOT USED		
	D11	NOT USED		
	D12	NOT USED		
	D13	NOT USED		
	D14	NOT USED		
	D15	NOT USED		
	D16	NOT USED		

1 Varies from 60 to battery voltage depending on position of drive wheels
2 Varies with temperature
* Less than 5 volts

91A13631

Courtesy of General Motors Corp.

Fig. 12: ECM Terminal Identification & Pin Voltages ("R" & "V" Series 6.2L Diesel w/o 4L80-E Transmission)

1991 ENGINE PERFORMANCE
Sensor Operating Range Charts

Astro, Blazer, Bravada, Jimmy, Lumina APV, Safari, Sierra, Silhouette, Sonoma, Syclone, Trans Sport, "C" & "K" Series, "G" Series, "P" Series, "R" & "V" Series, "S" & "T" Series

INTRODUCTION

Sensor operating range information can help determine if a sensor is out of calibration. An out-of-calibration sensor may not set a trouble code, but it will cause driveability problems.

NOTE: Perform all voltage tests with a Digital Volt-Ohmmeter (DVOM) with a minimum 10-megohm input impedance, unless stated otherwise in testing procedures.

COOLANT TEMPERATURE RESISTANCE VALUES [1]

°F (°C)	Ohms
210 (99)	185
160 (70)	450
100 (38)	1800
70 (20)	3400
20 (-7)	13,500
0 (-18)	25,000
-40 (-40)	100,700

[1] – Measure resistance across sensor terminals.

MANIFOLD AIR TEMPERATURE SENSOR RESISTANCE VALUES [1]

°F (°C)	Ohms
210 (99)	185
160 (70)	450
100 (38)	1800
70 (20)	3400
40 (4)	7500
20 (-7)	13,500
0 (-18)	25,000
-40 (-40)	100,700

[1] – Measure resistance across sensor terminals.

MAP SENSOR VOLTAGE RANGE [1]

Altitude (Ft.)	Volts
Below 1000	3.8-5.5
1000-2000	3.6-5.3
2000-3000	3.5-5.1
3000-4000	3.3-5.0
4000-5000	3.2-4.8
5000-6000	3.0-4.6
6000-7000	2.9-4.5
7000-8000	2.8-4.3
8000-9000	2.6-4.2
9000-10,000	2.5-4.0

[1] – Measured at sensor, or as seen on Scan tester.

OXYGEN SENSOR VOLTAGE TEST [1]

Condition	Volts
Lean	.1
Rich	.9

[1] – Measure voltage between O_2 sensor ground and signal terminals at ECM.

1991 ENGINE PERFORMANCE
Wiring Diagrams

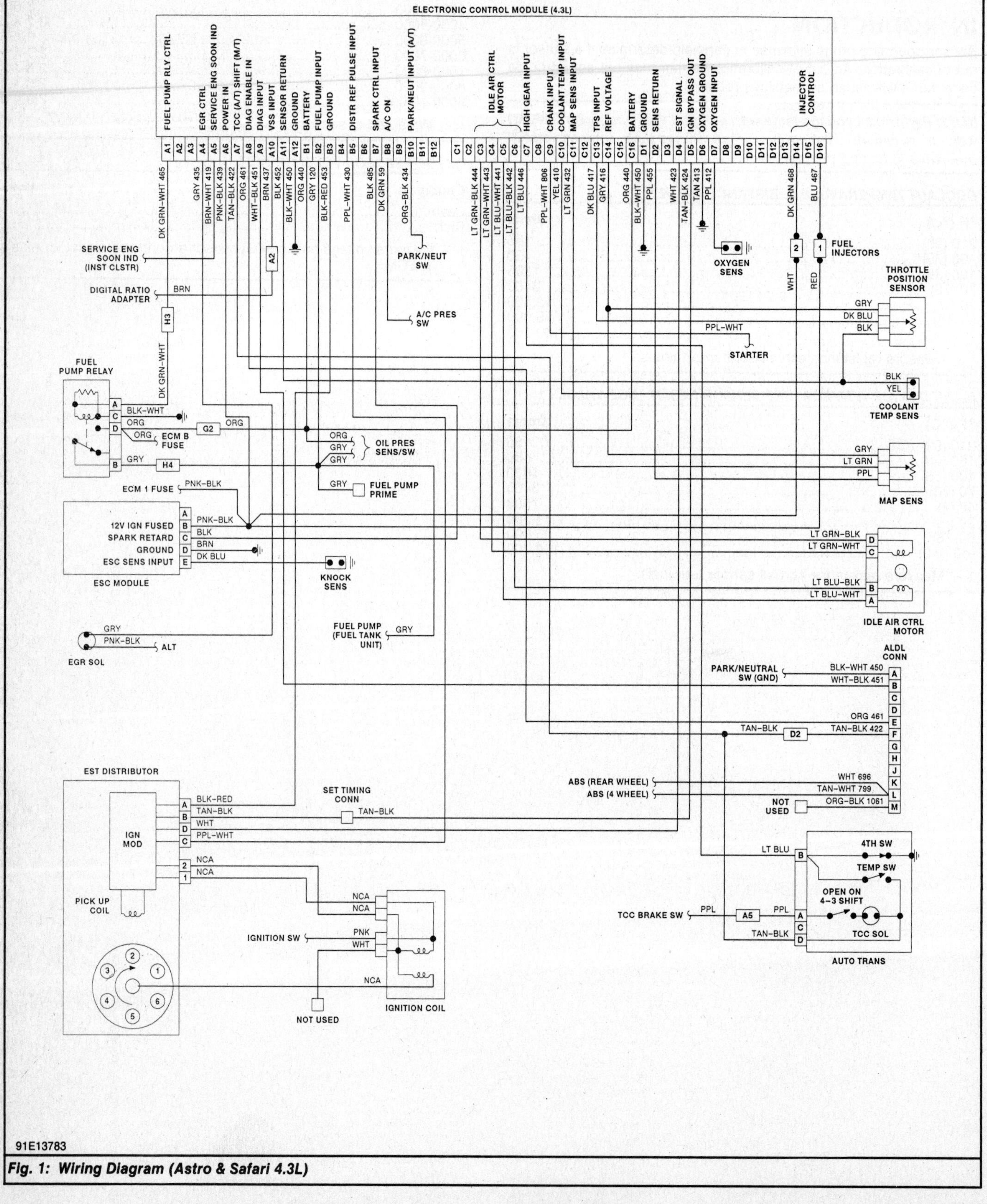
ELECTRONIC CONTROL MODULE (4.3L)
FUEL PUMP RLY CTRL
EGR CTRL
SERVICE ENG SOON IND
POWER IN
TCC (A/T) SHIFT (M/T)
DIAG ENABLE IN
DIAG INPUT
VSS INPUT
SENSOR RETURN
GROUND
BATTERY
FUEL PUMP INPUT
GROUND
DISTR REF PULSE INPUT
SPARK CTRL INPUT
A/C ON
PARK/NEUT INPUT (A/T)
IDLE AIR CTRL MOTOR
HIGH GEAR INPUT
CRANK INPUT
COOLANT TEMP INPUT
MAP SENS INPUT
TPS INPUT
REF VOLTAGE
BATTERY
GROUND
SENS RETURN
EST SIGNAL
IGN BYPASS OUT
OXYGEN GROUND
OXYGEN INPUT
INJECTOR CONTROL
SERVICE ENG SOON IND (INST CLSTR)
DIGITAL RATIO ADAPTER
FUEL PUMP RELAY
ECM B FUSE
OIL PRES SENS/SW
FUEL PUMP PRIME
ECM 1 FUSE
12V IGN FUSED
SPARK RETARD
GROUND
ESC SENS INPUT
ESC MODULE
KNOCK SENS
EGR SOL
ALT
FUEL PUMP (FUEL TANK UNIT)
PARK/NEUT SW
A/C PRES SW
OXYGEN SENS
FUEL INJECTORS
THROTTLE POSITION SENSOR
STARTER
COOLANT TEMP SENS
MAP SENS
IDLE AIR CTRL MOTOR
ALDL CONN
PARK/NEUTRAL SW (GND)
ABS (REAR WHEEL)
ABS (4 WHEEL)
NOT USED
EST DISTRIBUTOR
IGN MOD
PICK UP COIL
SET TIMING CONN
IGNITION SW
IGNITION COIL
NOT USED
4TH SW
TEMP SW
OPEN ON 4-3 SHIFT
TCC SOL
TCC BRAKE SW
AUTO TRANS
91E13783

Fig. 1: Wiring Diagram (Astro & Safari 4.3L)

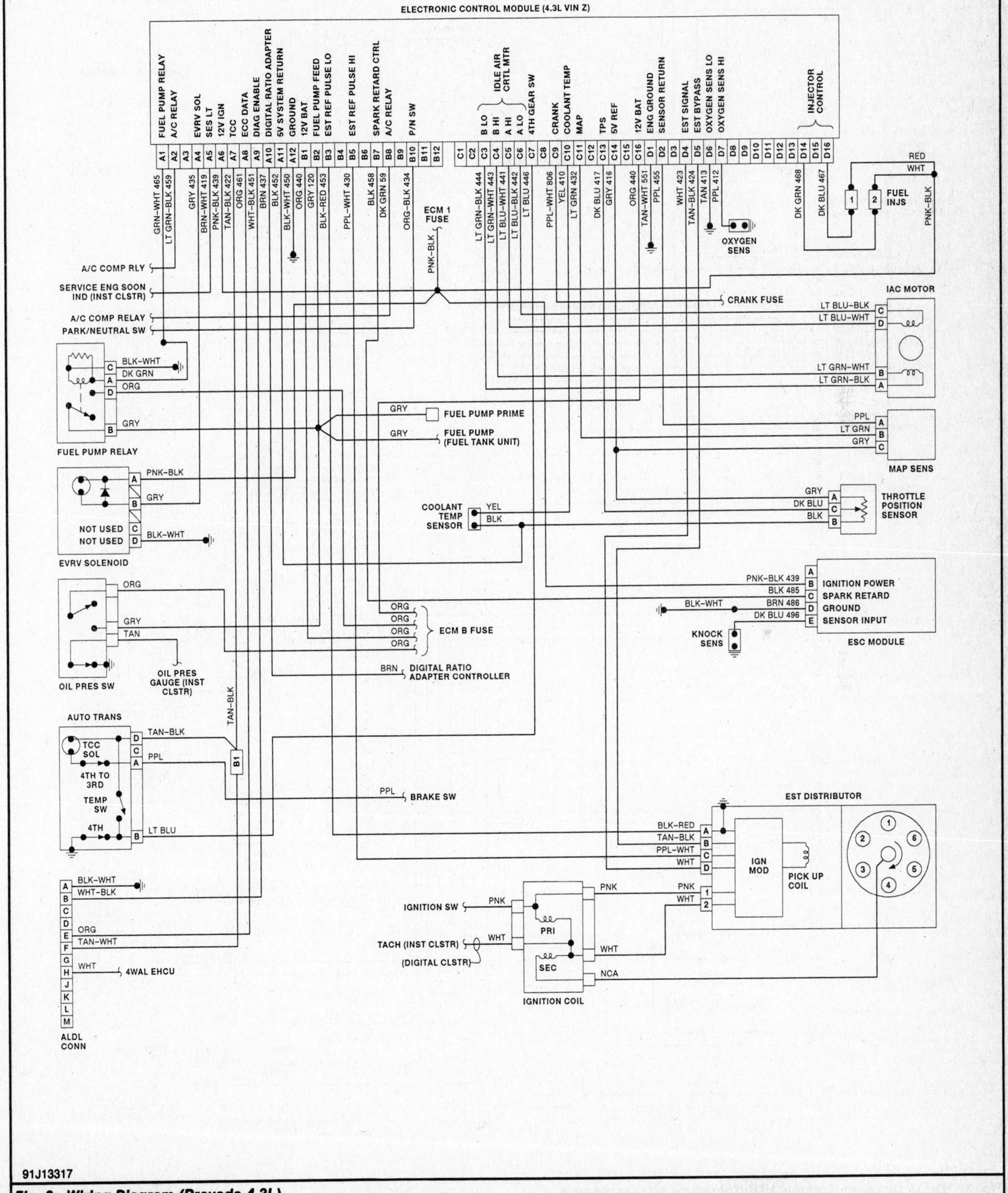
ELECTRONIC CONTROL MODULE (4.3L VIN Z)
FUEL PUMP RELAY
A/C RELAY
EVRV SOL
SES LT
12V IGN
TCC
ECC DATA
DIAG ENABLE
DIGITAL RATIO ADAPTER
5V SYSTEM RETURN
GROUND
12V BAT
FUEL PUMP FEED
EST REF PULSE LO
EST REF PULSE HI
SPARK RETARD CTRL
A/C RELAY
P/N SW
IDLE AIR CRTL MTR
B LO
B HI
A HI
A LO
4TH GEAR SW
CRANK
COOLANT TEMP
MAP
TPS
5V REF
12V BAT
ENG GROUND
SENSOR RETURN
EST SIGNAL
EST BYPASS
OXYGEN SENS LO
OXYGEN SENS HI
INJECTOR CONTROL
ECM 1 FUSE
OXYGEN SENS
FUEL INJS
A/C COMP RLY
SERVICE ENG SOON IND (INST CLSTR)
A/C COMP RELAY
PARK/NEUTRAL SW
CRANK FUSE
IAC MOTOR
FUEL PUMP RELAY
FUEL PUMP PRIME
FUEL PUMP (FUEL TANK UNIT)
MAP SENS
NOT USED
NOT USED
EVRV SOLENOID
COOLANT TEMP SENSOR
THROTTLE POSITION SENSOR
IGNITION POWER
SPARK RETARD
GROUND
SENSOR INPUT
ESC MODULE
KNOCK SENS
ECM B FUSE
OIL PRES SW
OIL PRES GAUGE (INST CLSTR)
DIGITAL RATIO ADAPTER CONTROLLER
AUTO TRANS
TCC SOL
4TH TO 3RD
TEMP SW
4TH
BRAKE SW
EST DISTRIBUTOR
IGN MOD
PICK UP COIL
IGNITION SW
TACH (INST CLSTR)
(DIGITAL CLSTR)
PRI
SEC
IGNITION COIL
4WAL EHCU
ALDL CONN
91J13317

Fig. 2: Wiring Diagram (Bravada 4.3L)

1991 ENGINE PERFORMANCE
Wiring Diagrams (Cont.)

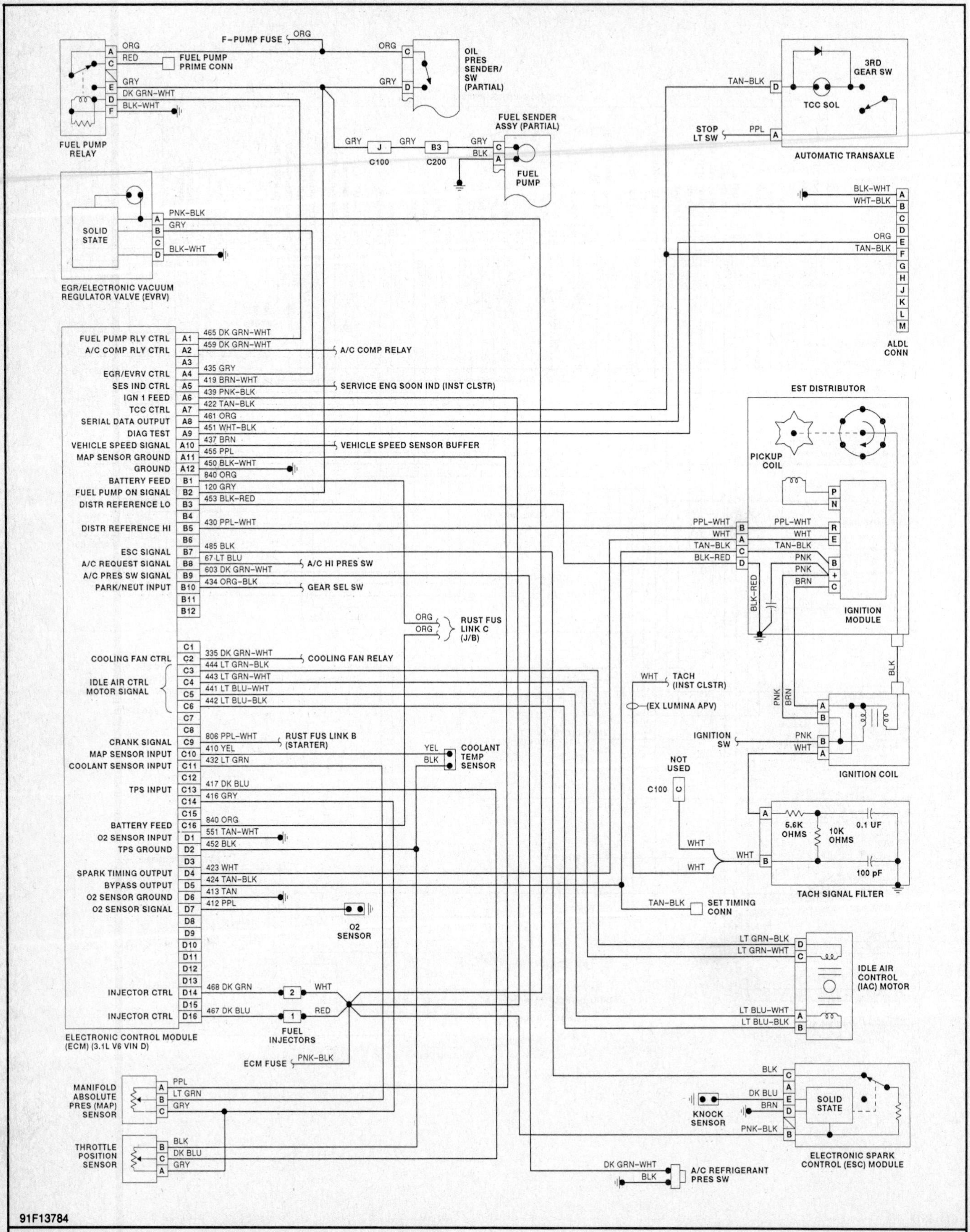
F-PUMP FUSE
ORG
RED
GRY
DK GRN-WHT
BLK-WHT
FUEL PUMP PRIME CONN
FUEL PUMP RELAY
OIL PRES SENDER/ SW (PARTIAL)
FUEL SENDER ASSY (PARTIAL)
FUEL PUMP
C100
C200
TAN-BLK
3RD GEAR SW
TCC SOL
STOP LT SW
PPL
AUTOMATIC TRANSAXLE
SOLID STATE
PNK-BLK
EGR/ELECTRONIC VACUUM REGULATOR VALVE (EVRV)
WHT-BLK
ALDL CONN
FUEL PUMP RLY CTRL
A/C COMP RLY CTRL
EGR/EVRV CTRL
SES IND CTRL
IGN 1 FEED
TCC CTRL
SERIAL DATA OUTPUT
DIAG TEST
VEHICLE SPEED SIGNAL
MAP SENSOR GROUND
GROUND
BATTERY FEED
FUEL PUMP ON SIGNAL
DISTR REFERENCE LO
DISTR REFERENCE HI
ESC SIGNAL
A/C REQUEST SIGNAL
A/C PRES SW SIGNAL
PARK/NEUT INPUT
465 DK GRN-WHT
459 DK GRN-WHT
435 GRY
419 BRN-WHT
439 PNK-BLK
422 TAN-BLK
461 ORG
451 WHT-BLK
437 BRN
455 PPL
450 BLK-WHT
840 ORG
120 GRY
453 BLK-RED
430 PPL-WHT
485 BLK
67 LT BLU
603 DK GRN-WHT
434 ORG-BLK
A/C COMP RELAY
SERVICE ENG SOON IND (INST CLSTR)
VEHICLE SPEED SENSOR BUFFER
A/C HI PRES SW
GEAR SEL SW
RUST FUS LINK C (J/B)
EST DISTRIBUTOR
PICKUP COIL
PPL-WHT
WHT
BLK-RED
PNK
BRN
IGNITION MODULE
COOLING FAN CTRL
IDLE AIR CTRL MOTOR SIGNAL
CRANK SIGNAL
MAP SENSOR INPUT
COOLANT SENSOR INPUT
TPS INPUT
BATTERY FEED
O2 SENSOR INPUT
TPS GROUND
SPARK TIMING OUTPUT
BYPASS OUTPUT
O2 SENSOR GROUND
O2 SENSOR SIGNAL
INJECTOR CTRL
INJECTOR CTRL
335 DK GRN-WHT
444 LT GRN-BLK
443 LT GRN-WHT
441 LT BLU-WHT
442 LT BLU-BLK
806 PPL-WHT
410 YEL
432 LT GRN
417 DK BLU
416 GRY
840 ORG
551 TAN-WHT
452 BLK
423 WHT
424 TAN-BLK
413 TAN
412 PPL
468 DK GRN
467 DK BLU
COOLING FAN RELAY
RUST FUS LINK B (STARTER)
YEL
BLK
COOLANT TEMP SENSOR
O2 SENSOR
FUEL INJECTORS
ELECTRONIC CONTROL MODULE (ECM) (3.1L V6 VIN D)
ECM FUSE
WHT TACH (INST CLSTR)
(EX LUMINA APV)
IGNITION SW
IGNITION COIL
NOT USED
C100
5.6K OHMS
10K OHMS
0.1 UF
100 pF
TACH SIGNAL FILTER
SET TIMING CONN
LT GRN-BLK
LT GRN-WHT
LT BLU-WHT
LT BLU-BLK
IDLE AIR CONTROL (IAC) MOTOR
MANIFOLD ABSOLUTE PRES (MAP) SENSOR
PPL
LT GRN
GRY
THROTTLE POSITION SENSOR
BLK
DK BLU
KNOCK SENSOR
ELECTRONIC SPARK CONTROL (ESC) MODULE
DK GRN-WHT
A/C REFRIGERANT PRES SW
91F13784

Fig. 3: Wiring Diagram (Lumina APV, Silhouette & Trans Sport 3.1L)

1991 ENGINE PERFORMANCE
Wiring Diagrams (Cont.)

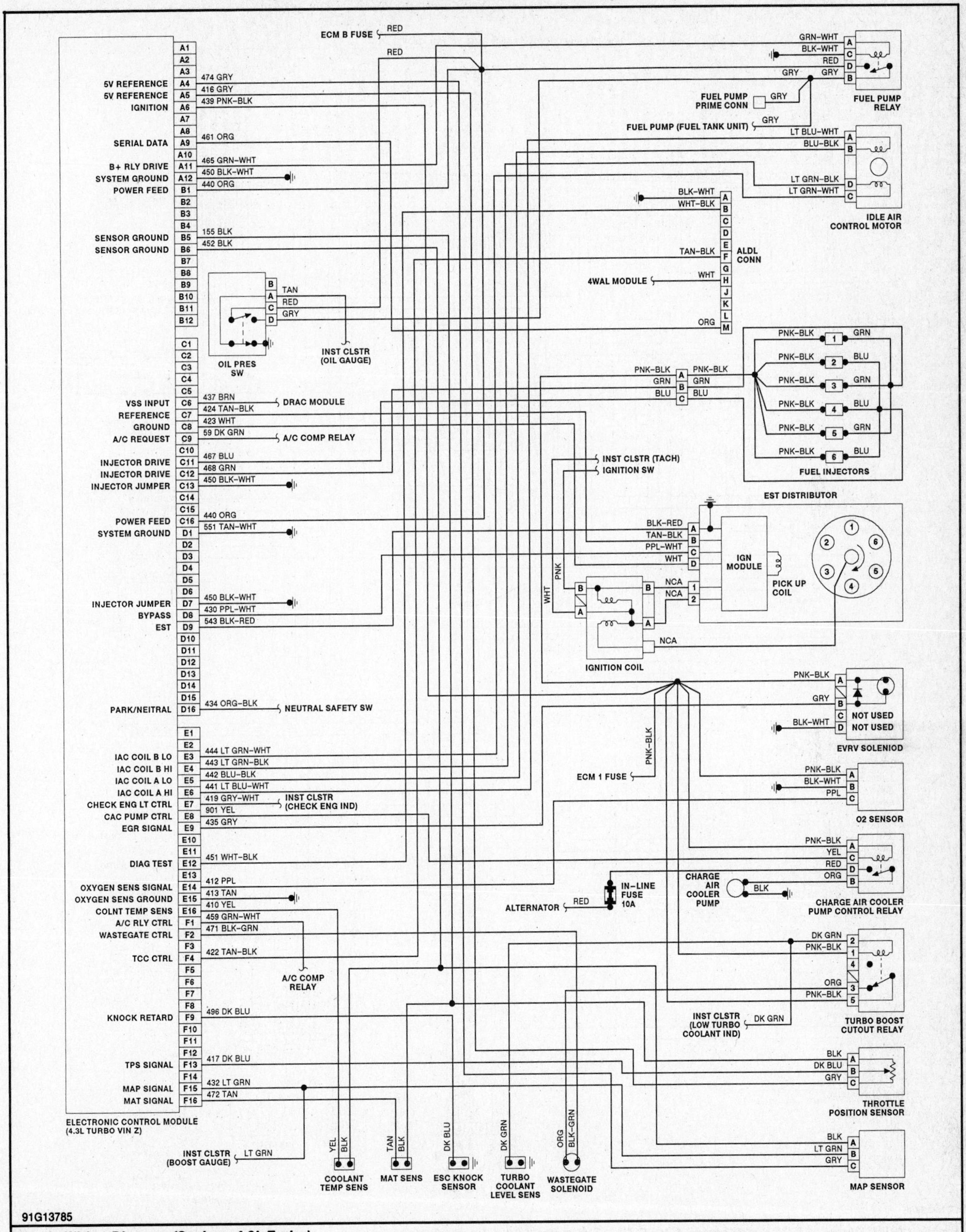
ECM B FUSE
RED
5V REFERENCE
5V REFERENCE
IGNITION
SERIAL DATA
B+ RLY DRIVE
SYSTEM GROUND
POWER FEED
SENSOR GROUND
SENSOR GROUND
VSS INPUT
REFERENCE
GROUND
A/C REQUEST
INJECTOR DRIVE
INJECTOR DRIVE
INJECTOR JUMPER
POWER FEED
SYSTEM GROUND
INJECTOR JUMPER
BYPASS
EST
PARK/NEITRAL
IAC COIL B LO
IAC COIL B HI
IAC COIL A LO
IAC COIL A HI
CHECK ENG LT CTRL
CAC PUMP CTRL
EGR SIGNAL
DIAG TEST
OXYGEN SENS SIGNAL
OXYGEN SENS GROUND
COLNT TEMP SENS
A/C RLY CTRL
WASTEGATE CTRL
TCC CTRL
KNOCK RETARD
TPS SIGNAL
MAP SIGNAL
MAT SIGNAL
474 GRY
416 GRY
439 PNK-BLK
461 ORG
465 GRN-WHT
450 BLK-WHT
440 ORG
155 BLK
452 BLK
437 BRN
424 TAN-BLK
423 WHT
59 DK GRN
467 BLU
468 GRN
450 BLK-WHT
440 ORG
551 TAN-WHT
450 BLK-WHT
430 PPL-WHT
543 BLK-RED
434 ORG-BLK
444 LT GRN-WHT
443 LT GRN-BLK
442 BLU-BLK
441 LT BLU-WHT
419 GRY-WHT
901 YEL
435 GRY
451 WHT-BLK
412 PPL
413 TAN
410 YEL
459 GRN-WHT
471 BLK-GRN
422 TAN-BLK
496 DK BLU
417 DK BLU
432 LT GRN
472 TAN
OIL PRES SW
TAN
RED
GRY
INST CLSTR (OIL GAUGE)
DRAC MODULE
A/C COMP RELAY
NEUTRAL SAFETY SW
INST CLSTR (CHECK ENG IND)
A/C COMP RELAY
ELECTRONIC CONTROL MODULE (4.3L TURBO VIN Z)
INST CLSTR (BOOST GAUGE)
LT GRN
YEL
BLK
TAN
BLK
DK BLU
DK GRN
ORG
BLK-GRN
COOLANT TEMP SENS
MAT SENS
ESC KNOCK SENSOR
TURBO COOLANT LEVEL SENS
WASTEGATE SOLENOID
GRN-WHT
BLK-WHT
RED
GRY
FUEL PUMP RELAY
FUEL PUMP PRIME CONN
FUEL PUMP (FUEL TANK UNIT)
LT BLU-WHT
BLU-BLK
LT GRN-BLK
LT GRN-WHT
IDLE AIR CONTROL MOTOR
BLK-WHT
WHT-BLK
TAN-BLK
ALDL CONN
4WAL MODULE
WHT
ORG
PNK-BLK
GRN
BLU
FUEL INJECTORS
INST CLSTR (TACH)
IGNITION SW
EST DISTRIBUTOR
BLK-RED
TAN-BLK
PPL-WHT
WHT
IGN MODULE
PICK UP COIL
NCA
IGNITION COIL
PNK
EVRV SOLENIOD
NOT USED
NOT USED
ECM 1 FUSE
O2 SENSOR
PPL
YEL
CHARGE AIR COOLER PUMP
CHARGE AIR COOLER PUMP CONTROL RELAY
IN-LINE FUSE 10A
ALTERNATOR
BLK
DK GRN
TURBO BOOST CUTOUT RELAY
INST CLSTR (LOW TURBO COOLANT IND)
DK BLU
THROTTLE POSITION SENSOR
LT GRN
MAP SENSOR
91G13785

Fig. 4: Wiring Diagram (Syclone 4.3L Turbo)

1991 ENGINE PERFORMANCE
Wiring Diagrams (Cont.)

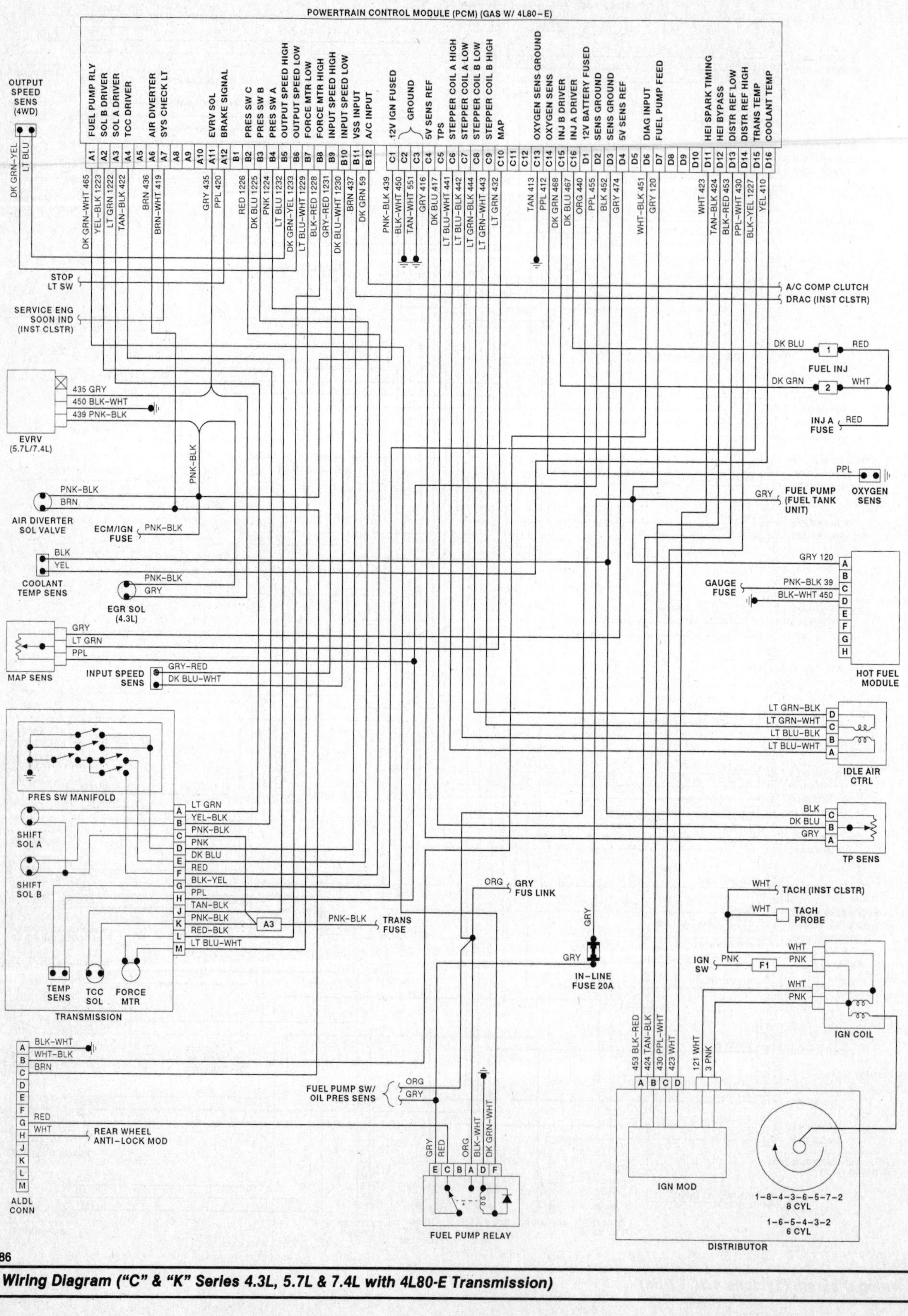
POWERTRAIN CONTROL MODULE (PCM) (GAS W/ 4L80-E)
FUEL PUMP RLY
SOL B DRIVER
SOL A DRIVER
TCC DRIVER
AIR DIVERTER
SYS CHECK LT
EVRV SOL
BRAKE SIGNAL
PRES SW C
PRES SW B
PRES SW A
OUTPUT SPEED HIGH
OUTPUT SPEED LOW
FORCE MTR LOW
FORCE MTR HIGH
INPUT SPEED HIGH
INPUT SPEED LOW
VSS INPUT
A/C INPUT
12V IGN FUSED
GROUND
5V SENS REF
TPS
STEPPER COIL A HIGH
STEPPER COIL A LOW
STEPPER COIL B LOW
STEPPER COIL B HIGH
MAP
OXYGEN SENS GROUND
OXYGEN SENS
INJ B DRIVER
INJ A DRIVER
12V BATTERY FUSED
SENS GROUND
SENS GROUND
5V SENS REF
DIAG INPUT
FUEL PUMP FEED
HEI SPARK TIMING
HEI BYPASS
DISTR REF LOW
DISTR REF HIGH
TRANS TEMP
COOLANT TEMP
A1 A2 A3 A4 A5 A6 A7 A8 A9 A10 A11 A12 B1 B2 B3 B4 B5 B6 B7 B8 B9 B10 B11 B12 C1 C2 C3 C4 C5 C6 C7 C8 C9 C10 C11 C12 C13 C14 C15 C16 D1 D2 D3 D4 D5 D6 D7 D8 D9 D10 D11 D12 D13 D14 D15 D16
DK GRN-WHT 465
YEL-BLK 1223
LT GRN 1222
TAN-BLK 422
BRN 436
BRN-WHT 419
GRY 435
PPL 420
RED 1226
DK BLU 1225
PNK 1224
LT BLU 1232
DK GRN-YEL 1233
LT BLU-WHT 1229
BLK-RED 1228
GRY-RED 1231
DK BLU-WHT 1230
BRN 437
DK GRN 59
PNK-BLK 439
BLK-WHT 450
TAN-WHT 551
GRY 416
DK BLU 417
LT BLU-WHT 441
LT BLU-BLK 442
LT GRN-BLK 444
LT GRN-WHT 443
LT GRN 432
TAN 413
PPL 412
DK GRN 468
DK BLU 467
ORG 440
PPL 455
BLK 452
GRY 474
WHT-BLK 451
GRY 120
WHT 423
TAN-BLK 424
BLK-RED 453
PPL-WHT 430
BLK-YEL 1227
YEL 410
OUTPUT SPEED SENS (4WD)
DK GRN-YEL
LT BLU
STOP LT SW
SERVICE ENG SOON IND (INST CLSTR)
A/C COMP CLUTCH
DRAC (INST CLSTR)
DK BLU
RED
FUEL INJ
DK GRN
WHT
INJ A FUSE
435 GRY
450 BLK-WHT
439 PNK-BLK
EVRV (5.7L/7.4L)
PNK-BLK
PPL
OXYGEN SENS
GRY
FUEL PUMP (FUEL TANK UNIT)
PNK-BLK
BRN
AIR DIVERTER SOL VALVE
ECM/IGN FUSE
BLK
YEL
COOLANT TEMP SENS
PNK-BLK
GRY
EGR SOL (4.3L)
GRY 120
GAUGE FUSE
PNK-BLK 39
BLK-WHT 450
A B C D E F G H
HOT FUEL MODULE
GRY
LT GRN
PPL
MAP SENS
INPUT SPEED SENS
GRY-RED
DK BLU-WHT
LT GRN-BLK
LT GRN-WHT
LT BLU-BLK
LT BLU-WHT
IDLE AIR CTRL
PRES SW MANIFOLD
SHIFT SOL A
SHIFT SOL B
LT GRN
YEL-BLK
PNK-BLK
PNK
DK BLU
RED
BLK-YEL
PPL
TAN-BLK
PNK-BLK
RED-BLK
LT BLU-WHT
A3
TRANS FUSE
BLK
DK BLU
GRY
TP SENS
ORG
GRY FUS LINK
GRY
IN-LINE FUSE 20A
WHT
TACH (INST CLSTR)
TACH PROBE
IGN SW
PNK
F1
IGN COIL
TEMP SENS
TCC SOL
FORCE MTR
TRANSMISSION
BLK-WHT
WHT-BLK
BRN
RED
WHT
REAR WHEEL ANTI-LOCK MOD
ALDL CONN
FUEL PUMP SW/ OIL PRES SENS
ORG
GRY
RED
BLK-WHT
DK GRN-WHT
E C B A D F
FUEL PUMP RELAY
453 BLK-RED
424 TAN-BLK
430 PPL-WHT
423 WHT
121 WHT
3 PNK
IGN MOD
1-8-4-3-6-5-7-2 8 CYL
1-6-5-4-3-2 6 CYL
DISTRIBUTOR

91H13786

Fig. 5: Wiring Diagram ("C" & "K" Series 4.3L, 5.7L & 7.4L with 4L80-E Transmission)

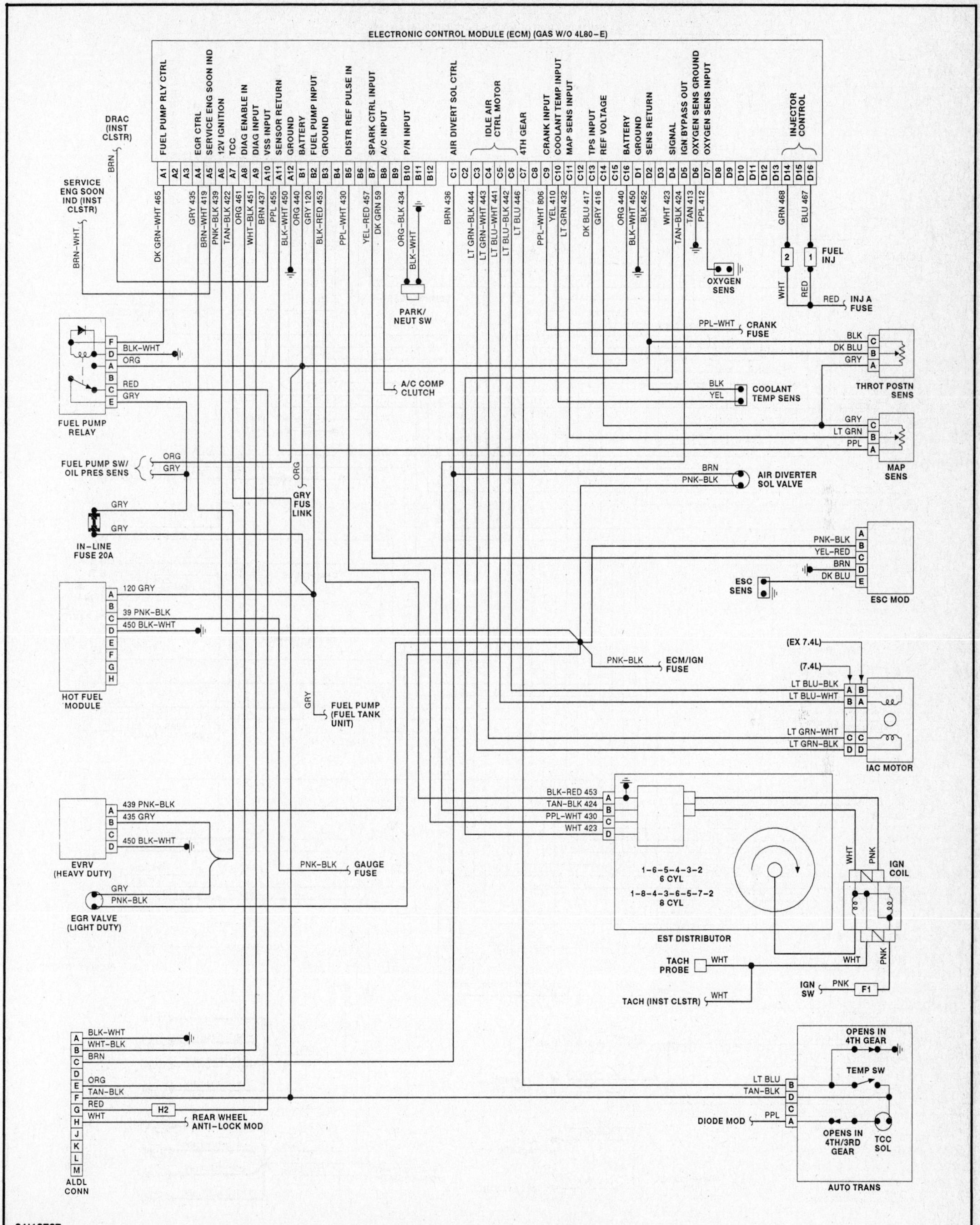

ELECTRONIC CONTROL MODULE (ECM) (GAS W/O 4L80-E)
FUEL PUMP RLY CTRL
EGR CTRL
SERVICE ENG SOON IND
12V IGNITION
TCC
DIAG ENABLE IN
DIAG INPUT
VSS INPUT
SENSOR RETURN
GROUND
BATTERY
FUEL PUMP INPUT
GROUND
DISTR REF PULSE IN
SPARK CTRL INPUT
A/C INPUT
P/N INPUT
AIR DIVERT SOL CTRL
IDLE AIR CTRL MOTOR
4TH GEAR
CRANK INPUT
COOLANT TEMP INPUT
MAP SENS INPUT
TPS INPUT
REF VOLTAGE
BATTERY
GROUND
SENS RETURN
SIGNAL
IGN BYPASS OUT
OXYGEN SENS GROUND
OXYGEN SENS INPUT
INJECTOR CONTROL
DRAC (INST CLSTR)
SERVICE ENG SOON IND (INST CLSTR)
FUEL PUMP RELAY
FUEL PUMP SW/ OIL PRES SENS
IN-LINE FUSE 20A
GRY FUS LINK
HOT FUEL MODULE
FUEL PUMP (FUEL TANK UNIT)
EVRV (HEAVY DUTY)
EGR VALVE (LIGHT DUTY)
GAUGE FUSE
ALDL CONN
REAR WHEEL ANTI-LOCK MOD
PARK/ NEUT SW
A/C COMP CLUTCH
OXYGEN SENS
FUEL INJ
INJ A FUSE
CRANK FUSE
THROT POSTN SENS
COOLANT TEMP SENS
MAP SENS
AIR DIVERTER SOL VALVE
ESC SENS
ESC MOD
ECM/IGN FUSE
(EX 7.4L)
(7.4L)
IAC MOTOR
EST DISTRIBUTOR
1-6-5-4-3-2 6 CYL
1-8-4-3-6-5-7-2 8 CYL
IGN COIL
TACH PROBE
TACH (INST CLSTR)
IGN SW
DIODE MOD
OPENS IN 4TH GEAR
TEMP SW
OPENS IN 4TH/3RD GEAR
TCC SOL
AUTO TRANS
91I13787

Fig. 6: Wiring Diagram ("C" & "K" Series 4.3L, 5.0L & 5.7L without 4L80-E Transmission)

1991 ENGINE PERFORMANCE
Wiring Diagrams (Cont.)

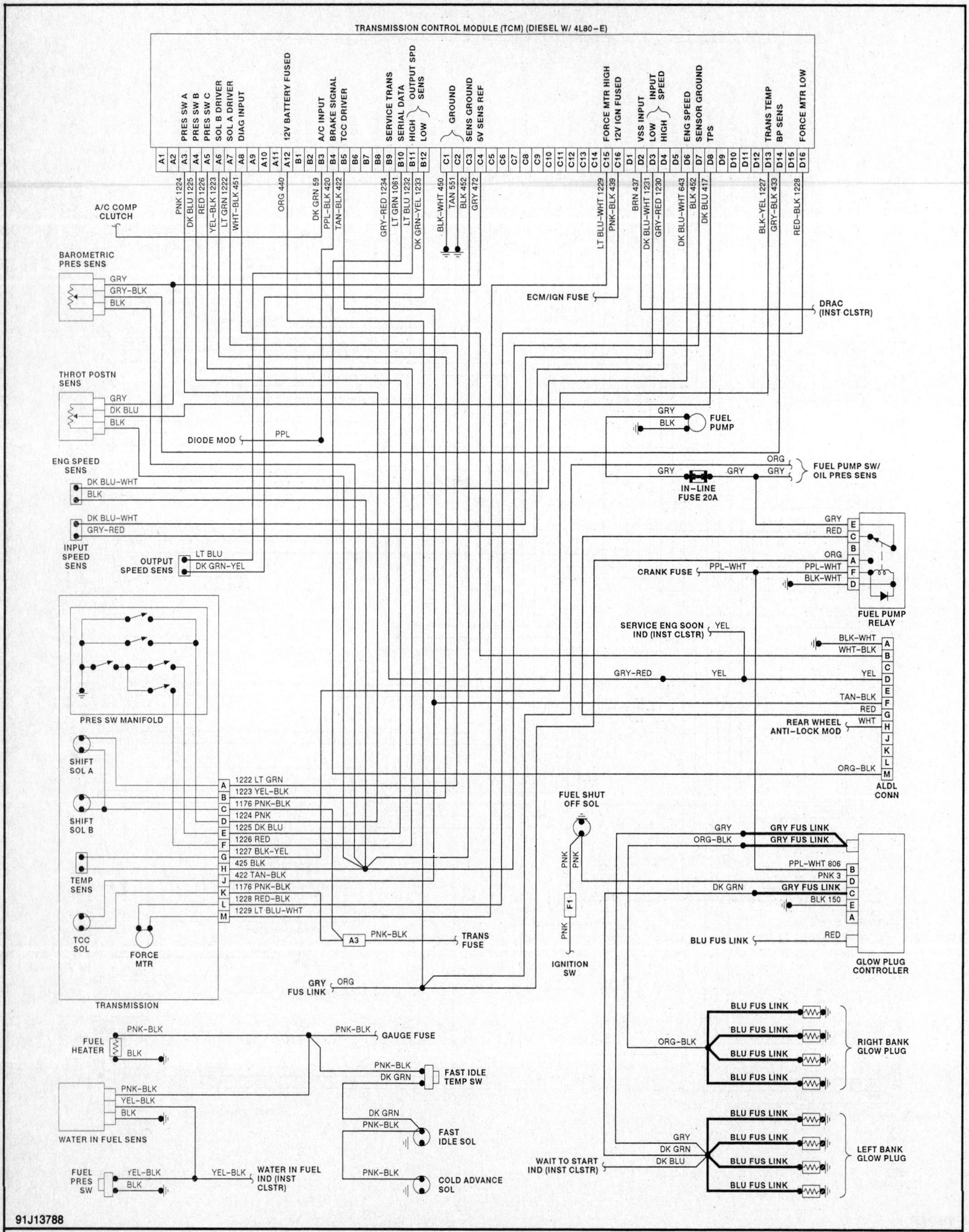
TRANSMISSION CONTROL MODULE (TCM) (DIESEL W/ 4L80-E)
A/C COMP CLUTCH
BAROMETRIC PRES SENS
THROT POSTN SENS
DIODE MOD
ENG SPEED SENS
INPUT SPEED SENS
OUTPUT SPEED SENS
PRES SW MANIFOLD
SHIFT SOL A
SHIFT SOL B
TEMP SENS
TCC SOL
FORCE MTR
TRANSMISSION
TRANS FUSE
GRY FUS LINK
ECM/IGN FUSE
DRAC (INST CLSTR)
FUEL PUMP
FUEL PUMP SW/ OIL PRES SENS
IN-LINE FUSE 20A
FUEL PUMP RELAY
CRANK FUSE
SERVICE ENG SOON IND (INST CLSTR)
REAR WHEEL ANTI-LOCK MOD
ALDL CONN
FUEL SHUT OFF SOL
IGNITION SW
GLOW PLUG CONTROLLER
BLU FUS LINK
RIGHT BANK GLOW PLUG
LEFT BANK GLOW PLUG
WAIT TO START IND (INST CLSTR)
FUEL HEATER
GAUGE FUSE
FAST IDLE TEMP SW
FAST IDLE SOL
COLD ADVANCE SOL
WATER IN FUEL SENS
FUEL PRES SW
WATER IN FUEL IND (INST CLSTR)
91J13788

Fig. 7: Wiring Diagram ("C" & "K" Series 6.2L Diesel with 4L80-E Transmission)

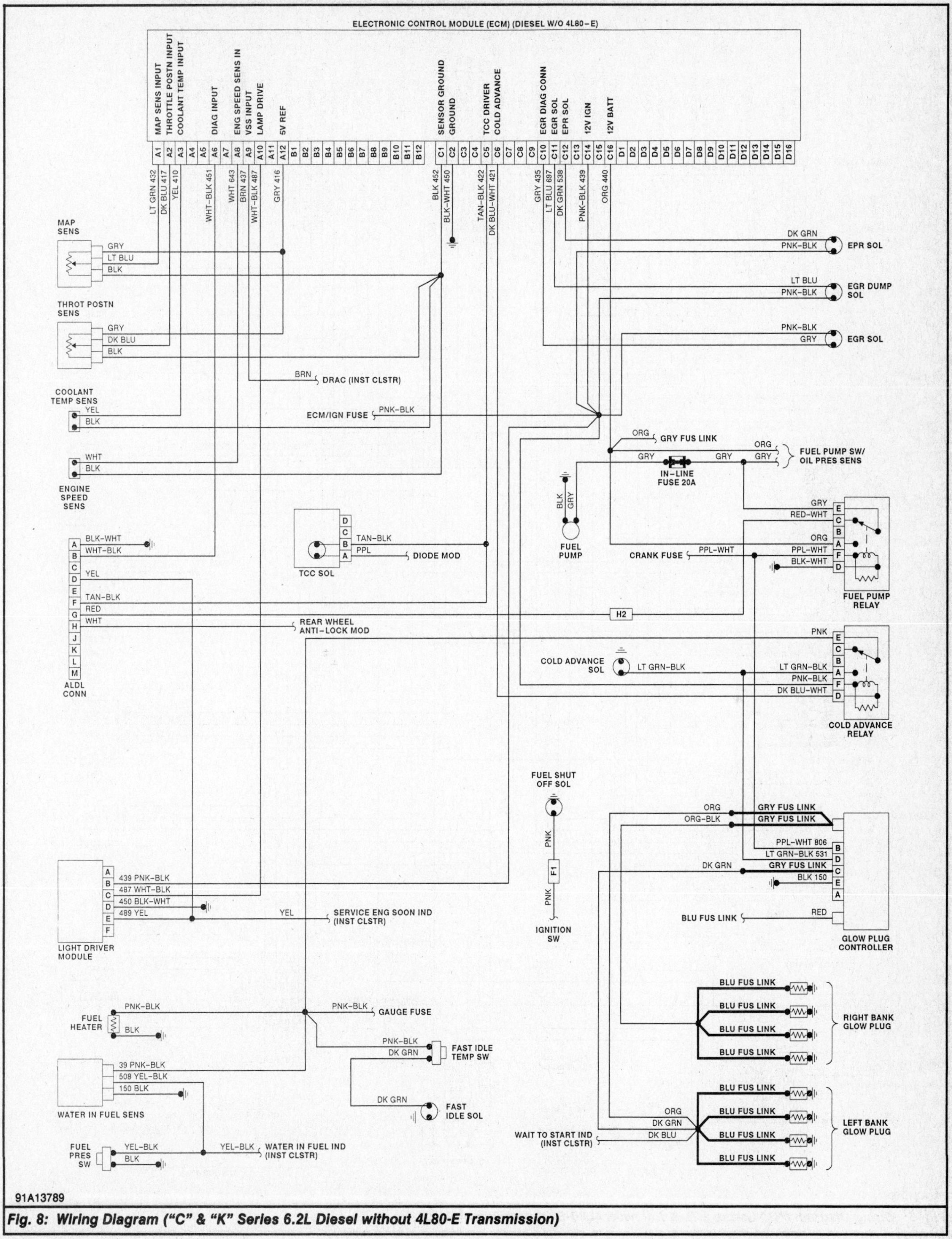

ELECTRONIC CONTROL MODULE (ECM) (DIESEL W/O 4L80-E)
MAP SENS INPUT
THROTTLE POSTN INPUT
COOLANT TEMP INPUT
DIAG INPUT
ENG SPEED SENS IN
VSS INPUT
LAMP DRIVE
5V REF
SENSOR GROUND
GROUND
TCC DRIVER
COLD ADVANCE
EGR DIAG CONN
EGR SOL
EPR SOL
12V IGN
12V BATT
MAP SENS
THROT POSTN SENS
COOLANT TEMP SENS
ENGINE SPEED SENS
DRAC (INST CLSTR)
ECM/IGN FUSE
TCC SOL
DIODE MOD
ALDL CONN
REAR WHEEL ANTI-LOCK MOD
EPR SOL
EGR DUMP SOL
EGR SOL
GRY FUS LINK
FUEL PUMP SW/ OIL PRES SENS
IN-LINE FUSE 20A
FUEL PUMP
CRANK FUSE
FUEL PUMP RELAY
COLD ADVANCE SOL
COLD ADVANCE RELAY
FUEL SHUT OFF SOL
IGNITION SW
GLOW PLUG CONTROLLER
BLU FUS LINK
LIGHT DRIVER MODULE
SERVICE ENG SOON IND (INST CLSTR)
FUEL HEATER
GAUGE FUSE
FAST IDLE TEMP SW
FAST IDLE SOL
WATER IN FUEL SENS
FUEL PRES SW
WATER IN FUEL IND (INST CLSTR)
WAIT TO START IND (INST CLSTR)
RIGHT BANK GLOW PLUG
LEFT BANK GLOW PLUG
91A13789

Fig. 8: Wiring Diagram ("C" & "K" Series 6.2L Diesel without 4L80-E Transmission)

1991 ENGINE PERFORMANCE
Wiring Diagrams (Cont.)

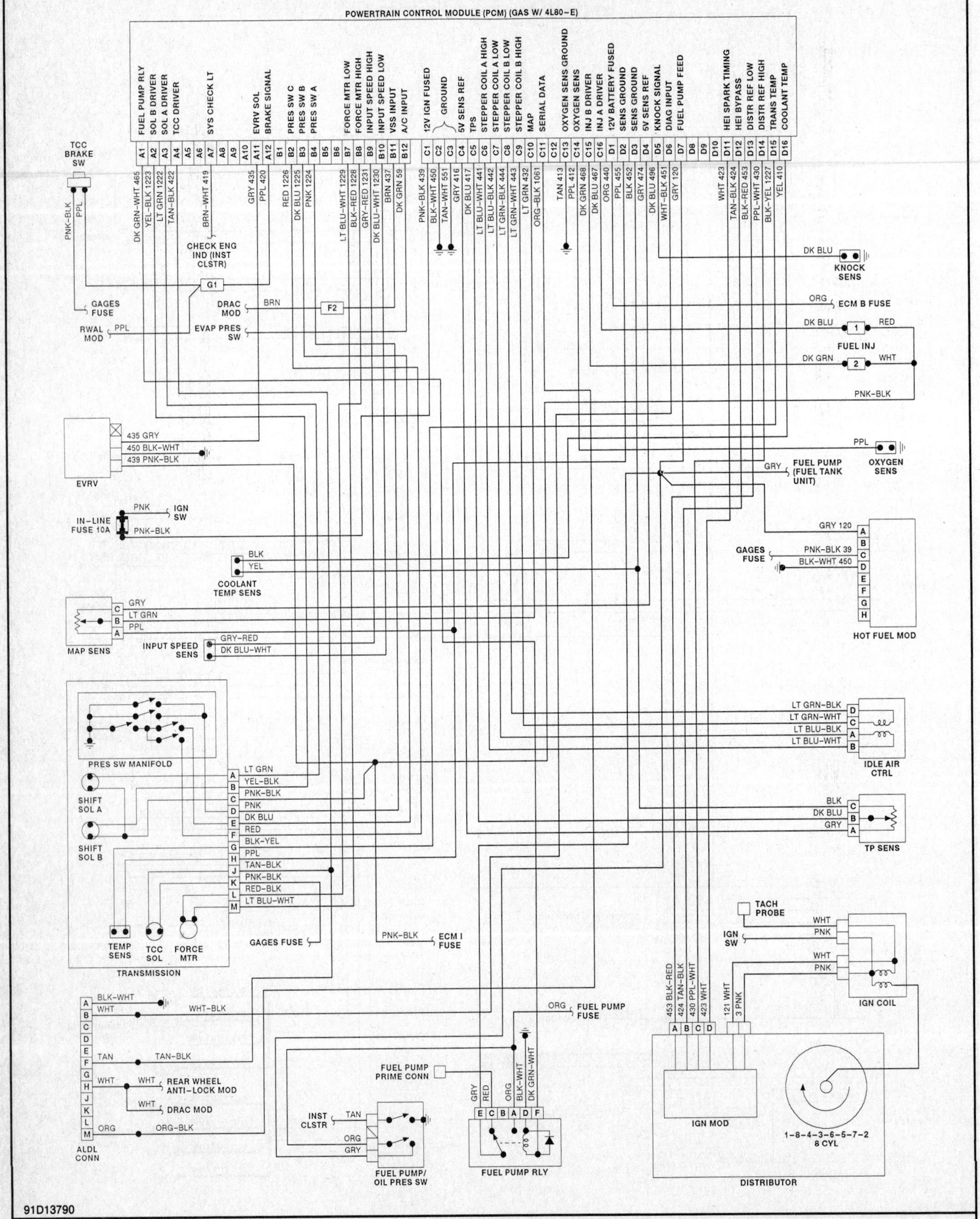
POWERTRAIN CONTROL MODULE (PCM) (GAS W/ 4L80-E)
FUEL PUMP RLY
SOL B DRIVER
SOL A DRIVER
TCC DRIVER
SYS CHECK LT
EVRV SOL
BRAKE SIGNAL
PRES SW C
PRES SW B
PRES SW A
FORCE MTR LOW
FORCE MTR HIGH
INPUT SPEED HIGH
INPUT SPEED LOW
VSS INPUT
A/C INPUT
12V IGN FUSED
GROUND
5V SENS REF
TPS
STEPPER COIL A HIGH
STEPPER COIL A LOW
STEPPER COIL B LOW
STEPPER COIL B HIGH
MAP
SERIAL DATA
OXYGEN SENS GROUND
OXYGEN SENS
INJ B DRIVER
INJ A DRIVER
12V BATTERY FUSED
SENS GROUND
SENS GROUND
5V SENS REF
KNOCK SIGNAL
DIAG INPUT
FUEL PUMP FEED
HEI SPARK TIMING
HEI BYPASS
DISTR REF LOW
DISTR REF HIGH
TRANS TEMP
COOLANT TEMP
A1 A2 A3 A4 A5 A6 A7 A8 A9 A10 A11 A12
B1 B2 B3 B4 B5 B6 B7 B8 B9 B10 B11 B12
C1 C2 C3 C4 C5 C6 C7 C8 C9 C10 C11 C12 C13 C14 C15 C16
D1 D2 D3 D4 D5 D6 D7 D8 D9 D10 D11 D12 D13 D14 D15 D16
DK GRN-WHT 465
YEL-BLK 1223
LT GRN 1222
TAN-BLK 422
BRN-WHT 419
GRY 435
PPL 420
RED 1226
DK BLU 1225
PNK 1224
LT BLU-WHT 1229
BLK-RED 1228
GRY-RED 1231
DK BLU-WHT 1230
BRN 437
DK GRN 59
PNK-BLK 439
BLK-WHT 450
TAN-WHT 551
GRY 416
DK BLU 417
LT BLU-WHT 441
LT BLU-BLK 442
LT GRN-BLK 444
LT GRN-WHT 443
LT GRN 432
ORG-BLK 1061
TAN 413
PPL 412
DK GRN 468
DK BLU 467
ORG 440
PPL 455
BLK 452
GRY 474
DK BLU 496
WHT-BLK 451
GRY 120
WHT 423
TAN-BLK 424
BLK-RED 453
PPL-WHT 430
BLK-YEL 1227
YEL 410
TCC BRAKE SW
PNK-BLK
PPL
CHECK ENG IND (INST CLSTR)
G1
GAGES FUSE
DRAC MOD
BRN
F2
RWAL MOD
PPL
EVAP PRES SW
DK BLU
KNOCK SENS
ORG
ECM B FUSE
DK BLU
RED
1
FUEL INJ
DK GRN
WHT
2
PNK-BLK
435 GRY
450 BLK-WHT
439 PNK-BLK
EVRV
PPL
OXYGEN SENS
GRY
FUEL PUMP (FUEL TANK UNIT)
PNK
IGN SW
IN-LINE FUSE 10A
PNK-BLK
GRY 120
GAGES FUSE
PNK-BLK 39
BLK-WHT 450
A B C D E F G H
HOT FUEL MOD
BLK
YEL
COOLANT TEMP SENS
GRY
LT GRN
PPL
C B A
MAP SENS
INPUT SPEED SENS
GRY-RED
DK BLU-WHT
LT GRN-BLK
LT GRN-WHT
LT BLU-BLK
LT BLU-WHT
D C A B
IDLE AIR CTRL
PRES SW MANIFOLD
SHIFT SOL A
SHIFT SOL B
A LT GRN
B YEL-BLK
C PNK-BLK
D PNK
E DK BLU
F RED
G BLK-YEL
H PPL
J TAN-BLK
K PNK-BLK
L RED-BLK
M LT BLU-WHT
BLK
DK BLU
GRY
C B A
TP SENS
TEMP SENS
TCC SOL
FORCE MTR
TRANSMISSION
GAGES FUSE
PNK-BLK
ECM I FUSE
TACH PROBE
IGN SW
WHT
PNK
WHT
PNK
IGN COIL
BLK-WHT
WHT
WHT-BLK
ORG
FUEL PUMP FUSE
TAN
TAN-BLK
WHT
WHT
REAR WHEEL ANTI-LOCK MOD
WHT
DRAC MOD
ORG
ORG-BLK
A B C D E F G H J K L M
ALDL CONN
FUEL PUMP PRIME CONN
INST CLSTR
TAN
ORG
GRY
FUEL PUMP/ OIL PRES SW
GRY
RED
ORG
BLK-WHT
DK GRN-WHT
E C B A D F
FUEL PUMP RLY
453 BLK-RED
424 TAN-BLK
430 PPL-WHT
423 WHT
121 WHT
3 PNK
A B C D
IGN MOD
1-8-4-3-6-5-7-2 8 CYL
DISTRIBUTOR
91D13790

Fig. 9: Wiring Diagram ("G" Series 5.7L & 7.4L with 4L80-E Transmission)

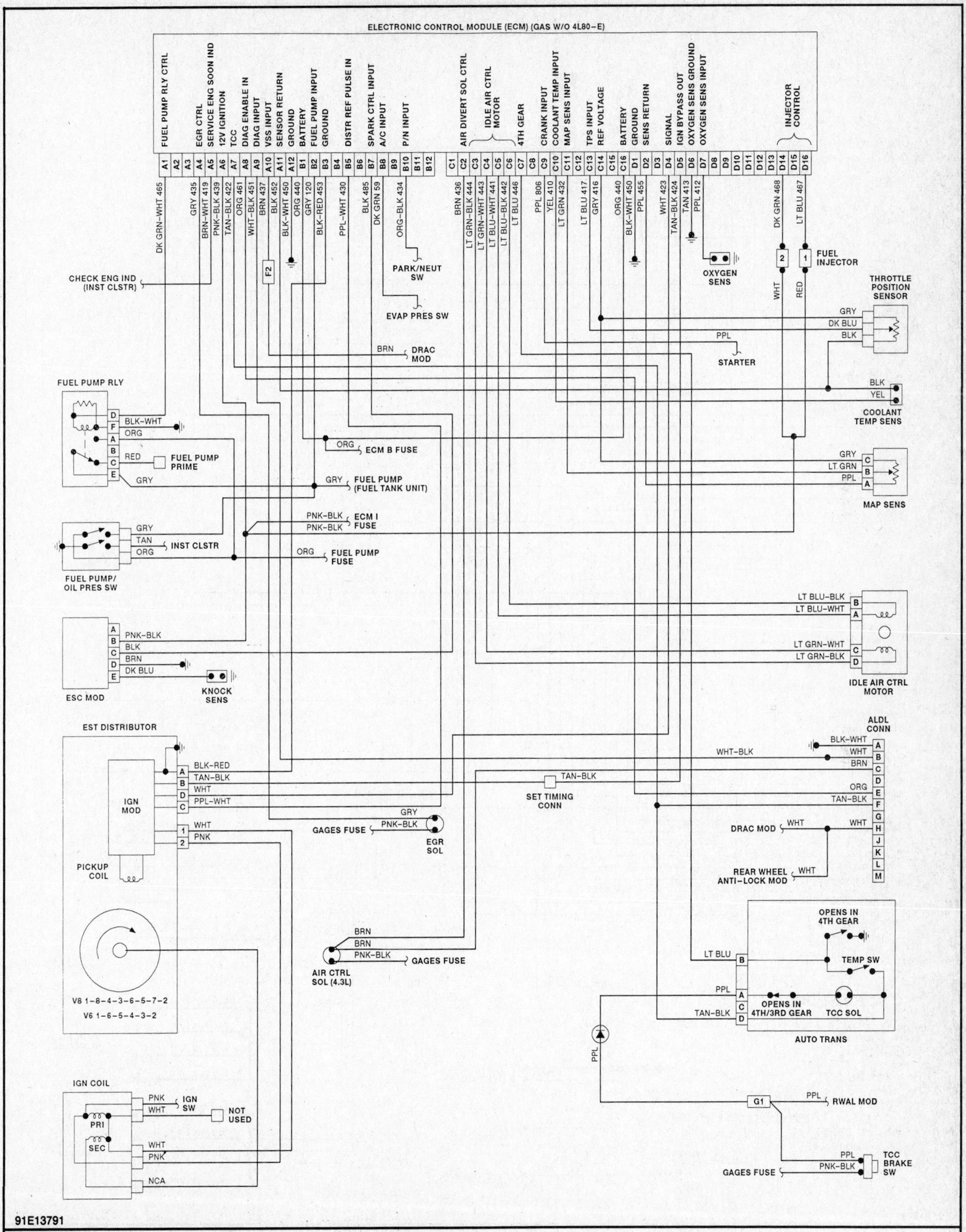

ELECTRONIC CONTROL MODULE (ECM) (GAS W/O 4L80-E)
FUEL PUMP RLY CTRL
EGR CTRL
SERVICE ENG SOON IND
12V IGNITION
TCC
DIAG ENABLE IN
DIAG INPUT
VSS INPUT
SENSOR RETURN
GROUND
BATTERY
FUEL PUMP INPUT
GROUND
DISTR REF PULSE IN
SPARK CTRL INPUT
A/C INPUT
P/N INPUT
AIR DIVERT SOL CTRL
IDLE AIR CTRL MOTOR
4TH GEAR
CRANK INPUT
COOLANT TEMP INPUT
MAP SENS INPUT
TPS INPUT
REF VOLTAGE
BATTERY GROUND
SENS RETURN
SIGNAL
IGN BYPASS OUT
OXYGEN SENS GROUND
OXYGEN SENS INPUT
INJECTOR CONTROL
CHECK ENG IND (INST CLSTR)
PARK/NEUT SW
EVAP PRES SW
DRAC MOD
STARTER
OXYGEN SENS
FUEL INJECTOR
THROTTLE POSITION SENSOR
FUEL PUMP RLY
ECM B FUSE
FUEL PUMP PRIME
FUEL PUMP (FUEL TANK UNIT)
COOLANT TEMP SENS
MAP SENS
ECM I FUSE
INST CLSTR
FUEL PUMP FUSE
FUEL PUMP/ OIL PRES SW
IDLE AIR CTRL MOTOR
ESC MOD
KNOCK SENS
EST DISTRIBUTOR
IGN MOD
PICKUP COIL
V8 1-8-4-3-6-5-7-2
V6 1-6-5-4-3-2
SET TIMING CONN
GAGES FUSE
EGR SOL
ALDL CONN
DRAC MOD
REAR WHEEL ANTI-LOCK MOD
OPENS IN 4TH GEAR
TEMP SW
OPENS IN 4TH/3RD GEAR
TCC SOL
AUTO TRANS
AIR CTRL SOL (4.3L)
IGN COIL
PRI
SEC
IGN SW
NOT USED
NCA
RWAL MOD
G1
TCC BRAKE SW
91E13791

Fig. 10: Wiring Diagram ("G" Series 4.3L & 5.7L without 4L80-E Transmission)

1991 ENGINE PERFORMANCE
Wiring Diagrams (Cont.)

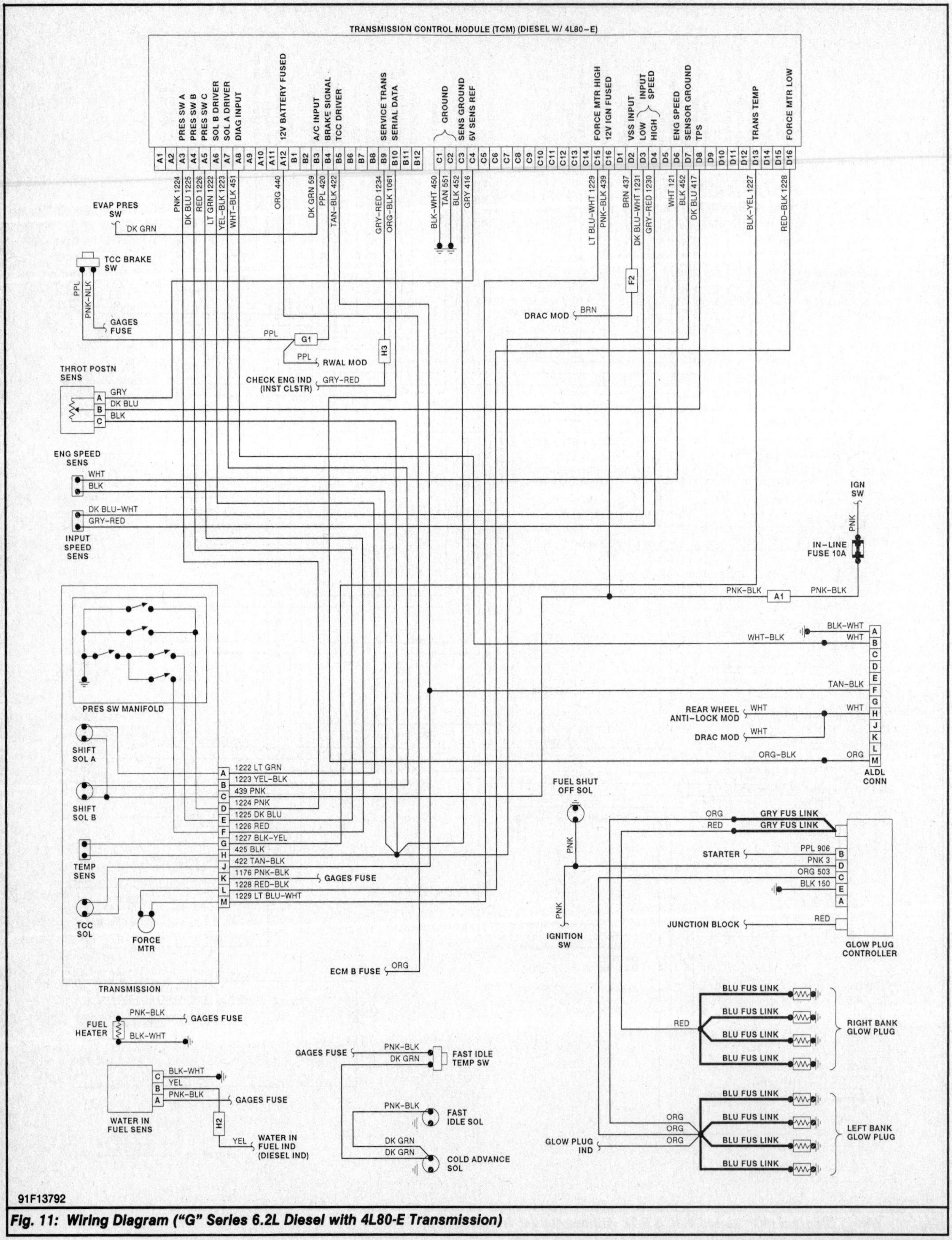
TRANSMISSION CONTROL MODULE (TCM) (DIESEL W/ 4L80-E)
PRES SW A
PRES SW B
PRES SW C
SOL B DRIVER
SOL A DRIVER
DIAG INPUT
12V BATTERY FUSED
A/C INPUT
BRAKE SIGNAL
TCC DRIVER
SERVICE TRANS
SERIAL DATA
GROUND
SENS GROUND
5V SENS REF
FORCE MTR HIGH
12V IGN FUSED
VSS INPUT
LOW
HIGH
INPUT SPEED
ENG SPEED
SENSOR GROUND
TPS
TRANS TEMP
FORCE MTR LOW
PNK 1224
DK BLU 1225
RED 1226
LT GRN 1222
YEL-BLK 1223
WHT-BLK 451
ORG 440
DK GRN 59
PPL 420
TAN-BLK 422
GRY-RED 1234
ORG-BLK 1061
BLK-WHT 450
TAN 551
BLK 452
GRY 416
LT BLU-WHT 1229
PNK-BLK 439
BRN 437
DK BLU-WHT 1231
GRY-RED 1230
WHT 121
BLK 452
DK BLU 417
BLK-YEL 1227
RED-BLK 1228
EVAP PRES SW
TCC BRAKE SW
GAGES FUSE
G1
RWAL MOD
H3
F2
DRAC MOD
CHECK ENG IND (INST CLSTR)
THROT POSTN SENS
ENG SPEED SENS
INPUT SPEED SENS
IGN SW
IN-LINE FUSE 10A
PNK-BLK
A1
PRES SW MANIFOLD
SHIFT SOL A
SHIFT SOL B
TEMP SENS
TCC SOL
FORCE MTR
TRANSMISSION
1222 LT GRN
1223 YEL-BLK
439 PNK
1224 PNK
1225 DK BLU
1226 RED
1227 BLK-YEL
425 BLK
422 TAN-BLK
1176 PNK-BLK
1228 RED-BLK
1229 LT BLU-WHT
REAR WHEEL ANTI-LOCK MOD
ALDL CONN
FUEL SHUT OFF SOL
IGNITION SW
GRY FUS LINK
STARTER
PPL 906
PNK 3
ORG 503
BLK 150
JUNCTION BLOCK
GLOW PLUG CONTROLLER
ECM B FUSE
FUEL HEATER
FAST IDLE TEMP SW
FAST IDLE SOL
COLD ADVANCE SOL
WATER IN FUEL SENS
H2
WATER IN FUEL IND (DIESEL IND)
BLU FUS LINK
RIGHT BANK GLOW PLUG
LEFT BANK GLOW PLUG
GLOW PLUG IND
91F13792

Fig. 11: Wiring Diagram ("G" Series 6.2L Diesel with 4L80-E Transmission)

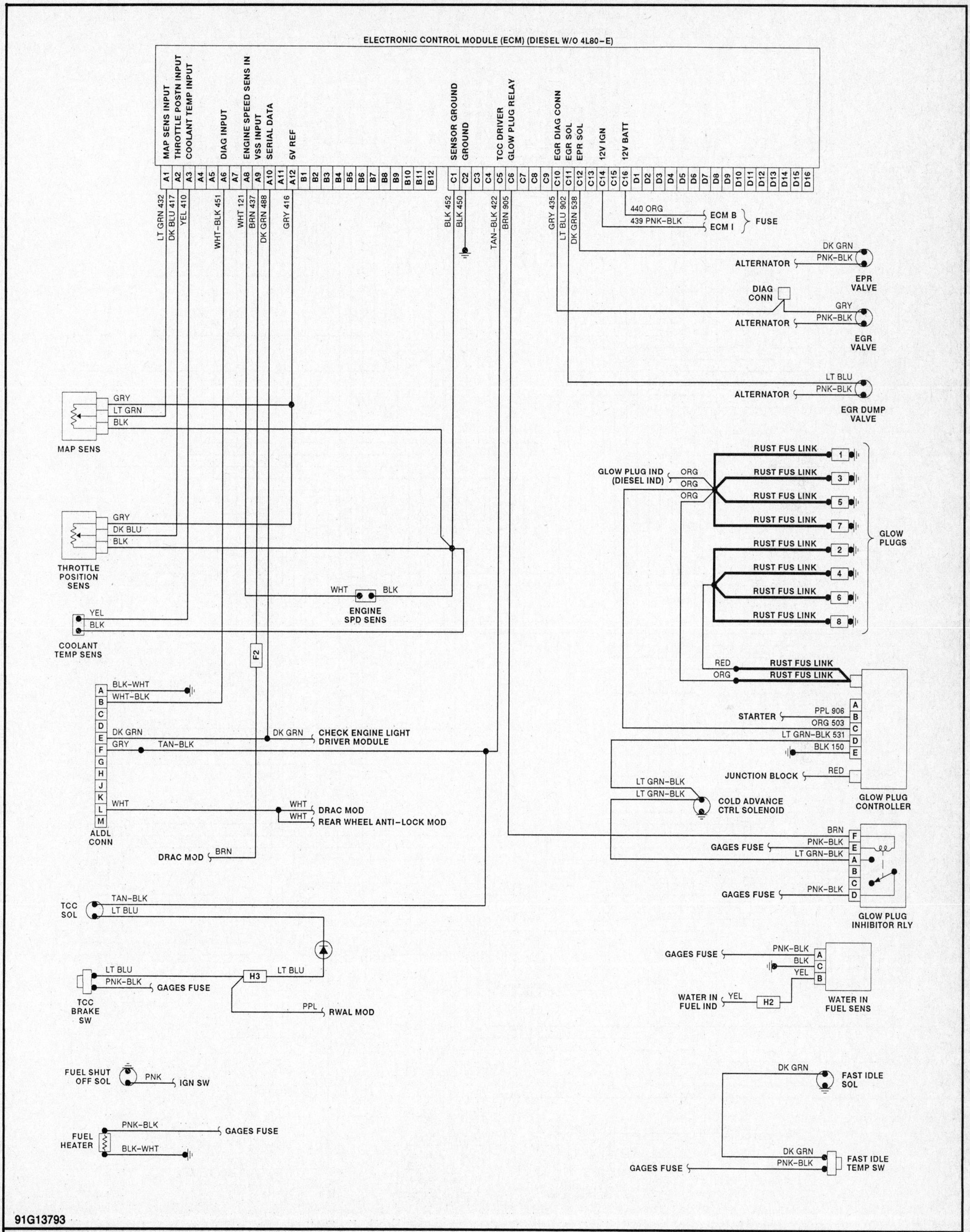
ELECTRONIC CONTROL MODULE (ECM) (DIESEL W/O 4L80-E)
MAP SENS INPUT
THROTTLE POSTN INPUT
COOLANT TEMP INPUT
DIAG INPUT
ENGINE SPEED SENS IN
VSS INPUT
SERIAL DATA
5V REF
SENSOR GROUND
GROUND
TCC DRIVER
GLOW PLUG RELAY
EGR DIAG CONN
EGR SOL
EPR SOL
12V IGN
12V BATT
ECM B
ECM I
FUSE
ALTERNATOR
EPR VALVE
DIAG CONN
EGR VALVE
EGR DUMP VALVE
MAP SENS
THROTTLE POSITION SENS
ENGINE SPD SENS
COOLANT TEMP SENS
GLOW PLUG IND (DIESEL IND)
RUST FUS LINK
GLOW PLUGS
STARTER
JUNCTION BLOCK
GLOW PLUG CONTROLLER
COLD ADVANCE CTRL SOLENOID
GAGES FUSE
GLOW PLUG INHIBITOR RLY
CHECK ENGINE LIGHT DRIVER MODULE
DRAC MOD
REAR WHEEL ANTI-LOCK MOD
ALDL CONN
TCC SOL
TCC BRAKE SW
RWAL MOD
WATER IN FUEL IND
WATER IN FUEL SENS
FUEL SHUT OFF SOL
IGN SW
FUEL HEATER
FAST IDLE SOL
FAST IDLE TEMP SW
91G13793

Fig. 12: Wiring Diagram ("G" Series 6.2L Diesel without 4L80-E Transmission)

1991 ENGINE PERFORMANCE
Wiring Diagrams (Cont.)

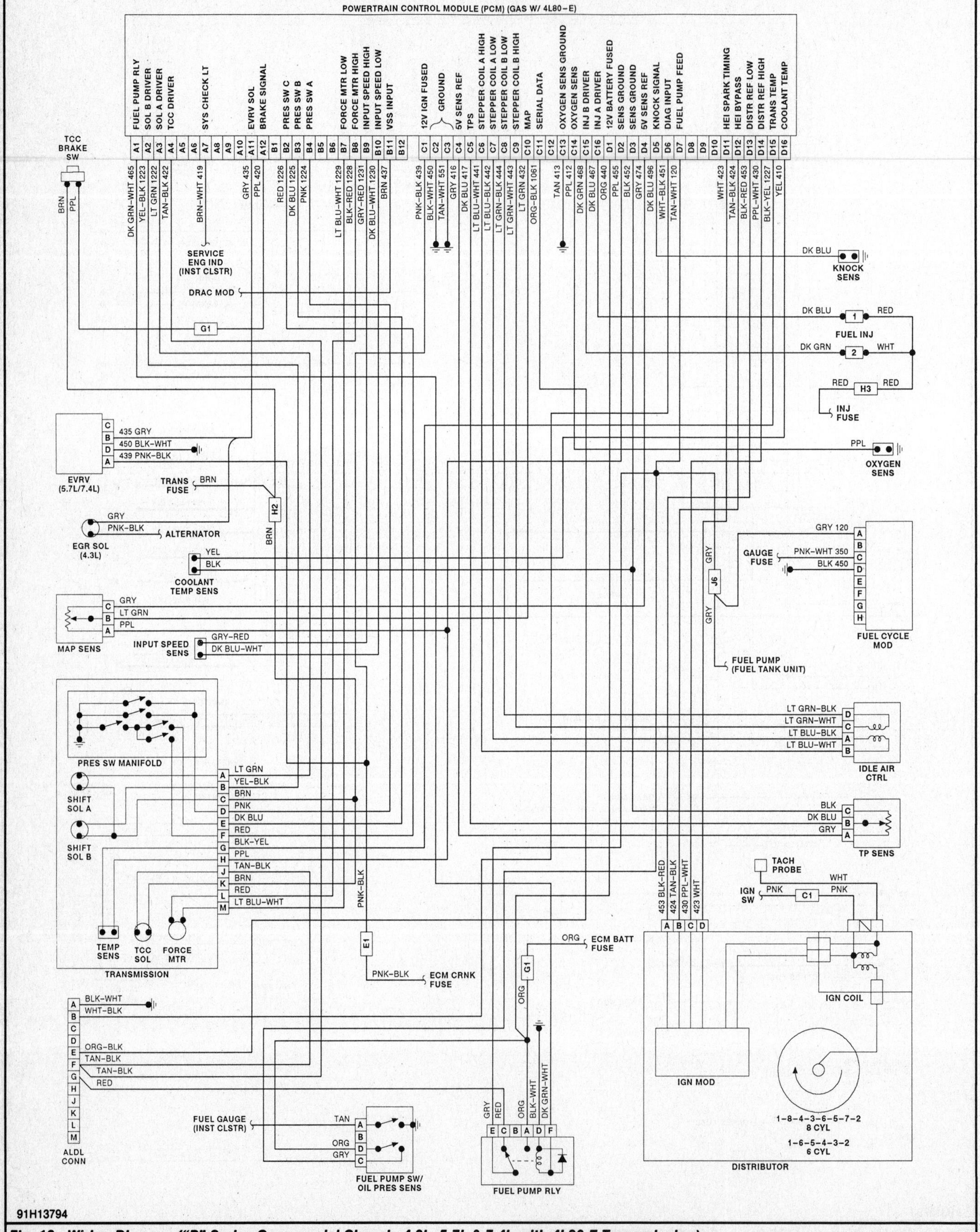
POWERTRAIN CONTROL MODULE (PCM) (GAS W/ 4L80-E)
FUEL PUMP RLY
SOL B DRIVER
SOL A DRIVER
TCC DRIVER
SYS CHECK LT
EVRV SOL
BRAKE SIGNAL
PRES SW C
PRES SW B
PRES SW A
FORCE MTR LOW
FORCE MTR HIGH
INPUT SPEED HIGH
INPUT SPEED LOW
VSS INPUT
12V IGN FUSED
GROUND
5V SENS REF
TPS
STEPPER COIL A HIGH
STEPPER COIL A LOW
STEPPER COIL B LOW
STEPPER COIL B HIGH
MAP
SERIAL DATA
OXYGEN SENS GROUND
OXYGEN SENS
INJ B DRIVER
INJ A DRIVER
12V BATTERY FUSED
SENS GROUND
SENS GROUND
5V SENS REF
KNOCK SIGNAL
DIAG INPUT
FUEL PUMP FEED
HEI SPARK TIMING
HEI BYPASS
DISTR REF LOW
DISTR REF HIGH
TRANS TEMP
COOLANT TEMP
TCC BRAKE SW
SERVICE ENG IND (INST CLSTR)
DRAC MOD
KNOCK SENS
FUEL INJ
INJ FUSE
EVRV (5.7L/7.4L)
TRANS FUSE
ALTERNATOR
EGR SOL (4.3L)
OXYGEN SENS
GAUGE FUSE
FUEL CYCLE MOD
COOLANT TEMP SENS
MAP SENS
INPUT SPEED SENS
FUEL PUMP (FUEL TANK UNIT)
PRES SW MANIFOLD
IDLE AIR CTRL
SHIFT SOL A
SHIFT SOL B
TP SENS
TACH PROBE
IGN SW
TEMP SENS
TCC SOL
FORCE MTR
TRANSMISSION
ECM BATT FUSE
ECM CRNK FUSE
IGN COIL
IGN MOD
1-8-4-3-6-5-7-2 8 CYL
1-6-5-4-3-2 6 CYL
ALDL CONN
FUEL GAUGE (INST CLSTR)
FUEL PUMP SW/ OIL PRES SENS
FUEL PUMP RLY
DISTRIBUTOR
91H13794

Fig. 13: Wiring Diagram ("P" Series Commercial Chassis 4.3L, 5.7L & 7.4L with 4L80-E Transmission)

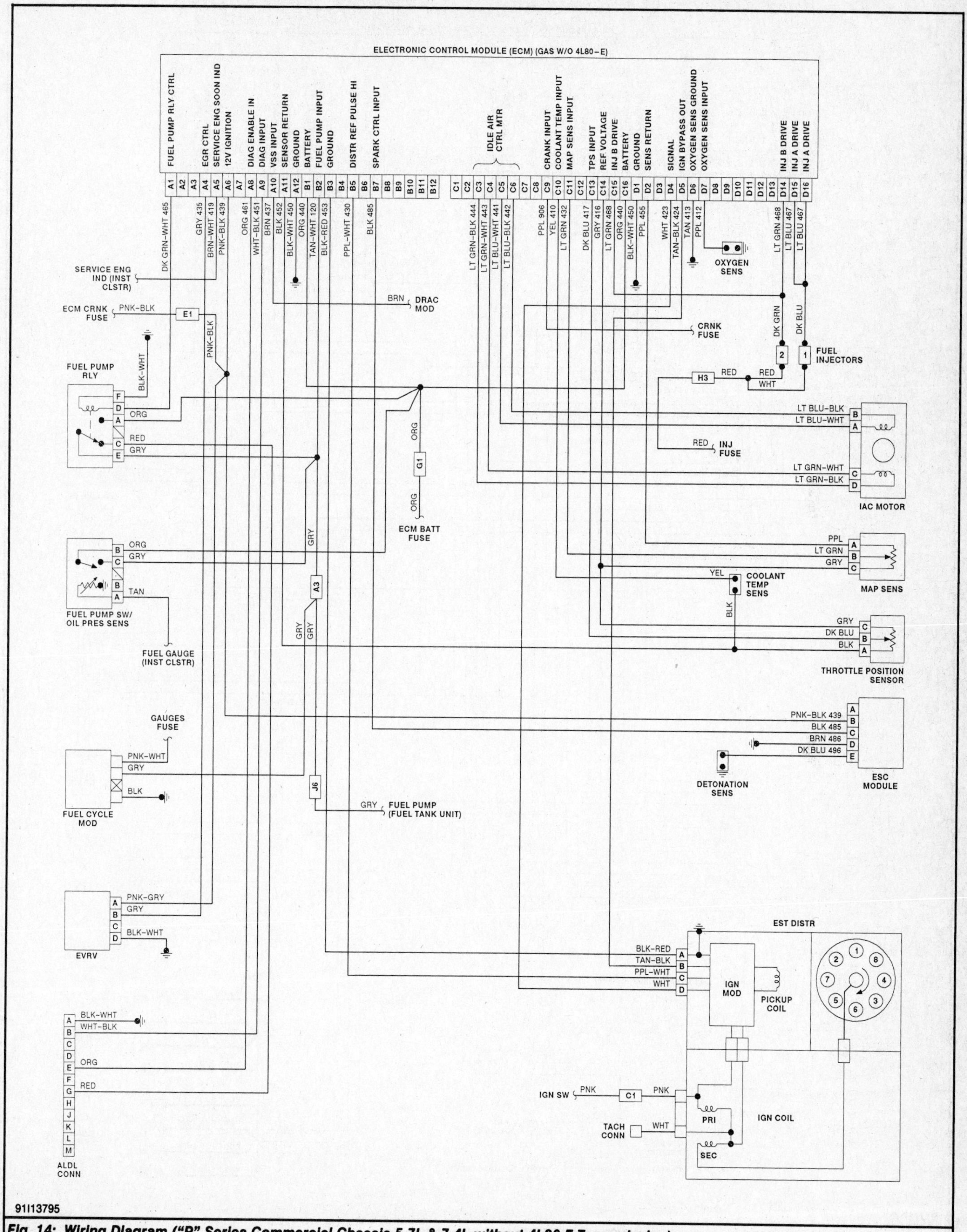
ELECTRONIC CONTROL MODULE (ECM) (GAS W/O 4L80-E)
FUEL PUMP RLY CTRL
EGR CTRL
SERVICE ENG SOON IND
12V IGNITION
DIAG ENABLE IN
DIAG INPUT
VSS INPUT
SENSOR RETURN
GROUND
BATTERY
FUEL PUMP INPUT
GROUND
DISTR REF PULSE HI
SPARK CTRL INPUT
IDLE AIR CTRL MTR
CRANK INPUT
COOLANT TEMP INPUT
MAP SENS INPUT
TPS INPUT
REF VOLTAGE
INJ B DRIVE
BATTERY
GROUND
SENS RETURN
SIGNAL
IGN BYPASS OUT
OXYGEN SENS GROUND
OXYGEN SENS INPUT
INJ B DRIVE
INJ A DRIVE
INJ A DRIVE
SERVICE ENG IND (INST CLSTR)
ECM CRNK FUSE
FUEL PUMP RLY
FUEL PUMP SW/ OIL PRES SENS
FUEL GAUGE (INST CLSTR)
GAUGES FUSE
FUEL CYCLE MOD
EVRV
ALDL CONN
DRAC MOD
ECM BATT FUSE
FUEL PUMP (FUEL TANK UNIT)
OXYGEN SENS
CRNK FUSE
FUEL INJECTORS
INJ FUSE
IAC MOTOR
MAP SENS
COOLANT TEMP SENS
THROTTLE POSITION SENSOR
ESC MODULE
DETONATION SENS
EST DISTR
IGN MOD
PICKUP COIL
IGN SW
TACH CONN
IGN COIL
PRI
SEC
91I13795

Fig. 14: Wiring Diagram ("P" Series Commercial Chassis 5.7L & 7.4L without 4L80-E Transmission)

1991 ENGINE PERFORMANCE
Wiring Diagrams (Cont.)

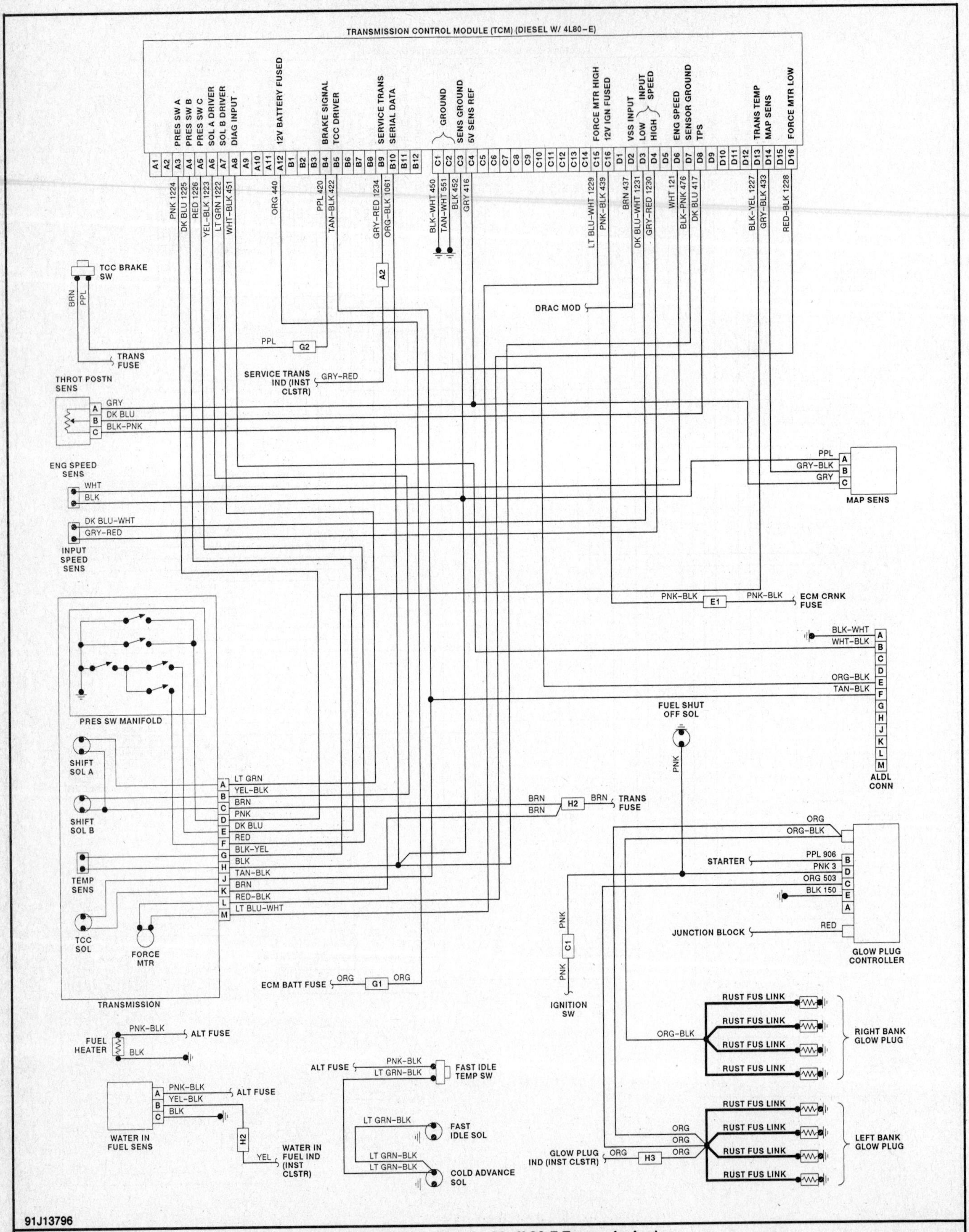
TRANSMISSION CONTROL MODULE (TCM) (DIESEL W/ 4L80-E)
PRES SW A
PRES SW B
PRES SW C
SOL A DRIVER
SOL B DRIVER
DIAG INPUT
12V BATTERY FUSED
BRAKE SIGNAL
TCC DRIVER
SERVICE TRANS
SERIAL DATA
GROUND
SENS GROUND
5V SENS REF
FORCE MTR HIGH
12V IGN FUSED
VSS INPUT
LOW
HIGH
INPUT SPEED
ENG SPEED
SENSOR GROUND
TPS
TRANS TEMP
MAP SENS
FORCE MTR LOW
A1 A2 A3 A4 A5 A6 A7 A8 A9 A10 A11 A12 B1 B2 B3 B4 B5 B6 B7 B8 B9 B10 B11 B12
C1 C2 C3 C4 C5 C6 C7 C8 C9 C10 C11 C12 C13 C14 C15 C16 D1 D2 D3 D4 D5 D6 D7 D8 D9 D10 D11 D12 D13 D14 D15 D16
PNK 1224
DK BLU 1225
RED 1226
YEL-BLK 1223
LT GRN 1222
WHT-BLK 451
ORG 440
PPL 420
TAN-BLK 422
GRY-RED 1234
ORG-BLK 1061
BLK-WHT 450
TAN-WHT 551
BLK 452
GRY 416
LT BLU-WHT 1229
PNK-BLK 439
BRN 437
DK BLU-WHT 1231
GRY-RED 1230
WHT 121
BLK-PNK 476
DK BLU 417
BLK-YEL 1227
GRY-BLK 433
RED-BLK 1228
TCC BRAKE SW
BRN
PPL
A2
DRAC MOD
PPL
G2
TRANS FUSE
SERVICE TRANS IND (INST CLSTR)
GRY-RED
THROT POSTN SENS
A
B
C
GRY
DK BLU
BLK-PNK
PPL
GRY-BLK
GRY
MAP SENS
ENG SPEED SENS
WHT
BLK
DK BLU-WHT
GRY-RED
INPUT SPEED SENS
PNK-BLK
E1
PNK-BLK
ECM CRNK FUSE
BLK-WHT
WHT-BLK
ORG-BLK
TAN-BLK
A B C D E F G H J K L M
ALDL CONN
FUEL SHUT OFF SOL
PNK
PRES SW MANIFOLD
SHIFT SOL A
SHIFT SOL B
TEMP SENS
TCC SOL
FORCE MTR
LT GRN
YEL-BLK
BRN
PNK
DK BLU
RED
BLK-YEL
BLK
TAN-BLK
BRN
RED-BLK
LT BLU-WHT
BRN
BRN
H2
BRN
TRANS FUSE
ORG
ORG-BLK
STARTER
PPL 906
PNK 3
ORG 503
BLK 150
JUNCTION BLOCK
RED
GLOW PLUG CONTROLLER
PNK
C1
PNK
IGNITION SW
ECM BATT FUSE
ORG
G1
ORG
TRANSMISSION
RUST FUS LINK
RUST FUS LINK
RUST FUS LINK
RUST FUS LINK
RIGHT BANK GLOW PLUG
ORG-BLK
RUST FUS LINK
RUST FUS LINK
RUST FUS LINK
RUST FUS LINK
LEFT BANK GLOW PLUG
ORG
ORG
ORG
GLOW PLUG IND (INST CLSTR)
ORG
H3
FUEL HEATER
PNK-BLK
BLK
ALT FUSE
ALT FUSE
PNK-BLK
LT GRN-BLK
FAST IDLE TEMP SW
LT GRN-BLK
FAST IDLE SOL
LT GRN-BLK
LT GRN-BLK
COLD ADVANCE SOL
WATER IN FUEL SENS
PNK-BLK
YEL-BLK
BLK
ALT FUSE
H2
YEL
WATER IN FUEL IND (INST CLSTR)
91J13796

Fig. 15: Wiring Diagram ("P" Series Commercial Chassis 6.2L Diesel with 4L80-E Transmission)

1991 ENGINE PERFORMANCE
Wiring Diagrams (Cont.)

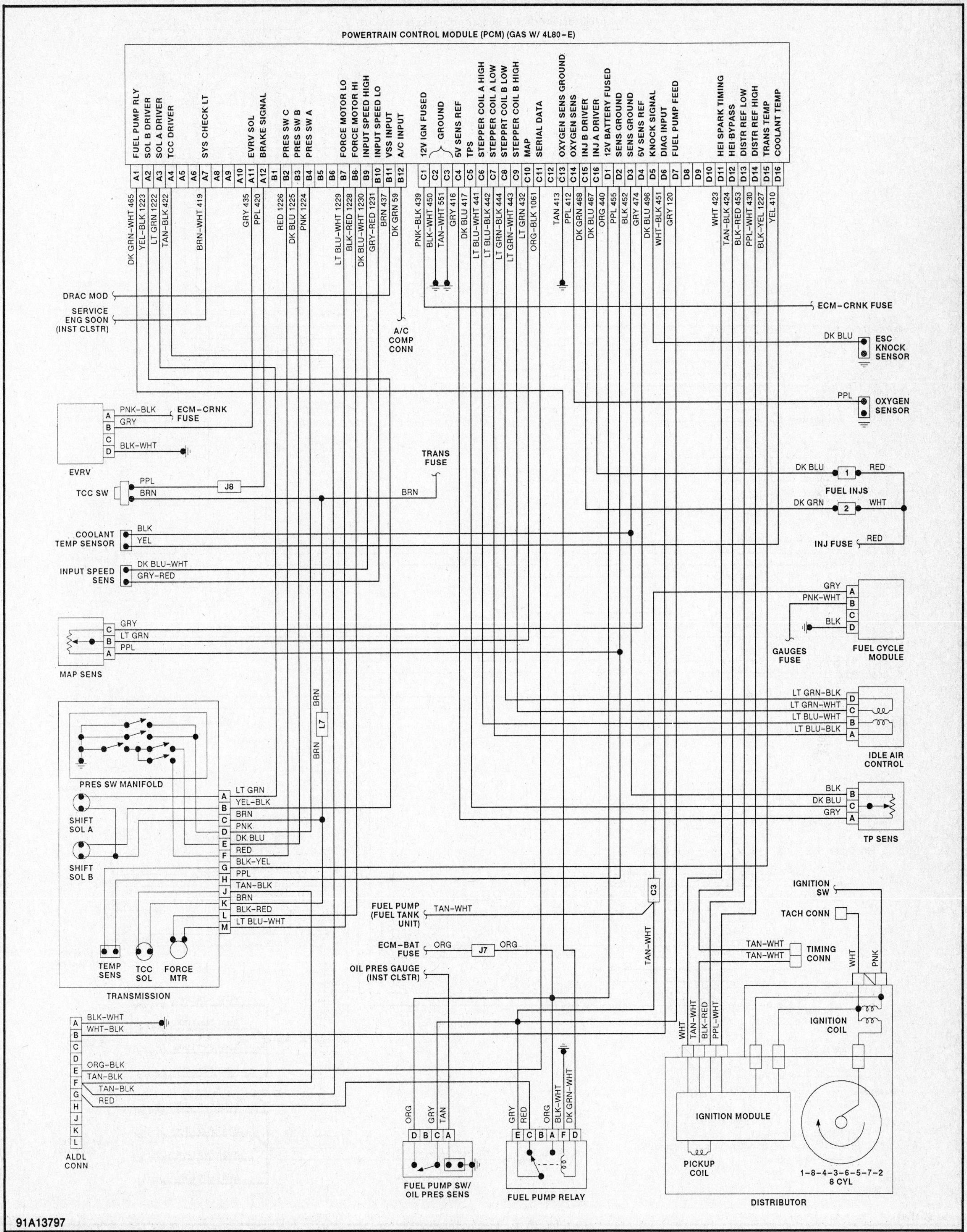
POWERTRAIN CONTROL MODULE (PCM) (GAS W/ 4L80-E)
FUEL PUMP RLY
SOL B DRIVER
SOL A DRIVER
TCC DRIVER
SYS CHECK LT
EVRV SOL
BRAKE SIGNAL
PRES SW C
PRES SW B
PRES SW A
FORCE MOTOR LO
FORCE MOTOR HI
INPUT SPEED HIGH
INPUT SPEED LO
VSS INPUT
A/C INPUT
12V IGN FUSED
GROUND
5V SENS REF
TPS
STEPPER COIL A HIGH
STEPPER COIL A LOW
STEPPRT COIL B LOW
STEPPER COIL B HIGH
MAP
SERIAL DATA
OXYGEN SENS GROUND
OXYGEN SENS
INJ B DRIVER
INJ A DRIVER
12V BATTERY FUSED
SENS GROUND
SENS GROUND
5V SENS REF
KNOCK SIGNAL
DIAG INPUT
FUEL PUMP FEED
HEI SPARK TIMING
HEI BYPASS
DISTR REF LOW
DISTR REF HIGH
TRANS TEMP
COOLANT TEMP
DRAC MOD
SERVICE ENG SOON (INST CLSTR)
A/C COMP CONN
ECM-CRNK FUSE
ESC KNOCK SENSOR
OXYGEN SENSOR
EVRV
TCC SW
TRANS FUSE
FUEL INJS
INJ FUSE
COOLANT TEMP SENSOR
INPUT SPEED SENS
MAP SENS
GAUGES FUSE
FUEL CYCLE MODULE
IDLE AIR CONTROL
PRES SW MANIFOLD
SHIFT SOL A
SHIFT SOL B
TP SENS
FUEL PUMP (FUEL TANK UNIT)
ECM-BAT FUSE
OIL PRES GAUGE (INST CLSTR)
IGNITION SW
TACH CONN
TIMING CONN
IGNITION COIL
TEMP SENS
TCC SOL
FORCE MTR
TRANSMISSION
ALDL CONN
IGNITION MODULE
PICKUP COIL
1-8-4-3-6-5-7-2 8 CYL
FUEL PUMP SW/ OIL PRES SENS
FUEL PUMP RELAY
DISTRIBUTOR
91A13797

Fig. 16: Wiring Diagram ("P" Series Motorhome 5.7L & 7.4L with 4L80-E Transmission)

1991 ENGINE PERFORMANCE
Wiring Diagrams (Cont.)

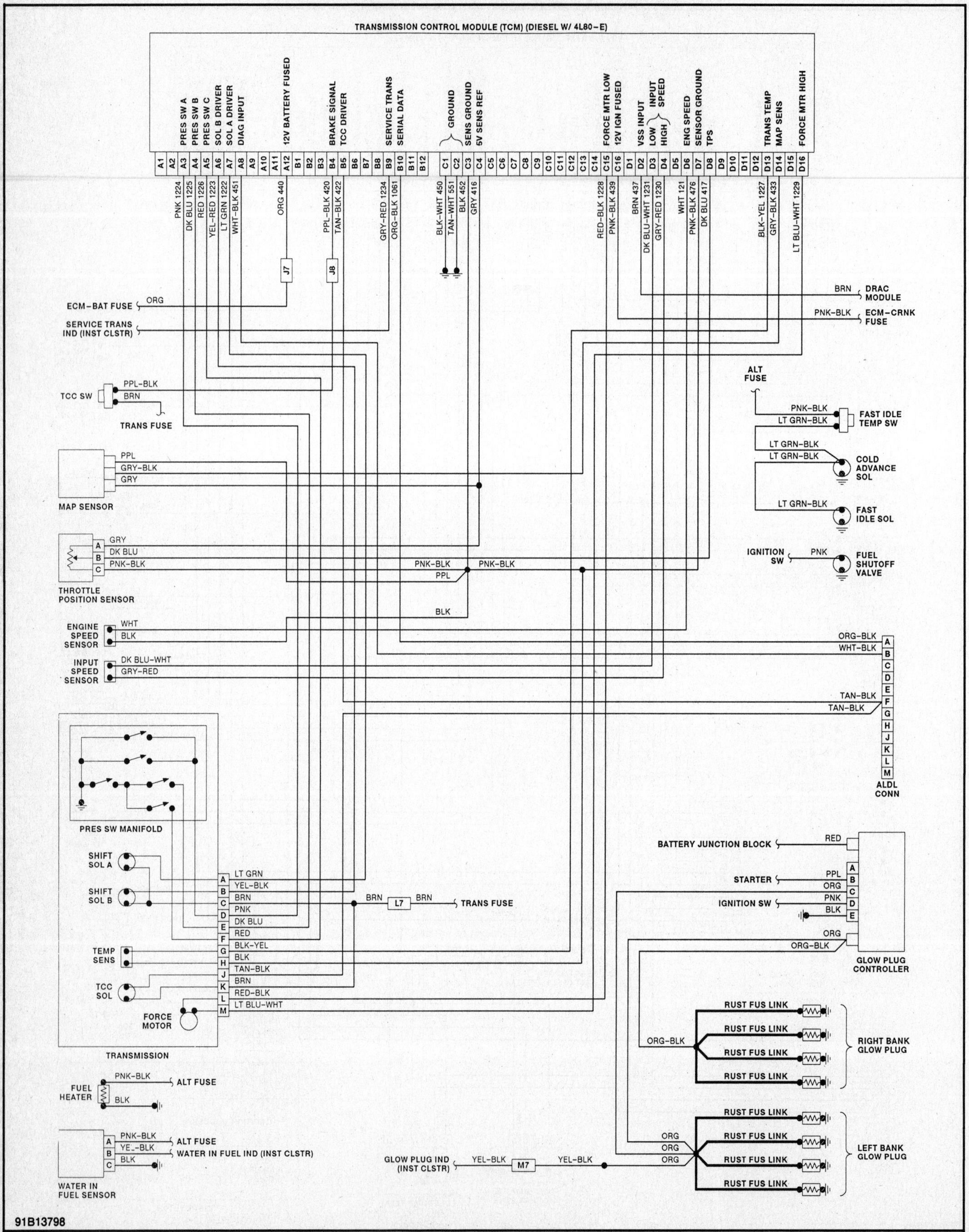
TRANSMISSION CONTROL MODULE (TCM) (DIESEL W/ 4L80-E)
PRES SW A
PRES SW B
PRES SW C
SOL B DRIVER
SOL A DRIVER
DIAG INPUT
12V BATTERY FUSED
BRAKE SIGNAL
TCC DRIVER
SERVICE TRANS
SERIAL DATA
GROUND
SENS GROUND
5V SENS REF
FORCE MTR LOW
12V IGN FUSED
VSS INPUT
LOW
HIGH
INPUT SPEED
ENG SPEED
SENSOR GROUND
TPS
TRANS TEMP
MAP SENS
FORCE MTR HIGH
A1 A2 A3 A4 A5 A6 A7 A8 A9 A10 A11 A12 B1 B2 B3 B4 B5 B6 B7 B8 B9 B10 B11 B12 C1 C2 C3 C4 C5 C6 C7 C8 C9 C10 C11 C12 C13 C14 C15 C16 D1 D2 D3 D4 D5 D6 D7 D8 D9 D10 D11 D12 D13 D14 D15 D16
PNK 1224
DK BLU 1225
RED 1226
YEL-RED 1223
LT GRN 1222
WHT-BLK 451
ORG 440
PPL-BLK 420
TAN-BLK 422
GRY-RED 1234
ORG-BLK 1061
BLK-WHT 450
TAN-WHT 551
BLK 452
GRY 416
RED-BLK 1228
PNK-BLK 439
BRN 437
DK BLU-WHT 1231
GRY-RED 1230
WHT 121
PNK-BLK 476
DK BLU 417
BLK-YEL 1227
GRY-BLK 433
LT BLU-WHT 1229
J7
J8
ECM-BAT FUSE
SERVICE TRANS IND (INST CLSTR)
DRAC MODULE
ECM-CRNK FUSE
TCC SW
PPL-BLK
BRN
TRANS FUSE
ALT FUSE
FAST IDLE TEMP SW
LT GRN-BLK
COLD ADVANCE SOL
FAST IDLE SOL
MAP SENSOR
PPL
GRY-BLK
GRY
IGNITION SW
PNK
FUEL SHUTOFF VALVE
THROTTLE POSITION SENSOR
DK BLU
ENGINE SPEED SENSOR
WHT
BLK
INPUT SPEED SENSOR
DK BLU-WHT
GRY-RED
ORG-BLK
WHT-BLK
TAN-BLK
ALDL CONN
PRES SW MANIFOLD
SHIFT SOL A
SHIFT SOL B
TEMP SENS
TCC SOL
FORCE MOTOR
TRANSMISSION
LT GRN
YEL-BLK
RED
BLK-YEL
RED-BLK
LT BLU-WHT
L7
BATTERY JUNCTION BLOCK
STARTER
ORG
GLOW PLUG CONTROLLER
RUST FUS LINK
RIGHT BANK GLOW PLUG
LEFT BANK GLOW PLUG
GLOW PLUG IND (INST CLSTR)
M7
FUEL HEATER
WATER IN FUEL IND (INST CLSTR)
YEL-BLK
WATER IN FUEL SENSOR
91B13798

Fig. 17: Wiring Diagram ("P" Series Motorhome 6.2L Diesel with 4L80-E Transmission)

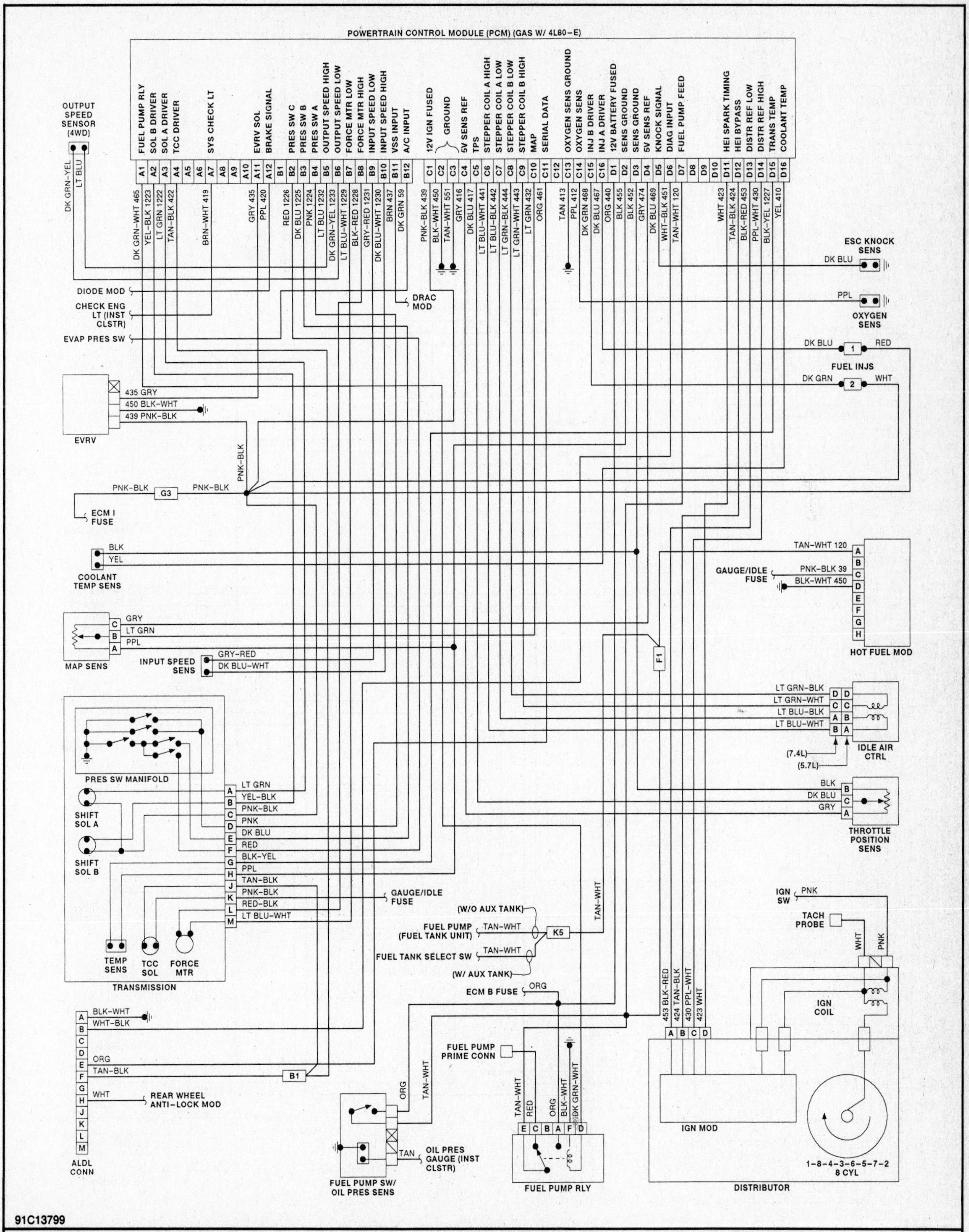

POWERTRAIN CONTROL MODULE (PCM) (GAS W/ 4L80-E)
OUTPUT SPEED SENSOR (4WD)
ESC KNOCK SENS
OXYGEN SENS
FUEL INJS
DIODE MOD
CHECK ENG LT (INST CLSTR)
EVAP PRES SW
DRAC MOD
EVRV
ECM I FUSE
COOLANT TEMP SENS
GAUGE/IDLE FUSE
HOT FUEL MOD
MAP SENS
INPUT SPEED SENS
IDLE AIR CTRL
PRES SW MANIFOLD
SHIFT SOL A
SHIFT SOL B
THROTTLE POSITION SENS
TEMP SENS
TCC SOL
FORCE MTR
TRANSMISSION
FUEL PUMP (FUEL TANK UNIT)
FUEL TANK SELECT SW
(W/O AUX TANK)
(W/ AUX TANK)
ECM B FUSE
IGN SW
TACH PROBE
IGN COIL
ALDL CONN
REAR WHEEL ANTI-LOCK MOD
FUEL PUMP PRIME CONN
OIL PRES GAUGE (INST CLSTR)
FUEL PUMP SW/ OIL PRES SENS
FUEL PUMP RLY
IGN MOD
DISTRIBUTOR
1-8-4-3-6-5-7-2 8 CYL
91C13799

Fig. 18: Wiring Diagram ("R" & "V" Series 5.7L & 7.4L with 4L80-E Transmission)

1991 ENGINE PERFORMANCE
Wiring Diagrams (Cont.)

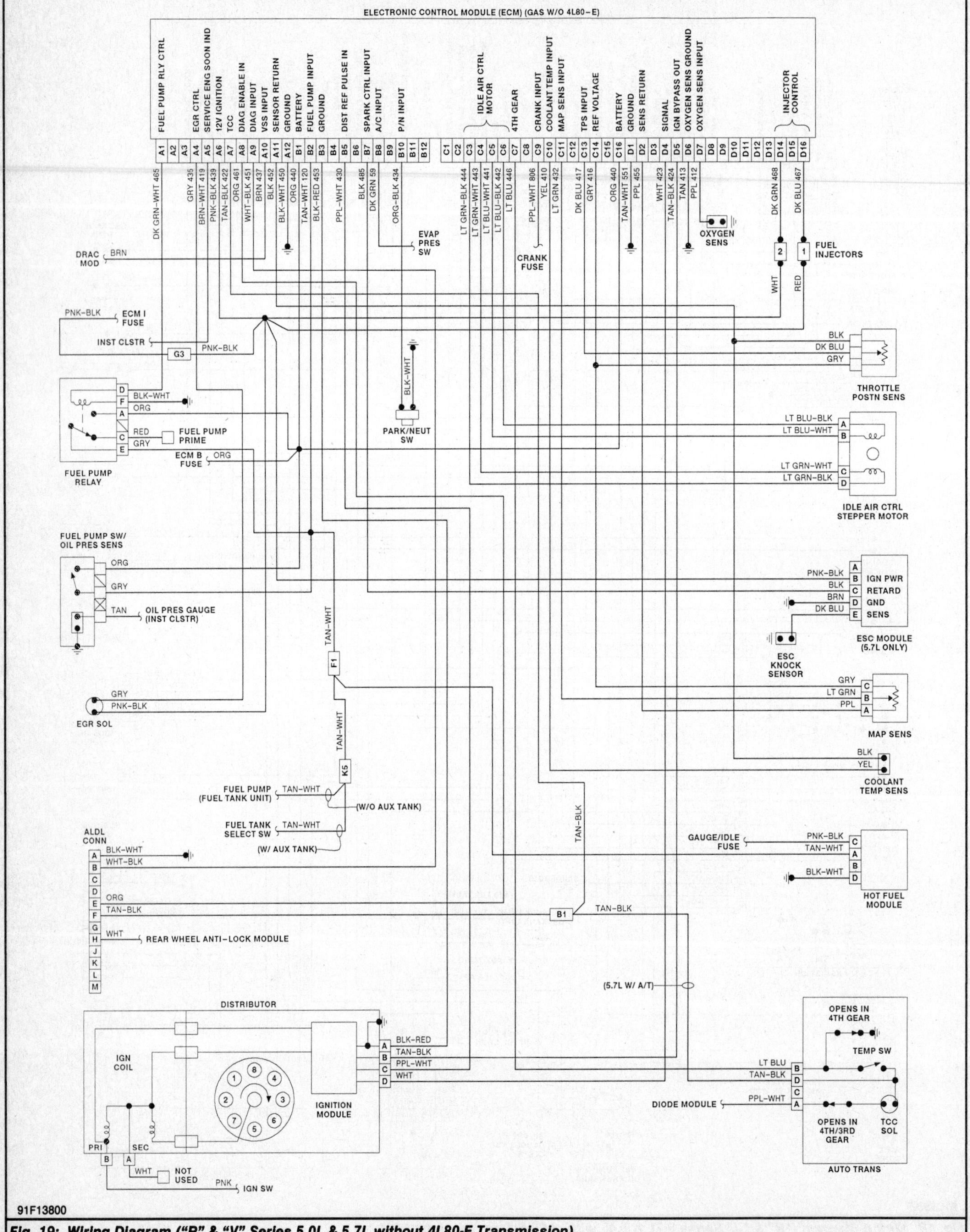
ELECTRONIC CONTROL MODULE (ECM) (GAS W/O 4L80-E)
FUEL PUMP RLY CTRL
EGR CTRL
SERVICE ENG SOON IND
12V IGNITION
TCC
DIAG ENABLE IN
DIAG INPUT
VSS INPUT
SENSOR RETURN
GROUND
BATTERY
FUEL PUMP INPUT
GROUND
DIST REF PULSE IN
SPARK CTRL INPUT
A/C INPUT
P/N INPUT
IDLE AIR CTRL MOTOR
4TH GEAR
CRANK INPUT
COOLANT TEMP INPUT
MAP SENS INPUT
TPS INPUT
REF VOLTAGE
BATTERY
GROUND
SENS RETURN
SIGNAL
IGN BYPASS OUT
OXYGEN SENS GROUND
OXYGEN SENS INPUT
INJECTOR CONTROL
OXYGEN SENS
FUEL INJECTORS
EVAP PRES SW
CRANK FUSE
DRAC MOD
ECM I FUSE
INST CLSTR
G3
THROTTLE POSTN SENS
FUEL PUMP PRIME
FUEL PUMP RELAY
ECM B FUSE
PARK/NEUT SW
IDLE AIR CTRL STEPPER MOTOR
FUEL PUMP SW/ OIL PRES SENS
OIL PRES GAUGE (INST CLSTR)
IGN PWR RETARD GND SENS
ESC MODULE (5.7L ONLY)
ESC KNOCK SENSOR
EGR SOL
MAP SENS
COOLANT TEMP SENS
FUEL PUMP (FUEL TANK UNIT)
(W/O AUX TANK)
FUEL TANK SELECT SW
(W/ AUX TANK)
ALDL CONN
GAUGE/IDLE FUSE
HOT FUEL MODULE
REAR WHEEL ANTI-LOCK MODULE
(5.7L W/ A/T)
DISTRIBUTOR
IGN COIL
IGNITION MODULE
PRI
SEC
NOT USED
IGN SW
OPENS IN 4TH GEAR
TEMP SW
DIODE MODULE
OPENS IN 4TH/3RD GEAR
TCC SOL
AUTO TRANS
91F13800

Fig. 19: Wiring Diagram ("R" & "V" Series 5.0L & 5.7L without 4L80-E Transmission)

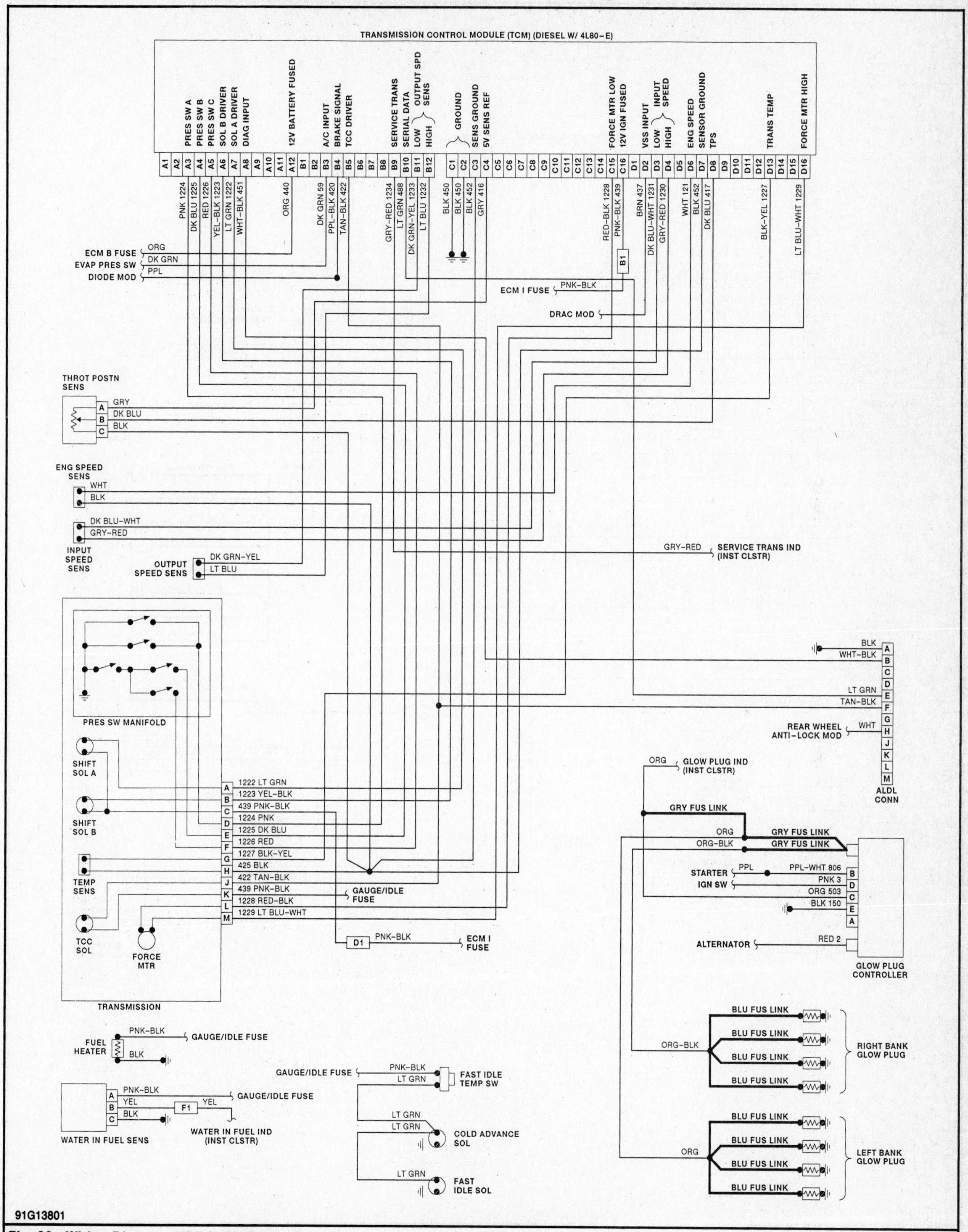
TRANSMISSION CONTROL MODULE (TCM) (DIESEL W/ 4L80-E)
PRES SW A
PRES SW B
PRES SW C
SOL B DRIVER
SOL A DRIVER
DIAG INPUT
12V BATTERY FUSED
A/C INPUT
BRAKE SIGNAL
TCC DRIVER
SERVICE TRANS
SERIAL DATA
LOW
HIGH
OUTPUT SPD SENS
GROUND
SENS GROUND
5V SENS REF
FORCE MTR LOW
12V IGN FUSED
VSS INPUT
INPUT SPEED
ENG SPEED
SENSOR GROUND
TPS
TRANS TEMP
FORCE MTR HIGH
PNK 1224
DK BLU 1225
RED 1226
YEL-BLK 1223
LT GRN 1222
WHT-BLK 451
ORG 440
DK GRN 59
PPL-BLK 420
TAN-BLK 422
GRY-RED 1234
LT GRN 488
DK GRN-YEL 1233
LT BLU 1232
BLK 450
BLK 450
BLK 452
GRY 416
RED-BLK 1228
PNK-BLK 439
BRN 437
DK BLU-WHT 1231
GRY-RED 1230
WHT 121
BLK 452
DK BLU 417
BLK-YEL 1227
LT BLU-WHT 1229
ECM B FUSE
EVAP PRES SW
DIODE MOD
ECM I FUSE
DRAC MOD
THROT POSTN SENS
ENG SPEED SENS
INPUT SPEED SENS
OUTPUT SPEED SENS
SERVICE TRANS IND (INST CLSTR)
PRES SW MANIFOLD
SHIFT SOL A
SHIFT SOL B
TEMP SENS
TCC SOL
FORCE MTR
TRANSMISSION
1222 LT GRN
1223 YEL-BLK
439 PNK-BLK
1224 PNK
1225 DK BLU
1226 RED
1227 BLK-YEL
425 BLK
422 TAN-BLK
439 PNK-BLK
1228 RED-BLK
1229 LT BLU-WHT
GAUGE/IDLE FUSE
ECM I FUSE
REAR WHEEL ANTI-LOCK MOD
ALDL CONN
GLOW PLUG IND (INST CLSTR)
GRY FUS LINK
STARTER
IGN SW
PPL-WHT 806
PNK 3
ORG 503
BLK 150
RED 2
ALTERNATOR
GLOW PLUG CONTROLLER
BLU FUS LINK
RIGHT BANK GLOW PLUG
LEFT BANK GLOW PLUG
FUEL HEATER
FAST IDLE TEMP SW
COLD ADVANCE SOL
FAST IDLE SOL
WATER IN FUEL SENS
WATER IN FUEL IND (INST CLSTR)
91G13801

Fig. 20: Wiring Diagram ("R" & "V" Series 6.2L Diesel with 4L80-E Transmission)

1991 ENGINE PERFORMANCE
Wiring Diagrams (Cont.)

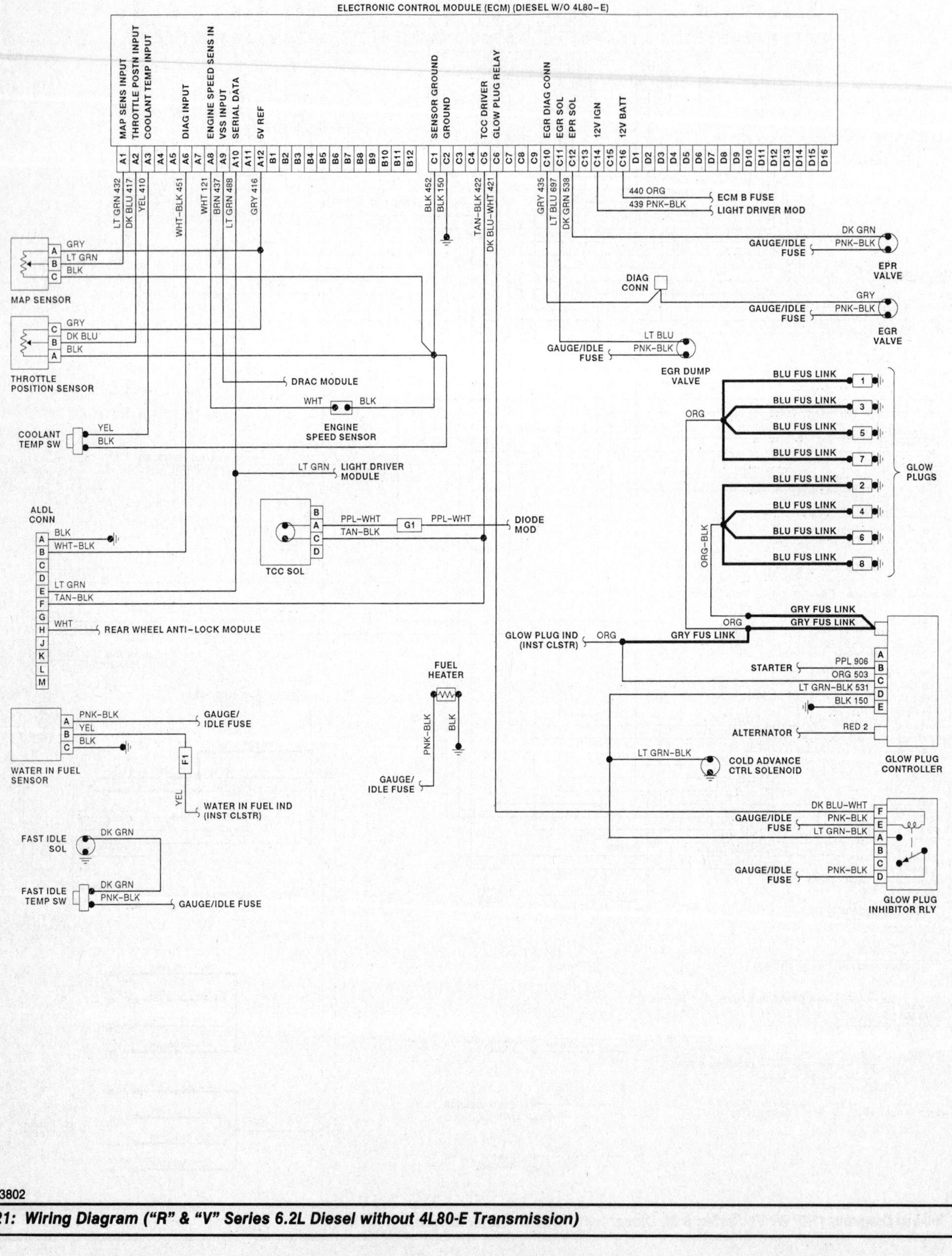
ELECTRONIC CONTROL MODULE (ECM) (DIESEL W/O 4L80-E)
MAP SENS INPUT
THROTTLE POSTN INPUT
COOLANT TEMP INPUT
DIAG INPUT
ENGINE SPEED SENS IN
VSS INPUT
SERIAL DATA
5V REF
SENSOR GROUND
GROUND
TCC DRIVER
GLOW PLUG RELAY
EGR DIAG CONN
EGR SOL
EPR SOL
12V IGN
12V BATT
A1 A2 A3 A4 A5 A6 A7 A8 A9 A10 A11 A12 B1 B2 B3 B4 B5 B6 B7 B8 B9 B10 B11 B12 C1 C2 C3 C4 C5 C6 C7 C8 C9 C10 C11 C12 C13 C14 C15 C16 D1 D2 D3 D4 D5 D6 D7 D8 D9 D10 D11 D12 D13 D14 D15 D16
LT GRN 432
DK BLU 417
YEL 410
WHT-BLK 451
WHT 121
BRN 437
LT GRN 488
GRY 416
BLK 452
BLK 150
TAN-BLK 422
DK BLU-WHT 421
GRY 435
LT BLU 697
DK GRN 538
440 ORG
ECM B FUSE
439 PNK-BLK
LIGHT DRIVER MOD
DK GRN
GAUGE/IDLE FUSE
PNK-BLK
EPR VALVE
DIAG CONN
GRY
EGR VALVE
LT BLU
EGR DUMP VALVE
GRY
LT GRN
BLK
MAP SENSOR
DK BLU
THROTTLE POSITION SENSOR
DRAC MODULE
WHT
ENGINE SPEED SENSOR
COOLANT TEMP SW
YEL
LT GRN
LIGHT DRIVER MODULE
BLU FUS LINK
ORG
ORG-BLK
GLOW PLUGS
ALDL CONN
WHT-BLK
TAN-BLK
REAR WHEEL ANTI-LOCK MODULE
PPL-WHT
TAN-BLK
G1
DIODE MOD
TCC SOL
GRY FUS LINK
GLOW PLUG IND (INST CLSTR)
FUEL HEATER
STARTER
PPL 906
ORG 503
LT GRN-BLK 531
BLK 150
ALTERNATOR
RED 2
GLOW PLUG CONTROLLER
PNK-BLK
GAUGE/IDLE FUSE
WATER IN FUEL SENSOR
F1
WATER IN FUEL IND (INST CLSTR)
LT GRN-BLK
COLD ADVANCE CTRL SOLENOID
DK BLU-WHT
GLOW PLUG INHIBITOR RLY
FAST IDLE SOL
DK GRN
FAST IDLE TEMP SW
91H13802

Fig. 21: Wiring Diagram ("R" & "V" Series 6.2L Diesel without 4L80-E Transmission)

1991 ENGINE PERFORMANCE
Wiring Diagrams (Cont.)

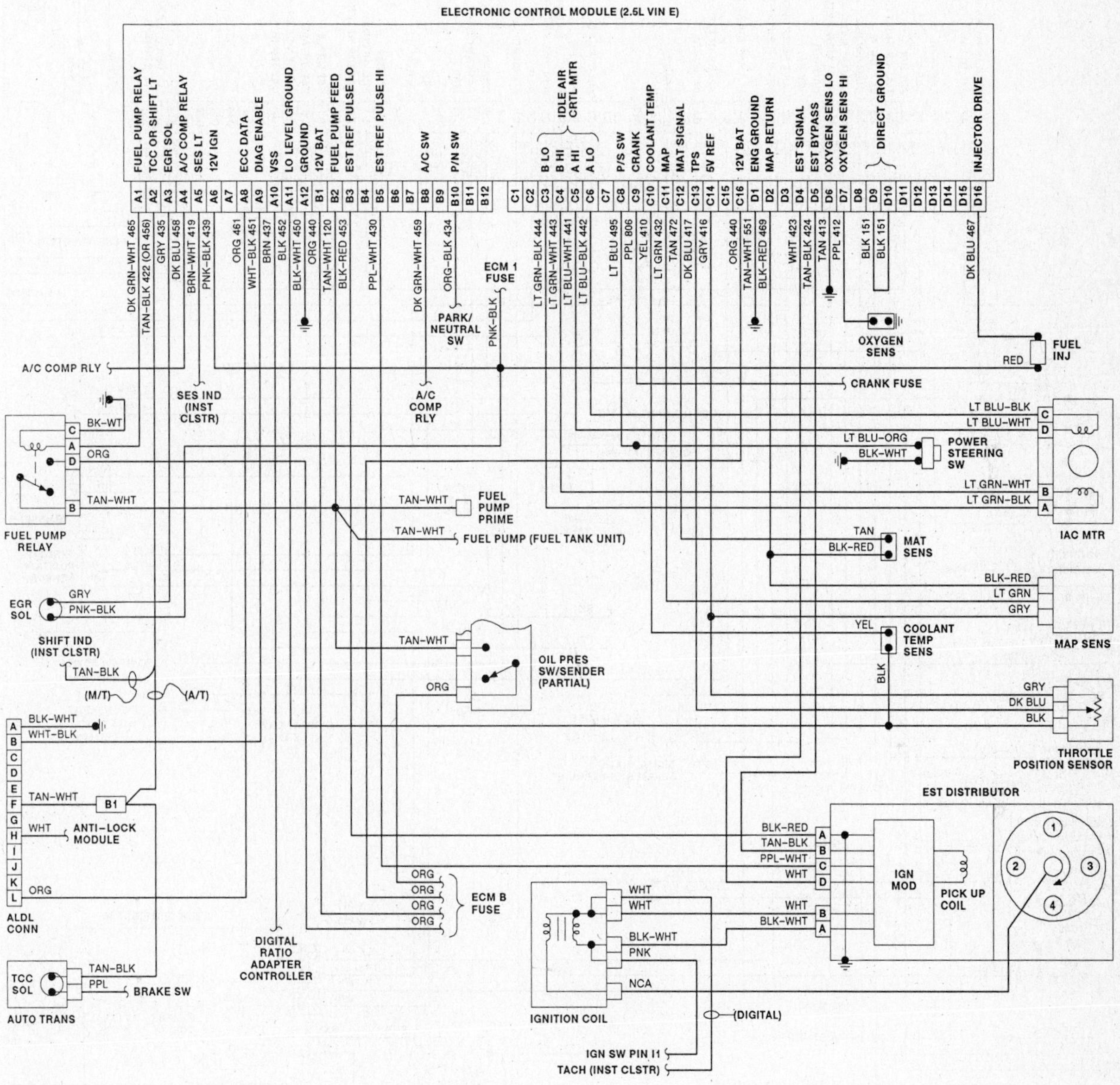
ELECTRONIC CONTROL MODULE (2.5L VIN E)
FUEL PUMP RELAY
TCC OR SHIFT LT
EGR SOL
A/C COMP RELAY
SES LT
12V IGN
ECC DATA
DIAG ENABLE
VSS
LO LEVEL GROUND
GROUND
12V BAT
FUEL PUMP FEED
EST REF PULSE LO
EST REF PULSE HI
A/C SW
P/N SW
IDLE AIR CRTL MTR
B LO
B HI
A HI
A LO
P/S SW
CRANK
COOLANT TEMP
MAP
MAT SIGNAL
TPS
5V REF
12V BAT
ENG GROUND
MAP RETURN
EST SIGNAL
EST BYPASS
OXYGEN SENS LO
OXYGEN SENS HI
DIRECT GROUND
INJECTOR DRIVE
A1 A2 A3 A4 A5 A6 A7 A8 A9 A10 A11 A12 B1 B2 B3 B4 B5 B6 B7 B8 B9 B10 B11 B12
C1 C2 C3 C4 C5 C6 C7 C8 C9 C10 C11 C12 C13 C14 C15 C16 D1 D2 D3 D4 D5 D6 D7 D8 D9 D10 D11 D12 D13 D14 D15 D16
DK GRN-WHT 465
TAN-BLK 422 (OR 456)
GRY 435
DK BLU 458
BRN-WHT 419
PNK-BLK 439
ORG 461
WHT-BLK 451
BRN 437
BLK 452
BLK-WHT 450
ORG 440
TAN-WHT 120
BLK-RED 453
PPL-WHT 430
DK GRN-WHT 459
ORG-BLK 434
ECM 1 FUSE
PNK-BLK
PARK/ NEUTRAL SW
LT GRN-BLK 444
LT GRN-WHT 443
LT BLU-WHT 441
LT BLU-BLK 442
LT BLU 495
PPL 806
YEL 410
LT GRN 432
TAN 472
DK BLU 417
GRY 416
ORG 440
TAN-WHT 551
BLK-RED 469
WHT 423
TAN-BLK 424
TAN 413
PPL 412
BLK 151
BLK 151
DK BLU 467
OXYGEN SENS
FUEL INJ
RED
A/C COMP RLY
SES IND (INST CLSTR)
A/C COMP RLY
CRANK FUSE
BK-WT
ORG
TAN-WHT
FUEL PUMP RELAY
TAN-WHT
FUEL PUMP PRIME
TAN-WHT
FUEL PUMP (FUEL TANK UNIT)
LT BLU-BLK
LT BLU-WHT
LT BLU-ORG
BLK-WHT
POWER STEERING SW
LT GRN-WHT
LT GRN-BLK
IAC MTR
TAN
BLK-RED
MAT SENS
BLK-RED
LT GRN
GRY
MAP SENS
YEL
COOLANT TEMP SENS
BLK
GRY
DK BLU
BLK
THROTTLE POSITION SENSOR
EGR SOL
GRY
PNK-BLK
SHIFT IND (INST CLSTR)
TAN-BLK
(M/T)
(A/T)
TAN-WHT
OIL PRES SW/SENDER (PARTIAL)
ORG
BLK-WHT
WHT-BLK
TAN-WHT
B1
WHT
ANTI-LOCK MODULE
ORG
ALDL CONN
DIGITAL RATIO ADAPTER CONTROLLER
ORG
ORG
ORG
ORG
ECM B FUSE
EST DISTRIBUTOR
BLK-RED
TAN-BLK
PPL-WHT
WHT
IGN MOD
PICK UP COIL
WHT
BLK-WHT
WHT
WHT
BLK-WHT
PNK
NCA
IGNITION COIL
(DIGITAL)
IGN SW PIN I1
TACH (INST CLSTR)
TCC SOL
TAN-BLK
PPL
BRAKE SW
AUTO TRANS

91I13803

Fig. 22: Wiring Diagram ("S" Series 2.5L)

1991 ENGINE PERFORMANCE
Wiring Diagrams (Cont.)

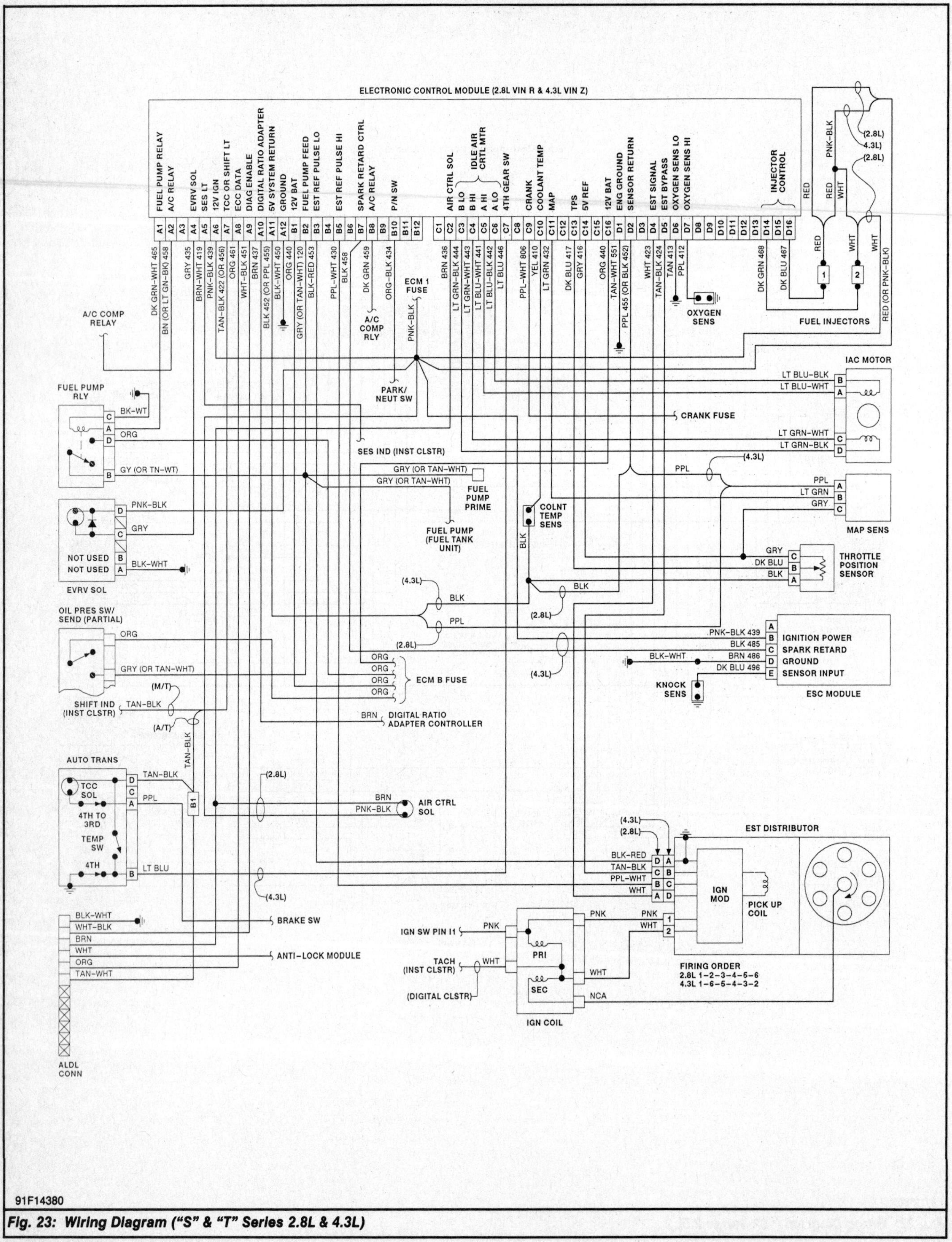
ELECTRONIC CONTROL MODULE (2.8L VIN R & 4.3L VIN Z)
FUEL PUMP RELAY
A/C RELAY
EVRV SOL
SES LT
12V IGN
TCC OR SHIFT LT
ECC DATA
DIAG ENABLE
DIGITAL RATIO ADAPTER
5V SYSTEM RETURN
GROUND
12V BAT
FUEL PUMP FEED
EST REF PULSE LO
EST REF PULSE HI
SPARK RETARD CTRL
A/C RELAY
P/N SW
AIR CTRL SOL
IDLE AIR CRTL MTR
4TH GEAR SW
CRANK
COOLANT TEMP
MAP
TPS
5V REF
12V BAT
ENG GROUND
SENSOR RETURN
EST SIGNAL
EST BYPASS
OXYGEN SENS LO
OXYGEN SENS HI
INJECTOR CONTROL
A/C COMP RELAY
FUEL PUMP RLY
EVRV SOL
NOT USED
OIL PRES SW/ SEND (PARTIAL)
SHIFT IND (INST CLSTR)
AUTO TRANS
TCC SOL
4TH TO 3RD
TEMP SW
ALDL CONN
BRAKE SW
ANTI-LOCK MODULE
ECM 1 FUSE
A/C COMP RLY
PARK/ NEUT SW
SES IND (INST CLSTR)
FUEL PUMP PRIME
FUEL PUMP (FUEL TANK UNIT)
ECM B FUSE
DIGITAL RATIO ADAPTER CONTROLLER
AIR CTRL SOL
COLNT TEMP SENS
OXYGEN SENS
FUEL INJECTORS
IAC MOTOR
CRANK FUSE
MAP SENS
THROTTLE POSITION SENSOR
IGNITION POWER
SPARK RETARD
GROUND
SENSOR INPUT
ESC MODULE
KNOCK SENS
EST DISTRIBUTOR
IGN MOD
PICK UP COIL
IGN SW PIN I1
TACH (INST CLSTR)
(DIGITAL CLSTR)
PRI
SEC
IGN COIL
FIRING ORDER
2.8L 1-2-3-4-5-6
4.3L 1-6-5-4-3-2
91F14380

Fig. 23: Wiring Diagram ("S" & "T" Series 2.8L & 4.3L)

1991 ENGINE PERFORMANCE
Vacuum Diagrams

Blazer, Bravada, Jimmy, Lumina APV, Sierra, Silhouette, Sonoma, Trans Sport, "C" & "K" Series, "G" Series, "P" Series, "R" & "V" Series, "S" & "T" Series

NOTE: Information is not available for models not listed.

INTRODUCTION

This article contains underhood views or schematics of vacuum hose routing. Use these vacuum diagrams during the visual inspection in BASIC DIAGNOSTIC PROCEDURES article. This will assist in identifying improperly routed vacuum hoses, which can cause driveability and/or computer-indicated malfunction.

MODEL IDENTIFICATION

Vehicle model can be identified by the fifth character of Vehicle Identification Number (VIN). See MODEL IDENTIFICATION table. VIN is stamped on a metal pad at top left of instrument panel, near windshield.

MODEL IDENTIFICATION

Series [1]	Model
"C"	2WD Pickup & Sierra
"G"	Van (Except Lumina APV, Silhouette & Trans Sport)
"K"	4WD Pickup & Sierra
"P"	Forward Control Chassis
"R"	2WD Blazer [2], Jimmy [2], Pickup & Suburban
"S"	2WD Blazer [2], Jimmy [2], Pickup & Sonoma
"T"	Bravada, 4WD Blazer [2], Jimmy [2], Pickup & Sonoma
"U"	Lumina APV, Silhouette & Trans Sport
"V"	4WD Blazer [2], Jimmy [2], Pickup & Suburban

[1] – Vehicle Series is the fifth character of VIN.
[2] – Blazer and Jimmy are available in two sizes: "S" and "T" Series (smaller version), and "R" and "V" Series (larger version).

VACUUM DIAGRAM REFERENCE CHART

Engine & Vehicle Series	Application	Transmission	Fig. No.
2.5L 4-Cyl.			
"S" Series	Calif. & Fed.	All	1
"S" Series	Calif. & Fed.	Manual	2
3.1L V6			
"U" Series	Calif. & Fed.	Automatic	3
4.3L V6			
"C" & "K" Series	Calif.	All	4
"C" & "K" Series	Calif. & Fed.	All	5
"C" & "K" Series	Calif.	All	6
"G" Series	Calif./Fed./High Alt.	Automatic	7
"G" Series	Calif.	All	8
"P" Series	Calif./Fed./High Alt. H.D.	All	9
"S" & "T" Series	Calif.	All	10
"S" & "T" Series	Calif. & Fed.	All	11
5.0L V8			
"C" & "K" Series	Fed.	All	12
"C" & "K" Series	Calif.	Automatic	13
"G" Series	Calif. & Fed.	Automatic	14
5.7L V8			
"C" & "K" Series	Calif.	Automatic	15
"C" & "K" Series	Calif.	Manual	16
"C" & "K" Series	Calif. & Fed.	All	17
"G" Series	Calif.	Automatic	18
"G" Series	Calif. & Fed. Heavy Duty	Automatic	19
"P" Series	Calif. & Fed. Heavy Duty	All	20
"R" & "V" Series	Calif. Light & Medium Duty	Automatic	21
"R" & "V" Series	Calif. & Fed. Heavy Duty	All	22
6.2L V8			
"C" & "K" Series	Fed. & High Alt.	Automatic	23
"G" Series	Fed. & High Alt.	Automatic	24
"R" & "V" Series	Fed. & High Alt.	Automatic	25
7.4L V8			
"C" & "K" Series	Calif. & Fed. Heavy Duty	All	26
"C" & "K" Series	Calif. & Fed.	Automatic	27
"G" Series	Calif. & Fed. Heavy Duty	Automatic	28
"P", "R" & "V" Series	Calif. & Fed. Heavy Duty	All	29
"P" Series	Calif./Fed./High Alt. H.D.	All	30

1991 ENGINE PERFORMANCE
Vacuum Diagrams (Cont.)

EMISSION CONTROL DEVICE ABBREVIATIONS

A/CL – Air Cleaner
AIR – Air Injection Reactor
A/T – Automatic Transmission
DISTR – Distributor
DVTR – Diverter Valve
EFE – Early Fuel Evaporation
EGR – Exhaust Gas Recirculation
EGR SOL – EGR Solenoid
EPR – Exhaust Pressure Regulator
ESC – Electronic Spark Control
MAP – Manifold Air Pressure Sensor
M/T – Manual Transmission
PCV – Positive Crankcase Ventilation
TBI – Throttle Body Injection
TRC – Throttle Return Control
TVS – Thermal Vacuum Switch
VAC – Vacuum

VACUUM DIAGRAMS

***NOTE:** The following vacuum diagrams are courtesy of General Motors Corp. Information is not available for models not listed. Letters in parenthesis are the emission calibration code, located on underhood label.*

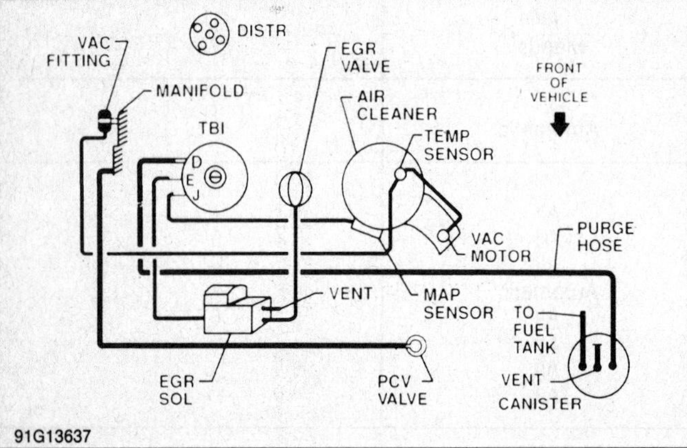
DISTR
VAC FITTING
MANIFOLD
EGR VALVE
FRONT OF VEHICLE
AIR CLEANER
TBI
TEMP SENSOR
D
E
J
VAC MOTOR
PURGE HOSE
VENT
MAP SENSOR
TO FUEL TANK
EGR SOL
PCV VALVE
VENT
CANISTER
91G13637

***Fig. 1:** 2.5L 4-Cyl. "S" Series Light Duty Calif./Fed. All Trans. (LCT, LCU & LDA)*

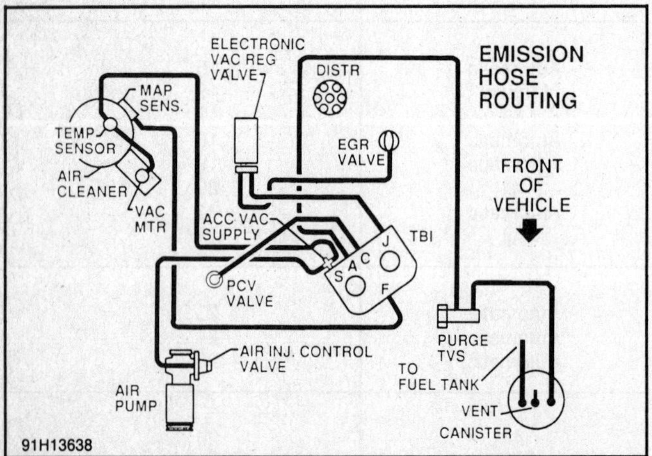
ELECTRONIC VAC REG VALVE
DISTR
EMISSION HOSE ROUTING
MAP SENS.
TEMP SENSOR
AIR CLEANER
VAC MTR
EGR VALVE
FRONT OF VEHICLE
ACC VAC SUPPLY
TBI
J
C
A
S
F
PCV VALVE
AIR INJ. CONTROL VALVE
PURGE TVS
AIR PUMP
TO FUEL TANK
VENT
CANISTER
91H13638

***Fig. 2:** 2.5L 4-Cyl. "S" Series Light Duty Calif./Fed. M/T (LDB & LDC)*

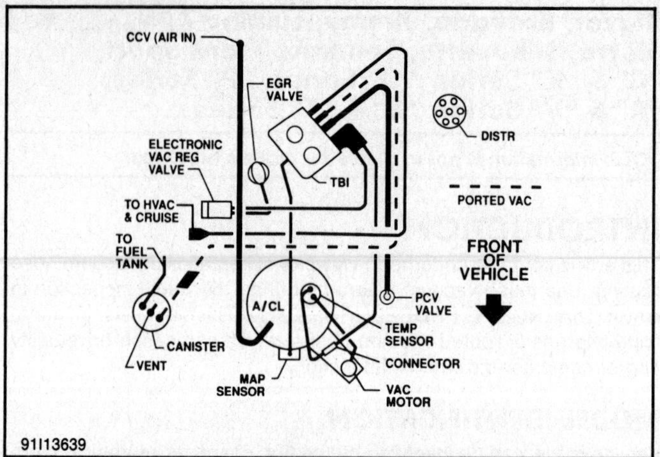
CCV (AIR IN)
EGR VALVE
DISTR
ELECTRONIC VAC REG VALVE
TBI
PORTED VAC
TO HVAC & CRUISE
TO FUEL TANK
FRONT OF VEHICLE
A/CL
PCV VALVE
TEMP SENSOR
CANISTER
CONNECTOR
VENT
MAP SENSOR
VAC MOTOR
91I13639

***Fig. 3:** 3.1L V6 "U" Series Light Duty Calif. A/T (LDR & LDS) & Light Duty Fed. A/T (LDP)*

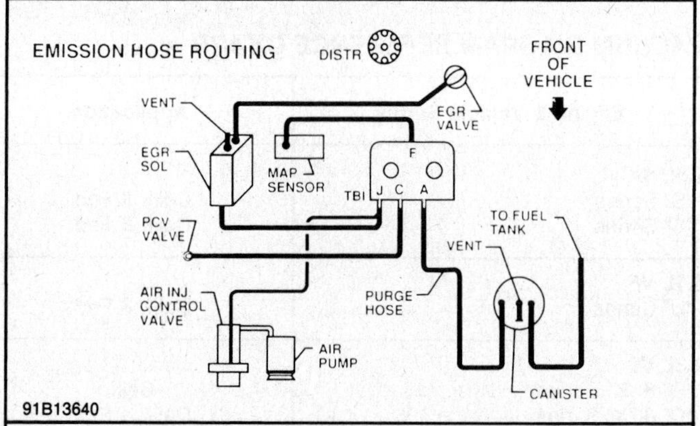
EMISSION HOSE ROUTING
DISTR
FRONT OF VEHICLE
VENT
EGR VALVE
EGR SOL
F
MAP SENSOR
TBI
J
C
A
PCV VALVE
TO FUEL TANK
VENT
AIR INJ. CONTROL VALVE
PURGE HOSE
AIR PUMP
CANISTER
91B13640

***Fig. 4:** 4.3L V6 "C" & "K" Series Light Duty Calif. All Trans. (LDW)*

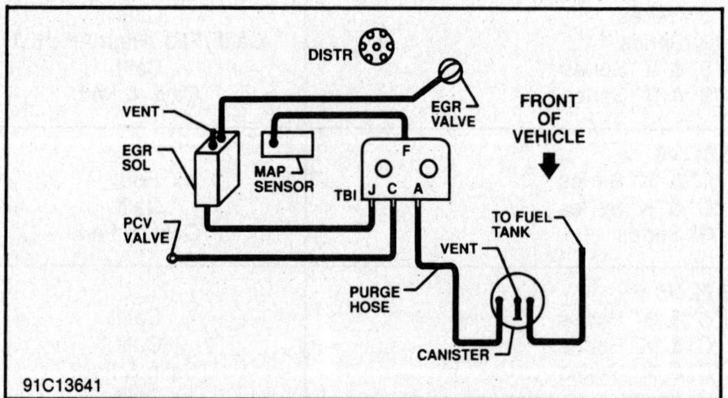
DISTR
VENT
EGR VALVE
FRONT OF VEHICLE
EGR SOL
F
MAP SENSOR
TBI
J
C
A
PCV VALVE
TO FUEL TANK
VENT
PURGE HOSE
CANISTER
91C13641

***Fig. 5:** 4.3L V6 "C" & "K" Series Light Duty Calif./Fed. All Trans. (LHM)*

1991 ENGINE PERFORMANCE
Vacuum Diagrams (Cont.)

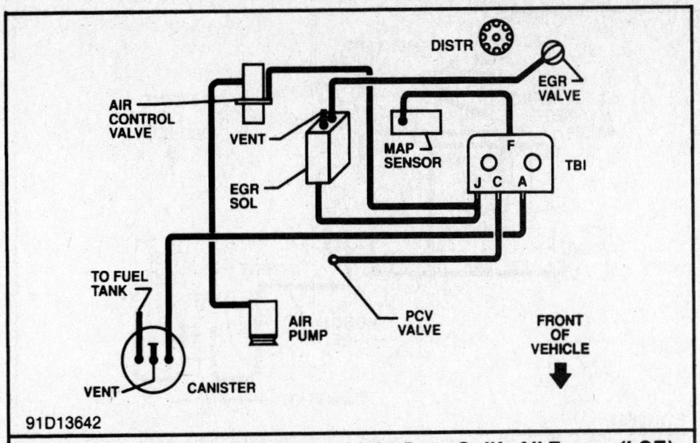
DISTR
AIR CONTROL VALVE
EGR VALVE
VENT
MAP SENSOR
F
J C A
TBI
EGR SOL
TO FUEL TANK
AIR PUMP
PCV VALVE
FRONT OF VEHICLE
VENT
CANISTER
91D13642

Fig. 6: 4.3L V6 "C" & "K" Series Light Duty Calif. All Trans. (LCZ)

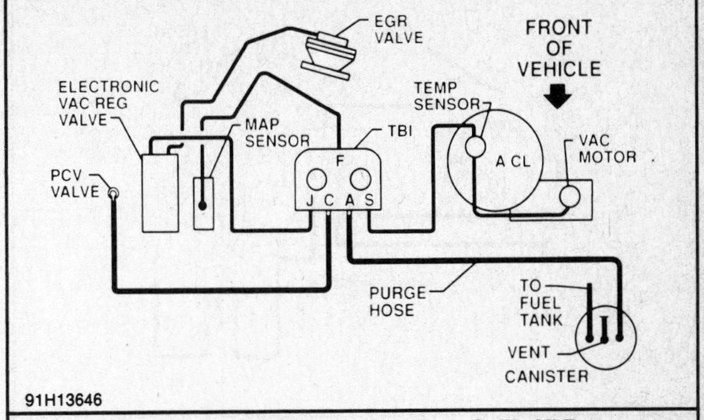
EGR VALVE
FRONT OF VEHICLE
ELECTRONIC VAC REG VALVE
TEMP SENSOR
MAP SENSOR
TBI
F
J C A S
A CL
VAC MOTOR
PCV VALVE
PURGE HOSE
TO FUEL TANK
VENT
CANISTER
91H13646

Fig. 10: 4.3L V6 "S" & "T" Series Light Duty Calif. All Trans. (LDF & LDH)

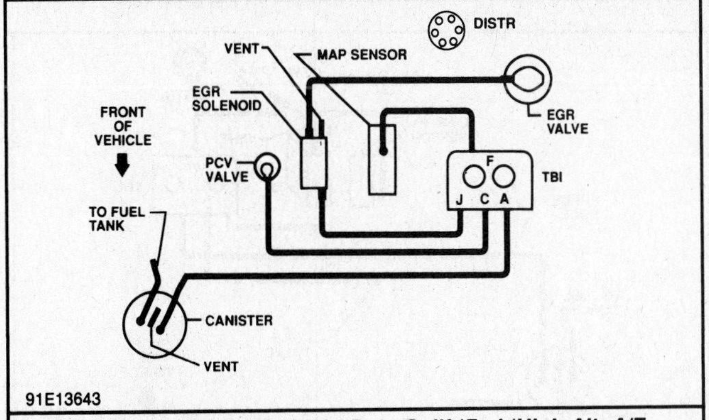
DISTR
VENT
MAP SENSOR
EGR SOLENOID
EGR VALVE
FRONT OF VEHICLE
PCV VALVE
F
J C A
TBI
TO FUEL TANK
CANISTER
VENT
91E13643

Fig. 7: 4.3L V6 "G" Series Light Duty Calif./Fed./High Alt. A/T (LNK)

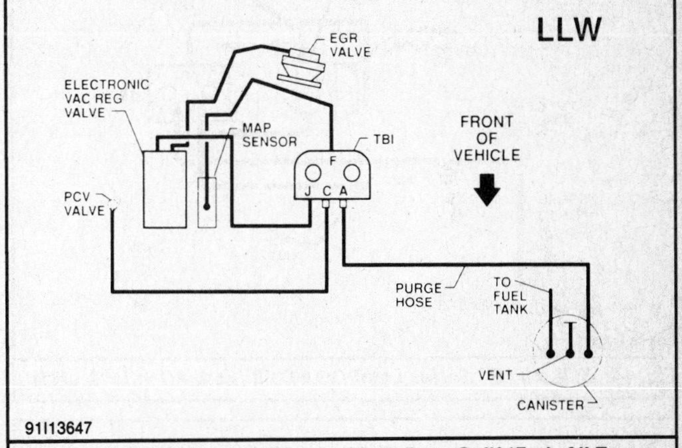
LLW
EGR VALVE
ELECTRONIC VAC REG VALVE
MAP SENSOR
TBI
F
J C A
FRONT OF VEHICLE
PCV VALVE
PURGE HOSE
TO FUEL TANK
VENT
CANISTER
91I13647

Fig. 11: 4.3L V6 "S" & "T" Series Light Duty Calif./Fed. All Trans. (LLW, LLY & LLZ)

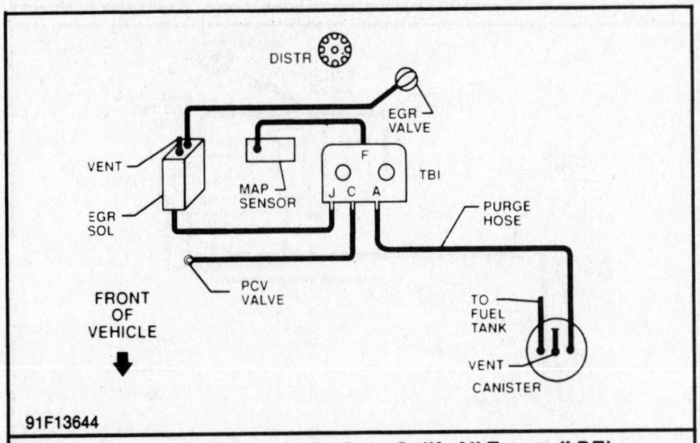
DISTR
EGR VALVE
F
VENT
TBI
MAP SENSOR
J C A
EGR SOL
PURGE HOSE
FRONT OF VEHICLE
PCV VALVE
TO FUEL TANK
VENT
CANISTER
91F13644

Fig. 8: 4.3L V6 "G" Series Light Duty Calif. All Trans. (LDZ)

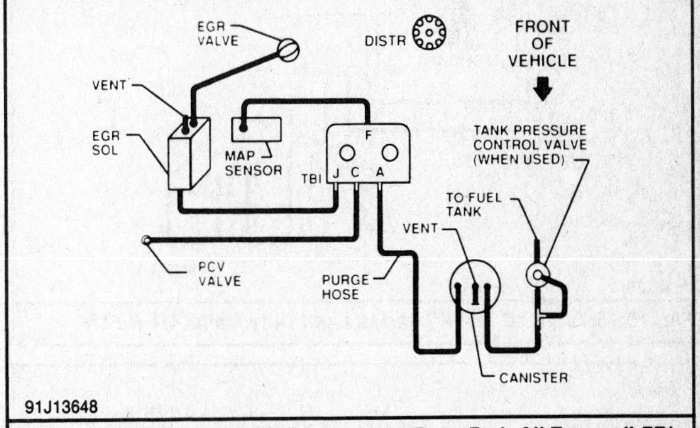
EGR VALVE
DISTR
FRONT OF VEHICLE
VENT
EGR SOL
F
MAP SENSOR
TBI
J C A
TANK PRESSURE CONTROL VALVE (WHEN USED)
TO FUEL TANK
VENT
PCV VALVE
PURGE HOSE
CANISTER
91J13648

Fig. 12: 5.0L V8 "C" & "K" Series Light Duty Fed. All Trans. (LFB)

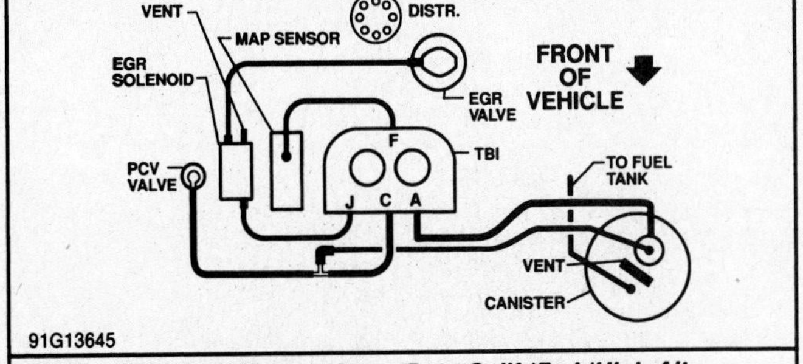
VENT
DISTR.
MAP SENSOR
EGR SOLENOID
FRONT OF VEHICLE
EGR VALVE
F
TBI
PCV VALVE
J C A
TO FUEL TANK
VENT
CANISTER
91G13645

Fig. 9: 4.3L V6 "P" Series Heavy Duty Calif./Fed./High Alt. All Trans. (LHP & LHR)

1991 ENGINE PERFORMANCE
Vacuum Diagrams (Cont.)

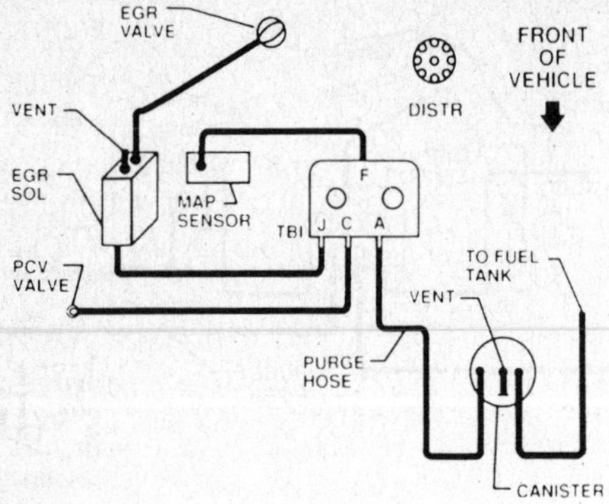
EGR VALVE
VENT
EGR SOL
FRONT OF VEHICLE
DISTR
MAP SENSOR
F
TBI
J C A
PCV VALVE
TO FUEL TANK
VENT
PURGE HOSE
CANISTER
91A13649

Fig. 13: 5.0L V8 "C" & "K" Series Light Duty Calif. A/T (LFD)

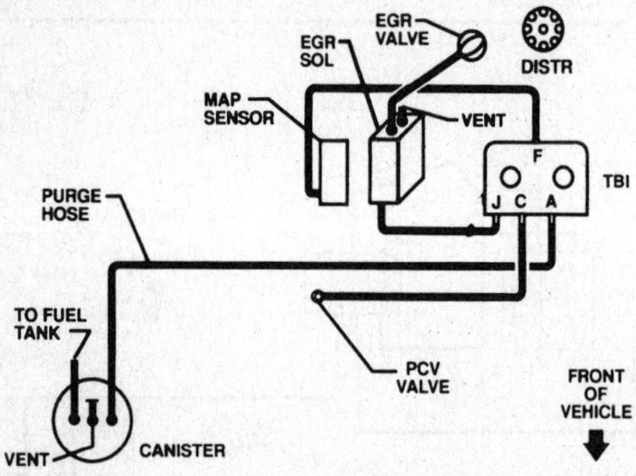
EGR VALVE
EGR SOL
DISTR
MAP SENSOR
VENT
F
TBI
J C A
PURGE HOSE
TO FUEL TANK
PCV VALVE
FRONT OF VEHICLE
VENT
CANISTER
91E13650

Fig. 14: 5.0L V8 "G" Series Light Duty Calif./Fed. A/T (LFF & LFH)

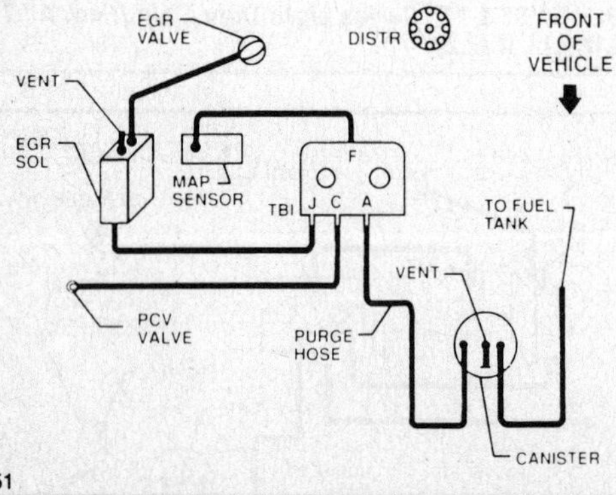
EGR VALVE
DISTR
FRONT OF VEHICLE
VENT
EGR SOL
MAP SENSOR
F
TBI
J C A
TO FUEL TANK
VENT
PCV VALVE
PURGE HOSE
CANISTER
91F13651

Fig. 15: 5.7L V8 "C" & "K" Series Light Duty Calif. A/T (LFM)

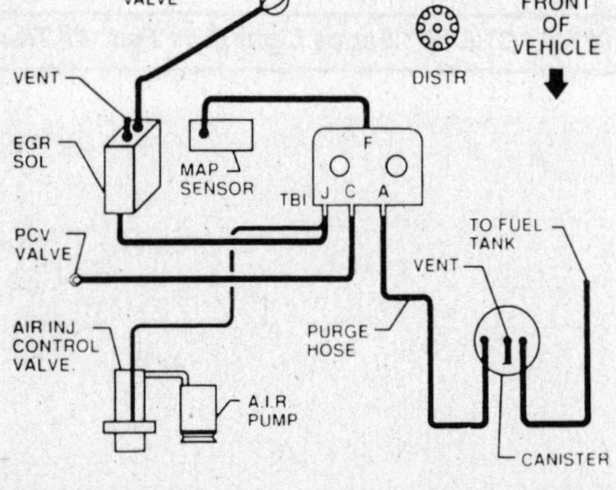
EGR VALVE
FRONT OF VEHICLE
DISTR
VENT
EGR SOL
MAP SENSOR
F
TBI
J C A
PCV VALVE
TO FUEL TANK
VENT
AIR INJ. CONTROL VALVE.
PURGE HOSE
A.I.R. PUMP
CANISTER
91G13652

Fig. 16: 5.7L V8 "C" & "K" Series Light Duty Calif. M/T (LFL)

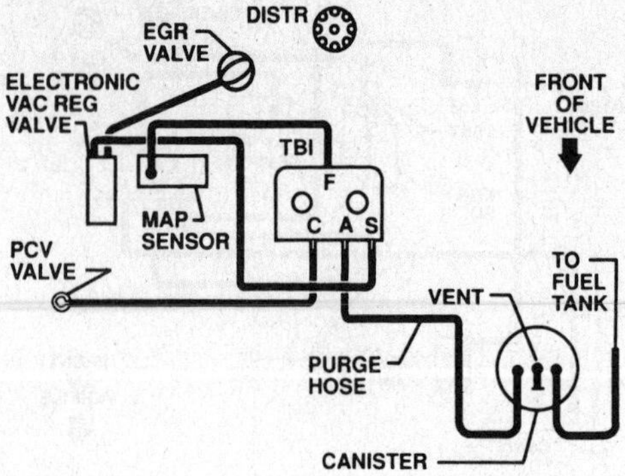
DISTR
EGR VALVE
ELECTRONIC VAC REG VALVE
FRONT OF VEHICLE
TBI
F
C A S
MAP SENSOR
PCV VALVE
TO FUEL TANK
VENT
PURGE HOSE
CANISTER
91H13653

Fig. 17: 5.7L V8 "C" & "K" Series Light Duty Calif./Fed. All Trans. (LHT & LMJ)

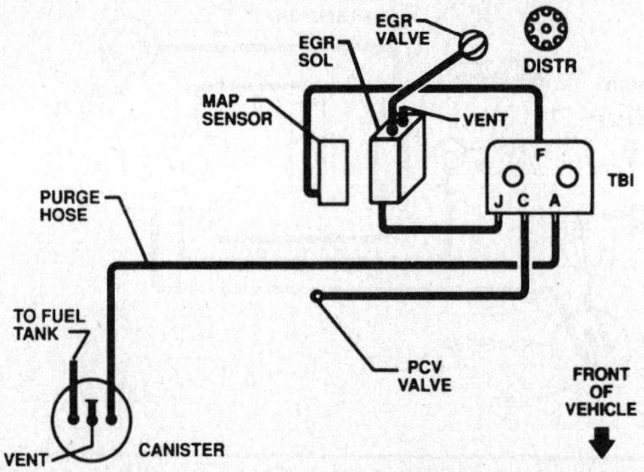
EGR VALVE
EGR SOL
DISTR
MAP SENSOR
VENT
F
TBI
J C A
PURGE HOSE
TO FUEL TANK
PCV VALVE
FRONT OF VEHICLE
VENT
CANISTER
91I13654

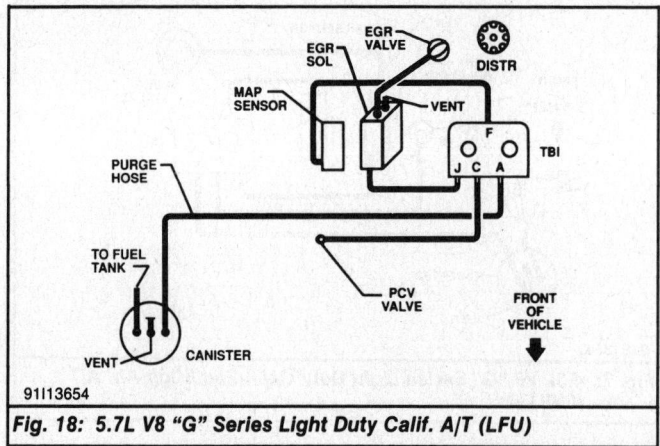

Fig. 18: 5.7L V8 "G" Series Light Duty Calif. A/T (LFU)

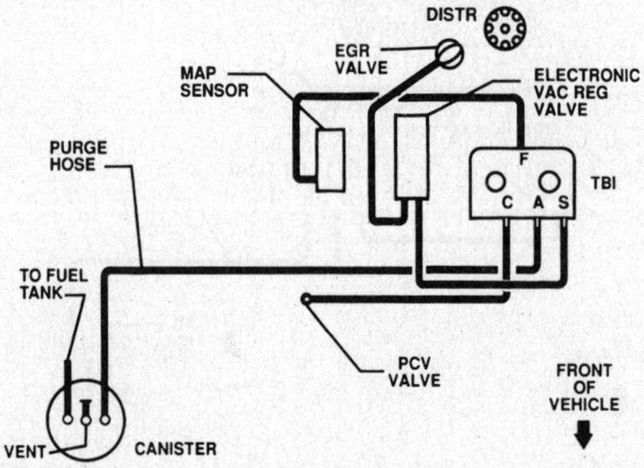
DISTR
EGR VALVE
MAP SENSOR
ELECTRONIC VAC REG VALVE
PURGE HOSE
F
TBI
C A S
TO FUEL TANK
PCV VALVE
FRONT OF VEHICLE
VENT
CANISTER
91J13655

Fig. 19: 5.7L V8 "G" Series Heavy Duty Calif./Fed. A/T (LJM)

1991 ENGINE PERFORMANCE
Vacuum Diagrams (Cont.)

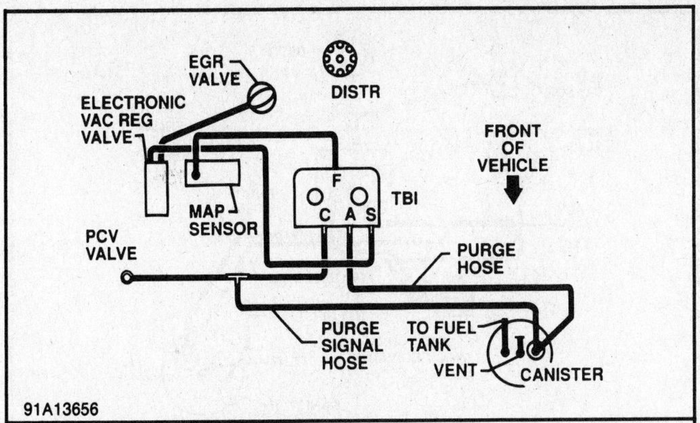
EGR VALVE
DISTR
ELECTRONIC VAC REG VALVE
FRONT OF VEHICLE
MAP SENSOR
TBI
PCV VALVE
PURGE HOSE
PURGE SIGNAL HOSE
TO FUEL TANK
VENT
CANISTER
91A13656

Fig. 20: 5.7L V8 "P" Series Heavy Duty Calif./Fed. All Trans. (LJB, LJC, LJD & LJF)

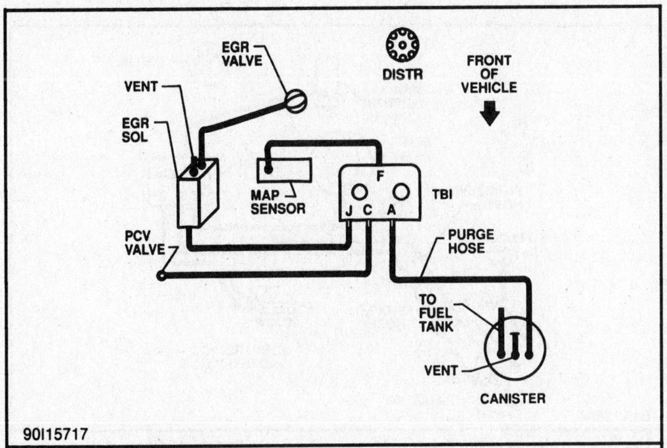
EGR VALVE
DISTR
FRONT OF VEHICLE
VENT
EGR SOL
MAP SENSOR
TBI
PCV VALVE
PURGE HOSE
TO FUEL TANK
VENT
CANISTER
90I15717

Fig. 21: 5.7L V8 "R" & "V" Series Light & Medium Duty Calif. A/T (LFP & LFS)

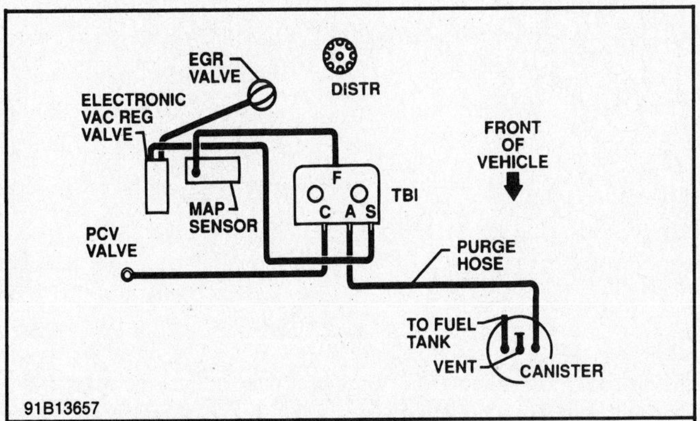
EGR VALVE
DISTR
ELECTRONIC VAC REG VALVE
FRONT OF VEHICLE
MAP SENSOR
TBI
PCV VALVE
PURGE HOSE
TO FUEL TANK
VENT
CANISTER
91B13657

Fig. 22: 5.7L V8 "R" & "V" Series Heavy Duty Calif./Fed. All Trans. (LHY)

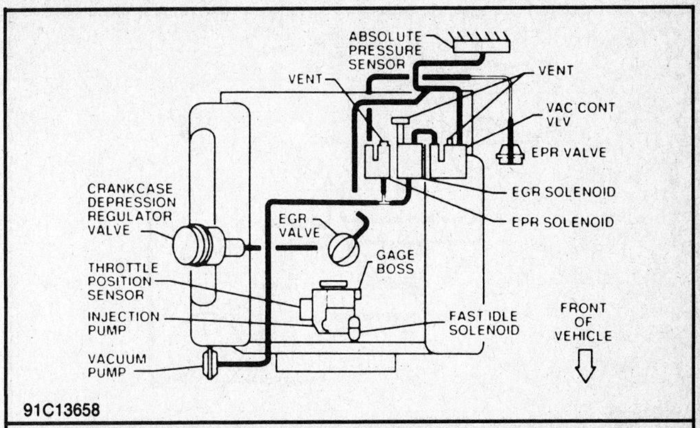
ABSOLUTE PRESSURE SENSOR
VENT
VENT
VAC CONT VLV
EPR VALVE
CRANKCASE DEPRESSION REGULATOR VALVE
EGR SOLENOID
EPR SOLENOID
EGR VALVE
GAGE BOSS
THROTTLE POSITION SENSOR
INJECTION PUMP
FAST IDLE SOLENOID
FRONT OF VEHICLE
VACUUM PUMP
91C13658

Fig. 23: 6.2L Diesel "C" & "K" Series Light Duty Fed./High Alt. A/T (LPZ & LHA)

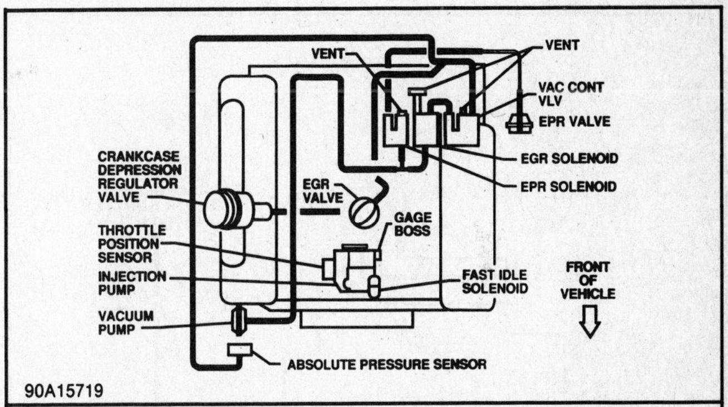
VENT
VENT
VAC CONT VLV
EPR VALVE
CRANKCASE DEPRESSION REGULATOR VALVE
EGR SOLENOID
EPR SOLENOID
EGR VALVE
GAGE BOSS
THROTTLE POSITION SENSOR
INJECTION PUMP
FAST IDLE SOLENOID
FRONT OF VEHICLE
VACUUM PUMP
ABSOLUTE PRESSURE SENSOR
90A15719

Fig. 24: 6.2L Diesel "G" Series Light Duty Fed./High Alt. A/T (LHF & LHH)

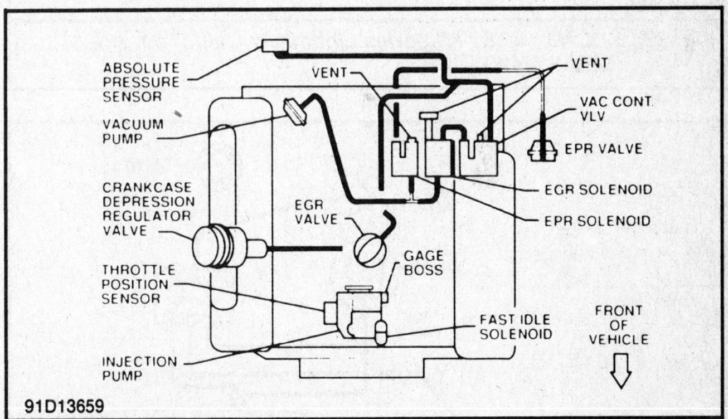
ABSOLUTE PRESSURE SENSOR
VENT
VENT
VAC CONT. VLV
VACUUM PUMP
EPR VALVE
CRANKCASE DEPRESSION REGULATOR VALVE
EGR SOLENOID
EPR SOLENOID
EGR VALVE
GAGE BOSS
THROTTLE POSITION SENSOR
FAST IDLE SOLENOID
FRONT OF VEHICLE
INJECTION PUMP
91D13659

Fig. 25: 6.2L Diesel "R" & "V" Series Light Duty Fed./High Alt. A/T (LHC & LHD)

1991 ENGINE PERFORMANCE
Vacuum Diagrams (Cont.)

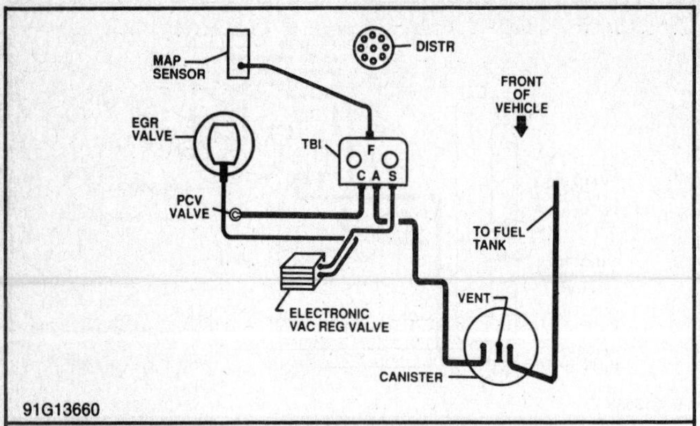
MAP SENSOR
DISTR
FRONT OF VEHICLE
EGR VALVE
TBI
F
C A S
PCV VALVE
TO FUEL TANK
ELECTRONIC VAC REG VALVE
VENT
CANISTER
91G13660

Fig. 26: 7.4L V8 "C" & "K" Series Heavy Duty Calif./Fed. All Trans. (LMS & LMX)

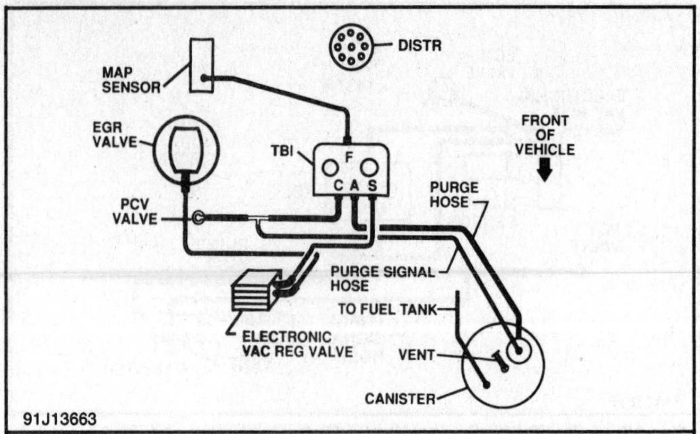
DISTR
MAP SENSOR
EGR VALVE
TBI
F
C A S
FRONT OF VEHICLE
PURGE HOSE
PCV VALVE
PURGE SIGNAL HOSE
TO FUEL TANK
ELECTRONIC VAC REG VALVE
VENT
CANISTER
91J13663

Fig. 29: 7.4L V8 "P", "R" & "V" Series Heavy Duty Calif./Fed. All Trans. (LPA, LPC & LPF)

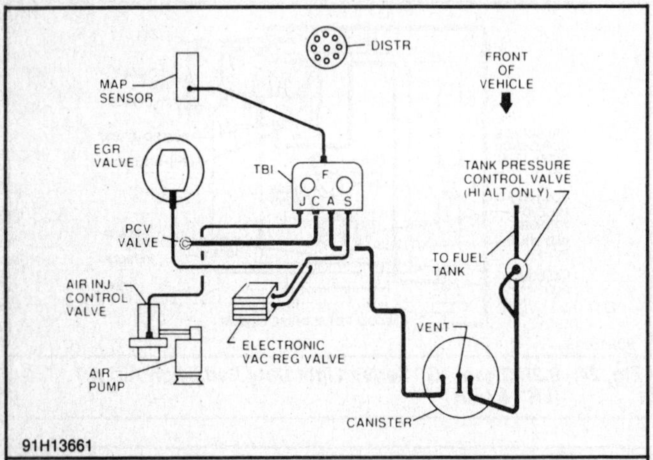
DISTR
FRONT OF VEHICLE
MAP SENSOR
EGR VALVE
TBI
F
J C A S
TANK PRESSURE CONTROL VALVE (HI ALT ONLY)
PCV VALVE
TO FUEL TANK
AIR INJ. CONTROL VALVE
VENT
ELECTRONIC VAC REG VALVE
AIR PUMP
CANISTER
91H13661

Fig. 27: 7.4L V8 "C" & "K" Series Light Duty Calif./Fed. A/T (LMU & LMW)

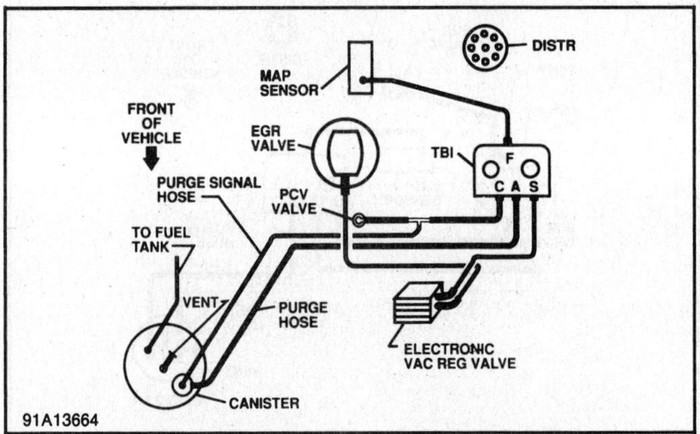
DISTR
MAP SENSOR
FRONT OF VEHICLE
EGR VALVE
TBI
F
C A S
PURGE SIGNAL HOSE
PCV VALVE
TO FUEL TANK
VENT
PURGE HOSE
ELECTRONIC VAC REG VALVE
CANISTER
91A13664

Fig. 30: 7.4L V8 "P" Series Heavy Duty Calif./Fed./High Alt. All Trans. (LMZ & LPB)

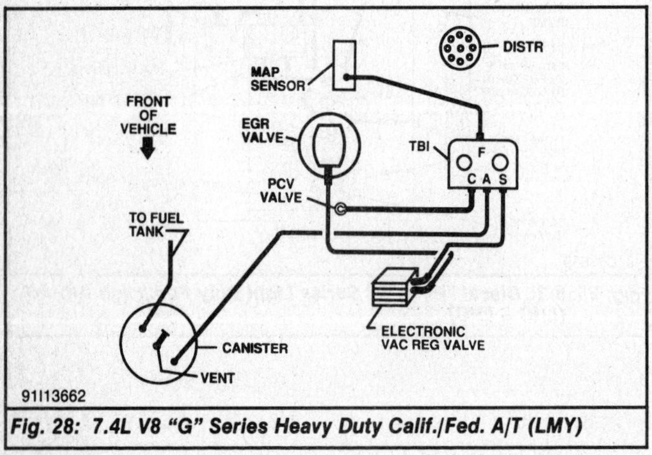
DISTR
MAP SENSOR
FRONT OF VEHICLE
EGR VALVE
TBI
F
C A S
PCV VALVE
TO FUEL TANK
CANISTER
ELECTRONIC VAC REG VALVE
VENT
91I13662

Fig. 28: 7.4L V8 "G" Series Heavy Duty Calif./Fed. A/T (LMY)

1991 ENGINE PERFORMANCE
Removal, Overhaul & Installation

Astro, Blazer, Bravada, Jimmy, Lumina APV, Safari, Sierra, Silhouette, Sonoma, Syclone, Trans Sport, "C" & "K" Series, "G" Series, "P" Series, "R" & "V" Series, "S" & "T" Series

INTRODUCTION

Removal, overhaul and installation procedures (when given by manufacturer) are covered in this article. If component removal and installation is primarily an unbolt and bolt-on procedure, only a simple torque specification may be supplied.

ON-VEHICLE ADJUSTMENTS

NOTE: For adjustments, see ON-VEHICLE ADJUSTMENTS article.

ELECTRONIC CONTROL MODULE (ECM)

CONTROL UNIT

CAUTION: When certain materials rub together, a transfer of electrons from one material to another may occur under special conditions. This causes electrostatic charge (static electricity) build up in one of the materials. When any conducting material comes in contact with the charged material, electrostatic discharge occurs, transferring electrons to the third material. Electronic components used in control systems are designed to carry very low voltages; a 30-volt charge created by static electricity can cause a total or degrading failure in ECM or other electronic components containing integrated circuits. Before servicing ECM, ground yourself, and ground the work area to discharge stored electricity.

STATIC CHARGE (VOLTS)

Movement	Relative Humidity 10-20%	Relative Humidity 65-90%
Walking Across Carpet	35,000	1500
Handling Clear Plastic Bag	20,000	1200
Sliding Across Velour Seat	15,000	400
Walking Across Tile/Vinyl	12,000	50
Handling Vinyl Envelope	7000	600

CAUTION: Static electricity can destroy integrated circuits within ECM. Before servicing ECM, ground yourself and the work area to discharge stored electricity.

CAUTION: DO NOT remove ECM from packaging until ready to install. Ground static-proof package BEFORE opening. DO NOT touch electrical terminals of components unless properly grounded. DO NOT lay electrical components on car seat, carpeting or dashboard. Use electrostatic protection mat and ground strap whenever possible. See Fig. 1.

NOTE: Before replacing ECM, carefully inspect all wiring and control components. Ignition switch must be in OFF position when connecting or disconnecting ECM connector.

Removal – Disconnect negative battery terminal. Unplug connectors from ECM. *See Fig. 1.* Remove ECM from vehicle. Remove PROM and CALPAC (if equipped) or MEM-CAL from ECM. See CALPAC, MEM-CAL, or PROGRAMMABLE READ-ONLY MEMORY (PROM).

Installation – Install PROM and CALPAC (if equipped) or MEM-CAL in new ECM. See CALPAC, MEM-CAL, or PROGRAMMABLE READ-ONLY MEMORY (PROM). Install ECM into vehicle. Connect electrical connectors to ECM. Install access panels. Connect negative battery terminal to battery.

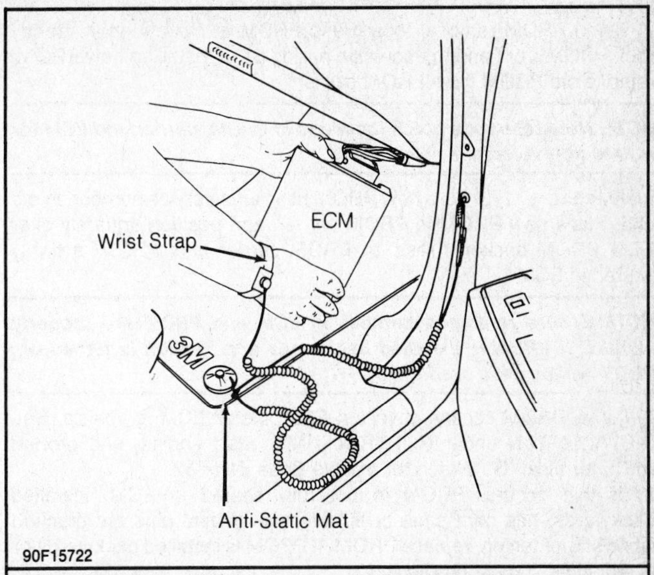
ECM
Wrist Strap
3M
Anti-Static Mat
90F15722

Fig. 1: Replacing ECM While Using 3M Anti-Static Mat

CALPAC

Removal & Installation – Some ECM's use a CALPAC as well as a PROM. *See Fig. 2.* The CALPAC must also be removed from old ECM and installed in new one. Removal and replacement procedures for CALPAC are same as for PROM. See PROGRAMMABLE READ-ONLY MEMORY (PROM) in this article. If units are installed improperly, grounding diagnostic test lead will set Code 52.

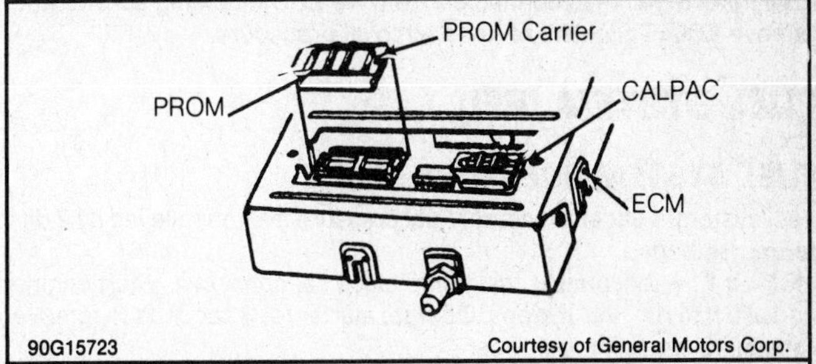
PROM Carrier
PROM
CALPAC
ECM
90G15723
Courtesy of General Motors Corp.

Fig. 2: ECM with PROM & CALPAC

MEM-CAL

Removal – Disconnect negative battery terminal. Remove ECM from vehicle. See REMOVAL under CONTROL UNIT. Using 2 fingers, push retaining clips back from MEM-CAL. At the same time, grasp it at both ends and lift out of socket. DO NOT remove MEM-CAL cover.

Installation – **1)** Carefully align MEM-CAL pins with ECM pin holes. DO NOT press in middle of MEM-CAL. Push downward evenly on ends of MEM-CAL until retaining clips on ends of MEM-CAL snap into place.

2) Install ECM. Reconnect negative battery terminal. Turn ignition on and ground ALDL terminal "B". Code 12 should be flashed at least 4 times. If Code 12 is not flashed at least 4 times, other codes are present. If Code(s) 42, 43, 51 or 52 are present, or if CHECK ENGINE light stays on constantly with code(s) present, MEM-CAL is not fully seated, or is defective.

PROGRAMMABLE READ-ONLY MEMORY (PROM)

Removal – **1)** Remove ECM from vehicle. See REMOVAL under CONTROL UNIT. Position ECM so bottom cover is facing upward. Remove slide-off PROM access cover by depressing locking tab.

1991 ENGINE PERFORMANCE
Removal, Overhaul & Installation (Cont.)

2) Using PROM removal tool, grasp PROM at narrow ends. Gently rock PROM from end to end while pulling up. If installing new PROM, remove old PROM from PROM carrier.

NOTE: Note reference notch locations in PROM, carrier and ECM for reassembly reference.

Installation - 1) Ensure new PROM has same service number as old one. Place new PROM in PROM carrier, and position squarely over ECM PROM socket. Press on PROM carrier until PROM is firmly seated in ECM.

NOTE: Ensure reference notches in ECM and PROM are properly aligned. If PROM is installed backwards and ignition is turned on, PROM will be destroyed.

2) Install PROM access cover on ECM. Install ECM in vehicle. See INSTALLATION under CONTROL UNIT. Start engine, and ground ALDL terminal "B". Watch for trouble Code 51 or 52.
3) If this occurs, PROM is not fully seated in ECM, installed backwards, has bent pins, or is defective. If bent pins are cracked while straightening, replace PROM. If PROM is installed backwards or is defective, it must be replaced.

ELECTRONIC SPARK CONTROL (ESC) MODULE

NOTE: The ESC is located on a bracket behind the distributor, mounted to firewall.

Removal & Installation - Turn ignition off. Remove bracket-to-firewall screws. Rotate bracket to access ESC module. Disconnect ESC module harness connector. Remove ESC mounting screws and remove ESC. To install, reverse removal procedure.

FUEL SYSTEM (PFI)

FUEL SYSTEM PRESSURE RELIEF

Fuel system is under pressure. Fuel pressure may be relieved by 2 different methods.
Method 1 - Disconnect fuel pump electrical connector. Start engine and allow to run until it stops. Operate starter for 3 seconds to remove remaining fuel from fuel lines.
Method 2 - Install Fuel Pressure Gauge (J-34730-1) on fuel pressure connection. Wrap shop towel around pressure connection when installing fuel pressure gauge to absorb fuel leakage. Place gauge bleed hose in container. Open bleed valve to bleed fuel pressure.

THROTTLE BODY

NOTE: Identification number is stamped on throttle body near throttle shaft. Identification number must be used for ordering replacement components.

Removal - 1) Relieve fuel pressure. See FUEL SYSTEM PRESSURE RELIEF under FUEL SYSTEM (PFI). Disconnect negative battery terminal. Loosen charge air cooler mounting bolts, and reposition charge air cooler unit to access throttle body.
2) Disconnect electrical connectors, vacuum lines, accelerator cable, throttle valve cable, and cruise control cable (if equipped). Remove throttle body screws. Remove throttle body assembly from manifold.
Installation - 1) To install, reverse removal procedure using new gasket. Ensure throttle and cruise control cables do not hold throttle valve open. Tighten retaining bolts to specification. See appropriate TORQUE SPECIFICATIONS table at end of article. Reset IAC valve pintle position.
2) To reset IAC valve pintle position, depress accelerator pedal slightly. Start and run engine for 5 seconds. Turn ignition off for 10 seconds. Restart engine and check for proper idle operation.

FUEL RAIL & INJECTORS

NOTE: Upper intake manifold must be removed in order to remove fuel rail and injectors.

Removal - 1) Move air cleaner and duct aside. Drain coolant from radiator. Drain charge air cooler radiator. Relief fuel pressure. See FUEL PRESSURE RELIEF under FUEL SYSTEM (PFI).
2) Disconnect negative battery terminal. Disconnect charge air cooler ducts and hoses. Remove charge air cooler center support bracket. Disconnect electrical connectors and hoses from EVRV solenoid, ignition coil and MAP sensor.
3) Remove multi-use bracket from lower intake manifold. Disconnect upper manifold electrical connectors and hoses. Remove throttle body from upper manifold. See THROTTLE BODY under FUEL SYSTEM (PFI).
4) Remove upper intake manifold mounting bolts. Remove upper intake manifold assembly and gasket. Disconnect heater hose at lower intake manifold. Disconnect charge air cooler inlet pipe.
5) Disconnect fuel injector electrical connectors. Disconnect fuel line at fuel rail. Remove fuel rail retaining bolts. Remove fuel rail and injectors.
Installation - To install, reverse removal procedure. Lubricate injector "O" rings with oil. Tighten fuel rail retaining bolts. See appropriate TORQUE SPECIFICATIONS table at end of article.

FUEL SYSTEM (TBI)

FUEL SYSTEM PRESSURE RELIEF

TBI Unit Model 700 - Place transmission gear selector in Park (Neutral on M/T). Set parking brake and block drive wheels. Loosen fuel filler cap to relieve tank pressure. Disconnect 3-terminal electrical connector at fuel tank. Start engine and allow to run until engine stalls. Crank engine for 3 seconds to relieve any residual pressure left in fuel lines. Fuel lines are now safe for servicing.
TBI Unit Model 220 - Fuel pressure is relieved and drops to zero when ignitions is turned off. To minimize risk of fire and personal injury, cover area to be disconnected with a shop rag.

THROTTLE BODY

Identification - An 8-digit unit identification number is stamped on throttle body assembly. On TBI model 220, number is stamped vertically on front of throttle body, at Throttle Position Sensor (TPS) side. On TBI model 700, number can be found on TPS side of mounting flange. Letter codes are stamped on throttle body at external tube locations to identify vacuum hose connections.
Removal - 1) Disconnect air cleaner (THERMAC) hose from engine vacuum fitting (if equipped). Remove air cleaner, adapter, and gasket. Relieve fuel pressure. See FUEL SYSTEM PRESSURE RELIEF under FUEL SYSTEM (TBI).
2) Disconnect electrical leads at IAC valve, throttle position sensor, and fuel injector(s). Disconnect fuel lines from throttle body. Discard fuel line "O" rings. Disconnect grommet with wires from throttle body.

NOTE: On TBI model 220, squeeze plastic tabs on injectors and pull connector straight up.

3) Disconnect throttle linkage, return spring and cruise control linkage (if equipped). Label and disconnect all vacuum hoses from throttle body. Remove throttle body mount bolts/nut. Remove throttle body.

NOTE: Disassembling throttle body unit for immersion in cleaning solvent requires removal of throttle body cover or fuel meter assembly, TPS and IAC assembly. Throttle valve screws are staked in position and should NOT be removed.

CAUTION: Pressure regulator spring is under heavy tension, and may cause personal injury if released. DO NOT immerse cover in any type of cleaning solvent.

1991 ENGINE PERFORMANCE
Removal, Overhaul & Installation (Cont.)

Disassembly (Throttle Body Cover – Model 220) – 1) Place throttle body on Holding Fixture (J-9789-118 or BT 30-15) to prevent damage to throttle valve. Remove cover-to-throttle body screws; note location of 2 short screws. Remove throttle body cover. *See Fig. 3*. Throttle body cover and pressure regulator are serviced as an assembly. DO NOT remove pressure regulator-to-cover screws.

2) Remove TPS, IAC, fuel injector, fuel filter, rubber parts, and diaphragms. Clean all remaining (metal) parts in a cold immersion-type cleaner such as Carbon X (X-55). Blow dry with compressed air. Inspect mating surfaces for damage which may prevent gasket sealing. Repair or replace faulty components.

Disassembly (Fuel Meter Assembly – Model 700) – 1) Remove fuel meter-to-throttle body retaining screws. Remove fuel meter assembly. *See Fig. 3*. Discard gasket. If fuel pressure regulator cover is removed, regulator diaphragm must be replaced to prevent fuel leaks.

2) Remove TPS, IAC, pressure regulator assembly, fuel injector, fuel filter, rubber parts, and diaphragms. Clean all remaining (metal) parts in a cold immersion-type cleaner such as Carbon X (X-55). Blow dry with compressed air. Inspect mating surfaces for damage which may prevent gasket sealing. Repair or replace faulty components.

Reassembly (Throttle Body Cover – Model 220) – 1) Install new dust seal into recess of throttle body. Install fuel outlet passage gasket on cover. Install throttle body cover gasket on throttle body. Install cover, making sure pressure regulator dust seal and cover gaskets are in place.

2) Apply thread locking compound to cover attaching screws. Install cover screws and lock washers. Tighten screws. Connect electrical lead to fuel injector, and install air cleaner.

Reassembly (Fuel Meter Assembly – Model 700) – 1) Install new fuel meter-to-throttle body assembly gasket. Match cutout portions of gasket with openings in throttle body assembly.

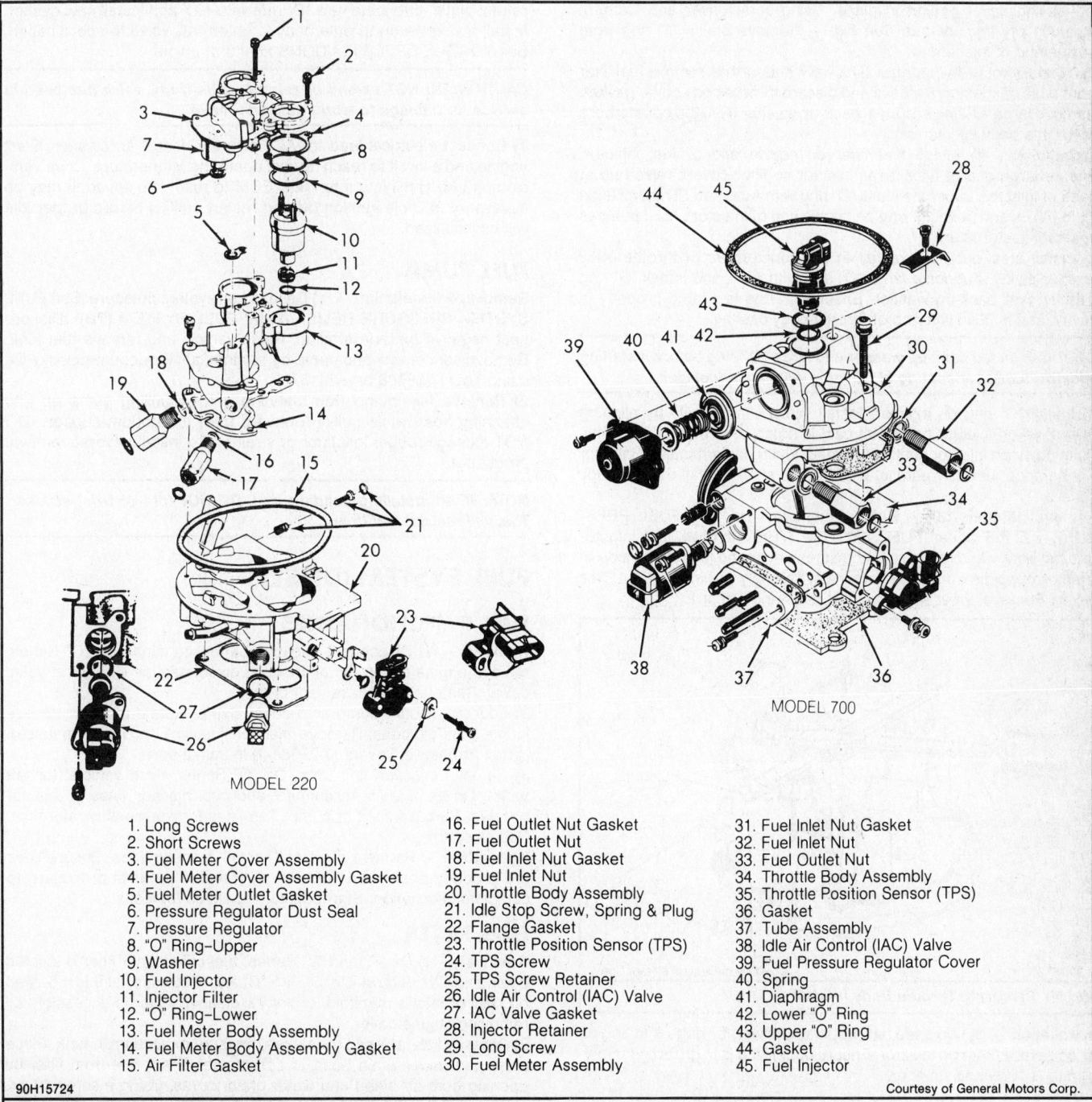

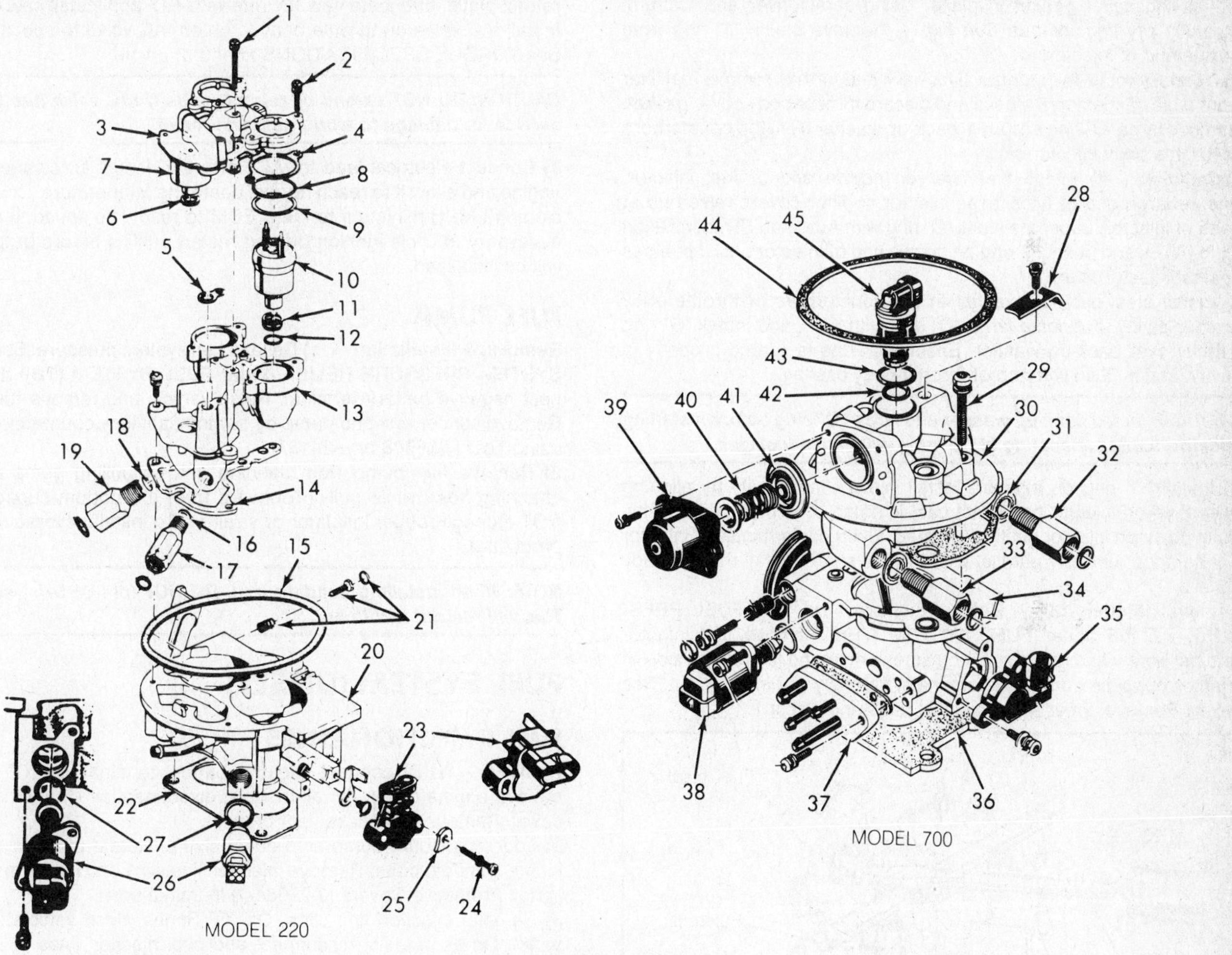
MODEL 220
MODEL 700

1. Long Screws
2. Short Screws
3. Fuel Meter Cover Assembly
4. Fuel Meter Cover Assembly Gasket
5. Fuel Meter Outlet Gasket
6. Pressure Regulator Dust Seal
7. Pressure Regulator
8. "O" Ring–Upper
9. Washer
10. Fuel Injector
11. Injector Filter
12. "O" Ring–Lower
13. Fuel Meter Body Assembly
14. Fuel Meter Body Assembly Gasket
15. Air Filter Gasket
16. Fuel Outlet Nut Gasket
17. Fuel Outlet Nut
18. Fuel Inlet Nut Gasket
19. Fuel Inlet Nut
20. Throttle Body Assembly
21. Idle Stop Screw, Spring & Plug
22. Flange Gasket
23. Throttle Position Sensor (TPS)
24. TPS Screw
25. TPS Screw Retainer
26. Idle Air Control (IAC) Valve
27. IAC Valve Gasket
28. Injector Retainer
29. Long Screw
30. Fuel Meter Assembly
31. Fuel Inlet Nut Gasket
32. Fuel Inlet Nut
33. Fuel Outlet Nut
34. Throttle Body Assembly
35. Throttle Position Sensor (TPS)
36. Gasket
37. Tube Assembly
38. Idle Air Control (IAC) Valve
39. Fuel Pressure Regulator Cover
40. Spring
41. Diaphragm
42. Lower "O" Ring
43. Upper "O" Ring
44. Gasket
45. Fuel Injector

90H15724

Courtesy of General Motors Corp.

Fig. 3: Exploded View of Throttle Body Assemblies

1991 ENGINE PERFORMANCE
Removal, Overhaul & Installation (Cont.)

2) Place fuel meter assembly on throttle body. Install fuel meter-to-throttle body retaining screws and washers (screws should be coated with locking compound). Tighten screws to specification. See TORQUE SPECIFICATIONS at end of article.
3) Install new "O" rings on fuel lines. Using a back-up wrench on fuel fittings, tighten fuel line nuts to 20 ft. lbs. (27 N.m). To complete reassembly, reverse disassembly procedure.
Installation – To install, reverse removal procedure. Ensure throttle body and intake manifold sealing surfaces are clean. Always use new throttle body gasket and fuel line "O" rings. Check fuel system for leaks by turning ignition on, but DO NOT start engine.

THROTTLE BODY INJECTOR

Removal (Model 220) – **1)** Relieve fuel pressure. See FUEL PRESSURE RELIEF under FUEL SYSTEM (TBI). Remove throttle body cover, leaving cover gasket in place. Using screwdriver and fulcrum, carefully pry injector out. *See Fig. 4*. Remove small "O" ring from nozzle end of injector.
2) Carefully rotate injector fuel filter back and forth to remove fuel filter from base of injector. Remove and discard throttle body cover gasket. Remove large "O" ring and steel back-up washer from top counterbore of throttle body injector cavity.
Installation – **1)** Install fuel filter on nozzle end of fuel injector. Ensure large end of filter faces injector so filter covers raised rib at base of injector. Lubricate small "O" ring with Automatic Transmission Fluid (ATF), and push "O" ring on nozzle end of injector until it presses against injector filter.
2) Install steel back-up washer in top counterbore of throttle body injector cavity. Lubricate large "O" ring with ATF, and install "O" ring directly over back-up washer. Ensure "O" ring is seated properly in cavity, and is flush with top of throttle body casting.

CAUTION: Install back-up washer and large "O" ring before installing injector. Improper seating of "O" ring will cause fuel leak.

3) Install "O" ring on injector. Install injector into cavity by aligning raised lug on injector base with cast-in notch of throttle body cavity. Push down on injector until fully seated. Electrical terminals of injector will be approximately parallel with throttle shaft. Install throttle body cover.
Removal (Model 700) – Relieve fuel pressure. See FUEL PRESSURE RELIEF under FUEL SYSTEM (TBI). Remove fuel injector retainer screw and retainer. Using screwdriver and fulcrum on side of injector opposite connector terminals, carefully pry injector out. *See Fig. 4*. Remove upper and lower "O" rings and discard.

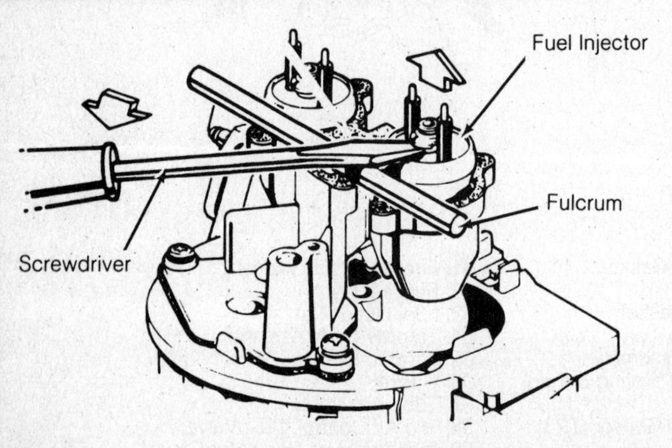
Fuel Injector
Fulcrum
Screwdriver

90I15725 Courtesy of General Motors Corp.

Fig. 4: Removing Throttle Body Injector

Installation – **1)** Lubricate new upper and lower "O" rings with engine oil and place them on injector. Ensure upper ring is in groove and lower ring is flush against filter.
2) Position injector in fuel meter assembly with electrical connector facing cutout for wire grommet.
3) Push injector down to seat in cavity. Install injector retainer. Coat injector retainer screw with thread locking compound and install. Tighten screw to 27 INCH lbs. (3.0 N.m).

IDLE AIR CONTROL (IAC) VALVE

Removal – Remove air cleaner and related ducting. Remove Idle Air Control (IAC) electrical connector. On model 220, unscrew IAC valve. On model 700, remove IAC retaining screws and remove IAC valve. Replace if necessary.
Installation – **1)** Inspect gasket or "O" ring for damage. Replace if necessary. Measure distance from IAC contact flange to tip of pintle. Distance should not exceed 1 1/8" (28 mm). If valve is extended too far, damage to valve will result during installation.
2) To set IAC pintle length on a new IAC, use finger pressure to slowly retract pintle. Lubricate new "O" ring with ATF and install new gasket. Install IAC valve on throttle body. Tighten IAC valve to specification. See TORQUE SPECIFICATIONS at end of article.

CAUTION: DO NOT extend or retract pintle if IAC valve has been in service, or damage to worm gear will result.

3) Connect electrical lead to IAC valve and install air cleaner. Start engine and allow it to reach normal operating temperature. Drive vehicle at 43 MPH minimum to allow ECM to reset idle speed. It may be necessary to cycle ignition off and restart vehicle before proper idle will be initialized.

FUEL PUMP

Removal & Installation – **1)** Relieve fuel system pressure. See FUEL SYSTEM PRESSURE RELIEF under FUEL SYSTEM (TBI). Disconnect negative battery terminal. Raise vehicle and remove fuel tank. Remove sender unit and pump by turning cam lock counterclockwise using Tool (J-36608 or J-24187).
2) Remove fuel pump from sending unit by pulling pump up into attaching hose while pulling outward from the bottom support. DO NOT damage rubber insulator or strainer. To install, reverse removal procedure.

NOTE: When installing sending unit, DO NOT fold or twist strainer. This will restrict fuel flow.

FUEL SYSTEM (DIESEL)

FUEL INJECTION LINES

Removal – **1)** Disconnect negative battery terminal. On "G" Series, remove engine cover. On all models, disconnect air cleaner at valve cover. Remove crankcase vent bracket.
2) Loosen vacuum pump hold-down clamp. Rotate pump to access intake manifold bolts. Remove injection line clips and intake manifold. Install Protective Covers (J-29664-1) in intake ports.
3) Remove injection line clips. On "G" Series, raise vehicle (for left bank). On all models, disconnect and cap injection lines at injector nozzles. Remove lines at pump. Tag lines for reassembly reference. Cap all openings.
Installation – Remove caps and install injection lines. Ensure lines are properly positioned. *See Fig. 5*. Reverse removal procedure to complete installation. Start engine and check for leaks.

FUEL FILTER

Removal – **1)** On "R" and "V" Series, fuel conditioner filter is located on engine side of cowl. On "C", "K", "G" and "P" Series, filter is mounted on rear of intake manifold, under air cleaner. Filter is accessible by removing engine cover.
2) Remove fuel tank cap to release pressure or vacuum in tank. Place drain pan under drain hose to collect fuel. Drain fuel from filter by opening both air bleed and water drain valves. Using a screwdriver, release fuel conditioner bail wires. Remove filter. *See Fig. 6*.

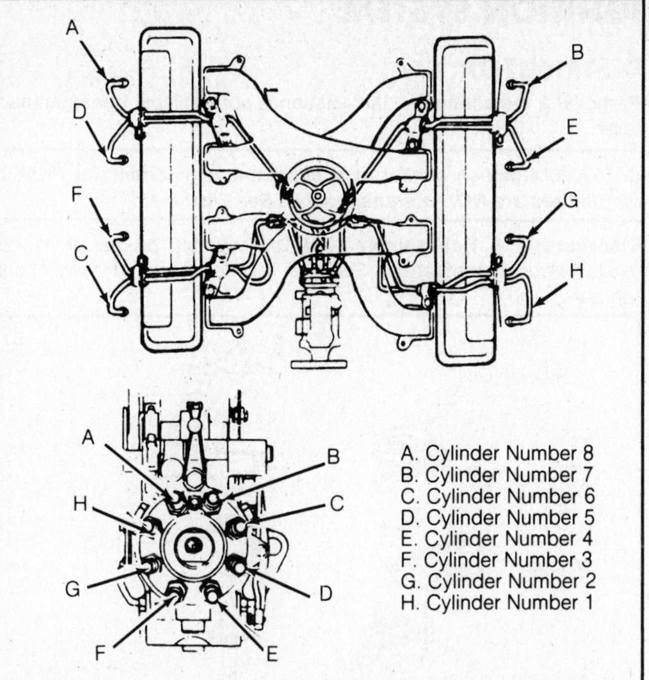
A
B
D
E
F
G
C
H
A
B
H
C
G
D
F
E
A. Cylinder Number 8
B. Cylinder Number 7
C. Cylinder Number 6
D. Cylinder Number 5
E. Cylinder Number 4
F. Cylinder Number 3
G. Cylinder Number 2
H. Cylinder Number 1

90J15726 Courtesy of General Motors Corp.

Fig. 5: Routing Diesel Fuel Injection Line

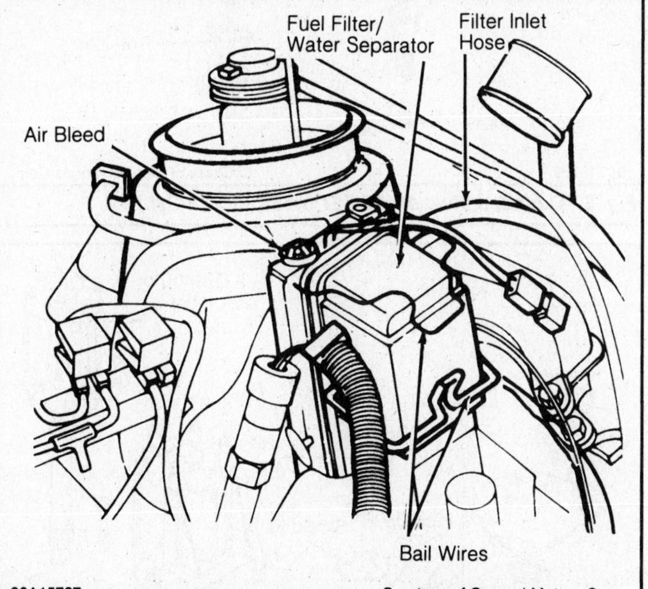
Fuel Filter/
Water Separator
Filter Inlet
Hose
Air Bleed
Bail Wires

90A15727 Courtesy of General Motors Corp.

Fig. 6: Locating Diesel Fuel Filter Assembly Components

Installation - 1) Clean filter mount pad. Install new filter element and snap on bail wires. Close water drain valve. Attach a 1/8" I.D. hose to air bleed, and place other end in drain pan.
2) Disconnect fuel injection pump shutoff solenoid wire. Crank engine for 10-15 seconds. Allow starter to cool for one minute. Repeat procedure until clear fuel comes out of air bleed hose.
3) Close air bleed. Connect injection pump shutoff solenoid wire, and install fuel tank cap. Start engine and allow to idle for 5 minutes. Check fuel conditioner filter for leaks.

FUEL PUMP

Removal & Installation - 1) Disconnect negative battery terminal. Disconnect electrical wiring from fuel pump and fuel pump support bracket.
2) Disconnect fuel lines from fuel pump. Remove support bracket screws and remove support bracket from fuel lines. Remove fuel pump and bracket from frame rail.
3) To install, reverse removal procedure. Check for fuel leak at fuel line fittings.

INJECTION PUMP

Removal ("C", "K", "P", "R" & "V" Series) - 1) Disconnect negative battery terminal. Remove intake manifold. Install Protective Covers (J-29664-1) in intake ports. Remove fuel injection lines. Disconnect throttle cable and detent cable (if equipped). Disconnect wiring, fuel return line, fuel supply line, and fuel injection lines at pump. Cap all openings.
2) Remove A/C hose retainer bracket (if equipped). Remove oil filler tube and vent hose assembly. Remove grommet. Scribe or paint alignment mark on front cover and injection pump flange.
3) Rotate engine to remove injection pump-to-drive gear retaining bolts accessible through oil filler neck hole. Remove injection pump mount nuts. Remove injection pump and gasket. *See Fig. 7.*
Installation - 1) Install new injection pump gasket. Align locating pin on injection pump hub with slot in injection pump driven gear. At the same time, align injection pump timing marks. Cylinder No. 1 must be set at TDC.
2) Attach injection pump to front cover. Alignment marks made during removal must be aligned. Tighten nuts. Attach pump to drive gear and

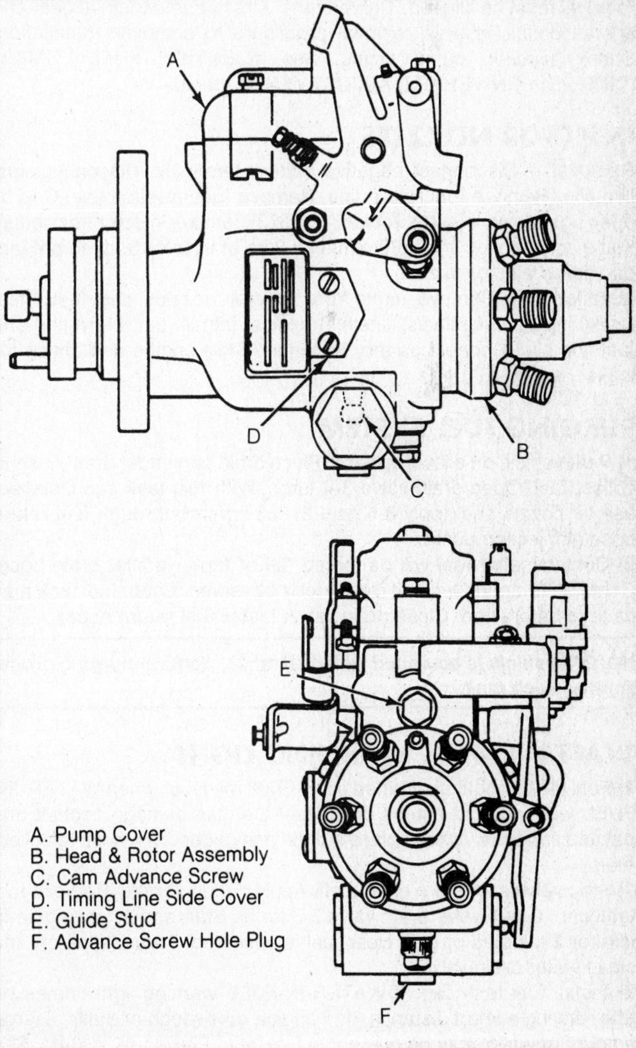
A
D
C
B
E
F
A. Pump Cover
B. Head & Rotor Assembly
C. Cam Advance Screw
D. Timing Line Side Cover
E. Guide Stud
F. Advance Screw Hole Plug

90B15728 Courtesy of General Motors Corp.

Fig. 7: Identifying Diesel Injection Pump Components

1991 ENGINE PERFORMANCE
Removal, Overhaul & Installation (Cont.)

tighten bolts. Reverse removal procedure to complete installation. Check injection pump timing. See INJECTION PUMP TIMING (DIESEL) in ON-VEHICLE ADJUSTMENTS article.

Removal ("G" Series) - 1) Disconnect negative battery terminals. Remove engine cover and intake manifold. Rotate snorkel up, and remove air cleaner inlet hose. Remove hood latch. Disconnect cable and move aside.

2) Remove windshield washer bottle, fan shroud bolts, and upper fan shroud. Disconnect rubber hose from oil fill tube. Disconnect oil fill tube attaching nuts, and remove oil fill tube. Remove oil fill tube grommet.

3) Rotate engine as necessary and remove pump drive gear bolts. Remove fuel filter and bracket, including line to injection pump. Disconnect wire looms from injection lines, and injection lines at brackets.

4) Disconnect oil pan dipstick tube from left cylinder head. Disconnect electrical connections at injection pump. Disconnect detent cable (if equipped). Disconnect accelerator cable.

5) Remove injection lines. Tag lines for reassembly reference. Cap all openings. Disconnect fuel return line. Scribe or paint mark on front cover and pump flange. Remove injection pump mount nuts. Remove injection pump. *See Fig. 7*. Cap all openings.

Installation - 1) Install new injection pump gasket. Align locating pin on injection pump hub with slot in injection pump driven gear while aligning injection pump timing marks.

2) Attach injection pump to front cover. Alignment marks made during removal must be aligned. Tighten nuts. Attach pump to drive gear and tighten bolts. Reverse removal procedure to complete installation. Check injection pump timing. See INJECTION PUMP TIMING (DIESEL) in ON-VEHICLE ADJUSTMENTS article.

INJECTOR NOZZLES

Removal - Disconnect negative battery terminals. Disconnect fuel line clip. Remove fuel return line. Remove fuel injection line. Cap all openings. Using Injector Socket (J-29873), remove injector nozzles(s). Place socket on 1 3/16" (30 mm) hex flats of injector body to prevent damaging injector nozzle.

Installation - Remove caps from injector nozzles and fuel lines. Install injector nozzles(s). Install fuel line. Install fuel return line and fuel line clip. Connect battery terminals. Start engine and check for leaks.

PURGING FUEL SYSTEM

1) Park vehicle on a level surface. Place drain pan under drain hose to collect fuel. Open drain valve 3-4 turns. With fuel tank cap installed, use air nozzle and apply 3-5 psi (.21-.35 kg/cm²) through fuel return hose at injection pump.

2) Contaminated fuel will be forced out of tank via filter drain hose. Continue to drain fuel until clear fuel is observed. Entire fuel tank may have to be drained. Close drain valve. Install fuel return hose.

NOTE: If vehicle is equipped with dual tanks, perform purging procedure on each tank.

WATER-IN-FUEL WARNING LIGHT

1) Fuel filter should be drained every 5000 miles, or when WATER-IN-FUEL warning light comes on. Diesel fuel can damage asphalt and painted surfaces. Always place a drain pan under drain hose to collect fuel.

2) Stop vehicle and turn engine off. Apply parking brake. Remove fuel tank cap. Open water drain valve 2-3 turns. Start and allow engine to idle for 2 minutes or until clear fuel is observed. Turn engine off and close water drain valve.

3) Install fuel tank cap. If WATER-IN-FUEL warning light comes on after driving a short distance, or if engine runs rough or stalls, a large amount of water may be present in fuel tank. Purge fuel system. See PURGING FUEL SYSTEM under FUEL SYSTEM (DIESEL).

IGNITION SYSTEM

DISTRIBUTOR

Removal & Installation - Information is not available from manufacturer.

CAUTION: Although similar in appearance, components of HEI/EST distributors are NOT interchangeable. See Figs. 8-10.

Disassembly & Reassembly - 1) Disassembly procedure is not available from manufacturer. *See Figs. 8-10* for exploded views of distributors.

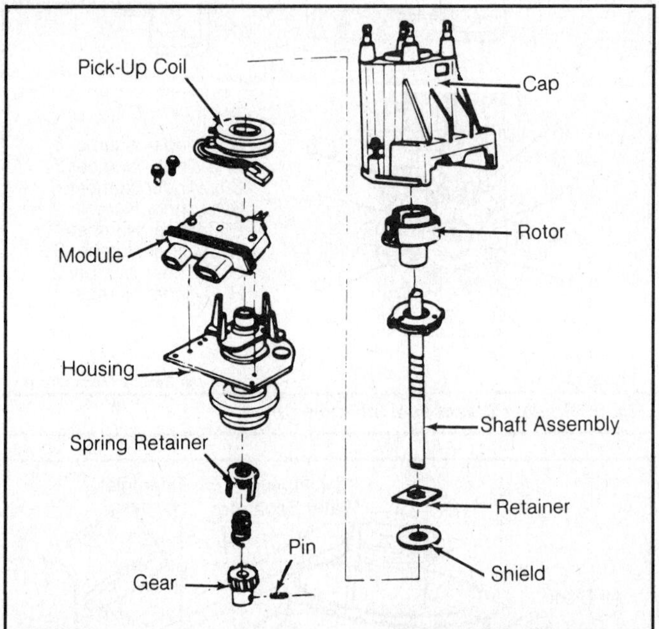
Pick-Up Coil
Cap
Module
Rotor
Housing
Shaft Assembly
Spring Retainer
Retainer
Pin
Gear
Shield
90C15729
Courtesy of General Motors Corp.

Fig. 8: Exploded View of HEI-EST Distributor (4-Cyl.)

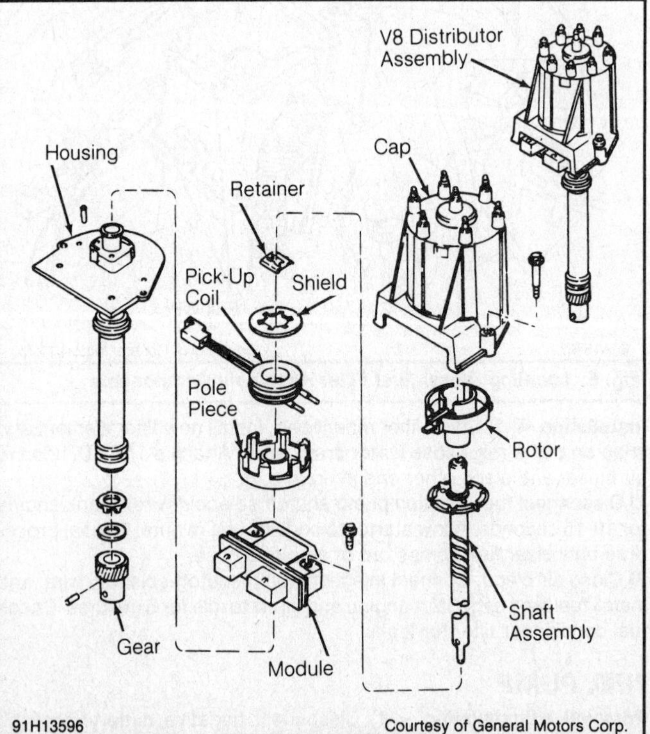
V8 Distributor
Assembly
Housing
Cap
Retainer
Pick-Up
Coil
Shield
Pole
Piece
Rotor
Shaft
Assembly
Gear
Module
91H13596
Courtesy of General Motors Corp.

Fig. 9: Exploded View of HEI-EST Distributor (V6 & V8)

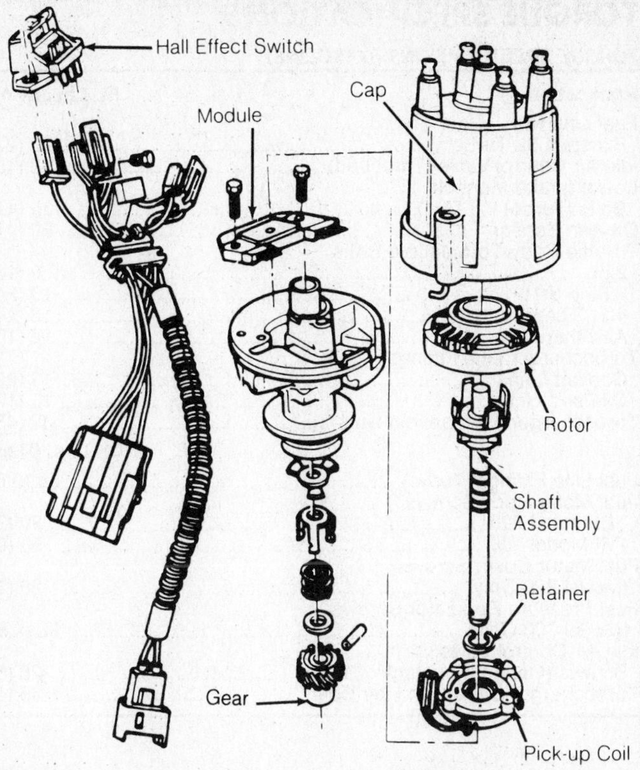
Hall Effect Switch
Cap
Module
Rotor
Shaft
Assembly
Retainer
Gear
Pick-up Coil

90G15731 Courtesy of General Motors Corp.

Fig. 10: Exploded View of HEI/EST Distributor with Hall Effect

2) When reassembling, ensure pick-up assembly arm is correctly installed on pin. If not, arm can float and cause ignition timing to vary. To prevent corrosion, lubricate terminals with petroleum jelly before installation.

3) To prevent heat damage, coat bottom of module and module rest pad in housing with silicone grease. Before installing roll pin in driven gear, ensure timing mark on roll pin and rotor tip align. *See Figs. 8-10.*

THROTTLE POSITION SENSOR (TPS)

GASOLINE

Removal & Installation – 1) Remove air cleaner assembly. Disconnect electrical lead from TPS. Remove attaching screws, lock washers, retainers, and TPS.

2) To install, reverse removal procedure. Adjust TPS to specification. See ON-VEHICLE ADJUSTMENTS article. When replacing a TPS, ensure correct part number is used. Use Loctite on TPS attaching screws.

DIESEL

Removal & Installation – 1) Remove air cleaner assembly and related hoses. Disconnect TPS connector. Remove 2 screws and throttle position sensor from injection pump. *See Fig. 11*.

2) To install, reverse removal procedure. Lightly tighten screws and adjust TPS. See ON-VEHICLE ADJUSTMENTS article.

OXYGEN (O_2) SENSOR

CAUTION: O_2 sensor is equipped with a permanent pigtail, which must be protected to prevent damage when removing sensor.

Removal – 1) O_2 sensor is mounted in the exhaust pipe, below exhaust manifold. Ensure sensor is free of contaminants. DO NOT use cleaning solvents of any type. Sensor may be difficult to remove when engine temperature is less than 120°F (48°C). Excessive removal force may damage threads in exhaust manifold or pipe.

2) Disconnect negative battery terminal. Disconnect electrical connector from O_2 sensor. Carefully remove O_2 sensor from exhaust pipe.

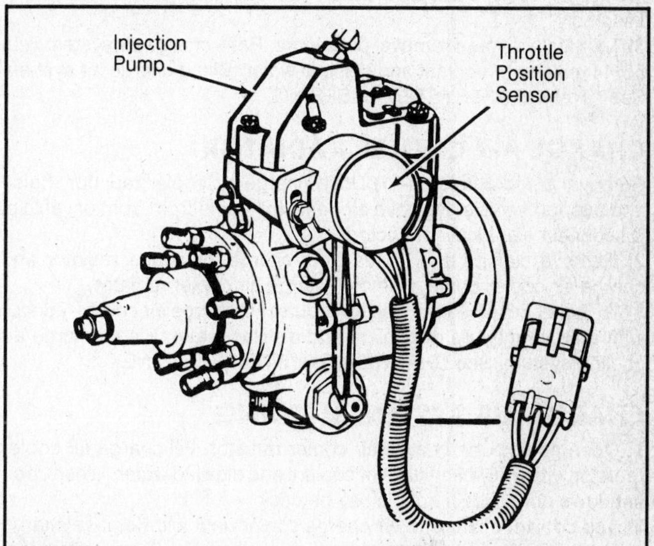
Injection
Pump
Throttle
Position
Sensor

90H15732 Courtesy of General Motors Corp.

Fig. 11: Locating Diesel Throttle Position Sensor (TPS)

CAUTION: Correct torque of O_2 sensor is critical to prevent crushing glass beads in graphite anti-seize compound. Crushing glass beads will cause sensor to seize in exhaust manifold. This may require replacement of exhaust manifold upon next removal.

Installation – 1) Whenever O_2 sensor is removed, coat threads with anti-seize compound before reinstalling. New O_2 sensors already have this compound applied to threads.

2) Install O_2 sensor in exhaust pipe and tighten sensor to 30 ft. lbs. (41 N.m). Reconnect electrical connector to O_2 sensor. Reconnect negative battery terminal.

TURBOCHARGER

4.3L PFI TURBO

Removal & Installation – 1) Drain coolant from radiator. Remove intake air duct and turbocharger air intake duct. Remove battery, battery tray, and vacuum reservoir tank.

2) Disconnect turbocharger oil feed line and electrical connector at solenoid. Remove turbocharger coolant return line assembly.

3) Raise and support vehicle. Remove wheel assembly. Remove right-hand wheelhouse panel. Remove turbocharger outlet pipe. Remove turbocharger oil return pipe, mounting nuts and coolant feed line assembly. Remove turbocharger assembly.

4) To install, reverse removal procedure. Ensure bolts and nuts are installed in same location from which they were removed. Tighten to specification. See appropriate TORQUE SPECIFICATIONS table at end of article.

CHARGE AIR COOLER

Removal & Installation – 1) Drain charge air cooler radiator. Remove hoses from charge air cooler. Remove charge air cooler assembly.

2) To install, reverse removal procedure. Fill charge air cooler radiator through the charge air cooler with a 56/44 mixture of coolant and distilled water. Bleed charge air cooling system. See CHARGE AIR SYSTEM BLEEDING.

1991 ENGINE PERFORMANCE
Removal, Overhaul & Installation (Cont.)

CHARGE AIR COOLER PUMP

Removal & Installation – 1) Drain charge air cooler radiator. Remove charge air cooler radiator. See CHARGE AIR COOLER RADIATOR.

2) Remove charge air cooler pump mounting bolts, coolant hoses, and charge air cooler radiator bracket. Remove charge air cooler pump assembly.

3) To install, reverse removal procedure. Refill charge air system with 56/44 mixture of coolant and distilled water. Bleed charge air system. See CHARGE AIR SYSTEM BLEEDING.

CHARGE AIR COOLER RADIATOR

Removal & Installation – 1) Drain charge air cooler radiator. Raise and support vehicle. Remove air deflector shield from front of vehicle. Disconnect electrical connectors.

2) Remove clamps and hoses from charge air cooler radiator and charge air cooler pump. Remove charge air cooler radiator.

3) To install, reverse removal procedure. Fill charge air cooler radiator with a 56/44 mixture of coolant and distilled water. Bleed charge air cooling system. See CHARGE AIR SYSTEM BLEEDING.

CHARGE AIR SYSTEM BLEEDING

1) Open petcock on charge air cooler radiator. Fill charge air cooler radiator with a 56/44 mixture of coolant and distilled water. When coolant flows out of drain hole, close petcock.

2) Add coolant mixture to air charge cooler until full. Remove charge air cooler pump relay located near coil assembly. Turn ignition on. Install jumper wire between charge air cooler relay terminals "A" and "B" to operate charge air cooler pump.

3) While pump is operating, add coolant mixture to system until system is full. Install charge air cooler pressure cap.

WASTEGATE ACTUATOR REPLACEMENT

Removal & Installation – 1) Remove passenger-side wheelhouse panel. Remove retaining pin to wastegate actuator rod. Remove vacuum hose to actuator, and remove bolts securing actuator to turbocharger unit.

2) Remove wastegate actuator from turbocharger unit. To install, reverse removal procedure.

TORQUE SPECIFICATIONS

TORQUE SPECIFICATIONS (GASOLINE)

Application	Ft. Lbs. (N.m)
Fuel Line Nut	
Except 4.3L Turbo	20 (27)
Idle Air Control Valve (Threaded)	13 (18)
Lower Intake Manifold	
Bolts (Turbo)	35 (47)
Oxygen Sensor	30 (41)
Throttle Body-To-Manifold Bolts	
2.5L	12.5 (17)
2.8L & 3.1L	18 (24)
4.3L Turbo	18 (24)
All Others	12 (16)
Turbocharger Line Fittings	
Coolant Lines	16 (22)
Oil Feed Line	13 (17)
Turbocharger-To-Manifold Nuts	33 (45)
	INCH Lbs. (N.m)
Fuel Line Fittings (Turbo)	58 (6.5)
Fuel Meter Body Screws	
TBI Model 220	30 (3)
TBI Model 700	53 (6)
Fuel Meter Cover Screws	
(Model 220 Only)	28 (3)
Fuel Pressure Regulator Screws	
(Model 700 Only)	22 (2.5)
Idle Air Control Valve	
Screws (Flange Mounted)	28 (3)
Turbocharger Oil Return Line Bolt	35 (4)

TORQUE SPECIFICATIONS (DIESEL)

Application	Ft. Lbs. (N.m)
Glow Plugs	13 (18)
Injection Line Fittings	20 (27)
Injection Nozzles	50 (68)
Injection Pump Gear Attaching Bolts	20 (27)
Injection Pump Mounting Nuts	30 (41)
Intake Manifold Bolts	30 (41)
	INCH Lbs. (N.m)
Advance Pin Hole Plug	90 (10)
Head Locating Screw	17 (23)
Injection Pump Cover Screws	33 (3.7)
Injection Pump Guide Stud	85 (9.5)
Side Cover Screws	18 (2)
Solenoid Terminal Nuts	12 (1.2)

1991 ELECTRICAL
Alternators & Regulators – Delco-Remy

Astro, Blazer, Bravada, Jimmy, Lumina APV, Safari, Sierra, Silhouette, Sonoma, Trans Sport, "C" & "K" Series, "G" Series, "P" Series, "R" & "V" Series, "S" & "T" Series

DESCRIPTION

Two types of alternators are used: 12SI series and CS130/144 series. The first series is designated SI (Systems Integral) because of the built-in regulator. The solid state regulator is enclosed in a solid mold. This unit, along with brush holder assembly, is attached to the slip ring end frame. Regulator voltage setting cannot be adjusted. All 12SI alternators have "Y" type stator windings. A condenser, mounted in the end frame, protects the rectifier bridge and diode trio from high voltages and suppresses radio noise.

The CS130/144 (Charging System) alternators have a high amperage output. The 130 or 144 designation is the outside diameter of the stator laminations, measured in millimeters. This alternator series also has an integral regulator but does not have a diode trio. The delta wound stator, rectifier bridge, rotor with slip rings, and brushes are similar to other alternators.

The CS130 alternator should not be disassembled for any reason. The alternator requires no periodic maintenance or adjustment and is serviceable only by complete replacement. The CS144, however, is serviceable.

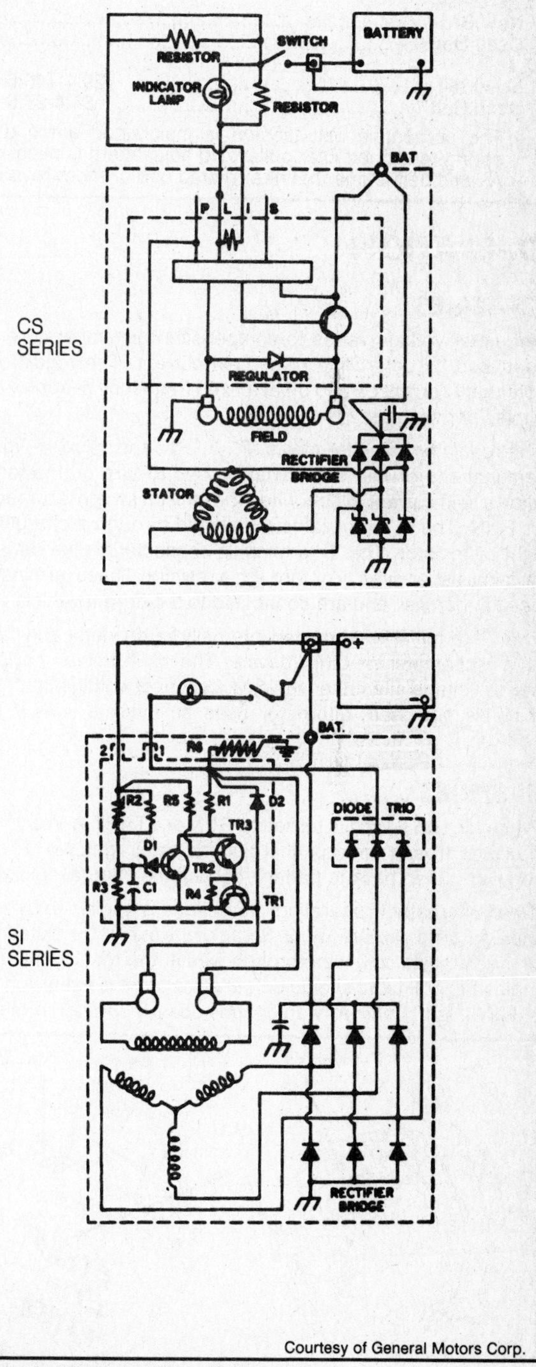
RESISTOR
SWITCH
BATTERY
INDICATOR LAMP
RESISTOR
BAT
P L I S
REGULATOR
FIELD
RECTIFIER BRIDGE
STATOR
CS SERIES
BAT.
R6
R2
R5
R1
D2
TR3
D1
TR2
R3
C1
R4
TR1
DIODE TRIO
SI SERIES
RECTIFIER BRIDGE
91G13520
Courtesy of General Motors Corp.

Fig. 1: Charging System Wiring Schematic

ALTERNATOR IDENTIFICATION & OUTPUT

ALTERNATOR IDENTIFICATION & OUTPUT

Application	Alternator Part No.	Rated Output Amps
Astro & Safari		
CS130	1101500	100
CS130	1101521	85
"C" & "K" Series		
CS130	1101110	85
CS130	1101111	100
CS130	1101293	100
CS130	1101317	85
CS130	1101318	105
CS130	1105688	100
CS130	1105712	85
CS130	1105716	105
"G", "P", "R" & "V" Series		
CS130	1101293	100
CS130	1101317	85
CS130	1101318	105
CS144	1101493	120
CS130	1101571	105
CS130	1101623	124
CS130	1101634	85
CS130	1101635	100
CS130	1101636	105
CS130	1101806	105
CS130	1101812	100
CS130	1101814	100
CS144	1102635	124
12SI	1105632	70
CS130	1105688	100
CS130	1105710	85
CS130	1105711	100
CS130	1105712	85
CS130	1105715	105
CS130	1105716	105
CS130	1105718	105
CS130	1105720	105
CS144	10479809	124
CS144	10479812	124
Lumina APV, Silhouette & Trans Sport		
CS130	1105694	100
Bravada, "S" & "T" Series		
CS130	1101259	85
CS130	1101293	100
CS130	1101317	85
CS130	1101346	96
CS130	110479808	85

1991 ELECTRICAL
Alternators & Regulators – Delco-Remy (Cont.)

ADJUSTMENTS

BELT TENSION

BELT ADJUSTMENT

Application	[1] Tension Lbs. (kg)
2.5L, 2.8L & 3.1L	[1]
4.3L, 5.0L & 5.7L	
New Belt	135 (61.2)
Used Belt [2]	90 (40.8)
6.2L Diesel	
New Belt	146 (66.2)
Used Belt [2]	67 (30.4)
7.4L	
New Belt	129.4-140.6 (58.7-63.8)
Used Belt [2]	84.4-95.6 (38.3-43.4)

[1] – The serpentine belt tension is maintained automatically by a spring-tensioned idler pulley. No adjustment is necessary.
[2] – A used belt is one that has rotated one or more revolutions.

OPERATION

CS SERIES

Regulator voltage varies to compensate for temperature. Voltage is regulated by controlling rotor field current. The regulator switches rotor field current on and off at a fixed frequency of approximately 400 cycles per second.

The regulator has 4 terminals "P", "L", "I", and "S". *See Fig. 2.* The "L" terminal and/or the "I" terminal is used to turn on the regulator and allows field current to flow when the ignition switch is turned to START or RUN. The "L" terminal is connected through a charging indicator light or resistor. The "I" terminal is connected to the battery positive terminal either directly or through a resistor. These terminals are often used in parallel, and are connected to 2 different vehicle circuits.

The "P" terminal is connected internally to the stator and may be wired to a tachometer or other device. The "S" terminal may be used to sense voltage at another vehicle location for voltage control. If "S" terminal is not used, alternator uses an internal sensor for voltage control.

SI SERIES

When ignition switch is turned to RUN or START, current from battery flows to ground through charging indicator light, No. 1 terminal and regulator, then back to battery, lighting the charge indicator light.

When alternator is operating, DC voltage is applied to battery through the BAT terminal. *See Fig. 2.* Some of the current is routed through the diode into field coil, then through wire at the No. 1 terminal to charge indicator light. Light should go out since there is equal voltage on both sides of light. Vehicles with gauges use a voltmeter in this circuit.

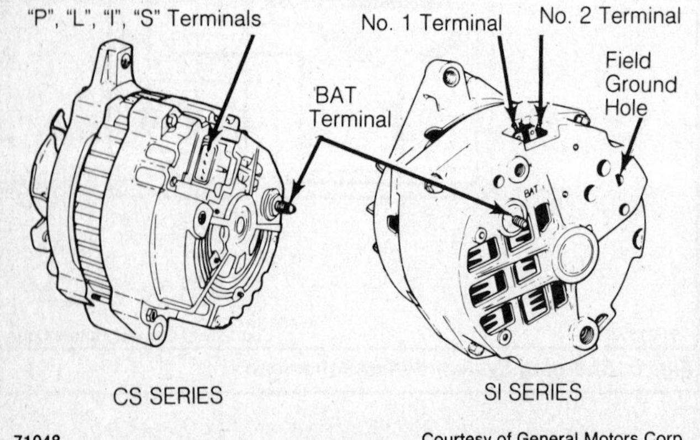
"P", "L", "I", "S" Terminals
No. 1 Terminal
No. 2 Terminal
Field Ground Hole
BAT Terminal
CS SERIES
SI SERIES
71048
Courtesy of General Motors Corp.

Fig. 2: Identifying Alternator Terminals & Locations

ON-VEHICLE TESTING

NOTE: Before making electrical checks, visually inspect all terminals for clean, tight connections. Check alternator mounting bolts and drive belt tension. Battery must be in good condition to test charging system.

CS SERIES

Overcharged Or Undercharged Battery – 1) If an overcharging condition is suspected, run engine at moderate speed. Connect voltmeter across battery terminals. If voltmeter indicates more than 16 volts, replace alternator.

2) If an undercharging condition is suspected, disconnect 4-wire connector from alternator. Turn ignition on with engine off. Connect a voltmeter between terminal "L" in wiring harness and ground. *See Fig. 2.* Record reading.

3) If terminal "I" is used, connect voltmeter between terminal "I" and ground. Record reading. If voltmeter reads battery voltage, circuits are okay. If voltmeter reads zero, this indicates an open circuit between terminal checked and battery. Repair as necessary.

Alternator Output Test – 1) Connect an ammeter in series circuit at BAT terminal of alternator. *See Fig. 2.* Turn on all available accessories. Connect a carbon pile across battery. Operate engine at 2000 RPM, and adjust carbon pile (as required) to obtain maximum current output while maintaining 13 volts or more.

2) Ampere output must be within 15 amps of rated output. If output is not within 15 amps of rated output, replace alternator. See ALTERNATOR IDENTIFICATION & OUTPUT table at beginning of article.

SI SERIES

Overcharged Or Undercharged Battery – 1) If an overcharging condition is suspected, attach a voltmeter across battery terminals. Run engine at a moderate speed with all accessories off. If voltmeter reads 15.5 volts or more, remove alternator for repair.

2) If an undercharging condition is suspected, turn ignition on. Connect a voltmeter from alternator BAT terminal to ground. *See Fig. 2.* Voltmeter should read 12 volts. Connect voltmeter between No. 1 terminal and ground. Voltmeter should read 12 volts.

3) Connect voltmeter between No. 2 terminal and ground. Voltmeter should read 12 volts. A zero reading on any connection indicates an open between connection and battery. Proceed to Alternator Output Test if checks are normal.

Alternator Output Test – 1) Connect an ammeter in series circuit at BAT terminal of alternator. *See Fig. 2.* Turn on all available accessories. Connect a carbon pile across battery. Operate engine at 2000 RPM and adjust carbon pile as required to obtain maximum current output.

2) Ampere output must be within 10 amps of rated output. See ALTERNATOR IDENTIFICATION & OUTPUT table at beginning of this article. If output is not within 10 amps of rated output, ground field winding by inserting a screwdriver into test hole. Repeat step **1)**.

NOTE: Tab is within 3/4" of casting surface. DO NOT force tool into end frame beyond 1". If test hole is not accessible, proceed to BENCH TESTING.

3) If output increases to within 10 amps of rated output with field grounded, regulator is defective. If output remains more than 10 amps below rated output, check field winding, diode trio, rectifier bridge, and stator. See BENCH TESTING in this article.

BENCH TESTING

NOTE: The CS130 is not serviceable. Altnernator replacement is required.

CS144 SERIES

Rotor Field Winding Test – 1) To check for grounds, attach one ohmmeter lead to shaft and remaining ohmmeter lead to either slip ring. *See Fig. 3*. If reading is low (not infinity), replace rotor.
2) To test for open field, attach ohmmeter leads to each slip ring. *See Fig. 3*. Resistance should be low (not infinity). If reading is high (infinity), replace rotor.
Stator Inspection – 1) To check for ground, connect one ohmmeter lead to any stator lead. Connect remaining ohmmeter lead to stator frame. Ohmmeter reading should be infinity. *See Fig. 4*.
2) Delco CS series alternators have delta stator windings and cannot be tested for short or open circuits with ohmmeter. A noticeable discoloration anywhere on the stator usually indicates stator failure.

NOTE: Some digital ohmmeters cannot be used to check the diodes in the rectifier bridge. Consult ohmmeter manufacturer to determine ohmmeter's capabilities.

Rectifier Bridge Test – 1) Position ohmmeter with one lead touching grounded heat sink and the other lead pressed firmly against flat metal on one of the 3 terminals or threaded studs. Observe reading and reverse test lead connections. *See Fig. 6*.
2) If both readings are the same, replace rectifier bridge. A good bridge will give a high and low reading. Repeat tests for remaining terminals. There should be 6 tests altogether (2 tests at each terminal).
3) Connect test leads to insulated heat sink and one of the 3 terminals. *See Fig. 6*. Observe reading and reverse connections. Repeat tests for remaining terminals. There should be a total of 6 tests (2 at each terminal).
4) Testing is complete when all 12 tests have been made. If any terminals have same readings for both connections (leads reversed), replace rectifier bridge.

SI SERIES

Rotor Field Winding Test – 1) To check for grounds, attach one ohmmeter lead to shaft and remaining lead to either slip ring. *See Fig. 3*. If ohmmeter does not read infinity, replace rotor.

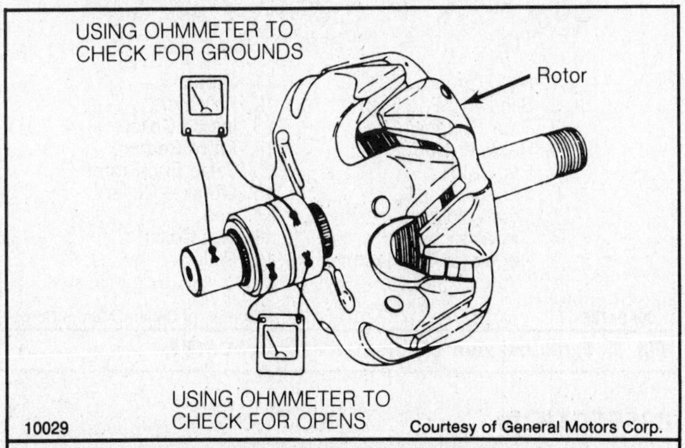
USING OHMMETER TO CHECK FOR GROUNDS
Rotor
USING OHMMETER TO CHECK FOR OPENS
10029
Courtesy of General Motors Corp.

Fig. 3: Bench Testing Rotor for Open or Short Circuit

2) To test for open field, attach ohmmeter leads to each slip ring. *See Fig. 3*. Resistance should measure 2.4-2.8 ohms. If resistance is not as specified, replace rotor.
Stator Test – 1) To test 12SI series alternator for open, measure resistance between the stator leads by connecting ohmmeter leads to stator leads (in pair). *See Fig. 4*. If resistance is infinite, replace stator.
2) To check for ground, connect one ohmmeter lead to any stator lead. Connect remaining lead to stator frame. Ohmmeter reading should be infinity. *See Fig. 4*.

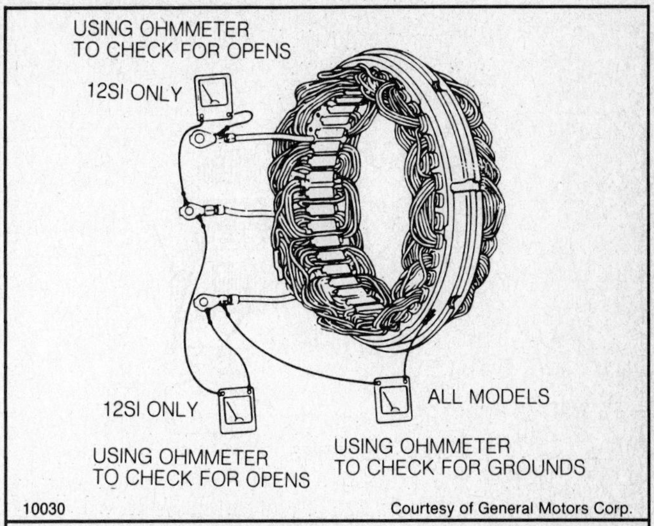
USING OHMMETER TO CHECK FOR OPENS
12SI ONLY
12SI ONLY
ALL MODELS
USING OHMMETER TO CHECK FOR OPENS
USING OHMMETER TO CHECK FOR GROUNDS
10030
Courtesy of General Motors Corp.

Fig. 4: Bench Testing Stator for Open or Grounded Circuits

Diode Trio Test – 1) Remove diode trio from end frame. Connect one ohmmeter lead to the single connector, and connect remaining lead to one of the 3 connectors. *See Fig. 5*. Note reading and reverse leads. If readings are the same, replace diode trio.

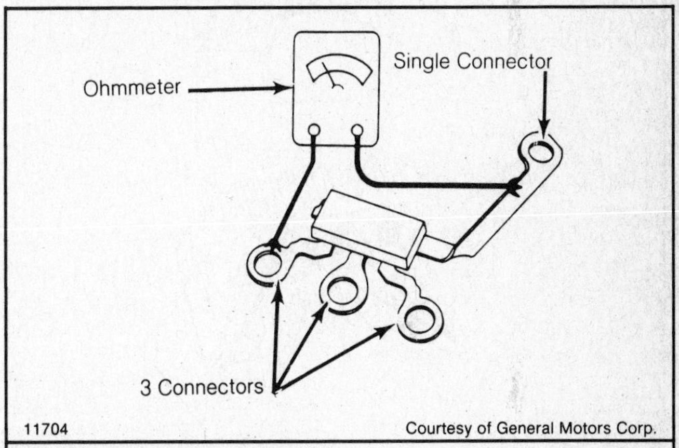
Ohmmeter
Single Connector
3 Connectors
11704
Courtesy of General Motors Corp.

Fig. 5: Bench Testing Diode Trio

2) A good diode trio will give a high and low reading. Repeat tests for remaining connectors. Also, connect ohmmeter leads to the 3 connectors (in pair). If any reading is zero, replace diode trio.
Rectifier Bridge Test – 1) Position ohmmeter with one lead touching grounded heat sink and the other lead pressed firmly against flat metal on one of the 3 terminals or threaded studs. Observe reading and reverse test lead connections. *See Fig. 6*.
2) If both readings are the same, replace rectifier bridge. A good bridge will give a high and low reading. Test all terminals (6 tests).
3) Connect test leads to insulated heat sink and one of the 3 terminals. Observe reading and reverse connections. Repeat tests for remaining terminals. There should be a total of 6 tests (2 at each terminals).
4) Testing is complete when all 12 tests have been made. If readings at any of the terminals are same for both connections (leads reversed), replace the diode trio or rectifier bridge.

1991 ELECTRICAL
Alternators & Regulators – Delco-Remy (Cont.)

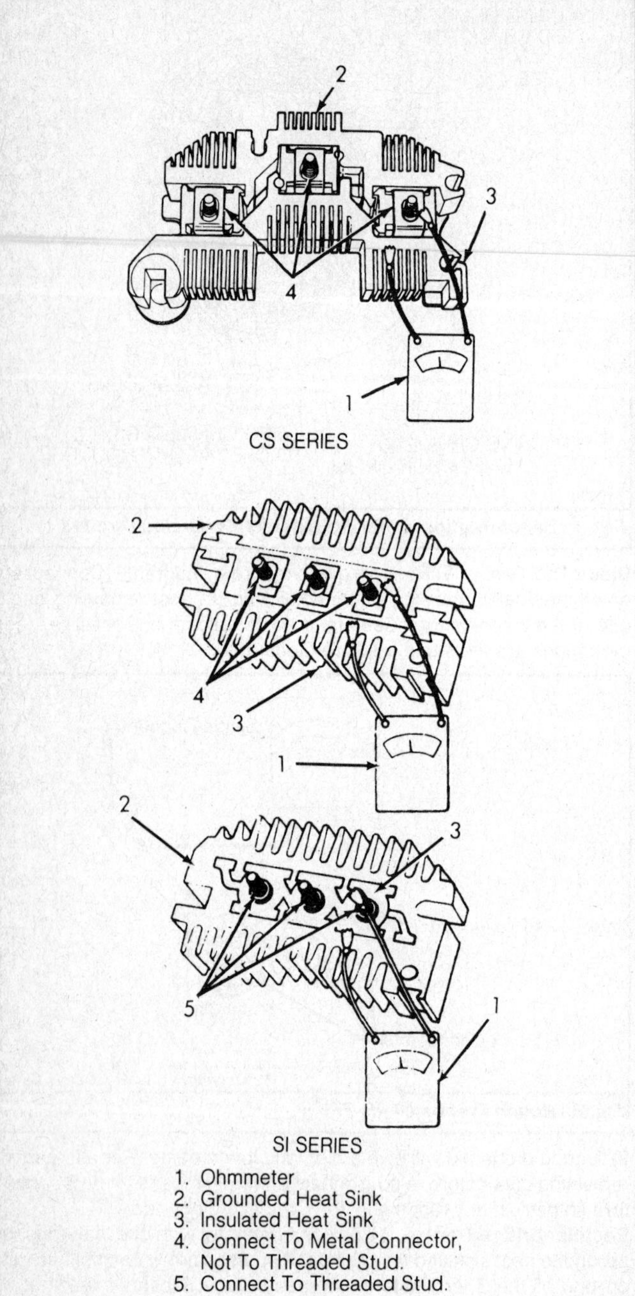
2
3
4
1
CS SERIES
2
4
3
1
2
3
5
1
SI SERIES
1. Ohmmeter
2. Grounded Heat Sink
3. Insulated Heat Sink
4. Connect To Metal Connector, Not To Threaded Stud.
5. Connect To Threaded Stud.

91C13518 Courtesy of General Motors Corp.

Fig. 6: Bench Testing Rectifier Bridge

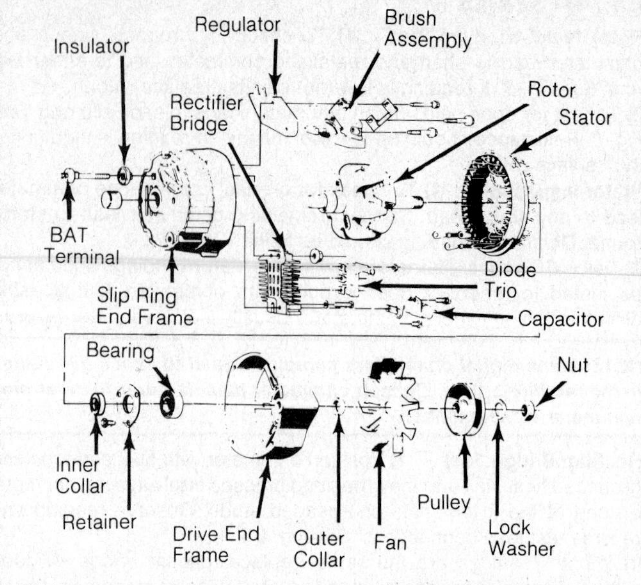
Insulator
Regulator
Brush Assembly
Rectifier Bridge
Rotor
Stator
BAT Terminal
Slip Ring End Frame
Diode Trio
Capacitor
Bearing
Nut
Inner Collar
Retainer
Drive End Frame
Outer Collar
Fan
Pulley
Lock Washer

15357 Courtesy of General Motors Corp.

Fig. 7: Exploded View of Alternator (Model 12SI)

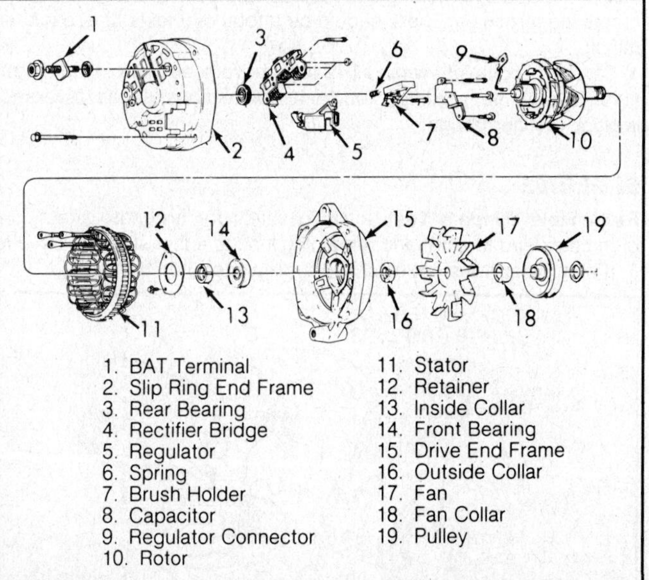
1. BAT Terminal
2. Slip Ring End Frame
3. Rear Bearing
4. Rectifier Bridge
5. Regulator
6. Spring
7. Brush Holder
8. Capacitor
9. Regulator Connector
10. Rotor
11. Stator
12. Retainer
13. Inside Collar
14. Front Bearing
15. Drive End Frame
16. Outside Collar
17. Fan
18. Fan Collar
19. Pulley

90A04786 Courtesy of General Motors Corp.

Fig. 8: Exploded View of Alternator (Model CS144)

OVERHAUL

NOTE: Step by step overhaul procedures are not available from manufacturer. Use Figs. 7 and 8 to assist you with DISASSEMBLY & REASSEMBLY procedures. Since CS130 alternator is not serviceable, no exploded view is provided.

INSPECTION

Using clean solvent, wash all metal parts except voltage regulator, rectifier bridge, bearings, stator and rotor. Inspect rotor slip rings. They may be cleaned with 400 grit or finer polishing cloth while rotor is being rotated. Slip rings may be lathe turned to maximum indicator reading of .002" (.05mm). Slip rings are not replaceable. Replace rotor if slip rings are excessively damaged. Inspect brushes for wear. Replace if they are worn to less than 50 percent of original length.

1991 ELECTRICAL
Starters – Delco-Remy

Astro, Blazer, Bravada, Jimmy, Lumina APV, Safari, Sierra, Silhouette, Sonoma, Trans Sport, "C" & "K" Series, "G" Series, "P" Series, "R" & "V" Series, "S" & "T" Series

DESCRIPTION

For identification, starter part numbers are stamped on the outside of the frame or on an identification label attached to the frame.

Five types of starters are used: SD-200/210/260/300 and 28MT series. The first series is designated SD (Straight Drive) because the pinion is driven directly by the armature shaft. Wound field coils energize pole pieces that are arranged around the armature. These are used on gasoline engines.

The 28MT starter has a pinion that is driven by a gear reduction system. This starter is used on the 6.2L diesel engine. The 28MT starter should not be dissembled for any reason and is serviceable only by complete replacement.

ON-VEHICLE TESTING

SOLENOID WINDING TESTS

NOTE: Tests are performed with all leads disconnected from solenoid. Complete tests in minimum amount of time to prevent solenoid from overheating.

Hold-In Windings – 1) Connect an ammeter, voltmeter, carbon pile and battery into starter circuit. *See Fig. 1.* Using carbon pile, decrease battery voltage to 10 volts.

2) Refer to SOLENOID HOLD-IN WINDING SPECIFICATIONS table for correct amperage reading. A higher reading indicates windings are shorted or grounded; a lower reading indicates excessive resistance.

SOLENOID HOLD-IN WINDING SPECIFICATIONS

Part No.	Amps	Volts
1114520	13-19	10
1114530	13-19	10
1114563	14-18	10
10469039	13-15	10

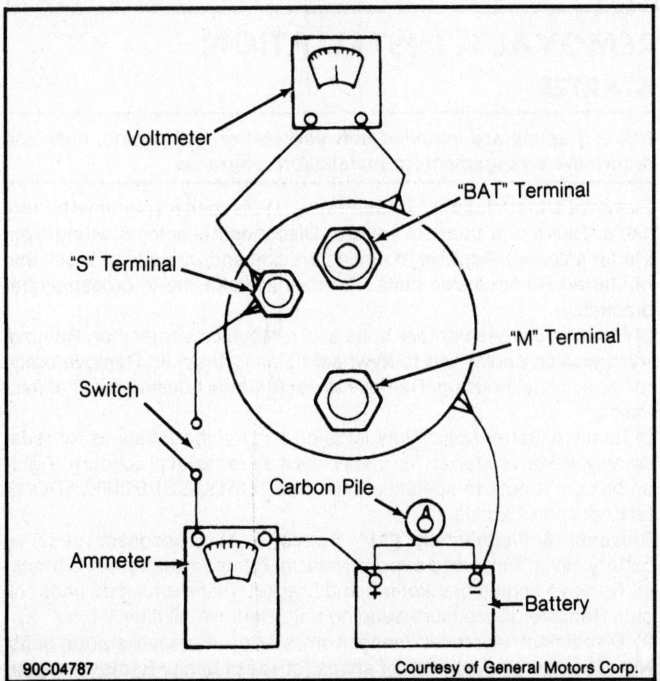
Voltmeter
"BAT" Terminal
"S" Terminal
"M" Terminal
Switch
Carbon Pile
Ammeter
Battery
90C04787
Courtesy of General Motors Corp.

Fig. 1: Testing Solenoid Hold-In Windings

Pull-In Windings – Using solenoid test connections shown in illustration, decrease battery voltage to 5 volts. *See Fig. 2.* Refer to SOLENOID PULL-IN WINDING SPECIFICATIONS table for correct amperage draw. A higher reading indicates windings are shorted or grounded; a lower reading indicates excessive resistance.

NOTE: To prevent overheating of pull-in windings, DO NOT energize for more than 15 seconds. Current draw will decrease as winding temperature increases.

SOLENOID PULL-IN WINDING SPECIFICATIONS

Part No.	Amps	Volts
1114520	23-30	5
1114530	23-30	5
1114563	26-30	5
10469039	31-36	5

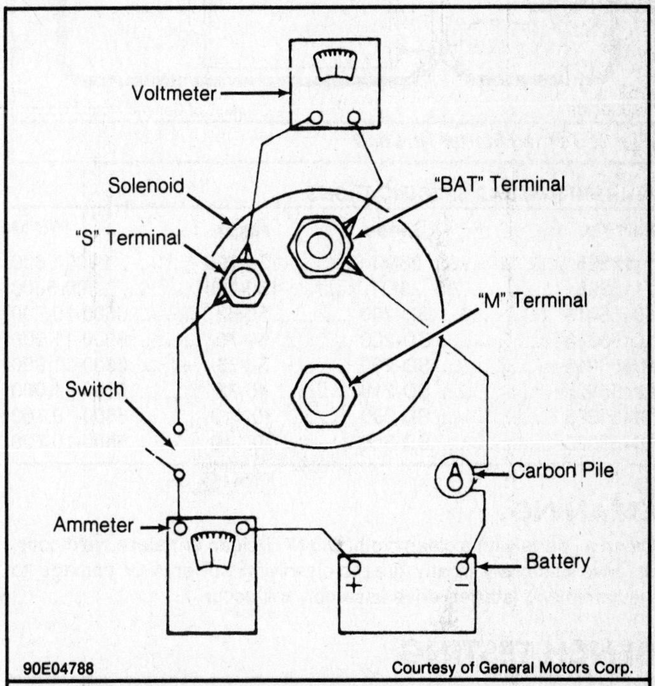
Voltmeter
Solenoid
"BAT" Terminal
"S" Terminal
"M" Terminal
Switch
Carbon Pile
Ammeter
Battery
90E04788
Courtesy of General Motors Corp.

Fig. 2: Testing Solenoid Pull-In Windings

STARTER NO-LOAD TEST

1) Connect a tachometer, ammeter and voltmeter into start circuit. *See Fig. 3.* Using carbon pile, adjust voltage to 10 volts and engage starter motor.

2) Read amperage draw and armature speed to ensure they are within specification. See STARTER NO-LOAD SPECIFICATIONS table. If exact voltage cannot be obtained and voltage is slightly higher than specification, RPM should also be slightly higher. Alternatively, carbon pile may be adjusted to reduce voltage.

3) Low free speed (no load) and high current draw indicates too much friction, shorted armature, or grounded armature or fields. Failure to operate with high current draw indicates a direct ground in terminal or fields, or frozen bearings.

4) Failure to operate with no current draw indicates an open field, open armature coils, broken brush springs, worn brushes, or high commutator insulation.

5) If free speed (no load) is low and there is low current draw, suspect high internal resistance due to poor connection, defective leads, or dirty commutator. A high free speed and high current draw usually indicates shorted fields.

1991 ELECTRICAL
Starters – Delco-Remy (Cont.)

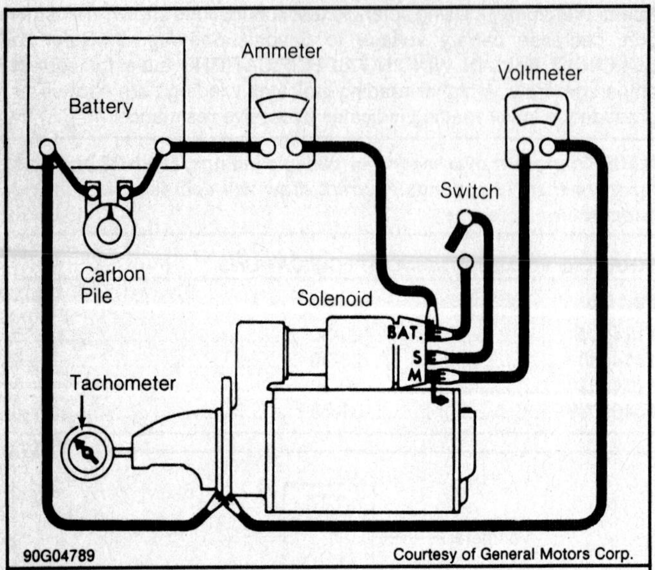
Ammeter
Voltmeter
Battery
Switch
Carbon
Pile
Solenoid
BAT.
S
M
Tachometer
90G04789
Courtesy of General Motors Corp.

Fig. 3: Testing Starter No-Load

STARTER NO-LOAD SPECIFICATIONS

Part No.	Series	Amps	RPM
1113295	28MT	130-190	2300-5600
1113296	28MT	130-190	2300-5600
10455013	SD-260	50-62	8500-10,700
10455016	SD-200	50-75	6000-11,900
10455018	SD-200	50-75	6500-11,900
10455025	SD-210	45-75	6000-11,000
10455305	SD-300	70-110	6500-10,700
10455306	SD-300	70-110	6500-10,700

CLEANING

Clean all parts with a clean cloth. DO NOT clean armature, field coils, or drive assembly in any grease-dissolving solvents or damage to insulation and (starter) drive assembly will occur.

BENCH TESTING

NOTE: The 28MT is not serviceable; starter replacement is required.

ARMATURE

Test armature for shorted coils with a growler. Check for grounded coils using a self-powered test light. Place one test lead on armature core or shaft, and other test lead on commutator. Light should not illuminate. If light illuminates, armature is grounded and must be replaced.

FIELD COILS (ENCLOSED HOUSING)

1) Disconnect field coil ground connections. Using self-powered test light, place one test lead on field coil frame and connect other test lead to field coil connector. If light illuminates, one or more coils are grounded and must be repaired or replaced.
2) Check for opens by placing test light across coil ends. Light should illuminate. If light does not illuminate, coils are open.
3) On SD-200 and SD-260 starters, coils cannot be replaced separately. The frame and fields must be replaced as a unit. On SD-300, a pole shoe spreader and pole shoe screwdriver should be used to replace a defective field coil. Assemble pole shoe with long lip (if equipped) facing the direction of armature rotation.

BRUSHES, SPRINGS & HOLDERS

Replace brushes if worn to 1/2 original length, oil-soaked or pitted. Check brush spring tension and replace springs if weak or distorted.

NOTE: The entire frame and field assembly must be replaced for the SD-210 & SD-260. The brushes and brush holders are integral parts of the assembly.

DRIVE & PINION

Pinion should turn freely in overrun direction and should not slip in drive direction. Check spring for correct tension and drive collar for wear. These parts can be removed for replacement by forcing collar toward clutch and removing lock ring from end of tube. Replace drive assembly if pinion teeth are worn, chipped or cracked.

PINION CLEARANCE

1) Disconnect motor field coil connector from solenoid "M" terminal and insulate it carefully. Connect a battery from solenoid "S" terminal to solenoid frame. Momentarily flash a jumper lead from "M" terminal to solenoid frame.
2) This shifts pinion into cranking position. Push pinion back toward commutator end to eliminate slack. Distance between pinion and pinion stop should be .010-.160" (.25-4.06 mm). Clearance is not adjustable. If clearance is not within specification, check for worn parts.

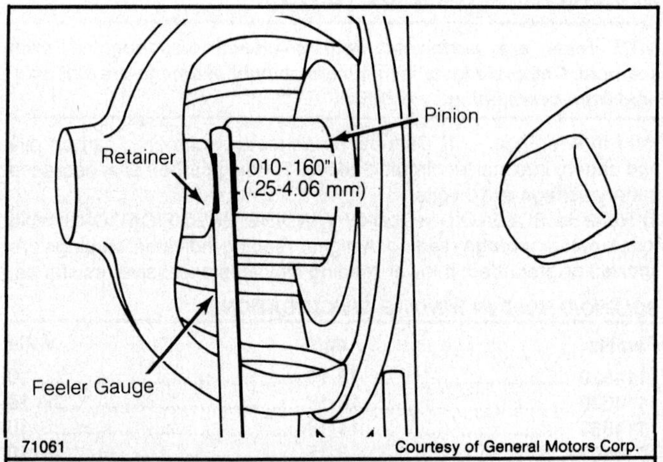
Pinion
Retainer
.010-.160"
(.25-4.06 mm)
Feeler Gauge
71061
Courtesy of General Motors Corp.

Fig. 4: Checking Pinion-to-Housing Clearance

REMOVAL & INSTALLATION

STARTER

NOTE: If shims are installed between starter and engine, note and record the arrangement for installation reference.

Removal & Installation ("T" Series) – 1) Disconnect negative battery cable. Raise and support vehicle. Disconnect electrical wiring from starter solenoid. Remove mounting bracket and wiring from brush end of starter. Remove skid plate. Remove 2 brake line-to-crossmember brackets.
2) Remove 6 crossmember bolts and remove crossmember. Remove transmission cooler line-to-flywheel housing bracket. Remove brace rod to flywheel housing. Remove lower flywheel housing cover (if necessary).
3) Remove starter bolts. Note location and number of shims for reassembly. Remove starter. To install, reverse removal procedure. Tighten bolts and nuts to specifications. See TORQUE SPECIFICATIONS table at end of article.
Removal & Installation ("U" Series) – 1) Disconnect negative battery cable. Raise and support vehicle. Remove nut from A/C bracket. Remove engine bracket nut and bracket. Place drain pan under oil pan. Remove oil pressure sending unit. Remove oil filter.
2) Disconnect electrical wiring from starter. Remove starter bolts. Note location and number of shims for reassembly. Remove starter. To install, reverse removal procedure. Tighten bolts and nuts to specifications. See TORQUE SPECIFICATIONS table at end of article.

Removal & Installation (Except "T" & "U" Series) – 1) Disconnect negative battery cable. Raise and support vehicle. Remove starter braces and shields (if equipped). Remove brush end mounting bracket (if equipped). Disconnect electrical wiring from starter solenoid.

2) Remove starter mounting bolts. Remove shims and note arrangement for reassembly. Remove starter. To install, reverse removal procedure. Ensure shims are installed in original location. Tighten bolts or nuts to specifications. See TORQUE SPECIFICATIONS table.

OVERHAUL

NOTE: Overhaul procedures are not available from manufacturer. See Figs. 5-7 for exploded views of starters. The 28MT starter is not serviceable.

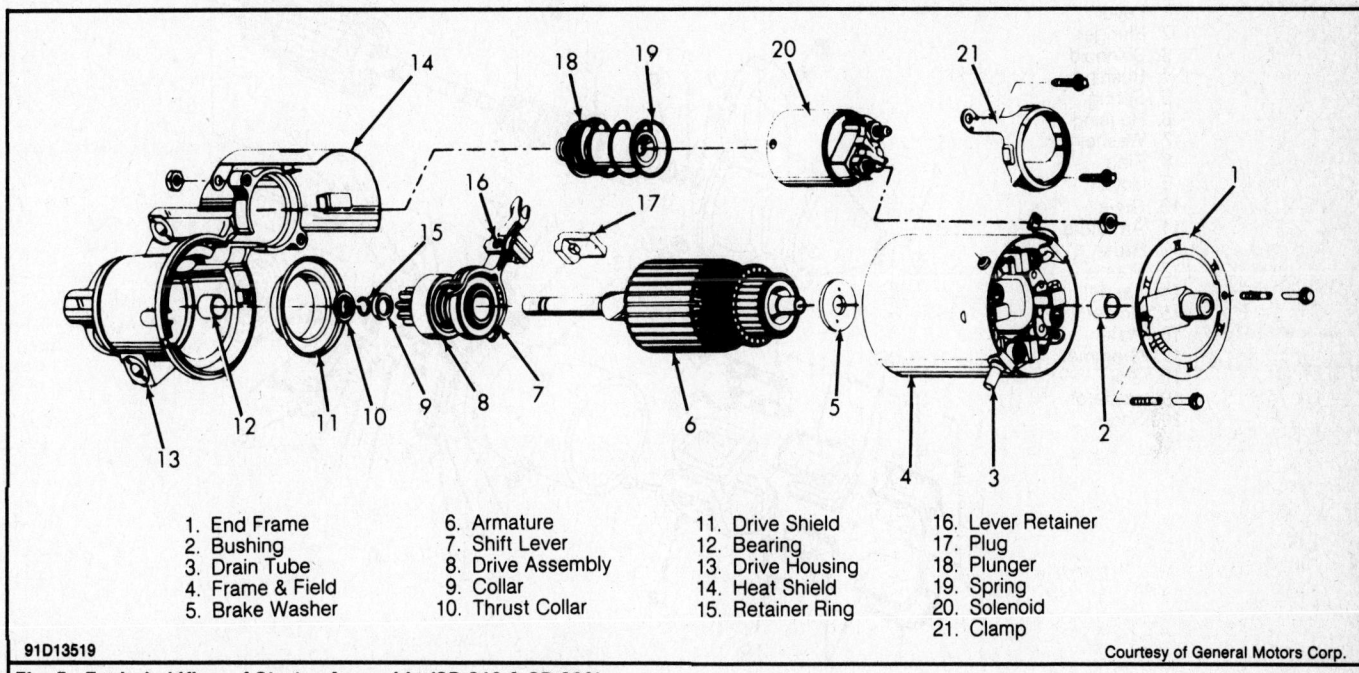

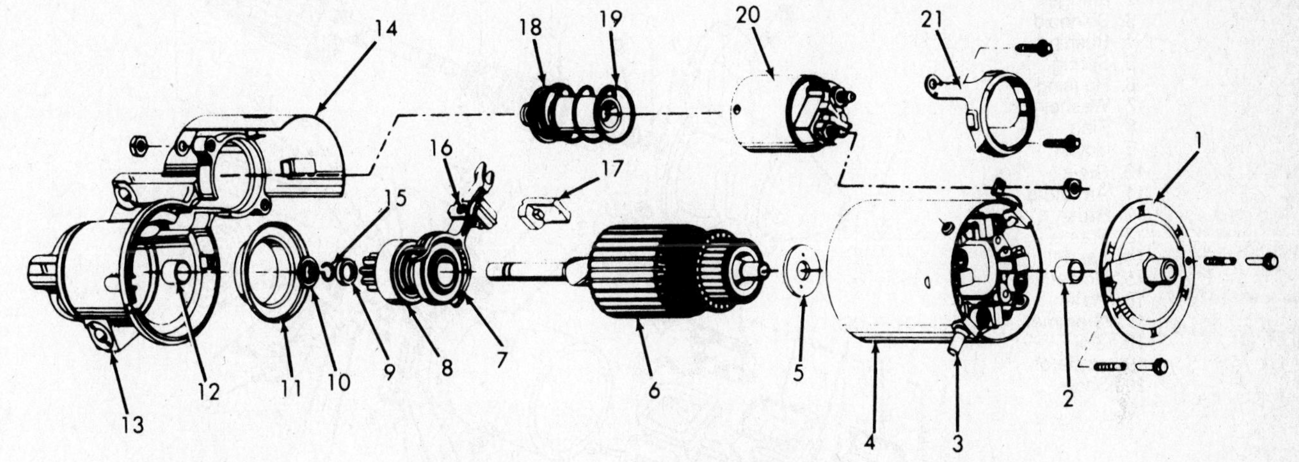
1
2
3
4
5
6
7
8
9
10
11
12
13
14
15
16
17
18
19
20
21

1. End Frame
2. Bushing
3. Drain Tube
4. Frame & Field
5. Brake Washer
6. Armature
7. Shift Lever
8. Drive Assembly
9. Collar
10. Thrust Collar
11. Drive Shield
12. Bearing
13. Drive Housing
14. Heat Shield
15. Retainer Ring
16. Lever Retainer
17. Plug
18. Plunger
19. Spring
20. Solenoid
21. Clamp

91D13519

Courtesy of General Motors Corp.

Fig. 5: Exploded View of Starter Assembly (SD-210 & SD-260)

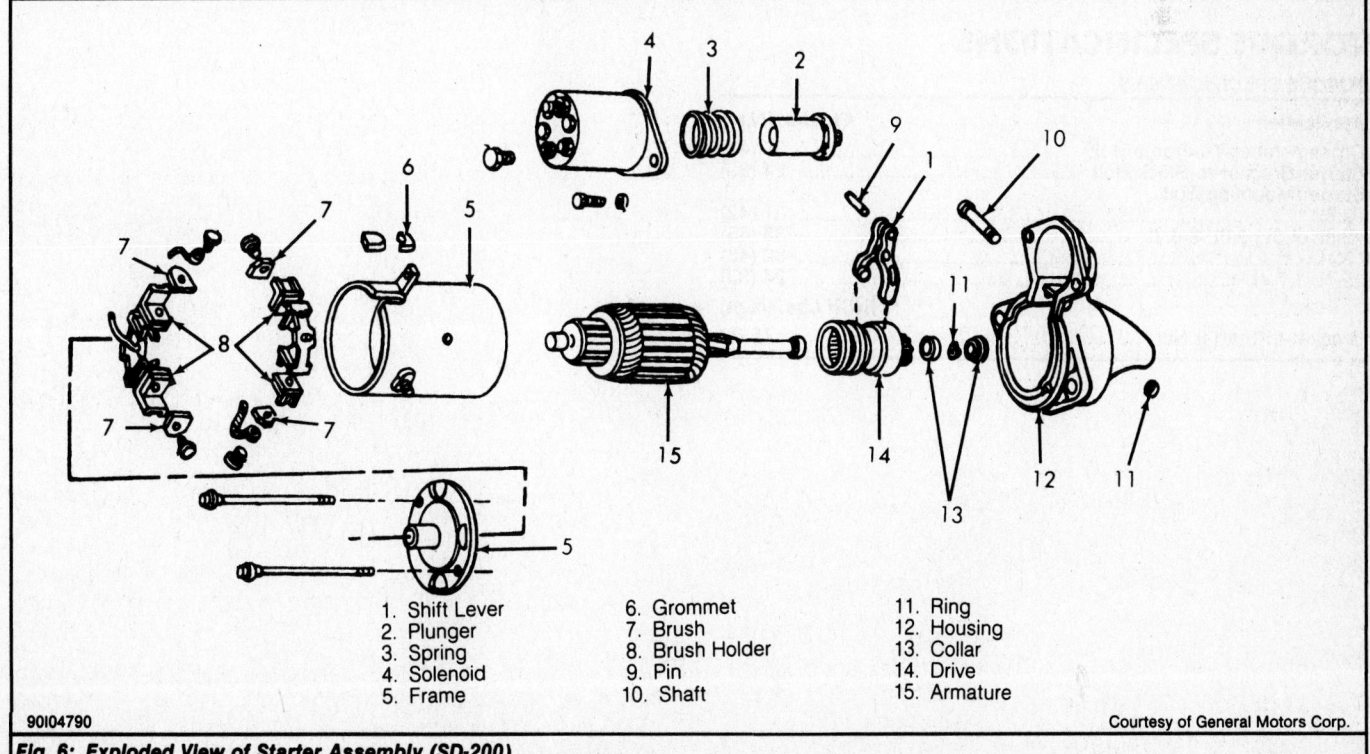

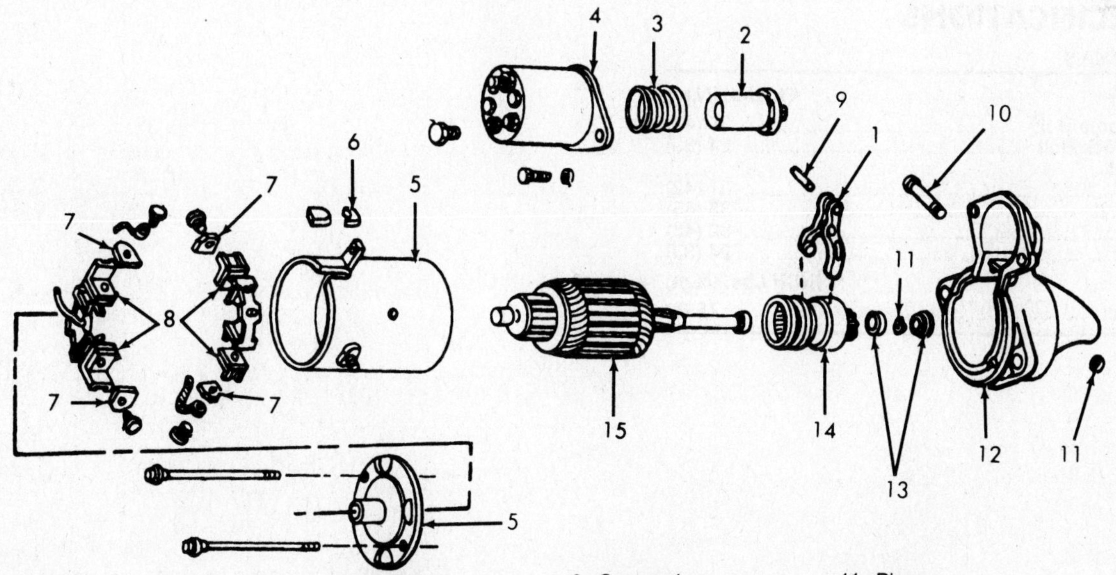
1
2
3
4
5
6
7
8
9
10
11
12
13
14
15

1. Shift Lever
2. Plunger
3. Spring
4. Solenoid
5. Frame
6. Grommet
7. Brush
8. Brush Holder
9. Pin
10. Shaft
11. Ring
12. Housing
13. Collar
14. Drive
15. Armature

90I04790

Courtesy of General Motors Corp.

Fig. 6: Exploded View of Starter Assembly (SD-200)

1991 ELECTRICAL
Starters – Delco-Remy (Cont.)

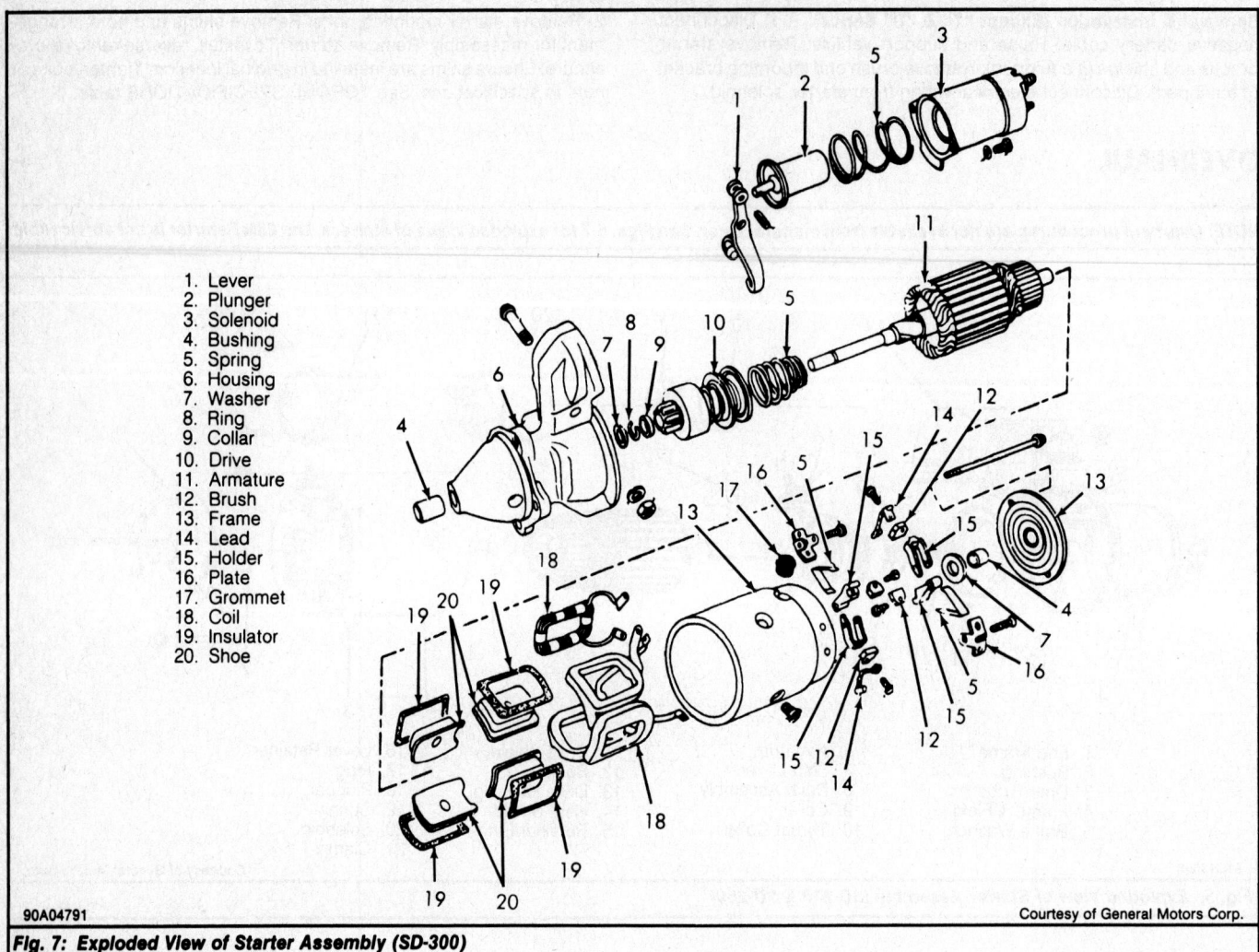

1. Lever
2. Plunger
3. Solenoid
4. Bushing
5. Spring
6. Housing
7. Washer
8. Ring
9. Collar
10. Drive
11. Armature
12. Brush
13. Frame
14. Lead
15. Holder
16. Plate
17. Grommet
18. Coil
19. Insulator
20. Shoe

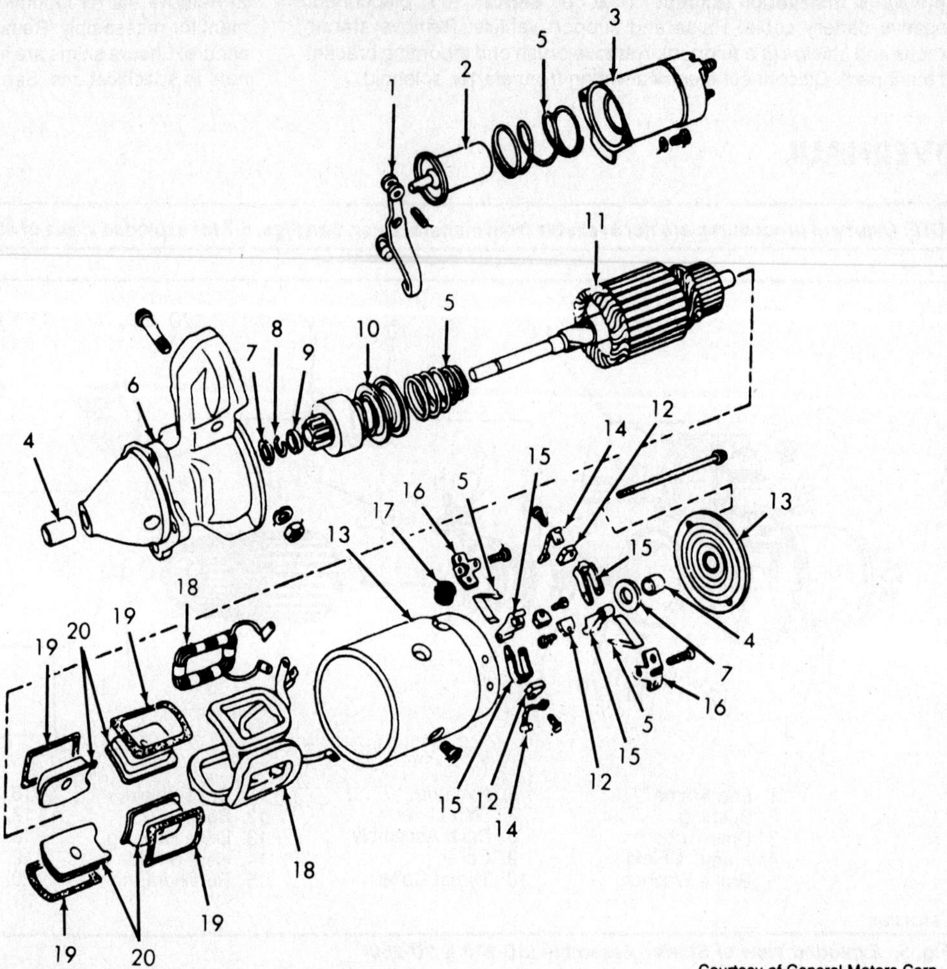

90A04791

Courtesy of General Motors Corp.

Fig. 7: Exploded View of Starter Assembly (SD-300)

TORQUE SPECIFICATIONS

TORQUE SPECIFICATIONS

Application	Ft. Lbs. (N.m)
Crossmember-To-Frame Bolt	35 (47)
Starter Bracket-to-Block Bolt	24 (33)
Starter Mounting Bolt	
2.5L	31 (42)
2.8L, 4.3L, 5.0L & 6.2L	33 (45)
3.1L	32 (43)
5.7L & 7.4L	24 (33)
	INCH Lbs. (N.m)
Bracket-to-Starter Nut	75 (8)

1991 WIRING DIAGRAMS
Astro & Safari

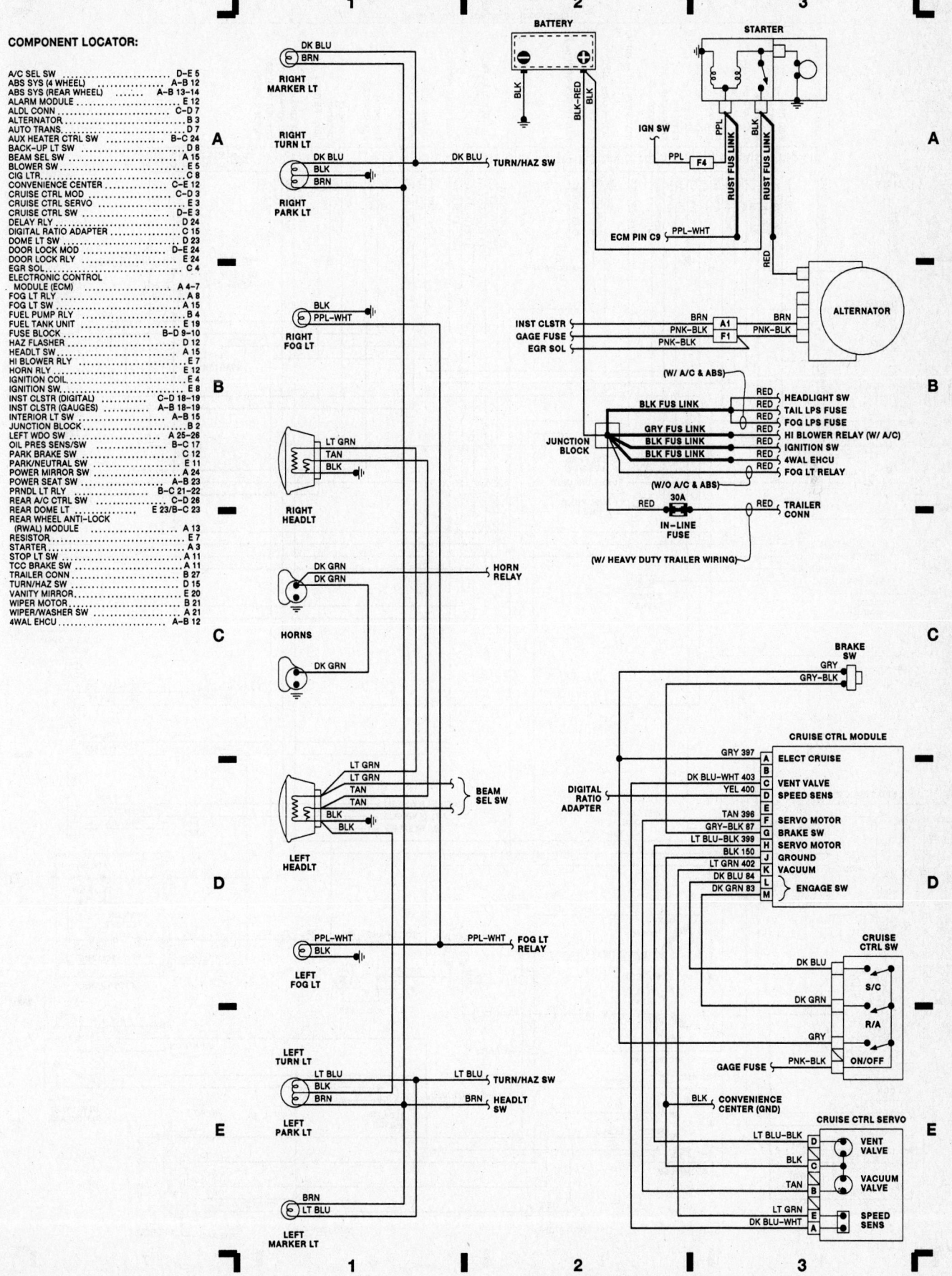

COMPONENT LOCATOR:

A/C SEL SW	D–E 5
ABS SYS (4 WHEEL)	A–B 12
ABS SYS (REAR WHEEL)	A–B 13–14
ALARM MODULE	E 12
ALDL CONN	C–D 7
ALTERNATOR	B 3
AUTO TRANS.	D 7
AUX HEATER CTRL SW	B–C 24
BACK–UP LT SW	D 8
BEAM SEL SW	A 15
BLOWER SW	E 5
CIG LTR.	C 8
CONVENIENCE CENTER	C–E 12
CRUISE CTRL MOD	C–D 3
CRUISE CTRL SERVO	E 3
CRUISE CTRL SW	D–E 3
DELAY RLY	D 24
DIGITAL RATIO ADAPTER	C 15
DOME LT SW	D 23
DOOR LOCK MOD	D–E 24
DOOR LOCK RLY	E 24
EGR SOL.	C 4
ELECTRONIC CONTROL MODULE (ECM)	A 4–7
FOG LT RLY	A 8
FOG LT SW	A 15
FUEL PUMP RLY	B 4
FUEL TANK UNIT	E 19
FUSE BLOCK	B–D 9–10
HAZ FLASHER	D 12
HEADLT SW	A 15
HI BLOWER RLY	E 7
HORN RLY	E 12
IGNITION COIL.	E 4
IGNITION SW.	E 8
INST CLSTR (DIGITAL)	C–D 18–19
INST CLSTR (GAUGES)	A–B 18–19
INTERIOR LT SW	A–B 15
JUNCTION BLOCK	B 2
LEFT WDO SW	A 25–26
OIL PRES SENS/SW	B–C 17
PARK BRAKE SW	C 12
PARK/NEUTRAL SW	E 11
POWER MIRROR SW	A 24
POWER SEAT SW	A–B 23
PRNDL LT RLY	B–C 21–22
REAR A/C CTRL SW	C–D 26
REAR DOME LT	E 23/B–C 23
REAR WHEEL ANTI–LOCK (RWAL) MODULE	A 13
RESISTOR	E 7
STARTER	A 3
STOP LT SW	A 11
TCC BRAKE SW	A 11
TRAILER CONN	B 27
TURN/HAZ SW	D 15
VANITY MIRROR	E 20
WIPER MOTOR	B 21
WIPER/WASHER SW	A 21
4WAL EHCU	A–B 12

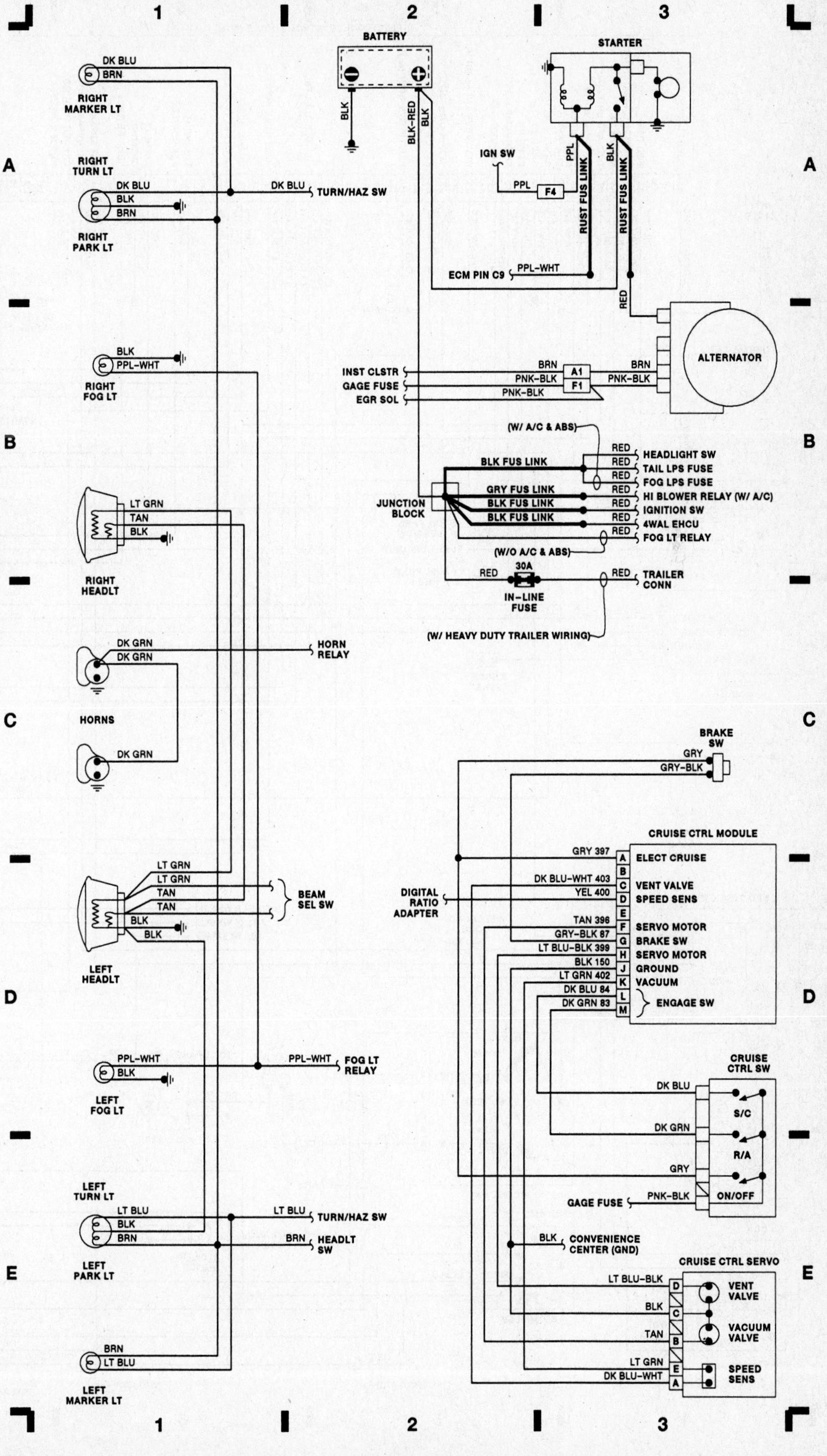
1
2
3
A
B
C
D
E
RIGHT MARKER LT
DK BLU
BRN
RIGHT TURN LT
RIGHT PARK LT
BLK
TURN/HAZ SW
RIGHT FOG LT
PPL-WHT
RIGHT HEADLT
LT GRN
TAN
HORNS
DK GRN
HORN RELAY
LEFT HEADLT
BEAM SEL SW
LEFT FOG LT
FOG LT RELAY
LEFT TURN LT
LT BLU
LEFT PARK LT
HEADLT SW
LEFT MARKER LT
BATTERY
BLK-RED
STARTER
IGN SW
PPL
F4
RUST FUS LINK
ECM PIN C9
RED
ALTERNATOR
INST CLSTR
GAGE FUSE
EGR SOL
A1
F1
PNK-BLK
(W/ A/C & ABS)
HEADLIGHT SW
TAIL LPS FUSE
FOG LPS FUSE
HI BLOWER RELAY (W/ A/C)
IGNITION SW
4WAL EHCU
FOG LT RELAY
BLK FUS LINK
GRY FUS LINK
JUNCTION BLOCK
(W/O A/C & ABS)
30A
IN-LINE FUSE
TRAILER CONN
(W/ HEAVY DUTY TRAILER WIRING)
BRAKE SW
GRY
GRY-BLK
CRUISE CTRL MODULE
GRY 397
DK BLU-WHT 403
YEL 400
TAN 396
GRY-BLK 87
LT BLU-BLK 399
BLK 150
LT GRN 402
DK BLU 84
DK GRN 83
ELECT CRUISE
VENT VALVE
SPEED SENS
SERVO MOTOR
BRAKE SW
GROUND
VACUUM
ENGAGE SW
DIGITAL RATIO ADAPTER
CRUISE CTRL SW
S/C
R/A
ON/OFF
GAGE FUSE
CONVENIENCE CENTER (GND)
CRUISE CTRL SERVO
LT BLU-BLK
VENT VALVE
VACUUM VALVE
SPEED SENS
DK BLU-WHT

1991 WIRING DIAGRAMS
Astro & Safari (Cont.)

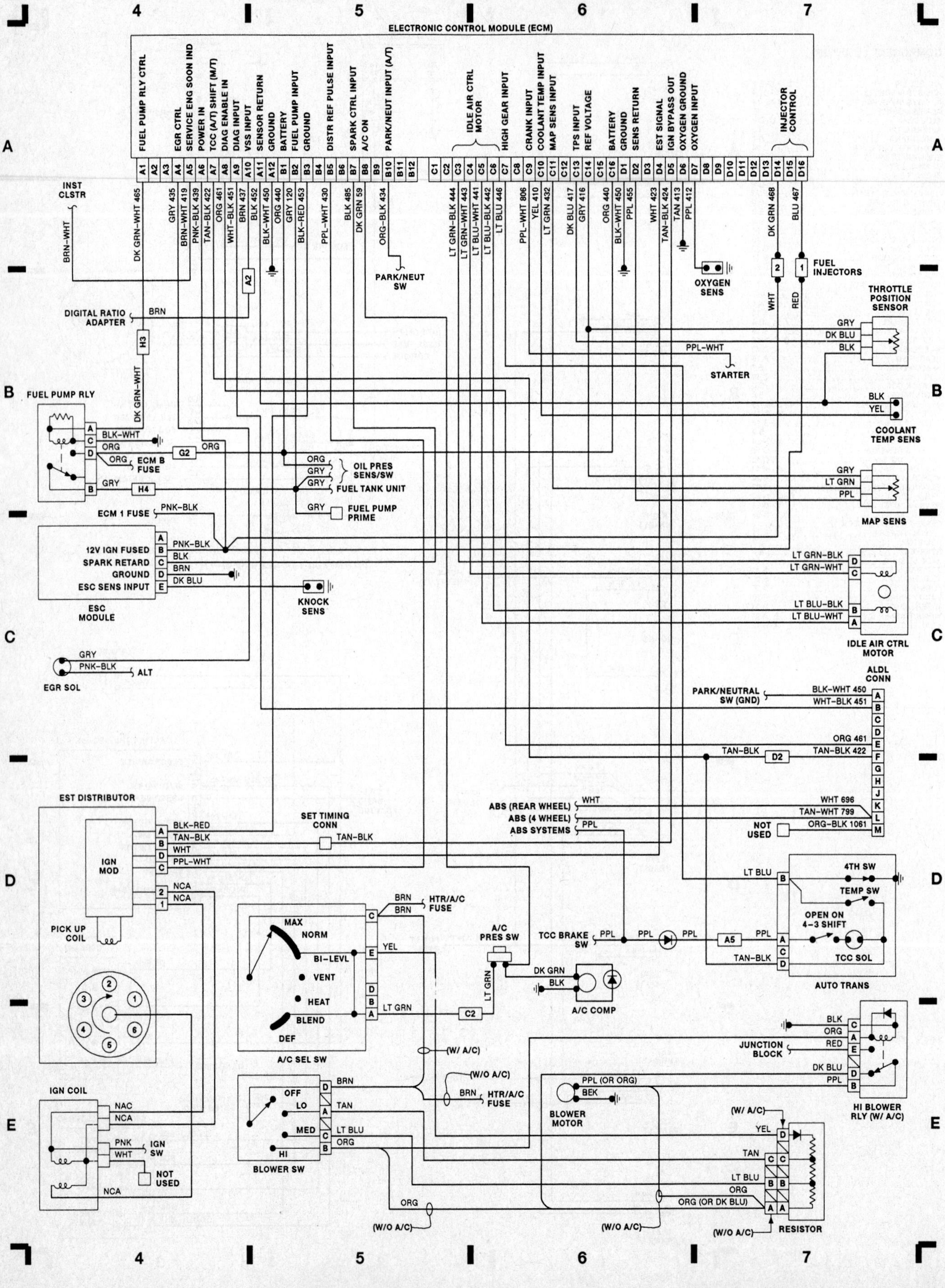
ELECTRONIC CONTROL MODULE (ECM)
FUEL PUMP RLY CTRL
EGR CTRL
SERVICE ENG SOON IND
POWER IN
TCC (A/T) SHIFT (M/T)
DIAG ENABLE IN
DIAG INPUT
VSS INPUT
SENSOR RETURN
GROUND
BATTERY
FUEL PUMP INPUT
GROUND
DISTR REF PULSE INPUT
SPARK CTRL INPUT
A/C ON
PARK/NEUT INPUT (A/T)
IDLE AIR CTRL MOTOR
HIGH GEAR INPUT
CRANK INPUT
COOLANT TEMP INPUT
MAP SENS INPUT
TPS INPUT
REF VOLTAGE
BATTERY
GROUND
SENS RETURN
EST SIGNAL
IGN BYPASS OUT
OXYGEN GROUND
OXYGEN INPUT
INJECTOR CONTROL
INST CLSTR
PARK/NEUT SW
OXYGEN SENS
FUEL INJECTORS
THROTTLE POSITION SENSOR
DIGITAL RATIO ADAPTER
STARTER
FUEL PUMP RLY
COOLANT TEMP SENS
ECM B FUSE
OIL PRES SENS/SW
FUEL TANK UNIT
FUEL PUMP PRIME
MAP SENS
ECM 1 FUSE
12V IGN FUSED
SPARK RETARD
GROUND
ESC SENS INPUT
ESC MODULE
KNOCK SENS
IDLE AIR CTRL MOTOR
EGR SOL
ALT
ALDL CONN
PARK/NEUTRAL SW (GND)
ABS (REAR WHEEL)
ABS (4 WHEEL)
ABS SYSTEMS
NOT USED
EST DISTRIBUTOR
IGN MOD
SET TIMING CONN
PICK UP COIL
4TH SW
TEMP SW
OPEN ON 4-3 SHIFT
TCC SOL
AUTO TRANS
HTR/A/C FUSE
MAX
NORM
BI-LEVL
VENT
HEAT
BLEND
DEF
A/C SEL SW
A/C PRES SW
TCC BRAKE SW
A/C COMP
(W/ A/C)
(W/O A/C)
JUNCTION BLOCK
HI BLOWER RLY (W/ A/C)
IGN COIL
OFF
LO
MED
HI
BLOWER SW
BLOWER MOTOR
IGN SW
NOT USED
RESISTOR

1991 WIRING DIAGRAMS
Astro & Safari (Cont.)

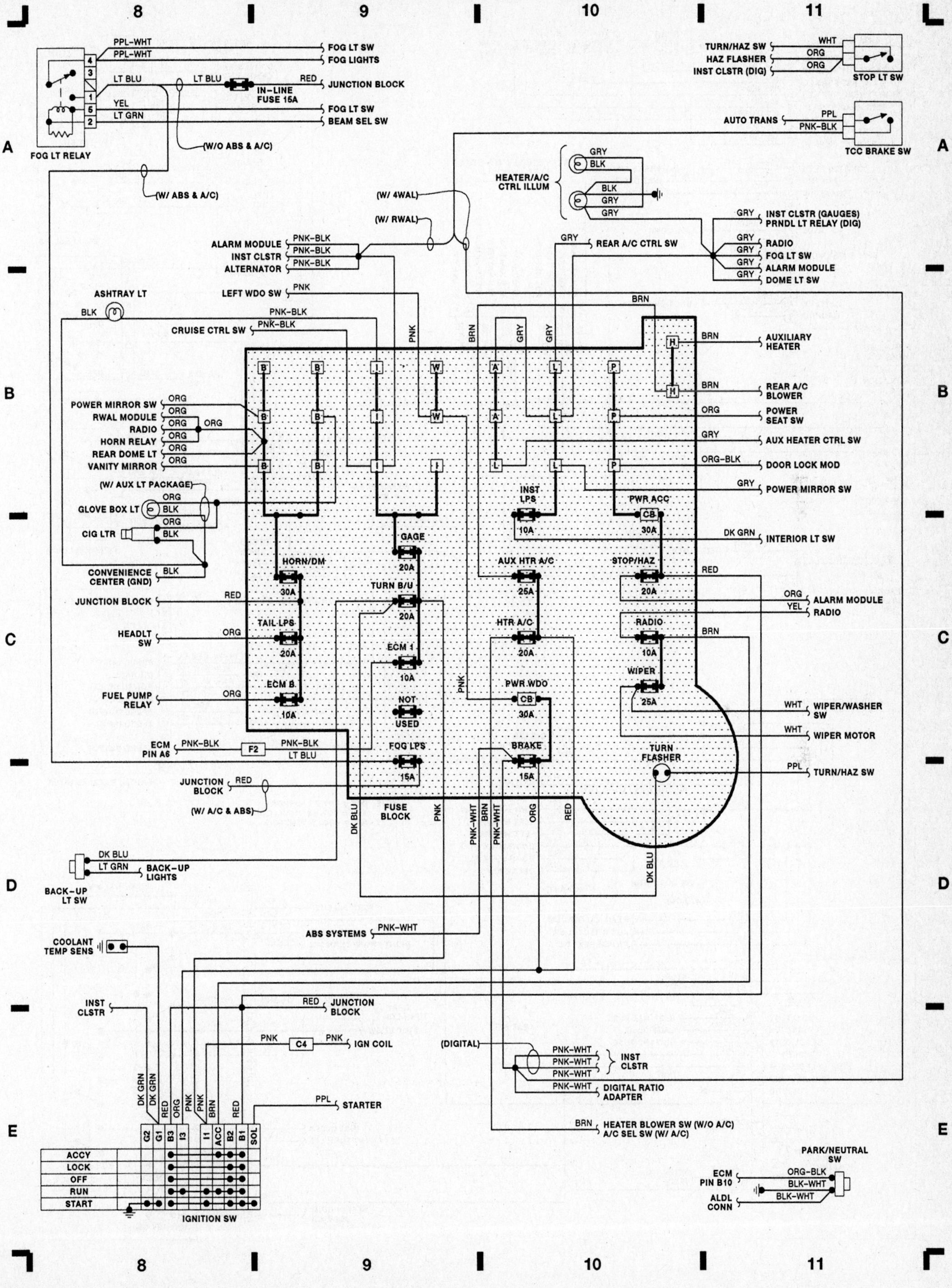

8
9
10
11
A
B
C
D
E
FOG LT RELAY
PPL-WHT
FOG LT SW
FOG LIGHTS
LT BLU
RED
JUNCTION BLOCK
IN-LINE FUSE 15A
YEL
LT GRN
BEAM SEL SW
(W/O ABS & A/C)
(W/ ABS & A/C)
TURN/HAZ SW
HAZ FLASHER
INST CLSTR (DIG)
WHT
ORG
STOP LT SW
AUTO TRANS
PPL
PNK-BLK
TCC BRAKE SW
HEATER/A/C CTRL ILLUM
GRY
BLK
INST CLSTR (GAUGES)
PRNDL LT RELAY (DIG)
RADIO
ALARM MODULE
DOME LT SW
REAR A/C CTRL SW
(W/ 4WAL)
(W/ RWAL)
INST CLSTR
ALTERNATOR
LEFT WDO SW
PNK
ASHTRAY LT
CRUISE CTRL SW
BRN
AUXILIARY HEATER
REAR A/C BLOWER
POWER SEAT SW
AUX HEATER CTRL SW
ORG-BLK
DOOR LOCK MOD
POWER MIRROR SW
RWAL MODULE
HORN RELAY
REAR DOME LT
VANITY MIRROR
(W/ AUX LT PACKAGE)
GLOVE BOX LT
CIG LTR
CONVENIENCE CENTER (GND)
INST LPS
10A
PWR ACC
CB
30A
DK GRN
INTERIOR LT SW
GAGE
20A
HORN/DM
AUX HTR A/C
25A
STOP/HAZ
TURN B/U
TAIL LPS
HTR A/C
HEADLT SW
ECM 1
ECM B
FUEL PUMP RELAY
PWR WDO
WIPER
WIPER/WASHER SW
WIPER MOTOR
NOT USED
FOG LPS
15A
BRAKE
TURN FLASHER
ECM PIN A6
F2
(W/ A/C & ABS)
FUSE BLOCK
DK BLU
PNK-WHT
BACK-UP LIGHTS
BACK-UP LT SW
ABS SYSTEMS
COOLANT TEMP SENS
INST CLSTR
IGN COIL
C4
(DIGITAL)
DIGITAL RATIO ADAPTER
STARTER
HEATER BLOWER SW (W/O A/C)
A/C SEL SW (W/ A/C)
G2
G1
B3
I3
I1
ACC
B2
B1
SOL
ACCY
LOCK
OFF
RUN
START
IGNITION SW
PARK/NEUTRAL SW
ECM PIN B10
ALDL CONN
BLK-WHT

1991 WIRING DIAGRAMS
Astro & Safari (Cont.)

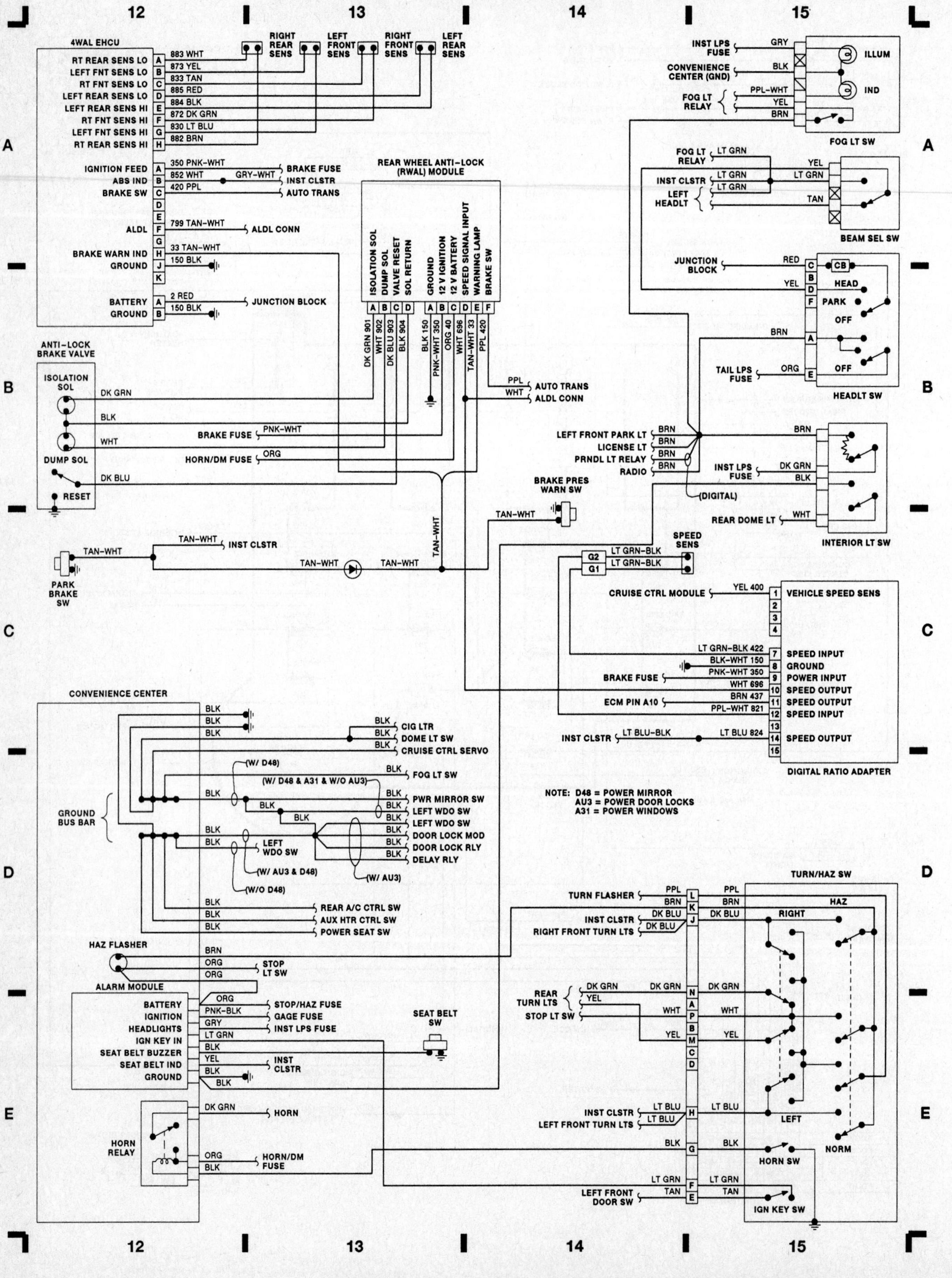
12
13
14
15
A
B
C
D
E
4WAL EHCU
RT REAR SENS LO
LEFT FNT SENS LO
RT FNT SENS LO
LEFT REAR SENS LO
LEFT REAR SENS HI
RT FNT SENS HI
LEFT FNT SENS HI
RT REAR SENS HI
883 WHT
873 YEL
833 TAN
885 RED
884 BLK
872 DK GRN
830 LT BLU
882 BRN
RIGHT REAR SENS
LEFT FRONT SENS
RIGHT FRONT SENS
LEFT REAR SENS
IGNITION FEED
ABS IND
BRAKE SW
350 PNK-WHT
852 WHT
420 PPL
GRY-WHT
BRAKE FUSE
INST CLSTR
AUTO TRANS
ALDL
799 TAN-WHT
ALDL CONN
BRAKE WARN IND
GROUND
33 TAN-WHT
150 BLK
BATTERY
GROUND
2 RED
150 BLK
JUNCTION BLOCK
REAR WHEEL ANTI-LOCK (RWAL) MODULE
ISOLATION SOL
DUMP SOL
VALVE RESET
SOL RETURN
GROUND
12 V IGNITION
12 V BATTERY
SPEED SIGNAL INPUT
WARNING LAMP
BRAKE SW
DK GRN 901
WHT 902
DK BLU 903
BLK 904
BLK 150
PNK-WHT 350
ORG 40
WHT 696
TAN-WHT 33
PPL 420
PPL
WHT
AUTO TRANS
ALDL CONN
ANTI-LOCK BRAKE VALVE
ISOLATION SOL
DK GRN
BLK
WHT
DUMP SOL
DK BLU
RESET
BRAKE FUSE
PNK-WHT
HORN/DM FUSE
ORG
TAN-WHT
INST CLSTR
PARK BRAKE SW
BRAKE PRES WARN SW
INST LPS FUSE
GRY
CONVENIENCE CENTER (GND)
BLK
FOG LT RELAY
PPL-WHT
YEL
BRN
ILLUM
IND
FOG LT SW
FOG LT RELAY
LT GRN
INST CLSTR
LEFT HEADLT
TAN
BEAM SEL SW
JUNCTION BLOCK
RED
CB
HEAD
PARK
OFF
TAIL LPS FUSE
ORG
HEADLT SW
LEFT FRONT PARK LT
LICENSE LT
PRNDL LT RELAY
RADIO
(DIGITAL)
DK GRN
REAR DOME LT
INTERIOR LT SW
SPEED SENS
G2
G1
LT GRN-BLK
CRUISE CTRL MODULE
YEL 400
VEHICLE SPEED SENS
LT GRN-BLK 422
BLK-WHT 150
PNK-WHT 350
WHT 696
BRN 437
PPL-WHT 821
LT BLU-BLK
LT BLU 824
ECM PIN A10
SPEED INPUT
GROUND
POWER INPUT
SPEED OUTPUT
DIGITAL RATIO ADAPTER
CONVENIENCE CENTER
CIG LTR
DOME LT SW
CRUISE CTRL SERVO
(W/ D48)
(W/ D48 & A31 & W/O AU3)
FOG LT SW
PWR MIRROR SW
LEFT WDO SW
DOOR LOCK MOD
DOOR LOCK RLY
DELAY RLY
GROUND BUS BAR
LEFT WDO SW
(W/ AU3 & D48)
(W/O D48)
(W/ AU3)
REAR A/C CTRL SW
AUX HTR CTRL SW
POWER SEAT SW
NOTE: D48 = POWER MIRROR
AU3 = POWER DOOR LOCKS
A31 = POWER WINDOWS
HAZ FLASHER
STOP LT SW
ALARM MODULE
BATTERY
IGNITION
HEADLIGHTS
IGN KEY IN
SEAT BELT BUZZER
SEAT BELT IND
PNK-BLK
STOP/HAZ FUSE
GAGE FUSE
INST LPS FUSE
SEAT BELT SW
HORN
HORN RELAY
HORN/DM FUSE
TURN/HAZ SW
TURN FLASHER
RIGHT FRONT TURN LTS
HAZ
RIGHT
REAR TURN LTS
STOP LT SW
LEFT FRONT TURN LTS
LEFT
NORM
HORN SW
LEFT FRONT DOOR SW
IGN KEY SW

1991 WIRING DIAGRAMS
Astro & Safari (Cont.)

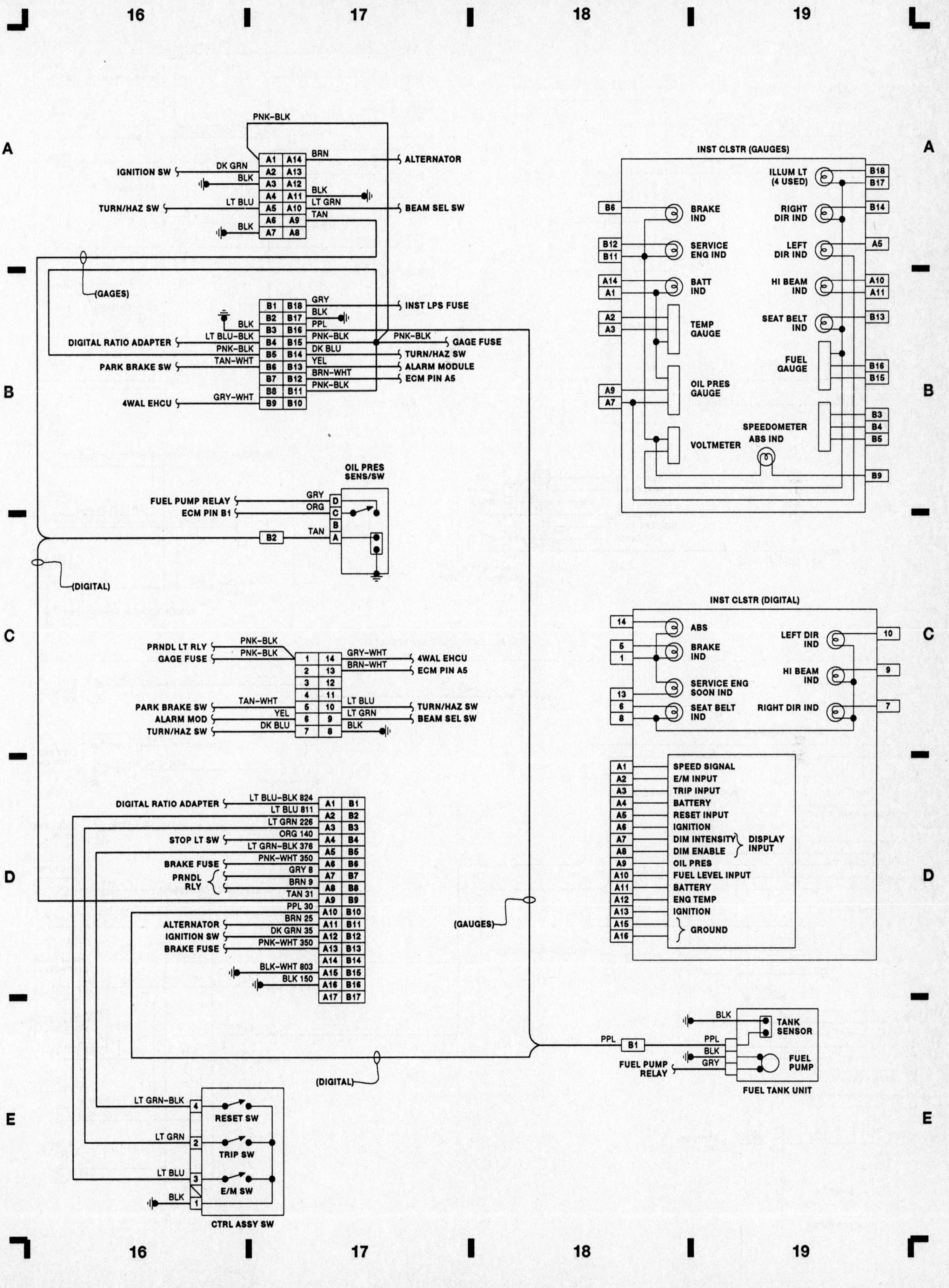
16
17
18
19
A
B
C
D
E
PNK-BLK
BRN
ALTERNATOR
IGNITION SW
DK GRN
BLK
TURN/HAZ SW
LT BLU
LT GRN
BEAM SEL SW
TAN
(GAGES)
GRY
INST LPS FUSE
PPL
DIGITAL RATIO ADAPTER
LT BLU-BLK
PNK-BLK
GAGE FUSE
DK BLU
TURN/HAZ SW
PARK BRAKE SW
TAN-WHT
YEL
ALARM MODULE
BRN-WHT
ECM PIN A5
4WAL EHCU
GRY-WHT
OIL PRES SENS/SW
FUEL PUMP RELAY
ECM PIN B1
ORG
(DIGITAL)
PRNDL LT RLY
GAGE FUSE
GRY-WHT
4WAL EHCU
BRN-WHT
ECM PIN A5
PARK BRAKE SW
ALARM MOD
TURN/HAZ SW
DK BLU
LT BLU
TURN/HAZ SW
BEAM SEL SW
DIGITAL RATIO ADAPTER
LT BLU-BLK 824
LT BLU 811
LT GRN 226
STOP LT SW
ORG 140
LT GRN-BLK 376
BRAKE FUSE
PNK-WHT 350
GRY 8
PRNDL RLY
BRN 9
TAN 31
PPL 30
ALTERNATOR
BRN 25
IGNITION SW
DK GRN 35
BRAKE FUSE
PNK-WHT 350
BLK-WHT 803
BLK 150
(GAUGES)
LT GRN-BLK
RESET SW
TRIP SW
E/M SW
CTRL ASSY SW
INST CLSTR (GAUGES)
ILLUM LT (4 USED)
BRAKE IND
RIGHT DIR IND
SERVICE ENG IND
LEFT DIR IND
BATT IND
HI BEAM IND
TEMP GAUGE
SEAT BELT IND
FUEL GAUGE
OIL PRES GAUGE
SPEEDOMETER
ABS IND
VOLTMETER
INST CLSTR (DIGITAL)
ABS
BRAKE IND
LEFT DIR IND
HI BEAM IND
SERVICE ENG SOON IND
SEAT BELT IND
RIGHT DIR IND
SPEED SIGNAL
E/M INPUT
TRIP INPUT
BATTERY
RESET INPUT
IGNITION
DIM INTENSITY
DIM ENABLE
DISPLAY INPUT
OIL PRES
FUEL LEVEL INPUT
BATTERY
ENG TEMP
IGNITION
GROUND
TANK SENSOR
FUEL PUMP
FUEL PUMP RELAY
FUEL TANK UNIT

1991 WIRING DIAGRAMS
Astro & Safari (Cont.)

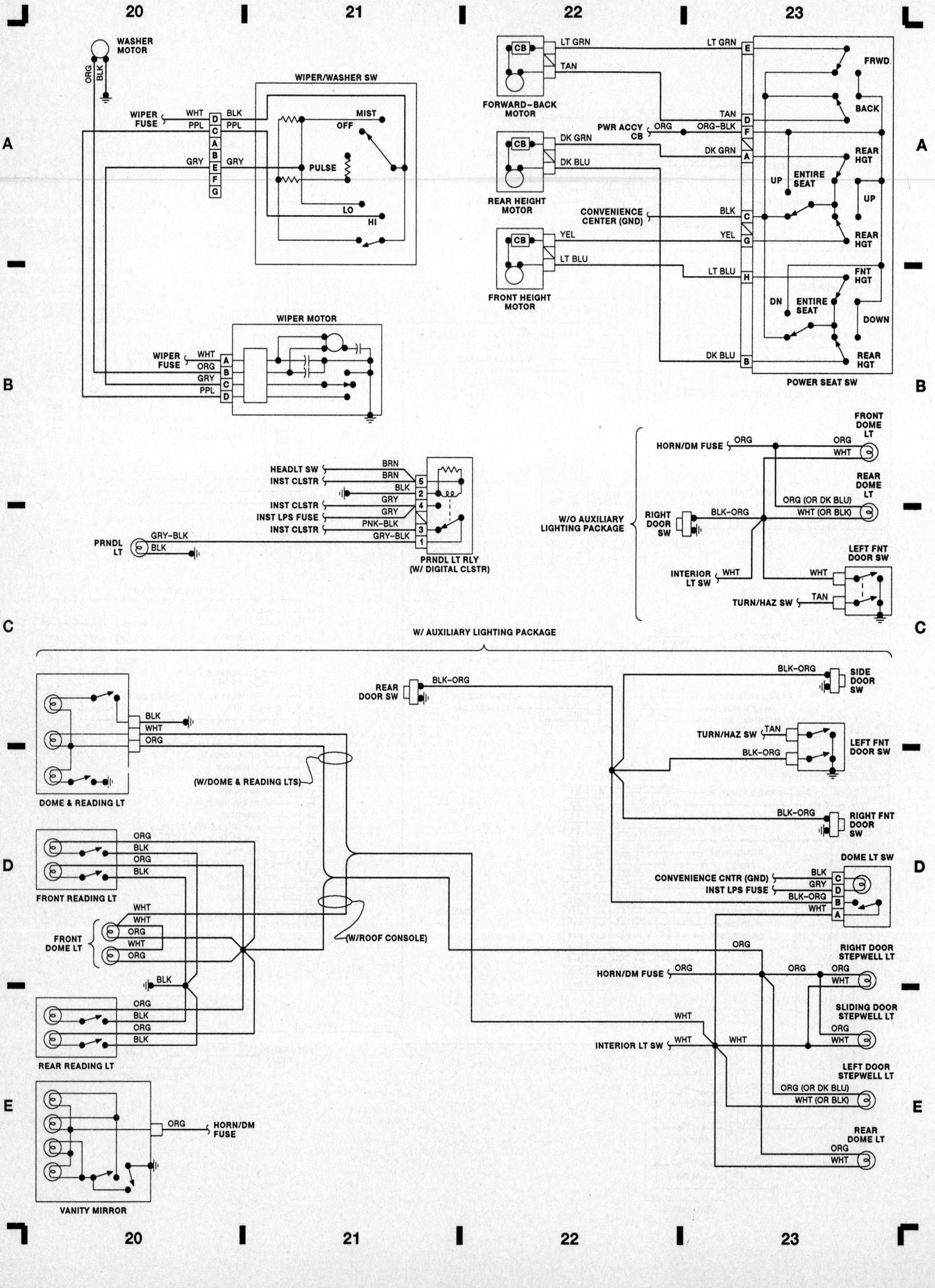
20
21
22
23
A
B
C
D
E
WASHER MOTOR
ORG
BLK
WIPER/WASHER SW
WIPER FUSE
WHT
PPL
BLK
GRY
MIST
OFF
PULSE
LO
HI
WIPER MOTOR
ORG
FORWARD-BACK MOTOR
CB
LT GRN
TAN
PWR ACCY CB
ORG-BLK
REAR HEIGHT MOTOR
DK GRN
DK BLU
CONVENIENCE CENTER (GND)
FRONT HEIGHT MOTOR
YEL
LT BLU
FRWD
BACK
REAR HGT
UP
ENTIRE SEAT
FNT HGT
DN
DOWN
POWER SEAT SW
HEADLT SW
INST CLSTR
INST LPS FUSE
BRN
PNK-BLK
GRY-BLK
PRNDL LT
PRNDL LT RLY (W/ DIGITAL CLSTR)
HORN/DM FUSE
FRONT DOME LT
REAR DOME LT
ORG (OR DK BLU)
WHT (OR BLK)
W/O AUXILIARY LIGHTING PACKAGE
RIGHT DOOR SW
BLK-ORG
INTERIOR LT SW
LEFT FNT DOOR SW
TURN/HAZ SW
W/ AUXILIARY LIGHTING PACKAGE
DOME & READING LT
(W/DOME & READING LTS)
REAR DOOR SW
SIDE DOOR SW
RIGHT FNT DOOR SW
FRONT READING LT
FRONT DOME LT
(W/ROOF CONSOLE)
DOME LT SW
CONVENIENCE CNTR (GND)
INST LPS FUSE
RIGHT DOOR STEPWELL LT
SLIDING DOOR STEPWELL LT
LEFT DOOR STEPWELL LT
REAR READING LT
VANITY MIRROR
HORN/DM FUSE

1991 WIRING DIAGRAMS
Astro & Safari (Cont.)

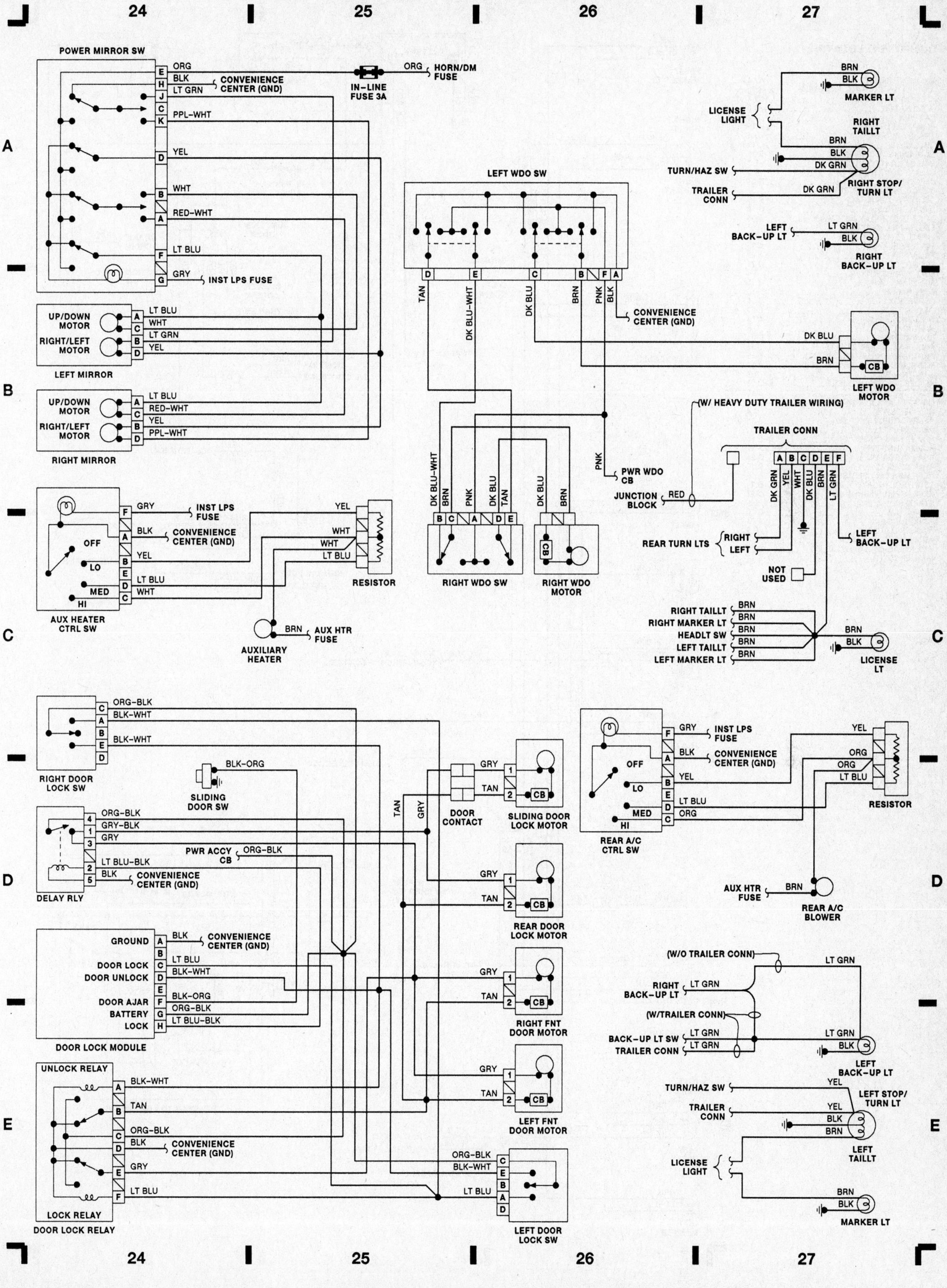
24
25
26
27
POWER MIRROR SW
ORG
BLK
LT GRN
CONVENIENCE CENTER (GND)
PPL-WHT
YEL
WHT
RED-WHT
LT BLU
GRY
INST LPS FUSE
IN-LINE FUSE 3A
HORN/DM FUSE
UP/DOWN MOTOR
RIGHT/LEFT MOTOR
LEFT MIRROR
RIGHT MIRROR
LEFT WDO SW
TAN
DK BLU-WHT
DK BLU
BRN
PNK
LEFT WDO MOTOR
PWR WDO CB
JUNCTION BLOCK
RED
(W/ HEAVY DUTY TRAILER WIRING)
TRAILER CONN
RIGHT WDO SW
RIGHT WDO MOTOR
MARKER LT
LICENSE LIGHT
RIGHT TAILLT
TURN/HAZ SW
DK GRN
RIGHT STOP/ TURN LT
LEFT BACK-UP LT
RIGHT BACK-UP LT
REAR TURN LTS
RIGHT
LEFT
NOT USED
HEADLT SW
LEFT TAILLT
LEFT MARKER LT
RIGHT MARKER LT
LICENSE LT
OFF
LO
MED
HI
AUX HEATER CTRL SW
RESISTOR
AUXILIARY HEATER
AUX HTR FUSE
RIGHT DOOR LOCK SW
ORG-BLK
BLK-WHT
BLK-ORG
SLIDING DOOR SW
DOOR CONTACT
SLIDING DOOR LOCK MOTOR
REAR DOOR LOCK MOTOR
RIGHT FNT DOOR MOTOR
LEFT FNT DOOR MOTOR
GRY-BLK
LT BLU-BLK
PWR ACCY CB
DELAY RLY
GROUND
DOOR LOCK
DOOR UNLOCK
DOOR AJAR
BATTERY
LOCK
DOOR LOCK MODULE
UNLOCK RELAY
LOCK RELAY
DOOR LOCK RELAY
LEFT DOOR LOCK SW
REAR A/C CTRL SW
REAR A/C BLOWER
(W/O TRAILER CONN)
(W/TRAILER CONN)
BACK-UP LT SW
LEFT STOP/ TURN LT
CB

1991 WIRING DIAGRAMS
Bravada

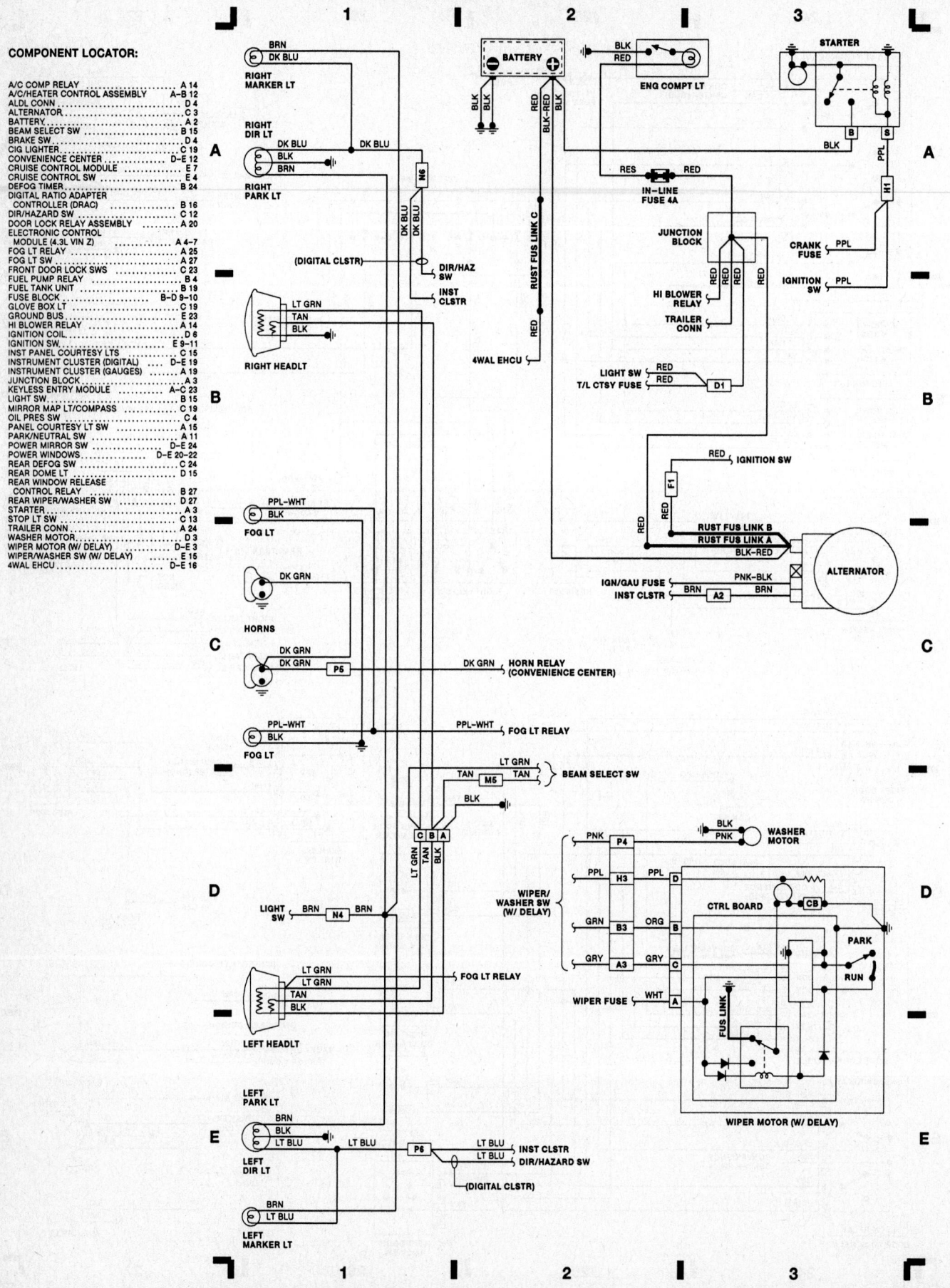

COMPONENT LOCATOR:

A/C COMP RELAY	A 14
A/C/HEATER CONTROL ASSEMBLY	A–B 12
ALDL CONN	D 4
ALTERNATOR	C 3
BATTERY	A 2
BEAM SELECT SW	B 15
BRAKE SW	D 4
CIG LIGHTER	C 19
CONVENIENCE CENTER	D–E 12
CRUISE CONTROL MODULE	E 7
CRUISE CONTROL SW	E 4
DEFOG TIMER	B 24
DIGITAL RATIO ADAPTER CONTROLLER (DRAC)	B 16
DIR/HAZARD SW	C 12
DOOR LOCK RELAY ASSEMBLY	A 20
ELECTRONIC CONTROL MODULE (4.3L VIN Z)	A 4–7
FOG LT RELAY	A 25
FOG LT SW	A 27
FRONT DOOR LOCK SWS	C 23
FUEL PUMP RELAY	B 4
FUEL TANK UNIT	B 19
FUSE BLOCK	B–D 9–10
GLOVE BOX LT	C 19
GROUND BUS	E 23
HI BLOWER RELAY	A 14
IGNITION COIL	D 6
IGNITION SW	E 9–11
INST PANEL COURTESY LTS	C 15
INSTRUMENT CLUSTER (DIGITAL)	D–E 19
INSTRUMENT CLUSTER (GAUGES)	A 19
JUNCTION BLOCK	A 3
KEYLESS ENTRY MODULE	A–C 23
LIGHT SW	B 15
MIRROR MAP LT/COMPASS	C 19
OIL PRES SW	C 4
PANEL COURTESY LT SW	A 15
PARK/NEUTRAL SW	A 11
POWER MIRROR SW	D–E 24
POWER WINDOWS	D–E 20–22
REAR DEFOG SW	C 24
REAR DOME LT	D 15
REAR WINDOW RELEASE CONTROL RELAY	B 27
REAR WIPER/WASHER SW	D 27
STARTER	A 3
STOP LT SW	C 13
TRAILER CONN	A 24
WASHER MOTOR	D 3
WIPER MOTOR (W/ DELAY)	D–E 3
WIPER/WASHER SW (W/ DELAY)	E 15
4WAL EHCU	D–E 16

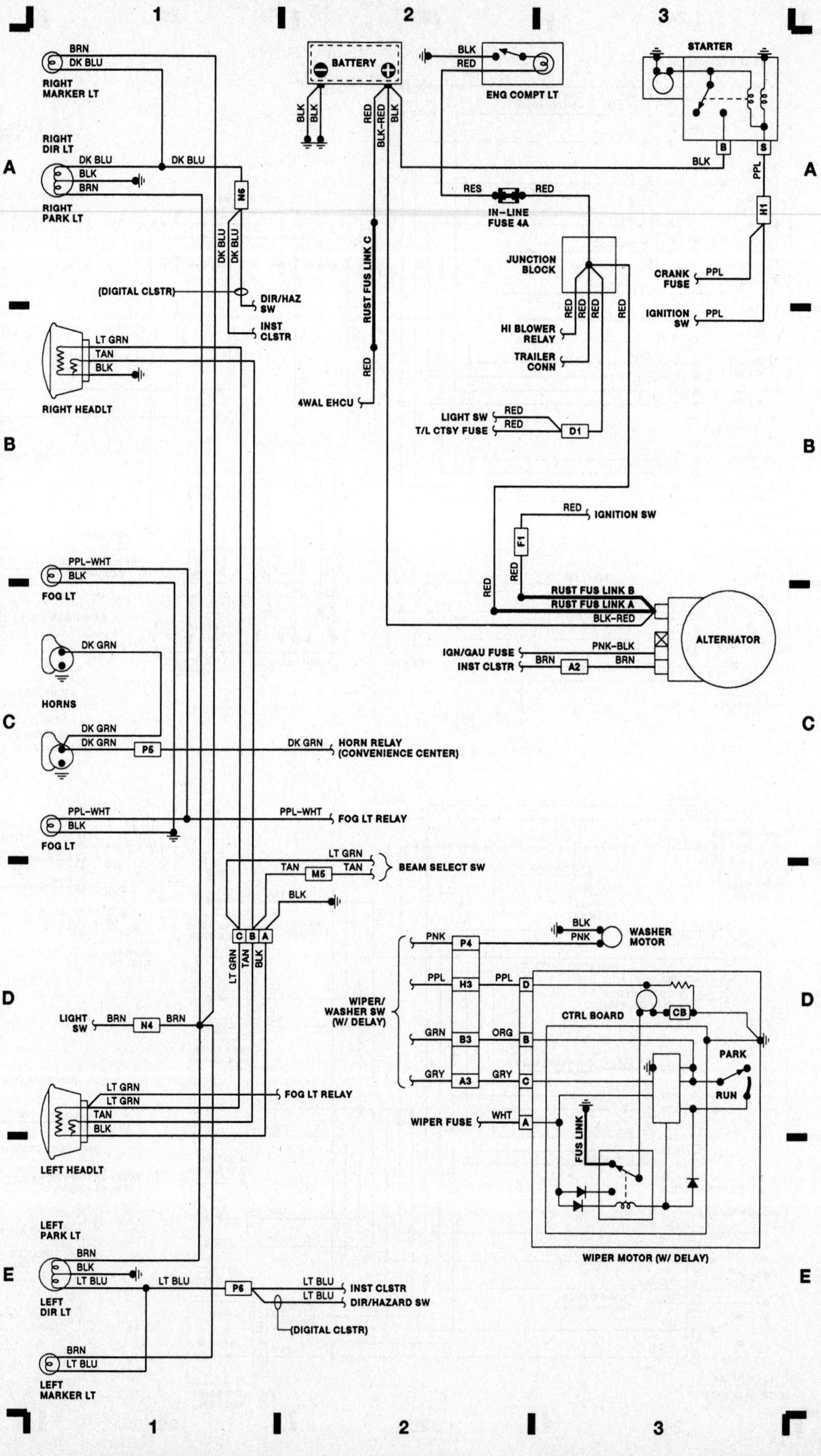
1
2
3
A
B
C
D
E
RIGHT MARKER LT
RIGHT DIR LT
RIGHT PARK LT
RIGHT HEADLT
FOG LT
HORNS
LEFT HEADLT
LEFT PARK LT
LEFT DIR LT
LEFT MARKER LT
BATTERY
ENG COMPT LT
STARTER
IN-LINE FUSE 4A
JUNCTION BLOCK
CRANK FUSE
IGNITION SW
HI BLOWER RELAY
TRAILER CONN
4WAL EHCU
LIGHT SW
T/L CTSY FUSE
RUST FUS LINK C
RUST FUS LINK B
RUST FUS LINK A
ALTERNATOR
IGN/GAU FUSE
INST CLSTR
(DIGITAL CLSTR)
DIR/HAZ SW
HORN RELAY (CONVENIENCE CENTER)
FOG LT RELAY
BEAM SELECT SW
WASHER MOTOR
WIPER/WASHER SW (W/ DELAY)
CTRL BOARD
PARK
RUN
WIPER FUSE
FUS LINK
WIPER MOTOR (W/ DELAY)
DIR/HAZARD SW

1991 WIRING DIAGRAMS
Bravada (Cont.)

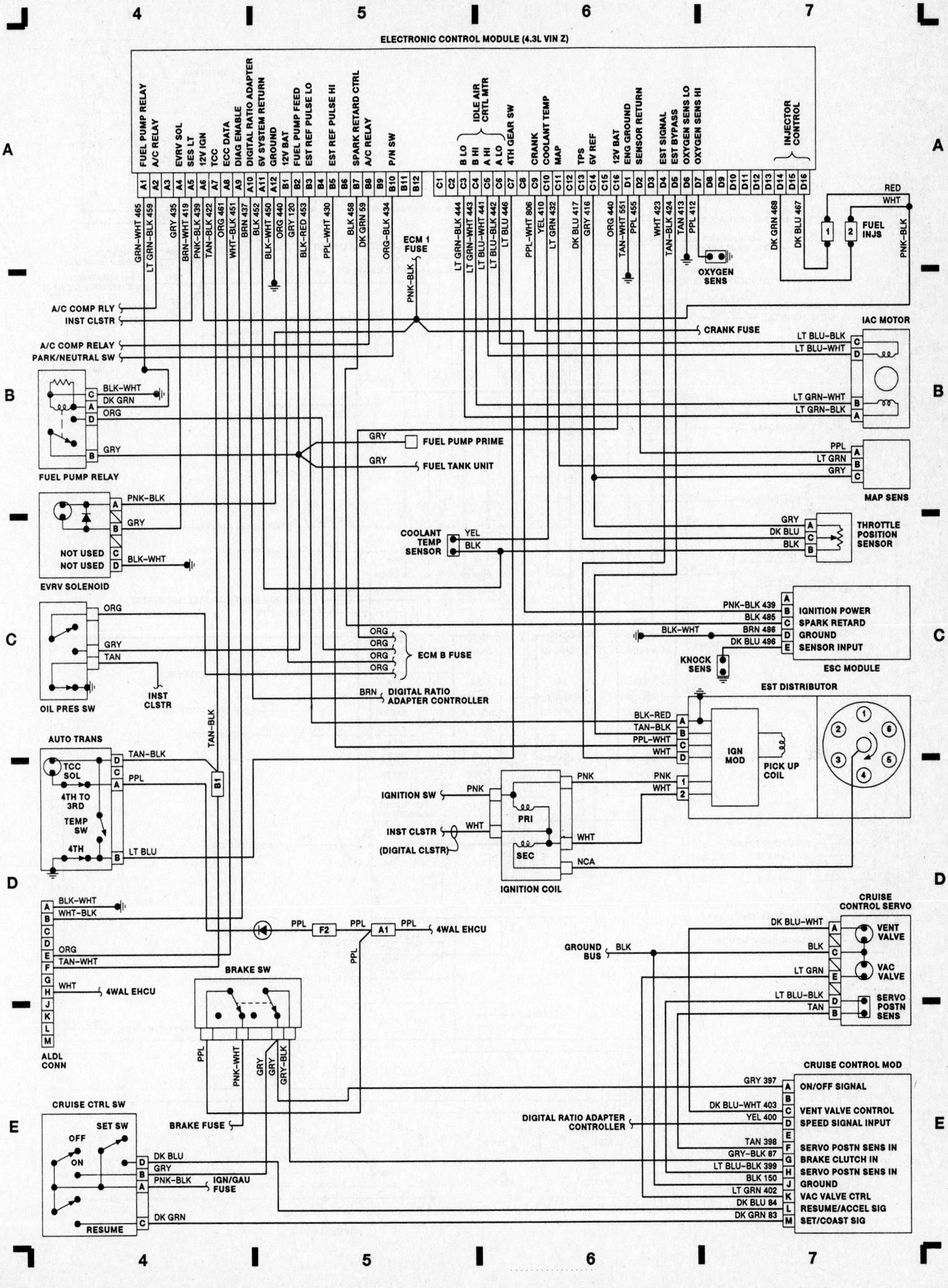
ELECTRONIC CONTROL MODULE (4.3L VIN Z)
FUEL PUMP RELAY
A/C RELAY
EVRV SOL
SES LT
12V IGN
TCC
ECC DATA
DIAG ENABLE
DIGITAL RATIO ADAPTER
5V SYSTEM RETURN
GROUND
12V BAT
FUEL PUMP FEED
EST REF PULSE LO
EST REF PULSE HI
SPARK RETARD CTRL
A/C RELAY
P/N SW
IDLE AIR CRTL MTR
B LO
B HI
A HI
A LO
4TH GEAR SW
CRANK
COOLANT TEMP
MAP
TPS
5V REF
12V BAT
ENG GROUND
SENSOR RETURN
EST SIGNAL
EST BYPASS
OXYGEN SENS LO
OXYGEN SENS HI
INJECTOR CONTROL
ECM 1 FUSE
OXYGEN SENS
FUEL INJS
A/C COMP RLY
INST CLSTR
A/C COMP RELAY
PARK/NEUTRAL SW
CRANK FUSE
IAC MOTOR
FUEL PUMP RELAY
FUEL PUMP PRIME
FUEL TANK UNIT
MAP SENS
EVRV SOLENOID
NOT USED
COOLANT TEMP SENSOR
THROTTLE POSITION SENSOR
IGNITION POWER
SPARK RETARD
GROUND
SENSOR INPUT
ESC MODULE
KNOCK SENS
OIL PRES SW
INST CLSTR
ECM B FUSE
DIGITAL RATIO ADAPTER CONTROLLER
EST DISTRIBUTOR
IGN MOD
PICK UP COIL
AUTO TRANS
TCC SOL
4TH TO 3RD TEMP SW
4TH
IGNITION SW
INST CLSTR
(DIGITAL CLSTR)
PRI
SEC
NCA
IGNITION COIL
CRUISE CONTROL SERVO
VENT VALVE
VAC VALVE
SERVO POSTN SENS
GROUND BUS
ALDL CONN
4WAL EHCU
BRAKE SW
BRAKE FUSE
CRUISE CTRL SW
OFF
ON
SET SW
RESUME
IGN/GAU FUSE
DIGITAL RATIO ADAPTER CONTROLLER
CRUISE CONTROL MOD
ON/OFF SIGNAL
VENT VALVE CONTROL
SPEED SIGNAL INPUT
SERVO POSTN SENS IN
BRAKE CLUTCH IN
SERVO POSTN SENS IN
GROUND
VAC VALVE CTRL
RESUME/ACCEL SIG
SET/COAST SIG

1991 WIRING DIAGRAMS
Bravada (Cont.)

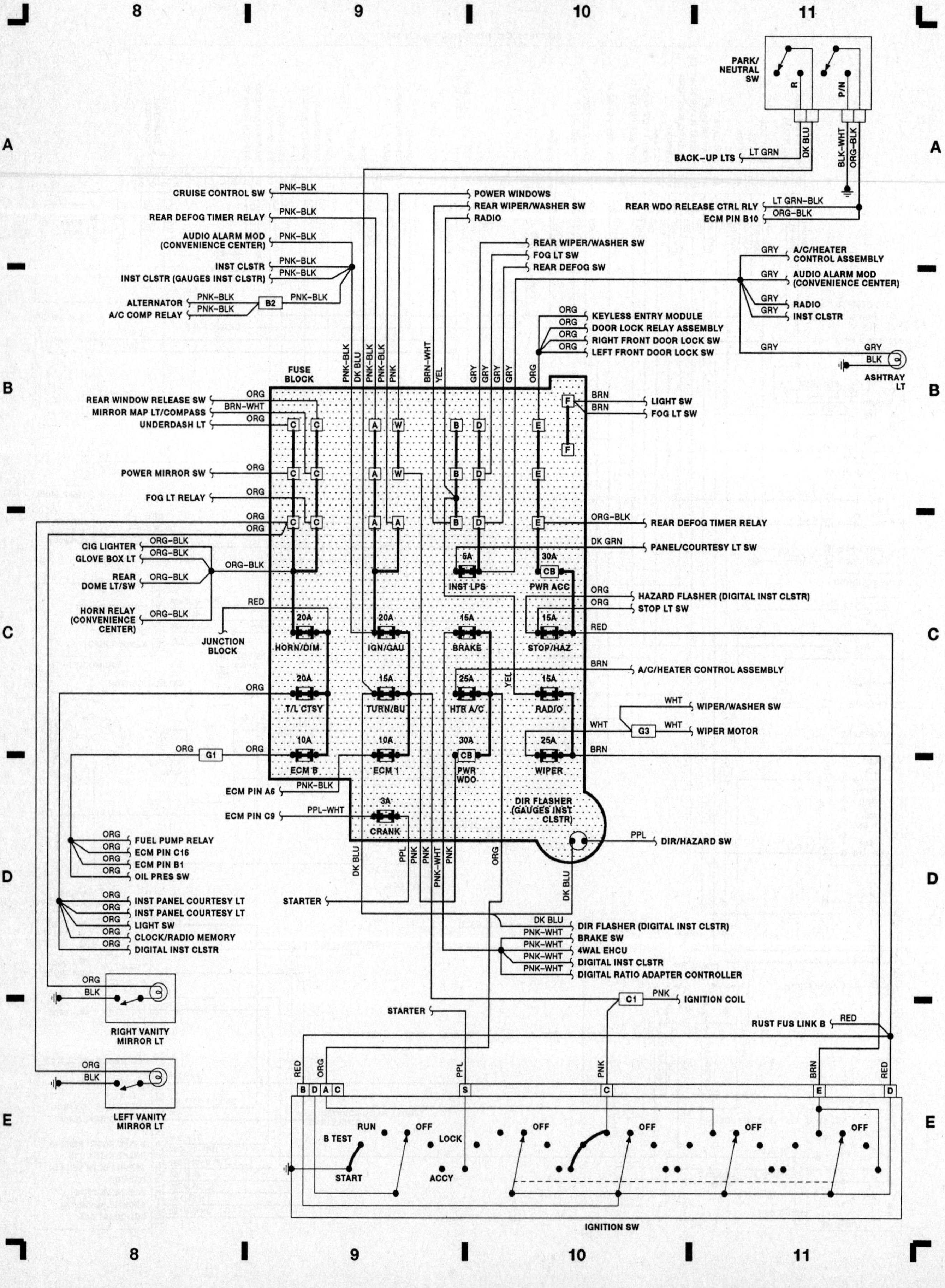
PARK/NEUTRAL SW
BACK-UP LTS
REAR WDO RELEASE CTRL RLY
ECM PIN B10
CRUISE CONTROL SW
REAR DEFOG TIMER RELAY
AUDIO ALARM MOD (CONVENIENCE CENTER)
INST CLSTR
INST CLSTR (GAUGES INST CLSTR)
ALTERNATOR
A/C COMP RELAY
POWER WINDOWS
REAR WIPER/WASHER SW
RADIO
FOG LT SW
REAR DEFOG SW
A/C/HEATER CONTROL ASSEMBLY
KEYLESS ENTRY MODULE
DOOR LOCK RELAY ASSEMBLY
RIGHT FRONT DOOR LOCK SW
LEFT FRONT DOOR LOCK SW
ASHTRAY LT
FUSE BLOCK
REAR WINDOW RELEASE SW
MIRROR MAP LT/COMPASS
UNDERDASH LT
LIGHT SW
POWER MIRROR SW
FOG LT RELAY
PANEL/COURTESY LT SW
CIG LIGHTER
GLOVE BOX LT
REAR DOME LT/SW
HORN RELAY (CONVENIENCE CENTER)
JUNCTION BLOCK
INST LPS
PWR ACC
HAZARD FLASHER (DIGITAL INST CLSTR)
STOP LT SW
HORN/DIM
IGN/GAU
BRAKE
STOP/HAZ
T/L CTSY
TURN/BU
HTR A/C
WIPER/WASHER SW
WIPER MOTOR
ECM B
ECM 1
PWR WDO
WIPER
ECM PIN A6
ECM PIN C9
CRANK
DIR FLASHER (GAUGES INST CLSTR)
DIR/HAZARD SW
FUEL PUMP RELAY
ECM PIN C16
ECM PIN B1
OIL PRES SW
INST PANEL COURTESY LT
INST PANEL COURTESY LT
LIGHT SW
CLOCK/RADIO MEMORY
DIGITAL INST CLSTR
STARTER
DIR FLASHER (DIGITAL INST CLSTR)
BRAKE SW
4WAL EHCU
DIGITAL INST CLSTR
DIGITAL RATIO ADAPTER CONTROLLER
RIGHT VANITY MIRROR LT
LEFT VANITY MIRROR LT
STARTER
IGNITION COIL
RUST FUS LINK B
B TEST
RUN
OFF
LOCK
START
ACCY
IGNITION SW

1991 WIRING DIAGRAMS
Bravada (Cont.)

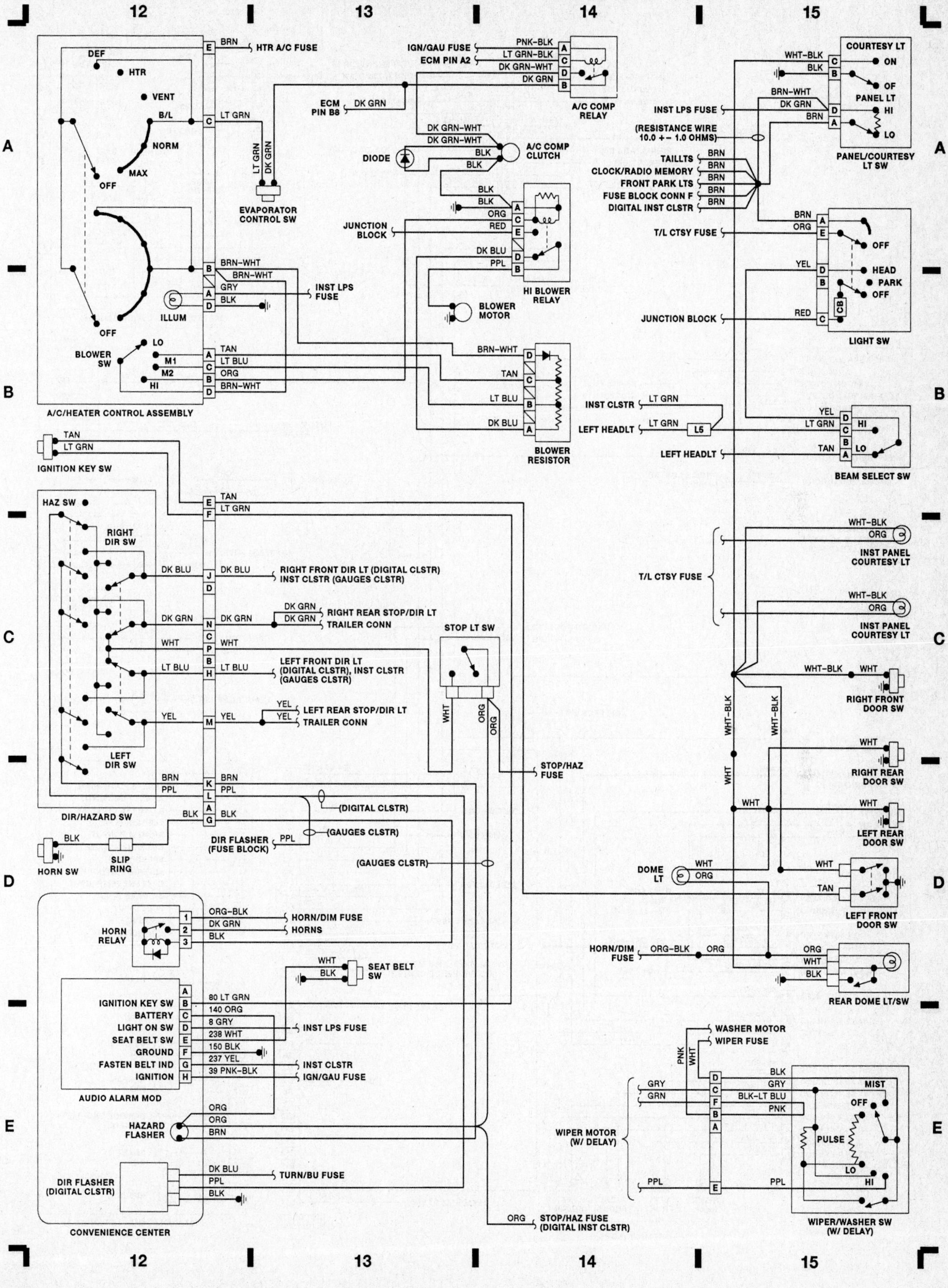
12
13
14
15
A
B
C
D
E
HTR A/C FUSE
DEF
HTR
VENT
B/L
NORM
MAX
OFF
OFF
ILLUM
BLOWER SW
LO
M1
M2
HI
A/C/HEATER CONTROL ASSEMBLY
BRN
LT GRN
BRN-WHT
GRY
BLK
TAN
LT BLU
ORG
EVAPORATOR CONTROL SW
ECM PIN B8
DK GRN
IGN/GAU FUSE
ECM PIN A2
PNK-BLK
LT GRN-BLK
DK GRN-WHT
A/C COMP RELAY
DIODE
A/C COMP CLUTCH
JUNCTION BLOCK
RED
DK BLU
PPL
HI BLOWER RELAY
BLOWER MOTOR
INST LPS FUSE
BLOWER RESISTOR
COURTESY LT
ON
OF
PANEL LT
HI
LO
PANEL/COURTESY LT SW
WHT-BLK
BRN-WHT
(RESISTANCE WIRE 10.0 +- 1.0 OHMS)
TAILLTS
CLOCK/RADIO MEMORY
FRONT PARK LTS
FUSE BLOCK CONN F
DIGITAL INST CLSTR
T/L CTSY FUSE
OFF
HEAD
PARK
YEL
CB
JUNCTION BLOCK
LIGHT SW
INST CLSTR
LEFT HEADLT
L5
BEAM SELECT SW
IGNITION KEY SW
HAZ SW
RIGHT DIR SW
LEFT DIR SW
DIR/HAZARD SW
RIGHT FRONT DIR LT (DIGITAL CLSTR)
INST CLSTR (GAUGES CLSTR)
RIGHT REAR STOP/DIR LT
TRAILER CONN
STOP LT SW
WHT
LEFT FRONT DIR LT (DIGITAL CLSTR), INST CLSTR (GAUGES CLSTR)
LEFT REAR STOP/DIR LT
TRAILER CONN
STOP/HAZ FUSE
(DIGITAL CLSTR)
(GAUGES CLSTR)
DIR FLASHER (FUSE BLOCK)
HORN SW
SLIP RING
INST PANEL COURTESY LT
INST PANEL COURTESY LT
RIGHT FRONT DOOR SW
RIGHT REAR DOOR SW
LEFT REAR DOOR SW
DOME LT
LEFT FRONT DOOR SW
HORN/DIM FUSE
ORG-BLK
REAR DOME LT/SW
HORN RELAY
HORN/DIM FUSE
HORNS
SEAT BELT SW
IGNITION KEY SW
BATTERY
LIGHT ON SW
SEAT BELT SW
GROUND
FASTEN BELT IND
IGNITION
80 LT GRN
140 ORG
8 GRY
238 WHT
150 BLK
237 YEL
39 PNK-BLK
INST LPS FUSE
INST CLSTR
IGN/GAU FUSE
AUDIO ALARM MOD
HAZARD FLASHER
DIR FLASHER (DIGITAL CLSTR)
TURN/BU FUSE
CONVENIENCE CENTER
STOP/HAZ FUSE (DIGITAL INST CLSTR)
WASHER MOTOR
WIPER FUSE
PNK
WIPER MOTOR (W/ DELAY)
GRN
BLK-LT BLU
MIST
OFF
PULSE
LO
HI
WIPER/WASHER SW (W/ DELAY)

1991 WIRING DIAGRAMS
Bravada (Cont.)

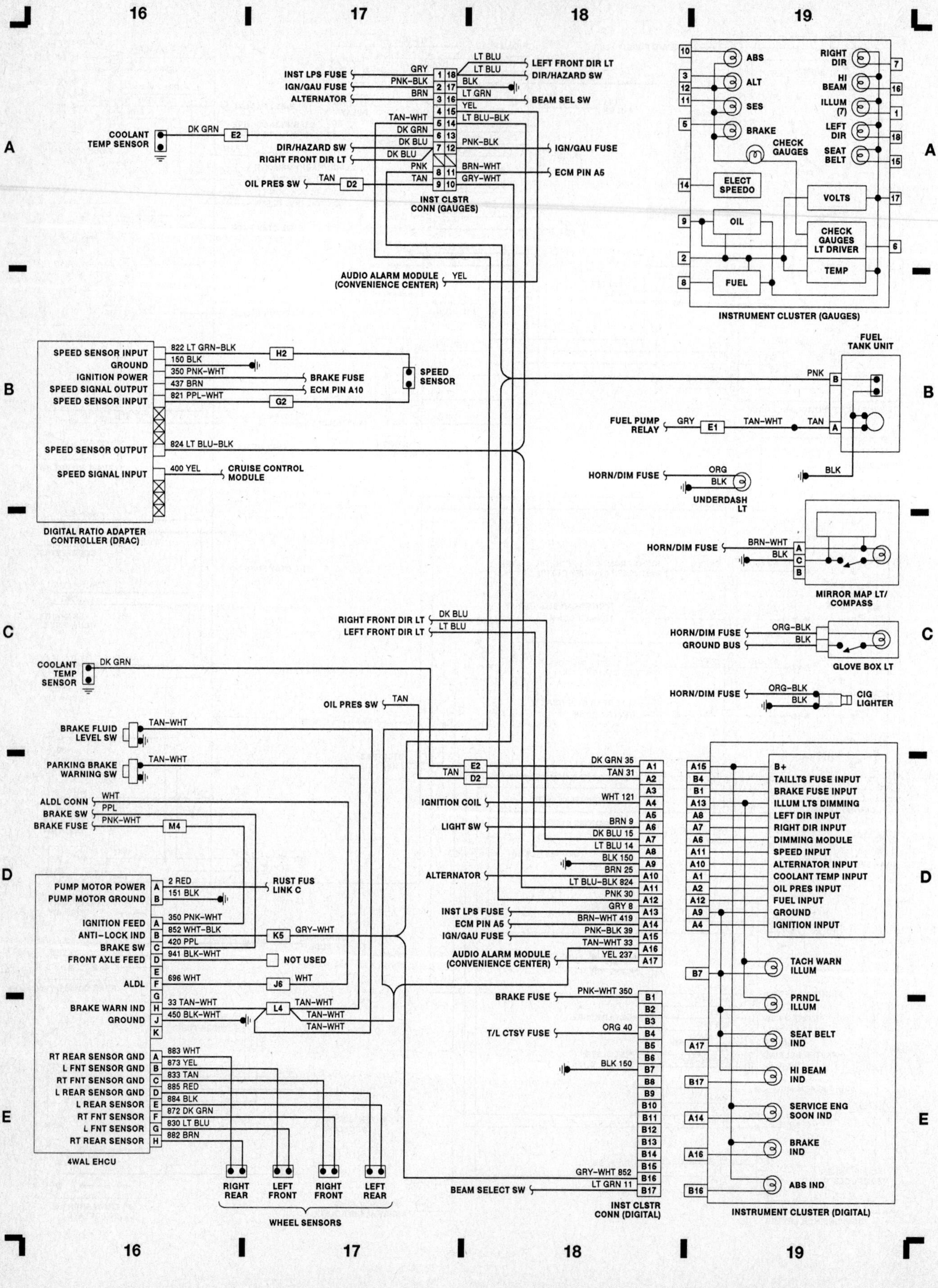
INST LPS FUSE
IGN/GAU FUSE
ALTERNATOR
LEFT FRONT DIR LT
DIR/HAZARD SW
BEAM SEL SW
COOLANT TEMP SENSOR
DIR/HAZARD SW
RIGHT FRONT DIR LT
IGN/GAU FUSE
ECM PIN A5
OIL PRES SW
INST CLSTR CONN (GAUGES)
AUDIO ALARM MODULE (CONVENIENCE CENTER)
ABS
ALT
SES
BRAKE
CHECK GAUGES
RIGHT DIR
HI BEAM
ILLUM (7)
LEFT DIR
SEAT BELT
ELECT SPEEDO
VOLTS
OIL
CHECK GAUGES LT DRIVER
TEMP
FUEL
INSTRUMENT CLUSTER (GAUGES)
SPEED SENSOR INPUT
GROUND
IGNITION POWER
SPEED SIGNAL OUTPUT
SPEED SENSOR INPUT
SPEED SENSOR OUTPUT
SPEED SIGNAL INPUT
DIGITAL RATIO ADAPTER CONTROLLER (DRAC)
BRAKE FUSE
ECM PIN A10
SPEED SENSOR
CRUISE CONTROL MODULE
FUEL TANK UNIT
FUEL PUMP RELAY
HORN/DIM FUSE
UNDERDASH LT
MIRROR MAP LT/ COMPASS
GLOVE BOX LT
GROUND BUS
CIG LIGHTER
RIGHT FRONT DIR LT
LEFT FRONT DIR LT
COOLANT TEMP SENSOR
OIL PRES SW
BRAKE FLUID LEVEL SW
PARKING BRAKE WARNING SW
ALDL CONN
BRAKE SW
BRAKE FUSE
IGNITION COIL
LIGHT SW
ALTERNATOR
INST LPS FUSE
ECM PIN A5
IGN/GAU FUSE
AUDIO ALARM MODULE (CONVENIENCE CENTER)
BRAKE FUSE
T/L CTSY FUSE
BEAM SELECT SW
INST CLSTR CONN (DIGITAL)
PUMP MOTOR POWER
PUMP MOTOR GROUND
IGNITION FEED
ANTI-LOCK IND
BRAKE SW
FRONT AXLE FEED
ALDL
BRAKE WARN IND
GROUND
RT REAR SENSOR GND
L FNT SENSOR GND
RT FNT SENSOR GND
L REAR SENSOR GND
L REAR SENSOR
RT FNT SENSOR
L FNT SENSOR
RT REAR SENSOR
4WAL EHCU
RUST FUS LINK C
NOT USED
RIGHT REAR
LEFT FRONT
RIGHT FRONT
LEFT REAR
WHEEL SENSORS
B+
TAILLTS FUSE INPUT
BRAKE FUSE INPUT
ILLUM LTS DIMMING
LEFT DIR INPUT
RIGHT DIR INPUT
DIMMING MODULE
SPEED INPUT
ALTERNATOR INPUT
COOLANT TEMP INPUT
OIL PRES INPUT
FUEL INPUT
GROUND
IGNITION INPUT
TACH WARN ILLUM
PRNDL ILLUM
SEAT BELT IND
HI BEAM IND
SERVICE ENG SOON IND
BRAKE IND
ABS IND
INSTRUMENT CLUSTER (DIGITAL)

1991 WIRING DIAGRAMS
Bravada (Cont.)

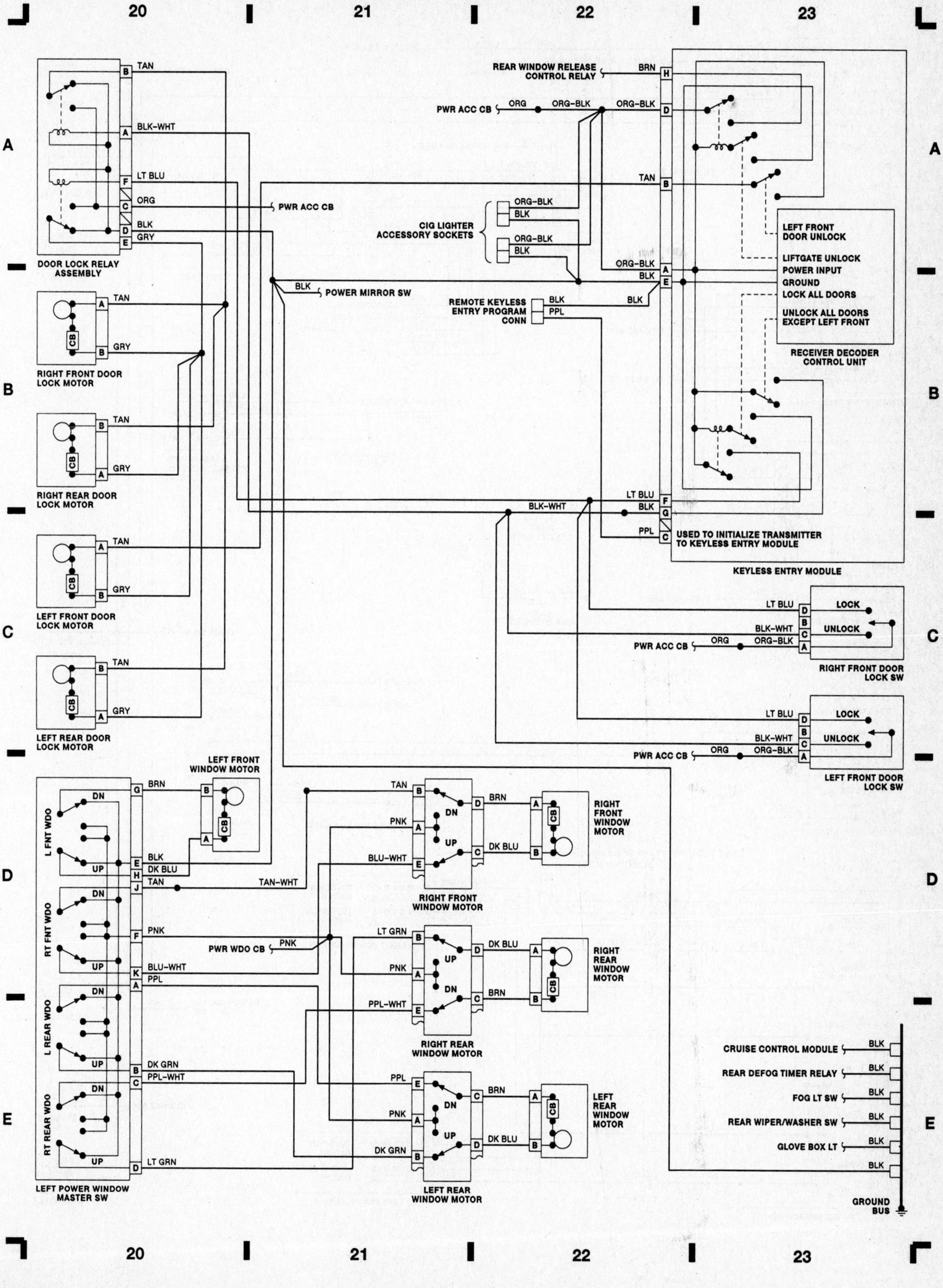
20
21
22
23
A
B
C
D
E
TAN
BLK-WHT
LT BLU
ORG
BLK
GRY
PWR ACC CB
DOOR LOCK RELAY ASSEMBLY
POWER MIRROR SW
RIGHT FRONT DOOR LOCK MOTOR
RIGHT REAR DOOR LOCK MOTOR
LEFT FRONT DOOR LOCK MOTOR
LEFT REAR DOOR LOCK MOTOR
CB
REAR WINDOW RELEASE CONTROL RELAY
BRN
ORG-BLK
CIG LIGHTER ACCESSORY SOCKETS
REMOTE KEYLESS ENTRY PROGRAM CONN
PPL
LEFT FRONT DOOR UNLOCK
LIFTGATE UNLOCK
POWER INPUT
GROUND
LOCK ALL DOORS
UNLOCK ALL DOORS EXCEPT LEFT FRONT
RECEIVER DECODER CONTROL UNIT
USED TO INITIALIZE TRANSMITTER TO KEYLESS ENTRY MODULE
KEYLESS ENTRY MODULE
LOCK
UNLOCK
RIGHT FRONT DOOR LOCK SW
LEFT FRONT DOOR LOCK SW
LEFT FRONT WINDOW MOTOR
L FNT WDO
RT FNT WDO
L REAR WDO
RT REAR WDO
DN
UP
DK BLU
TAN-WHT
PNK
BLU-WHT
PWR WDO CB
LT GRN
PPL-WHT
DK GRN
LEFT POWER WINDOW MASTER SW
RIGHT FRONT WINDOW MOTOR
RIGHT REAR WINDOW MOTOR
LEFT REAR WINDOW MOTOR
CRUISE CONTROL MODULE
REAR DEFOG TIMER RELAY
FOG LT SW
REAR WIPER/WASHER SW
GLOVE BOX LT
GROUND BUS

1991 WIRING DIAGRAMS
Bravada (Cont.)

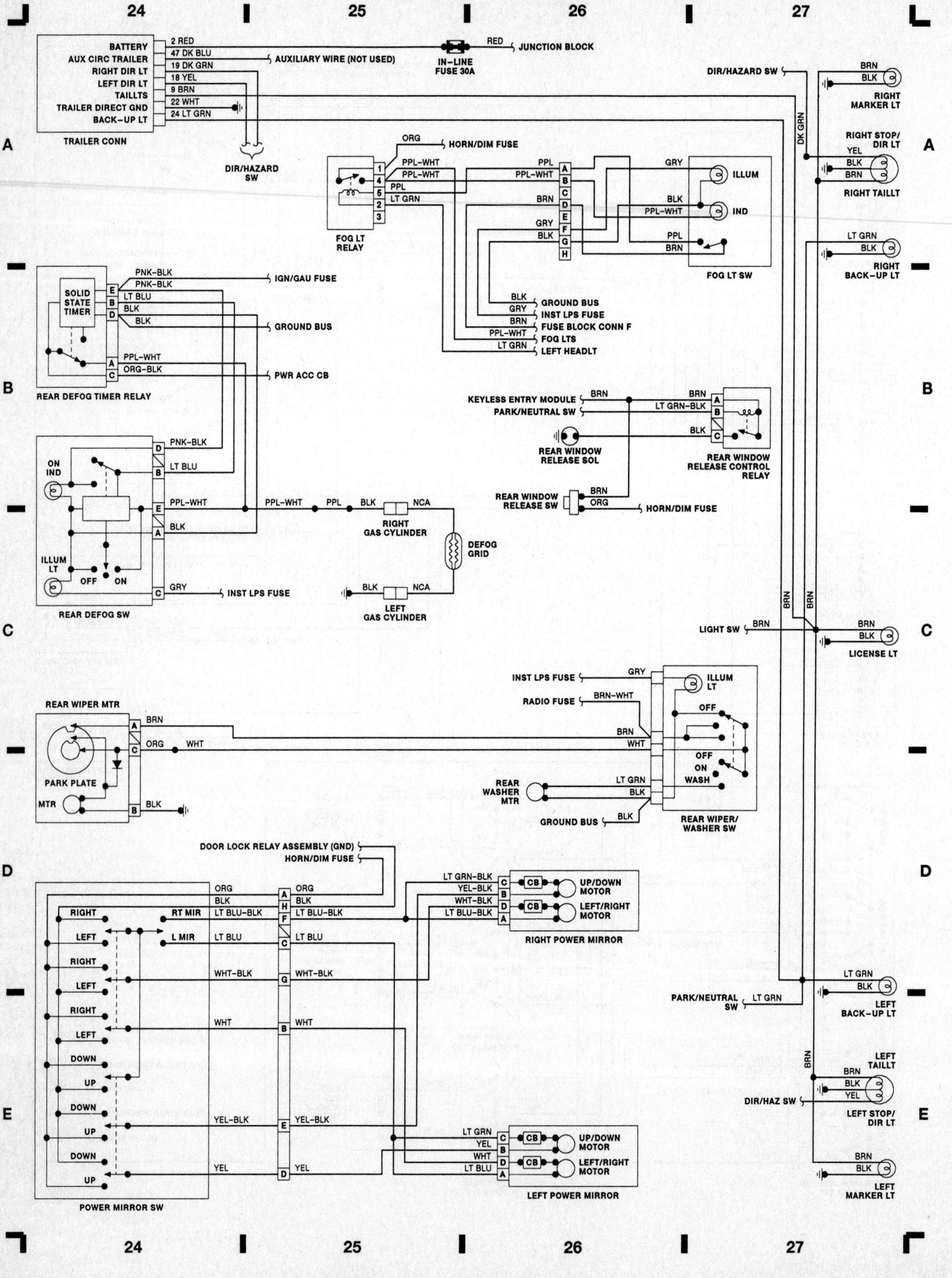
24
25
26
27
A
B
C
D
E
BATTERY
AUX CIRC TRAILER
RIGHT DIR LT
LEFT DIR LT
TAILLTS
TRAILER DIRECT GND
BACK-UP LT
2 RED
47 DK BLU
19 DK GRN
18 YEL
9 BRN
22 WHT
24 LT GRN
TRAILER CONN
AUXILIARY WIRE (NOT USED)
IN-LINE
FUSE 30A
RED
JUNCTION BLOCK
DIR/HAZARD
SW
DIR/HAZARD SW
DK GRN
RIGHT
MARKER LT
RIGHT STOP/
DIR LT
RIGHT TAILLT
RIGHT
BACK-UP LT
ORG
HORN/DIM FUSE
PPL-WHT
PPL
LT GRN
FOG LT
RELAY
GRY
BRN
BLK
ILLUM
IND
FOG LT SW
GROUND BUS
INST LPS FUSE
FUSE BLOCK CONN F
FOG LTS
LEFT HEADLT
SOLID
STATE
TIMER
PNK-BLK
LT BLU
IGN/GAU FUSE
ORG-BLK
PWR ACC CB
REAR DEFOG TIMER RELAY
KEYLESS ENTRY MODULE
PARK/NEUTRAL SW
LT GRN-BLK
REAR WINDOW
RELEASE SOL
REAR WINDOW
RELEASE CONTROL
RELAY
REAR WINDOW
RELEASE SW
ON
IND
ILLUM
LT
OFF
NCA
RIGHT
GAS CYLINDER
DEFOG
GRID
LEFT
GAS CYLINDER
REAR DEFOG SW
LIGHT SW
LICENSE LT
BRN-WHT
RADIO FUSE
REAR WIPER MTR
PARK PLATE
MTR
WHT
REAR
WASHER
MTR
WASH
REAR WIPER/
WASHER SW
DOOR LOCK RELAY ASSEMBLY (GND)
RT MIR
L MIR
LT BLU-BLK
WHT-BLK
YEL-BLK
YEL
RIGHT
LEFT
DOWN
UP
POWER MIRROR SW
CB
UP/DOWN
MOTOR
LEFT/RIGHT
MOTOR
RIGHT POWER MIRROR
LEFT POWER MIRROR
LEFT
BACK-UP LT
PARK/NEUTRAL
SW
LEFT
TAILLT
LEFT STOP/
DIR LT
DIR/HAZ SW
LEFT
MARKER LT

1991 WIRING DIAGRAMS
Lumina APV, Silhouette & Trans Sport

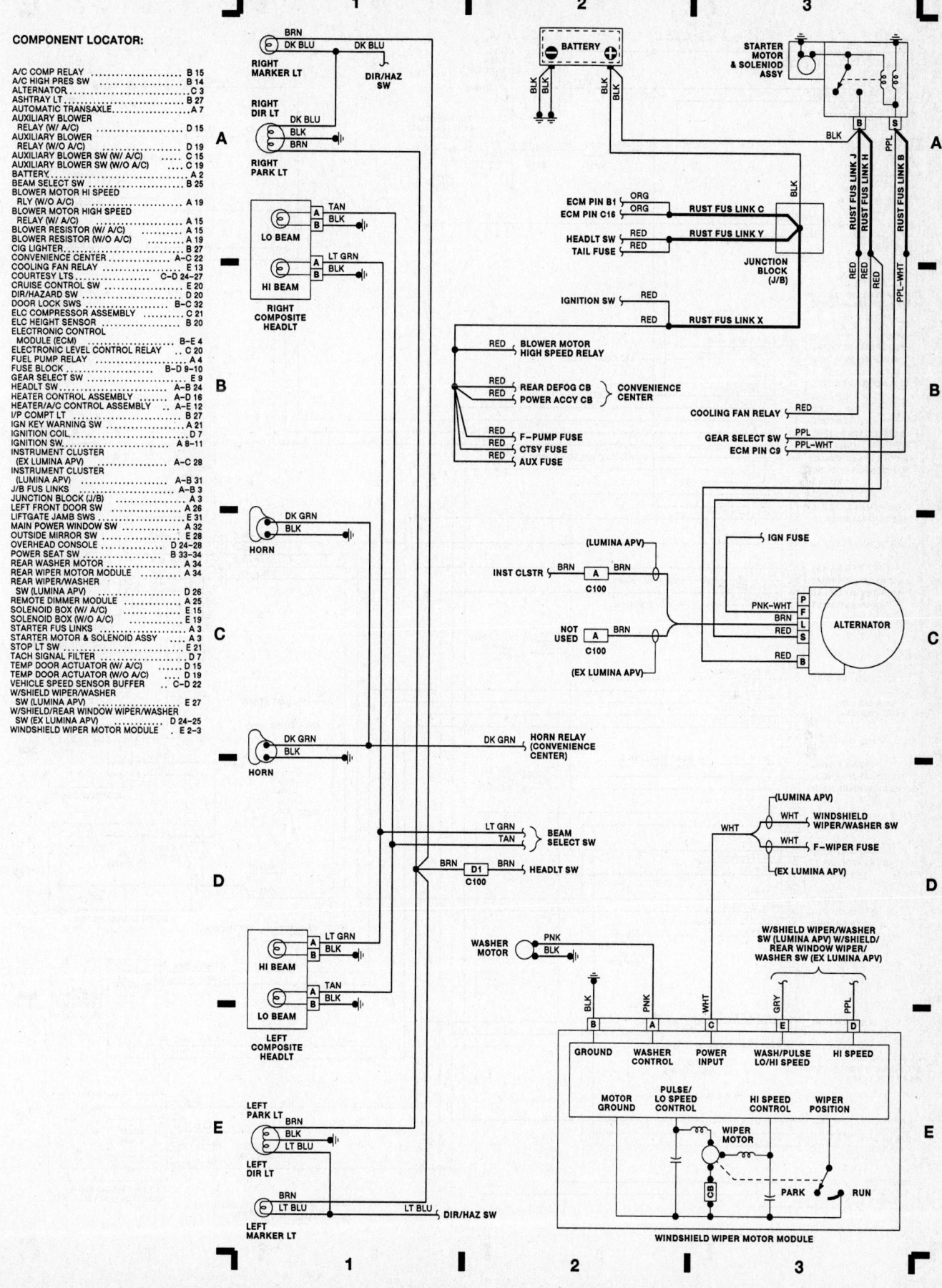

COMPONENT LOCATOR:

A/C COMP RELAY	B 15
A/C HIGH PRES SW	B 14
ALTERNATOR	C 3
ASHTRAY LT	B 27
AUTOMATIC TRANSAXLE	A 7
AUXILIARY BLOWER RELAY (W/ A/C)	D 15
AUXILIARY BLOWER RELAY (W/O A/C)	D 19
AUXILIARY BLOWER SW (W/ A/C)	C 15
AUXILIARY BLOWER SW (W/O A/C)	C 19
BATTERY	A 2
BEAM SELECT SW	B 25
BLOWER MOTOR HI SPEED RLY (W/O A/C)	A 19
BLOWER MOTOR HIGH SPEED RELAY (W/ A/C)	A 15
BLOWER RESISTOR (W/ A/C)	A 15
BLOWER RESISTOR (W/O A/C)	A 19
CIG LIGHTER	B 27
CONVENIENCE CENTER	A–C 22
COOLING FAN RELAY	E 13
COURTESY LTS	C–D 24–27
CRUISE CONTROL SW	E 20
DIR/HAZARD SW	D 20
DOOR LOCK SWS	B–C 32
ELC COMPRESSOR ASSEMBLY	C 21
ELC HEIGHT SENSOR	B 20
ELECTRONIC CONTROL MODULE (ECM)	B–E 4
ELECTRONIC LEVEL CONTROL RELAY	C 20
FUEL PUMP RELAY	A 4
FUSE BLOCK	B–D 9–10
GEAR SELECT SW	E 9
HEADLT SW	A–B 24
HEATER CONTROL ASSEMBLY	A–D 16
HEATER/A/C CONTROL ASSEMBLY	A–E 12
I/P COMPT LT	B 27
IGN KEY WARNING SW	A 21
IGNITION COIL	D 7
IGNITION SW	A 8–11
INSTRUMENT CLUSTER (EX LUMINA APV)	A–C 28
INSTRUMENT CLUSTER (LUMINA APV)	A–B 31
J/B FUS LINKS	A–B 3
JUNCTION BLOCK (J/B)	A 3
LEFT FRONT DOOR SW	A 26
LIFTGATE JAMB SWS	E 31
MAIN POWER WINDOW SW	A 32
OUTSIDE MIRROR SW	E 28
OVERHEAD CONSOLE	D 24–28
POWER SEAT SW	B 33–34
REAR WASHER MOTOR	A 34
REAR WIPER MOTOR MODULE	A 34
REAR WIPER/WASHER SW (LUMINA APV)	D 26
REMOTE DIMMER MODULE	A 25
SOLENOID BOX (W/ A/C)	E 15
SOLENOID BOX (W/O A/C)	E 19
STARTER FUS LINKS	A 3
STARTER MOTOR & SOLENOID ASSY	A 3
STOP LT SW	E 21
TACH SIGNAL FILTER	D 7
TEMP DOOR ACTUATOR (W/ A/C)	D 15
TEMP DOOR ACTUATOR (W/O A/C)	D 19
VEHICLE SPEED SENSOR BUFFER	C–D 22
W/SHIELD WIPER/WASHER SW (LUMINA APV)	E 27
W/SHIELD/REAR WINDOW WIPER/WASHER SW (EX LUMINA APV)	D 24–25
WINDSHIELD WIPER MOTOR MODULE	E 2–3

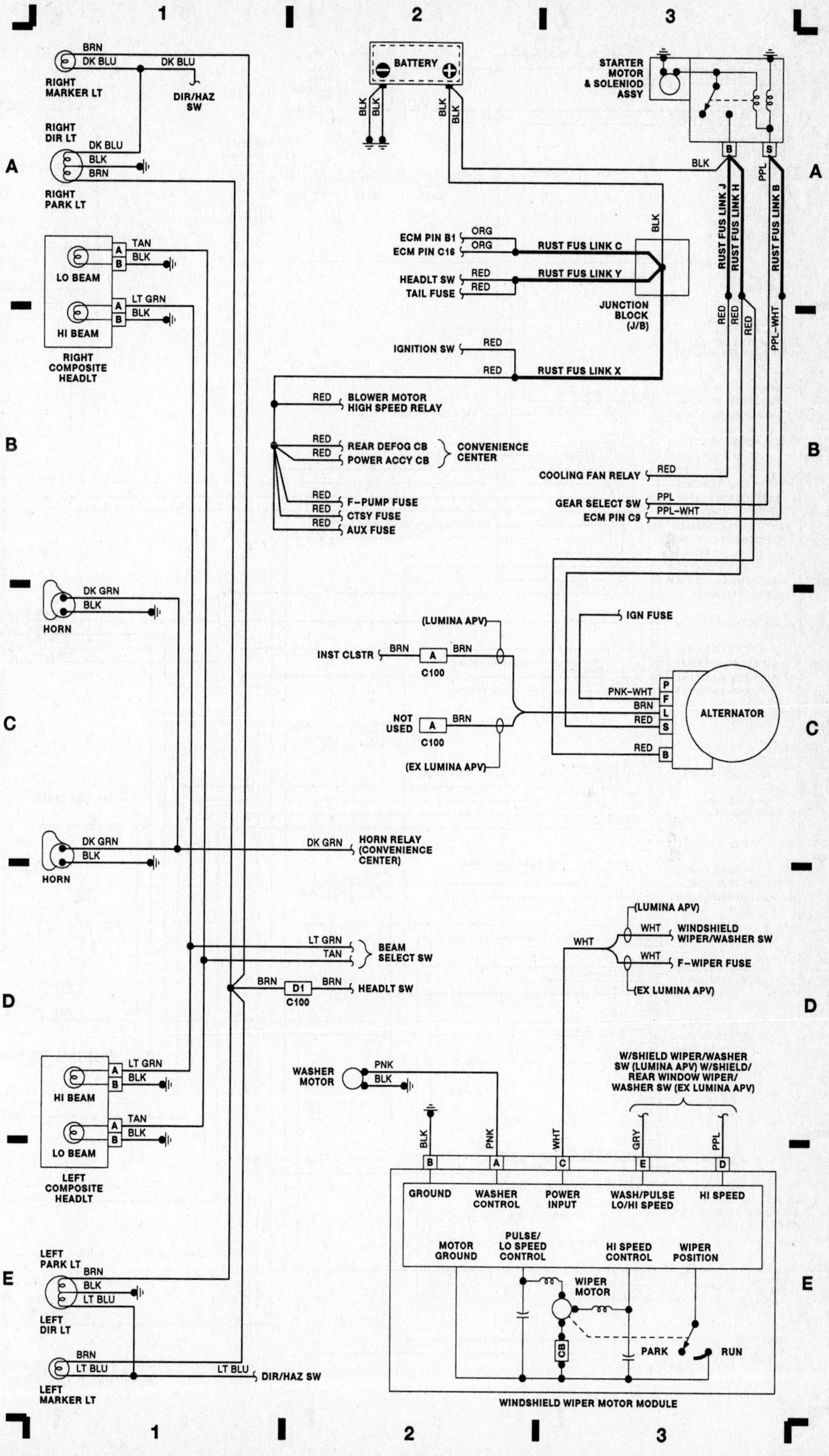
1
2
3
A
B
C
D
E
RIGHT MARKER LT
DIR/HAZ SW
RIGHT DIR LT
RIGHT PARK LT
LO BEAM
HI BEAM
RIGHT COMPOSITE HEADLT
BATTERY
STARTER MOTOR & SOLENIOD ASSY
ECM PIN B1
ECM PIN C16
RUST FUS LINK C
HEADLT SW
TAIL FUSE
RUST FUS LINK Y
JUNCTION BLOCK (J/B)
IGNITION SW
RUST FUS LINK X
RUST FUS LINK J
RUST FUS LINK H
RUST FUS LINK B
BLOWER MOTOR HIGH SPEED RELAY
REAR DEFOG CB
POWER ACCY CB
CONVENIENCE CENTER
COOLING FAN RELAY
GEAR SELECT SW
ECM PIN C9
F-PUMP FUSE
CTSY FUSE
AUX FUSE
HORN
IGN FUSE
(LUMINA APV)
INST CLSTR
C100
NOT USED
(EX LUMINA APV)
ALTERNATOR
HORN RELAY (CONVENIENCE CENTER)
BEAM SELECT SW
HEADLT SW
WINDSHIELD WIPER/WASHER SW
F-WIPER FUSE
WASHER MOTOR
W/SHIELD WIPER/WASHER SW (LUMINA APV) W/SHIELD/ REAR WINDOW WIPER/ WASHER SW (EX LUMINA APV)
LEFT COMPOSITE HEADLT
GROUND
WASHER CONTROL
POWER INPUT
WASH/PULSE LO/HI SPEED
HI SPEED
MOTOR GROUND
PULSE/ LO SPEED CONTROL
HI SPEED CONTROL
WIPER POSITION
WIPER MOTOR
PARK
RUN
LEFT PARK LT
LEFT DIR LT
LEFT MARKER LT
WINDSHIELD WIPER MOTOR MODULE

1991 WIRING DIAGRAMS
Lumina APV, Silhouette & Trans Sport (Cont.)

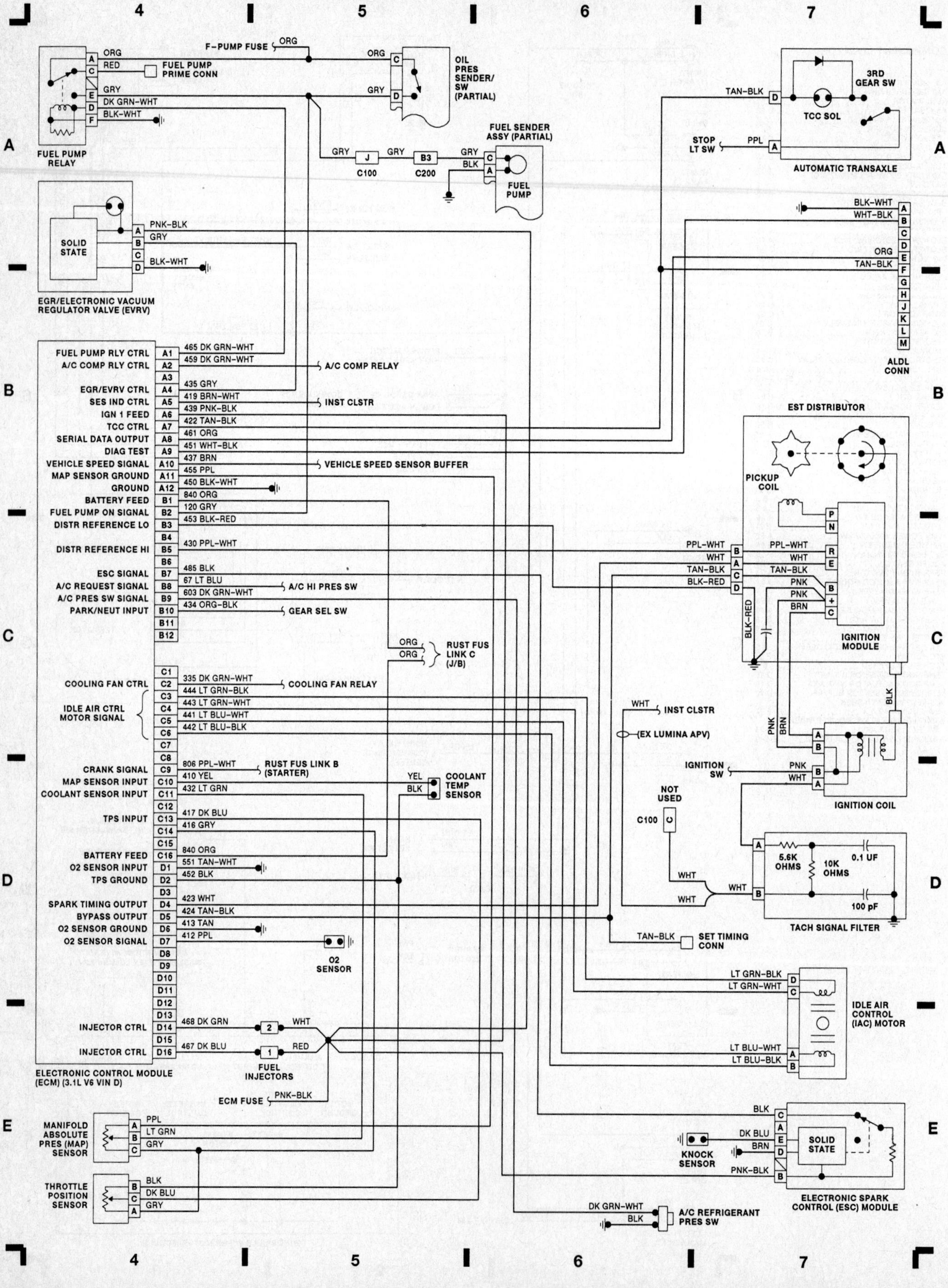
FUEL PUMP RELAY
F-PUMP FUSE
FUEL PUMP PRIME CONN
OIL PRES SENDER/ SW (PARTIAL)
FUEL SENDER ASSY (PARTIAL)
FUEL PUMP
C100
C200
3RD GEAR SW
TCC SOL
STOP LT SW
AUTOMATIC TRANSAXLE
SOLID STATE
EGR/ELECTRONIC VACUUM REGULATOR VALVE (EVRV)
ALDL CONN
FUEL PUMP RLY CTRL
A/C COMP RLY CTRL
EGR/EVRV CTRL
SES IND CTRL
IGN 1 FEED
TCC CTRL
SERIAL DATA OUTPUT
DIAG TEST
VEHICLE SPEED SIGNAL
MAP SENSOR GROUND
GROUND
BATTERY FEED
FUEL PUMP ON SIGNAL
DISTR REFERENCE LO
DISTR REFERENCE HI
ESC SIGNAL
A/C REQUEST SIGNAL
A/C PRES SW SIGNAL
PARK/NEUT INPUT
A/C COMP RELAY
INST CLSTR
VEHICLE SPEED SENSOR BUFFER
A/C HI PRES SW
GEAR SEL SW
RUST FUS LINK C (J/B)
EST DISTRIBUTOR
PICKUP COIL
IGNITION MODULE
COOLING FAN CTRL
IDLE AIR CTRL MOTOR SIGNAL
COOLING FAN RELAY
(EX LUMINA APV)
CRANK SIGNAL
MAP SENSOR INPUT
COOLANT SENSOR INPUT
RUST FUS LINK B (STARTER)
COOLANT TEMP SENSOR
IGNITION SW
IGNITION COIL
NOT USED
TPS INPUT
BATTERY FEED
O2 SENSOR INPUT
TPS GROUND
5.6K OHMS
10K OHMS
0.1 UF
100 pF
TACH SIGNAL FILTER
SPARK TIMING OUTPUT
BYPASS OUTPUT
O2 SENSOR GROUND
O2 SENSOR SIGNAL
O2 SENSOR
SET TIMING CONN
IDLE AIR CONTROL (IAC) MOTOR
INJECTOR CTRL
INJECTOR CTRL
FUEL INJECTORS
ELECTRONIC CONTROL MODULE (ECM) (3.1L V6 VIN D)
ECM FUSE
MANIFOLD ABSOLUTE PRES (MAP) SENSOR
KNOCK SENSOR
ELECTRONIC SPARK CONTROL (ESC) MODULE
THROTTLE POSITION SENSOR
A/C REFRIGERANT PRES SW

1991 WIRING DIAGRAMS
Lumina APV, Silhouette & Trans Sport (Cont.)

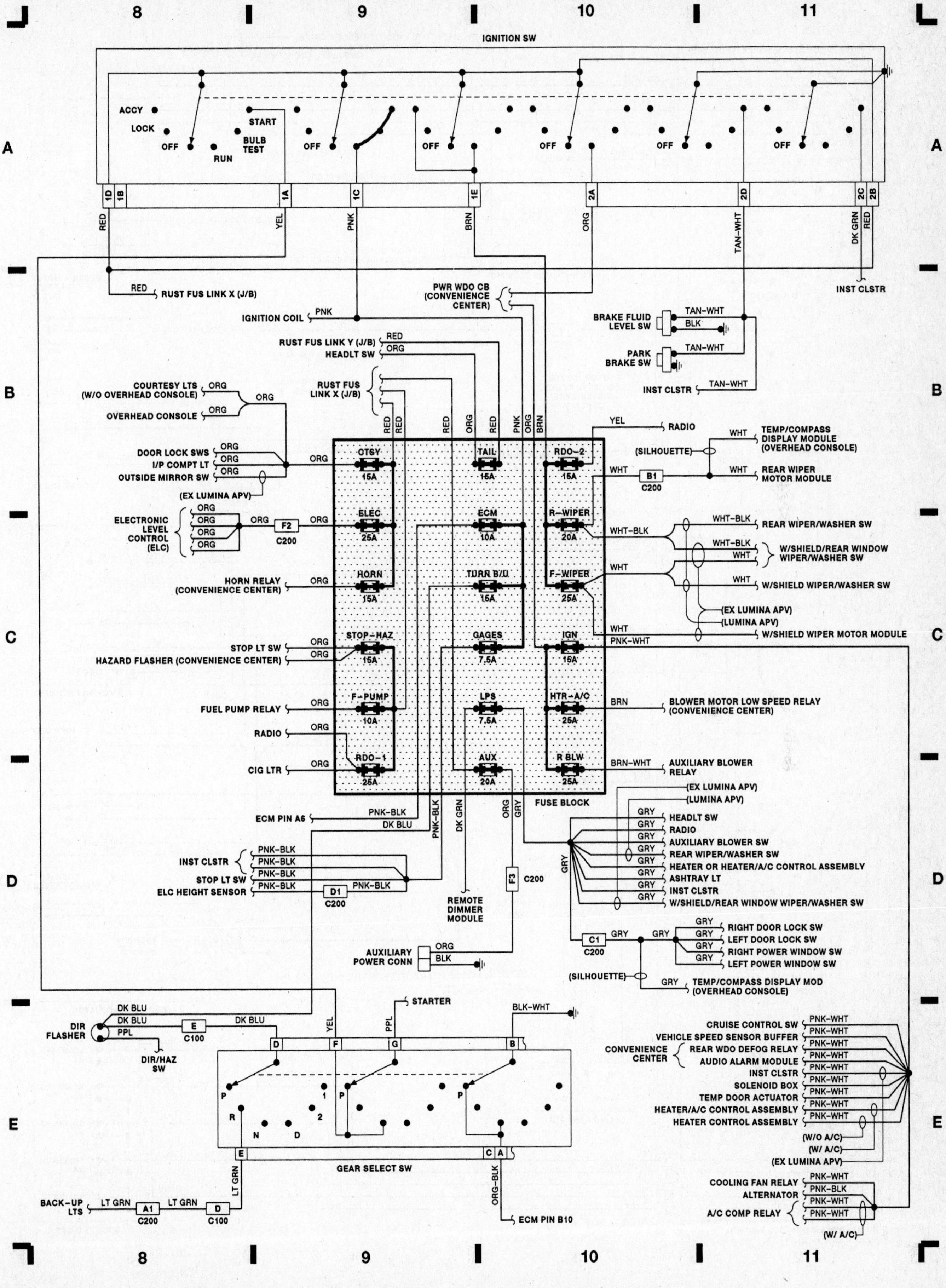
IGNITION SW
ACCY
LOCK
OFF
RUN
START
BULB TEST
RUST FUS LINK X (J/B)
IGNITION COIL
PWR WDO CB (CONVENIENCE CENTER)
RUST FUS LINK Y (J/B)
HEADLT SW
RUST FUS LINK X (J/B)
COURTESY LTS (W/O OVERHEAD CONSOLE)
OVERHEAD CONSOLE
BRAKE FLUID LEVEL SW
PARK BRAKE SW
INST CLSTR
DOOR LOCK SWS
I/P COMPT LT
OUTSIDE MIRROR SW
(EX LUMINA APV)
ELECTRONIC LEVEL CONTROL (ELC)
HORN RELAY (CONVENIENCE CENTER)
STOP LT SW
HAZARD FLASHER (CONVENIENCE CENTER)
FUEL PUMP RELAY
RADIO
CIG LTR
OTSY 15A
TAIL 15A
RDO-2 15A
ELEC 25A
ECM 10A
R-WIPER 20A
HORN 15A
TURN B/U 15A
F-WIPER 25A
STOP-HAZ 15A
GAGES 7.5A
IGN 15A
F-PUMP 10A
LPS 7.5A
HTR-A/C 25A
RDO-1 25A
AUX 20A
R BLW 25A
FUSE BLOCK
TEMP/COMPASS DISPLAY MODULE (OVERHEAD CONSOLE)
(SILHOUETTE)
REAR WIPER MOTOR MODULE
REAR WIPER/WASHER SW
W/SHIELD/REAR WINDOW WIPER/WASHER SW
W/SHIELD WIPER/WASHER SW
(EX LUMINA APV)
(LUMINA APV)
W/SHIELD WIPER MOTOR MODULE
BLOWER MOTOR LOW SPEED RELAY (CONVENIENCE CENTER)
AUXILIARY BLOWER RELAY
ECM PIN A6
INST CLSTR
STOP LT SW
ELC HEIGHT SENSOR
REMOTE DIMMER MODULE
AUXILIARY POWER CONN
HEADLT SW
RADIO
AUXILIARY BLOWER SW
REAR WIPER/WASHER SW
HEATER OR HEATER/A/C CONTROL ASSEMBLY
ASHTRAY LT
INST CLSTR
W/SHIELD/REAR WINDOW WIPER/WASHER SW
RIGHT DOOR LOCK SW
LEFT DOOR LOCK SW
RIGHT POWER WINDOW SW
LEFT POWER WINDOW SW
TEMP/COMPASS DISPLAY MOD (OVERHEAD CONSOLE)
DIR FLASHER
DIR/HAZ SW
STARTER
GEAR SELECT SW
BACK-UP LTS
ECM PIN B10
CONVENIENCE CENTER
CRUISE CONTROL SW
VEHICLE SPEED SENSOR BUFFER
REAR WDO DEFOG RELAY
AUDIO ALARM MODULE
INST CLSTR
SOLENOID BOX
TEMP DOOR ACTUATOR
HEATER/A/C CONTROL ASSEMBLY
HEATER CONTROL ASSEMBLY
(W/O A/C)
(W/ A/C)
(EX LUMINA APV)
COOLING FAN RELAY
ALTERNATOR
A/C COMP RELAY
(W/ A/C)

1991 WIRING DIAGRAMS
Lumina APV, Silhouette & Trans Sport (Cont.)

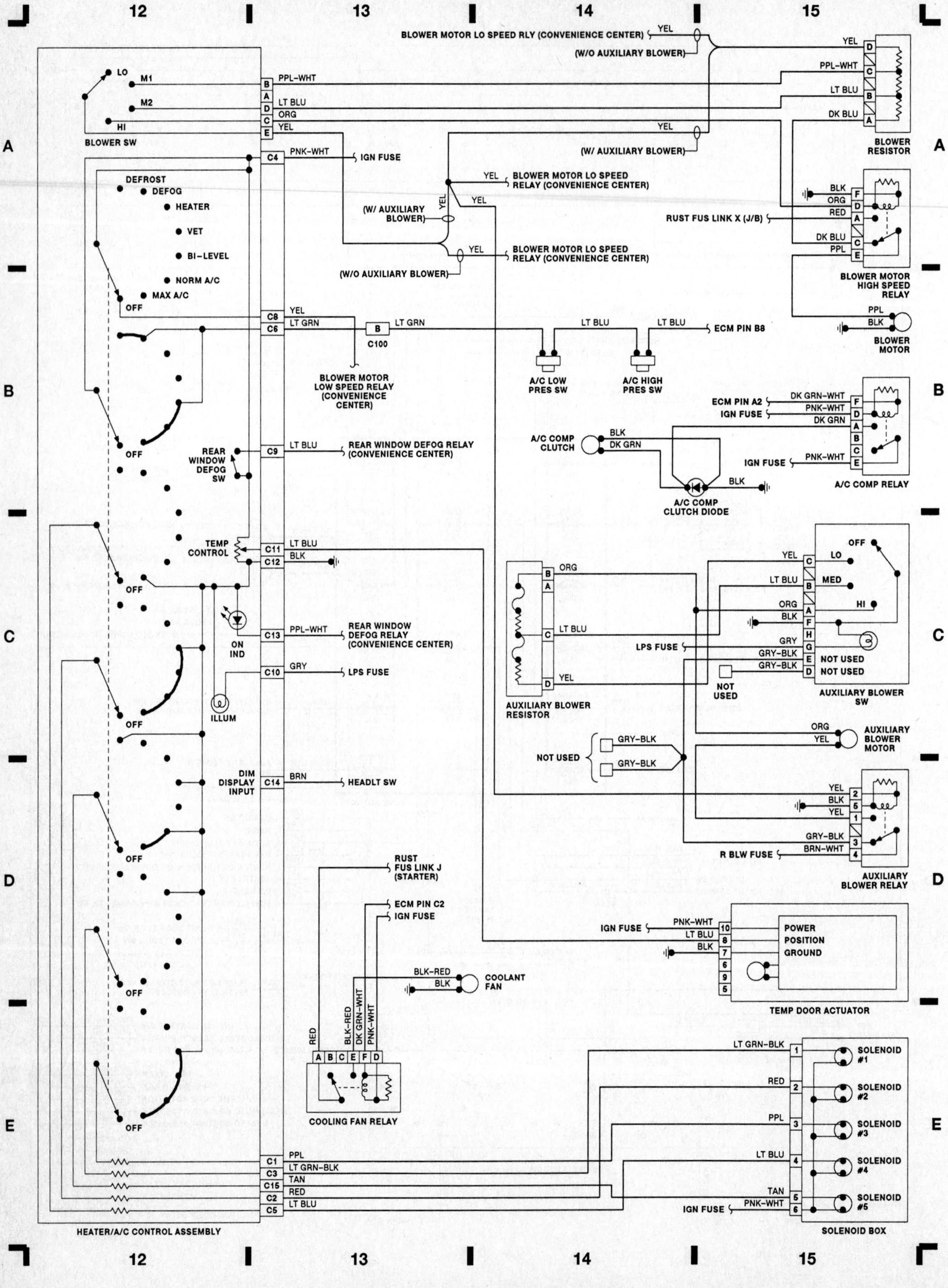
12
13
14
15
A
B
C
D
E
BLOWER MOTOR LO SPEED RLY (CONVENIENCE CENTER)
(W/O AUXILIARY BLOWER)
(W/ AUXILIARY BLOWER)
YEL
PPL-WHT
LT BLU
DK BLU
ORG
BLOWER RESISTOR
LO
M1
M2
HI
BLOWER SW
PNK-WHT
IGN FUSE
DEFROST
DEFOG
HEATER
VET
BI-LEVEL
NORM A/C
MAX A/C
OFF
BLOWER MOTOR LO SPEED RELAY (CONVENIENCE CENTER)
(W/ AUXILIARY BLOWER)
(W/O AUXILIARY BLOWER)
BLK
RED
RUST FUS LINK X (J/B)
PPL
BLOWER MOTOR HIGH SPEED RELAY
LT GRN
C100
ECM PIN B8
BLOWER MOTOR
BLOWER MOTOR LOW SPEED RELAY (CONVENIENCE CENTER)
A/C LOW PRES SW
A/C HIGH PRES SW
ECM PIN A2
DK GRN-WHT
DK GRN
A/C COMP CLUTCH
A/C COMP CLUTCH DIODE
A/C COMP RELAY
REAR WINDOW DEFOG SW
REAR WINDOW DEFOG RELAY (CONVENIENCE CENTER)
TEMP CONTROL
MED
ON IND
GRY
LPS FUSE
GRY-BLK
NOT USED
AUXILIARY BLOWER RESISTOR
AUXILIARY BLOWER SW
ILLUM
AUXILIARY BLOWER MOTOR
DIM DISPLAY INPUT
BRN
HEADLT SW
BRN-WHT
R BLW FUSE
AUXILIARY BLOWER RELAY
RUST FUS LINK J (STARTER)
ECM PIN C2
POWER
POSITION
GROUND
TEMP DOOR ACTUATOR
BLK-RED
COOLANT FAN
DK GRN-WHT
COOLING FAN RELAY
LT GRN-BLK
SOLENOID #1
SOLENOID #2
SOLENOID #3
SOLENOID #4
SOLENOID #5
TAN
SOLENOID BOX
HEATER/A/C CONTROL ASSEMBLY

1991 WIRING DIAGRAMS
Lumina APV, Silhouette & Trans Sport (Cont.)

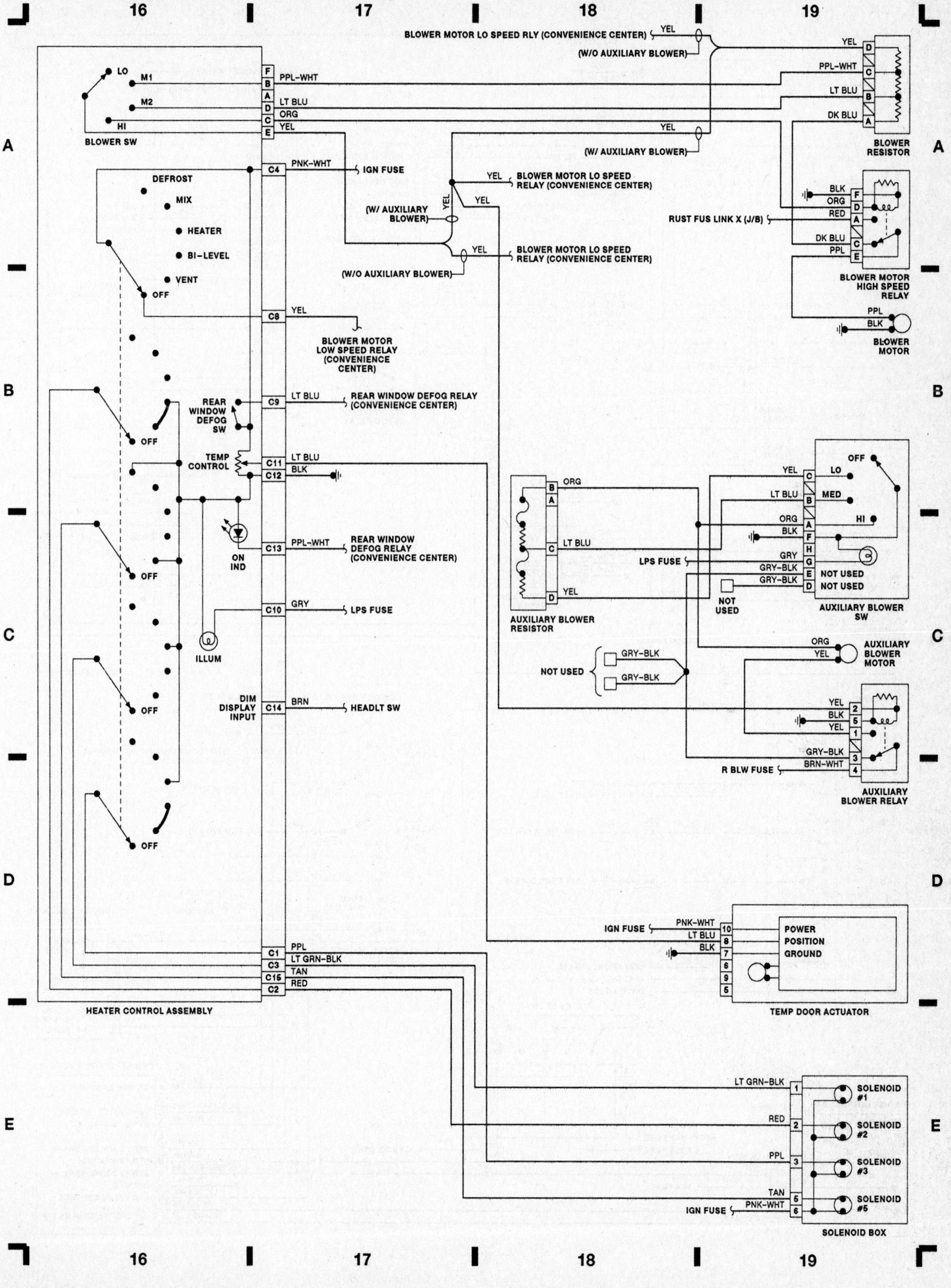
16
17
18
19
A
B
C
D
E
BLOWER MOTOR LO SPEED RLY (CONVENIENCE CENTER)
YEL
(W/O AUXILIARY BLOWER)
LO
M1
M2
HI
BLOWER SW
F
B
A
D
C
E
PPL-WHT
LT BLU
ORG
YEL
(W/ AUXILIARY BLOWER)
DK BLU
BLOWER RESISTOR
DEFROST
MIX
HEATER
BI-LEVEL
VENT
OFF
C4
PNK-WHT
IGN FUSE
BLOWER MOTOR LO SPEED RELAY (CONVENIENCE CENTER)
(W/ AUXILIARY BLOWER)
BLK
RED
RUST FUS LINK X (J/B)
PPL
BLOWER MOTOR HIGH SPEED RELAY
BLOWER MOTOR
C8
BLOWER MOTOR LOW SPEED RELAY (CONVENIENCE CENTER)
REAR WINDOW DEFOG SW
C9
REAR WINDOW DEFOG RELAY (CONVENIENCE CENTER)
TEMP CONTROL
C11
C12
ON IND
C13
C10
GRY
LPS FUSE
ILLUM
DIM DISPLAY INPUT
C14
BRN
HEADLT SW
AUXILIARY BLOWER RESISTOR
MED
GRY-BLK
NOT USED
AUXILIARY BLOWER SW
AUXILIARY BLOWER MOTOR
BRN-WHT
R BLW FUSE
AUXILIARY BLOWER RELAY
C1
C3
C15
C2
LT GRN-BLK
TAN
HEATER CONTROL ASSEMBLY
POWER
POSITION
GROUND
TEMP DOOR ACTUATOR
SOLENOID #1
SOLENOID #2
SOLENOID #3
SOLENOID #5
SOLENOID BOX

1991 WIRING DIAGRAMS
Lumina APV, Silhouette & Trans Sport (Cont.)

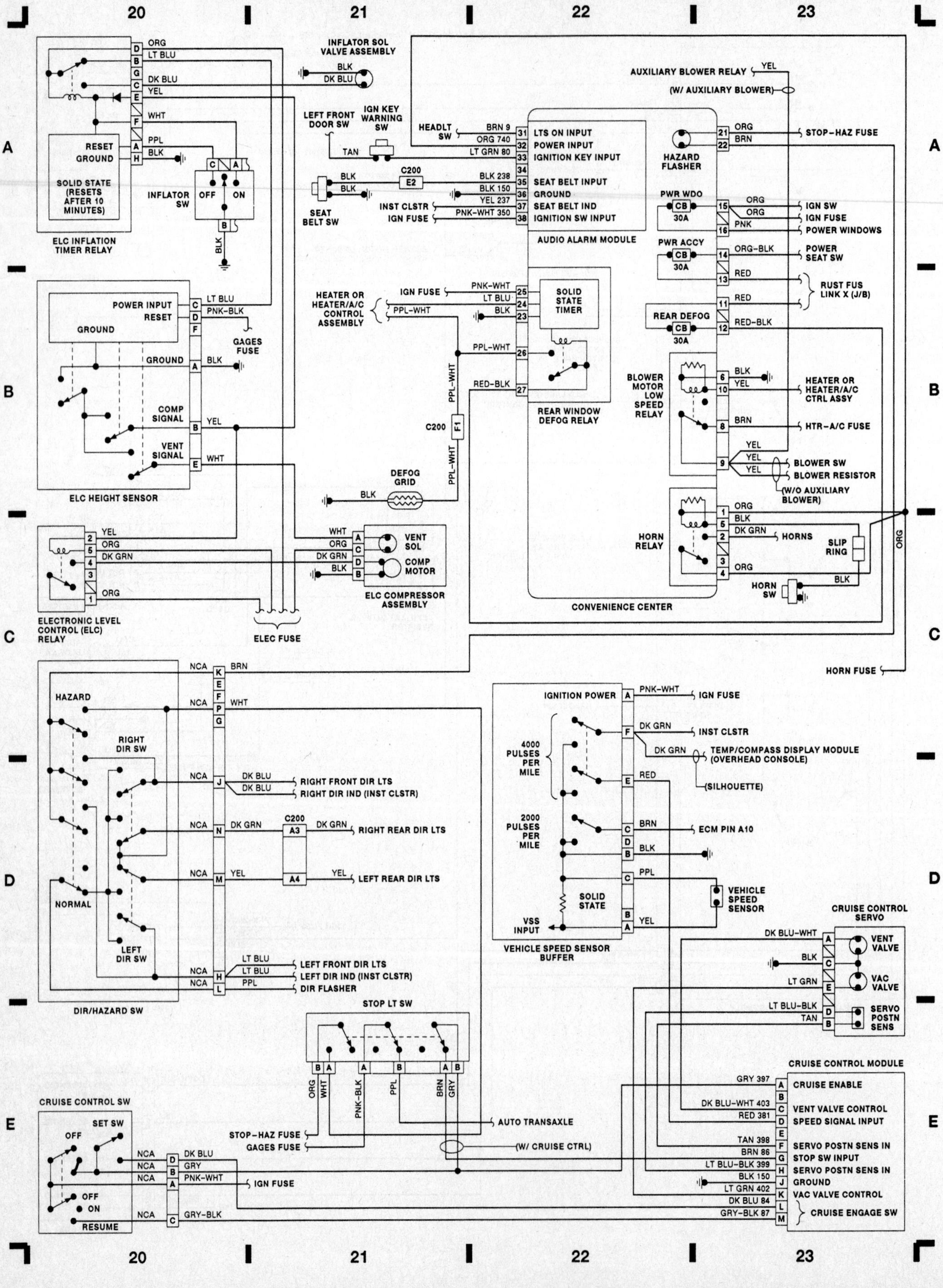
20
21
22
23
ELC INFLATION TIMER RELAY
SOLID STATE (RESETS AFTER 10 MINUTES)
INFLATOR SOL VALVE ASSEMBLY
INFLATOR SW
LEFT FRONT DOOR SW
IGN KEY WARNING SW
SEAT BELT SW
AUDIO ALARM MODULE
LTS ON INPUT
POWER INPUT
IGNITION KEY INPUT
SEAT BELT INPUT
GROUND
SEAT BELT IND
IGNITION SW INPUT
AUXILIARY BLOWER RELAY
(W/ AUXILIARY BLOWER)
HAZARD FLASHER
STOP-HAZ FUSE
PWR WDO
IGN SW
IGN FUSE
POWER WINDOWS
PWR ACCY
POWER SEAT SW
RUST FUS LINK X (J/B)
REAR DEFOG
ELC HEIGHT SENSOR
GAGES FUSE
HEATER OR HEATER/A/C CONTROL ASSEMBLY
SOLID STATE TIMER
REAR WINDOW DEFOG RELAY
BLOWER MOTOR LOW SPEED RELAY
HEATER OR HEATER/A/C CTRL ASSY
HTR-A/C FUSE
BLOWER SW
BLOWER RESISTOR
(W/O AUXILIARY BLOWER)
DEFOG GRID
HORN RELAY
HORNS
SLIP RING
HORN SW
CONVENIENCE CENTER
ELECTRONIC LEVEL CONTROL (ELC) RELAY
ELC COMPRESSOR ASSEMBLY
VENT SOL
COMP MOTOR
ELEC FUSE
HORN FUSE
DIR/HAZARD SW
HAZARD
RIGHT DIR SW
LEFT DIR SW
NORMAL
RIGHT FRONT DIR LTS
RIGHT DIR IND (INST CLSTR)
RIGHT REAR DIR LTS
LEFT REAR DIR LTS
LEFT FRONT DIR LTS
LEFT DIR IND (INST CLSTR)
DIR FLASHER
VEHICLE SPEED SENSOR BUFFER
IGNITION POWER
4000 PULSES PER MILE
2000 PULSES PER MILE
SOLID STATE
VSS INPUT
INST CLSTR
TEMP/COMPASS DISPLAY MODULE (OVERHEAD CONSOLE)
(SILHOUETTE)
ECM PIN A10
VEHICLE SPEED SENSOR
CRUISE CONTROL SERVO
VENT VALVE
VAC VALVE
SERVO POSTN SENS
STOP LT SW
AUTO TRANSAXLE
(W/ CRUISE CTRL)
CRUISE CONTROL SW
SET SW
OFF
ON
RESUME
CRUISE CONTROL MODULE
CRUISE ENABLE
VENT VALVE CONTROL
SPEED SIGNAL INPUT
SERVO POSTN SENS IN
STOP SW INPUT
SERVO POSTN SENS IN
GROUND
VAC VALVE CONTROL
CRUISE ENGAGE SW

1991 WIRING DIAGRAMS
Lumina APV, Silhouette & Trans Sport (Cont.)

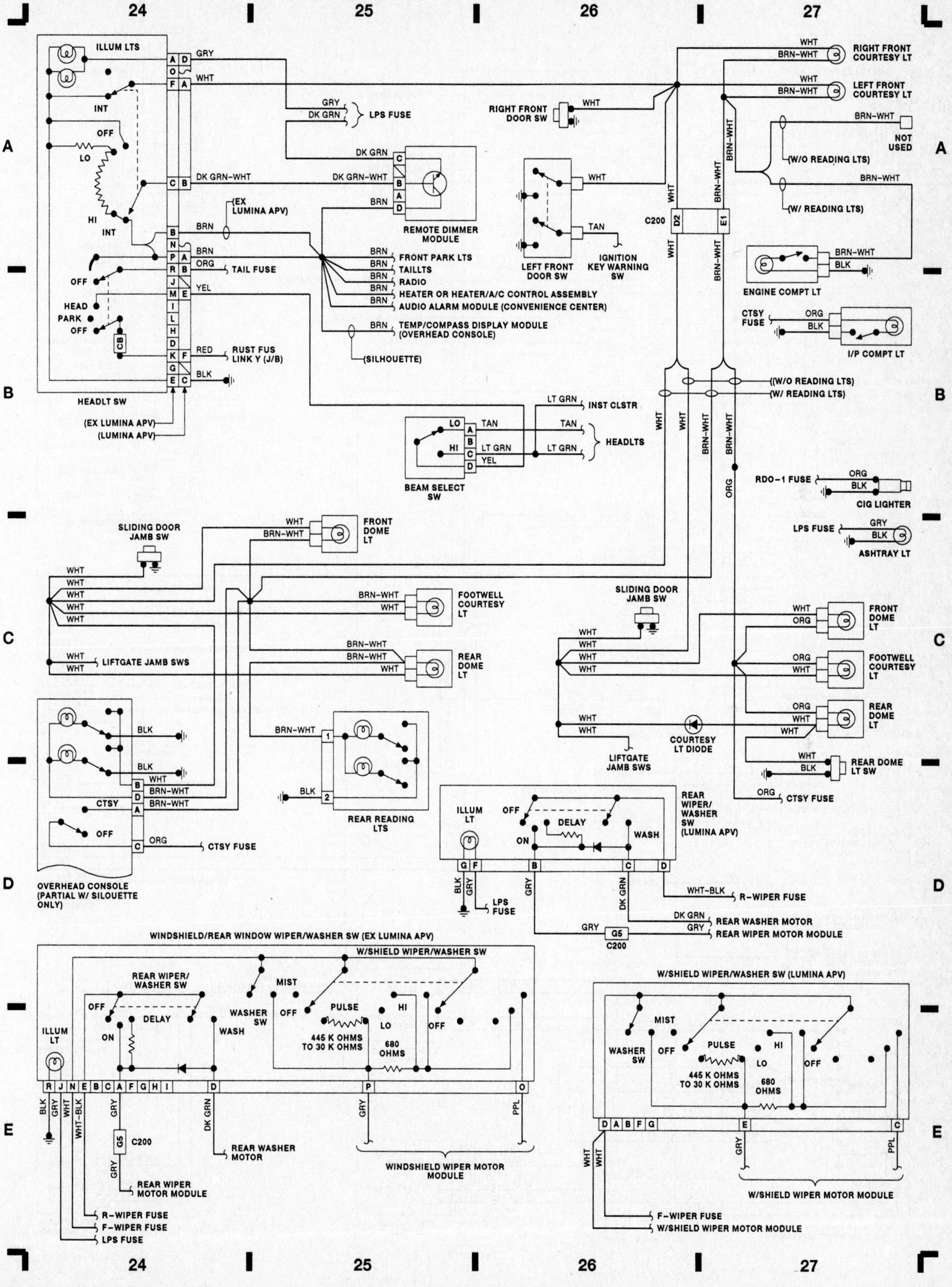

ILLUM LTS
HEADLT SW
(EX LUMINA APV)
(LUMINA APV)
LPS FUSE
TAIL FUSE
RUST FUS LINK Y (J/B)
REMOTE DIMMER MODULE
FRONT PARK LTS
TAILLTS
RADIO
HEATER OR HEATER/A/C CONTROL ASSEMBLY
AUDIO ALARM MODULE (CONVENIENCE CENTER)
TEMP/COMPASS DISPLAY MODULE (OVERHEAD CONSOLE)
(SILHOUETTE)
RIGHT FRONT DOOR SW
LEFT FRONT DOOR SW
IGNITION KEY WARNING SWS
RIGHT FRONT COURTESY LT
LEFT FRONT COURTESY LT
NOT USED
(W/O READING LTS)
(W/ READING LTS)
ENGINE COMPT LT
CTSY FUSE
I/P COMPT LT
INST CLSTR
HEADLTS
BEAM SELECT SW
RDO-1 FUSE
CIG LIGHTER
ASHTRAY LT
SLIDING DOOR JAMB SW
FRONT DOME LT
FOOTWELL COURTESY LT
REAR DOME LT
LIFTGATE JAMB SWS
COURTESY LT DIODE
REAR DOME LT SW
REAR READING LTS
OVERHEAD CONSOLE (PARTIAL W/ SILOUETTE ONLY)
REAR WIPER/WASHER SW (LUMINA APV)
R-WIPER FUSE
REAR WASHER MOTOR
REAR WIPER MOTOR MODULE
WINDSHIELD/REAR WINDOW WIPER/WASHER SW (EX LUMINA APV)
W/SHIELD WIPER/WASHER SW
445 K OHMS TO 30 K OHMS
680 OHMS
WINDSHIELD WIPER MOTOR MODULE
F-WIPER FUSE
W/SHIELD WIPER/WASHER SW (LUMINA APV)
W/SHIELD WIPER MOTOR MODULE

1991 WIRING DIAGRAMS
Lumina APV, Silhouette & Trans Sport (Cont.)

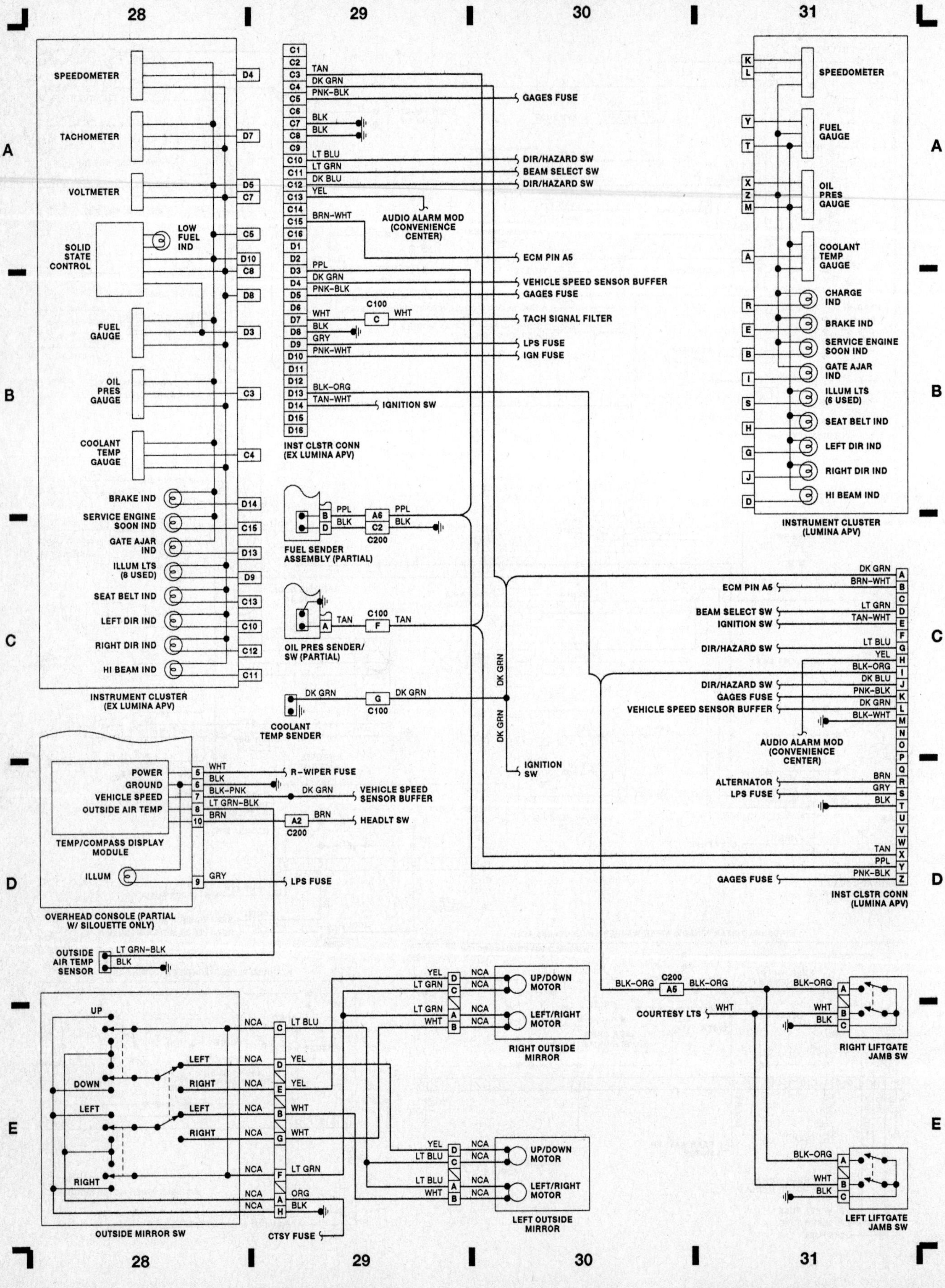
28
29
30
31
SPEEDOMETER
TACHOMETER
VOLTMETER
LOW FUEL IND
SOLID STATE CONTROL
FUEL GAUGE
OIL PRES GAUGE
COOLANT TEMP GAUGE
BRAKE IND
SERVICE ENGINE SOON IND
GATE AJAR IND
ILLUM LTS (8 USED)
SEAT BELT IND
LEFT DIR IND
RIGHT DIR IND
HI BEAM IND
INSTRUMENT CLUSTER (EX LUMINA APV)
GAGES FUSE
DIR/HAZARD SW
BEAM SELECT SW
AUDIO ALARM MOD (CONVENIENCE CENTER)
ECM PIN A5
VEHICLE SPEED SENSOR BUFFER
TACH SIGNAL FILTER
LPS FUSE
IGN FUSE
IGNITION SW
INST CLSTR CONN (EX LUMINA APV)
FUEL SENDER ASSEMBLY (PARTIAL)
OIL PRES SENDER/ SW (PARTIAL)
COOLANT TEMP SENDER
CHARGE IND
BRAKE IND
SERVICE ENGINE SOON IND
GATE AJAR IND
ILLUM LTS (6 USED)
SEAT BELT IND
LEFT DIR IND
RIGHT DIR IND
HI BEAM IND
INSTRUMENT CLUSTER (LUMINA APV)
ALTERNATOR
INST CLSTR CONN (LUMINA APV)
POWER
GROUND
VEHICLE SPEED
OUTSIDE AIR TEMP
TEMP/COMPASS DISPLAY MODULE
ILLUM
R-WIPER FUSE
HEADLT SW
OVERHEAD CONSOLE (PARTIAL W/ SILOUETTE ONLY)
OUTSIDE AIR TEMP SENSOR
UP/DOWN MOTOR
LEFT/RIGHT MOTOR
RIGHT OUTSIDE MIRROR
LEFT OUTSIDE MIRROR
OUTSIDE MIRROR SW
CTSY FUSE
COURTESY LTS
RIGHT LIFTGATE JAMB SW
LEFT LIFTGATE JAMB SW

1991 WIRING DIAGRAMS
Lumina APV, Silhouette & Trans Sport (Cont.)

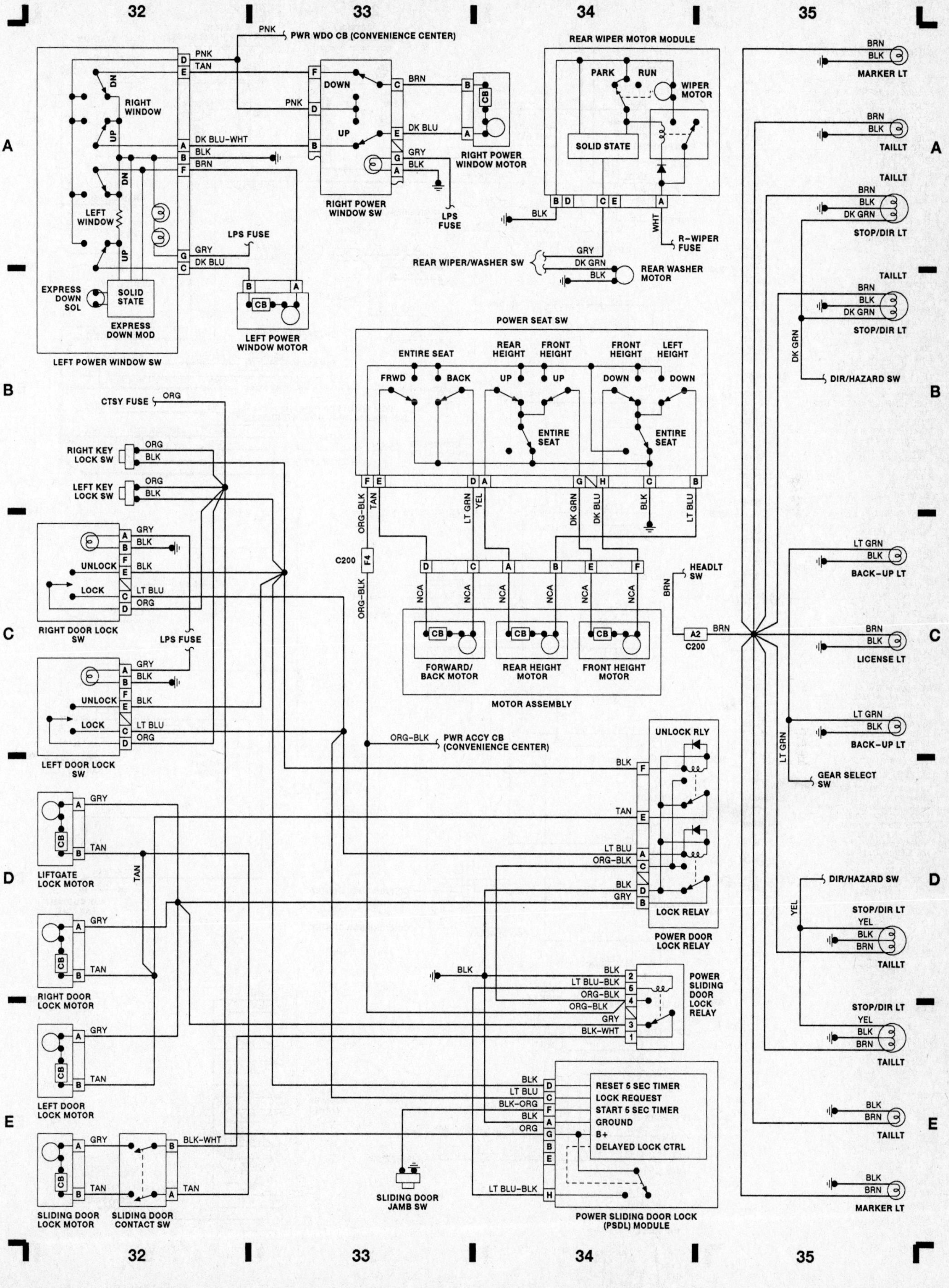

PWR WDO CB (CONVENIENCE CENTER)
RIGHT WINDOW
LEFT WINDOW
EXPRESS DOWN SOL
SOLID STATE
EXPRESS DOWN MOD
LEFT POWER WINDOW SW
LPS FUSE
LEFT POWER WINDOW MOTOR
RIGHT POWER WINDOW SW
RIGHT POWER WINDOW MOTOR
REAR WIPER MOTOR MODULE
PARK
RUN
WIPER MOTOR
R-WIPER FUSE
REAR WIPER/WASHER SW
REAR WASHER MOTOR
MARKER LT
TAILLT
STOP/DIR LT
DIR/HAZARD SW
POWER SEAT SW
ENTIRE SEAT
REAR HEIGHT
FRONT HEIGHT
LEFT HEIGHT
CTSY FUSE
RIGHT KEY LOCK SW
LEFT KEY LOCK SW
RIGHT DOOR LOCK SW
LEFT DOOR LOCK SW
FORWARD/ BACK MOTOR
REAR HEIGHT MOTOR
FRONT HEIGHT MOTOR
MOTOR ASSEMBLY
HEADLT SW
BACK-UP LT
LICENSE LT
GEAR SELECT SW
PWR ACCY CB (CONVENIENCE CENTER)
UNLOCK RLY
LOCK RELAY
POWER DOOR LOCK RELAY
LIFTGATE LOCK MOTOR
RIGHT DOOR LOCK MOTOR
LEFT DOOR LOCK MOTOR
POWER SLIDING DOOR LOCK RELAY
RESET 5 SEC TIMER
LOCK REQUEST
START 5 SEC TIMER
GROUND
B+
DELAYED LOCK CTRL
POWER SLIDING DOOR LOCK (PSDL) MODULE
SLIDING DOOR JAMB SW
SLIDING DOOR LOCK MOTOR
SLIDING DOOR CONTACT SW

1991 WIRING DIAGRAMS
"C" & "K" Series

COMPONENT LOCATOR:

A/C COMP RLY	D 34
ALDL CONN (DIESEL W/ 4L80–E)	C–D 19
ALDL CONN (DIESEL W/O 4L80–E)	C 12
ALDL CONN (GAS W/ 4L80–E)	E 8
ALDL CONN (GAS W/O 4L80–E)	D–E 4
ALTERNATOR	C 3
AUDIO ALARM MOD	C–D 28
AUTO TRANS	E 7
AUX BATT RLY	A 1
AUX COOLANT FAN RLY	C 3
BEAM SEL SW	A–B 24
BLOWER SW (W/O A/C)	A 33–34
CARGO LT	B 28
CARGO LT SW	C 29
CIG LTR	B 29
CONVENIENCE CENTER	D–E 21–22
COURTESY LT	A 29
CRUISE CTRL MOD	E 4
DEFOG CTRL	D 24
DIMMER SW	B 24
DIODE MOD	C 24
DIR FLASHER	A 25
DIR/HAZ SW	A–B 27
ELECTRONIC CONTROL MODLUE (ECM) (GAS W/O 4L80–E)	A 4–7
ELECTRONIC CONTROL MODULE (ECM) (DIESEL W/O 4L80–E)	A 12–15
ENG TEMP SENS	D 29–30
FOG LT RLY	D 1–2
FOG LT SW	B–C 24
FRONT AXLE SW	D 27
FUEL PUMP RLY (DIESEL W/ 4L80–E)	C 19
FUEL PUMP RLY (DIESEL W/O 4L08–E)	C 15
FUEL PUMP RLY (GAS W/ 4L80–E)	E 9–10
FUEL PUMP RLY (GAS W/O 4L80–E)	B 4
FUEL PUMP SW/OIL PRES SENS	B–C 28
FUEL SHUT OFF SOL (DIESEL W/ 4L80–E)	D 18
FUEL SHUT OFF SOL (DIESEL W/O 4L80–E)	D 14
FUEL TANK UNIT	B 28
FUSE BLOCK	B–C 21–22
GLOVE BOX LT	A 28
GLOW PLUG CTRL (DIESEL W/ 4L80–E)	D 19
GLOW PLUG CTRL (DIESEL W/O 4L80–E)	D 15
HAZARD FLASHER	C 27
HEATER & A/C CTRL	D–E 32
HORN RLY	A 28
HOT FUEL MOD (GAS W/ 4L80–E)	C 11
HOT FUEL MOD (GAS W/O 4L80–E)	C 4
IGN COIL (GAS W/ 4L80–E)	D–E 11
IGN COIL (GAS W/O 4L80–E)	D 7
IGN SW	A 20–23
INST CLSTR	A–C 30–31
LEFT BANK GLOW PLUG (DIESEL W/ 4L80–E)	E 19
LEFT BANK GLOW PLUG (DIESEL W/O 4L80–E)	E 15
LEFT FRONT DOOR SW	C 28
LEFT PWR LOCK SW	A 33
LEFT PWR WDO SW	A 32
LIGHT SW	A 24
LOW BLOWER RLY	C–D 32
LOW COOLANT MOD (DIESEL)	B 28
POWERTRAIN CONTROL MODULE (PCM) (GAS W/ 4L80–E)	A 8–11
REAR WHEEL ANTI–LOCK MOD	E 28
ROOF MARKER LTS	E 2–3
SPEED SENSOR	E 26
STARTER	A 3
STOP LT SW	C–D 27
TCC SOL (DIESEL W/O 4L80–E)	C 13
TRANSFER CASE RLY	D–E 27
TRANSMISSION (DIESEL W/ 4L80–E)	C–D 16
TRANSMISSION (GAS W/ 4L80–E)	C–D 8
TRANSMISSION CONTROL MODULE (TCM) (DIESEL W/ 4L80–E)	A 16–19
WATER IN FUEL SENS (DIESEL W/ 4L80–E)	E 16
WATER IN FUEL SENS (DIESEL W/O 4L80–E)	E 12
WIPER MTR	D–E 24
WIPER/WASHER SW	E 24
4WD CONSOLE LT	E 27

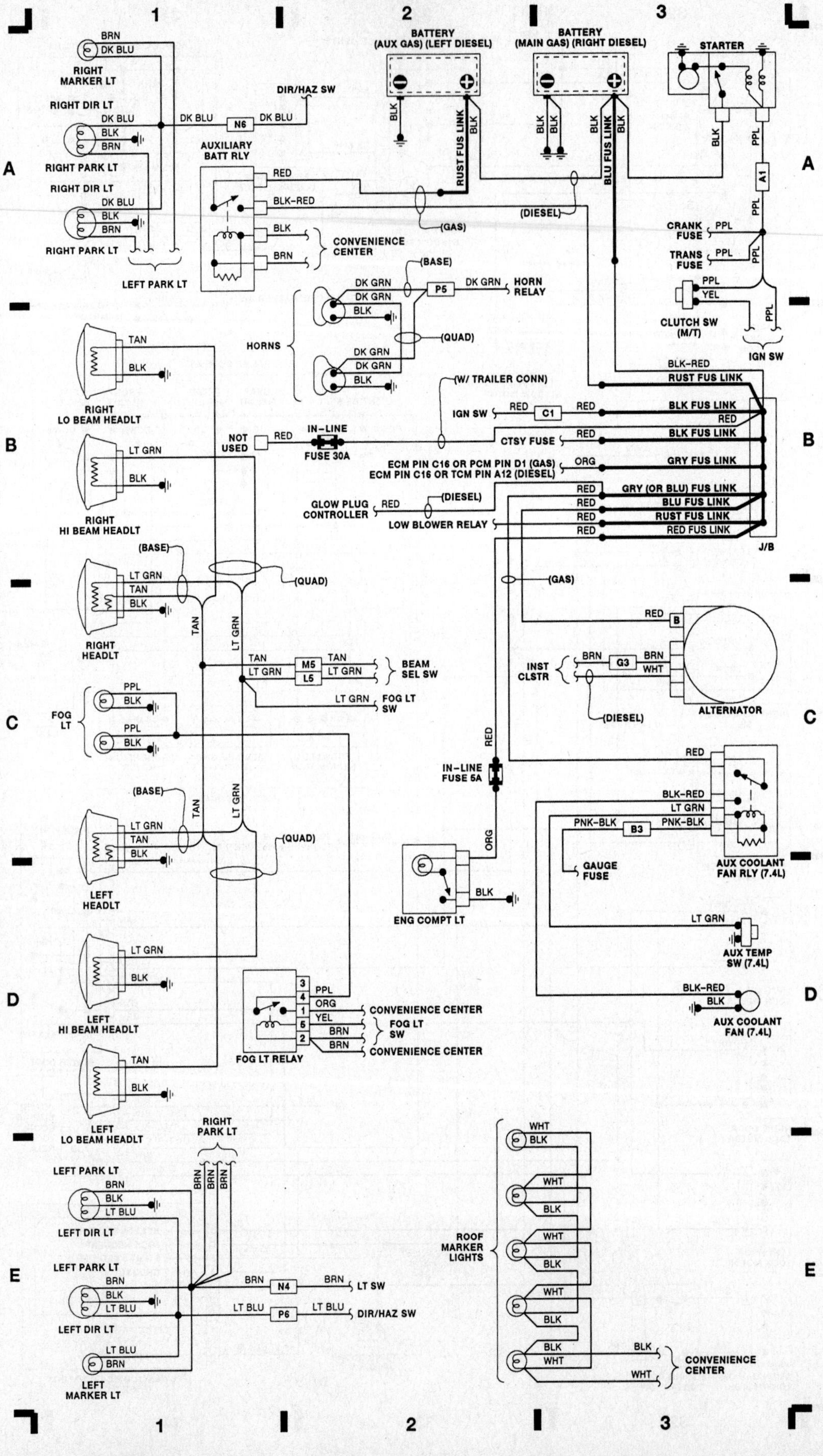
1
2
3
A
B
C
D
E
RIGHT MARKER LT
RIGHT DIR LT
RIGHT PARK LT
LEFT PARK LT
DIR/HAZ SW
AUXILIARY BATT RLY
CONVENIENCE CENTER
BATTERY (AUX GAS) (LEFT DIESEL)
BATTERY (MAIN GAS) (RIGHT DIESEL)
STARTER
RUST FUS LINK
BLU FUS LINK
(GAS)
(DIESEL)
CRANK FUSE
TRANS FUSE
CLUTCH SW (M/T)
IGN SW
HORNS
HORN RELAY
(BASE)
(QUAD)
(W/ TRAILER CONN)
RIGHT LO BEAM HEADLT
RIGHT HI BEAM HEADLT
RIGHT HEADLT
NOT USED
IN-LINE FUSE 30A
IGN SW
CTSY FUSE
ECM PIN C16 OR PCM PIN D1 (GAS)
ECM PIN C16 OR TCM PIN A12 (DIESEL)
GLOW PLUG CONTROLLER
LOW BLOWER RELAY
BLK FUS LINK
GRY FUS LINK
GRY (OR BLU) FUS LINK
RED FUS LINK
J/B
BEAM SEL SW
FOG LT SW
FOG LT
INST CLSTR
ALTERNATOR
IN-LINE FUSE 5A
LEFT HEADLT
ENG COMPT LT
GAUGE FUSE
AUX COOLANT FAN RLY (7.4L)
AUX TEMP SW (7.4L)
AUX COOLANT FAN (7.4L)
LEFT HI BEAM HEADLT
FOG LT RELAY
LEFT LO BEAM HEADLT
RIGHT PARK LT
LEFT DIR LT
LEFT MARKER LT
LT SW
ROOF MARKER LIGHTS

1991 WIRING DIAGRAMS
"C" & "K" Series (Cont.)

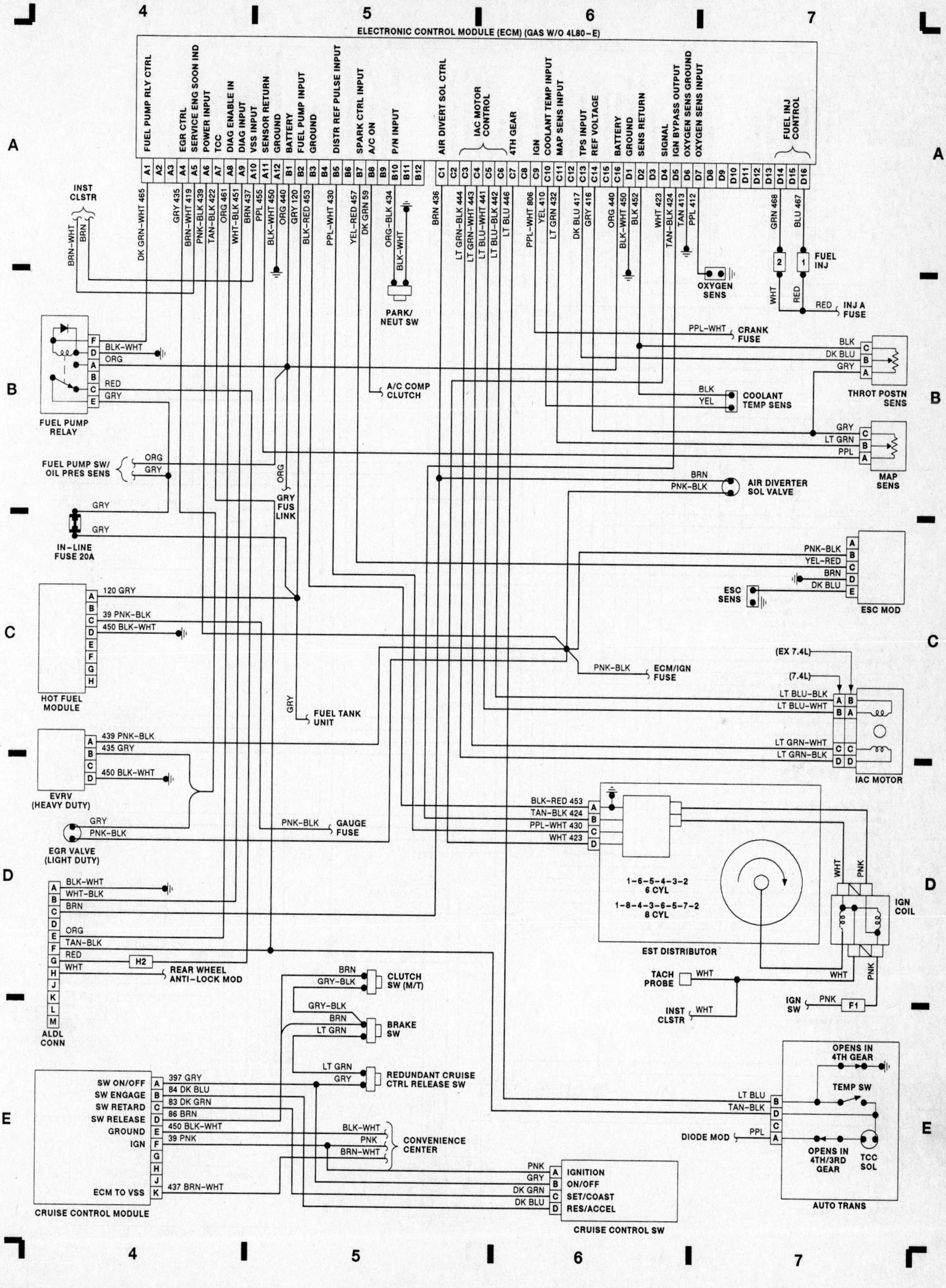
ELECTRONIC CONTROL MODULE (ECM) (GAS W/O 4L80-E)
FUEL PUMP RLY CTRL
EGR CTRL
SERVICE ENG SOON IND
POWER INPUT
TCC
DIAG ENABLE IN
DIAG INPUT
VSS INPUT
SENSOR RETURN
GROUND
BATTERY
FUEL PUMP INPUT
GROUND
DISTR REF PULSE INPUT
SPARK CTRL INPUT
A/C ON
P/N INPUT
AIR DIVERT SOL CTRL
IAC MOTOR CONTROL
4TH GEAR
IGN
COOLANT TEMP INPUT
MAP SENS INPUT
TPS INPUT
REF VOLTAGE
BATTERY
GROUND
SENS RETURN
SIGNAL
IGN BYPASS OUTPUT
OXYGEN SENS GROUND
OXYGEN SENS INPUT
FUEL INJ CONTROL
INST CLSTR
FUEL PUMP RELAY
FUEL PUMP SW/ OIL PRES SENS
IN-LINE FUSE 20A
GRY FUS LINK
PARK/ NEUT SW
A/C COMP CLUTCH
OXYGEN SENS
FUEL INJ
INJ A FUSE
CRANK FUSE
THROT POSTN SENS
COOLANT TEMP SENS
MAP SENS
AIR DIVERTER SOL VALVE
ESC SENS
ESC MOD
HOT FUEL MODULE
ECM/IGN FUSE
FUEL TANK UNIT
(EX 7.4L)
(7.4L)
IAC MOTOR
EVRV (HEAVY DUTY)
EGR VALVE (LIGHT DUTY)
GAUGE FUSE
1-6-5-4-3-2 6 CYL
1-8-4-3-6-5-7-2 8 CYL
EST DISTRIBUTOR
IGN COIL
TACH PROBE
INST CLSTR
IGN SW
ALDL CONN
REAR WHEEL ANTI-LOCK MOD
CLUTCH SW (M/T)
BRAKE SW
REDUNDANT CRUISE CTRL RELEASE SW
CONVENIENCE CENTER
SW ON/OFF
SW ENGAGE
SW RETARD
SW RELEASE
GROUND
IGN
ECM TO VSS
CRUISE CONTROL MODULE
IGNITION
ON/OFF
SET/COAST
RES/ACCEL
CRUISE CONTROL SW
OPENS IN 4TH GEAR
TEMP SW
DIODE MOD
OPENS IN 4TH/3RD GEAR
TCC SOL
AUTO TRANS

1991 WIRING DIAGRAMS
"C" & "K" Series (Cont.)

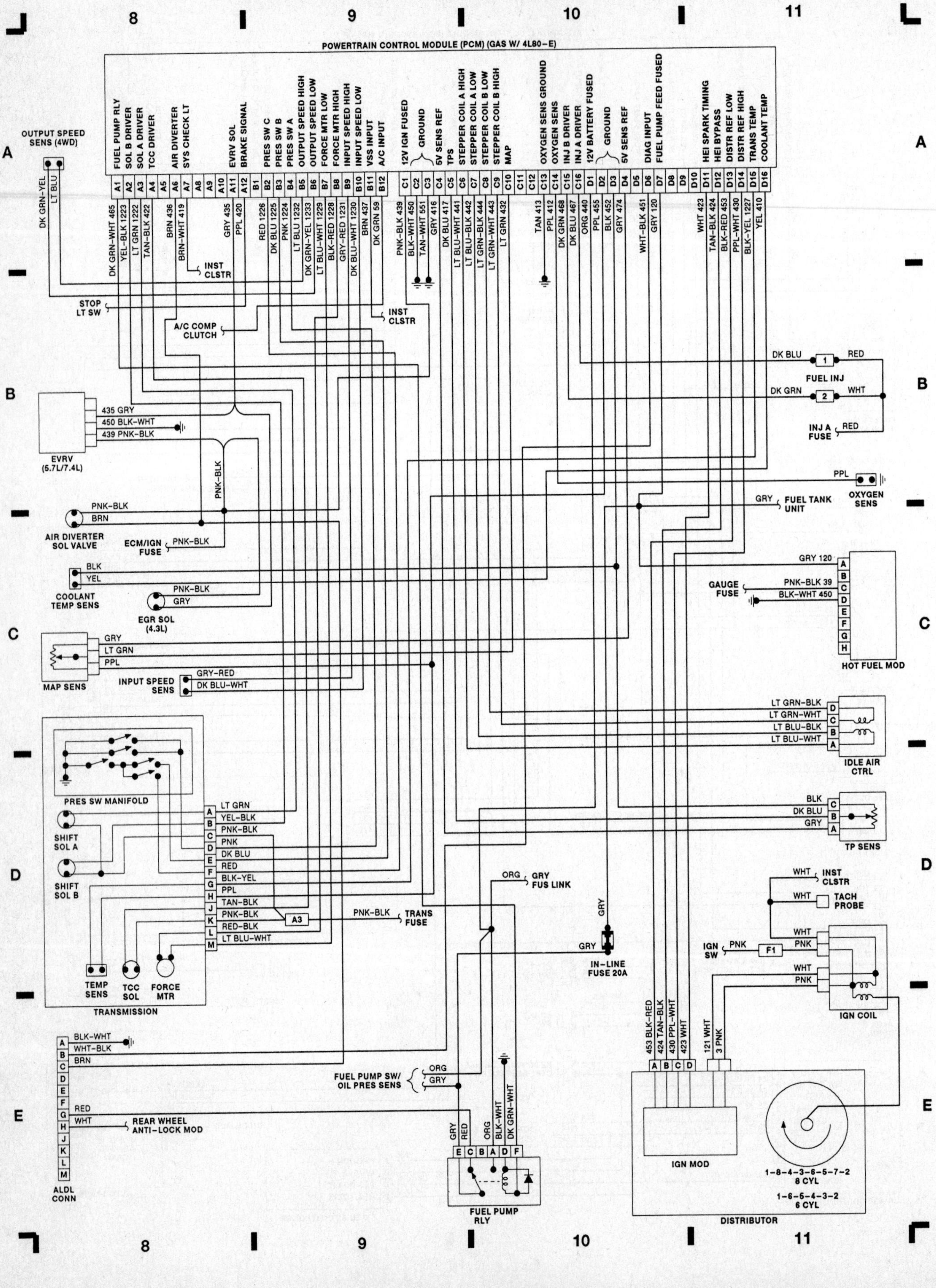
8
9
10
11
POWERTRAIN CONTROL MODULE (PCM) (GAS W/ 4L80-E)
OUTPUT SPEED SENS (4WD)
FUEL PUMP RLY
SOL B DRIVER
SOL A DRIVER
TCC DRIVER
AIR DIVERTER
SYS CHECK LT
EVRV SOL
BRAKE SIGNAL
PRES SW C
PRES SW B
PRES SW A
OUTPUT SPEED HIGH
OUTPUT SPEED LOW
FORCE MTR LOW
FORCE MTR HIGH
INPUT SPEED HIGH
INPUT SPEED LOW
VSS INPUT
A/C INPUT
12V IGN FUSED
GROUND
5V SENS REF
TPS
STEPPER COIL A HIGH
STEPPER COIL A LOW
STEPPER COIL B LOW
STEPPER COIL B HIGH
MAP
OXYGEN SENS GROUND
OXYGEN SENS
INJ B DRIVER
INJ A DRIVER
12V BATTERY FUSED
GROUND
5V SENS REF
DIAG INPUT
FUEL PUMP FEED FUSED
HEI SPARK TIMING
HEI BYPASS
DISTR REF LOW
DISTR REF HIGH
TRANS TEMP
COOLANT TEMP
STOP LT SW
INST CLSTR
A/C COMP CLUTCH
EVRV (5.7L/7.4L)
AIR DIVERTER SOL VALVE
ECM/IGN FUSE
COOLANT TEMP SENS
EGR SOL (4.3L)
MAP SENS
INPUT SPEED SENS
PRES SW MANIFOLD
SHIFT SOL A
SHIFT SOL B
TEMP SENS
TCC SOL
FORCE MTR
TRANSMISSION
TRANS FUSE
ORG GRY FUS LINK
IN-LINE FUSE 20A
FUEL INJ
INJ A FUSE
OXYGEN SENS
FUEL TANK UNIT
GAUGE FUSE
HOT FUEL MOD
IDLE AIR CTRL
TP SENS
INST CLSTR
TACH PROBE
IGN SW
IGN COIL
ALDL CONN
REAR WHEEL ANTI-LOCK MOD
FUEL PUMP SW/ OIL PRES SENS
FUEL PUMP RLY
IGN MOD
1-8-4-3-6-5-7-2 8 CYL
1-6-5-4-3-2 6 CYL
DISTRIBUTOR

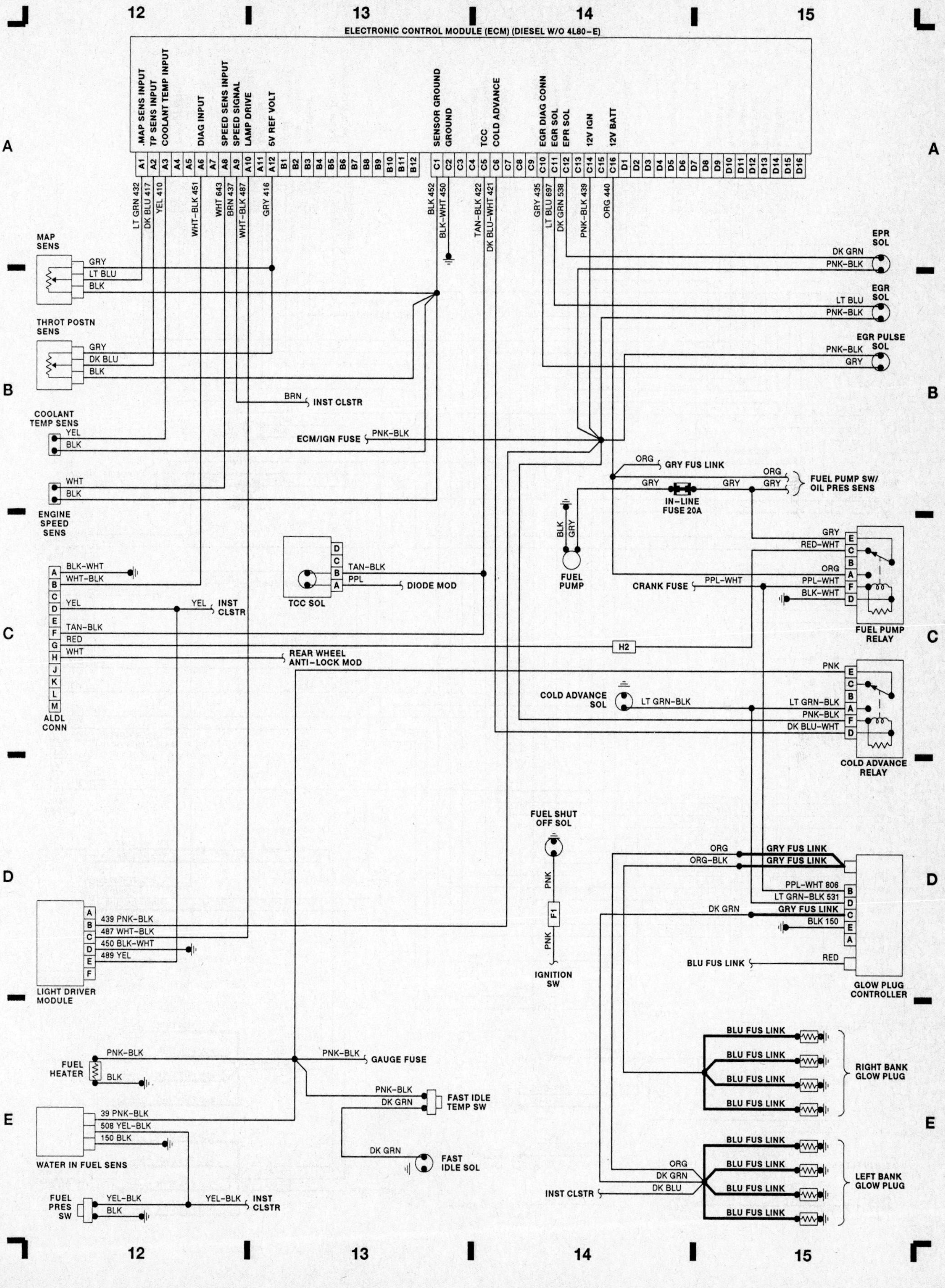

ELECTRONIC CONTROL MODULE (ECM) (DIESEL W/O 4L80-E)
MAP SENS INPUT
TP SENS INPUT
COOLANT TEMP INPUT
DIAG INPUT
SPEED SENS INPUT
SPEED SIGNAL
LAMP DRIVE
5V REF VOLT
SENSOR GROUND
GROUND
TCC
COLD ADVANCE
EGR DIAG CONN
EGR SOL
EPR SOL
12V IGN
12V BATT
LT GRN 432
DK BLU 417
YEL 410
WHT-BLK 451
WHT 643
BRN 437
WHT-BLK 487
GRY 416
BLK 452
BLK-WHT 450
TAN-BLK 422
DK BLU-WHT 421
GRY 435
LT BLU 697
DK GRN 538
PNK-BLK 439
ORG 440
MAP SENS
THROT POSTN SENS
COOLANT TEMP SENS
ENGINE SPEED SENS
EPR SOL
EGR SOL
EGR PULSE SOL
INST CLSTR
ECM/IGN FUSE
GRY FUS LINK
FUEL PUMP SW/ OIL PRES SENS
IN-LINE FUSE 20A
FUEL PUMP
CRANK FUSE
FUEL PUMP RELAY
TCC SOL
DIODE MOD
ALDL CONN
REAR WHEEL ANTI-LOCK MOD
H2
COLD ADVANCE SOL
COLD ADVANCE RELAY
FUEL SHUT OFF SOL
F1
IGNITION SW
GLOW PLUG CONTROLLER
PPL-WHT 806
LT GRN-BLK 531
BLK 150
BLU FUS LINK
LIGHT DRIVER MODULE
439 PNK-BLK
487 WHT-BLK
450 BLK-WHT
489 YEL
FUEL HEATER
GAUGE FUSE
FAST IDLE TEMP SW
FAST IDLE SOL
WATER IN FUEL SENS
39 PNK-BLK
508 YEL-BLK
150 BLK
FUEL PRES SW
RIGHT BANK GLOW PLUG
LEFT BANK GLOW PLUG

1991 WIRING DIAGRAMS "C" & "K" Series (Cont.)

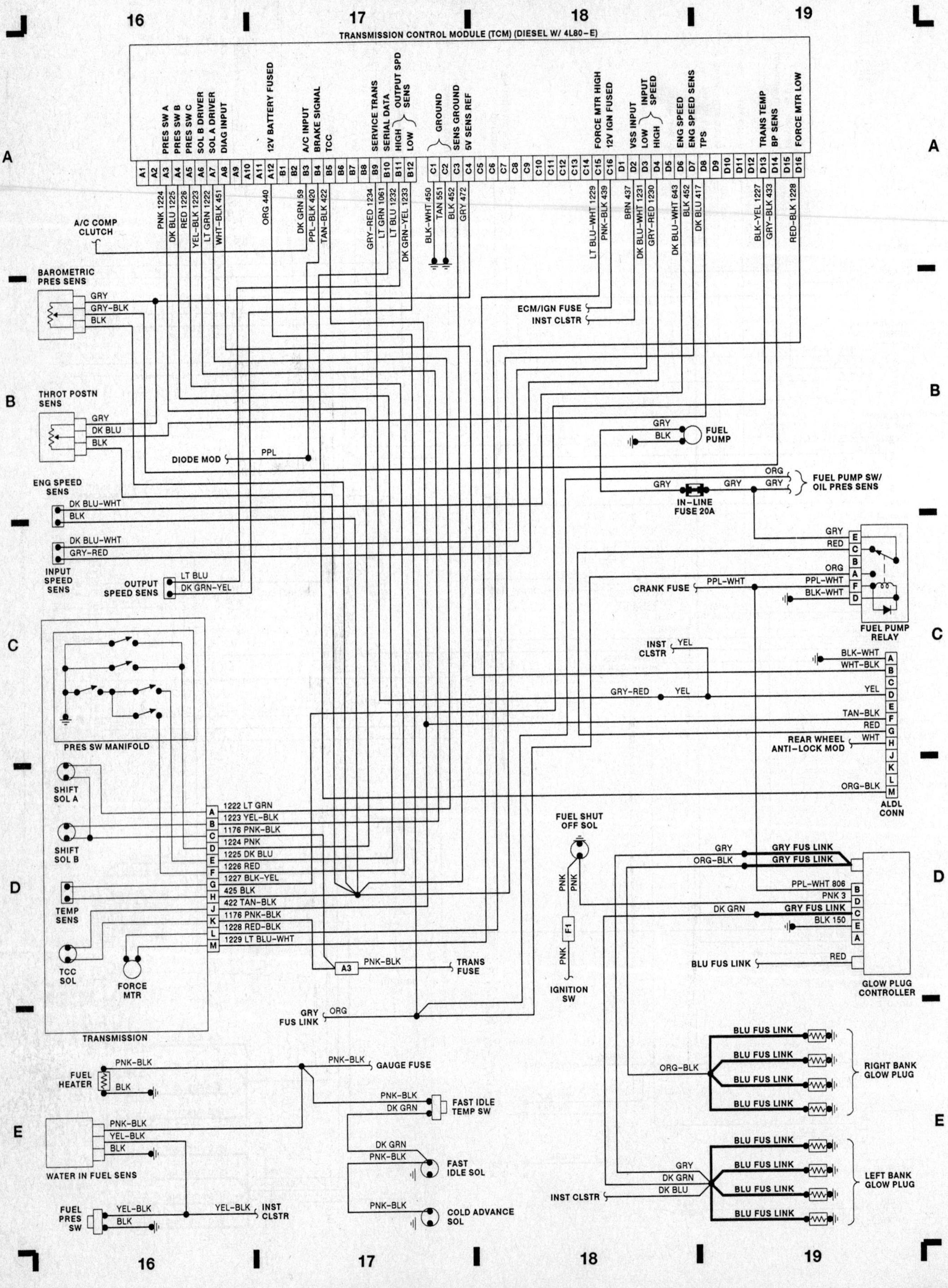
16
17
18
19
A
B
C
D
E
TRANSMISSION CONTROL MODULE (TCM) (DIESEL W/ 4L80-E)
PRES SW A
PRES SW B
PRES SW C
SOL B DRIVER
SOL A DRIVER
DIAG INPUT
12V BATTERY FUSED
A/C INPUT
BRAKE SIGNAL
TCC
SERVICE TRANS
SERIAL DATA
OUTPUT SPD SENS
HIGH
LOW
GROUND
SENS GROUND
5V SENS REF
FORCE MTR HIGH
12V IGN FUSED
VSS INPUT
INPUT SPEED
LOW
HIGH
ENG SPEED
ENG SPEED SENS
TPS
TRANS TEMP
BP SENS
FORCE MTR LOW
A1 A2 A3 A4 A5 A6 A7 A8 A9 A10 A11 A12 B1 B2 B3 B4 B5 B6 B7 B8 B9 B10 B11 B12 C1 C2 C3 C4 C5 C6 C7 C8 C9 C10 C11 C12 C13 C14 C15 C16 D1 D2 D3 D4 D5 D6 D7 D8 D9 D10 D11 D12 D13 D14 D15 D16
PNK 1224
DK BLU 1225
RED 1226
YEL-BLK 1223
LT GRN 1222
WHT-BLK 451
ORG 440
DK GRN 59
PPL-BLK 420
TAN-BLK 422
GRY-RED 1234
LT GRN 1061
LT BLU 1232
DK GRN-YEL 1233
BLK-WHT 450
TAN 551
BLK 452
GRY 472
LT BLU-WHT 1229
PNK-BLK 439
BRN 437
DK BLU-WHT 1231
GRY-RED 1230
DK BLU-WHT 643
BLK 452
DK BLU 417
BLK-YEL 1227
GRY-BLK 433
RED-BLK 1228
A/C COMP CLUTCH
BAROMETRIC PRES SENS
GRY
GRY-BLK
BLK
ECM/IGN FUSE
INST CLSTR
THROT POSTN SENS
GRY
DK BLU
BLK
GRY
BLK
FUEL PUMP
DIODE MOD
PPL
ORG
GRY
GRY
GRY
FUEL PUMP SW/ OIL PRES SENS
IN-LINE FUSE 20A
ENG SPEED SENS
DK BLU-WHT
BLK
DK BLU-WHT
GRY-RED
INPUT SPEED SENS
OUTPUT SPEED SENS
LT BLU
DK GRN-YEL
GRY
RED
ORG
CRANK FUSE
PPL-WHT
PPL-WHT
BLK-WHT
E C B A F D
FUEL PUMP RELAY
INST CLSTR
YEL
BLK-WHT
WHT-BLK
GRY-RED
YEL
YEL
TAN-BLK
RED
REAR WHEEL ANTI-LOCK MOD
WHT
ORG-BLK
A B C D E F G H J K L M
ALDL CONN
PRES SW MANIFOLD
SHIFT SOL A
SHIFT SOL B
TEMP SENS
TCC SOL
FORCE MTR
TRANSMISSION
1222 LT GRN
1223 YEL-BLK
1176 PNK-BLK
1224 PNK
1225 DK BLU
1226 RED
1227 BLK-YEL
425 BLK
422 TAN-BLK
1176 PNK-BLK
1228 RED-BLK
1229 LT BLU-WHT
A3
PNK-BLK
TRANS FUSE
GRY FUS LINK
ORG
FUEL SHUT OFF SOL
PNK
PNK
F1
PNK
IGNITION SW
GRY
ORG-BLK
GRY FUS LINK
GRY FUS LINK
PPL-WHT 806
PNK 3
DK GRN
GRY FUS LINK
BLK 150
BLU FUS LINK
RED
B D C E A
GLOW PLUG CONTROLLER
FUEL HEATER
PNK-BLK
BLK
PNK-BLK
GAUGE FUSE
PNK-BLK
DK GRN
FAST IDLE TEMP SW
WATER IN FUEL SENS
PNK-BLK
YEL-BLK
BLK
DK GRN
PNK-BLK
FAST IDLE SOL
PNK-BLK
COLD ADVANCE SOL
FUEL PRES SW
YEL-BLK
BLK
YEL-BLK
INST CLSTR
BLU FUS LINK
BLU FUS LINK
BLU FUS LINK
BLU FUS LINK
ORG-BLK
RIGHT BANK GLOW PLUG
BLU FUS LINK
BLU FUS LINK
BLU FUS LINK
BLU FUS LINK
GRY
DK GRN
DK BLU
INST CLSTR
LEFT BANK GLOW PLUG

1991 WIRING DIAGRAMS
"C" & "K" Series (Cont.)

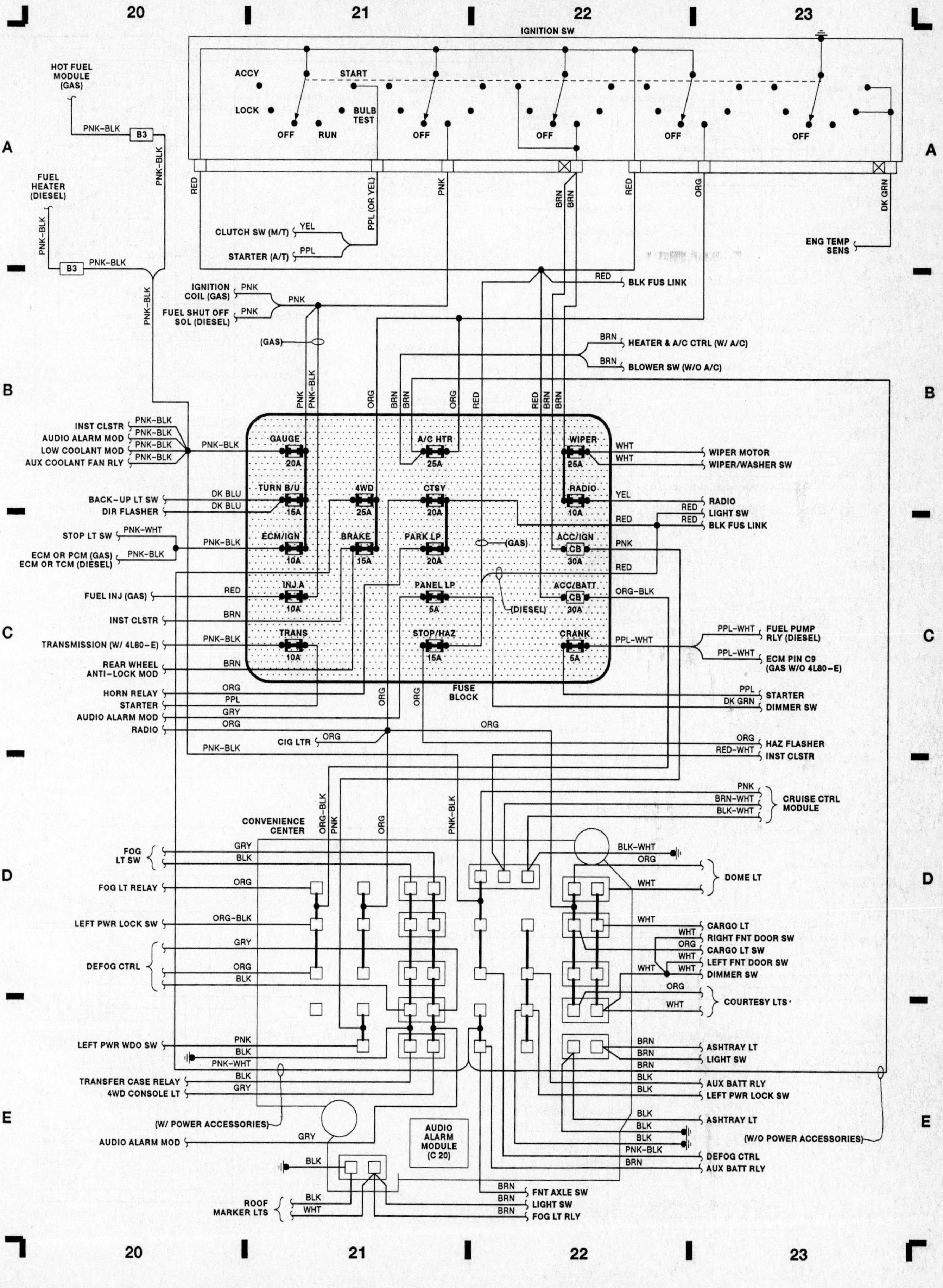
IGNITION SW
ACCY
START
LOCK
BULB TEST
OFF
RUN
HOT FUEL MODULE (GAS)
PNK-BLK
B3
FUEL HEATER (DIESEL)
RED
PPL (OR YEL)
PNK
BRN
ORG
DK GRN
CLUTCH SW (M/T)
YEL
STARTER (A/T)
PPL
ENG TEMP SENS
BLK FUS LINK
IGNITION COIL (GAS)
FUEL SHUT OFF SOL (DIESEL)
(GAS)
HEATER & A/C CTRL (W/ A/C)
BLOWER SW (W/O A/C)
INST CLSTR
AUDIO ALARM MOD
LOW COOLANT MOD
AUX COOLANT FAN RLY
GAUGE 20A
A/C HTR 25A
WIPER 25A
WHT
WIPER MOTOR
WIPER/WASHER SW
BACK-UP LT SW
DIR FLASHER
DK BLU
TURN B/U 15A
4WD 25A
CTSY 20A
RADIO 10A
RADIO
LIGHT SW
STOP LT SW
PNK-WHT
ECM OR PCM (GAS)
ECM OR TCM (DIESEL)
ECM/IGN 10A
BRAKE 15A
PARK LP 20A
ACC/IGN CB 30A
FUEL INJ (GAS)
INJ A 10A
PANEL LP 5A
ACC/BATT CB 30A
(DIESEL)
ORG-BLK
TRANSMISSION (W/ 4L80-E)
TRANS 10A
STOP/HAZ 15A
CRANK 5A
PPL-WHT
FUEL PUMP RLY (DIESEL)
ECM PIN C9 (GAS W/O 4L80-E)
REAR WHEEL ANTI-LOCK MOD
HORN RELAY
STARTER
RADIO
GRY
FUSE BLOCK
DIMMER SW
CIG LTR
HAZ FLASHER
RED-WHT
CRUISE CTRL MODULE
BRN-WHT
BLK-WHT
CONVENIENCE CENTER
FOG LT SW
BLK
FOG LT RELAY
DOME LT
LEFT PWR LOCK SW
CARGO LT
RIGHT FNT DOOR SW
CARGO LT SW
LEFT FNT DOOR SW
DEFOG CTRL
COURTESY LTS
LEFT PWR WDO SW
ASHTRAY LT
AUX BATT RLY
LEFT PWR LOCK SW
TRANSFER CASE RELAY
4WD CONSOLE LT
(W/ POWER ACCESSORIES)
(W/O POWER ACCESSORIES)
AUDIO ALARM MOD
AUDIO ALARM MODULE (C 20)
ROOF MARKER LTS
FNT AXLE SW
FOG LT RLY
20
21
22
23
A
B
C
D
E

1991 WIRING DIAGRAMS
"C" & "K" Series (Cont.)

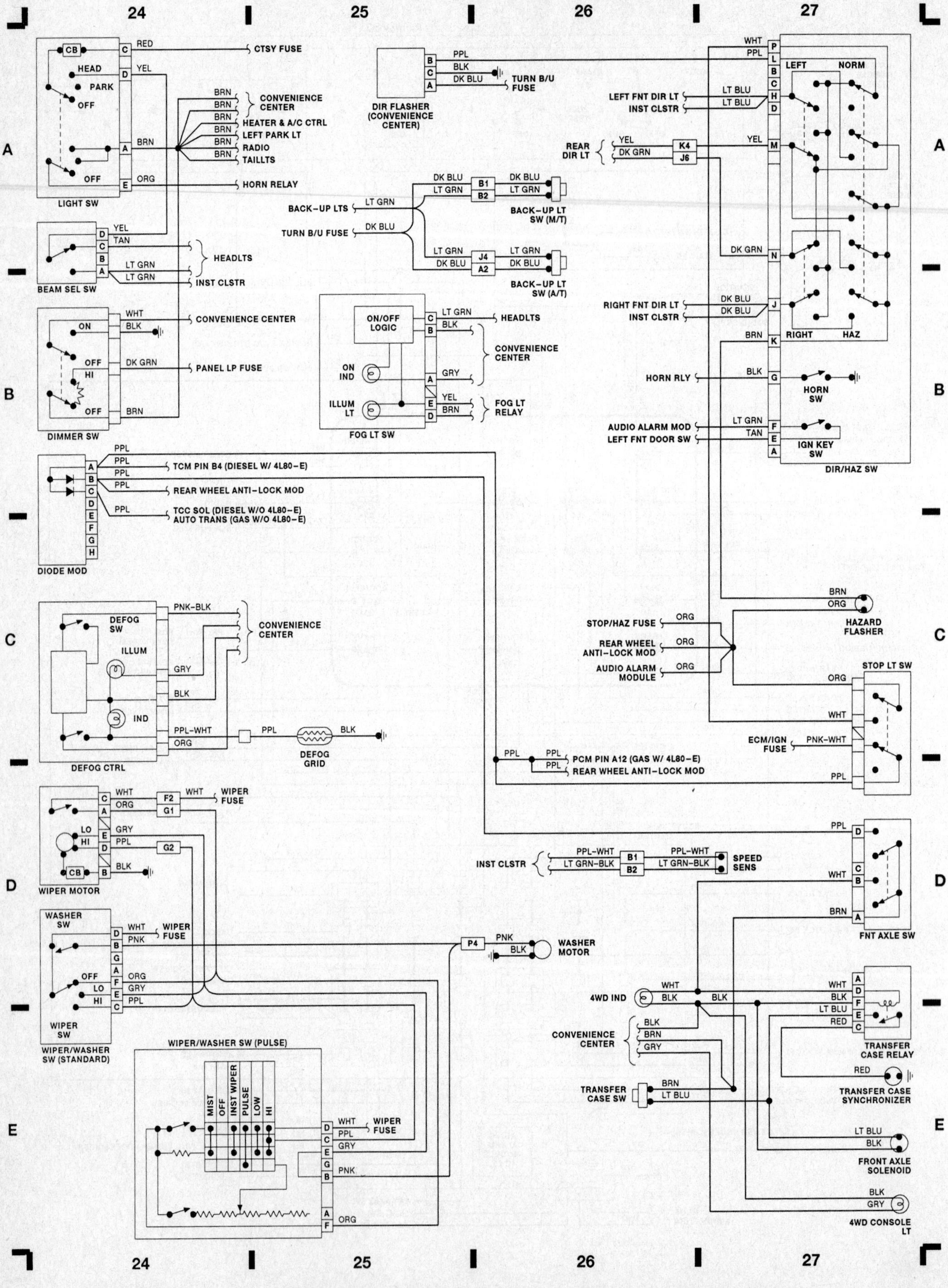
24
25
26
27
LIGHT SW
CTSY FUSE
HEAD
PARK
OFF
CONVENIENCE CENTER
HEATER & A/C CTRL
LEFT PARK LT
RADIO
TAILLTS
HORN RELAY
BEAM SEL SW
HEADLTS
INST CLSTR
DIMMER SW
CONVENIENCE CENTER
PANEL LP FUSE
DIR FLASHER (CONVENIENCE CENTER)
TURN B/U FUSE
BACK-UP LTS
BACK-UP LT SW (M/T)
BACK-UP LT SW (A/T)
ON/OFF LOGIC
ON IND
ILLUM LT
FOG LT SW
FOG LT RELAY
LEFT FNT DIR LT
INST CLSTR
REAR DIR LT
RIGHT FNT DIR LT
HORN RLY
HORN SW
AUDIO ALARM MOD
LEFT FNT DOOR SW
IGN KEY SW
DIR/HAZ SW
LEFT
NORM
RIGHT
HAZ
DIODE MOD
TCM PIN B4 (DIESEL W/ 4L80-E)
REAR WHEEL ANTI-LOCK MOD
TCC SOL (DIESEL W/O 4L80-E)
AUTO TRANS (GAS W/O 4L80-E)
DEFOG SW
ILLUM
IND
DEFOG CTRL
DEFOG GRID
HAZARD FLASHER
STOP/HAZ FUSE
REAR WHEEL ANTI-LOCK MOD
AUDIO ALARM MODULE
STOP LT SW
ECM/IGN FUSE
PCM PIN A12 (GAS W/ 4L80-E)
REAR WHEEL ANTI-LOCK MOD
WIPER FUSE
WIPER MOTOR
INST CLSTR
SPEED SENS
FNT AXLE SW
WASHER SW
WASHER MOTOR
WIPER SW
WIPER/WASHER SW (STANDARD)
4WD IND
CONVENIENCE CENTER
TRANSFER CASE RELAY
TRANSFER CASE SYNCHRONIZER
TRANSFER CASE SW
WIPER/WASHER SW (PULSE)
MIST
OFF
INST WIPER
PULSE
LOW
HI
FRONT AXLE SOLENOID
4WD CONSOLE LT

1991 WIRING DIAGRAMS
"C" & "K" Series (Cont.)

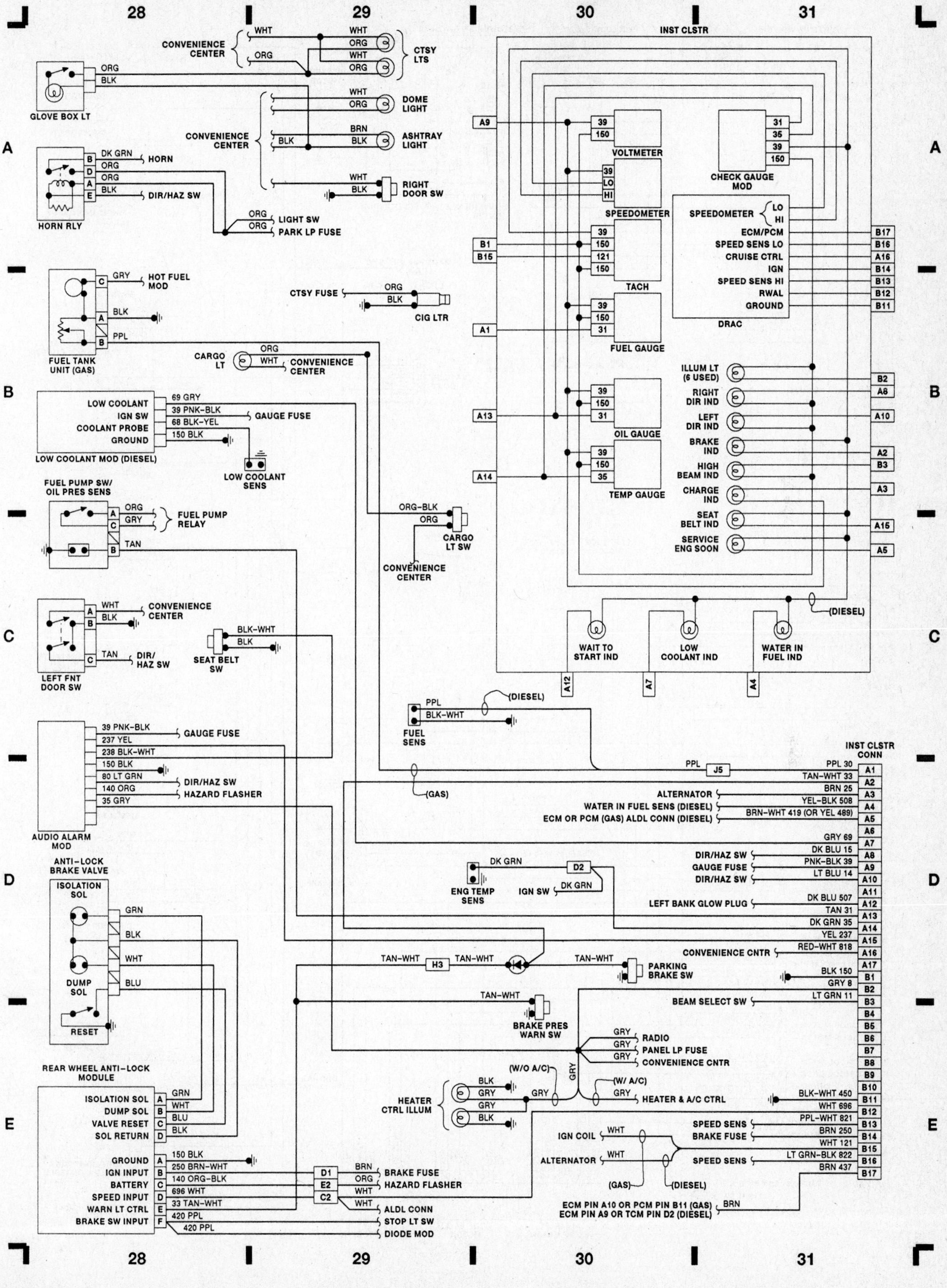
28
29
30
31
INST CLSTR
CONVENIENCE CENTER
CTSY LTS
GLOVE BOX LT
DOME LIGHT
ASHTRAY LIGHT
RIGHT DOOR SW
HORN
DIR/HAZ SW
HORN RLY
LIGHT SW
PARK LP FUSE
VOLTMETER
SPEEDOMETER
CHECK GAUGE MOD
TACH
FUEL GAUGE
OIL GAUGE
TEMP GAUGE
ECM/PCM
SPEED SENS LO
CRUISE CTRL
IGN
SPEED SENS HI
RWAL
GROUND
DRAC
HOT FUEL MOD
CTSY FUSE
CIG LTR
FUEL TANK UNIT (GAS)
CARGO LT
ILLUM LT (6 USED)
RIGHT DIR IND
LEFT DIR IND
BRAKE IND
HIGH BEAM IND
CHARGE IND
SEAT BELT IND
SERVICE ENG SOON
LOW COOLANT
IGN SW
COOLANT PROBE
GROUND
GAUGE FUSE
LOW COOLANT MOD (DIESEL)
LOW COOLANT SENS
FUEL PUMP SW/ OIL PRES SENS
FUEL PUMP RELAY
CARGO LT SW
WAIT TO START IND
LOW COOLANT IND
WATER IN FUEL IND
(DIESEL)
LEFT FNT DOOR SW
SEAT BELT SW
FUEL SENS
AUDIO ALARM MOD
HAZARD FLASHER
INST CLSTR CONN
ALTERNATOR
WATER IN FUEL SENS (DIESEL)
ECM OR PCM (GAS) ALDL CONN (DIESEL)
ENG TEMP SENS
LEFT BANK GLOW PLUG
ANTI-LOCK BRAKE VALVE
ISOLATION SOL
DUMP SOL
RESET
CONVENIENCE CNTR
PARKING BRAKE SW
BRAKE PRES WARN SW
BEAM SELECT SW
RADIO
PANEL LP FUSE
REAR WHEEL ANTI-LOCK MODULE
HEATER CTRL ILLUM
HEATER & A/C CTRL
IGN COIL
SPEED SENS
BRAKE FUSE
ISOLATION SOL
DUMP SOL
VALVE RESET
SOL RETURN
IGN INPUT
BATTERY
SPEED INPUT
WARN LT CTRL
BRAKE SW INPUT
ALDL CONN
STOP LT SW
DIODE MOD
ECM PIN A10 OR PCM PIN B11 (GAS)
ECM PIN A9 OR TCM PIN D2 (DIESEL)

1991 WIRING DIAGRAMS
"C" & "K" Series (Cont.)

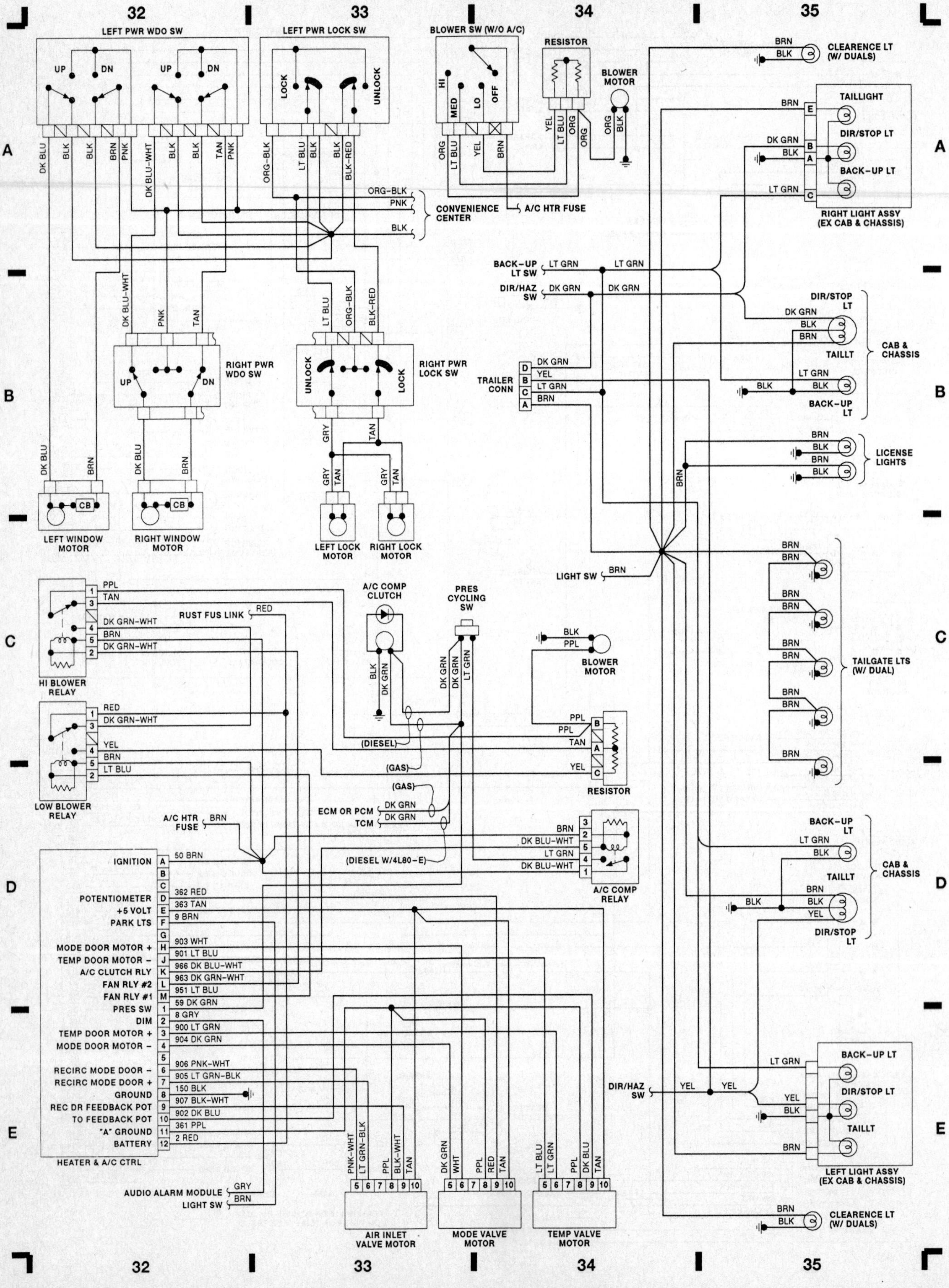
32
33
34
35
LEFT PWR WDO SW
LEFT PWR LOCK SW
BLOWER SW (W/O A/C)
RESISTOR
BLOWER MOTOR
CLEARENCE LT (W/ DUALS)
TAILLIGHT
DIR/STOP LT
BACK-UP LT
RIGHT LIGHT ASSY (EX CAB & CHASSIS)
CONVENIENCE CENTER
A/C HTR FUSE
BACK-UP LT SW
DIR/HAZ SW
CAB & CHASSIS
TRAILER CONN
RIGHT PWR WDO SW
RIGHT PWR LOCK SW
LICENSE LIGHTS
LEFT WINDOW MOTOR
RIGHT WINDOW MOTOR
LEFT LOCK MOTOR
RIGHT LOCK MOTOR
LIGHT SW
A/C COMP CLUTCH
PRES CYCLING SW
RUST FUS LINK
HI BLOWER RELAY
LOW BLOWER RELAY
TAILGATE LTS (W/ DUAL)
ECM OR PCM
TCM
A/C COMP RELAY
IGNITION
POTENTIOMETER
+5 VOLT
PARK LTS
MODE DOOR MOTOR +
TEMP DOOR MOTOR −
A/C CLUTCH RLY
FAN RLY #2
FAN RLY #1
PRES SW
DIM
TEMP DOOR MOTOR +
MODE DOOR MOTOR −
RECIRC MODE DOOR −
RECIRC MODE DOOR +
GROUND
REC DR FEEDBACK POT
TO FEEDBACK POT
"A" GROUND
BATTERY
HEATER & A/C CTRL
50 BRN
362 RED
363 TAN
9 BRN
903 WHT
901 LT BLU
966 DK BLU-WHT
963 DK GRN-WHT
951 LT BLU
59 DK GRN
8 GRY
900 LT GRN
904 DK GRN
906 PNK-WHT
905 LT GRN-BLK
150 BLK
907 BLK-WHT
902 DK BLU
361 PPL
2 RED
AUDIO ALARM MODULE
LEFT LIGHT ASSY (EX CAB & CHASSIS)
AIR INLET VALVE MOTOR
MODE VALVE MOTOR
TEMP VALVE MOTOR
(DIESEL)
(GAS)
(DIESEL W/4L80-E)

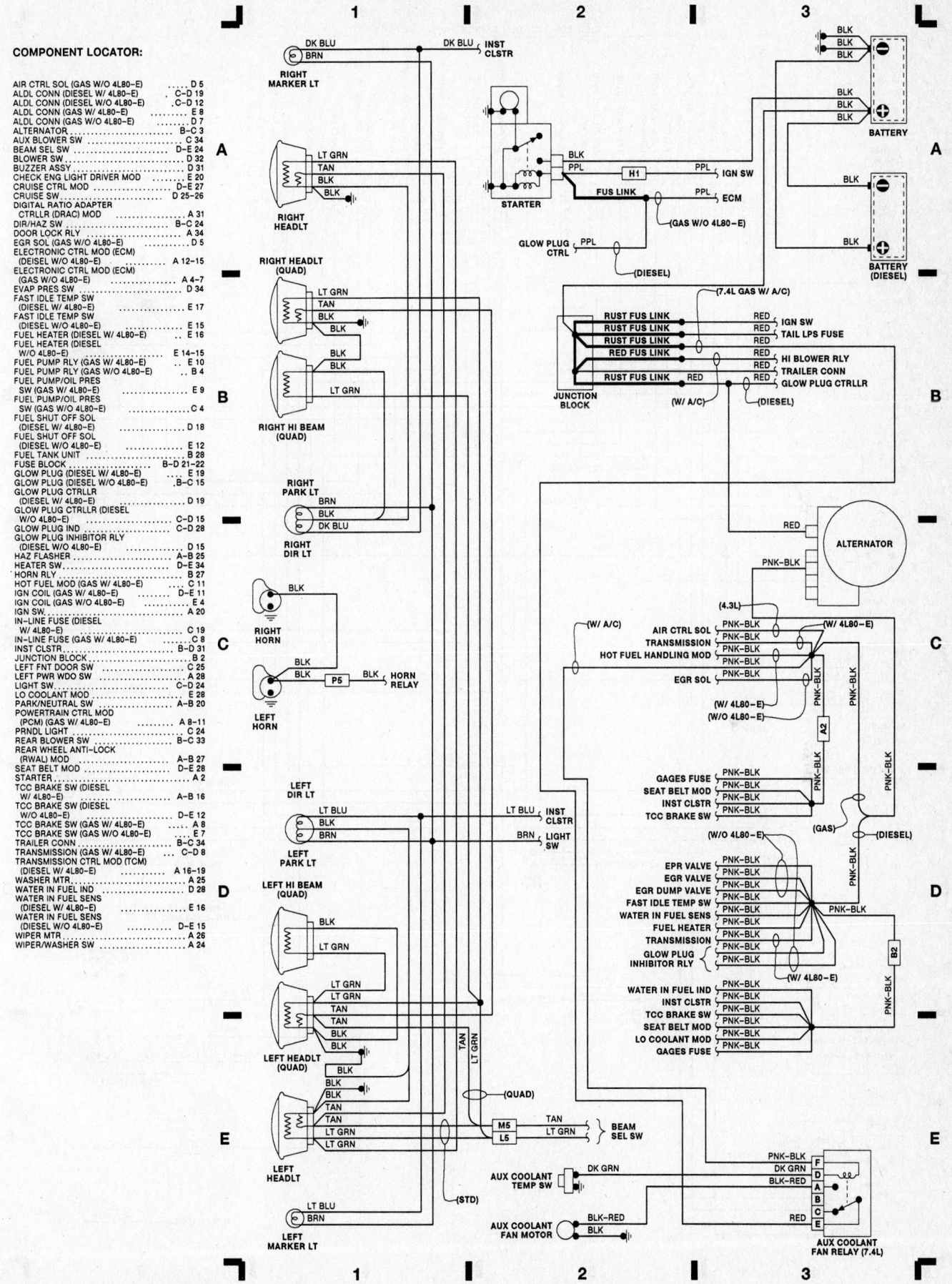

COMPONENT LOCATOR:

AIR CTRL SOL (GAS W/O 4L80-E)	D 5
ALDL CONN (DIESEL W/ 4L80-E)	C-D 19
ALDL CONN (DIESEL W/O 4L80-E)	C-D 12
ALDL CONN (GAS W/ 4L80-E)	E 8
ALDL CONN (GAS W/O 4L80-E)	D 7
ALTERNATOR	B-C 3
AUX BLOWER SW	C 34
BEAM SEL SW	D-E 24
BLOWER SW	D 32
BUZZER ASSY	D 31
CHECK ENG LIGHT DRIVER MOD	E 20
CRUISE CTRL MOD	D-E 27
CRUISE SW	D 25-26
DIGITAL RATIO ADAPTER CTRLLR (DRAC) MOD	A 31
DIR/HAZ SW	B-C 24
DOOR LOCK RLY	A 34
EGR SOL (GAS W/O 4L80-E)	D 5
ELECTRONIC CTRL MOD (ECM) (DEISEL W/O 4L80-E)	A 12-15
ELECTRONIC CTRL MOD (ECM) (GAS W/O 4L80-E)	A 4-7
EVAP PRES SW	D 34
FAST IDLE TEMP SW (DIESEL W/ 4L80-E)	E 17
FAST IDLE TEMP SW (DIESEL W/O 4L80-E)	E 15
FUEL HEATER (DIESEL W/ 4L80-E)	E 16
FUEL HEATER (DIESEL W/O 4L80-E)	E 14-15
FUEL PUMP RLY (GAS W/ 4L80-E)	E 10
FUEL PUMP RLY (GAS W/O 4L80-E)	B 4
FUEL PUMP/OIL PRES SW (GAS W/ 4L80-E)	E 9
FUEL PUMP/OIL PRES SW (GAS W/O 4L80-E)	C 4
FUEL SHUT OFF SOL (DIESEL W/ 4L80-E)	D 18
FUEL SHUT OFF SOL (DIESEL W/O 4L80-E)	E 12
FUEL TANK UNIT	B 28
FUSE BLOCK	B-D 21-22
GLOW PLUG (DIESEL W/ 4L80-E)	E 19
GLOW PLUG (DIESEL W/O 4L80-E)	B-C 15
GLOW PLUG CTRLLR (DIESEL W/ 4L80-E)	D 19
GLOW PLUG CTRLLR (DIESEL W/O 4L80-E)	C-D 15
GLOW PLUG IND	C-D 28
GLOW PLUG INHIBITOR RLY (DIESEL W/O 4L80-E)	D 15
HAZ FLASHER	A-B 25
HEATER SW	D-E 34
HORN RLY	B 27
HOT FUEL MOD (GAS W/ 4L80-E)	C 11
IGN COIL (GAS W/ 4L80-E)	D-E 11
IGN COIL (GAS W/O 4L80-E)	E 4
IGN SW	A 20
IN-LINE FUSE (DIESEL W/ 4L80-E)	C 19
IN-LINE FUSE (GAS W/ 4L80-E)	C 8
INST CLSTR	B-D 31
JUNCTION BLOCK	B 2
LEFT FNT DOOR SW	C 25
LEFT PWR WDO SW	A 28
LIGHT SW	C-D 24
LO COOLANT MOD	E 28
PARK/NEUTRAL SW	A-B 20
POWERTRAIN CTRL MOD (PCM) (GAS W/ 4L80-E)	A 8-11
PRNDL LIGHT	C 24
REAR BLOWER SW	B-C 33
REAR WHEEL ANTI-LOCK (RWAL) MOD	A-B 27
SEAT BELT MOD	D-E 28
STARTER	A 2
TCC BRAKE SW (DIESEL W/ 4L80-E)	A-B 16
TCC BRAKE SW (DIESEL W/O 4L80-E)	D-E 12
TCC BRAKE SW (GAS W/ 4L80-E)	A 8
TCC BRAKE SW (GAS W/O 4L80-E)	E 7
TRAILER CONN	B-C 34
TRANSMISSION (GAS W/ 4L80-E)	C-D 8
TRANSMISSION CTRL MOD (TCM) (DIESEL W/ 4L80-E)	A 16-19
WASHER MTR	A 25
WATER IN FUEL IND	D 28
WATER IN FUEL SENS (DIESEL W/ 4L80-E)	E 16
WATER IN FUEL SENS (DIESEL W/O 4L80-E)	D-E 15
WIPER MTR	A 26
WIPER/WASHER SW	A 24

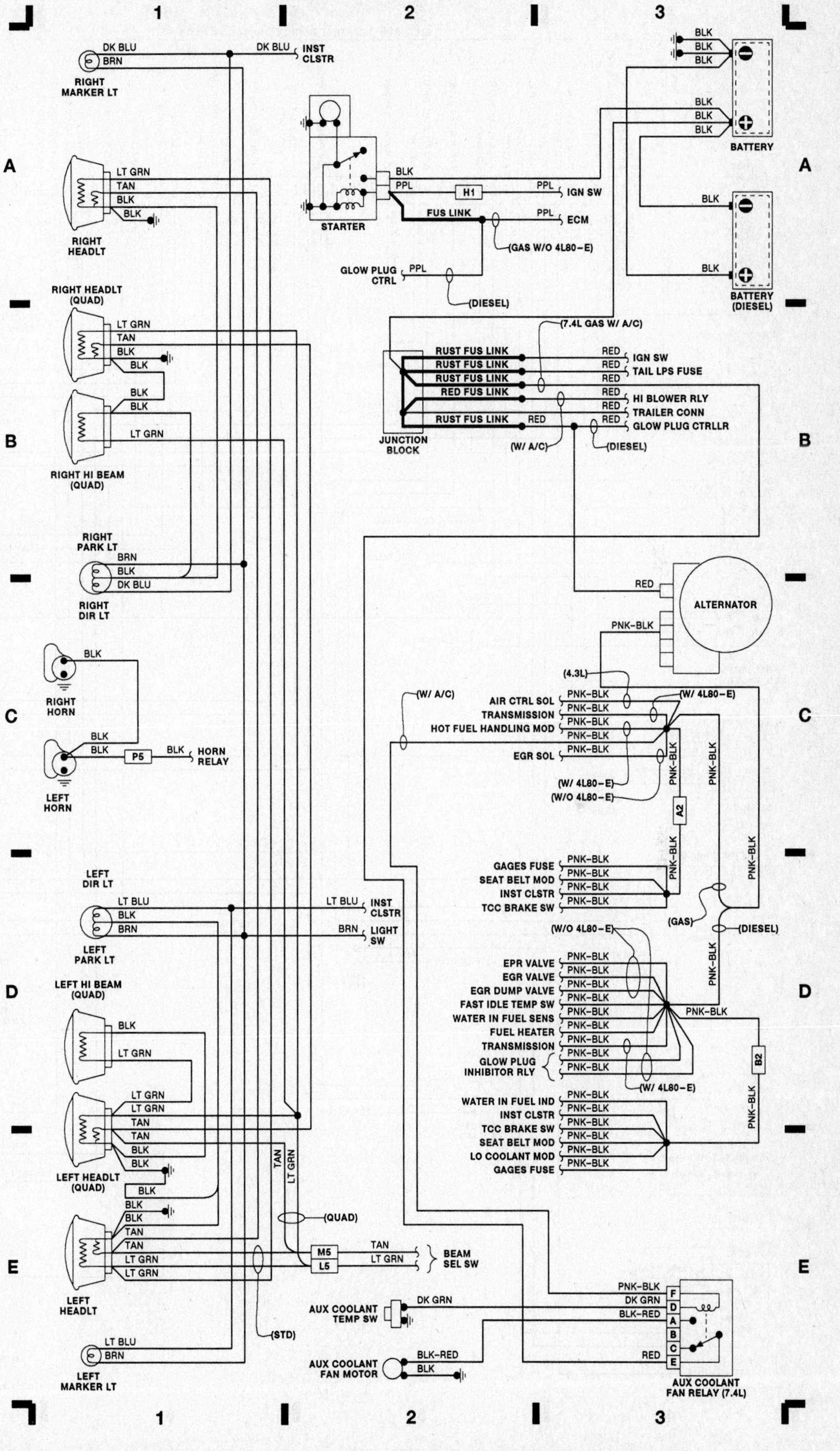

RIGHT MARKER LT
INST CLSTR
RIGHT HEADLT
STARTER
IGN SW
FUS LINK
ECM
(GAS W/O 4L80-E)
GLOW PLUG CTRL
(DIESEL)
BATTERY
BATTERY (DIESEL)
RIGHT HEADLT (QUAD)
RIGHT HI BEAM (QUAD)
(7.4L GAS W/ A/C)
RUST FUS LINK
RED FUS LINK
TAIL LPS FUSE
HI BLOWER RLY
TRAILER CONN
GLOW PLUG CTRLLR
JUNCTION BLOCK
(W/ A/C)
RIGHT PARK LT
RIGHT DIR LT
ALTERNATOR
RIGHT HORN
LEFT HORN
HORN RELAY
(4.3L)
AIR CTRL SOL
TRANSMISSION
HOT FUEL HANDLING MOD
EGR SOL
(W/ 4L80-E)
(W/O 4L80-E)
GAGES FUSE
SEAT BELT MOD
TCC BRAKE SW
LEFT DIR LT
LIGHT SW
LEFT PARK LT
(GAS)
(DIESEL)
EPR VALVE
EGR VALVE
EGR DUMP VALVE
FAST IDLE TEMP SW
WATER IN FUEL SENS
FUEL HEATER
GLOW PLUG INHIBITOR RLY
LEFT HI BEAM (QUAD)
WATER IN FUEL IND
LO COOLANT MOD
LEFT HEADLT (QUAD)
(QUAD)
BEAM SEL SW
LEFT HEADLT
(STD)
AUX COOLANT TEMP SW
AUX COOLANT FAN MOTOR
AUX COOLANT FAN RELAY (7.4L)
LEFT MARKER LT

1991 WIRING DIAGRAMS
"G" Series (Cont.)

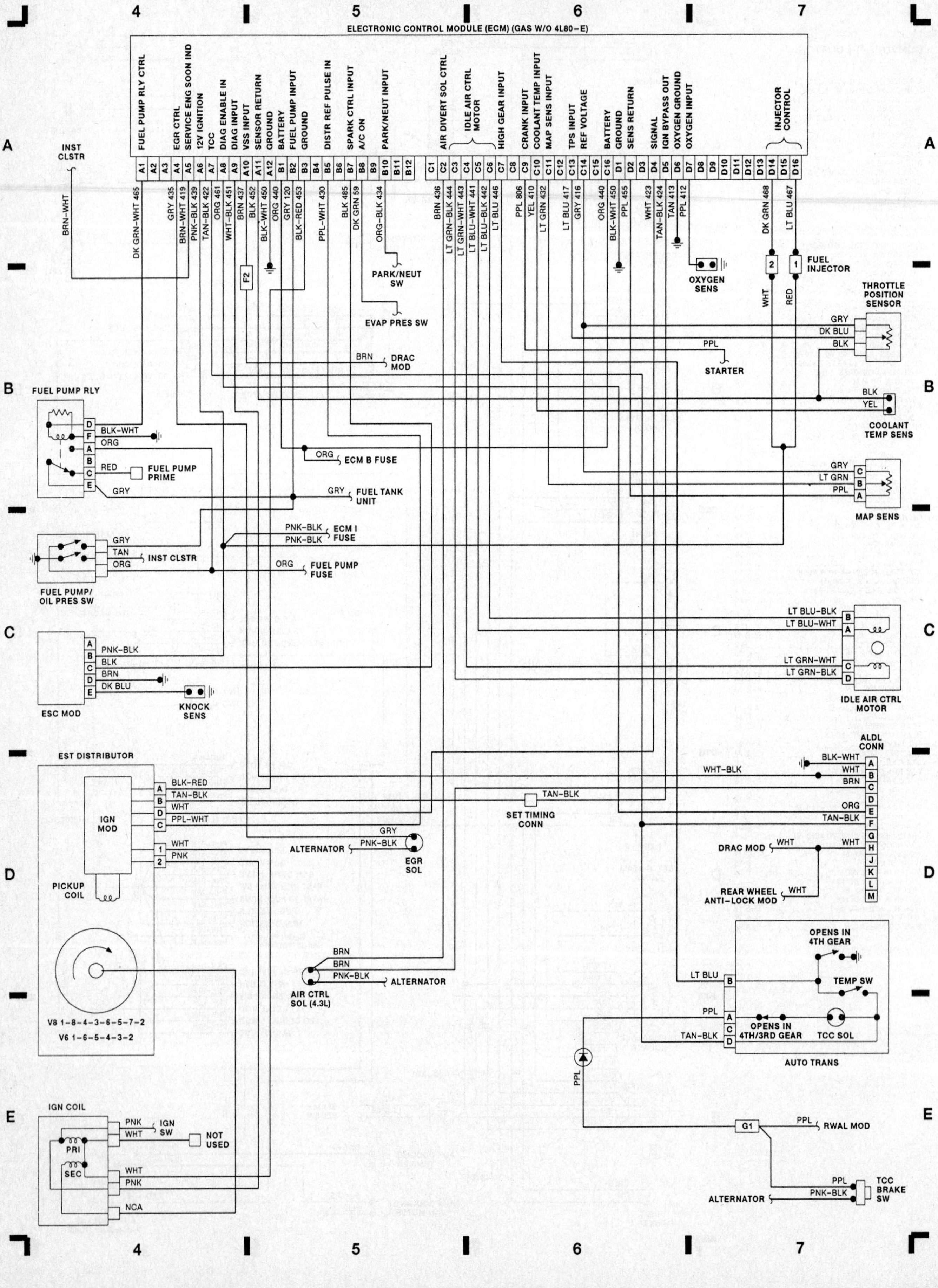
ELECTRONIC CONTROL MODULE (ECM) (GAS W/O 4L80-E)
FUEL PUMP RLY CTRL
EGR CTRL
SERVICE ENG SOON IND
12V IGNITION
TCC
DIAG ENABLE IN
DIAG INPUT
VSS INPUT
SENSOR RETURN
GROUND
BATTERY
FUEL PUMP INPUT
GROUND
DISTR REF PULSE IN
SPARK CTRL INPUT
A/C ON
PARK/NEUT INPUT
AIR DIVERT SOL CTRL
IDLE AIR CTRL MOTOR
HIGH GEAR INPUT
CRANK INPUT
COOLANT TEMP INPUT
MAP SENS INPUT
TPS INPUT
REF VOLTAGE
BATTERY
GROUND
SENS RETURN
SIGNAL
IGN BYPASS OUT
OXYGEN GROUND
OXYGEN INPUT
INJECTOR CONTROL
INST CLSTR
BRN-WHT
DK GRN-WHT 465
GRY 435
BRN-WHT 419
PNK-BLK 439
TAN-BLK 422
ORG 461
WHT-BLK 451
BRN 437
BLK 452
BLK-WHT 450
ORG 440
GRY 120
BLK-RED 453
PPL-WHT 430
BLK 485
DK GRN 59
ORG-BLK 434
BRN 436
LT GRN-BLK 444
LT GRN-WHT 443
LT BLU-WHT 441
LT BLU-BLK 442
LT BLU 446
PPL 806
YEL 410
LT GRN 432
LT BLU 417
GRY 416
ORG 440
BLK-WHT 450
PPL 455
WHT 423
TAN-BLK 424
TAN 413
PPL 412
DK GRN 468
LT BLU 467
F2
PARK/NEUT SW
EVAP PRES SW
OXYGEN SENS
FUEL INJECTOR
WHT
RED
THROTTLE POSITION SENSOR
GRY
DK BLU
BLK
PPL
STARTER
DRAC MOD
FUEL PUMP RLY
BLK-WHT
ORG
RED
FUEL PUMP PRIME
GRY
COOLANT TEMP SENS
YEL
ECM B FUSE
FUEL TANK UNIT
LT GRN
MAP SENS
PNK-BLK
ECM I FUSE
TAN
INST CLSTR
FUEL PUMP FUSE
FUEL PUMP/ OIL PRES SW
LT BLU-BLK
LT BLU-WHT
LT GRN-WHT
LT GRN-BLK
IDLE AIR CTRL MOTOR
ESC MOD
BRN
DK BLU
KNOCK SENS
EST DISTRIBUTOR
IGN MOD
BLK-RED
WHT
PPL-WHT
PNK
PICKUP COIL
SET TIMING CONN
ALTERNATOR
EGR SOL
ALDL CONN
WHT-BLK
REAR WHEEL ANTI-LOCK MOD
V8 1-8-4-3-6-5-7-2
V6 1-6-5-4-3-2
AIR CTRL SOL (4.3L)
OPENS IN 4TH GEAR
TEMP SW
OPENS IN 4TH/3RD GEAR
TCC SOL
AUTO TRANS
IGN COIL
IGN SW
NOT USED
PRI
SEC
NCA
G1
RWAL MOD
TCC BRAKE SW

1991 WIRING DIAGRAMS
"G" Series (Cont.)

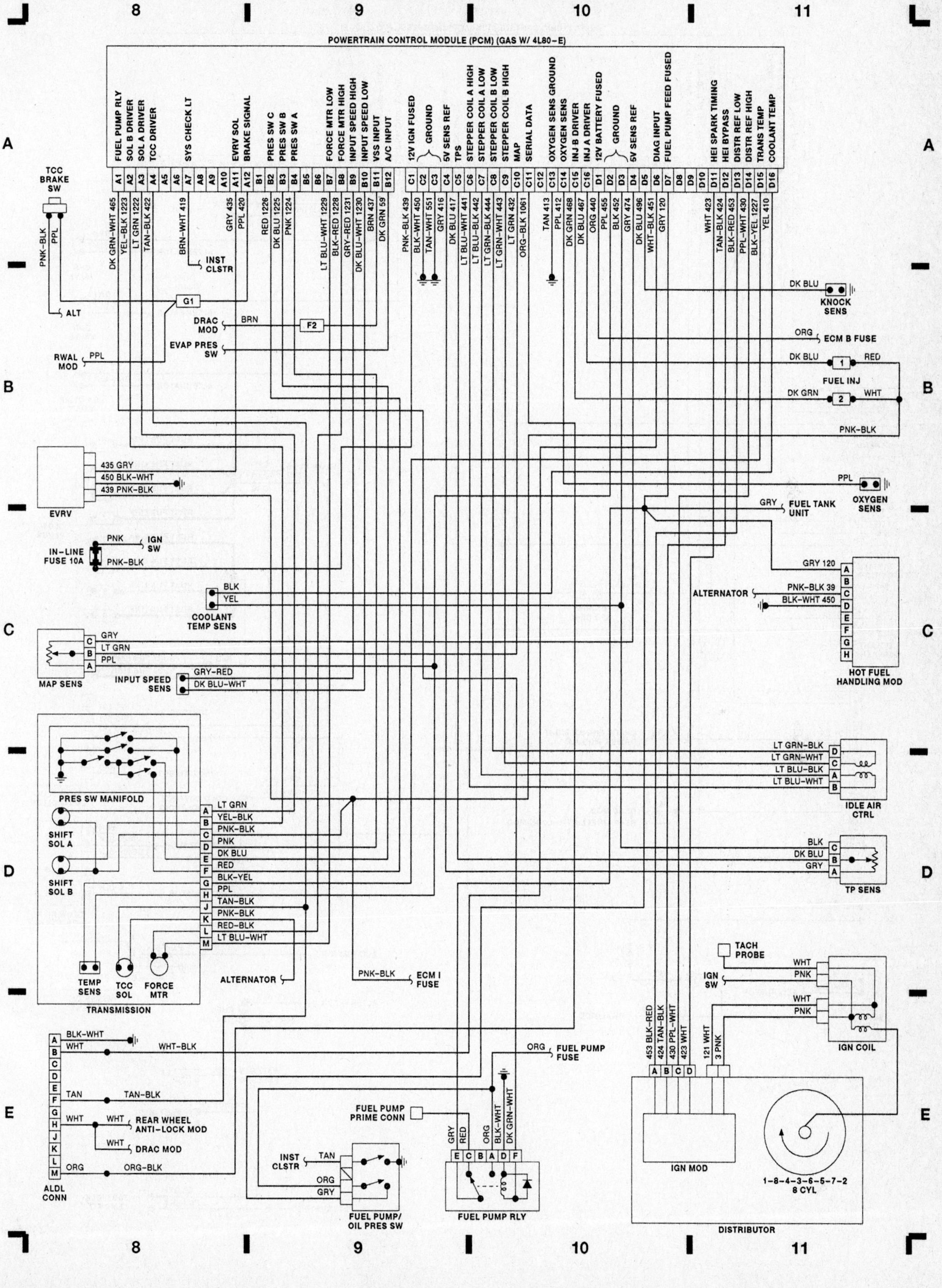
8
9
10
11
A
B
C
D
E
POWERTRAIN CONTROL MODULE (PCM) (GAS W/ 4L80-E)
FUEL PUMP RLY
SOL B DRIVER
SOL A DRIVER
TCC DRIVER
SYS CHECK LT
EVRV SOL
BRAKE SIGNAL
PRES SW C
PRES SW B
PRES SW A
FORCE MTR LOW
FORCE MTR HIGH
INPUT SPEED HIGH
INPUT SPEED LOW
VSS INPUT
A/C INPUT
12V IGN FUSED
GROUND
5V SENS REF
TPS
STEPPER COIL A HIGH
STEPPER COIL A LOW
STEPPER COIL B LOW
STEPPER COIL B HIGH
MAP
SERIAL DATA
OXYGEN SENS GROUND
OXYGEN SENS
INJ B DRIVER
INJ A DRIVER
12V BATTERY FUSED
GROUND
5V SENS REF
DIAG INPUT
FUEL PUMP FEED FUSED
HEI SPARK TIMING
HEI BYPASS
DISTR REF LOW
DISTR REF HIGH
TRANS TEMP
COOLANT TEMP
A1 A2 A3 A4 A5 A6 A7 A8 A9 A10 A11 A12 B1 B2 B3 B4 B5 B6 B7 B8 B9 B10 B11 B12 C1 C2 C3 C4 C5 C6 C7 C8 C9 C10 C11 C12 C13 C14 C15 C16 D1 D2 D3 D4 D5 D6 D7 D8 D9 D10 D11 D12 D13 D14 D15 D16
DK GRN-WHT 465
YEL-BLK 1223
LT GRN 1222
TAN-BLK 422
BRN-WHT 419
GRY 435
PPL 420
RED 1226
DK BLU 1225
PNK 1224
LT BLU-WHT 1229
BLK-RED 1228
GRY-RED 1231
DK BLU-WHT 1230
BRN 437
DK GRN 59
PNK-BLK 439
BLK-WHT 450
TAN-WHT 551
GRY 416
DK BLU 417
LT BLU-WHT 441
LT BLU-BLK 442
LT GRN-BLK 444
LT GRN-WHT 443
LT GRN 432
ORG-BLK 1061
TAN 413
PPL 412
DK GRN 468
DK BLU 467
ORG 440
PPL 455
BLK 452
GRY 474
DK BLU 496
WHT-BLK 451
GRY 120
WHT 423
TAN-BLK 424
BLK-RED 453
PPL-WHT 430
BLK-YEL 1227
YEL 410
TCC BRAKE SW
PNK-BLK
PPL
INST CLSTR
ALT
G1
DRAC MOD
BRN
F2
EVAP PRES SW
RWAL MOD
PPL
DK BLU
KNOCK SENS
ORG
ECM B FUSE
DK BLU
RED
1
FUEL INJ
DK GRN
WHT
2
PNK-BLK
435 GRY
450 BLK-WHT
439 PNK-BLK
EVRV
PPL
OXYGEN SENS
GRY
FUEL TANK UNIT
PNK
IGN SW
IN-LINE FUSE 10A
PNK-BLK
GRY 120
ALTERNATOR
PNK-BLK 39
BLK-WHT 450
BLK
YEL
COOLANT TEMP SENS
A B C D E F G H
HOT FUEL HANDLING MOD
GRY
LT GRN
PPL
MAP SENS
GRY-RED
DK BLU-WHT
INPUT SPEED SENS
LT GRN-BLK
LT GRN-WHT
LT BLU-BLK
LT BLU-WHT
IDLE AIR CTRL
PRES SW MANIFOLD
LT GRN
YEL-BLK
PNK-BLK
PNK
DK BLU
RED
BLK-YEL
PPL
TAN-BLK
PNK-BLK
RED-BLK
LT BLU-WHT
SHIFT SOL A
SHIFT SOL B
BLK
DK BLU
GRY
TP SENS
TEMP SENS
TCC SOL
FORCE MTR
TRANSMISSION
ALTERNATOR
PNK-BLK
ECM I FUSE
TACH PROBE
WHT
PNK
IGN SW
WHT
PNK
IGN COIL
BLK-WHT
WHT
WHT-BLK
ORG
FUEL PUMP FUSE
TAN
TAN-BLK
453 BLK-RED
424 TAN-BLK
430 PPL-WHT
423 WHT
121 WHT
3 PNK
WHT
WHT
REAR WHEEL ANTI-LOCK MOD
WHT
DRAC MOD
FUEL PUMP PRIME CONN
GRY
RED
ORG
BLK-WHT
DK GRN-WHT
INST CLSTR
TAN
ORG
GRY
ORG
ORG-BLK
ALDL CONN
FUEL PUMP/ OIL PRES SW
E C B A D F
FUEL PUMP RLY
IGN MOD
1-8-4-3-6-5-7-2
8 CYL
DISTRIBUTOR

1991 WIRING DIAGRAMS
"G" Series (Cont.)

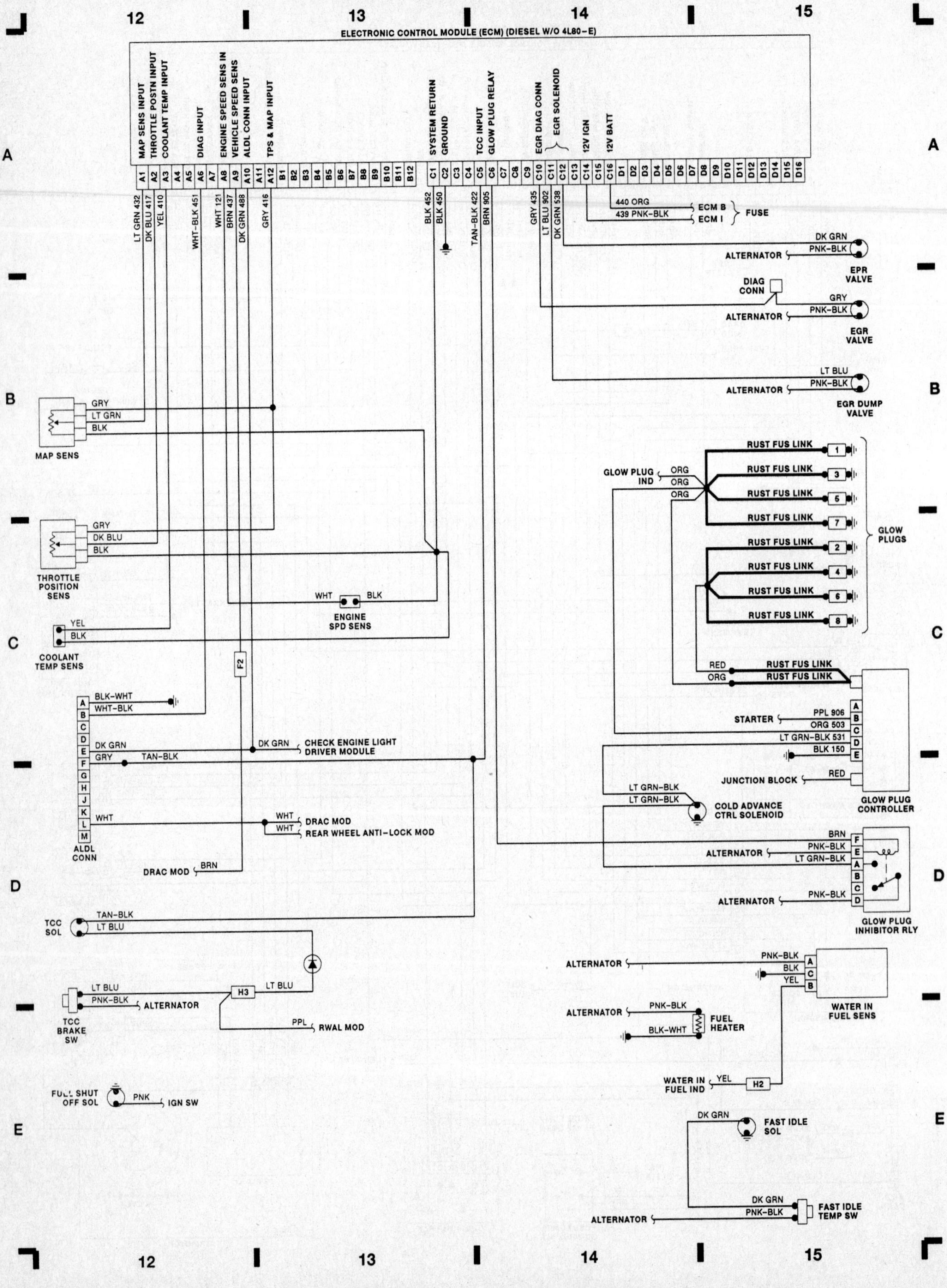
12
13
14
15
ELECTRONIC CONTROL MODULE (ECM) (DIESEL W/O 4L80-E)
MAP SENS INPUT
THROTTLE POSTN INPUT
COOLANT TEMP INPUT
DIAG INPUT
ENGINE SPEED SENS IN
VEHICLE SPEED SENS
ALDL CONN INPUT
TPS & MAP INPUT
SYSTEM RETURN
GROUND
TCC INPUT
GLOW PLUG RELAY
EGR DIAG CONN
EGR SOLENOID
12V IGN
12V BATT
A1 A2 A3 A4 A5 A6 A7 A8 A9 A10 A11 A12 B1 B2 B3 B4 B5 B6 B7 B8 B9 B10 B11 B12 C1 C2 C3 C4 C5 C6 C7 C8 C9 C10 C11 C12 C13 C14 C15 C16 D1 D2 D3 D4 D5 D6 D7 D8 D9 D10 D11 D12 D13 D14 D15 D16
LT GRN 432
DK BLU 417
YEL 410
WHT-BLK 451
WHT 121
BRN 437
DK GRN 488
GRY 416
BLK 452
BLK 450
TAN-BLK 422
BRN 905
GRY 435
LT BLU 902
DK GRN 538
440 ORG
439 PNK-BLK
ECM B
ECM I
FUSE
A
B
C
D
E
DK GRN
PNK-BLK
ALTERNATOR
EPR VALVE
DIAG CONN
GRY
EGR VALVE
LT BLU
EGR DUMP VALVE
GRY
LT GRN
BLK
MAP SENS
DK BLU
THROTTLE POSITION SENS
WHT
BLK
ENGINE SPD SENS
YEL
COOLANT TEMP SENS
F2
BLK-WHT
WHT-BLK
DK GRN
GRY
TAN-BLK
CHECK ENGINE LIGHT DRIVER MODULE
WHT
DRAC MOD
REAR WHEEL ANTI-LOCK MOD
A B C D E F G H J K L M
ALDL CONN
DRAC MOD
BRN
TCC SOL
H3
TCC BRAKE SW
RWAL MOD
PPL
FUEL SHUT OFF SOL
PNK
IGN SW
GLOW PLUG IND
ORG
RUST FUS LINK
1 3 5 7 2 4 6 8
GLOW PLUGS
RED
STARTER
PPL 906
ORG 503
LT GRN-BLK 531
BLK 150
JUNCTION BLOCK
GLOW PLUG CONTROLLER
LT GRN-BLK
COLD ADVANCE CTRL SOLENOID
GLOW PLUG INHIBITOR RLY
WATER IN FUEL SENS
FUEL HEATER
BLK-WHT
WATER IN FUEL IND
H2
FAST IDLE SOL
FAST IDLE TEMP SW

1991 WIRING DIAGRAMS
"G" Series (Cont.)

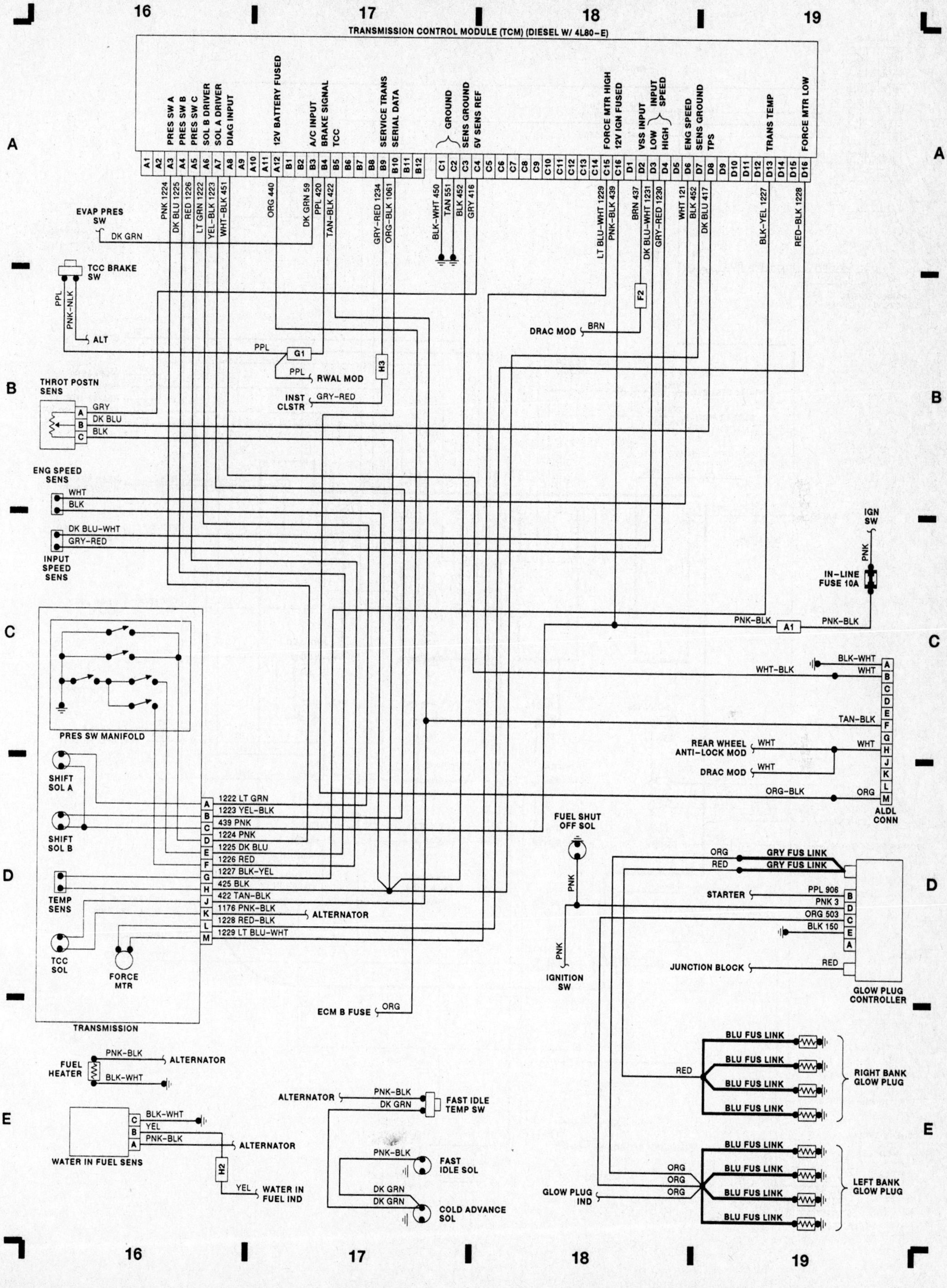
16
17
18
19
TRANSMISSION CONTROL MODULE (TCM) (DIESEL W/ 4L80-E)
PRES SW A
PRES SW B
PRES SW C
SOL B DRIVER
SOL A DRIVER
DIAG INPUT
12V BATTERY FUSED
A/C INPUT
BRAKE SIGNAL
TCC
SERVICE TRANS
SERIAL DATA
GROUND
SENS GROUND
5V SENS REF
FORCE MTR HIGH
12V IGN FUSED
VSS INPUT
LOW
HIGH
INPUT SPEED
ENG SPEED
SENS GROUND
TPS
TRANS TEMP
FORCE MTR LOW
EVAP PRES SW
TCC BRAKE SW
ALT
THROT POSTN SENS
ENG SPEED SENS
INPUT SPEED SENS
DRAC MOD
RWAL MOD
INST CLSTR
IGN SW
IN-LINE FUSE 10A
PRES SW MANIFOLD
SHIFT SOL A
SHIFT SOL B
TEMP SENS
TCC SOL
FORCE MTR
TRANSMISSION
ALTERNATOR
ECM B FUSE
REAR WHEEL ANTI-LOCK MOD
ALDL CONN
FUEL SHUT OFF SOL
IGNITION SW
STARTER
JUNCTION BLOCK
GLOW PLUG CONTROLLER
GRY FUS LINK
BLU FUS LINK
RIGHT BANK GLOW PLUG
LEFT BANK GLOW PLUG
GLOW PLUG IND
FUEL HEATER
WATER IN FUEL SENS
WATER IN FUEL IND
FAST IDLE TEMP SW
FAST IDLE SOL
COLD ADVANCE SOL
1222 LT GRN
1223 YEL-BLK
439 PNK
1224 PNK
1225 DK BLU
1226 RED
1227 BLK-YEL
425 BLK
422 TAN-BLK
1176 PNK-BLK
1228 RED-BLK
1229 LT BLU-WHT

1991 WIRING DIAGRAMS
"G" Series (Cont.)

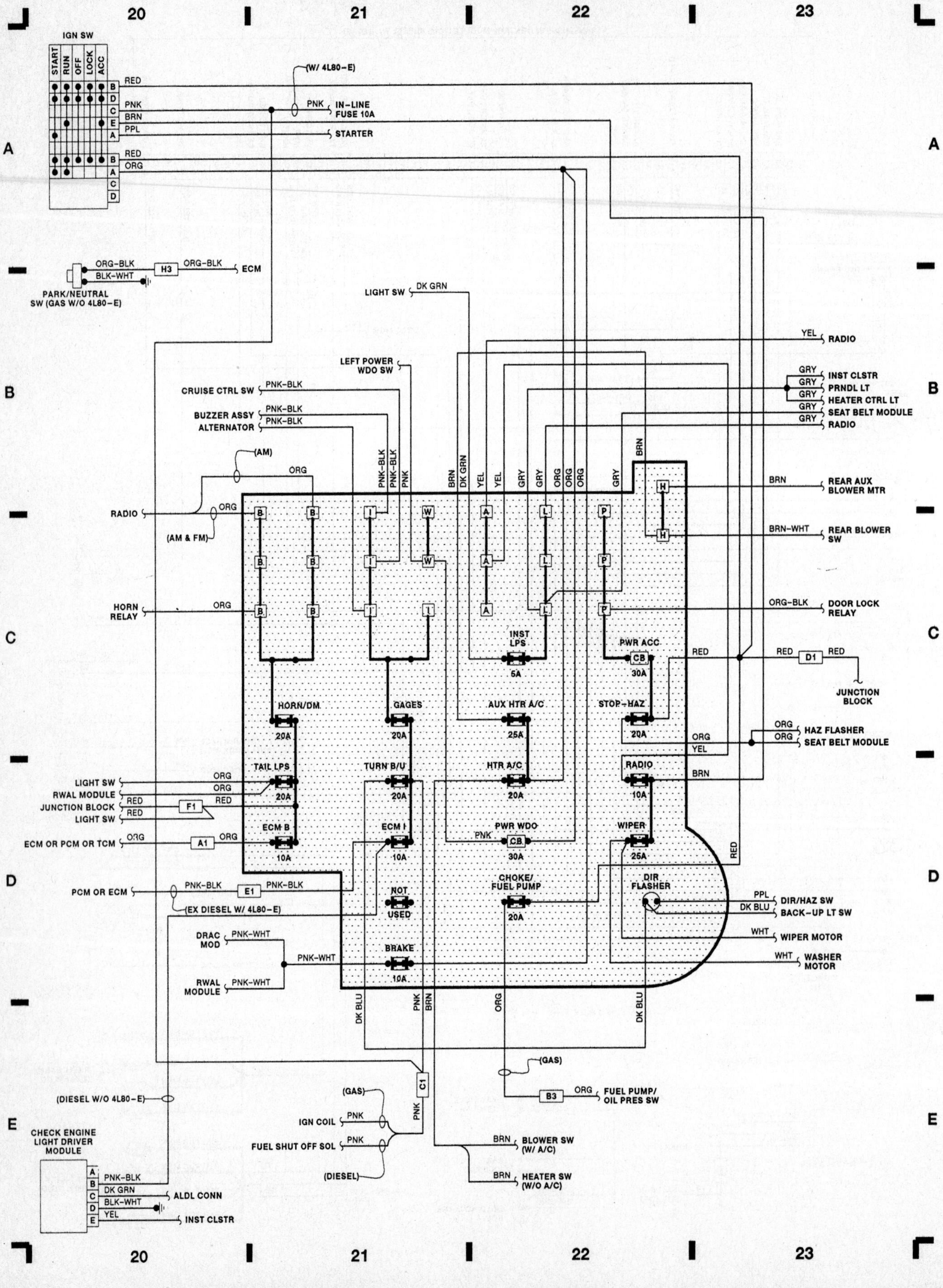
20
21
22
23
A
B
C
D
E
IGN SW
START
RUN
OFF
LOCK
ACC
RED
PNK
BRN
PPL
(W/ 4L80-E)
IN-LINE FUSE 10A
STARTER
ORG
ORG-BLK
BLK-WHT
H3
ECM
PARK/NEUTRAL SW (GAS W/O 4L80-E)
LIGHT SW
DK GRN
YEL
RADIO
LEFT POWER WDO SW
GRY
INST CLSTR
PRNDL LT
HEATER CTRL LT
SEAT BELT MODULE
CRUISE CTRL SW
PNK-BLK
BUZZER ASSY
ALTERNATOR
(AM)
(AM & FM)
REAR AUX BLOWER MTR
BRN-WHT
REAR BLOWER SW
HORN RELAY
DOOR LOCK RELAY
INST LPS
5A
PWR ACC
CB
30A
D1
JUNCTION BLOCK
HORN/DM
20A
GAGES
AUX HTR A/C
25A
STOP-HAZ
HAZ FLASHER
TAIL LPS
TURN B/U
HTR A/C
10A
RWAL MODULE
F1
ECM B
ECM I
PWR WDO
WIPER
ECM OR PCM OR TCM
A1
PCM OR ECM
E1
(EX DIESEL W/ 4L80-E)
NOT USED
CHOKE/ FUEL PUMP
DIR FLASHER
DIR/HAZ SW
DK BLU
BACK-UP LT SW
WHT
WIPER MOTOR
WASHER MOTOR
DRAC MOD
PNK-WHT
BRAKE
(GAS)
C1
B3
FUEL PUMP/ OIL PRES SW
(DIESEL W/O 4L80-E)
IGN COIL
FUEL SHUT OFF SOL
(DIESEL)
BLOWER SW (W/ A/C)
HEATER SW (W/O A/C)
CHECK ENGINE LIGHT DRIVER MODULE
ALDL CONN

1991 WIRING DIAGRAMS
"G" Series (Cont.)

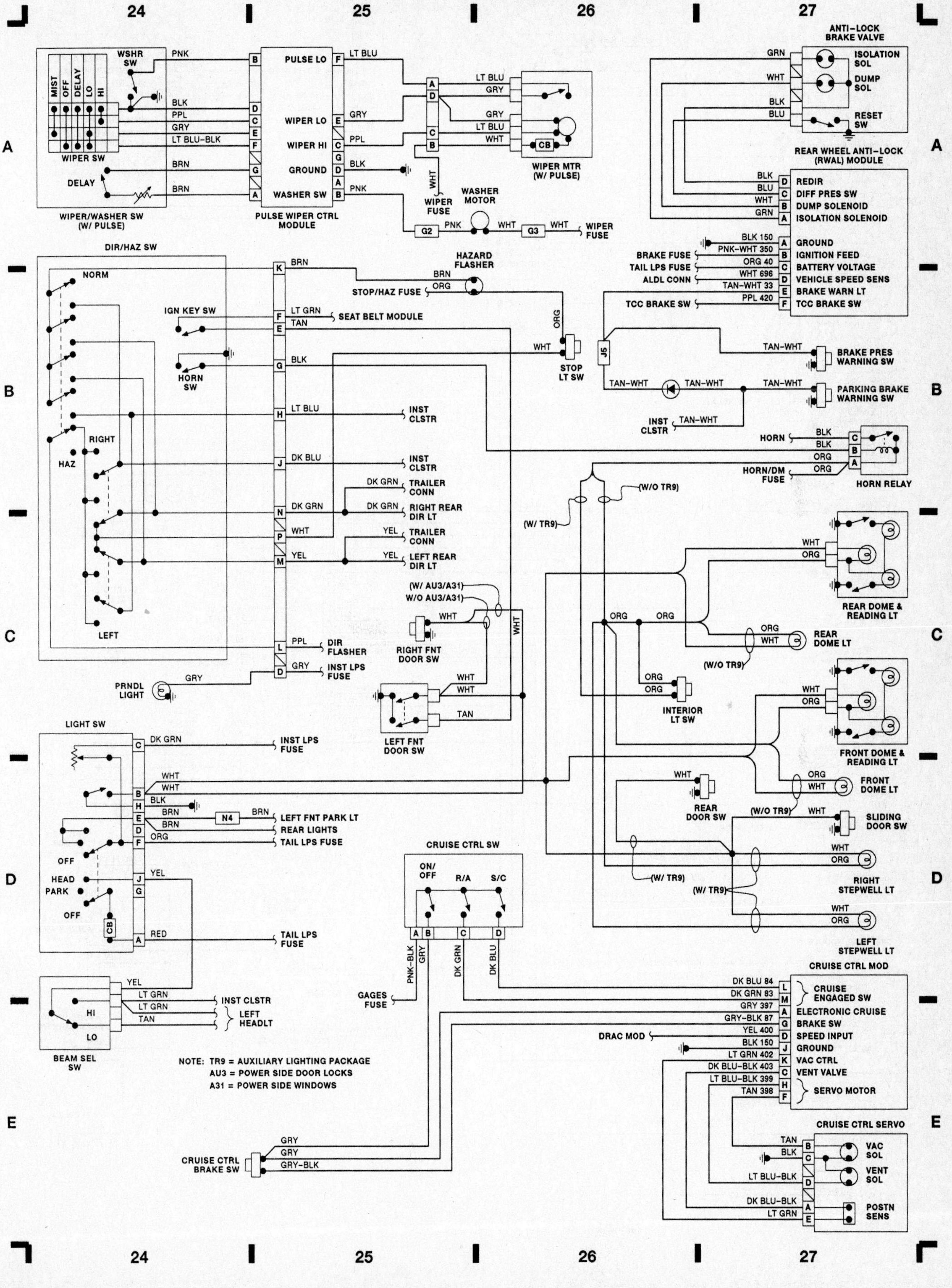
WIPER/WASHER SW (W/ PULSE)
PULSE WIPER CTRL MODULE
WIPER MTR (W/ PULSE)
WASHER MOTOR
WIPER FUSE
ANTI-LOCK BRAKE VALVE
ISOLATION SOL
DUMP SOL
RESET SW
REAR WHEEL ANTI-LOCK (RWAL) MODULE
REDIR
DIFF PRES SW
DUMP SOLENOID
ISOLATION SOLENOID
GROUND
IGNITION FEED
BATTERY VOLTAGE
VEHICLE SPEED SENS
BRAKE WARN LT
TCC BRAKE SW
BRAKE FUSE
TAIL LPS FUSE
ALDL CONN
DIR/HAZ SW
HAZARD FLASHER
STOP/HAZ FUSE
IGN KEY SW
SEAT BELT MODULE
HORN SW
STOP LT SW
BRAKE PRES WARNING SW
PARKING BRAKE WARNING SW
INST CLSTR
HORN
HORN/DM FUSE
HORN RELAY
TRAILER CONN
RIGHT REAR DIR LT
LEFT REAR DIR LT
RIGHT FNT DOOR SW
LEFT FNT DOOR SW
DIR FLASHER
INST LPS FUSE
PRNDL LIGHT
REAR DOME & READING LT
REAR DOME LT
INTERIOR LT SW
FRONT DOME & READING LT
FRONT DOME LT
REAR DOOR SW
SLIDING DOOR SW
RIGHT STEPWELL LT
LEFT STEPWELL LT
LIGHT SW
LEFT FNT PARK LT
REAR LIGHTS
TAIL LPS FUSE
CRUISE CTRL SW
GAGES FUSE
CRUISE CTRL MOD
CRUISE ENGAGED SW
ELECTRONIC CRUISE BRAKE SW
SPEED INPUT
VAC CTRL
VENT VALVE
SERVO MOTOR
DRAC MOD
BEAM SEL SW
LEFT HEADLT
CRUISE CTRL BRAKE SW
CRUISE CTRL SERVO
VAC SOL
VENT SOL
POSTN SENS
NOTE: TR9 = AUXILIARY LIGHTING PACKAGE
AU3 = POWER SIDE DOOR LOCKS
A31 = POWER SIDE WINDOWS

1991 WIRING DIAGRAMS
"G" Series (Cont.)

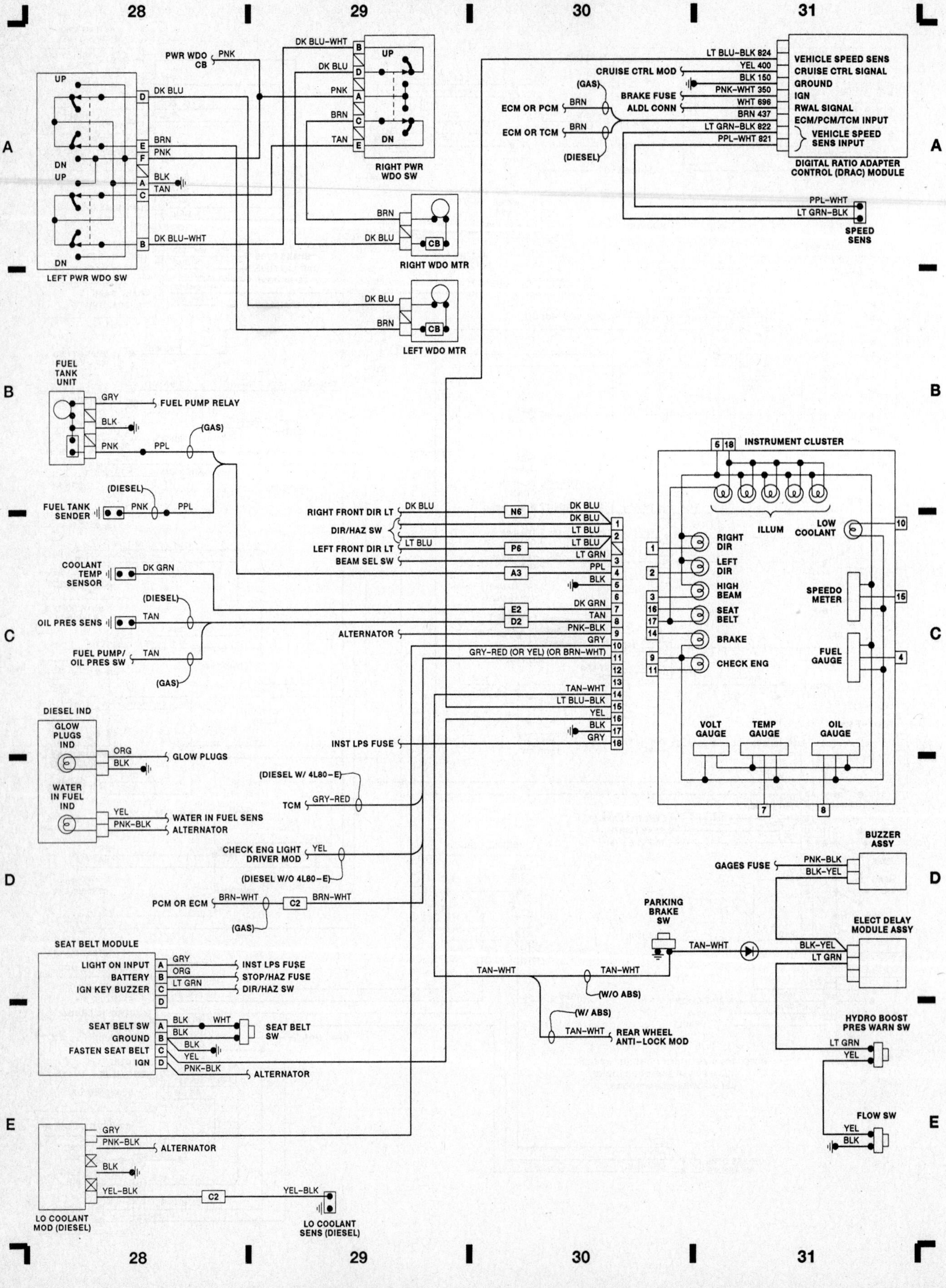
28
29
30
31
A
B
C
D
E
PWR WDO CB
PNK
DK BLU-WHT
DK BLU
BRN
TAN
UP
DN
RIGHT PWR WDO SW
LEFT PWR WDO SW
DK BLU
BRN
PNK
BLK
TAN
DK BLU-WHT
RIGHT WDO MTR
LEFT WDO MTR
CB
LT BLU-BLK 824
YEL 400
BLK 150
PNK-WHT 350
WHT 696
BRN 437
LT GRN-BLK 822
PPL-WHT 821
CRUISE CTRL MOD
(GAS)
BRAKE FUSE
ALDL CONN
ECM OR PCM
ECM OR TCM
(DIESEL)
VEHICLE SPEED SENS
CRUISE CTRL SIGNAL
GROUND
IGN
RWAL SIGNAL
ECM/PCM/TCM INPUT
VEHICLE SPEED SENS INPUT
DIGITAL RATIO ADAPTER CONTROL (DRAC) MODULE
PPL-WHT
LT GRN-BLK
SPEED SENS
FUEL TANK UNIT
GRY
FUEL PUMP RELAY
BLK
PNK
PPL
FUEL TANK SENDER
COOLANT TEMP SENSOR
DK GRN
OIL PRES SENS
FUEL PUMP/ OIL PRES SW
RIGHT FRONT DIR LT
DIR/HAZ SW
LEFT FRONT DIR LT
BEAM SEL SW
LT BLU
N6
P6
A3
E2
D2
LT GRN
PNK-BLK
ALTERNATOR
GRY-RED (OR YEL) (OR BRN-WHT)
TAN-WHT
LT BLU-BLK
YEL
INST LPS FUSE
INSTRUMENT CLUSTER
ILLUM
RIGHT DIR
LEFT DIR
HIGH BEAM
SEAT BELT
BRAKE
CHECK ENG
LOW COOLANT
SPEEDO METER
FUEL GAUGE
VOLT GAUGE
TEMP GAUGE
OIL GAUGE
DIESEL IND
GLOW PLUGS IND
ORG
GLOW PLUGS
WATER IN FUEL IND
WATER IN FUEL SENS
(DIESEL W/ 4L80-E)
TCM
GRY-RED
CHECK ENG LIGHT DRIVER MOD
(DIESEL W/O 4L80-E)
PCM OR ECM
BRN-WHT
C2
SEAT BELT MODULE
LIGHT ON INPUT
BATTERY
IGN KEY BUZZER
SEAT BELT SW
GROUND
FASTEN SEAT BELT
IGN
INST LPS FUSE
STOP/HAZ FUSE
DIR/HAZ SW
WHT
SEAT BELT SW
PARKING BRAKE SW
TAN-WHT
(W/O ABS)
(W/ ABS)
REAR WHEEL ANTI-LOCK MOD
BUZZER ASSY
GAGES FUSE
BLK-YEL
ELECT DELAY MODULE ASSY
HYDRO BOOST PRES WARN SW
FLOW SW
LO COOLANT MOD (DIESEL)
YEL-BLK
LO COOLANT SENS (DIESEL)

1991 WIRING DIAGRAMS
"G" Series (Cont.)

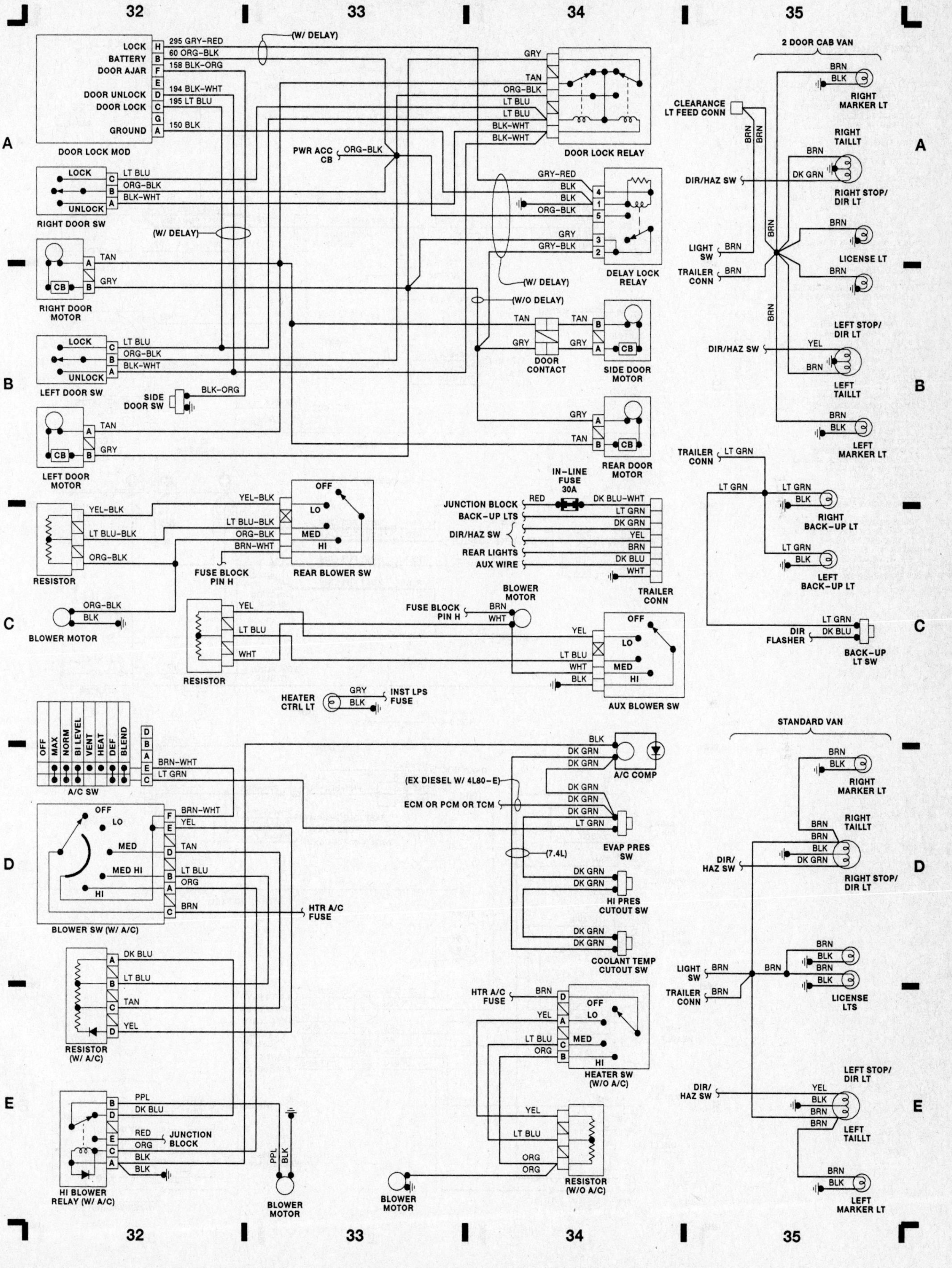
32
33
34
35
DOOR LOCK MOD
LOCK
BATTERY
DOOR AJAR
DOOR UNLOCK
DOOR LOCK
GROUND
295 GRY-RED
60 ORG-BLK
158 BLK-ORG
194 BLK-WHT
195 LT BLU
150 BLK
(W/ DELAY)
PWR ACC CB
DOOR LOCK RELAY
RIGHT DOOR SW
LEFT DOOR SW
RIGHT DOOR MOTOR
LEFT DOOR MOTOR
DELAY LOCK RELAY
(W/O DELAY)
DOOR CONTACT
SIDE DOOR MOTOR
SIDE DOOR SW
REAR DOOR MOTOR
2 DOOR CAB VAN
CLEARANCE LT FEED CONN
RIGHT MARKER LT
RIGHT TAILLT
DIR/HAZ SW
RIGHT STOP/DIR LT
LIGHT SW
TRAILER CONN
LICENSE LT
LEFT STOP/DIR LT
LEFT TAILLT
LEFT MARKER LT
RIGHT BACK-UP LT
LEFT BACK-UP LT
DIR FLASHER
BACK-UP LT SW
RESISTOR
REAR BLOWER SW
FUSE BLOCK PIN H
BLOWER MOTOR
JUNCTION BLOCK
BACK-UP LTS
REAR LIGHTS
AUX WIRE
IN-LINE FUSE 30A
TRAILER CONN
AUX BLOWER SW
HEATER CTRL LT
INST LPS FUSE
A/C SW
OFF MAX NORM BI LEVEL VENT HEAT DEF BLEND
A/C COMP
(EX DIESEL W/ 4L80-E)
ECM OR PCM OR TCM
EVAP PRES SW
(7.4L)
HI PRES CUTOUT SW
COOLANT TEMP CUTOUT SW
BLOWER SW (W/ A/C)
HTR A/C FUSE
RESISTOR (W/ A/C)
HI BLOWER RELAY (W/ A/C)
HEATER SW (W/O A/C)
RESISTOR (W/O A/C)
STANDARD VAN
LICENSE LTS
OFF
LO
MED
MED HI
HI

1991 WIRING DIAGRAMS
"P" Series – Commercial

COMPONENT LOCATOR:

ALARM	E 20
ALDL CONN (DIESEL W/ 4L80–E)	C–D 15
ALDL CONN (GAS W/ 4L80–E)	E 8
ALDL CONN (GAS W/O 4L80–E)	D–E 4
ALTERNATOR (DIESEL)	C–D 3
ALTERNATOR (GAS)	B 3
BACK–UP LT SW	A 25
BEAM SEL SW	B 24
CLUTCH SW (GAS)	B 1
DIGITAL RATIO ADAPTER CONTROLLER (DRAC) MOD	D 24
DIR/HAZ SW	B–D 24
EGR SOL (4.3L) (GAS W/ 4L80–E)	C 8
ELECTRONIC CONTROL MODULE (ECM) (GAS W/O 4L80–E)	A 4–7
FAST IDLE TEMP SW (DIESEL W/ 4L80–E)	E 13
FLASHER UNIT	E 20
FUEL CYCLE MOD (GAS W/ 4L80–E)	C 11
FUEL CYCLE MOD (GAS W/O 4L80–E)	C 4
FUEL HEATER (DIESEL W/ 4L80–E)	E 12
FUEL INJ (GAS W/O 4L80–E)	B 7
FUEL PUMP RLY (GAS W/ 4L80–E)	E 10
FUEL PUMP RLY (GAS W/O 4L80–E)	B 4
FUEL PUMP SW/OIL PRES SENS (GAS W/ 4L80–E)	E 9
FUEL PUMP SW/OIL PRES SENS (GAS W/O 4L80–E)	C 4
FUEL TANK UNIT	C 23
GLOW PLUG CTRLLR (DIESEL W/ 4L80–E)	D 15
GLOW PLUGS (DIESEL W/ 4L80–E)	E 15
HAZ FLASHER	C 25–26
HORN RLY	C–D 27
IGN COIL (GAS W/ 4L80–E)	E 11
IGN COIL (GAS W/O 4L80–E)	E 6–7
INST CLSTR	A–B 21–22
JUNCTION BLOCK (DIESEL)	C 2
JUNCTION BLOCK (GAS)	A 2
LIGHT SW	A 24
LO COOLANT MOD (DIESEL)	B–C 21–22
POWERTRAIN CONTROL MODULE (PCM) (GAS W/ 4L80–E)	A 8–11
STARTER (DIESEL)	C 3
STARTER (GAS)	A 3
STOP LT SW	B 25–26
TRANSMISSION (DIESEL W/ 4L80–E)	C–D 12
TRANSMISSION (GAS W/ 4L80–E)	C–D 8
TRANSMISSION CONTROL MODULE (TCM) (DIESEL W/ 4L80–E)	A 12–15
WATER IN FUEL SENS (DIESEL W/ 4L80–E)	E 12
WIPER/WASHER MOTOR	E 3
WIPER/WASHER SW	D–E 23

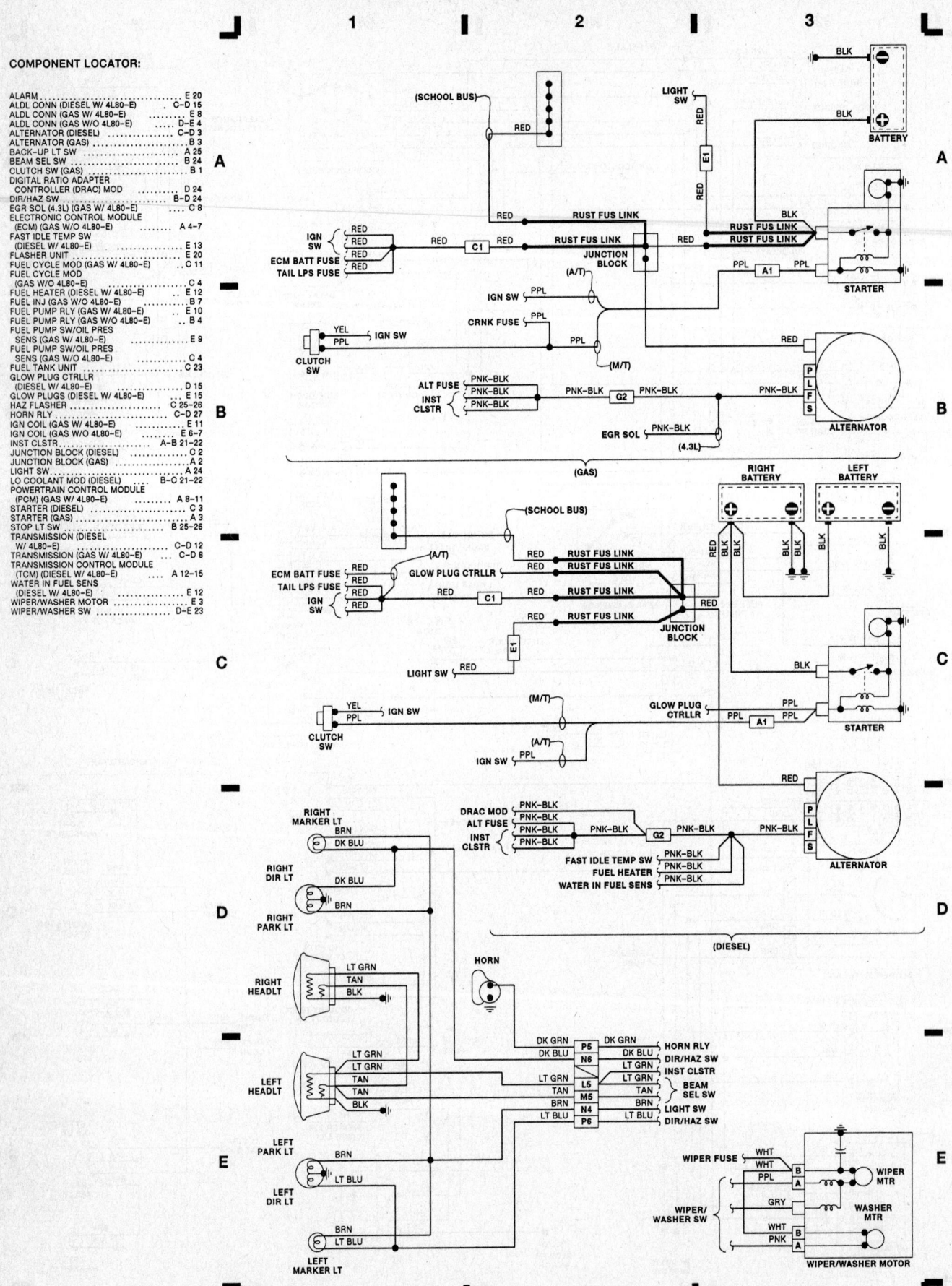

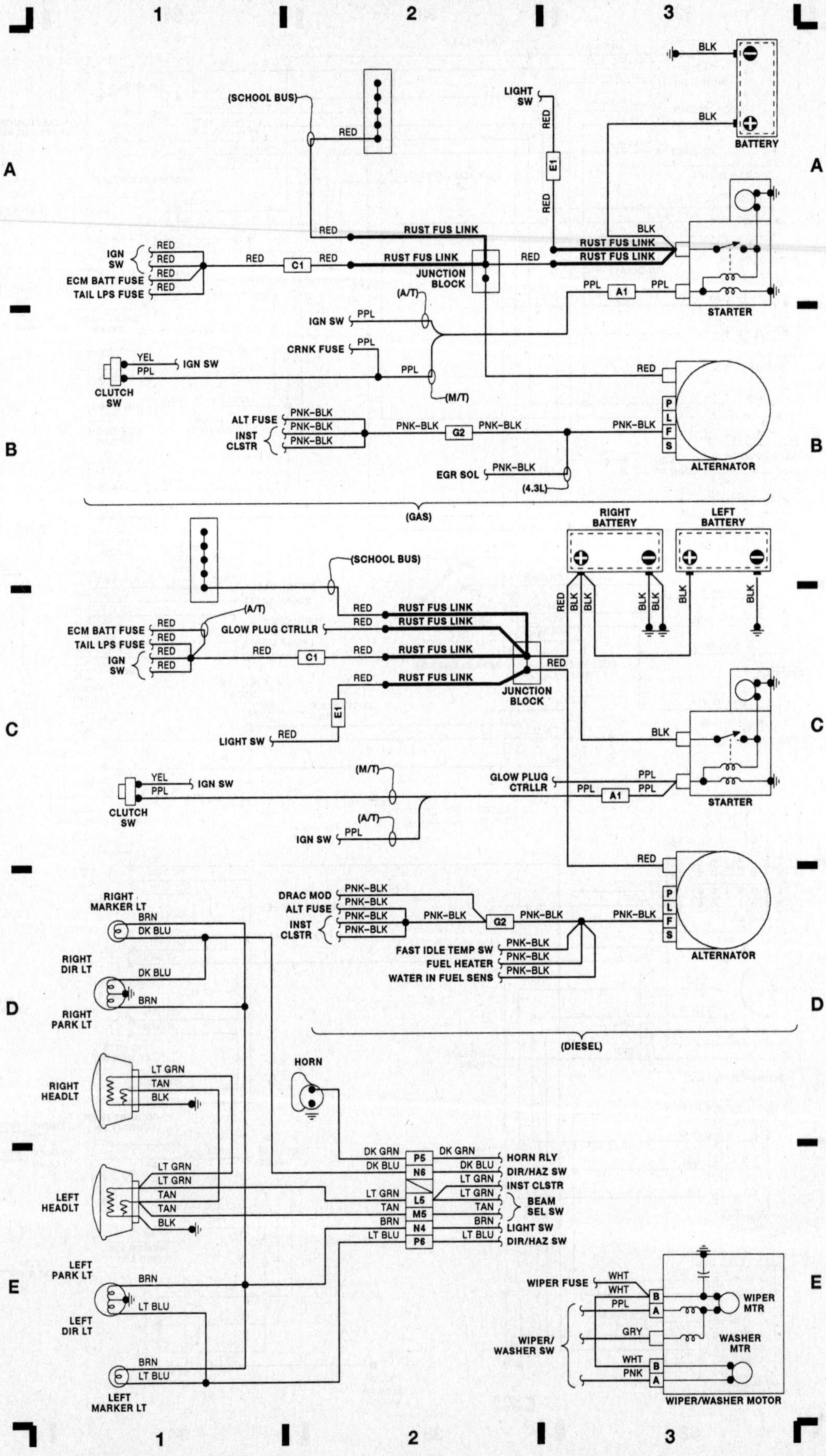
1
2
3
A
B
C
D
E
(SCHOOL BUS)
LIGHT SW
BATTERY
IGN SW
ECM BATT FUSE
TAIL LPS FUSE
RUST FUS LINK
JUNCTION BLOCK
STARTER
CRNK FUSE
CLUTCH SW
ALT FUSE
INST CLSTR
ALTERNATOR
EGR SOL
(4.3L)
(GAS)
RIGHT BATTERY
LEFT BATTERY
GLOW PLUG CTRLLR
DRAC MOD
FAST IDLE TEMP SW
FUEL HEATER
WATER IN FUEL SENS
(DIESEL)
RIGHT MARKER LT
RIGHT DIR LT
RIGHT PARK LT
HORN
RIGHT HEADLT
LEFT HEADLT
HORN RLY
DIR/HAZ SW
INST CLSTR
BEAM SEL SW
LIGHT SW
LEFT PARK LT
LEFT DIR LT
LEFT MARKER LT
WIPER FUSE
WIPER MTR
WIPER/WASHER SW
WASHER MTR
WIPER/WASHER MOTOR

1991 WIRING DIAGRAMS
"P" Series – Commercial (Cont.)

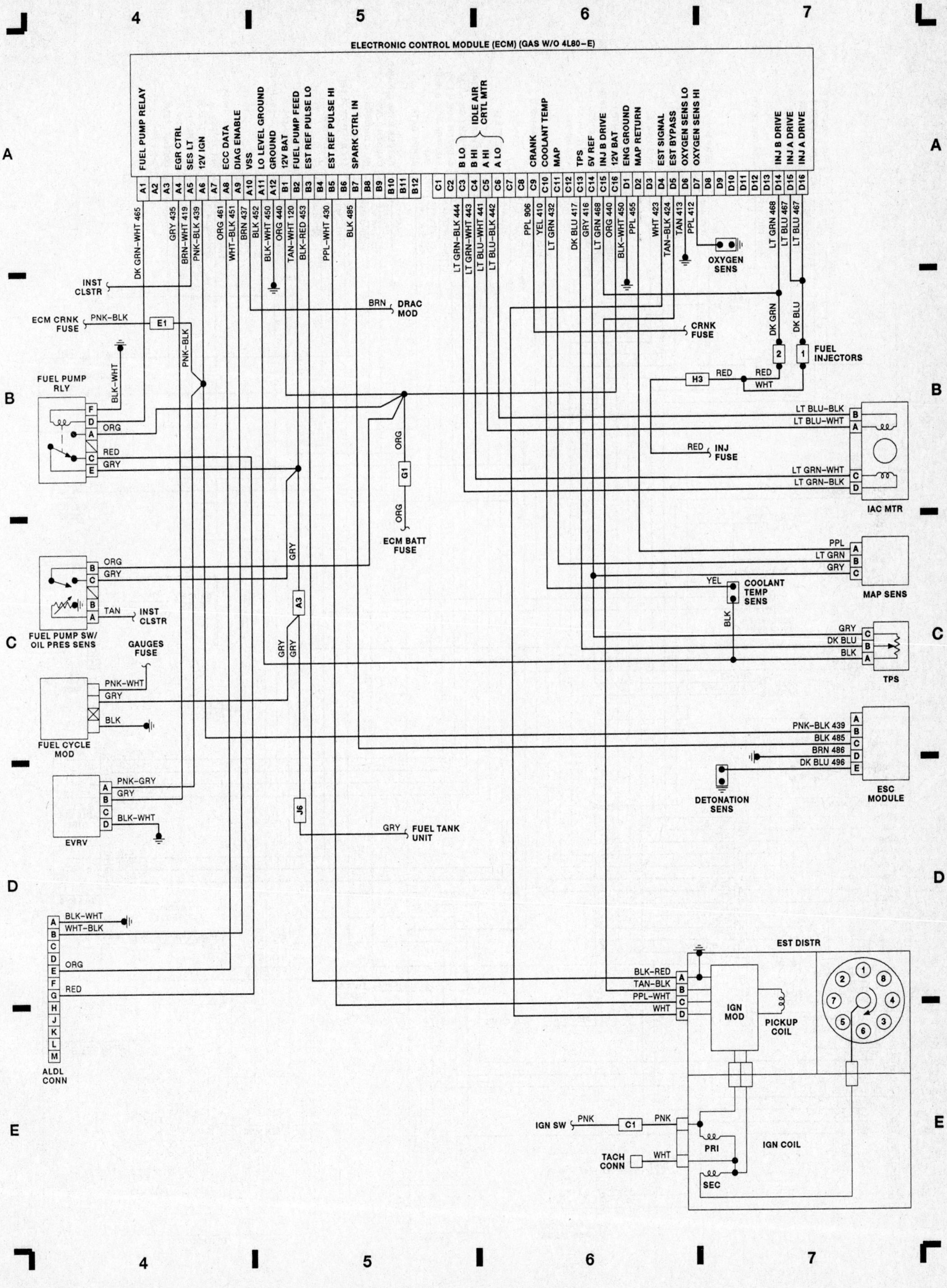
ELECTRONIC CONTROL MODULE (ECM) (GAS W/O 4L80–E)
FUEL PUMP RELAY
EGR CTRL
SES LT
12V IGN
ECC DATA
DIAG ENABLE
VSS
LO LEVEL GROUND
GROUND
12V BAT
FUEL PUMP FEED
EST REF PULSE LO
EST REF PULSE HI
SPARK CTRL IN
IDLE AIR CRTL MTR
B LO
B HI
A HI
A LO
CRANK
COOLANT TEMP
MAP
TPS
5V REF
INJ B DRIVE
12V BAT
ENG GROUND
MAP RETURN
EST SIGNAL
EST BYPASS
OXYGEN SENS LO
OXYGEN SENS HI
INJ B DRIVE
INJ A DRIVE
INJ A DRIVE
DK GRN–WHT 465
GRY 435
BRN–WHT 419
PNK–BLK 439
ORG 461
WHT–BLK 451
BRN 437
BLK 452
BLK–WHT 450
ORG 440
TAN–WHT 120
BLK–RED 453
PPL–WHT 430
BLK 485
LT GRN–BLK 444
LT GRN–WHT 443
LT BLU–WHT 441
LT BLU–BLK 442
PPL 906
YEL 410
LT GRN 432
DK BLU 417
GRY 416
LT GRN 468
ORG 440
BLK–WHT 450
PPL 455
WHT 423
TAN–BLK 424
TAN 413
PPL 412
LT GRN 468
LT BLU 467
LT BLU 467
OXYGEN SENS
INST CLSTR
BRN DRAC MOD
ECM CRNK FUSE
PNK–BLK
E1
CRNK FUSE
DK GRN
DK BLU
FUEL INJECTORS
FUEL PUMP RLY
BLK–WHT
H3
RED
WHT
LT BLU–BLK
LT BLU–WHT
ORG
GRY
INJ FUSE
LT GRN–WHT
LT GRN–BLK
G1
IAC MTR
ECM BATT FUSE
PPL
LT GRN
MAP SENS
YEL
COOLANT TEMP SENS
TAN
INST CLSTR
A3
FUEL PUMP SW/ OIL PRES SENS
GAUGES FUSE
DK BLU
BLK
TPS
PNK–WHT
FUEL CYCLE MOD
PNK–BLK 439
BLK 485
BRN 486
DK BLU 496
ESC MODULE
DETONATION SENS
PNK–GRY
J6
BLK–WHT
EVRV
GRY FUEL TANK UNIT
WHT–BLK
ALDL CONN
EST DISTR
BLK–RED
TAN–BLK
PPL–WHT
WHT
IGN MOD
PICKUP COIL
IGN SW
PNK
C1
PRI
IGN COIL
TACH CONN
SEC

1991 WIRING DIAGRAMS
"P" Series – Commercial (Cont.)

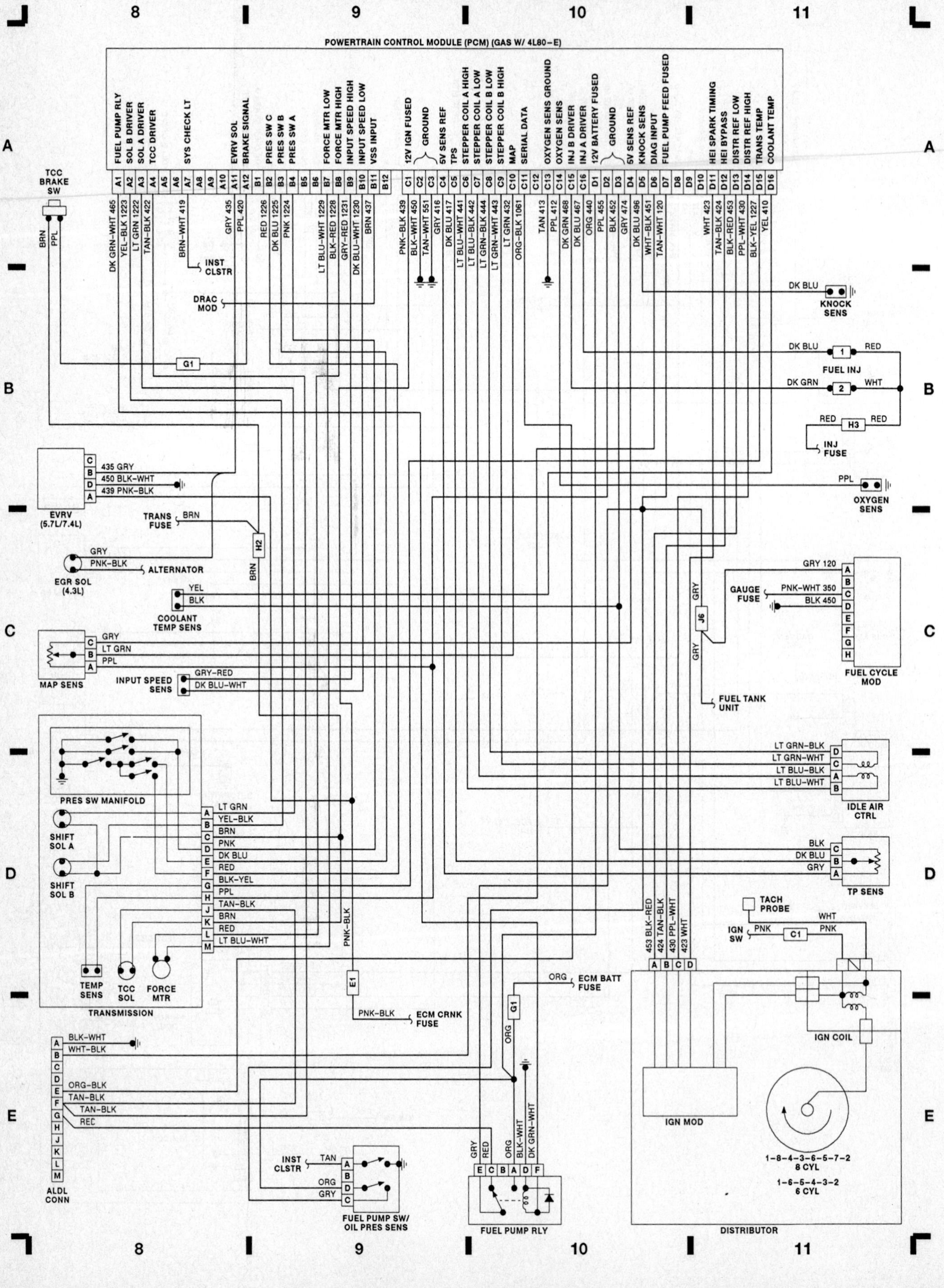
8
9
10
11
A
B
C
D
E
POWERTRAIN CONTROL MODULE (PCM) (GAS W/ 4L80–E)
FUEL PUMP RLY
SOL B DRIVER
SOL A DRIVER
TCC DRIVER
SYS CHECK LT
EVRV SOL
BRAKE SIGNAL
PRES SW C
PRES SW B
PRES SW A
FORCE MTR LOW
FORCE MTR HIGH
INPUT SPEED HIGH
INPUT SPEED LOW
VSS INPUT
12V IGN FUSED
GROUND
5V SENS REF
TPS
STEPPER COIL A HIGH
STEPPER COIL A LOW
STEPPER COIL B LOW
STEPPER COIL B HIGH
MAP
SERIAL DATA
OXYGEN SENS GROUND
OXYGEN SENS
INJ B DRIVER
INJ A DRIVER
12V BATTERY FUSED
GROUND
5V SENS REF
KNOCK SENS
DIAG INPUT
FUEL PUMP FEED FUSED
HEI SPARK TIMING
HEI BYPASS
DISTR REF LOW
DISTR REF HIGH
TRANS TEMP
COOLANT TEMP
A1 A2 A3 A4 A5 A6 A7 A8 A9 A10 A11 A12 B1 B2 B3 B4 B5 B6 B7 B8 B9 B10 B11 B12
C1 C2 C3 C4 C5 C6 C7 C8 C9 C10 C11 C12 C13 C14 C15 C16 D1 D2 D3 D4 D5 D6 D7 D8 D9 D10 D11 D12 D13 D14 D15 D16
DK GRN–WHT 465
YEL–BLK 1223
LT GRN 1222
TAN–BLK 422
BRN–WHT 419
GRY 435
PPL 420
RED 1226
DK BLU 1225
PNK 1224
LT BLU–WHT 1229
BLK–RED 1228
GRY–RED 1231
DK BLU–WHT 1230
BRN 437
PNK–BLK 439
BLK–WHT 450
TAN–WHT 551
GRY 416
DK BLU 417
LT BLU–WHT 441
LT BLU–BLK 442
LT GRN–BLK 444
LT GRN–WHT 443
LT GRN 432
ORG–BLK 1061
TAN 413
PPL 412
DK GRN 468
DK BLU 467
ORG 440
PPL 455
BLK 452
GRY 474
DK BLU 496
WHT–BLK 451
TAN–WHT 120
WHT 423
TAN–BLK 424
BLK–RED 453
PPL–WHT 430
BLK–YEL 1227
YEL 410
TCC BRAKE SW
BRN
PPL
INST CLSTR
DRAC MOD
G1
KNOCK SENS
DK BLU
FUEL INJ
RED
DK GRN
WHT
H3
INJ FUSE
EVRV (5.7L/7.4L)
435 GRY
450 BLK–WHT
439 PNK–BLK
TRANS FUSE
H2
OXYGEN SENS
EGR SOL (4.3L)
GRY
PNK–BLK
ALTERNATOR
COOLANT TEMP SENS
YEL
BLK
GRY 120
GAUGE FUSE
PNK–WHT 350
BLK 450
J6
FUEL CYCLE MOD
MAP SENS
LT GRN
INPUT SPEED SENS
GRY–RED
DK BLU–WHT
FUEL TANK UNIT
LT GRN–BLK
LT GRN–WHT
LT BLU–BLK
LT BLU–WHT
IDLE AIR CTRL
PRES SW MANIFOLD
SHIFT SOL A
SHIFT SOL B
YEL–BLK
BRN
PNK
DK BLU
RED
BLK–YEL
TAN–BLK
LT BLU–WHT
TP SENS
TACH PROBE
IGN SW
C1
TEMP SENS
TCC SOL
FORCE MTR
TRANSMISSION
E1
ECM CRNK FUSE
ORG
ECM BATT FUSE
453 BLK–RED
424 TAN–BLK
430 PPL–WHT
423 WHT
IGN COIL
ALDL CONN
BLK–WHT
WHT–BLK
ORG–BLK
TAN–BLK
REC
INST CLSTR
TAN
FUEL PUMP SW/ OIL PRES SENS
FUEL PUMP RLY
IGN MOD
1–8–4–3–6–5–7–2
8 CYL
1–6–5–4–3–2
6 CYL
DISTRIBUTOR

1991 WIRING DIAGRAMS
"P" Series – Commercial (Cont.)

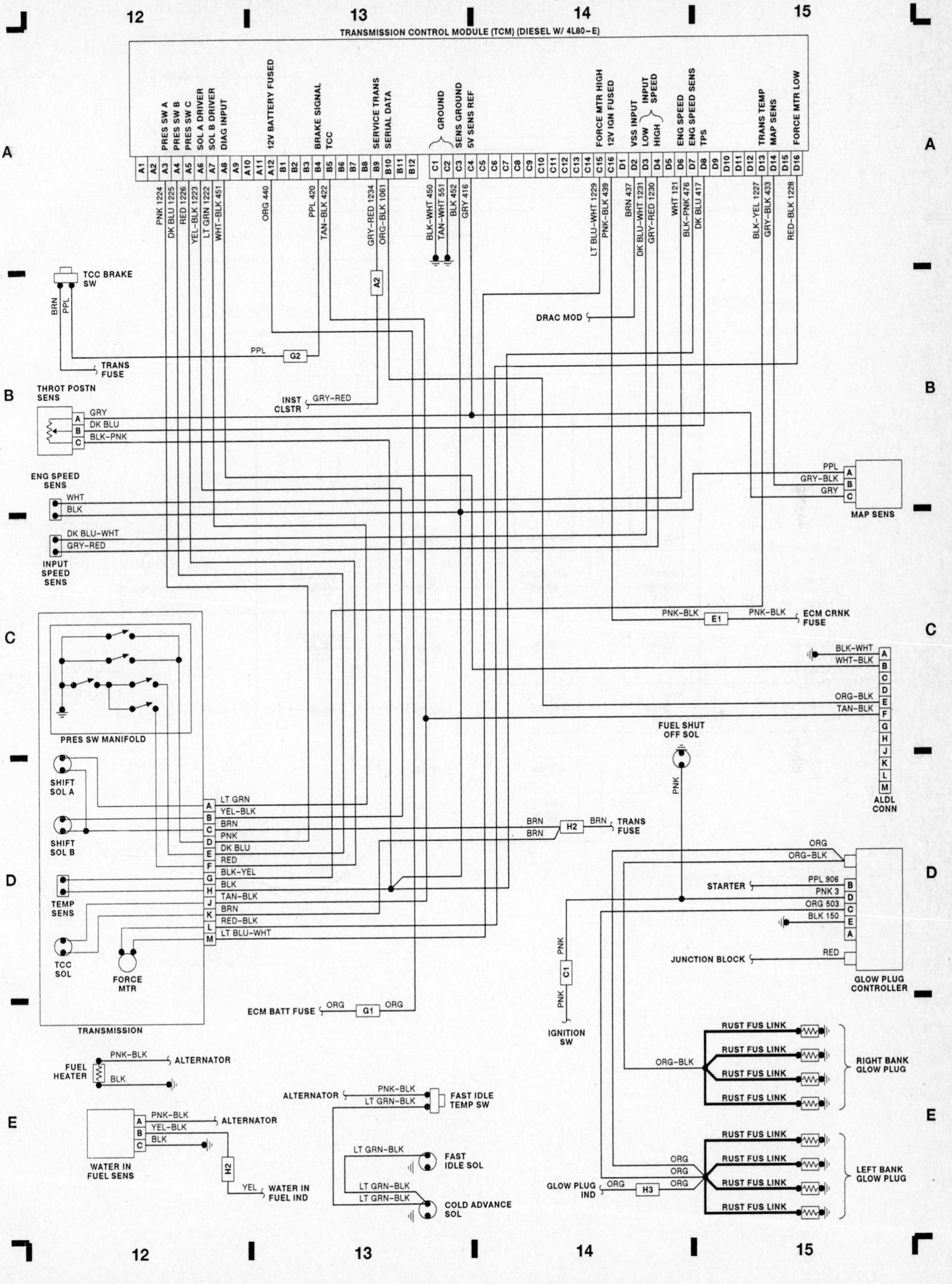
TRANSMISSION CONTROL MODULE (TCM) (DIESEL W/ 4L80-E)
PRES SW A
PRES SW B
PRES SW C
SOL A DRIVER
SOL B DRIVER
DIAG INPUT
12V BATTERY FUSED
BRAKE SIGNAL
TCC
SERVICE TRANS
SERIAL DATA
GROUND
SENS GROUND
5V SENS REF
FORCE MTR HIGH
12V IGN FUSED
VSS INPUT
LOW
HIGH
INPUT SPEED
ENG SPEED
ENG SPEED SENS
TPS
TRANS TEMP
MAP SENS
FORCE MTR LOW
PNK 1224
DK BLU 1225
RED 1226
YEL-BLK 1223
LT GRN 1222
WHT-BLK 451
ORG 440
PPL 420
TAN-BLK 422
GRY-RED 1234
ORG-BLK 1061
BLK-WHT 450
TAN-WHT 551
BLK 452
GRY 416
LT BLU-WHT 1229
PNK-BLK 439
BRN 437
DK BLU-WHT 1231
GRY-RED 1230
WHT 121
BLK-PNK 476
DK BLU 417
BLK-YEL 1227
GRY-BLK 433
RED-BLK 1228
TCC BRAKE SW
TRANS FUSE
DRAC MOD
INST CLSTR
THROT POSTN SENS
ENG SPEED SENS
INPUT SPEED SENS
MAP SENS
ECM CRNK FUSE
ALDL CONN
FUEL SHUT OFF SOL
PRES SW MANIFOLD
SHIFT SOL A
SHIFT SOL B
TEMP SENS
TCC SOL
FORCE MTR
TRANSMISSION
ECM BATT FUSE
STARTER
JUNCTION BLOCK
GLOW PLUG CONTROLLER
IGNITION SW
RUST FUS LINK
RIGHT BANK GLOW PLUG
LEFT BANK GLOW PLUG
GLOW PLUG IND
FUEL HEATER
ALTERNATOR
WATER IN FUEL SENS
WATER IN FUEL IND
FAST IDLE TEMP SW
FAST IDLE SOL
COLD ADVANCE SOL

1991 WIRING DIAGRAMS
"P" Series – Commercial (Cont.)

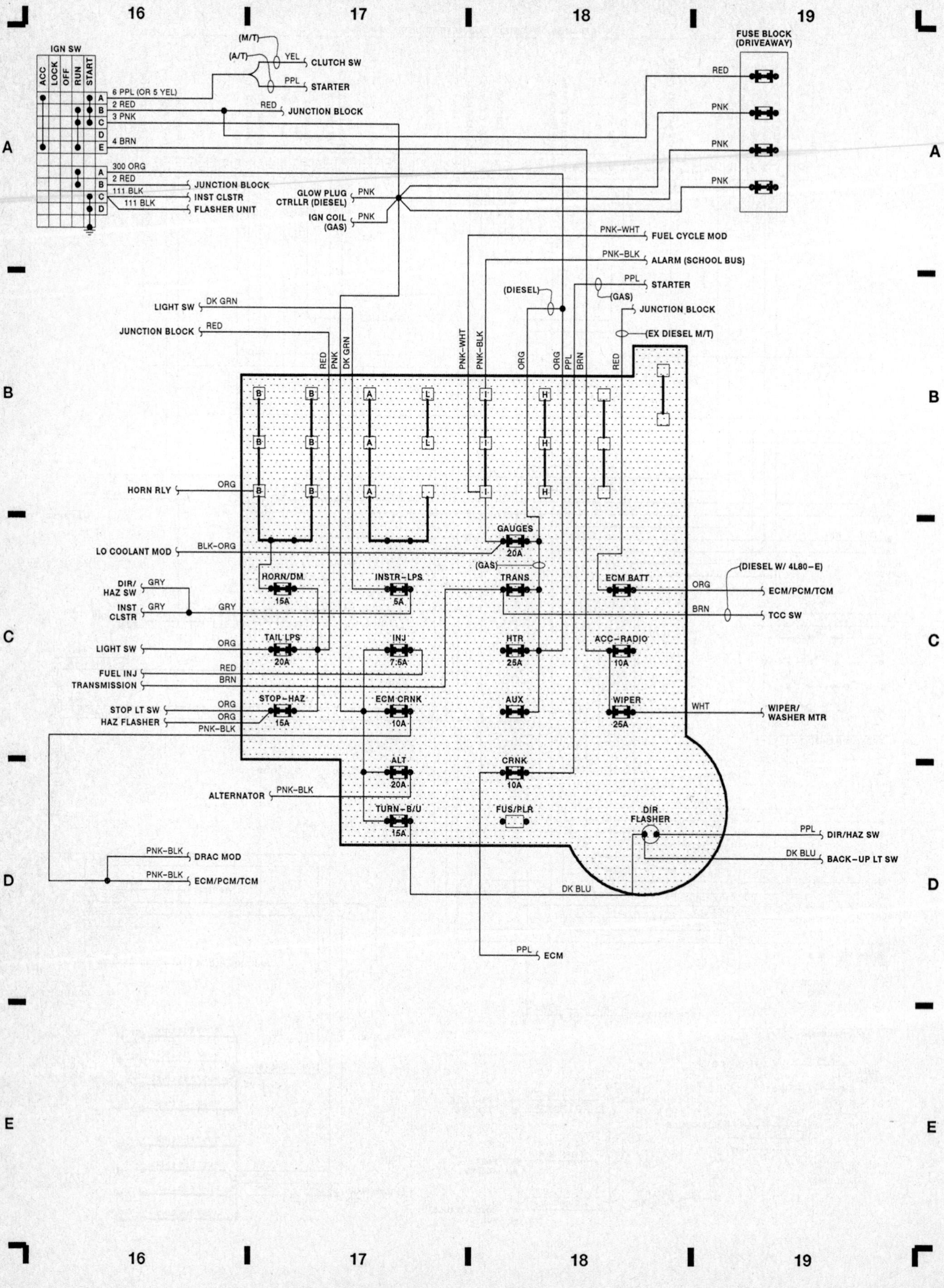
16
17
18
19
A
B
C
D
E
IGN SW
ACC
LOCK
OFF
RUN
START
6 PPL (OR 5 YEL)
2 RED
3 PNK
4 BRN
300 ORG
2 RED
111 BLK
111 BLK
(M/T)
(A/T)
YEL
CLUTCH SW
PPL
STARTER
RED
JUNCTION BLOCK
INST CLSTR
FLASHER UNIT
GLOW PLUG CTRLLR (DIESEL)
IGN COIL (GAS)
PNK
FUSE BLOCK (DRIVEAWAY)
PNK-WHT
FUEL CYCLE MOD
PNK-BLK
ALARM (SCHOOL BUS)
(DIESEL)
(GAS)
STARTER
(EX DIESEL M/T)
LIGHT SW
DK GRN
ORG
PPL
BRN
HORN RLY
LO COOLANT MOD
BLK-ORG
GAUGES 20A
HORN/DM 15A
INSTR-LPS 5A
TRANS
ECM BATT
(DIESEL W/ 4L80-E)
ECM/PCM/TCM
TCC SW
DIR/ HAZ SW
GRY
INST CLSTR
TAIL LPS 20A
INJ 7.5A
HTR 25A
ACC-RADIO 10A
FUEL INJ
TRANSMISSION
STOP LT SW
HAZ FLASHER
STOP-HAZ 15A
ECM CRNK 10A
AUX
WIPER 25A
WHT
WIPER/ WASHER MTR
ALT 20A
CRNK 10A
ALTERNATOR
TURN-B/U 15A
FUS/PLR
DIR FLASHER
DIR/HAZ SW
DK BLU
BACK-UP LT SW
DRAC MOD
ECM

1991 WIRING DIAGRAMS
"P" Series – Commercial (Cont.)

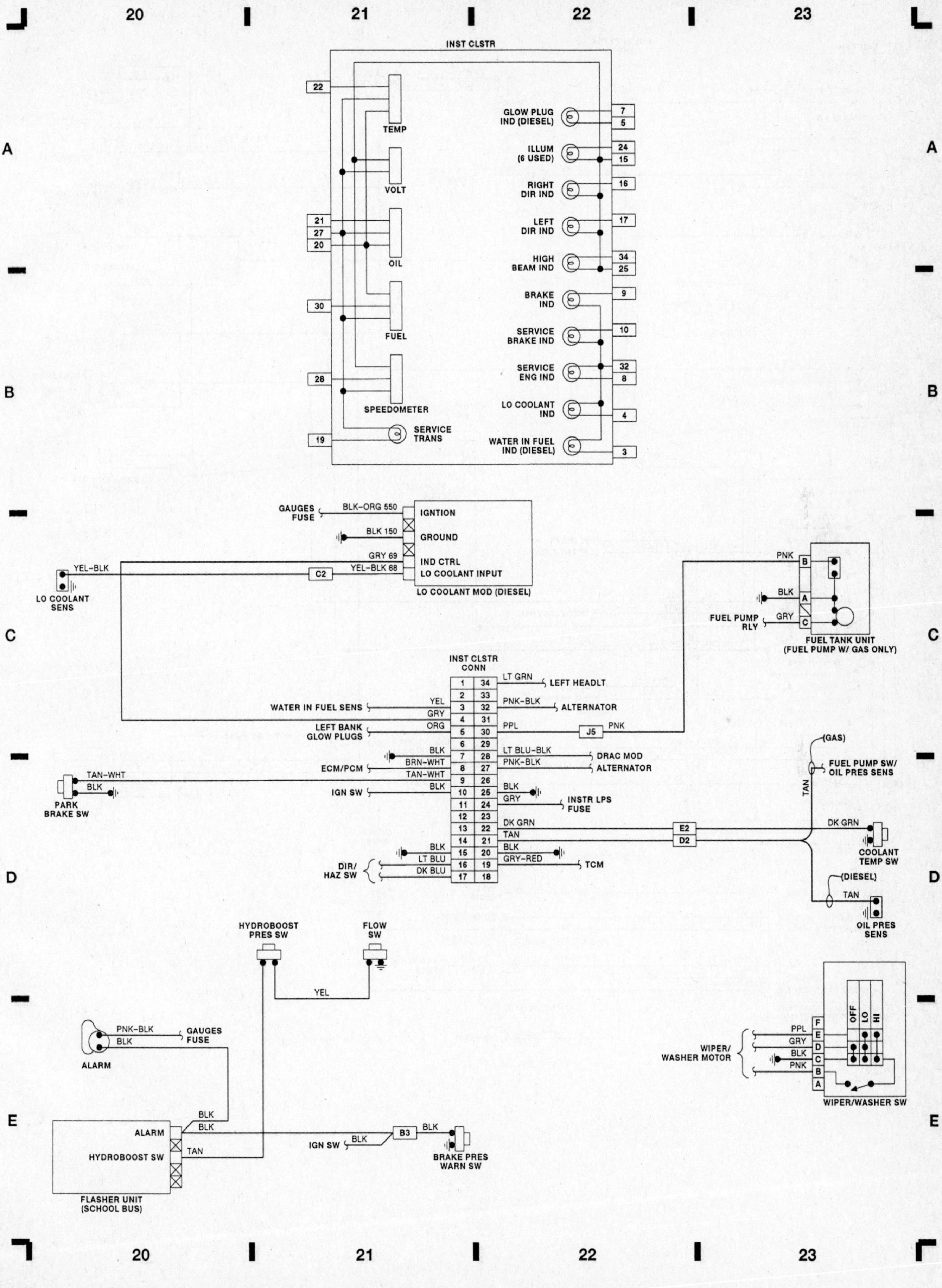
INST CLSTR
TEMP
VOLT
OIL
FUEL
SPEEDOMETER
SERVICE TRANS
GLOW PLUG IND (DIESEL)
ILLUM (6 USED)
RIGHT DIR IND
LEFT DIR IND
HIGH BEAM IND
BRAKE IND
SERVICE BRAKE IND
SERVICE ENG IND
LO COOLANT IND
WATER IN FUEL IND (DIESEL)
GAUGES FUSE
BLK-ORG 550
BLK 150
GRY 69
YEL-BLK 68
IGNTION
GROUND
IND CTRL
LO COOLANT INPUT
LO COOLANT MOD (DIESEL)
YEL-BLK
LO COOLANT SENS
FUEL PUMP RLY
FUEL TANK UNIT (FUEL PUMP W/ GAS ONLY)
INST CLSTR CONN
LEFT HEADLT
ALTERNATOR
WATER IN FUEL SENS
LEFT BANK GLOW PLUGS
DRAC MOD
ECM/PCM
PARK BRAKE SW
IGN SW
INSTR LPS FUSE
DIR/ HAZ SW
TCM
(GAS)
FUEL PUMP SW/ OIL PRES SENS
COOLANT TEMP SW
(DIESEL)
OIL PRES SENS
HYDROBOOST PRES SW
FLOW SW
ALARM
FLASHER UNIT (SCHOOL BUS)
HYDROBOOST SW
BRAKE PRES WARN SW
WIPER/ WASHER MOTOR
WIPER/WASHER SW
OFF
LO
HI

1991 WIRING DIAGRAMS
"P" Series – Commercial (Cont.)

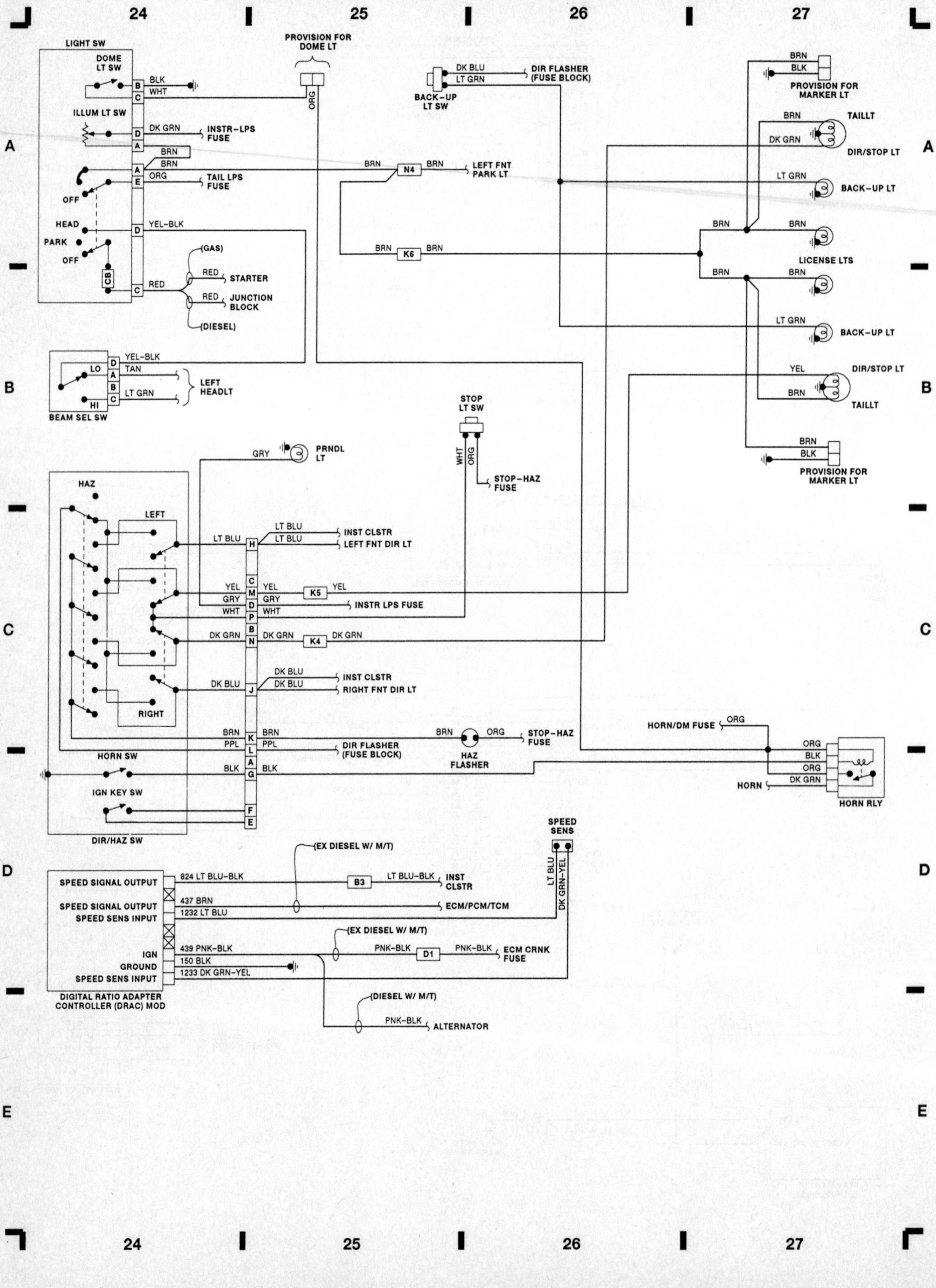
24
25
26
27
A
B
C
D
E
LIGHT SW
DOME LT SW
ILLUM LT SW
OFF
HEAD
PARK
OFF
CB
BLK
WHT
DK GRN
INSTR-LPS FUSE
BRN
BRN
ORG
TAIL LPS FUSE
YEL-BLK
(GAS)
RED
STARTER
RED
JUNCTION BLOCK
(DIESEL)
PROVISION FOR DOME LT
ORG
DK BLU
LT GRN
DIR FLASHER (FUSE BLOCK)
BACK-UP LT SW
N4
LEFT FNT PARK LT
K6
BRN
PROVISION FOR MARKER LT
TAILLT
DK GRN
DIR/STOP LT
LT GRN
BACK-UP LT
LICENSE LTS
BACK-UP LT
YEL
DIR/STOP LT
TAILLT
PROVISION FOR MARKER LT
LO
HI
TAN
LT GRN
LEFT HEADLT
BEAM SEL SW
STOP LT SW
WHT
ORG
STOP-HAZ FUSE
GRY
PRNDL LT
HAZ
LEFT
RIGHT
LT BLU
INST CLSTR
LEFT FNT DIR LT
YEL
K5
GRY
INSTR LPS FUSE
WHT
DK GRN
K4
DK BLU
INST CLSTR
RIGHT FNT DIR LT
PPL
DIR FLASHER (FUSE BLOCK)
HAZ FLASHER
STOP-HAZ FUSE
HORN SW
IGN KEY SW
DIR/HAZ SW
HORN/DM FUSE
HORN
HORN RLY
SPEED SENS
(EX DIESEL W/ M/T)
SPEED SIGNAL OUTPUT
SPEED SIGNAL OUTPUT
SPEED SENS INPUT
IGN
GROUND
SPEED SENS INPUT
824 LT BLU-BLK
437 BRN
1232 LT BLU
439 PNK-BLK
150 BLK
1233 DK GRN-YEL
B3
LT BLU-BLK
INST CLSTR
ECM/PCM/TCM
D1
PNK-BLK
ECM CRNK FUSE
LT BLU
DK GRN-YEL
(DIESEL W/ M/T)
ALTERNATOR
DIGITAL RATIO ADAPTER CONTROLLER (DRAC) MOD

1991 WIRING DIAGRAMS
"P" Series – Motorhome

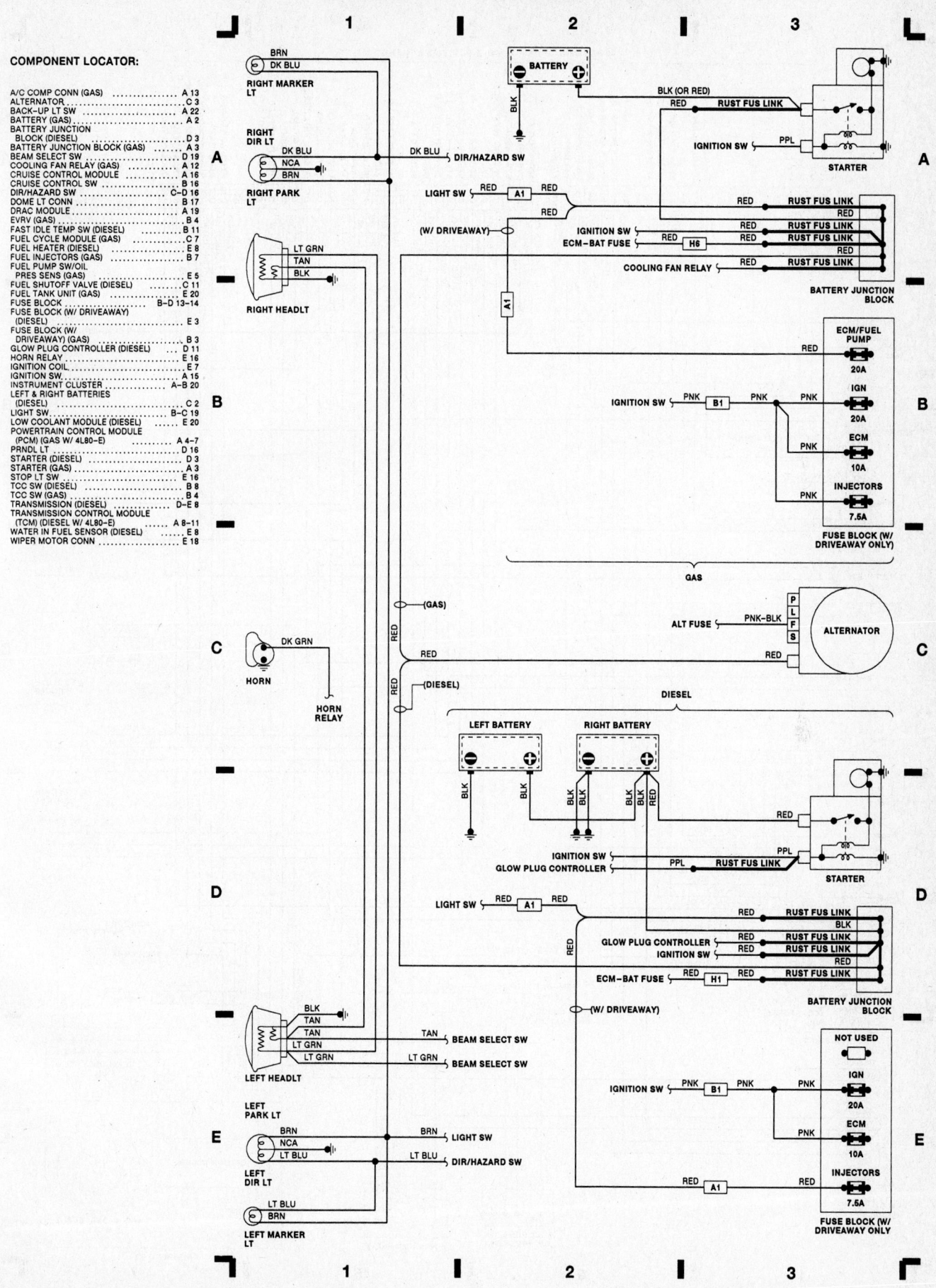

COMPONENT LOCATOR:

A/C COMP CONN (GAS) .... A 13
ALTERNATOR .... C 3
BACK-UP LT SW .... A 22
BATTERY (GAS) .... A 2
BATTERY JUNCTION
  BLOCK (DIESEL) .... D 3
BATTERY JUNCTION BLOCK (GAS) .... A 3
BEAM SELECT SW .... D 19
COOLING FAN RELAY (GAS) .... A 12
CRUISE CONTROL MODULE .... A 16
CRUISE CONTROL SW .... B 16
DIR/HAZARD SW .... C–D 16
DOME LT CONN .... B 17
DRAC MODULE .... A 19
EVRV (GAS) .... B 4
FAST IDLE TEMP SW (DIESEL) .... B 11
FUEL CYCLE MODULE (GAS) .... C 7
FUEL HEATER (DIESEL) .... E 8
FUEL INJECTORS (GAS) .... B 7
FUEL PUMP SW/OIL
  PRES SENS (GAS) .... E 5
FUEL SHUTOFF VALVE (DIESEL) .... C 11
FUEL TANK UNIT (GAS) .... E 20
FUSE BLOCK .... B–D 13–14
FUSE BLOCK (W/ DRIVEAWAY)
  (DIESEL) .... E 3
FUSE BLOCK (W/
  DRIVEAWAY) (GAS) .... B 3
GLOW PLUG CONTROLLER (DIESEL) .... D 11
HORN RELAY .... E 16
IGNITION COIL .... E 7
IGNITION SW .... A 15
INSTRUMENT CLUSTER .... A–B 20
LEFT & RIGHT BATTERIES
  (DIESEL) .... C 2
LIGHT SW .... B–C 19
LOW COOLANT MODULE (DIESEL) .... E 20
POWERTRAIN CONTROL MODULE
  (PCM) (GAS W/ 4L80–E) .... A 4–7
PRNDL LT .... D 16
STARTER (DIESEL) .... D 3
STARTER (GAS) .... A 3
STOP LT SW .... E 16
TCC SW (DIESEL) .... B 8
TCC SW (GAS) .... B 4
TRANSMISSION (DIESEL) .... D–E 8
TRANSMISSION CONTROL MODULE
  (TCM) (DIESEL W/ 4L80–E) .... A 8–11
WATER IN FUEL SENSOR (DIESEL) .... E 8
WIPER MOTOR CONN .... E 18

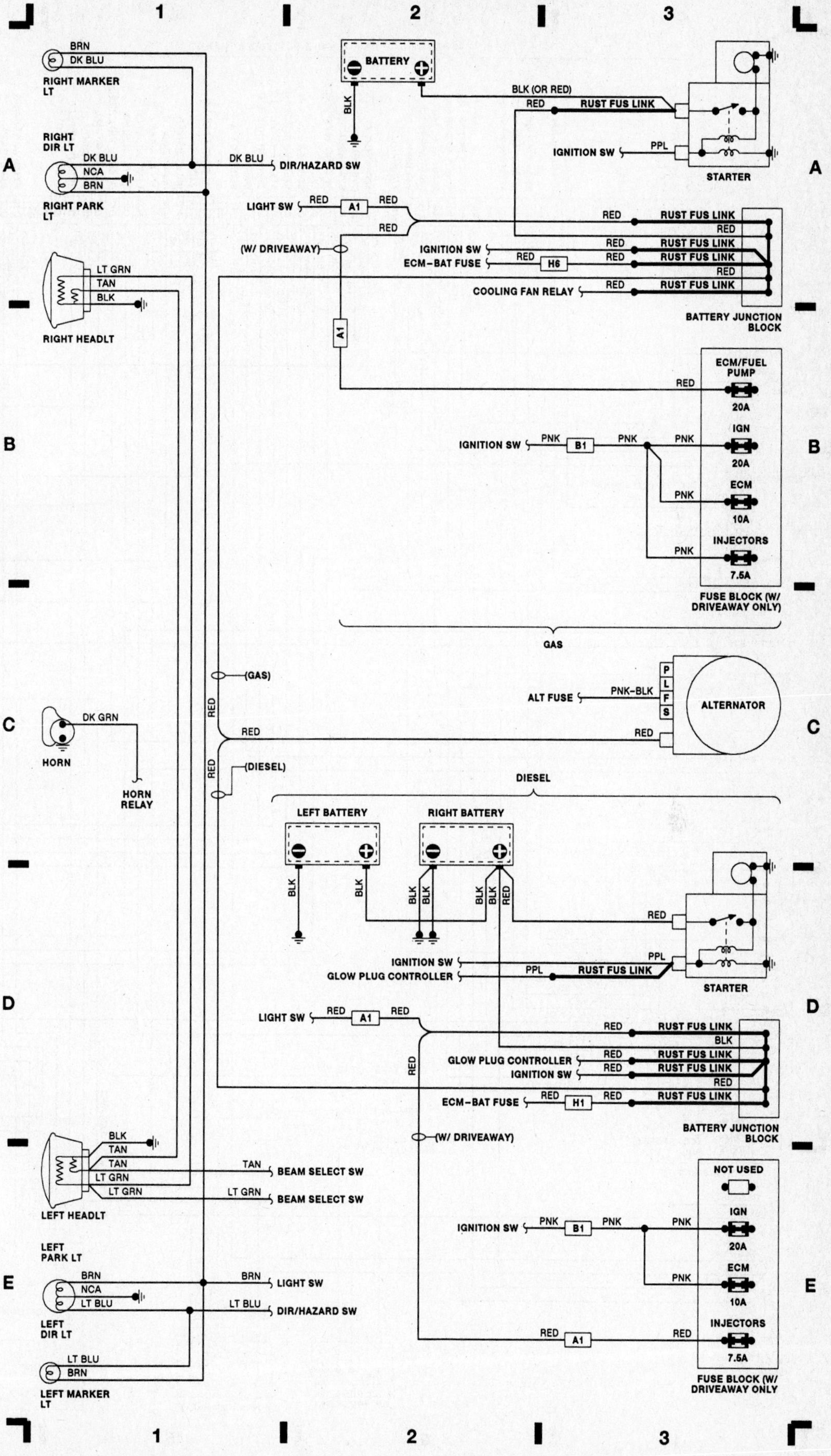
1
2
3
A
B
C
D
E
BRN
DK BLU
RIGHT MARKER LT
RIGHT DIR LT
DK BLU
NCA
BRN
DIR/HAZARD SW
RIGHT PARK LT
LT GRN
TAN
BLK
RIGHT HEADLT
BATTERY
BLK
BLK (OR RED)
RED
RUST FUS LINK
IGNITION SW
PPL
STARTER
LIGHT SW
A1
RED
(W/ DRIVEAWAY)
ECM–BAT FUSE
H6
COOLING FAN RELAY
BATTERY JUNCTION BLOCK
ECM/FUEL PUMP
20A
IGN
ECM
10A
INJECTORS
7.5A
B1
PNK
FUSE BLOCK (W/ DRIVEAWAY ONLY)
GAS
(GAS)
ALT FUSE
PNK–BLK
P
L
F
S
ALTERNATOR
HORN
DK GRN
HORN RELAY
(DIESEL)
DIESEL
LEFT BATTERY
RIGHT BATTERY
GLOW PLUG CONTROLLER
H1
BEAM SELECT SW
LEFT HEADLT
LEFT PARK LT
LT BLU
LIGHT SW
LEFT DIR LT
LEFT MARKER LT
NOT USED
FUSE BLOCK (W/ DRIVEAWAY ONLY

1991 WIRING DIAGRAMS
"P" Series – Motorhome (Cont.)

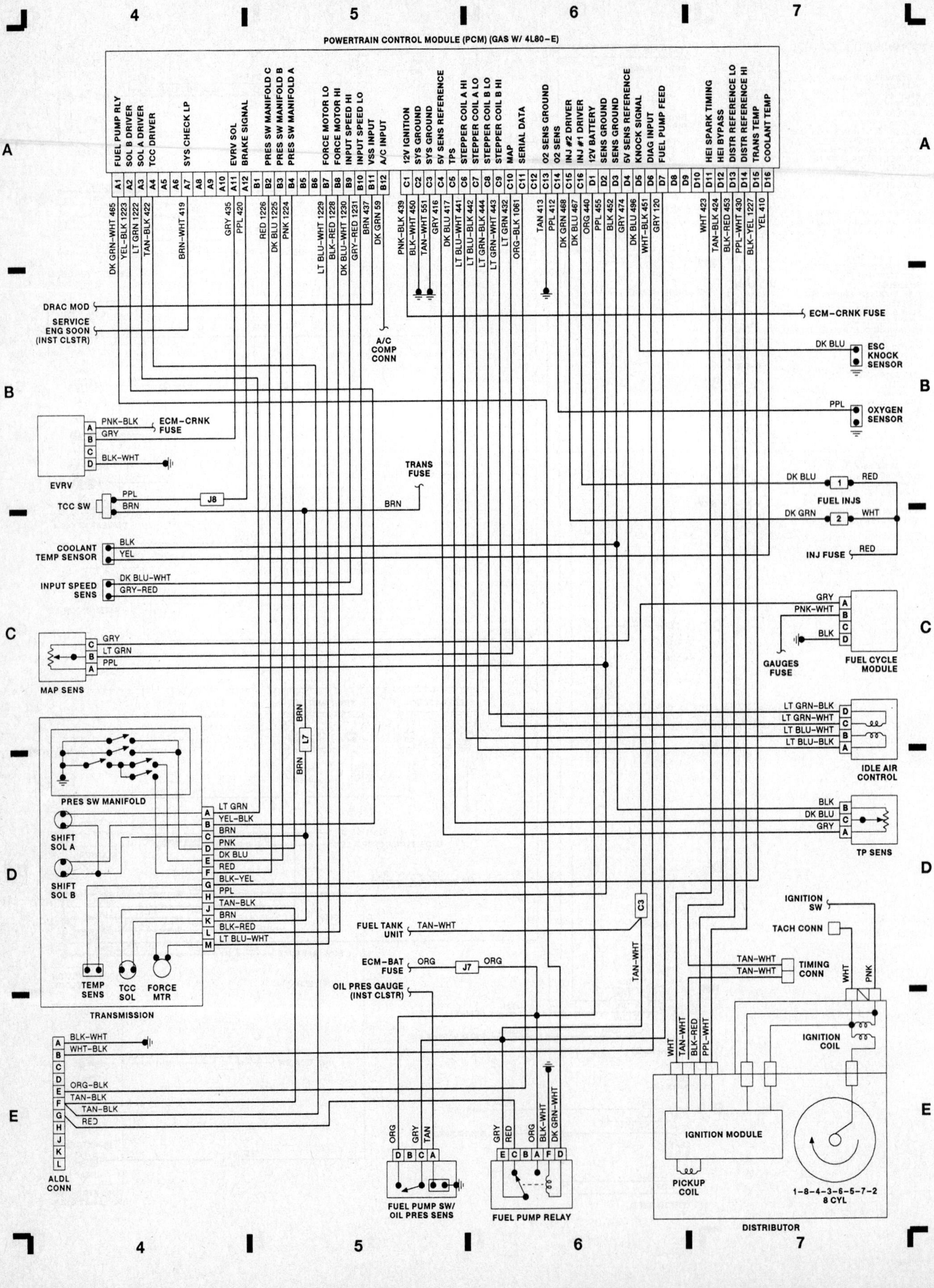
POWERTRAIN CONTROL MODULE (PCM) (GAS W/ 4L80-E)
FUEL PUMP RLY
SOL B DRIVER
SOL A DRIVER
TCC DRIVER
SYS CHECK LP
EVRV SOL
BRAKE SIGNAL
PRES SW MANIFOLD C
PRES SW MANIFOLD B
PRES SW MANIFOLD A
FORCE MOTOR LO
FORCE MOTOR HI
INPUT SPEED HI
INPUT SPEED LO
VSS INPUT
A/C INPUT
12V IGNITION
SYS GROUND
SYS GROUND
5V SENS REFERENCE
TPS
STEPPER COIL A HI
STEPPER COIL A LO
STEPPER COIL B LO
STEPPER COIL B HI
MAP
SERIAL DATA
O2 SENS GROUND
O2 SENS
INJ #2 DRIVER
INJ #1 DRIVER
12V BATTERY
SENS GROUND
SENS GROUND
5V SENS REFERENCE
KNOCK SIGNAL
DIAG INPUT
FUEL PUMP FEED
HEI SPARK TIMING
HEI BYPASS
DISTR REFERENCE LO
DISTR REFERENCE HI
TRANS TEMP
COOLANT TEMP
DK GRN-WHT 465
YEL-BLK 1223
LT GRN 1222
TAN-BLK 422
BRN-WHT 419
GRY 435
PPL 420
RED 1226
DK BLU 1225
PNK 1224
LT BLU-WHT 1229
BLK-RED 1228
DK BLU-WHT 1230
GRY-RED 1231
BRN 437
DK GRN 59
PNK-BLK 439
BLK-WHT 450
TAN-WHT 551
GRY 416
DK BLU 417
LT BLU-WHT 441
LT BLU-BLK 442
LT GRN-BLK 444
LT GRN-WHT 443
LT GRN 432
ORG-BLK 1061
TAN 413
PPL 412
DK GRN 468
DK BLU 467
ORG 440
PPL 455
BLK 452
GRY 474
DK BLU 496
WHT-BLK 451
GRY 120
WHT 423
TAN-BLK 424
BLK-RED 453
PPL-WHT 430
BLK-YEL 1227
YEL 410
DRAC MOD
SERVICE ENG SOON (INST CLSTR)
A/C COMP CONN
ECM-CRNK FUSE
ESC KNOCK SENSOR
OXYGEN SENSOR
EVRV
TCC SW
J8
TRANS FUSE
FUEL INJS
INJ FUSE
COOLANT TEMP SENSOR
INPUT SPEED SENS
MAP SENS
GAUGES FUSE
FUEL CYCLE MODULE
IDLE AIR CONTROL
TP SENS
PRES SW MANIFOLD
SHIFT SOL A
SHIFT SOL B
TEMP SENS
TCC SOL
FORCE MTR
TRANSMISSION
L7
C3
FUEL TANK UNIT
ECM-BAT FUSE
J7
OIL PRES GAUGE (INST CLSTR)
IGNITION SW
TACH CONN
TIMING CONN
IGNITION COIL
ALDL CONN
FUEL PUMP SW/ OIL PRES SENS
FUEL PUMP RELAY
IGNITION MODULE
PICKUP COIL
1-8-4-3-6-5-7-2 8 CYL
DISTRIBUTOR

1991 WIRING DIAGRAMS
"P" Series – Motorhome (Cont.)

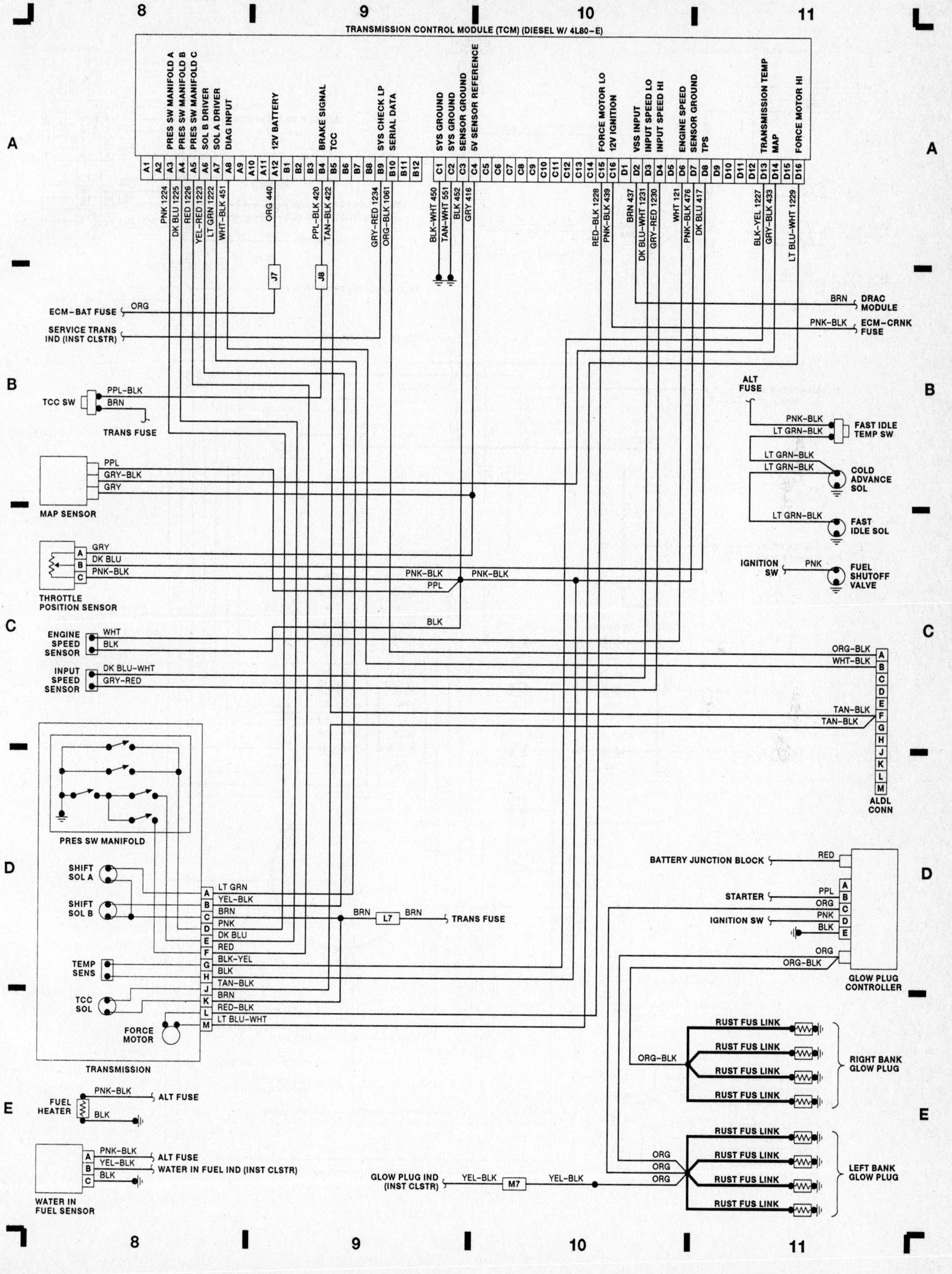
TRANSMISSION CONTROL MODULE (TCM) (DIESEL W/ 4L80-E)
PRES SW MANIFOLD A
PRES SW MANIFOLD B
PRES SW MANIFOLD C
SOL B DRIVER
SOL A DRIVER
DIAG INPUT
12V BATTERY
BRAKE SIGNAL
TCC
SYS CHECK LP
SERIAL DATA
SYS GROUND
SYS GROUND
SENSOR GROUND
5V SENSOR REFERENCE
FORCE MOTOR LO
12V IGNITION
VSS INPUT
INPUT SPEED LO
INPUT SPEED HI
ENGINE SPEED
SENSOR GROUND
TPS
TRANSMISSION TEMP
MAP
FORCE MOTOR HI
PNK 1224
DK BLU 1225
RED 1226
YEL-RED 1223
LT GRN 1222
WHT-BLK 451
ORG 440
PPL-BLK 420
TAN-BLK 422
GRY-RED 1234
ORG-BLK 1061
BLK-WHT 450
TAN-WHT 551
BLK 452
GRY 416
RED-BLK 1228
PNK-BLK 439
BRN 437
DK BLU-WHT 1231
GRY-RED 1230
WHT 121
PNK-BLK 476
DK BLU 417
BLK-YEL 1227
GRY-BLK 433
LT BLU-WHT 1229
J7
J8
ECM-BAT FUSE
SERVICE TRANS IND (INST CLSTR)
DRAC MODULE
ECM-CRNK FUSE
TCC SW
TRANS FUSE
ALT FUSE
FAST IDLE TEMP SW
COLD ADVANCE SOL
FAST IDLE SOL
IGNITION SW
FUEL SHUTOFF VALVE
MAP SENSOR
THROTTLE POSITION SENSOR
ENGINE SPEED SENSOR
INPUT SPEED SENSOR
ALDL CONN
PRES SW MANIFOLD
SHIFT SOL A
SHIFT SOL B
TEMP SENS
TCC SOL
FORCE MOTOR
TRANSMISSION
L7
TRANS FUSE
BATTERY JUNCTION BLOCK
STARTER
IGNITION SW
GLOW PLUG CONTROLLER
RUST FUS LINK
RIGHT BANK GLOW PLUG
LEFT BANK GLOW PLUG
FUEL HEATER
ALT FUSE
WATER IN FUEL SENSOR
WATER IN FUEL IND (INST CLSTR)
GLOW PLUG IND (INST CLSTR)
M7

1991 WIRING DIAGRAMS
"P" Series – Motorhome (Cont.)

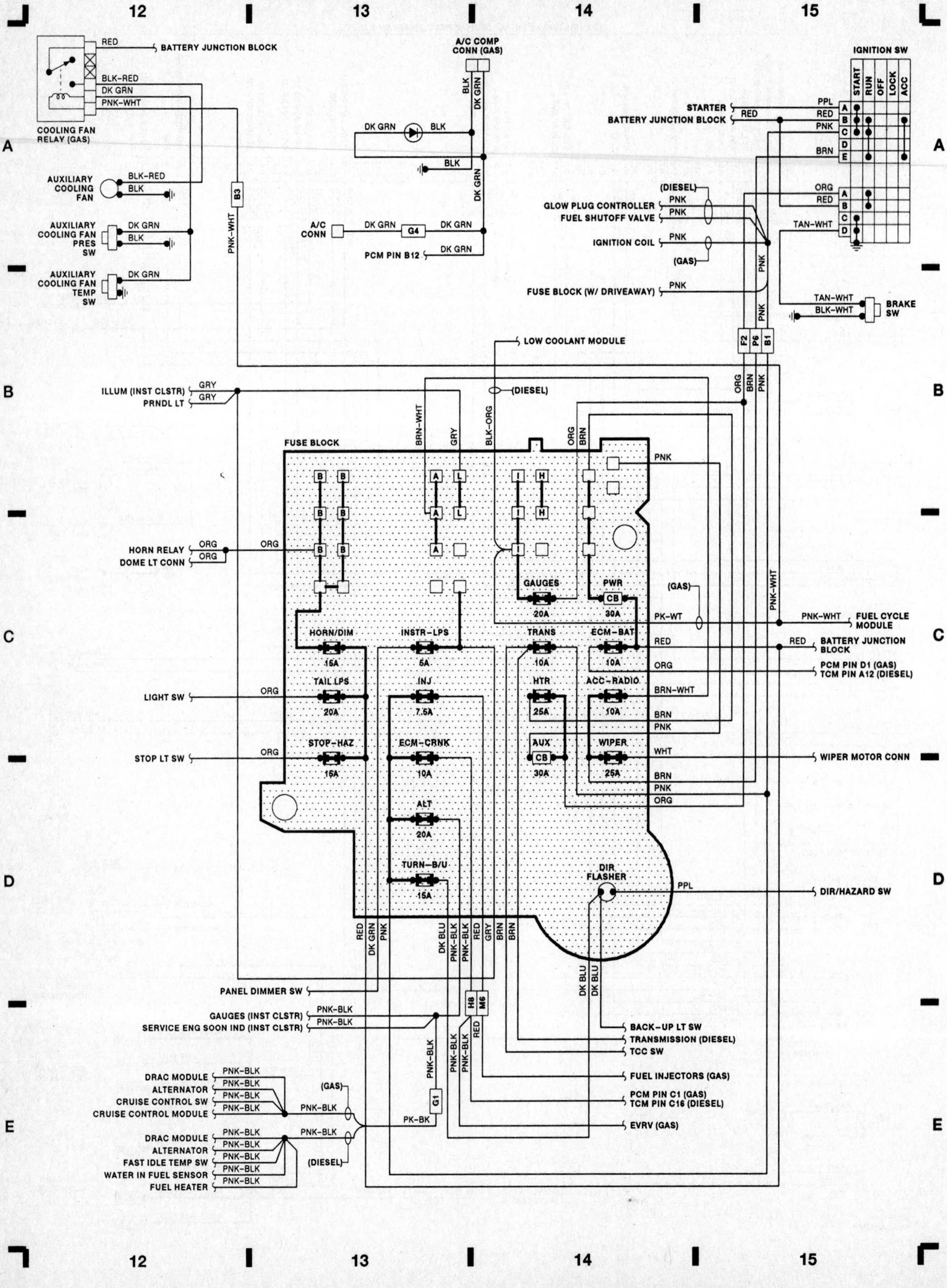
12
13
14
15
A
B
C
D
E
COOLING FAN RELAY (GAS)
RED
BATTERY JUNCTION BLOCK
BLK-RED
DK GRN
PNK-WHT
AUXILIARY COOLING FAN
BLK-RED
BLK
AUXILIARY COOLING FAN PRES SW
DK GRN
BLK
AUXILIARY COOLING FAN TEMP SW
DK GRN
B3
PNK-WHT
A/C COMP CONN (GAS)
BLK
DK GRN
DK GRN
BLK
A/C CONN
G4
PCM PIN B12
IGNITION SW
START
RUN
OFF
LOCK
ACC
STARTER
BATTERY JUNCTION BLOCK
PPL
RED
PNK
BRN
ORG
TAN-WHT
(DIESEL)
GLOW PLUG CONTROLLER
FUEL SHUTOFF VALVE
IGNITION COIL
(GAS)
FUSE BLOCK (W/ DRIVEAWAY)
BRAKE SW
BLK-WHT
F2
P6
B1
LOW COOLANT MODULE
ILLUM (INST CLSTR)
PRNDL LT
GRY
BRN-WHT
BLK-ORG
FUSE BLOCK
HORN RELAY
DOME LT CONN
ORG
GAUGES
20A
PWR
CB
30A
HORN/DIM
15A
INSTR-LPS
5A
TRANS
10A
ECM-BAT
10A
TAIL LPS
20A
INJ
7.5A
HTR
25A
ACC-RADIO
10A
STOP-HAZ
15A
ECM-CRNK
10A
AUX
CB
30A
WIPER
25A
ALT
20A
TURN-B/U
15A
DIR FLASHER
LIGHT SW
STOP LT SW
PK-WT
PNK-WHT
FUEL CYCLE MODULE
BATTERY JUNCTION BLOCK
PCM PIN D1 (GAS)
TCM PIN A12 (DIESEL)
WHT
WIPER MOTOR CONN
PPL
DIR/HAZARD SW
DK BLU
PNK-BLK
H8
M6
PANEL DIMMER SW
GAUGES (INST CLSTR)
SERVICE ENG SOON IND (INST CLSTR)
BACK-UP LT SW
TRANSMISSION (DIESEL)
TCC SW
FUEL INJECTORS (GAS)
PCM PIN C1 (GAS)
TCM PIN C16 (DIESEL)
EVRV (GAS)
G1
PK-BK
DRAC MODULE
ALTERNATOR
CRUISE CONTROL SW
CRUISE CONTROL MODULE
FAST IDLE TEMP SW
WATER IN FUEL SENSOR
FUEL HEATER

1991 WIRING DIAGRAMS
"P" Series – Motorhome (Cont.)

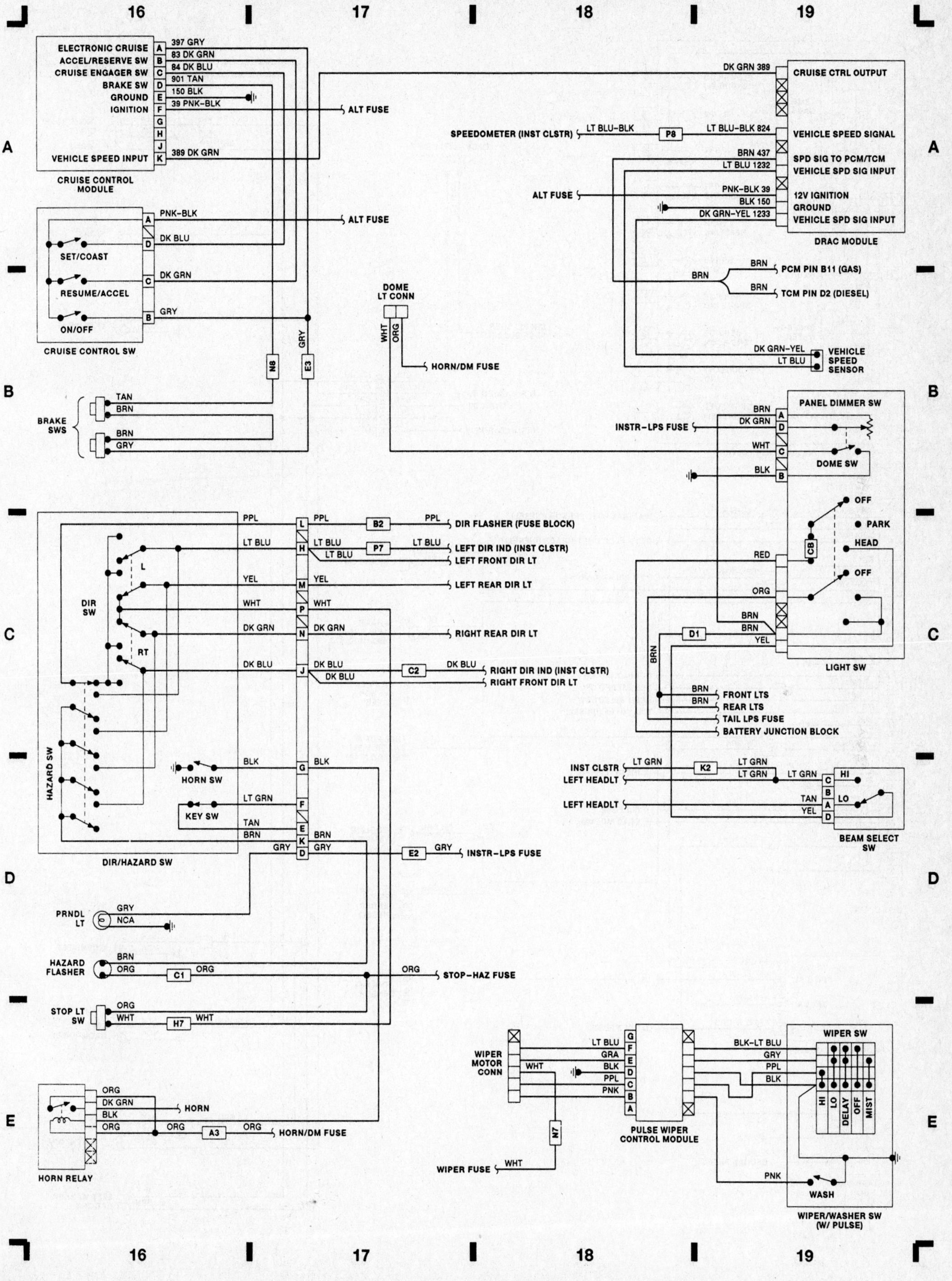
16
17
18
19
A
B
C
D
E
ELECTRONIC CRUISE
ACCEL/RESERVE SW
CRUISE ENGAGER SW
BRAKE SW
GROUND
IGNITION
VEHICLE SPEED INPUT
CRUISE CONTROL MODULE
397 GRY
83 DK GRN
84 DK BLU
901 TAN
150 BLK
39 PNK-BLK
389 DK GRN
ALT FUSE
DK GRN 389
CRUISE CTRL OUTPUT
SPEEDOMETER (INST CLSTR)
LT BLU-BLK
P8
LT BLU-BLK 824
VEHICLE SPEED SIGNAL
BRN 437
LT BLU 1232
SPD SIG TO PCM/TCM
VEHICLE SPD SIG INPUT
PNK-BLK 39
BLK 150
DK GRN-YEL 1233
12V IGNITION
GROUND
VEHICLE SPD SIG INPUT
DRAC MODULE
PNK-BLK
DK BLU
DK GRN
GRY
SET/COAST
RESUME/ACCEL
ON/OFF
CRUISE CONTROL SW
BRN
PCM PIN B11 (GAS)
TCM PIN D2 (DIESEL)
DOME LT CONN
WHT
ORG
HORN/DM FUSE
N8
E3
DK GRN-YEL
LT BLU
VEHICLE SPEED SENSOR
TAN
BRAKE SWS
PANEL DIMMER SW
INSTR-LPS FUSE
DOME SW
BLK
OFF
PARK
HEAD
CB
RED
PPL
B2
DIR FLASHER (FUSE BLOCK)
LT BLU
P7
LEFT DIR IND (INST CLSTR)
LEFT FRONT DIR LT
YEL
LEFT REAR DIR LT
DIR SW
L
RT
RIGHT REAR DIR LT
C2
RIGHT DIR IND (INST CLSTR)
RIGHT FRONT DIR LT
D1
LIGHT SW
FRONT LTS
REAR LTS
TAIL LPS FUSE
BATTERY JUNCTION BLOCK
HAZARD SW
HORN SW
KEY SW
LT GRN
INST CLSTR
LEFT HEADLT
K2
HI
LO
BEAM SELECT SW
E2
DIR/HAZARD SW
PRNDL LT
NCA
HAZARD FLASHER
C1
STOP-HAZ FUSE
STOP LT SW
H7
WIPER MOTOR CONN
GRA
PNK
WIPER SW
BLK-LT BLU
MIST
DELAY
HORN
HORN RELAY
A3
N7
PULSE WIPER CONTROL MODULE
WIPER FUSE
WASH
WIPER/WASHER SW (W/ PULSE)

1991 WIRING DIAGRAMS
"P" Series – Motorhome (Cont.)

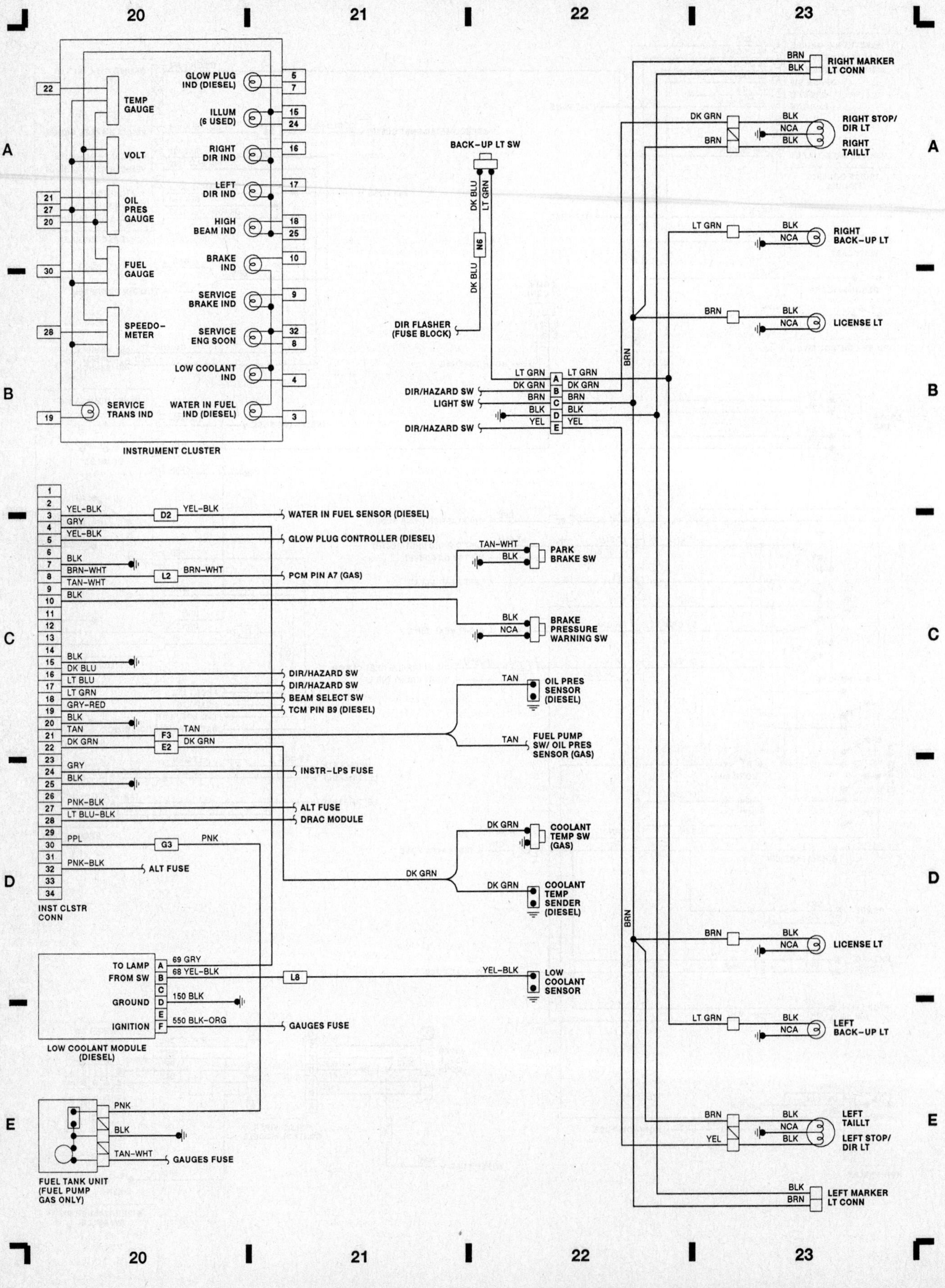
20
21
22
23
A
B
C
D
E
GLOW PLUG IND (DIESEL)
TEMP GAUGE
ILLUM (6 USED)
VOLT
RIGHT DIR IND
LEFT DIR IND
OIL PRES GAUGE
HIGH BEAM IND
FUEL GAUGE
BRAKE IND
SERVICE BRAKE IND
SPEEDO-METER
SERVICE ENG SOON
LOW COOLANT IND
SERVICE TRANS IND
WATER IN FUEL IND (DIESEL)
INSTRUMENT CLUSTER
BACK-UP LT SW
DK BLU
LT GRN
N6
DIR FLASHER (FUSE BLOCK)
DIR/HAZARD SW
LIGHT SW
DIR/HAZARD SW
RIGHT MARKER LT CONN
RIGHT STOP/ DIR LT
RIGHT TAILLT
RIGHT BACK-UP LT
LICENSE LT
WATER IN FUEL SENSOR (DIESEL)
GLOW PLUG CONTROLLER (DIESEL)
PCM PIN A7 (GAS)
PARK BRAKE SW
BRAKE PRESSURE WARNING SW
DIR/HAZARD SW
DIR/HAZARD SW
BEAM SELECT SW
TCM PIN B9 (DIESEL)
OIL PRES SENSOR (DIESEL)
FUEL PUMP SW/ OIL PRES SENSOR (GAS)
INSTR-LPS FUSE
ALT FUSE
DRAC MODULE
ALT FUSE
COOLANT TEMP SW (GAS)
COOLANT TEMP SENDER (DIESEL)
INST CLSTR CONN
TO LAMP FROM SW
GROUND
IGNITION
69 GRY
68 YEL-BLK
150 BLK
550 BLK-ORG
GAUGES FUSE
LOW COOLANT MODULE (DIESEL)
LOW COOLANT SENSOR
LICENSE LT
LEFT BACK-UP LT
LEFT TAILLT
LEFT STOP/ DIR LT
LEFT MARKER LT CONN
FUEL TANK UNIT (FUEL PUMP GAS ONLY)
GAUGES FUSE

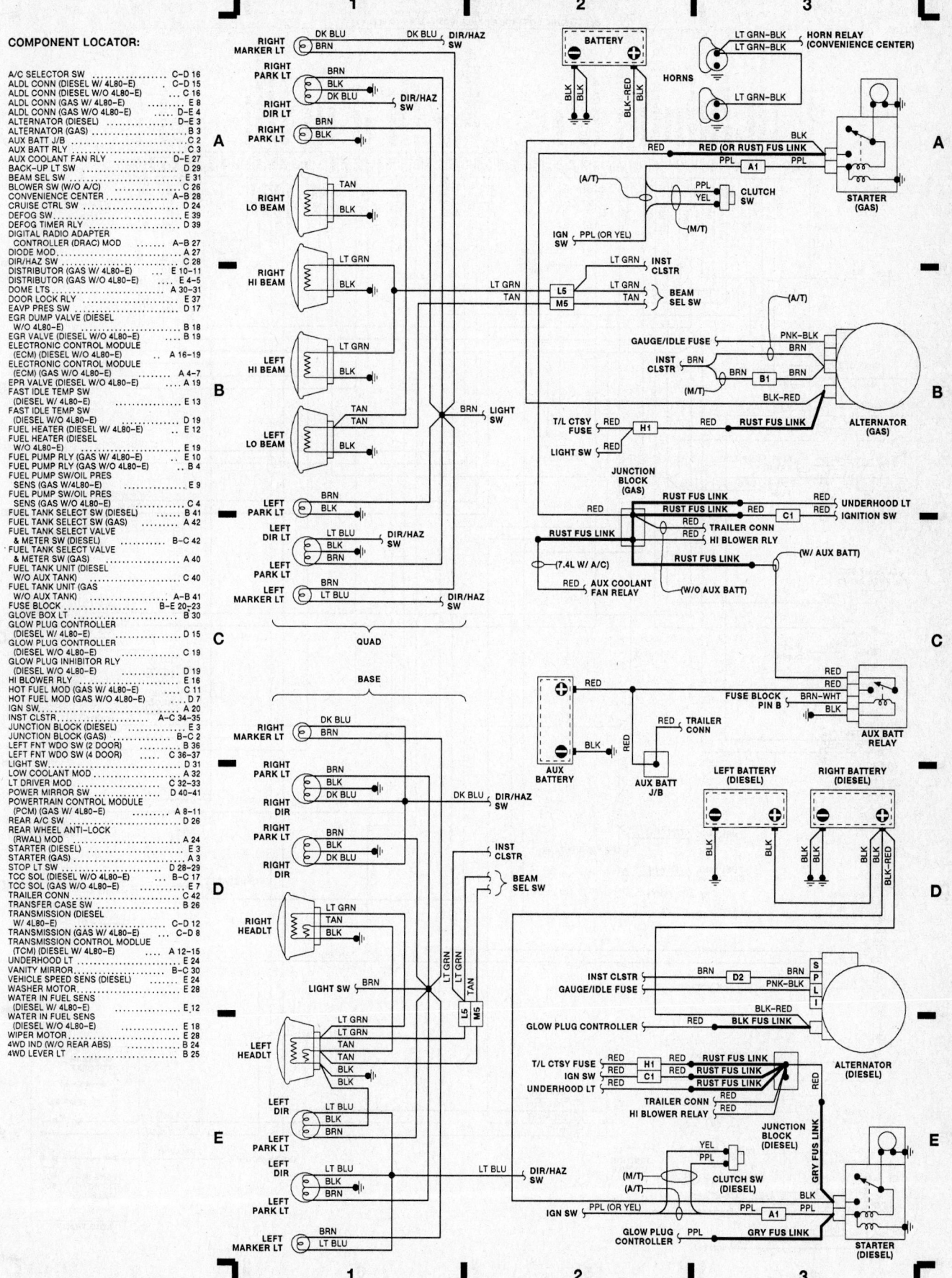

COMPONENT LOCATOR:

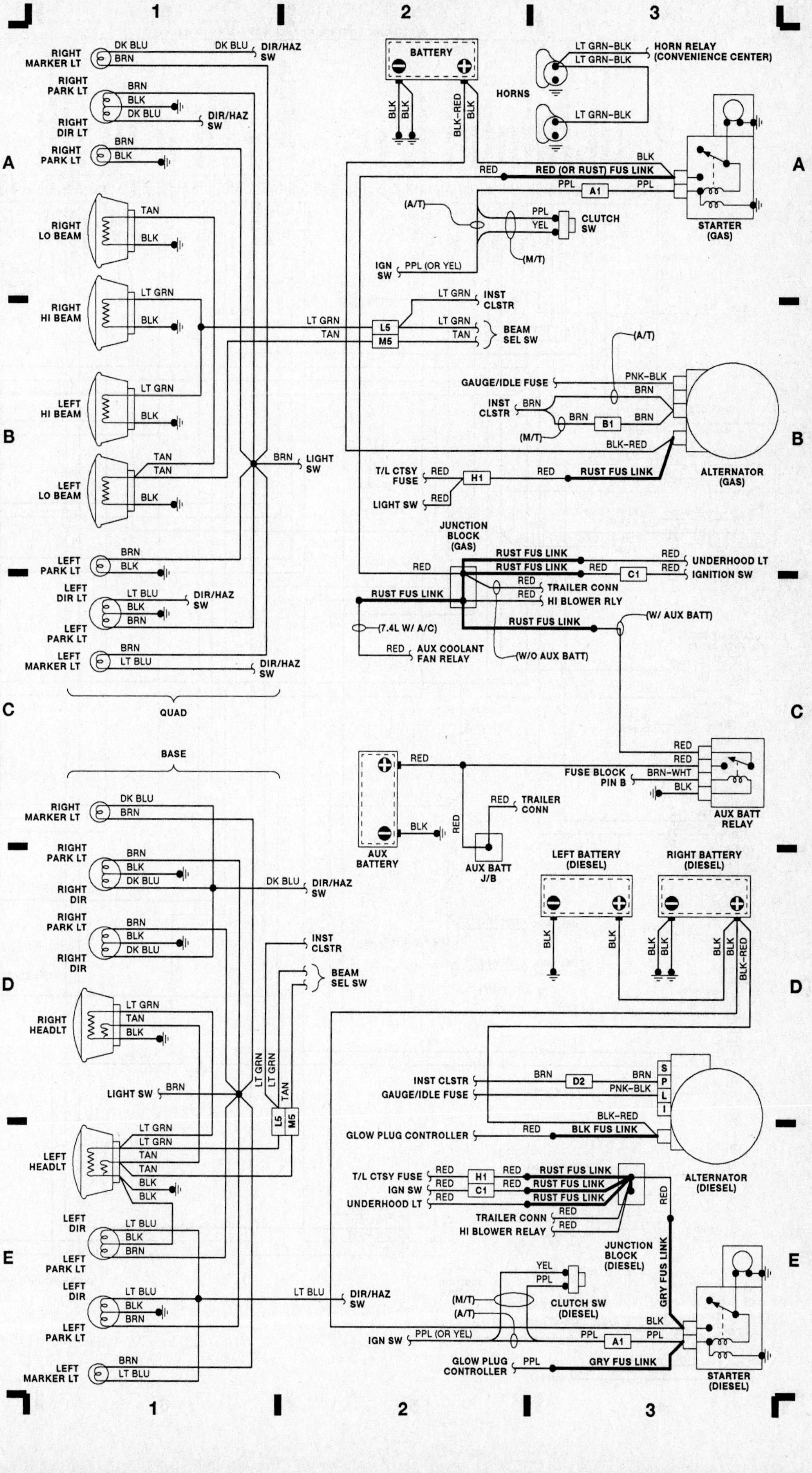

1
2
3
A
B
C
D
E
RIGHT MARKER LT
RIGHT PARK LT
RIGHT DIR LT
RIGHT LO BEAM
RIGHT HI BEAM
LEFT HI BEAM
LEFT LO BEAM
LEFT PARK LT
LEFT DIR LT
LEFT MARKER LT
DIR/HAZ SW
LIGHT SW
QUAD
BASE
RIGHT DIR
RIGHT HEADLT
LEFT HEADLT
LEFT DIR
INST CLSTR
BEAM SEL SW
BATTERY
HORNS
HORN RELAY (CONVENIENCE CENTER)
RED (OR RUST) FUS LINK
CLUTCH SW
STARTER (GAS)
IGN SW
GAUGE/IDLE FUSE
ALTERNATOR (GAS)
T/L CTSY FUSE
JUNCTION BLOCK (GAS)
RUST FUS LINK
UNDERHOOD LT
IGNITION SW
TRAILER CONN
HI BLOWER RLY
(W/ AUX BATT)
(7.4L W/ A/C)
AUX COOLANT FAN RELAY
(W/O AUX BATT)
FUSE BLOCK PIN B
AUX BATT RELAY
AUX BATTERY
AUX BATT J/B
LEFT BATTERY (DIESEL)
RIGHT BATTERY (DIESEL)
GLOW PLUG CONTROLLER
BLK FUS LINK
ALTERNATOR (DIESEL)
JUNCTION BLOCK (DIESEL)
GRY FUS LINK
CLUTCH SW (DIESEL)
STARTER (DIESEL)

1991 WIRING DIAGRAMS
"R" & "V" Series (Cont.)

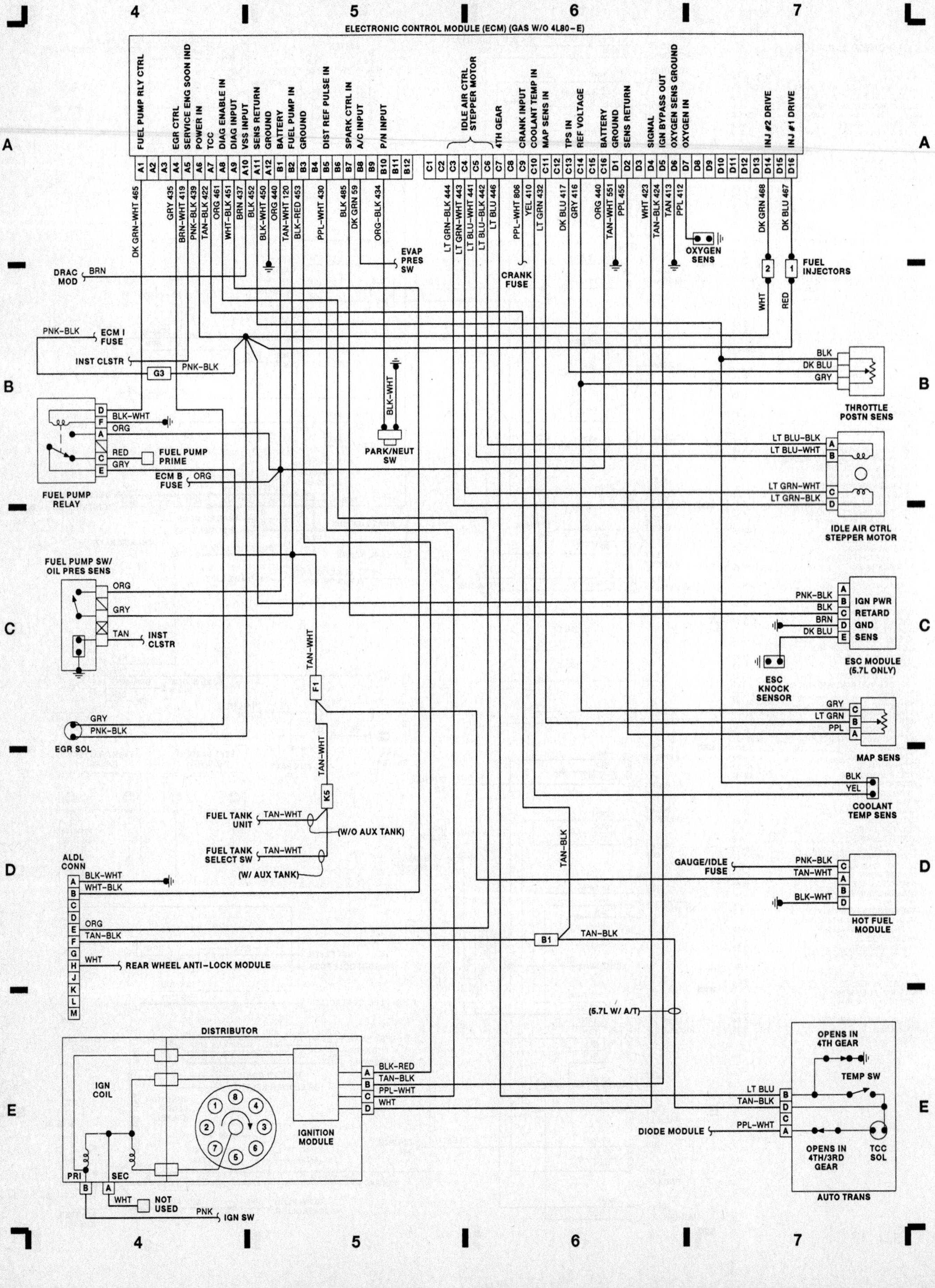
ELECTRONIC CONTROL MODULE (ECM) (GAS W/O 4L80-E)
FUEL PUMP RLY CTRL
EGR CTRL
SERVICE ENG SOON IND
POWER IN
TCC
DIAG ENABLE IN
DIAG INPUT
VSS INPUT
SENS RETURN
GROUND
BATTERY
FUEL PUMP IN
GROUND
DIST REF PULSE IN
SPARK CTRL IN
A/C INPUT
P/N INPUT
IDLE AIR CTRL STEPPER MOTOR
4TH GEAR
CRANK INPUT
COOLANT TEMP IN
MAP SENS IN
TPS IN
REF VOLTAGE
BATTERY
GROUND
SENS RETURN
SIGNAL
IGN BYPASS OUT
OXYGEN SENS GROUND
OXYGEN IN
INJ #2 DRIVE
INJ #1 DRIVE
DK GRN-WHT 465
GRY 435
BRN-WHT 419
PNK-BLK 439
TAN-BLK 422
ORG 461
WHT-BLK 451
BRN 437
BLK 452
BLK-WHT 450
ORG 440
TAN-WHT 120
BLK-RED 453
PPL-WHT 430
BLK 485
DK GRN 59
ORG-BLK 434
LT GRN-BLK 444
LT GRN-WHT 443
LT BLU-WHT 441
LT BLU-BLK 442
LT BLU 446
PPL-WHT 806
YEL 410
LT GRN 432
DK BLU 417
GRY 416
ORG 440
TAN-WHT 551
PPL 455
WHT 423
TAN-BLK 424
TAN 413
PPL 412
DK GRN 468
DK BLU 467
EVAP PRES SW
OXYGEN SENS
FUEL INJECTORS
DRAC MOD
CRANK FUSE
ECM I FUSE
INST CLSTR
G3
THROTTLE POSTN SENS
FUEL PUMP PRIME
FUEL PUMP RELAY
ECM B FUSE
PARK/NEUT SW
IDLE AIR CTRL STEPPER MOTOR
FUEL PUMP SW/ OIL PRES SENS
IGN PWR
RETARD
GND
SENS
ESC MODULE (5.7L ONLY)
ESC KNOCK SENSOR
EGR SOL
MAP SENS
COOLANT TEMP SENS
FUEL TANK UNIT
(W/O AUX TANK)
FUEL TANK SELECT SW
(W/ AUX TANK)
ALDL CONN
REAR WHEEL ANTI-LOCK MODULE
GAUGE/IDLE FUSE
HOT FUEL MODULE
(5.7L W/ A/T)
DISTRIBUTOR
IGN COIL
IGNITION MODULE
PRI
SEC
NOT USED
IGN SW
OPENS IN 4TH GEAR
TEMP SW
DIODE MODULE
OPENS IN 4TH/3RD GEAR
TCC SOL
AUTO TRANS

1991 WIRING DIAGRAMS
"R" & "V" Series (Cont.)

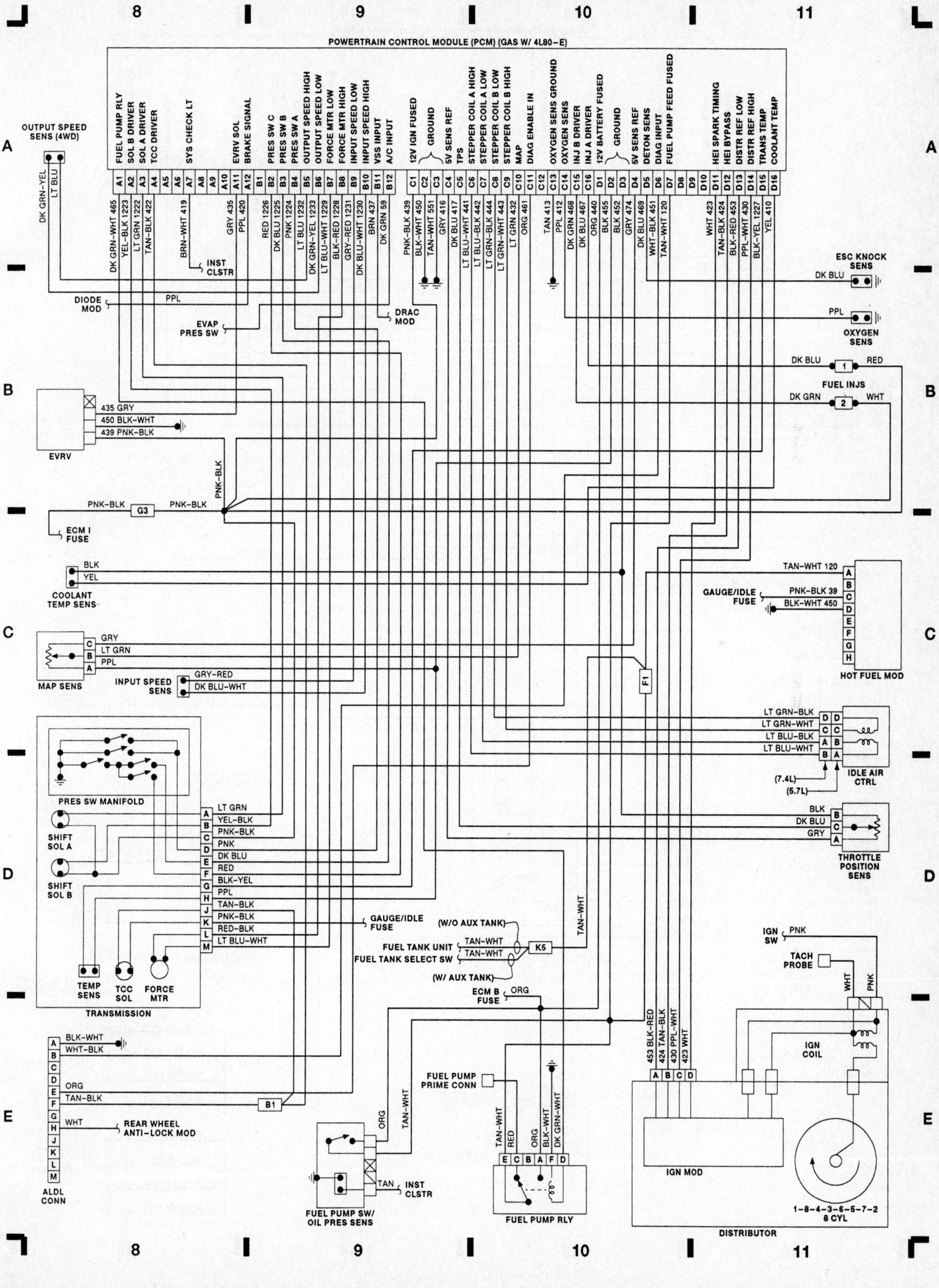
POWERTRAIN CONTROL MODULE (PCM) (GAS W/ 4L80-E)
FUEL PUMP RLY
SOL B DRIVER
SOL A DRIVER
TCC DRIVER
SYS CHECK LT
EVRV SOL
BRAKE SIGNAL
PRES SW C
PRES SW B
PRES SW A
OUTPUT SPEED HIGH
OUTPUT SPEED LOW
FORCE MTR LOW
FORCE MTR HIGH
INPUT SPEED LOW
INPUT SPEED HIGH
VSS INPUT
A/C INPUT
12V IGN FUSED
GROUND
5V SENS REF
TPS
STEPPER COIL A HIGH
STEPPER COIL A LOW
STEPPER COIL B LOW
STEPPER COIL B HIGH
MAP
DIAG ENABLE IN
OXYGEN SENS GROUND
OXYGEN SENS
INJ B DRIVER
INJ A DRIVER
12V BATTERY FUSED
GROUND
5V SENS REF
DETON SENS
DIAG INPUT
FUEL PUMP FEED FUSED
HEI SPARK TIMING
HEI BYPASS
DISTR REF LOW
DISTR REF HIGH
TRANS TEMP
COOLANT TEMP
A1 A2 A3 A4 A5 A6 A7 A8 A9 A10 A11 A12 B1 B2 B3 B4 B5 B6 B7 B8 B9 B10 B11 B12
C1 C2 C3 C4 C5 C6 C7 C8 C9 C10 C11 C12 C13 C14 C15 C16 D1 D2 D3 D4 D5 D6 D7 D8 D9 D10 D11 D12 D13 D14 D15 D16
DK GRN-WHT 465
YEL-BLK 1223
LT GRN 1222
TAN-BLK 422
BRN-WHT 419
GRY 435
PPL 420
RED 1226
DK BLU 1225
PNK 1224
LT BLU 1232
DK GRN-YEL 1233
LT BLU-WHT 1229
BLK-RED 1228
GRY-RED 1231
DK BLU-WHT 1230
BRN 437
DK GRN 59
PNK-BLK 439
BLK-WHT 450
TAN-WHT 551
GRY 416
DK BLU 417
LT BLU-WHT 441
LT BLU-BLK 442
LT GRN-BLK 444
LT GRN-WHT 443
LT GRN 432
ORG 461
TAN 413
PPL 412
DK GRN 468
DK BLU 467
ORG 440
BLK 452
GRY 474
DK BLU 469
WHT-BLK 451
TAN-WHT 120
WHT 423
TAN-BLK 424
BLK-RED 453
PPL-WHT 430
BLK-YEL 1227
YEL 410
OUTPUT SPEED SENS (4WD)
DK GRN-YEL
LT BLU
INST CLSTR
DIODE MOD
PPL
EVAP PRES SW
DRAC MOD
ESC KNOCK SENS
DK BLU
PPL
OXYGEN SENS
DK BLU
RED
FUEL INJS
DK GRN
WHT
435 GRY
450 BLK-WHT
439 PNK-BLK
EVRV
PNK-BLK
PNK-BLK
G3
PNK-BLK
ECM I FUSE
BLK
YEL
COOLANT TEMP SENS
TAN-WHT 120
GAUGE/IDLE FUSE
PNK-BLK 39
BLK-WHT 450
HOT FUEL MOD
GRY
LT GRN
PPL
MAP SENS
INPUT SPEED SENS
GRY-RED
DK BLU-WHT
F1
LT GRN-BLK
LT GRN-WHT
LT BLU-BLK
LT BLU-WHT
(7.4L)
(5.7L)
IDLE AIR CTRL
PRES SW MANIFOLD
SHIFT SOL A
SHIFT SOL B
LT GRN
YEL-BLK
PNK-BLK
PNK
DK BLU
RED
BLK-YEL
PPL
TAN-BLK
PNK-BLK
RED-BLK
LT BLU-WHT
BLK
DK BLU
GRY
THROTTLE POSITION SENS
GAUGE/IDLE FUSE
(W/O AUX TANK)
FUEL TANK UNIT
TAN-WHT
FUEL TANK SELECT SW
TAN-WHT
K5
(W/ AUX TANK)
TAN-WHT
TEMP SENS
TCC SOL
FORCE MTR
TRANSMISSION
IGN SW
PNK
TACH PROBE
WHT
PNK
ECM B FUSE
ORG
BLK-WHT
WHT-BLK
ORG
TAN-BLK
B1
WHT
REAR WHEEL ANTI-LOCK MOD
ALDL CONN
FUEL PUMP PRIME CONN
TAN-WHT
ORG
TAN
INST CLSTR
FUEL PUMP SW/ OIL PRES SENS
TAN-WHT
RED
ORG
BLK-WHT
DK GRN-WHT
FUEL PUMP RLY
453 BLK-RED
424 TAN-BLK
430 PPL-WHT
423 WHT
IGN COIL
IGN MOD
1-8-4-3-6-5-7-2
8 CYL
DISTRIBUTOR

1991 WIRING DIAGRAMS
"R" & "V" Series (Cont.)

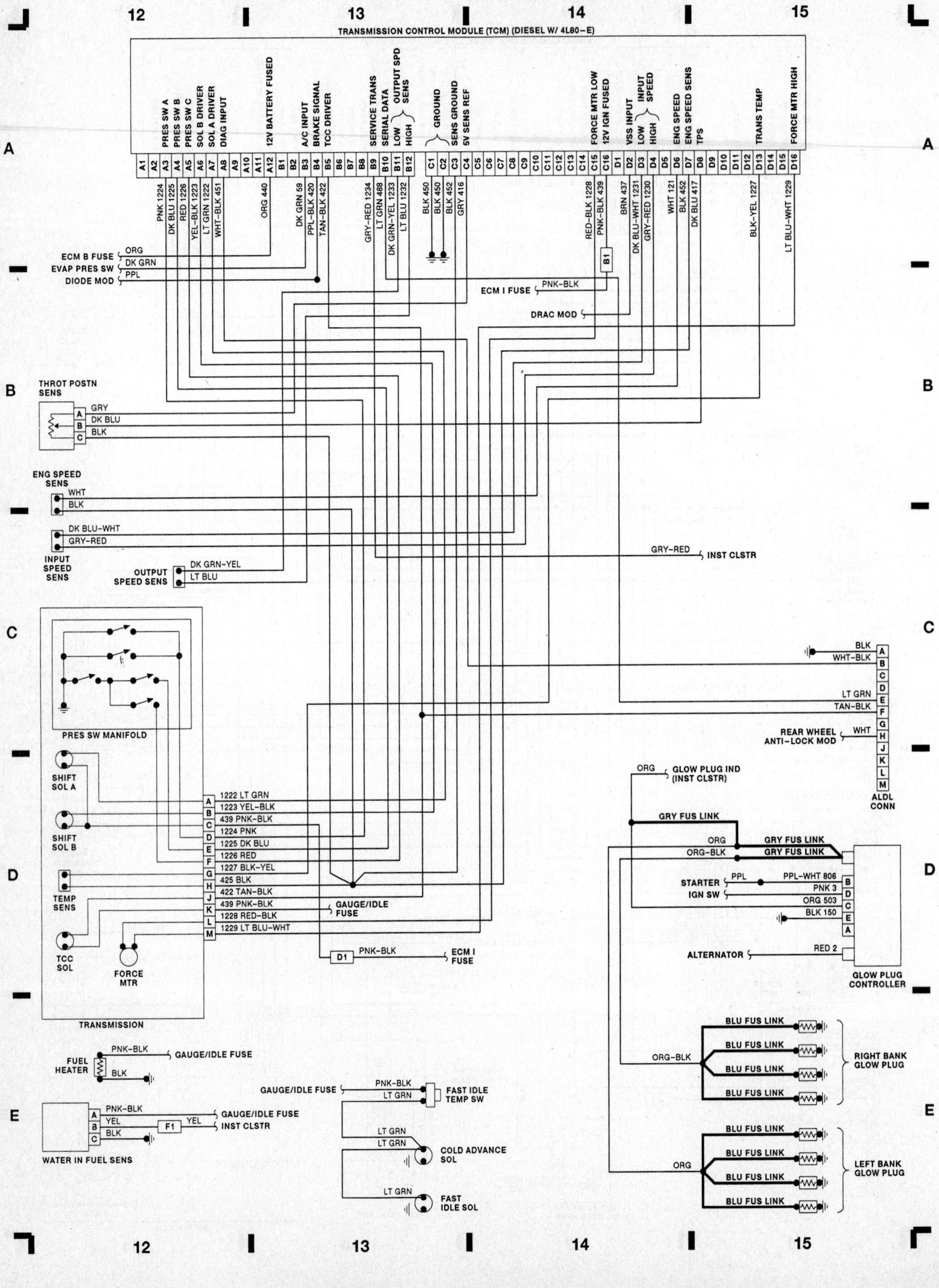
12
13
14
15
TRANSMISSION CONTROL MODULE (TCM) (DIESEL W/ 4L80-E)
PRES SW A
PRES SW B
PRES SW C
SOL B DRIVER
SOL A DRIVER
DIAG INPUT
12V BATTERY FUSED
A/C INPUT
BRAKE SIGNAL
TCC DRIVER
SERVICE TRANS
SERIAL DATA
OUTPUT SPD SENS LOW HIGH
GROUND
SENS GROUND
5V SENS REF
FORCE MTR LOW
12V IGN FUSED
VSS INPUT
INPUT SPEED LOW HIGH
ENG SPEED
ENG SPEED SENS
TPS
TRANS TEMP
FORCE MTR HIGH
PNK 1224
DK BLU 1225
RED 1226
YEL-BLK 1223
LT GRN 1222
WHT-BLK 451
ORG 440
DK GRN 59
PPL-BLK 420
TAN-BLK 422
GRY-RED 1234
LT GRN 488
DK GRN-YEL 1233
LT BLU 1232
BLK 450
BLK 450
BLK 452
GRY 416
RED-BLK 1228
PNK-BLK 439
BRN 437
DK BLU-WHT 1231
GRY-RED 1230
WHT 121
BLK 452
DK BLU 417
BLK-YEL 1227
LT BLU-WHT 1229
ECM B FUSE
EVAP PRES SW
DIODE MOD
ECM I FUSE
DRAC MOD
THROT POSTN SENS
ENG SPEED SENS
INPUT SPEED SENS
OUTPUT SPEED SENS
INST CLSTR
PRES SW MANIFOLD
SHIFT SOL A
SHIFT SOL B
TEMP SENS
TCC SOL
FORCE MTR
TRANSMISSION
1222 LT GRN
1223 YEL-BLK
439 PNK-BLK
1224 PNK
1225 DK BLU
1226 RED
1227 BLK-YEL
425 BLK
422 TAN-BLK
439 PNK-BLK
1228 RED-BLK
1229 LT BLU-WHT
GAUGE/IDLE FUSE
ECM I FUSE
REAR WHEEL ANTI-LOCK MOD
ALDL CONN
GLOW PLUG IND (INST CLSTR)
GRY FUS LINK
STARTER
IGN SW
PPL-WHT 806
PNK 3
ORG 503
BLK 150
RED 2
ALTERNATOR
GLOW PLUG CONTROLLER
BLU FUS LINK
RIGHT BANK GLOW PLUG
LEFT BANK GLOW PLUG
FUEL HEATER
WATER IN FUEL SENS
FAST IDLE TEMP SW
COLD ADVANCE SOL
FAST IDLE SOL

1991 WIRING DIAGRAMS
"R" & "V" Series (Cont.)

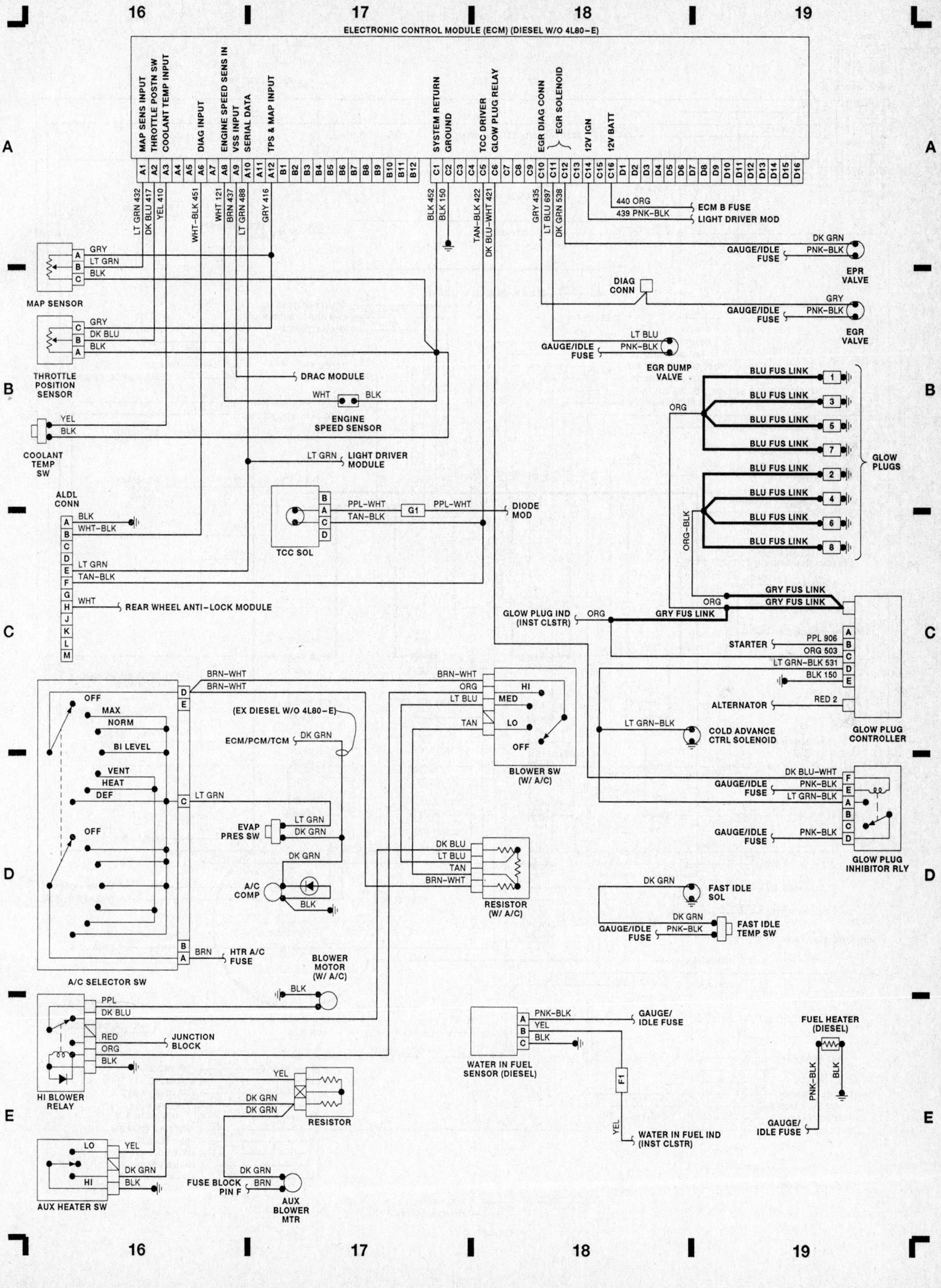
ELECTRONIC CONTROL MODULE (ECM) (DIESEL W/O 4L80-E)
MAP SENS INPUT
THROTTLE POSTN SW
COOLANT TEMP INPUT
DIAG INPUT
ENGINE SPEED SENS IN
VSS INPUT
SERIAL DATA
TPS & MAP INPUT
SYSTEM RETURN
GROUND
TCC DRIVER
GLOW PLUG RELAY
EGR DIAG CONN
EGR SOLENOID
12V IGN
12V BATT
440 ORG
ECM B FUSE
439 PNK-BLK
LIGHT DRIVER MOD
MAP SENSOR
THROTTLE POSITION SENSOR
COOLANT TEMP SW
DRAC MODULE
ENGINE SPEED SENSOR
LIGHT DRIVER MODULE
ALDL CONN
TCC SOL
DIODE MOD
REAR WHEEL ANTI-LOCK MODULE
EPR VALVE
EGR VALVE
DIAG CONN
EGR DUMP VALVE
GAUGE/IDLE FUSE
BLU FUS LINK
GLOW PLUGS
GRY FUS LINK
GLOW PLUG IND (INST CLSTR)
STARTER
ALTERNATOR
GLOW PLUG CONTROLLER
COLD ADVANCE CTRL SOLENOID
GLOW PLUG INHIBITOR RLY
FAST IDLE SOL
FAST IDLE TEMP SW
(EX DIESEL W/O 4L80-E)
ECM/PCM/TCM
EVAP PRES SW
A/C COMP
BLOWER SW (W/ A/C)
RESISTOR (W/ A/C)
A/C SELECTOR SW
HTR A/C FUSE
BLOWER MOTOR (W/ A/C)
JUNCTION BLOCK
HI BLOWER RELAY
RESISTOR
AUX HEATER SW
FUSE BLOCK PIN F
AUX BLOWER MTR
WATER IN FUEL SENSOR (DIESEL)
GAUGE/ IDLE FUSE
WATER IN FUEL IND (INST CLSTR)
FUEL HEATER (DIESEL)

1991 WIRING DIAGRAMS
"R" & "V" Series (Cont.)

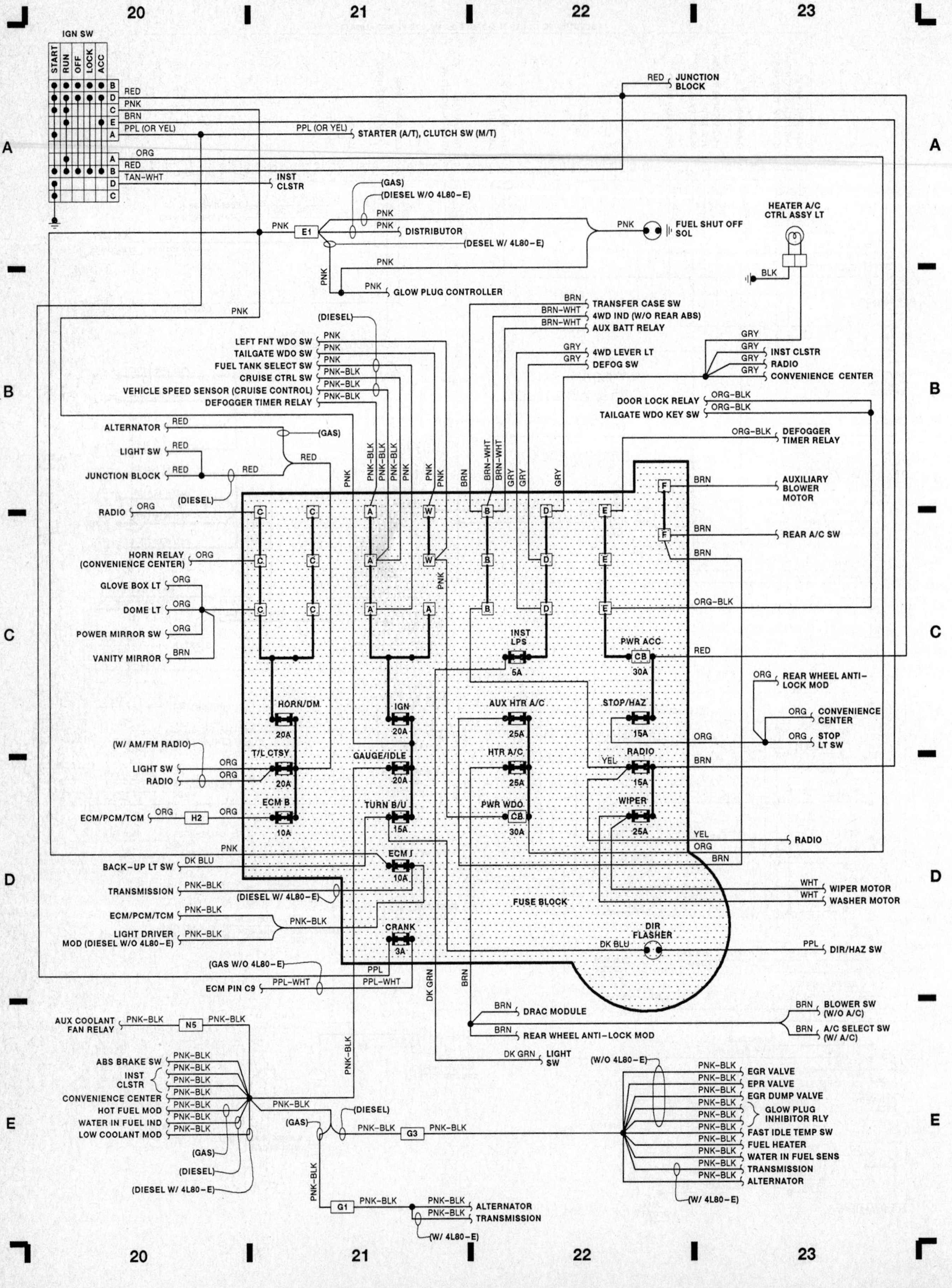
20
21
22
23
A
B
C
D
E
IGN SW
START
RUN
OFF
LOCK
ACC
RED
PNK
BRN
PPL (OR YEL)
ORG
TAN-WHT
PPL (OR YEL)
STARTER (A/T), CLUTCH SW (M/T)
INST
CLSTR
RED
JUNCTION
BLOCK
(GAS)
(DIESEL W/O 4L80-E)
PNK
E1
DISTRIBUTOR
(DESEL W/ 4L80-E)
FUEL SHUT OFF
SOL
GLOW PLUG CONTROLLER
HEATER A/C
CTRL ASSY LT
BLK
TRANSFER CASE SW
4WD IND (W/O REAR ABS)
AUX BATT RELAY
BRN-WHT
4WD LEVER LT
DEFOG SW
GRY
INST CLSTR
RADIO
CONVENIENCE CENTER
(DIESEL)
LEFT FNT WDO SW
TAILGATE WDO SW
FUEL TANK SELECT SW
CRUISE CTRL SW
VEHICLE SPEED SENSOR (CRUISE CONTROL)
DEFOGGER TIMER RELAY
PNK-BLK
DOOR LOCK RELAY
TAILGATE WDO KEY SW
ORG-BLK
DEFOGGER
TIMER RELAY
ALTERNATOR
LIGHT SW
JUNCTION BLOCK
RADIO
(GAS)
(DIESEL)
AUXILIARY
BLOWER
MOTOR
REAR A/C SW
HORN RELAY
(CONVENIENCE CENTER)
GLOVE BOX LT
DOME LT
POWER MIRROR SW
VANITY MIRROR
INST
LPS
5A
PWR ACC
CB
30A
REAR WHEEL ANTI-
LOCK MOD
CONVENIENCE
CENTER
STOP
LT SW
HORN/DM
20A
IGN
20A
AUX HTR A/C
25A
STOP/HAZ
15A
(W/ AM/FM RADIO)
LIGHT SW
RADIO
T/L CTSY
20A
GAUGE/IDLE
20A
HTR A/C
25A
RADIO
15A
YEL
ECM B
10A
TURN B/U
15A
PWR WDO
CB
30A
WIPER
25A
ECM/PCM/TCM
H2
BACK-UP LT SW
DK BLU
ECM I
10A
TRANSMISSION
(DIESEL W/ 4L80-E)
ECM/PCM/TCM
LIGHT DRIVER
MOD (DIESEL W/O 4L80-E)
FUSE BLOCK
WIPER MOTOR
WASHER MOTOR
WHT
CRANK
3A
DIR
FLASHER
DIR/HAZ SW
PPL
(GAS W/O 4L80-E)
ECM PIN C9
PPL-WHT
DK GRN
DRAC MODULE
REAR WHEEL ANTI-LOCK MOD
BLOWER SW
(W/O A/C)
A/C SELECT SW
(W/ A/C)
LIGHT
SW
AUX COOLANT
FAN RELAY
N5
ABS BRAKE SW
INST
CLSTR
CONVENIENCE CENTER
HOT FUEL MOD
WATER IN FUEL IND
LOW COOLANT MOD
(GAS)
(DIESEL)
(DIESEL W/ 4L80-E)
G3
G1
ALTERNATOR
TRANSMISSION
(W/ 4L80-E)
(W/O 4L80-E)
EGR VALVE
EPR VALVE
EGR DUMP VALVE
GLOW PLUG
INHIBITOR RLY
FAST IDLE TEMP SW
FUEL HEATER
WATER IN FUEL SENS
TRANSMISSION
ALTERNATOR
(W/ 4L80-E)

1991 WIRING DIAGRAMS
"R" & "V" Series (Cont.)

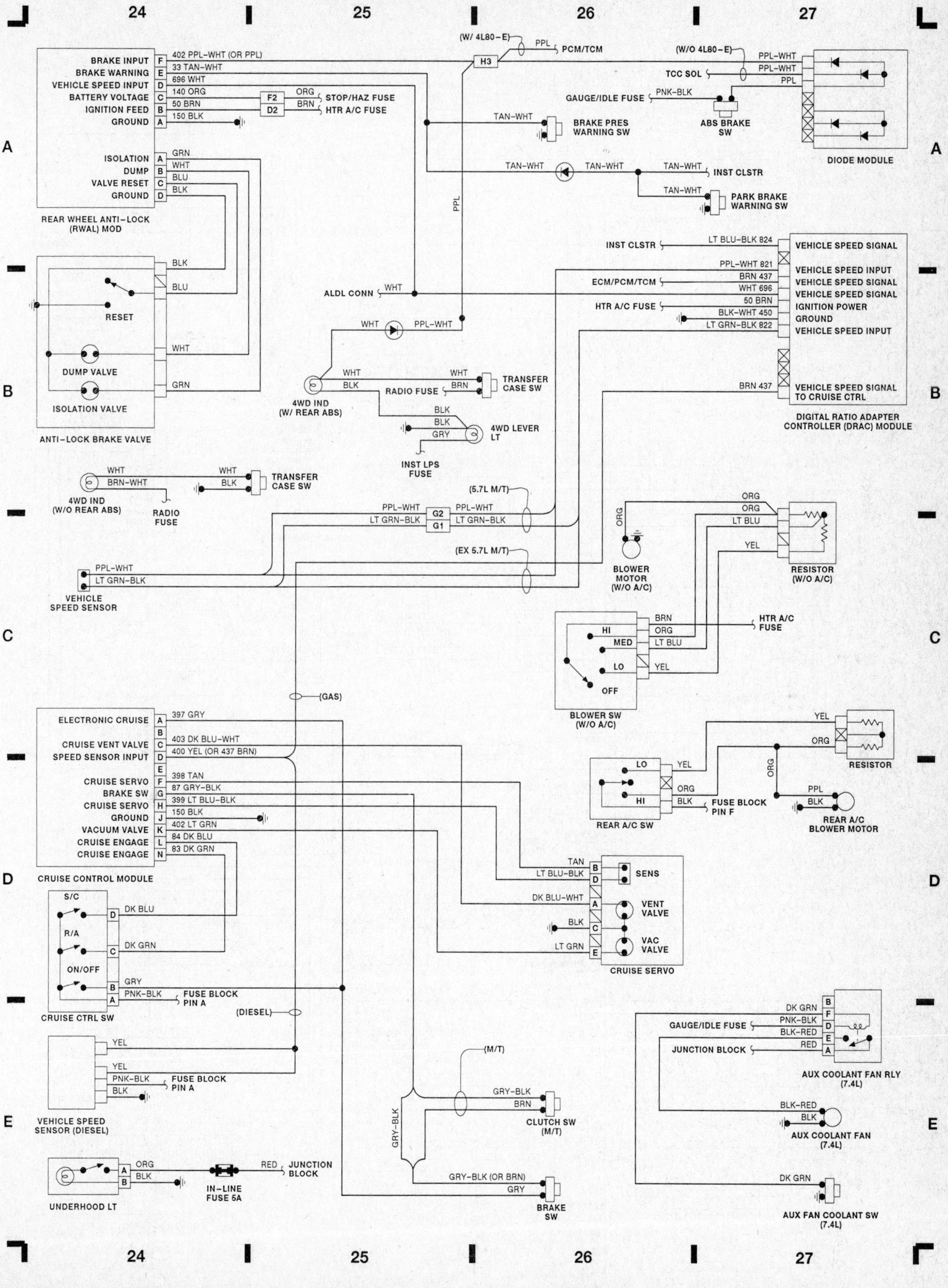
24
25
26
27
A
B
C
D
E
BRAKE INPUT
BRAKE WARNING
VEHICLE SPEED INPUT
BATTERY VOLTAGE
IGNITION FEED
GROUND
402 PPL-WHT (OR PPL)
33 TAN-WHT
696 WHT
140 ORG
50 BRN
150 BLK
STOP/HAZ FUSE
HTR A/C FUSE
ISOLATION
DUMP
VALVE RESET
GROUND
REAR WHEEL ANTI-LOCK (RWAL) MOD
(W/ 4L80-E)
PCM/TCM
(W/O 4L80-E)
TCC SOL
GAUGE/IDLE FUSE
ABS BRAKE SW
DIODE MODULE
BRAKE PRES WARNING SW
INST CLSTR
PARK BRAKE WARNING SW
RESET
DUMP VALVE
ISOLATION VALVE
ANTI-LOCK BRAKE VALVE
ALDL CONN
4WD IND (W/ REAR ABS)
RADIO FUSE
TRANSFER CASE SW
4WD LEVER LT
INST LPS FUSE
LT BLU-BLK 824
PPL-WHT 821
BRN 437
WHT 696
50 BRN
BLK-WHT 450
LT GRN-BLK 822
ECM/PCM/TCM
VEHICLE SPEED SIGNAL
VEHICLE SPEED INPUT
IGNITION POWER
GROUND
VEHICLE SPEED SIGNAL TO CRUISE CTRL
DIGITAL RATIO ADAPTER CONTROLLER (DRAC) MODULE
4WD IND (W/O REAR ABS)
(5.7L M/T)
(EX 5.7L M/T)
VEHICLE SPEED SENSOR
BLOWER MOTOR (W/O A/C)
RESISTOR (W/O A/C)
HI
MED
LO
OFF
BLOWER SW (W/O A/C)
(GAS)
ELECTRONIC CRUISE
CRUISE VENT VALVE
SPEED SENSOR INPUT
CRUISE SERVO
BRAKE SW
CRUISE SERVO
GROUND
VACUUM VALVE
CRUISE ENGAGE
CRUISE ENGAGE
397 GRY
403 DK BLU-WHT
400 YEL (OR 437 BRN)
398 TAN
87 GRY-BLK
399 LT BLU-BLK
150 BLK
402 LT GRN
84 DK BLU
83 DK GRN
CRUISE CONTROL MODULE
REAR A/C SW
FUSE BLOCK PIN F
RESISTOR
REAR A/C BLOWER MOTOR
SENS
VENT VALVE
VAC VALVE
CRUISE SERVO
S/C
R/A
ON/OFF
FUSE BLOCK PIN A
CRUISE CTRL SW
(DIESEL)
VEHICLE SPEED SENSOR (DIESEL)
AUX COOLANT FAN RLY (7.4L)
JUNCTION BLOCK
AUX COOLANT FAN (7.4L)
(M/T)
CLUTCH SW (M/T)
GRY-BLK (OR BRN)
BRAKE SW
AUX FAN COOLANT SW (7.4L)
UNDERHOOD LT
IN-LINE FUSE 5A

1991 WIRING DIAGRAMS
"R" & "V" Series (Cont.)

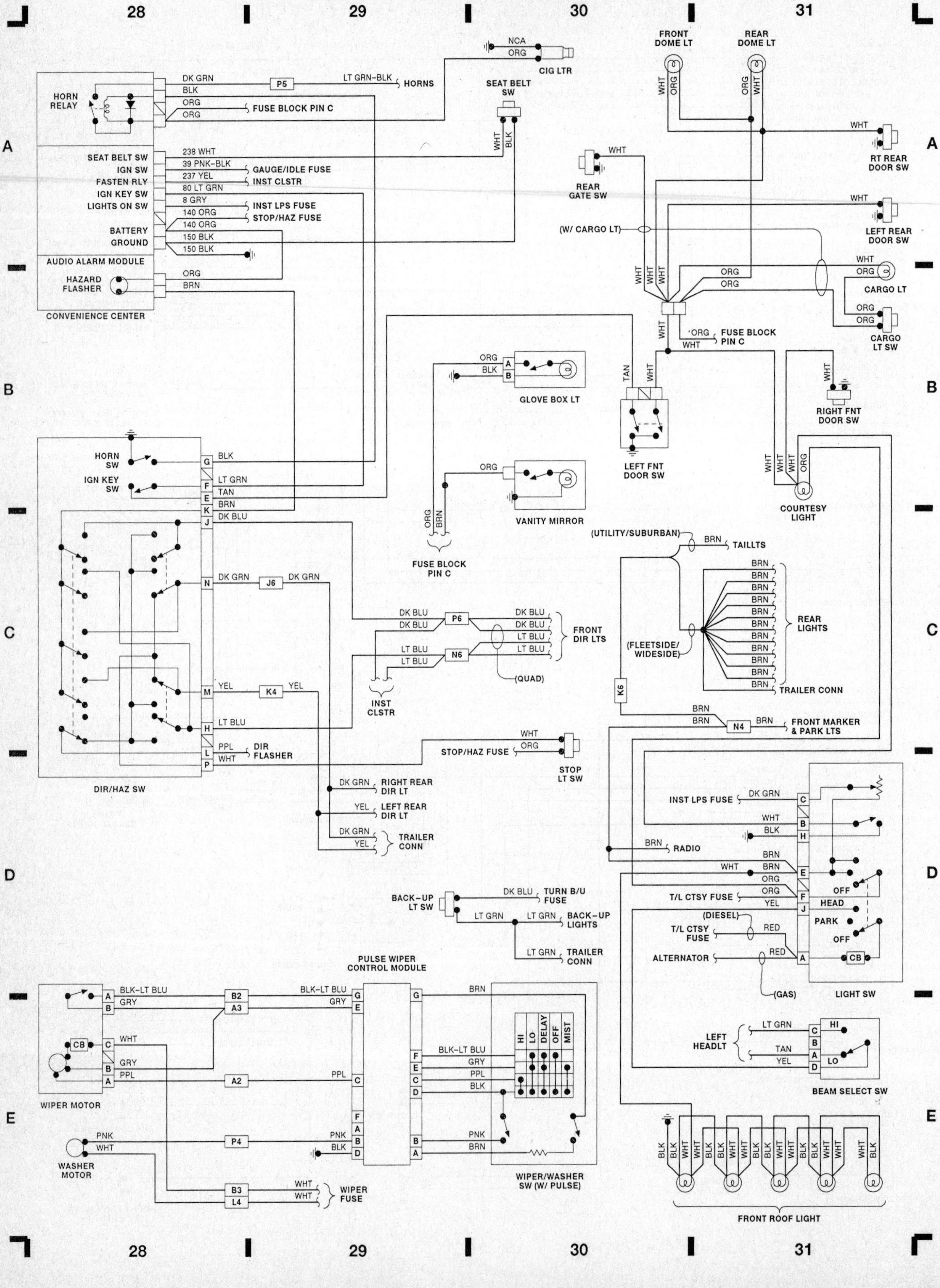
28
29
30
31
HORN RELAY
DK GRN
BLK
ORG
ORG
P5
LT GRN-BLK
HORNS
FUSE BLOCK PIN C
NCA
ORG
CIG LTR
SEAT BELT SW
SEAT BELT SW
IGN SW
FASTEN RLY
IGN KEY SW
LIGHTS ON SW
BATTERY
GROUND
238 WHT
39 PNK-BLK
237 YEL
80 LT GRN
8 GRY
140 ORG
140 ORG
150 BLK
150 BLK
GAUGE/IDLE FUSE
INST CLSTR
INST LPS FUSE
STOP/HAZ FUSE
AUDIO ALARM MODULE
HAZARD FLASHER
BRN
CONVENIENCE CENTER
FRONT DOME LT
REAR DOME LT
WHT
RT REAR DOOR SW
REAR GATE SW
(W/ CARGO LT)
LEFT REAR DOOR SW
CARGO LT
CARGO LT SW
FUSE BLOCK PIN C
TAN
GLOVE BOX LT
LEFT FNT DOOR SW
RIGHT FNT DOOR SW
COURTESY LIGHT
HORN SW
IGN KEY SW
LT GRN
DK BLU
VANITY MIRROR
FUSE BLOCK PIN C
(UTILITY/SUBURBAN)
TAILLTS
REAR LIGHTS
(FLEETSIDE/ WIDESIDE)
TRAILER CONN
J6
P6
N6
FRONT DIR LTS
LT BLU
(QUAD)
INST CLSTR
YEL
K4
K6
N4
FRONT MARKER & PARK LTS
PPL
DIR FLASHER
STOP/HAZ FUSE
STOP LT SW
DIR/HAZ SW
RIGHT REAR DIR LT
LEFT REAR DIR LT
TRAILER CONN
INST LPS FUSE
RADIO
T/L CTSY FUSE
OFF
HEAD
PARK
(DIESEL)
T/L CTSY FUSE
RED
ALTERNATOR
CB
(GAS)
LIGHT SW
BACK-UP LT SW
TURN B/U FUSE
BACK-UP LIGHTS
TRAILER CONN
PULSE WIPER CONTROL MODULE
BLK-LT BLU
GRY
B2
A3
A2
HI
LO
DELAY
MIST
WIPER MOTOR
LEFT HEADLT
BEAM SELECT SW
PNK
P4
WASHER MOTOR
B3
L4
WIPER FUSE
WIPER/WASHER SW (W/ PULSE)
FRONT ROOF LIGHT
A
B
C
D
E

1991 WIRING DIAGRAMS
"R" & "V" Series (Cont.)

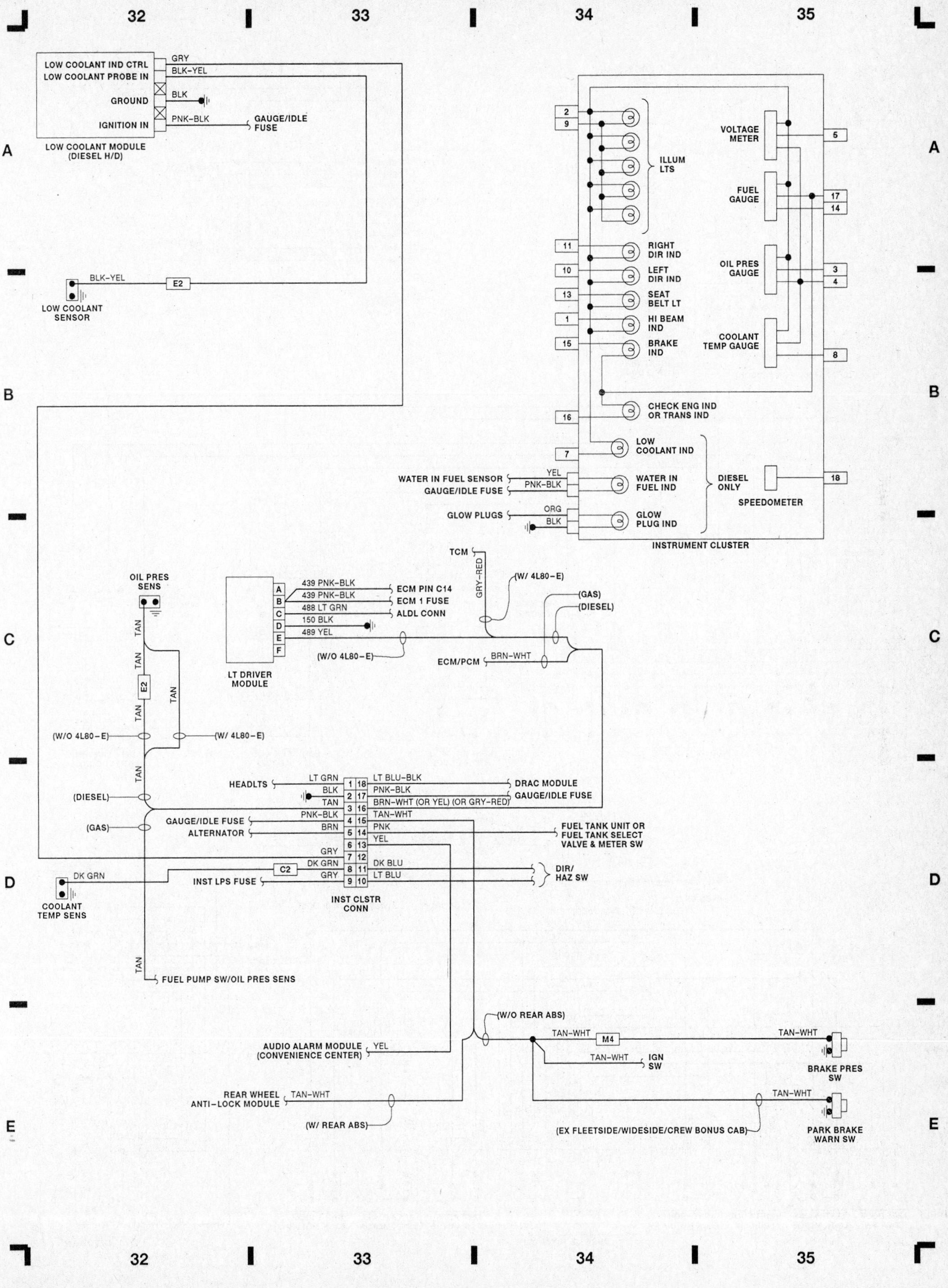
32
33
34
35
A
B
C
D
E
LOW COOLANT IND CTRL
LOW COOLANT PROBE IN
GROUND
IGNITION IN
GRY
BLK-YEL
BLK
PNK-BLK
GAUGE/IDLE FUSE
LOW COOLANT MODULE (DIESEL H/D)
BLK-YEL
E2
LOW COOLANT SENSOR
2
9
ILLUM LTS
VOLTAGE METER
5
FUEL GAUGE
17
14
11
RIGHT DIR IND
10
LEFT DIR IND
OIL PRES GAUGE
3
4
13
SEAT BELT LT
1
HI BEAM IND
COOLANT TEMP GAUGE
15
BRAKE IND
8
CHECK ENG IND OR TRANS IND
16
LOW COOLANT IND
7
WATER IN FUEL SENSOR
YEL
GAUGE/IDLE FUSE
PNK-BLK
WATER IN FUEL IND
DIESEL ONLY
18
SPEEDOMETER
GLOW PLUGS
ORG
BLK
GLOW PLUG IND
INSTRUMENT CLUSTER
TCM
GRY-RED
(W/ 4L80-E)
(GAS)
(DIESEL)
OIL PRES SENS
A
B
C
D
E
F
439 PNK-BLK
439 PNK-BLK
488 LT GRN
150 BLK
489 YEL
ECM PIN C14
ECM 1 FUSE
ALDL CONN
(W/O 4L80-E)
ECM/PCM
BRN-WHT
LT DRIVER MODULE
TAN
E2
(W/O 4L80-E)
(W/ 4L80-E)
(DIESEL)
(GAS)
HEADLTS
LT GRN
BLK
TAN
PNK-BLK
BRN
GRY
DK GRN
GRY
GAUGE/IDLE FUSE
ALTERNATOR
1 18
2 17
3 16
4 15
5 14
6 13
7 12
8 11
9 10
LT BLU-BLK
PNK-BLK
BRN-WHT (OR YEL) (OR GRY-RED)
TAN-WHT
PNK
YEL
DK BLU
LT BLU
DRAC MODULE
GAUGE/IDLE FUSE
FUEL TANK UNIT OR FUEL TANK SELECT VALVE & METER SW
DIR/ HAZ SW
DK GRN
C2
INST LPS FUSE
COOLANT TEMP SENS
INST CLSTR CONN
FUEL PUMP SW/OIL PRES SENS
(W/O REAR ABS)
TAN-WHT
M4
TAN-WHT
TAN-WHT
IGN SW
BRAKE PRES SW
AUDIO ALARM MODULE (CONVENIENCE CENTER)
YEL
REAR WHEEL ANTI-LOCK MODULE
TAN-WHT
(W/ REAR ABS)
TAN-WHT
(EX FLEETSIDE/WIDESIDE/CREW BONUS CAB)
PARK BRAKE WARN SW

1991 WIRING DIAGRAMS
"R" & "V" Series (Cont.)

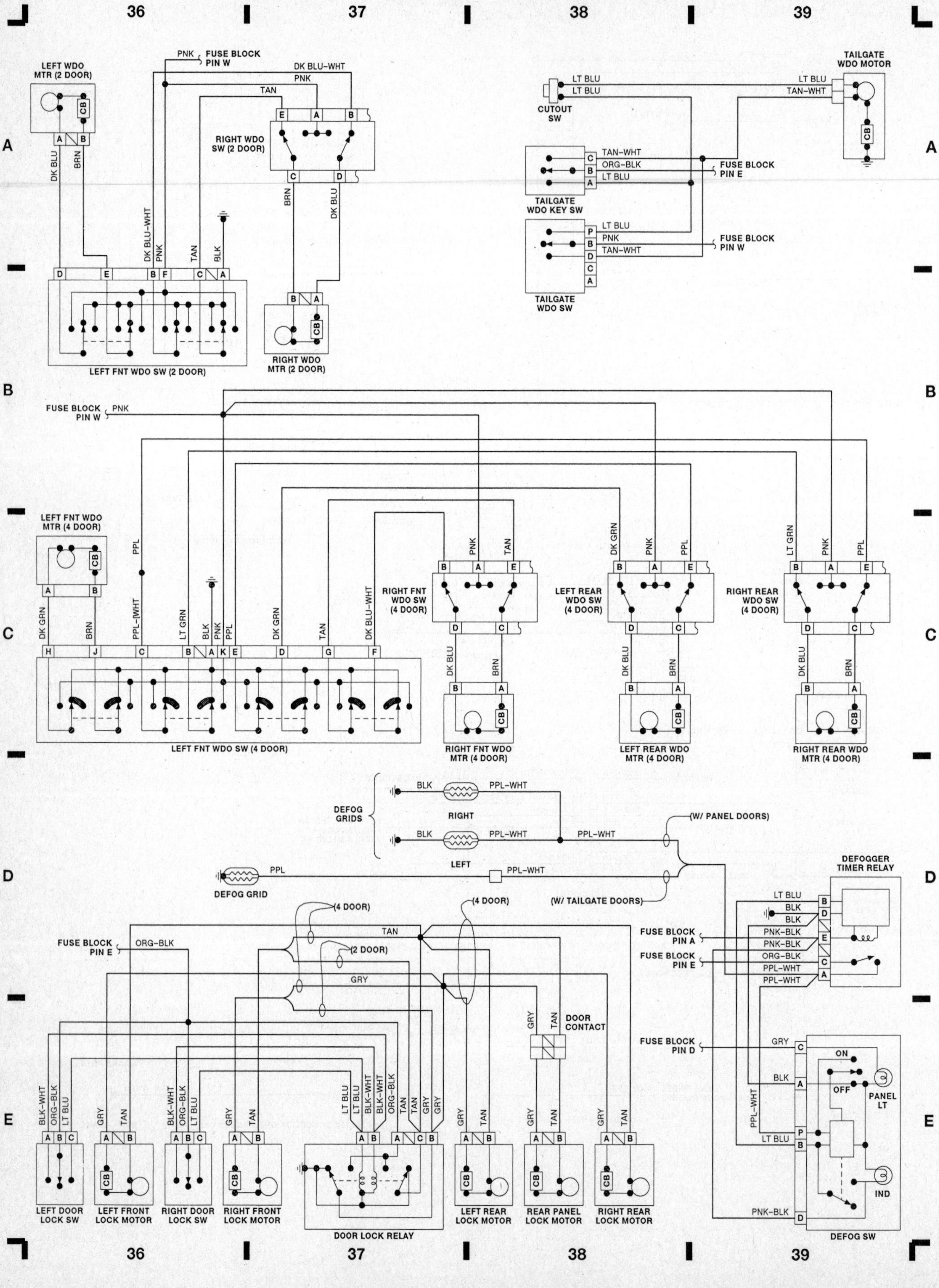
36
37
38
39
A
B
C
D
E
LEFT WDO MTR (2 DOOR)
CB
DK BLU
BRN
PNK
FUSE BLOCK PIN W
DK BLU-WHT
PNK
TAN
RIGHT WDO SW (2 DOOR)
DK BLU-WHT
PNK
TAN
BLK
LEFT FNT WDO SW (2 DOOR)
RIGHT WDO MTR (2 DOOR)
LT BLU
LT BLU
CUTOUT SW
TAILGATE WDO MOTOR
LT BLU
TAN-WHT
TAN-WHT
ORG-BLK
LT BLU
FUSE BLOCK PIN E
TAILGATE WDO KEY SW
LT BLU
PNK
TAN-WHT
FUSE BLOCK PIN W
TAILGATE WDO SW
FUSE BLOCK PIN W
PNK
LEFT FNT WDO MTR (4 DOOR)
PPL
DK GRN
BRN
PPL-WHT
LT GRN
BLK
PNK
PPL
DK GRN
TAN
DK BLU-WHT
LEFT FNT WDO SW (4 DOOR)
RIGHT FNT WDO SW (4 DOOR)
LEFT REAR WDO SW (4 DOOR)
RIGHT REAR WDO SW (4 DOOR)
DK GRN
LT GRN
RIGHT FNT WDO MTR (4 DOOR)
LEFT REAR WDO MTR (4 DOOR)
RIGHT REAR WDO MTR (4 DOOR)
DEFOG GRIDS
BLK
PPL-WHT
RIGHT
LEFT
PPL-WHT
(W/ PANEL DOORS)
DEFOG GRID
PPL
PPL-WHT
(W/ TAILGATE DOORS)
DEFOGGER TIMER RELAY
LT BLU
BLK
BLK
PNK-BLK
PNK-BLK
ORG-BLK
PPL-WHT
PPL-WHT
FUSE BLOCK PIN A
FUSE BLOCK PIN E
(4 DOOR)
(4 DOOR)
(2 DOOR)
TAN
GRY
FUSE BLOCK PIN E
ORG-BLK
GRY
TAN
DOOR CONTACT
FUSE BLOCK PIN D
GRY
ON
OFF
PANEL LT
IND
LT BLU
PNK-BLK
DEFOG SW
BLK-WHT
ORG-BLK
LT BLU
LEFT DOOR LOCK SW
LEFT FRONT LOCK MOTOR
RIGHT DOOR LOCK SW
RIGHT FRONT LOCK MOTOR
DOOR LOCK RELAY
LEFT REAR LOCK MOTOR
REAR PANEL LOCK MOTOR
RIGHT REAR LOCK MOTOR

1991 WIRING DIAGRAMS
"R" & "V" Series (Cont.)

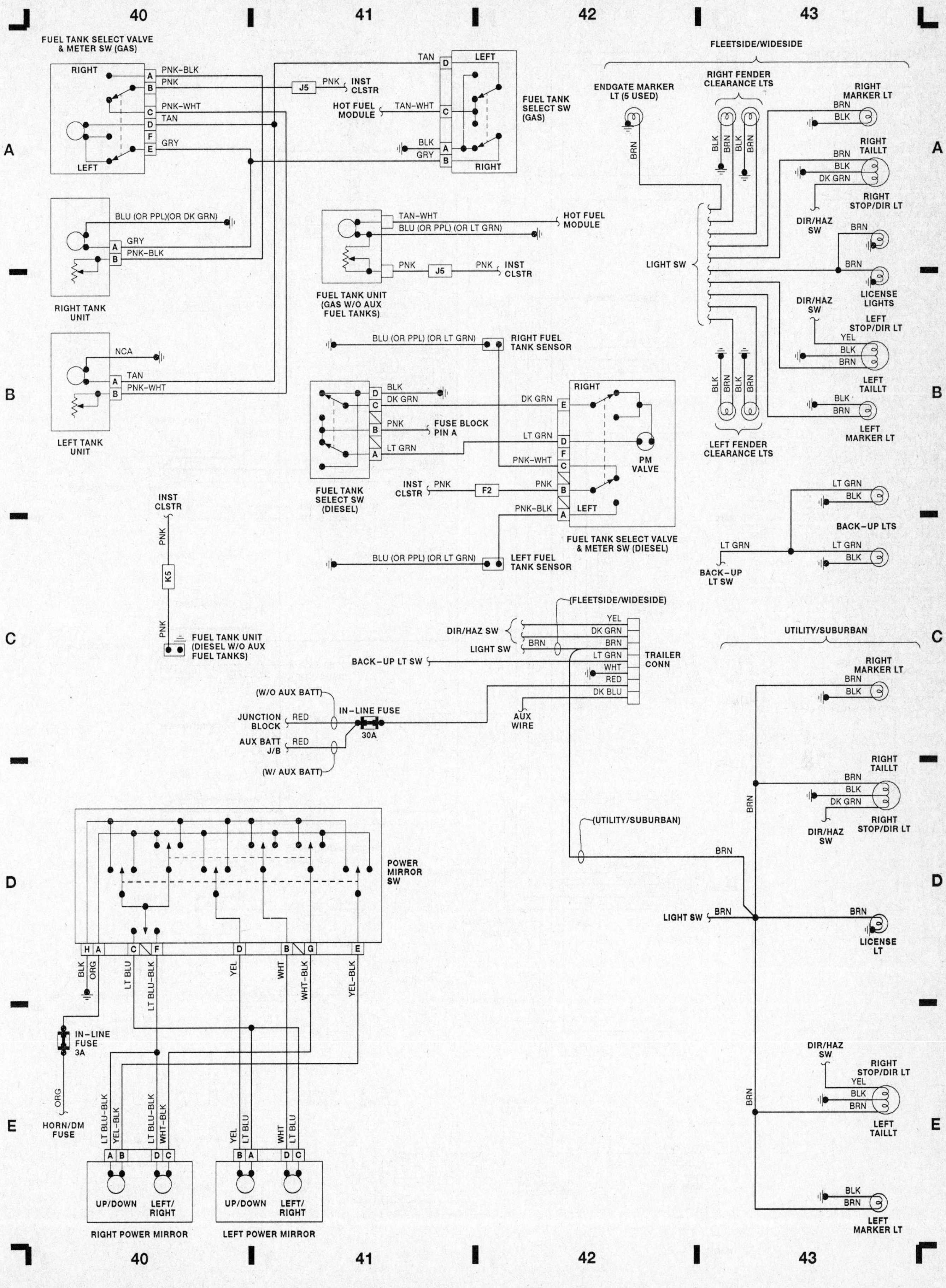

40
41
42
43
A
B
C
D
E
FUEL TANK SELECT VALVE & METER SW (GAS)
RIGHT
LEFT
PNK-BLK
PNK
PNK-WHT
TAN
GRY
J5
INST CLSTR
HOT FUEL MODULE
TAN-WHT
BLK
LEFT
RIGHT
FUEL TANK SELECT SW (GAS)
BLU (OR PPL)(OR DK GRN)
RIGHT TANK UNIT
TAN-WHT
BLU (OR PPL) (OR LT GRN)
FUEL TANK UNIT (GAS W/O AUX FUEL TANKS)
NCA
LEFT TANK UNIT
RIGHT FUEL TANK SENSOR
DK GRN
FUSE BLOCK PIN A
LT GRN
FUEL TANK SELECT SW (DIESEL)
PM VALVE
F2
FUEL TANK SELECT VALVE & METER SW (DIESEL)
LEFT FUEL TANK SENSOR
K5
FUEL TANK UNIT (DIESEL W/O AUX FUEL TANKS)
FLEETSIDE/WIDESIDE
ENDGATE MARKER LT (5 USED)
RIGHT FENDER CLEARANCE LTS
BRN
RIGHT MARKER LT
RIGHT TAILLT
RIGHT STOP/DIR LT
DIR/HAZ SW
LIGHT SW
LICENSE LIGHTS
LEFT STOP/DIR LT
YEL
LEFT TAILLT
LEFT MARKER LT
LEFT FENDER CLEARANCE LTS
BACK-UP LTS
BACK-UP LT SW
(FLEETSIDE/WIDESIDE)
WHT
RED
DK BLU
TRAILER CONN
AUX WIRE
(W/O AUX BATT)
IN-LINE FUSE
JUNCTION BLOCK
AUX BATT J/B
30A
(W/ AUX BATT)
UTILITY/SUBURBAN
(UTILITY/SUBURBAN)
LICENSE LT
POWER MIRROR SW
ORG
LT BLU
LT BLU-BLK
WHT-BLK
YEL-BLK
IN-LINE FUSE 3A
HORN/DM FUSE
UP/DOWN
LEFT/ RIGHT
RIGHT POWER MIRROR
LEFT POWER MIRROR

1991 WIRING DIAGRAMS
"S" & "T" Series

COMPONENT LOCATOR:

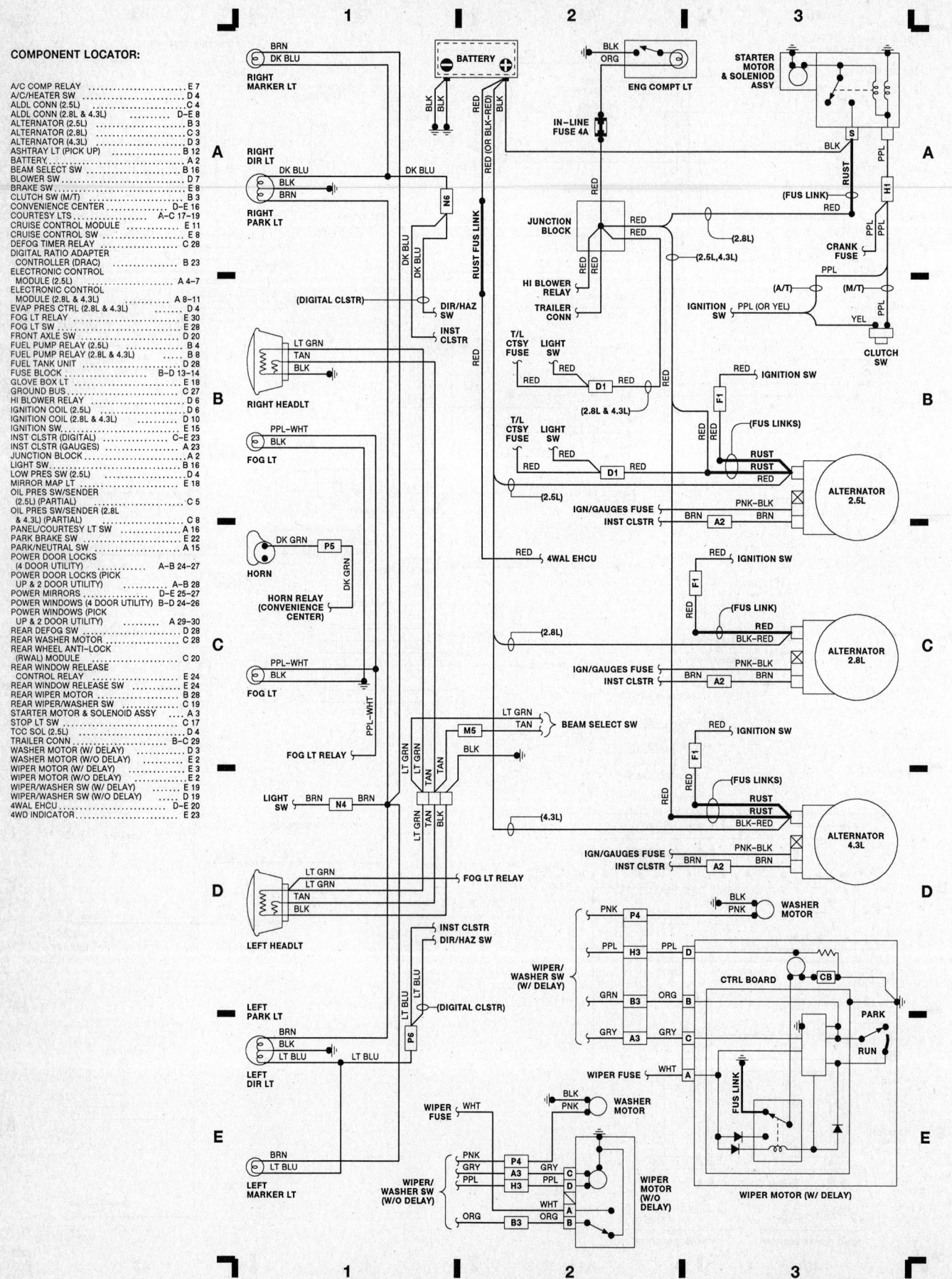

A/C COMP RELAY	E 7
A/C/HEATER SW	D 4
ALDL CONN (2.5L)	C 4
ALDL CONN (2.8L & 4.3L)	D–E 8
ALTERNATOR (2.5L)	B 3
ALTERNATOR (2.8L)	C 3
ALTERNATOR (4.3L)	D 3
ASHTRAY LT (PICK UP)	B 12
BATTERY	A 2
BEAM SELECT SW	B 16
BLOWER SW	D 7
BRAKE SW	E 8
CLUTCH SW (M/T)	B 3
CONVENIENCE CENTER	D–E 16
COURTESY LTS	A–C 17–19
CRUISE CONTROL MODULE	E 11
CRUISE CONTROL SW	E 8
DEFOG TIMER RELAY	C 28
DIGITAL RATIO ADAPTER CONTROLLER (DRAC)	B 23
ELECTRONIC CONTROL MODULE (2.5L)	A 4–7
ELECTRONIC CONTROL MODULE (2.8L & 4.3L)	A 8–11
EVAP PRES CTRL (2.8L & 4.3L)	D 4
FOG LT RELAY	E 30
FOG LT SW	E 28
FRONT AXLE SW	D 20
FUEL PUMP RELAY (2.5L)	B 4
FUEL PUMP RELAY (2.8L & 4.3L)	B 8
FUEL TANK UNIT	D 28
FUSE BLOCK	B–D 13–14
GLOVE BOX LT	E 18
GROUND BUS	C 27
HI BLOWER RELAY	D 6
IGNITION COIL (2.5L)	D 6
IGNITION COIL (2.8L & 4.3L)	D 10
IGNITION SW	E 15
INST CLSTR (DIGITAL)	C–E 23
INST CLSTR (GAUGES)	A 23
JUNCTION BLOCK	A 2
LIGHT SW	B 16
LOW PRES SW (2.5L)	D 4
MIRROR MAP LT	E 18
OIL PRES SW/SENDER (2.5L) (PARTIAL)	C 5
OIL PRES SW/SENDER (2.8L & 4.3L) (PARTIAL)	C 8
PANEL/COURTESY LT SW	A 16
PARK BRAKE SW	E 22
PARK/NEUTRAL SW	A 15
POWER DOOR LOCKS (4 DOOR UTILITY)	A–B 24–27
POWER DOOR LOCKS (PICK UP & 2 DOOR UTILITY)	A–B 28
POWER MIRRORS	D–E 25–27
POWER WINDOWS (4 DOOR UTILITY)	B–D 24–26
POWER WINDOWS (PICK UP & 2 DOOR UTILITY)	A 29–30
REAR DEFOG SW	D 28
REAR WASHER MOTOR	C 28
REAR WHEEL ANTI-LOCK (RWAL) MODULE	C 20
REAR WINDOW RELEASE CONTROL RELAY	E 24
REAR WINDOW RELEASE SW	E 24
REAR WIPER MOTOR	B 28
REAR WIPER/WASHER SW	C 19
STARTER MOTOR & SOLENOID ASSY	A 3
STOP LT SW	C 17
TCC SOL (2.5L)	D 4
TRAILER CONN	B–C 29
WASHER MOTOR (W/ DELAY)	D 3
WASHER MOTOR (W/O DELAY)	E 2
WIPER MOTOR (W/ DELAY)	E 3
WIPER MOTOR (W/O DELAY)	E 2
WIPER/WASHER SW (W/ DELAY)	E 19
WIPER/WASHER SW (W/O DELAY)	D 19
4WAL EHCU	D–E 20
4WD INDICATOR	E 23

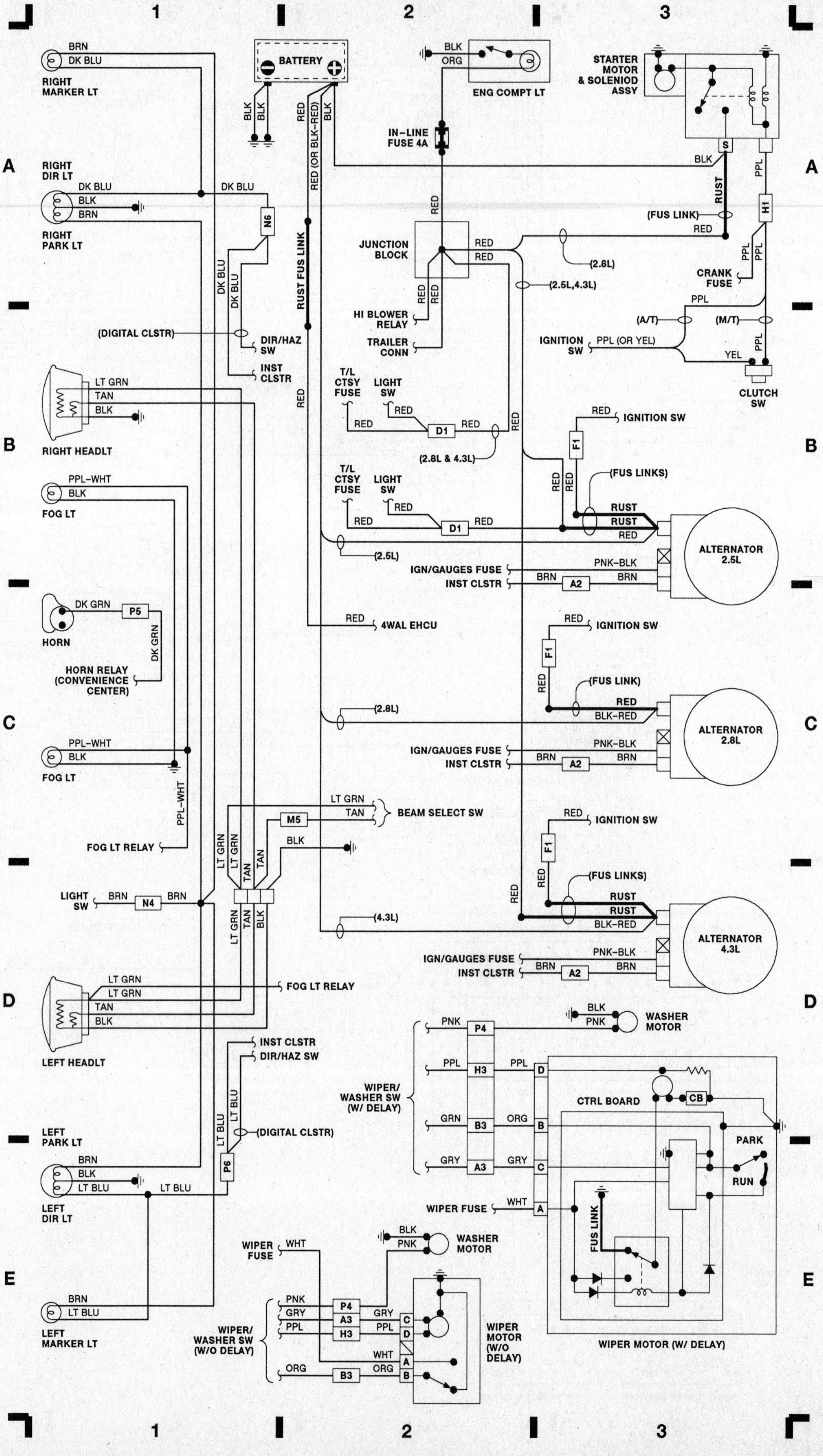
1
2
3
A
B
C
D
E
BATTERY
RIGHT MARKER LT
RIGHT DIR LT
RIGHT PARK LT
RIGHT HEADLT
FOG LT
HORN
HORN RELAY (CONVENIENCE CENTER)
FOG LT RELAY
LIGHT SW
LEFT HEADLT
LEFT PARK LT
LEFT DIR LT
LEFT MARKER LT
ENG COMPT LT
IN-LINE FUSE 4A
JUNCTION BLOCK
HI BLOWER RELAY
TRAILER CONN
DIR/HAZ SW
INST CLSTR
(DIGITAL CLSTR)
RUST FUS LINK
4WAL EHCU
BEAM SELECT SW
STARTER MOTOR & SOLENIOD ASSY
(FUS LINK)
CRANK FUSE
IGNITION SW
CLUTCH SW
T/L CTSY FUSE
LIGHT SW
ALTERNATOR 2.5L
ALTERNATOR 2.8L
ALTERNATOR 4.3L
IGN/GAUGES FUSE
INST CLSTR
(FUS LINKS)
WASHER MOTOR
WIPER/WASHER SW (W/ DELAY)
CTRL BOARD
PARK
RUN
FUS LINK
WIPER FUSE
WIPER MOTOR (W/ DELAY)
WIPER/WASHER SW (W/O DELAY)
WIPER MOTOR (W/O DELAY)

1 2 3

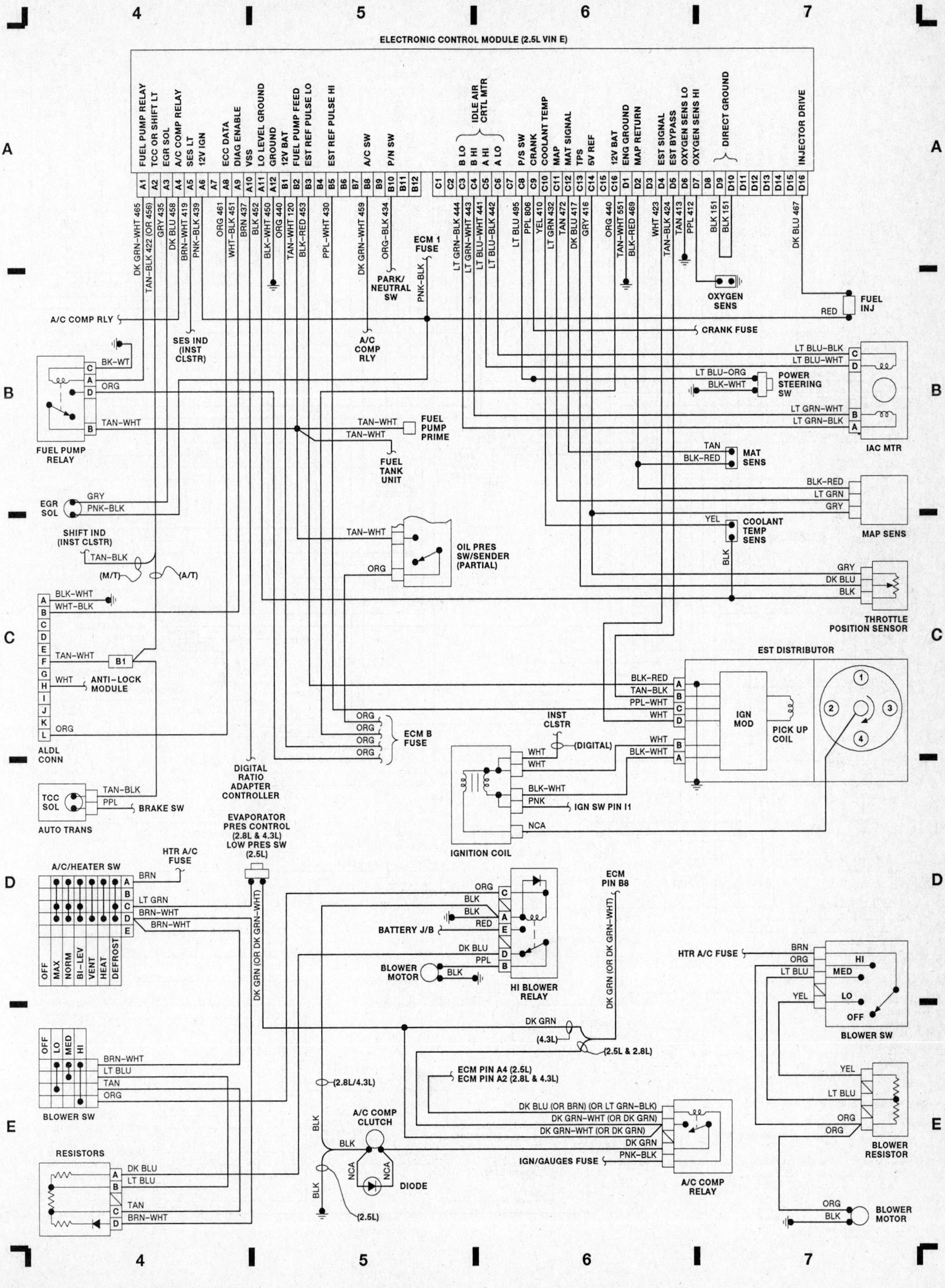

ELECTRONIC CONTROL MODULE (2.5L VIN E)
FUEL PUMP RELAY
TCC OR SHIFT LT
EGR SOL
A/C COMP RELAY
SES LT
12V IGN
ECC DATA
DIAG ENABLE
VSS
LO LEVEL GROUND
GROUND
12V BAT
FUEL PUMP FEED
EST REF PULSE LO
EST REF PULSE HI
A/C SW
P/N SW
IDLE AIR CRTL MTR
B LO
B HI
A HI
A LO
P/S SW
CRANK
COOLANT TEMP
MAP
MAT SIGNAL
TPS
5V REF
12V BAT
ENG GROUND
MAP RETURN
EST SIGNAL
EST BYPASS
OXYGEN SENS LO
OXYGEN SENS HI
DIRECT GROUND
INJECTOR DRIVE
DK GRN-WHT 465
TAN-BLK 422 (OR 456)
GRY 435
DK BLU 458
BRN-WHT 419
PNK-BLK 439
ORG 461
WHT-BLK 451
BRN 437
BLK 452
BLK-WHT 450
ORG 440
TAN-WHT 120
BLK-RED 453
PPL-WHT 430
DK GRN-WHT 459
ORG-BLK 434
LT GRN-BLK 444
LT GRN-WHT 443
LT BLU-WHT 441
LT BLU-BLK 442
LT BLU 495
PPL 806
YEL 410
LT GRN 432
TAN 472
DK BLU 417
GRY 416
ORG 440
TAN-WHT 551
BLK-RED 469
WHT 423
TAN-BLK 424
TAN 413
PPL 412
BLK 151
BLK 151
DK BLU 467
ECM 1 FUSE
PARK/NEUTRAL SW
OXYGEN SENS
FUEL INJ
A/C COMP RLY
SES IND (INST CLSTR)
A/C COMP RLY
CRANK FUSE
POWER STEERING SW
IAC MTR
FUEL PUMP RELAY
FUEL PUMP PRIME
FUEL TANK UNIT
MAT SENS
EGR SOL
MAP SENS
SHIFT IND (INST CLSTR)
(M/T)
(A/T)
COOLANT TEMP SENS
OIL PRES SW/SENDER (PARTIAL)
THROTTLE POSITION SENSOR
ANTI-LOCK MODULE
ALDL CONN
EST DISTRIBUTOR
IGN MOD
PICK UP COIL
ECM B FUSE
INST CLSTR
(DIGITAL)
IGN SW PIN I1
IGNITION COIL
TCC SOL
AUTO TRANS
BRAKE SW
DIGITAL RATIO ADAPTER CONTROLLER
EVAPORATOR PRES CONTROL (2.8L & 4.3L) LOW PRES SW (2.5L)
HTR A/C FUSE
A/C/HEATER SW
OFF
MAX
NORM
BI-LEV
VENT
HEAT
DEFROST
BATTERY J/B
BLOWER MOTOR
HI BLOWER RELAY
ECM PIN B8
HTR A/C FUSE
BLOWER SW
HI
MED
LO
OFF
(4.3L)
(2.5L & 2.8L)
ECM PIN A4 (2.5L)
ECM PIN A2 (2.8L & 4.3L)
BLOWER SW
(2.8L/4.3L)
A/C COMP CLUTCH
DK BLU (OR BRN) (OR LT GRN-BLK)
DK GRN-WHT (OR DK GRN)
DK GRN-WHT (OR DK GRN)
IGN/GAUGES FUSE
A/C COMP RELAY
BLOWER RESISTOR
RESISTORS
DIODE
(2.5L)
BLOWER MOTOR

1991 WIRING DIAGRAMS
"S" & "T" Series (Cont.)

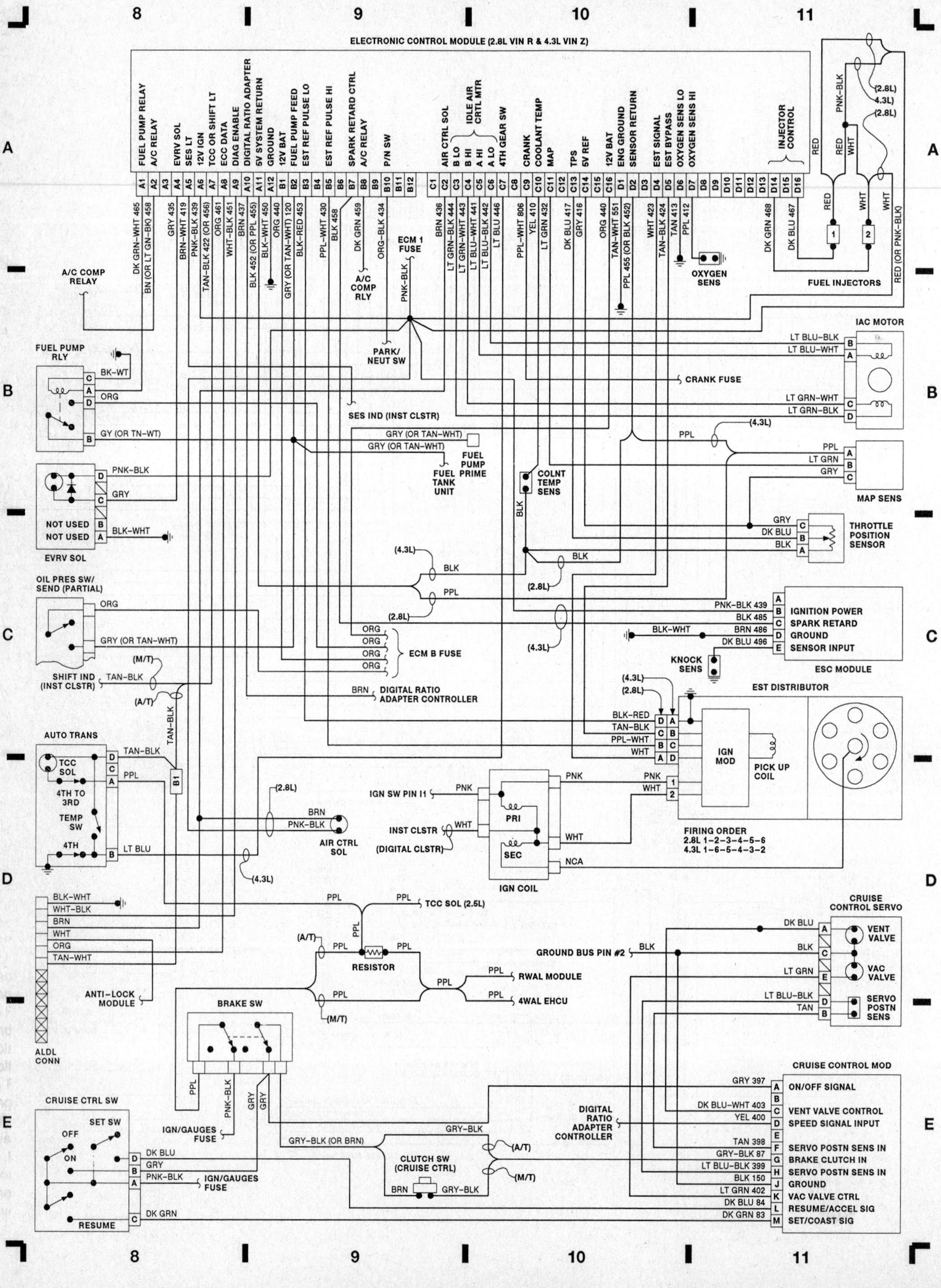
ELECTRONIC CONTROL MODULE (2.8L VIN R & 4.3L VIN Z)
FUEL PUMP RELAY
A/C RELAY
EVRV SOL
SES LT
12V IGN
TCC OR SHIFT LT
ECC DATA
DIAG ENABLE
DIGITAL RATIO ADAPTER
5V SYSTEM RETURN
GROUND
12V BAT
FUEL PUMP FEED
EST REF PULSE LO
EST REF PULSE HI
SPARK RETARD CTRL
A/C RELAY
P/N SW
AIR CTRL SOL
IDLE AIR CRTL MTR
4TH GEAR SW
CRANK
COOLANT TEMP
MAP
TPS
5V REF
12V BAT
ENG GROUND
SENSOR RETURN
EST SIGNAL
EST BYPASS
OXYGEN SENS LO
OXYGEN SENS HI
INJECTOR CONTROL
A/C COMP RELAY
FUEL PUMP RLY
EVRV SOL
OIL PRES SW/ SEND (PARTIAL)
SHIFT IND (INST CLSTR)
AUTO TRANS
ALDL CONN
ANTI-LOCK MODULE
BRAKE SW
CRUISE CTRL SW
IGN/GAUGES FUSE
CLUTCH SW (CRUISE CTRL)
ECM 1 FUSE
A/C COMP RLY
PARK/ NEUT SW
SES IND (INST CLSTR)
FUEL PUMP PRIME
FUEL TANK UNIT
COLNT TEMP SENS
ECM B FUSE
DIGITAL RATIO ADAPTER CONTROLLER
AIR CTRL SOL
IGN SW PIN I1
INST CLSTR (DIGITAL CLSTR)
IGN COIL
TCC SOL (2.5L)
RESISTOR
RWAL MODULE
4WAL EHCU
GROUND BUS PIN #2
OXYGEN SENS
FUEL INJECTORS
IAC MOTOR
CRANK FUSE
MAP SENS
THROTTLE POSITION SENSOR
IGNITION POWER
SPARK RETARD
GROUND
SENSOR INPUT
ESC MODULE
KNOCK SENS
EST DISTRIBUTOR
IGN MOD
PICK UP COIL
FIRING ORDER
2.8L 1-2-3-4-5-6
4.3L 1-6-5-4-3-2
CRUISE CONTROL SERVO
VENT VALVE
VAC VALVE
SERVO POSTN SENS
CRUISE CONTROL MOD
ON/OFF SIGNAL
VENT VALVE CONTROL
SPEED SIGNAL INPUT
SERVO POSTN SENS IN
BRAKE CLUTCH IN
SERVO POSTN SENS IN
GROUND
VAC VALVE CTRL
RESUME/ACCEL SIG
SET/COAST SIG

1991 WIRING DIAGRAMS
"S" & "T" Series (Cont.)

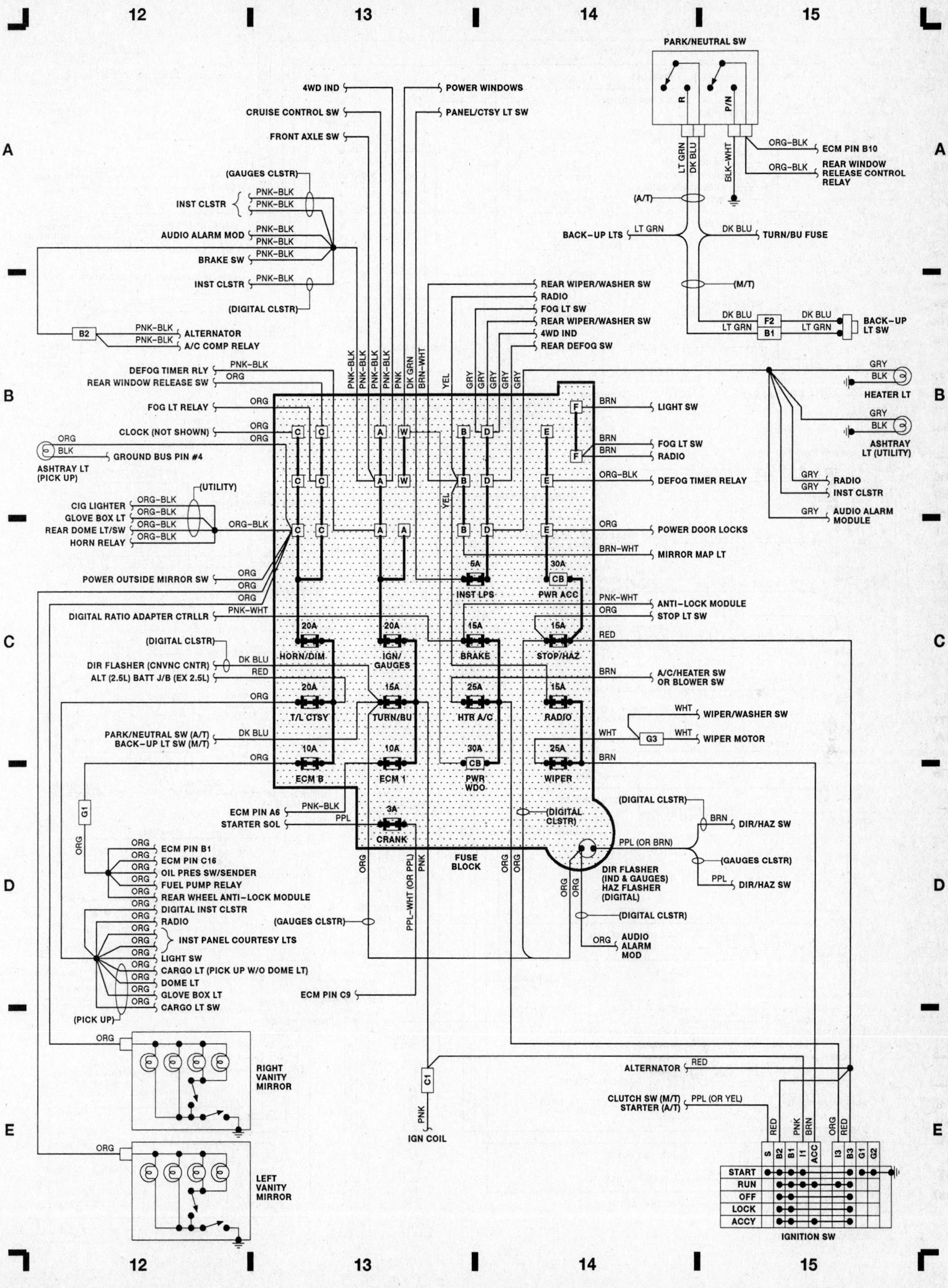
PARK/NEUTRAL SW
R
P/N
LT GRN
DK BLU
BLK-WHT
ORG-BLK
ECM PIN B10
REAR WINDOW RELEASE CONTROL RELAY
(A/T)
BACK-UP LTS
TURN/BU FUSE
(M/T)
BACK-UP LT SW
F2
B1
HEATER LT
ASHTRAY LT (UTILITY)
RADIO
INST CLSTR
AUDIO ALARM MODULE
4WD IND
POWER WINDOWS
CRUISE CONTROL SW
PANEL/CTSY LT SW
FRONT AXLE SW
(GAUGES CLSTR)
INST CLSTR
AUDIO ALARM MOD
BRAKE SW
(DIGITAL CLSTR)
B2
ALTERNATOR
A/C COMP RELAY
REAR WIPER/WASHER SW
FOG LT SW
REAR DEFOG SW
DEFOG TIMER RLY
REAR WINDOW RELEASE SW
FOG LT RELAY
CLOCK (NOT SHOWN)
ASHTRAY LT (PICK UP)
GROUND BUS PIN #4
(UTILITY)
CIG LIGHTER
GLOVE BOX LT
REAR DOME LT/SW
HORN RELAY
LIGHT SW
FOG LT SW
DEFOG TIMER RELAY
POWER DOOR LOCKS
MIRROR MAP LT
POWER OUTSIDE MIRROR SW
DIGITAL RATIO ADAPTER CTRLLR
ANTI-LOCK MODULE
STOP LT SW
DIR FLASHER (CNVNC CNTR)
ALT (2.5L) BATT J/B (EX 2.5L)
A/C-HEATER SW OR BLOWER SW
WIPER/WASHER SW
WIPER MOTOR
G3
PARK/NEUTRAL SW (A/T)
BACK-UP LT SW (M/T)
5A INST LPS
30A CB PWR ACC
20A HORN/DIM
20A IGN/GAUGES
15A BRAKE
15A STOP/HAZ
20A T/L CTSY
15A TURN/BU
25A HTR A/C
15A RADIO
10A ECM B
10A ECM 1
30A CB PWR WDO
25A WIPER
3A CRANK
FUSE BLOCK
ECM PIN A6
STARTER SOL
G1
ECM PIN B1
ECM PIN C16
OIL PRES SW/SENDER
FUEL PUMP RELAY
REAR WHEEL ANTI-LOCK MODULE
DIGITAL INST CLSTR
INST PANEL COURTESY LTS
CARGO LT (PICK UP W/O DOME LT)
DOME LT
CARGO LT SW
(PICK UP)
DIR/HAZ SW
DIR FLASHER (IND & GAUGES) HAZ FLASHER (DIGITAL)
AUDIO ALARM MOD
ECM PIN C9
RIGHT VANITY MIRROR
LEFT VANITY MIRROR
C1
IGN COIL
ALTERNATOR
CLUTCH SW (M/T)
STARTER (A/T)
S B2 B1 I1 ACC I3 B3 G1 G2
START
RUN
OFF
LOCK
ACCY
IGNITION SW

1991 WIRING DIAGRAMS
"S" & "T" Series (Cont.)

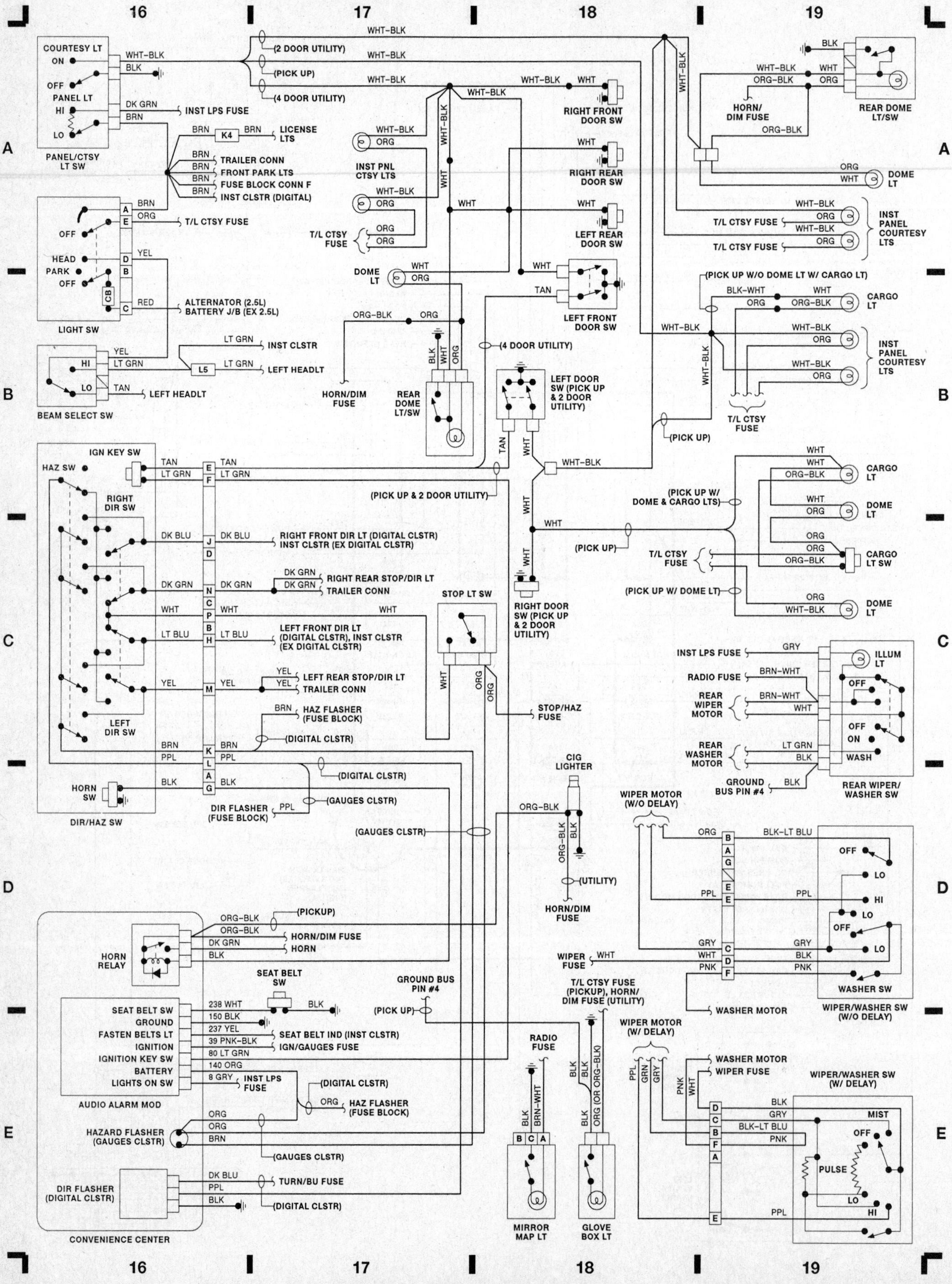
16
17
18
19
A
B
C
D
E
COURTESY LT
PANEL/CTSY LT SW
LIGHT SW
BEAM SELECT SW
IGN KEY SW
HAZ SW
RIGHT DIR SW
LEFT DIR SW
HORN SW
DIR/HAZ SW
INST LPS FUSE
LICENSE LTS
TRAILER CONN
FRONT PARK LTS
FUSE BLOCK CONN F
INST CLSTR (DIGITAL)
T/L CTSY FUSE
ALTERNATOR (2.5L) BATTERY J/B (EX 2.5L)
INST CLSTR
LEFT HEADLT
(2 DOOR UTILITY)
(PICK UP)
(4 DOOR UTILITY)
INST PNL CTSY LTS
DOME LT
HORN/DIM FUSE
REAR DOME LT/SW
RIGHT FRONT DOOR SW
RIGHT REAR DOOR SW
LEFT REAR DOOR SW
LEFT FRONT DOOR SW
LEFT DOOR SW (PICK UP & 2 DOOR UTILITY)
RIGHT DOOR SW (PICK UP & 2 DOOR UTILITY)
STOP LT SW
STOP/HAZ FUSE
INST PANEL COURTESY LTS
CARGO LT
CARGO LT SW
(PICK UP W/O DOME LT W/ CARGO LT)
(PICK UP W/ DOME & CARGO LTS)
(PICK UP W/ DOME LT)
RIGHT FRONT DIR LT (DIGITAL CLSTR)
INST CLSTR (EX DIGITAL CLSTR)
RIGHT REAR STOP/DIR LT
LEFT FRONT DIR LT (DIGITAL CLSTR), INST CLSTR (EX DIGITAL CLSTR)
LEFT REAR STOP/DIR LT
HAZ FLASHER (FUSE BLOCK)
(DIGITAL CLSTR)
(GAUGES CLSTR)
DIR FLASHER (FUSE BLOCK)
CIG LIGHTER
(UTILITY)
INST LPS FUSE
RADIO FUSE
REAR WIPER MOTOR
REAR WASHER MOTOR
GROUND BUS PIN #4
ILLUM LT
REAR WIPER/WASHER SW
WIPER MOTOR (W/O DELAY)
WIPER/WASHER SW (W/O DELAY)
WASHER SW
WASHER MOTOR
WIPER FUSE
WIPER MOTOR (W/ DELAY)
WIPER/WASHER SW (W/ DELAY)
MIST
PULSE
HORN RELAY
SEAT BELT SW
SEAT BELT SW
GROUND
FASTEN BELTS LT
IGNITION
IGNITION KEY SW
BATTERY
LIGHTS ON SW
AUDIO ALARM MOD
238 WHT
150 BLK
237 YEL
39 PNK-BLK
80 LT GRN
140 ORG
8 GRY
SEAT BELT IND (INST CLSTR)
IGN/GAUGES FUSE
GROUND BUS PIN #4
T/L CTSY FUSE (PICKUP), HORN/DIM FUSE (UTILITY)
HAZARD FLASHER (GAUGES CLSTR)
DIR FLASHER (DIGITAL CLSTR)
TURN/BU FUSE
CONVENIENCE CENTER
MIRROR MAP LT
GLOVE BOX LT

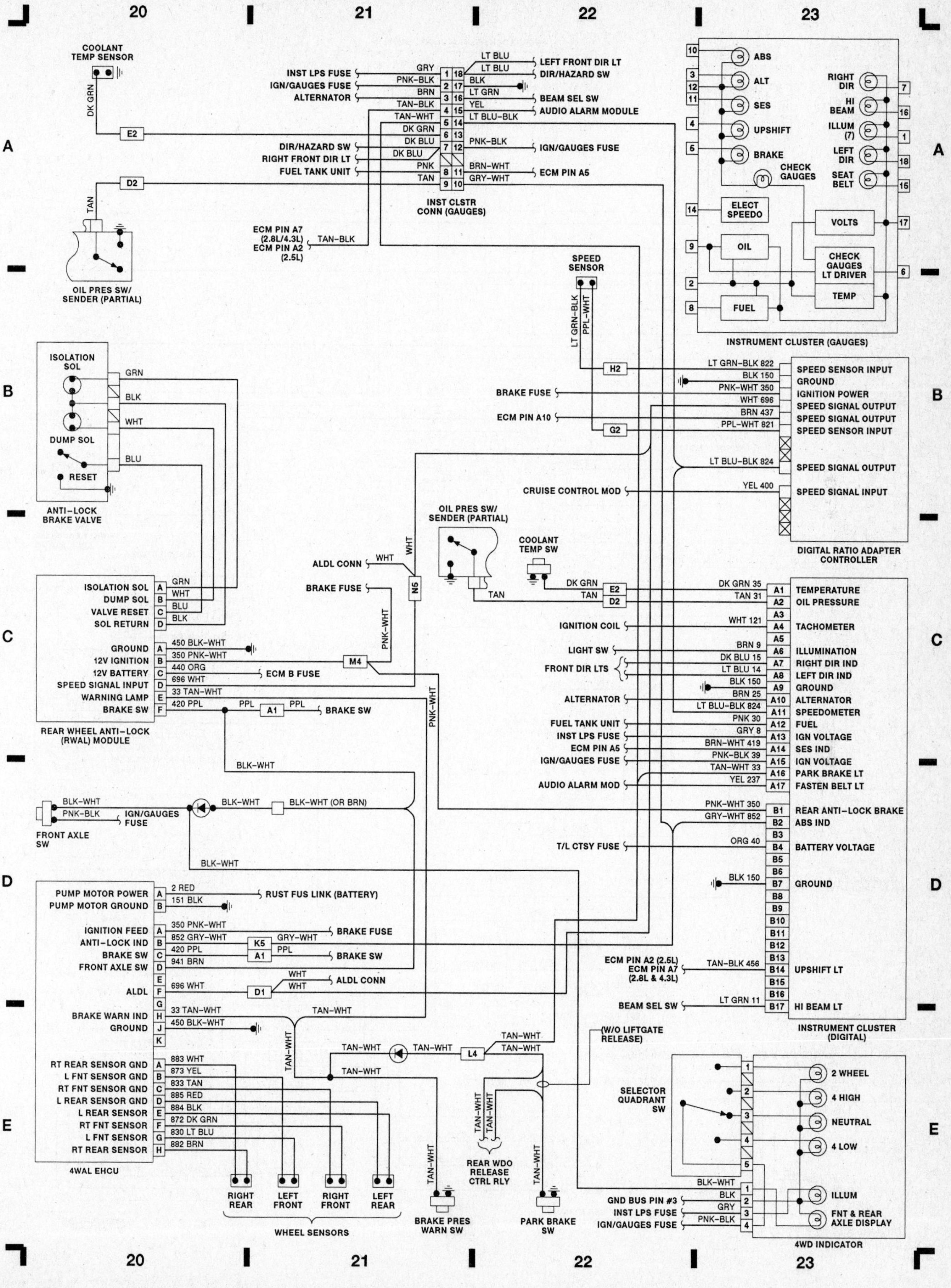
COOLANT TEMP SENSOR
OIL PRES SW/ SENDER (PARTIAL)
INST LPS FUSE
IGN/GAUGES FUSE
ALTERNATOR
DIR/HAZARD SW
RIGHT FRONT DIR LT
FUEL TANK UNIT
LEFT FRONT DIR LT
DIR/HAZARD SW
BEAM SEL SW
AUDIO ALARM MODULE
IGN/GAUGES FUSE
ECM PIN A5
INST CLSTR CONN (GAUGES)
ECM PIN A7 (2.8L/4.3L) ECM PIN A2 (2.5L)
SPEED SENSOR
INSTRUMENT CLUSTER (GAUGES)
ABS
ALT
SES
UPSHIFT
BRAKE
CHECK GAUGES
RIGHT DIR
HI BEAM
ILLUM (7)
LEFT DIR
SEAT BELT
ELECT SPEEDO
VOLTS
OIL
CHECK GAUGES LT DRIVER
TEMP
FUEL
ISOLATION SOL
DUMP SOL
RESET
ANTI-LOCK BRAKE VALVE
BRAKE FUSE
ECM PIN A10
CRUISE CONTROL MOD
SPEED SENSOR INPUT
GROUND
IGNITION POWER
SPEED SIGNAL OUTPUT
SPEED SIGNAL OUTPUT
SPEED SENSOR INPUT
SPEED SIGNAL OUTPUT
SPEED SIGNAL INPUT
DIGITAL RATIO ADAPTER CONTROLLER
COOLANT TEMP SW
ALDL CONN
BRAKE FUSE
ISOLATION SOL
DUMP SOL
VALVE RESET
SOL RETURN
GROUND
12V IGNITION
12V BATTERY
SPEED SIGNAL INPUT
WARNING LAMP
BRAKE SW
REAR WHEEL ANTI-LOCK (RWAL) MODULE
ECM B FUSE
BRAKE SW
TEMPERATURE
OIL PRESSURE
TACHOMETER
ILLUMINATION
RIGHT DIR IND
LEFT DIR IND
GROUND
ALTERNATOR
SPEEDOMETER
FUEL
IGN VOLTAGE
SES IND
IGN VOLTAGE
PARK BRAKE LT
FASTEN BELT LT
REAR ANTI-LOCK BRAKE
ABS IND
BATTERY VOLTAGE
GROUND
UPSHIFT LT
HI BEAM LT
INSTRUMENT CLUSTER (DIGITAL)
IGNITION COIL
LIGHT SW
FRONT DIR LTS
ALTERNATOR
FUEL TANK UNIT
INST LPS FUSE
ECM PIN A5
IGN/GAUGES FUSE
AUDIO ALARM MOD
T/L CTSY FUSE
ECM PIN A2 (2.5L)
ECM PIN A7 (2.8L & 4.3L)
BEAM SEL SW
FRONT AXLE SW
IGN/GAUGES FUSE
PUMP MOTOR POWER
PUMP MOTOR GROUND
RUST FUS LINK (BATTERY)
IGNITION FEED
ANTI-LOCK IND
BRAKE SW
FRONT AXLE SW
ALDL
BRAKE WARN IND
GROUND
BRAKE FUSE
BRAKE SW
ALDL CONN
RT REAR SENSOR GND
L FNT SENSOR GND
RT FNT SENSOR GND
L REAR SENSOR GND
L REAR SENSOR
RT FNT SENSOR
L FNT SENSOR
RT REAR SENSOR
4WAL EHCU
RIGHT REAR
LEFT FRONT
RIGHT FRONT
LEFT REAR
WHEEL SENSORS
BRAKE PRES WARN SW
REAR WDO RELEASE CTRL RLY
PARK BRAKE SW
(W/O LIFTGATE RELEASE)
SELECTOR QUADRANT SW
2 WHEEL
4 HIGH
NEUTRAL
4 LOW
ILLUM
FNT & REAR AXLE DISPLAY
GND BUS PIN #3
INST LPS FUSE
IGN/GAUGES FUSE
4WD INDICATOR

1991 WIRING DIAGRAMS
"S" & "T" Series (Cont.)

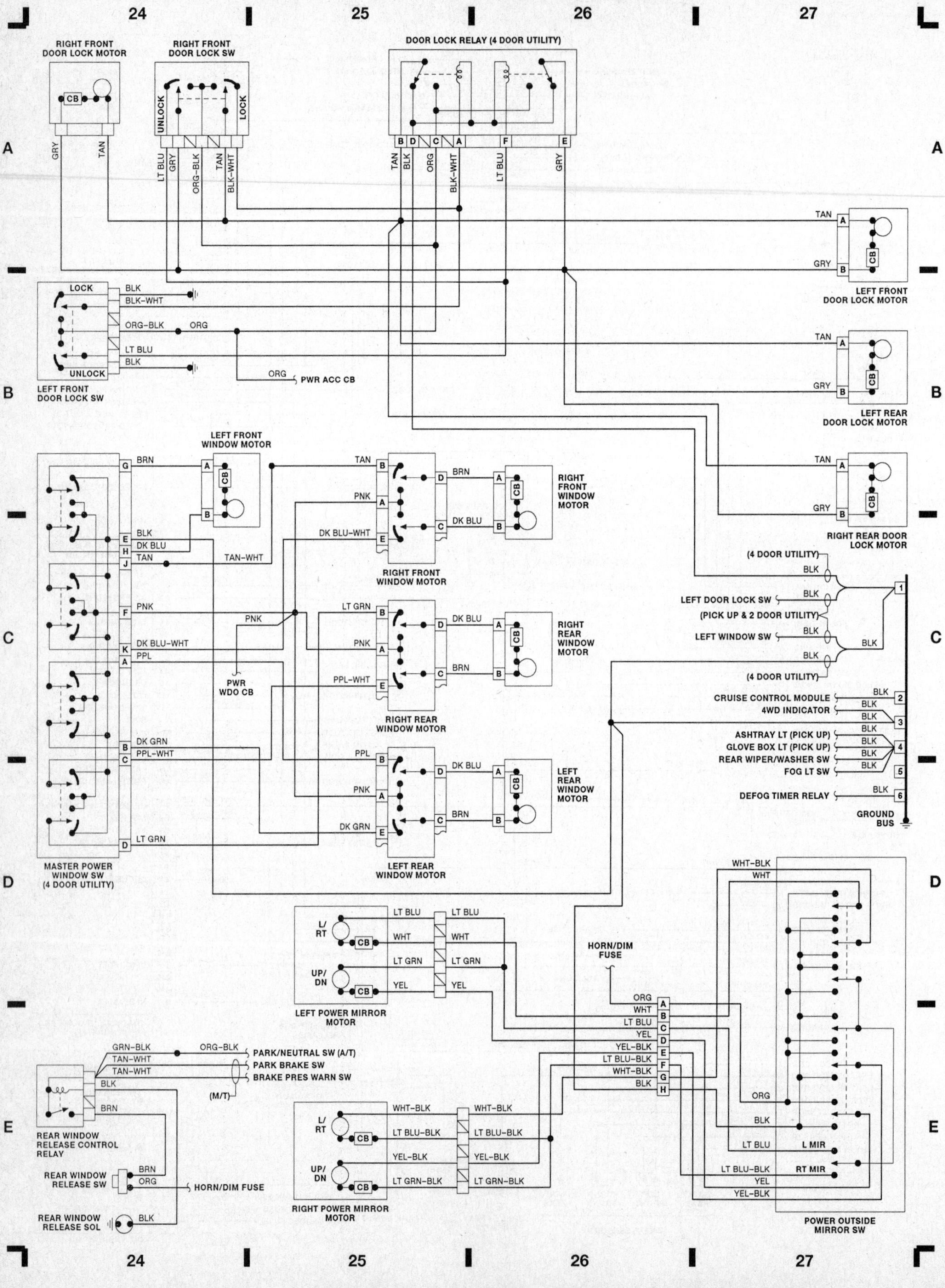
24
25
26
27
A
B
C
D
E
RIGHT FRONT DOOR LOCK MOTOR
RIGHT FRONT DOOR LOCK SW
DOOR LOCK RELAY (4 DOOR UTILITY)
UNLOCK
LOCK
CB
GRY
TAN
LT BLU
ORG-BLK
BLK-WHT
BLK
ORG
LEFT FRONT DOOR LOCK MOTOR
LEFT REAR DOOR LOCK MOTOR
RIGHT REAR DOOR LOCK MOTOR
LEFT FRONT DOOR LOCK SW
PWR ACC CB
LEFT FRONT WINDOW MOTOR
RIGHT FRONT WINDOW MOTOR
RIGHT REAR WINDOW MOTOR
LEFT REAR WINDOW MOTOR
MASTER POWER WINDOW SW (4 DOOR UTILITY)
BRN
DK BLU
PNK
DK BLU-WHT
TAN-WHT
PPL
DK GRN
PPL-WHT
LT GRN
PWR WDO CB
(4 DOOR UTILITY)
LEFT DOOR LOCK SW
(PICK UP & 2 DOOR UTILITY)
LEFT WINDOW SW
CRUISE CONTROL MODULE
4WD INDICATOR
ASHTRAY LT (PICK UP)
GLOVE BOX LT (PICK UP)
REAR WIPER/WASHER SW
FOG LT SW
DEFOG TIMER RELAY
GROUND BUS
L/RT
UP/DN
LEFT POWER MIRROR MOTOR
RIGHT POWER MIRROR MOTOR
HORN/DIM FUSE
WHT
YEL
WHT-BLK
LT BLU-BLK
YEL-BLK
LT GRN-BLK
L MIR
RT MIR
POWER OUTSIDE MIRROR SW
GRN-BLK
PARK/NEUTRAL SW (A/T)
PARK BRAKE SW
BRAKE PRES WARN SW
(M/T)
REAR WINDOW RELEASE CONTROL RELAY
REAR WINDOW RELEASE SW
REAR WINDOW RELEASE SOL

1991 WIRING DIAGRAMS
"S" & "T" Series (Cont.)

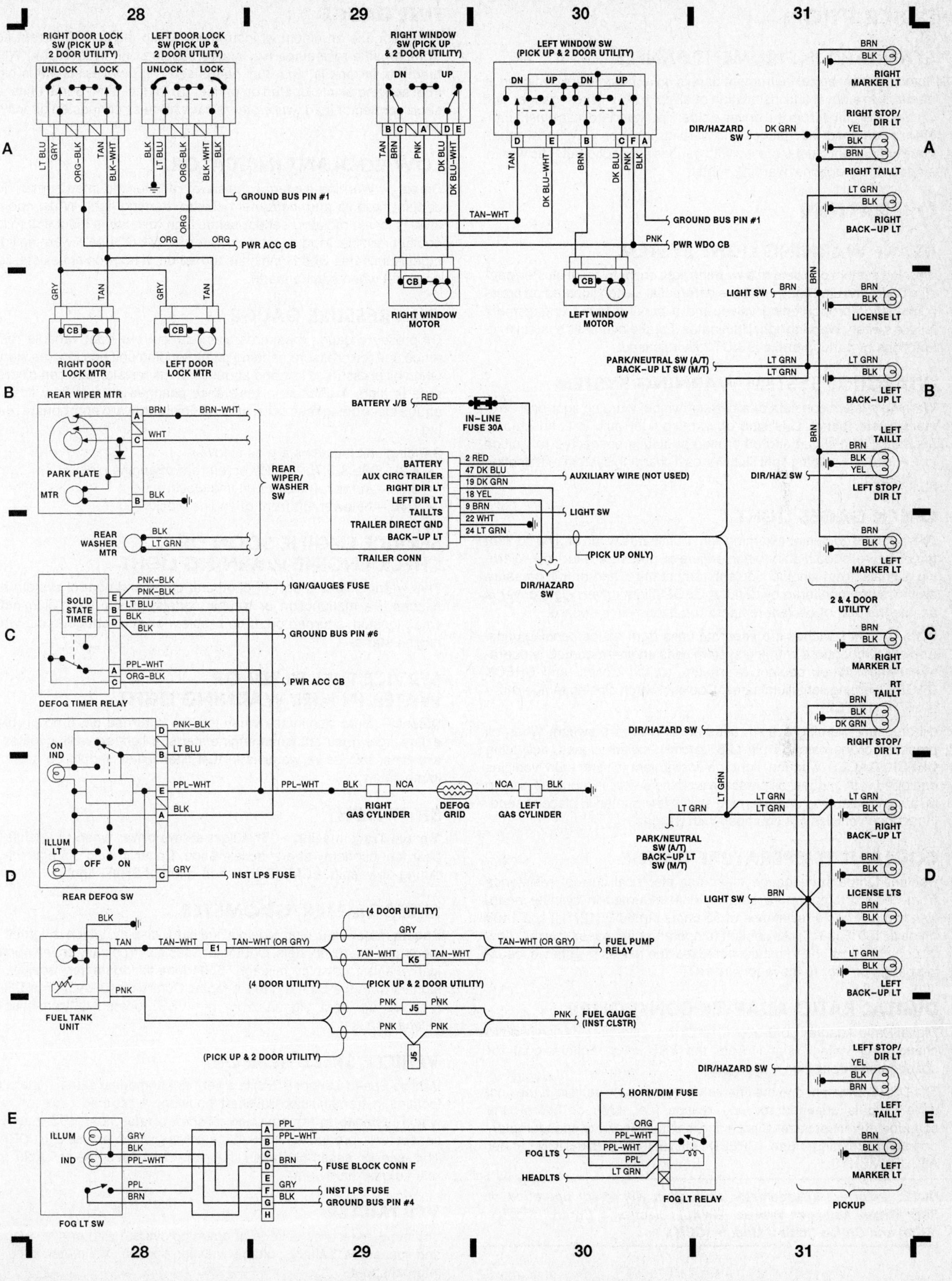
RIGHT DOOR LOCK SW (PICK UP & 2 DOOR UTILITY)
LEFT DOOR LOCK SW (PICK UP & 2 DOOR UTILITY)
RIGHT WINDOW SW (PICK UP & 2 DOOR UTILITY)
LEFT WINDOW SW (PICK UP & 2 DOOR UTILITY)
GROUND BUS PIN #1
PWR ACC CB
PWR WDO CB
RIGHT DOOR LOCK MTR
LEFT DOOR LOCK MTR
RIGHT WINDOW MOTOR
LEFT WINDOW MOTOR
REAR WIPER MTR
PARK PLATE
MTR
REAR WIPER/ WASHER SW
REAR WASHER MTR
BATTERY J/B
IN-LINE FUSE 30A
BATTERY
AUX CIRC TRAILER
RIGHT DIR LT
LEFT DIR LT
TAILLTS
TRAILER DIRECT GND
BACK-UP LT
TRAILER CONN
AUXILIARY WIRE (NOT USED)
LIGHT SW
(PICK UP ONLY)
DIR/HAZARD SW
SOLID STATE TIMER
DEFOG TIMER RELAY
IGN/GAUGES FUSE
GROUND BUS PIN #6
PWR ACC CB
ON IND
ILLUM LT
OFF ON
REAR DEFOG SW
INST LPS FUSE
RIGHT GAS CYLINDER
DEFOG GRID
LEFT GAS CYLINDER
FUEL TANK UNIT
(4 DOOR UTILITY)
(PICK UP & 2 DOOR UTILITY)
FUEL PUMP RELAY
FUEL GAUGE (INST CLSTR)
ILLUM
IND
FOG LT SW
FUSE BLOCK CONN F
INST LPS FUSE
GROUND BUS PIN #4
HORN/DIM FUSE
FOG LTS
HEADLTS
FOG LT RELAY
RIGHT MARKER LT
RIGHT STOP/ DIR LT
RIGHT TAILLT
RIGHT BACK-UP LT
LICENSE LT
PARK/NEUTRAL SW (A/T) BACK-UP LT SW (M/T)
LEFT BACK-UP LT
LEFT TAILLT
LEFT STOP/ DIR LT
LEFT MARKER LT
2 & 4 DOOR UTILITY
RT TAILLT
LICENSE LTS
PICKUP

1991 SAFETY EQUIPMENT
Instrument Panels – "C" & "K" Series

DESCRIPTION

STANDARD INSTRUMENT PANELS

Standard mechanical instrument panels on all models are designed to permit the removal and installation of all control switches, gauges and illuminating bulbs from the driver's side. The standard instrument panels are equipped with gauges and warning lights only. Optional equipment instrument cluster comes with gauges and tachometer as well as standard and optional warning lights.

OPERATION

BRAKE WARNING LIGHT SYSTEM

Warning system consists of a warning light on instrument cluster/panel, a brake warning light/pressure differential switch (located on brake combination/proportioning valve) and a parking brake engagement telltale switch. Warning light illuminates if brake hydraulic system malfunctions or parking brake is NOT fully released.

CHARGING SYSTEM WARNING SYSTEM

Warning system consists of a battery symbol warning light on instrument cluster/panel. One side of warning light bulb is connected to alternator field circuit and other side of bulb is connected to ignition power circuit. Warning light illuminates if charging system malfunction is detected.

CHECK GAGES LIGHT

This optional equipment warning light illuminates when engine coolant temperature is too high or when engine oil pressure is too low. Warning signals from engine coolant temperature and/or oil pressure switches are monitored by CHECK GAGES light driver. Light driver is an integral part of coolant temperature gauge circuit board.

Warning light switches are separate units from gauge sending units. Coolant temperature warning system uses engine-mounted temperature switch. When coolant overheats, switch closes, and CHECK GAGES warning light illuminates. Coolant switch closing temperature is 257°F (125°C).

Oil pressure warning system uses an oil pressure switch. When oil pressure drops below 4 psi (.28 kg/cm²), switch closes, activating CHECK GAGES warning light on instrument cluster. On vehicles equipped with gauges, oil pressure warning switch is mounted next to oil pressure sending unit. Warning switch is mounted in place of sending unit on vehicles not equipped with gauges.

COOLANT TEMPERATURE GAUGE

Coolant temperature gauge measures electrical current resistance from coolant temperature sending unit, mounted in cylinder head. Sending unit has a resistance of 55 ohms at 260°F (127°C) and 1400 ohms at 100°F (38°C). As coolant temperature increases, current flow through sending unit to gauge increases due to less resistance, causing gauge pointer to move toward HOT.

DIGITAL RATIO ADAPTER CONTROLLER

Digital Ratio Adapter Controller (DRAC) is a solid-state device used to change AC voltage signal from the VSS to a digital signal for speedometer operation.

The DRAC is matched to the final drive ratio of each vehicle. If the final drive ratio is changed for any reason (i.e., tires or gears), the speedometer must be recalibrated to maintain accurate speedometer/odometer reading. See SPEEDOMETER CALIBRATION under ADJUSTMENTS.

NOTE: Incorrect speedometer calibration will affect operation of Rear Wheel Anti-Lock Brakes (RWAL), Electronic Control Module (ECM) and Cruise Control Module (CCM).

FUEL GAUGE

Fuel gauge is an electrical instrument which measures current flow from variable-resistance fuel gauge sending unit in fuel tank. When fuel level in tank is high, fuel gauge sending unit resistance is high. Fuel sending unit is located on or near top of fuel tank. Some units use short connector lead, while others have harness connected directly to unit.

LOW COOLANT INDICATOR

Diesel – Warning system consists of radiator mounted sensor, low coolant module and instrument cluster warning light. When coolant level is low in radiator, sensor sends high resistance feedback to low coolant module. Module then activates LOW COOLANT warning light. Light illuminates when ignition is turned on. If no problem exists, light goes out when engine starts.

OIL PRESSURE GAUGE

Oil pressure gauge measures electrical current from variable resistance unit (oil pressure sending unit). Sending unit has low resistance when oil pressure is low and about 90 ohms resistance when oil pressure is high. A change in resistance changes current flow through gauge electromagnetic coils, moving pointer toward appropriate reading.

Sending unit locations are as follows:

- 4.3L, 5.0L & 5.7L – At lower left rear of engine block.
- 6.2L – At top left rear of engine block.
- 7.4L – At lower left front of engine block.

SERVICE ENGINE SOON OR CHECK ENGINE WARNING LIGHT

This warning light is part of computer command control system and flashes if a malfunction or trouble code(s) exists. Light illuminates when ignition is turned on. If no problem exists, light goes out when engine starts.

SERVICE FUEL FILTER OR WATER IN FUEL WARNING LIGHT

Diesel – Light illuminates when ignition is turned on. If no problem exists, light goes out when engine starts. If light stays illuminated at any time, excessive water is in fuel filter. Filter should be serviced immediately.

SHIFT LIGHT

Manual Transmission – This light shows driver when to upshift for best fuel economy at any acceleration. Driver should disregard light during downshift. ECM controls activation of SHIFT light.

SPEEDOMETER/ODOMETER

Speedometer uses disc-type dial indicator display, which is lighted by electronic quartz crystals. Odometer uses electronically driven numerical wheels to display mileage. Speedometer/odometer receives its signals from the Digital Ratio Adapter Controller (DRAC). The DRAC receives its input signals from the VSS, located in transmission tailshaft housing.

VEHICLE SPEED SENSOR

Vehicle Speed Sensor (VSS) is a permanent magnet signal generator, located in transmission tailshaft housing. A toothed rotor or tone wheel fastened to transmission tailshaft rotates near VSS magnetic sensor coil, producing AC voltage pulses which are sent to DRAC. This sensor assembly takes the place of speedometer cable and related gear hardware.

VOLTMETER

Voltmeter measures voltage of charging system with engine running and measures battery voltage with ignition on. Voltmeter uses an internal shunt.

1991 SAFETY EQUIPMENT
Instrument Panels – "C" & "K" Series (Cont.)

WAIT OR GLOW PLUGS LIGHT

Diesel – Light illuminates when ignition is turned on, showing glow plugs are warming cylinder combustion area to ease starting. When light goes out, engine is ready to be started. During cranking or after starting, light normally cycles on and off a few times, showing glow plugs are still warming cylinder.

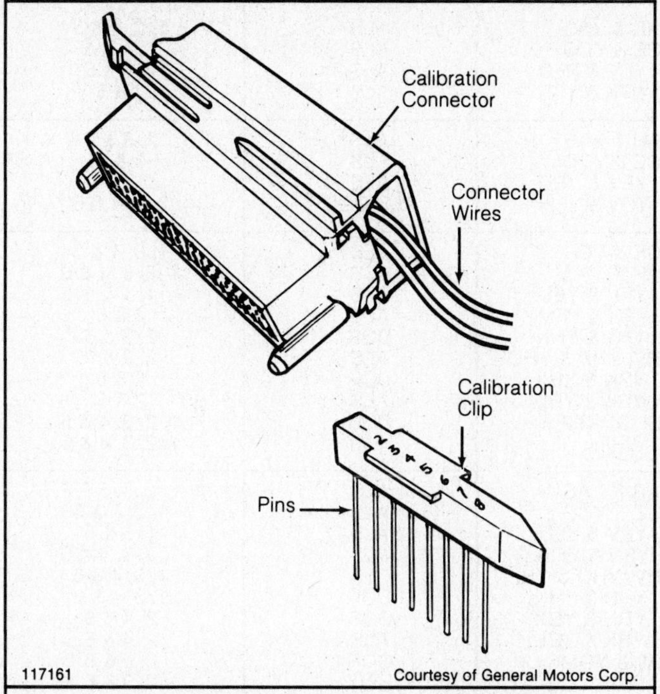
Calibration
Connector
Connector
Wires
Calibration
Clip
Pins
117161
Courtesy of General Motors Corp.

Fig. 1: Identifying Speedometer Calibration Components

ADJUSTMENTS

SPEEDOMETER CALIBRATION

CAUTION: DO NOT touch calibration clip pins at back of instrument cluster as immediate electrostatic discharge damage to cluster will result.

NOTE: Speedometer must be replaced or recalibrated when rear axle ratio or tire size is changed.

NOTE: The calibration connector from Service Kit (25085515) should be used a maximum of 10 times. If speedometer has been previously recalibrated, it is not necessary to perform step 1). Follow instructions provided with service kit.

Calibration – 1) Remove instrument cluster from vehicle. SEE INSTRUMENT CLUSTER under REMOVAL & INSTALLATION. Plug speedometer calibration connector from Service Kit (25085515) into back of instrument cluster, and momentarily touch calibration connector wires to battery terminals. *See Figs. 1 and 2.*

2) Use vehicle axle ratio, tire size and tread type to determine appropriate pins to remove from calibration clip. See SPEEDOMETER CALIBRATION TABLE. Pins are numbered 1 through 8 from top (rectangular end) to bottom (tapered end). *See Fig. 1.*

3) Remove pins by bending them back and forth using long needle-nose pliers. Insert modified calibration clip into 8 holes in rectangular slot on back of instrument cluster. *See Fig. 2.* Install cluster in vehicle.

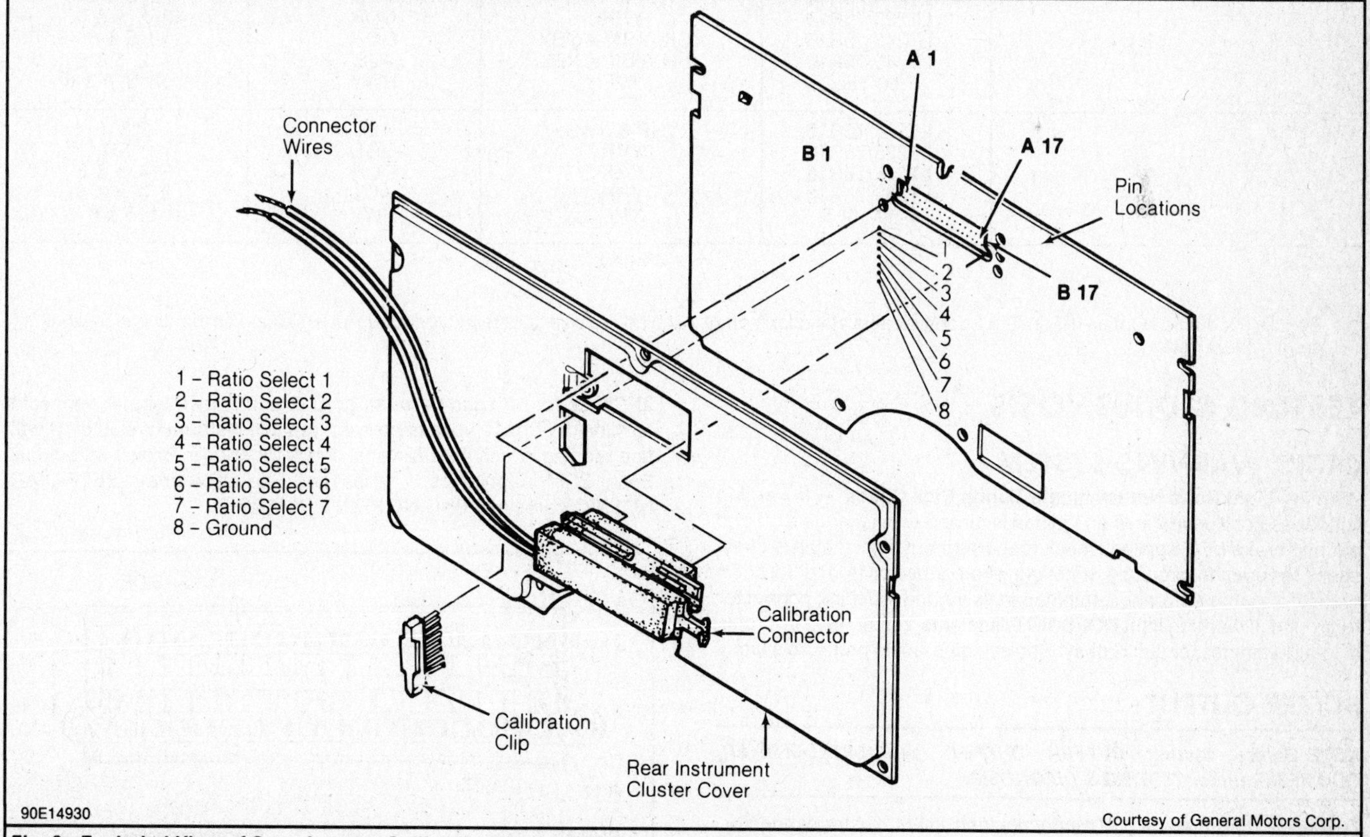
A 1
B 1
A 17
Pin
Locations
B 17
Connector
Wires
1
2
3
4
5
6
7
8
1 - Ratio Select 1
2 - Ratio Select 2
3 - Ratio Select 3
4 - Ratio Select 4
5 - Ratio Select 5
6 - Ratio Select 6
7 - Ratio Select 7
8 - Ground
Calibration
Connector
Calibration
Clip
Rear Instrument
Cluster Cover
90E14930
Courtesy of General Motors Corp.

Fig. 2: Exploded View of Speedometer Calibration Service Kit Components & Locations

1991 SAFETY EQUIPMENT
Instrument Panels – "C" & "K" Series (Cont.)

SPEEDOMETER CALIBRATION TABLE

Axle Ratio	Tire Size	RPO [1]	HWY, On-Off Road, All Season	Pins To Remove
2.73 (GU2)	P195/75R15	YAR & YAS	ALS	1, 2, 4 & 5
	P205/75R15	YCE & YCG	ALS	1, 4 & 5
	P225/75R15	YET, YEV & YEU	ALS	2, 3 & 5
	P235/75R15	YFL, YFM & YFN	ALS	3 & 5
3.08 (GU4)	P195/75R15	YAR & YAS	ALS	2, 3 & 6
	P205/75R15	YCE & YCG	ALS	3 & 6
	P225/75R15	YET, YEV & YEU	ALS	6
	P235/75R15	YFL, YFN & YFM	ALS/OOR	2, 3, 4 & 5
3.42 (GU6)	P205/75R15	YCE & YCG	ALS	1, 3, 4 & 6
	P195/75R15	YAR & YAS	ALS	1, 2, 3, 4 & 6
	P225/75R15	YET, YEV & YEU	ALS	1, 4 & 6
	P235/75R15	YFL, YFN & YFM	ALS	4 & 6
	LT225/75R16	YHR, YHJ & YHN	OOR	2, 3 & 6
	LT225/75R16	YHE, YHV, YHP & YHQ	ALS	2, 3 & 6
	LT245/75R16	YGK, YBN & YBX	OOR	2 & 6
	LT245/75R16	YHH, YBK & YBL	ALS	2 & 6
	LT265/75R16	YGL & YGM	OOR	1, 2, 3, 4 & 5
	7.50-16LT	YPF	HWY	1, 2, 3, 4 & 5
3.73 (GT4)	P195/75R15	YAR & YAS	ALS	1, 2, 3, 5 & 6
	P205/75R15	YCE & YCG	ALS	1, 3, 5 & 6
	P225/75R15	YET, YEV & YEU	ALS	1, 5 & 6
	P235/75R15	YFL, YFN & YFM	ALS	1, 2, 3, 4 & 6
	LT225/75R16	YHE, YHV, YHQ & YHP	ALS	1, 3, 4 & 6
	LT225/75R16	YHR, YHS & YHN	OOR	1, 3, 4 & 6
	LT245/75R16	YGK, YBN & YBX	OOR	2, 4 & 6
	LT245/75R16	YHH, YBK & YBL	ALS	2, 4 & 6
	LT265/75R16	YGL & YGM	OOR	2, 3 & 6
	7.50-16LT	YPF	HWY	2, 3 & 6
4.10 (GT5)	LT225/75R16	YGL & YGM	OOR	1, 2, 3, 4 & 6
	LT225/75R16	YHP & YHQ	ALS	1, 2, 3, 5 & 6
	LT225/75R16	YHR	OOR	2, 3, 5 & 6
	LT245/75R16	YGK, YBN & YBX	OOR	2, 5 & 6
	LT245/75R16	YHH, YBK & YBL	ALS	1, 2, 5 & 6
	7.50-16LT	YPF	HWY	1, 2, 3, 4 & 6
4.56 (HC4)	LT225/75R16	YHP & YHQ	ALS	2 & 7
	LT225/75R16	YHR	OOR	1 & 7
	LT245/75R16	YGK	OOR	3, 4, 5 & 6
	LT245/75R16	YHH	ALS	3, 4, 5 & 6
	7.50-16LT	YPF	HWY	4, 5 & 6

[1] – Regular Production Option (RPO)/Tire Codes: Letters stand for factory-installed tire size and tread type. Code letters found on identification label on glove box door.

TESTING & DIAGNOSIS

BRAKE WARNING SYSTEM

Warning Light Does Not Illuminate During Bulb Check – If warning light does not illuminate when ignition is turned on with engine off and parking brake NOT applied, check for burned-out bulb. If bulb is okay, check for open in circuit by removing wire connector from differential pressure switch on brake combination valve and touching connector to ground. If warning light DOES NOT illuminate, repair open in circuit. If light illuminates, circuit is okay. Replace differential pressure switch.

BUFFER OUTPUT

NOTE: Before testing BUFFER OUTPUT, see SPEEDOMETER/ ODOMETER under TESTING & DIAGNOSIS.

Testing & Diagnosis – 1) Disconnect instrument cluster connector. Turn ignition on. Check for 12 volts between ground and Red/White wire at instrument cluster connector terminal A16. *See Fig. 3.* If 12 volts is present, go to next step. If voltage reading is less than 12 volts, check for open in Red/White wire (cruise control circuit).

2) Check for 12 volts between ground and Brown wire at connector terminal B17. If 12 volts is present, replace instrument cluster. If voltage reading is less than 12 volts, check for open in Brown wire circuit. Enter ECM diagnostics if necessary. See appropriate SELF-DIAGNOSTICS article in ENGINE PERFORMANCE.

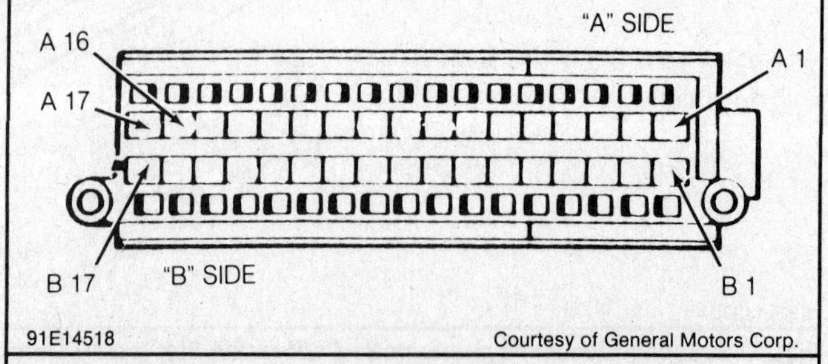
"A" SIDE
A 16
A 1
A 17
B 17
"B" SIDE
B 1
91E14518
Courtesy of General Motors Corp.

Fig. 3: Identifying Instrument Cluster Connector Terminals

BUFFER POWER

***NOTE:** Before testing BUFFER POWER, see SPEEDOMETER/ ODOMETER under TESTING & DIAGNOSIS.*

Testing & Diagnosis – 1) Disconnect instrument cluster connector. Turn ignition on. Turn on cruise control (if equipped). Using a DVOM, check for 12 volts between ground and Pink/Black wire at cluster harness connector terminal A9. *See Fig. 3.* If voltage reading is 12 volts, go to step **2)**. If voltage reading is less than 12 volts, check for blown GAGES fuse. If fuse is okay, check for open in Pink/Black wire.
2) Check for 12 volts between ground and Brown wire at harness connector terminal B14. *See Fig. 3.* If voltage reading is 12 volts, go to step **3)**. If voltage reading is less than 12 volts, check for blown BRAKE fuse. If fuse is okay, check for open in Brown wire.
3) Check for 12 volts between Brown wire at connector terminal B14 and White wire at cluster harness connector terminal B15. If voltage reading is 12 volts, go to step **4)**. If voltage reading is less than 12 volts, check for open in White wire.
4) Check for 12 volts between Brown wire at connector terminal B14 and Black wire at harness connector terminal B1. If voltage reading is 12 volts, check for problem in VSS circuit. See VEHICLE SPEED SENSOR under TESTING & DIAGNOSIS. If voltage reading is less than 12 volts, repair open in Black wire.

CHECK GAGES LIGHT

Light Inoperative – 1) Turn ignition on. Check for burned-out bulb. If bulb is okay, check for open in Dark Green wire from cluster connector A14 to ground terminal of ignition switch. If wire is okay, check for voltage to bulb socket.
2) If voltage is NOT present, problem is in coolant temperature gauge circuit board power circuit to CHECK GAGES light driver. Repair/ replace temperature gauge and circuit as necessary. Light driver is an integral part of coolant temperature gauge circuit board. Replace defective instrument cluster if necessary.
Light Inoperative With High Coolant Temperature – Check for inoperative coolant temperature gauge and circuit. Repair/replace as necessary. If temperature gauge and circuit are okay, replace defective instrument cluster.
Light Inoperative With Low Oil Pressure – Check for inoperative oil pressure gauge switch circuit. Repair/replace as necessary. If gauge and circuit are okay, replace defective instrument cluster.
Light Always On – Check for inoperative coolant temperature and oil pressure gauge circuits. Replace coolant temperature and/or oil pressure gauge if necessary. If coolant temperature and oil pressure gauges and circuits are okay, replace defective instrument cluster.

COOLANT TEMPERATURE GAUGE

Gauge Reads Cold When Engine Is Hot – 1) Check for blown GAGES fuse. If fuse is okay, disconnect lead connector from coolant temperature sending unit, and turn ignition on. Turn engine control switch key on. Connect sending unit lead to ground. Gauge should read 260 (HOT). If gauge reads 260, go to next step. If gauge does not read 260, check for open in sending unit lead circuit. If sending unit lead circuit is okay, replace gauge.
2) Reconnect connector to sending unit. If gauge now reads 100, ensure sending unit connection is correct. If connection is okay, replace sending unit. After replacing sending unit, if gauge still reads near 100 with hot engine, gauge is also damaged. Replace gauge.
Gauge Reads Hot When Engine Is Cold – 1) Turn ignition on. Remove connector from temperature gauge sending unit. If gauge reading goes down to 100 (COLD), replace externally shorted sending unit.
2) If temperature gauge continues to read 260, check for short to ground in wiring circuit between sending unit and gauge. If circuit is okay, replace temperature gauge.
Gauge Readings Are Inaccurate – 1) Check wiring for corroded or loose connections. Clean and tighten terminals and connections as necessary. Also check resistance in temperature sending unit ground circuit. If terminals, connections and ground circuit are okay, go to next step.
2) Disconnect lead connector from temperature gauge sending unit. Using an ohmmeter, test sending unit resistance. See TEMPERATURE GAUGE SENDING UNIT RESISTANCE table. If sending unit values are incorrect, replace temperature gauge sending unit.

TEMPERATURE GAUGE SENDING UNIT RESISTANCE

Degrees °F (°C)	Ohms
104 (40)	1365
257 (125)	55

FUEL GAUGE

Gauge Stays At EMPTY Position – Check for fuel in tank. Turn ignition on. Disconnect lead at fuel tank. If gauge now reads past FULL mark, replace fuel gauge sending unit. If gauge does not read past FULL mark, check for short to ground between gauge and fuel tank. Repair as necessary. If ground is okay, replace gauge.
Gauge Stays At FULL Position – 1) Turn ignition on. Check for open circuit between gauge and sending unit by disconnecting sending unit lead at fuel tank. Connect sending unit lead to ground, and note gauge reading.
2) If fuel gauge now reads EMPTY, replace fuel gauge sending unit. If fuel gauge still reads FULL or beyond, repair open in wire between gauge and fuel tank.
Gauge Reading Is Inaccurate –1) Check wiring for corroded or loose connections. Clean and tighten as required. If wiring and connections are okay, remove fuel gauge sending unit. Using an ohmmeter, test sending unit resistance. See FUEL GAUGE SENDING UNIT RESISTANCE table.
2) If sending unit resistance values are correct, disconnect front body wiring harness connector at engine firewall. Connect Gauge Tester (J-24538-A) to instrument cluster terminal A1. *See Fig. 3.*
3) Turn ignition on, and test gauge using tester. See FUEL GAUGE SENDING UNIT RESISTANCE table. If gauge reads accurately when connected to gauge tester, check wiring between fuel tank and front connector. If gauge reads between 1/4 and 1/2 full when tester is set at 90 ohms, replace fuel gauge.

FUEL GAUGE SENDING UNIT RESISTANCE

Position	Ohms
Empty	1
1/2	44
Full	88

OIL PRESSURE GAUGE

Gauge Reads "0" When Engine Running – 1) Check oil level, and add oil if necessary. Test oil pressure using manual gauge and adapter. If oil pressure reading is good on manual gauge tester, check for grounded gauge circuit by disconnecting lead at sending unit.
2) Turn ignition on. Oil pressure gauge should now read 80. If gauge stays at zero, disconnect lead from gauge. If gauge now reads 80, find and repair short to ground between gauge and sending unit. If gauge still reads zero, replace gauge, and test oil pressure gauge sending unit resistance. See OIL PRESSURE GAUGE SENDING UNIT RESISTANCE table. Replace sending unit if it reads one ohm with engine running.

OIL PRESSURE GAUGE SENDING UNIT RESISTANCE

Position	Ohms
Engine Off	1
Engine Running	[1] 44

[1] – With oil pressure at about 40 psi (2.8 kg/cm²).

Gauge Constantly Reads 80 Or More – 1) Check for open circuit between gauge and sending unit by disconnecting lead at sending unit. Connect lead to ground, and note reading on gauge.
2) If oil pressure gauge reads zero, replace oil pressure gauge sending unit. If oil pressure gauge still reads 80 or beyond, find open wire between gauge and sending unit.

1991 SAFETY EQUIPMENT
Instrument Panels – "C" & "K" Series (Cont.)

Gauge Reading Inaccurate – Disconnect lead from oil pressure sending unit. Connect Gauge Tester (J-24538-A) to lead and ground. Turn ignition on. If gauge reads accurately when connected to tester, replace oil pressure sending unit. If gauge still reads inaccurately, replace oil pressure gauge.

SPEEDOMETER/ODOMETER

Buzzing Sound With Manual Transmission – Check transmission shift linkage, and adjust as necessary.
Tick Or Ringing Sound With Jumpy Pointer At 0-30 MPH – Replace speedometer.
Sticky Speedometer Pointer – Check for bent speedometer disc dial, and straighten if necessary. Recheck speedometer operation.
Incorrect Calibration – Check rear axle ratio and rear tire size listed on factory identification label on glove box door. If rear axle ratio and tire size are same as factory equipped, check vehicle speed sensor circuit. See VEHICLE SPEED SENSOR under TESTING & DIAGNOSIS. If vehicle speed sensor circuit is okay, check speedometer calibration using correct tire size. See SPEEDOMETER CALIBRATION under ADJUSTMENTS.

VEHICLE SPEED SENSOR

Sensor Resistance Test – Disconnect vehicle speed sensor harness connector at transmission, and test resistance of sensor. If sensor resistance is 900-2000 ohms, reconnect harness, and go to FUNCTIONAL TEST. If sensor resistance is not 900-2000 ohms, replace vehicle speed sensor, and recheck system.
Functional Test – **1)** Lift and support rear of vehicle. Disconnect instrument cluster connector. Start engine, and place transmission in Drive. Using a voltmeter, measure voltage between instrument cluster connector terminals B13 (Purple/White wire) and B16 (Light Green/Black wire) while varying engine speed.
2) If voltage varies with engine speed, vehicle speed sensor is okay. If no voltage is present, check wires for opens and connectors for tightness. If still no voltage is present, replace vehicle speed sensor.

VOLTMETER

Voltmeter Reads 9 Volts Or Less – **1)** Measure voltage across battery terminals. Voltage should be about 12 volts. If battery is discharged, recharge battery, and perform load test. Repair cause of discharged battery.
2) With ignition on and battery terminals cleaned and connected, observe voltmeter with battery charger in operation. Voltmeter gauge should read 12 volts or more. If gauge does not read 12 volts or more, check for high resistance in voltmeter gauge terminal connections. Clean and tighten connections.
3) If voltmeter reading is still low, apply 12 volts directly to positive terminal of gauge. If voltmeter does not respond accurately, replace gauge.

REMOVAL & INSTALLATION

GAUGES

Removal & Installation – Remove instrument cluster. See INSTRUMENT CLUSTER under REMOVAL & INSTALLATION. Remove cluster case retainer screws and retainer (if equipped). *See Fig. 4.* Remove individual gauge mounting screws. Carefully remove gauge. To install, reverse removal procedure.

INSTRUMENT CLUSTER

CAUTION: Static electricity can destroy integrated circuits within instrument cluster. Before servicing, ground yourself and work area to discharge stored electricity.

Removal & Installation – Disconnect negative battery cable. Remove radio and heater control units. Remove 4 retainer screws. Remove trim plate (A/T only). Touch hands to ground to discharge static electricity before removing instrument cluster. Being extremely careful NOT to touch circuit board pins, disconnect 34-pin connector. To install, reverse removal procedure.

SPEEDOMETER

Removal & Installation – Remove instrument cluster. See INSTRUMENT CLUSTER under REMOVAL & INSTALLATION. Remove lens screws, lens, faceplate/applique and retainer. Remove speedometer head retainer screws and retainer. *See Fig. 4.* Carefully remove speedometer without touching circuitry. To install, reverse removal procedure.

VEHICLE SPEED SENSOR

Removal & Installation – Raise and support vehicle. At transmission tailshaft housing, unplug vehicle speed sensor harness. Remove hold-down bolt or unscrew vehicle speed sensor. Catch transmission fluid in suitable container. Remove "O" ring. To install, reverse removal procedure, and recheck fluid level.

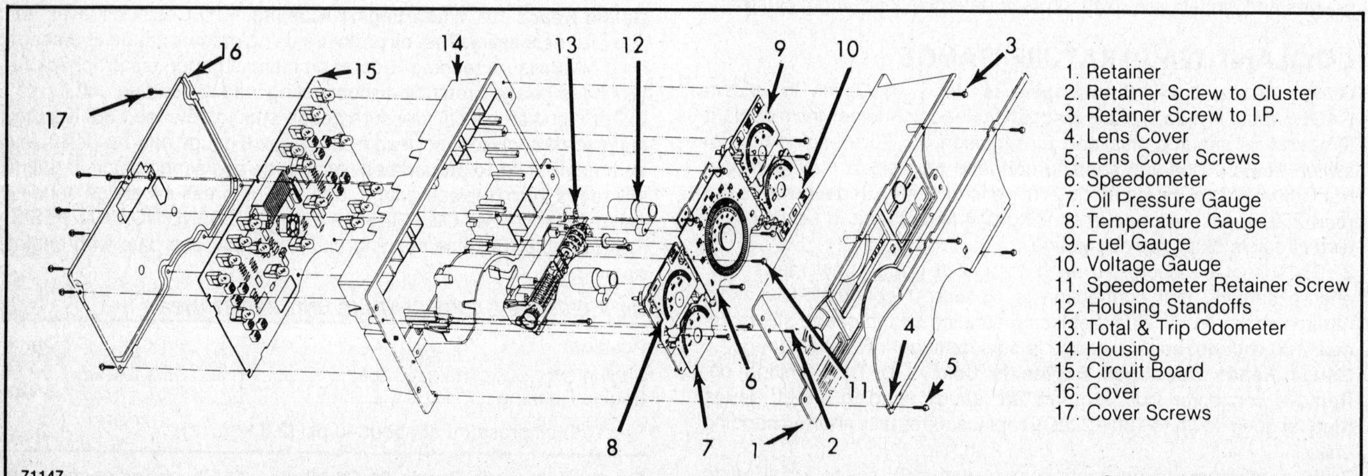
16
15
14
13
12
9
10
3
17
4
5
6
11
8
7
1
2
1. Retainer
2. Retainer Screw to Cluster
3. Retainer Screw to I.P.
4. Lens Cover
5. Lens Cover Screws
6. Speedometer
7. Oil Pressure Gauge
8. Temperature Gauge
9. Fuel Gauge
10. Voltage Gauge
11. Speedometer Retainer Screw
12. Housing Standoffs
13. Total & Trip Odometer
14. Housing
15. Circuit Board
16. Cover
17. Cover Screws
71147
Courtesy of General Motors Corp.

Fig. 4: Exploded View of Deluxe Instrument Cluster with Gauges

1991 SAFETY EQUIPMENT
Instrument Panels – "G", "P", "R" & "V" Series

DESCRIPTION

INSTRUMENT PANELS

Standard instrument panels are designed to allow removal and installation of all control switches, gauges and illuminating bulbs from the driver's side. Instrument panels are equipped with gauges, analog speedometer, and warning lights.

OPERATION

BRAKE WARNING LIGHT SYSTEM

Warning system consists of a warning light on instrument cluster/panel, a brake warning light/pressure differential switch (located on brake combination valve), and a parking brake engagement telltale switch. If brake hydraulic system malfunctions, or if parking brake is NOT fully released, warning light will illuminate.

CHARGING SYSTEM WARNING SYSTEM

Warning system consists of a battery symbol warning light on instrument cluster. One side of warning light bulb is connected to alternator field circuit, and other side of bulb is connected to ignition power circuit. If charging system malfunction is detected, warning light will illuminate.

COOLANT TEMPERATURE GAUGE

Coolant temperature gauge measures electrical current flow from coolant temperature sending unit mounted in cylinder head. Sending unit has a resistance of 55 ohms at 260°F (127°C), and 1400 ohms at 100°F (38°C). As coolant temperature increases, current flow through sending unit to gauge increases due to lower resistance, causing gauge pointer to move toward HOT position.

FUEL GAUGE

Fuel gauge is an electrical instrument that measures current flow from variable-resistance fuel gauge sending unit in fuel tank. When fuel level in tank is high, fuel gauge sending unit resistance is high. Fuel sending unit is located on, or near top of fuel tank. Some units use short connector lead, while others have harness connected directly to unit.

LOW COOLANT INDICATOR (6.2L DIESEL)

Warning system consists of radiator-mounted sensor, low coolant module, and instrument cluster warning light. When coolant level in radiator is low, sensor sends high resistance feedback to low coolant module. Module then illuminates LOW COOLANT warning light. Light will illuminate when ignition is turned on, and if no problem exists, it will go out when engine is started.

OIL PRESSURE GAUGE

Oil pressure gauge measures electrical current flow from variable-resistance oil pressure sending unit. Sending unit resistance is low when oil pressure is low, and is about 90 ohms when oil pressure is high. A change in resistance changes current flow through gauge electromagnetic coils, causing pointer to move from low to high.

OIL PRESSURE SENDING UNIT LOCATIONS

Application	Location
4.3L, 5.0L & 5.7L	Lower Left Rear Of Engine Block
6.2L	Top Left Rear Of Engine Block
7.4L	Lower Left Front Of Engine Block

PARK BRAKE WARNING LIGHT

"P" Series (A/T) – Vehicles NOT equipped with Park position are equipped with warning light/buzzer system. If vehicle is stopped, shifted into Neutral, and parking brake is NOT immediately applied, warning light illuminates and buzzer sounds until parking brake is applied.

SERVICE ENGINE SOON

This warning light is part of computerized engine control system, and will flash when a malfunction or trouble code(s) exists. As a bulb check, light will illuminate when ignition is turned on. If no problem exists, light will go out when engine is started.

SERVICE FUEL FILTER OR WATER IN FUEL WARNING LIGHT (6.2L DIESEL)

As a bulb check, light will illuminate when ignition is turned on. If no problem exists, light will go out when engine is started. If light stays on at any time, excessive water in fuel filter is indicated. Service filter immediately.

SPEEDOMETER/ODOMETER

Integrated circuits control needle-type air core speedometer, and stepper motor-driven odometer. Speedometer/odometer receives its signals from the Digital Ratio Adapter Controller (DRAC), which receives its input signals from the Vehicle Speed Sensor (VSS).

VEHICLE SPEED SENSOR (VSS)

The VSS is a permanent magnet signal generator located in transmission tailshaft housing. A toothed rotor, or tone wheel fastened to transmission tailshaft rotates near VSS magnetic sensor coil, producing AC voltage pulses that are sent to the DRAC. This sensor assembly takes the place of speedometer cable and related gear hardware.

VOLTMETER

Voltmeter gauge on instrument panel measures voltage of charging system with engine running, and measures battery voltage with ignition on and engine not running. When engine is running, state of charge should be higher than when engine is off. If indicator enters either Red zone, charging system malfunction is indicated.

WAIT OR GLOW PLUGS LIGHT (6.2L DIESEL)

Light will illuminate when ignition is turned on to indicate glow plugs are warming up the cylinder combustion area to ease starting. When light goes out, engine is ready to be started. During cranking or after starting, it is normal for light to cycle on and off a few times, indicating glow plugs are still operating to warm cylinder.

TESTING

BRAKE WARNING SYSTEM

If warning light does not illuminate with ignition switch on, engine off and parking brake NOT applied, check for burned out light bulb. If bulb is okay, check for open in circuit. Remove wire connector from differential pressure switch on brake combination valve, and touch connector to ground. If warning light DOES NOT illuminate, repair open in circuit. If light illuminates, circuit is okay. Replace differential pressure switch.

COOLANT TEMPERATURE GAUGE

Gauge Inaccurate – 1) Disconnect temperature gauge sending unit connector. Connect Red lead of Gauge Tester (J 33431-B) to sending unit connector Dark Green wire. Connect other wire to ground. Adjust tester resistance dials to 1400 ohms, then adjust to 55 ohms.

2) Temperature gauge should read cold, then hot. If gauge responds correctly, replace temperature sending unit. If gauge does not respond as described, check for open circuit in Dark Green wire. If circuit is okay, replace temperature gauge.

TEMPERATURE GAUGE SENDING UNIT RESISTANCE

Temperature °F (°C)	Ohms
100 (38)	1400
260 (127)	55

1991 SAFETY EQUIPMENT
Instrument Panels – "G", "P", "R" & "V" Series (Cont.)

Gauge Always Reads Cold – Disconnect temperature gauge sending unit connector. Connect Dark Green wire to ground. If temperature gauge reads hot, replace temperature sending unit. If temperature gauge does not read hot, check for open circuit in Dark Green wire. If circuit is okay, replace temperature gauge.

Gauge Reads Too Hot – Disconnect temperature gauge sending unit lead connector. Turn ignition on. If gauge reads cold, replace temperature gauge sending unit. If gauge does not read cold, check for open circuit in Dark Green wire. If circuit is okay, see GAUGE INACCURATE under COOLANT TEMPERATURE GAUGE.

FUEL GAUGE

Gauge Reading Is Inaccurate – **1)** Disconnect fuel gauge sending unit wire. Connect Red lead of Gauge Tester (J 33431-B) to sending unit connector Pink wire. Connect other wire to ground. Adjust tester resistance dials to zero ohm, then to 90 ohms.

2) Temperature gauge should read empty, then full. If gauge responds correctly, check fuel tank ground wire for high resistance and repair if necessary. If ground circuit resistance is not high, replace fuel tank sending unit.

Gauge Always Reads Empty – Disconnect fuel gauge sending unit wire. Turn ignition on. If gauge reads full, check fuel gauge ground circuit. If circuit is okay, replace fuel gauge sending unit. If gauge reads empty, check for short circuit in Pink wire. If circuit is okay, replace fuel gauge.

Gauge Always Reads Full – Disconnect fuel gauge sending unit wire. Turn ignition on. Connect a fused jumper wire from sending unit Pink wire to ground. If gauge reads full, check for short circuit in Pink wire. If fuel gauge reads empty, check fuel gauge ground circuit. If circuit is okay, replace fuel gauge sending unit.

OIL PRESSURE GAUGE

Gauge Reads Low Or No Pressure – Check oil level and add oil if necessary. Test oil pressure with manual gauge and adapter. If oil pressure reading is good on manual gauge tester, disconnect lead at sending unit. Turn ignition on. If gauge still reads low, check for short in Tan wire. If wire is okay, replace oil pressure gauge. If gauge reads high with sending unit lead disconnected, replace sending unit.

Gauge Reads High Pressure – Disconnect lead at sending unit. Turn ignition on. Connect a fused jumper wire from sending unit Tan wire to ground. If gauge reads low pressure, replace oil pressure sending unit. If fuel gauge reads high pressure, check for open circuit in Tan wire. If circuit is okay, replace oil pressure gauge.

Gauge Reading Is Inaccurate – **1)** Disconnect oil pressure sending unit connector. Connect Red lead of Gauge Tester (J 33431-B) to sending unit connector Tan wire. Connect other wire to ground. Adjust tester resistance dials to zero ohm, then adjust to 90 ohms.

2) Oil pressure gauge should read low, then high pressure. If gauge responds correctly, replace oil pressure sending unit. If gauge does not respond as described, check for open circuit in Tan wire. If circuit is okay, replace oil pressure gauge.

SPEEDOMETER/ODOMETER

Speedometer Inoperative Or Inaccurate – **1)** Disconnect instrument cluster connector. Turn ignition on. Connect voltmeter between Light Blue/Black wire and ground. If battery voltage is present, go to next step. If battery voltage is not present, check HTR-A/C fuse and replace if necessary. If fuse is okay, repair open circuit in Light Blue/Black wire.

2) Turn ignition on. Connect voltmeter between Light Blue/Black wire and Black wire of instrument cluster connector. If battery voltage is not present, repair open circuit in Black wire between instrument cluster connector and ground. If battery voltage is present, go to VEHICLE SPEED SENSOR (VSS) & DIGITAL RATIO ADAPTER CONTROLLER (DRAC).

VEHICLE SPEED SENSOR (VSS) & DIGITAL RATIO ADAPTER CONTROLLER (DRAC)

Speedometer & Odometer Are Inaccurate – Ensure correct DRAC is installed.

Speedometer & Odometer Do Not Operate Properly – Perform the following test(s).

- **DRAC Inoperative** – Disconnect DRAC harness connector and turn ignition on. See DRAC MODULE LOCATIONS table. Check voltage between Pink/Black wire of harness connector and ground. If voltage is less than battery voltage, check for open or short in Pink/Black wire.
- **Poor Ground Path** – Check voltage between Pink/Black wire and Black/White wire of DRAC harness connector. If voltage is less than battery voltage, check for open or short in Black/White wire.
- **No VSS Signal** – Raise and support vehicle. Connect voltmeter between Purple/White wire and Light Green/Black wire at DRAC. Start engine and place transmission in Drive. Ensure AC voltage changes with vehicle speed. If AC voltage does not vary with vehicle speed, check for open or short in both wires. If both wires are okay, replace VSS located in transmission tailshaft housing.
- **No Speedometer Output** - Raise and support vehicle. Connect voltmeter between Pink/Black wire and Black/White wire at DRAC harness connector. Start engine and place transmission in Drive. Ensure AC voltage changes with vehicle speed. If AC voltage does not vary with vehicle speed, replace DRAC.
- **No Cruise Control Output** – Raise and support vehicle. Connect voltmeter between Yellow wire and Black/White wire at DRAC harness connector. Start engine and place transmission in Drive. Ensure AC voltage changes with vehicle speed. If AC voltage does not vary with vehicle speed, replace DRAC.

DRAC MODULE LOCATIONS

Model	Location
"G" Series	On Parking Brake Bracket
"P" Series	Inside Left Shipping Panel
"R" & "V" Series	Below Instrument Panel, Near Steering Column

VOLTMETER GAUGE

Voltmeter Not Accurate – Turn ignition on. Using voltmeter, measure voltage across battery terminals. If reading is the same as vehicle's voltmeter, gauge is okay. If reading is not the same as vehicle's voltmeter, check instrument cluster connector Pink/Black and Black wires for open circuit. If circuits are okay, replace voltmeter.

REMOVAL & INSTALLATION

DIGITAL RATIO ADAPTER CONTROLLER (DRAC)

CAUTION: Static electricity can destroy integrated circuits within DRAC. Before servicing DRAC, ground yourself and the work area to discharge stored electricity.

Removal & Installation – Disconnect negative battery terminal. Unplug instrument panel harness from DRAC. See DRAC MODULE LOCATIONS table under VEHICLE SPEED SENSOR (VSS) & DIGITAL RATIO ADAPTER CONTROLLER (DRAC) under TESTING. Remove DRAC retaining screws and remove DRAC. *See Figs. 1 and 2*. To install, reverse removal procedure.

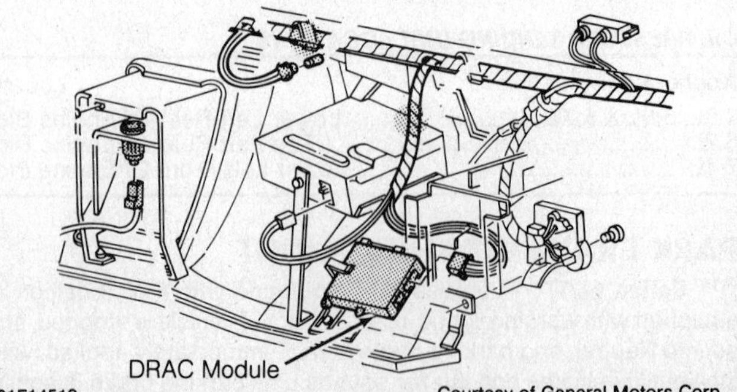
DRAC Module
91F14519
Courtesy of General Motors Corp.

Fig. 1: Locating DRAC Module ("G" Series)

Instrument Panels – "G", "P", "R" & "V" Series (Cont.)

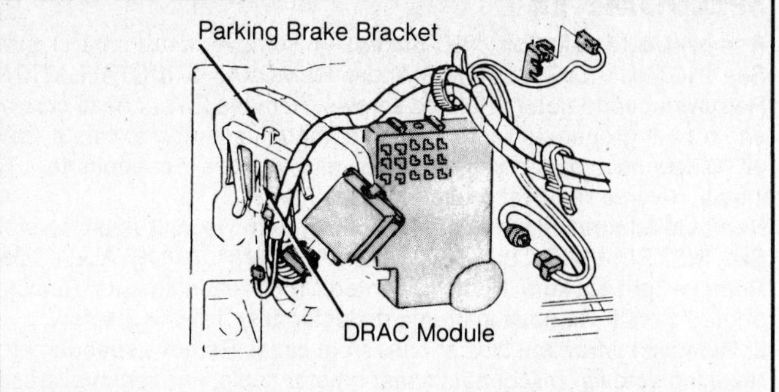
Parking Brake Bracket
DRAC Module

91I14520 Courtesy of General Motors Corp.

Fig. 2: Locating DRAC Module ("R" & "V" Series)

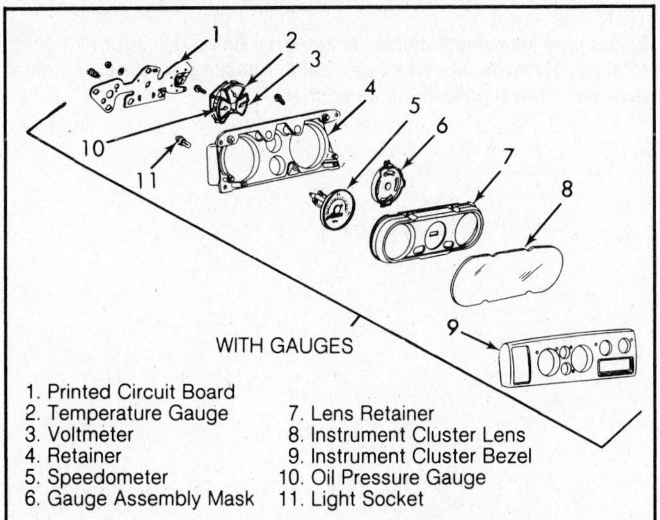
WITH GAUGES
1. Printed Circuit Board
2. Temperature Gauge
3. Voltmeter
4. Retainer
5. Speedometer
6. Gauge Assembly Mask
7. Lens Retainer
8. Instrument Cluster Lens
9. Instrument Cluster Bezel
10. Oil Pressure Gauge
11. Light Socket

90F14913 Courtesy of General Motors Corp.

Fig. 3: Exploded View of Instrument Cluster ("G" Series)

GAUGES

Removal & Installation ("R" & "V" Series) – 1) Remove instrument cluster. See INSTRUMENT CLUSTER under REMOVAL & INSTALLATION.

2) Remove instrument cluster case front cover or retainer. Remove screws from gauge being serviced. Remove gauge(s). *See Fig. 4*. To install, reverse removal procedure.

Removal & Installation ("G" Series) – Remove instrument cluster. See INSTRUMENT CLUSTER under REMOVAL & INSTALLATION. Remove instrument cluster lens and lens retainer. Remove printed circuit board. Remove nuts from gauge being serviced. Remove gauge(s). *See Fig. 3*. To install, reverse removal procedure.

Removal & Installation ("P" Series) – Remove instrument cluster. See INSTRUMENT CLUSTER under REMOVAL & INSTALLATION. Remove light socket assemblies. Remove printed circuit board. See PRINTED CIRCUIT under REMOVAL & INSTALLATION. Remove instrument cluster case retaining screws. Remove instrument cluster case from bezel. Remove screws from gauge being serviced. Remove gauge(s). To install, reverse removal procedure.

INSTRUMENT CLUSTER

Removal & Installation ("G" Series) – 1) Disconnect negative battery cable. Disconnect speedometer cable by depressing spring clip on rear of speedometer head and pulling cable free. Remove clock reset knob.

2) Remove instrument cluster bezel retaining screws, and remove bezel. *See Fig. 3*. Remove lower instrument cluster retaining screws. Pull top of cluster away from dash panel, and lift cluster out. Disconnect instrument cluster harness, and remove cluster. To install, reverse removal procedure.

Removal & Installation ("P" Series) – 1) Disconnect negative battery terminal. Disconnect speedometer cable by depressing spring clip on rear of speedometer head and pulling cable free. Remove clock adjustment stem.

2) Remove instrument cluster bezel retaining screws, and remove bezel. Disconnect instrument cluster harness and remove cluster. To install, reverse removal procedure.

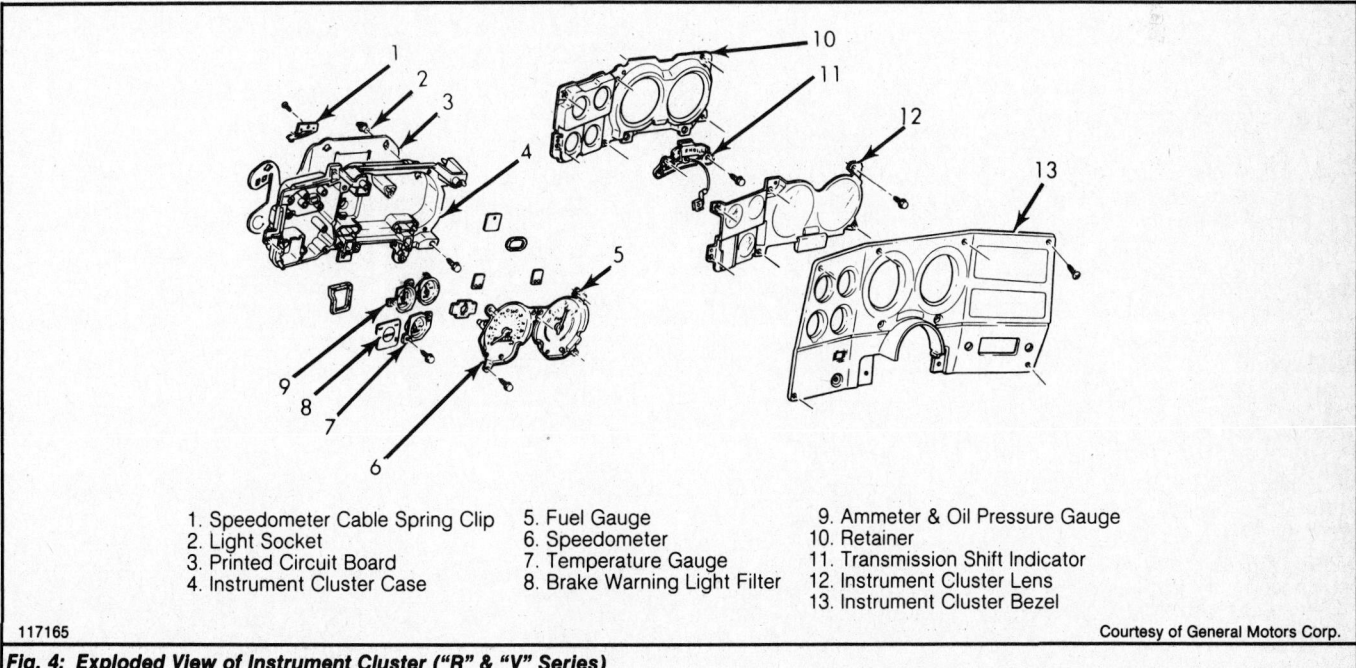

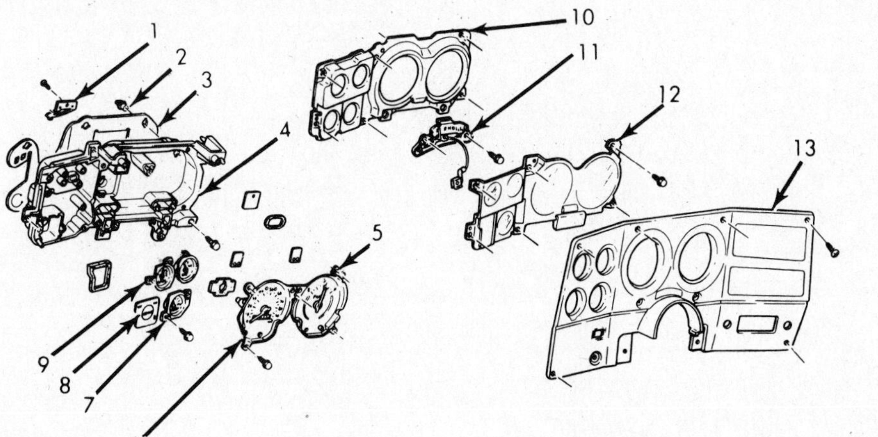
1. Speedometer Cable Spring Clip
2. Light Socket
3. Printed Circuit Board
4. Instrument Cluster Case
5. Fuel Gauge
6. Speedometer
7. Temperature Gauge
8. Brake Warning Light Filter
9. Ammeter & Oil Pressure Gauge
10. Retainer
11. Transmission Shift Indicator
12. Instrument Cluster Lens
13. Instrument Cluster Bezel

117165 Courtesy of General Motors Corp.

Fig. 4: Exploded View of Instrument Cluster ("R" & "V" Series)

1991 SAFETY EQUIPMENT
Instrument Panels – "G", "P", "R" & "V" Series (Cont.)

Removal & Installation ("R" & "V" Series) – 1) Disconnect negative battery cable. Remove headlight switch knob and radio control knobs. Remove lower steering column cover from instrument bezel. On A/T models, remove shift indicator clip from steering column. Remove 8 bezel screws, and remove bezel.

2) Disconnect speedometer cable by depressing spring clip on rear of speedometer head and pulling cable free. *See Fig. 4*. Remove instrument cluster retaining screws. Pull cluster out enough to disconnect instrument cluster harness and remove cluster. To install, reverse removal procedure.

PRINTED CIRCUIT

Removal & Installation – 1) Remove instrument cluster. See INSTRUMENT CLUSTER under REMOVAL & INSTALLATION. Remove instrument cluster light sockets. Remove printed circuit board retaining screws.

2) On "G" and "P" Series, remove fuel, temperature and ammeter gauge terminal nuts. On all models, remove printed circuit board. To install, reverse removal procedure. Ensure all gauge terminal nuts are tightened securely.

SPEEDOMETER

Removal & Installation ("G" Series) – Remove instrument cluster. See INSTRUMENT CLUSTER under REMOVAL & INSTALLATION. Remove speedometer retaining screws. Remove 2 Torx head screws and rubber grommets securing speedometer assembly to cluster cover. Disconnect speedometer cable, and remove speedometer. To install, reverse removal procedure. *See Fig. 3*.

Removal & Installation ("P" Series) – 1) Remove instrument cluster. See INSTRUMENT CLUSTER under REMOVAL & INSTALLATION. Remove light sockets. Remove printed circuit retaining nuts. Remove printed circuit. Remove instrument cluster case retaining screws.

2) Remove instrument cluster case from bezel. Remove speedometer retaining screws. Disconnect speedometer cable, and remove speedometer. To install, reverse removal procedure.

Removal & Installation ("R" & "V" Series) – 1) Remove instrument cluster. See INSTRUMENT CLUSTER under REMOVAL & INSTALLATION.

2) Remove instrument cluster bezel/lens. Remove instrument gauge retainer. Remove speedometer head retaining screws. To install, reverse removal procedure. *See Fig. 4*.

1991 SAFETY EQUIPMENT
Instrument Panels – Lumina APV

DESCRIPTION

INSTRUMENT PANELS

Standard mechanical instrument panels are designed to allow removal and installation of all control switches, gauges, and illuminating bulbs from the driver's side. The instrument panels are equipped with gauges and analog speedometer, as well as warning lights.

OPERATION

BRAKE/PARK WARNING LIGHT SYSTEM

Warning system consists of a warning light on instrument cluster, a brake warning light switch (located on brake combination valve), and a parking brake engagement telltale switch. If brake hydraulic system malfunctions, or if parking brake is NOT fully released, warning light will illuminate.

CHARGING SYSTEM WARNING SYSTEM

Warning system consists of a battery symbol warning light on instrument cluster. One side of warning light bulb is connected to alternator field circuit, and other side of bulb is connected to ignition power circuit. If charging system malfunction is detected, warning light will illuminate.

COOLANT TEMPERATURE GAUGE

Coolant temperature gauge measures electrical resistance from coolant temperature sending unit mounted in cylinder head. Sending unit has a resistance of 55 ohms at 260°F (127°C), and 1400 ohms at 100°F (38°C). As coolant temperature increases, the current flow through sending unit to gauge increases due to less resistance, causing gauge pointer to move toward HOT position.

FUEL GAUGE

Fuel gauge measures current flow from a fuel gauge sending unit with variable resistance. When fuel level in tank is high, fuel gauge sending unit resistance is high. Fuel gauge sending unit is located on, or near top of fuel tank.

OIL PRESSURE GAUGE

Oil pressure gauge measures electrical current from an oil pressure sending unit with variable resistance. Sending unit resistance is low when oil pressure is low, and is about 90 ohms when oil pressure is high. A change in resistance changes current flow through gauge electromagnetic coils, causing pointer to move from low to high. Sending unit is located at bottom left of engine block, on oil filter housing.

SERVICE ENGINE SOON LIGHT

This warning light is part of computer command control system, and will flash when a malfunction or trouble code(s) exists. Light will illuminate when ignition is turned on. If no problem exists, light will go out when engine is started.

SPEEDOMETER/ODOMETER

Integrated circuits control the needle-type air core speedometer, and the stepper motor-driven odometer. Speedometer/odometer receives its signals from the Vehicle Speed Sensor (VSS) buffer, which receives its input signals from the VSS.

VEHICLE SPEED SENSOR (VSS)

The VSS is mounted in the transaxle. VSS produces an A/C signal proportional to the speed of transaxle rotation. The signal is amplified and converted to DC signal by VSS buffer. Signal is transmitted to ECM, cruise control module, and speedometer. The ECM, cruise control module, and speedometer convert electrical signal to determine vehicle speed.

TESTING

NOTE: Check GAGES fuse and replace if blown. If fuse blows again, check for short to ground in Pink/Black wire.

INSTRUMENT CLUSTER

All Gauges Inaccurate – Connect jumper wire from instrument cluster connector terminals "M" and "T" to ground. *See Fig. 1.* If all gauges are still inaccurate, replace instrument cluster.

All Gauges Inoperative – **1)** Remove instrument cluster. Turn ignition on. Connect test light between instrument cluster connector terminal "Z" and ground. *See Fig. 1.* If test light does not come on, repair open in Pink/Black wire. If test light comes on, go to next step.

2) Connect test light between instrument cluster connector terminal "K" and ground. If light does not come on, repair open in Pink/Black wire. If test light comes on, connect test light between connector terminals "K" and "M". If test light comes on, repair open in Black/White wire. If test light does not come on, go to next step.

3) Connect test light between instrument cluster connector terminals "K" and "T". If light does not come on, repair open in Black wire. If test light comes on, check for poor connections at instrument cluster. If connections are okay, replace instrument cluster.

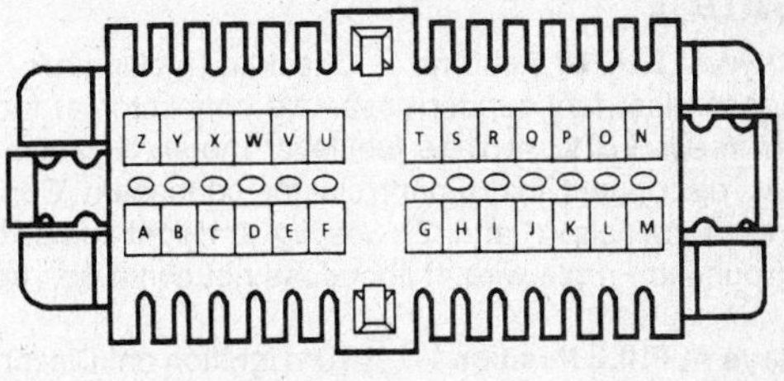
Z Y X W V U
T S R Q P O N
A B C D E F
G H I J K L M

**CAVITIES NOT LISTED ARE NOT USED

CAVITY	WIRE COLOR	CKT	DESCRIPTION
A	DK GRN	35	COOLANT TEMPERATURE SIGNAL
B	BRN/WHT	419	SERVICE ENGINE SOON INDICATOR
D	LT GRN	11	HI BEAM INDICATOR (WITHOUT DRL) (WITH DRL)
E	TAN/WHT	33	BRAKE INDICATOR
G	LT BLU	14	LEFT TURN INDICATOR
H	YEL	237	FASTEN BELTS INDICATOR
I	BLK/ORN	158	GATE AJAR INDICATOR
J	DK BLU	15	RIGHT TURN INDICATOR
K	PNK/BLK	39	IGNITION 1 – HOT IN RUN, BULB TEST OR START
L	DK GRN	389	VEHICLE SPEED INPUT
M	BLK/WHT	450	GROUND
R	BRN	25	CHARGE INDICATOR CONTROL
S	GRY	8	INSTRUMENT CLUSTER DIMMABLE BACKLIGHTING
T	BLK	151	GROUND
X	TAN	31	OIL PRESSURE SIGNAL
Y	PPL	30	FUEL LEVEL SIGNAL
Z	PNK/BLK	39	IGNITION 1 – HOT IN RUN, BULB TEST OR START

91I14512 Courtesy of General Motors Corp.

Fig. 1: Identifying Instrument Cluster Connector Terminals

1991 SAFETY EQUIPMENT
Instrument Panels – Lumina APV (Cont.)

BRAKE WARNING SYSTEM

If warning light does not illuminate with ignition switch on, engine off and parking brake NOT applied, check for burned out light bulb. If bulb is okay, check for open in circuit. Remove wire connector from differential pressure switch on brake combination valve, and touch connector to ground. If warning light DOES NOT illuminate, repair open in circuit. If light illuminates, circuit is okay. Replace differential pressure switch.

COOLANT TEMPERATURE GAUGE

1) Turn ignition on. If coolant gauge does not indicate high, go to next step. If coolant gauge indicates high, remove terminal lead from coolant temperature sending unit. If coolant temperature gauge indicates low, replace coolant temperature gauge sending unit. If coolant temperature gauge does not indicate low, check for short circuit in Dark Green wire. If wire is okay, replace gauge.

2) Remove terminal lead from coolant temperature sending unit. Turn ignition to RUN position. Using voltmeter, measure voltage between coolant temperature sending unit and ground. If voltage is present, replace sending unit. If voltage is not present, check for open circuit in Dark Green wire between sending unit and instrument cluster connector terminal "A". If wire is okay, replace coolant temperature gauge.

FUEL GAUGE

Gauge Stays At EMPTY Position – Check for fuel in tank. Turn ignition on. Disconnect fuel sender assembly connector at fuel tank. If gauge now reads FULL, replace fuel lever meter. If gauge does not read FULL, disconnect instrument cluster connector. Connect test light between terminals "Y" and "Z". *See Fig. 1.* If light comes on, repair short to ground in Purple wire. If light does not come on, replace fuel gauge.

Gauge Stays At FULL Position – **1)** Turn ignition on. Disconnect fuel sender assembly connector. Connect test light between battery positive and connector terminal "D" (Black wire). If test light comes on, go to next step. If test light does not come on, repair open circuit in Black wire.

2) Connect a fused jumper wire between fuel sender assembly connector terminal "B" (Purple wire) and ground. If fuel gauge reads EMPTY, check for damaged or corroded fuel sender assembly connector and repair if necessary. If fuel sender assembly connector is okay, replace fuel lever meter. If fuel gauge does not read EMPTY, check for open in Purple wire between fuel sender assembly and instrument cluster. If wire is okay, replace fuel gauge.

FUEL GAUGE SENDING UNIT RESISTANCE

Position	Ohms
Empty	1
1/4 Full	33
1/2 Full	50
3/4 Full	83
Full	88

Gauge Reading Is Inaccurate – Note fuel level indicated by gauge. Disconnect fuel gauge connector at instrument cluster. Using DVOM, measure resistance between terminal "Y" (Purple wire) and ground. If resistance is within specification, replace fuel gauge. If resistance is not within specification, replace fuel lever meter. See FUEL GAUGE SENDING UNIT RESISTANCE table.

OIL PRESSURE GAUGE

Gauge Reads Low or No Pressure – Check oil level and add if necessary. Test oil pressure with manual gauge and adapter. If oil pressure reading is good on manual gauge tester, disconnect lead at sending unit. If gauge still reads low, check for open in Tan wire. If wire is okay, replace oil pressure gauge. If gauge reads high with sending unit lead disconnected, replace sending unit.

Gauge Reads High Pressure – Disconnect lead at sending unit. Using voltmeter, measure voltage between terminal "A" (Tan wire) and ground. If battery voltage is not present, check for open circuit in Tan wire. If wire is okay, replace oil pressure gauge. If battery voltage is present, check connector at oil pressure sending unit. If connector is okay, replace oil pressure sending unit.

Gauge Reading Is Inaccurate – Disconnect instrument cluster connector. Using DVOM, measure resistance between connector terminal "X" and ground. If resistance is approximately one ohm, replace oil pressure gauge. If resistance is not approximately one ohm, replace oil pressure sending unit.

SPEEDOMETER/ODOMETER

Speedometer Is Inoperative Or Inaccurate – **1)** Disconnect Vehicle Speed Sensor (VSS) from top of transaxle. Connect Instrument Panel Tester (J 33431-B) to VSS connector. Set tester to 54 MPH. Turn ignition on. If speedometer reads 6 MPH, check for poor connection at VSS. If connection is okay, replace VSS. If speedometer does not reads 6 MPH, go to next step.

2) Turn ignition off. Remove tester from VSS. Disconnect VSS buffer located behind instrument panel, above convenience center. *See Fig. 2.* Connect Instrument Panel Tester (J 33431-B) to terminal "F" (Dark Green wire) of VSS buffer connector C1.

3) Set tester to 54 MPH. Turn ignition on. If speedometer reads 54 MPH, check for poor connection at VSS buffer. If connection is okay, replace VSS buffer. If speedometer does not read 54 MPH, check for open or short circuit in Dark Green wire. If wire is okay, replace speedometer.

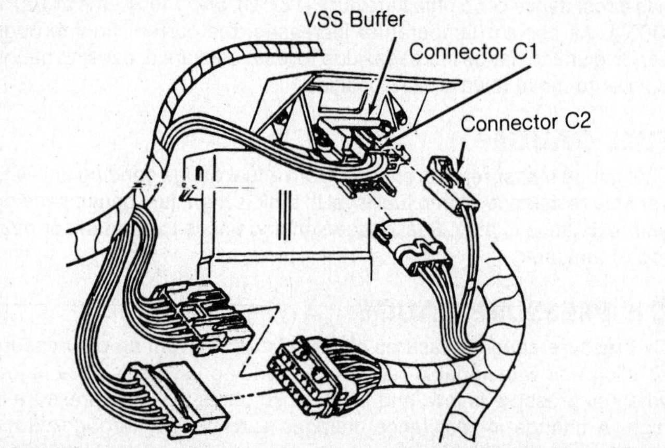
VSS Buffer
Connector C1
Connector C2
91J14513
Courtesy of General Motors Corp.

Fig. 2: Locating VSS Buffer

Speedometer Is Inaccurate & ECM Code 24 Is Set – **1)** Turn ignition on. Connect voltmeter between terminal "A" (Pink/White wire) of VSS buffer connector C1 and ground. If battery voltage is present, go to next step. If battery voltage is not present, repair open in Pink/White wire.

2) Connect voltmeter between terminals "A" (Pink/White wire) and "B" (Black wire) of VSS buffer connector C1. If battery voltage is present, go to next step. If battery voltage is not present, repair open in Black wire.

3) Turn ignition on. Place transaxle in Neutral. Raise drive wheels. Set voltmeter on AC scale. Measure voltage between terminals "A" (Purple wire) and "C" (Yellow wire) of VSS buffer connector C2 while rotating drive wheels by hand. If voltage varies between zero and one volt, check connectors C1 and C2. If connectors are okay, replace VSS buffer. If voltage remains at zero volt, check for open circuit in Yellow or Purple wire. If wire is okay, replace VSS.

1991 SAFETY EQUIPMENT
Instrument Panels – Silhouette & Trans Sport

DESCRIPTION

INSTRUMENT PANELS

Standard mechanical instrument panels are designed to allow removal and installation of all control switches, gauges and illuminating bulbs from the driver's side. The instrument panels are equipped with gauges and analog speedometer, as well as warning lights.

OPERATION

BRAKE/PARK WARNING LIGHT SYSTEM

Warning system consists of a warning light on instrument cluster, a brake warning light switch (located on brake combination valve), and a parking brake engagement telltale switch. If brake hydraulic system malfunctions, or if parking brake is NOT fully released, warning light will illuminate.

VOLTMETER

Voltmeter gauge on instrument panel shows battery's state of charge at all times. When engine is running, state of charge will be higher than when engine is off. If indicator enters either Red zone, charging system malfunction is indicated.

COOLANT TEMPERATURE GAUGE

Coolant temperature gauge measures current flow from coolant temperature sending unit mounted in cylinder head. Sending unit has a resistance of 55 ohms at 260°F (127°C), and 1400 ohms at 100°F (38°C). As coolant temperature increases, the current flow through sending unit to gauge increases due to less resistance, causing gauge pointer to move toward HOT position.

FUEL GAUGE

Fuel gauge measures current flow from a fuel gauge sending unit with variable resistance. When fuel level in tank is high, fuel gauge sending unit resistance is high. Fuel gauge sending unit is located on, or near top of fuel tank.

OIL PRESSURE GAUGE

Oil pressure gauge measures electrical current from an oil pressure sending unit with variable resistance. Sending unit resistance is low when oil pressure is low, and is about 90 ohms when oil pressure is high. A change in resistance changes current flow through gauge electromagnetic coils, causing pointer to move from low to high. Sending unit is located at bottom left of engine block, on oil filter housing.

SERVICE ENGINE SOON LIGHT

This warning light is part of computer command control system and will flash when a malfunction or trouble code(s) exists. As a bulb check, light will illuminate when ignition is turned on. If no problem exists, light will go out when engine is started.

SPEEDOMETER/ODOMETER

Integrated circuits control the needle-type air core speedometer, and the stepper motor-driven odometer. Speedometer/odometer receives its signals from Vehicle Speed Sensor (VSS) buffer, which receives its input signals from the VSS.

VEHICLE SPEED SENSOR (VSS)

The VSS is mounted in the transaxle. VSS produces an A/C signal proportional to the speed of transaxle rotation. The signal is amplified and converted to DC signal by VSS buffer. Signal is transmitter to ECM, cruise control module, and speedometer. The ECM, cruise control module, and speedometer convert electrical signal to determine vehicle speed.

TESTING

NOTE: Check GAGES fuse and replace if blown. If fuse blows again, check for short to ground in Pink/White wire.

INSTRUMENT CLUSTER

All Gauges Inaccurate – Connect jumper wire from instrument cluster connector terminals C7, C8 and D8 to ground. *See Fig. 1.* If all gauges are still inaccurate, replace instrument cluster.

All Gauges Inoperative – **1)** Remove instrument cluster. Turn ignition on. Connect test light between instrument cluster connector terminal D10 and ground. *See Fig. 1.* If test light does not come on, repair open in Pink/White wire. If test light comes on, go to next step.

2) Connect test light between instrument cluster connector terminal C5 and ground. If test light does not come on, repair open in Pink/Black wire. If test light comes on, connect test light between connector terminal D5 and ground. If test light does not come on, repair open in Pink/Black wire. If test light comes on, go to next step.

3) Connect test light between instrument cluster connector terminals C7 and D10. If test light does not come on, repair open in Black wire to terminal C7. If test light comes on, connect test light between instrument cluster connector terminals C8 and D10. If test light does not come on, repair open in Black wire to terminal C8. If test light comes on, connect test light between connector terminals D8 and D10. If test light does not come on, repair open in Black wire to terminal D8. If test light comes on, check connections at instrument cluster connector. If connections are okay, replace instrument cluster printed circuit board.

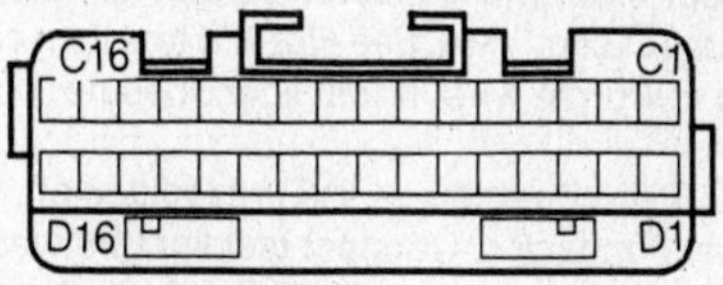
C16
C1
D16
D1

** CAVITIES NOT LISTED ARE NOT USED

CAVITY	WIRE COLOR	CKT	DESCRIPTION
C3	TAN	31	OIL PRESSURE SIGNAL
C4	DK GRN	35	COOLANT TEMPERATURE SIGNAL
C5	PNK/BLK	39	IGNITION 1 - HOT IN RUN, BULB TEST OR START
C7	BLK	151	GROUND
C8	BLK	151	GROUND
C10	LT BLU	14	LEFT TURN SIGNAL
C11	LT GRN	11	HI BEAM SIGNAL
C12	DK BLU	15	RIGHT TURN SIGNAL
C13	YEL	237	FASTEN BELTS INDICATOR POWER FEED
C15	BRN/WHT	419	SERVICE ENGINE SOON INDICATOR CONTROL
D3	PPL	30	FUEL LEVEL SIGNAL
D4	DK GRN	389	VEHICLE SPEED INPUT
D5	PNK/BLK	39	IGNITION 1 - HOT IN RUN, BULB TEST OR START
D7	WHT	121	TACH SIGNAL
D8	BLK	151	GROUND
D9	GRY	8	INSTRUMENT CLUSTER DIMMABLE BACKLIGHTING
D10	PNK/WHT	350	IGNITION 3 - HOT IN RUN
D13	BLK/ORN	158	LIFTGATE AJAR INDICATOR CONTROL
D14	TAN/WHT	33	BRAKE WARNING INDICATOR CONTROL

91B14515 Courtesy of General Motors Corp.

Fig. 1: Identifying Instrument Cluster Connector Terminals

1991 SAFETY EQUIPMENT
Instrument Panels – Silhouette & Trans Sport (Cont.)

BRAKE WARNING SYSTEM

If warning light does not illuminate with ignition switch on, engine off and parking brake NOT applied, check for burned out light bulb. If bulb is okay, check for open in circuit. Remove wire connector from differential pressure switch on brake combination valve, and touch connector to ground. If warning light DOES NOT illuminate, repair open in circuit. If light illuminates, circuit is okay. Replace differential pressure switch.

COOLANT TEMPERATURE GAUGE

1) Turn ignition on. If coolant gauge does not indicate high, go to next step. If coolant gauge indicates high, remove terminal lead from coolant temperature sending unit. If coolant temperature gauge indicates low, replace coolant temperature gauge sending unit. If coolant temperature gauge does not indicate low, check for short circuit in Dark Green wire. If wire is okay, replace coolant temperature gauge.

2) Remove terminal lead from coolant temperature sending unit. Turn ignition to RUN position. Using voltmeter, measure voltage between coolant temperature sending unit and ground. If voltage is present, replace sending unit. If voltage is not present, check for open circuit in Dark Green wire between sending unit and instrument cluster connector terminal C4. If wire is okay, replace coolant temperature gauge.

FUEL GAUGE

Gauge Stays At EMPTY Position – Check for fuel in tank. Turn ignition on. Disconnect fuel sender assembly connector at fuel tank. If gauge now reads FULL, replace fuel sender. If gauge does not read FULL, disconnect instrument cluster connector. Connect test light between terminals D3 and D10. *See Fig. 1.* If test light comes on, repair short to ground in Purple wire. If test light does not come on, replace fuel gauge.

Gauge Stays At FULL Position – **1)** Turn ignition on. Disconnect fuel sender assembly connector. Connect test light between battery positive terminal and connector terminal "D" (Black wire). If test light comes on, go to next step. If test light does not come on, repair open circuit in Black wire.

2) Connect a fused jumper wire between fuel sender assembly connector terminal "B" (Purple wire) and ground. If gauge reads EMPTY, check for damaged or corroded fuel sender assembly connector and repair if necessary. If connector is okay, replace fuel sender. If fuel gauge does not read EMPTY, check for open in Purple wire between fuel sender assembly and instrument cluster. If wire is okay, replace fuel gauge.

Gauge Reading Is Inaccurate – Note fuel level indicated by gauge. Disconnect fuel gauge connector at instrument cluster. Using DVOM, measure resistance between terminal D3 (Purple wire) and ground. If resistance is within specification, replace fuel gauge. If resistance is not within specification, replace fuel lever meter. See FUEL GAUGE SENDING UNIT RESISTANCE table.

FUEL GAUGE SENDING UNIT RESISTANCE

Position	Ohms
Empty	1
1/4 Full	33
1/2 Full	50
3/4 Full	83
Full	88

OIL PRESSURE GAUGE

Gauge Reads Low Or No Pressure – Check oil level and add if necessary. Test oil pressure with manual gauge and adapter. If oil pressure reading is good on manual gauge tester, disconnect lead at sending unit. Turn ignition on. If gauge still reads low, check for open in Tan wire. If wire is okay, replace oil pressure gauge. If gauge reads high with sending unit lead disconnected, replace oil pressure sending unit.

Gauge Reads High Pressure – Disconnect lead at sending unit. Using voltmeter, measure voltage between terminal "A" (Tan wire) and ground. Turn ignition on. If battery voltage is not present, check for open circuit in Tan wire. If wire is okay, replace oil pressure gauge. If battery voltage is present, check connector at oil pressure sending unit. If connector is okay, replace oil pressure sending unit.

Gauge Reading Is Inaccurate – Turn ignition off. Disconnect instrument cluster connector. Using DVOM, measure resistance between connector terminal C3 and ground. If resistance is approximately one ohm, replace oil pressure gauge. If resistance is not approximately one ohm, replace oil pressure sending unit.

SPEEDOMETER/ODOMETER

Speedometer Is Inoperative Or Inaccurate – **1)** Disconnect Vehicle Speed Sensor (VSS) from top of transaxle. Connect Instrument Panel Tester (J 33431-B) to VSS connector. Set tester to 54 MPH. Turn ignition on. If speedometer reads 6 MPH, check for poor connection at VSS. If connection is okay, replace VSS. If speedometer does not reads 6 MPH, go to next step.

2) Turn ignition off. Remove tester from VSS. Disconnect VSS buffer located behind instrument panel, above convenience center. *See Fig. 2.* Connect Instrument Panel Tester (J 33431-B) to terminal "F" (Dark Green wire) of VSS buffer connector C1.

3) Set tester to 54 MPH. Turn ignition on. If speedometer reads 54 MPH, check for poor connection at VSS buffer. If connection is okay, replace VSS buffer. If speedometer does not read 54 MPH, check for open or short circuit in Dark Green wire. If wire is okay, replace speedometer.

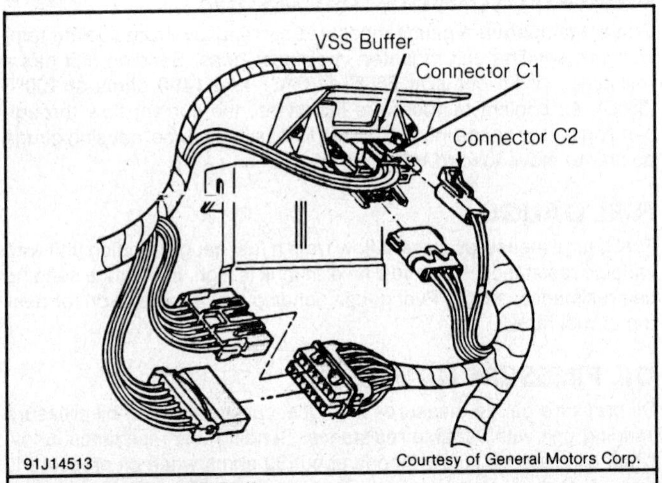
VSS Buffer
Connector C1
Connector C2
91J14513
Courtesy of General Motors Corp.

Fig. 2: Locating VSS Buffer

Speedometer Is Inaccurate & ECM Code 24 Is Set – **1)** Turn ignition on. Connect voltmeter between terminal "A" (Pink/White wire) of VSS buffer connector C1 and ground. If battery voltage is present, go to next step. If battery voltage is not present, repair open in Pink/White wire.

2) Connect voltmeter between terminals "A" (Pink/White wire) and "B" (Black wire) of VSS buffer connector C1. If battery voltage is present, go to next step. If battery voltage is not present, repair open in Black wire.

3) Turn ignition on. Place transaxle in Neutral. Raise drive wheels. Set voltmeter on AC scale. Measure voltage between terminals "A" (Purple wire) and "C" (Yellow wire) of VSS buffer connector C2 while rotating drive wheels by hand. If voltage varies between zero and one volt, check for poor connection at connectors C1 and C2. If connection is okay, replace VSS buffer. If voltage remains at zero volt, check for open circuit in Yellow or Purple wire. If wire is okay, replace VSS.

TACHOMETER

Tachometer Is Inoperative Or Inaccurate – **1)** Disconnect tachometer signal filter connector. *See Fig. 3.* Turn ignition on. Using voltmeter, measure voltage between terminal "A" (White wire) and ground. If battery voltage is present, go to next step. If battery voltage is not present, check for open circuit in White wire between tachometer signal filter and ignition coil. If wire is okay, replace ignition coil.

2) Turn ignition off. Connect tachometer signal filter connector. Remove instrument cluster connector. Turn ignition on. Measure voltage between connector terminal D10 (Pink/White wire) and ground. *See Fig. 1.* If battery voltage is present, go to next step. If battery voltage is not present, check for open circuit in Pink/White wire.

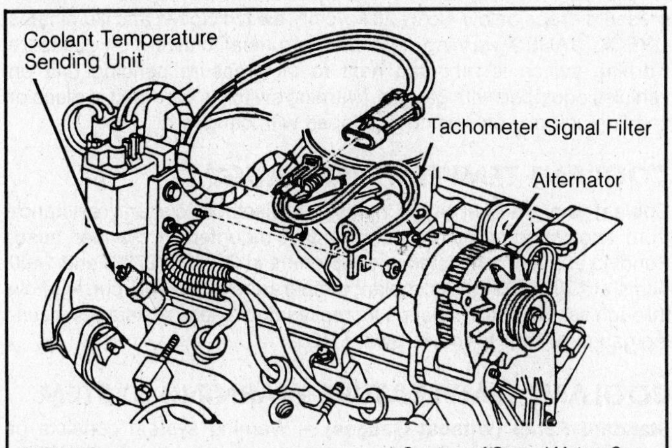

Coolant Temperature
Sending Unit
Tachometer Signal Filter
Alternator
91C14516
Courtesy of General Motors Corp.

Fig. 3: Locating Tachometer Signal Filter

3) Measure voltage between instrument cluster connector terminal D7 (White wire) and ground. If battery voltage is present, check for poor connection at connector or instrument cluster printed circuit board. If connection is okay, replace tachometer. If battery voltage is not present, check for open circuit in White wire between tachometer signal filter and instrument cluster. If wire is okay, replace tachometer signal filter.

WIRING DIAGRAMS

See appropriate chassis wiring diagram in WIRING DIAGRAMS.

1991 SAFETY EQUIPMENT
Instrument Panels – All Others

Astro, Safari, "S" & "T" Series

DESCRIPTION

STANDARD INSTRUMENT PANELS

Standard mechanical instrument panels on all models are designed to permit the removal and installation of all control switches, gauges and illuminating bulbs from the driver's side. The standard instrument panels are equipped with warning lights only. Optional equipment instrument clusters come equipped with gauges and digital speedometer, as well as standard and optional warning lights.

ELECTRONIC INSTRUMENT CLUSTER

This instrument cluster is a solid-state device that uses a digital display for speedometer/odometer information and bar graph displays for gauge information. This electronic device receives input signals from the following components and systems.

- English/Metric switch
- Odometer trip/reset switch
- Battery, charging, ignition and lighting systems
- Oil, fuel and temperature sending units
- Digital Ratio Adapter Controller (DRAC)
- Vehicle speed sensor

Vehicle speed sensor (VSS) signal originates at transmission tone wheel on tailshaft. This AC voltage signal is changed to a digital signal for speedometer use by Digital Ratio Adapter Controller (DRAC). The electronic instrument cluster does not contain any serviceable components and is serviced as a complete assembly.

OPERATION

BRAKE WARNING LIGHT SYSTEM

Warning system consists of a Red BRAKE warning light on instrument cluster/panel, a BRAKE warning light/pressure differential switch (located on brake combination/proportioning valve) and a parking brake engagement telltale switch. If brake hydraulic system malfunctions, or if parking brake is NOT fully released, BRAKE warning light will illuminate.

ABS (OR ANTI-LOCK) WARNING LIGHT SYSTEM

An Amber ABS or ANTI-LOCK warning light will illuminate when ignition is turned on, and if no problem exists, light will go out when engine starts. If amber ABS warning light stays on at any time, conventional brake system will still be operational, but without anti-lock assistance. If both BRAKE and ABS warning lights illuminate at same time while driving, stop vehicle carefully and park vehicle until systems can be repaired.

CHARGING SYSTEM WARNING SYSTEM

Standard Panel – Warning system consists of a battery symbol warning light on instrument cluster/panel. One side of warning light bulb is connected to alternator field circuit and other side of bulb is connected to ignition power circuit. If charging system malfunction is detected, warning light will illuminate.

Electronic Digital Instrument Cluster – If charging system malfunctions, signal box around voltmeter gauge battery symbol will illuminate and flash at full intensity.

CHECK GAGES LIGHT

"S" & "T" Series (Gauge Cluster) – This optional equipment warning light illuminates when engine coolant temperature is too high or when engine oil pressure is too low. Warning signals from engine coolant temperature and/or oil pressure switches are monitored by CHECK GAGES light driver. Light driver is an integral part of coolant temperature gauge circuit board.

Warning light switches are separate units from gauge sending units. Coolant temperature warning system uses engine mounted temperature switch. When coolant overheats, switch closes and CHECK GAGES warning light illuminates. Coolant switch closing temperature is 257°F (125°C).

Oil pressure warning system uses an oil pressure switch. When oil pressure drops below 4 psi (.28 kg/cm²), switch closes and illuminates CHECK GAGES warning light on instrument cluster. Oil pressure warning switch is mounted next to oil pressure sending unit on vehicles equipped with gauges. Warning switch is mounted in place of sending unit on vehicles not equipped with gauges.

COOLANT TEMPERATURE GAUGE

Coolant temperature gauge measures electrical current resistance from coolant temperature sending unit mounted in cylinder head. Sending unit has a resistance of 55 ohms at 260°F (127°C) and 1400 ohms at 100°F (38°C). As coolant temperature increases, current flow through sending unit to gauge increases due to less resistance, causing gauge pointer to move toward HOT.

COOLANT TEMPERATURE WARNING SYSTEM

Standard Panel (Without Gauges) – Warning system consists of temperature switch and instrument cluster warning light. When coolant overheats, switch closes and warning light illuminates. Switch closing temperature is 257°F (125°C).

Standard Panel (With Gauges) – See CHECK GAGES LIGHT.

Electronic Digital Instrument Cluster – If coolant temperature reaches 245°F (118°C), engine mounted coolant temperature switch signals box around temperature gauge thermometer symbol to illuminate and flash at full intensity.

DIGITAL RATIO ADAPTER CONTROLLER

Digital Ratio Adapter Controller (DRAC) is a solid-state device used to change AC voltage signal from the VSS to a digital signal for speedometer operation.

DRAC is matched to the final drive ratio of each vehicle. If the final drive ratio is changed for any reason (i.e. tires or gears), DRAC must be replaced to maintain accurate speedometer/odometer reading.

NOTE: Incorrect DRAC calibration may adversely affect Rear Wheel Anti-Lock Brakes (RWAL), Electronic Control Module (ECM), and Cruise Control Module (CCM).

FUEL GAUGE

Fuel gauge is an electrical instrument that measures current flow from variable-resistance fuel gauge sending unit in fuel tank. When fuel level in tank is high, fuel gauge sending unit resistance is high. Fuel sending unit is located on or near top of fuel tank. Some units use short connector lead, while others have harness connected directly to unit.

LOW FUEL WARNING

Electronic Digital Instrument Cluster – When fuel level in tank is less than 3.0 gals. (11L), or fuel gauge is at or below fourth segment from bottom of display, this signals warning box around fuel gauge gas pump symbol to illuminate and flash at full intensity.

LOW OIL PRESSURE WARNING SYSTEM

Standard Panel – Warning system consists of an oil pressure switch and a warning light on instrument cluster. Oil pressure switch closes when oil pressure drops to less than 4 psi (.28 kg/cm²) and illuminates warning light on instrument cluster. Oil pressure warning switch is mounted next to oil pressure sending unit on vehicles equipped with gauges. Warning switch is mounted in place of sending unit on vehicles NOT equipped with gauges. Light will illuminate when ignition is turned on, and if no problem exists, light will go out when engine starts.

Electronic Digital Instrument Cluster – If engine oil pressure drops to less than 10 psi (.70 kg/cm²), oil pressure switch closes and signals warning box around oil pressure gauge oil can symbol to illuminate and flash at full intensity. Oil pressure warning switch is mounted next to oil pressure sending unit.

OIL PRESSURE GAUGE

Oil pressure gauge measures electrical current from variable-resistance oil pressure sending unit. Sending unit has low resistance when oil pressure is low and has about 90 ohms resistance when oil pressure is high. A change in resistance changes current flow through gauge electromagnetic coils, causing pointer to move from low to high.

Sending unit locations are as follows:

- 2.5L – In right side of block, under intake manifold.
- 2.8L – At bottom left of engine block, on oil filter housing.
- 4.3L – At top rear of engine block.

SERVICE ENGINE SOON OR CHECK ENGINE WARNING LIGHT

This warning light is part of computer command control system and will flash or stay on when a malfunction or trouble code(s) exists. Light will illuminate when ignition is turned on, and if no problem exists, light will go out when engine starts.

SHIFT LIGHT

"S" & "T" Series (M/T) – This light shows when to upshift for best fuel economy at any acceleration. Disregard light during downshift. SHIFT light is controlled by ECM.

SPEEDOMETER/ODOMETER

Integrated circuits control the needle type air core speedometer and the stepper motor driven odometer. Speedometer/odometer receives its signals from the Digital Ratio Adapter Controller (DRAC), which receives its input signals from Vehicle Speed Sensor (VSS).

VEHICLE SPEED SENSOR

Vehicle Speed Sensor (VSS) is a permanent magnet signal generator located in transmission tailshaft housing. A toothed rotor or tone wheel fastened to transmission tailshaft rotates near VSS magnetic sensor coil, producing AC voltage pulses that are sent to the DRAC. This sensor assembly takes the place of speedometer cable and related gear hardware.

VOLTMETER

Voltmeter measures voltage of charging system with engine running and measures battery voltage with ignition on. Voltmeter uses an internal shunt. On electronic digital instrument clusters, if charging system malfunctions, signal box around voltmeter gauge battery symbol will illuminate and flash at full intensity.

TESTING & DIAGNOSIS

BRAKE WARNING SYSTEM

If warning light does not illuminate when ignition switch is turned on, engine off and parking brake NOT applied, check for burned out light bulb. If bulb is okay, check for open in circuit by removing wire connector from differential pressure switch on brake combination valve and touch connector to ground. If warning light DOES NOT illuminate, repair open in circuit. If light does illuminate, circuit is okay. Replace differential pressure switch.

CHECK GAGES LIGHT ("S" & "T" SERIES)

Light Inoperative – Turn ignition on. Check for burned out bulb and/or check for opens in printed circuit between oil pressure gauge and temperature gauge and between temperature gauge and CHECK GAGES light. If opens are found in printed circuit, replace instrument cluster. If printed circuit if okay, replace temperature gauge.

Light Inoperative With High Coolant Temperature – Check for inoperative coolant temperature gauge circuit, repair/replace temperature gauge/circuit as necessary. If temperature gauge circuit is okay, replace defective instrument cluster.

Light Inoperative With Low Oil Pressure –Check for inoperative oil pressure gauge/switch circuit, repair/replace as necessary. If gauge circuit is okay, replace defective instrument cluster.

Light Always On – Check for inoperative coolant temperature and oil pressure gauge circuits. Replace coolant temperature and/or oil pressure gauge if necessary. If coolant temperature and oil pressure gauge circuits are okay, replace defective instrument cluster.

COOLANT TEMPERATURE GAUGE (ASTRO & SAFARI)

NOTE: If vehicle is equipped with electronic coolant temperature gauge, see ELECTRONIC INSTRUMENT CLUSTER (ASTRO & SAFARI) under TESTING & DIAGNOSIS.

Gauge Reads Cold When Engine Is Hot – 1) Check for blown GAGE fuse. If fuse is okay, remove terminal connector from sending unit. Turn ignition on. Connect test light between sending unit harness connector and ground. If test light DOES NOT illuminate, go to step **3)**.

2) If test light illuminates and temperature gauge reads HOT, wiring circuit to gauge is okay. Check/repair sending unit lead connector. If wire lead and connector are okay, replace sending unit. If gauge still reads COLD, replace coolant temperature gauge.

3) With ignition off, ground sending unit harness connector and check continuity between sending unit terminal at gauge and ground and between gauge ignition terminal and ground. Also check temperature gauge case ground. If all checks are okay, replace coolant temperature gauge.

Gauge Reads Hot When Engine Is Cold – 1) Turn ignition on. Disconnect terminal connector from temperature gauge sending unit. Gauge reading should go to COLD. If it does, replace sending unit.

2) If gauge continues to read HOT after replacing sending unit, check for short in wiring between sending unit and gauge. If no short is found, replace coolant temperature gauge.

Gauge Readings Are Inaccurate – 1) Check wiring for corroded or loose connections. If necessary, clean and tighten terminals and connections. Also check for resistance in temperature sending unit ground circuit. If terminals, connections and ground circuit are okay, go to next step.

2) Disconnect lead from temperature gauge sending unit. Using ohmmeter, test sending unit resistance. See TEMPERATURE GAUGE SENDING UNIT RESISTANCE table. If sending unit values are incorrect, replace sending unit.

TEMPERATURE GAUGE SENDING UNIT RESISTANCE

Degrees °F (°C)	Ohms
104 (40)	1365
257 (125)	55

COOLANT TEMPERATURE GAUGE ("S" & "T" SERIES)

Gauge Reads Cold When Engine Is Hot – 1) Check for blown GAGES fuse. If fuse is okay, disconnect connector from coolant temperature sending unit and turn ignition on. Connect test light from sending unit lead connector to ground. Gauge should read 260 (hot). If not, go to step **3)**.

2) If gauge reads 260, gauge is okay. Reconnect connector to sending unit. If gauge now reads 100, and engine is still hot, replace sending unit. If after replacing sending unit, gauge still reads near 100 with hot engine, gauge is also damaged and must be replaced.

3) If test light illuminates, circuit is okay. Replace gauge. If test light DOES NOT illuminate, connect test light to ignition terminal of gauge. If test light does illuminate, gauge is receiving voltage.

1991 SAFETY EQUIPMENT
Instrument Panels – All Others (Cont.)

4) Connect test light to gauge sending unit terminal, gauge reading should go to 260. If not, gauge is defective. If gauge does go to hot, repair open in circuit between gauge and sending unit.

Gauge Reads Hot When Engine Is Cold – 1) Turn ignition on. Remove connector from temperature gauge sensor. If gauge goes down to 100 (cold), replace externally shorted sending unit.

2) If temperature gauge continues to read 260, check for short to ground in wiring circuit between sending unit and gauge. If short is NOT found, replace temperature gauge.

Gauge Readings Are Inaccurate – 1) Check wiring for corroded or loose connections. Clean and tighten terminals and connections as necessary. Also check resistance in temperature sending unit ground circuit. If terminals, connections and ground circuit are okay, go to next step.

2) Disconnect connector from temperature gauge sending unit. Using an ohmmeter, test sending unit resistance. See TEMPERATURE GAUGE SENDING UNIT RESISTANCE table. If sending unit values are incorrect, replace temperature gauge sending unit.

COOLANT TEMPERATURE WARNING SYSTEM

Warning Light Inoperative – If warning light does not come on during bulb check, check or replace burned out light bulb. If bulb is okay, check for an open in circuit. Remove terminal lead from coolant temperature switch and ground lead. If warning light does not come on, repair open in circuit. If light does come on, replace switch.

ELECTRONIC INSTRUMENT CLUSTER (ASTRO & SAFARI)

NOTE: Replace electronic instrument cluster if any one of the following conditions exists; Cluster display is always dim, speedometer is inoperative or inaccurate (odometer operating correctly), one or both odometers do not operate properly (speedometer operating correctly), low fuel indicator does not light with low fuel level, temperature indicator does not light with engine coolant overheated or oil pressure indicator does not light at all.

Cluster Display Does Not Light – 1) Check ignition power to cluster, cluster ground and for an inoperative cluster. Disconnect large 17-pin connector from cluster.

2) Using a DVOM, measure voltage from harness connector pin terminal A13 to ground with ignition on. *See Fig. 1.* If battery voltage is present, go to next step. If DVOM reads less than battery voltage or zero, repair Pink/White wire from ignition.

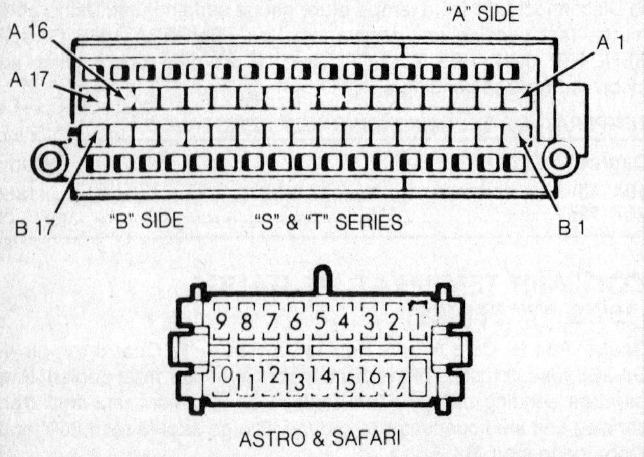
"A" SIDE
A 16
A 1
A 17
B 17
"B" SIDE
"S" & "T" SERIES
B 1
9 8 7 6 5 4 3 2 1
10 11 12 13 14 15 16 17
ASTRO & SAFARI
91A14514
Courtesy of General Motors Corp.

Fig. 1: Identifying Electronic Instrument Cluster Connector Terminals

3) Turn ignition off. Using an ohmmeter, measure resistance from harness connector pin terminals A15 and A16 to ground. If ohmmeter reads anything but 0-0.5 ohm, repair Black wires at pin terminals A15 and A16 to ground. If resistance is correct, go to next step.

4) If ignition power feed and ground circuits are okay, replace inoperative instrument cluster.

Cluster Display Does Not Dim With Lights On – 1) Check for open or shorted parking light power circuit, bad parking light switch and for an inoperative cluster. Turn parking lights and ignition on.

2) Using a DVOM, measure voltage between ground and pin terminal A8 of large 17-pin connector. If voltage reading is less than battery voltage, repair open or short in Brown wire. If voltage reading is okay, go to next step.

3) Using a DVOM, measure voltage between ground and pin terminal A8 of large 17-pin connector while adjusting panel light dimmer switch from high intensity to low intensity.

4) DVOM should read between zero and battery voltage. If not, repair Gray wire or replace parking light switch. If no problem is found, replace inoperative instrument cluster.

Cluster Display Does Not Switch Between English & Metric – 1) Check for inoperative cluster control switch, wiring, or inoperative cluster. Disconnect large 17-pin connector at cluster. Measure cluster control switch resistance between connector pin terminal A2 and ground. *See Fig. 1.*

2) Resistance should be zero in one position and open in the other. If switch does not respond as indicated, repair Light Blue wire between cluster and switch, switch or Black wire from switch to ground.

3) If switch and related wiring are okay, replace inoperative instrument cluster.

Speedometer & Odometer Do Not Operate – 1) Check for VSS signal. Disconnect large 17-pin connector from cluster and disconnect connector from Digital Ratio Adapter Controller (DRAC) that is mounted behind dash on bracket near radio.

2) Measure resistance of wire between connector pin terminal A1 of cluster connector and Light Blue/Black wire terminal of DRAC harness connector. If resistance is greater than zero ohms and the VSS circuit is working properly, replace inoperative instrument cluster.

Cluster Display Does Not Switch Between Total & Trip Odometer – 1) Check for inoperative cluster control switch or wiring. Disconnect large 17-pin connector from cluster. Using an ohmmeter, measure resistance between cluster connector pin A3 and ground. *See Fig. 1.*

2) Resistance should be zero in one position and open in the other. If switch does not respond as indicated, repair Light Green wire between cluster and switch, or replace switch, or repair Black wire from switch to ground.

3) If switch and related wiring are okay, replace inoperative instrument cluster.

Trip Odometer Does Not Reset – 1) Check for inoperative cluster control switch or wiring. Disconnect large 17-pin connector from cluster. Using an ohmmeter, measure resistance between cluster connector pin A5 and ground. *See Fig. 1.*

2) Resistance should be zero in one position and open in the other. If switch does not respond as indicated, repair Light Green/Black wire between cluster and switch, replace switch, or repair Black wire from switch to ground.

3) If switch and related wiring are okay, replace inoperative instrument cluster.

Fuel Gauge Is Inaccurate – 1) Check for shorts or opens in wiring between fuel tank sending unit and cluster, or for an inoperative fuel tank sending unit. Disconnect fuel gauge sending unit at fuel tank. Connect one lead of Instrument Panel Tester (J-33431) to Pink wire and other lead to ground.

2) Turn ignition on. Set tester resistance dial to zero ohms. Fuel gauge should read empty. Now set resistance dial to 35 ohms. Fuel gauge should read half full or have 7-8 segments illuminated. Next, set resistance dial to 90 ohms. Fuel gauge should read full or fully illuminated (digital gauge).

3) If fuel gauge responds correctly to tester, check Black wire to ground at fuel gauge sending unit. If Black wire is okay, replace fuel gauge sending unit.

4) If gauge does not respond as indicated, check Pink wire between fuel gauge sending unit and cluster. If wire is okay, replace inoperative cluster.

Temperature Gauge Is Inaccurate – 1) Check for shorts or opens in wiring between temperature sending unit and cluster, or for an inoperative temperature sending unit. Disconnect temperature sending unit at engine. Connect one lead of Instrument Panel Tester (J-33431) to Dark Green wire and other lead to ground.

2) Turn ignition on. Set tester resistance dials to 1400 ohms. Temperature gauge should read cold. Now set resistance dials to 400 ohms. Temperature gauge should read half or have 7-8 segments illuminated. Next, set resistance dials to zero ohms. Temperature gauge should read hot.

3) If temperature gauge responds correctly, replace temperature gauge sending unit. If gauge does not respond as indicated, check Dark Green wire between temperature gauge sending unit and cluster connector. If wire is okay, replace inoperative cluster.

Oil Pressure Gauge Inaccurate – 1) Check for shorts or opens in wiring between oil pressure sending unit and cluster or for inoperative oil pressure sending unit. Disconnect oil pressure sending unit at engine. Connect one lead of Instrument Panel Tester (J-33431) to Tan wire and other lead to ground.

2) Turn ignition on. Set tester resistance dial to zero ohms. Oil pressure should read low. Now set resistance dial to 35 ohms. Oil pressure gauge should read half or have 7-8 segments illuminated. Set resistance dial to 90 ohms. Oil pressure gauge should read high.

3) If fuel gauge responds correctly, replace oil pressure gauge sending unit. If gauge does not respond as indicated, check Tan wire between fuel gauge sending unit and cluster connector. If wire is okay, replace inoperative cluster.

Voltmeter Is Inaccurate – 1) Check for short, open, or high resistance between alternator Brown wire and cluster. Using a DVOM, measure voltage between battery terminals and measure voltage between Brown wire and ground.

2) If readings are different, repair Brown wire. If readings are the same, check Black ground wire for high resistance to ground. If Black wire is okay, replace inoperative instrument cluster.

ELECTRONIC INSTRUMENT CLUSTER ("S" & "T" SERIES)

NOTE: Replace electronic instrument cluster if any one of the following conditions exists; Cluster display is always dim, speedometer is inoperative or inaccurate (odometer operating correctly), one or both odometers do not operate properly (speedometer operating correctly), low fuel indicator does not light with low fuel level, temperature indicator does not light with engine coolant overheated or oil pressure indicator does not light at all.

Cluster Display Does Not Light – 1) Check ignition feed to cluster. Disconnect 34-pin connector from cluster. Using a voltmeter, measure voltage between instrument cluster connector terminal A15 and ground with ignition on. *See Fig. 1*.

2) If battery voltage is not present, repair open in Pink/White wire from ignition. If battery voltage is present, measure voltage between instrument cluster connector terminals A15 and B7.

3) If battery voltage is present, replace cluster. If battery voltage is not present, repair open in Black wire between ground and instrument cluster connector B7.

Cluster Display Does Not Dim With Lights On – 1) Disconnect 34-pin connector from cluster. Using a voltmeter, measure voltage between instrument cluster connector terminal A6 and ground with ignition and parking lights on. *See Fig. 1*.

2) If reading is less than battery voltage, repair open or short in Brown wire to instrument cluster connector terminal A6. If battery voltage is present, go to next step.

3) While still measuring voltage between terminal A6 and ground, adjust instrument panel light dimmer switch from high intensity to low intensity. If voltage does not drop as switch is turned from high to low intensity, check Brown wire between instrument cluster connector terminal A6 and park light switch. Repair as necessary.

4) If Brown wire is okay, check park light switch. Replace as necessary. If park light switch is okay, replace instrument cluster.

Speedometer & Odometers Do Not Operate – 1) Disconnect 34-pin connector from cluster. Disconnect Digital Ratio Adapter Controller (DRAC) connector. Using an ohmmeter, measure resistance between terminal A11 of instrument cluster connector and Light Blue/Black wire terminal of DRAC connector. *See Fig. 1*.

2) If resistance is greater than zero ohms, check vehicle speed sensor and ensure correct DRAC is installed. See VEHICLE SPEED SENSOR & DIGITAL RATIO ADAPTER CONTROLLER (DRAC) under TESTING & DIAGNOSIS. If vehicle speed sensor and DRAC are okay, replace instrument cluster.

Fuel Gauge Is Inaccurate – 1) Disconnect fuel gauge sending unit at fuel tank. Connect one lead of Signal Generator & Instrument Panel Tester (J-33431) to Pink wire of sending unit connector and other lead to ground. Turn ignition on and adjust resistance dials of tester to different settings and check fuel gauge. See FUEL GAUGE SENDER RESISTANCE SPECIFICATIONS table.

FUEL GAUGE SENDER RESISTANCE SPECIFICATIONS

Resistance Setting	Fuel Gauge Reading
Zero Ohms	Empty
35 Ohms	Half Full (7-8 Segments Lit)
90 Ohms	Full

2) If fuel gauge responds correctly, check Black (ground) wire from fuel sending unit and repair as necessary. If Black wire is okay, replace fuel tank sending unit.

3) If fuel gauge does not respond correctly, check Pink wire between fuel sending unit and instrument cluster connector terminal A12. *See Fig. 1*. Repair as necessary. If Pink wire is okay, replace instrument cluster.

Temperature Gauge Is Inaccurate – 1) Disconnect temperature sending unit and connect one lead of Signal Generator & Instrument Panel Tester (J-33431) to Dark Green wire of temperature sending unit connector and other lead to ground. Turn ignition on and adjust resistance dials of tester to different settings and check temperature gauge. See TEMPERATURE GAUGE SENDER RESISTANCE SPECIFICATIONS table.

TEMPERATURE GAUGE SENDER RESISTANCE SPECIFICATIONS

Resistance Setting	Temperature Gauge Reading
1400 Ohms	Cold
400 Ohms	Warm (7-8 Segments Lit)
55 Ohms	Hot

2) If gauge responds correctly, replace temperature sending unit. If gauge does not respond correctly, check Dark Green wire between temperature sending unit and instrument cluster connector terminal A1. *See Fig. 1*. Repair as necessary. If Dark Green wire is okay, replace instrument cluster.

Oil Pressure Gauge Is Inaccurate – 1) Disconnect oil pressure sending unit and connect one lead of Signal Generator & Instrument Panel Tester (J-33431) to Tan wire of oil pressure sending unit connector and other lead to ground. Turn ignition on and adjust resistance dials of tester to different settings and check oil pressure gauge. See OIL PRESSURE GAUGE SENDER RESISTANCE SPECIFICATIONS table.

OIL PRESSURE GAUGE SENDER RESISTANCE SPECIFICATIONS

Resistance Setting	Oil Pressure Gauge Reading
Zero Ohms	Low
35 Ohms	Half (7-8 Segments Lit)
90 Ohms	High

2) If gauge responds correctly, replace oil pressure sending unit. If gauge does not respond correctly, check Tan wire between oil pressure sending unit and instrument cluster connector terminal A2. *See Fig. 1*. Repair as necessary. If Tan wire is okay, replace instrument cluster.

Voltmeter Is Inaccurate – 1) Measure and record voltage between battery terminals. Disconnect 34-pin instrument cluster connector. Measure voltage between instrument cluster connector terminal A15

1991 SAFETY EQUIPMENT
Instrument Panels – All Others (Cont.)

and chassis ground. *See Fig. 1*. If voltage readings are different, repair Pink/Black wire from instrument cluster connector terminal A15. If voltage readings are the same, go to next step.

2) Using an ohmmeter, measure resistance between ground and instrument cluster terminals A9 and B7. If high resistance is present in either circuit, repair open or short in appropriate Black wire. If wires are okay, replace instrument cluster.

FUEL GAUGE

NOTE: If vehicle is equipped with electronic fuel gauge, see appropriate ELECTRONIC INSTRUMENT CLUSTER under TESTING & DIAGNOSIS.

Gauge Stays At EMPTY Position – Check for fuel in tank. Turn ignition on. Check for a grounded fuel gauge circuit by disconnecting lead at fuel tank. Fuel gauge should now read past FULL mark. If gauge does not read past FULL mark, replace fuel gauge sending unit in tank. If gauge still reads EMPTY, repair short to ground between gauge and fuel tank.

Gauge Stays At FULL Position – 1) Turn ignition on. Check for open circuit between gauge and sending unit by disconnecting sending unit lead at fuel tank. Jumper wire sending unit lead to ground and note gauge reading.

2) If fuel gauge now reads EMPTY, replace fuel gauge sending unit. If fuel gauge still reads FULL or beyond, repair open in wire between gauge and fuel tank.

Gauge Reading Is Inaccurate –1) Check wiring for corroded or loose connections. Clean and tighten as required. If wiring and connections are okay, remove fuel gauge sending unit. Using an ohmmeter, test sending unit resistance. See FUEL GAUGE SENDING UNIT RESISTANCE table.

2) If sending unit values are correct, disconnect front body wiring harness connector at engine firewall. Connect Gauge Tester (J-24538-A) to terminal No. 30 (Purple wire). Turn ignition on. If gauge reads accurately when connected to Gauge Tester, check wiring between fuel tank and front connector.

3) If gauge reads between 1/4 and 1/2 full with tester set at 90 ohms, replace fuel gauge.

FUEL GAUGE SENDING UNIT RESISTANCE

Position	Ohms
Empty	1
1/2 Full	44
Full	88

OIL PRESSURE GAUGE

NOTE: If vehicle is equipped with electronic oil pressure gauge, see appropriate ELECTRONIC INSTRUMENT CLUSTER under TESTING & DIAGNOSIS.

Gauge Reads "0" With Engine Running – 1) Check oil level and add if necessary. Test oil pressure with manual gauge and adapter. If oil pressure reading is good on manual gauge tester, check for grounded gauge circuit by disconnecting lead at sending unit.

2) Turn ignition on. Oil pressure gauge should now read 80. If gauge stays at zero, disconnect lead from gauge. Gauge should now read 80. If gauge reads 80, find short to ground between gauge and sending unit. If gauge still reads zero, replace gauge and test oil pressure gauge sending unit resistance. See OIL PRESSURE GAUGE SENDING UNIT RESISTANCE table. Replace sending unit if it reads one ohm with engine running.

Gauge Constantly Reads 80 Or More – 1) Check for open circuit between gauge and sending unit by disconnecting lead at sending unit. Connect lead to ground and note reading on gauge.

2) If oil pressure gauge reads zero, replace oil pressure gauge sending unit. If oil pressure gauge still reads 80 or more, find open wire between gauge and sending unit.

Gauge Reading Is Inaccurate – Disconnect lead from oil pressure sending unit. Connect Gauge Tester (J-24538-A) for Astro and Safari or (J-33431) for "S" & "T" Series to lead and ground. Turn ignition on. If gauge reads accurately, replace oil pressure sending unit. If gauge still reads inaccurately, replace oil pressure gauge.

OIL PRESSURE GAUGE SENDING UNIT RESISTANCE

Position	Ohms
Engine Off	1
Engine Running	[1] 44

[1] – With oil pressure at about 40 psi (2.8 kg/cm²).

OIL PRESSURE WARNING SYSTEM

Turn ignition on. If warning light does not come on, check for burned-out bulb. If bulb is okay, check for an open in warning switch circuit (NOT same circuit as sending unit). Remove lead connector from oil pressure switch and connect to ground. If warning light DOES NOT come on, find open in circuit. If light does come on, replace warning switch.

VEHICLE SPEED SENSOR & DIGITAL RATIO ADAPTER CONTROLLER (DRAC)

Speedometer & Odometer Are Inaccurate – Ensure that correct digital ratio adapter controller is installed for specific final drive ratio. Replace if necessary.

Speedometer & Odometer Do Not Operate Properly – 1) Disconnect Digital Ratio Adapter Controller (DRAC). Turn ignition on. Measure voltage between Pink/Black wire of DRAC harness connector and good chassis ground.

2) If battery voltage is present, go to next step. If voltage is less than battery voltage, check for blown BRAKE fuse and replace if necessary. If fuse is okay, check for an open or short in Pink/Black wire between fuse block and DRAC harness connector. Repair as necessary.

3) On Astro and Safari, measure voltage between Pink/Black wire terminal and Black/White wire terminal of DRAC harness connector. If battery voltage is present, go to step **5)**. If battery voltage is not present, check for open or short in Black/White wire and repair as necessary.

4) On "S" and "T" Series, measure voltage between Light Blue/Black wire terminal and Black wire terminal of DRAC harness connector. If battery voltage is present, go to next step. If battery voltage is not present, check for open or short in Black wire and repair as necessary.

5) Raise and support vehicle. Start engine and place transmission in Drive. Measure voltage between Purple/White wire terminal and Light Green/Black wire terminal of DRAC harness connector.

6) If voltage is present, go to next step. If voltage is not present, check both wires for shorts or opens and repair as necessary. If wires are okay, replace vehicle speed sensor.

7) With vehicle still raised, engine running and transmission in Drive, connect DRAC harness connector to digital ratio adapter controller. Backprobe DRAC harness connector and measure voltage changes between Pink/Black wire terminal (Light Blue/Black wire terminal on "S" and "T" Series) and Black/White wire terminal (Black wire terminal on "S" and "T" Series) while varying vehicle speed.

8) If voltage does not change with vehicle speed, go to next step. If voltage varies with vehicle speed, replace DRAC.

9) Measure voltage between DRAC harness connector Yellow wire terminal and Black/White wire terminal (Black wire terminal on "S" and "T" Series) while varying vehicle speed.

10) If voltage does not vary with vehicle speed, test instrument cluster. See appropriate ELECTRONIC INSTRUMENT CLUSTER tests under TESTING & DIAGNOSIS. If voltage varies with vehicle speed, replace DRAC.

VOLTMETER

NOTE: If vehicle is equipped with electronic voltmeter, see appropriate ELECTRONIC INSTRUMENT CLUSTER tests under TESTING & DIAGNOSIS.

1) Measure voltage across battery terminals. Voltage should be approximately 12 volts. If battery is discharged, recharge battery and perform load test. Repair cause of discharged battery.

2) With ignition on and battery terminals cleaned and connected, observe voltmeter with battery charger in operation. Voltmeter should read 12 volts or more. If not, check for high resistance in voltmeter terminal connections. Clean and tighten connections.

3) If voltmeter reading is still low, apply 12 volts directly to positive terminal of voltmeter. If voltmeter does not respond accurately, replace voltmeter.

REMOVAL & INSTALLATION

DIGITAL RATIO ADAPTER CONTROLLER

CAUTION: Static electricity can destroy integrated circuits within DRAC. Before servicing DRAC, ground yourself and work area to discharge stored electricity.

Removal & Installation – Disconnect negative battery cable. Unplug instrument panel harness from DRAC. See DRAC LOCATIONS table. To install, reverse removal procedure.

DRAC LOCATIONS

Model	Location
Astro	Under dash, right of steering column
Safari	Mounted on bracket, on left side of radio
"S" & "T" Series	Behind glove box, mounted on ECM bracket

GAUGES

NOTE: If vehicle is equipped with electronic gauges, instrument cluster is NOT serviceable and is to be replaced as complete assembly. See INSTRUMENT CLUSTER under REMOVAL & INSTALLATION.

Removal & Installation (Astro & Safari) – Remove instrument cluster. See INSTRUMENT CLUSTER under REMOVAL & INSTALLATION. Remove cluster case retainer screws and retainer (if equipped). Remove individual gauge mounting screws. Carefully remove gauge. *See Fig. 2.* To install, reverse removal procedure.

INSTRUMENT CLUSTER

Removal & Installation (Astro & Safari) – **1)** Disconnect negative battery terminal. Remove instrument cluster trim plate screws. *See Fig. 2.* Remove lower steering column trim plate and instrument cluster trim plate.

2) Remove instrument cluster screws. Touch hands to ground to discharge static electricity before pulling out cluster to disconnect instrument cluster harness and speedometer cable. Remove instrument cluster. To install, reverse removal procedure.

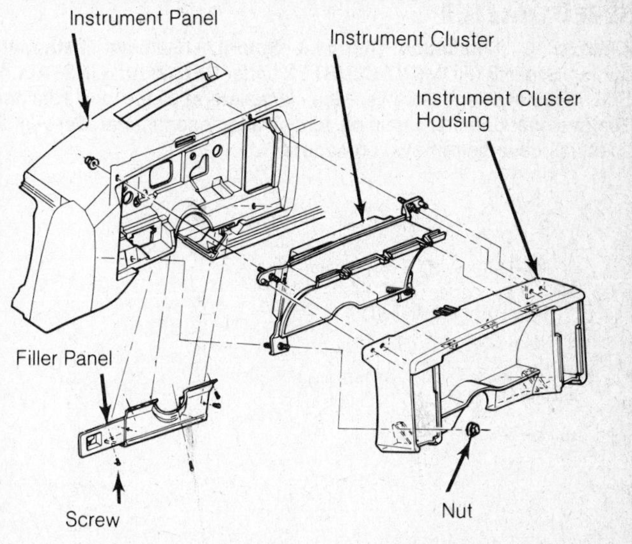

Instrument Panel
Instrument Cluster
Instrument Cluster Housing
Filler Panel
Screw
Nut

16142 Courtesy of General Motors Corp.

Fig. 3: Exploded View of Instrument Cluster ("S" & "T" Series)

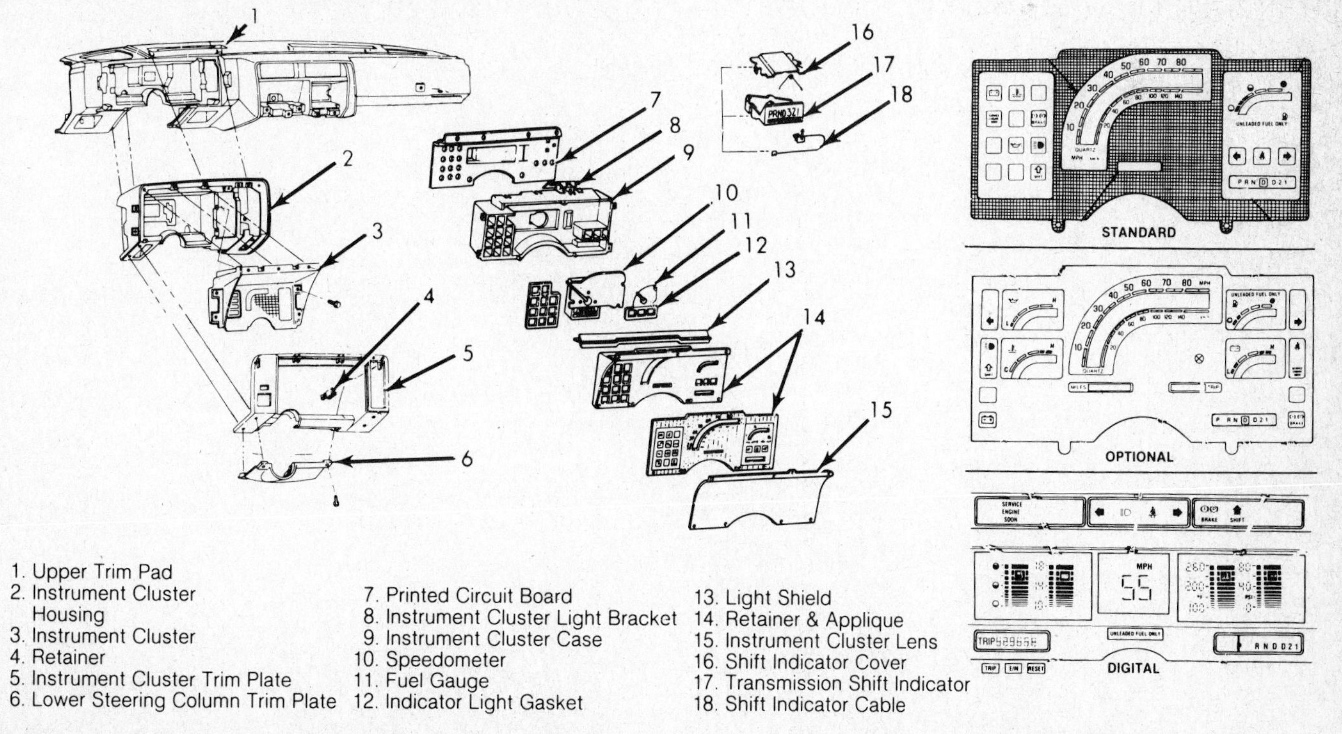

1. Upper Trim Pad
2. Instrument Cluster Housing
3. Instrument Cluster
4. Retainer
5. Instrument Cluster Trim Plate
6. Lower Steering Column Trim Plate
7. Printed Circuit Board
8. Instrument Cluster Light Bracket
9. Instrument Cluster Case
10. Speedometer
11. Fuel Gauge
12. Indicator Light Gasket
13. Light Shield
14. Retainer & Applique
15. Instrument Cluster Lens
16. Shift Indicator Cover
17. Transmission Shift Indicator
18. Shift Indicator Cable
STANDARD
OPTIONAL
DIGITAL

71143 Courtesy of General Motors Corp.

Fig. 2: Exploded View of Instrument Clusters (Astro & Safari)

1991 SAFETY EQUIPMENT
Instrument Panels – All Others (Cont.)

Removal & Installation ("S" & "T" Series) – 1) Disconnect negative battery terminal. Remove light switch trim plate and disconnect light switch harness. Remove A/C-heater control assembly and disconnect A/C-heater control assembly harness.

2) Remove filler panel (lower steering column panel). *See Fig. 3.* Remove instrument cluster housing nuts and cluster. Touch hands to ground to discharge static electricity before pulling out instrument cluster to disconnect harness connections and remove cluster. To install, reverse removal procedure.

SPEEDOMETER

Removal & Installation (Astro & Safari) – Remove instrument cluster. See INSTRUMENT CLUSTER under REMOVAL & INSTALLATION. Remove lens screws, lens, faceplate/applique and retainer. Remove speedometer retaining screws and speedometer. *See Fig. 2.* To install, reverse removal procedure.

ELECTRONIC CLUSTER TRIP SWITCH

Removal & Installation (Astro & Safari) – Disconnect negative battery terminal. Remove instrument cluster. See INSTRUMENT CLUSTER under REMOVAL & INSTALLATION. Disconnect instrument cluster harness from trip switch panel. Remove screws and trip switch panel. To install, reverse removal procedure.

VEHICLE SPEED SENSOR

Removal & Installation – Raise and support vehicle. Unplug vehicle speed sensor harness at transmission tailshaft housing. Remove hold-down bolt, or unscrew vehicle speed sensor. Catch transmission fluid in a container. Remove "O" ring. To install, reverse removal procedure and recheck fluid level.

1991 SAFETY EQUIPMENT
Rear Window Defogger

Lumina APV, Silhouette, Trans Sport, "C" & "K" Series, "R" & "V" Series, "S" & "T" Series

DESCRIPTION & OPERATION

Rear window defogger consists of control switch on dash panel, timer relay and heating element grid. On "C" and "K" Series, timer relay is incorporated in control switch. On all other models, timer relay is a separate unit. For timer relay location, see TIMER RELAY LOCATION table. Grid is bonded to inside surface of rear window. Current enters grid on left side and is grounded on right side of cab. *See Fig. 1.*

Ignition switch must be in RUN position to operate system. If control switch is left on, timer relay allows current to flow to grid for 10 minutes, then stops current flow to grid. The first time the control switch is activated, timer relay allows current flow to grid for 10 minutes.

Each time control switch is activated after initially activating control switch, timer relay will allow current flow to grid for 5 minutes. If ignition switch is turned off then back on, timer relay resets to 10 minute cycle. Any time control switch or ignition switch is turned off, current stops flowing to grid.

TIMER RELAY LOCATION

Application	Location
Lumina APV, Silhouette & Trans Sport	Connected to relay panel, under right side of dash panel
"C" & "K" Series	Incorporated in control switch
"R" & "V" Series	Below fuse block
"S" & "T" Series	On brake pedal support bracket

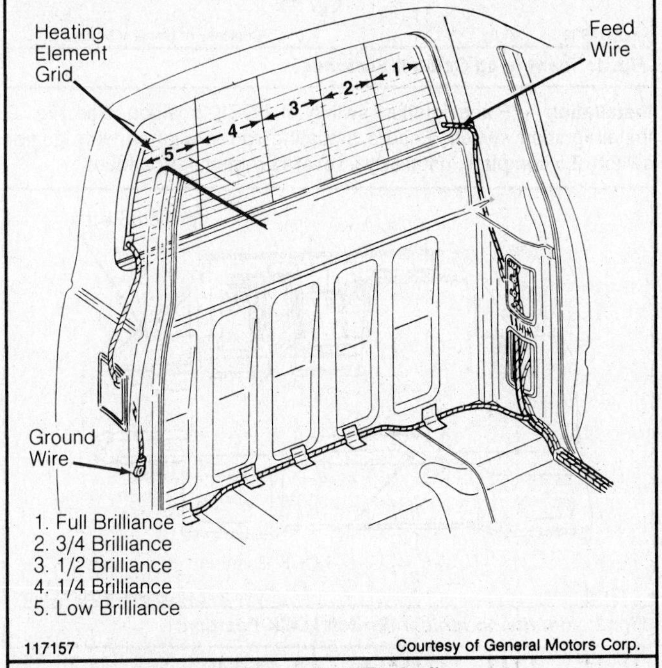
Heating Element Grid
Feed Wire
1
2
3
4
5
Ground Wire
1. Full Brilliance
2. 3/4 Brilliance
3. 1/2 Brilliance
4. 1/4 Brilliance
5. Low Brilliance
117157
Courtesy of General Motors Corp.

Fig. 1: Rear Window Defogger Grid (Typical)

TROUBLE SHOOTING

DEFOGGER DOES NOT HEAT WINDOW

Check circuit breaker:
- 30 amp ACC/BATT on "C" and "K" Series
- 30 amp REAR DEFOG on Lumina APV, Silhouette and Trans Sport
- 30 amp PWR/ACC on "R" and "V" Series and "S" and "T" Series

Check fuse:
- 20 amp GAGES on "C" and "K" Series
- 10 amp IGN on Lumina APV, Silhouette and Trans Sport
- 20 amp IGN on "R" and "V" Series
- 20 amp IGN/GAGES on "S" and "T" Series

Check control switch for proper operation. Check for voltage at left grid connection. Check grid ground circuit. Check for open circuits in grid. See GRID TEST & REPAIR.

GRID TEST & REPAIR

1) Start engine and turn defogger system on. Ground test light and lightly probe each grid line. Move test light from feed wire side of grid to ground side. *See Fig. 1.*

2) Test light should gradually dim as it is moved across grid. Be sure to check each grid in at least 2 places to avoid the possibility of bridging a gap with test light.

3) If test light shows full brilliance at both ends of grid, check for loose ground wire contact at cab body. If test light goes out as it is moved across grid, a break has been detected. Use a grease pencil to mark break(s) on outside of window.

4) To repair grid, turn system off and disconnect negative battery cable. Clean area to be repaired with steel wool. Wipe area clean with denatured alcohol. Be sure to clean 1/4" (6 mm) beyond each side of break.

5) With glass at room temperature of 70-90°F (20-32°C), position repair template over area to be repaired. Apply grid repair material to grid and remove template. Allow repair area to air dry for at least 24 hours.

6) Test defogger operation to verify repair. If repair appears discolored, apply a coating of tincture of iodine. Allow iodine to dry for 30 seconds and carefully wipe off excess.

WIRING DIAGRAMS

See appropriate chassis wiring diagram in WIRING DIAGRAMS.

1991 SAFETY & EQUIPMENT
Steering Column Switches

Astro, Blazer, Bravada, Jimmy, Lumina APV, Safari, Sierra, Silhouette, Sonoma, Trans Sport, "C" & "K" Series, "G" Series, "P" Series, "R" & "V" Series, "S" & "T" Series

TESTING

HAZARD WARNING SWITCH

1) Turn ignition on and operate turn signals. If turn signals operate, check stop/hazard fuse. If fuse is okay, replace hazard flasher. Operate hazard flasher system. If system does not operate, go to step **2)**. If fuse is blown, replace stop/hazard fuse. If new fuse blows, repair short to ground in turn signal circuit(s) or in stoplight circuit.

2) Using a test light, check for voltage at Brown wire at turn signal steering column connector under dash. If no voltage is present, repair open circuit between flasher and connector.

3) If voltage is present and connections at steering column connector are okay, check output voltage from turn signal switch at Light Blue, Blue, Yellow, and Dark Green wires. If there is no output voltage, replace turn signal switch.

HORN

Horn Inoperative - Disconnect turn signal switch connector. Connect jumper wire between Black wire at connector and ground. If horn sounds, replace horn switch. If horn does not sound, check horn relay or check horn circuit from convenience center. See appropriate chassis diagram in WIRING DIAGRAMS.

Horn Sounds Continuously - Disconnect turn signal switch connector. If horn stops, replace horn switch. If horn does not stop, check for a defective horn relay or short to ground in horn circuit. Replace or repair as necessary.

TURN SIGNAL SWITCH

One Side Inoperative - **1)** Turn hazard warning system on. If one or more bulbs are inoperative, use a test light to check circuit at light bulb sockets. If test light illuminates, check bulb socket ground circuit.

2) If bulb socket is properly grounded, repair open wiring between bulb socket and turn signal switch. If flasher can be heard, but bulbs do not light, disconnect each circuit to locate and repair open or short circuit to ground.

Both Sides Inoperative - **1)** Turn hazard warning system on. If all turn signals come on, replace turn signal fuse. If replacement fuse blows, repair short to ground in turn signal circuit(s).

2) If turn signal fuse is okay and hazard warning system operates turn signals, replace turn signal flasher. If turn signals still fail to operate, check steering column connector. If connector is okay, replace turn signal switch.

WIPER SWITCH

For testing information on wiper switch, see appropriate WIPER/WASHER SYSTEMS article.

REMOVAL & INSTALLATION

IGNITION SWITCH

***NOTE:** It is not necessary to remove steering wheel. Ignition switch is mounted on top of steering column, near front of dash.*

Removal - **1)** Remove steering column-to-dash panel bracket. Lower steering column. Remove ignition switch retaining screws. Place ignition switch lock cylinder in LOCK position.

2) If cylinder lock was removed, the actuating rod to the switch should be pulled up until there is a definite stop, then moved down one detent, which is the LOCK position. Disconnect electrical harness connectors. Remove ignition switch assembly. *See Fig. 1*.

***NOTE:** Use only specified screws. Using screws that are too long may prevent column from compressing under impact.*

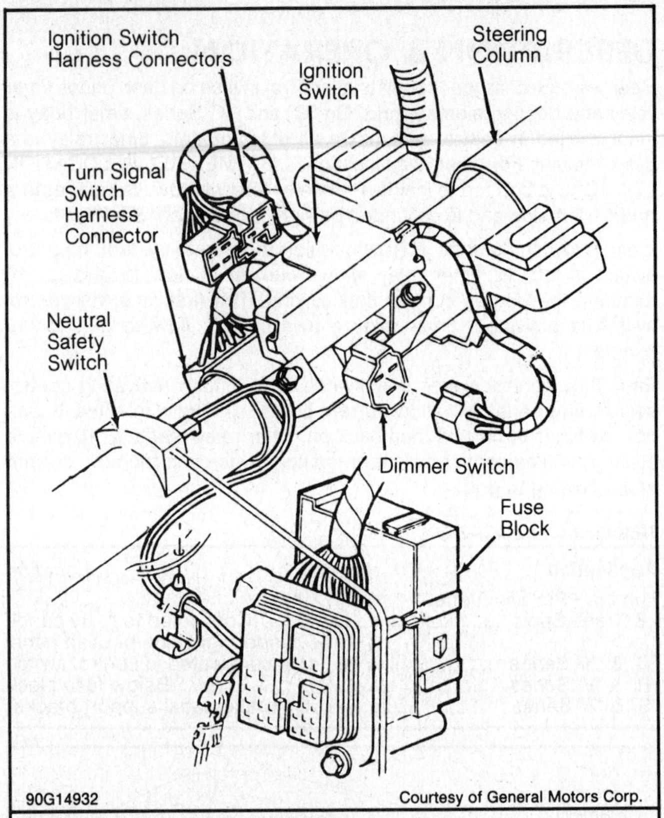
Ignition Switch Harness Connectors
Steering Column
Ignition Switch
Turn Signal Switch Harness Connector
Neutral Safety Switch
Dimmer Switch
Fuse Block
90G14932
Courtesy of General Motors Corp.

Fig. 1: Identifying Column Switches

Installation - Place ignition switch in LOCK position. *See Fig. 2.* Install ignition switch. Ensure actuating rod is aligned with ignition switch. To complete installation, reverse removal procedure.

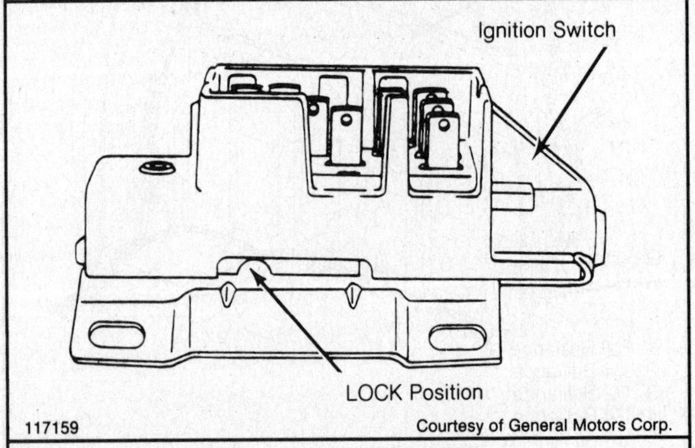
Ignition Switch
LOCK Position
117159
Courtesy of General Motors Corp.

Fig. 2: Identifying Ignition Switch LOCK Position

LOCK CYLINDER

Removal - **1)** Disconnect negative battery terminal. Remove steering wheel. Using Lock Plate Compressor (J-23653-A), compress lock plate and pry snap ring from groove. *See Fig. 3.* Discard snap ring. Remove lock plate. Lift turn signal switch far enough to slip over end of shaft. It is not necessary to remove turn signal switch completely.

2) Place key in lock cylinder. Turn key to RUN position. Remove lock retaining screw, being careful not to drop screw down column. Rotate lock cylinder to align cylinder key with keyway in housing. *See Fig. 4.* Pull cylinder from housing.

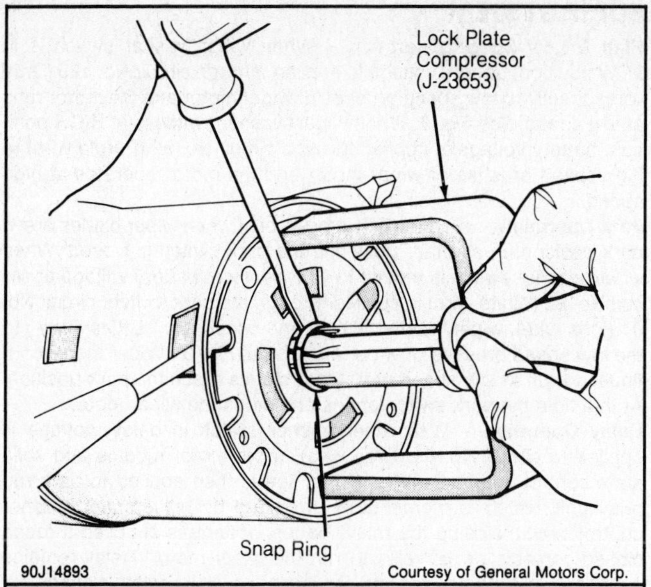
Lock Plate
Compressor
(J-23653)
Snap Ring
90J14893
Courtesy of General Motors Corp.

Fig. 3: Removing Lock Plate & Snap Ring

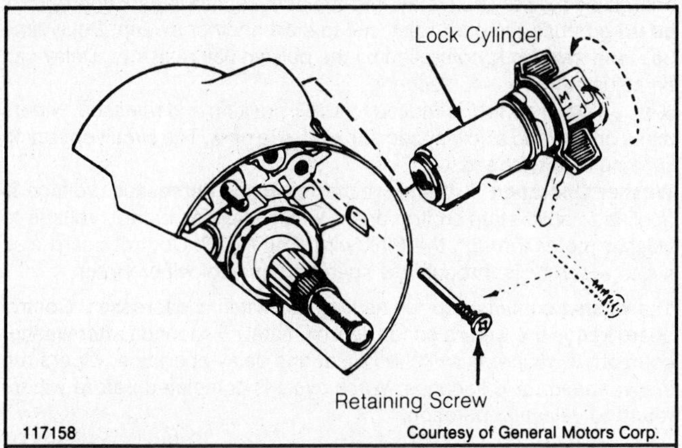
Lock Cylinder
Retaining Screw
117158
Courtesy of General Motors Corp.

Fig. 4: Removing Lock Cylinder Assembly

Installation - To install, hold lock cylinder while rotating key clockwise to stop. Align cylinder key and housing keyway. Insert cylinder into cylinder key/housing keyway assembly. To complete installation, reverse removal procedure.

TURN SIGNAL/COMBINATION SWITCH

Removal - 1) Remove steering wheel and instrument panel trim cover. Remove lock plate cover. Screw center post of Lock Plate Compressor (J-23653-A) onto steering shaft as far as it will go. Compress lock plate by turning center post nut clockwise. *See Fig. 3.*

2) Pry retaining ring out of shaft. Remove lock plate compressor. Remove lock plate and remove turn signal lever. Press hazard warning knob inward and unscrew. Remove hazard warning knob.

3) Remove turn signal switch mounting screws. Pull switch connector out of bracket and feed switch connector through column support bracket and pull turn signal switch straight up. Guide wiring harness through column housing and wire protector. Remove wire protector.

4) Position turn signal and shifter housing in low position. Remove harness cover by pulling toward the lower end of column. Pull turn signal switch straight up, guiding wiring harness and cover through the column housing.

NOTE: Use only specified screws. Using screws that are too long may prevent column from compressing under impact.

Installation - 1) On tilt columns, feed connector down through the housing and under mounting bracket. Install cover on harness. On all columns, position turn signal switch in neutral position. Pull out on hazard warning knob.

2) Install turn signal switch lever. Install mounting screws, instrument panel trim plate, hazard warning knob, washer, upper bearing preload spring and cancelling cam onto the upper end of shaft.

3) Screw center post of Lock Plate Compressor (J-23653-C) onto steering shaft as far as it will go. Install NEW retaining ring over center post. Place "C" bar over the center post. Compress lock plate by turning nut clockwise.

4) Slide new retaining ring down the tapered center post into the shaft groove. Remove lock plate compressor. Install cover on lock plate and snap into position. Install steering wheel.

WIPER SWITCH

See TURN SIGNAL/COMBINATION SWITCH under REMOVAL & INSTALLATION.

TORQUE SPECIFICATIONS

TORQUE SPECIFICATIONS

Application	Ft. Lbs. (N.m)
Steering Column Support Bracket Nuts/Bolts	22 (30)
Steering Wheel Retaining Nut	30 (41)
	INCH Lbs. (N.m)
Ignition Switch-To-Column Screws	35 (4.0)
Lock Cylinder Retaining Screw	22 (2.5)
Turn Signal Switch Screws	35 (4.0)

1991 SAFETY EQUIPMENT
Wiper/Washer Systems – Astro & Safari

DESCRIPTION

The wiper system consists of a permanent magnet, positive park wiper motor; radio frequency interference suppressor; multi-function switch and wiring harness. Wiper motor drives a crank arm attached to a transmission and link assembly mounted in front of the windshield in fresh air plenum.

The transmission transfers rotary motion from wiper motor into reciprocating motion at the wiper drive shaft. Wiper motor is protected by circuit breaker for protection from blade blockage. Circuit breaker resets automatically after cooling off.

Two different systems are available. The base system uses a windshield wiper motor with a high, low and mist mode. The optional system motor includes an additional pulse mode.

Pulse system uses an integrated circuit board, positioned inside wiper housing cover, to control the pulse function. The multi-function switch used in the pulse system incorporates a variable resistor (rheostat) to set rate of pulse to wiper motor circuit board.

When pulse system is in pulse mode, wipers make single strokes with an adjustable time interval between strokes. Time interval is controlled by a solid state pulse/speed/wash control, located in the wiper motor module. Duration of the relay interval is determined by the delay resistance in wiper/washer switch.

OPERATION

BASE SYSTEM

High & Low Speed Operation – The motor has 3 brushes, referred to as common, low speed and high speed. With ignition on, battery voltage is applied to both the low and high speed fixed contacts of the column switch. Low and high speed brushes of the wiper motor are connected to column switch through terminals "C" and "D". *See Fig. 1.*

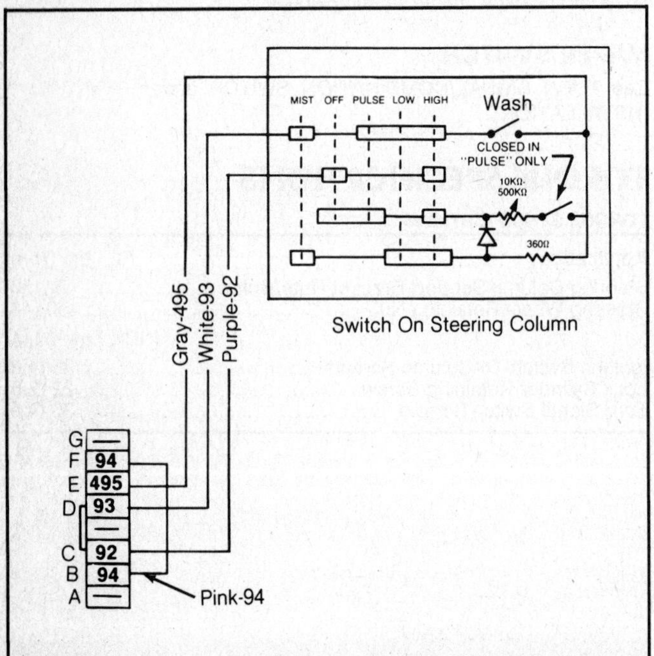
MIST OFF PULSE LOW HIGH
Wash
CLOSED IN "PULSE" ONLY
10KΩ-500KΩ
360Ω
Switch On Steering Column
Gray-495
White-93
Purple-92
G
F 94
E 495
D 93
C 92
B 94
A
Pink-94

90J04620 Courtesy of General Motors Corp.

Fig. 1: Wiper/Washer Switch Wiring Diagram

Armature is grounded through a common brush by a ground strap. Moving column switch to LOW or HIGH speed position, completes respective brush circuit to 12 volts at column switch and the wiper motor runs at selected speed.

Washer Operation – Actuating washer portion of column switch completes washer pump motor circuit to ground. With column switch in WASH position, wiper switch is mechanically moved to LOW position. This dual function simultaneously starts wiper motor and washer operation.

PULSE SYSTEM

High & Low Speed Operation – When wiper/washer switch is in LOW position, battery voltage is applied through circuit No. 495 (Gray wire) directly to low speed brushes of wiper motor and the motor runs at low speed. *See Fig. 3.* When wiper/washer switch is in HIGH position, battery voltage is applied through circuit No. 92 (Purple wire) to high speed brushes of wiper motor and the motor operates at high speed.

Park Operation – Park switch is open only when wiper blades are in park position. In all other positions the park switch is closed. When wiper/washer switch is moved to OFF position, battery voltage at circuit No. 93 (White wire) is applied through the park switch, circuit No. 94 (Pink wire), wiper/washer switch and circuit No. 91 (Gray wire) to the low speed brushes of wiper motor. *See Fig. 3* . Wiper motor continues to run at low speed until wiper blades reach the park position. At that time the park switch opens and stops the wiper motor.

Delay Operation – With wiper/washer switch in delay, voltage is applied to circuit No. 91 (Gray wire), wiper motor module and solid state control board. *See Fig. 3.* Voltage is then applied to park/run relay coil, which is momentarily grounded by pulse/speed/washer control circuit, closing the relay. Battery voltage is supplied through closed contacts of the relay to run the wiper motor. Relay remains energized as long as contacts of park/run switch remain closed.

When wiper blades have reached park, park/run switch opens, de-energizing the park/run relay. Wiper blades remain in park until control board grounds the park/relay coil to start another sweep. Delay time between sweeps is controlled by the pulse delay resistors. Delay can be adjusted from 0-43 seconds.

Mist – When control is moved to MIST position and released, wipers make one sweep at low speed and return to park. The circuit operation is same as low speed.

Washer Operation – When washer switch is depressed, voltage is applied to solid state control board which supplies battery voltage to washer motor through the Pink wire. *See Fig. 3.* Control board also starts wiper cycle through low speed brushes of wiper motor.

The washer continues to run as long as switch is depressed. Control board keeps the wipers on for approximately 6 seconds after washer goes off. If washer is switched on during delay operation, wipers run in low speed for 6 seconds. Wash cycle is completed before wipers return to delayed operation.

TESTING

NOTE: Ensure wiper fuse is not blown. Replace if necessary.

WIPERS INOPERATIVE IN ANY MODE

1) Disconnect pulse wiper switch connector No. C236. *See Fig. 2* . Connect voltmeter between circuit No. 93 (White wire) at wiper/washer switch connector C236 to ground. *See Fig. 3.* If battery voltage is present, go to step **3)**.

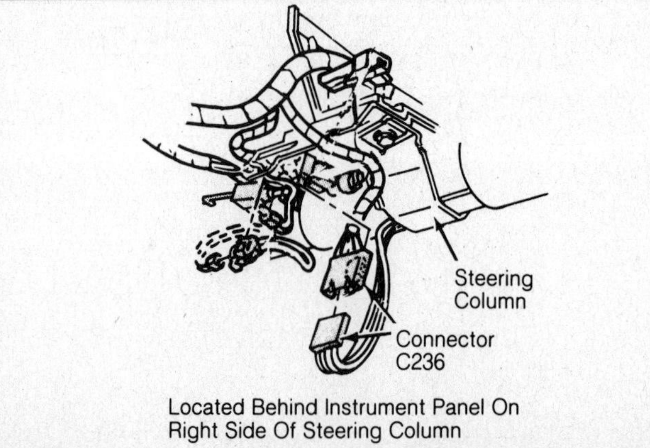
Steering Column
Connector C236
Located Behind Instrument Panel On Right Side Of Steering Column

90D04622 Courtesy of General Motors Corp.

Fig. 2: Locating Pulse Windshield Connector C236

Wiper/Washer Systems – Astro & Safari (Cont.)

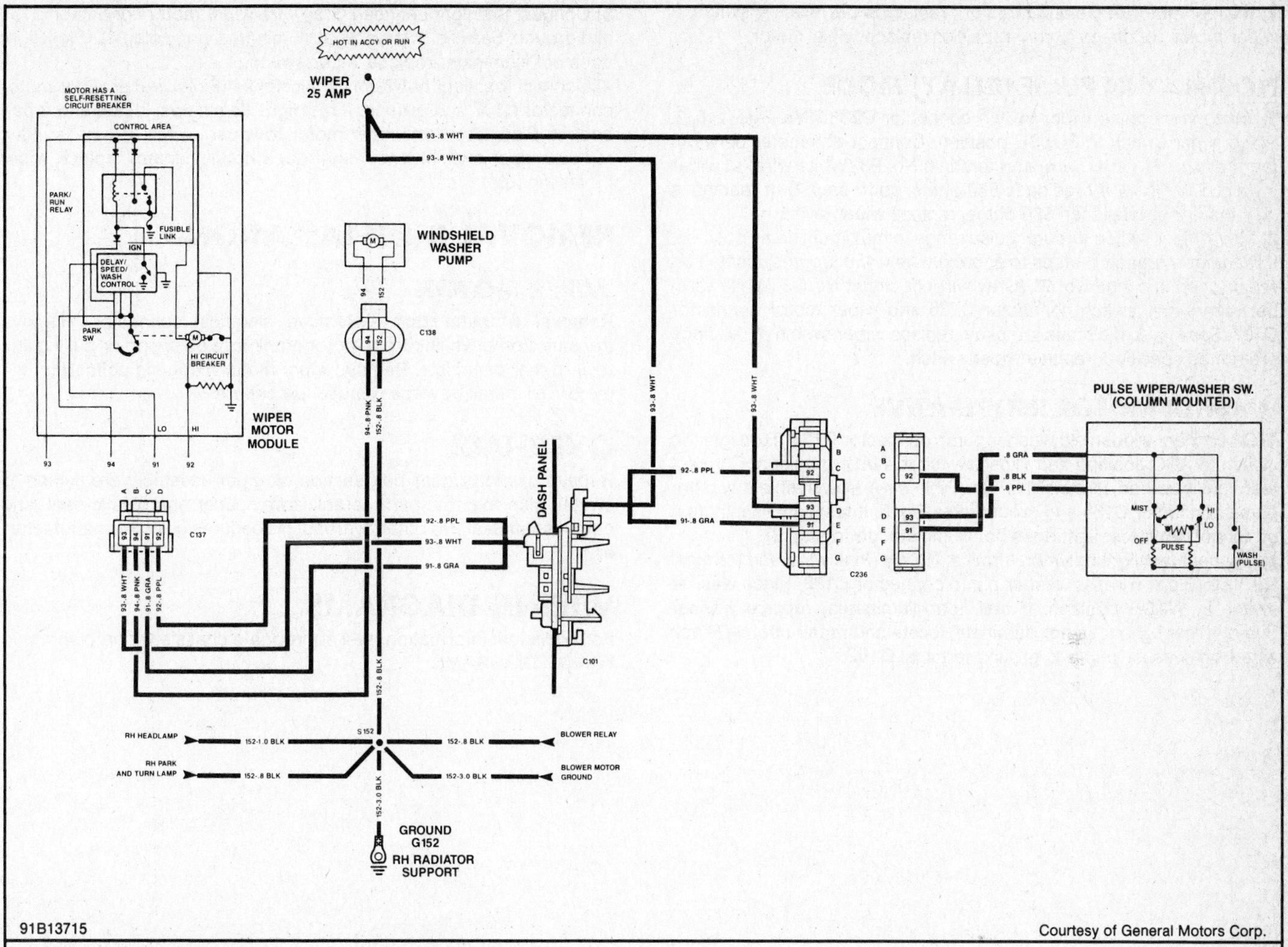

HOT IN ACCY OR RUN
WIPER
25 AMP
MOTOR HAS A SELF-RESETTING CIRCUIT BREAKER
CONTROL AREA
PARK/ RUN RELAY
FUSIBLE LINK
IGN
DELAY/ SPEED/ WASH CONTROL
PARK SW
HI CIRCUIT BREAKER
LO
HI
WIPER MOTOR MODULE
93
94
91
92
93-.8 WHT
WINDSHIELD WASHER PUMP
C138
94-.8 PNK
152-.8 BLK
C137
93-.8 WHT
94-.8 PNK
91-.8 GRA
92-.8 PPL
DASH PANEL
92-.8 PPL
93-.8 WHT
91-.8 GRA
C101
S152
RH HEADLAMP
152-1.0 BLK
152-.8 BLK
BLOWER RELAY
RH PARK AND TURN LAMP
152-.8 BLK
152-3.0 BLK
BLOWER MOTOR GROUND
152-3.0 BLK
GROUND
G152
RH RADIATOR SUPPORT
C236
PULSE WIPER/WASHER SW. (COLUMN MOUNTED)
.8 GRA
.8 BLK
.8 PPL
MIST
HI
LO
OFF
PULSE
WASH (PULSE)
91B13715
Courtesy of General Motors Corp.

Fig. 3: Windshield Wiper/Washer System Wiring Diagram

2) If battery voltage was not present, locate and repair open in White wire from switch to fuse block. If wire is okay, go to step **3)**.

3) Connect voltmeter between circuit No. C236 (Gray wire) and ground. Move wiper switch to LO position. Repeat test at Purple wire with wiper switch in HI position. If battery voltage exists at both wires, go to next step. If battery voltage does not exist at one or both wires, replace wiper/washer switch.

4) Disconnect wiper motor connector C137. Connect fused jumper between battery junction block and wiper motor terminal C91 (Gray wire). *See Fig. 3*. If wipers operate, locate and repair open in White or Purple wire between wiper/washer switch and wiper motor. If wipers fail to operate, repair or replace wiper motor.

WIPERS RUN AT LOW SPEED ONLY

1) Disconnect pulse wiper motor connector C137. *See Fig. 3*. Turn ignition switch to ACC position and wiper switch to HI position. Connect test light between wiper connector C236, terminal No. 92 (Purple wire) and ground. *See Fig. 3*. If test light illuminates, replace wiper motor. If test light does not illuminate, go to step **2)**.

2) Connect test light between wiper switch connector terminal No. 92 (Purple wire) of wiper switch connector C236 and ground. *See Figs. 2 & 3*. If test light illuminates, locate and repair open in circuit No. 92 (Purple wire) from wiper switch to wiper motor. If test light does not illuminate, replace wiper switch.

WIPERS RUN AT HIGH SPEED ONLY

1) Disconnect pulse wiper motor connector C137. *See Fig. 3*. Place ignition switch in ACC position and wiper switch in LO position. Connect test light between circuit No. 91 (Gray wire) of wiper motor connector C137 to ground. *See Fig. 3*. If test light illuminates, replace wiper motor. If test light does not illuminate, go to step **2)**.

2) Connect test light between circuit No. 91 (Gray wire) of wiper switch connector C236 and ground. *See Figs. 2 & 3*. If test light illuminates, locate and repair open in circuit No. 91 (Gray wire) from wiper switch to wiper motor. If test light does not illuminate, replace wiper switch.

WIPERS DO NOT PARK

1) Turn ignition switch to RUN position. Connect test light between White wire at wiper motor connector C137 and ground. *See Fig. 3*. If test light illuminates, go to step **2)**. If test light did not illuminate, repair open in White wire between wiper motor and fuse block.

2) Connect test light between Pink wire at wiper motor connector C137 and ground. *See Fig. 3*. If test light illuminates, go to step **3)**. If test light did not illuminate, repair or replace wiper motor.

3) Disconnect wiper/washer switch connector C236. Connect test light between Pink wire at circuit C236 and ground. *See Fig. 3*. If test light illuminates, replace wiper/washer switch. If test light did not illuminate, locate and repair open in Pink wire between wiper motor and wiper/washer switch.

WIPERS RUN CONTINUOUSLY

1) Disconnect wiper motor connector C137. *See Fig. 3*. Connect a fused jumper between terminal No. 94 (Pink wire) and terminal No. 91 (Gray wire) of wiper motor. Connect fused jumper from terminal No. 93 (White wire) of wiper module and battery junction block.

1991 SAFETY EQUIPMENT
Wiper/Washer Systems – Astro & Safari (Cont.)

2) If wiper motor parks and turns off, replace wiper/washer switch. If wiper motor continues to run, repair or replace wiper motor.

NO DELAY IN PULSE (DELAY) MODE

1) Disconnect pulse wiper switch connector C236. *See Figs. 2 & 3*. Place wiper switch in PULSE position. Connect ohmmeter between terminal No. 91 (Gray wire) and terminal No. 93 (White wire) at wiper switch. *See Fig. 3*. If reading is 680 ohms, go to step **2)**. If reading is less than or greater than 680 ohms, replace wiper switch.
2) Move wiper switch through pulse range to maximum delay position. If readings increase in steps to approximately 450 k/ohms, locate and repair open in circuit No. 91 (Gray wire) or circuit No. 93 (White wire) between wiper switch connector C236 and wiper motor connector C137. *See Fig. 3*. If circuits are okay, replace wiper switch. If readings are not as specified, replace wiper switch.

WASHER MOTOR INOPERATIVE

1) Disconnect windshield washer pump connector C138. Turn ignition switch to ACC position and wiper switch to WASH position. Connect test light between terminal No. 94 (Pink wire) at windshield washer pump connector C138 and ground. *See Fig. 3*. If test light illuminates, go to step **2)**. If test light does not illuminate, go to step **3)**.
2) Connect test light between terminal No. 94 (Pink wire) and terminal No. 150 (Black wire) at washer pump connector C138. Place washer switch in WASH position. If test light illuminates, replace washer pump. If test light does not illuminate, locate and repair open in Black wire from washer pump to ground terminal G152.
3) Connect test light between Gray wire wiper motor connector C137 and ground. *See Fig. 3*. If test light illuminates, go to step **4)**. If test light does not illuminate, replace wiper switch.
4) Connect test light between circuit No. 94 (Pink wire) at wiper motor connector C137 and ground. If test light illuminates, locate and repair open in Pink wire from wiper motor to wiper switch. If wire is okay, replace wiper switch. If test light does not illuminate, replace wiper motor module.

REMOVAL & INSTALLATION

WIPER MOTOR

Removal & Installation – Remove electrical connector. Remove transmission drive link from motor crank arm by prying or pulling link toward rear of vehicle. Remove wiper motor mounting bolts. Remove motor. To install, reverse removal procedure.

OVERHAUL

Repairs to motor/gear box section of wiper assembly are limited to switch, plus external parts, crank arm, spacer and plastic seal, and output shaft seal. No other overhaul procedures given by manufacturer.

WIRING DIAGRAMS

For additional information, see appropriate chassis wiring diagram in WIRING DIAGRAMS.

1991 SAFETY EQUIPMENT
Wiper/Washer Systems – "C" & "K" Series

DESCRIPTION

Wiper system consists of a permanent magnet, positive-park wiper motor mounted on engine compartment side of firewall. Motor drives a crank arm, which is attached to individual transmission links for both the left and right sides.

Transmissions are mounted in front of the windshield, in the fresh air plenum. Wiper motor is sealed and no service parts are available. Delay module is also sealed and attached directly to wiper motor. Module is replaced as a unit during service.

Windshield washer is a reservoir-mounted electric pump. Windshield washer reservoir is mounted on the inner engine compartment fender.

TESTING

WIPER MOTOR INOPERATIVE

1) Disconnect wiper switch connector C266. Connect test light between White wire at wiper switch connector C266 and ground. *See Fig. 1*. If test light illuminates, go to step **2)**. If test light does not illuminate, check wiper fuse. If fuse is good, check and repair open in White wire from wiper switch to fuse block.

2) Reconnect wiper switch connector C266. Move wiper switch to LO position. Connect test light between Gray wire at wiper switch connector C266 and ground. *See Fig. 1*. If test light illuminates, check and repair open in Gray wire from wiper switch to wiper motor module. If test light does not illuminate, replace wiper switch.

WIPERS RUN AT LOW SPEED ONLY

1) Disconnect wiper motor module connector C177. Turn ignition to ACC position and wiper switch to HI position. Connect test light between Purple wire at wiper module connector C177 and ground. *See Fig. 1*. If test light illuminates, replace wiper motor module. If test light does not illuminate, go to step **2)**.

2) Connect test light between Purple wire at wiper switch connector C266 and ground. *See Fig. 1*. If test light illuminates, check and repair open in Purple wire from wiper switch to wiper motor module. If test light does not illuminate, replace wiper switch.

WIPERS RUN AT HIGH SPEED ONLY

1) Disconnect wiper motor module connector C177. *See Fig. 1*. Turn ignition to ACC position and wiper switch to LO position. Connect test light between Gray wire at wiper motor module connector C177 and ground. If test light illuminates, replace wiper motor module. If test light does not illuminate, go to step **2)**.

2) Connect test light between Gray wire at wiper switch connector C266 and ground. *See Fig. 1*. If test light illuminates, check and repair open in Gray wire from wiper switch to wiper motor module. If test light does not illuminate, repair wiper switch.

WIPER MOTOR RUNS CONTINUOUSLY

1) Disconnect wiper motor module connector C177. Turn ignition to ACC position and wiper switch to LO position. Connect test light between Gray wire at wiper module connector C177 and ground. *See Fig. 1*. If test light illuminates, go to step **2)**. If test light does not illuminate, check and repair open in Gray wire from wiper motor module to wiper switch.

2) Move wiper switch to HI position. Connect test light between Purple wire at wiper motor module connector C177 and ground. *See Fig. 1*. If test light illuminates, go to step **3)**. If test light does not illuminate, check and repair open in Purple wire from wiper motor module to wiper switch.

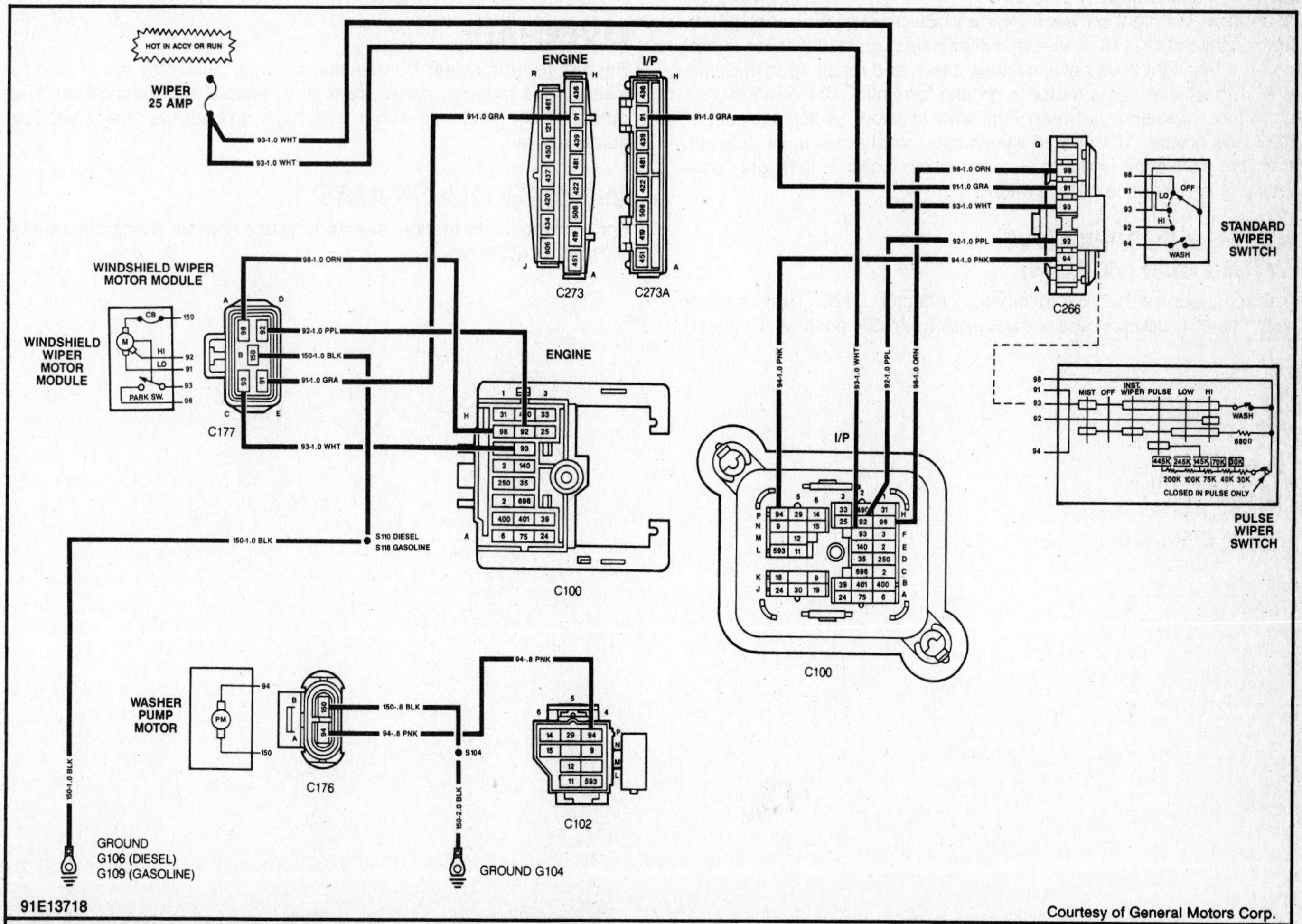
HOT IN ACCY OR RUN
WIPER 25 AMP
93-1.0 WHT
ENGINE
I/P
91-1.0 GRA
C273
C273A
98-1.0 ORN
93-1.0 WHT
92-1.0 PPL
94-1.0 PNK
STANDARD WIPER SWITCH
C266
WINDSHIELD WIPER MOTOR MODULE
WINDSHIELD WIPER MOTOR MODULE
PARK SW.
150-1.0 BLK
C177
ENGINE
C100
S110 DIESEL
S118 GASOLINE
I/P
C100
MIST OFF INST. WIPER PULSE LOW HI
WASH
CLOSED IN PULSE ONLY
PULSE WIPER SWITCH
WASHER PUMP MOTOR
C176
94-.8 PNK
150-.8 BLK
S104
C102
150-2.0 BLK
GROUND G106 (DIESEL) G109 (GASOLINE)
GROUND G104
91E13718
Courtesy of General Motors Corp.

Fig. 1: Wiper/Washer System Wiring Diagram ("C" & "K" Series)

1991 SAFETY EQUIPMENT

Wiper/Washer Systems – "C" & "K" Series (Cont.)

3) Connect test light between White wire at wiper motor module connector C177 and ground. If test light illuminates, replace wiper motor module (with pulse wipers), or go to step **4)** (without pulse wipers). On all systems, if test light does not illuminate, check and repair open in White wire from wiper motor module to ground.
4) Turn ignition and wiper switches off. Connect ohmmeter between Orange and Gray wires at wiper motor module connector C177. *See Fig. 1*. If ohmmeter reads zero ohm, replace wiper motor module. If ohmmeter reads greater than zero ohm, check and repair open in Orange wire from wiper motor module to wiper switch.

NO DELAY IN PULSE (DELAY) MODE

1) Disconnect wiper connector C266. Place wiper switch in LO position. Connect ohmmeter between Gray wire terminal to White wire terminal at wiper switch. If ohmmeter reads approximately 680 ohms, go to step **2)**. If ohmmeter reads less than or greater than 680 ohms, replace wiper switch.
2) Move wiper switch through delay range to maximum delay position. If ohmmeter readings increase in steps to approximately 450 k/ohms, check and repair open in Gray or White wire from wiper switch connector C266 to wiper switch motor module C177. *See Fig. 1*. If wiring is okay, replace wiper switch. If readings are not as specified, replace wiper switch.

WASHER INOPERATIVE (WITHOUT PULSE WIPERS)

1) Disconnect washer pump motor connector C176. Turn ignition switch to ACC position and wiper switch to WASH position. Connect test light between Pink wire at washer pump motor connector C176 and ground. *See Fig. 1*. If test light illuminates, go to step **2)**. If test light does not illuminate, go to step **3)**.
2) Connect test light between Pink and Black wire at washer pump motor connector C176. If test light illuminates, replace washer pump motor. If test light does not illuminate, check and repair open in Black wire from washer pump motor to ground terminal G104. *See Fig. 1*.
3) Connect test light between Pink wire at wiper switch connector C266 and ground. If test light illuminates, check and repair open in Pink wire from wiper switch to washer pump motor. If test light does not illuminate, replace wiper switch.

WASHER INOPERATIVE (WITH PULSE WIPERS)

1) Disconnect washer pump motor connector C176. Turn ignition switch to ACC position and wiper switch to WASH position. Connect test light between Pink wire at washer pump motor connector C176 and ground. *See Fig. 1*. If test light illuminates, go to step **2)**. If test light does not illuminate, go to step **3)**.
2) Connect test light between Pink and Black wires at washer pump motor connector C176. If test light illuminates, replace washer pump motor. If test light does not illuminate, check and repair open in Black wire from washer pump motor to ground terminal G104. *See Fig. 1*.
3) Connect test light between Gray wire at wiper motor module connector C177 and ground. If test light illuminates, go to step **4)**. If test light does not illuminate, check and repair open in Gray wire from wiper motor module to wiper switch. If wire is okay, replace wiper switch.
4) Connect test light between Orange wire at wiper motor module connector C177 and ground. If test light illuminates, check and repair open in Orange wire from wiper motor module to wiper switch. If wire is okay, replace wiper switch. If test light does not illuminate, replace wiper motor module.

REMOVAL & INSTALLATION

WIPER MOTOR

Removal – 1) Ensure wipers are in Park position. Disconnect negative battery cable. Remove cowl vent grille. Disconnect electrical harness connector at motor.
2) Remove drive link sockets from motor crank arm. DO NOT remove crank arm. Loosen socket screws, and slide links off crank arm. Remove screws attaching wiper motor to firewall, and remove motor assembly.
Installation – To install, reverse removal procedure. Lubricate crank arm pivot before installation.

OVERHAUL

Repairs to motor/gear box section of wiper assembly are limited to switch, plus external parts, crank arm, spacer and plastic seal, and output shaft seal. No other overhaul procedures are given by manufacturer.

WIRING DIAGRAMS

For additional information, see appropriate chassis wiring diagram in WIRING DIAGRAMS.

1991 SAFETY EQUIPMENT
Wiper/Washer Systems – "G" Series

DESCRIPTION

Wiper system consists of (1) a 2-speed, permanent magnet motor enclosed in an upper and lower housing and (2) a pulse/control module attached to motor. Assembly is located on firewall. Wiper motor is protected by an automatic reset circuit breaker located on the motor brush holder assembly. Vehicle wiring is fuse protected.

Windshield washer is a reservoir-mounted electric pump. Windshield washer reservoir is mounted on engine compartment firewall.

TESTING

NOTE: To locate connectors in following tests, refer to Fig. 1.

WIPER MOTOR INOPERATIVE

1) Turn ignition to RUN position and wiper switch to HI position. Connect test light between White wire at wiper motor connector C248 and ground. *See Fig. 1*. If test light illuminates, go to step **2)**. If test light does not illuminate, check wiper fuse or repair open in White wire between wiper motor connector C277 and fuse block.
2) Connect a fused jumper wire from Black wire at wiper switch connector C259 to ground. If wiper motor runs, locate and repair open between wiper switch connector C259 and ground. If wiper motor fails to run, replace wiper motor.

WIPERS INOPERATIVE IN HI

1) Turn ignition to RUN position and wiper switch to HI position. Connect a fused jumper wire from Purple wire at pulse wiper module connector C224 to ground. *See Fig. 1*. If wiper motor runs, go to step **2)**. If wiper motor fails to run, check and repair open in Purple wire between wiper motor and wiper module connectors. If wire is okay, replace wiper motor.
2) Connect a fused jumper wire from Purple wire at wiper switch connector C259 to ground. If wiper motor runs, replace wiper/washer switch. If wiper motor fails to run, check and repair open in Purple wire between wiper motor and wiper motor module connector. If wire is okay, replace wiper motor.

WIPERS INOPERATIVE IN LO OR DELAY

1) Turn ignition to RUN position and wiper switch to LO position. Connect a fused jumper from Gray wire at pulse wiper module connector C224 to ground. *See Fig. 1*. If wiper motor runs, go to step **2)**. If wiper motor fails to run, check and repair open in Gray wire between wiper motor and wiper module connector. If wire is okay, replace wiper motor.
2) Connect a fused jumper wire from Gray wire at wiper switch connector C259 to ground. If wiper motor runs, replace wiper/washer switch. If wiper motor fails to run, check and repair open in Gray wire between wiper switch connector C259 and wiper module connector C226. If wire is okay, replace wiper washer switch.

WASHER MOTOR RUNS CONTINUOUSLY

1) Turn ignition to RUN position and wiper switch to WASH position. Disconnect wiper switch connector C259. *See Fig. 1*. If washer motor stops pumping, replace wiper switch. If washer motor continues pumping, go to step **2)**.
2) Disconnect wiper control module connector C224. If washer motor stops pumping, replace wiper control module. If washer motor continues pumping, check and repair short in Pink wire between pulse wiper control module connector C224 and washer pump connector C137.

WASHER INOPERATIVE

1) Turn ignition to RUN position and wiper switch to WASH position. Connect test light between White wire at washer pump connector C137 and ground. *See Fig. 1*. If test light illuminates, go to step **2)**. If test light does not illuminate, check and repair open in White wire between washer pump connector C137 and fuse block.
2) Connect test light between Pink and White wires at washer pump connector C137. If test light illuminates, replace washer pump. If test light does not illuminate, go to step **3)**.
3) Connect a fused jumper wire from Pink wire at wiper control module to ground. If washer motor pumps, go to step **4)**. If washer motor fails to pump, check and repair open in Pink wire between washer pump connector C137 and wiper control module connector C224. *See Fig. 1*.
4) Connect a fused jumper wire from Pink wire at wiper switch connector C259 to ground. If washer motor pumps, go to step **5)**. If washer pump fails to pump, check and repair open in Pink wire between wiper control module and wiper switch.
5) Connect a fused jumper from Black wire at wiper switch connector C259 to ground. If washer motor pumps, check and repair open in Black wire between wiper switch connector C259 and ground. If washer motor fails to pump, replace wiper switch.

REMOVAL & INSTALLATION

WIPER MOTOR

Removal – 1) Ensure wipers are in park position. Disconnect negative battery cable. Remove wiper arms from wiper linkage. Remove cowl panel cover. Remove drive rod from wiper motor crank arm. Loosen nuts holding drive rod to wiper motor and remove drive rod. Disconnect wiring to motor.
2) Remove left defroster outlet from flex hose and position hose to one side. Remove screw securing left heater duct to engine cover shroud and slip heater duct down and out. Remove washer hoses. Remove screws securing wiper motor to firewall. Remove wiper motor.
Installation – To install, reverse removal procedure. Ensure wipers are in park position before installing. Lubricate wiper motor crank arm pivot prior to installation.

OVERHAUL

Repairs to motor/gear box section of wiper assembly are limited to switch, plus external parts, crank arm, spacer and plastic seal, and output shaft seal. No other overhaul procedures are given by manufacturer.

WIRING DIAGRAMS

For additional information, see appropriate chassis wiring diagram in WIRING DIAGRAMS.

1991 SAFETY EQUIPMENT
Wiper/Washer Systems – "G" Series (Cont.)

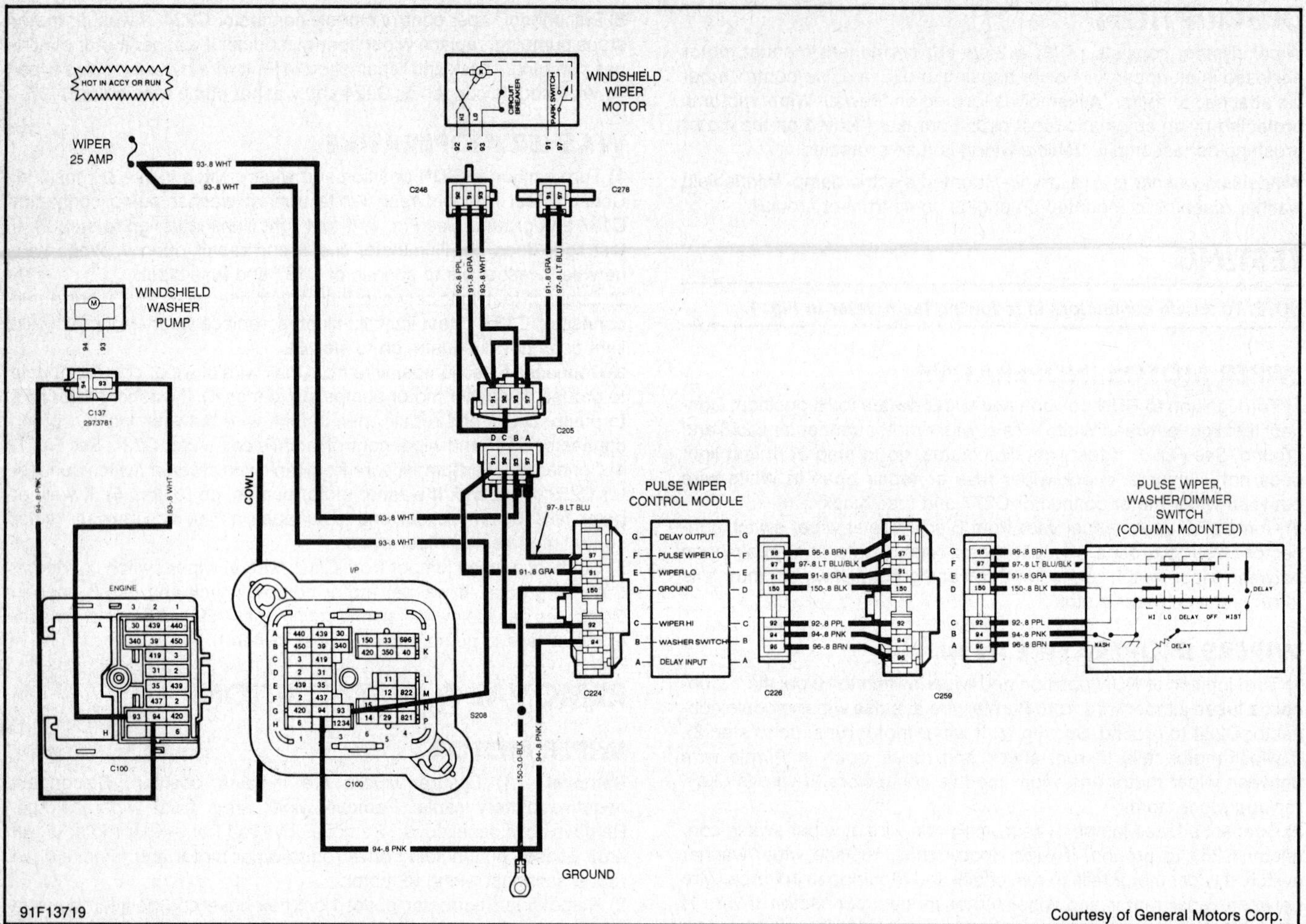
HOT IN ACCY OR RUN
WIPER
25 AMP
WINDSHIELD
WIPER
MOTOR
CIRCUIT BREAKER
PARK SWITCH
C248
C278
93-.8 WHT
92-.8 PPL
91-.8 GRA
91-.8 GRA
97-.8 LT BLU
WINDSHIELD
WASHER
PUMP
C137
2973781
94-.8 PNK
COWL
C205
97-.8 LT BLU
ENGINE
I/P
C100
S208
150-.5 G BLK
94-.8 PNK
GROUND
PULSE WIPER
CONTROL MODULE
DELAY OUTPUT
PULSE WIPER LO
WIPER LO
GROUND
WIPER HI
WASHER SWITCH
DELAY INPUT
C224
96-.8 BRN
97-.8 LT BLU/BLK
91-.8 GRA
150-.8 BLK
92-.8 PPL
94-.8 PNK
96-.8 BRN
C226
C259
PULSE WIPER,
WASHER/DIMMER
SWITCH
(COLUMN MOUNTED)
DELAY
HI
LO
DELAY
OFF
MIST
WASH
91F13719

Courtesy of General Motors Corp.

Fig. 1: Wiper/Washer System Wiring Diagram ("G" Series)

1991 SAFETY EQUIPMENT
Wiper/Washer Systems – FWD Vans

Lumina APV, Silhouette, Trans Sport

DESCRIPTION

Front wiper/washer system is a 3-speed system with a pulse wipe mode. Front system consists of wiper motor, printed circuit board and linkage assembled in a tubular frame bracket.

Rear wiper/washer system is a one-speed system with a pulse wipe mode. Rear system consists of wiper motor, gear box and linkage. Both front and rear wiper/washer switches are integrated in one combination switch. Separate front and rear washer pumps are located on washer reservoir in engine compartment.

OPERATION

FRONT WIPER SYSTEM

Front wiper speeds are controlled by front wiper switch, which supplies voltage to specified wiper motor assembly terminal. *See Figs. 1 and 2.* In pulse operation, single stroke time interval is determined by timer in wiper motor assembly. Length of wiper delay is determined by pulse delay resistor in wiper switch.

REAR WIPER SYSTEM

Rear wiper is controlled by rear wiper switch, which supplies voltage to the appropriate terminals of wiper motor. In pulse operation, pulse module of motor controls wiper stroke.

TROUBLE SHOOTING

WIPER MOTOR INOPERATIVE

Front & Rear Wipers – Ensure fuse is good. If fuse is defective, check for short or open to ground in White wire from fuse block to wiper switch terminal "N" (front wiper) or terminal "E" (rear wiper) and respective wiper motor.

WASHER INOPERATIVE

Front & Rear Washers – Ensure reservoir is full and hoses are connected. Check for clogged spray nozzles. Check for missing or damaged connector seal at washer motor. If front washer does not operate and wipers operate in HI only, check for open in Gray wire between front wiper switch and windshield wiper motor.

TESTING & DIAGNOSIS

COMPONENT TESTING

Front Wiper/Washer Switch Test – **1)** Disconnect electrical connector at front wiper motor. Using voltmeter or ohmmeter, check for voltage or continuity at designated terminals of electrical connector as specified. *See Fig. 2.*

2) Check for voltage with ignition on. Check for continuity with ignition off. If switch is okay, remove wiper motor and test. Perform FRONT WIPER MOTOR TEST.

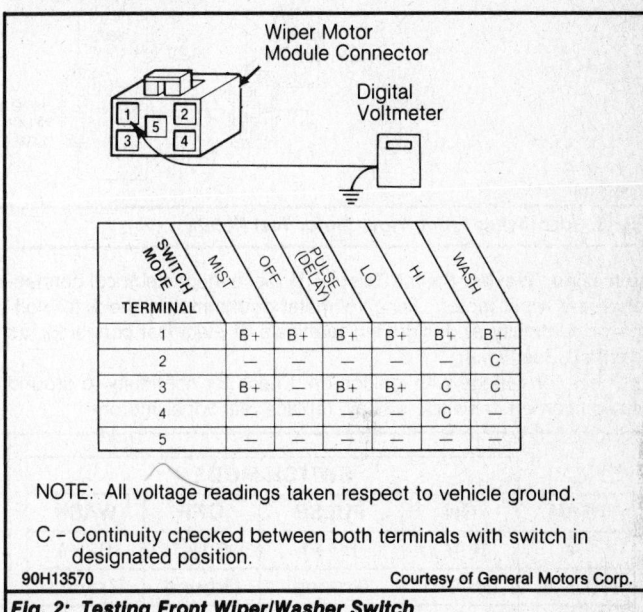

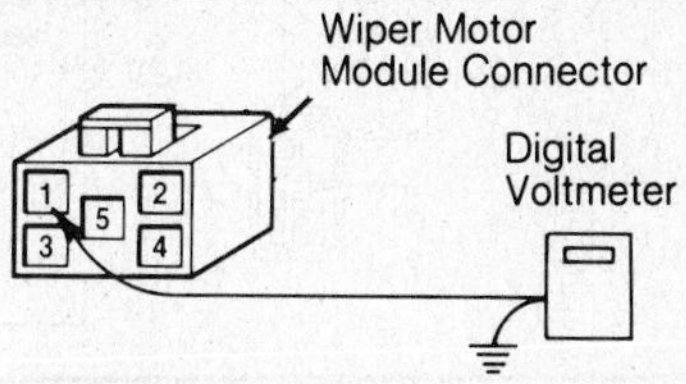
Wiper Motor
Module Connector
Digital
Voltmeter
1
2
3
4
5

TERMINAL \ SWITCH MODE	MIST	OFF	PULSE (DELAY)	LO	HI	WASH
1	B+	B+	B+	B+	B+	B+
2	—	—	—	—	—	C
3	B+	—	B+	B+	C	C
4	—	—	—	—	C	—
5	—	—	—	—	—	—

NOTE: All voltage readings taken respect to vehicle ground.

C – Continuity checked between both terminals with switch in designated position.

90H13570 Courtesy of General Motors Corp.

Fig. 2: Testing Front Wiper/Washer Switch

Front Wiper Motor Test – **1)** Remove wiper motor. See FRONT WIPER MOTOR & DRIVE ARM ASSEMBLY under REMOVAL & INSTALLATION. Apply battery voltage and ground to designated terminals in specified switch positions. It may be necessary to use a 1/2 watt (680 ohm) resistor. *See Fig. 3.*

2) A test washer pump may be connected during test procedure. DO NOT use pump from vehicle. When using washer pump, DO NOT hold WASH button longer than 15 seconds in each 2 minute interval. If wiper motor fails to operate in all modes, replace wiper motor.

WIPER SWITCH POSITION	WASH BUTTON POSITION: OFF	WASH BUTTON POSITION: BUTTON HELD MORE THAN ONE SECOND
MIST	Wiper runs instantaneously or, if held, runs continuously in low speed.	Wiper continues to run in low speed during wash cycle, then resumes in low speed.
OFF	Wiper and washer are off—blades are at park position.	Wiper starts, runs and washes in low speed. Fluid flows as long as button is held, then approx. six seconds of drying wipes and wiper returns to park position and shuts off.
DELAY	Wiper runs one low speed wipe. Blades stop at inner wipe position, next wipe is delayed for period of time of 0-30 seconds (depending upon rheostat setting), then cycle repeats.	Delay function is overridden and followed by wash and dry cycle above. Blades then return to inner wipe position and delay function resumes.
LO	Wiper runs in continuous low speed.	Wiper continues to run in low during wash cycle above, and remains in low speed after wash.
HI	Wiper runs in continuous high speed.	Same as low speed wash above except motor running in high speed.

90E13569 Courtesy of General Motors Corp.

Fig. 1: Identifying Front Wiper System Operating Modes

1991 SAFETY EQUIPMENT
Wiper/Washer Systems – FWD Vans (Cont.)

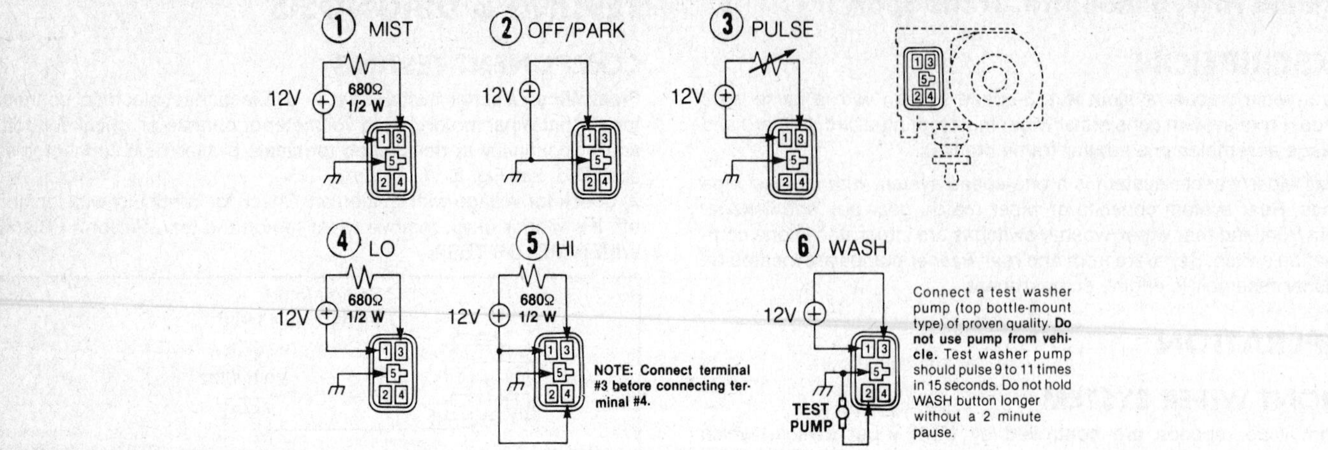
1 MIST
2 OFF/PARK
3 PULSE
4 LO
5 HI
6 WASH
12V
680Ω
1/2 W
NOTE: Connect terminal #3 before connecting terminal #4.
Connect a test washer pump (top bottle-mount type) of proven quality. Do not use pump from vehicle. Test washer pump should pulse 9 to 11 times in 15 seconds. Do not hold WASH button longer without a 2 minute pause.
TEST PUMP

90I13571 Courtesy of General Motors Corp.

Fig. 3: Identifying Front Wiper Motor Test Points

Rear Wiper/Washer Switch Test – 1) Disconnect electrical connector at rear wiper motor. Using voltmeter or ohmmeter, check for voltage or continuity at designated terminals of electrical connector as specified. *See Fig. 4.*

2) Check for voltage with ignition on. Check for continuity to ground with ignition off. If switch is okay, replace rear wiper motor.

	SWITCH MODE			
TERM.	ON	PULSE	OFF	WASH
A	B (+)	B (+)	B (+)	B (+)
B	Ground	Ground	Ground	Ground
C	B (+)	B (+)	0V	B (+)

91A14506 Courtesy of General Motors Corp.

Fig. 4: Rear Wiper/Washer Switch Test Chart

SYSTEM TESTING

NOTE: Check front wiper system operation before testing front wiper system. See Fig. 1.

Front Wipers Inoperative In All Modes – 1) Turn ignition on. Using a voltmeter, check for battery voltage between White wire (terminal "N") at front wiper switch and ground. If voltage exists, proceed to next step. If voltage does not exist, check for defective fuse or open in White wire between fuse block and wiper switch terminal "N".

2) Remove electrical connector from wiper motor. Using test light, check for battery voltage between White wire of wiper motor connector and ground. If voltage exists, proceed to next step. If voltage does not exist, check for defective connection at wiper motor or open in White wire between fuse block and wiper motor connector.

3) Place wiper switch in LO position. Using voltmeter, measure voltage between Gray wire of wiper motor connector and ground. If battery voltage exists, proceed to next step. If battery voltage does not exist, check for open in Gray wire between wiper switch and front wiper motor. If wiring circuit is okay, replace wiper switch.

4) Place wiper switch in high speed. Using voltmeter, measure voltage between Purple wire of wiper motor connector and ground. If battery voltage exists, proceed to next step. If battery voltage does not exist, check for open in Purple wire between wiper switch and front wiper motor. If wiring is okay, replace wiper switch.

5) Measure voltage between Purple wire and Black wire of wiper motor connector. If battery voltage does not exist, check for open in Black wire between front wiper motor connector and ground. If battery voltage exists, check for defective connections at wiper motor. If connections are okay, replace front wiper motor.

Front Wipers Operate In High Speed Only – 1) Remove connector from wiper motor. Turn ignition on. Place wiper switch in LO position. Using a voltmeter, measure voltage from Gray wire of wiper motor connector to ground. If battery voltage exists, check for defective connection at Gray wire connection of wiper motor. If connection is okay, replace front wiper motor.

2) If battery voltage does not exist, check for open in Gray wire between wiper switch and front wiper motor. Check for defective connection at Gray wire of wiper switch. If all connections are okay, replace wiper switch.

Front Wipers Operate In Low Speed Only – 1) Remove connector from wiper motor. Turn ignition on. Place wiper switch in HI position. Using a voltmeter, measure voltage from Purple wire of wiper motor connector to ground. If battery voltage exists, check for defective connection at Purple wire connection of wiper motor. If connection is okay, replace wiper motor.

2) If battery voltage does not exist, check for open in Purple wire between wiper switch and front wiper motor. Check for defective connection at Purple wire of wiper switch. If wire and connection are okay, replace wiper switch.

Front Wipers Run Continuously – 1) Remove electrical connector from wiper motor. Turn ignition on. Ensure wiper switch is off. Using a voltmeter, measure voltage between Gray wire of front wiper motor connector and ground.

2) If battery voltage exists, proceed to next step. If battery voltage does not exist, measure voltage between Purple wire of wiper motor connector and ground. If battery voltage does not exist, replace wiper motor. If battery voltage exists, check for short to battery voltage in Purple wire between wiper switch and wiper motor. If no short exists, replace wiper switch.

3) Check for short to battery voltage in Gray wire between wiper motor and wiper switch terminal "P". If no short exists, replace wiper switch.

Front Wiper Pulse Delay Inoperative Or Operates Incorrectly – 1) With ignition off, remove connector from front wiper switch. Place wiper switch in Pulse position. Using an ohmmeter, measure resistance between terminal "N" (White wire) and terminal "P" (Gray wire) of wiper switch. Move wiper switch through delay range and note resistance readings.

2) Resistance range should be 30,000-445,000 ohms. If resistance is not within specification, replace wiper switch. If resistance is within specification, check for open or defective connection in Gray wire between wiper switch terminal "P" and wiper motor. If wiring is okay, replace wiper motor.

Front Washer Inoperative – 1) Remove electrical connector at washer motor. Turn ignition on. Connect test light between Black wire and Pink wire of washer motor connector.

2) Turn washer on and note test light. If voltage exists, replace washer motor. If no voltage exists, connect test light between Black wire terminal of washer motor connector and ground.

3) Turn washer on and note test light. If voltage exists, repair open in Black wire from washer motor to ground.
4) If voltage does not exist, install electrical connector on washer motor. Remove connector from wiper motor. Connect test light between Gray wire of wiper motor harness and ground. Turn washer on and observe test light.
5) If voltage exists, check for open in Pink wire between wiper motor and washer motor. If wire is okay, replace wiper motor. If voltage does not exist, check for open in Gray wire between wiper switch terminal "P" and wiper motor. If wire is okay, replace wiper switch.
Rear Wiper Inoperative In All Modes – 1) Turn ignition on. Using test light, check for battery voltage between terminal "E" (White wire) at rear wiper switch and ground. If test light comes on, proceed to next step. If test light does not come on, check for defective fuse or open in White wire between fuse block and wiper switch terminal "E".
2) Place rear wiper switch in ON position. Using a test light, check for voltage between terminal "A" (Gray wire) of wiper switch and ground. If test light comes on, go to next step. If test light does not come on, check connections at wiper switch terminals "E" (White wire) and "A" (Gray wire). If connections are okay, replace wiper switch.
3) Using a test light, backprobe terminal "C" (Gray wire) of wiper motor module connector to ground. If test light comes on, go to next step. If test light does not come on, check for faulty connections or open in Gray wire between wiper motor module connector terminal "C" and wiper switch terminal "A". Repair as necessary.
4) Using a test light, backprobe terminal "A" (White wire) of wiper motor module connector to ground. If test light comes on, go to next step. If test light does not come on, check for faulty connections or open in White wire between wiper motor module connector terminal "A" and fuse block. Repair as necessary.
5) Using a test light, backprobe between terminals "A" (White wire) and "B" (Black wire) of wiper motor module connector. If test light comes on, check for faulty connection at wiper motor module. If connection is okay, replace wiper motor module. If test light does not come on, repair open in Black (ground) wire between wiper motor module connector terminal "B" and ground.
Rear Wiper Delay Operates Incorrectly Or Not At All – 1) Remove wiper switch from console and then reconnect electrical connector. Place rear wiper switch in DELAY position. Using an ohmmeter, measure the resistance between terminals "A" and "E" of wiper switch.
2) If resistance is approximately 750,000 ohms, replace rear window wiper motor module. If resistance is not as specified, replace wiper switch.
Rear Washer Inoperative – 1) Disconnect rear washer motor at washer reservoir. Turn ignition on. Connect a test light between terminals "A" (Dark Green wire) and "B" (Black wire) of washer motor harness connector. Activate wash switch while observing test light.
2) If test light does not come on while activating wash switch, go to next step. If test light does come on while activating wash switch, check for faulty connections at rear washer motor and repair as necessary. If connections are okay, replace washer motor.
3) Connect test light between terminal "A" (Dark Green wire) of rear washer motor harness connector and ground. If test light does not come on while activating wash switch, go to next step. If test light does come on while activating wash switch, repair open in Black wire between washer motor and ground.
4) Check for open or faulty connections in Dark Green wire between washer motor and wiper switch. Repair as necessary. If Dark Green wire is okay, replace wiper switch.

REMOVAL & INSTALLATION

FRONT WIPER ARMS

Removal – Disconnect washer hoses. Remove wiper arm retaining nut. Lift wiper arm and insert a small pin through both holes next to pivot area of wiper arm. Using Puller (J-22888-D), remove wiper arm.
Installation – 1) Ensure wiper motor is in Park position. Install wiper arm. Install retaining nut finger tight. Remove pin from pivot area of wiper arm.
2) On driver side applications, measure from tip of wiper blade to bottom edge of windshield at the glass junction panel. Glass junction panel is located at bottom of windshield. Distance must be approximately 5.8" (147 mm). If distance is correct, tighten retaining nut to specification.
3) On passenger side applications, measure from tip of wiper blade to bottom edge of windshield. Distance must be approximately 1.3" (33 mm). If distance is correct, tighten retaining nut to specification. On all applications, reconnect washer hoses.

FRONT WIPER MOTOR & DRIVE ARM ASSEMBLY

Removal – 1) Remove wiper arms. See FRONT WIPER ARMS under REMOVAL & INSTALLATION. Remove air cleaner. Remove electrical connector from wiper motor.
2) Remove drive arm retaining bolts. Remove wiper motor assembly retaining nuts. *See Fig. 5.* Remove wiper motor assembly with drive arms. Disconnect wiper motor from drive arms.
Installation – To install, reverse removal procedure. Install center nut on wiper motor frame first, followed by remaining wiper motor frame retaining nuts. Install drive arm housing bolts last. Tighten bolts/nuts to specification. See TORQUE SPECIFICATIONS table at end of article.

FRONT WIPER LINKAGE

Removal – Remove wiper motor assembly. See FRONT WIPER MOTOR & DRIVE ARM ASSEMBLY under REMOVAL & INSTALLATION. Loosen bolts until linkage is released from ball on drive arms. Remove bellcrank bolts. *See Fig. 5.*
Installation – To install, reverse removal procedure. Ensure linkage is positioned correctly.

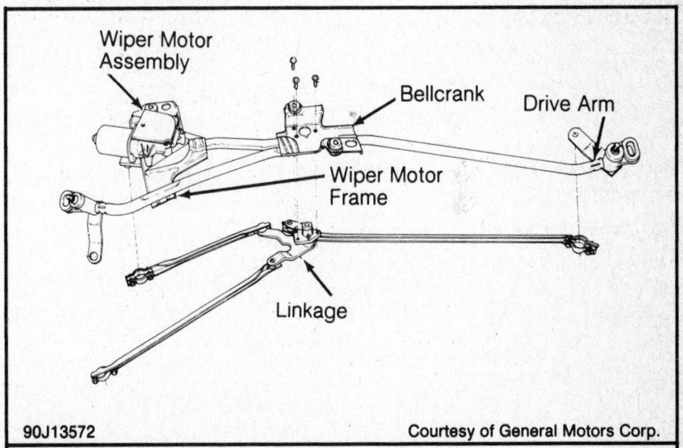
Wiper Motor
Assembly
Bellcrank
Drive Arm
Wiper Motor
Frame
Linkage
90J13572
Courtesy of General Motors Corp.
Fig. 5: Identifying Front Wiper Motor & Linkage

FRONT WIPER MOTOR PRINTED CIRCUIT BOARD

NOTE: Remove front wiper motor assembly to service printed circuit board (if necessary).

Removal & Installation – Disconnect electrical connector at front wiper motor. Remove cover retaining bolts on wiper motor. Lift circuit board from front wiper motor assembly. To install, reverse removal procedure.

REAR WIPER ARM

Removal – Lift wiper arm from back glass and pull retaining latch. Remove arm from wiper pivot shaft.
Installation – With wiper motor in PARK position, install head of wiper arm on serrated wiper pivot shaft in a position where wiper blade will rest in proper parked position. Install left arm extension and push in retaining latch when head is fully seated on pivot shaft.

1991 SAFETY EQUIPMENT
Wiper/Washer Systems – FWD Vans (Cont.)

REAR WIPER MOTOR

Removal & Installation – Disconnect motor electrical connector. Remove rear wiper arm. See REAR WIPER ARM under REMOVAL & INSTALLATION. Remove nut securing pivot shaft to back glass. Remove motor mounting screws from inside vehicle. Remove motor. To install, reverse removal procedure.

WIRING DIAGRAMS

See appropriate chassis wiring diagram in WIRING DIAGRAMS.

TORQUE SPECIFICATIONS

NOTE: Torque specifications for rear wiper/washer system components are not available from manufacturer.

TORQUE SPECIFICATIONS (FRONT WIPER/WASHER SYSTEM)

Application	Ft. Lbs. (N.m)
Wiper Arm Nut	30 (41)
	INCH Lbs. (N.m)
Drive Arm Housing Bolt	72-84 (8-9)
Linkage Bellcrank Bolt	48-72 (5-8)
Linkage-To-Ball Bolt	48-72 (5-8)
Linkage-To-Wiper Motor Bolt	48-72 (5-8)
Wiper Motor Bolt	48-72 (5-8)
Wiper Motor Frame Nut	72-84 (8-9)

1991 SAFETY EQUIPMENT
Wiper/Washer Systems – "P", "R" & "V" Series

DESCRIPTION

Wiper system consists of (1) a 2-speed, permanent magnet motor enclosed in an upper and lower housing and (2) a pulse/control module attached to motor. Assembly is located on firewall. Wiper motor is protected by an automatic reset circuit breaker located on the motor brush holder assembly. Vehicle wiring is fuse protected.

Windshield washer is a reservoir-mounted electric pump. Windshield washer reservoir is mounted in engine compartment.

TESTING

WIPER MOTOR INOPERATIVE

1) Turn ignition switch to RUN position and wiper switch to HI position. Connect test light between ground and White wire at wiper motor connector C187 on "P" Series or C188 on "R" and "V" Series. If test light illuminates, go to step **2)**. If test light does not illuminate, check and repair open in White wire between fuse block and connector C187 on "P" Series or C188 on "R" and "V" Series. *See Fig. 1 or 2*.

2) On all models, connect a fused jumper wire between Black wire at wiper switch connector C207 and ground. If wiper motor runs, repair open circuit between ground and Black wire at wiper switch connector C221 on "P" Series or C207 on "R" and "V" Series. *See Fig. 1 or 2*. If wiper motor does not run, replace wiper motor.

WIPERS DO NOT OPERATE IN HI

1) Place ignition switch in RUN or ACC position and wiper switch in HI position. Connect a fused jumper between ground and Purple wire at wiper module connector C221 on "P" Series or C207 on "R" and "V" Series. *See Fig. 1 or 2*.

2) On "P" Series, if wiper motor runs, replace wiper/washer switch. If wiper motor fails to run, repair open in Purple wire between wiper motor and wiper/washer switch connector. If wire is okay, replace wiper motor.

3) On "R" and "V" Series, if wiper motor does not run, repair open in Purple wire between wiper motor connector C188 and wiper module connector. If wire is okay, replace wiper motor. If wiper motor runs, go to step **4)**.

4) Connect a fused jumper wire from Purple wire at wiper switch connector C204 to ground. If wiper motor runs, replace wiper/washer switch. If wiper motor fails to run, check and repair open in Purple wire between wiper switch connector C204 and wiper module connector C207. If wire is okay, repair wiper control module. *See Fig. 2*.

WIPERS DO NOT OPERATE IN LO OR DELAY

1) Turn ignition to RUN of ACC position and wiper switch in LO position. Connect a fused jumper between ground and Gray wire at wiper switch connector C221 on "P" Series or at wiper module connector C207 on "R" and "V" Series. *See Fig. 1 or 2*.

2) On "P" Series, if wiper motor runs, replace wiper/washer switch. If wiper motor fails to run, repair open in Purple wire between wiper motor and wiper/washer switch connector. If wire is okay, replace wiper motor. *See Fig. 1*.

3) On "R" and "V" Series, if wiper motor runs, go to step **4)**. If wiper motor fails to run, repair open in Gray wire between wiper motor connector C188 and wiper module connector C207. *See Fig. 2*. If wire is okay, replace wiper motor.

4) Connect a fused jumper wire from Gray wire at wiper switch connector C204 to ground. If wiper motor runs, replace wiper/washer switch. If wiper motor fails to run, check and repair open in Gray wire

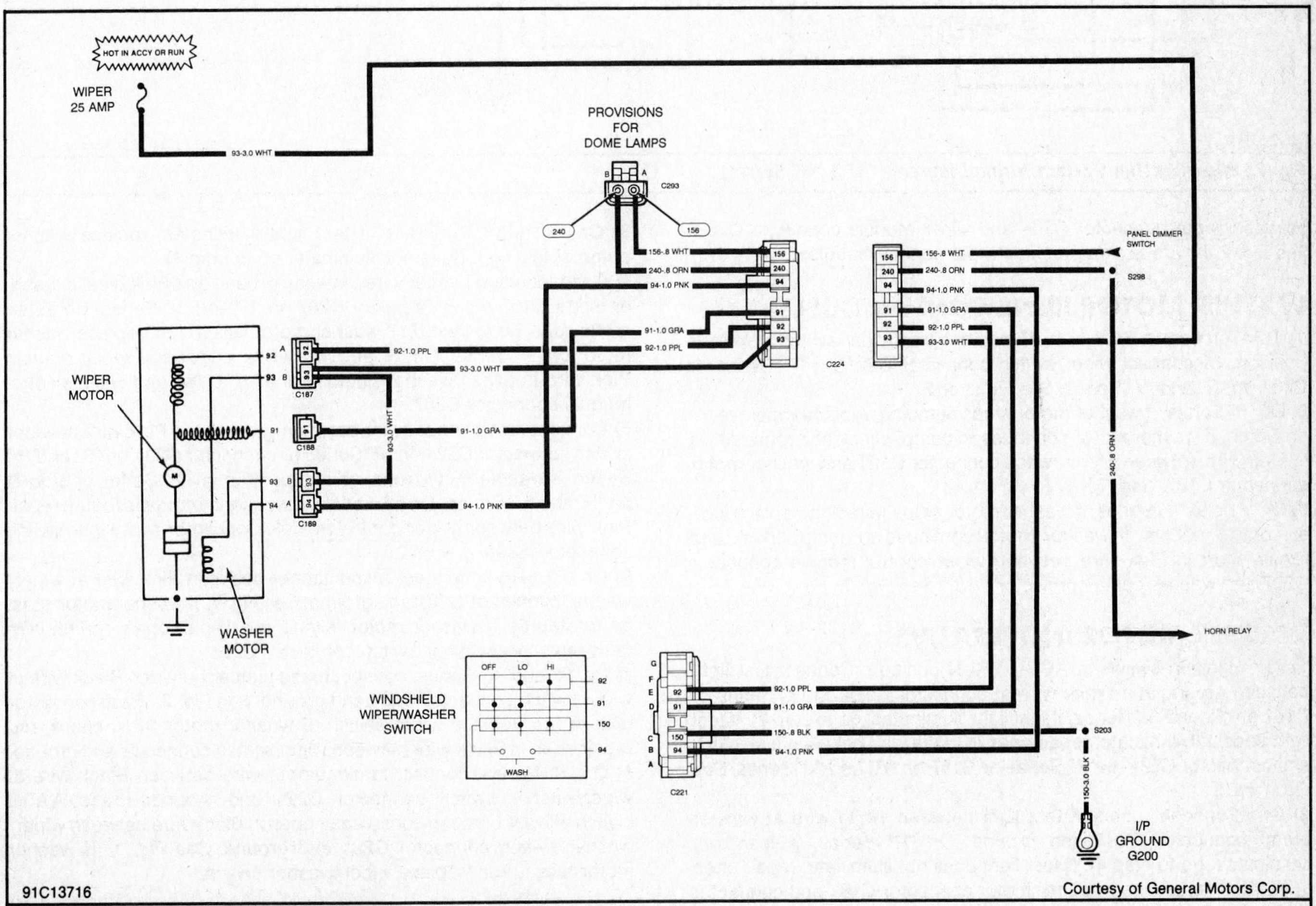
HOT IN ACCY OR RUN
WIPER
25 AMP
93-3.0 WHT
PROVISIONS
FOR
DOME LAMPS
C293
240
156
156-.8 WHT
240-.8 ORN
94-1.0 PNK
91-1.0 GRA
92-1.0 PPL
93-3.0 WHT
C224
PANEL DIMMER
SWITCH
S298
WIPER
MOTOR
C187
C188
C189
WASHER
MOTOR
240-.8 ORN
HORN RELAY
WINDSHIELD
WIPER/WASHER
SWITCH
OFF
LO
HI
WASH
C221
150-.8 BLK
S203
150-3.0 BLK
I/P
GROUND
G200
91C13716
Courtesy of General Motors Corp.

Fig. 1: Wiper/Washer System Wiring Diagram ("P" Series)

1991 SAFETY EQUIPMENT

Wiper/Washer Systems – "P", "R" & "V" Series (Cont.)

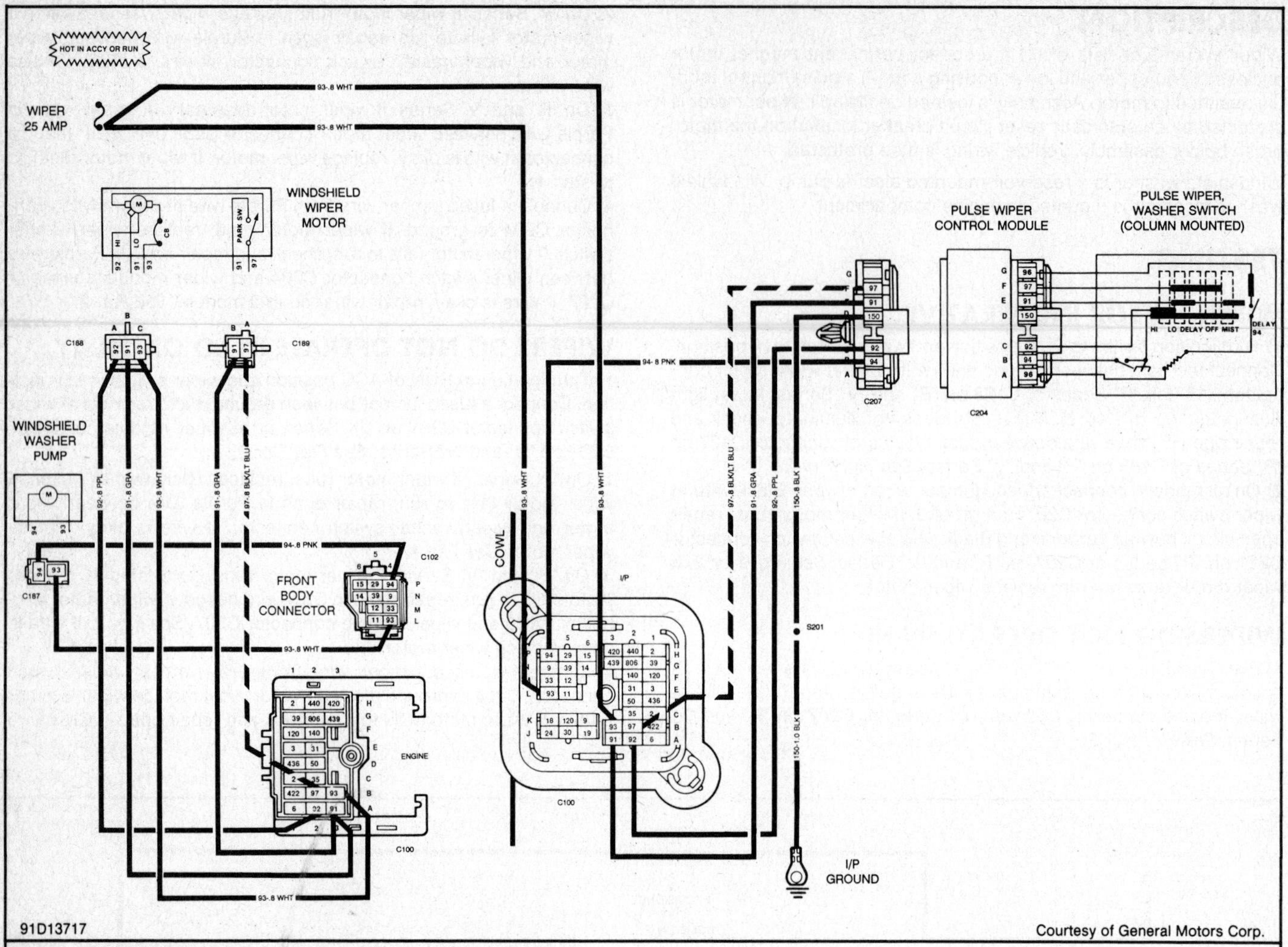
HOT IN ACCY OR RUN
WIPER
25 AMP
WINDSHIELD
WIPER
MOTOR
PULSE WIPER
CONTROL MODULE
PULSE WIPER,
WASHER SWITCH
(COLUMN MOUNTED)
C188
C189
C207
C204
WINDSHIELD
WASHER
PUMP
C187
FRONT
BODY
CONNECTOR
C102
COWL
I/P
S201
ENGINE
C100
I/P
GROUND
91D13717
Courtesy of General Motors Corp.

Fig. 2: Wiper/Washer System Wiring Diagram ("R" & "V" Series)

between wiper connector C204 and wiper module connector C207. *See Fig. 2*. If wire is okay, replace wiper control module.

WASHER MOTOR RUNS CONTINUOUSLY

1) Turn ignition to RUN or ACC position and wiper switch to WASH position. Disconnect wiper switch connector C221 on "P" Series or C207 on "R" and "V" Series. *See Fig. 1 or 2*.

2) On "P" Series, if washer motor stops pumping, replace wiper washer switch. If washer motor continues to pump, check and repair short in Pink wire between wiper switch connector C221 and washer motor connector C187. *See Fig. 1*.

3) On "R" and "V" Series, if washer motor stops pumping, replace wiper control module. If washer motor continues to pump, check and repair short in Pink wire between wiper control module connector C207 and washer pump connector C187. *See Fig. 2*.

WASHER MOTOR INOPERATIVE

1) Turn ignition switch to ACC or RUN position. Connect test light between ground and White wire at connector C224 on "P" Series or C187 on "R" and "V" Series. If test light illuminates, go to step **2)**. If test light does not illuminate, repair open in White wire between fuse block and connector C224 on "P" Series or C187 on "R" and "V" Series. *See Fig. 1 or 2*.

2) On all models, connect test light between White wire at washer pump connector C187 and ground. On "P" Series, if test light illuminates, go to step **4)**. If test light does not illuminate, repair open in White wire between washer motor connector C187 and connector C224. *See Fig. 1*.

3) On "R" and "V" models, if test light illuminates, replace washer pump. If test light does not illuminate, go to step **4)**.

4) Connect fused jumper wire between ground and Pink wire at washer motor C187 on "P" Series or C207 on "R" and "V" Series. If washer motor runs, go to step **5)**. If washer motor fails to run, replace washer motor on "P" Series. On "R" and "V" Series, check and repair open in Pink wire between washer pump connector C187 and wiper control module connector C207.

5) Connect fused jumper wire between ground and Pink wire at wiper switch connector C224 on "P" Series or connector C204 on "R" and "V" Series. If washer motor runs, go to next step on "P" Series or step **7)** on "R" and "V" Series. On all models, if washer motor fails to run, repair Pink wire between wiper control module connector and wiper switch connector. *See Fig. 1 or 2*.

6) On "P" Series, connect fused jumper between Pink wire at wiper/washer connector C221 and ground. *See Fig. 1*. If washer motor runs, go to step **8)**. If washer motor fails to run, repair open in Pink wire between wiper/washer switch connector C221.

7) On "R" and "V" Series, connect fused jumper between Black wire at wiper switch connector C204 and ground. *See Fig. 2*. If washer motor fails to run, replace wiper switch. If washer motor runs, check and repair open in Black wire between wiper switch connector and ground.

8) On "P" Series, connect fused jumper wire between Black wire at wiper/washer switch connector C221 and ground. Press WASH switch. If washer motor runs, repair open in Black wire between wiper/washer switch connector C221 and ground. *See Fig. 1*. If washer motor fails to run, replace wiper/washer switch.

Wiper/Washer Systems – "P", "R" & "V" Series (Cont.)

REMOVAL & INSTALLATION

WIPER MOTOR

NOTE: Wiper motor removal and installation information is not available from manufacturer for "P" Series vehicles.

Removal ("R" & "V" Series) – 1) Ensure wipers are in park position and negative battery cable is disconnected. Disconnect electrical harness at motor.

2) Remove wiper motor mounting screws through access hole. Pull wiper motor away from firewall, far enough to gain access to crank arm attaching nut. Remove crank arm attaching nut and crank arm from motor.

Installation – To install, reverse removal procedure. Lubricate crank arm pivot prior to installation.

OVERHAUL

Repairs to motor/gear box section of wiper assembly are limited to switch, plus external parts, crank arm, spacer and plastic seal, and output shaft seal. No other overhaul procedures are given by manufacturer.

WIRING DIAGRAMS

For additional information, see appropriate chassis wiring diagram in WIRING DIAGRAMS.

1991 SAFETY EQUIPMENT
Wiper/Washer Systems – "S" & "T" Series

DESCRIPTION

The 2 wiper/washer systems available on "S" & "T" Series include a base system and an optional system. Base system uses a low, high, and mist mode. In additiion to a low, high and mist mode, the optional system uses a pulse mode. It has an additional integrated circuit board to control pulse function, as well as a rheostat (built into the switch) to control the rate of pulse.

TESTING

WIPER SYSTEM

Wiper Inoperative – 1) Check wiper fuse at box, and replace if necessary. If fuse is okay, connect voltmeter between terminal No. 93 (White wire) of connector C340 and ground. *See Fig. 1 or 2.* Turn ignition to ACCY position. If battery voltage is not present, repair open circuit in White wire. If battery voltage is present, go to next step.

2) With ignition on, turn wiper switch to LO. Connect voltmeter between terminal No. 91 (Gray wire) of connector C340 and ground. Turn wiper switch to HI. Connect voltmeter between terminal No. 92 (Purple wire) of connector C340 and ground. If battery voltage is not present at both terminals, replace wiper/washer switch. If battery voltage is present at both terminals, go to next step.

3) Disconnect wiper motor wiring harness connector (C155). Connect fused jumper wire between terminal No. 91 (Gray wire) and battery positive terminal. If wipers operate, repair open circuit in White and/or Purple wire. If wipers do not operate, repair or replace wiper motor.

Wiper Has Low Speed Only – 1) Disconnect wiper motor wiring harness connector (C155). *See Fig. 1 or 2.* Turn ignition to ACCY position. Turn wiper switch to HI. Connect test light between terminal No. 92 (Purple wire) and ground. If test light comes on, replace or repair motor. If test light does not come on, go to next step.

2) Connect test light between terminal No. 92 (Purple wire) of switch connector C340 and ground. Turn ignition to ACCY position. Connect voltmeter between Purple wire of connector C340 and ground. If test light comes on, repair open circuit in Purple wire between wiper switch and wiper motor. If test light does not come on, repair or replace wiper switch.

Wiper Has High Speed Only – 1) Disconnect wiper motor wiring harness connector (C155). *See Fig. 1 or 2.* Turn ignition to ACCY position. Turn wiper switch to LO. Connect test light between terminal No. 91 (Gray wire) and ground. If test light comes on, replace or repair motor. If test light does not come on, go to next step.

2) Connect test light between terminal No. 91 (Gray wire) of switch connector C340 and ground. Turn ignition to ACCY position. Connect voltmeter between Purple wire of connector C340 and ground. If test light comes on, repair open circuit in Gray wire between wiper switch and wiper motor. If test light does not come on, repair or replace wiper switch.

Wiper Will Not Park – 1) Turn ignition on. Connect test light between terminal No. 93 (White wire) of wiper motor wiring harness connector (C155) and ground. *See Fig. 1 or 2.* If test light does not come on, repair open circuit in White wire between wiper motor and instrument panel. If test light does come on, go to next step.

2) Connect test light between terminal No. 98 (Orange wire) of wiper motor wiring harness connector (C155) and ground. If test light does not come on, repair or replace wiper switch. If test light does come on, go to next step.

3) Disconnect wiper/washer switch connector (C340). Connect test light between terminal No. 98 (Orange wire) of wiper/washer switch connector (C340) and ground. If test light does not comes on, repair open circuit in Orange wire between wiper switch and wiper motor. If test light does come on, repair or replace wiper switch.

Wiper Will Not Shut Off – 1) Disconnect wiper motor wiring harness connector (C155). *See Fig. 1 or 2.* Connect fused jumper wire between terminal No. 98 (Orange wire) and terminal No. 91 (Gray wire) of wiper motor wiring harness connector (C155).

2) Connect fused jumper wire between terminal No. 93 (White wire) and battery positive terminal. If wiper motor parks and turns off, replace wiper/washer switch. If wiper motor continues to run, repair or replace wiper motor module.

Windshield Washer Pump Inoperative (Pulse Wiper System) – 1) Disconnect windshield washer pump wiring harness connector (C154). *See Fig. 1.* Turn ignition to ACCY position. Turn wiper switch to WASH. Connect test light between windshield washer pump wiring harness connector (C154) terminal No. 94 (Pink wire) and ground. If test light comes on, go to next step. If test light does not come on, go to step **3)**.

2) Connect test light between windshield washer pump wiring harness connector (C154) terminal No. 94 (Pink wire) and terminal No. 150 (Black wire). Turn wiper switch to WASH position. If test light does not comes on, repair open circuit in Black wire from windshield washer pump to ground. If test light does come on, repair or replace windshield washer pump.

3) Connect test light between wiper motor connector (C155) terminal No. 91 (Gray wire) and ground. Turn wiper switch to WASH position. Turn ignition to ACCY position. If test light does not come on, repair or replace wiper switch. If test light comes on, go to next step.

4) Connect test light between wiper motor connector (C155) terminal No. 98 (Orange wire) and ground. Turn ignition to ACCY position. If test light does not come on, repair or replace wiper motor. If test light comes on, repair open circuit in Orange wire between wiper motor and switch. If wire is not open, replace wiper switch.

Windshield Washer Pump Inoperative (Except Pulse Wiper System) – 1) Disconnect windshield washer pump wiring harness connector (C154). *See Fig. 2.* Turn ignition to ACCY position. Turn washer switch on. Connect test light between windshield washer pump wiring harness connector (C154) terminal No. 94 (Pink wire) and ground. If test light comes on, go to next step. If test light does not come on, go to step **3)**.

2) Connect test light between windshield washer pump wiring harness connector (C154) terminal No. 94 (Pink wire) and terminal No. 150 (Black wire). If test light does not comes on, repair open circuit in Black wire to ground. If test light does come on, repair or replace windshield washer pump.

3) Connect test light between wiper/washer switch connector (C340) terminal No. 94 (Pink wire) and terminal No. 150 (Black wire). Turn wiper switch to WASH. Turn ignition to ACCY position. If test light comes on, repair open circuit in Pink wire between wiper switch and windshield washer pump. If test light does not come on, replace wiper switch.

Rear Wiper Inoperative – 1) Disconnect rear wiper switch connector (C362). *See Fig. 3.* Turn ignition to ACCY position. Connect test light between terminal No. 141 (Brown/White wire) and ground. If test light does not come on, check RADIO fuse. If fuse is okay, repair open circuit in Brown/White wire between wiper switch and fuse block. If test light comes on, go to next step.

2) Connect rear wiper switch (C362). Turn wiper switch on. Connect test light between wiper switch connector terminal No. 393 (White or Orange wire) and ground. If test light does not come on, replace wiper switch. If test light does come on, go to next step.

3) Connect test light between wiper motor wiring harness connector (C901) terminal No. 393 (White or Orange wire) and ground. If test light comes on, repair open in (White or Orange wire) between wiper motor and wiper switch. If test light does not comes on, go to next step.

4) Connect test light between wiper motor wiring harness connector (C901) terminal No. 393 and terminal No. 150 (Black wire). If test light does not comes on, repair open in circuit 150 between wiper motor and ground. If test light comes on, repair or replace wiper motor.

Rear Windshield Washer Inoperative – 1) Disconnect windshield washer pump wiring harness connector (C162). *See Fig. 3.* Turn ignition to ACCY position. Connect test light between windshield washer pump wiring harness connector terminal No. 392 (Green wire) and ground. Push washer switch button on. If test light comes on, go to next step. If test light does not come on, go to step **3)**.

2) Connect test light between windshield washer pump wiring harness connector (C162) terminal No. 392 and terminal No. 150 (Black wire). If test light does not come on, repair open circuit in Black wire to ground. If test light does come on, repair or replace windshield washer pump.

3) Connect test light between wiper switch connector (C362) terminal No. 392 (Green wire) and ground. Push washer switch button on. If

Wiper/Washer Systems – "S" & "T" Series (Cont.)

test light comes on, repair open circuit in Green wire between wiper switch and wiper motor. If test light comes on, repair or replace wiper switch.

REMOVAL & INSTALLATION

WIPER MOTOR (FRONT)

Removal & Installation – 1) Disconnect battery negative cable. Remove wiper arms. Remove cowl vent and grille. Loosen but do not remove transmission drive link to motor crank arm attaching nuts. *See Fig. 4.*

2) Detach drive link from motor crank arm. Disconnect motor electrical leads. Remove motor attaching screws. Rotate motor upward and outward to remove. To install, reverse removal procedure.

WIPER MOTOR COVER

Removal – Remove wiper motor. From housing side, drill ends off 7 rivets holding cover to housing. Remove cover.

Installation – To install, reverse removal procedure. Attach cover to housing with self-tapping screws.

WIPER HOUSING

Removal – 1) Remove wiper motor. Remove wiper motor cover. Remove crank gear lock nut, crank arm, shaft seal, thrust collar and washer. Push end of gear shaft through housing and remove gear assembly and washer.

2) File burr from retaining ring groove and where crank arm seats on shaft. Remove intermediate gear and washers. Drill ends off 4 rivets holding bearings and bearing straps in place.

CAUTION: DO NOT let metal chips fall into wiper motor.

3) Remove 6-point socket screws holding brush assembly in place. Remove armature, brush and magnet assembly together to avoid necessary realignment of brushes.

Installation – To install, reverse removal procedure. Use new housing retaining ring and self-tapping screws. Position thrust pin casing with insert about 1/32" above rear of pin.

WIPER MOTOR (REAR)

Removal & Installation – 1) Disconnect battery negative cable. Remove wiper cover retaining screws. Remove wiper motor retaining screws. Install 1/8" pin in wiper arm to hold detent spring. Remove wiper arm. *See Fig. 5.*

2) Support end gate glass. Remove end gate glass support arm. Remove wiper motor hinge bolt. Remove nuts and spacers and flat seals from wiper motor. Remove wiper motor. To install, reverse removal procedure.

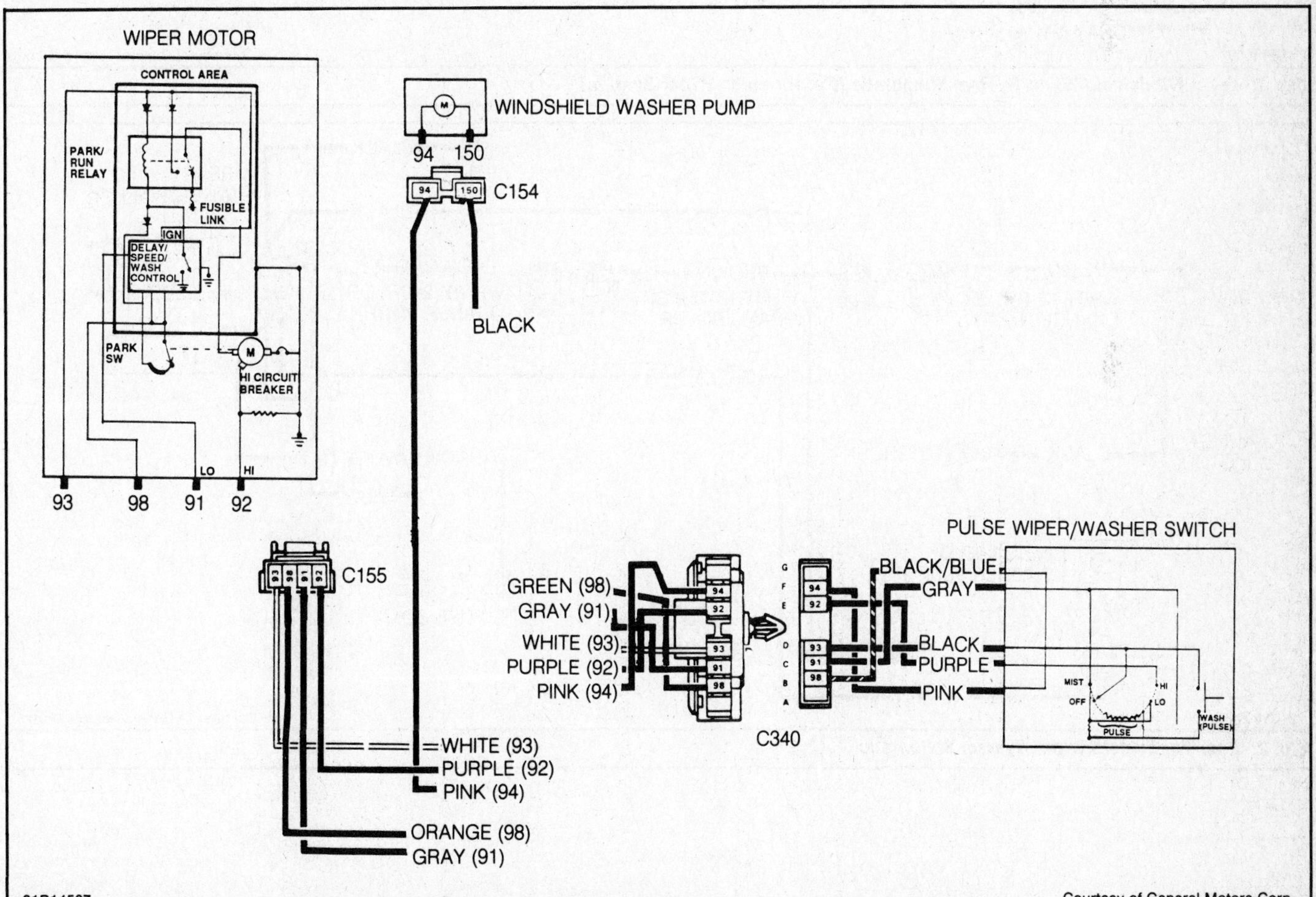
WIPER MOTOR
CONTROL AREA
PARK/RUN RELAY
FUSIBLE LINK
IGN
DELAY/SPEED/WASH CONTROL
PARK SW
M
HI CIRCUIT BREAKER
LO
HI
93
98
91
92
M
WINDSHIELD WASHER PUMP
94
150
C154
BLACK
C155
GREEN (98)
GRAY (91)
WHITE (93)
PURPLE (92)
PINK (94)
C340
PULSE WIPER/WASHER SWITCH
BLACK/BLUE
GRAY
BLACK
PURPLE
PINK
MIST
OFF
HI
LO
PULSE
WASH (PULSE)
WHITE (93)
PURPLE (92)
PINK (94)
ORANGE (98)
GRAY (91)
91B14507
Courtesy of General Motors Corp.

Fig. 1: Front Windshield Wiper System Schematic (Pulse Wiper System)

1991 SAFETY EQUIPMENT
Wiper/Washer Systems – "S" & "T" Series (Cont.)

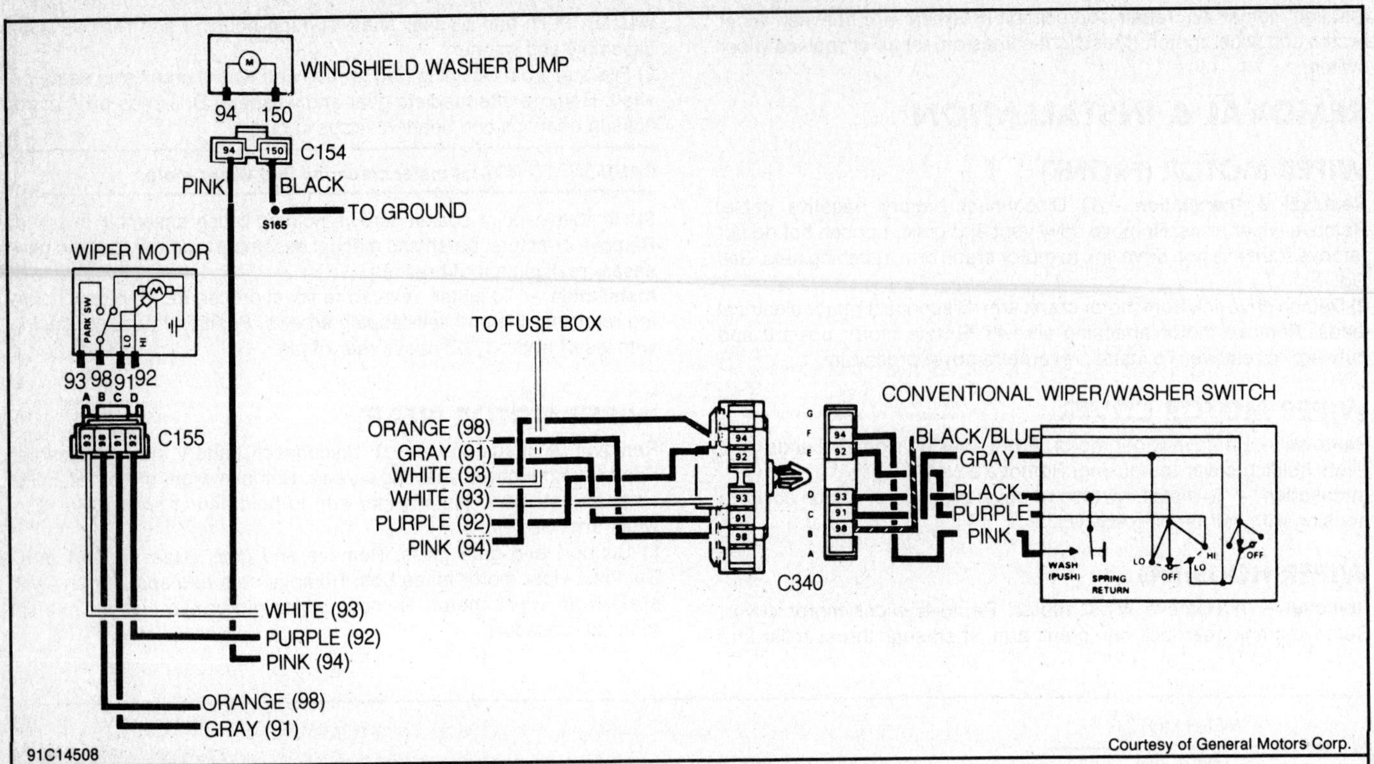
WINDSHIELD WASHER PUMP
94 150
C154
PINK BLACK
S165
TO GROUND
WIPER MOTOR
93 98 91 92
A B C D
C155
TO FUSE BOX
ORANGE (98)
GRAY (91)
WHITE (93)
WHITE (93)
PURPLE (92)
PINK (94)
C340
CONVENTIONAL WIPER/WASHER SWITCH
BLACK/BLUE
GRAY
BLACK
PURPLE
PINK
WASH (PUSH)
SPRING RETURN
WHITE (93)
PURPLE (92)
PINK (94)
ORANGE (98)
GRAY (91)
91C14508
Courtesy of General Motors Corp.

Fig. 2: Front Windshield Wiper System Schematic (Except Pulse Wiper System)

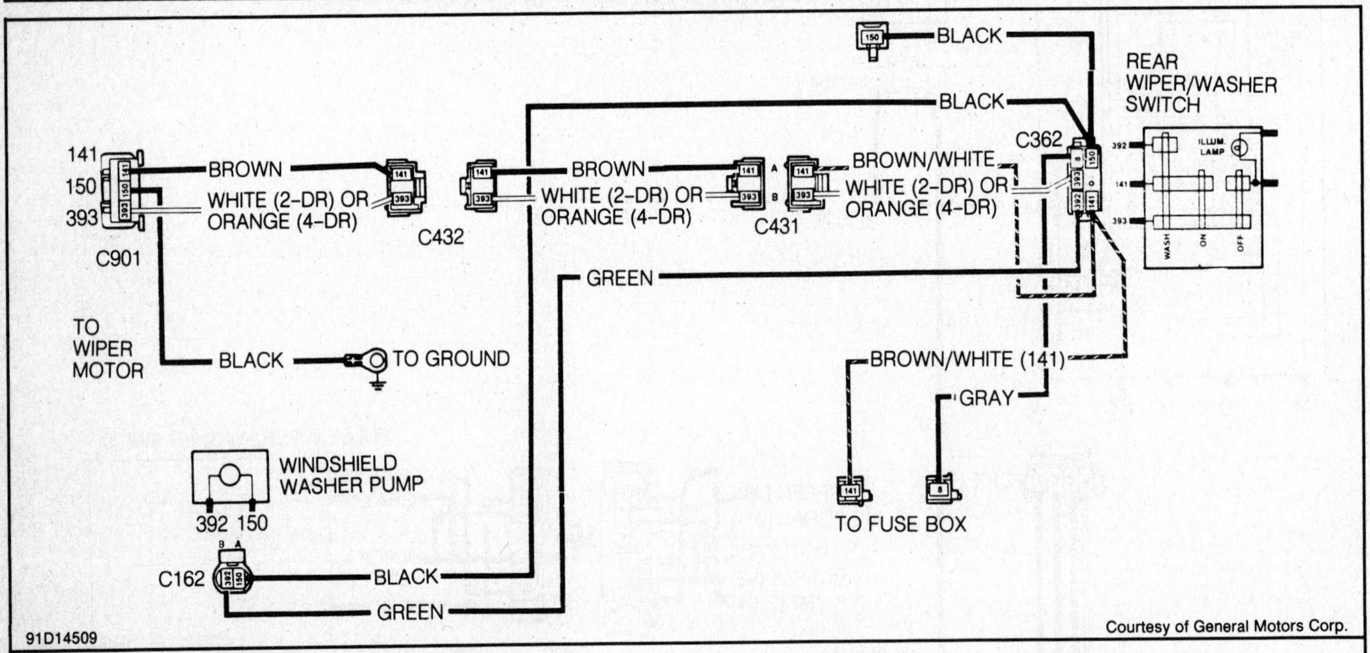
BLACK
REAR WIPER/WASHER SWITCH
BLACK
C362
141
150
393
BROWN
WHITE (2-DR) OR ORANGE (4-DR)
C901
C432
BROWN
WHITE (2-DR) OR ORANGE (4-DR)
C431
BROWN/WHITE
WHITE (2-DR) OR ORANGE (4-DR)
GREEN
TO WIPER MOTOR
BLACK
TO GROUND
BROWN/WHITE (141)
GRAY
WINDSHIELD WASHER PUMP
392 150
C162
BLACK
GREEN
TO FUSE BOX
91D14509
Courtesy of General Motors Corp.

Fig. 3: Rear Windshield Wiper System Schematic

1991 SAFETY EQUIPMENT
Wiper/Washer Systems – "S" & "T" Series (Cont.)

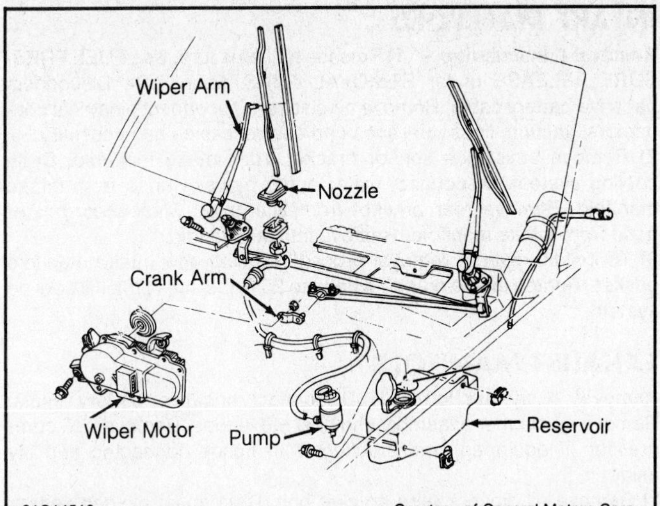
Wiper Arm
Nozzle
Crank Arm
Wiper Motor
Pump
Reservoir
91G14510
Courtesy of General Motors Corp.

Fig. 4: Exploded View of Front Wiper System

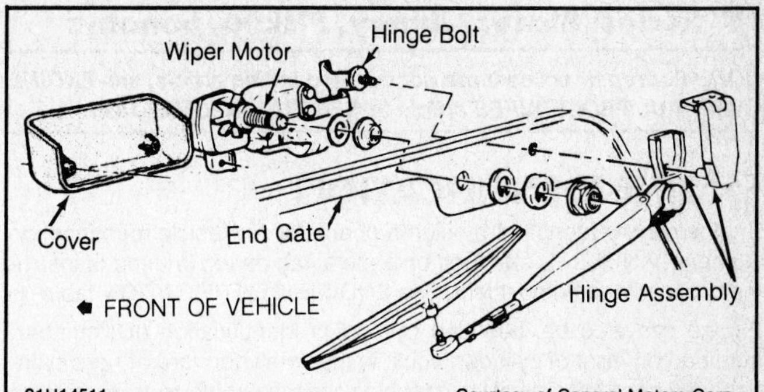
Wiper Motor
Hinge Bolt
Cover
End Gate
FRONT OF VEHICLE
Hinge Assembly
91H14511
Courtesy of General Motors Corp.

Fig. 5: Exploded View of Rear Wiper System

WIRING DIAGRAMS

For additional information, see appropriate chassis wiring diagram in WIRING DIAGRAMS.

1991 ENGINES
2.5L 4-Cylinder

"S" Series: Blazer, Jimmy, Pickup, Sonoma

NOTE: For repair procedures not covered in this article, see ENGINE OVERHAUL PROCEDURES article in GENERAL INFORMATION.

ENGINE IDENTIFICATION

Engine can be identified by eighth character of Vehicle Identification Number (VIN). VIN is stamped on a metal tag on top left end of instrument panel, near windshield. See ENGINE IDENTIFICATION table.

Engine can also be identified by engine identification (ID) number, stamped on front of cylinder block, immediately forward of right cylinder head or on left side of cylinder block on the engine-to-transmission mounting flange.

ENGINE IDENTIFICATION

Engine	VIN Code [1]	Engine ID No.
2.5L (151") TBI	A [2]	[2] L38
	E	LN8

[1] – Eighth character of Vehicle Identification Number (VIN).
[2] – High output.

ADJUSTMENTS

VALVE CLEARANCE ADJUSTMENT

Valve clearance is nonadjustable. Engine is equipped with hydraulic valve lifters.

REMOVAL & INSTALLATION

NOTE: For reassembly reference, label all electrical connectors, vacuum hoses and fuel lines before removal. Also, place mating marks on engine hood and other assemblies before removal.

FUEL PRESSURE RELEASE

Loosen fuel tank filler cap to release tank pressure. Disconnect 3-wire electrical connector at fuel tank. Operate engine until it stalls. Crank engine for an additional 3 seconds. Turn ignition off. Connect 3-wire electrical connector.

ENGINE

Removal & Installation – 1) Release fuel pressure. See FUEL PRESSURE RELEASE under REMOVAL & INSTALLATION. Remove hood. Disconnect negative battery cable. Drain cooling system.

2) Remove power steering reservoir from fan shroud (if equipped). Remove upper fan shroud, fan and radiator. Remove A/C compressor and power steering pump (if equipped) with hoses connected and lay aside. Remove air cleaner.

3) Remove fuel line bracket near fuel filter. Disconnect electrical connectors, vacuum lines, fuel lines and control cables as necessary. Disconnect heater hoses.

4) Remove strut rod. Disconnect exhaust pipe from converter hanger and exhaust manifold. Remove flexplate/flywheel cover, drive belt splash shield (if equipped) and starter. Remove flexplate-to-converter bolts (A/T). Remove 2 outer air dam bolts (left side).

5) Remove lower fan shroud. For access to upper transmission-to-engine bolts, remove body-to-chassis mounting bolts (left side), raise left side of body and support with wood blocks. Remove upper transmission-to-engine bolts. Lower body.

6) Remove remaining transmission-to-engine bolts. Remove motor mount through bolts. Lower vehicle. Support transmission. Pull engine forward slightly and turn sideways. Remove engine. To install, reverse removal procedure. Fill cooling system.

INTAKE MANIFOLD

Removal & Installation – 1) Release fuel pressure. See FUEL PRESSURE RELEASE under REMOVAL & INSTALLATION. Disconnect negative battery cable. Remove air cleaner. Disconnect electrical connectors, vacuum lines, fuel lines and control cables as necessary.

2) Remove emissions sensor bracket from intake manifold. Drain cooling system. Disconnect water pump by-pass hose from intake manifold. Remove rear bracket from alternator. Disconnect heater hose from intake manifold. Remove intake manifold.

3) To install, reverse removal procedure using new intake manifold gasket. Tighten intake manifold bolts to 25 ft. lbs. (34 N.m). Fill cooling system.

EXHAUST MANIFOLD

Removal & Installation – 1) Disconnect negative battery cable. Remove air cleaner assembly and heat stove tube. Remove A/C compressor (if equipped) and brackets with hoses connected and lay aside.

2) Remove oil dipstick tube bracket bolt. Disconnect oxygen sensor electrical connector. Disconnect exhaust pipe from manifold. Remove exhaust manifold.

3) To install, reverse removal procedure using new exhaust manifold gasket. Tighten exhaust manifold bolts in sequence. *See Fig. 1.* Tighten bolt Nos. 1, 2 and 7 to 36 ft. lbs. (49 N.m). Tighten bolt Nos. 3, 4, 5 and 6 to 32 ft. lbs. (43 N.m).

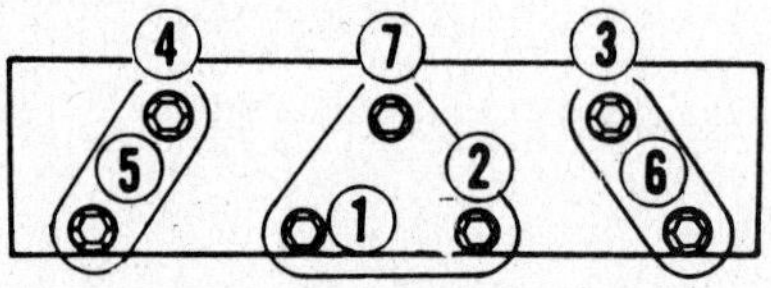
4
7
3
5
2
6
1

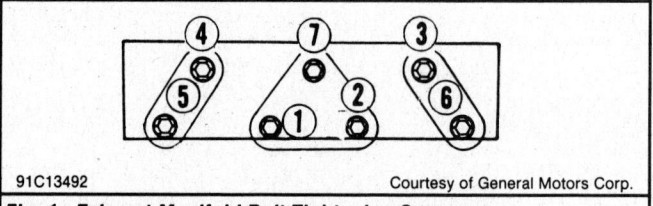

91C13492 Courtesy of General Motors Corp.

Fig. 1: Exhaust Manifold Bolt Tightening Sequence

CYLINDER HEAD

Removal – 1) Release fuel pressure. See FUEL PRESSURE RELEASE under REMOVAL & INSTALLATION. Disconnect negative battery cable. Drain cooling system. Remove air cleaner.

2) Remove A/C compressor (if equipped) and brackets with hoses connected and lay aside. Remove rocker arm cover. Loosen rocker arm nuts, rotate rocker arms to one side and remove push rods.

3) Disconnect electrical connectors, vacuum lines, fuel lines and control cables as necessary. Remove alternator and brackets. Disconnect water pump by-pass hose and heater hose from intake manifold. Disconnect exhaust pipe from exhaust manifold.

4) Remove upper radiator hose. Remove fuel filter and fuel line bracket from rear of cylinder head. Remove dipstick tube. Remove cylinder head bolts and cylinder head.

Installation – 1) Clean cylinder head bolt threads and cylinder block holes. Apply thread sealing compound (1052080) to cylinder head bolt No. 9. Install gasket over dowel pins and ensure all holes align with cylinder block.

2) Install cylinder head with all bolts finger tight. Tighten all bolts in sequence to 18 ft. lbs. (24 N.m). *See Fig. 2.* Then tighten all bolts EXCEPT bolt No. 9 to 26 ft. lbs. (35 N.m). Tighten bolt No. 9 to 18 ft. lbs. (24 N.m).

3) Repeat sequence, tightening all bolts an additional 1/4 turn (90 degrees). To install remaining components, reverse removal procedure. Tighten rocker arm bolts with lifter on base circle of camshaft. Fill cooling system.

FRONT CRANKSHAFT SEAL

Removal – Disconnect negative battery cable. Remove serpentine drive belt. Remove crankshaft damper hub bolt. Remove pulley and hub using puller. Replace hub if oil seal contact area is grooved or rough. Carefully pry out front crankshaft seal using large screwdriver (DO NOT distort timing gear cover).

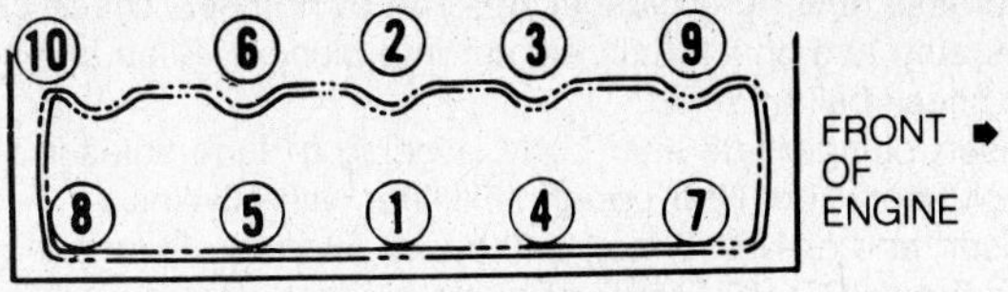
10
6
2
3
9
8
5
1
4
7
FRONT OF ENGINE

91D13493 Courtesy of General Motors Corp.

Fig. 2: Cylinder Head Bolt Tightening Sequence

Installation - Coat seal-to-hub sealing lip with oil. Install seal using Seal Installer (J-34995). Tighten crankshaft damper hub bolt to 160 ft. lbs. (217 N.m). To complete installation, reverse removal procedure.

TIMING GEARS & CAMSHAFT

NOTE: Camshaft gear is pressed onto camshaft. Camshaft gear and camshaft must be removed as an assembly.

Removal - 1) Disconnect negative battery cable. Remove power steering reservoir from fan shroud (if equipped). Remove upper fan shroud. Remove serpentine drive belt, fan and water pump pulley. Remove crankshaft pulley and damper hub.

2) Remove timing gear cover. Remove distributor. Remove cover plate, bearing and oil pump drive shaft and gear assembly from right side of cylinder block. *See Fig. 3.* Remove hydraulic valve lifters. See HYDRAULIC VALVE LIFTERS under REMOVAL & INSTALLATION.

3) Remove radiator. Discharge A/C refrigerant and remove A/C condenser. Remove grille. Rotate crankshaft until thrust plate screws are visible through holes in camshaft gear. Remove thrust plate screws, thrust plate and spacer ring. Remove camshaft.

Inspection - 1) Measure camshaft end play. If end play exceeds .005" (.13 mm), replace thrust plate. If end play is less than .0015" (.038 mm), replace spacer ring.

2) Measure journal diameter and out-of-round. If journal diameter is not 1.869" (47.47 mm) or out-of-round exceeds .001" (.03 mm), replace camshaft.

Installation - Coat camshaft lobes and journals with engine oil supplement. Install camshaft, ensuring timing marks on camshaft gear and crankshaft gear are aligned. To install remaining components, reverse removal procedure. Fill cooling system. Evacuate and charge A/C refrigerant system.

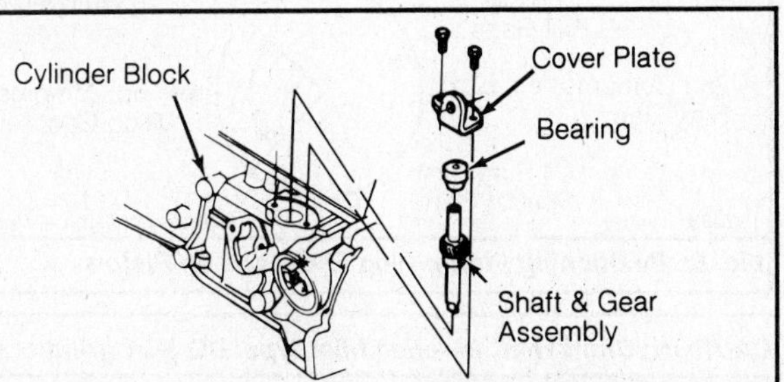
Cylinder Block
Cover Plate
Bearing
Shaft & Gear Assembly

91742 Courtesy of General Motors Corp.

Fig. 3: Exploded View of Oil Pump Drive Shaft Assembly

PUSH ROD SIDE COVER

Removal - 1) Disconnect negative battery cable. Drain cooling system. Remove lower radiator hose and water pump by-pass hose. Remove alternator and bracket. Remove spark plug wires and bracket from intake manifold.

2) Remove fuel line bracket bolt from side cover. Remove oil pressure sending unit. Remove wiring harness brackets from side cover. Remove 4 nuts from side cover studs. Reverse and reinstall 2 nuts onto 2 inner studs. Install 2 remaining nuts onto same inner studs.

3) Using 2 wrenches, hold inner nut stationary. Jam 2 nuts tightly together. Using a wrench on inner nut, alternately unscrew studs until side cover breaks loose. Remove jammed nuts from studs. Remove studs from side cover.

Installation - Clean side cover-to-cylinder block sealing surfaces. Replace damaged studs and rubber washers. Tighten studs to 90 INCH lbs. (10 N.m). Apply a 3/16" diameter (5 mm) bead of RTV sealant to side cover. Install side cover. To complete installation, reverse removal procedure. Tighten side cover studs/nuts to 90 INCH lbs. (10 N.m). Fill cooling system.

ROCKER ARMS & PUSH RODS

Removal - 1) Disconnect negative battery cable. Remove air cleaner, PCV valve and crankcase ventilation pipe. Remove EGR valve. Disconnect vacuum lines as necessary. Remove spark plug wires and clip from cover.

CAUTION: To prevent sealing surface damage, DO NOT pry rocker arm cover from cylinder head.

2) Remove rocker arm cover bolts. Install Rocker Arm Cover Remover (J-34144-A) in place of each rocker arm cover bolt. Rotate rocker arm cover remover until rocker arm cover is lifted from cylinder head. Remove rocker arm cover.

3) Mark component location for reassembly reference. Remove rocker arm bolt and ball. Remove rocker arm, push rod and guide.

CAUTION: Push rod guides are different and must be installed in their original locations.

Installation - 1) If installing new rocker arms or balls, coat components with Molykote. Install push rod guides, push rods, rocker arms, balls and rocker arm bolts. Ensure push rods seat in lifters. Tighten rocker arm bolt to 22 ft. lbs. (30 N.m) with lifter on base circle of camshaft lobe.

2) Apply a 3/16" (5 mm) diameter bead of RTV sealant to rocker arm cover, inboard of bolt holes. DO NOT allow sealant to enter rocker arm cover bolt holes in cylinder head. Install rocker arm cover. Tighten rocker arm cover bolts to 75 INCH pounds (8 N.m). To install remaining components, reverse removal procedure.

HYDRAULIC VALVE LIFTERS

Removal - 1) Remove rocker arms and push rods. See ROCKER ARMS & PUSH RODS under REMOVAL & INSTALLATION. Remove push rod side cover. See PUSH ROD SIDE COVER under REMOVAL & INSTALLATION.

2) Remove lifter retainer, guide and lifter. *See Fig. 4.* Mark component location for reassembly reference.

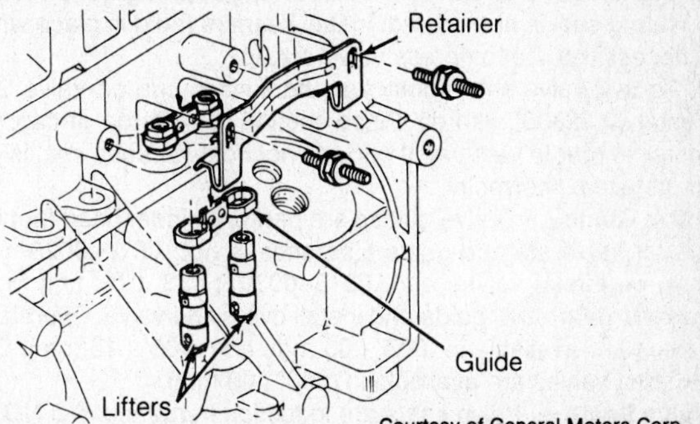
Retainer
Guide
Lifters

91740 Courtesy of General Motors Corp.

Fig. 4: Exploded View of Lifter Retainer Assembly

Inspection - Measure lifter diameter and lifter bore diameter. Determine lifter oil clearance. Replace lifter if oil clearance is not within specification. See VALVE LIFTERS table under ENGINE SPECIFICATIONS at end of article.

Installation - Lubricate lifter surfaces with oil and install in bore. To install remaining components, reverse removal procedure. Tighten lifter retainer stud to 90 INCH lbs. (10 N.m).

REAR CRANKSHAFT SEAL

Removal - Remove transmission and flywheel/flexplate. See appropriate AUTOMATIC TRANSMISSION SERVICING article (A/T) or

1991 ENGINES
2.5L 4-Cylinder (Cont.)

CLUTCHES article (M/T). Note direction of seal for installation. Carefully pry seal from housing. DO NOT scratch sealing surface on crankshaft outer diameter.

Installation - Coat inner and outer seal surfaces with engine oil. Using Seal Installer (J-34924), install seal. To install remaining components, reverse removal procedure.

WATER PUMP

Removal - Drain cooling system. Remove serpentine belt. Remove upper fan shroud, fan/clutch assembly and water pump pulley. Disconnect hose(s) from water pump. Remove water pump bolts and water pump.

Installation - To install, reverse removal procedure. Apply Sealant (1052080) to water pump bolt threads. Tighten water pump bolts to 22 ft. lbs. (30 N.m). Fill cooling system.

OIL PAN

Removal - **1)** Disconnect negative battery cable. Remove power steering fluid reservoir from fan shroud (if equipped). Remove upper fan shroud. Raise and support vehicle. Drain crankcase. Remove strut rods.

2) Disconnect exhaust pipe from manifold and catalytic converter as necessary. Remove flywheel/flexplate cover, starter and brace. Disconnect brake line bracket from crossmember. Remove front engine mount bolts. Remove oil pan.

Installation - **1)** Apply a bead of RTV sealant to sealing surface of oil pan (inboard of oil pan bolt holes), rear main bearing cap-to-cylinder block junction and front cover-to-cylinder block junction. Install oil pan.

2) Tighten oil pan bolts to 90 INCH lbs. (10 N.m). To install remaining components, reverse removal procedure.

OVERHAUL

CYLINDER HEAD

Valve Springs - Replace valve spring if free length, installed height and pressure are not within specification. See VALVES & VALVE SPRINGS table under ENGINE SPECIFICATIONS at end of article.

Valve Stem Oil Seals - **1)** Valve stem uses an upper "O" ring seal and a lower cone seal. To install valve stem oil seals, slide cone seal over valve stem until seated against cylinder head. Install spring/damper, shield and cap. Apply engine oil to "O" ring seal.

2) Compress valve spring. Install "O" ring seal in groove in valve stem, ensuring seal is not twisted. Install keepers (hold in place with grease if necessary). Decompress valve spring.

3) To test valve seal, lightly wet the suction cup on Valve Stem Seal Tester (J-22330) with oil. Place suction cup on top of cap. Press on tester to create vacuum. If cup will not hold vacuum, seal is damaged or installed incorrectly.

Valve Guides - Valve guides are part of cylinder head (not replaceable). If valve stem-to-guide clearance is not .0010-.0025" (.025-.064 mm) on intake valves and .0013-.0030" (.033-.076 mm) on exhaust valves, ream valve guide and install oversized valve. Oversized intake valves are available in .003" (.08 mm) and .005" (.13 mm). Oversized exhaust valves are available in .003" (.08 mm).

Valve Seats - Valve seats are induction hardened. DO NOT remove an excessive amount of material from seat.

Valves - Replace valve if margin is less than 1/32" (.8 mm).

VALVE TRAIN

Hydraulic Valve Lifter - **1)** To disassemble, press down on push rod seat with screwdriver and remove retainer. *See Fig. 5.* Remove push rod seat, metering valve, plunger and plunger spring (if plunger is stuck, turn lifter upside down and tap against flat surface to dislodge).

2) Using small screwdriver, pry check ball retainer from plunger. Remove check ball spring and check ball from plunger. Remove plunger spring from lifter body.

CAUTION: DO NOT interchange parts between lifters.

3) To assemble, turn plunger upside-down. Insert check ball, check ball spring and check ball retainer into plunger. Slide plunger spring over check ball retainer.

4) Insert plunger into lifter body, aligning oil feed holes in lifter body and plunger. Turn lifter upright. Fill lifter with 10W oil.

5) Insert end of 1/8" (3 mm) drift punch into top of plunger and press down firmly (DO NOT force or pump plunger). Insert a 1/16" (1.5 mm) drift punch through both oil holes to hold plunger down against spring pressure. Remove 1/8" (3 mm) drift punch.

6) Refill lifter with 10W oil. Install metering valve, push rod seat and retainer. Push down on push rod seat using a push rod. Remove 1/16" (1.5 mm) drift punch.

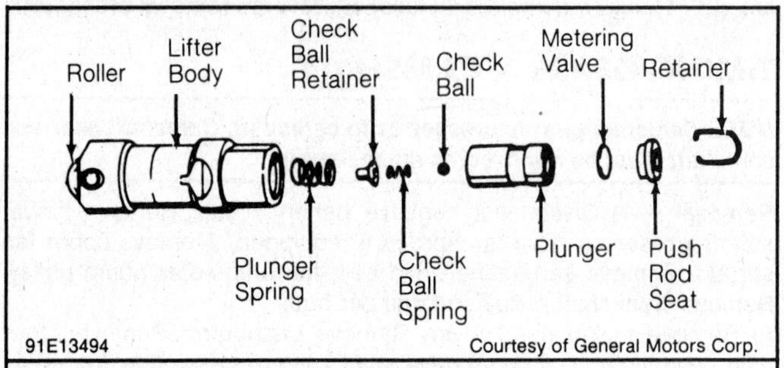
Roller
Lifter Body
Check Ball Retainer
Check Ball
Metering Valve
Retainer
Plunger Spring
Check Ball Spring
Plunger
Push Rod Seat
91E13494
Courtesy of General Motors Corp.

Fig. 5: Exploded View of Hydraulic Valve Lifter

CYLINDER BLOCK ASSEMBLY

Piston & Rod Assembly - Mark piston position in relation to connecting rod before separating components. Install piston in cylinder block with mark on top of piston toward front of engine.

Fitting Pistons - Measure piston diameter at 90-degree angle to piston pin bore, on center line of piston pin bore (1 13/16" below top of piston). Measure cylinder bore diameter 2.25" (57.2 mm) from cylinder block deck surface.

Piston Rings - Install piston rings with end gaps properly spaced around circumference of piston. *See Fig. 6.*

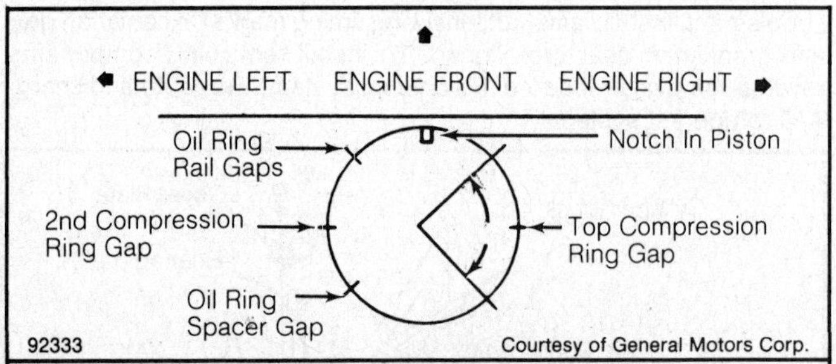
ENGINE LEFT
ENGINE FRONT
ENGINE RIGHT
Oil Ring Rail Gaps
Notch In Piston
2nd Compression Ring Gap
Top Compression Ring Gap
Oil Ring Spacer Gap
92333
Courtesy of General Motors Corp.

Fig. 6: Positioning Piston Ring End Gaps on Piston

CAUTION: Crankshaft is rolled fillet type. DO NOT grind crankshaft.

Rod Bearings - Undersized bearings are available in .001" (.025 mm).

Crankshaft & Main Bearings - Mark main bearing caps for reassembly reference. Undersize bearings are available in .001" (.025 mm).

Thrust Bearing - Rear main bearing is thrust bearing. To measure crankshaft end play, tighten main bearing cap bolts to 10 ft. lbs. (14 N.m). Tap end of crankshaft rearward then forward with lead hammer to align rear main bearing and crankshaft thrust surfaces. Tighten main bearing cap bolts to 65 ft. lbs. (88 N.m). Measure end play between front end of rear main bearing cap and crankshaft.

Cylinder Block - If cylinder block deck surface warpage exceeds .004" (.10 mm), machine surface. Replace cylinder block if more than .010" (.25 mm) material is removed from deck surface.

ENGINE OILING

ENGINE LUBRICATION SYSTEM

Oil pump is gear-driven from camshaft. *See Fig. 7.* Pump draws oil from pan, feeding it through oil filter and into passage along right side of block, where it intersects lifter bosses. Oil is then routed to camshaft and crankshaft bearings through smaller drilled passages. Oil is supplied to rocker arms through hydraulic lifters and push rods. By-pass valves are located in pick-up screen, oil filter mounting and oil pump. Oil returns to pan through return holes in cylinder head and cylinder block.

Crankcase Capacity – Oil capacity is approximately 3.5 qts. (3.3L) with filter change.

Oil Pressure – Oil pressure is 36-41 psi (2.53-2.88 kg/cm²) at 2000 RPM at normal operating temperature.

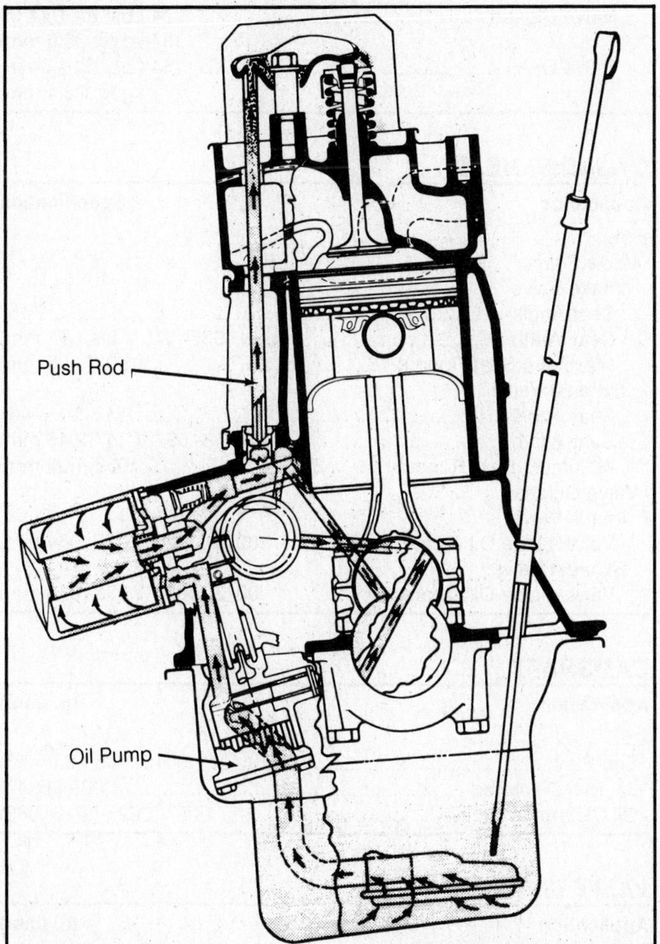
Push Rod
Oil Pump
91F13495
Courtesy of General Motors Corp.

Fig. 7: Cross-Sectional View of Engine Oiling Circuit

OIL PUMP

Removal & Disassembly – **1)** Remove oil pan. See OIL PAN under REMOVAL & INSTALLATION. Remove oil pump bolts and pick-up tube nut. Remove oil pump.

2) Remove oil pump cover screws, cover and gasket. *See Fig. 8.* Mark gear teeth for reassembly reference. Remove drive gear and shaft. Remove idler gear. Remove spring retainer, pressure regulator spring and pressure regulator valve.

Inspection – **1)** Replace oil pump if pick-up tube is loose. Ensure pressure regulator valve slides freely in its bore. With gears removed, measure gear length and diameter, and gear pocket depth and diameter.

2) Install gears. Measure gear lash, side clearance and end clearance. Replace oil pump if any measurements are not within specification. See OIL PUMP SPECIFICATIONS table.

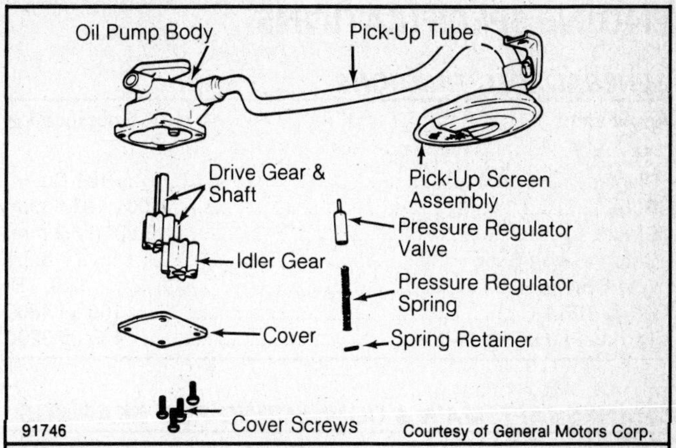
Oil Pump Body
Pick-Up Tube
Drive Gear & Shaft
Pick-Up Screen Assembly
Pressure Regulator Valve
Idler Gear
Pressure Regulator Spring
Cover
Spring Retainer
Cover Screws
91746
Courtesy of General Motors Corp.

Fig. 8: Exploded View of Oil Pump

OIL PUMP SPECIFICATIONS

Application	Specification In. (mm)
Gear	
Diameter	1.496-1.500 (38.00-38.10)
End Clearance	.002-.005 (.05-.13)
Lash	.009-.015 (.23-.38)
Length	.999-1.002 (25.37-25.45)
Side Clearance (Maximum)	.004 (.10)
Gear Pocket	
Depth	.995-.998 (25.27-25.35)
Diameter	1.503-1.506 (38.18-38.25)

Reassembly & Installation – To reassemble, reverse disassembly procedure. Align marks on gears when installing in pump body. Tighten pump cover screws to 10 ft. lbs. (14 N.m). To install, reverse removal procedure. Tighten oil pump bolts to 18 ft. lbs. (24 N.m). Tighten pick-up tube nut to 22 ft. lbs. (30 N.m).

TORQUE SPECIFICATIONS

TORQUE SPECIFICATIONS

Application	Ft. Lbs. (N.m)
Connecting Rod Cap Nut	30 (41)
Crankshaft Damper Hub Bolt	160 (217)
Crankshaft Pulley-To-Damper Hub Bolt	26 (34)
Cylinder Head Bolt	[1]
Exhaust Manifold Bolt [2]	
Bolts No. 1, 2 & 7	36 (49)
Bolts No. 3, 4, 5 & 6	32 (43)
Flexplate Bolt (A/T)	55 (75)
Flywheel Bolt (M/T)	65 (88)
Intake Manifold Bolt	25 (34)
Main Bearing Cap Bolt	65 (88)
Oil Pump Cover Bolt	10 (14)
Oil Pump-To-Block Bolt	18 (24)
Oil Pump Pick-Up Tube Nut	22 (30)
Rocker Arm Bolt	22 (30)
Water Pump Bolt	22 (30)
	INCH Lbs. (N.m)
Camshaft Thrust Plate Bolt	90 (10)
Front Timing Gear Cover Bolt	90 (10)
Lifter Retainer Bolt/Stud	90 (10)
Oil Pan Bolt	90 (10)
Push Rod Cover Nut & Stud	90 (10)
Rocker Arm Cover Bolt	75 (8.5)

[1] – See CYLINDER HEAD under REMOVAL & INSTALLATION for cylinder head bolt tightening procedures. Tighten bolts in sequence. *See Fig. 2.*

[2] – Tighten cylinder head bolt in sequence and to specification. *See Fig. 1.*

1991 ENGINES
2.5L 4-Cylinder (Cont.)

ENGINE SPECIFICATIONS

GENERAL SPECIFICATIONS

Application	Specification
2.5L	
Displacement	151 Cu. In.
Bore	4.00" (101.6 mm)
Stroke	3.00" (76.2 mm)
Compression Ratio	8.3:1
Fuel System	TBI
HP @ RPM	105 @ 4800
Torque Ft. Lbs. @ RPM	135 @ 3200

CRANKSHAFT, MAIN & CONNECTING ROD BEARINGS

Application	In. (mm)
2.5L	
Crankshaft End Play	.0035-.0085 (.089-.216)
Main Bearings	
Journal Diameter	2.300 (58.42)
Journal Out-Of-Round	.0005 (.013)
Journal Taper	.0005 (.013)
Oil Clearance	.0005-.0022 (.013-.056)
Connecting Rod Bearings	
Journal Diameter	2.000 (50.80)
Journal Out-Of-Round	.0005 (.013)
Journal Taper	.0005 (.013)
Oil Clearance	.0005-.0026 (.013-.066)

CONNECTING RODS

Application	In. (mm)
2.5L	
Side Play	.006-.020 (.15-.51)

PISTONS, PINS & RINGS

Application	In. (mm)
2.5L	
Pistons	
Clearance	.0014-.0022 (.036-.056)
Pins	
Diameter	.938-.942 (23.83-23.93)
Piston Fit	.0002-.0004 (.005-.010)
Rod Fit	Press Fit
Rings	
No. 1	
End Gap	.010-.020 (.25-.51)
Side Clearance	.002-.003 (.05-.08)
No. 2	
End Gap	.010-.020 (.25-.51)
Side Clearance	.001-.003 (.03-.08)
No. 3 (Oil)	
End Gap	.020-.060 (.51-1.52)
Side Clearance	.015-.055 (.38-1.40)

CYLINDER BLOCK

Application	In. (mm)
2.5L	
Cylinder Bore	
Diameter	4.00 (101.6)
Maximum Taper	.005 (.13)
Maximum Out-Of-Round	.001 (.03)
Maximum Deck Warpage	.004 (.10)

VALVES & VALVE SPRINGS

Application	Specification
2.5L	
Intake Valves	
Face Angle	45°
Minimum Margin	1/32" (.8 mm)
Stem Diameter	.3133-.3138" (7.958-7.971 mm)
Exhaust Valves	
Face Angle	45°
Minimum Margin	1/32" (.8 mm)
Stem Diameter	.3128-3135" (7.945-7.963 mm)
Valve Springs	
Free Length	1.78" (45.2 mm)
Installed Height	1.44" (36.6 mm)
Pressure	
Valve Closed	74 Lbs. @ 1.44 In. (34 kg @ 36.6 mm)
Valve Open	164 Lbs. @ 1.04 In. (74 kg @ 26.4 mm)

CYLINDER HEAD

Application	Specification
2.5L	
Valve Seats	
Intake Valve	
Seat Angle	46°
Seat Width	.035-.075" (.89-1.91 mm)
Maximum Seat Runout	.002" (.05 mm)
Exhaust Valve	
Seat Angle	46°
Seat Width	.058-.097" (1.47-2.46 mm)
Maximum Seat Runout	.002" (.05 mm)
Valve Guides	
Intake Valve	
Valve Guide Oil Clearance	.0010-.0025" (.025-.064 mm)
Exhaust Valve	
Valve Guide Oil Clearance	.0013-.0030" (.033-.076 mm)

CAMSHAFT

Application	In. (mm)
2.5L	
End Play	.0015-.005 (.038-.13)
Journal Diameter	1.869 (47.47)
Oil Clearance	.0007-.0027 (.018-.069)

VALVE LIFTERS

Application	In. (mm)
2.5L	
Bore Diameter	.8435-.8445 (21.425-21.450)
Lifter Diameter	.8420-.8427 (21.387-21.405)
Oil Clearance	.0025 (.064)

1991 ENGINES
2.8L V6

"S" Series: Blazer, Jimmy, Pickup, Sonoma

NOTE: For repair procedures not covered in this article, see ENGINE OVERHAUL PROCEDURES article in GENERAL INFORMATION.

ENGINE IDENTIFICATION

Engine may be identified by the eighth character of Vehicle Identification Number (VIN) on top of instrument panel, near lower left corner of windshield. Eighth character R identifies 2.8L TBI engine.

Engine may also be identified by engine identification number stamped on right side of cylinder block below cylinder No. 1 exhaust manifold port, or on front of cylinder block above timing chain cover (to left of center). Engine ID number LL2 identifies 2.8L TBI engine.

ADJUSTMENTS

VALVE CLEARANCE ADJUSTMENT

NOTE: Although valve clearance adjustment is not usually required (engine uses hydraulic valve lifters), perform the following procedures after servicing valve train.

1) Remove rocker arm cover. Rotate crankshaft until cylinder No. 1 is at TDC of compression stroke. Grasp cylinder No. 1 intake valve push rod with thumb and forefinger, and attempt to rotate.

2) Loosen adjusting nut until push rod rotates freely. Continue to rotate push rod back and forth while slowly tightening adjusting nut. When resistance is felt while rotating push rod, stop tightening adjusting nut. Valve train is now at zero lash. Tighten adjusting nut 1 1/2 turns.

3) Repeat step **2)** for intake valves of cylinders No. 5 and 6, and exhaust valves of cylinders No. 1, 2 and 3. Rotate crankshaft one revolution (until cylinder No. 4 is at TDC of compression stroke).

4) Repeat step **2)** for intake valves of cylinders No. 2, 3 and 4, and exhaust valves of cylinders No. 4, 5 and 6. Install rocker arm cover and gasket.

REMOVAL & INSTALLATION

NOTE: For reassembly reference, label all electrical connectors, vacuum hoses and fuel lines before removal. Also, place mating marks on engine hood and other major assemblies before removal.

FUEL PRESSURE RELEASE

Disconnect negative battery cable. Loosen fuel tank cap to relieve tank pressure. Internal constant bleed feature relieves fuel system pressure in fuel lines and TBI unit when ignition switch is turned off. No further pressure release is required.

ENGINE

Removal & Installation – 1) Release fuel pressure. See FUEL PRESSURE RELEASE under REMOVAL & INSTALLATION. Disconnect negative battery cable. Remove hood. Drain cooling system. Disconnect upper radiator hose from radiator.

2) Remove coolant overflow hose, upper fan shroud, radiator and fan/clutch assembly. Remove air cleaner. Disconnect fuel lines, electrical connectors, vacuum hoses, coolant hoses and control cables as necessary. Remove distributor cap. Raise and support vehicle.

3) Remove exhaust pipe between converter and exhaust manifolds. Remove engine strut rods from bell housing. Remove flexplate/flywheel cover (if equipped). Remove torque converter bolts (A/T). Remove rear shield from converter.

4) Disconnect converter hanger at exhaust pipe. Remove lower fan shroud and 2 outer air dam bolts. Remove left body mount bolts. Raise body to access bell housing bolts. Remove bell housing bolts. Lower body. Remove motor mount through bolts.

5) Lower vehicle. Remove A/C compressor and P/S pump with hoses connected and lay aside (if equipped). Support transmission and remove engine. To install, reverse removal procedure. Fill cooling system.

INTAKE MANIFOLD

Removal – 1) Release fuel pressure. See FUEL PRESSURE RELEASE under REMOVAL & INSTALLATION. Drain cooling system. Disconnect negative battery cable. Remove air cleaner.

2) Disconnect fuel lines, electrical connectors, vacuum hoses, coolant hoses and control cables as necessary. Mark distributor position and remove distributor. Remove rocker arm covers. Remove intake manifold bolts and nuts. Remove intake manifold and gaskets.

Installation – 1) Inspect intake manifold-to-cylinder head gasket surface warpage. If warpage exceeds .005" (.13 mm), replace intake manifold. Apply 3/16" (5 mm) bead of RTV sealant to front and rear intake manifold-to-cylinder block sealing surfaces; extend RTV sealant bead 1/4" (6 mm) beyond cylinder block-to-cylinder head junctions.

2) Position new intake manifold gaskets on cylinder heads, cutting gaskets as necessary to fit behind push rods. Ensure all holes are aligned. Install intake manifold. Tighten intake manifold bolts in sequence to 23 ft. lbs. (31 N.m). *See Fig. 1.* To install remaining components, reverse removal procedure.

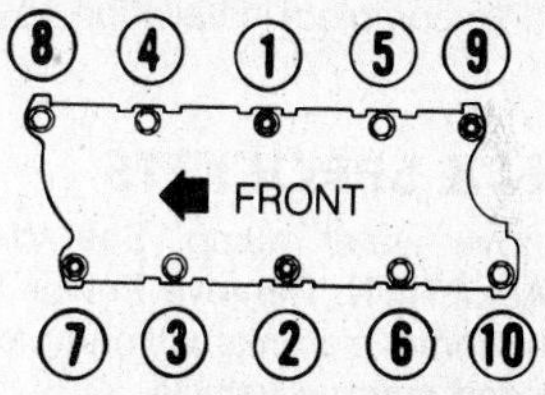
8
4
1
5
9
FRONT
7
3
2
6
10

91G13496 Courtesy of General Motors Corp.

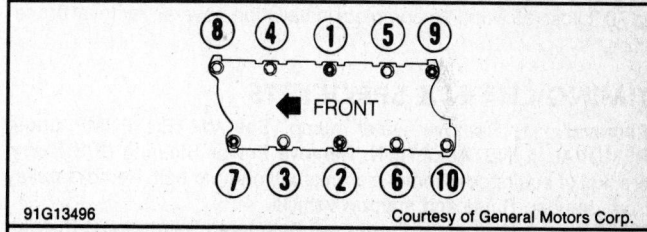

Fig. 1: Intake Manifold Bolt Tightening Sequence

EXHAUST MANIFOLD

Removal – 1) Disconnect negative battery cable. Raise and support vehicle. Disconnect exhaust pipe from manifold. Remove 4 bolts from rear end of exhaust manifold. Lower vehicle.

2) For right manifold, remove heat shield, diverter valve, air pump and alternator brackets. For left manifold, remove heat stove pipe and P/S pump bracket. Remove remaining manifold bolts. Remove manifold and gasket.

Installation – Inspect exhaust manifold-to-cylinder head gasket surface warpage. If warpage exceeds .005" (.13 mm), replace exhaust manifold. To install, reverse removal procedure using new gasket. Tighten exhaust manifold bolts to 25 ft. lbs. (34 N.m).

CYLINDER HEAD

Removal – 1) Remove intake manifold. See INTAKE MANIFOLD under REMOVAL & INSTALLATION. Drain coolant from cylinder block. Raise and support vehicle. Disconnect exhaust pipe from manifold. Lower vehicle.

2) Remove oil dipstick tube (if removing left cylinder head). Disconnect fuel lines, electrical connectors, vacuum hoses, coolant hoses and control cables as necessary.

3) Remove serpentine belt, alternator and air pump with bracket (if removing right cylinder head). Remove rocker arm nut, rocker arm, pivot ball and push rods. Keep components in order for reassembly. Remove cylinder head bolts. Remove cylinder head and gasket.

Installation – 1) Ensure cylinder head bolt threads and cylinder block holes are clean. Install cylinder head. Apply GM Sealant (1052080) to head bolt threads. Install head bolts and tighten in sequence to 40 ft. lbs. (54 N.m). *See Fig. 2.* Tighten head bolts an additional 90 degrees (1/4 turn).

2) To install remaining components, reverse removal procedure. Adjust valves. See VALVE CLEARANCE ADJUSTMENT under ADJUSTMENTS. Fill cooling system.

1991 ENGINES
2.8L V6 (Cont.)

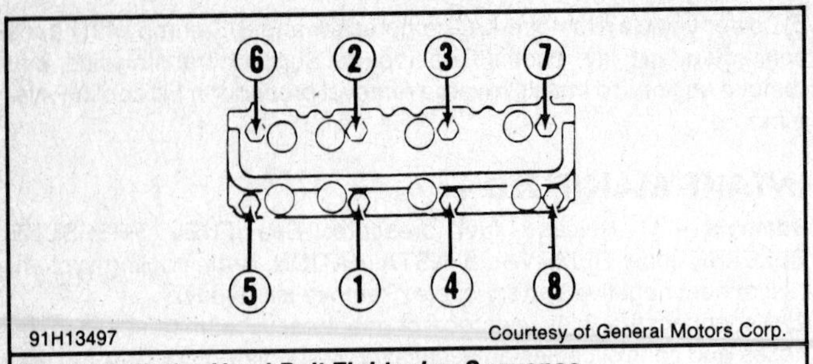
6
2
3
7
5
1
4
8
91H13497
Courtesy of General Motors Corp.

Fig. 2: Cylinder Head Bolt Tightening Sequence

FRONT CRANKSHAFT OIL SEAL

Removal – Disconnect negative battery cable. Remove serpentine belt. Remove crankshaft damper bolt. Remove pulley from damper. Raise and support vehicle. Remove damper using Crankshaft Damper Puller (J-24420-B) or (J-23523-E). Using large screwdriver, carefully pry out seal.

Installation – Coat sealing lip and damper surface with oil. Install seal using Seal Installer (J-35468). Clean damper key and keyway. Apply GM Sealant (1052336) to keyway. Install damper using Crankshaft Damper Installer (J-29113). Install damper bolt and tighten to 70 ft. lbs. (95 N.m). To complete installation, reverse removal procedure.

TIMING CHAIN & SPROCKETS

Removal – 1) Remove water pump. See WATER PUMP under REMOVAL & INSTALLATION. Remove Power Steering (P/S) pump bracket (if equipped). Remove crankshaft damper bolt. Remove pulley from damper. Raise and support vehicle.

2) Remove damper using Crankshaft Damper Puller (J-24420-B) or (J-23523-E). Disconnect lower radiator hose from timing chain cover. Remove timing chain cover bolts. Remove cover and gasket.

3) Rotate crankshaft until timing marks on camshaft and crankshaft sprockets align. *See Fig. 3.* Check timing chain deflection. If timing chain deflects more than 3/8" (9.5 mm) from timing chain damper, replace chain.

4) Remove camshaft sprocket bolts. Remove camshaft sprocket and timing chain. Remove crankshaft sprocket (if necessary).

Installation – 1) Install crankshaft sprocket (if removed). Apply Molykote to camshaft sprocket thrust surface. Install timing chain over camshaft sprocket. Hold sprocket vertically with chain hanging downward. Align timing marks. *See Fig. 3.*

2) Install timing chain and camshaft sprocket on camshaft, ensuring sprocket dowel pin hole aligns with camshaft dowel pin. Install and tighten camshaft sprocket bolts to 20 ft. lbs. (27 N.m). Lubricate timing chain with engine oil.

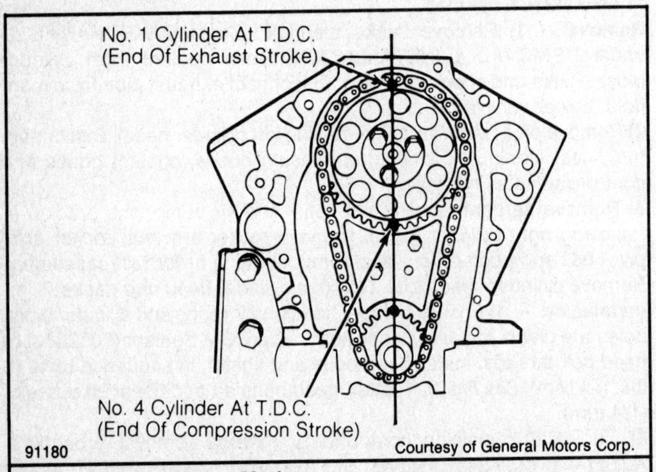
No. 1 Cylinder At T.D.C.
(End Of Exhaust Stroke)
No. 4 Cylinder At T.D.C.
(End Of Compression Stroke)
91180
Courtesy of General Motors Corp.

Fig. 3: Aligning Timing Marks

3) Lightly coat both sides of new timing chain cover gasket with anaerobic sealer. Install timing chain cover. Tighten cover bolts to 18 ft. lbs. (24 N.m). To install remaining components, reverse removal procedure. Fill cooling system.

VALVE LIFTERS

Removal – Remove intake manifold. See INTAKE MANIFOLD under REMOVAL & INSTALLATION. Remove rocker arm nut. Remove rocker arm, pivot ball and push rods. Keep components in order for reassembly. Remove valve lifters.

NOTE: Some engines are equipped with standard and oversize valve lifters. Oversize lifter usage is indicated by small, White paint dot and/or ".25 mm O.S." stamped near lifter bore.

Installation – If installing new lifter, coat bottom of lifter with Molykote. Install lifter in original bore. To complete installation, reverse removal procedure. Adjust valves. See VALVE CLEARANCE ADJUSTMENT under ADJUSTMENTS.

CAMSHAFT

Removal – 1) Drain cooling system. Remove radiator. Remove upper fan shroud. Remove valve lifters. See VALVE LIFTERS under REMOVAL & INSTALLATION.

2) Remove timing chain and camshaft sprocket. See TIMING CHAIN & SPROCKETS under REMOVAL & INSTALLATION. Carefully remove camshaft.

Inspection – Measure camshaft journal diameter, lobe lift and oil clearance. See CAMSHAFT table under ENGINE SPECIFICATIONS at end of article. Replace components if measurements are not within specification.

Installation – 1) Lubricate camshaft bearings and camshaft lobes with GM Lubricant (1051396). Install camshaft. To install remaining components, reverse removal procedure. Ensure timing marks are aligned. *See Fig. 3.* Install valve lifters and push rods in original location.

2) Adjust valves. See VALVE CLEARANCE ADJUSTMENT under ADJUSTMENTS. If camshaft is replaced, add GM Engine Oil Supplement (1052367) to engine oil.

REAR CRANKSHAFT OIL SEAL

Removal – Remove transmission and flexplate/flywheel. Note direction of seal installation. Using screwdriver, carefully pry seal from housing in rear main bearing. DO NOT scratch crankshaft sealing surface.

Installation – 1) Coat inner and outer seal surfaces with engine oil. Install seal on mandrel of Seal Installer (J-34686) until dust lip bottoms against tool collar. *See Fig. 4.*

2) Align seal installer dowel pin with alignment hole of crankshaft. Install seal installer on crankshaft. Hand tighten seal installer bolts or torque to 36 INCH lbs. (4 N.m).

3) To install seal in housing, tighten seal installer handle until seal installer collar is even with cylinder block. Remove seal installer. To install remaining components, reverse removal procedure.

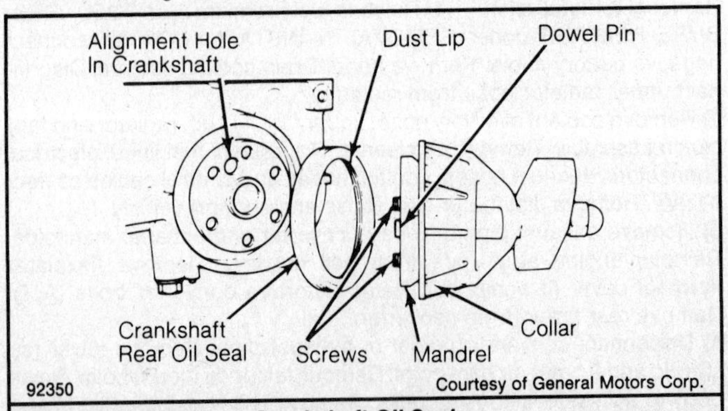
Alignment Hole
In Crankshaft
Dust Lip
Dowel Pin
Crankshaft
Rear Oil Seal
Screws
Mandrel
Collar
92350
Courtesy of General Motors Corp.

Fig. 4: Installing Rear Crankshaft Oil Seal

WATER PUMP

Removal – Disconnect negative battery cable. Drain coolant. Remove serpentine belt and upper fan shroud. Remove fan/clutch assembly and water pump pulley. Disconnect necessary coolant hoses. Remove water pump bolts and nut. Note bolt lengths and location. Remove water pump and gasket.

Installation – Apply GM Sealant (1052080) to bolts. To install, reverse removal procedure using new gasket. Tighten water pump bolts and nut to 22 ft. lbs. (30 N.m). Fill cooling system.

OIL PAN

Removal & Installation – **1)** Remove engine. See ENGINE under REMOVAL & INSTALLATION. Remove oil pan bolts. Remove oil pan and gasket.

2) To install, apply GM Sealer (1052914) to half-round section at rear end of oil pan. Install oil pan with new gasket. Tighten 2 bolts at rear end of oil pan to 18 ft. lbs. (24 N.m). Tighten all other bolts to 84 INCH lbs. (10 N.m).

OVERHAUL

CYLINDER HEAD

Valve Springs – Replace valve spring if free length, installed height and pressure are not within specification. Replace valve spring damper if free length is not within specification. See VALVES & VALVE SPRINGS table under ENGINE SPECIFICATIONS at end of article.

Valve Stem Oil Seals – Intake valve uses an upper "O" ring seal and a lower seal. *See Fig. 5.* Exhaust valve uses only an upper "O" ring seal and an oil shedder/rotator. When installing intake valve lower seal, slide seal over valve stem and valve guide boss. Coat "O" ring seal with engine oil before installation. Ensure seal is not twisted when installed.

Valve Guides – Valve guides are part of cylinder head (not replaceable). If valve stem-to-guide clearance is not .0026-.0068" (.066-.172 mm), ream valve guide and install oversize valve. Oversize valves are available in .003" (.08 mm), .015" (.38 mm) and .030" (.76 mm).

Valves – Replace valve if margin is less than 1/32" (.8 mm).

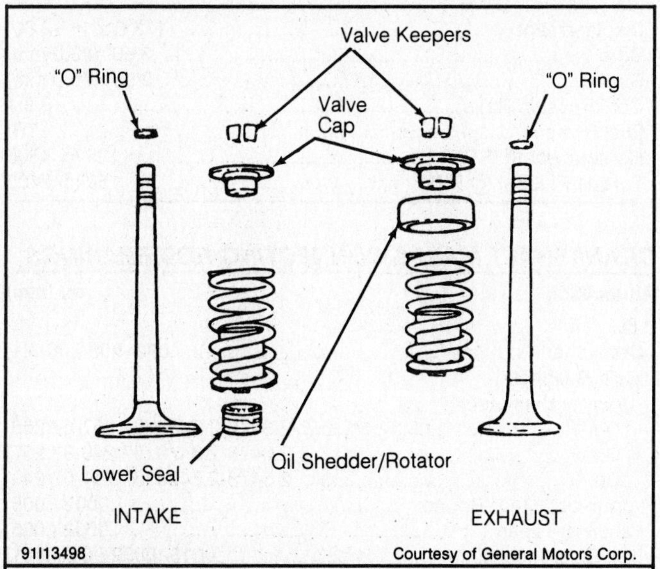
Valve Keepers
"O" Ring
"O" Ring
Valve Cap
Lower Seal
Oil Shedder/Rotator
INTAKE
EXHAUST
91I13498
Courtesy of General Motors Corp.

Fig. 5: Exploded View of Intake & Exhaust Valve/Spring Assemblies

VALVE TRAIN

Rocker Arm Assembly – Clean push rods, rocker arms, balls and nuts with solvent then blow dry. Inspect rocker arms and balls at mating surface for damage. Inspect push rods for bends or wear. Ensure push rod oil passages are clear.

CYLINDER BLOCK ASSEMBLY

Cylinder Block – If cylinder block deck surface warpage exceeds .004" (.10 mm), machine surface. Replace cylinder block if more than .010" (.25 mm) material is removed from deck surface.

Piston & Rod Assembly – Mark piston position in relation to connecting rod before separating components. Replace piston and pin as matched set. Install piston in cylinder block, with mark on top of piston toward front of engine.

Fitting Pistons – **1)** Mark piston and cylinder for reassembly reference. Remove rings from piston. Ensure piston and cylinder are clean. Insert piston into cylinder bore upside down.

2) Piston should free fall in cylinder bore when bottom of piston skirt is 1/2 - 1" (12-25 mm) from top of deck surface. Try piston in different bore if piston fails to free fall.

3) If piston free falls, correct fit must be determined. Install piston and a .0025" (.060 mm) feeler gauge for used pistons, or .0020" (.050 mm) feeler gauge for new pistons in cylinder bore. Feeler gauge must be at least 6" (152 mm) long and no more than 1/2" (12 mm) wide. Position feeler gauge at 90-degree angle to piston pin.

4) With piston 1/2 - 1" (12-25 mm) from top of deck surface, note if piston free falls. If piston fails to free fall, piston is correctly fitted for that cylinder. If piston free falls, select a larger diameter piston.

Piston Rings – Ensure ring end gap and side clearance are within specification. See PISTONS, PINS & RINGS table under ENGINE SPECIFICATIONS at end of article. Install rings with mark on top of ring facing top of piston, and with ring end gaps properly spaced around the piston. *See Fig. 6.*

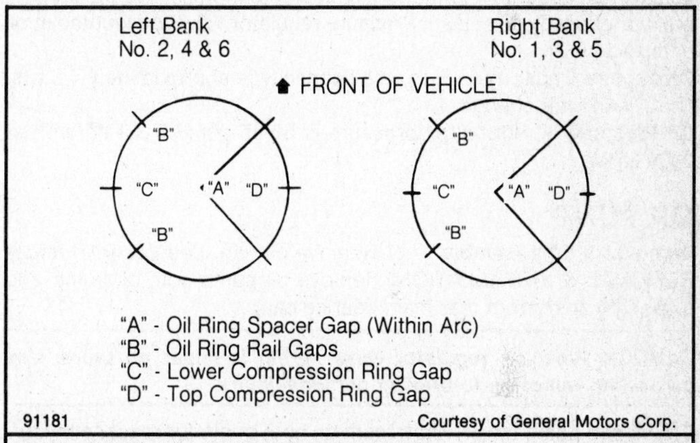
Left Bank
No. 2, 4 & 6
Right Bank
No. 1, 3 & 5
FRONT OF VEHICLE
"B"
"C"
"A"
"D"
"B"
"B"
"C"
"A"
"D"
"B"
"A" - Oil Ring Spacer Gap (Within Arc)
"B" - Oil Ring Rail Gaps
"C" - Lower Compression Ring Gap
"D" - Top Compression Ring Gap
91181
Courtesy of General Motors Corp.

Fig. 6: Positioning Piston Rings End Gaps

Rod Bearings – Mark rods and rod bearing caps for reassembly reference. Rod bearings of .001" (.26 mm) undersize are available. Install rod bearing cap on rod, with bearing tang slot facing away from center of engine. Ensure rod side clearance is .006-.025" (.16-.64 mm).

CAUTION: Crankshaft is rolled fillet type. DO NOT grind crankshaft. DO NOT scrape, shim or file bearings.

Crankshaft & Main Bearings – **1)** Mark main bearing caps for reassembly reference. Main bearings of .0006" (.016 mm) and .0013" (.032 mm) undersize are available.

2) Apply thin coats of GM Anaerobic Sealant (1052756) and RTV sealant to rear main bearing cap in specified areas. *See Fig. 7.* Install main bearing caps with arrows facing front of engine. Ensure crankshaft end play is .002-.008" (.06-.21 mm). See THRUST BEARING.

Thrust Bearing – **1)** Main bearing cap No. 3 is thrust bearing. Tighten main bearing cap bolts, except No. 3 main bearing cap, to 70 ft. lbs. (95 N.m). Tighten No. 3 main bearing cap bolts to 11 ft. lbs. (15 N.m).

2) Using lead hammer, tap crankshaft toward rear of engine then toward front of engine to align crankshaft thrust surfaces. Tighten No. 3 main bearing cap bolts to 70 ft. lbs. (95 N.m). Measure crankshaft end play between front side of No. 3 main bearing and crankshaft thrust surface.

Valve Lifter Bores – Some engines may be equipped with oversize valve lifters. Oversize lifter usage is indicated by small, White paint dot and/or ".25 mm O.S." stamped near lifter bore.

1991 ENGINES
2.8L V6 (Cont.)

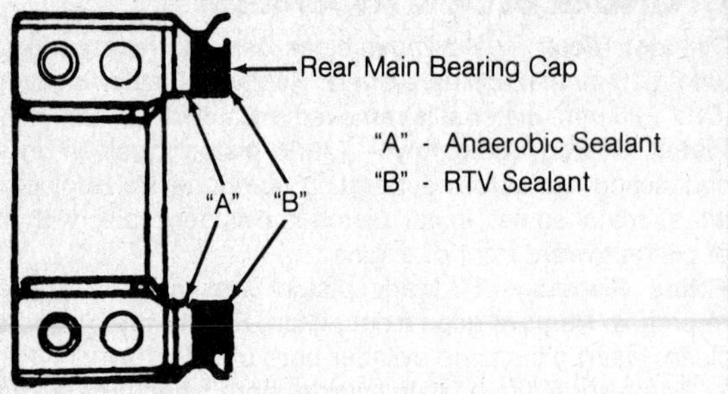
Rear Main Bearing Cap
"A" - Anaerobic Sealant
"B" - RTV Sealant
"A"
"B"
91J13499
Courtesy of General Motors Corp.

Fig. 7: Applying Anaerobic & RTV Sealants to Rear Main Bearing Cap

ENGINE OILING

ENGINE LUBRICATION SYSTEM

The camshaft-driven gear-type oil pump provides pressurized lubrication through the oil filter, to main gallery above left side of camshaft center line. The main gallery provides lubrication to valve lifters on left bank, camshaft bearings, crankshaft bearings and right gallery.

The right gallery supplies oil to valve lifters on right bank. Rocker arms are lubricated by passages in the push rods. Slot in front camshaft bearing provides lubrication to timing chain. Pistons and piston pins are lubricated by oil splash. Pressure regulator valve is mounted in oil pump body.

Crankcase Capacity – Engine oil capacity is approximately 4.5 qts. (4.3L) with filter change.

Oil Pressure – Normal oil pressure is 50-55 psi (3.5-3.9 kg/cm²) at 2000 RPM.

OIL PUMP

Removal & Disassembly – **1)** Remove oil pan. See OIL PAN under REMOVAL & INSTALLATION. Remove oil pump bolt, oil pump and extension shaft from rear main bearing cap.

CAUTION: Pressure regulator valve spring is under pressure. Use care when removing to prevent personal injury.

2) Remove pump cover. Mark teeth on both gears for reassembly reference. Remove idler gear, drive gear and shaft from pump body. Remove pressure regulator valve retaining pin, valve and spring.

Inspection – Pump is serviced as an assembly. Replace pump if damaged or excessively worn. Replace pick-up screen tube if loose.

CAUTION: Use only original equipment oil pump cover gasket, as gasket thickness is critical.

Reassembly & Installation – Coat all internal components with engine oil. To reassemble, reverse disassembly procedure using new cover gasket. Ensure reference mark is aligned on gears. To install, reverse removal procedure. Ensure pump extension shaft is fully engaged.

TORQUE SPECIFICATIONS

TORQUE SPECIFICATIONS

Application	Ft. Lbs. (N.m)
Camshaft Sprocket Bolt	20 (27)
Connecting Rod Cap Nut	39 (53)
Crankshaft Damper Bolt	70 (95)
Cylinder Head Bolt	[1]
Exhaust Manifold Bolt	25 (34)
Flexplate/Flywheel Bolt	52 (71)
Intake Manifold Bolt	[2] 23 (31)
Main Bearing Cap Bolt	70 (95)
Oil Filter Adapter Bolt	63 (85)
Oil Pan Bolt (Rear 2)	18 (24)
Oil Pump Bolt	30 (41)
Rocker Arm Stud	48 (65)
Timing Chain Cover Bolt	18 (24)
Timing Chain Damper Bolt	15 (20)
Water Pump Bolt & Nut [3]	22 (30)
	INCH Lbs. (N.m)
Oil Pan Bolt/Nut (Except Rear 2)	7 (10)
Rocker Arm Cover Bolt	72 (8)

[1] – Apply GM Sealant (1052080) to bolt threads. Tighten bolts in sequence to 40 ft. lbs. (54 N.m), then tighten an additional 90 degrees (1/4 turn). *See Fig. 2*.

[2] – Tighten in sequence to specification then repeat procedure. *See Fig. 1*.

[3] – Apply GM Sealant (1052080) to bolt threads.

ENGINE SPECIFICATIONS

GENERAL SPECIFICATIONS

Application	Specification
2.8L	
Displacement	173 Cu. In. (2.8L)
Bore	3.50" (89.0 mm)
Stroke	2.99" (76.0 mm)
Compression Ratio	8.9:1
Fuel System	TBI
Horsepower @ RPM	125 @ 4800
Torque Ft. Lbs. @ RPM	150 @ 2400

CRANKSHAFT MAIN & CONNECTING ROD BEARINGS

Application	In. (mm)
2.8L	
Crankshaft End Play	.002-.008 (.06-.21)
Main Bearings	
Journal Diameter	
Dot 1	2.6479-2.6482 (67.257-67.265)
Dot 2	2.6476-2.6479 (67.249-67.257)
Dot 3	2.6473-2.6476 (67.241-67.249)
Journal Out-Of-Round	.0002 (.005)
Journal Taper	.0002 (.005)
Oil Clearance	.0016-.0032 (.041-.081)
Connecting Rod Bearings	
Journal Diameter	
Dot 1	1.9989-1.9994 (50.771-50.784)
Dot 2	1.9983-1.9989 (50.758-50.771)
Journal Out-Of-Round	.0002 (.005)
Journal Taper	.0002 (.005)
Oil Clearance	.0014-.0037 (.035-.095)

1991 ENGINES
2.8L V6 (Cont.)

CONNECTING RODS

Application	In. (mm)
2.8L	
Side Play	.006-.025 (.16-.64)

PISTONS, PINS & RINGS

Application	In. (mm)
2.8L	
Pistons	
Clearance	.0007-.0017 (.017-.043)
Pins	
Diameter	.9053-.9056 (22.994-23.002)
Piston Fit	.0003-.0004 (.007-.009)
Rod Fit	.0007-.0020 (.019-.052)
Rings	
No. 1	
End Gap	.010-.020 (.25-.50)
Side Clearance	.001-.003 (.03-.07)
No. 2	
End Gap	.010-.020 (.25-.50)
Side Clearance	.002-.004 (.04-.10)
No. 3 (Oil)	
End Gap	.002-.055 (.05-1.40)
Side Clearance (Max.)	.008 (.20)

CYLINDER BLOCK

Application	In. (mm)
2.8L	
Cylinder Bore	
Diameter	3.504-3.507 (88.99-89.07)
Maximum Taper	.0008 (.02)
Maximum Out-Of-Round	.0008 (.02)

VALVES & VALVE SPRINGS

Application	Specification
2.8L	
Intake Valves	
Face Angle	45°
Exhaust Valves	
Face Angle	45°
Valve Springs	
Free Length	1.91" (48.5 mm)
Installed Height	1.57" (40.0 mm)
Pressure	
Valve Closed	88 Lbs. @ 1.57 In. (40 kg @ 40.0 mm)
Valve Open	194 Lbs. @ 1.18 In. (88 kg @ 30.0 mm)

CYLINDER HEAD

Application	Specification
2.8L	
Valve Seats	
Intake Valve	
Seat Angle	46°
Seat Width	.049-.059" (1.25-1.50 mm)
Maximum Seat Runout	.002" (.05 mm)
Exhaust Valve	
Seat Angle	46°
Seat Width	.063-.075" (1.60-1.90 mm)
Maximum Seat Runout	.002" (.05 mm)
Valve Guides	
Intake Valve	
Valve Guide Oil Clearance	.001-.003" (.03-.07 mm)
Exhaust Valve	
Valve Guide Oil Clearance	.001-.003" (.03-.07 mm)

CAMSHAFT

Application	In. (mm)
2.8L	
Journal Diameter	1.868-1.870 (47.44-47.49)
Lobe Lift	
Intake	.262 (6.65)
Exhaust	.273 (6.94)
Oil Clearance	.001-.004 (.03-.10)

1991 ENGINES
3.1L V6

Lumina APV, Silhouette, Trans Sport

NOTE: For repair procedures not covered in this article, see ENGINE OVERHAUL PROCEDURES article in GENERAL INFORMATION.

ENGINE IDENTIFICATION

Engine may be identified by eighth character of Vehicle Identification Number (VIN) stamped on pad on top of instrument panel, near lower left corner of windshield. Eighth character, "D", identifies 3.1L TBI engine.

Engine may also be identified by engine identification (ID) number stamped on left side of cylinder block, on engine-to-transaxle mating flange. Engine ID number, LG6, identifies 3.1L TBI engine.

ADJUSTMENTS

VALVE CLEARANCE ADJUSTMENT

NOTE: Although valve clearance adjustment is not usually required (engine uses hydraulic valve lifters), perform the following procedures after servicing valve train.

1) Remove rocker arm covers. Rotate crankshaft until cylinder No. 1 is at TDC of compression stroke.
2) Grasp cylinder No. 1 intake valve push rod with thumb and forefinger, and loosen adjusting nut until push rod rotates freely. Continue to rotate push rod back and forth while tightening adjusting nut. When push rod can no longer be rotated, stop tightening adjusting nut. Valve train is now at zero lash. Turn adjusting nut 1 1/2 turns.
3) Repeat step **2)** for intake valves of cylinders No. 5 and 6, and exhaust valves of cylinders No. 1, 2 and 3. Rotate crankshaft one revolution (until cylinder No. 4 is at TDC of compression stroke).
4) Repeat step **2)** for intake valves of cylinders No. 2, 3 and 4, and exhaust valves of cylinders No. 4, 5 and 6. Install rocker arm covers and gaskets.

REMOVAL & INSTALLATION

NOTE: For reassembly reference, label all electrical connectors, vacuum hoses and fuel lines before removal. Also, place mating marks on engine hood and other major assemblies before removal.

FUEL PRESSURE RELEASE

Disconnect negative battery cable. Loosen fuel tank cap to relieve tank pressure. Internal constant bleed feature relieves fuel system pressure in fuel lines and TBI unit when ignition switch is turned off. No further pressure release is required.

COOLING SYSTEM BLEEDING

CAUTION: On vehicles with rear heater, turn off rear blower switch while filling cooling system to ensure maximum coolant flow to rear heater system.

ENGINE

NOTE: Manufacturer's engine removal procedure states removing engine, transaxle and frame as an assembly.

Removal – 1) Release fuel pressure. See FUEL PRESSURE RELEASE under REMOVAL & INSTALLATION. Disconnect battery cables. Drain cooling system.
2) Remove air intake tube from air cleaner and radiator support. Disconnect ECM electrical connectors from ECM, and push harness through hole in firewall, into engine compartment. Disconnect necessary harness-to-chassis fasteners. Lay harness on engine.
3) Disconnect engine harness from block connector near left hood hinge. Lay harness on engine. Disconnect fuel lines, electrical connectors, vacuum hoses, coolant hoses and control cables as necessary. Discharge A/C refrigerant system.
4) Remove A/C compressor from mounting bracket with hoses attached. Disconnect refrigerant hoses from A/C compressor. Remove upper engine strut rod mount. Raise and support vehicle. Remove front wheels. Remove stabilizer shaft.
5) Disconnect tie rod ends from steering knuckles. Disconnect lower control arm ball joints from steering knuckles. Remove drive axles from transaxle, and hang aside with wire. Remove intermediate steering shaft pinch bolt.
6) Remove starter, flexplate cover and torque converter bolts. Disconnect exhaust downpipe from right manifold. Support engine/transaxle/frame assembly. Remove frame bolts. Lower engine/transaxle/frame assembly from vehicle.
Installation – To install, reverse removal procedure. Fill cooling system. Evacuate and charge A/C system.

INTAKE MANIFOLD

Removal – 1) Release fuel pressure. See FUEL PRESSURE RELEASE under REMOVAL & INSTALLATION. Drain cooling system. Disconnect negative battery cable. Remove air cleaner.
2) Disconnect fuel lines, electrical connectors, vacuum hoses, coolant hoses and control cables as necessary. Remove engine strut rod mount. Remove coolant by-pass tube between timing chain cover and thermostat housing. Remove Throttle Body Injection (TBI) unit. Remove left rocker arm cover.
3) Remove serpentine belt, alternator and alternator brackets. Remove right rocker arm cover. Remove P/S pump with hoses attached and lay aside. Remove distributor. Remove intake manifold.
Installation – 1) Apply 3/16" (5 mm) bead of RTV sealant to front and rear intake manifold-to-cylinder block sealing surfaces; extend RTV sealant 1/4" (6 mm) beyond cylinder block-to-cylinder head junctions. Position new intake manifold gaskets on cylinder heads.
2) Install intake manifold. Tighten intake manifold bolts in sequence to 13 ft. lbs. (18 N.m), then tighten again to 19 ft. lbs. (26 mm). *See Fig. 1.* To install remaining components, reverse removal procedure. Fill cooling system.

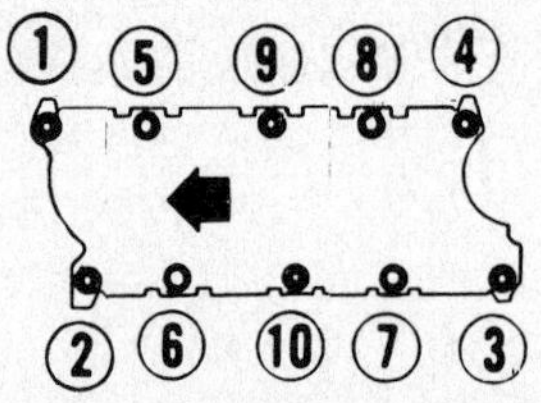
1
5
9
8
4
2
6
10
7
3

91C13500 Courtesy of General Motors Corp.

Fig. 1: Intake Manifold Bolt Tightening Sequence

EXHAUST MANIFOLD

Removal (Left) – Disconnect negative battery cable. Remove serpentine belt. Remove A/C compressor with hoses attached and lay aside. Remove engine strut rod mount. Disconnect exhaust crossover pipe from manifold. Remove manifold.
Removal (Right) – Disconnect negative battery cable and oxygen sensor wire. Disconnect exhaust crossover pipe from manifold. Raise and support vehicle. Disconnect exhaust downpipe from manifold. Support rear center of frame. Remove rear center frame mount bolts. Lower frame 8-10" (203-254 mm). Remove manifold.
Installation (Left & Right) – Install manifold. Tighten manifold-to-cylinder head bolts to 24 ft. lbs. (33 N.m). To install remaining components, reverse removal procedure.

CYLINDER HEAD

Removal – 1) Remove intake manifold. See INTAKE MANIFOLD under REMOVAL & INSTALLATION. Remove exhaust manifold. See EXHAUST MANIFOLD under REMOVAL & INSTALLATION.

2) Loosen push rod nuts enough to remove push rods. Keep components in order for reassembly. Remove cylinder head bolts. Remove cylinder head and gasket.

Installation - 1) Clean cylinder head bolt threads and cylinder block holes. Install cylinder head and new gasket. Apply GM Sealant (1052080) to head bolt threads. Install head bolts and tighten in sequence to 41 ft. lbs. (56 N.m). *See Fig. 2.* Tighten head bolts an additional 90 degrees (1/4 turn).

2) To install remaining components, reverse removal procedure. Adjust valves. See VALVE CLEARANCE ADJUSTMENT under ADJUSTMENTS. Fill cooling system.

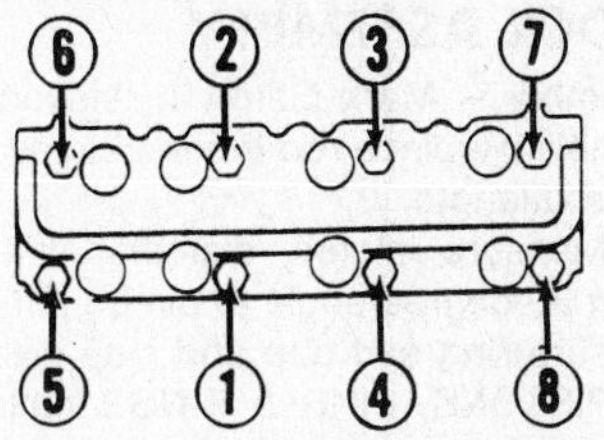
6
2
3
7
5
1
4
8

91H13497 Courtesy of General Motors Corp.

Fig. 2: Cylinder Head Bolt Tightening Sequence

FRONT CRANKSHAFT OIL SEAL

Removal - Disconnect negative battery cable. Remove serpentine belt. Raise and support vehicle. Remove right inner fender splash shield. Remove crankshaft damper bolt. Remove damper using Crankshaft Damper Puller (J-24420-B). Using large screwdriver, carefully pry out seal.

Installation - Coat sealing lip and damper surface with oil. Install seal using Seal Installer (J-35468). Clean damper key and keyway. Apply GM Sealant (1052336) to keyway. Install damper using Crankshaft Damper Installer (J-29113). Install damper bolt and tighten to 75 ft. lbs. (102 N.m). To complete installation, reverse removal procedure.

TIMING CHAIN & SPROCKETS

Removal - 1) Disconnect negative battery cable. Drain coolant. Remove serpentine belt. Remove P/S pump with hoses attached and lay aside. Raise and support vehicle. Remove right inner fender splash shield.

2) Remove crankshaft damper bolt. Remove damper using Crankshaft Damper Puller (J-24420-B). Remove starter. Remove 2 front engine mount-to-frame nuts. Raise and support engine. Remove front engine mount.

3) Remove timing chain cover bolts. Remove oil pan bolts and lower the oil pan as necessary. Disconnect lower radiator hose and coolant by-pass hose from timing chain cover. Remove serpentine belt pulley. Remove timing chain cover.

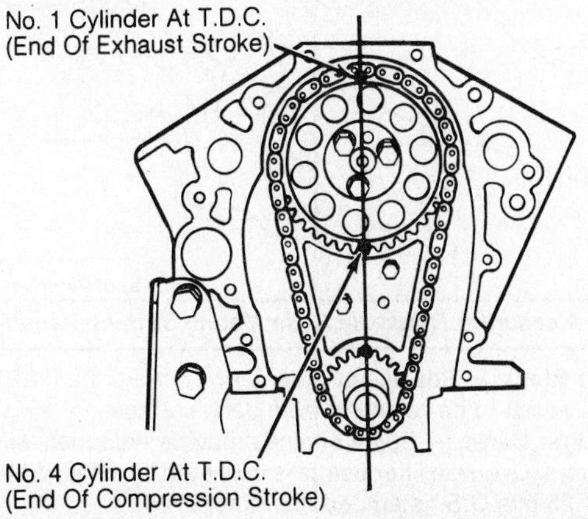
No. 1 Cylinder At T.D.C.
(End Of Exhaust Stroke)
No. 4 Cylinder At T.D.C.
(End Of Compression Stroke)

91180 Courtesy of General Motors Corp.

Fig. 3: Aligning Timing Marks

4) Rotate crankshaft until timing marks on camshaft and crankshaft sprockets align. *See Fig. 3.* Remove camshaft sprocket bolts. Remove camshaft sprocket and timing chain. Remove crankshaft sprocket (if necessary).

Installation - 1) If crankshaft sprocket was removed, install using Crankshaft Sprocket Installer (J-5590). Install timing chain over camshaft sprocket. Hold sprocket vertically with chain hanging down. Align timing marks. *See Fig. 3.*

2) Install timing chain and camshaft sprocket on camshaft, ensuring sprocket dowel pin hole aligns with camshaft dowel pin. Install and tighten camshaft sprocket bolts to 18 ft. lbs. (24 N.m). Lubricate timing chain with engine oil.

3) Apply GM Sealer (1052080) to timing chain cover-to-oil pan sealing surface. Install timing chain cover with new gasket. Tighten cover bolts to 18 ft. lbs. (24 N.m). To install remaining components, reverse removal procedure. Fill cooling system.

VALVE LIFTERS

Removal - Remove intake manifold. See INTAKE MANIFOLD under REMOVAL & INSTALLATION. Loosen rocker arm nuts, rotate rocker arms and remove push rods. Keep push rods in order for reassembly. Remove valve lifters.

NOTE: Some engines are equipped with standard and oversize valve lifters. Oversize lifter usage is indicated by small, White paint dot and/or ".25 mm O.S." stamped near lifter bore.

Installation - If installing new lifter, coat bottom of lifter with Molykote. Install lifter in original bore. To complete installation, reverse removal procedure. Adjust valves. See VALVE CLEARANCE ADJUSTMENT under ADJUSTMENTS.

CAMSHAFT

NOTE: To remove camshaft, engine must be removed from vehicle.

Removal - 1) Remove engine. See ENGINE under REMOVAL & INSTALLATION. Remove valve lifters. See VALVE LIFTERS under REMOVAL & INSTALLATION.

2) Remove timing chain and camshaft sprocket. See TIMING CHAIN & SPROCKETS under REMOVAL & INSTALLATION. Carefully remove camshaft.

Inspection - Measure camshaft journal diameter, lobe lift and oil clearance. Replace components if measurements are not within specification. See CAMSHAFT table under ENGINE SPECIFICATIONS at end of article.

Installation - 1) Lubricate camshaft bearings and camshaft lobes with GM Lubricant (1051396). Install camshaft. To install remaining components, reverse removal procedure. Ensure timing marks are aligned. *See Fig. 3.* Install valve lifters and push rods in original location.

2) Adjust valves. See VALVE CLEARANCE ADJUSTMENT under ADJUSTMENTS. If camshaft was replaced, add GM Engine Oil Supplement (1052367) to engine oil.

REAR CRANKSHAFT OIL SEAL

Removal - Remove transaxle and flexplate. Note direction of seal installation. Using screwdriver, carefully pry seal from housing in rear main bearing. DO NOT scratch sealing surface of crankshaft.

Installation - 1) Coat inner and outer seal surfaces with engine oil. Install seal on mandrel of Seal Installer (J-34686) until dust lip bottoms against tool collar. *See Fig. 4.*

2) Align seal installer dowel pin with alignment hole of crankshaft. Install seal installer on crankshaft. Hand tighten seal installer bolts, or torque to 36 INCH lbs. (4 N.m).

3) To install seal in housing, tighten seal installer handle until seal installer collar is even with cylinder block. Remove seal installer. To install remaining components, reverse removal procedure.

1991 ENGINES
3.1L V6 (Cont.)

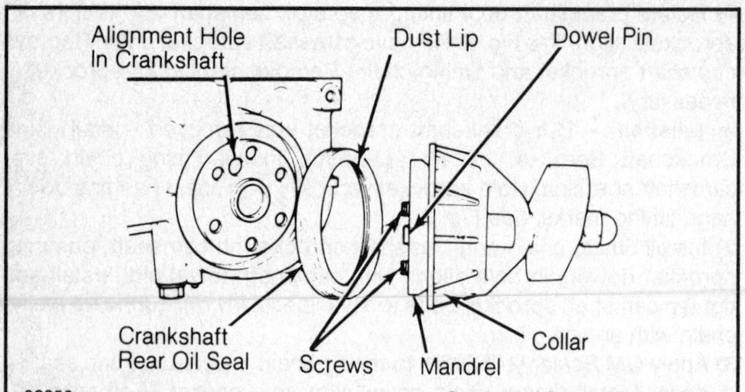
Alignment Hole
In Crankshaft
Dust Lip
Dowel Pin
Crankshaft
Rear Oil Seal
Screws
Mandrel
Collar
92350
Courtesy of General Motors Corp.

Fig. 4: Installing Rear Crankshaft Oil Seal

WATER PUMP

Removal – Disconnect negative battery cable. Drain coolant. Remove serpentine belt. Remove water pump pulley. Note locator tab near 12 o'clock position at top of water pump housing for installation reference. Remove water pump and gasket.

Installation – Apply thread sealant to water pump bolts. Install water pump with new gasket, ensuring locator tab at top of water pump housing is positioned vertically.

OIL PAN

Removal – **1)** Disconnect negative battery cable. Remove serpentine belt. Raise and support vehicle. Remove right inner fender splash shield. Remove crankshaft damper bolt. Remove damper using Crankshaft Damper Puller (J-24420-B).

2) Drain crankcase. Remove flexplate cover and starter. Remove 2 front engine mount-to-frame nuts. Raise and support engine. Remove oil pan bolts. Remove oil pan and gasket.

Installation – Apply GM Sealer (1052914) to half-round section at rear end of oil pan. Install oil pan with new gasket.

OVERHAUL

CYLINDER HEAD

Valve Springs – Replace valve spring if free length, installed height and pressure are not within specification. See VALVES & VALVE SPRINGS table under ENGINE SPECIFICATIONS at end of article.

Valve Stem Oil Seals – Intake valve uses an upper "O" ring seal and a lower seal. *See Fig. 5.* Exhaust valve uses upper "O" ring seal only.

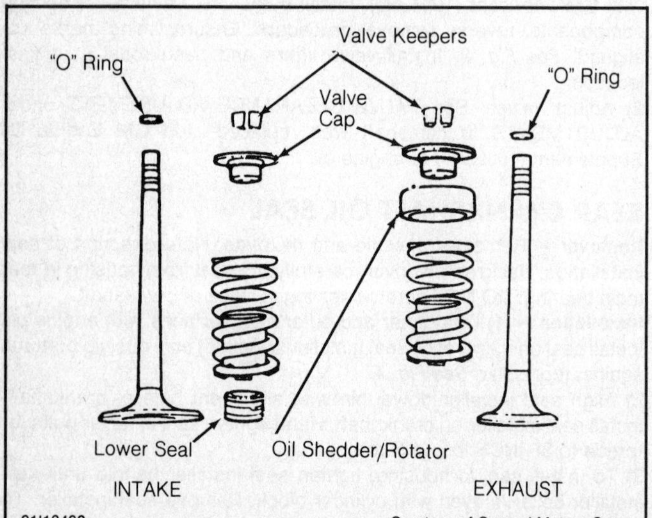
Valve Keepers
"O" Ring
"O" Ring
Valve
Cap
Lower Seal
Oil Shedder/Rotator
INTAKE
EXHAUST
91I13498
Courtesy of General Motors Corp.

Fig. 5: Exploded View of Intake & Exhaust Valve/Spring Assemblies

When installing intake valve lower seal, slide seal over valve stem and valve guide boss. Exhaust valve uses oil shedder/rotator. Coat "O" ring seal with engine oil before installation; ensure seal is not twisted when installed.

VALVE TRAIN

Rocker Arm Assembly – Clean push rods, rocker arms, balls and nuts with solvent then blow dry. Inspect rocker arms and balls at mating surface for damage. Inspect push rods for bends or wear. Ensure push rod oil passages are clear.

CYLINDER BLOCK ASSEMBLY

Piston & Rod Assembly – Mark piston in relation to cylinder bore and rod for reassembly. Replace rod if bend exceeds .010" (.25 mm) per 3" (76.2 mm) of rod length.

Fitting Pistons – Measure piston diameter with pin removed. Measure diameter at 90-degree angle to pin on pin centerline.

Piston Rings – Ensure ring end gap and side clearance are within specification. See PISTONS, PINS & RINGS table under ENGINE SPECIFICATIONS at end of article.

Rod Bearings – Ensure rod side clearance is .014-.027" (.36-.68 mm).

Crankshaft & Main Bearings – Ensure crankshaft journal diameter, runout and taper are within specification. See CRANKSHAFT, MAIN & CONNECTING ROD BEARINGS under ENGINE SPECIFICATIONS at end of article.

Thrust Bearing – With main bearing cap bolts loosely tightened, pry crankshaft rearward to align main bearing caps. Pry crankshaft forward to align rear face of thrust bearing. Tighten main bearing cap bolts to 72 ft. lbs. (98 mm), and measure crankshaft end play between thrust bearing rear face and crankshaft thrust surface.

CAUTION: If transaxle case mating surface is not flat, a broken flywheel may result.

Transaxle Case Mating Surface – **1)** Mount dial indicator gauge plate flat against crankshaft flange. Place dial indicator stem on lower left transaxle mounting bolt boss (flat area around bolt hole). *See Fig. 6.*

2) Adjust dial indicator to zero. Record readings obtained on all mounting bolt hole bosses. If variation between mounting bolt bosses exceeds .010" (.25 mm), replace crankshaft or cylinder block as necessary.

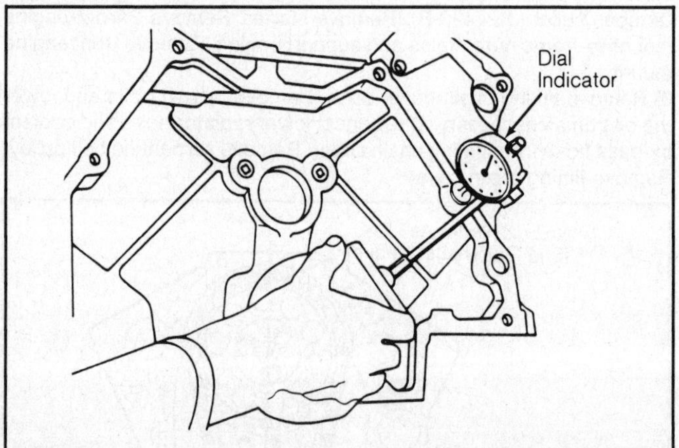
Dial
Indicator
91D13501
Courtesy of General Motors Corp.

Fig. 6: Measuring Transaxle Case Mating Surface Variation

Cylinder Block – Replace cylinder block if more than .010" (.25 mm) material needs to be removed from deck surface.

Valve Lifter Bores – Some engines may be equipped with oversize valve lifters. Oversize lifter usage is indicated by small, White paint dot and/or ".25 mm O.S." stamped near lifter bore.

ENGINE OILING

ENGINE LUBRICATION SYSTEM

The camshaft-driven gear-type oil pump provides pressurized lubrication through the oil filter, to main gallery above left side of camshaft center line. The main gallery provides lubrication to valve lifters on left bank, camshaft bearings, crankshaft bearings and right gallery.

The right gallery supplies oil to valve lifters on right bank. Rocker arms are lubricated by passages in push rods. Slot in front camshaft bearing provides lubrication to timing chain. Pistons and piston pins are lubricated by oil splash. Pressure regulator valve is mounted in oil pump body.

Crankcase Capacity – Engine oil capacity is approximately 4.0 qts. (3.8L). More oil may need to be added when changing oil filter.

Oil Pressure – Normal oil pressure is 15 psi (1.1 kg/cm²) at 1100 RPM.

OIL PUMP

WARNING: Pressure regulator valve spring is under pressure. Use care when removing to prevent personal injury.

Removal & Disassembly – 1) Remove oil pan. See OIL PAN under REMOVAL & INSTALLATION. Remove oil pump mounting bolt. Remove oil pump and drive shaft extension.

2) Remove oil pump cover screws. Remove cover and gasket. Mark gear teeth for reassembly reference. Remove drive gear and idler gear. Remove spring retaining pin, spring and pressure relief valve.

Inspection – 1) Replace pick-up tube if loose. Ensure pressure regulator valve slides freely in its bore. With gears removed, measure gear length and diameter, and measure gear pocket depth and diameter.

2) Install gears. Measure gear lash, side clearance and end clearance. Replace oil pump if any measurements are not within specification. See OIL PUMP SPECIFICATIONS table.

Reassembly & Installation – To reassemble, reverse disassembly procedure. Align marks on gears when installing in pump body. To install, reverse removal procedure. Tighten oil pump mounting bolt to 30 ft. lbs. (41 N.m). Tighten pick-up tube nut to 22 ft. lbs. (30 N.m).

OIL PUMP SPECIFICATIONS

Application	Specification In. (mm)
Gear	
Diameter	1.498-1.500 (38.05-38.10)
End Clearance	
Iron Body	.001-.004 (.03-.10)
Aluminum Body	.002-.005 (.05-.13)
Lash	.009-.015 (.23-.38)
Length	1.199-1.200 (30.45-30.48)
Side Clearance	
Iron Body	.001-.003 (.03-.08)
Aluminum Body	.003-.004 (.08-.10)
Gear Pocket	
Depth	
Iron Body	1.201-1.203 (30.51-30.56)
Aluminum Body	1.195-1.198 (30.35-30.43)
Diameter	
Iron Body	1.502-1.504 (38.15-38.20)
Aluminum Body	1.503-1.506 (38.18-38.25)

TORQUE SPECIFICATIONS

TORQUE SPECIFICATIONS

Application	Ft. Lbs. (N.m)
Camshaft Sprocket Bolt	18 (24)
Connecting Rod Cap Nut	39 (53)
Crankshaft Damper Bolt	75 (102)
Cylinder Head Bolt [1]	
Step 1	41 (56)
Step 2	Additional 90 degrees (1/4 turn).
Exhaust Manifold Bolt	24 (33)
Flexplate Bolt	52 (71)
Intake Manifold Bolt [2]	
Step 1	13 (18)
Step 2	19 (26)
Main Bearing Cap Bolt	72 (98)
Oil Pan Bolt	15 (20)
Oil Pump Bolt	30 (41)
Rocker Arm Stud	48 (65)
Timing Chain Cover Bolt	
Small Diameter	20 (27)
Large Diameter	28 (38)
Timing Chain Damper Bolt	15 (20)
	INCH Lbs. (N.m)
Oil Pan Stud Nuts	89 (10)
Oil Pump Cover Bolt	89 (10)
Rocker Arm Cover Bolt	89 (10)
Water Pump Bolt	89 (10)

[1] – Apply thread sealant to bolts. Tighten bolts in sequence. *See Fig. 2.*

[2] – Tighten bolts in sequence. *See Fig. 1.*

ENGINE SPECIFICATIONS

GENERAL SPECIFICATIONS

Application	Specification
3.1L	
Displacement	189 Cu. In. (3.1L)
Bore	3.50" (89.0 mm)
Stroke	3.31" (84.0 mm)
Compression Ratio	8.9:1
Fuel System	TBI
Horsepower @ RPM	120 @ 4200
Torque Ft. Lbs. @ RPM	170 @ 2200

CRANKSHAFT, MAIN & CONNECTING ROD BEARINGS

Application	In. (mm)
3.1L	
Crankshaft End Play	.002-.008 (.06-.21)
Main Bearings	
Journal Diameter	2.6473-2.6479 (67.241-67.257)
Journal Out-Of-Round	.0002 (.005)
Journal Taper	.0002 (.005)
Oil Clearance	.0013-.0029 (.032-.074)
Connecting Rod Bearings	
Journal Diameter	1.9987-1.9994 (50.768-50.784)
Journal Out-Of-Round	.0002 (.005)
Journal Taper	.0002 (.005)
Oil Clearance	.0011-.0033 (.028-.083)

1991 ENGINES
3.1L V6 (Cont.)

CONNECTING RODS

Application	In. (mm)
3.1L	
Maximum Bend	[1] .010 (.25)
Side Play	.004-.015 (.36-.68)

[1] – Specification is per 3" of rod length.

PISTONS, PINS & RINGS

Application	In. (mm)
3.1L	
Pins	
Diameter	.9052-.9054 (22.992-22.996)
Piston Fit	.0004-.0009 (.010-.022)
Rod Fit	.0007-.0018 (.018-.046)
Rings	
No. 1	
End Gap	.010-.020 (.25-.50)
Side Clearance	.002-.004 (.05-.09)
No. 2	
End Gap	.020-.028 (.50-.71)
Side Clearance	.002-.004 (.05-.09)
No. 3 (Oil)	
End Gap	.010-.030 (.25-.75)
Side Clearance (Max.)	.008 (.20)

CYLINDER BLOCK

Application	In. (mm)
3.1L	
Cylinder Bore	
Diameter	3.5036-3.5067 (88.992-89.070)
Maximum Taper	.0005 (.013)
Maximum Out-Of-Round	.0005 (.013)

VALVES & VALVE SPRINGS

Application	Specification
3.1L	
Intake Valves	
Face Angle	45°
Exhaust Valves	
Face Angle	45°
Valve Springs	
Free Length	1.91" (48.5 mm)
Installed Height	1.58" (40.0 mm)
Out-Of-Square	1/16" (1.6 mm)
Pressure	
Valve Closed	81 Lbs. @ 1.57 In. (37 kg @ 40.0 mm)
Valve Open	192 Lbs. @ 1.18 In. (87 kg @ 30.0 mm)

CYLINDER HEAD

Application	Specification
3.1L	
Valve Seats	
Intake Valve	
Seat Angle	46°
Seat Width	.061-.073" (1.55-1.85 mm)
Maximum Seat Runout	.002" (.05 mm)
Exhaust Valve	
Seat Angle	46°
Seat Width	.067-.079" (1.70-2.00 mm)
Maximum Seat Runout	.002" (.05 mm)
Valve Guides	
Intake Valve	
Valve Guide Oil Clearance	.001-.003" (.03-.07 mm)
Exhaust Valve	
Valve Guide Oil Clearance	.001-.003" (.03-.07 mm)

CAMSHAFT

Application	In. (mm)
3.1L	
Journal Diameter	1.8677-1.8815 (47.440-47.790)
Lobe Lift	
Intake	.2306 (5.858)
Exhaust	.2620 (6.654)
Oil Clearance	.001-.004 (.03-.10)

1991 ENGINES
4.3L V6, 5.0L, 5.7L & 7.4L V8

Astro, Bravada, Safari, "C" & "K" Series, "G" Series, "P" Series, "R" & "V" Series, "S" & "T" Series

NOTE: For repair procedures not covered in this article, see ENGINE OVERHAUL PROCEDURES article in GENERAL INFORMATION.

ENGINE IDENTIFICATION

Engine can be identified by eighth character of Vehicle Identification Number (VIN). VIN is stamped on a metal tag on top left end of instrument panel, near windshield. See ENGINE IDENTIFICATION table.

Engine can also be identified by engine identification (ID) number, stamped on front of cylinder block, immediately forward of right cylinder head *or* on left side of cylinder block, on engine-to-transmission mating flange.

ENGINE IDENTIFICATION

Engine	[1] VIN Code	Engine ID No.
4.3L TBI	[2] 1B	[2] LU2
	Z	LB4
5.0L TBI	H	LO3
5.7L TBI	K	LO5
7.4L TBI	N	L19

[1] – Eighth character of VIN.
[2] – High Output.

ADJUSTMENTS

VALVE CLEARANCE ADJUSTMENT

NOTE: Although valve clearance adjustment is not usually required (engine uses hydraulic valve lifters), perform the following procedures after servicing valve train.

1) Rotate engine until No. 1 piston is on TDC of compression stroke. Go to step **2)** and adjust specified valves as listed in appropriate VALVE CLEARANCE ADJUSTMENT table.
2) Loosen rocker arm adjusting nut until lash is present. Tighten adjusting nut until lash is removed (under this condition, push rod cannot be rotated with fingers). On all engines except 7.4L, tighten adjusting nut one full turn. On 7.4L, tighten adjusting nut 3/4 turn.
3) Rotate crankshaft 360 degrees to bring No. 4 piston (4.3L) or No. 6 piston (5.0L, 5.7L and 7.4L) to TDC of compression stroke. Adjust remaining valves. See appropriate VALVE CLEARANCE ADJUSTMENT table

4.3L VALVE CLEARANCE ADJUSTMENT

Piston at TDC	Adjust Intake	Adjust Exhaust
No. 1	No. 1, 2 & 3	No. 1, 5 & 6
No. 4	No. 4, 5 & 6	No. 2, 3 & 4

5.0L, 5.7L & 7.4L VALVE CLEARANCE ADJUSTMENT

Piston at TDC	Adjust Intake	Adjust Exhaust
No. 1	No. 1, 2, 5 & 7	No. 1, 3, 4 & 8
No. 6	No. 3, 4, 6 & 8	No. 2, 5, 6 & 7

REMOVAL & INSTALLATION

NOTE: For reassembly reference, label all electrical connectors, vacuum hoses and fuel lines before removal. Also place mating marks on engine hood and other major assemblies before removal.

FUEL PRESSURE RELEASE

Disconnect battery terminals. Loosen fuel tank cap to relieve tank pressure. Internal constant bleed feature in throttle body injection unit relieves fuel system pressure when ignition switch is turned off. No further pressure relief is required.

ENGINE (4.3L)

CAUTION: Minimal clearance exists between oil pump pick-up tube and bottom of oil pan. DO NOT place jack under oil pan, crankshaft pulley or any sheet metal when lifting engine.

Removal & Installation (Astro & Safari) – 1) Release fuel system pressure. See FUEL PRESSURE RELEASE under REMOVAL & INSTALLATION. Disconnect battery. Drain cooling system. Raise and support vehicle.
2) Disconnect exhaust pipes from manifolds. Remove flywheel cover, torque converter bolts (A/T), starter and oil filter. Disconnect engine wiring harness from transmission and frame.
3) Disconnect fuel lines from frame. Disconnect transmission fluid lines and engine oil cooler lines from radiator. Remove lower fan shroud bolts. Remove motor mount through-bolts. Lower vehicle.
4) Remove headlight bezels and grille. Remove lower radiator close-out panel, radiator support braces and radiator cross brace. Remove hood latch mechanism. Discharge A/C system (if equipped). Remove master cylinder, upper fan shroud, upper radiator core support and radiator.
5) Remove radiator filler panels. Remove engine cover. Disconnect A/C hose from accumulator. Remove A/C compressor and bracket. Remove power steering pump.
6) Disconnect vacuum hoses as necessary. Disconnect engine wiring harness clips from firewall. Remove right kick panel. Disconnect engine wiring harness connector from ESC module. Push connector and harness through firewall. Remove distributor cap and A/C accumulator. Disconnect fuel line from TBI unit.
7) Remove transmission dipstick tube. Disconnect heater hose from heater core. Remove horn. Support transmission. Support engine with adjustable jack. Remove bellhousing bolts. Lower engine from vehicle.
8) To install, reverse removal procedure. Fill crankcase and cooling system. Evacuate and charge A/C system.
Removal & Installation ("C" & "K" Series) – 1) Release fuel system pressure. See FUEL PRESSURE RELEASE under REMOVAL & INSTALLATION. Disconnect battery. Remove hood. Remove air cleaner, accessory drive belt, fan and water pump pulley.
2) Drain cooling system. Remove fan shroud and radiator. Disconnect heater hoses from engine. Disconnect fuel lines, electrical connectors, vacuum hoses, coolant hoses and control cables as necessary. Remove A/C compressor and power steering pump with hoses attached and position out of way (if equipped).
3) Raise and support vehicle. Drain crankcase. Disconnect exhaust pipes from manifolds. Disconnect strut rods. Remove flywheel cover. Remove starter. Remove torque converter bolts (A/T). Lower vehicle.
4) Support transmission. Attach engine hoist. Remove bellhousing bolts. Remove front engine mount-to-frame bolts. Remove engine. To install, reverse removal procedure. Fill crankcase and cooling system. Evacuate and charge A/C system.
Removal & Installation ("G" Series) – 1) Release fuel system pressure. See FUEL PRESSURE RELEASE under REMOVAL & INSTALLATION. Disconnect battery. Drain cooling system. Remove engine cover and air cleaner. Remove power steering fluid reservoir.
2) Remove upper fan shroud, fan, fan pulley, radiator and lower fan shroud. Discharge A/C refrigerant system. Remove A/C condenser. Remove A/C compressor and brace. Remove alternator. Remove cruise control servo (if equipped).
3) Disconnect fuel lines, electrical connectors, vacuum hoses, coolant hoses and control cables as necessary. Remove throttle body injection unit. Remove distributor cap with wires attached. Remove diverter valve assembly and pipe.
4) Remove ignition coil and manifold absolute pressure sensor. Remove upper half of engine oil dipstick tube. Remove engine oil filler

1991 ENGINES
4.3L V6, 5.0L, 5.7L & 7.4L V8 (Cont.)

tube. Remove headlight bezels, grille and upper radiator support (sheet metal cross panel support).
5) Raise and support vehicle. Drain crankcase. Disconnect exhaust pipes from manifolds. Remove strut rods. Remove flywheel cover. Disconnect oil cooler lines from engine. Remove starter, torque converter bolts (A/T) and engine mount through-bolts.
6) Lower vehicle. Attach engine hoist. Remove bellhousing bolts. Support transmission. Remove engine. To install, reverse removal procedure. Fill crankcase and cooling system. Evacuate and charge A/C system.

NOTE: On "P" Series, engine and transmission are removed as an assembly through the side door.

Removal & Installation ("P" Series & "R" & "V" Series) – 1) Release fuel system pressure. See FUEL PRESSURE RELEASE under REMOVAL & INSTALLATION. Disconnect battery. Drain cooling system. On "P" Series, remove engine cover and floor panel sections.
2) On all vehicles, remove air cleaner, duct and exhaust heat stove pipe. Remove distributor cap and set aside. Disconnect all engine harness electrical connectors and set aside. Disconnect fuel lines from throttle body injection unit. Remove fuel line clamps from transmission and set fuel lines aside.
3) Disconnect ground strap from rear end of left cylinder head. Disconnect all transmission harness electrical connectors and set harness aside. Remove transmission shifter (if necessary). Remove upper radiator hose, all accessory drive belts, fan, fan pulley, fan shroud and lower radiator hose.
4) Remove engine oil filler tube. Remove clutch adjuster rod, return spring and pivot arm assembly (M/T). Disconnect exhaust pipes from manifolds. Disconnect battery cable from clamp on cylinder block. Disconnect drive shaft from transmission. Remove transmission mount.
5) Disconnect oil cooler lines from oil filter adapter and oil cooler line clamps from engine. Attach engine hoist. Remove engine mount through-bolts. Remove engine and transmission assembly (through side door on "P" Series). To install, reverse removal procedure. Fill crankcase and cooling system.
Removal & Installation ("S" Series) – 1) Release fuel system pressure. See FUEL PRESSURE RELEASE under REMOVAL & INSTALLATION. Disconnect battery. Remove hood. Drain cooling system.
2) Disconnect upper radiator hose from radiator. Remove coolant overflow hose and upper fan shroud. Disconnect transmission fluid lines and engine oil cooler lines (if equipped). Remove radiator and fan. Disconnect heater hoses. Remove air cleaner.
3) Disconnect fuel lines, electrical connectors, vacuum hoses, coolant hoses and control cables as necessary. Remove distributor cap. Raise and support vehicle. Disconnect exhaust pipe from converter and manifolds. Remove strut rods and flywheel cover.
4) Remove torque converter bolts (A/T). Remove shield from rear of catalytic converter. Disconnect converter hanger from exhaust pipe. Remove 2 outer air dam bolts. Remove left body mount bolts, raise and support body and remove bellhousing bolts. Lower body.
5) Remove motor mount through-bolts. Lower vehicle. Remove A/C compressor and power steering pump with hoses attached and set aside (if equipped). Attach engine hoist. Support transmission. Remove engine. To install, reverse removal procedure. Fill crankcase and cooling system.
Removal & Installation ("T" Series Except Bravada) – 1) Release fuel system pressure. See FUEL PRESSURE RELEASE under REMOVAL & INSTALLATION. Disconnect battery. Remove hood. Raise and support vehicle.
2) Loosen or remove body mount bolts. Raise and support body. Remove upper bellhousing bolts and front air dam end bolts. Lower body. Remove remaining bellhousing bolts. Remove No. 2 frame crossmember. Disconnect exhaust pipes from manifolds.
3) Disconnect catalytic converter hanger. Remove flywheel cover bolts. Disconnect front driveshaft from differential. Remove flywheel cover. Disconnect transmission cooler lines from engine clips. Remove motor mount bolts.
4) Remove torque converter bolts. Remove front splash shield and lower fan shroud bolts. Lower vehicle. Drain cooling system. Remove upper fan shroud. Disconnect radiator hoses from radiator. Disconnect oil filter pipe from remote oil filter.
5) Remove radiator, fan and air cleaner. Remove A/C compressor and power steering pump with hoses attached and lay aside (if equipped). Disconnect fuel lines, electrical connectors, vacuum hoses, coolant hoses and control cables as necessary.
6) Support transmission. Attach engine hoist. Remove engine. To install, reverse removal procedure. Fill crankcase and cooling system.
Removal & Installation (Bravada) – 1) Release fuel system pressure. See FUEL PRESSURE RELEASE under REMOVAL & INSTALLATION. Disconnect battery. Remove hood. Raise and support vehicle. Drain cooling system and crankcase.
2) Disconnect exhaust pipes from manifolds. Disconnect drive shaft from front differential. Remove starter. Remove flywheel cover and torque converter bolts. Remove engine mount through-bolts. Remove oil filter adapter.
3) Remove strut rod. Remove bellhousing bolts. Disconnect transmission fluid cooler lines from clips. Lower vehicle. Remove air cleaner, upper fan shroud, accessory drive belt and fan/clutch assembly.
4) Remove A/C compressor with hoses attached and set aside (if equipped). Remove radiator. Disconnect power steering hoses from power steering pump. Disconnect fuel lines, electrical connectors, vacuum hoses, coolant hoses and control cables as necessary.
5) Remove alternator. Disconnect spark plug wires from distributor cap. Remove cap. Support transmission. Remove bracket from oil cooler. Attach engine hoist. Remove engine.
6) To install, reverse removal procedure. Fill crankcase and cooling system. Bleed power steering fluid system.

ENGINE (5.0L & 5.7L)

CAUTION: Minimal clearance exists between oil pump pick-up tube and bottom of oil pan. DO NOT place jack under oil pan, crankshaft pulley or any sheet metal when lifting engine.

Removal & Installation ("C" & "K" Series & "R" & "V" Series) – 1) Release fuel system pressure. See FUEL PRESSURE RELEASE under REMOVAL & INSTALLATION. Disconnect battery. Remove hood. Drain cooling system.
2) Remove air cleaner, accessory drive belt, fan and water pump pulley. Remove radiator and fan shroud. Disconnect heater hoses from engine. Disconnect fuel lines, electrical connectors, vacuum hoses, coolant hoses and control cables as necessary.
3) Remove A/C compressor and power steering pump with hoses attached and set aside (if equipped). Raise and support vehicle. Drain crankcase. Disconnect exhaust pipes from manifolds. Remove strut rods (if equipped). Remove flywheel cover and starter. Remove torque converter bolts (A/T).
4) Lower vehicle. Support transmission. Attach engine hoist. Remove bellhousing bolts. Remove engine mount through-bolts. Remove engine. To install, reverse removal procedure. Fill crankcase and cooling system.

NOTE: On "G" Series, engine and transmission are removed as an assembly.

Removal & Installation ("G" Series) – 1) Release fuel system pressure. See FUEL PRESSURE RELEASE under REMOVAL & INSTALLATION. Disconnect battery negative cable. Drain cooling system.
2) Remove coolant recovery reservoir. Remove grille, lower grille valance and upper radiator support. Discharge A/C refrigerant system. Remove A/C condenser and radiator. Remove power steering pump with hoses attached and set aside (if equipped).
3) Remove engine cover, air cleaner and throttle body injection unit. Disconnect fuel lines, electrical connectors, vacuum hoses, coolant hoses and control cables as necessary. Remove thermostat housing and oil filler tube. Raise and support vehicle. Disconnect exhaust pipes from manifolds.
4) Disconnect drive shaft from transmission. Disconnect transmission shift linkage and vehicle speed sensor connector from transmission. Drain crankcase. Remove transmission mount bolts. Support engine with jack.

5) Remove front engine mounts and place wood blocks between cylinder block and frame. Lower vehicle. Attach engine hoist. Remove engine and transmission as an assembly. To install, reverse removal procedure. Fill crankcase and cooling system. Evacuate and charge A/C system.

NOTE: On "P" Series, engine and transmission are removed as an assembly through the side door.

Removal & Installation ("P" Series) - 1) Release fuel system pressure. See FUEL PRESSURE RELEASE under REMOVAL & INSTALLATION. Disconnect battery. Drain cooling system. Remove engine cover and floor panel sections from inside vehicle.
2) Remove air cleaner, duct and exhaust heat stove pipe. Remove distributor cap and set aside. Disconnect all engine harness electrical connectors and set harness aside. Disconnect fuel lines from throttle body injection unit. Remove fuel line clamps from transmission and set fuel lines aside.
3) Disconnect hydraulic line from clutch slave cylinder. Disconnect ground strap from rear end of left cylinder head. Disconnect all transmission harness electrical connectors and set harness aside. Remove transmission shift lever (M/T).
4) Remove upper radiator hose, all accessory drive belts, fan, fan pulley, fan shroud and lower radiator hose. Remove engine oil filler tube. Raise and support vehicle. Disconnect exhaust pipes from manifolds. Disconnect battery cable from clamp on cylinder block.
5) Disconnect drive shaft from transmission. Remove transmission mount. Disconnect oil cooler lines from oil filter adapter. Disconnect oil cooler line clamps from engine. Attach engine hoist.
6) Remove engine mount through-bolts. Remove engine and transmission assembly through side door. To install, reverse removal procedure. Fill crankcase and cooling system.

ENGINE (7.4L)

CAUTION: Minimal clearance exists between oil pump pick-up tube and bottom of oil pan. DO NOT place jack under oil pan, crankshaft pulley or any sheet metal when lifting engine.

Removal & Installation ("C" & "K" Series, "P" Series & "R" & "V" Series) - 1) Release fuel system pressure. See FUEL PRESSURE RELEASE under REMOVAL & INSTALLATION. Disconnect battery. Remove hood. Drain cooling system.
2) Remove air cleaner, accessory drive belt, fan and water pump pulley. Remove radiator and fan shroud. Disconnect heater hoses from engine. Disconnect fuel lines, electrical connectors, vacuum hoses, coolant hoses and control cables as necessary.
3) Remove A/C compressor and power steering pump with hoses attached and set aside (if equipped). Raise and support vehicle. Drain crankcase. Disconnect exhaust pipes from manifolds. Remove starter. Remove flywheel cover. Remove torque converter bolts (A/T).
4) Remove bellhousing bolts and engine mount through-bolts. Lower vehicle. Support transmission. Attach engine hoist. Remove engine. To install, reverse removal procedure. Fill crankcase and cooling system.
Removal & Installation ("G" Series) - 1) Release fuel system pressure. See FUEL PRESSURE RELEASE under REMOVAL & INSTALLATION. Disconnect battery. Remove engine cover. Drain crankcase and cooling system.
2) Remove air intake duct and air cleaner. Disconnect fuel lines, electrical connectors, vacuum hoses, coolant hoses and control cables as necessary. Remove distributor cap, distributor and ignition coil.
3) Remove transmission and engine oil dipstick tubes. Remove EGR purge valve. Remove 2 A/C compressor brackets. Remove throttle body injection unit. Remove headlight bezels, grille, bumper filler panel and cruise control servo (if equipped). Remove hood latch, coolant reservoir and upper radiator brackets.
4) Remove front end sheet metal cross panel. Discharge A/C refrigerant system. Remove A/C condenser, windshield washer fluid reservoir and washer pump. Remove upper fan shroud, engine oil cooler and transmission oil cooler. Remove radiator, lower fan shroud, fan, serpentine drive belt and water pump pulley.
5) Disconnect A/C refrigerant line from accumulator and alternator bracket. Remove A/C compressor and idler pulley. Remove alternator and belt tensioner. Remove exhaust crossover pipe from manifolds. Remove starter. Disconnect drive shaft and shift linkage from transmission.
6) Remove engine mount through-bolts. Support transmission. Remove transmission crossmember. Lower vehicle. Attach engine hoist. Remove engine and transmission as an assembly.
7) To install, reverse removal procedure. Fill crankcase and cooling system. Evacuate and charge A/C refrigerant system.

INTAKE MANIFOLD

Removal - 1) Release fuel system pressure. See FUEL PRESSURE RELEASE under REMOVAL & INSTALLATION. Disconnect battery. Drain cooling system. Remove air cleaner.
2) Disconnect fuel lines, electrical connectors, vacuum hoses, coolant hoses and control cables as necessary. Remove alternator bracket, A/C compressor (with hoses attached), throttle body injection unit and cruise control servo as necessary.
3) Remove distributor cap. Mark distributor rotor in relation to distributor housing. Mark base of distributor housing in relation to intake manifold. Remove distributor. Remove intake manifold bolts, intake manifold and gaskets.
Installation - 1) On all engines except 7.4L, install gaskets on cylinder heads. Apply a 3/16" (5 mm) bead of RTV sealant to front and rear intake
manifold-to-cylinder block mounting surfaces. *See Fig. 1.* Extend bead 1/2" (13 mm) beyond cylinder block-to-cylinder head junction.
2) On 7.4L, install front and rear intake manifold seals on cylinder block. Install gaskets on cylinder heads. *See Fig. 2.*
3) On all models, install intake manifold and bolts. Tighten bolts in sequence to specification. *See Fig. 3.* See TORQUE SPECIFICATIONS table at end of article. To complete installation, reverse removal procedure. Fill cooling system.

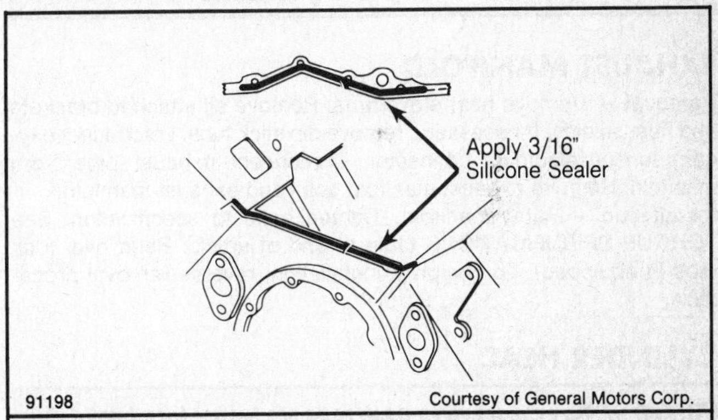
Apply 3/16"
Silicone Sealer
91198
Courtesy of General Motors Corp.

Fig. 1: Applying RTV Sealant Before Installing Intake Manifold (Except 7.4L)

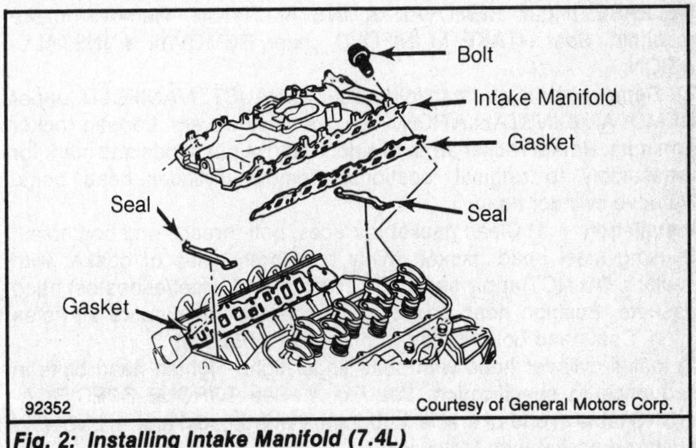
Bolt
Intake Manifold
Gasket
Seal
Seal
Gasket
92352
Courtesy of General Motors Corp.

Fig. 2: Installing Intake Manifold (7.4L)

1991 ENGINES
4.3L V6, 5.0L, 5.7L & 7.4L V8 (Cont.)

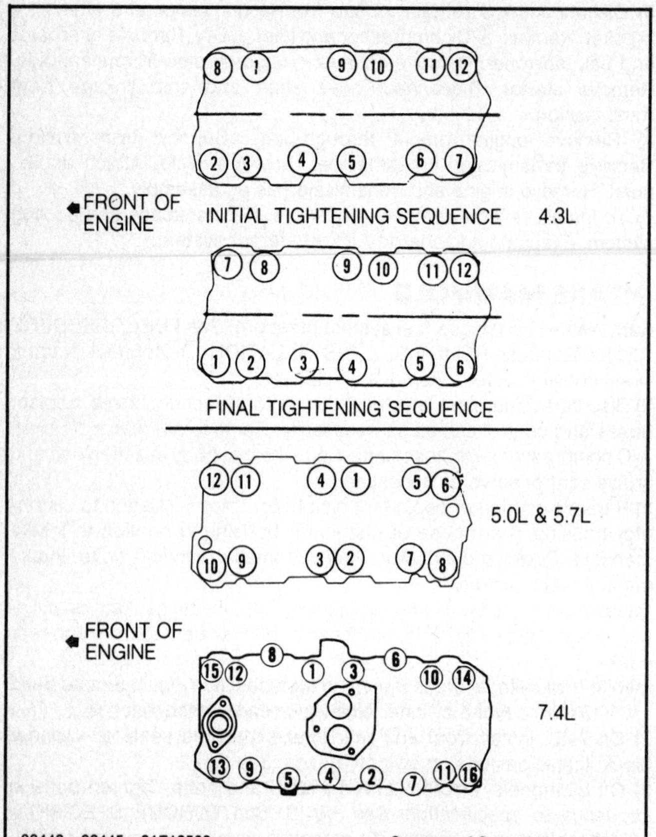
FRONT OF ENGINE
INITIAL TIGHTENING SEQUENCE
4.3L
FINAL TIGHTENING SEQUENCE
5.0L & 5.7L
FRONT OF ENGINE
7.4L
92442 92445 91E13503
Courtesy of General Motors Corp.

Fig. 3: Intake Manifold Bolt Tightening Sequence

EXHAUST MANIFOLD

Removal – Remove heat stove tube. Remove all attached brackets and heat shields. If necessary, remove dip stick tube. Disconnect oxygen sensor electrical connector. Disconnect exhaust pipe from manifold. Remove exhaust manifold bolts and exhaust manifold.

Installation – Install manifold. Tighten bolts to specification. See TORQUE SPECIFICATIONS table at end of article. Bend over lock tabs (if equipped). To complete installation, reverse removal procedure.

CYLINDER HEAD

NOTE: On 7.4L, exhaust valve push rods are longer than intake valve push rods.

Removal – **1)** Release fuel system pressure. See FUEL PRESSURE RELEASE under REMOVAL & INSTALLATION. Remove intake manifold. See INTAKE MANIFOLD under REMOVAL & INSTALLATION.

2) Remove exhaust manifold. See EXHAUST MANIFOLD under REMOVAL & INSTALLATION. Remove valve covers. Loosen rocker arm nuts. Rotate rocker arms to side. Remove push rods and mark for reassembly to original locations. Remove cylinder head bolts. Remove cylinder head.

Installation – **1)** Clean gasket surfaces, bolt threads and bolt holes. If using steel head gasket, thinly coat both sides of gasket with sealant. DO NOT apply sealant to composition (steel/asbestos) head gaskets. Position head gasket on cylinder block. Ensure all holes align. Coat head bolt threads with Sealant (1052080).

2) Install cylinder head with bolts finger-tight. Tighten head bolts in sequence to specification. *See Fig. 4.* See TORQUE SPECIFICATIONS table at end of article. Lubricate valve tip, rocker arm pivot and push rod socket with Molykote.

3) To complete installation, reverse removal procedure. Adjust valves. See VALVE CLEARANCE ADJUSTMENT under ADJUSTMENTS.

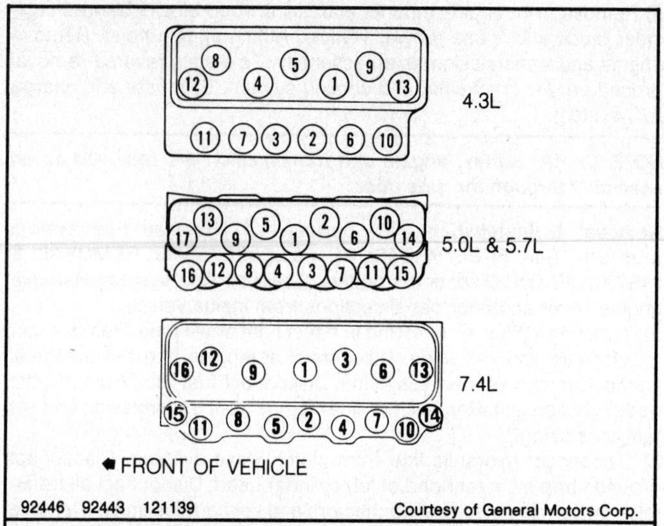
4.3L
5.0L & 5.7L
7.4L
FRONT OF VEHICLE
92446 92443 121139
Courtesy of General Motors Corp.

Fig. 4: Cylinder Head Bolt Tightening Sequence

FRONT COVER OIL SEAL

Removal – Remove accessory drive belt(s) and pulley. Remove crankshaft damper bolt. Using Damper Puller/Installer (J-23523-E), remove crankshaft damper. Carefully pry seal from cover with screwdriver. DO NOT distort front cover.

Installation – **1)** Coat seal lip with engine oil. Using Seal Installer (J-22102) on 7.4L and (J-35468) on all others, install new seal in front cover with seal lip facing engine. Apply RTV sealant to Woodruff keyway in crankshaft damper.

2) Install crankshaft damper. Install crankshaft damper bolt and tighten to specification. See TORQUE SPECIFICATIONS table at end of article. To install remaining components, reverse removal procedure.

TIMING CHAIN & SPROCKETS

Removal – **1)** Disconnect battery. Drain cooling system. If necessary, remove radiator shroud. Remove accessory drive belts, fan and pulley. Remove crankshaft damper bolt. Using Damper Puller/Installer (J-23523-E), remove crankshaft damper.

2) Remove all mounting brackets and coolant hoses attached to water pump. Remove water pump. Remove oil pan. See OIL PAN under REMOVAL & INSTALLATION. Remove front cover and gasket.

3) Rotate crankshaft until timing marks on camshaft and crankshaft sprockets are aligned. *See Fig. 5.* Remove camshaft sprocket and timing chain. To remove crankshaft sprocket, use Sprocket Puller (J-1619) on 7.4L and (J-5825-A) on all others.

Installation – **1)** Install Woodruff key in crankshaft (if removed). Using Crankshaft Sprocket Installer (J-22102) on 7.4L and (J-5590) on all others, install crankshaft sprocket. Install camshaft sprocket and timing chain, ensuring timing marks on sprockets are aligned. *See Fig. 5.*

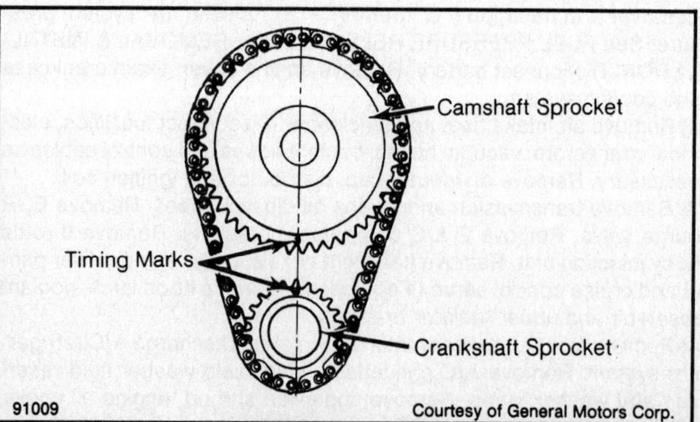
Camshaft Sprocket
Timing Marks
Crankshaft Sprocket
91009
Courtesy of General Motors Corp.

Fig. 5: Aligning Timing Marks

2) Install and tighten camshaft sprocket bolts to specification. See TORQUE SPECIFICATIONS table at end of article. Install gasket to front cover with gasket sealant. Install front cover and gasket.
3) Apply RTV sealant to Woodruff keyway in crankshaft damper. Install crankshaft damper. Install crankshaft damper bolt and tighten to specification. See TORQUE SPECIFICATIONS table at end of article. To install remaining components, reverse removal procedure.

ROCKER ARM STUDS (EXCEPT 7.4L)

CAUTION: Ream rocker arm stud bore before installing oversize rocker arm stud or cylinder head may be damaged.

Removal & Installation – 1) Rocker arm studs are pressed into cylinder head. Using Stud Remover (J-5802-01), place remover over stud. Install flat washer and nut. Tighten nut to remove stud from cylinder head.
2) If stud is loose in cylinder head, ream stud bore for oversize stud using Reamer (J-5715) for .003" (.08 mm) oversize stud and (J-6036) for .013" (.33 mm) oversize stud.
3) Coat press-fit area of stud with hypoid axle lubricant. Using Stud Driver (J-6880), drive stud into bore until driver bottoms against cylinder head.

VALVE LIFTERS

NOTE: On 7.4L, exhaust valve push rods are longer than intake valve push rods.

Removal – 1) Remove intake manifold. See INTAKE MANIFOLD under REMOVAL & INSTALLATION. Remove valve covers. Loosen all rocker arm nuts and rotate rockers to one side.
2) Remove push rods, noting location for reassembly reference. On 4.3L, remove lifter retainer. On all engines, remove lifters, noting location for reassembly reference.
Installation – Coat lifter feet and body with High Viscosity Oil/Zinc (12345501). Install lifters in original location. To install remaining components, reverse removal procedure.

CAMSHAFT

Removal – Remove radiator, A/C condenser (if equipped) and grille. Remove valve lifters. See VALVE LIFTERS under REMOVAL & INSTALLATION. Remove timing chain and camshaft sprocket. See TIMING CHAIN & SPROCKETS under REMOVAL & INSTALLATION. If necessary, raise engine. Remove camshaft.
Installation – Coat camshaft lobes and bearing journals with High Viscosity Oil/Zinc (12345501). Install camshaft. To install remaining components, reverse removal procedure.

REAR CRANKSHAFT OIL SEAL

Removal – Remove transmission, clutch (M/T) and flywheel. Using screwdriver, pry seal from housing. DO NOT scratch crankshaft sealing surface. Note direction of seal lip.
Installation – 1) Lubricate inner and outer diameter of seal with engine oil. Place seal on Seal Installer (J-35621) or (J-38841 on 7.4L). Position seal installer against crankshaft.
2) Thread the attaching screws into crankshaft flange and tighten with screwdriver. This squares the seal with the crankshaft. Rotate seal installer handle until it bottoms. Remove seal installer. Install flywheel, clutch (M/T) and transmission.

WATER PUMP

Removal – Disconnect battery. Drain cooling system. Remove all drive belts, coolant hoses and mounting brackets attached to water pump. If necessary, remove fan shroud. Remove fan and pulley. Remove water pump and gaskets.
Installation – Install water pump with new gaskets. Tighten water pump bolts to specification. See TORQUE SPECIFICATIONS table at end of article. To install remaining components, reverse removal procedure.

OIL PAN

CAUTION: Minimal clearance exists between oil pump pick-up tube and bottom of oil pan. DO NOT place jack under oil pan, crankshaft pulley or any sheet metal when lifting engine.

Removal (Astro, Safari, "C" & "K" Series, "P" Series, & "R" & "V" Series With 4.3L, 5.0L & 5.7L) – 1) Disconnect battery. Raise and support vehicle. Drain crankcase. Remove exhaust crossover pipe, strut rods, strut rod brackets and flywheel cover.
2) Remove starter. Remove or disconnect engine oil cooler lines and/or transmission fluid lines as necessary. Remove oil pan bolts, oil pan and gasket.
Removal (Bravada) – 1) Disconnect battery. Remove engine oil dipstick. Raise and support vehicle. Remove accessory drive belt splash shield. Drain crankcase. Remove flywheel cover. Remove front engine mount through-bolts.
2) Raise engine. Support in place with wood blocks. Disconnect oil cooler line. Remove oil filter adapter. Remove pitman arm and idler arm. Remove front differential mount through-bolts. Remove front drive shaft. Roll differential forward. Remove starter. Remove oil pan bolts, oil pan and gasket.

CAUTION: On "C" & "K" Series, "P" Series and "R" & "V" Series with 7.4L, disconnect oil pressure tube from side of engine to prevent damage to tube when engine is raised.

Removal ("C" & "K" Series With 7.4L) – 1) Disconnect battery. Remove fan shroud bolts. Move shroud rearward. Remove air cleaner and distributor cap. Raise and support vehicle. Drain crankcase. Remove starter (M/T). Remove flywheel cover and oil filter.
2) Disconnect oil pressure line from side of cylinder block. Remove front engine mount through-bolts. Raise and support engine. Remove oil pan bolts, oil pan and gasket.
Removal ("G" Series With 7.4L) – 1) Disconnect battery. Remove engine cover. Raise and support vehicle. Drain crankcase. Disconnect front drive shaft from differential. Remove transmission. Remove flywheel and engine oil dipstick tube.
2) Remove front engine mount through-bolts. Raise engine enough to allow room for oil pan removal. Remove oil pan bolts (DO NOT remove oil pan). Remove oil pump and allow to rest in oil pan. Remove oil pump and oil pan.

CAUTION: On "C" & "K" Series, "P" Series and "R" & "V" Series with 7.4L, disconnect oil pressure tube from side of engine to prevent damage to tube when engine is raised.

Removal ("P" Series & "R" & "V" Series With 7.4L) – 1) Disconnect battery. Disconnect oil pressure tube from side of engine. Raise and support vehicle. Drain crankcase. Remove strut rods and flywheel cover. Disconnect oil cooler lines from oil filter housing.
2) Disconnect vent hose from front differential (4WD). Remove starter. Remove front engine mount through-bolts. Raise and support engine. Remove oil pan bolts, oil pan and gasket.
Removal ("S" Series) – Raise and support vehicle. Drain crankcase. Remove engine. See ENGINE under REMOVAL & INSTALLATION. Remove oil pan bolts, oil pan and gasket.
Removal ("T" Series Except Bravada) – 1) Disconnect battery. Remove engine oil dipstick and accessory drive belt splash shield. Raise and support vehicle. Drain crankcase. Remove front axle shield and transfer case shield. Remove brake line clips from crossmember.
2) Remove second crossmember. Remove converter hanger bolts and exhaust pipe clamp from converter. Disconnect exhaust pipes from manifolds. Slide exhaust pipe rearward. Disconnect front drive shaft from differential.
3) Remove flywheel cover. Remove starter motor. Remove idler arm-to-frame bolts. Remove differential housing mounting bolts from bracket (right side) and frame (left side).
4) Move differential housing forward. Remove front engine mount through-bolts. Raise and support engine. Remove oil pan bolts, oil pan and gasket.

1991 ENGINES
4.3L V6, 5.0L, 5.7L & 7.4L V8 (Cont.)

Installation (All Models) – **1)** On all engines except 7.4L, apply RTV sealant to front cover-to-cylinder block junction and rear main bearing-to-cylinder block junction. On 7.4L, apply RTV sealant to both sides of oil pan gasket.
2) On all engines, install oil pan. Tighten oil pan bolts to specification. See TORQUE SPECIFICATIONS table at end of article. To install remaining components, reverse removal procedure. Fill crankcase.

OVERHAUL

CYLINDER HEAD

Valve Springs – **1)** Measure valve spring free length, installed height and pressure (tension). Replace valve spring if not within specification. See VALVES & VALVE SPRINGS table under ENGINE SPECIFICATIONS at end of article.
2) Measure installed height between cylinder head spring seat (or top of shim, if shimmed) and top of spring shield (top of spring on 7.4L). If installed height exceeds specification, install shims as necessary to bring installed height to specification. Ensure installed height is not less than specified.
Valve Stem Oil Seals – **1)** On 4.3L, intake valve uses upper "O" ring seal and lower umbrella seal; exhaust valve uses upper "O" ring seal. On 5.0L and 5.7L, intake and exhaust valves use upper "O" ring seal and lower umbrella seal. On 7.4L, intake and exhaust valves use lower umbrella seal.
2) When installing umbrella seal, seat the seal against valve guide boss on cylinder head. Coat upper "O" ring seal with engine oil before installation and ensure seal is not twisted when installed.
Valve Guides – Valve guides are part of cylinder head (not replaceable). Measure valve guide oil clearance. See CYLINDER HEAD table under ENGINE SPECIFICATIONS at end of article. If not within specification, ream valve guide and install valves with oversize stems.
Valves – Replace valve if margin is less than 1/32" (.8 mm).

VALVE TRAIN

Rocker Arm Assembly – Clean push rods, rocker arms, balls and nuts with solvent and blow dry. Inspect rocker arms and balls at mating surface. The surface should be smooth and free of damage. Inspect push rods for bends or wear. Ensure oil passages are clear.

CYLINDER BLOCK ASSEMBLY

Piston & Rod Assembly – **1)** Mark piston in relation to cylinder bore before removal. Piston pin is press-fitted in connecting rod. Mark piston in relation to connecting rod before separating components.
2) Replace piston and piston pin as matched set. Install piston in bore with notch (dimple on 7.4L) on top of piston toward front of engine.
Fitting Pistons – **1)** Measure piston diameter at 90 degree angle to piston pin, on piston pin centerline. Measure cylinder bore diameter 2 1/2" below cylinder block deck. Determine piston clearance.
2) If piston clearance is not within specification, replace piston and/or machine cylinder bore as necessary. See CYLINDER BLOCK table and PISTONS, PINS & RINGS table under ENGINE SPECIFICATIONS at end of article.
Piston Rings – Measure piston ring end gap and side clearance. If not within specification, replace piston and/or rings as necessary. See PISTONS, PINS & RINGS table under ENGINE SPECIFICATIONS at end of article. Install rings with mark on ring facing upward. Position ring end gaps around circumference of piston as specified. *See Fig. 6.*
Rod Bearings – **1)** Measure rod bearing journal out-of-round, taper and oil clearance. If not within specification, replace rod bearings and/or machine crankshaft. See CRANKSHAFT, MAIN & CONNECTING ROD BEARINGS table under ENGINE SPECIFICATIONS at end of article.
2) Ensure rod side play is within specification. See CONNECTING RODS table under ENGINE SPECIFICATIONS at end of article.

NOTE: On 7.4L, if rear main bearing cap is removed, rear crankshaft oil seal must be replaced (transmission must be removed to replace seal).

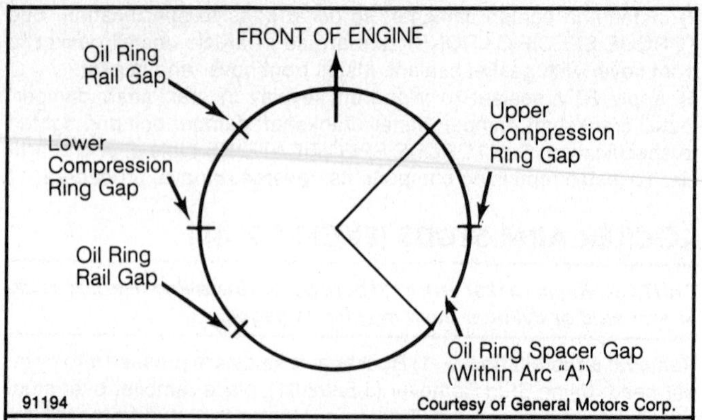
FRONT OF ENGINE
Oil Ring
Rail Gap
Upper
Compression
Ring Gap
Lower
Compression
Ring Gap
Oil Ring
Rail Gap
Oil Ring Spacer Gap
(Within Arc "A")
91194
Courtesy of General Motors Corp.

Fig. 6: Positioning Piston Ring End Gaps

Crankshaft & Main Bearings – **1)** Mark bearing caps for reassembly. Measure journal diameter, out-of-round, taper and oil clearance. If not within specification, replace main bearings and/or machine crankshaft. See CRANKSHAFT, MAIN & CONNECTING ROD BEARINGS table under ENGINE SPECIFICATIONS at end of article.
2) Align thrust bearing surfaces and measure crankshaft end play. See THRUST BEARING.

NOTE: The distance between rear main bearing thrust faces on some 4.3L, 5.0L and 5.7L engines is .008" (.20 mm) wider than standard. When replacing rear main bearings on these engines (identified by .008" stamped on crankshaft rear counterweight), use only .008" (.20 mm) wider bearings.

Thrust Bearing – **1)** Install main bearing caps (except rear) and tighten cap bolts to specification. See TORQUE SPECIFICATIONS table at end of article. On 7.4L, apply anaerobic sealant to cap-to-cylinder block mating surfaces. On all engines, Install rear main bearing cap and tighten cap bolts to 10 ft. lbs. (14 N.m).
2) Tap crankshaft rearward then forward to align thrust surfaces. Tighten rear main bearing cap bolts to specification. Measure crankshaft end play at forward thrust surface of rear main bearing cap. See CRANKSHAFT, MAIN & CONNECTING ROD BEARINGS table under ENGINE SPECIFICATIONS at end of article.
Cylinder Block – Measure cylinder bore out-of-round and taper. If not within specification, machine cylinder bore and/or replace piston. See CYLINDER BLOCK table under ENGINE SPECIFICATIONS at end of article.

ENGINE OILING

ENGINE LUBRICATION SYSTEM

Gear-type oil pump delivers full pressure lubrication through full-flow oil filter to main oil gallery. Main oil gallery feeds crankshaft and camshaft bearings through drilled passages in block.

Valve lifter oil gallery feeds valve lifters. From lifters, oil is routed through hollow push rods to upper valve train components. Timing chain and sprockets are lubricated by oil drainage from No. 1 camshaft bearing. Pistons and piston pins are lubricated by oil splash. Non-adjustable oil pressure regulator is located in oil pump body.
Crankcase Capacity – See CRANKCASE CAPACITY table.

CRANKCASE CAPACITY [1]

Application	Qts. (L)
Except 7.4L	5 (4.7)
7.4L	7 (6.6)

[1] – Capacity includes oil filter.

Oil Pressure – Measure oil pressure with engine at operating temperature and specified RPM. See OIL PRESSURE SPECIFICATIONS table.

OIL PRESSURE SPECIFICATIONS [1]

Application	psi (kg/cm²) @ RPM
Except 7.4L	6 (.4) @ 1000 18 (1.3) @ 2000 24 (1.7) @ 4000
7.4L	10 (.7) @ 500 40-60 (2.8-4.2) @ 2000

1 - Minimum specification.

OIL PUMP

***NOTE:** On all engines except 7.4L, pick-up tube is serviceable, however, DO NOT remove tube from pump body unless tube is damaged. On 7.4L, pick-up tube and pump are serviced as an assembly.*

Removal & Disassembly - 1) Remove oil pan. See OIL PAN under REMOVAL & INSTALLATION. Remove oil pump bolt. Remove pump and extension shaft. On all engines except 7.4L, remove pick-up tube (if necessary).

2) Remove pump cover. Mark relationship between gears at a meshing point for reassembly. Remove gears. Remove pressure regulator valve retaining pin. Remove pressure regulator valve and spring.

Inspection - Inspect pump body and cover for cracks or excessive wear. Inspect pump gears for damage or wear. Check drive gear shaft for looseness in pump body. Check pressure regulator valve for fit in bore. Replace entire pump assembly if damaged. Inspect inlet tube and screen assembly for damage.

Reassembly & Installation - 1) Install pump gears into pump body with marked gear teeth indexed. If pick-up tube was removed, apply sealant to tube end. Tap tube end into pump using plastic hammer. Reassemble remaining components in reverse order of disassembly.

2) Prime oil pump with engine oil. Install pump and extension shaft, ensuring slot on top of extension shaft engages with drive tang on end of distributor shaft. Tighten oil pump bolt to specification. See TORQUE SPECIFICATIONS table at end of article. Install oil pan.

TORQUE SPECIFICATIONS

TORQUE SPECIFICATIONS (4.3L, 5.0L & 5.7L)

Application	Ft. Lbs. (N.m)
Bellhousing Bolt	32 (43)
Camshaft Sprocket Bolt	21 (28)
Connecting Rod Cap Nut	
4.3L	1
5.0L & 5.7L	45 (61)
Crankshaft Damper Bolt	70 (95)
Cylinder Head Bolt 2	
Step 1	25 (34)
Step 2	45 (61)
Step 3	65 (88)
Exhaust Manifold Bolt	
Center 2	26 (35)
All Others	20 (27)
Flywheel Bolt	75 (102)
Front Cover Bolt (4.3L)	10 (14)
Intake Manifold Bolt	3 35 (47)
Main Bearing Cap Bolt	
4.3L	75 (102)
5.0L & 5.7L	
Outer Bolts Of Caps No. 2, 3 & 4	70 (95)
All Others	80 (108)
Oil Filter Adapter Bolt (4.3L)	15 (20)
Oil Filter By-Pass Valve Bolt (5.0L & 5.7L)	20 (27)

1 - Tighten to 20 ft. lbs. (27 N.m) then tighten an additional 60 degrees.

2 - Apply GM Sealer (1052080) to head bolt threads. Tighten in sequence. *See Fig. 4.*

3 - Tighten in sequence. *See Fig. 3.*

TORQUE SPECIFICATIONS (4.3L, 5.0L & 5.7L Cont.)

Application	Ft. Lbs.
Oil Pan Nut	17 (23)
Oil Pump Bolt	65 (88)
Rear Crankshaft Oil Seal Retainer Bolt	11 (15)
Valve Lifter Retainer Bolt (4.3L)	12 (16)
Water Pump Bolt	30 (41)
	INCH Lbs. (N.m)
Front Cover Bolt (5.0L & 5.7L)	8 (11)
Oil Pan Bolt	100 (11)
Oil Pump Cover Bolt	80 (9)
Valve Cover Bolt	90 (10)

TORQUE SPECIFICATIONS (7.4L)

Application	Ft. Lbs. (N.m)
Bellhousing Bolt	30 (41)
Camshaft Sprocket Bolt	20 (27)
Connecting Rod Cap Nut	48 (65)
Crankshaft Damper Bolt	85 (115)
Cylinder Head Bolt 1	
Step 1	30 (41)
Step 2	60 (81)
Step 3	80 (108)
Exhaust Manifold Bolt	40 (54)
Flywheel Bolt	65 (88)
Intake Manifold Bolt	2 30 (41)
Main Bearing Cap Bolt	100 (136)
Oil Pan Bolt	13 (18)
Oil Pump Bolt	65 (88)
Rocker Arm Bolt	40 (54)
Water Pump Bolt	30 (41)
	INCH Lbs. (N.m)
Front Cover Bolt	96 (11)
Oil Pump Cover Bolt	80 (9)
Valve Cover Bolt	60 (7)

1 - Apply GM Sealer (1052080) to head bolt threads. Tighten in sequence. *See Fig. 4.*

2 - Tighten in sequence. *See Fig. 3.*

ENGINE SPECIFICATIONS

GENERAL SPECIFICATIONS

Application	Specification
4.3L	
Displacement	262 (4.3L)
Bore	4.00" (101.6 mm)
Stroke	3.48" (88.4 mm)
Compression Ratio	9.3:1
Fuel System	TBI
Horsepower @ RPM	155 @ 4000
Torque Ft. Lbs. @ RPM	235 @ 2400
5.0L	
Displacement	305 Cu. In. (5.0L)
Bore	3.74" (95.0 mm)
Stroke	3.48" (88.4 mm)
Compression Ratio	1 9.3:1
Fuel System	TBI
HP @ RPM	170 @ 4000
Torque Ft. Lbs. @ RPM	255 @ 2400

1 - On vehicles over 8500 lbs. GVW, compression ratio is 8.3:1.

1991 ENGINES
4.3L V6, 5.0L, 5.7L & 7.4L V8 (Cont.)

GENERAL SPECIFICATIONS (Cont.)

Application	Specification
5.7L	
Displacement	350 Cu. In. (5.7L)
Bore	4.00" (101.6 mm)
Stroke	3.48" (88.4 mm)
Compression Ratio	[1] 9.3:1
Fuel System	TBI
Horsepower @ RPM	190 @ 4000
Torque Ft. Lbs. @ RPM	295 @ 2400
7.4L	
Displacement	454 Cu. In. (7.4L)
Bore	4.25" (108.0 mm)
Stroke	4.00" (101.6 mm)
Compression Ratio	7.9:1
Fuel System	TBI
Horsepower @ RPM	230 @ 3600
Torque Ft. Lbs. @ RPM	385 @ 1600

CRANKSHAFT, MAIN & CONNECTING ROD BEARINGS

Application	In. (mm)
4.3L	
Crankshaft End Play	.002-.006 (.05-.15)
Main Bearings	
Journal Diameter	
No. 1	2.4484-2.4493 (62.189-62.212)
No. 2 & 3	2.4481-2.4490 (62.182-62.205)
No. 4	2.4479-2.4488 (62.177-62.200)
Journal Out-Of-Round	.002 (.05)
Journal Taper	.001 (.03)
Oil Clearance	
Standard	
No. 1	.0008-.0020 (.020-.051)
No. 2 & 3	.0011-.0023 (.028-.059)
No. 4	.0017-.0032 (.043-.081)
Service Limit	
No. 1	.0010-.0015 (.025-.038)
No. 2 & 3	.0010-.0025 (.025-.064)
No. 4	.0025-.0035 (.064-.089)
Connecting Rod Bearings	
Journal Diameter	2.2487-2.2497 (57.117-57.142)
Journal Out-Of-Round	.002 (.05)
Journal Taper	.001 (.03)
Oil Clearance	.0013-.0035 (.033-.089)
5.0L & 5.7L	
Crankshaft End Play	.002-.006 (.05-.15)
Main Bearings	
Journal Diameter	
No. 1	2.4484-2.4493 (62.189-62.212)
No. 2, 3 & 4	2.4481-2.4490 (62.182-62.205)
No. 5	2.4479-2.4488 (62.177-62.200)
Journal Out-Of-Round	.001 (.03)
Journal Taper	.001 (.03)
Oil Clearance	
No. 1	.0010-.0015 (.025-.038)
No. 2, 3 & 4	.0010-.0025 (.025-.064)
No. 5	.0025-.0035 (.064-.089)
Connecting Rod Bearings	
Journal Diameter	2.0988-2.0998 (53.310-53.335)
Journal Out-Of-Round	.001 (.03)
Journal Taper	.001 (.03)
Oil Clearance	.0013-.0035 (.033-.089)

CRANKSHAFT, MAIN & CONNECTING ROD BEARINGS (Cont.)

Application	In. (mm)
7.4L	
Crankshaft End Play	.006-.010 (.15-.25)
Main Bearings	
Journal Diameter	2.7482-2.7489 (69.804-69.822)
Journal Out-Of-Round	.001 (.03)
Journal Taper	.001 (.03)
Oil Clearance	
Standard	
No. 1, 2, 3 & 4	.0017-.0030 (.043-.076)
No. 5	.0025-.0038 (.064-.097)
Service Limit	
No. 1, 2, 3 & 4	.0010-.0030 (.025-.076)
No. 5	.0025-.0040 (.064-.102)
Connecting Rod Bearings	
Journal Diameter	2.1990-2.1996 (55.855-55.870)
Journal Out-Of-Round	.001 (.03)
Journal Taper	.001 (.03)
Oil Clearance	.0011-.0029 (.028-.074)

CONNECTING RODS

Application	In. (mm)
4.3L, 5.0L & 5.7L	
Side Play	.006-.014 (.15-.36)
7.4L	
Side Play	.013-.023 (.33-.58)

PISTONS, PINS & RINGS

Application	In. (mm)
4.3L, 5.0L & 5.7L	
Pistons	
Clearance	.0007-.0017 (.018-.043)
Pins	
Diameter	
4.3L	.9270-.9273 (23.546-23.553)
5.0L & 5.7L	.9269-.9271 (23.543-23.548)
Piston Fit	.0002-.0007 (.005-.018)
Rod Fit	.0008-.0016 (.020-.041) Interference
Rings	
No. 1	
End Gap	.010-.020 (.25-.51)
Side Clearance	.001-.003 (.03-.08)
No. 2	
End Gap	.010-.025 (.25-.64)
Side Clearance	.001-.003 (.03-.08)
No. 3 (Oil)	
End Gap	.015-.055 (.38-1.40)
Side Clearance	.002-.007 (.05-.18)
7.4L	
Pistons	
Clearance	[1] .003-.004 (.08-.10)
Pins	
Diameter	.9895-.9897 (2.513-2.514)
Piston Fit	.0002-.0007 (.005-.018)
Rod Fit	.0021-.0031 (.053-.079) Interference
Rings	
No. 1	
End Gap	.010-.018 (.25-.46)
Side Clearance	.001-.003 (.03-.07)
No. 2	
End Gap	.016-.024 (.41-.61)
Side Clearance	.001-.003 (.03-.07)
No. 3 (Oil)	
End Gap	.010-.030 (.25-.76)
Side Clearance	.005-.007 (.127-.178)

[1] – Maximum service limit is .005" (.13 mm).

1991 ENGINES
4.3L V6, 5.0L, 5.7L & 7.4L V8 (Cont.)

CYLINDER BLOCK

Application	In. (mm)
4.3L	
Cylinder Bore	
Diameter	4.0007-4.0017 (101.618-101.643)
Maximum Taper	[1] .0005 (.013)
Maximum Out-Of-Round	[2] .001 (.03)
5.0L	
Cylinder Bore	
Diameter	3.7350-3.7385 (94.869-94.958)
Maximum Taper	[1] .0005 (.013)
Maximum Out-Of-Round	[2] .001 (.03)
5.7L	
Cylinder Bore	
Diameter	3.9995-4.0025 (101.587-101.664)
Maximum Taper	[1] .0005 (.013)
Maximum Out-of-Round	[2] .001 (.03)
7.4L	
Cylinder Bore	
Diameter	4.2500-4.2507 (107.950-107.968)
Maximum Taper	[1] .0005 (.013)
Maximum Out-Of-Round	[2] .001 (.03)

[1] – Specification is for thrust side. Relief side is .001" (.03 mm).
[2] – Production specification is given. Maximum service specification is .002" (.05 mm).

VALVES & VALVE SPRINGS

Application	Specification
4.3L, 5.0L, & 5.7L	
Intake Valves	
Face Angle	45°
Minimum Margin	.031" (.79 mm)
Exhaust Valves	
Face Angle	45°
Minimum Margin	.031" (.79 mm)
Valve Springs	
Free Length	2.03" (51.6 mm)
Installed Height	1.69-1.75" (42.9-44.5 mm)
Pressure	
Valve Closed	76-84 Lbs. @ 1.70 In. (34-38 kg @ 43.2 mm)
Valve Open	194-206 Lbs. @ 1.25 In. (88-93 kg @ 31.8 mm)
7.4L	
Intake Valves	
Face Angle	45°
Exhaust Valves	
Face Angle	45°
Valve Springs	
Free Length	2.12 (53.8)
Installed Height	1.80 (45.7)
Pressure	
Valve Closed	74-86 Lbs. @ 1.80 In. (34-39 kg @ 45.7 mm)
Valve Open	195-215 Lbs. @ 1.40 In. (88-98 kg @ 35.6 mm)

CYLINDER HEAD

Application	Specification
4.3L, 5.0L, 5.7L & 7.4L	
Valve Seats	
Intake Valve	
Seat Angle	46°
Seat Width	.031-.063" (.79-1.60 mm)
Maximum Seat Runout	.002" (.05 mm)
Exhaust Valve	
Seat Angle	46°
Seat Width	.063-.094" (1.60-2.39 mm)
Maximum Seat Runout	.002" (.05 mm)
Valve Guides	
Intake Valve	
Valve Guide Oil Clearance	.001-.003" (.03-.08 mm)
Exhaust Valve	
Valve Guide Oil Clearance	.001-.003" (.03-.08 mm)

CAMSHAFT

Application	In. (mm)
4.3L	
End Play	.004-.012 (.10-.30)
Journal Diameter	1.8682-1.8692 (47.452-47.478)
Lobe Lift	
VIN Z	
Intake	[1] .234 (5.94)
Exhaust	[1] .257 (6.53)
VIN B	
Intake	[1] .269 (6.83)
Exhaust	[1] .276 (7.01)
5.0L	
End Play	.004-.012 (.10-.30)
Journal Diameter	1.8682-1.8692 (47.452-47.478)
Lobe Lift	
Intake	[1] .2336 (5.933)
Exhaust	[1] .2565 (6.515)
5.7L	
End Play	.004-.012 (.10-.30)
Journal Diameter	1.8682-1.8692 (47.452-47.478)
Lobe Lift	
Intake	[1] .2565 (6.515)
Exhaust	[1] .2690 (6.833)
7.4L	
Journal Diameter	1.9482-1.9492 (49.484-49.510)
Lobe Lift	
Intake	[1] .2343 (5.951)
Exhaust	[1] .2530 (6.426)

[1] – Plus or minus .002" (.05 mm).

1991 ENGINES
6.2L V8 Diesel

"C" & "K" Series, "G" Series, "P" Series, "R" & "V" Series

NOTE: For repair procedures not covered in this article, see ENGINE OVERHAUL PROCEDURES article in GENERAL INFORMATION.

ENGINE IDENTIFICATION

Engine can be identified by eighth character of Vehicle Identification Number (VIN). VIN is stamped on a metal plate on top left end of instrument panel, near windshield. See ENGINE IDENTIFICATION table.

Engine can also be identified by engine identification (ID) number, stamped on cylinder block in one the following locations:

- On right side of timing chain case casting.
- On engine-to-transmission mating flange, near left cylinder head.
- At left front of engine block, near cylinder head-to-block mating surface.

ENGINE IDENTIFICATION

Application	VIN Code	Engine ID
6.2L		
Light Duty Emissions	C	LH6
Heavy Duty Emissions	J	LL4

ADJUSTMENTS

VALVE CLEARANCE ADJUSTMENT

Engine is equipped with hydraulic valve lifters. No valve adjustment is required.

REMOVAL & INSTALLATION

NOTE: For reassembly reference, label all electrical connectors, vacuum hoses and fuel lines before removal. Also place mating marks on engine hood and other major assemblies before removal.

ENGINE

NOTE: Removal and installation information on "P" Series is not available from manufacturer.

Removal & Installation ("C" & "K" Series & "R" & "V" Series) – 1) Disconnect batteries. Raise and support vehicle. Remove flywheel cover. Remove torque converter bolts (A/T). Disconnect exhaust pipes from manifolds. Remove starter, bellhousing bolts and engine mount through-bolts.

2) Disconnect cylinder block heater wires. Remove wiring harness, automatic transmission cooler lines and front battery cable from clamp on oil pan. Disconnect fuel return and oil cooler lines from engine. Lower vehicle. Remove hood. Drain cooling system.

3) Remove air cleaner. Disconnect alternator wires and clips. Disconnect injection pump wiring. Disconnect wiring from valve cover clips and glow plugs. Remove EGR/EPR solenoids, glow plug controller and temperature solenoid. Move harness aside. Disconnect engine-to-chassis ground strap.

4) Remove upper fan shroud and fan. Remove power steering pump and reservoir and lay aside. Disconnect control cables from injection pump. Disconnect heater hose from engine. Disconnect radiator hoses. Remove radiator. Support transmission. Remove engine. To install, reverse removal procedure. Fill cooling system.

Removal & Installation ("G" Series) – 1) Disconnect batteries. Remove headlight bezels, grille, bumper and lower valance panel. Remove hood latch, coolant recovery bottle, upper fan shroud and tie bar. Remove engine cover. Discharge A/C system, disconnect A/C condenser lines and remove condenser (if equipped).

2) Drain cooling system. Remove radiator, fan and lower shroud. Remove intake manifold. See INTAKE MANIFOLD under REMOVAL & INSTALLATION. Remove injection pump. See INJECTION PUMP under REMOVAL & INSTALLATION.

3) Raise and support vehicle. Remove P/S pump with hoses attached and lay aside. Disconnect exhaust pipes from manifolds. Remove flywheel cover, torque converter bolts (A/T) and engine mount through-bolts. Disconnect cylinder block heater wires.

4) Remove starter. Disconnect fuel line from fuel pump. Lower vehicle. Remove bellhousing bolts. Discharge A/C refrigerant and remove A/C compressor (if equipped). Remove oil filler tube upper bracket.

5) Disconnect engine harness electrical connectors and lay harness aside. Remove air cleaner resonator and bracket. Remove transmission dipstick tube. Disconnect heater hoses from engine. Remove alternator upper bracket.

6) Remove coolant crossover pipe. Attach Engine Lifting Fixture (J-33888) to center intake manifold bolt holes. Support transmission. Remove engine. To install, reverse removal procedure. Fill cooling system. Evacuate and charge A/C system.

INTAKE MANIFOLD

Removal – 1) Disconnect batteries. Remove air cleaner. Remove PCV and EGR hoses. Remove fuel line bracket and ground strap. Remove A/C compressor rear bracket (if equipped). On "C" & "K" Series and "G" Series, remove EPR/EGR solenoids and bracket. On "G" Series, remove crankcase depression relief valve.

2) On all models, loosen vacuum pump hold-down clamp (if equipped). Rotate pump to gain access to intake manifold bolt. Remove intake manifold bolts and fuel line clips. Remove intake manifold and gaskets.

CAUTION: Engines with light duty emissions rating (VIN C) use intake manifold gaskets that have openings for EGR ports; engines with heavy duty emissions rating (VIN J) DO NOT have openings. Use correct gaskets according to vehicle emissions rating.

Installation – 1) Install new manifold gaskets according to emissions rating. Install intake manifold. Tighten intake manifold bolts in sequence to 32 ft. lbs. (43 N.m). *See Fig. 1.*

2) To complete installation, reverse removal procedure. Rotate vacuum pump to correct position and tighten hold-down clamp (if equipped). *See Fig. 2.*

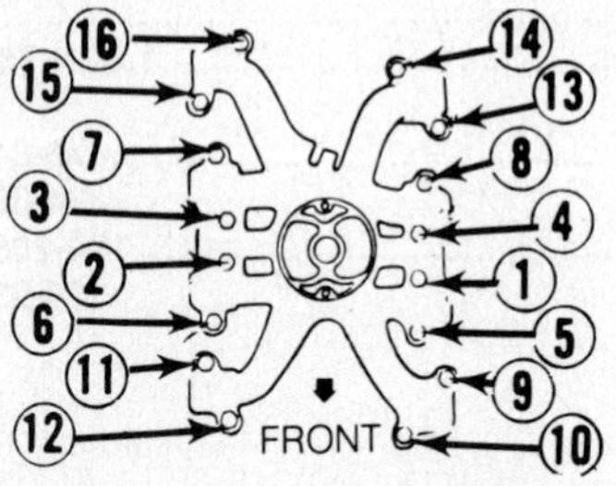
16
15
7
3
2
6
11
12
14
13
8
4
1
5
9
10
FRONT

91209 Courtesy of General Motors Corp.

Fig. 1: Intake Manifold Bolt Tightening Sequence

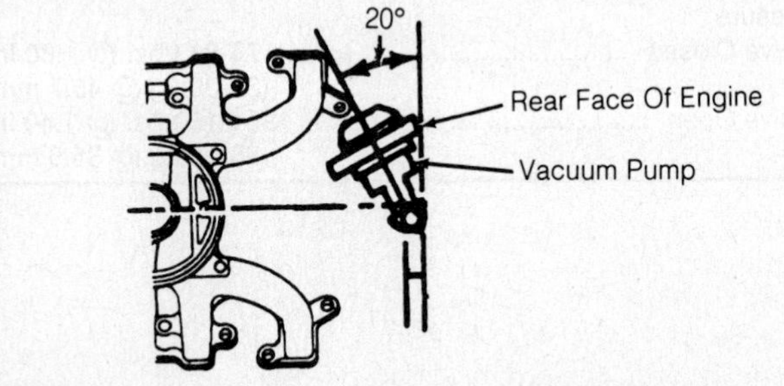
20°
Rear Face Of Engine
Vacuum Pump

91G13504 Courtesy of General Motors Corp.

Fig. 2: Positioning Vacuum Pump

EXHAUST MANIFOLD

Removal – Disconnect batteries. Raise vehicle. Disconnect exhaust pipe from manifold. Lower vehicle. On "G" Series, "P" Series and "R" & "V" Series, disconnect glow plug wires. Remove glow plugs. On all models, remove air cleaner duct bracket. If removing left manifold, remove dipstick tube (if necessary). Remove air conditioning bracket (if equipped). Remove exhaust manifold.

Installation – Install exhaust manifold. Tighten bolts to 26 ft. lbs. (35 N.m). To complete installation, reverse removal procedure.

CYLINDER HEAD

NOTE: Removal and Installation information on "P" Series is not available from manufacturer

Removal (Except "G" Series) – 1) Remove intake manifold. See INTAKE MANIFOLD under REMOVAL & INSTALLATION. Remove injection line clips from brackets. Disconnect injection lines from injector nozzles.

2) Disconnect injection lines from injection pump. Remove injection lines. Remove valve covers. Drain coolant. Raise and support vehicle. Disconnect exhaust pipe from manifold. Lower vehicle.

3) Remove A/C compressor, ground strap from rear of cylinder head, power steering pump and alternator as necessary. Disconnect necessary wiring. Remove glow plug relay and dipstick tube.

4) Disconnect glow plug wires. Remove rocker arm bolts and rocker arm shafts. Mark component location for reassembly reference. Note hardened upper end of push rod, indicated by paint stripe. Mark push rods if no paint stripe is visible. Remove push rods.

5) Disconnect necessary coolant hoses and ground straps. Remove coolant crossover pipe. Remove cylinder head bolts (rear bolt in left cylinder head may need to remain in head during removal). Remove cylinder head.

Removal ("G" Series) – 1) Remove intake manifold. See INTAKE MANIFOLD under REMOVAL & INSTALLATION. Remove injection line clips from brackets. Disconnect injection lines from injector nozzles.

2) Disconnect injection lines from injection pump. Remove injection lines. Remove upper fan shroud. Raise and support vehicle. Disconnect exhaust pipe from manifold. Lower vehicle.

3) Remove valve covers. Mark component location for reassembly reference, including crankshaft position. Remove rocker arm bolts and rocker arm shafts. Note hardened upper end of push rod, indicated by paint stripe. Mark push rods if no paint stripe is visible. Remove push rods.

4) Drain coolant. Remove air cleaner resonator and bracket. Remove transmission fluid and engine oil dipstick tubes. Disconnect necessary coolant hoses. Remove alternator and upper bracket. Remove coolant crossover pipe.

5) Disconnect necessary coolant hoses and ground straps. Remove coolant crossover pipe. Remove cylinder head bolts (rear bolt in left cylinder head may need to remain in head during removal). Remove cylinder head bolts, cylinder head and gasket.

Inspection – See CYLINDER HEAD under OVERHAUL.

Installation – 1) Clean cylinder head and cylinder block gasket surfaces. Clean cylinder head bolt thread and bolt holes. Apply Sealant (1052080) to head bolt threads and underside of bolt heads. DO NOT apply sealant to head gasket surface. Install rear head bolt in left cylinder head. Install cylinder head.

***CAUTION: Install push rods with hardened end (indicated by paint stripe) upward or engine damage may result. To prevent valve and piston contact during rocker arm shaft installation, rotate crankshaft until positioned as noted in step 3)** before tightening rocker arm shaft bolts.*

2) Install head bolts and tighten to specification. See TORQUE SPECIFICATIONS table at end of article. Tighten in sequence. *See Fig. 3*. Install push rods in original location with hardened end upward.

3) Rotate crankshaft until timing mark on crankshaft damper aligns with 0 mark on timing tab, then rotate crankshaft counterclockwise 3 1/2" (estimate this distance by aligning crankshaft damper mark with first lower water pump bolt). *See Fig. 8*.

4) Install rocker arm shafts, ensuring push rods are seated in rocker arms. Alternately tighten shaft bolts to 40 ft. lbs. (54 N.m). To complete installation, reverse removal procedure.

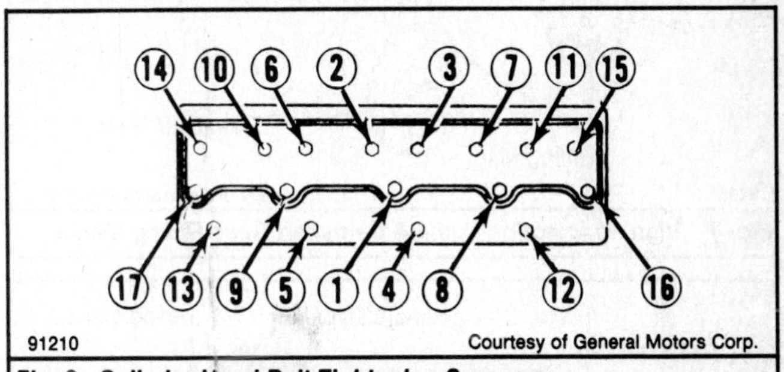
14
10
6
2
3
7
11
15
17
13
9
5
1
4
8
12
16
91210
Courtesy of General Motors Corp.

Fig. 3: Cylinder Head Bolt Tightening Sequence

FRONT COVER OIL SEAL

Removal – Disconnect batteries. Remove drive belts. Raise and support vehicle. Remove crankshaft pulley bolts and pulley. Remove crankshaft damper bolt and washer. Using Damper Puller (J-23523-E), remove crankshaft damper. Pry seal from cover using screwdriver. Note direction of seal lip.

Installation – Ensure seal area is free of burrs. Coat seal lip and crankshaft damper sealing surface with engine oil. Install new seal using Seal Installer (J-22101). Install crankshaft damper, washer and bolt. Tighten crankshaft damper bolt to 200 ft. lbs. (269 N.m). To complete installation, reverse removal procedure.

TIMING CHAIN & SPROCKETS

NOTE: Adjust injection pump timing if timing chain, sprockets or injection pump gears are replaced.

Removal – 1) Disconnect batteries. Drain coolant. Remove water pump and plate. See WATER PUMP under REMOVAL & INSTALLATION. Remove intake manifold. See INTAKE MANIFOLD under REMOVAL & INSTALLATION.

2) Remove crankshaft pulley bolts and pulley. Remove crankshaft damper bolt and washer. Using Damper Puller (J-23523-E), remove crankshaft damper. Pry front cover oil seal from front cover using screwdriver.

3) Rotate crankshaft until mark on crankshaft damper aligns with 0 mark on timing tab with injection pump gear-to-camshaft gear timing marks aligned. *See Fig. 4*. Remove injection pump gear-to-injection pump bolts. Remove injection pump gear.

4) Remove baffle (if equipped). Scribe mark the injection pump flange in relation to the front cover (if unmarked). Remove injection pump mounting nuts. Pull pump from front cover and lay on cylinder block. Remove oil pan-to-front cover bolts and front cover-to-cylinder block bolts.

5) Remove front cover. Measure timing chain free play. See TIMING CHAIN FREE PLAY. Remove camshaft gear from camshaft sprocket. *See Fig. 5*. Note alignment of timing marks on crankshaft and camshaft sprockets. Remove camshaft sprocket and timing chain. Remove crankshaft sprocket (if necessary).

Timing Chain Free Play – 1) Position dial indicator on front of cylinder block with dial indicator tip in contact with center of timing chain between sprockets. Pull chain away from crankshaft and adjust dial indicator to zero.

2) Push chain toward crankshaft and note indicator reading. If chain deflection exceeds .80" (20.3 mm) on used parts or .50" (12.7 mm) on new parts, replace chain. Replace sprockets if worn.

1991 ENGINES
6.2L V8 Diesel (Cont.)

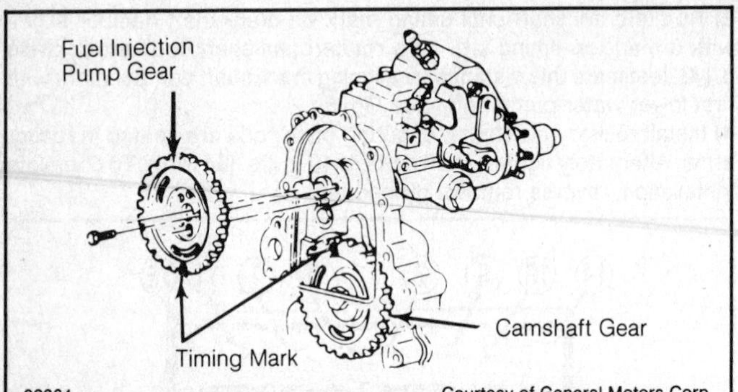
Fuel Injection
Pump Gear
Camshaft Gear
Timing Mark
92364
Courtesy of General Motors Corp.

Fig. 4: Aligning Injection Pump & Camshaft Gear Timing Marks

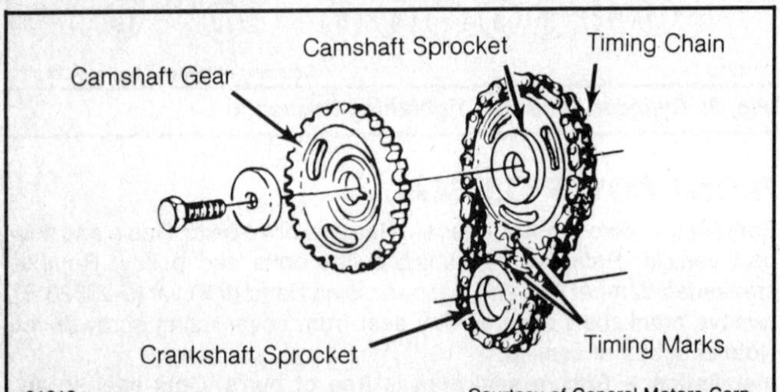
Camshaft Sprocket
Timing Chain
Camshaft Gear
Crankshaft Sprocket
Timing Marks
91213
Courtesy of General Motors Corp.

Fig. 5: Aligning Crankshaft & Camshaft Sprocket Timing Marks

Installation – **1)** Install crankshaft sprocket (if removed). Install camshaft sprocket and timing chain as an assembly, ensuring timing marks are aligned. *See Fig. 5*. Install camshaft gear, washer and bolt. Tighten camshaft gear bolt to specification. See TORQUE SPECIFICATIONS table at end of article.

2) Install new front cover oil seal using Seal Installer (J-22102). Coat seal lip and crankshaft damper sealing surface with engine oil. Apply 3/32" (2 mm) bead of anaerobic sealant to front cover at front cover-to-cylinder block sealing surface. Apply 3/16" (5 mm) bead of RTV sealant to front cover at front cover-to-oil pan sealing surface.

3) Install front cover. Tighten front cover bolts and oil pan bolts to specification. Install baffle (if equipped). If installing new front cover, place a timing mark on new front cover. See MARKING TDC ON FRONT COVER.

4) Install injection pump gasket and injection pump, aligning timing marks on injection pump flange and front cover. Install injection pump gear, ensuring timing marks on injection pump gear and camshaft gear are aligned. *See Fig. 4*. Tighten gear bolts to specification.

5) Ensure .040" (1.0 mm) minimum clearance exists between baffle and injection pump gear. To complete installation, reverse removal procedure. Fill cooling system. Adjust injection pump timing if timing chain, sprockets or injection pump gears were replaced.

Marking TDC On Front Cover – **1)** Rotate crankshaft until cylinder No. 1 is on TDC of compression stroke (timing marks on injection pump gear and camshaft gear will be aligned and slot in injection pump gear will be in 6 o'clock position). *See Figs. 4 and 6*.

2) Install Timing Fixture (J-33042) in place of injection pump without gasket. Install injection pump gear bolts to fasten gear to timing fixture. Install nut finger tight on upper front cover stud to secure timing fixture.

3) Tighten large bolt (18 mm head) on timing fixture to 35 ft. lbs. (47 N.m). Tighten nut on upper front cover stud. Ensure crankshaft did not rotate and timing fixture is not binding. Strike scriber with hammer to mark TDC indicator on front housing. Remove timing fixture.

INJECTION PUMP

Removal – **1)** Disconnect batteries. Remove intake manifold. See INTAKE MANIFOLD under REMOVAL & INSTALLATION. Remove fuel injection lines. Disconnect control cables from injection pump.

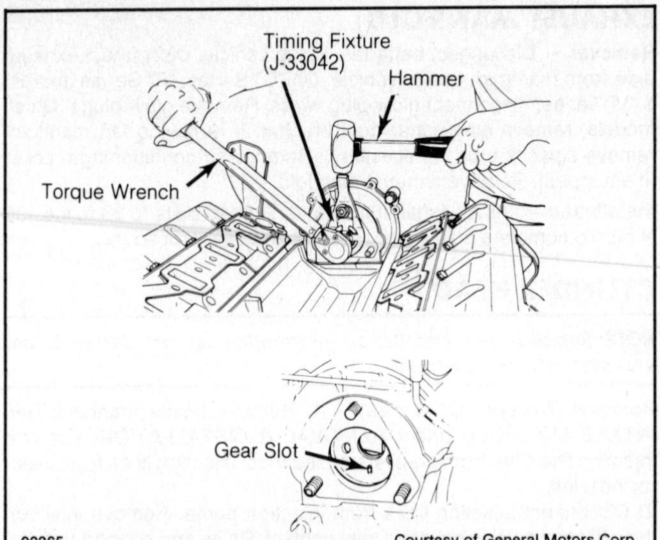
Timing Fixture
(J-33042)
Hammer
Torque Wrench
Gear Slot
92365
Courtesy of General Motors Corp.

Fig. 6: Marking TDC on Front Cover

2) Disconnect wiring, fuel return line and fuel supply line from injection pump. Cap all fuel line openings. Remove A/C hose retainer bracket (if equipped). Remove oil filler tube and vent hose assembly. Remove grommet.

3) Scribe an alignment mark on front cover and injection pump flange. Remove injection pump gear-to-injection pump bolts, accessible through oil filler neck hole (rotate crankshaft as necessary). Remove injection pump mounting nuts. Remove injection pump and gasket.

Installation – **1)** Install new injection pump gasket. Install injection pump, aligning locating pin on injection pump hub with slot in injection pump gear. Loosely install injection pump mounting nuts.

2) Align timing marks on injection pump flange and front cover. Tighten injection pump mounting nuts to 30 ft. lbs. (41 N.m). Install injection pump gear-to-injection pump bolts. Tighten bolts to 20 ft. lbs. (27 N.m).

3) To complete installation, reverse removal procedure. Ensure fuel lines are properly connected to ports on injection pump. *See Fig. 7*.

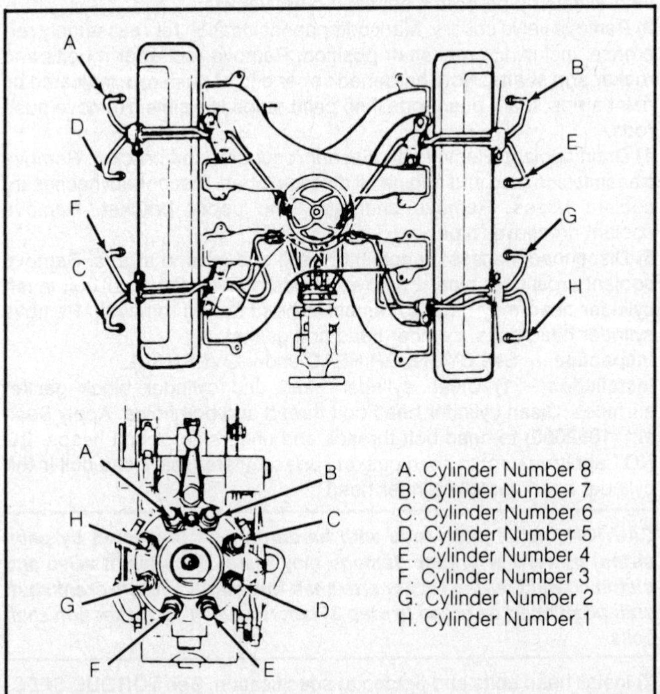
A
B
D
E
F
G
C
H
A
B
H
C
G
D
F
E
A. Cylinder Number 8
B. Cylinder Number 7
C. Cylinder Number 6
D. Cylinder Number 5
E. Cylinder Number 4
F. Cylinder Number 3
G. Cylinder Number 2
H. Cylinder Number 1
90J15726
Courtesy of General Motors Corp.

Fig. 7: Identifying Fuel Injection Lines

ROCKER ARM ASSEMBLY

Removal - 1) Remove intake manifold. See INTAKE MANIFOLD under REMOVAL & INSTALLATION. Remove fuel injection lines and valve covers.

2) Remove rocker arm shaft bolts and rocker arm shaft. Mark component location for reassembly reference. To disassemble rocker arm shaft, see ROCKER ARM ASSEMBLY under OVERHAUL.

3) If removing push rods, note paint stripe on hardened end of push rod (end closest to rocker arm). If no paint stripe is present, mark hardened end of push rod for reassembly reference.

CAUTION: Follow installation procedure to prevent piston and valve damage.

Installation - 1) Rotate crankshaft until timing mark on crankshaft damper aligns with 0 mark on timing tab. Rotate crankshaft counterclockwise 3 1/2" (estimate this distance by aligning crankshaft damper mark with first lower water pump bolt). *See Fig. 8*.

2) Install push rods with hardened end upward in original location (if removed). Install rocker arm assembly in original location, ensuring push rods are seated in rocker arms. Install rocker arm shaft bolts. Alternately tighten shaft bolts to 40 ft. lbs. (54 N.m). To complete installation, reverse removal procedure.

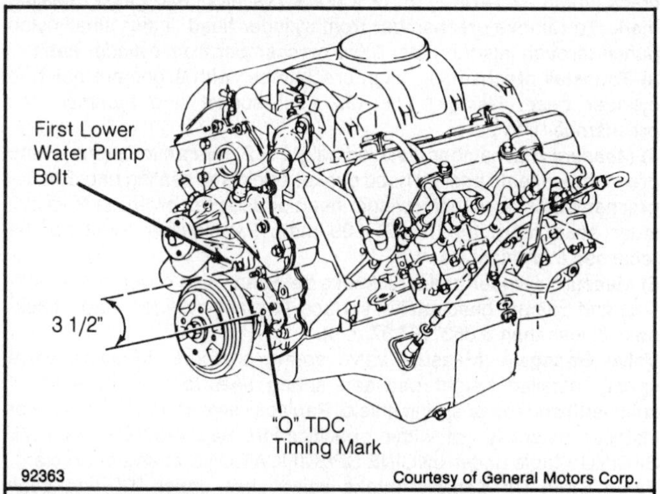
First Lower
Water Pump
Bolt
3 1/2"
"O" TDC
Timing Mark
92363
Courtesy of General Motors Corp.

Fig. 8: Positioning Crankshaft Before Installing Rocker Arm Assembly

HYDRAULIC VALVE LIFTERS

Removal - 1) Remove intake manifold. See INTAKE MANIFOLD under REMOVAL & INSTALLATION. Remove rocker arm assembly. See ROCKER ARM ASSEMBLY under REMOVAL & INSTALLATION. On "G" Series, remove cylinder head. Remove guide plate clamps, guide plates and lifters.

2) On all except "G" Series, remove guide plate clamps and guide plates through access holes in cylinder head using mechanical fingers. Remove lifters using Lifter Remover (J-29834) and magnet. Mark lifter location.

NOTE: Some engines are equipped with standard size and .010" (.25 mm) oversize diameter lifters. Bores fitted with oversize lifters are identified by O.S. stamped on cylinder block pad adjacent to lifter bore and on top rail of cylinder case above lifter bore. Oversize lifters are identified by 10 stamped on side of lifter.

Inspection - 1) Check for nicks, burrs or scoring on parts. Ensure lifter roller operates smoothly without excessive play and contains no flat spots.

2) Measure lifter oil clearance. If oil clearance is not within specification, replace lifter with .010" (mm) oversize lifter if resulting oil clearance is within specification. See VALVE LIFTERS table under ENGINE SPECIFICATIONS at end of article.

CAUTION: Prime new lifters in kerosene or diesel fuel before installation to prevent damage to lifter when engine is started. After installing guide plate clamps, rotate crankshaft by hand 2 complete turns to ensure free movement of lifters in guide plates.

Installation - 1) Submerge new lifters in clean kerosene or diesel fuel and operate plunger several times. Coat lifter roller and bearings with Assembly Lubricant (1052365). Install lifter into original bore. Install guide plate and guide plate clamp. Tighten clamp bolts to 18 ft. lbs. (24 N.m).

2) After all clamps are installed, rotate crankshaft by hand 2 complete turns to ensure free movement of lifters in guide plates. If crankshaft will not rotate, lifter(s) may be binding in guide plate.

3) Install rocker arm assemblies in proper sequence to prevent piston and valve damage. See installation procedure under ROCKER ARM ASSEMBLY. To complete installation, reverse removal procedure.

CAMSHAFT

Removal (Except "G" Series) - 1) Disconnect batteries. Drain cooling system. Remove alternator, grille, A/C compressor, condenser, radiator and power steering pump as necessary. Remove vacuum pump, engine speed sensor or oil pump drive unit from top of engine.

2) Remove hydraulic valve lifters. See HYDRAULIC VALVE LIFTERS under REMOVAL & INSTALLATION. Remove timing chain and sprockets. See TIMING CHAIN & SPROCKETS under REMOVAL & INSTALLATION.

3) Remove front engine mount through-bolts. Raise and support engine to ease camshaft removal. Remove camshaft thrust plate and spacer. Remove camshaft.

Removal ("G" Series) - 1) Disconnect batteries. Drain cooling system. Remove grille, bumper, lower valance, coolant bottle and upper tie bar. Remove engine cover. Remove A/C compressor, condenser, radiator, shroud and fan. Remove vacuum pump, oil pump drive or engine speed sensor. Remove cylinder heads. See CYLINDER HEAD under REMOVAL & INSTALLATION.

2) Remove timing chain and sprockets. See TIMING CHAIN & SPROCKETS under REMOVAL & INSTALLATION. Remove valve lifters. See VALVE LIFTERS under REMOVAL & INSTALLATION. Remove camshaft thrust plate and spacer (if equipped). Remove camshaft.

Inspection - Inspect camshaft lobes for signs of flaking or flat spots. Measure camshaft journal diameter. Determine oil clearance. Replace camshaft and/or bearings as necessary if not within specification. See CAMSHAFT table under ENGINE SPECIFICATIONS at end of article.

NOTE: Replace hydraulic lifters if installing new camshaft.

Installation - 1) If replacing camshaft bearings, see CAMSHAFT BEARINGS under REMOVAL & INSTALLATION. Coat camshaft journals with engine oil and lobes with High Viscosity Oil/Zinc (12345501). Install camshaft. Install thrust spacer with inside chamfer toward camshaft. Install thrust plate.

2) Ensure camshaft end play is .002-.012" (.05-.31 mm). Install camshaft sprocket and timing chain, ensuring timing marks are aligned. *See Fig. 5*. To complete installation, reverse removal procedure.

CAMSHAFT BEARINGS

Removal - Remove rear camshaft plug. Remove inner camshaft bearings using Bearing Remover/Installer (J-6098-01) and Adapter (J-6098-10). Rear inner bearing must be removed with pilot fitted in rear camshaft bearing. Remove front and rear camshaft bearings.

CAUTION: Camshaft bearing bores are different sizes. Install bearings with bearing seam in upper half of bore (cylinder block). Install front bearing with notch on bearing facing front of cylinder block. Front bearing contains 2 oil holes. Ensure oil holes in all bearings align with oil holes in block.

1991 ENGINES
6.2L V8 Diesel (Cont.)

Installation – Install rear camshaft bearings, then front camshaft bearings to act as guides for remover/installer pilot. Install inner camshaft bearings. Coat new rear camshaft bore plug with Loctite Sealer (592). Install plug from even with block surface to 1/32" (.8 mm) below surface.

REAR CRANKSHAFT OIL SEAL

Removal & Installation – **1)** Remove oil pan and oil pump. See OIL PAN under REMOVAL & INSTALLATION. Remove rear main bearing cap. Remove lower half of seal from cap. Tap end of upper half of seal with a small drift punch to remove seal from block. Clean block surface and seal grooves.

2) Lubricate new crankshaft seal lips with engine oil. Carefully insert end of one half of new seal into block seal groove. Push this piece into the groove until one end of seal extends 1/2" (13 mm) from block.

3) Insert other half of seal into block seal groove. The contact ends of the seal halves will be at 4 and 10 o'clock, or 8 and 2 o'clock positions. This provides proper alignment of main cap with seal lips. Lightly coat seal groove of main bearing cap with Loctite (414).

4) Apply a thin film of anaerobic sealant to bearing cap in specified areas. *See Fig. 9*. Lightly oil the cap bolt threads. Tap main bearing cap into place with brass or leather mallet. Install cap bolts and tighten to specification. See TORQUE SPECIFICATIONS table at end of article. To install remaining components, reverse removal procedure.

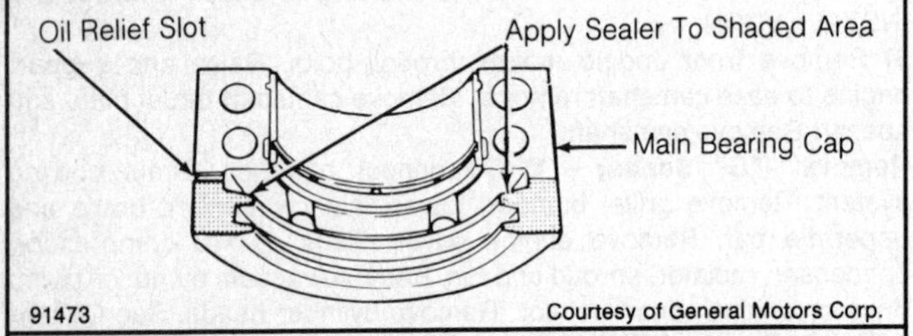
Oil Relief Slot
Apply Sealer To Shaded Area
Main Bearing Cap
91473
Courtesy of General Motors Corp.

Fig. 9: Applying Anaerobic Sealant to Rear Main Bearing Cap

WATER PUMP

Removal – **1)** Disconnect batteries. Drain coolant. Remove accessory drive belts, fan, fan shroud and pulley. Remove alternator, power steering pump and related brackets as necessary.

2) Disconnect coolant by-pass hose and lower radiator hose from water pump. Remove water pump bolts. Remove water pump and water pump plate as an assembly. Remove water pump plate-to-water pump bolt. Separate water pump from plate.

Installation – **1)** Apply anaerobic sealant to sealing surface of plate and water pump. Install plate to pump with new gasket. Coat water pump bolt threads with Sealant (1052080).

2) Install pump and plate assembly to front cover with new gasket. Tighten bolts to specification. See TORQUE SPECIFICATIONS table at end of article. To complete installation, reverse removal procedure.

OIL PAN

Removal ("C" & "K" Series) – Disconnect batteries. Raise and support vehicle. Drain crankcase. Remove flywheel cover. Disconnect exhaust pipes from manifolds. Remove front engine mount through-bolts. Raise and support engine. Remove oil pan bolts, oil pan and oil pan rear seal.

Removal ("G" Series) – **1)** Disconnect batteries. Remove engine cover. Remove engine oil dipstick and tube from valve cover. Raise and support vehicle. Remove flywheel cover. Drain crankcase. Disconnect engine oil cooler lines from cylinder block.

2) Remove starter. Remove battery cables, automatic transmission fluid lines and clamps from oil pan. Remove oil pan bolts. Lower oil pan from engine (DO NOT attempt to remove oil pan).

3) Rotate crankshaft until forward crankshaft throw for connecting rods No. 1 and 2 are up. Remove oil pump bolt. Allow oil pump and extension shaft to fall into oil pan. Remove oil pan and oil pump. Remove oil pan rear seal.

Removal ("P" Series & "R" & "V" Series) – **1)** Disconnect batteries. Raise and support vehicle. Drain crankcase. Remove oil filter. Remove flywheel cover. Remove left front engine mount through-bolt. Raise and support engine. Remove strut rods.

2) Remove battery cables, automatic transmission fluid cooler lines and clamps from oil pan. Move cylinder block heater wire aside (if equipped). Raise and support engine. Remove oil pan bolts, oil pan and oil pan rear seal.

Installation (All Models) – **1)** Submerge new lifters in clean kerosene or diesel fuel and operate plunger several times. Coat lifter roller and bearings with Assembly Lubricant (1052365). Install lifter into original bore. Install guide plate and guide plate clamp. Tighten clamp bolts to 18 ft. lbs. (24 N.m).

OVERHAUL

CYLINDER HEAD

Cylinder Head – **1)** Replace cylinder head if surface warpage exceeds .006" (.15 mm) across its length or .003" (.08 mm) across its width. DO NOT machine cylinder head surface.

2) Inspect prechamber for facial cracks. Replace prechamber if facial crack length exceeds 3/16" or if crack reaches head gasket sealing mark. To remove prechamber from cylinder head, insert small nylon punch through injector hole. Drive prechamber from cylinder head.

3) To install prechamber, align prechamber with alignment notch in cylinder head. Using 1 1/4" (32 mm) socket and hammer, tap prechamber into bore.

4) Measure prechamber installed height in 2 or more locations where prechamber seats against head gasket shield and sealing ring. Ensure prechamber is even with cylinder head or does not protrude from cylinder head more than .002" (.05 mm). Prechamber must not be recessed in cylinder head.

5) Measure cylinder head thickness between valve cover gasket surface and cylinder head gasket surface. Replace cylinder head if thickness is less than 3.853" (97.87 mm).

Valve Springs – Measure valve spring pressure. Measure valve spring installed height between spring seat (or top of shim, if shimmed) and top of spring shield. Replace valve spring if pressure or installed height is not within specification. See VALVES & VALVE SPRINGS table under ENGINE SPECIFICATIONS at end of article.

Valve Stem Oil Seals – Intake valve uses upper "O" ring seal. Exhaust valve uses upper "O" ring seal and lower umbrella seal, seated against cylinder head.

Valve Guides – **1)** Valve guides are part of cylinder head (not replaceable). Measure valve stem-to-guide oil clearance. See CYLINDER HEAD table under ENGINE SPECIFICATIONS at end of article.

2) If not within specification, ream valve guides using Reamer Set (J-7049) and install oversize valves. Oversize valves are available in .003" (.08 mm) and .015" (.38 mm) oversize.

Valve Seat – No replacement procedure is available from manufacturer. Valve seats are induction hardened. Excessive removal of material may damage valve seat. Measure seat width and runout. See CYLINDER HEAD table under ENGINE SPECIFICATIONS at end of article.

Valves – Valves with .003" (.08 mm) and .015" (.38 mm) oversize stems are available for worn valve guides.

VALVE TRAIN

CAUTION: Note paint stripe on hardened end of push rod (end closest to rocker arm). If no paint stripe is present, mark hardened end of push rod for reassembly reference.

Rocker Arm Assembly – **1)** To disassemble rocker arm assembly, insert screwdriver into rocker arm shaft bore. Break off end of retainer. Pull out retainer with pliers. Mark rocker arms for reassembly to original location on shaft. Remove rocker arms from shaft.

2) Inspect rocker arms and rocker arm shaft at mating surface for damage. Inspect push rods for bend and wear. Ensure oil passages are clear.

3) To assemble rocker arm assembly, coat rocker arms with engine oil and install on shaft in original locations. Center rocker arms with their corresponding holes on shaft. Install retainers with a 1/2" (13 mm) minimum diameter drift punch.

Hydraulic Valve Lifters – Engine is equipped with roller type hydraulic valve lifters. Lifters are serviced as complete assemblies only. Parts are not interchangeable between lifters.

CYLINDER BLOCK ASSEMBLY

Piston & Rod Assembly – **1)** Mark piston and rod assembly for installation to original bore. Mark rod and cap in relation to piston. Assemble rod to piston with rod bearing tang on same side of piston as piston crown indent.

2) Properly position ring end gaps around circumference of piston. *See Fig. 10.* Install piston and rod assembly in bore with piston crown indent toward outside of engine.

NOTE: Engine is equipped with either Bohn or Zollner pistons, identified by B or Z stamped inside piston skirt. Piston clearance requirements differ between piston manufacturer.

Fitting Pistons – **1)** Measure cylinder bore diameter 2 1/2" (63.5 mm) below cylinder block deck surface. Measure piston diameter at 90 degree angle to piston pin, on pin centerline. Determine piston clearance.

2) If clearance is not within specification, replace piston and/or machine cylinder bore. See CYLINDER BLOCK table and PISTON, PINS & RINGS table under ENGINE SPECIFICATIONS at end of article.

Piston Rings – Measure piston ring end gap and side clearance. If not within specification, replace piston and/or rings as necessary. See PISTONS, PINS & RINGS table under ENGINE SPECIFICATIONS at end of article. Install rings with mark on ring facing upward. Position ring end gaps around circumference of piston as specified. *See Fig. 10.*

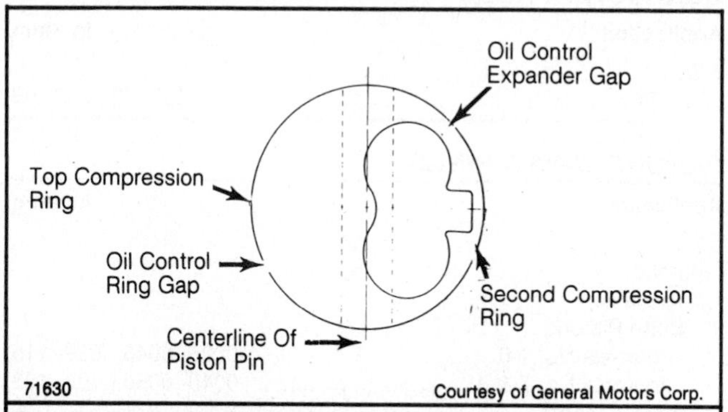

Oil Control
Expander Gap
Top Compression
Ring
Oil Control
Ring Gap
Second Compression
Ring
Centerline Of
Piston Pin
71630
Courtesy of General Motors Corp.

Fig. 10: Positioning Piston Ring End Gaps

CAUTION: Crankshaft is rolled fillet type. DO NOT machine crankshaft.

Rod Bearings – **1)** Mark rod caps in relation to rod for reassembly reference. Measure rod bearing journal out-of-round, taper and oil clearance. If not within specification, install new rod bearings. See CRANKSHAFT, MAIN & CONNECTING ROD BEARINGS table under ENGINE SPECIFICATIONS at end of article.

2) Undersize bearings may be used in combination with standard to produce correct clearance. If not within specification after installing new bearings, replace crankshaft. DO NOT machine crankshaft. Ensure rod side play is .007-.025" (.17-.63 mm).

NOTE: Some VIN C engines may contain both standard and .003" (.08 mm) oversize connecting rod bearings, identified by O.S. stamped on bearing cap lower end.

CAUTION: Crankshaft is rolled fillet type. DO NOT machine crankshaft.

Crankshaft & Main Bearings – **1)** Mark main bearing caps in relation to cylinder block. Measure crankshaft journal diameter, out-of-round and taper. Determine oil clearance.

2) If not within specification, replace main bearings. DO NOT machine crankshaft. See CRANKSHAFT, MAIN & CONNECTING ROD BEARINGS table under ENGINE SPECIFICATIONS at end of article.

3) For rear main bearing installation, see REAR CRANKSHAFT OIL SEAL under REMOVAL & INSTALLATION. Align thrust bearing surfaces and measure crankshaft end play. See THRUST BEARING.

Thrust Bearing – **1)** Main bearing No. 3 is thrust bearing. Tighten all other main bearing caps to specification. Tighten thrust bearing to 10 ft. lbs. (14 N.m). Tap crankshaft rearward, then forward.

2) Tighten thrust bearing cap to specification. Measure crankshaft end play at front face of thrust bearing. If crankshaft end play is not .004-.010" (.10-.25 mm), replace thrust bearing or crankshaft.

Cylinder Block – **1)** Measure cylinder block deck surface warpage. If warpage exceeds .006" (.15 mm) over its length or .003" (.08) across its width, replace cylinder block. DO NOT machine cylinder block deck surface.

2) Measure cylinder bore taper and out-of-round. If not within specification, machine cylinder bore and/or replace piston. See CYLINDER BLOCK table under ENGINE SPECIFICATIONS at end of article.

ENGINE OILING

ENGINE LUBRICATION SYSTEM

Pressurized lubrication is provided by gear-type oil pump. Camshaft drives oil pump through the shaft of a gear-driven vacuum pump and/or engine speed sensor, depending on engine application. Lubrication flows through external oil cooler then into full-flow oil filter. Non-adjustable oil pressure regulator valve is located in oil pump body. *See Fig. 11.*

Main oil gallery supplies oil through drilled passages to camshaft and crankshaft bearings. Oil flows through galleries to valve lifters then through hollow push rods to rocker arms.

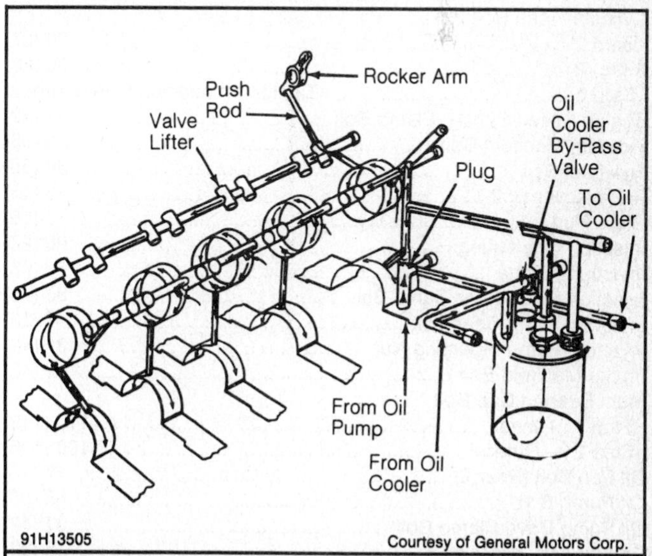

Rocker Arm
Push
Rod
Valve
Lifter
Oil
Cooler
By-Pass
Valve
Plug
To Oil
Cooler
From Oil
Pump
From Oil
Cooler
91H13505
Courtesy of General Motors Corp.

Fig. 11: Cross-Sectional View of Engine Oiling Circuit

NOTE: Manufacturer recommends changing oil filter at EVERY oil change.

Crankcase Capacity – Crankcase capacity is 7 qts. (6.6L) including oil filter change.

Oil Pressure – Normal oil pressure is 40-45 psi (2.81-3.16 kg/cm²) at 2000 RPM.

1991 ENGINES
6.2L V8 Diesel (Cont.)

OIL PUMP

Removal & Disassembly – 1) Remove oil pan, oil pump and extension shaft. See OIL PAN under REMOVAL & INSTALLATION. Remove pump cover screws and pump cover. Mark gears so they may be reassembled with same tooth indexed. Remove idler gear, drive gear and shaft from pump housing.

2) Remove pressure regulator valve retaining pin from pump cover. Remove regulator valve components from pump cover. Note order of removal. DO NOT disassemble pick-up screen and pipe. Screen and pipe are serviced only as an assembly with pump.

Inspection – 1) Inspect pump body and cover for cracks or excessive wear. Inspect pump gears for damage or wear. Check drive gear shaft for looseness in pump body.

2) Check pressure regulator valve for fit in bore. Inspect inlet tube and screen assembly for damage. Replace entire pump assembly if damaged.

Reassembly & Installation – 1) Install pump gears into pump body with marked gear teeth indexed. Reassemble remaining components in reverse order of disassembly. On "G" Series, place pump and extension shaft inside oil pan. Position oil pan in place.

2) On all models, install pump and extension shaft on engine, ensuring slot on top of extension shaft engages with drive tang on end of pump drive or vacuum pump. Tighten mounting bolt to 65 ft. lbs. (88 N.m). Install oil pan.

TORQUE SPECIFICATIONS

TORQUE SPECIFICATIONS

Application	Ft. Lbs. (N.m)
Bellhousing Bolt	30 (41)
Camshaft Gear Bolt	75 (102)
Camshaft Thrust Plate Bolt	17 (23)
Connecting Rod Nut	48 (65)
Coolant Crossover Pipe Bolt	31 (42)
Crankshaft Damper Bolt	200 (271)
Crankshaft Pulley Bolt	30 (41)
Cylinder Head Bolt [1]	
Step 1	20 (27)
Step 2	50 (68)
Step 3	Tighten an additional 90 degrees.
Engine Speed Sensor Clamp Bolt	31 (42)
Exhaust Manifold Bolt	26 (35)
Flywheel Bolt	65 (88)
Front Cover Bolt	33 (45)
Glow Plug	13 (18)
Injection Line Fitting	20 (27)
Injection Nozzle	50 (68)
Injection Pump Gear Baffle Bolt	33 (45)
Injection Pump Gear Bolt	17 (23)
Injection Pump Mounting Nut	31 (42)
Intake Manifold Bolt [2]	32 (43)
Main Bearing Cap Bolt	
Step 1 – Inner	110 (149)
Step 2 – Outer	100 (136)
Oil Pan Bolt (Rear 2)	17 (23)
Oil Pump Bolt	65 (88)
Oil Pump Drive Clamp Bolt	31 (42)
Rocker Arm Cover Bolt	16 (22)
Rocker Arm Shaft Bolt	40 (54)
Thermostat Housing-To-Coolant Crossover Pipe Bolt	31 (42)
Vacuum Pump Clamp Bolt	31 (42)
Valve Lifter Guide Plate Clamp Bolt	18 (24)
Water Pump Plate-To- Front Cover Bolt	17 (23)
Water Pump Plate-To-Pump Bolt	17 (23)
Water Pump-to-Cylinder Block Bolt	31 (42)
	INCH Lbs. (N.m)
Oil Pan Bolt (Except Rear 2)	84 (10)

[1] – Tighten in sequence. See Figure 2.
[2] – Tighten in sequence. See Figure 1.

ENGINE SPECIFICATIONS

GENERAL SPECIFICATIONS

Application	Specification
6.2L	
Displacement	378 Cu. In.
Bore	3.98 (101)
Stroke	3.82 (97)
Compression Ratio	21.3:1
Fuel System	Diesel
Horsepower @ RPM	140 @ 3600
Torque Ft. Lbs. @ RPM	270 @ 2000

CRANKSHAFT, MAIN & CONNECTING ROD BEARINGS

Application	In. (mm)
6.2L	
Crankshaft End Play	.004-.010 (.10-.25)
Main Bearings	
Journal Diameter	
Journals No. 1-4	2.9495-2.9504 (74.917-74.941)
Journal No. 5	2.9496-2.9502 (74.912-74.936)
Journal Out-Of-Round	.0002 (.005)
Journal Taper	.0002 (.005)
Oil Clearance	
Journals No. 1-4	.0018-.0033 (.045-.083)
Journal No. 5	.0022-.0037 (.055-.093)
Connecting Rod Bearings	
Journal Diameter	2.3981-2.3992 (60.913-60.939)
Journal Out-Of-Round	.0002 (.005)
Journal Taper	.0002 (.005)
Oil Clearance	.0018-.0039 (.045-.100)

CONNECTING RODS

Application	In. (mm)
6.2L	
Side Play	.007-.025 (.17-.63)

PISTONS, PINS & RINGS

Application	In. (mm)
6.2L	
Pistons	
Clearance	
Bohn Pistons	
Journals No. 1-6	.0035-.0045 (.089-.115)
Journals No. 7 & 8	.0040-.0050 (.102-.128)
Zollner Pistons	
Journals No. 1-6	.0044-.0054 (.112-.138)
Journals No. 7 & 8	.0049-.0059 (.125-.151)
Pins	
Diameter	1.2203-1.2206 (30.996-31.004)
Piston Fit	.0003-.0012 (.008-.031)
Rod Fit	.0003-.0012 (.008-.031)
Rings	
No. 1	
End Gap	.012-.022 (.30-.55)
Side Clearance	.0030-.0070 (.076-.178)
No. 2	
End Gap	.030-.040 (.75-1.00)
Side Clearance	.0015-.0031 (.039-.080)
No. 3 (Oil)	
End Gap	.010-.020 (.25-.51)
Side Clearance	.0016-.0038 (.040-.096)

1991 ENGINES
6.2L V8 Diesel (Cont.)

CYLINDER BLOCK

Application	In. (mm)
6.2L	
Maximum Deck Warpage [1]	
Across Block Length	.006" (.15 mm)
Across Block Width	.003" (.08 mm)
Cylinder Bore	
Diameter	3.9759-3.9789 (100.987-101.065)
Maximum Taper	.0008 (.020)
Maximum Out-Of-Round	.0008 (.020)

[1] – DO NOT resurface cylinder block deck.

VALVES & VALVE SPRINGS

Application	Specification
6.2L	
Intake Valves	
Face Angle	45°
Exhaust Valves	
Face Angle	45°
Valve Springs	
Installed Height	1.8 (46 mm)
Out-Of-Square	.062" (1.58 mm)
Pressure	
Valve Closed	79 Lbs. @ 1.81 In. (36 kg @ 46.0 mm)
Valve Open	231 Lbs. @ 1.39 In. (105 kg @ 35.3 mm)

CYLINDER HEAD

Application	Specification
6.2L	
Maximum Warpage [1]	
Across Head Length	.006" (.15 mm)
Across Head Width	.003" (.08 mm)
Valve Seats	
Intake Valve	
Seat Angle	46°
Seat Width	.035-.060" (.89-1.53 mm)
Maximum Seat Runout	.002" (.05 mm)
Exhaust Valve	
Seat Angle	46°
Seat Width	.062-.093" (1.57-2.36 mm)
Maximum Seat Runout	.002" (.05 mm)
Valve Guides	
Intake Valve	
Valve Guide Oil Clearance	.0010-.0027" (.026-.069 mm)
Exhaust Valve	
Valve Guide Oil Clearance	.0010-.0027" (.026-.069 mm)

[1] – DO NOT resurface cylinder head.

CAMSHAFT

Application	In. (mm)
6.2L	
End Play	.0020-.0120 (.051-.305)
Journal Diameter	
Journals No. 1-4	2.1642-2.1663 (54.970-55.025)
Journal No. 5	2.0067-2.0089 (50.970-51.025)
Lobe Lift	
Intake	[1] .2808 (7.133)
Exhaust	[1] .2808 (7.133)
Oil Clearance	.0010-.0046 (.025-.118)

[1] – Plus or minus .002" (.05 mm).

VALVE LIFTERS

Application	In. (mm)
6.2L	
Bore Diameter	
Standard	.923-.924 (23.45-23.47)
Oversize	.933-.934 (23.70-23.72)
Lifter Diameter	
Standard	.921-.922 (23.39-23.41)
Oversize	.931-.932 (23.64-23.66)
Oil Clearance [1]	.0016-.0031 (.040-.080)

[1] – Oversized lifter can be used to replace standard if resulting clearance is within specification.

1991 ENGINE COOLING
Specifications & Electric Cooling Fans

Astro, Blazer, Bravada, Jimmy, Lumina APV, Safari, Sierra, Silhouette, Sonoma, Trans Sport, "C" & "K" Series, "G" Series, "P" Series, "R" & "V" Series, "S" & "T" Series

SPECIFICATIONS

BELT ADJUSTMENT

For serpentine belt routing, *see Figs. 1-4*.

BELT ADJUSTMENT

Application	[1] Tension Lbs. (kg)
2.5L, 2.8L & 3.1L	[1]
4.3L, 5.0L & 5.7L	
New Belt	135 (61.2)
Old Belt	90 (40.8)
6.2L Diesel	
New Belt	146 (66.2)
Old Belt	67 (30.4)
7.4L	
New Belt	129.4-140.6 (58.7-63.8)
Old Belt	84.4-95.6 (38.3-43.4)

[1] – Serpentine belt tension is maintained automatically by a spring-tensioned idler pulley. No adjustment is necessary.

COOLING SYSTEM SPECIFICATIONS

COOLING SYSTEM SPECIFICATIONS

Application	Specification
Coolant Replacement Interval	30,000 Miles
Coolant Capacity [1]	
2.5L (VIN E)	11.5 (11.0)
2.8L (VIN R)	10.5 (10.0)
3.1L (VIN D)	[2] 13.0 (12.3)
4.3L (VIN Z)	
"C" & "K" Series	10.9 (10.3)
Except "C" & "K" Series	13.5 (12.8)
5.0L (VIN H)	17.0 (16.0)
5.7L (VIN K)	17.0 (16.0)
6.2L (VIN C & J)	25.0 (23.5)
7.4L (VIN N)	23.0 (22.0)
Pressure Cap	15 psi
Thermostat Opens	
Starts	188°F (87°C)
Fully Open	206° (97°C)

[1] – Specification is approximate and includes heater capacity.
[2] – Add extra 3 qts. (2.8L) coolant to vehicles with rear heater.

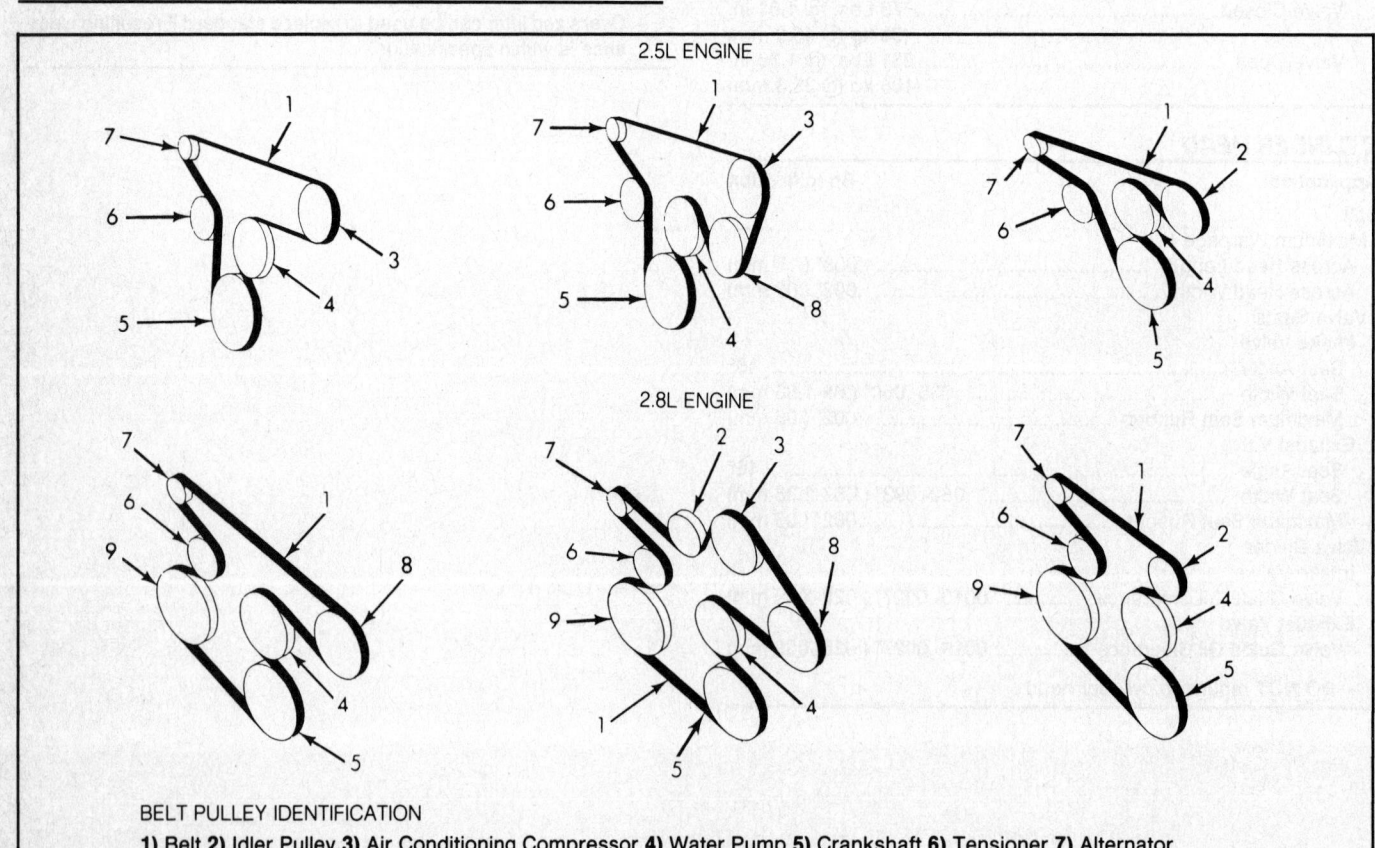

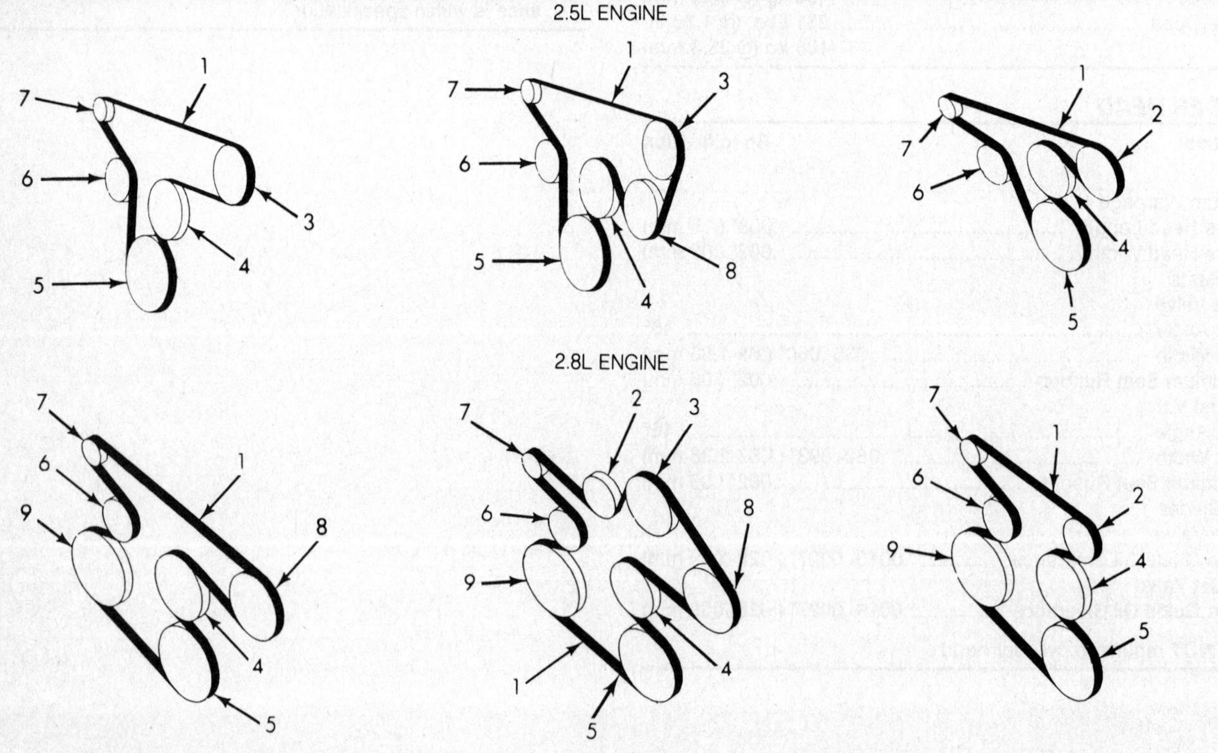
2.5L ENGINE
2.8L ENGINE

BELT PULLEY IDENTIFICATION

1) Belt **2)** Idler Pulley **3)** Air Conditioning Compressor **4)** Water Pump **5)** Crankshaft **6)** Tensioner **7)** Alternator **8)** Power Steering Pump **9)** AIR Pump

71684 71685

Courtesy of General Motors Corp.

Fig. 1: Serpentine Belt Routing (2.5L & 2.8L)

1991 ENGINE COOLING
Specifications & Electric Cooling Fans (Cont.)

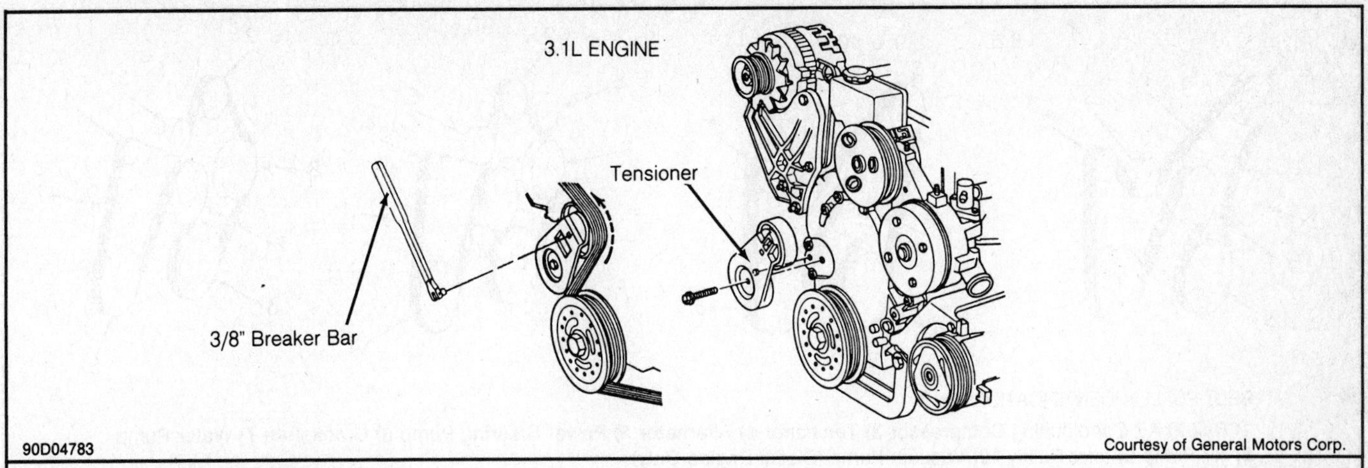
3.1L ENGINE
Tensioner
3/8" Breaker Bar
90D04783
Courtesy of General Motors Corp.

Fig. 2: Serpentine Belt Installation (3.1L)

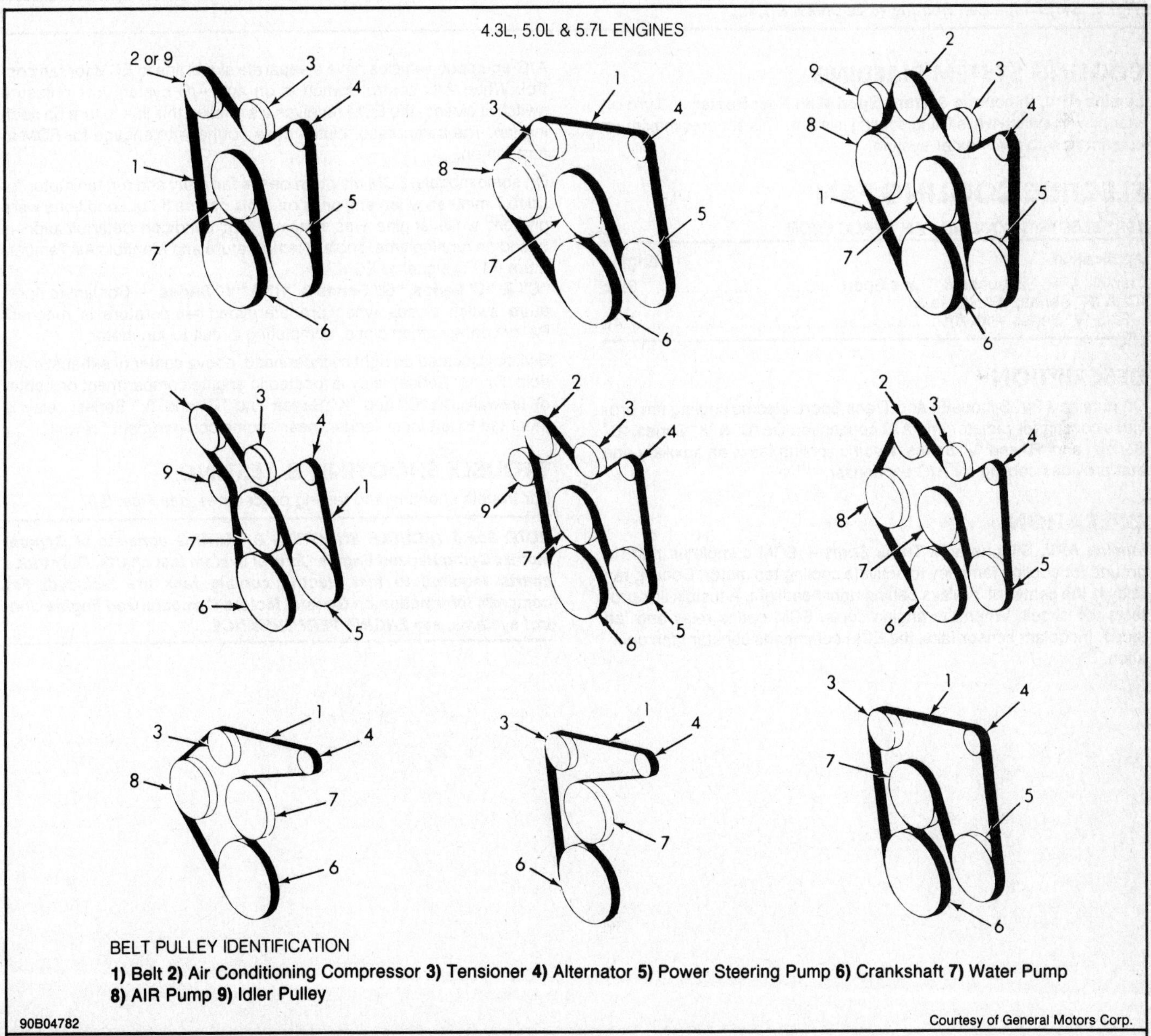
4.3L, 5.0L & 5.7L ENGINES
BELT PULLEY IDENTIFICATION
1) Belt 2) Air Conditioning Compressor 3) Tensioner 4) Alternator 5) Power Steering Pump 6) Crankshaft 7) Water Pump
8) AIR Pump 9) Idler Pulley
90B04782
Courtesy of General Motors Corp.

Fig. 3: Serpentine Drive Belt Routing (4.3L, 5.0L & 5.7L)

1991 ENGINE COOLING
Specifications & Electric Cooling Fans (Cont.)

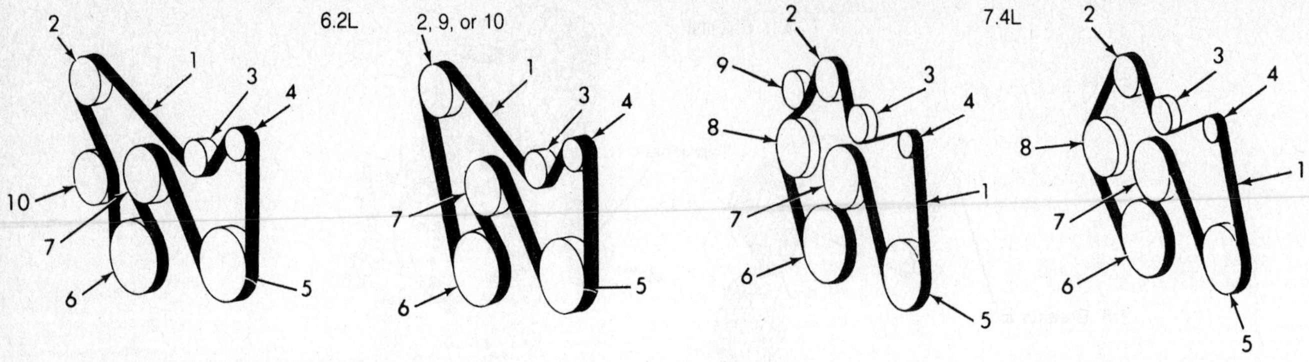
6.2L
7.4L
2
1
3
4
10
7
6
5
2, 9, or 10
9
8

BELT PULLEY IDENTIFICATION

1) Belt **2)** Air Conditioning Compressor **3)** Tensioner **4)** Alternator **5)** Power Steering Pump **6)** Crankshaft **7)** Water Pump **8)** Air Pump **9)** Idler Pulley **10)** Vacuum Pump (Diesel Engine Only)

121142 121185

Courtesy of General Motors Corp.

Fig. 4: Serpentine Belt Routing (6.2L Diesel & 7.4L)

COOLING SYSTEM BLEEDING

Lumina APV, Silhouette & Trans Sport With Rear Heater – Turn off rear blower switch while filling cooling system. This ensures maximum coolant flow to rear heater system.

ELECTRIC COOLING FAN

1991 ELECTRIC COOLING FAN APPLICATION

Application	Engine
Lumina APV, Silhouette & Trans Sport	3.1L
"C" & "K" Series, "G" Series & "R" & "V" Series With A/C	7.4L

DESCRIPTION

On Lumina APV, Silhouette and Trans Sport, electric cooling fan provides cooling for radiator and A/C condenser. On "C" & "K" Series, "G" Series , and "R" and "V" Series, electric cooling fan is an auxiliary unit that provides cooling for A/C condenser.

OPERATION

Lumina APV, Silhouette & Trans Sport – ECM completes path to ground for cooling fan relay to activate cooling fan motor. Cooling fan relay is the center of 3 relays behind right headlight. A fusible link protects the circuit. When the engine cools, ECM opens relay and fan stops. If coolant sensor fails, the ECM commands constant fan operation.

A/C-equipped vehicles have a separate signal line to ECM for fan control. When A/C control switch is on and A/C system low pressure switch is closed, the ECM receives a signal on this line to turn on cooling fan. The compressor clutch does not have to engage for ECM to turn fan on.

On some models, ECM may turn on the fan relay and run fan motor for up to 7 minutes when engine is off. This occurs if hot conditions were present while engine was running. Hot condition determination is based on running time, coolant temperature and Manifold Air Temperature (MAT) signal to ECM.

"C" & "K" Series, "G" Series & "R" & "V" Series – Coolant temperature switch closes when predetermined temperature is reached. Relay contacts then close, completing circuit to fan motor.

Switch is located on right cylinder head, above center of exhaust manifold. On "G" Series, relay is located in engine compartment on center of firewall. On "C" and "K" Series and "R" and "V" Series, relay is mounted to left inner fender, near engine compartment firewall.

TROUBLE SHOOTING & TESTING

For trouble shooting and testing procedures, *see Figs. 5-8*.

NOTE: Some TROUBLE SHOOTING & TESTING consists of General Motors Computerized Engine Control system test charts. Only those charts required to test electric cooling fans are included. For complete information on General Motors Computerized Engine Control systems, see ENGINE PERFORMANCE.

1991 ENGINE COOLING
Specifications & Electric Cooling Fans (Cont.)

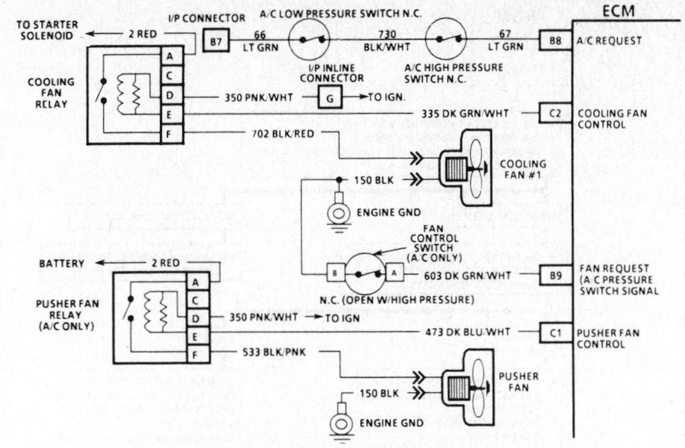
TO STARTER SOLENOID
2 RED
I/P CONNECTOR
A/C LOW PRESSURE SWITCH N.C.
B7
66 LT GRN
730 BLK/WHT
67 LT GRN
B8
A/C REQUEST
ECM
COOLING FAN RELAY
A
C
D
E
F
I/P INLINE CONNECTOR
A/C HIGH PRESSURE SWITCH N.C.
350 PNK/WHT
G
TO IGN.
335 DK GRN/WHT
C2
COOLING FAN CONTROL
702 BLK/RED
COOLING FAN #1
150 BLK
ENGINE GND
FAN CONTROL SWITCH (A/C ONLY)
BATTERY
2 RED
B
A
603 DK GRN/WHT
B9
FAN REQUEST (A/C PRESSURE SWITCH SIGNAL
PUSHER FAN RELAY (A/C ONLY)
N.C. (OPEN W/HIGH PRESSURE)
350 PNK/WHT
TO IGN
473 DK BLU/WHT
C1
PUSHER FAN CONTROL
533 BLK/PNK
PUSHER FAN
150 BLK
ENGINE GND

DIAGNOSTIC AIDS

If an overheating condition is suspected, verify if this is due to actual boilover. If gauge or light indicates an overheat condition, and no boilover is in evidence, inspect the gauge/light circuit for malfunction.

If vehicle is overheating and the gauge or light indicates the same, but cooling fan is not operating, and Scan tester indicates normal readings, coolant temperature sensor is out of calibration and should be replaced. If engine is overheating and cooling fan is on, check cooling system.

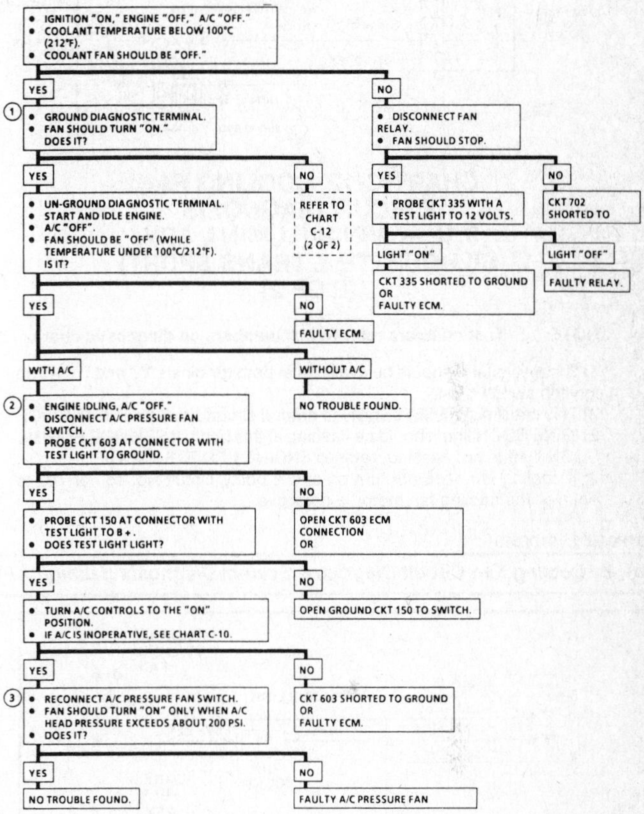
• IGNITION "ON," ENGINE "OFF," A/C "OFF."
• COOLANT TEMPERATURE BELOW 100°C (212°F).
• COOLANT FAN SHOULD BE "OFF."
YES
NO
1
• GROUND DIAGNOSTIC TERMINAL.
• FAN SHOULD TURN "ON."
DOES IT?
• DISCONNECT FAN RELAY.
• FAN SHOULD STOP.
YES
NO
YES
NO
• UN-GROUND DIAGNOSTIC TERMINAL.
• START AND IDLE ENGINE.
• A/C "OFF".
• FAN SHOULD BE "OFF" (WHILE TEMPERATURE UNDER 100°C/212°F).
IS IT?
REFER TO CHART C-12 (2 OF 2)
• PROBE CKT 335 WITH A TEST LIGHT TO 12 VOLTS.
CKT 702 SHORTED TO
LIGHT "ON"
LIGHT "OFF"
CKT 335 SHORTED TO GROUND OR FAULTY ECM.
FAULTY RELAY.
YES
NO
FAULTY ECM.
WITH A/C
WITHOUT A/C
2
• ENGINE IDLING, A/C "OFF."
• DISCONNECT A/C PRESSURE FAN SWITCH.
• PROBE CKT 603 AT CONNECTOR WITH TEST LIGHT TO GROUND.
NO TROUBLE FOUND.
YES
NO
• PROBE CKT 150 AT CONNECTOR WITH TEST LIGHT TO B+.
• DOES TEST LIGHT LIGHT?
OPEN CKT 603 ECM CONNECTION OR
YES
NO
• TURN A/C CONTROLS TO THE "ON" POSITION.
• IF A/C IS INOPERATIVE, SEE CHART C-10.
OPEN GROUND CKT 150 TO SWITCH.
YES
NO
3
• RECONNECT A/C PRESSURE FAN SWITCH.
• FAN SHOULD TURN "ON" ONLY WHEN A/C HEAD PRESSURE EXCEEDS ABOUT 200 PSI.
• DOES IT?
CKT 603 SHORTED TO GROUND OR FAULTY ECM.
YES
NO
NO TROUBLE FOUND.
FAULTY A/C PRESSURE FAN

CHART C-12, COOLING FAN CIRCUIT DIAGNOSIS
3.1L - VIN D (LUMINA APV, SILHOUETTE & TRANS SPORT) (1 OF 2)

The ECM controls cooling fan based on inputs from coolant temperature sensor (located in front of distributor on left side of engine), A/C fan control switch and vehicle speed. The ECM grounds the circuit to the cooling fan control relay. This energizes fan control relay for fan operation. Wiring circuit to fan control relay is grounded when coolant temperature exceeds 223°F (106°F) or when A/C is operating and A/C fan control switch opens with high A/C pressure of approximately 200 psi (14.1 kg/cm²).

NOTE: Test numbers refer to test numbers on diagnostic charts.

1) With ALDL diagnostic terminal grounded, cooling fan driver closes and energizes fan control relay.
2) If A/C fan control switch or circuit is open, cooling fan operates whenever A/C is operating.
3) With A/C clutch energized, A/C fan control switch should open when A/C high pressure exceeds 200 psi (14.1 kg/cm²). This signal indicates that ECM should energize fan control relay.

91H05548 91J05549

Courtesy of General Motors Corp.

Fig. 5: Cooling Fan Circuit Diagram & System Diagnosis (Lumina APV, Silhouette & Trans Sport) (1 of 2)

1991 ENGINE COOLING
Specifications & Electric Cooling Fans (Cont.)

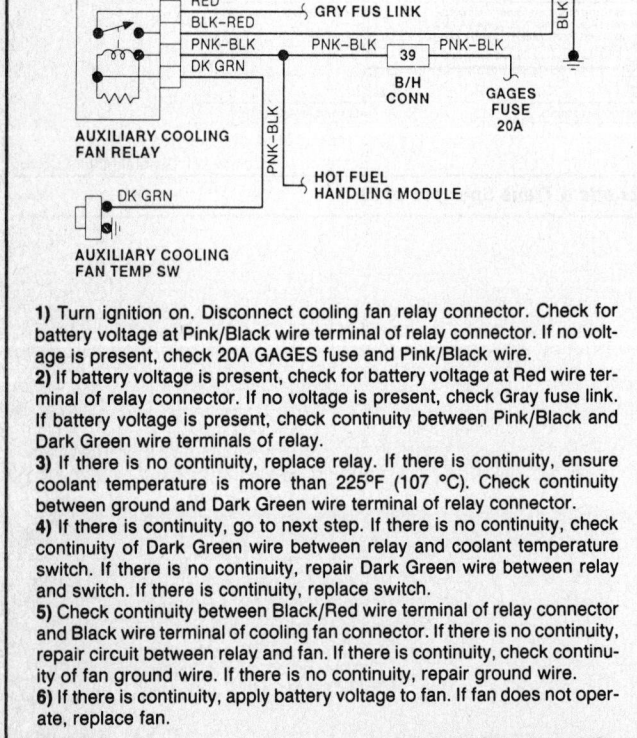

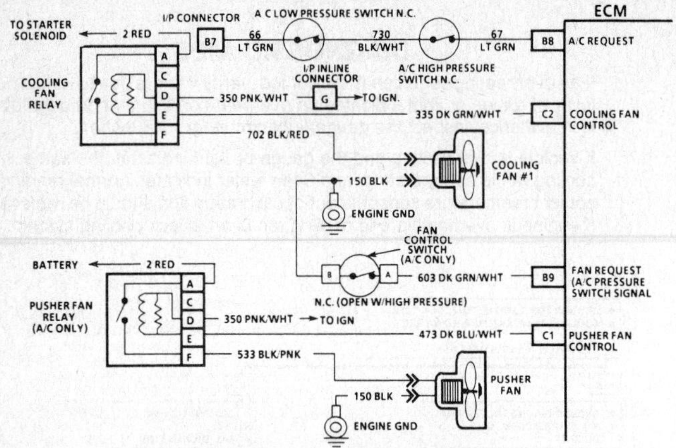
TO STARTER SOLENOID
2 RED
I/P CONNECTOR
B7
A C LOW PRESSURE SWITCH N.C.
66 LT GRN
730 BLK/WHT
67 LT GRN
ECM
B8
A/C REQUEST
I/P INLINE CONNECTOR
A/C HIGH PRESSURE SWITCH N.C.
COOLING FAN RELAY
350 PNK/WHT
G
TO IGN.
335 DK GRN/WHT
C2
COOLING FAN CONTROL
702 BLK/RED
COOLING FAN #1
150 BLK
ENGINE GND
FAN CONTROL SWITCH (A/C ONLY)
BATTERY
2 RED
603 DK GRN/WHT
B9
FAN REQUEST (A/C PRESSURE SWITCH SIGNAL
N.C. (OPEN W/HIGH PRESSURE)
PUSHER FAN RELAY (A/C ONLY)
350 PNK/WHT
TO IGN
473 DK BLU/WHT
C1
PUSHER FAN CONTROL
533 BLK/PNK
PUSHER FAN
150 BLK
ENGINE GND

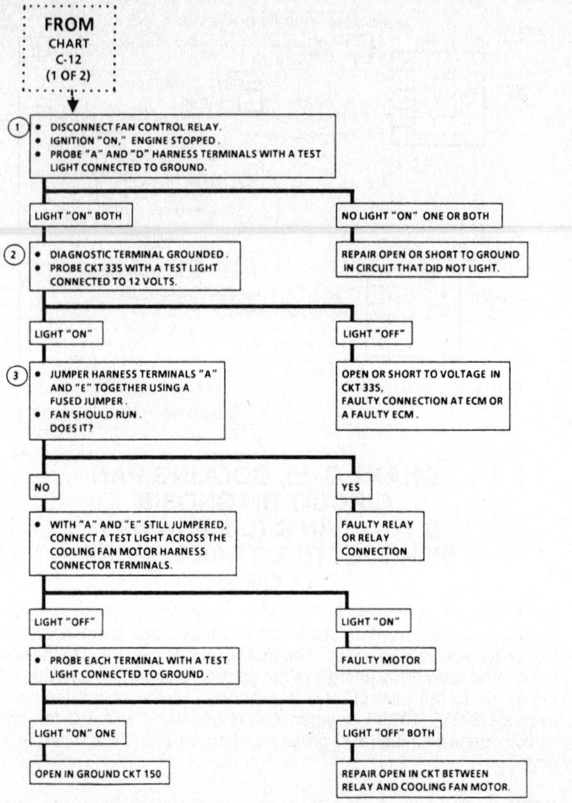
FROM CHART C-12 (1 OF 2)
1 • DISCONNECT FAN CONTROL RELAY.
• IGNITION "ON," ENGINE STOPPED.
• PROBE "A" AND "D" HARNESS TERMINALS WITH A TEST LIGHT CONNECTED TO GROUND.
LIGHT "ON" BOTH
NO LIGHT "ON" ONE OR BOTH
2 • DIAGNOSTIC TERMINAL GROUNDED.
• PROBE CKT 335 WITH A TEST LIGHT CONNECTED TO 12 VOLTS.
REPAIR OPEN OR SHORT TO GROUND IN CIRCUIT THAT DID NOT LIGHT.
LIGHT "ON"
LIGHT "OFF"
3 • JUMPER HARNESS TERMINALS "A" AND "E" TOGETHER USING A FUSED JUMPER.
• FAN SHOULD RUN.
DOES IT?
OPEN OR SHORT TO VOLTAGE IN CKT 335, FAULTY CONNECTION AT ECM OR A FAULTY ECM.
NO
YES
• WITH "A" AND "E" STILL JUMPERED, CONNECT A TEST LIGHT ACROSS THE COOLING FAN MOTOR HARNESS CONNECTOR TERMINALS.
FAULTY RELAY OR RELAY CONNECTION
LIGHT "OFF"
LIGHT "ON"
• PROBE EACH TERMINAL WITH A TEST LIGHT CONNECTED TO GROUND.
FAULTY MOTOR
LIGHT "ON" ONE
LIGHT "OFF" BOTH
OPEN IN GROUND CKT 150
REPAIR OPEN IN CKT BETWEEN RELAY AND COOLING FAN MOTOR.

CHART C-12, COOLING FAN CIRCUIT DIAGNOSIS 3.1L – VIN D (LUMINA APV, SILHOUETTE & TRANS SPORT) (2 OF 2)

NOTE: **Test numbers refer to test numbers on diagnostic charts.**

1) Battery voltage should be available at both terminals "A" and "D" when ignition switch is on.
2) This checks the ECM's ability to ground circuit No. 335. The SERVICE ENGINE SOON light should be flashing at this point. If SERVICE ENGINE SOON light is not flashing, refer to ENGINE PERFORMANCE.
3) If cooling fan does not turn on at this point, circuit No. 150 or 702 is open or the cooling fan motor is defective.

91B05550 91D05551

Courtesy of General Motors Corp.

Fig. 6: Cooling Fan Circuit Diagram & System Diagnosis (Lumina APV, Silhouette & Trans Sport) (2 of 2)

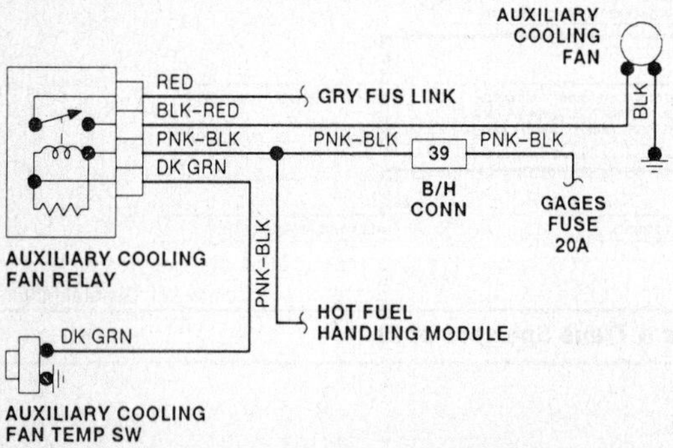
AUXILIARY COOLING FAN
RED
BLK-RED
PNK-BLK
DK GRN
GRY FUS LINK
PNK-BLK
39
PNK-BLK
BLK
B/H CONN
GAGES FUSE 20A
AUXILIARY COOLING FAN RELAY
PNK-BLK
HOT FUEL HANDLING MODULE
DK GRN
AUXILIARY COOLING FAN TEMP SW

1) Turn ignition on. Disconnect cooling fan relay connector. Check for battery voltage at Pink/Black wire terminal of relay connector. If no voltage is present, check 20A GAGES fuse and Pink/Black wire.
2) If battery voltage is present, check for battery voltage at Red wire terminal of relay connector. If no voltage is present, check Gray fuse link. If battery voltage is present, check continuity between Pink/Black and Dark Green wire terminals of relay.
3) If there is no continuity, replace relay. If there is continuity, ensure coolant temperature is more than 225°F (107 °C). Check continuity between ground and Dark Green wire terminal of relay connector.
4) If there is continuity, go to next step. If there is no continuity, check continuity of Dark Green wire between relay and coolant temperature switch. If there is no continuity, repair Dark Green wire between relay and switch. If there is continuity, replace switch.
5) Check continuity between Black/Red wire terminal of relay connector and Black wire terminal of cooling fan connector. If there is no continuity, repair circuit between relay and fan. If there is continuity, check continuity of fan ground wire. If there is no continuity, repair ground wire.
6) If there is continuity, apply battery voltage to fan. If fan does not operate, replace fan.

91B05395

Courtesy of General Motors Corp.

Fig. 7: Cooling Fan Circuit Diagram & System Diagnosis ("C" & "K" Series with 7.4L)

1991 ENGINE COOLING
Specifications & Electric Cooling Fans (Cont.)

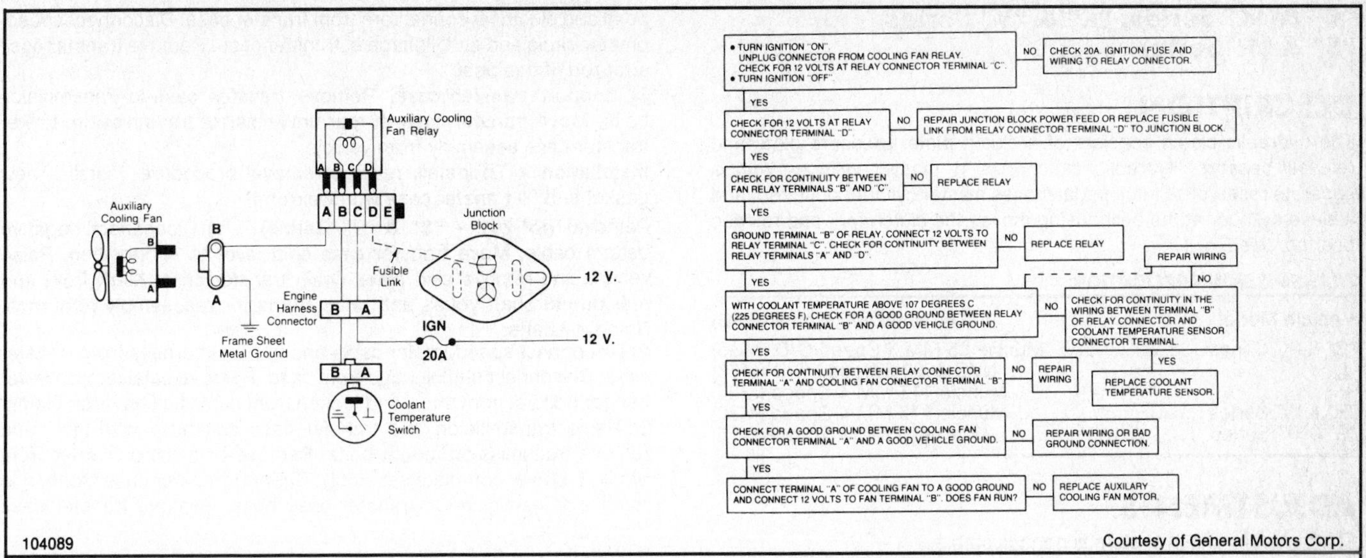
Auxiliary Cooling Fan Relay
Auxiliary Cooling Fan
Junction Block
Fusible Link
12 V.
Engine Harness Connector
Frame Sheet Metal Ground
IGN
20A
12 V.
Coolant Temperature Switch
• TURN IGNITION "ON".
UNPLUG CONNECTOR FROM COOLING FAN RELAY.
CHECK FOR 12 VOLTS AT RELAY CONNECTOR TERMINAL "C".
• TURN IGNITION "OFF".
NO
CHECK 20A. IGNITION FUSE AND WIRING TO RELAY CONNECTOR.
YES
CHECK FOR 12 VOLTS AT RELAY CONNECTOR TERMINAL "D".
NO
REPAIR JUNCTION BLOCK POWER FEED OR REPLACE FUSIBLE LINK FROM RELAY CONNECTOR TERMINAL "D" TO JUNCTION BLOCK.
YES
CHECK FOR CONTINUITY BETWEEN FAN RELAY TERMINALS "B" AND "C".
NO
REPLACE RELAY
YES
GROUND TERMINAL "B" OF RELAY. CONNECT 12 VOLTS TO RELAY TERMINAL "C". CHECK FOR CONTINUITY BETWEEN RELAY TERMINALS "A" AND "D".
NO
REPLACE RELAY
REPAIR WIRING
NO
YES
WITH COOLANT TEMPERATURE ABOVE 107 DEGREES C (225 DEGREES F), CHECK FOR A GOOD GROUND BETWEEN RELAY CONNECTOR TERMINAL "B" AND A GOOD VEHICLE GROUND.
NO
CHECK FOR CONTINUITY IN THE WIRING BETWEEN TERMINAL "B" OF RELAY CONNECTOR AND COOLANT TEMPERATURE SENSOR CONNECTOR TERMINAL.
YES
YES
CHECK FOR CONTINUITY BETWEEN RELAY CONNECTOR TERMINAL "A" AND COOLING FAN CONNECTOR TERMINAL "B".
NO
REPAIR WIRING
REPLACE COOLANT TEMPERATURE SENSOR.
YES
CHECK FOR A GOOD GROUND BETWEEN COOLING FAN CONNECTOR TERMINAL "A" AND A GOOD VEHICLE GROUND.
NO
REPAIR WIRING OR BAD GROUND CONNECTION.
YES
CONNECT TERMINAL "A" OF COOLING FAN TO A GOOD GROUND AND CONNECT 12 VOLTS TO FAN TERMINAL "B". DOES FAN RUN?
NO
REPLACE AUXILARY COOLING FAN MOTOR.
104089
Courtesy of General Motors Corp.

Fig. 8: Cooling Fan Circuit Diagram & System Diagnosis ("G" Series & "R" & "V" Series with 7.4L)

WIRING DIAGRAMS

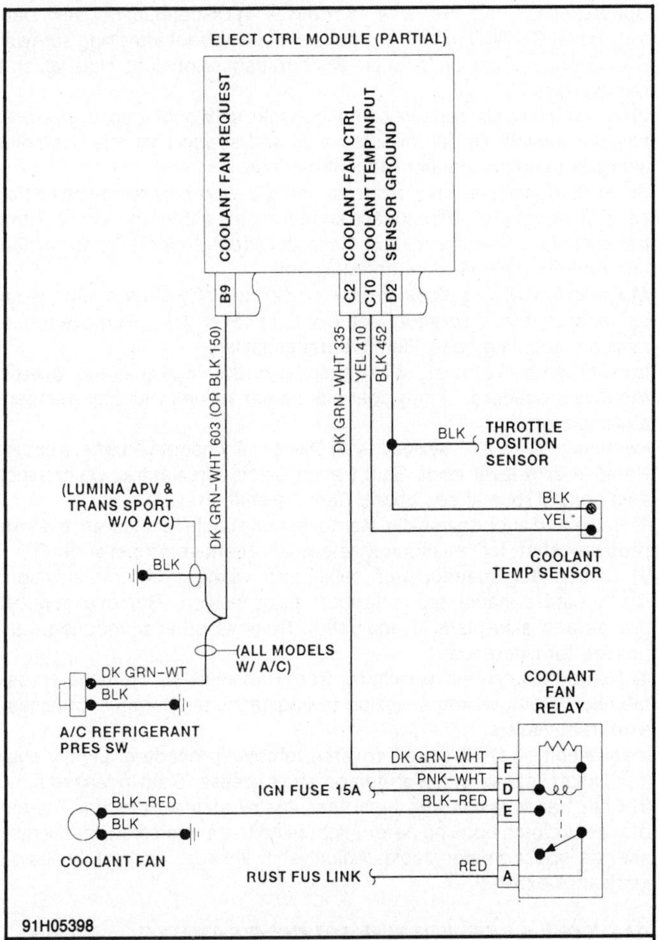
ELECT CTRL MODULE (PARTIAL)
COOLANT FAN REQUEST
COOLANT FAN CTRL
COOLANT TEMP INPUT
SENSOR GROUND
B9
C2
C10
D2
DK GRN–WHT 603 (OR BLK 150)
DK GRN–WHT 335
YEL 410
BLK 452
BLK
THROTTLE POSITION SENSOR
(LUMINA APV & TRANS SPORT W/O A/C)
BLK
YEL
COOLANT TEMP SENSOR
BLK
(ALL MODELS W/ A/C)
DK GRN–WT
BLK
A/C REFRIGERANT PRES SW
COOLANT FAN RELAY
DK GRN–WHT
PNK–WHT
IGN FUSE 15A
BLK–RED
BLK–RED
BLK
COOLANT FAN
RED
RUST FUS LINK
91H05398

Fig. 9: Cooling Fan Circuit Wiring Diagram (Lumina APV, Trans Sport & Silhouette)

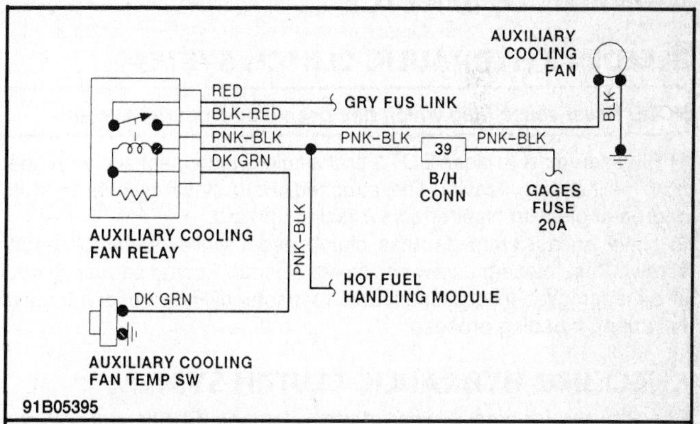
AUXILIARY COOLING FAN
RED
GRY FUS LINK
BLK–RED
BLK
PNK–BLK
PNK–BLK
39
PNK–BLK
DK GRN
B/H CONN
GAGES FUSE 20A
AUXILIARY COOLING FAN RELAY
PNK–BLK
HOT FUEL HANDLING MODULE
DK GRN
AUXILIARY COOLING FAN TEMP SW
91B05395

Fig. 10: Cooling Fan Circuit Wiring Diagram ("C" & "K" Series with 7.4L with A/C)

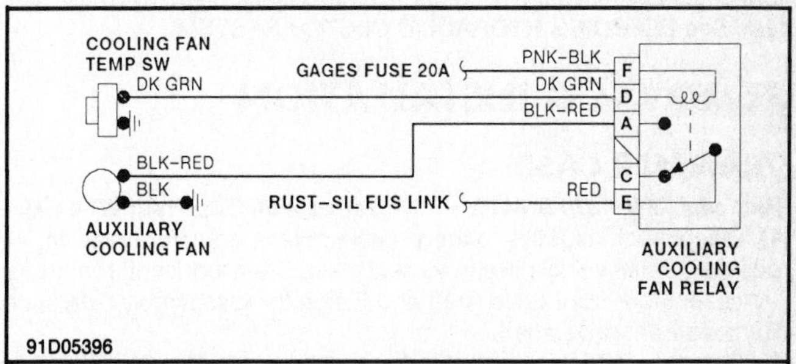
COOLING FAN TEMP SW
DK GRN
GAGES FUSE 20A
PNK–BLK
DK GRN
BLK–RED
BLK–RED
BLK
RUST–SIL FUS LINK
RED
AUXILIARY COOLING FAN
AUXILIARY COOLING FAN RELAY
91D05396

Fig. 11: Cooling Fan Circuit Wiring Diagram ("G" Series with 7.4L with A/C)

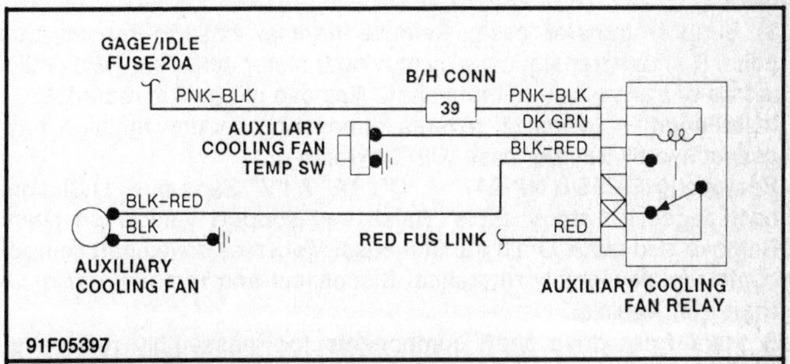
GAGE/IDLE FUSE 20A
B/H CONN
PNK–BLK
39
PNK–BLK
AUXILIARY COOLING FAN TEMP SW
DK GRN
BLK–RED
BLK–RED
BLK
RED FUS LINK
RED
AUXILIARY COOLING FAN
AUXILIARY COOLING FAN RELAY
91F05397

Fig. 12: Cooling Fan Circuit Wiring Diagram ("R" & "V" Series with 7.4L with A/C)

1991 CLUTCHES
Hydraulic

"C" & "K" Series, "R" & "V" Series, "S" & "T" Series

DESCRIPTION

The hydraulic clutch consists of a clutch plate, pressure plate and release bearing. Hydraulic clutch has a master cylinder with a separate reservoir. Clutch pedal moves master cylinder push rod, and a slave cylinder at the bellhousing moves the clutch fork and release bearing. *See Fig. 1.*

TRANSMISSION APPLICATION

Vehicle Model	Transmission Model (RPO)
"C" & "K" Series	Muncie 85 MM 5-Speed O/D (MG5)
	NVG 4500 5-Speed O/D (MT8)
	Muncie 117 MM 4-Speed (M20)
"R" & "V" Series	Muncie 117 MM 4-Speed (M20)
"S" & "T" Series	Warner 77 MM 5-Speed (T5)

ADJUSTMENTS

The hydraulic clutch system is nonadjustable.

IN-VEHICLE SERVICE

BLEEDING HYDRAULIC CLUTCH SYSTEM

NOTE: Never reuse fluid which has been bled from the system.

1) Fill reservoir with clean DOT 3 brake fluid. Disconnect slave cylinder from bellhousing, leaving line attached. Hold slave cylinder at a 45 degree angle with bleeder screw facing upward.
2) Have an assistant depress clutch pedal while opening bleeder screw. Close bleeder screw and release pedal. Repeat sequence until all air is removed from system. Ensure master cylinder reservoir stays full during bleeding process.

CHECKING HYDRAULIC CLUTCH SYSTEM

Check hoses for cracks, wear or other damage. Check hydraulic cylinders for loose mounting and signs of leakage. Clutch pedal travel should be at least 6" (152.5 mm). Secondary push rod travel at clutch fork should be at least .75" (19 mm). If necessary, bleed hydraulic system. See BLEEDING HYDRAULIC CLUTCH SYSTEM.

REMOVAL & INSTALLATION

TRANSFER CASE

Removal (BW-1370 & 4470 – "K" Series With Dual Rear Wheels) – 1) Disconnect negative battery cable. Place transfer case in 4H position. Raise vehicle. Remove skid plate. Drain lubricant from transfer case. Mark front drive shaft and flange for reassembly reference. Remove front drive shaft.
2) Remove left strut rod. Mark rear drive shaft and flange for reassembly reference. Remove rear drive shaft. Disconnect electrical connectors from transfer case. Disconnect shift linkage at transfer case.
3) Support transfer case. Remove transfer case-to-transmission bolts. Remove transfer case by moving transfer case rearward until it is free of transmission output shaft. Remove old gasket material.
Installation – To install, reverse removal procedure. Install a new gasket and fill transfer case with Dexron-II.
Removal (NP-205 & NP-241 – "C", "K" & "V" Series) – 1) Disconnect negative battery cable. Raise and support vehicle on hoist. Remove skid plate. Drain transfer case. Mark rear drive shaft components for reassembly reference. Disconnect and remove rear drive shaft from vehicle.
2) Mark front drive shaft components for reassembly reference. Disconnect and remove front drive shaft from vehicle. Disconnect vent hose and electrical connectors from transfer case. Disconnect speedometer cable and shift linkage at transfer case. Remove transfer case strut rod (if equipped).
3) Support transfer case. Remove transfer case-to-transmission bolts. Move transfer case to rear until clear of transmission. Lower transfer case assembly from vehicle.
Installation – To install, reverse removal procedure. Install a new gasket and fill transfer case with Dexron-II.
Removal (NP-231 – "S" & "T" Series) – 1) Disconnect negative battery cable. Move transfer case shift lever to 4H position. Raise vehicle and remove skid plate. Drain transfer case. Mark front and rear output shaft yokes and drive shafts for reassembly reference. Remove shafts.
2) Disconnect speedometer cable and vacuum harness from transfer case. Disconnect shift linkage from case. Remove catalytic converter hanger bolts at converter, and loosen front catalytic converter clamp.
3) Raise transmission and transfer case assembly with jack, and remove transmission mount bolts. Remove catalytic converter front bracket. Lower complete assembly. Support transfer case alone, and remove transmission-to-transfer case bolts. Remove transfer case from vehicle.
Installation – To install, reverse removal procedure. Install a new gasket and fill transfer case with Dexron-II.

TRANSMISSION

Removal ("C", "K", "R" & "V" Series) – 1) Disconnect negative battery cable. On 2WD models, remove shift lever boot attaching screws. Slide boot up the shift lever. Shift transmission into Neutral and remove lever.
2) On 4WD models, remove center console, shift boot, boot bridge and selector switch. On all models, raise and support vehicle. Remove skid plate and disconnect vacuum harness.
3) On all models, remove propeller shaft(s). Carefully remove transfer case (if equipped). Disconnect speedometer cable and wiring from transmission. Remove clutch slave cylinder. Support transmission and remove transmission mounting bolts.
4) Remove exhaust pipes, crossmember and any other components as necessary for clearance. Remove dust cover bolts. Remove transmission mounting bolts. Remove transmission.
Installation – To install, shift transmission into high gear and reverse removal procedure. Lightly coat input shaft splines with high-temperature grease.
Removal ("S" & "T" Series) – 1) Disconnect negative battery cable. Remove shift lever boot. Shift transmission into Neutral. Disconnect shift control rods (if equipped). Remove shift lever.
2) Raise and support vehicle. Remove brake cable for clearance. Mark propeller shaft for reassembly reference. Remove propeller shaft.
3) Disconnect speedometer cable and wiring from transmission. Disconnect exhaust pipe. Support transmission. Remove support braces and skid plate (if equipped). Remove other components as needed for clearance.
4) Remove clutch slave cylinder from transmission. Remove crossmember. Remove transmission-to-engine bolts. Remove transmission from vehicle.
Installation – 1) To install, reverse removal procedure. Lightly coat input shaft splines with high-temperature grease to aid in reassembly.
2) Shift transmission into high gear. Install support braces. Tighten braces to clutch housing before tightening to transmission. Install new seal on speedometer cable. Adjust shift linkage. Add transmission lubricant Dexron-II.

CLUTCH ASSEMBLY & PILOT BEARING

NOTE: DO NOT use compressor air to clean clutch parts. The clutch disc contains asbestos which is harmful if inhaled.

Removal – 1) Remove transmission. See TRANSMISSION under REMOVAL & INSTALLATION. Remove slave cylinder from bellhousing. *See Fig. 1.* Remove screws and flywheel cover. Remove bellhousing. Remove clutch fork and release bearing. Remove ball stud or clutch fork retainer if worn or damaged.

1991 CLUTCHES
Hydraulic (Cont.)

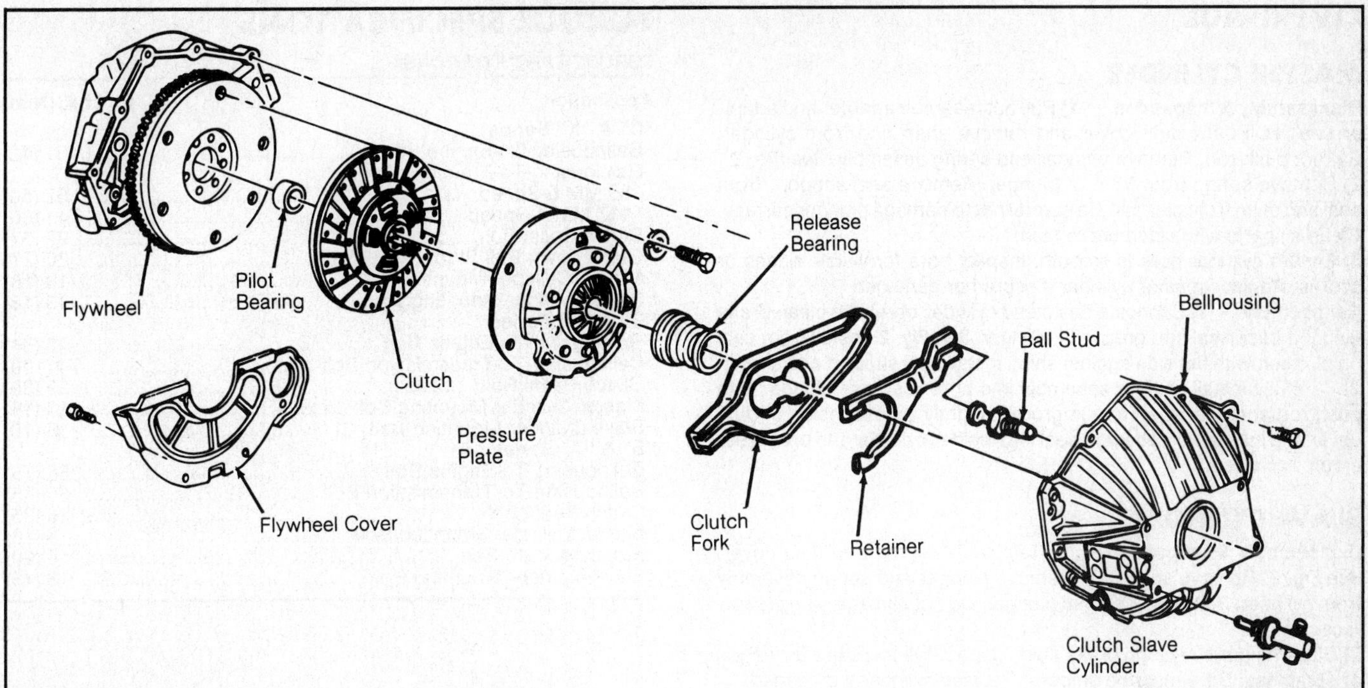
Release Bearing
Bellhousing
Ball Stud
Flywheel
Pilot Bearing
Clutch
Pressure Plate
Flywheel Cover
Clutch Fork
Retainer
Clutch Slave Cylinder

31613 Courtesy of General Motors Corp.

Fig. 1: Exploded View of Clutch Assembly & Pilot Bearing

2) Install clutch pilot in clutch disc during removal. Mark flywheel and pressure plate for reassembly reference. Evenly loosen pressure plate bolts 1-2 turns at a time until clutch plate spring tension is released. Remove clutch pilot, pressure plate and clutch disc.

Installation - 1) Support clutch disc and pressure plate on flywheel with clutch pilot. Ensure reference marks are aligned. Tighten bolts evenly to avoid distortion.

2) Remove pilot. Lubricate ball stud and fork fingers with high-temperature grease. Lubricate O.D. groove and pack grease into I.D. recess of release bearing.

3) If replacing clutch fork retainer, install retainer so fingers and tabs fit into release bearing groove, and retainer wraps around flat side of ball stud. *See Fig. 1.* Reverse removal procedure to complete installation.

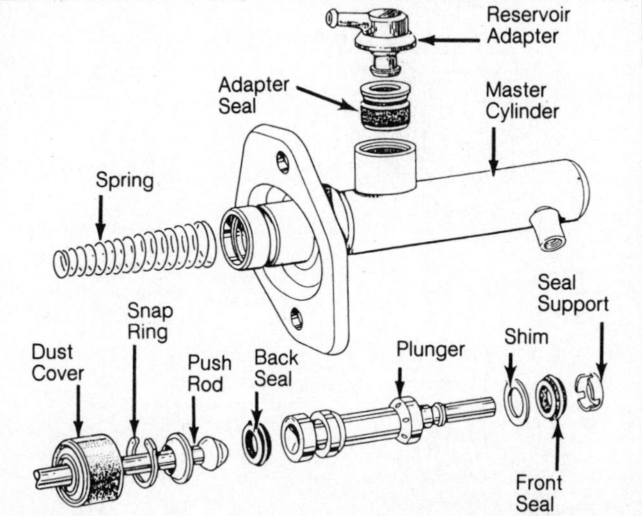
Reservoir Adapter
Adapter Seal
Master Cylinder
Spring
Seal Support
Snap Ring
Dust Cover
Push Rod
Back Seal
Plunger
Shim
Front Seal

29175 Courtesy of General Motors Crop.

Fig. 2: Exploded View of Clutch Master Cylinder

MASTER CYLINDER & RESERVOIR

Removal - 1) Disconnect negative battery cable. Remove steering column covers or panel. On "C", "K" and "S" Series, remove A/C duct from lower left side of instrument panel.

2) On all models, disconnect push rod from clutch pedal. Disconnect reservoir hose at master cylinder. Remove master cylinder retaining nuts. Remove master cylinder.

Installation - To install, reverse removal procedure. Bleed system. See BLEEDING HYDRAULIC CLUTCH SYSTEM under IN-VEHICLE SERVICE.

SLAVE CYLINDER

Removal & Installation - Disconnect negative battery cable. Raise and support vehicle. Disconnect and cap hydraulic line at slave cylinder. Remove slave cylinder. To install, reverse removal procedure. Bleed hydraulic system. See BLEEDING HYDRAULIC CLUTCH SYSTEM under IN-VEHICLE SERVICE.

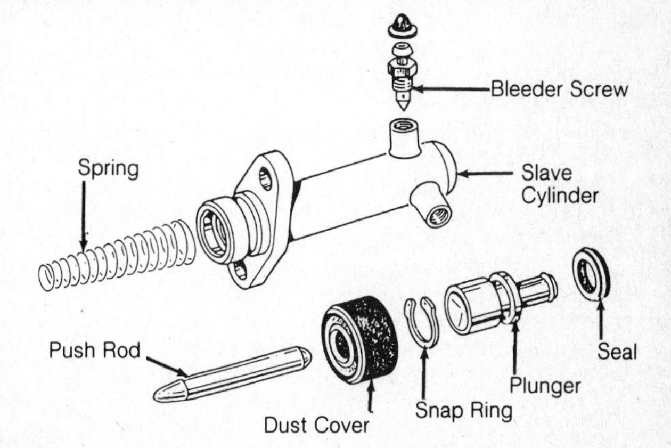
Bleeder Screw
Spring
Slave Cylinder
Push Rod
Seal
Plunger
Snap Ring
Dust Cover

29176 Courtesy of General Motors Corp.

Fig. 3: Exploded View of Clutch Slave Cylinder

1991 CLUTCHES
Hydraulic (Cont.)

OVERHAUL

MASTER CYLINDER

Disassembly & Inspection - **1)** Pull out reservoir adapter and adapter seal. Pull back dust cover and remove snap ring from cylinder. Extract push rod. Remove plunger and spring assembly. *See Fig. 2.*
2) Remove spring from front of plunger. Remove seal support, front seal and shim from plunger. Be careful not to damage plunger surface. Clean all parts with clean brake fluid.
3) Ensure cylinder bore is smooth. Inspect bore for visible ridges or scores. Replace master cylinder if scored or damaged.
Reassembly - **1)** Lubricate seals and cylinder bore with clean brake fluid. Fit back seal into groove in plunger. *See Fig. 2.* Install front seal on plunger, with flat side against shim. Install seal support and spring.
2) Carefully install plunger assembly into bore. Depress plunger with push rod and seat snap ring in groove. Lightly grease inside of dust cover and install. Put reservoir seal into master cylinder and press reservoir into place.

SLAVE CYLINDER

Disassembly & Inspection - **1)** Remove push rod and dust cover. *See Fig. 3.* Remove snap ring. Remove plunger and spring assembly from cylinder. Remove seal from plunger. Do not damage plunger surface.
2) Clean all parts in clean brake fluid. Inspect cylinder bore for ridges or scratches. Bore must be smooth. Replace cylinder if damaged.
Reassembly - Place seal in groove on plunger. *See Fig. 3.* Lubricate bore and seal with clean brake fluid. Slide spring and plunger assembly into cylinder bore. Depress plunger far enough to install snap ring in groove. Lightly grease inside of dust cover and install boot. Install push rod.

TORQUE SPECIFICATIONS

TORQUE SPECIFICATIONS

Application	Ft. Lbs. (N.m)
"C" & "K" Series	
Bellhousing-To-Engine Bolt	31 (42)
Bellhousing-To-Transmission Bolt	
85 MM 5-Speed	37 (50)
117 MM 4-Speed	74 (100)
Clutch Pedal Bolt	27 (37)
Cross Lever Ball Stud	20 (27)
Master Cylinder Mounting Bolt	13 (18)
Slave Cylinder Mounting Bolt	13 (18)
"R" & "V" Series	
Bellhousing-To-Engine Bolt	40 (54)
Bellhousing-To-Transmission Bolt	74 (100)
Clutch Pedal Bolt	29 (39)
Master Cylinder Mounting Bolt	13 (18)
Slave Cylinder Mounting Bolt	13 (18)
"S" & "T" Series	
Bellhousing-To-Engine Bolt	55 (75)
Bellhousing-To-Transmission Bolt	55 (75)
Clutch Pedal Bolt	26 (35)
Master Cylinder Mounting Bolt	13 (18)
Pressure Plate Bolt	15 (20)
Slave Cylinder Mounting Bolt	13 (18)

1991 CLUTCHES
Mechanical

"P" Series

DESCRIPTION

The mechanical clutch consists of a clutch disc, pressure plate and a release bearing. All "P" Series have an upper pull rod from clutch pedal to bellcrank, and a lower pull rod from bellcrank to cross lever. The cross lever moves the clutch fork and release bearing with an adjustable rod.

TRANSMISSION APPLICATION

Vehicle Model	Transmission Model (RPO)
"P" Series	NVG 4500 5-Speed O/D (MT8)

ADJUSTMENTS

CLUTCH PEDAL FREE PLAY

4-Wheel Disc Brakes - 1) Hold clutch pedal against bumper. Disconnect return spring at clutch fork. Loosen lock nut and swivel. Move clutch fork back until clutch spring pressure is felt.

2) Loosen nut "B". Turn nut "A" until it is 0.29" (7.4 mm) away from rod shoulder. *See Fig. 1.* Tighten nut "B" against clutch fork. Tighten swivel lock nut until all free play is removed. Install return spring and check pedal free play. Free play should be 1.50" (38.1 mm).

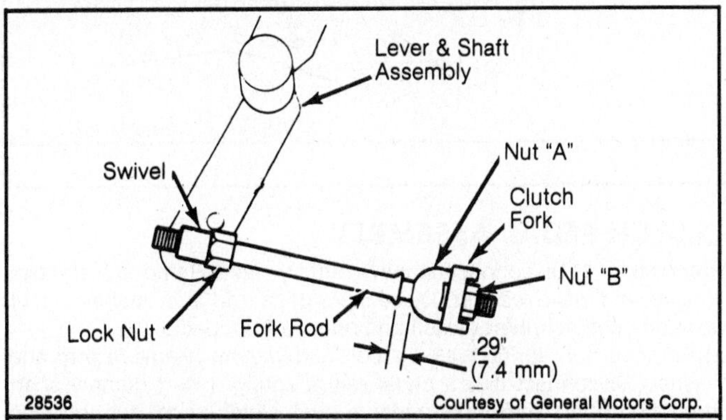
Lever & Shaft
Assembly
Nut "A"
Swivel
Clutch
Fork
Nut "B"
Lock Nut
Fork Rod
.29"
(7.4 mm)
28536
Courtesy of General Motors Corp.

Fig. 1: Adjusting Free Play (4-Wheel Disc Brakes)

Except 4-Wheel Disc Brakes - 1) Hold clutch pedal against bumper. Disconnect return spring at clutch fork. Loosen lock nut and swivel. Remove swivel from lever and shaft assembly. Move clutch fork back until clutch spring pressure is felt.

2) Adjust fork rod length until swivel can be easily inserted in gauge hole. *See Fig. 2.* Increase fork rod length until all free play is removed. Remove swivel from gauge hole and insert it in lower hole on lever and shaft assembly.

3) Secure swivel with wave washer and cotter pin. Tighten lock nut. Ensure fork rod length does not change. Install return spring and check pedal free play. Free play should be 1.38" (34.1 mm).

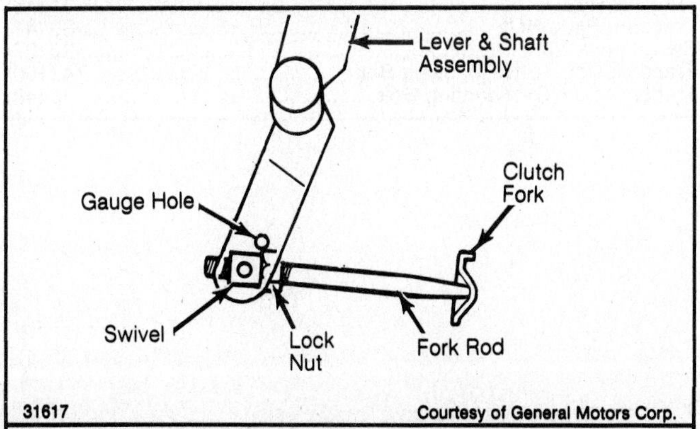
Lever & Shaft
Assembly
Clutch
Fork
Gauge Hole
Swivel
Lock
Nut
Fork Rod
31617
Courtesy of General Motors Corp.

Fig. 2: Adjusting Free Play (Except 4-Wheel Disc Brakes)

IN-VEHICLE SERVICE

CLUTCH RELEASE

Start engine and apply brakes. Depress and hold clutch pedal approximately 1/2" (13 mm) from floor mat. Shift back and forth between 1st and Reverse. If shifts are smooth, clutch is working properly. If shifts are not smooth, clutch is not releasing fully. Adjust clutch pedal free play. See CLUTCH PEDAL FREE PLAY under ADJUSTMENTS.

LINKAGE

Check linkage for bending or damage. Check for worn swivels, or loose or damaged mount brackets. Inspect clutch lever for bending, wear or damage. Ensure clearance exists between clutch and mount brackets, and between ball studs. If linkage is okay, lubricate clutch linkage.

REMOVAL & INSTALLATION

TRANSMISSION

Removal - 1) Raise and support vehicle. Drain transmission lubricant. Disconnect shift rods and/or shift lever. Disconnect parking brake lever and controls (if equipped). Mark propeller shaft for reassembly reference. Remove propeller shaft.

2) Disconnect speedometer cable and wiring from transmission. Disconnect exhaust pipe. Support transmission and remove crossmember. Remove other parts, if needed, for clearance.

3) Remove transmission mounting bolts. Move transmission rearward to free from engine. DO NOT allow transmission to hang from clutch. Remove transmission. Note condition and location of bellhousing plugs. Remove if damaged.

Installation - To install, reverse removal procedure. Lightly coat input shaft splines with high-temperature grease before installation. Install new seal on speedometer cable. Adjust shift linkage. Fill with Dexron-II automatic transmission fluid.

CLUTCH

Removal - 1) With transmission removed, disconnect rod and return spring at clutch fork. Remove bellhousing. Pry against release fork until it is released from ball pivot. Remove release bearing from clutch fork. Mark position of pressure plate on flywheel for reassembly reference.

2) Install clutch alignment tool to support clutch assembly during removal. Remove pressure plate bolts evenly, 1-2 turns at a time, to avoid warping pressure plate. Remove bolts until spring tension is released. Remove clutch alignment tool, pressure plate and clutch disc.

Installation - To install, reverse removal procedure. Lubricate clutch fork ball seat and recess in release bearing before installation. Ensure reference marks on pressure plate and flywheel are aligned.

CLUTCH LINKAGE & CROSS LEVER

Removal - 1) Disconnect negative battery cable. From inside cab, remove cotter pins, washers and wave washers. Disconnect pedal rod and bushing. Remove screws and floor pan dust boot. Disconnect lower pedal rod.

2) Disconnect pull-back spring. Remove cotter pins, washers and wave washers from adjusting rod. Note position of adjusting rod and remove rod. *See Fig. 3.*

3) Remove hardware holding cross lever bracket to frame. Remove bracket and remove cross lever. Remove ball stud, nut and star washer from bracket. Remove engine-side ball stud if worn or damaged. *See Fig. 4.*

Installation - To install, reverse removal procedure. Lubricate linkage. Adjust clutch pedal free play. See CLUTCH PEDAL FREE PLAY under ADJUSTMENTS.

1991 CLUTCHES
Mechanical (Cont.)

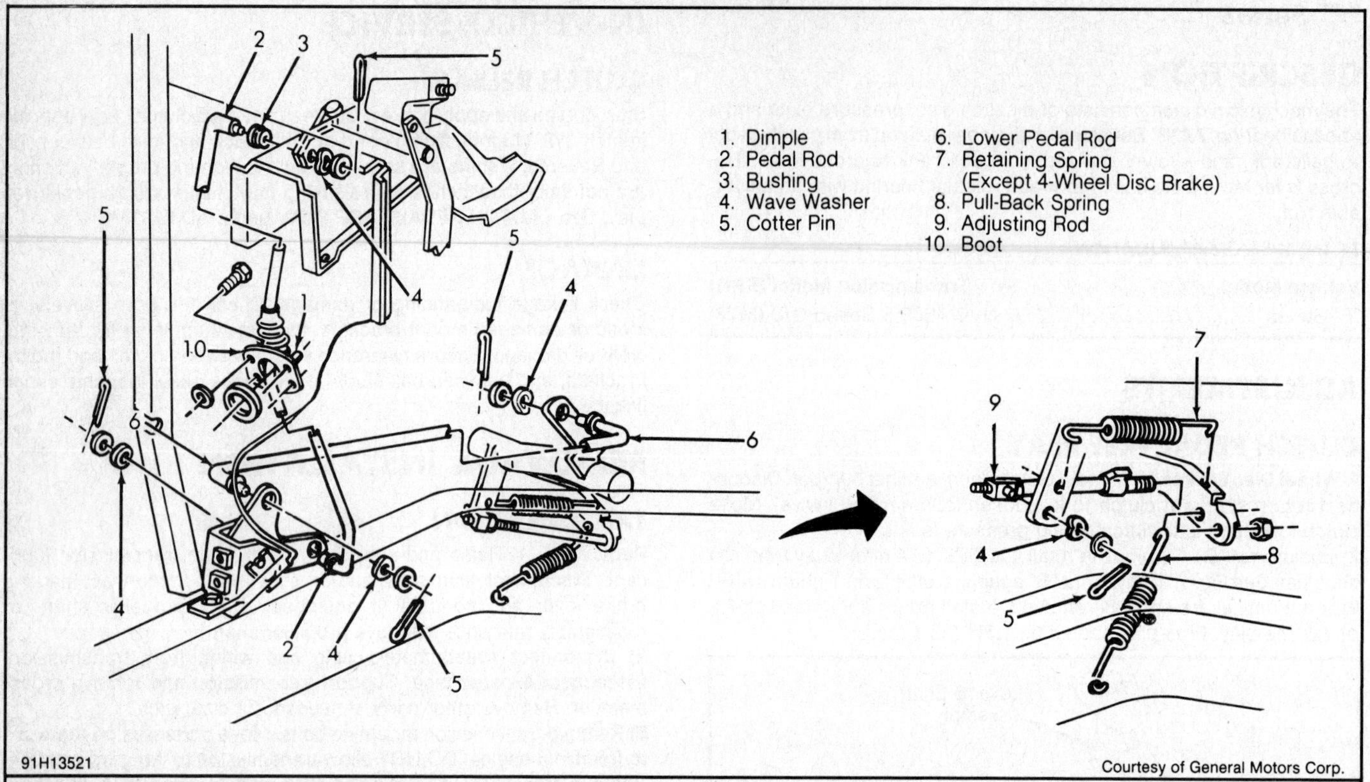
1. Dimple
2. Pedal Rod
3. Bushing
4. Wave Washer
5. Cotter Pin
6. Lower Pedal Rod
7. Retaining Spring
(Except 4-Wheel Disc Brake)
8. Pull-Back Spring
9. Adjusting Rod
10. Boot
91H13521
Courtesy of General Motors Corp.

Fig. 3: Exploded View of Clutch Linkage

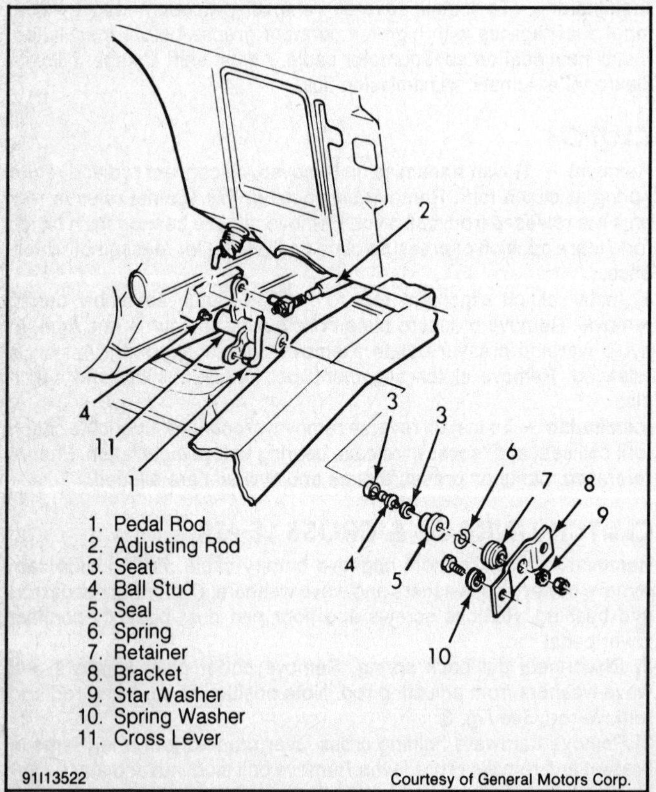
1. Pedal Rod
2. Adjusting Rod
3. Seat
4. Ball Stud
5. Seal
6. Spring
7. Retainer
8. Bracket
9. Star Washer
10. Spring Washer
11. Cross Lever
91I13522
Courtesy of General Motors Corp.

Fig. 4: Exploded View of Cross Lever

CLUTCH PEDAL ASSEMBLY

Removal – 1) Disconnect negative battery cable. Remove cotter pin, washer and wave washer. Disconnect pedal rod and bushing. Note position on clutch/start switch and remove from pedal.

2) Remove nut, spring washer, bolt and washer. Remove arm and washer. Disconnect clutch pedal return spring. Insert dummy shaft through support and brake pedal to push clutch pedal out and hold components in place. Remove bushings.

Installation – To install, reverse removal procedure. Lubricate bushings with petroleum jelly. If necessary, adjust clutch pedal free play. See CLUTCH PEDAL FREE PLAY under ADJUSTMENTS.

TORQUE SPECIFICATIONS

TORQUE SPECIFICATIONS

Application	Ft. Lbs. (N.m)
Bellhousing-To-Engine Bolt	40 (54)
Cross Lever Ball Stud	
Bracket Side	20 (27)
Engine Side	34 (46)
Pressure Plate Bolt	30 (41)
Swivel Lock Nut	20 (27)
Transmission-To-Bellhousing Bolt	74 (100)
Transmission-To-Mounting Bolt	35 (48)

1991 DRIVE AXLES
Axle Ratio Identification

Astro, Blazer, Bravada, Jimmy, Safari, Sierra, "C" & "K" Series, "G" Series, "P" Series, "R" & "V" Series

CORPORATE BUILT AXLES

Axle identification code for rear axles is stamped on forward surface of right axle tube, 3-5" outboard of carrier (6-8" on 20 and 30 series trucks). Location of identification code for front axles is not available from manufacturer.

DANA BUILT AXLES

Identification code is stamped on rear surface of right axle tube. In addition, the 3-digit axle code appears on tape strip attached to outboard end of axle tube.

ROCKWELL BUILT AXLES

Identification code is stamped on carrier assembly.

ASTRO & SAFARI REAR AXLE RATIO IDENTIFICATION

Application & Code	Ratio
7.625" Ring Gear	
SGF, SGS, SGG [1], SGT [1]	3.23:1
SGH, SGU, SGJ [1], SGW [1]	3.42:1
SGK, SGX, SGL [1], SGY [1]	3.73:1
SGM, SHL, SGN [1], SHM [1]	4.10:1

[1] – With positive traction, limited slip differential.

"C" SERIES REAR AXLE RATIO IDENTIFICATION

Application & Code	Ratio
8.5" Ring Gear	
PDB, PDL, PDU, PFA PDG [1], PDR [1], PDX [1], PFD [1]	3.08:1
PDC, PDM, PDW, PFB, PDH [1], PDS [1], PDU [1], PFF [1]	3.42:1
PDD, PDN, PDJ [1], PDT [1]	3.73:1
9.5" Ring Gear	
PGJ, PGY, PSM [1], PHC [1]	3.42:1
PGK, PGZ, PGH [1], PHD [1]	3.73:1
PGL, PHA, RNN, PGP [1], PHF [1]	4.10:1
PHB, PHG [1]	4.56:1
10.5" Ring Gear	
TFA, TFD [1]	3.42:1
RWY, RXF, RXM, SKG, TFB, RXB [1], RXT [1], RXR [1], TFF [1]	3.73:1
RWZ, RXG, RXN, SKH, TFC, RXC [1], RXK [1], RXS [1], SKL [1], TFG [1]	4.10:1
RXA, RXH, RXP, RXD [1], RXL [1], RXT [1]	4.56:1
10.5" Ring Gear (ROCKWELL)	
TFW	4.56:1
TFX	5.13:1

[1] – With positive traction, limited slip differential.

"G" SERIES REAR AXLE RATIO IDENTIFICATION

Application & Code	Ratio
8.5" Ring Gear	
PNK, PNL [1]	3.08:1
PNM, PNN [1]	3.42:1
PNP, PNR [1]	3.73:1
9.5" Ring Gear	
HBG, KCT [1]	3.23:1
PYR, RAP, PYN [1], RAR [1]	3.73:1
PYS, RBS, PYP [1], RBT [1]	4.10:1
HBJ, KCU [1]	4.56:1
9.75" Ring Gear (DANA)	
SJJ, SJK	4.10:1
SJG, SJH	4.56:1
10.5" Ring Gear	
RGU	3.42:1
RGW	3.73:1
10.5" Ring Gear (DANA)	
RGG	3.42:1
RGH, SKP	3.73:1
RGJ, SKM, SKR	4.10:1
SKN	4.56:1

[1] – With positive traction, limited slip differential.

"K" SERIES REAR AXLE RATIO IDENTIFICATION

Application & Code	Ratio
8.5" Ring Gear	
PFG, PFL, PFT, PFY, PFJ [1], PFP [1], PRW [1]	3.42:1
PFH, PFM, PFU, PFZ, PFK [1], PFR [1], PFX [1], PGA [1], PGB [1]	3.73:1
PFN, PSF [1]	4.10:1
9.5" Ring Gear	
PHS, PJG, PHW [1], PJL [1]	3.42:1
PHT, PJH, PHX [1], PJM [1]	3.73:1
PHU, PJJ, PHY [1], PJN [1]	4.10:1
PJK, PJP [1]	4.56:1
10.5" Ring Gear	
TFH, TFL [1]	3.42:1
RWY, RXF, RXM, SKG, TFJ	3.73:1
RWZ, RXG, RXN, SKH, TFK, RXB [1], RXJ [1], RXR [1], TFM [1]	4.10:1
RXA, RXH, RXP, RXD [1], RXL [1], RXT [1], RXC [1], RXK [1], RXS [1], SKL [1], TFN [1]	4.56:1

[1] – With positive traction, limited slip differential.

"K" SERIES FRONT AXLE RATIO IDENTIFICATION

Code	Ratio
ZBK, ZCP, ZGS, ZHW	3.42:1
ZBL, ZCR, ZGT, ZGX, ZHX	3.73:1
ZBM, ZCS, ZGU, ZHY	4.10:1
ZHZ, ZGZ	4.56:1

"P" SERIES REAR AXLE RATIO IDENTIFICATION

Application & Code	Ratio
10.5" Ring Gear	
HJN, PXR, RPP, HJS [1], PXU [1]	3.73:1
HJP, PXS, RPR	4.10:1
HJR, PXT, PXW, RPS, SWT, SWX, RPU [1], HJT [1]	4.56:1
SWU, SWY	4.88:1
PLX, RPT	5.13:1
10.5" Ring Gear (ROCKWELL)	
RLL	5.13:1

[1] – With positive traction, limited slip differential.

"R" SERIES REAR AXLE RATIO IDENTIFICATION

Application & Code	Ratio
8.5" Ring Gear	
PNT, PNY [1]	3.08:1
PNU, PNZ [1]	3.42:1
PNW, PPA [1]	3.73:1
9.5" Ring Gear	
KBW, KBX [1]	3.42:1
RAA, RAB [1]	3.73:1
RBW, RCK [1]	4.10:1
GUN	4.56:1
10.5" Ring Gear	
KMV, KMX [1]	3.42:1
GDP, HFP, HFY, HKP, HKS [1], HFT [1], HHL [1]	3.73:1
GDR, HFR, HFZ, HKT [1], HFU [1], HHM [1]	4.10:1
GDS, HFS, HFW [1], HHN [1], KDC [1]	4.56:1

[1] – With positive traction, limited slip differential.

"S" & "T" SERIES REAR AXLE RATIO IDENTIFICATION

Application & Code	Ratio
7.5" Ring Gear	
GAJ	3.42:1
GAK, HZP [1]	3.73:1
GAL, HZR [1],	4.11:1
7.625" Ring Gear	
RNB	2.73:1
KUK, KUN, RNC, RND [1], RNH, RPW, RPZ, RRA, RRC, RRD, RRG, RRH	3.08:1
PLM [1], PMM, KUR, KUS [1], RNE, RNG RNJ, RNK [1], RPY [1], RRB [1], RRF [1], RRJ [1], RPX	3.42:1

[1] – With positive traction, limited slip differential.

1991 DRIVE AXLES
Axle Ratio Identification (Cont.)

"T" SERIES FRONT AXLE RATIO IDENTIFICATION

Code	Ratio
ZAH	3.08:1
SKY, ZAD, ZAK, ZXC, ZYD	3.42:1

"V" SERIES REAR AXLE RATIO IDENTIFICATION

Application & Code	Ratio
8.5" Ring Gear	
PPB, PPJ, PPF [1], PPM [1]	3.08:1
PPC, PPK, PPG [1], PPN [1]	3.42:1
PPD, PPH [1]	3.73:1
9.5" Ring Gear	
RAC, RAD [1]	3.73:1
RBY, RCL [1]	4.10:1
10.5" Ring Gear	
GDP, HHP, HHX, HHT [1], HJK [1]	3.73:1
GDR, HHR, HHY, HHU [1], HJL [1]	4.10:1
GDS, HHS, HHZ, HHW [1], HJM [1]	4.56:1

[1] – With positive traction, limited slip differential.

"V" SERIES FRONT AXLE RATIO IDENTIFICATION

Code	Ratio
ZDC, ZDP, ZGC, ZHC, ZHD, ZGD	3.08:1
ZDK, ZDU, ZGH, ZHH, ZMH	3.42:1
ZDX, ZDZ, ZFB, ZFD, ZFF, ZFM, ZGK, ZGM, ZGN, ZHK, ZHN, ZFR [1], ZFS [1], ZFP, ZFN, ZFT [1], ZFU [1],	3.73:1
ZGP, ZGR, ZHP, ZHR	4.10:1
ZFW [1], ZFX [1]	4.56:1

[1] – DANA built front axle.

1991 DRIVE AXLES
Axle Shafts – FWD Van

Lumina APV, Silhouette, Trans Sport

DESCRIPTION

Drive axles are completely flexible assemblies consisting of an inner and an outer Constant Velocity (CV) joint connected by an axle shaft. Inner tripot CV joint is capable of moving in and out. Outer ball/cage CV joint is flexible but cannot move in and out.

All drive axles, except left hand inboard end on automatic transaxle, incorporate a male spline and interlock with transaxles gears through the use of barrel-type snap rings. Left-hand inboard shaft attachment on automatic transaxle uses a female spline. Female spline is installed over a stub shaft extending out from transaxle.

Drive axle spline end mating with knuckle and hub assembly is a helical spline. Spline provides a tight press fit and assures end play does not exist between hub bearing and drive shaft assembly. Intermediate shaft assemblies are used on models with manual transaxles.

REMOVAL & INSTALLATION

DRIVE AXLES

Removal & Installation – 1) Raise and support vehicle. Remove tire and wheel assembly. Remove tie rod end cotter pin and tie rod nut. Separate tie rod end from steering knuckle.

2) Remove axle nut and washer. Insert a long punch through brake caliper and into brake rotor fins to aid in axle nut removal. Discard axle nut. Remove lower ball joint pinch bolt. Install modified (inner tabs removed) Seal Protector (J 34754) over drive axle seal.

NOTE: Drive Axle Seal Protector (J 34754) should be modified and installed on any drive axle before performing services on or near drive axle. Failure to do so may result in seal damage and possible future joint failure.

3) Separate ball joint from steering knuckle. To remove axle shaft from hub/bearing assembly, press axle shaft inward using Axle Remover (J 28733). DO NOT allow axle shaft to drop or hang freely when removing from hub/bearing assembly.

4) Remove axle remover. Remove axle shaft from transaxle using slide hammer. To install axle shaft, reverse removal procedure. Seat drive axle into transaxle by placing screwdriver into groove on joint housing and tap until seated. Use a new axle shaft nut. Torque all nuts and bolts to specification. See TORQUE SPECIFICATIONS table.

TORQUE SPECIFICATIONS

TORQUE SPECIFICATIONS

Application	Ft. Lbs. (N.m)
Axle Shaft (Hub) Nut	185 (251)
Brake Caliper Bolts	38 (52)
Hub & Bearing Bolts	62 (84)
Large Seal Clamp	130 (176)
Lower Ball Joint Pinch Bolt	33 (45)
Small Seal Clamp	100 (136)
Wheel Lug Nuts	100 (136)

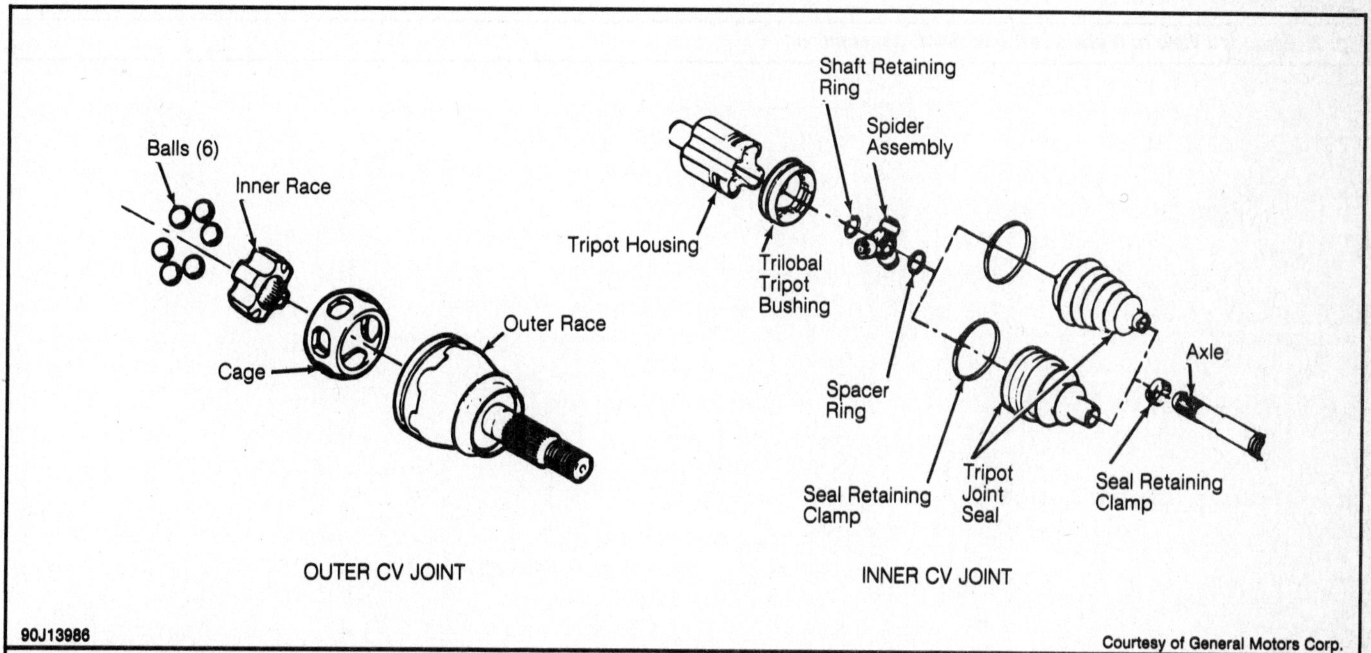
Balls (6)
Inner Race
Cage
Outer Race
OUTER CV JOINT
Shaft Retaining Ring
Spider Assembly
Tripot Housing
Trilobal Tripot Bushing
Spacer Ring
Seal Retaining Clamp
Tripot Joint Seal
Seal Retaining Clamp
Axle
INNER CV JOINT
90J13986
Courtesy of General Motors Corp.

Fig. 1: Exploded View of Inner & Outer CV Joints

1991 DRIVE AXLES
Axle Shafts – FWD Van (Cont.)

OVERHAUL

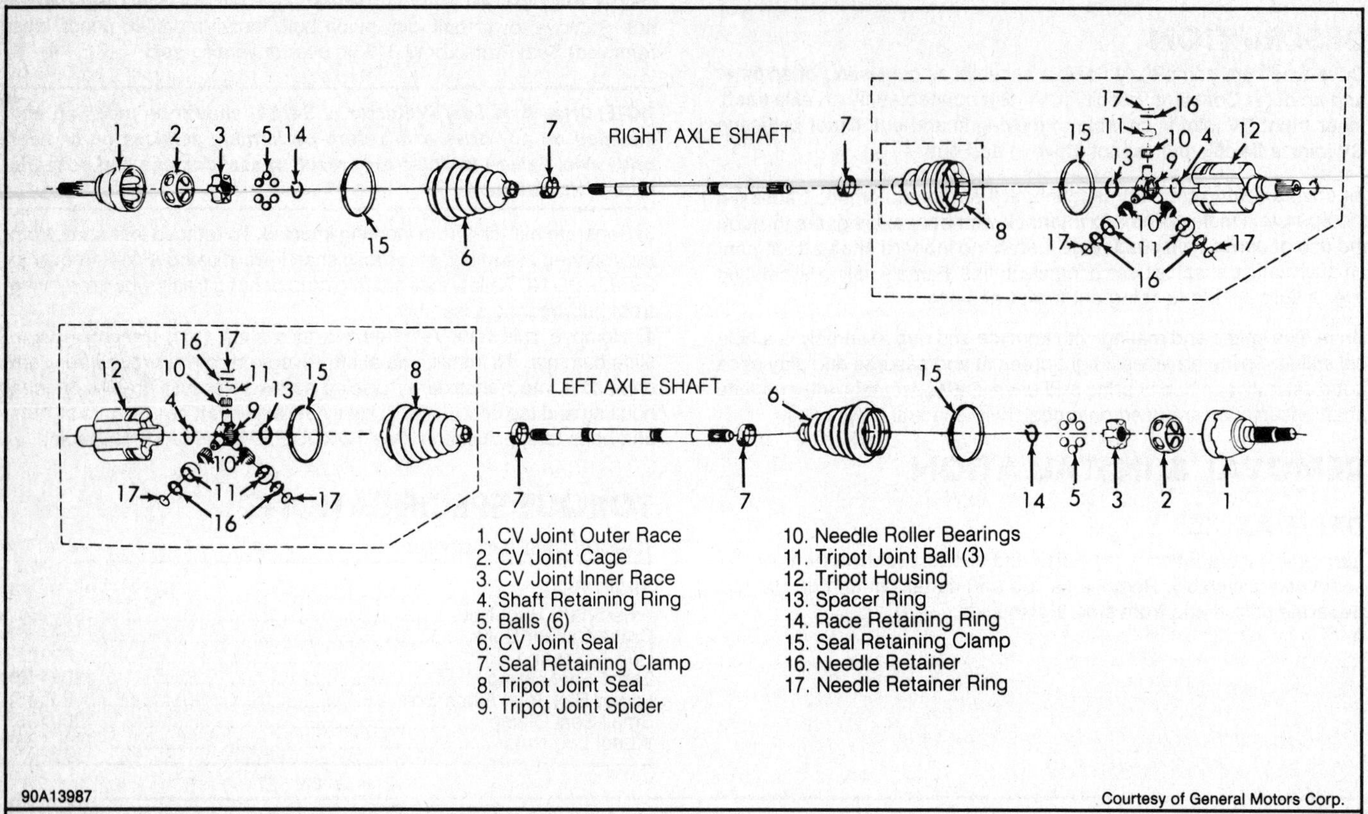
RIGHT AXLE SHAFT
LEFT AXLE SHAFT
1. CV Joint Outer Race
2. CV Joint Cage
3. CV Joint Inner Race
4. Shaft Retaining Ring
5. Balls (6)
6. CV Joint Seal
7. Seal Retaining Clamp
8. Tripot Joint Seal
9. Tripot Joint Spider
10. Needle Roller Bearings
11. Tripot Joint Ball (3)
12. Tripot Housing
13. Spacer Ring
14. Race Retaining Ring
15. Seal Retaining Clamp
16. Needle Retainer
17. Needle Retainer Ring
90A13987
Courtesy of General Motors Corp.

Fig. 2: Exploded View of Right & Left Axle Shaft Assemblies

1991 DRIVE AXLES
"K" Series Front Axle

DESCRIPTION

Axle used on "K" Series models has a 4WD center disconnect feature which allows shifting in or out of 4WD under most conditions while vehicle is in motion. Axle is shifted by a thermal actuator solenoid contained within right axle tube. *See Figs. 2 and 3.*

Right drive axle consists of a solid axle shaft which rides inside of a stationary axle tube. A short stub shaft with a CV joint is bolted to inner axle shaft flange. Left drive axle consists of a flexible drive shaft using an inner tripod joint and outer CV joint. Left axle tripod joint housing bolts to axle carrier drive flange. CV joint/spindle on outer end of drive shaft slips through steering knuckle/hub assembly. *See Fig. 1.*

Axle uses a conventional ring and pinion gear set to transmit the driving force of engine to the wheels. Gear set transfers driving force at a 90 degree angle from propeller shaft to drive shafts.

Axle is produced with 8 1/4" ring gear (K15/25 Series) or 9 1/4" ring gear (K35 Series), with minor differences between the 2.

AXLE RATIO & IDENTIFICATION

To determine drive axle ratio, see AXLE RATIO IDENTIFICATION article.

REMOVAL & INSTALLATION

LEFT DRIVE AXLE

Removal & Installation – 1) Raise and support vehicle on safety stands. Remove skid plate (if equipped). Remove wheel and tire assembly. Remove stabilizer bar hardware and remove stabilizer bar from lower control arm. DO NOT mix left and right side components if both sides are being removed.

2) Disconnect left inner tie rod from steering relay rod. Insert a long drift through disc rotor vanes to prevent axle from turning. Loosen hub nut and remove nut and washer from end of drive axle. Disconnect drive axle flange bolts retaining inner tripod joint housing to axle carrier output shaft.

3) Pull down on inner end of axle shaft. DO NOT allow axle shaft to hang free. Using suitable puller, or a brass drift, push outboard end of axle shaft out of hub assembly. Remove drive axle from vehicle.

4) To install axle shaft, reverse removal procedure. Tighten all bolts and nuts to specifications. See TORQUE SPECIFICATIONS table at end of article.

RIGHT AXLE TUBE & INNER SHAFT

Removal – 1) Disconnect negative battery cable. Raise and support vehicle on safety stands. Remove skid plate (if equipped). Remove wheel and tire assembly.

2) Remove stabilizer bar hardware and remove stabilizer bar from lower control arm. DO NOT mix left and right side components if both sides are being removed. Disconnect right inner tie rod from steering relay rod.

3) Disconnect stub shaft flange bolts retaining stub axle to drive axle flange. Turn wheel outward to loosen stub shaft from drive axle flange. Push stub shaft toward front of vehicle and wire aside.

4) Disconnect actuator solenoid connector at axle tube. Disconnect indicator light switch connector at axle tube. Remove actuator solenoid and indicator light switch if these components are to be serviced. Place suitable container under drive axle. Remove drain plug and washer and drain lubricant. Remove nuts and washers retaining axle tube to frame.

5) Remove bolts attaching axle tube to axle carrier. Remove axle tube from axle carrier. Ensure that open end of tube is pointed upward.

Installation – 1) If internal carrier components have been changed, see reassembly steps **4)** through **9)** of RIGHT AXLE TUBE ASSEMBLY under OVERHAUL. Apply sealant to carrier sealing surface. Install axle tube to carrier housing. Install 6 retaining bolts and tighten to 30 ft. lbs. (40 N.m). Connect stub shaft to inner shaft flange and install bolts. Tighten bolts to 59 ft. lbs. (80 N.m).

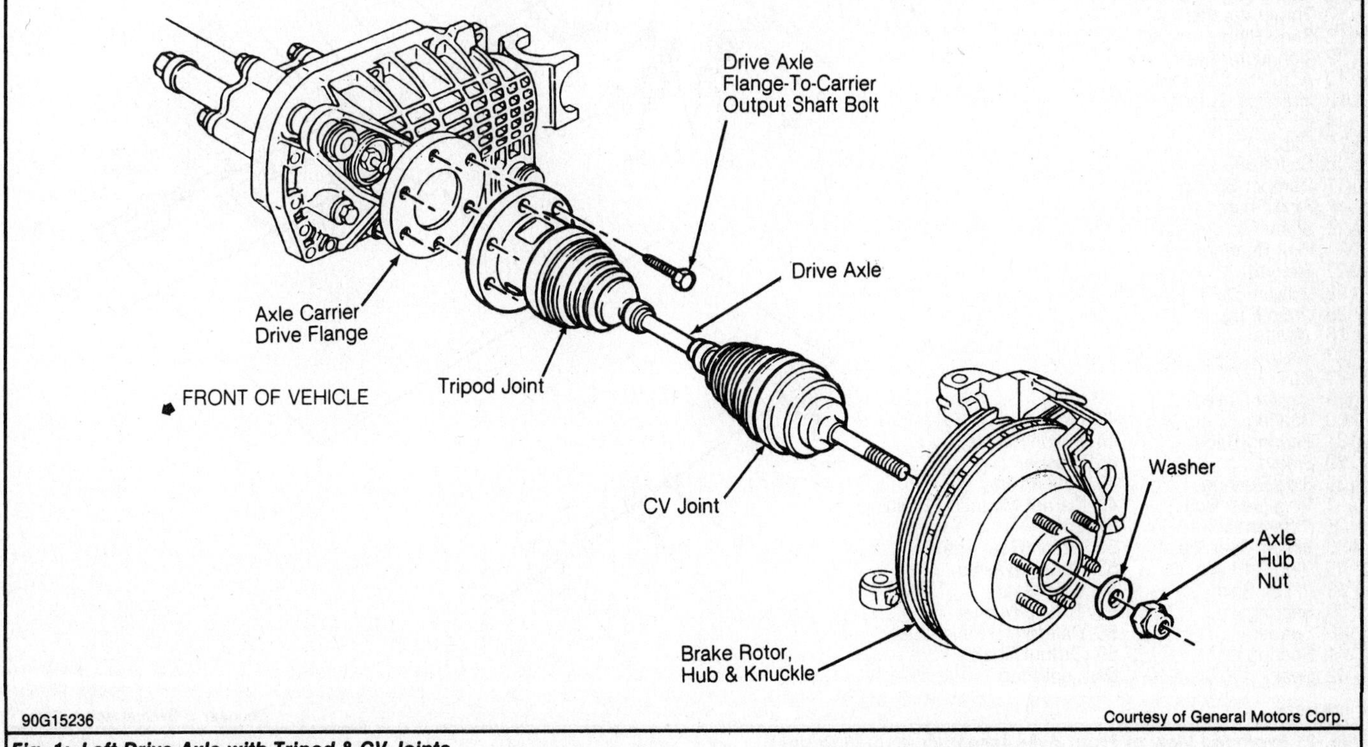
Drive Axle
Flange-To-Carrier
Output Shaft Bolt
Drive Axle
Axle Carrier
Drive Flange
FRONT OF VEHICLE
Tripod Joint
CV Joint
Washer
Axle
Hub
Nut
Brake Rotor,
Hub & Knuckle
90G15236
Courtesy of General Motors Corp.

Fig. 1: Left Drive Axle with Tripod & CV Joints

1991 DRIVE AXLES
"K" Series Front Axle (Cont.)

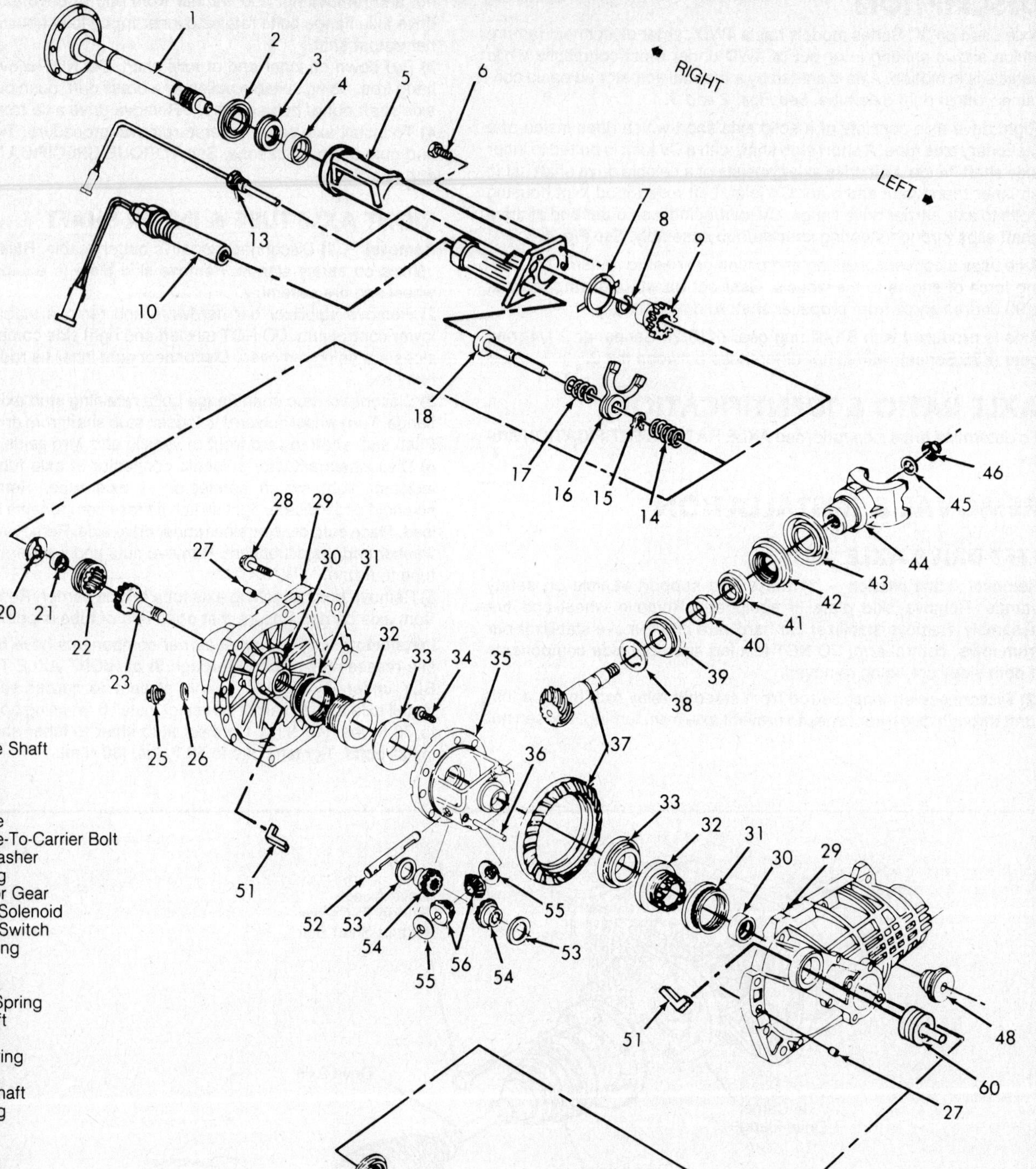
RIGHT
LEFT

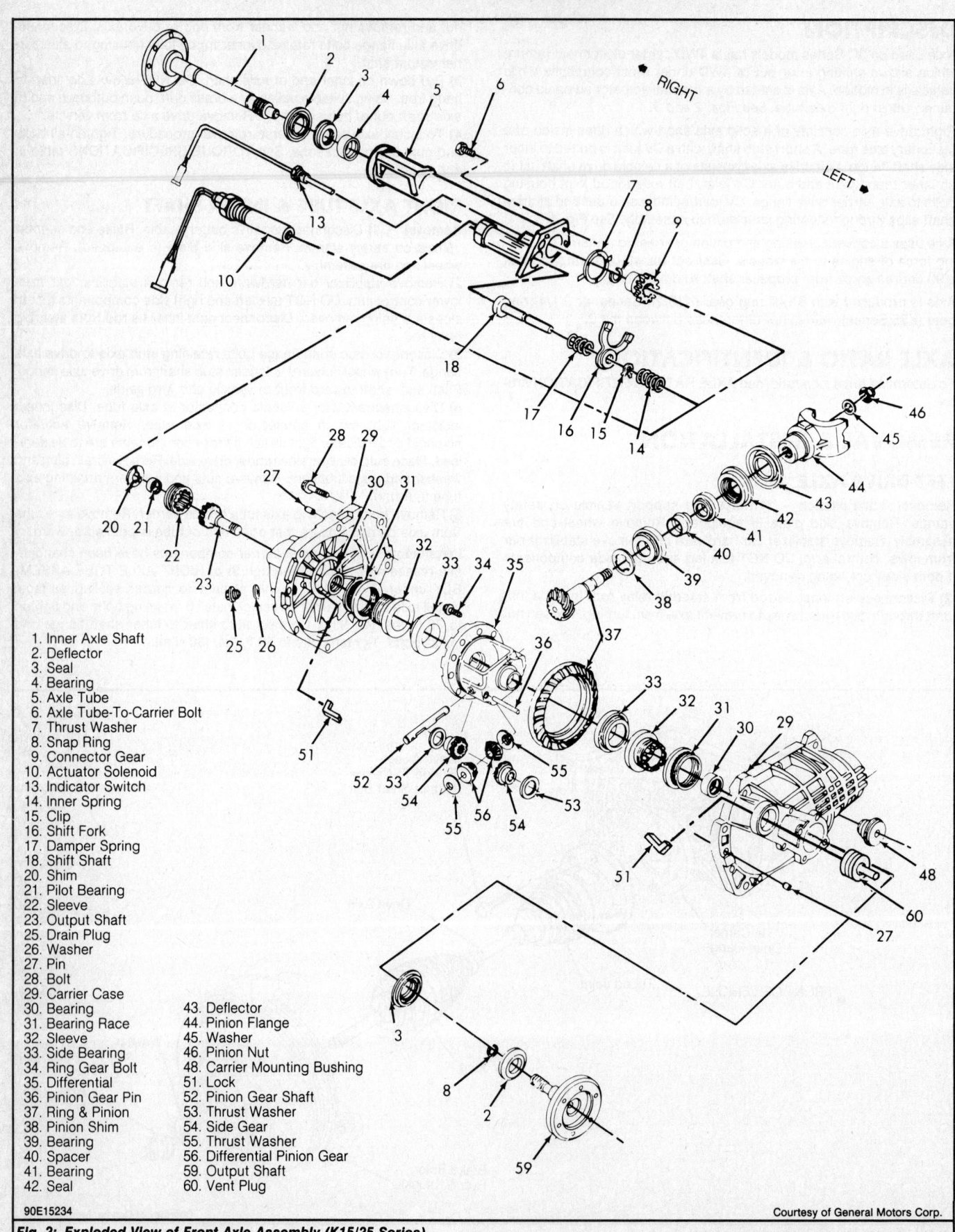

1. Inner Axle Shaft
2. Deflector
3. Seal
4. Bearing
5. Axle Tube
6. Axle Tube-To-Carrier Bolt
7. Thrust Washer
8. Snap Ring
9. Connector Gear
10. Actuator Solenoid
13. Indicator Switch
14. Inner Spring
15. Clip
16. Shift Fork
17. Damper Spring
18. Shift Shaft
20. Shim
21. Pilot Bearing
22. Sleeve
23. Output Shaft
25. Drain Plug
26. Washer
27. Pin
28. Bolt
29. Carrier Case
30. Bearing
31. Bearing Race
32. Sleeve
33. Side Bearing
34. Ring Gear Bolt
35. Differential
36. Pinion Gear Pin
37. Ring & Pinion
38. Pinion Shim
39. Bearing
40. Spacer
41. Bearing
42. Seal
43. Deflector
44. Pinion Flange
45. Washer
46. Pinion Nut
48. Carrier Mounting Bushing
51. Lock
52. Pinion Gear Shaft
53. Thrust Washer
54. Side Gear
55. Thrust Washer
56. Differential Pinion Gear
59. Output Shaft
60. Vent Plug

90E15234

Courtesy of General Motors Corp.

Fig. 2: Exploded View of Front Axle Assembly (K15/25 Series)

1991 DRIVE AXLES
"K" Series Front Axle (Cont.)

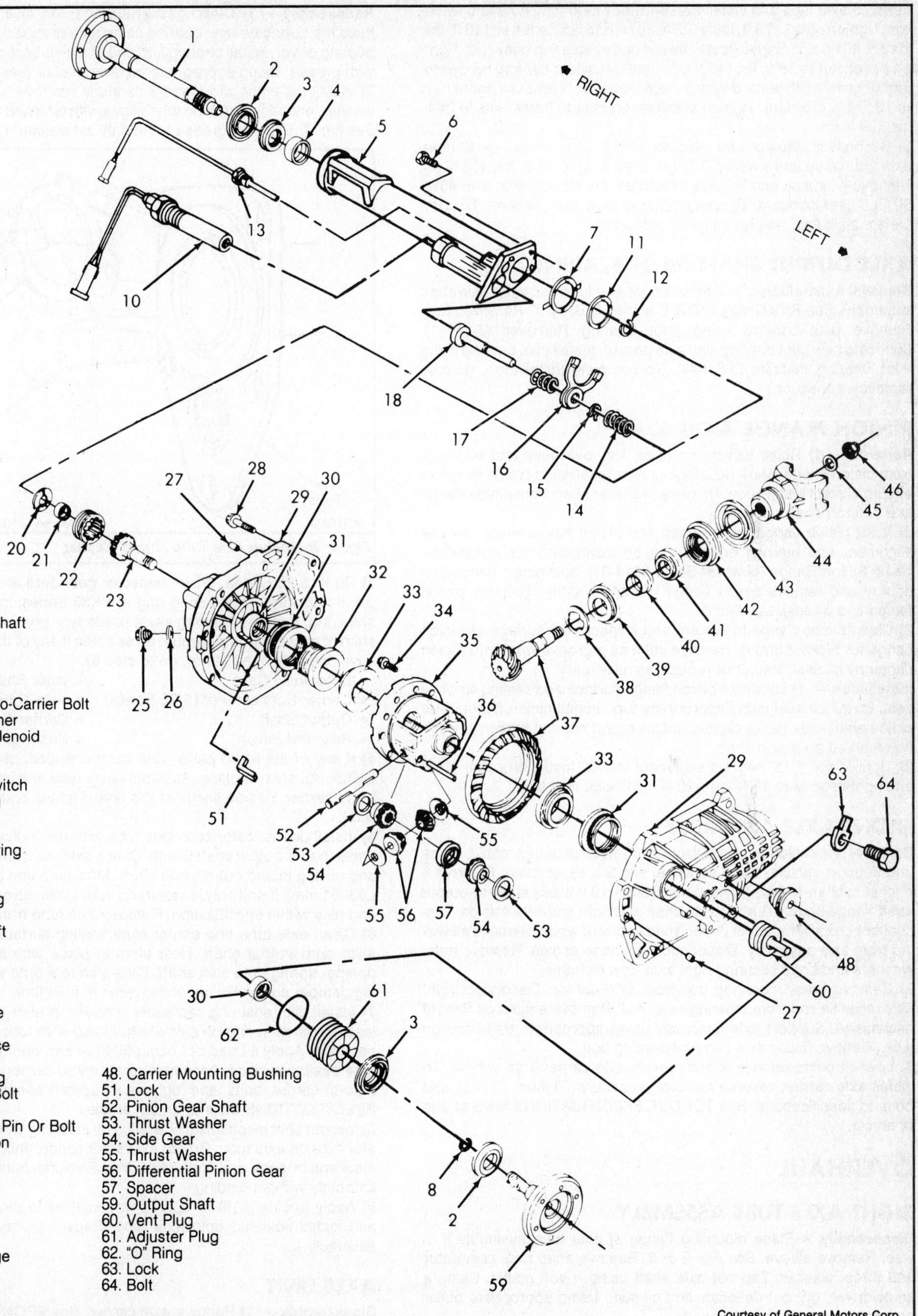
RIGHT
LEFT
1
2
3
4
5
6
7
8
10
11
12
13
14
15
16
17
18
20
21
22
23
25
26
27
28
29
30
31
32
33
34
35
36
37
38
39
40
41
42
43
44
45
46
48
51
52
53
54
55
56
57
59
60
61
62
63
64

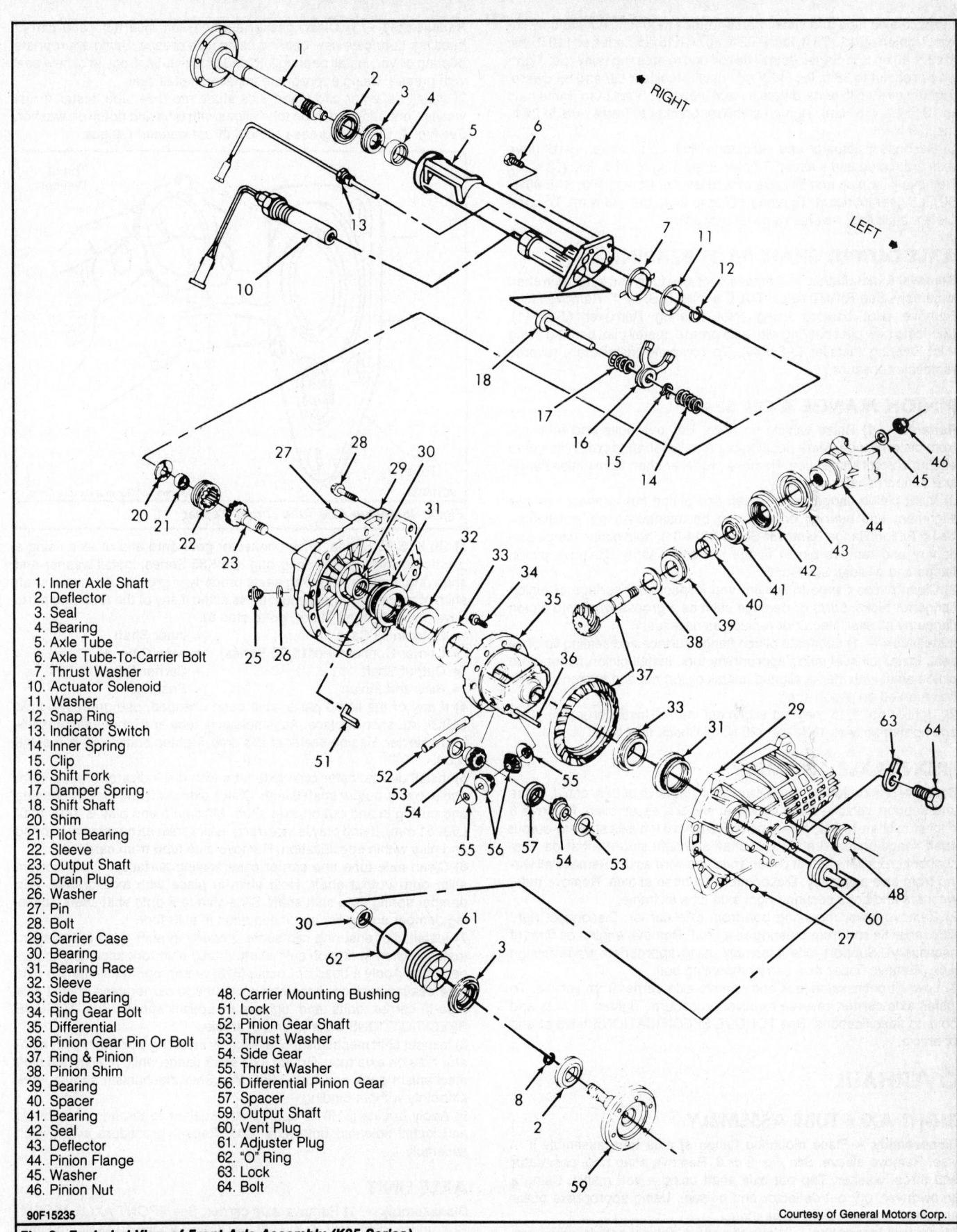

1. Inner Axle Shaft
2. Deflector
3. Seal
4. Bearing
5. Axle Tube
6. Axle Tube-To-Carrier Bolt
7. Thrust Washer
10. Actuator Solenoid
11. Washer
12. Snap Ring
13. Indicator Switch
14. Inner Spring
15. Clip
16. Shift Fork
17. Damper Spring
18. Shift Shaft
20. Shim
21. Pilot Bearing
22. Sleeve
23. Output Shaft
25. Drain Plug
26. Washer
27. Pin
28. Bolt
29. Carrier Case
30. Bearing
31. Bearing Race
32. Sleeve
33. Side Bearing
34. Ring Gear Bolt
35. Differential
36. Pinion Gear Pin Or Bolt
37. Ring & Pinion
38. Pinion Shim
39. Bearing
40. Spacer
41. Bearing
42. Seal
43. Deflector
44. Pinion Flange
45. Washer
46. Pinion Nut
48. Carrier Mounting Bushing
51. Lock
52. Pinion Gear Shaft
53. Thrust Washer
54. Side Gear
55. Thrust Washer
56. Differential Pinion Gear
57. Spacer
59. Output Shaft
60. Vent Plug
61. Adjuster Plug
62. "O" Ring
63. Lock
64. Bolt

90F15235

Courtesy of General Motors Corp.

Fig. 3: Exploded View of Front Axle Assembly (K35 Series)

1991 DRIVE AXLES
"K" Series Front Axle (Cont.)

2) Raise axle tube and install frame-to-tube mounting nuts and washers. Tighten nuts to 75 ft. lbs. (102 N.m) on K15/25 Series or 110 ft. lbs. (149 N.m) on K35 Series. Install tie rod end to steering relay rod. Tighten tie rod nut to 35 ft. lbs (48 N.m). Install stabilizer bar and hardware. Tighten all stabilizer hardware except stabilizer bracket to frame nuts to 13 ft. lbs. (18 N.m). Tighten stabilizer bracket to frame nuts to 24 ft. lbs. (33 N.m).

3) Reconnect actuator and indicator switch connectors. Install drive axle drain plug and washer. Tighten drain plug to 24 ft. lbs. (33 N.m). Remove filler plug and fill drive axle to level of fill plug with SAE 80W-90 GL5 gear lubricant. Tighten fill plug to 24 ft. lbs. (33 N.m). To complete installation, reverse removal procedure.

AXLE OUTPUT SHAFT PILOT BEARING

Removal & Installation – Remove right axle tube and inner axle shaft assembly. See RIGHT AXLE TUBE & INNER SHAFT. Remove shim. Remove pilot bearing using Pilot Bearing Remover (J-34011). Lubricate new pilot bearing with axle grease. Install pilot bearing using Pilot Bearing Installer (J-33842). To complete installation, reverse removal procedure.

PINION FLANGE & OIL SEAL

Removal – **1)** Raise vehicle on hoist. Remove bolts and retainers from pinion flange. Mark position of propeller shaft to pinion flange to ensure correct installation. Remove propeller shaft from pinion flange and support shaft out of way.

2) Mark pinion flange, pinion shaft and pinion nut to ensure proper alignment and bearing preload can be maintained on installation. Using Pinion Flange Remover Set (J-8614-01), hold pinion flange stationary and remove pinion flange nut and washer. Remove pinion flange and oil seal. *See Fig. 8.*

3) Clean pinion flange in solvent and inspect seal surface of pinion flange for nicks, burrs or damage such as a groove worn into pinion flange by oil seal. Repair or replace as necessary.

Installation – **1)** Lubricate pinion flange surface and sealing lip of oil seal. Install oil seal using appropriate tool. Install pinion flange onto pinion shaft with marks aligned. Install pinion nut and tighten to position marked on pinion shaft.

2) Tighten nut 1/16" beyond alignment marks. Install propeller shaft and tighten bolts to 15 ft. lbs. (20 N.m). Check fluid level.

FRONT AXLE ASSEMBLY

Removal & Installation – **1)** Disconnect negative battery cable. Raise and support vehicle. Remove wheel and tire assemblies. Remove 6 right stub shaft-to-axle flange bolts. Remove 6 left axle shaft-to-output shaft flange bolts. Wire left axle shaft and right stub shaft aside. Disconnect propeller shaft at pinion yoke and wire aside. Remove all wiring from axle assembly. Disconnect vent hose at axle. Remove nuts, washers and bolts securing right axle tube to frame.

2) Remove lower mounting bolt from axle carrier. Disconnect right side inner tie rod from steering relay rod. Remove engine oil filter (if necessary). Support axle assembly using appropriate transmission jack. Remove upper axle carrier mounting bolt.

3) Lower transmission jack and remove axle carrier from vehicle. To install axle carrier, reverse removal procedure. Tighten all nuts and bolts to specifications. See TORQUE SPECIFICATIONS table at end of article.

OVERHAUL

RIGHT AXLE TUBE ASSEMBLY

Disassembly – Place mounting flange of axle tube assembly in a vise. Remove sleeve. *See Fig. 2 or 3.* Remove snap ring, connector and thrust washer. Tap out axle shaft using a soft mallet. Using a screwdriver, pry out deflector and oil seal. Using appropriate puller and slide hammer, remove bearing.

Cleaning & Inspection – Wash all parts in solvent and dry with compressed air. Inspect all parts for excessive wear and scoring. Inspect splined stub shaft for wear, cracks and twisted splines.

Reassembly – **1)** Clean gasket surfaces on axle tube and carrier housing. Lubricate new bearing using axle grease. Using appropriate bearing driver, install bearing into end of axle tube. Coat lip of new seal with grease. Using appropriate installer, install seal.

2) Install deflector and insert axle shaft into axle tube. Install thrust washer, ensuring notch on tube aligns with tabs and notch on washer. *See Fig. 4.* Use axle grease to hold thrust washer in place.

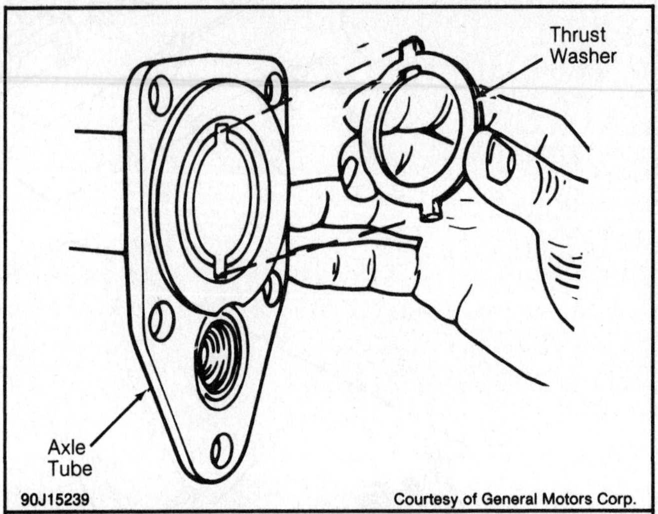
Thrust
Washer
Axle
Tube
90J15239
Courtesy of General Motors Corp.

Fig. 4: Installing Axle Tube Thrust Washer

3) On K15/25 Series, drive connector gear onto end of axle using a plastic hammer. Install snap ring. On K35 Series, install washer and snap ring. Ensure snap ring seats properly in groove. An output shaft shim of proper thickness must be selected if any of the following parts have been changed. If not, go to step **6)**.

- Differential Case
- Carrier Connector (K15/25 Series)
- Output Shaft
- Ring and Pinion
- Inner Shaft
- Axle Tube
- Carrier Case
- Bearings

4) If any of the listed parts have been changed, use grease to hold ORIGINAL shim in place. Assemble axle tube and inner shaft assembly to carrier. Use no sealer at this time. Tighten bolts to 30 ft. lbs. (40 N.m).

5) Install dial indicator onto axle tube with dial indicator shaft at right angle to axle output shaft flange. Check axle shaft end play by pushing and pulling in and out on axle shaft. Maximum end play is .001-.020" (.03-.51 mm). If end play is incorrect, select shim as necessary to bring end play within specification. Remove axle tube from carrier.

6) Clean axle tube and carrier case sealing surfaces. Place correct shim onto output shaft. Hold shim in place with axle grease. Slip damper spring onto shift shaft. Slide shift fork onto shift shaft, ensuring damper spring fits into indentation in shift fork.

7) Install clip, ensuring clip seats properly in shift shaft indentation. Install tension spring on shift shaft. Attach shift fork assembly to carrier case. Apply a bead of Loctite (518) or appropriate sealant to axle tube sealing surface. Assemble axle tube to carrier case. Install axle tube-to-carrier bolts and tighten to specifications. See TORQUE SPECIFICATIONS table at end of article.

8) Inspect shift mechanism operation by inserting a drift into shift actuator hole on axle tube. Rotate axle shaft flange while moving the shift mechanism back and forth with drift. Shift mechanism should work smoothly without binding.

9) Apply Loctite (518) or appropriate sealant to threads of solenoid and install solenoid onto axle tube. Repeat procedure with switch assembly.

AXLE UNIT

Disassembly – **1)** Remove axle carrier. See FRONT AXLE ASSEMBLY under REMOVAL & INSTALLATION. Remove solenoid and indicator switch from right axle tube. Remove tube and inner shaft

1991 DRIVE AXLES
"K" Series Front Axle (Cont.)

assembly. See RIGHT AXLE TUBE & INNER SHAFT under REMOVAL & INSTALLATION.

2) Remove sleeve, shift shaft, damper spring, shift fork, clip and inner spring. *See Fig. 2 or 3.* Remove shim. Remove output shaft from right side of carrier assembly. Remove left output flange from carrier assembly by prying on one side with a screwdriver while simultaneously tapping outward on other side with a soft faced hammer. *See Fig. 5.* Remove deflector.

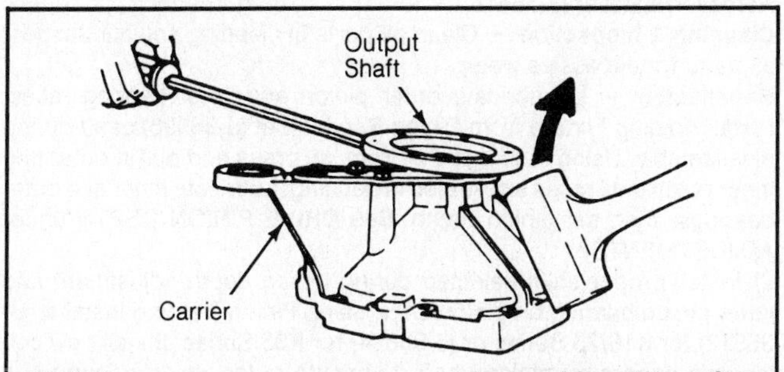
Output
Shaft
Carrier
90C15240
Courtesy of General Motors Corp.

Fig. 5: Removing Left Output Flange

3) Pry out left output flange seal with a screwdriver. Remove left and right output shaft bearings using Bearing Remover (J-29369-1) for K15/25 Series or (J-29369-2) for K35 Series. Remove bolts holding carrier halves together. Tap on lugs provided to separate carrier halves. Pry up on left and right side bearing locks (right side only on K35 Series) and remove differential assembly from carrier. On K35 Series, remove adjuster plug bolt and lock at left half of carrier.

4) Using Sleeve Adjuster (J-36599), rotate sleeve and push side bearings (right side only on K35 Series) out of bores. *See Fig. 6.* On K35 Series, remove adjuster plug, bearing and "O" ring from left side of carrier by rotating adjuster plug using Adjuster Plug Remover (J-36615). *See Fig. 7.*

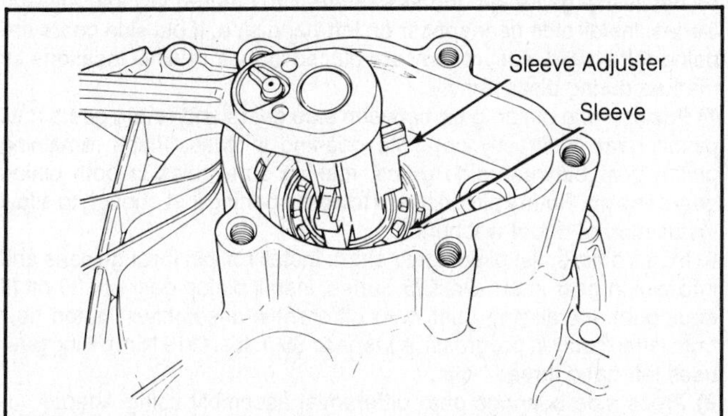
Sleeve Adjuster
Sleeve
90D15241
Courtesy of General Motors Corp.

Fig. 6: Removing Bearing Using Sleeve Adjuster

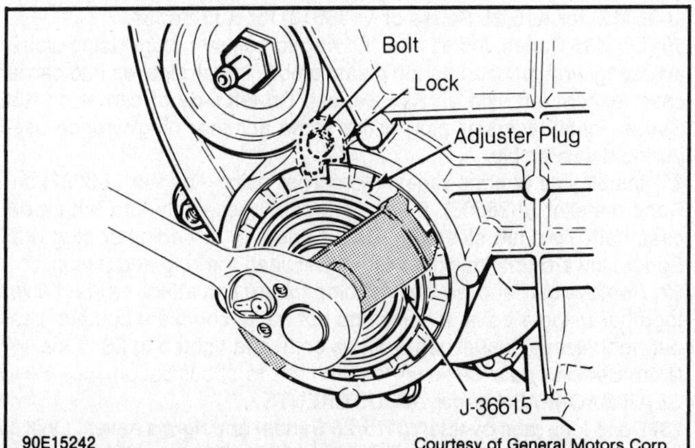
Bolt
Lock
Adjuster Plug
J-36615
90E15242
Courtesy of General Motors Corp.

Fig. 7: Removing Bearing Using Adjuster Plug Remover

5) Using Pinion Flange Remover Set (J-8614-01), hold pinion flange stationary and remove pinion nut, flat washer and pinion yoke. *See Fig. 8.* Remove pinion deflector. Mount left carrier case half in Holding Fixture from Pinion Service Tool Set (J-36598). Remove pinion with shim, inner bearing and spacer as an assembly. *See Fig. 9.* Remove bearing spacer.

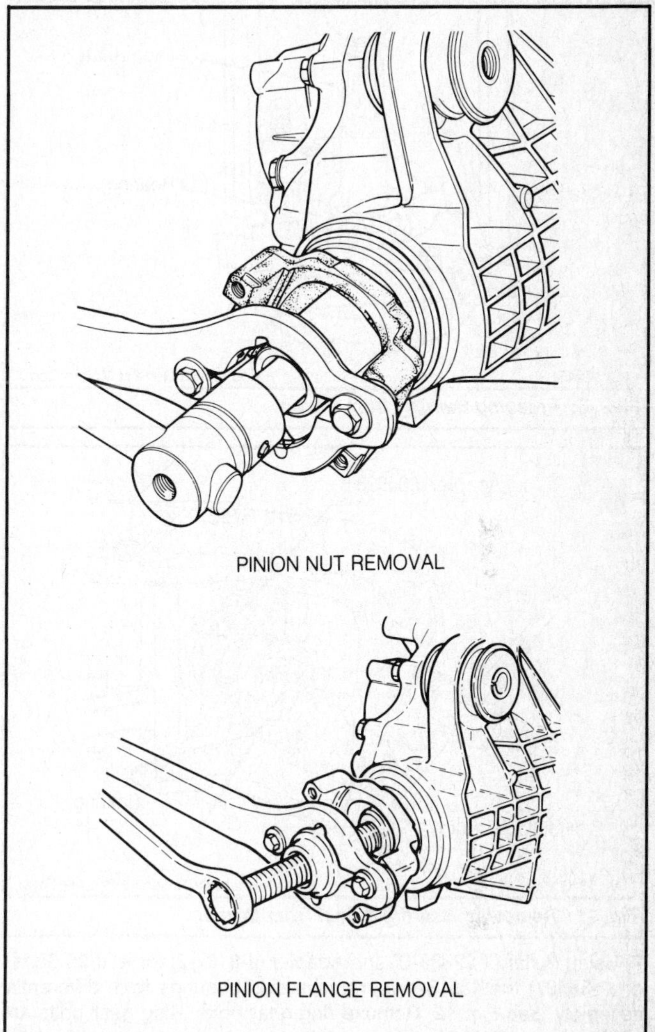
PINION NUT REMOVAL
PINION FLANGE REMOVAL
90F15243
Courtesy of General Motors Corp.

Fig. 8: Removing Pinion Nut & Flange

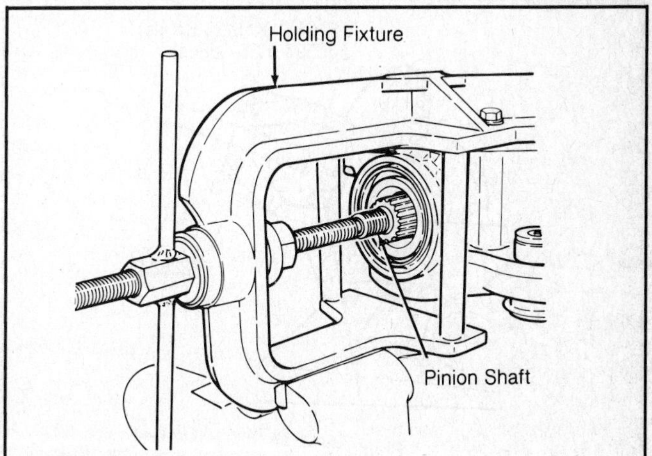
Holding Fixture
Pinion Shaft
90G15244
Courtesy of General Motors Corp.

Fig. 9: Pressing Pinion from Carrier

1991 DRIVE AXLES
"K" Series Front Axle (Cont.)

6) Using Pinion Bearing Remover (J-8612-B) for K15/25 Series or (J-36606) for K35 Series, press bearing from pinion. *See Fig. 10.* Remove shim from pinion. Using Holding Fixture and Pinion Service Tool Set (J-36598), remove seal and outer bearing from left half of carrier. *See Fig. 11.* Use Adapter Plate (J-36598-6) on K15/25 Series. Remove bearing races using same service tool set.

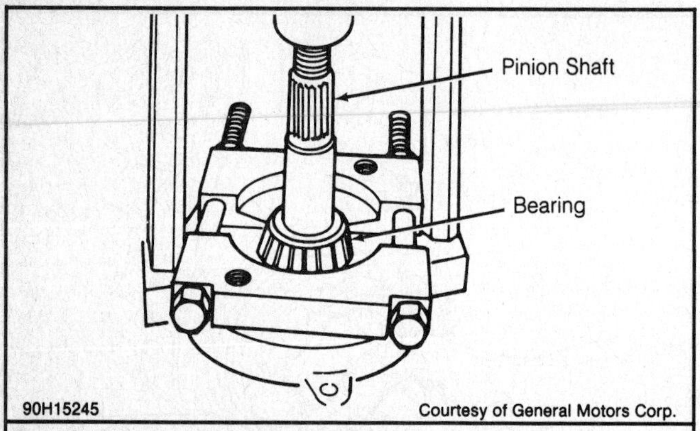
Pinion Shaft
Bearing
90H15245
Courtesy of General Motors Corp.

Fig. 10: Pressing Bearing from Pinion

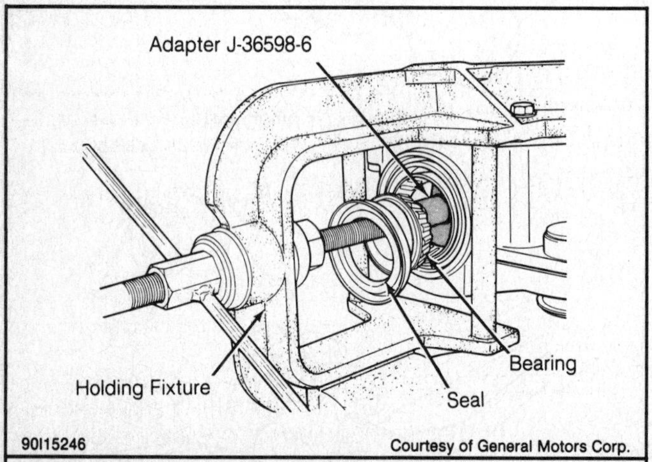
Adapter J-36598-6
Bearing
Holding Fixture
Seal
90I15246
Courtesy of General Motors Corp.

Fig. 11: Removing Bearing & Seal from Carrier

7) Using Puller (J-22888-D) and Adapter (J-8107-2) for K15/25 Series or (J-36597) for K35 Series, remove side bearings from differential assembly. *See Fig. 12.* Remove ring gear bolts. Ring gear bolts are left-hand thread. Using a brass drift, drive ring gear from differential case. DO NOT pry ring gear from case. This will damage ring gear and case.

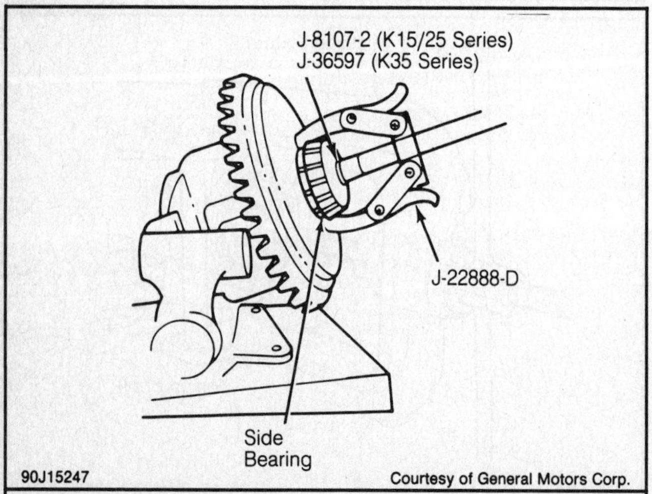
J-8107-2 (K15/25 Series)
J-36597 (K35 Series)
J-22888-D
Side
Bearing
90J15247
Courtesy of General Motors Corp.

Fig. 12: Removing Side Bearing from Differential

8) Using a punch and hammer, drive out roll pin from differential pinion gear shaft. Remove pinion gear shaft. On K35 Series, a bolt may be used in place of a roll pin. Roll pinion gears and thrust washers out of differential case.

9) Remove side gears and thrust washers, marking side gears and differential case as left and right for reassembly reference. On K35 Series, remove spacer. Using a 6-point socket, remove vent plug. Upper and lower carrier mounting bushings may be replaced using Remover/Installer (J-36616).

Cleaning & Inspection – Clean all parts in cleaning solvent. Inspect all parts for excessive wear.

Reassembly – **1)** Lubricate outer pinion and inner bearing races. Install Holding Fixture from Pinion Service Set (J-36598) used during disassembly. Using race installer from kit, press and pull in outer and inner races until races are seated in housing. Lubricate inner and outer bearings, then set pinion depth. See DRIVE PINION DEPTH under ADJUSTMENTS.

2) Install proper shim selected during pinion depth adjustment and inner pinion bearing on pinion shaft using Pinion Bearing Installer (J-35512) for K15/25 Series or (J-36614) for K35 Series. Install new collapsible spacer on pinion shaft. Lubricate outer pinion bearing and install bearing and pinion seal into carrier. Insert pinion with inner bearing and spacer into carrier.

3) Install deflector, pinion flange, washer and nut. Install flange holder used when removing flange and hold flange while torquing pinion flange nut. Tighten nut until no end play is present. DO NOT tighten further.

4) Rotate pinion several times to ensure bearings have been seated. Set final preload to 15-25 INCH lbs. (1.7-2.8 N.m) by tightening pinion nut in small increments. Each tightening increases preload by several INCH pounds.

5) If preload specification is exceeded, pinion must be removed and collapsible spacer replaced. Once preload has been obtained, rotate pinion several times to ensure bearings have seated and recheck preload. Readjust if necessary.

6) Install side gears and thrust washers into differential case. On K35 Series, install side gear spacer on left-hand side. If old side gears are being reinstalled, ensure they are placed in their original locations as marked during disassembly.

7) Position one pinion gear between side gears and rotate gears until pinion gear is directly opposite opening in case. Place remaining pinion gear between side gears, making sure holes in both pinion gears line up. Rotate pinion gears toward opening just enough to allow installation of thrust washers.

8) Install differential pinion gear shaft. Install roll pin through case and into pinion gear shaft. On K35 Series, install pinion gear shaft bolt (if equipped). Install ring gear onto differential assembly. Tighten new bolts alternately in progressive steps to 88 ft. lbs. (119 N.m). Ring gear uses left-hand thread bolts.

9) Press side bearings onto differential assembly using Adapter (J-8092) and Side Bearing Installer (J-22761) for K15/25 Series or (J-29710) for K35 Series. Press bearings onto sleeves (and adjuster plug on left side of K35 Series) using Adapter (J-8092) and Bearing Installer (J-36612) for K15/25 Series or (J-36613) for K35 Series.

10) On K35 Series, install new "O" ring to adjuster plug. Using sleeve adjusting wrench used during disassembly, install sleeves into carrier case (except left side on K35 Series). On left side of carrier on K35 Series, install adjuster plug using same adjuster plug wrench used during disassembly.

11) Install side bearing races into carrier using Adapter (J-8092) and Race Installer (J-36603). Place differential assembly into left carrier case half. Turn left sleeve (K15/25 Series) or left adjuster plug (K35 Series) inward until backlash is felt between the ring and pinion.

12) Remove carrier case from holding fixture and attach carrier halves together using 4 bolts. If halves do not make complete contact, back out right sleeve. Install carrier case bolts and tighten to 35 ft. lbs. (47 N.m). Set ring gear backlash adjustment to specification. See RING GEAR BACKLASH under ADJUSTMENTS.

13) Bend lock tabs over left (K15/25 Series) and right sleeves. On K35 Series, install left adjuster plug lock and bolt. Remove 4 bolts holding

1991 DRIVE AXLES
"K" Series Front Axle (Cont.)

axle carrier halves together and separate housing halves. Apply Loctite (518) or appropriate sealant to one carrier housing surface.

14) Reconnect axle carrier housing halves. Install 10 attaching bolts and tighten to specification. See TORQUE SPECIFICATIONS table at end of article. Using appropriate seal installer, install seal into left side of carrier case. Place deflector onto left output shaft and insert into left side of carrier. Drive into place with a soft-faced hammer.

15) Install new pilot bearing into right output shaft using Pilot Bearing Installer (J-33842). Insert right output shaft into right side of carrier. Apply Loctite (518) or appropriate sealant to threads of vent plug. Install vent plug into left side of carrier.

16) Install right axle tube and inner shaft assembly. See RIGHT AXLE TUBE & INNER SHAFT under REMOVAL & INSTALLATION.

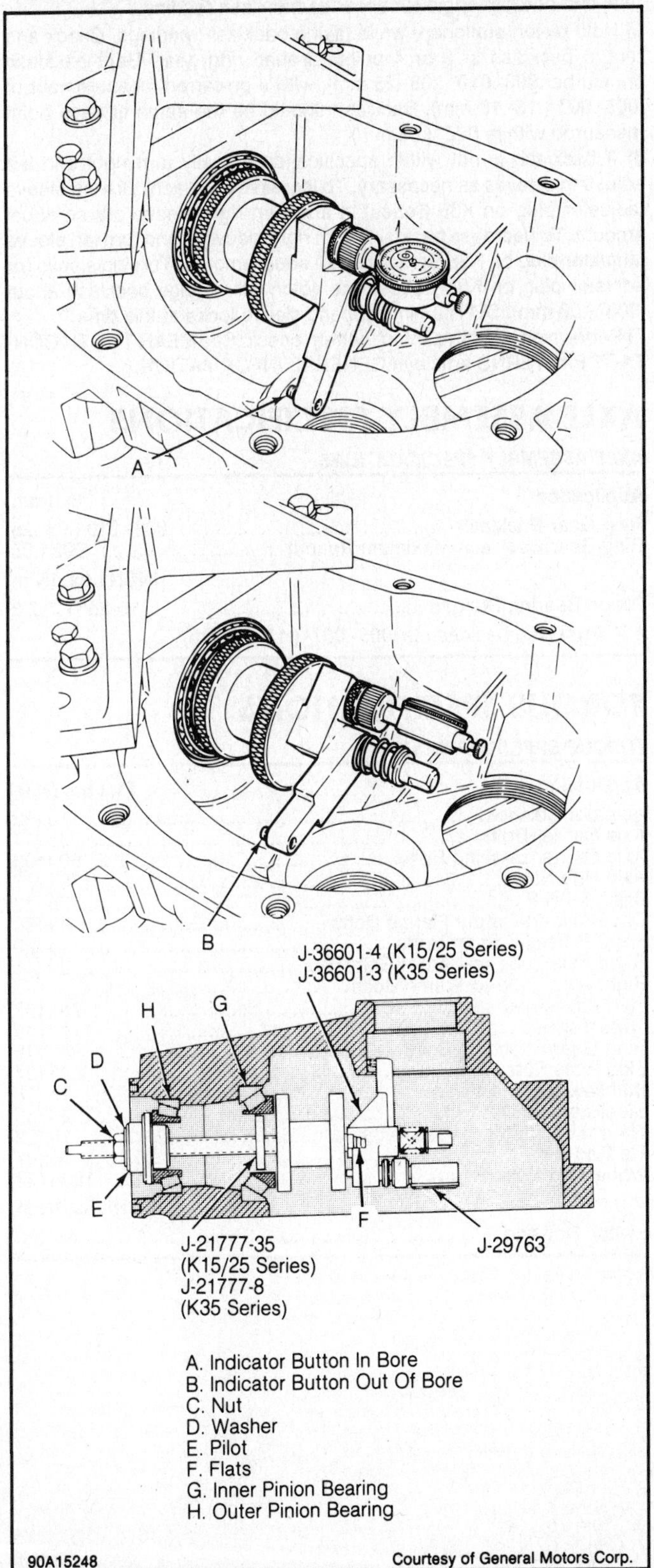
A
B
J-36601-4 (K15/25 Series)
J-36601-3 (K35 Series)
H
G
D
C
E
F
J-21777-35
(K15/25 Series)
J-21777-8
(K35 Series)
J-29763
A. Indicator Button In Bore
B. Indicator Button Out Of Bore
C. Nut
D. Washer
E. Pilot
F. Flats
G. Inner Pinion Bearing
H. Outer Pinion Bearing
90A15248
Courtesy of General Motors Corp.

Fig. 13: Pinion Shim Setting Gauge & Dial Indicator Installation & Measurement

ADJUSTMENTS

DRIVE PINION DEPTH

1) Lubricate inner and outer pinion bearings liberally with axle lubricant. Hold pinion bearings in position and install Pinion Shim Setting Gauge (J-36601-4) for K15/25 Series or (J-36601-3) for K35 Series. Install Dial Indicator (J-29763) onto gauge. *See Fig. 13.* With gauge installed, preload inner and outer pinion bearings to 10-15 INCH lbs. (1.0-1.6 N.m) by tightening shim setting gauge mounting bolt while holding end of gauge shaft with a wrench. Rotate shaft several times to ensure bearings have seated. Recheck preload.

2) Push dial indicator downward until needle rotates approximately 3 turns clockwise. Tighten dial indicator in this position. Set button of pinion shim setting gauge on differential bearing bore.

NOTE: The 4WD front axle drive pinions are nominal or zero, and are not marked. Shim thickness will equal dial indicator gauge reading.

3) Rotate gauge slowly back and forth until dial indicator reads lowest point of bore. Set dial indicator to zero. Repeat rocking action of gauge to verify zero setting.

4) After zero setting is obtained and verified, move gauge button out of differential side bearing bore. Record dial indicator reading. Use a shim that is exactly the same size as indicator reading.

5) Remove dial indicator and gauge from carrier. Position correct shim on drive pinion. Install drive pinion.

RING GEAR BACKLASH

1) Using sleeve adjusting wrench, tighten right adjusting sleeve until no backlash is present, which is approximately 100 ft. lbs. (136 N.m).

2) Using sleeve adjusting wrench (K15/25 Series) or adjuster plug wrench (K35 Series), tighten left adjusting sleeve until no backlash is present, which is approximately 100 ft. lbs. (136 N.m).

3) Mark location of adjusting sleeves or adjuster plug in relation to carrier halves so notches in sleeves or adjuster plug can be counted when turned. Turn right sleeve out 2 notches using sleeve adjusting wrench. Turn left sleeve (K15/25 Series) or adjuster plug (K35 Series) in one notch.

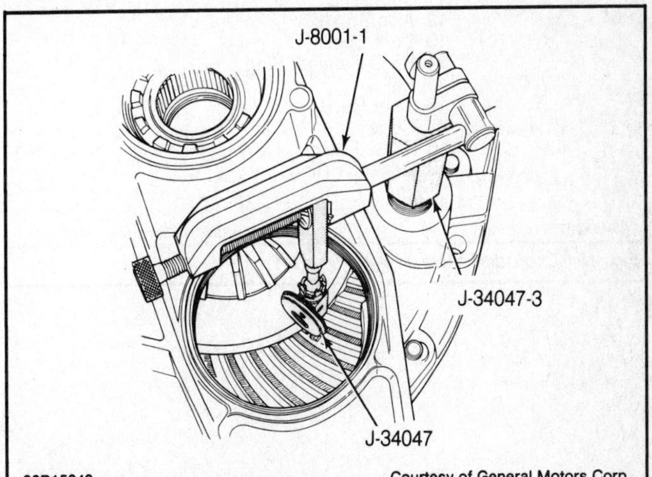
J-8001-1
J-34047-3
J-34047
90B15249
Courtesy of General Motors Corp.

Fig. 14: Checking Ring Gear Backlash

1991 DRIVE AXLES
"K" Series Front Axle (Cont.)

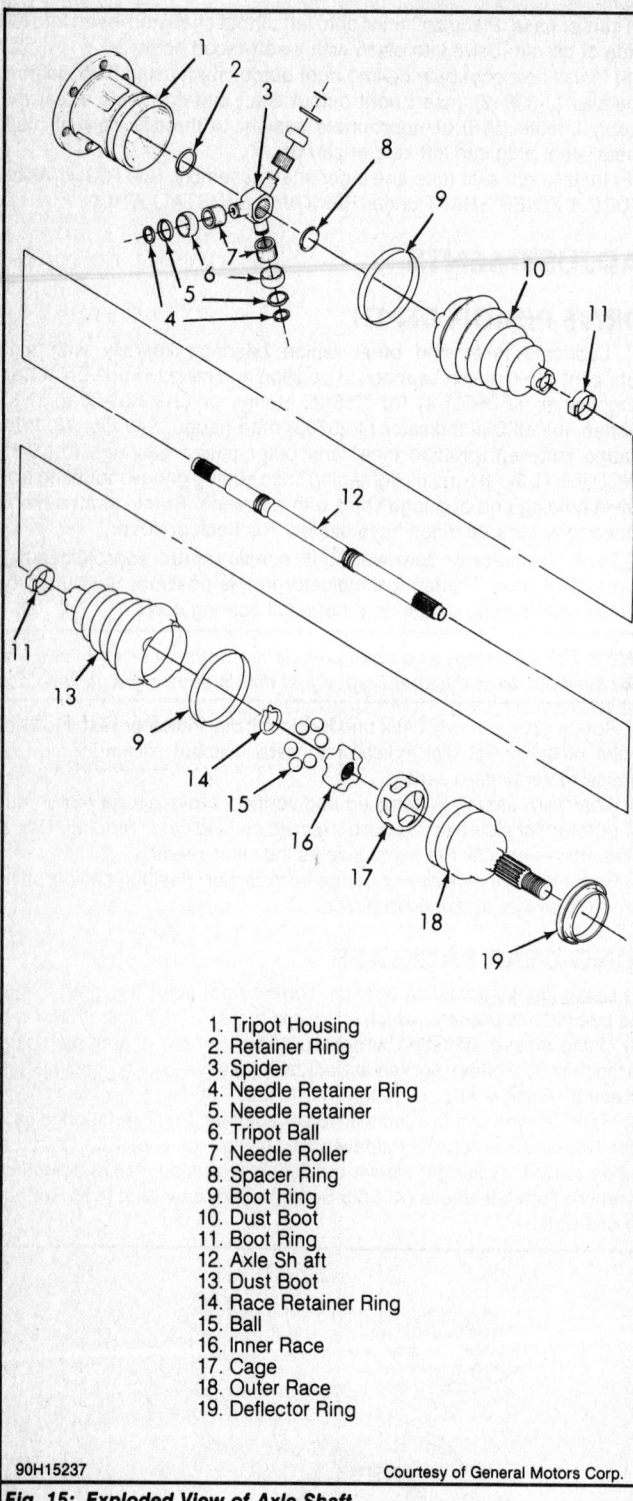

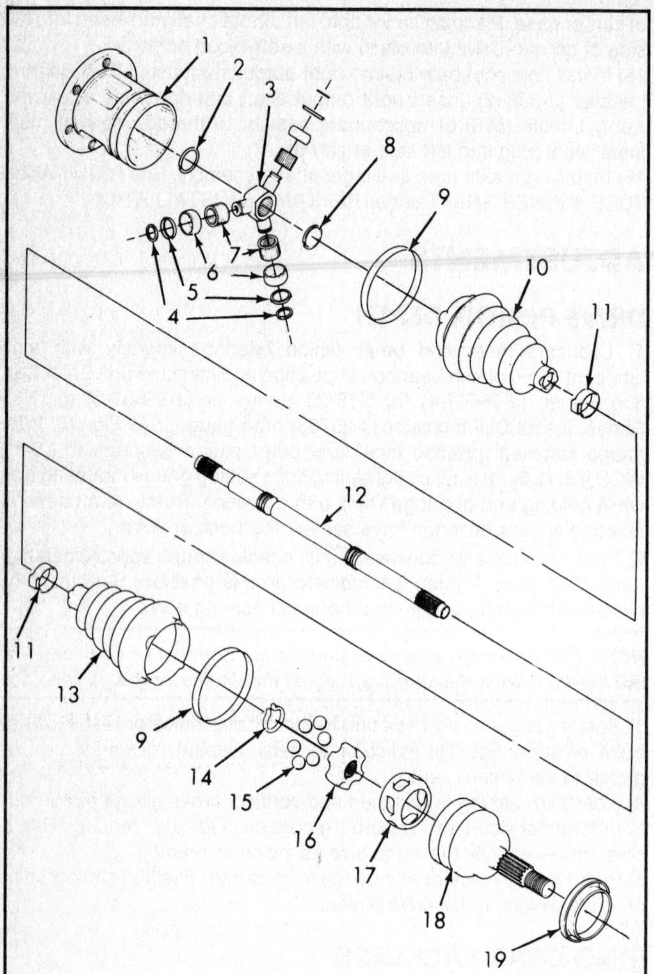
1
2
3
8
9
7
6
5
4
10
11
12
11
13
9
14
15
16
17
18
19
1. Tripot Housing
2. Retainer Ring
3. Spider
4. Needle Retainer Ring
5. Needle Retainer
6. Tripot Ball
7. Needle Roller
8. Spacer Ring
9. Boot Ring
10. Dust Boot
11. Boot Ring
12. Axle Sh aft
13. Dust Boot
14. Race Retainer Ring
15. Ball
16. Inner Race
17. Cage
18. Outer Race
19. Deflector Ring
90H15237
Courtesy of General Motors Corp.

Fig. 15: Exploded View of Axle Shaft

4) Rotate pinion several times to seat bearings. Mount Dial Indicator Base (J-34047-3) in oil filler plug hole on left side of carrier case. Mount Dial Indicator (J-34047) and Adapter (J-8001-1) through oil vent plug hole so that indicator stem is touching a ring gear tooth. *See Fig. 14.* Use a small button on indicator stem so contact can be made near heel end of tooth angle for accurate backlash reading.

5) Hold pinion stationary while taking backlash readings. Check and record backlash at 3 or 4 points around ring gear. Gear backlash should be .003-.010" (.08-.25 mm), with a preferred measurement of .005-.007 (.13-.18 mm). Backlash should be the same at each point measured within .002" (.05 mm).

6) If backlash is not within specification, equally turn right and left adjusting sleeves as necessary. To increase backlash, turn left sleeve (adjuster plug on K35 Series) in and turn right sleeve out an equal amount. To decrease backlash, turn right sleeve in and turn left sleeve (adjuster plug on K35 Series) out an equal amount. Turning sleeve (or adjuster plug on K35 Series) one notch will change backlash about .003" (.08 mm). DO NOT install/bend sleeve locks at this time.

7) Perform gear tooth contact pattern check. See GEAR TOOTH CONTACT PATTERNS article in GENERAL INFORMATION.

AXLE ASSEMBLY SPECIFICATIONS

AXLE ASSEMBLY SPECIFICATIONS

Application	In. (mm)
Ring Gear Backlash	[1] .003-.010 (.08-.25)
Ring Gear Backlash Maximum Runout	.002 (.05)
	INCH Lbs. (N.m)
Pinion Bearing Preload	15-25 (1.7-2.8)

[1] – Preferred backlash is .005-.007" (.13-.18 mm).

TORQUE SPECIFICATIONS

TORQUE SPECIFICATIONS

Application	Ft. Lbs. (N.m)
Actuator Solenoid	16 (22)
Axle Carrier Bolts	35 (47)
Axle Carrier Bushing Bolts	80 (108)
Axle Hub Nut	175 (237)
Drain & Fill Plugs	24 (33)
Drive Axle-to-Output Flange Bolts	59 (80)
Front Propeller Shaft Bolts	15 (20)
Right Axle Tube-to-Carrier Bolts	30 (41)
Right Axle Tube-to-Frame Bolts	
K15/25 Series	75 (102)
K35 Series	110 (149)
Ring Gear Attaching Bolts	88 (119)
Skid Plate Screws	25 (34)
Stabilizer Bar Hardware	13 (18)
Stabilizer Bracket Nuts	24 (33)
Thermal Actuator to Axle Tube	16 (22)
Tie Rod Nut	35 (47)
Wheel Lug Nuts (Front)	120 (163)
	INCH Lbs. (N.m)
Switch Housing	45 (5.0)

1991 DRIVE AXLES
"T" Series 4WD Front Axle

Blazer, Jimmy, Pickup, Sonoma

DESCRIPTION & OPERATION

NOTE: "T" Series Bravada is equipped with an All-Wheel Drive (AWD) front axle. For information on this axle, see ALL-WHEEL DRIVE FRONT AXLE article in DRIVE AXLES.

Chevrolet and GMC "T" Series (4WD) models use an independent front drive axle with a vacuum actuation system. Axle consists of a transfer case with a synchronized input shaft, and a front axle unit with central locking clutch and vacuum operated cable shift control.

The vacuum actuation system consists of a vacuum switch and vacuum actuator. *See Fig. 1*. The shift mechanism in transfer case triggers vacuum switch to apply engine vacuum to vacuum actuator, after about a 3-second delay. The vacuum actuator, in turn, pulls on shift cable which pulls on shift fork in axle. This connects the right axle output shaft to the front axle differential. Torque is now available to front wheels.

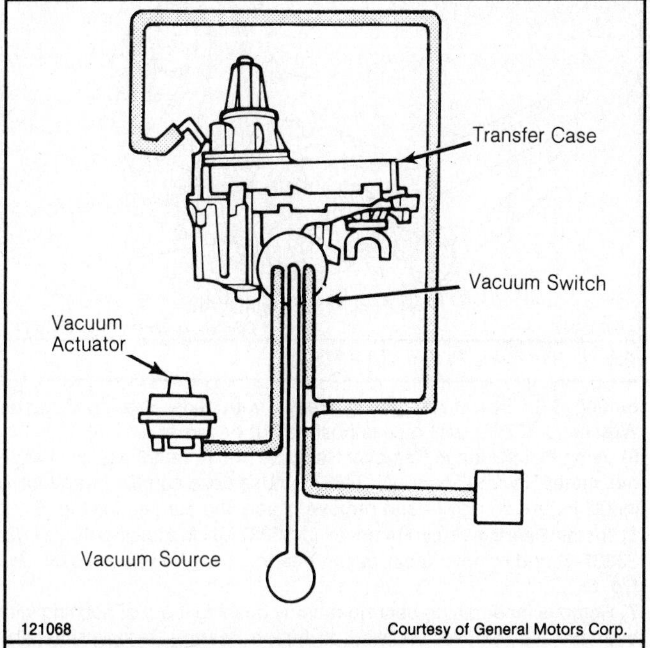
Transfer Case
Vacuum Switch
Vacuum Actuator
Vacuum Source
121068
Courtesy of General Motors Corp.

Fig. 1: Vacuum Actuation System

AXLE RATIO & IDENTIFICATION

To determine drive axle ratio, see AXLE RATIO IDENTIFICATION article.

REMOVAL & INSTALLATION

AXLE SHAFTS

Removal & Installation - 1) Raise and support vehicle on safety stands. Remove wheel and brake caliper and flex hoses at brackets. Remove tie rods at steering knuckle using Puller (J-24319). Remove shock lower bolts and push shocks out of way.

2) Remove drive axle-to-axle tube bolts. Remove axle shaft cotter pin, nut and washer. Position inner part of drive axle forward and support away from frame. Remove shaft from hub using Puller (J-28733). Remove axle shaft from vehicle.

3) Install axle shaft into hub. Tighten nut and washer to specifications. See TORQUE SPECIFICATIONS table at end of article. Install retainer and install cotter pin. To complete installation, reverse removal procedure.

RIGHT AXLE TUBE & INNER SHAFT

Removal - 1) Disconnect negative battery cable. Remove shift cable from vacuum actuator by disengaging lock spring. Push in actuator diaphragm to release cable.

2) Unlock steering wheel. Raise and support vehicle. Remove front wheels, engine drive belt shield and front axle skid plate (if equipped).

3) Place a support under right lower control arm and disconnect right upper ball joint. Remove support so control arm can hang free. Disconnect right drive axle shaft from differential output shaft.

4) Remove 4WD indicator light connection from switch. Remove 3 bolts securing cable and switch housing. Pull housing away to gain access to cable locking spring. DO NOT unscrew cable coupling nut unless cable is being replaced. See SHIFT CABLE removal.

5) Disconnect shift cable from shift fork shaft by lifting spring over slot in shift fork. Remove bolts securing tube bracket to frame bracket. Remove bolts securing tube assembly to carrier.

6) Remove tube assembly by working around drive axle. DO NOT allow sleeve, thrust washers, connector and output shaft to fall out of carrier while removing tube. *See Fig. 4*.

Installation - 1) Install sleeve, thrust washers, connector and output shaft in carrier. Apply Loctite (514) on axle tube to differential surface. Be sure to install thrust washer with notch aligned with tab on washer. *See Fig. 2*.

2) Install tube and shaft assembly to differential and install one bolt at one o'clock position but do not tighten. Pull assembly down and install cable, switch housing and remaining 4 bolts. Tighten bolts to specification. See TORQUE SPECIFICATIONS table at end of article.

3) Install and tighten 2 bolts securing tube to frame. Check shift unit operation. To complete installation, reverse removal procedure.

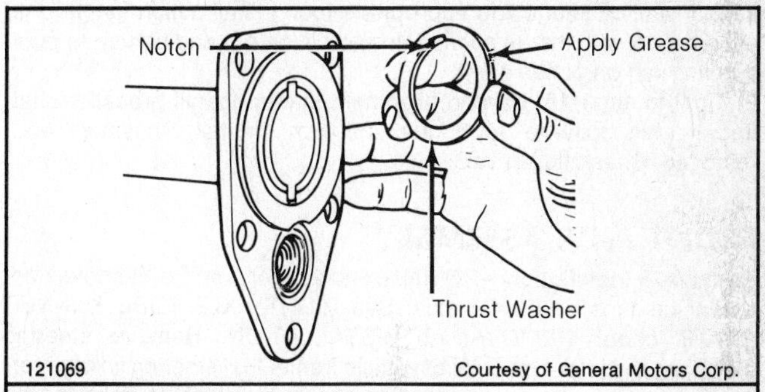
Notch
Apply Grease
Thrust Washer
121069
Courtesy of General Motors Corp.

Fig. 2: Installing Axle Tube Thrust Washer

SHIFT CABLE

Removal - 1) Disengage shift cable from vacuum actuator by disengaging locking spring. Push actuator diaphragm in to release cable. Squeeze 2 locking fingers of cable with pliers. Pull cable out of bracket hole.

2) Raise and support vehicle. Remove bolts securing cable and switch housing to carrier. Do not unscrew coupling nut at this time. Remove shift cable housing from carrier assembly. Pull out about 3/4" (19 mm) of cable. Remove cable end from shift fork shaft. Bend tang of lock spring, then pull cable end from shift fork shaft.

3) Note cable routing for installation. Unscrew coupler nut and remove shift cable from shift cable housing. Remove cable from vehicle.

Installation - 1) Install cable and switch housing to carrier. Tighten mounting bolts to 36 ft. lbs. (48 N.m).

2) Guide cable though switch housing into fork shaft hole and push cable in. Cable will snap into place. Start coupling nut by hand to avoid cross threading. Tighten nut to 90 INCH lbs. (10 N.m). DO NOT overtighten nut.

3) Connect shift cable to vacuum actuator by pressing cable into bracket hole. Cable and housing will snap into place. Check cable operation.

1991 DRIVE AXLES
"T" Series 4WD Front Axle (Cont.)

VACUUM ACTUATOR

Removal & Installation - Disconnect vacuum line from actuator. Remove shift cable. See SHIFT CABLE under REMOVAL & INSTALLATION. Remove vacuum actuator bolts and actuator. To install, reverse removal procedure.

AXLE OUTPUT SHAFT PILOT BEARING

Removal & Installation - Remove right extension tube and inner axle shaft. See RIGHT AXLE TUBE & INNER SHAFT under REMOVAL & INSTALLATION. Remove pilot bearing using Output Shaft Pilot Bearing Remover (J-34011). Install new pilot bearing using Output Shaft Pilot Bearing Installer (J-33842). To complete installation, reverse removal procedure.

PINION FLANGE & OIL SEAL

Removal - 1) Remove crossmember if necessary. Remove bolts and retainers from pinion flange. Mark position of propeller shaft to pinion flange to ensure correct installation. Remove propeller shaft from pinion flange and support shaft out of way.

2) Mark pinion flange, pinion shaft and pinion nut to ensure proper alignment and bearing preload are maintained on installation. Using Pinion Flange Remover Set (J-8614-01), hold pinion flange stationary and remove pinion flange nut and washer. Remove pinion flange and oil seal. *See Fig. 3.*

3) Clean pinion flange in solvent and inspect seal surface of pinion flange for nicks, burrs or damage such as a groove worn into pinion flange by oil seal. Repair or replace as necessary.

Installation - 1) Lubricate pinion flange surface and sealing lip of oil seal. Install oil seal using appropriate tool. Install pinion flange onto pinion shaft with marks aligned. Install pinion nut and tighten to position marked on pinion shaft.

2) Tighten nut 1/16" beyond alignment marks. Install propeller shaft and tighten bolts to 15 ft. lbs. (20 N.m). Install crossmember if removed. Check fluid level.

FRONT AXLE ASSEMBLY

Removal & Installation - 1) Raise and support vehicle. Remove right extension tube and inner axle. See RIGHT AXLE TUBE & INNER SHAFT under REMOVAL & INSTALLATION. Remove steering stabilizer and idler arm bolts at vehicle frame. Pull steering linkage forward. Remove axle vent hose. Remove inner attaching bolts for the left drive axle.

2) Mark front propeller shaft to ensure proper installation. Remove bolts and clamps. Working through hole in frame, remove axle-to-frame mounting bolts. Tip axle assembly counterclockwise while lifting to gain clearance from mounting ears and remove axle assembly. To install, reverse removal procedure. Tighten all bolts and nuts to specifications. See TORQUE SPECIFICATIONS table at end of article.

OVERHAUL

AXLE UNIT

Disassembly - 1) Remove axle output shaft and thrust washer. Remove left output shaft by prying between shaft flange and carrier bolt head with a screwdriver and simultaneously striking shaft flange with a soft-faced hammer.

2) Remove 6 cover-to-carrier bolts securing left side. Tap cover to loosen and remove. While supporting cover, drive out left seal using a punch.

3) Remove 10 bolts holding axle housing halves together. Insert screwdriver in slots provided (one next to fill plug, and 180 degrees from fill plug) and pry axle housing halves apart. *See Fig. 10.*

4) Remove differential from housing. Remove both side bearing adjusting locks. Remove race for both differential side bearings by turning side bearing adjusting sleeve with Side Bearing Adjuster Wrench (J-33792) until race is pushed out of carrier.

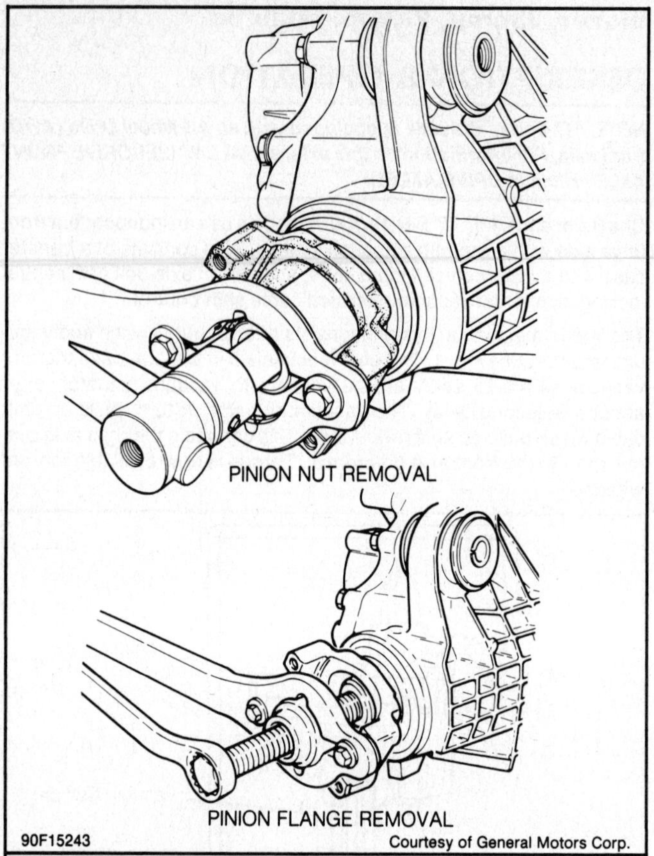
PINION NUT REMOVAL
PINION FLANGE REMOVAL
90F15243
Courtesy of General Motors Corp.

Fig. 3: Removing Pinion Nut & Flange

5) Using Pinion Flange Remover Set (J-8614-01), remove pinion flange nut. Install Holding Fixture (J-33837-1). Use bolts supplied with tool to install fixture on carrier and remove pinion and flange. *See Fig. 5.*

6) Install Bearing Race Remover (J-33837-6) on Holding Fixture (J-33837-1) and remove outer pinion bearing, race and pinion seal. *See Fig. 6.*

7) Remove inner pinion bearing race by pushing it out of housing with bearing race remover installed on Pinion Bearing Remover/Installer (J-33837). Remove inner drive pinion bearing using Differential Side/Pinion Bearing Remover (J-22912-01).

Cleaning & Inspection - Clean all parts in cleaning solvent. Inspect all parts for excessive wear.

Reassembly - 1) Lubricate outer pinion and inner bearing races. Install using Holding Fixture (J-33837-1) and Bearing Race Installer (J-33837-4) until races are seated in housing. *See Fig. 7.* Lubricate inner and outer bearings, then set pinion depth. See DRIVE PINION DEPTH under ADJUSTMENTS.

2) Install inner pinion bearing on shaft using Pinion Bearing Installer (J33785). Install new collapsible spacer on pinion shaft and position assembly in carrier. Lubricate outer pinion bearing and install in housing.

3) Lubricate pinion bearing seal with axle lube. Using Pinion Seal Installer (J-33782), install seal. Install pinion flange, washer and nut.

4) Install Flange Holder (J-8614-01) on pinion flange and hold flange while tightening pinion flange nut. Tighten nut until no end play is present. Do not tighten further as preload specifications are being approached. For preload procedure, see DRIVE PINION DEPTH under ADJUSTMENTS.

5) Rotate pinion several times to ensure bearings have been seated. Set final preload to 15-25 INCH lbs. (1.7-2.8 N.m).

6) Assemble output shaft bearings and adjusting sleeves into inserts in carrier and finger tighten. Install differential side bearing race into housing using Differential Side Bearing Race Installer (J-23423-A).

1991 DRIVE AXLES
"T" Series 4WD Front Axle (Cont.)

7) Using new output shaft bearings, adjusting sleeve inserts and Output Shaft Bearing Installer (J-33788), press output shaft bearings into adjusting sleeves from inner side of sleeves.

8) Install adjusting sleeve and bearing into insert and finger tighten. Using Differential Side Bearing Race Installer (J-23423-A), press assembly into axle housing.

9) Install differential into housing and set ring gear backlash adjustment to specification. See RING GEAR BACKLASH under ADJUSTMENTS.

10) Install left differential housing seal. Support housing to prevent distorting or bending of housing. Apply gasket sealer to housing surface and install housing cover.

DIFFERENTIAL HOUSING

Disassembly – 1) Using Differential Side/Pinion Bearing Remover (J-22912-01), remove side bearings. Remove pinion shaft lock screw and pinion. Remove pinions, side gears and thrust washers from housing. Mark side gears and housing for reassembly reference.

2) If ring gear is to be replaced and is tight on housing after removing right-hand thread bolts, drive off ring gear using a brass drift and hammer. DO NOT pry between ring gear and housing.

Reassembly – 1) Lubricate all parts with axle lubricant. Place side gear thrust washers over side gear hubs. Install side gears in housing. Ensure all original parts are installed in original positions.

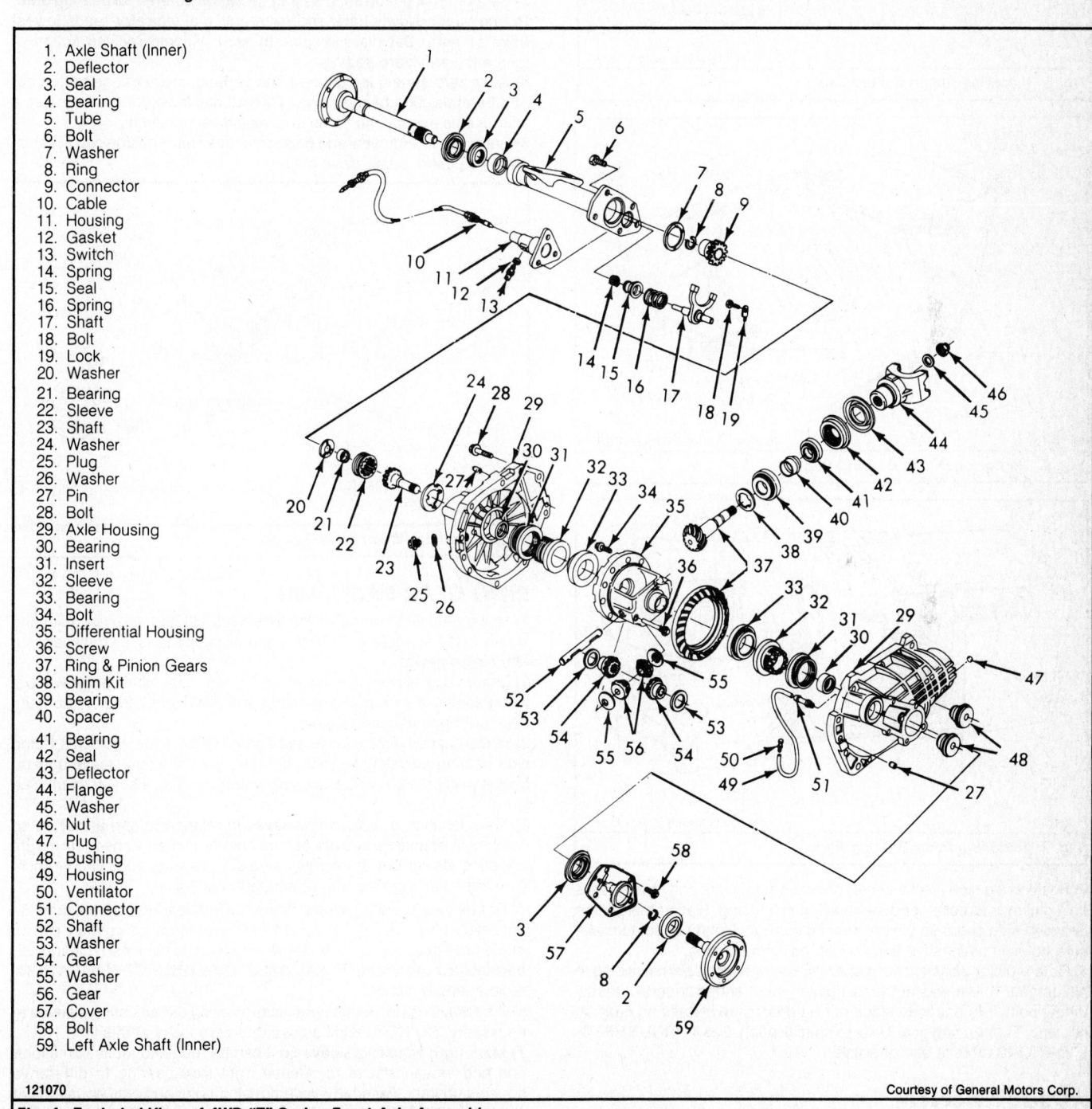

1. Axle Shaft (Inner)
2. Deflector
3. Seal
4. Bearing
5. Tube
6. Bolt
7. Washer
8. Ring
9. Connector
10. Cable
11. Housing
12. Gasket
13. Switch
14. Spring
15. Seal
16. Spring
17. Shaft
18. Bolt
19. Lock
20. Washer
21. Bearing
22. Sleeve
23. Shaft
24. Washer
25. Plug
26. Washer
27. Pin
28. Bolt
29. Axle Housing
30. Bearing
31. Insert
32. Sleeve
33. Bearing
34. Bolt
35. Differential Housing
36. Screw
37. Ring & Pinion Gears
38. Shim Kit
39. Bearing
40. Spacer
41. Bearing
42. Seal
43. Deflector
44. Flange
45. Washer
46. Nut
47. Plug
48. Bushing
49. Housing
50. Ventilator
51. Connector
52. Shaft
53. Washer
54. Gear
55. Washer
56. Gear
57. Cover
58. Bolt
59. Left Axle Shaft (Inner)

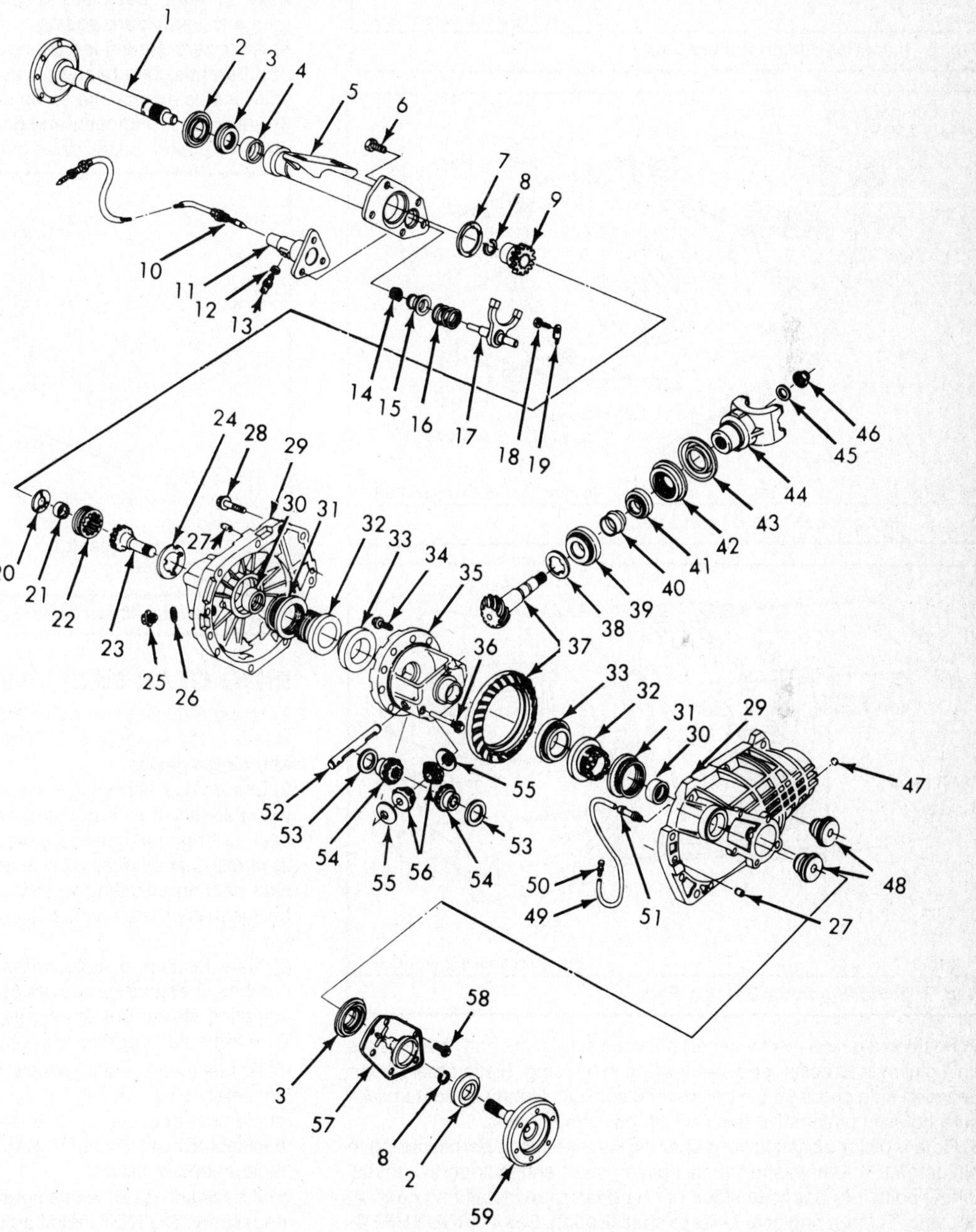
1
2
3
4
5
6
7
8
9
10
11
12
13
14
15
16
17
18
19
20
21
22
23
24
25
26
27
28
29
30
31
32
33
34
35
36
37
38
39
40
41
42
43
44
45
46
47
48
49
50
51
52
53
54
55
56
57
58
59

121070

Courtesy of General Motors Corp.

Fig. 4: Exploded View of 4WD "T" Series Front Axle Assembly

1991 DRIVE AXLES
"T" Series 4WD Front Axle (Cont.)

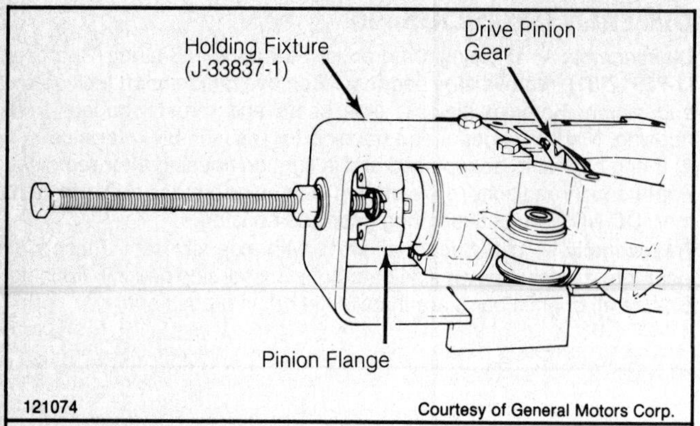
Holding Fixture
(J-33837-1)
Drive Pinion
Gear
Pinion Flange
121074
Courtesy of General Motors Corp.

Fig. 5: Installing Pinion Fixture Tool

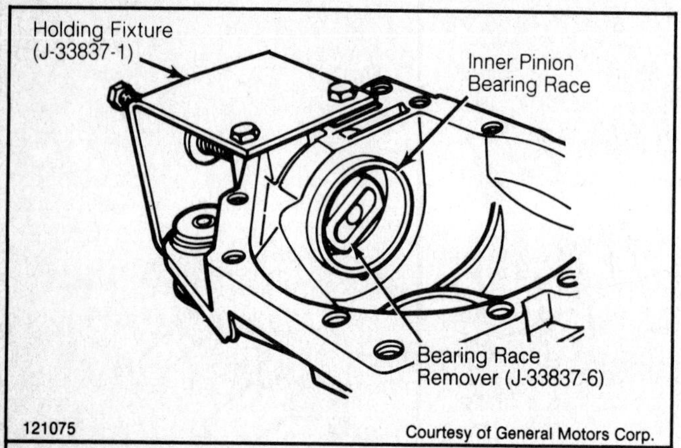
Holding Fixture
(J-33837-1)
Inner Pinion
Bearing Race
Bearing Race
Remover (J-33837-6)
121075
Courtesy of General Motors Corp.

Fig. 6: Removing Pinion Bearing Race

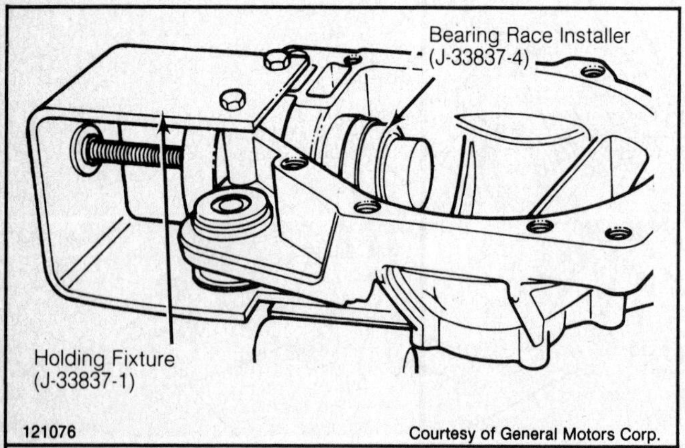
Bearing Race Installer
(J-33837-4)
Holding Fixture
(J-33837-1)
121076
Courtesy of General Motors Corp.

Fig. 7: Installing Inner Bearing Race

2) Position a pinion (with washer) between side gears and rotate gears until pinion is directly opposite opening in housing. Place other pinion between side gears so pinion shaft holes align. Rotate gears to make sure holes in pinions will line up with holes in housing.

3) Rotate pinions back toward opening just enough to permit sliding in pinion gear thrust washer. Install pinion shaft and lock screw. Install 2 new bolts into opposite sides of ring gear, then install ring gear on housing. Tighten ring gear bolts to specification. See TORQUE SPECIFICATIONS table at end of article.

ADJUSTMENTS

DRIVE PINION DEPTH

1) Lubricate inner and outer pinion bearings liberally with axle lubricant. Hold pinion bearings in position and install Pinion Shim Setting Gauge (J-33838). With gauge installed, preload inner and outer pinion bearing to 15-25 INCH lbs. (1.7-2.8 N.m) by tightening mounting bolt while holding end of gauge shaft with a wrench.

2) Using Dial Indicator (J-29763), set reading to zero, then position dial indicator on pinion shim setting gauge. Push dial indicator downward until needle rotates approximately 3 turns clockwise. Tighten dial indicator in this position. *See Fig. 8.*

NOTE: All "T" series 4WD front axle drive pinions are nominal or zero, and are not marked. Shim thickness will equal dial indicator gauge reading.

3) Set button of pinion shim setting gauge on differential bearing bore. Rotate gauge slowly back and forth until dial indicator reads lowest point of bore. Set dial indicator to zero. Repeat rocking action of gauge to verify zero setting.

4) After zero setting is obtained and verified, move gauge button out of differential side bearing bore. Record dial indicator reading. Use a shim that is exactly the same size as indicator reading.

5) Remove dial indicator and gauge from carrier. Position correct shim on drive pinion. Install drive pinion.

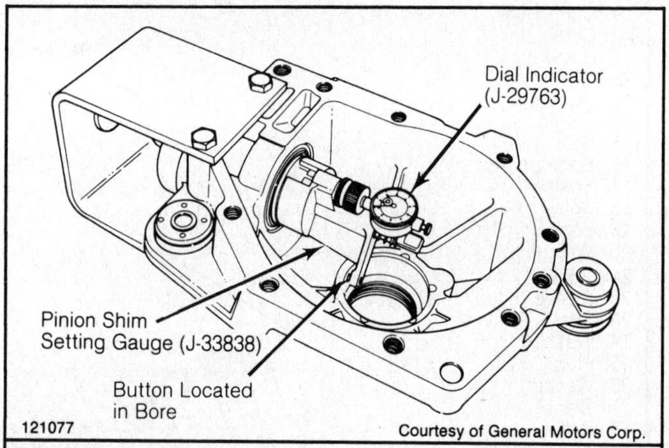
Dial Indicator
(J-29763)
Pinion Shim
Setting Gauge (J-33838)
Button Located
in Bore
121077
Courtesy of General Motors Corp.

Fig. 8: Setting Pinion Shim Gauge

RING GEAR BACKLASH

1) Using Side Bearing Adjusting Wrench (J-33792), turn left adjusting sleeve in toward differential housing until backlash is felt between ring and pinion gears.

2) Ensure carrier mating surfaces are clean. Assemble carrier without using sealer. If axle housing halves will not make complete contact, back out right adjusting sleeve.

3) Install 4 axle housing bolts and tighten to 37 ft. lbs. (50 N.m). Using side bearing adjusting wrench, tighten right adjusting sleeve until no backlash is present, which is approximately 100 ft. lbs. (140 N.m). *See Fig. 9.*

4) Mark location of adjusting sleeves in relation to carrier halves so notches in adjusting sleeves can be counted when turned. Turn right adjusting sleeve out 2 notches using side bearing adjusting wrench. Turn left adjusting sleeve in one notch. *See Fig. 10.*

5) Rotate axle housing several times to seat bearings, then mount dial indicator. Use a small button on indicator stem so contact can be made near heel end of tooth angle for accurate backlash reading. Set backlash to specification. See AXLE ASSEMBLY SPECIFICATIONS table at end of article.

6) If backlash is not within specification, readjust adjusting sleeves as necessary. DO NOT install adjusting sleeve locks at this time.

7) Mark right adjusting sleeve so it can be repositioned in same location and loosen sleeve to release right side bearing to differential housing contact. Remove 4 axle housing bolts and axle housing half. Apply Loctite (514) on one axle housing surface.

8) Reinstall axle housing halves. Install 10 attaching bolts and tighten to specification. Reposition right adjusting sleeve in previous marked position and install both adjusting sleeve locks.

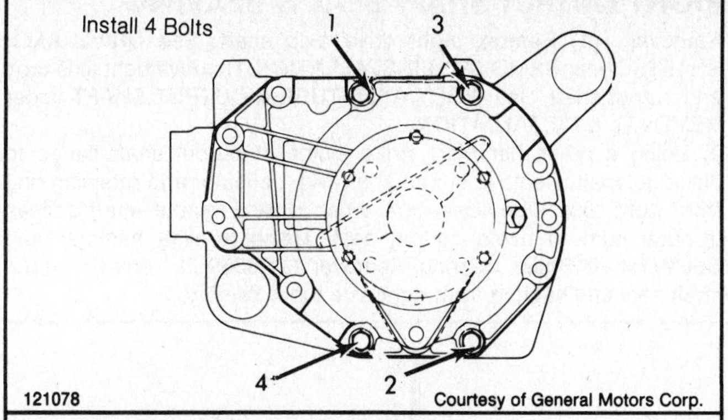

Install 4 Bolts
1
3
4
2

121078 Courtesy of General Motors Corp.

Fig. 9: Position of Bolts in Axle Housing

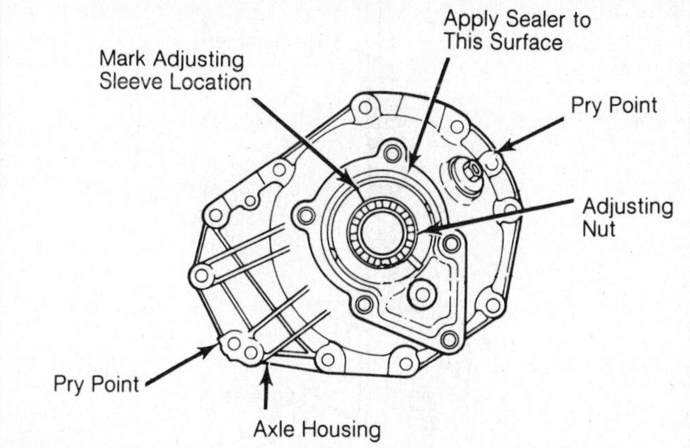

Apply Sealer to
This Surface
Mark Adjusting
Sleeve Location
Pry Point
Adjusting
Nut
Pry Point
Axle Housing

121079 Courtesy of General Motors Corp.

Fig. 10: Marking Adjusting Sleeve Location

9) Perform gear tooth contact pattern check. See GEAR TOOTH CONTACT PATTERNS article in GENERAL INFORMATION.

AXLE ASSEMBLY SPECIFICATIONS

AXLE ASSEMBLY SPECIFICATIONS

Application	In. (mm)
Ring Gear Backlash	.003-.010 (.08-.25)
Ring Gear Backlash Runout	.003 (.08)
	INCH Lbs. (N.m)
Pinion Bearing Preload	15-25 (1.7-2.8)

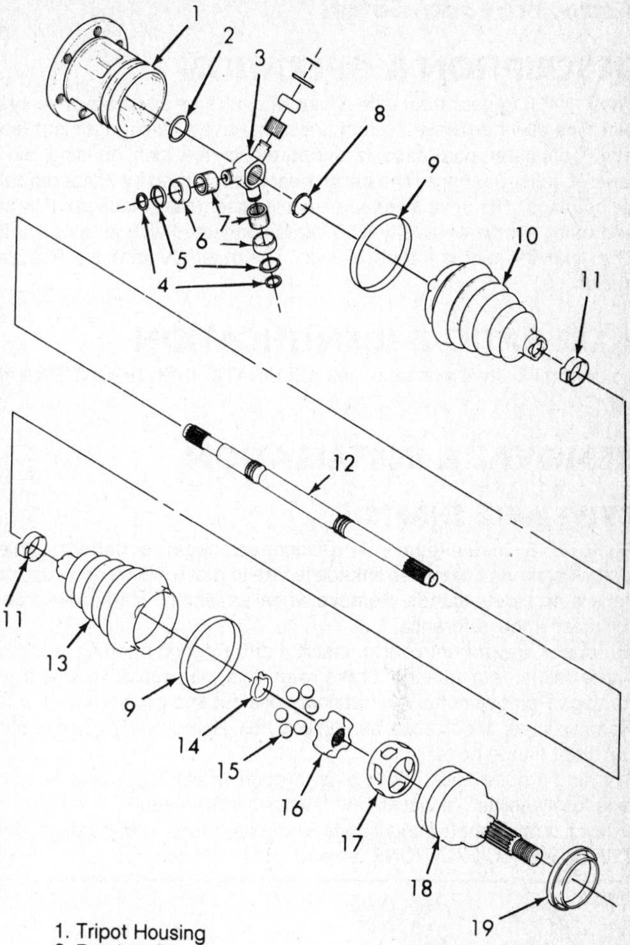

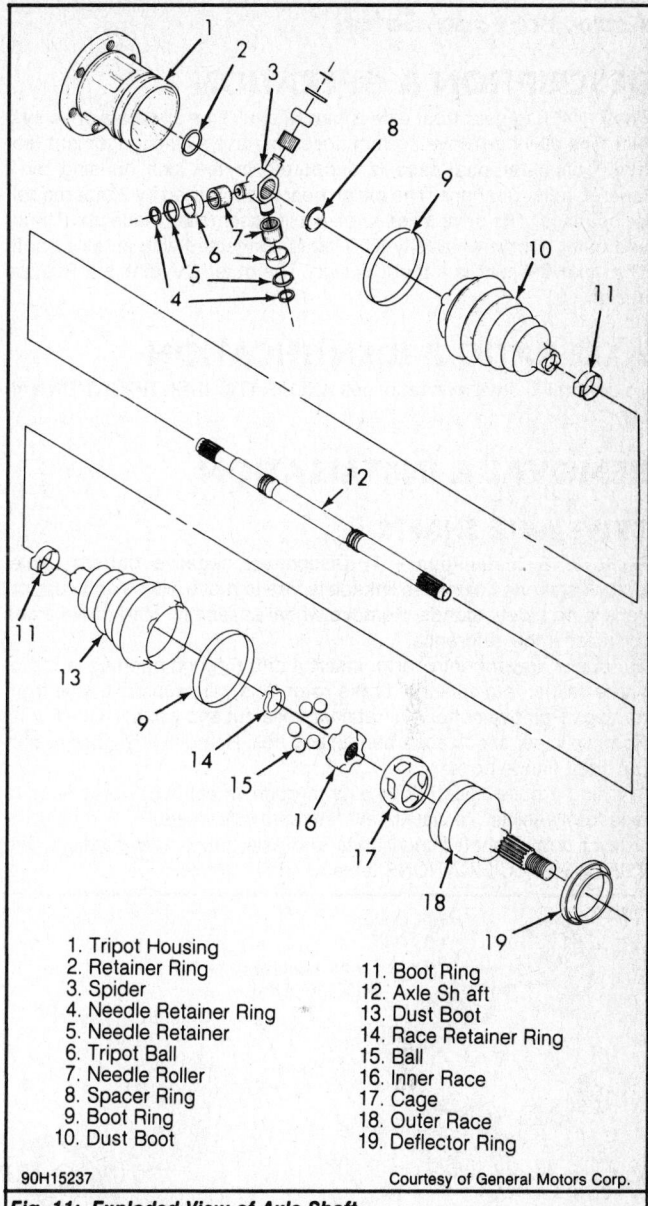

1. Tripot Housing
2. Retainer Ring
3. Spider
4. Needle Retainer Ring
5. Needle Retainer
6. Tripot Ball
7. Needle Roller
8. Spacer Ring
9. Boot Ring
10. Dust Boot
11. Boot Ring
12. Axle Sh aft
13. Dust Boot
14. Race Retainer Ring
15. Ball
16. Inner Race
17. Cage
18. Outer Race
19. Deflector Ring

90H15237 Courtesy of General Motors Corp.

Fig. 11: Exploded View of Axle Shaft

TORQUE SPECIFICATIONS

TORQUE SPECIFICATIONS

Application	Ft. Lbs. (N.m)
Adjusting Sleeve Lock Nut	14 (19)
Axle Housing Bolts	30-40 (40-54)
Axle Housing-To-Frame Bolts	65 (88)
Axle Hub Nut	160-200 (217-271)
Cable Switch Housing Bolts	30-40 (40-54)
Drive Axle-To-Output Flange Bolts	60 (81)
Front Propeller Shaft Bolts	15 (20)
Idler Arm-To-Frame Bolts	60 (81)
Lower Shock Bolt	54 (73)
Right Axle Tube-To-Housing Nuts	55 (75)
Ring Gear Attaching Bolts	52-66 (71-89)
Tie Rod Nut	35 (47)
Upper Ball Joint Nut	61 (83)
Wheel Lug Nuts	
Aluminum	90 (122)
Steel	73 (99)
	INCH Lbs. (N.m)
Shift Cable Coupling Nut	90 (10)

1991 DRIVE AXLES
All-Wheel Drive Front Axle

Astro, Bravada, Safari

DESCRIPTION & OPERATION

The 7 1/4" ring gear front axle is part of a full time all-wheel drive system. The all-wheel drive system does not have a disengagement feature. The differential case is supported in the axle housing by 2 tapered roller bearings. The pinion gear is supported by 2 tapered roller bearings. The drive axles are flexible assemblies made up of inner and outer constant velocity (CV) joints connected with an axle shaft. The inner CV joint is a tripot design. The outer CV joint is a Rzeppa design.

AXLE RATIO & IDENTIFICATION

To determine drive axle ratio, see AXLE RATIO IDENTIFICATION article.

REMOVAL & INSTALLATION

DRIVE AXLE SHAFTS

Removal & Installation - 1) Disconnect negative battery cable. Unlock steering column so linkage is free to move. Raise and support vehicle on safety stands. Remove wheel assembly. Mark drive axles for reassembly reference.

2) Support lower control arm. Insert a drift through opening in top of brake caliper into vanes of brake rotor (this will keep drive axle from turning). Remove cotter pin, retainer, axle nut and washer. *See Fig. 1.* Remove lower shock absorber nut and bolt. Remove drive axle to output shaft flange bolts.

3) Using a puller, push drive axle through wheel hub. Remove drive axle from vehicle. To install, reverse removal procedure. Torque drive axle to output shaft flange bolts and axle nut to specification. See TORQUE SPECIFICATIONS table at end of article.

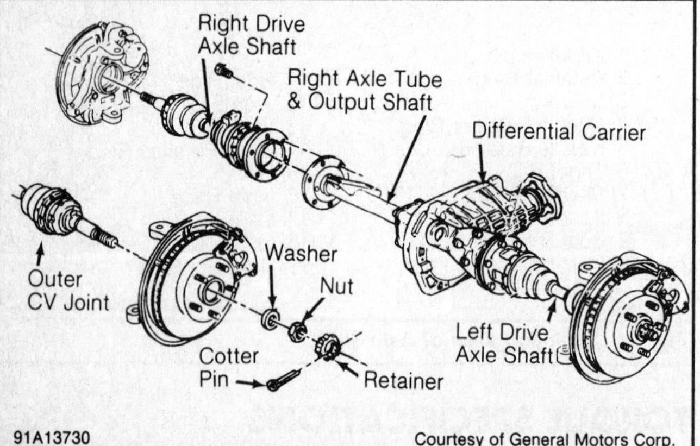
Right Drive
Axle Shaft
Right Axle Tube
& Output Shaft
Differential Carrier
Outer
CV Joint
Washer
Nut
Cotter
Pin
Retainer
Left Drive
Axle Shaft
91A13730
Courtesy of General Motors Corp.

Fig. 1: Exploded View of All-Wheel Drive Front Axle Assembly

RIGHT AXLE TUBE & OUTPUT SHAFT

NOTE: If differential fluid is not drained prior to removal of right axle tube, some differential fluid may spill out when axle tube is removed.

Removal - Remove right drive axle shaft. See DRIVE AXLE SHAFTS under REMOVAL & INSTALLATION. Remove right axle tube support bracket bolts and nuts from vehicle frame. Remove axle tube to differential carrier bolts. Remove right axle tube and output shaft from differential carrier.

Installation - Apply Loctite (514) on axle tube to differential surface. Align splines on output axle shaft to differential splines. Install right axle tube and output axle shaft to differential carrier. To complete installation, reverse removal procedure. Torque bolts and nuts to specification. See TORQUE SPECIFICATIONS table at end of article. Ensure differential fluid level is full.

RIGHT OUTPUT SHAFT SEAL & BEARING

Removal - 1) Remove right drive axle shaft. See DRIVE AXLE SHAFTS under REMOVAL & INSTALLATION. Remove right axle tube and output shaft. See RIGHT AXLE TUBE & OUTPUT SHAFT under REMOVAL & INSTALLATION.

2) Using a brass hammer, strike inside of output shaft flange to dislodge shaft. Remove output shaft with deflector and retaining ring from right axle tube. Use care when pulling output shaft splines through seal to avoid cutting seal. Using a slide hammer and Countershaft Roller Bearing Remover (J-29369-2), remove output shaft seal and bearing from right axle tube. *See Fig. 2.*

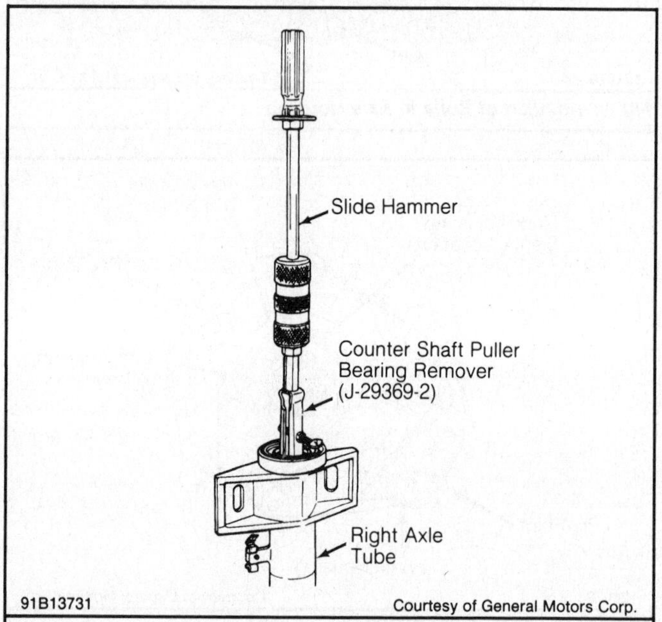
Slide Hammer
Counter Shaft Puller
Bearing Remover
(J-29369-2)
Right Axle
Tube
91B13731
Courtesy of General Motors Corp.

Fig. 2: Removing Right Axle Tube Bearing & Seal

Installation - 1) Lubricate seal lips, bearings and bearing surfaces with axle lubricant. Using Axle Tube Bearing Installer (J-33844), install bearing into axle tube.

2) Using Output Shaft Seal Installer (J-33893), install seal into axle tube. Install axle shaft into axle tube using care to not cut seal with splines of axle shaft. To complete installation, reverse removal procedure.

PINION FLANGE & OIL SEAL

Removal - 1) Unlock steering column so linkage is free to move. Raise and support vehicle on safety stands. Place a reference mark on propeller shaft and pinion flange for reassembly reference. Remove bolts from pinion flange. Remove propeller shaft from pinion flange and support shaft out of way.

2) Using an INCH lb. torque wrench, check and record pinion preload. This measurement gives combined pinion bearing, seal, carrier bearing, axle bearing and seal preload.

3) Mark pinion flange, pinion shaft and pinion nut to ensure proper alignment and bearing preload can be maintained on installation. Using Pinion Flange Remover Set (J-8614-01), hold pinion flange stationary and remove pinion flange nut and washer. Place a container under pinion flange opening to catch differential fluid. Remove pinion flange and oil seal.

4) Clean pinion flange in solvent and inspect seal surface of pinion flange for nicks, burrs or damage such as a groove worn into pinion flange by oil seal. Repair or replace as necessary.

Installation - 1) Lubricate pinion flange surface and sealing lip of oil seal. Using Seal Installer (J-33782), install pinion oil seal. Install pinion flange onto pinion shaft with marks aligned. Install pinion nut. Tighten pinion nut a little at a time. Turn pinion flange several times after each turn of pinion nut to ensure bearings are seated. Tighten pinion nut to position marked on pinion shaft.

2) Check pinion bearing preload. If preload is 3-5 INCH lbs. (.3-.6 N.m) more than preload recorded before disassembly, installation of pinion nut is complete. If preload is not 3-5 INCH lbs. (.3-.6 N.m) more than preload recorded before disassembly, tighten pinion nut until preload is 3-5 INCH lbs. (.3-.6 N.m) more than preload before disassembly. DO NOT overtighten pinion nut.

DIFFERENTIAL CARRIER

Removal & Installation – 1) Remove drive axle shafts. See DRIVE AXLE SHAFTS under REMOVAL & INSTALLATION. Remove right axle tube and output shaft. See RIGHT AXLE TUBE & OUTPUT SHAFT under REMOVAL & INSTALLATION.

2) Place a reference mark on propeller shaft and pinion flange for reassembly reference. Remove bolts from pinion flange. Remove propeller shaft from pinion flange and support shaft out of way.

3) Support differential carrier assembly. Remove upper mounting bolt and nut. Remove lower mounting bolt and nut. Slide front carrier assembly to the right. Drop right side of carrier assembly and twist to clear mounting brackets, oil pan and steering linkage. Remove differential carrier assembly from vehicle.

OVERHAUL

DIFFERENTIAL & CARRIER

Disassembly – 1) Using a slide hammer and Adapter (J-21579), remove left output shaft and deflector. *See Fig. 3*. Remove cover-to-carrier bolts securing left cover. Tap cover to loosen and remove.

2) Remove 10 bolts holding differential carrier halves together. Insert screwdriver in slots provided (one next to fill plug and one 180 degrees from fill plug) and pry differential carrier halves apart.

3) Remove differential from differential carrier. Remove side bearing bolts and lock tabs from both differential carrier halves. Remove race for both differential side bearings by turning side bearing adjusting sleeve with Side Bearing Adjuster Wrench (J-33792) until race is pushed out of carrier.

4) Using Pinion Flange Remover Set (J-8614-01), remove pinion flange nut and washer. Install Holding Fixture (J-33837-1) on left carrier case half. Thread Bolt (J-33837-3) into Fixture (J-33837-1). Turn Bolt (J-33837-3) to remove pinion flange and deflector.

5) Remove pinion shaft with spacer, pinion bearings and shim from left carrier half. Remove outer bearing and spacer from pinion shaft. Using a press, remove inner bearing and shim from pinion shaft.

6) Install Holding Fixture (J-33837-1) onto left carrier half. Thread Bolt (J-33837-3) into Fixture (J-33837-1). Place Driver (J-33837-6) in front of bearing race in left carrier half. *See Fig. 4*. Turn Bolt (J-33837-3) to press outer pinion shaft bearing race from carrier half.

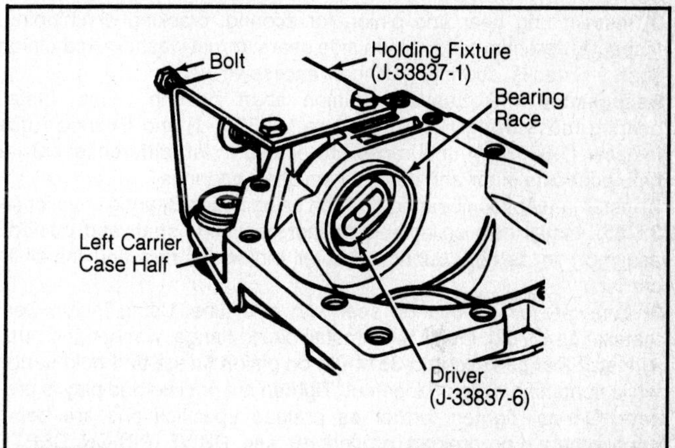
Bolt
Holding Fixture
(J-33837-1)
Bearing
Race
Left Carrier
Case Half
Driver
(J-33837-6)

91D13733 Courtesy of General Motors Corp.

Fig. 4: Removing Pinion Shaft Bearing Race

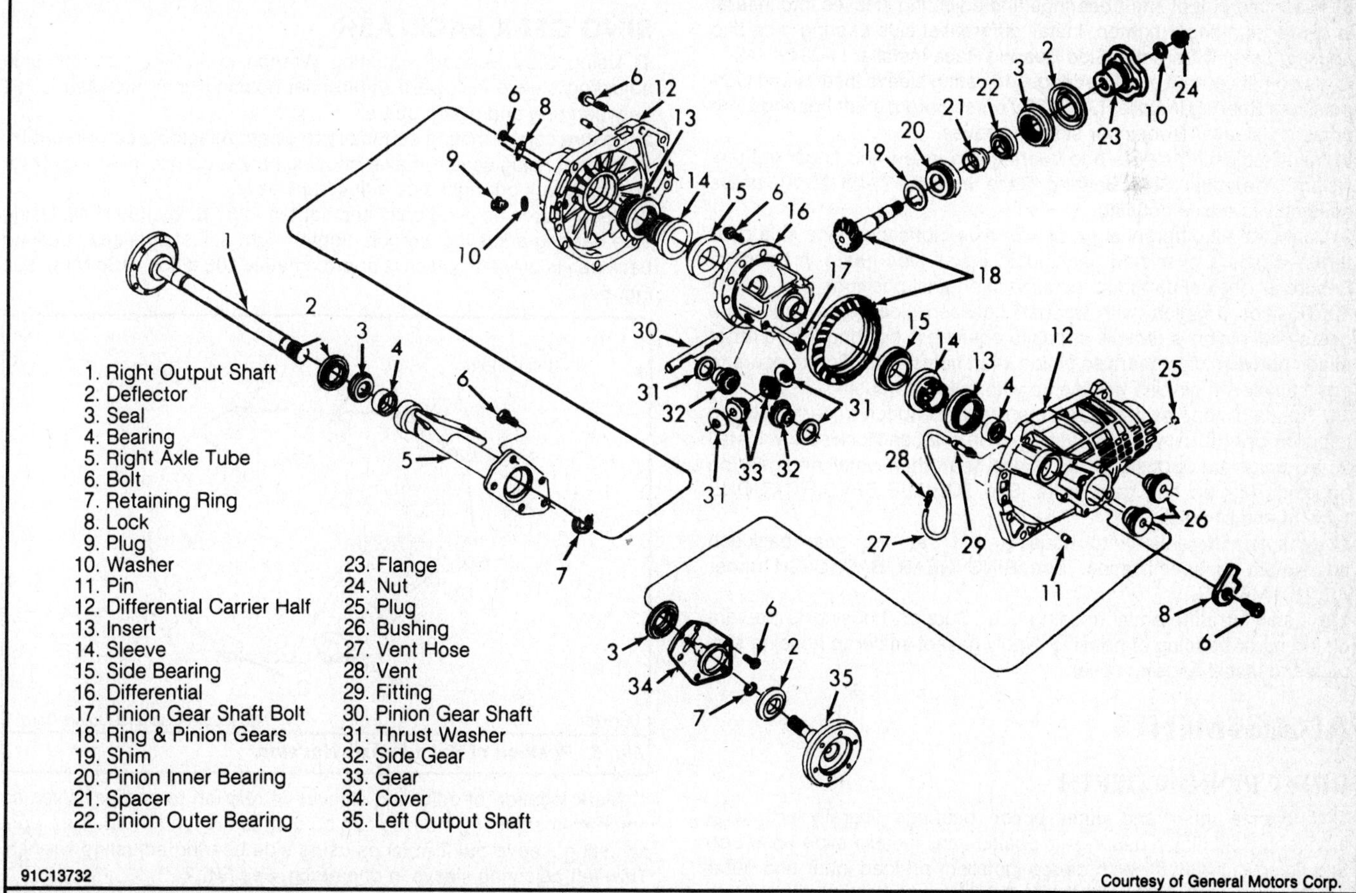
1. Right Output Shaft
2. Deflector
3. Seal
4. Bearing
5. Right Axle Tube
6. Bolt
7. Retaining Ring
8. Lock
9. Plug
10. Washer
11. Pin
12. Differential Carrier Half
13. Insert
14. Sleeve
15. Side Bearing
16. Differential
17. Pinion Gear Shaft Bolt
18. Ring & Pinion Gears
19. Shim
20. Pinion Inner Bearing
21. Spacer
22. Pinion Outer Bearing
23. Flange
24. Nut
25. Plug
26. Bushing
27. Vent Hose
28. Vent
29. Fitting
30. Pinion Gear Shaft
31. Thrust Washer
32. Side Gear
33. Gear
34. Cover
35. Left Output Shaft

91C13732 Courtesy of General Motors Corp.

Fig. 3: Exploded View of All-Wheel Drive Front Axle Assembly

1991 DRIVE AXLES
All-Wheel Drive Front Axle (Cont.)

7) Remove pinion gear shaft bolt. *See Fig. 3*. Remove pinion gear shaft. Remove pinion gears, side gears and thrust washers. Mark pinion gears and side gears for reassembly reference.
8) Remove ring gear bolts. Remove ring gear, using a brass drift and hammer if necessary. Using Side Bearing Remover (J-22912-01), remove side bearings. Using Bushing Remover (J-33791), remove side bearing bushings.
Cleaning & Inspection – 1) Clean all parts in cleaning solvent. Inspect all bearings, bearing races and rollers for scoring, chipping or excessive wear. Inspect axle shaft and side gear splines for excessive wear.

NOTE: DO NOT steam clean any parts having a ground and polished surface, such as bearings, gears and shafts.

2) Inspect ring gear and pinion for scoring, cracking or chipping. Inspect differential case, pinion side gears, thrust washers and pinion shaft for cracks, scoring, galling or excessive wear.
Reassembly – 1) Lubricate pinion shaft bearing races. Install bearing races using Holding Fixture (J-33837-1) and Bearing Race Installer (J-33837-4) until races are seated in left differential carrier half. Lubricate inner and outer pinion shaft bearings.
2) Install inner pinion bearing on shaft using Pinion Bearing Installer (J-33785). Install new collapsible spacer on pinion shaft and position assembly in carrier. Lubricate outer pinion bearing and install in carrier.
3) Lubricate pinion bearing seal with axle lube. Using Pinion Seal Installer (J-33782), install seal. Install pinion flange, washer and nut.
4) Install Flange Holder (J-8614-01) on pinion flange and hold flange while tightening pinion flange nut. Tighten nut until no end play is present. Do not tighten further as preload specifications are being approached. For preload procedure, see DRIVE PINION DEPTH under ADJUSTMENTS.
5) Rotate pinion several times to ensure bearings have been seated. Set final preload to 15-25 INCH lbs. (1.7-2.8 N.m).
6) Assemble output shaft bearings and adjusting sleeves into inserts in carrier and finger tighten. Install differential side bearing race into housing using Differential Side Bearing Race Installer (J-23423-A).
7) Using new output shaft bearings, adjusting sleeve inserts and Output Shaft Bearing Installer (J-33788), press output shaft bearings into adjusting sleeves from inner side of sleeves.
8) Install adjusting sleeve and bearing into insert and finger tighten. Using Differential Side Bearing Race Installer (J-23423-A), press assembly into axle housing.
9) Lubricate all differential parts with axle lubricant. Place side gear thrust washers over side gear hubs. Install side gears in housing. Ensure all original parts are installed in original positions.
10) Position a pinion (with washer) between side gears and rotate gears until pinion is directly opposite opening in housing. Place other pinion between side gears so pinion shaft holes align. Rotate gears to ensure holes in pinions will line up with holes in housing.
11) Rotate pinions back toward opening just enough to permit sliding in pinion gear thrust washer. Install pinion shaft and lock screw. Install 2 new bolts into opposite sides of ring gear, then install ring gear on housing. Tighten ring gear bolts. See TORQUE SPECIFICATIONS table at end of article.
12) Install differential into housing and set ring gear backlash adjustment to specification. See RING GEAR BACKLASH under ADJUSTMENTS.
13) Install left differential housing seal. Support housing to prevent distorting or bending of housing. Apply gasket sealer to housing surface and install housing cover.

ADJUSTMENTS

DRIVE PINION DEPTH

1) Lubricate inner and outer pinion bearings liberally with axle lubricant. Hold pinion bearings in position and install Pinion Shim Setting Gauge (J-33838). With gauge installed, preload inner and outer pinion bearing to 15-25 INCH lbs. (1.7-2.8 N.m) by tightening mounting bolt while holding end of gauge shaft with a wrench.
2) Using Dial Indicator (J-29763), set reading to zero, then position dial indicator on pinion shim setting gauge. Push dial indicator downward until needle rotates approximately 3 turns clockwise. Tighten dial indicator in this position. *See Fig. 5*.

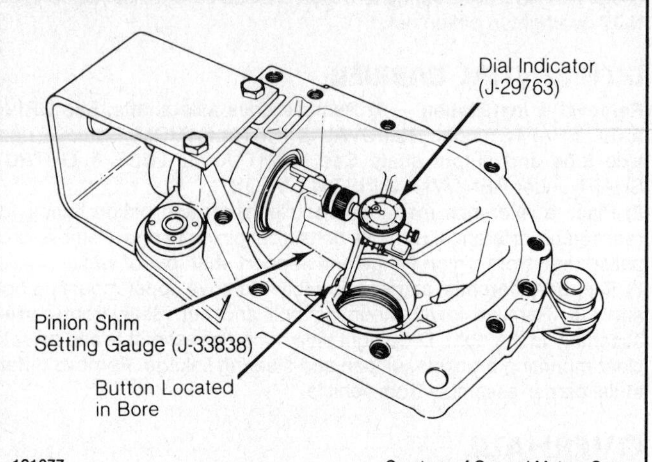
Dial Indicator
(J-29763)
Pinion Shim
Setting Gauge (J-33838)
Button Located
in Bore
121077
Courtesy of General Motors Corp.
Fig. 5: Setting Pinion Shim Gauge

3) Set button of pinion shim setting gauge on differential bearing bore. Rotate gauge slowly back and forth until dial indicator reads lowest point of bore. Set dial indicator to zero. Repeat rocking action of gauge to verify zero setting.
4) After zero setting is obtained and verified, move gauge button out of differential side bearing bore. Record dial indicator reading. Use a shim that is exactly the same size as indicator reading.
5) Remove dial indicator and gauge from carrier. Position correct shim on drive pinion. Install drive pinion.

RING GEAR BACKLASH

1) Using Side Bearing Adjusting Wrench (J-33792), turn left side adjusting sleeve in toward differential housing until backlash is felt between ring and pinion gears.
2) Ensure carrier mating surfaces are clean. Assemble carrier together without using sealer. If axle housing halves do not make complete contact, back out right side adjusting sleeve.
3) Install 4 axle housing bolts and tighten to 37 ft. lbs. (50 N.m). Using side bearing adjusting wrench, tighten right adjusting sleeve until no backlash is present, which is approximately 100 ft. lbs. (136 N.m). *See Fig. 6*.

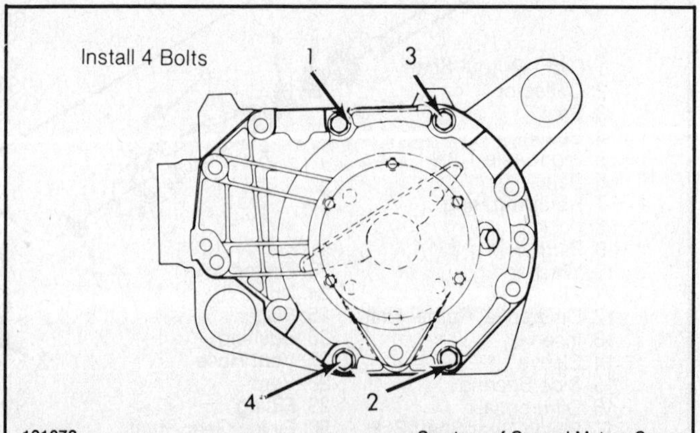
Install 4 Bolts
1
3
4
2
121078
Courtesy of General Motors Corp.
Fig. 6: Position of Bolts in Axle Housing

4) Mark location of adjusting sleeves in relation to carrier halves so notches in adjusting sleeves can be counted when turned. Turn right adjusting sleeve out 2 notches using side bearing adjusting wrench. Turn left adjusting sleeve in one notch. *See Fig. 7*.

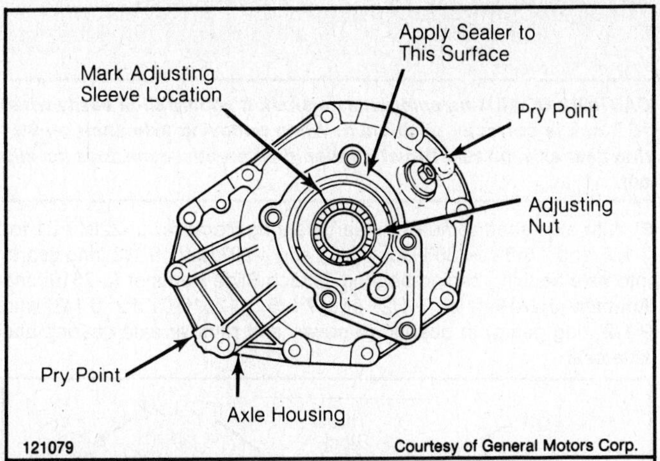

Apply Sealer to
This Surface
Mark Adjusting
Sleeve Location
Pry Point
Adjusting
Nut
Pry Point
Axle Housing
121079
Courtesy of General Motors Corp.

Fig. 7: Marking Adjusting Sleeve Location

5) Rotate axle housing several times to seat bearings, then mount dial indicator. Use small button on indicator stem so contact can be made near heel end of tooth angle for accurate backlash reading. Set backlash to specification. See AXLE ASSEMBLY SPECIFICATIONS table at end of article.

6) If backlash is not within specification, readjust adjusting sleeves as necessary. DO NOT install adjusting sleeve locks at this time.

7) Mark right adjusting sleeve so it can be repositioned in same location and loosen sleeve to release right side bearing to differential housing contact. Remove 4 axle housing bolts and axle housing half. Apply Loctite (514) on one axle housing surface.

8) Reinstall axle housing halves. Install 10 attaching bolts and tighten to specification. Reposition right adjusting sleeve in previous marked position and install both adjusting sleeve locks.

9) Perform gear tooth contact pattern check. See GEAR TOOTH CONTACT PATTERNS article in GENERAL INFORMATION.

AXLE ASSEMBLY SPECIFICATIONS

AXLE ASSEMBLY SPECIFICATIONS

Application	In. (mm)
Ring Gear Backlash	.003-.010 (.08-.25)
Ring Gear Backlash Runout	.003 (.08)
	INCH Lbs. (N.m)
Pinion Bearing Preload	15-25 (1.7-2.8)

TORQUE SPECIFICATIONS

TORQUE SPECIFICATIONS

Application	Ft. Lbs. (N.m)
Differential Carrier Case Bolts	35 (47)
Drive Axle Nut	160-200 (217-271)
Drive Axle-To-Output Flange Bolts	60 (81)
Front Axle Mounting Bolts	65 (88)
Idler Arm-To-Frame Bolts	60 (81)
Lower Shock Bolt	18 (24)
Pinion Flange Bolts	55 (75)
Right Axle Tube-To-Differential Carrier Bolts	36 (49)
Right Axle Tube-To-Support Bracket Bolts	55 (75)
Ring Gear Attaching Bolts	60 (81)
Wheel Lug Nuts	90 (122)
	INCH Lbs. (N.m)
Adjusting Sleeve Lock Bolt	71 (8)

1991 DRIVE AXLES
7 1/2", 7 5/8", 8 1/2" & 9 1/2" Ring Gears

Astro, Safari, "C" & "K" Series, "G" Series, "R" & "V" Series, "S" & "T" Series

***NOTE:** The 8 1/2" ring gear differential is also used as front drive axle on K15/25 models. These models may also be equipped with a Dana front drive axle. See appropriate article in DRIVE AXLES.*

DESCRIPTION

Axle assembly is hypoid gear type with integral carrier housing. It is used on Light Duty emission vehicles with semi-floating axles. Pinion bearing preload is made with a collapsible spacer. Differential side bearing preload adjustment and drive pinion depth adjustment are made by using shims.

A removable housing cover permits inspection and minor servicing of differential without removing axle from vehicle. Service procedures are same for all assemblies, except for torque specifications and special tool numbers. Astro and Safari use 7 5/8" ring gear. "S" and "T" series use 7 1/2" and 7 5/8" ring gears. All other models use 8 1/2" and 9 1/2" ring gears.

AXLE RATIO & IDENTIFICATION

To determine drive axle ratio, see AXLE RATIO IDENTIFICATION article.

REMOVAL & INSTALLATION

AXLE SHAFT & BEARING

Removal - 1) Raise vehicle. Support with jack stands. Remove wheels and brake drums. Place drain pan below cover. Loosen but do not remove differential cover bolts. Break cover loose and catch lubricant in drain pan. Remove differential cover bolts and remove cover.
2) Remove differential pinion shaft lock bolt. On axles without locking differential, remove differential pinion shaft. Push flanged end of axle shaft toward center of vehicle. Remove "C" lock from button end of axle shaft.
3) Remove axle shaft from axle housing, being careful not to damage seal. Repeat procedure for other side. *See Fig. 1.*

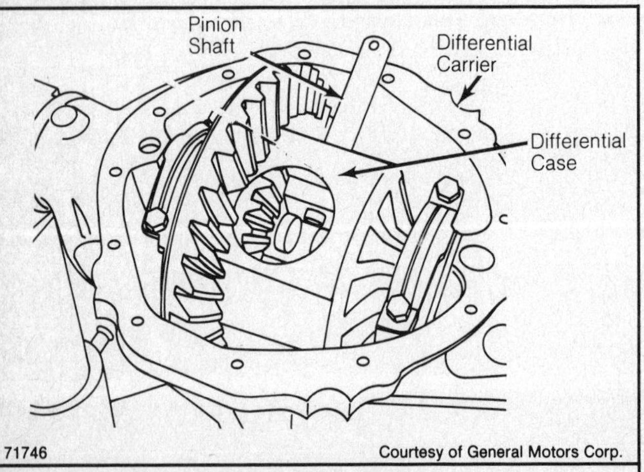
Pinion Shaft
Differential Carrier
Differential Case
71746
Courtesy of General Motors Corp.

Fig. 1: Positioning Case for Axle Removal

4) On axles with locking differential, partially remove pinion shaft. Rotate differential case until pinion shaft touches edge of housing. Reach into case with screwdriver and rotate "C" lock until its open end points directly inward. When "C" lock is correctly positioned, axle shaft can be pushed inward, allowing "C" lock to be removed. Remove axle shaft. *See Fig. 2.*

***CAUTION:** DO NOT hammer on axle shaft. It should slide easily when "C" lock is correctly positioned. When removing axle shaft on 9½" ring gear axle, be sure thrust washer in differential case does not slip out.*

5) With axle shaft removed, insert Bearing Remover (J-22813-01 for 7 1/2" and 7 5/8"; J-23689 for 8 1/2"; and J-29712 for 9 1/2" ring gears) into axle housing behind bearing. Attach Slide Hammer (J-2619) and Adapter (J-2619-4 for 7 1/2" and 7 5/8"; J-2619-01 for 8 1/2" and 9 1/2" ring gears) to bearing remover, and remove axle bearing and axle seal.

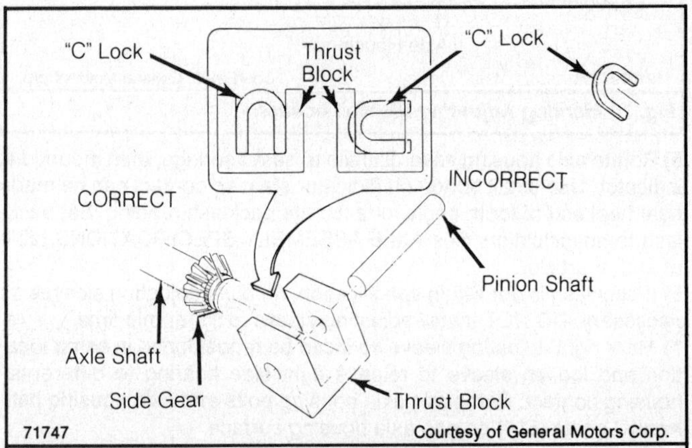
"C" Lock
Thrust Block
"C" Lock
CORRECT
INCORRECT
Pinion Shaft
Axle Shaft
Side Gear
Thrust Block
71747
Courtesy of General Motors Corp.

Fig. 2: Removing Locking Differential "C" Lock

Installation - 1) To install, reverse removal procedure. Using Bearing Installer (J-23765 for 7 1/2" and 7 5/8"; J-23690 for 8 1/2"; and J-29709 for 9 1/2" ring gears), install axle shaft housing bearing until bearing installer bottoms against housing shoulder.
2) Using Seal Installer (J-23771 for 7 1/2" and 7 5/8"; J-21128 for 8 1/2"; and J-29713 for 9 1/2" ring gears), install axle shaft housing seal until it is flush with outer edge of axle tube. After installing axle shaft and "C" lock, pull axle shaft outward so "C" lock seats in side gear counterbore. Install pinion shaft and pinion shaft lock bolt. Tighten bolt to specification. See TORQUE SPECIFICATIONS table at end of article.

PINION FLANGE & OIL SEAL

Removal - 1) Raise vehicle and allow axle assembly to hang free. Remove pinion flange bolts and position propeller shaft out of way.
2) Rotate pinion shaft through several revolutions using an INCH lb. torque wrench. Note and record pinion bearing preload. Mark relationship of pinion flange and shaft for reassembly. Count number of exposed threads on pinion shaft.
3) Hold flange with Companion Flange Holder (J-8614-01) and remove self-locking nut. Using Pinion Flange Remover (J-8614-1, 2 and 3 for 7 1/2" and 7 5/8"; and J-8614-01 for 8 1/2" and 9 1/2" ring gears), remove pinion flange. Pry pinion seal from housing.

***CAUTION:** Be careful not to damage differential carrier when removing pinion seal.*

Installation - 1) Inspect pinion flange oil seal surface, drive splines, ears and bearing contact surface. Replace pinion flange (if necessary). Pack oil seal lip cavity with lithium base extreme pressure lubricant. Place pinion seal in bore.
2) Using Seal Installer (J-23911 for 7 1/2" and 7 5/8" ring gears), Gauge Plate (J-22804-1 for 9 1/2" ring gear) and Seal Installer (J-23836 for 8 1/2" and 9 1/2" ring gears), drive pinion seal into place.
3) Make sure oil seal is square in carrier. Pack cavity between end of pinion splines and pinion flange with a non-hardening sealer. Using Companion Flange Holder (J-8614-01), install flange on pinion shaft.

1991 DRIVE AXLES
7 1/2", 7 5/8", 8 1/2" & 9 1/2" Ring Gears (Cont.)

4) Install washer and nut in original position, taking note of scribe marks and number of exposed threads. Measure pinion preload. Tighten nut in small increments until preload exceeds original figure by 3-5 INCH lbs. (.3-.6 N.m). Install propeller shaft and lower vehicle.

CAUTION: DO NOT hammer flange onto pinion shaft, as ring gear and pinion will be damaged.

AXLE ASSEMBLY

Removal & Installation – 1) Raise vehicle. Using jack stands, support vehicle at frame. Allow differential to hang free. Drain lubricant. Remove rear wheels and brake drums. Remove parking brake cable. Disconnect propeller shaft and brake lines. Disconnect vent hose from vent fitting at axle housing. Support axle housing with floor jack under center of carrier. Disconnect shock absorbers at axle housing.

2) Disconnect height sensing and brake proportional valve linkage (if equipped). Remove stabilizer shaft (if equipped). Remove "U" bolt, nuts, washers, spacers and spring plates from axle assembly. Slowly lower floor jack. Remove axle assembly from vehicle. To install axle assembly, reverse removal procedure. Bleed brake system.

OVERHAUL

DIFFERENTIAL ASSEMBLY

NOTE: Check and record ring gear backlash and pinion bearing preload before disassembly.

Disassembly – 1) Remove axle shafts as previously described. Roll out differential pinions and thrust washers. Mark pinions and thrust washers (left and right) for reassembly. Remove side gears and thrust washers. Mark side gears and thrust washers (left and right) for reassembly.

2) Mark differential bearing caps and housing for reassembly. Loosen bearing cap bolts and tap bearing cap surfaces to loosen caps. Using pry bar inserted in differential carrier, pry against housing at differential window to remove carrier.

CAUTION: Be careful, as carrier bearings are preloaded. Carrier will fall free after being pried past a certain point.

3) After removing carrier, place shims with appropriate bearing cups. Install bearing caps onto housing in their original position before removal. Using Differential Side Bearing Remover (J-22888) and Adapter (J-8107-2 for 7 1/2" and 7 5/8" ring gears; J-8107-4 for 8 1/2"; and J-8107-3 for 9 1/2" ring gears), remove differential side bearings.

NOTE: Ring gear bolts have left-hand threads.

4) Remove ring gear bolts. Tap ring gear off carrier using a soft drift and hammer. Using an INCH lb. torque wrench, check torque required to rotate drive pinion. If no preload reading is obtained, check for looseness of pinion assembly. Looseness indicates pinion bearings should be replaced.

5) Install Companion Flange Holder (J-8614-01) on flange, with holder notches toward flange. Remove pinion nut and washer. Remove flange. Install pinion nut halfway on pinion. Install differential cover using 2 bolts. Tap end of pinion (using soft drift and hammer) to remove pinion.

CAUTION: DO NOT damage pinion bearings when removing pinion from differential housing.

6) Remove differential cover and pinion assembly. Remove pinion oil seal and front bearing from housing. Remove collapsible spacer from pinion. Remove inner bearing and shim from pinion. Using Bearing Remover (J-25320 for 7 1/2" and 7 5/8"; J-8612-B for 8 1/2"; and J-22912-01 on 9 1/2" ring gears), press bearing from pinion.

7) Remove bearing cups from axle housing using hammer and punch in slotted areas. Inspect bearings and bearing cups, and replace them as required. Discard oil seal, pinion nut and collapsible spacer.

Cleaning & Inspection – Clean all parts in cleaning solvent. Inspect all bearings, bearing cups, races and rollers for chipping or excessive wear. Inspect axle shaft, ring gear and pinion for scoring, cracking or chipping. Inspect differential case, pinion side gears, thrust washers and pinion shaft for cracks or excessive wear.

Reassembly – 1) Lubricate all parts with gear oil. Install side gears and thrust washers into case as marked in disassembly. Install pinion gears into case without thrust washers. Install one pinion gear onto side gears and rotate gears until pinion gear is exactly opposite from pinion shaft opening in case. Place second pinion gear onto side gears so that pinion gear hole is exactly opposite from pinion shaft opening in case.

2) Verify that pinion shaft fits through pinion gears. Install pinion gear thrust washers. Install pinion shaft and pinion shaft lock bolt. Tighten bolt to specification. Install ring gear squarely onto case. Tighten ring gear bolts evenly and alternately to specification. See TORQUE SPECIFICATIONS table at end of article.

3) Install inner pinion bearing onto pinion using Bearing Installer (J-5590). Drive bearing onto pinion until bearing is seated on pinion shims. Install a new collapsible spacer. Install pinion into axle housing. Install outer bearing onto pinion using Bearing Installer (J-5590). Hold pinion forward from inside housing while driving bearing onto pinion.

4) If new ring and pinion or bearings were installed, see DRIVE PINION DEPTH and SIDE BEARING PRELOAD under ADJUSTMENTS. Install pinion oil seal and pinion flange. See PINION FLANGE & OIL SEAL under REMOVAL & INSTALLATION. To complete installation, see BACKLASH & FINAL ASSEMBLY under ADJUSTMENTS.

ADJUSTMENTS

DRIVE PINION DEPTH

1) Drive pinion rear bearing shim thickness must be determined whenever a new axle housing, ring and pinion set, or pinion bearings are installed. Shim pack thickness is determined by using Pinion Setting Gauge Set (J-21777).

2) If removed, install pinion bearing cups into housing. Place lubricated pinion bearings into cups. Position Gauging Plate (J-23597-11 for 7 1/2" and 7 5/8"; J-21777-29 for 8 1/2"; and J-21777-85 for 9 1/2" ring gears) and rear pinion bearing pilot on preloaded stud.

3) Install pinion bearing through rear of housing. Install front pinion bearings and Bearing Disc (J-21777-42). Tighten hex nut until snug. Rotate bearings to insure proper seating. Hold preload stud stationary with a wrench on flats. Tighten hex nut until 20 INCH lbs. (2.2 N.m) are required to rotate bearings. *See Fig. 3.*

4) Mount side bearing Gauging Discs (J-21777-45 for 7 1/2", 7 5/8" and 8 1/2"; and J-21777-86 for 9 1/2" ring gears) on ends of arbor. Place arbor into carrier making sure discs are properly seated. Install side bearing caps and bolts. Tighten bolts to avoid movement.

5) Position dial indicator on mounting post of arbor, with contact button resting on top surface of plunger. Set dial indicator at zero. Push indicator down on indicator shaft until needle rotates 3 to 4 revolutions to right, then tighten in this position.

6) Place plunger onto gauging area of gauge plate. Rock plunger rod slowly back and forth across gauging area until dial indicator reads greatest deflection.

7) Set indicator to zero. Repeat rocking action several times to verify setting. Once zero reading is obtained, swing plunger until it is removed from gauging area.

8) Dial indicator will now read required pinion shim thickness for a nominal pinion. Record this reading. Check drive pinion for painted or stamped markings on pinion stems, or for a stamped code number on small end of pinion gear.

9) If marking is a plus (+), add that many thousandths of an inch from indicator reading. If marking is a minus (-), subtract that many

1991 DRIVE AXLES
7 1/2", 7 5/8", 8 1/2" & 9 1/2" Ring Gears (Cont.)

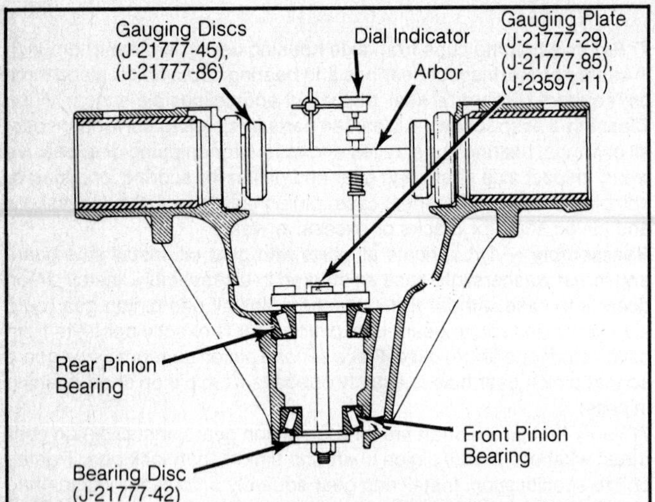
Gauging Discs
(J-21777-45),
(J-21777-86)
Dial Indicator
Gauging Plate
(J-21777-29),
(J-21777-85),
(J-23597-11)
Arbor
Rear Pinion
Bearing
Front Pinion
Bearing
Bearing Disc
(J-21777-42)
71748
Courtesy of General Motors Corp.

Fig. 3: Sectional View of Pinion Setting Gauge Set

thousandths of an inch from indicator reading. This will then be required thickness of rear pinion bearing shim pack.

NOTE: If no markings are found on pinion, use dial indicator reading as shim thickness.

10) Remove bearing caps and gauging tool from housing. Place selected shim pack on pinion gear. Using a press, install lubricated pinion bearing onto pinion shaft.
11) Install a new collapsible spacer over pinion gear shaft. Position pinion assembly in housing. While holding pinion forward, carefully drive front pinion bearing onto pinion gear shaft until a few threads are exposed.
12) Install seal, pinion flange, washer and nut. Tighten nut until all end play is removed. Rotate pinion several times to seat bearings. Check preload using an INCH lb. torque wrench.
13) Continue tightening nut and checking preload until specified preload is obtained. See AXLE ASSEMBLY SPECIFICATIONS table at end of article. DO NOT back off nut to lessen preload.
14) If preload is exceeded, a new collapsible spacer must be installed, and nut must be retightened until proper preload is obtained.

SIDE BEARING PRELOAD

7 1/2", 7 5/8" & 8 1/2" Ring Gears – 1) Side bearing preload is adjusted by varying the thickness of both left and right side bearing shims equally. Lubricate bearings and place differential assembly into position in housing. Hold in place by hand.
2) Install Bearing Strap (J-22779-6) on left bearing. Tighten bolts evenly to a snug fit. Install right bearing cap. Tighten bolts to a snug fit.
3) Position ring gear tight against pinion so backlash is .000-.001" (0-.025 mm). Insert Gauge (J-22779) between left bearing cup and carrier housing.
4) While moving gauge up and down, tighten adjusting nut on end of gauge until a slight drag is felt. Tighten lock bolt on side of tool.
5) Install adjustment spacer and shim between right bearing cup and axle housing. Determine bearing preload by inserting progressively larger feeler gauges between carrier and shim. The point just before drag begins is the correct feeler gauge thickness. This is the zero setting without preload.
6) Remove bearing strap, gauge, spacer, shim, feeler gauge and differential case from axle housing. Using a micrometer, measure and average readings in 3 places on gauge. Record measurement.
7) Add together dimensions of shim, spacer and feeler gauge. Subtract .010" (.25 mm) from ring gear (left) side measurement and add .010" (.25 mm) to opposite (right) side measurement. This allows for correct backlash adjustment.
8) To obtain correct preload, add .004" (.10 mm) to both measurements. The total is correct shim pack thickness for each side.

Example:

Ring Gear Side (Left) Shim Pack
.250" (Gauging Tool Measurement)
-.010" (Backlash Adjustment)
+.004" (Bearing Preload)
=.244" (Ring Gear Side Shim Pack)

Opposite Ring Gear Side (Right) Shim Pack
.265" (Combined Measurement Total)
+.010" (Backlash Adjustment)
+.004" (Bearing Preload)
=.279" (Opposite Ring Gear Side Shim Pack)

9) Install ring gear side shim first. Wedge opposite side shim between bearing cup and spacer. Install shim so chamfered side is against spacer.

NOTE: If shim is not chamfered enough and scrapes spacer when it is installed, file or grind chamfer before installation.

10) It may be necessary to partially remove differential when right side shim is installed. Tap shim into place with a soft-faced hammer. Tighten bearing cap bolts to specifications. Check backlash. See BACKLASH & FINAL ASSEMBLY.

9 1/2" Ring Gear – 1) Differential side bearing preload is adjusted by adjusting nut in differential bearing bore (right side). The bore and bearing cap provide the mating threads for the bearing nut. Install bearing cups to differential bearings in original locations.
2) Install differential case into axle housing assembly. Install bearing shims. Push case away from pinion towards axle housing and install adjusting nut. Tighten nut with Spanner Wrench (J-24429). Turn pinion to seat bearings.
3) Back off adjusting nut. Install bearing caps and bolts loosely in their original positions. Turn adjusting nut until nut contacts shim. Tighten nut 3 additional slots.
4) Tighten bearing cap bolts to specifications. Install adjusting nut lock bolt. Tighten to specification. Check backlash adjustment. See BACKLASH & FINAL ASSEMBLY.

BACKLASH & FINAL ASSEMBLY

1) Rotate case several times to seat bearings. Check backlash at 4 locations around outside edge of ring gear using a dial indicator mounted to axle housing. Install indicator in line with gear rotation and perpendicular to tooth angle. Pinion must be held steady while taking readings. Variation should not exceed .002" (.05 mm).
2) If backlash is incorrect, adjust side bearing shims as necessary. After adjustment is completed, perform gear tooth contact pattern check. See GEAR TOOTH CONTACT PATTERNS article in GENERAL INFORMATION. Install axle shafts and housing cover. *See Fig. 4.*

NOTE: Total shim pack thickness for right and left side combined must not be changed. If a shim is removed from one side, same thickness shim must be added to other side.

AXLE ASSEMBLY SPECIFICATIONS

AXLE ASSEMBLY SPECIFICATIONS

Application	Specification In. (mm)
Ring Gear Backlash	.005-.009 (.13-.23)
Side Bearing Preload	.008 (.20)
	INCH Lbs. (N.m)
Pinion Bearing Preload	
7 1/2" & 7 5/8" Ring Gear	
Used Bearings	8-12 (1.0-1.4)
New Bearings	24-32 (2.7-3.6)
8 1/2" & 9 1/2" Ring Gear	
Used Bearings	10-15 (1.1-1.7)
New Bearings	20-25 (2.3-2.8)

1991 DRIVE AXLES
7 1/2", 7 5/8", 8 1/2" & 9 1/2" Ring Gears (Cont.)

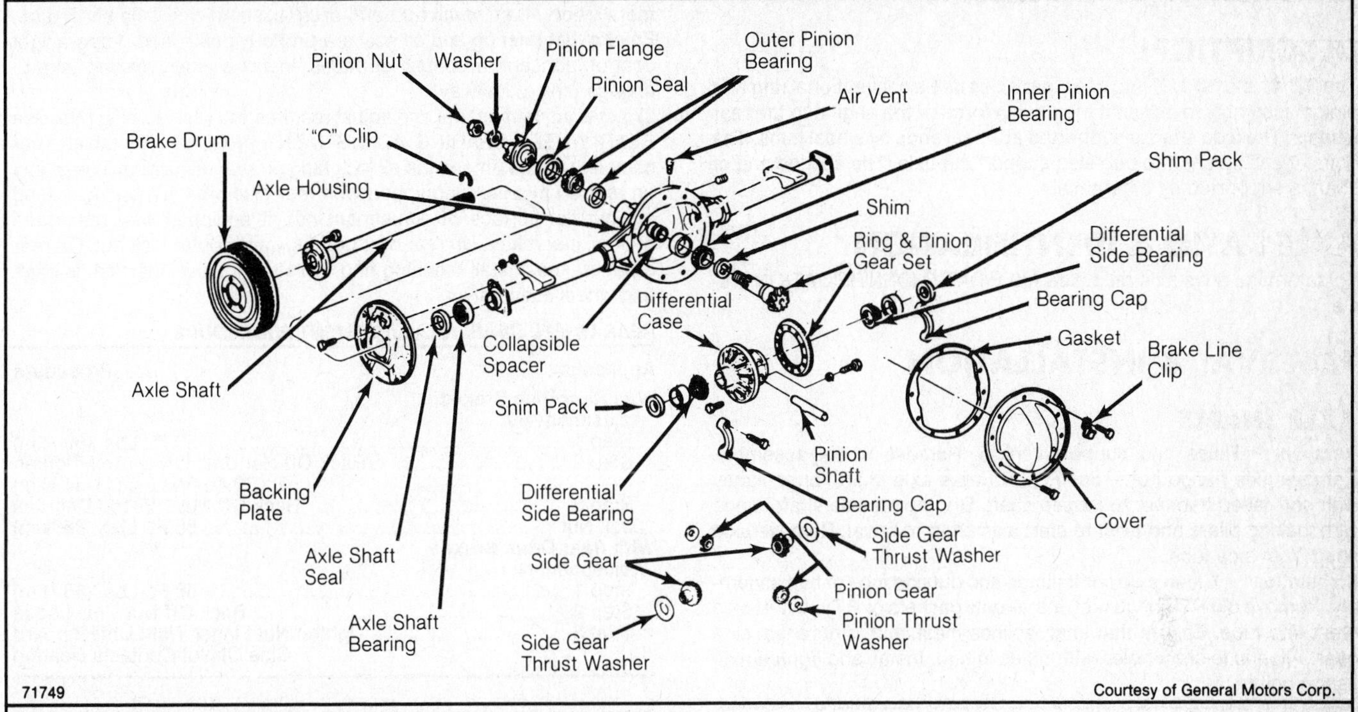
Pinion Nut
Washer
Pinion Flange
Pinion Seal
Outer Pinion Bearing
Air Vent
Inner Pinion Bearing
Shim Pack
Brake Drum
"C" Clip
Axle Housing
Shim
Ring & Pinion Gear Set
Differential Side Bearing
Bearing Cap
Gasket
Brake Line Clip
Differential Case
Collapsible Spacer
Axle Shaft
Shim Pack
Pinion Shaft
Backing Plate
Differential Side Bearing
Bearing Cap
Cover
Side Gear Thrust Washer
Axle Shaft Seal
Side Gear
Pinion Gear
Axle Shaft Bearing
Pinion Thrust Washer
Side Gear Thrust Washer
71749
Courtesy of General Motors Corp.

Fig. 4: Exploded View of Typical Ring Gear Axle Assembly (8 1/2" Shown)

TORQUE SPECIFICATIONS

TORQUE SPECIFICATIONS

Application	Ft. Lbs. (N.m)
Differential Bearing Adjusting Lock Bolt	
9 1/2" Ring Gear	22 (30)
Differential Cover Bolts	20 (27)
Pinion Shaft Lock Bolt	25 (34)
Ring Gear-To-Differential Case Bolt [1]	
7 1/2" & 7 5/8" Ring Gear	90 (122)
8 1/2" Ring Gear	60 (81)
9 1/2" Ring Gear	105 (142)
Side Bearing Cap Bolt	
7 1/2" Ring Gear	55 (75)
8 1/2" Ring Gear	60 (81)
9 1/2" Ring Gear	60 (81)
Side Bearing Preload Adjusting Nut Lock Bolt	
9 1/2" Ring Gear	22 (30)

[1] – Left-hand thread. Use new bolts.

1991 DRIVE AXLES
Dana 9 3/4" & 10 1/2" Full-Floating Axles

"C" & "K" Series, "G" Series, "P" Series, "R" & "V" Series

DESCRIPTION

The 9 3/4" and 10 1/2" ring gear rear axles use a conventional ring and pinion assembly to transmit the driving force of the engine to the rear wheels. The axle shaft is supported at wheel ends by wheel hubs. The bolts attaching shaft to hub also support the axle. The splined end of shaft is supported by differential.

AXLE RATIO & IDENTIFICATION

To determine drive axle ratio, see AXLE RATIO IDENTIFICATION article.

REMOVAL & INSTALLATION

AXLE SHAFTS

Removal - Raise and support vehicle. Remove wheel assembly. Remove axle flange bolts. *See Fig. 1.* Strike axle shaft flange lightly with soft-faced hammer to loosen shaft. Grip rib on axle shaft flange with locking pliers and twist to start axle shaft removal. Remove axle shaft from axle tube.

Installation - Clean axle shaft flange and outside face of hub assembly. Remove old RTV or gasket. Install new gaskets or RTV. Insert axle shaft into tube. Ensure that shaft splines mesh with differential side gear. Align axle shaft holes with holes in hub. Install and tighten axle flange bolts.

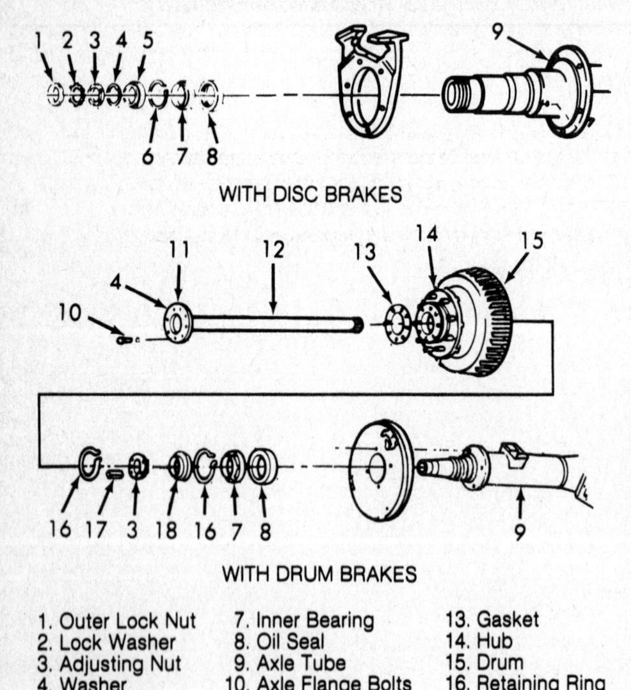
1 2 3 4 5
9
6 7 8
WITH DISC BRAKES
11
12
13
14
15
4
10
16 17 3 18 16 7 8
9
WITH DRUM BRAKES
1. Outer Lock Nut
2. Lock Washer
3. Adjusting Nut
4. Washer
5. Outer Bearing
6. Retaining Ring
7. Inner Bearing
8. Oil Seal
9. Axle Tube
10. Axle Flange Bolts
11. Axle Shaft Flange
12. Axle Shaft
13. Gasket
14. Hub
15. Drum
16. Retaining Ring
17. Key
18. Outer Bearing
91I13316
Courtesy of General Motors Corp.

Fig. 1: Exploded View of Axle & Hub Assembly

HUB & DRUM ASSEMBLY

Removal - Raise and support vehicle. Remove wheel assembly. Remove axle shaft. See AXLE SHAFTS under REMOVAL & INSTALLATION. Using Wheel Bearing Nut Wrench (J-2222-C), remove wheel bearing nut if equipped with rear disc brakes, or retaining ring if equipped with rear drum brakes. If equipped with rear disc brakes, remove lock tang. If equipped with rear disc brakes, remove key. On all rear axles, remove adjustment nut and washer. Remove hub and drum assembly.

Installation - **1)** Install hub and drum assembly on axle shaft tube. Ensure that bearing and oil seal are properly positioned. Apply a light coat of lubricant to contact surfaces. Install washer, making sure to engage tang in keyway.

2) Install adjustment nut and adjust rear bearing while turning hub. See REAR WHEEL BEARING ADJUSTMENT PROCEDURE table. After completing adjustment, install lock tang on rear disc brake axle or key on rear drum axle. If equipped with rear disc brakes, bend lock tang against flat surface of adjustment nut. If equipped with rear drum brakes, insert key. On rear disc brakes, install outer lock nut. On rear drum brakes, install retaining ring. On all rear axles, install axle shaft and wheel assembly.

REAR WHEEL BEARING ADJUSTMENT PROCEDURE

Application	Procedure
With Rear Disc Brakes	
Adjustment Nut	
Step 1	50 Ft. Lbs. (68 N.m)
Step 2	Back Off Nut Until Loose And Tighten To 30-40 Ft. Lbs. (41-54 N.m)
Step 3	Back Off Nut 135-150 Degrees
Lock Nut	65 Ft. Lbs. (88 N.m)
With Rear Drum Brakes	
Adjustment Nut	
Step 1	50 Ft. Lbs. (68 N.m)
Step 2	Back Off Nut Until Loose
Step 3	Tighten Nut Finger Tight Until Inboard Side Of Nut Contacts Bearing

PINION FLANGE & PINION SEAL

Removal - Raise and support vehicle. Remove propeller shaft. Mark pinion flange and drive pinion nut for reassembly reference. Using Pinion Flange Holder/Remover (J-8614-01), remove drive pinion nut and pinion flange. Pry drive pinion seal from bore, being careful not to damage machined surfaces.

Installation - **1)** Thoroughly clean machined surfaces. Lubricate inside diameter of seal. Pack cavity between pinion stem, pinion flange, and pinion nut washer with a non-hardening sealer.

2) Using Pinion Seal Installer (J-24384), drive oil seal into place. Using pinion flange holder/remover, install pinion flange and drive pinion nut. Ensure mark made during removal is aligned. Install propeller shaft.

REAR AXLE HOUSING ASSEMBLY

Removal - **1)** Raise and support vehicle. Place jack stands under frame side rails for support. Drain lubricant from axle. Remove propeller shaft. Remove wheel assemblies.

2) Remove hub and drum assembly. On models with rear disc brakes, see HUB & DRUM ASSEMBLY under REMOVAL & INSTALLATION. On all models, disconnect parking brake cable from lever and at brake flange plates. Remove hydraulic brake lines. Detach height-sensing/brake proportioning valve linkage, if equipped. Remove shock absorbers.

3) Remove stabilizer bar (if equipped). Disconnect hose from axle vent fitting (if equipped). Support rear axle assembly with floor jack and remove leaf spring "U" bolts. Carefully lower rear axle assembly and remove from vehicle.

Installation - Place rear axle assembly on floor jack. Raise rear axle assembly and install "U" bolts and nuts. To complete installation, reverse removal procedure.

DIFFERENTIAL ASSEMBLY

Removal & Installation - Removal and installation of differential assembly is covered as part of overhaul procedure. See DIFFERENTIAL ASSEMBLY under OVERHAUL.

1991 DRIVE AXLES
Dana 9 3/4" & 10 1/2" Full-Floating Axles (Cont.)

OVERHAUL

DIFFERENTIAL ASSEMBLY

Disassembly - 1) Properly support rear axle assembly. Remove differential cover bolts and cover. Drain lubricant from axle. Remove axle shafts. See AXLE SHAFTS under REMOVAL & INSTALLATION.
2) Remove bearing cap bolts. Note letters on caps and drive axle housing for reassembly reference. Remove differential bearing caps. *See Fig. 3 or 4*. Mount dial indicator on differential housing. *See Fig. 2*. Preload dial indicator to .020" (.51 mm), then rotate gauge to zero dial.

CAUTION: DO NOT spread housing more than .015" (.38 mm) as housing will be damaged.

3) Use Drive Axle Housing Spreader (J-24385-01) to spread drive axle housing out .015" (.38 mm). *See Fig. 2*. Using 2 prybars, pry differential case out of housing.
4) Remove drive axle housing spreader. Use Differential Bearing Remover (J-29721), Adapters (J-29721-70), and Removal Plug (J-8107-03) to remove differential bearings and shims. Store bearings with matching bearing cups. Mark bearing sets and shims left or right for reassembly reference.
5) Place differential case in soft-jawed vise and remove ring gear bolts. Using a soft-faced hammer, tap ring gear off differential case. Remove pinion shaft lock pin. Remove pinion shaft, pinion gears and thrust washers. Remove differential side gears and thrust washers. Mark gears and washers for reassembly reference.
6) Check drive pinion bearing preload. If drive pinion bearings need to be replaced, mark pinion flange and drive pinion nut for reassembly reference. Using Pinion Flange Holder/Remover (J-8614-01), remove drive pinion nut and pinion flange.
7) Install differential cover with 2 bolts to keep drive pinion from falling out of housing during removal. Tap drive pinion out of differential housing. Remover cover and retrieve drive pinion and shims. Save shims for reassembly.
8) Pry drive pinion oil seal from bore, being careful not to damage machined surfaces. Remove outer drive pinion bearing and oil slinger. Remove drive pinion bearing cups from drive axle housing.
9) Remove drive pinion adjustment shims and baffle. Keep shims and baffle together for reassembly. Using Differential Bearing Remover (J-29721) and Adapters (J-29721-70), remove inner drive pinion bearing.

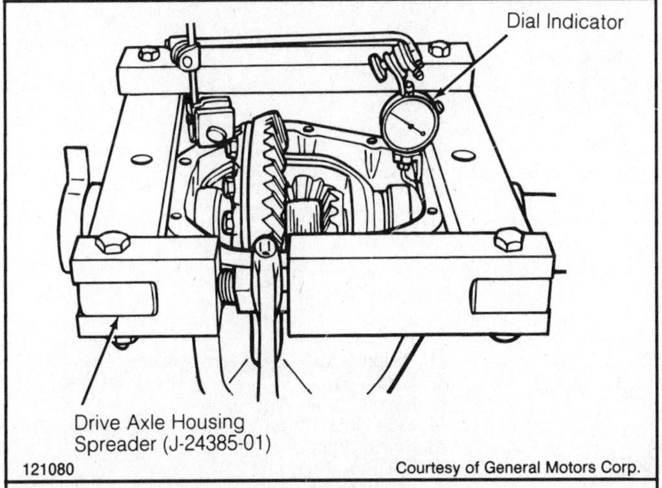
Dial Indicator
Drive Axle Housing
Spreader (J-24385-01)
121080
Courtesy of General Motors Corp.

Fig. 2: Spreading Drive Axle Housing

NOTE: DO NOT steam clean any parts having a ground and polished surface, such as bearings, gears and shafts.

Cleaning & Inspection - 1) Use cleaning solvent to rinse gears and bearings. Check bearing rollers for wear. Check pinion and flange splines for excessive wear. Ensure ring gear teeth are in good condition.
2) Check differential case for cracks, scoring of side gears, thrust washers and pinion thrust faces. Check fit of side gears to case and to axle shaft splines.

Differential Case Reassembly - 1) Apply lubricant to all differential parts. Assemble new side gear thrust washers with side gears. Install side gear assembly in differential case. Ensure side gears are installed on same side as removed.
2) Place pinion gears onto side gears so that holes in pinion gears are 180 degrees apart. Rotate pinion gears into place and verify that pinion gears line up with pinion shaft holes.
3) Rotate pinion gears toward differential opening just enough to slide new pinion thrust washers into place. Align lock pin holes in case and pinion shaft. Install pinion shaft lock pin. Peen lock pin into place.
4) Ensure that differential case and ring gear mating surfaces are clean and free of burrs. Thread 2 studs on opposite sides of ring gear. Press ring gear onto differential case, making sure to align ring gear bolt holes. Install and tighten NEW ring gear bolts in a crisscross pattern.

Determining Total Differential Shim Pack - 1) Ensure drive pinion is out of drive axle housing. On 9 3/4" drive axle, install assembled differential case, with Master Differential Bearings (D-117) installed, in drive axle housing. On 10 1/2" drive axle, install assembled differential case, with Master Differential Bearings (D-136) installed, in drive axle housing. Mount dial indicator on ring gear bolt side of differential case. *See Fig. 5*.
2) On 10 1/2" heavy duty drive axles, install outboard spacer between master bearing (ring gear side) and drive axle housing. On all axles, force differential assembly toward dial indicator as far as possible.
3) Preload dial indicator to one half of its travel. Place tip of dial indicator on a machined (flat) differential surface, just next to ring gear bolt. Mark this location with chalk. Set dial indicator to zero.
4) Force differential assembly in opposite direction of dial indicator as far as it will go. Repeat this step until same reading is obtained. Record the number of thousandths that the dial indicator traveled, NOT the reading on dial.
5) On 9 3/4" and 10 1/2" light duty (model "B" and "U") drive axles, the reading obtained in step **4)** will determine the thickness of shim pack to be used without any bearing preload, which will be added later.
6) On 10 1/2" heavy duty drive axles, the reading obtained in step **4)** plus the spacer thickness will determine the thickness of shims and spacer to be used.
7) On all axles, remove dial indicator from drive axle housing. Remove differential case from drive axle housing. DO NOT remove master bearings from differential case assembly.

Pinion Depth Adjustment - 1) Clean all drive axle housing bores. The drive pinion bore must be free of nicks and dirt. Install Master Drive Pinion Block (D-120) or (D-137) on heavy duty axles, in pinion bore. Install Master Drive Pinion Block (D-120) or (D-137) in pinion bore. Assemble Master Discs (D-116-2) onto Arbor (D-115-3). Install arbor and disc assembly into drive axle housing.
2) Place Pinion Height Block (D-116-1) on top of master drive pinion block and against arbor. *See Fig. 6*. Place Dial Indicator Block (D-115) on lowest step of pinion height block. While applying a downward pressure on dial indicator block, set dial indicator to zero.
3) Slide dial indicator block over to arbor. Move dial indicator block back and forth (perpendicular to arbor) to get highest reading. This reading, plus or minus value etched on drive pinion head, is thickness of shim pack necessary for proper pinion depth adjustment.
4) Using a micrometer, measure each shim thickness separately. Add shim thicknesses together to obtain total shim pack thickness. If a baffle or slinger is used, its thickness must be measured and included in shim pack.

NOTE: A positive (+) value on drive pinion head indicates the distance between ring gear centerline and drive pinion must be increased by the number of thousandths marked on pinion. A negative (-) indicates that distance must be decreased. A zero (0) etched drive pinion will use the shim thickness determined by this procedure.

1991 DRIVE AXLES
Dana 9 3/4" & 10 1/2" Full-Floating Axles (Cont.)

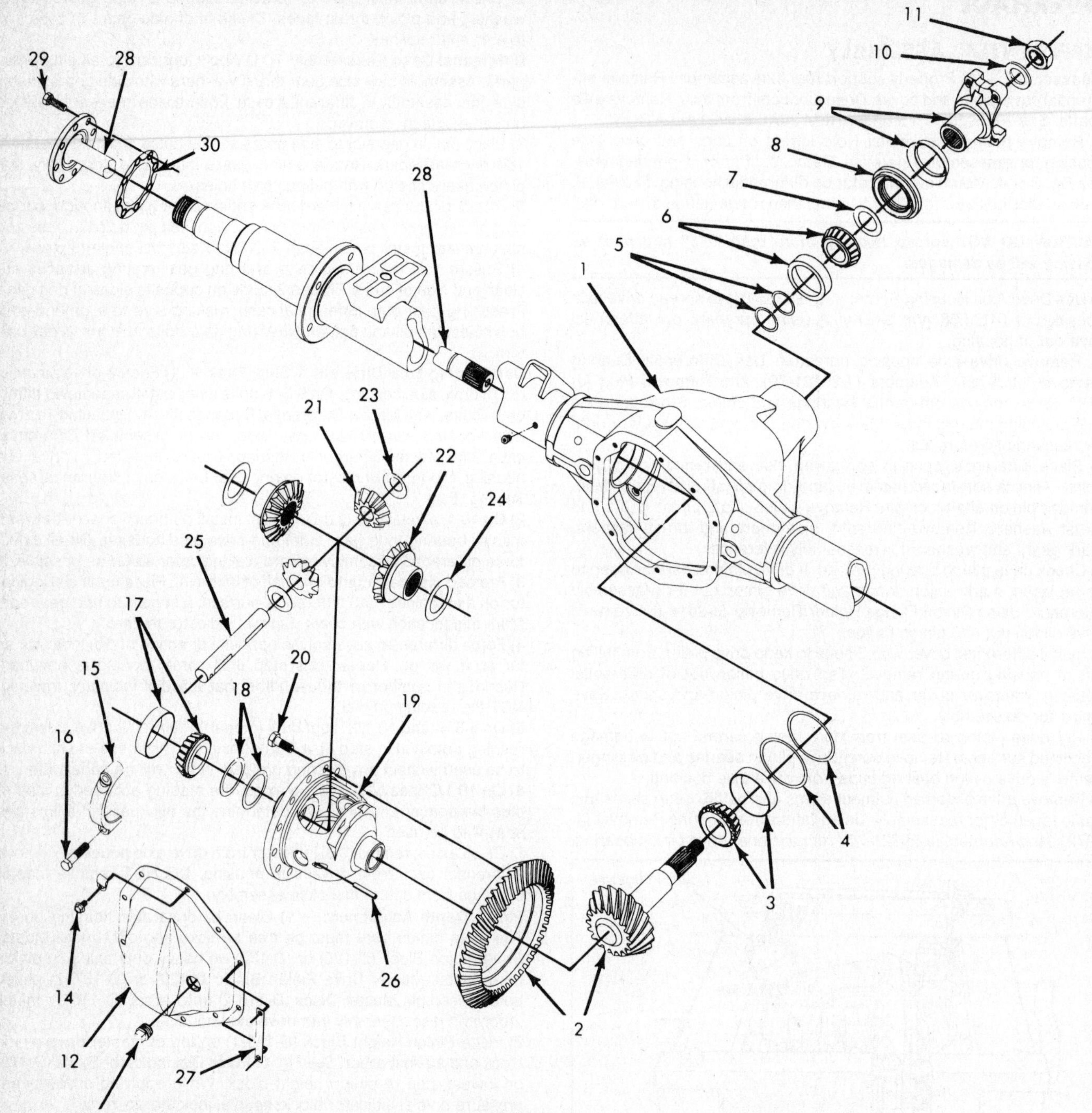
1
2
3
4
5
6
7
8
9
10
11
12
13
14
15
16
17
18
19
20
21
22
23
24
25
26
27
28
28
29
30

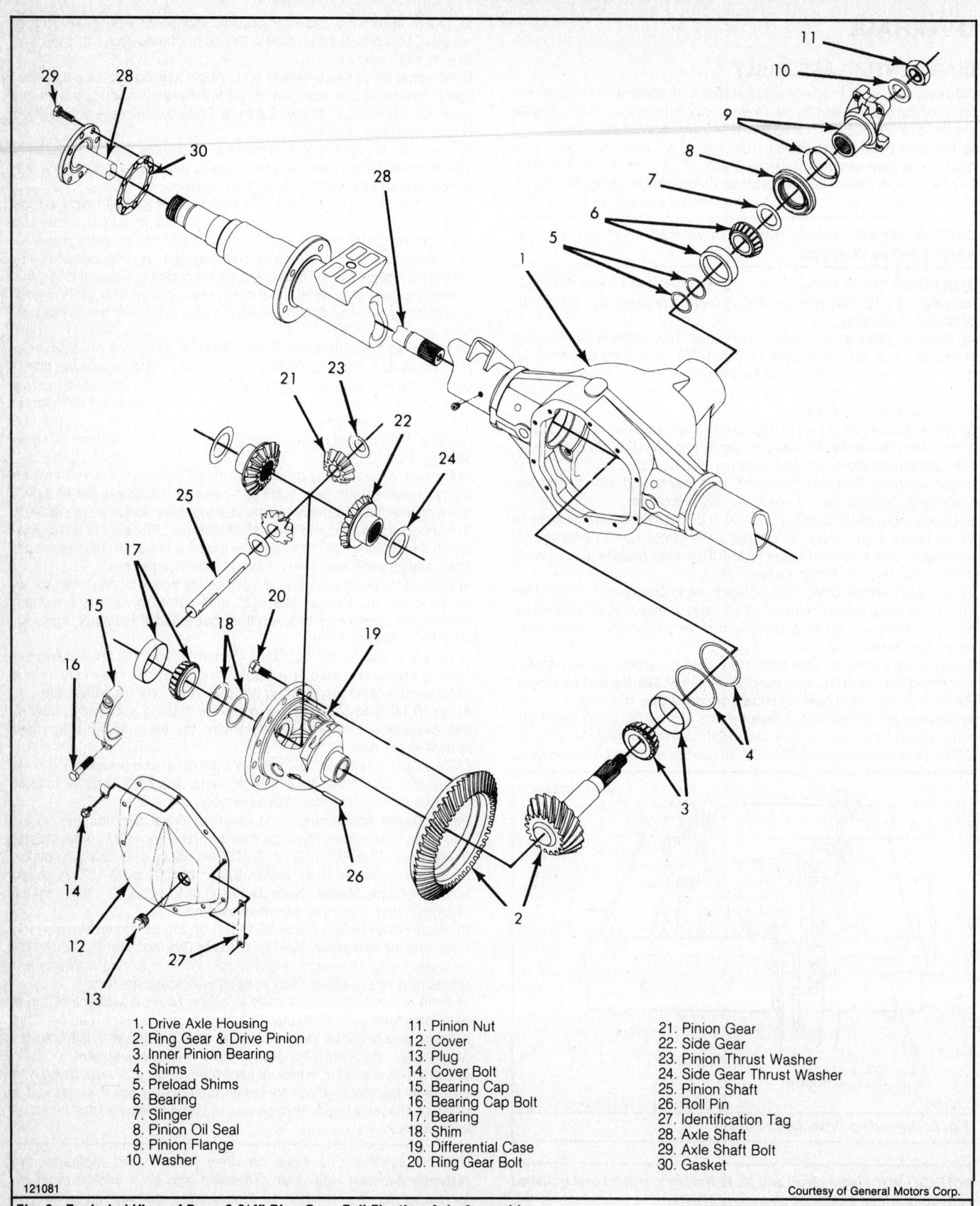

1. Drive Axle Housing
2. Ring Gear & Drive Pinion
3. Inner Pinion Bearing
4. Shims
5. Preload Shims
6. Bearing
7. Slinger
8. Pinion Oil Seal
9. Pinion Flange
10. Washer
11. Pinion Nut
12. Cover
13. Plug
14. Cover Bolt
15. Bearing Cap
16. Bearing Cap Bolt
17. Bearing
18. Shim
19. Differential Case
20. Ring Gear Bolt
21. Pinion Gear
22. Side Gear
23. Pinion Thrust Washer
24. Side Gear Thrust Washer
25. Pinion Shaft
26. Roll Pin
27. Identification Tag
28. Axle Shaft
29. Axle Shaft Bolt
30. Gasket

121081

Courtesy of General Motors Corp.

Fig. 3: Exploded View of Dana 9 3/4" Ring Gear Full-Floating Axle Assembly

1991 DRIVE AXLES
Dana 9 3/4" & 10 1/2" Full-Floating Axles (Cont.)

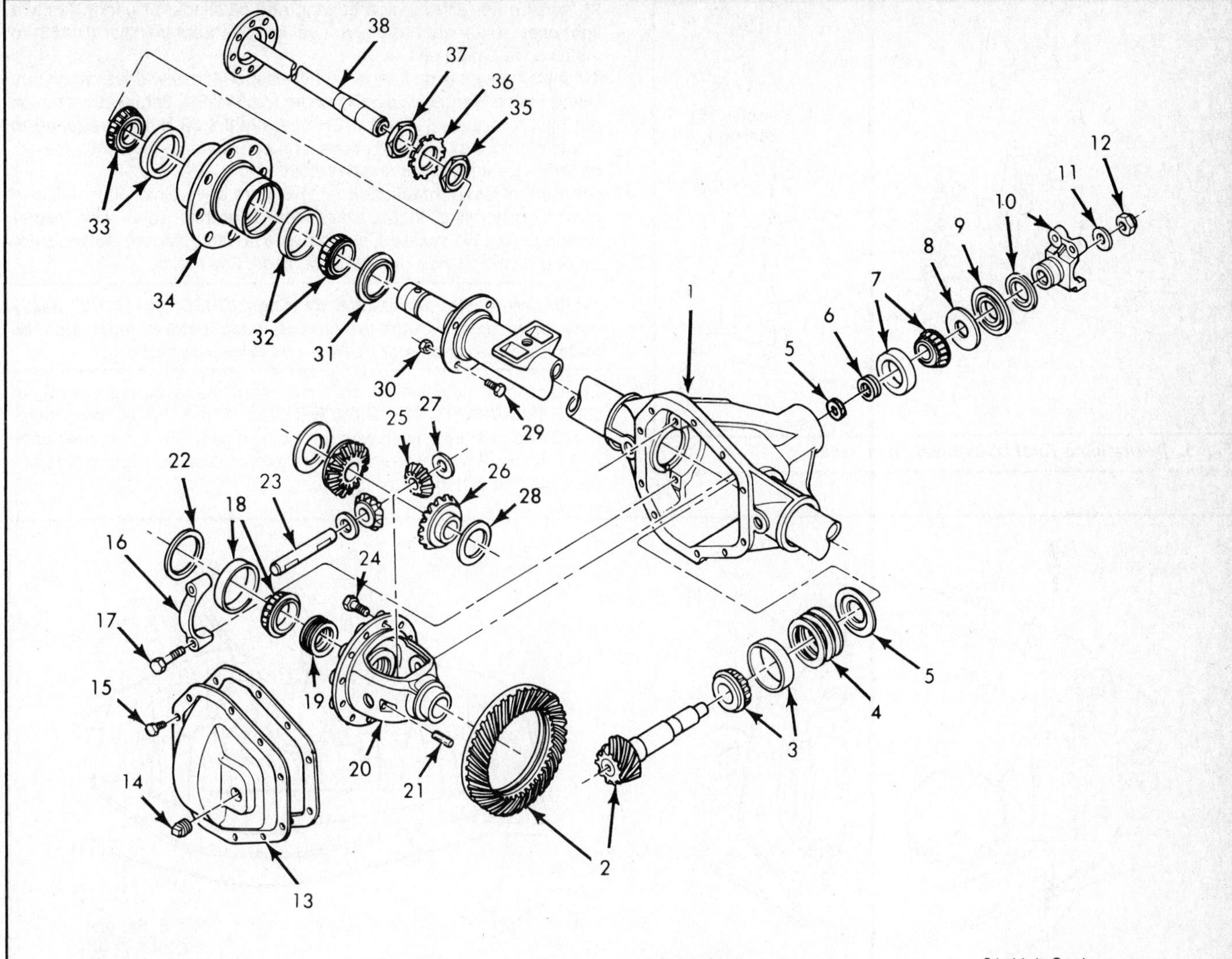
1
2
3
4
5
6
7
8
9
10
11
12
13
14
15
16
17
18
19
20
21
22
23
24
25
26
27
28
29
30
31
32
33
34
35
36
37
38

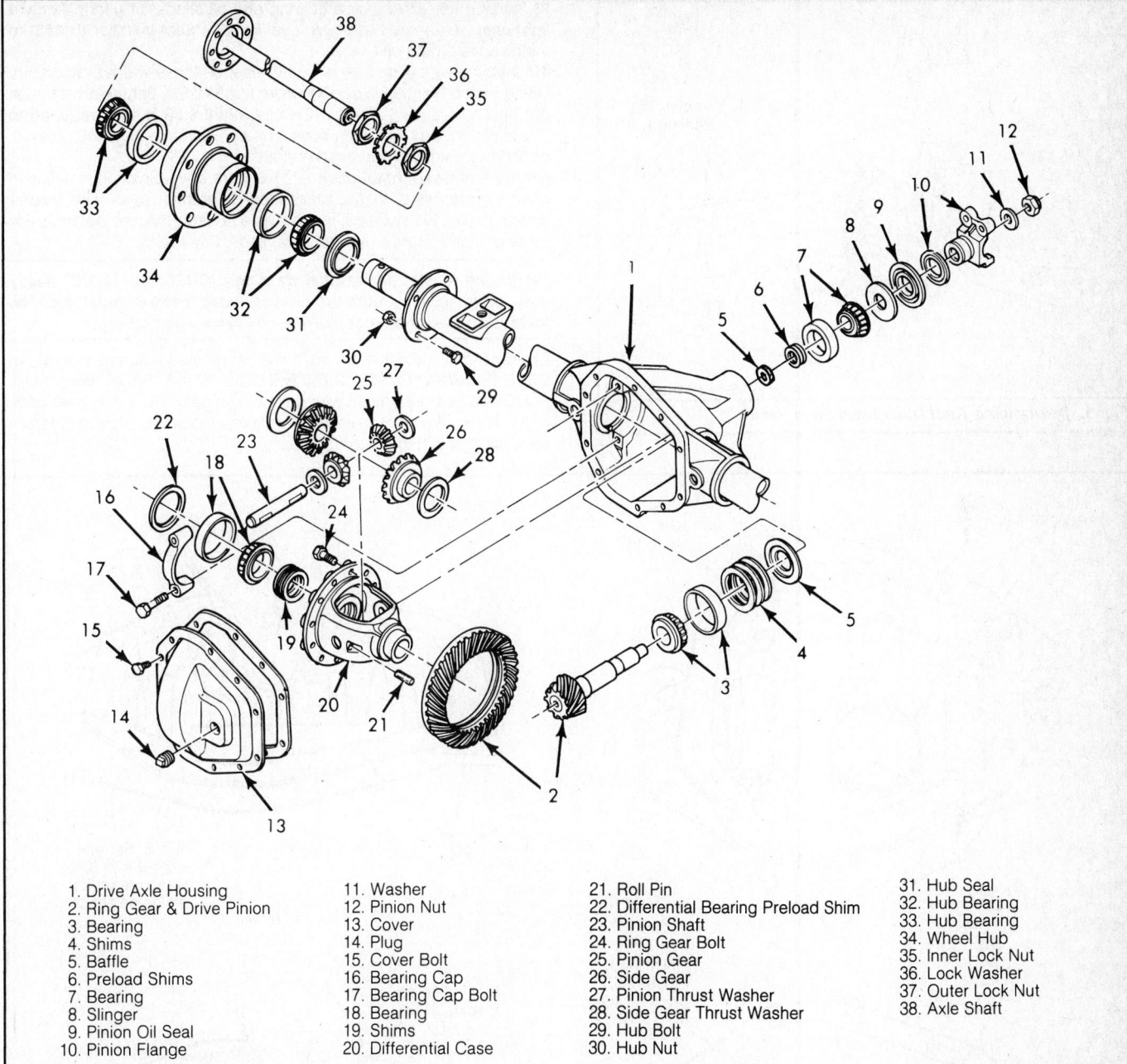

1. Drive Axle Housing
2. Ring Gear & Drive Pinion
3. Bearing
4. Shims
5. Baffle
6. Preload Shims
7. Bearing
8. Slinger
9. Pinion Oil Seal
10. Pinion Flange
11. Washer
12. Pinion Nut
13. Cover
14. Plug
15. Cover Bolt
16. Bearing Cap
17. Bearing Cap Bolt
18. Bearing
19. Shims
20. Differential Case
21. Roll Pin
22. Differential Bearing Preload Shim
23. Pinion Shaft
24. Ring Gear Bolt
25. Pinion Gear
26. Side Gear
27. Pinion Thrust Washer
28. Side Gear Thrust Washer
29. Hub Bolt
30. Hub Nut
31. Hub Seal
32. Hub Bearing
33. Hub Bearing
34. Wheel Hub
35. Inner Lock Nut
36. Lock Washer
37. Outer Lock Nut
38. Axle Shaft

121082

Courtesy of General Motors Corp.

Fig. 4: Exploded View of Dana 10 1/2" Full-Floating Axle Assembly

Drive Pinion Assembly & Preload – 1) Place required shims and baffle, if used, in inner bearing bore. Use Pinion Bearing Cup Installer (D-111) on 9 3/4" axles or (C-4204) on 10 1/2" axles, and Handle (C-4171) to install drive pinion inner bearing cup into drive axle housing. Ensure cup is seated on shims.

2) Use Pinion Bearing Cup Installer (J-7818) and Handle (J-8092) to install drive pinion outer bearing cup into drive axle housing. Use Pinion Bearing Installer (J-5590) to install inner bearing and oil slinger (if used) on drive pinion.

3) Install drive pinion in drive axle housing. Install outer drive pinion bearing and slinger (if used). DO NOT install preload shims and oil seal at this time.

4) Install drive pinion flange. Install washer and drive pinion nut. Using Pinion Flange Holder/Remover (J-8614-01), tighten drive pinion nut until a torque of 10 INCH Lbs. (1.13 N.m) is required to rotate drive pinion. Rotate drive pinion several times to seat bearings.

5) Assemble Master Discs (D-116-2) onto Arbor (D-115-3). Install arbor and disc assembly into drive axle housing. Place Pinion Height Block (D-116-1) on top of drive pinion and against arbor. Place Dial Indicator Block (D-115) on lowest step of pinion height block. While applying a downward pressure on dial indicator block, set dial indicator to zero.

6) Slide dial indicator block over to arbor. *See Fig. 6.* Move dial indicator block back and forth (perpendicular to arbor) to get highest reading. If reading is within .002" (.05 mm) of drive pinion marking, drive pinion depth is set correctly.

7) If depth is not within drive pinion marking, change shim pack by the amount indicator needle is deflected away from drive pinion marking. Dial indicator needle will move to left if drive pinion has a positive (+) value etched on it. Needle will move to right if pinion head has a negative (-) value etched on it.

8) Remove drive pinion nut, washer, pinion flange and bearing. Remove preload shims. Install shims that were removed, or measure old shims and replace them with new shims if necessary.

Dana 9 3/4" & 10 1/2" Full-Floating Axles (Cont.)

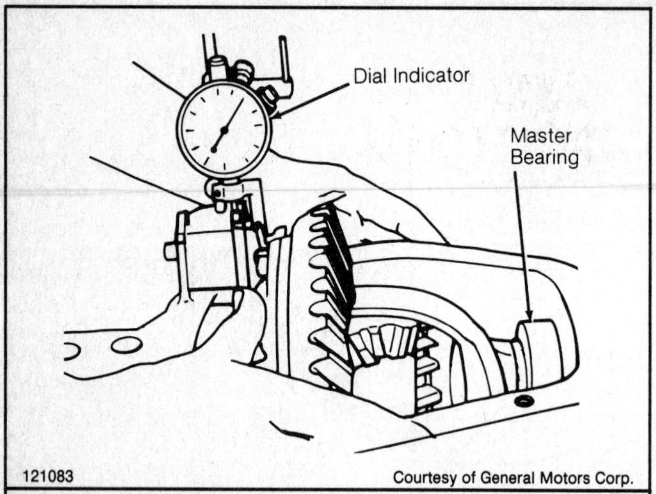
Dial Indicator
Master
Bearing
121083
Courtesy of General Motors Corp.

Fig. 5: Determining Total Differential Shim Pack

9) Install outer drive pinion bearing and oil slinger (if used). Apply a light coat of lubricant to pinion seal lip. Use Seal Installer (D-163) to install drive pinion oil seal.

10) Install drive pinion flange. Install washer and new drive pinion nut. Using Pinion Flange Holder/Remover (J-8614-01), tighten drive pinion nut until a torque of 20-40 INCH Lbs. (2.26-4.53 N.m) is required to rotate pinion. *See Fig. 7*. If necessary, add shims to increase preload, or remove shims to decrease preload.

Differential Case Installation – 1) Ensure drive pinion is installed in drive axle housing. Install assembled differential case, with Master Bearings (D-117) installed, in drive axle housing. Mount dial indicator on ring gear bolt side of differential case. *See Fig. 5*.

NOTE: Use Master Differential Bearings (D-136) on 10 1/2" heavy duty drive axles. Outboard spacer, used before, must also be installed between master bearing and drive axle housing.

2) Place dial indicator tip on chalk mark made during step **3)** of DETERMINING TOTAL DIFFERENTIAL SHIM PACK procedure. Force ring gear into mesh with drive pinion gear. Rock ring gear back and forth to allow teeth to mesh. While force is still applied to differential case, set dial indicator to zero.

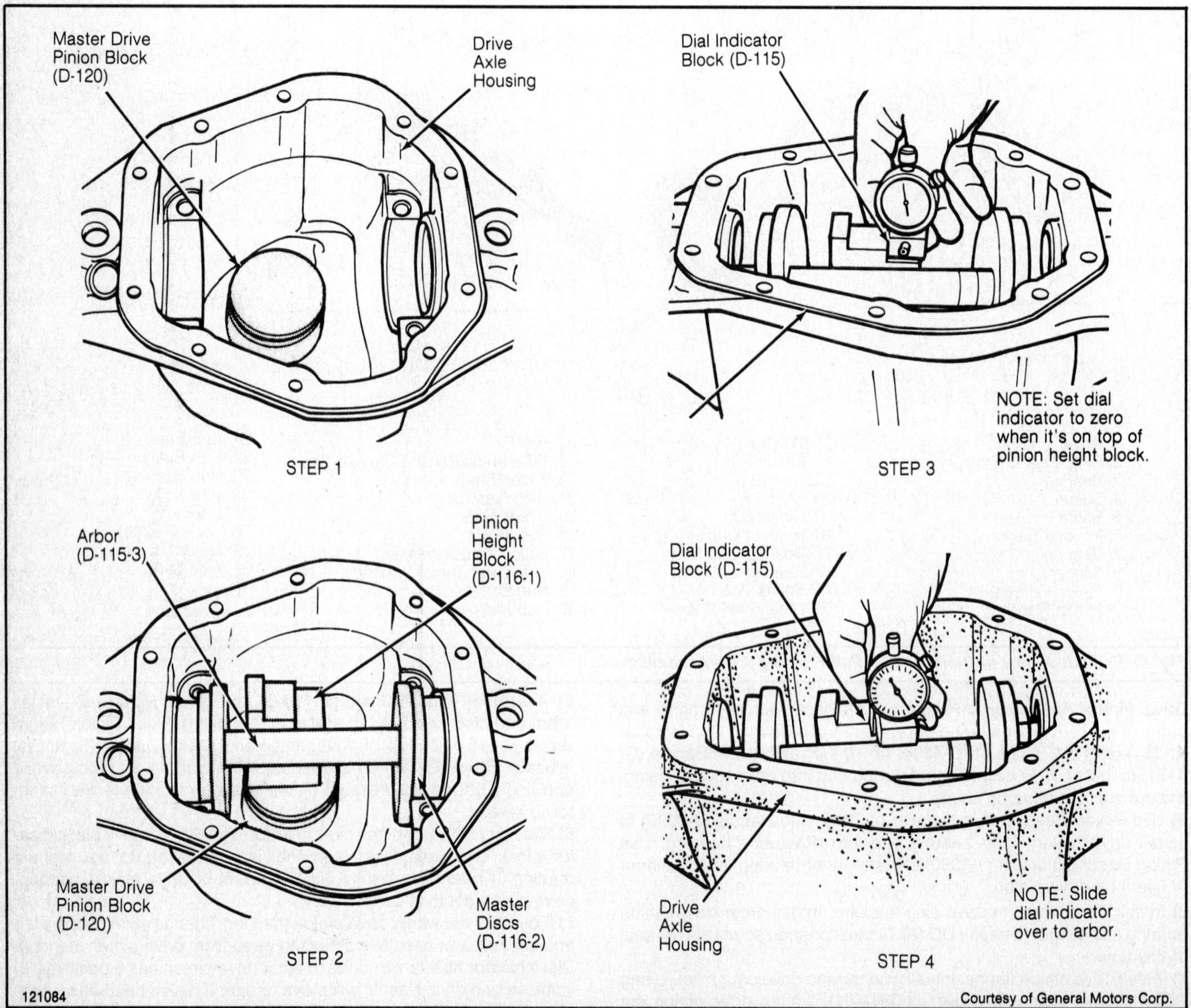
Master Drive
Pinion Block
(D-120)
Drive
Axle
Housing
STEP 1
Dial Indicator
Block (D-115)
NOTE: Set dial
indicator to zero
when it's on top of
pinion height block.
STEP 3
Arbor
(D-115-3)
Pinion
Height
Block
(D-116-1)
Master Drive
Pinion Block
(D-120)
Master
Discs
(D-116-2)
STEP 2
Dial Indicator
Block (D-115)
Drive
Axle
Housing
NOTE: Slide
dial indicator
over to arbor.
STEP 4
121084
Courtesy of General Motors Corp.

Fig. 6: Adjusting Pinion Depth

Dana 9 3/4" & 10 1/2" Full-Floating Axles (Cont.)

3) Force differential case away from drive pinion gear to obtain an indicator reading. Repeat this action until a constant reading is obtained. Record reading. Remove dial indicator and differential case from drive axle housing.
4) Remove master bearings from differential case. Subtract reading found in step **3)** of this procedure from total shim pack reading obtained under DETERMINING TOTAL DIFFERENTIAL SHIM PACK procedure.

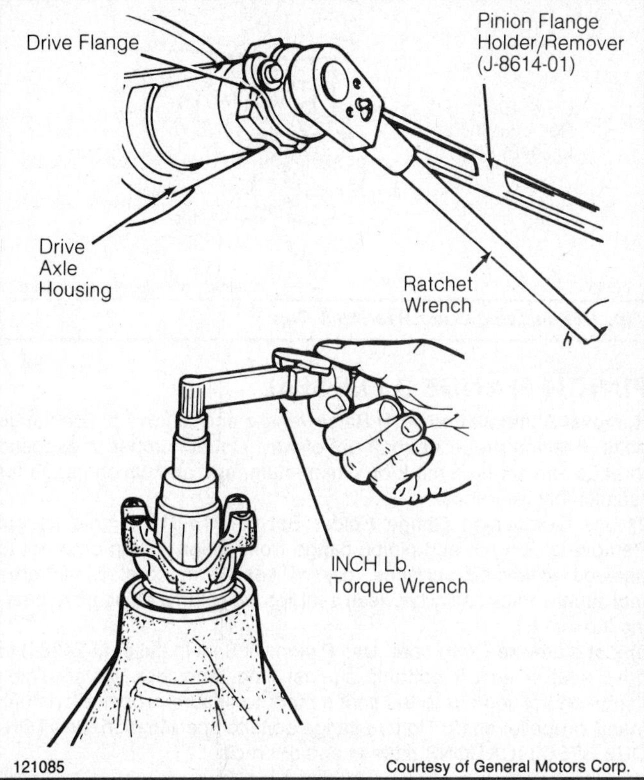
Drive Flange
Pinion Flange Holder/Remover (J-8614-01)
Drive Axle Housing
Ratchet Wrench
INCH Lb. Torque Wrench
121085
Courtesy of General Motors Corp.
Fig. 7: Checking Drive Pinion Preload

NOTE: The reading found in step 3) of this procedure will determine shim size to be used on ring gear side. The remaining portion of the shim pack will be used on the opposite side of ring gear. Add an additional .015" (.38 mm) to the side opposite the ring gear to preload bearings.

5) Place proper amount of shims on differential bearing hub (ring gear side) and drive differential bearing onto hub using Differential Bearing Installer (J-23690) and Handle (J-8092).
6) Place proper amount of shims on differential bearing hub (opposite ring gear side) and drive differential bearing onto hub using differential bearing installer and handle.
7) Mount dial indicator on differential housing. *See Fig. 2*. Preload dial indicator to .020" (.51 mm), then rotate gauge to zero dial. Use Drive Axle Housing Spreader (J-24385-01) to spread drive axle housing to .015" (.38 mm). DO NOT spread housing more than specified, as housing will be damaged.
8) Remove dial indicator. Install cups on differential case bearings. Install differential case in drive axle housing. If necessary, use a rawhide mallet to properly seat differential case in housing.
9) On 10 1/2" heavy duty drive axles, use Preload Shim Installer (J-4205) and Handle (C-4171) to tap outboard spacer into place. On all drive axles, remove drive axle housing spreader. Install bearing caps and tighten to specification. See TORQUE SPECIFICATIONS table at end of article.
Checking Ring Gear Backlash – 1) Mount dial indicator on drive axle housing. *See Fig. 8*. Place dial indicator tip at heel end of ring gear tooth. Check backlash at 3 equally spaced locations.
2) Backlash should be .005-.009" (.13-.23 mm). Variation between points checked must not vary more than .002" (.05 mm). High backlash is corrected by moving ring gear closer to drive pinion. Low backlash is corrected by moving ring gear away from drive pinion.
3) To adjust ring gear backlash, remove differential case from housing; remove differential bearings and move proper amount of shims from one side to another.
4) When backlash adjustment is completed, check ring gear tooth contact pattern. See GEAR TOOTH CONTACT PATTERNS article in GENERAL INFORMATION. Pattern should be correct if assembly and adjustments were done properly.
5) With differential assembled and correctly adjusted, install new cover gasket and cover. Tighten cover bolts to specification. Install axle shafts and fill drive axle with lubricant.

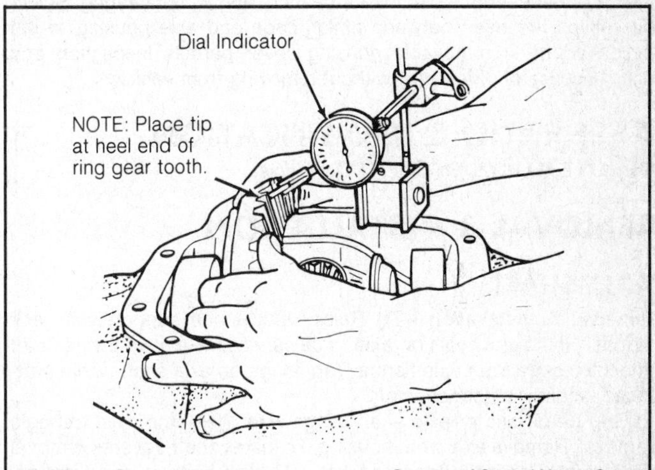
Dial Indicator
NOTE: Place tip at heel end of ring gear tooth.
121086
Courtesy of General Motors Corp.
Fig. 8: Checking Ring Gear Backlash

AXLE ASSEMBLY SPECIFICATIONS

DRIVE AXLE ASSEMBLY SPECIFICATIONS [1]

Application	Specifications
Ring Gear Backlash	.005-.009" (.13-.23 mm)
Pinion Bearing Preload	20-40 INCH lbs. (2.26-4.53 N.m)
10 1/2" Ring Gear Inner Pinion Bearings	
"B" & Heavy Duty Models	1.4375" Wide
"U" Models	1.1875" Wide
10 1/2" Ring Gear Differential Bearings	
"B" & "U" Models	1.0000" Wide
Heavy Duty Models	1.1875" Wide

[1] – Adjustment shims are available in .003", .005", .010", and .030" thicknesses.

TORQUE SPECIFICATIONS

TORQUE SPECIFICATIONS

Applications	Ft. Lbs. (N.m)
Axle Cover Bolts	35 (47)
Axle Shaft-To-Hub Bolts	115 (156)
Bearing Cap Bolts	85 (115)
Brake Backing Plate Bolts	105 (142)
Filler Plug	25 (34)
Leaf Spring "U" Bolt Nut	114 (155)
Lower Shock Mount Nut	75 (102)
Propeller Shaft Bolt	15 (20)
Ring Gear Bolts	
9 3/4" Ring Gear	110 (150)
10 1/2" Ring Gear	105 (142)
Wheel Lug Nut	
Single Rear Wheels	120 (163)
Dual Real Wheels	140 (190)

1991 DRIVE AXLES
10 1/2" Ring Gear

"C" & "K" Series, "G" Series, "P" Series, "R" & "V" Series

NOTE: "G" Series may also be equipped with a Dana drive axle. See appropriate article in DRIVE AXLES.

DESCRIPTION

The axle assembly is a hypoid gear type with integral carrier housing, which is used with full floating axles. The drive pinion bearing preload adjustment is made with a collapsible spacer. The differential side bearing preload adjustment is made with side bearing adjusting nuts. Pinion drive gear is supported in separate cage by three bearings: a pinion front bearing, a pinion rear bearing, and a pilot bearing. Selective shims are used between pinion cage and axle housing to set pinion depth. A removable housing cover permits inspection and minor service of differential without removing from vehicle.

AXLE RATIO & IDENTIFICATION

See AXLE RATIO IDENTIFICATION article.

REMOVAL & INSTALLATION

AXLE SHAFT

Removal & Installation – 1) Raise vehicle and support with jack stands. Remove wheels on axle to be serviced. Remove 8 axle shaft attaching bolts from axle flange. Tap flange on axle shaft with a soft-faced hammer to loosen shaft.

2) Grip rib on end of axle shaft flange with pliers and twist to begin removal. Remove axle from housing. To install shaft, reverse removal procedure. Use new flange gaskets. Tighten bolts to specification. See TORQUE SPECIFICATIONS table at end of article.

HUB & DRUM ASSEMBLY

Removal & Installation – 1) Remove axle shaft. See AXLE SHAFT under REMOVAL & INSTALLATION. Remove lock nut retainer ring, key, and lock nut. Pull hub and drum assembly straight off axle housing.

2) Thoroughly clean seal contact area. Apply a thin coat of bearing lubricant to contact surface on outside of axle tube. To install, reverse removal procedure. See WHEEL BEARINGS for bearing adjustment procedure.

WHEEL BEARINGS

Removal – 1) Remove axle shaft and hub/drum assembly. See AXLE SHAFT and HUB & DRUM ASSEMBLY under REMOVAL & INSTALLATION. Use a long drift or punch to drive inner bearing, cup, and oil seal from hub. Remove outer bearing retaining ring.

NOTE: Remove inner bearing cup and outer bearing retaining ring before removing outer bearing cup.

2) Use Driver Handle (J-8092) and Outer Bearing Cup Remover/Installer (J-24426) to drive outer bearing and cup out of hub. *See Fig. 1.*

Installation – 1) Lubricate bearings with gear oil. Place outer bearing cup into hub from rear. Using Driver Handle (J-8092) and Bearing Cup Installer (J-8608), drive cup into hub beyond retaining ring groove.

NOTE: Ensure Bearing Cup Installer (J-8608) is installed upside down on Driver Handle (J-8092) so chamfer does not contact bearing cup.

2) Install outer bearing retaining ring. Using Outer Bearing Cup Remover/Installer (J-24426), drive outer cup back against retaining ring until seated. Place inner bearing cup into hub. Using Driver Handle (J-8092) and Inner Bearing Cup Installer (J-24427), drive cup into hub until seated against hub shoulder.

3) Install inner bearing. Pack cavity between seal lips with high melting point wheel bearing lubricant. Position seal in hub bore. Using Seal Installer (J-24428), carefully drive seal into hub until seal is flush with edge of hub. Place hub assembly onto axle housing. Install outer bearing. Using Wheel Bearing Nut Wrench (J-2222L), install adjusting nut.

4) Tighten adjusting nut to 50 ft. lbs. (70 N.m) while rotating hub. Ensure bearing cones are seated and in contact with spindle shoulder. Back off nut. Tighten finger tight against bearing. Install key and retaining ring.

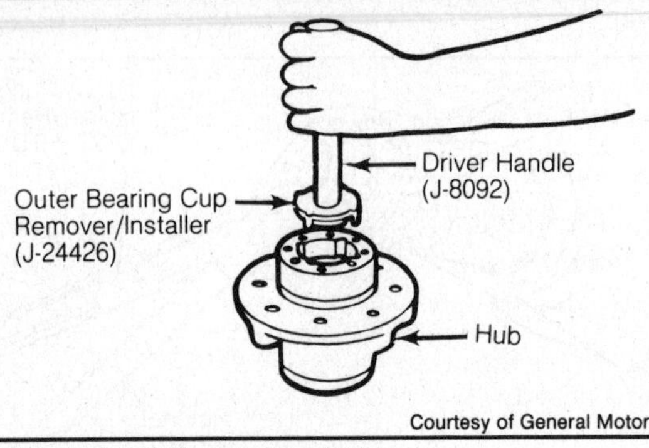
Driver Handle
(J-8092)
Outer Bearing Cup
Remover/Installer
(J-24426)
Hub

71750 Courtesy of General Motors Corp.

Fig. 1: Removing Outer Bearing & Cup

PINION FLANGE & OIL SEAL

Removal & Installation – 1) Raise vehicle and remove pinion flange bolts. Position propeller shaft out of way. Count number of exposed threads and scribe a mark on pinion stem, nut, and pinion flange for reassembly reference.

2) Use Companion Flange Holder Set (J-8614-01) to hold flange. Remove pinion nut and pinion flange from pinion. Using care not to damage machined surfaces, pry oil seal from bore. Clean area thoroughly. Pack cavity between seal lips with high melting point bearing lubricant.

3) Place new seal into bore. Use Pinion Oil Seal Installer (J-24384) to drive seal in until it bottoms against inner shoulder. Install pinion flange and pinion nut to the scribe mark to ensure proper alignment. Install propeller shaft. Tighten flange bolts to specification. See TORQUE SPECIFICATIONS table at end of article.

AXLE ASSEMBLY

Removal & Installation – 1) Raise vehicle and support at frame side rails with jack stands. Remove rear wheels. Remove pinion flange bolts and position propeller shaft out of way. Remove wheel hub. Disconnect parking brake cable at lever and at backing plate.

2) Disconnect hydraulic brake hose at connector on axle housing. Remove stabilizer bar (if equipped). Disconnect shock absorbers at axle brackets. Using floor jack, raise axle assembly slightly to relieve tension on springs. Remove spring "U" bolts, and lower floor jack. Remove axle assembly from vehicle. To install axle assembly, reverse removal procedure. Tighten bolts to specifications. See TORQUE SPECIFICATIONS table at end of article.

OVERHAUL

DIFFERENTIAL ASSEMBLY

Disassembly – 1) Place drain pan under differential carrier cover. Loosen housing cover bolts and drain lubricant. Remove housing cover and axle shafts. See AXLE SHAFT under REMOVAL & INSTALLATION. Remove pinion flange bolts, and position propeller shaft out of way. Note and record ring gear backlash, and pinion bearing preload for reassembly reference. Mark bearing caps for reassembly reference.

2) Remove adjusting nut locks and lock bolts from bearing caps. Remove bearing caps. Use Adjusting Nut Wrench (J-24429) to loosen side bearing adjusting nuts, and remove differential case assembly from axle housing. Remove differential side bearings using Puller (J-22888) and Plug (J-8107).

NOTE: Jaws of Puller (J-22888) must pull from beneath bearing cone, not cage.

3) Scribe mark across differential case halves. Remove left-hand thread ring gear bolts. Remove ring gear using brass drift if necessary. Split case halves. Remove differential side gears and thrust washers. Mark case halves and gears as left or right for reassembly.

4) Remove differential pinion spider gear. Remove pinion gears and thrust washers from spider. Check pinion bearing preload using an INCH-lb. torque wrench. Looseness indicates excessive wear. See AXLE ASSEMBLY SPECIFICATIONS table.

5) Remove 6 pinion cage assembly bolts and washers. Remove pinion assembly. It may be necessary to tap on pinion gear with a brass drift to free cage. Remove pinion cage and cage shims. Ensure shims are marked as right or left for side identification. Set shims aside for later measurement.

6) Place pinion cage assembly in a soft-jawed vise. Using Companion Flange Holder Set (J-8614-01), remove pinion nut and flange. *See Fig. 2.* Place pinion cage in press and press pinion from cage. DO NOT let pinion fall to floor.

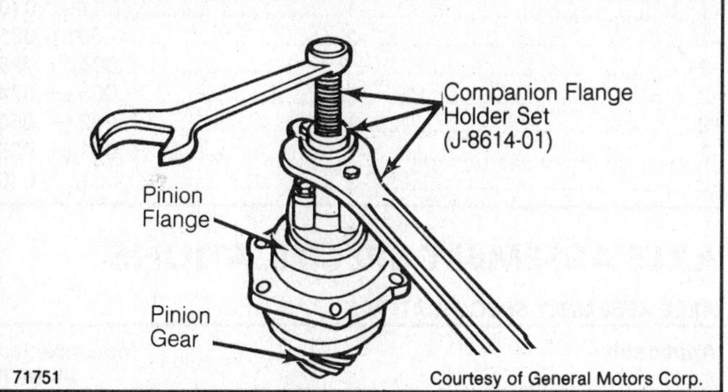

Companion Flange
Holder Set
(J-8614-01)
Pinion
Flange
Pinion
Gear
71751
Courtesy of General Motors Corp.

Fig. 2: Removing Pinion Flange

7) Remove collapsible spacer from pinion. Using Press and Bearing Remover (J-22912-01), press inner bearing from pinion. Using a hammer and punch, remove pinion seal from pinion cage. Remove outer bearing from pinion cage.

8) Remove bearing cups from pinion cage. Using a hammer and brass drift, remove pilot bearing from axle housing.

Cleaning & Inspection – 1) Clean all parts in cleaning solvent. Inspect all bearings, bearing cups, races, and rollers for scoring, chipping or excessive wear. Inspect axle shaft and side gear splines for excessive wear.

2) Inspect ring gear and pinion for scoring, cracking or chipping. Inspect differential case, pinion side gears, thrust washers, and pinion shaft for cracks, scoring or excessive wear.

Reassembly (Pinion Assembly) – 1) Lubricate all parts with hypoid gear oil. Using press and Pinion Bearing Installer (J-24433), press pinion inner bearing onto pinion. Using Driver Handle (J-8092) and Outer Bearing Cup Installer (J-8608), install outer bearing cup. Using driver and Inner Bearing Cup Installer (J-24432), install inner cup.

2) Install new collapsible spacer to pinion. Insert pinion into pinion cage. Press outer bearing onto pinion shaft. Install new pinion oil seal using driver handle and Seal Installer (J-24434). Install pinion flange oil deflector and pinion flange.

3) Install pinion washer and new pinion nut. Place pinion cage in soft-jawed vise. Install Companion Flange Holder Set (J-8614-01) to pinion flange. While rotating pinion gear, tighten pinion nut until there is no end play left at pinion. Rotate pinion several times and check pinion preload. Tighten pinion nut in small steps, rotating pinion between adjustments until preload is adjusted to specification. See AXLE ASSEMBLY SPECIFICATIONS table.

NOTE: If pinion preload limits are exceeded, pinion will have to be removed and a new collapsible spacer have to be installed.

4) If reinstalling original ring and pinion gears, use new pinion shims of same number and thickness as those removed. If installing new gears, compare pinion depth code number of new pinion gear with that of original pinion gear. From these 2 codes, determine correction factor by referring to PINION DEPTH CODES table.

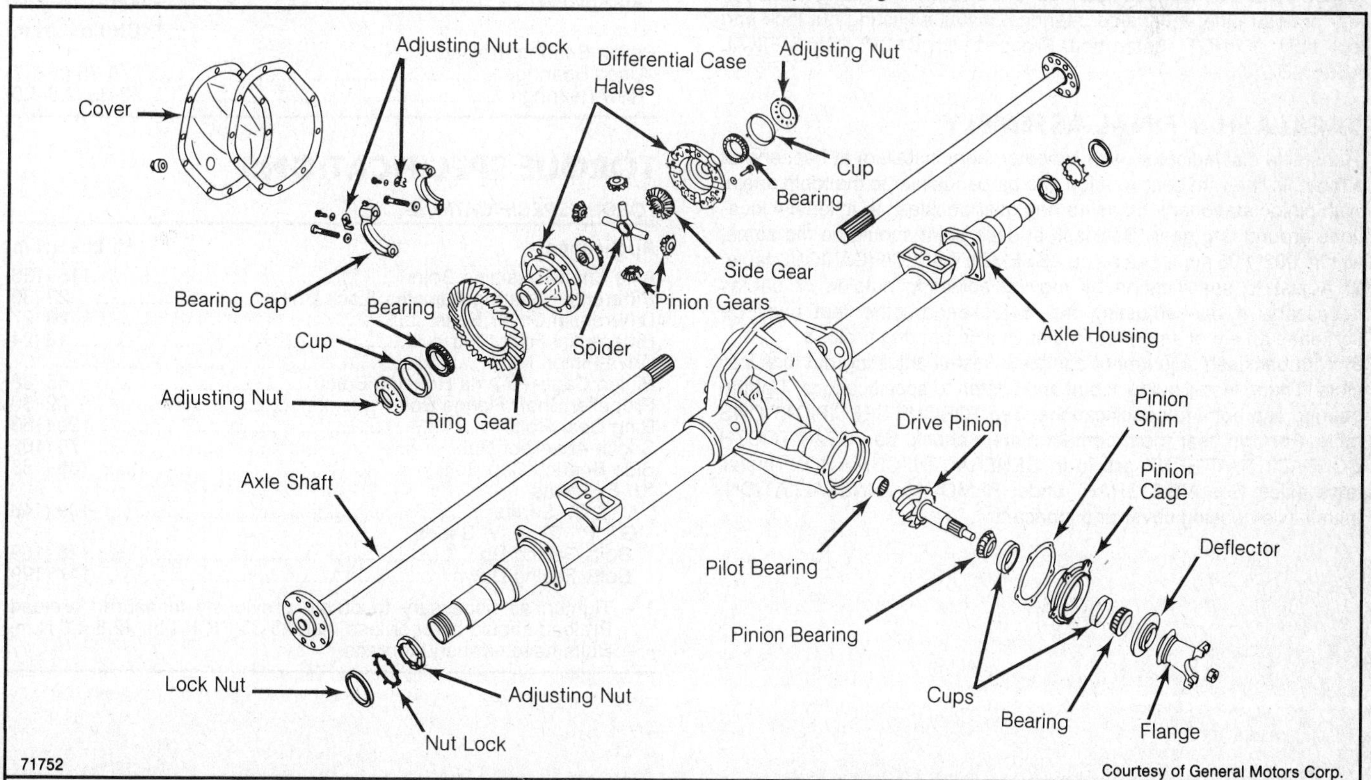

Adjusting Nut Lock
Differential Case
Halves
Adjusting Nut
Cover
Cup
Bearing
Side Gear
Bearing Cap
Pinion Gears
Bearing
Spider
Axle Housing
Cup
Adjusting Nut
Ring Gear
Pinion
Shim
Drive Pinion
Pinion
Cage
Axle Shaft
Deflector
Pilot Bearing
Pinion Bearing
Lock Nut
Adjusting Nut
Cups
Bearing
Flange
Nut Lock
71752
Courtesy of General Motors Corp.

Fig. 3: Exploded View of 10 1/2" Ring Gear Axle Assembly

1991 DRIVE AXLES
10 1/2" Ring Gear (Cont.)

5) Combine correction factor with thickness of new shim pack. Place new shim pack onto carrier housing. Install new pinion pilot bearing into axle housing using driver handle and Pilot Bearing Installer (J-34943). Install pinion cage to axle housing. Tighten 6 cage retaining bolts to specification in a crosswise sequence. See TORQUE SPECIFICATIONS table at end of article.

Reassembly (Case Assembly) – 1) Lubricate all parts with hypoid gear oil. Place pinion gears and thrust washers on differential spider. Install side gears and thrust washers to case halves in their original locations. Install differential spider to differential.

2) Assemble case halves, aligning marks previously scribed on case. Obtain and install 2 left-hand threaded studs in ring gear, directly opposite each other to ease in alignment/installation process of ring gear.

3) Install ring gear onto studs. Tap ring gear lightly with soft-faced hammer until new ring gear attaching bolts can be installed. Tighten bolts evenly until ring gear is flush with case flange.

4) Remove threaded studs. Install 2 remaining bolts and tighten all ring gear bolts alternately and evenly to specification. See TORQUE SPECIFICATIONS table at end of article. Install differential side bearings using driver handle and Bearing Installer (J-24449).

ADJUSTMENTS

SIDE BEARING PRELOAD

1) Place lubricated bearing cups onto differential side bearings in original locations, and place differential assembly into carrier. Install bearing caps in their original positions, and tighten cap bolts until just snug.

2) Using Bearing Backlash Wrench (J-24429), loosen right side bearing adjusting nut, and tighten left side adjusting nut until ring gear just contacts drive pinion (zero lash point). Back off left adjusting nut 2 slots to locking position. Install left adjusting nut lock and lock bolt. DO NOT tighten bolt.

3) Tighten right adjusting nut until case is in firm contact with left adjusting nut. Loosen right adjusting nut until it is free of bearing. Retighten right nut until it just contacts bearing. Tighten right adjusting nut an additional 2 slots (used bearings) or 3 slots (new bearings) to properly preload differential side bearings. Install adjusting nut lock and lock bolt. DO NOT tighten bolt. Proceed with BACKLASH & FINAL ASSEMBLY.

BACKLASH & FINAL ASSEMBLY

1) Install a dial indicator (with indicator stem installed) at heel end of a tooth, in line with gear rotation and perpendicular to the tooth angle. With pinion stationary, measure ring gear backlash in at least 4 locations around ring gear. Backlash at each point should be the same, within .002" (.05 mm). See AXLE ASSEMBLY SPECIFICATIONS table.

2) Adjust to specification by moving adjusting nuts in or out as necessary. If one adjusting nut is loosened, other nut must be tightened an equal amount to maintain side bearing preload.

3) With backlash adjustment complete, install adjusting nut lock into slots in nuts. Install nut lock bolt and tighten to specifications. Tighten bearing cap bolts to specifications. See TORQUE SPECIFICATIONS table. Perform gear tooth contact pattern check. See GEAR TOOTH CONTACT PATTERNS article in GENERAL INFORMATION. Install drive axles. See AXLE SHAFT under REMOVAL & INSTALLATION. Install axle housing cover and lubricant.

PINION DEPTH CODES

Original Code	Service Code	Correction In. (mm)
+2	+2	0 (0)
+2	+1	-.001 (-.025)
+2	0	-.002 (-.050)
+2	-1	-.003 (-.074)
+2	-2	-.004 (-.098)
+1	+2	+.001 (+.025)
+1	+1	0 (0)
+1	0	-.001 (-.025)
+1	-1	-.002 (-.050)
+1	-2	-.003 (-.074)
0	+2	+.002 (+.050)
0	+1	+.001 (+.025)
0	0	0 (0)
0	-1	-.001 (-.025)
0	-2	-.002 (-.050)
-1	+2	+.003 (+.074)
-1	+1	+.002 (+.050)
-1	0	+.001 (+.025)
-1	-1	0 (0)
-1	-2	-.001 (-.025)
-2	+2	+.004 (+.098)
-2	+1	+.003 (+.074)
-2	0	+.002 (+.050)
-2	-1	+.001 (+.025)
-2	-2	0 (0)

AXLE ASSEMBLY SPECIFICATIONS

AXLE ASSEMBLY SPECIFICATIONS

Application	Measurement In. (mm)
Ring Gear Backlash	
Preferred	.005-.008 (.127-.203)
Acceptable	.003-.008 (.076-.203)
	INCH Lbs. (N.m)
Pinion Bearing Preload	
Used Bearings	5-15 (.6-1.7)
New Bearings	23-35 (2.6-4.0)

TORQUE SPECIFICATIONS

TORQUE SPECIFICATIONS

Application	Ft. Lbs. (N.m)
Axle Shaft Retaining Bolts	115 (156)
Differential Bearing Adjusting Lock Bolts	22 (30)
Differential Cover Bolts	20 (27)
Differential Filler Plug	18 (24)
Drive Pinion Nut	1
Pinion Cage-To-Axle Housing Bolts	65 (88)
Propeller Shaft Flange Bolts	22 (30)
Ring Gear Bolts 2	120 (163)
Shock Absorber Nuts	75 (102)
Side Bearing Cap Bolts	135 (183)
"U" Bolt Nuts	
"C" & "K" Series	109 (148)
"G", "P", "R" & "V" Series	
Bolts Facing Up	125 (169)
Bolts Facing Down	147 (199)

1 – Tighten as necessary to obtain previously measured preload. Preload should be at or less than 25-35 INCH Lbs. (2.8-4.0 N.m).

2 – Bolts have left-hand threads.

1991 DRIVE AXLES
Rockwell 12" Ring Gear

"P" Series

DESCRIPTION

Rockwell 12" ring gear uses a full-floating axle. Axle shaft is supported by wheel hubs at the wheel ends of axle and is held in the axle housing by an axle cap bolted to the wheel hub. Splined end of the axle shaft is supported by the differential. Axle is sealed with a pinion seal, a gasket at each axle shaft end, and a gasket between the axle housing and differential carrier.

AXLE RATIO & IDENTIFICATION

To determine drive axle ratio, see AXLE RATIO IDENTIFICATION article.

ADJUSTMENTS

HUB BEARINGS

1) Raise and support vehicle. Remove axle shaft. See AXLE SHAFT under REMOVAL & INSTALLATION. Remove wheel hub assembly nut and lock washer. *See Fig. 1*. Using Wheel Hub Bearing Nut Wrench (J-25510), tighten hub bearing adjusting nut to 50 ft. lbs. (68 N.m) while rotating hub.
2) Ensure bearings are seated. Loosen adjusting nut 1/8 turn. Install lock washer and axle shaft nut. Tighten axle shaft nut to specification. Bend tang on lock washer. Install axle shaft and hub cover.

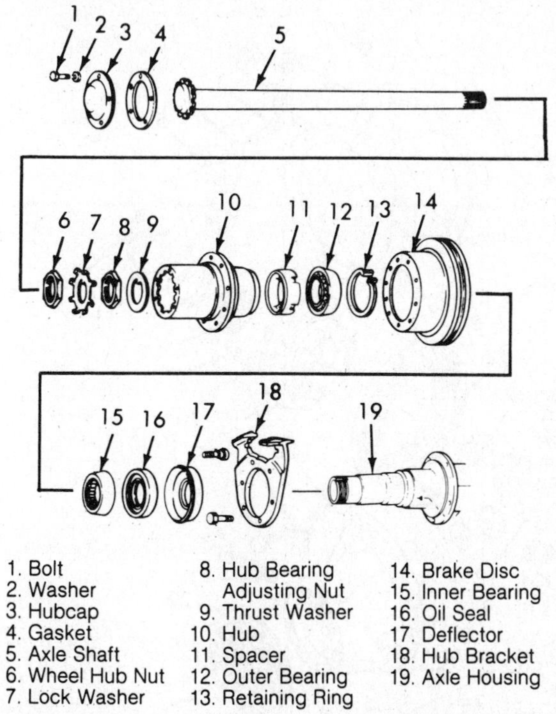
1
2
3
4
5
6
7
8
9
10
11
12
13
14
15
16
17
18
19
1. Bolt
2. Washer
3. Hubcap
4. Gasket
5. Axle Shaft
6. Wheel Hub Nut
7. Lock Washer
8. Hub Bearing Adjusting Nut
9. Thrust Washer
10. Hub
11. Spacer
12. Outer Bearing
13. Retaining Ring
14. Brake Disc
15. Inner Bearing
16. Oil Seal
17. Deflector
18. Hub Bracket
19. Axle Housing

91H13307 Courtesy of General Motors Corp.

Fig. 1: Exploded View of Axle & Hub Assembly

REMOVAL & INSTALLATION

AXLE SHAFT

Removal – Raise and support vehicle. Remove axle shaft hubcap bolts and washers. Remove hubcap with gasket. *See Fig. 1*. Thread an adapter into wheel hub end of axle shaft. Attach a slide hammer to adapter. Using slide hammer, remove axle shaft from axle housing.

Installation – Index splines on axle shaft and wheel hub. Using a slide hammer, tap axle shaft into axle housing. Ensure old hubcap gasket material is removed from wheel hub assembly. Install a new hubcap gasket. Install hubcap with bolts and washers.

WHEEL HUB & SEAL

Removal & Installation – 1) Remove caliper and support with wire. Remove axle shaft. See AXLE SHAFT under REMOVAL & INSTALLATION. Using Wheel Hub Bearing Nut Wrench (J-25510), remove wheel hub assembly nut. *See Fig. 1*. Remove lock washer.
2) Using Wheel Hub Bearing Nut Wrench (J-25510), remove hub bearing adjusting nut and thrust washer. Remove hub and rotor assembly from axle housing. Remove deflector. Pry oil seal from wheel hub, using care not to damage bore surface. Thoroughly clean seal contact surface area.
3) To install, pack cavity between seal lips with high melting point wheel bearing lubricant. Using Seal Installer (J-24428), carefully press seal into hub until seal is flush with edge of hub. To complete installation, reverse removal procedure.

HUB BEARINGS

Removal & Installation – 1) Remove wheel hub assembly. See WHEEL HUB & SEAL under REMOVAL & INSTALLATION. Use a long drift or punch to drive inner bearing and race from hub. Remove outer bearing retaining ring. Drive outer bearing out of hub.

NOTE: Inner bearing race and outer bearing retaining ring must be removed before attempting to remove outer bearing.

2) To install, place outer bearing assembly into hub. Drive bearing past retaining ring groove in hub. Ensure chamfer of bearing race installer does not contact bearing race.
3) Install outer bearing retaining ring, and drive race into hub until seated. Drive inner race into hub until seated against shoulder. Install inner bearing and NEW oil seal. Place hub assembly onto axle housing. Install adjusting nut, and adjust hub bearing.

PINION FLANGE & OIL SEAL

Removal & Installation – 1) Disconnect propeller shaft. Scribe a line down pinion nut, pinion stem and pinion flange for reassembly reference. Remove pinion nut cotter pin and pinion nut. Using a puller, remove pinion flange from stem. *See Fig. 2*.

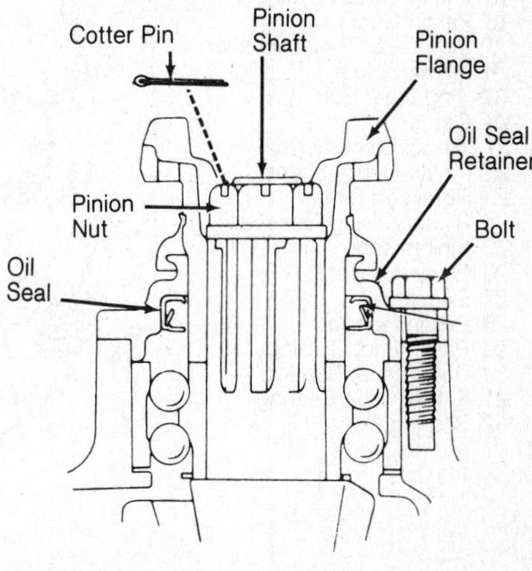
Cotter Pin
Pinion Shaft
Pinion Flange
Oil Seal Retainer
Pinion Nut
Bolt
Oil Seal

91I13308 Courtesy of General Motors Corp.

Fig. 2: Cut-Away View of Pinion Flange & Oil Seal

2) Remove bolts securing oil seal retainer to differential carrier. Remove oil seal retainer. Pry oil seal from bore, using care not to damage machined surface.

1991 DRIVE AXLES
Rockwell 12" Ring Gear (Cont.)

3) Lubricate inside cavity of new oil seal with extreme pressure lubricant. Install new pinion oil seal into bore. Ensure seal bottoms against shoulder in bore. Install oil seal retainer and bolts to carrier.

4) Pack cavity between pinion stem and pinion flange with a non-hardening sealer such as Permatex type A. *See Fig. 2*. Discard old pinion shaft nut. Using reference marks scribed during removal, install pinion flange, new pinion nut, pinion nut cotter pin and propeller shaft. Torque pinion nut to specification.

DIFFERENTIAL ASSEMBLY

Removal & Installation – 1) Drain differential. Remove axle shafts. See AXLE SHAFT under REMOVAL & INSTALLATION in this article. Disconnect propeller shaft. To prevent differential carrier from falling out during removal, loosen (but do not remove) 2 top carrier to housing bolts. Remove remaining carrier to housing bolts and washers.

2) Break carrier loose from axle housing with soft mallet. Remove 2 top bolts and washers, and work carrier free. Use a roller jack to safely remove carrier from housing. To install, reverse removal procedure.

OVERHAUL

DIFFERENTIAL ASSEMBLY

NOTE: Check and record ring gear backlash and pinion bearing preload BEFORE disassembly. See REASSEMBLY (DRIVE PINION & CAGE) and RING GEAR BACKLASH under OVERHAUL.

Disassembly (Differential Case & Gear) – 1) With carrier in holding fixture, loosen jam nut and back off thrust block adjusting screw. *See Fig. 3*. Center punch one differential carrier leg and bearing cap for reassembly reference.

2) Remove bearing cap bolts and bearing caps. Remove adjusting nuts. Remove differential and ring gear assembly from carrier. Scribe a reference mark across differential case halves.

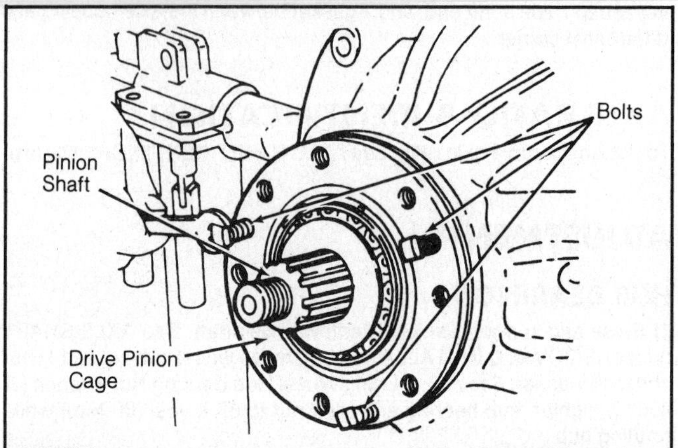
Bolts
Pinion Shaft
Drive Pinion Cage
91C13310

Courtesy of General Motors Corp.

Fig. 4: Removing Pinion Cage

1. Axle Housing
2. Axle Vent
3. Bolt
4. Washer
5. Bearing Cap
6. Bracket
7. Nut
8. Plug
9. Gasket
10. Pin
11. Adjusting Nut
12. Bearing
13. Differential Case
14. Side Gears
15. Pinion Thrust Washers
16. Pinion Gears
17. Side Gear Thrust Washer
18. Pinion Spider
19. Ring Gear Bolt
20. Carrier
21. Thrust Block Screw
22. Pinion Depth Shims
23. Retaining Ring
24. Pinion & Ring Gear Set
25. Pinion Cage
26. Pinion Oil Seal
27. Deflector
28. Pinion Flange
29. Pinion Pilot Bearing
30. Rear Pinion Bearing
31. Front Pinion Bearing
32. Bearing Race

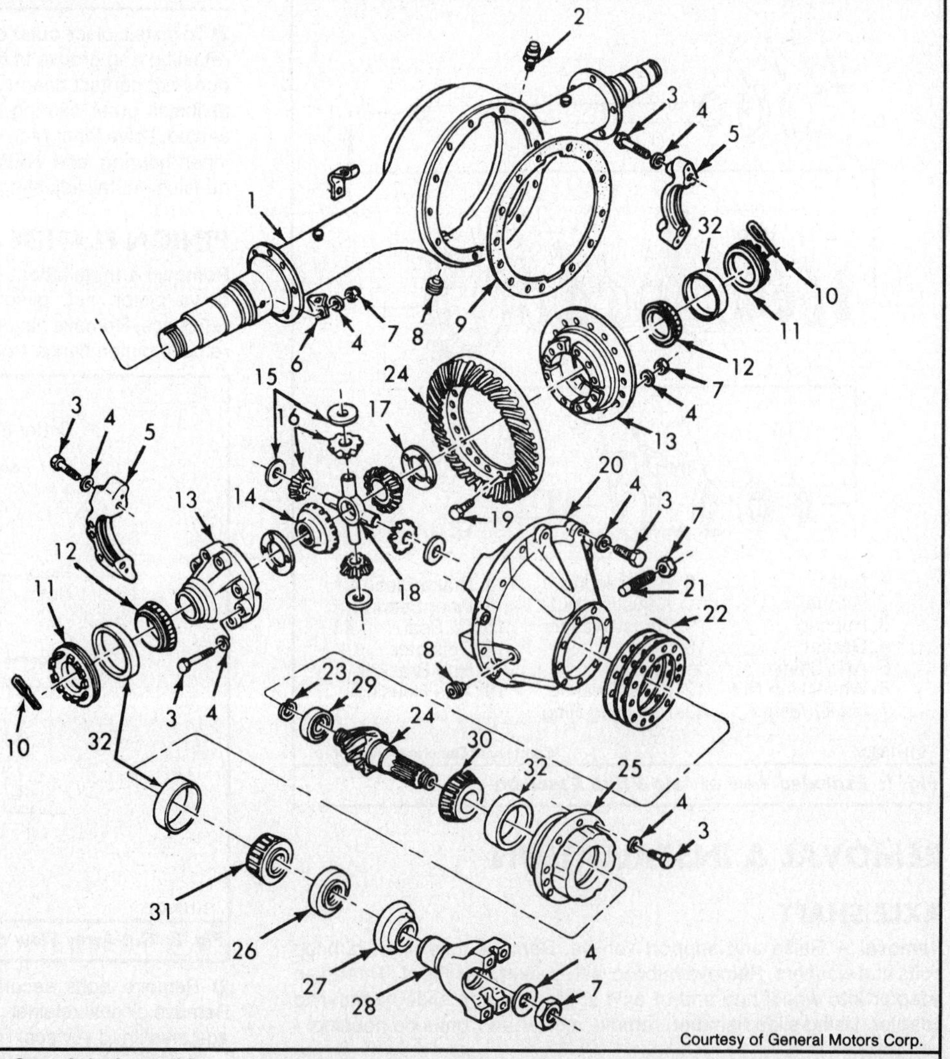
91J13309

Courtesy of General Motors Corp.

Fig. 3: Exploded View of Rockwell 12" Ring Gear Axle Assembly

3) Remove differential case bolts. *See Fig. 3.* Separate case halves. Remove pinion spider. Remove side gears with thrust washers and pinion gears with thrust washers from pinion spider. *See Fig. 3.*
4) Remove ring gear nuts and washers from differential case. Remove ring gear bolts. Separate ring gear from differential case. *See Fig. 3.* Using a press, remove differential side bearings. Identify bearings for reassembly reference.

Disassembly (Drive Pinion & Cage) - 1) Hold pinion flange and remove pinion nut and washer. Using a puller, remove flange. Remove pinion cage cover bolts. Using bolts from a puller, thread bolts into pinion cage holes to push cage away from carrier. *See Fig. 4.* Remove drive pinion cage. Wire shim pack together and save for reassembly reference.

2) Using a press, remove pinion gear from cage. Remove pinion oil seal from cage. Remove outer bearing from cage. Using a press, remove inner bearing from cage. Remove pilot bearing retaining ring. Using a puller, remove pilot bearing from pinion gear.
Cleaning & Inspection — 1) Clean all parts in cleaning solvent. Inspect all bearings, bearing races and rollers for scoring, chipping or excessive wear. Inspect axle shaft and side gear splines for excessive wear.

NOTE: DO NOT steam clean any parts having a ground and polished surface, such as bearings, gears and shafts.

2) Inspect ring gear and pinion for scoring, cracking or chipping. Inspect differential case, pinion side gears, thrust washers and pinion shaft for cracks, scoring, galling or excessive wear.
Reassembly (Drive Pinion & Cage) - 1) Lubricate bearings and races with axle lubricant. Using a press, install rear and pilot bearings firmly against pinion shoulders. *See Fig. 3.*
2) Using pliers, install pilot bearing snap ring and squeeze ring into pinion shaft groove. Insert pinion and bearing assembly in pinion cage and position spacer(s) over pinion shaft. Using a press, install front pinion gear bearing firmly against spacer(s).
3) Rotate cage several revolutions to ensure bearings seat. Using a press, apply 11 tons of pressure to pinion assembly. To check bearing preload torque, wrap soft wire around cage. Attach wire to a pound scale. Pull in horizontal line with pound scale. Record rotating torque, not starting torque. *See Fig. 5.*

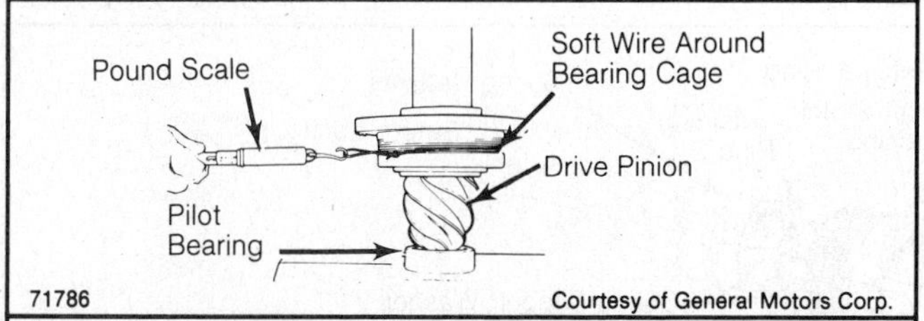
Pound Scale
Soft Wire Around Bearing Cage
Drive Pinion
Pilot Bearing
71786
Courtesy of General Motors Corp.

Fig. 5: Checking Pinion Gear Preload Torque

4) Preload (rotating) torque should be 5-15 INCH lbs. To determine inch pounds of torque, determine diameter of pinion cage in inches. Divide diameter by 2 to find radius in inches. Multiply radius by number of pounds on scale. Use a thinner spacer to increase bearing preload, and a thicker spacer to decrease bearing preload.
5) Press pinion flange against forward bearing and install washer and old pinion shaft nut. Hold flange and tighten pinion shaft nut to 240 ft. lbs. (325 N.m). Recheck pinion bearing preload torque. If preload is within specification, go to step **7)**. If preload is not within specification, go to next step.
6) Hold flange and remove pinion shaft nut and flange. Add or remove spacers as necessary to achieve 5-15 INCH lbs. of preload.
7) Discard old pinion shaft nut. Cover outer edge of seal body with a non-hardening sealing compound. Using a seal installer, drive pinion seal against cover shoulder. Install pinion flange deflector.
8) Press flange against outer bearing, and install washer and new pinion shaft nut. Torque pinion shaft nut to 240 ft. lbs. (325 N.m).
Reassembly (Differential Case & Gear) - 1) DO NOT press or drive ring gear onto differential case, or damage to components may result. Ensure ring gear is clean and free of burrs. Heat ring gear in water to 160-180°F (71-82°C) for 10 minutes before assembly. Place ring gear onto differential case. Install new ring gear bolts. Torque ring gear bolts gradually in an alternating pattern to pull ring gear onto differential case.
2) Position thrust washers and side gears in case halves assembly. Place spider with pinions and thrust washers in position. Align scribe (reference) marks on differential case made during disassembly. Install differential case bolts. Torque to specification. Ensure differential case assembly rotates freely. Using a press, install bearings onto differential case.
3) Temporarily install bearing races, threaded adjusting rings and bearing caps. Tighten bearing cap bolts to proper torque. Bearing races must have a hand fit in bores. If bearing races do not have a hand fit in bores, use emery cloth on bearing bores until a hand fit is obtained.
4) Once races fit, remove bearing caps. Coat differential bearings and races with rear axle lubricant. Place bearing races over assembled differential bearing. Position differential assembly in carrier. Insert bearing adjusting nuts and turn hand tight against bearing races.
5) If bearing caps do not position properly, adjusting nuts may be cross threaded. Remove caps and reposition adjusting nuts. Install bearing cap washers and bolts. Torque bearing cap bolts to specification. See TORQUE SPECIFICATIONS table at end of article.
Adjusting Pinion Gear Depth - To accurately install a new pinion and cage assembly into carrier, mathematically calculate the proper pinion cage shim pack thickness using variation number on pinion head of original and new drive pinion:

Example:

Original Pack Thickness	.030"
Original Variation Number (+2)	-.002"
Standard Pack Thickness	.028"
New Variation Number (+5)	+.005"
New Pack Thickness	.033"

Ring Gear Runout & Side Bearing Preload - 1) Use a dial indicator at back face of ring gear. Loosen bearing adjusting nut on side opposite ring gear, but only enough to notice end play on dial indicator. Tighten same adjusting nut until zero end play is obtained.
2) Rotate ring gear and check runout. If runout exceeds .008" (.20 mm), remove differential and check for cause. Tighten adjusting nuts one notch each from zero end play to preload differential bearings.
Ring Gear Backlash - 1) If drive gear is not going to be replaced, use established backlash recorded before disassembly. For new gears, backlash should be set at .008-.015" (.20-.38 mm) initially.
2) Adjust backlash by moving ring gear only. Back off one adjusting nut and tighten opposite adjusting nut the same amount. *See Fig. 3.*

NOTE: Preload will change if adjusting nuts are not moved exactly the same amount.

3) Install adjusting nut pins. Install thrust block screw and lock nut. Torque thrust block screw sufficiently to place thrust block firmly against back face of ring gear.
4) To secure correct adjustment of .008-.015" (.20-.38 mm) clearance, loosen thrust block screw 1/4 turn and lock securely with nut. Recheck to ensure there is a clearance of .008-.015" (.20-.38 mm) during full rotation of ring gear.

TORQUE SPECIFICATIONS

TORQUE SPECIFICATIONS

Application	Ft. Lbs. (N.m)
Axle Shaft Lock Nut	250 (339)
Bearing Cap Bolt	130 (176)
Caliper Mounting Bolt	35 (47)
Differential Case Bolt	45 (61)
Pinion Bearing Cage Bolt	35 (47)
Pinion Shaft Nut	240 (325)
Ring Gear Bolt	100 (136)
Thrust Block Screw Nut	150-190 (203-257)
Wheel Hub Bearing Nut	50 (68)

1991 DRIVE AXLES
4WD Automatic Locking Hubs

"V" Series

DESCRIPTION

Automatic locking hub engages or disengages front axle shaft with front hub. Shifting transfer case into 4WD engages automatic locking hubs. Hub will remain engaged during coasting or downhill operation. Hub disengages when transfer case is shifted into 2WD, and when vehicle is slowly moved rearward several feet.

REMOVAL & INSTALLATION

LOCKING HUB

Removal - 1) Remove cover-to-outer clutch housing screws. Remove "O" rings. Remove cover, sealing ring and bearing race spring. Remove bearing inner race, bearing and bearing retainer clip. *See Fig. 1.*

2) Remove seal bridge retainer from outer clutch housing. Remove wire retainer ring by compressing it with needle nose pliers.

3) To aid in locking hub unit removal, loosely install 2 cover screws in the outer clutch housing. Pull locking hub unit from hub.

Installation - 1) To install, reverse removal procedure. Lubricate housing splines with Lubricant (1052750) before installing components. Ensure wire retainer ring fully seats in groove in hub assembly. Pack bearing with Lubricant (1052750) before installing.

2) When installing bearing race spring, apply small amount of grease on spring to retain spring in locator area of the cover. Replace "O" ring and install cover screws. Tighten screws to 45 INCH lbs. (5 N.m).

OVERHAUL

LOCKING HUB

Disassembly - 1) Remove retaining ring and small spacer from inboard end of hub sleeve. Rotate drag sleeve and detent with brake band until components release from locking unit. *See Fig. 1.*

CAUTION: DO NOT remove brake band from drag sleeve and detent, as spring tension of brake band will be altered.

2) Carefully remove shield to prevent damage during removal. Remove snap ring from groove in outer clutch housing. Place outer clutch housing on bench, with inner cage end of clutch housing down.

3) Remove retaining ring, return spring, spring retainers and spring support washer. Place opposite end of outer clutch housing on a socket with outside diameter of approximately 1 7/16".

4) Press downward on outer clutch housing to expose White plastic tab of outer cage. Remove inner cage by prying plastic tab of outer cage from opening in inner cage. DO NOT use excessive force or plastic tab will be damaged.

5) Remove outer cage. Pry outer legs on cam follower from flat areas of clutch gear to release hub sleeve and conical spring. Remove outer clutch housing. Remove "C" type retaining ring from hub sleeve.

Cleaning & Inspection - Wash all parts with cleaning solvent and blow dry. Check cover for cracks or pitting condition. Replace worn or damaged components.

Reassembly - 1) Install conical spring on cam follower, with smaller end of conical spring toward cam follower. Pack hub sleeve with Lubricant (1052750). Install clutch gear over splines of hub sleeve.

2) Install cam follower on clutch gear. Ensure legs on cam follower engage with flat areas of clutch gear. Lubricate splines of hub sleeve with lubricant.

CAUTION: Ensure clutch gear and conical spring slide freely over hub sleeve splines.

3) Install "C" type retaining ring on hub sleeve. Install hub sleeve assembly in outer clutch housing. Install outer cage by seating it under rim of outer clutch housing.

4) Install inner cage and snap ring. Install spring support washer, spring retainer, return spring and remaining spring retainer in outer clutch housing. Install retaining ring in outer clutch housing.

5) Lubricate outer diameter of brake band with Lubricant (1052750). Install shield on brake band. Install drag sleeve and detent, and install brake band assembly. Install small spacer and retaining ring.

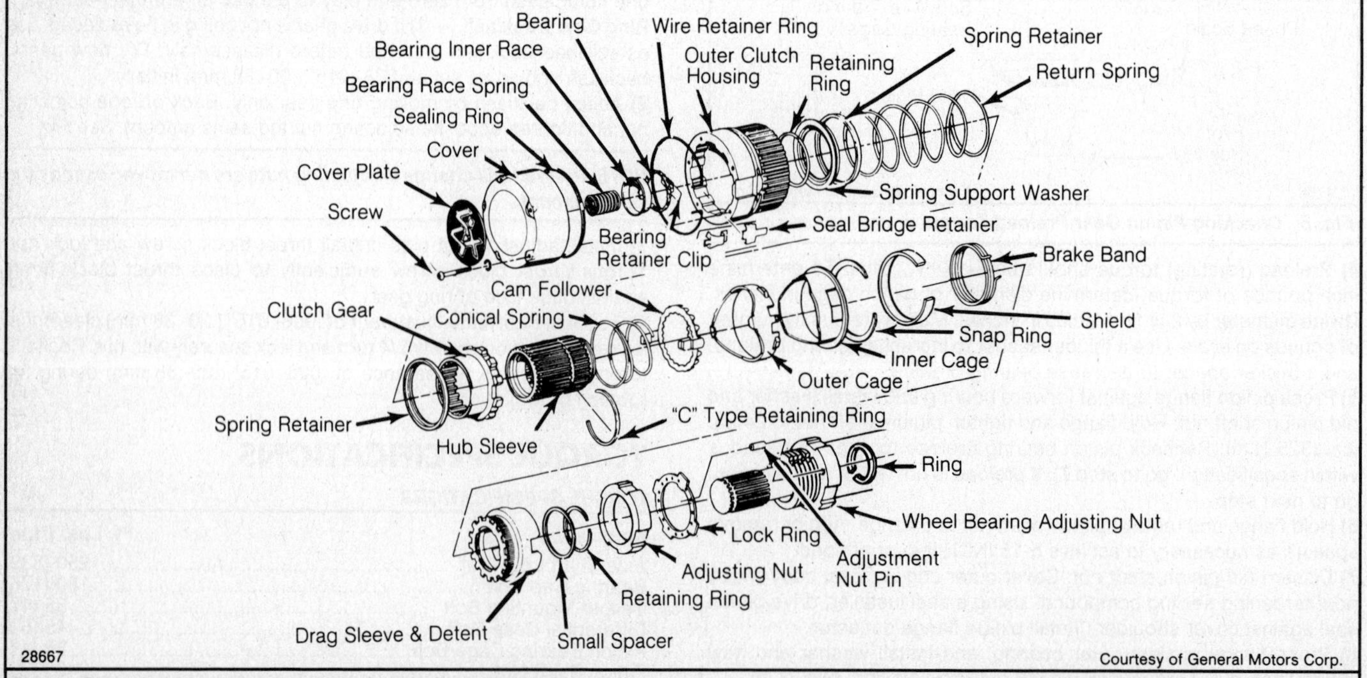
Bearing
Wire Retainer Ring
Bearing Inner Race
Outer Clutch Housing
Retaining Ring
Spring Retainer
Return Spring
Bearing Race Spring
Sealing Ring
Cover
Cover Plate
Screw
Spring Support Washer
Seal Bridge Retainer
Bearing Retainer Clip
Brake Band
Cam Follower
Clutch Gear
Conical Spring
Shield
Snap Ring
Inner Cage
Outer Cage
Spring Retainer
"C" Type Retaining Ring
Hub Sleeve
Ring
Wheel Bearing Adjusting Nut
Lock Ring
Adjustment Nut Pin
Adjusting Nut
Retaining Ring
Drag Sleeve & Detent
Small Spacer

28667

Courtesy of General Motors Corp.

Fig. 1: Exploded View of Automatic Locking Hub (Typical)

1991 DRIVE AXLES
4WD Manual Locking Hubs

"V" Series

DESCRIPTION

Locking hubs provide a means of engagement of front wheels on vehicles with front drive axle. When hub is engaged, full power is transmitted to both front wheels. When hubs are disengaged, front wheels are free to turn, but axle shafts and differential will remain idle.

Engagement is accomplished through action of gears within hub. With hub in engaged position, clutch body and hub body act as one piece to connect axle shaft to wheel hub.

REMOVAL & INSTALLATION

LOCKING HUB

Removal - 1) Remove screws and tabbed lock washers attaching hub lock-knob cover assembly to axle hub (if equipped). *See Fig. 1.* Remove hub lock-knob cover assembly. Remove lock ring from axle hub and axle shaft snap ring from axle shaft. Remove hub body assembly.

2) Clean hub components in solvent. Dry components, using compressed air or clean shop towel. Ensure old lubricant, dirt, water and other foreign materials are flushed out.

CAUTION: DO NOT turn hub control dial until hub has been installed. Hub clutch nut and cup can be damaged if dial is rotated while hub is off vehicle. DO NOT disassemble hub lock-knob assembly. If assembly is faulty, replace as a unit only. Inner drive gear and hub body assembly may be disassembled for cleaning and component replacement.

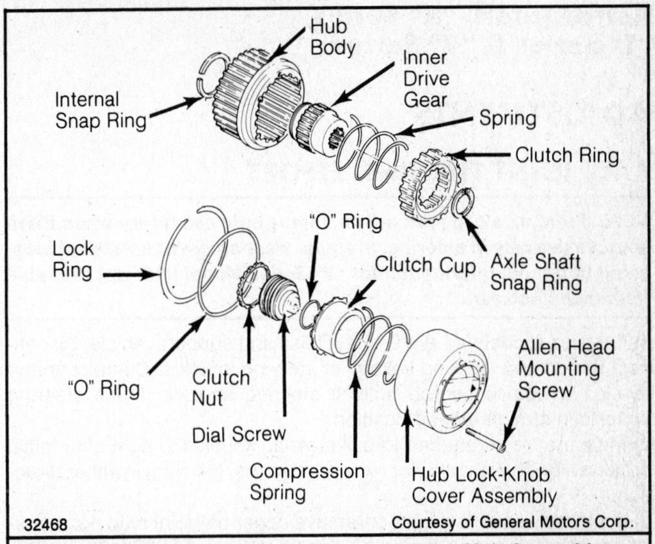
Hub Body
Inner Drive Gear
Internal Snap Ring
Spring
Clutch Ring
"O" Ring
Lock Ring
Clutch Cup
Axle Shaft Snap Ring
Allen Head Mounting Screw
"O" Ring
Clutch Nut
Dial Screw
Compression Spring
Hub Lock-Knob Cover Assembly
32468
Courtesy of General Motors Corp.

Fig. 1: Exploded View of Warn Manual Locking Hub Assembly

Installation - 1) Apply a light coat of multipurpose grease to hub components. DO NOT pack hub with lubricant.

2) Install hub body assembly and axle shaft snap ring on axle shaft. Install large lock ring in axle hub. Install new "O" ring if hub body is being replaced.

3) Position hub body in clutch. Align screw holes in axle and hub body. Install screws and tabbed lock washers (if equipped). Tighten screws to 45 INCH lbs. (5.1 N.m).

4) Raise vehicle front end. Turn hub control dials to FREE position and rotate wheels. Wheels should rotate freely. Ensure control dials fully engage in LOCK position. If wheels drag or dials will not fully engage, recheck hub assembly and installation.

1991 DRIVE AXLES
4WD Steering Knuckles

Astro, Safari, "K" Series, "T" Series & "V" Series

ADJUSTMENTS

BALL JOINT TURNING EFFORT

NOTE: Front axle ball joint adjustment is only necessary when there is excessive play in steering, irregular wear on tire or persistent loosening of tie rod. Information for "V" Series Model V3 is not available from manufacturer.

"V" Series Models V1 & V2 – 1) Raise and support vehicle. Disconnect tie rod and steering linkage at steering knuckle. Connect spring tension gauge to tie rod hole in steering knuckle. Place steering knuckle in straight-ahead position.

2) Measure force required to pull steering knuckle to right after initial break-away. Pull should not exceed 25 ft. lbs. (34 N.m) in either direction.

3) If excessive pull is required, remove upper ball joint stud nut. Loosen adjusting sleeve as required using Stud Wrench (J-23447). *See Fig. 1.* Reconnect tie rod and steering linkage.

REMOVAL & INSTALLATION

STEERING KNUCKLE

Removal (Astro, Safari, "K" Series & "T" Series) – 1) Raise and support vehicle. Remove wheel and tire assembly. Install Axle Shaft Boot Seal Protector (J-28712) on axle shaft boot to protect boot during repair. Depress brake caliper piston, detach brake caliper and move aside. Remove brake rotor.

2) Remove cotter pin and retainer (if equipped) from nut for axle shaft. *See Fig. 2.* Remove nut and washer from axle shaft. Remove cotter pin and tie rod end nut. Separate tie rod end from steering knuckle.

3) Attach puller to hub. Tighten pressure screw and force axle shaft from hub and bearing assembly. Remove hub and bearing assembly from steering knuckle. Remove splash shield. Support lower control arm with floor jack or jack stand.

CAUTION: Lower control arm must be supported with floor jack or jack stand to maintain tension on torsion bar.

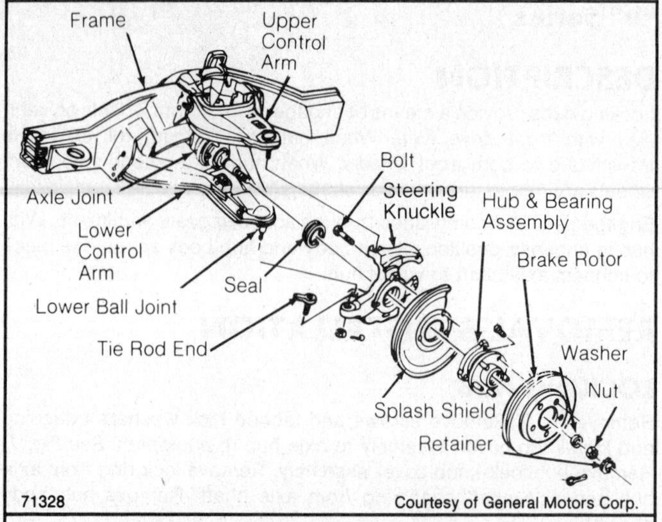
Frame
Upper Control Arm
Bolt
Axle Joint
Steering Knuckle
Hub & Bearing Assembly
Lower Control Arm
Brake Rotor
Seal
Lower Ball Joint
Tie Rod End
Washer
Nut
Splash Shield
Retainer
71328
Courtesy of General Motors Corp.

Fig. 2: Exploded View of Hub & Steering Knuckle Assembly ("K" Series Shown; Others Are Similar)

4) Remove cotter pins from ball joint studs. On "T" Series, place Ball Joint Separator (J-34026) over upper or lower ball joint. Loosen ball joint nut. *See Fig. 3.* Back off until nut contacts ball joint separator. Continue backing off nut until nut forces ball stud out of steering knuckle.

5) On all other models, separate ball joint from steering knuckle using Ball Joint Separator (J-36607). On all models, remove steering knuckle from vehicle without damaging or moving axle shaft. Remove seal from steering knuckle.

Installation – 1) To install, reverse removal procedure. Using seal installer, install NEW seal in steering knuckle. Use Seal Installer (J-36605 for Astro and Safari, J-36606 for "K" Series or J-28574 for "T" Series).

2) On "T" series, ensure spacer is installed on steering knuckle at upper ball joint stud hole. On all models, tighten bolts/nuts to specification. See TORQUE SPECIFICATIONS table at end of article. If necessary, tighten tie rod and ball joint nuts to align cotter key hole. DO NOT loosen nuts for alignment. Remove boot protector from axle shaft.

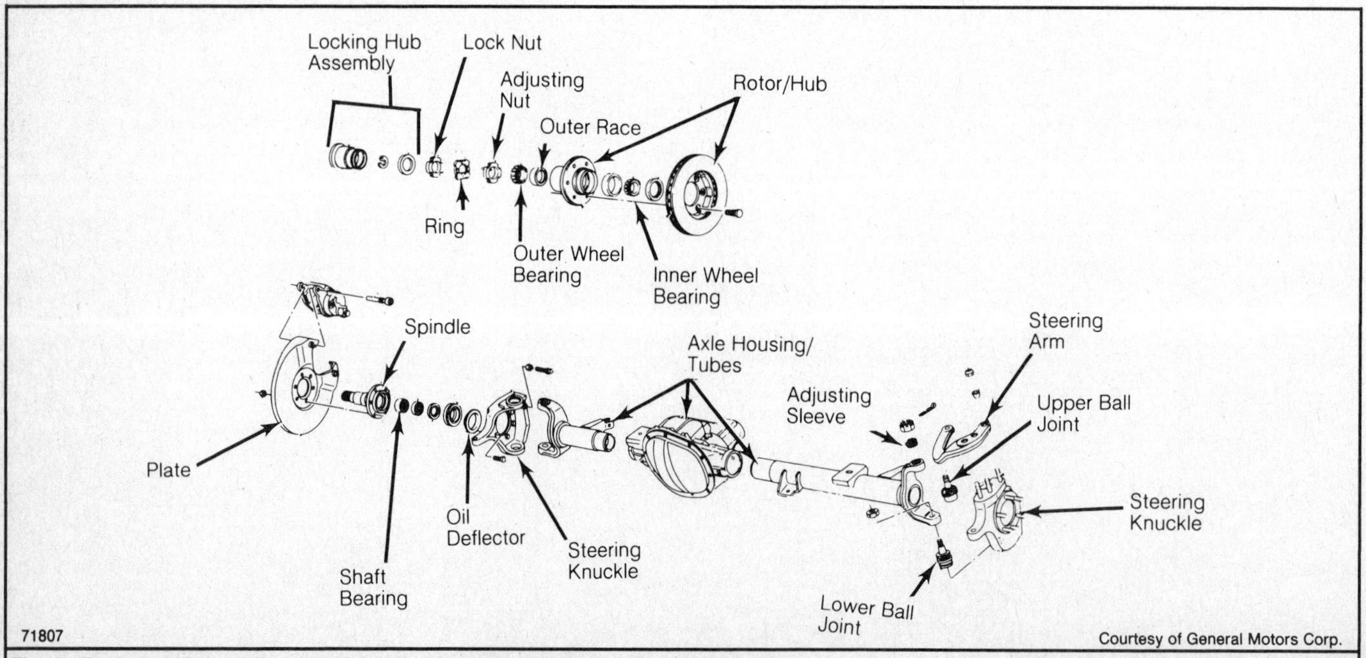
Locking Hub Assembly
Lock Nut
Adjusting Nut
Rotor/Hub
Outer Race
Ring
Outer Wheel Bearing
Inner Wheel Bearing
Spindle
Axle Housing/ Tubes
Steering Arm
Adjusting Sleeve
Upper Ball Joint
Plate
Steering Knuckle
Oil Deflector
Steering Knuckle
Shaft Bearing
Lower Ball Joint
71807
Courtesy of General Motors Corp.

Fig. 1: Exploded View of Steering Knuckle Assembly ("V" Series Models V1 & V2)

1991 DRIVE AXLES
4WD Steering Knuckles (Cont.)

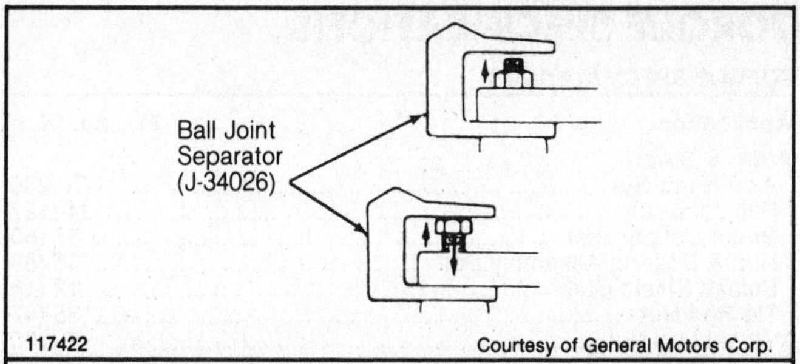
Ball Joint
Separator
(J-34026)
117422
Courtesy of General Motors Corp.

Fig. 3: Separating Ball Joint from Steering Knuckle ("T" Series)

NOTE: For locking hub and wheel bearing service procedures, see appropriate article in SUSPENSION.

Removal ("V" Series Models V1 & V2) – 1) Raise and support vehicle. Remove wheel and tire assembly. Remove brake caliper. Remove locking hubs (if equipped) and rotor and hub. See appropriate article in SUSPENSION.

2) Remove spindle nuts and lightly tap spindle with soft-face hammer to free it from steering knuckle. Disconnect tie rod end from steering knuckle.

3) Remove steering arm-to-steering knuckle nuts and adapters. Remove steering arm from steering knuckle. Remove upper and lower ball joint nuts from steering knuckle.

CAUTION: DO NOT remove adjusting sleeve unless new ball joints are to be installed. See Fig. 1. If necessary to loosen adjusting sleeve for steering knuckle removal use Stud Wrench (J-23447). DO NOT loosen more than 2 threads.

4) Separate ball joints from steering knuckle. Remove steering knuckle.

Installation – 1) To install, reverse removal procedure. Lubricate bearing in spindle with wheel bearing grease. Install spindle using NEW retaining nuts. Tighten nuts to specification. See TORQUE SPECIFICATIONS table at end of this article.

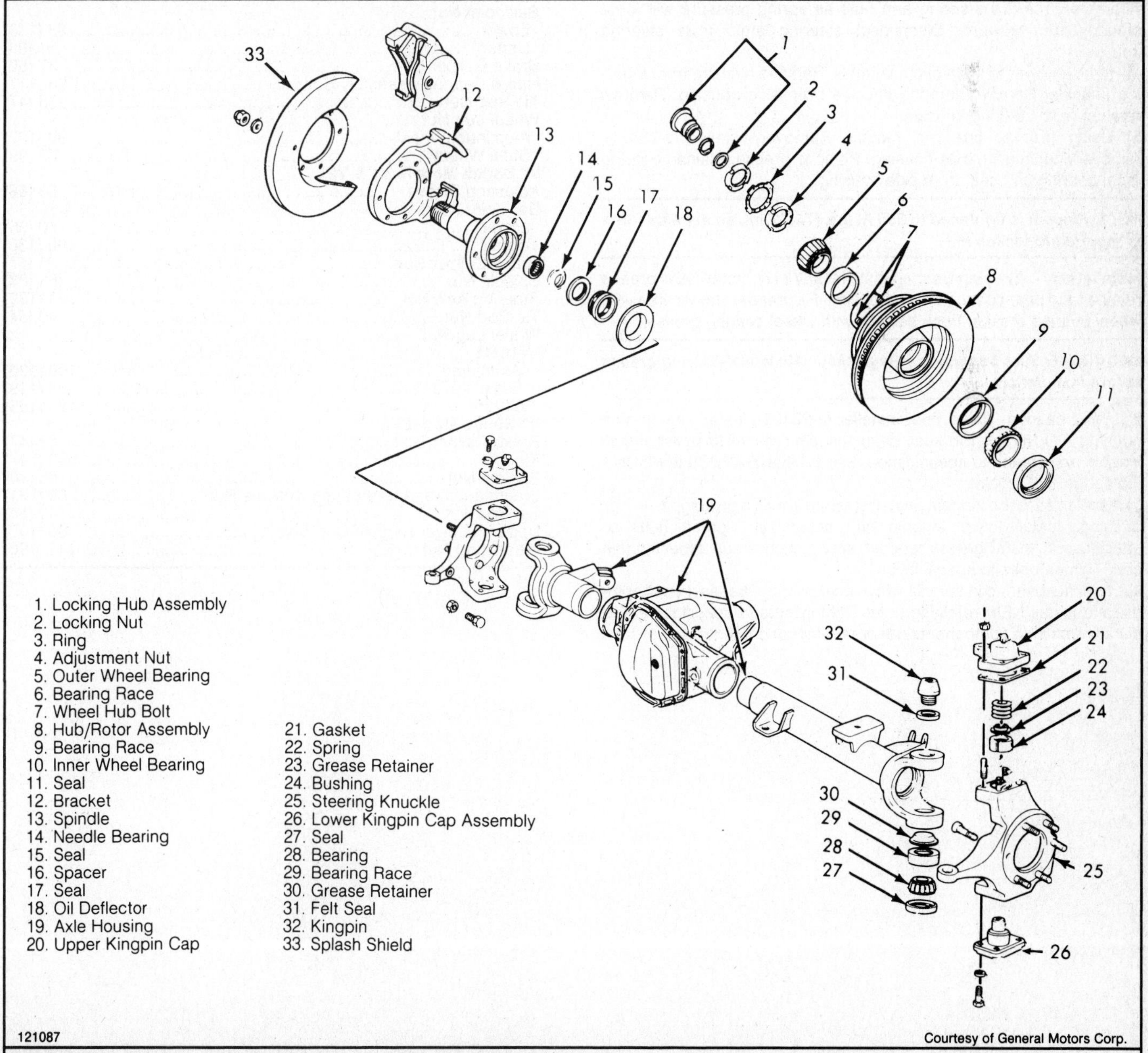
1. Locking Hub Assembly
2. Locking Nut
3. Ring
4. Adjustment Nut
5. Outer Wheel Bearing
6. Bearing Race
7. Wheel Hub Bolt
8. Hub/Rotor Assembly
9. Bearing Race
10. Inner Wheel Bearing
11. Seal
12. Bracket
13. Spindle
14. Needle Bearing
15. Seal
16. Spacer
17. Seal
18. Oil Deflector
19. Axle Housing
20. Upper Kingpin Cap
21. Gasket
22. Spring
23. Grease Retainer
24. Bushing
25. Steering Knuckle
26. Lower Kingpin Cap Assembly
27. Seal
28. Bearing
29. Bearing Race
30. Grease Retainer
31. Felt Seal
32. Kingpin
33. Splash Shield
121087
Courtesy of General Motors Corp.

Fig. 4: Exploded View of Steering Knuckle Assembly ("V" Series Model V3)

1991 DRIVE AXLES
4WD Steering Knuckles (Cont.)

2) Install NEW steering arm-to-steering knuckle retaining nuts. DO NOT reuse steering arm retaining nuts. Tighten bolts/nuts to specification. When aligning upper ball joint nut with cotter pin hole, always tighten nut. DO NOT loosen nut.

NOTE: On V1 and V2 models, it may be necessary to check ball joint turning effort when excessive play exists or irregular tire wear exists. See BALL JOINT TURNING EFFORT under ADJUSTMENTS.

NOTE: For locking hub and wheel bearing service procedures, see appropriate article in SUSPENSION.

Removal ("V" Series Model V3) – 1) Raise and support vehicle. Remove wheel and tire assembly. Remove brake caliper. Remove locking hubs (if equipped) and rotor/hub assembly. See appropriate article in SUSPENSION.

2) Remove nuts, washers, splash shield, bracket and spindle. It may be necessary to lightly tap spindle with soft-face hammer to free it from steering knuckle.

3) Alternately remove upper kingpin cap bolts as spring pressure will force cap upward. Remove kingpin cap, gasket and spring. *See Fig. 4.* Alternately remove steering arm nuts as spring pressure will force steering arm upward. Disconnect steering arms from steering knuckle.

4) Remove lower kingpin cap assembly. Remove bushing from steering knuckle. Remove steering knuckle from axle housing. Remove retainer from steering knuckle.

5) Using breaker bar and Kingpin Remover/Installer (J-26871), remove kingpin from axle housing. Remove grease retainer, bearing race, bearing and seal from axle housing.

NOTE: Kingpin is tightened to 550 ft. lbs. (747 N.m), so extreme force is required to loosen it.

Installation – 1) Using Bearing Installer (J-7817), install NEW grease retainer and bearing race in axle housing. Fill grease retainer area with wheel bearing grease. Pack bearing with wheel bearing grease.

CAUTION: Ensure bearing is fully packed with wheel bearing grease before installation.

2) Install bearing. Using Seal Installer (J-22301), install seal in axle housing. DO NOT distort seal. Using kingpin remover/installer, install kingpin and tighten to specification. See TORQUE SPECIFICATIONS table at end of article.

3) Install felt seal on kingpin. Install steering knuckle on kingpin. Install bushing. Install lower kingpin cap assembly. Tighten bolts to specification. Install grease retainer, spring, gasket and upper kingpin cap. Tighten bolts to specification.

4) Lubricate bearing in spindle with wheel bearing grease. Install spindle and install NEW retaining nuts. Tighten nuts to specification. To install remaining components, reverse removal procedure.

TORQUE SPECIFICATIONS

TORQUE SPECIFICATIONS

Application	Ft. Lbs. (N.m)
Astro & Safari	
Axle Shaft Nut	173 (235)
Ball Joint Nut	94 (127)
Brake Caliper Bolt	37 (50)
Hub & Bearing Assembly Bolt	66 (89)
Splash Shield Bolt	12 (16)
Tie Rod Nut	35 (47)
Wheel Lug Nut	92 (125)
"K" Series	
Axle Shaft Nut	173 (235)
Ball Joint Nut	94 (127)
Brake Caliper Bolt	28 (38)
Hub & Bearing Assembly Bolt	66 (89)
Splash Shield Bolt	12 (16)
Tie Rod Nut	35 (47)
Wheel Lug Nut	
Single Wheel	90 (122)
Dual Wheel	125 (169)
"T" Series	
Axle Shaft Nut	181 (245)
Ball Joint Nut	
Lower	83 (113)
Upper	61 (83)
Brake Caliper Bolt	37 (50)
Hub & Bearing Assembly Bolt	86 (117)
Tie Rod Nut	35 (47)
Wheel Lug Nut	
Aluminum Wheel	90 (122)
Steel Wheel	73 (99)
"V" Series Models V1 & V2	
Adjusting Sleeve	50 (68)
Ball Joint Nut	
Lower	70 (95)
Upper	100 (136)
Brake Caliper Bolt	35 (47)
Spindle Nut	65 (88)
Steering Arm Nut	90 (122)
Tie Rod Nut	40 (54)
Wheel Lug Nut	
V10/15	
Aluminum	100 (136)
Steel	88 (119)
V20/25	120 (163)
"V" Series Model V3	
Brake Caliper Bolt	35 (47)
Kingpin	550 (747)
Spindle Nut	65 (88)
Steering Linkage-to-Steering Knuckle Nut	89 (121)
Tie Rod Nut	40 (54)
Upper & Lower Kingpin Cap Bolt	80 (108)
Wheel Lug Nut	140 (190)

1991 DRIVE AXLES
Eaton Locking Differential

Astro, Safari, "C" & "K" Series, "G" Series, "P" Series, "R" & "V" Series, "S" & "T" Series

DESCRIPTION

Locking differential consist of either a 1-piece case or 2-piece case. The 1-piece case is used on all axles except models with 10 1/2" ring gear axle. The 10 1/2" ring gear axle uses the 2-piece case. The 1-piece case has 2 pinion gears. The 2-piece case has 3-pinion gears. Both types have a clutch disc pack behind each of the side gears.

AXLE RATIO & IDENTIFICATION

To determine drive axle ratio, see AXLE RATIO IDENTIFICATION article.

REMOVAL & INSTALLATION

Removal and installation procedures are covered in conventional differential article. See appropriate article in DRIVE AXLES.

OVERHAUL

1-PIECE CASE

Disassembly (Differential) – **1)** Using Governor Remover (J-26252), remove governor bushing. Remove "C" clips holding latching bracket in position on governor shaft. Move latching bracket down shaft.

2) Using governor remover, remove latching bracket bushing. *See Fig. 1.* Remove latching bracket, shaft, spring and governor from case. Remove stop pin on 9 1/2" ring gear units. *See Fig. 1.* Remove lock screw and pinion shaft on all models. Remove pinion gears and thrust washers from case by rotating a side gear.

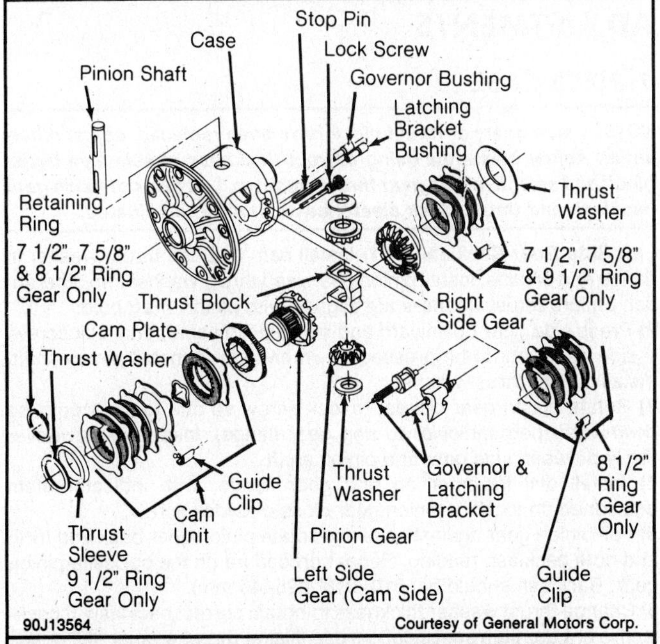
Stop Pin
Case
Lock Screw
Pinion Shaft
Governor Bushing
Latching Bracket Bushing
Retaining Ring
Thrust Washer
7 1/2", 7 5/8" & 8 1/2" Ring Gear Only
7 1/2", 7 5/8" & 9 1/2" Ring Gear Only
Thrust Block
Right Side Gear
Cam Plate
Thrust Washer
Guide Clip
Thrust Washer
Governor & Latching Bracket
8 1/2" Ring Gear Only
Cam Unit
Thrust Sleeve 9 1/2" Ring Gear Only
Pinion Gear
Left Side Gear (Cam Side)
Guide Clip
90J13564
Courtesy of General Motors Corp.

Fig. 1: Exploded View of 1-Piece Case Locking Differential

3) Remove thrust block, right side gear, clutch pack and thrust washer. Remove left side gear, cam plate and cam unit (clutch pack) as an assembly. Remove thrust washer.

Disassembly (Cam Unit With 7 1/2", 7 5/8" Or 8 1/2" Ring Gear) – Remove retaining ring, clutch plates, guide clips and wave spring. Remove cam plate and left side gear.

Disassembly (Cam Unit With 9 1/2" Ring Gear) – Measure and record overall length of gear assembly from front of gear to back of thrust sleeve, including thrust washer. Remove guide clips. Using press and Bearing Remover (J-22912-01), press thrust sleeve from left side gear. Remove lock plates, wave spring and cam plate from left side gear.

Inspection – Clean all parts in solvent. Inspect all gears for cracks or scoring. Inspect all clutch components and thrust washers for damage. Check fit of side gears on axle shafts. Inspect thrust sleeve for wear. Replace components as necessary.

NOTE: If side gears or thrust block were replaced, adjust differential. Check side gear backlash and thrust block clearance. See 1-PIECE CASE under ADJUSTMENTS.

Reassembly (Cam Unit With 7 1/2", 7 5/8" Or 8 1/2" Ring Gear) – Install cam plate on left side gear. Install wave spring. On units with 7 1/2" or 7 5/8" ring gear, install 8 clutch plates. Install 10 clutch plates on 8 1/2" ring gear units. Clutch plates must be installed in alternating sequence. *See Fig. 1.* Install retaining ring. Use grease to hold guide clips in place; install guide clips on clutch plates.

Reassembly (Cam Unit With 9 1/2" Ring Gear) – **1)** Install cam plate on left side gear. Install wave spring. Install clutch plates. Clutch plates must be installed in alternating sequence. *See Fig. 1.* Press thrust sleeve on left side gear until sleeve is even with left side gear disc splines' surface.

2) Use grease to hold guide clips in place; install guide clips on clutch plates. If side gear or thrust sleeve were replaced, measure and record overall length of gear assembly from front of gear to back of thrust sleeve and thrust washer.

3) Compare new measurement with original measurement taken during disassembly. If difference between the 2 measurements is .003" (.07 mm) or more, install new thrust washer to obtain measurement nearest to original measurement.

Reassembly (Differential) – **1)** Install thrust washer and left side gear (cam unit) in case. Install thrust washer for right side gear in case. Install clutch pack for right side gear. Clutch plates must be installed in alternating sequence. *See Fig. 1.*

2) Use grease to hold guide clips in place, and install guide clips on clutch plates. Install right side gear, thrust block, thrust washers and pinion gears. Install pinion gears in case, 180 degrees apart.

3) Rotate pinion gears and thrust block into the case. Ensure open side of thrust block faces small window opening.

4) Install pinion shaft and NEW lock screw. DO NOT tighten lock screw to specification at this time.

NOTE: Once unit is installed in differential housing, tighten lock screw to specification.

5) Place governor assembly and latching bracket into case. Place straight end of latching bracket spring over governor assembly shaft. *See Fig. 2.*

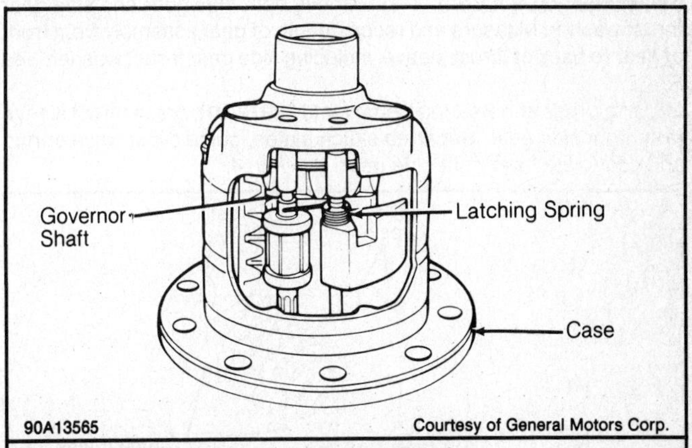
Governor Shaft
Latching Spring
Case
90A13565
Courtesy of General Motors Corp.

Fig. 2: Installing Governor & Latching Bracket

6) On 9 1/2" ring gear units, install stop pin until pin is even with surface of case.

7) Latching bracket bushing has a tapered hole, and governor bushing has a straight hole. Press governor bushing into case until shaft end play of .004-.020" (.10-.51 mm) exists. Press latching bracket bushing into case so no shaft end play exists. Once unit is installed, tighten lock screw to 37 ft. lbs. (51 N.m) on 9 1/2" ring gear, or 27 ft. lbs. (37 N.m) on all others.

1991 DRIVE AXLES
Eaton Locking Differential (Cont.)

2-PIECE CASE

Disassembly (Differential) – 1) With differential removed from housing, remove ring gear and side bearings. Remove screws from front face of ring gear flange. Place differential on differential case's right half.
2) Using a screwdriver, gently pry differential case halves apart at yoke hole locations. Remove differential case's left half. Hold thumb against inside of gear hub when separating differential case halves to prevent left side gear from falling out.
3) Remove governor and latching bracket assembly. *See Fig. 3.* Remove left side gear, clutch plates, guide clips and side gear thrust washer. Remove reaction blocks, pinion yoke, pinion gears and pinion thrust washers.

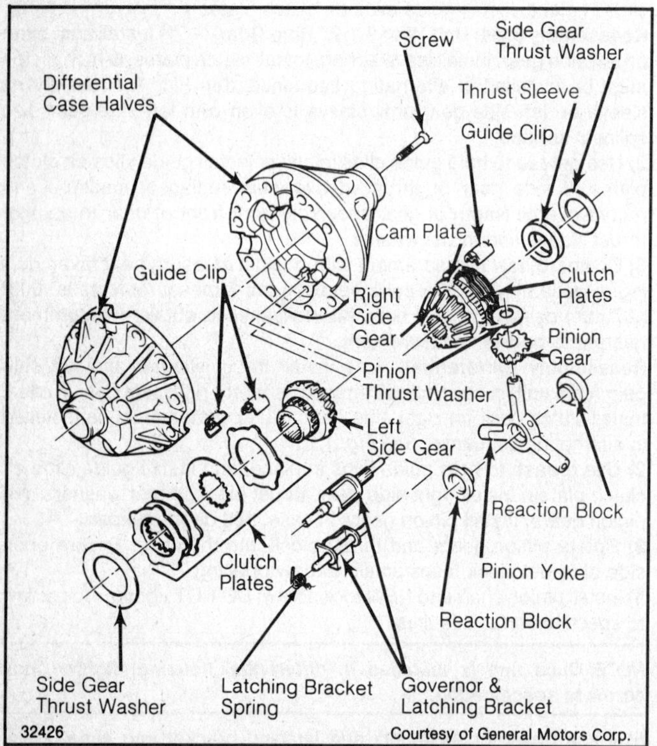
Screw
Side Gear Thrust Washer
Differential Case Halves
Thrust Sleeve
Guide Clip
Cam Plate
Guide Clip
Clutch Plates
Right Side Gear
Pinion Gear
Pinion Thrust Washer
Left Side Gear
Reaction Block
Clutch Plates
Pinion Yoke
Reaction Block
Side Gear Thrust Washer
Latching Bracket Spring
Governor & Latching Bracket
32426
Courtesy of General Motors Corp.

Fig. 3: Exploded View of 2-Piece Case Locking Differential

Disassembly (Cam Unit) – 1) Remove right side gear and side gear thrust washer. Measure and record length of gear assembly from front of gear to back of thrust sleeve, including side gear thrust washer. *See Fig. 3.*
2) Using press and Bearing Remover (J 22912-01), press thrust sleeve from right side gear. Separate clutch plates, guide clips, wave spring and cam plate from right side gear. *See Fig. 4.*

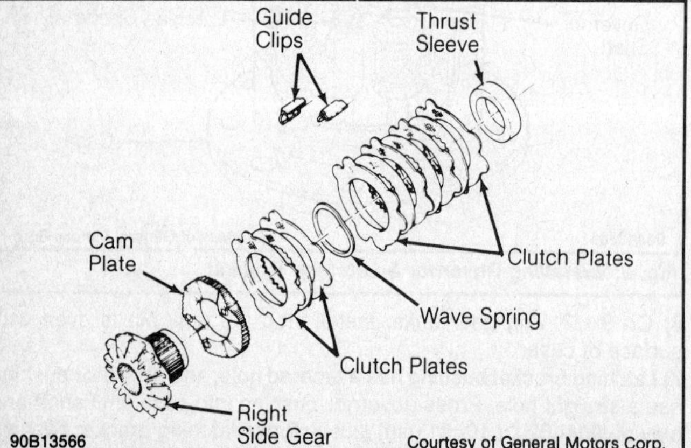
Guide Clips
Thrust Sleeve
Cam Plate
Clutch Plates
Wave Spring
Clutch Plates
Right Side Gear
90B13566
Courtesy of General Motors Corp.

Fig. 4: Exploded View of Right Side Gear (Cam Unit) & Components

Inspection – Clean all parts in solvent. Inspect all gears for cracks or scoring. Inspect all clutch components and thrust washers for damage. Check fit of side gears on axle shafts. Inspect thrust sleeve for wear. Replace components as necessary.

NOTE: If side gears or reaction blocks were replaced, adjust differential. Check side gear backlash and reaction block clearance. See 2-PIECE CASE under ADJUSTMENTS.

Reassembly (Cam Unit) – 1) Install cam plate on right side gear. Install wave spring and clutch plates. Install clutch plates. Clutch plates must be installed in alternating sequence. *See Fig. 4.*
2) Press thrust sleeve on right side gear until sleeve is even with surface of right side gear disc splines.
3) Use grease to hold guide clips in place, and install guide clips on clutch plates. If side gear or thrust sleeve were replaced, measure and record overall length of gear assembly from front of gear to back of thrust sleeve and thrust washer.
4) Compare new measurement with original measurement taken during disassembly. If difference between the 2 measurements is .003" (.07 mm) or more, install new thrust washer to obtain measurement nearest to original measurement.
Reassembly (Differential) – 1) Install side gear thrust washer and right side gear in differential case half. Install reaction blocks, pinion yoke, pinion gears and pinion thrust washers.
2) Install left side gear thrust washer and clutch plates in differential case half. Ensure clutch plates are installed in alternating sequence. *See Fig. 3.* Install left side gear and latching bracket assembly.
3) Install governor assembly. Ensure straight end of latching bracket spring is over governor assembly shaft. *See Fig. 2.* Hold left side gear in differential case half and install cases together. Install retaining bolts and tighten.

ADJUSTMENTS

1-PIECE CASE

NOTE: If side gears or thrust block have been replaced, adjust differential. Adjust clearance using correct thickness of selective thrust block and selective side gear thrust washers. Left and right side gear backlash and thrust block clearance must also be adjusted.

Left Side Gear Backlash – 1) Install cam unit and thrust washer in flange end of case. Install pinion gears and thrust washer into differential. Ensure thrust washers are aligned with pinion shaft hole.
2) Press side gear downward and install pinion shaft and lock screw. If side gear cannot be pressed down enough to install pinion shaft, install thinner thrust washer.
3) Rotate pinion gear closest to lock screw so one tooth is pointing downward (perpendicular to ring gear flange). Insert a screwdriver firmly between side gear and pinion shaft.
4) Install dial indicator on ring gear flange, with indicator stem positioned on tooth of pinion gear closest to lock screw.
5) Pull pinion gear against case and rotate pinion gear back and forth and note backlash reading. Repeat procedure on the opposite pinion gear. Backlash should be .010-.018" (.25-.46 mm).
6) Change thrust washer thickness to obtain correct backlash. If backlash is greater than specification, use thicker thrust washer. If it is less than specification, use thinner thrust washer.
Right Side Gear Backlash – 1) Alternately assemble clutch plates. *See Fig. 1.* Use grease to hold guide clips in place, and install guide clips on clutch plates.
2) Install thrust washer, clutch plates and right side gear into case. Install pinion gears and thrust washers. Ensure they align with pinion shaft hole.
3) Press side gear downward and install pinion shaft and lock screw. If side gear cannot be pressed down enough to install pinion shaft, install thinner thrust washer.
4) Rotate pinion gear closest to lock screw or stop pin so one tooth is pointing downward (perpendicular to ring gear flange). Insert a screwdriver firmly between side gear and pinion shaft.

1991 DRIVE AXLES
Eaton Locking Differential (Cont.)

5) Install dial indicator on ring gear flange, with indicator stem positioned on tooth of pinion gear closest to lock screw.
6) Pull pinion gear against case and rotate pinion gear back and forth and note backlash reading. Repeat procedure on the opposite pinion gear. Backlash should be .002-.010" (.05-.25 mm).
7) Change thrust washer thickness to obtain correct backlash. If backlash is greater than specification, use thicker thrust washer. If it is less than specification, use thinner thrust washer.
Thrust Block Clearance - 1) Install thrust washer, left side gear (cam unit), thrust washer, clutch plates and right side gear in case. Install pinion shaft and lock screw.
2) Insert a screwdriver firmly between each side gear and pinion shaft. Using a 1-2" telescoping gauge, measure distance between the faces (not gear teeth) of both side gears.
3) Remove telescoping gauge and measure with a micrometer. This is the side gear spread. With micrometer, measure original thrust block at outer corner. Thrust block thickness should be 0-.006" (0-.15 mm) less than side gear spread.
4) To adjust clearance, select thrust block with different thickness, or reshim right clutch pack. Ensure right side gear backlash remains at .002-.010" (.05-.25 mm).

2-PIECE CASE

NOTE: If side gears or thrust block have been replaced, adjust differential. Adjust clearance using correct thickness of selective thrust block and selective side gear thrust washers. Left and right side gear backlash and thrust block clearance must also be adjusted.

Right Side Gear Clearance - 1) Install right side gear (cam unit) and side gear thrust washer in differential case's right half. Using washers, long bolt and nut, clamp right side gear unit in differential case.
2) Install pinion gears and thrust washers on pinion yoke. Install pinion yoke in differential case half. Loosen nut on the bolt. Position one pinion gear tooth facing downward (perpendicular to ring gear flange) and tighten nut.
3) Install dial indicator on ring gear flange, with indicator stem positioned on one tooth of pinion gear. Pull pinion gear against differential case half. Rotate pinion gear back and forth and note backlash reading.
4) Ensure pinion yoke remains seated while checking backlash. Repeat procedure on the remaining pinion gears. Backlash should be .010-.018" (.25-.46 mm).
5) Change thrust washer thickness to obtain correct backlash. If backlash is greater than specification, use thicker thrust washer. If it is less than specification, use thinner thrust washer.
Left Side Gear Clearance - 1) Assemble clutch plates in alternating sequence. *See Fig. 3.* Use grease to hold guide clips in place, and install guide clips on clutch plates.
2) Install thrust washer, clutch plates and left side gear in differential case half. Using washers, long bolt and nut, clamp left side gear in differential case.
3) Install pinion gears and thrust washers on pinion yoke. Install pinion yoke in differential case half. Loosen nut on bolt. Position one pinion gear tooth facing downward (perpendicular to ring gear flange) and tighten nut.
4) Install dial indicator on ring gear flange, with indicator stem positioned on one tooth of pinion gear. Pull pinion gear against differential case. Rotate pinion gear back and forth and note backlash reading.
5) Ensure pinion yoke remains seated while checking backlash. Repeat procedure on the remaining pinion gears. Backlash should be .002-.010" (.05-.25 mm).
6) Change thrust washer thickness to obtain correct backlash. If backlash is greater than specification, use thicker thrust washer. If it is less than specification, use thinner thrust washer.
Reaction Block Clearance - 1) Install left thrust washer, right thrust washer, side gears and clutch plates in differential case halves. Using washers, long bolt and nut, clamp both side gears in differential case.
2) Place straightedge across top of both side gears. Using depth micrometer, measure distance from face of straightedge to surface of differential case half. Subtract straightedge thickness from this measurement.
3) Add measurement of both sides together. This is the side gear spread. Assemble both original reaction blocks together and measure thickness of both reaction blocks.
4) Reaction block thickness should be 0-.006" (0-.15 mm) less than side gear spread. To adjust clearance, select reaction block with different thickness, or reshim left clutch pack. Ensure left side gear backlash remains within specification.

AXLE ASSEMBLY SPECIFICATIONS

AXLE ASSEMBLY SPECIFICATIONS

Application	Measurement In. (mm)
Governor Shaft End Play	.004-.020" (.10-.51)
Pinion Gear Backlash	
1-Piece Case	
Left Side Gear	.010-.018" (.25-.46)
Right Side Gear	.002-.010" (.05-.25)
2-Piece Case	
Left Side Gear	.002-.010" (.05-.25)
Right Side Gear	.010-.018" (.25-.46)

TORQUE SPECIFICATIONS

TORQUE SPECIFICATIONS

Application	Ft. Lbs. (N.m)
Pinion Shaft Lock Screw	
9 1/2" Ring Gear	37 (51)
All Others	27 (37)

1991 DRIVE AXLES
Propeller Shafts & Universal Joints

Astro, Blazer, Bravada, Jimmy, Safari, Sierra, Sonoma, "C" & "K" Series, "G" Series, "P" Series, "R" & "V" Series, "S" & "T" Series

DESCRIPTION

PROPELLER SHAFTS

Propeller shafts may have one shaft, 2 shafts with a center bearing or 3 shafts with slip joints. Three shafts are used on 4WD vehicles. Location of slip joints vary with model application. *See Fig. 1.*

UNIVERSAL JOINTS

Universal joints compensate for the effects of vehicle loading and axle windup present during acceleration. When operated within designed angle variations, a universal joint will operate effectively. When the designed angle is changed or exceeded, the operational life of the joint will decrease.

On a driveline with a designed deep angle, a Constant Velocity (CV) Joint is used in place of a simple universal joint. A CV joint is composed of 2 universal joints, coupled by a yoke and phased for constant velocity. A ball socket between the 2 universal joints serves as a centering device. *See Fig. 2.* This causes each of the 2 units to operate through half of the complete angle between propeller shaft and differential carrier.

Needle roller bearings are used in universal joints. Needles are held in place on the trunnions by round bearing cups. Bearing cups are held in the yokes either by snap rings or injected plastic retainers, depending on manufacturer.

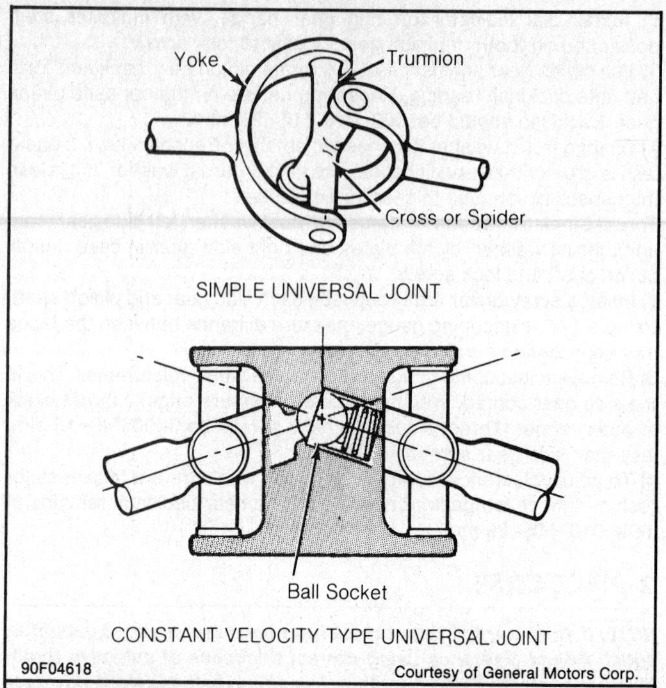
Yoke
Trunnion
Cross or Spider
SIMPLE UNIVERSAL JOINT
Ball Socket
CONSTANT VELOCITY TYPE UNIVERSAL JOINT
90F04618
Courtesy of General Motors Corp.

Fig. 2: Identifying Simple Universal Joint & Constant Velocity (CV) Joint

INSPECTION

If abnormal vibration or driveline noise is present, check these sources of possible vibration before overhauling driveline:

Propeller Shaft – Check propeller shaft for damage or dents. Check for undercoating adhering to shaft. If present, clean shaft thoroughly.

Universal Joints – Check for foreign material stuck in joints. Check for loose bolts, worn bearings aand rust showing lack of grease.

Center Bearing – Tighten propeller shaft center bearing mounting bolts. If bearing insulator is deteriorated or oil-soaked, replace it.

Engine & Transmission Mounts – Tighten mounting bolts. If mounts are deteriorated, replace them.

Tires & Wheels – Check tire inflation and wheel balance. Check for foreign objects in tread, damaged tread, mismatched tread patterns or incorrect tire size.

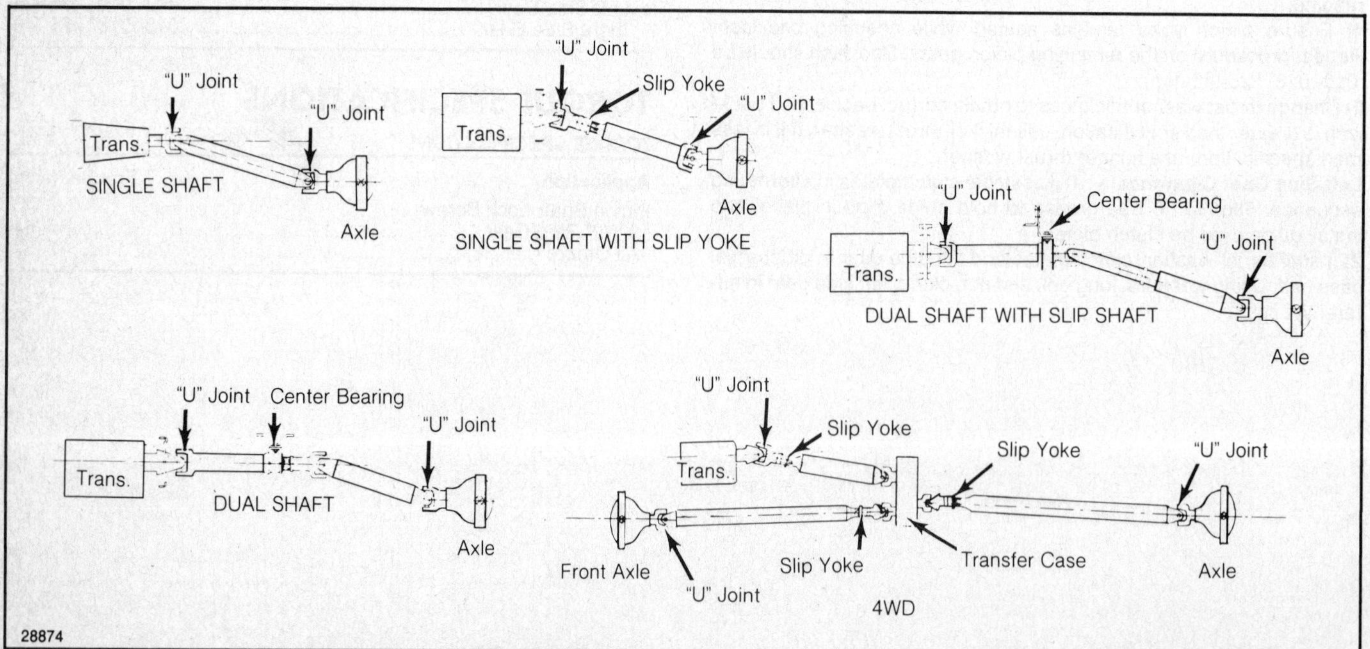
"U" Joint
"U" Joint
Trans.
SINGLE SHAFT
Axle
"U" Joint
Slip Yoke
"U" Joint
Trans.
Axle
SINGLE SHAFT WITH SLIP YOKE
"U" Joint
Center Bearing
"U" Joint
Trans.
DUAL SHAFT WITH SLIP SHAFT
Axle
"U" Joint
Center Bearing
"U" Joint
Trans.
DUAL SHAFT
Axle
"U" Joint
Slip Yoke
Trans.
Slip Yoke
"U" Joint
Front Axle
Slip Yoke
Transfer Case
Axle
"U" Joint
4WD
28874

Fig. 1: Identifying Commonly Used Propeller Shaft Combinations

ADJUSTMENTS

PROPELLER SHAFT PHASING

1-Piece Shafts - Ensure flange on each end of propeller shaft is in same plane. Check for arrows on slip joint and propeller shaft to aid in alignment. If flanges are not in same plane, disassemble universal joint and align. *See Fig. 3.*

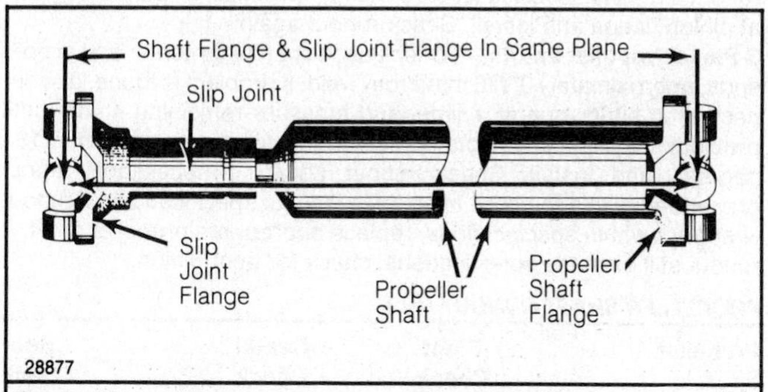
Shaft Flange & Slip Joint Flange In Same Plane
Slip Joint
Slip Joint Flange
Propeller Shaft
Propeller Shaft Flange
28877

Fig. 3: Phase Alignment of 1-Piece Propeller Shaft

2-Piece Or 3-Piece Shafts - **1)** Rotate transmission until yoke ears are on a horizontal plane. If propeller shaft is correctly installed, center line of yoke ears at each end of individual shafts will be parallel. If flanges are not in same plane, remove propeller shaft. Install propeller shaft with yokes aligned to a horizontal plane. *See Fig. 4.*

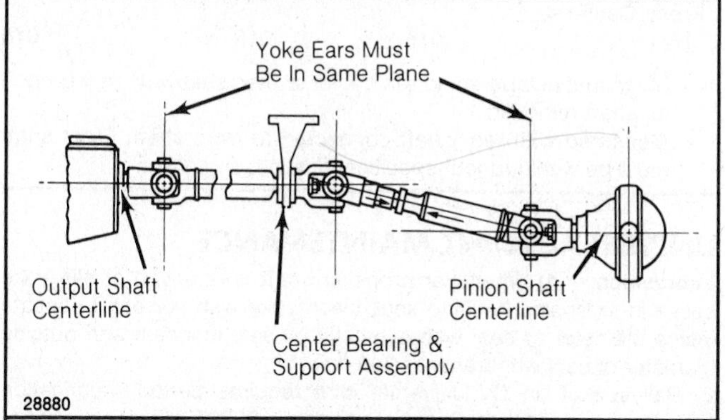
Yoke Ears Must Be In Same Plane
Output Shaft Centerline
Pinion Shaft Centerline
Center Bearing & Support Assembly
28880

Fig. 4: Phase Alignment of 2-Piece Propeller Shaft (3-Piece Shaft Similar)

2) On models with 2-piece shafts, rotate transmission yoke until trunnion is in horizontal plane. Install front propeller shaft with "U" joint trunnion in vertical plane. Connect bearing support to crossmember.
3) Ensure that front face of bearing support is perpendicular (90 degrees) to centerline of propeller shaft. Install rear propeller shaft with "U" joint trunnion of slip joint in vertical plane.
4) Set differential pinion yoke trunnion in vertical plane. Connect rear propeller shaft to pinion yoke. If 2-piece shaft is correctly installed, centerline of trunnions at each end of individual shafts will be parallel. *See Fig. 4.*

PROPELLER SHAFT BALANCING

Adjustment - **1)** Propeller shaft imbalance may often be cured by disconnecting shaft and rotating it 180 degrees in relation to other components. Test by raising rear wheels off ground, and turning shaft with engine.

NOTE: DO NOT run engine without ram airflow across radiator for prolonged periods, as overheating of engine or transmission may occur.

2) On most models, balance testing may be done by marking shaft in 4 positions, 90 degrees apart. Place marks approximately 6" (152 mm) forward of weld, at rear end of shaft. Number marks 1, 2, 3 and 4.
3) Place screw-type hose clamp so clamp head is in No. 1 position, and rotate shaft with engine. If there is little or no change, move clamp head to No. 2 position, and repeat test.
4) Continue procedure until vibration is at lowest level. If no difference is noted with clamp head moved to all 4 positions, vibrations may not be propeller shaft imbalance.
5) If vibration is lessened but not completely gone, place 2 clamps at that point, and run test again. Combined weight of clamps in one position may increase vibration. If so, rotate clamps 1/2" apart, above and below best position, and repeat test.
6) Continue to rotate clamps as necessary, until vibration is at lowest point. If vibration level is still unacceptable, leave rear clamp(s) in position and repeat procedure at front end of propeller shaft. If vibration can be eliminated or reduced to acceptable levels using this test procedure, send propeller shaft to balance shop for permanent balancing.

FLANGE ALIGNMENT & RUNOUT

Adjustment - **1)** All flanges must be perpendicular in both vertical and horizontal planes to engine crankshaft. Only exception is "broken back" type driveline, which has flanges that are not perpendicular in vertical plane. *See Fig. 5.*

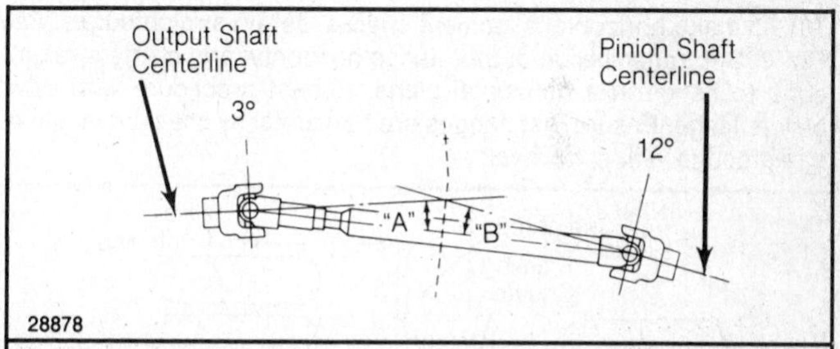
Output Shaft Centerline
Pinion Shaft Centerline
3°
12°
"A"
"B"
28878

Fig. 5: "Broken Back" Type Propeller Shaft Alignment (Typical)

2) With nonparallel or "broken back" type installation, working angles of universal joints of a given propeller shaft should be equal. Angle "A" = angle "B".
3) This is calculated as follows: angle of output shaft centerline is subtracted from angle of propeller shaft. Difference should equal angle of propeller shaft subtracted from pinion shaft angle.
4) Parallel type joints maintain constant velocity between output shaft and pinion shaft. Vibration is minimized and component life maximized when universal joints are parallel.
5) Using dial indicator, measure runout of transmission flange, center bearing flange and pinion flange. If runout exceeds .003-.005" (.08-.13 mm), replace flange.
6) If dial indicator cannot be used, push rod with snug fit through flange bearing bore. See if it aligns with opposite flange bore. If not, replace flange. *See Fig. 6.*

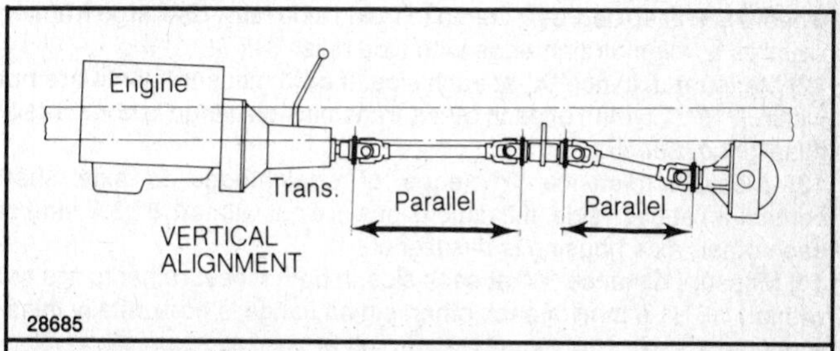
Engine
Trans.
Parallel
Parallel
VERTICAL ALIGNMENT
28685

Fig. 6: Vertical Alignment of Propeller Shaft

7) Rotate transmission flange until it is vertical, measuring from side. Check center bearing and pinion flanges. They cannot be more than one degree off vertical. See PROPELLER SHAFT PHASING under ADJUSTMENTS.
8) Rotate transmission flange until it is vertical, measured from side. Measure angle from end and record it. Check all other flanges for same angle. They must be within 1/2 degree of each other. Adjust as required.

1991 DRIVE AXLES
Propeller Shafts & Universal Joints (Cont.)

9) If difficulty is encountered when making these adjustments, horizontal alignment should be checked. Even though vertical alignment is correct, horizontal alignment can be badly out of adjustment. This is often found after major component replacement or repair of serious accident damage. *See Fig. 7.*

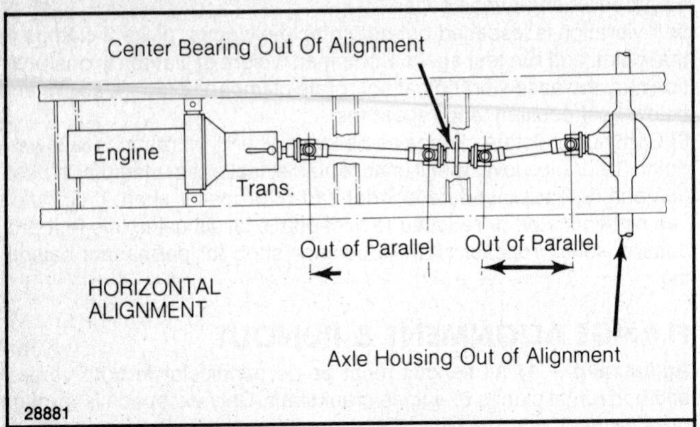
Center Bearing Out Of Alignment
Engine
Trans.
Out of Parallel
Out of Parallel
HORIZONTAL
ALIGNMENT
Axle Housing Out of Alignment
28881

Fig. 7: Horizontal Alignment of Propeller Shaft

10) To make horizontal alignment checks, set up straightedges. *See Fig. 8.* Set transmission output flange horizontal and clamp straightedge to flange in a horizontal plane. Repeat procedure with drive pinion flange. Ensure that flanges are horizontal by checking angle of straightedge with spirit level.

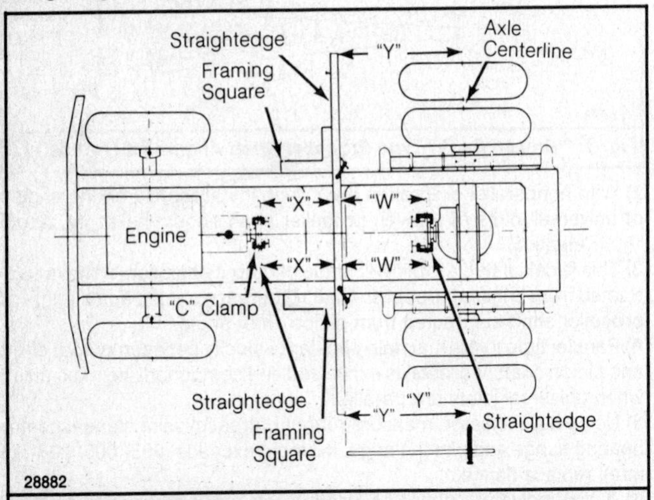
Straightedge
Framing
Square
"Y"
Axle
Centerline
"X"
"W"
Engine
"X"
"W"
"C" Clamp
Straightedge
"Y"
"Y"
Straightedge
Framing
Square
28882

Fig. 8: Checking Horizontal Alignment

11) Using straightedge that is 12" (305 mm) longer than width of rear wheel track at 90 degrees, clamp to frame side rails. Use large framing squares to align straightedge with side rails.

12) Measure distance "X" at each side. If both measurements are not within 1/16" (1.6 mm) of each other, transmission flange is horizontally misaligned. *See Fig. 8.*

13) Measure distance "Y" (edge of straightedge to axle shaft centerline) at each side. If 2 dimensions are not within 1/8" (3.2 mm) of each other, axle housing is misaligned.

14) Measure distance "W" at each side. If both measurements are not within 1/16" (1.6 mm) of each other, pinion flange is horizontally misaligned.

PROPELLER SHAFT RUNOUT

Raise vehicle so rear wheels can spin. Attach dial indicator to smooth place on vehicle underbody. A magnetic base dial gauge is recommended. Do not attach dial indicator base at a weld. With transmission in Neutral, hand rotate axle pinion flange or transmission and take required dial indicator readings on propeller shaft. See PROPELLER SHAFT RUNOUT (IN.) table.

1-Piece Propeller Shafts – If runout exceeds specifications, rotate propeller shaft 180 degrees at pinion flange and install. Check runout again.

2-Piece Propeller Shafts – Measure rear propeller shaft runout. Reference mark position of rear propeller shaft yoke to the pinion flange. Remove rear propeller shaft and measure front propeller shaft runout, both on the tube and at the tapered hole on the splined end. If the runout exceeds specifications, rotate rear propeller shaft 180 degrees at pinion flange and install. Check runout again.

3-Piece Propeller Shafts – Check each shaft at its center and at both ends, approximately 3" (76 mm) from weld. If problem is found, disconnect each shaft, one at a time, and measure remaining shafts until problem shaft is found. Rotate shaft connected to problem shaft 180 degrees and install. Check runout again. If necessary, repeat procedure in an attempt to bring the runout to specifications. If runout is still not within specifications, replace appropriate propeller shaft. If runout still exceeds specifications, check for bent pinion.

PROPELLER SHAFT RUNOUT (IN.)

Propeller Shaft	Front Check	Center Check	Rear Check
1-Piece			
Astro & Safari	.024	.024	.024
All Others	.040	.050	.055
2-Piece			
Front	.020	.....	[1] .008
Rear	[2] .030	.030	.035
3-Piece			
Front, Center & Rear	.015	.010	.015

1 – Measured at tapered hole in end of splined shaft with rear propeller shaft removed.

2 – Measured with rear shaft connected to front shaft. Front shaft must be within runout specifications.

UNIVERSAL JOINT MAINTENANCE

Lubrication – 1) Whenever propeller shaft is removed or slip yoke sticks in extension housing seal, clean yoke with solvent. Lubricate inside diameter of seal with synthetic oil seal lubricant and outside diameter of seal with transmission fluid.

2) Ball socket on CV universal joint requires periodic lubrication through provided fitting. Special Lubricant (1050679) is recommended by manufacturer. If lubrication fitting cannot be seen from beneath vehicle, CV joint may be lubricated from above using Adapter (J-25512-2) attached to end of a flex hose. *See Fig. 9.*

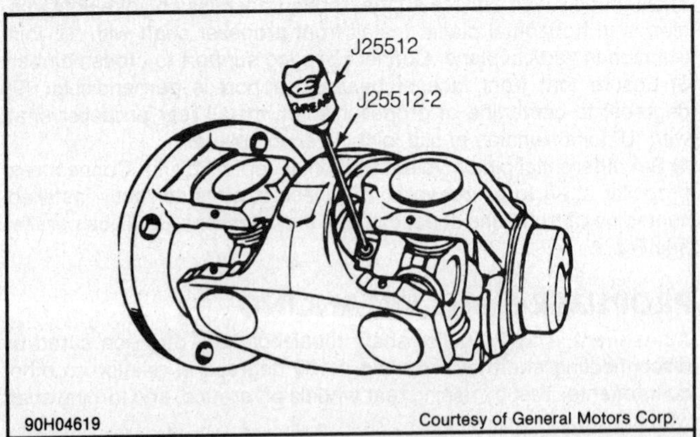
J25512
J25512-2
GREASE
90H04619
Courtesy of General Motors Corp.

Fig. 9: Lubricating Ball Socket of CV Joint

OVERHAUL

NOTE: DO NOT disassemble universal joints unless external leakage or damage has occurred.

1991 DRIVE AXLES
Propeller Shafts & Universal Joints (Cont.)

Before disassembly, scribe alignment marks on yoke and shaft for reassembly. If joints are rusted or corroded, apply penetrating oil before pressing out bearing cups or trunnion pin.

CROSS SHAFT & ROLLER TYPE UNIVERSAL JOINTS

Snap rings or injected plastic retainers may be used to retain bearing cups. Joints with snap rings may be disassembled and reassembled using same cross shaft and bearings. Joints with nylon retainers are disassembled by breaking nylon retainers; install new nylon retainers after service, or replace joints with joints that use snap rings.

Removal & Disassembly - 1) Disconnect yoke or flange attaching bolts and remove propeller shaft from vehicle. DO NOT use a pry bar to hold propeller shaft while loosening bolts; damage to bearing seals may result. Scribe marks on yoke and shaft for reassembly reference.

2) Remove retaining strap (if equipped). Remove bushing retainers/ snap rings from yoke. Press out bearing cups. Remove last bearing cup by pressing on end of cross shaft.

3) Remove cross shaft assembly from yoke. DO NOT remove seal retainers from cross shaft. Cross shaft and retainers are serviced as an assembly.

Reassembly & Installation - 1) Coat roller bearings with lubricant. Fill bearing cups with grease. Place cross assembly in propeller shaft yoke. Place bearing cups in position.

2) Press both bearing cups into yoke until retainers/snap rings can be installed. Ensure cross stays aligned in center of bearing cups while pressing into place. Install retainers/snap rings. Repeat procedure for remaining bearing caps. Install strap (if equipped). Install propeller shaft in vehicle; ensure scribed marks are aligned.

CONSTANT VELOCITY (CV) TYPE UNIVERSAL JOINTS

Removal & Disassembly - 1) Disconnect yoke and flange attaching bolts. Remove propeller shaft from vehicle. Index mark joint, yoke flange and cross shafts for reassembly. *See Fig. 10.*

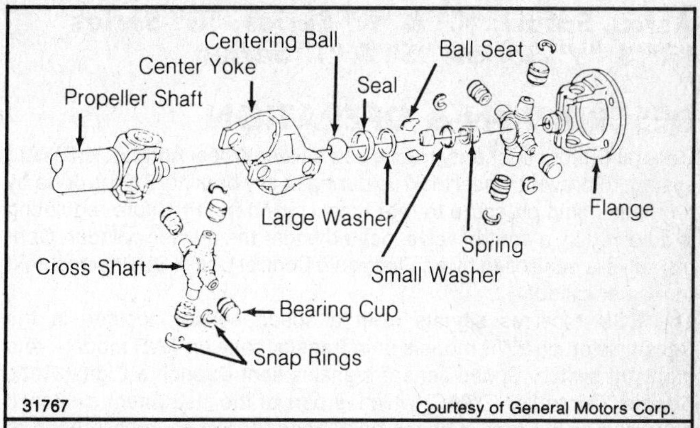
Centering Ball
Center Yoke
Ball Seat
Seal
Propeller Shaft
Large Washer
Flange
Spring
Small Washer
Cross Shaft
Bearing Cup
Snap Rings
31767
Courtesy of General Motors Corp.

Fig. 10: Exploded View of CV Type Universal Joint

2) Pry out all snap rings and press bearing out far enough to allow bearing cup end to be clamped in vise. Tap on yoke until free of bearing cup.

3) Repeat procedure for remaining bearings. Remove remaining parts from center yoke assembly.

Reassembly - 1) Pack all bearings with special Lubricant (1050679). Assemble center yoke components in reverse order of disassembly.

2) Using arbor press or vise, press 2 opposing bearing cups into position at same time until all bearing cups are installed. Ensure cross shafts and yokes remain aligned during this process.

3) Check for free movement of joint. If bind exists, seat bearings by sharply rapping yokes with brass hammer. DO NOT hammer directly on bearings.

Installation - 1) Before installing propeller shaft, clean yoke and inspect machined surface for scratches, nicks or burrs.

2) Provide support for propeller shaft during installation to prevent damage to universal joints. Position front end of shaft and align marks made during removal.

3) Install and attach 2 clamps to pinion yoke. Install 4 screws and lock washer assemblies on CV joint at transfer case. Use press bar to prevent assembly from rotating while attaching screw assemblies.

1991 BRAKES
Anti-Lock – RWAL

Astro, Safari, "C" & "K" Series, "G" Series, "R" & "V" Series, "S" & "T" Series

DESCRIPTION & OPERATION

General Motors light duty trucks use a Rear Wheel Anti-Lock (RWAL) system to prevent wheel lock-up during heavy braking. This is done by regulating fluid pressure to rear wheel cylinders. Pressure regulating is adjusted by a control valve located under the master cylinder. Control valve is controlled by an Electronic Control Unit (ECU) located next to master cylinder.

The ECU receives signals from a speed sensor, located in the transmission on 2WD models or in transfer case on 4WD models, and stoplight switch. Speed sensor signal is sent through a Digital Ratio Adapter Controller (DRAC) which is part of the instrument cluster. If axle ratio or tire size changes on "C" and "K" Series, recalibration of the DRAC must be performed. On all other models, DRAC must be replaced. The system is disabled when vehicle is in 4WD.

On models equipped with automatic transmission, an in-line resistor, located between module and stoplight switch, prevents battery voltage from energizing the transmission converter clutch solenoid. The RWAL system is connected to the existing brake warning light on the instrument panel. When ignition is turned on, warning light should come on for approximately 2 seconds to indicate system is operating.

ADJUSTMENTS

DRAC CALIBRATION

CAUTION: DO NOT touch pins on rear of instrument cluster or damage will occur.

"C" & "K" Series – Remove instrument panel. Plug Digital Ratio Adapter Calibration Service Kit (25085515) connector into rear of instrument panel. *See Fig. 1.* Momentarily touch wires across vehicle's battery terminals. See INSTRUMENT PANEL CALIBRATION TABLE in this article. Remove appropriate pins from clip. Install clip in instrument panel. Install instrument panel.

TESTING & DIAGNOSIS

NOTE: Ensure brake warning light is on before trying to retrieve trouble code. If light is not on, grounding ALDL connector will lead to false CODE 9.

1) System can be diagnosed through trouble codes. To activate trouble codes, connect a jumper wire between terminals "A" and "H" on ALDL connector and observe flashing on brake warning light. Sequence should be one long flash followed by short flashes (i.e. one long flash followed by 4 short flashes indicates CODE 5).

2) System will repeat code as long as ALDL connector is grounded. Long flash after short flashes indicates repeat of code. If there is more than one failure, only the first failure code will be stored and displayed. See TROUBLE SHOOTING CHARTS in this article.

3) On "C" and "K" Series trucks with dual rear wheels, a "chirping" noise may occur when applying brakes. This is a mechanical problem, not RWAL. To correct, remove brake drums and spray two coats of Graphite Compound (12345268) onto brake linings. Allow compound to dry between coats.

NOTE: If ECU connector retaining clip is broken when unplugging connector, service clips are available from manufacturer.

BRAKE BLEEDING PROCEDURE

Brake system may be bled the same as a conventional system. If manual bleeding, wait 15 seconds between strokes. If pressure bleeding, pressurize brake bleeder to 20-25 psi (kg/cm²). Brake bleeding sequence is as follows: right rear, left rear, right front, left front, isolation dump valve. Use DOT 3 brake fluid only.

TORQUE SPECIFICATIONS

TORQUE SPECIFICATIONS

Application	Ft. Lbs. (N.m)
Brake Line Fittings	10 (14)
Isolation Dump Valve Mounting Bolts	21 (28)
Speed Sensor Mounting Bolt	
Transmission Mounted	10 (14)
Transfer Case Mounted	32 (43)

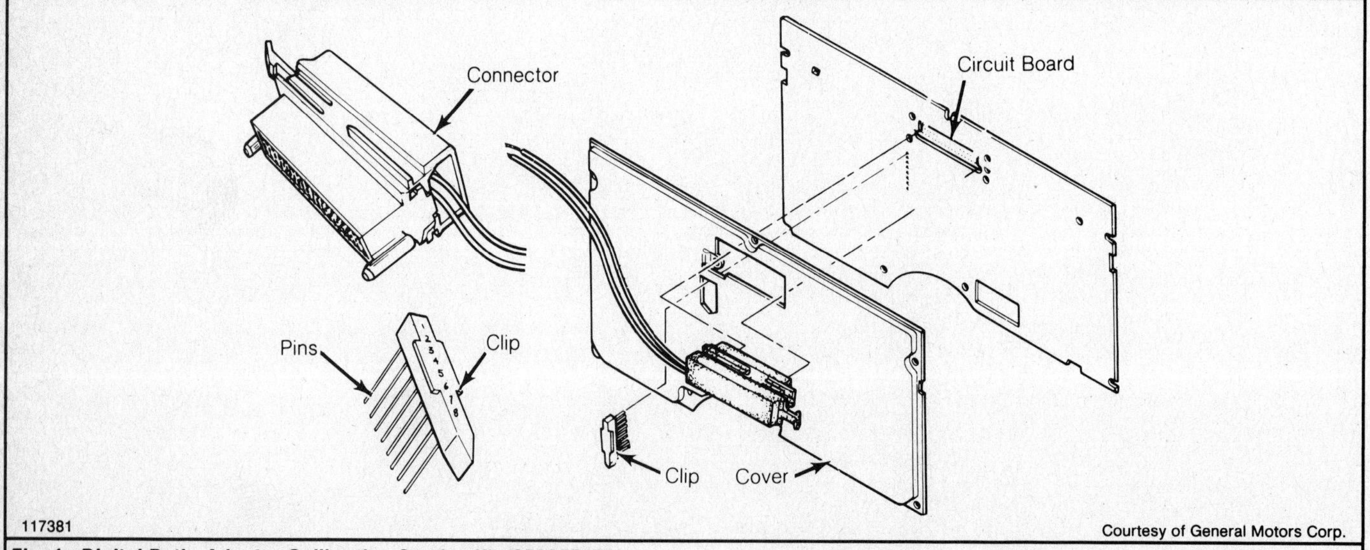
Connector
Circuit Board
Pins
Clip
Clip
Cover
117381
Courtesy of General Motors Corp.

Fig. 1: Digital Ratio Adapter Calibration Service Kit (25085515)

1991 BRAKES
Anti-Lock – RWAL (Cont.)

INSTRUMENT PANEL CALIBRATION TABLE

Axle Ratio	Tire Size	RPO	HWY/OOR AT/ALS	Pins To Remove
2.73 (GU2)	P195/75R15	YAR & YAS	ALS	1, 2, 4 & 5
	P205/75R15	YCE, YCG	ALS	1, 4 & 5
	P225/75R15	YET, YEV & YEU	ALS	2,3 & 5
	P235/75R15	YFL, YFM & YFN	ALS	3 & 5
3.08 (GU4)	P195/75R15	YAR & YAS	ALS	2, 3 & 6
	P205/75R15	YCE & YCG	ALS	3 & 6
	P225/75R15	YET, YEV & YEU	ALS	6
	P235/75R15	YFL, YFN & YFM	ALS/OOR	2, 3, 4 & 5
3.42 (GU6)	P205/75R15	YCE, YCG	ALS	1, 3, 4 & 6
	P195/75R15	YAR & YAS	ALS	1, 2, 3, 4 & 6
	P225/75R15	YET, YEV & YEU	ALS	1, 4 & 6
	P235/75R15	YFL, YFN & YFM	ALS	4 & 6
	LT225/75R16	YHR, YHJ & YHN	OOR	2, 3 & 6
	LT225/75R16	YHE, YHV, YHP & YHQ	ALS	2, 3 & 6
	LT245/75R16	YGK, YBN & YBX	OOR	2 & 6
	LT245/75R16	YHH, YBK & YBL	ALS	2 & 6
	LT265/75R16	YGL & YGM	OOR	1, 2, 3, 4 & 5
	7.50-16LT	YPF	HWY	1, 2, 3, 4 & 5
3.73 (GT4)	P195/75R15	YAR & YAS	ALS	1, 2, 3, 5 & 6
	P205/75R15	YCE & YCG	ALS	1, 3, 5 & 6
	P225/75R15	YET, YEV & YEU	ALS	1, 5 & 6
	P235/75R15	YFL, YFN & YFM	ALS	1, 2, 3, 4 & 6
	LT225/75R16	YHE, YHV, YHQ & YHP	OOR	1, 3, 4 & 6
	LT225/75R16	YHR, YHS & YHN	OOR	1, 3, 4 & 6
	LT245/75R16	YGK, YBN & YBX	OOR	2, 4 & 6
	LT245/75R16	YHH, YBK & YBL	ALS	2, 4 & 6
	LT265/75R16	YGL & YGM	OOR	2, 3 & 6
	7.50-16LT	YPF	HWY	2, 3 & 6
4.10 (GT5)	LT225/75R16	YGL & YGM	OOR	1, 2, 3, 4 & 6
	LT225/75R16	YHP & YHQ	ALS	1, 2, 3, 5 & 6
	LT225/75R16	YHR	OOR	2, 3, 5 & 6
	LT245/75R16	YGK, YBN & YBX	OOR	2, 5 & 6
	LT245/75R16	YGK, YBN & YBX	OOR	2, 5 & 6
	LT245/75R16	YHH, YBK & YBL	ALS	1, 2, 5 & 6
	7.50-16LT	YPF	HWY	1, 2, 3, 4 & 6
4.56 (HC4)	LT225/75R16	YHP & YHQ	ALS	2 & 7
	LT225/75R16	YHR	OOR	1 & 7
	LT245/75R16	YGK	OOR	3, 4, 5 & 6
	LT245/75R16	YHH	ALS	3, 4, 5 & 6
	7.50-16LT	YPF	HWY	4, 5 & 6

1991 BRAKES
Anti-Lock – RWAL (Cont.)

TROUBLE SHOOTING CHARTS

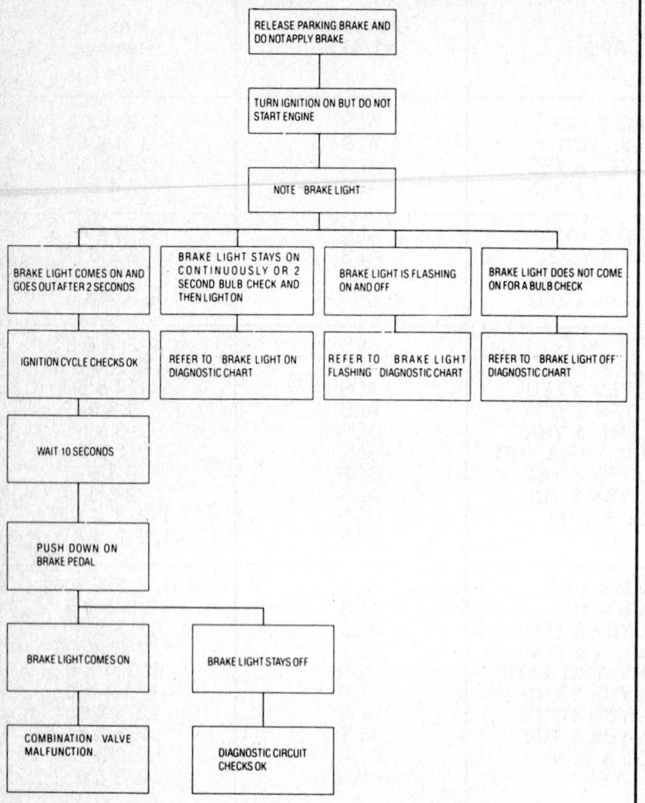
RELEASE PARKING BRAKE AND DO NOT APPLY BRAKE
TURN IGNITION ON BUT DO NOT START ENGINE
NOTE BRAKE LIGHT
BRAKE LIGHT COMES ON AND GOES OUT AFTER 2 SECONDS
BRAKE LIGHT STAYS ON CONTINUOUSLY OR 2 SECOND BULB CHECK AND THEN LIGHT ON
BRAKE LIGHT IS FLASHING ON AND OFF
BRAKE LIGHT DOES NOT COME ON FOR A BULB CHECK
IGNITION CYCLE CHECKS OK
REFER TO "BRAKE LIGHT ON" DIAGNOSTIC CHART
REFER TO "BRAKE LIGHT FLASHING" DIAGNOSTIC CHART
REFER TO "BRAKE LIGHT OFF" DIAGNOSTIC CHART
WAIT 10 SECONDS
PUSH DOWN ON BRAKE PEDAL
BRAKE LIGHT COMES ON
BRAKE LIGHT STAYS OFF
COMBINATION VALVE MALFUNCTION
DIAGNOSTIC CIRCUIT CHECKS OK

90J06148 Courtesy of General Motors Corp.

Fig. 2: Diagnostic Circuit Check (All Models)

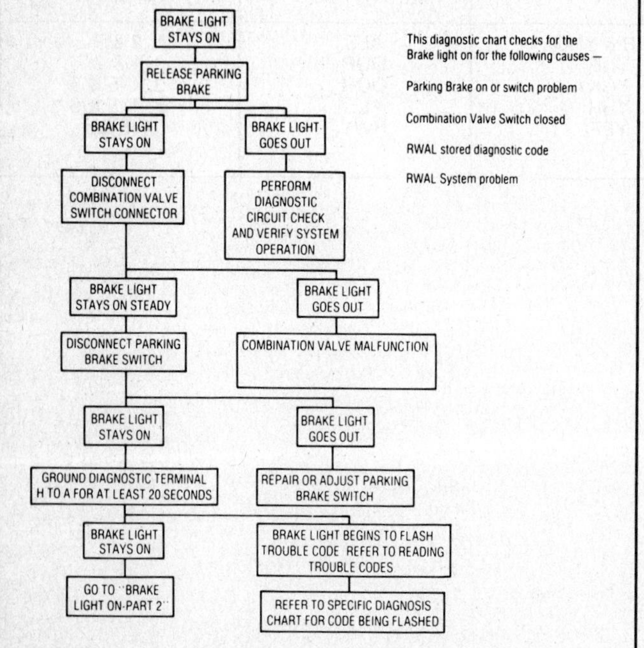
BRAKE LIGHT STAYS ON
RELEASE PARKING BRAKE
BRAKE LIGHT STAYS ON
BRAKE LIGHT GOES OUT
DISCONNECT COMBINATION VALVE SWITCH CONNECTOR
PERFORM DIAGNOSTIC CIRCUIT CHECK AND VERIFY SYSTEM OPERATION
BRAKE LIGHT STAYS ON STEADY
BRAKE LIGHT GOES OUT
DISCONNECT PARKING BRAKE SWITCH
COMBINATION VALVE MALFUNCTION
BRAKE LIGHT STAYS ON
BRAKE LIGHT GOES OUT
GROUND DIAGNOSTIC TERMINAL H TO A FOR AT LEAST 20 SECONDS
REPAIR OR ADJUST PARKING BRAKE SWITCH
BRAKE LIGHT STAYS ON
BRAKE LIGHT BEGINS TO FLASH TROUBLE CODE REFER TO READING TROUBLE CODES
GO TO "BRAKE LIGHT ON-PART 2"
REFER TO SPECIFIC DIAGNOSIS CHART FOR CODE BEING FLASHED
This diagnostic chart checks for the Brake light on for the following causes –
Parking Brake on or switch problem
Combination Valve Switch closed
RWAL stored diagnostic code
RWAL System problem

90B06149 Courtesy of General Motors Corp.

Fig. 3: Brake Light On – Part 1 (All Models)

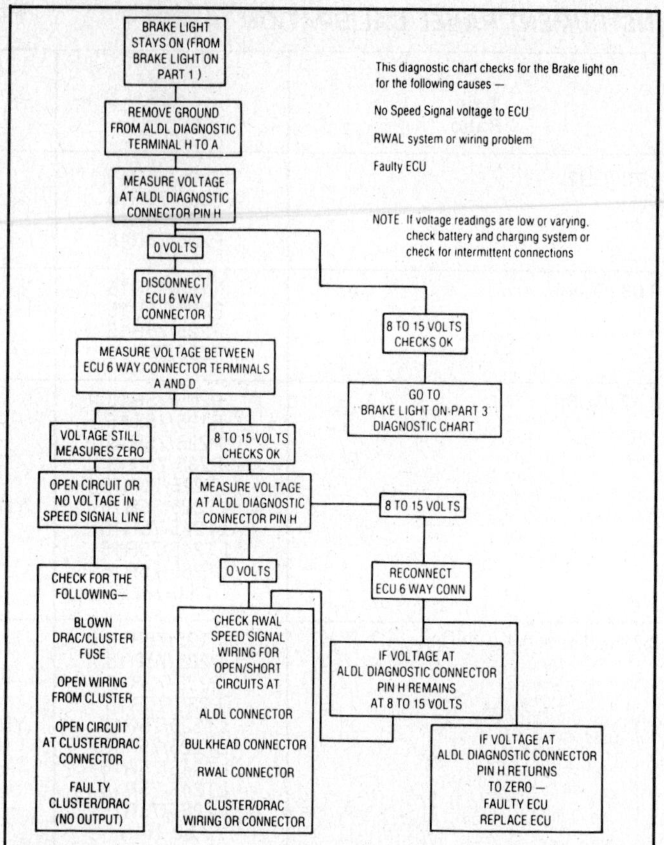
BRAKE LIGHT STAYS ON (FROM BRAKE LIGHT ON PART 1)
REMOVE GROUND FROM ALDL DIAGNOSTIC TERMINAL H TO A
MEASURE VOLTAGE AT ALDL DIAGNOSTIC CONNECTOR PIN H
0 VOLTS
DISCONNECT ECU 6 WAY CONNECTOR
8 TO 15 VOLTS CHECKS OK
MEASURE VOLTAGE BETWEEN ECU 6 WAY CONNECTOR TERMINALS A AND D
GO TO BRAKE LIGHT ON-PART 3 DIAGNOSTIC CHART
VOLTAGE STILL MEASURES ZERO
8 TO 15 VOLTS CHECKS OK
OPEN CIRCUIT OR NO VOLTAGE IN SPEED SIGNAL LINE
MEASURE VOLTAGE AT ALDL DIAGNOSTIC CONNECTOR PIN H
8 TO 15 VOLTS
0 VOLTS
RECONNECT ECU 6 WAY CONN
CHECK FOR THE FOLLOWING—
BLOWN DRAC/CLUSTER FUSE
OPEN WIRING FROM CLUSTER
OPEN CIRCUIT AT CLUSTER/DRAC CONNECTOR
FAULTY CLUSTER/DRAC (NO OUTPUT)
CHECK RWAL SPEED SIGNAL WIRING FOR OPEN/SHORT CIRCUITS AT
ALDL CONNECTOR
BULKHEAD CONNECTOR
RWAL CONNECTOR
CLUSTER/DRAC WIRING OR CONNECTOR
IF VOLTAGE AT ALDL DIAGNOSTIC CONNECTOR PIN H REMAINS AT 8 TO 15 VOLTS
IF VOLTAGE AT ALDL DIAGNOSTIC CONNECTOR PIN H RETURNS TO ZERO – FAULTY ECU REPLACE ECU
This diagnostic chart checks for the Brake light on for the following causes –
No Speed Signal voltage to ECU
RWAL system or wiring problem
Faulty ECU
NOTE If voltage readings are low or varying, check battery and charging system or check for intermittent connections

90D06150 Courtesy of General Motors Corp.

Fig. 4: Brake Light On – Part 2 (All Models)

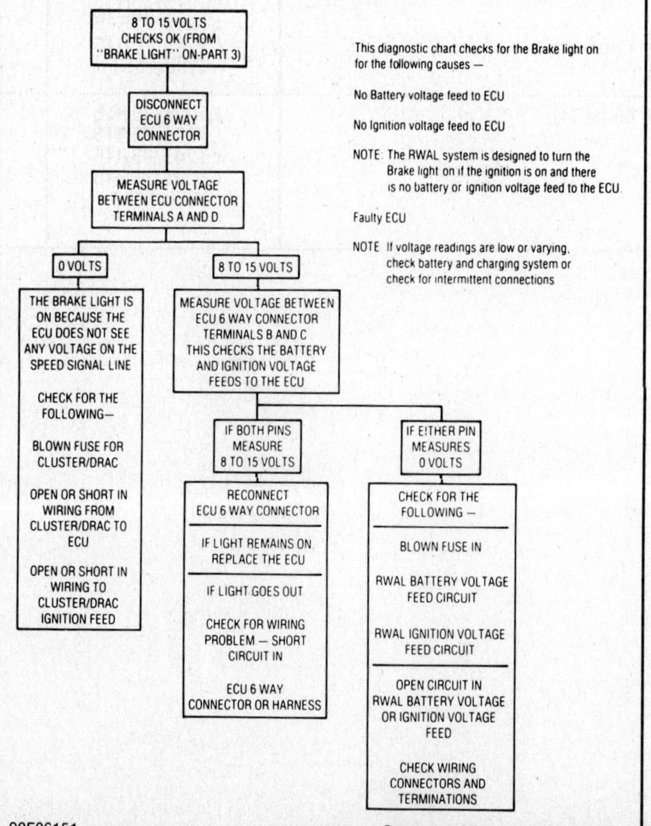
8 TO 15 VOLTS CHECKS OK (FROM "BRAKE LIGHT" ON-PART 3)
DISCONNECT ECU 6 WAY CONNECTOR
MEASURE VOLTAGE BETWEEN ECU CONNECTOR TERMINALS A AND D
0 VOLTS
8 TO 15 VOLTS
THE BRAKE LIGHT IS ON BECAUSE THE ECU DOES NOT SEE ANY VOLTAGE ON THE SPEED SIGNAL LINE
CHECK FOR THE FOLLOWING—
BLOWN FUSE FOR CLUSTER/DRAC
OPEN OR SHORT IN WIRING FROM CLUSTER/DRAC TO ECU
OPEN OR SHORT IN WIRING TO CLUSTER/DRAC IGNITION FEED
MEASURE VOLTAGE BETWEEN ECU 6 WAY CONNECTOR TERMINALS B AND C THIS CHECKS THE BATTERY AND IGNITION VOLTAGE FEEDS TO THE ECU
IF BOTH PINS MEASURE 8 TO 15 VOLTS
IF EITHER PIN MEASURES 0 VOLTS
RECONNECT ECU 6 WAY CONNECTOR
IF LIGHT REMAINS ON REPLACE THE ECU
IF LIGHT GOES OUT
CHECK FOR WIRING PROBLEM – SHORT CIRCUIT IN
ECU 6 WAY CONNECTOR OR HARNESS
CHECK FOR THE FOLLOWING –
BLOWN FUSE IN
RWAL BATTERY VOLTAGE FEED CIRCUIT
RWAL IGNITION VOLTAGE FEED CIRCUIT
OPEN CIRCUIT IN RWAL BATTERY VOLTAGE OR IGNITION VOLTAGE FEED
CHECK WIRING CONNECTORS AND TERMINATIONS
This diagnostic chart checks for the Brake light on for the following causes –
No Battery voltage feed to ECU
No Ignition voltage feed to ECU
NOTE The RWAL system is designed to turn the Brake light on if the ignition is on and there is no battery or ignition voltage feed to the ECU.
Faulty ECU
NOTE If voltage readings are low or varying, check battery and charging system or check for intermittent connections

90F06151 Courtesy of General Motors Corp.

Fig. 5: Brake Light On – Part 3 (All Models)

1991 BRAKES
Anti-Lock – RWAL (Cont.)

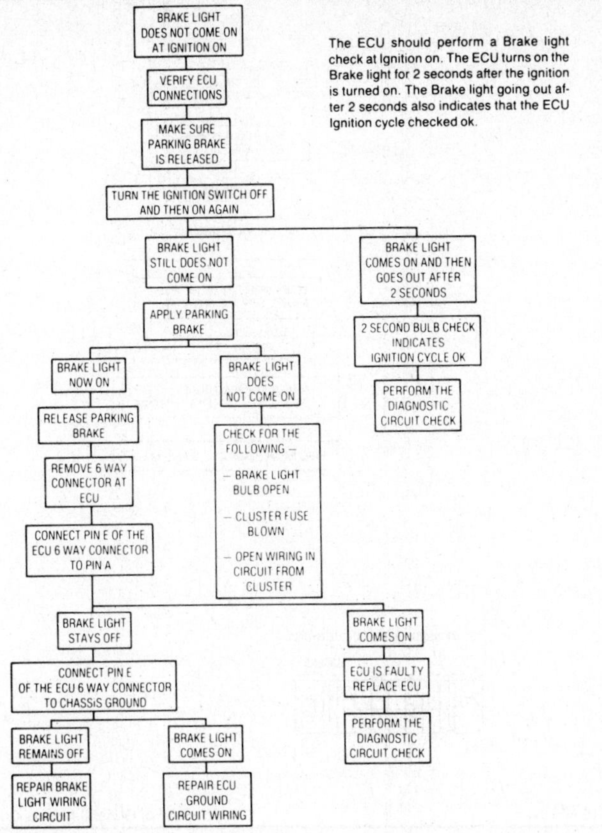
BRAKE LIGHT DOES NOT COME ON AT IGNITION ON
VERIFY ECU CONNECTIONS
MAKE SURE PARKING BRAKE IS RELEASED
TURN THE IGNITION SWITCH OFF AND THEN ON AGAIN
BRAKE LIGHT STILL DOES NOT COME ON
BRAKE LIGHT COMES ON AND THEN GOES OUT AFTER 2 SECONDS
APPLY PARKING BRAKE
2 SECOND BULB CHECK INDICATES IGNITION CYCLE OK
PERFORM THE DIAGNOSTIC CIRCUIT CHECK
BRAKE LIGHT NOW ON
BRAKE LIGHT DOES NOT COME ON
RELEASE PARKING BRAKE
CHECK FOR THE FOLLOWING –
– BRAKE LIGHT BULB OPEN
– CLUSTER FUSE BLOWN
– OPEN WIRING IN CIRCUIT FROM CLUSTER
REMOVE 6 WAY CONNECTOR AT ECU
CONNECT PIN E OF THE ECU 6 WAY CONNECTOR TO PIN A
BRAKE LIGHT STAYS OFF
BRAKE LIGHT COMES ON
CONNECT PIN E OF THE ECU 6 WAY CONNECTOR TO CHASSIS GROUND
ECU IS FAULTY REPLACE ECU
PERFORM THE DIAGNOSTIC CIRCUIT CHECK
BRAKE LIGHT REMAINS OFF
BRAKE LIGHT COMES ON
REPAIR BRAKE LIGHT WIRING CIRCUIT
REPAIR ECU GROUND CIRCUIT WIRING

The ECU should perform a Brake light check at Ignition on. The ECU turns on the Brake light for 2 seconds after the ignition is turned on. The Brake light going out after 2 seconds also indicates that the ECU Ignition cycle checked ok.

90H06152 Courtesy of General Motors Corp.

Fig. 6: Brake Light Off (All Models)

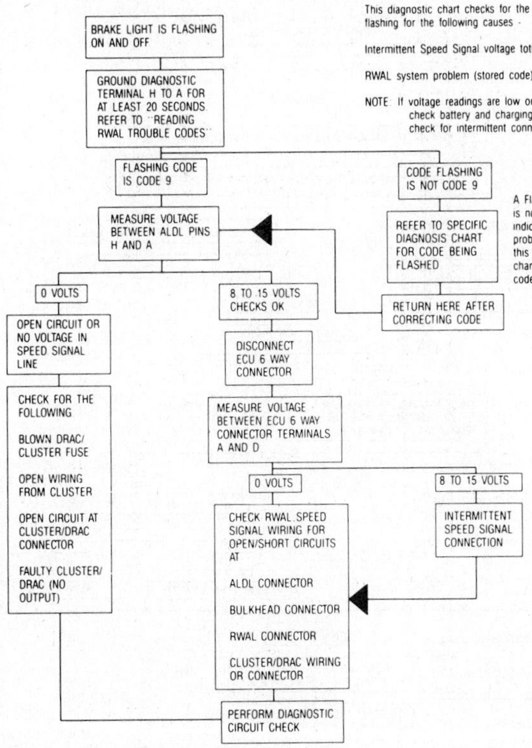
BRAKE LIGHT IS FLASHING ON AND OFF
GROUND DIAGNOSTIC TERMINAL H TO A FOR AT LEAST 20 SECONDS. REFER TO "READING RWAL TROUBLE CODES"
FLASHING CODE IS CODE 9
CODE FLASHING IS NOT CODE 9
MEASURE VOLTAGE BETWEEN ALDL PINS H AND A
REFER TO SPECIFIC DIAGNOSIS CHART FOR CODE BEING FLASHED
RETURN HERE AFTER CORRECTING CODE
0 VOLTS
8 TO 15 VOLTS CHECKS OK
OPEN CIRCUIT OR NO VOLTAGE IN SPEED SIGNAL LINE
DISCONNECT ECU 6 WAY CONNECTOR
CHECK FOR THE FOLLOWING
BLOWN DRAC/ CLUSTER FUSE
OPEN WIRING FROM CLUSTER
OPEN CIRCUIT AT CLUSTER/DRAC CONNECTOR
FAULTY CLUSTER/ DRAC (NO OUTPUT)
MEASURE VOLTAGE BETWEEN ECU 6 WAY CONNECTOR TERMINALS A AND D
0 VOLTS
8 TO 15 VOLTS
CHECK RWAL SPEED SIGNAL WIRING FOR OPEN/SHORT CIRCUITS AT
ALDL CONNECTOR
BULKHEAD CONNECTOR
RWAL CONNECTOR
CLUSTER/DRAC WIRING OR CONNECTOR
INTERMITTENT SPEED SIGNAL CONNECTION
PERFORM DIAGNOSTIC CIRCUIT CHECK

This diagnostic chart checks for the Brake light flashing for the following causes -

Intermittent Speed Signal voltage tothe ECU

RWAL system problem (stored code)

NOTE: If voltage readings are low or varying, check battery and charging system or check for intermittent connections

A Flashing code that is not code 9 indicates two problems - return to this point in this chart after correcting code that was read

90J06153 Courtesy of General Motors Corp.

Fig. 7: Brake Light Flashing (All Models)

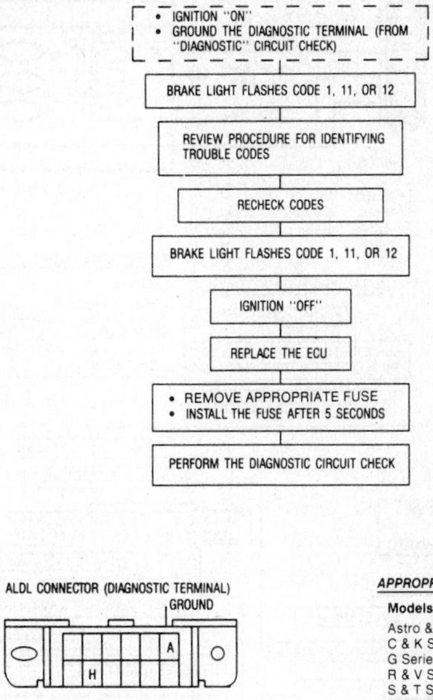
• IGNITION "ON"
• GROUND THE DIAGNOSTIC TERMINAL (FROM "DIAGNOSTIC" CIRCUIT CHECK)
BRAKE LIGHT FLASHES CODE 1, 11, OR 12
REVIEW PROCEDURE FOR IDENTIFYING TROUBLE CODES
RECHECK CODES
BRAKE LIGHT FLASHES CODE 1, 11, OR 12
IGNITION "OFF"
REPLACE THE ECU
• REMOVE APPROPRIATE FUSE
• INSTALL THE FUSE AFTER 5 SECONDS
PERFORM THE DIAGNOSTIC CIRCUIT CHECK
ALDL CONNECTOR (DIAGNOSTIC TERMINAL)
GROUND
A
H

APPROPRIATE FUSE

Models	Fuse
Astro & Safari	BRAKE
C & K Series	STOP/HAZARD
G Series	TAIL LPS
R & V Series	STOP/HAZARD
S & T Series	ECMB

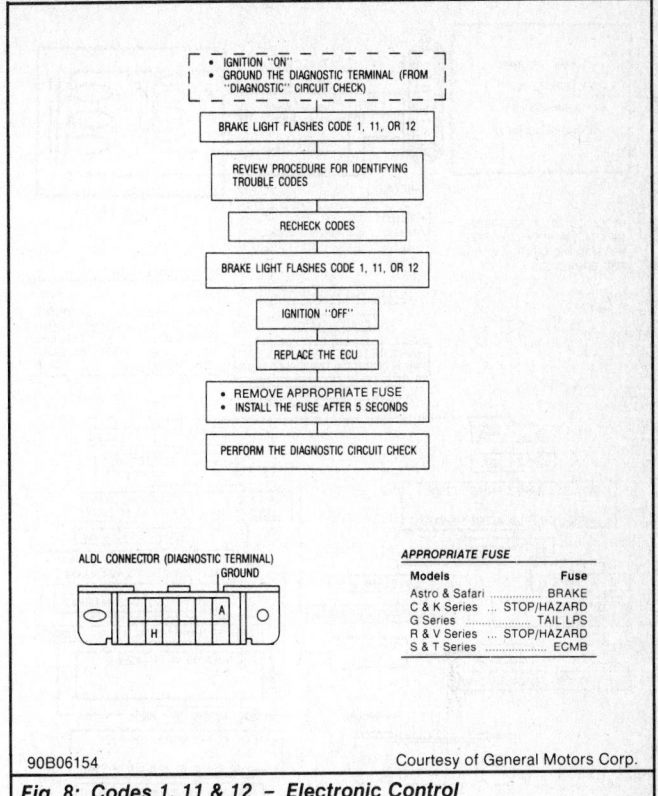

90B06154 Courtesy of General Motors Corp.

Fig. 8: Codes 1, 11 & 12 – Electronic Control Unit Malfunction (All Models)

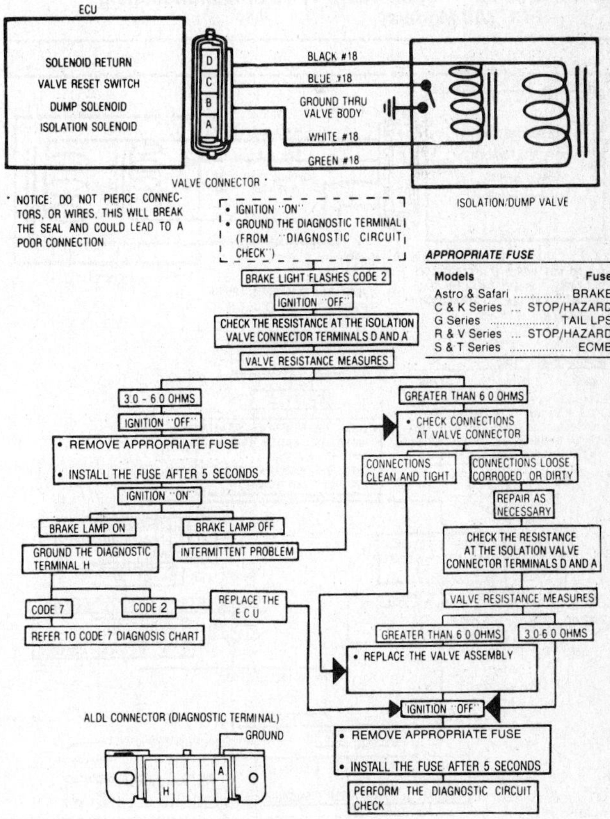
ECU
SOLENOID RETURN
VALVE RESET SWITCH
DUMP SOLENOID
ISOLATION SOLENOID
D
C
B
A
BLACK #18
BLUE #18
GROUND THRU VALVE BODY
WHITE #18
GREEN #18
VALVE CONNECTOR *
ISOLATION/DUMP VALVE
* NOTICE: DO NOT PIERCE CONNECTORS, OR WIRES, THIS WILL BREAK THE SEAL AND COULD LEAD TO A POOR CONNECTION
• IGNITION "ON"
• GROUND THE DIAGNOSTIC TERMINAL (FROM "DIAGNOSTIC CIRCUIT CHECK")
BRAKE LIGHT FLASHES CODE 2
IGNITION "OFF"
CHECK THE RESISTANCE AT THE ISOLATION VALVE CONNECTOR TERMINALS D AND A
VALVE RESISTANCE MEASURES
3.0 - 6.0 OHMS
GREATER THAN 6.0 OHMS
IGNITION "OFF"
• CHECK CONNECTIONS AT VALVE CONNECTOR
• REMOVE APPROPRIATE FUSE
• INSTALL THE FUSE AFTER 5 SECONDS
CONNECTIONS CLEAN AND TIGHT
CONNECTIONS LOOSE, CORRODED, OR DIRTY
REPAIR AS NECESSARY
IGNITION "ON"
BRAKE LAMP ON
BRAKE LAMP OFF
CHECK THE RESISTANCE AT THE ISOLATION VALVE CONNECTOR TERMINALS D AND A
GROUND THE DIAGNOSTIC TERMINAL H
INTERMITTENT PROBLEM
VALVE RESISTANCE MEASURES
CODE 7
CODE 2
REPLACE THE ECU
REFER TO CODE 7 DIAGNOSIS CHART
GREATER THAN 6.0 OHMS
3.0-6.0 OHMS
• REPLACE THE VALVE ASSEMBLY
IGNITION "OFF"
ALDL CONNECTOR (DIAGNOSTIC TERMINAL)
GROUND
A
H
• REMOVE APPROPRIATE FUSE
• INSTALL THE FUSE AFTER 5 SECONDS
PERFORM THE DIAGNOSTIC CIRCUIT CHECK

APPROPRIATE FUSE

Models	Fuse
Astro & Safari	BRAKE
C & K Series	STOP/HAZARD
G Series	TAIL LPS
R & V Series	STOP/HAZARD
S & T Series	ECMB

90E06155 Courtesy of General Motors Corp.

Fig. 9: Code 2 – Open Isolation Valve or Malfunctioning ECU (All Models)

1991 BRAKES
Anti-Lock – RWAL (Cont.)

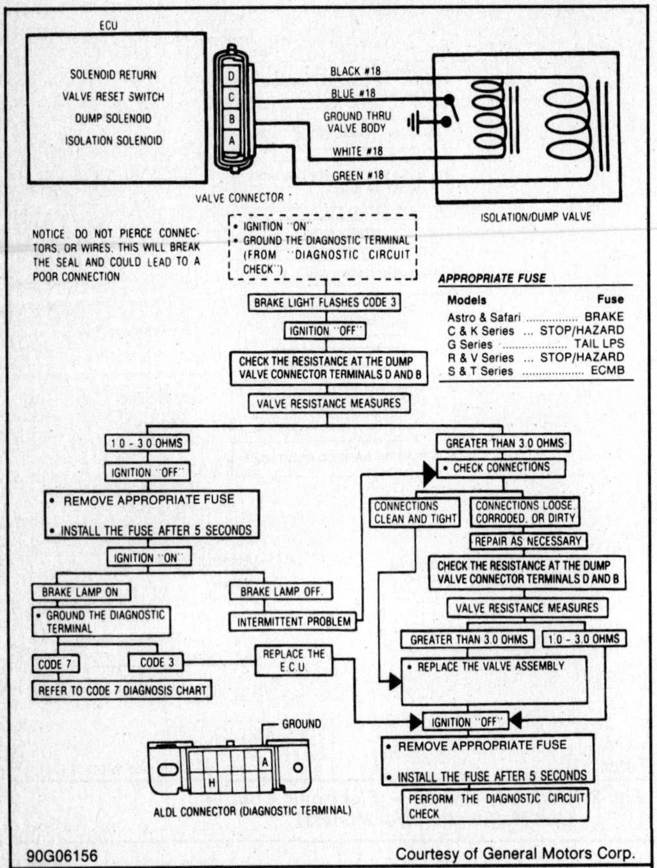
ECU
SOLENOID RETURN
VALVE RESET SWITCH
DUMP SOLENOID
ISOLATION SOLENOID
D
C
B
A
BLACK #18
BLUE #18
GROUND THRU VALVE BODY
WHITE #18
GREEN #18
VALVE CONNECTOR
ISOLATION/DUMP VALVE
NOTICE: DO NOT PIERCE CONNECTORS OR WIRES. THIS WILL BREAK THE SEAL AND COULD LEAD TO A POOR CONNECTION.
• IGNITION "ON"
• GROUND THE DIAGNOSTIC TERMINAL (FROM "DIAGNOSTIC CIRCUIT CHECK")
APPROPRIATE FUSE
Models / Fuse
Astro & Safari .... BRAKE
C & K Series ... STOP/HAZARD
G Series .... TAIL LPS
R & V Series ... STOP/HAZARD
S & T Series .... ECMB
BRAKE LIGHT FLASHES CODE 3
IGNITION "OFF"
CHECK THE RESISTANCE AT THE DUMP VALVE CONNECTOR TERMINALS D AND B
VALVE RESISTANCE MEASURES
1.0 - 3.0 OHMS
GREATER THAN 3.0 OHMS
IGNITION "OFF"
• CHECK CONNECTIONS
• REMOVE APPROPRIATE FUSE
• INSTALL THE FUSE AFTER 5 SECONDS
CONNECTIONS CLEAN AND TIGHT
CONNECTIONS LOOSE, CORRODED, OR DIRTY
REPAIR AS NECESSARY
IGNITION "ON"
CHECK THE RESISTANCE AT THE DUMP VALVE CONNECTOR TERMINALS D AND B
BRAKE LAMP ON
BRAKE LAMP OFF
• GROUND THE DIAGNOSTIC TERMINAL
INTERMITTENT PROBLEM
VALVE RESISTANCE MEASURES
GREATER THAN 3.0 OHMS
1.0 - 3.0 OHMS
CODE 7
CODE 3
REPLACE THE E.C.U.
• REPLACE THE VALVE ASSEMBLY
REFER TO CODE 7 DIAGNOSIS CHART
IGNITION "OFF"
GROUND
• REMOVE APPROPRIATE FUSE
• INSTALL THE FUSE AFTER 5 SECONDS
PERFORM THE DIAGNOSTIC CIRCUIT CHECK
ALDL CONNECTOR (DIAGNOSTIC TERMINAL)
A
H
90G06156
Courtesy of General Motors Corp.

Fig. 10: Code 3 – Open Dump Valve or Malfunctioning ECU (All Models)

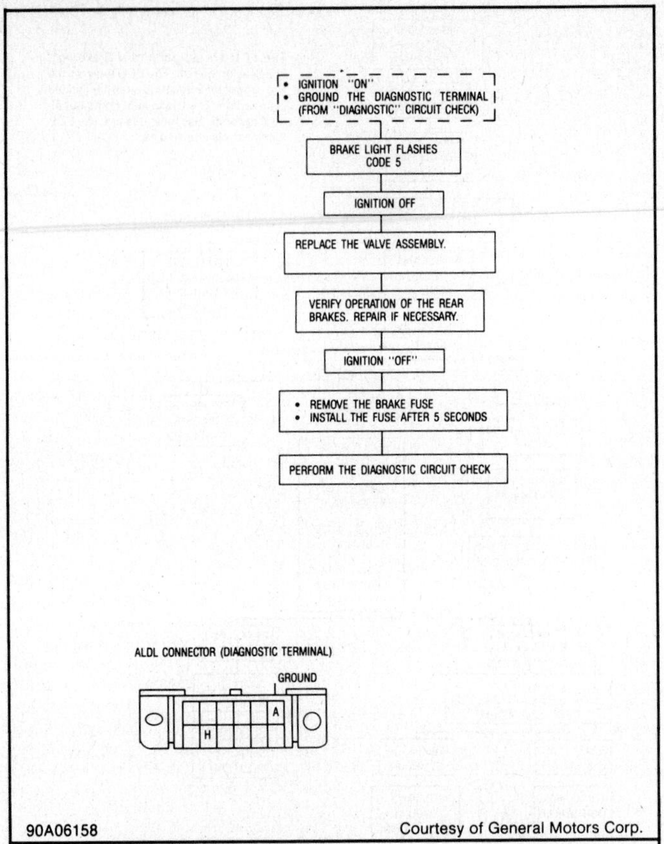
• IGNITION "ON"
• GROUND THE DIAGNOSTIC TERMINAL (FROM "DIAGNOSTIC" CIRCUIT CHECK)
BRAKE LIGHT FLASHES CODE 5
IGNITION OFF
REPLACE THE VALVE ASSEMBLY.
VERIFY OPERATION OF THE REAR BRAKES. REPAIR IF NECESSARY.
IGNITION "OFF"
• REMOVE THE BRAKE FUSE
• INSTALL THE FUSE AFTER 5 SECONDS
PERFORM THE DIAGNOSTIC CIRCUIT CHECK
ALDL CONNECTOR (DIAGNOSTIC TERMINAL)
GROUND
A
H
90A06158
Courtesy of General Motors Corp.

Fig. 12: Code 5 – Excessive Actuations of the Dump Valve During Anti-Lock Stop (Astro & Safari)

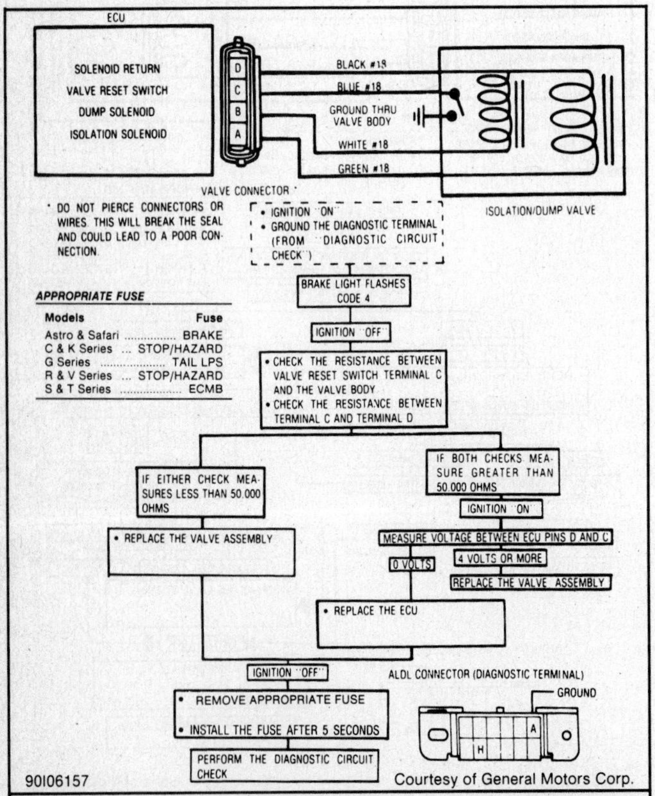
ECU
SOLENOID RETURN
VALVE RESET SWITCH
DUMP SOLENOID
ISOLATION SOLENOID
D
C
B
A
BLACK #18
BLUE #18
GROUND THRU VALVE BODY
WHITE #18
GREEN #18
VALVE CONNECTOR
ISOLATION/DUMP VALVE
DO NOT PIERCE CONNECTORS OR WIRES. THIS WILL BREAK THE SEAL AND COULD LEAD TO A POOR CONNECTION.
• IGNITION "ON"
• GROUND THE DIAGNOSTIC TERMINAL (FROM "DIAGNOSTIC CIRCUIT CHECK")
APPROPRIATE FUSE
Models / Fuse
Astro & Safari .... BRAKE
C & K Series ... STOP/HAZARD
G Series .... TAIL LPS
R & V Series ... STOP/HAZARD
S & T Series .... ECMB
BRAKE LIGHT FLASHES CODE 4
IGNITION "OFF"
• CHECK THE RESISTANCE BETWEEN VALVE RESET SWITCH TERMINAL C AND THE VALVE BODY
• CHECK THE RESISTANCE BETWEEN TERMINAL C AND TERMINAL D
IF EITHER CHECK MEASURES LESS THAN 50,000 OHMS
IF BOTH CHECKS MEASURE GREATER THAN 50,000 OHMS
IGNITION "ON"
• REPLACE THE VALVE ASSEMBLY
MEASURE VOLTAGE BETWEEN ECU PINS D AND C
4 VOLTS OR MORE
0 VOLTS
REPLACE THE VALVE ASSEMBLY
• REPLACE THE ECU
IGNITION "OFF"
• REMOVE APPROPRIATE FUSE
• INSTALL THE FUSE AFTER 5 SECONDS
PERFORM THE DIAGNOSTIC CIRCUIT CHECK
ALDL CONNECTOR (DIAGNOSTIC TERMINAL)
GROUND
A
H
90I06157
Courtesy of General Motors Corp.

Fig. 11: Code 4 – Grounded Anti-Lock Valve Switch (All Models)

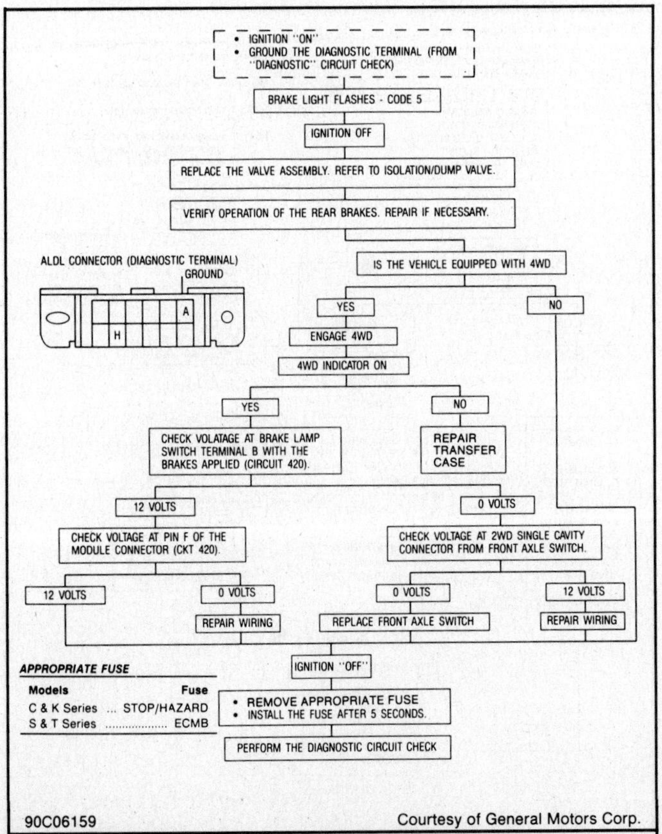
• IGNITION "ON"
• GROUND THE DIAGNOSTIC TERMINAL (FROM "DIAGNOSTIC" CIRCUIT CHECK)
BRAKE LIGHT FLASHES - CODE 5
IGNITION OFF
REPLACE THE VALVE ASSEMBLY. REFER TO ISOLATION/DUMP VALVE.
VERIFY OPERATION OF THE REAR BRAKES. REPAIR IF NECESSARY.
ALDL CONNECTOR (DIAGNOSTIC TERMINAL)
GROUND
A
H
IS THE VEHICLE EQUIPPED WITH 4WD
YES
NO
ENGAGE 4WD
4WD INDICATOR ON
YES
NO
CHECK VOLATAGE AT BRAKE LAMP SWITCH TERMINAL B WITH THE BRAKES APPLIED (CIRCUIT 420).
REPAIR TRANSFER CASE
12 VOLTS
0 VOLTS
CHECK VOLTAGE AT PIN F OF THE MODULE CONNECTOR (CKT 420).
CHECK VOLTAGE AT 2WD SINGLE CAVITY CONNECTOR FROM FRONT AXLE SWITCH.
12 VOLTS
0 VOLTS
0 VOLTS
12 VOLTS
REPAIR WIRING
REPLACE FRONT AXLE SWITCH
REPAIR WIRING
APPROPRIATE FUSE
Models / Fuse
C & K Series ... STOP/HAZARD
S & T Series .... ECMB
IGNITION "OFF"
• REMOVE APPROPRIATE FUSE
• INSTALL THE FUSE AFTER 5 SECONDS.
PERFORM THE DIAGNOSTIC CIRCUIT CHECK
90C06159
Courtesy of General Motors Corp.

Fig. 13: Code 5 – Excessive Actuations of the Dump Valve During Anti-Lock Stop ("C", "K", "S" & "T" Series)

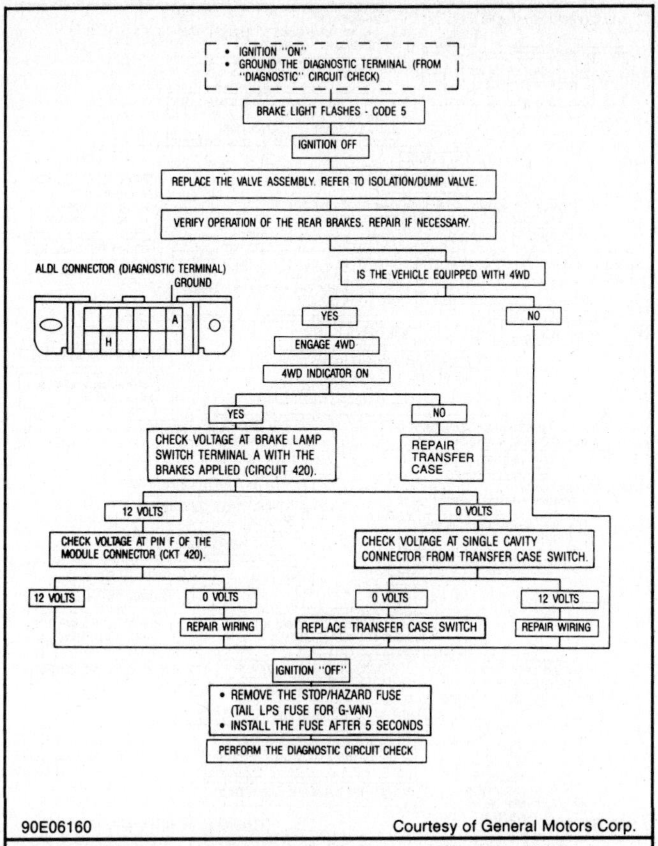

• IGNITION "ON"
• GROUND THE DIAGNOSTIC TERMINAL (FROM "DIAGNOSTIC" CIRCUIT CHECK)
BRAKE LIGHT FLASHES - CODE 5
IGNITION OFF
REPLACE THE VALVE ASSEMBLY. REFER TO ISOLATION/DUMP VALVE.
VERIFY OPERATION OF THE REAR BRAKES. REPAIR IF NECESSARY.
ALDL CONNECTOR (DIAGNOSTIC TERMINAL)
GROUND
A
H
IS THE VEHICLE EQUIPPED WITH 4WD
YES
NO
ENGAGE 4WD
4WD INDICATOR ON
YES
NO
CHECK VOLTAGE AT BRAKE LAMP SWITCH TERMINAL A WITH THE BRAKES APPLIED (CIRCUIT 420).
REPAIR TRANSFER CASE
12 VOLTS
0 VOLTS
CHECK VOLTAGE AT PIN F OF THE MODULE CONNECTOR (CKT 420).
CHECK VOLTAGE AT SINGLE CAVITY CONNECTOR FROM TRANSFER CASE SWITCH.
12 VOLTS
0 VOLTS
0 VOLTS
12 VOLTS
REPAIR WIRING
REPLACE TRANSFER CASE SWITCH
REPAIR WIRING
IGNITION "OFF"
• REMOVE THE STOP/HAZARD FUSE (TAIL LPS FUSE FOR G-VAN)
• INSTALL THE FUSE AFTER 5 SECONDS
PERFORM THE DIAGNOSTIC CIRCUIT CHECK
90E06160
Courtesy of General Motors Corp.

Fig. 14: Code 5 – Excessive Actuations of the Dump Valve During Anti-Lock Stop ("G", "R" & "V" Series)

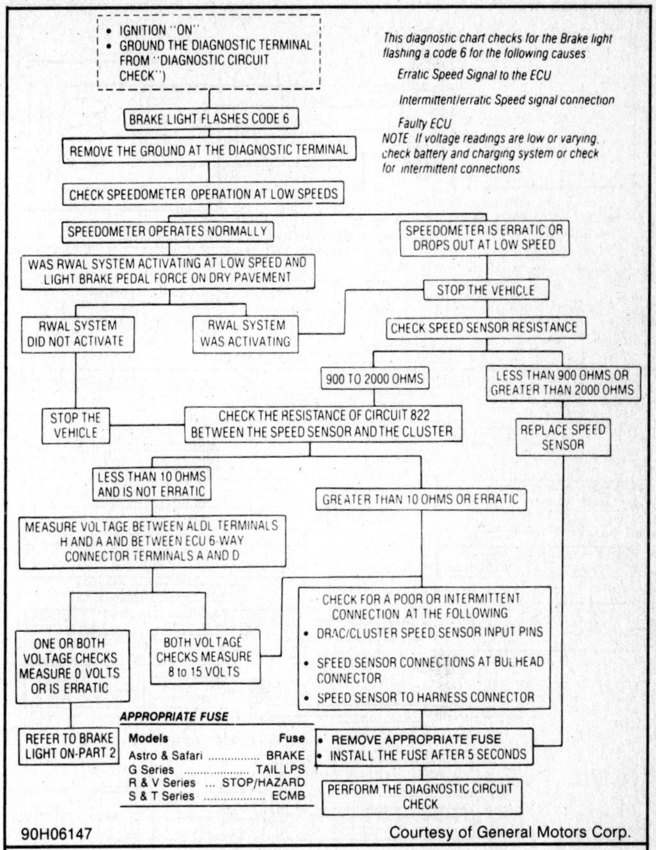

• IGNITION "ON"
• GROUND THE DIAGNOSTIC TERMINAL FROM "DIAGNOSTIC CIRCUIT CHECK")
This diagnostic chart checks for the Brake light flashing a code 6 for the following causes
Erratic Speed Signal to the ECU
Intermittent/erratic Speed signal connection
Faulty ECU
NOTE If voltage readings are low or varying, check battery and charging system or check for intermittent connections
BRAKE LIGHT FLASHES CODE 6
REMOVE THE GROUND AT THE DIAGNOSTIC TERMINAL
CHECK SPEEDOMETER OPERATION AT LOW SPEEDS
SPEEDOMETER OPERATES NORMALLY
SPEEDOMETER IS ERRATIC OR DROPS OUT AT LOW SPEED
WAS RWAL SYSTEM ACTIVATING AT LOW SPEED AND LIGHT BRAKE PEDAL FORCE ON DRY PAVEMENT
STOP THE VEHICLE
RWAL SYSTEM DID NOT ACTIVATE
RWAL SYSTEM WAS ACTIVATING
CHECK SPEED SENSOR RESISTANCE
900 TO 2000 OHMS
LESS THAN 900 OHMS OR GREATER THAN 2000 OHMS
STOP THE VEHICLE
CHECK THE RESISTANCE OF CIRCUIT 822 BETWEEN THE SPEED SENSOR AND THE CLUSTER
REPLACE SPEED SENSOR
LESS THAN 10 OHMS AND IS NOT ERRATIC
GREATER THAN 10 OHMS OR ERRATIC
MEASURE VOLTAGE BETWEEN ALDL TERMINALS H AND A AND BETWEEN ECU 6-WAY CONNECTOR TERMINALS A AND D
CHECK FOR A POOR OR INTERMITTENT CONNECTION AT THE FOLLOWING
• DRAC/CLUSTER SPEED SENSOR INPUT PINS
• SPEED SENSOR CONNECTIONS AT BULHEAD CONNECTOR
• SPEED SENSOR TO HARNESS CONNECTOR
ONE OR BOTH VOLTAGE CHECKS MEASURE 0 VOLTS OR IS ERRATIC
BOTH VOLTAGE CHECKS MEASURE 8 to 15 VOLTS
APPROPRIATE FUSE
Models Fuse
Astro & Safari .... BRAKE
G Series .... TAIL LPS
R & V Series ... STOP/HAZARD
S & T Series .... ECMB
REFER TO BRAKE LIGHT ON-PART 2
• REMOVE APPROPRIATE FUSE
• INSTALL THE FUSE AFTER 5 SECONDS
PERFORM THE DIAGNOSTIC CIRCUIT CHECK
90H06147
Courtesy of General Motors Corp.

Fig. 16: Code 6 – Erratic Speed Signal (All Others)

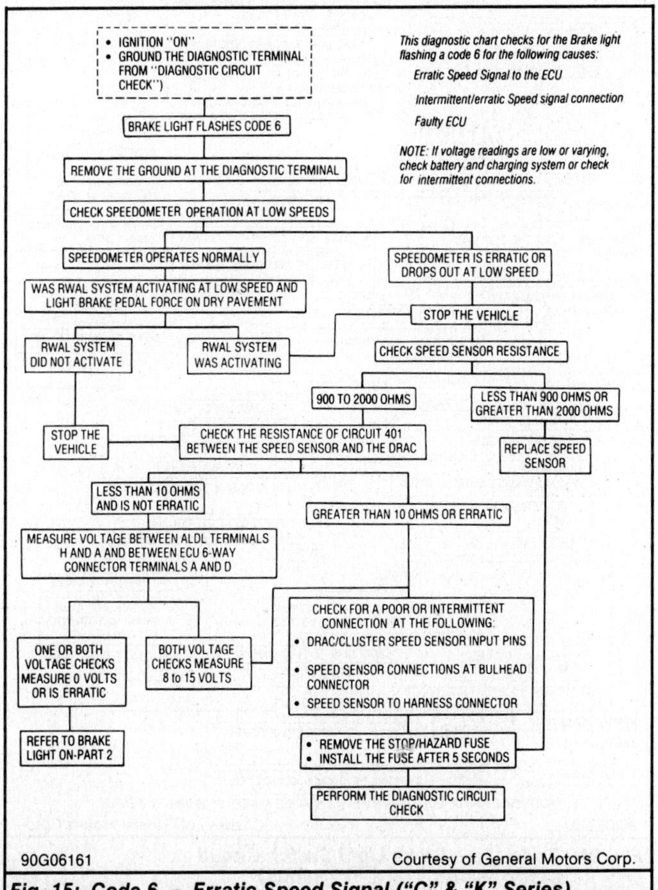

• IGNITION "ON"
• GROUND THE DIAGNOSTIC TERMINAL FROM "DIAGNOSTIC CIRCUIT CHECK")
This diagnostic chart checks for the Brake light flashing a code 6 for the following causes:
Erratic Speed Signal to the ECU
Intermittent/erratic Speed signal connection
Faulty ECU
NOTE: If voltage readings are low or varying, check battery and charging system or check for intermittent connections.
BRAKE LIGHT FLASHES CODE 6
REMOVE THE GROUND AT THE DIAGNOSTIC TERMINAL
CHECK SPEEDOMETER OPERATION AT LOW SPEEDS
SPEEDOMETER OPERATES NORMALLY
SPEEDOMETER IS ERRATIC OR DROPS OUT AT LOW SPEED
WAS RWAL SYSTEM ACTIVATING AT LOW SPEED AND LIGHT BRAKE PEDAL FORCE ON DRY PAVEMENT
STOP THE VEHICLE
RWAL SYSTEM DID NOT ACTIVATE
RWAL SYSTEM WAS ACTIVATING
CHECK SPEED SENSOR RESISTANCE
900 TO 2000 OHMS
LESS THAN 900 OHMS OR GREATER THAN 2000 OHMS
STOP THE VEHICLE
CHECK THE RESISTANCE OF CIRCUIT 401 BETWEEN THE SPEED SENSOR AND THE DRAC
REPLACE SPEED SENSOR
LESS THAN 10 OHMS AND IS NOT ERRATIC
GREATER THAN 10 OHMS OR ERRATIC
MEASURE VOLTAGE BETWEEN ALDL TERMINALS H AND A AND BETWEEN ECU 6-WAY CONNECTOR TERMINALS A AND D
CHECK FOR A POOR OR INTERMITTENT CONNECTION AT THE FOLLOWING:
• DRAC/CLUSTER SPEED SENSOR INPUT PINS
• SPEED SENSOR CONNECTIONS AT BULHEAD CONNECTOR
• SPEED SENSOR TO HARNESS CONNECTOR
ONE OR BOTH VOLTAGE CHECKS MEASURE 0 VOLTS OR IS ERRATIC
BOTH VOLTAGE CHECKS MEASURE 8 to 15 VOLTS
REFER TO BRAKE LIGHT ON-PART 2
• REMOVE THE STOP/HAZARD FUSE
• INSTALL THE FUSE AFTER 5 SECONDS
PERFORM THE DIAGNOSTIC CIRCUIT CHECK
90G06161
Courtesy of General Motors Corp.

Fig. 15: Code 6 – Erratic Speed Signal ("C" & "K" Series)

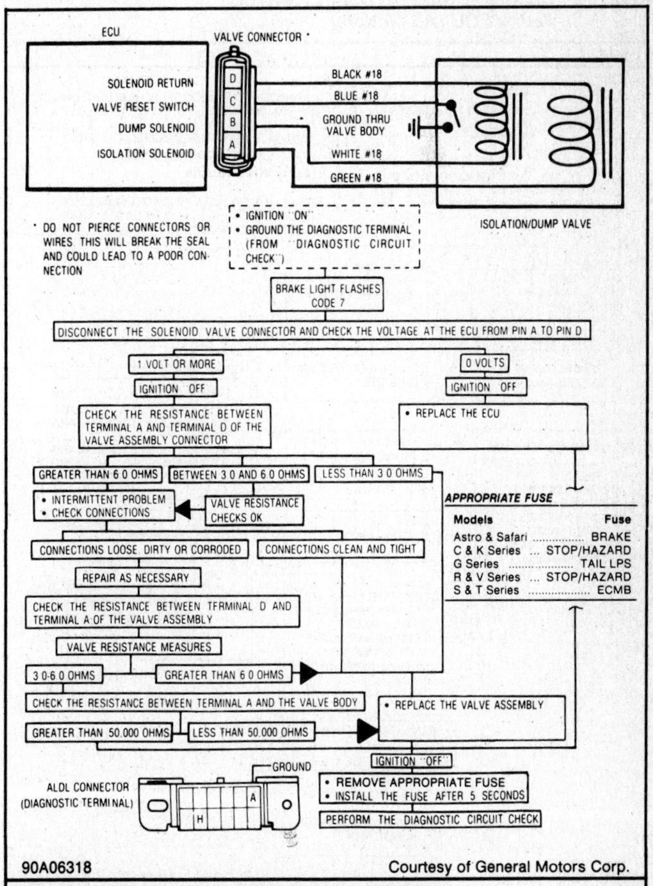

ECU
VALVE CONNECTOR *
SOLENOID RETURN
VALVE RESET SWITCH
DUMP SOLENOID
ISOLATION SOLENOID
D
C
B
A
BLACK #18
BLUE #18
GROUND THRU VALVE BODY
WHITE #18
GREEN #18
ISOLATION/DUMP VALVE
* DO NOT PIERCE CONNECTORS OR WIRES. THIS WILL BREAK THE SEAL AND COULD LEAD TO A POOR CONNECTION
• IGNITION "ON"
• GROUND THE DIAGNOSTIC TERMINAL (FROM "DIAGNOSTIC CIRCUIT CHECK")
BRAKE LIGHT FLASHES CODE 7
DISCONNECT THE SOLENOID VALVE CONNECTOR AND CHECK THE VOLTAGE AT THE ECU FROM PIN A TO PIN D
1 VOLT OR MORE
0 VOLTS
IGNITION OFF
IGNITION OFF
CHECK THE RESISTANCE BETWEEN TERMINAL A AND TERMINAL D OF THE VALVE ASSEMBLY CONNECTOR
• REPLACE THE ECU
GREATER THAN 6.0 OHMS
BETWEEN 3.0 AND 6.0 OHMS
LESS THAN 3.0 OHMS
• INTERMITTENT PROBLEM
• CHECK CONNECTIONS
VALVE RESISTANCE CHECKS OK
APPROPRIATE FUSE
Models Fuse
Astro & Safari .... BRAKE
C & K Series ... STOP/HAZARD
G Series .... TAIL LPS
R & V Series ... STOP/HAZARD
S & T Series .... ECMB
CONNECTIONS LOOSE, DIRTY OR CORRODED
CONNECTIONS CLEAN AND TIGHT
REPAIR AS NECESSARY
CHECK THE RESISTANCE BETWEEN TERMINAL D AND TERMINAL A OF THE VALVE ASSEMBLY
VALVE RESISTANCE MEASURES
3.0-6.0 OHMS
GREATER THAN 6.0 OHMS
CHECK THE RESISTANCE BETWEEN TERMINAL A AND THE VALVE BODY
• REPLACE THE VALVE ASSEMBLY
GREATER THAN 50,000 OHMS
LESS THAN 50,000 OHMS
GROUND
IGNITION "OFF"
ALDL CONNECTOR (DIAGNOSTIC TERMINAL)
A
H
• REMOVE APPROPRIATE FUSE
• INSTALL THE FUSE AFTER 5 SECONDS
PERFORM THE DIAGNOSTIC CIRCUIT CHECK
90A06318
Courtesy of General Motors Corp.

Fig. 17: Code 7 – Shorted Isolation Valve or Faulty ECU (All Models)

1991 BRAKES
Anti-Lock – RWAL (Cont.)

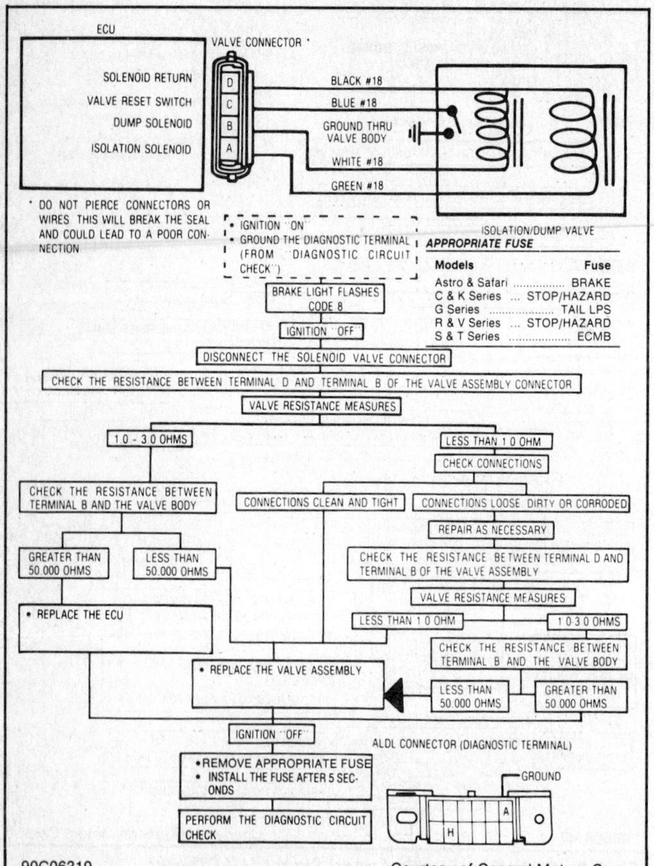
ECU
VALVE CONNECTOR *
SOLENOID RETURN
VALVE RESET SWITCH
DUMP SOLENOID
ISOLATION SOLENOID
D
C
B
A
BLACK #18
BLUE #18
GROUND THRU VALVE BODY
WHITE #18
GREEN #18
* DO NOT PIERCE CONNECTORS OR WIRES THIS WILL BREAK THE SEAL AND COULD LEAD TO A POOR CONNECTION
• IGNITION "ON"
• GROUND THE DIAGNOSTIC TERMINAL (FROM "DIAGNOSTIC CIRCUIT CHECK")
ISOLATION/DUMP VALVE
APPROPRIATE FUSE
Models / Fuse
Astro & Safari .... BRAKE
C & K Series ... STOP/HAZARD
G Series .... TAIL LPS
R & V Series ... STOP/HAZARD
S & T Series .... ECMB
BRAKE LIGHT FLASHES CODE 8
IGNITION "OFF"
DISCONNECT THE SOLENOID VALVE CONNECTOR
CHECK THE RESISTANCE BETWEEN TERMINAL D AND TERMINAL B OF THE VALVE ASSEMBLY CONNECTOR
VALVE RESISTANCE MEASURES
1.0 - 3.0 OHMS
LESS THAN 1.0 OHM
CHECK CONNECTIONS
CHECK THE RESISTANCE BETWEEN TERMINAL B AND THE VALVE BODY
CONNECTIONS CLEAN AND TIGHT
CONNECTIONS LOOSE, DIRTY OR CORRODED
REPAIR AS NECESSARY
GREATER THAN 50,000 OHMS
LESS THAN 50,000 OHMS
CHECK THE RESISTANCE BETWEEN TERMINAL D AND TERMINAL B OF THE VALVE ASSEMBLY
VALVE RESISTANCE MEASURES
• REPLACE THE ECU
LESS THAN 1.0 OHM
1.0-3.0 OHMS
CHECK THE RESISTANCE BETWEEN TERMINAL B AND THE VALVE BODY
• REPLACE THE VALVE ASSEMBLY
LESS THAN 50,000 OHMS
GREATER THAN 50,000 OHMS
IGNITION "OFF"
ALDL CONNECTOR (DIAGNOSTIC TERMINAL)
•REMOVE APPROPRIATE FUSE
• INSTALL THE FUSE AFTER 5 SECONDS
GROUND
A
H
PERFORM THE DIAGNOSTIC CIRCUIT CHECK

90C06319 Courtesy of General Motors Corp.

Fig. 18: Code 8 – Shorted Dump Valve or Faulty ECU (All Models)

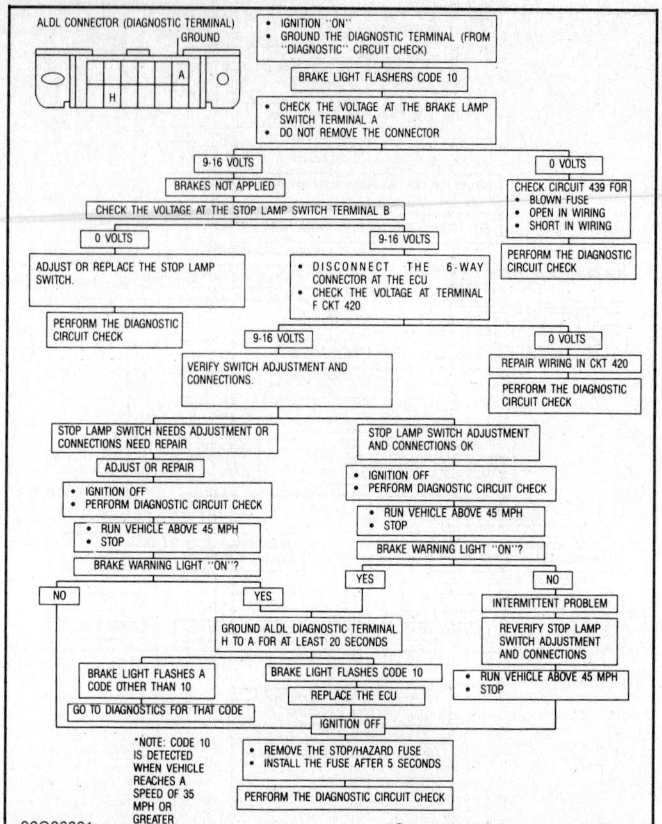
ALDL CONNECTOR (DIAGNOSTIC TERMINAL)
GROUND
A
H
• IGNITION "ON"
• GROUND THE DIAGNOSTIC TERMINAL (FROM "DIAGNOSTIC" CIRCUIT CHECK)
BRAKE LIGHT FLASHERS CODE 10
• CHECK THE VOLTAGE AT THE BRAKE LAMP SWITCH TERMINAL A
• DO NOT REMOVE THE CONNECTOR
9-16 VOLTS
0 VOLTS
BRAKES NOT APPLIED
CHECK CIRCUIT 439 FOR
• BLOWN FUSE
• OPEN IN WIRING
• SHORT IN WIRING
CHECK THE VOLTAGE AT THE STOP LAMP SWITCH TERMINAL B
0 VOLTS
9-16 VOLTS
PERFORM THE DIAGNOSTIC CIRCUIT CHECK
ADJUST OR REPLACE THE STOP LAMP SWITCH.
• DISCONNECT THE 6-WAY CONNECTOR AT THE ECU
• CHECK THE VOLTAGE AT TERMINAL F CKT 420
PERFORM THE DIAGNOSTIC CIRCUIT CHECK
9-16 VOLTS
0 VOLTS
VERIFY SWITCH ADJUSTMENT AND CONNECTIONS.
REPAIR WIRING IN CKT 420
PERFORM THE DIAGNOSTIC CIRCUIT CHECK
STOP LAMP SWITCH NEEDS ADJUSTMENT OR CONNECTIONS NEED REPAIR
STOP LAMP SWITCH ADJUSTMENT AND CONNECTIONS OK
ADJUST OR REPAIR
• IGNITION OFF
• PERFORM DIAGNOSTIC CIRCUIT CHECK
• IGNITION OFF
• PERFORM DIAGNOSTIC CIRCUIT CHECK
• RUN VEHICLE ABOVE 45 MPH
• STOP
• RUN VEHICLE ABOVE 45 MPH
• STOP
BRAKE WARNING LIGHT "ON"?
BRAKE WARNING LIGHT "ON"?
YES
NO
NO
YES
INTERMITTENT PROBLEM
GROUND ALDL DIAGNOSTIC TERMINAL H TO A FOR AT LEAST 20 SECONDS
REVERIFY STOP LAMP SWITCH ADJUSTMENT AND CONNECTIONS
BRAKE LIGHT FLASHES A CODE OTHER THAN 10
BRAKE LIGHT FLASHES CODE 10
• RUN VEHICLE ABOVE 45 MPH
• STOP
REPLACE THE ECU
GO TO DIAGNOSTICS FOR THAT CODE
IGNITION OFF
*NOTE: CODE 10 IS DETECTED WHEN VEHICLE REACHES A SPEED OF 35 MPH OR GREATER
• REMOVE THE STOP/HAZARD FUSE
• INSTALL THE FUSE AFTER 5 SECONDS
PERFORM THE DIAGNOSTIC CIRCUIT CHECK

90G06321 Courtesy of General Motors Corp.

Fig. 20: Code 10 – Brake Light Switch Circuit ("C" & "K" Series)

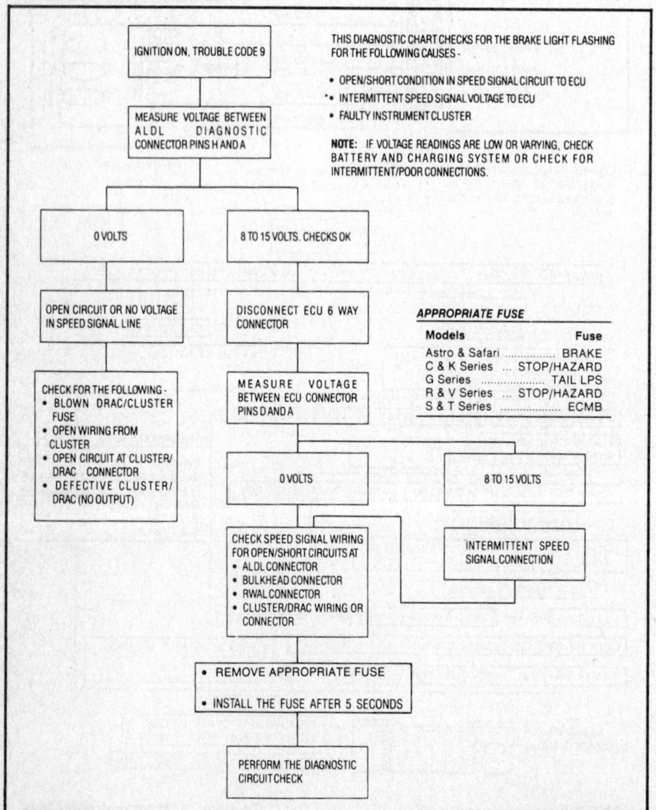
IGNITION ON, TROUBLE CODE 9
THIS DIAGNOSTIC CHART CHECKS FOR THE BRAKE LIGHT FLASHING FOR THE FOLLOWING CAUSES -
• OPEN/SHORT CONDITION IN SPEED SIGNAL CIRCUIT TO ECU
• INTERMITTENT SPEED SIGNAL VOLTAGE TO ECU
• FAULTY INSTRUMENT CLUSTER
MEASURE VOLTAGE BETWEEN ALDL DIAGNOSTIC CONNECTOR PINS H AND A
NOTE: IF VOLTAGE READINGS ARE LOW OR VARYING, CHECK BATTERY AND CHARGING SYSTEM OR CHECK FOR INTERMITTENT/POOR CONNECTIONS.
0 VOLTS
8 TO 15 VOLTS. CHECKS OK
OPEN CIRCUIT OR NO VOLTAGE IN SPEED SIGNAL LINE
DISCONNECT ECU 6 WAY CONNECTOR
APPROPRIATE FUSE
Models / Fuse
Astro & Safari .... BRAKE
C & K Series ... STOP/HAZARD
G Series .... TAIL LPS
R & V Series ... STOP/HAZARD
S & T Series .... ECMB
CHECK FOR THE FOLLOWING -
• BLOWN DRAC/CLUSTER FUSE
• OPEN WIRING FROM CLUSTER
• OPEN CIRCUIT AT CLUSTER/DRAC CONNECTOR
• DEFECTIVE CLUSTER/DRAC (NO OUTPUT)
MEASURE VOLTAGE BETWEEN ECU CONNECTOR PINS D AND A
0 VOLTS
8 TO 15 VOLTS
CHECK SPEED SIGNAL WIRING FOR OPEN/SHORT CIRCUITS AT
• ALDL CONNECTOR
• BULKHEAD CONNECTOR
• RWAL CONNECTOR
• CLUSTER/DRAC WIRING OR CONNECTOR
INTERMITTENT SPEED SIGNAL CONNECTION
• REMOVE APPROPRIATE FUSE
• INSTALL THE FUSE AFTER 5 SECONDS
PERFORM THE DIAGNOSTIC CIRCUIT CHECK

90E06320 Courtesy of General Motors Corp.

Fig. 19: Code 9 – Open Circuit to Speed Sensor (All Models)

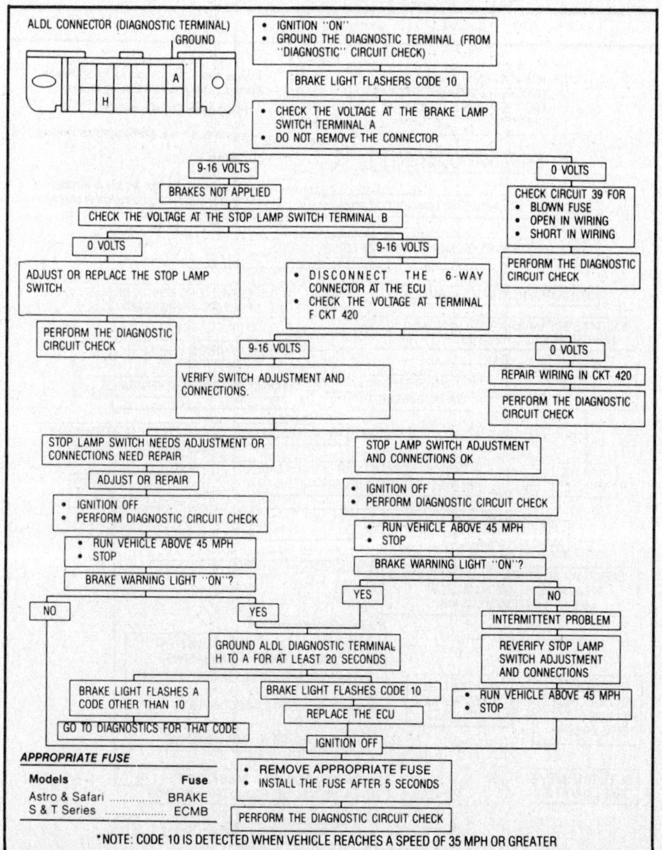
ALDL CONNECTOR (DIAGNOSTIC TERMINAL)
GROUND
A
H
• IGNITION "ON"
• GROUND THE DIAGNOSTIC TERMINAL (FROM "DIAGNOSTIC" CIRCUIT CHECK)
BRAKE LIGHT FLASHERS CODE 10
• CHECK THE VOLTAGE AT THE BRAKE LAMP SWITCH TERMINAL A
• DO NOT REMOVE THE CONNECTOR
9-16 VOLTS
0 VOLTS
BRAKES NOT APPLIED
CHECK CIRCUIT 39 FOR
• BLOWN FUSE
• OPEN IN WIRING
• SHORT IN WIRING
CHECK THE VOLTAGE AT THE STOP LAMP SWITCH TERMINAL B
0 VOLTS
9-16 VOLTS
PERFORM THE DIAGNOSTIC CIRCUIT CHECK
ADJUST OR REPLACE THE STOP LAMP SWITCH.
• DISCONNECT THE 6-WAY CONNECTOR AT THE ECU
• CHECK THE VOLTAGE AT TERMINAL F CKT 420
PERFORM THE DIAGNOSTIC CIRCUIT CHECK
9-16 VOLTS
0 VOLTS
VERIFY SWITCH ADJUSTMENT AND CONNECTIONS.
REPAIR WIRING IN CKT 420
PERFORM THE DIAGNOSTIC CIRCUIT CHECK
STOP LAMP SWITCH NEEDS ADJUSTMENT OR CONNECTIONS NEED REPAIR
STOP LAMP SWITCH ADJUSTMENT AND CONNECTIONS OK
ADJUST OR REPAIR
• IGNITION OFF
• PERFORM DIAGNOSTIC CIRCUIT CHECK
• IGNITION OFF
• PERFORM DIAGNOSTIC CIRCUIT CHECK
• RUN VEHICLE ABOVE 45 MPH
• STOP
• RUN VEHICLE ABOVE 45 MPH
• STOP
BRAKE WARNING LIGHT "ON"?
BRAKE WARNING LIGHT "ON"?
YES
NO
NO
YES
INTERMITTENT PROBLEM
GROUND ALDL DIAGNOSTIC TERMINAL H TO A FOR AT LEAST 20 SECONDS
REVERIFY STOP LAMP SWITCH ADJUSTMENT AND CONNECTIONS
BRAKE LIGHT FLASHES A CODE OTHER THAN 10
BRAKE LIGHT FLASHES CODE 10
• RUN VEHICLE ABOVE 45 MPH
• STOP
REPLACE THE ECU
GO TO DIAGNOSTICS FOR THAT CODE
IGNITION OFF
APPROPRIATE FUSE
Models / Fuse
Astro & Safari .... BRAKE
S & T Series .... ECMB
• REMOVE APPROPRIATE FUSE
• INSTALL THE FUSE AFTER 5 SECONDS
PERFORM THE DIAGNOSTIC CIRCUIT CHECK
*NOTE: CODE 10 IS DETECTED WHEN VEHICLE REACHES A SPEED OF 35 MPH OR GREATER

90I06322 Courtesy of General Motors Corp.

Fig. 21: Code 10 – Brake Light Switch Circuit (Astro, Safari, "S" & "T" Series)

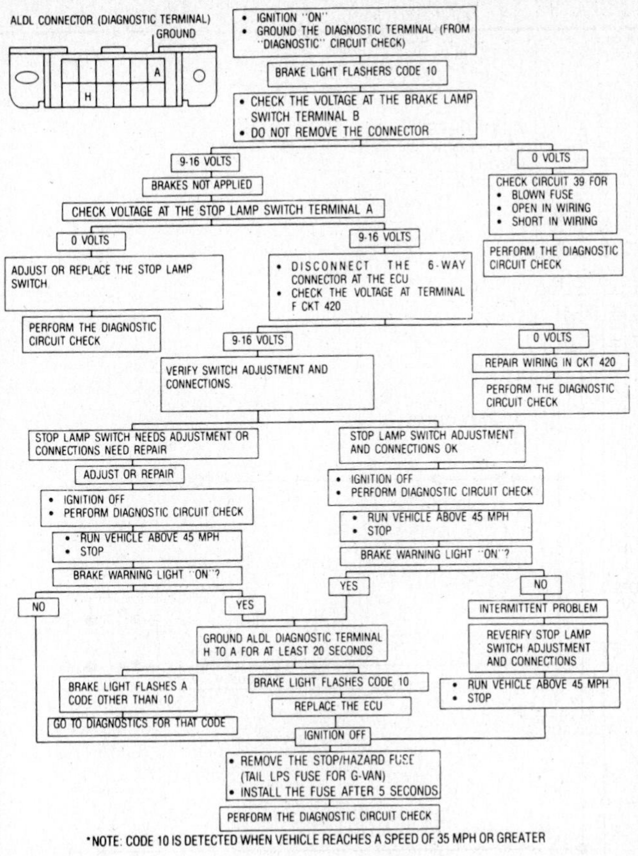

ALDL CONNECTOR (DIAGNOSTIC TERMINAL)
GROUND
A
H
• IGNITION "ON"
• GROUND THE DIAGNOSTIC TERMINAL (FROM "DIAGNOSTIC" CIRCUIT CHECK)
BRAKE LIGHT FLASHERS CODE 10
• CHECK THE VOLTAGE AT THE BRAKE LAMP SWITCH TERMINAL B
• DO NOT REMOVE THE CONNECTOR
9-16 VOLTS
0 VOLTS
BRAKES NOT APPLIED
CHECK CIRCUIT 39 FOR
• BLOWN FUSE
• OPEN IN WIRING
• SHORT IN WIRING
CHECK VOLTAGE AT THE STOP LAMP SWITCH TERMINAL A
0 VOLTS
9-16 VOLTS
PERFORM THE DIAGNOSTIC CIRCUIT CHECK
ADJUST OR REPLACE THE STOP LAMP SWITCH
• DISCONNECT THE 6-WAY CONNECTOR AT THE ECU
• CHECK THE VOLTAGE AT TERMINAL F CKT 420
PERFORM THE DIAGNOSTIC CIRCUIT CHECK
9-16 VOLTS
0 VOLTS
REPAIR WIRING IN CKT 420
VERIFY SWITCH ADJUSTMENT AND CONNECTIONS
PERFORM THE DIAGNOSTIC CIRCUIT CHECK
STOP LAMP SWITCH NEEDS ADJUSTMENT OR CONNECTIONS NEED REPAIR
STOP LAMP SWITCH ADJUSTMENT AND CONNECTIONS OK
ADJUST OR REPAIR
• IGNITION OFF
• PERFORM DIAGNOSTIC CIRCUIT CHECK
• IGNITION OFF
• PERFORM DIAGNOSTIC CIRCUIT CHECK
• RUN VEHICLE ABOVE 45 MPH
• STOP
• RUN VEHICLE ABOVE 45 MPH
• STOP
BRAKE WARNING LIGHT "ON"?
BRAKE WARNING LIGHT "ON"?
YES
NO
NO
YES
INTERMITTENT PROBLEM
GROUND ALDL DIAGNOSTIC TERMINAL H TO A FOR AT LEAST 20 SECONDS
REVERIFY STOP LAMP SWITCH ADJUSTMENT AND CONNECTIONS
BRAKE LIGHT FLASHES A CODE OTHER THAN 10
BRAKE LIGHT FLASHES CODE 10
• RUN VEHICLE ABOVE 45 MPH
• STOP
REPLACE THE ECU
GO TO DIAGNOSTICS FOR THAT CODE
IGNITION OFF
• REMOVE THE STOP/HAZARD FUSE (TAIL LPS FUSE FOR G-VAN)
• INSTALL THE FUSE AFTER 5 SECONDS
PERFORM THE DIAGNOSTIC CIRCUIT CHECK
*NOTE: CODE 10 IS DETECTED WHEN VEHICLE REACHES A SPEED OF 35 MPH OR GREATER

90A06323 Courtesy of General Motors Corp.

Fig. 22: Code 10 – Brake Light Switch Circuit ("G", "R" & "V" Series)

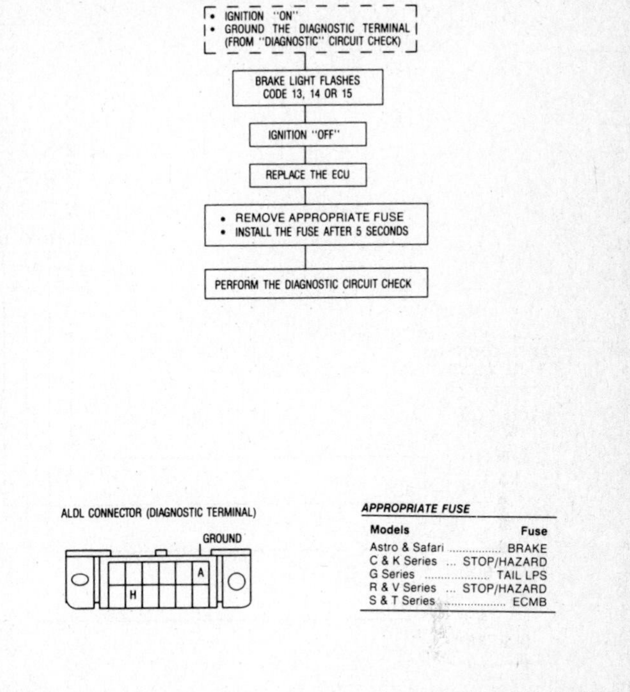

• IGNITION "ON"
• GROUND THE DIAGNOSTIC TERMINAL (FROM "DIAGNOSTIC" CIRCUIT CHECK)
BRAKE LIGHT FLASHES CODE 13, 14 OR 15
IGNITION "OFF"
REPLACE THE ECU
• REMOVE APPROPRIATE FUSE
• INSTALL THE FUSE AFTER 5 SECONDS
PERFORM THE DIAGNOSTIC CIRCUIT CHECK
ALDL CONNECTOR (DIAGNOSTIC TERMINAL)
GROUND
A
H
APPROPRIATE FUSE
Models
Fuse
Astro & Safari .... BRAKE
C & K Series ... STOP/HAZARD
G Series .... TAIL LPS
R & V Series ... STOP/HAZARD
S & T Series .... ECMB

90C06324 Courtesy of General Motors Corp.

Fig. 23: Codes 13, 14 & 15 – Electronic Control Unit Malfunction (All Models)

1991 BRAKES
Anti-Lock – RWAL (Cont.)

WIRING DIAGRAMS

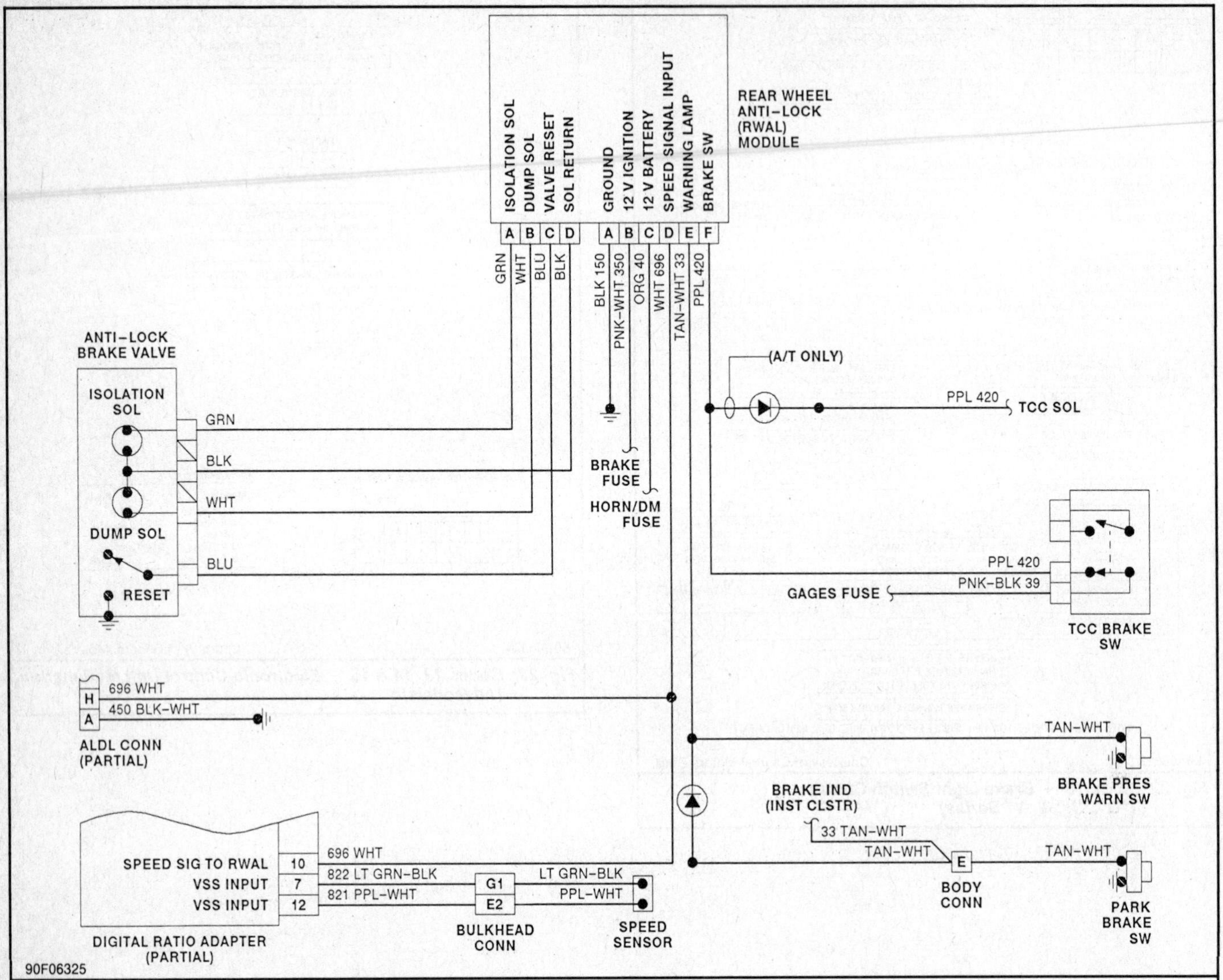
REAR WHEEL
ANTI-LOCK
(RWAL)
MODULE
ISOLATION SOL
DUMP SOL
VALVE RESET
SOL RETURN
GROUND
12 V IGNITION
12 V BATTERY
SPEED SIGNAL INPUT
WARNING LAMP
BRAKE SW
A B C D
A B C D E F
GRN
WHT
BLU
BLK
BLK 150
PNK-WHT 350
ORG 40
WHT 696
TAN-WHT 33
PPL 420
ANTI-LOCK
BRAKE VALVE
ISOLATION
SOL
GRN
BLK
WHT
DUMP SOL
BLU
RESET
BRAKE
FUSE
HORN/DM
FUSE
(A/T ONLY)
PPL 420
TCC SOL
PPL 420
PNK-BLK 39
GAGES FUSE
TCC BRAKE
SW
H
A
696 WHT
450 BLK-WHT
ALDL CONN
(PARTIAL)
TAN-WHT
BRAKE PRES
WARN SW
BRAKE IND
(INST CLSTR)
33 TAN-WHT
TAN-WHT
E
TAN-WHT
BODY
CONN
PARK
BRAKE
SW
SPEED SIG TO RWAL
VSS INPUT
VSS INPUT
10
7
12
696 WHT
822 LT GRN-BLK
821 PPL-WHT
G1
E2
LT GRN-BLK
PPL-WHT
BULKHEAD
CONN
SPEED
SENSOR
DIGITAL RATIO ADAPTER
(PARTIAL)
90F06325

Fig. 24: RWAL Wiring Diagram (Astro & Safari)

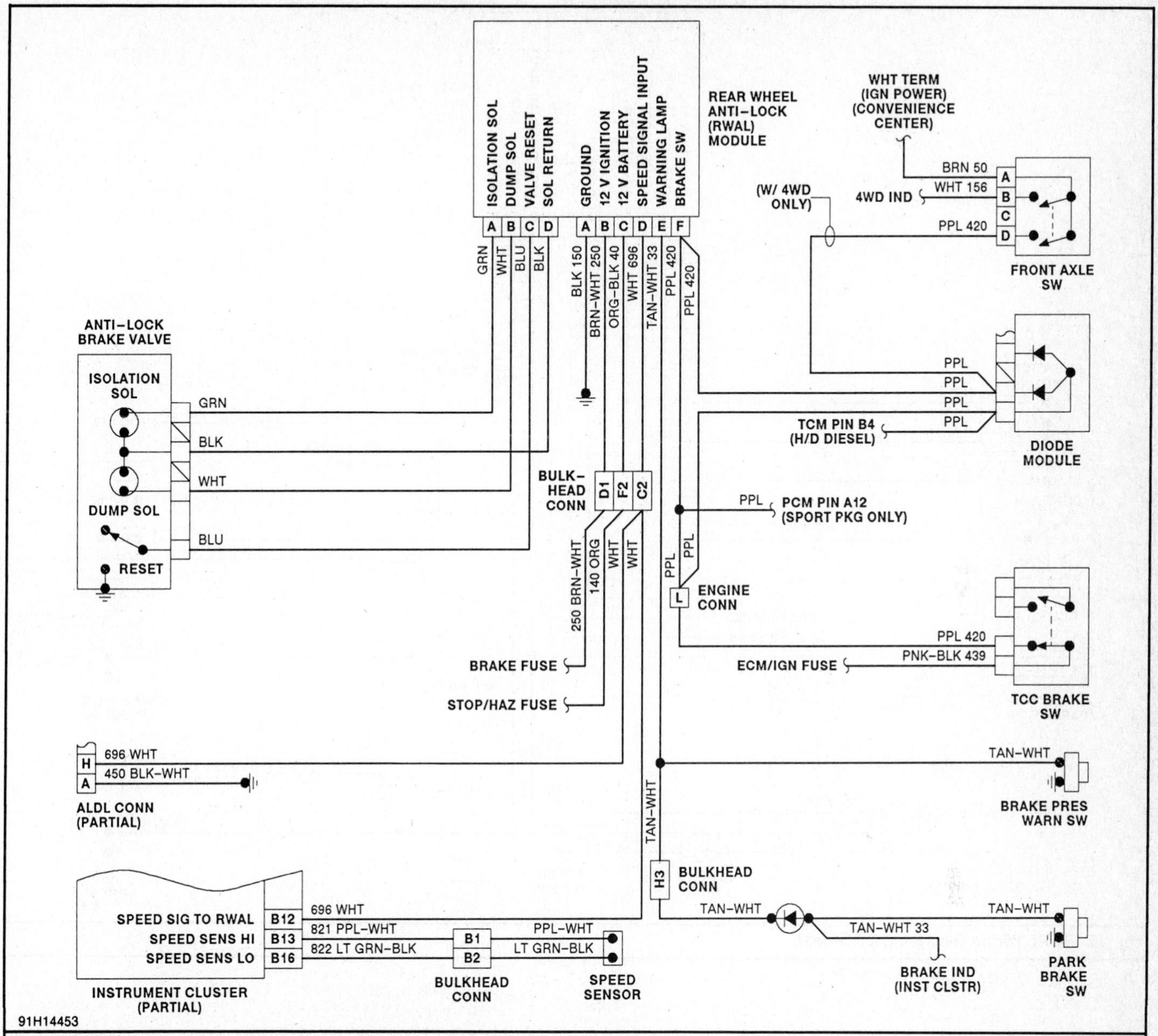
REAR WHEEL ANTI-LOCK (RWAL) MODULE
ISOLATION SOL
DUMP SOL
VALVE RESET
SOL RETURN
GROUND
12 V IGNITION
12 V BATTERY
SPEED SIGNAL INPUT
WARNING LAMP
BRAKE SW
GRN
WHT
BLU
BLK
BLK 150
BRN-WHT 250
ORG-BLK 40
WHT 696
TAN-WHT 33
PPL 420
WHT TERM (IGN POWER) (CONVENIENCE CENTER)
BRN 50
WHT 156
4WD IND
(W/ 4WD ONLY)
FRONT AXLE SW
ANTI-LOCK BRAKE VALVE
ISOLATION SOL
DUMP SOL
RESET
PPL
TCM PIN B4 (H/D DIESEL)
DIODE MODULE
BULK-HEAD CONN
PCM PIN A12 (SPORT PKG ONLY)
250 BRN-WHT
140 ORG
ENGINE CONN
BRAKE FUSE
STOP/HAZ FUSE
PNK-BLK 439
ECM/IGN FUSE
TCC BRAKE SW
696 WHT
450 BLK-WHT
ALDL CONN (PARTIAL)
TAN-WHT
BRAKE PRES WARN SW
BULKHEAD CONN
SPEED SIG TO RWAL
SPEED SENS HI
SPEED SENS LO
821 PPL-WHT
822 LT GRN-BLK
PPL-WHT
LT GRN-BLK
INSTRUMENT CLUSTER (PARTIAL)
BULKHEAD CONN
SPEED SENSOR
TAN-WHT 33
BRAKE IND (INST CLSTR)
PARK BRAKE SW
91H14453

Fig. 25: RWAL Wiring Diagram ("C" & "K" Series)

1991 BRAKES
Anti-Lock – RWAL (Cont.)

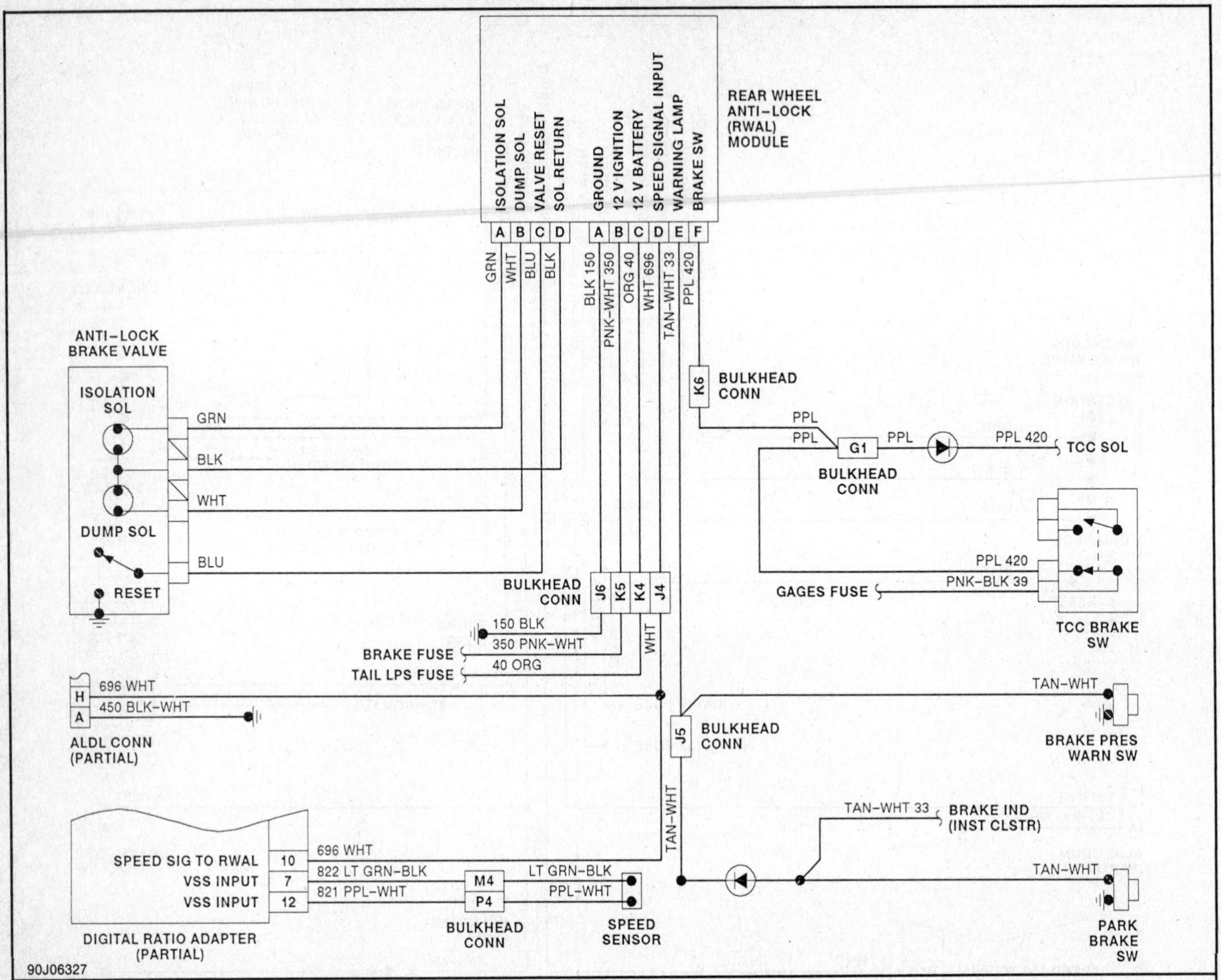
REAR WHEEL ANTI-LOCK (RWAL) MODULE
ISOLATION SOL
DUMP SOL
VALVE RESET
SOL RETURN
GROUND
12 V IGNITION
12 V BATTERY
SPEED SIGNAL INPUT
WARNING LAMP
BRAKE SW
GRN
WHT
BLU
BLK
BLK 150
PNK-WHT 350
ORG 40
WHT 696
TAN-WHT 33
PPL 420
ANTI-LOCK BRAKE VALVE
ISOLATION SOL
DUMP SOL
RESET
BULKHEAD CONN
TCC SOL
TCC BRAKE SW
GAGES FUSE
PNK-BLK 39
BRAKE FUSE
TAIL LPS FUSE
150 BLK
350 PNK-WHT
40 ORG
696 WHT
450 BLK-WHT
ALDL CONN (PARTIAL)
TAN-WHT
BRAKE PRES WARN SW
BRAKE IND (INST CLSTR)
SPEED SIG TO RWAL
VSS INPUT
VSS INPUT
822 LT GRN-BLK
821 PPL-WHT
LT GRN-BLK
PPL-WHT
DIGITAL RATIO ADAPTER (PARTIAL)
SPEED SENSOR
PARK BRAKE SW
90J06327

Fig. 26: RWAL Wiring Diagram ("G" Series)

1991 BRAKES
Anti-Lock – RWAL (Cont.)

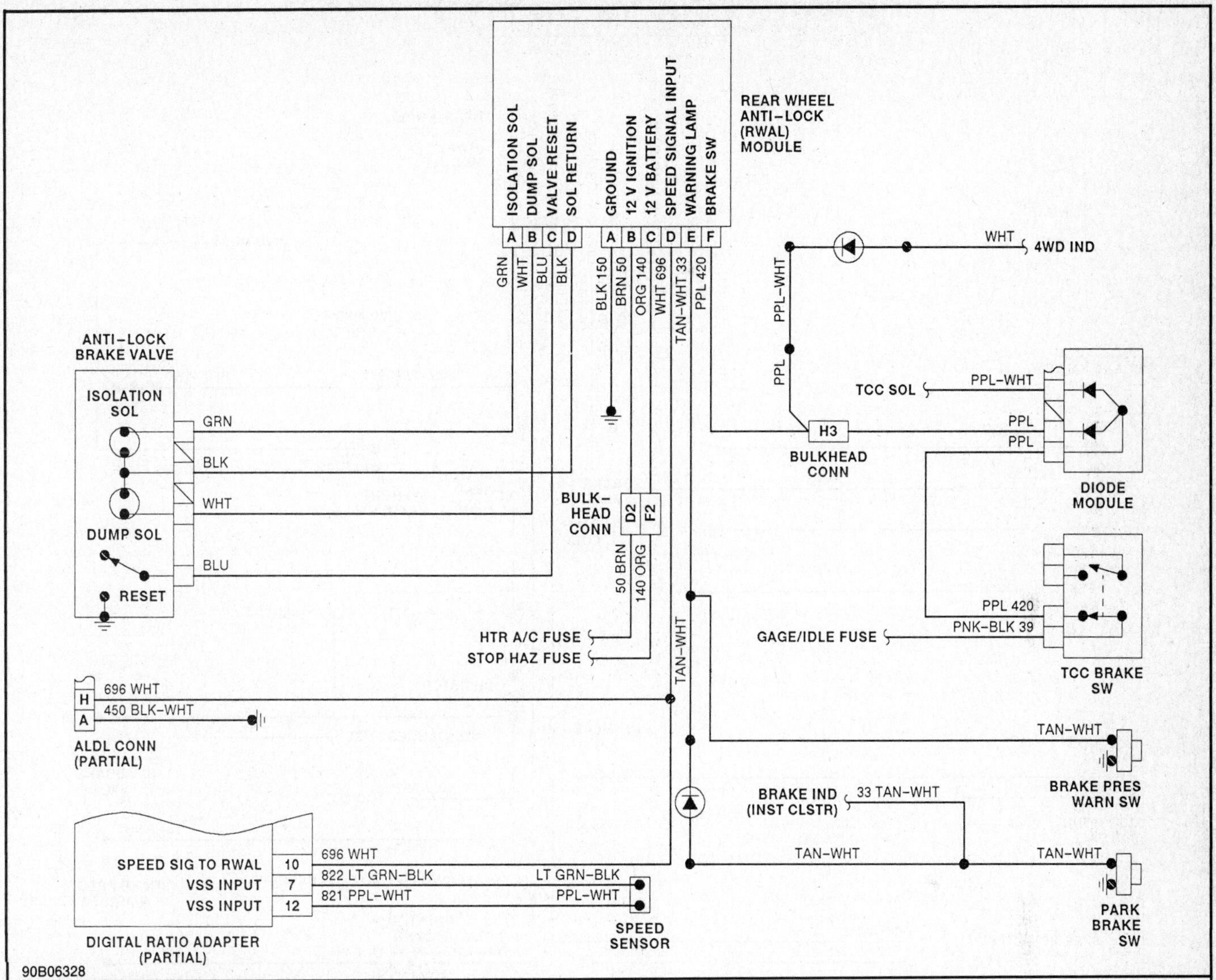
REAR WHEEL ANTI-LOCK (RWAL) MODULE
ISOLATION SOL
DUMP SOL
VALVE RESET
SOL RETURN
GROUND
12 V IGNITION
12 V BATTERY
SPEED SIGNAL INPUT
WARNING LAMP
BRAKE SW
A B C D
A B C D E F
GRN
WHT
BLU
BLK
BLK 150
BRN 50
ORG 140
WHT 696
TAN-WHT 33
PPL 420
ANTI-LOCK BRAKE VALVE
ISOLATION SOL
DUMP SOL
RESET
GRN
BLK
WHT
BLU
BULK-HEAD CONN
D2
F2
50 BRN
140 ORG
HTR A/C FUSE
STOP HAZ FUSE
TAN-WHT
WHT
4WD IND
PPL-WHT
PPL
TCC SOL
PPL-WHT
H3
BULKHEAD CONN
PPL
PPL
DIODE MODULE
PPL 420
PNK-BLK 39
GAGE/IDLE FUSE
TCC BRAKE SW
H
A
696 WHT
450 BLK-WHT
ALDL CONN (PARTIAL)
TAN-WHT
BRAKE PRES WARN SW
BRAKE IND (INST CLSTR)
33 TAN-WHT
TAN-WHT
TAN-WHT
PARK BRAKE SW
SPEED SIG TO RWAL
VSS INPUT
VSS INPUT
10
7
12
696 WHT
822 LT GRN-BLK
821 PPL-WHT
LT GRN-BLK
PPL-WHT
SPEED SENSOR
DIGITAL RATIO ADAPTER (PARTIAL)
90B06328

Fig. 27: RWAL Wiring Diagram ("R" & "V" Series)

1991 BRAKES
Anti-Lock – RWAL (Cont.)

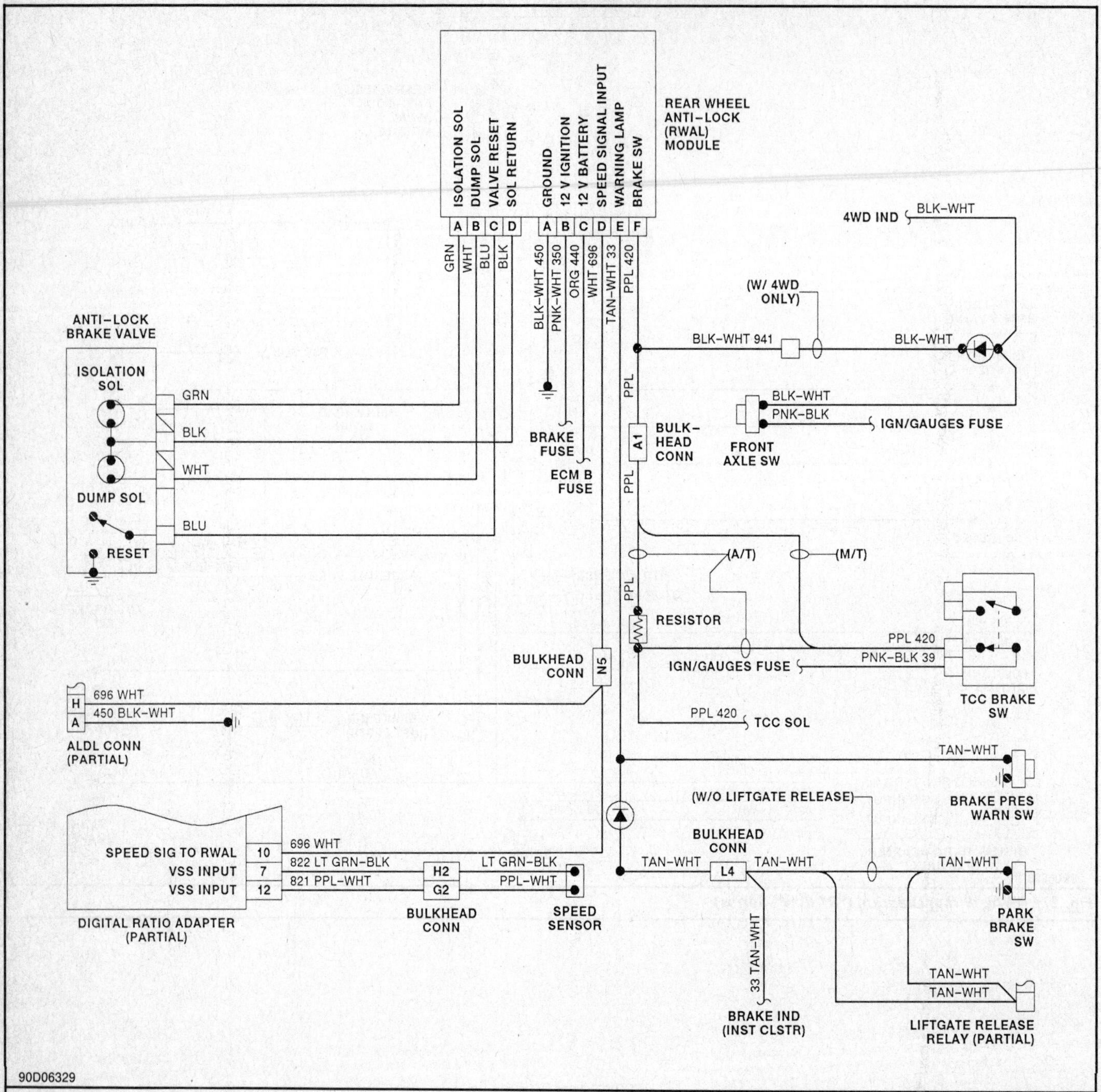
REAR WHEEL ANTI-LOCK (RWAL) MODULE
ISOLATION SOL
DUMP SOL
VALVE RESET
SOL RETURN
GROUND
12 V IGNITION
12 V BATTERY
SPEED SIGNAL INPUT
WARNING LAMP
BRAKE SW
A B C D
A B C D E F
GRN
WHT
BLU
BLK
BLK-WHT 450
PNK-WHT 350
ORG 440
WHT 696
TAN-WHT 33
PPL 420
ANTI-LOCK BRAKE VALVE
ISOLATION SOL
DUMP SOL
RESET
BRAKE FUSE
ECM B FUSE
4WD IND
BLK-WHT
(W/ 4WD ONLY)
BLK-WHT 941
PPL
BULK-HEAD CONN
A1
PNK-BLK
IGN/GAUGES FUSE
FRONT AXLE SW
(A/T)
(M/T)
RESISTOR
PPL 420
PNK-BLK 39
TCC BRAKE SW
TCC SOL
BULKHEAD CONN
N5
696 WHT
450 BLK-WHT
H
A
ALDL CONN (PARTIAL)
TAN-WHT
BRAKE PRES WARN SW
(W/O LIFTGATE RELEASE)
BULKHEAD CONN
L4
PARK BRAKE SW
SPEED SIG TO RWAL
VSS INPUT
VSS INPUT
10
7
12
822 LT GRN-BLK
821 PPL-WHT
H2
G2
LT GRN-BLK
PPL-WHT
DIGITAL RATIO ADAPTER (PARTIAL)
SPEED SENSOR
33 TAN-WHT
BRAKE IND (INST CLSTR)
LIFTGATE RELEASE RELAY (PARTIAL)
90D06329

Fig. 28: RWAL Wiring Diagram ("S" & "T" Series)

1991 BRAKES
Anti-Lock – 4WAL

Astro, Bravada, Safari, "S" & "T" Series

DESCRIPTION

The Kelsey-Hayes 4-Wheel Anti-Lock (4WAL) brake system is used to prevent wheel lock-up during heavy braking. This allows driver to maintain steering control while stopping the vehicle in the shortest distance. The system consists of: Electro-Hydraulic Control Unit (EHCU), 4 wheel sensors, warning lights, electrical wiring and hydraulic lines. *See Fig. 1.*

The EHCU is located on firewall, under the master cylinder. It consists of an Electronic Control Unit (ECU), hydraulic control unit, 2 accumulators, pump motor and a relay. The hydraulic control unit consists of an Isolation Solenoid Valve (ISO), Pulse-Width Modulated (PVM) valve, a High Pressure Accumulator (HPA), Low Pressure Accumulator (LPA) and a reset switch of each channel. If overhaul or repair to any component on the EHCU is necessary, complete assembly must be replaced.

OPERATION

When ignition is turned on, the EHCU performs a self-check of the 4WAL electrical system. The Yellow ANTILOCK and Red BRAKE warning lights will come on for 2 seconds. The ANTILOCK light should turn off if no electrical faults are found. The ANTILOCK light should only stay on when the EHCU has detected a problem with the 4WAL system. The Red BRAKE light may come on or stay on if the parking brake is applied or a mechanical brake problem is detected.

Once the vehicle has exceeded 8 MPH and the driver has fully released the brake pedal, the EHCU performs a self-check on the electro-hydraulic portion of the system. This includes the pump, control valves and reset switches. If the EHCU detects a problem during this self-check or the initial self-test, an indicator light will come on and the 4WAL system will be disabled, and a trouble code will be stored.

When the brake pedal is depressed, voltage to the EHCU drops from 12 volts to one volt. At this point, the EHCU monitors wheel speed through AC signal from a speed sensor located at each wheel. If the deceleration rate of a wheel speed reaches a preprogrammed rate,

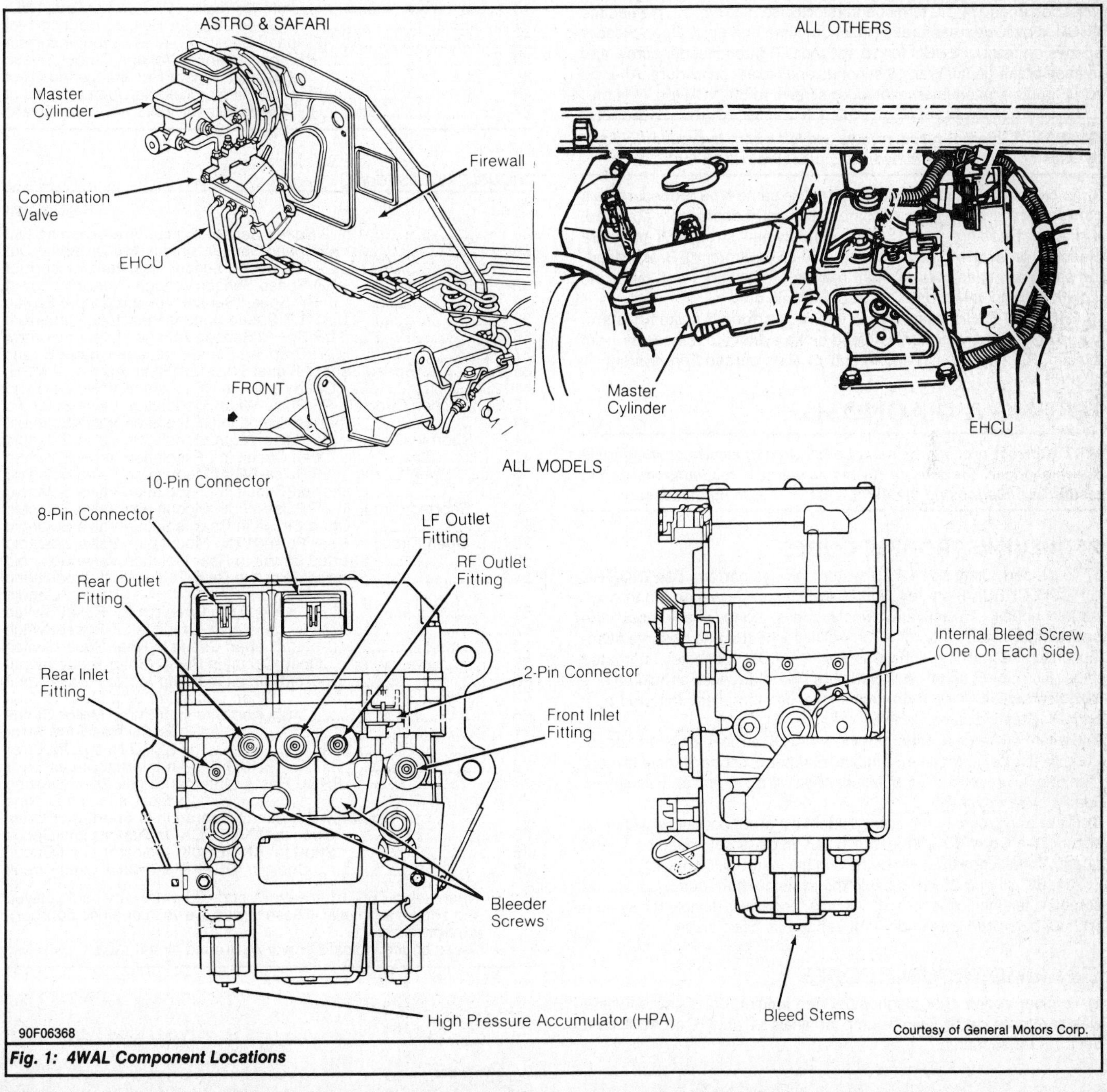
ASTRO & SAFARI
Master Cylinder
Firewall
Combination Valve
EHCU
FRONT
ALL OTHERS
Master Cylinder
EHCU
ALL MODELS
10-Pin Connector
8-Pin Connector
LF Outlet Fitting
RF Outlet Fitting
Rear Outlet Fitting
Rear Inlet Fitting
2-Pin Connector
Front Inlet Fitting
Internal Bleed Screw (One On Each Side)
Bleeder Screws
High Pressure Accumulator (HPA)
Bleed Stems
90F06368
Courtesy of General Motors Corp.

Fig. 1: 4WAL Component Locations

1991 BRAKES
Anti-Lock – 4WAL (Cont.)

the EHCU will activate various control valves to prevent wheel lock-up by increasing or decreasing hydraulic pressure to each channel: left front, right front or rear wheels.

On 4WD models, a front axle mounted switch is used to inform the EHCU when the vehicle is in 2WD or 4WD mode. This switch is a open during 2WD operation, thus sending an one volt or less signal. During 4WD operation, switch closes, sending a 12-volt signal to the EHCU. This signal changes the anti-lock braking program for 4WD operation.

BLEEDING BRAKE SYSTEM

NOTE: It is not necessary to bleed EHCU during normal brake system bleeding. If EHCU is replaced, it will be necessary to bleed EHCU first.

1) Install 2 Combination Valve Depressors (J-35856) on High Pressure Accumulator (HPA) bleed valves. *See Fig. 1*. Install one Combination Valve Depressor (J-35856) on combination bleed valve.

2) Before beginning bleeding procedure, the internal bleeder screws must be turned 1/4-1/2 turn counterclockwise. *See Fig. 1*. To bleed the EHCU, slowly depress brake pedal one time and hold. Open bleeder screws on front of EHCU for 15 seconds. Tighten bleeder screw and release brake pedal. Wait 15 seconds and repeat procedure. After no air is found, tighten internal bleeder screws to 60 INCH lbs. (7 N.m).

CAUTION: If internal bleed screws are left open, hydraulic fluid will by-pass accumulator and hydraulic pressure will be lost.

3) To bleed mechanical brake system, use same type procedure as a conventional system. Ensure combination valve depressors are used. If manual bleeding, wait 15 seconds between strokes. If pressure bleeding, pressurize brake bleeder to 20-25 psi (kg/cm²). Brake bleeding sequence is as follows: right rear, left rear, right front, left front, isolation dump valve. Use DOT 3 brake fluid only.

4) Connect TECH-1 scan tool to vehicle. Perform 3 system tests to purge any air from EHCU. Re-bleed brake system to remove air from system. Repeat steps **3)** and **4)** until all air is purged from system.

TESTING & DIAGNOSIS

NOTE: Correct procedures must be followed to ensure misdiagnosis does not occur. The use of a TECH 1 scan tool is recommended when testing and diagnosing the 4WAL system, but is not necessary.

RETRIEVING TROUBLE CODES

1) To properly diagnose 4WAL system, always perform DIAGNOSTIC CIRCUIT CHECK first. *See Fig. 3*. System can be diagnosed through trouble codes. To activate trouble codes, connect a jumper wire between terminals "A" and "H" on ALDL connector and observe flashing on brake warning light. *See Fig. 2*. ALDL connector is located under instrument panel on the driver's side. Sequence should be one long flash followed by short flashes (i.e. one long flash followed by 4 short flashes indicates Code 5).

2) System will repeat code as long as ALDL connector is grounded. Long flash after short flashes indicates repeat of code. If there is more than one failure, only the first failure code will be stored and displayed. *See Figs. 3 through 31*.

3) If the ALDL connector was accidentally grounded twice within 10 seconds, a Code 65 will be set. If this code is set, clear code and retest. Not all codes set will be held in the memory. Codes 21, 22, 25, 26, 31, 32, 35 and 36 will disable the system when found, but will be erased when ignition is turn off. All other codes will disable the system and will be stored in memory until repair has been made.

CLEARING TROUBLE CODES

1) To clear codes after diagnosing, turn ignition on. Using a jumper wire or remote starter switch, jump terminals "A" and "H" on ALDL connector for 2 seconds.

2) Remove jumper wire for 2 seconds, then reconnect for 2 seconds. Do this sequence 2 more times. Be careful not to set a false Code 65. Check for codes. If no codes are found, turn ignition off. If codes are found, recheck system.

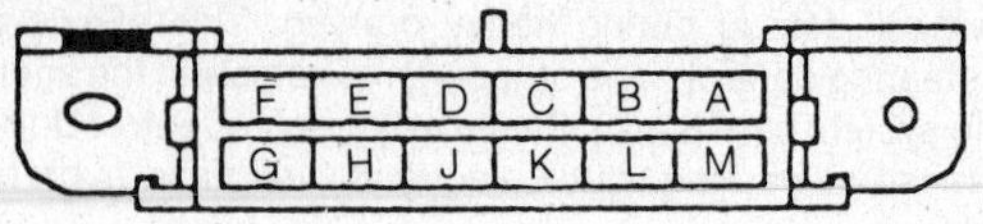
F
E
D
C
B
A
G
H
J
K
L
M

90H06369 Courtesy of General Motors Corp.

Fig. 2: ALDL Connector Terminals

TROUBLE CODES

Code	Breakdown
12	System Normal (2WD)
13	System Normal – Brakes Applied (2WD)
14	System Normal (4WD)
15	System Normal – Brakes Applied (4WD)
21	RF Speed Sensor Resistance Incorrect
22	RF Speed Sensor Voltage Output Incorrect
23	RF Speed Sensor Voltage Output Erratic
25	LF Speed Sensor Resistance Incorrect
26	LF Speed Sensor Voltage Output Incorrect
27	LF Speed Sensor Voltage Output Erratic

TROUBLE CODES (Cont.)

Code	Breakdown
28 [1]	1 or 2 Speed Sensor Signals Are Dropping Out
29 [1]	All Speed Sensor Signals Are Dropping Out
31	RR Speed Sensor Resistance Incorrect
32	RR Speed Sensor Voltage Output Incorrect
33	RR Speed Sensor Voltage Output Erratic
35	LR Speed Sensor Resistance Incorrect
36	LR Speed Sensor Voltage Output Incorrect
37	LR Speed Sensor Voltage Output Erratic
38	Speed Sensor Signal Error (2:1 Ratio Above 12 MPH)
41	Open Circuit in RF Isolation Valve Solenoid
42	Open Circuit in RF Pulse-Width Modulation Valve Solenoid
43 [2]	Shorted Circuit in RF Isolation Valve Solenoid
44 [2]	Shorted Circuit in RF Pulse-Width Modulation Valve Solenoid
45	Open Circuit in LF Isolation Valve Solenoid
46	Open Circuit in LF Pulse-Width Modulation Valve Solenoid
47 [2]	Shorted Circuit in LF Isolation Valve Solenoid
48 [2]	Shorted Circuit in LF Pulse-Width Modulation Valve Solenoid
51	Open Circuit in Rear Isolation Valve Solenoid
52	Open Circuit in Rear Pulse-Width Modulation Valve Solenoid
53 [2]	Shorted Circuit in Rear Isolation Valve Solenoid
54 [2]	Shorted Circuit in Rear Pulse-Width Modulation Valve Solenoid
61	Open Circuit in RF Reset Switch
62	Open Circuit in LF Reset Switch
63	Open Circuit in Rear Reset Switch
65	Open Circuit in Pump Motor Relay Circuit
66	Shorted Circuit in Pump Motor Relay Circuit
67	Open Circuit in Pump Motor Circuit
68 [2]	Shorted Circuit in Pump Motor Circuit
71	EHCU Has RAM Error
72	EHCU Has ROM Error
73	EHCU Has An Internal Circuit Error
74	EHCU Has An Internal Circuit Error Causing Excessive Isolation Time
81	Brake Switch Circuit Operation Is Shorted or Open
85	Open in "ANTILOCK" Indicator Light Circuit
86	Short in "ANTILOCK" Indicator Light Circuit
88	Short in "BRAKE" Indicator Light Circuit

[1] – When using TECH 1 scan tool, code 28 or 29 may be displayed and shown as invalid. These codes are valid and use appropriate flow chart.

[2] – These codes indicate power or ground circuit fault.

REMOVAL & INSTALLATION

ELECTRO-HYDRAULIC CONTROL UNIT (EHCU)

NOTE: Before replacing EHCU Module, bleed down brake booster by depressing brake pedal several times.

Astro & Safari – 1) Ensure front wheels are in straight ahead position. Index upper and lower "U" joints on steering shaft. Remove pinch bolt from each "U" joint. Index steering gear position. Separate steering gear from frame rail. It is not necessary to disconnect pitman arm from steering gear.

2) Remove intermediate shaft from steering column. Disconnect hydraulic lines from EHCU and combination valve. Disconnect electrical connectors from EHCU. Remove EHCU and bracket from vehicle. To install, reverse removal procedure. Align all index marks. Bleed brake system, including EHCU. See BLEEDING BRAKE SYSTEM in this article.

Bravada & "S"/"T" Models – 1) Remove washer tank reservoir bolts, set reservoir to one side and remove the 3 electrical connectors from EHCU module. Remove brake lines from EHCU, taking care not to get brake fluid on paint or electrical connections.

2) Remove bolts connecting upper bracket assembly to lower bracket assembly. Remove EHCU module and upper braket assembly from vehicle. Remove 6 bolts and remove mounting bracket from EHCU module. To install, reverse removal procedure. Bleed brake system, including EHCU. See BLEEDING BRAKE SYSTEM in this article.

FRONT WHEEL SPEED SENSOR

NOTE: Ensure speed sensor wire routing is noted before removing for installation purposes. Misrouted wiring may cause electromagnetic interference type faults.

Removal & Installation – 1) Remove wheel and tire assembly. Remove brake caliper and wire out of the way. On 2WD models, remove hub and rotor assembly. Remove splash shield and speed sensor assembly. To install, reverse removal procedure. Tighten wheel bearing nut to 12 ft. lbs. (16 N.m), then back off. Hand tighten nut until hub end play is .001-.005" (.03-.13 mm).

2) On 4WD models, remove brake rotor. Remove drive axle nut. Remove bolts retaining hub and bearing assembly. Using a puller, remove hub and bearing assembly. Remove splash shield and speed sensor assembly. On all models, reverse removal procedure for installation. Air gap between sensor and exciter ring should be .050" (1.27 mm) and is non-adjustable.

REAR WHEEL SPEED SENSOR

Removal & Installation – Remove wheel assembly. Remove brake drum. Remove primary brake shoe. Remove sensor wire connector and sensor wire. Remove bolts and remove speed sensor by pulling wire through hole in backing plate. To install, reverse removal procedure.

TORQUE SPECIFICATIONS

TORQUE SPECIFICATIONS

Application	Ft. Lbs. (N.m)
EHCU Hydraulic Fittings	14-22 (19-30)
EHCU Mounting Bracket-to-Body Bolt	14-24 (19-33)
Front Axle Shaft Nut (AWD)	94 (128)
Intermediate Steering Shaft	
"U" Joint Pinch Bolt	30 (41)
Splash Shield Bolt	11 (15)
Steering Gear Bolt	55 (75)
Wheel Speed Sensor Bolt	
Front	10 (14)
Rear	26 (35)
Wheel Lug Nut	90 (122)
	INCH Lbs. (N.m)
EHCU-to-Mounting Bracket Bolt	72-96 (8-10)
EHCU Internal Bleeder Screw	60 (7)

TROUBLE SHOOTING CHARTS

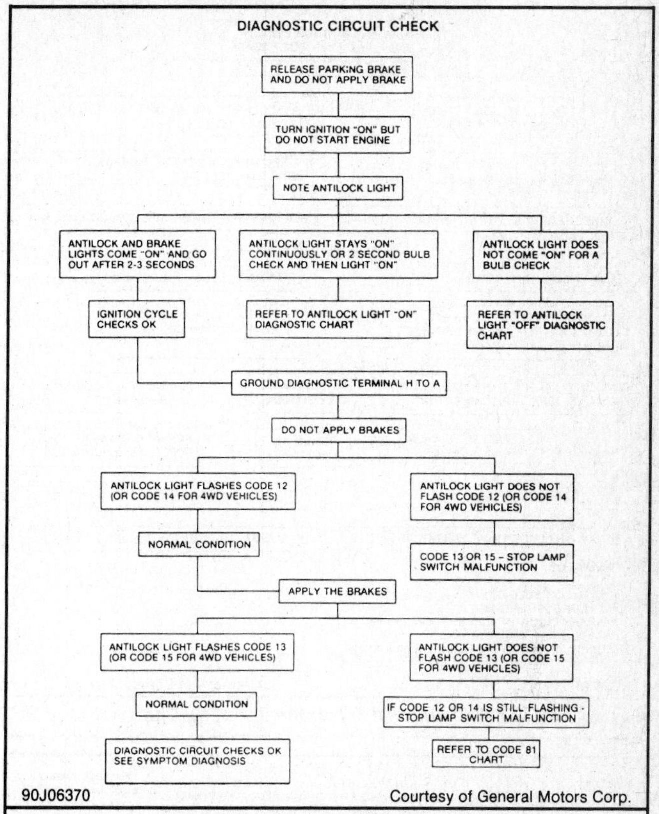
DIAGNOSTIC CIRCUIT CHECK
RELEASE PARKING BRAKE AND DO NOT APPLY BRAKE
TURN IGNITION "ON" BUT DO NOT START ENGINE
NOTE ANTILOCK LIGHT
ANTILOCK AND BRAKE LIGHTS COME "ON" AND GO OUT AFTER 2-3 SECONDS
ANTILOCK LIGHT STAYS "ON" CONTINUOUSLY OR 2 SECOND BULB CHECK AND THEN LIGHT "ON"
ANTILOCK LIGHT DOES NOT COME "ON" FOR A BULB CHECK
IGNITION CYCLE CHECKS OK
REFER TO ANTILOCK LIGHT "ON" DIAGNOSTIC CHART
REFER TO ANTILOCK LIGHT "OFF" DIAGNOSTIC CHART
GROUND DIAGNOSTIC TERMINAL H TO A
DO NOT APPLY BRAKES
ANTILOCK LIGHT FLASHES CODE 12 (OR CODE 14 FOR 4WD VEHICLES)
ANTILOCK LIGHT DOES NOT FLASH CODE 12 (OR CODE 14 FOR 4WD VEHICLES)
NORMAL CONDITION
CODE 13 OR 15 – STOP LAMP SWITCH MALFUNCTION
APPLY THE BRAKES
ANTILOCK LIGHT FLASHES CODE 13 (OR CODE 15 FOR 4WD VEHICLES)
ANTILOCK LIGHT DOES NOT FLASH CODE 13 (OR CODE 15 FOR 4WD VEHICLES)
NORMAL CONDITION
IF CODE 12 OR 14 IS STILL FLASHING - STOP LAMP SWITCH MALFUNCTION
DIAGNOSTIC CIRCUIT CHECKS OK SEE SYMPTOM DIAGNOSIS
REFER TO CODE 81 CHART
90J06370
Courtesy of General Motors Corp.

Fig. 3: Diagnostic Circuit Check Trouble Shooting Chart

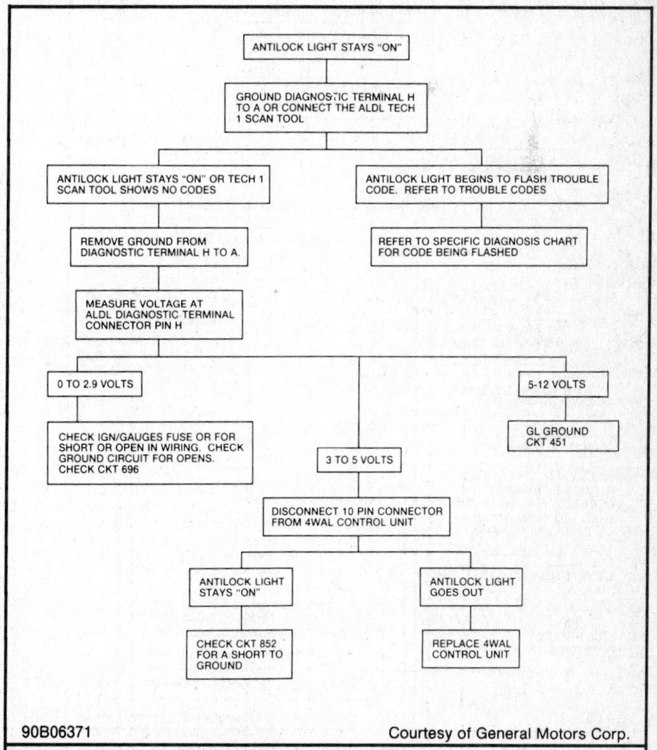
ANTILOCK LIGHT STAYS "ON"
GROUND DIAGNOSTIC TERMINAL H TO A OR CONNECT THE ALDL TECH 1 SCAN TOOL
ANTILOCK LIGHT STAYS "ON" OR TECH 1 SCAN TOOL SHOWS NO CODES
ANTILOCK LIGHT BEGINS TO FLASH TROUBLE CODE. REFER TO TROUBLE CODES
REMOVE GROUND FROM DIAGNOSTIC TERMINAL H TO A.
REFER TO SPECIFIC DIAGNOSIS CHART FOR CODE BEING FLASHED
MEASURE VOLTAGE AT ALDL DIAGNOSTIC TERMINAL CONNECTOR PIN H
0 TO 2.9 VOLTS
5-12 VOLTS
CHECK IGN/GAUGES FUSE OR FOR SHORT OR OPEN IN WIRING. CHECK GROUND CIRCUIT FOR OPENS. CHECK CKT 696
3 TO 5 VOLTS
GL GROUND CKT 451
DISCONNECT 10 PIN CONNECTOR FROM 4WAL CONTROL UNIT
ANTILOCK LIGHT STAYS "ON"
ANTILOCK LIGHT GOES OUT
CHECK CKT 852 FOR A SHORT TO GROUND
REPLACE 4WAL CONTROL UNIT
90B06371
Courtesy of General Motors Corp.

Fig. 4: "ANTILOCK" Light ON Trouble Shooting Chart

1991 BRAKES
Anti-Lock – 4WAL (Cont.)

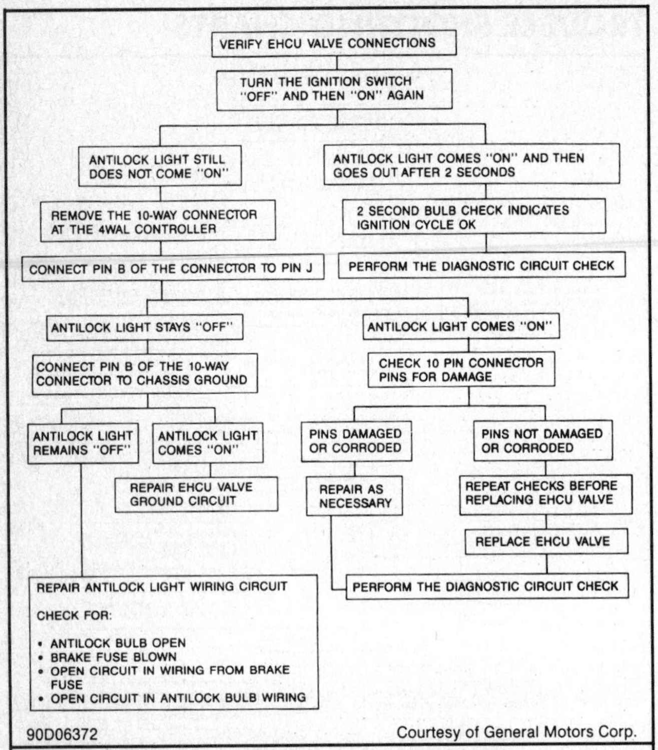
VERIFY EHCU VALVE CONNECTIONS
TURN THE IGNITION SWITCH "OFF" AND THEN "ON" AGAIN
ANTILOCK LIGHT STILL DOES NOT COME "ON"
ANTILOCK LIGHT COMES "ON" AND THEN GOES OUT AFTER 2 SECONDS
REMOVE THE 10-WAY CONNECTOR AT THE 4WAL CONTROLLER
2 SECOND BULB CHECK INDICATES IGNITION CYCLE OK
CONNECT PIN B OF THE CONNECTOR TO PIN J
PERFORM THE DIAGNOSTIC CIRCUIT CHECK
ANTILOCK LIGHT STAYS "OFF"
ANTILOCK LIGHT COMES "ON"
CONNECT PIN B OF THE 10-WAY CONNECTOR TO CHASSIS GROUND
CHECK 10 PIN CONNECTOR PINS FOR DAMAGE
ANTILOCK LIGHT REMAINS "OFF"
ANTILOCK LIGHT COMES "ON"
PINS DAMAGED OR CORRODED
PINS NOT DAMAGED OR CORRODED
REPAIR EHCU VALVE GROUND CIRCUIT
REPAIR AS NECESSARY
REPEAT CHECKS BEFORE REPLACING EHCU VALVE
REPLACE EHCU VALVE
REPAIR ANTILOCK LIGHT WIRING CIRCUIT
CHECK FOR:
• ANTILOCK BULB OPEN
• BRAKE FUSE BLOWN
• OPEN CIRCUIT IN WIRING FROM BRAKE FUSE
• OPEN CIRCUIT IN ANTILOCK BULB WIRING
PERFORM THE DIAGNOSTIC CIRCUIT CHECK
90D06372
Courtesy of General Motors Corp.

Fig. 5: "ANTILOCK" Light OFF Trouble Shooting Chart

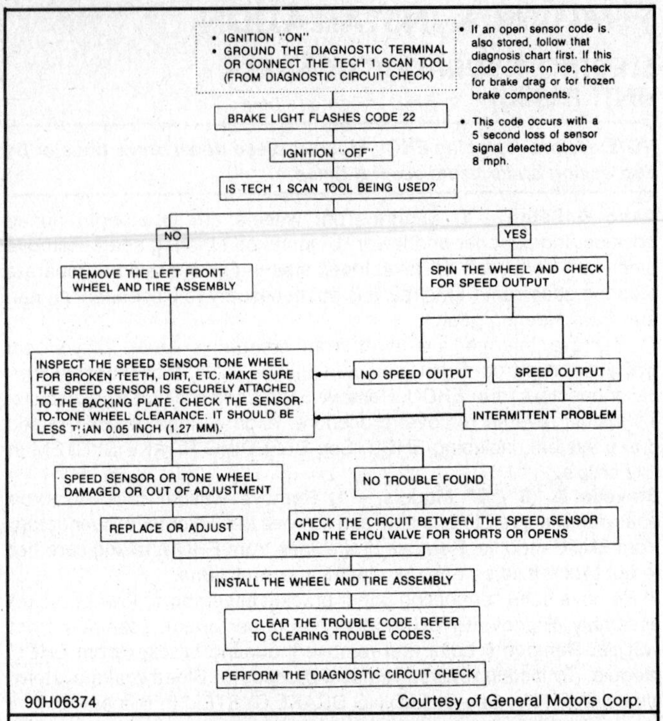
• IGNITION "ON"
• GROUND THE DIAGNOSTIC TERMINAL OR CONNECT THE TECH 1 SCAN TOOL (FROM DIAGNOSTIC CIRCUIT CHECK)
• If an open sensor code is also stored, follow that diagnosis chart first. If this code occurs on ice, check for brake drag or for frozen brake components.
BRAKE LIGHT FLASHES CODE 22
• This code occurs with a 5 second loss of sensor signal detected above 8 mph.
IGNITION "OFF"
IS TECH 1 SCAN TOOL BEING USED?
NO
YES
REMOVE THE LEFT FRONT WHEEL AND TIRE ASSEMBLY
SPIN THE WHEEL AND CHECK FOR SPEED OUTPUT
INSPECT THE SPEED SENSOR TONE WHEEL FOR BROKEN TEETH, DIRT, ETC. MAKE SURE THE SPEED SENSOR IS SECURELY ATTACHED TO THE BACKING PLATE. CHECK THE SENSOR-TO-TONE WHEEL CLEARANCE. IT SHOULD BE LESS THAN 0.05 INCH (1.27 MM).
NO SPEED OUTPUT
SPEED OUTPUT
INTERMITTENT PROBLEM
SPEED SENSOR OR TONE WHEEL DAMAGED OR OUT OF ADJUSTMENT
NO TROUBLE FOUND
REPLACE OR ADJUST
CHECK THE CIRCUIT BETWEEN THE SPEED SENSOR AND THE EHCU VALVE FOR SHORTS OR OPENS
INSTALL THE WHEEL AND TIRE ASSEMBLY
CLEAR THE TROUBLE CODE. REFER TO CLEARING TROUBLE CODES.
PERFORM THE DIAGNOSTIC CIRCUIT CHECK
90H06374
Courtesy of General Motors Corp.

Fig. 7: Code 22 – RF Speed Sensor Voltage Output Incorrect Trouble Shooting Chart

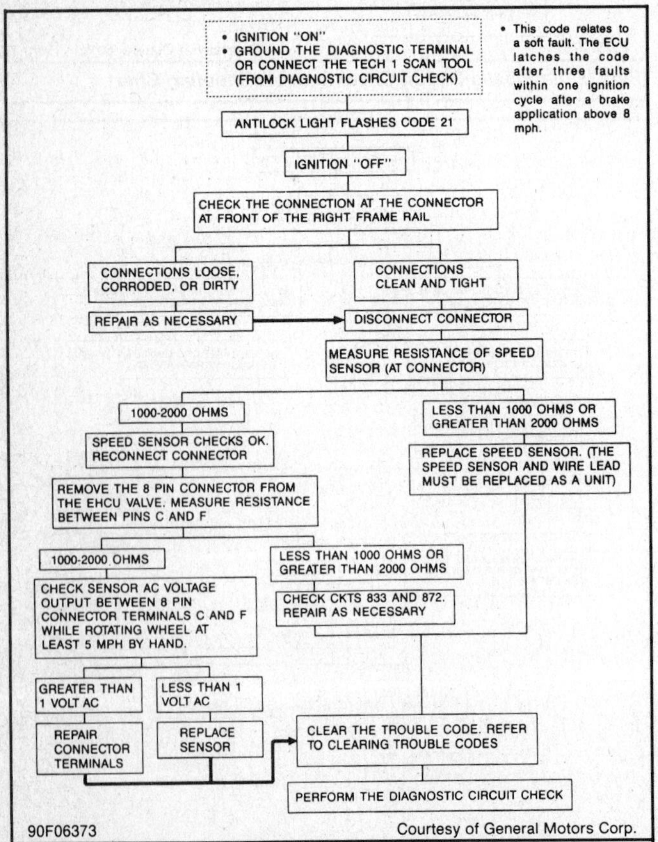
• IGNITION "ON"
• GROUND THE DIAGNOSTIC TERMINAL OR CONNECT THE TECH 1 SCAN TOOL (FROM DIAGNOSTIC CIRCUIT CHECK)
• This code relates to a soft fault. The ECU latches the code after three faults within one ignition cycle after a brake application above 8 mph.
ANTILOCK LIGHT FLASHES CODE 21
IGNITION "OFF"
CHECK THE CONNECTION AT THE CONNECTOR AT FRONT OF THE RIGHT FRAME RAIL
CONNECTIONS LOOSE, CORRODED, OR DIRTY
CONNECTIONS CLEAN AND TIGHT
REPAIR AS NECESSARY
DISCONNECT CONNECTOR
MEASURE RESISTANCE OF SPEED SENSOR (AT CONNECTOR)
1000-2000 OHMS
LESS THAN 1000 OHMS OR GREATER THAN 2000 OHMS
SPEED SENSOR CHECKS OK. RECONNECT CONNECTOR
REPLACE SPEED SENSOR. (THE SPEED SENSOR AND WIRE LEAD MUST BE REPLACED AS A UNIT)
REMOVE THE 8 PIN CONNECTOR FROM THE EHCU VALVE. MEASURE RESISTANCE BETWEEN PINS C AND F
1000-2000 OHMS
LESS THAN 1000 OHMS OR GREATER THAN 2000 OHMS
CHECK SENSOR AC VOLTAGE OUTPUT BETWEEN 8 PIN CONNECTOR TERMINALS C AND F WHILE ROTATING WHEEL AT LEAST 5 MPH BY HAND.
CHECK CKTS 833 AND 872. REPAIR AS NECESSARY
GREATER THAN 1 VOLT AC
LESS THAN 1 VOLT AC
REPAIR CONNECTOR TERMINALS
REPLACE SENSOR
CLEAR THE TROUBLE CODE. REFER TO CLEARING TROUBLE CODES
PERFORM THE DIAGNOSTIC CIRCUIT CHECK
90F06373
Courtesy of General Motors Corp.

Fig. 6: Code 21 – RF Speed Sensor Resistance Incorrect Trouble Shooting Chart

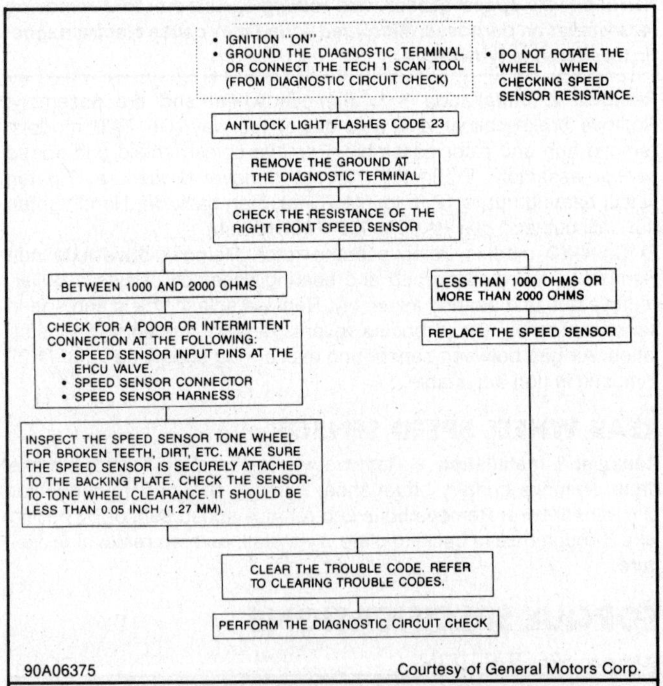
• IGNITION "ON"
• GROUND THE DIAGNOSTIC TERMINAL OR CONNECT THE TECH 1 SCAN TOOL (FROM DIAGNOSTIC CIRCUIT CHECK)
• DO NOT ROTATE THE WHEEL WHEN CHECKING SPEED SENSOR RESISTANCE.
ANTILOCK LIGHT FLASHES CODE 23
REMOVE THE GROUND AT THE DIAGNOSTIC TERMINAL
CHECK THE RESISTANCE OF THE RIGHT FRONT SPEED SENSOR
BETWEEN 1000 AND 2000 OHMS
LESS THAN 1000 OHMS OR MORE THAN 2000 OHMS
REPLACE THE SPEED SENSOR
CHECK FOR A POOR OR INTERMITTENT CONNECTION AT THE FOLLOWING:
• SPEED SENSOR INPUT PINS AT THE EHCU VALVE.
• SPEED SENSOR CONNECTOR
• SPEED SENSOR HARNESS
INSPECT THE SPEED SENSOR TONE WHEEL FOR BROKEN TEETH, DIRT, ETC. MAKE SURE THE SPEED SENSOR IS SECURELY ATTACHED TO THE BACKING PLATE. CHECK THE SENSOR-TO-TONE WHEEL CLEARANCE. IT SHOULD BE LESS THAN 0.05 INCH (1.27 MM).
CLEAR THE TROUBLE CODE. REFER TO CLEARING TROUBLE CODES.
PERFORM THE DIAGNOSTIC CIRCUIT CHECK
90A06375
Courtesy of General Motors Corp.

Fig. 8: Code 23 – RF Speed Sensor Voltage Output Erratic Trouble Shooting Chart

1991 BRAKES
Anti-Lock – 4WAL (Cont.)

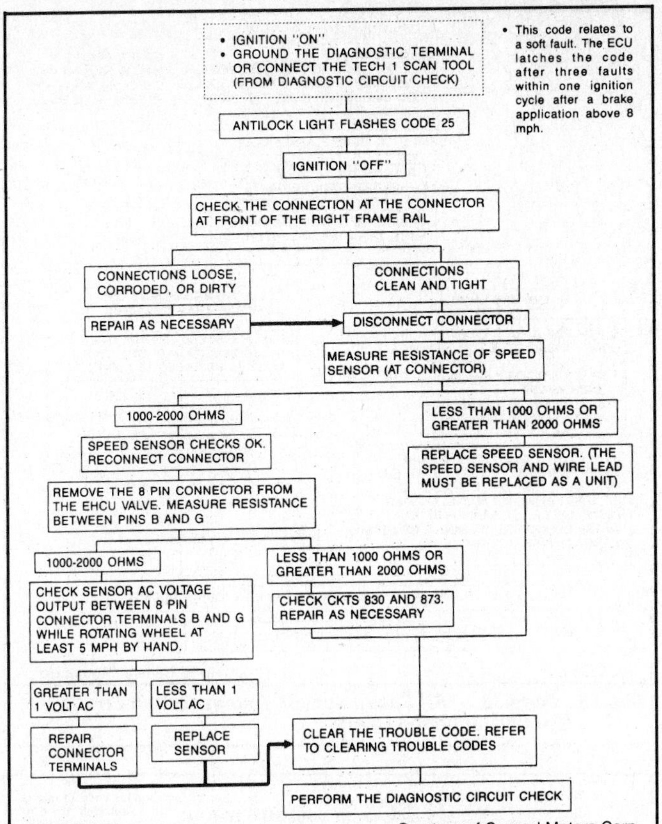
• IGNITION "ON"
• GROUND THE DIAGNOSTIC TERMINAL OR CONNECT THE TECH 1 SCAN TOOL (FROM DIAGNOSTIC CIRCUIT CHECK)
• This code relates to a soft fault. The ECU latches the code after three faults within one ignition cycle after a brake application above 8 mph.
ANTILOCK LIGHT FLASHES CODE 25
IGNITION "OFF"
CHECK THE CONNECTION AT THE CONNECTOR AT FRONT OF THE RIGHT FRAME RAIL
CONNECTIONS LOOSE, CORRODED, OR DIRTY
CONNECTIONS CLEAN AND TIGHT
REPAIR AS NECESSARY
DISCONNECT CONNECTOR
MEASURE RESISTANCE OF SPEED SENSOR (AT CONNECTOR)
1000-2000 OHMS
LESS THAN 1000 OHMS OR GREATER THAN 2000 OHMS
SPEED SENSOR CHECKS OK. RECONNECT CONNECTOR
REPLACE SPEED SENSOR. (THE SPEED SENSOR AND WIRE LEAD MUST BE REPLACED AS A UNIT)
REMOVE THE 8 PIN CONNECTOR FROM THE EHCU VALVE. MEASURE RESISTANCE BETWEEN PINS B AND G
1000-2000 OHMS
LESS THAN 1000 OHMS OR GREATER THAN 2000 OHMS
CHECK SENSOR AC VOLTAGE OUTPUT BETWEEN 8 PIN CONNECTOR TERMINALS B AND G WHILE ROTATING WHEEL AT LEAST 5 MPH BY HAND.
CHECK CKTS 830 AND 873. REPAIR AS NECESSARY
GREATER THAN 1 VOLT AC
LESS THAN 1 VOLT AC
REPAIR CONNECTOR TERMINALS
REPLACE SENSOR
CLEAR THE TROUBLE CODE. REFER TO CLEARING TROUBLE CODES
PERFORM THE DIAGNOSTIC CIRCUIT CHECK

90C06376 Courtesy of General Motors Corp.

Fig. 9: Code 25 – LF Speed Sensor Resistance Incorrect Trouble Shooting Chart

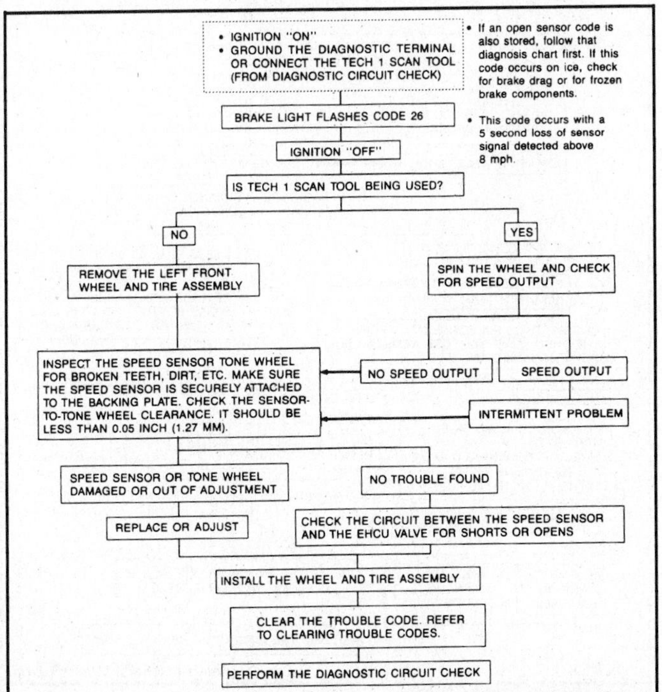
• IGNITION "ON"
• GROUND THE DIAGNOSTIC TERMINAL OR CONNECT THE TECH 1 SCAN TOOL (FROM DIAGNOSTIC CIRCUIT CHECK)
• If an open sensor code is also stored, follow that diagnosis chart first. If this code occurs on ice, check for brake drag or for frozen brake components.
• This code occurs with a 5 second loss of sensor signal detected above 8 mph.
BRAKE LIGHT FLASHES CODE 26
IGNITION "OFF"
IS TECH 1 SCAN TOOL BEING USED?
NO
YES
REMOVE THE LEFT FRONT WHEEL AND TIRE ASSEMBLY
SPIN THE WHEEL AND CHECK FOR SPEED OUTPUT
INSPECT THE SPEED SENSOR TONE WHEEL FOR BROKEN TEETH, DIRT, ETC. MAKE SURE THE SPEED SENSOR IS SECURELY ATTACHED TO THE BACKING PLATE. CHECK THE SENSOR-TO-TONE WHEEL CLEARANCE. IT SHOULD BE LESS THAN 0.05 INCH (1.27 MM).
NO SPEED OUTPUT
SPEED OUTPUT
INTERMITTENT PROBLEM
SPEED SENSOR OR TONE WHEEL DAMAGED OR OUT OF ADJUSTMENT
NO TROUBLE FOUND
REPLACE OR ADJUST
CHECK THE CIRCUIT BETWEEN THE SPEED SENSOR AND THE EHCU VALVE FOR SHORTS OR OPENS
INSTALL THE WHEEL AND TIRE ASSEMBLY
CLEAR THE TROUBLE CODE. REFER TO CLEARING TROUBLE CODES.
PERFORM THE DIAGNOSTIC CIRCUIT CHECK

90E06377 Courtesy of General Motors Corp.

Fig. 10: Code 26 – LF Speed Sensor Voltage Output Incorrect Trouble Shooting Chart

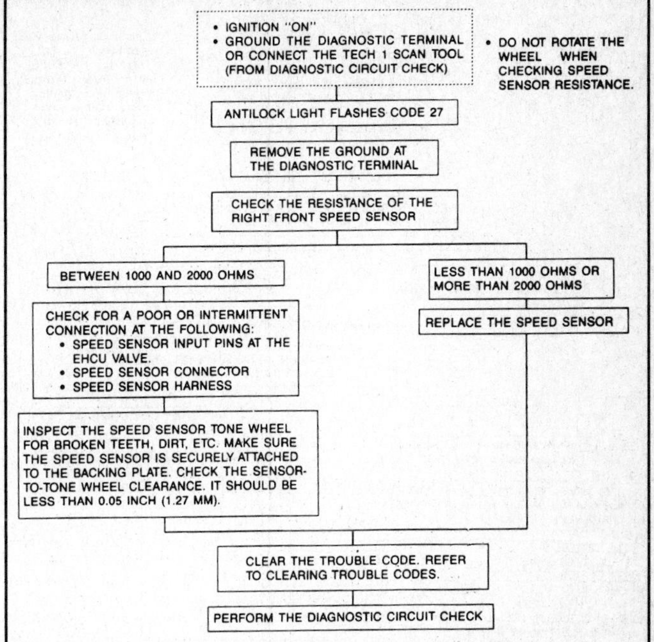
• IGNITION "ON"
• GROUND THE DIAGNOSTIC TERMINAL OR CONNECT THE TECH 1 SCAN TOOL (FROM DIAGNOSTIC CIRCUIT CHECK)
• DO NOT ROTATE THE WHEEL WHEN CHECKING SPEED SENSOR RESISTANCE.
ANTILOCK LIGHT FLASHES CODE 27
REMOVE THE GROUND AT THE DIAGNOSTIC TERMINAL
CHECK THE RESISTANCE OF THE RIGHT FRONT SPEED SENSOR
BETWEEN 1000 AND 2000 OHMS
LESS THAN 1000 OHMS OR MORE THAN 2000 OHMS
CHECK FOR A POOR OR INTERMITTENT CONNECTION AT THE FOLLOWING:
• SPEED SENSOR INPUT PINS AT THE EHCU VALVE.
• SPEED SENSOR CONNECTOR
• SPEED SENSOR HARNESS
REPLACE THE SPEED SENSOR
INSPECT THE SPEED SENSOR TONE WHEEL FOR BROKEN TEETH, DIRT, ETC. MAKE SURE THE SPEED SENSOR IS SECURELY ATTACHED TO THE BACKING PLATE. CHECK THE SENSOR-TO-TONE WHEEL CLEARANCE. IT SHOULD BE LESS THAN 0.05 INCH (1.27 MM).
CLEAR THE TROUBLE CODE. REFER TO CLEARING TROUBLE CODES.
PERFORM THE DIAGNOSTIC CIRCUIT CHECK

90G06378 Courtesy of General Motors Corp.

Fig. 11: Code 27 – LF Speed Sensor Voltage Output Erratic Trouble Shooting Chart

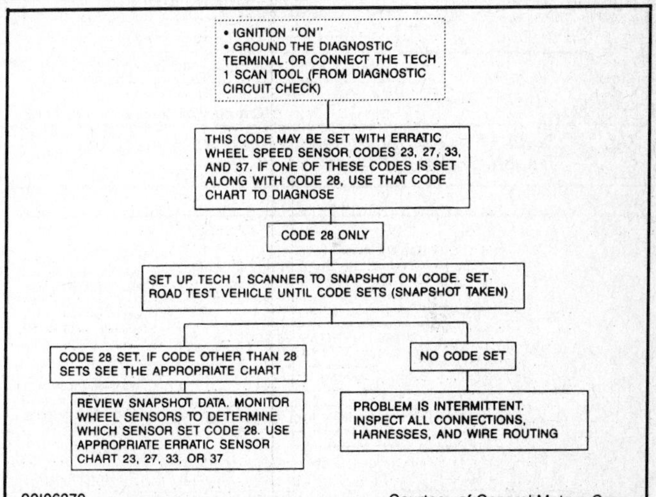
• IGNITION "ON"
• GROUND THE DIAGNOSTIC TERMINAL OR CONNECT THE TECH 1 SCAN TOOL (FROM DIAGNOSTIC CIRCUIT CHECK)
THIS CODE MAY BE SET WITH ERRATIC WHEEL SPEED SENSOR CODES 23, 27, 33, AND 37. IF ONE OF THESE CODES IS SET ALONG WITH CODE 28, USE THAT CODE CHART TO DIAGNOSE
CODE 28 ONLY
SET UP TECH 1 SCANNER TO SNAPSHOT ON CODE. SET ROAD TEST VEHICLE UNTIL CODE SETS (SNAPSHOT TAKEN)
CODE 28 SET. IF CODE OTHER THAN 28 SETS SEE THE APPROPRIATE CHART
NO CODE SET
REVIEW SNAPSHOT DATA. MONITOR WHEEL SENSORS TO DETERMINE WHICH SENSOR SET CODE 28. USE APPROPRIATE ERRATIC SENSOR CHART 23, 27, 33, OR 37
PROBLEM IS INTERMITTENT. INSPECT ALL CONNECTIONS, HARNESSES, AND WIRE ROUTING

90I06379 Courtesy of General Motors Corp.

Fig. 12: Code 28 – 1 or 2 Speed Sensor Signals Are Dropping Out Trouble Shooting Chart

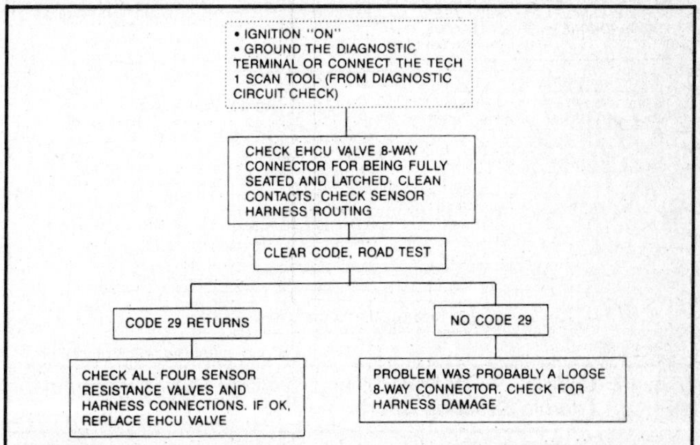
• IGNITION "ON"
• GROUND THE DIAGNOSTIC TERMINAL OR CONNECT THE TECH 1 SCAN TOOL (FROM DIAGNOSTIC CIRCUIT CHECK)
CHECK EHCU VALVE 8-WAY CONNECTOR FOR BEING FULLY SEATED AND LATCHED. CLEAN CONTACTS. CHECK SENSOR HARNESS ROUTING
CLEAR CODE, ROAD TEST
CODE 29 RETURNS
NO CODE 29
CHECK ALL FOUR SENSOR RESISTANCE VALVES AND HARNESS CONNECTIONS. IF OK, REPLACE EHCU VALVE
PROBLEM WAS PROBABLY A LOOSE 8-WAY CONNECTOR. CHECK FOR HARNESS DAMAGE

90A06380 Courtesy of General Motors Corp.

Fig. 13: Code 29 – All Speed Sensor Signals Are Dropping Out Trouble Shooting Chart

1991 BRAKES
Anti-Lock – 4WAL (Cont.)

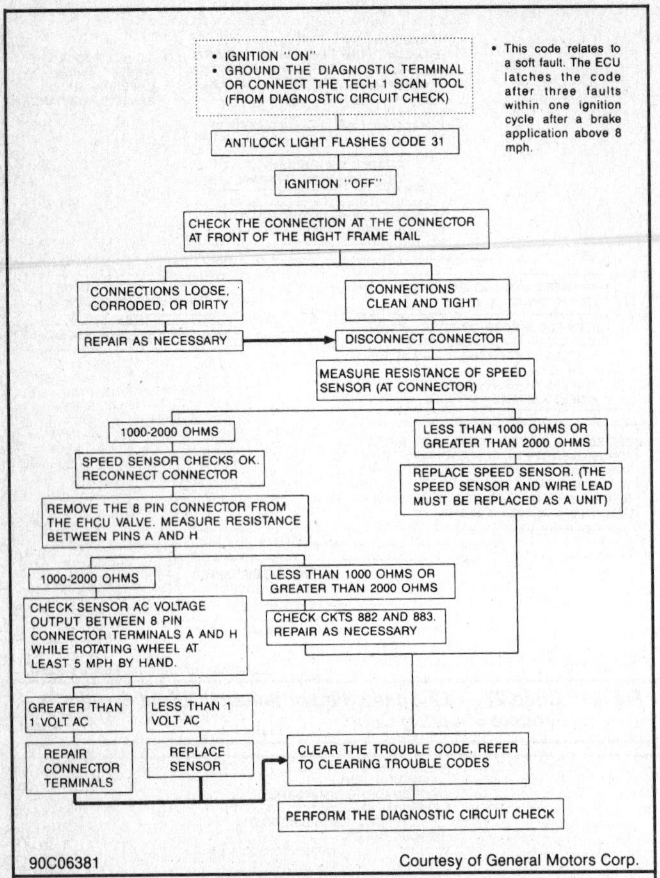
• IGNITION "ON"
• GROUND THE DIAGNOSTIC TERMINAL OR CONNECT THE TECH 1 SCAN TOOL (FROM DIAGNOSTIC CIRCUIT CHECK)
• This code relates to a soft fault. The ECU latches the code after three faults within one ignition cycle after a brake application above 8 mph.
ANTILOCK LIGHT FLASHES CODE 31
IGNITION "OFF"
CHECK THE CONNECTION AT THE CONNECTOR AT FRONT OF THE RIGHT FRAME RAIL
CONNECTIONS LOOSE, CORRODED, OR DIRTY
CONNECTIONS CLEAN AND TIGHT
REPAIR AS NECESSARY
DISCONNECT CONNECTOR
MEASURE RESISTANCE OF SPEED SENSOR (AT CONNECTOR)
1000-2000 OHMS
LESS THAN 1000 OHMS OR GREATER THAN 2000 OHMS
SPEED SENSOR CHECKS OK. RECONNECT CONNECTOR
REPLACE SPEED SENSOR. (THE SPEED SENSOR AND WIRE LEAD MUST BE REPLACED AS A UNIT)
REMOVE THE 8 PIN CONNECTOR FROM THE EHCU VALVE. MEASURE RESISTANCE BETWEEN PINS A AND H
1000-2000 OHMS
LESS THAN 1000 OHMS OR GREATER THAN 2000 OHMS
CHECK SENSOR AC VOLTAGE OUTPUT BETWEEN 8 PIN CONNECTOR TERMINALS A AND H WHILE ROTATING WHEEL AT LEAST 5 MPH BY HAND.
CHECK CKTS 882 AND 883. REPAIR AS NECESSARY
GREATER THAN 1 VOLT AC
LESS THAN 1 VOLT AC
REPAIR CONNECTOR TERMINALS
REPLACE SENSOR
CLEAR THE TROUBLE CODE. REFER TO CLEARING TROUBLE CODES
PERFORM THE DIAGNOSTIC CIRCUIT CHECK
90C06381
Courtesy of General Motors Corp.

Fig. 14: Code 31 – RR Speed Sensor Resistance Incorrect Trouble Shooting Chart

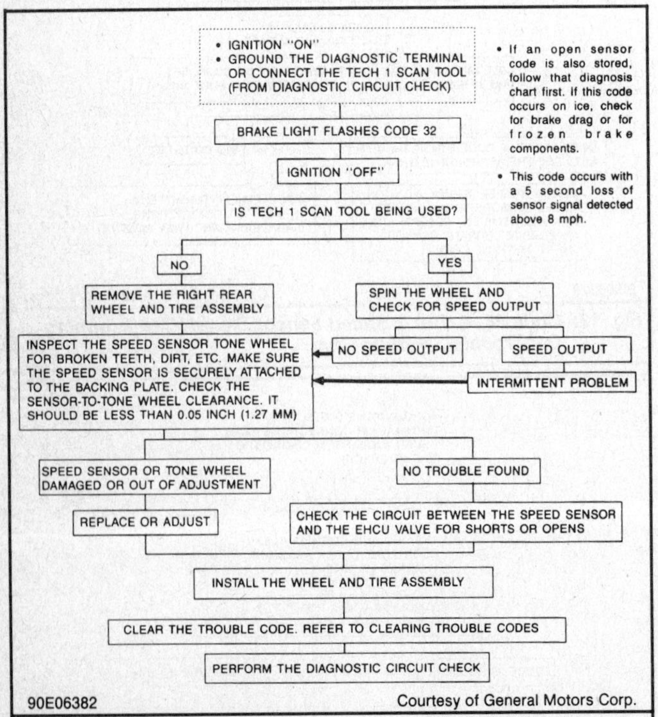
• IGNITION "ON"
• GROUND THE DIAGNOSTIC TERMINAL OR CONNECT THE TECH 1 SCAN TOOL (FROM DIAGNOSTIC CIRCUIT CHECK)
• If an open sensor code is also stored, follow that diagnosis chart first. If this code occurs on ice, check for brake drag or for frozen brake components.
• This code occurs with a 5 second loss of sensor signal detected above 8 mph.
BRAKE LIGHT FLASHES CODE 32
IGNITION "OFF"
IS TECH 1 SCAN TOOL BEING USED?
NO
YES
REMOVE THE RIGHT REAR WHEEL AND TIRE ASSEMBLY
SPIN THE WHEEL AND CHECK FOR SPEED OUTPUT
INSPECT THE SPEED SENSOR TONE WHEEL FOR BROKEN TEETH, DIRT, ETC. MAKE SURE THE SPEED SENSOR IS SECURELY ATTACHED TO THE BACKING PLATE. CHECK THE SENSOR-TO-TONE WHEEL CLEARANCE. IT SHOULD BE LESS THAN 0.05 INCH (1.27 MM)
NO SPEED OUTPUT
SPEED OUTPUT
INTERMITTENT PROBLEM
SPEED SENSOR OR TONE WHEEL DAMAGED OR OUT OF ADJUSTMENT
NO TROUBLE FOUND
REPLACE OR ADJUST
CHECK THE CIRCUIT BETWEEN THE SPEED SENSOR AND THE EHCU VALVE FOR SHORTS OR OPENS
INSTALL THE WHEEL AND TIRE ASSEMBLY
CLEAR THE TROUBLE CODE. REFER TO CLEARING TROUBLE CODES
PERFORM THE DIAGNOSTIC CIRCUIT CHECK
90E06382
Courtesy of General Motors Corp.

Fig. 15: Code 32 – RR Speed Sensor Voltage Output Incorrect Trouble Shooting Chart

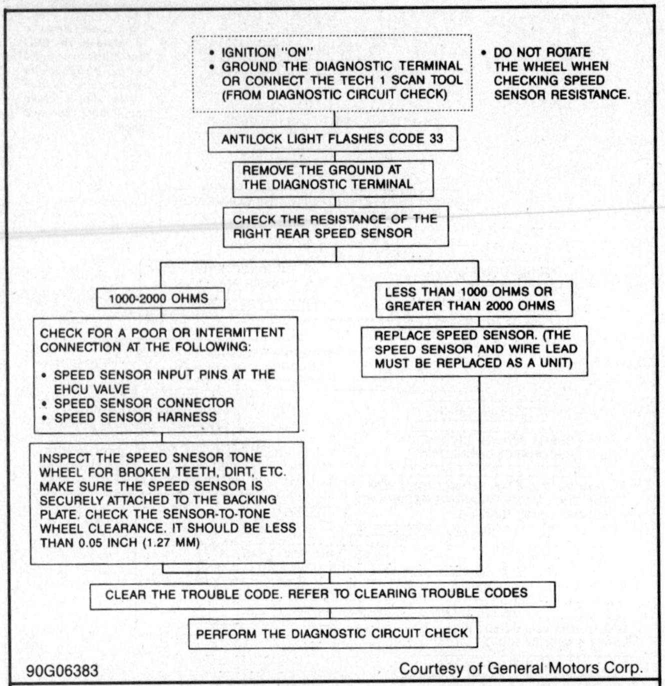
• IGNITION "ON"
• GROUND THE DIAGNOSTIC TERMINAL OR CONNECT THE TECH 1 SCAN TOOL (FROM DIAGNOSTIC CIRCUIT CHECK)
• DO NOT ROTATE THE WHEEL WHEN CHECKING SPEED SENSOR RESISTANCE.
ANTILOCK LIGHT FLASHES CODE 33
REMOVE THE GROUND AT THE DIAGNOSTIC TERMINAL
CHECK THE RESISTANCE OF THE RIGHT REAR SPEED SENSOR
1000-2000 OHMS
LESS THAN 1000 OHMS OR GREATER THAN 2000 OHMS
CHECK FOR A POOR OR INTERMITTENT CONNECTION AT THE FOLLOWING:
• SPEED SENSOR INPUT PINS AT THE EHCU VALVE
• SPEED SENSOR CONNECTOR
• SPEED SENSOR HARNESS
REPLACE SPEED SENSOR. (THE SPEED SENSOR AND WIRE LEAD MUST BE REPLACED AS A UNIT)
INSPECT THE SPEED SNESOR TONE WHEEL FOR BROKEN TEETH, DIRT, ETC. MAKE SURE THE SPEED SENSOR IS SECURELY ATTACHED TO THE BACKING PLATE. CHECK THE SENSOR-TO-TONE WHEEL CLEARANCE. IT SHOULD BE LESS THAN 0.05 INCH (1.27 MM)
CLEAR THE TROUBLE CODE. REFER TO CLEARING TROUBLE CODES
PERFORM THE DIAGNOSTIC CIRCUIT CHECK
90G06383
Courtesy of General Motors Corp.

Fig. 16: Code 33 – RR Speed Sensor Voltage Output Erratic Trouble Shooting Chart

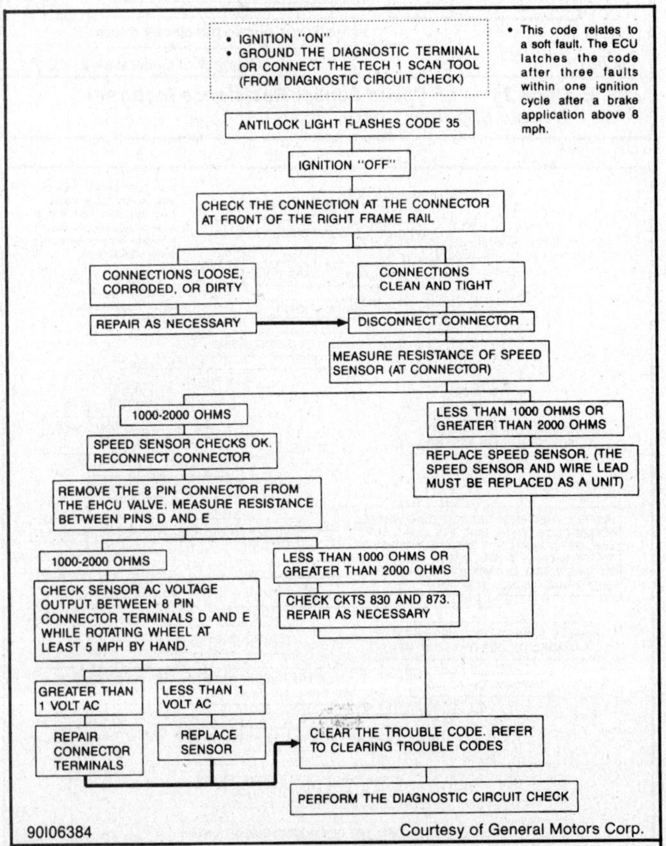
• IGNITION "ON"
• GROUND THE DIAGNOSTIC TERMINAL OR CONNECT THE TECH 1 SCAN TOOL (FROM DIAGNOSTIC CIRCUIT CHECK)
• This code relates to a soft fault. The ECU latches the code after three faults within one ignition cycle after a brake application above 8 mph.
ANTILOCK LIGHT FLASHES CODE 35
IGNITION "OFF"
CHECK THE CONNECTION AT THE CONNECTOR AT FRONT OF THE RIGHT FRAME RAIL
CONNECTIONS LOOSE, CORRODED, OR DIRTY
CONNECTIONS CLEAN AND TIGHT
REPAIR AS NECESSARY
DISCONNECT CONNECTOR
MEASURE RESISTANCE OF SPEED SENSOR (AT CONNECTOR)
1000-2000 OHMS
LESS THAN 1000 OHMS OR GREATER THAN 2000 OHMS
SPEED SENSOR CHECKS OK. RECONNECT CONNECTOR
REPLACE SPEED SENSOR. (THE SPEED SENSOR AND WIRE LEAD MUST BE REPLACED AS A UNIT)
REMOVE THE 8 PIN CONNECTOR FROM THE EHCU VALVE. MEASURE RESISTANCE BETWEEN PINS D AND E
1000-2000 OHMS
LESS THAN 1000 OHMS OR GREATER THAN 2000 OHMS
CHECK SENSOR AC VOLTAGE OUTPUT BETWEEN 8 PIN CONNECTOR TERMINALS D AND E WHILE ROTATING WHEEL AT LEAST 5 MPH BY HAND.
CHECK CKTS 830 AND 873. REPAIR AS NECESSARY
GREATER THAN 1 VOLT AC
LESS THAN 1 VOLT AC
REPAIR CONNECTOR TERMINALS
REPLACE SENSOR
CLEAR THE TROUBLE CODE. REFER TO CLEARING TROUBLE CODES
PERFORM THE DIAGNOSTIC CIRCUIT CHECK
90I06384
Courtesy of General Motors Corp.

Fig. 17: Code 35 – LR Speed Sensor Resistance Incorrect Trouble Shooting Chart

1991 BRAKES
Anti-Lock – 4WAL (Cont.)

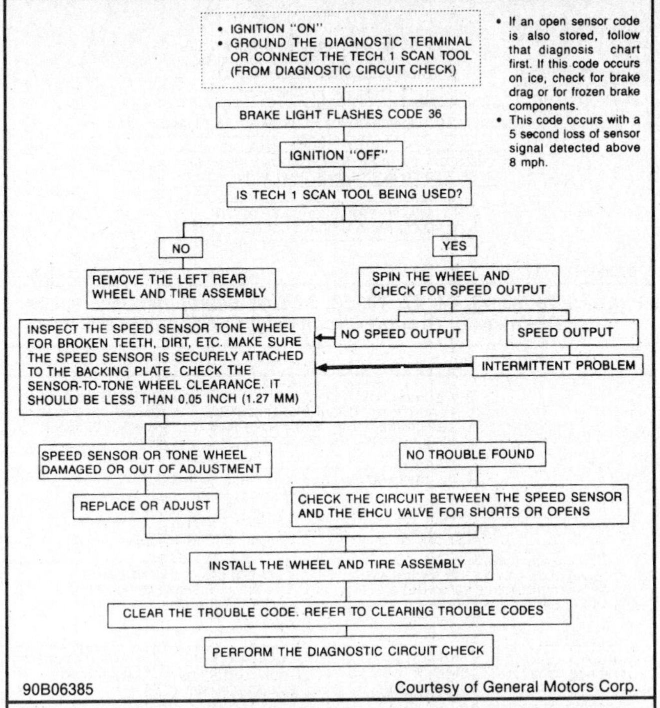
• IGNITION "ON"
• GROUND THE DIAGNOSTIC TERMINAL OR CONNECT THE TECH 1 SCAN TOOL (FROM DIAGNOSTIC CIRCUIT CHECK)
• If an open sensor code is also stored, follow that diagnosis chart first. If this code occurs on ice, check for brake drag or for frozen brake components.
• This code occurs with a 5 second loss of sensor signal detected above 8 mph.
BRAKE LIGHT FLASHES CODE 36
IGNITION "OFF"
IS TECH 1 SCAN TOOL BEING USED?
NO
YES
REMOVE THE LEFT REAR WHEEL AND TIRE ASSEMBLY
SPIN THE WHEEL AND CHECK FOR SPEED OUTPUT
INSPECT THE SPEED SENSOR TONE WHEEL FOR BROKEN TEETH, DIRT, ETC. MAKE SURE THE SPEED SENSOR IS SECURELY ATTACHED TO THE BACKING PLATE. CHECK THE SENSOR-TO-TONE WHEEL CLEARANCE. IT SHOULD BE LESS THAN 0.05 INCH (1.27 MM)
NO SPEED OUTPUT
SPEED OUTPUT
INTERMITTENT PROBLEM
SPEED SENSOR OR TONE WHEEL DAMAGED OR OUT OF ADJUSTMENT
NO TROUBLE FOUND
REPLACE OR ADJUST
CHECK THE CIRCUIT BETWEEN THE SPEED SENSOR AND THE EHCU VALVE FOR SHORTS OR OPENS
INSTALL THE WHEEL AND TIRE ASSEMBLY
CLEAR THE TROUBLE CODE. REFER TO CLEARING TROUBLE CODES
PERFORM THE DIAGNOSTIC CIRCUIT CHECK

90B06385 Courtesy of General Motors Corp.

Fig. 18: Code 36 – LR Speed Sensor Voltage Output incorrect Trouble Shooting Chart

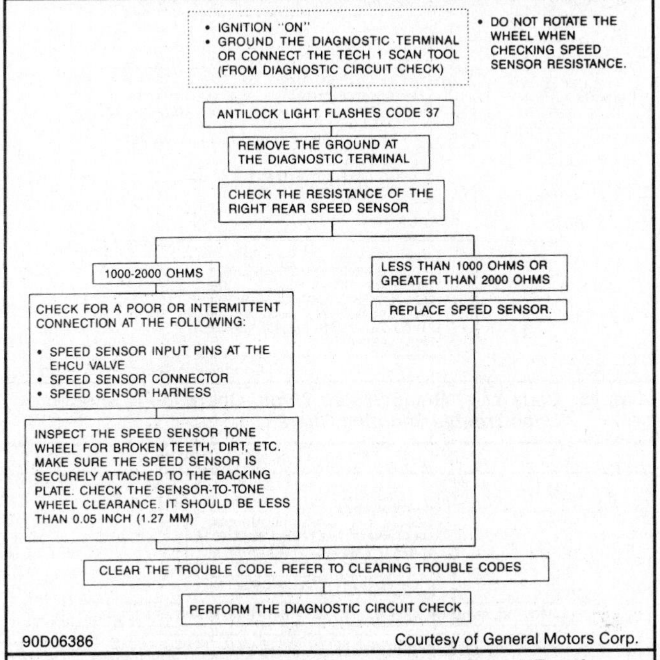
• IGNITION "ON"
• GROUND THE DIAGNOSTIC TERMINAL OR CONNECT THE TECH 1 SCAN TOOL (FROM DIAGNOSTIC CIRCUIT CHECK)
• DO NOT ROTATE THE WHEEL WHEN CHECKING SPEED SENSOR RESISTANCE.
ANTILOCK LIGHT FLASHES CODE 37
REMOVE THE GROUND AT THE DIAGNOSTIC TERMINAL
CHECK THE RESISTANCE OF THE RIGHT REAR SPEED SENSOR
1000-2000 OHMS
LESS THAN 1000 OHMS OR GREATER THAN 2000 OHMS
CHECK FOR A POOR OR INTERMITTENT CONNECTION AT THE FOLLOWING:
• SPEED SENSOR INPUT PINS AT THE EHCU VALVE
• SPEED SENSOR CONNECTOR
• SPEED SENSOR HARNESS
REPLACE SPEED SENSOR.
INSPECT THE SPEED SENSOR TONE WHEEL FOR BROKEN TEETH, DIRT, ETC. MAKE SURE THE SPEED SENSOR IS SECURELY ATTACHED TO THE BACKING PLATE. CHECK THE SENSOR-TO-TONE WHEEL CLEARANCE. IT SHOULD BE LESS THAN 0.05 INCH (1.27 MM)
CLEAR THE TROUBLE CODE. REFER TO CLEARING TROUBLE CODES
PERFORM THE DIAGNOSTIC CIRCUIT CHECK

90D06386 Courtesy of General Motors Corp.

Fig. 19: Code 37 – LR Speed Sensor Voltage Output Erratic Trouble Shooting Chart

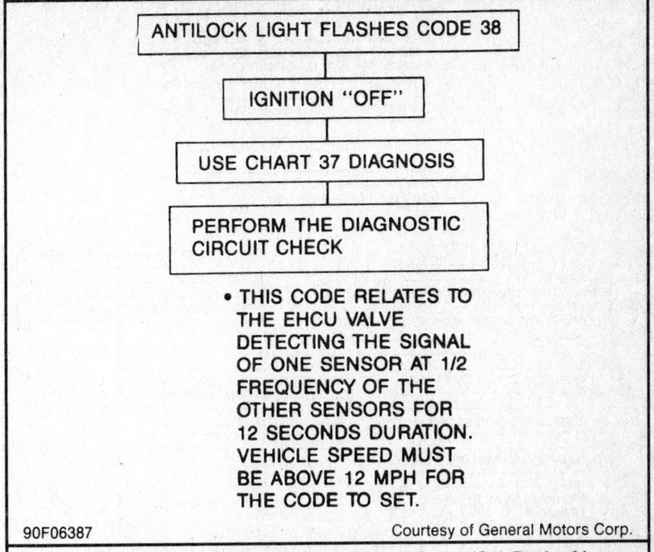
ANTILOCK LIGHT FLASHES CODE 38
IGNITION "OFF"
USE CHART 37 DIAGNOSIS
PERFORM THE DIAGNOSTIC CIRCUIT CHECK
• THIS CODE RELATES TO THE EHCU VALVE DETECTING THE SIGNAL OF ONE SENSOR AT 1/2 FREQUENCY OF THE OTHER SENSORS FOR 12 SECONDS DURATION. VEHICLE SPEED MUST BE ABOVE 12 MPH FOR THE CODE TO SET.

90F06387 Courtesy of General Motors Corp.

Fig. 20: Code 38 – Speed Sensor Signal Error (2:1 Ratio Above 12 MPH) Trouble Shooting Chart

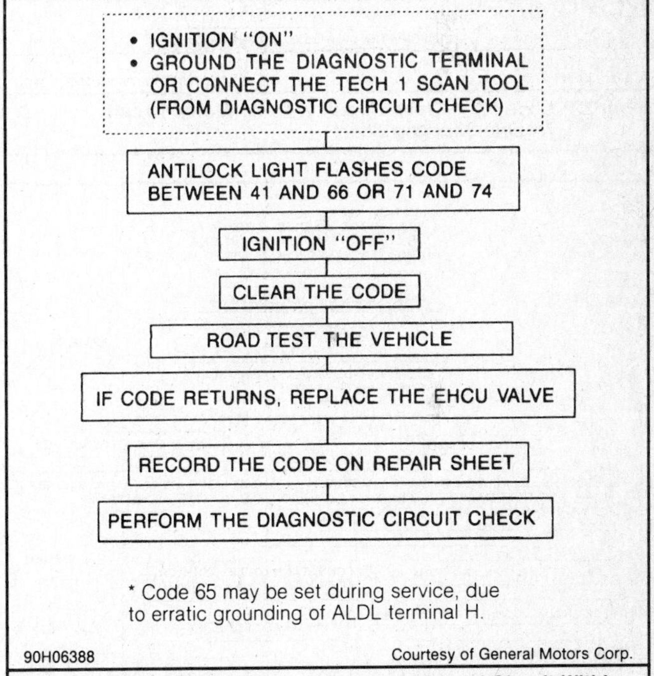
• IGNITION "ON"
• GROUND THE DIAGNOSTIC TERMINAL OR CONNECT THE TECH 1 SCAN TOOL (FROM DIAGNOSTIC CIRCUIT CHECK)
ANTILOCK LIGHT FLASHES CODE BETWEEN 41 AND 66 OR 71 AND 74
IGNITION "OFF"
CLEAR THE CODE
ROAD TEST THE VEHICLE
IF CODE RETURNS, REPLACE THE EHCU VALVE
RECORD THE CODE ON REPAIR SHEET
PERFORM THE DIAGNOSTIC CIRCUIT CHECK
* Code 65 may be set during service, due to erratic grounding of ALDL terminal H.

90H06388 Courtesy of General Motors Corp.

Fig. 21: Codes 41-66 & 71-74 – Open or Shorted Circuit Within EHCU Trouble Shooting Chart

1991 BRAKES
Anti-Lock – 4WAL (Cont.)

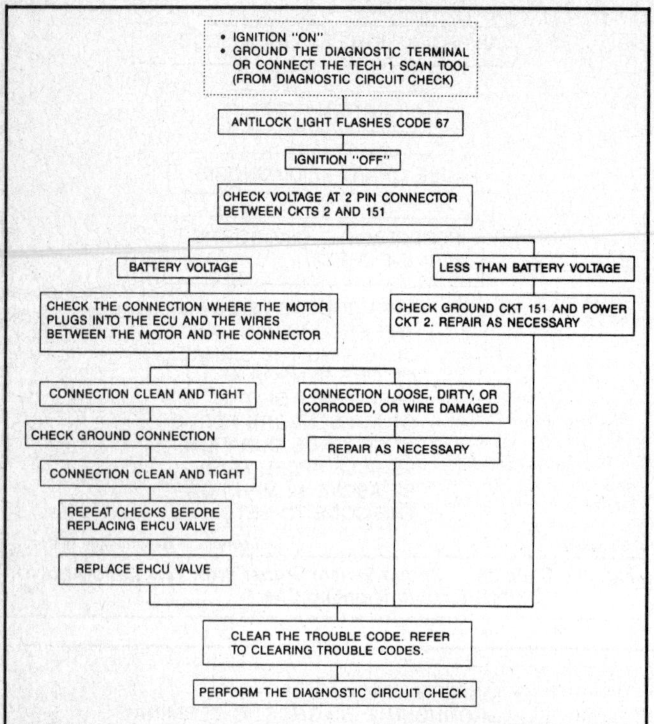
• IGNITION "ON"
• GROUND THE DIAGNOSTIC TERMINAL OR CONNECT THE TECH 1 SCAN TOOL (FROM DIAGNOSTIC CIRCUIT CHECK)
ANTILOCK LIGHT FLASHES CODE 67
IGNITION "OFF"
CHECK VOLTAGE AT 2 PIN CONNECTOR BETWEEN CKTS 2 AND 151
BATTERY VOLTAGE
LESS THAN BATTERY VOLTAGE
CHECK THE CONNECTION WHERE THE MOTOR PLUGS INTO THE ECU AND THE WIRES BETWEEN THE MOTOR AND THE CONNECTOR
CHECK GROUND CKT 151 AND POWER CKT 2. REPAIR AS NECESSARY
CONNECTION CLEAN AND TIGHT
CONNECTION LOOSE, DIRTY, OR CORRODED, OR WIRE DAMAGED
CHECK GROUND CONNECTION
REPAIR AS NECESSARY
CONNECTION CLEAN AND TIGHT
REPEAT CHECKS BEFORE REPLACING EHCU VALVE
REPLACE EHCU VALVE
CLEAR THE TROUBLE CODE. REFER TO CLEARING TROUBLE CODES.
PERFORM THE DIAGNOSTIC CIRCUIT CHECK

90J06389 Courtesy of General Motors Corp.

***Fig. 22:* Code 67 – Open Circuit in Pump Motor Circuit Trouble Shooting Chart**

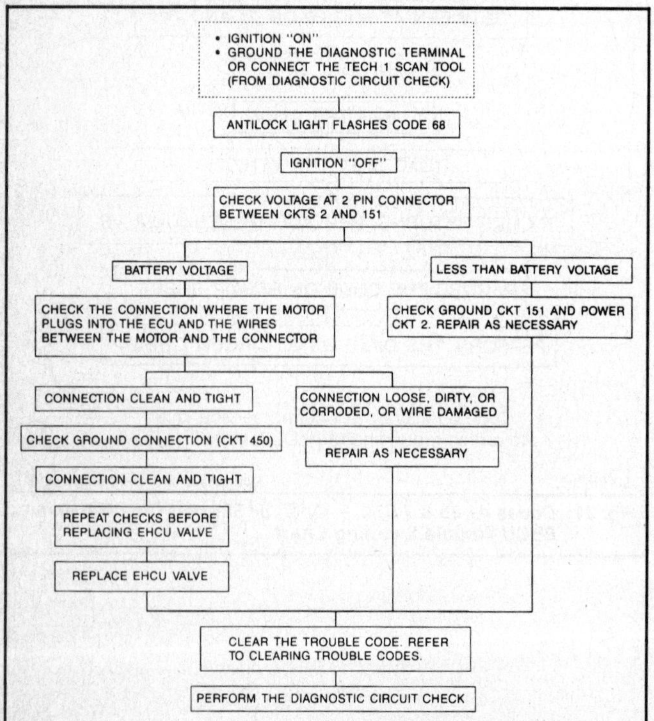
• IGNITION "ON"
• GROUND THE DIAGNOSTIC TERMINAL OR CONNECT THE TECH 1 SCAN TOOL (FROM DIAGNOSTIC CIRCUIT CHECK)
ANTILOCK LIGHT FLASHES CODE 68
IGNITION "OFF"
CHECK VOLTAGE AT 2 PIN CONNECTOR BETWEEN CKTS 2 AND 151
BATTERY VOLTAGE
LESS THAN BATTERY VOLTAGE
CHECK THE CONNECTION WHERE THE MOTOR PLUGS INTO THE ECU AND THE WIRES BETWEEN THE MOTOR AND THE CONNECTOR
CHECK GROUND CKT 151 AND POWER CKT 2. REPAIR AS NECESSARY
CONNECTION CLEAN AND TIGHT
CONNECTION LOOSE, DIRTY, OR CORRODED, OR WIRE DAMAGED
CHECK GROUND CONNECTION (CKT 450)
REPAIR AS NECESSARY
CONNECTION CLEAN AND TIGHT
REPEAT CHECKS BEFORE REPLACING EHCU VALVE
REPLACE EHCU VALVE
CLEAR THE TROUBLE CODE. REFER TO CLEARING TROUBLE CODES.
PERFORM THE DIAGNOSTIC CIRCUIT CHECK

90B06390 Courtesy of General Motors Corp.

***Fig. 23:* Code 68 – Shorted Circuit in Pump Motor Circuit Trouble Shooting Chart**

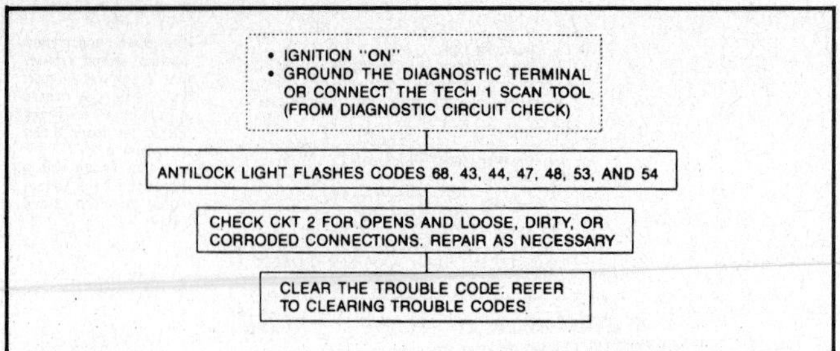
• IGNITION "ON"
• GROUND THE DIAGNOSTIC TERMINAL OR CONNECT THE TECH 1 SCAN TOOL (FROM DIAGNOSTIC CIRCUIT CHECK)
ANTILOCK LIGHT FLASHES CODES 68, 43, 44, 47, 48, 53, AND 54
CHECK CKT 2 FOR OPENS AND LOOSE, DIRTY, OR CORRODED CONNECTIONS. REPAIR AS NECESSARY
CLEAR THE TROUBLE CODE. REFER TO CLEARING TROUBLE CODES

90D06391 Courtesy of General Motors Corp.

***Fig. 24:* Codes 43, 44, 47, 48, 53, 54 & 68 Simultaneously – Loss Of Power or Ground Circuit Trouble Shooting Chart**

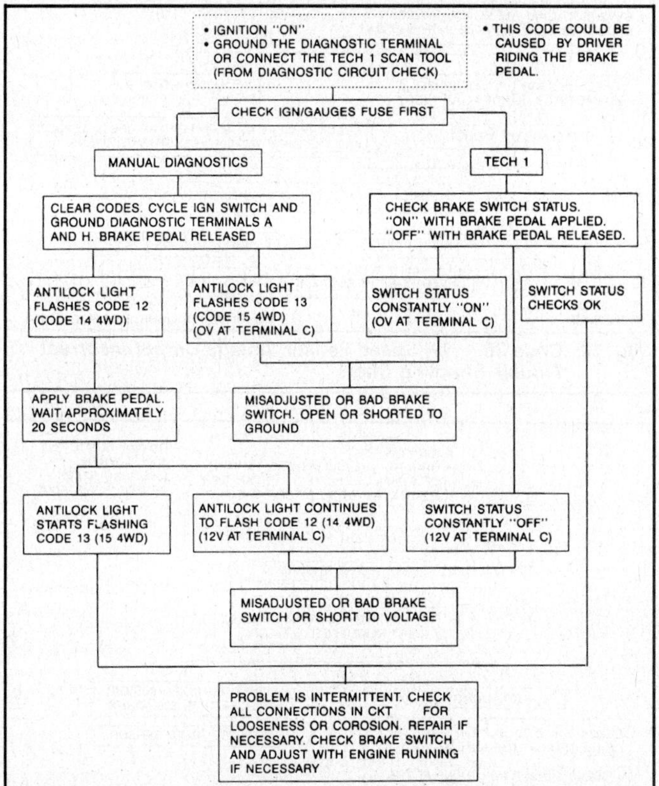
• IGNITION "ON"
• GROUND THE DIAGNOSTIC TERMINAL OR CONNECT THE TECH 1 SCAN TOOL (FROM DIAGNOSTIC CIRCUIT CHECK)
• THIS CODE COULD BE CAUSED BY DRIVER RIDING THE BRAKE PEDAL.
CHECK IGN/GAUGES FUSE FIRST
MANUAL DIAGNOSTICS
TECH 1
CLEAR CODES. CYCLE IGN SWITCH AND GROUND DIAGNOSTIC TERMINALS A AND H. BRAKE PEDAL RELEASED
CHECK BRAKE SWITCH STATUS. "ON" WITH BRAKE PEDAL APPLIED. "OFF" WITH BRAKE PEDAL RELEASED.
ANTILOCK LIGHT FLASHES CODE 12 (CODE 14 4WD)
ANTILOCK LIGHT FLASHES CODE 13 (CODE 15 4WD) (OV AT TERMINAL C)
SWITCH STATUS CONSTANTLY "ON" (OV AT TERMINAL C)
SWITCH STATUS CHECKS OK
APPLY BRAKE PEDAL. WAIT APPROXIMATELY 20 SECONDS
MISADJUSTED OR BAD BRAKE SWITCH. OPEN OR SHORTED TO GROUND
ANTILOCK LIGHT STARTS FLASHING CODE 13 (15 4WD)
ANTILOCK LIGHT CONTINUES TO FLASH CODE 12 (14 4WD) (12V AT TERMINAL C)
SWITCH STATUS CONSTANTLY "OFF" (12V AT TERMINAL C)
MISADJUSTED OR BAD BRAKE SWITCH OR SHORT TO VOLTAGE
PROBLEM IS INTERMITTENT. CHECK ALL CONNECTIONS IN CKT FOR LOOSENESS OR COROSION. REPAIR IF NECESSARY. CHECK BRAKE SWITCH AND ADJUST WITH ENGINE RUNNING IF NECESSARY

90F06392 Courtesy of General Motors Corp.

***Fig. 25:* Code 81 – Brake Switch Circuit Operation Is Shorted or Open Trouble Shooting Chart**

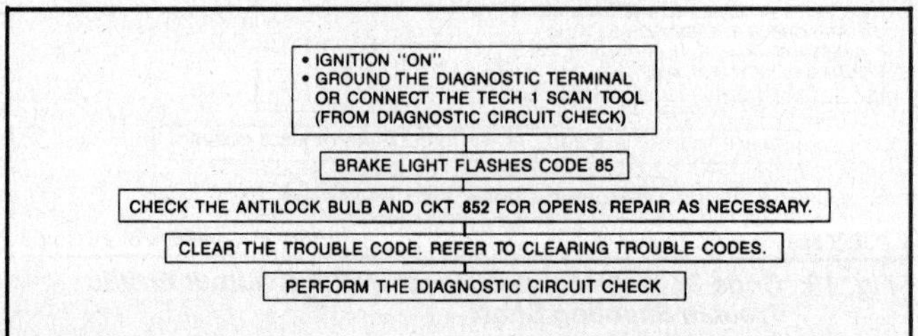
• IGNITION "ON"
• GROUND THE DIAGNOSTIC TERMINAL OR CONNECT THE TECH 1 SCAN TOOL (FROM DIAGNOSTIC CIRCUIT CHECK)
BRAKE LIGHT FLASHES CODE 85
CHECK THE ANTILOCK BULB AND CKT 852 FOR OPENS. REPAIR AS NECESSARY.
CLEAR THE TROUBLE CODE. REFER TO CLEARING TROUBLE CODES.
PERFORM THE DIAGNOSTIC CIRCUIT CHECK

90H06393 Courtesy of General Motors Corp.

***Fig. 26:* Code 85 – Open in "ANTILOCK" Indicator Light Circuit Trouble Shooting Chart**

1991 BRAKES
Anti-Lock – 4WAL (Cont.)

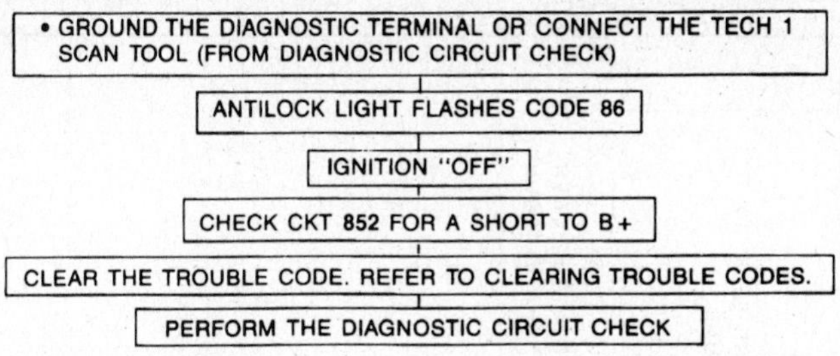
• GROUND THE DIAGNOSTIC TERMINAL OR CONNECT THE TECH 1 SCAN TOOL (FROM DIAGNOSTIC CIRCUIT CHECK)
ANTILOCK LIGHT FLASHES CODE 86
IGNITION "OFF"
CHECK CKT 852 FOR A SHORT TO B+
CLEAR THE TROUBLE CODE. REFER TO CLEARING TROUBLE CODES.
PERFORM THE DIAGNOSTIC CIRCUIT CHECK

90J06394 Courtesy of General Motors Corp.

Fig. 27: Code 86 – Short in "ANTILOCK" Indicator Light Circuit Trouble Shooting Chart

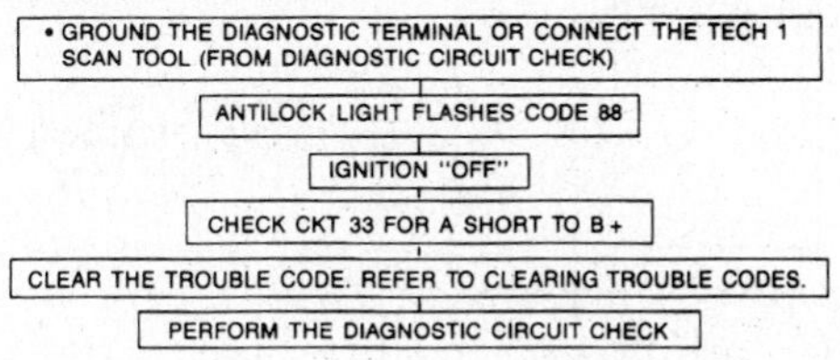
• GROUND THE DIAGNOSTIC TERMINAL OR CONNECT THE TECH 1 SCAN TOOL (FROM DIAGNOSTIC CIRCUIT CHECK)
ANTILOCK LIGHT FLASHES CODE 88
IGNITION "OFF"
CHECK CKT 33 FOR A SHORT TO B+
CLEAR THE TROUBLE CODE. REFER TO CLEARING TROUBLE CODES.
PERFORM THE DIAGNOSTIC CIRCUIT CHECK

90C06395 Courtesy of General Motors Corp.

Fig. 28: Code 88 – Short in "BRAKE" Indicator Light Circuit Trouble Shooting Chart

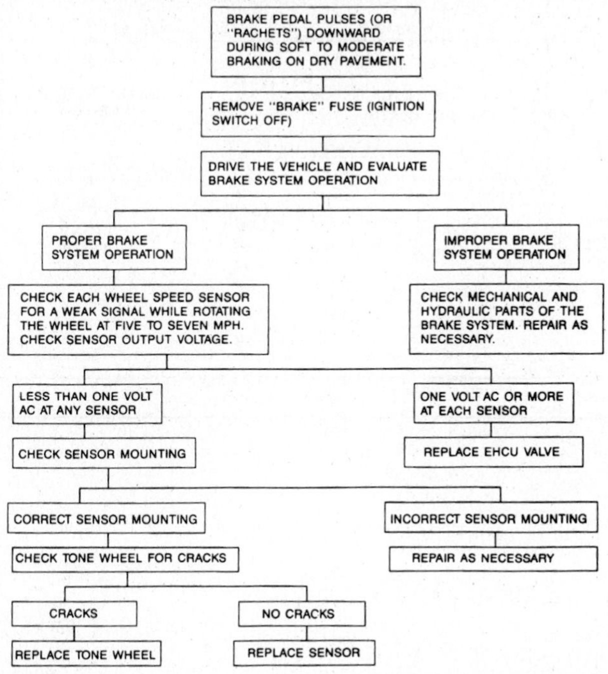
BRAKE PEDAL PULSES (OR "RACHETS") DOWNWARD DURING SOFT TO MODERATE BRAKING ON DRY PAVEMENT.
REMOVE "BRAKE" FUSE (IGNITION SWITCH OFF)
DRIVE THE VEHICLE AND EVALUATE BRAKE SYSTEM OPERATION
PROPER BRAKE SYSTEM OPERATION
IMPROPER BRAKE SYSTEM OPERATION
CHECK EACH WHEEL SPEED SENSOR FOR A WEAK SIGNAL WHILE ROTATING THE WHEEL AT FIVE TO SEVEN MPH. CHECK SENSOR OUTPUT VOLTAGE.
CHECK MECHANICAL AND HYDRAULIC PARTS OF THE BRAKE SYSTEM. REPAIR AS NECESSARY.
LESS THAN ONE VOLT AC AT ANY SENSOR
ONE VOLT AC OR MORE AT EACH SENSOR
CHECK SENSOR MOUNTING
REPLACE EHCU VALVE
CORRECT SENSOR MOUNTING
INCORRECT SENSOR MOUNTING
CHECK TONE WHEEL FOR CRACKS
REPAIR AS NECESSARY
CRACKS
NO CRACKS
REPLACE TONE WHEEL
REPLACE SENSOR

90J06416 Courtesy of General Motors Corp.

Fig. 29: No Code – Brake Pedal Pulses Trouble Shooting Chart

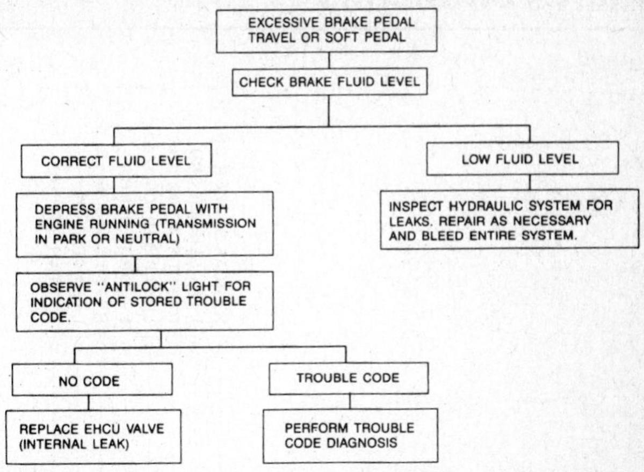
EXCESSIVE BRAKE PEDAL TRAVEL OR SOFT PEDAL
CHECK BRAKE FLUID LEVEL
CORRECT FLUID LEVEL
LOW FLUID LEVEL
DEPRESS BRAKE PEDAL WITH ENGINE RUNNING (TRANSMISSION IN PARK OR NEUTRAL)
INSPECT HYDRAULIC SYSTEM FOR LEAKS. REPAIR AS NECESSARY AND BLEED ENTIRE SYSTEM.
OBSERVE "ANTILOCK" LIGHT FOR INDICATION OF STORED TROUBLE CODE.
NO CODE
TROUBLE CODE
REPLACE EHCU VALVE (INTERNAL LEAK)
PERFORM TROUBLE CODE DIAGNOSIS

90A06417 Courtesy of General Motors Corp.

Fig. 30: No Code – Excessive Brake Pedal Travel or Soft Pedal Trouble Shooting Chart

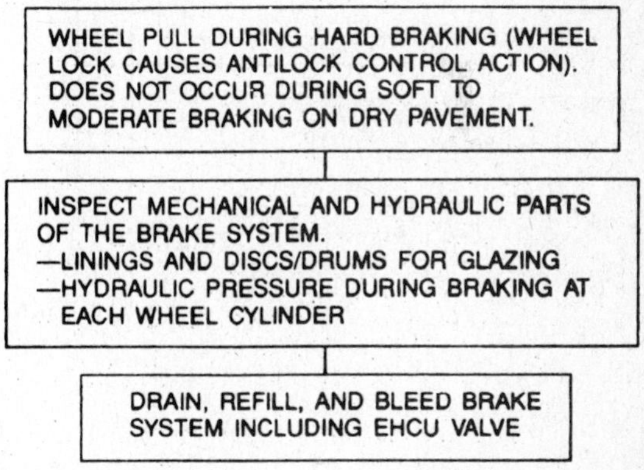
WHEEL PULL DURING HARD BRAKING (WHEEL LOCK CAUSES ANTILOCK CONTROL ACTION). DOES NOT OCCUR DURING SOFT TO MODERATE BRAKING ON DRY PAVEMENT.
INSPECT MECHANICAL AND HYDRAULIC PARTS OF THE BRAKE SYSTEM.
—LININGS AND DISCS/DRUMS FOR GLAZING
—HYDRAULIC PRESSURE DURING BRAKING AT EACH WHEEL CYLINDER
DRAIN, REFILL, AND BLEED BRAKE SYSTEM INCLUDING EHCU VALVE

90B06418 Courtesy of General Motors Corp.

Fig. 31: No Code – Wheel Pull During Hard Braking Trouble Shooting Chart

1991 BRAKES
Anti-Lock – 4WAL (Cont.)

WIRING DIAGRAMS

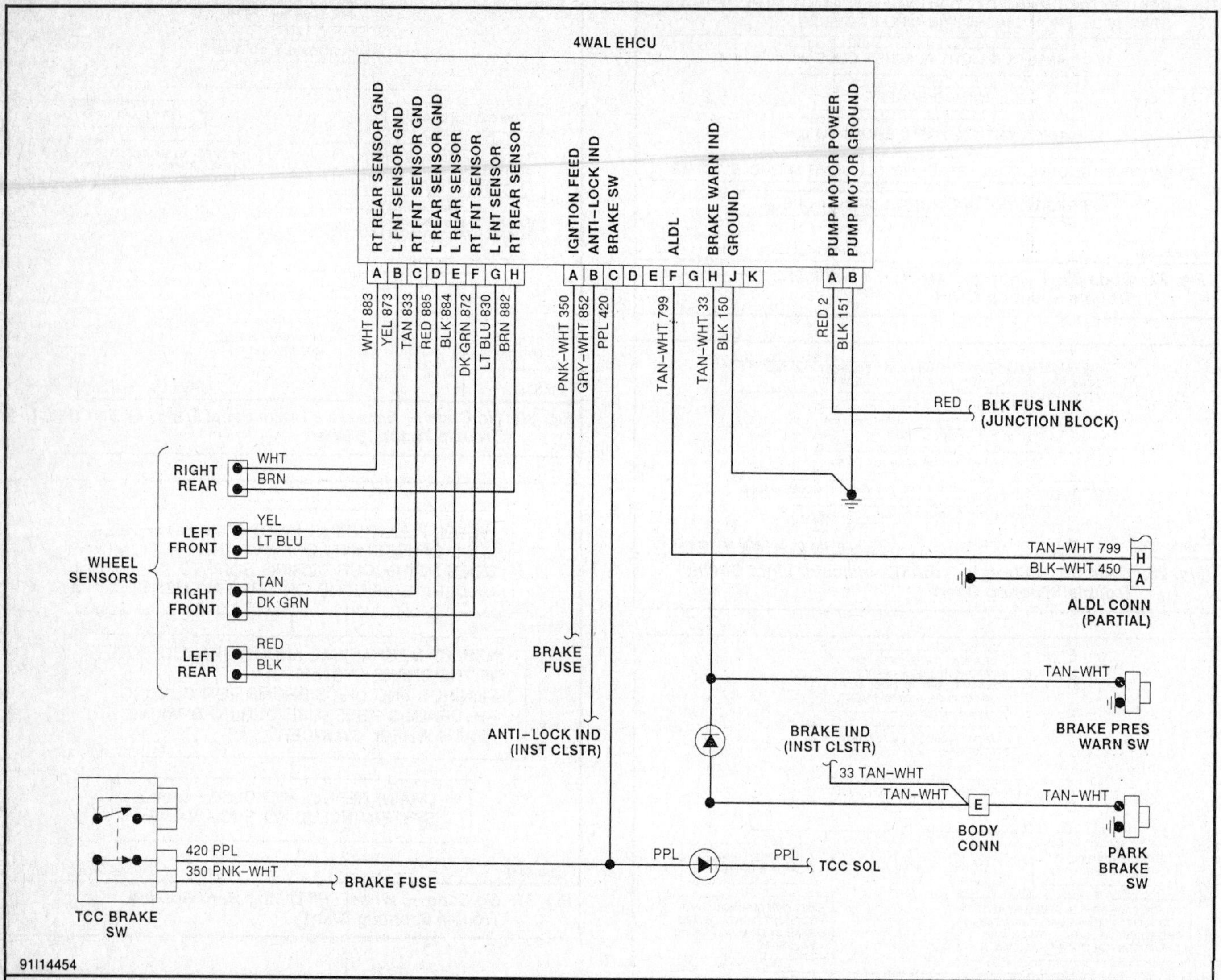
4WAL EHCU
RT REAR SENSOR GND
L FNT SENSOR GND
RT FNT SENSOR GND
L REAR SENSOR GND
L REAR SENSOR
RT FNT SENSOR
L FNT SENSOR
RT REAR SENSOR
IGNTION FEED
ANTI-LOCK IND
BRAKE SW
ALDL
BRAKE WARN IND
GROUND
PUMP MOTOR POWER
PUMP MOTOR GROUND
WHT 883
YEL 873
TAN 833
RED 885
BLK 884
DK GRN 872
LT BLU 830
BRN 882
PNK-WHT 350
GRY-WHT 852
PPL 420
TAN-WHT 799
TAN-WHT 33
BLK 150
RED 2
BLK 151
RED
BLK FUS LINK
(JUNCTION BLOCK)
WHEEL SENSORS
RIGHT REAR
WHT
BRN
LEFT FRONT
YEL
LT BLU
RIGHT FRONT
TAN
DK GRN
LEFT REAR
RED
BLK
BRAKE FUSE
ANTI-LOCK IND
(INST CLSTR)
TAN-WHT 799
BLK-WHT 450
ALDL CONN
(PARTIAL)
TAN-WHT
BRAKE PRES
WARN SW
BRAKE IND
(INST CLSTR)
33 TAN-WHT
TAN-WHT
BODY
CONN
PARK
BRAKE
SW
420 PPL
350 PNK-WHT
BRAKE FUSE
PPL
TCC SOL
TCC BRAKE
SW
91I14454

Fig. 32: 4WAL Brake System Wiring Diagram (Astro & Safari)

1991 BRAKES
Anti-Lock – 4WAL (Cont.)

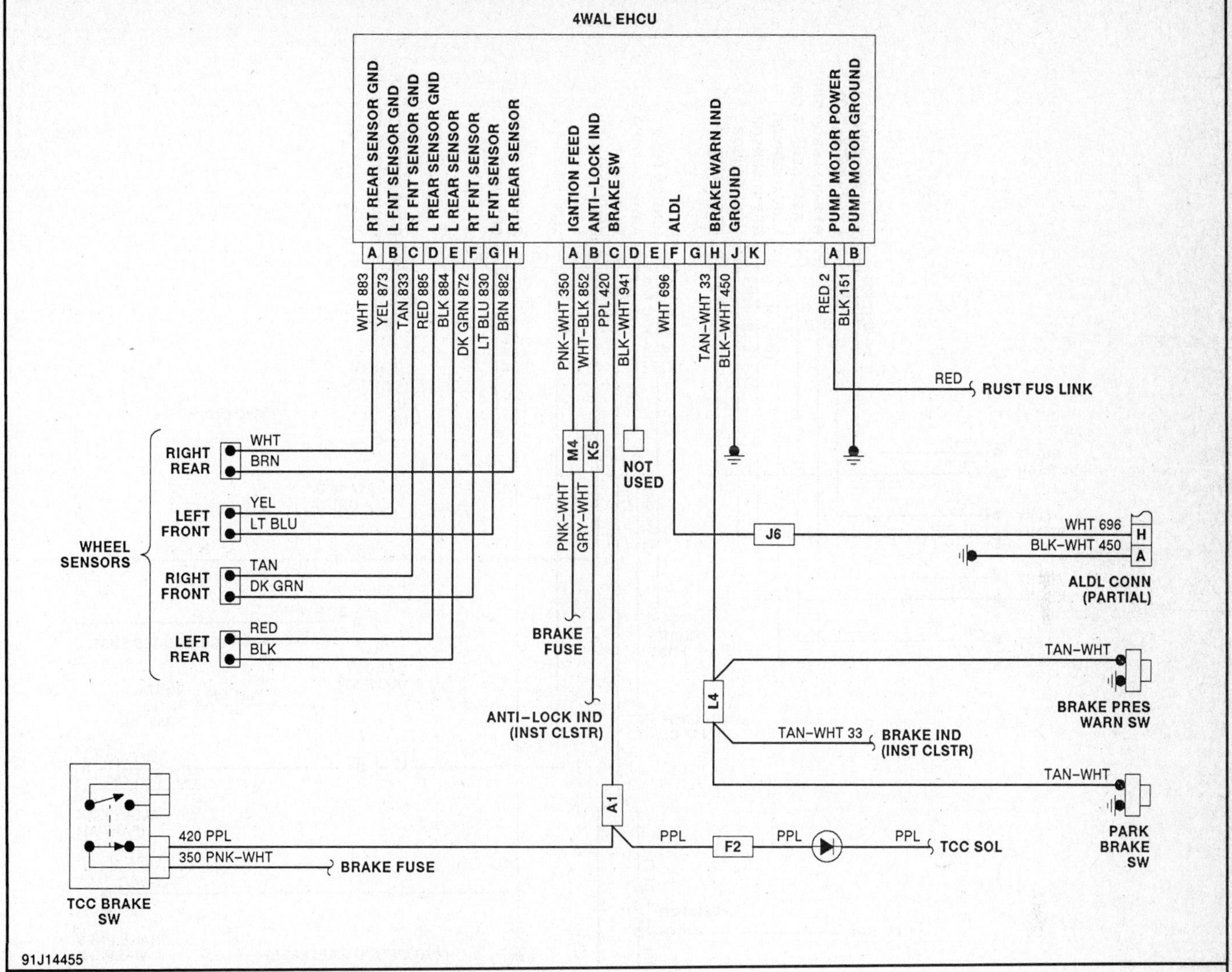
4WAL EHCU
RT REAR SENSOR GND
L FNT SENSOR GND
RT FNT SENSOR GND
L REAR SENSOR GND
L REAR SENSOR
RT FNT SENSOR
L FNT SENSOR
RT REAR SENSOR
IGNTION FEED
ANTI-LOCK IND
BRAKE SW
ALDL
BRAKE WARN IND
GROUND
PUMP MOTOR POWER
PUMP MOTOR GROUND
WHT 883
YEL 873
TAN 833
RED 885
BLK 884
DK GRN 872
LT BLU 830
BRN 882
PNK-WHT 350
WHT-BLK 852
PPL 420
BLK-WHT 941
WHT 696
TAN-WHT 33
BLK-WHT 450
RED 2
BLK 151
RED
RUST FUS LINK
M4
K5
NOT USED
RIGHT REAR
WHT
BRN
LEFT FRONT
YEL
LT BLU
WHEEL SENSORS
RIGHT FRONT
TAN
DK GRN
LEFT REAR
RED
BLK
PNK-WHT
GRY-WHT
BRAKE FUSE
ANTI-LOCK IND (INST CLSTR)
J6
WHT 696
BLK-WHT 450
H
A
ALDL CONN (PARTIAL)
TAN-WHT
BRAKE PRES WARN SW
L4
TAN-WHT 33
BRAKE IND (INST CLSTR)
TAN-WHT
PARK BRAKE SW
A1
420 PPL
350 PNK-WHT
BRAKE FUSE
PPL
F2
PPL
PPL
TCC SOL
TCC BRAKE SW
91J14455

Fig. 33: 4WAL Brake System Wiring Diagram (Bravada)

1991 BRAKES
Anti-Lock – 4WAL (Cont.)

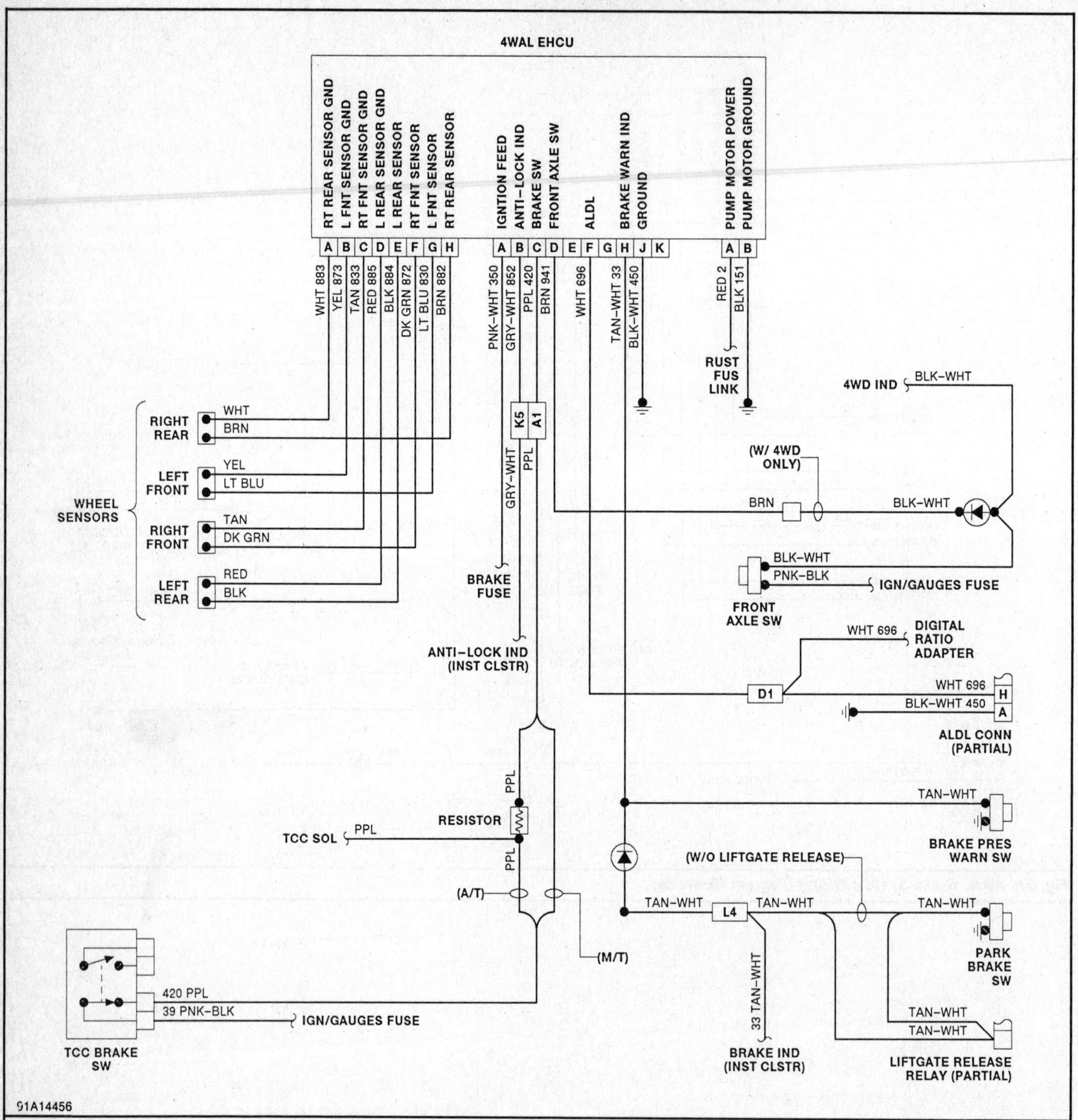
4WAL EHCU
RT REAR SENSOR GND
L FNT SENSOR GND
RT FNT SENSOR GND
L REAR SENSOR GND
L REAR SENSOR
RT FNT SENSOR
L FNT SENSOR
RT REAR SENSOR
IGNTION FEED
ANTI-LOCK IND
BRAKE SW
FRONT AXLE SW
ALDL
BRAKE WARN IND
GROUND
PUMP MOTOR POWER
PUMP MOTOR GROUND
WHT 883
YEL 873
TAN 833
RED 885
BLK 884
DK GRN 872
LT BLU 830
BRN 882
PNK-WHT 350
GRY-WHT 852
PPL 420
BRN 941
WHT 696
TAN-WHT 33
BLK-WHT 450
RED 2
BLK 151
RUST FUS LINK
4WD IND
BLK-WHT
WHEEL SENSORS
RIGHT REAR
LEFT FRONT
RIGHT FRONT
LEFT REAR
WHT
BRN
YEL
LT BLU
TAN
DK GRN
RED
BLK
K5
A1
GRY-WHT
PPL
(W/ 4WD ONLY)
BRN
BLK-WHT
PNK-BLK
IGN/GAUGES FUSE
FRONT AXLE SW
BRAKE FUSE
ANTI-LOCK IND (INST CLSTR)
WHT 696
DIGITAL RATIO ADAPTER
D1
WHT 696
BLK-WHT 450
ALDL CONN (PARTIAL)
TAN-WHT
BRAKE PRES WARN SW
RESISTOR
TCC SOL
PPL
(W/O LIFTGATE RELEASE)
(A/T)
TAN-WHT
L4
PARK BRAKE SW
(M/T)
33 TAN-WHT
420 PPL
39 PNK-BLK
IGN/GAUGES FUSE
TCC BRAKE SW
BRAKE IND (INST CLSTR)
LIFTGATE RELEASE RELAY (PARTIAL)
91A14456
Fig. 34: 4WAL Brake System Wiring Diagram ("S" & "T" Series)

1991 BRAKES
Disc & Drum

Astro, Blazer, Bravada, Jimmy, Lumina APV, Safari, Sierra, Silhouette, Sonoma, Trans Sport, "C" & "K" Series, "G" Series, "P" Series, "R" & "V" Series, "S" & "T" Series

NOTE: Information in this article also applies to vehicles equipped with Anti-Lock Brake System (ABS); however, not all information on ABS is included in this article. See Anti-Lock – RWAL or Anti-Lock – 4WAL article.

DESCRIPTION & OPERATION

NOTE: On vehicles with full-floating axle, axle shaft and hub must be removed to remove brake disc or drum. See Figs. 10 and 11. On vehicles with semi-floating axle, brake drum can be removed without removing axle shaft.

MODEL IDENTIFICATION

Vehicle model can be identified by fifth character of Vehicle Identification Number (VIN), stamped on metal pad on top of left end of instrument panel, near windshield. See MODEL IDENTIFICATION table.

MODEL IDENTIFICATION

Series [1]	Model
"C"	2WD Pickup & Sierra
"G"	RWD Van
"K"	4WD Pickup & Sierra
"L"	2WD Astro & Safari
"M"	All-Wheel Drive Astro & Safari
"P"	Forward Control Chassis
"R"	[2] 2WD Blazer, [2] Jimmy, Pickup & Suburban
"S"	[2] 2WD Blazer, [2] Jimmy, Pickup & Sonoma
"T"	Bravada, [2] 4WD Blazer, [2] Jimmy, Pickup & Sonoma
"U"	Lumina APV, Silhouette & Trans Sport
"V"	[2] 4WD Blazer, [2] Jimmy, Pickup & Suburban

[1] – Vehicle series is fifth character of VIN.
[2] – Blazer and Jimmy are available in "S" and "T" Series (smaller version) and "R" and "V" Series (larger version).

AUTOMATIC PARKING BRAKE

"P" Series Motorhome – On the automatic apply parking brake system, when shift lever is in Park, engine running, and manual parking brake foot lever in released position, fluid flows from steering gear to port SR on relay valve and out to port TW to the control valve supply port SC. *See Fig. 1.* Once the system is charged, pressure should range between 130-150 psi (9.1-10.5 kg/cm²). Any excess fluid will be discharged through port "R" and back to the pump. The supply port or charge port SC is blocked off due to control valve position in Park mode.

Any previously pressure built-up in control valve flows through control valve out port EC back through the relay valve, triggering release of pressure from port "D" of relay valve through port ER to reservoir. *See Fig. 1.* This allows the spring controlled actuator to apply parking brake. The spring will apply brake by travelling as far as the brake adjustment demand requires to balance brake apply and spring force.

When valve is released from Park position, fluid charge at shift control valve port SC is diverted to port DC. The shift control port EC is blocked off. Fluid charge at relay valve port SR is diverted to port "D", pressurizing parking brake system and actuator. *See Fig. 1.* Fluid pressure working against the spring pressure in actuator, releases parking brake.

The manual foot lever should still be applied whenever vehicle is shifted into Park. This will alert operator of need for adjustment in the parking brake system.

BRAKE SHOE ASSEMBLY

Some "C" and "K" Series vehicles are equipped with leading/trailing brakes, identified by adjuster screw hole in backing plate, located above horizontal centerline of rear axle. All other "C" and "K" Series vehicles and all other models are equipped with dual-servo brakes, identified by adjuster screw hole at bottom of backing plate.

Brake assembly consists of backing plate, brake shoes, return springs, automatic adjusting assembly and a wheel cylinder.

Automatic adjusting assembly consist of an actuator lever, return spring, actuator link, adjusting screw and spring. Automatic adjustment is accomplished through movement of actuating lever and secondary shoe.

BRAKE WARNING LIGHT

Lumina APV, Silhouette & Trans Sport – Brake warning light is energized when ignition is on and parking brake is applied or when master cylinder fluid level is low. Brake warning light is not energized if hydraulic pressure is lost; system is not equipped with pressure differential switch.

Except Lumina APV, Silhouette & Trans Sport – Pressure differential warning switch in combination valve energizes brake warning light

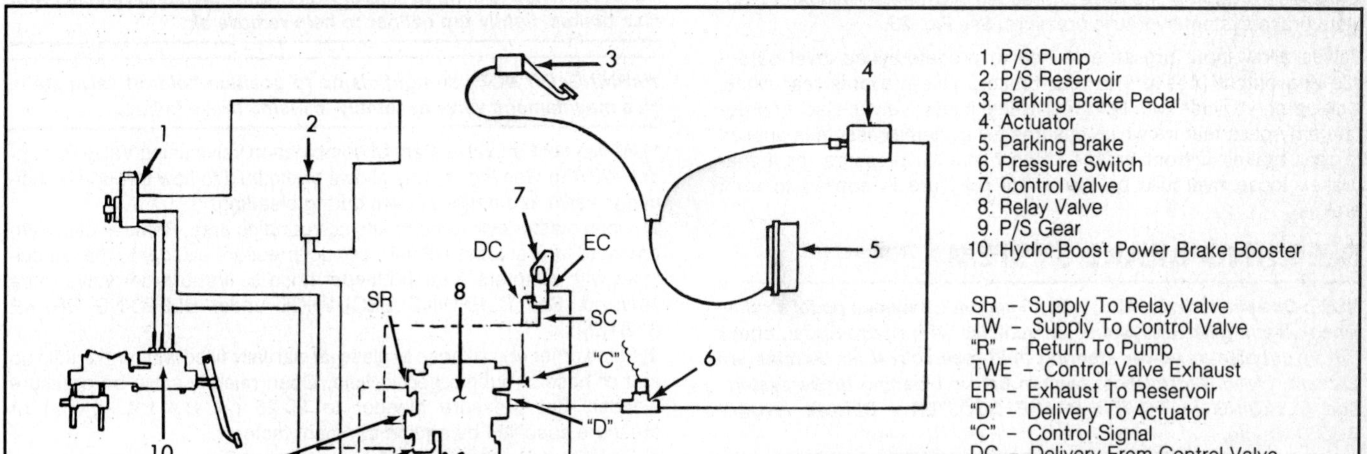
1
2
3
4
5
6
7
8
9
10
DC
EC
SR
SC
"C"
"D"
TW
"R"
TWE
ER
1. P/S Pump
2. P/S Reservoir
3. Parking Brake Pedal
4. Actuator
5. Parking Brake
6. Pressure Switch
7. Control Valve
8. Relay Valve
9. P/S Gear
10. Hydro-Boost Power Brake Booster
SR – Supply To Relay Valve
TW – Supply To Control Valve
"R" – Return To Pump
TWE – Control Valve Exhaust
ER – Exhaust To Reservoir
"D" – Delivery To Actuator
"C" – Control Signal
DC – Delivery From Control Valve
SC – Supply To Control Valve
EC – Exhaust From Control Valve
91A13755
Courtesy of General Motors Corp.

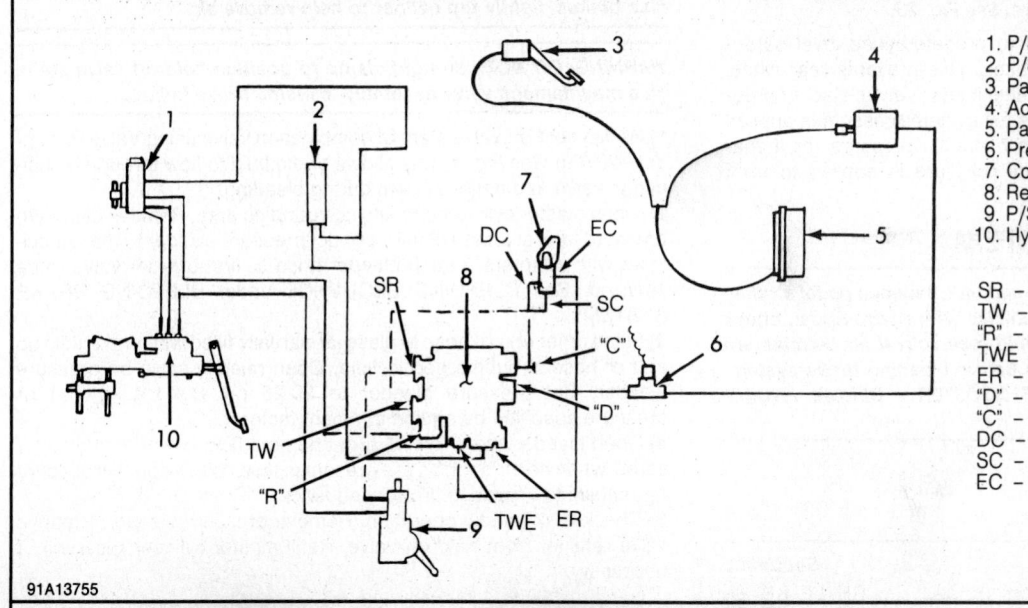

Fig. 1: Schematic of Automatic Parking Brake System ("P" Series Motorhome)

1991 BRAKES
Disc & Drum (Cont.)

on instrument panel when front or rear brakes loose hydraulic pressure. After repairing failed side of hydraulic system, depress brake pedal with moderate to heavy pressure to hydraulically center the piston. This will turn off brake warning light.

CALIPERS

Front brakes are floating caliper or sliding caliper design. *See Figs. 14 and 15*. Rear brakes are sliding caliper design. Caliper is attached to caliper mount. Caliper is mounted to steering knuckle or caliper adapter, depending on application. Caliper assembly slides back and forth in machined cut-outs.

HYDRAULIC CONTROL VALVES

Combination Valve (Except Lumina APV, Silhouette & Trans Sport) – System uses a combination valve to regulate brake system hydraulic pressure. Combination valve, located in brake lines between master cylinder and wheels, has 3 pressure control functions:

- **Metering** (or hold off) section of valve limits pressure to front brakes until pressure of rear brake shoe retractor springs is overcome, then allows pressure to front brakes.
- **Proportioning** section of valve allows input pressure to rise to predetermined level before allowing output pressure to rear brakes. This prevents rear wheel lock-up on vehicles with light rear wheel loads.
- **By-Pass** section of valve ensures full system pressure is applied to rear brakes if front brakes looses hydraulic pressure (or if rear brakes loose hydraulic pressure, full pressure is applied to front brakes).

Combination valve also contains a pressure differential warning switch. See BRAKE WARNING LIGHT under DESCRIPTION & OPERATION.

Height-Sensing Proportioning Valve ("C" & "K" Series, "P" Series & "R" & "V" Series) – Valve senses vehicle load conditions through relative movement between rear axle and body. *See Figs. 4 and 5*. As vehicle load increases (resulting in decreased vehicle height), valve allows higher pressure to rear brakes, resulting in optimum front-to-rear brake pressure balance.

WARNING: On vehicles with height sensing proportioning valve, use of aftermarket load leveling kits, air shocks, or modifications that change axle-to-frame distance will provide a false reading to valve. False readings may result in unsatisfactory brake performance.

Proportioning Valves (Lumina APV, Silhouette & Trans Sport) –System uses 2 proportioning valves, threaded into master cylinder, to regulate brake system hydraulic pressure. *See Fig. 23*.

Valves allow input pressure to rise to predetermined level before allowing output pressure to rear brakes. This prevents rear wheel lock-up on vehicles with light rear wheel loads. Valves also incorporate a by-pass feature which ensures full system pressure is applied to rear brakes if front brakes loose hydraulic pressure (or if rear brakes loose hydraulic pressure, full pressure is applied to front brakes).

BLEEDING BRAKE SYSTEM

NOTE: On vehicles with ABS, wait 15 seconds between pedal strokes when bleeding brake system. On vehicles with Hydro-Boost, check for air bubbles in power steering fluid reservoir. If air bubbles are present, bleed Hydro-Boost system before bleeding brake system. See BLEEDING in POWER BRAKE BOOSTER - BENDIX HYDRO-BOOST article.

BLEEDING SEQUENCE

BLEEDING SEQUENCE

Application	Sequence
Lumina APV, Silhouette & Trans Sport	RR, LF, LR, RF
All Others	RR, LR, RF, LF

MASTER CYLINDER BLEEDING

NOTE: To prevent air from entering brake system, bench bleed master cylinder before installing.

1) Place master cylinder in soft-jawed vise. DO NOT overtighten vise. Install bleeder tubes in both outlets of master cylinder. *See Fig. 2*. Fill master cylinder reservoir. Ensure ends of bleeder tubes are submerged in brake fluid.
2) Using screwdriver or drift punch at end of master cylinder bore, press and release piston assembly until air bubbles are no longer present in fluid flow. Leave bleeder tubes installed on master cylinder. Install master cylinder.
3) Remove bleeder tubes. Connect brake lines at master cylinder. DO NOT fully tighten brake lines at this time. Slowly press brake pedal to floor and hold. Tighten brake lines. Release brake pedal. Bleed brake system. See MANUAL BLEEDING, PRESSURE BLEEDING or VACUUM BLEEDING.

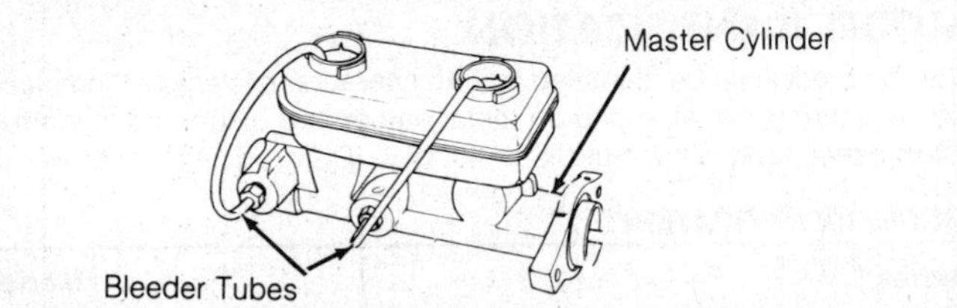
Master Cylinder
Bleeder Tubes

117379 Courtesy of General Motors Corp.

Fig. 2: Bench Bleeding Master Cylinder

MANUAL BLEEDING

NOTE: Air tends to cling to caliper walls. When bleeding vehicles with disc brakes, lightly tap caliper to help remove air.

1) Fill master cylinder. Install bleeder hose to bleeder screw at first wheel to be serviced. See BLEEDING SEQUENCE under BLEEDING BRAKE SYSTEM. Submerge other end of hose in glass jar partially filled with brake fluid.
2) Open bleeder screw 3/4 - 1 turn. Slowly press brake pedal to floor. Note fluid flow. Close bleeder screw. Release pedal. Repeat procedure until air bubbles are no longer present in fluid flow.

PRESSURE BLEEDING

NOTE: Air tends to cling to caliper walls. When bleeding vehicles with disc brakes, lightly tap caliper to help remove air.

WARNING: DO NOT use rigid clamp to position hold off valve stem. This may damage valve assembly, causing brake failure.

1) Retain hold off valve stem of combination valve using Valve Retainer (J-23709). *See Fig. 3*. This allows brake fluid to flow through combination valve and entire system during bleeding.
2) Clean master cylinder cap and surrounding area. Remove cap. With pressure tank at least 1/2 full, connect pressure bleeder to master cylinder with adapters. Attach bleeder hose to first bleeder valve to be serviced. See BLEEDING SEQUENCE under BLEEDING BRAKE SYSTEM.
3) Place other end of hose in glass jar partially filled with brake fluid so end of hose is submerged in fluid. Open release valve on pressure bleeder. Set pressure bleeder to 20-25 psi (1.4-1.8 kg/cm²) or pressure specified by equipment manufacturer.
4) Open bleeder screw 3/4 - 1 turn and note fluid flow. Close bleeder screw when no air bubbles are present in fluid flow. Repeat procedure on remaining wheels in proper sequence.
5) Check brake pedal operation. Remove pressure bleeder. Remove valve retainer from hold off valve. Refill master cylinder reservoir, if necessary.

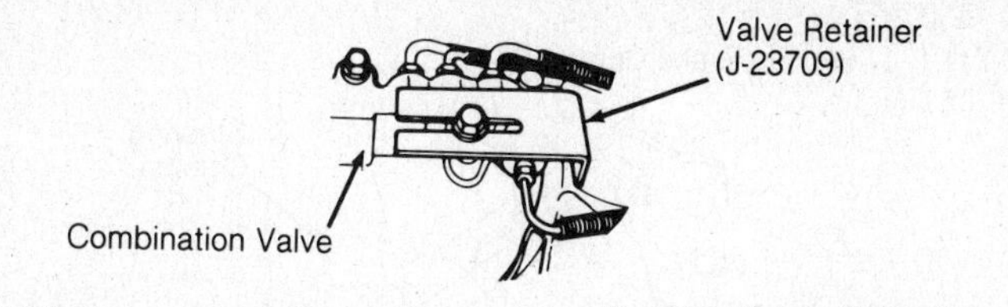
Valve Retainer
(J-23709)
Combination Valve
117380
Courtesy of General Motors Corp.

Fig. 3: Positioning Hold Off Valve On Combination Valve (Typical)

VACUUM BLEEDING

NOTE: Air tends to cling to caliper walls. When bleeding vehicles with disc brakes, lightly tap caliper to help remove air.

1) Fill master cylinder reservoir. Install vacuum bleed equipment to first bleeder valve to be serviced. See BLEEDING SEQUENCE under BLEEDING BRAKE SYSTEM.
2) Open bleeder valve 3/4 - 1 turn. Press vacuum pump to draw fluid into reservoir jar until no air bubbles are present in fluid flow. Close bleeder screw. Repeat procedure on remaining wheels in sequence.

ADJUSTMENTS

HEIGHT-SENSING PROPORTIONING VALVE

NOTE: If front wheel lock-up is experienced during braking when vehicle is near maximum GVWR, adjust height-sensing proportioning valve.

"C" & "K" Series - Ensure rear axle is hanging free and valve is securely bolted to frame when lever is attached to valve before height-sensing proportioning valve is adjusted. *See Fig. 4*.
"P" Series & "R" & "V" Series - 1) Raise vehicle at frame rails, allowing rear axle to hang free. Remove nut and lever from valve shaft. *See Fig. 5*. Select appropriate adjustment gauge (available from manufacturer). Rotate valve shaft to permit installation of gauge.
2) Install gauge with flat on valve shaft indexed to flat on gauge, and tang on gauge inserted in valve mounting hole. Install lever (DO NOT pull lever onto shaft using nut). Install nut. Break off tang on gauge. Lower and test-drive vehicle.

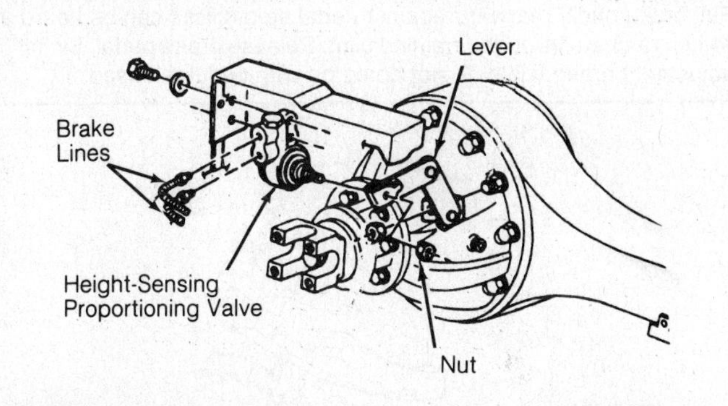
Lever
Brake
Lines
Height-Sensing
Proportioning Valve
Nut
91B13756
Courtesy of General Motors Corp.

Fig. 4: Height-Sensing Proportioning Valve ("C" & "K" Series)

PARKING BRAKE

NOTE: On all models except "C" and "K" Series with leading/trailing brakes, ensure rear brake shoes are adjusted before adjusting parking brake. See REAR BRAKE SHOES under ADJUSTMENTS.

Astro & Safari - 1) Raise and support vehicle. Loosen parking brake cable adjusting nut. Apply parking brake pedal 2 notches from fully released position.

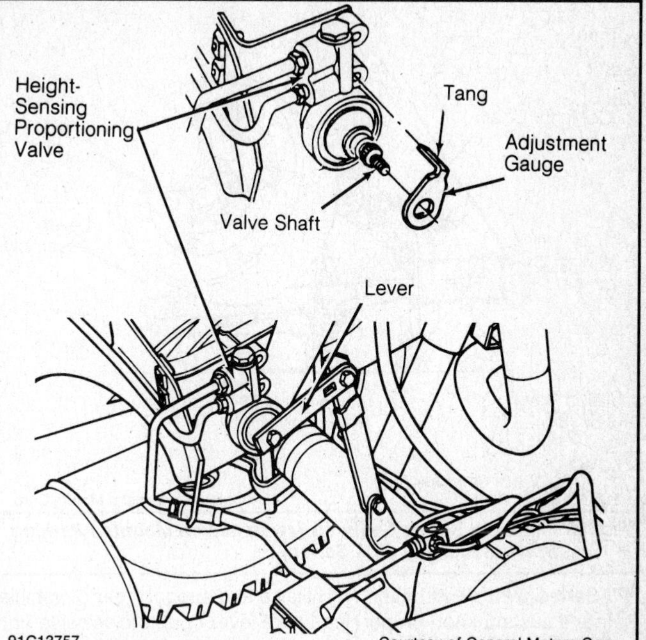
Height-
Sensing
Proportioning
Valve
Tang
Adjustment
Gauge
Valve Shaft
Lever
91C13757
Courtesy of General Motors Corp.

Fig. 5: Height-Sensing Proportioning Valve ("P" Series & "R" & "V" Series)

2) Tighten adjusting nut until left rear wheel can be turned rearward using 2 hands, but not forward. Release parking brake and ensure wheels rotate freely. Lower vehicle.
Lumina APV, Silhouette & Trans Sport - Apply parking brake pedal 3 notches from fully released position. Raise and support vehicle. Tighten parking brake cable adjusting nut until right rear wheel can be turned rearward but not forward. Release parking brake and ensure wheels rotate freely. Lower vehicle.
"C" & "K" Series With Leading/Trailing Brakes - 1) Raise and support rear of vehicle. Remove rear wheels. Remove brake drums. Rotate parking brake adjusting screw until clearance between brake drum and shoes is .010-.020" (.25-.51 mm). Use brake drum diameter gauge to determine clearance.
2) Ensure stop on parking brake lever is in contact with edge of brake shoe web. If parking brake cable is holding stops off of shoe web, loosen cable adjusting nut. Tighten cable adjusting nut until lever stop begins to move off of shoe web.
3) Loosen cable adjusting nut until lever stop moves back toward lever stop and barely contacts the stop. Clearance should be no more than .020" (.51 mm) between lever stop and shoe web.
4) Install brake drums and wheels. Apply and release service brake pedal 30-35 times with normal pedal force, pausing about one second between pedal applications. Apply parking brake pedal 6 notches from fully released position.
5) Rear wheels should not be able to be rotated. Release parking brake and ensure wheels rotate freely. Lower vehicle.
"C" Series with Transmission-Mounted Parking Brake - 1) Remove clevis pin from lever assembly. *See Fig. 6.* Apply parking brake pedal 4 notches from fully released position.
2) Using small length of cable or chain and a turnbuckle, install Spring Scale (J-35999) between lever assembly and vehicle frame. Tighten turnbuckle until spring scale indicates 50 lbs. (22.7 kg).
3) Loosen clevis nut (at cable end). Turn clevis until clevis pin slides freely into lever assembly with all slack removed from cable. Install clevis pin and retain with a cotter pin. Tighten clevis nut. Remove spring scale. Release parking brake.
"C" & "K" Series With Dual-Servo Brakes, "G" Series, "P" Series With Foot Pedal, "R" & "V" Series - Raise and support vehicle. Loosen parking brake cable adjusting nut. Apply parking brake pedal 4 notches from fully released position. Tighten adjusting nut until wheels rotate forward with moderate drag. Release parking brake and ensure wheels rotate freely. Lower vehicle.

1991 BRAKES
Disc & Drum (Cont.)

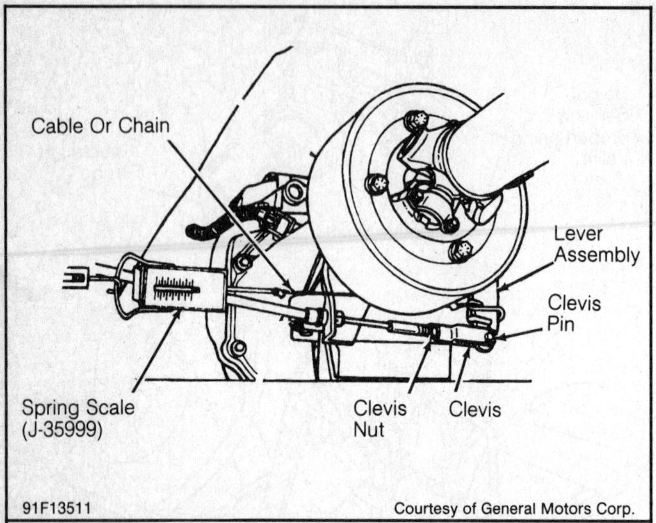
Cable Or Chain
Lever Assembly
Clevis Pin
Spring Scale (J-35999)
Clevis Nut
Clevis
91F13511
Courtesy of General Motors Corp.

Fig. 6: Installing Spring Scale on Transmission-Mounted Parking Brake Assembly ("C" Series)

"P" Series With Hand Lever – 1) Raise and support rear of vehicle. Rotate adjusting knob on parking brake lever counterclockwise until it stops. Apply parking brake. Loosen parking brake cable adjusting nut.

2) Tighten adjusting nut until slight drag is felt when rotating rear wheels forward. Tighten adjusting knob on parking brake lever until definite snap-over-center pressure is felt when parking brake lever is applied. Release parking brake. Ensure wheels rotate freely. Lower vehicle.

"P" Series With Transmission-Mounted Parking Brake – 1) Raise and support rear of vehicle. For preferred method of adjustment, perform steps **2)** and **3)**. For alternate method of adjustment, perform step **4)**.

2) Remove drive shaft. Install parking brake drum over first rivet section of brake shoes. Insert .010" (.25 mm) shims between both shoes and drum, spaced 140-180 degrees apart.

3) Rotate adjuster screw until no clearance exists. Remove shims. Install drum and drive shaft. Drum should rotate freely with light drag.

4) Rotate adjuster screw through hole in backing plate until brake drum just locks up. Back off adjuster screw until drum spins freely with light drag. Lower vehicle.

"S" & "T" Series – 1) Raise and support vehicle. Loosen parking brake cable adjusting nut. Apply parking brake pedal 2 notches (2WD) or 3 notches (Bravada and 4WD) from fully released position.

2) Tighten adjusting nut until wheels will not rotate forward without excessive force. Back off adjusting nut until slight drag exists when wheels are rotated forward. Release parking brake and ensure wheels rotate freely. Lower vehicle.

PARKING BRAKE CONTROL ROD

"P" Series Motorhome – 1) Disconnect parking brake control rod from control valve lever and transmission control equalizer. *See Fig. 7.* Place control valve lever in park position. Place transmission selector in Park.

2) Connect parking brake control rod to control valve lever. Loosen parking brake control rod jam nuts. Rotate rod as necessary to align hole at end of rod with hole in transmission control equalizer lever. Install and tighten bolt.

REAR BRAKE SHOES

Lumina APV, Silhouette & Trans Sport – 1) Ensure parking brake is released. Raise and support vehicle. Remove rear wheels. Rotate adjusting screw until clearance between brake drum and shoes is .050" (1.27 mm). Use brake drum diameter gauge to determine clearance.

2) Install brake drum. Install wheels. Operate vehicle for several forward and reverse stops while firmly applying brakes. Repeat procedure until ample brake pedal reserve is obtained.

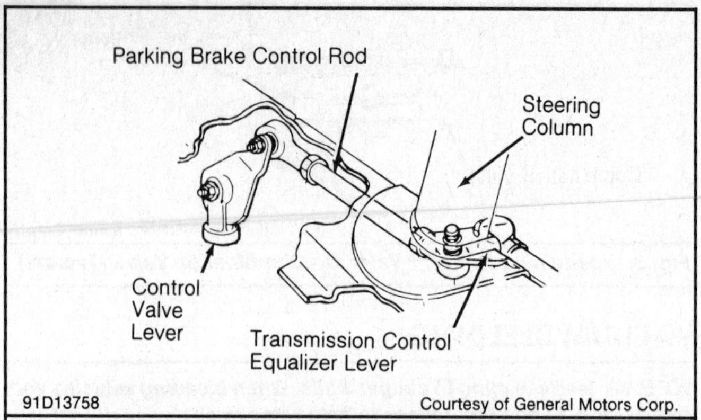
Parking Brake Control Rod
Steering Column
Control Valve Lever
Transmission Control Equalizer Lever
91D13758
Courtesy of General Motors Corp.

Fig. 7: Adjusting Automatic Parking Brake Control Rod ("P" Series Motorhome)

"C" & "K" Series With Leading/Trailing Brakes – Brake shoe adjustment is accomplished by adjusting parking brake. See PARKING BRAKE under ADJUSTMENTS.

Except "C" & "K" Series With Leading/Trailing Brakes – 1) Ensure parking brake is released. Raise and support vehicle. Knock out lanced area in backing plate with a punch (if not already removed) and remove from brake assembly.

2) Working through hole in backing plate, rotate adjusting screw until brake shoes expand and brake drums can just be turned by hand. Ensure drag is equal at both wheels. Back off adjusting screw 24 notches (Astro, Safari and "S" & "T" Series) or 33 notches (all others) at each wheel.

3) If heavy drag is present after adjusting screw is backed off 12 notches (Astro, Safari and "S" & "T" Series) or 15 notches (all others), check parking brake adjustment. See PARKING BRAKE under ADJUSTMENTS. To complete procedure, install plug in backing plate. Check parking brake adjustment.

STOPLIGHT SWITCH

"C" & "K" Series With Cruise Control – Depress and hold brake pedal. Pull lever on stoplight switch back to its stop. *See Fig. 8.* Pull brake pedal against pedal stop. Release brake pedal. Switch is adjusted if brake lights do not come on with pedal released.

Except "C" & "K" Series With Cruise Control – Depress and hold brake pedal. Push switch forward until firmly seated in retaining clip. Pull brake pedal rearward against pedal stop (clicks can be heard as switch ratchets through retaining clip). Release brake pedal. Switch is adjusted if brake lights do not come on with pedal released.

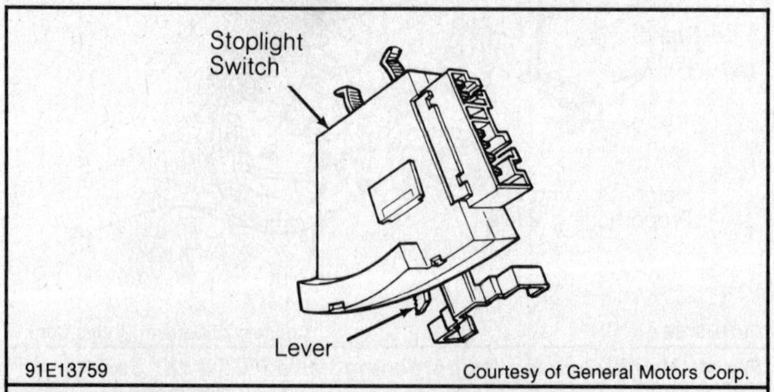
Stoplight Switch
Lever
91E13759
Courtesy of General Motors Corp.

Fig. 8: Stoplight Switch ("C" &"K" Series With Cruise Control)

TESTING

BRAKE WARNING LIGHT

Electrical Circuit – Disconnect wire from switch terminal on combination valve. Connect wire to ground. Turn ignition on. If brake warning light does not come on, repair brake warning light bulb or wiring circuit. If light operates, brake warning light electrical circuit is okay.

NOTE: On Astro and Safari, system is not equipped with pressure differential switch.

Warning Light Switch – 1) Fill master cylinder reservoir. Attach bleeder hose to bleeder screw at either rear wheel. Immerse other end of hose in container of brake fluid. Turn ignition on.
2) While depressing brake pedal, open bleeder screw (close bleeder screw before releasing pedal). On all models except Astro and Safari, if light comes on, go to step **3)**. If light does not come on, switch is defective; replace combination valve.
3) Close bleeder screw. Depress brake pedal with moderate to heavy pressure. If light goes out, switch is okay. If light stays on, switch is defective, replace combination valve. Repeat test on front brake system. System should function in same manner as rear.

REMOVAL & INSTALLATION

AUTOMATIC PARKING BRAKE ("P" SERIES MOTORHOME)

NOTE: Adjust parking brake control rod after removing and installing control valve. See PARKING BRAKE CONTROL ROD under ADJUSTMENTS. Adjust parking brake after removing and installing actuator. See PARKING BRAKE under ADJUSTMENTS. If any parking brake system fluid lines are disconnected, bleed parking brake system.

System Bleeding – 1) Place transmission in Park to set control valve in Park mode. Start engine. Turn steering wheel from stop to stop to bleed power steering system. Place transmission in Neutral.
2) Open bleed screw on actuator until fluid flow is free of air, then close bleed screw (bleed screw is near fluid hose connection, on top of actuator). Loosen exhaust line fitting (port EC) at control valve. *See Fig. 1*. Place transmission in Park. Allow small amount of fluid to bleed from fitting, then tighten fitting.
3) Cycle the system. If noisy, repeat bleeding procedure. Check power steering fluid level with transmission in Neutral and parking brake applied manually. Fluid level should be 7.12" (180.9 mm) from top of reservoir.

FRONT BRAKE CALIPER

NOTE: For front disc pad removal and installation, perform FRONT BRAKE CALIPER removal and installation procedures but do not disconnect brake hose from caliper (hang caliper out of way with wire). Replace all pads on an axle if wear indicator on any pad contacts rotor or if pad is worn to within 1/32" (.8 mm) of pad backing.

Removal (Floating Caliper) – 1) Remove two-thirds of brake fluid from master cylinder. Raise and support vehicle. Remove wheel. Using "C" clamp or large pliers, compress caliper piston until it bottoms in its bore.
2) Disconnect brake hose from caliper. Remove caliper guide pins. *See Fig. 14*. Remove caliper. Remove pads from caliper. Note retainer spring on inner pad (some models) and remove if replacing pads.
Installation – 1) Remove caliper sleeves from caliper. *See Fig. 14*. Apply silicone grease to outer diameter of caliper sleeves and inner diameter of bushings. Insert caliper sleeves into bushings.
2) Install retainer spring on inner pad (if removed). Install pads in caliper. Install caliper. Install guide pins and tighten to specification. See TORQUE SPECIFICATIONS table at end of article.
3) Connect brake hose to caliper and tighten hose bolt to 32 ft. lbs. (43 N.m). Bleed brake system. See MANUAL BLEEDING, PRESSURE BLEEDING or VACUUM BLEEDING under BLEEDING BRAKE SYSTEM.
4) If outer pads are equipped with locking ears, bend ears toward caliper until ears touch caliper. This prevents movement of outer pad in caliper. *See Fig. 9*. Install wheel.
Removal (Sliding Caliper) – 1) Remove two-thirds of brake fluid from master cylinder. Raise and support vehicle. Remove wheel. Using "C" clamp or large pliers, compress caliper piston until it bottoms in its bore.

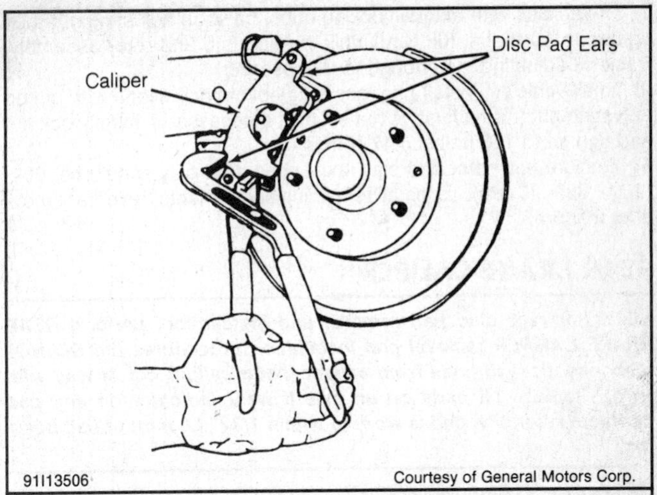
Disc Pad Ears
Caliper
91I13506
Courtesy of General Motors Corp.
Fig. 9: Bending Outer Pad Ears Toward Caliper

2) Disconnect brake hose from caliper. Remove caliper support key bolt. *See Fig. 15*. Using hammer and brass punch, drive out caliper support key and spring. Remove caliper. Remove inner and outer pads.
Installation – 1) Using wire brush, clean corrosion from machined ways on caliper and caliper mount. Apply silicone grease to these surfaces. Install inner pad and anti-rattle spring on caliper mount. *See Fig. 15*. Install outer pad in caliper. Place caliper on caliper mount.
2) Using a hammer and brass punch, install caliper support key and spring. Install caliper support key bolt, ensuring bolt boss fits into circular cutout on caliper support key. Tighten bolt to 15 ft. lbs. (20 N.m).
3) Connect brake hose to caliper and tighten hose bolt to specification. See TORQUE SPECIFICATIONS table at end of article. Bleed brake system. See MANUAL BLEEDING, PRESSURE BLEEDING or VACUUM BLEEDING under BLEEDING BRAKE SYSTEM. Install wheel.

FRONT BRAKE ROTOR

Removal (All 2WD Vehicles Except Lumina APV, Silhouette & Trans Sport) – Remove brake caliper (DO NOT disconnect brake hose). See FRONT BRAKE CALIPER under REMOVAL & INSTALLATION. Remove grease cap from end of hub. Remove cotter pin, nut, washer and outer bearing. Remove rotor and hub assembly.
Installation – 1) Clean and pack wheel bearings. Install rotor and hub assembly. Install outer bearing, washer and nut. Tighten nut to 12 ft. lbs. (16 N.m) while rotating rotor and hub assembly. This seats bearings.
2) Back off nut until it just begins to loosen. Finger-tighten nut. Back off nut until hole in spindle aligns with hole in nut (DO NOT back off more than 1/2 of a flat). Install new cotter pin, bend over ends and ensure ends will not contact grease cap when installed. To complete installation, reverse removal procedure.
Removal & Installation (AWD Astro & Safari, Bravada, Lumina APV, Silhouette, Trans Sport & All 4WD Vehicles Except "V" Series) – Remove brake caliper (DO NOT disconnect brake hose). See FRONT BRAKE CALIPER under REMOVAL & INSTALLATION. Remove rotor. To install, reverse removal procedure.
Removal ("V" Series) – 1) Remove brake caliper (DO NOT disconnect brake hose). See FRONT BRAKE CALIPER under REMOVAL & INSTALLATION. Remove locking hub. See appropriate 4WD LOCKING HUBS article in DRIVE AXLES.
2) Using Wheel Bearing Nut Wrench (J-6893-D) on V15 and V25 models, or (J-26878-A) on V35 models, remove wheel bearing lock nut, ring and adjusting nut (note how hole in ring is aligned with pin on adjusting nut). Remove hub and rotor assembly.
Installation – 1) Install hub and rotor assembly. Install wheel bearing adjusting nut and tighten to 50 ft. lbs. (68 N.m) while turning hub and rotor assembly. This seats wheel bearings.
2) On vehicles with automatic locking hubs, back off adjusting nut then tighten to 35 ft. lbs. (47 N.m) while turning hub and rotor assembly. Back off adjusting nut 3/8 turn maximum.

1991 BRAKES
Disc & Drum (Cont.)

3) On vehicles with manual locking hubs, back off adjusting nut then tighten to 50 ft. lbs. (68 N.m) while turning hub and rotor assembly. Back off adjusting nut enough to free bearing.
4) On all vehicles, install ring, ensuring hole in ring aligns with pin on adjusting nut (turn adjusting nut slightly, if necessary). Install lock nut and tighten to 160 ft. lbs. (217 N.m).
5) Measure hub/rotor end play (axial play). End play should be .001-.010" (.025-.25 mm). To install remaining components, reverse removal procedure.

REAR BRAKE CALIPER

NOTE: For rear disc pad removal and installation, perform REAR BRAKE CALIPER removal and installation procedures but DO NOT disconnect brake hose from caliper (hang caliper out of way with wire). Replace all pads on an axle if wear indicator on any pad contacts rotor or if pad is worn to within 1/32" (.8 mm) of pad backing.

Removal – 1) Remove two-thirds of brake fluid from master cylinder. Raise and support vehicle. Remove wheel. Using "C" clamp or large pliers, compress caliper piston until it bottoms in its bore.
2) Disconnect brake hose from caliper. Remove caliper support key bolt. *See Fig. 15.* Using hammer and brass punch, drive out caliper support key and spring. Remove caliper. Remove inner and outer pads.
Installation – 1) Using wire brush, clean corrosion from machined ways on caliper and caliper mount. Apply silicone grease to these surfaces. Install inner pad and anti-rattle spring on caliper mount. Install outer pad in caliper. Install caliper.
2) Using hammer and brass punch, install caliper support key and spring. Install caliper support key bolt, ensuring bolt boss fits into circular cutout on caliper support key. Tighten bolt to 15 ft. lbs. (20 N.m).
3) Connect brake hose to caliper and tighten hose bolt to specification. See TORQUE SPECIFICATIONS table at end of article. Bleed brake system. See MANUAL BLEEDING, PRESSURE BLEEDING or VACUUM BLEEDING under BLEEDING BRAKE SYSTEM. Install wheel.

REAR BRAKE ROTOR

Removal (9 3/4" & 10 1/2" Full-Floating Axle) – 1) Raise and support vehicle. Remove brake caliper (DO NOT disconnect brake hose). See REAR BRAKE CALIPER under REMOVAL & INSTALLATION. Remove bolts from end of axle shaft.
2) Lightly tap axle shaft flange with soft hammer to loosen shaft. Grip rib on axle shaft flange with locking pliers. Twist axle shaft to start shaft removal. Pull axle shaft from axle housing.
3) Bend lock washer tab away from lock nut. Using Wheel Bearing Nut Wrench (J-2222-C), remove lock nut. Remove lock washer. Remove adjusting nut and washer. Remove hub and rotor assembly.

Installation – 1) Install hub and rotor assembly. Install washer and adjusting nut. Using Wheel Bearing Nut Wrench (J-2222-C), tighten adjusting nut to 50 ft. lbs. (68 N.m) while turning hub and rotor assembly.
2) Back off adjusting nut and tighten to 30-40 ft. lbs. (41-54 N.m) while turning hub and rotor assembly. Back off adjusting nut 135-150 degrees. Install lock washer and lock nut finger tight. Bend lock washer tab over adjusting nut flat at a minimum angle of 30 degrees.
3) Tighten lock nut to 65 ft. lbs. (88 N.m) minimum. Bend lock washer tab over lock nut flat at a minimum angle of 60 degrees. To install remaining components, reverse removal procedure.
Removal (12" Full-Floating Axle) – 1) Raise and support vehicle. Remove brake caliper (DO NOT disconnect brake hose). See REAR BRAKE CALIPER under REMOVAL & INSTALLATION. Remove hub cap and gasket from hub. *See Fig. 10.* Install Adapter (J-2619-01) in tapped hole on axle shaft flange.
2) Using slide hammer and adapter, remove axle shaft. Bend lock washer tab away from lock nut. Using Wheel Bearing Nut Wrench (J-25510), remove lock nut. Remove lock washer, adjusting nut and washer. Remove hub and rotor assembly.
Installation – 1) Install hub and rotor assembly. Install washer and adjusting nut. *See Fig. 10.* Using Wheel Bearing Nut Wrench (J-25510), tighten adjusting nut to 50 ft. lbs. (68 N.m) while turning hub and rotor assembly. Back off adjusting nut 1/8 turn.
2) Install lock washer and lock nut finger tight. Bend lock washer tab over adjusting nut flat. Tighten lock nut to 250 ft. lbs. (339 N.m). Bend lock washer long tab over lock nut flat. To install remaining components, reverse removal procedure.

REAR BRAKE DRUM

Removal & Installation (Semi-Floating Axle) – Ensure parking brake is released. Raise and support rear of vehicle. Remove wheel. Remove brake drum (if necessary, back off adjuster wheel before removing brake drum). To install, reverse removal procedure. Adjust rear brake shoes. See REAR BRAKE SHOES under ADJUSTMENTS.
Removal (Full-Floating Axle) – 1) Ensure parking brake is released. Raise and support rear of vehicle. Remove wheel. Remove bolts from end of axle shaft. *See Fig. 11.*
2) Lightly tap axle shaft flange with soft hammer to loosen shaft. Grip rib on axle shaft flange with locking pliers. Twist axle shaft to start shaft removal. Pull axle shaft from axle housing.
3) Remove retaining ring and key. Using Wheel Bearing Nut Wrench (J-2222-C), remove adjusting nut. Remove washer. Remove hub and brake drum assembly (if necessary, back off adjuster wheel before removing brake drum).
Installation – 1) Apply light coat of bearing lubricant to axle tube. Install hub and brake drum assembly. Install washer and adjusting nut. Using Wheel Bearing Nut Wrench (J-2222-C), tighten adjusting nut 50 ft. lbs. (68 N.m), while turning hub and rotor assembly.

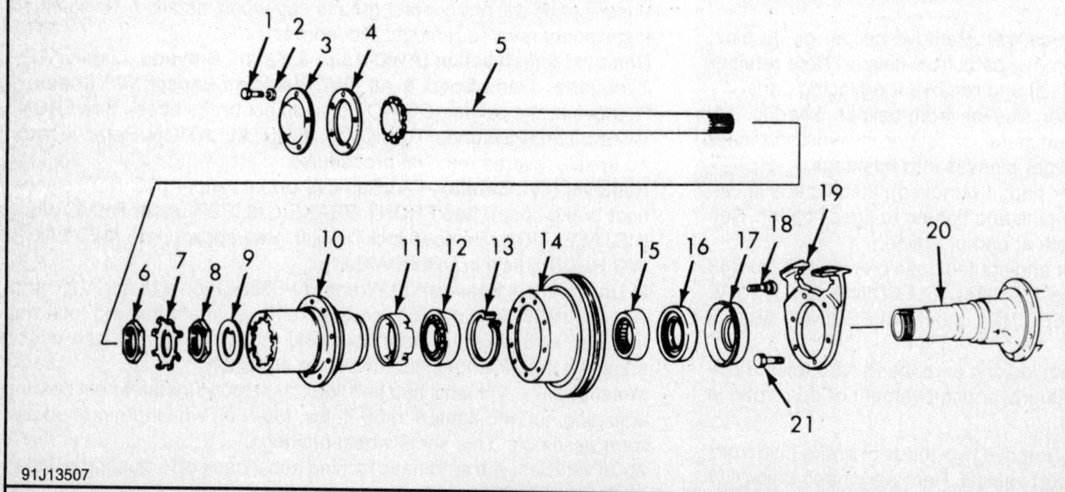
1
2
3
4
5
6
7
8
9
10
11
12
13
14
15
16
17
18
19
20
21
91J13507

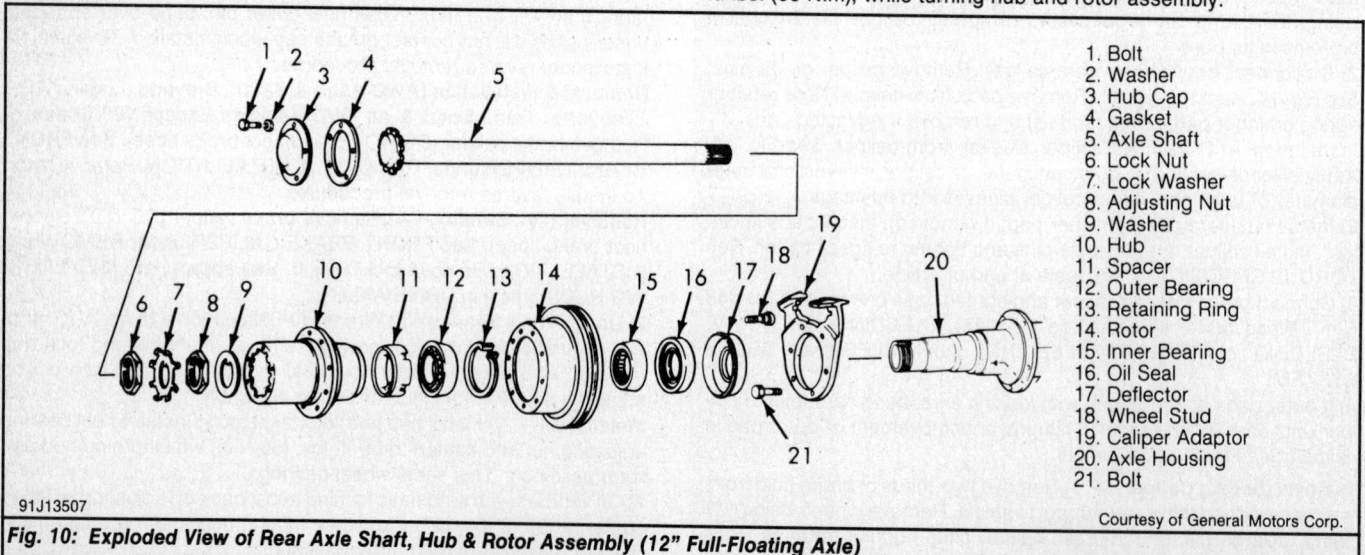

1. Bolt
2. Washer
3. Hub Cap
4. Gasket
5. Axle Shaft
6. Lock Nut
7. Lock Washer
8. Adjusting Nut
9. Washer
10. Hub
11. Spacer
12. Outer Bearing
13. Retaining Ring
14. Rotor
15. Inner Bearing
16. Oil Seal
17. Deflector
18. Wheel Stud
19. Caliper Adaptor
20. Axle Housing
21. Bolt

Courtesy of General Motors Corp.

Fig. 10: Exploded View of Rear Axle Shaft, Hub & Rotor Assembly (12" Full-Floating Axle)

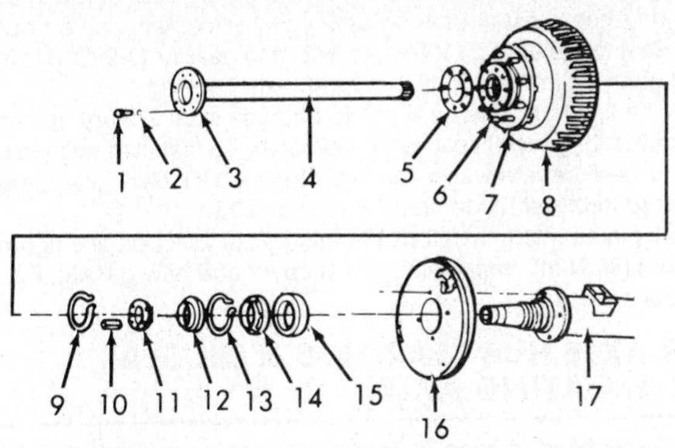
1
2
3
4
5
6
7
8
9
10
11
12
13
14
15
16
17

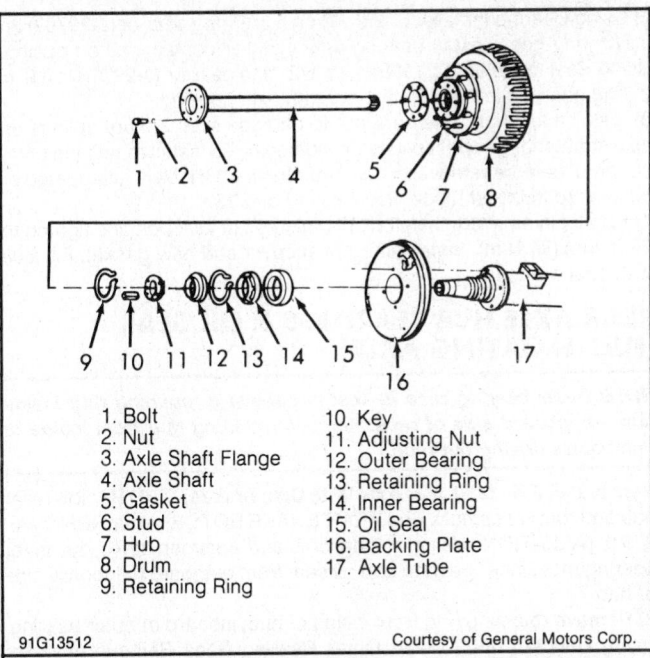

1. Bolt
2. Nut
3. Axle Shaft Flange
4. Axle Shaft
5. Gasket
6. Stud
7. Hub
8. Drum
9. Retaining Ring
10. Key
11. Adjusting Nut
12. Outer Bearing
13. Retaining Ring
14. Inner Bearing
15. Oil Seal
16. Backing Plate
17. Axle Tube

91G13512 Courtesy of General Motors Corp.

Fig. 11: Exploded View of Rear Axle Shaft, Hub & Brake Drum Assembly (Full-Floating Axle)

2) Back off adjusting nut until just loose, then tighten until nut's inboard face contacts outer bearing cone shoulder (torque on nut MUST be zero or finger-tight).
3) Insert key into adjusting nut slot. If slot is in alignment with axle spindle keyway, loosen nut slightly but not more than one slot to align key. Install retaining ring. Install axle shaft and wheel. Lower vehicle.

REAR BRAKE SHOES

NOTE: For rear brake shoe removal and installation, see Figs. 16-18. DO NOT interchange left and right adjusting screw assemblies as one side is right-hand thread and other is left-hand thread.

WHEEL CYLINDER

Removal & Installation – Remove rear brake shoes. See REAR BRAKE SHOES under REMOVAL & INSTALLATION. Disconnect brake line from wheel cylinder. Remove brake cylinder retaining bolts and brake cylinder. To install, reverse removal procedure. Bleed brake system. See MANUAL BLEEDING, PRESSURE BLEEDING or VACUUM BLEEDING under BLEEDING BRAKE SYSTEM.

MASTER CYLINDER

Removal – **1)** With engine off, press brake pedal several times to release vacuum in power brake unit. Clean dirt and grease from master cylinder brake line fittings. Disconnect brake lines from master cylinder and plug line ends.
2) On vehicles with combination valve and bracket attached to master cylinder mounting studs, remove combination valve and bracket. On vehicles without power brake unit, disconnect brake pedal push rod at brake pedal. On all vehicles, remove master cylinder retaining nuts and master cylinder.
Installation – **1)** Bench bleed master cylinder before installing. See MASTER CYLINDER under BLEEDING BRAKE SYSTEM. Position master cylinder on mounting studs. Position combination valve and bracket on mounting studs (if applicable). Loosely install master cylinder retaining nuts. Connect brake lines to master cylinder but DO NOT tighten.
2) Tighten master cylinder retaining nuts. Tighten brake lines. Connect brake pedal push rod (if disconnected). Fill fluid reservoir. Bleed brake system. See MANUAL BLEEDING, PRESSURE BLEEDING or VACUUM BLEEDING under BLEEDING BRAKE SYSTEM.

POWER BRAKE BOOSTER

NOTE: For Hydro-Boost removal and installation, see POWER BRAKE BOOSTER – BENDIX HYDRO-BOOST article.

Removal & Installation – **1)** Remove master cylinder. See MASTER CYLINDER under REMOVAL & INSTALLATION. Ensure no brake fluid contacts ABS control unit (if equipped) or related electrical connectors and wiring.
2) Disconnect vacuum hose from booster. Disconnect booster push rod from brake pedal. Remove booster mounting nuts from inside vehicle. Remove booster and gasket.
3) To install, reverse removal procedure. Bleed brake system if lines were disconnected from master cylinder. See MANUAL BLEEDING, PRESSURE BLEEDING or VACUUM BLEEDING under BLEEDING BRAKE SYSTEM.

HEIGHT-SENSING PROPORTIONING VALVE

Removal & Installation ("C" & "K" Series) – Raise vehicle by frame, allowing rear axle to hang free. Remove bracket that covers valve. Remove nut and lever from valve shaft. *See Fig. 4*. Clean area around brake line fittings at valve. Disconnect brake lines from valve. Remove valve-to-frame bolts and valve.
2) To install, reverse removal procedure, ensuring rear axle is hanging free and valve is securely bolted to frame when lever is attached to valve (this ensures correct valve adjustment). Bleed brake system. See MANUAL BLEEDING, PRESSURE BLEEDING or VACUUM BLEEDING under BLEEDING BRAKE SYSTEM.
Removal & Installation ("P" Series & "R" & "V" Series) – Raise vehicle by frame, allowing rear axle to hang free. Clean area around brake line fittings at valve. *See Fig. 5*. Disconnect brake lines from valve. Remove nut and lever from valve shaft. Remove valve-to-frame bolts and valve.
2) To install, reverse removal procedure. If installing new valve, adjust the new valve. See HEIGHT-SENSING PROPORTIONING VALVE under ADJUSTMENTS. Bleed brake system. See MANUAL BLEEDING, PRESSURE BLEEDING or VACUUM BLEEDING under BLEEDING BRAKE SYSTEM.

COMBINATION VALVE

Removal – Disconnect brake warning light electrical connector from combination valve switch. Disconnect brake lines from valve. Cap brake line ends. Remove valve mounting bolts. Remove valve.
Installation – To install, reverse removal procedure. Bleed brake system. See MANUAL BLEEDING, PRESSURE BLEEDING or VACUUM BLEEDING under BLEEDING BRAKE SYSTEM. Center the brake warning light switch piston by applying moderate to heavy force on brake pedal.

REAR AXLE BEARING & OIL SEAL (SEMI-FLOATING AXLE)

Removal (Astro, Safari & "S" & "T" Series) – **1)** Raise and support vehicle. Remove wheels and brake drums. Loosen differential cover plate and drain lubricant from axle. Remove cover plate.
2) Remove pinion shaft lock bolt. *See Figs. 12 and 13.* Remove pinion shaft. Push axle shaft toward center of vehicle and remove "C" lock from end of axle shaft. Remove axle shaft.
3) Pry seal from axle housing. Using Slide Hammer (J-2619-01) and Axle Bearing Puller (J-22813-01), remove bearing from axle housing.
Installation – **1)** Lubricate bearing with axle lubricant. Using Handle (J-8092) and Bearing Installer (J-23765), install bearing in axle housing until bearing installer bottoms against shoulder of axle housing.
2) Using Seal Installer (J-23771), install seal until even with surface of axle housing. Lubricate seal lips with axle lubricant. Install axle shaft and "C" lock. *See Figs. 12 and 13.* Pull axle shaft outward to ensure "C" lock seats in side gear.
3) Install pinion shaft. Install NEW pinion shaft lock bolt. Tighten lock bolt to 25 ft. lbs. (34 N.m). Install differential cover and new gasket. Fill drive axle with axle lubricant.

1991 BRAKES
Disc & Drum (Cont.)

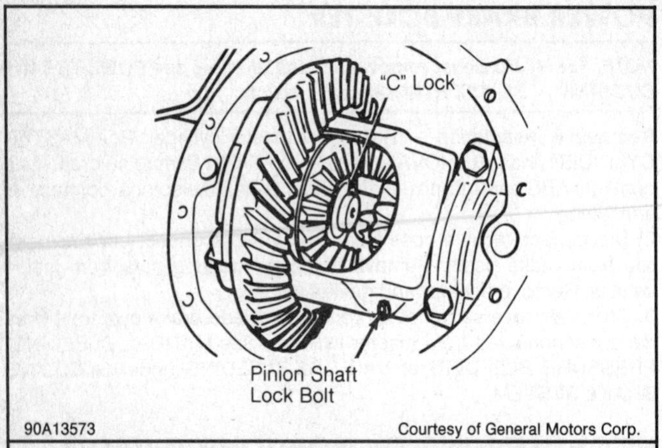
"C" Lock
Pinion Shaft
Lock Bolt
90A13573
Courtesy of General Motors Corp.

Fig. 12: Locating "C" Lock & Pinion Shaft Lock Bolt (Astro, Safari & "S" & "T" Series Shown; Others Similar)

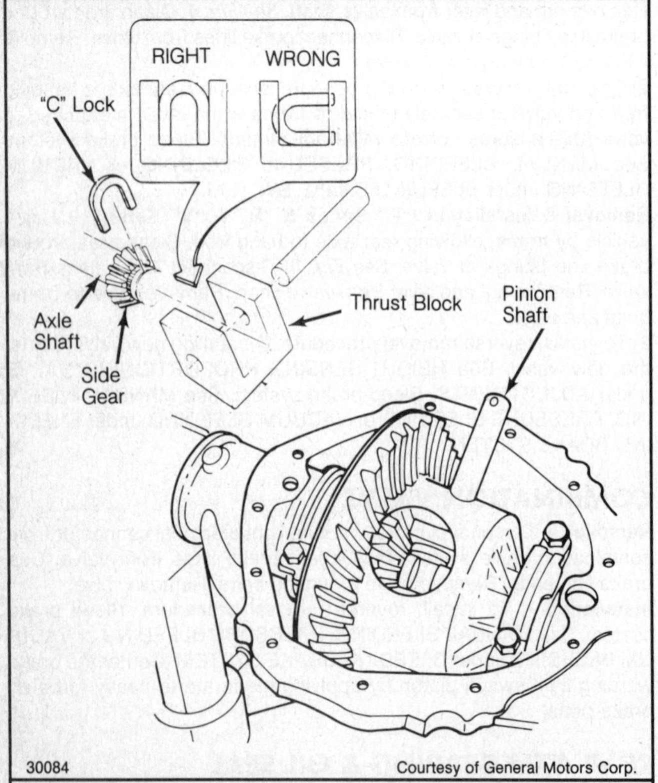
RIGHT
WRONG
"C" Lock
Thrust Block
Pinion
Shaft
Axle
Shaft
Side
Gear
30084
Courtesy of General Motors Corp.

Fig. 13: Removing & Installing "C" Lock & Pinion Shaft On Locking Differential (Typical)

Removal (Except Astro, Safari & "S" & "T" Series) – 1) Raise and support vehicle. Remove wheel and brake drum. Loosen differential cover plate and drain lubricant from axle. Remove cover plate. Remove pinion shaft lock bolt. *See Figs. 12 and 13.*

2) On locking differential models, remove pinion shaft part way. Rotate differential case until pinion shaft contacts axle housing. Using screwdriver, rotate "C" lock until it aligns with thrust block. On all models, push axle shaft toward center of vehicle and remove "C" lock from end of axle shaft.

3) Remove axle shaft from axle housing. Using Seal Remover (J-23689), remove seal from axle housing. Remove bearing using Slide Hammer (J-2619-01) and Bearing Puller (J-23689) on 8 1/2" ring gear, or (J-29712) on 9 1/2" ring gear.

Installation – 1) Lubricate bearing and seal lips with wheel bearing grease. Fill axle cavity between seal and axle with wheel bearing grease.

2) Using Bearing Installer (J-23690) on 8 1/2" ring gear or (J-29709) on 9 1/2" ring gear, install bearing until installer contacts axle housing. Using Seal Installer (J-21128) on 8 1/2" ring gear or (J-29713) on 9 1/2" ring gear, install seal until even with axle housing.

3) Install axle shaft. Use care not to damage seal. Ensure splines on axle shaft engage with splines on side gear. To install remaining components, reverse removal procedure. Ensure "C" lock is fully seated or positioned in thrust block. *See Figs. 12 and 13.*

4) Install pinion shaft, install NEW pinion shaft lock bolt and tighten to 25 ft. lbs. (34 N.m). Install differential cover and new gasket. Fill axle with gear lubricant.

REAR AXLE HUB BEARINGS & OIL SEAL (FULL-FLOATING AXLE)

NOTE: Outer bearing race is seated against a retaining ring inside hub, on inboard side of race. Remove retaining ring from inside of hub before driving out race.

Removal (9 3/4" & 10 1/2" Axle With Disc Brakes) – 1) Remove rear hub and rotor assembly. See REAR BRAKE ROTOR under REMOVAL & INSTALLATION. Using a long drift and hammer, drive out inner bearing race, inner bearing and oil seal from outboard to inboard side of hub.

2) Remove retaining ring from inside of hub, inboard of outer bearing. Using Handle (J-8092) and Outer Bearing Race Remover/Installer (J-24426), drive out outer bearing race from outboard to inboard side of hub.

Installation – 1) Clean and pack bearings with Wheel Bearing Lubricant (1051344). Using handle and Bearing Race Installer (J-8608), drive outer wheel bearing race into hub from inboard side of hub (ensure chamfered edge of bearing race installer is facing upward so that it does not contact bearing race).

2) Install retaining ring on inboard side of outer bearing race. Turn hub and rotor assembly inboard side down. Using Outer Bearing Race Remover/Installer (J-24426), seat outer bearing race against retaining ring.

3) Using Inner Bearing Race Remover/Installer (J-24427), drive inner bearing race into hub from inboard side of hub. Install inner bearing. Install new oil seal using Axle Shaft Seal Installer (J-24428).

4) To complete installation, reverse removal procedure. To adjust wheel bearings, follow REAR BRAKE ROTOR installation procedure under REMOVAL & INSTALLATION.

Removal (9 3/4" & 10 1/2" Axle With Drum Brakes) – 1) Remove rear hub and drum assembly. See REAR BRAKE DRUM under REMOVAL & INSTALLATION. Using a long drift and hammer, drive out inner bearing race, inner bearing and oil seal from outboard to inboard side of hub. *See Fig. 11.*

2) Remove retaining ring from inside of hub, inboard of outer bearing. Using Handle (J-8092) and Outer Bearing Race Remover/Installer (J-24426), drive out outer bearing race from outboard to inboard side of hub.

Installation – 1) Clean and pack bearings with Wheel Bearing Lubricant (1051344). Using handle and Bearing Race Installer (J-8608), drive outer wheel bearing race into hub from inboard side of hub (ensure chamfered edge of bearing race installer is facing upward so it does not contact bearing race). *See Fig. 11.*

2) Install retaining ring on inboard side of outer bearing race. Turn hub and rotor assembly inboard side down. Using Outer Bearing Race Remover/Installer (J-24426), seat outer bearing race against retaining ring.

3) Using Inner Bearing Race Remover/Installer (J-24427), drive inner bearing race into hub from inboard side of hub. Install inner bearing. Install new oil seal using Axle Shaft Seal Installer (J-24428).

4) To complete installation, reverse removal procedure. To adjust wheel bearing, follow REAR BRAKE DRUM installation procedure under REMOVAL & INSTALLATION.

Removal & Installation (12" Axle) – Remove rear hub and rotor assembly. See REAR BRAKE ROTOR under REMOVAL & INSTALLATION. Note how outer bearing race is seated against retaining ring inside hub, on inboard side of race. *See Fig. 10.* Hub bearing removal and installation procedure is not available from manufacturer.

OVERHAUL

WARNING: DO NOT hone composite master cylinder bore. Honing destroys hardened surface, causing premature piston seal failure. If bore surface is rough or pitted, replace master cylinder.

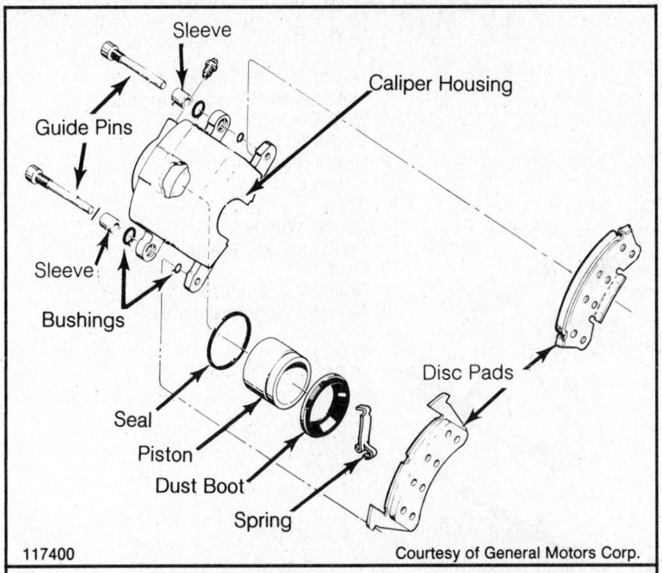
Sleeve
Guide Pins
Caliper Housing
Sleeve
Bushings
Seal
Piston
Dust Boot
Spring
Disc Pads
117400
Courtesy of General Motors Corp.

Fig. 14: Exploded View of Floating Caliper Assembly (Typical)

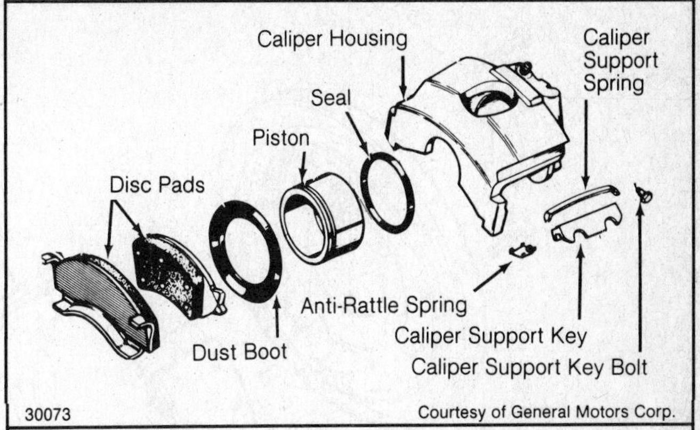
Caliper Housing
Caliper Support Spring
Seal
Piston
Disc Pads
Anti-Rattle Spring
Caliper Support Key
Dust Boot
Caliper Support Key Bolt
30073
Courtesy of General Motors Corp.

Fig. 16: Exploded View of Sliding Caliper Assembly (Typical)

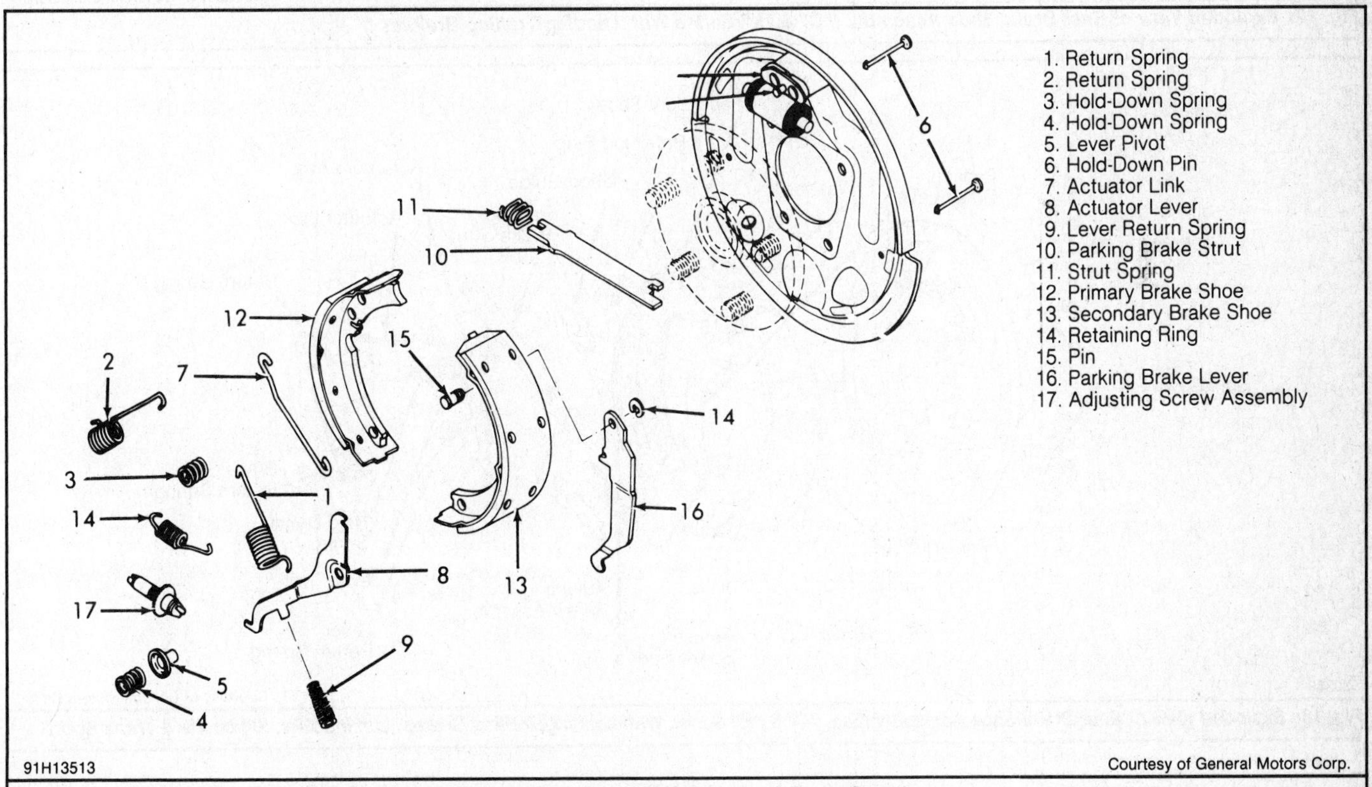
1. Return Spring
2. Return Spring
3. Hold-Down Spring
4. Hold-Down Spring
5. Lever Pivot
6. Hold-Down Pin
7. Actuator Link
8. Actuator Lever
9. Lever Return Spring
10. Parking Brake Strut
11. Strut Spring
12. Primary Brake Shoe
13. Secondary Brake Shoe
14. Retaining Ring
15. Pin
16. Parking Brake Lever
17. Adjusting Screw Assembly
91H13513
Courtesy of General Motors Corp.

Fig. 15: Exploded View of Rear Brake Shoe Assembly (Lumina APV, Silhouette & Trans Sport)

1991 BRAKES
Disc & Drum (Cont.)

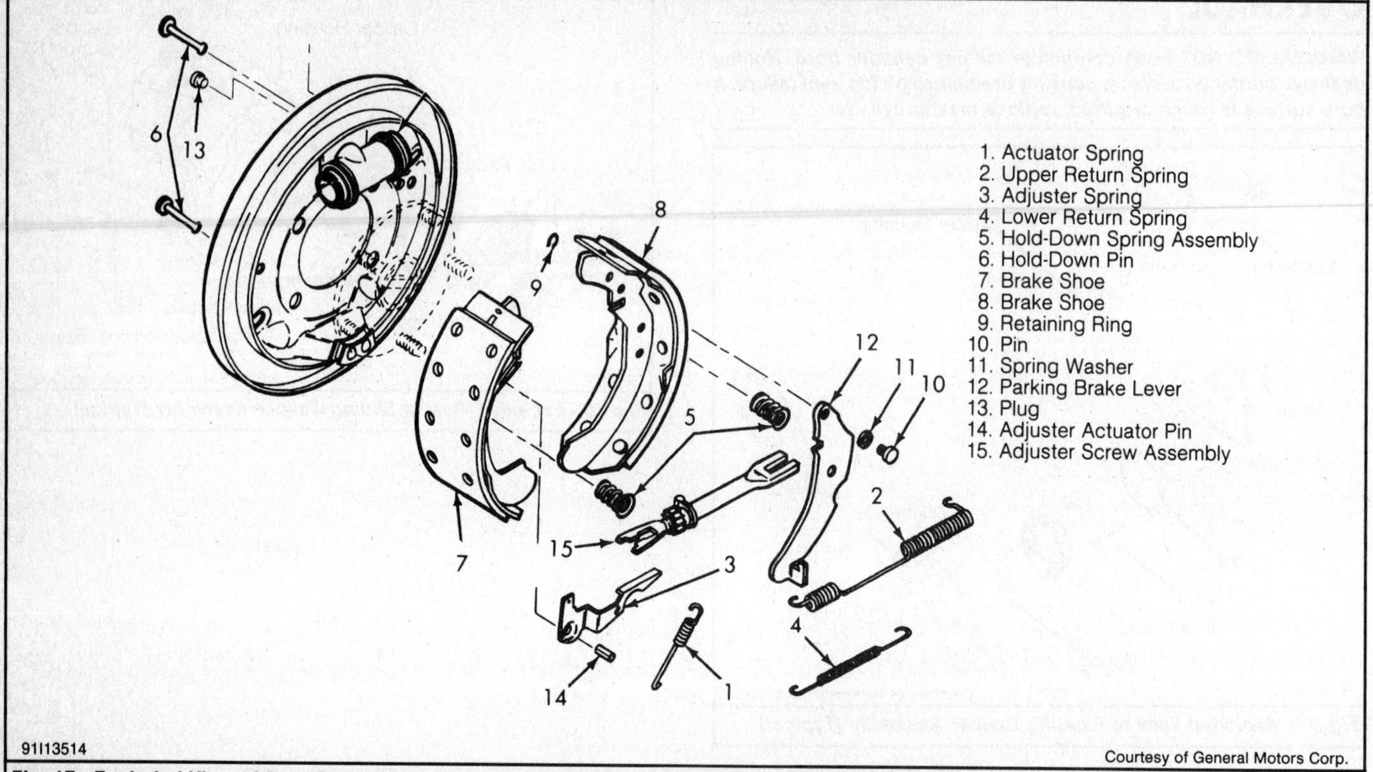
6
13
8
9
12
11
10
5
2
15
7
3
4
14
1
1. Actuator Spring
2. Upper Return Spring
3. Adjuster Spring
4. Lower Return Spring
5. Hold-Down Spring Assembly
6. Hold-Down Pin
7. Brake Shoe
8. Brake Shoe
9. Retaining Ring
10. Pin
11. Spring Washer
12. Parking Brake Lever
13. Plug
14. Adjuster Actuator Pin
15. Adjuster Screw Assembly
91I13514
Courtesy of General Motors Corp.

Fig. 17: Exploded View of Rear Brake Shoe Assembly ("C" & "K" Series With Leading/Trailing Brakes)

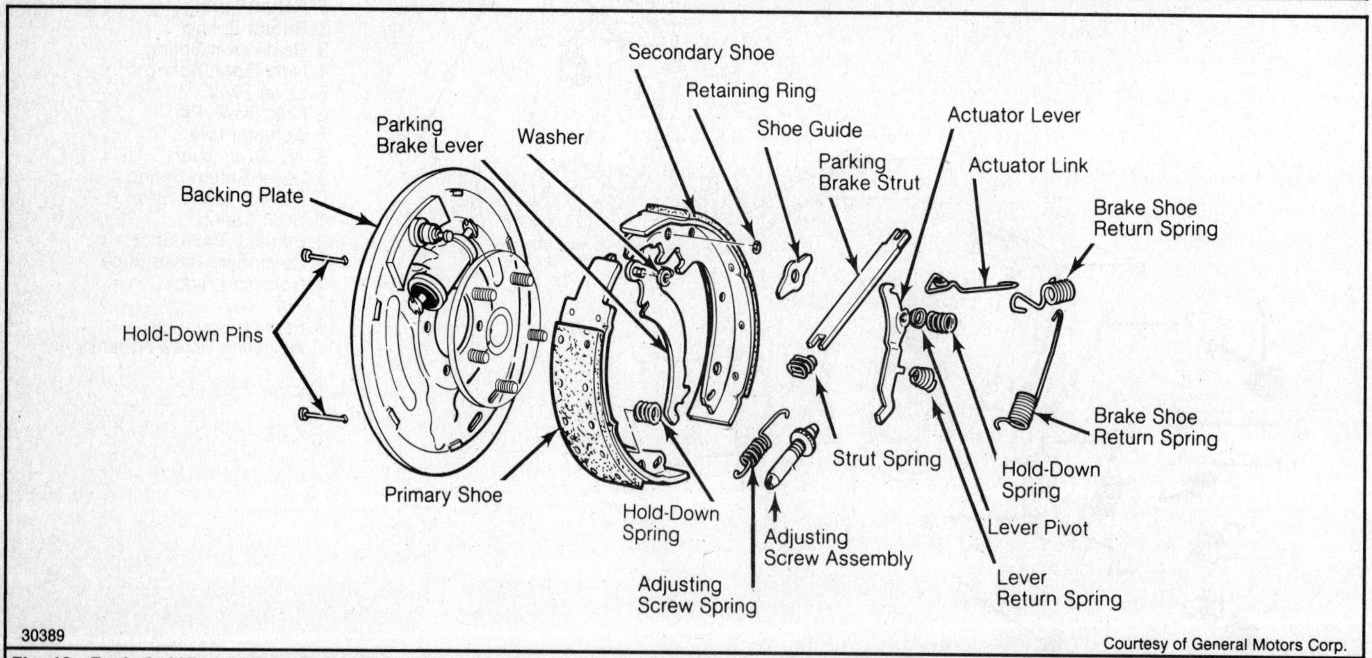
Secondary Shoe
Retaining Ring
Shoe Guide
Actuator Lever
Parking Brake Lever
Washer
Parking Brake Strut
Actuator Link
Backing Plate
Brake Shoe Return Spring
Hold-Down Pins
Brake Shoe Return Spring
Strut Spring
Hold-Down Spring
Primary Shoe
Hold-Down Spring
Lever Pivot
Adjusting Screw Assembly
Lever Return Spring
Adjusting Screw Spring
30389
Courtesy of General Motors Corp.

Fig. 18: Exploded View of Rear Brake Shoe Assembly (Exc. "C" & "K" Series With Leading/Trailing Brakes, Lumina APV, Silhouette & Trans Sport)

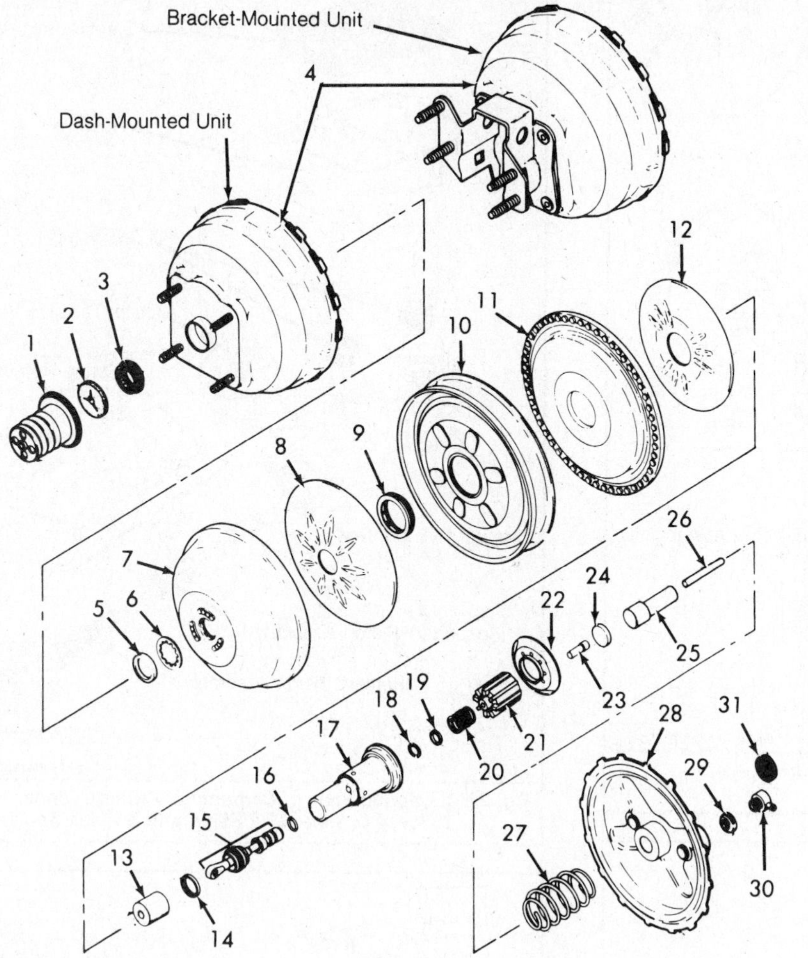

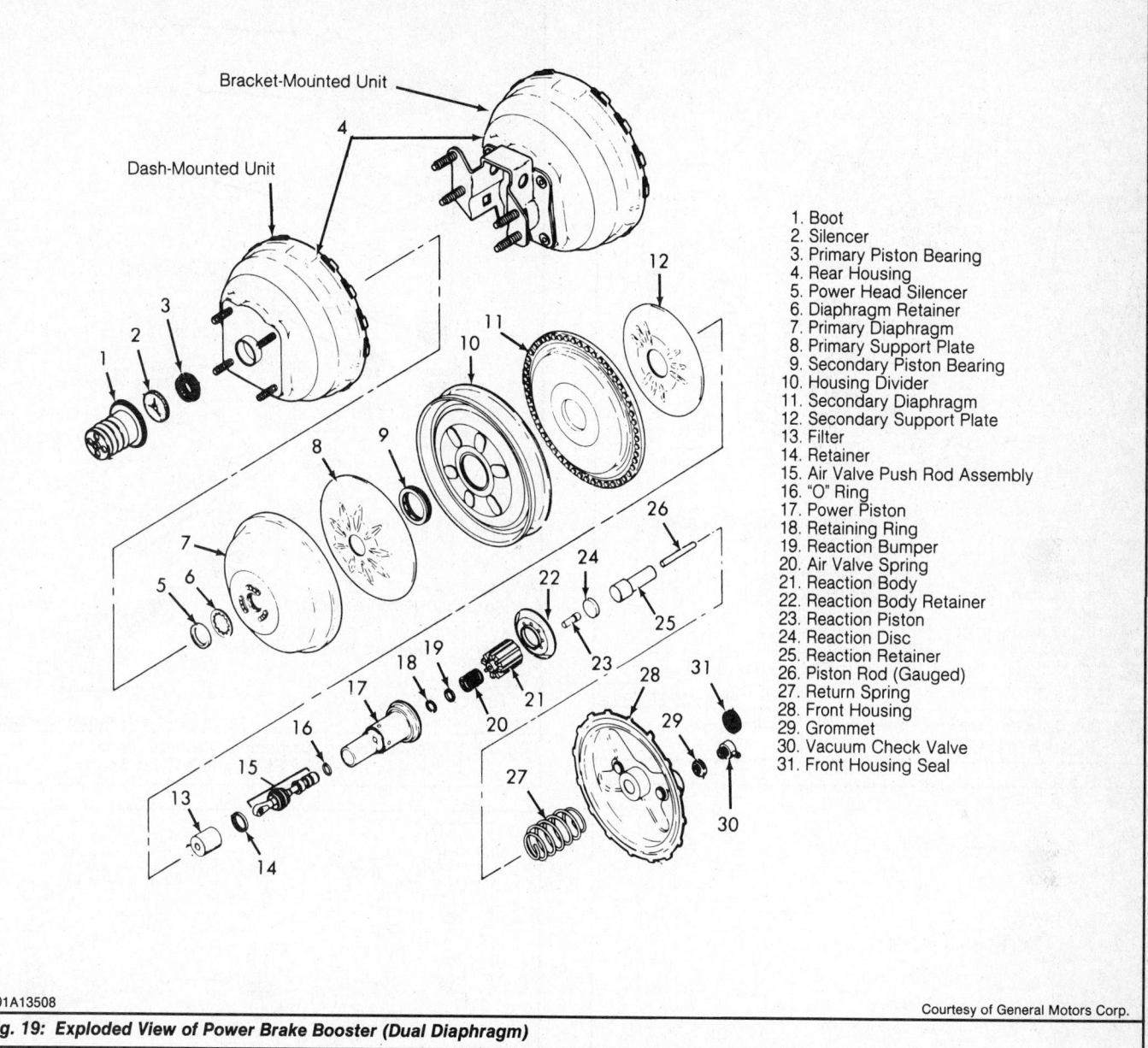

Bracket-Mounted Unit
Dash-Mounted Unit
4
1
2
3
5
6
7
8
9
10
11
12
13
14
15
16
17
18
19
20
21
22
23
24
25
26
27
28
29
30
31

1. Boot
2. Silencer
3. Primary Piston Bearing
4. Rear Housing
5. Power Head Silencer
6. Diaphragm Retainer
7. Primary Diaphragm
8. Primary Support Plate
9. Secondary Piston Bearing
10. Housing Divider
11. Secondary Diaphragm
12. Secondary Support Plate
13. Filter
14. Retainer
15. Air Valve Push Rod Assembly
16. "O" Ring
17. Power Piston
18. Retaining Ring
19. Reaction Bumper
20. Air Valve Spring
21. Reaction Body
22. Reaction Body Retainer
23. Reaction Piston
24. Reaction Disc
25. Reaction Retainer
26. Piston Rod (Gauged)
27. Return Spring
28. Front Housing
29. Grommet
30. Vacuum Check Valve
31. Front Housing Seal

91A13508

Courtesy of General Motors Corp.

Fig. 19: Exploded View of Power Brake Booster (Dual Diaphragm)

1991 BRAKES
Disc & Drum (Cont.)

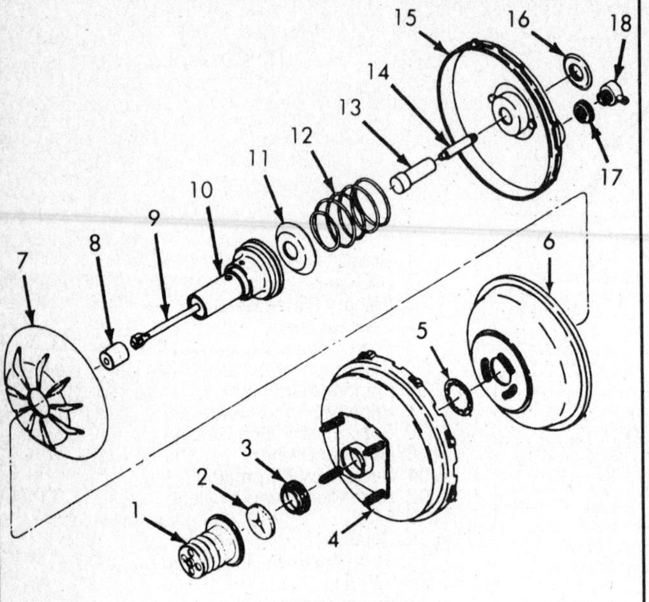
15
16
18
14
13
12
11
10
17
9
8
7
6
5
3
2
1
4

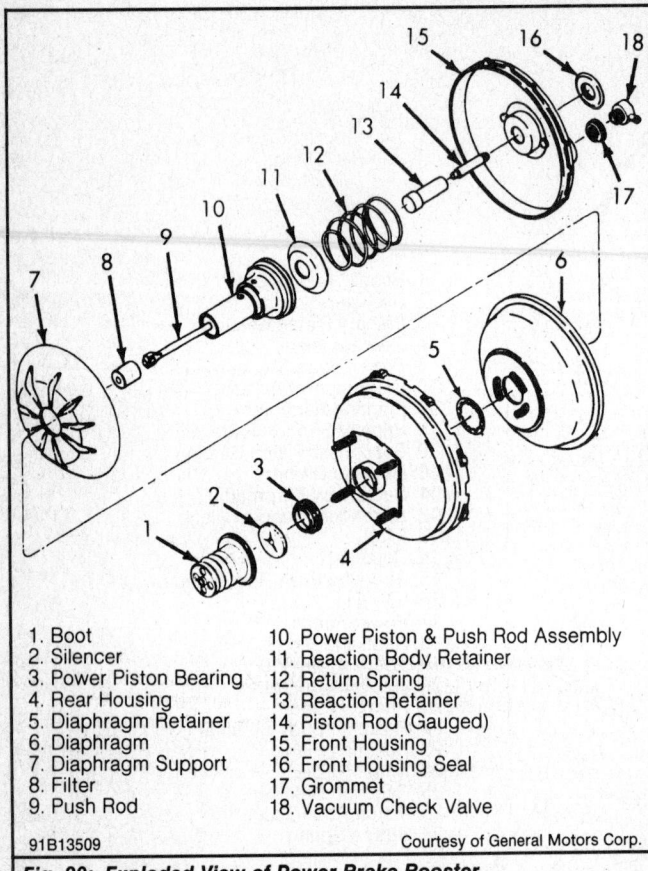

1. Boot
2. Silencer
3. Power Piston Bearing
4. Rear Housing
5. Diaphragm Retainer
6. Diaphragm
7. Diaphragm Support
8. Filter
9. Push Rod
10. Power Piston & Push Rod Assembly
11. Reaction Body Retainer
12. Return Spring
13. Reaction Retainer
14. Piston Rod (Gauged)
15. Front Housing
16. Front Housing Seal
17. Grommet
18. Vacuum Check Valve

91B13509 Courtesy of General Motors Corp.

Fig. 20: Exploded View of Power Brake Booster (Single Diaphragm)

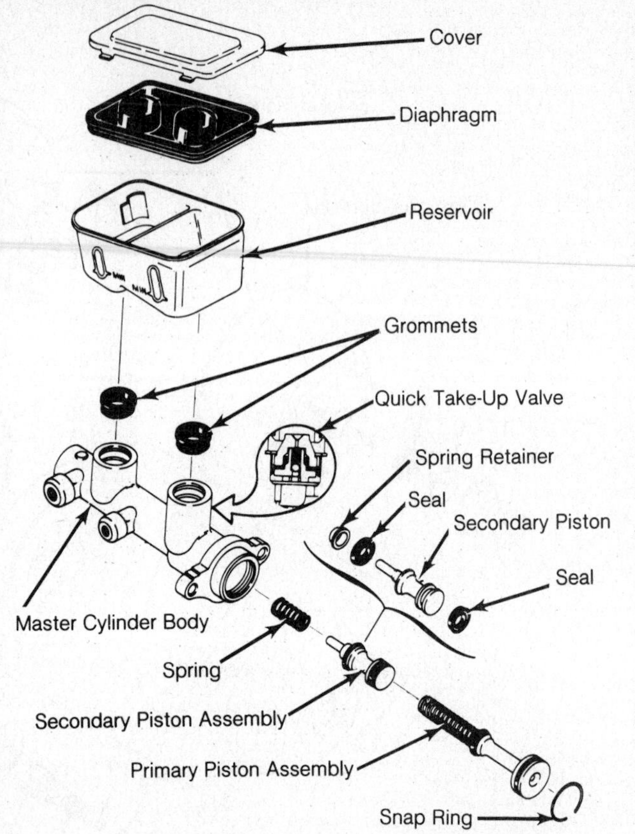
Cover
Diaphragm
Reservoir
Grommets
Quick Take-Up Valve
Spring Retainer
Seal
Secondary Piston
Seal
Master Cylinder Body
Spring
Secondary Piston Assembly
Primary Piston Assembly
Snap Ring

30354 Courtesy of General Motors Corp.

Fig. 22: Exploded View of Composite Master Cylinder (Except Lumina APV, Silhouette & Trans Sport)

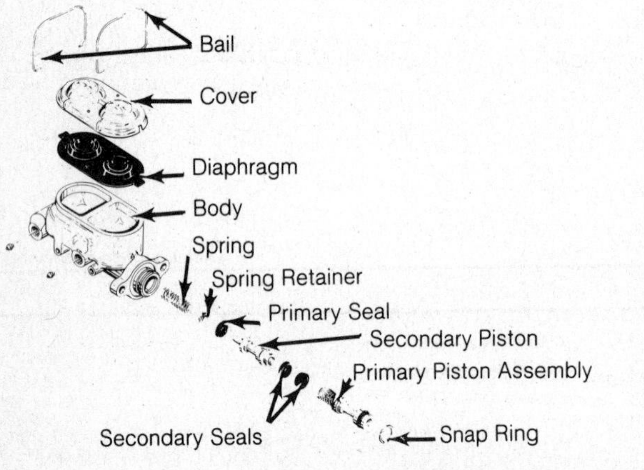
Bail
Cover
Diaphragm
Body
Spring
Spring Retainer
Primary Seal
Secondary Piston
Primary Piston Assembly
Secondary Seals
Snap Ring

30349 Courtesy of General Motors Corp.

Fig. 21: Exploded View of Cast Iron Master Cylinder

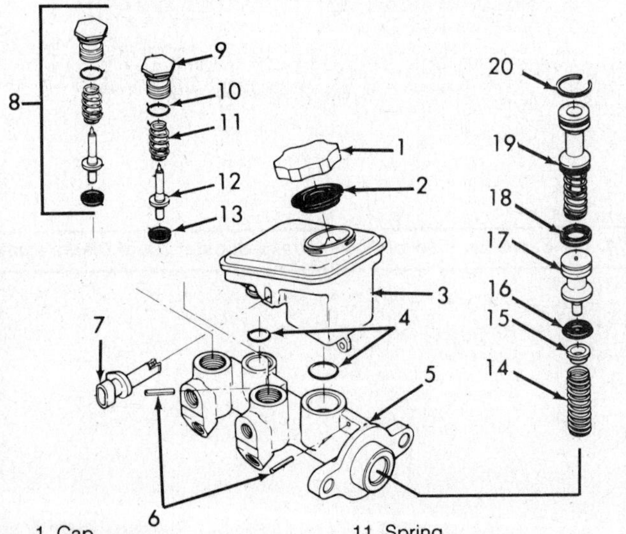
8
9
10
11
12
13
1
2
3
4
5
6
7
20
19
18
17
16
15
14

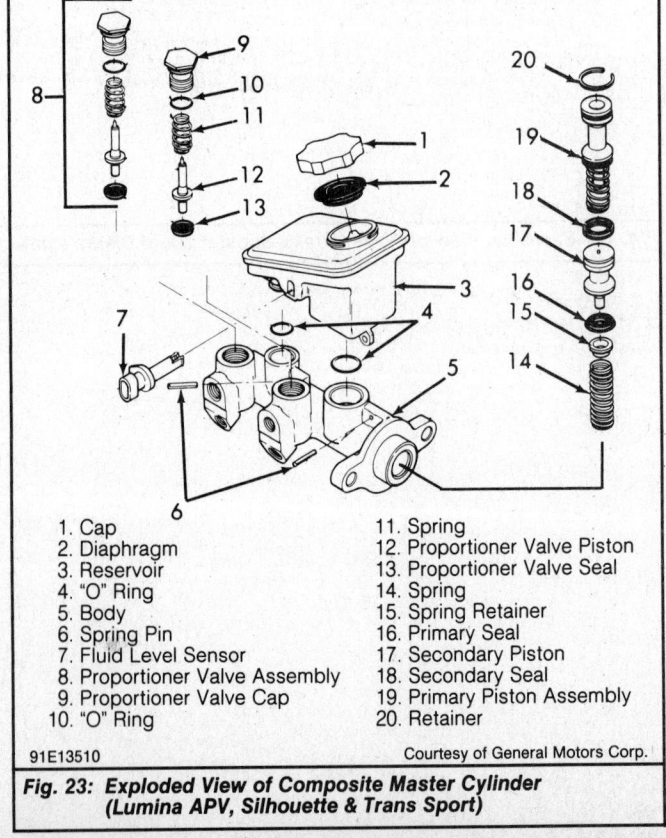

1. Cap
2. Diaphragm
3. Reservoir
4. "O" Ring
5. Body
6. Spring Pin
7. Fluid Level Sensor
8. Proportioner Valve Assembly
9. Proportioner Valve Cap
10. "O" Ring
11. Spring
12. Proportioner Valve Piston
13. Proportioner Valve Seal
14. Spring
15. Spring Retainer
16. Primary Seal
17. Secondary Piston
18. Secondary Seal
19. Primary Piston Assembly
20. Retainer

91E13510 Courtesy of General Motors Corp.

Fig. 23: Exploded View of Composite Master Cylinder (Lumina APV, Silhouette & Trans Sport)

TORQUE SPECIFICATIONS

TORQUE SPECIFICATIONS

Application	Ft. Lbs. (N.m)
Axle Shaft-To-Hub Bolt (9 3/4" & 10 1/2" Ring Gear)	115 (156)
Caliper Guide Pin (Floating Caliper)	
"C" & "K" Series	28 (38)
Except "C" & "K" Series	37 (50)
Caliper Support Key Bolt (Sliding Caliper)	15 (20)
Differential Cover Bolt	20 (27)
Front Brake Hose-To-Caliper Bolt	32 (43)
Pinion Shaft Lock Bolt [1]	25 (34)
Rear Wheel Bearing Lock Nut	
9 3/4" & 10 1/2" Ring Gear	65 (88)
12" Ring Gear	250 (339)
Wheel Lug Nut	
Astro, Bravada & Safari	90 (122)
Lumina APV, Silhouette & Trans Sport	100 (136)
"C" & "K" Series	
With Dual Rear Wheels	
Light Duty	140 (190)
Heavy Duty	175 (237)
With Single Rear Wheels	120 (163)
"G" Series	
G15 & G25	100 (136)
G35	
With Dual Rear Wheels	140 (190)
With Single Rear Wheels	120 (163)
"P" Series & "R" & "V" Series	
With Dual Rear Wheels	
8 Lug	140 (190)
10 Lug	175 (237)
With Single Rear Wheels	
5 Lug	100 (136)
6 Lug	
Aluminum Wheels	100 (136)
Steel Wheels	88 (119)
8 Lug	120 (163)
"S" & "T" Series Except Bravada	
With Aluminum Wheels	90 (122)
With Steel Wheels	73 (99)

[1] – Use NEW pinion shaft lock bolt. DO NOT reuse bolt.

DRUM BRAKE SPECIFICATIONS

DRUM BRAKE SPECIFICATIONS

Application	In. (mm)
Astro, Safari & "S" & "T" Series	
Drum	
Original Diameter	9.50 (241.3)
Discard Diameter	9.56 (242.8)
Maximum Refinish Diameter	9.59 (243.6)
Width	2.00 (50.8)
Lumina APV, Silhouette & Trans Sport	
Drum	
Original Diameter	8.86 (225.0)
Discard Diameter	8.91 (226.3)
Maximum Refinish Diameter	8.89 (225.8)
Wheel Cylinder Diameter	.748 (19.00)
All Others	
Drum	
Original Diameter	10.00 (254.0) 11.15 (283.2) 12.00 (304.8) 13.00 (330.2)
Discard Diameter	
10.00" Drum	10.09 (256.3)
11.15" Drum	11.24 (285.5)
12.00" Drum	12.090 (307.09)
13.00" Drum	13.09 (332.5)
Maximum Refinish Diameter	
10.00" Drum	10.05 (255.3)
11.15" Drum	11.21 (284.7)
12.00" Drum	12.060 (306.32)
13.00" Drum	13.06 (331.7)
Width	
10.00" Drum	2.25 (57.0)
11.15" Drum	2.75 (69.9)
12.00" Drum	[1]
13.00" Drum	2.50 (63.5) Or 3.50 (88.9)

[1] – Information is not available from manufacturer.

DISC BRAKE SPECIFICATIONS

DISC BRAKE SPECIFICATIONS

Application	In. (mm)
Lateral Runout	
All Models	.004 (.10)
Parallelism	
All Models	.0005 (.013)
Original Thickness	
Astro & Safari	1.04 (26.4)
Lumina APV, Silhouette & Trans Sport	1.043 (26.49)
"S" & "T" Series	1.03 (26.2)
All Others	
11.57" Rotor	
4600 Lbs. GVW	1.00 (25.4)
6400 & 7200 Lbs. GVW	1.25 (31.8)
11.86" Rotor	1.29 (32.8)
12.50" Rotor	
"C" & "K" Series	1.26 (32.0)
Except "C" & "K" Series	
8400 Lbs. GVW	1.28 (32.5)
10,000 Lbs. GVW	1.54 (39.1)
13.75" Rotor	1.54 (39.1)
14.25" Rotor	1.54 (39.1)
Minimum Refinish Thickness [1]	
Astro, Safari & "S" & "T" Series	.980 (24.89)
Lumina APV, Silhouette & Trans Sport	.972 (24.69)
All Others	
11.57 X 1.00" Rotor	.980 (24.89)
11.57 X 1.25" Rotor	1.230 (31.24)
11.86 X 1.29" Rotor	1.230 (31.24)
12.50 X 1.26" Rotor	1.230 (31.24)
12.50 X 1.28" Rotor	1.230 (31.24)
12.50 X 1.54" Rotor	1.480 (37.59)
13.75 X 1.54" Rotor	1.480 (37.59)
14.25 X 1.54" Rotor	1.480 (37.59)
Discard Thickness	
Astro, Safari & "S" & "T" Series	.965 (24.51)
Lumina APV, Silhouette & Trans Sport	.957 (24.31)
All Others	
11.57 X 1.00" Rotor	.965 (24.51)
11.57 X 1.25" Rotor	1.215 (30.86)
11.86 X 1.29" Rotor	1.215 (30.86)
12.50 X 1.26" Rotor	1.215 (30.86)
12.50 X 1.28" Rotor	1.215 (30.86)
12.50 X 1.54" Rotor	1.465 (37.21)
13.75 X 1.54" Rotor	1.465 (37.21)
14.25 X 1.54" Rotor	1.465 (37.21)

[1] – Use specification stamped on rotor (if available).

1991 BRAKES
Power Brake Booster – Bendix Hydro-Boost

Astro, Safari, "C" & "K" Series, "G" Series, "P" Series, "R" & "V" Series

DESCRIPTION

System uses power steering pump fluid pressure to operate booster. Master cylinder is mounted to output push rod of booster. Booster also has reserve system to provide at least 2 assisted braking applications. If reserve system is depleted, brakes can be applied manually.

OPERATION

BRAKES RELEASED

With pedal released, spool valve return spring holds spool valve open. Spool valve allows fluid flow between power steering pump and power steering gear.

Fluid pressure is blocked from entering boost pressure chamber by lands on spool valve. Boost pressure chamber is vented through spool valve, to pump return port, and back to power steering pump.

BRAKES APPLIED

Pressing pedal moves pedal rod and spool valve. This closes fluid return to pump and admits fluid into boost chamber from pressure port. Additional valve movement restricts flow between power steering pump and power steering gear.

As fluid pressure increases in boost chamber, it forces piston forward, actuating master cylinder piston and applying brakes. If steering is required while braking, power steering pump pressure will rise and spool valve will shift open, allowing more fluid to flow to power steering gear.

RESERVE SYSTEM

System consists of charging valve, accumulator valve and spring-loaded accumulator. Accumulator is integral with booster. System is open to pressure port of booster.

Charging valve has an orifice and ball check valve. Fluid from pump passes through orifice in valve, unseats ball check valve and enters accumulator. Ball check valve prevents reverse flow.

Accumulator valve is poppet-type valve held closed by accumulator pressure. If no pump pressure is available, an actuator on spool valve sleeve opens accumulator valve. Fluid pressure can also enter accumulator from boost chamber through accumulator valve, when boost chamber pressure exceeds accumulator pressure.

Pressure relief valve vents accumulator to pump return port when pressure in accumulator exceeds approximately 1600 psi (112 kg/cm²).

TROUBLE SHOOTING

For trouble shooting information, refer to charts in Fig. 6 at end of article.

TESTING

NOTE: Inoperative Hydro-Boost cannot cause noisy brakes, fading brake pedal or pulling brakes. If one of these conditions exists, other components of brake system are at fault.

PRELIMINARY CHECKS

1) Check engine idle speed. Check all power steering hoses and brake lines for leaks or restrictions. Fill master cylinder with brake fluid. Fill power steering pump reservoir with power steering fluid.

2) Check for air in power steering fluid reservoir. Check power steering belt tension and condition. Check power steering pump pressure.

BOOSTER FUNCTIONAL TEST

With engine off, press brake pedal several times to deplete accumulator reserve. Press and hold brake pedal with about 40 lbs. (18 kg) pressure. Start engine. Brake pedal should fall slightly, then push back against foot. If no action is felt, booster is not operating properly.

ACCUMULATOR LEAK-DOWN TEST

1) Start engine. Charge accumulator by applying brakes or turning steering wheel from stop-to-stop. Turn engine off. Allow vehicle to sit for one hour. Apply and release brake pedal. There should be at least 2 power-assisted applications. This indicates the accumulator is retaining a charge.

2) If accumulator does not retain charge for one hour but functions normally immediately after charging, replace accumulator valve. If accumulator can be heard charging and discharging but does not hold a charge, replace accumulator valve. See OVERHAUL.

3) Discharge accumulator by pressing brake pedal several times. Attempt to rotate accumulator can in respect to housing. If it is possible to rotate can, accumulator has lost its gas charge. Replace accumulator assembly.

REMOVAL & INSTALLATION

POWER BRAKE BOOSTER

Removal – 1) Press brake pedal several times to exhaust pressure from accumulator. Clean dirt from hydraulic line connections at booster and at master cylinder. Disconnect hydraulic lines from booster and plug all openings.

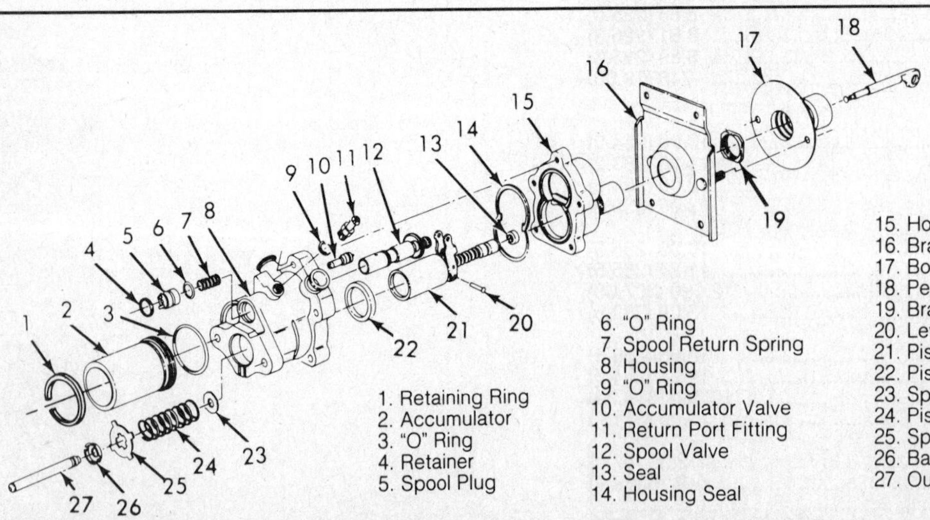
1
2
3
4
5
6
7
8
9
10
11
12
13
14
15
16
17
18
19
20
21
22
23
24
25
26
27

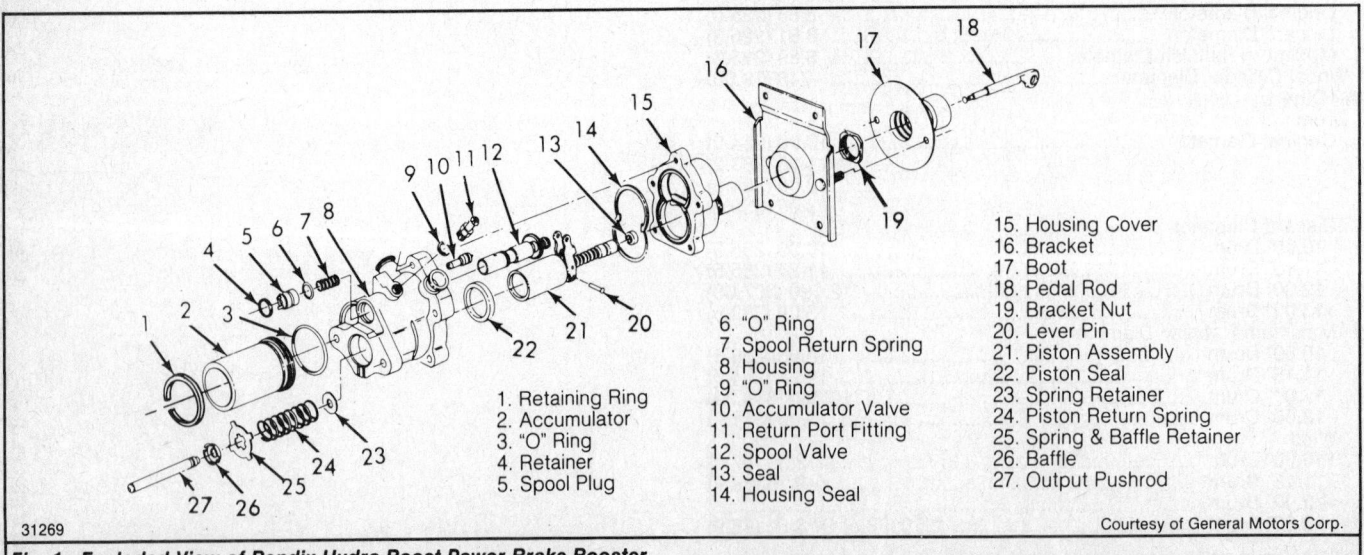

1. Retaining Ring
2. Accumulator
3. "O" Ring
4. Retainer
5. Spool Plug
6. "O" Ring
7. Spool Return Spring
8. Housing
9. "O" Ring
10. Accumulator Valve
11. Return Port Fitting
12. Spool Valve
13. Seal
14. Housing Seal
15. Housing Cover
16. Bracket
17. Boot
18. Pedal Rod
19. Bracket Nut
20. Lever Pin
21. Piston Assembly
22. Piston Seal
23. Spring Retainer
24. Piston Return Spring
25. Spring & Baffle Retainer
26. Baffle
27. Output Pushrod

31269

Courtesy of General Motors Corp.

Fig. 1: Exploded View of Bendix Hydro-Boost Power Brake Booster

NOTE: In most cases, it is not necessary to disconnect master cylinder brake lines to remove booster.

2) Remove and support master cylinder. Disconnect booster push rod from brake pedal. Remove booster-to-firewall nuts from inside vehicle. Remove booster and gaskets.

Installation – To install, reverse removal procedure. Lubricate pedal rod and linkage pivot bolts, pins, sleeves and bushings. Bleed hydro-boost system. See BLEEDING HYDRO-BOOST SYSTEM. Check stoplight switch adjustment.

OVERHAUL

POWER BRAKE BOOSTER

WARNING: DO NOT attempt to repair or apply heat to accumulator. Before discarding defective accumulator, drill a 1/16" hole through end of accumulator can at end opposite of "O" ring.

Disassembly – **1)** Install Accumulator Piston Compressor (J-26889) on master cylinder mounting stud and retain with nut. *See Figs. 1 and 2*. Compress accumulator using "C" clamp.

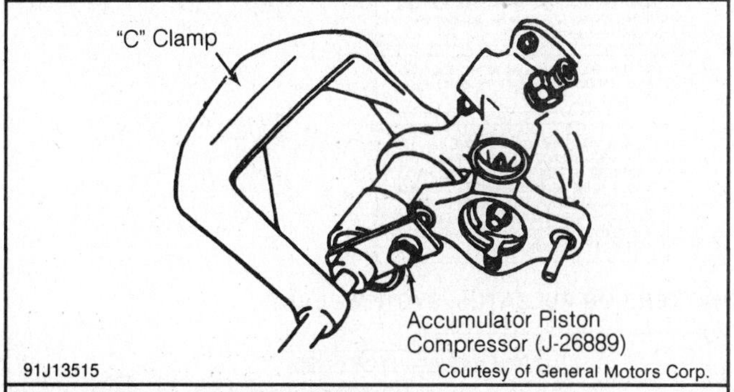
"C" Clamp
Accumulator Piston Compressor (J-26889)
91J13515
Courtesy of General Motors Corp.

Fig. 2: Compressing Accumulator

2) Insert punch into hole in housing. Release clamp and remove accumulator piston compressor. Remove accumulator and "O" ring. Remove retainer, spool plug, "O" ring and spool return spring from spool plug bore.

3) Remove baffle, output pushrod, spring and baffle retainer, piston return spring and spring retainer. Saw off eyelet on pedal rod. Remove pedal rod boot, bracket nut and bracket. Remove housing cover bolts. Separate cover from housing.

4) Remove seal from end of rod on piston assembly. Remove housing seal. Remove piston assembly and piston seal. Remove spool valve. Remove accumulator valve using wire hook. *See Fig. 3*. Remove return port fitting and "O" ring.

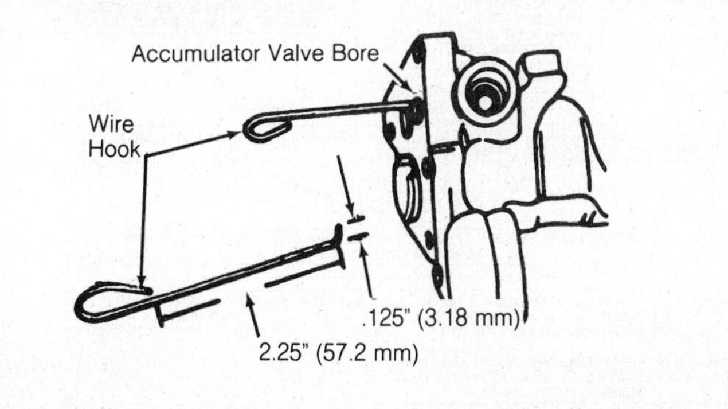
Accumulator Valve Bore
Wire Hook
.125" (3.18 mm)
2.25" (57.2 mm)
91A13516
Courtesy of General Motors Co:p.

Fig. 3: Removing Accumulator Valve Using Fabricated Tool

Cleaning & Inspection – **1)** Clean all parts with power steering fluid. DO NOT use any other cleaner. If any accumulator valve components are damaged or lost, replace all valve components.

2) Inspect tube seats from burrs or nicks. If damaged, remove tube seat using a No. 4 bolt extractor. Install tube seat using hammer and Tube Seat Installer (J-6217). *See Fig. 4*.

Reassembly – **1)** Lubricate all seals, "O" rings and metal friction points with power steering fluid. Install "O" ring and return port fitting. Install accumulator valve and spool valve.

2) Lubricate Seal Protector (J-24551-A) or (J-25083) with power steering fluid. Install piston seal and piston assembly. *See Fig. 5*. Install seal on end of piston assembly. Install housing seal in groove.

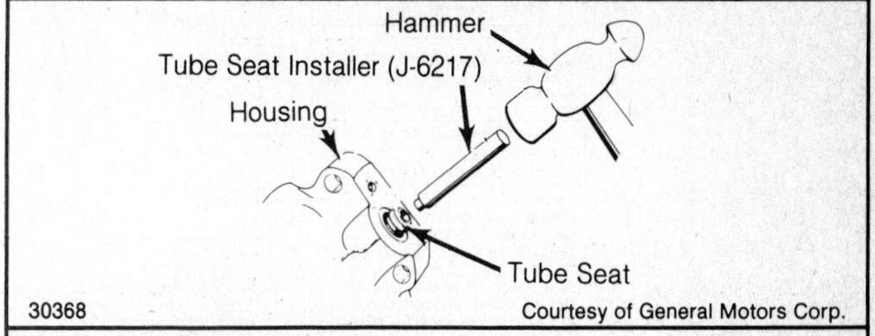
Hammer
Tube Seat Installer (J-6217)
Housing
Tube Seat
30368
Courtesy of General Motors Corp.

Fig. 4: Installing Tube Seat

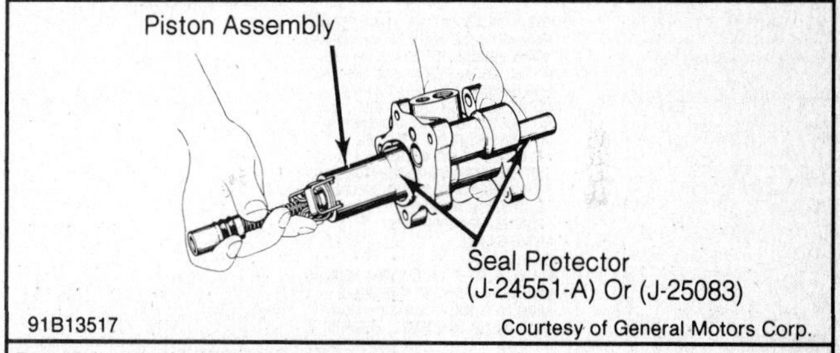
Piston Assembly
Seal Protector (J-24551-A) Or (J-25083)
91B13517
Courtesy of General Motors Corp.

Fig. 5: Installing Piston Assembly

3) Mate housing to cover. Install housing-to-cover bolts and tighten to 22 ft. lbs. (30 N.m). Install bracket and bracket nut. Tighten bracket nut to 110 ft. lbs. (149 N.m). Install boot.

4) Install spring retainer, piston return spring, baffle and output push rod using seal protector. Install spring and baffle retainer. Install "O" ring on spool plug. Install spool return spring, spool plug and retainer in spool plug bore.

5) Install "O" ring on accumulator. Install accumulator using Accumulator Piston Compressor (J-26889) and "C" clamp. *See Fig. 2*. Install accumulator retaining ring. Install jam nut and eyelet from repair kit onto pedal rod.

BLEEDING HYDRO-BOOST SYSTEM

1) Fill power steering pump reservoir and leave undisturbed for at least 2 minutes. Start engine and run momentarily. Add fluid if necessary. Repeat until fluid level remains constant with engine running.

2) Stop engine. Raise front wheels off the ground. Turn steering wheel from stop-to-stop. Add fluid if necessary. Lower vehicle.

3) Start engine. Press brake pedal several times while turning steering wheel from stop-to-stop. Turn engine off. Press brake pedal several times to exhaust accumulator pressure. Check fluid level. Add fluid (if necessary).

4) If fluid is foamy, let vehicle stand for several minutes, then repeat step **3)**. Air in system will cause fluid level to rise with engine off. Continue to bleed system until all air is expelled. If all air is not expelled after bleeding system, check power steering system for problem.

TORQUE SPECIFICATIONS

TORQUE SPECIFICATIONS

Application	Ft. Lbs. (N.m)
Booster-To-Cowl Nut	20 (27)
Bracket Nut	110 (149)
Housing-To-Cover Bolts	22 (30)
Master Cylinder-To-Booster Nut	20 (27)
Power Steering-To-Booster Line	25 (34)

Power Brake Booster – Bendix Hydro-Boost (Cont.)

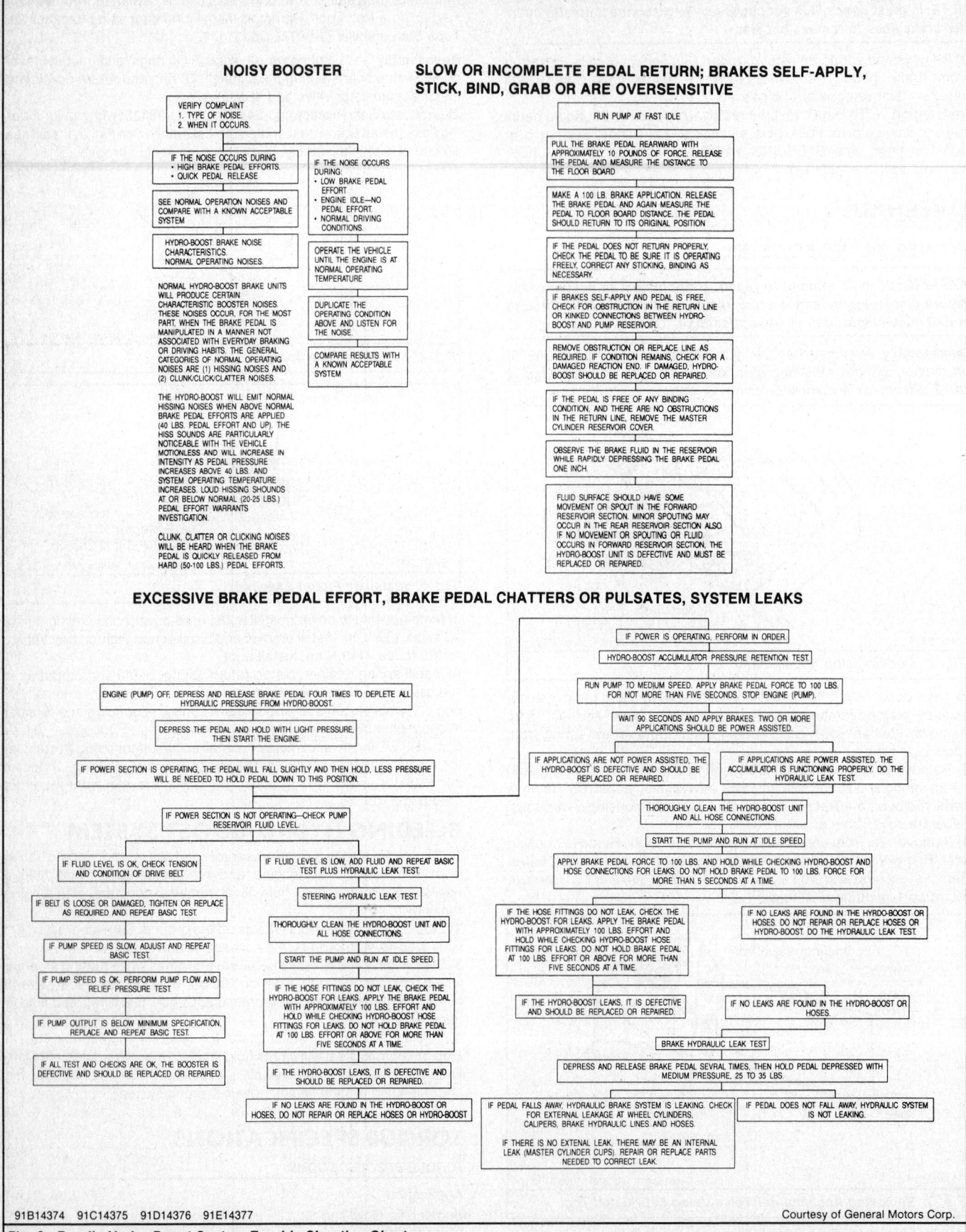

NOISY BOOSTER

VERIFY COMPLAINT
1. TYPE OF NOISE.
2. WHEN IT OCCURS.

IF THE NOISE OCCURS DURING
• HIGH BRAKE PEDAL EFFORTS.
• QUICK PEDAL RELEASE

SEE NORMAL OPERATION NOISES AND COMPARE WITH A KNOWN ACCEPTABLE SYSTEM

HYDRO-BOOST BRAKE NOISE CHARACTERISTICS. NORMAL OPERATING NOISES.

NORMAL HYDRO-BOOST BRAKE UNITS WILL PRODUCE CERTAIN CHARACTERISTIC BOOSTER NOISES. THESE NOISES OCCUR, FOR THE MOST PART, WHEN THE BRAKE PEDAL IS MANIPULATED IN A MANNER NOT ASSOCIATED WITH EVERYDAY BRAKING OR DRIVING HABITS. THE GENERAL CATEGORIES OF NORMAL OPERATING NOISES ARE (1) HISSING NOISES AND (2) CLUNK/CLICK/CLATTER NOISES.

THE HYDRO-BOOST WILL EMIT NORMAL HISSING NOISES WHEN ABOVE NORMAL BRAKE PEDAL EFFORTS ARE APPLIED (40 LBS. PEDAL EFFORT AND UP). THE HISS SOUNDS ARE PARTICULARLY NOTICEABLE WITH THE VEHICLE MOTIONLESS AND WILL INCREASE IN INTENSITY AS PEDAL PRESSURE INCREASES ABOVE 40 LBS. AND SYSTEM OPERATING TEMPERATURE INCREASES. LOUD HISSING SHOUNDS AT OR BELOW NORMAL (20-25 LBS.) PEDAL EFFORT WARRANTS INVESTIGATION.

CLUNK, CLATTER OR CLICKING NOISES WILL BE HEARD WHEN THE BRAKE PEDAL IS QUICKLY RELEASED FROM HARD (50-100 LBS.) PEDAL EFFORTS.

IF THE NOISE OCCURS DURING:
• LOW BRAKE PEDAL EFFORT
• ENGINE IDLE—NO PEDAL EFFORT.
• NORMAL DRIVING CONDITIONS.

OPERATE THE VEHICLE UNTIL THE ENGINE IS AT NORMAL OPERATING TEMPERATURE

DUPLICATE THE OPERATING CONDITION ABOVE AND LISTEN FOR THE NOISE.

COMPARE RESULTS WITH A KNOWN ACCEPTABLE SYSTEM

SLOW OR INCOMPLETE PEDAL RETURN; BRAKES SELF-APPLY, STICK, BIND, GRAB OR ARE OVERSENSITIVE

RUN PUMP AT FAST IDLE

PULL THE BRAKE PEDAL REARWARD WITH APPROXIMATELY 10 POUNDS OF FORCE. RELEASE THE PEDAL AND MEASURE THE DISTANCE TO THE FLOOR BOARD

MAKE A 100 LB. BRAKE APPLICATION. RELEASE THE BRAKE PEDAL AND AGAIN MEASURE THE PEDAL TO FLOOR BOARD DISTANCE. THE PEDAL SHOULD RETURN TO ITS ORIGINAL POSITION

IF THE PEDAL DOES NOT RETURN PROPERLY, CHECK THE PEDAL TO BE SURE IT IS OPERATING FREELY, CORRECT ANY STICKING, BINDING AS NECESSARY.

IF BRAKES SELF-APPLY AND PEDAL IS FREE, CHECK FOR OBSTRUCTION IN THE RETURN LINE OR KINKED CONNECTIONS BETWEEN HYDRO-BOOST AND PUMP RESERVOIR.

REMOVE OBSTRUCTION OR REPLACE LINE AS REQUIRED. IF CONDITION REMAINS, CHECK FOR A DAMAGED REACTION END. IF DAMAGED, HYDRO-BOOST SHOULD BE REPLACED OR REPAIRED.

IF THE PEDAL IS FREE OF ANY BINDING CONDITION, AND THERE ARE NO OBSTRUCTIONS IN THE RETURN LINE, REMOVE THE MASTER CYLINDER RESERVOIR COVER.

OBSERVE THE BRAKE FLUID IN THE RESERVOIR WHILE RAPIDLY DEPRESSING THE BRAKE PEDAL ONE INCH.

FLUID SURFACE SHOULD HAVE SOME MOVEMENT OR SPOUT IN THE FORWARD RESERVOIR SECTION. MINOR SPOUTING MAY OCCUR IN THE REAR RESERVOIR SECTION ALSO. IF NO MOVEMENT OR SPOUTING OR FLUID OCCURS IN FORWARD RESERVOIR SECTION, THE HYDRO-BOOST UNIT IS DEFECTIVE AND MUST BE REPLACED OR REPAIRED.

EXCESSIVE BRAKE PEDAL EFFORT, BRAKE PEDAL CHATTERS OR PULSATES, SYSTEM LEAKS

ENGINE (PUMP) OFF, DEPRESS AND RELEASE BRAKE PEDAL FOUR TIMES TO DEPLETE ALL HYDRAULIC PRESSURE FROM HYDRO-BOOST.

DEPRESS THE PEDAL AND HOLD WITH LIGHT PRESSURE, THEN START THE ENGINE.

IF POWER SECTION IS OPERATING, THE PEDAL WILL FALL SLIGHTLY AND THEN HOLD, LESS PRESSURE WILL BE NEEDED TO HOLD PEDAL DOWN TO THIS POSITION.

IF POWER SECTION IS NOT OPERATING—CHECK PUMP RESERVOIR FLUID LEVEL.

IF FLUID LEVEL IS OK, CHECK TENSION AND CONDITION OF DRIVE BELT.

IF BELT IS LOOSE OR DAMAGED, TIGHTEN OR REPLACE AS REQUIRED AND REPEAT BASIC TEST.

IF PUMP SPEED IS SLOW, ADJUST AND REPEAT BASIC TEST.

IF PUMP SPEED IS OK, PERFORM PUMP FLOW AND RELIEF PRESSURE TEST.

IF PUMP OUTPUT IS BELOW MINIMUM SPECIFICATION, REPLACE AND REPEAT BASIC TEST.

IF ALL TEST AND CHECKS ARE OK, THE BOOSTER IS DEFECTIVE AND SHOULD BE REPLACED OR REPAIRED.

IF FLUID LEVEL IS LOW, ADD FLUID AND REPEAT BASIC TEST PLUS HYDRAULIC LEAK TEST.

STEERING HYDRAULIC LEAK TEST.

THOROUGHLY CLEAN THE HYDRO-BOOST UNIT AND ALL HOSE CONNECTIONS.

START THE PUMP AND RUN AT IDLE SPEED.

IF THE HOSE FITTINGS DO NOT LEAK, CHECK THE HYDRO-BOOST FOR LEAKS. APPLY THE BRAKE PEDAL WITH APPROXIMATELY 100 LBS. EFFORT AND HOLD WHILE CHECKING HYDRO-BOOST HOSE FITTINGS FOR LEAKS. DO NOT HOLD BRAKE PEDAL AT 100 LBS. EFFORT OR ABOVE FOR MORE THAN FIVE SECONDS AT A TIME.

IF THE HYDRO-BOOST LEAKS, IT IS DEFECTIVE AND SHOULD BE REPLACED OR REPAIRED.

IF NO LEAKS ARE FOUND IN THE HYDRO-BOOST OR HOSES, DO NOT REPAIR OR REPLACE HOSES OR HYDRO-BOOST

IF POWER IS OPERATING, PERFORM IN ORDER.

HYDRO-BOOST ACCUMULATOR PRESSURE RETENTION TEST.

RUN PUMP TO MEDIUM SPEED. APPLY BRAKE PEDAL FORCE TO 100 LBS. FOR NOT MORE THAN FIVE SECONDS. STOP ENGINE (PUMP).

WAIT 90 SECONDS AND APPLY BRAKES. TWO OR MORE APPLICATIONS SHOULD BE POWER ASSISTED.

IF APPLICATIONS ARE NOT POWER ASSISTED, THE HYDRO-BOOST IS DEFECTIVE AND SHOULD BE REPLACED OR REPAIRED.

IF APPLICATIONS ARE POWER ASSISTED. THE ACCUMULATOR IS FUNCTIONING PROPERLY. DO THE HYDRAULIC LEAK TEST.

THOROUGHLY CLEAN THE HYDRO-BOOST UNIT AND ALL HOSE CONNECTIONS.

START THE PUMP AND RUN AT IDLE SPEED.

APPLY BRAKE PEDAL FORCE TO 100 LBS. AND HOLD WHILE CHECKING HYDRO-BOOST AND HOSE CONNECTIONS FOR LEAKS. DO NOT HOLD BRAKE PEDAL TO 100 LBS. FORCE FOR MORE THAN 5 SECONDS AT A TIME.

IF THE HOSE FITTINGS DO NOT LEAK, CHECK THE HYDRO-BOOST. FOR LEAKS. APPLY THE BRAKE PEDAL WITH APPROXIMATELY 100 LBS. EFFORT AND HOLD WHILE CHECKING HYDRO-BOOST HOSE FITTINGS FOR LEAKS. DO NOT HOLD BRAKE PEDAL AT 100 LBS. EFFORT OR ABOVE FOR MORE THAN FIVE SECONDS AT A TIME.

IF THE HYDRO-BOOST LEAKS, IT IS DEFECTIVE AND SHOULD BE REPLACED OR REPAIRED.

IF NO LEAKS ARE FOUND IN THE HYDRO-BOOST OR HOSES.

IF NO LEAKS ARE FOUND IN THE HYDRO-BOOST OR HOSES. DO NOT REPAIR OR REPLACE HOSES OR HYDRO-BOOST. DO THE HYDRAULIC LEAK TEST.

BRAKE HYDRAULIC LEAK TEST

DEPRESS AND RELEASE BRAKE PEDAL SEVRAL TIMES, THEN HOLD PEDAL DEPRESSED WITH MEDIUM PRESSURE, 25 TO 35 LBS.

IF PEDAL FALLS AWAY, HYDRAULIC BRAKE SYSTEM IS LEAKING. CHECK FOR EXTERNAL LEAKAGE AT WHEEL CYLINDERS, CALIPERS, BRAKE HYDRAULIC LINES AND HOSES.

IF THERE IS NO EXTENAL LEAK, THERE MAY BE AN INTERNAL LEAK (MASTER CYLINDER CUPS). REPAIR OR REPLACE PARTS NEEDED TO CORRECT LEAK.

IF PEDAL DOES NOT FALL AWAY, HYDRAULIC SYSTEM IS NOT LEAKING.

91B14374 91C14375 91D14376 91E14377

Courtesy of General Motors Corp.

Fig. 6: Bendix Hydro-Boost System Trouble Shooting Charts

1991 WHEEL ALIGNMENT
Specifications & Procedures

Astro, Blazer, Bravada, Jimmy, Lumina APV, Safari, Sierra, Silhouette, Sonoma, Trans Sport, "C" & "K" Series, "G" Series, "P" Series, "R" & "V" Series, "S" & "T" Series

PRE-ALIGNMENT

VEHICLE CHECKS

Before making wheel alignment adjustments, check or adjust the following:

1) Tire pressure must be inflated to manufacturer's recommended specification. Tires should be equal in size and type. Runout must not be excessive. Tires and wheels should be in balance.

2) Wheel bearings must be properly adjusted. Steering linkage and suspension must not have excessive wear and/or looseness. Check for wear in tie rod ends and ball joints.

3) Steering gear box must not have excessive play. Check and adjust to manufacturer's specification.

4) Vehicle must be at correct ride height with full fuel load and spare tire in vehicle. No extra load should be on vehicle. See RIDE HEIGHT under ALIGNMENT PROCEDURES.

5) Vehicle must be level with floor and with suspension settled. Jounce front and rear of vehicle several times and allow it to settle to normal ride height.

6) Ensure steering wheel spokes are centered with front wheels in straight-ahead position. Correct by shortening one tie rod adjusting sleeve and lengthening opposite sleeve in equal amounts.

7) Ensure wheel lug nuts are tightened to proper specification. See TORQUE SPECIFICATIONS at end of article.

JACKING & HOISTING

Vehicle may be raised by floor jack or vehicle hoist. Ensure hoist or jack supports vehicle at proper lifting points. *See Figs. 1-6*. If vehicle is to be raised on a twin-post hoist, use caution not to damage suspension, rear axle cover and/or steering linkage components.

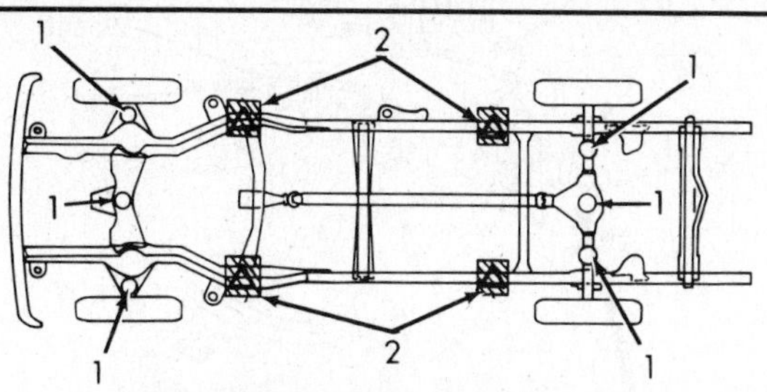

1 - Vehicle Jack or Floor Jack
2 - Hoist or Vehicle Jack

90E04477 Courtesy of General Motors Corp.

Fig. 1: Hoisting & Jacking Locations (Astro, Safari, "S" & "T" Series)

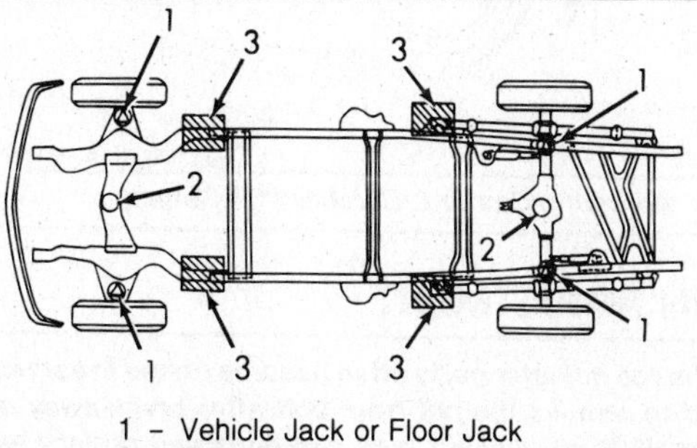

1 - Vehicle Jack or Floor Jack
2 - Floor Jack
3 - Hoist

90G04478 Courtesy of General Motors Corp.

Fig. 2: Hoisting & Jacking Locations ("C" & "K" Series)

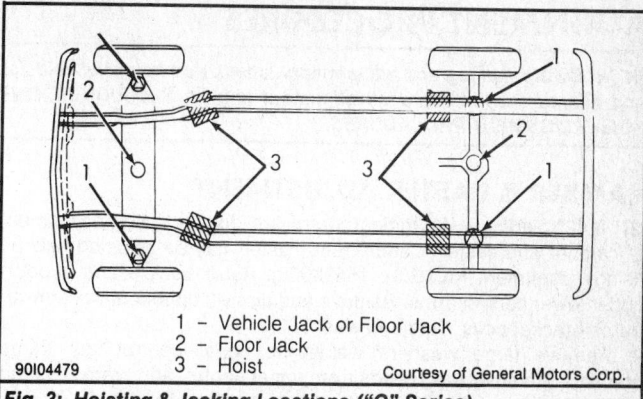

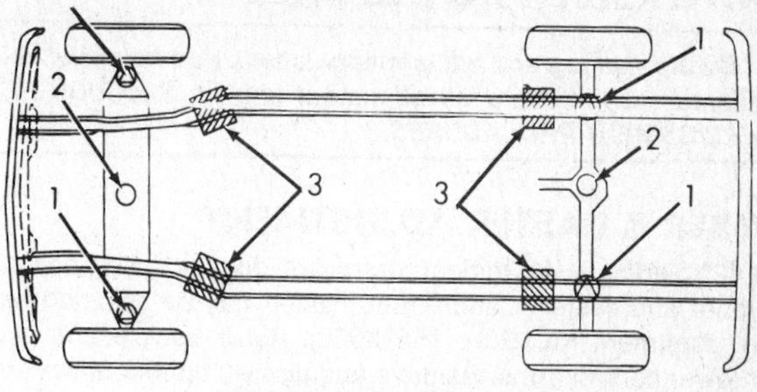

1 - Vehicle Jack or Floor Jack
2 - Floor Jack
3 - Hoist

90I04479 Courtesy of General Motors Corp.

Fig. 3: Hoisting & Jacking Locations ("G" Series)

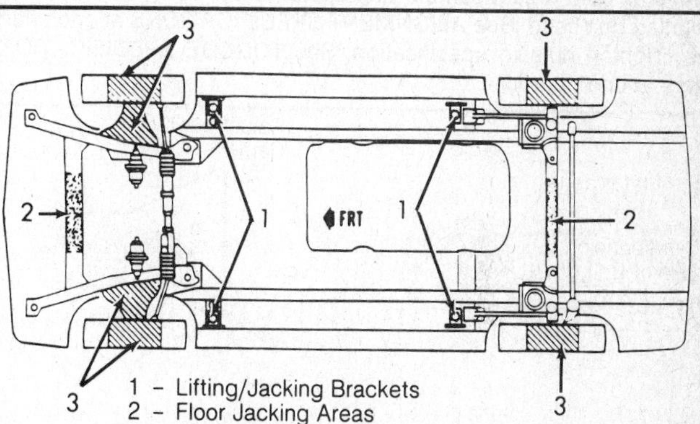
FRT

1 - Lifting/Jacking Brackets
2 - Floor Jacking Areas
3 - Suspension Contact Hoist Areas

90A04480 Courtesy of General Motors Corp.

Fig. 4: Hoisting & Jacking Locations (Lumina APV, Silhouette & Trans Sport)

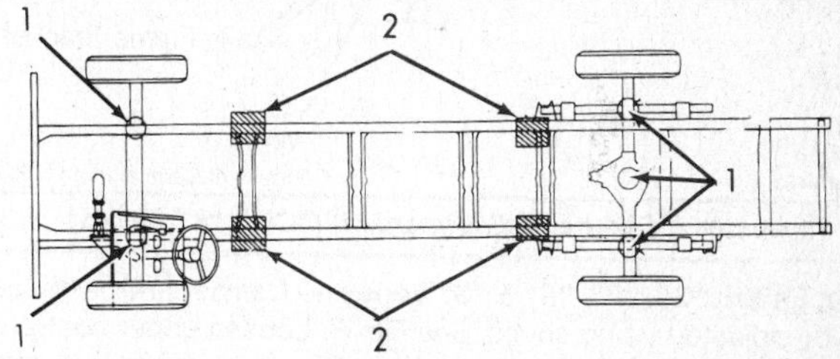

1 - Floor Jack
2 - Hoist

90C04481 Courtesy of General Motors Corp.

Fig. 5: Hoisting & Jacking Locations ("P" Series)

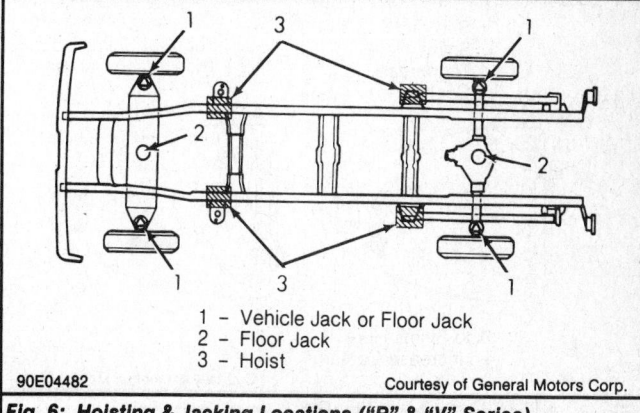

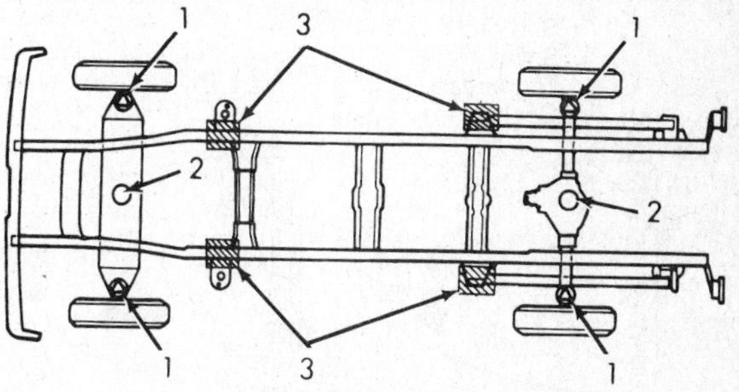

1 - Vehicle Jack or Floor Jack
2 - Floor Jack
3 - Hoist

90E04482 Courtesy of General Motors Corp.

Fig. 6: Hoisting & Jacking Locations ("R" & "V" Series)

1991 WHEEL ALIGNMENT
Specifications & Procedures (Cont.)

ALIGNMENT PROCEDURES

NOTE: Before making any adjustments, check ride height of vehicle, and measure and record all alignment angles. See RIDE HEIGHT under ALIGNMENT PROCEDURES.

CAMBER & CASTER ADJUSTMENT

"C" & "K" Series - 1) Original control arm does not allow adjustment of camber and caster. Camber and caster may be adjusted only by using Adjustment Kit (G.M. 15538596). Raise vehicle and support under lower control arms. Remove and discard upper control arm-to-frame bracket bolts, nuts and washer.

2) Remove large washers welded to upper control arm frame brackets. Remove weld beads from upper control arm bracket. Grind area smooth. Install adjustment cams to bracket. *See Fig. 7.*

3) Install bolt. Adjust camber and caster to correct specifications by rotating bolt head. See ALIGNMENT SPECIFICATIONS at end of article. Tighten nuts to specification. See TORQUE SPECIFICATIONS table at end of article.

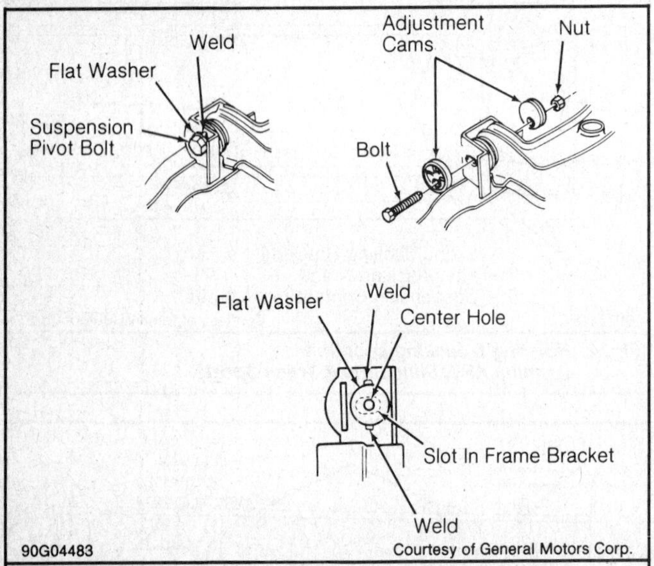
Weld
Adjustment Cams
Nut
Flat Washer
Suspension Pivot Bolt
Bolt
Flat Washer
Weld
Center Hole
Slot In Frame Bracket
Weld
90G04483
Courtesy of General Motors Corp.

Fig. 7: Caster & Camber Adjustment Kit ("C" & "K" Series)

Astro, Safari, "G", "P", "R" & "S" Series - Camber and caster angle may be adjusted using shims. *See Fig. 8.* Loosen upper control arm shaft-to-frame nuts. Remove original shims from bolts and add or remove shims to meet specification. See ALIGNMENT SPECIFICATIONS at end of article. Tighten nuts to specification when servicing is complete. See TORQUE SPECIFICATIONS table at end of article.

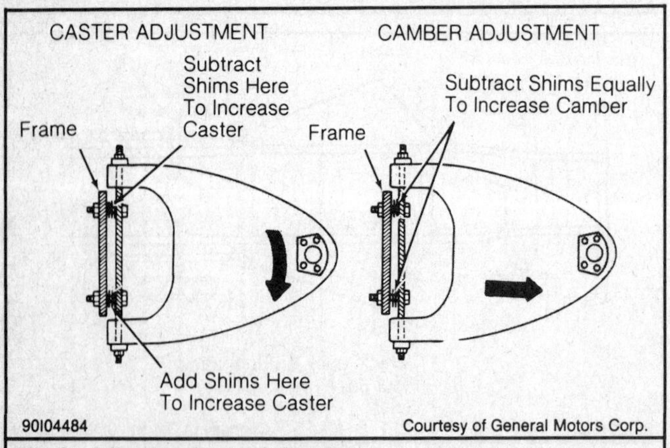
CASTER ADJUSTMENT
CAMBER ADJUSTMENT
Subtract Shims Here To Increase Caster
Subtract Shims Equally To Increase Camber
Frame
Frame
Add Shims Here To Increase Caster
90I04484
Courtesy of General Motors Corp.

Fig. 8: Adjusting Caster & Camber (Astro, Safari, "G", "P", "R" & "S" Series)

Lumina APV, Silhouette & Trans Sport - 1) Caster is not adjustable. Measure caster to check for bent or damaged parts. See ALIGNMENT SPECIFICATIONS at end of article. Replace damaged components if necessary.

2) For camber adjustment, loosen both strut-to-knuckle bolts enough to allow movement. *See Fig. 9.* Adjust camber to specification by moving top of wheel in or out. See ALIGNMENT SPECIFICATIONS at end of article. Tighten strut-to-knuckle bolts to specification. See TORQUE SPECIFICATIONS table at end of article.

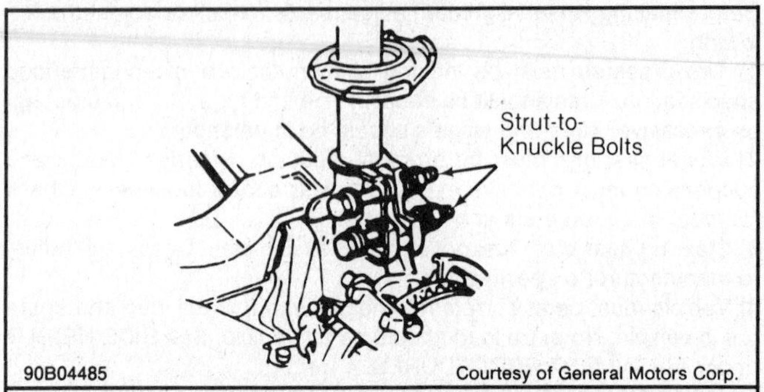
Strut-to-Knuckle Bolts
90B04485
Courtesy of General Motors Corp.

Fig. 9: Adjusting Camber (Lumina APV, Silhouette & Trans Sport)

"V" Series - Caster and camber are not adjustable.

"T" Series - Caster and camber adjustments are made by means of cams on upper control arm frame attaching bolts. *See Fig. 10.* Loosen upper control arm-to-frame attaching nuts. Rotate cam by rotating bolt head. Adjust caster and camber to specification. See ALIGNMENT SPECIFICATIONS at end of article. Tighten nuts to specification. See TORQUE SPECIFICATIONS table at end of article.

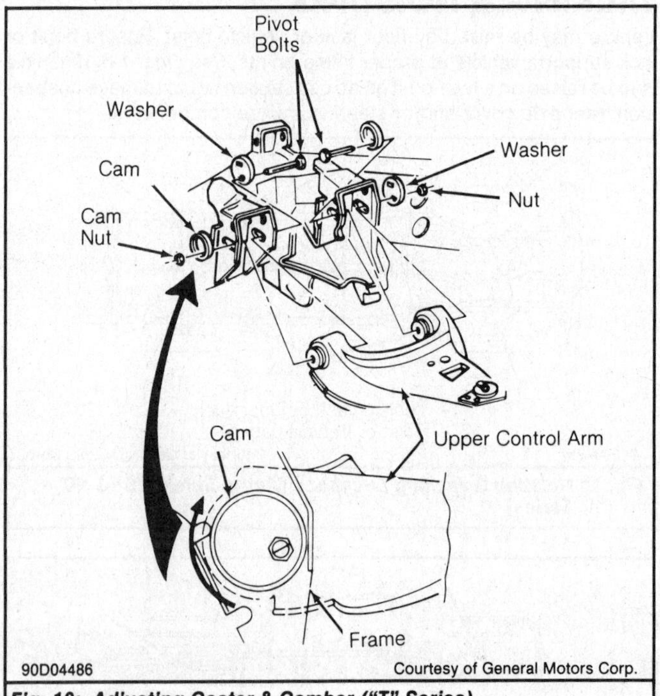
Pivot Bolts
Washer
Washer
Cam
Nut
Cam Nut
Cam
Upper Control Arm
Frame
90D04486
Courtesy of General Motors Corp.

Fig. 10: Adjusting Caster & Camber ("T" Series)

TOE-IN ADJUSTMENT

NOTE: Tie rod adjuster parts often become rusted in service. If torque required to remove the nut from bolt after break-away exceeds 84 INCH lbs. (9 N.m), discard nuts and bolts and replace with correct numbered parts.

1) Center the steering wheel and hold with steering wheel clamp. Loosen tie rod lock nuts or adjustment sleeve clamp bolts. Rotate inner tie rods or adjustment sleeves to align toe to specification. See ALIGNMENT SPECIFICATIONS at end of article.

2) Ensure the number of threads showing on each tie rod or inside each adjustment sleeve is nearly equal. Ensure tie rod ends are square before tightening lock nuts. Tighten tie rod lock nuts or adjustment sleeve clamp bolts to specification. See TORQUE SPECIFICATIONS table at end of article.

RIDE HEIGHT

1) Proper ride height is necessary for correct wheel alignment. Ensure tires are correctly inflated, cargo compartment is empty and fuel tank is full. Bounce vehicle several times to normalize ride height.

2) Most vehicles provide front wheel alignment specifications which allow camber and caster adjustment for a large range of ride heights. See RIDE HEIGHT SPECIFICATIONS table. Ride height measurement points are shown in illustrations. *See Figs. 11-16.*

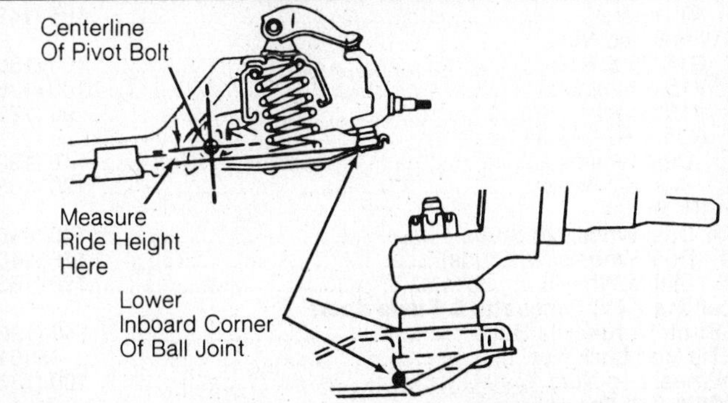

Centerline
Of Pivot Bolt
Measure
Ride Height
Here
Lower
Inboard Corner
Of Ball Joint
117408
Courtesy of General Motors Corp.

Fig. 11: Measuring Points (Astro, Safari & "S" Series)

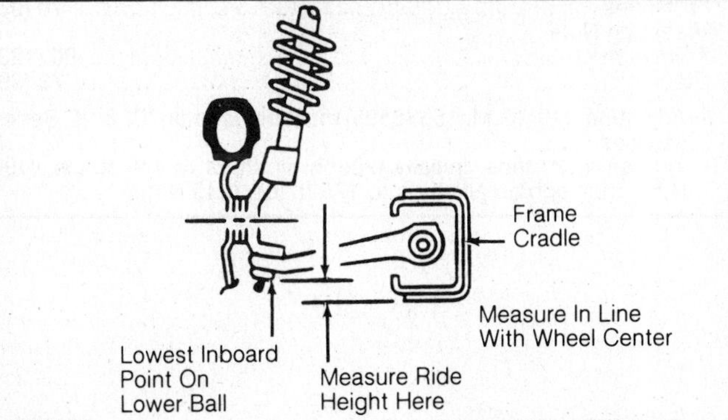

Frame
Cradle
Measure In Line
With Wheel Center
Lowest Inboard
Point On
Lower Ball
Measure Ride
Height Here
90F04487
Courtesy of General Motors Corp.

Fig. 12: Measuring Points (Lumina APV, Silhouette & Trans Sport)

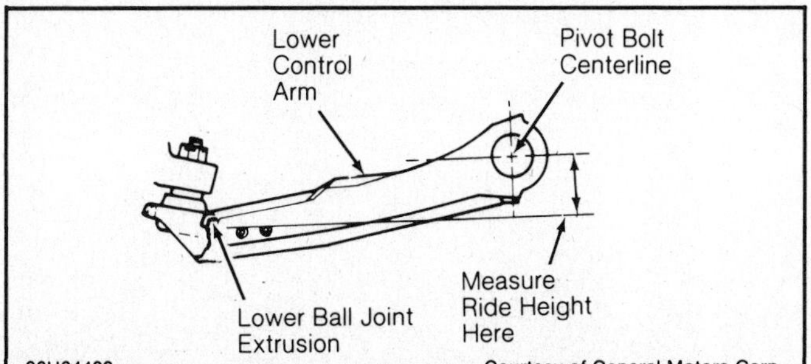

Lower
Control
Arm
Pivot Bolt
Centerline
Measure
Ride Height
Here
Lower Ball Joint
Extrusion
90H04488
Courtesy of General Motors Corp.

Fig. 13: Measuring Points ("C" Series)

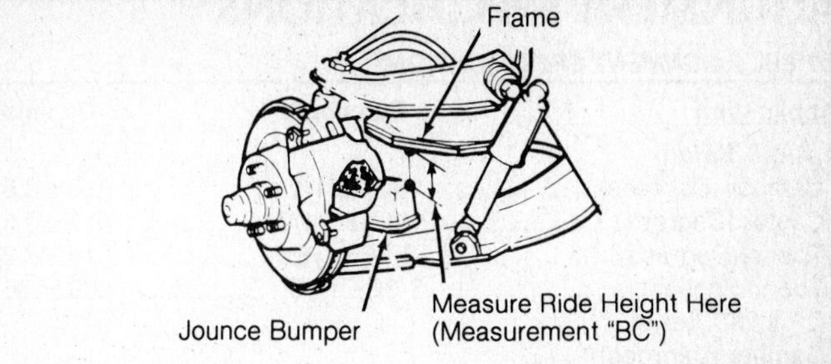

Frame
Measure Ride Height Here
(Measurement "BC")
Jounce Bumper
117410
Courtesy of General Motors Corp.

Fig. 14: Measuring Points ("G","P" & "R" Series)

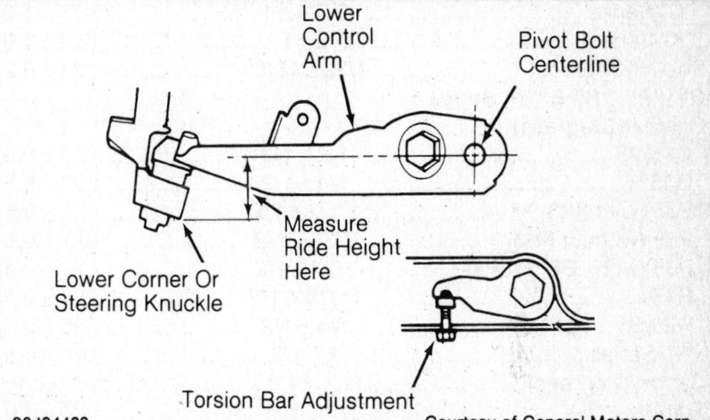

Lower
Control
Arm
Pivot Bolt
Centerline
Measure
Ride Height
Here
Lower Corner Or
Steering Knuckle
Torsion Bar Adjustment
90J04489
Courtesy of General Motors Corp.

Fig. 15: Measuring Points ("K" Series)

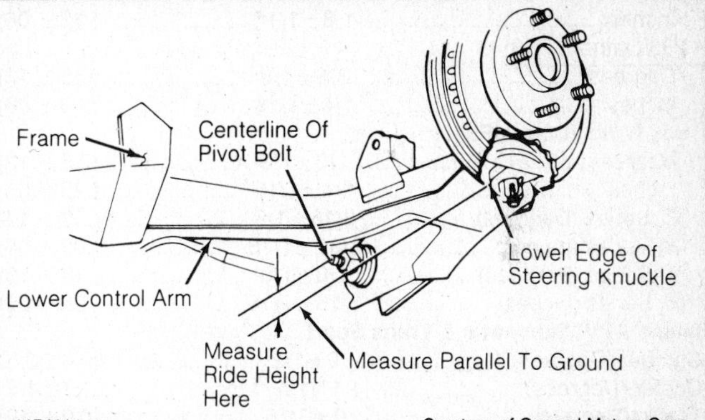

Frame
Centerline Of
Pivot Bolt
Lower Edge Of
Steering Knuckle
Lower Control Arm
Measure
Ride Height
Here
Measure Parallel To Ground
117411
Courtesy of General Motors Corp.

Fig. 16: Measuring Points ("T" Series)

RIDE HEIGHT SPECIFICATIONS

Application	Ride Height Dimension INCH (mm)
Astro & Safari	
2WD	3.1 ± 0.2 (80 ± 6.0)
4WD	5.4 ± 0.2 (136 ± 6.0)
"C" & "K" Series	
C15/35	3.7 ± 0.2 (95 ± 6.0)
K15/25	6.2 ± 0.2 (157 ± 6.0)
K35	5.7 ± 0.2 (145 ± 6.0)
"G", "P", "R" & "V" Series	[1]
Lumina APV, Silhouette & Trans Sport	0 ± .04 (0 ± 1)
"S" Series	2.8 ± 0.2 (73 ± 6.0)
"T" Series	4.8 ± 0.2 (122 ± 6.0)

[1] – Ride height is not adjustable.

1991 WHEEL ALIGNMENT
Specifications & Procedures (Cont.)

ALIGNMENT SPECIFICATIONS

WHEEL ALIGNMENT SPECIFICATIONS

Application	Fraction	Decimal
Astro & Safari		
Camber (Degrees) [1]	13/16±1/2	(0.8±0.5)
Caster (Degrees) [1]	2 11/16±1/2	(2.7±0.5)
Toe-in (Degrees)	3/16±1/8	(.19±.13)
Toe-in (Inches)	3/32±1/16	(.09±.06)
"C" & "K" Series		
Camber (Degrees) [1]		
"C" & K35	1/2±1/2	(0.5±0.5)
K15/25	21/32±1/2	(.65±0.5)
Caster (Degrees) [1]		
"C" Series	3 3/4±1	(3.75±1.0)
"K" Series	3±1	(3.0±1.0)
Toe-in (Degrees) [2]	7/32±13/64	(.24±0.2)
"G", "P", "R" & "V" Series		
Camber (Degrees)		
G15/25	1/2±1/2	(0.5±0.5)
G35	1/4±1/2	(.25±0.5)
P35 (with FS3) [3] [4]	1 1/2±1/2	(1.5±0.5)
P35 (without FS3) [3]	3/32±1/2	(0.1±0.5)
P35 (with JB8 or JF9) [3]	3/32±1/2	(0.1±0.5)
R15	11/16±1/2	(0.7±0.5)
R25/35	1/4±1/2	(.25±0.5)
"V" Series [4]	1±1/2	(1.0±0.5)
Caster (Degrees)	[5]	[5]
Toe-in		
"G" Series (Degrees)	0±3/16	(0.0±.19)
P35 (With FS3) [3]		
Degrees	1/16±1/8	(.07±.12)
Inches	1/8±1/16	(.12±.06)
P35 (without FS3) [3]		
Degrees	3/8±1/8	(.38±.13)
Inches	1/4±1/16	(.18±.06)
P35 (With JB8 or JF9) [3]		
Degrees	1/2±1/8	(0.5±.12)
Inches	1/4±1/16	(.25±.06)
"R" Series (Degrees)	3/16±1/8	(.19±.13)
"R" Series (Inches)	3/32±1/16	(.09±.06)
"V" Series (Degrees)	1/8±1/8	(.13±.13)
"V" Series (Inches)	1/16±1/16	(.06±.06)
Lumina APV, Silhouette & Trans Sport		
Camber (Degrees) [6]	0±1/2	(0.0±0.5)
Caster (Degrees)	1 11/16±1	(1.7±1.0)
Toe-in (Degrees)	0±3/16	(0.0±.19)
"S" & "T" Series		
Camber (Degrees) [1]	13/16±1/2	(0.8±0.5)
Caster (Degrees) [1]	2±1/2	(2.0±0.5)
Toe-in (Degrees)	5/16±3/32	(.31±.09)

1 – Left and right adjustments must be within 0.5 degree of each other.
2 – Toe-in on left and right side must be set equally per wheel. Steering wheel must be held in straight-ahead position within plus or minus 5.0 degrees.
3 – *See Fig. 17* for explanation of Regular Production Option (RPO) codes.
4 – For reference only. No means of adjustment is provided.
5 – *See Figs. 17 & 18* for caster specifications.
6 – Left and right adjustments must be within .07 degree of each other.

TORQUE SPECIFICATIONS

TORQUE SPECIFICATIONS

Application	Ft. Lbs. (N.m)
Astro & Safari	
Tie Rod Adjustment Sleeve Clamp Bolts	13 (18)
Upper Control Arm Nuts	
2WD	85 (115)
4WD	99 (135)
Wheel Lug Nuts	90 (122)
"C" & "K" Series	
Tie Rod Adjustment Sleeve Clamp Bolts	14 (19)
Upper Control Arm Nuts [1]	75-90 (100-122)
Wheel Lug Nuts	
Dual Rear Wheels	140 (190)
Single Wheels	120 (163)
"G", "P", "R" & "V" Series	
Tie Rod Adjustment Sleeve Clamp Bolts	
"V" Series	40 (54)
All Others	14 (19)
Upper Control Arm Nuts	
G15/25 & R15	70 (95)
All Others	105 (142)
Wheel Lug Nuts	
G15/25 & R15	100 (136)
V15 (Aluminum)	100 (136)
V15 (Steel)	90 (122)
G35 & R/V 25/35	
Dual Wheels	140 (190)
Single Wheels	120 (163)
"P" Series	
Dual Wheels (8 Studs)	140 (190)
Dual Wheels (10 Studs)	[2] 175 (240)
Single Wheels	120 (163)
Lumina APV, Silhouette & Trans Sport	
Strut-To-Knuckle Bolts	140 (190)
Tie Rod Lock Nut	45 (61)
Wheel Lug Nuts	100 (136)
"S" & "T" Series	
Tie Rod Adjustment Sleeve Clamp Bolts	14 (19)
Upper Control Arm Nuts	
"S" Series	65 (88)
"T" Series	70 (95)
Wheel Lug Nuts	
Aluminum	90 (122)
Steel	73 (99)

1 – Adjustment Kit (G.M. 15538596) must be used on "C" & "K" Series vehicles.
2 – Tighten in 2 steps. Initially tighten all studs to 140 ft. lbs. (190 N.m), then tighten all studs to 175 ft. lbs. (240 N.m).

1991 WHEEL ALIGNMENT
Specifications & Procedures (Cont.)

Caster Specification Table – Measure ride height. *See Fig. 14*. Use ride height measurement (measurement "BC") with the following table to find the proper caster setting for vehicle.

Dimension "BC" MM	Dimension "BC" Inches	R1	R2 + 3	P3 (42) Except FS3, R05, JB8 or JF9	P3 (42) w/R05 Except FS3, JB8 or JF9	P3 (42) w/JB8 or JF9 Except FS3	P3 (32) w/JB8 or JF9 Except FS3	P3 (32, 42) w/FS3	V1 + 2 + 3
38.1	1.50	—	—	—	—	—	—	+5° NOMINAL (References only, no means of adjustment provided.)	+8° NOMINAL (References only, no means of adjustment provided.)
44.5	1.75	—	—	—	—	—	—		
50.8	2.00	—	—	3.0°	2.5°	3.2°	—		
57.2	2.25	—	—	2.6°	2.2°	2.9°	—		
63.5	2.50	3.7°	1.5°	2.3°	1.9°	2.6°	5.5°		
70	2.75	3.5°	1.2°	2.0°	1.6°	2.4°	5.3°		
76.2	3.00	3.2°	0.9°	1.7°	1.3°	2.1°	5.0°		
82.5	3.25	2.9°	0.6°	1.4°	1.1°	1.8°	4.7°		
88.9	3.50	2.6°	0.3°	1.2°	0.8°	1.5°	4.4°		
95.3	3.75	2.4°	0.1°	0.9°	0.5°	1.2°	4.1°		
101.6	4.00	2.1°	−0.01°	0.6°	0.3°	1.0°	3.8°		
108	4.25	1.8°	−0.15°	0.4°	0.0°	0.7°	3.6°		
114.3	4.50	1.5°	−0.7°	0.2°	−0.2°	0.5°	3.3°		
120.7	4.75	1.3°	−1.0°	−0.1°	−0.4°	0.2°	3.1°		
127	5.00	1.0°	−1.6°	—	—	−0.1°	2.9°		
133.4	5.25	0.8°	−1.85°	—	—	−0.3°	2.6°		
139.7	5.50	0.5°	−1.25°	—	—	−0.5°	2.4°		
146	5.75	0.3°	−1.4°	—	—	−0.7°	2.2°		
152.4	6.00	0°	—	—	—	—	2.0°		

FS3 – I-Beam Front Axle (5000 lbs.)
JB8 – Hydraulic Power Disc Brakes
JF9 – Hydraulic Power 4-Wheel Disc Brakes
R05 – Dual Rear Wheels

91C13526

Courtesy of General Motors Corp.

Fig. 17: Caster Specifications ("P", "R" & "V" Series)

1991 WHEEL ALIGNMENT
Specifications & Procedures (Cont.)

Caster Specification Table - Measure ride height. *See Fig. 14*. Use ride height measurement (measurement "BC") with the following table to find the proper caster setting for vehicle.

Dimension "BC" MM	Dimension "BC" Inches	G100 + 200	G300
38.1	1.50	3.4°	3.1°
44.5	1.75	3.2°	3.0°
50.8	2.00	3.0°	2.7°
57.2	2.25	2.9°	2.4°
63.5	2.50	2.7°	2.1°
70	2.75	2.5°	1.8°
76.2	3.00	2.3°	1.5°
82.5	3.25	2.2°	1.2°
88.9	3.50	2.0°	1.0°
95.3	3.75	1.8°	0.7°
101.6	4.00	1.7°	0.7°
108	4.25	1.5°	0.2°
114.3	4.50	1.4°	−0.03°
120.7	4.75	—	—
127	5.00	—	—
133.4	5.25	—	—
139.7	5.50	—	—
146	5.75	—	—
152.4	6.00	—	—

91D13527

Courtesy of General Motors Corp.

Fig. 18: Caster Specifications ("G" Series)

1991 SUSPENSION
Front – FWD

Lumina APV, Silhouette, Trans Sport

DESCRIPTION

Front suspension is a combination strut and spring design. The control arms pivot from the frame. *See Fig. 1.* The frame has isolation mounts to the body and conventional rubber bushing for control arm pivots. The upper end of the strut is isolated by a rubber mount and contains a bearing to allow for wheel turning.

The lower end of the steering knuckle pivots on a ball joint riveted to the control arm. The ball joint is fastened to the steering knuckle with a pinch bolt.

ADJUSTMENTS & INSPECTION

WHEEL ALIGNMENT SPECIFICATIONS & PROCEDURES

NOTE: See SPECIFICATIONS & PROCEDURES article in WHEEL ALIGNMENT.

FRONT WHEEL BEARINGS

Front bearings are pre-adjusted and lubricated, requiring no routine maintenance or adjustment. Front wheel bearings are serviceable only by complete replacement of hub and bearing assembly.

BALL JOINT CHECKING

Raise and support vehicle. Allow suspension to hang freely. Inspect ball joint seals for cracks or tears. Replace ball joint if seal is damaged. Grasp tire at top and bottom. Note horizontal movement of the knuckle relative to the control arm. Replace ball joint if any looseness exists. Ball stud tightness in steering knuckle boss should be checked by shaking wheel and looking for looseness at stud end.

REMOVAL & INSTALLATION

BALL JOINT

CAUTION: When servicing suspension, use Drive Axle Boot Protector (J-34754). Modify boot protector by removing 3 tabs on inside surface. DO NOT overextend drive axle joint, or internal parts may separate.

Removal – 1) Raise vehicle and support with jack stands under frame or suspension. Allow weight to rest on jack stands, not on control arms. Remove wheels. Place drive axle boot protectors on drive axle joint.

2) Remove pinch bolt from steering knuckle securing ball joint stud. Separate ball joint from steering knuckle. Tap stud with mallet to loosen (if necessary).

3) Drill out ball joint retaining rivets. DO NOT damage drive axle seals when removing rivet. Loosen stabilizer bar bushing assembly nut. Remove ball joint from steering knuckle and control arm.

Installation – 1) Install ball joint in control arm. Install and tighten retaining bolts as shown in instructions included with ball joint kit.

2) Position steering knuckle over ball joint stud. Use NEW pinch bolt and nut whenever ball joint is separated from steering knuckle.

3) Align notch in ball joint stud with steering knuckle bolt hole, and install new pinch bolt. Install new pinch bolt nut. Tighten stabilizer bar bushing assembly nut. Tighten bolts to specification. See TORQUE SPECIFICATIONS table at end of article. Remove drive axle boot protectors. Install wheel. Lower vehicle and check wheel alignment. See SPECIFICATIONS & PROCEDURES article in WHEEL ALIGNMENT.

STEERING KNUCKLE

Removal – 1) Raise vehicle and support with jack stands under frame or suspension. Allow weight to rest on jack stands, not on control arms. Remove wheels. Place drive axle boot protectors on drive axle joint. Disconnect stabilizer bar from control arm. See STABILIZER BAR & BUSHING ASSEMBLY under REMOVAL & INSTALLATION.

2) Remove hub and bearing assembly. See HUB & BEARING ASSEMBLY under REMOVAL & INSTALLATION. *See Fig. 1.* Separate ball joint from steering knuckle. See BALL JOINT under REMOVAL & INSTALLATION.

CAUTION: DO NOT overextend drive axle CV joints or internal parts may separate.

3) With a sharp tool, scribe reference marks on steering knuckle along lower outboard strut radius. See *Fig. 2* (VIEW A). Also, scribe reference marks on inboard side of strut flange along curve of steering knuckle (VIEW B), and on strut lower mount clamp and steering knuckle (VIEW C).

4) Remove strut-to-steering knuckle retaining bolts. Remove steering knuckle.

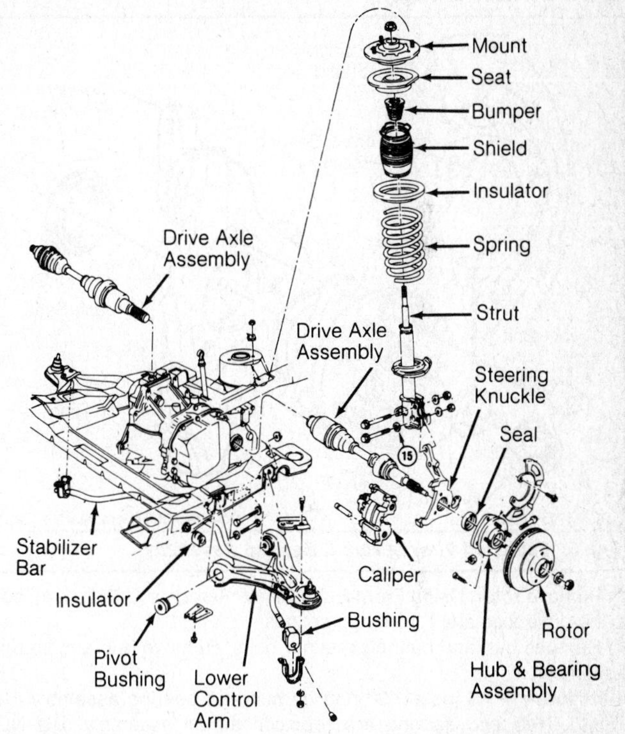
Mount
Seat
Bumper
Shield
Insulator
Spring
Strut
Drive Axle Assembly
Drive Axle Assembly
Steering Knuckle
Seal
15
Stabilizer Bar
Insulator
Caliper
Bushing
Rotor
Pivot Bushing
Lower Control Arm
Hub & Bearing Assembly

90E04793 Courtesy of General Motors Corp.

Fig. 1: Exploded View of Front Suspension Components

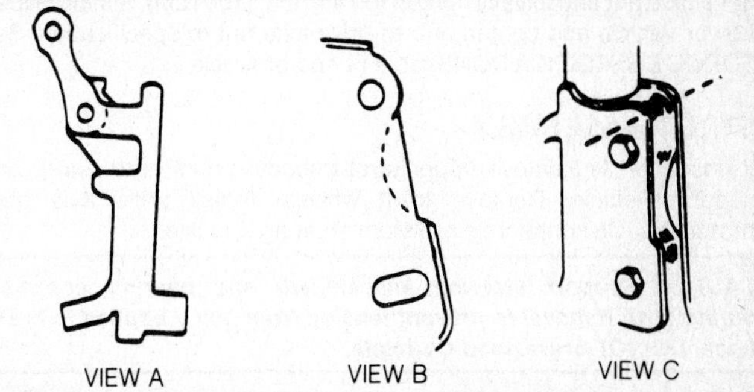
VIEW A
VIEW B
VIEW C

90G04794 Courtesy of General Motors Corp.

Fig. 2: Scribing Reference Marks on Strut & Knuckle

Installation – 1) Install new bearing seal (if removed). Loosely install steering knuckle to strut. Install steering knuckle on ball joint. Tighten ball joint-to-steering knuckle pinch bolt to specification (always use NEW pinch bolt and nut). See TORQUE SPECIFICATIONS table at end of article.

1991 SUSPENSION
Front – FWD (Cont.)

2) Check drive axle boot protector. Raise assembly with floor jack to align steering knuckle and strut bolt holes. Align reference mark on strut and steering knuckle. Install strut-to-steering knuckle retaining bolts. Tighten to specification. See TORQUE SPECIFICATIONS table.
3) Install hub assembly on steering knuckle and tighten to specification. Initially tighten hub-to-drive axle nut to 74 ft. lbs. (100 N.m). Install rotor, caliper, wheel and lug nuts. Tighten wheel lug nuts to specification. See TORQUE SPECIFICATIONS table. Lower vehicle and tighten hub-to-drive axle nut to specification.

HUB & BEARING ASSEMBLY

Removal – 1) Raise vehicle and support with jack stands under frame or suspension. Allow weight to rest on jack stands, not on control arms. Remove wheels. Place drive axle boot protectors on drive axle joint.
2) Remove hub-to-drive axle nut and washer. *See Fig. 3.* Remove disc brake caliper. DO NOT disconnect brake line. Support caliper to prevent brake hose damage.

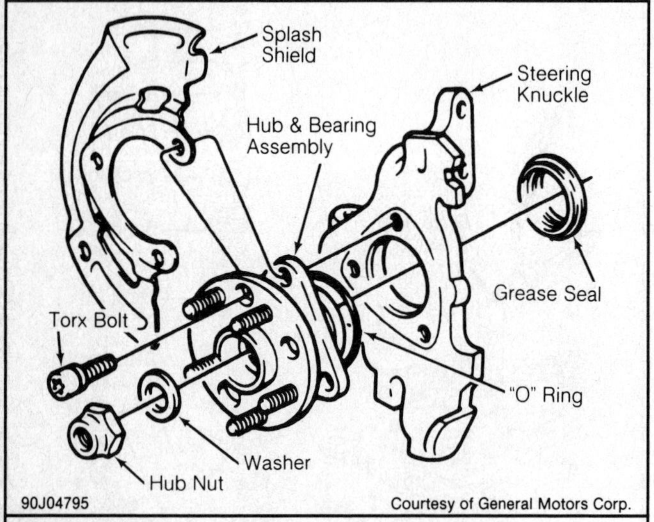
Splash
Shield
Steering
Knuckle
Hub & Bearing
Assembly
Grease Seal
Torx Bolt
"O" Ring
Washer
Hub Nut
90J04795
Courtesy of General Motors Corp.

Fig. 3: Exploded View of Hub & Bearing Assembly

3) Remove rotor. Using Front Hub Spindle Remover (J-28733-A), separate drive axle shaft from hub splines.
4) Remove hub and bearing retainer bolts. Remove hub and bearing assembly.
Installation – 1) Install "O" ring on hub and bearing assembly. *See Fig. 3.* Hub and bearing are replaced as an assembly. DO NOT damage seal during axle shaft, and hub and bearing assembly installation.
2) Install hub and bearing assembly. Install rotor. Install NEW hub-to-drive axle nut and initially tighten to 74 ft. lbs. (100 N.m). Install caliper. Lower vehicle and tighten hub-to-drive axle nut to specification. See TORQUE SPECIFICATIONS table at end of article.

STRUT ASSEMBLY

Removal – 1) Remove upper strut-to-body mount nuts. Raise and support vehicle. Remove front wheels. Install drive axle boot protectors. Disconnect tie rod from steering knuckle.

CAUTION: Support steering knuckle/hub and bearing assembly during strut removal to prevent tension from being applied to brake hose. DO NOT overextend CV joints.

2) Remove brake line clip or bracket bolt from strut. Scribe strut-to-mount clamp outline on steering knuckle for reassembly reference. *See Fig. 2.*
3) Remove lower strut mounting bolts and remove strut assembly from vehicle. DO NOT chip or scratch coil spring coating. Support steering knuckle/hub and bearing assembly to prevent overextending axle shaft CV joints.

Disassembly – 1) Mount strut assembly in strut/spring compressor. Wear eye protection while performing this operation. Compress strut/spring to approximately 1/2 its height. DO NOT bottom spring or strut rod. Using a socket, hold strut rod stationary while removing nut from top of shaft.
2) Install Guide Rod (J-34013-27) on strut shaft to guide shaft down through bearing cap of top mount assembly. Loosen strut/spring compressor screw while guiding strut shaft from assembly. Continue to loosen screw until spring tension is removed. Remove strut and spring from compressor.

CAUTION: DO NOT chip or crack coil spring coating. Coil spring damage may occur if coating is damaged.

Reassembly – Upper spring seat flat must be aligned with lower strut-to-steering knuckle mounting flange. Reverse disassembly procedure. Tighten strut top nut to specification. See TORQUE SPECIFICATIONS table at end of article.

NOTE: Check alignment after strut installation.

Installation – To install, reverse removal procedure. When installing strut assembly in steering knuckle, ensure scribe marks on steering knuckle align with strut for proper lower adjusting cam bolt position. Tighten bolts to specification. See TORQUE SPECIFICATIONS table at end of article.

CONTROL ARM

Removal – 1) Raise vehicle and support with jack stands under frame or suspension. Allow weight to rest on jack stands, not on control arms. Remove wheels. Place drive axle boot protectors on inner and outer drive axle joints. Remove stabilizer bar from control arm. See STABILIZER BAR & BUSHING ASSEMBLY under REMOVAL & INSTALLATION.
2) Separate ball joint from control arm. See BALL JOINT under REMOVAL & INSTALLATION. Remove control arm bolts and remove control arm.
Installation – To install, reverse removal procedure. On pinch-type ball joints, install new bolt and nut. Tighten control arm bolts with vehicle weight on control arms. Check wheel alignment. See SPECIFICATIONS & PROCEDURES article in WHEEL ALIGNMENT.

NOTE: Control arm bolts must be tightened to specification with vehicle weight on control arms. See TORQUE SPECIFICATIONS table.

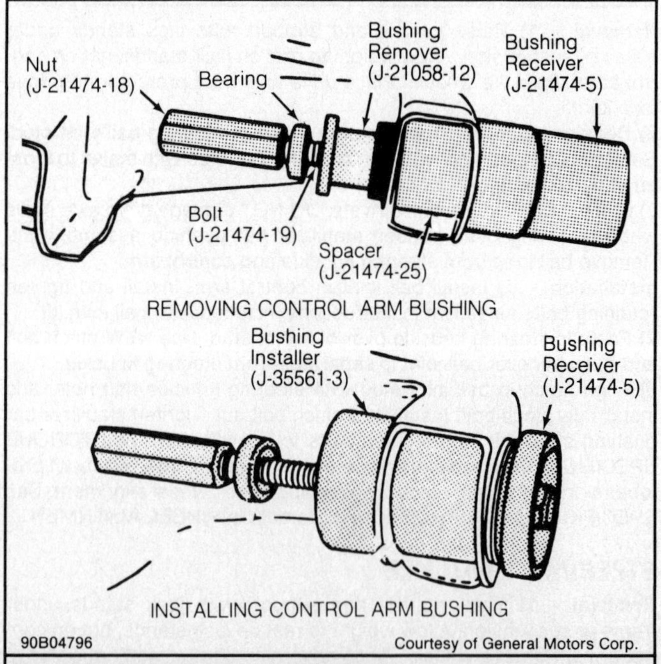
Nut
(J-21474-18)
Bearing
Bushing
Remover
(J-21058-12)
Bushing
Receiver
(J-21474-5)
Bolt
(J-21474-19)
Spacer
(J-21474-25)
REMOVING CONTROL ARM BUSHING
Bushing
Installer
(J-35561-3)
Bushing
Receiver
(J-21474-5)
INSTALLING CONTROL ARM BUSHING
90B04796
Courtesy of General Motors Corp.

Fig. 4: Replacing Control Arm Bushings

1991 SUSPENSION
Front – FWD (Cont.)

CONTROL ARM BUSHINGS

Removal & Installation – Remove control arm. See CONTROL ARM under REMOVAL & INSTALLATION. Use control arm bushing service tools to change bushings in control arm. *See Fig. 4*.

STABILIZER BAR & BUSHING ASSEMBLY

Removal – **1)** Raise and support vehicle. Allow suspension to hang freely. Remove wheels. Disconnect stabilizer bar bushings and clamps from control arms.

2) Remove stabilizer bar mounting plates from frame. Remove stabilizer bar and bushings from vehicle. Inspect and replace all rubber bushings showing signs of wear, damage or deterioration.

Installation – To install, reverse removal procedure. During installation, loosely assemble all fasteners and ensure stabilizer bar is centered from side to side. Tighten stabilizer bar nut and bolt to specification. See TORQUE SPECIFICATIONS table.

TORQUE SPECIFICATIONS

TORQUE SPECIFICATIONS

Application	Ft. Lbs. (N.m)
Ball Joint-To-Steering Knuckle Pinch Bolt	33 (45)
Brake Caliper Bolt	38 (51)
Control Arm-To-Crossmember Pivot Bolt	61 (83)
Hub & Bearing Retainer Bolt	70 (95)
Hub-To-Drive Axle Nut	[1] 185 (260)
Stabilizer Bar	
Bar-To-Control Arm Clamp Nut	33 (45)
Plate-To-Frame Bolt	40 (55)
Strut Assembly	
Strut-To-Steering Knuckle Bolt	140 (190)
Strut-To-Upper Body Mount Nut	18 (25)
Top Nut	65 (85)
Wheel Nut	100 (140)

[1] – Tighten to 74 ft. lbs. (100 N.m) during initial assembly. After installing wheels and lowering vehicle to ground, tighten nut to specification.

1991 SUSPENSION
Front – 2WD Coil Spring – "G", "P" & "R" Series

NOTE: Vehicle series numbers in this article list Chevrolet models first, followed by GMC. Example: G15/1500. Chevrolet/GMC equivalent models are as follows: 15 = 1500, 25 = 2500 and 35 = 3500.

DESCRIPTION

Independent front suspension consists of upper and lower control arms with steering knuckle mounted between ball joints. Control arms are mounted on inner shafts. Coil springs are mounted between lower control arm and a formed seat in suspension crossmember. Some models have urethane air cylinders inside the coil springs. Hydraulic or gas-charged shock absorbers fit between lower control arm and frame. A stabilizer bar is mounted to frame side rails, and is connected to lower control arms by links.

ADJUSTMENTS & INSPECTION

WHEEL ALIGNMENT SPECIFICATIONS & PROCEDURES

NOTE: See SPECIFICATIONS & PROCEDURES article in WHEEL ALIGNMENT.

FRONT WHEEL BEARINGS

CAUTION: Never preload tapered roller bearings, or damage to bearings will result. Bearings are designed to have a slightly loose feel when properly adjusted.

1) Raise and support vehicle. Remove hub dust cap and cotter pin. Tighten spindle bearing nut to 12 ft. lbs. (16 N.m) while turning wheel forward by hand. Back off nut until it is just loose.
2) Finger tighten nut until snug. Loosen nut slightly (no more than 1/2 flat) until new cotter pin can be installed. Hub play (in and out) should be .001-.005" (.03-.13 mm) when properly adjusted. Install dust cap and wheel cover.

BALL JOINT CHECKING

Upper Ball Joint – 1) Upper ball joint stud is spring-loaded in the socket to minimize looseness and compensate for normal wear. Raise vehicle and support at lower control arm. Remove front wheel assembly.
2) Inspect ball joint stud for lateral shake by gripping hub assembly at top and bottom, and moving spindle inward and outward. Replace ball joint if any lateral movement exists.
3) Check ball joint, only with ball joint disconnected from steering knuckle, to see if stud can be rotated by finger pressure. Replace ball joint if stud can be twisted. Inspect upper ball joint rubber grease seal for cuts or tears. Replace ball joint if damage is found.
Lower Ball Joint – 1) Lower ball joint wear may be checked without disassembling ball stud. Raise and support vehicle at wheel and hub with jack stand.
2) Measure distance between top of ball joint stud and tip of lower grease fitting. *See Fig. 2.* Move support to lower control arm and allow wheel and hub to hang free.

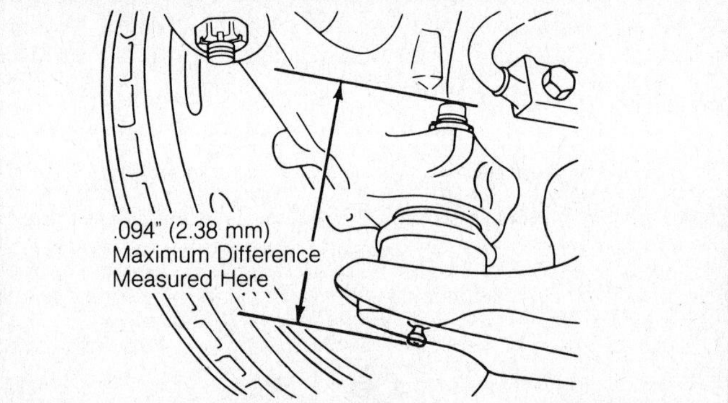
.094" (2.38 mm)
Maximum Difference
Measured Here

30190 Courtesy of General Motors Corp.

Fig. 2: Checking Lower Ball Joint Wear

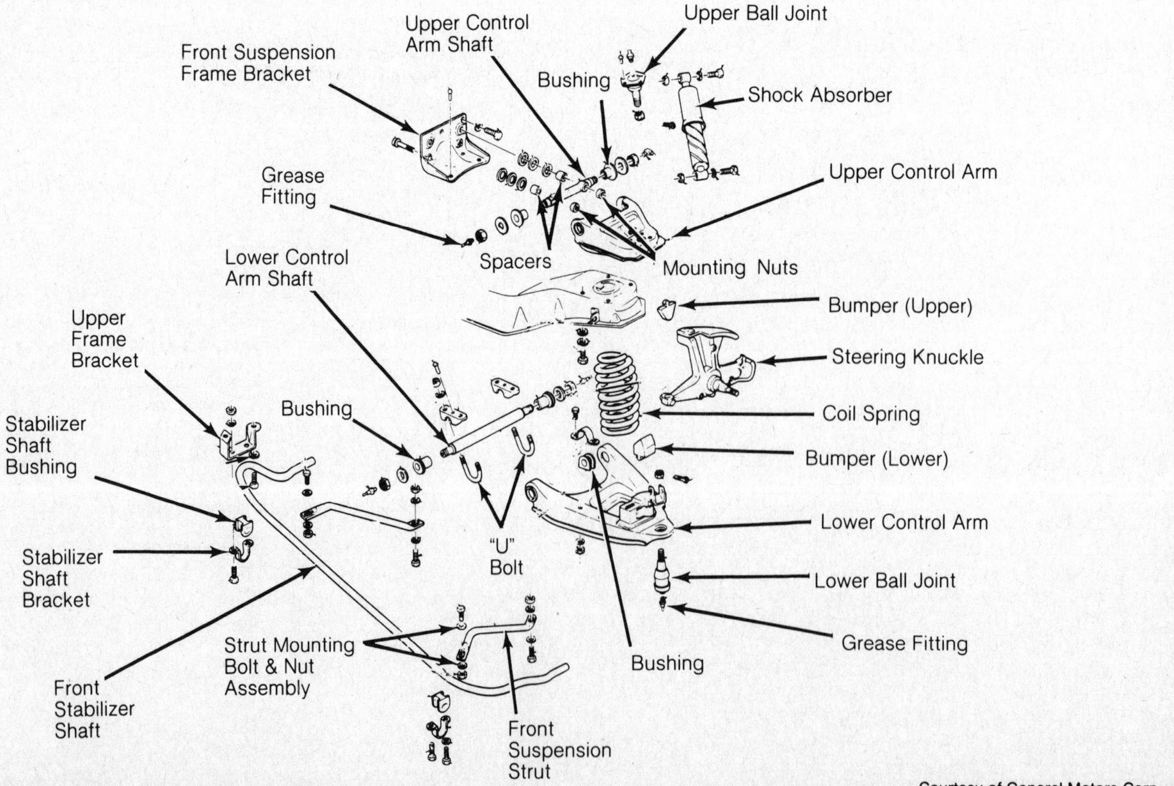
Upper Control Arm Shaft
Upper Ball Joint
Front Suspension Frame Bracket
Bushing
Shock Absorber
Grease Fitting
Upper Control Arm
Spacers
Mounting Nuts
Lower Control Arm Shaft
Bumper (Upper)
Upper Frame Bracket
Steering Knuckle
Bushing
Coil Spring
Stabilizer Shaft Bushing
Bumper (Lower)
Lower Control Arm
Stabilizer Shaft Bracket
"U" Bolt
Lower Ball Joint
Grease Fitting
Strut Mounting Bolt & Nut Assembly
Bushing
Front Stabilizer Shaft
Front Suspension Strut

30189 Courtesy of General Motors Corp.

Fig. 1: Exploded View of Typical Front Suspension

3) Recheck distance. If difference between measurements exceeds .094" (2.38 mm), replace ball joint. Inspect lower ball joint rubber grease seal for cuts or tears. Replace ball joint if damage is found.

REMOVAL & INSTALLATION

WHEEL BEARINGS

Removal – 1) Raise and support vehicle. Remove wheel and tire assembly. Remove brake caliper and hang aside. DO NOT allow brake caliper to hang by brake hose.

2) Remove dust cap, cotter pin, spindle nut and washer. Remove hub and rotor assembly. Remove outer bearing, inner grease seal and inner bearing.

3) Clean bearings and inspect bearing and races for damage. If races require removal from hub, drive old races from hub using a hammer and a brass drift inserted through notches of hub.

Installation – 1) To install, reverse removal procedure. Install outer race using Race Installers (J-8457) and (J-8449) for inner bearing race. Pack bearings with proper lubricant.

2) Install grease seal until seal is even with hub surface. Lubricate seal lip and hub cavity with wheel bearing grease. To complete installation, reverse removal procedure. Adjust wheel bearings. See FRONT WHEEL BEARINGS under ADJUSTMENTS & INSPECTION.

SHOCK ABSORBERS

Removal – Raise and support vehicle. Remove shock absorber retaining bolts. Remove shock absorber.

Inspection – 1) On fluid-filled shock, purge air from pressure chamber by mounting shock in vise (top end up) and fully extending unit. Reverse position (top end down) and fully collapse unit. Repeat procedure several times.

2) Bench check shock unit by mounting in vise with top end up (top end down on gas-charged shocks). DO NOT clamp vise on reservoir tube or mounting threads. Check rubber grommets for deterioration and replace as needed. Operate shock by hand at various rates of speed and note resistance. If resistance is not smooth and constant, replace shock.

Installation – To install, reverse removal procedure. Tighten all bolts and nuts to specification. See TORQUE SPECIFICATIONS table at end of article.

STABILIZER BAR

Removal – Raise and support vehicle. Remove wheel and tire assembly. Remove stabilizer bar-to-frame retaining bolts and clamps. Disconnect stabilizer bar from lower control arms. Remove stabilizer bar and bushings. Check all rubber bushings for excessive wear or damage.

Installation – To install, reverse removal procedure. Bushings should be installed with slit area toward front of vehicle. Apply rubber lubricant to bushings to aid in installation.

COIL SPRINGS

Removal – 1) Raise and support vehicle under frame, with control arms hanging free. Remove wheel and tire assembly. Disconnect shock absorber and stabilizer bar at lower control arm. Install Lower Control Arm Shaft Support (J-23028-01) on a jack. *See Fig. 3*. Position assembly under lower control arm so shaft seats in grooves of lower control arm shaft support.

WARNING: Securely bolt Lower Control Arm Shaft Support (J-23028-01) to jack, and install safety chain through lower control arm and coil spring to prevent personal injury.

2) If air bags are installed in coil springs, remove valve cap and valve core. Pry on air cylinder to release air pressure. Reinstall valve core and valve cap to retain vacuum condition. Push air cylinder upward as far as possible. Install safety chain around coil spring and through lower control arm.

3) Raise jack to release tension from lower control arm shaft. Remove control arm shaft-to-crossmember "U" bolts. Carefully lower jack until all tension is released from coil spring. Remove safety chain and coil spring. Remove air cylinder.

4) Check air cylinder for leaks. Inflate air cylinder to 20 psi (1.4 kg/cm²) and submerge in water. Check for air bubbles. Replace air cylinder if leaks exist.

Installation – To install, reverse removal procedure. Install air cylinder so protector plate is positioned toward upper control arm, and air valve protrudes through hole in lower control arm. Ensure front indexing hole in lower control arm shaft aligns with crossmember attaching stud.

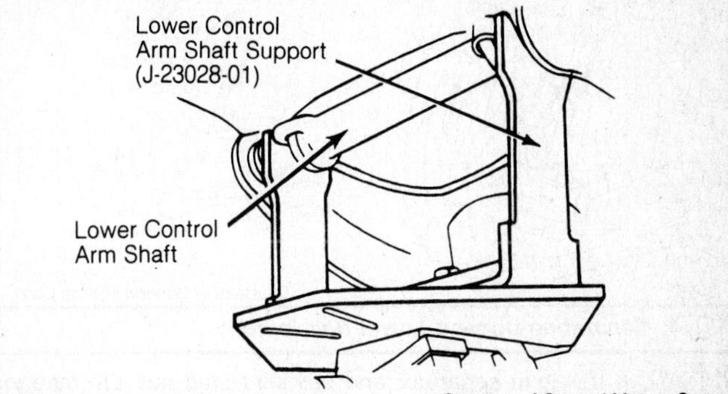
Lower Control
Arm Shaft Support
(J-23028-01)
Lower Control
Arm Shaft
30191
Courtesy of General Motors Corp.

Fig. 3: Installing Lower Control Arm Support

STEERING KNUCKLE

Removal – 1) Raise and support vehicle near ball joint so coil spring remains compressed. Remove wheel and tire assembly. Remove brake caliper, hub and brake rotor assembly. Remove rotor splash shield.

2) Remove cotter pin and nut from tie rod end. Use Tie Rod Remover (J-6627-A) to remove tie rod stud from steering knuckle arm.

3) Support lower control arm with floor jack. Remove upper and lower ball joint cotter pins, and loosen ball joint stud nuts. Using Ball Joint Separator (J-23742), separate steering knuckle from ball joint studs. *See Fig. 4*. Remove ball joint stud nuts and remove steering knuckle.

Inspection – Inspect tapered holes in steering knuckle for out-of-round, deformation or damage. Replace steering knuckle if damaged.

Installation – To install, reverse removal procedure. Tighten nuts to specification. See TORQUE SPECIFICATIONS table at end of article. Tighten ball joint and tie rod end stud nut to align cotter pin holes as necessary. Adjust wheel bearings. See FRONT WHEEL BEARINGS under ADJUSTMENTS & INSPECTION.

UPPER BALL JOINT

Removal – 1) Raise and support vehicle. Support lower control arm with floor jack. Remove wheel and tire assembly. Remove cotter pin from upper ball joint stud. Loosen nut 2 turns. DO NOT remove at this time.

2) Remove brake caliper. Install Ball Joint Separator (J-23742) between ball joint studs. *See Fig. 4*.

3) Extend bolt on ball joint separator to loosen ball joint stud from steering knuckle. Remove ball joint separator and ball joint stud nut. Drill out rivets and remove ball joint assembly.

CAUTION: When installing upper and lower ball joint stud nuts, NEVER loosen nut to install cotter pin. Tighten nuts only.

Installation – To install, reverse removal procedure. Use NEW nuts and bolts to install ball joint. Install grease fitting and lubricate new ball joint.

LOWER BALL JOINT

Removal – 1) Raise and support vehicle. Support lower control arm with floor jack. Remove wheel and tire assembly. Remove lower ball

1991 SUSPENSION
Front – 2WD Coil Spring – "G", "P" & "R" Series (Cont.)

joint stud cotter pin. Loosen ball joint stud nut 2 turns. DO NOT remove at this time.
2) Remove brake caliper. Install Ball Joint Separator (J-23742) between ball joint studs. *See Fig. 4*. Extend bolt on ball joint separator to loosen ball stud.

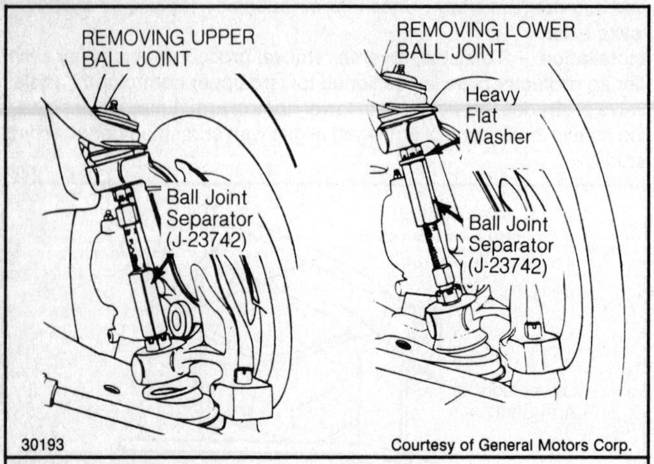
REMOVING UPPER BALL JOINT
REMOVING LOWER BALL JOINT
Heavy Flat Washer
Ball Joint Separator (J-23742)
Ball Joint Separator (J-23742)
30193
Courtesy of General Motors Corp.

Fig. 4: Separating Upper & Lower Ball Joints

3) Remove ball joint separator and ball joint stud nut. Lift steering knuckle assembly from lower ball joint stud. Support upper control arm with block of wood.
4) Assemble on the control arm, a "C" Clamp (J-9519-30) and Removers (J-9519-7 and J-9519-28) from Ball Joint Remover/Installer Set (J-9519-D). *See Fig. 5*. Remove ball joint.
Installation – Assemble the "C" Clamp (J-9519-30) and Installer (J-9519-16) from ball joint remover/installer set. *See Fig. 5*. Reverse removal procedure to install. Ensure bleed vent in rubber boot is facing forward. Install grease fitting and lubricate new ball joint with chassis lubricant.

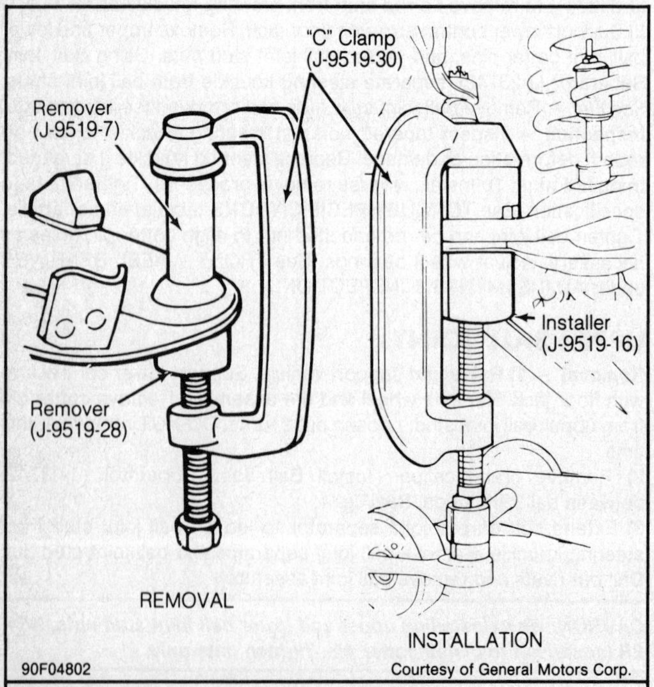
"C" Clamp (J-9519-30)
Remover (J-9519-7)
Installer (J-9519-16)
Remover (J-9519-28)
REMOVAL
INSTALLATION
90F04802
Courtesy of General Motors Corp.

Fig. 5: Removing & Installing Lower Ball Joint

UPPER CONTROL ARM

Removal – 1) Raise and support vehicle. Support lower control arm with floor jack. Remove wheel and tire assembly.
2) Remove brake caliper and suspend aside. Remove cotter pin from upper ball joint stud and loosen nut.
3) Using Ball Joint Separator (J-23742), loosen ball joint stud from steering knuckle. *See Fig. 4*. Remove ball joint separator and ball joint stud nut. Raise control arm from steering knuckle. Support steering knuckle assembly.
4) Remove upper control arm shaft-to-frame nuts. Remove upper control arm and alignment shims. Tape alignment shims together and tag location for reassembly.
Installation – To install, reverse removal procedure. Ensure alignment shims are installed in original location, with concave and convex sides together. To complete installation, reverse removal procedure. Check wheel alignment. See SPECIFICATIONS & PROCEDURES article in WHEEL ALIGNMENT.

NOTE: Normal shim pack will leave at least 2 bolt threads exposed beyond nut. If 2 bolt threads are not exposed, check for damaged control arms and components. Thickness difference between front and rear shim packs must not exceed .30" (7.6 mm). Front shim pack thickness must be at least .24" (6.1 mm). Tighten thinner shim pack nut first.

UPPER CONTROL ARM BUSHINGS

Bushing Replacement (G15/1500, G25/2500 & R15/1500) – 1) Mount control arm assembly in a vise. Remove nuts from ends of control arm shaft. Using components from Control Arm Bushing Service Set (J-24435-A), remove bushing from control arm.
2) Remove shaft from control arm. Note direction of shaft installation. Repeat procedure to remove remaining bushing. Reverse removal order to install bushings. Ensure bushings are fully seated.
Bushing Replacement (G35/3500, P25/2500, P35/3500, R25/2500 & R35/3500) – 1) Components can be changed with control arm in vehicle. To remove components, disconnect upper control arm from frame. See UPPER CONTROL ARM under REMOVAL & INSTALLATION. Unscrew bushings and slide control arm shaft out of control arm. Remove inner seals from between bushings and shaft.
2) To install, slide NEW seal onto each end of upper control arm shaft. Install shaft into upper control arm. Adjust shaft until centered in control arm, then tighten bushing nuts to specification. *See Fig. 6*. See TORQUE SPECIFICATIONS table at end of article. Check shaft for free rotation. Install grease fittings and lubricate bushings.

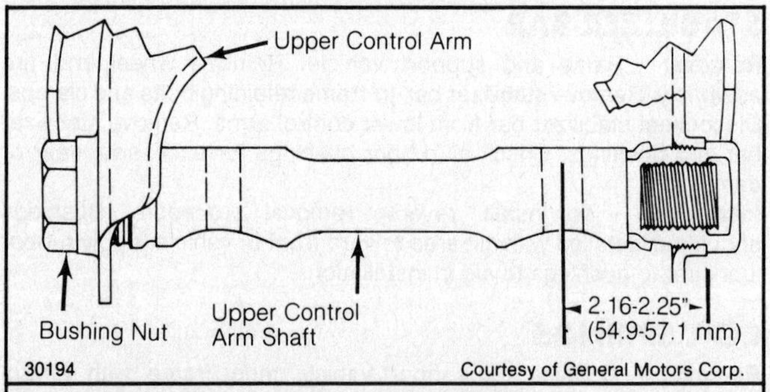
Upper Control Arm
Bushing Nut
Upper Control Arm Shaft
2.16-2.25"
(54.9-57.1 mm)
30194
Courtesy of General Motors Corp.

Fig. 6: Positioning Upper Control Arm Shaft (G35/3500, P25/2500, P35/3500, R25/2500 & R35/3500)

LOWER CONTROL ARM

WARNING: Securely bolt Lower Control Arm Shaft Support (J-23028-01) to jack, and install safety chain through lower control arm and coil spring to prevent personal injury.

Removal – 1) Raise and support vehicle. Support lower control arm with floor jack. Remove wheel and tire assembly.
2) Remove brake caliper and suspend aside. Remove coil spring. See COIL SPRINGS under REMOVAL & INSTALLATION. Support inboard end of control arm. Remove cotter pin from lower ball joint stud, then loosen ball joint stud nut one turn.

3) Using Ball Joint Separator (J-23742), position large cupped end of separator over upper ball stud nut, and position pilot-threaded end of tool onto lower ball stud. *See Fig. 4.*
4) Extend bolt of ball joint separator to separate ball stud from steering knuckle. Remove ball joint separator and stud nut. Remove control arm-to-frame nuts. Remove control arm.
Installation – To install, reverse removal procedure. Ensure front indexing hole in lower control arm shaft aligns with crossmember attaching stud.

LOWER CONTROL ARM BUSHINGS

Bushing Replacement (R15/1500) – 1) Bushings and control arm shaft can be replaced without removing control arm. Raise and support vehicle under frame, with control arms hanging free.
2) Remove wheel and tire assembly. Disconnect shock absorber and stabilizer bar bracket at lower control arm. Install Lower Control Arm Shaft Support (J-23028-01) onto a suitable jack. *See Fig. 3.* Position assembly under lower control arm so shaft seats in grooves of lower control arm shaft support.

WARNING: Securely bolt Lower Control Arm Shaft Support (J-23028-01) to jack, and install safety chain through lower control arm and coil spring to prevent personal injury.

3) Remove control arm shaft-to-crossmember "U" bolts. Loosen control arm shaft bushing nuts. DO NOT remove nuts. Remove control arm-to-frame "U" bolts. Carefully lower jack until all spring tension is released. Remove nuts and "U" bolts. Lower control arm from frame.
4) Remove staked area from front bushing. Use Control Arm Bushing Set (J-24435-A) for bushing replacement. Using Spacer (J-24435-6), Bushing Remover (J-24435-3) and "C" Clamp (J-24435-7), remove one bushing from control arm. With control arm shaft still in control arm, remove remaining bushing from control arm.
5) Reverse removal order to install. Using Installer (J-24435-4), Spacer (J-24435-6) and "C" Clamp (J-24435-7), install one bushing. Install lower control arm shaft and install remaining bushing. *See Fig. 7.* Stake front control arm bushing in at least 2 areas on control arm.
6) Install lower control arm. Ensure front indexing hole in lower control arm shaft aligns with crossmember attaching stud. Tighten all fasteners to specification. See TORQUE SPECIFICATIONS table at end of article. Check wheel alignment. See SPECIFICATIONS & PROCEDURES article in WHEEL ALIGNMENT.
Bushing Replacement (G15/1500 & G25/2500 Except 6.2L Diesel) – 1) Remove lower control arm. See LOWER CONTROL ARM under REMOVAL & INSTALLATION. Remove nuts and washers from control arm shaft.
2) Install control arm in press for rear bushing removal. Press on front of lower control arm shaft and remove rear bushing. Remove lower control arm shaft.
3) Using Bushing Remover (J-24435-3), Spacer (J-24435-2 and J-24435-6) and "C" Clamp (J-24435-7), remove front bushing.

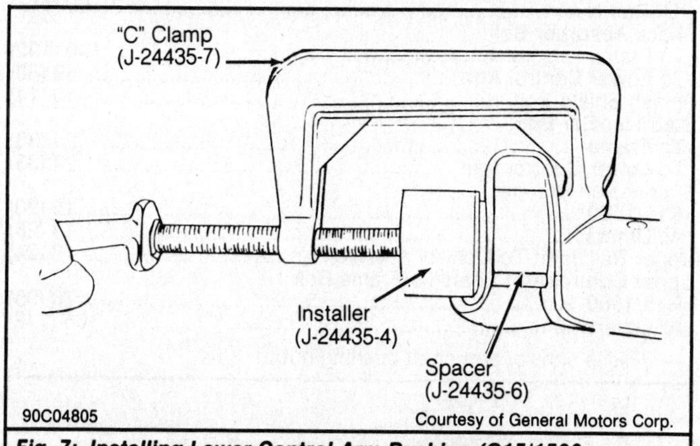
"C" Clamp
(J-24435-7)
Installer
(J-24435-4)
Spacer
(J-24435-6)
90C04805
Courtesy of General Motors Corp.

Fig. 7: Installing Lower Control Arm Bushing (G15/1500, G25/2500 Except 6.2L Diesel & R15/1500)

4) Use Installer (J-24435-4), Spacer (J-24435-6) and "C" Clamp (J-24435-7) to install front bushing. *See Fig. 7.* Stake front bushing in at least 2 areas.
5) Align outer tube hole so it faces front or toward staked bushing. Install lower control arm shaft and repeat procedure to install remaining bushing. Install washers and nuts on lower control arm shaft. Install lower control arm.
Bushing Replacement (G25/2500 6.2L Diesel) – 1) Remove lower control arm. See LOWER CONTROL ARM under REMOVAL & INSTALLATION. Remove nuts and washers from control arm shaft.
2) Use Control Arm Bushing Set (J-24435-A) for bushing replacement. Using Removers (J-24435-1 and J-24435-3) and "C" Clamp (J-24435-7), remove one bushing from control arm. *See Fig. 8.* Remove control arm shaft. Repeat procedure to remove remaining bushing.
3) To install bushings, use Installers (J-24435-4 and J-24435-5) and "C" Clamp (J-24435-7). *See Fig. 9.* Install one bushing. Install control arm shaft, and repeat procedure to install remaining bushing. Install lower control arm.

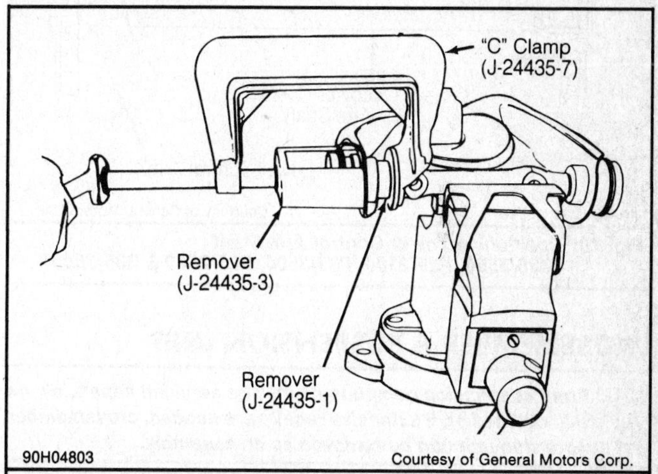
"C" Clamp
(J-24435-7)
Remover
(J-24435-3)
Remover
(J-24435-1)
90H04803
Courtesy of General Motors Corp.

Fig. 8: Removing Lower Control Arm Bushing (G25/2500 6.2L Diesel)

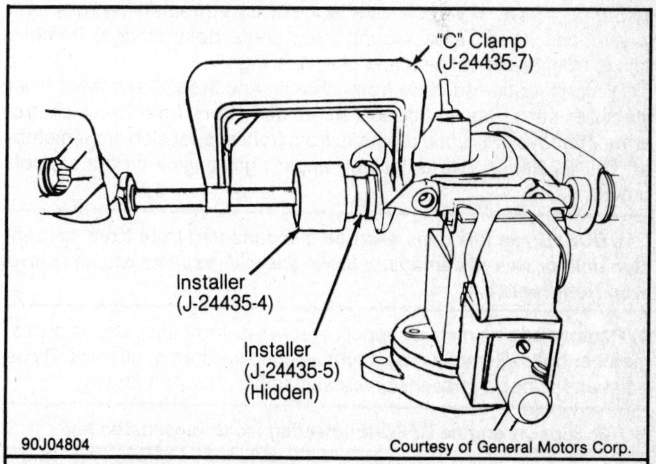
"C" Clamp
(J-24435-7)
Installer
(J-24435-4)
Installer
(J-24435-5)
(Hidden)
90J04804
Courtesy of General Motors Corp.

Fig. 9: Installing Lower Control Arm Bushing (G25/2500 6.2L Diesel)

Bushing Replacement (G35/3500, P25/2500, P35/3500, R25/2500 & R35/3500) – 1) Raise and support vehicle under frame, with control arms hanging free. Remove wheel and tire assembly. Disconnect shock absorber and stabilizer bar bracket at lower control arm.
2) Place floor jack under lower control arm. Jack must be positioned inward of coil spring and in depression areas of control arm. Install safety chain over upper control arm on inside of stabilizer bar and outside of shock absorber.

1991 SUSPENSION
Front – 2WD Coil Spring – "G", "P" & "R" Series (Cont.)

3) Remove lower control arm "U" bolt nuts and washers. Lower the control arm. Remove grease fittings. Remove bushing nuts and remove lower control arm shaft from control arm. Remove seals located between bushing and lower control arm shaft.

4) To install, slide NEW seals onto lower control arm shaft. Install shaft into lower control arm. Adjust shaft until centered in control arm, then tighten bushing nuts to specification. *See Fig. 10.* See TORQUE SPECIFICATIONS table at end of article. Check shaft for free rotation. Install grease fittings and lubricate bushings.

5) Install lower control arm. Ensure front indexing hole in lower control arm shaft aligns with crossmember attaching stud. Tighten all fasteners to specification. See TORQUE SPECIFICATIONS table at end of article. Check wheel alignment. See SPECIFICATIONS & PROCEDURES article in WHEEL ALIGNMENT.

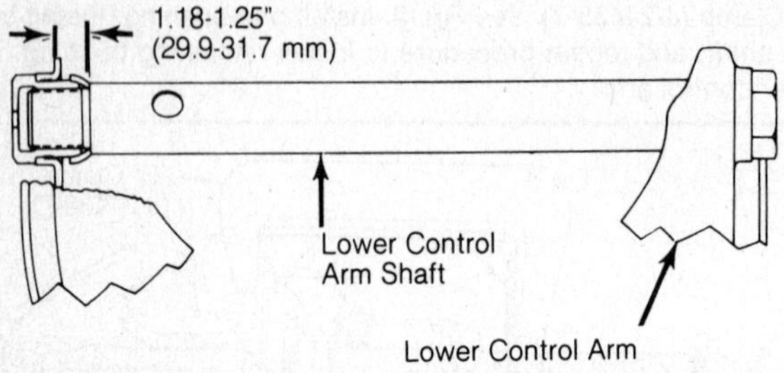
1.18-1.25"
(29.9-31.7 mm)
Lower Control
Arm Shaft
Lower Control Arm

117421 Courtesy of General Motors Corp.

Fig. 10: Positioning Lower Control Arm Shaft (G35/3500, P25/2500, P35/3500, R25/2500 & R35/3500)

CROSSMEMBER & SUSPENSION UNIT

NOTE: Front suspension components may be serviced separately as previously outlined or, if extensive repairs are needed, crossmember and suspension unit can be removed as an assembly.

Removal – 1) Disconnect negative battery cable. Raise and support vehicle. Remove front wheel and tire assemblies. Disconnect front brake hose clip from each upper control arm.

2) Support front of vehicle with jack stands at frame side rails, and lower hoist. Clean area around front brake hose fittings. Remove hoses from brake calipers and plug openings.

3) Disconnect tie rod ends from steering knuckles. Disconnect front stabilizer bar (if equipped) and shock absorbers from lower control arms. Remove brake line clip bolts from front suspension crossmember. On "R" Series, clip is located under right engine mount support bracket.

CAUTION: Brake line clips must be disconnected from front suspension unit, or severe damage to brake line will result when unit is lowered from vehicle.

4) Remove engine mount support bracket-to-front suspension crossmember bolts. Remove crossmember-to-lower frame rail bolts. Raise hoist and support suspension crossmember. Support engine.

NOTE: Support engine BEFORE lowering front suspension unit.

5) Remove upper control arm bracket-to-frame side rail bolts. Suspension unit is now disconnected. Lower hoist and remove front suspension unit from vehicle.

Installation – To install, reverse removal procedure. Lubricate suspension components. Bleed brake system.

TORQUE SPECIFICATION

TORQUE SPECIFICATIONS

Application	Ft. Lbs. (N.m)
"G" Series	
Ball Joint-To-Steering Knuckle Nut	
Lower	90 (122)
Upper	
G35/3500	90 (122)
All Others	50 (68)
Control Arm Shaft Bolt/Nut	
Lower Control Arm	
G35/3500	[1] 280 (380)
All Others	115 (156)
Upper Control Arm	
G35/3500	[1] 190 (257)
All Others	115 (156)
Crossmember-To-Bottom Frame Rail Bolt	90 (122)
Crossmember-To-Frame Side Rail Bolt	65 (88)
Crossmember-To-Support Strut Bolt	60 (81)
Lower Control Arm Shaft-To-Frame	
"U" Bolt Nut	
G35/3500	85 (115)
All Others	65 (88)
Shock Absorber Bolt	
To Frame	80 (108)
To Lower Control Arm	80 (108)
Splash Shield Bolt	10 (14)
Stabilizer Bar Bolt	
To Frame	21 (28)
To Lower Control Arm	24 (33)
Suspension Bumper	15 (20)
Upper Ball Joint-To-Control Arm Bolt	18 (24)
Upper Control Arm Shaft-To-Frame Bolt	
G35/3500	105 (142)
All Others	70 (95)
"P" & "R" Series	
Ball Joint-To-Steering Knuckle Nut	
Lower	90 (122)
Upper	
R15/1500	50 (68)
All Others	90 (122)
Control Arm Shaft Bolt/Nut	
Lower Control Arm	
R15/1500	70 (95)
All Others	[1] 280 (380)
Upper Control Arm	
R15/1500	115 (156)
All Others	[1] 190 (257)
Crossmember-To-Bottom Frame Rail Bolt	
Motorhome	215 (291)
"P" Series With Disc Brakes	130 (176)
R35/3500 With Heavy Duty Suspension	130 (176)
All Others	90 (122)
Crossmember-To-Frame Side Rail Bolt	
"P" Series With Disc Brakes & Motorhome	100 (136)
R35/3500 With Heavy Duty Suspension	100 (136)
All Others	65 (88)
Crossmember-To-Support Strut Bolt	60 (81)
Lower Control Arm Shaft-To-Frame	
"U" Bolt Nut	85 (115)
Shock Absorber Bolt	
To Frame	140 (190)
To Lower Control Arm	59 (80)
Splash Shield Bolt	10 (14)
Stabilizer Bar Bolt	
To Frame	24 (33)
To Lower Control Arm	24 (33)
Suspension Bumper	
R15/1500	15 (20)
All Others	19 (26)
Upper Ball Joint-To-Control Arm Bolt	18 (24)
Upper Control Arm Shaft-To-Frame Bolt	
R15/1500	70 (95)
All Others	105 (142)

[1] – This is control arm shaft bushing nut.

1991 SUSPENSION
Front – 2WD Coil Spring – All Others

Astro, Safari, "C" & "S" Series

NOTE: Vehicle series numbers in this article list Chevrolet model first, followed by GMC. Example: "C" Series model 15/1500. Chevrolet/GMC equivalent models are as follows: 15 = 1500, 25 = 2500 and 35 = 3500.

DESCRIPTION

Independent front suspension consists of upper and lower control arms with steering knuckle mounted by ball joints. The upper and lower control arms are mounted with pivot shafts or bolts through rubber bushings. Coil springs are mounted between lower control arm and a formed seat in suspension crossmember. A stabilizer bar is mounted by bracket to frame side rails, and connected to lower control arms by link bolts.

The front wheels are held in proper relation to each other by 2 tie rods connected to steering arms on the knuckles at one end, and to intermediate shaft at the other.

ADJUSTMENTS & INSPECTION

WHEEL ALIGNMENT SPECIFICATIONS & PROCEDURES

NOTE: See SPECIFICATIONS & PROCEDURES article in WHEEL ALIGNMENT.

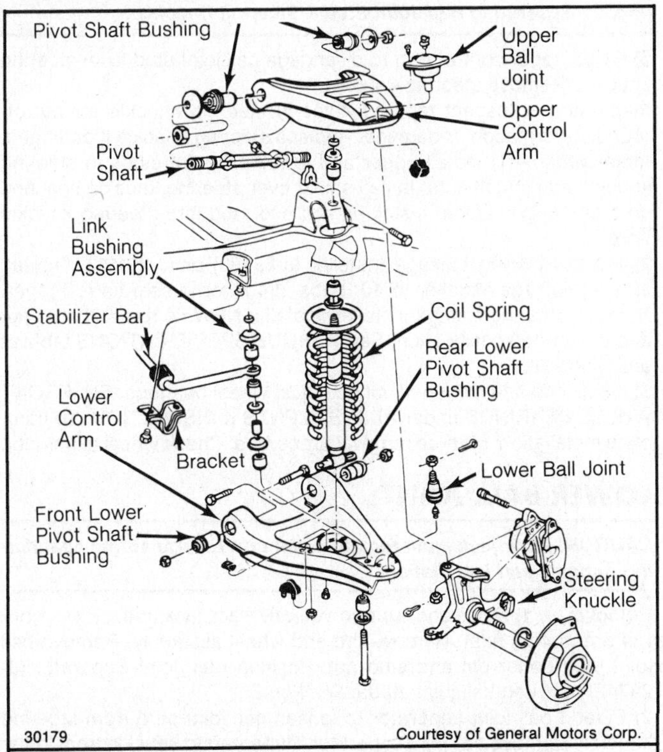
Pivot Shaft Bushing
Upper Ball Joint
Upper Control Arm
Pivot Shaft
Link Bushing Assembly
Stabilizer Bar
Coil Spring
Rear Lower Pivot Shaft Bushing
Lower Control Arm
Bracket
Lower Ball Joint
Front Lower Pivot Shaft Bushing
Steering Knuckle
30179
Courtesy of General Motors Corp.

Fig. 1: Exploded View of Typical Coil Spring Suspension

FRONT WHEEL BEARINGS

CAUTION: Never preload tapered roller bearings, or damage to roller ends will result. Bearings are designed to have a slightly loose feel when properly adjusted.

1) Raise and support vehicle. Rotate wheel by hand to check bearings for excessive tightness, looseness, noise or roughness. Grip wheel assembly at top and bottom and check hub play. If movement is not .001-.005" (.03-.13 mm), adjust bearings.

2) Tighten spindle bearing nut to 12 ft. lbs. (16 N.m) while turning wheel forward by hand. Back off nut until it is just loose. Finger tighten nut until snug. Loosen nut slightly (no more than 1/2 a flat) until new cotter pin can be installed. Recheck hub play.

BALL JOINT CHECKING

NOTE: Ensure wheel bearings are properly adjusted before checking ball joints. Replace ball joint rubber grease seal if cut or damaged.

Upper & Lower Ball Joints ("C" Series) – 1) Raise and support vehicle with a jack stand near lower ball joint. Place a dial indicator on spindle hub.

2) Pry tire and wheel assembly up and down, and note dial indicator reading. If reading exceeds .08" (2.0 mm), replace loose ball joint.

Upper Ball Joint (Astro, Safari & "S" Series) – 1) Raise and support vehicle with jack stands under lower control arms, as close as possible to each lower ball joint. Ensure upper control arm bumper does not contact frame. Place dial indicator against lower part of wheel rim. Push in on bottom of tire while pulling outward at the top. Read dial indicator, then reverse push/pull procedure.

2) Lateral (horizontal) deflection should not exceed .125" (3.18 mm). If deflection is excessive, replace ball joint.

Lower Ball Joint (Astro, Safari & "S" Series) – 1) Wear indicator is built into the ball joint. Wear is indicated by the position of the 1/2" diameter round boss that the grease fitting is threaded into. A new ball joint has a boss projection of .050" (1.27 mm) beyond cover surface.

2) With vehicle weight on wheels, ensure wear indicator protrudes beyond surface of ball joint cover. Replace ball joint if wear indicator is recessed or even with housing.

REMOVAL & INSTALLATION

WHEEL BEARINGS

Removal – 1) Raise and support vehicle. Remove tire and wheel assembly. Remove brake caliper and wire aside. DO NOT hang caliper by flexible hose. Remove hub dust cap, cotter pin, retainer nut and washer. Remove hub and rotor assembly.

2) Remove outer wheel bearing. Pry out inner bearing grease seal and discard. Remove inner bearing. Inspect bearings for damage or excessive wear. Replace as needed. If necessary, drive out bearing races using hammer and Wheel Bearing Race Remover (J-29117).

Inspection – Wash wheel bearings and hub in solvent and dry with compressed air. DO NOT spin bearings with air.

Installation – 1) If bearing races are removed, drive bearing races into position using hammer and brass drift. Lubricate bearings thoroughly.

2) To complete installation, reverse removal procedure. Adjust wheel bearings. See FRONT WHEEL BEARINGS under ADJUSTMENTS & INSPECTION.

SHOCK ABSORBERS

Removal – Raise and support vehicle. Hold upper stem from turning while removing upper stem retaining nut, retainer and rubber grommet at top of shock absorber. Remove shock absorber-to-lower control arm bolt. Remove shock absorber.

Inspection – 1) On fluid-filled shock, purge air from pressure chamber by mounting in vise (top end up) and fully extending unit. Reverse position (top end down) and fully collapse unit. Repeat procedure several times.

2) Bench check shock unit by mounting in vise with top end up (top end down on gas-charged shocks). DO NOT clamp on reservoir tube or mounting threads. Check rubber grommets for damage or deterioration and replace as needed. Operate shock by hand at various rates of speed and note resistance. If resistance is not smooth and constant, replace shocks.

Installation – To install, reverse removal procedure. Tighten attaching nut and bolts to specification. See TORQUE SPECIFICATIONS table at end of article.

1991 SUSPENSION
Front – 2WD Coil Spring – All Others (Cont.)

STABILIZER BAR

Removal – 1) Raise and support vehicle. Remove bolt and link bushing assembly from each side of stabilizer bar. *See Fig. 1.* Mark components for installation to original location.

2) Remove bracket-to-frame (or body) mounting bolts. Remove stabilizer bar with rubber insulator bushings and brackets attached. Inspect insulator bushings and link bolt grommets for damage or deterioration; replace as necessary.

Installation – 1) Apply rubber lubricant to insulator bushing contact areas of stabilizer bar. Install all components in original location. Install insulator bushings onto bar, with bushing slit toward front of vehicle.

NOTE: On Astro and Safari, install stabilizer bar with identification forming on right of vehicle, and offset of bar in downward position.

2) Install bushing brackets squarely onto bushings. Loosely install mounting bolts. On Astro and Safari, install link bolt components at lower control arms. Lower vehicle. Tighten all nuts and bolts to specification. See TORQUE SPECIFICATIONS table at end of article.

3) On all other models, tighten bolts to specification. Ensure link bushing assembly nut is even with bottom of bolt. Lower vehicle.

COIL SPRINGS

Removal – 1) Raise vehicle and support under frame, allowing control arms hang free. Remove lower shock absorber mounting bolts. Push shock absorber upward through control arm and into coil spring.

2) Secure Front Coil Spring Compressor (J-23028-01) onto an adjustable jack. Position spring compressor and jack under lower control arm to cradle lower control arm inner bushings.

WARNING: Failure to secure Front Coil Spring Compressor (J-23028-01) to appropriate jack may cause personal injury.

3) Remove stabilizer bar-to-lower control arm link bolt components. Raise jack to release spring tension on lower control arm pivot bolts. Install a safety chain around spring, through lower control arm.

4) Remove lower control arm pivot bolts (rear bolt first). Carefully lower jack until all tension is released from coil spring. Remove safety chain and coil spring from vehicle.

NOTE: DO NOT apply force on lower control arm and ball joint to remove coil spring. Coil spring can easily be removed by maneuvering spring.

Installation – 1) Position coil spring on control arm. Ensure spring insulator is in place. Lift control arm with spring compressor and jack. Ensure coil spring is properly positioned, with end of lower spring coil covering one drain hole, and clear of or partially covering the other.

NOTE: Coil spring must be positioned with tape at lowest position. Bottom of spring is coiled helical, and top is coiled flat with a gripper notch near end of spring coil.

2) Install lower control arm pivot bolts (front bolt first). Pivot bolts must be installed with nuts toward rear of vehicle. To install remaining components, reverse removal procedure.

STEERING KNUCKLE

Removal – 1) Raise and support vehicle with jack stands at front lift points. Remove wheel and tire assembly. Remove brake caliper and move aside.

NOTE: DO NOT place jack stands under lower control arm. Spring tension is needed to break loose ball joint stud.

2) Remove hub and rotor assembly. Remove splash shield. Separate tie rod end stud from steering knuckle using Tie Rod Remover (J-6627).

CAUTION: Lower control arm must be supported with floor jack during removal and installation of steering knuckle.

3) If replacing steering knuckle, carefully remove steering knuckle grease seal. Position jack under lower control arm, near spring seat. Raise jack until lower control arm is just supported.

4) Remove cotter pins and nuts from ball joints. Using Ball Joint Separator (J-23742), separate ball joint studs from steering knuckle. *See Fig. 2.*

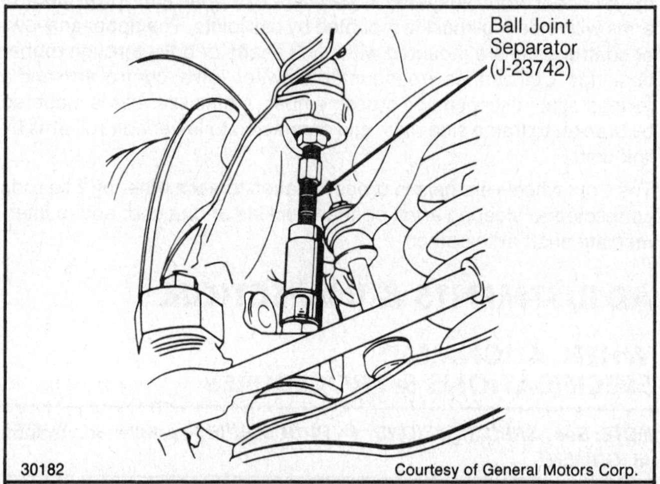
Ball Joint
Separator
(J-23742)
30182
Courtesy of General Motors Corp.

Fig. 2: Separating Ball Joint Stud & Steering Knuckle

5) Raise upper control arm to disengage ball joint stud from steering knuckle. Remove steering knuckle.

Inspection – Inspect tapered holes in steering knuckle for out-of-round, deformation or damage. Replace steering knuckle if damaged.

Installation – 1) Install upper and lower ball joint studs in steering knuckle and install nuts. Install shield over steering knuckle seal and onto steering knuckle. Install tie rod end stud into steering knuckle bore.

2) Install Steering Linkage Installer (J-29193) or (J-29194). Tighten steering linkage installer to 40 ft. lbs. (54 N.m) to seat tie rod taper. Remove steering linkage installer. Install a NEW tie rod end stud nut and tighten to specification. See TORQUE SPECIFICATIONS table at end of article.

3) Install hub and rotor assembly. Adjust wheel bearings. See FRONT WHEEL BEARINGS under ADJUSTMENTS & INSPECTION. To complete installation, reverse removal procedure. Check wheel alignment.

LOWER BALL JOINT

CAUTION: Floor jack must remain under control arm spring seat during removal and installation.

Removal – 1) Raise and support vehicle. Place jack under lower control arm spring seat. Remove tire and wheel assembly. Remove ball joint stud cotter pin and stud nut. Position Ball Joint Separator (J-23742) between ball joint studs. *See Fig. 2.*

2) Extend ball joint separator to loosen ball joint stud from steering knuckle. Remove ball joint separator. Pull steering knuckle from lower ball joint.

3) Place a wooden block between upper control arm and frame to keep steering knuckle assembly out of the way. Ensure no tension exists on brake caliper hose. Remove grease seal and grease fitting from ball joint.

4) Install, from the Ball Joint Remover and Installer Set (J-9519-D), a "C" Clamp (J-9519-30), Adapter (J-9519-7) and Remover/Installer (J-9519-28) on the lower ball joint. *See Fig. 3.* Rotate forcing screw on "C" clamp to press lower ball joint from control arm bore. Remove ball joint.

Installation – 1) Position new ball joint in lower control arm bore. Using "C" clamp and Installer (J-9519-16), press ball joint into bore until it bottoms on control arm. *See Fig. 3.* Remove installer tools.

1991 SUSPENSION
Front – 2WD Coil Spring – All Others (Cont.)

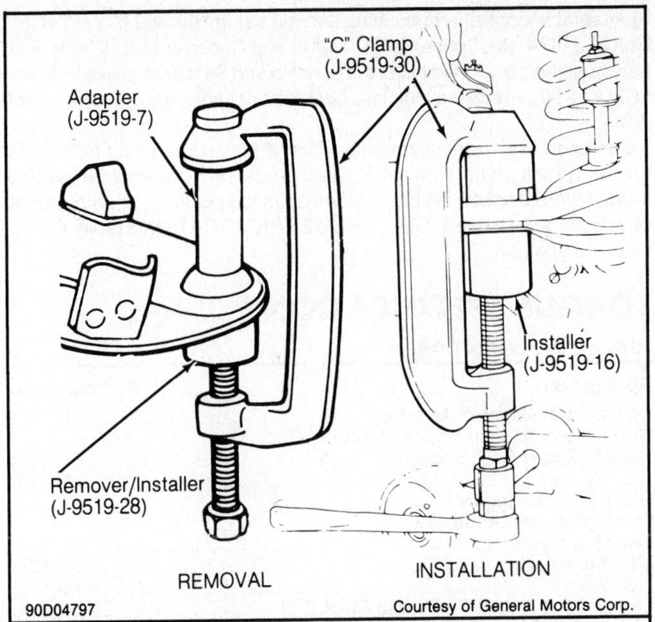
"C" Clamp
(J-9519-30)
Adapter
(J-9519-7)
Installer
(J-9519-16)
Remover/Installer
(J-9519-28)
REMOVAL
INSTALLATION
90D04797
Courtesy of General Motors Corp.

Fig. 3: Removing & Installing Lower Ball Joint

2) Position grease seal on ball joint so grease purge hole faces inward. Press grease seal on ball joint. Ensure grease seal is fully seated on ball joint. To install remaining components, reverse removal procedure. Lubricate ball joint fitting. Check and adjust wheel alignment.

UPPER BALL JOINT

Removal – 1) Raise and support front of vehicle with jack stands positioned under lower control arms near ball joint. Jack stands must remain under lower control arm during upper ball joint servicing.
2) Remove wheel and tire assembly. Remove cotter pin and upper ball joint stud nut. Install Ball Joint Separator (J-23742) between the ball studs. *See Fig. 2.* Extend ball joint separator to separate ball joint stud from steering knuckle.
3) Remove ball joint separator. Remove ball joint stud from steering knuckle. Support steering knuckle assembly to prevent damage to brake line.
4) Using drill and a 1/8" (3.18 mm) drill bit, drill a 1/4" (6.35 mm) deep hole in ball joint retaining rivets. Using a 1/2" (12.70 mm) drill bit, drill out the rivet heads. Using a hammer and small punch, drive out rivets and remove ball joint assembly.
Installation – To install, reverse removal procedure. Use nuts and bolts in place of rivets to attach ball joint to control arm. Lubricate new ball joint. Check wheel alignment.

UPPER CONTROL ARM & PIVOT SHAFT BUSHINGS

Removal (Upper Control Arm) – 1) Raise and support front of vehicle under lower control arms, between spring seats and ball joints. Remove wheel and tire. Place floor jack under lower control arm spring seat.
2) Note location of alignment shims for reassembly. Remove control arm retaining nuts and remove alignment shims. Remove cotter pin and upper ball joint stud nut. Install Ball Joint Separator (J-23742) between ball studs. *See Fig. 2.* Extend ball joint separator to separate ball joint stud from steering knuckle.
3) Support rotor and hub assembly to prevent damage to brake hose. Lift upper control arm, and remove upper control arm mounting bolts. Remove upper control arm.

NOTE: Upper control arm bushings are not replaceable on "C" Series models 15/1500 and 25/2500; control arm and bushings are serviced as a unit. Bushing replacement procedures for other "C" Series are not available from manufacturer.

Pivot Shaft Bushing Replacement (Astro, Safari & "S" Series) – 1) With upper control arm removed from vehicle, remove nuts from ends of pivot shaft. Position control arm assembly in a soft-jawed vise.
2) Using Bushing Remover (J-22269-1), a slotted washer and a short piece of pipe (slightly larger than bushing), press bushing and pivot shaft from control arm. Repeat procedure for opposite bushing.
3) To install bushings, place pivot shaft in control arm. Using Bushing Installer (J-22269-1) and small piece of pipe with the same O.D. as bushing, press new bushing into control arm bore and onto pivot shaft.
4) Ensure each bushing is positioned .48-.52" (12.8-13.8 mm) from face of control arm to bushing outer sleeve. Repeat procedure for bushing on opposite side. Install nuts onto pivot shaft ends.
Installation – To Install, reverse removal procedure. On "C" Series without pivot shaft, upper control arm pivot bushing bolt heads MUST face each other, and should be tightened to specification with vehicle at riding height. See TORQUE SPECIFICATIONS table at end of article. ON "S" Series, left-side upper control arm shaft MUST have depression facing inboard. Check wheel alignment.

LOWER CONTROL ARM & PIVOT BUSHINGS

Removal (Lower Control Arm) – Remove coil spring. See COIL SPRINGS under REMOVAL & INSTALLATION in this article. Remove cotter pin, nut and separate lower ball joint stud from steering knuckle. Remove steering knuckle from lower control arm. Remove bolts and lower control arm.

NOTE: Bushing replacement procedure for "C" Series is not available from manufacturer.

Pivot Bushing Replacement (Astro, Safari & "S" Series) – 1) Using a blunt chisel, drive front bushing flare down even with rubber of bushing. Install control arm bushing service set. On Astro and Safari, service set includes Receiver (J-21474-5), Nut (J-21474-18), Bolt (J-21474-19), Remover (J-21474-23) and Spacer (J-23737). *See Fig. 4.*
2) On "S" Series, service set includes Receiver (J-21474-5), Nut (J-21474-18), Bolt (J-21474-19), Remover (J-21474-23) and Spacer (J-22222-5). *See Fig. 4.* On all models, press front bushing from control arm.

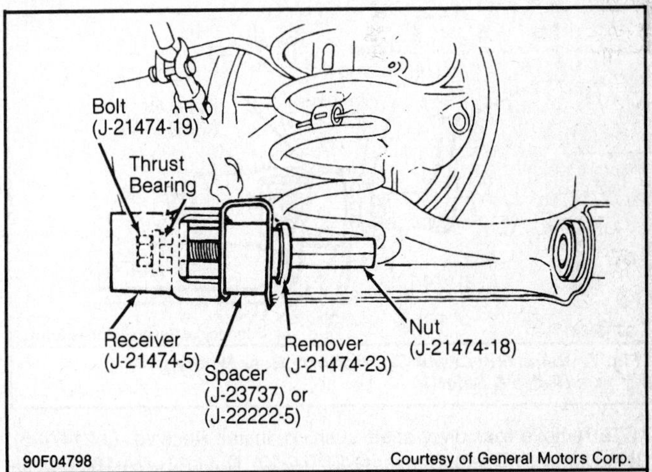
Bolt
(J-21474-19)
Thrust
Bearing
Receiver
(J-21474-5)
Spacer
(J-23737) or
(J-22222-5)
Remover
(J-21474-23)
Nut
(J-21474-18)
90F04798
Courtesy of General Motors Corp.

Fig. 4: Removing Lower Control Arm Front Bushing

3) To install front bushing, assemble control arm bushing service set. On Astro and Safari, use Installer (J-21474-20) and Spacer (J-21474-12) with other removal components of service set. *See Fig. 5.*
4) On "S" Series, use Washer (J-21474-8) with other removal components of service set to install new bushing. *See Fig. 4.* Position new bushing in control arm bore. Press bushing into bore.
5) Installed front bushings must be flared. On Astro and Safari, install Flaring Die (J-21474-2), Installer (J-21474-13), Nut (J-21474-18), Bolt (J-21474-19) and Spacer (J-23737). Flaring procedure for Astro and Safari is similar to flaring procedure for "S" Series. *See Fig. 6.*

1991 SUSPENSION
Front – 2WD Coil Spring – All Others (Cont.)

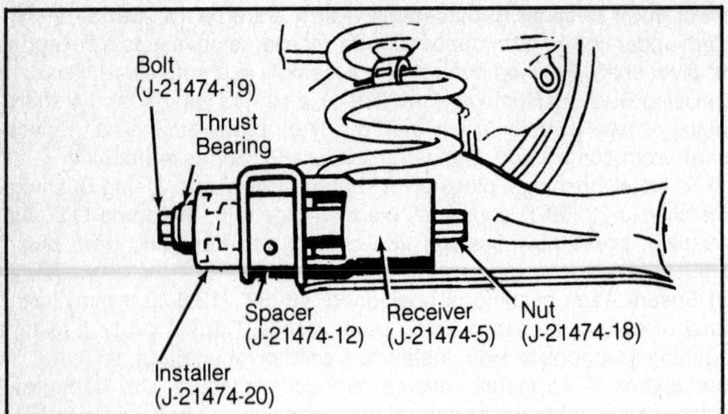
Bolt
(J-21474-19)
Thrust
Bearing
Spacer
(J-21474-12)
Receiver
(J-21474-5)
Nut
(J-21474-18)
Installer
(J-21474-20)
90H04799
Courtesy of General Motors Corp.

Fig. 5: Installing Lower Control Arm Front Bushing (Astro & Safari)

6) On "S" Series, install Flaring Die (J-21474-2), Spacer (J-21474-12), Installer (J-21474-13) and Nut (J-21474-18). *See Fig. 6.* On all models, turn nut on flaring component until bushing is flared approximately 45 degrees. Remove bushing flaring die and components.

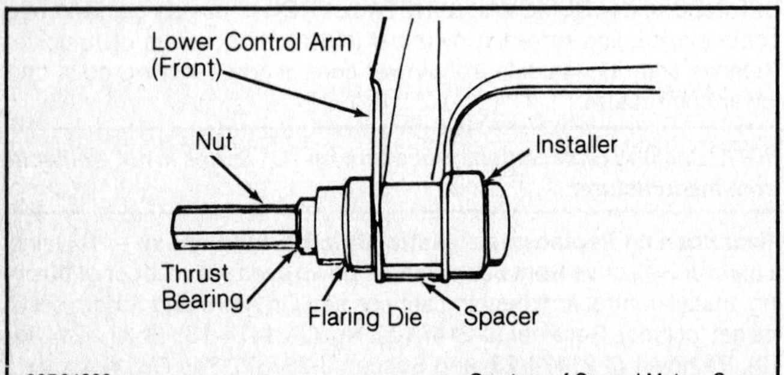
Lower Control Arm
(Front)
Nut
Installer
Thrust
Bearing
Flaring Die
Spacer
90B04800
Courtesy of General Motors Corp.

Fig. 6: Flaring Lower Control Arm Front Bushing

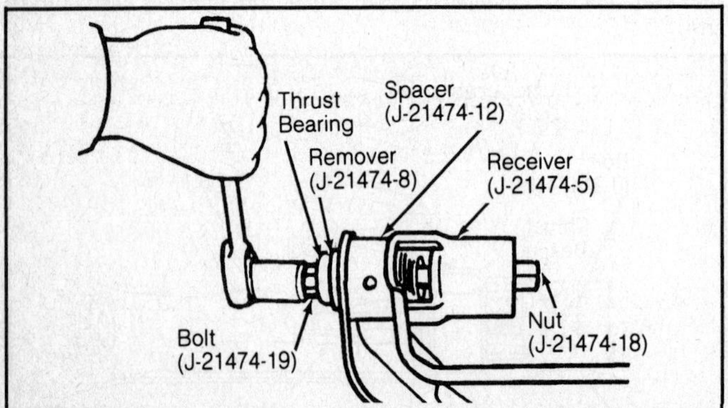
Thrust
Bearing
Spacer
(J-21474-12)
Remover
(J-21474-8)
Receiver
(J-21474-5)
Bolt
(J-21474-19)
Nut
(J-21474-18)
90D04801
Courtesy of General Motors Corp.

Fig. 7: Removing Lower Control Arm Rear Bushing (Astro & Safari)

7) To remove rear pivot shaft bushing, install Receiver (J-21474-5), Remover (J-21474-8), Spacer (J-21474-12), Nut (J-21474-18), Bolt (J-21474-19). *See Fig. 7.* Press bushing from bore.

8) Assemble control arm bushing service set. Install Nut (J-21474-18), Bolt (J-21474-19), Spacer (J-21474-12) and Receiver (J-21474-5) over new bushing positioned in bore. On Astro and Safari, also use Installer (J-21474-20). Press bushing into position until bottoms against control arm.

Installation – To install, reverse removal procedure using NEW nuts on control arm bolts. Control arm bolts must be installed with the bolt head toward front of vehicle. Tighten bolts to specification with weight of vehicle on its wheels. See TORQUE SPECIFICATIONS table. Check wheel alignment.

TORQUE SPECIFICATIONS

TORQUE SPECIFICATIONS

Application	Ft. Lbs. (N.m)
Ball Joint-To-Control Arm Bolt	17 (23)
Brake Rotor Splash Shield Mounting Bolt	
Astro, Safari & "S" Series	10 (14)
"C" Series	19 (26)
Bumper Mounting Bolt	20 (27)
Lower Ball Joint Stud Nut	
Astro & Safari	90 (122)
"C" Series	94 (127)
"S" Series	83 (112)
Lower Control Arm-To-Frame Pivot Bolt	
Astro & Safari	[1] 90 (122)
"C" Series	[1] 121 (164)
"S" Series	
Front Bolt	[1] 94 (127)
Rear Bolt	[1] 66 (89)
Shock Absorber-To-Lower Control Arm Mounting Bolt	
Astro & Safari	18 (25)
"C" & "S" Series	20 (27)
Shock Absorber Upper Mounting Nut	
Astro & Safari	11 (15)
"C" & "S" Series	8 (11)
Stabilizer Bar	
Insulator Bracket-To-Frame Mounting Bolt	
Astro & Safari	27 (37)
"C" & "S" Series	[1] 24 (33)
Link Mounting Bolt	[2] 13 (18)
Tie Rod End Stud Nut	
Astro & Safari	35 (47)
"C" & "S" Series	40 (54)
Upper Ball Joint Stud Nut	
Astro & Safari	65 (88)
"C" Series	70 (95)
"S" Series	61 (83)
Upper Control Arm Pivot Mounting Nut	85 (115)
Upper Control Arm-To-Frame Mounting Bolt	
Astro & Safari	75 (102)
"C" Series	90 (122)
"S" Series	65 (88)
Wheel Lug Nut	
Astro, Safari & "S" Series	90 (122)
"C" Series	
Dual Wheels	140 (190)
Single Wheels	120 (163)

[1] – Tighten to specifications with weight of vehicle on its wheels.
[2] – Obtain torque by running nut to unthreaded portion of bolt.

1991 SUSPENSION
Front – Leaf Spring

"P" & "V" Series

***NOTE:** Vehicle series numbers in this article list Chevrolet models first followed by GMC models. Example: V15/1500. Chevrolet/GMC equivalent models are: 15 = 1500, 25 = 2500 and 35 = 3500.*

DESCRIPTION

Leaf spring assembly attaches to front axle with "U" bolts. At wheel ends of V15/25 models, steering knuckle is attached with ball joints. "P" Series and V35/3500 models use kingpin attachments. On V35/3500 models, tapered upper kingpin fits in a tapered nylon bushing. Lower kingpin is part of bearing cap and rides in a tapered roller bearing. *See Figs. 1 and 2.*

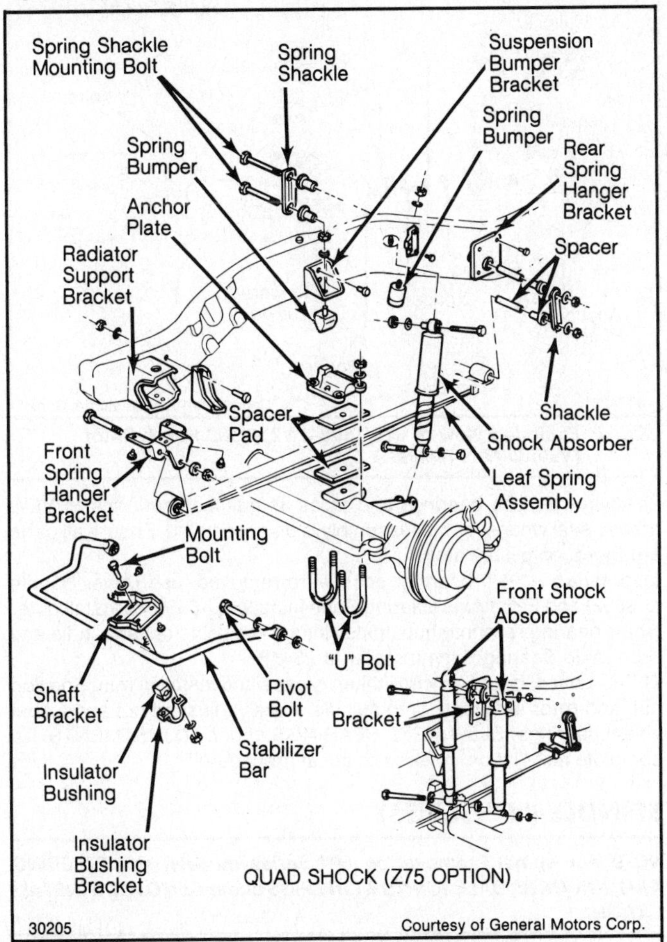
Spring Shackle Mounting Bolt
Spring Shackle
Suspension Bumper Bracket
Spring Bumper
Spring Bumper
Rear Spring Hanger Bracket
Anchor Plate
Radiator Support Bracket
Spacer
Spacer Pad
Shackle
Shock Absorber
Front Spring Hanger Bracket
Leaf Spring Assembly
Mounting Bolt
Front Shock Absorber
"U" Bolt
Shaft Bracket
Pivot Bolt
Bracket
Stabilizer Bar
Insulator Bushing
Insulator Bushing Bracket
QUAD SHOCK (Z75 OPTION)
30205
Courtesy of General Motors Corp.

***Fig. 1:** Exploded View of "V" Series Front Suspension*

ADJUSTMENTS

WHEEL ALIGNMENT SPECIFICATIONS & PROCEDURES

Caster and camber are designed into front axle assembly and are non-adjustable. Toe-in can be adjusted. See SPECIFICATIONS & PROCEDURES article in WHEEL ALIGNMENT.

WHEEL BEARINGS

"P" Series – Raise and support vehicle. Remove bearing cap and cotter pin. To seat bearing, tighten adjusting nut to 12 ft. lbs. (16 N.m) while rotating wheel. Back off adjusting nut approximately one flat. Check rotor and hub end play. End play should be .0005-.0080" (.013-.203 mm). Install cotter pin and bearing cap.

"V" Series – **1)** Remove locking hub. See LOCKING HUBS under REMOVAL & INSTALLATION. Remove wheel bearing lock nut and ring. *See Fig. 4*. To seat bearings, tighten adjusting nut to 50 ft. lbs. (68 N.m) while rotating hub.

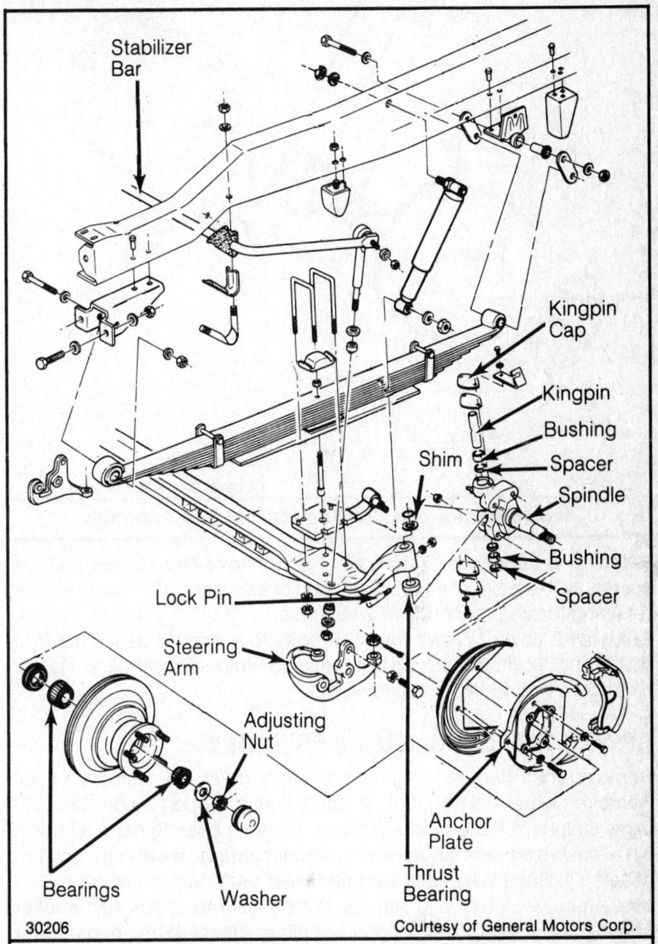
Stabilizer Bar
Kingpin Cap
Kingpin
Bushing
Shim
Spacer
Spindle
Bushing
Spacer
Lock Pin
Steering Arm
Adjusting Nut
Anchor Plate
Thrust Bearing
Bearings
Washer
30206
Courtesy of General Motors Corp.

***Fig. 2:** Exploded View of Front Suspension ("P" Series)*

2) Back off adjusting nut. Rotate hub and retighten to 35 ft. lbs. (47 N.m) on automatic hubs or 50 ft. lbs. (68 N.m) on manual hubs. Back off adjusting nut enough to free bearing on manual hubs, or 3/8 turn maximum on automatic hubs.

3) On automatic and manual locking hubs, install ring and wheel bearing lock nut. Ensure hole in ring aligns with pin on lock nut. Move adjusting nut to align pin. Install and tighten wheel bearing lock nut to 160 ft. lbs. (217 N.m).

4) Hub and rotor assembly end play should be .001-.010" (.03-.25 mm). If not to specification, repeat adjustment procedure. If end play is within specification, install locking hub assembly.

REMOVAL & INSTALLATION

LOCKING HUBS

Removal & Installation (Automatic) – **1)** Raise and support vehicle. Remove wheels. Remove automatic locking hub cover screws. Lift off cover and "O" ring. *See Fig. 3.*

2) Remove spring, inner race, bearing and retainer ring. Remove keeper from outer clutch housing. Remove ring with needle nose-pliers.

3) Install 2 cover screws in outer clutch housing and withdraw the assembly from wheel hub. To install locking hub, reverse removal procedure. Clean and lubricate bearing and race. Use new "O" ring and tighten cover screws to 45 INCH lbs. (5 N.m).

1991 SUSPENSION
Front – Leaf Spring (Cont.)

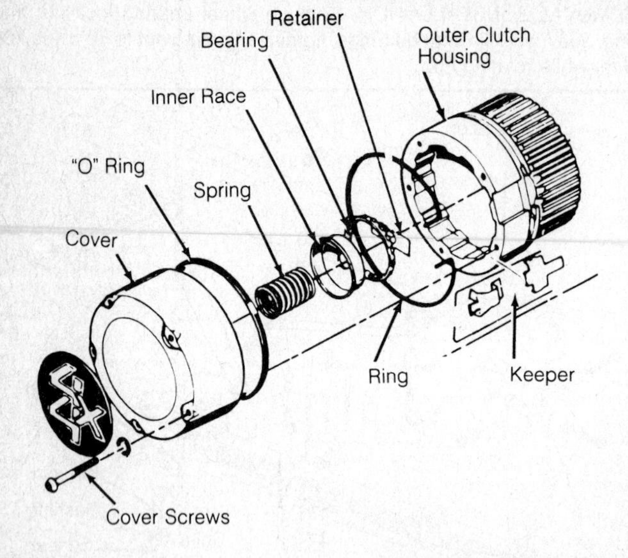
Retainer
Bearing
Outer Clutch Housing
Inner Race
"O" Ring
Spring
Cover
Ring
Keeper
Cover Screws
117425
Courtesy of General Motors Corp.

Fig. 3: Exploded View of Automatic Locking Hub Assembly

Removal & Installation (Manual) – 1) Remove cap screws and cap assembly. Remove snap ring from end of axle shaft. Remove lock ring retaining locking hub body in wheel hub.

2) Install 2 cover screws into hub body to withdraw assembly from wheel hub. To install locking hub, reverse removal procedure. Tighten cap screws to 45 INCH lbs. (5 N.m).

BRAKE ROTOR & HUB ASSEMBLY

Removal ("P" Series) – Raise and support vehicle. Remove wheel. Remove caliper from mounting bracket and support aside. DO NOT allow caliper to hang by brake hose. Remove bearing cap and cotter pin. Remove adjusting nut, washer, outer bearing, brake rotor and hub assembly. Remove grease seal and inner bearing if necessary.

Inspection – Wash all bearings in solvent and check for cracked bearing cages and worn, chipped or pitted rollers. Wash hub I.D. and inspect bearing races for cracks, scoring or looseness in hub. Replace components as needed.

NOTE: Always replace bearings and races as matched sets. Install new grease seal whenever wheel hub is disassembled. Before assembly, ensure all parts are thoroughly lubricated.

Installation – Install outer bearing race using Bearing Installer (J-29040). Install inner bearing race, using 3" (76.2 mm) diameter rod. Pack wheel bearings with wheel bearing grease. To complete installation, reverse removal procedure. Adjust wheel bearings. See WHEEL BEARINGS under ADJUSTMENTS.

Removal ("V" Series) – 1) Raise and support vehicle. Remove wheel. Remove brake caliper from mounting anchor plate and support aside. DO NOT allow caliper to hang by brake hose. Remove locking hub assembly. See LOCKING HUBS under REMOVAL & INSTALLATION.

2) Using Wheel Bearing Nut Wrench (J-26878-A) on V35/3500 or (J-6893-D) on all others, remove wheel bearing lock nut, ring and adjusting nut. *See Fig. 4*. Remove hub assembly and outer wheel bearing from spindle. Using a brass drift, remove inner wheel bearing and grease seal by tapping out with hammer.

3) If bearing(s) and/or race(s) require replacement, press races out with arbor press, or they may be driven out. To drive out races, insert brass drift, through hub, behind race. Using hammer, strike drift (alternating on each side of race) until race is removed.

Inspection – 1) Wash all bearings in solvent. Check for cracked bearing cages and worn, chipped or pitted rollers. Wash hub I.D. and inspect bearing races for cracks, scoring or looseness in hub. Replace components as needed.

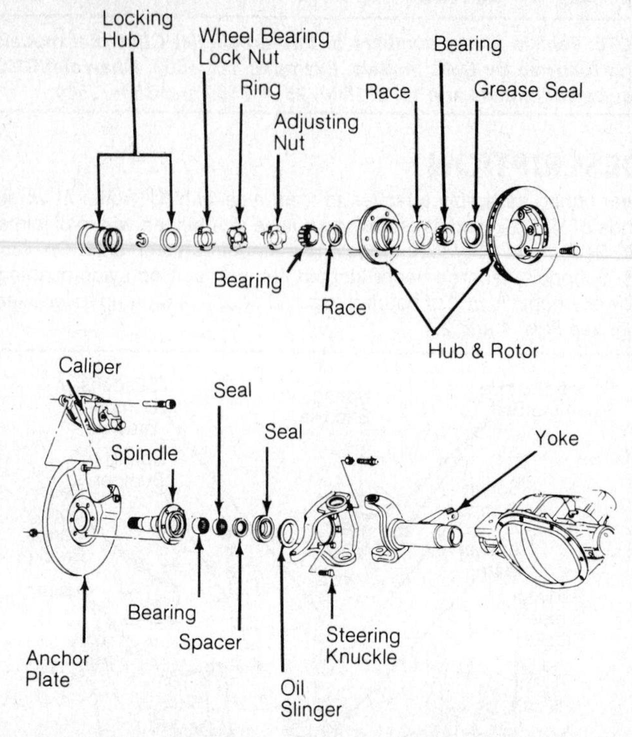
Locking Hub
Wheel Bearing Lock Nut
Ring
Adjusting Nut
Bearing
Race
Grease Seal
Bearing
Race
Hub & Rotor
Caliper
Seal
Seal
Spindle
Yoke
Bearing
Spacer
Steering Knuckle
Anchor Plate
Oil Slinger
117426
Courtesy of General Motors Corp.

Fig. 4: Exploded View of V15/1500 & V25/2500 Hub & Rotor (V35/3500 is Similar.)

2) Always replace bearings and races as matched sets. Install NEW grease seal whenever hub assembly is disassembled. Ensure all parts are thoroughly lubricated.

Installation – 1) If bearing races were removed, use Driver Handle (J-8092) and Front Axle Bearing Race Installer (J-6368) to install outer wheel bearing race into hub. Install inner race using driver handle and Front Axle Bearing Race Installer (J-23448).

2) Pack wheel bearings with lithium grease and install in hub. Position hub and rotor assembly onto spindle. Install adjusting nut and adjust wheel bearings. See WHEEL BEARINGS under ADJUSTMENTS. To complete installation, reverse removal procedure.

SPINDLE ("P" SERIES)

NOTE: For spindle removal on "P" Series models, see STEERING ARM, KNUCKLE, BALL JOINTS & KINGPINS under REMOVAL & INSTALLATION.

SPINDLE ("V" SERIES)

Removal – 1) Raise and support vehicle. Remove wheel. Remove locking hub. See LOCKING HUBS under REMOVAL & INSTALLATION. Remove brake caliper from mounting bracket and support aside. DO NOT allow caliper to hang by brake hose.

2) Remove hub and rotor assembly. Remove anchor plate and discard retaining nuts. NEW nuts must be used on reassembly. *See Fig. 4*. Detach spindle retaining bolts.

3) Remove spindle by tapping end of spindle lightly with soft-faced hammer. If necessary, remove seal, spacer, bearing seal and bearing from spindle. Replace spacer, bearing and seals if worn or damaged. DO NOT clamp machined surface of spindle in vise.

Installation – 1) If necessary, lubricate and install new bearing into spindle using Driver Handle (J-8092) and Needle Bearing Installer (J-23445-A) for V15/1500 and 25/2500, or (J-21465-17) for V35/3500. Install bearing seal ("V" block) with groove facing spacer. *See Fig. 5*.

1991 SUSPENSION
Front – Leaf Spring (Cont.)

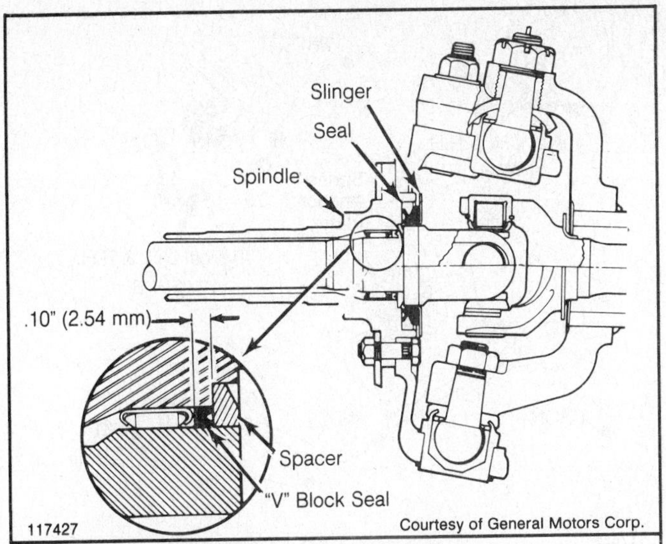
Slinger
Seal
Spindle
.10" (2.54 mm)
Spacer
"V" Block Seal
117427
Courtesy of General Motors Corp.

Fig. 5: Cross-Sectional View of Front Spindle

2) Install new grease seal onto slinger with slinger lip facing spindle. Install slinger, seal and spacer (chamfer toward slinger) onto axle shaft.
3) Install spindle, anchor plate and bracket (if equipped) onto steering knuckle. Using NEW nuts, tighten nuts to 65 ft. lbs. (88 N.m). Install hub and rotor assembly with locking hub in reverse of removal procedure. Adjust wheel bearings. See WHEEL BEARINGS under ADJUSTMENTS.

STEERING ARM, KNUCKLE, BALL JOINTS & KINGPINS

Removal ("P" Series With Kingpins) – 1) Raise and support vehicle. Remove wheel. Remove disc brake caliper without disconnecting brake hose. Suspend caliper on body. Remove hub and rotor assembly.
2) Remove mounting bolts, anchor plate, steering arm and splash shield. Steering arm can hang by tie rod end. Remove kingpin caps. Remove lock pin nut and washer. Tap out lock pin. Using a drift, remove kingpin, spacers and bushings. Remove steering knuckle and spindle assembly. Remove dust seal, shim and thrust bearing. *See Fig. 2.*

Installation – 1) Install new kingpin bushings. Ream bushings to 1.1804-1.1820" (29.982-30.023 mm). Lubricate thrust bearing. Install steering knuckle, thrust bearing, shim and dust seal. Lubricate kingpin.
2) Install kingpin and spacers. Install lock pin, washer and nut. Install kingpin caps. To complete installation, reverse removal procedure.

NOTE: Remove lower ball joint before servicing upper ball joint. Remove left knuckle steering arm to service upper ball joint.

Removal ("V" Series With Ball Joints) – 1) Raise and support vehicle. Remove wheels. Remove locking hub, hub and rotor assembly, and spindle components. Detach tie rod end from steering knuckle.
2) Remove left side steering arm only if ball joints are being replaced on that side. Remove steering arm nuts and adapters. *See Fig. 10.* Discard self-locking nuts for steering arm. NEW nuts must be used on installation. Remove steering arm.

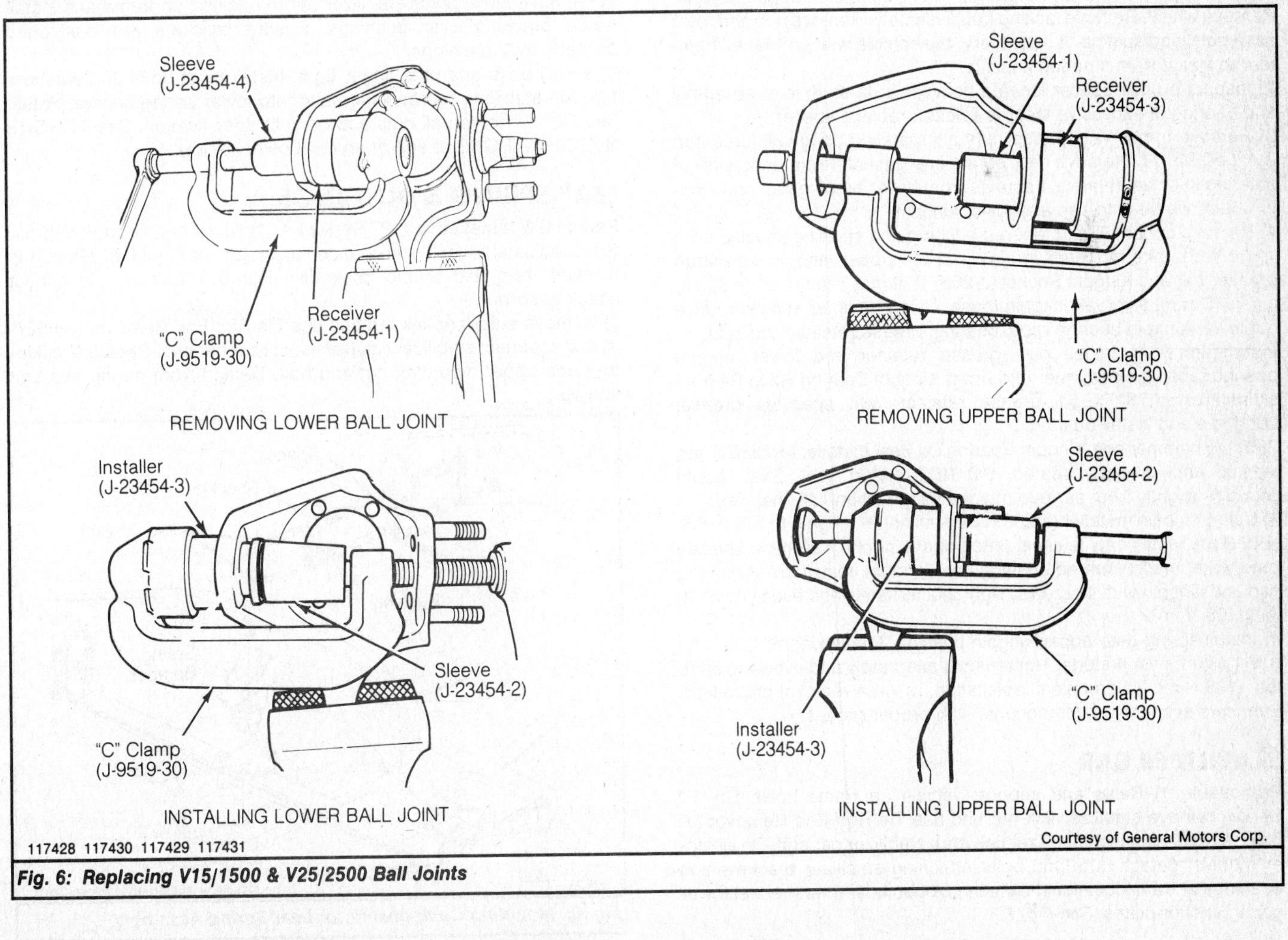
Sleeve
(J-23454-4)
Receiver
(J-23454-1)
"C" Clamp
(J-9519-30)
REMOVING LOWER BALL JOINT
Sleeve
(J-23454-1)
Receiver
(J-23454-3)
"C" Clamp
(J-9519-30)
REMOVING UPPER BALL JOINT
Installer
(J-23454-3)
Sleeve
(J-23454-2)
"C" Clamp
(J-9519-30)
INSTALLING LOWER BALL JOINT
Sleeve
(J-23454-2)
"C" Clamp
(J-9519-30)
Installer
(J-23454-3)
INSTALLING UPPER BALL JOINT
117428 117430 117429 117431
Courtesy of General Motors Corp.

Fig. 6: Replacing V15/1500 & V25/2500 Ball Joints

1991 SUSPENSION
Front – Leaf Spring (Cont.)

3) Remove cotter pins and nuts from ball joint studs. Separate steering knuckle assembly from ball joints.

CAUTION: DO NOT remove yoke upper ball joint stud adjusting ring unless new ball joints are being installed. If it is necessary to loosen adjusting ring to remove knuckle, DO NOT loosen more than 2 threads using Ball Stud Nut Wrench (J-23447). Non-hardened threads in yoke can be easily damaged by hardened threads of adjusting ring.

Ball Joint Replacement – 1) Remove snap ring from lower ball joint. Lower ball joint must be removed before servicing upper ball joint. Install steering knuckle assembly in vise.
2) Replace ball joints using "C" clamp and appropriate adapters.*See Fig. 6.* Install snap ring in lower ball joint.
Installation – 1) Tighten upper ball joint adjusting ring to 50 ft. lbs. (68 N.m) using Spanner Wrench (J-23447). Position steering knuckle and ball joints into yoke. Install stud nuts (finger tight) onto studs.
2) Push up on steering knuckle (to keep stud from turning) while tightening lower ball joint stud nut to 30 ft. lbs. (41 N.m). Tighten upper ball joint stud nut to 100 ft. lbs. (136 N.m). Install new cotter pin. DO NOT loosen stud nut to insert cotter pin. Tighten only enough to align slot in nut with stud hole.
3) Final tighten lower ball joint stud nut to 70 ft. lbs. (95 N.m). If tie rod and steering arm were removed, assemble steering arm to knuckle. Install 3 adapters. Tighten 3 NEW self-locking mounting nuts to 90 ft. lbs. (122 N.m).
4) Install tie rod end stud in knuckle arm bore. Tighten stud nut to 40 ft. lbs. (54 N.m). Install new cotter pin. To complete installation, reverse removal procedure. Lubricate suspension components with proper grease.
Removal (V35/3500 With Kingpins) – 1) Raise and support vehicle. Remove wheel. Remove locking hub assembly. Remove hub and rotor assembly, and spindle. If necessary, tap spindle with soft-faced hammer to free it from steering knuckle.
2) Inspect bronze spacer located between axle shaft joint assembly and bearing. If excessive wear is evident, replace spacer.
3) Remove upper kingpin cap nuts alternately (spring will force cap up). *See Fig. 11.* Remove cap, spring and gasket. From underside of steering knuckle, remove 4 screws from lower bearing cap and kingpin. Remove bearing cap and lower kingpin.
4) Remove upper kingpin tapered bushing and steering knuckle from yoke. With yoke mounted in vise, remove upper kingpin with large breaker bar and Kingpin Socket (J-26871). It may require up to 600 ft. lbs. (813 N.m) to break kingpin loose. Using hammer and drift, drive out lower kingpin bearing race, bearing, grease retainer and seal.
Installation – 1) Install new grease retainer and lower kingpin bearing race using hammer and Front Kingpin Bearing Race Remover/Installer (J-7817). Fill grease retainer with specified grease. Lubricate and install bearing.
2) Using hammer and Kingpin Bearing Oil Seal Installer (J-22301), tap in seal until properly seated. DO NOT distort seal. Seal should protrude slightly from surface of yoke flange when fully installed.
3) Using Kingpin Installer (J-28871), install upper kingpin to 550 ft. lbs. (745 N.m). Install new felt seal onto upper kingpin. Assemble knuckle onto yoke. Install tapered bushing over kingpin. Install lower bearing cap and kingpin with 4 screws. Tighten alternately and evenly to 80 ft. lbs. (108 N.m).
4) Install spring onto upper kingpin bushing. Install kingpin cap, with new gasket, over 4 studs. Tighten nuts alternately and evenly to 80 ft. lbs. (108 N.m). To complete installation, reverse removal procedure. Lubricate suspension components with proper grease.

STABILIZER BAR

Removal – 1) Raise and support vehicle on frame hoist. On "P" Series, remove stabilizer link nut and use Tie Rod End Remover (J-6627-A) to disconnect stabilizer link from stabilizer bar end. On all other models, detach nuts and bolts attaching stabilizer brackets and bushings at frame locations. Detach pivot bolts and washers at lower spring anchor plates. *See Fig. 7.*

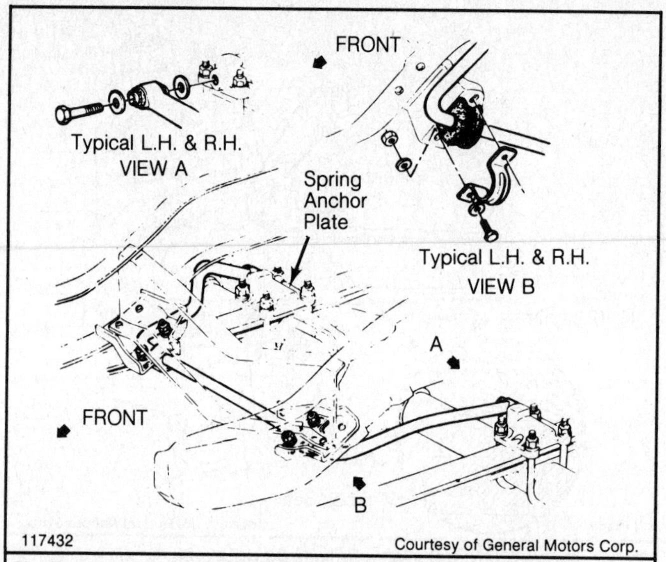
FRONT
Typical L.H. & R.H.
VIEW A
Spring
Anchor
Plate
Typical L.H. & R.H.
VIEW B
A
FRONT
B
117432
Courtesy of General Motors Corp.

Fig. 7: Mounting Attachments for Stabilizer Bar (Typical)

2) Remove stabilizer bar from vehicle. Inspect rubber bushings for excessive wear or deterioration. Check bar for damage. Replace components as necessary.
Installation – 1) On "V" Series, apply rubber grease to stabilizer bar bushing locations. Position bar-to-frame bushings with slit toward front of vehicle. On "P" Series, install stabilizer link into stabilizer bar end and install link nut.
2) On all models, place stabilizer bar in position on frame and install frame brackets over bushings. Ensure brackets are positioned properly over bushings.
3) Install bolts and nuts finger tight. Install pivot bolts and washers through stabilizer bar bushings and into lower spring anchor plates. *See Fig. 7.* Tighten all nuts and bolts to specification. See TORQUE SPECIFICATIONS at end of article. Lower vehicle.

LEAF SPRING & BUSHINGS

Removal & Installation ("P" Series) – 1) Raise and support vehicle. Place adjustable jack stand under axle. Lift axle until all tension is relieved from leaf spring assembly. Remove wheels. Disconnect shock absorber.
2) Remove stabilizer link nut and use Tie Rod End Remover (J-6627-A) to disconnect stabilizer link from stabilizer bar end. Detach shackle-to-frame upper mounting nut and bolt. Detach front spring eye bolt and nut.

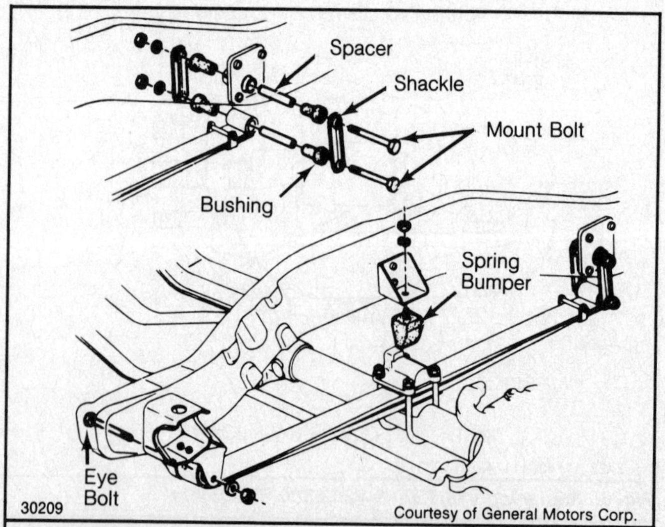
Spacer
Shackle
Mount Bolt
Bushing
Spring
Bumper
Eye
Bolt
30209
Courtesy of General Motors Corp.

Fig. 8: Mounting Components for Leaf Spring Assembly

1991 SUSPENSION
Front – Leaf Spring (Cont.)

3) Detach "U" bolt mounting nuts and remove spring-to-axle "U" bolts. Remove spring leafs, upper anchor plate and spring spacer pads. Detach shackle-to-spring lower mounting nut and bolt.
4) Remove bushings, spacers and shackles. *See Fig. 8.* Inspect bushings for excessive wear or deterioration. Check spring leafs for cracks, damage or loss of arc. Replace components as necessary.
5) To install leaf spring, reverse removal procedure. Tighten "U" bolt nuts in a diagonal sequence. See TORQUE SPECIFICATIONS at end of article.
Removal ("V" Series) – 1) Raise and support vehicle. Place adjustable jack stand under axle. Lift axle until all tension is relieved from leaf spring assembly. Remove wheels. Detach shackle-to-frame upper mounting nut and bolt. Detach front spring eye bolt and nut.
2) On V15/1500 & V25/2500 and left side of V35/3500 models, remove nuts, washers, "U" bolts, plate and spacers. On right side of V35/3500 models, remove bolts, nuts, washers, "U" bolts, plate and spacers. Remove spring. Remove shackle from springs.
Bushing Replacement – Place spring leaf on hydraulic press and press out bushing using proper sized rod, pipe or remover. Press in new bushing using proper sized rod, pipe or installer. Ensure installer presses on steel outer shell of bushing. Install bushing until it protrudes an equal amount on each side of spring.
Installation – To install leaf spring, reverse removal procedure. Tighten spring-to-axle bolts and "U" bolt nuts in proper sequence to 150 ft. lbs. (203 N.m). *See Fig. 9.*

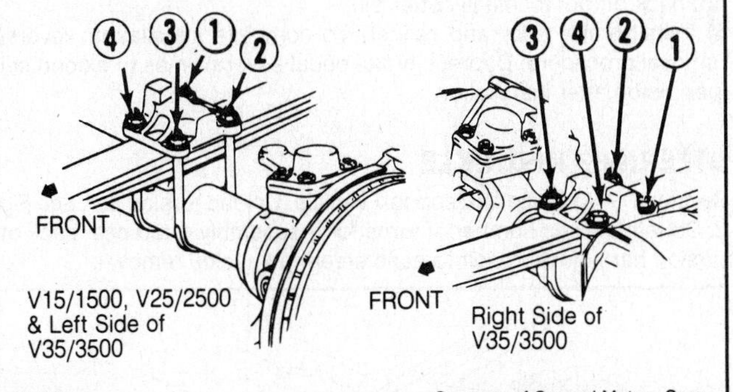
4
3
1
2
FRONT
V15/1500, V25/2500
& Left Side of
V35/3500
3
4
2
1
FRONT
Right Side of
V35/3500
30210
Courtesy of General Motors Corp.

Fig. 9: Tightening Sequence for Leaf Spring "U" Bolts ("V" Series)

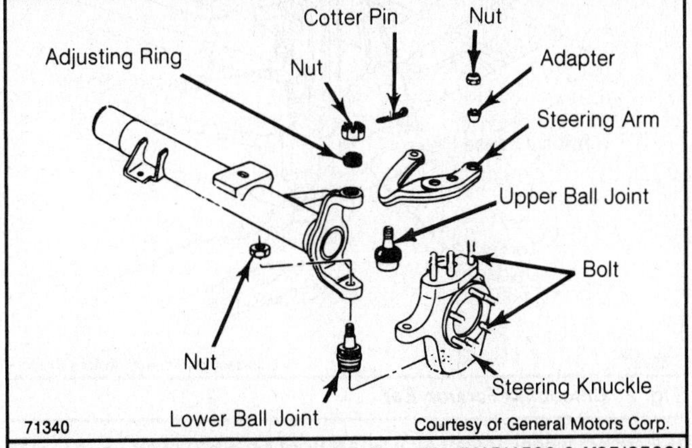
Cotter Pin
Nut
Adjusting Ring
Nut
Adapter
Steering Arm
Upper Ball Joint
Bolt
Nut
Steering Knuckle
71340
Lower Ball Joint
Courtesy of General Motors Corp.

Fig. 10: Exploded View of Steering Knuckle (V15/1500 & V25/2500)

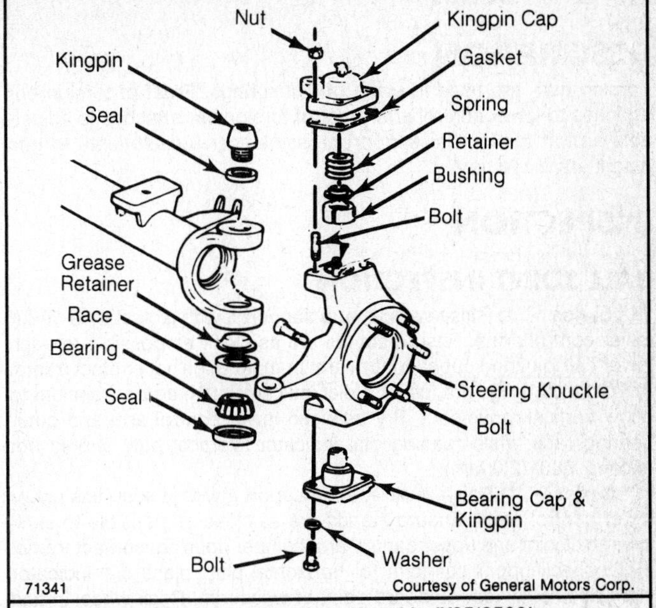
Nut
Kingpin Cap
Kingpin
Gasket
Seal
Spring
Retainer
Bushing
Bolt
Grease
Retainer
Race
Bearing
Seal
Steering Knuckle
Bolt
Bearing Cap &
Kingpin
Washer
Bolt
71341
Courtesy of General Motors Corp.

Fig. 11: Exploded View of Steering Knuckle (V35/3500)

TORQUE SPECIFICATIONS

TORQUE SPECIFICATIONS

Application	Ft. Lbs. (N.m)
"P" Series	
Anchor Plate & Steering Arm-To-Steering Knuckle Nut	230 (312)
Kingpin Cap Bolt	5 (7)
Kingpin Lock Pin Nut	29 (39)
Leaf Spring	
Axle "U" Bolt	80 (108)
Eye Bolt	90 (122)
Shackle Nut	92 (125)
Shackle-To-Frame Nut	92 (125)
Splash Shield-To-Anchor Plate Bolt	12 (16)
Stabilizer Bar-To-Frame Bolt	21 (28)
Stabilizer Bar-To-Link Nut	47 (64)
Tie Rod End Stud Nut	162 (220)
"V" Series	
Anchor Plate-To-Steering Knuckle Nut	[1] 65 (88)
Ball Joint	
Lower Ball Joint Stud Nut	70 (95)
Upper Ball Joint Stud Nut	[2] 100 (136)
Adjusting Ring-To-Spindle	50 (68)
Kingpin Cap Bolt	80 (108)
Kingpin-To-Steering Knuckle	550 (745)
Leaf Spring	
Axle "U" Bolt	150 (203)
Shackle Nut	90 (120)
Shackle-To-Frame Nut	50 (70)
Stabilizer Bar-To-Frame Bracket Bolt	
V35/3500	52 (71)
All Other Models	70 (95)
Stabilizer Bar-To-Spring Plate Bolt	133 (180)
Steering Arm-To-Steering Knuckle Nut [1]	90 (120)
Tie Rod End Stud Nut	40 (55)
	INCH Lbs. (N.m)
Kingpin Cap Bolt ("P" Series)	5 (7)

[1] – Use new mounting nuts whenever spindle is removed from knuckle.
[2] – Plus additional torque to align cotter pin, not to exceed 130 ft. lbs. (176 N.m).

1991 SUSPENSION
Front – 4WD Torsion Bar

"K" & "T" Series

DESCRIPTION

Torsion bars are used in place of coil springs. Front of torsion bar attaches to lower control arm. Rear of torsion bar attaches to adjustable arm at torsion bar support crossmember. Adjustments to trim height are made here.

INSPECTION

BALL JOINT INSPECTION

"K" Series – 1) Raise vehicle, and support it with jack stands under lower control arms. Ensure stands are as close as possible to each lower ball joint and upper control arm bumper does not contact frame.
2) To check ball joints, place a dial indicator stem against spindle to show vertical movement. Pry between lower control arm and outer bearing race while reading dial indicator. Vertical play should not exceed .080" (2.0 mm).
"T" Series – 1) Raise vehicle, and support it with jack stands under lower control arms. Ensure stands are as close as possible to each lower ball joint and upper control arm bumper does not contact frame.
2) To check upper ball joint for horizontal play, place dial indicator stem against lowest outboard point of wheel rim. Rock wheel in and out. Horizontal play should not exceed .125" (3.18 mm). If upper ball joint stud can be rotated, replace ball joint.
3) To check lower ball joint, place dial indicator against the spindle to show vertical movement. Pry between lower control arm and outer wheel bearing race portion of hub assembly. The reading should not exceed .125" (3.18 mm). If lower ball joint is within specification, check upper ball joint for excessive play.

ADJUSTMENTS

WHEEL ALIGNMENT SPECIFICATIONS & PROCEDURES

NOTE: See SPECIFICATIONS & PROCEDURES article in WHEEL ALIGNMENT.

WHEEL BEARING ADJUSTMENT

Front wheel bearings are sealed, pre-adjusted and require no maintenance unless wheel hub and bearing carrier is removed. See WHEEL HUB & BEARING ASSEMBLY under REMOVAL & INSTALLATION.

REMOVAL & INSTALLATION

WHEEL HUB & BEARING ASSEMBLY

NOTE: Darkened areas on bearing assembly are caused by heat treatment process and do not indicate a need for replacement.

Removal – 1) Raise and support vehicle. Remove wheel. Depress brake caliper piston. Detach brake caliper mounting bolts and move aside. Remove disc brake rotor. *See Fig. 1.*
2) Detach dust cover and remove cotter pin, nut retainer, nut and washer. Slide hub/bearing carrier off front axle shaft splines. Inspect steering knuckle grease seal and hub bearing for excessive wear or damage and replace as necessary. If hub wheel stud must be replaced, use Wheel Stud Remover (J-6627-A).
Installation – 1) To install new wheel stud, lubricate stud bore and install stud. Place 4 washers on stud and install stud nut with flat side to washers. Tighten stud nut to draw stud into hub bore. Remove nut and washers. Install hub and bearing assembly onto axle shaft, if removed. Install and tighten hub and bearing bolts to specification. See TORQUE SPECIFICATIONS table at end of article.
2) With hub and bearing assembly installed, tighten drive axle nut to 181 ft. lbs. (245 N.m) on "K" Series, or 173 ft. lbs. (234 N.m) on "T" Series. Install drive axle nut cover, new cotter pin and dust cover. Do not back off nut to install cotter pin.
3) Install brake rotor and caliper. To complete installation, reverse removal procedure. Depress brake pedal several times to extend caliper piston after installation.

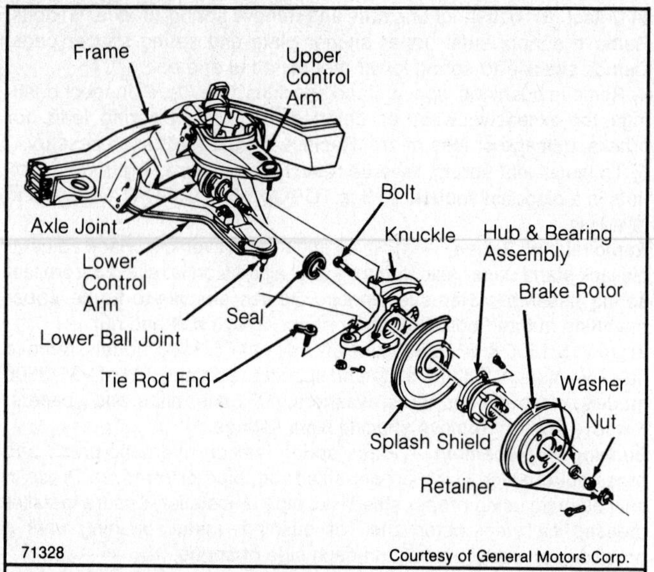
Frame
Upper Control Arm
Bolt
Axle Joint
Knuckle
Hub & Bearing Assembly
Lower Control Arm
Brake Rotor
Seal
Lower Ball Joint
Tie Rod End
Washer
Nut
Splash Shield
Retainer
71328
Courtesy of General Motors Corp.

Fig. 1: Exploded View of "T" Series Hub & Knuckle Assembly ("K" Series Is Similar)

STEERING KNUCKLE

Removal – 1) Raise and support vehicle. Unload torsion bar. *See Fig. 2.* Counting exact number of turns for reassembly reference, back off torsion bar adjusting bolt to ease steering knuckle removal.

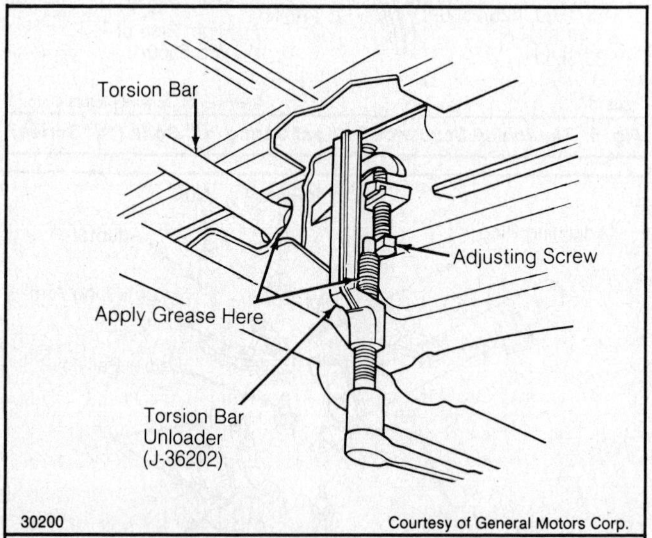
Torsion Bar
Adjusting Screw
Apply Grease Here
Torsion Bar Unloader (J-36202)
30200
Courtesy of General Motors Corp.

Fig. 2: Unloading Torsion Bar

2) Remove wheel. Install Axle Shaft Boot Seal Protector (J-28712) to protect drive axle boot during repair. Depress caliper piston, detach brake caliper and wire aside. Remove brake rotor.
3) Remove dust cover, drive axle nut cover, axle nut and washer. Slide hub and bearing assembly off axle shaft. Remove splash shield and tie rod end nut. Separate tie rod end from steering knuckle.
4) On "T" Series, place Ball Joint Separator (J-34026) over upper or lower ball joint. Loosen ball joint retainer nut. *See Fig. 3.* Back off until nut contacts tool. Continue backing off nut until nut forces ball stud out of knuckle. On "K" Series, separate ball joint from steering knuckle using Ball Joint Separator (J-36607).

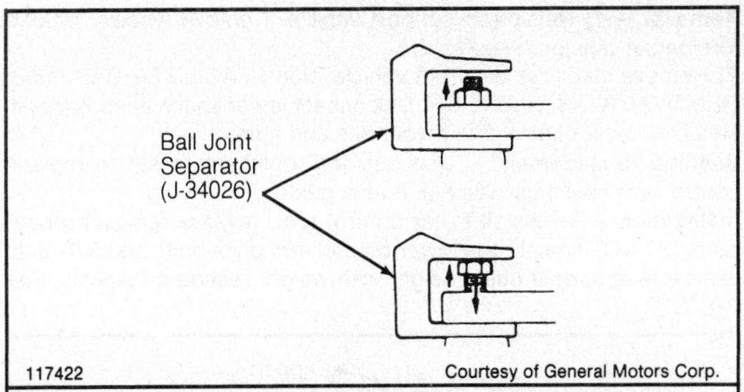

Ball Joint
Separator
(J-34026)
117422
Courtesy of General Motors Corp.

Fig. 3: Separating "T" Series Ball Joint from Steering Knuckle

5) On all models, remove steering knuckle from vehicle without damaging or moving axle shaft. Inspect knuckle grease seal for cuts, distortion and wear. Check steering knuckle, bearing carrier and wheel bearing for damage. Replace components as necessary.

Installation – 1) Install new knuckle grease seal using hammer and Front Hub Knuckle Inner Seal Installer (J-28574). Install spacer. Install knuckle onto ball joint studs.

2) Attach ball joint mounting nuts. Install tie rod nut. Install hub and bearing assembly onto axle shaft and into knuckle. Tighten drive axle nut. See TORQUE SPECIFICATIONS table at end of article.

3) To complete installation, reverse removal procedure. Check and adjust ride height. *See Fig. 6 or 7.* Check front end alignment as necessary. See SPECIFICATIONS & PROCEDURES article in WHEEL ALIGNMENT.

UPPER & LOWER BALL JOINTS

Removal – 1) Raise and support vehicle under lower control arms. Remove wheel. Depress caliper piston, detach brake caliper and wire aside. Remove brake rotor. Remove dust cover, cotter pin, drive axle nut cover, drive axle nut and washer.

2) Slide hub and bearing assembly off of axle shaft. Separate tie rod end and ball joints from steering knuckle. For "T" Series, use Ball Joint Separator (J-34026). *See Fig. 3.* On "K" Series, use Ball Joint Separator (J-36607).

3) On all models, remove steering knuckle as previously described. To remove upper or lower ball joint, use a drill and a 1/8" (3.18 mm) drill bit to drill pilot hole in rivet.

4) Drill a 1/4" (6.35 mm) deep pilot hole in ball joint retaining rivets. Using a 1/2" (12.70 mm) drill bit, drill out the rivet heads. Using a hammer and small punch, drive out rivets and remove ball joint assembly.

Installation – 1) Install new ball joint using bolts and nuts in place of rivets. Tighten upper and lower ball joint mounting nuts to specification. See TORQUE SPECIFICATIONS table at end of article.

2) To complete installation, reverse removal procedure. DO NOT tighten ball joint stud nuts more than an additional 1/6 turn to align cotter pin hole.

3) Lubricate ball joints and tie rods with grease. Check and adjust ride height. *See Fig. 6 or 7.* Check front end alignment as necessary. See SPECIFICATIONS & PROCEDURES article in WHEEL ALIGNMENT.

UPPER CONTROL ARM & BUSHINGS

Removal – 1) Raise and support vehicle under lower control arms. Remove wheel. Remove upper ball joint cotter pin and nut. Separate ball joint from steering knuckle. For "T" Series, use Ball Joint Separator (J-34026). *See Fig. 3.* For "K" Series, use Ball Joint Separator (J-36607).

2) On all models, mark alignment adjustment cams for realignment reference. Remove upper control arm pivot bolts, cams/washers and nuts. Discard nuts. Note component locations for reassembly reference. Remove control arm. *See Fig. 4 or 5.*

3) Replace bushings and/or bumper as needed. Mount control arm in vise and note bushing installed position for reassembly reference. Press bushing out of control arm.

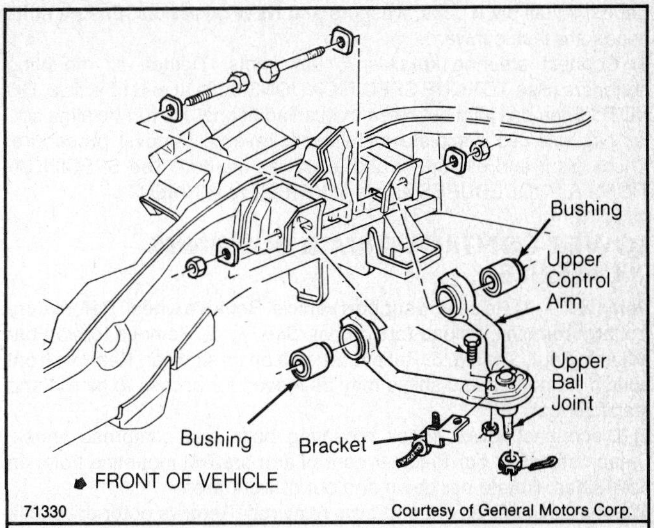

Bushing
Upper
Control
Arm
Upper
Ball
Joint
Bushing
Bracket
FRONT OF VEHICLE
71330
Courtesy of General Motors Corp.

Fig. 4: Exploded View of "K" Series Upper Control Arm

Installation – 1) If upper control arm bumper is deteriorated or damaged, install new bumper. On "T" Series, install upper control arm bushings with bushing service set. *See Fig. 5.* Press in bushing until properly seated in control arm.

NOTE: On "K" Series, alignment angles are preset at factory. Adjusting cams are available for installation.

2) On all models, mount control arm on vehicle. On "T" Series, install pivot bolts, alignment adjustment cams and NEW pivot nuts. On "K"

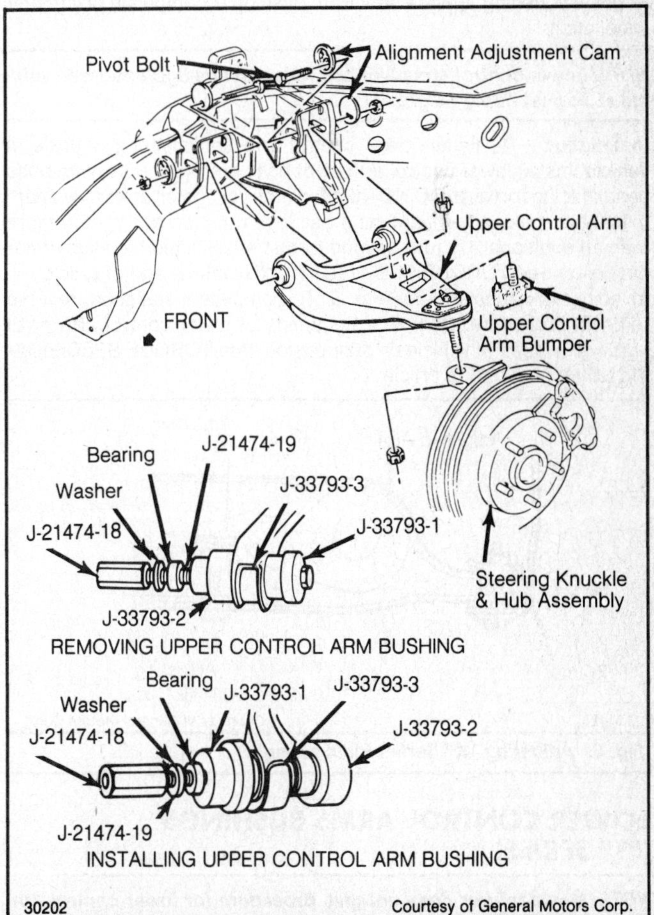

Pivot Bolt
Alignment Adjustment Cam
Upper Control Arm
FRONT
Upper Control
Arm Bumper
Steering Knuckle
& Hub Assembly
Bearing
J-21474-19
Washer
J-33793-3
J-21474-18
J-33793-1
J-33793-2
REMOVING UPPER CONTROL ARM BUSHING
Bearing
J-33793-1
J-33793-3
Washer
J-21474-18
J-33793-2
J-21474-19
INSTALLING UPPER CONTROL ARM BUSHING
30202
Courtesy of General Motors Corp.

Fig. 5: Replacing "T" Series Upper Control Arm & Bushings

1991 SUSPENSION
Front – 4WD Torsion Bar (Cont.)

Series, install pivot bolts, washers and NEW pivot nuts. Ensure bolts heads are facing inward.

3) Connect steering knuckle to ball joints. Tighten all mounting fasteners. See TORQUE SPECIFICATIONS table at end of article. DO NOT tighten ball joint nut more than an additional 1/6 turn to align cotter pin hole. To complete installation, reverse removal procedure. Check front end alignment and adjust as needed. See SPECIFICATIONS & PROCEDURES article in WHEEL ALIGNMENT.

LOWER CONTROL ARM & BUSHINGS ("K" SERIES)

Removal – 1) Raise and support vehicle. Remove wheel. Before control arm removal, unload torsion bar. *See Fig. 2*. Remove torsion bar adjusting nut. *See Fig. 6*. Relieve tension on torsion bar. Remove front splash shield bolts so shield may be moved for access to tie rod and stabilizer bar.

2) Disconnect lower shock mounting bolts and compress shock. Detach stabilizer bar-to-lower control arm bracket mounting bolts on both sides. Rotate bar down and out of work area.

3) Separate inner tie rod end from relay rod. Remove outer drive axle shaft nut and washer. Remove bolts connecting drive axle shaft to differential drive flange. Press drive axle shaft splines out of hub. Remove drive axle shaft from vehicle.

4) Remove cotter pin and nut from upper ball joint. Separate upper ball joint from steering knuckle using Ball Joint Separator (J-36607).

5) Remove lower control arm pivot mounting bolts with nuts. Remove lower control arm and knuckle as a unit. Separate lower control arm from steering knuckle.

Bushing Replacement – On 1/2 ton and 3/4 ton vehicles (K1 and K2 Series), replace lower control arm if bushings are worn or damaged. On 1 ton vehicles (K3 Series), use a press or Bushing Service Set (J-36618) to replace bushings. On front bushing, unbend crimps before removing bushing. Ensure new front bushing is crimped in place after installation.

NOTE: Lower control arm pivot bolt nuts must be tightened with vehicle at normal riding height.

Installation – 1) Install lower control arm and steering knuckle in vehicle. Install lower control arm pivot bolts and NEW nuts, with bolts heads facing forward. DO NOT tighten nuts yet. Install drive axle shaft. Install ball joint. When tightening ball joint nuts, do not tighten more than an additional 1/6 turn beyond torque specification to align cotter pin holes. See TORQUE SPECIFICATIONS table at end of article.

2) Adjust riding height. *See Fig. 6*. To complete installation, reverse removal procedure. Complete tightening of lower control arm pivot nuts with weight of vehicle on suspension. See TORQUE SPECIFICATIONS table at end of article.

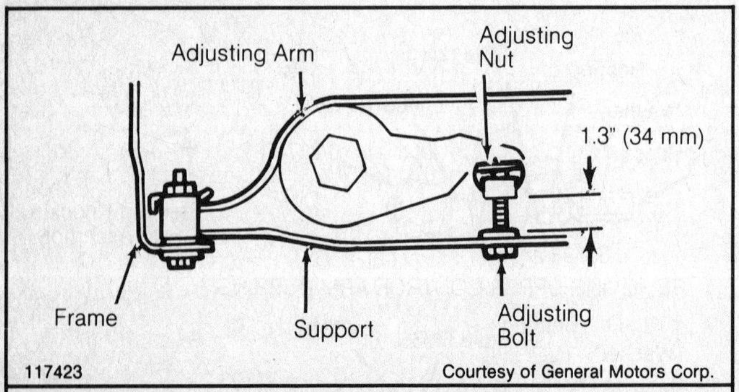
Adjusting Arm
Adjusting Nut
1.3" (34 mm)
Frame
Support
Adjusting Bolt
117423
Courtesy of General Motors Corp.

Fig. 6: Adjusting "K" Series Riding Height

LOWER CONTROL ARMS BUSHINGS ("T" SERIES)

NOTE: Manufacturer does not give procedure for lower control arm removal.

Removal – 1) Raise and support vehicle. Remove wheels. Unload torsion bar tension. *See Fig. 2*.

2) Remove stabilizer bar from vehicle. See STABILIZER BAR under REMOVAL & INSTALLATION. Disconnect lower shock absorber bolt. Remove lower control arm pivot bolts and nuts.

Bushing Replacement – Use bushing replacement set to replace control arm bushings, *See Fig. 8* as a guide.

Installation – To install lower control arm, reverse removal procedure. DO NOT final torque lower control arm pivot bolts and nuts until vehicle is at normal riding height with weight resting on wheels. *See Fig. 7*.

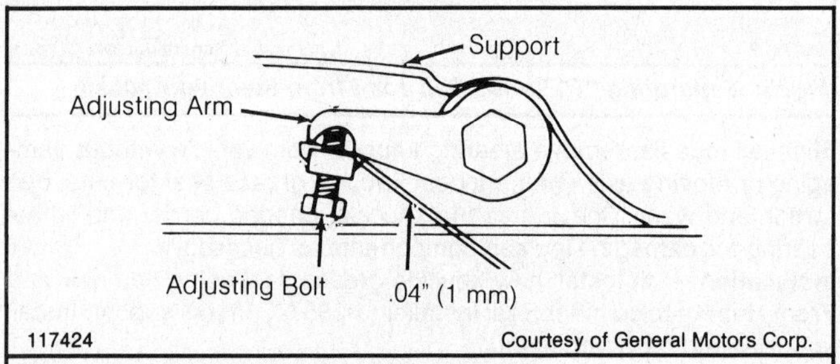
Support
Adjusting Arm
Adjusting Bolt
.04" (1 mm)
117424
Courtesy of General Motors Corp.

Fig. 7: Adjusting "T" Series Riding Height

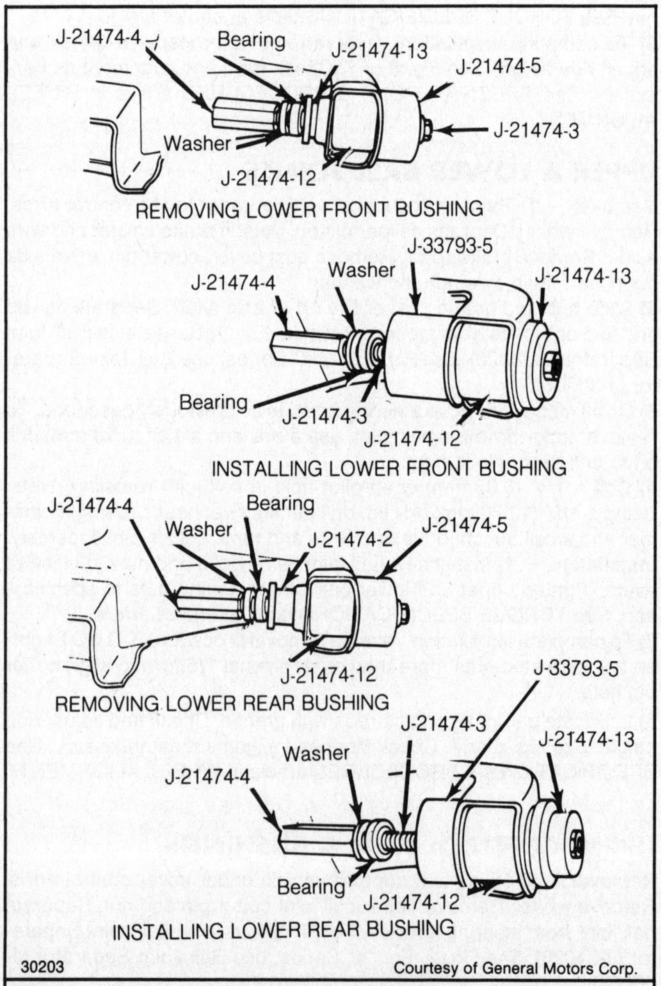
J-21474-4
Bearing
J-21474-13
J-21474-5
J-21474-3
Washer
J-21474-12
REMOVING LOWER FRONT BUSHING
J-33793-5
Washer
J-21474-4
J-21474-13
Bearing
J-21474-3
J-21474-12
INSTALLING LOWER FRONT BUSHING
J-21474-4
Bearing
Washer
J-21474-2
J-21474-5
J-21474-12
REMOVING LOWER REAR BUSHING
J-33793-5
J-21474-3
J-21474-13
Washer
J-21474-4
Bearing
J-21474-12
INSTALLING LOWER REAR BUSHING
30203
Courtesy of General Motors Corp.

Fig. 8: Replacing "T" Series Lower Control Arm Bushings

TORSION BARS & CROSSMEMBER SUPPORT

Removal – 1) Raise and support vehicle. Remove wheel. Unload torsion bar tension. *See Fig. 2*. Remove torsion bar adjusting bolt, counting number of turns for reassembly reference. Slowly relieve torsion bar tension.

1991 SUSPENSION
Front – 4WD Torsion Bar (Cont.)

2) Remove unloader tool. Detach torsion bar support mounting bolts and nuts. Remove retainers and rubber insulators. *See Fig. 9*. On "K" Series, slide torsion bar support rearward. Pull torsion bar down and slide back to remove bar from control arm. "K" Series torsion bars must be reinstalled in the same location and direction as removed.

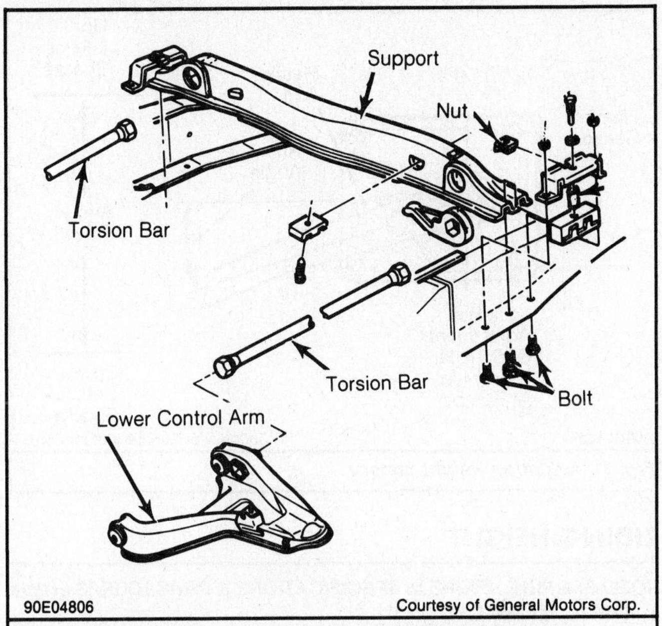
Support
Nut
Torsion Bar
Torsion Bar
Bolt
Lower Control Arm
90E04806
Courtesy of General Motors Corp.

Fig. 9: Exploded View of Torsion Bar & Support Assembly

3) On "T" Series, slide torsion bars forward into lower control arm to clear support crossmember. Lower torsion bars and remove from vehicle. Remove crossmember support and adjusting arms (if necessary). Inspect torsion bars, adjusting arms, retainers, rubber support cushions and crossmember support for bend, cracks, deterioration or damage. Check adjusting screw and nut for damage or stripped threads. Replace components as necessary.

Installation – 1) Ensure torsion bar support, rubber insulators and retainers are in place on frame, slightly behind mounting holes. Slide torsion bar into lower control arm in original position.

2) Slide torsion bar support forward, engaging rear of torsion bars in adjusting arms. Install and tighten torsion bar retainer bolts and nuts. See TORQUE SPECIFICATIONS table at end of article.

3) Install adjusting bolt and nut on each torsion bar. Add tension to torsion bar with Torsion Bar Unloader (J-36202). Tighten adjusting bolt until correct ride height is obtained. *See Fig. 6 or 7*. Install wheels and lower vehicle.

STABILIZER BAR

NOTE: Keep right and left side front end parts separated for reinstallation in original locations.

Removal – 1) Raise and support vehicle. Remove both wheel and tire assemblies. Unload torsion bar. *See Fig. 2*. Detach stabilizer bar frame bracket mounting bolts. Detach bar-to-lower control arm bracket mounting bolts.

2) Install frame bracket mounting bolts and tighten to specification. Tighten remaining mounting bolts. See TORQUE SPECIFICATIONS table. To complete installation, reverse removal procedure. Reset riding height. *See Fig. 6 or 7*.

Installation – 1) Install new insulator bushings on stabilizer bar (with split toward front) and brackets onto bushings. Position bar and partially start lower control arm bracket mounting bolts.

2) Install frame bracket mounting bolts and tighten to specification. Tighten remaining mounting bolts. See TORQUE SPECIFICATIONS table. To complete installation, reverse removal procedure. Reset riding height. *See Figs. 6 and 7*.

TORQUE SPECIFICATIONS

TORQUE SPECIFICATIONS

Application	Ft. Lbs. (N.m)
"K" Series	
Ball Joint-To-Control Arm Nuts	
1/2 & 3/4 Ton	17 (23)
1 Ton	52 (70)
Ball Joint Stud Nuts [1]	94 (127)
Brake Caliper Mount Bolt	28 (38)
Drive Axle-To-Hub & Bearing Nut	173 (234)
Hub & Bearing/Shield & Knuckle Bolts	66 (89)
Lower Control Arm-To-Frame Nuts [2] [3]	96 (130)
Lug Nut	
Dual Wheel	140 (190)
Single Wheel	120 (163)
Retainer-To-Torsion Bar Support Bolts	35 (47)
Shock Absorber Nut [4]	66 (89)
Stabilizer Bar Clamp-To-Frame Bolts	12 (16)
Stabilizer Bar Link Bolt	13 (18)
Tie Rod End-To-Steering Knuckle Nut	35 (47)
Torsion Bar Retainer Nut	33 (45)
Upper Control Arm-To-Frame Nuts [2]	139 (188)
"T" Series	
Joint-To-Control Arm Nuts [1]	17 (23)
Ball Joint Stud Nuts [1]	
Lower	83 (112)
Upper	61 (83)
Brake Caliper Mount Bolt	37 (50)
Drive Axle Nut-To-Hub & Bearing	181 (245)
Hub & Bearing/Shield & Knuckle Nuts	86 (117)
Lower Control Arm-To-Frame Bolts	148 (201)
Lower Control Arm-To-Frame Nuts	92 (125)
Lug Nut	
Aluminum Wheel	90 (122)
Steel Wheel	73 (99)
Retainer-To-Torsion Bar Support Bolts	26 (35)
Shock Absorber Nut [3]	54 (73)
Stabilizer Bar Clamp-To-Frame Bolts	35 (47)
Stabilizer Bar Link Bolt	24 (33)
Tie Rod End-To-Steering Knuckle Nut	35 (47)
Torsion Bar Retainer Bolt	25 (34)
Upper Control Arm-To-Frame Nuts	70 (95)

1 – DO NOT back off retainer nut to install new cotter pin. After reaching proper torque, tighten nut only enough to align slot.
2 – Use new nuts during reassembly.
3 – Install both mounting bolts with their nuts facing rearward.
4 – Install shock absorber mounting bolt with nut to rear of vehicle. Install lower mounting bolt with nut facing forward.

1991 SUSPENSION
Rear – Electronic Level Control

Lumina APV, Silhouette, Trans Sport

DESCRIPTION

Rear level control automatically adjusts rear height of vehicle regardless of load. System is activated when ignition is on and weight is added or removed from vehicle.

Electronic Level Control (ELC) consists of a compressor, air drier, exhaust solenoid, compressor relay, height sensor, air adjustable shock absorbers and connecting air lines. Air drier contains a moisture absorbing chemical and pressure maintaining valves. Valves maintain minimum system pressure of approximately 7-14 psi (.5-.9 kg/cm²).

A provision is made so ELC compressor can be used for other purposes, such as inflating tires, etc. The inflation equipment consists of inflator switch, inflator solenoid valve assembly and inflation timer relay.

OPERATION

RAISING VEHICLE

When weight is added to vehicle, height sensor arm rotates upward, grounding compressor relay circuit. After a time delay of approximately 8-15 seconds, compressor relay turns air compressor on, causing vehicle to rise.

As vehicle rises, height sensor rotates downward to curb height position. When vehicle is within 1" (25.4 mm) of curb height, height sensor opens ground circuit to compressor relay, turning compressor off.

LOWERING VEHICLE

When weight is removed from vehicle, height sensor arm rotates downward, After a time delay of approximately 8-15 seconds, downward rotation of the arm grounds exhaust solenoid valve circuit. Energizing exhaust solenoid valve causes air to vent through air drier and out of exhaust solenoid valve.

As vehicle lowers, height sensor arm rotates upward to curb height position. When vehicle is within 1" (25.4 mm) of curb height, height sensor opens exhaust solenoid valve circuit, causing exhaust solenoid valve to close.

AIR REPLENISHMENT

In order to ensure the system is operating with at least minimum air pressure, the height sensor commands an air replenishment cycle each time the ignition is cycled on. An internal timer circuit is activated when ignition is turned on. After a delay of approximately 35-45 seconds, compressor turns on for 3-5 seconds to ensure residual system pressure.

If weight is added or removed from vehicle during 35-45 second delay, air replenishment cycle will be overridden and vehicle will rise or lower after normal time delay.

INFLATOR

When inflator switch is turned on, it grounds the inflation timer relay. This operates the inflator solenoid valve assembly, turning on the compressor through the ELC relay. The inflator solenoid valve assembly redirects compressed air from the suspension to the inflator hose.

The inflation timer relay limits inflation operation to 10 minutes each time the inflator switch is operated.

ADJUSTMENTS

HEIGHT SENSOR

1) Place vehicle on level surface, with gas tank full and NO load in vehicle. Turn ignition switch to ON position. Bounce vehicle 3 times to normalize suspension. To increase vehicle riding height, loosen lock bolt on sensor arm. Move plastic arm upward, and tighten lock nut.

2) To lower riding height, loosen lock nut, move plastic arm down and tighten lock nut. There is a total of 5 degrees adjustment on sensor. One degree adjustment provides 1/4" change in height at bumper. If adjustment cannot be made, problem is with rear springs or suspension. *See Fig. 1.*

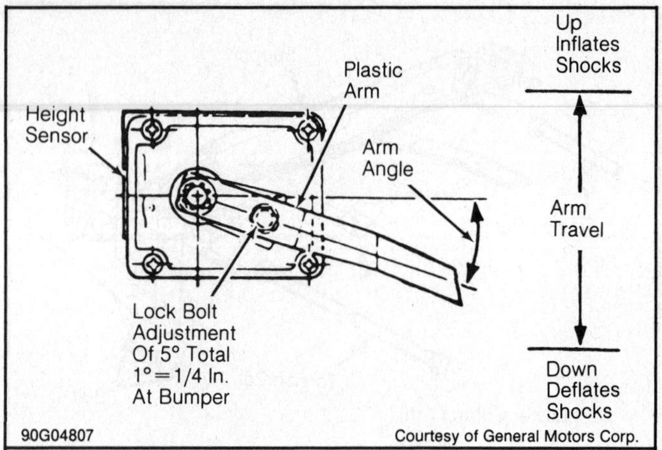
Up
Inflates
Shocks
Plastic
Arm
Height
Sensor
Arm
Angle
Arm
Travel
Lock Bolt
Adjustment
Of 5° Total
1° = 1/4 In.
At Bumper
Down
Deflates
Shocks
90G04807
Courtesy of General Motors Corp.

Fig. 1: Adjusting Height Sensor

RIDING HEIGHT

NOTE: See RIDE HEIGHT in SPECIFICATIONS & PROCEDURES article in WHEEL ALIGNMENT.

TROUBLE SHOOTING

Perform SYSTEM OPERATIONAL TEST and SYSTEM LEAK TEST under TESTING to determine if electrical fault exists. Refer to WIRING DIAGRAM, ELC COMPONENT LOCATION table and ELC CIRCUIT/CONNECTOR IDENTIFICATION table to locate and identify circuits, components, etc.

VEHICLE LOADED, WILL NOT RISE

Leaks in air lines, fittings or shock absorbers. Pinched lines between compressor and shock absorbers. Defective height sensor. Compressor inoperative. Loose or damaged electrical connections to sensor or compressor.

VEHICLE LOADED, RISES, THEN LEAKS DOWN

Severe leak in lines, fittings or shock absorbers. Internal leak in motor.

VEHICLE LOADED, RISES PARTIALLY

Height sensor out of adjustment. Compressor or wiring defective.

VEHICLE RISES WHEN LOADED, LEAKS DOWN WHEN DRIVING

Defective drier or compressor. Pinched air lines or leaks in fittings or air lines.

VEHICLE RIDES HIGH

Height sensor out of adjustment. Drier plugged or air lines pinched. Poor electrical connections.

TESTING

SYSTEM OPERATIONAL TEST

1) Unload vehicle. With ignition off, check riding height. Turn ignition on. Add 300 lbs. (136 kg) load to rear passenger compartment. Compressor should start operating after a time delay of approximately 8-15 seconds. Vehicle should rise to within 1" (25.4 mm) of curb height.

2) Remove load from passenger compartment. Exhaust should start within 8-15 seconds. Within 2 minutes, exhaust should stop and vehicle should be within 1" (25.4 mm) of curb height.

SYSTEM LEAK TEST

1) Install Pressure Gauge (J-22124A) in line between air drier assembly and existing line to shocks. *See Fig. 2.* Install gauge so shut-off valve is on compressor side of gauge. With shut-off valve open, apply shop air pressure through the fill valve until gauge reaches 100 psi (7.03 kg/cm²).

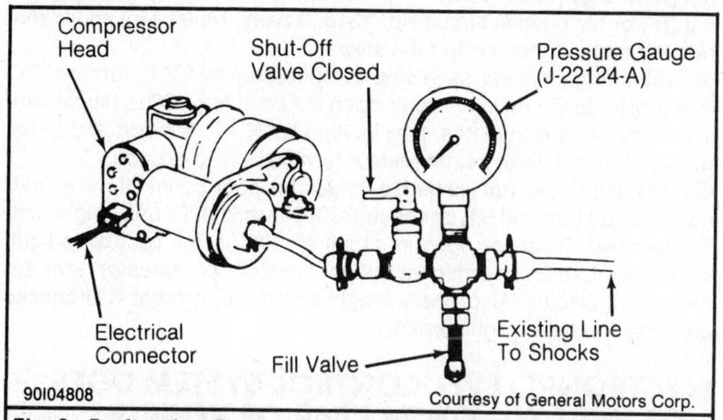
Compressor Head
Shut-Off Valve Closed
Pressure Gauge (J-22124-A)
Electrical Connector
Existing Line To Shocks
Fill Valve
90I04808
Courtesy of General Motors Corp.

Fig. 2: Performing Electronic Level Control (ELC) Leak Test

2) If a leak is indicated, close shut-off valve and continue to watch for a pressure drop. If pressure continues to drop, leak is external from the compressor. Leak test all connections. If pressure stops decreasing after shut-off valve is closed, leak is in the compressor assembly.
3) Check compressor for leaks. If pressure builds up rapidly but vehicle does not rise, check for pinched air line, or stuck or binding shocks.

COMPRESSOR PERFORMANCE TEST

1) Disconnect pressure line from air drier and attach Pressure Gauge (J-22124-A) to air drier fitting. Disconnect electrical connector from compressor motor and exhaust solenoid terminals. *See Fig. 2.*
2) Connect 12-volt power supply to compressor through ammeter. Current draw must not exceed 14 amps. Replace compressor if current draw is greater than 14 amps. Allow pressure to reach 100 psi (7.03 kg/cm²) minimum, and shut off compressor. Allow pressure to stabilize.
3) If pressure leaks down below 90 psi (6.33 kg/cm²) before holding steady but does not reach zero psi, replace head assembly. If pressure leaks down to zero psi, perform compressor/drier leak test. Repair as necessary.
4) If compressor output is less than 110 psi (7.73 kg/cm²), perform compressor/drier leak test. If no is leak found, replace compressor. See COMPRESSOR/DRIER LEAK TEST under TESTING.
5) If compressor does not operate, replace compressor. If compressor operates correctly, reconnect wiring and air lines.

NOTE: If compressor is allowed to run to maximum output pressure of 180 psi (12.7 kg/cm²), solenoid exhaust valve will act as a relief valve. This gives a false indication of system leakage.

COMPRESSOR/DRIER LEAK TEST

1) Attach Pressure Gauge (J-22124-A) to drier fitting. Allow pressure to reach 100 psi (7.03 kg/cm²) minimum and shut off compressor.
2) Using soap and water solution. Check for pressure leaks at locations shown. *See Fig. 3.* Torque compressor head bolts if necessary. See TORQUE SPECIFICATIONS table at end of article.

HEIGHT SENSOR OPERATION TEST

1) Cycle ignition on. Raise vehicle on hoist. Ensure axle housing is supported as close to ride height specification as possible. Check all wiring for good connections. Disconnect link from height sensor arm.
2) Move sensor arm upward. After an 8-15 second delay, the compressor should run and shock absorbers should start to inflate. As soon as shock absorber air boots fill, stop compressor by moving sensor actuator arm down.
3) Move sensor arm below position where compressor stopped running. There should be an 8-15 second delay before shock absorbers start to deflate, and lower vehicle. Replace height sensor if it does not function correctly.

SENSOR ACTUATOR ARM TEST

Raise vehicle. Ensure link is attached to actuator arm correctly, and actuator arm is properly aligned. *See Fig. 1.*

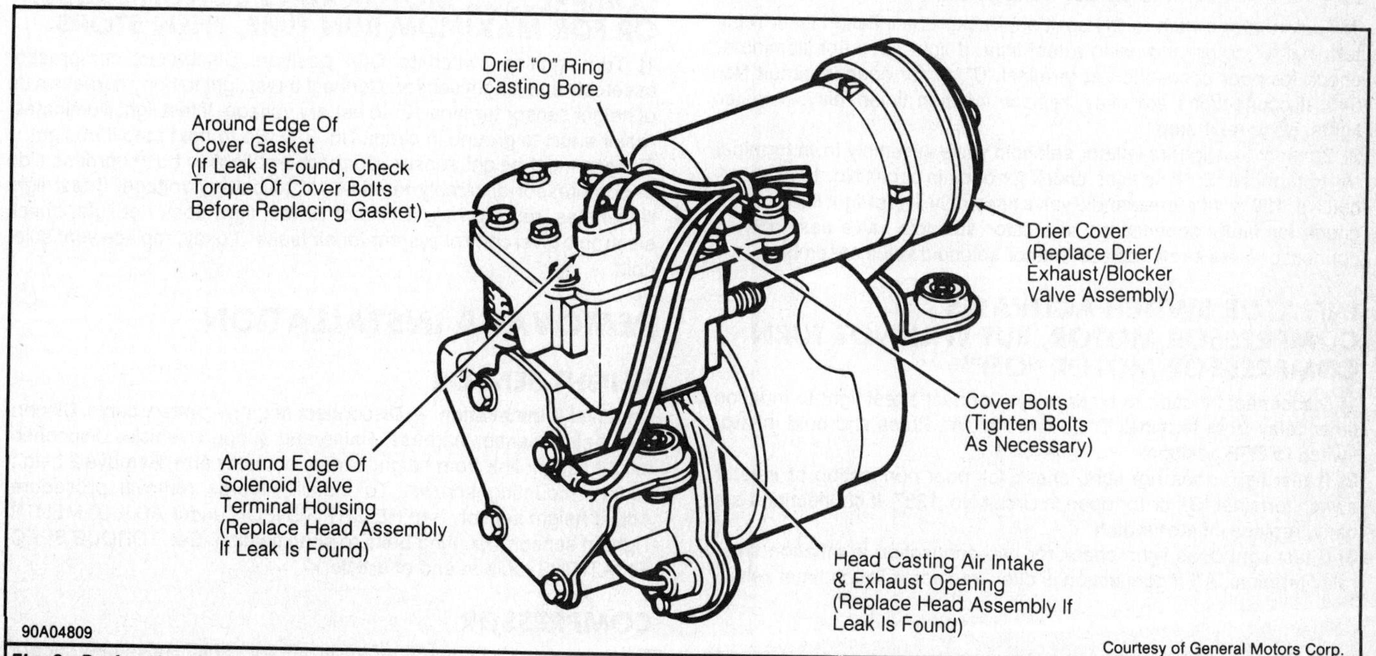
Drier "O" Ring Casting Bore
Around Edge Of Cover Gasket (If Leak Is Found, Check Torque Of Cover Bolts Before Replacing Gasket)
Drier Cover (Replace Drier/ Exhaust/Blocker Valve Assembly)
Cover Bolts (Tighten Bolts As Necessary)
Around Edge Of Solenoid Valve Terminal Housing (Replace Head Assembly If Leak Is Found)
Head Casting Air Intake & Exhaust Opening (Replace Head Assembly If Leak Is Found)
90A04809
Courtesy of General Motors Corp.

Fig. 3: Performing Compressor/Drier Leak Test

1991 SUSPENSION
Rear – Electronic Level Control (Cont.)

INFLATOR SWITCH DOES NOT ACTIVATE COMPRESSOR MOTOR

1) Using voltmeter, measure voltage from timer relay terminal "E" to ground. If there is no voltage, go to next step. If voltage reads battery voltage, go to step **6)**.
2) Measure voltage at relay terminal No. 2 to ground. If reading is battery voltage, repair open in circuit No. 321. If there is zero volts, go to next step.
3) Using test light, backprobe relay terminals No. 1 & 5 to ground. If test light does not illuminate, repair open in circuit No. 340. If light is on, go to next step.
4) Connect a fused jumper from terminal No. 1 to terminal No. 4 of relay. If compressor motor starts, check for faulty connections at relay. If relay connections are okay, replace relay. If compressor motor does not run with jumper still connected, disconnect compressor. Use test light to probe body harness side of compressor from terminal "B" to ground. If test light does not light, repair open in circuit No. 322. If test light illuminates, go to next step.
5) With fused jumper connected as in step **4)**, connect test light to body harness side of compressor from terminal "B" to terminal "D". If test light does not light, repair open in circuit No. 150. If test light lights, check for poor connections at both terminals. If connections are okay, replace compressor motor.
6) Using a voltmeter, measure voltage from timer relay terminal "D" to ground. If there is zero volts, check for bad connection at terminal "D", or for open in circuit No. 340. Using a voltmeter, measure voltage from timer relay terminal "D" to terminal "H". If there is zero volts, repair open in circuit No. 150. If there is voltage, go to next step.
7) Disconnect inflator switch. Connect a fused jumper to inflator switch from terminal "A" to terminal "B". If compressor motor starts, check for faulty connection at switch. If connection is okay, replace inflator switch. If compressor does not run, go to next step.
8) With jumper connected as in step **7)**, measure voltage from timer relay terminal "F" to ground using voltmeter. If no voltage, check for poor connections at timer relay terminals "F", "E" and "H". If connections are okay, replace inflation timer relay. If voltage reads battery voltage, check for open in circuit No. 1250 or circuit No. 150 to inflator switch.

INFLATOR SWITCH ACTIVATES COMPRESSOR MOTOR, BUT HIGH PRESSURE AIR IS NOT AVAILABLE AT AIR HOSE

1) Turn inflator switch to ON position. Backprobe inflation timer relay terminal "C" to ground using a test light. If light does not illuminate, check for poor connection at terminal "C", or for open in circuit No. 340. If connections are okay, replace inflation timer relay. If tester lights, go to next step.
2) Connect test light to inflator solenoid valve assembly from terminal "A" to terminal "B". If no light, check for open in circuit No. 1249 or circuit No. 150 to inflator solenoid valve assembly. If test light illuminates, check for faulty connections at inflator solenoid valve assembly. If connections are okay, replace inflator solenoid valve assembly.

INFLATOR SWITCH ACTIVATES COMPRESSOR MOTOR, BUT WILL NOT TURN COMPRESSOR MOTOR "OFF"

1) Disconnect inflation to timer relay. Connect a test light to inflation timer relay from terminal "D" to terminal "A". Press and hold inflator switch to OFF position.
2) If test light does not light, check for poor connection at inflator switch terminal "C", or for open in circuit No. 1267. If connections are okay, replace inflator switch.
3) If test light does light, check for bad connection at inflation timer relay terminal "A". If connection is okay, replace inflation timer relay.

COMPRESSOR MOTOR DOES NOT TURN "ON" TO RAISE REAR OF VEHICLE, BUT INFLATOR SWITCH OPERATES NORMALLY

1) Disconnect height sensor. Connect a fused jumper to body harness side of height sensor from terminal "B" to ground. If compressor motor does not run, repair open in circuit No. 321. If motor runs, go to next step.
2) Remove jumper. Using a test light, probe body harness side of height sensor from terminal "C" to terminal ground. If test light does not illuminate, check for faulty connection at inflation timer relay terminal "B", or for open in circuit No. 1248. If okay, replace inflation timer relay. If tester lights, go to next step.
3) Probe height sensor as in step **2)** from terminal "C" to terminal "A". If test light does not light, repair open in circuit No. 150 to height sensor. If test light illuminates, turn ignition to "RUN" position and probe body harness side of height sensor terminal "D" to ground.
4) If test light does not illuminate, check for poor connections at connector C200 terminal D1, connector C302 terminal "B" and height sensor terminal "B" or for open in circuit No. 39. If test light does light, check for bad connection at height sensor, or actuator arm for damage or binding. Also, check height sensor adjustment. If all checks are okay, replace height sensor.

ELECTRONIC LEVEL CONTROL SYSTEM DOES NOT VENT TO LOWER REAR OF VEHICLE

1) Disconnect height sensor. Connect a fused jumper to body harness side of height sensor terminal "E" to ground. Vent solenoid should click and vent air. If vent solenoid operates, check for poor connection at height sensor terminal "E", or actuator arm for damage or binding. Also, check height sensor adjustment. If all checks are okay, replace height sensor. If vent solenoid does not operate, go to next step.
2) Does fuse in fused jumper blow? If fuse blows, repair short to voltage on circuit No. 320. If fuse does not blow, with jumper still connected, disconnect compressor assembly. Connect test light to body harness side of compressor assembly from terminal "C" to terminal "A".
3) If light illuminates, check for faulty connections at compressor assembly terminal "A" and terminal "C". If connections are okay, replace vent solenoid. If tester does not light, check for open in circuit No. 320 or No. 340 to compressor assembly.

COMPRESSOR MOTOR RUNS CONTINUOUSLY OR FOR MAXIMUM RUN TIME, THEN STOPS

1) Turn ignition switch to OFF position. Disconnect compressor assembly and height sensor. Connect a test light to body harness side of height sensor terminal "E" to battery voltage. If test light illuminates, repair short to ground in circuit No. 320. Go to next step if no light.
2) Reconnect height sensor. Connect test light to body harness side of compressor assembly terminal "A" to battery voltage. If test light illuminates, replace height sensor. If test light does not light, check electronic level control system for air leaks. If okay, replace vent solenoid.

REMOVAL & INSTALLATION

HEIGHT SENSOR

Removal & Installation – Disconnect negative battery cable. Disconnect height sensor harness. Raise and support vehicle. Disconnect height sensor link from height sensor actuator arm. Remove 2 height sensor mounting screws. To install, reverse removal procedure. Adjust height sensor. See HEIGHT SENSOR under ADJUSTMENTS. Tighten sensor mounting bolts to specification. See TORQUE SPECIFICATIONS table at end of article.

COMPRESSOR

Removal – 1) Disconnect negative battery cable. Raise and support vehicle. Deflate system through service valve. Disconnect high pressure line at drier by rotating spring 90 degrees while holding connector end. Remove tube assembly. *See Fig. 4.*

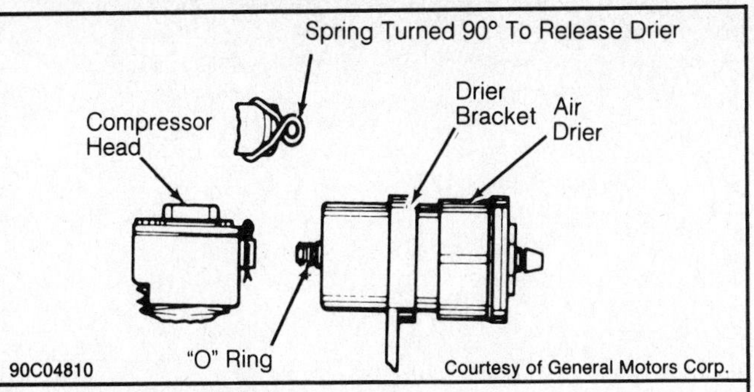
Spring Turned 90° To Release Drier
Compressor Head
Drier Bracket
Air Drier
"O" Ring
90C04810
Courtesy of General Motors Corp.

Fig. 4: Removing Air Drier

2) Disconnect solenoid and motor connectors. Remove support bracket screws. Remove compressor-to-bracket screws. Remove compressor and bracket as an assembly.

Installation – To install, reverse removal procedure. Tighten screws to specification. See TORQUE SPECIFICATIONS table at end of article. Turn ignition on and allow system to cycle. Check for leaks using soap and water solution.

AIR DRIER

Removal – Disconnect high pressure line by turning spring 90 degrees and removing tube assembly. Disconnect air drier from compressor by turning spring and sliding air drier and "O" ring from compressor head assembly.

Installation – Lubricate "O" ring and install in port of compressor head. Return spring to its original position. Install air drier on compressor head assembly. If difficulty arises when installing air drier in compressor head assembly, rotate slightly while apply pressure. Check system for leaks.

AIR LINE REPAIR

If a leak is found in air line, it is not necessary to replace entire line. Air line can be repaired by splicing in a service coupling at leak area. Inflate system to 100 psi (7.03 kg/cm²). Use a soap and water solution to locate leak. Deflate system through service valve and cut out leaking area. Install service coupling and tighten tube nuts to 72 INCH lbs. (8 N.m). *See Fig. 5.* Inflate system and check for leaks using a soap and water solution.

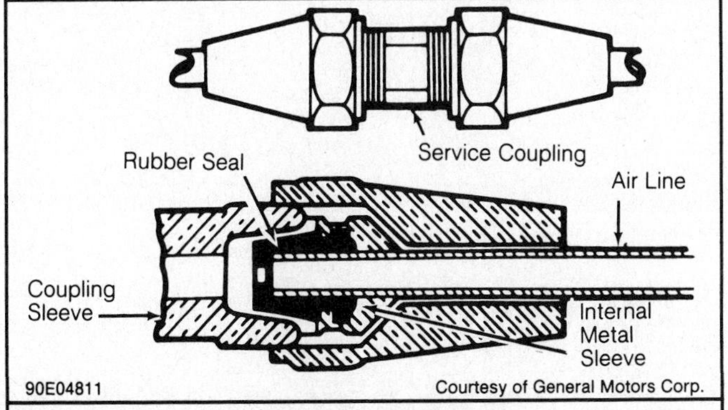
Service Coupling
Rubber Seal
Air Line
Coupling Sleeve
Internal Metal Sleeve
90E04811
Courtesy of General Motors Corp.

Fig. 5: Repairing Air Line With Service Coupling

ELC COMPONENT & CONNECTOR LOCATION

Component	Location
Compressor Assembly	Behind Left Side Rear Wheel
ELC Relay	Behind Left Side Rear Wheel Well
Fuse Block	Behind Instrument Panel Compartment Door
Height Sensor	Mounted to Center of Rear Crossmember
Inflation Timer Relay	Behind Left Side Rear Wheel Well
Inflator Solenoid Valve	Behind Left Side Rear Wheel Well
Inflator Switch	Behind Left Side Rear Wheel Well
Connectors	
C200 (26 Cavities)	Near Base Front Pillar, Left of Parking Brake
C302 (2 Cavities)	Above Left Side Rear Wheel Well
G401	Above Left Side Rear Wheel Well
P300	Behind Left Side Rear Wheel Well
S208	Instrument Panel Wiring Harness, Near Instrument Cluster
S300, S303 & S407	Body Harness, Behind Left Side Rear Wheel Well

ELC CIRCUIT IDENTIFICATION

Circuit Number	Wire Color	Location
39	Pink/Black	Fuse Block to Height Sensor
150	Black	Compressor to Inflator Solenoid to Inflator Switch to Timer Relay to Height Sensor to Ground
320	White	Compressor to Height Sensor
321	Yellow	ELC Relay to Height Sensor to Timer Relay
322	Dark Green	ELC Relay to Compressor
340	Orange	ELC Fuse to ELC Relay to Compressor to Timer Relay
1248	Light Blue	Timer Relay to Height Sensor
1249	Dark Blue	Timer Relay to Inflator Solenoid
1250	White	Timer Relay to Inflator Switch
1267	Purple	Timer Relay to Inflator Switch

TORQUE SPECIFICATIONS

TORQUE SPECIFICATIONS

Application	INCH Lbs. (N.m)
Compressor Bracket Mounting Screws	35 (4.0)
Compressor Head Bolts	35 (4.0)
Compressor Mounting Screws	35 (4.0)
Compressor Relay Mounting Screws	27 (3.0)
Height Sensor Link Nuts	53 (6.0)
Height Sensor Mounting Screws	35 (4.0)

1991 SUSPENSION
Rear – Electronic Level Control (Cont.)

WIRING DIAGRAM

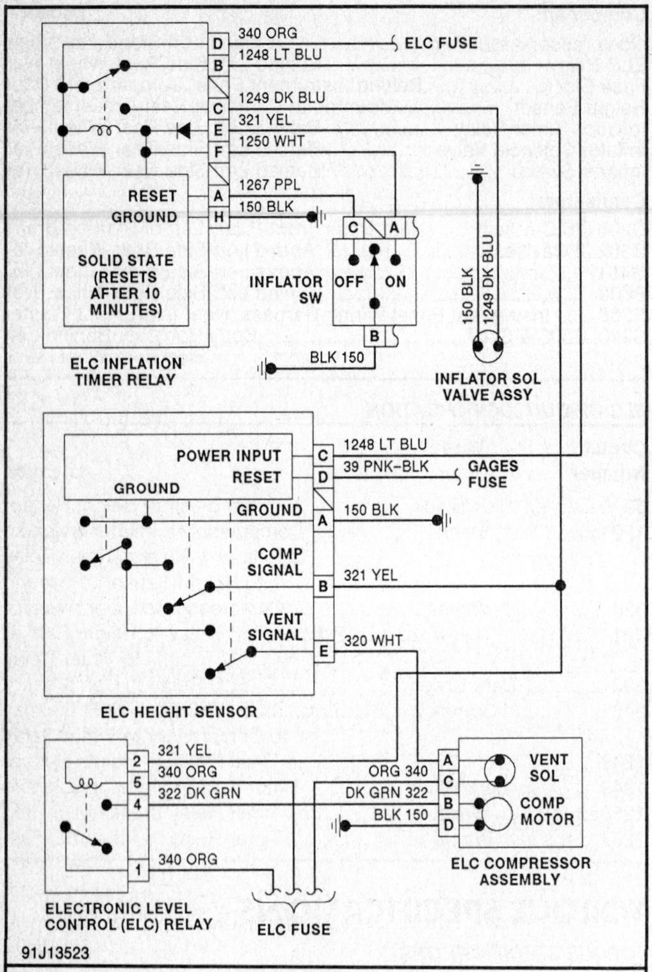
340 ORG
ELC FUSE
1248 LT BLU
1249 DK BLU
321 YEL
1250 WHT
RESET
GROUND
1267 PPL
150 BLK
SOLID STATE (RESETS AFTER 10 MINUTES)
INFLATOR SW
OFF
ON
150 BLK
1249 DK BLU
BLK 150
ELC INFLATION TIMER RELAY
INFLATOR SOL VALVE ASSY
POWER INPUT
RESET
GROUND
1248 LT BLU
39 PNK-BLK
GAGES FUSE
150 BLK
COMP SIGNAL
321 YEL
VENT SIGNAL
320 WHT
ELC HEIGHT SENSOR
321 YEL
340 ORG
322 DK GRN
340 ORG
ORG 340
DK GRN 322
BLK 150
VENT SOL
COMP MOTOR
ELC COMPRESSOR ASSEMBLY
ELECTRONIC LEVEL CONTROL (ELC) RELAY
ELC FUSE
91J13523

Fig. 6: Electronic Level Control (ELC) Wiring Diagram

1991 STEERING
Steering Columns

Astro, Blazer, Bravada, Jimmy, Lumina APV, Safari, Sierra, Silhouette, Sonoma, Trans Sport, "C" & "K" Series, "G" Series, "P" Series, "R" & "V" Series, "S" & "T" Series

DESCRIPTION

All models use collapsible steering columns. All columns have integral ignition switch and locking device. Optional tilt wheel is available with both automatic and manual transmissions.

ADJUSTMENTS

LOWER BEARING

Manual Transmission (Column Shift) - Place transmission in Neutral position. Disconnect transmission rods. Test rotational drag by turning 2-3 shift lever through shifting arc. *See Fig. 1.* Drag must not measure more than 2 lbs. (9 N). Loosen 3 clamping screws. Increase clearance by sliding clamping screws counterclockwise until first reverse lever is free of drag.

Decrease clearance by sliding clamping screws clockwise until slight drag is felt at first reverse shift lever. Install a .005 INCH (.13 mm) shim between space on either side of shift levers. Slide clamp screws counterclockwise until system is loose. Slide screws clockwise until drag is felt in first reverse shift lever. Tighten clamping screws. Remove shim. Install transmission rods.

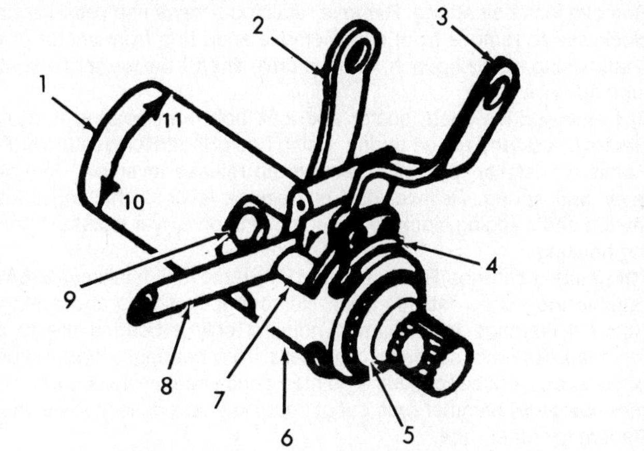
1
2
3
4
5
6
7
8
9
10
11

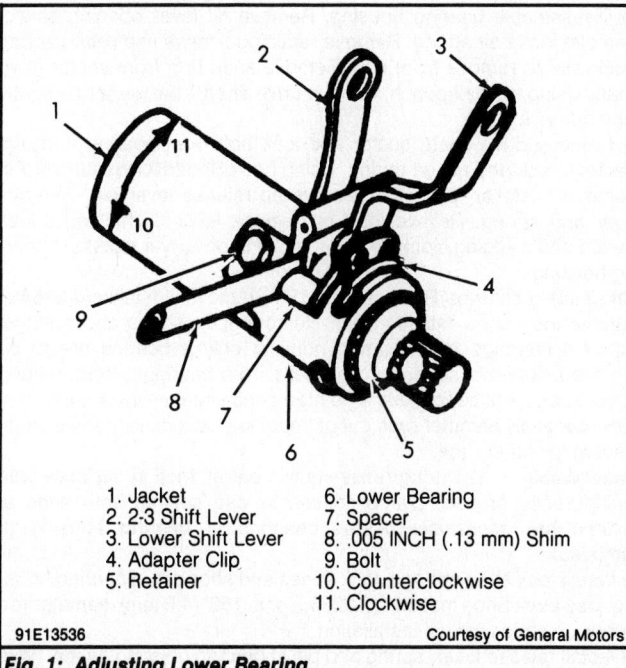

1. Jacket
2. 2-3 Shift Lever
3. Lower Shift Lever
4. Adapter Clip
5. Retainer
6. Lower Bearing
7. Spacer
8. .005 INCH (.13 mm) Shim
9. Bolt
10. Counterclockwise
11. Clockwise

91E13536 Courtesy of General Motors

Fig. 1: Adjusting Lower Bearing

REMOVAL & INSTALLATION

NOTE: For removal and installation procedures of column mounted switches, see STEERING COLUMN SWITCHES article in SAFETY EQUIPMENT.

INTERMEDIATE SHAFT

Removal - Set front wheels in straight-ahead position. Mark pot joint to steering gear position. Mark rag joint to steering gear wormshaft position. Remove intermediate shaft bolt and pinch bolt. Remove intermediate shaft.

Installation - To install, reverse removal procedure. Tighten bolts to specifications. See TORQUE SPECIFICATIONS table at end of article.

STEERING COLUMN

NOTE: Although steering column removal and installation procedures cover all models, some procedures may not apply to all models.

Removal - 1) Disconnect battery negative terminal. Disconnect transmission shift linkage from column shift tube levers. Mark position of pot joint to steering shaft. Remove pot joint bolt from steering shaft.

2) Remove steering column bracket nuts and screws. Remove bracket. Remove steering column seal. Remove steering wheel. See STEERING WHEEL under REMOVAL & INSTALLATION. Disconnect wiring connectors at column harness.

3) Disconnect start/neutral switch and back-up light switch connectors (if equipped). Disconnect transmission indicator cable (if equipped). Rotate column allowing shift lever to clear dash opening. Remove steering column assembly.

Installation - To install, reverse removal procedure. Tighten bolts and screws to specifications. See TORQUE SPECIFICATIONS table at end of article.

HORN BUTTON

Removal & Installation - Disconnect battery negative terminal. Remove horn button. To install, reverse removal procedure.

STEERING WHEEL

Removal - Disconnect negative battery cable. Remove horn pad. Remove snap ring and steering wheel retaining nut. Remove horn lead assembly (if equipped). Mark steering wheel and shaft for reassembly reference. Using Steering Wheel Puller (J-1859-03), remove steering wheel.

NOTE: Turn signal switch must be in neutral position prior to installing steering wheel to prevent damage to canceling cam and switch assembly.

Installation - Before installing steering wheel, ensure turn signal switch is in neutral position. To complete installation, reverse removal procedure. Tighten retaining nut to 30 ft. lbs. (41 N.m). Install snap ring.

FLEXIBLE COUPLING

Removal - Remove Intermediate shaft. See INTERMEDIATE SHAFT under REMOVAL & INSTALLATION. Secure intermediate shaft in vise. Remove coupling-to-flange nuts and washers.

Installation - To install, reverse removal procedure. Tighten nuts to specification. See TORQUE SPECIFICATIONS table at end of article.

POT COUPLING

Removal - Remove Intermediate shaft. See INTERMEDIATE SHAFT under REMOVAL & INSTALLATION. Secure intermediate shaft in vise. Remove retainer clip, coupling and washer. Remove bearings and spring. Remove shaft from vise. Using a socket and press, removing pin. When pin is flush with bushing, complete pin removal using a bolt with a diameter smaller than pin. Remove clamp and seal.

Installation - To install, reverse removal procedure. Inspect all parts for wear and replace as needed. Pack bearing and coupling with high temperature grease. Pin must extend equal length from either side of shaft.

OVERHAUL

STANDARD COLUMN

NOTE: All columns are similar except for appearance of covers. Some models use ignition key light, while others do not. Disassembly and reassembly procedures cover all models. Some procedures may not apply to every steering column.

1991 STEERING
Steering Columns (Cont.)

Disassembly - 1) Remove dash panel bracket and screws from column. Secure lower end of steering column jacket in vise. Remove steering wheel. See STEERING WHEEL in REMOVAL & INSTALLATION. Remove all column switches. See STEERING COLUMN SWITCHES article in SAFETY EQUIPMENT. On column shift models, remove shift lever pivot pin and lever.
2) Remove upper bearing washer. Remove turn signal and ignition lock housing screws. Remove housing assembly. Remove bushing and retainer from lower end of housing. Remove ignition switch actuating rod, rack assembly, rack preload spring, shaft lock bolt and spring assembly from housing. Remove shift lever detent plate.
3) Using a blunt punch or screwdriver, remove ignition switch actuator sector through lock cylinder hole by firmly pushing on block tooth of sector. Remove gear shift lever housing and shroud from jacket assembly. On floor shift models, remove transmission control lock tube housing and shroud. Remove shift lever spring from gear shift lever housing. On floor shift models, remove lock tube spring.
4) Remove steering shaft from lower end of jacket. Disconnect back-up switch or neutral/safety switch. Remove lower bearing retaining clip. Remove lower bearing retainer, bearing adapter assembly, shift tube spring and washer. Using light pressure on bearing outer race, remove lower bearing from adapter. Slide out shift tube assembly.
Reassembly - 1) Coat all friction surfaces with grease. Clamp column in vise so that both ends of column are accessible. Install ignition switch actuator sector into lock cylinder hole over sector shaft with tang end to outside of hole. Using a blunt instrument, press ignition switch actuator sector over shaft.
2) Install shift lever detent plate onto turn signal and ignition lock housing. Rack preload spring into housing from bottom with long section toward handwheel and hook onto edge of housing. Install locking bolt onto crossover arm on rack. Insert rack and lock bolt assembly into bottom of housing with teeth up and toward centerline of column. Align first tooth of rack and sector. Block teeth will line up when rack assembly is seated.
3) Install lower gear shift housing bushing and retainer. Insert lower housing bearing from end of jacket. Align bearing and jacket marks so that bearing rests on stops. Install shift lever spring into housing.
4) Install housing and shroud assemblies into upper end of mast jacket rotating housing until seated in bearing. Install turn signal and lock cylinder housing into jacket. Gear shift housing should be in Park position with rack pulled downward. Seat turn signal housing and install 4 screws. Install lower bearing into adapter assembly.
5) Install shift tube assembly into lower end of jacket. Rotate until upper shift tube key seats into housing keyway. Install spring and lower bearing adapter assembly into bottom of jacket. Holding adapter in place, install lower bearing reinforcement and retainer clip. Snap clip into jacket and reinforcement into jacket slots.
6) Connect back-up light switch or neutral/safety switch. Install steering shaft into column. Install upper bearing washer. Install all column switches. See STEERING COLUMN SWITCHES article in SAFETY EQUIPMENT. Install steering wheel. See STEERING WHEEL under REMOVAL & INSTALLATION. On column shift models, install shift lever pivot pin and lever. Install dash panel bracket and screws on column. Remove steering column jacket from vise. Tighten bolts and screws to specifications. See TORQUE SPECIFICATIONS table at end of article.

TILT WHEEL COLUMN

Disassembly - 1) Remove dash panel bracket and screws from column. Secure lower end of steering column jacket in vise. Remove steering wheel. See STEERING WHEEL under REMOVAL & INSTALLATION. Remove all column switches. See STEERING COLUMN SWITCHES article in SAFETY EQUIPMENT. Remove tilt release lever. Remove shift lever pivot pin and lever.
2) Remove housing cover screws and cover. Reinstall tilt lever release and place column in Up position. Using a screwdriver, turn retainer until aligned with groves in housing. Remove tilt lever spring retainer, spring and guide. Remove pot joint-to-steering shaft clamp bolt. Remove intermediate shaft and pot joint assembly.
3) Push in upper steering shaft and remove upper bearing inner race and seat. Remove lower bearing retainer clip. Remove lower bearing reinforcement, lower bearing and adapter assembly from lower end of mast jacket. Using Pivot Pin Remover (J-21854-01), remove upper bearing housing pivot pins. Disengage lock shoes with tilt release lever installed.
4) Remove bearing housing by pulling upward to extend rack fully downward. Rotate housing to left, disengaging ignition switch rack from actuator rod. Remove steering shaft assembly from upper end of column. Remove steering shaft by removing centering spheres and anti-lash spring. Remove transmission indicator wire (if equipped).
5) Remove bearing housing support-to-gear shift housing screws. Remove bearing housing support. Remove ignition switch actuator rod. Remove shift tube retaining ring and washer.

NOTE: DO NOT allow shift tube to interfere with jacket or damage to shift tube and jacket could result. Guide shift tube carefully through lower end of slotted opening in jacket.

6) Install Shift Tube Remover (J-23072) into lock plate with threads tightly secured to lock plate. Rotate center screw clockwise forcing shift tube from housing. Remove shift tube from lower end of mast jacket. On floor shift models, remove transmission lock tube from lower end of mast jacket. Remove shift tube remover.
7) Remove lock plate and washer. Tip lock plate down toward housing hub and out of jacket notches. Slide lock plate under jacket opening. Remove shift lever housing from mast jacket. On floor shift models, remove transmission control lock tube housing.
8) Disassemble bearing housing. Remove tilt lever opening shield. Remove lock bolt spring. Remove retaining screws and rotate spring clockwise to remove from bolt. Remove snap ring from sector drive shaft. Using a small punch, remove drive shaft from sector by lightly tapping drive shaft.
9) Remove drive shaft, sector and lock bolt from bearing housing. Remove rack and pinion spring. Using Lock Shoe/Release Lever Pin Remover/Installer (J-22635), remove tilt release lever pin. Remove lever and spring. Relieve load on release lever by holding shoes inward and wedging block between top of shoes (over slots)and bearing housing.
10) Using Lock Shoe/Release Lever Pin Remover/Installer (J-22635), remove lock shoe retaining pin. Remove lock shoes and springs. Remove bearings from bearing housing only if bearing are to be replaced. Remove separator and balls from bearings. With bearing housing on work bench, use a pointed punch against back surface of race. Carefully hammer race out of housing until a puller can be used. Repeat for other race.
Reassembly - 1) During reassembly, coat all friction surfaces with multipurpose grease. Clamp column in vise so that both ends of column are accessible. Install bearings in bearing housing (if removed).
2) Install lock shoe springs, lock shoes and shoe pin in bearing housing. Use Lock Shoe Installer (J-22635) or a .180" (4.6 mm) diameter rod to line up shoes for pin installation.
3) Install release lever, spring and pin in bearing housing. Install drive shaft in housing. Lightly tap sector onto drive shaft far enough to install snap ring. Install snap ring. Install lock bolt. Engage lock bolt with sector cam surface. Install rack and spring. Block tooth on rack should engage block tooth on sector.
4) Install tilt release lever. Install lock bolt spring and spring retaining screw. Tighten to 35 INCH lbs. (4 N.m). Install shift lever spring into housing by winding spring up with pliers and pushing in. On floor shift models, install plunger and slide gear shift lever housing into mast jacket.

NOTE: DO NOT push or tap on end of shift tube. Shift tube lever must be aligned with slotted opening at lower end of mast jacket to prevent damage to shift tube and mast jacket.

5) Install washer and lock plate. Slide lock plate into notches in jacket. Carefully install shift tube in lower end of jacket. Align key in tube with keyway in shift lever housing. Using Shift Tube Installer (J-23073-01),

1. Cover
2. Retainer
3. Shaft Lock
4. Turn Signal Cancelling Cam
5. Upper Bearing Spring
6. Turn Signal Switch Screw
7. Turn Signal Switch
8. Wiring Protector
9. Upper Bearing Inner Race Seat
10. Upper Bearing Race
11. Housing Cover Screw
12. Cylinder Lock Screw
13. Lock Housing Cover
14. Ignition Lock
15. Upper, Lower Bearing
16. Steering Shaft Lock Bolt
17. Lock Bolt Spring
18. Column Lock Shoe
19. Ignition Switch Selector Drive Shaft
20. Lock Shoe Retaining Pin
21. Pivot/Tilt Pin
22. Lock Shoe Retaining Spring
23. Shoe Release Spring
24. Shoe Releasing Lever Pin
25. Ignition Switch Actuator
26. Shoe Release Lever
27. Ignition Switch Actuator Rack Kit
28. Ignition Switch Rack Preload Spring
29. Housing
30. Ignition Switch Actuator Sector
31. Lock Bolt Spring Bolt
32. Steering Wheel Tilt Spring Guide
33. Steering Wheel Tilt Spring
34. Tilt Spring Retainer
35. Tilt Lever Operating Shield
36. Upper Steering Shaft
37. Sphere Kit
38. Sphere Spring
39. Lower Steering Shaft
40. Shaft
41. Housing Support
42. Dowel Pin
43. Shift Lever Gate
44. Shift Lever Detent Plate Screw
45. Support Retaining Ring
46. Bowl Thrust Washer
47. Support Lock Plate
48. Support Wave Washer
49. Steering Column Gear Shift Lever Housing
50. Gear Shift Lever Bowl
51. Gear Shift Bowl Shroud
52. Shroud Retaining Plate
53. Key Release Lever
54. Key Release Spring
55. Housing Shroud
56. Ignition Switch Screw
57. Ignition Switch
58. Steering Column Jacket
59. Lower Bearing Adapter Clip
60. Dash Seal
61. Shift Tube
62. Lower Bearing Adapter
63. Lower Shift Tube Bearing
64. Lower Bearing Adapter Reinforcement
65. Coupling Shield
66. Coupling Shaft Bolt
67. Upper Intermediate Shaft Kit
68. Pin Preload Spring
69. Intermediate Shaft Slip Seal
70. Lower Intermediate Shaft Kit
71. Intermediate Shaft Coupling Bolt
72. Dimmer Switch
73. Dimmer Switch Rod
74. Turn Signal Switch Actuator Arm
75. Housing Cover End Cap
76. Pin Preload Spring
77. Wiper Switch
78. Switch Rod Actuator
79. Switch Actuator Pivot Pin

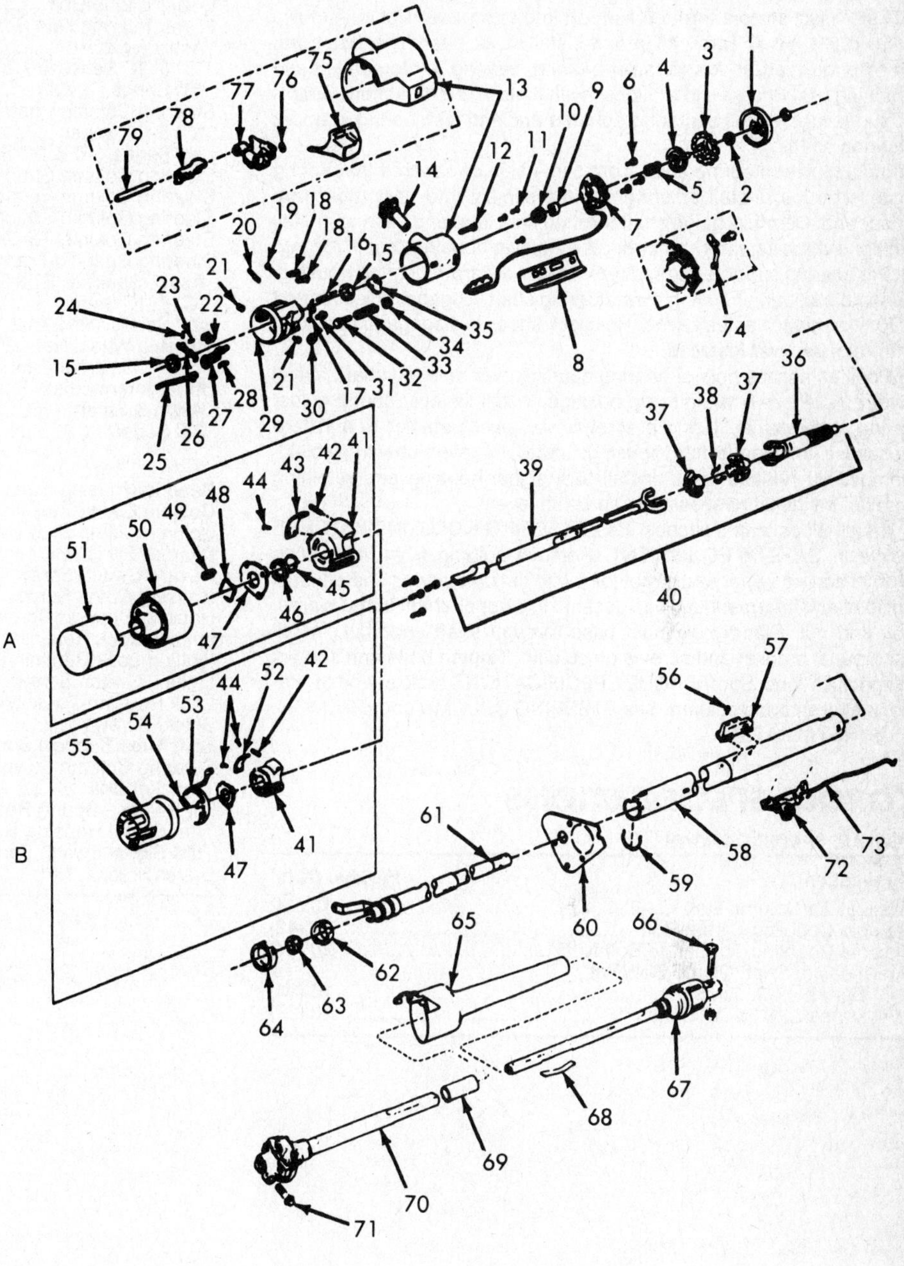

A
B

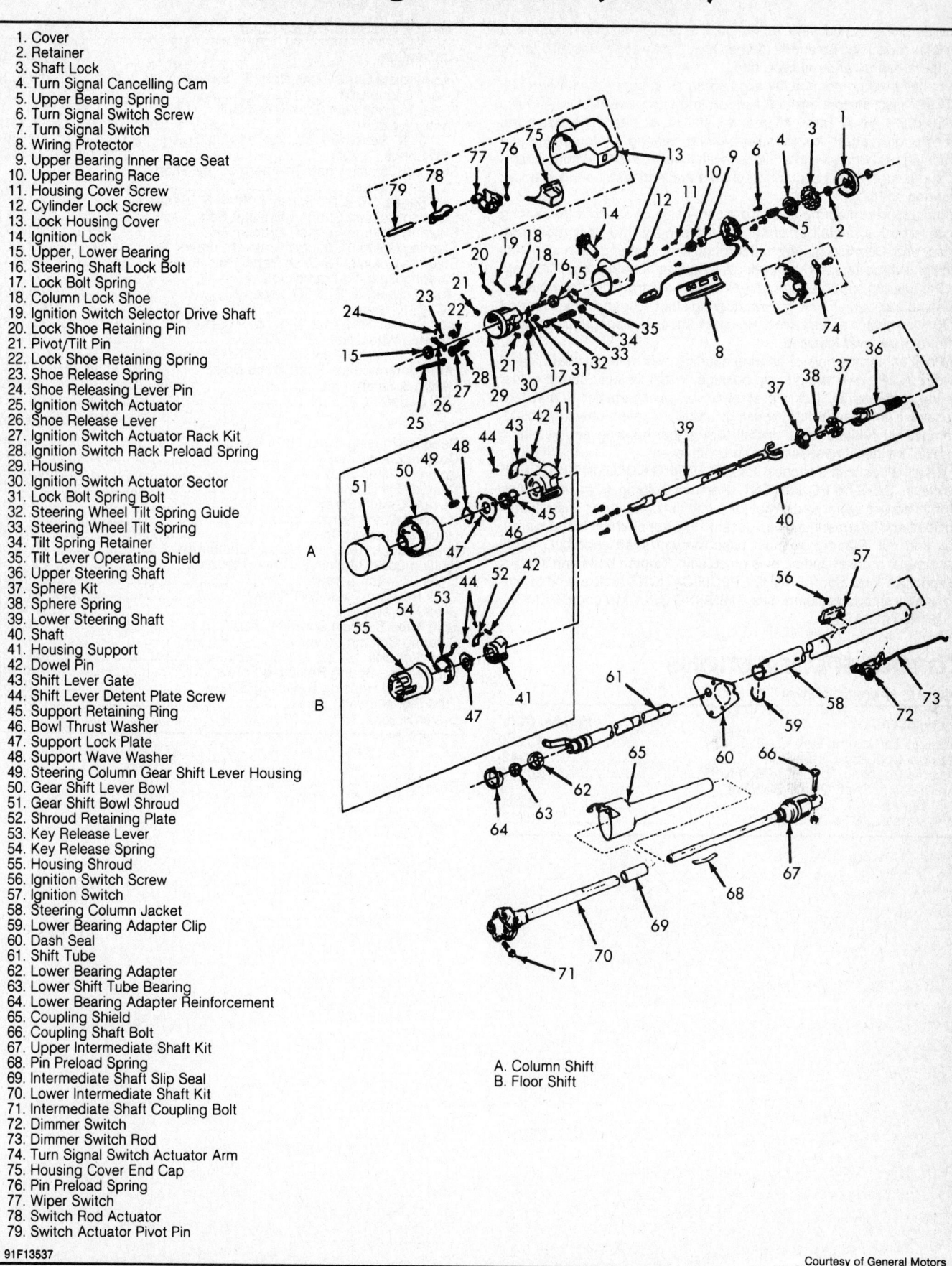

A. Column Shift
B. Floor Shift

91F13537

Courtesy of General Motors

Fig. 2: Exploded View of Tilt Steering Column

1991 STEERING
Steering Columns (Cont.)

pull shift tube into housing. Do not push or tap on end of shift tube. Pull shift lever housing up and compress lock plate washer. Install bearing support washer and retaining ring.

6) Install bearing support by aligning notch in support with notch in jacket. Insert screws through support into lock plate. Tighten screws to 60 INCH lbs. (7 N.m). Align and install lower bearing adapter into lower end of jacket. Install lower bearing, bearing reinforcement and retaining clip. Ensure clip is aligned with slots in reinforcement, adapter and jacket. Install centering spheres and anti-lash spring in upper steering shaft.

7) Install lower steering shaft from same side of spheres that spring ends protrude. Install steering shaft assembly into shift tube from upper end. Carefully guide shaft through shift tube and bearing. Install ignition switch actuator rod through shift lever housing. Insert rod into slot in bearing support. Extend rack downward from bearing housing. Assemble bearing housing over steering shaft. Engage rack over end of ignition switch actuator rod. Hold lock shoes in disengaged position with release lever installed.

8) Position access hole of bearing housing over steering shaft. Install pivot pins. Place bearing in Up position. Install tilt lever spring guide, spring and retainer. Using a screwdriver, push retainer in and turn clockwise to engage into housing. Install tilt lever opening shield. Remove tilt release lever. Install turn signal housing and retaining screws. Install tilt release lever and shift lever.

9) Install all column switches. See STEERING COLUMN SWITCHES article in SAFETY EQUIPMENT. Remove column from vise. Align groove across upper end of pot joint with flat on steering shaft. Install pot joint and intermediate shaft assembly to upper shaft. Install clamp, bolt and nut. Clamp bolt must pass through shaft undercut. Install dash panel bracket and screws on column. Tighten bolts and screws to specifications. See TORQUE SPECIFICATIONS table at end of article. Install steering column. See STEERING COLUMN under REMOVAL & INSTALLATION.

TORQUE SPECIFICATIONS

TORQUE SPECIFICATIONS

Application	Ft. Lbs. (N.m)
Bracket-To-Column Bolt	10 (14)
Flexible Coupling Clamp Bolt	31 (42)
Flexible Coupling-To-Flange Bolt Nut	20 (27)
Intermediate Shaft Clamp Bolt/Nut	
"G" Series	10 (14)
"P" Series & "R" & "V" Series	20 (27)

TORQUE SPECIFICATIONS (Cont.)

Application	Ft. Lbs. (N.m)
Intermediate Shaft Pinch Bolt ("P" Series)	75 (102)
Lower Clamp Bolt	26 (35)
Lower Intermediate Shaft Pinch Bolt	
Astro & Safari	30 (41)
"C" & "K" Series	22 (30)
"G" Series	46 (62)
Steering Column Shaft-To-Intermediate Shaft	
"C" & "K" Series	46 (62)
"P" Series, "R" & "V" Series & "S" & "T" Series	44 (59)
Steering Column Support Bracket Bolt	22 (30)
Steering Column Support Bracket Nut	20 (27)
Steering Column Support Bracket Screws	22 (30)
Steering Column-To-Dash Panel Bolt	10 (14)
Steering Gear-To-Frame Bolt	
Astro, Safari & "S" & "T" Series	55 (75)
"C" & "K" Series	100 (136)
"G" Series, "P" Series & "R" & "V" Series	65 (88)
Steering Wheel Nut	30 (41)
Upper Clamp Nut Bolt	45 (61)
Upper Intermediate Shaft Pinch Bolt	
Astro & Safari	30 (41)
"G" Series	35 (47)
	INCH Lbs. (N.m)
Bearing Housing-To-Lock Housing Screw	35 (4)
Column Clamp Stud	20 (2)
Column Clamp Stud Nut	106 (12)
Dimmer Switch Screw	35 (4)
Hazard Switch Screw	27 (3)
Housing Cover Screw	100 (11)
Housing Support Screw	5 (6.8)
Ignition Lock Retaining Screw (Standard)	40 (4.5)
Ignition Lock Retaining Screw (Tilt)	22 (2.5)
Ignition Switch Screw	35 (4)
Lock Housing-To-Jacket Screw	90 (10)
Shield Screw	4 (6)
Shift Tube Support Screw	60 (7)
Steering Column Lower	
Bracket Bolt	106 (12)
Tilt Release Spring Retaining Screw	35 (4)
Turn Signal Housing Retaining Screw	45 (5)
Turn Signal Switch Screw	35 (4)
Upper Bracket Nut	106 (12)

1991 STEERING
Manual Recirculating Ball

"S" & "T" Series

DESCRIPTION & OPERATION

Steering gear is a recirculating ball-type consisting of a ball nut connected to steering worm and in-mesh with sector gear. Proper engagement between sector and ball nut is obtained by adjusting screw. Worm bearing adjuster can be turned to provide proper preloading of upper and lower bearings.

STEERING SERVICE PRECAUTIONS

Replacement fasteners must have the same part numbers as the originals. Tighten all fasteners to specification. Always use NEW cotter pins. When installing cotter pins, DO NOT back off castle nuts to align cotter pin hole. Tighten nut to next slot that lines up with hole.

DO NOT hammer on ball studs, or damage to threads may result. If threads are not clean and smooth, ball studs may turn in joint when nuts are tightened. Tie rod sleeve clamps must always be positioned as specified before tightening bolts.

ADJUSTMENTS

NOTE: Adjust worm bearing preload prior to performing over-center preload adjustment. If steering gear is removed, install INCH lb. torque wrench on worm shaft to check preload adjustments.

WORM BEARING PRELOAD

1) Place reference marks on pitman arm and sector shaft. Using Pitman Arm Remover (J-6632-01), remove pitman arm from sector shaft. Loosen worm bearing adjuster lock nut. Back off worm bearing adjuster 1/4 turn. *See Fig. 1.*

CAUTION: DO NOT turn wheel hard against stop with steering linkage disconnected or steering gear may be damaged.

2) Remove horn button. Turn wheel to right stop and back off 1/2 turn. Install INCH lb. torque wrench on steering shaft nut. Rotate steering shaft 90 degrees and note torque wrench reading.
3) Torque required to maintain wheel movement should be 5-8 INCH lbs. (.6-.9 N.m). If not within specification, tighten worm bearing adjuster clockwise to increase preload or counterclockwise to decrease preload.
4) Adjust and hold worm bearing adjuster while tightening lock nut. Recheck worm bearing preload.

OVER-CENTER PRELOAD

1) With worm bearing preload adjusted, turn worm shaft slowly from stop-to-stop while counting total number of turns. Turn shaft back to the exact center position.
2) Loosen lock nut and turn sector shaft adjuster screw (located in center of sector shaft cover) in until all lash is taken out of sector shaft. Tighten lock nut. Rotate worm shaft slightly off center then attach an INCH lb. torque wrench to worm shaft or steering wheel nut.
3) Rotate worm shaft back through center position and note rotating torque. Rotating torque should be 4-10 INCH lbs. (.5-1.1 N.m) in excess of worm bearing preload. Maximum torque should not exceed 16 INCH lbs. (1.8 N.m). If rotating torque is not within specification, adjust sector shaft adjuster screw.

CAUTION: If maximum torque is exceeded, rotate sector shaft adjuster screw counterclockwise, and adjust by rotating lock nut clockwise.

REMOVAL & INSTALLATION

NOTE: Replacement fasteners must have the same part numbers as originals. Torque all fasteners and install NEW cotter pin.

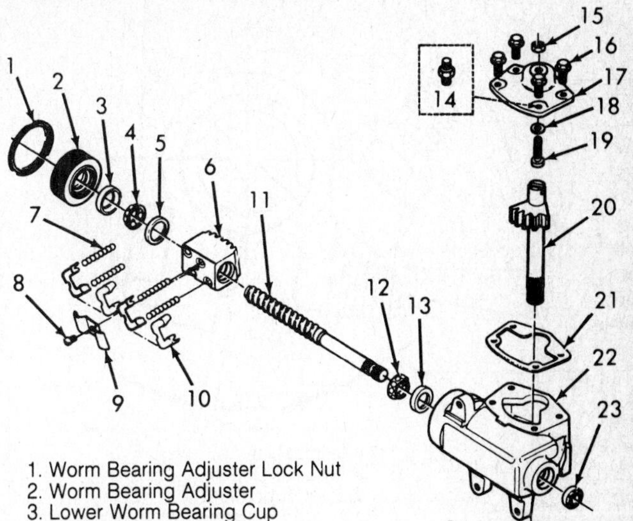
1
2
3
4
5
6
7
8
9
10
11
12
13
14
15
16
17
18
19
20
21
22
23
24
25
26
27

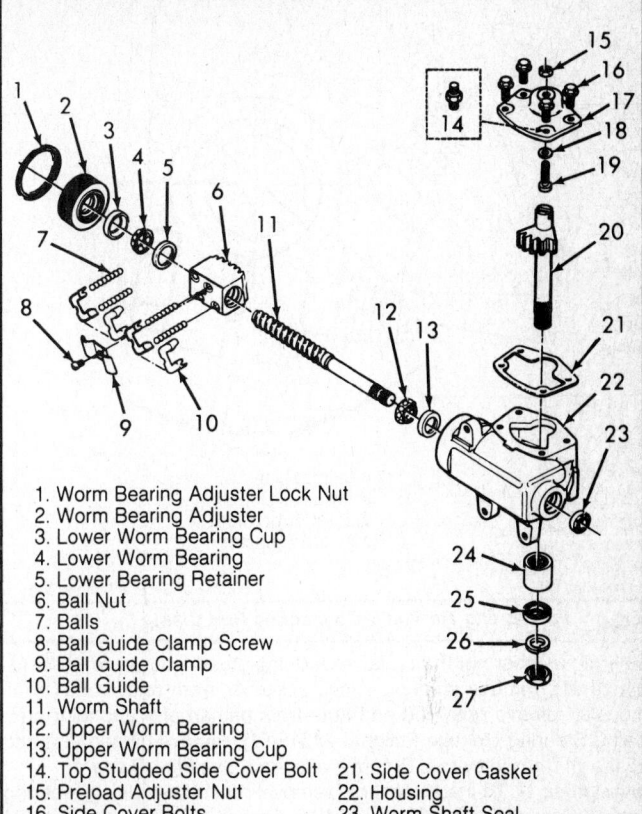

1. Worm Bearing Adjuster Lock Nut
2. Worm Bearing Adjuster
3. Lower Worm Bearing Cup
4. Lower Worm Bearing
5. Lower Bearing Retainer
6. Ball Nut
7. Balls
8. Ball Guide Clamp Screw
9. Ball Guide Clamp
10. Ball Guide
11. Worm Shaft
12. Upper Worm Bearing
13. Upper Worm Bearing Cup
14. Top Studded Side Cover Bolt
15. Preload Adjuster Nut
16. Side Cover Bolts
17. Side Cover
18. Preload Adjuster Shim
19. Preload Adjuster
20. Pitman Shaft
21. Side Cover Gasket
22. Housing
23. Worm Shaft Seal
24. Pitman Shaft Needle Bearing
25. Pitman Shaft Seal
26. Spring Washer
27. Pitman Arm Nut

91F13529 Courtesy of General Motors Corp.

Fig. 1: Exploded View of Steering Gear

STEERING GEAR

Removal – 1) Set front wheels in straight-ahead position. Disconnect negative battery cable. Remove flexible coupling-to-steering shaft pinch bolt. Remove flexible coupling cover on "T" Series or shield on "S" Series. Place reference marks on coupling and shaft for reassembly reference. Remove lower clamp bolt and lower clamp from worm shaft.
2) Mark relationship of pitman arm-to-sector shaft. Remove pitman arm retaining nut. Remove pitman arm using Puller (J-6632-01). Remove steering gear mounting bolts and remove gear assembly.
Installation – To install, reverse removal procedure. Ensure all reference marks are aligned and flexible coupling pinch bolt is aligned with groove of the shaft.

INNER AND OUTER TIE ROD ENDS

Removal – Raise and support vehicle. Remove cotter pins and outer tie rod end nut. Using Wheel Stud and Tie Rod Remover (J-6627-A), remove outer tie rod ball studs from steering knuckle and inner tie rod ball studs from relay rod. Remove tie rod ends from adjuster tube. Loosen clamp bolts and unscrew assemblies.
Installation – To install, reverse removal procedure. Lubricate tie rod threads with chassis lubricant before installing. Inner and outer tie rod end threads must be adjusted equally within 3 threads. Adjust toe-in. See SPECIFICATIONS & PROCEDURES article in WHEEL ALIGNMENT. Tie rod ends must rotate full travel and travel must be maintained during clamp tightening. *See Fig. 2.*

RELAY ROD

Removal – Raise and support vehicle. Remove inner tie rod end nuts. Remove inner tie rod ends from relay rod. On "T" Series, remove

1991 STEERING
Manual Recirculating Ball (Cont.)

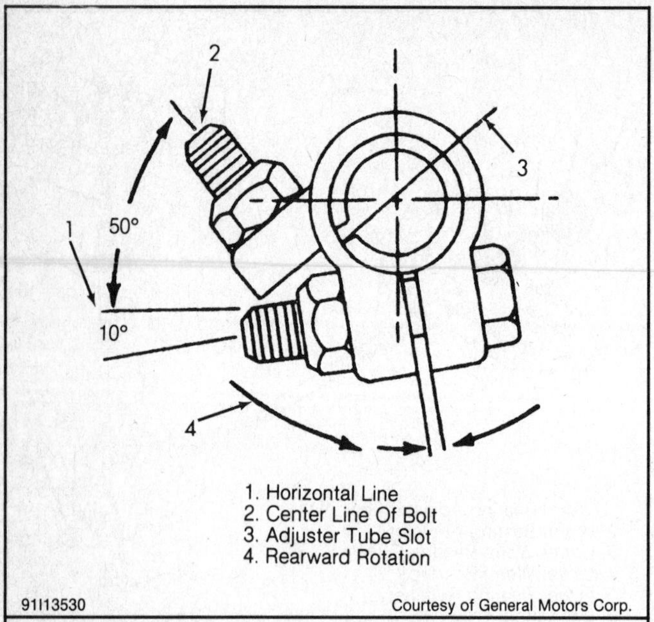
1
2
3
4
50°
10°
1. Horizontal Line
2. Center Line Of Bolt
3. Adjuster Tube Slot
4. Rearward Rotation
91I13530
Courtesy of General Motors Corp.

Fig. 2: Positioning Tie Rod & Connecting Rod Clamp

steering damper nut from relay rod. Using Steering Linkage Puller (J-24319-01), remove steering shock absorber from relay rod. On all models, remove relay rod end nuts from pitman arm and idler arm. Using Steering Linkage Puller (J-24319-01), remove pitman arm and idler arm from relay rod. Remove relay rod. *See Figs. 3 and 4.*

Installation – To install, reverse removal procedure. Using Steering Linkage Installer (J-29193 or J-29194), seat all tapers to 40 ft. lbs. (54 N.m). Tighten nuts to specifications. See TORQUE SPECIFICATIONS table at end of this article. Adjust toe-in. See SPECIFICATIONS & PROCEDURES article in WHEEL ALIGNMENT.

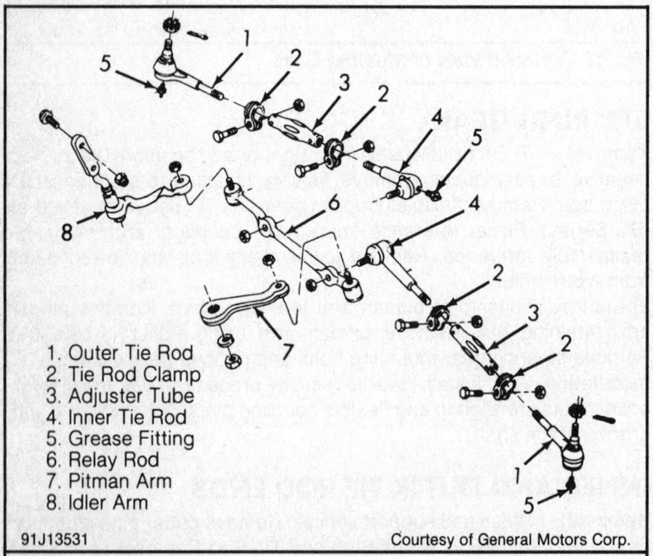
1. Outer Tie Rod
2. Tie Rod Clamp
3. Adjuster Tube
4. Inner Tie Rod
5. Grease Fitting
6. Relay Rod
7. Pitman Arm
8. Idler Arm
91J13531
Courtesy of General Motors Corp.

Fig. 3: Exploded View of Steering Linkage ("S" Series)

IDLER ARM

NOTE: Replace idler arm assembly if an up and down force of 25 lbs. (11 kg), applied at relay rod end of idler arm, produces a lash of more than 1/8" (3 mm) in straight-ahead position.

Removal – Raise and support vehicle. Remove idler arm nut and bolt from tie rod end. Remove idler arm nut and spring washer from relay rod. Using Steering Linkage Puller (J-24319-01) remove idler arm from relay rod. Remove idler arm. *See Fig. 5.*

Installation – To install, reverse removal procedure. Using Steering Linkage Installer (J-29193 or J-29194) seat all tapers to 40 ft. lbs. (54

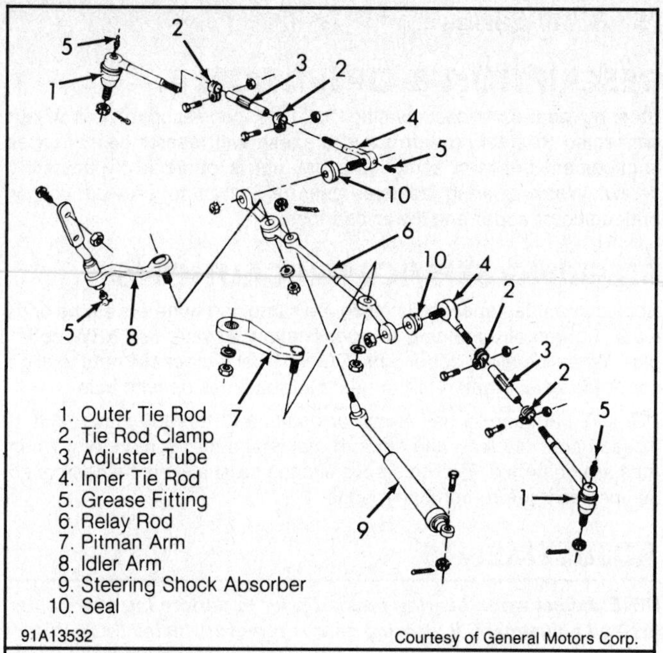
1. Outer Tie Rod
2. Tie Rod Clamp
3. Adjuster Tube
4. Inner Tie Rod
5. Grease Fitting
6. Relay Rod
7. Pitman Arm
8. Idler Arm
9. Steering Shock Absorber
10. Seal
91A13532
Courtesy of General Motors Corp.

Fig. 4: Exploded View of Steering Linkage ("T" Series)

N.m). Tighten nuts to specifications. See TORQUE SPECIFICATIONS table at end of article. Adjust toe-in. See SPECIFICATIONS & PROCEDURES article in WHEEL ALIGNMENT.

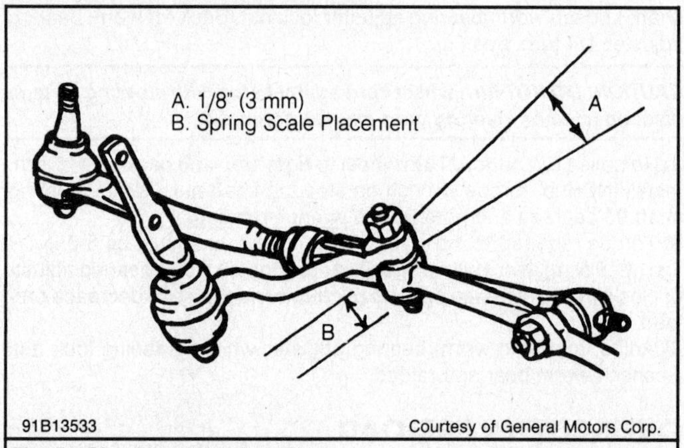
A. 1/8" (3 mm)
B. Spring Scale Placement
A
B
91B13533
Courtesy of General Motors Corp.

Fig. 5: Checking Idler Arm Play

PITMAN ARM

Removal – **1)** Disconnect air induction assembly. Slide up intermediate shaft cover. Mark intermediate shaft for reassembly, Remove intermediate shaft. Disconnect oil filter lines at crossmember bracket. Remove splash shield.

2) Remove pitman arm nut and spring washer from relay rod. Using Steering Linkage Puller (J-24319-01), remove pitman arm from relay rod.

3) Remove lower steering gear bolts. LOOSEN upper steering gear bolt. Rotate steering gear for pitman arm clearance at crossmember and support with block of wood.

4) Remove pitman arm nut and spring washer from sector shaft. Index mark arm-to-shaft position. Using Remover (J-6632-01) or Puller (J-29107), remove pitman arm from shaft. *See Figs. 3 and 4.*

Installation – To install, reverse removal procedure. Tighten nuts to specifications. See TORQUE SPECIFICATIONS table at end of article. DO NOT hammer on pitman arm, or damage to steering gear may result. Be sure to reinstall hardened steel washer before installing nut.

1991 STEERING
Manual Recirculating Ball (Cont.)

STEERING SHOCK ABSORBER

Removal ("T" Series) – Remove steering shock damper nut from relay rod. Using Steering Linkage Puller (J-24319-01), remove steering shock damper form relay rod. Remove cotter pin, nut and bolt from frame mount end. Remove steering shock damper. *See Fig. 4.*

Installation – To install, reverse removal procedure. Using Steering Linkage Installer (J-29193 or J-29194), seat all tapers to 40 ft. lbs. (54 N.m). Tighten nuts to specifications. See TORQUE SPECIFICATIONS table at end of this article. Adjust toe-in. See SPECIFICATIONS & PROCEDURES article in WHEEL ALIGNMENT.

SECTOR SHAFT SEAL

Removal – **1)** Seal may be replaced with steering gear installed. *See Fig. 1.* Set front wheels in straight-ahead position. Mark relationship of pitman arm-to-sector shaft. Using Puller (J-6632-01), remove pitman arm.

2) Remove sector shaft cover bolts. Lift sector shaft and side cover assembly from housing. Pry sector shaft seal from housing using a screwdriver. DO NOT scratch housing bore. Remove sector shaft adjuster screw lock nut. Remove sector shaft cover from sector shaft assembly by turning adjuster screw clockwise.

3) Inspect gear lubricant for contamination. If lubricant is contaminated in any way, gear should be completely rebuilt.

Installation – **1)** Lubricate new sector shaft seal with steering gear lubricant. Position seal in sector shaft bore and tap it into place using a socket.

2) Install sector shaft in gear so center tooth of sector enters center tooth space of ball nut. Fill gear housing with lubricant and install new side cover gasket on gear housing. Install side cover over sector shaft by reaching through cover hole with a screwdriver.

3) Turn sector shaft adjuster screw counterclockwise until screw bottoms and then back off screw 1/4 turn. Install sector shaft cover bolts and sector shaft adjuster lock nut. Adjust worm bearing preload and over-center preload. See WORM BEARING PRELOAD and OVER-CENTER PRELOAD under ADJUSTMENTS.

4) Install pitman arm on sector shaft using marks made at removal. Tighten pitman shaft-to-sector shaft nut to specification. See TORQUE SPECIFICATIONS table at end of article.

OVERHAUL

DISASSEMBLY

1) Place steering gear in a vise, clamping onto one mounting tab. Worm shaft should be in a horizontal position. Rotate worm shaft from stop-to-stop while counting total number of turns. Turn shaft back to the exact center position.

2) Loosen sector shaft adjuster screw lock nut. Remove sector shaft cover bolts. Lift sector shaft cover and sector shaft from housing.

3) Loosen worm bearing adjuster lock nut. Remove worm bearing adjuster with bearing and bearing race. *See Fig. 1.* Remove ball nut and worm shaft assembly.

CAUTION: DO NOT allow ball nut to rotate down to either end of worm shaft, as ball guide ends may be damaged.

4) Remove remaining bearing from housing. Using screwdriver, pry bearing retainer from worm bearing adjuster assembly and remove bearing. Remove sector shaft adjuster screw lock nut.

5) Hold sector shaft cover and turn sector shaft adjuster screw clockwise to remove sector shaft cover. Remove sector shaft adjuster screw and shim from sector shaft. Pry out and discard both sector shaft and worm shaft seals.

CLEANING & INSPECTION

Clean components with solvent and dry with compressed air. Inspect bearings and races for signs of wear. Inspect sector shaft fit at side cover. Check ball nut and worm shaft assembly for wear and straightness.

COMPONENT SERVICE

Sector Shaft Bearing Replacement – Support steering gear in an arbor press. Using Bearing Remover (J-6278), drive sector shaft bearing from housing. Using Bearing Installer (J-35469 and J-8092), install new bearing into housing. Replacement bushings are machined to size and require no reaming.

Worm Shaft Bearing Race (In Worm Bearing Adjuster) – Using Slide Hammer (J-29369-1), remove bearing race from worm bearing adjuster. Using Bearing Race Installer (J-35365), install bearing race in worm bearing adjuster.

Worm Shaft Bearing Race (In Housing) – Using a hammer and punch, remove bearing race from housing. Using Bearing Race Installer (J-35365), install new bearing race in housing.

Ball Nut & Worm Shaft Assembly – Ball nut disassembly is only necessary if binding or tightness exists while rotating worm shaft. If disassembly is required, proceed to step **1)**.

CAUTION: Note number of balls located in each circuit of ball nut. Correct amount must be installed in each circuit. Note direction of ball nut installation on worm shaft.

1) Remove ball guides retaining clamp. Pull guides from ball nut while catching balls in clean pan. Turn nut over and rotate worm shaft until all balls have been removed.

2) Remove worm shaft from the ball nut. Wash parts and inspect worm, nut grooves, and ball bearings for indentations. Check ball guides for damage at ends where they deflect or pick up balls from helical path on worm shaft.

3) Measure distance between ball grooves of worm gear. Distance between grooves determines amount of balls to be installed in each circuit. See BALL USAGE table.

BALL USAGE

Groove Distance In. (mm)	Balls Per Circuit
.04 (1.0)	25
.10 (2.5)	27
.20 (5.0)	27

4) To reassemble ball nut and worm shaft, install ball nut with narrow end of ball nut teeth upward on right side (looking from steering wheel end of worm shaft). Install worm shaft. Ensure worm shaft is aligned with grooves in ball nut.

5) Install guides in ball nut. Install proper amount of balls in one guide hole while rotating the worm shaft. Repeat procedure for the remaining guide. Install guide clamps and bolts.

REASSEMBLY

1) Place gear housing in a vise with worm shaft bore horizontal and side cover opening facing upward. All seals, bushings and worm shaft bearing races should be installed.

2) Place upper ball bearing over worm shaft. Install worm shaft and ball nut assembly into housing and up through the upper ball bearing race and seal. Install bearing and retainer in worm bearing adjuster.

3) Install worm shaft and worm bearing adjuster in housing. Tighten worm bearing adjuster until a slight amount of worm shaft end play exists. Install sector shaft adjuster screw and shim in slotted end of sector shaft.

4) Using feeler gauge, check clearance between adjuster screw and sector shaft when holding adjuster screw upward. Clearance should not exceed .002" (.05 mm). If clearance exceeds specification, a different thickness shim should be installed.

5) Rotate worm shaft until ball nut is at center of its travel. Install sector shaft assembly so center tooth of sector teeth enters center tooth space in ball nut.

6) Install side cover gasket. Install side cover over sector shaft by reaching through cover with a screwdriver.

7) Turn adjuster screw counterclockwise until screw bottoms and then back off screw 1/2 turn. Loosely install a new lock nut onto adjuster screw.

1991 STEERING
Manual Recirculating Ball (Cont.)

8) Install sector shaft cover bolts. Adjust worm bearing preload and over-center preload. See WORM BEARING PRELOAD and OVER-CENTER PRELOAD under ADJUSTMENTS.

TORQUE SPECIFICATIONS

TORQUE SPECIFICATIONS

Application	Ft. Lbs. (N.m)
Idler Arm-To-Frame Nut	60 (81)
Inner Tie Rod-To-Relay Rod Nut	35 (47)
Outer Tie Rod-To-Steering Knuckle Nut	35 (47)
Pitman Arm-To-Sector Shaft Nut	185 (249)
Relay Rod-To-Idler Arm Nut	
"S" Series	35 (47)
"T" Series	60 (81)
Relay Rod-To-Pitman Arm Nut	
"S" Series	35 (47)
"T" Series	60 (81)
Sector Shaft Adjuster Screw Lock Nut	22 (30)
Sector Shaft Cover Bolt	32 (43)
Steering Gear Lower Clamp Bolt	30 (41)
Steering Gear-To-Frame Nut	55 (75)
Steering Shock Absorber	
To-Front Crossmember Nut	26 (35)
To-Relay Rod Nut	45 (61)
Tie Rod Adjuster Tube Clamp Bolt	14 (19)
	INCH Lbs. (N.m)
Flexible Coupling Pinch Bolt	50 (5.6)

1991 STEERING
Power Steering – General Servicing

Astro, Blazer, Bravada, Jimmy, Safari, Sierra, Sonoma, "C" & "K" Series, "G" Series, "P" Series, "R" & "V" Series, "S" & "T" Series

LUBRICATION

SERVICE INTERVALS

Check fluid at every oil change.

CHECKING FLUID LEVEL

Check fluid with engine stopped and fluid hot or cold. Fluid level must be at FULL-HOT or FULL-COLD mark on dipstick. On models with remote reservoir, fluid level must be .5-1.0" from top of reservoir with wheels turned fully left.

RECOMMENDED FLUID

Application	Part No. or Type
All Models	GM 1050017

REFILLING & BLEEDING SYSTEM

1) Fill reservoir to correct level. Let oil settle 2 minutes. Start engine, and run it 4-5 seconds. Check reservoir. Add fluid (if necessary). Repeat procedure until level in reservoir remains constant.

2) Raise vehicle so both front wheels leave ground. Start engine, and increase engine speed to 1500 RPM. Turn wheels right and left, lightly contacting stops. Check fluid level. Add fluid (if necessary).

3) Lower vehicle. Turn wheels right and left. Check fluid level. Add fluid (if necessary). If fluid is foamy, proceed to step **4)**.

4) Turn off engine. After letting vehicle sit for a few minutes, repeat steps **1)** through **3)**. Check fluid for air in system. If fluid level is low and air is apparent, repeat complete procedure.

TESTING

PREPARATION

1) Ensure belt tension is correct. Disconnect power steering pump pressure hose. Keep hose end raised to prevent fluid loss. Connect Pressure Gauge (J-5176-D) hose to power steering pump fitting. Connect other hose from valve side of tester to steering gear inlet.

2) Open valve. Run engine until fluid reaches normal operating temperature of 150-170°F (66-77°C). Check fluid level. Add fluid (if necessary).

PRESSURE TEST

1) Note pressure reading with valve open and engine idling. Pressure should be 80-125 psi (6-9 kg/cm²). If pressure is above 200 psi (14 kg/cm²), check hoses for restrictions and poppet valve for proper assembly.

Note: Idle pressure is 80-125 psi (6-9 kg/cm²).

PUMP SPECIFICATIONS

			Minimum Output [1]		Maximum Output [2]		Relief Valve Settings			
							Minimum		Maximum	
Vehicle	Part Number	Model	GPM [3]	L/Min. [4]	GPM [3]	L/Min. [4]	PSI	kPa	PSI	kPa
R/V Model	7838933	132-P-122	1.32	5.00	3.1-3.5	11.7-13.2	1200	8274	1300	8964
	7838934	132-P-123	1.32	5.00	3.1-3.5	11.7-13.2	1350	9308	1450	9998
	7838935	132-P-124	1.32	5.00	3.1-3.5	11.7-13.2	1200	8274	1300	8964
	7838936	132-P-125	1.32	5.00	3.1-3.5	11.7-13.2	1350	9308	1450	9998
	7839798	132-P-144	1.32	5.00	3.1-3.5	11.7-13.2	1350	9308	1450	9998
	7839800	132-P-146	1.32	5.00	3.1-3.5	11.7-13.2	1200	8274	1300	8964
	7839801	132-P-147	1.32	5.00	3.1-3.5	11.7-13.2	1200	8274	1300	8964
	7839802	132-P-148	1.32	5.00	3.1-3.5	11.7-13.2	1200	8274	1300	8964
	7839804	132-P-150	1.32	5.00	3.1-3.5	11.7-13.2	1200	8274	1300	8964
	7839813	132-P-159	1.32	5.00	3.1-3.5	11.7-13.2	1350	9308	1450	9998
	7839816	132-P-161	1.32	5.00	3.1-3.5	11.7-13.2	1350	9308	1450	9998
	26000518	132-P-260	1.32	5.00	3.1-3.5	11.7-13.2	1200	8274	1300	8964
	26003926	132-P-280	1.32	5.00	3.1-3.5	11.7-13.2	1200	8274	1300	8964
	26010182	132-P-290	1.32	5.00	3.1-3.5	11.7-13.2	1200	8274	1300	8964
	26010183	132-P-291	1.32	5.00	3.1-3.5	11.7-13.2	1350	9308	1450	9998
G Model	7841731	132-P-222	1.32	5.00	3.1-3.5	11.7-13.2	1350	9308	1450	9998
	26001536	132-P-267	1.32	5.00	3.1-3.5	11.7-13.2	1200	8274	1300	8964
P Model	7839808	132-P-154	1.32	5.00	2.4-2.8	9.1-10.6	1200	8274	1300	8964
	7839809	132-P-155	1.32	5.00	2.4-2.8	9.1-10.6	1200	8274	1300	8964
	7839812	132-P-158	1.32	5.00	2.4-2.8	9.1-10.6	1350	9308	1450	9998
	7842032	132-P-226	1.32	5.00	3.1-3.5	11.7-13.2	1200	8274	1300	8964
	7842033	132-P-227	1.32	5.00	3.1-3.5	11.7-13.2	1200	8274	1300	8964
	7842490	132-P-231	1.32	5.00	2.4-2.8	9.1-10.6	1350	9308	1450	9998
	7842491	132-P-232	1.32	5.00	3.1-3.5	11.7-13.2	1200	8274	1300	8964

1 – Output of Power Steering Fluid at 32°C (90°F) temperature when operating pump at 465 rpm against 4585-5068 kPa (665-735 psi) pressure.

2 – Output of Power Steering Fluid at 32°C (90°F) temperature when operating pump at 1500 rpm against 345 kPa (50 psi) pressure.

3 – Gallons Per Minutes

4 – Liters Per Minute

117434

Courtesy of General Motors Corp.

Fig. 1: Pump Pressure Specifications ("G", "P" and "R" & "V" Series)

1991 STEERING
Power Steering – General Servicing (Cont.)

2) Completely close and reopen gate valve 3 times. Record highest reading each time. DO NOT close valve longer than 5 seconds. Readings should be within specifications. On "G", "P" and "R" & "V" Series, see *Fig. 1.* On all other models, see PRESSURE TEST SPECIFICATIONS table.

3) If readings are within specifications and within 50 psi (4 kg/cm²) of each other, pump is operating properly. On "G", "P" and "R" & "V" Series, see *Fig. 1.* On all other models, see PRESSURE TEST SPECIFICATIONS table.

4) If readings are higher than specifications and not within 50 psi (4 kg/cm²) of each other, flow control valve in pump is sticking. Remove and clean or replace flow control valve.

5) If pressure is constant but more than 100 psi (7 kg/cm²) below specifications, clean or replace flow control valve in pump. If readings are still low, replace pump.

6) If pump is within specifications, open valve, and turn steering wheel from right to left stops. Record pressure. DO NOT hold wheel against either stop longer than 5 seconds.

7) Pressure should be within specifications. On "G", "P" and "R" & "V" Series, see *Fig. 1.* On all other models, see PRESSURE TEST SPECIFICATIONS table. If pressure is low, steering gear is leaking internally and must be repaired.

PRESSURE TEST SPECIFICATIONS

Application	Idle Pressure psi (kg/cm²)	Relief Pressure psi (kg/cm²)
Astro & Safari	80-125 (6-9)	1250-1350 (87-95)
C15/25 & "K" Series	80-125 (6-9)	1200-1300 (84-91)
C35	80-125 (6-9)	1350-1450 (95-102)
C35 (with Hydro-Boost)	80-125 (6-9)	1465-1515 (103-106)
"S" & "T" Series	80-125 (6-9)	1100-1200 (77-84)

BELT TENSION (Tension in Lbs. Using Burroughs Tension Gauge)

Application	New Belt	Used Belt
Serpentine Belt	[1]	[1]
"V" Belt	146	67

[1] – Serpentine belts are equipped with self-tensioner and no adjustment is required.

1991 STEERING
Power Rack & Pinion

Lumina APV, Silhouette, Trans Sport

STEERING SERVICE PRECAUTIONS

Replacement fasteners must be of same part number or equivalent. Tighten all fasteners to specification. Always use new cotter pins. When installing cotter pins, DO NOT back off castle nuts to align cotter pin hole. Tighten nut to next slot that lines up with hole.
DO NOT hammer on ball studs, or damage to threads may result. If threads are not clean and smooth, ball studs may turn in joint when nuts are tightened. Tie rod sleeve clamps must always be positioned as specified before tightening bolts.

ADJUSTMENTS

RACK BEARING PRELOAD

1) With steering gear installed, raise and support vehicle. Position wheels in straight-ahead position. Loosen adjuster plug lock nut. *See Fig. 1.* Rotate adjuster plug clockwise until it bottoms in the housing.
2) Back off adjuster plug 50-70 degrees (approximately one flat). Tighten adjuster plug lock nut to specification. See TORQUE SPECIFICATIONS table at end of article. DO NOT allow adjusting plug to rotate while tightening lock nut.

CAUTION: Ensure steering wheel returns to center position after adjusting rack bearing preload.

LUBRICATION, TROUBLE SHOOTING & TESTING

For lubrication and testing, see POWER STEERING - GENERAL SERVICING article. For trouble shooting, see TROUBLE SHOOTING tables in GENERAL INFORMATION.

REMOVAL & INSTALLATION

OUTER TIE ROD END

Removal - Remove cotter pin and nut from outer tie rod end at steering knuckle. Using Steering Linkage Remover (J-24319-01) separate tie rod end from steering knuckle. Loosen lock nut on inner tie rod. Unscrew outer tie rod from inner tie rod. Note number of turns required for removal.
Installation - To install, reverse removal procedure. Install tie rod to same number of turns required during removal. Adjust toe-in. See SPECIFICATIONS & PROCEDURES article in WHEEL ALIGNMENT. Ensure boot is not twisted. Tighten tie rod lock nut and tie rod-to-steering knuckle nut to specifications. See TORQUE SPECIFICATIONS table at end of article.

INNER TIE ROD END

Removal - **1)** Remove cotter pin and nut from outer tie rod end at steering knuckle. Using Steering Linkage Remover (J-24319-01) separate tie rod end from steering knuckle. Loosen lock nut on inner tie rod. Unscrew outer tie rod from inner tie rod. Note number of turns required for removal.
2) Remove tie rod end clamp. Using side cutters, remove boot clamp. Mark location of breather tube on housing. Remove breather tube and boot, Remove shock dampener from inner tie rod and slide back on rack.

CAUTION: Hold rack during inner tie rod removal to prevent damage to internal gears of rack.

3) Place wrenches on flats of rack assembly and inner tie rod housing. Rotate housing counterclockwise until tie rod separates from rack.
Installation - **1)** To install, ensure all surfaces are clean. Stake both sides of inner tie rod housing to flats on rack. Insert .01 inch (.25mm) feeler gauge between rack and tie rod housing stake. Feeler gauge must NOT pass between rack and housing stake.
2) Lubricate boot contact areas on inner tie rod end and housing with grease before installing boot. Install boot, aligning reference mark with mark on housing. Install new boot seal clamps. Using Clamp Pliers (J-22610), tighten boot clamps. Ensure boot is not twisted. To complete installation, reverse removal procedure.

BOOT

Removal - Remove outer tie rod end. See OUTER TIE ROD END. Remove lock nut for outer tie rod from inner tie rod. Remove boot clamps and boot.

CAUTION: Mark location of breather tube on housing for reassembly reference before removing boot. See Fig. 1.

Installation - **1)** To install, ensure all surfaces are clean. Lubricate boot contact areas on inner tie rod end and housing with grease before installing boot. Install boot, aligning reference mark with mark on housing.
2) Install new boot seal clamps. Using Clamp Pliers (J-22610), tighten boot clamps. Ensure boot is not twisted. To complete installation, reverse removal procedure.

STEERING GEAR

CAUTION: Disconnect steering column intermediate shaft before removing steering gear.

Removal - **1)** Remove air cleaner. Remove dust boot from steering gear (if equipped). Remove bolt from intermediate shaft at steering gear pinion shaft. Separate intermediate shaft from steering gear pinion shaft.

NOTE: It may be necessary to remove intermediate shaft-to-steering column shaft bolt. Separate intermediate shaft from steering column shaft before disconnecting intermediate shaft from steering gear pinion shaft.

2) Disconnect pressure and return hydraulic line assemblies at steering gear. Raise and support vehicle. Remove front wheels and tires. Remove cotter pin and nut from tie rod end at steering knuckle. Separate tie rod end from steering knuckle.
3) Remove remaining brackets and clips on crossmember. Support body with jack stands to allow for lowering of the frame approximately 5" (127 mm) for steering gear removal. Support frame with jack. Remove rear frame-to-body bolts.
4) Disconnect stabilizer bar before rear of frame can be lowered (if necessary). Lower rear of frame approximately 5" (127 mm). DO NOT lower rear of frame too far or engine components will be damaged by contacting the cowl.
5) Remove steering gear mounting bolts. Remove steering gear through left wheel opening.
Installation - To install, reverse removal procedure. Install NEW frame-to-body bolts. Tighten all bolts to specification. See TORQUE SPECIFICATIONS table at end of article.

CAUTION: Install NEW frame-to-body bolts. DO NOT reuse old bolts.

OVERHAUL

INNER TIE ROD END

Disassembly - **1)** Remove steering gear and boot. See STEERING GEAR and BOOT under REMOVAL & INSTALLATION in this article. Remove shock damper ring from inner tie rod.
2) Place wrench on flat area of rack assembly and wrench on flat of inner tie rod housing. *See Fig. 2.* Rotate inner tie rod housing counterclockwise and separate inner tie rod from the rack.

1991 STEERING
Power Rack & Pinion (Cont.)

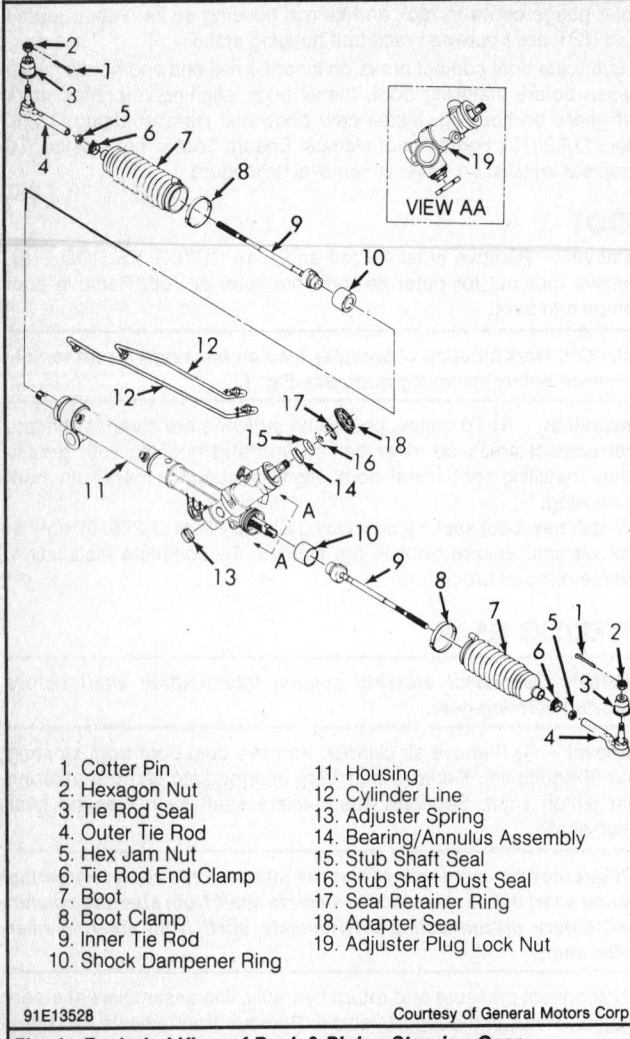

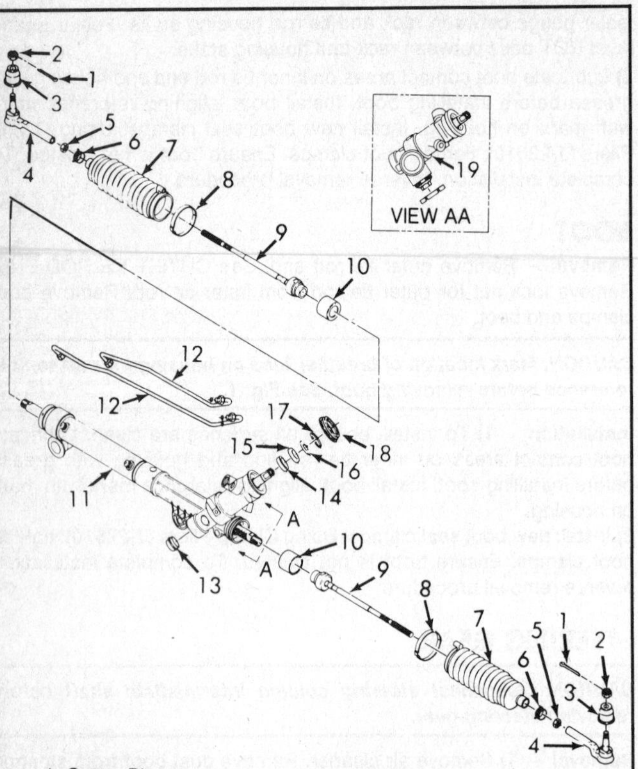
VIEW AA
1. Cotter Pin
2. Hexagon Nut
3. Tie Rod Seal
4. Outer Tie Rod
5. Hex Jam Nut
6. Tie Rod End Clamp
7. Boot
8. Boot Clamp
9. Inner Tie Rod
10. Shock Dampener Ring
11. Housing
12. Cylinder Line
13. Adjuster Spring
14. Bearing/Annulus Assembly
15. Stub Shaft Seal
16. Stub Shaft Dust Seal
17. Seal Retainer Ring
18. Adapter Seal
19. Adjuster Plug Lock Nut
91E13528
Courtesy of General Motors Corp.

Fig. 1: Exploded View of Rack & Pinion Steering Gear

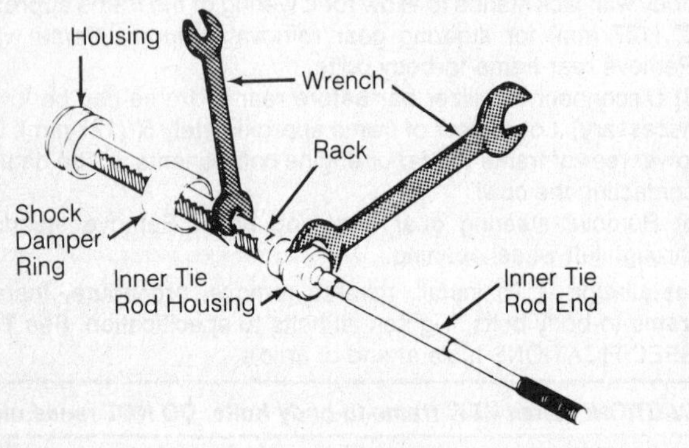
Housing
Wrench
Rack
Shock Damper Ring
Inner Tie Rod Housing
Inner Tie Rod End
90D13568
Courtesy of General Motors Corp.

Fig. 2: Separating Inner Tie Rod From Rack

Reassembly – 1) Install shock damper ring on rack. Install inner tie rod on rack. Tighten inner tie rod to specification. See TORQUE SPECIFICATIONS table at end of article. Ensure inner tie rod moves freely in housing.

2) Support inner tie rod housing. Stake BOTH sides of inner tie rod housing to flat areas on the rack. Ensure a .010" (.25 mm) feeler gauge will not slide between rack and staked area on inner tie rod housing.

3) Slide shock damper ring onto inner tie rod housing until it engages. To reassemble remaining components, reverse disassembly procedure.

PINION SEAL, DUST SEAL & BEARING/ANNULUS ASSEMBLY

Disassembly – 1) Remove steering gear. See STEERING GEAR under REMOVAL & INSTALLATION in this article. Remove adjuster plug lock nut, adjuster plug, spring and rack bearing. *See Fig. 1.*

2) Remove seal retainer ring from top of housing. Remove dust cover. Hold pinion shaft and remove nut from bottom of pinion shaft.

NOTE: DO NOT remove pinion from housing. Press pinion assembly far enough to only allow seals & bearing/annulus assembly removal. Removal of pinion assembly is not required.

3) Arbor press must be used to remove seals and bearing/annulus assembly. DO NOT hammer on pinion shaft, as drive pin in pinion shaft will be damaged. Using arbor press, press on threaded end of pinion.

4) Press pinion shaft, dust seal, shaft seal and bearings from housing. Remove seal rings from pinion shaft. *See Fig. 1.*

Reassembly – 1) Install nut on bottom of pinion shaft. Tighten nut to specification while holding pinion shaft. See TORQUE SPECIFICATIONS table at end of article. Install dust cover.

2) Install annulus bearing and needle bearing on pinion shaft. Install Seal Protector (J-29810) on pinion shaft. Apply small amount of grease between stub shaft seal and dust seal. Install stub shaft seal and dust seal over seal protector and slide into housing. Install seal retainer ring.

3) Coat rack bearing, spring and adjuster plug with lithium grease. Install rack bearing, spring and adjuster plug in housing.

4) Position rack in center of housing. Rotate adjuster plug clockwise until it bottoms in the housing. Back off adjuster plug 50-70 degrees (approximately one flat). *See Fig. 1.*

5) Using INCH lb. torque wrench, check torque required to rotate pinion. Maximum torque should be 16 INCH lbs. (1.8 N.m). Tighten adjuster plug lock nut to specification. DO NOT allow adjusting plug to rotate while tightening lock nut.

TORQUE SPECIFICATIONS

TORQUE SPECIFICATIONS

Application	Ft. Lbs. (N.m)
Adjuster Plug Lock Nut	50 (68)
Frame-To-Body Bolt	[1] 103 (140)
Inner Tie Rod	70 (95)
Intermediate Shaft Bolt	35 (47)
Lines-To-Steering Gear	18 (24)
Pinion Shaft Nut	26 (35)
Steering Gear Mounting Bolt	70 (95)
Tie Rod End Lock Nut	50 (68)
Tie Rod-To-Steering Knuckle Nut	[2] 30 (41)
Wheel Lug Nut	100 (136)

[1] – Use NEW bolt. DO NOT reuse bolts.
[2] – Maximum torque to align cotter key hole is 52 ft. lbs. (71 N.m).

1991 STEERING
Power Recirculating Ball

Astro, Blazer, Bravada, Jimmy, Safari, Sierra, Sonoma, "C" & "K" Series, "G" Series, "P" Series, "R" & "V" Series, "S" & "T" Series

DESCRIPTION

Steering gear is a variable ratio, recirculating ball type. The wormshaft is supported at the lower end by a thrust bearing with 2 races. It is supported at the upper end by a bearing assembly in the adjuster plug. Control valves, located inside steering gear housing, direct power steering fluid to either side of rack piston. A 4-character build date is stamped on the cover. *See Fig. 1.*

LUBRICATION & TESTING

See POWER STEERING – GENERAL SERVICING article.

TROUBLE SHOOTING

See TROUBLE SHOOTING article in GENERAL INFORMATION.

STEERING SERVICE PRECAUTIONS

Replacement fasteners must be of same part number as original. Tighten all fasteners to specification. Always use NEW cotter pins. When installing cotter pins, DO NOT back off castle nuts to align cotter pin hole. Tighten nut to next slot that lines up with hole.

DO NOT hammer on ball studs, or damage to threads may result. If threads are not clean and smooth, ball studs may turn in joint when nuts are tightened. Position tie rod sleeve clamps as specified before tightening bolts. *See Fig. 4.*

ADJUSTMENTS

THRUST BEARING PRELOAD

1) Remove steering gear from vehicle. See REMOVAL & INSTALLATION. Rotate gear lock-to-lock several times to drain fluid. Loosen adjuster plug lock nut. Using spanner wrench, turn adjuster plug clockwise until plug is seated in housing. Torque should be approximately 20 ft. lbs. (27 N.m).

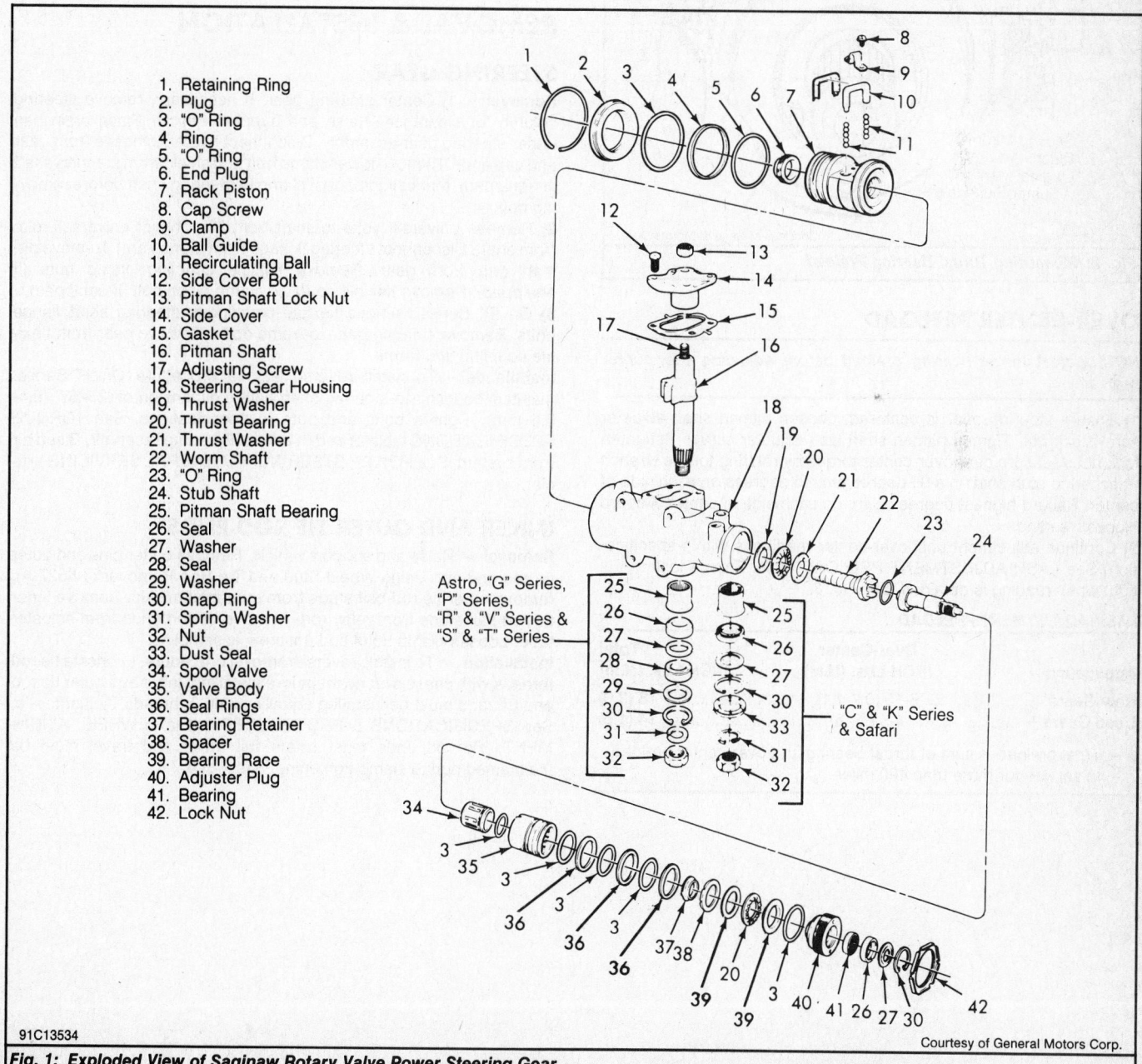

1. Retaining Ring
2. Plug
3. "O" Ring
4. Ring
5. "O" Ring
6. End Plug
7. Rack Piston
8. Cap Screw
9. Clamp
10. Ball Guide
11. Recirculating Ball
12. Side Cover Bolt
13. Pitman Shaft Lock Nut
14. Side Cover
15. Gasket
16. Pitman Shaft
17. Adjusting Screw
18. Steering Gear Housing
19. Thrust Washer
20. Thrust Bearing
21. Thrust Washer
22. Worm Shaft
23. "O" Ring
24. Stub Shaft
25. Pitman Shaft Bearing
26. Seal
27. Washer
28. Seal
29. Washer
30. Snap Ring
31. Spring Washer
32. Nut
33. Dust Seal
34. Spool Valve
35. Valve Body
36. Seal Rings
37. Bearing Retainer
38. Spacer
39. Bearing Race
40. Adjuster Plug
41. Bearing
42. Lock Nut

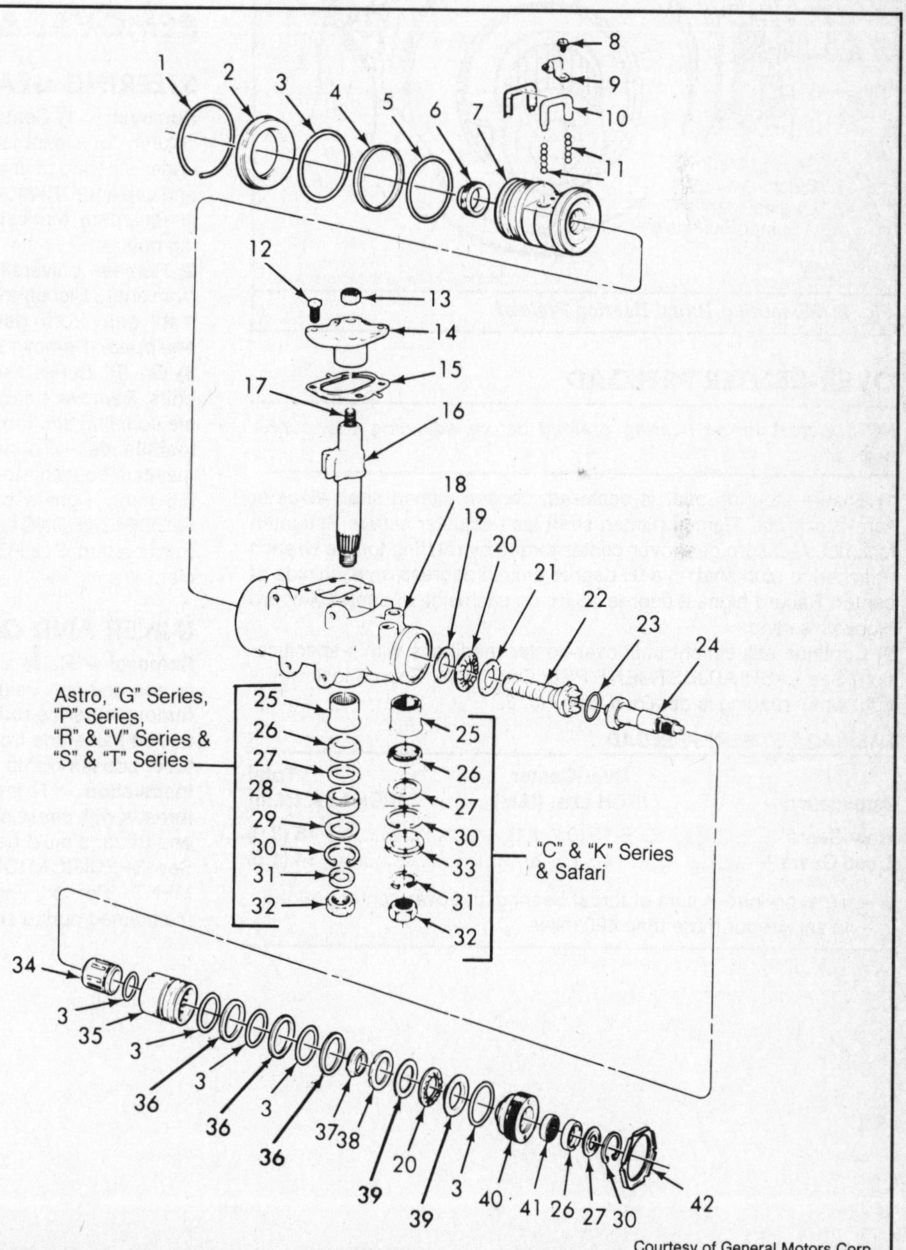
Astro, "G" Series,
"P" Series,
"R" & "V" Series &
"S" & "T" Series
"C" & "K" Series
& Safari

91C13534

Courtesy of General Motors Corp.

Fig. 1: Exploded View of Saginaw Rotary Valve Power Steering Gear

1991 STEERING
Power Recirculating Ball (Cont.)

2) Index mark housing opposite one hole in adjuster plug. *See Fig. 2.* Measure about 1/2" counterclockwise from mark. Mark housing. Rotate plug counterclockwise until hole in adjuster aligns with second mark.
3) Tighten lock nut. Ensure adjuster plug remains in position. Attach INCH lb. torque wrench to end of stub shaft. Turn stub shaft to right stop, then back 1/4 turn.
4) Using torque wrench, measure rotational torque required to turn shaft. Reading should be taken with handle of torque wrench near vertical while turning it counterclockwise at an even rate. Reading should be 4-10 INCH lbs. (.4-1.1 N.m). If not, repeat procedure.

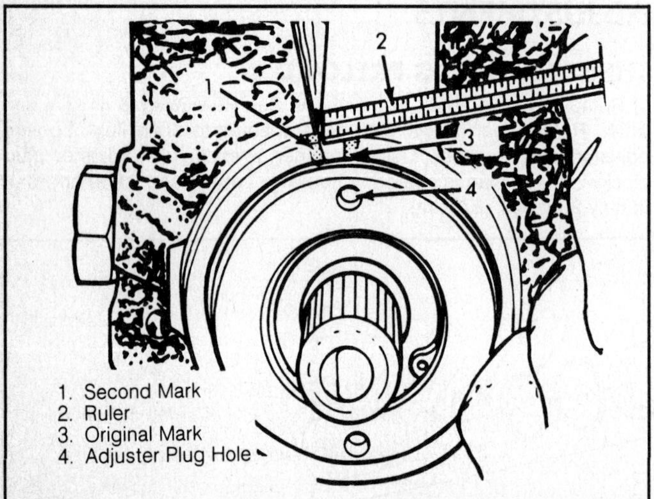
2
1
3
4
1. Second Mark
2. Ruler
3. Original Mark
4. Adjuster Plug Hole
117436
Courtesy of General Motors Corp.
Fig. 2: Measuring Thrust Bearing Preload

OVER-CENTER PRELOAD

NOTE: Adjust thrust bearing preload before adjusting over-center preload.

1) Ensure steering gear is centered. Loosen pitman shaft adjuster screw lock nut. Tighten pitman shaft lash adjuster screw. Retighten lock nut. Measure gear over-center torque by rotating torque wrench attached to stub shaft in a 90 degree arc, 45 degrees on each side of center. Record highest degree of arc on each side of center. Record highest reading.
2) Continue adjustment until over-center reading is within specification. See LASH ADJUSTMENT PRELOAD table. Ensure lock nut is tight when reading is obtained. *See Fig. 3.*

LASH ADJUSTMENT PRELOAD

Application	Over-Center INCH Lbs. (N.m)	[1] Total INCH Lbs. (N.m)
New Gears	6-10 (0.7-1.1)	18 (2.0)
Used Gears [2]	4-5 (.5-.6)	14 (1.6)

[1] – Total preload is sum of thrust bearing and over-center preload.
[2] – In service for more than 400 miles.

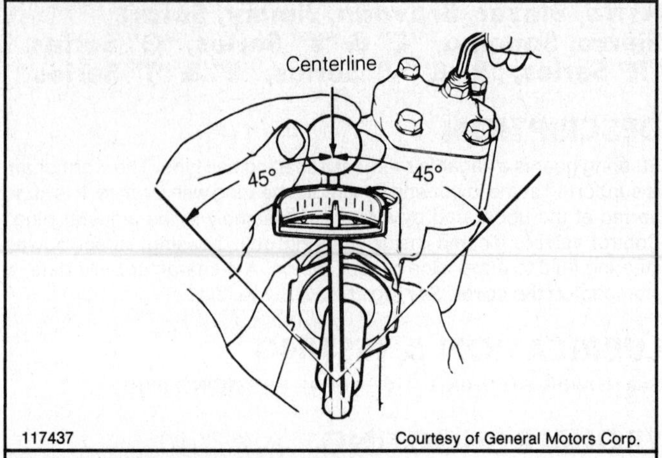
Centerline
45°
45°
117437
Courtesy of General Motors Corp.
Fig. 3: Adjusting Over-Center Preload

REMOVAL & INSTALLATION

STEERING GEAR

Removal – 1) Center steering gear. If necessary, remove steering column for clearance. Raise and support vehicle. Place drain pan under steering gear assembly. Disconnect hydraulic hoses from gear and cap ends. Remove lower clamp bolt and shield from steering shaft (if equipped). Mark alignment of clamp to steering shaft before removing bolt.
2) Remove universal yoke-to-shaft bolt. Disconnect universal yoke from shaft. Disconnect steering linkage from pitman arm. Remove pitman arm from gear. Remove flexible coupling clamp nuts (if equipped). Remove flexible coupling clamp pinch bolt (if equipped).
3) On "P" Series, remove flexible coupling-to-steering shaft flange bolts. Remove steering gear-to-frame bolts. Remove gear from flexible coupling and frame.
Installation – To install, reverse removal procedure. On "P" Series, maintain coupling-to-steering shaft flange dimension of .25-.37" (6.4-9.5 mm). Tighten bolts and nuts to specifications. See TORQUE SPECIFICATIONS table at end of article. Fill pump reservoir. Bleed air from system. See POWER STEERING – GENERAL SERVICING article.

INNER AND OUTER TIE ROD ENDS

Removal – Raise and support vehicle. Remove cotter pins and outer tie rod end nut. Using Wheel Stud and Tie Rod Remover (J-6627-A), remove outer tie rod ball studs from steering knuckle. Remove inner tie rod ball studs from relay rod. Remove tie rod ends from adjuster tube. Loosen clamp bolts and unscrew assemblies.
Installation – To install, reverse removal procedure. Lubricate tie rod threads with chassis lubricant before installing. Inner and outer tie rod end threads must be installed equally within 3 threads. Adjust toe-in. See SPECIFICATIONS & PROCEDURES article in WHEEL ALIGNMENT. Tie rod ends must rotate full travel and travel must be maintained during clamp tightening. *See Fig. 4.*

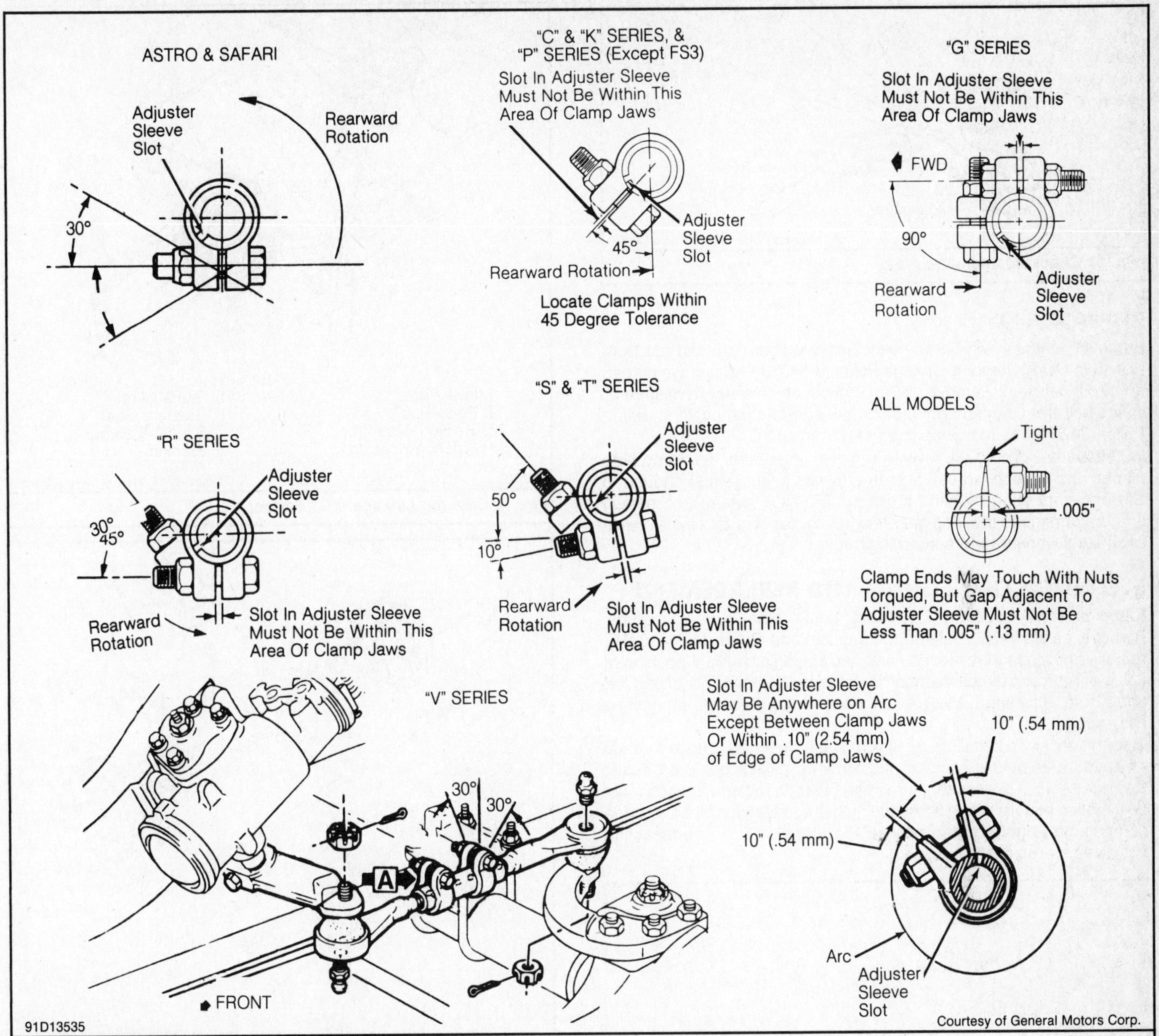
ASTRO & SAFARI
Adjuster Sleeve Slot
Rearward Rotation
30°
"C" & "K" SERIES, & "P" SERIES (Except FS3)
Slot In Adjuster Sleeve Must Not Be Within This Area Of Clamp Jaws
Adjuster Sleeve Slot
45°
Rearward Rotation
Locate Clamps Within 45 Degree Tolerance
"G" SERIES
Slot In Adjuster Sleeve Must Not Be Within This Area Of Clamp Jaws
FWD
90°
Rearward Rotation
Adjuster Sleeve Slot
"R" SERIES
Adjuster Sleeve Slot
30°
45°
Rearward Rotation
Slot In Adjuster Sleeve Must Not Be Within This Area Of Clamp Jaws
"S" & "T" SERIES
Adjuster Sleeve Slot
50°
10°
Rearward Rotation
Slot In Adjuster Sleeve Must Not Be Within This Area Of Clamp Jaws
ALL MODELS
Tight
.005"
Clamp Ends May Touch With Nuts Torqued, But Gap Adjacent To Adjuster Sleeve Must Not Be Less Than .005" (.13 mm)
"V" SERIES
30°
30°
A
FRONT
Slot In Adjuster Sleeve May Be Anywhere on Arc Except Between Clamp Jaws Or Within .10" (2.54 mm) of Edge of Clamp Jaws
10" (.54 mm)
10" (.54 mm)
Arc
Adjuster Sleeve Slot
91D13535
Courtesy of General Motors Corp.

Fig. 4: Positioning Tie Rod & Connecting Rod Clamp

RELAY ROD

Removal – Raise and support vehicle. Remove inner tie rod end nuts. Remove inner tie rod ends from relay rod. On "C" & "K" Series and "T" Series, remove steering damper nut from relay rod . Using Steering Linkage Puller (J-24319-01), remove steering damper from relay rod. Remove relay rod end nuts from pitman arm and idler arm. Using Steering Linkage Puller (J-24319-01), remove pitman arm and idler arm from relay rod. Remove relay rod.

Installation – To install, reverse removal procedure. Using Steering Linkage Installer (J-29193 or J-29194), seat all tapers to 40 ft. lbs. (54 N.m). Tighten nuts to specifications. See TORQUE SPECIFICATIONS table at end of article. Adjust toe-in. See SPECIFICATIONS & PROCEDURES article in WHEEL ALIGNMENT.

IDLER ARM

NOTE: Replace idler arm assembly if an up and down force (forward and rearward on "G" Series) of 25 lbs. (11 kg), applied at relay rod end of idler arm, produces a lash of more than 1/8" (3 mm) in straight-ahead position.

Removal – Raise and support vehicle. Remove idler arm nut and bolt from tie rod end. Remove idler arm nut and spring washer from relay rod. Using Steering Linkage Puller (J-24319-01), remove idler arm from relay rod. Remove idler arm. *See Fig. 5.*

Installation – To install, reverse removal procedure. Using Steering Linkage Installer (J-29193 or J-29194), seat all tapers to 40 ft. lbs. (54 N.m). Tighten nuts to specifications. See TORQUE SPECIFICATIONS table at end of article. Adjust toe-in. See SPECIFICATIONS & PROCEDURES article in WHEEL ALIGNMENT.

1991 STEERING
Power Recirculating Ball (Cont.)

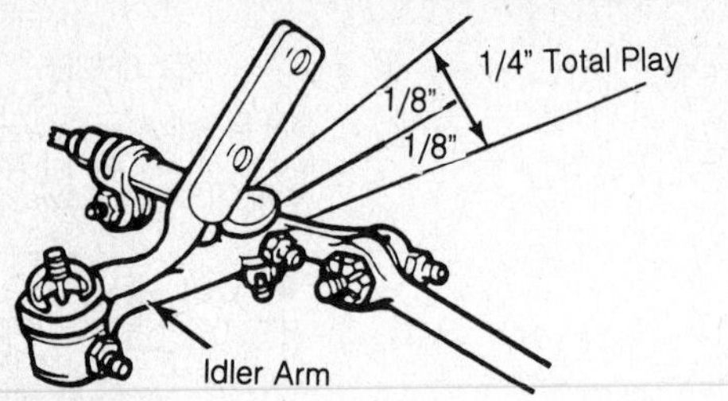
1/4" Total Play
1/8"
1/8"
Idler Arm

30283 Courtesy of General Motors Corp.

Fig. 5: Checking Idler Arm Play

PITMAN ARM

Removal - Place vehicle on hoist. Remove cotter pin and nut from ball stud. Using Steering Linkage Puller (J-24319-01), remove pitman arm from ball stud. Remove pitman arm nut and washer from shaft or clamp bolt from pitman arm. Index mark arm-to-shaft position. Using Puller (J-6632-01), remove pitman arm from shaft.

Installation - To install, reverse removal procedure. If a clamp-type pitman arm is used, spread pitman arm with a wedge just enough to slip arm onto shaft by hand pressure. DO NOT hammer on pitman arm, or damage to steering gear may result. Be sure to reinstall hardened steel washer before installing nut.

STEERING CONNECTING ROD REPLACEMENT

Removal (4WD Models) - Remove cotter pins from ball studs. Remove castle nuts. Using Steering Linkage Puller (J-24319-01), remove ball studs from steering arm and pitman arm. Mark position of adjuster tube and direction of bolt installation. Remove connecting rod ends from adjusting tube. Loosen clamp bolts. Remove connecting rod ends.

Installation - To install, reverse removal procedure. Ensure threads on studs and nuts are clean and smooth. Check ball stud seals. Replace seals (if necessary). Inner and outer tie rod end threads must be installed equally within 3 threads. Install connecting rod on steering components. Tighten nuts. Install NEW cotter pins. Ensure connecting rod clamps are properly aligned.

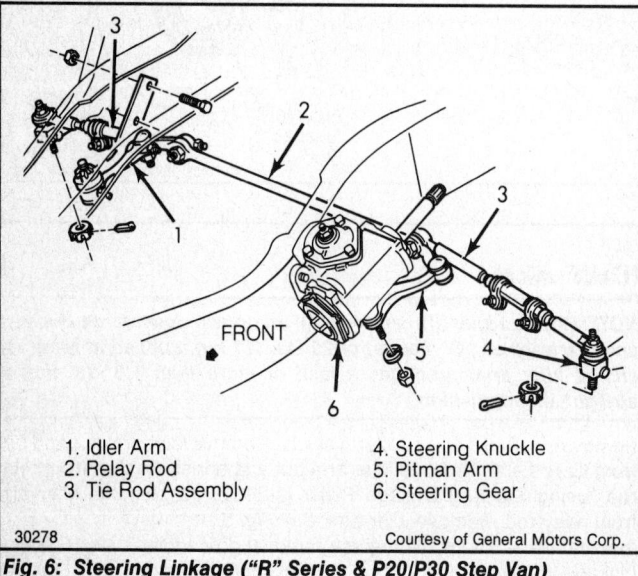

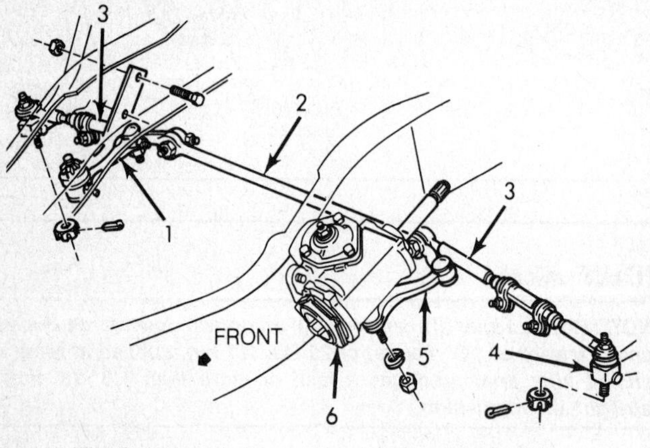
FRONT

1. Idler Arm
2. Relay Rod
3. Tie Rod Assembly
4. Steering Knuckle
5. Pitman Arm
6. Steering Gear

30278 Courtesy of General Motors Corp.

Fig. 6: Steering Linkage ("R" Series & P20/P30 Step Van)

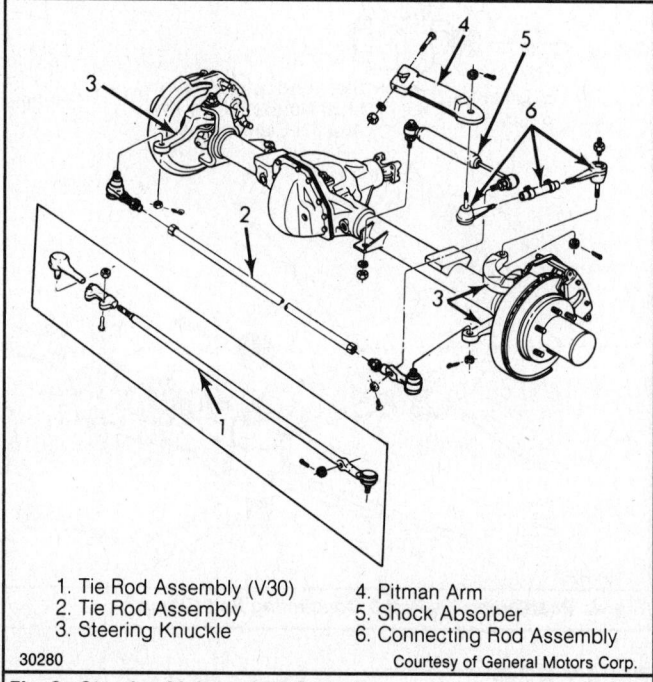

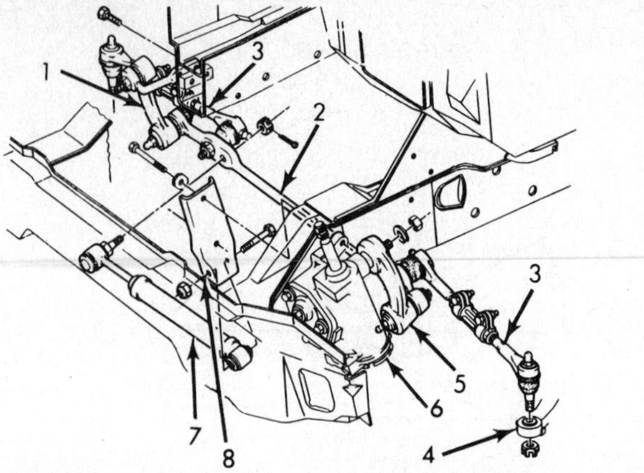

1. Idler Arm
2. Relay Rod
3. Tie Rod Assembly
4. Steering Knuckle
5. Pitman Arm
6. Steering Gear
7. Shock Absorber
8. Bracket

30279 Courtesy of General Motors Corp.

Fig. 7: Steering Linkage ("G" Series)

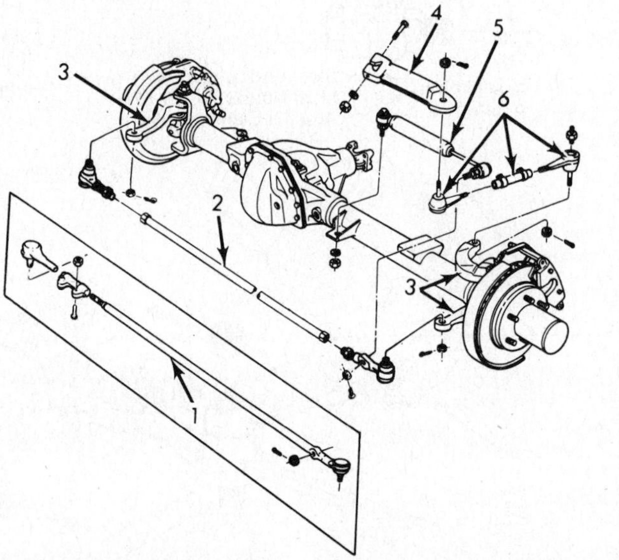

1. Tie Rod Assembly (V30)
2. Tie Rod Assembly
3. Steering Knuckle
4. Pitman Arm
5. Shock Absorber
6. Connecting Rod Assembly

30280 Courtesy of General Motors Corp.

Fig. 8: Steering Linkage ("V" Series)

1991 STEERING
Power Recirculating Ball (Cont.)

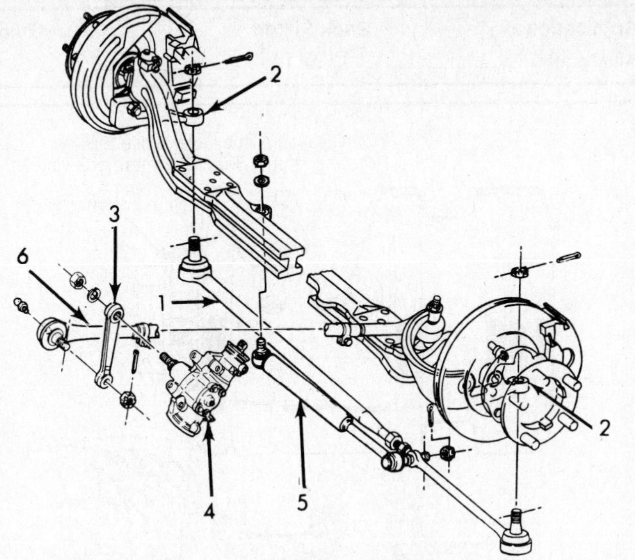

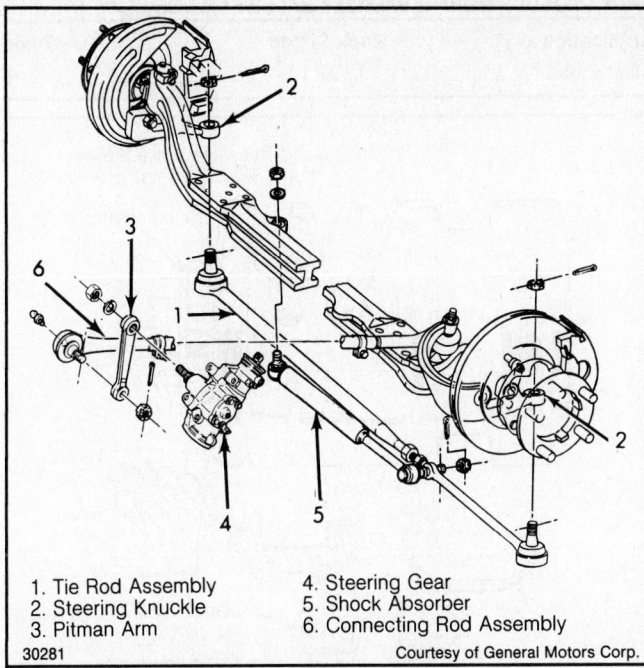

1. Tie Rod Assembly
2. Steering Knuckle
3. Pitman Arm
4. Steering Gear
5. Shock Absorber
6. Connecting Rod Assembly

30281 Courtesy of General Motors Corp.

Fig. 9: Steering Linkage with I-Beam Axle (P30)

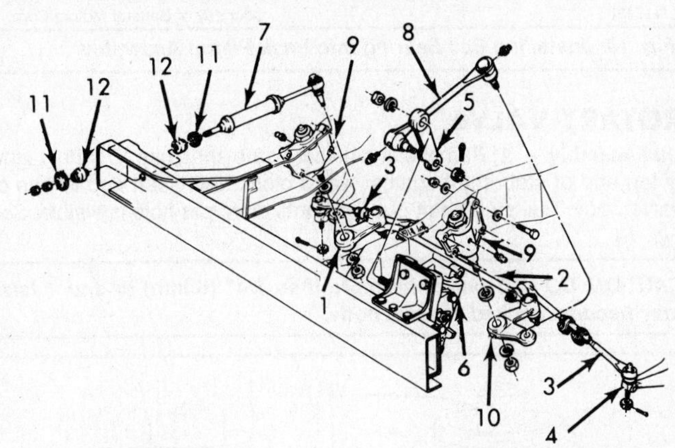

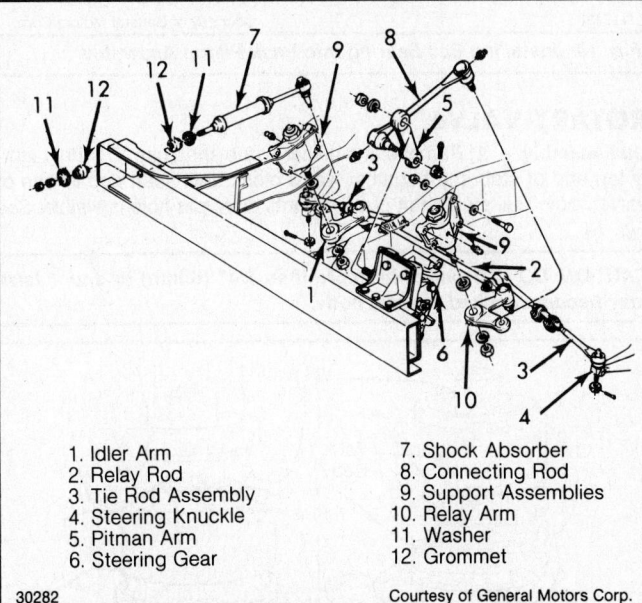

1. Idler Arm
2. Relay Rod
3. Tie Rod Assembly
4. Steering Knuckle
5. Pitman Arm
6. Steering Gear
7. Shock Absorber
8. Connecting Rod
9. Support Assemblies
10. Relay Arm
11. Washer
12. Grommet

30282 Courtesy of General Motors Corp.

Fig. 10: Steering Linkage (P30 Motorhome)

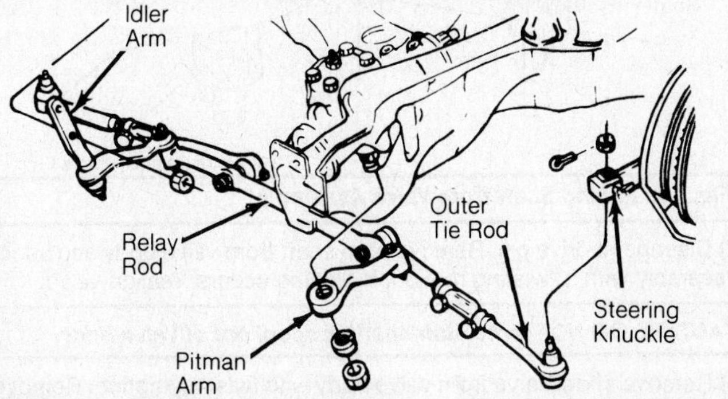
Idler Arm
Relay Rod
Outer Tie Rod
Steering Knuckle
Pitman Arm

30508 Courtesy of General Motors Corp.

Fig. 11: Steering Linkage ("S" Series)

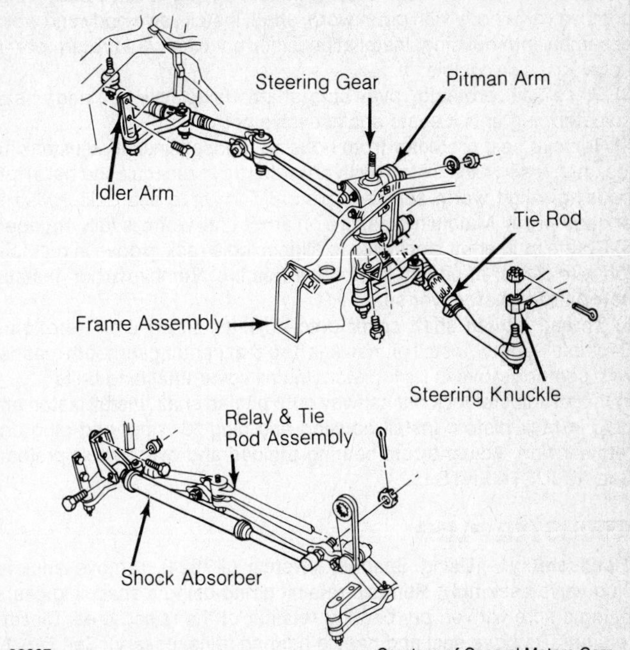
Steering Gear
Pitman Arm
Idler Arm
Tie Rod
Frame Assembly
Steering Knuckle
Relay & Tie Rod Assembly
Shock Absorber

30287 Courtesy of General Motors Corp.

Fig. 12: Steering Linkage (Astro & Safari)

OVERHAUL

STEERING GEAR

Disassembly – 1) Cap all openings in gear. Clean gear exterior completely. Mount gear in vise so that pitman shaft points downward. Rotate housing end plug retainer ring until one end of plug is over hole in housing.

2) Force end of ring from groove in housing. Remove ring. Rotate stub shaft counterclockwise to force housing end plug from housing. Rotate stub shaft 1/2 turn clockwise to draw rack piston inward.

CAUTION: DO NOT rotate stub shaft more than necessary to remove plug, as ball bearings will fall out of worm and rack piston assembly.

3) Remove rack piston end plug. Remove lock nut from pitman shaft adjuster. Remove pitman shaft cover. Remove and discard "O" ring or gasket from cover. Turn stub shaft until pitman shaft teeth are centered in housing.

4) Using a soft-faced hammer, tap end of pitman shaft to free shaft from housing. Remove pitman shaft. Remove adjuster plug lock nut. Using a spanner wrench, remove adjuster plug.

5) Insert Rack Piston Arbor (J-21552) into end of rack piston assembly until arbor just contacts worm shaft. Threaded arbor will keep recirculating balls from falling out of rack piston. Turn stub shaft counterclockwise to force rack piston onto arbor. Remove rack piston and arbor as an assembly.

6) Ensure arbor is fully inserted so recirculating balls will not fall out. Remove stub shaft and control valve assembly from housing. Remove worm, wormshaft lower thrust bearing, and races from housing.

Inspection – 1) Clean all internal parts in solvent and dry with compressed air. Avoid wiping valve parts with cloth. Lint may cause binding of mechanism.

2) DO NOT steam clean hydraulic parts. If further disassembly is required, see appropriate sub-heading under OVERHAUL in this article.

Reassembly – 1) Lubricate all parts with power steering fluid before reassembly. Install lower thrust bearing and races on worm shaft. *See Fig. 1.*

NOTE: If conical thrust races are used, ensure tapered surfaces are parallel to each other and that cupped sides face toward stub shaft.

1991 STEERING
Power Recirculating Ball (Cont.)

2) Place worm shaft in valve body. Install "O" ring in valve body. Align notch in valve body with pin in worm shaft. Install valve body and worm assembly into housing. Installation is correct when fluid return port in housing is fully visible.
3) Place seal protector over stub shaft. Using new "O" ring, install adjuster plug until it seats against valve body.
4) Remove seal protector from housing. Loosely install adjuster plug lock nut. Insert rack piston (with arbor to retain recirculating balls) into housing. Align worm and rack piston. Turn stub shaft clockwise to engage worm. Maintain pressure on arbor until worm is fully engaged.
5) Rotate stub shaft clockwise to align middle rack groove in rack piston with center of pitman shaft roller bearing. Remove arbor. Install a new pitman shaft cover seal.
6) Thread pitman shaft cover onto adjuster screw until it bottoms. Back off 1/2 turn. Install pitman shaft so that center gear tooth meshes with center groove in rack piston. Install cover attaching bolts.
7) Install adjuster lock nut halfway onto pitman shaft. Install piston and plug in rack piston. Install housing end plug "O" ring, end plug and retainer ring. Adjust thrust bearing preload and over-center preload. See ADJUSTMENTS.

ADJUSTER PLUG

Disassembly – Using Spanner Wrench (J-7624), remove adjuster plug valve assembly. Remove retaining ring using a snap ring pliers. Using a screwdriver, pry bearing retainer at the raised area. Discard retainer. Remove seal and needle bearing (if necessary). *See Fig. 1.*
Inspection – Inspect bearing for cracks. Check for pitting, scoring, or cracking. Check thrust races and spacer for damage. Replace parts as necessary.
Reassembly – **1)** Using adjuster plug Bearing Installer (J-8524-1) and Driver (J-7079-2), seat needle bearing in adjuster plug assembly. Lubricate oil seal with power steering fluid. Install oil seal, washer and retaining ring into adjuster plug.
2) Ensure retainer projections must not extend beyond washer, when retainer ring is seated. Washer must be free to rotate.

RACK PISTON & WORM

Disassembly – If installed, remove Rack Piston Arbor (J-21552) from rack piston. If arbor is not used, remove worm shaft, lower thrust bearing and bearing races from rack piston. Remove piston ring and back-up "O" ring from rack piston. Remove ball guide clamp and ball guides. Remove all recirculating balls from rack piston.
Inspection – **1)** Clean and dry all parts. Inspect worm shaft and rack piston grooves for scoring. Inspect ball bearings for damage. If any ball bearings are damaged, replace entire set. Check ball guides for pinching of ends.
2) Inspect lower thrust bearing races for cracking, scoring, or pitting. If either part is damaged, replace wormshaft and rack piston as an assembly. Inspect rack piston teeth for chips, cracks, dents or scoring.
Reassembly – **1)** Lubricate Teflon seal and "O" ring with power steering fluid and carefully install onto rack piston. Install worm shaft into rack piston until worm shaft touches piston shoulder. While turning worm shaft counterclockwise, insert ball bearings into rack piston.

NOTE: See RACK PISTON & WORM ASSEMBLY BALL BEARINGS table for number of balls to be installed. ENSURE light and dark colored balls are installed alternately, as Black balls are .0005" (.013 mm) smaller than Silver balls.

2) Install correct number of balls in ball guide, alternating ball colors. Bearings in guide must be in sequence with bearings in rack piston. Hold balls in place with chassis lubricant. Install return ball guide assembly into position.
3) Install clamp. Tighten cap screws. *See Fig. 13.* Insert Rack Piston Arbor (J-21552) into rack piston until it contacts worm shaft. Maintain pressure on arbor, and back worm out of rack piston. DO NOT allow ball bearings to drop out.

RACK PISTON & WORM ASSEMBLY BALL BEARINGS

Application	Rack Piston	Guide
All Models	17 or 19	5

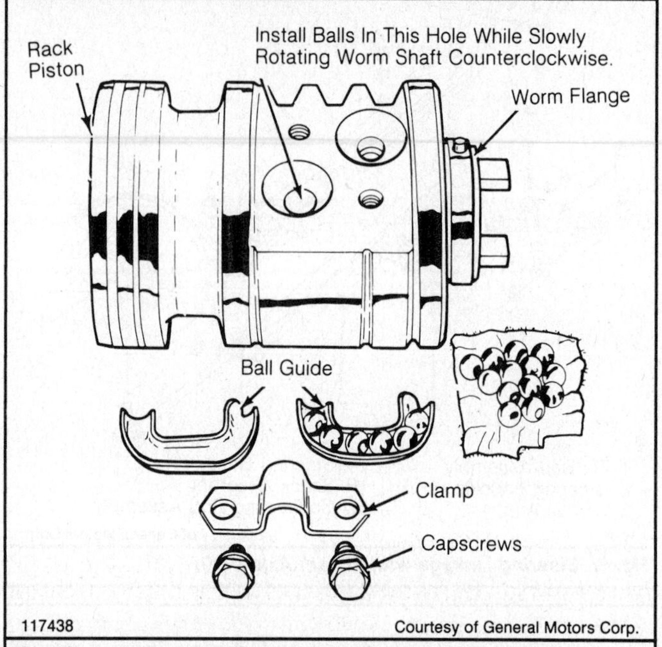
Rack Piston
Install Balls In This Hole While Slowly Rotating Worm Shaft Counterclockwise.
Worm Flange
Ball Guide
Clamp
Capscrews
117438
Courtesy of General Motors Corp.

Fig. 13: Installing Ball Bearing into Rack Piston Assembly

ROTARY VALVE

Disassembly – **1)** Remove and discard stub shaft cap "O" ring. Lightly tap end of stub shaft against wood block until shaft cap is free of valve body. Pull stub shaft outward until drive pin hole is visible. *See Fig. 14.*

CAUTION: DO NOT pull shaft more than 1/4" (6 mm) or spool valve may become cocked in valve body.

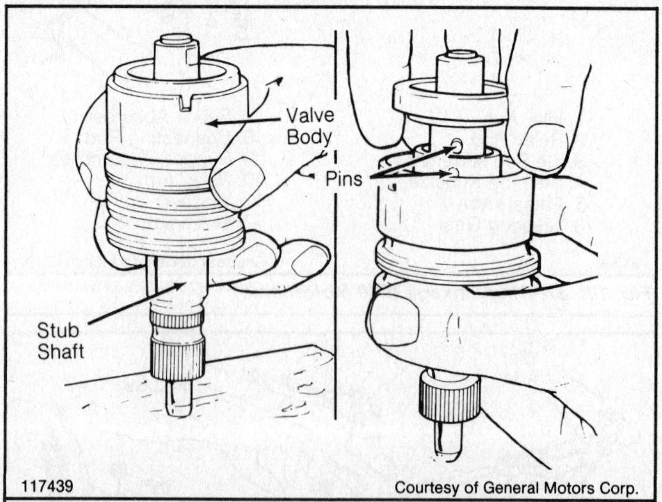
Valve Body
Pins
Stub Shaft
117439
Courtesy of General Motors Corp.

Fig. 14: Pulling Shaft from Valve Assembly

2) Disengage drive pin. Remove stub shaft from valve body and spool assembly with a twisting motion. If binding occurs, realign valve.

CAUTION: DO NOT force stub shaft or spool out of valve body.

3) Remove spool valve from valve body with twisting motion. Remove and discard all "O" rings and Teflon rings.
Inspection – **1)** Wash all parts in solvent and blow dry. Check for leaks between stub shaft and torsion bar. Check for nicks and scores

on stub shaft. Sand down with Crocus cloth if possible. Check notch valve body skirt for wear.

2) Check spool valve fit in valve body. With "O" ring removed, lubricate spool valve with power steering fluid. Rotate spool valve in valve body. If valve does not rotate freely, replace complete valve.

3) Valve assembly is balanced during assembly. If replacing any parts other than rings or seals, replace complete assembly.

Reassembly – 1) Lubricate valve body components with power steering fluid. Install new "O" rings in seal grooves. Install new Teflon rings over "O" rings. Take care not to damage seal rings during installation.

NOTE: Teflon seal rings may appear to be distorted after installation. However, heat of operation will straighten them.

2) Lubricate replacement spool valve damper "O" ring with petroleum jelly and install on spool valve. Carefully insert spool valve into valve body.

3) Push spool valve through valve body until locating pin hole is visible at opposite end of valve body, and spool valve is flush with notched end of valve. Install stub shaft into spool valve and valve body.

4) Align stub shaft locating pin with spool valve locating hole. Align notch in stub shaft cap with pin in valve body. Press stub shaft and spool valve into valve body. Install stub shaft cap "O" ring into valve body.

CAUTION: Before installing assembled valve body into gear housing, ensure valve body stub shaft locating pin is fully engaged in stub shaft cap notch. DO NOT allow stub shaft to disengage from valve body pin.

HOUSING ASSEMBLY

Disassembly – 1) Remove pitman shaft seal snap ring. Remove seals and washers. *See Fig. 1.* Press pitman shaft bearing out of housing from lower end.

2) If hose connector seat is being replaced, tap seat with a 5/16" x 18 thread tap. Thread connector seats ONLY 2-3 threads. Install bolt with flat washer and nut into seat. Hold bolt while tightening nut to extract seat.

Inspection – 1) If housing bore is severely worn, scored or pitted, replace housing. Minor scratches may be removed with crocus cloth.

2) Inspect all retaining ring, bearing and seal surfaces in housing. If any surface is worn or damaged, replace housing.

Reassembly – 1) Install pitman shaft bearing in steering housing using Handle (J-8092) and Adapter (J-22407). Position bearing so identification marks face away from tool. Press bearing in until tool bottoms against housing. DO NOT bottom bearing in housing.

2) Install seals with lips facing toward housing bore. Install snap ring.

TORQUE SPECIFICATIONS

TORQUE SPECIFICATIONS

Application	Ft. Lbs. (N.m)
Adjuster Plug Lock Nut	81 (110)
Connecting Rod-To-Pitman Arm Nut	
Astro & Safari	35 (47)
"P" Series (Motorhome & Forward Control Chassis)	70 (95)
"V" Series	89 (121)
Connecting Rod-To-Relay Arm Nut	
"P" Series (Motorhome)	70 (95)
Coupling Clamp Nuts	20 (27)
Coupling Clamp Pinch Bolt	
"G" Series	46 (62)
"P" Series	75 (102)
Coupling-To-Steering Shaft Flange Bolt	20 (27)
Idler Arm Mounting Bolt	
Astro & Safari	81 (106)
"C" Series	78 (105)
"G" Series	35 (47)
"R" Series & "P" Series	30 (41)
"S" Series	60 (81)
Idler Arm-To-Relay Rod Nut [1]	
Astro & Safari	35 (47)
"C" Series	40 (54)
"G" Series & "R" Series	66 (89)
"S" Series	35 (47)
"T" Series	60 (81)
Pitman Arm Attaching Nut	180 (244)
Pitman Arm-To-Relay Rod Nut [1]	
"C" Series	40 (54)
"G" Series & "R" Series	66 (89)
Pitman Arm-To-Steering Gear Nut	
Astro, Safari, "C", "G", "K", "P" Series Step Van & "R" Series	184 (249)
"P" Series (Motorhome & Forward Control Chassis)	125 (170)
"V" Series	92 (125)
Pitman Shaft Adjuster Lock Nut	
Astro & Safari	37 (50)
"C" & "K" Series	32 (43)
"S" & "T" Series	20 (27)
"G" Series, "P" Series & "R" & "V" Series	35 (47)
Rack Piston End Plug	50 (68)
Relay Rod-To-Relay Arm Nut	
"P" Series (Motorhome)	66 (89)
Side Cover Bolts	40 (54)
Steering Gear Lower Clamp Bolt	
"C" & "K" Series	22 (30)
"S" & "T" Series	26 (35)
Steering Gear-To-Frame Bolts	
Astro & Safari & "S" & "T" Series	55 (75)
"C" & "K" Series	100 (136)
"G" Series, "P" Series & "R" & "V" Series	66 (89)
Tie Rod Clamp Nut	
"V" Series	40 (54)
Except "V" Series	14 (19)
Tie Rod Jam Nut	
"P" Series (Forward Control Chassis)	277 (375)
"V" Series	175 (237)
Tie Rod-To-Relay Rod Nut	
Astro, Safari & "S" Series	35 (47)
"C" Series & "V" Series	40 (54)
"G" Series & "R" Series	66 (89)
Tie Rod-To-Steering Knuckle Nut	
Astro & Safari	35 (47)
"C" Series & "V" Series	40 (54)
"G" Series & "R" Series	46 (62)
"S" Series	35 (47)
Universal Yoke-To-Shaft Bolt	29 (40)

[1] – Seat the taper using a free-spinning nut, then install lock nut.

1991 STEERING
Power Steering Pumps

Astro, Blazer, Bravada, Jimmy, Lumina APV, Safari, Sierra, Silhouette, Sonoma, Trans Sport, "C" & "K" Series, "G" Series, "P" Series, "R" & "V" Series, "S" & "T" Series

DESCRIPTION

Two different types of Saginaw vane-type power steering pumps are used. The Model P pump is mounted inside the reservoir. *See Fig. 1*. The Model TC pump is mounted below the reservoir. *See Fig. 2*. On both models, the vanes are driven by a rotor, and move fluid from the intake to the pressure cavities of pump ring.

Centrifugal force moves vanes against inside surface of pump ring to pick up residual oil. As more oil is picked up, it is forced into cavities of thrust plate, into 2 crossover holes in pump ring and pressure plate, and into a high pressure area between pressure plate and housing end plate.

Filling the high pressure area causes oil to flow under the vanes, in slots of the rotor. This forces vanes to follow inside oval surface of pump ring. As vanes rotate to small area of pump ring, oil is forced out from between vanes.

LUBRICATION & TESTING

See POWER STEERING - GENERAL SERVICING article.

TROUBLE SHOOTING

See TROUBLE SHOOTING article in GENERAL INFORMATION.

REMOVAL & INSTALLATION

POWER STEERING PUMP

Removal & Installation - 1) Loosen pump adjusting bolt (or nut) and pump mounting bolts. Remove pump drive belt. Disconnect pressure and return hoses from pump. Cap ends to prevent loss of fluid or contamination.

2) Using Puller (J-29785-A), remove pulley from shaft. Remove bracket-to-engine bolts. Remove pump and mounting bracket as an assembly. To install, reverse removal procedure. Use Pulley Installer (J-25033-B) to install pulley. Fill and bleed system. See POWER STEERING - GENERAL SERVICING article.

OVERHAUL

Disassembly (Model P) - 1) Drain pump reservoir. Clean exterior of unit. Using Puller (J-29785-A), remove pulley from shaft if not previously removed.

2) Remove pressure line union and "O" ring. Remove reservoir retaining bolts. Remove reservoir and "O" rings from housing.

3) Using punch and screwdriver, remove end plate retaining ring. Remove end plate and pressure plate spring. *See Fig. 1.*

4) Remove "O" ring, flow control valve, and spring. Using soft-faced hammer, tap end of drive shaft to loosen pressure plate. Remove pressure plate, pump ring, vanes, retaining ring, rotor, and thrust plate assembly from body.

5) Remove drive shaft. Using a screwdriver, pry drive shaft oil seal from housing. Remove dowel pins and seals.

Cleaning & Inspection - 1) Clean all pump components in solvent and blow dry. Inspect flow control valve assembly for wear, scoring, burrs or other damage. Inspect seal bore for burrs, nicks or score marks.

2) Inspect machined surfaces of body for scratches or burrs. Check "O" ring mating surfaces. Inspect drive shaft for excessive wear.

3) Inspect pump ring for roughness. Check thrust plate and pressure plate for scoring and wear. Ensure vanes slide freely but fit snugly into slots. If vanes are loose in slots, replace rotor and/or vanes.

Reassembly - 1) Lubricate all "O" rings, seals, pump ring, rotor and vanes with power steering fluid. Using Seal Installer (J-7728), install new shaft seal.

2) Install dowel pins and all "O" rings. Install drive shaft and thrust plate. Install rotor over shaft splines, with counterbore toward drive shaft end of housing.

3) Install new rotor retaining ring. Ensure ring is seated in groove. Install vanes with rounded edges toward pump ring. Install pump ring and pressure plate. Install "O" ring, flow control valve, and spring.

4) Install pressure plate spring, end plate, and retaining ring. Install seals and reservoir. Install union, "O" ring, and reservoir retaining bolts.

Disassembly (Model TC) - 1) Clamp front hub in soft-jawed vise. Pry tab outward and remove reservoir clips (if equipped). *See Fig. 2.* Remove reservoir or return tube and "O" ring. Using Pulley Remover (J-25034-B), remove pulley from shaft if not previously removed.

2) Remove fitting, "O" ring, flow control valve and spring. Note location of beveled side of snap ring. Remove snap ring, drive shaft, and bearing. *See Fig. 2.* Using screwdriver, remove drive shaft seal from housing. Remove thrust plate retaining ring by inserting punch into access hole and disengaging retaining ring.

3) Using a brass drift, tap on thrust plate and remove. Remove "O" ring, pump ring, rotor and vanes. Remove dowel pins, pressure plate, "O" ring, and pressure plate spring. Remove "O" ring, dowel pin, and sleeve.

Cleaning & Inspection - 1) Clean all pump components in solvent and blow dry. Inspect flow control valve assembly for wear, scoring, burrs or other damage. Inspect seal bore for burrs, nicks or score marks.

2) Inspect machined surfaces of body for scratches or burrs. Check "O" ring mating surfaces. Inspect drive shaft for wear.

3) Inspect pump ring for roughness. Check thrust plate and pressure plate for scoring and wear. Ensure vanes slide freely but fit snugly into slots. If vanes are loose in slots, replace rotor and/or vanes.

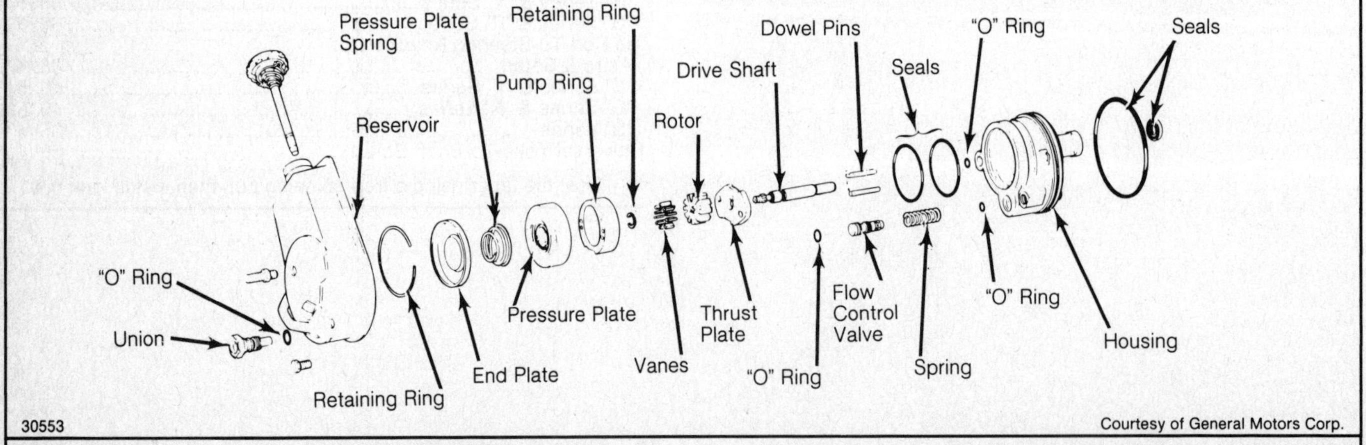
Pressure Plate Spring
Retaining Ring
Dowel Pins
"O" Ring
Seals
Pump Ring
Drive Shaft
Seals
Reservoir
Rotor
"O" Ring
Union
Pressure Plate
Thrust Plate
Flow Control Valve
"O" Ring
Housing
End Plate
Vanes
"O" Ring
Spring
Retaining Ring
30553
Courtesy of General Motors Corp.

Fig. 1: Exploded View of Pump Assembly (Model P)

1991 STEERING
Power Steering Pumps (Cont.)

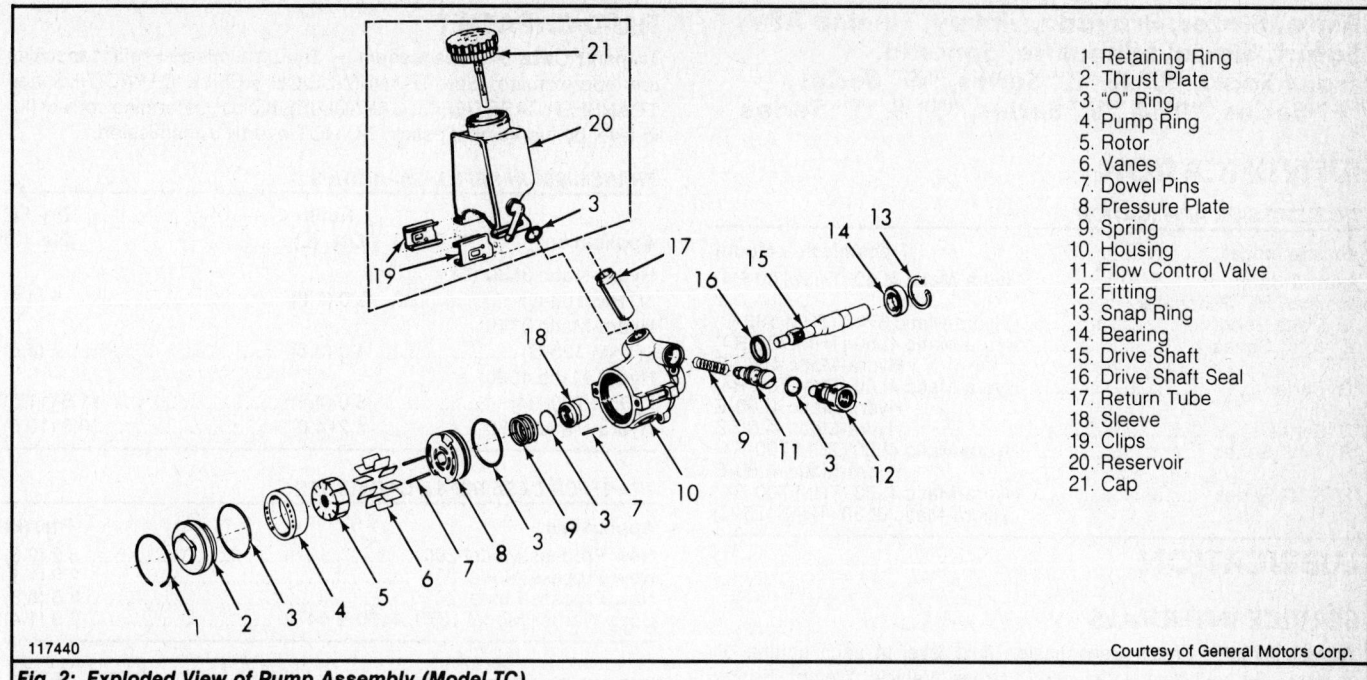

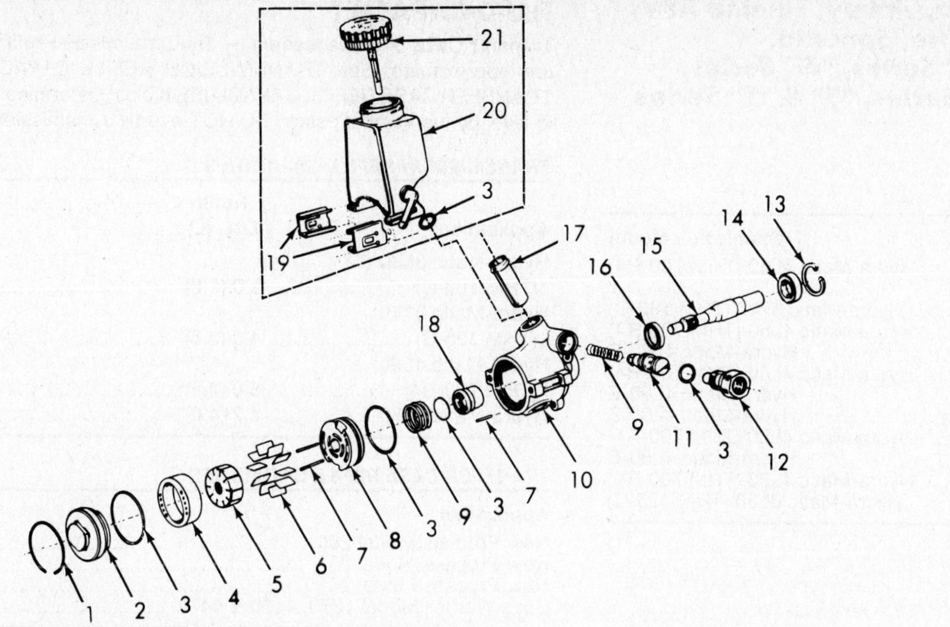
21
20
3
19
17
16
15
14
13
18
9
11
3
12
10
7
3
9
3
8
7
6
5
4
3
2
1
117440
Courtesy of General Motors Corp.

1. Retaining Ring
2. Thrust Plate
3. "O" Ring
4. Pump Ring
5. Rotor
6. Vanes
7. Dowel Pins
8. Pressure Plate
9. Spring
10. Housing
11. Flow Control Valve
12. Fitting
13. Snap Ring
14. Bearing
15. Drive Shaft
16. Drive Shaft Seal
17. Return Tube
18. Sleeve
19. Clips
20. Reservoir
21. Cap

Fig. 2: Exploded View of Pump Assembly (Model TC)

Reassembly – 1) Lubricate all "O" rings, seals, pump ring, rotor and vanes with power steering fluid.

CAUTION: Install pump ring with identification marks facing toward thrust plate end of housing. Thrust plate must be installed so indentations in thrust plate align with bolt holes of housing, and thrust plate engages with pump ring dowel pins.

2) Install sleeve and dowel pin. Install pressure plate spring and "O" ring. Install pressure plate with dowel pin hole aligned with that of the housing. Install dowel pins.
3) Install vanes with rounded edges toward pump ring. Install rotor with counterbore toward drive shaft end of housing. Install pump ring with identification marks facing toward thrust plate end of housing. Install "O" ring and thrust plate.
4) Place pump assembly in arbor press. Compress thrust plate and install retaining ring so opening of ring is centered with bolt hole of housing.
5) Using a socket, install drive shaft seal in housing until seal bottoms. Install bearing on drive shaft. Install drive shaft in housing. Rotate drive shaft during installation to align with rotor serrations.
6) Install snap ring. Ensure beveled edge seats properly. Install spring, flow control valve, and "O" rings. Install return tube or reservoir with new "O" ring.

TORQUE SPECIFICATIONS

TORQUE SPECIFICATIONS

Application	Ft. Lbs. (N.m)
Adjusting Bracket Bolt	64 (87)
Front Brace Bolt (6.2L)	30 (41)
Front Brace Nut (6.2L)	30 (41)
Mounting Bolt	
2.5L	20 (27)
2.8L, 4.3L, 5.0L, 5.7L & 7.4L	36 (50)
3.1L	18 (24)
6.2L	32 (44)
"O" Ring Union Fitting	55 (75)
Pressure Line Fitting	20 (27)
Rear Brace Bolt-To-Engine	
7.4L	24 (33)
Rear Brace Nut-To-Engine	
2.5L & 2.8L	33 (45)
4.3L, 5.0L & 5.7L	25 (34)
Rear Brace Nut-To-Pump	
2.5L & 2.8L	18 (24)
4.3L	24 (33)
5.0L, 5.7L & 7.4L	36 (50)
Rear Mounting Nut (6.2L)	17 (23)

1991 TRANSMISSION SERVICING
Automatic Transmission

Astro, Blazer, Bravada, Jimmy, Lumina APV, Safari, Sierra, Silhouette, Sonoma, Trans Sport, "C" & "K" Series, "G" Series, "P" Series, "R" & "V" Series, "S" & "T" Series

IDENTIFICATION

TRANSMISSION APPLICATION

Vehicle Model	Transmission Model
Astro & Safari	Hydra-Matic 4L60 (THM 700-R4)
Lumina APV, Silhouette & Trans Sport	Hydra-Matic 3T40 (THM 180-C)
"C" & "K" Series	Hydra-Matic 4L60 (THM 700-R4) Hydra-Matic 4L80-E
"G" Series	Hydra-Matic 4L60 (THM 700-R4) Hydra-Matic 4L80-E
"P" Series	Hydra-Matic 4L80-E
"R" & "V" Series	Hydra-Matic 4L60 (THM 700-R4) Hydra-Matic 4L80-E
"S" & "T" Series	Hydra-Matic 4L60 (THM 700-R4) Hydra-Matic 3L30 (THM 125-C)

LUBRICATION

SERVICE INTERVALS

Transmission – Check transmission fluid level at each engine oil change. On vehicles under 8600 Gross Vehicle Weight Rating (GVWR), change transmission fluid and filter at 30,000 mile intervals. On vehicles over 8600 GVWR, change transmission fluid and filter at 24,000 miles.

If vehicle is used in severe service conditions (commercial use, trailer pulling, constant stop-and-go driving), change fluid and filter every 15,000 miles on vehicles under 8600 GVWR and at 12,000 miles on vehicles over 8600 GVWR.

Transfer Case – Check transfer case lubricant every oil change or every 12 months. Check more frequently under severe conditions.

CHECKING FLUID LEVEL

NOTE: Vehicle must be at normal operating temperature when checking fluid level. One pint of fluid raises level from ADD to FULL mark on dipstick in a hot transmission. DO NOT overfill.

Transmission – With vehicle parked on a level surface and engine at idle, move selector lever through all positions, ending in Park. Remove dipstick, wipe clean and check fluid level. Fluid level should be between ADD and FULL marks on dipstick.

If vehicle has been operated for an extended time at high speed, in city traffic, or pulling a trailer, an accurate fluid level cannot be immediately determined. Transmission must cool for about 30 minutes after vehicle is parked before fluid level can be accurately checked.

Transfer Case – Remove fill plug. Check oil level. If level is not up to fill plug opening, add lubricant until it is.

RECOMMENDED FLUID

Transmissions and transfer cases use Dexron-II ATF.

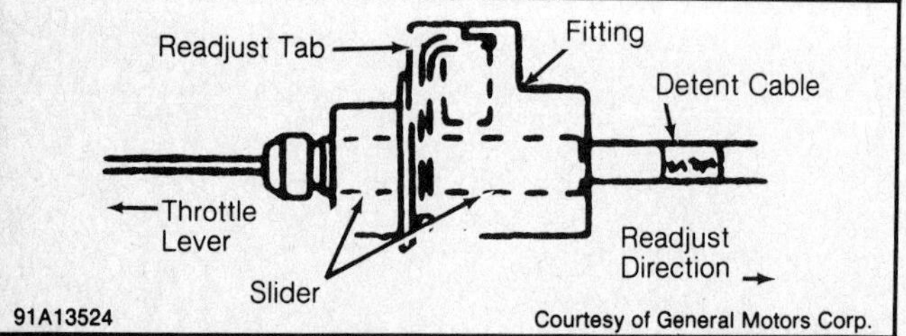
Readjust Tab
Fitting
Detent Cable
Throttle Lever
Slider
Readjust Direction
91A13524
Courtesy of General Motors Corp.

Fig. 1: Adjusting T.V. Cable

FLUID CAPACITY

Transfer Case & Transmission – The transmission refill capacities are approximate. See TRANSMISSION REFILL CAPACITIES and TRANSFER CASE REFILL CAPACITIES tables. Determine correct fluid level by marks on dipstick. DO NOT overfill transmission.

TRANSMISSION REFILL CAPACITIES

Application	Refill Qts. (L)	Dry Fill Qts. (L)
Hydra-Matic 3L30 (THM 180-C)	3.0 (2.8)	5 (4.9)
Hydra-Matic 3T40 (THM 125-C)	4.0 (3.8)	7 (6.6)
Hydra-Matic 4L60 (THM 700-R4)	5.0 (4.8)	11.6 (11.0)
Hydra-Matic 4L80-E	4.2 (4.0)	10.6 (10.0)

TRANSFER CASE REFILL CAPACITIES

Application	Pts. (L)
New Process Model 205	5.2 (2.5)
New Process Model 231	2.2 (1.1)
New Process Model 241	4.5 (8.5)
Borg-Warner Model 1370, 4470 & 4472	2.9 (1.4)

DRAINING & REFILLING

Transmission – **1)** Raise and support vehicle. Loosen transmission oil pan bolts. Slowly pry pan loose with a large screwdriver and allow fluid to drain. Remove oil pan and gasket. Remove filter or filter screen. Replace paper element filter (if used).

2) Clean filter screen (if equipped) and pan with solvent. Blow dry with compressed air. Install oil pan with new gasket.

3) Add 3 quarts of Dexron-II. Start engine and recheck level. Add fluid until level is between FULL and ADD marks on dipstick. Test drive vehicle and recheck fluid level.

Transfer Case – Remove drain plug from transfer case. Remove fill plug for easier draining. With fluid fully drained, reinstall drain plug. Fill transfer case to fill plug opening with Dexron-II.

ADJUSTMENTS

THROTTLE VALVE (T.V.) CABLE

Hydra-Matic 4L60 (THM 700-R4) – Depress readjust tab on cable adjuster and hold. *See Fig. 1.* Move slider back through fitting away from throttle body lever until slider stops at fitting. Release readjust tab and open throttle body lever to full throttle stop. This automatically adjusts slider to correct setting.

VACUUM REGULATOR VALVE (VRV)

Diesel – **1)** Loosen vacuum regulator valve-to-injection pump bolts enough to allow for regulator valve rotation. Attach vacuum pump to bottom vacuum port of valve (vacuum gauge to top port). *See Fig. 2.*

2) Insert .646" (16.4 mm) Gauge Block (J-33043) between gauge boss on injection pump and wide open stop screw on throttle lever. Rotate throttle shaft against block.

3) Apply 18-21 in. Hg vacuum to VRV. Slowly rotate VRV body clockwise (facing valve) until vacuum gauge reads 10.9-12.1 in. Hg. Hold valve body in this position and tighten mounting screws.

NOTE: Set valve while rotating in a CLOCKWISE direction only.

4) Check adjustment by allowing throttle shaft to return to idle position, then rotate shaft back against gauge block. If vacuum gauge reading is not 10.9-12.1 in. Hg, readjust valve.

5) With vacuum regulator valve vacuum set, confirm detent switch point by reading resistance between ignition terminal and detent terminal. Attach an ohmmeter across ignition terminal (Pink/Black wire) and detent terminal (Orange wire).

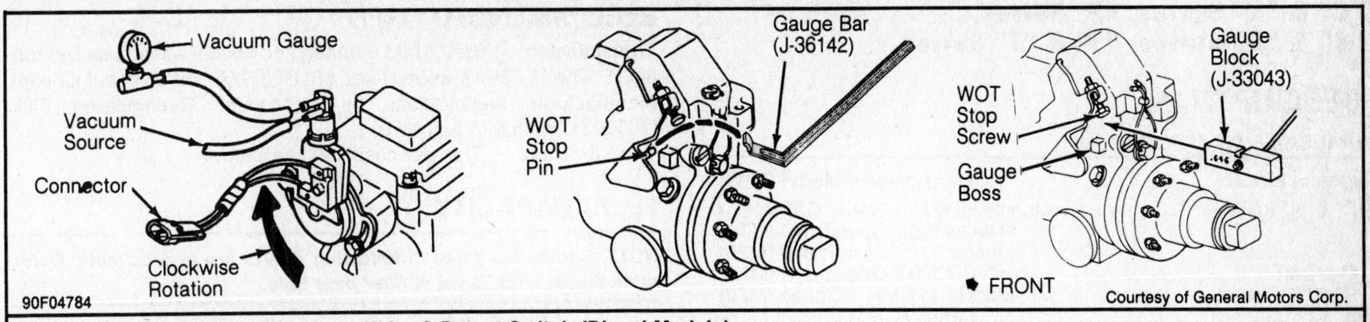

Vacuum Gauge
Vacuum Source
Connector
Clockwise Rotation
90F04784
WOT Stop Pin
Gauge Bar (J-36142)
WOT Stop Screw
Gauge Boss
Gauge Block (J-33043)
FRONT
Courtesy of General Motors Corp.

Fig. 2: Adjusting Vacuum Regulator Valve & Detent Switch (Diesel Models)

6) Insert Gauge Bar (J-36142) between gauge boss on pump and wide open stop screw on throttle shaft. *See Fig. 2.* Rotate and hold throttle lever against gauge bar. There should be no continuity (infinite resistance).

7) Release throttle lever and allow it to return to idle position. Remove gauge bar. Rotate throttle lever to Wide Open Throttle (WOT) position. Check switch for continuity. There should be continuity before throttle reaches WOT position. If switch does not meet specification, return to step 1).

SHIFT LINKAGE

Lumina APV, Silhouette & Trans Sport – 1) To adjust shift cable, place shift lever in Neutral. Turn transaxle lever clockwise from Park through Reverse to Neutral.

2) Place shift control assembly in Neutral position. Push tab on cable adjuster to adjust cable in cable mounting bracket.

Except Lumina APV, Silhouette & Trans Sport – 1) Ensure shift tube and lever are free in steering column. To adjust linkage, remove screw and spring washer from swivel. Turn transmission lever clockwise to stop, then counterclockwise 2 detents. This is Neutral position.

2) Place selector lever in Neutral. Locate proper position using mechanical stops, NOT shift indicator pointer. Hold swivel against shift lever. Install spring washer and screw and tighten finger tight. Avoid applying force in either direction (along shift rod or lever) while tightening screw to 17 ft. lbs. (23 N.m).

NEUTRAL SAFETY SWITCH

Column-Mounted Switch – 1) Place gearshift selector lever in Neutral, and loosen switch attaching screws. Rotate switch on column until a 3/32" (2.5 mm) drill bit will insert into switch gauge hole to a depth of .4" (10 mm).

2) Tighten switch attaching screws and remove gauge pin. Check for engine starting in Neutral and Park only.

Transmission-Mounted Switch – 1) Raise and support vehicle. Loosen neutral safety switch mounting bolts. Align hole in switch lever with hole in switch assembly. Insert a 3/32" (2.5 mm) drill bit through switch holes to hold switch in Neutral.

2) With selector lever on transmission in Neutral detent position, tighten switch mounting bolts and remove gauge pin. Lower vehicle and check switch operation, ensuring vehicle will NOT start in any forward or reverse gear.

OIL PAN GASKET IDENTIFICATION

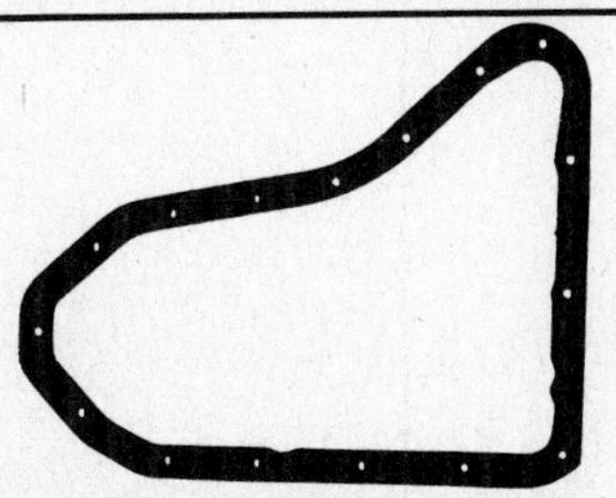

35217

Fig. 3: Identifying Hydra-Matic 3T40 (THM 125-C) Oil Pan Gasket

35218

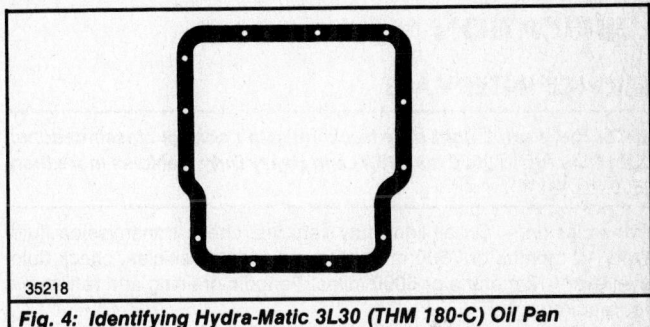

Fig. 4: Identifying Hydra-Matic 3L30 (THM 180-C) Oil Pan Gasket

91B13525

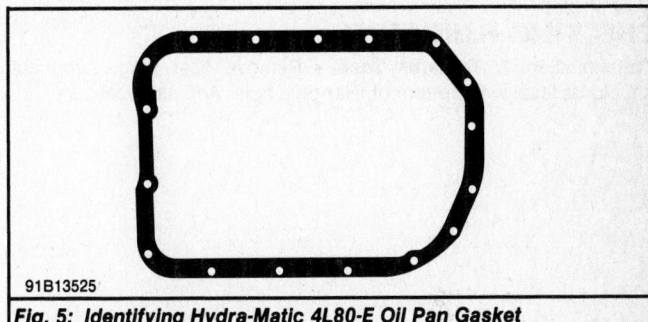

Fig. 5: Identifying Hydra-Matic 4L80-E Oil Pan Gasket

121173

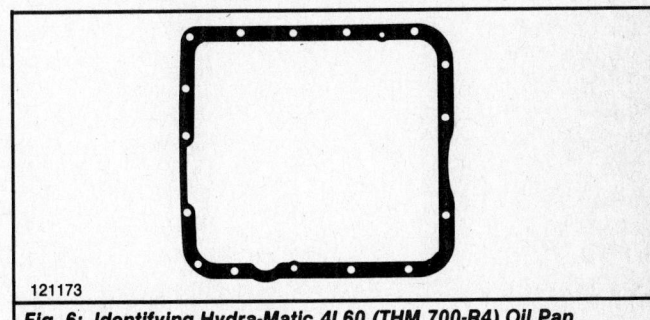

Fig. 6: Identifying Hydra-Matic 4L60 (THM 700-R4) Oil Pan Gasket

1991 TRANSMISSION SERVICING
Manual Transmission

"C" & "K" Series, "P" Series, "R" & "V" Series, "S" & "T" Series

DESCRIPTION

TRANSMISSION APPLICATION

Vehicle Model	Transmission Model (RPO)
"C" & "K" Series	Muncie 85 MM 5-Speed O/D (MG5)
	NVG 4500 5-Speed O/D (MT8)
	Muncie 117 MM 4-Speed (M20)
"P" Series	NVG 4500 5-Speed O/D (MT8)
"R" & "V" Series	Muncie 117 MM 4-Speed (M20)
"S" & "T" Series	Warner 77 MM 5-Speed (T5)

LUBRICATION

SERVICE INTERVALS

NOTE: There are 2 light duty truck emission control classifications: Light Duty (up to 8600 lbs. GVW) and Heavy Duty (vehicles more than 8600 lbs. GVW).

Transmission - On all light duty vehicles, check transmission fluid every 12 months or 7500 miles. On heavy duty vehicles, check fluid level every 12 months or 6000 miles. Periodic draining and refilling is not required.

Transfer Case - Check transfer case lubricant at every oil change or every 12 months. Under severe conditions, check more frequently

CHECKING FLUID LEVEL

Transmission & Transfer Case - Remove filler plug. Lubricant should be level with bottom of filler plug hole. Add as necessary.

RECOMMENDED FLUID

Transmission - The 77 MM 5-speed and 4500 5-speed use Dexron-II ATF. The 117 MM 4-speed uses API GL5 SAE 80W90 gear lubricant. Manufacturer recommends using Manual Transmission Fluid (1052931) in 85 MM 5-speed.

Transfer Case - Transfer cases all use Dexron-II ATF.

FLUID CAPACITY

NOTE: Capacities listed in following charts are approximate. Determine correct fluid level at filler plug hole.

TRANSMISSION REFILL CAPACITIES

Application	Pts. (L)
5-Speed (77 MM)	4.4 (2.1)
5-Speed (85 MM)	3.6 (1.7)
4-Speed (117 MM)	8.4 (4.0)
5-Speed (4500)	8.4 (4.0)

TRANSFER CASE REFILL CAPACITIES

Application	Pts. (L)
New Process Model 205	5.2 (2.5)
New Process Model 231	2.2 (1.1)
New Process Model 241	4.5 (2.1)
Borg-Warner Model 1370, 4470 & 4472	2.9 (1.4)

ADJUSTMENTS

NOTE: Manual transmissions have no shift rods. The shift lever mounts directly to top of transmission and is not adjustable.

Astro, Blazer, Bravada, Jimmy, Lumina APV, Safari, Sierra, Silhouette, Sonoma, Trans Sport, "C" & "K" Series, "G" Series, "P" Series, "R" & "V" Series, "S" & "T" Series

MANUAL TRANSMISSION

NOTE: For manual transmission replacement procedures, see appropriate CLUTCHES article.

TRANSFER CASE (A/T)

K30 SERIES WITH DUAL REAR WHEELS

Removal (BW-1370 & BW-4470) – 1) Disconnect negative battery cable. Place transfer case in 4H position. Raise vehicle. Remove skid plate. Drain lubricant from transfer case. Mark front drive shaft and flange for reassembly reference. Remove front drive shaft.

2) Remove left strut rod. Mark rear drive shaft and flange for reassembly reference. Remove rear drive shaft. Disconnect electrical connectors from transfer case. Disconnect shift linkage at transfer case.

3) Support transfer case and remove transfer case-to-transmission adapter bolts. Remove transfer case by moving transfer case rearward until it is free of transmission output shaft. Remove old gasket material.

Installation – To install, reverse removal procedure. Install a NEW gasket and fill transfer case with Dexron-II.

ASTRO, BRAVADA & SAFARI

Removal (BW-4472) – 1) Disconnect negative battery cable. Raise and support vehicle on hoist. Drain transfer case. Mark rear drive shaft components for reassembly reference. Disconnect rear drive shaft from differential and remove from vehicle.

2) Mark front drive shaft components for reassembly reference. Disconnect front drive shaft from transfer case and differential. Remove front drive shaft from vehicle. Disconnect breather hose and electrical connectors from transfer case.

3) Support transfer case and remove transfer case mount and support bracket. Remove transfer case-to-transmission adapter bolts. Move transfer case to rear and lower assembly from vehicle.

Installation – Position NEW gasket on transfer case adapter with gasket sealer. To complete installation, reverse removal procedure and fill transfer case with Dexron-II.

V10/15, V20/25, V30/35 & "C" & "K" SERIES

Removal (NP-205 & NP-241) – 1) Disconnect negative battery cable. Raise and support vehicle on hoist. Remove skid plate. Drain transfer case. Mark rear drive shaft components for reassembly reference. Disconnect and remove rear drive shaft from vehicle.

2) Mark front drive shaft components for reassembly reference. Disconnect and remove front drive shaft from vehicle. Disconnect vent hose and electrical connectors from transfer case. Disconnect speedometer cable and shift linkage at transfer case. Remove transfer case strut rod (if equipped).

3) Support transfer case and remove bolts attaching transfer case to transmission adapter. Move transfer case to rear until input shaft clears adapter. Lower transfer case assembly from vehicle.

Installation – To install, reverse removal procedure. Install a NEW gasket and fill transfer case with Dexron-II.

"S" & "T" SERIES

Removal (NP-231) – 1) Disconnect negative battery cable. Move transfer case shift lever to 4H position. Raise vehicle and remove skid plate. Drain transfer case. Mark front and rear output shaft yokes and drive shafts for reassembly reference and remove shafts.

2) Disconnect speedometer cable and vacuum harness from transfer case. Disconnect shift linkage from case. Remove catalytic converter hanger bolts at converter and loosen front catalytic converter clamp.

3) Raise transmission and transfer case assembly with jack and remove transmission mount bolts. Remove catalytic converter front bracket. Lower transmission and transfer case. Support transfer case alone and remove transmission-to-transfer case bolts.

4) Remove shift lever bracket from transfer case adapter in order to reach upper left attaching bolt. Separate transfer case from transmission adapter and remove from vehicle.

Installation – To install, reverse removal procedure. Always use a NEW gasket between transfer case and adapter and fill transfer case with Dexron-II.

AUTOMATIC TRANSMISSION

ASTRO, SAFARI, "C", "G", "K", "R", "S" "T" & "V" Series

Removal (Hydra-Matic 4L60/THM 700-R4) – 1) Open hood and disconnect negative battery cable. Remove air cleaner. Disconnect TV cable from throttle linkage. Raise vehicle. Drain transmission fluid. Disconnect shift linkage at transmission. Remove drive shaft.

2) Remove transmission support bracket attaching bolts at converter. Position transmission jack under transmission and raise slightly. Remove transmission crossmember-to-mount bolts, crossmember-to-frame bolts and vibration damper (if equipped). Slide crossmember rearward and remove from vehicle.

CAUTION: When lowering transmission to gain clearance for additional component removal, use care not to stretch or damage transmission lines, cables or wires.

3) Remove dipstick tube and seal. Cap openings. Disconnect speedometer cable at transmission. Disconnect vacuum modulator line (if equipped). Disconnect all electrical leads at transmission and electrical harness clips on transmission. Disconnect oil cooler lines and cap openings.

4) Disconnect transfer case shifter and move aside. Note location of transmission support brackets before removal for reassembly reference. Remove transmission support braces. Remove torque converter cover and mark flywheel and torque converter to maintain original balance. Remove torque converter-to-flywheel bolts.

5) Support engine and remove transmission-to-engine bolts. Disconnect transmission assembly, being careful not to damage any cables, lines or linkage. Install Torque Converter Holding Strap (J-21366) and remove transmission from vehicle.

Installation – To install, reverse removal procedure. Mount vibration damper (if equipped) at a 90 degree angle to centerline of transmission.

LUMINA APV, SILHOUETTE & TRANS SPORT

Removal (Hydra-Matic 3T40/THM 125-C) – 1) Place transmission gear selector in Park. Set parking brake and block drive wheels. Although fuel pressure drops to zero when ignition is turned off, loosen fuel filler cap to relieve tank pressure. To further minimize risk of fire and personal injury, cover surrounding areas with a shop rag while removing fuel lines.

WARNING: To avoid possible personal injury and fire danger, relieve fuel pressure as outlined in step 1).

2) Disconnect battery cables. Drain cooling system. Remove airflow tube from air cleaner and radiator core support. Disconnect wiring harness at ECM and pull through firewall. Separate engine wiring harness from body connectors and lay harness on engine.

3) Remove accelerator and throttle valve cables. Disconnect fuel lines and transmission shift linkage. Disconnect radiator and heater hoses. Disconnect transmission cooler lines at radiator.

4) Discharge A/C system. Remove A/C compressor and bracket. Disconnect A/C hose at rear of compressor. Cap disconnected hoses and compressor fittings. Remove upper engine strut. Raise and support vehicle.

1991 TRANSMISSION SERVICING
Transmission Removal & Installation (Cont.)

5) Remove front wheels and stabilizer shaft. Disconnect tie rod ends at steering knuckle. Remove lower control arm ball joints from steering knuckles. See appropriate article in SUSPENSION.
6) Remove drive axles from transaxle and wire out of way. See appropriate article in DRIVE AXLES. Remove intermediate steering shaft pinch bolt. Remove starter.
7) Remove torque converter cover. Remove converter-to-flex plate bolts. Separate exhaust pipe at rear manifold. Support engine/frame/transaxle assembly (with hydraulic table). Remove frame bolts. Lower engine/frame/transaxle assembly. Remove transaxle from assembly.
Installation – To install, reverse removal procedure. Always use a NEW gasket between transfer case and adapter and fill transfer case with Dexron-II.

"C", "G", "K", "R" & "V" SERIES

Removal (Hydra-Matic 4L80-E) – 1) Disconnect negative battery cable. Remove air cleaner. Raise vehicle. Drain transmission fluid. Disconnect shift linkage at transmission. Remove drive shaft.
2) Position transmission jack under transmission and raise slightly. Remove transmission crossmember-to-mount bolts, crossmember-to-frame bolts and vibration damper (if equipped). Slide crossmember rearward and remove from vehicle.

CAUTION: When lowering transmission to gain clearance for additional component removal, use care not to stretch or damage transmission lines, cables or wires.

3) Remove dipstick tube and seal. Cap openings. Disconnect cooler lines and cap openings. Disconnect transfer case shifter and move aside. Note location of transmission support brackets before removal for reassembly reference. Remove transmission support braces. Remove torque converter cover and mark flywheel and torque converter to maintain original balance. Remove torque converter-to-flywheel bolts.
4) Support engine and remove transmission-to-engine bolts. Disconnect transmission assembly, being careful not to damage any cables, lines or linkage. Install Torque Converter Holding Strap (J-21366) and remove transmission from vehicle.
Installation – To install, reverse removal procedure. Add Dexron-II Automatic Transmission Fluid.

"S" & "T" SERIES

NOTE: On 4WD models, refer to TRANSFER CASE procedures to remove transfer case.

Removal (Hydra-Matic 3L30/THM 180-C) – 1) Disconnect negative battery cable. Remove air cleaner and disconnect TV cable at throttle body. Raise and support vehicle. Drain transmission fluid.
2) Mark drive shaft(s) for reassembly reference and remove shaft(s). Disconnect speedometer cable, shift linkage and all electrical leads from transmission. On 4WD models, remove brake line from crossmember clips.
3) Remove transmission support bracket bolts. Disconnect catalytic converter support bracket. Support transmission and transfer case (if equipped). Remove crossmember. Lower transmission enough to provide clearance to reach other components.

CAUTION: When lowering transmission to gain clearance for additional component removal, use care not to stretch or damage transmission lines, cables or wires.

4) Remove dipstick tube and seal. Remove oil cooler lines and TV cable. Cap all disconnected lines and openings. Disconnect transfer case shifter and move out of the way. Remove vibration damper and support brackets (if equipped).
5) Remove torque convert cover and mark flywheel-to-torque converter position for reassembly reference. Remove flywheel-to-torque converter bolts. Support engine with jack and remove transmission-to-engine bolts. Slide transmission straight back from engine and install Torque Converter Holding Strap (J-21366) to prevent converter damage during removal. Remove transmission.
Installation – To install, reverse removal procedure. Before installing flex plate-to-converter bolts, make certain that weld nuts on converter are flush with the flex plate and converter rotates freely by hand in this position. Hand tighten all flex plate-to-torque converter bolts before tightening to specification.

TORQUE SPECIFICATIONS

TORQUE SPECIFICATIONS

Application	Ft. Lbs. (N.m)
Converter-To-Flex Plate	
Astro, Safari & "S" & "T" Series	62 (84)
All Others	46 (62)
Crossmember-To-Frame Bolts	
"G", "R" & "P" Series	63 (85)
"S" Series (Left Side Only)	30 (41)
"S" (Right Side Only) & "T" Series	35 (47)
"V" Series	52 (70)
All Others	56 (76)
Transaxle Bracket Bolts	
Lumina APV, Silhouette & Trans Sport	41 (56)
Transaxle Mount-To-Bracket Nut	
Lumina APV, Silhouette & Trans Sport	35 (47)
Transfer Case-To-Adapter Bolts	
Astro, Safari & "S" & "T" Series	38 (51)
All Others	24 (33)
Transmission-To-Adapter Bolts	
Astro & Safari	38 (51)
"S" & "T" Series	32 (43)
All Others	24 (33)
Transmission-To-Engine Bolts	
Lumina APV, Silhouette & Trans Sport	55 (75)
"S" & "T" Series	75 (102)
All Others	23 (31)
Transmission-To-Mount Bolts	
"S" & "T" Series	35 (47)
All Others	35 (47)
Transmission Mount-To-Crossmember Bolts	
"S" & "T" Series	25 (34)
All Others	35 (47)

JEEP

1991 JEEP CONTENTS

GENERAL INFORMATION [1]

1 – For all GENERAL INFORMATION, see front of this manual.

ENGINE PERFORMANCE

ENGINE PERFORMANCE (Cont.)

1991 JEEP CONTENTS (Cont.)

ENGINE PERFORMANCE (Cont.)

ELECTRICAL

WIRING DIAGRAMS

SAFETY EQUIPMENT

1991 JEEP CONTENTS (Cont.)

1991 JEEP CONTENTS (Cont.)

BRAKES

ANTI-LOCK BRAKE SYSTEMS

DISC & DRUM

WHEEL ALIGNMENT

SPECIFICATIONS & PROCEDURES

SUSPENSION

FRONT

STEERING

STEERING COLUMN

MANUAL RECIRCULATING BALL

POWER RECIRCULATING BALL

TRANSMISSION SERVICING

AUTOMATIC TRANSMISSION

MANUAL TRANSMISSION

TRANSMISSION REMOVAL & INSTALLATION

1991 ENGINE PERFORMANCE
Jeep Introduction

1991 MODEL COVERAGE

MODEL	BODY CODE	ENGINE [1]	ENGINE ID	FUEL SYSTEM	IGNITION SYSTEM
Cherokee	XJ	2.5L (HX)	P	PFI [2]	Magnetic
		4.0L (MX)	S	PFI [2]	Magnetic
Comanche	MJ	2.5L (HX)	P	PFI [2]	Magnetic
		4.0L (MX)	S	PFI [2]	Magnetic
Grand Wagoneer	SJ	6.0L (NX)	7	2-Bbl.	Magnetic
Wrangler	YJ	2.5L (HX)	P	PFI [2]	Magnetic
		4.0L (MX)	S	PFI [2]	Magnetic

[1] – Fourth and fifth characters of engine code (on block) identify engine. See ENGINE CODE LOCATION.
[2] – Sequential Multi-Point Fuel Injection.

VIN DEFINITION

1J4FJ35S9ML000001

① ② ③ ④ ⑤ ⑥ ⑦ ⑧ ⑨ ⑩ ⑪ ⑫ ⑬ ⑭ ⑮ ⑯ ⑰

① Indicates Nation of Origin.
② Indicates Manufacturer.
③ Indicates Vehicle Type.
④ Indicates GVWR.
⑤ Indicates Vehicle Line.
⑥ Indicates Vehicle Series.
⑦ Indicates Body Type.
⑧ **Indicates Engine Code.**
⑨ Indicates Check Digit.
⑩ **Indicates Model Year.**
⑪ Indicates Assembly Plant.
⑫ - ⑰ Indicates Plant Sequential Number.

MODEL YEAR VIN CODE APPLICATION

VIN Code	Model Year
L	1990
M	1991

ENGINE CODE LOCATION

2.5L (HX) – On machined surface, on right side of cylinder block, between cylinders No. 3 and No. 4.
4.0L (MX) – On machined surface, on right side of cylinder block, between cylinders No. 2 and No. 3.
6.0L (NX) – On plate, attached to right bank cylinder head cover.

1991 ENGINE PERFORMANCE
Emission Applications

1991 JEEP EMISSION SYSTEMS

Model, Engine & Fuel System	Emission Control Systems & Devices	Remarks
Cherokee, Comanche, Wrangler 2.5L (150") 4-Cyl. PFI	**CCV** [1], **TAC, EVAP, TWC, EGR, SPK, O_2, CEC, EMR, CE,** EVAP-PRRV, SPK-CC	[1] - No PCV valve is used. [2] - Upstream and downstream. [3] - AP and canister purge.
4.0L (242") 6-Cyl. PFI	**CCV** [1], **TAC, EVAP, TWC, EGR, SPK, O_2, CEC, EMR, CE,** EVAP-PRRV, SPK-CC	
Grand Wagoneer 6.0L (360") V8 2-Bbl.	**PCV, TAC, EVAP, OC, BP/EGR, SPK, AP,** AP-ACV, AP-CKV [2], EVAP-BVV, DCTO [3], EFE, BP/EGR-BPT, BP/EGR-CTO, BP/EGR-TVS, EVAP-VM, RDV, EVAP-PRRV, VA-CTO	

NOTE: Major emission control systems are listed above in bold type; components are listed in light type.

AP - Air Pump
AP-ACV - Air Control Valve
AP-CKV - Check Valve
BP/EGR - Backpressure EGR
BP/EGR-BPT - Backpressure Transducer
BP/EGR-TVS - Thermal Vacuum Switch
CCV - Crankcase Ventilation
CE - Check Engine Light
CEC - Computerized Engine Control
DCTO - Dual Coolant Temperature Override
EFE - Early Fuel Evaporation
EGR - Exhaust Gas Recirculation
EMR - Emission Maintenance Reminder Light
EVAP - Evaporative Emission Control
EVAP-BVV - Bowl Vent Valve
EVAP-PRRV - Pressure Relief/Rollover Valve
EVAP-VM - EVAP System Vacuum Motor
OC - Oxidation Catalyst
O_2 - Oxygen Sensor
PCV - Positive Crankcase Ventilation
PFI - Multi-Port Fuel Injection
RDV - Retard Delay Valves
SPK - Spark Controls
SPK-CC - SPK Computer Controlled
TAC - Thermostatic Air Cleaner
TWC - Three-Way Catalyst
VA-CTO - Vacuum Advance-Coolant Temp. Override

1991 ENGINE PERFORMANCE
Service & Adjustment Specifications

Cherokee, Comanche
Grand Wagoneer, Wrangler

INTRODUCTION

Use this article to quickly find specifications related to servicing and on-vehicle adjustments. This is a quick-reference article for when you are familiar with an adjustment procedure and only need a specification.

CAPACITIES

BATTERY SPECIFICATIONS

Application & Group [1]	Cold Crank Amps @ 0°F (-18°C)
2.5L & 4.0L	390
2.5L & 4.0L (Heavy Duty)	475
6.0L	475

[1] – All models use group 58 battery.

FLUID CAPACITIES

Application	[1] Quantity
Crankcase [2]	
2.5L	4.0 qts. (3.8L)
4.0L	6.0 qts. (5.7L)
6.0L	5.0 qts. (4.7L)
Cooling System (Includes Heater)	
2.5L (Cherokee & Comanche)	10.0 qts. (9.5L)
2.5L (Wrangler)	9.0 qts. (8.5L)
4.0L (Cherokee & Comanche)	12.0 qts. (11.4L)
4.0L (Wrangler)	10.5 qts. (9.9L)
6.0L	15.5 qts. (14.7L)
Automatic Transmission (Mercon or Dexron-II) [3]	
AW-4	8.5 pts. (4.0L)
727	8-10 pts. (3.8-4.7L)
999	8 pts. (3.8L)
Manual Transmission (API GL-5 75W-90)	
AX-4 (4-Speed)	7.8 pts. (3.7L)
AX-5 (2WD 5-Speed)	7.4 pts. (3.5L)
AX-5 (4WD 5-Speed)	7.0 pts. (3.3L)
AX-15 (5-Speed)	6.7 pts. (3.2L)
Front/Rear Axles (API GL-5 75W-90)	
Cherokee [4]	2.5 pts. (1.2L)
Comanche & Wrangler [5,6]	2.5 pts. (1.2L)
Comanche & Wrangler (H/D Axle) [5,6]	3.0 pts. (1.4L)
Grand Wagoneer [5,6]	3.8 pts. (1.8L)
Transfer Case (Mercon or Dexron-II)	
Command-Trac 231	2.2 pts. (1.0L)
Command-Trac 231 (Wrangler)	3.3 pts. (1.5L)
Model 229	6.0 pts. (2.8L)
Selec-Trac 242	3.0 pts. (1.4L)

[1] – Fluid capacities listed are approximate. Always fill to FULL mark.
[2] – Does not include oil filter.
[3] – Drain and refill capacity only. Does not include torque converter.
[4] – With trailer towing package (5000 lbs.), use 75W-140 synthetic gear oil.
[5] – With trailer towing package use API GL-5 80W-140.
[6] – With limited slip differential, add 2 ounces of friction modifier.

QUICK-SERVICE

SERVICE INTERVALS & SPECIFICATIONS

REPLACEMENT INTERVALS

Component	Miles
Oil & Filter	7500
Air Filter	30,000
Coolant	52,500
Fuel Filter	30,000
Oxygen Sensor	75,000
Spark Plugs	30,000

BELT ADJUSTMENT
(Tension In Lbs. (kg) Using Belt Tension Gauge)

Application	Tension
Serpentine Belt	
New Belts	180-200 (81.72-90.8)
Used Belts	140-160 (63.56-72.64)
V-Belt	
New Belts	120-160 (54.48-72.64)
Used Belts	90-115 (40.86-52.21)

MECHANICAL CHECKS

ENGINE COMPRESSION

Check engine compression with engine at normal operating temperature at specified cranking speed, all spark plugs removed (on dual plugs, remove exhaust side only) and throttle wide open.

NOTE: Compression pressure and cylinder pressure variation for 2.5L and 4.0L engines are not available from manufacturer.

2.5L & 4.0L COMPRESSION RATIO

Application	Specification
2.5L	9.2:1
4.0L	8.8:1

6.0L COMPRESSION SPECIFICATIONS

Application	Specification
Compression Ratio	8.25:1
Minimum Compression Pressure	120 psi (8.4 kg/cm²)
Maximum Variation Between Cylinders	30 psi (2.1 kg/cm²)

VALVE CLEARANCE

NOTE: All models are equipped with hydraulic lifters. No adjustments are required.

IGNITION SYSTEM

IGNITION COIL

IGNITION COIL RESISTANCE – Ohms @ 68°F (20°C)

Application	Primary Ohms	Secondary Ohms
2.5L & 4.0L	.95-1.20	[1] 11,300-15,300
6.0L	1.13-1.23	7700-9300

[1] – With Diamond coil. Toyodenso coil is 11,300-13,300 ohms.

DISTRIBUTOR SENSORS

DISTRIBUTOR SENSOR

Application	Ohms
6.0L	400-800

HIGH TENSION WIRE RESISTANCE

HIGH TENSION WIRE RESISTANCE

Application	Ohms
All Wires	250-1000 per inch

SPARK PLUGS

SPARK PLUG TYPE

Application	Specification
2.5L & 4.0L	Champion RC-12 LYC
6.0L	Champion RN-12 YC

1991 ENGINE PERFORMANCE
Service & Adjustment Specifications (Cont.)

SPARK PLUG SPECIFICATIONS

Application	Gap In. (mm)	Torque Ft. Lbs. (N.m)
2.5L, 4.0L & 6.0L	.035 (.89)	27 (36.6)

FIRING ORDER & TIMING MARKS

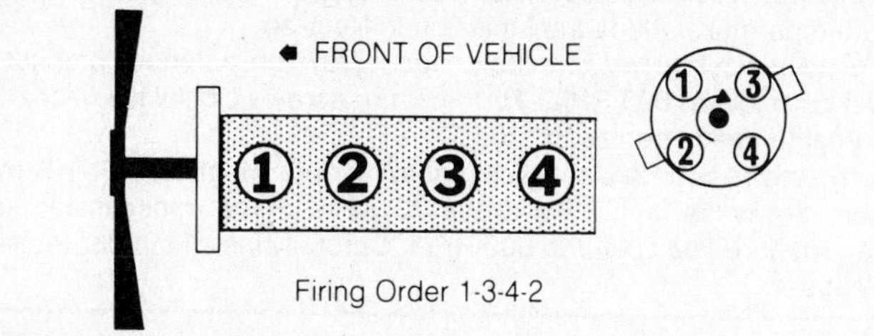
FRONT OF VEHICLE
Firing Order 1-3-4-2
9087

Fig. 1: Firing Order (2.5L)

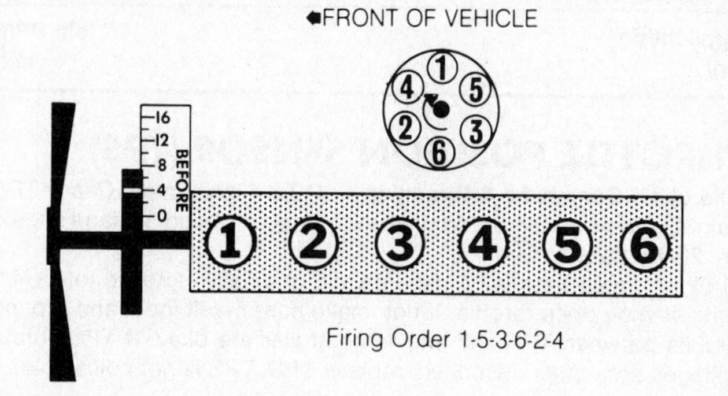
FRONT OF VEHICLE
BEFORE
Firing Order 1-5-3-6-2-4
71919

Fig. 2: Firing Order (4.0L)

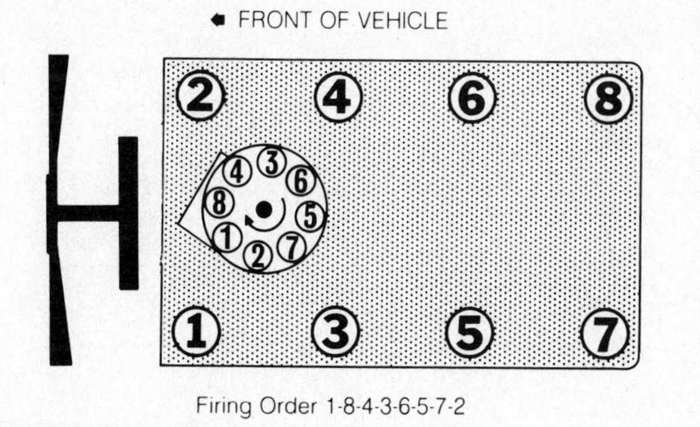
FRONT OF VEHICLE
Firing Order 1-8-4-3-6-5-7-2
8375

Fig. 3: Firing Order (6.0L)

IGNITION TIMING

NOTE: No adjustment is possible on 2.5L and 4.0L engines with Single Board Engine Controller II computerized ignition.

V8 IGNITION TIMING (Degrees BTDC @ RPM)

Application	Specification
6.0L 2-Bbl.	[1] 16 @ 600

[1] – Automatic transmission in Drive.

DISTRIBUTOR SPECIFICATIONS

Fuel injected models are equipped with Single Board Engine Controller II computerized ignition. The distributor's only function is to distribute high voltage to appropriate spark plug. No adjustments are required.

V8 TOTAL SPARK ADVANCE (Degrees BTDC @ 4000 RPM)

Application	Specification
6.0L	
With Vacuum Advance	32-42
Without Vacuum Advance	12-17

FUEL SYSTEM

FUEL PUMP

NOTE: Fuel pump performance refers to fuel pressure and volume availability, not regulated fuel pressure.

FUEL PUMP PERFORMANCE

Application	Pressure psi (kg/cm²)	Min. Vol. In 30 sec.
2.5L & 4.0L	39 (2.70)	1 pt. (.47L)
6.0L	5-6.5 (.35-.46)	1 pt. (.47L)

REGULATED FUEL PRESSURE

Application	psi (kg/cm²)
2.5L & 4.0L (At Idle)	
With Vacuum	31 (2.18)
Without Vacuum	39 (2.70)

INJECTOR RESISTANCE

INJECTOR RESISTANCE – Ohms @ 68°F (20°C)

Application	Specification
2.5L & 4.0L	12.8-15.2

IDLE SPEED & MIXTURE

NOTE: On vehicles with fuel injection, idle mixture is controlled by the Single Board Engine Controller II (SBEC-II). Idle mixture adjustment is not required or possible on fuel injected models. On carbureted models, mixture should be adjusted only if vehicle fails emission testing or carburetor has been disassembled.

V8 IDLE SPEED

Application	RPM
6.0L	[1] 600

[1] – Idle drop should be 20 RPM.

NOTE: If final RPM differs more than 30 RPM from specified curb idle, reset curb idle, and repeat mixture adjustment.

FAST IDLE SPEED

FAST IDLE SPECIFICATIONS

Application	RPM
6.0L	1500-1700

THROTTLE POSITION SENSOR (TPS)

2.5L & 4.0L – Output voltage (center terminal of TPS) should be .20-1.2 volts with closed throttle. TPS is not adjustable.

1991 ENGINE PERFORMANCE
On-Vehicle Adjustments

Cherokee, Comanche
Grand Wagoneer, Wrangler

ENGINE MECHANICAL

Before performing any on-vehicle adjustments to fuel or ignition systems, ensure engine mechanical condition is okay.

VALVE CLEARANCE

NOTE: All models use hydraulic lifters. No adjustments are required.

IGNITION TIMING

4 & 6-CYLINDER IGNITION TIMING

Ignition timing is not adjustable.

V8 IGNITION TIMING

Grand Wagoneer - 1) Set parking brake. Place transmission in Park. Turn A/C off. Warm engine to normal operating temperature. Connect timing light and tachometer to engine. Disconnect and plug distributor vacuum advance hose.
2) With engine idling, check and adjust timing. Tighten distributor hold down clamp and recheck ignition timing. Remove timing light and tachometer. Reconnect vacuum advance hose.

V8 IGNITION TIMING (Degrees BTDC @ RPM)

Application	Specification
Grand Wagoneer	16 @ 600

IDLE SPEED & MIXTURE

NOTE: Mixture adjustment is NOT a normal tune-up procedure and should not be performed unless mixture control unit is replaced or vehicle fails emissions testing.

NOTE: On vehicles with fuel injection, air/fuel mixture is controlled by Single Board Engine Controller-II (SBEC-II) and is not adjustable. On carbureted models, ensure idle speed and timing are set before adjusting idle mixture. If mixture adjustment procedure lasts 3 minutes, run engine at 2000 RPM in Neutral for one minute, and then resume adjustment.

COLD (FAST) IDLE

Grand Wagoneer - Warm engine to operating temperature. Place fast idle lever on second step of fast idle cam. Adjust fast idle speed to 1500-1700 RPM.

V8 IDLE SPEED & MIXTURE

Grand Wagoneer - 1) Remove carburetor. Remove idle mixture screw tamper resistant caps. Install carburetor. Warm engine to operating temperature. Place transmission in Neutral.
2) To adjust curb idle, turn hex-head screw on solenoid bracket. Adjust curb idle to 600 RPM. Turn mixture screws clockwise (leaner) until engine speed begins to drop.
3) Turn screws counterclockwise (richer) to obtain highest RPM. Turn screws clockwise until RPM drops 20 RPM. Place transmission in Drive. Set curb idle speed to 600 RPM. Carefully install tamper resistant caps.

NOTE: If final RPM is not 570-630 RPM, reset curb idle and repeat mixture adjustment.

V8 IDLE SPEED

Application	Idle RPM
6.0L	600

THROTTLE POSITION SENSOR (TPS)

Cherokee, Comanche & Wrangler - 1) Turn ignition on. Check TPS output voltage at center terminal. With throttle closed, voltage should be .20-1.5 volts.
2) Slowly open throttle. Voltage should gradually increase to 4.1-4.8 volts at wide open throttle. If not, make sure 5-volt input and ground circuits between TPS and engine controller are okay. If TPS output voltages are not as described, replace TPS. TPS is not adjustable.

1991 ENGINE PERFORMANCE
Theory & Operation

Cherokee, Comanche, Grand Wagoneer, Wrangler

INTRODUCTION

This article covers basic description and operation of engine performance-related systems and components. Read this article before diagnosing vehicles or systems with which you are not completely familiar.

COMPUTERIZED ENGINE CONTROLS

SINGLE BOARD ENGINE CONTROLLER-II

The Single Board Engine Controller-II (SBEC-II) is a dual microprocessor that receives various signals from engine sensors and provides the necessary signals to control engine sub-systems. The SBEC-II has a voltage converter that converts battery voltage to regulated 5-volt or 8-volt outputs. The regulated 5-volt output is used to power Manifold Absolute Pressure (MAP) sensor, Throttle Position Sensor (TPS) and logic circuits. The regulated 8-volt output is used to power crankshaft position sensor and synchronization signal generator in distributor.

The ignition and fuel injection systems are controlled by the SBEC-II. Based on present engine operating conditions, the engine controller is programmed to provide a precise amount of fuel and the correct ignition timing to meet existing engine speed and load requirements.

The engine controller adjusts ignition timing based on inputs it receives from synchronization sensor generator, MAP sensor, coolant temperature sensor, throttle position sensor, vehicle speed sensor, transmission gear selection (automatic transmissions only), and brake switch.

The engine controller adjusts idle speed based on inputs it receives from throttle position sensor, vehicle speed sensor, transmission gear selection (automatic transmissions only), A/C clutch switch, and brake switch.

The engine controller also controls the speed (cruise) control system and alternator charge rate by controlling the alternator field.

NOTE: Components are grouped into 2 categories. The first category covers INPUT DEVICES, which control or produce voltage signals that are monitored by the SBEC-II. The second category covers OUTPUT SIGNALS, which are components controlled by the SBEC-II.

INPUT DEVICES

Vehicles are equipped with different combinations of input devices. Not all devices are used on all models. To determine the input device usage on a specific model, see appropriate wiring diagram in WIRING DIAGRAMS article. The available input signals include the following:

A/C Pressure Switch & Evaporator Switch – When A/C switch is in ON position and A/C low pressure switch and evaporator switch are closed, an A/C select signal is sent to engine controller. If A/C low pressure switch or evaporator switch opens, the engine controller will not receive an A/C select signal.

When A/C function is selected (A/C switch on), the A/C request signal provides information to the engine controller from the A/C temperature control thermostat (evaporator switch). This signal indicates evaporator temperature is in the proper range for A/C operation.

The A/C request signal is used by engine controller to determine required Automatic Idle Speed (AIS) motor position and to activate or deactivate A/C compressor clutch. When engine controller receives an A/C request signal, it repositions the AIS motor to increase idle speed. The increased idle speed compensates for additional engine load caused by engagement of A/C compressor.

On 4.0L engine, whenever A/C compressor clutch is energized, engine controller also energizes the radiator (cooling) fan relay. This occurs regardless on engine coolant temperature.

Alternator Output – The engine controller keeps charging system voltage at 13.4-15.0 volts. Charging system voltage will be adjusted by engine controller based on battery temperature sensor, located within engine controller housing. The voltage determined by engine controller as final goal for charging system is called "control" voltage. The control voltage will be used to determine alternator field control and to detect if charging system is operating properly.

If sensed voltage is lower than "control" voltage, engine controller will alter duty cycle and ground alternator (rotor) field for a longer period of time and create a higher alternator output which should raise sensed voltage level. If sensed voltage is higher than "control" voltage, engine controller will alter duty cycle and lower alternator output which should lower sensed voltage level.

Battery Voltage Signal – The engine controller uses a battery voltage signal to determine vehicle's battery voltage level. The engine controller uses this information to determine injector pulse width and alternator field control.

The engine controller uses battery voltage level to regulate alternator field (rotor) duty cycle and alter fuel injector pulse width according to available voltage. If battery voltage drops, engine controller will increase injector on time to compensate for the reduced fuel flow of injector caused by the lower voltage. This will permit injector to deliver proper amount of fuel to the engine.

Brake Switch – The brake switch is mounted on steering column support bracket, under instrument panel. The engine controller uses the brake switch to determine when brakes are being applied or not. When brakes are applied (brake switch on) and if engine controller sees a TPS opening and a lower speed sensor rate, it recognizes a deceleration condition and opens up the Automatic Idle Speed (AIS) motor. The brake switch signal will also disengage speed (cruise) control operation, if it was engaged.

Coolant Temperature Sensor – The coolant temperature sensor is mounted on top of engine, next to thermostat housing. It provides an analog signal to the engine controller that is used to calculate injector pulse width and ignition timing when engine is cold. Input from the coolant temperature sensor will also affect Automatic Idle Speed (AIS) motor position and spark advance operation.

Crankshaft Position Sensor – The Hall Effect type crankshaft position sensor is mounted on transaxle bellhousing. The sensor reads slots (4 per cylinder) on flywheel/flex plate. The signal generated provides engine speed and crankshaft position information to engine controller. The engine controller uses this information to determine proper fuel injection and ignition timing.

When a flywheel/flex plate slot passes the crankshaft position sensor magnet, output voltage of the Hall Effect sensor goes high (5 volts). When the metal between the slots is aligned with sensor, output voltage goes low (.3 volts).

This high/low voltage signal is generated and sent to engine controller each time one of the slots passes the crankshaft position sensor. The engine controller uses this information to determine when to energize the injectors for fuel delivery to the proper cylinders.

Ignition Circuit – When ignition key is turned to the ON position, the engine controller receives a signal that the ignition circuit has been activated. The engine controller will start looking at the input signals.

Manifold Absolute Pressure (MAP) Sensor – The MAP sensor is mounted on engine compartment firewall. The MAP sensor is used by engine controller to calibrate amount of air/fuel mixture supplied to the engine. This sensor measures manifold absolute pressure and ambient barometric pressure when ignition switch is first turned on, during engine cranking, and at wide open throttle.

The MAP sensor transmits a low voltage signal (1.5-2.1 volts) at idle when manifold vacuum is high, and a higher voltage signal (3.9-4.8 volts) during open throttle when manifold vacuum is low.

Input voltage (from the engine controller) to MAP sensor ranges from 4.8-5.1 volts. Adjustments made as a result of this input will usually affect injector pulse width, ignition timing, idle speed, and upshift indicator light.

1991 ENGINE PERFORMANCE
Theory & Operation (Cont.)

Manifold Air Temperature (MAT) Sensor – The MAP sensor is located on intake manifold, with sensor element extending into the air stream. The sensor measures the temperature of air entering the intake manifold. This sensor provides an analog voltage signal to engine controller. This signal is used to compensate for changes in air density due to temperature.

The MAT sensor is a Negative Temperature Coefficient (NTC) thermistor-type sensor. Its internal resistance varies opposite with temperature. At cold temperatures, the resistance is high. As temperature increases, its resistance decreases.

Oxygen (O_2) Sensor – The heated oxygen sensor detects amount of oxygen content of the exhaust gases and produces a voltage signal. Engine controller uses this signal to monitor system output signals which control air/fuel mixture.

Variations in voltage signal from O_2 sensor serve as air/fuel ratio indicators. Changes occur because oxygen sensor voltage input to engine controller varies. When oxygen content is low (rich mixture), voltage signal will be approximately one volt. When oxygen content is high (lean mixture), voltage signal will be approximately 0.1 volt.

The O_2 sensor contains a ceramic heater in the sensor housing. The heater operates on 12 volts. The heater is used in cold starts to help O_2 sensor heat up quicker and to maintain the O_2 sensor's Zirconia semiconductor at its operational temperature of 932-1112°F (500-600°C).

In "closed loop" operation, engine controller monitors O_2 sensor input (along with other sensors) and adjusts the injector pulse width accordingly. During "open loop" operation, engine controller ignores O_2 sensor input and adjust injector pulse width to a pre-programmed value based on the other sensor inputs.

Park/Neutral Switch – On vehicles equipped with automatic transmission, a gear position indicator signal is sent to engine controller when gear selector lever has been moved to the Drive range. This signal comes from the Park/Neutral switch (Neutral safety switch on AW-4) and allows engine controller to adjust idle speed, fuel injector pulse width, and ignition timing advance.

Power Steering Switch – On 2.5L vehicles with power steering, a power steering switch is used. The switch is located on pressure line, next to power steering pump.

The power steering switch sends a signal to engine controller when pressures in system rise above 250-300 psi (17.6-21.1 kg/cm²) and engine RPM is low. The engine controller, through AIS motor, will raise the idle speed to prevent engine from stalling.

Serial Communications Interface Receive – The Serial Communications Interface (SCI) receive circuit is the serial data circuit that is used when diagnosing vehicle with Chrysler's Diagnostic Readout Box-II (DRB-II). The engine controller receives data from the DRB-II through this SCI receive circuit.

Speed (Cruise) Control Switches – The speed (cruise) control switches provide 3 separate inputs to the engine controller. The ON/OFF switch informs engine controller that speed control system has been activated. The SET switch informs engine controller that a set vehicle speed has been selected. The RESUME switch informs engine controller that the previously selected set speed has been selected.

Start (Cranking) Signal – The start (cranking) signal from starter relay signals engine controller when starter is engaged. When engine controller determines that starter is engaged, it starts looking at inputs from crankshaft position sensor and synchronization signal generator.

The engine controller then uses these signals to determine spark timing and whether the first fuel injection should occur at cylinder No. 4 or 1 (4-cylinder) or cylinder No. 3 or 4 (6-cylinder). Once synchronization has been established, the engine controller energizes the proper injector and provides the ignition output needed to start the engine.

Synchronization Signal Generator – The synchronization signal generator is located in distributor. This Hall Effect type sensor works in conjunction with engine speed signal of crankshaft position sensor providing engine controller with inputs necessary to establish and maintain proper fuel injector firing order.

When leading of pulse ring enters the sync signal generator, change in the magnetic field causes a 5-volt reference signal to be induced. On 4-cylinder engines, this indicates to the engine controller that piston No. 4 will be the next piston at Top Dead Center (TDC). On 6-cylinder engine, it indicates that piston No. 3 will be at TDC.

When trailing edge of pulse ring leaves the sync signal generator, the collapse of the magnetic field causes reference signal to drop to zero volts. On 4-cylinder engines, this indicates that piston No. 1 will be the next piston at TDC. On 6-cylinder engine, it indicates that piston No. 4 will be at TDC.

Throttle Position Sensor (TPS) – The TPS is mounted on throttle body and monitors opening angle of throttle valve. It contains a potentiometer operated by the opening and closing of throttle plate. Engine controller uses TPS input signal to determine throttle position under all operating conditions and adjust fuel injector pulse width and ignition timing accordingly.

The engine controller supplies a 5-volt reference signal to TPS. The TPS output voltage (input signal to engine controller) represents throttle blade position. The TPS output voltage varies from one volt at minimum throttle opening (idle) to 4 volts at wide open throttle.

Vehicle Speed Sensor – The vehicle speed sensor is located on transaxle extension housing (2WD models) or on transfer case extension housing (4WD models). The engine controller uses vehicle speed (distance) sensor to detect if vehicle is moving and at what speed it is moving.

The sensor is an 8-pole switch which provides a pulse or switching rate, proportional to vehicle speed, to the engine controller. By comparing the number of pulses to time elapsed, the controller determines vehicle speed and distance traveled.

The vehicle speed sensor generates 8 pulses per sensor revolution. This signal, along with a closed throttle signal from the TPS sensor, indicates a closed throttle deceleration to the engine controller.

Under deceleration conditions, engine controller adjusts the Automatic Idle Speed (AIS) motor to maintain desired MAP value. During idle (vehicle stopped), the engine controller adjusts the AIS motor to maintain a desired engine speed.

The vehicle speed (distance) sensor input is also used to maintain speed (cruise) control operation and as a reference for Emission Maintenance Reminder (EMR) light.

Vehicle Theft Alarm – Cherokee is equipped with vehicle theft alarm. The theft alarm module will provide a signal to engine controller to enable it to start the engine. With theft alarm module activated, no signal though the communication bus will be sensed by the engine controller and the engine will not start. The engine controller controls ignition and fuel delivery to the engine.

OUTPUT SIGNALS

NOTE: Vehicles are equipped with different combinations of computer-controlled components. Not all components listed below are used on every vehicle. For theory and operation on each output component, refer to the system indicated after component.

A/C Compressor Clutch Relay – See MISCELLANEOUS CONTROLS.
Alternator Light – See MISCELLANEOUS CONTROLS.
Automatic Shutdown Relay – See FUEL DELIVERY.
Automatic Idle Speed (AIS) Motor – See IDLE SPEED.
Ballast Resistor – See FUEL DELIVERY.
Ballast Resistor By-Pass Relay – See FUEL DELIVERY.
CHECK ENGINE Light – See SELF-DIAGNOSTIC SYSTEM.
Emission Maintenance Reminder (EMR) Light – See EMISSION SYSTEMS.
Fuel Injectors – See FUEL DELIVERY.
Fuel Pump Relay – See FUEL DELIVERY.
Ignition Coil – See IGNITION SYSTEM.
Injection Timing – See FUEL DELIVERY.
Radiator (Cooling) Fan Relay – See MISCELLANEOUS CONTROLS.

Serial Communication Interface Transmit - See MISCELLANEOUS CONTROLS.
Speed (Cruise) Control Solenoids - See MISCELLANEOUS CONTROLS.
Tachometer - See MISCELLANEOUS CONTROLS.
Upshift Light - See MISCELLANEOUS CONTROLS.

FUEL SYSTEM

FUEL DELIVERY

Automatic Shutdown Relay - The Automatic Shutdown (ASD) relay is located in power distribution center near the battery or next to radiator coolant recovery bottle.

The ASD relay is used by the engine controller to supply voltage to fuel pump, fuel injectors and ignition coil. The relay contacts are normally open.

Power is supplied to relay coil when the ignition switch is turned on. The engine controller controls the ground circuit, which energizes the coil and closes the relay contacts.

The engine controller will only ground the relay when ignition switch is in the RUN or START positions and some activity is sensed through the crankshaft position sensor and the synchronization signal in the distributor. If the engine controller senses the RPM signal has stopped, it will remove the ground from relay coil, which will cause the contacts to open and remove power from the circuit.

Ballast Resistor - Cherokee and Comanche models have a ballast resistor located between fuel pump relay and the fuel pump. Its purpose is to reduce voltage to the fuel pump. This reduces fuel pump noise during operation. Ballast resistor is mounted on fender panel, next to washer fluid reservoir.

When fuel pump relay is energized, voltage is supplied to fuel pump through the ballast resistor. During start and wide open throttle conditions, ballast resistor is by-passed and fuel pump receives its voltage from ballast resistor by-pass relay.

NOTE: Wrangler models DO NOT use a ballast resistor or ballast resistor by-pass relay in the fuel pump circuit. The engine controller operates fuel pump through the fuel pump relay during all operating conditions.

Ballast Resistor By-Pass Relay - Cherokee and Comanche models have a ballast resistor by-pass relay located on a bracket next to power distribution center (next to coolant recovery bottle). By switching the ground circuit on or off, the engine controller can control fuel pump (power) feed. The ballast resistor by-pass relay receives its voltage from fuel pump relay.

Normally, voltage is supplied to fuel pump through a ballast resistor. At wide open throttle, fuel pump receives voltage through the ballast resistor by-pass relay, which speeds up fuel pump to compensate for higher fuel demand.

Fuel Pump (Electric) - Cherokee, Comanche and Wrangler models are equipped with a gear/rotor type electric pump. Pump is driven by a permanent magnet, 12-volt electric motor that is immersed in fuel tank. The pump is an integral part of the fuel gauge sending unit.

Fuel system pressure is maintained at about 31 psi (2.2 kg/cm²) when pump is operating and vacuum applied to fuel pressure regulator. With no vacuum applied to fuel pressure regulator, fuel pressure should be 39-41 psi (2.7-2.9 kg/cm²) or higher. When fuel pump is not operating, fuel pressure is maintained at 19-39 psi (1.3-2.7 kg/cm²) by fuel pump outlet check valve and the fuel pressure regulator.

Fuel Pump (Mechanical) - The Grand Wagoneer is equipped with a single action mechanical fuel pump. The fuel pump is comprised of an actuating lever, an inlet valve, an outlet valve and a diaphragm and spring assembly. An eccentric cam on the engine camshaft operates the fuel pump lever, which is linked to the pump diaphragm. The lever pulls the diaphragm to its extended position to draw fuel past the inlet valve.

When the carburetor float needle valve closes, fuel pump output is limited to the amount of fuel that returns back to the fuel tank through the fuel return tube. The fuel accumulated in the fuel pump chamber prevents the diaphragm from relaxing. The actuating lever continues to move up and down, but is prevented from operating the diaphragm which is held in the extended position by fuel pressure. Fuel flow from the pump remains halted until excess pressure is released through the fuel return tube or until the carburetor float needle moves off its seat.

Fuel Pump Relay - Cherokee and Comanche models have a fuel pump relay located in the power distribution center, next to coolant recovery bottle. On Wrangler, the fuel pump relay is located in power distribution center next to battery.

The feed side of the relay coil is powered by the ignition switch. The relay is energized by the engine controller by grounding the other side of the relay coil. The relay contacts are normally open and will close when the engine controller provides a ground path for the relay coil.

The fuel pump circuit is completed during cranking and whenever the engine is running. If the ignition key is turned to the RUN position, the fuel pump will operate for 1-3 seconds and then shut off. If the engine controller DOES NOT receive a crank or run signal, it deactivates the fuel pump by opening the relay coil ground circuit. The 1-3 second time limit is used to prevent unnecessary operation of the fuel pump once the system is pressurized. If the engine were running, the engine controller would maintain the fuel pump relay coil ground allowing continuous operation of the fuel pump.

Fuel Return System - The Grand Wagoneer employs a fuel return system to reduce the possibility of high temperature fuel vapors. The fuel return system consists of a fuel filter equipped with a return nipple and a return tube to the fuel tank. During normal operation a small amount of liquid fuel is returned to the fuel tank. During periods of high under hood temperatures, vaporized fuel is returned to the fuel tank instead of being delivered to the carburetor. The fuel filter must be installed with the return fitting positioned upward to ensure proper fuel return system operation.

FUEL CONTROL

NOTE: The Grand Wagoneer 6.0L engine is equipped with a Motorcraft 2150, 2-barrel carburetor. Carburetor includes float (fuel inlet) circuit, bowl vents, idle metering (low speed) circuit, main metering (high speed) circuit, pump and power enrichment circuit, thermostatically controlled choke, and an altitude compensator circuit. Only the thermostatically controlled choke and altitude compensator circuit will be covered here.

Altitude Compensator Circuit - The altitude compensator supplies extra air necessary to lean out the air/fuel mixture at high altitudes. The compensator circuit parallels the carburetor main metering (high speed) circuit. The altitude compensator circuit has a small separate, nonadjustable choke valve that is linked directly with the primary choke valve. This small choke valve controls the airflow when the main choke is closed. *See Fig. 1.*

Air flows down through a passage in carburetor main body and into a plenum chamber located adjacent to the 2 main venturi bores. A spring-loaded valve regulates the amount of air passed from plenum into the compensator body. Air flows from altitude compensator body through 2 air passages bored into the main venturi tubes.

The opening and closing of the valve in the compensator body is controlled by an aneroid bellow that reacts to atmospheric pressure. At lower atmospheric pressures (high altitude), the bellow pushes on the end of the compensator valve stem, opening the valve. At lower altitudes, the aneroid bellow relaxes, automatically closing the valve. The aneroid bellow is calibrated during factory assembly and is NOT adjustable.

Fuel Injectors - The fuel injectors are controlled electronically by the engine controller. Because each injector is connected to 12 volts, the injector is energized when connected to ground through the engine controller. The engine controller also controls the amount of time the

1991 ENGINE PERFORMANCE
Theory & Operation (Cont.)

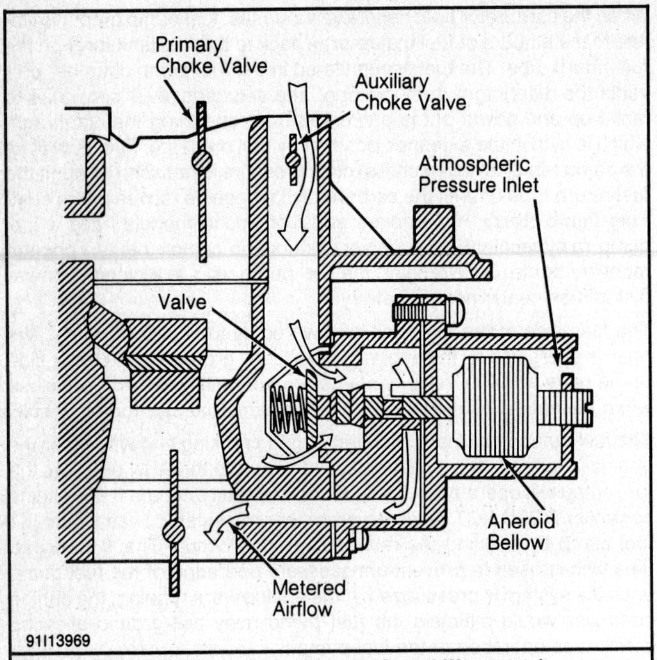
Primary
Choke Valve
Auxiliary
Choke Valve
Atmospheric
Pressure Inlet
Valve
Aneroid
Bellow
Metered
Airflow
91I13969

Fig. 1: Altitude Compensator Circuit (Grand Wagoneer)

injector is energized (pulse width). Pulse width is based on various inputs and is calculated by the engine controller. The fuel injectors are sequentially energized, by firing order, by the engine controller.

With injector connected to a pressurized fuel supply, a fine mist will spray from the injector nozzle into the intake manifold. The injector uses an electromagnet and spring pressure to open or close the fuel metering plunger. When connected to battery voltage, the coil of wire in the injector becomes an electromagnet. The magnetic field generated will overcome spring pressure and raise the plunger off its seat. When the injector circuit is opened by the engine controller, the magnetic field collapses and spring pressure forces the plunger against its seat.

Whenever an injector is opened, it will always spray a consistent amount of fuel for a given amount of pressure. Because pressure drop across the injector is fixed and the fuel flow rate constant, the only control variable is the amount of time injector is open. By controlling the time the injector is open (pulse width), the engine controller can decrease pulse width for engine idle or it can increase pulse width at wide open throttle.

Injection Timing – The 2.5L and 4.0L engine use a sequential port fuel injection system. This means that the injectors have a specific firing order and fuel injection is timed to piston movement. The spark plugs and injectors are fired in the same order: 1-3-4-2 on 2.5L and 1-5-3-6-2-4 on 4.0L.

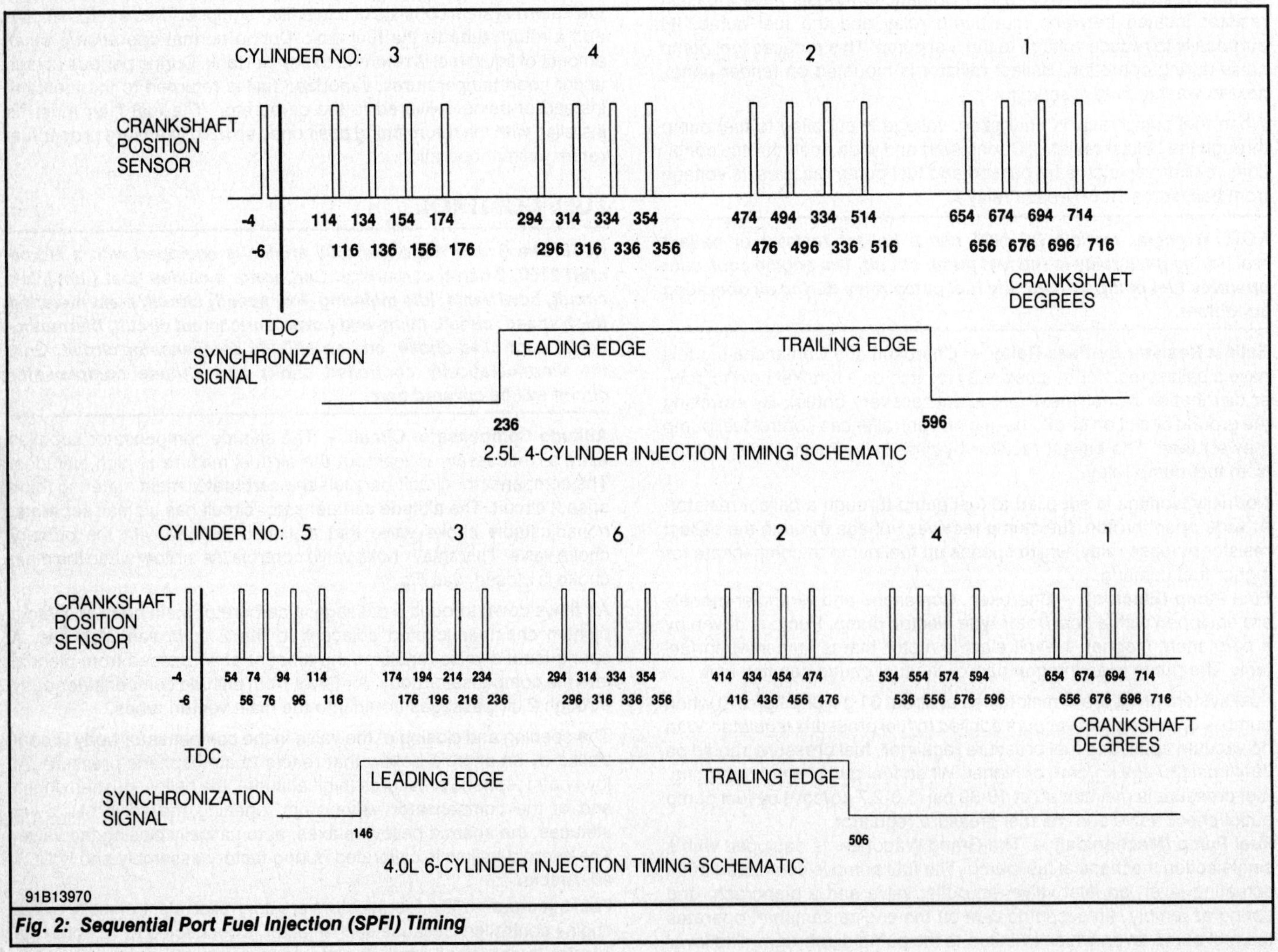
CYLINDER NO: 3 4 2 1
CRANKSHAFT
POSITION
SENSOR
-4 114 134 154 174 294 314 334 354 474 494 334 514 654 674 694 714
-6 116 136 156 176 296 316 336 356 476 496 336 516 656 676 696 716
CRANKSHAFT
DEGREES
TDC
SYNCHRONIZATION
SIGNAL
LEADING EDGE
TRAILING EDGE
236
596
2.5L 4-CYLINDER INJECTION TIMING SCHEMATIC
CYLINDER NO: 5 3 6 2 4 1
CRANKSHAFT
POSITION
SENSOR
-4 54 74 94 114 174 194 214 234 294 314 334 354 414 434 454 474 534 554 574 594 654 674 694 714
-6 56 76 96 116 176 196 216 236 296 316 336 356 416 436 456 476 536 556 576 596 656 676 696 716
CRANKSHAFT
DEGREES
TDC
SYNCHRONIZATION
SIGNAL
LEADING EDGE
TRAILING EDGE
146
506
4.0L 6-CYLINDER INJECTION TIMING SCHEMATIC
91B13970

Fig. 2: Sequential Port Fuel Injection (SPFI) Timing

1991 ENGINE PERFORMANCE
Theory & Operation (Cont.)

In order for the engine controller to fire the injectors in a specific order timed to crankshaft and piston movement, it has to establish a reference point. Establishing the reference point requires engine controller inputs from the crankshaft position sensor and synchronization signal generator.

The crankshaft position sensor is located on transmission bellhousing and provides the engine controller with crankshaft angle and speed. The engine controller converts crankshaft speed into engine RPM and crankshaft angle into piston position.

On 2.5L engine, the slotted flywheel/drive plate, rotating past the sensor, contains 2 groups of 4 slots located 180 degrees apart. Each group of slots represents the position of two of the pistons. Pistons No. 1 and 4 approach TDC at the same time and use the same flywheel slot, while piston No. 3 is matched with piston No. 2.

On 4.0L engine, the slotted flywheel/drive plate, rotating past the sensor, contains 3 groups of 4 slots located 120 degrees apart. Each group of slots represents the position of two of the pistons. Pistons No. 1 and 6 approach TDC at the same time and use the same flywheel slot. Pistons No. 2 and 5 are matched, while piston No. 3 is matched with piston No. 4.

The engine controller, through the crankshaft position sensor, knows that two pistons are approaching TDC and uses the sync signal generator to determine which injector/spark plug to fire. *See Fig. 2.*

Thermostatically Controlled Choke – The choke valve is located in the air horn assembly and provides a richer air/fuel mixture required for cold engine starting and operation. The choke shaft is connected by linkage to a bimetallic coil that winds up when cold and unwinds when warm.

When engine is cold, tension of the bimetallic coil holds the choke valve closed. When the engine is started, manifold vacuum is channeled through an opening at the base of the carburetor through a passage on the bottom side of the modulator diaphragm assembly, to move the diaphragm downward against the set screw. At the same time, the modulator arm contacts a tang on the choke shaft. The downward movement of the diaphragm assembly compresses the piston spring and exerts a pulling force on the modulator arm, causing the choke valve to open slightly.

The bimetallic coil is warmed by an electric heater element and, as the engine warms, heated air is routed from the exhaust crossover through a heat tube to the choke housing. The heater element and heated air entering the choke housing cause the bimetallic coil to begin unwinding and decrease the closing tension exerted against the choke valve. The coil gradually loses it tension and allows the choke valve to open.

A thermostatically controlled by-pass valve, helps prevent premature choke valve opening during an early part of engine warm-up period. The valve regulates temperature of the hot air flow to the choke housing by allowing unheated air to enter the heat tube. A thermostatic disc which is incorporated into the valve, is calibrated to close the valve at 75°F (24°C) and open the valve at 55°F (13°C).

The fast idle cam, actuated by the choke rod, contacts the fast idle speed adjustment screw and increases engine speed in proportion to choke valve opening. When the choke valve reaches the fully open position, the fast idle cam rotates free of the fast idle speed adjustment screw and allows the throttle lever to return to curb idle speed position.

IDLE SPEED

Automatic Idle Speed (AIS) Motor – The AIS motor is mounted on throttle body and is used by the engine controller to adjust engine idle speed. The throttle plate regulates off idle engine speed by controlling the amount of air allowed to enter the intake manifold and is mechanically operated by the accelerator cable.

The engine controller and idle stepper motor adjust engine idle by regulating the size of an air by-pass passage that routes air past the closed throttle plate. The amount of air flowing through the by-pass circuit depends on engine operating conditions at idle.

When the engine is cold, the engine controller increases engine speed by retracting the stepper motor pintle, thus allowing more air to enter the intake manifold. To maintain the proper air/fuel mixture, more fuel is also injected into the intake manifold. The increased air/fuel mixture, in turn, raises the engine idle speed. As the engine warms up, the engine controller will extend the stepper motor pintle into the air passage to reduce the amount of air by-passing the throttle plate.

IGNITION SYSTEM

SBEC-II CONTROLLED IGNITION SYSTEM

The Cherokee, Comanche, and Wrangler 2.5L or 4.0L engines use a Single Board Engine Controller-II (SBEC-II) based ignition system. Base ignition timing is NOT adjustable with this system. The SBEC-II controlled ignition system consists of coolant temperature sensor, crankshaft position sensor, distributor (includes rotor and synchronization sensor), ignition coil, manifold absolute pressure sensor, Single Board Engine Controller-II, and throttle position sensor.

Coolant Temperature Sensor – See INPUT DEVICES.

Crankshaft Position Sensor – See INPUT DEVICES.

Distributor – Distributor consists of cap, rotor, and synchronization signal generator. The distributor does not have built-in centrifugal or vacuum advance mechanisms to advance ignition timing. Ignition timing advance is electronically controlled by the engine controller. See SYNCHRONIZATION SIGNAL GENERATOR under INPUT DEVICES.

Ignition Coil – The ignition coil is constructed of epoxy-embedded windings and is not oil filled. Battery voltage is supplied to the ignition coil positive terminal. The engine controller receives inputs from the appropriate sensors. Based on these inputs, it then determines the proper ignition timing and interrupts the ignition coil ground signal to trigger secondary voltage of the ignition coil.

Manifold Absolute Pressure Sensor – See INPUT DEVICES.

Manifold Air Temperature Sensor – See INPUT DEVICES.

Single Board Engine Controller-II – The engine controller opens and closes the ignition coil ground circuit to adjust ignition timing according to engine operating conditions. The amount of electronic spark advance provided by the engine controller is determined by coolant temperature sensor, crankshaft position sensor (engine RPM), manifold absolute pressure sensor and throttle position sensor inputs. See COMPUTERIZED ENGINE CONTROLS for additional information.

Throttle Position Sensor – See INPUT DEVICES.

SOLID STATE IGNITION SYSTEM

The Grand Wagoneer 6.0L engine is equipped with a Solid State Ignition (SSI) system. The SSI system consists of ignition module, ignition coil, resistance wire, and distributor (pick-up coil and trigger wheel). Base ignition timing is adjustable with this system.

The ignition module is activated when ignition switch is in the START or ON position. The primary circuit is closed and current flows through the coil primary winding. When camshaft turns distributor, the trigger wheel teeth rotate past the pick-up coil assembly (in the distributor). As each tooth aligns with the pick-up coil, the resulting pulse triggers the ignition module which opens the coil primary circuit. A high voltage is then induced in the coil secondary winding and current flows to the distributor cap and rotor. As the rotor spins it distributes high voltage to the proper spark plug. Ignition timing is constantly changed by electronic, vacuum, and centrifugal advance mechanisms according to engine operating conditions.

Distributor – The distributor consist of cap, rotor, pick-up coil and trigger wheel, centrifugal and vacuum advance mechanisms. The distributor drive gear installed on the distributor shaft meshes with a spiral cut gear on the camshaft. The end of the distributor shaft is flattened and drives the oil pump. Flyweights connected to the distributor provide a means for centrifugal advance. Carburetor ported vacuum is used for vacuum advance.

Ignition Coil – The ignition coil is mounted on a bracket attached to intake manifold. Coil operation is controlled by the ignition module. Primary coil resistance is 1.11-1.25 ohms. Secondary coil resistance is 7650-9370 ohms.

1991 ENGINE PERFORMANCE
Theory & Operation (Cont.)

Ignition Module – The electronic ignition module is located in engine compartment on left wheelwell. It is a permanently sealed, solid state module that is not repairable. The ignition module processes ignition signals it receives from the distributor and then interrupts the primary circuit to the ignition coil causing spark to occur.

Pick-Up Coil & Trigger Wheel – The ignition coil primary circuit is opened and closed electronically by the ignition module. The pick-up coil and trigger wheel provide the input signal for the ignition module. The trigger wheel is installed on the distributor shaft and has one tooth for each cylinder. The pick-up coil has a magnetic field that is intensified by the presence of ferrous metal and reacts to the trigger wheel teeth as they pass.

As a trigger wheel tooth approaches and passes the pole piece of the pick-up coil, it reduces the reluctance to the magnetic field and increases field strength. Field strength decreases as the tooth moves away from the pole piece. The increase and decrease of field strength induces an alternating current in the pick-up coil, which triggers the ignition module. The ignition module opens or closes the coil primary circuit according to the position of the trigger wheel teeth.

Resistance Wire – A 1.35-ohm resistance wire is installed in the ignition system wiring to supply less than full battery voltage to the ignition coil after the starter motor solenoid is de-energized. During engine cranking, the resistance wire is by-passed and full battery voltage is applied to the ignition coil. The by-pass is accomplished through the "I" terminals of the starter motor solenoid.

EMISSION SYSTEMS

CRANKCASE VENTILATION (CCV) SYSTEM

Cherokee, Comanche, and Wrangler engines use a crankcase ventilation system. The CCV system performs the same function as a conventional PCV system, but does not use a vacuum controlled valve. On 2.5L engine, a fitting on the driver's side of the cylinder head cover contains a metered orifice that is connected to manifold vacuum. On 4.0L engine, a molded vacuum tube connects manifold vacuum to the top of the cylinder head cover. The molded vacuum tube contains a fixed, calibrated orifice that meters the amount of crankcase vapors drawn out of the engine.

On both engines, a fresh air supply hose from the air cleaner is connected to the cylinder head cover. When the engine is operating, fresh air enters the engine and mixes with crankcase vapors. Manifold vacuum then draws the crankcase vapors/air mixture through the fixed orifice and into the engine by intake manifold vacuum.

EMISSION MAINTENANCE REMINDER LIGHT

The Emission Maintenance Reminder (EMR) light on instrument cluster is an indicator to vehicle owner that components of the vehicle's emission system are scheduled for service or replacement.

The emission maintenance reminder function is built into the engine controller. The engine controller reads vehicle speed (distance) sensor and stores mileage information in a non-volatile, resettable memory. When the engine controller sees that the appropriate mileage has accumulated, about 82,500 miles (133,000 kilometers), it will turn on the EMR light.

The EMR light must be turned off and the engine controller reset by using Chrysler's Diagnostic Readout Box-II (DRB-II). If the engine controller has been replaced, the current EMR mileage must be installed into the replacement engine controller to maintain correct EMR light function. This procedure can only be accomplished by using the DRB-II diagnostic tester.

EVAPORATIVE EMISSION SYSTEM

This system stores fuel vapors from fuel tank, preventing vapors from reaching the atmosphere. As fuel evaporates inside fuel tank, vapors are routed inside vent hoses to evaporative canister, where they are stored until engine is started.

On Cherokee, Comanche and Wrangler, evaporative canister is equipped with a purge shutoff switch that controls canister purge operation. The switch is open when manifold vacuum is applied to it. The air cleaner contains a venturi as a purge line vacuum source. The effect of the venturi increases the speed of the intake air flowing by the slots in the venturi wall, creating a low pressure area around the slots. When the purge shutoff switch is open, vapors from the canister are drawn through slots and into the airstream flowing through the venturi. The vapors then pass through the intake manifold and into the engine combustion chambers.

On Grand Wagoneer, vacuum supply for the canister purge signal is controlled by coolant temperature. A Coolant Temperature Operated (CTO) valve restricts the purge signal vacuum flow to the canister until engine coolant temperature reaches 123-127°F (51-53°C). Once the CTO valve has opened, purge signal vacuum flows through the purge signal line to the canister. Vacuum from the purge signal line opens a one-way valve in the canister. When valve is open. fuel vapors stored in the canister are drawn into the engine by intake manifold vacuum.

Evaporative Canister – The evaporative canister used in Jeep vehicles is filled with granules of an activated carbon mixture. Fuel vapors entering the canister are absorbed by the granules. The evaporative canister has one inlet connected to the pressure relief/rollover valves of the fuel tank through hoses and tubes. On Grand Wagoneer, the evaporative canister has two inlet ports. One port connects to the fuel tank pressure relief/rollover valves and the other connect to the carburetor bowl vent valve.

Pressure Relief/Rollover Valves – All Jeep vehicle fuel tanks are equipped with two pressure relief/rollover valves. The dual function valves relieve fuel tank pressure and prevent fuel flow through fuel tank vent hoses in the event of a vehicle rollover. The valve consists of a plunger, spring, orifice and guide plate. The valve is normally open, allowing fuel vapors to vent to the canister where they are stored.

If bottom of plunger is contacted by sloshing fuel in fuel tank, the plunger seats in the guide plate, preventing liquid fuel from reaching the evaporative canister. In a vehicle rollover, the valve is inverted. This forces the plunger against the guide plate and fuel is prevented from flowing through the valve orifice and into fuel tank vent tube.

EXHAUST GAS RECIRCULATION (EGR) SYSTEM

The Grand Wagoneer 6.0L engine is equipped with an EGR system. System consists of EGR valve, EGR valve transducer, coolant temperature override valve, thermal vacuum switch, and connecting hoses.

Thermal Vacuum Switch (TVS) – The TVS is located in center of air cleaner. The TVS functions as an on/off switch and is controlled by air cleaner intake air temperature. At air temperatures below 40-50°F (4-10°C), the TVS prevents vacuum from opening the EGR valve thus improving cold engine driveability. If intake air temperature in air cleaner has reached 55°F (13°C), the thermal vacuum switch will open permitting vacuum to reach EGR valve transducer.

Coolant Temperature Override (CTO) Valve – The CTO valve is located at front of intake manifold, between oil filler tube and thermostat. When coolant temperature is lower than 155°F (68°C), no vacuum is applied to EGR valve. The CTO valve restricts vacuum flow to the thermal vacuum switch until coolant reaches 155°F (68°C). Once CTO valve opens, vacuum flows to thermal vacuum switch.

EGR Valve Transducer – The EGR valve transducer is connected to EGR valve by a vacuum hose and a backpressure hose. The transducer is controlled by exhaust system backpressure and is ported to exhaust manifold through a hose connecting it to the bottom of the EGR valve. When exhaust system backpressure is high enough, a bleed valve in the transducer will close, allowing vacuum to actuate the EGR valve. If backpressure does not close the bleed valve in the transducer, vacuum will be bled off.

When vacuum is applied to EGR valve, a metered amount of exhaust gas will be drawn into the intake manifold and mixed with air/fuel mixture.

POSITIVE CRANKCASE VENTILATION (PCV) SYSTEM

The Grand Wagoneer 6.0L engine is equipped with a PCV system. The PCV system prevents crankcase vapors from entering the atmosphere. Filtered air from the crankcase is routed through the PCV inlet hose and into the crankcase, forcing crankcase vapors through the PCV outlet hose into the engine by intake manifold vacuum.

Crankcase Vent Filter – The crankcase vent filter is used to filter fresh air before it enters crankcase through the PCV system. The filter is located on oil filler cap.

PCV Valve – The PCV valve contains a spring-loaded plunger that meters the amount of crankcase vapors routed into the engine combustion chambers based on intake manifold vacuum. When the engine is not running or during an engine backfire, the spring forces the plunger back against the seat preventing vapors from flowing through the PCV valve.

During periods of high manifold vacuum, such as idle or cruising speeds, manifold vacuum is high enough to completely compress the spring and pull the plunger to the top of the valve. In this position, there is minimal vapor flow through the PCV valve. During periods of moderate intake manifold vacuum, the plunger is pulled partially away from seat, resulting in maximum vapor flow through the PCV valve.

THERMOSTATIC AIR CLEANER (TAC)

The Grand Wagoneer 6.0L engine is equipped with a TAC system. The TAC system provides heated air for the carburetor during engine warm-up. The TAC system consists of heat stove, heated air tube, thermal switch, reverse delay valve, check valve, vacuum motor and air valve assembly.

SELF-DIAGNOSTIC SYSTEM

CHECK ENGINE LIGHT

The CHECK ENGINE light lets the driver know if the engine controller has recorded a system or sensor malfunctions. CHECK ENGINE light will come on if vehicle goes into a "limp-in" mode. The CHECK ENGINE can also be used to display fault codes. By cycling the ignition on, off, on, off and on within 5 seconds, the engine controller will display the fault codes in a series of flashes representing numbers. For additional information, see SELF-DIAGNOSTICS article.

MISCELLANEOUS CONTROLS

NOTE: Although not considered true engine performance-related systems, some controlled devices may affect driveability if they malfunction.

A/C COMPRESSOR CLUTCH RELAY

The engine controller controls the A/C compressor clutch through a relay. This allows the engine controller to receive an A/C select signal when driver moves mode lever into A/C position. The engine controller also receives a request signal from the A/C temperature control thermostat (evaporator switch).

The engine controller then adjusts idle speed using the AIS motor. Only then can the engine controller activate the A/C compressor clutch through the A/C compressor clutch relay. The increased idle speed will compensate for the additional load caused by the A/C compressor.

On 4.0L engine, whenever the A/C compressor clutch is energized, the engine controller also energizes the radiator (cooling) fan relay. This occurs regardless on engine coolant temperature.

ALTERNATOR LIGHT

The alternator (charging indicator) light on the standard (base) instrument cluster will come on if the engine controller senses a low charging condition or an overcharging condition. Once engine controller compensates for the accessory electrical load, alternator light should go out.

RADIATOR COOLING FAN RELAY

An electric radiator cooling fan is used on Cherokee and Comanche models with the 4.0L engine and A/C or heavy duty cooling. Normal operation of the radiator cooling fan is controlled by the engine controller through the coolant sensor input. Cooling fan will also operate whenever A/C compressor clutch is activated, regardless of temperature.

When engine coolant temperature reaches 217°F (103°C), engine controller supplies radiator cooling fan relay with a ground path which closes the radiator cooling fan relay contacts and allows battery voltage from the ignition switch to reach radiator cooling fan motor.

SPEED (CRUISE) CONTROL SOLENOIDS

The engine controller controls the vacuum vent, and dump solenoids when operating the cruise control system. When the SET button is pushed, the engine controller sees voltage on terminal No. 48. When button is released, the voltage signal is removed and the engine controller locks in a set speed for the system. The set speed becomes the target for the cruise control system to maintain. The cruise control system will not permit speeds higher than 85 MPH to be set.

The engine controller energizes the vacuum solenoids located in the cruise control servo assembly to open the throttle to maintain the set speed. To increase set speed, the engine controller grounds the vacuum solenoid through terminal No. 33 of the engine controller. The solenoid receives battery voltage with ignition on and as long as the brakes are off. The vacuum solenoid is spring loaded to block vacuum from getting into the servo diaphragm. When energized, vacuum solenoid is pulled open, allowing vacuum to enter servo diaphragm and open throttle.

At the same time vacuum solenoid is being commanded to open the throttle, the engine controller must supply a ground to the vent solenoid. The vent solenoid is spring loaded so that when it is not energized, it bleeds vacuum from the servo chamber. The vent solenoid receives battery voltage with ignition switch on and as long as the brakes are off. When the engine controller supplies the vent solenoid with a ground, the solenoid blocks the leakage of vacuum from the servo chamber. To increase throttle opening, the engine controller grounds the vacuum solenoid. To reduce throttle opening, the engine controller grounds the vent solenoid.

Anytime the brakes are applied, the brake switch will interrupt power supply to the dump solenoid which causes it to vent vacuum as the vent and vacuum solenoids return to their relaxed (non-energized) positions by opening their ground circuits. The dump solenoid is reset when the brakes are released but the engine controller will only reactivate the vacuum and vent solenoids when the RESUME switch is pushed.

UPSHIFT INDICATOR LIGHT

Vehicles equipped with a manual transmission have an upshift light located in the instrument cluster. The upshift light is controlled by the engine controller and will illuminate the light to inform the driver when to shift to the next higher gear for best fuel economy. The engine controller determines which gear should be used by observing and remembering RPM and manifold absolute pressure values. A high gear switch is NOT used in the transmission.

1991 ENGINE PERFORMANCE
Basic Diagnostic Procedures

Cherokee, Comanche, Grand Wagoneer, Wrangler

INTRODUCTION

The following diagnostic steps will help prevent overlooking a simple problem. This is also where to begin diagnosis for a no-start condition.

The first step in diagnosing any driveability problem is verifying the customer's complaint with a test drive under the conditions the problem reportedly occurred.

Before entering self-diagnostics (if equipped), perform a careful and complete visual inspection. Most engine control problems result from mechanical breakdowns, poor electrical connections or damaged/misrouted vacuum hoses. Before condemning the computerized system, perform each test listed in this article.

NOTE: Perform all voltage tests with a Digital Volt-Ohmmeter (DVOM) with a minimum 10-megohm input impedance, unless stated otherwise in test procedure.

PRELIMINARY INSPECTION & ADJUSTMENTS

VISUAL INSPECTION

Visually inspect all electrical wiring, looking for chafed, stretched, cut or pinched wiring. Ensure electrical connectors fit tightly and are not corroded. Ensure vacuum hoses are properly routed and are not pinched or cut. See VACUUM DIAGRAMS article to verify routing and connections (if necessary). Inspect air induction system for possible vacuum leaks.

MECHANICAL INSPECTION

Compression – Check engine mechanical condition with a compression gauge, vacuum gauge, or an engine analyzer. See engine analyzer manual for specific instructions.

WARNING: DO NOT use ignition switch during compression tests on fuel injected vehicles. Use a remote starter to crank engine. Fuel injectors on many models are triggered by ignition switch during cranking mode, which can create a fire hazard or contaminate the engine's oiling system.

2.5L & 4.0L COMPRESSION RATIO

Application	Specification
Compression Ratio	
2.5L	9.2:1
4.0L	8.8:1

NOTE: Compression pressure and cylinder pressure variation for 2.5L and 4.0L engines are not available from manufacturer.

6.0L COMPRESSION SPECIFICATIONS

Application	Specification
Compression Ratio	8.25:1
Minimum Compression Pressure	120 psi (8.4 kg/cm²)
Maximum Variation Between Cylinders	30 psi (2.1 kg/cm²)

Exhaust System Backpressure – The exhaust system can be checked with a vacuum or pressure gauge. Remove O_2 sensor or air injection check valve (if equipped). Connect a 0-5 psi pressure gauge and run engine at 2500 RPM. If exhaust system backpressure is greater than 1 3/4 - 2 psi, exhaust system or catalytic converter is plugged.

If a vacuum gauge is used, connect vacuum gauge hose to intake manifold vacuum port and start engine. Observe vacuum gauge. Open throttle part way and hold steady. If vacuum gauge reading slowly drops after stabilizing, check exhaust system for restriction.

FUEL SYSTEM

FUEL PRESSURE

Basic diagnosis of fuel system should begin with determining fuel system pressure.

WARNING: ALWAYS relieve fuel pressure before disconnecting any fuel injection-related component. DO NOT allow fuel to contact engine or electrical components.

Fuel Pressure Release (2.5L & 4.0L) – Disconnect negative battery cable. Remove fuel filler cap. Remove cap from pressure test port on fuel rail. Position shop towels to soak up any spilled fuel. Using a small screwdriver or pin punch, push test port valve in to relieve fuel pressure. *See Fig. 1.* Install cap over test port.

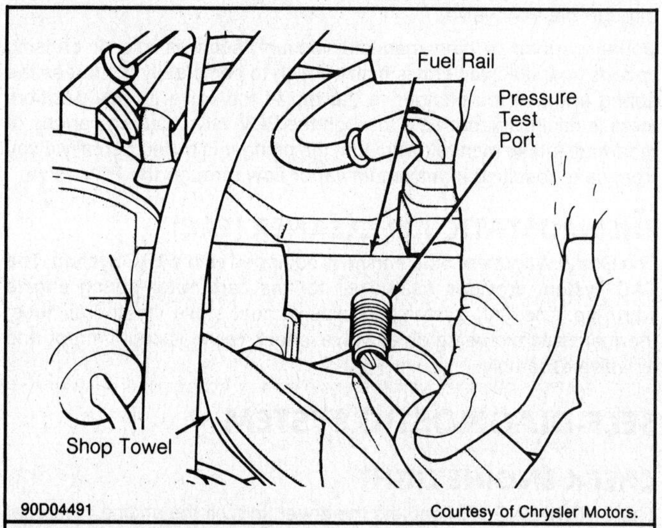
Fuel Rail
Pressure Test Port
Shop Towel
90D04491
Courtesy of Chrysler Motors.

Fig. 1: Releasing Fuel Pressure (2.5L & 4.0L)

Deadhead Pressure (2.5L & 4.0L) – **1)** Relieve fuel pressure. See FUEL PRESSURE RELEASE (2.5L & 4.0L). Connect a 0-60 psi (0-4.2 kg/cm²) fuel pressure gauge to the pressure test port fitting on fuel rail.

2) Remove fuel pump relay (located in power distribution center). Using a jumper wire, connect terminals No. 30 and 87. *See Fig. 2.* Note fuel pressure gauge, and momentarily pinch fuel return line.

3) Fuel pressure should be at least 53 psi (3.7 kg/cm²). DO NOT allow pressure to exceed 60 psi (4.2 kg/cm²). Release fuel return line.

Fuel System Pressure Test (2.5L & 4.0L) – **1)** Relieve fuel pressure. See FUEL PRESSURE RELEASE (25.L & 4.0L). Connect a 0-60 psi (0-4.2 kg/cm²) fuel pressure gauge to the pressure test port fitting on fuel rail.

2) Remove vacuum line from fuel pressure regulator. Start vehicle and note gauge reading. Reconnect vacuum line and note gauge reading. See FUEL SYSTEM PRESSURE SPECIFICATIONS table. Ensure pressure readings are as specified. If fuel pressure is not higher with vacuum line disconnected, inspect pressure regulator vacuum line for cause of no vacuum.

3) If fuel pressure is too high, inspect fuel return line for kinks and blockage. If fuel pressure is low, momentarily pinch fuel return line. If pressure remains low, inspect fuel supply line, fuel filter and fuel rail inlet for blockage. If fuel pressure rises, replace fuel pressure regulator.

FUEL SYSTEM PRESSURE SPECIFICATIONS

Application	psi (kg/cm²)
2.5L & 4.0L	
Vacuum Line Disconnected	39 (2.7)
Vacuum Line Connected	31 (2.2)

Fuel Pump Pressure Test (6.0L) – **1)** Disconnect fuel inlet fitting at carburetor. Connect pressure gauge between filter and carburetor.

2) Operate engine at idle speed. Note pressure reading on gauge. See FUEL PUMP PRESSURE SPECIFICATIONS table. If pump pressure is not within specification, replace pump. If pump pressure is within specification, perform capacity test. See CAPACITY (VOLUME) TEST (6.0L).

FUEL PUMP PRESSURE SPECIFICATIONS

Application	psi (kg/cm^2)
6.0L	5-6.5 (.34-.45)

Fuel System Rest Pressure (2.5L & 4.0L) – 1) Relieve fuel pressure. See FUEL PRESSURE RELEASE (2.5L & 4.0L). Connect a 0-60 psi (0-4.2 kg/cm^2) fuel pressure gauge to the pressure test port fitting on fuel rail. Start engine and note reading on pressure gauge. Shut engine off.
2) Wait 30 minutes and check fuel pressure. Fuel pressure should be within 20 psi (1.4 kg/cm^2) of first reading. If pressure is not as indicated, check fuel system for leaks at fuel pressure regulator, fuel pump check valve or fuel injectors.
Capacity (Volume) Test (2.5L & 4.0L) – 1) Relieve fuel pressure. SEE FUEL PRESSURE RELEASE (2.5L & 4.0L). Disconnect fuel line on fuel rail. Place fuel line into a graduated container.
2) Remove fuel pump relay (located in power distribution center). Using a jumper wire, connect terminals No. 30 and 87. *See Fig. 2.* Volume of fuel should be 1.05 quarts (1.0L) in one minute. If fuel volume is not as specified, check for a plugged fuel filter or fuel pump inlet sock.
Capacity (Volume) Test (6.0L) – Disconnect fuel inlet at carburetor. Run engine at idle. Allow fuel to flow into graduated container for 30 seconds. Volume of fuel should be one pint (.47L). If fuel volume is not as specified, check for restriction in fuel pipe from tank, and for proper fuel tank venting.
Fuel Pump Relay (2.5L & 4.0L) – 1) Disconnect negative battery cable. Remove Single-Board Engine Controller II (SBEC-II) harness connector. Reconnect battery cable.
2) Turn ignition on. Check for voltage at Dark Green/Yellow wire (Orange/Green wire on Wrangler) in SBEC-II harness connector. If voltage is not present, go to step **5)**. If voltage is present, ground the wire. Fuel pump should work.

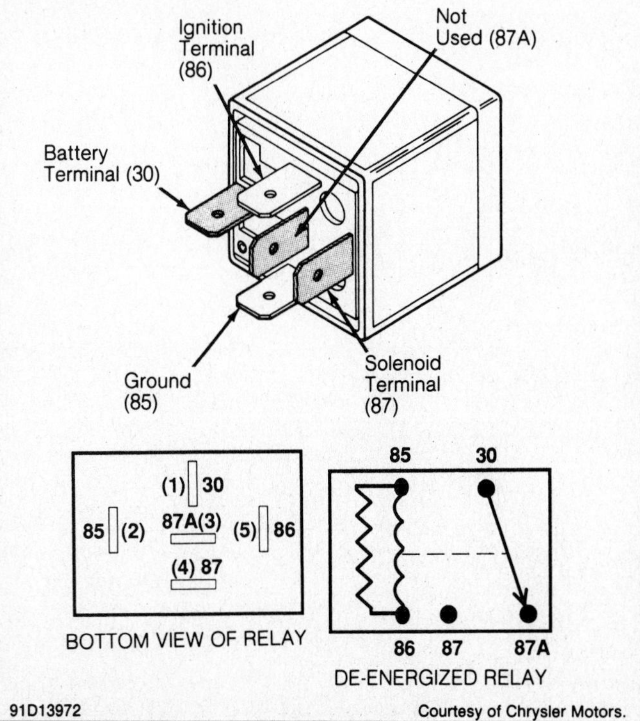
Ignition Terminal (86)
Not Used (87A)
Battery Terminal (30)
Ground (85)
Solenoid Terminal (87)
(1) 30
85 (2)
87A(3)
(5) 86
(4) 87
BOTTOM VIEW OF RELAY
85
30
86
87
87A
DE-ENERGIZED RELAY
91D13972
Courtesy of Chrysler Motors.

Fig. 2: Identifying Fuel Pump Relay Terminals

3) If fuel pump does not work, check if relay clicks. If relay does not click, go to step **6)**. If relay clicks, ensure voltage is present at relay terminals No. 30 (battery) and 87 (fuel pump), and at fuel pump. *See Fig. 2.*
4) If fuel pump still does not work, check ballast resistor (Cherokee and Comanche only) and fuel pump ground. If ballast resistor and ground are okay, replace fuel pump.
5) If no voltage is present, ensure wire has continuity to fuel pump relay terminal No. 85. Ensure voltage (from ignition switch) is present at relay terminal No. 86. *See Fig. 2.*
6) If all circuits are okay or fuel pump relay did not click in step **3)**, check resistance between relay terminals No. 86 and 85. *See Fig. 2.* Resistance should be 70-80 ohms. If resistance is not 70-80 ohms, replace relay.
7) Disconnect negative battery terminal. Reconnect SBEC-II harness connector. Connect battery cable. Check if fuel pump works. If fuel pump does not work, see appropriate SELF-DIAGNOSTICS article and check SBEC-II.

IGNITION CHECKS

SECONDARY SPARK

Spark Test – 1) Remove coil wire from distributor cap. Hold end of cable about 1/4" from ground. Crank engine. Spark should be present and constant. If spark is not present and constant, check coil and coil wire resistance. Perform IGNITION PRIMARY test under IGNITION CHECKS.
2) If coil wire spark is present, ensure spark reaches spark plugs. Check condition of rotor, cap, spark plug wires and spark plugs. Repair or replace if necessary.
Spark Plug & Coil Wire Resistance – Resistance should be 250-1000 ohms per inch.
Ignition Coil Resistance Test – 1) Remove primary and secondary leads from ignition coil. Using ohmmeter, check primary resistance between positive and negative terminals of coil. See IGNITION COIL RESISTANCE SPECIFICATIONS table.
2) Check secondary resistance between center tower and negative terminal of coil. See IGNITION COIL RESISTANCE SPECIFICATIONS table. Replace coil if readings are not within specification.

IGNITION COIL RESISTANCE SPECIFICATIONS

Application	Ohms
2.5L & 4.0L	
Primary Resistance	
75°F (24°C)	.95-1.20
Secondary Resistance	
75°F (24°C)	
Diamond	11,300-15,300
Toyodenso	11,300-13,300
6.0L	
Primary Resistance	
75°F (24°C)	1.13-1.23
200°F (93°C)	1.5
Secondary Resistance	
75°F (24°C)	7700-9300
200°F (93°C)	12,000

IGNITION PRIMARY

NOTE: Perform SECONDARY SPARK under IGNITION CHECKS before proceeding with test.

2.5L & 4.0L – 1) Ensure battery has a minimum of 12.5 volts (9.5 cranking volts) available to operate cranking and ignition systems.
2) Using an analog voltmeter, backprobe the following wires at distributor. Touch positive lead to Tan/Yellow wire (Gray/Black wire on Wrangler). Touch negative lead to the Black/Blue wire (Brown/Red wire on Wrangler).
3) Set voltmeter to 15-volt DC scale. Crank engine. Voltmeter needle should fluctuate between 0-5 volts. If voltmeter needle does not fluc-

1991 ENGINE PERFORMANCE
Basic Diagnostic Procedures (Cont.)

tuate between 0-5 volts, check related circuits or replace sync pulse generator. If sync pulse generator is okay, but engine does not start, see appropriate SELF-DIAGNOSTICS article and check SBEC-II.

6.0L – 1) Turn ignition on. Using voltmeter, check voltage between positive terminal of ignition coil and ground. If voltage is 5.5-6.5 volts, go to next step. If voltage is not 5.5-6.5 volts, check ignition switch, radio capacitor, connections and coil. Ensure resistance wire, between ignition switch and coil, is 1.3-1.4 ohms.

2) Turn ignition switch to START position while observing voltmeter. Battery voltage should exist. If battery voltage is not present, check wire attached to starter solenoid "I" terminal. Check starter solenoid for proper operation.

3) Disconnect 2-wire connector at ignition module. Turn ignition on. Ensure battery voltage is present at Yellow wire. Turn ignition switch to START position. Ensure battery voltage is present at Green wire. Repair or replace if necessary.

4) Disconnect 4-wire connector at ignition module. Resistance between terminals "C" (White wire) and "D" (Light Blue wire) should be 400-800 ohms. If resistance is not 400-800 ohms, check wiring and pick-up coil in distributor.

5) Ensure terminal "B" (Black wire) has continuity to ground. Repair or replace if necessary. Ensure terminal "A" (Green wire) has continuity to negative side of coil. If terminal "A" (Green wire) is shorted to ground, repair wire and replace ignition module.

6) Reconnect ignition module connectors. Repeat SECONDARY SPARK test under IGNITION CHECKS. If there is still no spark, replace ignition module.

IDLE SPEED & IGNITION TIMING

Ensure idle speed and ignition timing are set to specification. See CURB IDLE SPEED and IGNITION TIMING tables. For adjustment procedures, see ON-VEHICLE ADJUSTMENTS article.

NOTE: Curb idle speed and ignition timing on 2.5L and 4.0L are controlled by the Single-Board Engine Controller II (SBEC-II) and are not adjustable.

CURB IDLE SPEED

Application	Idle RPM
6.0L	600

IGNITION TIMING

Application	Specification (Degrees BTDC @ RPM)
6.0L	16 @ 600

SUMMARY

If no faults were found while performing BASIC DIAGNOSTIC PROCEDURES, proceed to SELF-DIAGNOSTICS article if applicable. If no hard codes are found in self-diagnostics, or if vehicle does not have a self-diagnostic system, proceed to TROUBLE SHOOTING – NO CODES article for diagnosis by symptom (i.e., ROUGH IDLE, NO-START, etc.), or intermittent diagnostic procedures.

1991 ENGINE PERFORMANCE
Self-Diagnostics

Cherokee, Comanche, Wrangler

INTRODUCTION

If no faults were found while performing BASIC DIAGNOSTIC PROCEDURES, proceed with self-diagnostics. If no fault codes or only pass codes are present after entering self-diagnostics, proceed to TROUBLE SHOOTING – NO CODES article for diagnosis by symptom (i.e. ROUGH IDLE, NO START, etc.).

MODEL IDENTIFICATION

VEHICLE BODY IDENTIFICATION

Model Name	Body Type
Cherokee	XJ
Comanche	MJ
Wrangler	YJ

SELF-DIAGNOSTIC SYSTEM

SYSTEM DIAGNOSIS

Self-diagnostic capabilities of this system, if properly utilized, can simplify testing. Single Board Engine Controller II (SBEC-II) monitors several different engine control system circuits.

If a problem is sensed with a monitored circuit, a fault code is stored in SBEC-II, CHECK ENGINE light illuminates and SBEC-II enters limp-in mode. In limp-in mode, SBEC compensates for component failure by substituting information from other sources, allowing vehicle operation until repairs can be made.

Once codes are known, refer to FAULT CODES to determine questionable circuit. Test circuits, and repair or replace components as required. If problem is repaired or ceases to exist, SBEC-II cancels fault code after 50 ignition on/off cycles. To clear codes, refer to CLEARING TROUBLE CODES.

A specific fault code results from a particular system failure. It is NOT necessarily reason for failure. Fault code does not condemn a specific component, but calls out a probable malfunction area.

Hard Failures – Hard failures cause CHECK ENGINE light to illuminate and remain on until the malfunction is repaired. If light comes on and remains on (light may flash) during vehicle operation, cause of malfunction must be determined using diagnostic (code) charts. If a sensor fails, SBEC-II will use a substitute value in its calculations, allowing engine operation in limp-in mode. In this condition, vehicle will run but driveability may be poor.

Intermittent Failures – Intermittent failures may cause CHECK ENGINE light to flicker or stay on until the intermittent fault goes away. However, the corresponding trouble code will be retained in SBEC-II memory. If related fault does not reoccur within a certain time frame, related trouble code will be erased from SBEC-II memory. Intermittent failures can be caused by faulty sensor, bad connector or wiring related problems. See INTERMITTENTS in TROUBLE SHOOTING – NO CODES article.

DIAGNOSTIC PROCEDURE

Refer to ENTERING ON-BOARD DIAGNOSTICS to obtain fault codes. If fault codes are NOT present and/or DRB-II (Diagnostic Readout Box-II) is used, proceed to one of the following tests:

- Go to NO START TEST 1A (NS-1A) chart if a no-start condition exists or engine stalls after start-up. Perform indicated VERIFICATION PROCEDURE after repairs. Ensure charts apply to engine being tested.
- Go to DRIVEABILITY TEST 1A (DR-1A) chart if engine runs but has performance problems. Perform indicated VERIFICATION PROCEDURE after repairs. Ensure charts apply to engine being tested.

NOTE: When using trouble shooting charts for diagnosis, DO NOT skip any steps in chart or incorrect diagnosis may result.

Before proceeding with diagnosis, the following precautions must be followed:

- Vehicle must have a fully charged battery and functional charging system.
- Probe SBEC-II connector from pin side. DO NOT backprobe SBEC-II connector.
- DO NOT cause short circuits when performing electrical tests. This will set additional fault codes, making diagnosis of original problem more difficult.
- DO NOT use a test light in place of a voltmeter.
- When checking for spark, ensure coil wire is NO more than 1/4" from ground. If coil wire is more than 1/4" from ground, damage to vehicle electronics and/or SBEC-II may result.
- DO NOT prolong testing of fuel injectors or engine may hydrostatically (liquid) lock.
- Always repair lowest fault code number (CHECK ENGINE light) or first fault displayed (DRB-II) first.
- Always perform indicated VERIFICATION PROCEDURE after repairs.
- Always disconnect DRB-II after use.
- Always disconnect DRB-II before charging battery.

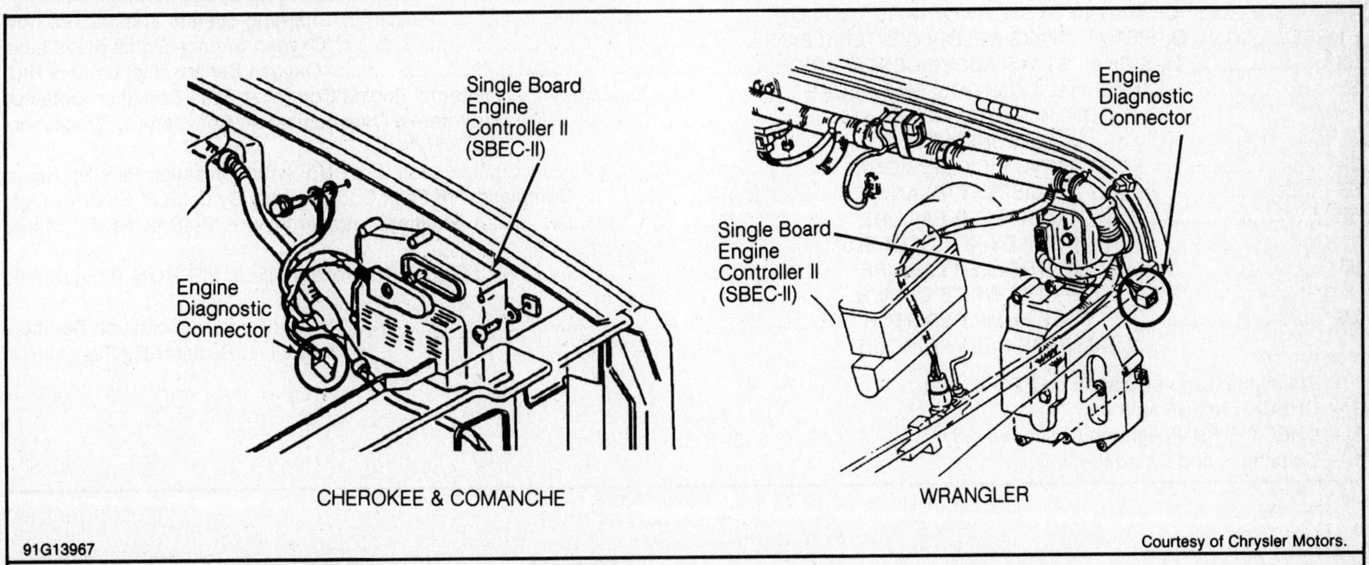
Single Board Engine Controller II (SBEC-II)
Engine Diagnostic Connector
CHEROKEE & COMANCHE
Engine Diagnostic Connector
Single Board Engine Controller II (SBEC-II)
WRANGLER
91G13967
Courtesy of Chrysler Motors.

Fig. 1: Locating Diagnostic Connector

1991 ENGINE PERFORMANCE
Self-Diagnostics (Cont.)

ENTERING ON-BOARD DIAGNOSTICS

NOTE: Manufacturer recommends using DRB-II (Diagnostic Readout Box-II) to diagnose the system. See DRB-II TEST FUNCTIONS for complete diagnostic instructions.

Obtaining Fault Codes – 1) Ensure ignition is off. Attach DRB-II to engine diagnostic connector. Connector is located on left side of engine compartment, near SBEC-II. *See Fig. 1*. Start engine (if possible). Turn A/C switch on, then off (if equipped).

2) Turn engine off. Without starting engine, turn ignition on and access READ FAULTS function of DRB-II FUEL/IGN MENU. See DRB-II DIAGNOSTIC MODE under DRB-II TEST FUNCTIONS if necessary.

3) Record all fault messages displayed by DRB-II, and observe CHECK ENGINE light on instrument cluster. CHECK ENGINE light should come on for 3 seconds and then go out (bulb check).

FAULT CODES

FAULT CODES

Code	Display On DRB-II [1]	Fault Condition
11	IGN REFERENCE SIGNAL	No Distributor Reference Signal Detected During Cranking
13 [2,3]	SLOW CHANGE IN MAP SIGNAL	No Difference In MAP Sensor Signal Is Detected
	NO CHANGE IN MAP (FROM START TO RUN)	No Difference Detected Between MAP And Barometric Pressure Readings
14 [2,3]	MAP VOLTAGE TOO LOW	MAP Sensor Input Less Than Minimum Acceptable Voltage
	MAP VOLTAGE TOO HIGH	MAP Sensor Input More Than Maximum Acceptable Voltage
15 [3]	NO VEHICLE SPEED SIGNAL	No Distance Sensor Signal Detected With Road Load Conditions
17	ENGINE IS COLD TOO LONG	Coolant Temperature Stays Below Normal Operating Temperature During Vehicle Operation
21 [3]	O_2 SIGNAL STAYS AT CENTER	Neither Rich Nor Lean Condition Is Detected From Oxygen Sensor Input
	O_2 SENSOR SHORTED TO VOLTAGE	Oxygen Sensor Input Voltage Maintained Above Normal Operating Range
22 [2,3]	COOLANT SENSOR VOLTAGE TOO LOW	Coolant Temperature Sensor Input Below Minimum Acceptable Voltage
	COOLANT SENSOR VOLTAGE TOO HIGH	Coolant Temperature Sensor Input Above Maximum Acceptable Voltage
23 [2,3]	CHARGE TEMP SENSOR VOLTAGE LOW	Charge Temperature Sensor Input Below Minimum Acceptable Voltage
	CHARGE TEMP SENSOR VOLTAGE HIGH	Charge Temperature Sensor Input Above Maximum Acceptable Voltage
24 [2,3]	TPS VOLTAGE LOW	TPS Sensor Output Less Than Minimum Acceptable Voltage
	TPS VOLTAGE HIGH	TPS Sensor Output More Than Maximum Acceptable Voltage
25 [3]	AUTOMATIC IDLE SPEED MOTOR CIRCUITS	A Shorted Or Open Circuit Detected In One Or More Automatic Idle Speed (AIS) Motor Circuits
27 [2,3]	INJECTOR (#) CONTROL CIRCUIT	Injector (Number) Output Driver Does Not Respond Correctly To SBEC Control Signal
33	A/C CLUTCH RELAY CIRCUIT	Open Or Shorted Condition Detected In A/C Clutch Relay Circuit
34 [4]	SPEED CONTROL SOLENOID CIRCUITS	Open Or Shorted Condition Detected In Speed (Cruise) Control Vacuum Or Vent Solenoid Circuits
35 [4]	RADIATOR FAN RELAY	Open Or Shorted Condition Detected In Radiator Fan Relay Circuit
41 [2,3]	ALTERNATOR FIELD NOT SWITCHING PROPERLY	An Open Or Shorted Condition Detected In Alternator Field Circuit
42	ASD RELAY CIRCUIT	An Open Or Shorted Condition Detected In ASD Relay Circuit
	NO ASD RELAY VOLTAGE SENSED AT CONTROLLER	No ASD Relay Voltage Sensed At SBEC Controller
44	BATTERY TEMP SENSOR VOLTAGE OUT OF LIMITS	Battery Temperature Sensor Voltage Out Of Limit
46 [2,3]	CHARGING SYSTEM VOLTAGE TOO HIGH	Charging System Voltage Too High
47 [2,3]	CHARGING SYSTEM VOLTAGE TOO LOW	Charging System Voltage Too Low
51 [3]	O_2 SIGNAL STAYS BELOW CENTER (LEAN)	Oxygen Sensor Signal Stays Lean
52 [3]	O_2 SIGNAL STAYS ABOVE CENTER (RICH)	Oxygen Sensor Signal Stays Rich
53	INTERNAL CONTROLLER FAILURE	Internal Engine Controller Fault Condition Detected
	CONTROLLER FAILURE SPI COMMUNICATIONS	No Internal Communication Between Co-Processors
54	NO SYNC PICK-UP SIGNAL	No Synchronization Pick-Up Signal
55	NO DISPLAY (BLANK)	Completion Of Fault Code Display By CHECK ENGINE Light
62	CONTROLLER FAILURE (EMR MILES NOT STORED)	Engine Controller Failure, EMR Miles Not Stored
63	CONTROLLER FAILURE EEPROM WRITE DENIED	Engine Controller Failure, EEPROM Write Denied
76 [4]	FUEL PUMP RESISTOR BYPASS RELAY CIRCUIT	An Open Or Shorted Condition Detected In The Ballast Resistor By-Pass Circuit

[1] – Actual message displayed on DRB-II.
[2] – CHECK ENGINE light on.
[3] – CHECK ENGINE light on (California only).
[4] – Comanche and Cherokee only.

CLEARING TROUBLE CODES

1) To clear trouble codes, ensure ignition is off. Connect DRB-II to engine diagnostic connector. Connector is located on left side of engine compartment, near SBEC-II. *See Fig. 1*. Turn ignition switch to RUN position.

2) The copyright information and diagnostic program version will appear on screen for a few seconds. After a few seconds DRB-II menu will appear. At FUEL/IGN menu, press "5" (ADJUSTMENTS) key. Press ENTER key. At ADJUSTMENTS menu, press "1" (ERASE FAULTS) key. Press ENTER key.

3) The DRB-II will display ERASE FAULTS ARE YOU SURE? (ENTER TO ERASE). Press ENTER key. When DRB-II is finished erasing fault codes, screen will display ERASE FAULTS, FAULTS ERASED.

DRB-II TEST FUNCTIONS

NOTE: DO NOT touch DRB-II keypad during DRB-II power-up sequence or an error message will result. If DRB-II screen is blank or any error messages appear, refer to DRB-II PROBLEMS & ERROR MESSAGES in this article.

DRB-II Diagnostic Mode – 1) In order to perform diagnostic tests using the DRB-II, the DRB-II must be in the FUEL/IGN MENU. At the FUEL/IGN MENU, fault codes and DRB-II test functions can be accessed.

2) To reach FUEL/IGN MENU, ensure ignition is off. Connect DRB-II to engine diagnostic connector. Connector is located on left side of engine compartment, near SBEC-II. *See Fig. 1*. Turn ignition switch to RUN position.

3) The copyright information and diagnostic program version will appear on screen for a few seconds. After a few seconds DRB-II menu will appear. At DRB-II menu, press "4" (SELECT SYSTEM) key. Press ENTER key.

4) At SELECT SYSTEM menu, press "1" (ENGINE) key. Press ENTER key. The DRB-II menu will appear indicating engine year, size, type of transmission and SBEC-II part number.

5) After a few seconds AIR COND menu will appear. Press "1" (WITH A/C) or press "2" (WITHOUT A/C). Press ENTER key. The DRB-II display will change to ENGINE SYSTEMS menu. At ENGINE SYSTEMS menu, press "1" (FUEL/IGNITION) key. Press ENTER key.

6) Display will change to FUEL/IGN MENU. At FUEL/IGN menu of engine diagnostic program, specific test functions programmed into DRB-II can be performed. The following DRB-II modes can be accessed: SYSTEM TEST, READ FAULTS, STATE DISPLAY, ACTUATOR TEST and ADJUSTMENTS.

SYSTEM TEST Mode – This function is not available in the engine diagnostics program.

READ FAULTS Mode – This function allows the user to read and erase fault codes. A fault counter will appear along with fault displayed on DRB-II. As an example, DRB-II will display 1 OF 2 FAULTS. SBEC-II will store up to 8 fault messages. Faults are numbered in reverse order of setting. The most recent fault to occur will be number one. Vehicles without air conditioning will always have A/C CLUTCH RELAY CKT (circuit) stored in memory. This fault will always be number one if vehicle is not equipped with A/C. If no fault messages are stored, DRB-II will display NO FAULTS DETECTED and start counter will show 0 STARTS SINCE ERS (Erased).

A start counter will appear below DRB-II fault counter display. Start counter counts the number of times vehicle is started since faults were last set, erased, or battery was disconnected. This helps determine if fault is intermittent. Memory space limits start counter to first 3 faults. Start counter of zero equals a hard fault. Start counter of more than zero indicates an intermittent fault. Start counter will count up to 255 starts. If no fault messages are stored, DRB-II will display NO FAULTS DETECTED and start counter will show 0 STARTS SINCE ERS (Erased).

STATE DISPLAY Mode – This function allows user to read states or values of a variety of sensors, inputs/outputs and components. The SBEC-II can only recognize high and low states on switch circuits. The SBEC-II cannot tell the difference between an open or short circuit or a defective switch. If DRB-II displays a change between INPUT HIGH and INPUT LOW, it can be assumed that the entire switch circuit to the SBEC-II is functioning.

ACTUATOR TEST Mode – This function allows the user to check for proper operation of output circuits or devices, which the SBEC-II cannot internally recognize. DRB-II allows SBEC-II to activate these outputs or devices, allowing an observer to verify proper operation.

Most of the tests available in this mode provide an audible or visual indication of device operation (click of relay contacts, spray fuel, etc.). With the exception of an intermittent condition, if a device functions properly during its test, it can be assumed that the device, wiring and its driver circuit are functioning properly.

ADJUSTMENTS Mode – This function allows the user to erase fault codes. Function also allows user to perform Emission Maintenance Reminder (EMR) memory test and reset Emission Maintenance Reminder (EMR) light and mileage.

DRB-II Volt/Ohmmeter Mode – 1) To access volt/ohmmeter mode of DRB-II, connect Red volt/ohmmeter test lead to Red port, located on top right side of DRB-II.

NOTE: Because DRB-II is grounded through engine diagnostic connector, only one volt/ohmmeter test lead is required when using volt/ohmmeter option. The DRB-II volt/ohmmeter mode should only be used when diagnostic flow charts require the use of this option.

2) To access voltmeter, press VOLT/OHM key once. DRB-II is now in voltmeter mode. Touch test probe to connector or wire to be measured. Read voltage on DRB-II display. When voltage testing is completed, press VOLT/OHM key 3 times to exit voltmeter mode.

3) To access ohmmeter, press VOLT/OHM key twice. DRB-II is now in ohmmeter mode. Touch test probe to connector or wire to be measured. Read resistance to circuit ground on DRB-II display. When resistance testing is complete, press VOLT/OHM key twice to exit ohmmeter mode.

DRB-II Continuity Meter Mode – To access continuity meter, press VOLT/OHM key 3 times. Display will read NO CONTINUITY. Touch test probe to connector or wire to be measured. Read continuity on DRB-II display. When continuity testing is complete, press VOLT/OHM key once to exit continuity meter mode.

VEHICLES TESTED Mode – 1) Vehicles tested mode is used to show what vehicles are covered by DRB-II cartridge. To access vehicles tested mode, ensure ignition is off.

2) Connect DRB-II to engine diagnostic connector. Connector is located on left side of engine compartment, near SBEC-II. *See Fig. 1*. Turn ignition switch to RUN position.

3) The copyright information and diagnostic program version will appear on screen for a few seconds. After a few seconds DRB-II menu will appear. At DRB-II menu, press "1" (VEHICLES TESTED) key. Press ENTER key. DRB-II will display vehicles covered by cartridge. Screen will display for 5 seconds and return to DRB-II menu.

HOW TO USE Mode – 1) To access how to use mode, ensure ignition is off. Attach DRB-II to engine diagnostic connector. Connector is located on left side of engine compartment, near SBEC-II. *See Fig. 1*. Turn ignition switch to RUN position.

2) The copyright information and diagnostic program version will appear on screen for a few seconds. After a few seconds DRB-II menu will appear. At DRB-II menu, press "2" (HOW TO USE) key. Press ENTER key. A series of screens will be displayed explaining the use of DRB-II keys used to move through engine diagnostic program.

CONFIGURE Mode – 1) Configure option allows user to VIEW or CHANGE DRB-II display to US/METRIC, KEY CLICK, KEY REPEAT, or REMOTE DISPLAY. All selections made under CONFIGURE option remain active until user changes selection.

2) To access how to use mode, ensure ignition is off. Attach DRB-II to engine diagnostic connector. Connector is located on left side of engine compartment, near SBEC-II. *See Fig. 1*. Turn ignition switch to RUN position.

3) The copyright information and diagnostic program version will appear on screen for a few seconds. After a few seconds DRB-II menu will appear. At DRB-II menu, press "3" (CONFIGURE) key. Press ENTER key. DRB-II will display CONFIGURE menu.

1991 ENGINE PERFORMANCE
Self-Diagnostics (Cont.)

4) Selecting VIEW from CONFIGURE menu allows user to view setting of CONFIGURE functions. Selecting CHANGE from CONFIGURE menu allows user to change setting of CONFIGURE functions.

5) Selecting US/METRIC function allows user to have sensor, input/output values displayed in either US/METRIC units. Selecting KEY CLICK allows user to have a Green light come on or have a beeper sound whenever a DRB-II key is pressed.

6) If REPEAT KEY function is on, the down/up arrow key will scroll the DRB-II display repeatedly. If the REPEAT KEY function is off, the down/up arrow will scroll the DRB-II display only one item at a time. Selecting REMOTE DISPLAY function allows user to have DRB-II screen displayed on another screen.

DRB-II PROBLEMS & ERROR MESSAGES

Blank DRB-II Message Screen – 1) Connect DRB-II to a different vehicle. If message screen is still blank, DRB-II or cable adapter are faulty. Substitute to find faulty component.

2) If message screen is not blank, DRB-II and cable adapter are functioning properly. Inspect diagnostic connector for proper wire placement, damaged terminals or pushed out pins. Repair as necessary.

3) If diagnostic connector is okay, use an ohmmeter to check resistance between Black/White or Black/Yellow wire and ground at engine diagnostic connector. If resistance is 10 ohms or more, repair open in Black/White or Black/Yellow wire.

NO RESPONSE Message – 1) Ensure ignition is OFF and disconnect DRB-II. Using an external ohmmeter, check resistance of Pink or Black/Red wire between SBEC-II pin No. 25 and engine diagnostic connector. *See Fig. 2*. If resistance is 10 ohms or more, repair open in Pink or Black/Red wire.

2) If resistance is less than 10 ohms, check resistance of Light Green or Black/Pink wire between SBEC-II pin No. 45 and engine diagnostic connector. If resistance is 10 ohms or more, repair open in Light Green/Orange or Black/Pink wire.

3) If resistance is less than 10 ohms, turn ignition off and disconnect DRB-II, DRB-II cartridge, and adapter cable. Find a second vehicle identical in equipment to vehicle being tested.

4) Connect DRB-II to substitute (second) vehicle and use DRB-II as you did on original vehicle. If message screen is still blank, adapter cable or DRB-II (including cartridge) is faulty. Substitute adapter cable with a known good cable to find faulty component.

5) If message screen is NOT blank, DRB-II and cable adapter are functioning properly. Inspect diagnostic connector on original vehicle for proper wire placement, corrosion, damaged terminals, or pushed-out pins. Repair as necessary.

RAM TEST FAILURE Message – Replace DRB-II.
CARTRIDGE ERROR Message – Replace DRB-II cartridge.
KEY PAD TEST FAILURE Message – Power up DRB-II again with fingers off the keypad. If error message returns, replace DRB-II.
HIGH OR LOW BATTERY Message – Correct condition of vehicle battery and reconnect DRB-II.

EMISSION MAINTENANCE REMINDER (EMR) MEMORY TEST

NOTE: Perform EMR memory test only if referred here by flow charts.

1) To perform EMR memory check, ensure ignition is off. Attach DRB-II to engine diagnostic connector. Connector is located on left side of engine compartment, near SBEC-II. *See Fig. 1*. Turn ignition switch to RUN position.

2) The copyright information and diagnostic program version will appear on screen for a few seconds. After a few seconds DRB-II menu will appear. At FUEL/IGN menu, press "5" (ADJUSTMENTS) key. Press ENTER key. At ADJUSTMENTS menu, press "4" (EMR MEMORY CHK) key. Press ENTER key. The DRB-II display will read EMR MEMORY CHECK ARE YOU SURE? (ENTER TO CONTINUE).

3) Press ENTER key. The DRB-II will display EMR MEMORY TEST WRITE TEST [-------] and after a few seconds IS INSTRUMENT PANEL MILEAGE BETWEEN XXXXX AND XXXXX? (PRESS YES OR NO). If vehicle mileage is within specification, EMR memory check is complete. Press YES key. If vehicle mileage is not within specification, go to next step.

4) Press NO key. DRB-II will display ENTER MILEAGE SHOWN ON INSTRUMENT PANEL (USE ENTER KEY TO END) XXXXXXX. Enter vehicle mileage. DO NOT enter tenths. When correct vehicle mileage is entered, press ENTER key.

5) DRB-II will ask for verification of mileage entry. If mileage entry was accurate, press ENTER key. DRB-II will display EMR MEMORY CHECK COMPLETE. Vehicle must travel at least 8 miles for reset to occur.

EMISSION MAINTENANCE REMINDER (EMR) LIGHT RESET PROCEDURE

The Emission Maintenance Reminder (EMR) light is designed to be a reminder to service the vehicle emissions control system. It is not an emissions warning system, only a reminder to perform necessary emissions servicing.

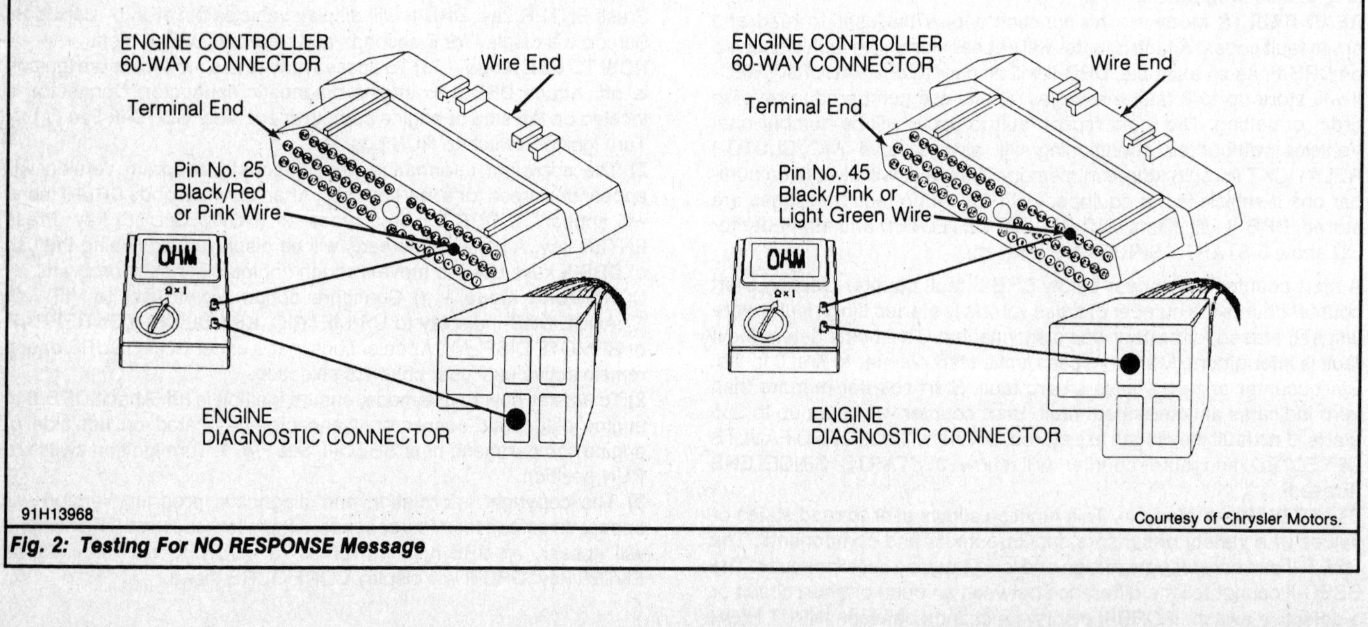
ENGINE CONTROLLER
60-WAY CONNECTOR
Wire End
Terminal End
Pin No. 25
Black/Red
or Pink Wire
OHM
ENGINE
DIAGNOSTIC CONNECTOR
ENGINE CONTROLLER
60-WAY CONNECTOR
Wire End
Terminal End
Pin No. 45
Black/Pink or
Light Green Wire
OHM
ENGINE
DIAGNOSTIC CONNECTOR
91H13968
Courtesy of Chrysler Motors.

Fig. 2: Testing For NO RESPONSE Message

The components to be serviced include PCV valve, oxygen sensor and some vacuum-operated components. EMR light will illuminate after a predetermined mileage.

1) To reset EMR light, ensure ignition is off. Connect DRB-II to engine diagnostic connector. Connector is located on left side of engine compartment, near SBEC-II. *See Fig. 1*. Turn ignition switch to RUN position.

2) The copyright information and diagnostic program version will appear on screen for a few seconds. After a few seconds DRB-II menu will appear. At FUEL/IGN menu, press "5" (ADJUSTMENTS) key. Press ENTER key.

3) At ADJUSTMENTS menu, press "3" (RESET EMR LIGHT) key. Press ENTER key. Display will read RESET EMR LIGHT ARE YOUR SURE? (ENTER TO RESET). Press ENTER key.

EMISSION MAINTENANCE REMINDER (EMR) MILEAGE TRANSFER

NOTE: Perform mileage transfer procedure only if SBEC-II is being replaced.

1) When SBEC-II is replaced, vehicle mileage must be copied from odometer to replacement SBEC-II memory. Transfer of vehicle mileage will enable new SBEC-II to operate EMR light properly.

2) To transfer mileage to SBEC-II, ensure ignition is off. Connect DRB-II to engine diagnostic connector. Connector is located on left side of engine compartment, near SBEC-II. *See Fig. 1*. Turn ignition switch to RUN position.

3) The copyright information and diagnostic program version will appear on screen for a few seconds. After a few seconds DRB-II menu will appear. At FUEL/IGN menu, press "5" (ADJUSTMENTS) key. Press ENTER key. At ADJUSTMENTS menu, press "4" (EMR MEMORY CHK) key. Press ENTER key. The DRB-II display will read EMR MEMORY CHECK ARE YOU SURE? (ENTER TO CONTINUE).

4) Press ENTER key. The DRB-II will display EMR MEMORY TEST WRITE TEST [-------] and after a few seconds IS INSTRUMENT PANEL MILEAGE BETWEEN XXXXX AND XXXXX? (PRESS YES OR NO). If vehicle mileage is within specification, EMR memory check is complete. Press YES key. If vehicle mileage is not within specification, go to next step.

5) Press NO key. DRB-II will display ENTER MILEAGE SHOWN ON INSTRUMENT PANEL (USE ENTER KEY TO END) XXXXXXX. Enter vehicle mileage. DO NOT enter tenths. When correct vehicle mileage is entered, press ENTER key.

6) The DRB-II will ask for verification of mileage entry. If mileage entry was accurate, press ENTER key. DRB-II will display EMR MEMORY CHECK COMPLETE. Vehicle must travel at least 8 miles for reset to occur.

THEFT ALARM TEST

NOTE: If SECURITY light comes and remains on with ignition on, the Chrysler Collision Detection (CCD) bus communication with the engine controller has been lost. After servicing vehicle ensure that system operates properly. A malfunctioning anti-theft system may keep engine from starting.

Cherokee – 1) Turn ignition switch to ACCY position 3 times and leave in ACCY position to activate Security Alarm Module (SAM) self-diagnostics. If parking lights and taillights do not flash, go to step **2)**. If headlights do not flash, go to step **6)**. If horn does not sound twice, go to step **7)**. If horn sounds and headlights, parking lights and tail lights flash, go to step **8)**.

2) Check accessory and parking light fuses. Replace if necessary. If fuses are okay, disconnect SAM connector. Security alarm module is located on driver's side of A/C-heater housing.

3) Check wiring side of SAM connector for battery voltage at battery, accessory, and headlight feed wires. Also check ground circuits for both ground wires.

4) If battery voltage and ground circuits are NOT okay, repair wiring harness and retest system. If battery voltage and ground circuits are okay, check for battery voltage at ignition feed wire of SAM connector.

5) If battery voltage is present, replace security alarm module and retest system. If battery voltage is NOT present, repair wiring harness and retest system.

6) Check headlight wiring harness and headlight relay. If wiring harness and relay are okay, replace security alarm module. If wiring harness and relay are NOT okay, repair wiring harness or replace relay and retest system.

7) Check horn, horn fuse and wiring harness. If horn, horn fuse and wiring harness are okay, replace security alarm module and retest system. If horn, horn fuse and wiring harness are NOT okay, repair wiring harness or replace fuse or horn and retest system.

8) Verify that SECURITY light is flashing. If SECURITY light is not flashing, check bulb and wiring harness. Repair or replace as necessary. If bulb and wiring are okay, replace security alarm module and retest system.

9) If SECURITY light is flashing, turn ignition switch to OFF position. Remove illuminated entry relay from vehicle. Relay is located on a bracket behind instrument panel.

10) Check theft alarm switches by opening and closing doors and liftgate. Replace switch(es) or repair wiring harness as necessary. If switches are okay, check hood switch by opening and closing hood.

11) Replace hood switch or repair wiring harness as necessary. If hood switch is okay, unlock (with key) each front door and liftgate one at a time to test disarm switches. Replace switch(es) or repair wiring harness as necessary and retest system.

12) If disarm switches are okay, cycle power door locks to lock position and then unlock. Replace door lock switch(es), lock/unlock relay(s) or repair wiring harness as necessary and retest system.

13) If power door locks operate properly, lock and unlock vehicle with keyless entry transmitter. Replace keyless entry transmitter, receiver or repair wiring harness as necessary and retest system.

14) If keyless entry system operates properly, turn ignition switch to ON position and wait 30 seconds. If SECURITY light comes on and stays on, repair or replace CCD bus and wiring as necessary and retest system. If SECURITY light remains off, theft alarm system is operating properly.

NOTE: A functional SBEC-II that has been used in a vehicle equipped with theft alarm system CANNOT be used in another vehicle that is NOT equipped with theft alarm system.

SUMMARY

If no hard fault codes or only pass codes are present, driveability symptoms exist or intermittent codes exist, proceed to TROUBLE SHOOTING – NO CODES article for diagnosis by symptom (i.e. ROUGH IDLE, NO START, etc.) or intermittent diagnostic procedures.

CODE CHARTS

NOTE: The following trouble shooting charts and illustrations are courtesy of Chrysler Motors.

1991 ENGINE PERFORMANCE
Self-Diagnostics (Cont.)

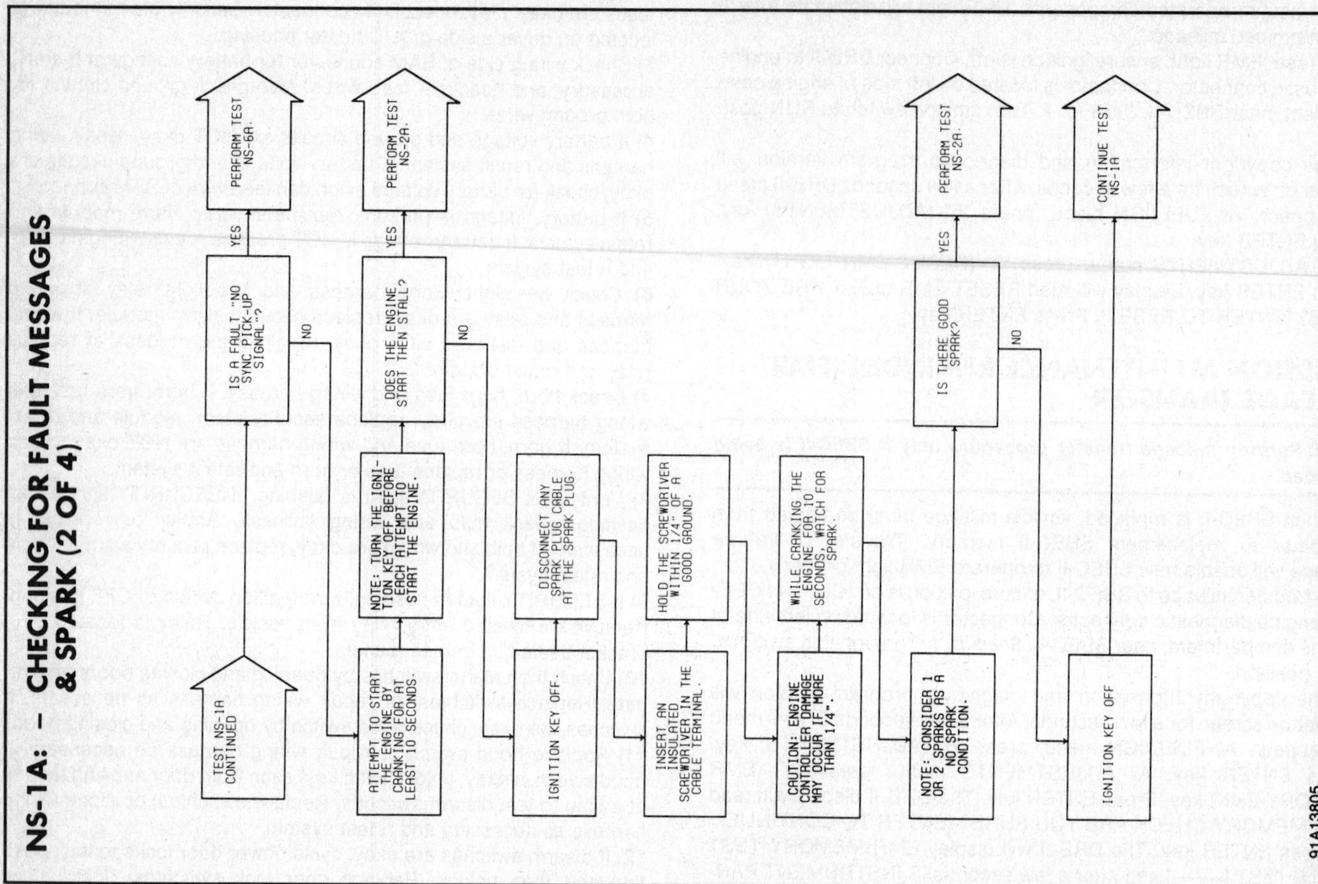
NS-1A: – CHECKING FOR FAULT MESSAGES & SPARK (2 OF 4)
TEST NS-1A CONTINUED
IS A FAULT "NO SYNC PICK-UP SIGNAL"?
YES
PERFORM TEST NS-6A.
NO
ATTEMPT TO START THE ENGINE BY CRANKING FOR AT LEAST 10 SECONDS.
NOTE: TURN THE IGNITION KEY OFF BEFORE EACH ATTEMPT TO START THE ENGINE.
DOES THE ENGINE START THEN STALL?
YES
PERFORM TEST NS-2A.
NO
IGNITION KEY OFF.
DISCONNECT ANY SPARK PLUG CABLE AT THE SPARK PLUG
INSERT AN INSULATED SCREWDRIVER IN THE CABLE TERMINAL.
HOLD THE SCREWDRIVER WITHIN 1/4" OF A GOOD GROUND.
CAUTION: ENGINE CONTROLLER DAMAGE MAY OCCUR IF MORE THAN 1/4".
WHILE CRANKING THE ENGINE FOR 10 SECONDS, WATCH FOR SPARK.
NOTE: CONSIDER 1 OR 2 SPARKS AS A NO SPARK CONDITION.
IS THERE GOOD SPARK?
YES
PERFORM TEST NS-2A.
NO
IGNITION KEY OFF
CONTINUE TEST NS-1A
91A13805

Fig. 4: No Start Test 1A – Checking For Fault Messages & Spark (2 of 4)

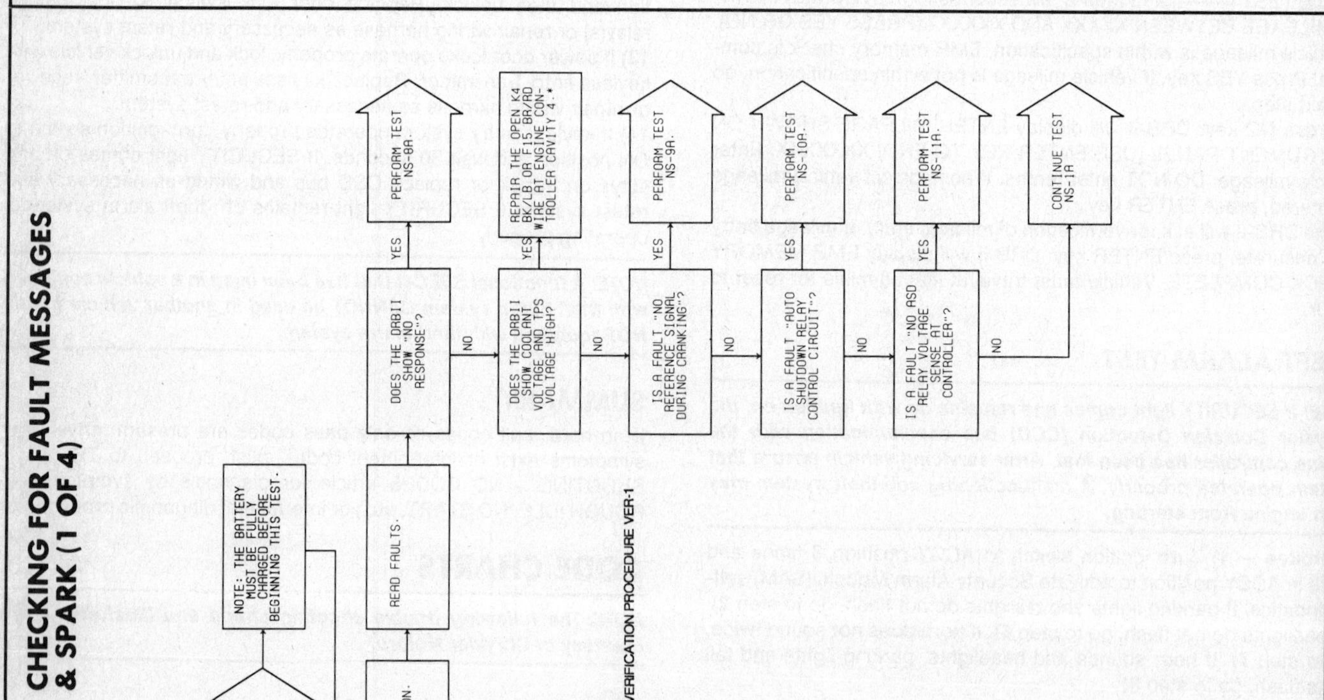
NS-1A: – CHECKING FOR FAULT MESSAGES & SPARK (1 OF 4)
START TEST NS-1A
NOTE: THE BATTERY MUST BE FULLY CHARGED BEFORE BEGINNING THIS TEST.
IGNITION KEY ON.
READ FAULTS.
DOES THE DRBII SHOW "NO RESPONSE"?
YES
PERFORM TEST NS-8A.
NO
DOES THE DRBII SHOW COOLANT VOLTAGE AND TPS VOLTAGE HIGH?
YES
REPAIR THE OPEN K4 BK/LB OR F15 BR/RD WIRE AT ENGINE CONTROLLER CAVITY 4.
NO
IS A FAULT "NO REFERENCE SIGNAL DURING CRANKING"?
YES
PERFORM TEST NS-5A.
NO
IS A FAULT "AUTO SHUTDOWN RELAY CONTROL CIRCUIT"?
YES
PERFORM TEST NS-10A.
NO
IS A FAULT "NO ASD RELAY VOLTAGE SENSE AT CONTROLLER"?
YES
PERFORM TEST NS-11A.
NO
CONTINUE TEST NS-1A
* - PERFORM VERIFICATION PROCEDURE VER-1
91J13804

Fig. 3: No Start Test 1A – Checking For Fault Messages & Spark (1 of 4)

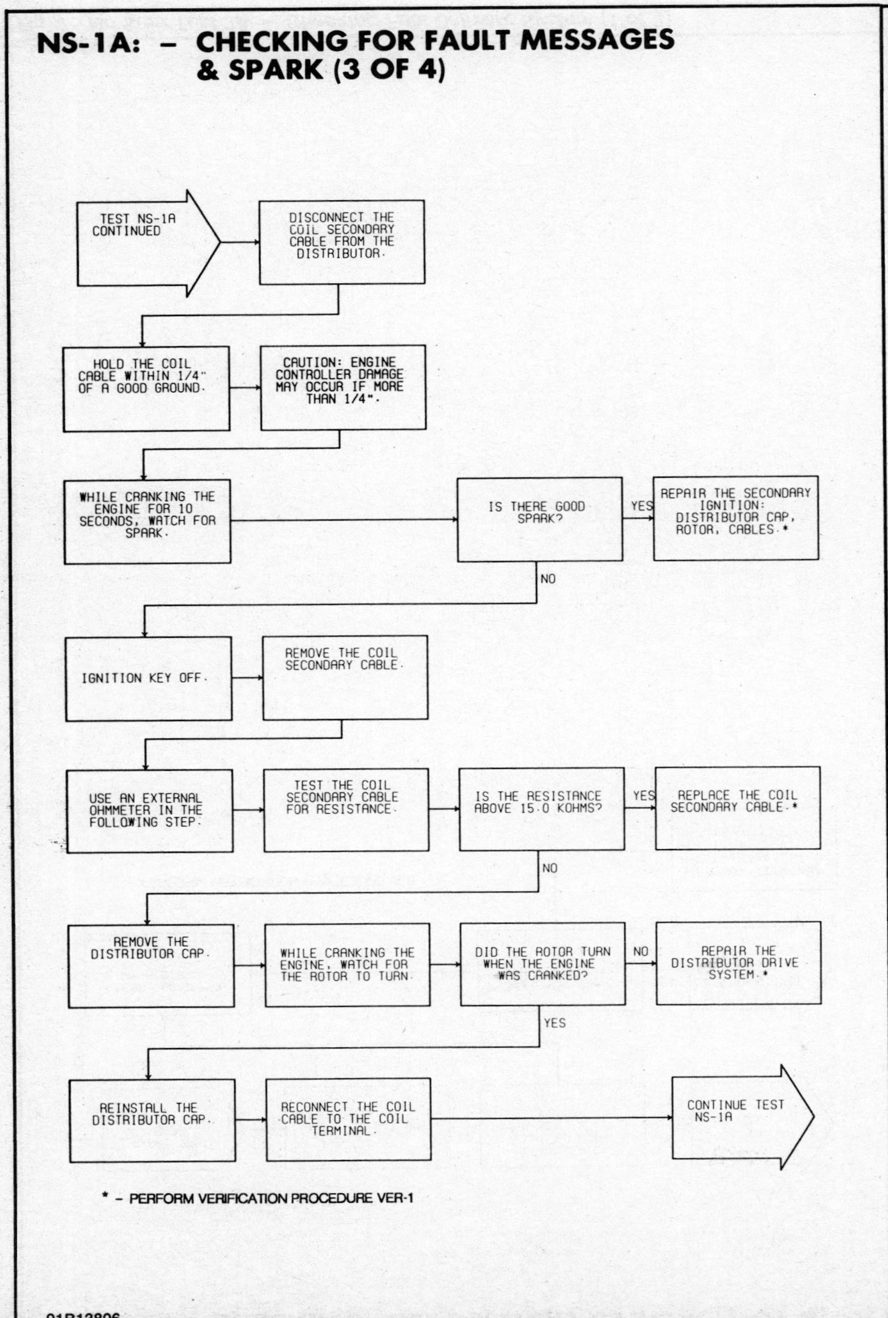
NS-1A: – CHECKING FOR FAULT MESSAGES & SPARK (3 OF 4)
TEST NS-1A CONTINUED
DISCONNECT THE COIL SECONDARY CABLE FROM THE DISTRIBUTOR.
HOLD THE COIL CABLE WITHIN 1/4" OF A GOOD GROUND.
CAUTION: ENGINE CONTROLLER DAMAGE MAY OCCUR IF MORE THAN 1/4".
WHILE CRANKING THE ENGINE FOR 10 SECONDS, WATCH FOR SPARK.
IS THERE GOOD SPARK?
YES
REPAIR THE SECONDARY IGNITION: DISTRIBUTOR CAP, ROTOR, CABLES.*
NO
IGNITION KEY OFF.
REMOVE THE COIL SECONDARY CABLE.
USE AN EXTERNAL OHMMETER IN THE FOLLOWING STEP.
TEST THE COIL SECONDARY CABLE FOR RESISTANCE.
IS THE RESISTANCE ABOVE 15.0 KOHMS?
YES
REPLACE THE COIL SECONDARY CABLE.*
NO
REMOVE THE DISTRIBUTOR CAP.
WHILE CRANKING THE ENGINE, WATCH FOR THE ROTOR TO TURN.
DID THE ROTOR TURN WHEN THE ENGINE WAS CRANKED?
NO
REPAIR THE DISTRIBUTOR DRIVE SYSTEM.*
YES
REINSTALL THE DISTRIBUTOR CAP.
RECONNECT THE COIL CABLE TO THE COIL TERMINAL.
CONTINUE TEST NS-1A
* – PERFORM VERIFICATION PROCEDURE VER-1
91B13806

Fig. 5: No Start Test 1A – Checking For Fault Messages & Spark (3 of 4)

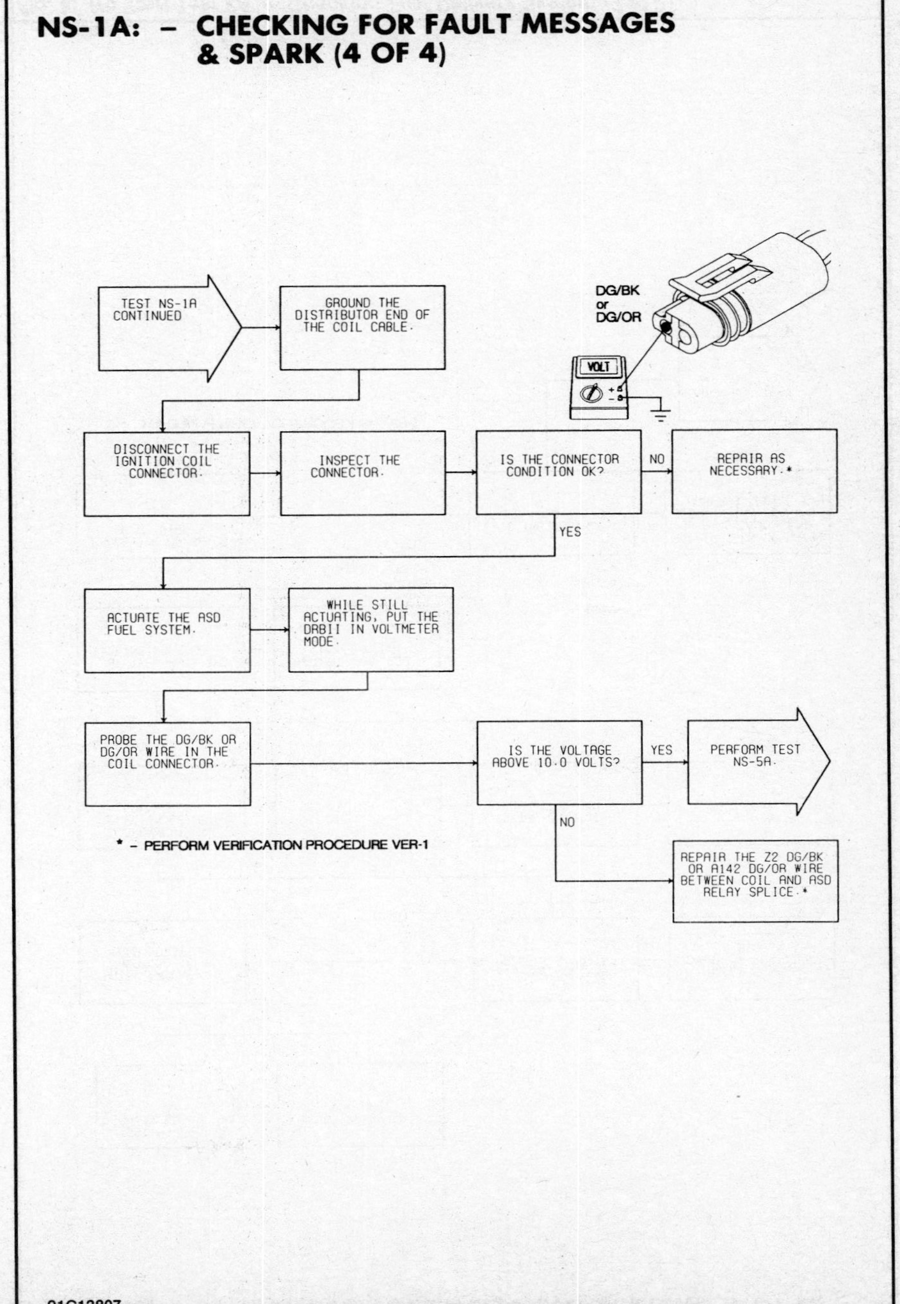
NS-1A: – CHECKING FOR FAULT MESSAGES & SPARK (4 OF 4)
TEST NS-1A CONTINUED
GROUND THE DISTRIBUTOR END OF THE COIL CABLE.
DG/BK or DG/OR
VOLT
DISCONNECT THE IGNITION COIL CONNECTOR.
INSPECT THE CONNECTOR.
IS THE CONNECTOR CONDITION OK?
NO
REPAIR AS NECESSARY.*
YES
ACTUATE THE ASD FUEL SYSTEM.
WHILE STILL ACTUATING, PUT THE DRBII IN VOLTMETER MODE.
PROBE THE DG/BK OR DG/OR WIRE IN THE COIL CONNECTOR.
IS THE VOLTAGE ABOVE 10.0 VOLTS?
YES
PERFORM TEST NS-5A.
NO
REPAIR THE Z2 DG/BK OR A142 DG/OR WIRE BETWEEN COIL AND ASD RELAY SPLICE.*
* – PERFORM VERIFICATION PROCEDURE VER-1
91C13807

Fig. 6: No Start Test 1A – Checking For Fault Messages & Spark (4 of 4)

1991 ENGINE PERFORMANCE
Self-Diagnostics (Cont.)

NS-2A: – CHECKING FUEL DELIVERY SYSTEM (1 OF 3)

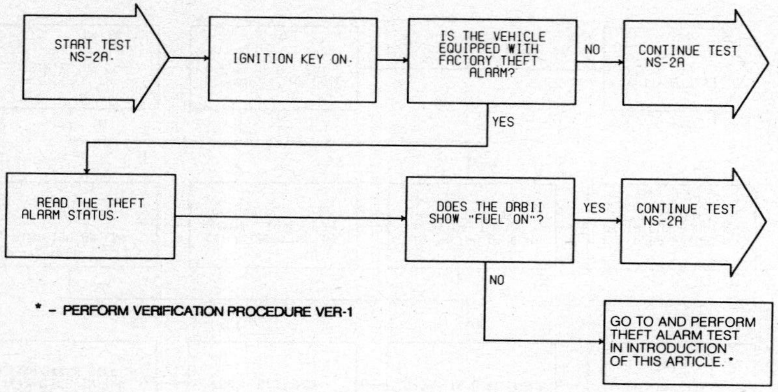
START TEST NS-2A.
IGNITION KEY ON.
IS THE VEHICLE EQUIPPED WITH FACTORY THEFT ALARM?
NO
CONTINUE TEST NS-2A
YES
READ THE THEFT ALARM STATUS.
DOES THE DRBII SHOW "FUEL ON"?
YES
CONTINUE TEST NS-2A
NO
GO TO AND PERFORM THEFT ALARM TEST IN INTRODUCTION OF THIS ARTICLE. *

* – PERFORM VERIFICATION PROCEDURE VER-1

91D13808

Fig. 7: No Start Test 2A – Checking Fuel Delivery System (1 of 3)

NS-2A: – CHECKING FUEL DELIVERY SYSTEM (2 OF 3)

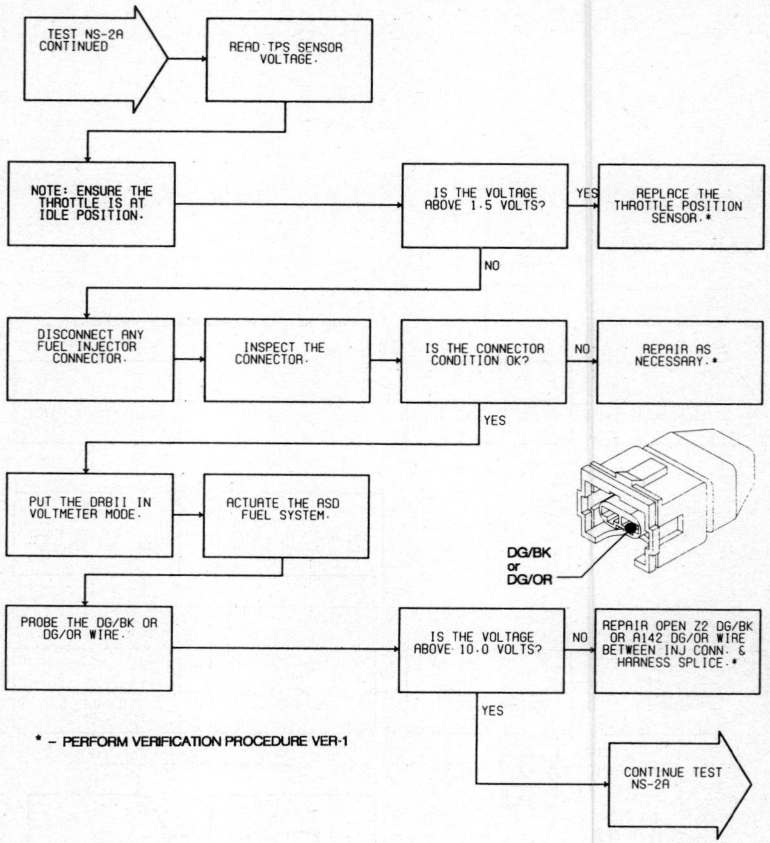
TEST NS-2A CONTINUED
READ TPS SENSOR VOLTAGE.
NOTE: ENSURE THE THROTTLE IS AT IDLE POSITION.
IS THE VOLTAGE ABOVE 1.5 VOLTS?
YES
REPLACE THE THROTTLE POSITION SENSOR. *
NO
DISCONNECT ANY FUEL INJECTOR CONNECTOR.
INSPECT THE CONNECTOR.
IS THE CONNECTOR CONDITION OK?
NO
REPAIR AS NECESSARY. *
YES
PUT THE DRBII IN VOLTMETER MODE.
ACTUATE THE ASD FUEL SYSTEM.
DG/BK
or
DG/OR
PROBE THE DG/BK OR DG/OR WIRE.
IS THE VOLTAGE ABOVE 10.0 VOLTS?
NO
REPAIR OPEN Z2 DG/BK OR A142 DG/OR WIRE BETWEEN INJ CONN. & HARNESS SPLICE. *
YES
CONTINUE TEST NS-2A

* – PERFORM VERIFICATION PROCEDURE VER-1

91E13809

Fig. 8: No Start Test 2A – Checking Fuel Delivery System (2 of 3)

NS-2A: – CHECKING FUEL DELIVERY SYSTEM (3 OF 3)

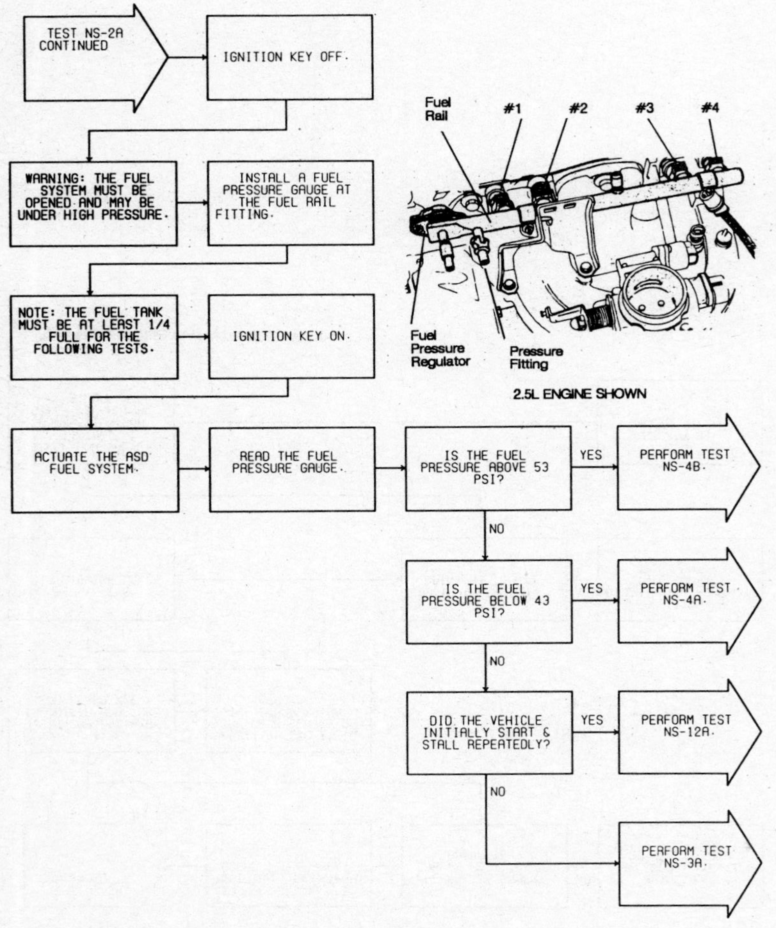
TEST NS-2A CONTINUED
IGNITION KEY OFF.
WARNING: THE FUEL SYSTEM MUST BE OPENED AND MAY BE UNDER HIGH PRESSURE.
INSTALL A FUEL PRESSURE GAUGE AT THE FUEL RAIL FITTING.
NOTE: THE FUEL TANK MUST BE AT LEAST 1/4 FULL FOR THE FOLLOWING TESTS.
IGNITION KEY ON.
ACTUATE THE ASD FUEL SYSTEM.
READ THE FUEL PRESSURE GAUGE.
IS THE FUEL PRESSURE ABOVE 53 PSI?
YES
PERFORM TEST NS-4B.
NO
IS THE FUEL PRESSURE BELOW 43 PSI?
YES
PERFORM TEST NS-4A.
NO
DID THE VEHICLE INITIALLY START & STALL REPEATEDLY?
YES
PERFORM TEST NS-12A.
NO
PERFORM TEST NS-3A.
Fuel Rail
#1
#2
#3
#4
Fuel Pressure Regulator
Pressure Fitting
2.5L ENGINE SHOWN

91H13810

Fig. 9: No Start Test 2A – Checking Fuel Delivery System (3 of 3)

NS-3A: – CHECKING SPARK DELIVERY & ENGINE MECHANICAL SYSTEMS (1 OF 2)

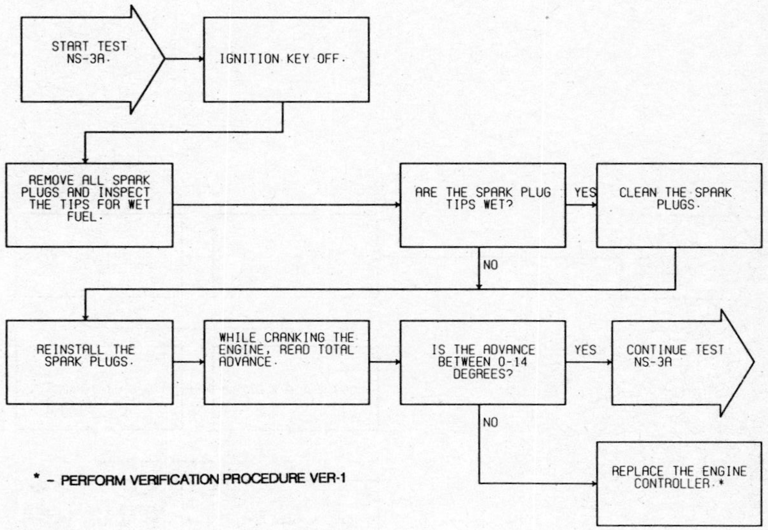
START TEST NS-3A.
IGNITION KEY OFF.
REMOVE ALL SPARK PLUGS AND INSPECT THE TIPS FOR WET FUEL.
ARE THE SPARK PLUG TIPS WET?
YES
CLEAN THE SPARK PLUGS.
NO
REINSTALL THE SPARK PLUGS.
WHILE CRANKING THE ENGINE, READ TOTAL ADVANCE.
IS THE ADVANCE BETWEEN 0-14 DEGREES?
YES
CONTINUE TEST NS-3A
NO
REPLACE THE ENGINE CONTROLLER.*

* – PERFORM VERIFICATION PROCEDURE VER-1

91I13811

Fig. 10: No Start Test NS-3A – Checking Spark Delivery & Engine Mechanical Systems (1 of 2)

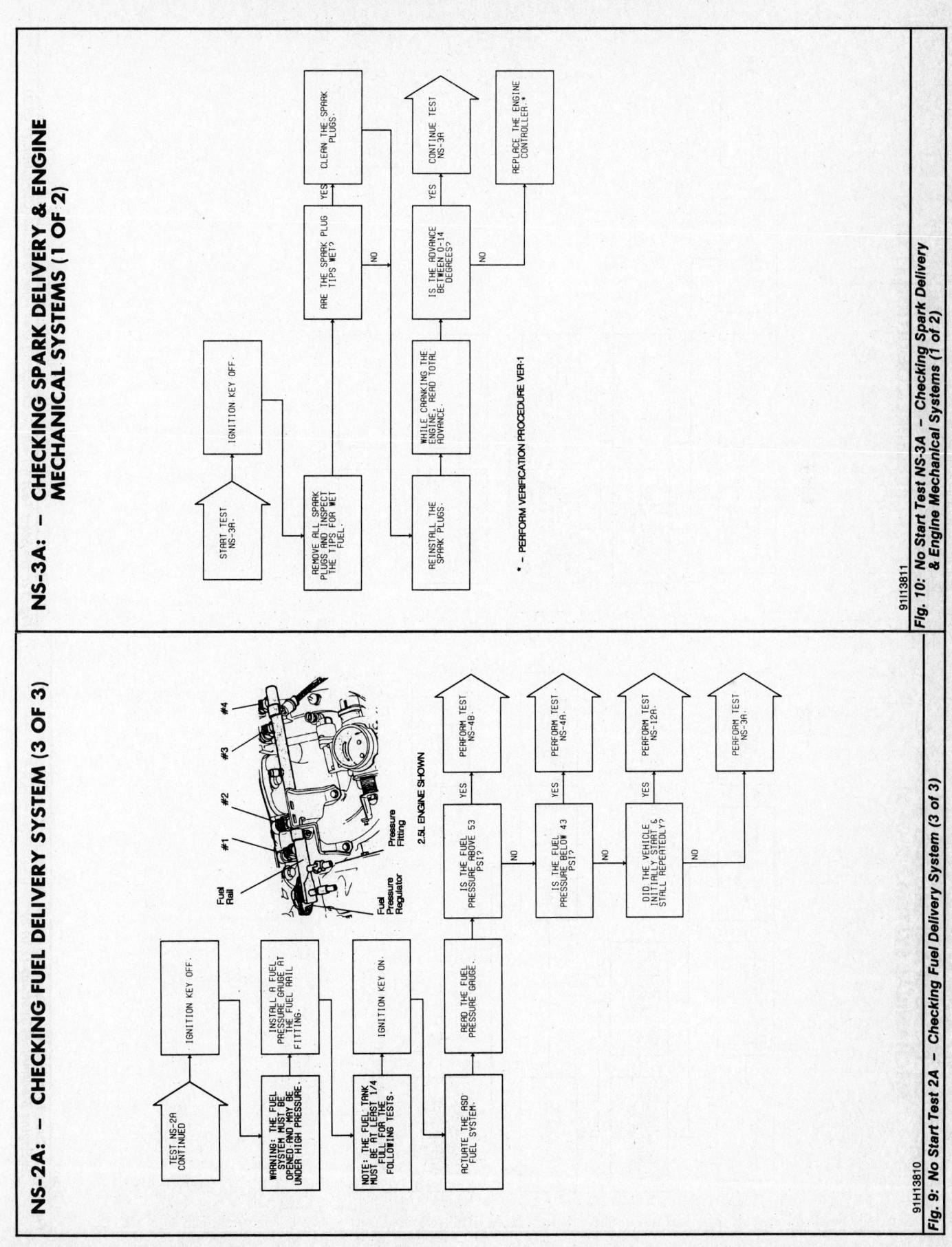

1991 ENGINE PERFORMANCE
Self-Diagnostics (Cont.)

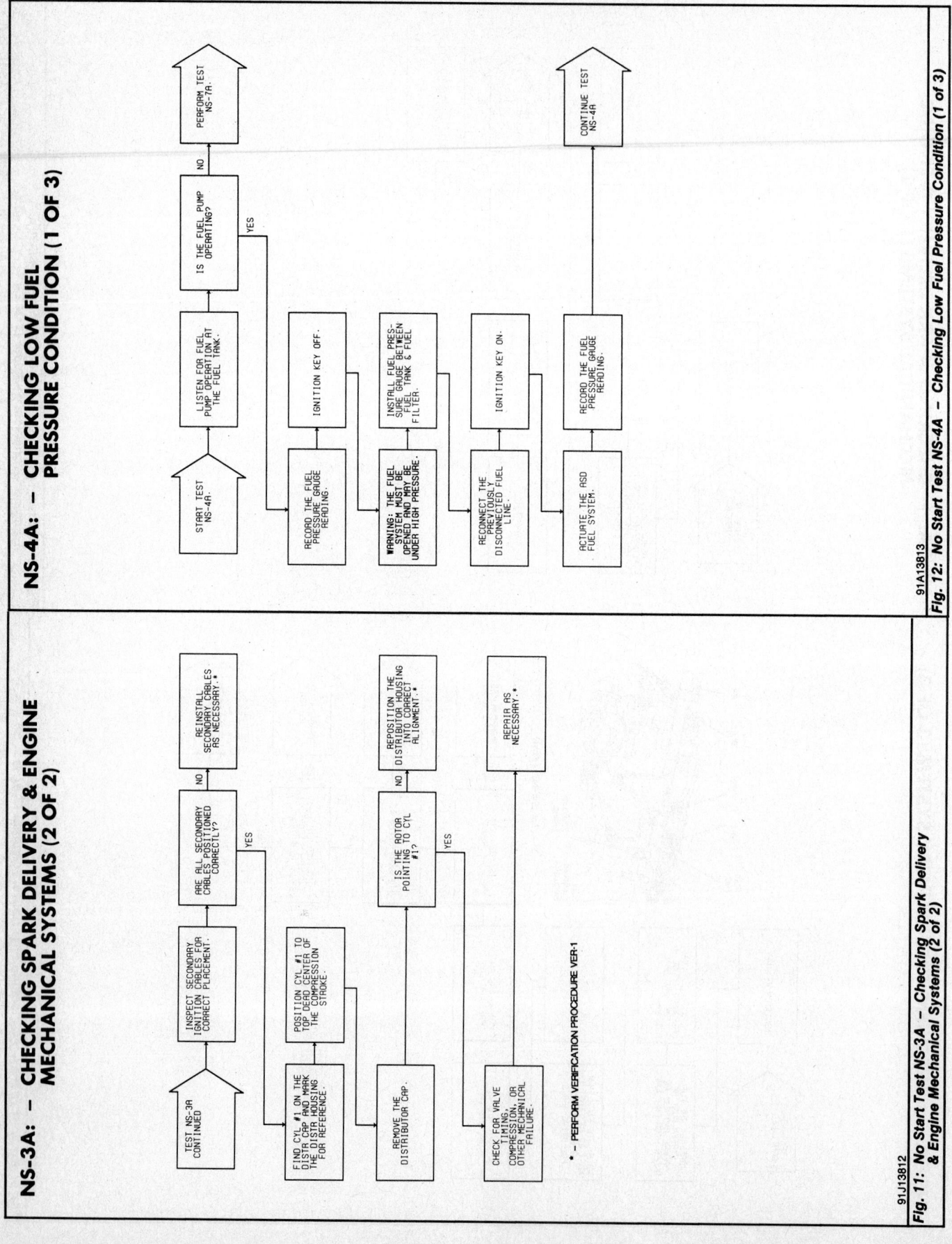

NS-3A: – CHECKING SPARK DELIVERY & ENGINE MECHANICAL SYSTEMS (2 OF 2)

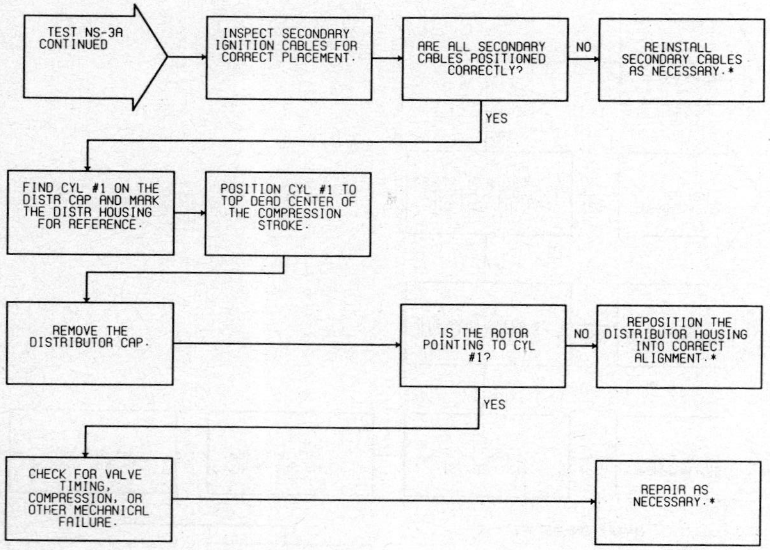
TEST NS-3A CONTINUED
INSPECT SECONDARY IGNITION CABLES FOR CORRECT PLACEMENT.
ARE ALL SECONDARY CABLES POSITIONED CORRECTLY?
NO
REINSTALL SECONDARY CABLES AS NECESSARY.*
YES
FIND CYL #1 ON THE DISTR CAP AND MARK THE DISTR HOUSING FOR REFERENCE.
POSITION CYL #1 TO TOP DEAD CENTER OF THE COMPRESSION STROKE.
REMOVE THE DISTRIBUTOR CAP.
IS THE ROTOR POINTING TO CYL #1?
NO
REPOSITION THE DISTRIBUTOR HOUSING INTO CORRECT ALIGNMENT.*
YES
CHECK FOR VALVE TIMING, COMPRESSION, OR OTHER MECHANICAL FAILURE.
REPAIR AS NECESSARY.*

* – PERFORM VERIFICATION PROCEDURE VER-1

91J13812

Fig. 11: No Start Test NS-3A – Checking Spark Delivery & Engine Mechanical Systems (2 of 2)

NS-4A: – CHECKING LOW FUEL PRESSURE CONDITION (1 OF 3)

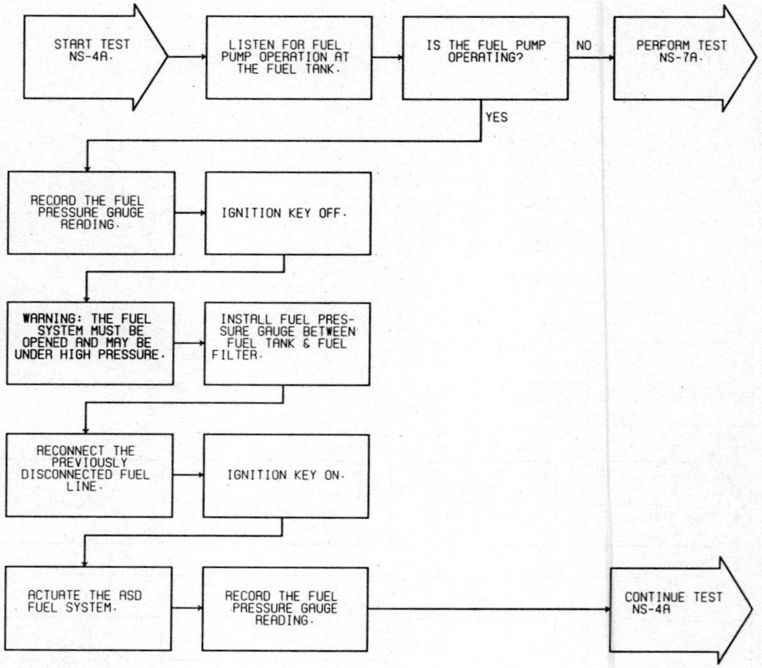
START TEST NS-4A.
LISTEN FOR FUEL PUMP OPERATION AT THE FUEL TANK.
IS THE FUEL PUMP OPERATING?
NO
PERFORM TEST NS-7A.
YES
RECORD THE FUEL PRESSURE GAUGE READING.
IGNITION KEY OFF.
WARNING: THE FUEL SYSTEM MUST BE OPENED AND MAY BE UNDER HIGH PRESSURE.
INSTALL FUEL PRESSURE GAUGE BETWEEN FUEL TANK & FUEL FILTER.
RECONNECT THE PREVIOUSLY DISCONNECTED FUEL LINE.
IGNITION KEY ON.
ACTUATE THE ASD FUEL SYSTEM.
RECORD THE FUEL PRESSURE GAUGE READING.
CONTINUE TEST NS-4A

91A13813

Fig. 12: No Start Test NS-4A – Checking Low Fuel Pressure Condition (1 of 3)

NS-4A: – CHECKING LOW FUEL PRESSURE CONDITION (2 OF 3)

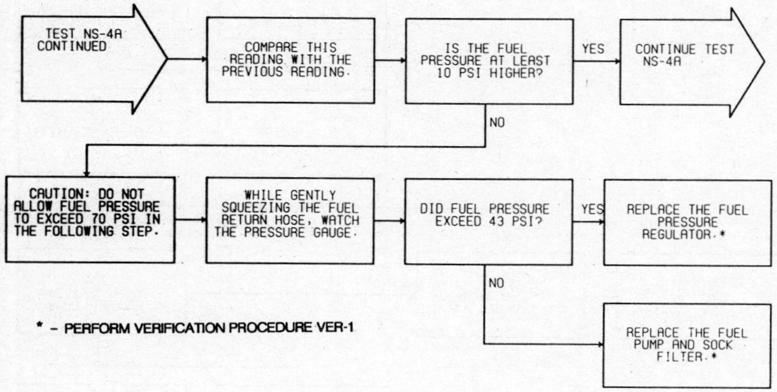
TEST NS-4A CONTINUED
COMPARE THIS READING WITH THE PREVIOUS READING.
IS THE FUEL PRESSURE AT LEAST 10 PSI HIGHER?
YES
CONTINUE TEST NS-4A
NO
CAUTION: DO NOT ALLOW FUEL PRESSURE TO EXCEED 70 PSI IN THE FOLLOWING STEP.
WHILE GENTLY SQUEEZING THE FUEL RETURN HOSE, WATCH THE PRESSURE GAUGE.
DID FUEL PRESSURE EXCEED 43 PSI?
YES
REPLACE THE FUEL PRESSURE REGULATOR.*
NO
REPLACE THE FUEL PUMP AND SOCK FILTER.*
* - PERFORM VERIFICATION PROCEDURE VER-1

91B13814

Fig. 13: No Start Test NS-4A – Checking Low Fuel Pressure Condition (2 of 3)

NS-4A: – CHECKING LOW FUEL PRESSURE CONDITION (3 OF 3)

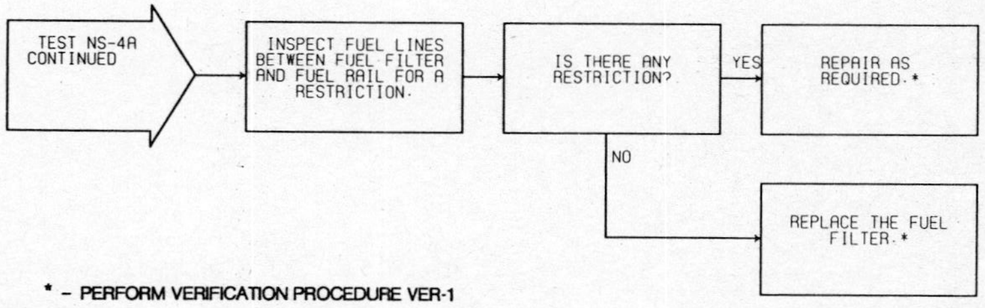
TEST NS-4A CONTINUED
INSPECT FUEL LINES BETWEEN FUEL FILTER AND FUEL RAIL FOR A RESTRICTION.
IS THERE ANY RESTRICTION?
YES
REPAIR AS REQUIRED.*
NO
REPLACE THE FUEL FILTER.*
* - PERFORM VERIFICATION PROCEDURE VER-1

91C13815

Fig. 14: No Start Test NS-4A – Checking Low Fuel Pressure Condition (3 of 3)

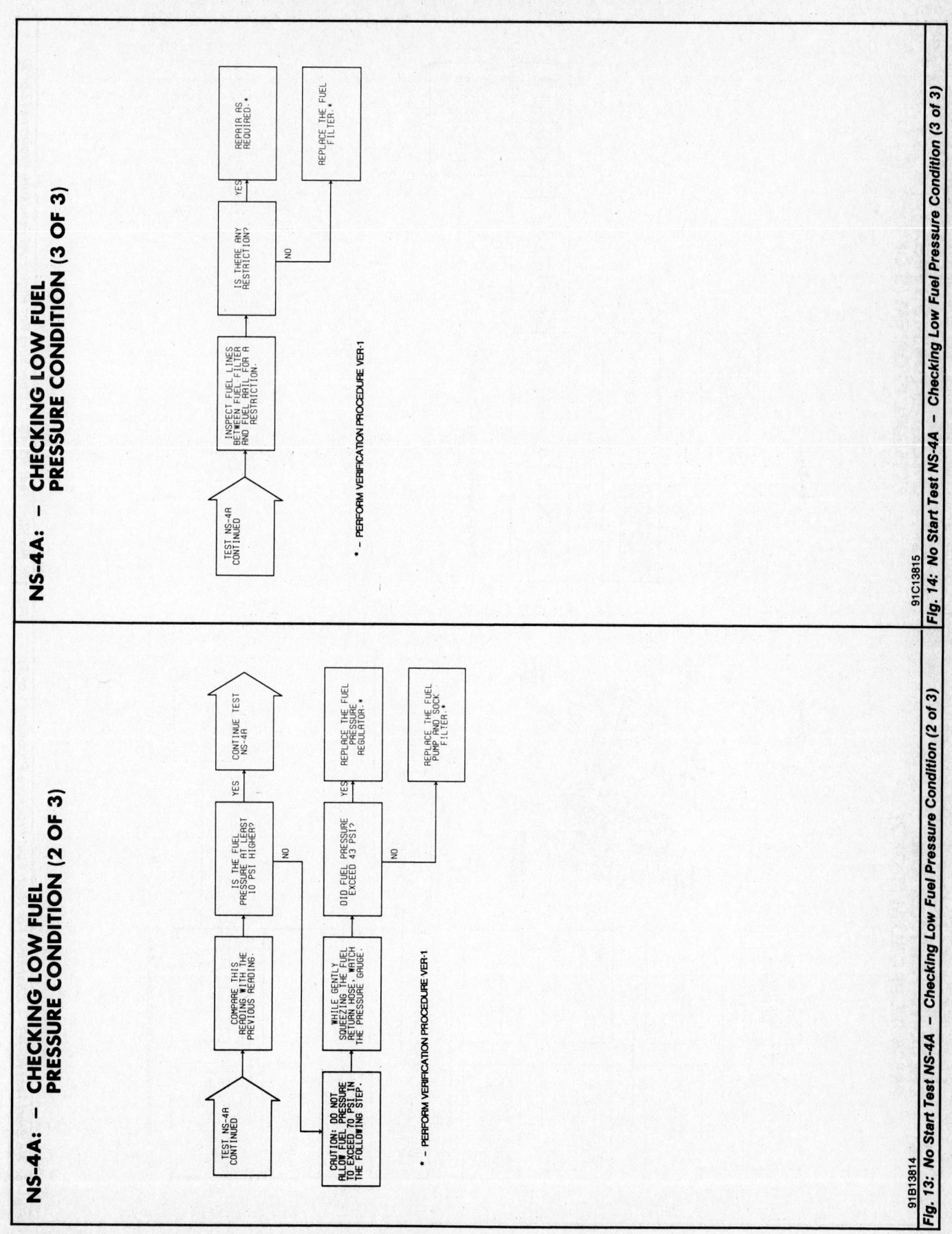

1991 ENGINE PERFORMANCE
Self-Diagnostics (Cont.)

NS-4B: – CHECKING FOR HIGH FUEL PRESSURE PROBLEM (1 OF 2)

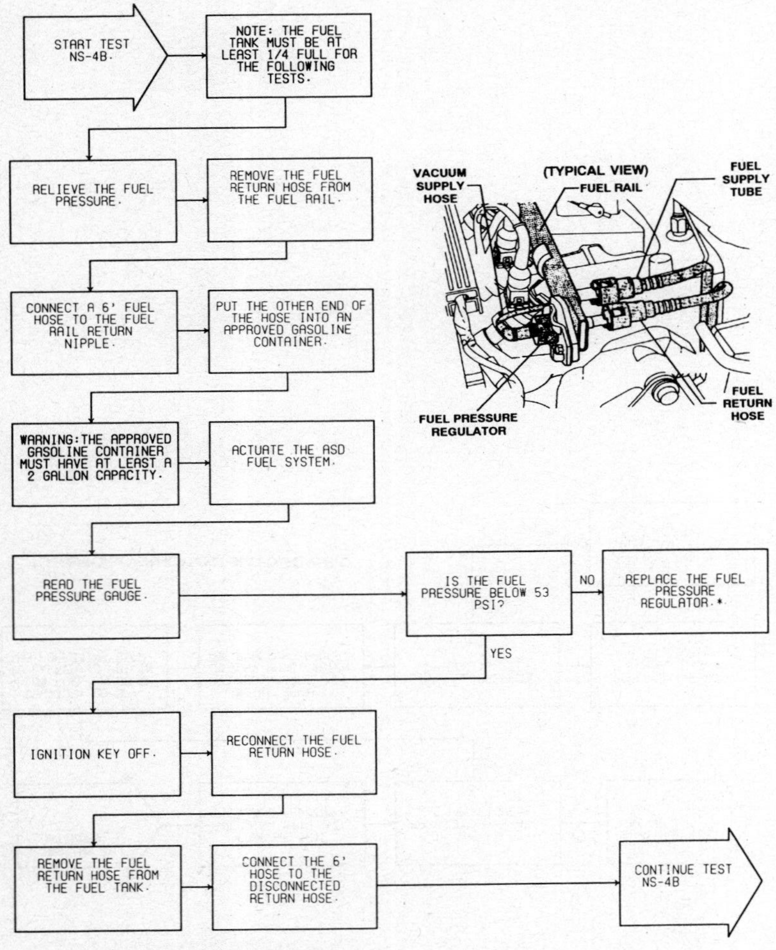
START TEST NS-4B.
NOTE: THE FUEL TANK MUST BE AT LEAST 1/4 FULL FOR THE FOLLOWING TESTS.
RELIEVE THE FUEL PRESSURE.
REMOVE THE FUEL RETURN HOSE FROM THE FUEL RAIL.
CONNECT A 6' FUEL HOSE TO THE FUEL RAIL RETURN NIPPLE.
PUT THE OTHER END OF THE HOSE INTO AN APPROVED GASOLINE CONTAINER.
WARNING: THE APPROVED GASOLINE CONTAINER MUST HAVE AT LEAST A 2 GALLON CAPACITY.
ACTUATE THE ASD FUEL SYSTEM.
READ THE FUEL PRESSURE GAUGE.
IS THE FUEL PRESSURE BELOW 53 PSI?
NO
REPLACE THE FUEL PRESSURE REGULATOR.*
YES
IGNITION KEY OFF.
RECONNECT THE FUEL RETURN HOSE.
REMOVE THE FUEL RETURN HOSE FROM THE FUEL TANK.
CONNECT THE 6' HOSE TO THE DISCONNECTED RETURN HOSE.
CONTINUE TEST NS-4B
VACUUM SUPPLY HOSE
(TYPICAL VIEW)
FUEL RAIL
FUEL SUPPLY TUBE
FUEL PRESSURE REGULATOR
FUEL RETURN HOSE

* – PERFORM VERIFICATION PROCEDURE VER-1

91D13816

Fig. 15: No Start Test NS-4B – Checking For High Fuel Pressure Problem (1 of 2)

NS-4B: – CHECKING FOR HIGH FUEL PRESSURE PROBLEM (2 OF 2)

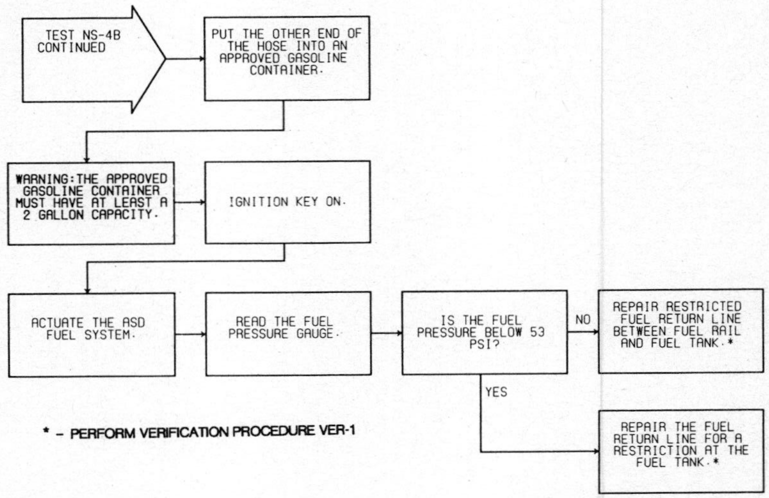
TEST NS-4B CONTINUED
PUT THE OTHER END OF THE HOSE INTO AN APPROVED GASOLINE CONTAINER.
WARNING: THE APPROVED GASOLINE CONTAINER MUST HAVE AT LEAST A 2 GALLON CAPACITY.
IGNITION KEY ON.
ACTUATE THE ASD FUEL SYSTEM.
READ THE FUEL PRESSURE GAUGE.
IS THE FUEL PRESSURE BELOW 53 PSI?
NO
REPAIR RESTRICTED FUEL RETURN LINE BETWEEN FUEL RAIL AND FUEL TANK.*
YES
REPAIR THE FUEL RETURN LINE FOR A RESTRICTION AT THE FUEL TANK.*

* – PERFORM VERIFICATION PROCEDURE VER-1

91E13817

Fig. 16: No Start Test NS-4B – Checking For High Fuel Pressure Problem (2 of 2)

NS-5A: – CHECKING FOR DEFECTIVE COIL OR CONTROL CIRCUIT (1 OF 2)

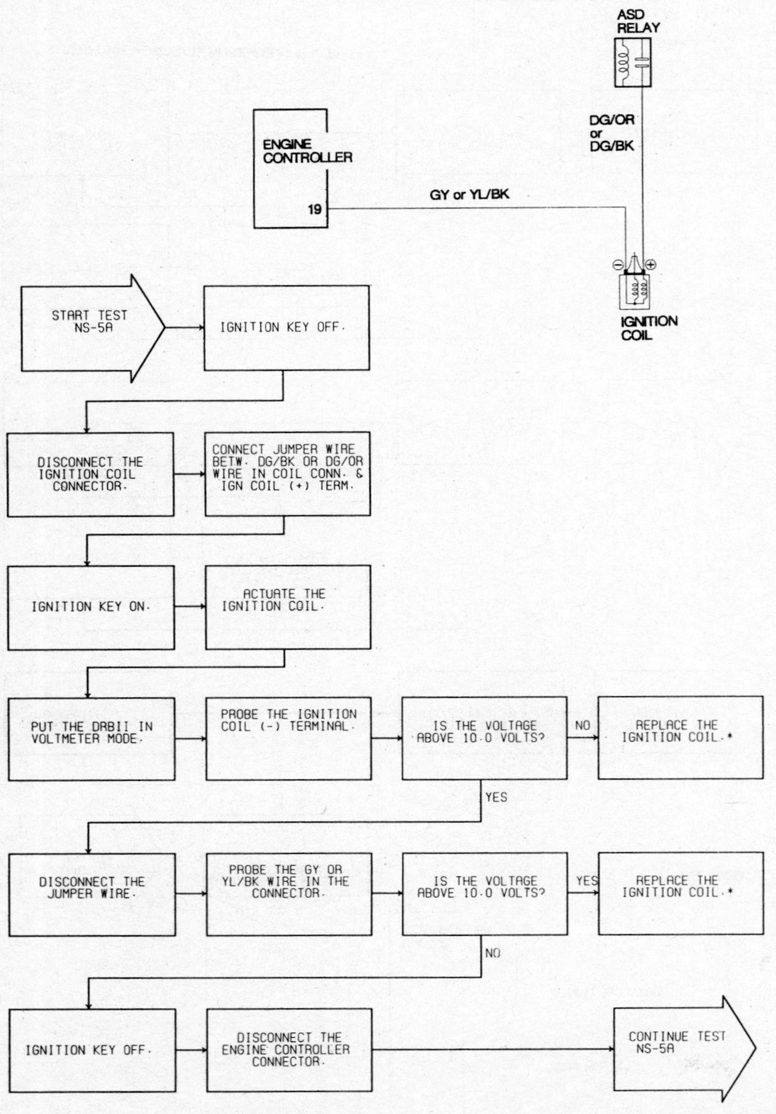
ASD RELAY
ENGINE CONTROLLER
19
GY or YL/BK
DG/OR or DG/BK
IGNITION COIL
START TEST NS-5A
IGNITION KEY OFF.
DISCONNECT THE IGNITION COIL CONNECTOR.
CONNECT JUMPER WIRE BETW. DG/BK OR DG/OR WIRE IN COIL CONN. & IGN COIL (+) TERM.
IGNITION KEY ON.
ACTUATE THE IGNITION COIL.
PUT THE DRBII IN VOLTMETER MODE.
PROBE THE IGNITION COIL (-) TERMINAL.
IS THE VOLTAGE ABOVE 10.0 VOLTS?
NO
REPLACE THE IGNITION COIL.*
YES
DISCONNECT THE JUMPER WIRE.
PROBE THE GY OR YL/BK WIRE IN THE CONNECTOR.
IS THE VOLTAGE ABOVE 10.0 VOLTS?
YES
REPLACE THE IGNITION COIL.*
NO
IGNITION KEY OFF.
DISCONNECT THE ENGINE CONTROLLER CONNECTOR.
CONTINUE TEST NS-5A

* – PERFORM VERIFICATION PROCEDURE VER-1

91G13934 91F13818

Fig. 17: *No Start Test NS-5A – Checking For Defective Coil Or Control Circuit (1 of 2)*

NS-5A: – CHECKING FOR DEFECTIVE COIL OR CONTROL CIRCUIT (2 OF 2)

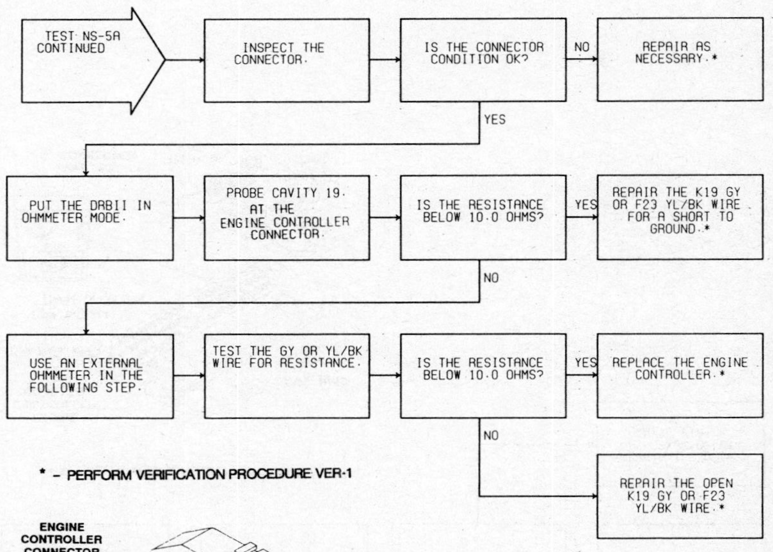
TEST NS-5A CONTINUED
INSPECT THE CONNECTOR.
IS THE CONNECTOR CONDITION OK?
NO
REPAIR AS NECESSARY.*
YES
PUT THE DRBII IN OHMMETER MODE.
PROBE CAVITY 19. AT THE ENGINE CONTROLLER CONNECTOR.
IS THE RESISTANCE BELOW 10.0 OHMS?
YES
REPAIR THE K19 GY OR F23 YL/BK WIRE FOR A SHORT TO GROUND.*
NO
USE AN EXTERNAL OHMMETER IN THE FOLLOWING STEP.
TEST THE GY OR YL/BK WIRE FOR RESISTANCE.
IS THE RESISTANCE BELOW 10.0 OHMS?
YES
REPLACE THE ENGINE CONTROLLER.*
NO
REPAIR THE OPEN K19 GY OR F23 YL/BK WIRE.*

* – PERFORM VERIFICATION PROCEDURE VER-1

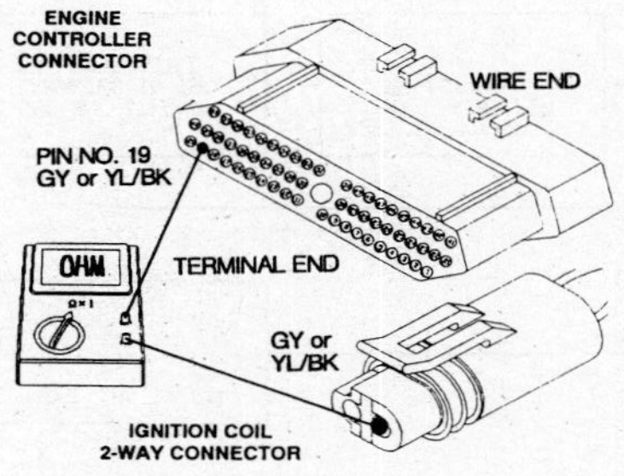
ENGINE CONTROLLER CONNECTOR
WIRE END
PIN NO. 19 GY or YL/BK
OHM
TERMINAL END
GY or YL/BK
IGNITION COIL 2-WAY CONNECTOR

91G13819

Fig. 18: *No Start Test NS-5A – Checking For Defective Coil Or Control Circuit (2 of 2)*

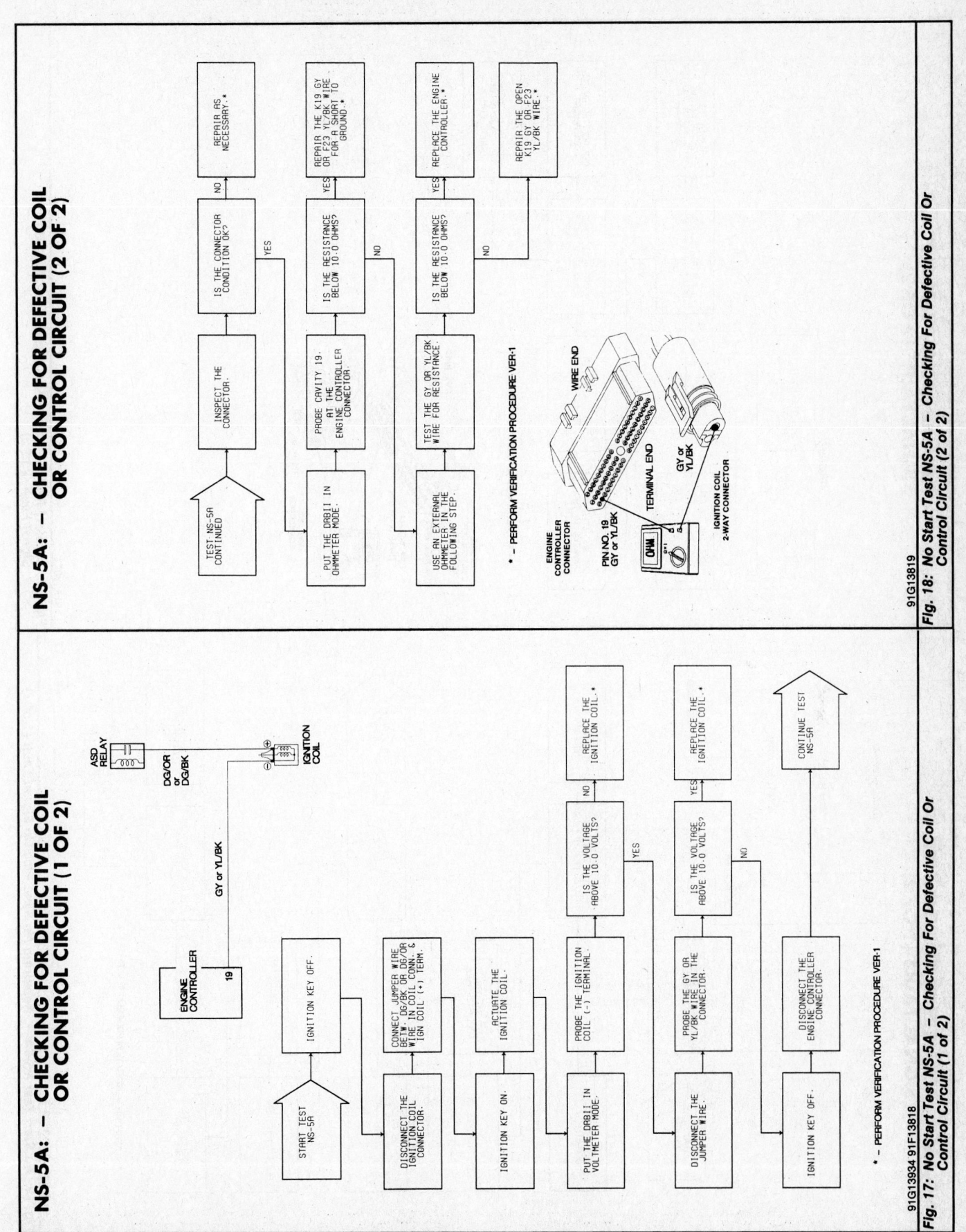

1991 ENGINE PERFORMANCE
Self-Diagnostics (Cont.)

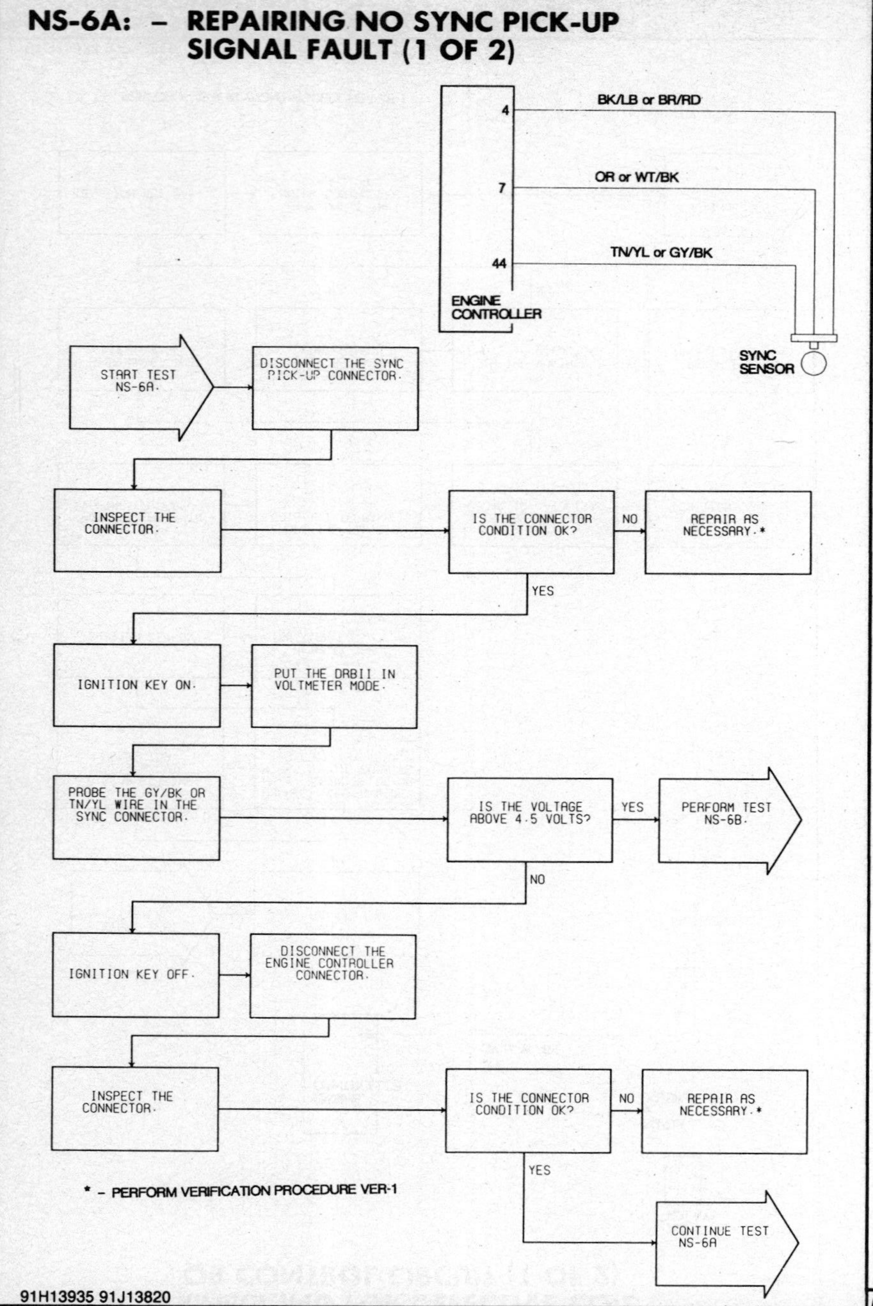
NS-6A: – REPAIRING NO SYNC PICK-UP SIGNAL FAULT (1 OF 2)
BK/LB or BR/RD
OR or WT/BK
TN/YL or GY/BK
4
7
44
ENGINE CONTROLLER
SYNC SENSOR
START TEST NS-6A.
DISCONNECT THE SYNC PICK-UP CONNECTOR.
INSPECT THE CONNECTOR.
IS THE CONNECTOR CONDITION OK?
NO
REPAIR AS NECESSARY.*
YES
IGNITION KEY ON.
PUT THE DRBII IN VOLTMETER MODE.
PROBE THE GY/BK OR TN/YL WIRE IN THE SYNC CONNECTOR.
IS THE VOLTAGE ABOVE 4.5 VOLTS?
YES
PERFORM TEST NS-6B.
NO
IGNITION KEY OFF.
DISCONNECT THE ENGINE CONTROLLER CONNECTOR.
INSPECT THE CONNECTOR.
IS THE CONNECTOR CONDITION OK?
NO
REPAIR AS NECESSARY.*
YES
CONTINUE TEST NS-6A
* – PERFORM VERIFICATION PROCEDURE VER-1
91H13935 91J13820

Fig. 19: No Start Test NS-6A – Repairing No Sync Pick-Up Signal Fault (1 of 2)

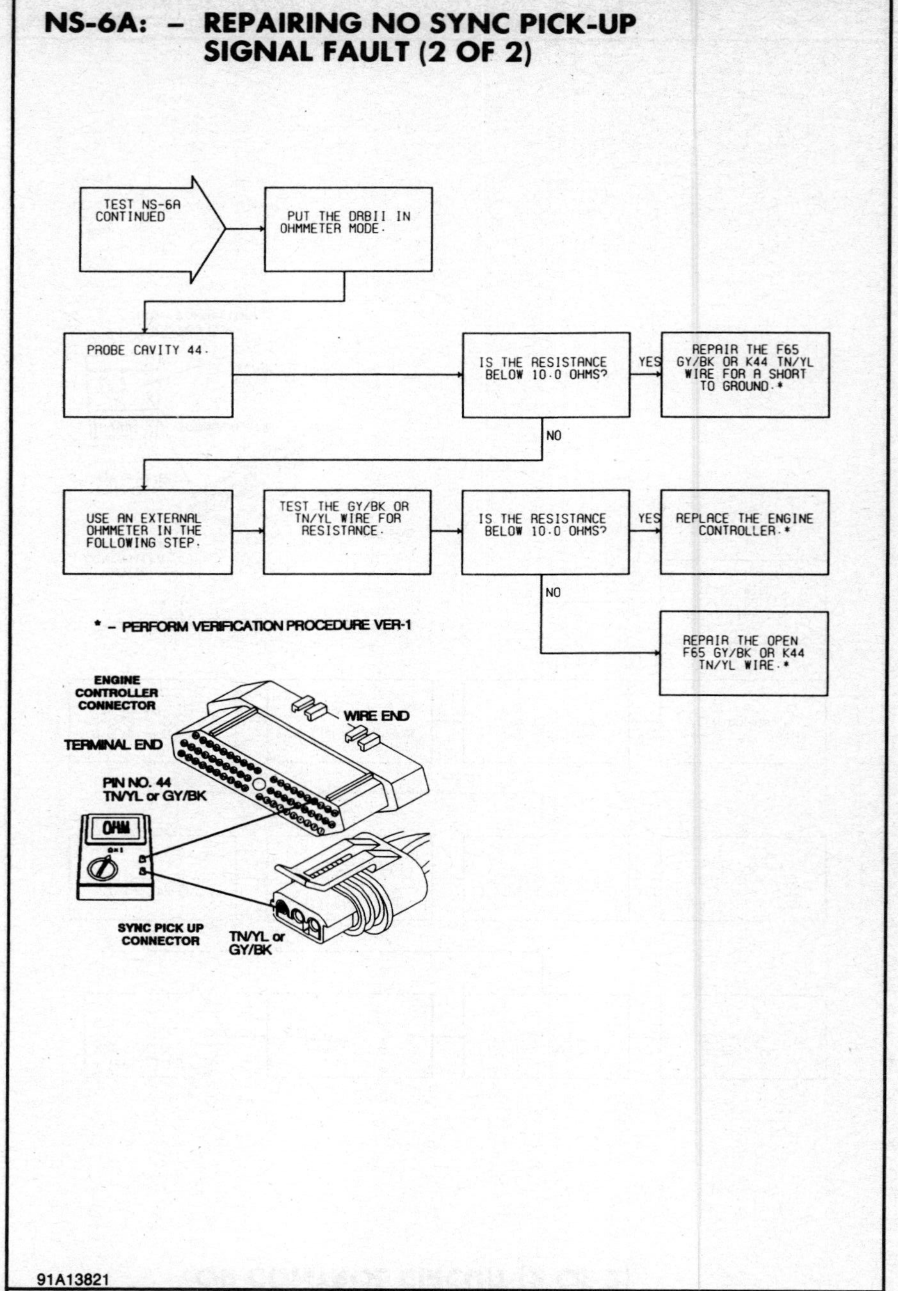
NS-6A: – REPAIRING NO SYNC PICK-UP SIGNAL FAULT (2 OF 2)
TEST NS-6A CONTINUED
PUT THE DRBII IN OHMMETER MODE.
PROBE CAVITY 44.
IS THE RESISTANCE BELOW 10.0 OHMS?
YES
REPAIR THE F65 GY/BK OR K44 TN/YL WIRE FOR A SHORT TO GROUND.*
NO
USE AN EXTERNAL OHMMETER IN THE FOLLOWING STEP.
TEST THE GY/BK OR TN/YL WIRE FOR RESISTANCE.
IS THE RESISTANCE BELOW 10.0 OHMS?
YES
REPLACE THE ENGINE CONTROLLER.*
NO
REPAIR THE OPEN F65 GY/BK OR K44 TN/YL WIRE.*
* – PERFORM VERIFICATION PROCEDURE VER-1
ENGINE CONTROLLER CONNECTOR
WIRE END
TERMINAL END
PIN NO. 44 TN/YL or GY/BK
OHM
SYNC PICK UP CONNECTOR
TN/YL or GY/BK
91A13821

Fig. 20: No Start Test NS-6A – Repairing No Sync Pick-Up Signal Fault (2 of 2)

NS-6B: – CHECKING DISTRIBUTOR SYNC CIRCUITS (1 OF 2)

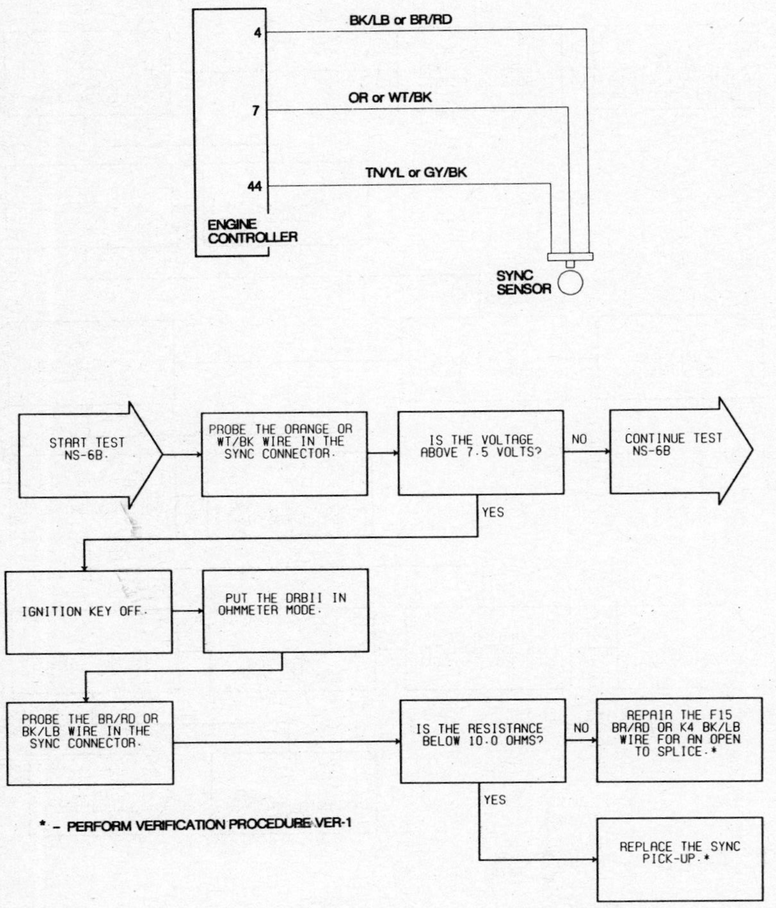
ENGINE CONTROLLER
4
7
44
BK/LB or BR/RD
OR or WT/BK
TN/YL or GY/BK
SYNC SENSOR
START TEST NS-6B.
PROBE THE ORANGE OR WT/BK WIRE IN THE SYNC CONNECTOR.
IS THE VOLTAGE ABOVE 7.5 VOLTS?
NO
CONTINUE TEST NS-6B
YES
IGNITION KEY OFF.
PUT THE DRBII IN OHMMETER MODE.
PROBE THE BR/RD OR BK/LB WIRE IN THE SYNC CONNECTOR.
IS THE RESISTANCE BELOW 10.0 OHMS?
NO
REPAIR THE F15 BR/RD OR K4 BK/LB WIRE FOR AN OPEN TO SPLICE.*
YES
REPLACE THE SYNC PICK-UP.*
* – PERFORM VERIFICATION PROCEDURE VER-1

91H13935 91B13822

Fig. 21: No Start Test NS-6B – Checking Distributor Sync Circuits (1 of 2)

NS-6B: – CHECKING DISTRIBUTOR SYNC CIRCUITS (2 OF 2)

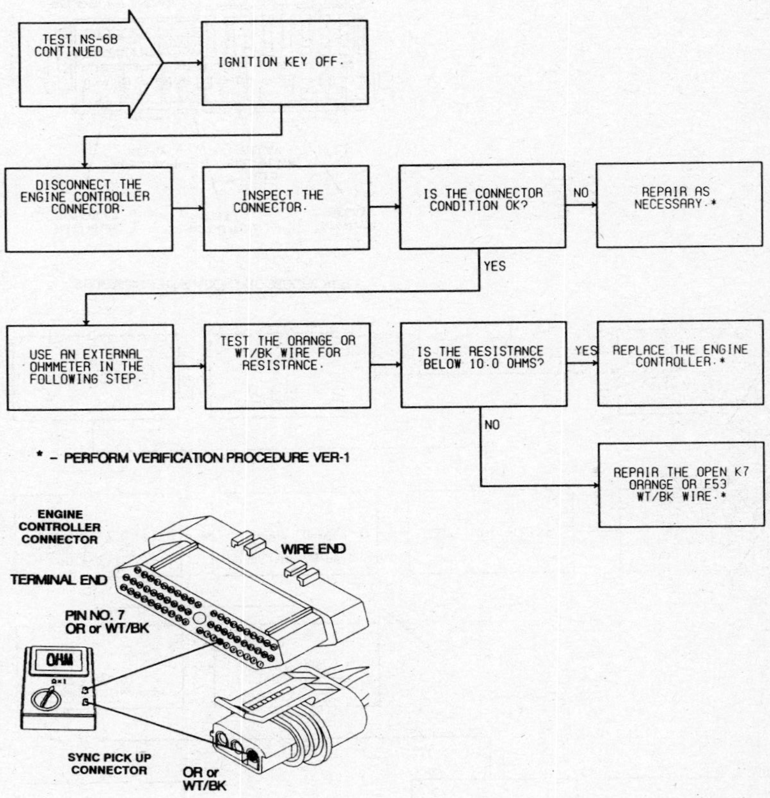
TEST NS-6B CONTINUED
IGNITION KEY OFF.
DISCONNECT THE ENGINE CONTROLLER CONNECTOR.
INSPECT THE CONNECTOR.
IS THE CONNECTOR CONDITION OK?
NO
REPAIR AS NECESSARY.*
YES
USE AN EXTERNAL OHMMETER IN THE FOLLOWING STEP.
TEST THE ORANGE OR WT/BK WIRE FOR RESISTANCE.
IS THE RESISTANCE BELOW 10.0 OHMS?
YES
REPLACE THE ENGINE CONTROLLER.*
NO
REPAIR THE OPEN K7 ORANGE OR F53 WT/BK WIRE.*
* – PERFORM VERIFICATION PROCEDURE VER-1
ENGINE CONTROLLER CONNECTOR
WIRE END
TERMINAL END
PIN NO. 7 OR or WT/BK
OHM
SYNC PICK UP CONNECTOR
OR or WT/BK

91C13823

Fig. 22: No Start Test NS-6B – Checking Distributor Sync Circuits (2 of 2)

1991 ENGINE PERFORMANCE
Self-Diagnostics (Cont.)

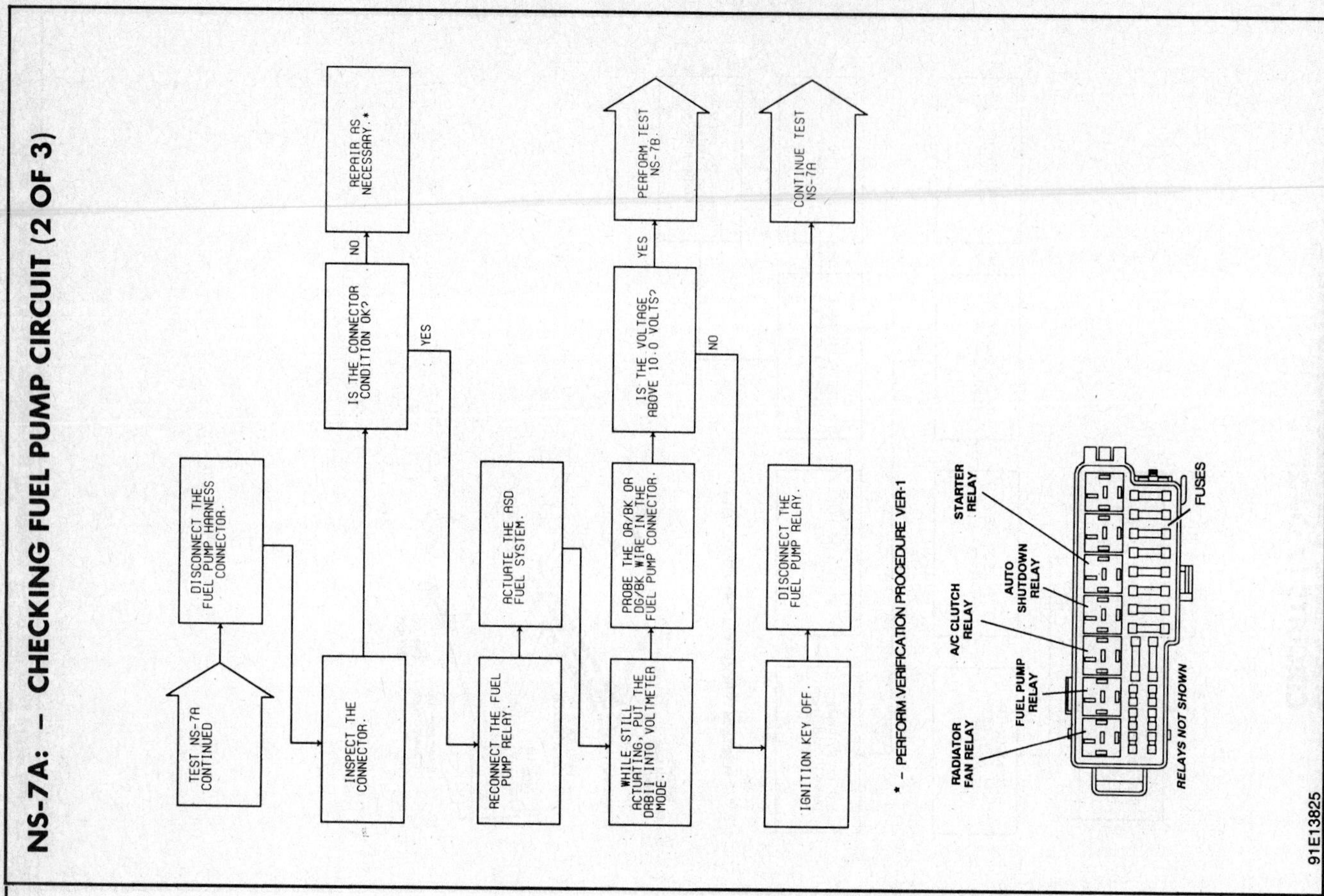
NS-7A: – CHECKING FUEL PUMP CIRCUIT (2 OF 3)
TEST NS-7A CONTINUED
DISCONNECT THE FUEL PUMP HARNESS CONNECTOR.
INSPECT THE CONNECTOR.
IS THE CONNECTOR CONDITION OK?
NO
REPAIR AS NECESSARY.*
YES
RECONNECT THE FUEL PUMP RELAY.
ACTUATE THE ASD FUEL SYSTEM.
WHILE STILL ACTUATING, PUT THE DRBII INTO VOLTMETER MODE.
PROBE THE OR/BK OR DG/BK WIRE IN THE FUEL PUMP CONNECTOR.
IS THE VOLTAGE ABOVE 10.0 VOLTS?
YES
PERFORM TEST NS-7B.
NO
IGNITION KEY OFF.
DISCONNECT THE FUEL PUMP RELAY.
CONTINUE TEST NS-7A
* – PERFORM VERIFICATION PROCEDURE VER-1
RADIATOR FAN RELAY
FUEL PUMP RELAY
A/C CLUTCH RELAY
AUTO SHUTDOWN RELAY
STARTER RELAY
FUSES
RELAYS NOT SHOWN
91E13825

Fig. 24: No Start Test NS-7A – Checking Fuel Pump Circuit (2 of 3)

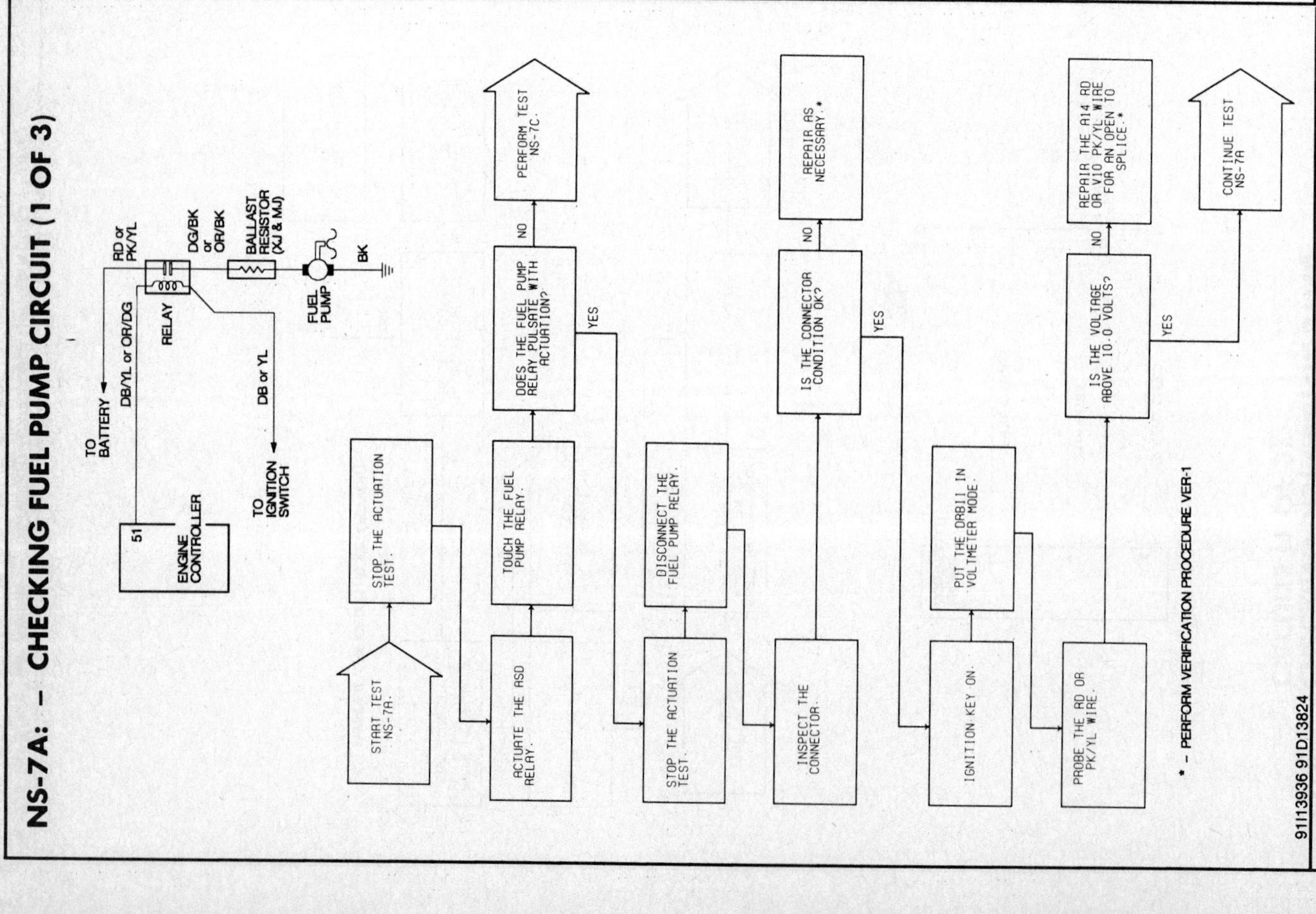
NS-7A: – CHECKING FUEL PUMP CIRCUIT (1 OF 3)
ENGINE CONTROLLER
51
TO BATTERY
DB/YL or OR/DG
RELAY
RD or PK/YL
DG/BK or OR/BK
BALLAST RESISTOR (XJ & MJ)
FUEL PUMP
BK
DB or YL
TO IGNITION SWITCH
START TEST NS-7A.
STOP THE ACTUATION TEST.
ACTUATE THE ASD RELAY.
TOUCH THE FUEL PUMP RELAY.
DOES THE FUEL PUMP RELAY PULSATE WITH ACTUATION?
NO
PERFORM TEST NS-7C.
YES
STOP THE ACTUATION TEST.
DISCONNECT THE FUEL PUMP RELAY.
INSPECT THE CONNECTOR.
IS THE CONNECTOR CONDITION OK?
NO
REPAIR AS NECESSARY.*
YES
IGNITION KEY ON.
PUT THE DRBII IN VOLTMETER MODE.
PROBE THE RD OR PK/YL WIRE.
IS THE VOLTAGE ABOVE 10.0 VOLTS?
NO
REPAIR THE A14 RD OR V10 PK/YL WIRE FOR AN OPEN TO SPLICE.*
YES
CONTINUE TEST NS-7A
* – PERFORM VERIFICATION PROCEDURE VER-1
91I13936 91D13824

Fig. 23: No Start Test NS-7A – Checking Fuel Pump Circuit (1 of 3)

NS-7A: – CHECKING FUEL PUMP CIRCUIT (3 OF 3)

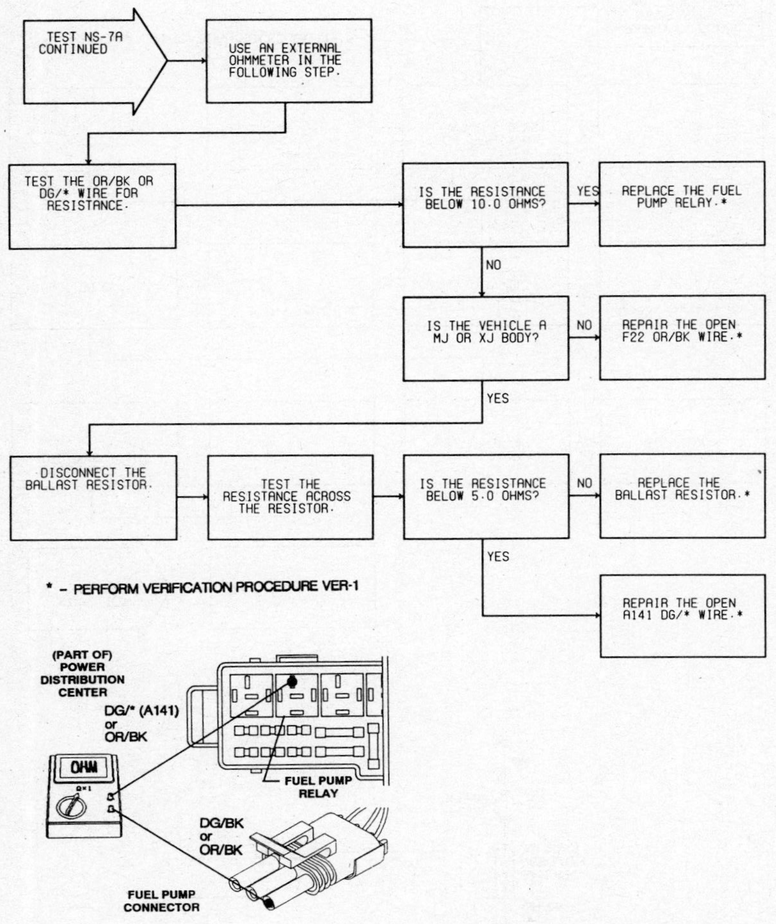
TEST NS-7A CONTINUED
USE AN EXTERNAL OHMMETER IN THE FOLLOWING STEP.
TEST THE OR/BK OR DG/* WIRE FOR RESISTANCE.
IS THE RESISTANCE BELOW 10.0 OHMS?
YES
REPLACE THE FUEL PUMP RELAY.*
NO
IS THE VEHICLE A MJ OR XJ BODY?
NO
REPAIR THE OPEN F22 OR/BK WIRE.*
YES
DISCONNECT THE BALLAST RESISTOR.
TEST THE RESISTANCE ACROSS THE RESISTOR.
IS THE RESISTANCE BELOW 5.0 OHMS?
NO
REPLACE THE BALLAST RESISTOR.*
YES
REPAIR THE OPEN A141 DG/* WIRE.*
* – PERFORM VERIFICATION PROCEDURE VER-1
(PART OF) POWER DISTRIBUTION CENTER
DG/* (A141) or OR/BK
OHM
FUEL PUMP RELAY
DG/BK or OR/BK
FUEL PUMP CONNECTOR

91F13826

Fig. 25: No Start Test NS-7A – Checking Fuel Pump Circuit (3 of 3)

NS-7B: – CHECKING FUEL PUMP GROUND CIRCUIT

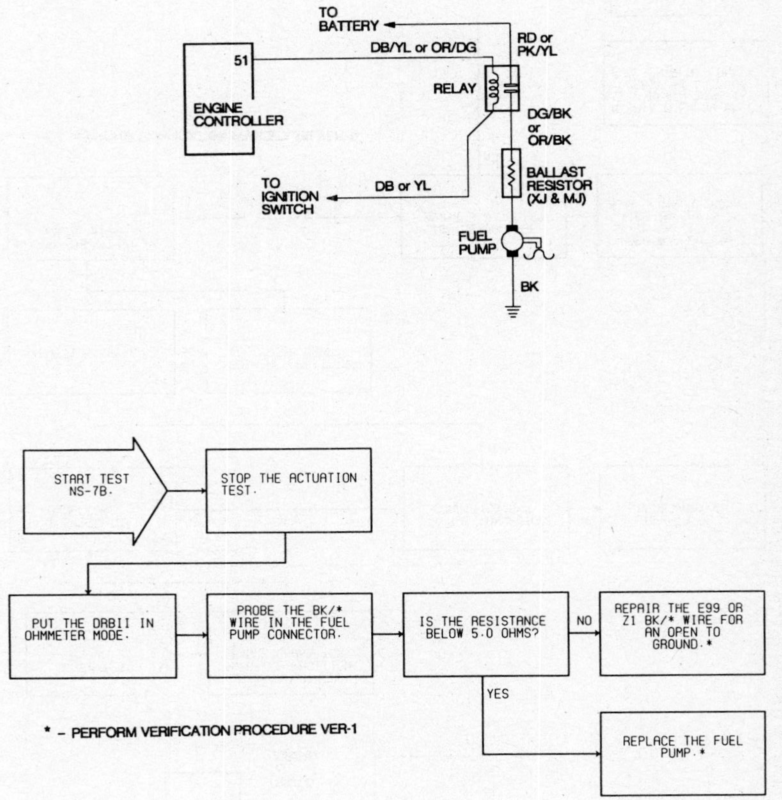
TO BATTERY
DB/YL or OR/DG
RD or PK/YL
51
ENGINE CONTROLLER
RELAY
DG/BK or OR/BK
TO IGNITION SWITCH
DB or YL
BALLAST RESISTOR (XJ & MJ)
FUEL PUMP
BK
START TEST NS-7B.
STOP THE ACTUATION TEST.
PUT THE DRBII IN OHMMETER MODE.
PROBE THE BK/* WIRE IN THE FUEL PUMP CONNECTOR.
IS THE RESISTANCE BELOW 5.0 OHMS?
NO
REPAIR THE E99 OR Z1 BK/* WIRE FOR AN OPEN TO GROUND.*
YES
REPLACE THE FUEL PUMP.*
* – PERFORM VERIFICATION PROCEDURE VER-1

91I13936 91G13827

Fig. 26: No Start Test NS-7B – Checking Fuel Pump Ground Circuit

1991 ENGINE PERFORMANCE
Self-Diagnostics (Cont.)

NS-7C: – CHECKING FUEL PUMP POWER CIRCUIT

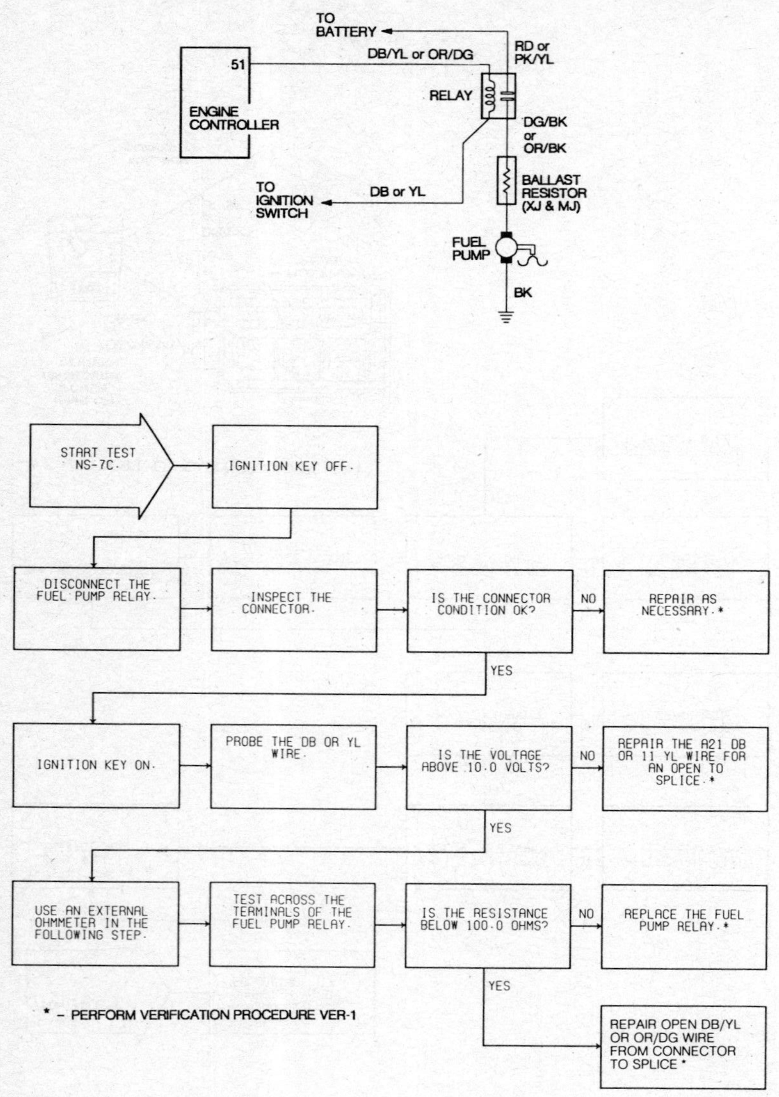
TO BATTERY
DB/YL or OR/DG
RD or PK/YL
51
ENGINE CONTROLLER
RELAY
DG/BK or OR/BK
TO IGNITION SWITCH
DB or YL
BALLAST RESISTOR (XJ & MJ)
FUEL PUMP
BK
START TEST NS-7C.
IGNITION KEY OFF.
DISCONNECT THE FUEL PUMP RELAY.
INSPECT THE CONNECTOR.
IS THE CONNECTOR CONDITION OK?
NO
REPAIR AS NECESSARY.*
YES
IGNITION KEY ON.
PROBE THE DB OR YL WIRE.
IS THE VOLTAGE ABOVE 10.0 VOLTS?
NO
REPAIR THE A21 DB OR 11 YL WIRE FOR AN OPEN TO SPLICE.*
YES
USE AN EXTERNAL OHMMETER IN THE FOLLOWING STEP.
TEST ACROSS THE TERMINALS OF THE FUEL PUMP RELAY.
IS THE RESISTANCE BELOW 100.0 OHMS?
NO
REPLACE THE FUEL PUMP RELAY.*
YES
REPAIR OPEN DB/YL OR OR/DG WIRE FROM CONNECTOR TO SPLICE *
* – PERFORM VERIFICATION PROCEDURE VER-1

91I13936 91H13828

Fig. 27: No Start Test NS-7C – Checking Fuel Pump Power Circuit

NS-8A: – REPAIRING NO RESPONSE CONDITION (1 OF 4)

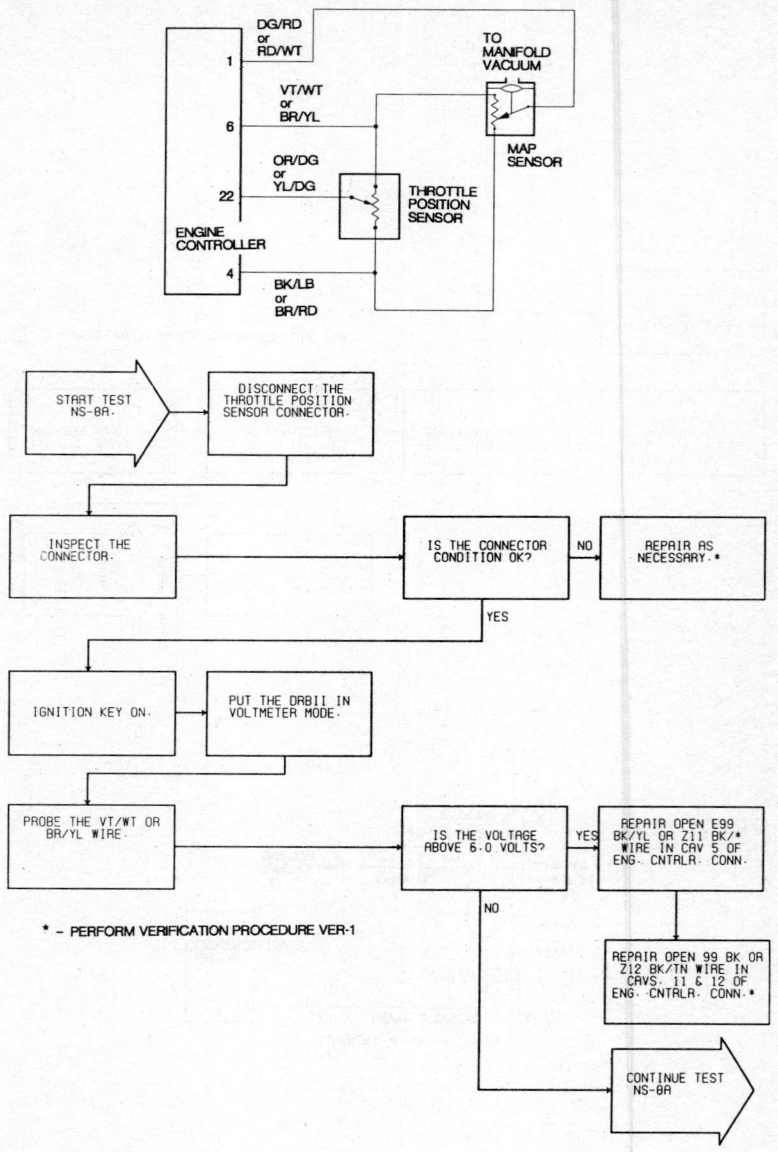
DG/RD or RD/WT
1
VT/WT or BR/YL
6
OR/DG or YL/DG
22
ENGINE CONTROLLER
4
BK/LB or BR/RD
TO MANIFOLD VACUUM
MAP SENSOR
THROTTLE POSITION SENSOR
START TEST NS-8A.
DISCONNECT THE THROTTLE POSITION SENSOR CONNECTOR.
INSPECT THE CONNECTOR.
IS THE CONNECTOR CONDITION OK?
NO
REPAIR AS NECESSARY.*
YES
IGNITION KEY ON.
PUT THE DRBII IN VOLTMETER MODE.
PROBE THE VT/WT OR BR/YL WIRE.
IS THE VOLTAGE ABOVE 6.0 VOLTS?
YES
REPAIR OPEN E99 BK/YL OR Z11 BK/* WIRE IN CAV 5 OF ENG. CNTRLR. CONN.
REPAIR OPEN 99 BK OR Z12 BK/TN WIRE IN CAVS. 11 & 12 OF ENG. CNTRLR. CONN.*
NO
CONTINUE TEST NS-8A
* – PERFORM VERIFICATION PROCEDURE VER-1

91J13937 91I13829

Fig. 28: No Start Test NS-8A – Repairing No Response Condition (1 of 4)

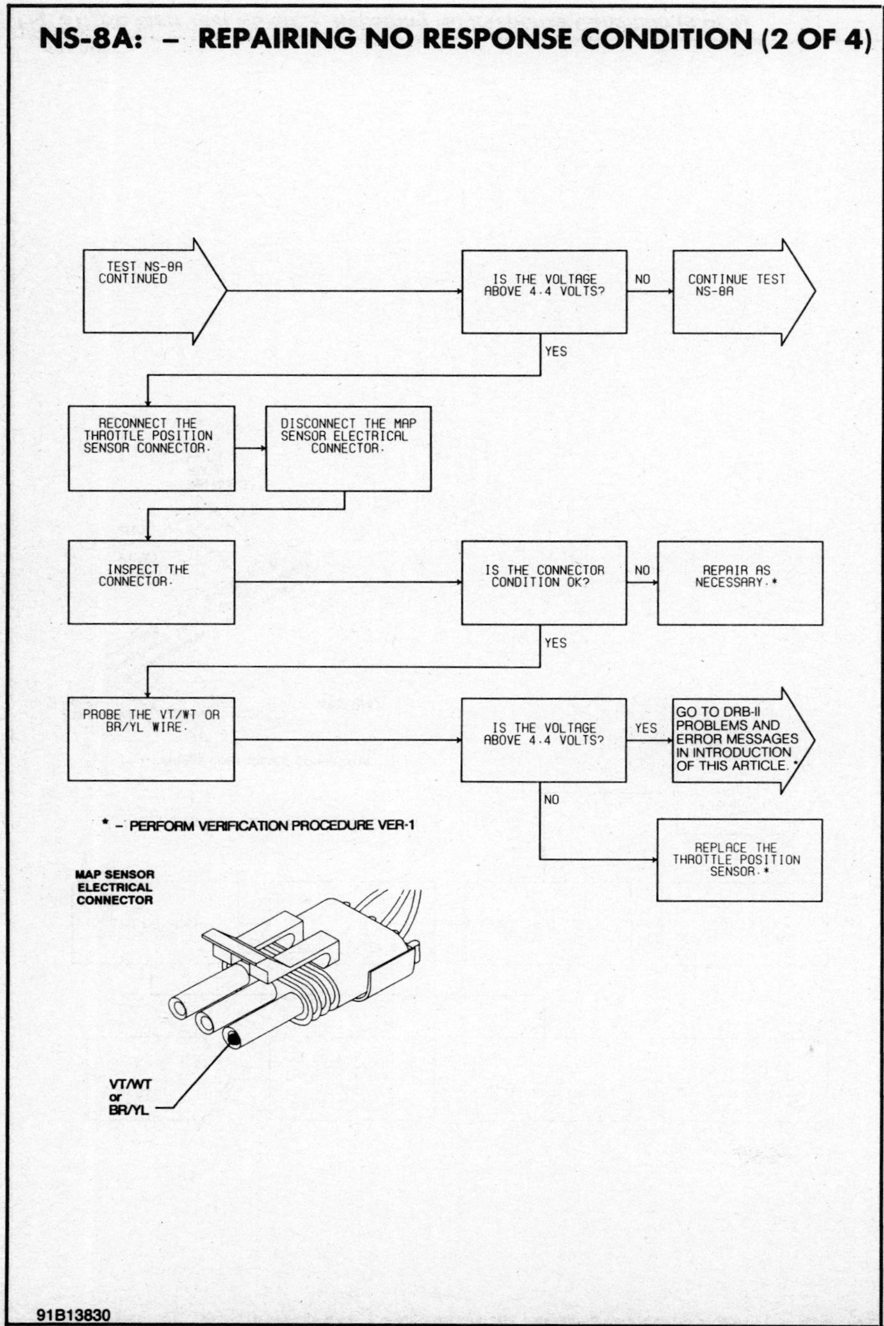
NS-8A: – REPAIRING NO RESPONSE CONDITION (2 OF 4)
TEST NS-8A CONTINUED
IS THE VOLTAGE ABOVE 4.4 VOLTS?
NO
CONTINUE TEST NS-8A
YES
RECONNECT THE THROTTLE POSITION SENSOR CONNECTOR.
DISCONNECT THE MAP SENSOR ELECTRICAL CONNECTOR.
INSPECT THE CONNECTOR.
IS THE CONNECTOR CONDITION OK?
NO
REPAIR AS NECESSARY.*
YES
PROBE THE VT/WT OR BR/YL WIRE.
IS THE VOLTAGE ABOVE 4.4 VOLTS?
YES
GO TO DRB-II PROBLEMS AND ERROR MESSAGES IN INTRODUCTION OF THIS ARTICLE.*
NO
REPLACE THE THROTTLE POSITION SENSOR.*
* – PERFORM VERIFICATION PROCEDURE VER-1
MAP SENSOR ELECTRICAL CONNECTOR
VT/WT or BR/YL
91B13830

Fig. 29: No Start Test NS-8A – Repairing No Response Condition (2 of 4)

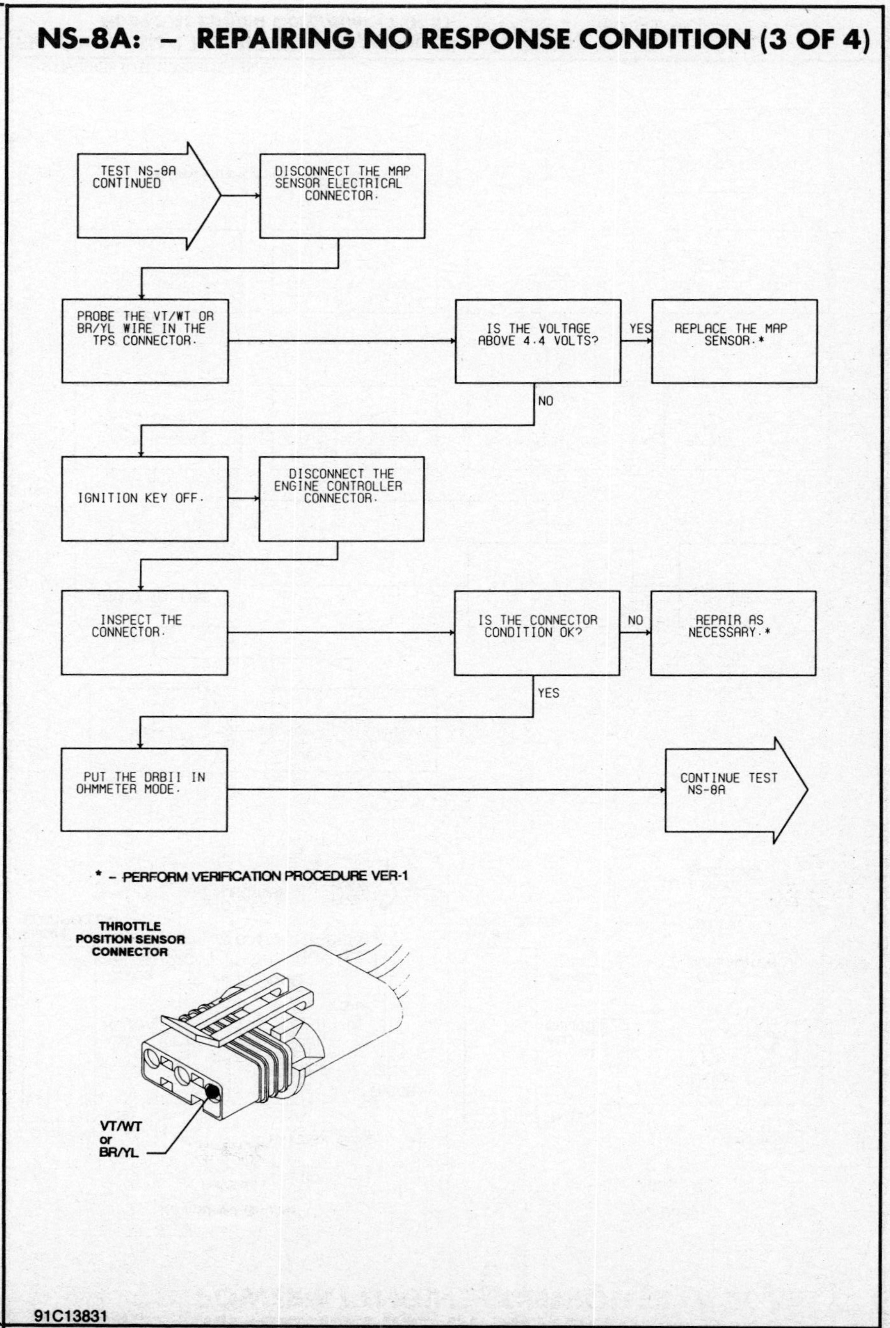
NS-8A: – REPAIRING NO RESPONSE CONDITION (3 OF 4)
TEST NS-8A CONTINUED
DISCONNECT THE MAP SENSOR ELECTRICAL CONNECTOR.
PROBE THE VT/WT OR BR/YL WIRE IN THE TPS CONNECTOR.
IS THE VOLTAGE ABOVE 4.4 VOLTS?
YES
REPLACE THE MAP SENSOR.*
NO
IGNITION KEY OFF.
DISCONNECT THE ENGINE CONTROLLER CONNECTOR.
INSPECT THE CONNECTOR.
IS THE CONNECTOR CONDITION OK?
NO
REPAIR AS NECESSARY.*
YES
PUT THE DRBII IN OHMMETER MODE.
CONTINUE TEST NS-8A
* – PERFORM VERIFICATION PROCEDURE VER-1
THROTTLE POSITION SENSOR CONNECTOR
VT/WT or BR/YL
91C13831

Fig. 30: No Start Test NS-8A – Repairing No Response Condition (3 of 4)

1991 ENGINE PERFORMANCE
Self-Diagnostics (Cont.)

NS-8A: – REPAIRING NO RESPONSE CONDITION (4 OF 4)

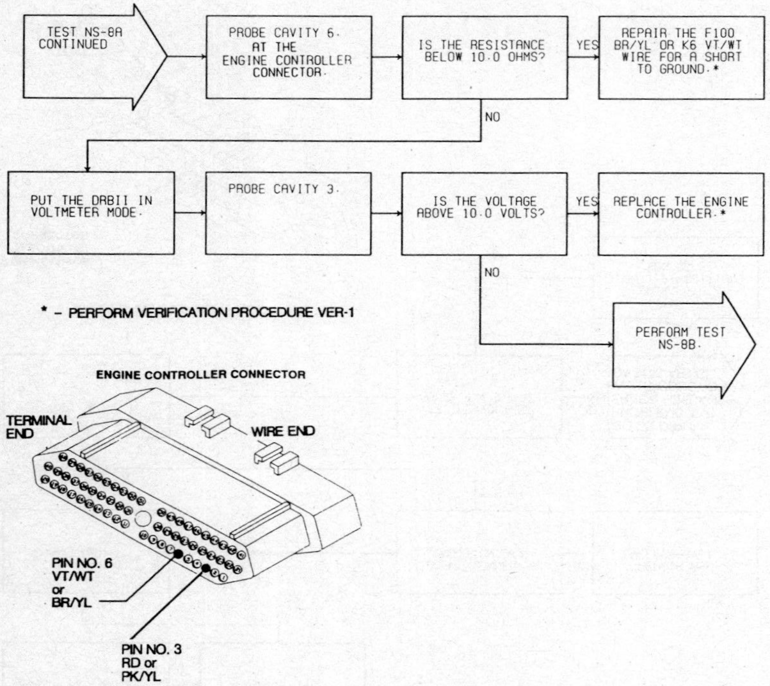
TEST NS-8A CONTINUED
PROBE CAVITY 6 AT THE ENGINE CONTROLLER CONNECTOR.
IS THE RESISTANCE BELOW 10.0 OHMS?
YES
REPAIR THE F100 BR/YL OR K6 VT/WT WIRE FOR A SHORT TO GROUND.*
NO
PUT THE DRBII IN VOLTMETER MODE.
PROBE CAVITY 3.
IS THE VOLTAGE ABOVE 10.0 VOLTS?
YES
REPLACE THE ENGINE CONTROLLER.*
NO
PERFORM TEST NS-8B.
* - PERFORM VERIFICATION PROCEDURE VER-1
ENGINE CONTROLLER CONNECTOR
TERMINAL END
WIRE END
PIN NO. 6 VT/WT or BR/YL
PIN NO. 3 RD or PK/YL

91D13832

Fig. 31: No Start Test NS-8A – Repairing No Response Condition (4 of 4)

NS-8B: – REPAIRING LOSS OF BATTERY POWER AT ENGINE CONTROLLER (1 OF 5)

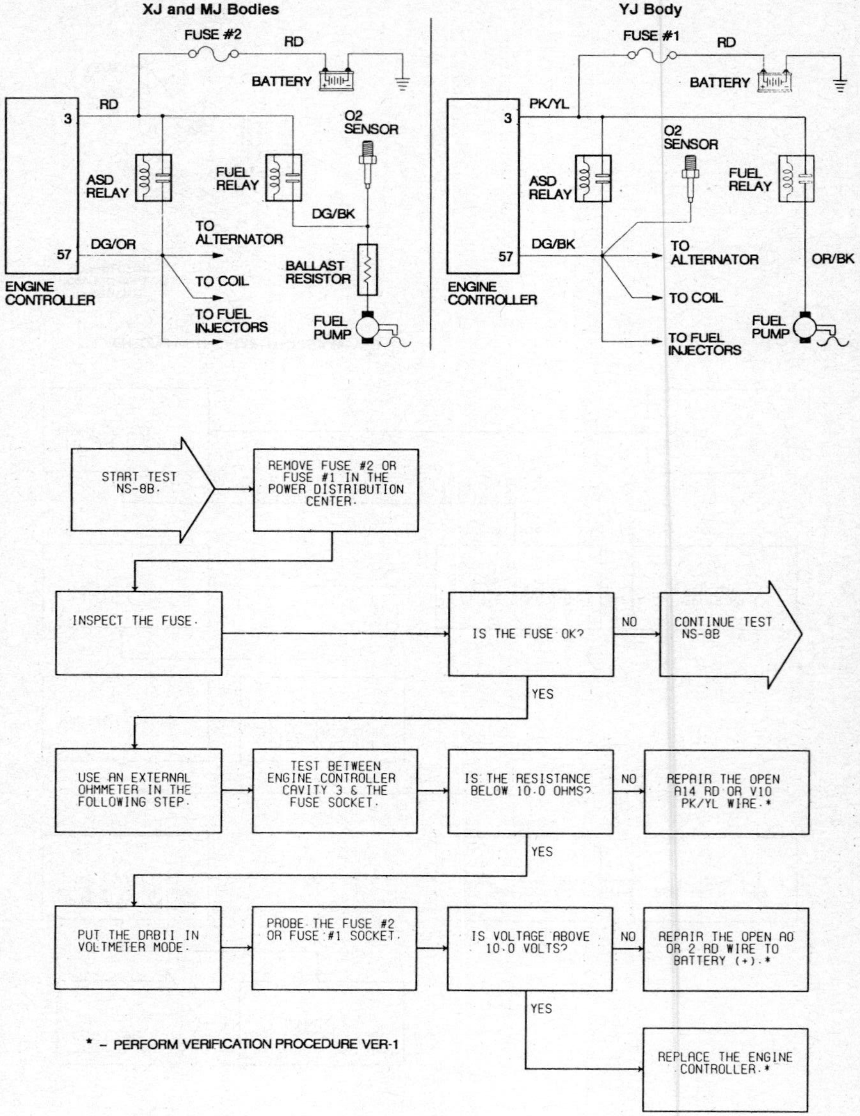
XJ and MJ Bodies
FUSE #2
RD
BATTERY
RD
3
ASD RELAY
FUEL RELAY
O2 SENSOR
DG/BK
TO ALTERNATOR
DG/OR
57
ENGINE CONTROLLER
TO COIL
BALLAST RESISTOR
TO FUEL INJECTORS
FUEL PUMP
YJ Body
FUSE #1
RD
BATTERY
PK/YL
3
ASD RELAY
O2 SENSOR
FUEL RELAY
DG/BK
57
ENGINE CONTROLLER
TO ALTERNATOR
OR/BK
TO COIL
FUEL PUMP
TO FUEL INJECTORS
START TEST NS-8B.
REMOVE FUSE #2 OR FUSE #1 IN THE POWER DISTRIBUTION CENTER.
INSPECT THE FUSE.
IS THE FUSE OK?
NO
CONTINUE TEST NS-8B
YES
USE AN EXTERNAL OHMMETER IN THE FOLLOWING STEP.
TEST BETWEEN ENGINE CONTROLLER CAVITY 3 & THE FUSE SOCKET.
IS THE RESISTANCE BELOW 10.0 OHMS?
NO
REPAIR THE OPEN A14 RD OR V10 PK/YL WIRE.*
YES
PUT THE DRBII IN VOLTMETER MODE.
PROBE THE FUSE #2 OR FUSE #1 SOCKET.
IS VOLTAGE ABOVE 10.0 VOLTS?
NO
REPAIR THE OPEN A0 OR 2 RD WIRE TO BATTERY (+).*
YES
REPLACE THE ENGINE CONTROLLER.*
* - PERFORM VERIFICATION PROCEDURE VER-1

91A13938 91B13939 91E13833

Fig. 32: No Start Test NS-8B – Repairing Loss Of Battery Power At Engine Controller (1 of 5)

NS-8B: – REPAIRING LOSS OF BATTERY POWER AT ENGINE CONTROLLER (2 OF 5)

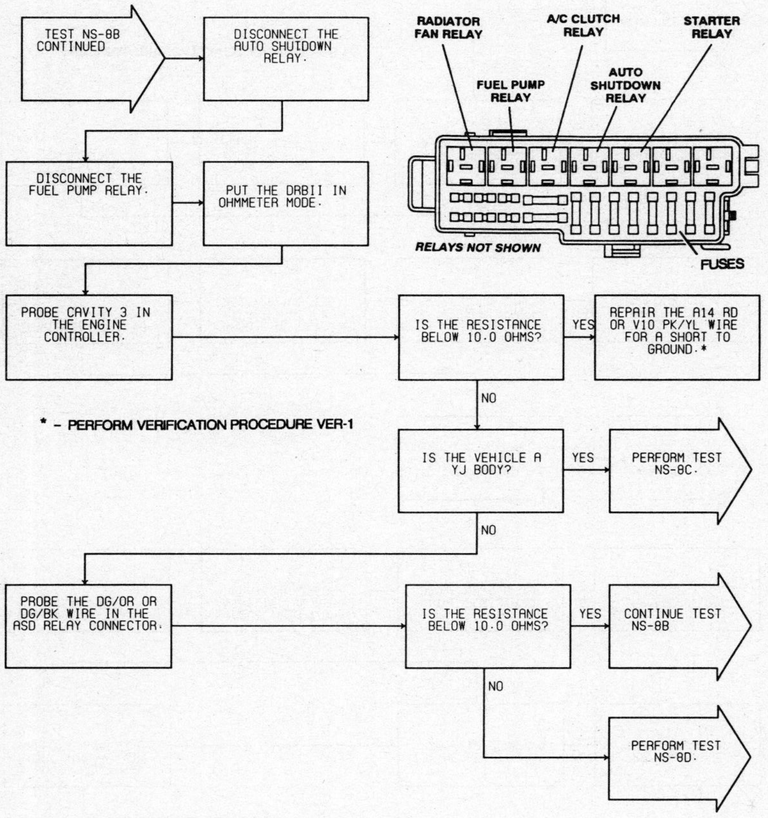
TEST NS-8B CONTINUED
DISCONNECT THE AUTO SHUTDOWN RELAY.
DISCONNECT THE FUEL PUMP RELAY.
PUT THE DRBII IN OHMMETER MODE.
PROBE CAVITY 3 IN THE ENGINE CONTROLLER.
IS THE RESISTANCE BELOW 10.0 OHMS?
YES
REPAIR THE A14 RD OR V10 PK/YL WIRE FOR A SHORT TO GROUND.*
NO
IS THE VEHICLE A YJ BODY?
YES
PERFORM TEST NS-8C.
NO
PROBE THE DG/OR OR DG/BK WIRE IN THE ASD RELAY CONNECTOR.
IS THE RESISTANCE BELOW 10.0 OHMS?
YES
CONTINUE TEST NS-8B
NO
PERFORM TEST NS-8D.
RADIATOR FAN RELAY
FUEL PUMP RELAY
A/C CLUTCH RELAY
AUTO SHUTDOWN RELAY
STARTER RELAY
RELAYS NOT SHOWN
FUSES
* – PERFORM VERIFICATION PROCEDURE VER-1

91F13834

Fig. 33: No Start Test NS-8B – Repairing Loss Of Battery Power At Engine Controller (2 of 5)

NS-8B: – REPAIRING LOSS OF BATTERY POWER AT ENGINE CONTROLLER (3 OF 5)

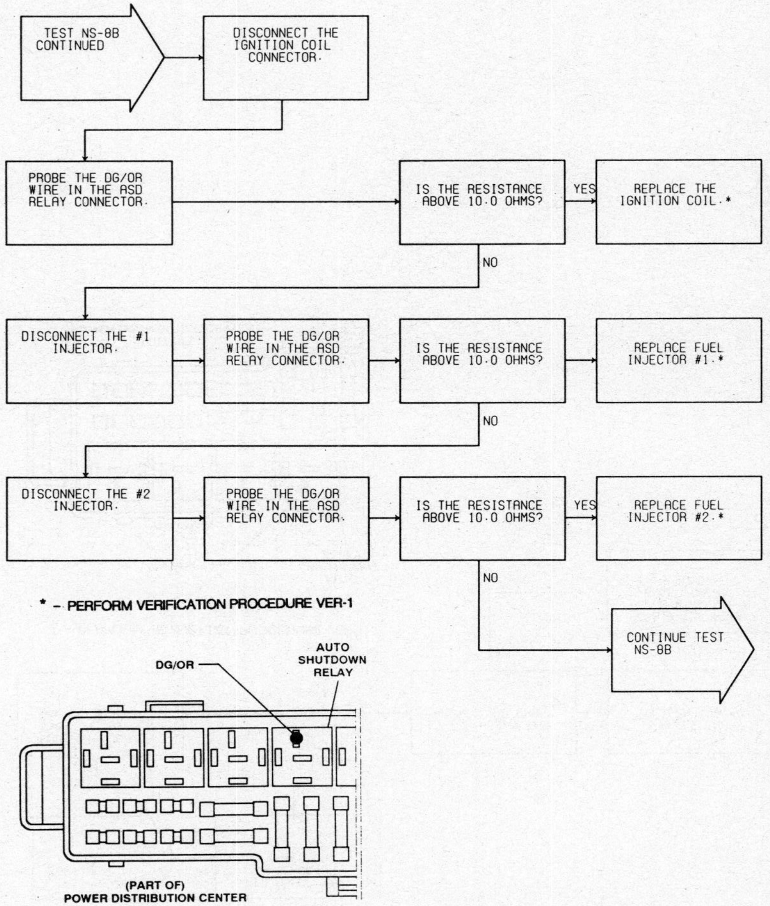
TEST NS-8B CONTINUED
DISCONNECT THE IGNITION COIL CONNECTOR.
PROBE THE DG/OR WIRE IN THE ASD RELAY CONNECTOR.
IS THE RESISTANCE ABOVE 10.0 OHMS?
YES
REPLACE THE IGNITION COIL.*
NO
DISCONNECT THE #1 INJECTOR.
PROBE THE DG/OR WIRE IN THE ASD RELAY CONNECTOR.
IS THE RESISTANCE ABOVE 10.0 OHMS?
REPLACE FUEL INJECTOR #1.*
NO
DISCONNECT THE #2 INJECTOR.
PROBE THE DG/OR WIRE IN THE ASD RELAY CONNECTOR.
IS THE RESISTANCE ABOVE 10.0 OHMS?
YES
REPLACE FUEL INJECTOR #2.*
NO
CONTINUE TEST NS-8B
* – PERFORM VERIFICATION PROCEDURE VER-1
DG/OR
AUTO SHUTDOWN RELAY
(PART OF) POWER DISTRIBUTION CENTER

91G13835

Fig. 34: No Start Test NS-8B – Repairing Loss Of Battery Power At Engine Controller (3 of 5)

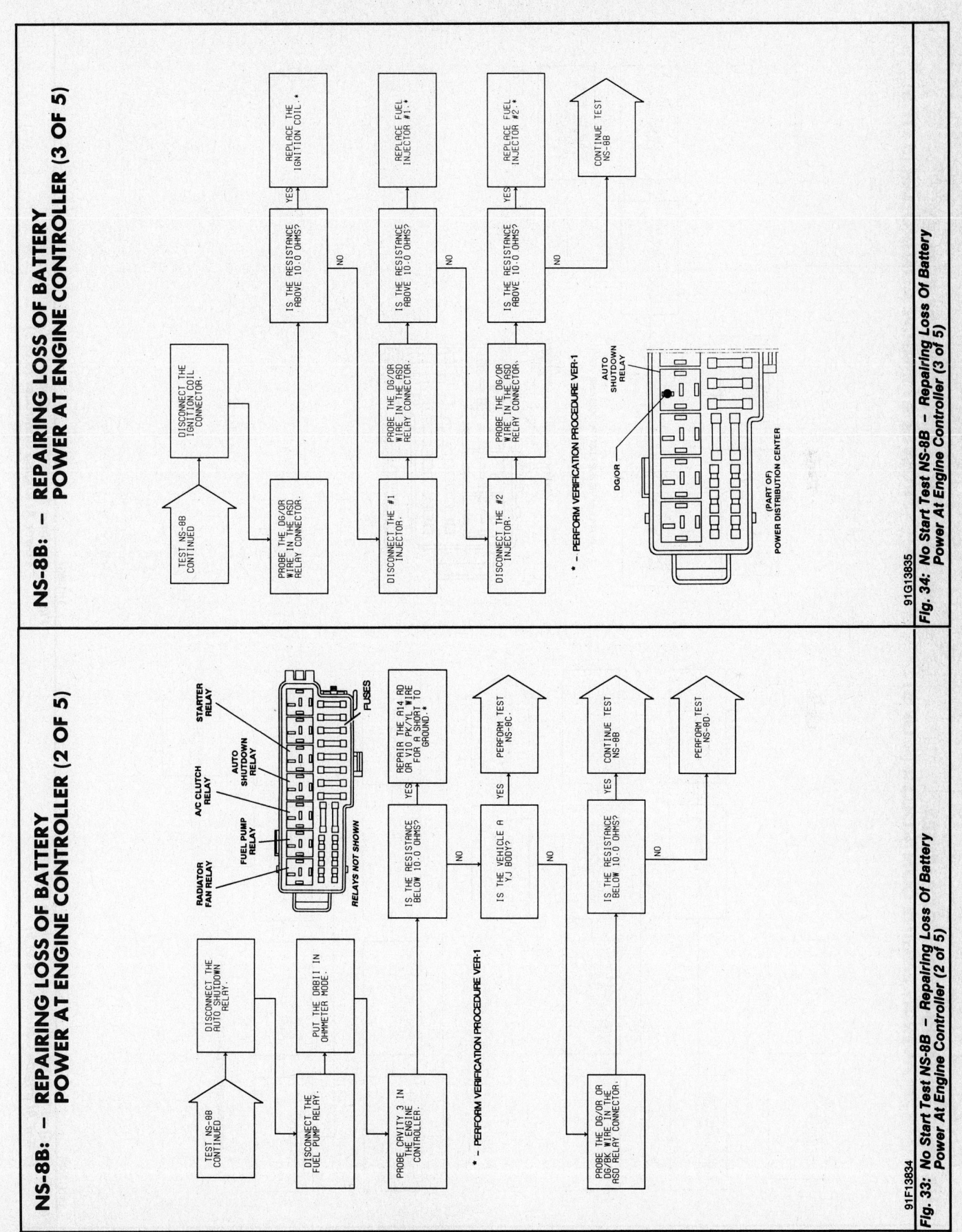

NS-8B: – REPAIRING LOSS OF BATTERY POWER AT ENGINE CONTROLLER (4 OF 5)

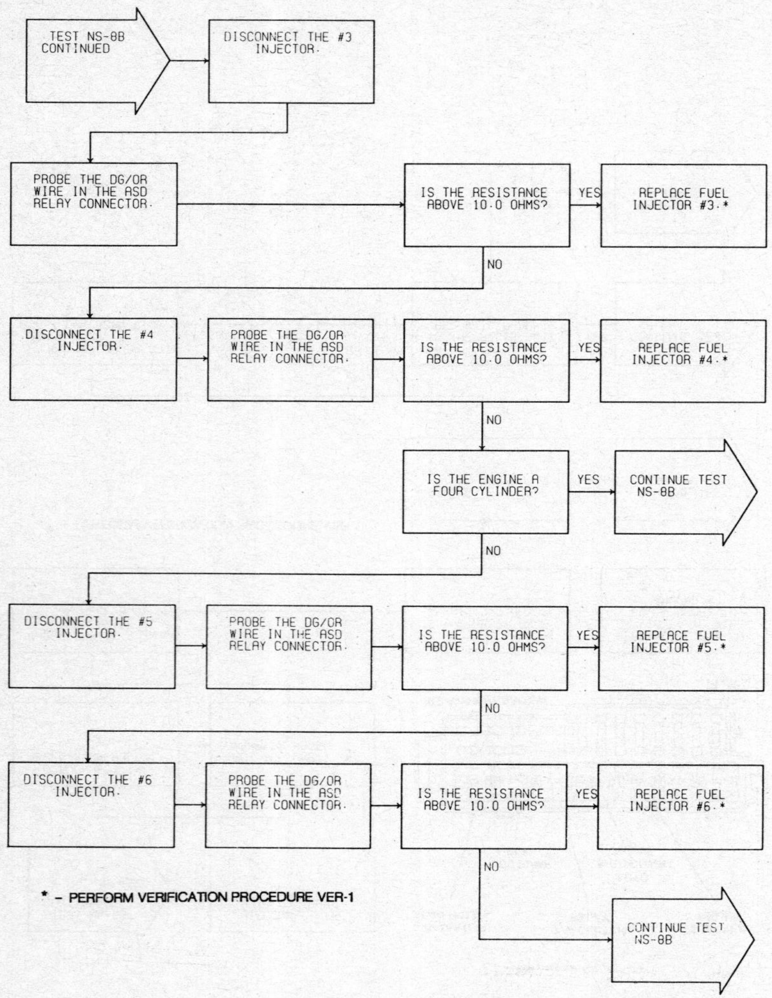
TEST NS-8B CONTINUED
DISCONNECT THE #3 INJECTOR.
PROBE THE DG/OR WIRE IN THE ASD RELAY CONNECTOR.
IS THE RESISTANCE ABOVE 10.0 OHMS?
YES
REPLACE FUEL INJECTOR #3.*
NO
DISCONNECT THE #4 INJECTOR.
PROBE THE DG/OR WIRE IN THE ASD RELAY CONNECTOR.
IS THE RESISTANCE ABOVE 10.0 OHMS?
YES
REPLACE FUEL INJECTOR #4.*
NO
IS THE ENGINE A FOUR CYLINDER?
YES
CONTINUE TEST NS-8B
NO
DISCONNECT THE #5 INJECTOR.
PROBE THE DG/OR WIRE IN THE ASD RELAY CONNECTOR.
IS THE RESISTANCE ABOVE 10.0 OHMS?
YES
REPLACE FUEL INJECTOR #5.*
NO
DISCONNECT THE #6 INJECTOR.
PROBE THE DG/OR WIRE IN THE ASD RELAY CONNECTOR.
IS THE RESISTANCE ABOVE 10.0 OHMS?
YES
REPLACE FUEL INJECTOR #6.*
NO
CONTINUE TEST NS-8B

* – PERFORM VERIFICATION PROCEDURE VER-1

91H13836

Fig. 35: No Start Test NS-8B – Repairing Loss Of Battery Power At Engine Controller (4 of 5)

NS-8B: – REPAIRING LOSS OF BATTERY POWER AT ENGINE CONTROLLER (5 OF 5)

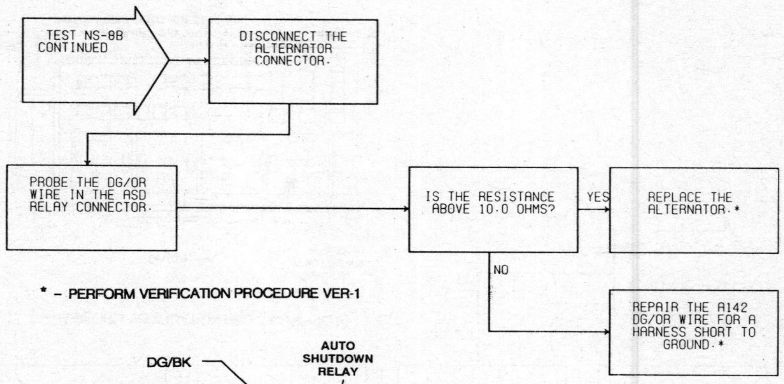
TEST NS-8B CONTINUED
DISCONNECT THE ALTERNATOR CONNECTOR.
PROBE THE DG/OR WIRE IN THE ASD RELAY CONNECTOR.
IS THE RESISTANCE ABOVE 10.0 OHMS?
YES
REPLACE THE ALTERNATOR.*
NO
REPAIR THE A142 DG/OR WIRE FOR A HARNESS SHORT TO GROUND.*

* – PERFORM VERIFICATION PROCEDURE VER-1

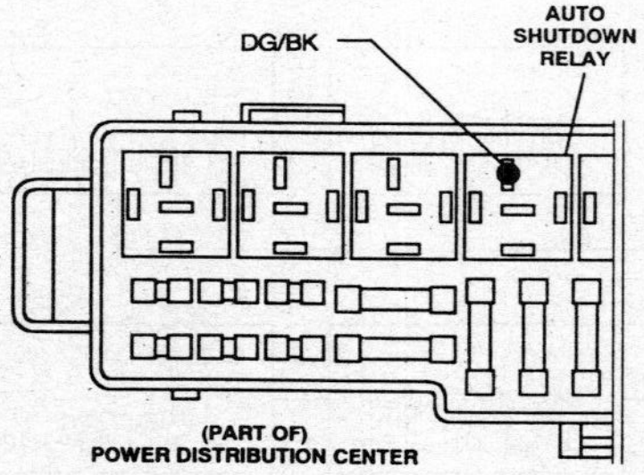
DG/BK
AUTO SHUTDOWN RELAY
(PART OF) POWER DISTRIBUTION CENTER

91I13837

Fig. 36: No Start Test NS-8B – Repairing Loss Of Battery Power At Engine Controller (5 of 5)

NS-8C: – REPAIRING LOSS OF BATTERY POWER AT ENGINE CONTROLLER (1 OF 3)

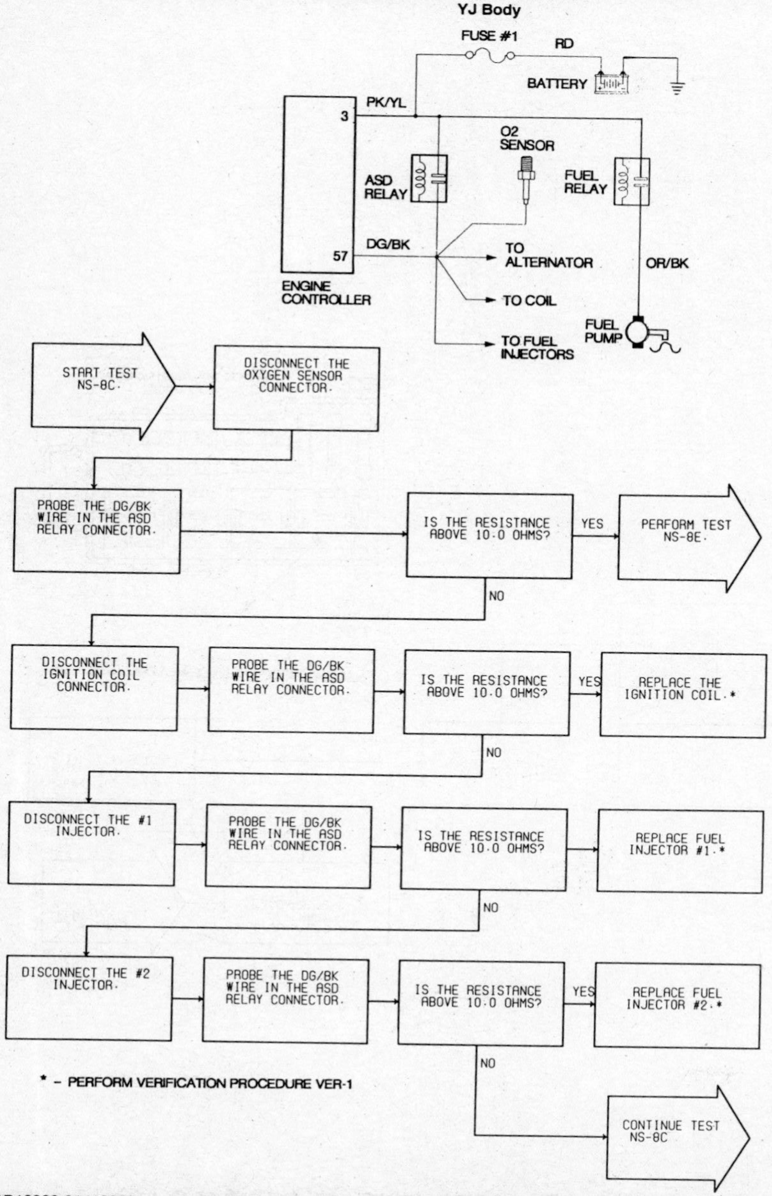
YJ Body
FUSE #1
RD
BATTERY
PK/YL
3
57
DG/BK
ENGINE CONTROLLER
ASD RELAY
O2 SENSOR
FUEL RELAY
TO ALTERNATOR
TO COIL
TO FUEL INJECTORS
OR/BK
FUEL PUMP
START TEST NS-8C.
DISCONNECT THE OXYGEN SENSOR CONNECTOR.
PROBE THE DG/BK WIRE IN THE ASD RELAY CONNECTOR.
IS THE RESISTANCE ABOVE 10.0 OHMS?
YES
PERFORM TEST NS-8E.
NO
DISCONNECT THE IGNITION COIL CONNECTOR.
PROBE THE DG/BK WIRE IN THE ASD RELAY CONNECTOR.
IS THE RESISTANCE ABOVE 10.0 OHMS?
YES
REPLACE THE IGNITION COIL.*
NO
DISCONNECT THE #1 INJECTOR.
PROBE THE DG/BK WIRE IN THE ASD RELAY CONNECTOR.
IS THE RESISTANCE ABOVE 10.0 OHMS?
REPLACE FUEL INJECTOR #1.*
NO
DISCONNECT THE #2 INJECTOR.
PROBE THE DG/BK WIRE IN THE ASD RELAY CONNECTOR.
IS THE RESISTANCE ABOVE 10.0 OHMS?
YES
REPLACE FUEL INJECTOR #2.*
NO
CONTINUE TEST NS-8C

* – PERFORM VERIFICATION PROCEDURE VER-1

91B13939 91J13838

Fig. 37: *No Start Test NS-8C – Repairing Loss Of Battery Power At Engine Controller (1 of 3)*

NS-8C: – REPAIRING LOSS OF BATTERY POWER AT ENGINE CONTROLLER (2 OF 3)

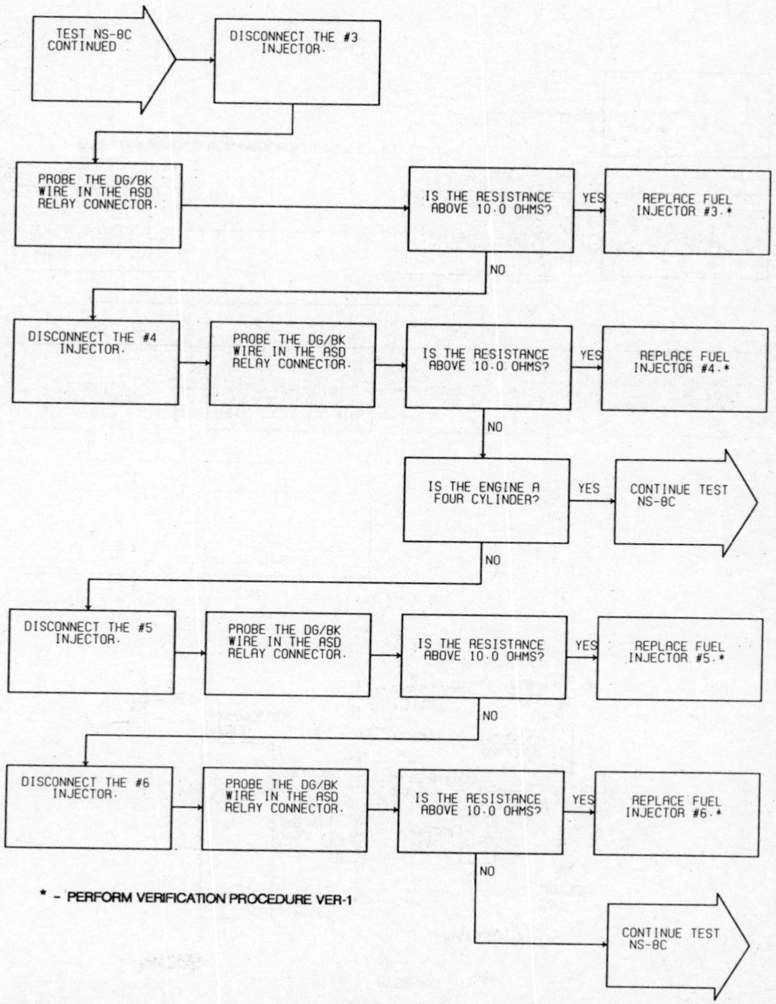
TEST NS-8C CONTINUED
DISCONNECT THE #3 INJECTOR.
PROBE THE DG/BK WIRE IN THE ASD RELAY CONNECTOR.
IS THE RESISTANCE ABOVE 10.0 OHMS?
YES
REPLACE FUEL INJECTOR #3.*
NO
DISCONNECT THE #4 INJECTOR.
PROBE THE DG/BK WIRE IN THE ASD RELAY CONNECTOR.
IS THE RESISTANCE ABOVE 10.0 OHMS?
YES
REPLACE FUEL INJECTOR #4.*
NO
IS THE ENGINE A FOUR CYLINDER?
YES
CONTINUE TEST NS-8C
NO
DISCONNECT THE #5 INJECTOR.
PROBE THE DG/BK WIRE IN THE ASD RELAY CONNECTOR.
IS THE RESISTANCE ABOVE 10.0 OHMS?
YES
REPLACE FUEL INJECTOR #5.*
NO
DISCONNECT THE #6 INJECTOR.
PROBE THE DG/BK WIRE IN THE ASD RELAY CONNECTOR.
IS THE RESISTANCE ABOVE 10.0 OHMS?
YES
REPLACE FUEL INJECTOR #6.*
NO
CONTINUE TEST NS-8C

* – PERFORM VERIFICATION PROCEDURE VER-1

91A13839

Fig. 38: *No Start Test NS-8C – Repairing Loss Of Battery Power At Engine Controller (2 of 3)*

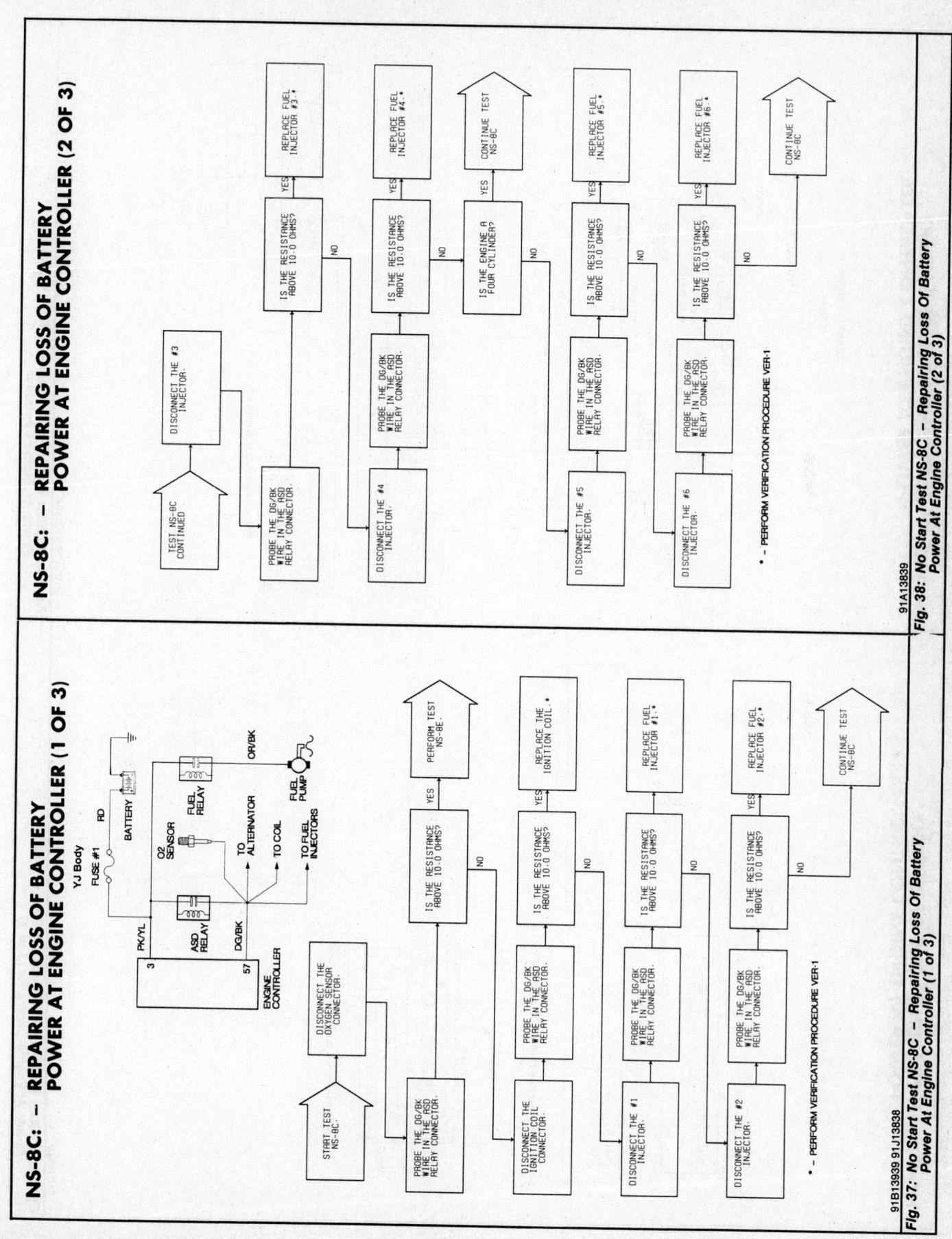

1991 ENGINE PERFORMANCE
Self-Diagnostics (Cont.)

NS-8C: – REPAIRING LOSS OF BATTERY POWER AT ENGINE CONTROLLER (3 OF 3)

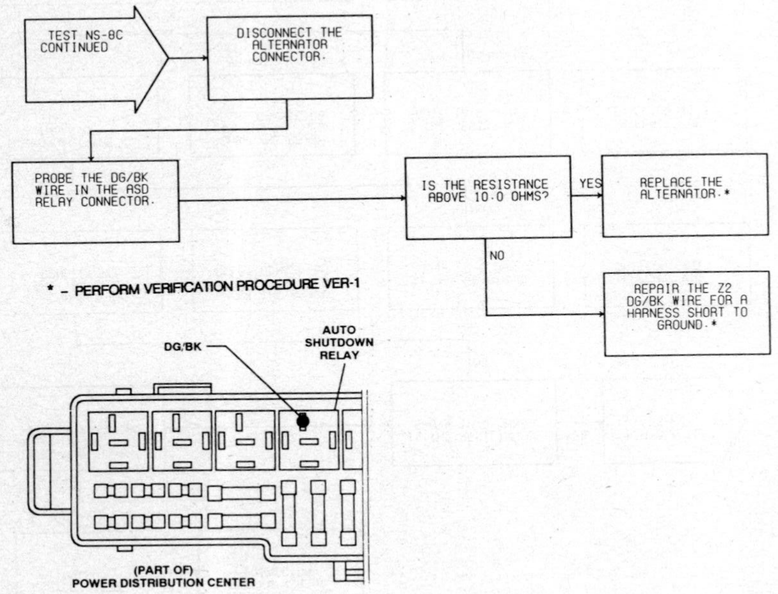
TEST NS-8C CONTINUED
DISCONNECT THE ALTERNATOR CONNECTOR.
PROBE THE DG/BK WIRE IN THE ASD RELAY CONNECTOR.
IS THE RESISTANCE ABOVE 10.0 OHMS?
YES
REPLACE THE ALTERNATOR.*
NO
REPAIR THE Z2 DG/BK WIRE FOR A HARNESS SHORT TO GROUND.*
* – PERFORM VERIFICATION PROCEDURE VER-1
DG/BK
AUTO SHUTDOWN RELAY
(PART OF) POWER DISTRIBUTION CENTER

91D13840

Fig. 39: No Start Test NS-8C – Repairing Loss Of Battery Power At Engine Controller (3 of 3)

NS-8D: – REPAIRING LOSS OF BATTERY POWER AT ENGINE CONTROLLER

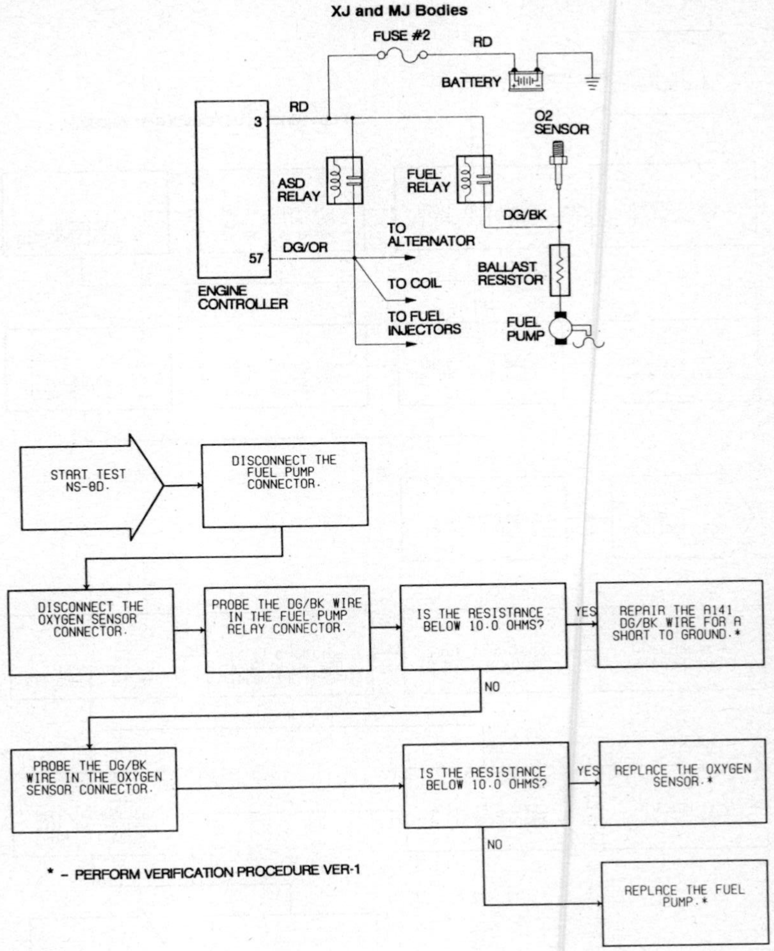
XJ and MJ Bodies
FUSE #2
RD
BATTERY
RD
3
ASD RELAY
FUEL RELAY
O2 SENSOR
DG/BK
TO ALTERNATOR
DG/OR
57
TO COIL
BALLAST RESISTOR
ENGINE CONTROLLER
TO FUEL INJECTORS
FUEL PUMP
START TEST NS-8D.
DISCONNECT THE FUEL PUMP CONNECTOR.
DISCONNECT THE OXYGEN SENSOR CONNECTOR.
PROBE THE DG/BK WIRE IN THE FUEL PUMP RELAY CONNECTOR.
IS THE RESISTANCE BELOW 10.0 OHMS?
YES
REPAIR THE A141 DG/BK WIRE FOR A SHORT TO GROUND.*
NO
PROBE THE DG/BK WIRE IN THE OXYGEN SENSOR CONNECTOR.
IS THE RESISTANCE BELOW 10.0 OHMS?
YES
REPLACE THE OXYGEN SENSOR.*
NO
REPLACE THE FUEL PUMP.*
* – PERFORM VERIFICATION PROCEDURE VER-1

91A13938 91E13841

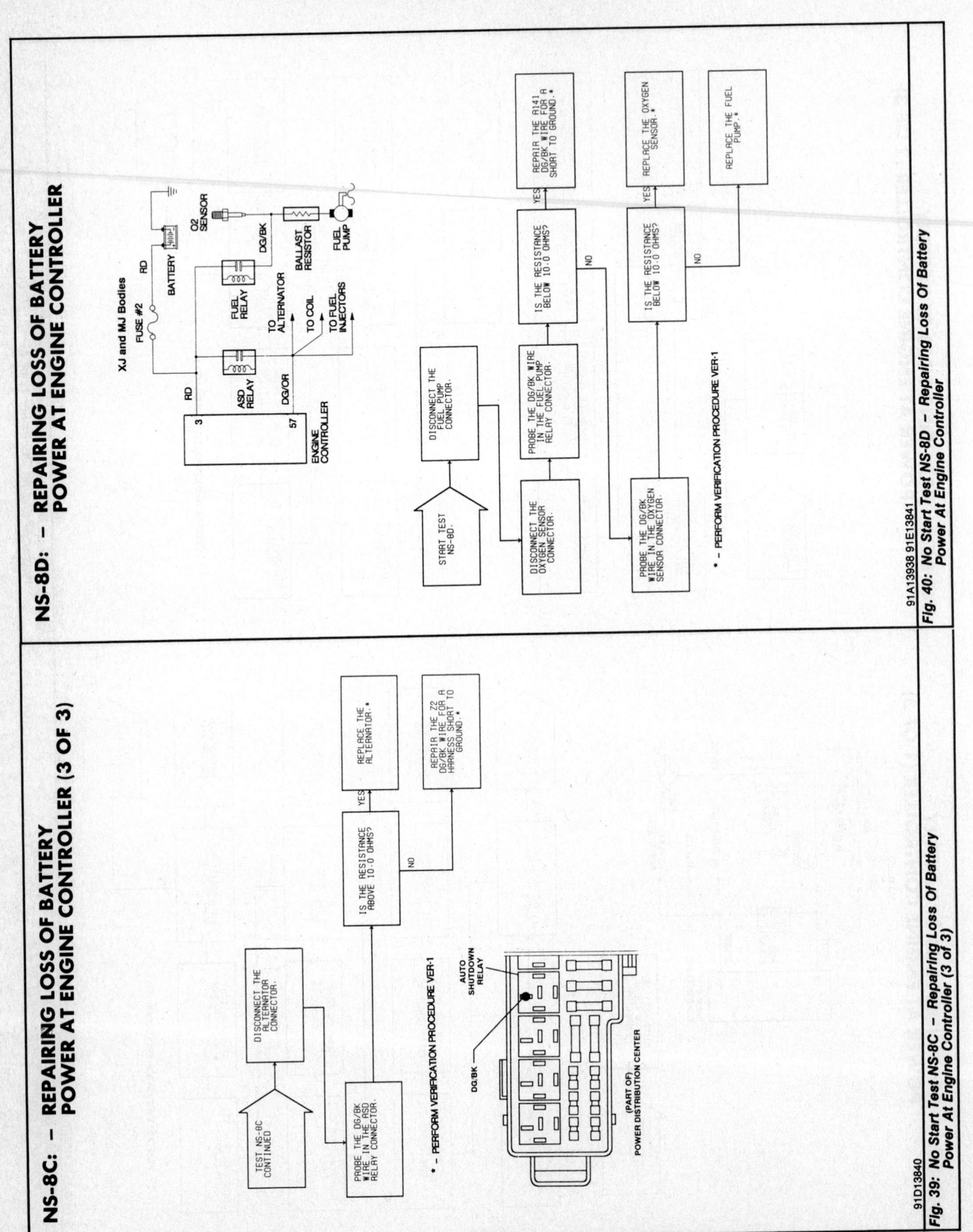

Fig. 40: No Start Test NS-8D – Repairing Loss Of Battery Power At Engine Controller

NS-8E: – REPAIRING LOSS OF BATTERY POWER AT ENGINE CONTROLLER

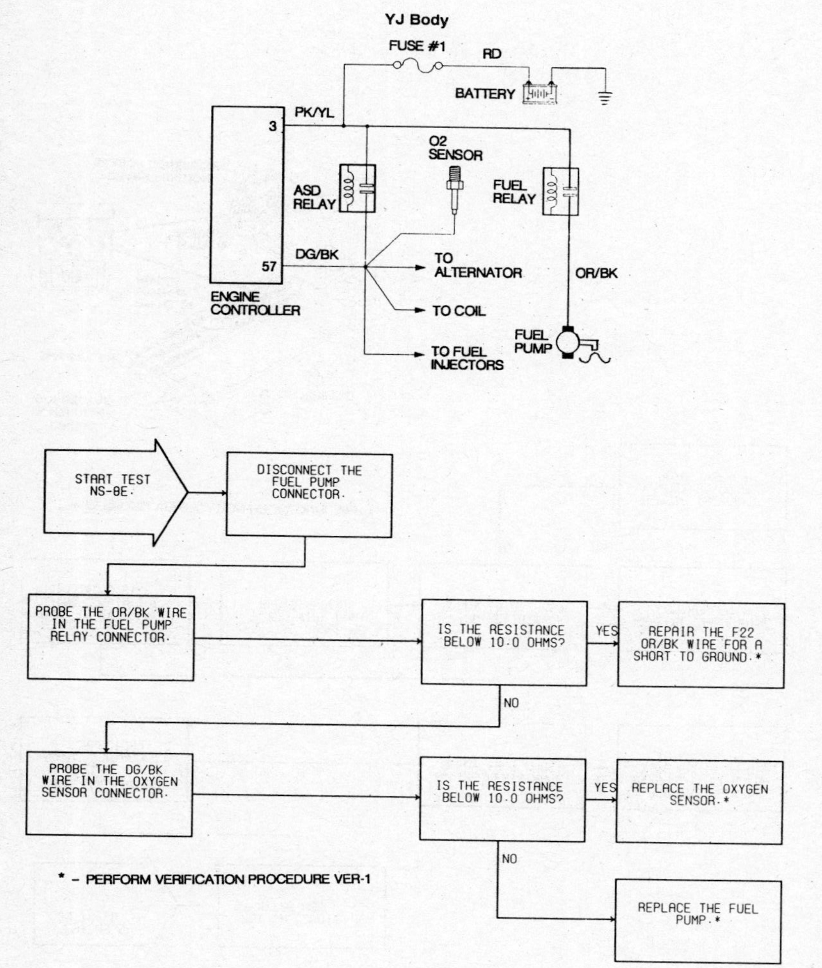
YJ Body
FUSE #1
RD
BATTERY
PK/YL
3
57
ENGINE CONTROLLER
ASD RELAY
O2 SENSOR
FUEL RELAY
DG/BK
TO ALTERNATOR
TO COIL
TO FUEL INJECTORS
OR/BK
FUEL PUMP
START TEST NS-8E.
DISCONNECT THE FUEL PUMP CONNECTOR.
PROBE THE OR/BK WIRE IN THE FUEL PUMP RELAY CONNECTOR.
IS THE RESISTANCE BELOW 10.0 OHMS?
YES
REPAIR THE F22 OR/BK WIRE FOR A SHORT TO GROUND.*
NO
PROBE THE DG/BK WIRE IN THE OXYGEN SENSOR CONNECTOR.
IS THE RESISTANCE BELOW 10.0 OHMS?
YES
REPLACE THE OXYGEN SENSOR.*
NO
REPLACE THE FUEL PUMP.*
* – PERFORM VERIFICATION PROCEDURE VER-1

91B13939 91F13842

Fig. 41: No Start Test NS-8E – Repairing Loss Of Battery Power At Engine Controller

NS-9A: – REPAIRING NO REFERENCE SIGNAL DURING CRANKING FAULT (1 OF 2)

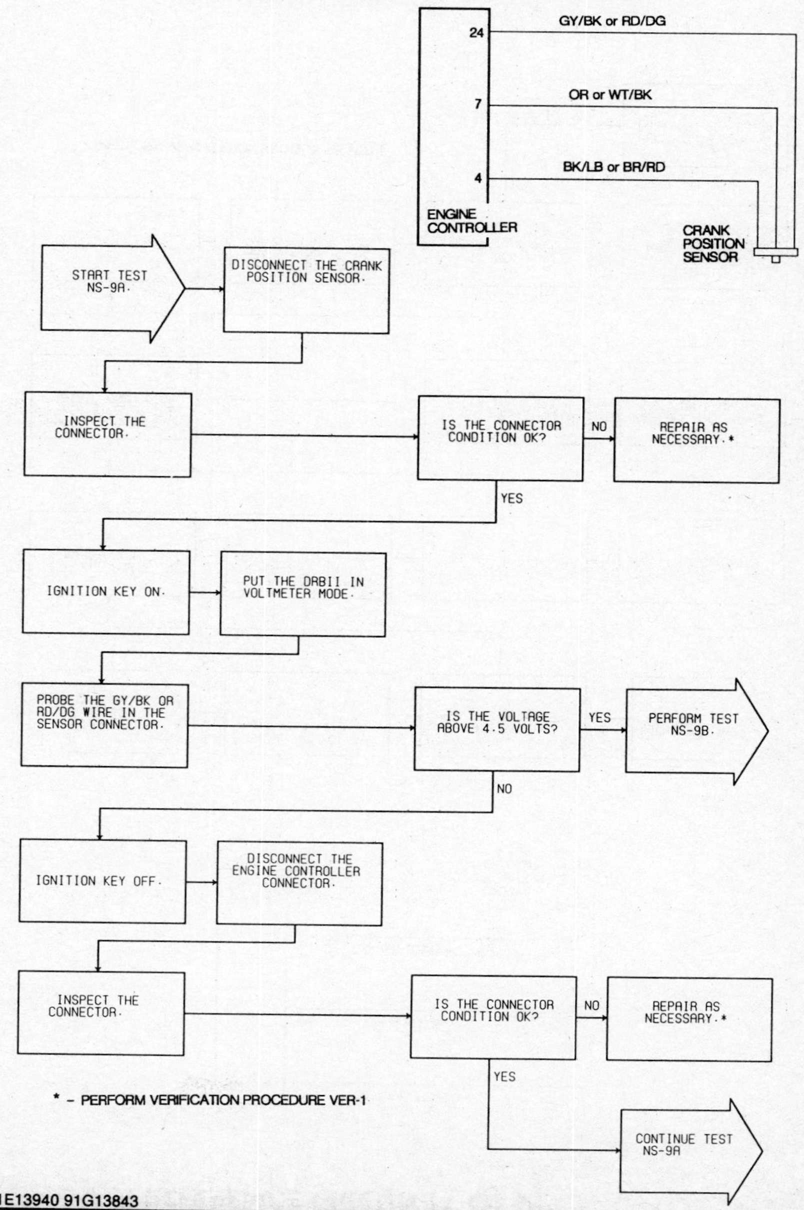
24
7
4
ENGINE CONTROLLER
GY/BK or RD/DG
OR or WT/BK
BK/LB or BR/RD
CRANK POSITION SENSOR
START TEST NS-9A.
DISCONNECT THE CRANK POSITION SENSOR.
INSPECT THE CONNECTOR.
IS THE CONNECTOR CONDITION OK?
NO
REPAIR AS NECESSARY.*
YES
IGNITION KEY ON.
PUT THE DRBII IN VOLTMETER MODE.
PROBE THE GY/BK OR RD/DG WIRE IN THE SENSOR CONNECTOR.
IS THE VOLTAGE ABOVE 4.5 VOLTS?
YES
PERFORM TEST NS-9B.
NO
IGNITION KEY OFF.
DISCONNECT THE ENGINE CONTROLLER CONNECTOR.
INSPECT THE CONNECTOR.
IS THE CONNECTOR CONDITION OK?
NO
REPAIR AS NECESSARY.*
YES
CONTINUE TEST NS-9A
* – PERFORM VERIFICATION PROCEDURE VER-1

91E13940 91G13843

Fig. 42: No Start Test NS-9A – Repairing No Reference Signal During Cranking Fault (1 of 2)

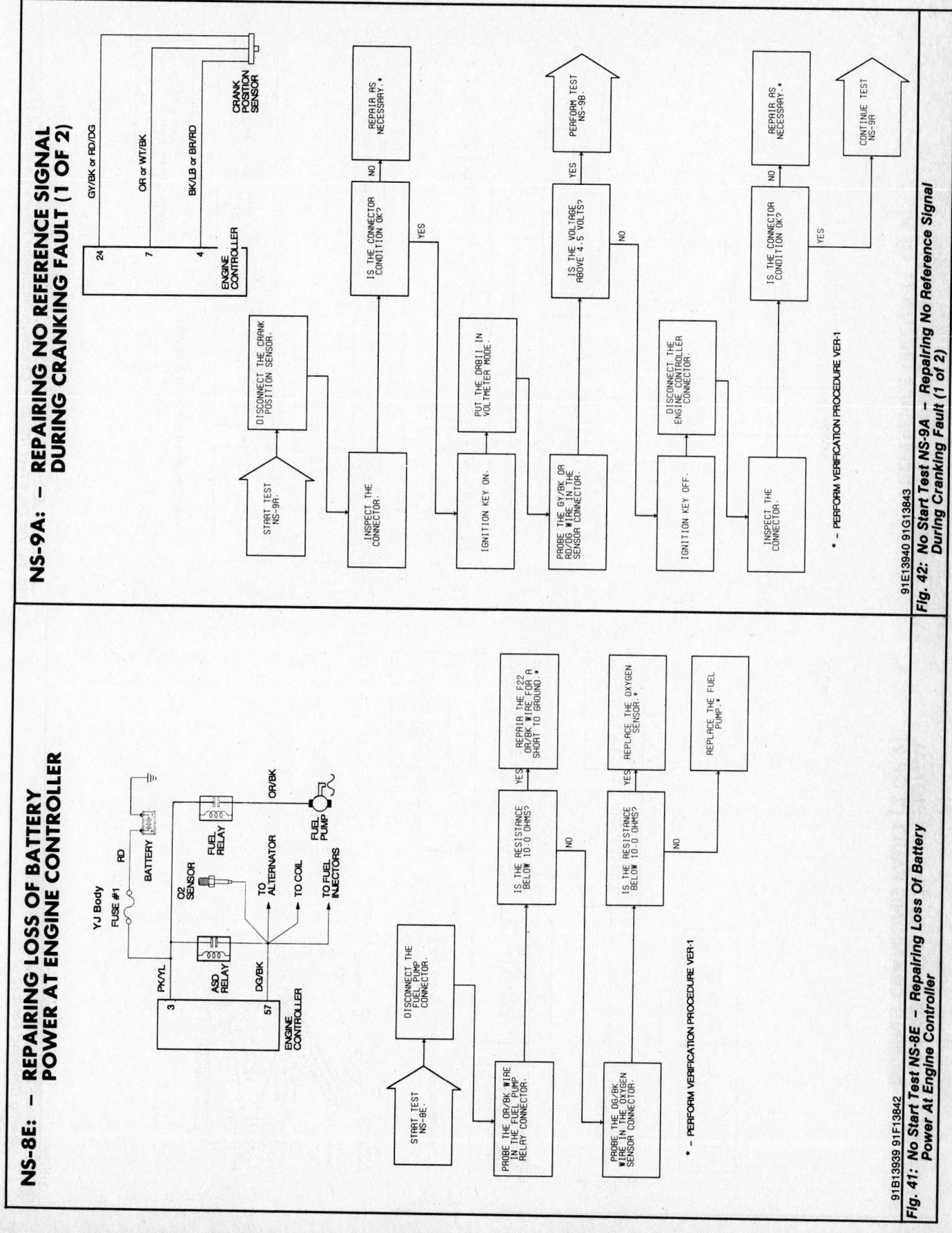

1991 ENGINE PERFORMANCE
Self-Diagnostics (Cont.)

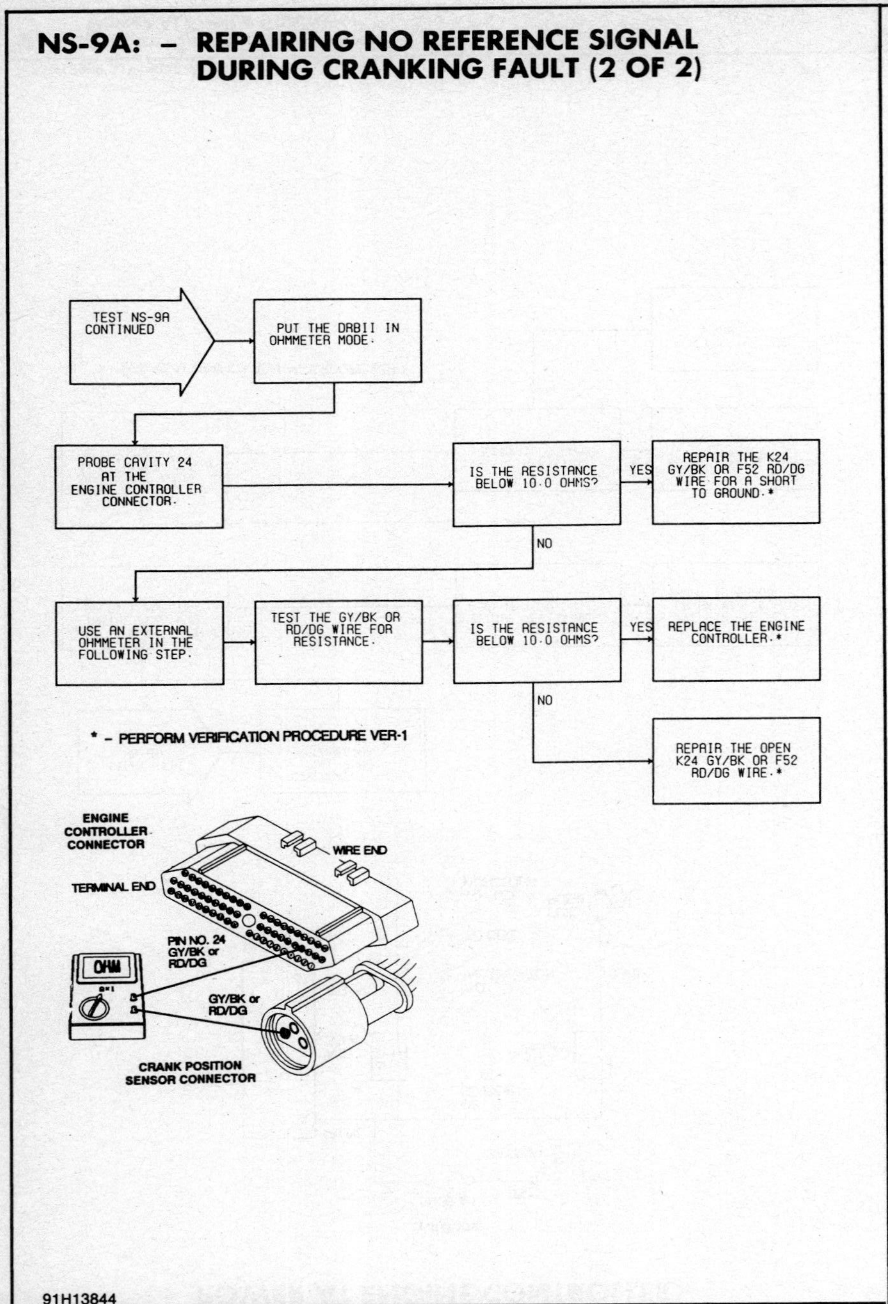
NS-9A: – REPAIRING NO REFERENCE SIGNAL DURING CRANKING FAULT (2 OF 2)
TEST NS-9A CONTINUED
PUT THE DRBII IN OHMMETER MODE.
PROBE CAVITY 24 AT THE ENGINE CONTROLLER CONNECTOR.
IS THE RESISTANCE BELOW 10.0 OHMS?
YES
REPAIR THE K24 GY/BK OR F52 RD/DG WIRE FOR A SHORT TO GROUND.*
NO
USE AN EXTERNAL OHMMETER IN THE FOLLOWING STEP.
TEST THE GY/BK OR RD/DG WIRE FOR RESISTANCE.
IS THE RESISTANCE BELOW 10.0 OHMS?
YES
REPLACE THE ENGINE CONTROLLER.*
NO
REPAIR THE OPEN K24 GY/BK OR F52 RD/DG WIRE.*
* – PERFORM VERIFICATION PROCEDURE VER-1
ENGINE CONTROLLER CONNECTOR
WIRE END
TERMINAL END
PIN NO. 24 GY/BK or RD/DG
OHM
GY/BK or RD/DG
CRANK POSITION SENSOR CONNECTOR
91H13844

Fig. 43: No Start Test NS-9A – Repairing No Reference Signal During Cranking Fault (2 of 2)

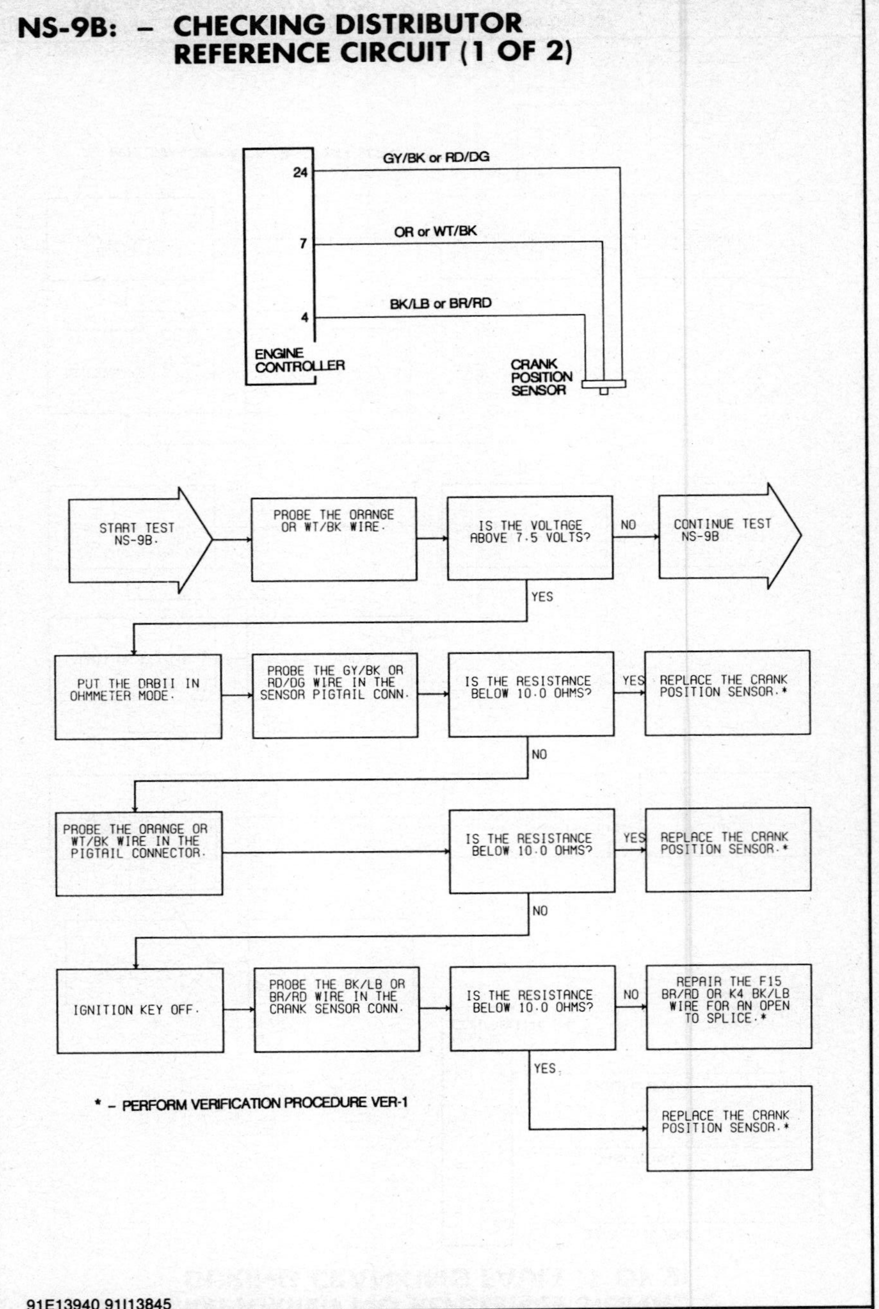
NS-9B: – CHECKING DISTRIBUTOR REFERENCE CIRCUIT (1 OF 2)
24
GY/BK or RD/DG
7
OR or WT/BK
4
BK/LB or BR/RD
ENGINE CONTROLLER
CRANK POSITION SENSOR
START TEST NS-9B.
PROBE THE ORANGE OR WT/BK WIRE.
IS THE VOLTAGE ABOVE 7.5 VOLTS?
NO
CONTINUE TEST NS-9B
YES
PUT THE DRBII IN OHMMETER MODE.
PROBE THE GY/BK OR RD/DG WIRE IN THE SENSOR PIGTAIL CONN.
IS THE RESISTANCE BELOW 10.0 OHMS?
YES
REPLACE THE CRANK POSITION SENSOR.*
NO
PROBE THE ORANGE OR WT/BK WIRE IN THE PIGTAIL CONNECTOR.
IS THE RESISTANCE BELOW 10.0 OHMS?
YES
REPLACE THE CRANK POSITION SENSOR.*
NO
IGNITION KEY OFF.
PROBE THE BK/LB OR BR/RD WIRE IN THE CRANK SENSOR CONN.
IS THE RESISTANCE BELOW 10.0 OHMS?
NO
REPAIR THE F15 BR/RD OR K4 BK/LB WIRE FOR AN OPEN TO SPLICE.*
YES
REPLACE THE CRANK POSITION SENSOR.*
* – PERFORM VERIFICATION PROCEDURE VER-1
91E13940 91I13845

Fig. 44: No Start Test NS-9B – Checking Distributor Reference Circuit (1 of 2)

NS-9B: – CHECKING DISTRIBUTOR REFERENCE CIRCUIT (2 OF 2)

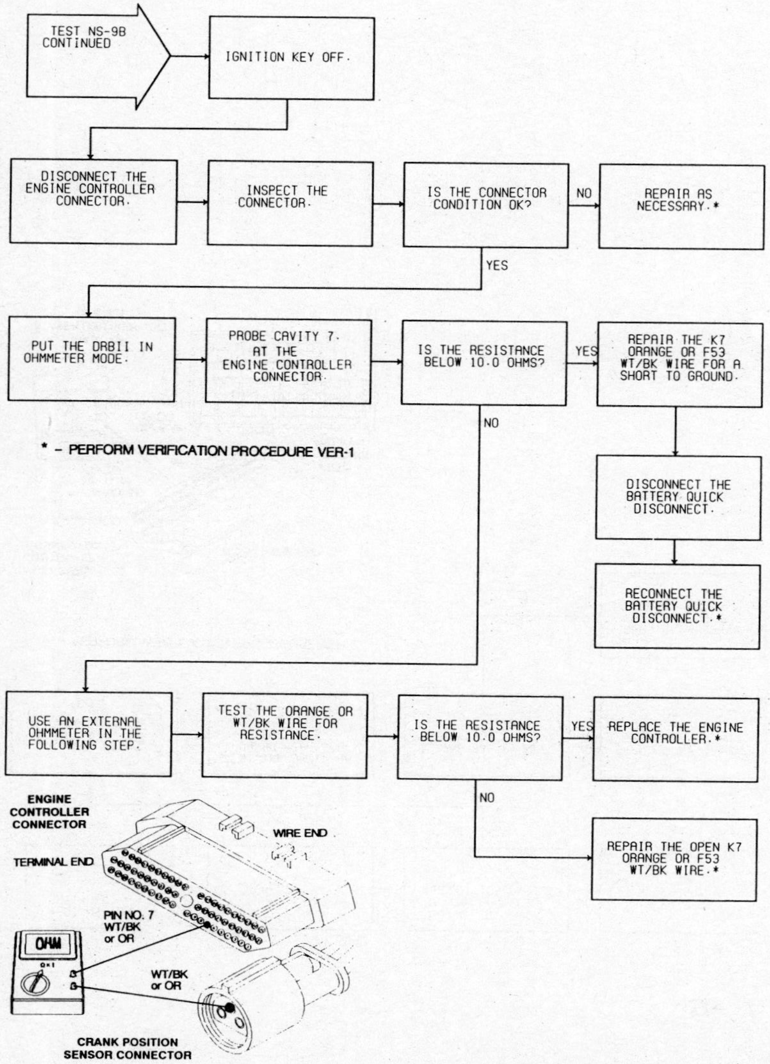
TEST NS-9B CONTINUED
IGNITION KEY OFF.
DISCONNECT THE ENGINE CONTROLLER CONNECTOR.
INSPECT THE CONNECTOR.
IS THE CONNECTOR CONDITION OK?
NO
REPAIR AS NECESSARY.*
YES
PUT THE DRBII IN OHMMETER MODE.
PROBE CAVITY 7. AT THE ENGINE CONTROLLER CONNECTOR.
IS THE RESISTANCE BELOW 10.0 OHMS?
YES
REPAIR THE K7 ORANGE OR F53 WT/BK WIRE FOR A SHORT TO GROUND.
NO
DISCONNECT THE BATTERY QUICK DISCONNECT.
RECONNECT THE BATTERY QUICK DISCONNECT.*
USE AN EXTERNAL OHMMETER IN THE FOLLOWING STEP.
TEST THE ORANGE OR WT/BK WIRE FOR RESISTANCE.
IS THE RESISTANCE BELOW 10.0 OHMS?
YES
REPLACE THE ENGINE CONTROLLER.*
NO
REPAIR THE OPEN K7 ORANGE OR F53 WT/BK WIRE.*
ENGINE CONTROLLER CONNECTOR
WIRE END
TERMINAL END
PIN NO. 7 WT/BK or OR
OHM
WT/BK or OR
CRANK POSITION SENSOR CONNECTOR

* – PERFORM VERIFICATION PROCEDURE VER-1

91J13846

Fig. 45: No Start Test NS-9B – Checking Distributor Reference Circuit (2 of 2)

NS-10A: – REPAIRING AUTO SHUTDOWN RELAY CONTROL CIRCUIT FAULT (1 OF 2)

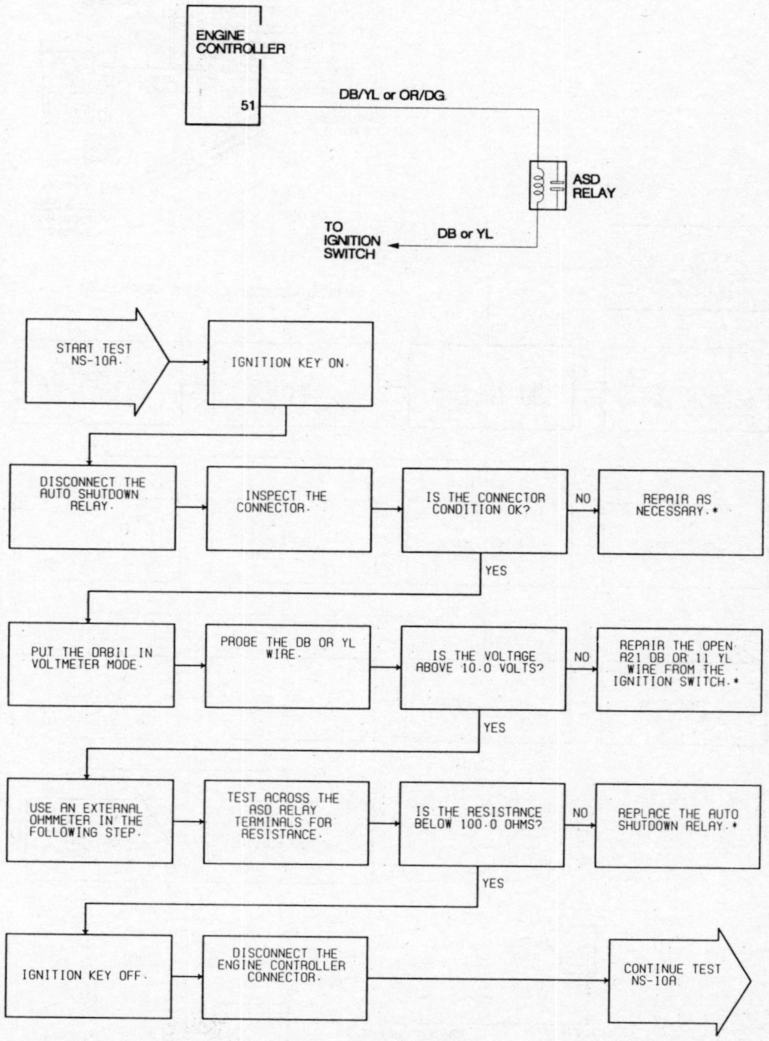
ENGINE CONTROLLER
51
DB/YL or OR/DG
ASD RELAY
TO IGNITION SWITCH
DB or YL
START TEST NS-10A.
IGNITION KEY ON.
DISCONNECT THE AUTO SHUTDOWN RELAY.
INSPECT THE CONNECTOR.
IS THE CONNECTOR CONDITION OK?
NO
REPAIR AS NECESSARY.*
YES
PUT THE DRBII IN VOLTMETER MODE.
PROBE THE DB OR YL WIRE.
IS THE VOLTAGE ABOVE 10.0 VOLTS?
NO
REPAIR THE OPEN A21 DB OR 11 YL WIRE FROM THE IGNITION SWITCH.*
YES
USE AN EXTERNAL OHMMETER IN THE FOLLOWING STEP.
TEST ACROSS THE ASD RELAY TERMINALS FOR RESISTANCE.
IS THE RESISTANCE BELOW 100.0 OHMS?
NO
REPLACE THE AUTO SHUTDOWN RELAY.*
YES
IGNITION KEY OFF.
DISCONNECT THE ENGINE CONTROLLER CONNECTOR.
CONTINUE TEST NS-10A

* – PERFORM VERIFICATION PROCEDURE VER-1

91F13941 91A13847

Fig. 46: No Start Test NS-10A – Repairing Auto Shutdown Relay Control Circuit Fault (1 of 2)

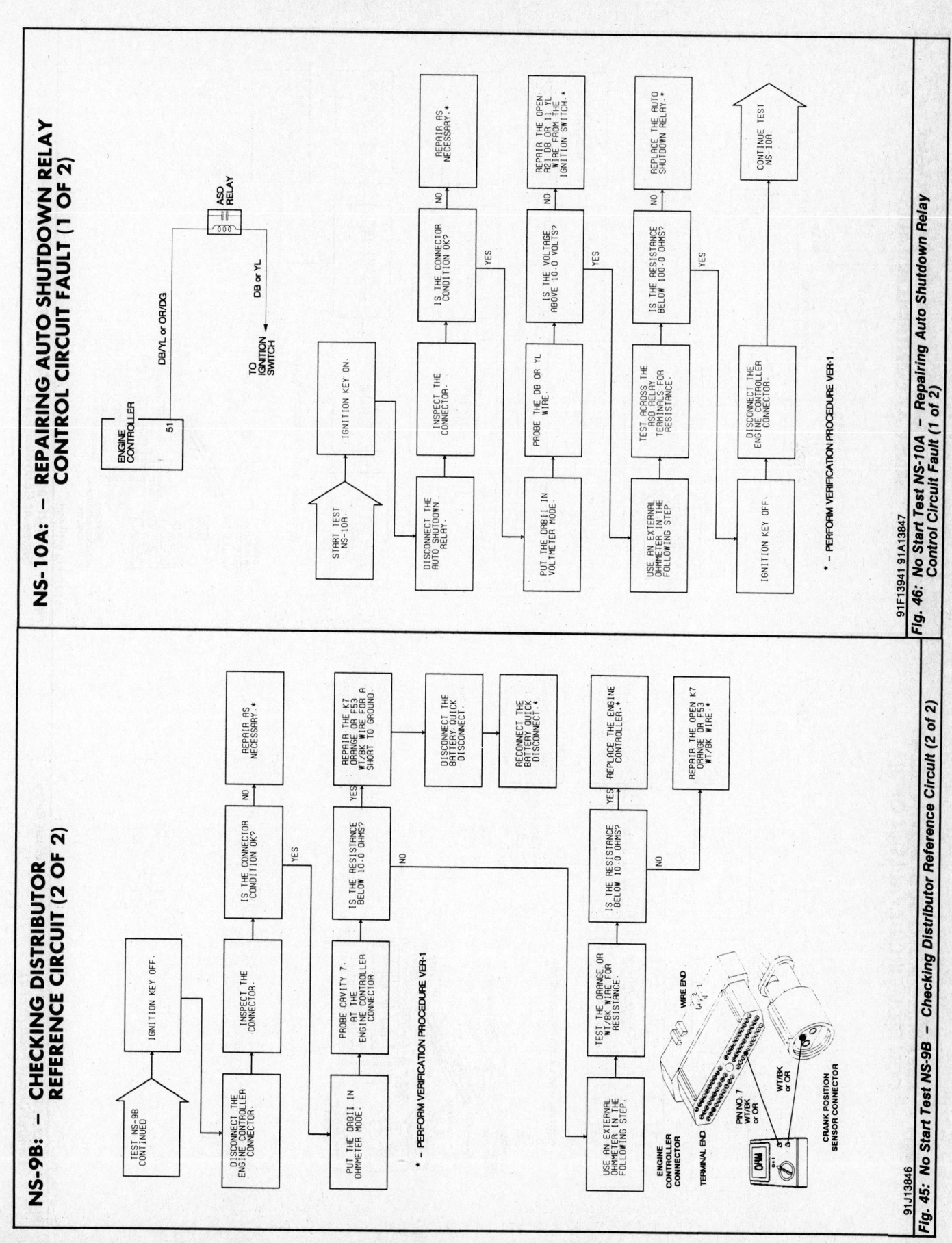

1991 ENGINE PERFORMANCE
Self-Diagnostics (Cont.)

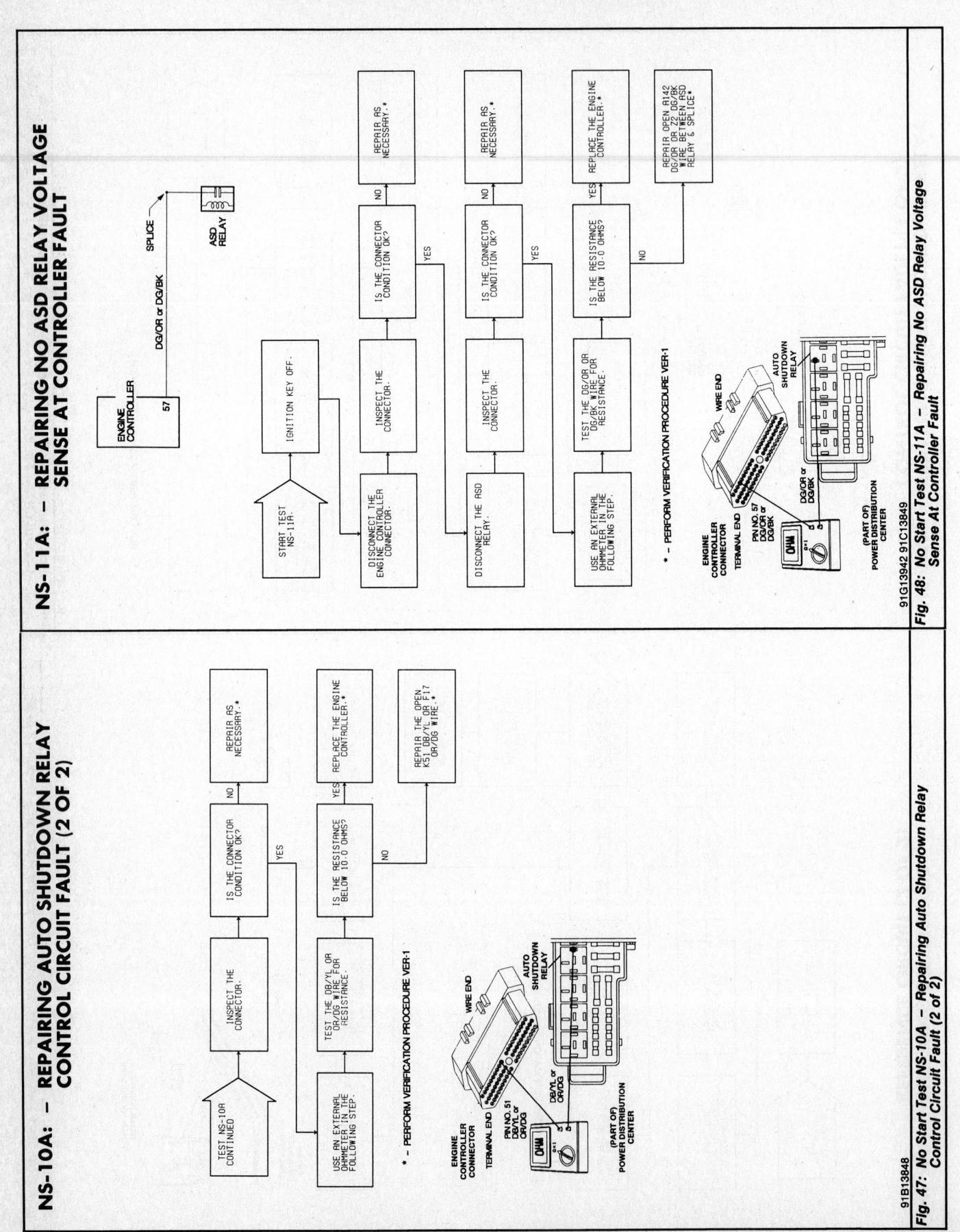

NS-10A: – REPAIRING AUTO SHUTDOWN RELAY CONTROL CIRCUIT FAULT (2 OF 2)

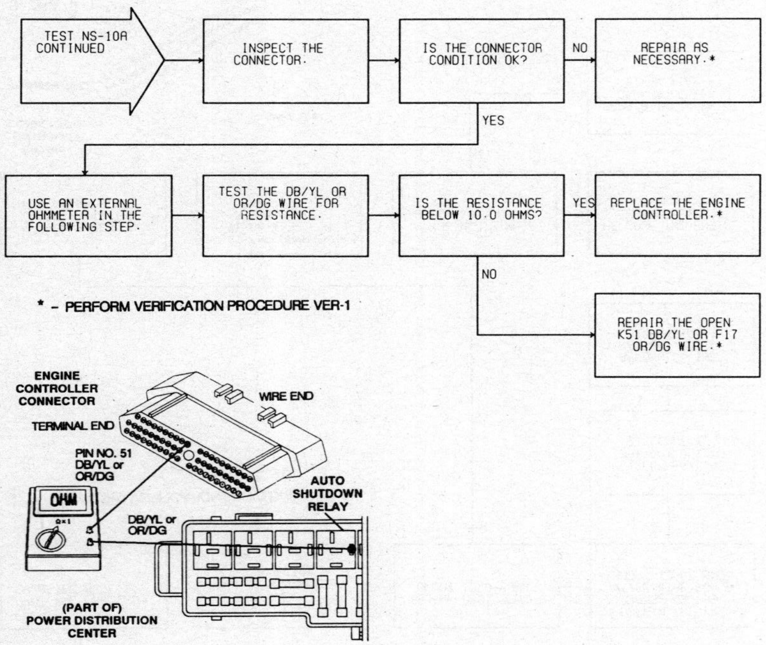
TEST NS-10A CONTINUED
INSPECT THE CONNECTOR.
IS THE CONNECTOR CONDITION OK?
NO
REPAIR AS NECESSARY.*
YES
USE AN EXTERNAL OHMMETER IN THE FOLLOWING STEP.
TEST THE DB/YL OR OR/DG WIRE FOR RESISTANCE.
IS THE RESISTANCE BELOW 10.0 OHMS?
YES
REPLACE THE ENGINE CONTROLLER.*
NO
REPAIR THE OPEN K51 DB/YL OR F17 OR/DG WIRE.*
* – PERFORM VERIFICATION PROCEDURE VER-1
ENGINE CONTROLLER CONNECTOR
WIRE END
TERMINAL END
PIN NO. 51 DB/YL or OR/DG
OHM
DB/YL or OR/DG
AUTO SHUTDOWN RELAY
(PART OF) POWER DISTRIBUTION CENTER

91B13848

Fig. 47: No Start Test NS-10A – Repairing Auto Shutdown Relay Control Circuit Fault (2 of 2)

NS-11A: – REPAIRING NO ASD RELAY VOLTAGE SENSE AT CONTROLLER FAULT

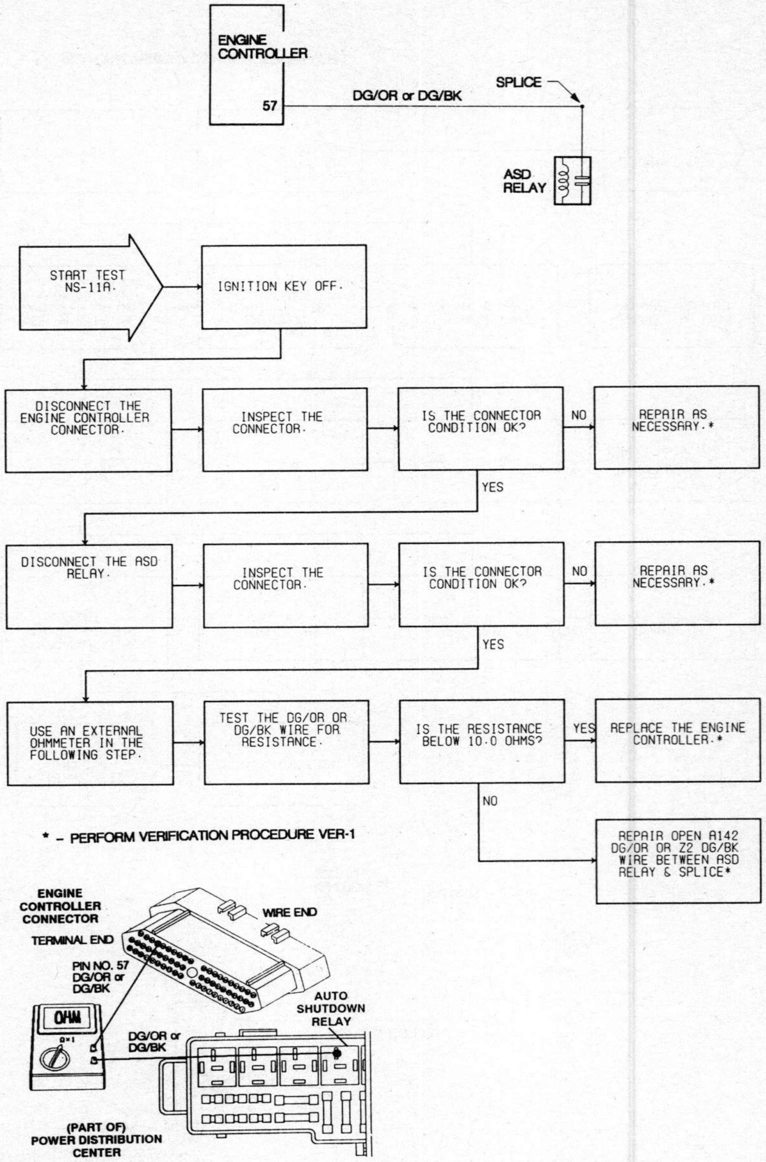
ENGINE CONTROLLER
57
DG/OR or DG/BK
SPLICE
ASD RELAY
START TEST NS-11A.
IGNITION KEY OFF.
DISCONNECT THE ENGINE CONTROLLER CONNECTOR.
INSPECT THE CONNECTOR.
IS THE CONNECTOR CONDITION OK?
NO
REPAIR AS NECESSARY.*
YES
DISCONNECT THE ASD RELAY.
INSPECT THE CONNECTOR.
IS THE CONNECTOR CONDITION OK?
NO
REPAIR AS NECESSARY.*
YES
USE AN EXTERNAL OHMMETER IN THE FOLLOWING STEP.
TEST THE DG/OR OR DG/BK WIRE FOR RESISTANCE.
IS THE RESISTANCE BELOW 10.0 OHMS?
YES
REPLACE THE ENGINE CONTROLLER.*
NO
REPAIR OPEN A142 DG/OR OR Z2 DG/BK WIRE BETWEEN ASD RELAY & SPLICE*
* – PERFORM VERIFICATION PROCEDURE VER-1
ENGINE CONTROLLER CONNECTOR
WIRE END
TERMINAL END
PIN NO. 57 DG/OR or DG/BK
OHM
DG/OR or DG/BK
AUTO SHUTDOWN RELAY
(PART OF) POWER DISTRIBUTION CENTER

91G13942 91C13849

Fig. 48: No Start Test NS-11A – Repairing No ASD Relay Voltage Sense At Controller Fault

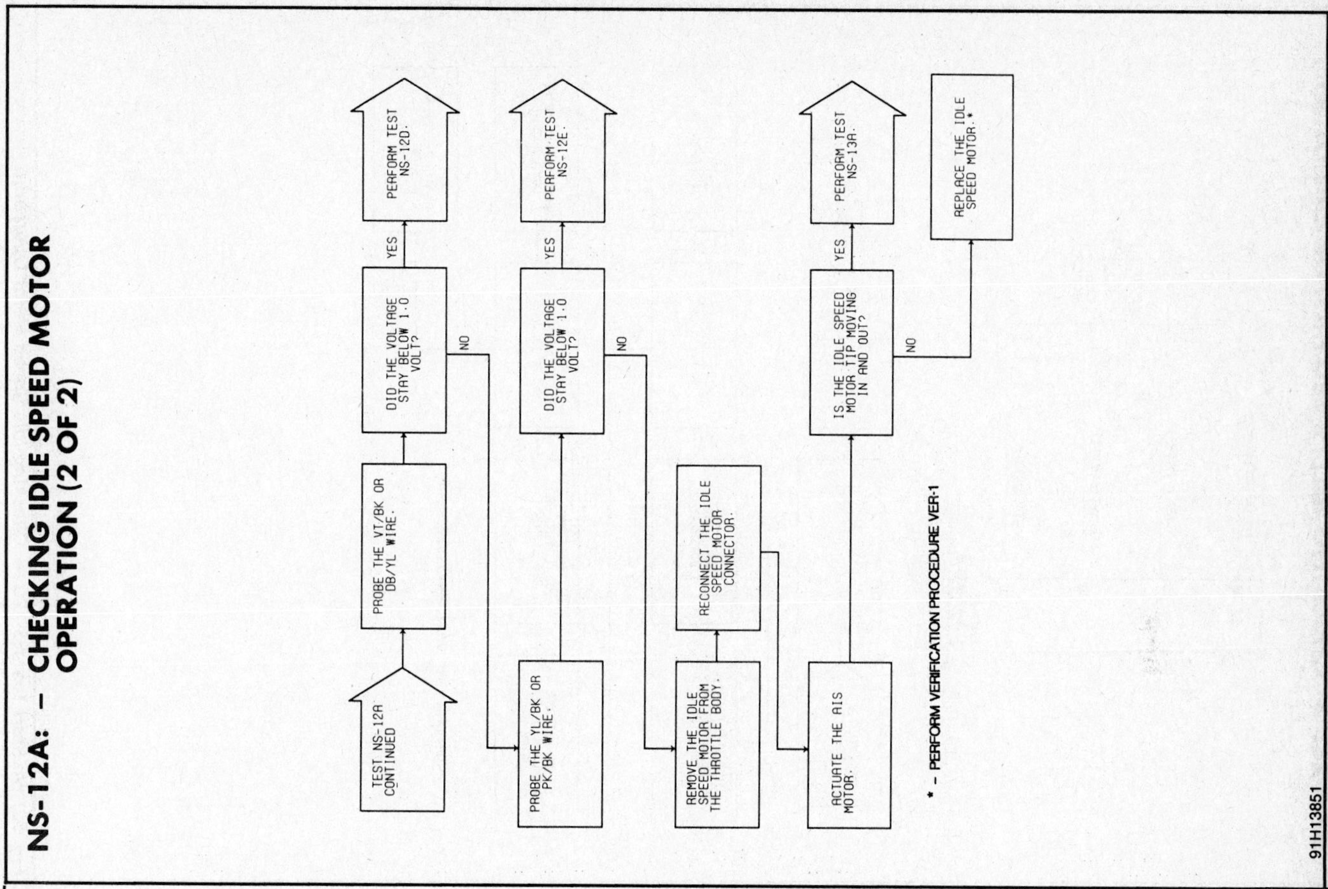

NS-12A: – CHECKING IDLE SPEED MOTOR OPERATION (2 OF 2)
TEST NS-12A CONTINUED
PROBE THE VT/BK OR DB/YL WIRE.
DID THE VOLTAGE STAY BELOW 1.0 VOLT?
YES
PERFORM TEST NS-12D.
NO
PROBE THE YL/BK OR PK/BK WIRE.
DID THE VOLTAGE STAY BELOW 1.0 VOLT?
YES
PERFORM TEST NS-12E.
NO
REMOVE THE IDLE SPEED MOTOR FROM THE THROTTLE BODY.
RECONNECT THE IDLE SPEED MOTOR CONNECTOR.
ACTUATE THE AIS MOTOR.
IS THE IDLE SPEED MOTOR TIP MOVING IN AND OUT?
YES
PERFORM TEST NS-13A.
NO
REPLACE THE IDLE SPEED MOTOR.*
* – PERFORM VERIFICATION PROCEDURE VER-1
91H13851

Fig. 50: No Start Test NS-12A – Checking Idle Speed Motor Operation (2 of 2)

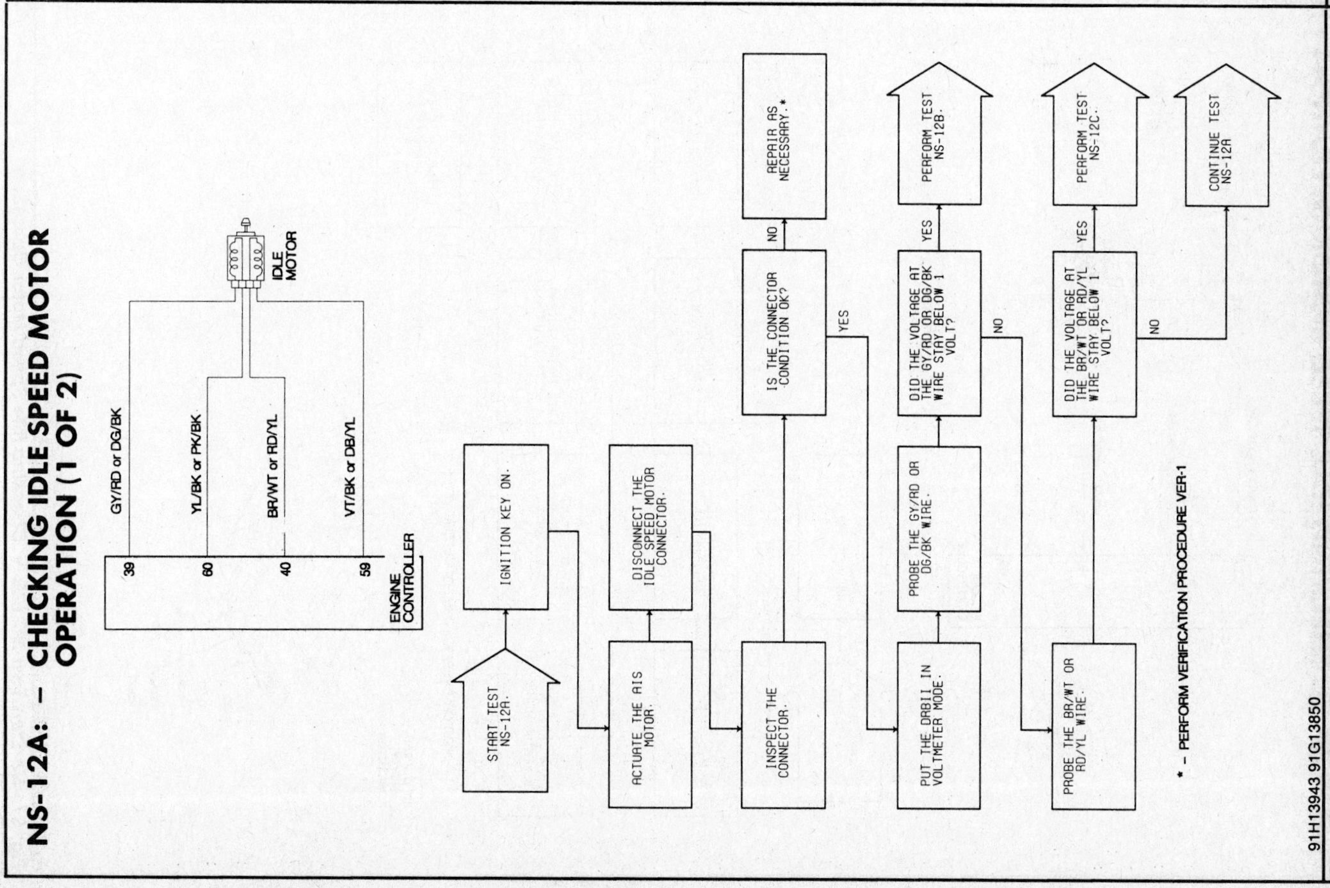

NS-12A: – CHECKING IDLE SPEED MOTOR OPERATION (1 OF 2)
GY/RD or DG/BK
YL/BK or PK/BK
BR/WT or RD/YL
VT/BK or DB/YL
39
60
40
59
ENGINE CONTROLLER
IDLE MOTOR
START TEST NS-12A.
IGNITION KEY ON.
ACTUATE THE AIS MOTOR.
DISCONNECT THE IDLE SPEED MOTOR CONNECTOR.
INSPECT THE CONNECTOR.
IS THE CONNECTOR CONDITION OK?
NO
REPAIR AS NECESSARY.*
YES
PUT THE DRBII IN VOLTMETER MODE.
PROBE THE GY/RD OR DG/BK WIRE.
DID THE VOLTAGE AT THE GY/RD OR DG/BK WIRE STAY BELOW 1 VOLT?
YES
PERFORM TEST NS-12B.
NO
PROBE THE BR/WT OR RD/YL WIRE.
DID THE VOLTAGE AT THE BR/WT OR RD/YL WIRE STAY BELOW 1 VOLT?
YES
PERFORM TEST NS-12C.
NO
CONTINUE TEST NS-12A
* – PERFORM VERIFICATION PROCEDURE VER-1
91H13943 91G13850

Fig. 49: No Start Test NS-12A – Checking Idle Speed Motor Operation (1 of 2)

1991 ENGINE PERFORMANCE
Self-Diagnostics (Cont.)

NS-12B: – CHECKING IDLE SPEED MOTOR OPERATION

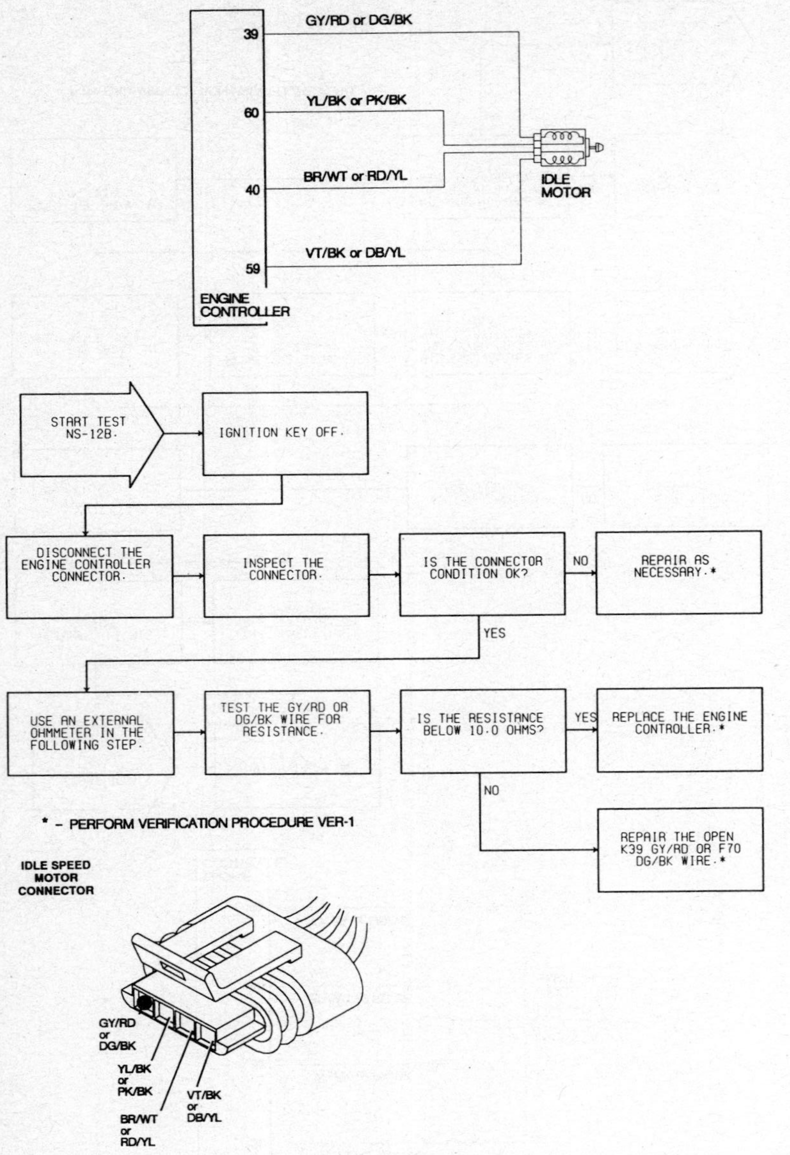
39
GY/RD or DG/BK
60
YL/BK or PK/BK
40
BR/WT or RD/YL
59
VT/BK or DB/YL
ENGINE CONTROLLER
IDLE MOTOR
START TEST NS-12B.
IGNITION KEY OFF.
DISCONNECT THE ENGINE CONTROLLER CONNECTOR.
INSPECT THE CONNECTOR.
IS THE CONNECTOR CONDITION OK?
NO
REPAIR AS NECESSARY.*
YES
USE AN EXTERNAL OHMMETER IN THE FOLLOWING STEP.
TEST THE GY/RD OR DG/BK WIRE FOR RESISTANCE.
IS THE RESISTANCE BELOW 10.0 OHMS?
YES
REPLACE THE ENGINE CONTROLLER.*
NO
REPAIR THE OPEN K39 GY/RD OR F70 DG/BK WIRE.*
* – PERFORM VERIFICATION PROCEDURE VER-1
IDLE SPEED MOTOR CONNECTOR
GY/RD or DG/BK
YL/BK or PK/BK
BR/WT or RD/YL
VT/BK or DB/YL

91H13943 91I13852

Fig. 51: No Start Test NS-12B – Checking Idle Speed Motor Operation

NS-12C: – CHECKING IDLE SPEED MOTOR OPERATION

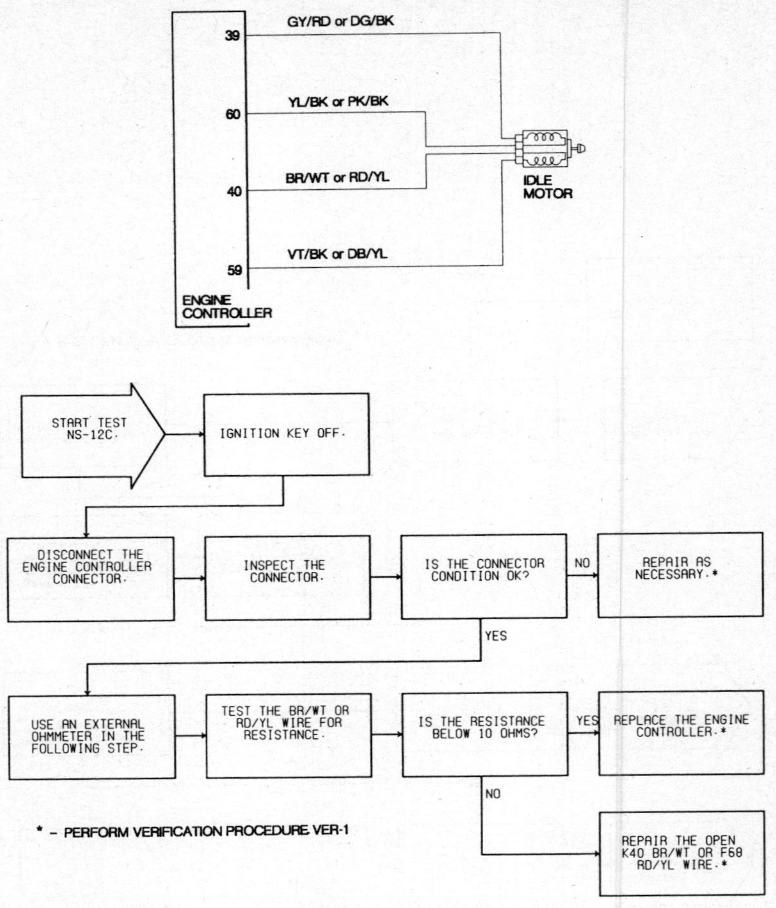
39
GY/RD or DG/BK
60
YL/BK or PK/BK
40
BR/WT or RD/YL
59
VT/BK or DB/YL
ENGINE CONTROLLER
IDLE MOTOR
START TEST NS-12C.
IGNITION KEY OFF.
DISCONNECT THE ENGINE CONTROLLER CONNECTOR.
INSPECT THE CONNECTOR.
IS THE CONNECTOR CONDITION OK?
NO
REPAIR AS NECESSARY.*
YES
USE AN EXTERNAL OHMMETER IN THE FOLLOWING STEP.
TEST THE BR/WT OR RD/YL WIRE FOR RESISTANCE.
IS THE RESISTANCE BELOW 10 OHMS?
YES
REPLACE THE ENGINE CONTROLLER.*
NO
REPAIR THE OPEN K40 BR/WT OR F68 RD/YL WIRE.*
* – PERFORM VERIFICATION PROCEDURE VER-1

91H13943 91J13853

Fig. 52: No Start Test NS-12C – Checking Idle Speed Motor Operation

NS-12D: – CHECKING IDLE SPEED MOTOR OPERATION

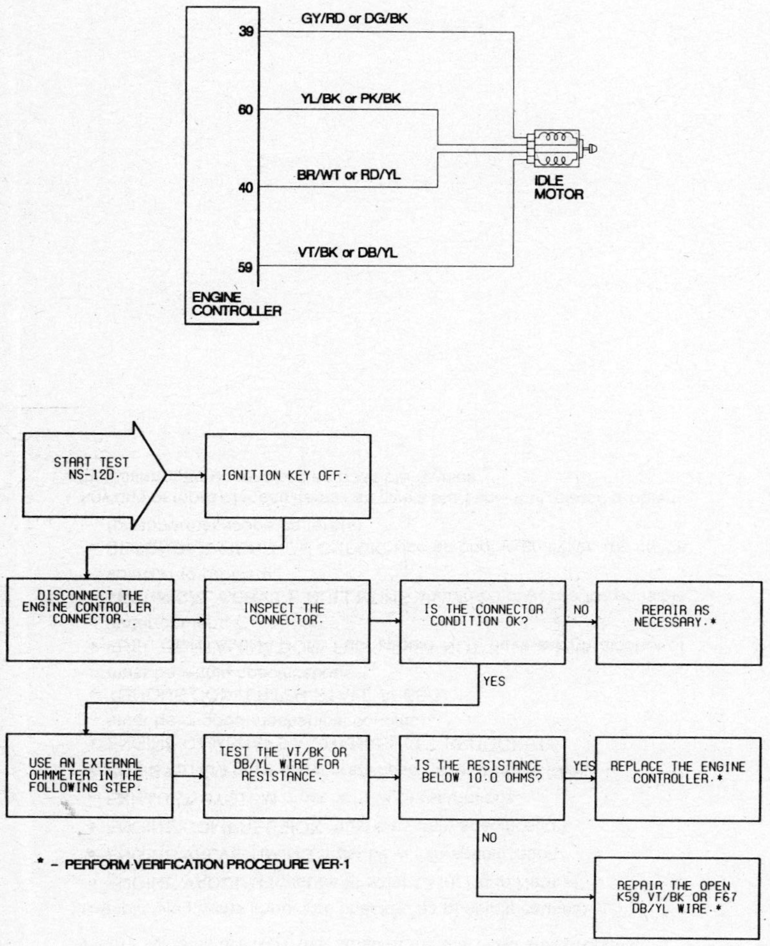
ENGINE CONTROLLER
39
GY/RD or DG/BK
60
YL/BK or PK/BK
40
BR/WT or RD/YL
59
VT/BK or DB/YL
IDLE MOTOR
START TEST NS-12D.
IGNITION KEY OFF.
DISCONNECT THE ENGINE CONTROLLER CONNECTOR.
INSPECT THE CONNECTOR.
IS THE CONNECTOR CONDITION OK?
NO
REPAIR AS NECESSARY.*
YES
USE AN EXTERNAL OHMMETER IN THE FOLLOWING STEP.
TEST THE VT/BK OR DB/YL WIRE FOR RESISTANCE.
IS THE RESISTANCE BELOW 10.0 OHMS?
YES
REPLACE THE ENGINE CONTROLLER.*
NO
REPAIR THE OPEN K59 VT/BK OR F67 DB/YL WIRE.*
* – PERFORM VERIFICATION PROCEDURE VER-1

91H13943 91A13854

Fig. 53: No Start Test NS-12D – Checking Idle Speed Motor Operation

NS-12E: – CHECKING IDLE SPEED MOTOR OPERATION

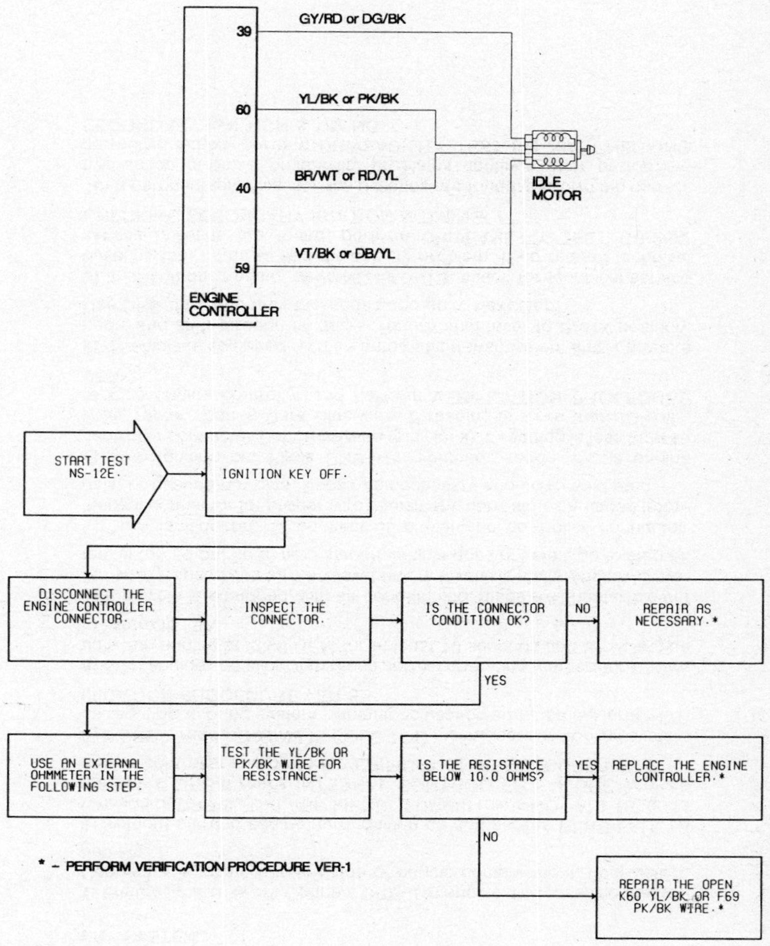
ENGINE CONTROLLER
39
GY/RD or DG/BK
60
YL/BK or PK/BK
40
BR/WT or RD/YL
59
VT/BK or DB/YL
IDLE MOTOR
START TEST NS-12E.
IGNITION KEY OFF.
DISCONNECT THE ENGINE CONTROLLER CONNECTOR.
INSPECT THE CONNECTOR.
IS THE CONNECTOR CONDITION OK?
NO
REPAIR AS NECESSARY.*
YES
USE AN EXTERNAL OHMMETER IN THE FOLLOWING STEP.
TEST THE YL/BK OR PK/BK WIRE FOR RESISTANCE.
IS THE RESISTANCE BELOW 10.0 OHMS?
YES
REPLACE THE ENGINE CONTROLLER.*
NO
REPAIR THE OPEN K60 YL/BK OR F69 PK/BK WIRE.*
* – PERFORM VERIFICATION PROCEDURE VER-1

91H13943 91B13855

Fig. 54: No Start Test NS-12E – Checking Idle Speed Motor Operation

NS-13A: PERFORMING NO FAULT CODE MECHANICAL TEST

At this point in the start and stall test procedure, you have determined that all of the engine control systems are operating properly. The engine control systems are NOT the cause of the start and stall problem.

The following items should be checked as possible causes:

- ENGINE VACUUM must be at least 13 in. Hg in Neutral.
- ENGINE VALVE TIMING must be within specification.
- ENGINE COMPRESSION must be within specification.
- EXHAUST SYSTEM must be free of restrictions.
- PCV SYSTEM must allow crankcase gases to flow freely.
- ENGINE CAMSHAFT & CRANKSHAFT SPROCKETS must be in good mechanical condition.
- TORQUE CONVERTER STALL SPEED must be within specifications.
- FUEL CONTAMINATION: Fuel should NOT have a high alcohol or water content.
- TECHNICAL SERVICE BULLETINS should be checked for possible solution to problem.
- SECONDARY IGNITION CHECK: Use an engine analyzer and check for abnormal scope pattern(s).

Any one or more of these items can give a start and stall related problem. they cannot be overlooked as possible causes.

Fig. 55: No Start Test NS-13A – Performing No Fault Code Mechanical Test

DR-1A: – CHECKING SYSTEM FOR FAULTS (1 OF 2)

NOTE: **Battery must be fully charged and at rated capacity before performing any driveability test procedure. If vehicle starts and stalls repeatedly, perform NO START TEST NS-2A: CHECKING FUEL DELIVERY SYSTEM.**

1) Ensure ignition is off. Connect DRB-II to engine diagnostic connector. Connector is located on left side of engine compartment, near SBEC. *See Fig. 1*.

2) Without starting engine, turn ignition on and access READ FAULTS function of DRB-II FUEL/IGN MENU. If DRB-II reads NO FAULTS, go to step **4)**. If DRB-II reads INTERNAL CONTROLLER FAILURE, replace engine controller and perform VERIFICATION PROCEDURE VER-2.

3) If DRB-II reads ENGINE IS COLD TOO LONG, service cooling system as required to bring system within specification and then perform VERIFICATION PROCEDURE VER-3.

4) Start engine and allow it to reach normal operating temperature. Manually run engine at 2000 RPM for at least 10 seconds and allow engine to return to idle.

5) If vehicle is equipped with air conditioning, place A/C-heater blower fan on low speed and turn A/C system on. If vehicle stalls when A/C system is turned on, go to next step. If vehicle does not stall, go to step **8)**.

6) Turn ignition off. Disconnect 60-pin engine controller connector. Inspect connector for proper wire placement, corrosion, damaged terminals, or pushed-out pins. Repair as necessary and go to next step.

7) Turn ignition on. Place DRB-II in voltmeter mode. Probe engine controller connector Dark Blue wire (pin No. 9). If reading is less than 10 volts, repair open in Dark Blue wire. If reading is more than 10 volts, replace engine controller and perform VERIFICATION PROCEDURE VER-2.

8) If vehicle is equipped with an automatic transmission, step on brake pedal and shift through all gears. Return shift lever to PARK position. Use DRB-II to read fault messages and go to next step.

9) If DRB-II once again reads NO FAULTS, check for technical service bulletins that relate to this driveability problem. If no related technical service bulletins are found, perform DRIVEABILITY TEST DR-26A: CHECKING SECONDARY IGNITION & TIMING.

10) If pertinent technical service bulletins are found, perform the corrective action given. If driveability problems continue after performing corrective action, perform DRIVEABILITY TEST DR-26A: CHECKING SECONDARY IGNITION & TIMING.

Fig. 56: Driveability Test DR-1A – Checking System For Faults (1 of 2)

DR-1A: – CHECKING SYSTEM FOR FAULTS (2 OF 2)

DRB-II FAULT MESSAGES

DRB-II Message	[1] Hard Fault	[2] Intermittent Fault
A/C Clutch Relay Circuit	DR-22A	DR-35A
Automatic Idle Speed Motor Circuits	DR-15A	DR-37A
Charge Temperature Sensor Voltage High	DR-11A	DR-36A
Charge Temperature Sensor Voltage Low	DR-12A	DR-36A
Controller Failure EEPROM Write Denied	DR-25A	DR-25A
Controller Failure EMR Miles Not Stored	DR-25A	DR-25A
Coolant Sensor Voltage Too High	DR-9A	DR-36A
Coolant Sensor Voltage Too Low	DR-10A	DR-36A
Injector No. 1 Control Circuit	DR-16A	DR-38A
Injector No. 2 Control Circuit	DR-17A	DR-38A
Injector No. 3 Control Circuit	DR-18A	DR-38A
Injector No. 4 Control Circuit	DR-19A	DR-38A
Injector No. 5 Control Circuit	DR-20A	DR-38A
Injector No. 6 Control Circuit	DR-21A	DR-38A
MAP Voltage Too High	DR-5A	DR-36A
MAP Voltage Too Low	DR-4A	DR-36A
No ASD Relay Voltage Sense At Controller	DR-24A	DR-24A
No Change In MAP From Start To Run	DR-3A	DR-36B
No Vehicle Speed Signal	DR-6A	DR-6A
O_2 Signal Shorted To Voltage	DR-8A	DR-8A
O_2 Signal Stays At Center	DR-7A	DR-7A
O_2 Signal Stays Below Center (Lean)	DR-26A	DR-26A
O_2 Signal Stays Above Center (Rich)	DR-26A	DR-26A
Radiator Fan Relay Circuit	DR-23A	DR-35A
Slow Change In Idle MAP Signal	DR-2A	DR-36A
Throttle Position Sensor Voltage High	DR-13A	DR-36A
Throttle Position Sensor Voltage Low	DR-14A	DR-36A

[1] – Key counter is "0".
[2] – Key counter is greater than "0".

Fig. 57: Driveability Test DR-1A – Checking System For Faults (2 of 2)

DR-2A: – REPAIRING SLOW CHANGE IN IDLE MAP SIGNAL FAULT (1 OF 2)

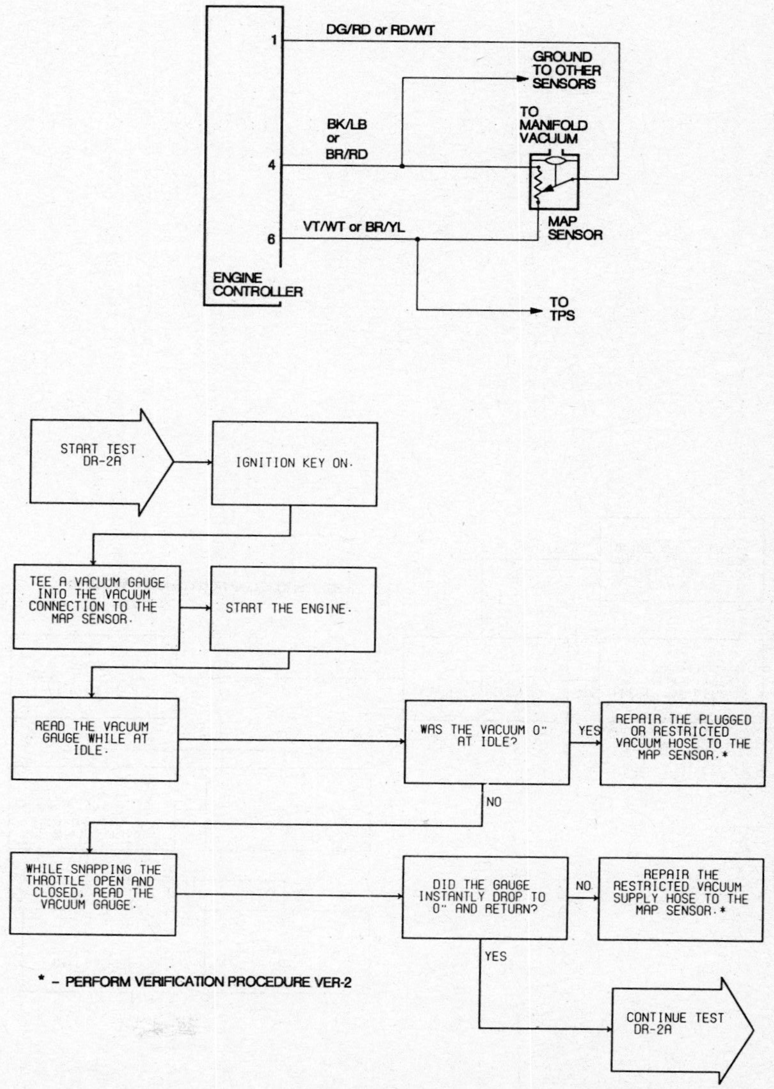
1
4
6
DG/RD or RD/WT
BK/LB or BR/RD
VT/WT or BR/YL
ENGINE CONTROLLER
GROUND TO OTHER SENSORS
TO MANIFOLD VACUUM
MAP SENSOR
TO TPS
START TEST DR-2A
IGNITION KEY ON.
TEE A VACUUM GAUGE INTO THE VACUUM CONNECTION TO THE MAP SENSOR.
START THE ENGINE.
READ THE VACUUM GAUGE WHILE AT IDLE.
WAS THE VACUUM 0" AT IDLE?
YES
REPAIR THE PLUGGED OR RESTRICTED VACUUM HOSE TO THE MAP SENSOR.*
NO
WHILE SNAPPING THE THROTTLE OPEN AND CLOSED, READ THE VACUUM GAUGE.
DID THE GAUGE INSTANTLY DROP TO 0" AND RETURN?
NO
REPAIR THE RESTRICTED VACUUM SUPPLY HOSE TO THE MAP SENSOR.*
YES
CONTINUE TEST DR-2A

* – PERFORM VERIFICATION PROCEDURE VER-2

91I13944 91C13856

Fig. 58: Driveability Test DR-2A – Repairing Slow Change In Idle Map Signal Fault (1 of 2)

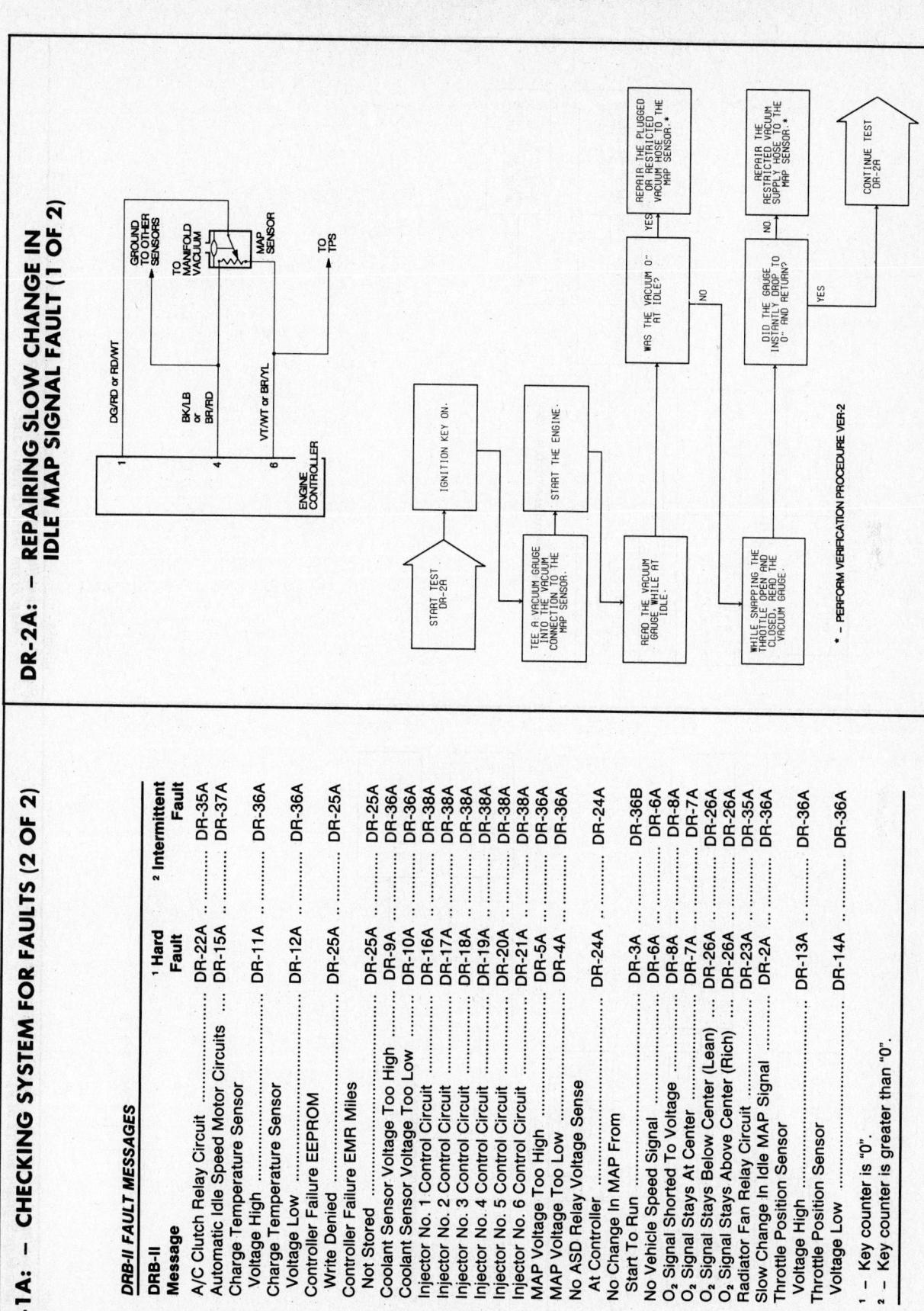

DR-2A: – REPAIRING SLOW CHANGE IN IDLE MAP SIGNAL FAULT (2 OF 2)

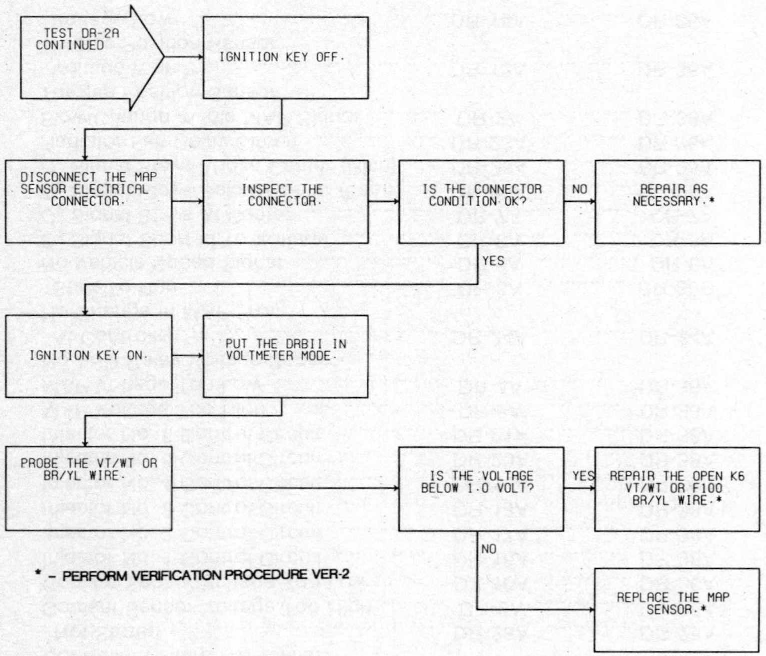
TEST DR-2A CONTINUED
IGNITION KEY OFF.
DISCONNECT THE MAP SENSOR ELECTRICAL CONNECTOR.
INSPECT THE CONNECTOR.
IS THE CONNECTOR CONDITION OK?
NO
REPAIR AS NECESSARY.*
YES
IGNITION KEY ON.
PUT THE DRBII IN VOLTMETER MODE.
PROBE THE VT/WT OR BR/YL WIRE.
IS THE VOLTAGE BELOW 1.0 VOLT?
YES
REPAIR THE OPEN K6 VT/WT OR F100 BR/YL WIRE.*
NO
REPLACE THE MAP SENSOR.*

* – PERFORM VERIFICATION PROCEDURE VER-2

91D13857

Fig. 59: Driveability Test DR-2A – Repairing Slow Change In Idle Map Signal Fault (2 of 2)

DR-3A: – REPAIRING NO CHANGE IN MAP FROM START TO RUN FAULT

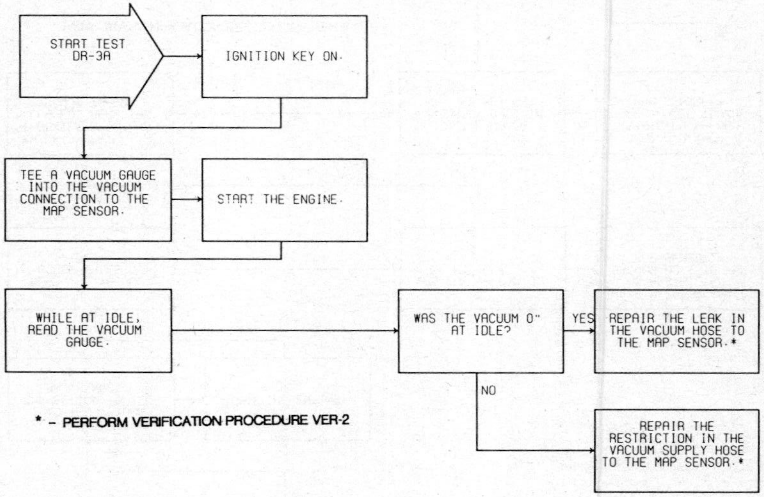
START TEST DR-3A
IGNITION KEY ON.
TEE A VACUUM GAUGE INTO THE VACUUM CONNECTION TO THE MAP SENSOR.
START THE ENGINE.
WHILE AT IDLE, READ THE VACUUM GAUGE.
WAS THE VACUUM 0" AT IDLE?
YES
REPAIR THE LEAK IN THE VACUUM HOSE TO THE MAP SENSOR.*
NO
REPAIR THE RESTRICTION IN THE VACUUM SUPPLY HOSE TO THE MAP SENSOR.*

* – PERFORM VERIFICATION PROCEDURE VER-2

91E13858

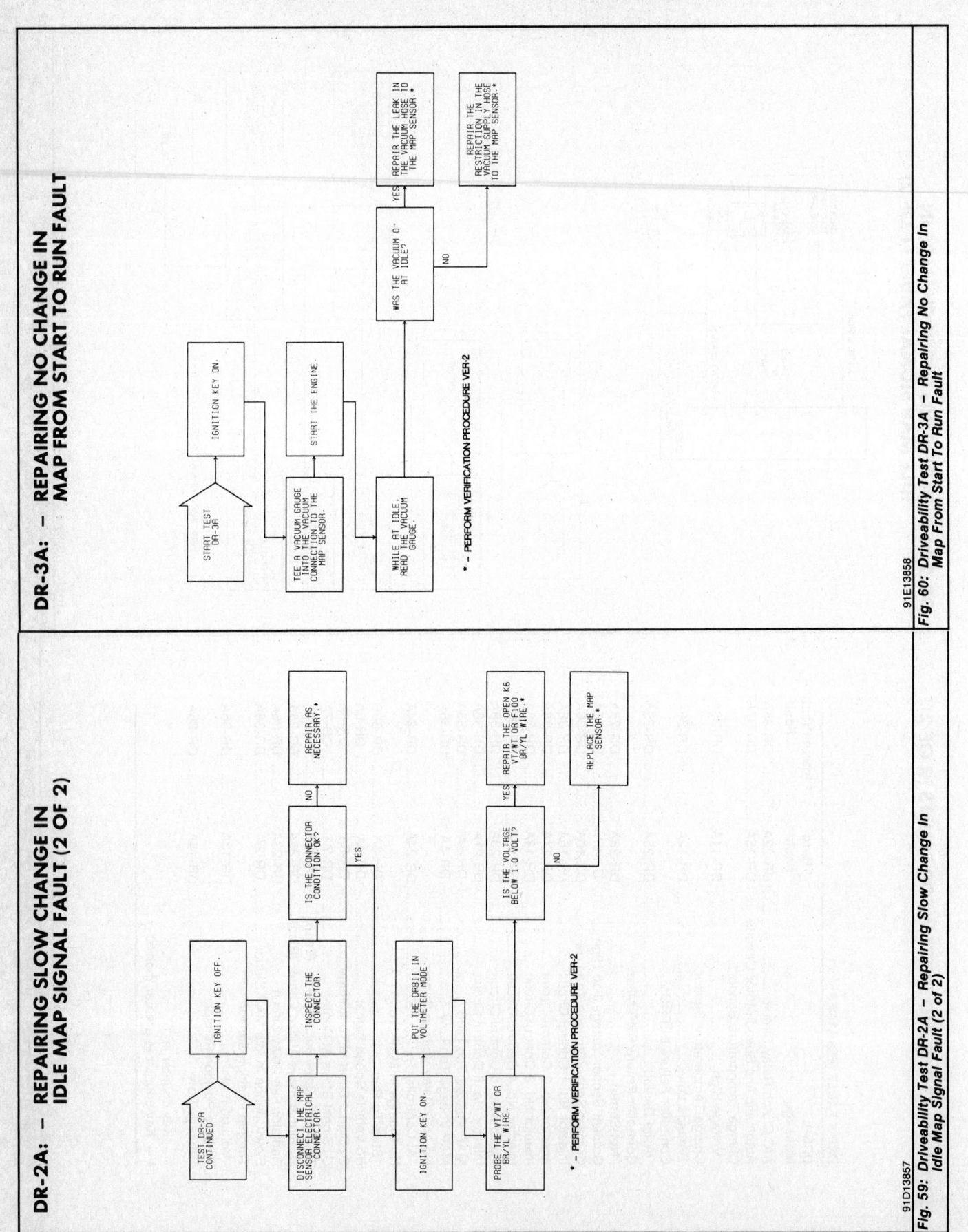

Fig. 60: Driveability Test DR-3A – Repairing No Change In Map From Start To Run Fault

DR-4A: – REPAIRING MAP VOLTAGE TOO LOW FAULT

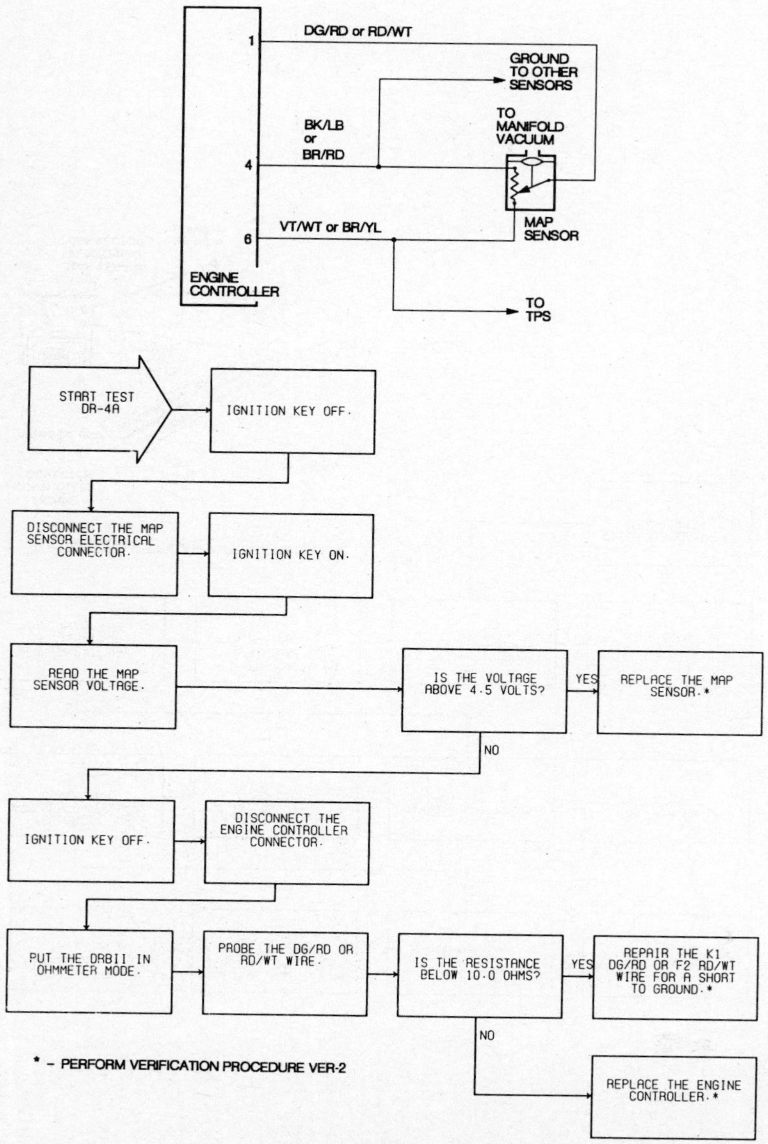
ENGINE CONTROLLER
1
4
6
DG/RD or RD/WT
BK/LB or BR/RD
VT/WT or BR/YL
GROUND TO OTHER SENSORS
TO MANIFOLD VACUUM
MAP SENSOR
TO TPS
START TEST DR-4A
IGNITION KEY OFF.
DISCONNECT THE MAP SENSOR ELECTRICAL CONNECTOR.
IGNITION KEY ON.
READ THE MAP SENSOR VOLTAGE.
IS THE VOLTAGE ABOVE 4.5 VOLTS?
YES
REPLACE THE MAP SENSOR.*
NO
IGNITION KEY OFF.
DISCONNECT THE ENGINE CONTROLLER CONNECTOR.
PUT THE DRBII IN OHMMETER MODE.
PROBE THE DG/RD OR RD/WT WIRE.
IS THE RESISTANCE BELOW 10.0 OHMS?
YES
REPAIR THE K1 DG/RD OR F2 RD/WT WIRE FOR A SHORT TO GROUND.*
NO
REPLACE THE ENGINE CONTROLLER.*
* – PERFORM VERIFICATION PROCEDURE VER-2

91I13944 91F13859

Fig. 61: Driveability Test DR-4A – Repairing Map Voltage Too Low Fault

DR-5A: – REPAIRING MAP VOLTAGE TOO HIGH FAULT (1 OF 2)

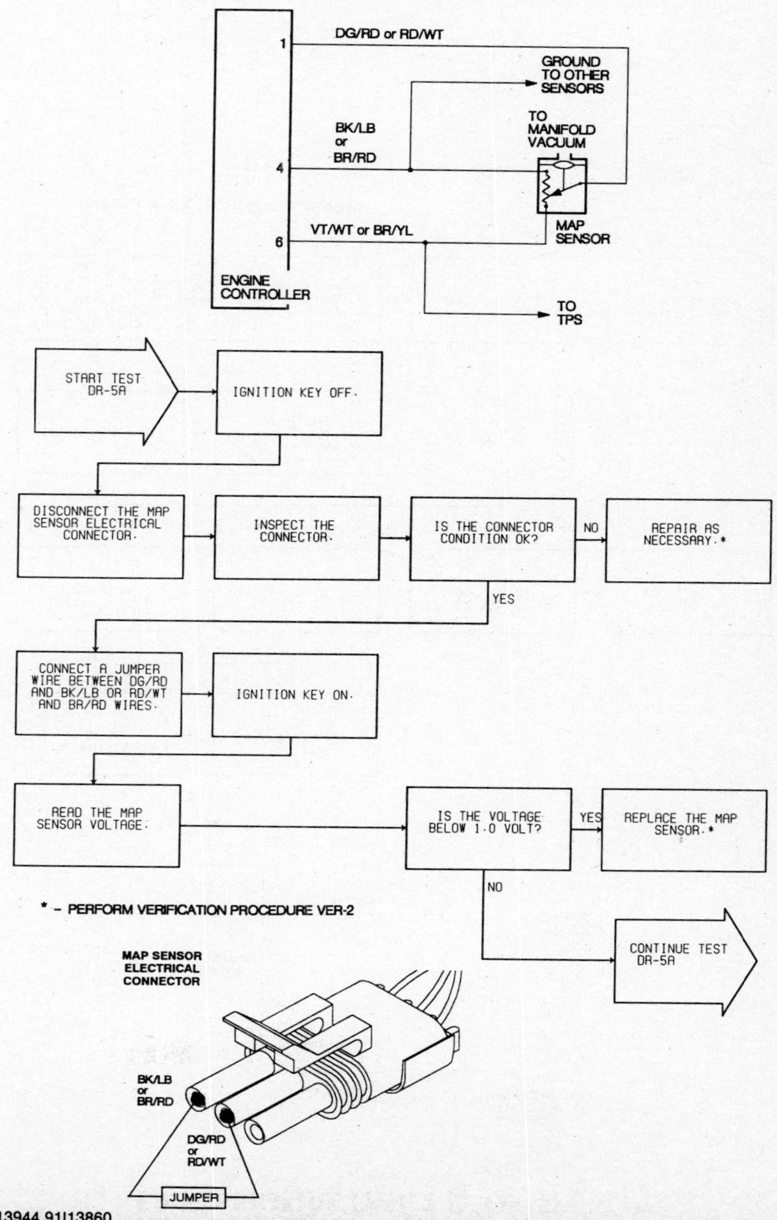
ENGINE CONTROLLER
1
4
6
DG/RD or RD/WT
BK/LB or BR/RD
VT/WT or BR/YL
GROUND TO OTHER SENSORS
TO MANIFOLD VACUUM
MAP SENSOR
TO TPS
START TEST DR-5A
IGNITION KEY OFF.
DISCONNECT THE MAP SENSOR ELECTRICAL CONNECTOR.
INSPECT THE CONNECTOR.
IS THE CONNECTOR CONDITION OK?
NO
REPAIR AS NECESSARY.*
YES
CONNECT A JUMPER WIRE BETWEEN DG/RD AND BK/LB OR RD/WT AND BR/RD WIRES.
IGNITION KEY ON.
READ THE MAP SENSOR VOLTAGE.
IS THE VOLTAGE BELOW 1.0 VOLT?
YES
REPLACE THE MAP SENSOR.*
NO
CONTINUE TEST DR-5A
* – PERFORM VERIFICATION PROCEDURE VER-2
MAP SENSOR ELECTRICAL CONNECTOR
BK/LB or BR/RD
DG/RD or RD/WT
JUMPER

91I13944 91I13860

Fig. 62: Driveability Test DR-5A – Repairing Map Voltage Too High Fault (1 of 2)

1991 ENGINE PERFORMANCE
Self-Diagnostics (Cont.)

DR-5A: – REPAIRING MAP VOLTAGE TOO HIGH FAULT (2 OF 2)

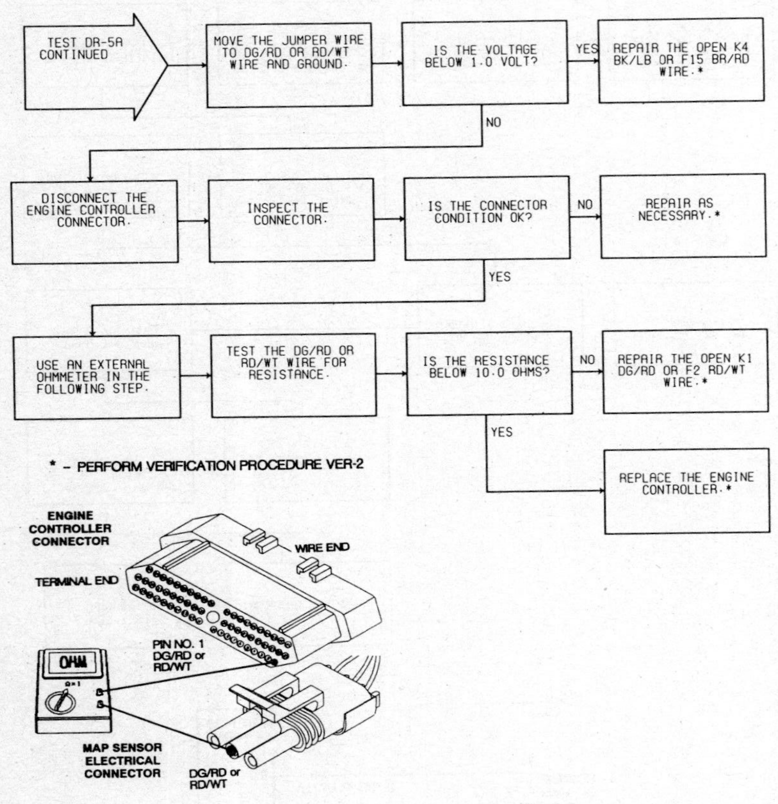
TEST DR-5A CONTINUED
MOVE THE JUMPER WIRE TO DG/RD OR RD/WT WIRE AND GROUND.
IS THE VOLTAGE BELOW 1.0 VOLT?
YES
REPAIR THE OPEN K4 BK/LB OR F15 BR/RD WIRE.*
NO
DISCONNECT THE ENGINE CONTROLLER CONNECTOR.
INSPECT THE CONNECTOR.
IS THE CONNECTOR CONDITION OK?
NO
REPAIR AS NECESSARY.*
YES
USE AN EXTERNAL OHMMETER IN THE FOLLOWING STEP.
TEST THE DG/RD OR RD/WT WIRE FOR RESISTANCE.
IS THE RESISTANCE BELOW 10.0 OHMS?
NO
REPAIR THE OPEN K1 DG/RD OR F2 RD/WT WIRE.*
YES
REPLACE THE ENGINE CONTROLLER.*
* - PERFORM VERIFICATION PROCEDURE VER-2
ENGINE CONTROLLER CONNECTOR
WIRE END
TERMINAL END
PIN NO. 1 DG/RD or RD/WT
OHM
MAP SENSOR ELECTRICAL CONNECTOR
DG/RD or RD/WT

91J13861

Fig. 63: Driveability Test DR-5A – Repairing Map Voltage Too High Fault (2 OF 2)

DR-6A: – REPAIRING NO VEHICLE SPEED SIGNAL FAULT (1 OF 4)

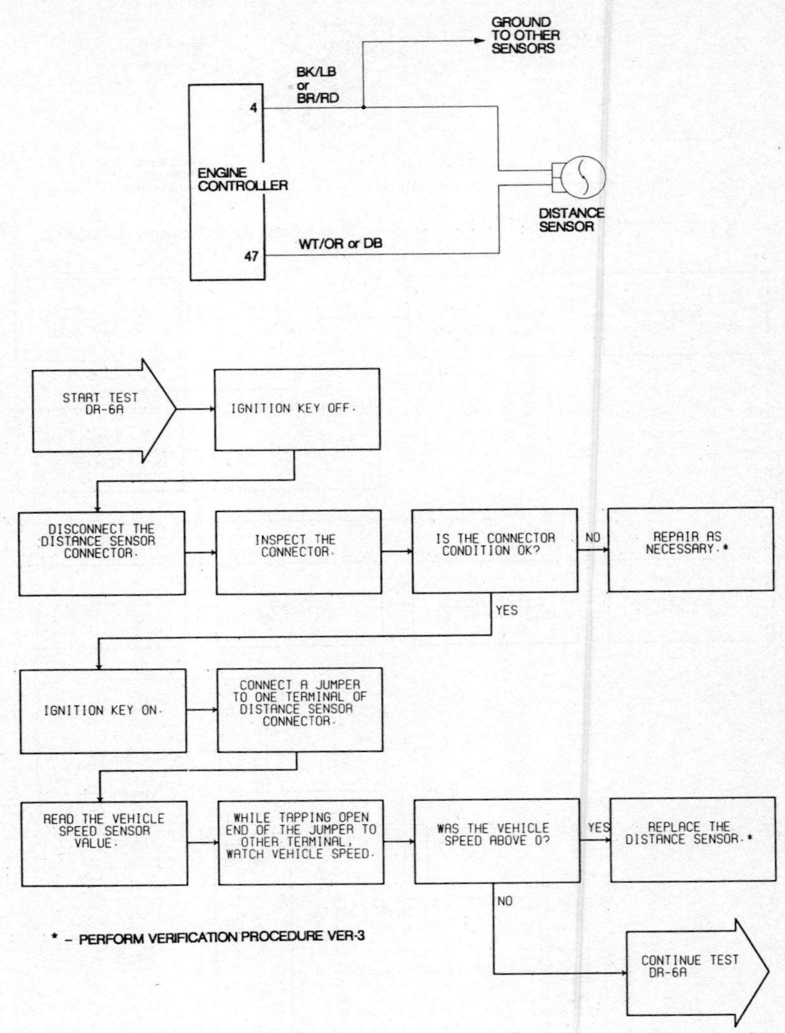
GROUND TO OTHER SENSORS
BK/LB or BR/RD
4
ENGINE CONTROLLER
47
WT/OR or DB
DISTANCE SENSOR
START TEST DR-6A
IGNITION KEY OFF.
DISCONNECT THE DISTANCE SENSOR CONNECTOR.
INSPECT THE CONNECTOR.
IS THE CONNECTOR CONDITION OK?
NO
REPAIR AS NECESSARY.*
YES
IGNITION KEY ON.
CONNECT A JUMPER TO ONE TERMINAL OF DISTANCE SENSOR CONNECTOR.
READ THE VEHICLE SPEED SENSOR VALUE.
WHILE TAPPING OPEN END OF THE JUMPER TO OTHER TERMINAL, WATCH VEHICLE SPEED.
WAS THE VEHICLE SPEED ABOVE 0?
YES
REPLACE THE DISTANCE SENSOR.*
NO
CONTINUE TEST DR-6A
* - PERFORM VERIFICATION PROCEDURE VER-3

91J13945 91A13862

Fig. 64: Driveability Test DR-6A – Repairing No Vehicle Speed Signal Fault (1 of 4)

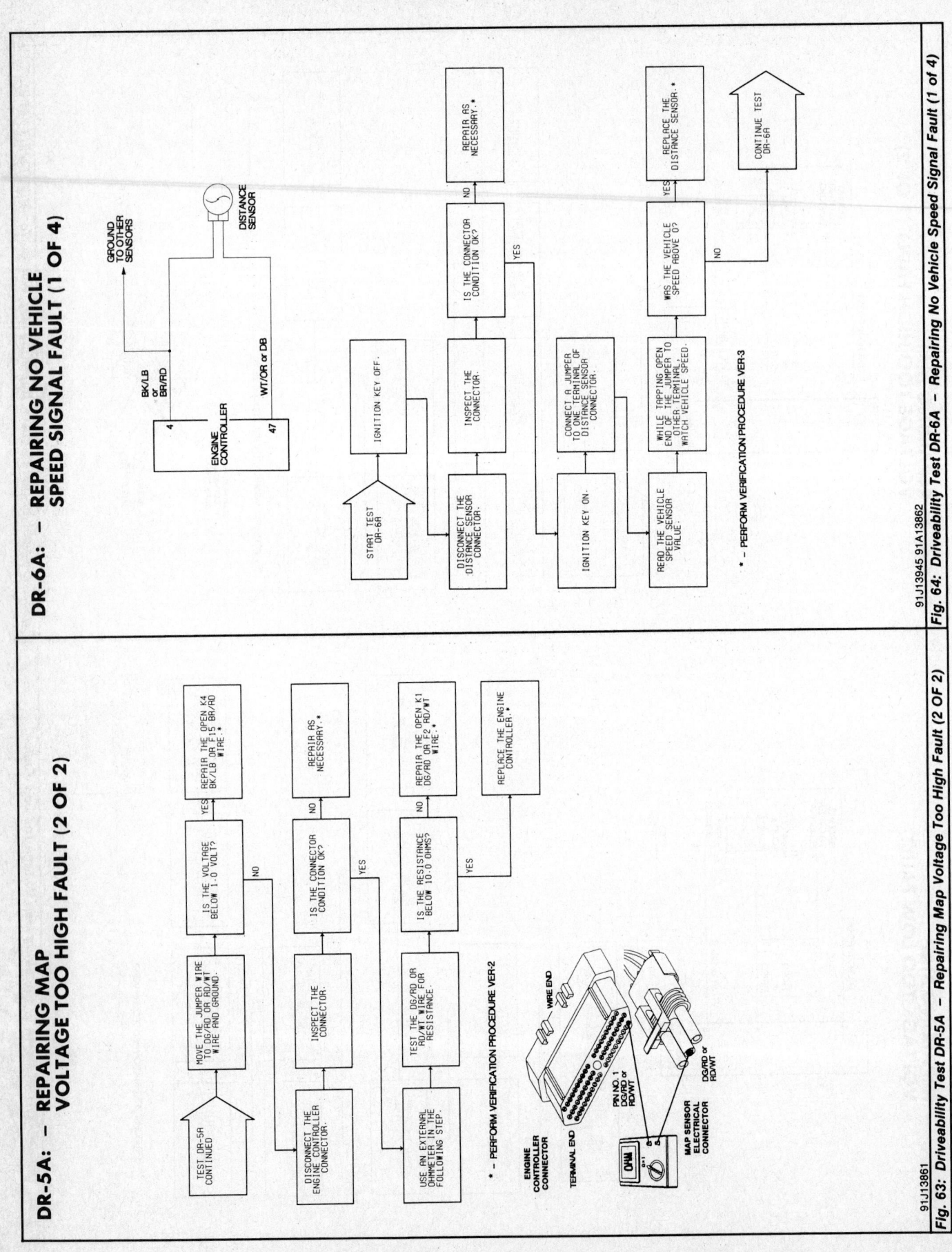

DR-6A: – REPAIRING NO VEHICLE SPEED SIGNAL FAULT (2 OF 4)

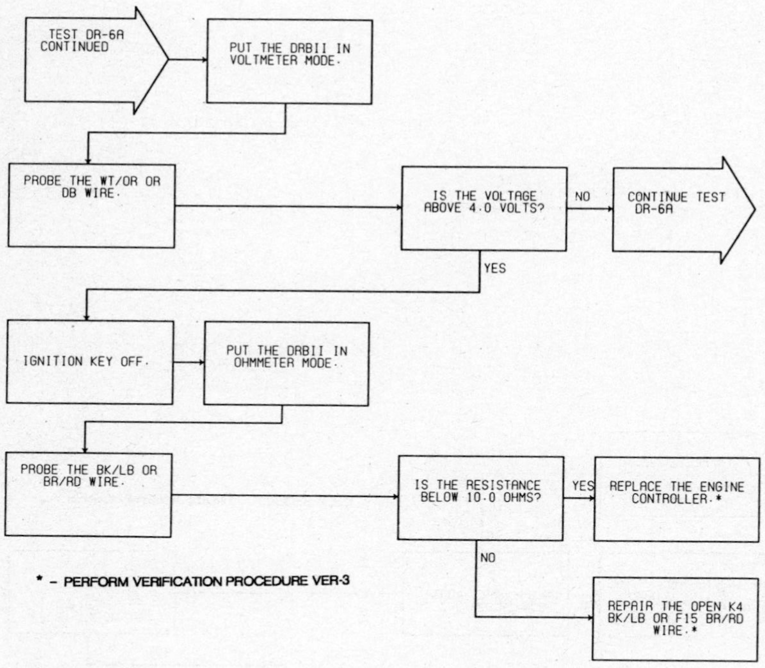
TEST DR-6A CONTINUED
PUT THE DRBII IN VOLTMETER MODE.
PROBE THE WT/OR OR DB WIRE.
IS THE VOLTAGE ABOVE 4.0 VOLTS?
NO
CONTINUE TEST DR-6A
YES
IGNITION KEY OFF.
PUT THE DRBII IN OHMMETER MODE.
PROBE THE BK/LB OR BR/RD WIRE.
IS THE RESISTANCE BELOW 10.0 OHMS?
YES
REPLACE THE ENGINE CONTROLLER.*
NO
REPAIR THE OPEN K4 BK/LB OR F15 BR/RD WIRE.*
* – PERFORM VERIFICATION PROCEDURE VER-3

91B13863

Fig. 65: Driveability Test DR-6A – Repairing No Vehicle Speed Signal Fault (2 of 4)

DR-6A: – REPAIRING NO VEHICLE SPEED SIGNAL FAULT (3 OF 4)

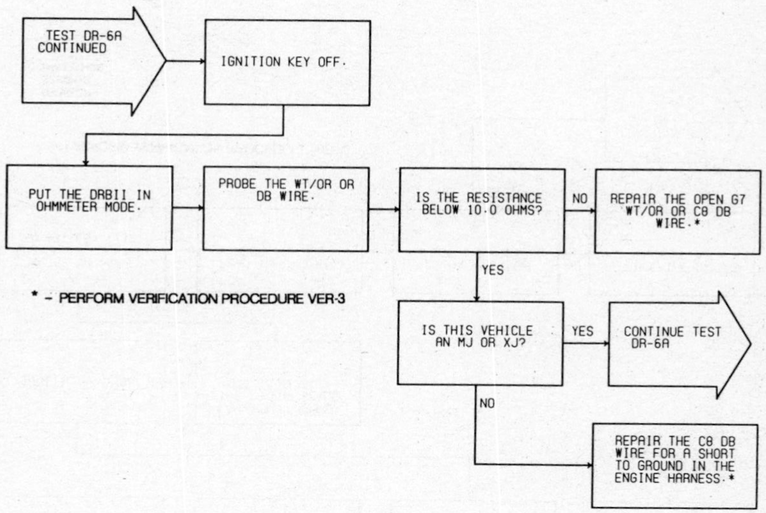
TEST DR-6A CONTINUED
IGNITION KEY OFF.
PUT THE DRBII IN OHMMETER MODE.
PROBE THE WT/OR OR DB WIRE.
IS THE RESISTANCE BELOW 10.0 OHMS?
NO
REPAIR THE OPEN G7 WT/OR OR C8 DB WIRE.*
YES
IS THIS VEHICLE AN MJ OR XJ?
YES
CONTINUE TEST DR-6A
NO
REPAIR THE C8 DB WIRE FOR A SHORT TO GROUND IN THE ENGINE HARNESS.*
* – PERFORM VERIFICATION PROCEDURE VER-3

91C13864

Fig. 66: Driveability Test DR-6A – Repairing No Vehicle Speed Signal Fault (3 of 4)

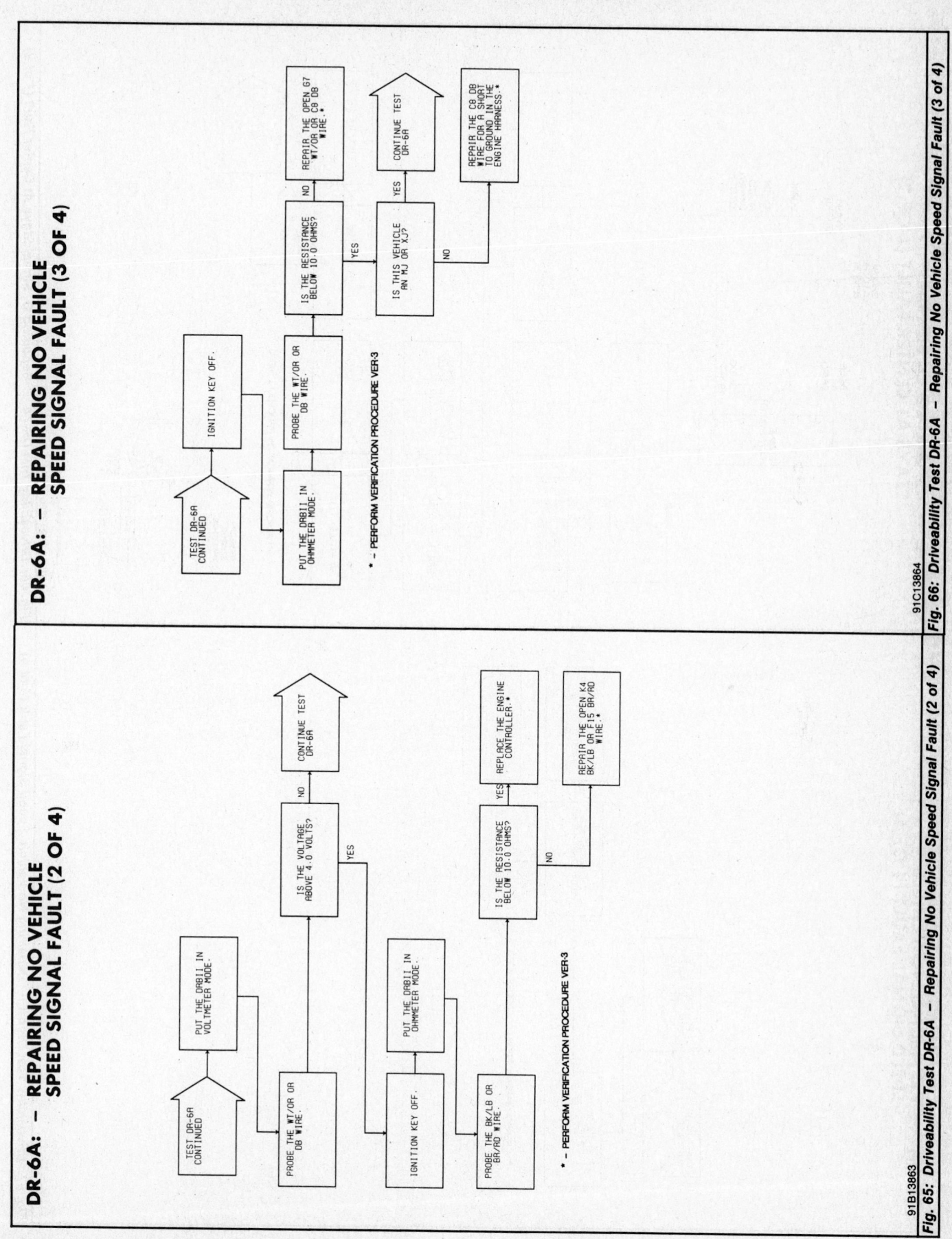

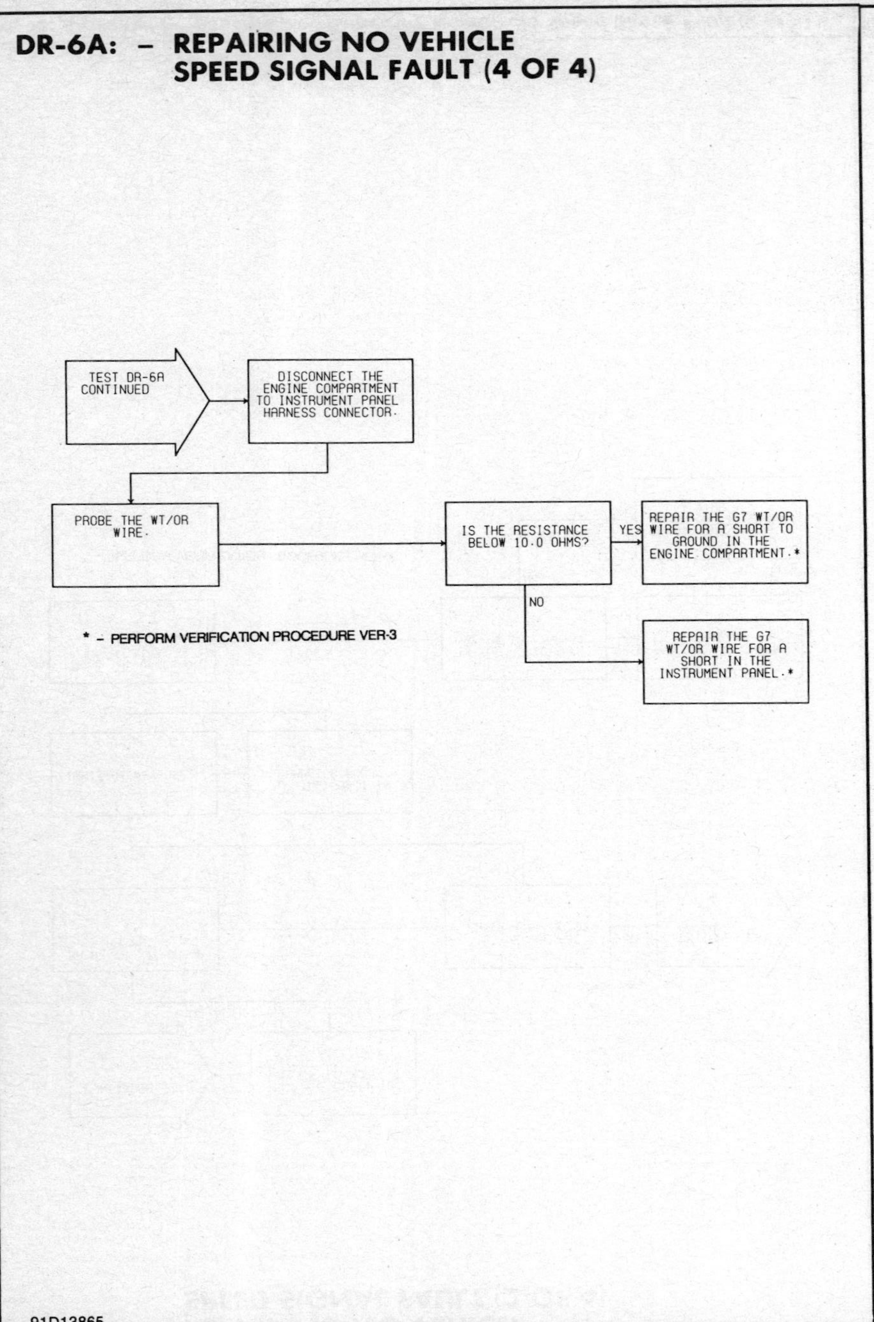
DR-6A: – REPAIRING NO VEHICLE SPEED SIGNAL FAULT (4 OF 4)
TEST DR-6A CONTINUED
DISCONNECT THE ENGINE COMPARTMENT TO INSTRUMENT PANEL HARNESS CONNECTOR.
PROBE THE WT/OR WIRE.
IS THE RESISTANCE BELOW 10.0 OHMS?
YES
REPAIR THE G7 WT/OR WIRE FOR A SHORT TO GROUND IN THE ENGINE COMPARTMENT.*
NO
REPAIR THE G7 WT/OR WIRE FOR A SHORT IN THE INSTRUMENT PANEL.*
* – PERFORM VERIFICATION PROCEDURE VER-3
91D13865

Fig. 67: Driveability Test DR-6A – Repairing No Vehicle Speed Signal Fault (4 of 4)

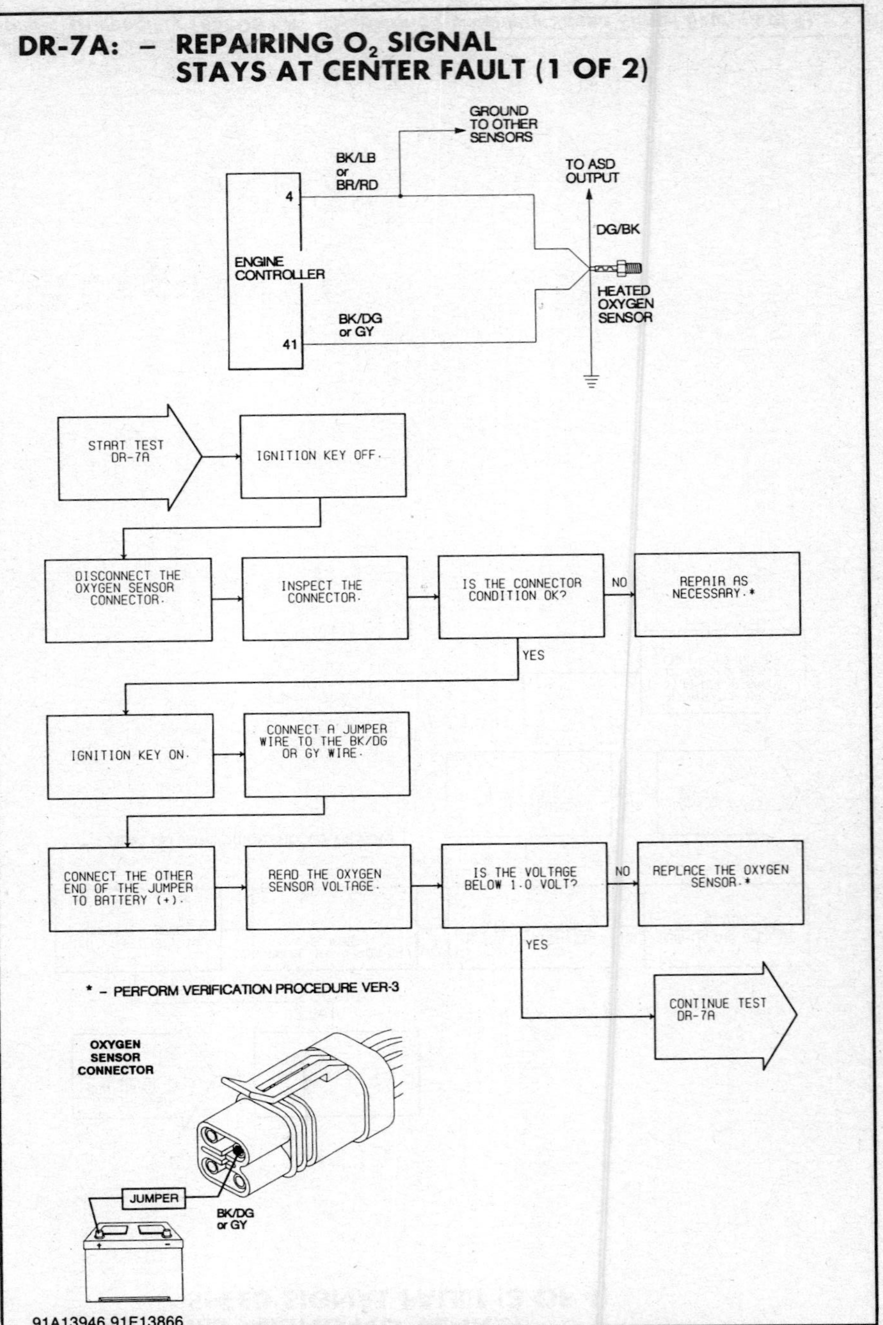
DR-7A: – REPAIRING O2 SIGNAL STAYS AT CENTER FAULT (1 OF 2)
GROUND TO OTHER SENSORS
BK/LB or BR/RD
TO ASD OUTPUT
4
DG/BK
ENGINE CONTROLLER
HEATED OXYGEN SENSOR
BK/DG or GY
41
START TEST DR-7A
IGNITION KEY OFF.
DISCONNECT THE OXYGEN SENSOR CONNECTOR.
INSPECT THE CONNECTOR.
IS THE CONNECTOR CONDITION OK?
NO
REPAIR AS NECESSARY.*
YES
IGNITION KEY ON.
CONNECT A JUMPER WIRE TO THE BK/DG OR GY WIRE.
CONNECT THE OTHER END OF THE JUMPER TO BATTERY (+).
READ THE OXYGEN SENSOR VOLTAGE.
IS THE VOLTAGE BELOW 1.0 VOLT?
NO
REPLACE THE OXYGEN SENSOR.*
YES
CONTINUE TEST DR-7A
* – PERFORM VERIFICATION PROCEDURE VER-3
OXYGEN SENSOR CONNECTOR
JUMPER
BK/DG or GY
91A13946 91E13866

Fig. 68: Driveability Test DR-7A – Repairing O_2 Signal Stays At Center Fault (1 of 2)

DR-7A: – REPAIRING O_2 SIGNAL STAYS AT CENTER FAULT (2 OF 2)

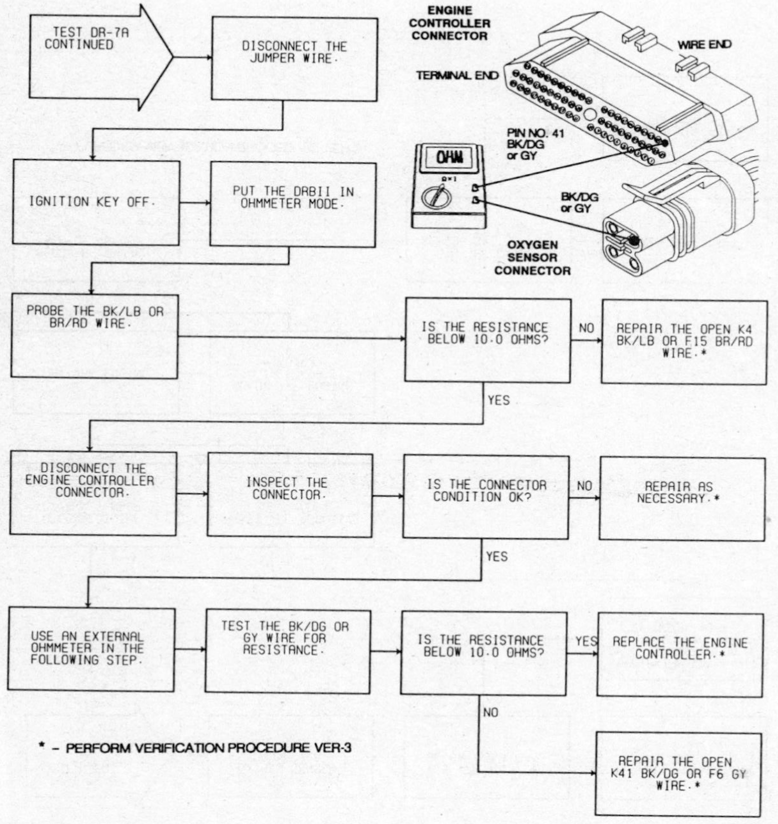
TEST DR-7A CONTINUED
DISCONNECT THE JUMPER WIRE.
IGNITION KEY OFF.
PUT THE DRBII IN OHMMETER MODE.
ENGINE CONTROLLER CONNECTOR
WIRE END
TERMINAL END
PIN NO. 41 BK/DG or GY
OHM
BK/DG or GY
OXYGEN SENSOR CONNECTOR
PROBE THE BK/LB OR BR/RD WIRE.
IS THE RESISTANCE BELOW 10.0 OHMS?
NO
REPAIR THE OPEN K4 BK/LB OR F15 BR/RD WIRE.*
YES
DISCONNECT THE ENGINE CONTROLLER CONNECTOR.
INSPECT THE CONNECTOR.
IS THE CONNECTOR CONDITION OK?
NO
REPAIR AS NECESSARY.*
YES
USE AN EXTERNAL OHMMETER IN THE FOLLOWING STEP.
TEST THE BK/DG OR GY WIRE FOR RESISTANCE.
IS THE RESISTANCE BELOW 10.0 OHMS?
YES
REPLACE THE ENGINE CONTROLLER.*
NO
REPAIR THE OPEN K41 BK/DG OR F6 GY WIRE.*
* – PERFORM VERIFICATION PROCEDURE VER-3

91F13867

Fig. 69: Driveability Test DR-7A – Repairing O_2 Signal Stays At Center Fault (2 of 2)

DR-8A: – REPAIRING O_2 SIGNAL SHORTED TO VOLTAGE FAULT (1 OF 2)

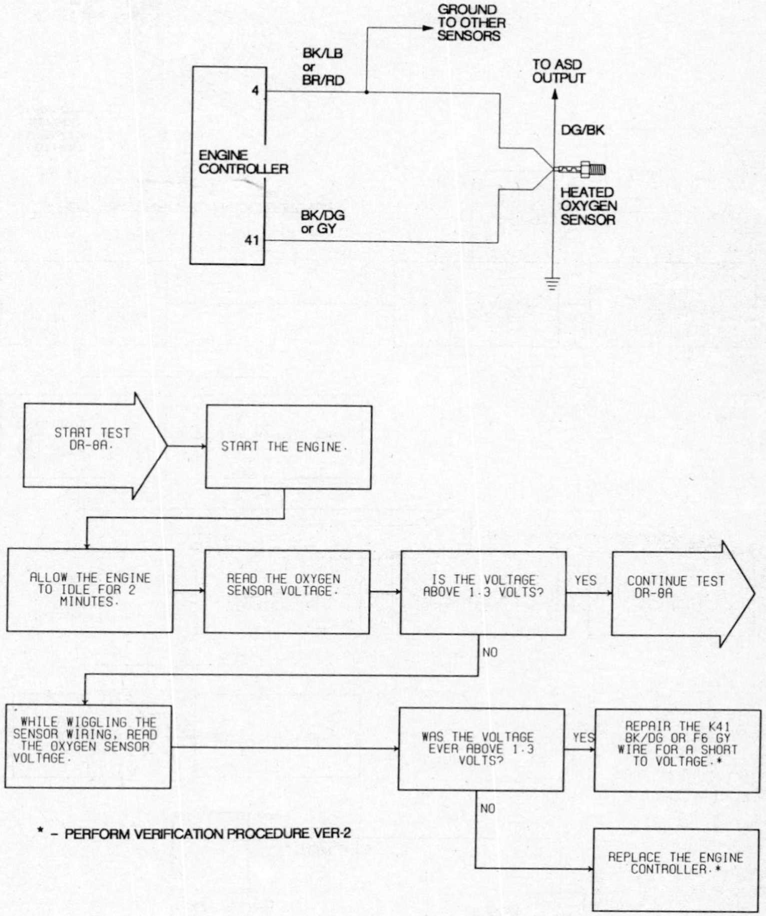
GROUND TO OTHER SENSORS
BK/LB or BR/RD
4
TO ASD OUTPUT
DG/BK
ENGINE CONTROLLER
HEATED OXYGEN SENSOR
BK/DG or GY
41
START TEST DR-8A.
START THE ENGINE.
ALLOW THE ENGINE TO IDLE FOR 2 MINUTES.
READ THE OXYGEN SENSOR VOLTAGE.
IS THE VOLTAGE ABOVE 1.3 VOLTS?
YES
CONTINUE TEST DR-8A
NO
WHILE WIGGLING THE SENSOR WIRING, READ THE OXYGEN SENSOR VOLTAGE.
WAS THE VOLTAGE EVER ABOVE 1.3 VOLTS?
YES
REPAIR THE K41 BK/DG OR F6 GY WIRE FOR A SHORT TO VOLTAGE.*
NO
REPLACE THE ENGINE CONTROLLER.*
* – PERFORM VERIFICATION PROCEDURE VER-2

91A13946 91G13868

Fig. 70: Driveability Test DR-8A – Repairing O_2 Signal Shorted To Voltage Fault (1 of 2)

DR-8A: – REPAIRING O_2 SIGNAL SHORTED TO VOLTAGE FAULT (2 OF 2)

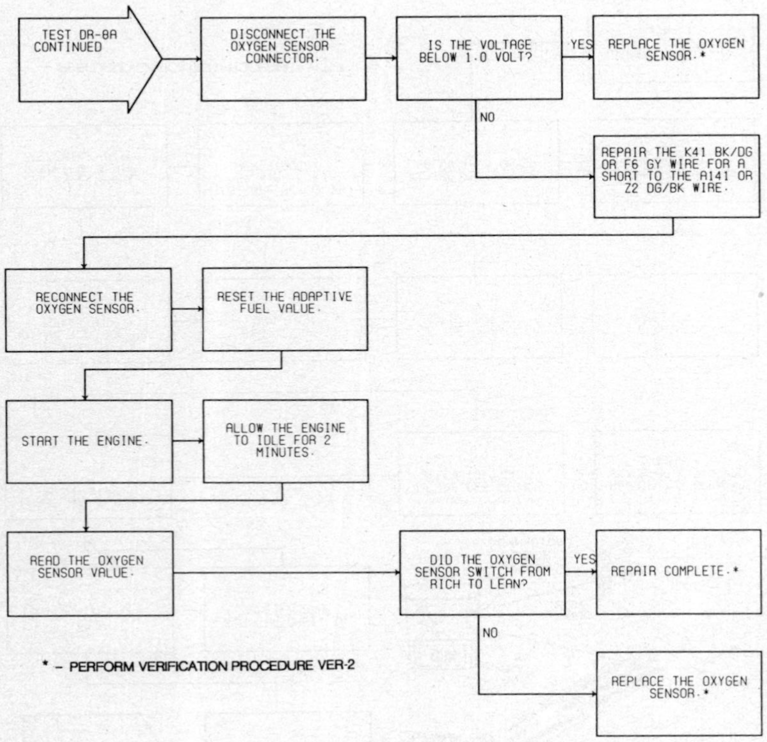
TEST DR-8A CONTINUED
DISCONNECT THE OXYGEN SENSOR CONNECTOR.
IS THE VOLTAGE BELOW 1.0 VOLT?
YES
REPLACE THE OXYGEN SENSOR.*
NO
REPAIR THE K41 BK/DG OR F6 GY WIRE FOR A SHORT TO THE A141 OR Z2 DG/BK WIRE.
RECONNECT THE OXYGEN SENSOR.
RESET THE ADAPTIVE FUEL VALUE.
START THE ENGINE.
ALLOW THE ENGINE TO IDLE FOR 2 MINUTES.
READ THE OXYGEN SENSOR VALUE.
DID THE OXYGEN SENSOR SWITCH FROM RICH TO LEAN?
YES
REPAIR COMPLETE.*
NO
REPLACE THE OXYGEN SENSOR.*
* – PERFORM VERIFICATION PROCEDURE VER-2

91H13869

Fig. 71: Driveability Test DR-8A – Repairing O_2 Signal Shorted To Voltage Fault (2 of 2)

DR-9A: – REPAIRING COOLANT SENSOR VOLTAGE TOO HIGH FAULT (1 OF 2)

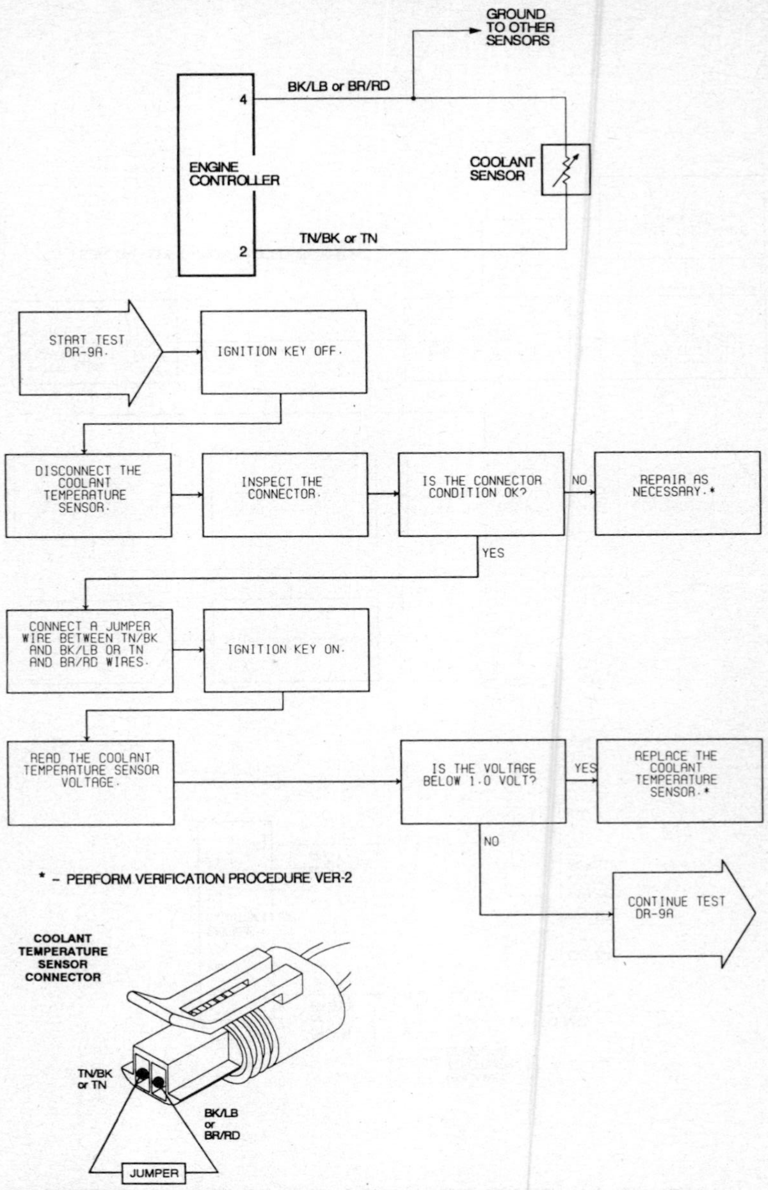
GROUND TO OTHER SENSORS
BK/LB or BR/RD
4
ENGINE CONTROLLER
COOLANT SENSOR
TN/BK or TN
2
START TEST DR-9A.
IGNITION KEY OFF.
DISCONNECT THE COOLANT TEMPERATURE SENSOR.
INSPECT THE CONNECTOR.
IS THE CONNECTOR CONDITION OK?
NO
REPAIR AS NECESSARY.*
YES
CONNECT A JUMPER WIRE BETWEEN TN/BK AND BK/LB OR TN AND BR/RD WIRES.
IGNITION KEY ON.
READ THE COOLANT TEMPERATURE SENSOR VOLTAGE.
IS THE VOLTAGE BELOW 1.0 VOLT?
YES
REPLACE THE COOLANT TEMPERATURE SENSOR.*
NO
CONTINUE TEST DR-9A
* – PERFORM VERIFICATION PROCEDURE VER-2
COOLANT TEMPERATURE SENSOR CONNECTOR
TN/BK or TN
BK/LB or BR/RD
JUMPER

91B13947 91A13870

Fig. 72: Driveability Test DR-9A – Repairing Coolant Sensor Voltage Too High Fault (1 of 2)

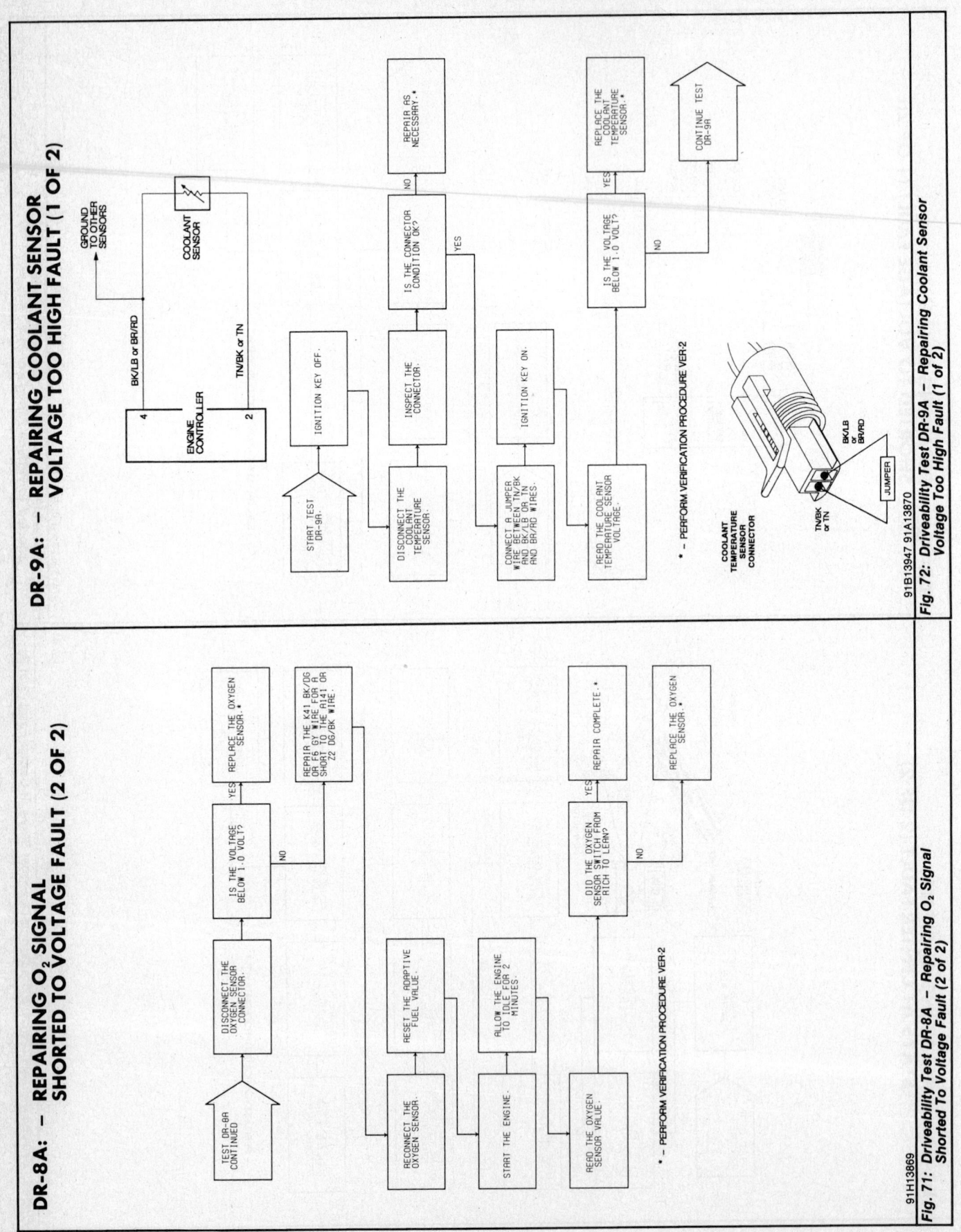

DR-9A: – REPAIRING COOLANT SENSOR VOLTAGE TOO HIGH FAULT (2 OF 2)

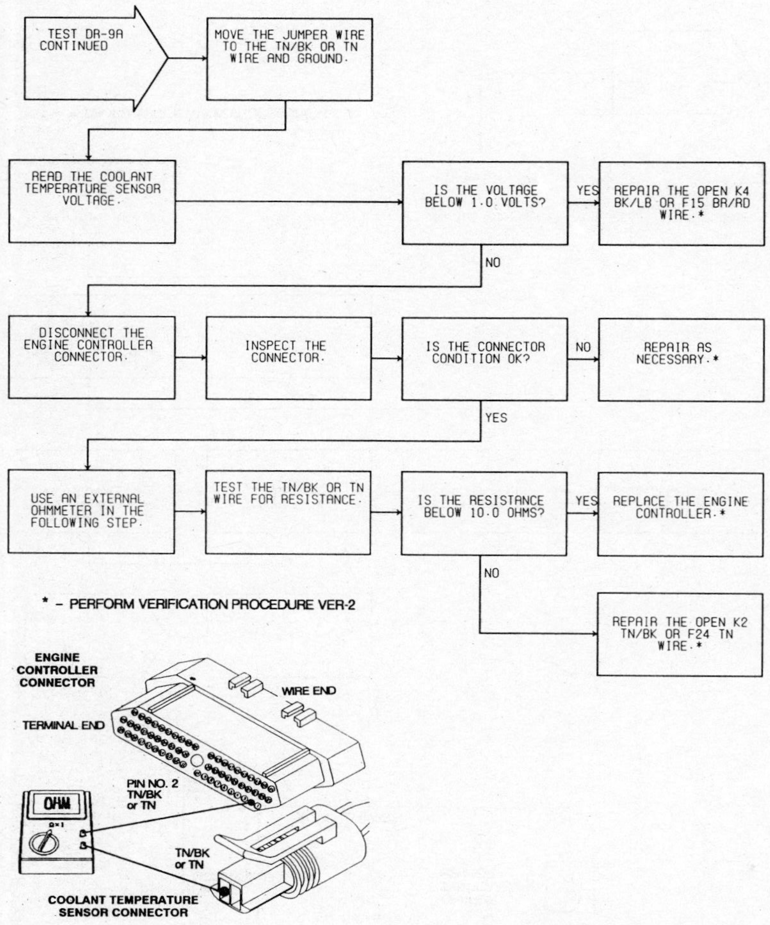
TEST DR-9A CONTINUED
MOVE THE JUMPER WIRE TO THE TN/BK OR TN WIRE AND GROUND.
READ THE COOLANT TEMPERATURE SENSOR VOLTAGE.
IS THE VOLTAGE BELOW 1.0 VOLTS?
YES
REPAIR THE OPEN K4 BK/LB OR F15 BR/RD WIRE.*
NO
DISCONNECT THE ENGINE CONTROLLER CONNECTOR.
INSPECT THE CONNECTOR.
IS THE CONNECTOR CONDITION OK?
NO
REPAIR AS NECESSARY.*
YES
USE AN EXTERNAL OHMMETER IN THE FOLLOWING STEP.
TEST THE TN/BK OR TN WIRE FOR RESISTANCE.
IS THE RESISTANCE BELOW 10.0 OHMS?
YES
REPLACE THE ENGINE CONTROLLER.*
NO
REPAIR THE OPEN K2 TN/BK OR F24 TN WIRE.*
* – PERFORM VERIFICATION PROCEDURE VER-2
ENGINE CONTROLLER CONNECTOR
WIRE END
TERMINAL END
PIN NO. 2 TN/BK or TN
OHM
TN/BK or TN
COOLANT TEMPERATURE SENSOR CONNECTOR

91B13871

Fig. 73: Driveability Test DR-9A – Repairing Coolant Sensor Voltage Too High Fault (2 of 2)

DR-10A: – REPAIRING COOLANT SENSOR VOLTAGE TOO LOW FAULT

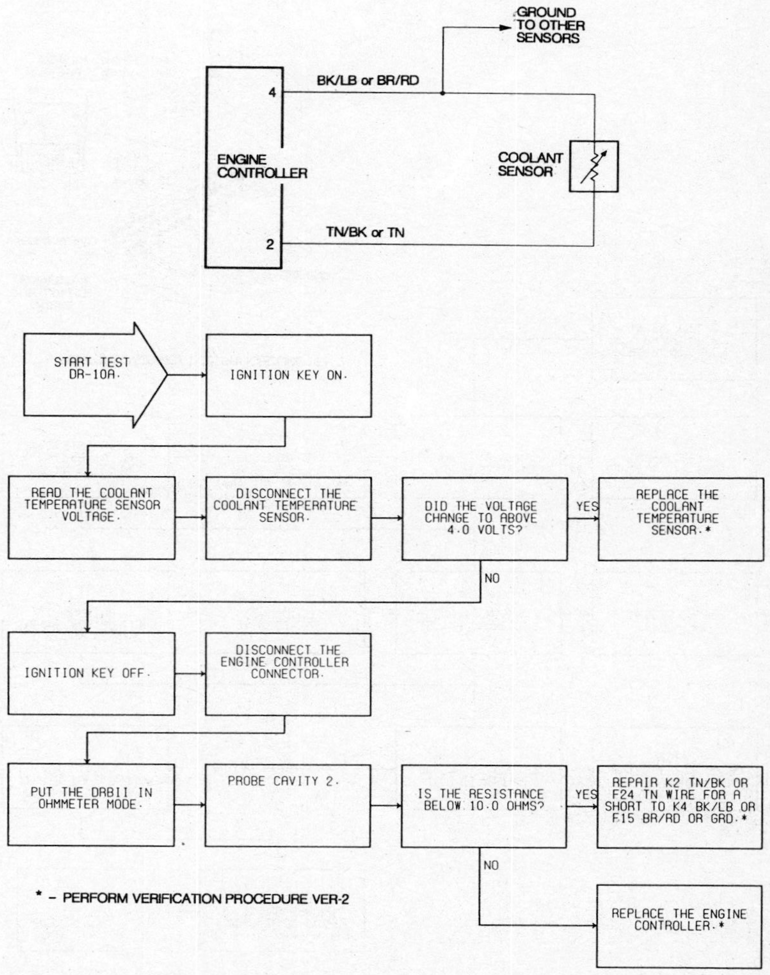
GROUND TO OTHER SENSORS
BK/LB or BR/RD
4
ENGINE CONTROLLER
COOLANT SENSOR
TN/BK or TN
2
START TEST DR-10A.
IGNITION KEY ON.
READ THE COOLANT TEMPERATURE SENSOR VOLTAGE.
DISCONNECT THE COOLANT TEMPERATURE SENSOR.
DID THE VOLTAGE CHANGE TO ABOVE 4.0 VOLTS?
YES
REPLACE THE COOLANT TEMPERATURE SENSOR.*
NO
IGNITION KEY OFF.
DISCONNECT THE ENGINE CONTROLLER CONNECTOR.
PUT THE DRBII IN OHMMETER MODE.
PROBE CAVITY 2.
IS THE RESISTANCE BELOW 10.0 OHMS?
YES
REPAIR K2 TN/BK OR F24 TN WIRE FOR A SHORT TO K4 BK/LB OR F15 BR/RD OR GRD.*
NO
REPLACE THE ENGINE CONTROLLER.*
* – PERFORM VERIFICATION PROCEDURE VER-2

91B13947 91A13961

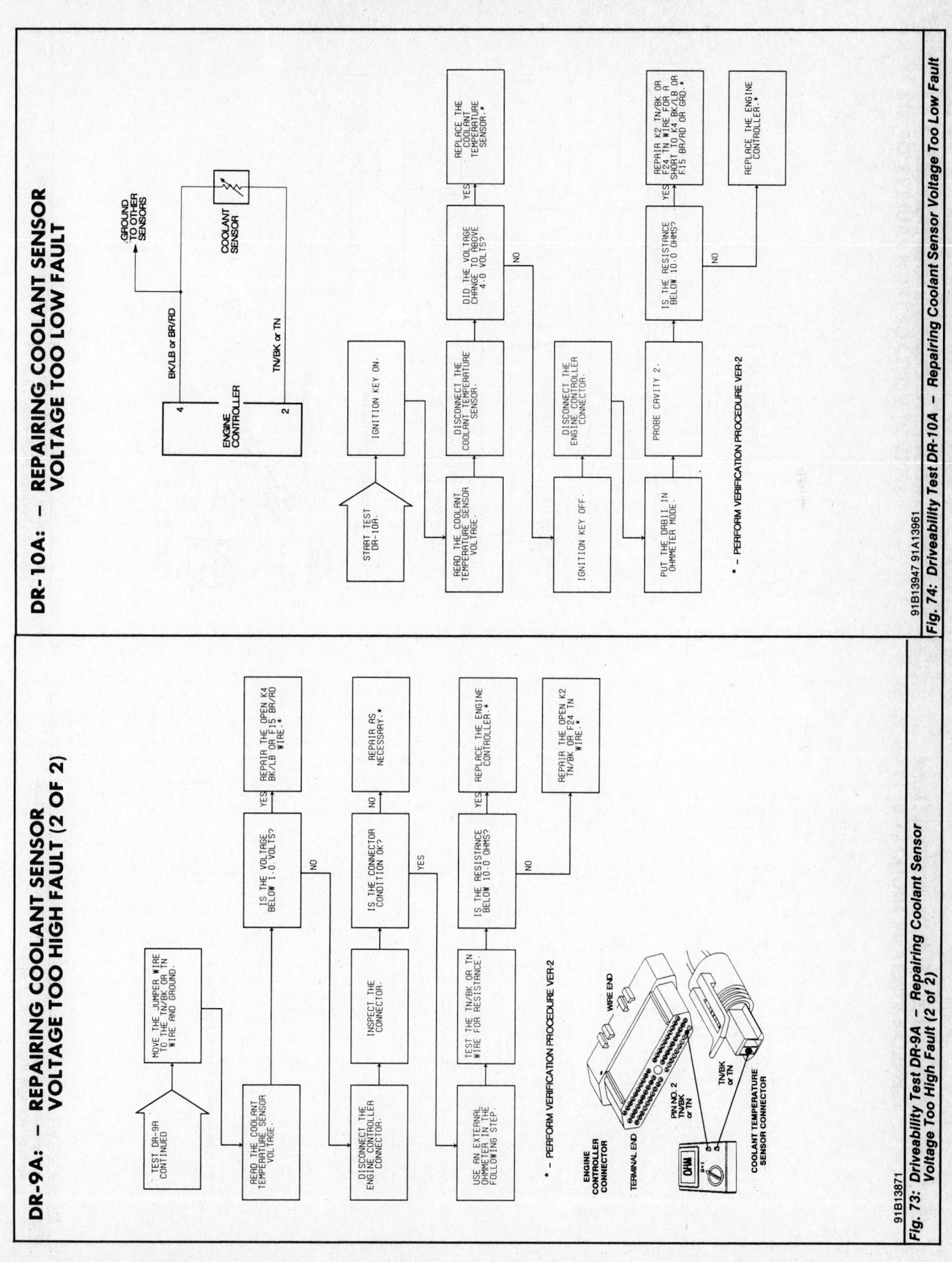

Fig. 74: Driveability Test DR-10A – Repairing Coolant Sensor Voltage Too Low Fault

DR-11A: – REPAIRING CHARGE TEMPERATURE SENSOR VOLTAGE HIGH FAULT (1 OF 2)

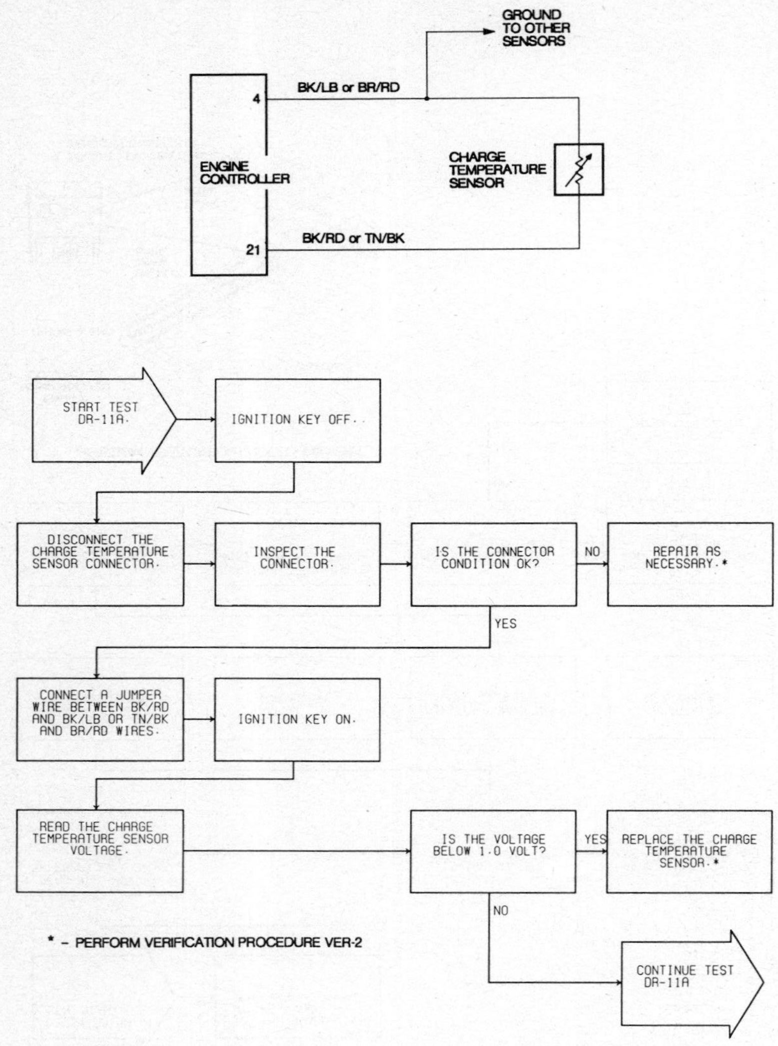
GROUND TO OTHER SENSORS
BK/LB or BR/RD
4
ENGINE CONTROLLER
CHARGE TEMPERATURE SENSOR
21
BK/RD or TN/BK
START TEST DR-11A.
IGNITION KEY OFF.
DISCONNECT THE CHARGE TEMPERATURE SENSOR CONNECTOR.
INSPECT THE CONNECTOR.
IS THE CONNECTOR CONDITION OK?
NO
REPAIR AS NECESSARY.*
YES
CONNECT A JUMPER WIRE BETWEEN BK/RD AND BK/LB OR TN/BK AND BR/RD WIRES.
IGNITION KEY ON.
READ THE CHARGE TEMPERATURE SENSOR VOLTAGE.
IS THE VOLTAGE BELOW 1.0 VOLT?
YES
REPLACE THE CHARGE TEMPERATURE SENSOR.*
NO
CONTINUE TEST DR-11A
* – PERFORM VERIFICATION PROCEDURE VER-2

91C13948 91C13872

Fig. 75: Driveability Test DR-11A – Repairing Charge Temperature Sensor Voltage High Fault (1 of 2)

DR-11A: – REPAIRING CHARGE TEMPERATURE SENSOR VOLTAGE HIGH FAULT (2 OF 2)

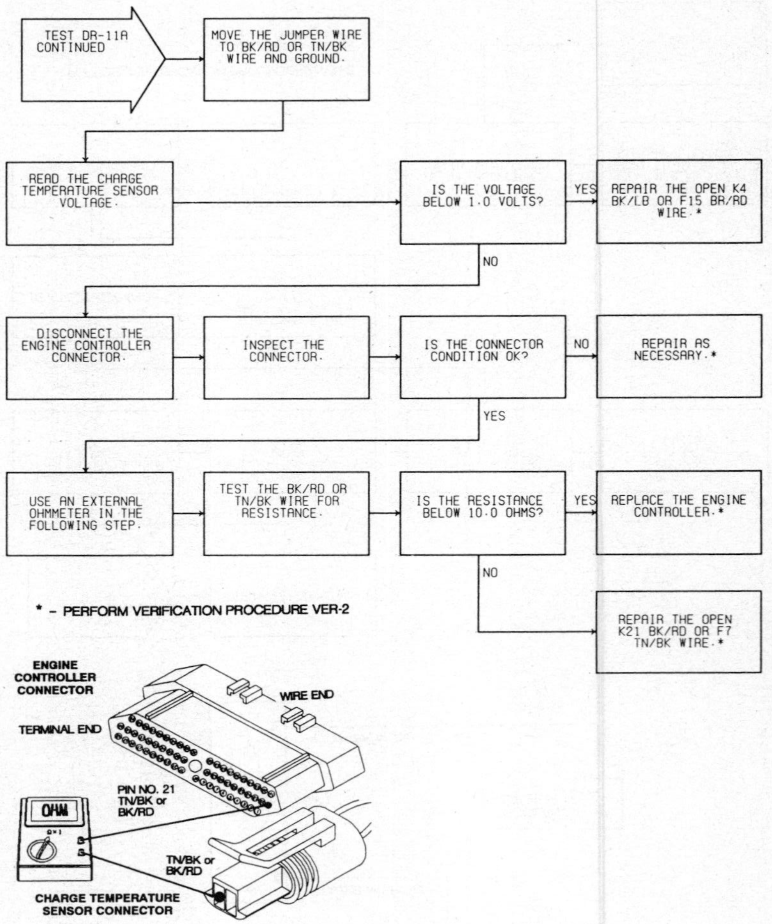
TEST DR-11A CONTINUED
MOVE THE JUMPER WIRE TO BK/RD OR TN/BK WIRE AND GROUND.
READ THE CHARGE TEMPERATURE SENSOR VOLTAGE.
IS THE VOLTAGE BELOW 1.0 VOLTS?
YES
REPAIR THE OPEN K4 BK/LB OR F15 BR/RD WIRE.*
NO
DISCONNECT THE ENGINE CONTROLLER CONNECTOR.
INSPECT THE CONNECTOR.
IS THE CONNECTOR CONDITION OK?
NO
REPAIR AS NECESSARY.*
YES
USE AN EXTERNAL OHMMETER IN THE FOLLOWING STEP.
TEST THE BK/RD OR TN/BK WIRE FOR RESISTANCE.
IS THE RESISTANCE BELOW 10.0 OHMS?
YES
REPLACE THE ENGINE CONTROLLER.*
NO
REPAIR THE OPEN K21 BK/RD OR F7 TN/BK WIRE.*
* – PERFORM VERIFICATION PROCEDURE VER-2
ENGINE CONTROLLER CONNECTOR
WIRE END
TERMINAL END
PIN NO. 21 TN/BK or BK/RD
OHM
TN/BK or BK/RD
CHARGE TEMPERATURE SENSOR CONNECTOR

91D13873

Fig. 76: Driveability Test DR-11A – Repairing Charge Temperature Sensor Voltage High Fault (2 of 2)

DR-12A: – REPAIRING CHARGE TEMPERATURE SENSOR VOLTAGE LOW FAULT

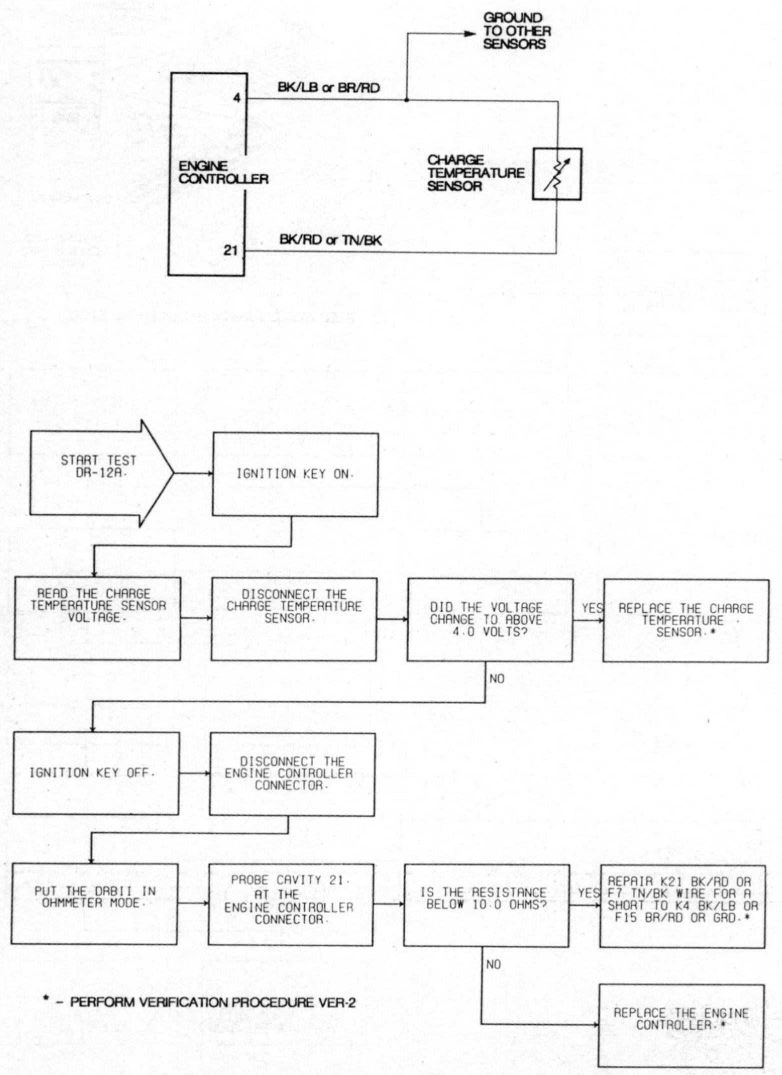
GROUND TO OTHER SENSORS
4
BK/LB or BR/RD
ENGINE CONTROLLER
CHARGE TEMPERATURE SENSOR
21
BK/RD or TN/BK
START TEST DR-12A.
IGNITION KEY ON.
READ THE CHARGE TEMPERATURE SENSOR VOLTAGE.
DISCONNECT THE CHARGE TEMPERATURE SENSOR.
DID THE VOLTAGE CHANGE TO ABOVE 4.0 VOLTS?
YES
REPLACE THE CHARGE TEMPERATURE SENSOR.*
NO
IGNITION KEY OFF.
DISCONNECT THE ENGINE CONTROLLER CONNECTOR.
PUT THE DRBII IN OHMMETER MODE.
PROBE CAVITY 21. AT THE ENGINE CONTROLLER CONNECTOR.
IS THE RESISTANCE BELOW 10.0 OHMS?
YES
REPAIR K21 BK/RD OR F7 TN/BK WIRE FOR A SHORT TO K4 BK/LB OR F15 BR/RD OR GRD.*
NO
REPLACE THE ENGINE CONTROLLER.*
* – PERFORM VERIFICATION PROCEDURE VER-2

91C13948 91E13874

Fig. 77: *Driveability Test DR-12A – Repairing Charge Temperature Sensor Voltage Low Fault*

DR-13A: – REPAIRING THROTTLE POSITION SENSOR VOLTAGE HIGH FAULT (1 OF 2)

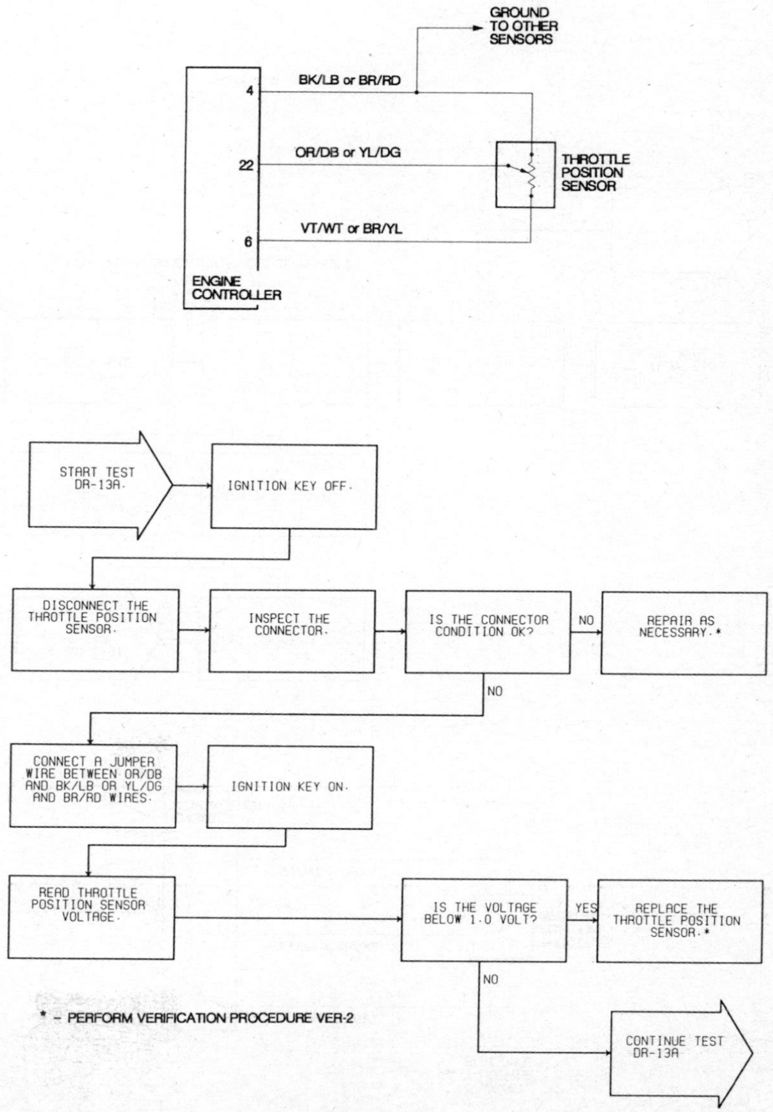
GROUND TO OTHER SENSORS
4
BK/LB or BR/RD
22
OR/DB or YL/DG
THROTTLE POSITION SENSOR
6
VT/WT or BR/YL
ENGINE CONTROLLER
START TEST DR-13A.
IGNITION KEY OFF.
DISCONNECT THE THROTTLE POSITION SENSOR.
INSPECT THE CONNECTOR.
IS THE CONNECTOR CONDITION OK?
NO
REPAIR AS NECESSARY.*
NO
CONNECT A JUMPER WIRE BETWEEN OR/DB AND BK/LB OR YL/DG AND BR/RD WIRES.
IGNITION KEY ON.
READ THROTTLE POSITION SENSOR VOLTAGE.
IS THE VOLTAGE BELOW 1.0 VOLT?
YES
REPLACE THE THROTTLE POSITION SENSOR.*
NO
CONTINUE TEST DR-13A
* – PERFORM VERIFICATION PROCEDURE VER-2

91D13949 91F13875

Fig. 78: *Driveability Test DR-13A – Repairing Throttle Position Sensor Voltage High Fault (1 of 2)*

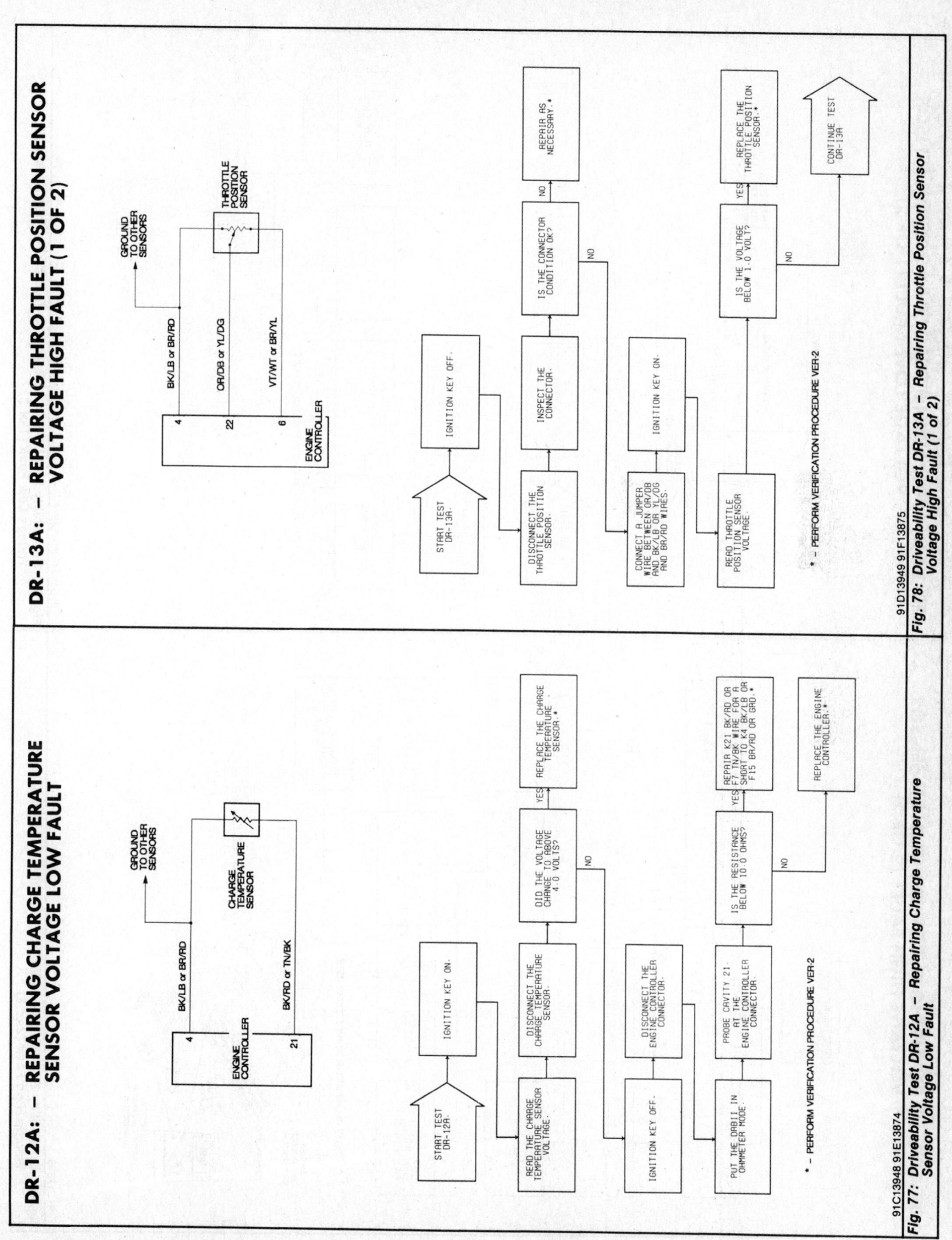

1991 ENGINE PERFORMANCE
Self-Diagnostics (Cont.)

DR-13A: – REPAIRING THROTTLE POSITION SENSOR VOLTAGE HIGH FAULT (2 OF 2)

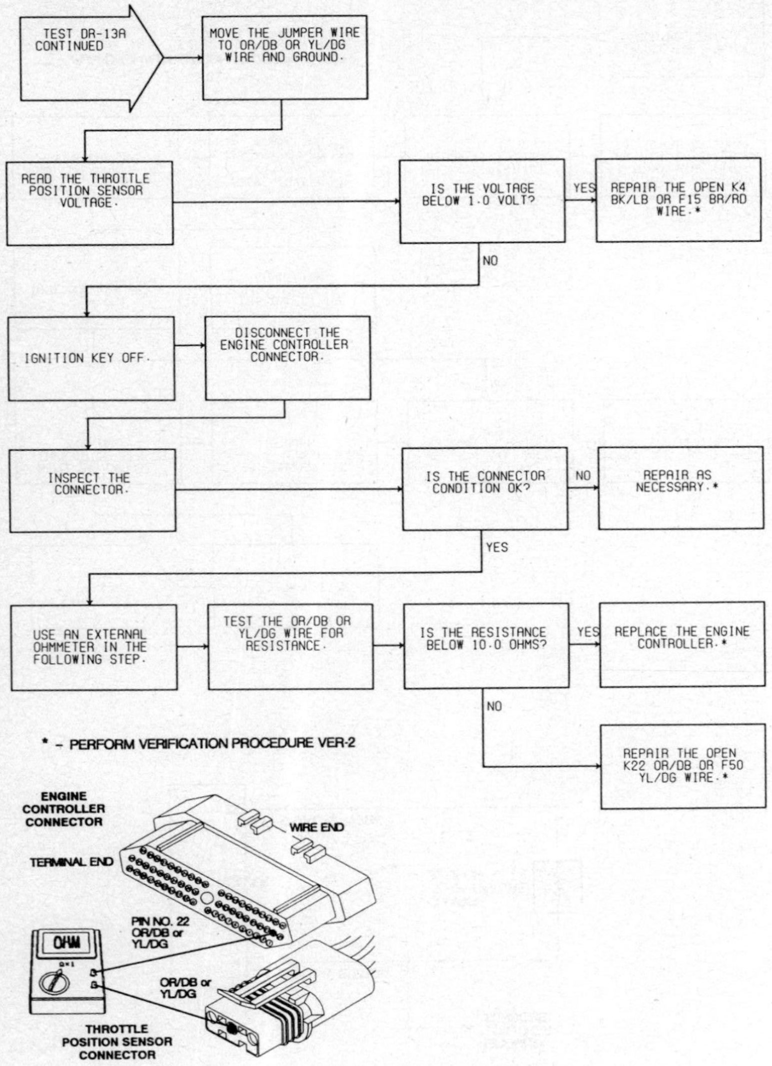
TEST DR-13A CONTINUED
MOVE THE JUMPER WIRE TO OR/DB OR YL/DG WIRE AND GROUND.
READ THE THROTTLE POSITION SENSOR VOLTAGE.
IS THE VOLTAGE BELOW 1.0 VOLT?
YES
REPAIR THE OPEN K4 BK/LB OR F15 BR/RD WIRE.*
NO
IGNITION KEY OFF.
DISCONNECT THE ENGINE CONTROLLER CONNECTOR.
INSPECT THE CONNECTOR.
IS THE CONNECTOR CONDITION OK?
NO
REPAIR AS NECESSARY.*
YES
USE AN EXTERNAL OHMMETER IN THE FOLLOWING STEP.
TEST THE OR/DB OR YL/DG WIRE FOR RESISTANCE.
IS THE RESISTANCE BELOW 10.0 OHMS?
YES
REPLACE THE ENGINE CONTROLLER.*
NO
REPAIR THE OPEN K22 OR/DB OR F50 YL/DG WIRE.*
* – PERFORM VERIFICATION PROCEDURE VER-2
ENGINE CONTROLLER CONNECTOR
WIRE END
TERMINAL END
PIN NO. 22 OR/DB or YL/DG
OHM
OR/DB or YL/DG
THROTTLE POSITION SENSOR CONNECTOR

91G13876

Fig. 79: Driveability Test DR-13A – Repairing Throttle Position Sensor Voltage High Fault (2 of 2)

DR-14A: – REPAIRING THROTTLE POSITION SENSOR VOLTAGE LOW FAULT (1 OF 2)

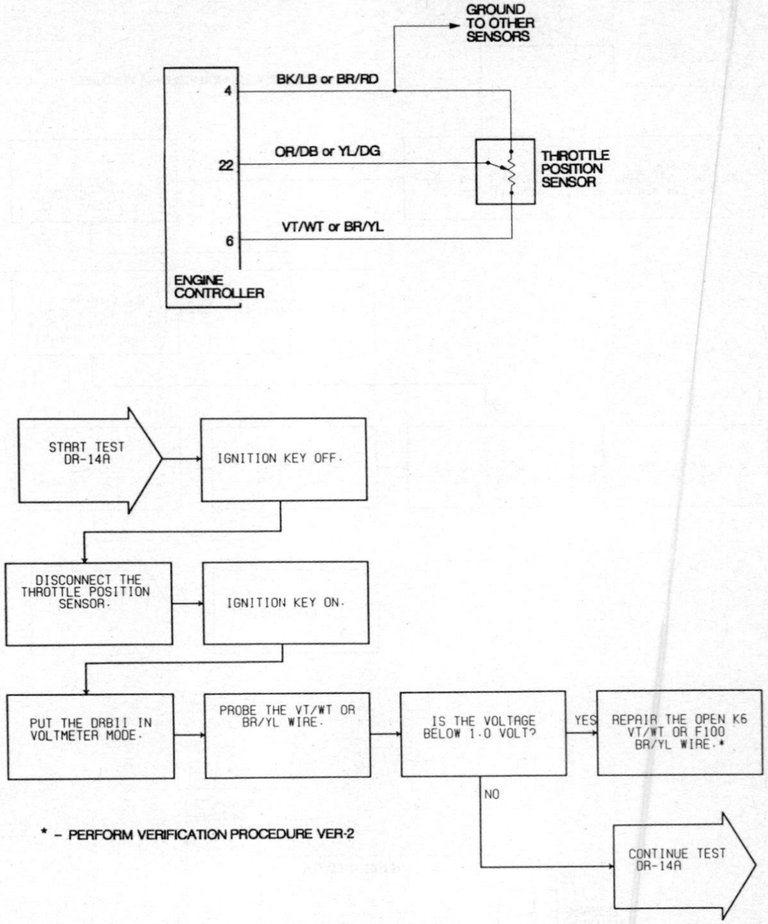
GROUND TO OTHER SENSORS
BK/LB or BR/RD
4
OR/DB or YL/DG
22
THROTTLE POSITION SENSOR
VT/WT or BR/YL
6
ENGINE CONTROLLER
START TEST DR-14A
IGNITION KEY OFF.
DISCONNECT THE THROTTLE POSITION SENSOR.
IGNITION KEY ON.
PUT THE DRBII IN VOLTMETER MODE.
PROBE THE VT/WT OR BR/YL WIRE.
IS THE VOLTAGE BELOW 1.0 VOLT?
YES
REPAIR THE OPEN K6 VT/WT OR F100 BR/YL WIRE.*
NO
* – PERFORM VERIFICATION PROCEDURE VER-2
CONTINUE TEST DR-14A

91D13949 91H13877

Fig. 80: Driveability Test DR-14A – Repairing Throttle Position Sensor Voltage Low Fault (1 of 2)

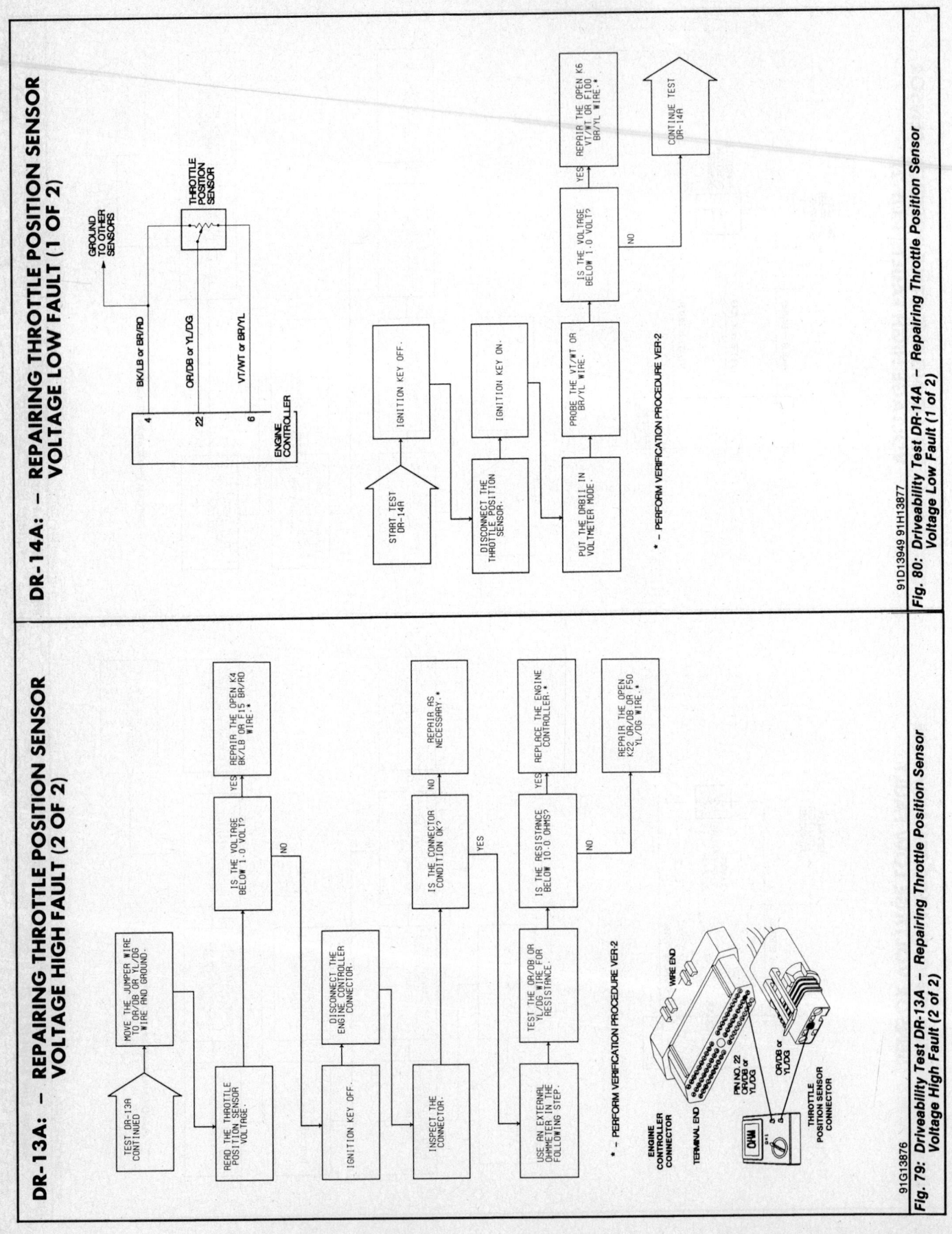

DR-14A: – REPAIRING THROTTLE POSITION SENSOR VOLTAGE LOW FAULT (2 OF 2)

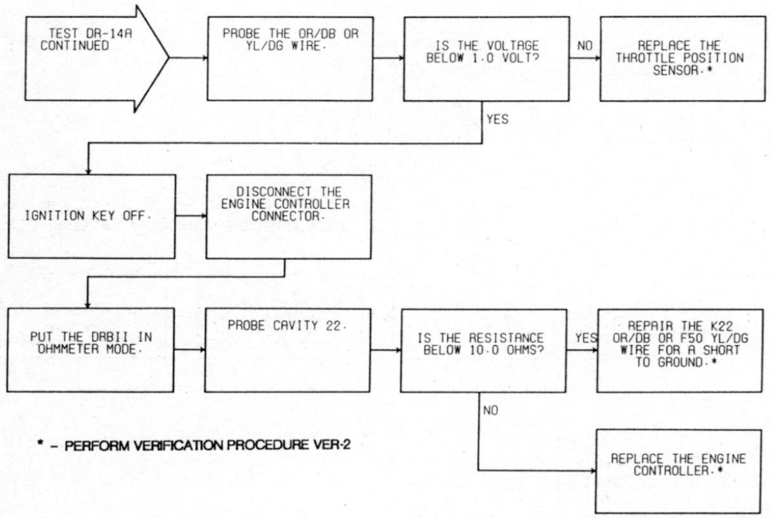
TEST DR-14A CONTINUED
PROBE THE OR/DB OR YL/DG WIRE.
IS THE VOLTAGE BELOW 1.0 VOLT?
NO
REPLACE THE THROTTLE POSITION SENSOR.*
YES
IGNITION KEY OFF.
DISCONNECT THE ENGINE CONTROLLER CONNECTOR.
PUT THE DRBII IN OHMMETER MODE.
PROBE CAVITY 22.
IS THE RESISTANCE BELOW 10.0 OHMS?
YES
REPAIR THE K22 OR/DB OR F50 YL/DG WIRE FOR A SHORT TO GROUND.*
NO
REPLACE THE ENGINE CONTROLLER.*

* – PERFORM VERIFICATION PROCEDURE VER-2

91I13878

Fig. 81: ***Driveability Test DR-14A – Repairing Throttle Position Sensor Voltage Low Fault (2 of 2)***

DR-15A: – REPAIRING AUTOMATIC IDLE SPEED MOTOR CIRCUITS FAULT (1 OF 5)

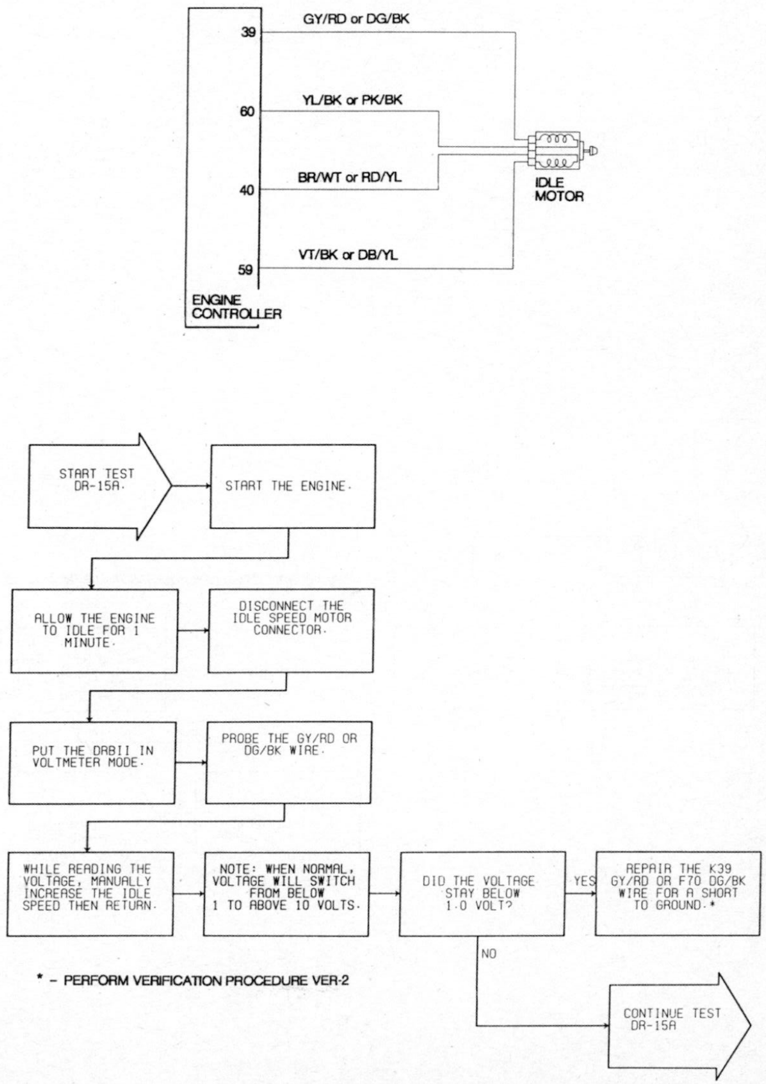
39
GY/RD or DG/BK
60
YL/BK or PK/BK
40
BR/WT or RD/YL
59
VT/BK or DB/YL
ENGINE CONTROLLER
IDLE MOTOR
START TEST DR-15A.
START THE ENGINE.
ALLOW THE ENGINE TO IDLE FOR 1 MINUTE.
DISCONNECT THE IDLE SPEED MOTOR CONNECTOR.
PUT THE DRBII IN VOLTMETER MODE.
PROBE THE GY/RD OR DG/BK WIRE.
WHILE READING THE VOLTAGE, MANUALLY INCREASE THE IDLE SPEED THEN RETURN.
NOTE: WHEN NORMAL, VOLTAGE WILL SWITCH FROM BELOW 1 TO ABOVE 10 VOLTS.
DID THE VOLTAGE STAY BELOW 1.0 VOLT?
YES
REPAIR THE K39 GY/RD OR F70 DG/BK WIRE FOR A SHORT TO GROUND.*
NO
CONTINUE TEST DR-15A

* – PERFORM VERIFICATION PROCEDURE VER-2

91H13943 91J13879

Fig. 82: ***Driveability Test DR-15A – Repairing Automatic Idle Speed Motor Circuits Fault (1 of 5)***

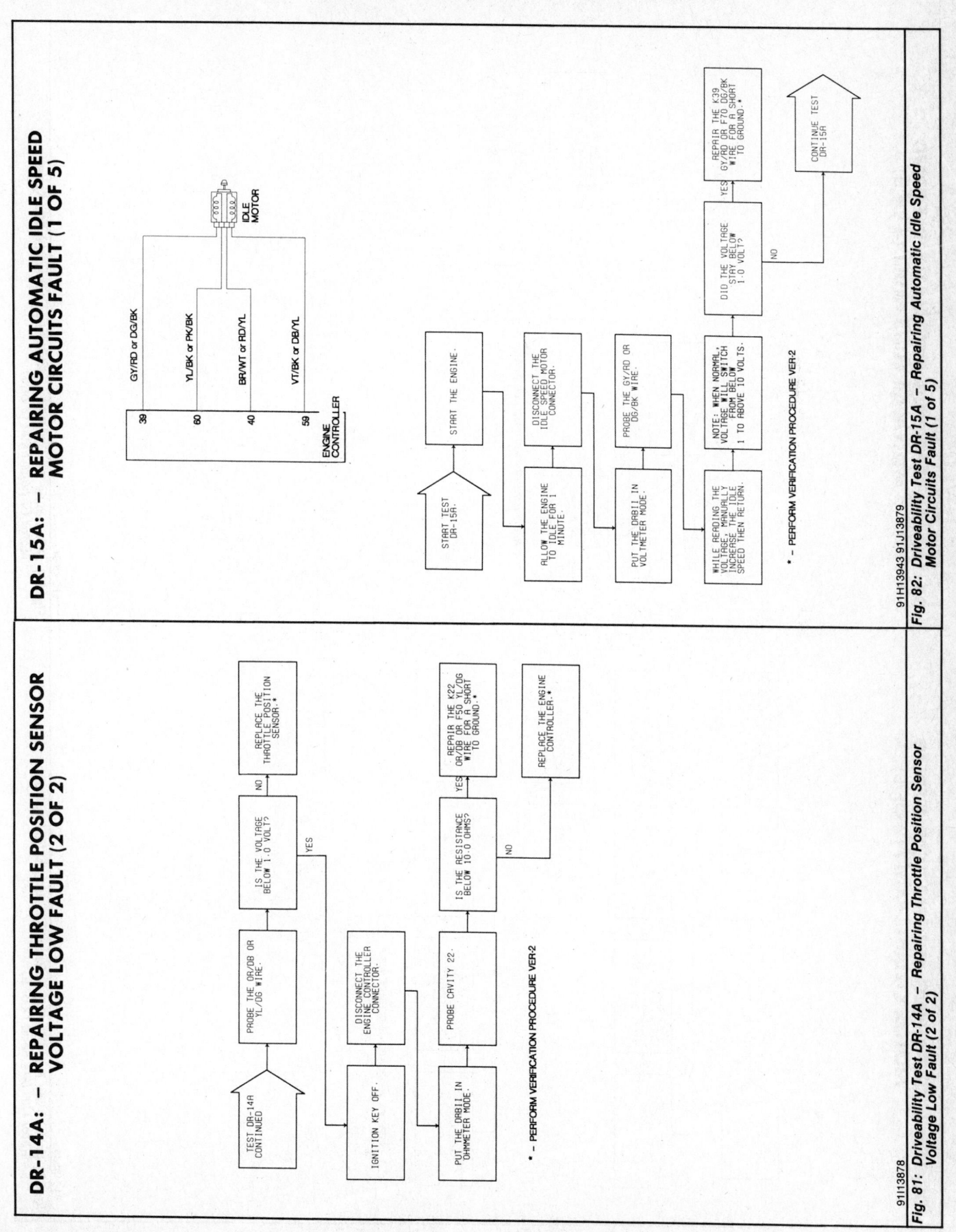

1991 ENGINE PERFORMANCE
Self-Diagnostics (Cont.)

DR-15A: – REPAIRING AUTOMATIC IDLE SPEED MOTOR CIRCUITS FAULT (2 OF 5)

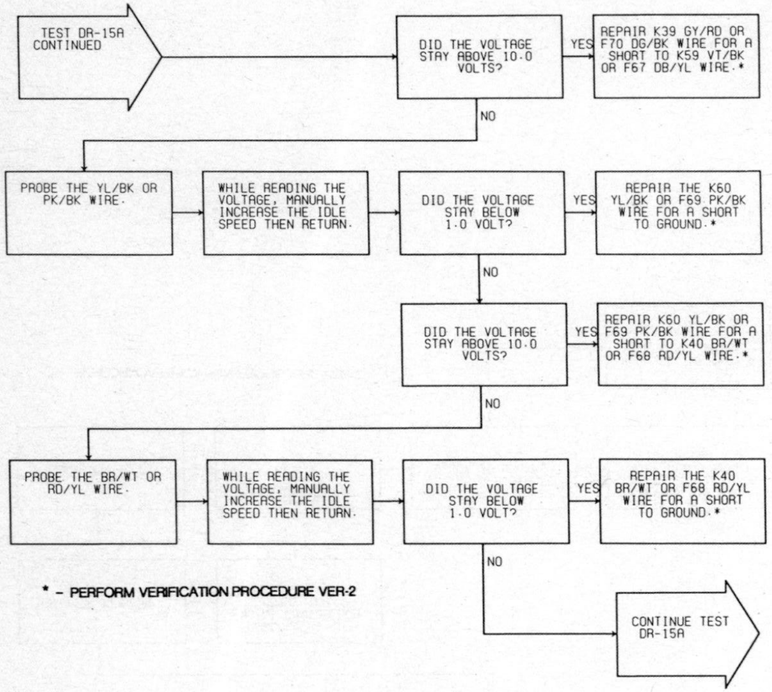
TEST DR-15A CONTINUED
DID THE VOLTAGE STAY ABOVE 10.0 VOLTS?
YES
REPAIR K39 GY/RD OR F70 DG/BK WIRE FOR A SHORT TO K59 VT/BK OR F67 DB/YL WIRE.*
NO
PROBE THE YL/BK OR PK/BK WIRE.
WHILE READING THE VOLTAGE, MANUALLY INCREASE THE IDLE SPEED THEN RETURN.
DID THE VOLTAGE STAY BELOW 1.0 VOLT?
YES
REPAIR THE K60 YL/BK OR F69 PK/BK WIRE FOR A SHORT TO GROUND.*
NO
DID THE VOLTAGE STAY ABOVE 10.0 VOLTS?
YES
REPAIR K60 YL/BK OR F69 PK/BK WIRE FOR A SHORT TO K40 BR/WT OR F68 RD/YL WIRE.*
NO
PROBE THE BR/WT OR RD/YL WIRE.
WHILE READING THE VOLTAGE, MANUALLY INCREASE THE IDLE SPEED THEN RETURN.
DID THE VOLTAGE STAY BELOW 1.0 VOLT?
YES
REPAIR THE K40 BR/WT OR F68 RD/YL WIRE FOR A SHORT TO GROUND.*
NO
CONTINUE TEST DR-15A

* – PERFORM VERIFICATION PROCEDURE VER-2

91C13880

Fig. 83: Driveability Test DR-15A – Repairing Automatic Idle Speed Motor Circuits Fault (2 of 5)

DR-15A: – REPAIRING AUTOMATIC IDLE SPEED MOTOR CIRCUITS FAULT (3 OF 5)

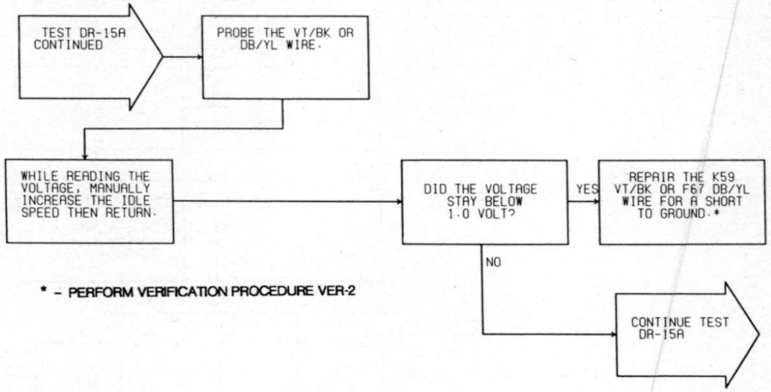
TEST DR-15A CONTINUED
PROBE THE VT/BK OR DB/YL WIRE.
WHILE READING THE VOLTAGE, MANUALLY INCREASE THE IDLE SPEED THEN RETURN.
DID THE VOLTAGE STAY BELOW 1.0 VOLT?
YES
REPAIR THE K59 VT/BK OR F67 DB/YL WIRE FOR A SHORT TO GROUND.*
NO
CONTINUE TEST DR-15A

* – PERFORM VERIFICATION PROCEDURE VER-2

91D13881

Fig. 84: Driveability Test DR-15A – Repairing Automatic Idle Speed Motor Circuits Fault (3 of 5)

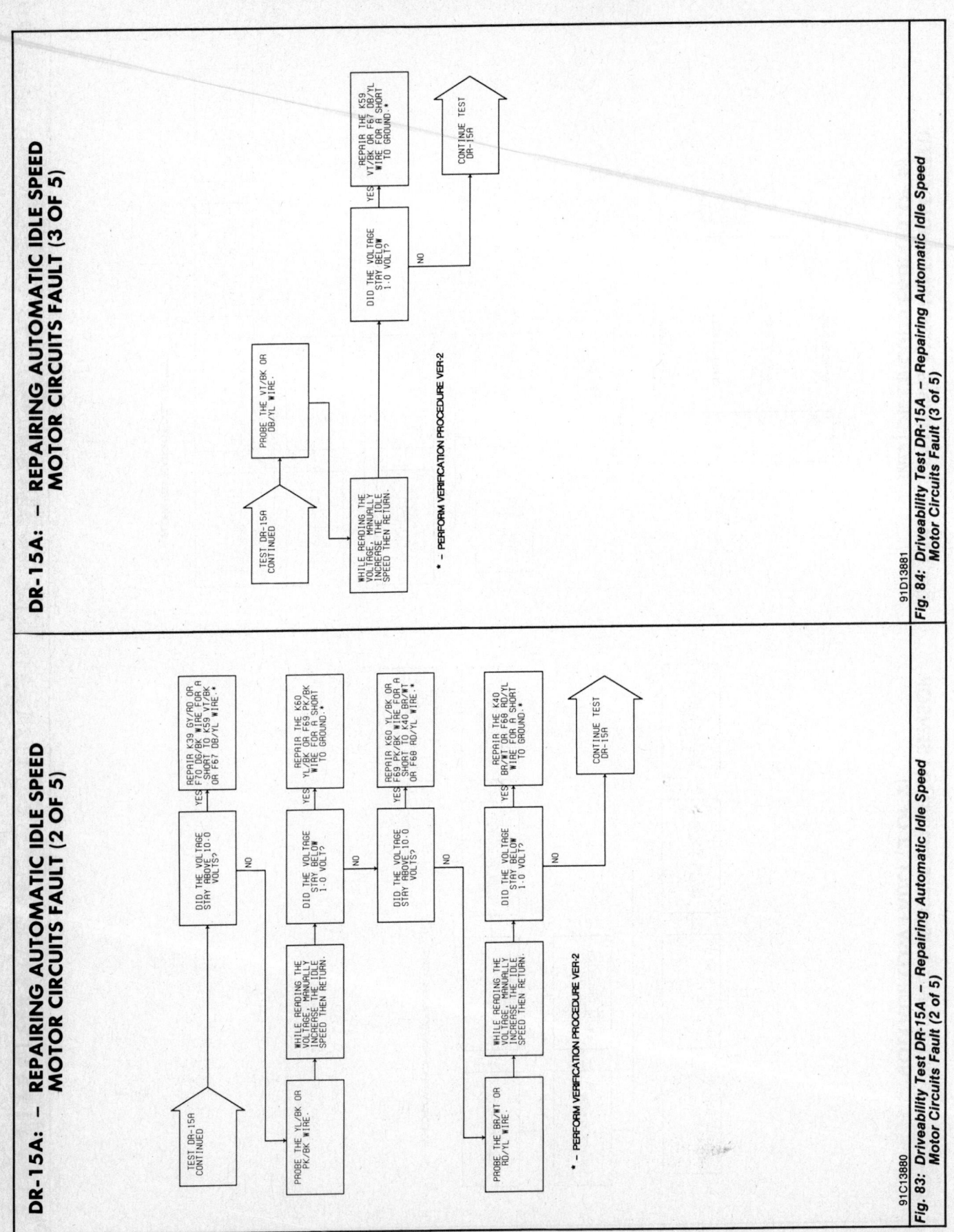

DR-15A: – REPAIRING AUTOMATIC IDLE SPEED MOTOR CIRCUITS FAULT (4 OF 5)

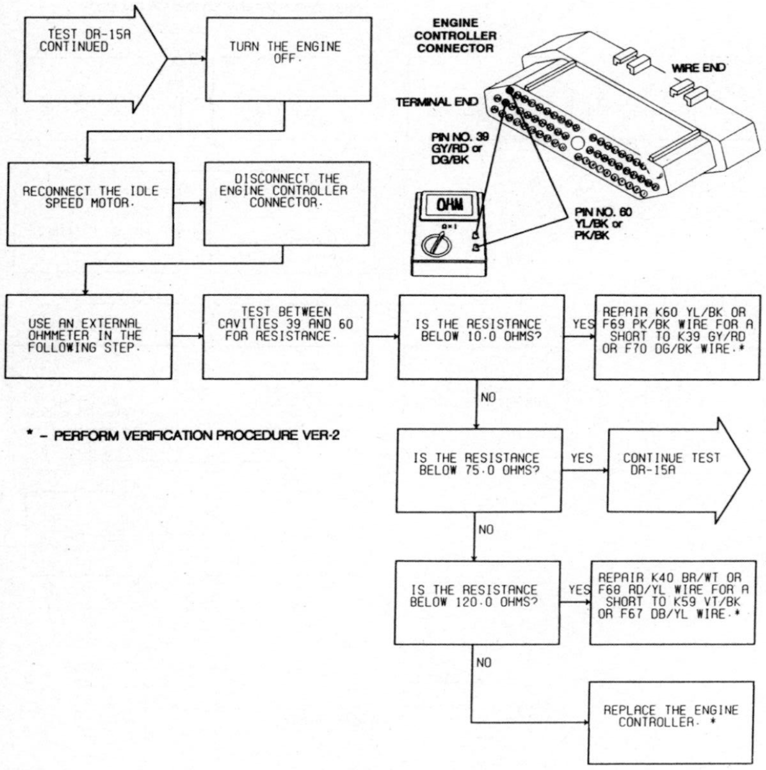
TEST DR-15A CONTINUED
TURN THE ENGINE OFF.
RECONNECT THE IDLE SPEED MOTOR.
DISCONNECT THE ENGINE CONTROLLER CONNECTOR.
USE AN EXTERNAL OHMMETER IN THE FOLLOWING STEP.
TEST BETWEEN CAVITIES 39 AND 60 FOR RESISTANCE.
IS THE RESISTANCE BELOW 10.0 OHMS?
YES
REPAIR K60 YL/BK OR F69 PK/BK WIRE FOR A SHORT TO K39 GY/RD OR F70 DG/BK WIRE.*
NO
IS THE RESISTANCE BELOW 75.0 OHMS?
YES
CONTINUE TEST DR-15A
NO
IS THE RESISTANCE BELOW 120.0 OHMS?
YES
REPAIR K40 BR/WT OR F68 RD/YL WIRE FOR A SHORT TO K59 VT/BK OR F67 DB/YL WIRE.*
NO
REPLACE THE ENGINE CONTROLLER. *
ENGINE CONTROLLER CONNECTOR
WIRE END
TERMINAL END
PIN NO. 39 GY/RD or DG/BK
PIN NO. 60 YL/BK or PK/BK
OHM

* – PERFORM VERIFICATION PROCEDURE VER-2

91E13882

Fig. 85: Driveability Test DR-15A – Repairing Automatic Idle Speed Motor Circuits Fault (4 of 5)

DR-15A: – REPAIRING AUTOMATIC IDLE SPEED MOTOR CIRCUITS FAULT (5 OF 5)

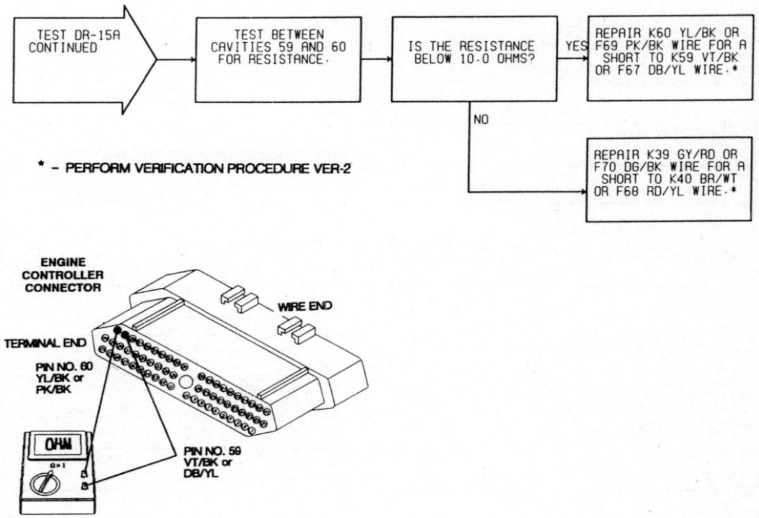
TEST DR-15A CONTINUED
TEST BETWEEN CAVITIES 59 AND 60 FOR RESISTANCE.
IS THE RESISTANCE BELOW 10.0 OHMS?
YES
REPAIR K60 YL/BK OR F69 PK/BK WIRE FOR A SHORT TO K59 VT/BK OR F67 DB/YL WIRE.*
NO
REPAIR K39 GY/RD OR F70 DG/BK WIRE FOR A SHORT TO K40 BR/WT OR F68 RD/YL WIRE.*
ENGINE CONTROLLER CONNECTOR
WIRE END
TERMINAL END
PIN NO. 60 YL/BK or PK/BK
PIN NO. 59 VT/BK or DB/YL
OHM

* – PERFORM VERIFICATION PROCEDURE VER-2

91F13883

Fig. 86: Driveability Test DR-15A – Repairing Automatic Idle Speed Motor Circuits Fault (5 of 5)

DR-16A: – REPAIRING INJECTOR #1 CONTROL CIRCUIT FAULT (1 OF 3)

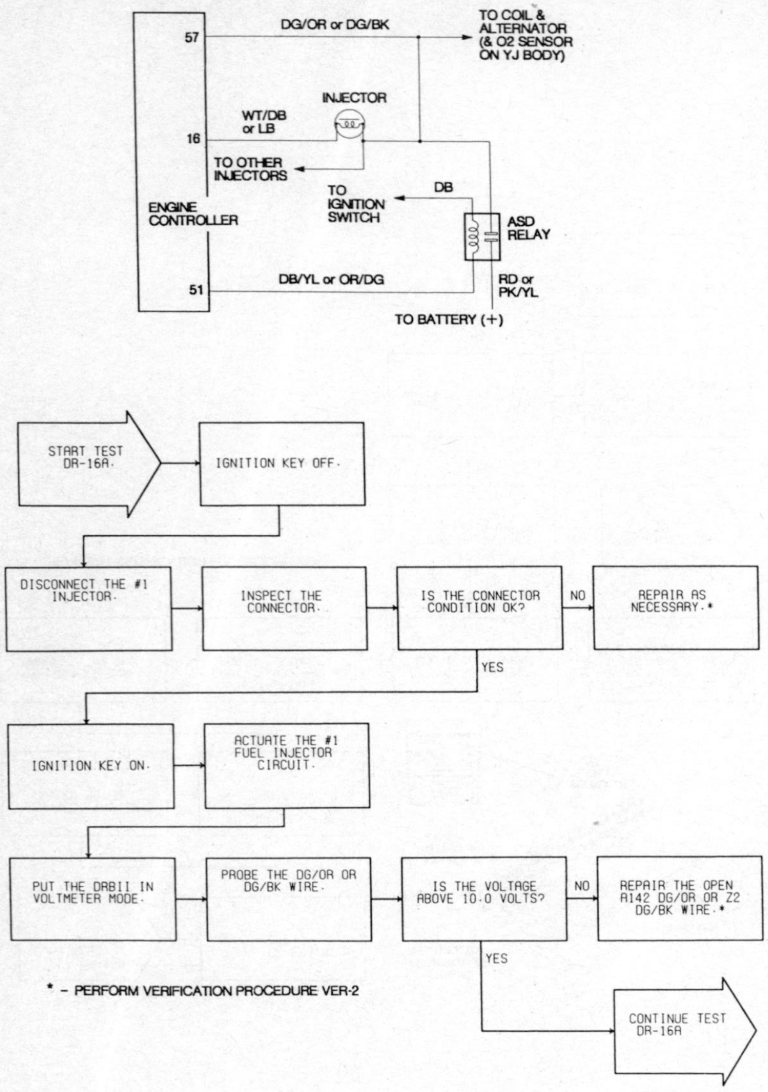
57
DG/OR or DG/BK
TO COIL & ALTERNATOR (& O2 SENSOR ON YJ BODY)
INJECTOR
WT/DB or LB
16
TO OTHER INJECTORS
TO IGNITION SWITCH
DB
ENGINE CONTROLLER
ASD RELAY
51
DB/YL or OR/DG
RD or PK/YL
TO BATTERY (+)
START TEST DR-16A.
IGNITION KEY OFF.
DISCONNECT THE #1 INJECTOR.
INSPECT THE CONNECTOR.
IS THE CONNECTOR CONDITION OK?
NO
REPAIR AS NECESSARY.*
YES
IGNITION KEY ON.
ACTUATE THE #1 FUEL INJECTOR CIRCUIT.
PUT THE DRBII IN VOLTMETER MODE.
PROBE THE DG/OR OR DG/BK WIRE.
IS THE VOLTAGE ABOVE 10.0 VOLTS?
NO
REPAIR THE OPEN A142 DG/OR OR Z2 DG/BK WIRE.*
YES
* – PERFORM VERIFICATION PROCEDURE VER-2
CONTINUE TEST DR-16A

91H13950 91G13884

Fig. 87: Driveability Test DR-16A – Repairing Injector #1 Control Circuit Fault (1 of 3)

DR-16A: – REPAIRING INJECTOR #1 CONTROL CIRCUIT FAULT (2 OF 3)

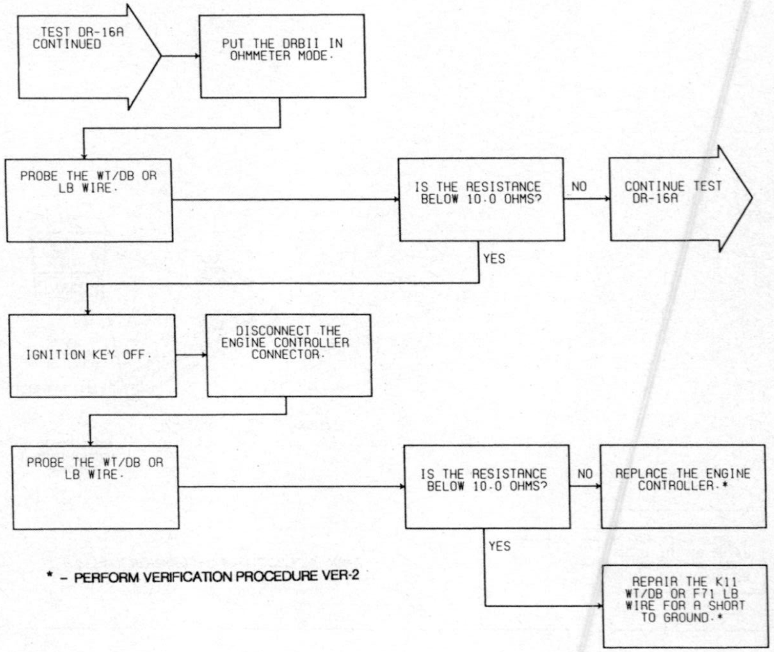
TEST DR-16A CONTINUED
PUT THE DRBII IN OHMMETER MODE.
PROBE THE WT/DB OR LB WIRE.
IS THE RESISTANCE BELOW 10.0 OHMS?
NO
CONTINUE TEST DR-16A
YES
IGNITION KEY OFF.
DISCONNECT THE ENGINE CONTROLLER CONNECTOR.
PROBE THE WT/DB OR LB WIRE.
IS THE RESISTANCE BELOW 10.0 OHMS?
NO
REPLACE THE ENGINE CONTROLLER.*
YES
REPAIR THE K11 WT/DB OR F71 LB WIRE FOR A SHORT TO GROUND.*
* – PERFORM VERIFICATION PROCEDURE VER-2

91H13885

Fig. 88: Driveability Test DR-16A – Repairing Injector #1 Control Circuit Fault (2 of 3)

DR-16A: – REPAIRING INJECTOR #1 CONTROL CIRCUIT FAULT (3 OF 3)

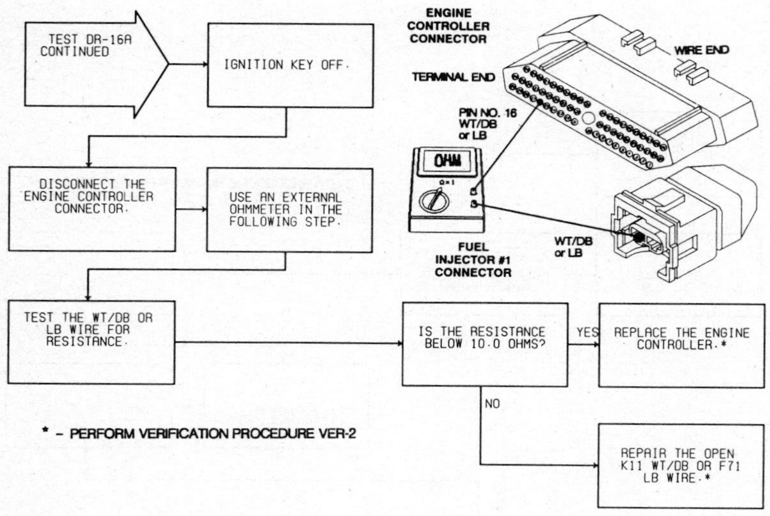
TEST DR-16A CONTINUED
IGNITION KEY OFF.
DISCONNECT THE ENGINE CONTROLLER CONNECTOR.
USE AN EXTERNAL OHMMETER IN THE FOLLOWING STEP.
TEST THE WT/DB OR LB WIRE FOR RESISTANCE.
IS THE RESISTANCE BELOW 10.0 OHMS?
YES
REPLACE THE ENGINE CONTROLLER.*
NO
REPAIR THE OPEN K11 WT/DB OR F71 LB WIRE.*
ENGINE CONTROLLER CONNECTOR
WIRE END
TERMINAL END
PIN NO. 16 WT/DB or LB
OHM
WT/DB or LB
FUEL INJECTOR #1 CONNECTOR
* – PERFORM VERIFICATION PROCEDURE VER-2

91I13886

Fig. 89: Driveability Test DR-16A – Repairing Injector #1 Control Circuit Fault (3 of 3)

DR-17A: – REPAIRING INJECTOR #2 CONTROL CIRCUIT FAULT (1 OF 3)

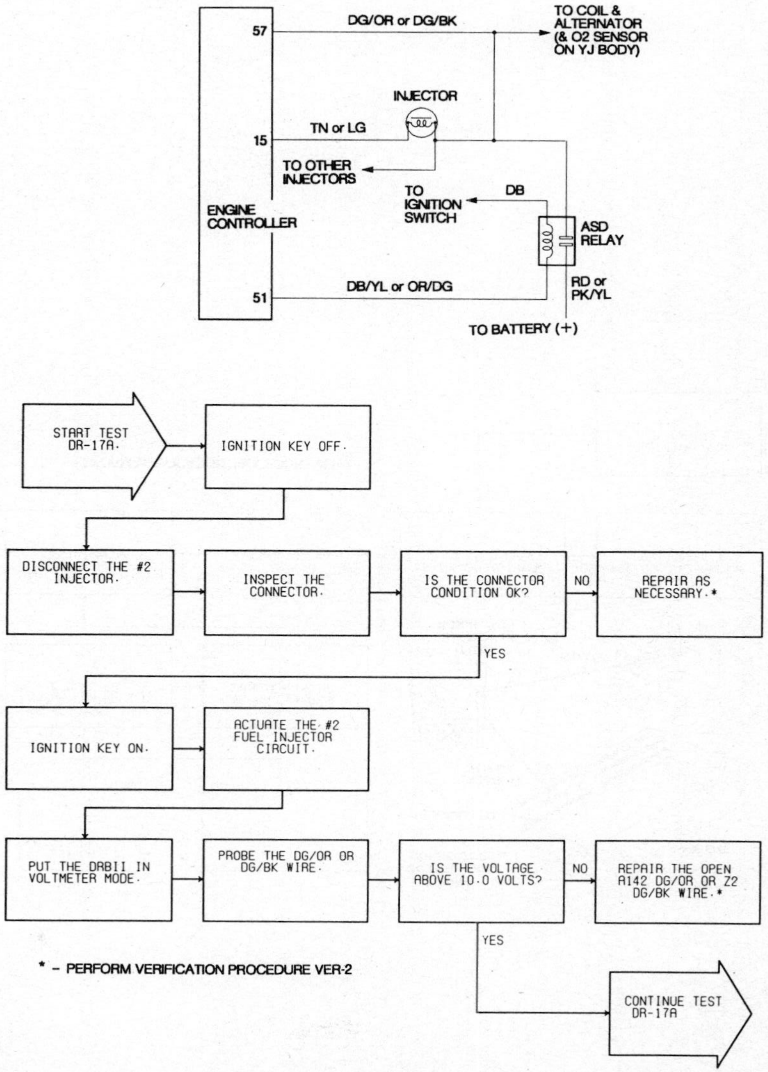
57
DG/OR or DG/BK
TO COIL & ALTERNATOR (& O2 SENSOR ON YJ BODY)
INJECTOR
15
TN or LG
TO OTHER INJECTORS
TO IGNITION SWITCH
DB
ENGINE CONTROLLER
ASD RELAY
51
DB/YL or OR/DG
RD or PK/YL
TO BATTERY (+)
START TEST DR-17A.
IGNITION KEY OFF.
DISCONNECT THE #2 INJECTOR.
INSPECT THE CONNECTOR.
IS THE CONNECTOR CONDITION OK?
NO
REPAIR AS NECESSARY.*
YES
IGNITION KEY ON.
ACTUATE THE #2 FUEL INJECTOR CIRCUIT.
PUT THE DRBII IN VOLTMETER MODE.
PROBE THE DG/OR OR DG/BK WIRE.
IS THE VOLTAGE ABOVE 10.0 VOLTS?
NO
REPAIR THE OPEN A142 DG/OR OR Z2 DG/BK WIRE.*
YES
CONTINUE TEST DR-17A
* – PERFORM VERIFICATION PROCEDURE VER-2

91I13951 91J13887

Fig. 90: Driveability Test DR-17A – Repairing Injector #2 Control Circuit Fault (1 of 3)

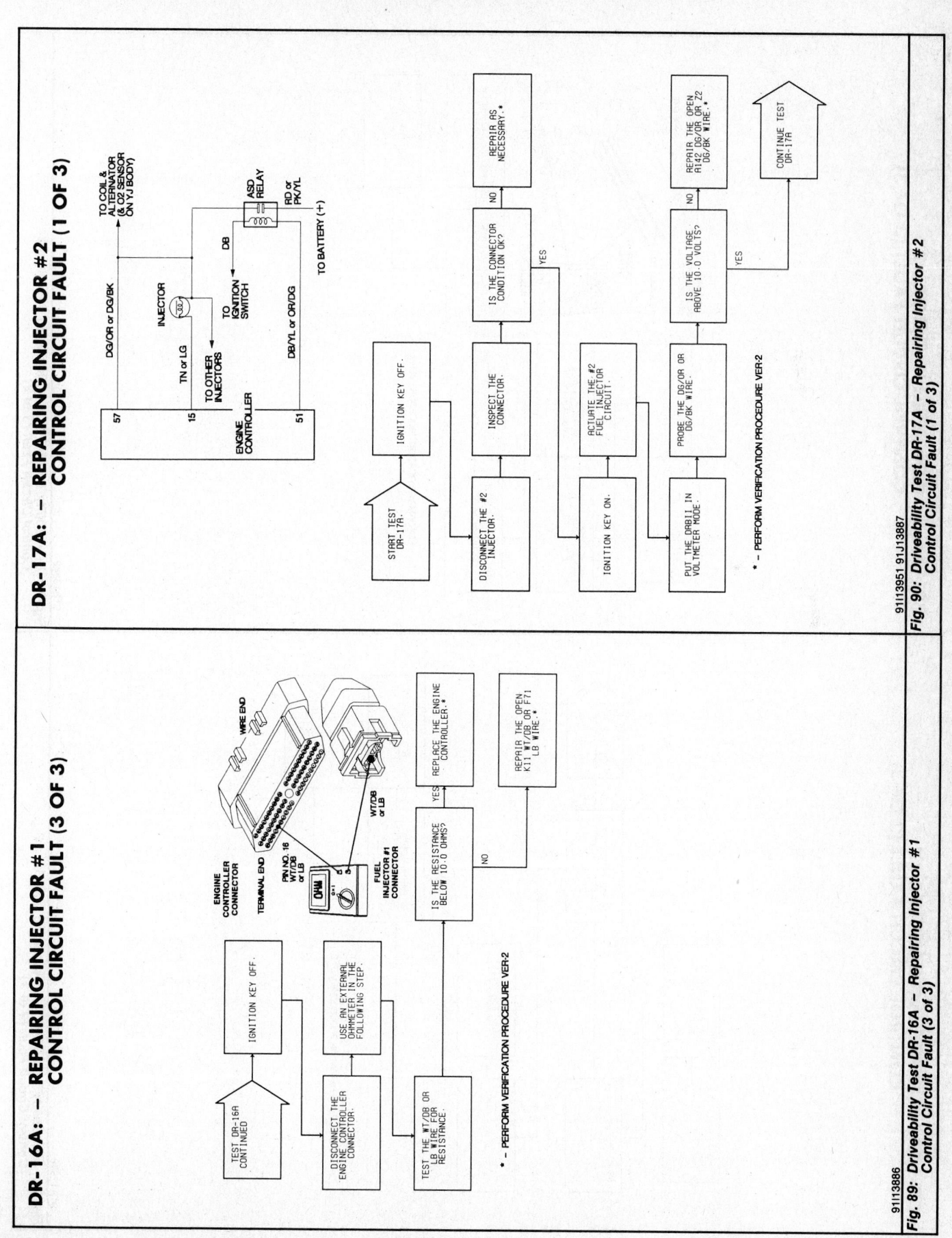

DR-17A: – REPAIRING INJECTOR #2 CONTROL CIRCUIT FAULT (2 OF 3)

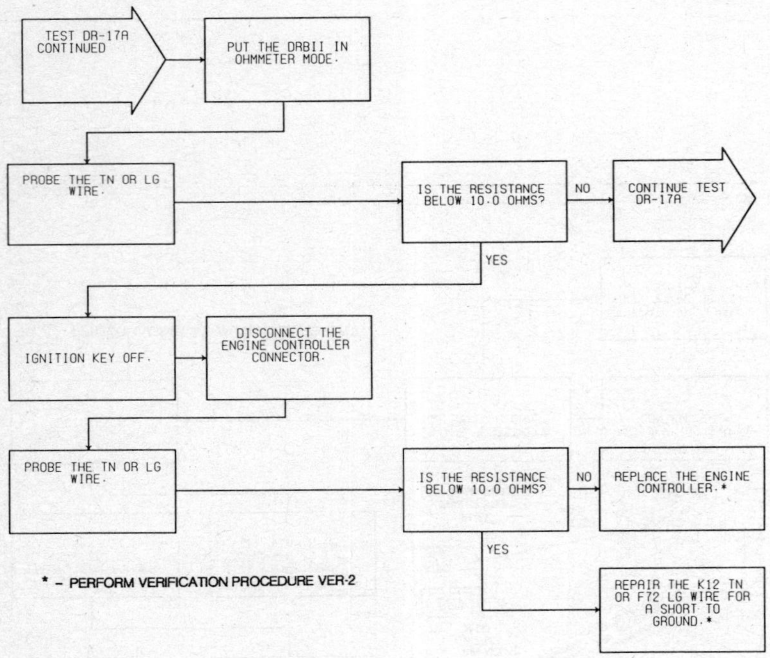
TEST DR-17A CONTINUED
PUT THE DRBII IN OHMMETER MODE.
PROBE THE TN OR LG WIRE.
IS THE RESISTANCE BELOW 10.0 OHMS?
NO
CONTINUE TEST DR-17A
YES
IGNITION KEY OFF.
DISCONNECT THE ENGINE CONTROLLER CONNECTOR.
PROBE THE TN OR LG WIRE.
IS THE RESISTANCE BELOW 10.0 OHMS?
NO
REPLACE THE ENGINE CONTROLLER.*
YES
REPAIR THE K12 TN OR F72 LG WIRE FOR A SHORT TO GROUND.*
* – PERFORM VERIFICATION PROCEDURE VER-2

91A13888

Fig. 91: Driveability Test DR-17A – Repairing Injector #2 Control Circuit Fault (2 of 3)

DR-17A: – REPAIRING INJECTOR #2 CONTROL CIRCUIT FAULT (3 OF 3)

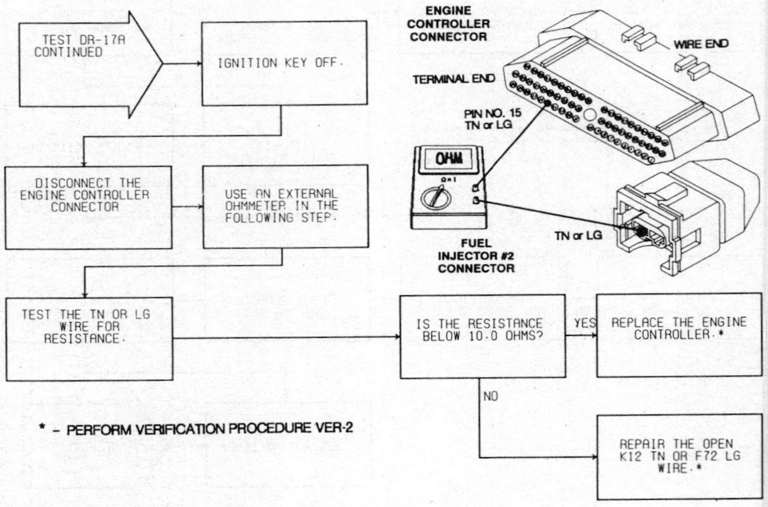
TEST DR-17A CONTINUED
IGNITION KEY OFF.
DISCONNECT THE ENGINE CONTROLLER CONNECTOR
USE AN EXTERNAL OHMMETER IN THE FOLLOWING STEP.
TEST THE TN OR LG WIRE FOR RESISTANCE.
ENGINE CONTROLLER CONNECTOR
WIRE END
TERMINAL END
PIN NO. 15 TN or LG
OHM
TN or LG
FUEL INJECTOR #2 CONNECTOR
IS THE RESISTANCE BELOW 10.0 OHMS?
YES
REPLACE THE ENGINE CONTROLLER.*
NO
REPAIR THE OPEN K12 TN OR F72 LG WIRE.*
* – PERFORM VERIFICATION PROCEDURE VER-2

91B13889

Fig. 92: Driveability Test DR-17A – Repairing Injector #2 Control Circuit Fault (3 of 3)

DR-18A: – REPAIRING INJECTOR #3 CONTROL CIRCUIT FAULT (1 OF 3)

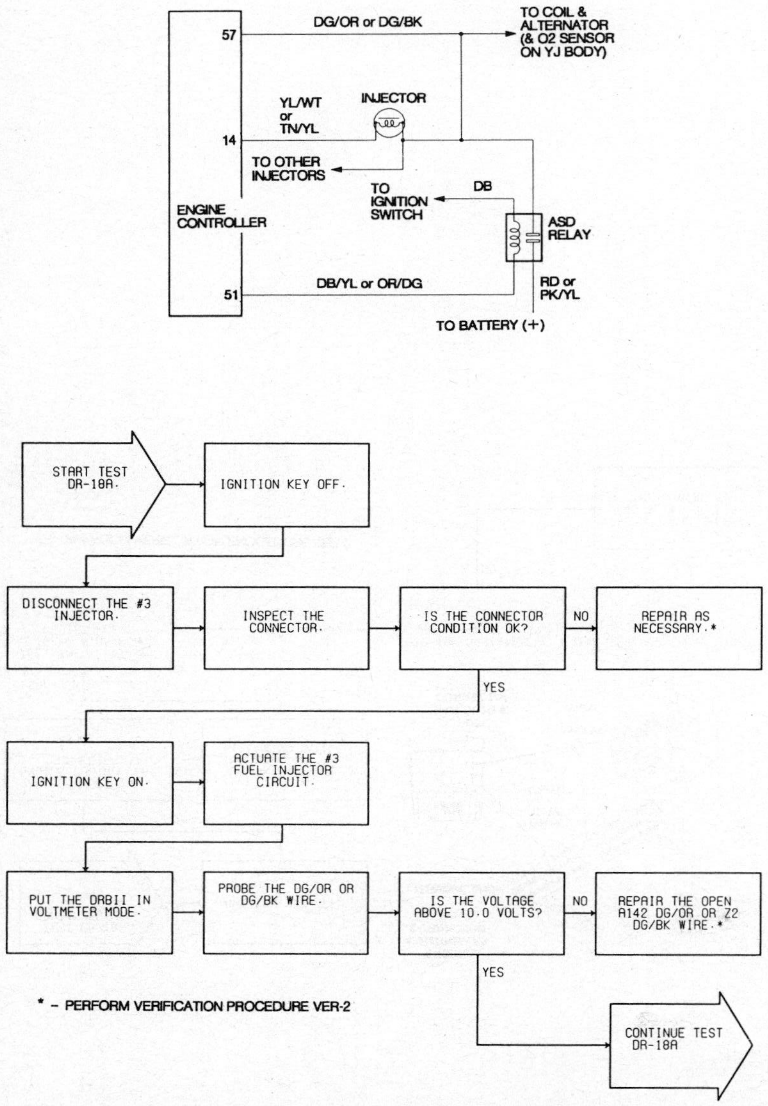
57
DG/OR or DG/BK
TO COIL & ALTERNATOR (& O2 SENSOR ON YJ BODY)
YL/WT or TN/YL
INJECTOR
14
TO OTHER INJECTORS
TO IGNITION SWITCH
DB
ENGINE CONTROLLER
ASD RELAY
51
DB/YL or OR/DG
RD or PK/YL
TO BATTERY (+)
START TEST DR-18A.
IGNITION KEY OFF.
DISCONNECT THE #3 INJECTOR.
INSPECT THE CONNECTOR.
IS THE CONNECTOR CONDITION OK?
NO
REPAIR AS NECESSARY.*
YES
IGNITION KEY ON.
ACTUATE THE #3 FUEL INJECTOR CIRCUIT.
PUT THE DRBII IN VOLTMETER MODE.
PROBE THE DG/OR OR DG/BK WIRE.
IS THE VOLTAGE ABOVE 10.0 VOLTS?
NO
REPAIR THE OPEN A142 DG/OR OR Z2 DG/BK WIRE.*
YES
CONTINUE TEST DR-18A

* – PERFORM VERIFICATION PROCEDURE VER-2

91J13952 91E13890

Fig. 93: Driveability Test DR-18A – Repairing Injector #3 Control Circuit Fault (1 of 3)

DR-18A: – REPAIRING INJECTOR #3 CONTROL CIRCUIT FAULT (2 OF 3)

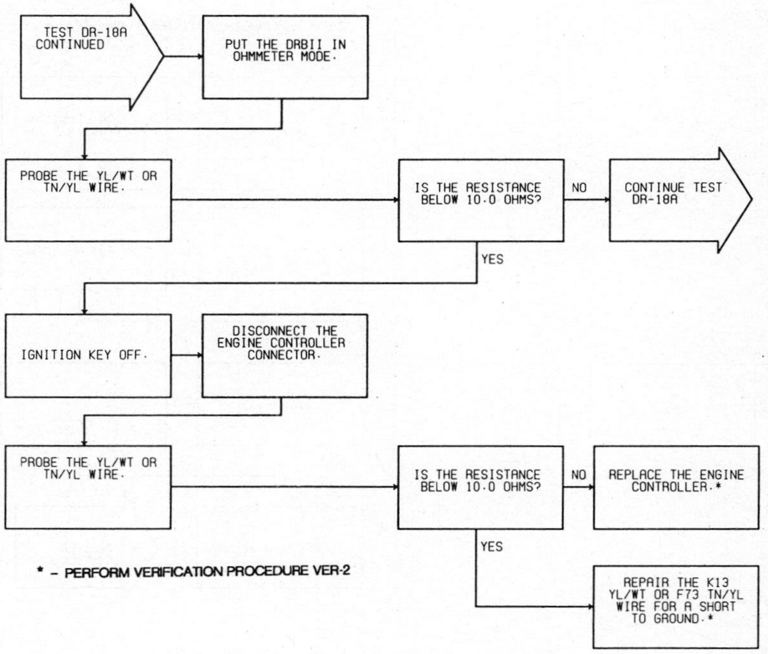
TEST DR-18A CONTINUED
PUT THE DRBII IN OHMMETER MODE.
PROBE THE YL/WT OR TN/YL WIRE.
IS THE RESISTANCE BELOW 10.0 OHMS?
NO
CONTINUE TEST DR-18A
YES
IGNITION KEY OFF.
DISCONNECT THE ENGINE CONTROLLER CONNECTOR.
PROBE THE YL/WT OR TN/YL WIRE.
IS THE RESISTANCE BELOW 10.0 OHMS?
NO
REPLACE THE ENGINE CONTROLLER.*
YES
REPAIR THE K13 YL/WT OR F73 TN/YL WIRE FOR A SHORT TO GROUND.*

* – PERFORM VERIFICATION PROCEDURE VER-2

91F13891

Fig. 94: Driveability Test DR-18A – Repairing Injector #3 Control Circuit Fault (2 of 3)

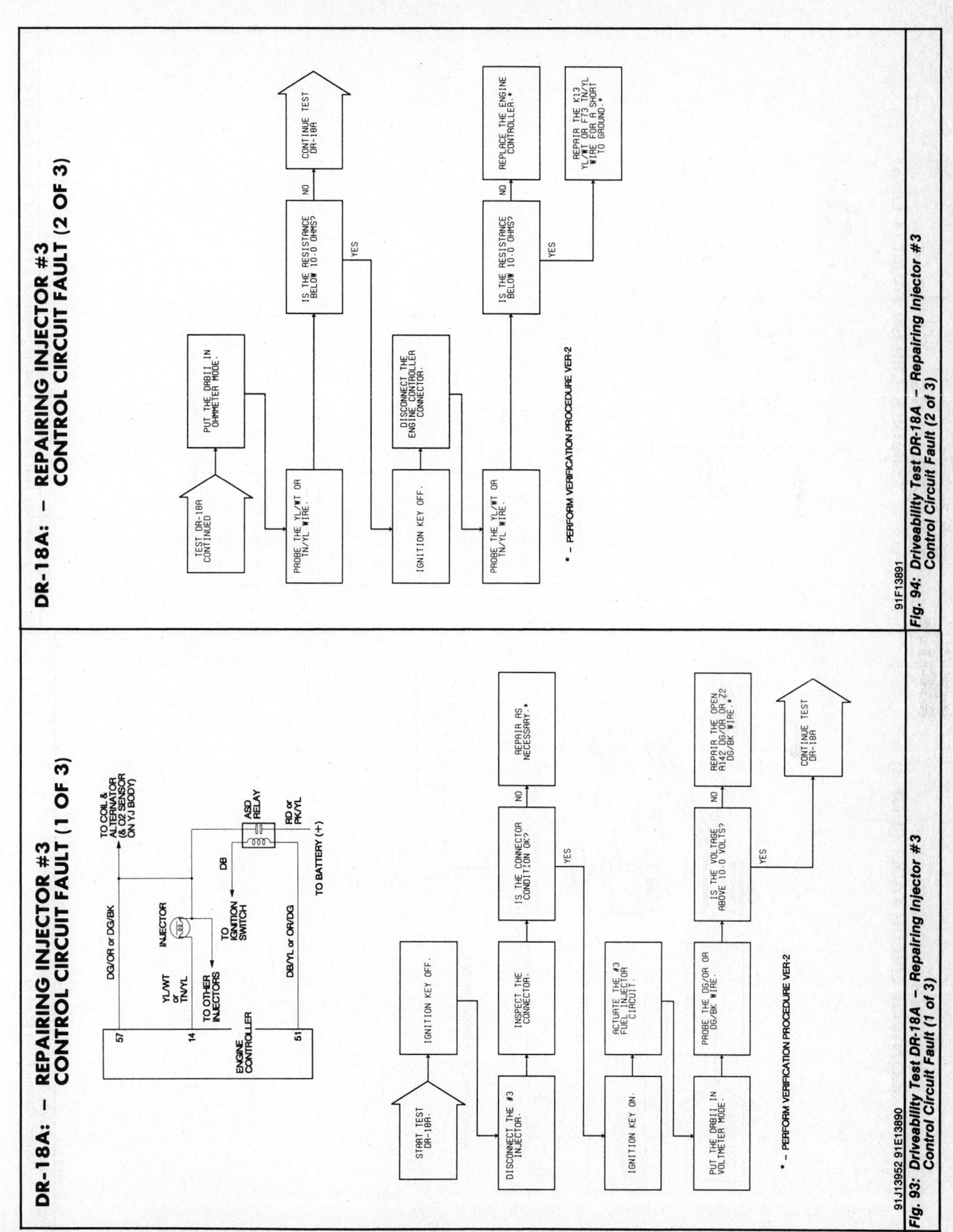

1991 ENGINE PERFORMANCE
Self-Diagnostics (Cont.)

DR-18A: – REPAIRING INJECTOR #3 CONTROL CIRCUIT FAULT (3 OF 3)

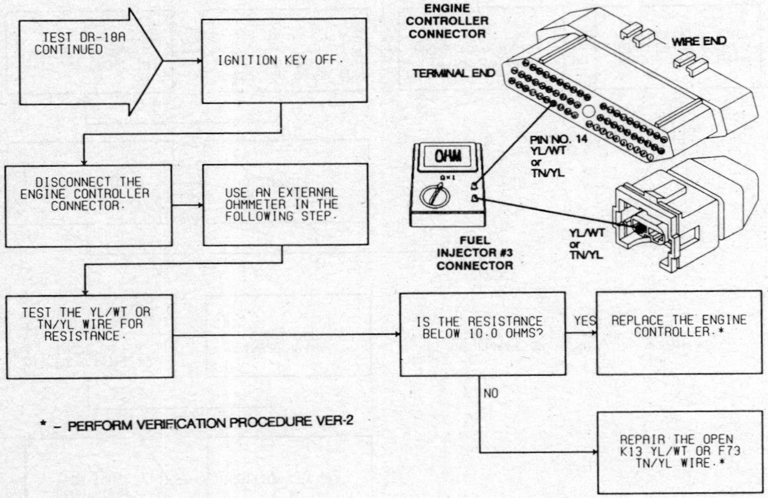
ENGINE CONTROLLER CONNECTOR
TERMINAL END
WIRE END
OHM
PIN NO. 14 YL/WT or TN/YL
YL/WT or TN/YL
FUEL INJECTOR #3 CONNECTOR
TEST DR-18A CONTINUED
IGNITION KEY OFF.
DISCONNECT THE ENGINE CONTROLLER CONNECTOR.
USE AN EXTERNAL OHMMETER IN THE FOLLOWING STEP.
TEST THE YL/WT OR TN/YL WIRE FOR RESISTANCE.
IS THE RESISTANCE BELOW 10.0 OHMS?
YES
REPLACE THE ENGINE CONTROLLER.*
NO
REPAIR THE OPEN K13 YL/WT OR F73 TN/YL WIRE.*
* – PERFORM VERIFICATION PROCEDURE VER-2

91G13892

Fig. 95: Driveability Test DR-18A – Repairing Injector #3 Control Circuit Fault (3 of 3)

DR-19A: – REPAIRING INJECTOR #4 CONTROL CIRCUIT FAULT (1 OF 3)

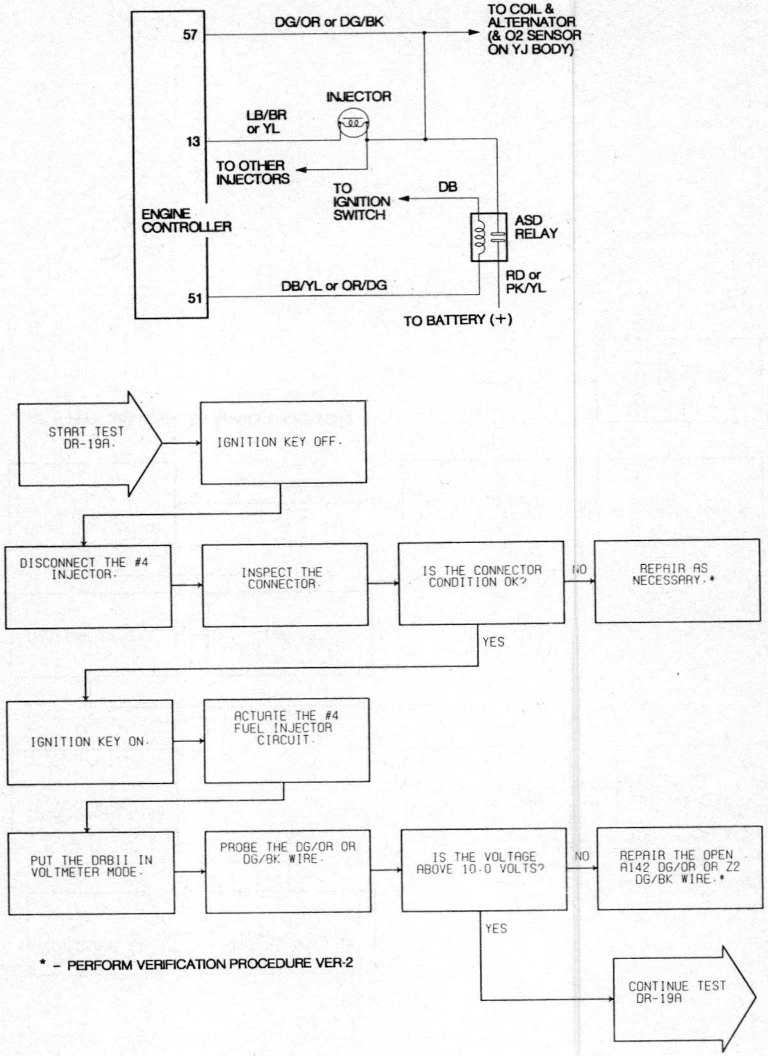
57
DG/OR or DG/BK
TO COIL & ALTERNATOR (& O2 SENSOR ON YJ BODY)
INJECTOR
LB/BR or YL
13
TO OTHER INJECTORS
TO IGNITION SWITCH
DB
ENGINE CONTROLLER
ASD RELAY
RD or PK/YL
51
DB/YL or OR/DG
TO BATTERY (+)
START TEST DR-19A.
IGNITION KEY OFF.
DISCONNECT THE #4 INJECTOR.
INSPECT THE CONNECTOR.
IS THE CONNECTOR CONDITION OK?
NO
REPAIR AS NECESSARY.*
YES
IGNITION KEY ON.
ACTUATE THE #4 FUEL INJECTOR CIRCUIT.
PUT THE DRBII IN VOLTMETER MODE.
PROBE THE DG/OR OR DG/BK WIRE.
IS THE VOLTAGE ABOVE 10.0 VOLTS?
NO
REPAIR THE OPEN A142 DG/OR OR Z2 DG/BK WIRE.*
YES
* – PERFORM VERIFICATION PROCEDURE VER-2
CONTINUE TEST DR-19A

91A13953 91H13893

Fig. 96: Driveability Test DR-19A Repairing Injector #4 Control Circuit Fault (1 of 3)

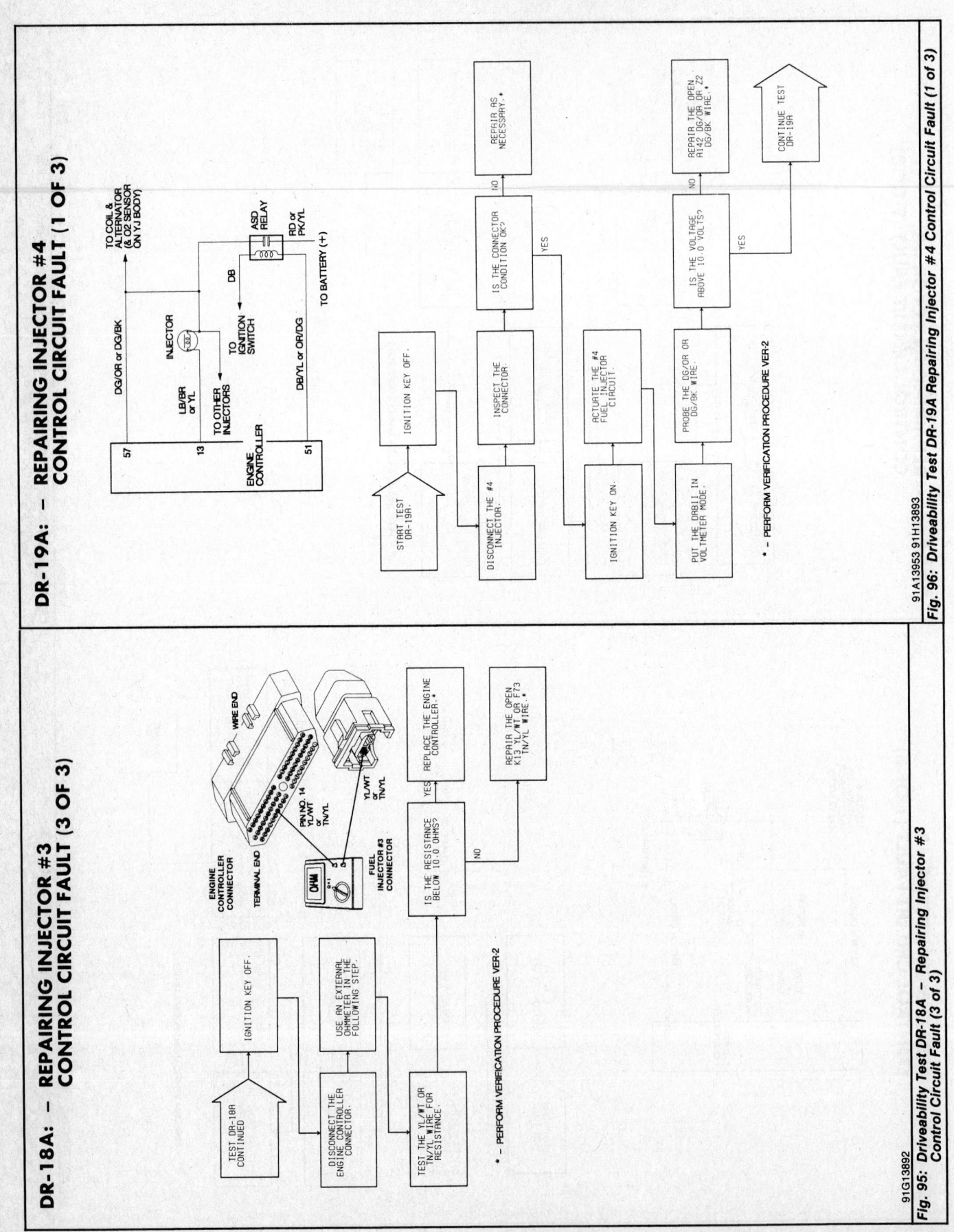

DR-19A: – REPAIRING INJECTOR #4 CONTROL CIRCUIT FAULT (2 OF 3)

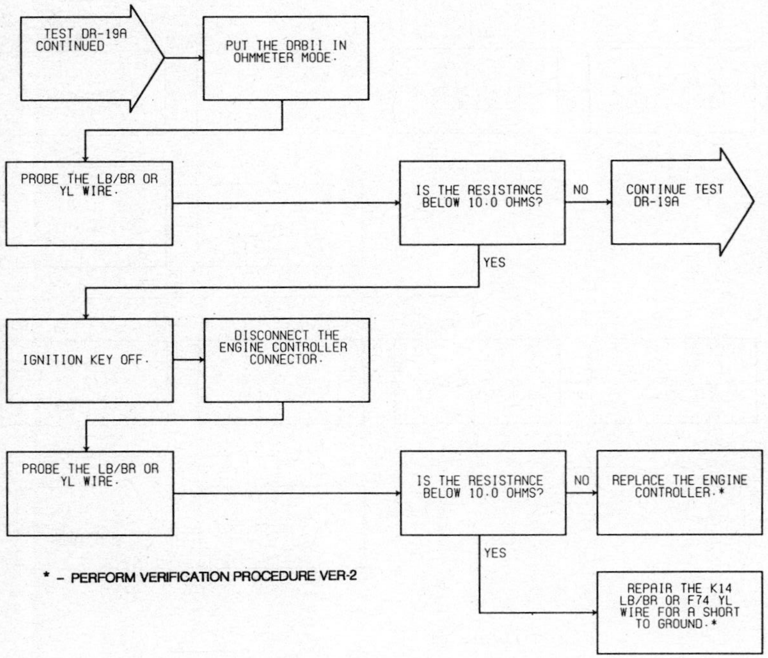
TEST DR-19A CONTINUED
PUT THE DRBII IN OHMMETER MODE.
PROBE THE LB/BR OR YL WIRE.
IS THE RESISTANCE BELOW 10.0 OHMS?
NO
CONTINUE TEST DR-19A
YES
IGNITION KEY OFF.
DISCONNECT THE ENGINE CONTROLLER CONNECTOR.
PROBE THE LB/BR OR YL WIRE.
IS THE RESISTANCE BELOW 10.0 OHMS?
NO
REPLACE THE ENGINE CONTROLLER.*
YES
REPAIR THE K14 LB/BR OR F74 YL WIRE FOR A SHORT TO GROUND.*
* - PERFORM VERIFICATION PROCEDURE VER-2

91I13894

Fig. 97: Driveability Test DR-19A Repairing Injector #4 Control Circuit Fault (2 of 3)

DR-19A: – REPAIRING INJECTOR #4 CONTROL CIRCUIT FAULT (3 OF 3)

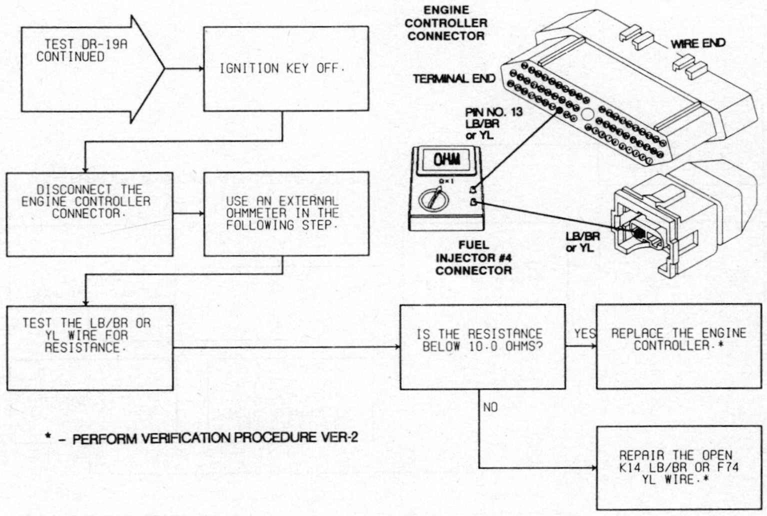
TEST DR-19A CONTINUED
IGNITION KEY OFF.
DISCONNECT THE ENGINE CONTROLLER CONNECTOR.
USE AN EXTERNAL OHMMETER IN THE FOLLOWING STEP.
TEST THE LB/BR OR YL WIRE FOR RESISTANCE.
IS THE RESISTANCE BELOW 10.0 OHMS?
YES
REPLACE THE ENGINE CONTROLLER.*
NO
REPAIR THE OPEN K14 LB/BR OR F74 YL WIRE.*
ENGINE CONTROLLER CONNECTOR
WIRE END
TERMINAL END
PIN NO. 13 LB/BR or YL
OHM
FUEL INJECTOR #4 CONNECTOR
LB/BR or YL
* - PERFORM VERIFICATION PROCEDURE VER-2

91J13895

Fig. 98: Driveability Test DR-19A Repairing Injector #4 Control Circuit Fault (3 of 3)

1991 ENGINE PERFORMANCE
Self-Diagnostics (Cont.)

DR-20A: – REPAIRING INJECTOR #5 CONTROL CIRCUIT FAULT (1 OF 3)

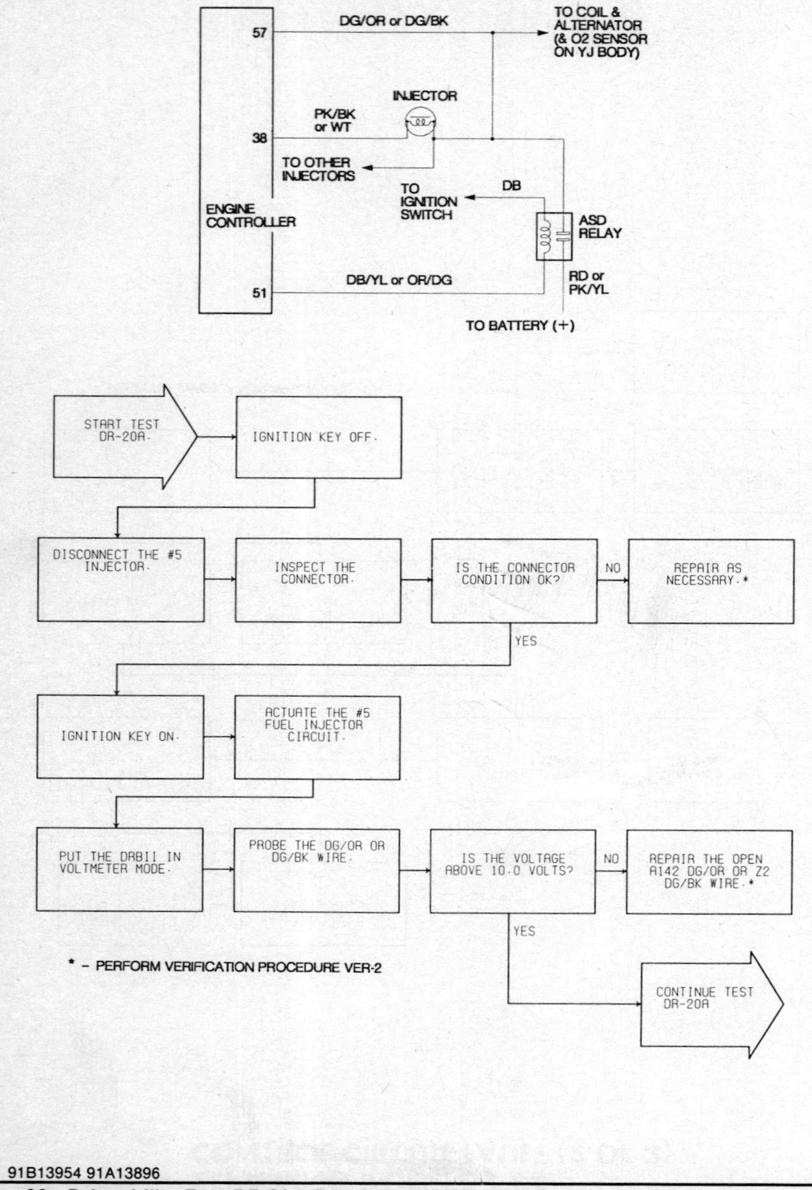
ENGINE CONTROLLER
57
38
51
DG/OR or DG/BK
TO COIL & ALTERNATOR (& O2 SENSOR ON YJ BODY)
INJECTOR
PK/BK or WT
TO OTHER INJECTORS
TO IGNITION SWITCH
DB
ASD RELAY
RD or PK/YL
DB/YL or OR/DG
TO BATTERY (+)
START TEST DR-20A.
IGNITION KEY OFF.
DISCONNECT THE #5 INJECTOR.
INSPECT THE CONNECTOR.
IS THE CONNECTOR CONDITION OK?
NO
REPAIR AS NECESSARY.*
YES
IGNITION KEY ON.
ACTUATE THE #5 FUEL INJECTOR CIRCUIT.
PUT THE DRBII IN VOLTMETER MODE.
PROBE THE DG/OR OR DG/BK WIRE.
IS THE VOLTAGE ABOVE 10.0 VOLTS?
NO
REPAIR THE OPEN A142 DG/OR OR Z2 DG/BK WIRE.*
YES
CONTINUE TEST DR-20A
* – PERFORM VERIFICATION PROCEDURE VER-2
91B13954 91A13896

Fig. 99: Driveability Test DR-20A Repairing Injector #5 Control Circuit Fault (1 of 3)

DR-20A: – REPAIRING INJECTOR #5 CONTROL CIRCUIT FAULT (2 OF 3)

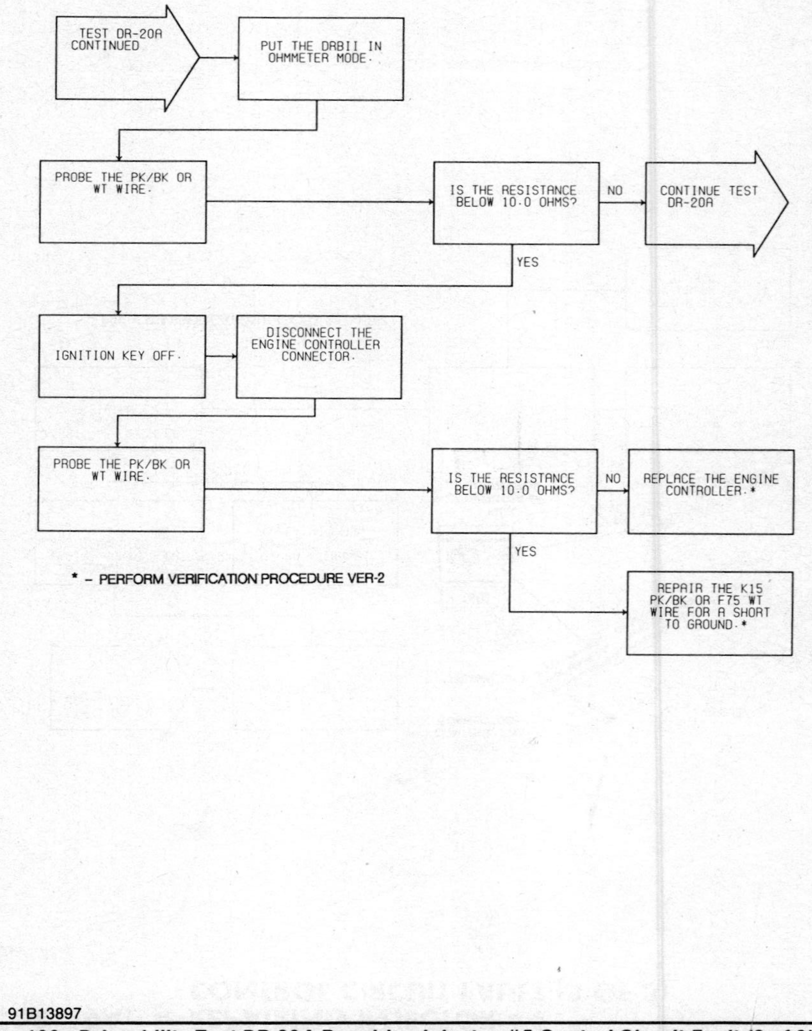
TEST DR-20A CONTINUED
PUT THE DRBII IN OHMMETER MODE.
PROBE THE PK/BK OR WT WIRE.
IS THE RESISTANCE BELOW 10.0 OHMS?
NO
CONTINUE TEST DR-20A
YES
IGNITION KEY OFF.
DISCONNECT THE ENGINE CONTROLLER CONNECTOR.
PROBE THE PK/BK OR WT WIRE.
IS THE RESISTANCE BELOW 10.0 OHMS?
NO
REPLACE THE ENGINE CONTROLLER.*
YES
REPAIR THE K15 PK/BK OR F75 WT WIRE FOR A SHORT TO GROUND.*
* – PERFORM VERIFICATION PROCEDURE VER-2
91B13897

Fig. 100: Driveability Test DR-20A Repairing Injector #5 Control Circuit Fault (2 of 3)

DR-20A: – REPAIRING INJECTOR #5 CONTROL CIRCUIT FAULT (3 OF 3)

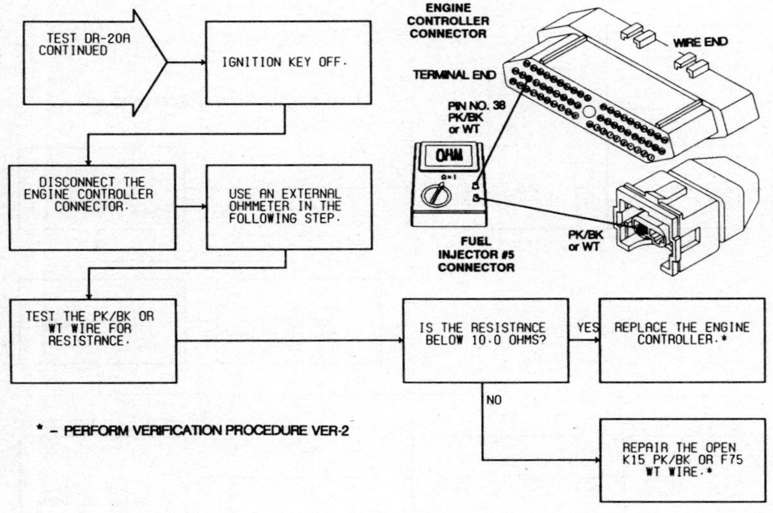
TEST DR-20A CONTINUED
IGNITION KEY OFF.
DISCONNECT THE ENGINE CONTROLLER CONNECTOR.
USE AN EXTERNAL OHMMETER IN THE FOLLOWING STEP.
TEST THE PK/BK OR WT WIRE FOR RESISTANCE.
IS THE RESISTANCE BELOW 10.0 OHMS?
YES
REPLACE THE ENGINE CONTROLLER.*
NO
REPAIR THE OPEN K15 PK/BK OR F75 WT WIRE.*
ENGINE CONTROLLER CONNECTOR
WIRE END
TERMINAL END
PIN NO. 38 PK/BK or WT
OHM
FUEL INJECTOR #5 CONNECTOR
PK/BK or WT

* – PERFORM VERIFICATION PROCEDURE VER-2

91C13898

Fig. 101: Driveability Test DR-20A Repairing Injector #5 Control Circuit Fault (3 of 3)

DR-21A: – REPAIRING INJECTOR #6 CONTROL CIRCUIT FAULT (1 OF 3)

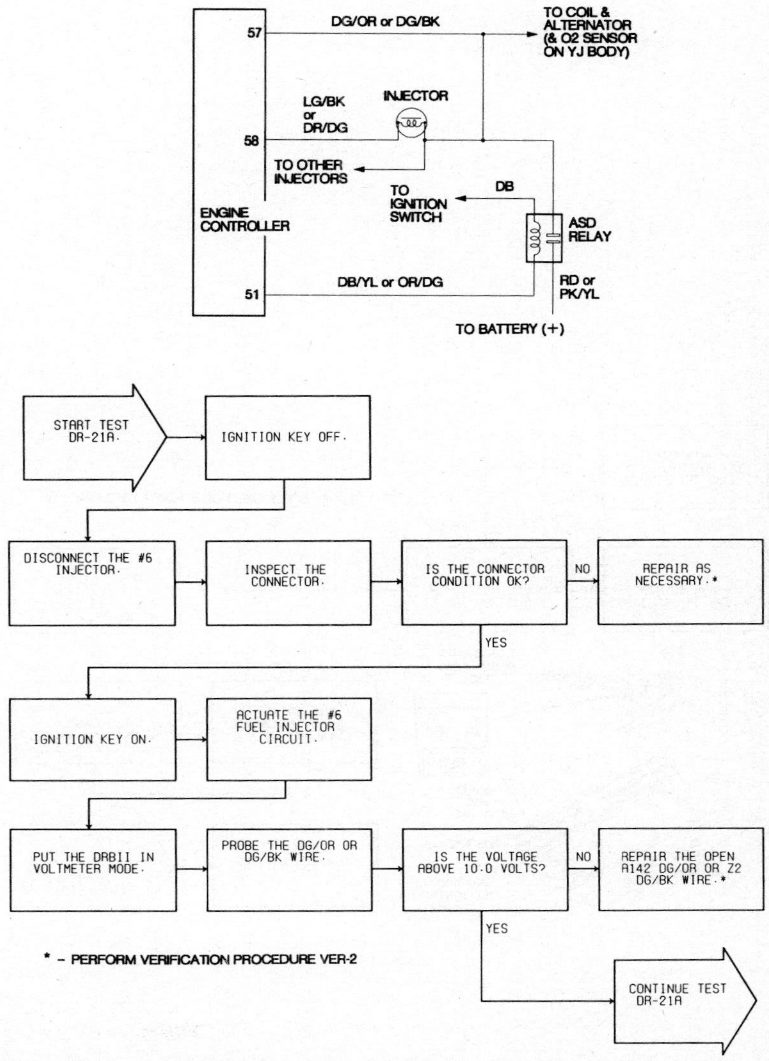
57
DG/OR or DG/BK
TO COIL & ALTERNATOR (& O2 SENSOR ON YJ BODY)
LG/BK or DR/DG
INJECTOR
58
TO OTHER INJECTORS
TO IGNITION SWITCH
DB
ENGINE CONTROLLER
ASD RELAY
51
DB/YL or OR/DG
RD or PK/YL
TO BATTERY (+)
START TEST DR-21A.
IGNITION KEY OFF.
DISCONNECT THE #6 INJECTOR.
INSPECT THE CONNECTOR.
IS THE CONNECTOR CONDITION OK?
NO
REPAIR AS NECESSARY.*
YES
IGNITION KEY ON.
ACTUATE THE #6 FUEL INJECTOR CIRCUIT.
PUT THE DRBII IN VOLTMETER MODE.
PROBE THE DG/OR OR DG/BK WIRE.
IS THE VOLTAGE ABOVE 10.0 VOLTS?
NO
REPAIR THE OPEN A142 DG/OR OR Z2 DG/BK WIRE.*
YES
CONTINUE TEST DR-21A

* – PERFORM VERIFICATION PROCEDURE VER-2

91C13955 91D13899

Fig. 102: Driveability Test DR-21A Repairing Injector #6 Control Circuit Fault (1 of 3)

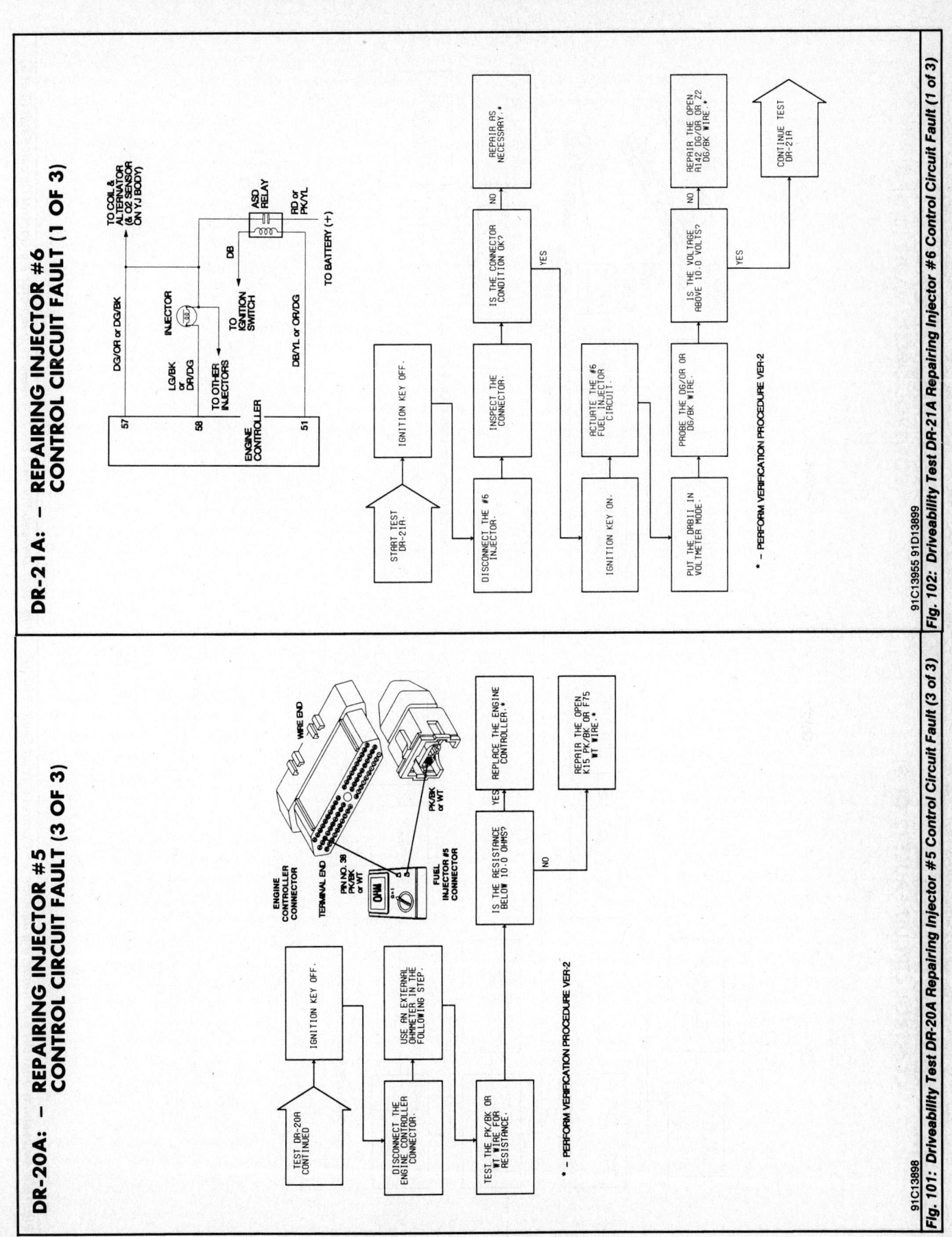

1991 ENGINE PERFORMANCE
Self-Diagnostics (Cont.)

DR-21A: – REPAIRING INJECTOR #6 CONTROL CIRCUIT FAULT (2 OF 3)

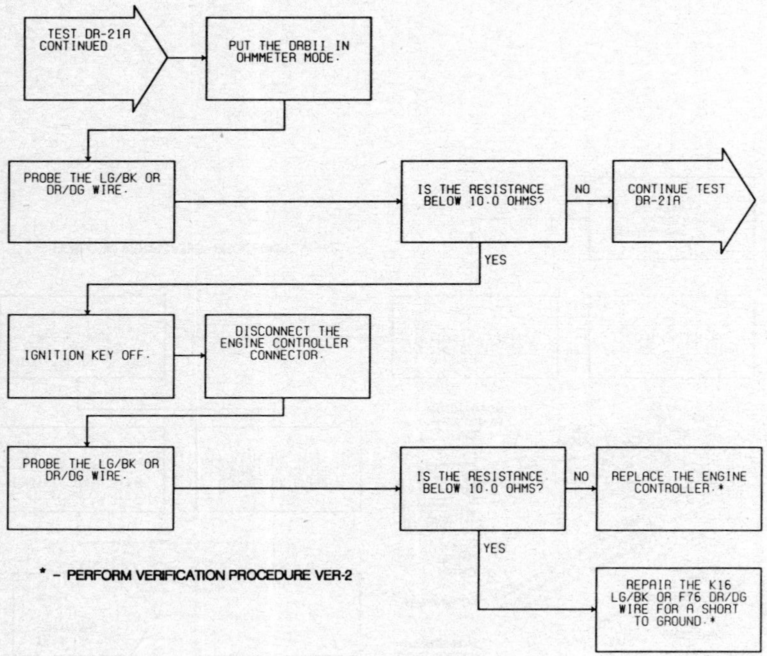
TEST DR-21A CONTINUED
PUT THE DRBII IN OHMMETER MODE.
PROBE THE LG/BK OR DR/DG WIRE.
IS THE RESISTANCE BELOW 10.0 OHMS?
NO
CONTINUE TEST DR-21A
YES
IGNITION KEY OFF.
DISCONNECT THE ENGINE CONTROLLER CONNECTOR.
PROBE THE LG/BK OR DR/DG WIRE.
IS THE RESISTANCE BELOW 10.0 OHMS?
NO
REPLACE THE ENGINE CONTROLLER.*
YES
REPAIR THE K16 LG/BK OR F76 DR/DG WIRE FOR A SHORT TO GROUND.*
* – PERFORM VERIFICATION PROCEDURE VER-2

91G13900

Fig. 103: Driveability Test DR-21A Repairing Injector #6 Control Circuit Fault (2 of 3)

DR-21A: – REPAIRING INJECTOR #6 CONTROL CIRCUIT FAULT (3 OF 3)

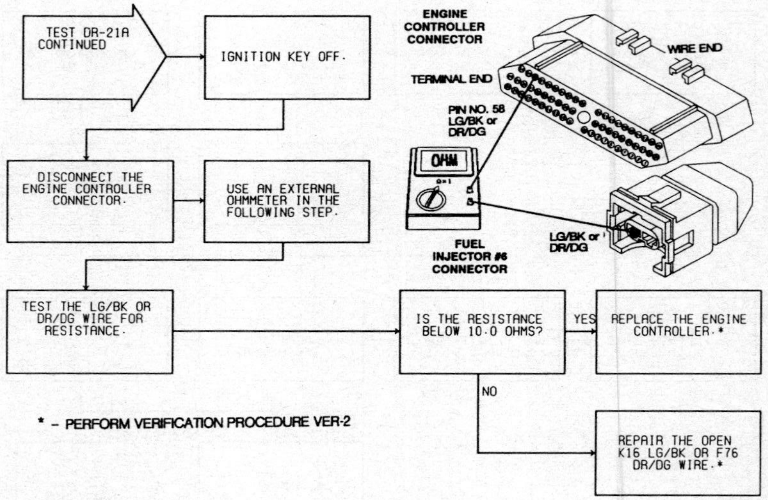
TEST DR-21A CONTINUED
IGNITION KEY OFF.
DISCONNECT THE ENGINE CONTROLLER CONNECTOR.
USE AN EXTERNAL OHMMETER IN THE FOLLOWING STEP.
TEST THE LG/BK OR DR/DG WIRE FOR RESISTANCE.
IS THE RESISTANCE BELOW 10.0 OHMS?
YES
REPLACE THE ENGINE CONTROLLER.*
NO
REPAIR THE OPEN K16 LG/BK OR F76 DR/DG WIRE.*
ENGINE CONTROLLER CONNECTOR
WIRE END
TERMINAL END
PIN NO. 58 LG/BK or DR/DG
OHM
LG/BK or DR/DG
FUEL INJECTOR #6 CONNECTOR
* – PERFORM VERIFICATION PROCEDURE VER-2

91H13901

Fig. 104: Driveability Test DR-21A Repairing Injector #6 Control Circuit Fault (3 of 3)

DR-22A: – REPAIRING A/C CLUTCH RELAY CIRCUIT FAULT (1 OF 2)

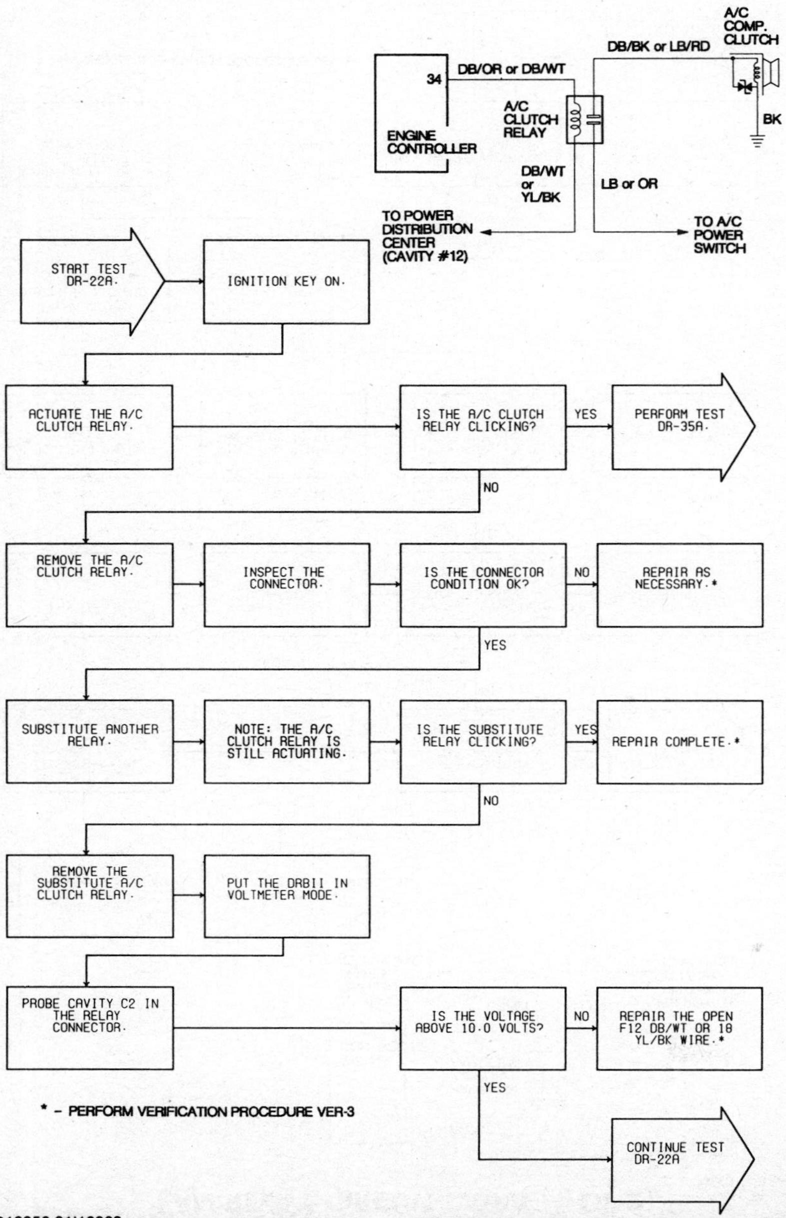
A/C COMP. CLUTCH
DB/BK or LB/RD
34
DB/OR or DB/WT
ENGINE CONTROLLER
A/C CLUTCH RELAY
BK
DB/WT or YL/BK
LB or OR
TO POWER DISTRIBUTION CENTER (CAVITY #12)
TO A/C POWER SWITCH
START TEST DR-22A.
IGNITION KEY ON.
ACTUATE THE A/C CLUTCH RELAY.
IS THE A/C CLUTCH RELAY CLICKING?
YES
PERFORM TEST DR-35A.
NO
REMOVE THE A/C CLUTCH RELAY.
INSPECT THE CONNECTOR.
IS THE CONNECTOR CONDITION OK?
NO
REPAIR AS NECESSARY.*
YES
SUBSTITUTE ANOTHER RELAY.
NOTE: THE A/C CLUTCH RELAY IS STILL ACTUATING.
IS THE SUBSTITUTE RELAY CLICKING?
YES
REPAIR COMPLETE.*
NO
REMOVE THE SUBSTITUTE A/C CLUTCH RELAY.
PUT THE DRBII IN VOLTMETER MODE.
PROBE CAVITY C2 IN THE RELAY CONNECTOR.
IS THE VOLTAGE ABOVE 10.0 VOLTS?
NO
REPAIR THE OPEN F12 DB/WT OR 18 YL/BK WIRE.*
YES
CONTINUE TEST DR-22A

* – PERFORM VERIFICATION PROCEDURE VER-3

91D13956 91I13902

Fig. 105: Driveability Test DR-22A Repairing A/C Clutch Relay Circuit Fault (1 of 2)

DR-22A: – REPAIRING A/C CLUTCH RELAY CIRCUIT FAULT (2 OF 2)

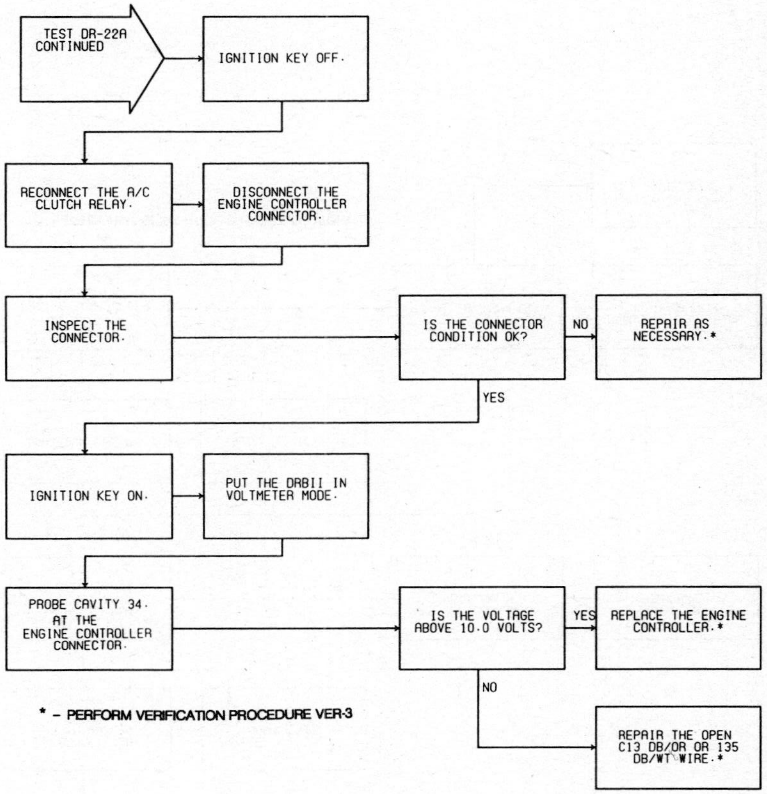
TEST DR-22A CONTINUED
IGNITION KEY OFF.
RECONNECT THE A/C CLUTCH RELAY.
DISCONNECT THE ENGINE CONTROLLER CONNECTOR.
INSPECT THE CONNECTOR.
IS THE CONNECTOR CONDITION OK?
NO
REPAIR AS NECESSARY.*
YES
IGNITION KEY ON.
PUT THE DRBII IN VOLTMETER MODE.
PROBE CAVITY 34. AT THE ENGINE CONTROLLER CONNECTOR.
IS THE VOLTAGE ABOVE 10.0 VOLTS?
YES
REPLACE THE ENGINE CONTROLLER.*
NO
REPAIR THE OPEN C13 DB/OR OR 135 DB/WT WIRE.*

* – PERFORM VERIFICATION PROCEDURE VER-3

91J13903

Fig. 106: Driveability Test DR-22A Repairing A/C Clutch Relay Circuit Fault (2 of 2)

1991 ENGINE PERFORMANCE
Self-Diagnostics (Cont.)

DR-23A: – REPAIRING RADIATOR FAN RELAY CIRCUIT FAULT (1 OF 2)

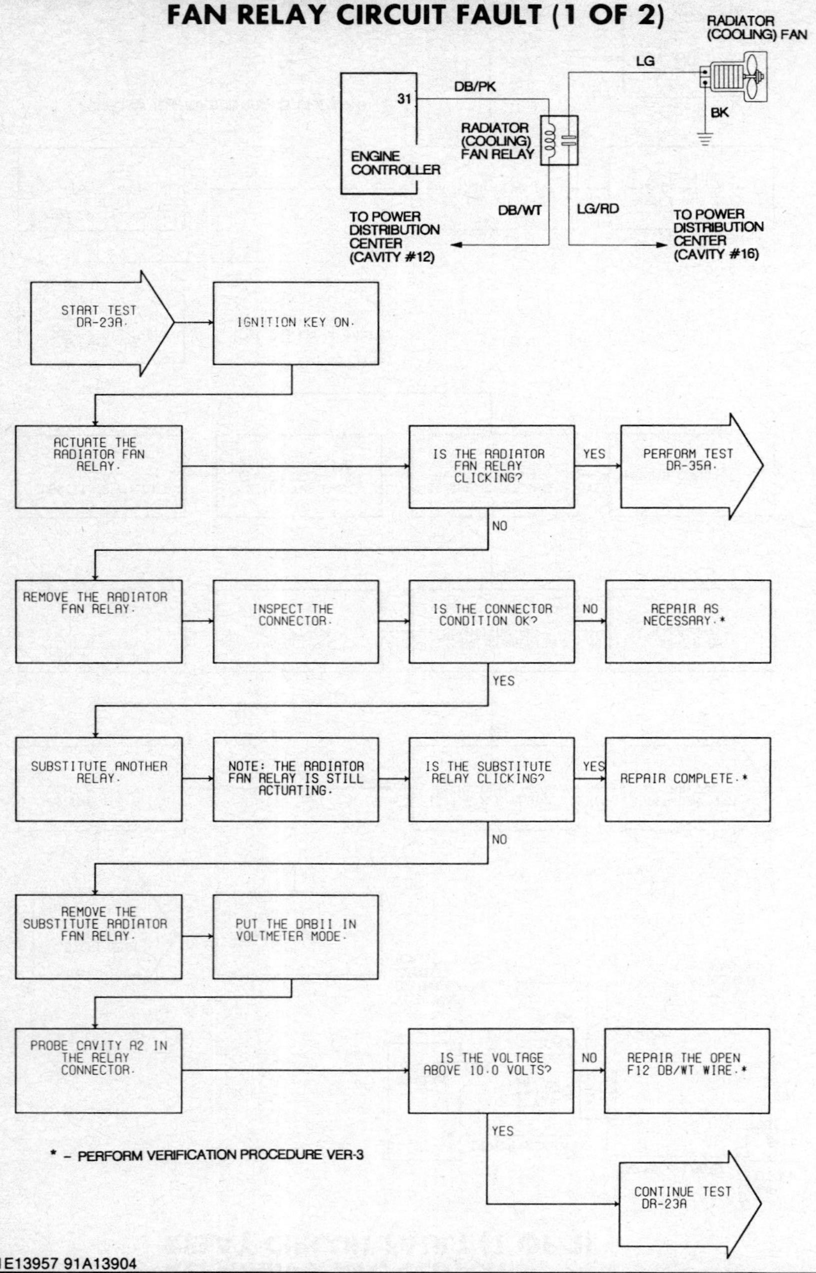
RADIATOR (COOLING) FAN
LG
31
DB/PK
BK
RADIATOR (COOLING) FAN RELAY
ENGINE CONTROLLER
TO POWER DISTRIBUTION CENTER (CAVITY #12)
DB/WT
LG/RD
TO POWER DISTRIBUTION CENTER (CAVITY #16)
START TEST DR-23A.
IGNITION KEY ON.
ACTUATE THE RADIATOR FAN RELAY.
IS THE RADIATOR FAN RELAY CLICKING?
YES
PERFORM TEST DR-35A.
NO
REMOVE THE RADIATOR FAN RELAY.
INSPECT THE CONNECTOR.
IS THE CONNECTOR CONDITION OK?
NO
REPAIR AS NECESSARY.*
YES
SUBSTITUTE ANOTHER RELAY.
NOTE: THE RADIATOR FAN RELAY IS STILL ACTUATING.
IS THE SUBSTITUTE RELAY CLICKING?
YES
REPAIR COMPLETE.*
NO
REMOVE THE SUBSTITUTE RADIATOR FAN RELAY.
PUT THE DRBII IN VOLTMETER MODE.
PROBE CAVITY A2 IN THE RELAY CONNECTOR.
IS THE VOLTAGE ABOVE 10.0 VOLTS?
NO
REPAIR THE OPEN F12 DB/WT WIRE.*
YES
CONTINUE TEST DR-23A
* – PERFORM VERIFICATION PROCEDURE VER-3

91E13957 91A13904

Fig. 107: Driveability Test DR-23A Repairing Radiator Fan Relay Circuit Fault (1 of 2)

DR-23A: – REPAIRING RADIATOR FAN RELAY CIRCUIT FAULT (2 OF 2)

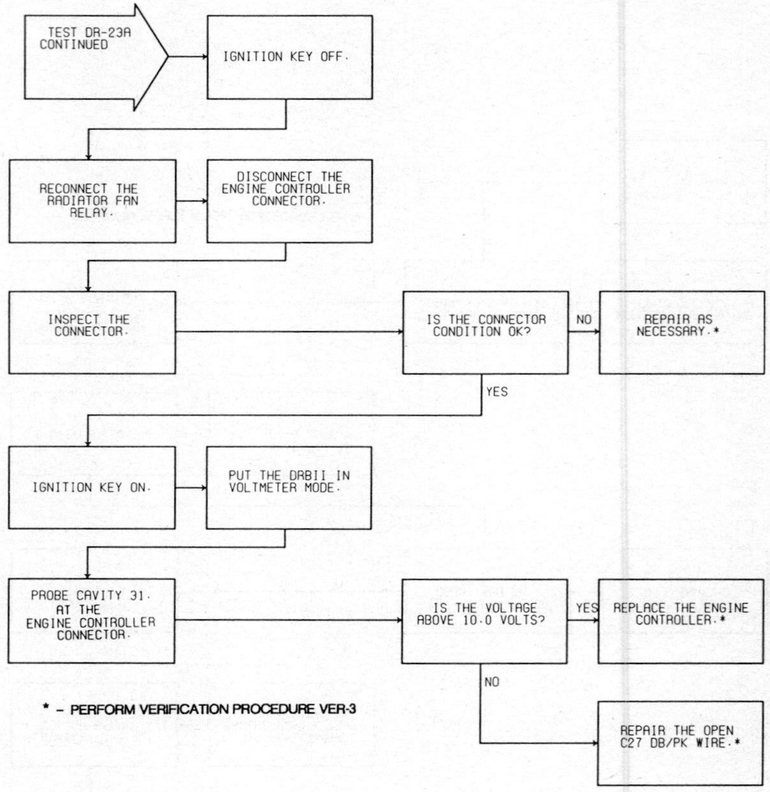
TEST DR-23A CONTINUED
IGNITION KEY OFF.
RECONNECT THE RADIATOR FAN RELAY.
DISCONNECT THE ENGINE CONTROLLER CONNECTOR.
INSPECT THE CONNECTOR.
IS THE CONNECTOR CONDITION OK?
NO
REPAIR AS NECESSARY.*
YES
IGNITION KEY ON.
PUT THE DRBII IN VOLTMETER MODE.
PROBE CAVITY 31. AT THE ENGINE CONTROLLER CONNECTOR.
IS THE VOLTAGE ABOVE 10.0 VOLTS?
YES
REPLACE THE ENGINE CONTROLLER.*
NO
REPAIR THE OPEN C27 DB/PK WIRE.*
* – PERFORM VERIFICATION PROCEDURE VER-3

91B13905

Fig. 108: Driveability Test DR-23A Repairing Radiator Fan Relay Circuit Fault (2 of 2)

DR-24A: – REPAIRING NO ASD RELAY VOLTAGE SENSE AT CONTROLLER FAULT (1 OF 2)

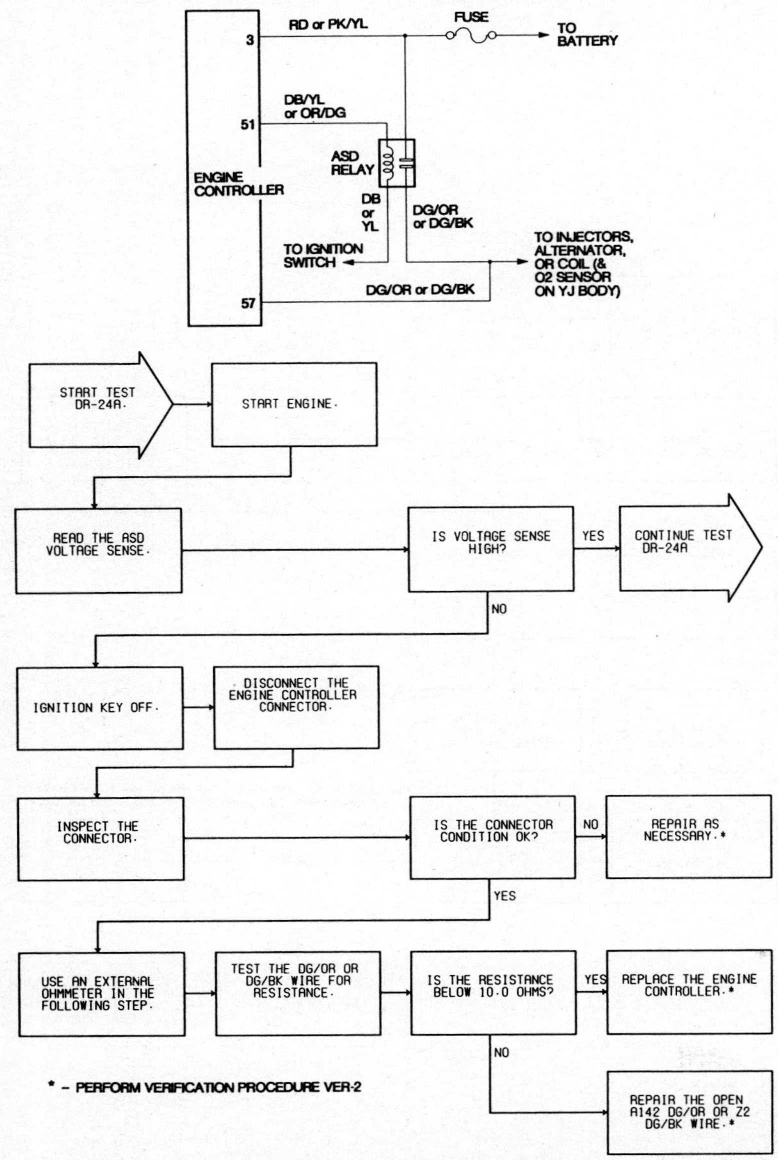
ENGINE CONTROLLER
3
51
57
RD or PK/YL
FUSE
TO BATTERY
DB/YL or OR/DG
ASD RELAY
DB or YL
DG/OR or DG/BK
TO IGNITION SWITCH
TO INJECTORS, ALTERNATOR, OR COIL (& O2 SENSOR ON YJ BODY)
DG/OR or DG/BK
START TEST DR-24A.
START ENGINE.
READ THE ASD VOLTAGE SENSE.
IS VOLTAGE SENSE HIGH?
YES
CONTINUE TEST DR-24A
NO
IGNITION KEY OFF.
DISCONNECT THE ENGINE CONTROLLER CONNECTOR.
INSPECT THE CONNECTOR.
IS THE CONNECTOR CONDITION OK?
NO
REPAIR AS NECESSARY.*
YES
USE AN EXTERNAL OHMMETER IN THE FOLLOWING STEP.
TEST THE DG/OR OR DG/BK WIRE FOR RESISTANCE.
IS THE RESISTANCE BELOW 10.0 OHMS?
YES
REPLACE THE ENGINE CONTROLLER.*
NO
REPAIR THE OPEN A142 DG/OR OR Z2 DG/BK WIRE.*
* – PERFORM VERIFICATION PROCEDURE VER-2

91F13958 91C13906

Fig. 109: *Driveability Test DR-24A Repairing No ASD Relay Voltage Sense At Controller Fault (1 of 2)*

DR-24A: – REPAIRING NO ASD RELAY VOLTAGE SENSE AT CONTROLLER FAULT (2 OF 2)

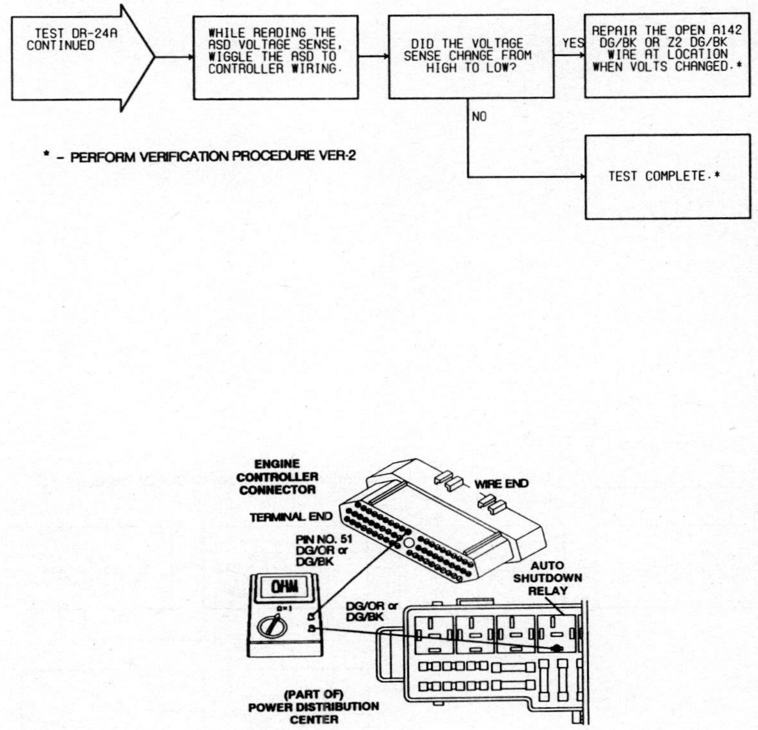
TEST DR-24A CONTINUED
WHILE READING THE ASD VOLTAGE SENSE, WIGGLE THE ASD TO CONTROLLER WIRING.
DID THE VOLTAGE SENSE CHANGE FROM HIGH TO LOW?
YES
REPAIR THE OPEN A142 DG/BK OR Z2 DG/BK WIRE AT LOCATION WHEN VOLTS CHANGED.*
NO
TEST COMPLETE.*
* – PERFORM VERIFICATION PROCEDURE VER-2
ENGINE CONTROLLER CONNECTOR
WIRE END
TERMINAL END
PIN NO. 51 DG/OR or DG/BK
OHM
AUTO SHUTDOWN RELAY
DG/OR or DG/BK
(PART OF) POWER DISTRIBUTION CENTER

91D13907

Fig. 110: *Driveability Test DR-24A Repairing No ASD Relay Voltage Sense At Controller Fault (2 of 2)*

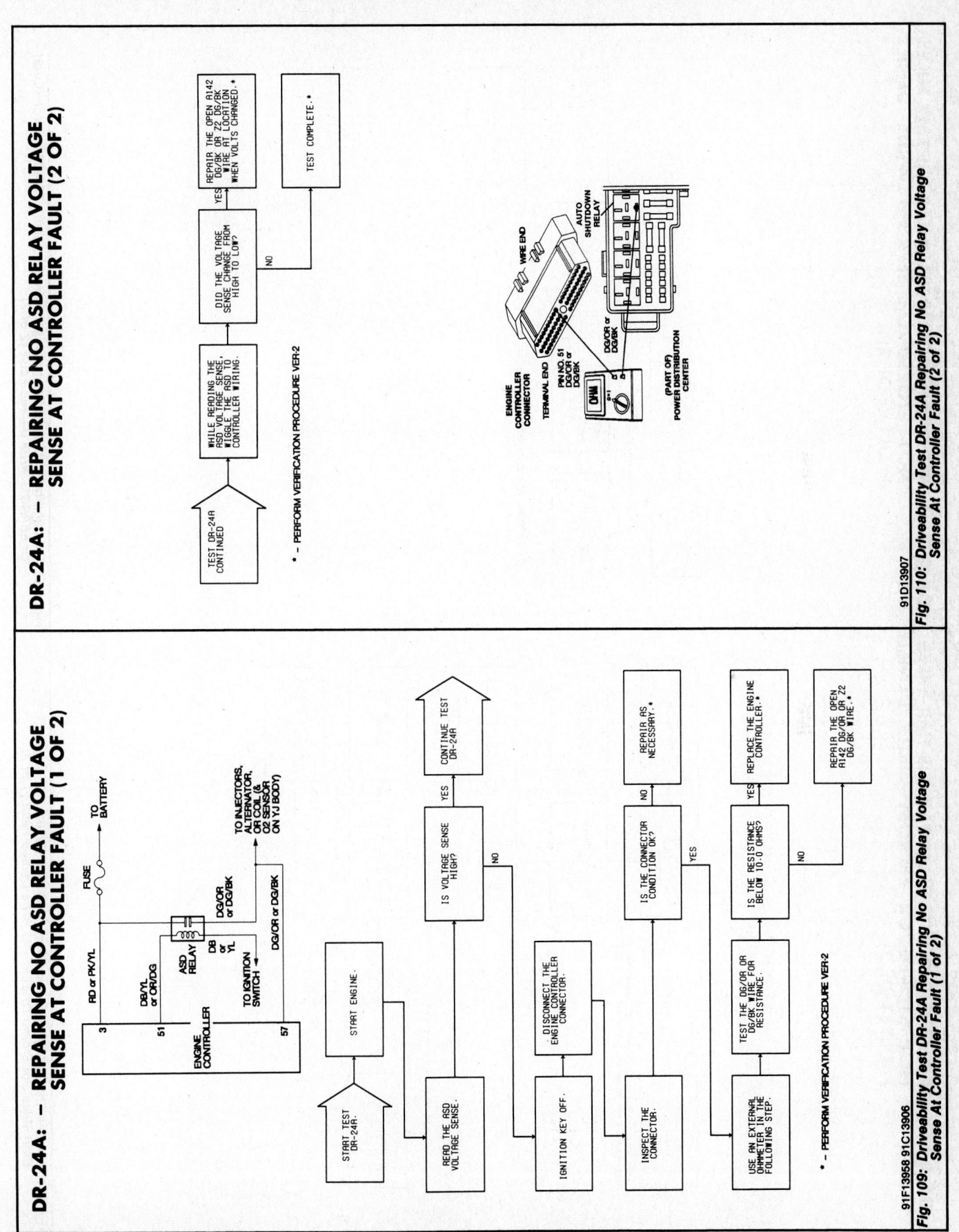

DR-25A: – REPAIRING CONTROLLER FAILURE EMR MILES NOT STORED OR EEPROM WRITE DENIED FAULT (1 OF 2)

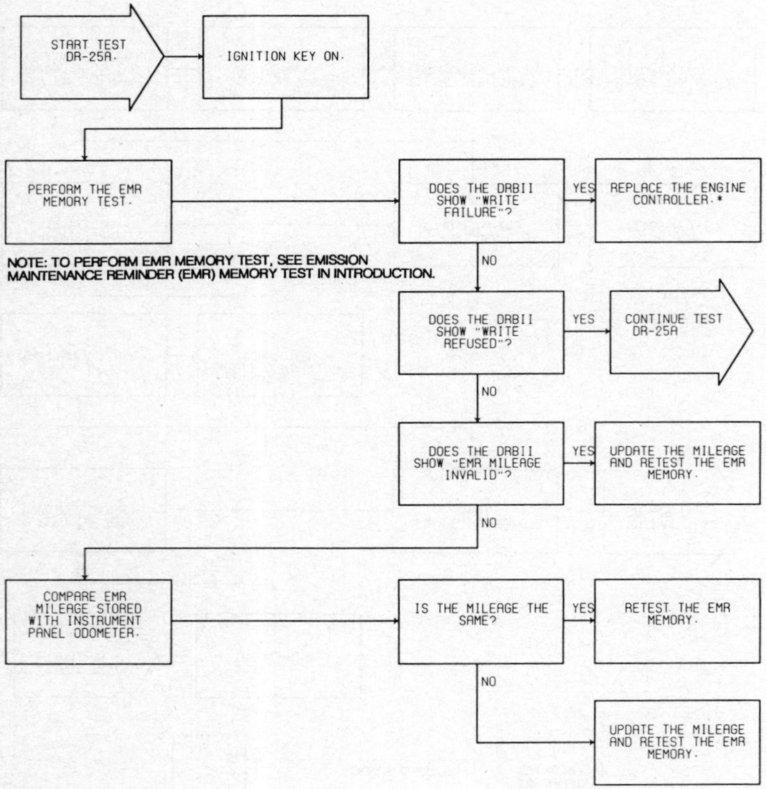
START TEST DR-25A.
IGNITION KEY ON.
PERFORM THE EMR MEMORY TEST.
DOES THE DRBII SHOW "WRITE FAILURE"?
YES
REPLACE THE ENGINE CONTROLLER.*
NO
DOES THE DRBII SHOW "WRITE REFUSED"?
YES
CONTINUE TEST DR-25A
NO
DOES THE DRBII SHOW "EMR MILEAGE INVALID"?
YES
UPDATE THE MILEAGE AND RETEST THE EMR MEMORY.
NO
COMPARE EMR MILEAGE STORED WITH INSTRUMENT PANEL ODOMETER.
IS THE MILEAGE THE SAME?
YES
RETEST THE EMR MEMORY.
NO
UPDATE THE MILEAGE AND RETEST THE EMR MEMORY.

NOTE: TO PERFORM EMR MEMORY TEST, SEE EMISSION MAINTENANCE REMINDER (EMR) MEMORY TEST IN INTRODUCTION.

91E13908

Fig. 111: Driveability Test DR-25A Repairing Controller Failure EMR Miles Not Stored Or EEPROM Write Denied Fault (1 of 2)

DR-25A: – REPAIRING CONTROLLER FAILURE EMR MILES NOT STORED OR EEPROM WRITE DENIED FAULT (2 OF 2)

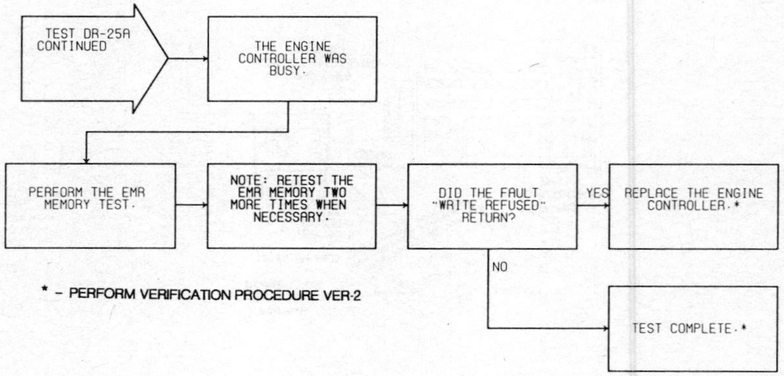
TEST DR-25A CONTINUED
THE ENGINE CONTROLLER WAS BUSY.
PERFORM THE EMR MEMORY TEST.
NOTE: RETEST THE EMR MEMORY TWO MORE TIMES WHEN NECESSARY.
DID THE FAULT "WRITE REFUSED" RETURN?
YES
REPLACE THE ENGINE CONTROLLER.*
NO
TEST COMPLETE.*

* – PERFORM VERIFICATION PROCEDURE VER-2

91F13909

Fig. 112: Driveability Test DR-25A Repairing Controller Failure EMR Miles Not Stored Or EEPROM Write Denied Fault (2 of 2)

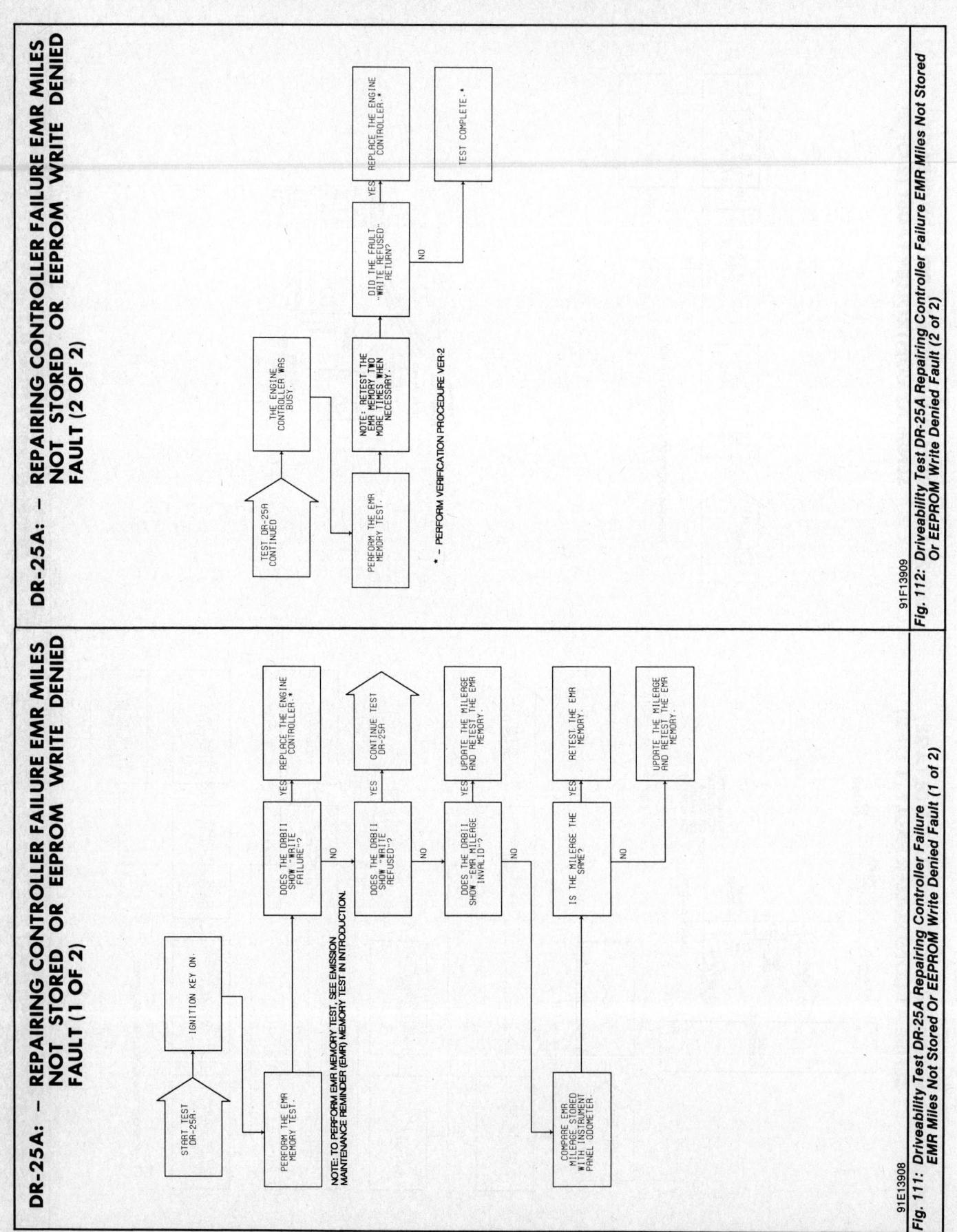

DR-26A: – CHECKING SECONDARY IGNITION & TIMING

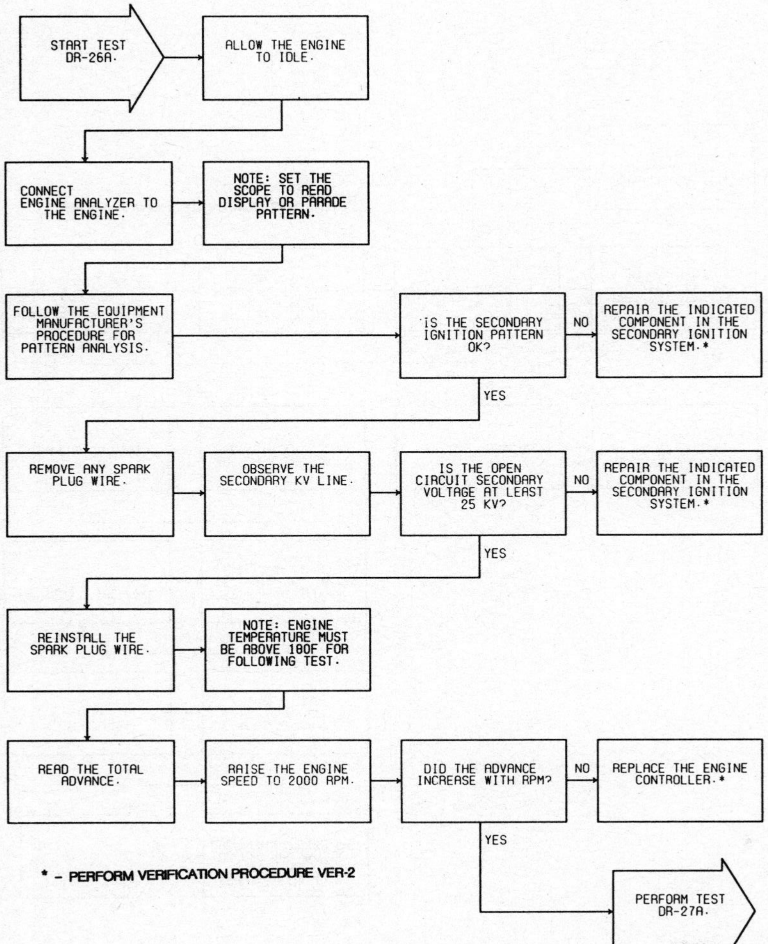

START TEST DR-26A.
ALLOW THE ENGINE TO IDLE.
CONNECT ENGINE ANALYZER TO THE ENGINE.
NOTE: SET THE SCOPE TO READ DISPLAY OR PARADE PATTERN.
FOLLOW THE EQUIPMENT MANUFACTURER'S PROCEDURE FOR PATTERN ANALYSIS.
IS THE SECONDARY IGNITION PATTERN OK?
NO
REPAIR THE INDICATED COMPONENT IN THE SECONDARY IGNITION SYSTEM.*
YES
REMOVE ANY SPARK PLUG WIRE.
OBSERVE THE SECONDARY KV LINE.
IS THE OPEN CIRCUIT SECONDARY VOLTAGE AT LEAST 25 KV?
NO
REPAIR THE INDICATED COMPONENT IN THE SECONDARY IGNITION SYSTEM.*
YES
REINSTALL THE SPARK PLUG WIRE.
NOTE: ENGINE TEMPERATURE MUST BE ABOVE 180F FOR FOLLOWING TEST.
READ THE TOTAL ADVANCE.
RAISE THE ENGINE SPEED TO 2000 RPM.
DID THE ADVANCE INCREASE WITH RPM?
NO
REPLACE THE ENGINE CONTROLLER.*
YES
PERFORM TEST DR-27A.
* - PERFORM VERIFICATION PROCEDURE VER-2

91I13910

Fig. 113: Driveability Test DR-26A Checking Secondary Ignition & Timing

DR-27A: – CHECKING FUEL PRESSURE (1 OF 2)

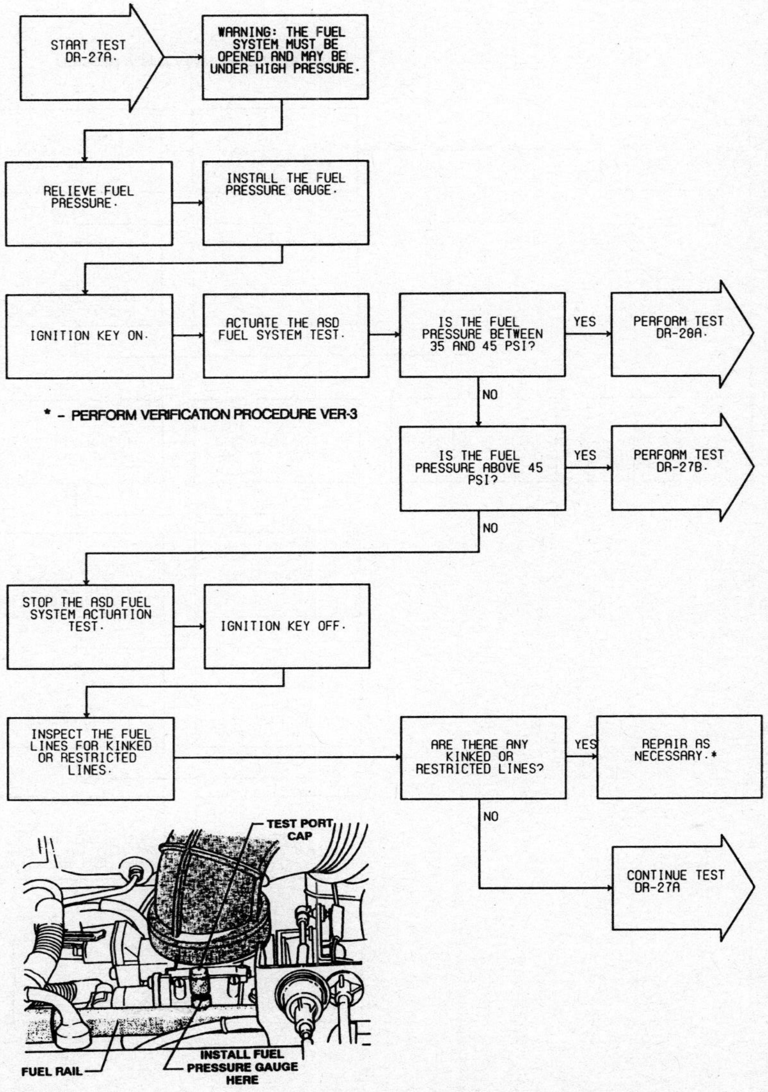

START TEST DR-27A.
WARNING: THE FUEL SYSTEM MUST BE OPENED AND MAY BE UNDER HIGH PRESSURE.
RELIEVE FUEL PRESSURE.
INSTALL THE FUEL PRESSURE GAUGE.
IGNITION KEY ON.
ACTUATE THE ASD FUEL SYSTEM TEST.
IS THE FUEL PRESSURE BETWEEN 35 AND 45 PSI?
YES
PERFORM TEST DR-28A.
NO
IS THE FUEL PRESSURE ABOVE 45 PSI?
YES
PERFORM TEST DR-27B.
NO
STOP THE ASD FUEL SYSTEM ACTUATION TEST.
IGNITION KEY OFF.
INSPECT THE FUEL LINES FOR KINKED OR RESTRICTED LINES.
ARE THERE ANY KINKED OR RESTRICTED LINES?
YES
REPAIR AS NECESSARY.*
NO
CONTINUE TEST DR-27A
* - PERFORM VERIFICATION PROCEDURE VER-3
TEST PORT CAP
FUEL RAIL
INSTALL FUEL PRESSURE GAUGE HERE

91J13911

Fig. 114: Driveability Test DR-27A Checking Fuel Pressure (1 of 2)

DR-27A: – CHECKING FUEL PRESSURE (2 OF 2)

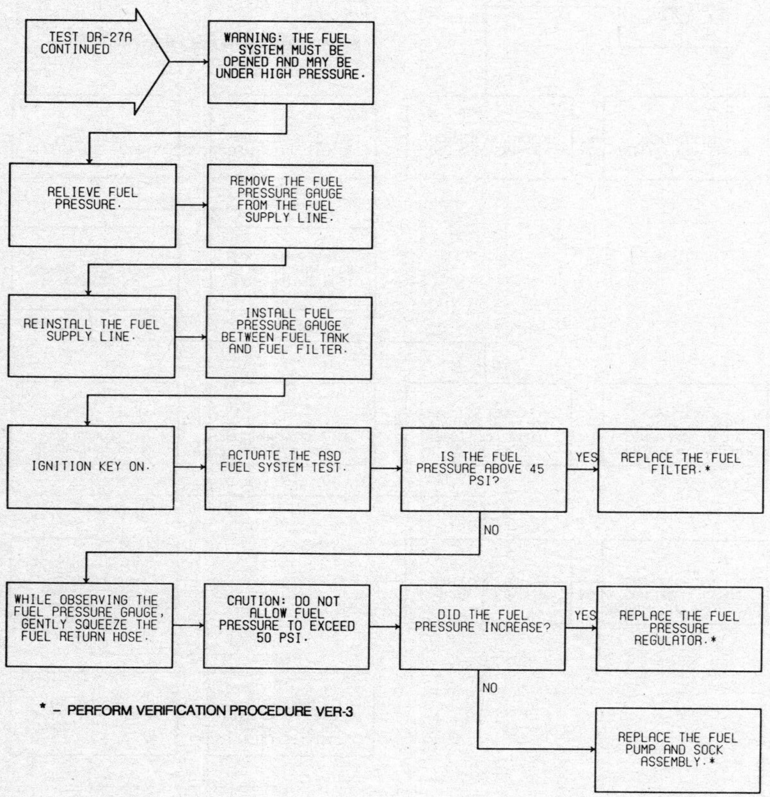
TEST DR-27A CONTINUED
WARNING: THE FUEL SYSTEM MUST BE OPENED AND MAY BE UNDER HIGH PRESSURE.
RELIEVE FUEL PRESSURE.
REMOVE THE FUEL PRESSURE GAUGE FROM THE FUEL SUPPLY LINE.
REINSTALL THE FUEL SUPPLY LINE.
INSTALL FUEL PRESSURE GAUGE BETWEEN FUEL TANK AND FUEL FILTER.
IGNITION KEY ON.
ACTUATE THE ASD FUEL SYSTEM TEST.
IS THE FUEL PRESSURE ABOVE 45 PSI?
YES
REPLACE THE FUEL FILTER.*
NO
WHILE OBSERVING THE FUEL PRESSURE GAUGE, GENTLY SQUEEZE THE FUEL RETURN HOSE.
CAUTION: DO NOT ALLOW FUEL PRESSURE TO EXCEED 50 PSI.
DID THE FUEL PRESSURE INCREASE?
YES
REPLACE THE FUEL PRESSURE REGULATOR.*
NO
REPLACE THE FUEL PUMP AND SOCK ASSEMBLY.*
* – PERFORM VERIFICATION PROCEDURE VER-3

91A13912

Fig. 115: Driveability Test DR-27A Checking Fuel Pressure (2 of 2)

DR-27B: – CHECKING FUEL PRESSURE (1 OF 2)

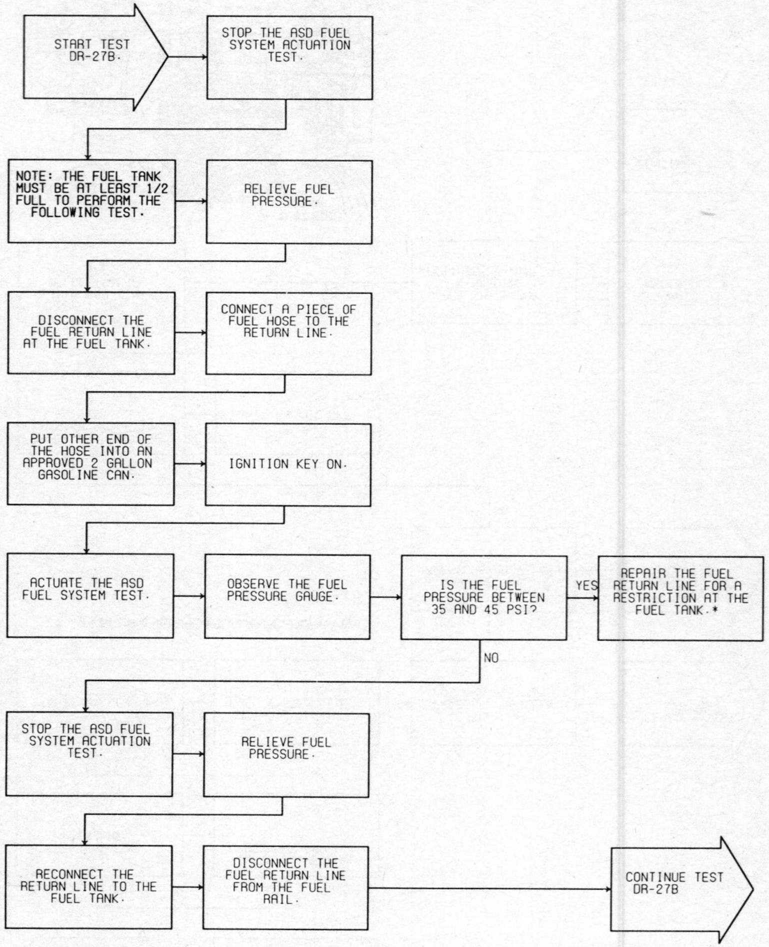
START TEST DR-27B.
STOP THE ASD FUEL SYSTEM ACTUATION TEST.
NOTE: THE FUEL TANK MUST BE AT LEAST 1/2 FULL TO PERFORM THE FOLLOWING TEST.
RELIEVE FUEL PRESSURE.
DISCONNECT THE FUEL RETURN LINE AT THE FUEL TANK.
CONNECT A PIECE OF FUEL HOSE TO THE RETURN LINE.
PUT OTHER END OF THE HOSE INTO AN APPROVED 2 GALLON GASOLINE CAN.
IGNITION KEY ON.
ACTUATE THE ASD FUEL SYSTEM TEST.
OBSERVE THE FUEL PRESSURE GAUGE.
IS THE FUEL PRESSURE BETWEEN 35 AND 45 PSI?
YES
REPAIR THE FUEL RETURN LINE FOR A RESTRICTION AT THE FUEL TANK.*
NO
STOP THE ASD FUEL SYSTEM ACTUATION TEST.
RELIEVE FUEL PRESSURE.
RECONNECT THE RETURN LINE TO THE FUEL TANK.
DISCONNECT THE FUEL RETURN LINE FROM THE FUEL RAIL.
CONTINUE TEST DR-27B

* – PERFORM VERIFICATION PROCEDURE VER-3

91B13913

Fig. 116: Driveability Test DR-27B Checking Fuel Pressure (1 of 2)

DR-27B: – CHECKING FUEL PRESSURE (2 OF 2)

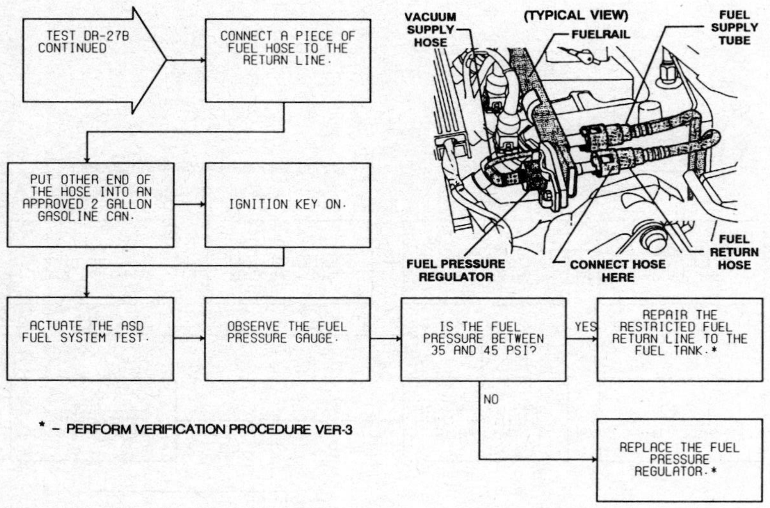
TEST DR-27B CONTINUED
CONNECT A PIECE OF FUEL HOSE TO THE RETURN LINE.
PUT OTHER END OF THE HOSE INTO AN APPROVED 2 GALLON GASOLINE CAN.
IGNITION KEY ON.
ACTUATE THE ASD FUEL SYSTEM TEST.
OBSERVE THE FUEL PRESSURE GAUGE.
IS THE FUEL PRESSURE BETWEEN 35 AND 45 PSI?
YES
REPAIR THE RESTRICTED FUEL RETURN LINE TO THE FUEL TANK.*
NO
REPLACE THE FUEL PRESSURE REGULATOR.*
VACUUM SUPPLY HOSE
(TYPICAL VIEW)
FUELRAIL
FUEL SUPPLY TUBE
FUEL RETURN HOSE
FUEL PRESSURE REGULATOR
CONNECT HOSE HERE

* – PERFORM VERIFICATION PROCEDURE VER-3

91C13914

Fig. 117: Driveability Test DR-27B Checking Fuel Pressure (2 of 2)

DR-28A: – CHECKING COOLANT & THROTTLE POSITION SENSOR CALIBRATIONS (1 OF 2)

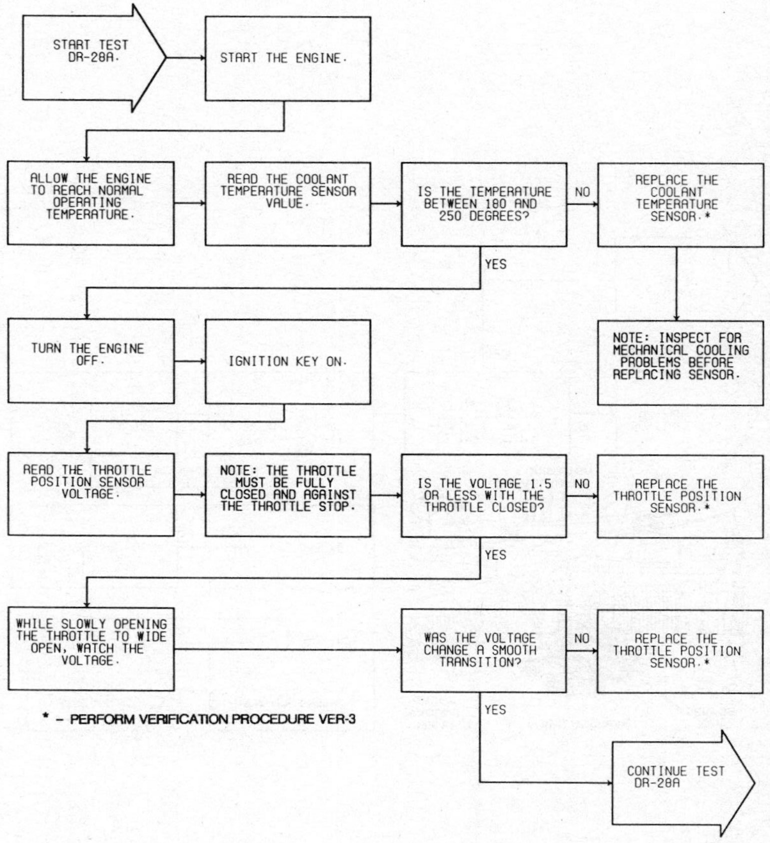
START TEST DR-28A.
START THE ENGINE.
ALLOW THE ENGINE TO REACH NORMAL OPERATING TEMPERATURE.
READ THE COOLANT TEMPERATURE SENSOR VALUE.
IS THE TEMPERATURE BETWEEN 180 AND 250 DEGREES?
NO
REPLACE THE COOLANT TEMPERATURE SENSOR.*
NOTE: INSPECT FOR MECHANICAL COOLING PROBLEMS BEFORE REPLACING SENSOR.
YES
TURN THE ENGINE OFF.
IGNITION KEY ON.
READ THE THROTTLE POSITION SENSOR VOLTAGE.
NOTE: THE THROTTLE MUST BE FULLY CLOSED AND AGAINST THE THROTTLE STOP.
IS THE VOLTAGE 1.5 OR LESS WITH THE THROTTLE CLOSED?
NO
REPLACE THE THROTTLE POSITION SENSOR.*
YES
WHILE SLOWLY OPENING THE THROTTLE TO WIDE OPEN, WATCH THE VOLTAGE.
WAS THE VOLTAGE CHANGE A SMOOTH TRANSITION?
NO
REPLACE THE THROTTLE POSITION SENSOR.*
YES
CONTINUE TEST DR-28A

* – PERFORM VERIFICATION PROCEDURE VER-3

91D13915

Fig. 118: Driveability Test DR-28A Checking Coolant & Throttle Position Sensor Calibrations (2 of 2)

DR-28A: – CHECKING COOLANT & THROTTLE POSITION SENSOR CALIBRATIONS (2 OF 2)

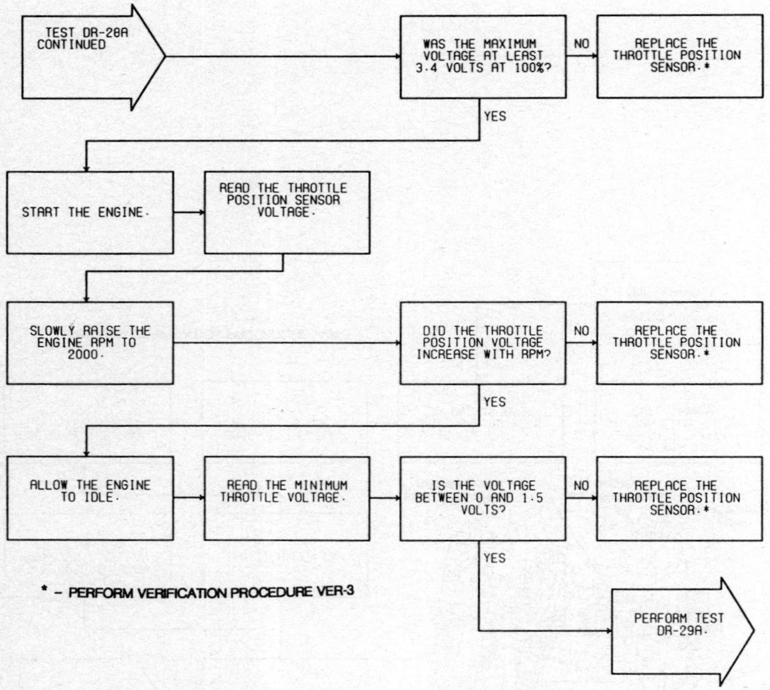
TEST DR-28A CONTINUED
WAS THE MAXIMUM VOLTAGE AT LEAST 3.4 VOLTS AT 100%?
NO
REPLACE THE THROTTLE POSITION SENSOR.*
YES
START THE ENGINE.
READ THE THROTTLE POSITION SENSOR VOLTAGE.
SLOWLY RAISE THE ENGINE RPM TO 2000.
DID THE THROTTLE POSITION VOLTAGE INCREASE WITH RPM?
NO
REPLACE THE THROTTLE POSITION SENSOR.*
YES
ALLOW THE ENGINE TO IDLE.
READ THE MINIMUM THROTTLE VOLTAGE.
IS THE VOLTAGE BETWEEN 0 AND 1.5 VOLTS?
NO
REPLACE THE THROTTLE POSITION SENSOR.*
YES
PERFORM TEST DR-29A.

* – PERFORM VERIFICATION PROCEDURE VER-3

91E13916

Fig. 119: Driveability Test DR-28A Checking Coolant & Throttle Position Sensor Calibrations (2 of 2)

DR-29A: – CHECKING MAP SENSOR CALIBRATION (1 OF 2)

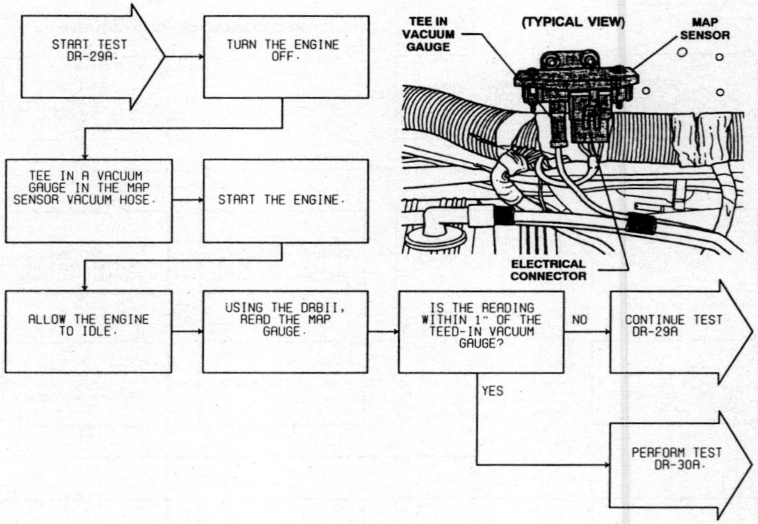
START TEST DR-29A.
TURN THE ENGINE OFF.
TEE IN A VACUUM GAUGE IN THE MAP SENSOR VACUUM HOSE.
START THE ENGINE.
ALLOW THE ENGINE TO IDLE.
USING THE DRBII, READ THE MAP GAUGE.
IS THE READING WITHIN 1" OF THE TEED-IN VACUUM GAUGE?
NO
CONTINUE TEST DR-29A
YES
PERFORM TEST DR-30A.
TEE IN VACUUM GAUGE
(TYPICAL VIEW)
MAP SENSOR
ELECTRICAL CONNECTOR

91F13917

Fig. 120: Driveability Test DR-29A Checking MAP Sensor Calibration (1 of 2)

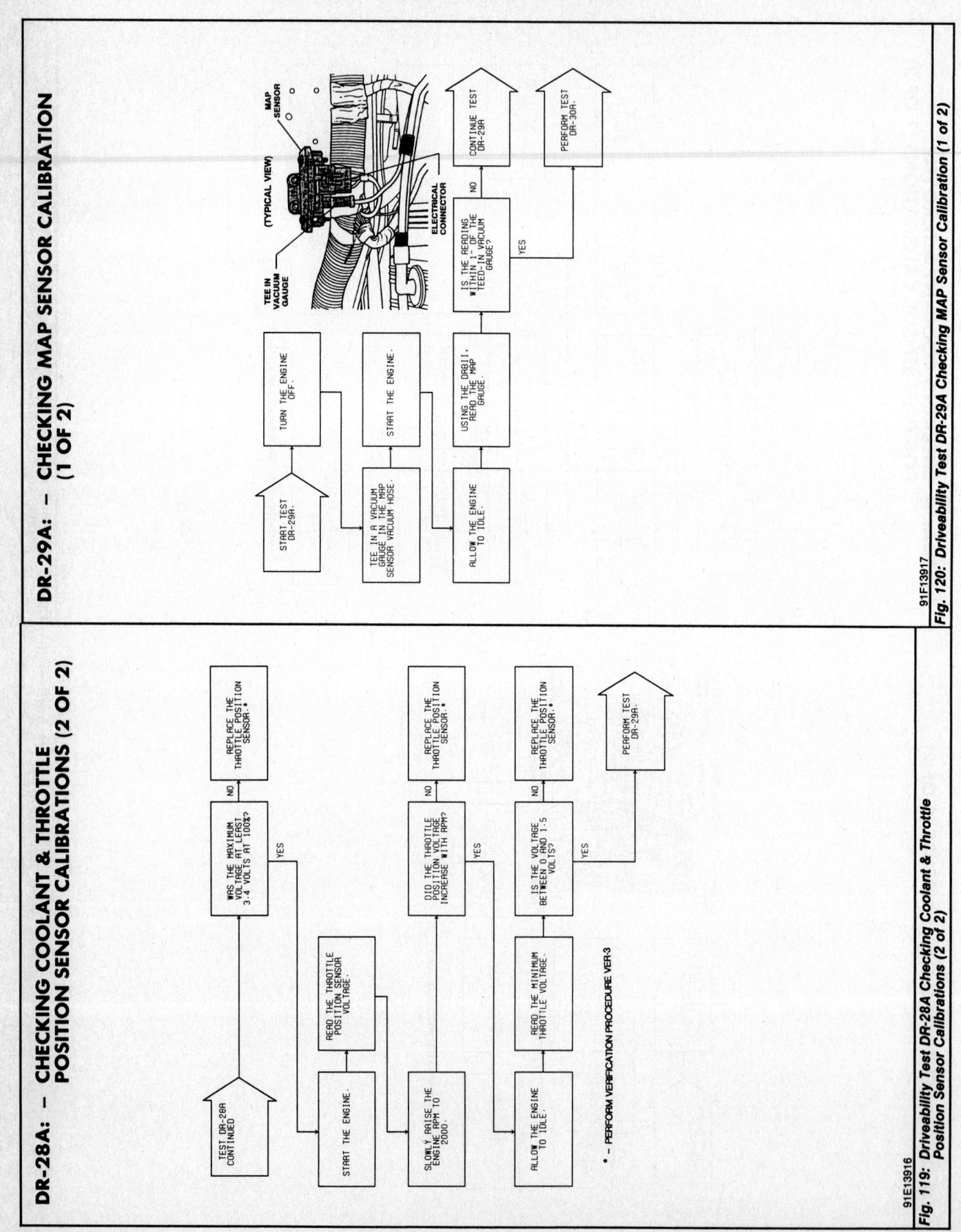

DR-29A: – CHECKING MAP SENSOR CALIBRATION (2 OF 2)

TEST DR-29A CONTINUED → TURN THE ENGINE OFF.

→ READ THE MAP SENSOR VOLTAGE. → DISCONNECT THE VACUUM GAUGE FROM THE MAP SENSOR.

→ CONNECT AN AUXILIARY VACUUM PUMP TO THE MAP SENSOR. → APPLY 5" OF VACUUM TO THE MAP SENSOR.

→ RECORD THE VOLTAGE. → INCREASE THE VACUUM TO 20".

→ RECORD THE VOLTAGE. → SUBTRACT THE VOLTAGE RECORDED AT 20" FROM THAT RECORDED AT 5". → WAS THE DIFFERENCE BETWEEN 2.3 AND 2.9 VOLTS?

- YES → REPAIR THE RESTRICTION IN THE VACUUM HOSE TO THE MAP SENSOR.*
- NO → REPLACE THE MAP SENSOR.*

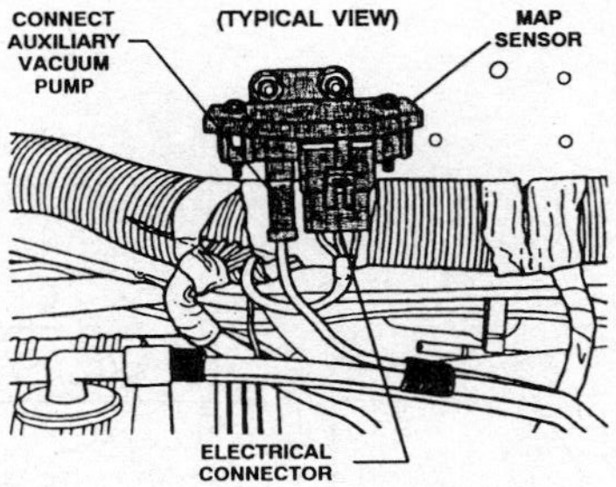
CONNECT AUXILIARY VACUUM PUMP
(TYPICAL VIEW)
MAP SENSOR
ELECTRICAL CONNECTOR

* – PERFORM VERIFICATION PROCEDURE VER-3

91G13918

Fig. 121: Driveability Test DR-29A Checking MAP Sensor Calibration (2 of 2)

DR-30A: – CHECKING OXYGEN SENSOR SWITCHING

START TEST DR-30A. → NOTE: THE ENGINE SHOULD BE AT NORMAL OPERATING TEMPERATURE.

→ READ THE OXYGEN SENSOR STATE. → ALLOW THE ENGINE TO IDLE FOR 1 MINUTE. → IS THE OXYGEN SENSOR SWITCHING RICH TO LEAN?

- YES → PERFORM TEST DR-31A.
- NO → IS THE OXYGEN SENSOR LOCKED ON LEAN?
  - YES → PERFORM TEST DR-30B.
  - NO → TURN THE ENGINE OFF. → LET THE VEHICLE HOT SOAK FOR 5 MINUTES.

→ REMOVE THE SPARK PLUGS KEEPING THEM IN ORDER ACCORDING TO THE CYLINDER. → INSPECT THE SPARK PLUGS FOR WET TIPS OR FOR FUEL FOULING. → ARE ANY OF THE SPARK PLUGS WET WITH FUEL OR FUEL FOULED?

- YES → REPLACE LEAKING INJECTOR(S) AT CORRESPONDING CYLINDER(S).*
- NO → INSPECT THE AIR CLEANER FILTER AND INLET DUCTS FOR RESTRICTION(S). → WHERE THERE ANY RESTRICTIONS?
  - YES → CLEAN RESTRICTED AIR INLET SYSTEM AS NECESSARY.*
  - NO → PERFORM TEST DR-34A.

* – PERFORM VERIFICATION PROCEDURE VER-3

91H13919

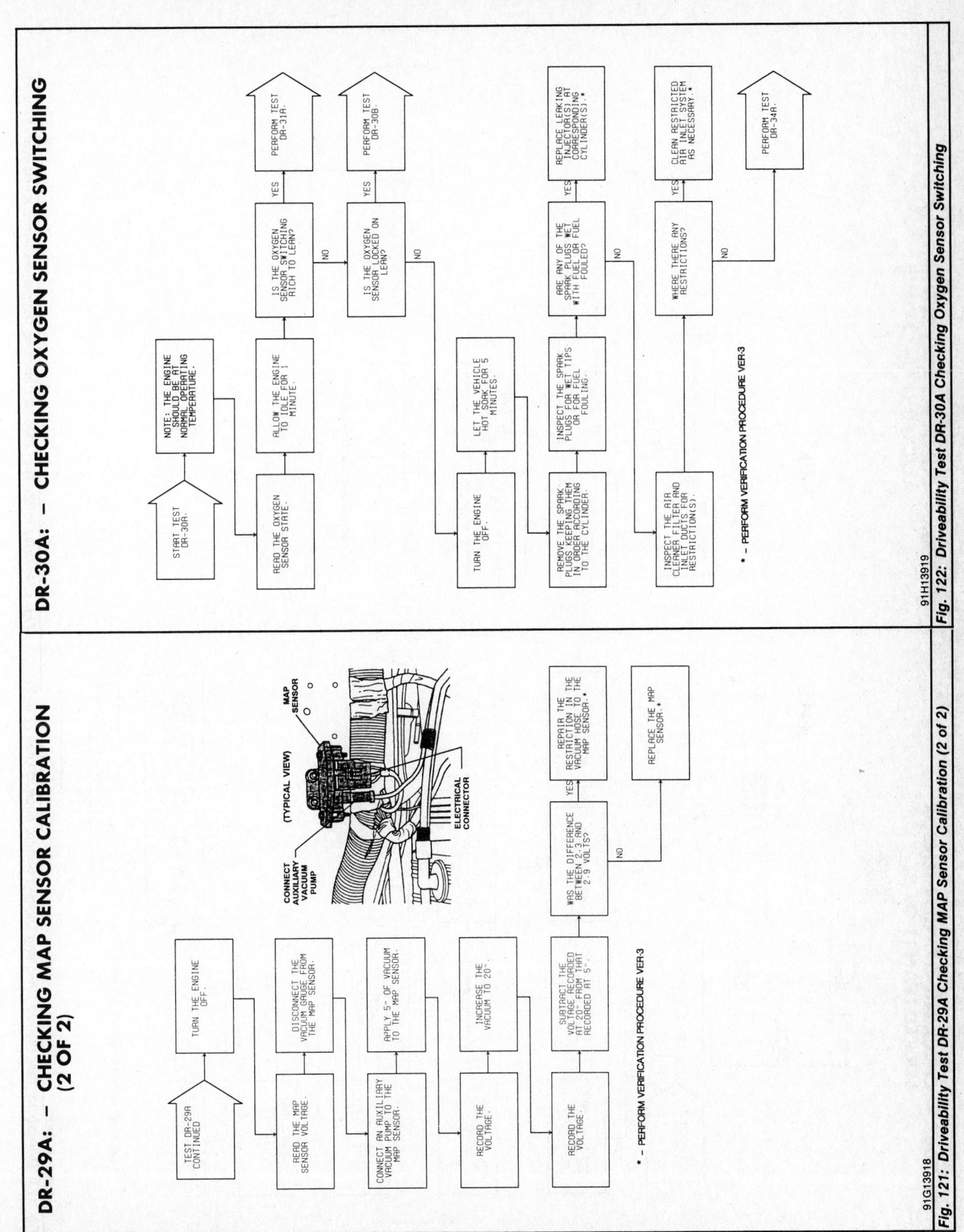

Fig. 122: Driveability Test DR-30A Checking Oxygen Sensor Switching

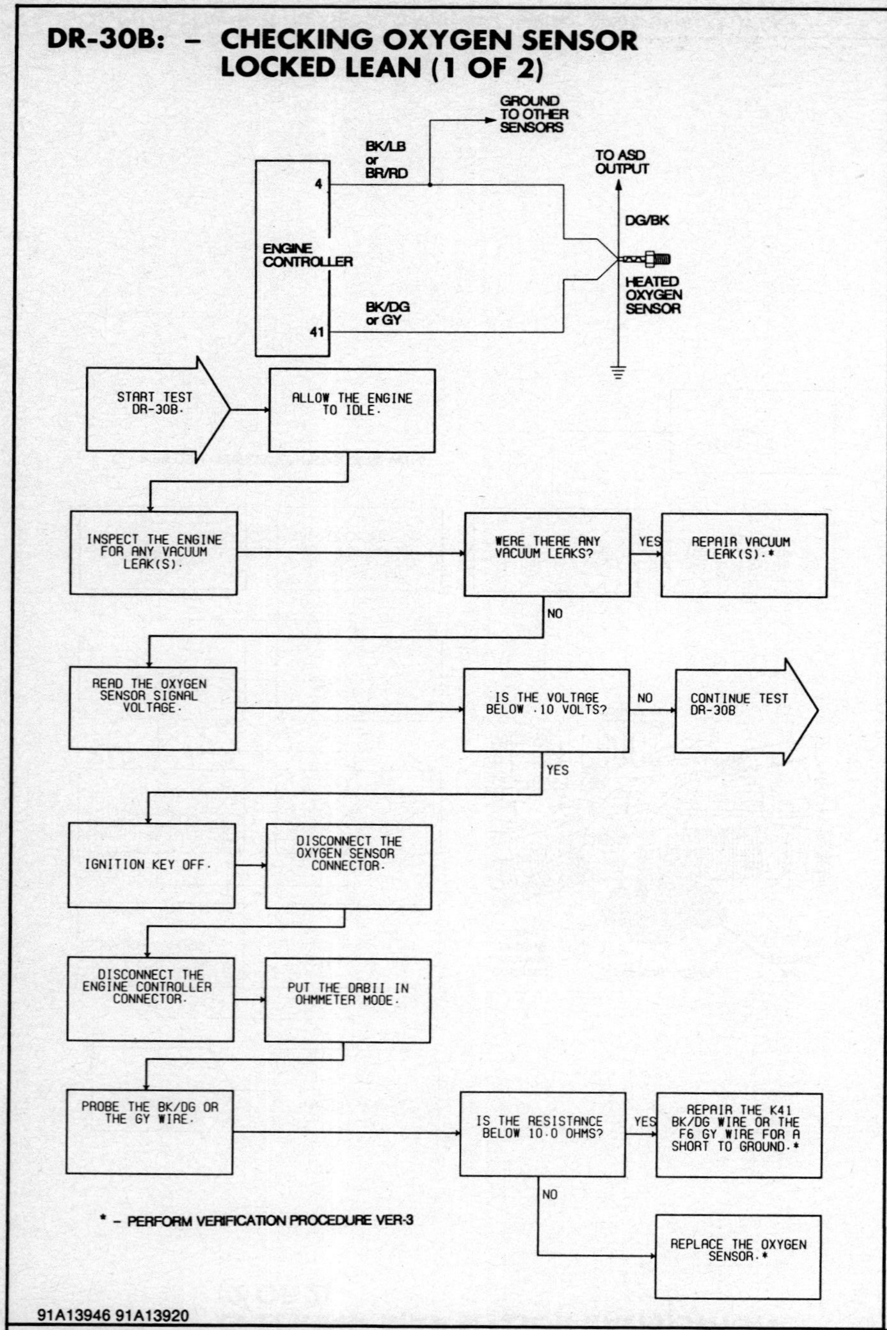
DR-30B: – CHECKING OXYGEN SENSOR LOCKED LEAN (1 OF 2)
GROUND TO OTHER SENSORS
BK/LB or BR/RD
TO ASD OUTPUT
4
DG/BK
ENGINE CONTROLLER
HEATED OXYGEN SENSOR
BK/DG or GY
41
START TEST DR-30B.
ALLOW THE ENGINE TO IDLE.
INSPECT THE ENGINE FOR ANY VACUUM LEAK(S).
WERE THERE ANY VACUUM LEAKS?
YES
REPAIR VACUUM LEAK(S).*
NO
READ THE OXYGEN SENSOR SIGNAL VOLTAGE.
IS THE VOLTAGE BELOW .10 VOLTS?
NO
CONTINUE TEST DR-30B
YES
IGNITION KEY OFF.
DISCONNECT THE OXYGEN SENSOR CONNECTOR.
DISCONNECT THE ENGINE CONTROLLER CONNECTOR.
PUT THE DRBII IN OHMMETER MODE.
PROBE THE BK/DG OR THE GY WIRE.
IS THE RESISTANCE BELOW 10.0 OHMS?
YES
REPAIR THE K41 BK/DG WIRE OR THE F6 GY WIRE FOR A SHORT TO GROUND.*
NO
REPLACE THE OXYGEN SENSOR.*
* – PERFORM VERIFICATION PROCEDURE VER-3
91A13946 91A13920

Fig. 123: Driveability Test DR-30B Checking Oxygen Sensor Locked Lean (1 of 2)

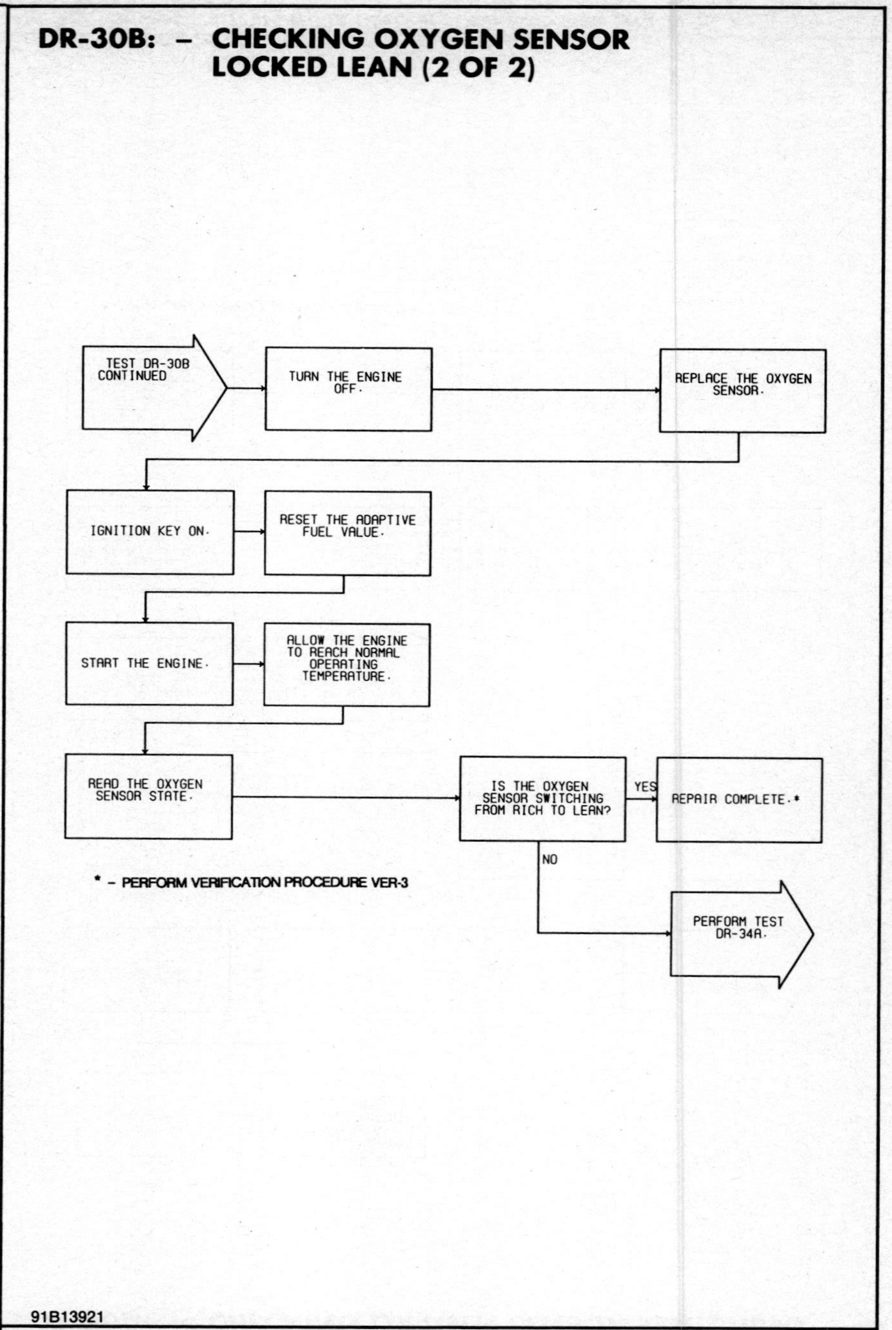
DR-30B: – CHECKING OXYGEN SENSOR LOCKED LEAN (2 OF 2)
TEST DR-30B CONTINUED
TURN THE ENGINE OFF.
REPLACE THE OXYGEN SENSOR.
IGNITION KEY ON.
RESET THE ADAPTIVE FUEL VALUE.
START THE ENGINE.
ALLOW THE ENGINE TO REACH NORMAL OPERATING TEMPERATURE.
READ THE OXYGEN SENSOR STATE.
IS THE OXYGEN SENSOR SWITCHING FROM RICH TO LEAN?
YES
REPAIR COMPLETE.*
NO
PERFORM TEST DR-34A.
* – PERFORM VERIFICATION PROCEDURE VER-3
91B13921

Fig. 124: Driveability Test DR-30B Checking Oxygen Sensor Locked Lean (2 of 2)

DR-31A: – CHECKING IDLE SPEED MOTOR OPERATION (1 OF 2)

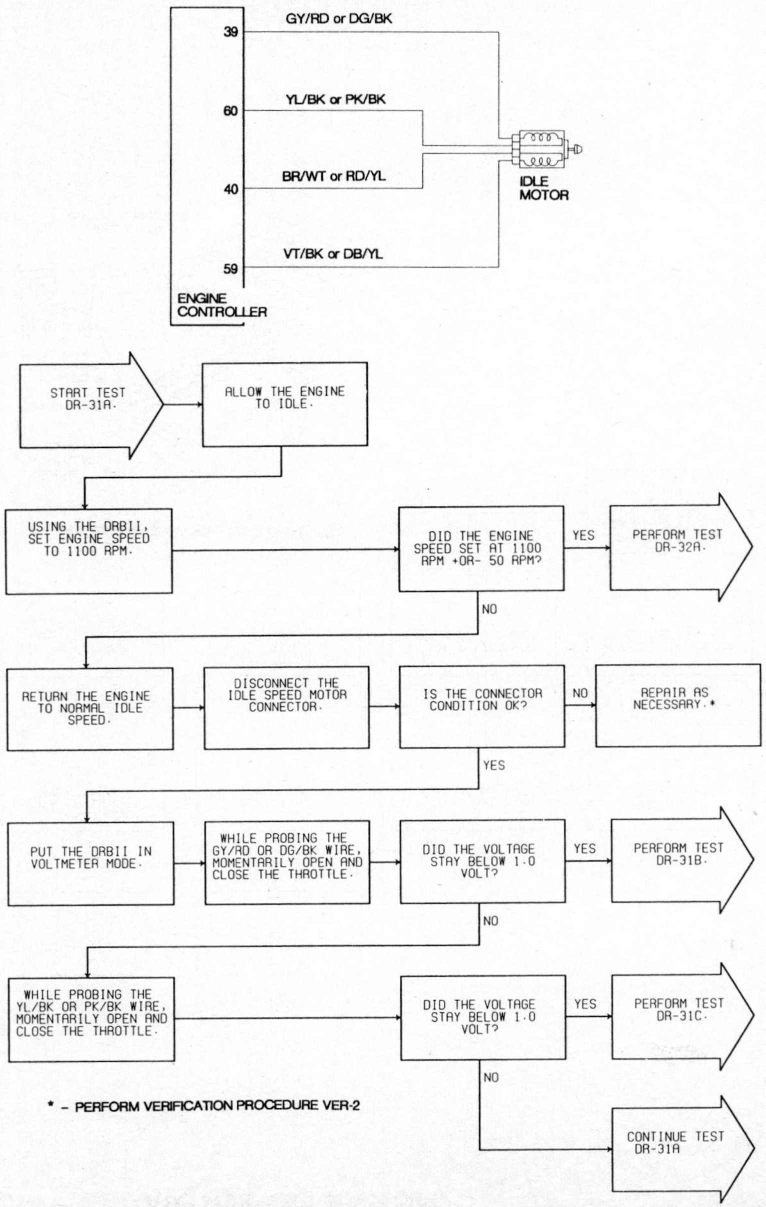
39
60
40
59
GY/RD or DG/BK
YL/BK or PK/BK
BR/WT or RD/YL
VT/BK or DB/YL
ENGINE CONTROLLER
IDLE MOTOR
START TEST DR-31A.
ALLOW THE ENGINE TO IDLE.
USING THE DRBII, SET ENGINE SPEED TO 1100 RPM.
DID THE ENGINE SPEED SET AT 1100 RPM +OR- 50 RPM?
YES
PERFORM TEST DR-32A.
NO
RETURN THE ENGINE TO NORMAL IDLE SPEED.
DISCONNECT THE IDLE SPEED MOTOR CONNECTOR.
IS THE CONNECTOR CONDITION OK?
NO
REPAIR AS NECESSARY.*
YES
PUT THE DRBII IN VOLTMETER MODE.
WHILE PROBING THE GY/RD OR DG/BK WIRE, MOMENTARILY OPEN AND CLOSE THE THROTTLE.
DID THE VOLTAGE STAY BELOW 1.0 VOLT?
YES
PERFORM TEST DR-31B.
NO
WHILE PROBING THE YL/BK OR PK/BK WIRE, MOMENTARILY OPEN AND CLOSE THE THROTTLE.
DID THE VOLTAGE STAY BELOW 1.0 VOLT?
YES
PERFORM TEST DR-31C.
NO
CONTINUE TEST DR-31A
* – PERFORM VERIFICATION PROCEDURE VER-2

91H13943 91C13922

Fig. 125: Driveability Test DR-31A Checking Idle Speed Motor Operation (1 of 2)

DR-31A: – CHECKING IDLE SPEED MOTOR OPERATION (2 OF 2)

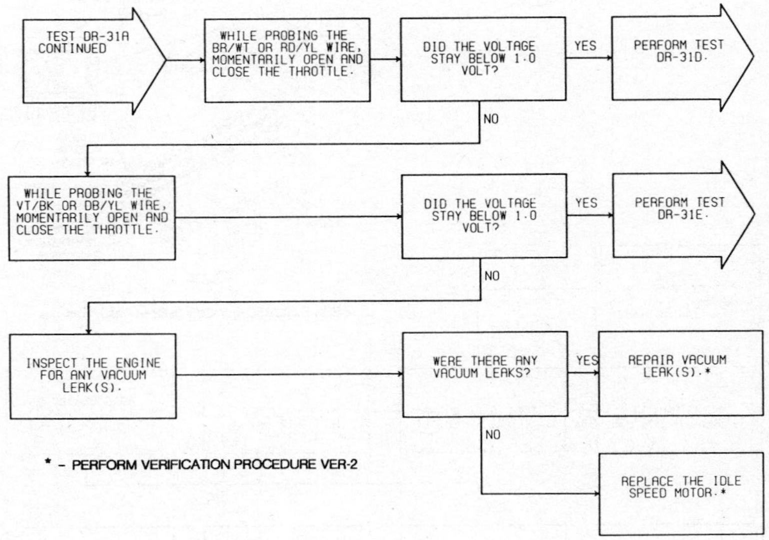
TEST DR-31A CONTINUED
WHILE PROBING THE BR/WT OR RD/YL WIRE, MOMENTARILY OPEN AND CLOSE THE THROTTLE.
DID THE VOLTAGE STAY BELOW 1.0 VOLT?
YES
PERFORM TEST DR-31D.
NO
WHILE PROBING THE VT/BK OR DB/YL WIRE, MOMENTARILY OPEN AND CLOSE THE THROTTLE.
DID THE VOLTAGE STAY BELOW 1.0 VOLT?
YES
PERFORM TEST DR-31E.
NO
INSPECT THE ENGINE FOR ANY VACUUM LEAK(S).
WERE THERE ANY VACUUM LEAKS?
YES
REPAIR VACUUM LEAK(S).*
NO
REPLACE THE IDLE SPEED MOTOR.*
* – PERFORM VERIFICATION PROCEDURE VER-2

91D13923

Fig. 126: Driveability Test DR-31A Checking Idle Speed Motor Operation (2 of 2)

1991 ENGINE PERFORMANCE
Self-Diagnostics (Cont.)

DR-31B: – CHECKING IDLE SPEED MOTOR OPERATION

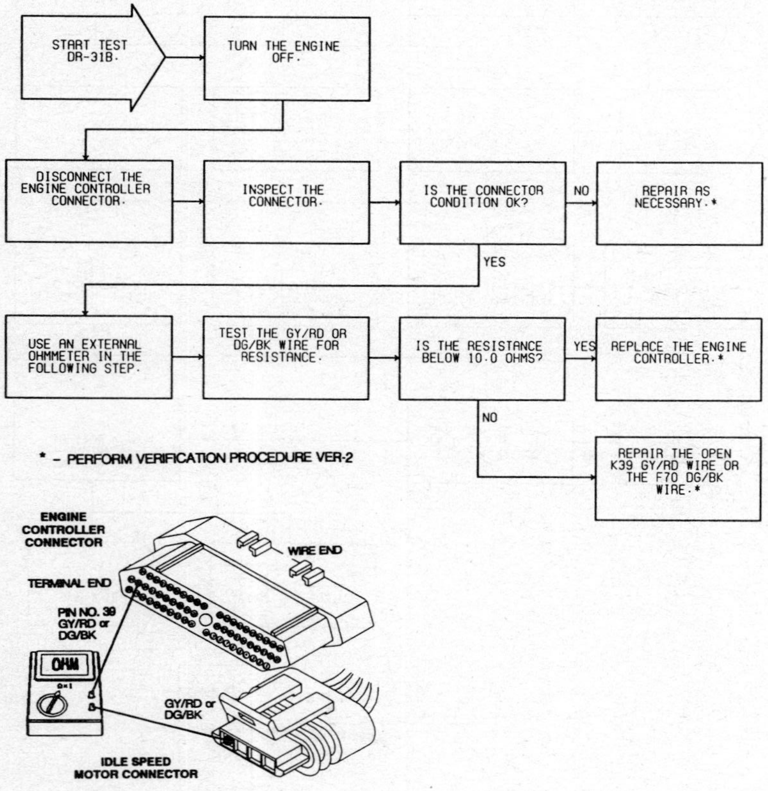
START TEST DR-31B.
TURN THE ENGINE OFF.
DISCONNECT THE ENGINE CONTROLLER CONNECTOR.
INSPECT THE CONNECTOR.
IS THE CONNECTOR CONDITION OK?
NO
REPAIR AS NECESSARY.*
YES
USE AN EXTERNAL OHMMETER IN THE FOLLOWING STEP.
TEST THE GY/RD OR DG/BK WIRE FOR RESISTANCE.
IS THE RESISTANCE BELOW 10.0 OHMS?
YES
REPLACE THE ENGINE CONTROLLER.*
NO
REPAIR THE OPEN K39 GY/RD WIRE OR THE F70 DG/BK WIRE.*
* – PERFORM VERIFICATION PROCEDURE VER-2
ENGINE CONTROLLER CONNECTOR
WIRE END
TERMINAL END
PIN NO. 39 GY/RD or DG/BK
OHM
GY/RD or DG/BK
IDLE SPEED MOTOR CONNECTOR

91E13924

Fig. 127: Driveability Test DR-31B Checking Idle Speed Motor Operation

DR-31C: – CHECKING IDLE SPEED MOTOR OPERATION

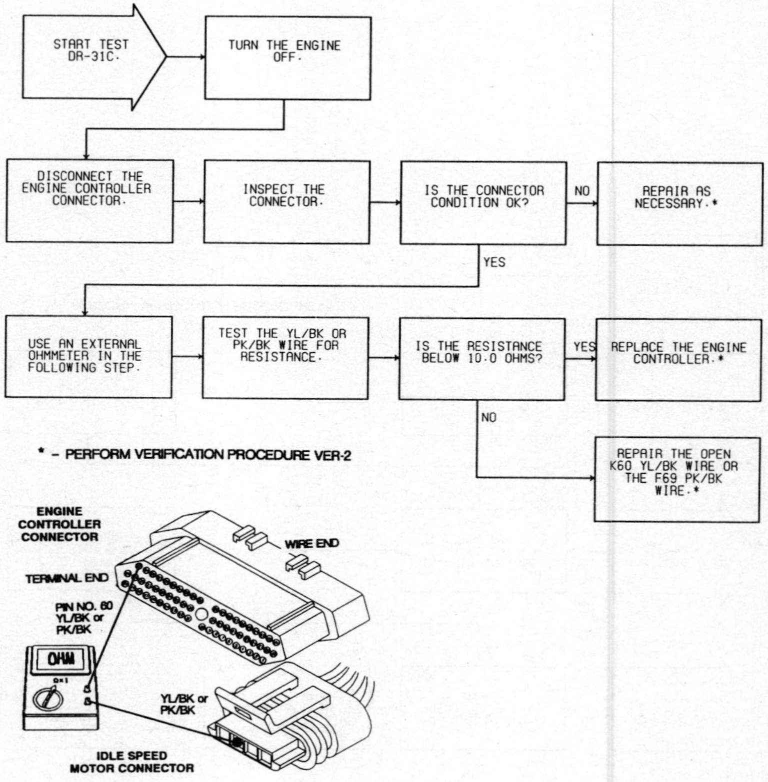
START TEST DR-31C.
TURN THE ENGINE OFF.
DISCONNECT THE ENGINE CONTROLLER CONNECTOR.
INSPECT THE CONNECTOR.
IS THE CONNECTOR CONDITION OK?
NO
REPAIR AS NECESSARY.*
YES
USE AN EXTERNAL OHMMETER IN THE FOLLOWING STEP.
TEST THE YL/BK OR PK/BK WIRE FOR RESISTANCE.
IS THE RESISTANCE BELOW 10.0 OHMS?
YES
REPLACE THE ENGINE CONTROLLER.*
NO
REPAIR THE OPEN K60 YL/BK WIRE OR THE F69 PK/BK WIRE.*
* – PERFORM VERIFICATION PROCEDURE VER-2
ENGINE CONTROLLER CONNECTOR
WIRE END
TERMINAL END
PIN NO. 60 YL/BK or PK/BK
OHM
YL/BK or PK/BK
IDLE SPEED MOTOR CONNECTOR

91F13925

Fig. 128: Driveability Test DR-31C Checking Idle Speed Motor Operation

DR-31D: – CHECKING IDLE SPEED MOTOR OPERATION

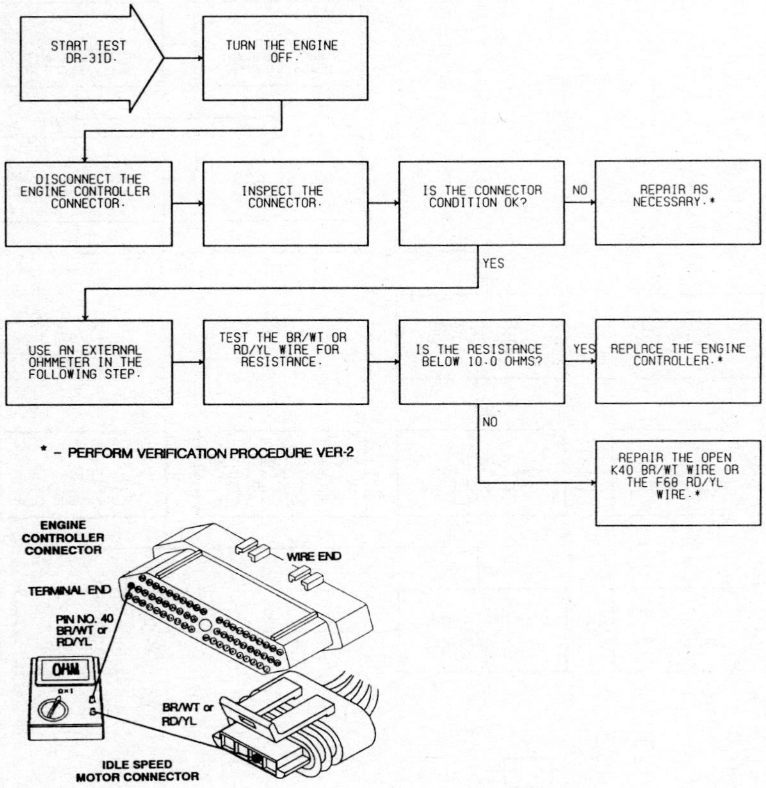
START TEST DR-31D.
TURN THE ENGINE OFF.
DISCONNECT THE ENGINE CONTROLLER CONNECTOR.
INSPECT THE CONNECTOR.
IS THE CONNECTOR CONDITION OK?
NO
REPAIR AS NECESSARY.*
YES
USE AN EXTERNAL OHMMETER IN THE FOLLOWING STEP.
TEST THE BR/WT OR RD/YL WIRE FOR RESISTANCE.
IS THE RESISTANCE BELOW 10.0 OHMS?
YES
REPLACE THE ENGINE CONTROLLER.*
NO
REPAIR THE OPEN K40 BR/WT WIRE OR THE F68 RD/YL WIRE.*
* – PERFORM VERIFICATION PROCEDURE VER-2
ENGINE CONTROLLER CONNECTOR
WIRE END
TERMINAL END
PIN NO. 40 BR/WT or RD/YL
OHM
BR/WT or RD/YL
IDLE SPEED MOTOR CONNECTOR

91G13926

Fig. 129: Driveability Test DR-31D Checking Idle Speed Motor Operation

DR-31E: – CHECKING IDLE SPEED MOTOR OPERATION

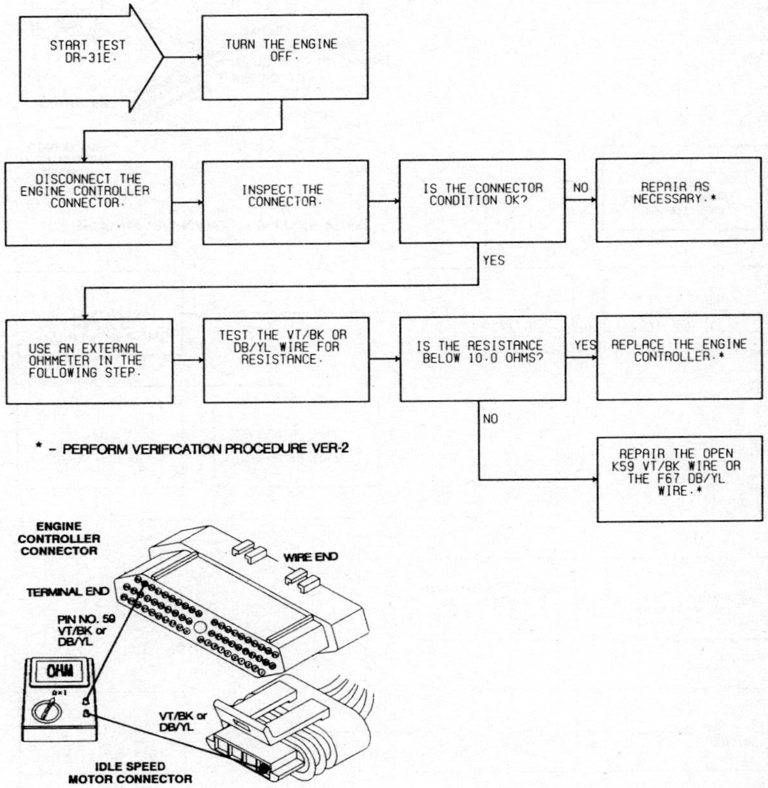
START TEST DR-31E.
TURN THE ENGINE OFF.
DISCONNECT THE ENGINE CONTROLLER CONNECTOR.
INSPECT THE CONNECTOR.
IS THE CONNECTOR CONDITION OK?
NO
REPAIR AS NECESSARY.*
YES
USE AN EXTERNAL OHMMETER IN THE FOLLOWING STEP.
TEST THE VT/BK OR DB/YL WIRE FOR RESISTANCE.
IS THE RESISTANCE BELOW 10.0 OHMS?
YES
REPLACE THE ENGINE CONTROLLER.*
NO
REPAIR THE OPEN K59 VT/BK WIRE OR THE F67 DB/YL WIRE.*
* – PERFORM VERIFICATION PROCEDURE VER-2
ENGINE CONTROLLER CONNECTOR
WIRE END
TERMINAL END
PIN NO. 59 VT/BK or DB/YL
OHM
VT/BK or DB/YL
IDLE SPEED MOTOR CONNECTOR

91H13927

Fig. 130: Driveability Test DR-31E Checking Idle Speed Motor Operation

1991 ENGINE PERFORMANCE
Self-Diagnostics (Cont.)

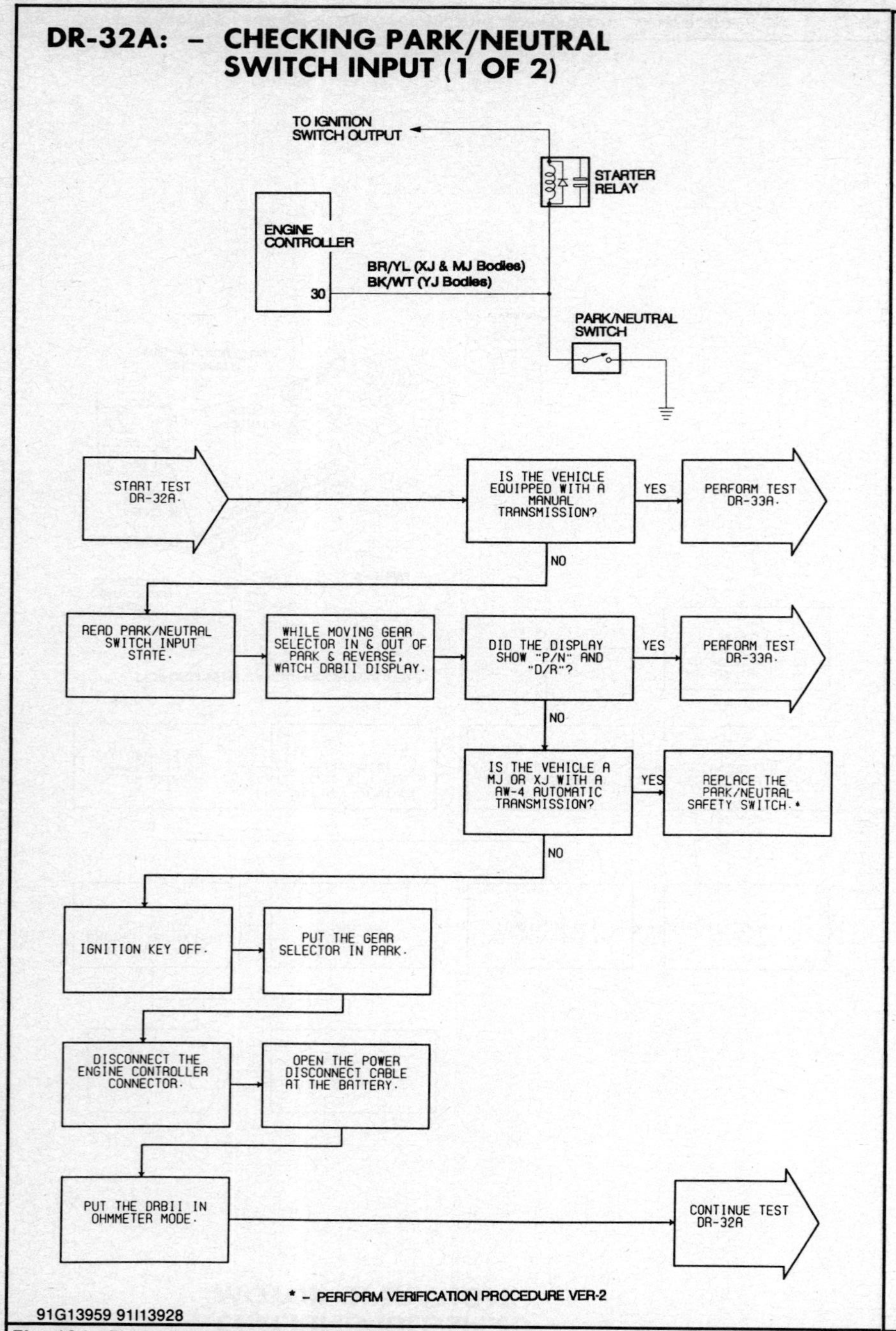
DR-32A: – CHECKING PARK/NEUTRAL SWITCH INPUT (1 OF 2)
TO IGNITION SWITCH OUTPUT
STARTER RELAY
ENGINE CONTROLLER
30
BR/YL (XJ & MJ Bodies)
BK/WT (YJ Bodies)
PARK/NEUTRAL SWITCH
START TEST DR-32A.
IS THE VEHICLE EQUIPPED WITH A MANUAL TRANSMISSION?
YES
PERFORM TEST DR-33A.
NO
READ PARK/NEUTRAL SWITCH INPUT STATE.
WHILE MOVING GEAR SELECTOR IN & OUT OF PARK & REVERSE, WATCH DRBII DISPLAY.
DID THE DISPLAY SHOW "P/N" AND "D/R"?
YES
PERFORM TEST DR-33A.
NO
IS THE VEHICLE A MJ OR XJ WITH A AW-4 AUTOMATIC TRANSMISSION?
YES
REPLACE THE PARK/NEUTRAL SAFETY SWITCH.*
NO
IGNITION KEY OFF.
PUT THE GEAR SELECTOR IN PARK.
DISCONNECT THE ENGINE CONTROLLER CONNECTOR.
OPEN THE POWER DISCONNECT CABLE AT THE BATTERY.
PUT THE DRBII IN OHMMETER MODE.
CONTINUE TEST DR-32A
* – PERFORM VERIFICATION PROCEDURE VER-2
91G13959 91I13928

Fig. 131: Driveability Test DR-32A Checking Park/Neutral Switch Input (1 of 2)

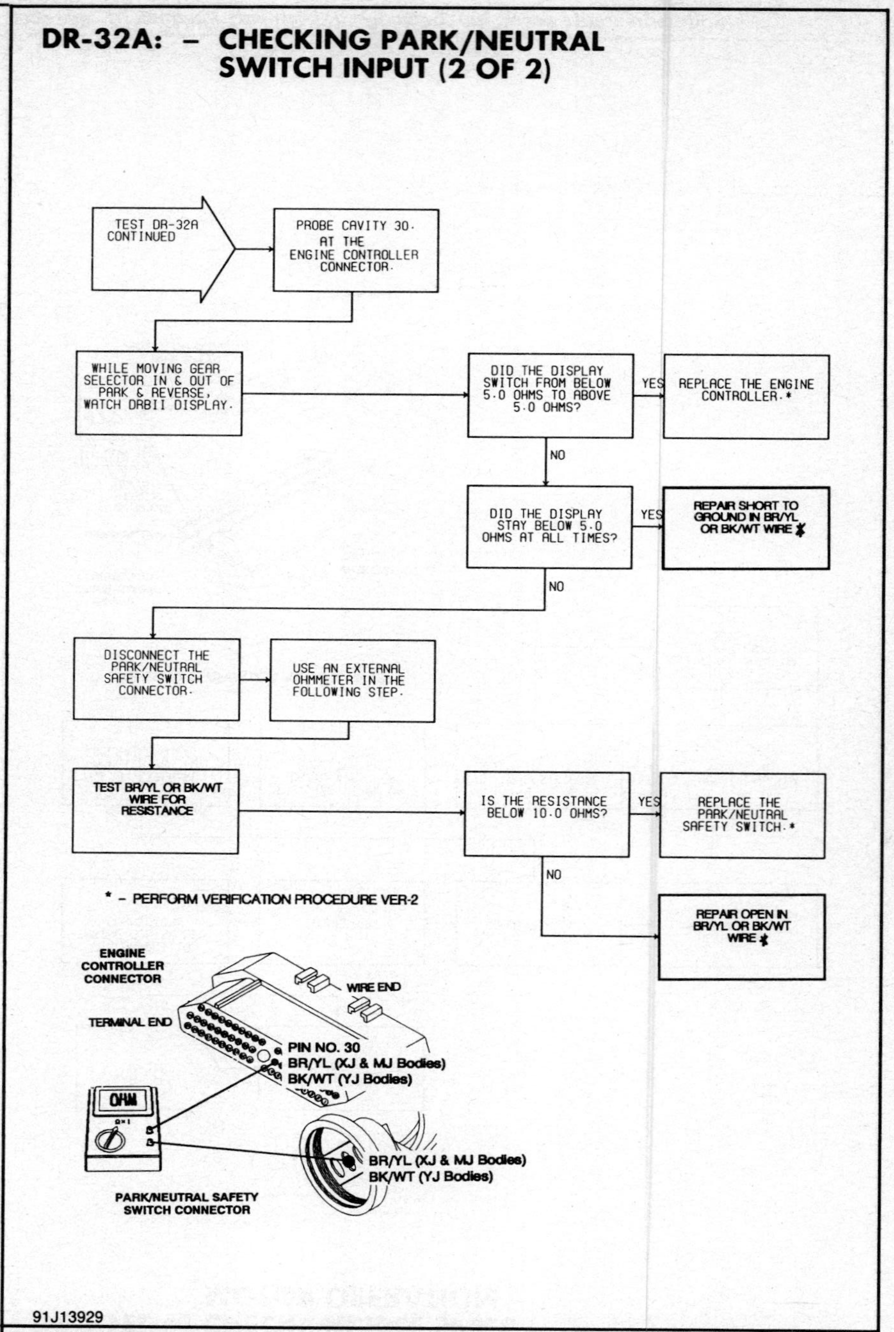
DR-32A: – CHECKING PARK/NEUTRAL SWITCH INPUT (2 OF 2)
TEST DR-32A CONTINUED
PROBE CAVITY 30. AT THE ENGINE CONTROLLER CONNECTOR.
WHILE MOVING GEAR SELECTOR IN & OUT OF PARK & REVERSE, WATCH DRBII DISPLAY.
DID THE DISPLAY SWITCH FROM BELOW 5.0 OHMS TO ABOVE 5.0 OHMS?
YES
REPLACE THE ENGINE CONTROLLER.*
NO
DID THE DISPLAY STAY BELOW 5.0 OHMS AT ALL TIMES?
YES
REPAIR SHORT TO GROUND IN BR/YL OR BK/WT WIRE ✱
NO
DISCONNECT THE PARK/NEUTRAL SAFETY SWITCH CONNECTOR.
USE AN EXTERNAL OHMMETER IN THE FOLLOWING STEP.
TEST BR/YL OR BK/WT WIRE FOR RESISTANCE
IS THE RESISTANCE BELOW 10.0 OHMS?
YES
REPLACE THE PARK/NEUTRAL SAFETY SWITCH.*
NO
REPAIR OPEN IN BR/YL OR BK/WT WIRE ✱
* – PERFORM VERIFICATION PROCEDURE VER-2
ENGINE CONTROLLER CONNECTOR
WIRE END
TERMINAL END
PIN NO. 30
BR/YL (XJ & MJ Bodies)
BK/WT (YJ Bodies)
OHM
BR/YL (XJ & MJ Bodies)
BK/WT (YJ Bodies)
PARK/NEUTRAL SAFETY SWITCH CONNECTOR
91J13929

Fig. 132: Driveability Test DR-32A Checking Park/Neutral Switch Input (2 of 2)

DR-33A: – CHECKING ENGINE CONTROLLER GROUNDS & POWER CIRCUITS (1 OF 2)

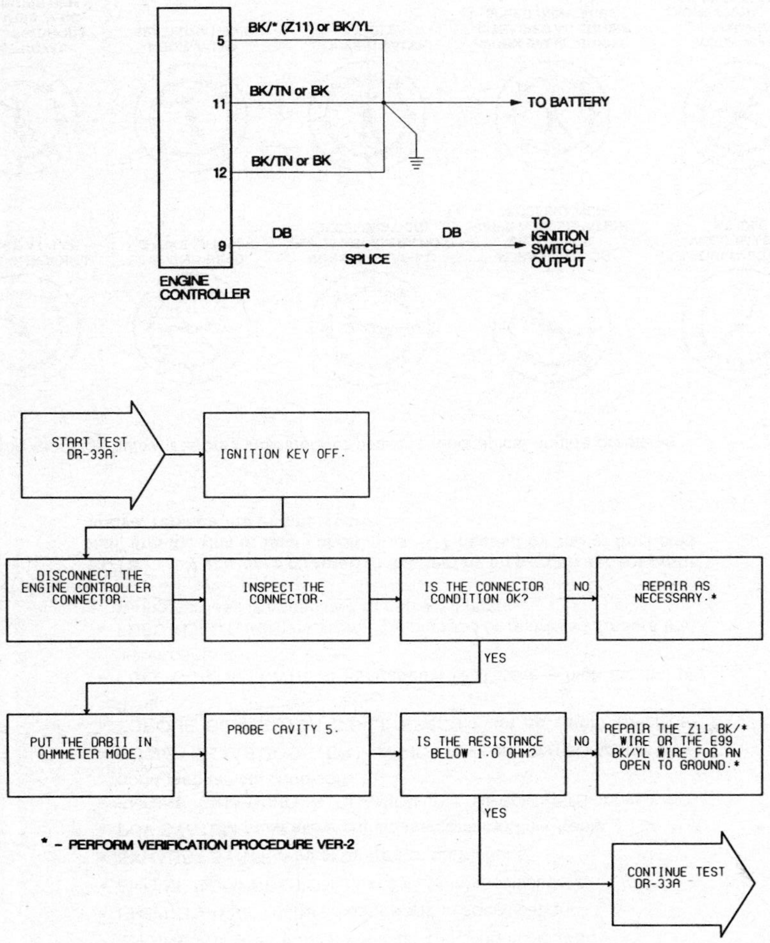
BK/* (Z11) or BK/YL
5
BK/TN or BK
11
TO BATTERY
BK/TN or BK
12
DB
9
SPLICE
DB
TO IGNITION SWITCH OUTPUT
ENGINE CONTROLLER
START TEST DR-33A.
IGNITION KEY OFF.
DISCONNECT THE ENGINE CONTROLLER CONNECTOR.
INSPECT THE CONNECTOR.
IS THE CONNECTOR CONDITION OK?
NO
REPAIR AS NECESSARY.*
YES
PUT THE DRBII IN OHMMETER MODE.
PROBE CAVITY 5.
IS THE RESISTANCE BELOW 1.0 OHM?
NO
REPAIR THE Z11 BK/* WIRE OR THE E99 BK/YL WIRE FOR AN OPEN TO GROUND.*
YES
CONTINUE TEST DR-33A
* – PERFORM VERIFICATION PROCEDURE VER-2

91J13960 91C13930

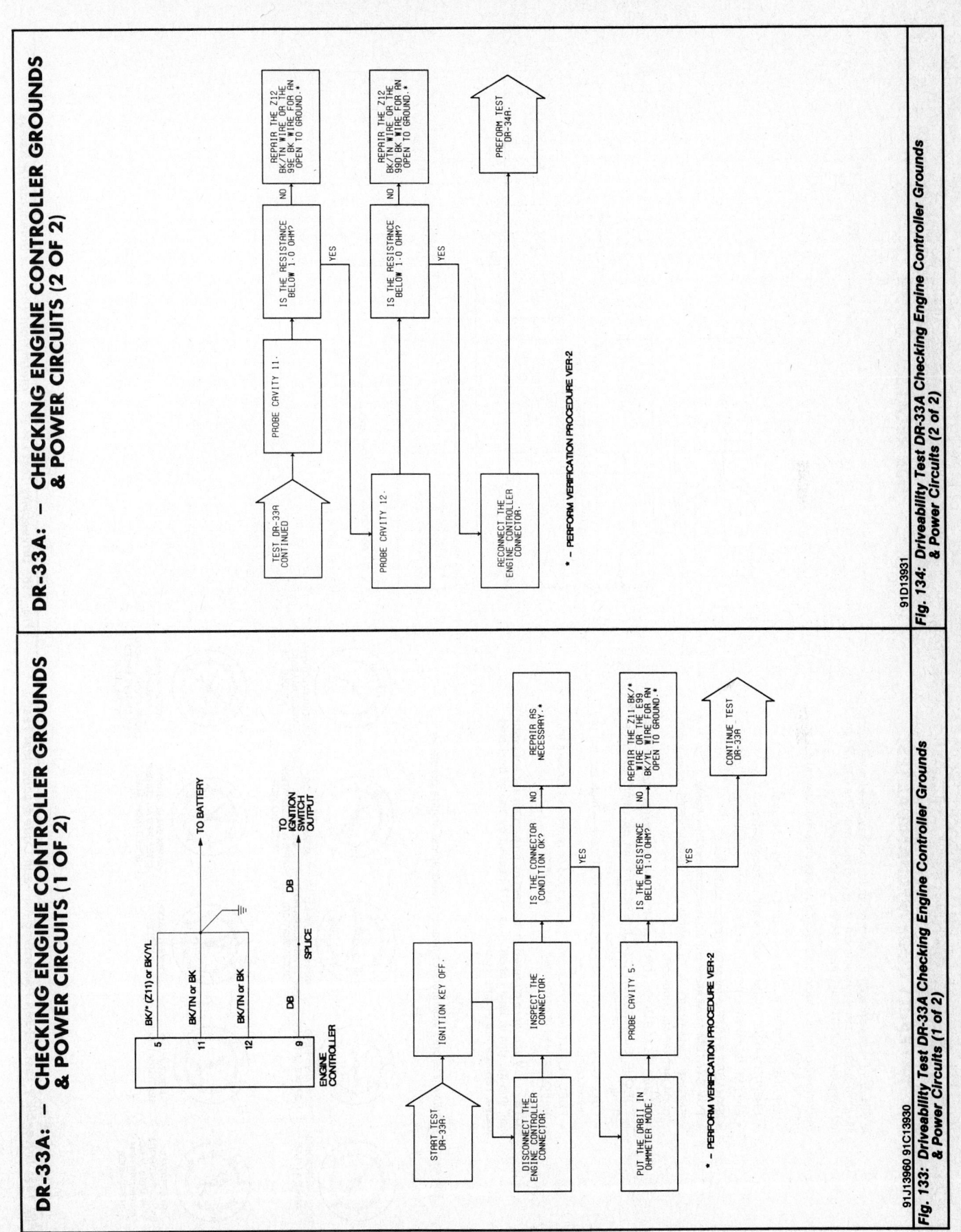

Fig. 133: Driveability Test DR-33A Checking Engine Controller Grounds & Power Circuits (1 of 2)

DR-33A: – CHECKING ENGINE CONTROLLER GROUNDS & POWER CIRCUITS (2 OF 2)

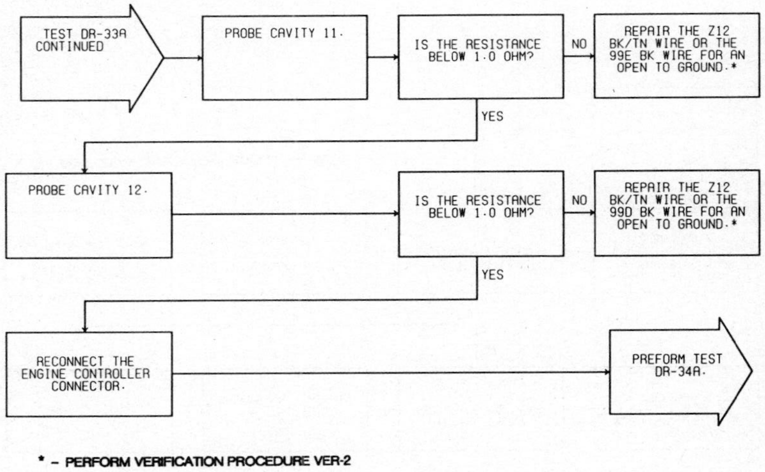
TEST DR-33A CONTINUED
PROBE CAVITY 11.
IS THE RESISTANCE BELOW 1.0 OHM?
NO
REPAIR THE Z12 BK/TN WIRE OR THE 99E BK WIRE FOR AN OPEN TO GROUND.*
YES
PROBE CAVITY 12.
IS THE RESISTANCE BELOW 1.0 OHM?
NO
REPAIR THE Z12 BK/TN WIRE OR THE 99D BK WIRE FOR AN OPEN TO GROUND.*
YES
RECONNECT THE ENGINE CONTROLLER CONNECTOR.
PREFORM TEST DR-34A.
* – PERFORM VERIFICATION PROCEDURE VER-2

91D13931

Fig. 134: Driveability Test DR-33A Checking Engine Controller Grounds & Power Circuits (2 of 2)

DR-34A: – PERFORMING NO FAULT CODE MECHANICAL TEST

At this point in the driveability test procedure, you have determined that all of the engine control systems are operating properly. The engine control systems are NOT the cause of the driveability problem.

The following items should be checked as possible mechanical causes of the problem:

- ENGINE VACUUM must be at least 13 in. Hg in Neutral.
- ENGINE VALVE TIMING must be within specification.
- ENGINE COMPRESSION must be within specification.
- EXHAUST SYSTEM must be free of restrictions.
- PCV SYSTEM must allow crankcase gases to flow freely.
- ENGINE CAMSHAFT & CRANKSHAFT SPROCKETS must be in good mechanical condition.
- POWER BRAKE BOOSTER must NOT have an internal vacuum leak.
- TORQUE CONVERTER STALL SPEED must be within specifications.
- FUEL CONTAMINATION: Fuel should NOT have a high alcohol or water content.
- FUEL INJECTOR(S) must NOT be plugged or restricted. Ensure that wiring harness is connected to correct injector.

NOTE: If you were directed to this test by an oxygen sensor problem, and the rich or lean condition is NOT caused by one of the items above, replace the engine controller.

* The readings below are only indicators of possible mechanical engine problems.

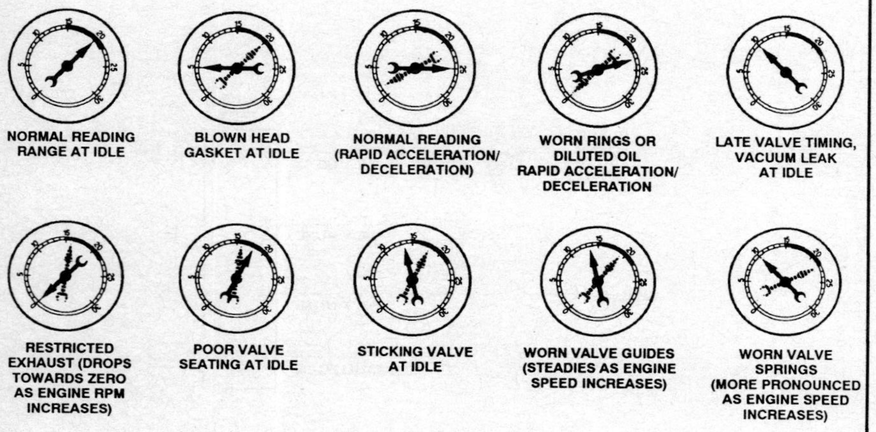
NORMAL READING RANGE AT IDLE
BLOWN HEAD GASKET AT IDLE
NORMAL READING (RAPID ACCELERATION/ DECELERATION)
WORN RINGS OR DILUTED OIL RAPID ACCELERATION/ DECELERATION
LATE VALVE TIMING, VACUUM LEAK AT IDLE
RESTRICTED EXHAUST (DROPS TOWARDS ZERO AS ENGINE RPM INCREASES)
POOR VALVE SEATING AT IDLE
STICKING VALVE AT IDLE
WORN VALVE GUIDES (STEADIES AS ENGINE SPEED INCREASES)
WORN VALVE SPRINGS (MORE PRONOUNCED AS ENGINE SPEED INCREASES)
91E13932 91F13933

Fig. 135: Driveability Test DR-34A Performing No Fault Code Mechanical Test

DR-35A: – INTERMITTENT TEST FOR SOLENOIDS OR RELAYS

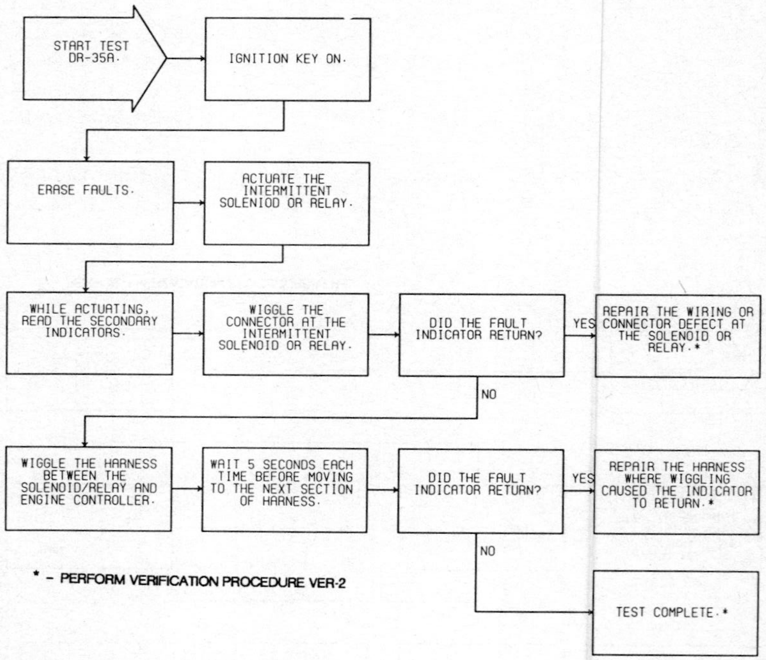
START TEST DR-35A.
IGNITION KEY ON.
ERASE FAULTS.
ACTUATE THE INTERMITTENT SOLENIOD OR RELAY.
WHILE ACTUATING, READ THE SECONDARY INDICATORS.
WIGGLE THE CONNECTOR AT THE INTERMITTENT SOLENOID OR RELAY.
DID THE FAULT INDICATOR RETURN?
YES
REPAIR THE WIRING OR CONNECTOR DEFECT AT THE SOLENOID OR RELAY. *
NO
WIGGLE THE HARNESS BETWEEN THE SOLENOID/RELAY AND ENGINE CONTROLLER.
WAIT 5 SECONDS EACH TIME BEFORE MOVING TO THE NEXT SECTION OF HARNESS.
DID THE FAULT INDICATOR RETURN?
YES
REPAIR THE HARNESS WHERE WIGGLING CAUSED THE INDICATOR TO RETURN. *
NO
TEST COMPLETE. *

* – PERFORM VERIFICATION PROCEDURE VER-2

91B13962

Fig. 136: Driveability Test DR-35A Intermittent Test For Solenoids Or Relays

DR-36A: – INTERMITTENT TEST FOR SENSORS

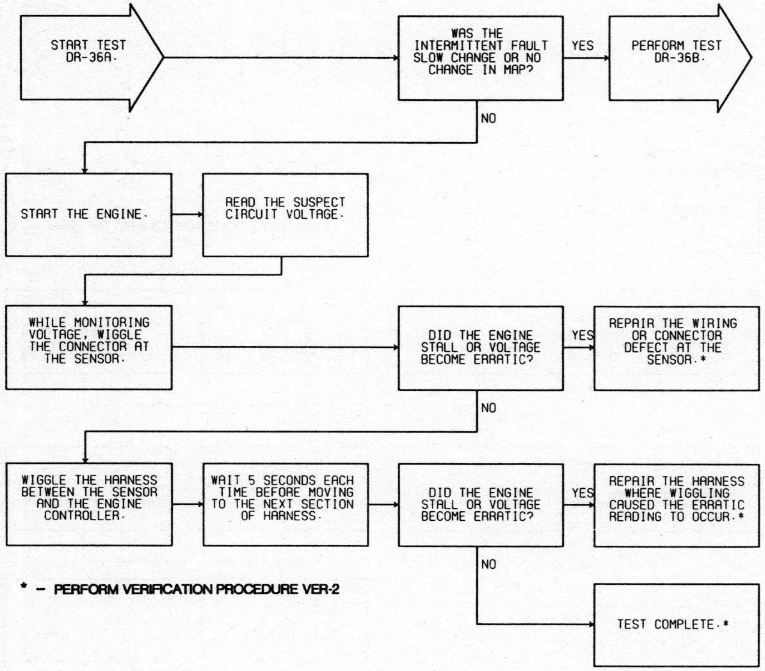
START TEST DR-36A.
WAS THE INTERMITTENT FAULT SLOW CHANGE OR NO CHANGE IN MAP?
YES
PERFORM TEST DR-36B.
NO
START THE ENGINE.
READ THE SUSPECT CIRCUIT VOLTAGE.
WHILE MONITORING VOLTAGE, WIGGLE THE CONNECTOR AT THE SENSOR.
DID THE ENGINE STALL OR VOLTAGE BECOME ERRATIC?
YES
REPAIR THE WIRING OR CONNECTOR DEFECT AT THE SENSOR.*
NO
WIGGLE THE HARNESS BETWEEN THE SENSOR AND THE ENGINE CONTROLLER.
WAIT 5 SECONDS EACH TIME BEFORE MOVING TO THE NEXT SECTION OF HARNESS.
DID THE ENGINE STALL OR VOLTAGE BECOME ERRATIC?
YES
REPAIR THE HARNESS WHERE WIGGLING CAUSED THE ERRATIC READING TO OCCUR.*
NO
TEST COMPLETE.*

* – PERFORM VERIFICATION PROCEDURE VER-2

91C13963

Fig. 137: Driveability Test DR-36A Intermittent Test For Sensors

DR-36B: – INTERMITTENT TEST FOR MAP SENSOR SIGNAL CHANGE

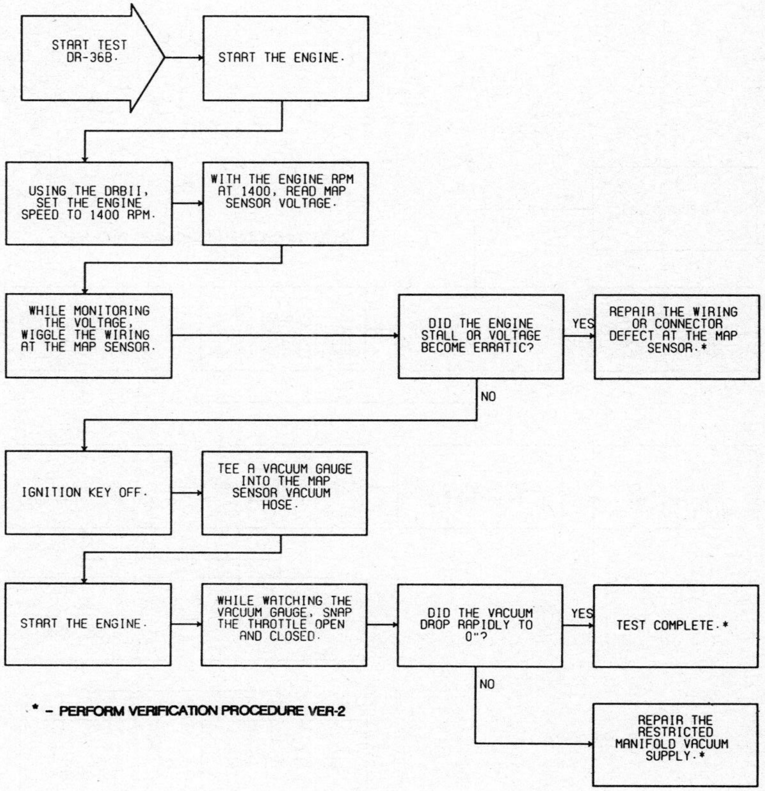
START TEST DR-36B.
START THE ENGINE.
USING THE DRBII, SET THE ENGINE SPEED TO 1400 RPM.
WITH THE ENGINE RPM AT 1400, READ MAP SENSOR VOLTAGE.
WHILE MONITORING THE VOLTAGE, WIGGLE THE WIRING AT THE MAP SENSOR.
DID THE ENGINE STALL OR VOLTAGE BECOME ERRATIC?
YES
REPAIR THE WIRING OR CONNECTOR DEFECT AT THE MAP SENSOR.*
NO
IGNITION KEY OFF.
TEE A VACUUM GAUGE INTO THE MAP SENSOR VACUUM HOSE.
START THE ENGINE.
WHILE WATCHING THE VACUUM GAUGE, SNAP THE THROTTLE OPEN AND CLOSED.
DID THE VACUUM DROP RAPIDLY TO 0"?
YES
TEST COMPLETE.*
NO
REPAIR THE RESTRICTED MANIFOLD VACUUM SUPPLY.*

* – PERFORM VERIFICATION PROCEDURE VER-2

91D13964

Fig. 138: Driveability Test DR-36B Intermittent Test For Map Sensor Signal Change

DR-37A: – INTERMITTENT TEST FOR AUTOMATIC IDLE SPEED MOTOR

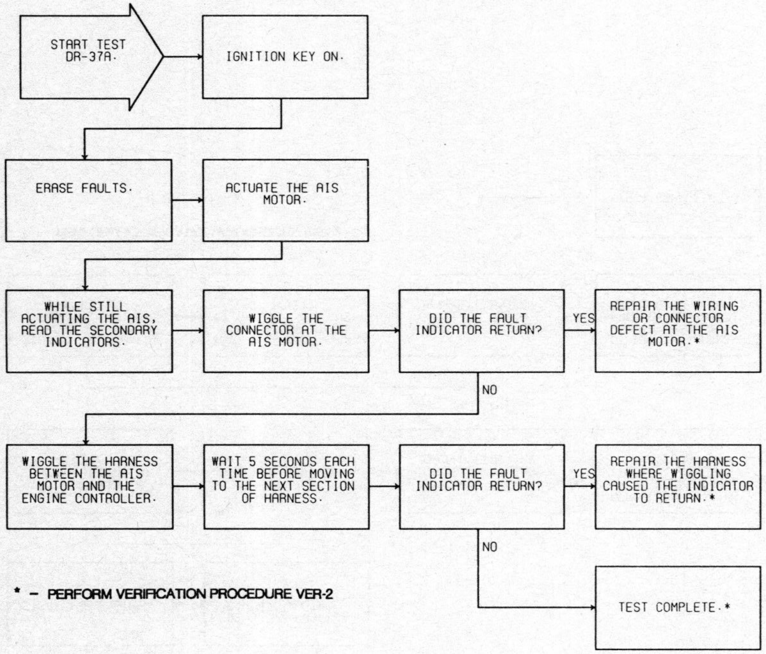
START TEST DR-37A.
IGNITION KEY ON.
ERASE FAULTS.
ACTUATE THE AIS MOTOR.
WHILE STILL ACTUATING THE AIS, READ THE SECONDARY INDICATORS.
WIGGLE THE CONNECTOR AT THE AIS MOTOR.
DID THE FAULT INDICATOR RETURN?
YES
REPAIR THE WIRING OR CONNECTOR DEFECT AT THE AIS MOTOR.*
NO
WIGGLE THE HARNESS BETWEEN THE AIS MOTOR AND THE ENGINE CONTROLLER.
WAIT 5 SECONDS EACH TIME BEFORE MOVING TO THE NEXT SECTION OF HARNESS.
DID THE FAULT INDICATOR RETURN?
YES
REPAIR THE HARNESS WHERE WIGGLING CAUSED THE INDICATOR TO RETURN.*
NO
TEST COMPLETE.*

* – PERFORM VERIFICATION PROCEDURE VER-2

91E13965

Fig. 139: Driveability Test DR-37A Intermittent Test For Automatic Idle Speed Motor

DR-38A: – INTERMITTENT TEST FOR FUEL INJECTORS

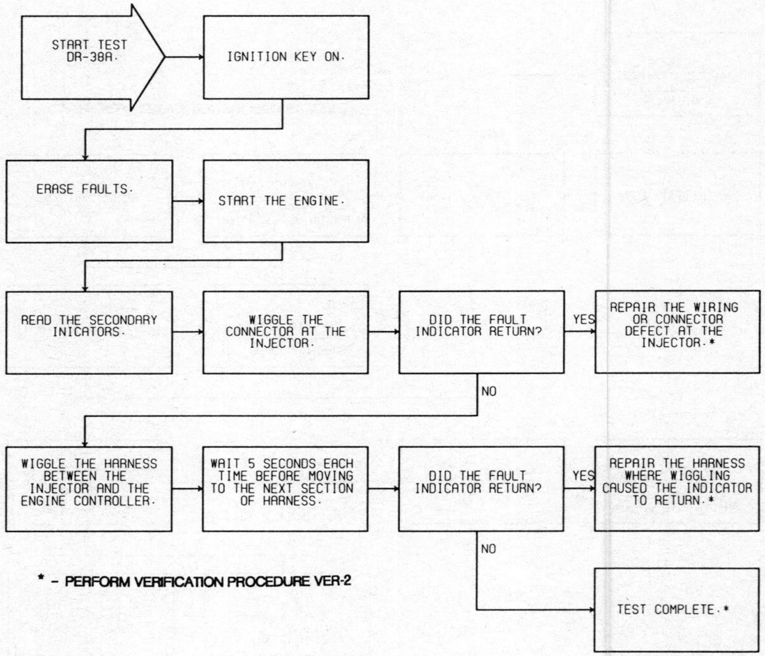
START TEST DR-38A.
IGNITION KEY ON.
ERASE FAULTS.
START THE ENGINE.
READ THE SECONDARY INICATORS.
WIGGLE THE CONNECTOR AT THE INJECTOR.
DID THE FAULT INDICATOR RETURN?
YES
REPAIR THE WIRING OR CONNECTOR DEFECT AT THE INJECTOR.*
NO
WIGGLE THE HARNESS BETWEEN THE INJECTOR AND THE ENGINE CONTROLLER.
WAIT 5 SECONDS EACH TIME BEFORE MOVING TO THE NEXT SECTION OF HARNESS.
DID THE FAULT INDICATOR RETURN?
YES
REPAIR THE HARNESS WHERE WIGGLING CAUSED THE INDICATOR TO RETURN.*
NO
TEST COMPLETE.*

* – PERFORM VERIFICATION PROCEDURE VER-2

91F13966

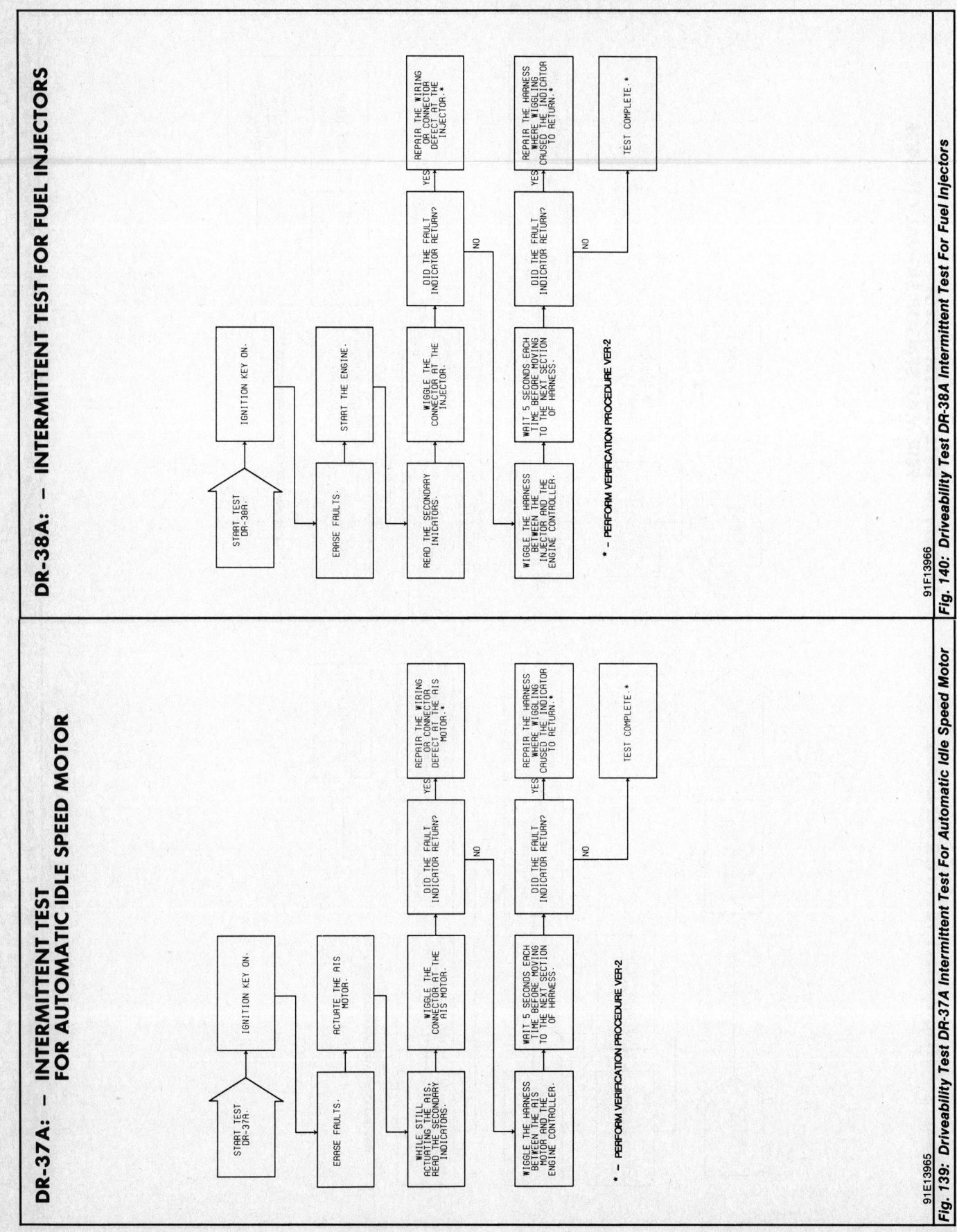

Fig. 140: Driveability Test DR-38A Intermittent Test For Fuel Injectors

VER-1: – VERIFICATION PROCEDURE VER-1

Inspect vehicle to ensure that all components are connected. Reassemble and reconnect components as necessary. Attempt to start engine. If engine does not start, perform NO START TEST NS-1A: CHECKING FOR FAULT MESSAGES & SPARK.

If engine starts and the engine controller has been replaced, perform the following steps.

1) If vehicle is equipped with a factory theft alarm system, start vehicle at least 20 TIMES so that the theft alarm system may be activated when desired.

2) Write (transfer) EMR mileage into new engine controller. See EMISSION MAINTENANCE REMINDER (EMR) MILEAGE TRANSFER. INTRODUCTION.

3) The no start condition has been corrected. The repair procedure is now complete.

If engine starts and the engine controller has NOT been replaced, perform the following steps:

1) Connect DRB-II to engine diagnostic connector and erase faults.

2) The no start condition has been corrected and the fault messages have been erased. The repair procedure is now complete.

Fig. 141: Verification Procedure VER-1

VER-2: – VERIFICATION PROCEDURE VER-2

NOTE: If VERIFICATION PROCEDURE VER-3 was performed previously, perform VERIFICATION PROCEDURE VER-3 once again.

Inspect vehicle to ensure that all components are connected. Reassemble and reconnect components as necessary. If there is another fault that has not been dealt with, return to DRIVEABILITY TEST DR-1A: CHECKING SYSTEM FOR FAULTS and perform the specified procedure for that fault.

If engine controller has been changed, perform the following steps:

1) If vehicle is equipped with a factory theft alarm system, start vehicle at least 20 TIMES so that the theft alarm system may be activated when desired.

2) Write (transfer) EMR mileage into new engine controller. See EMISSION MAINTENANCE REMINDER (EMR) MILEAGE TRANSFER. INTRODUCTION.

3) Connect DRB-II to engine diagnostic connector and erase faults. To ensure that no other faults remain, perform the following steps:

4) Start engine and allow it to reach normal operating temperature. Manually run engine at 2000 RPM of at least 10 seconds and allow engine to return to idle.

5) If vehicle is equipped with an automatic transmission, step on brake pedal and shift through all gears. Return shift lever to PARK position. If vehicle is equipped with air conditioning, place A/C-heater blower fan on low speed and turn A/C system on.

6) Turn ignition off. Restart engine and allow it to idle for at least 2 MINUTES. Turn ignition off. Connect DRB-II to engine diagnostic connector and check for faults. If there are no faults, the repair is now complete.

7) If the repaired fault has reset, the repair procedure is incomplete. Check for technical service bulletins that relate to this driveability problem and return to DRIVEABILITY TEST DR-1A: CHECKING SYSTEM FOR FAULTS if necessary.

8) If there is another fault that has not been dealt with, return to DRIVEABILITY TEST DR-1A: CHECKING SYSTEM FOR FAULTS and perform the specified procedure for that fault.

Fig. 142: Verification Procedure VER-2

1991 ENGINE PERFORMANCE
Self-Diagnostics (Cont.)

VER-3: – VERIFICATION PROCEDURE VER-3

Inspect vehicle to ensure that all components are connected. Reassemble and reconnect components as necessary. If there is another fault that has not been dealt with, return to DRIVEABILITY TEST DR-1A: CHECKING SYSTEM FOR FAULTS and perform the specified procedure for that fault.

If engine controller has been changed, perform the following steps:

1) If vehicle is equipped with a factory theft alarm system, start vehicle at least 20 TIMES so that the theft alarm system may be activated when desired.

2) Write (transfer) EMR mileage into new engine controller. See EMISSION MAINTENANCE REMINDER (EMR) MILEAGE TRANSFER. INTRODUCTION.

3) Connect DRB-II to engine diagnostic connector and erase faults. Disconnect DRB-II from vehicle. To ensure that no other faults remain, perform the following steps:

4) If vehicle is equipped with air conditioning, place A/C-heater blower fan on low speed and turn A/C system on. Road test vehicle for at least 5 MINUTES and at some point attain a speed of at least 40 MPH, ensuring that transmission shifts through all gears. Upon completion of road test, turn ignition off.

5) Restart engine and allow it to idle for at least 2 MINUTES. Turn ignition off. Connect DRB-II to engine diagnostic connector and check for faults. If there are no faults, the repair is now complete.

6) If the repaired fault has reset, the repair procedure is incomplete. Check for technical service bulletins that relate to this driveability problem and return to DRIVEABILITY TEST DR-1A: CHECKING SYSTEM FOR FAULTS if necessary.

7) If there is another fault that has not been dealt with, return to DRIVEABILITY TEST DR-1A: CHECKING SYSTEM FOR FAULTS and perform the specified procedure for that fault.

Fig. 143: Verification Procedure VER-3

1991 ENGINE PERFORMANCE
Trouble Shooting - No Codes

Cherokee, Comanche
Grand Wagoneer, Wrangler

INTRODUCTION

Before diagnosing symptoms or intermittent faults, perform steps in BASIC DIAGNOSTIC PROCEDURES and SELF-DIAGNOSTICS articles. Use this article to diagnose driveability problems existing when a hard fault code is not present or vehicle is not equipped with a self-diagnostic system.

NOTE: Some manufacturer driveability problems may have been corrected by manufacturer with a revised computer calibration chip or computer control unit. Check with manufacturer for latest chip or computer application.

Symptom checks can direct the technician to malfunctioning component(s) for further diagnosis. A symptom should lead to a specific component, system test or an adjustment.

Use intermittent test procedures to locate driveability problems that do not occur when the vehicle is being tested. These test procedures should also be used if a soft (intermittent) trouble code was present, but no problem was found during self-diagnostic testing.

NOTE: For specific testing procedures, see SYSTEM & COMPONENT TESTING article. For specifications, see ON-VEHICLE ADJUSTMENTS or SERVICE & ADJUSTMENT SPECIFICATIONS article.

SYMPTOMS

SYMPTOM DIAGNOSIS

Symptom checks cannot be used properly unless problem occurs while vehicle is being tested. To reduce diagnostic time, ensure steps in BASIC DIAGNOSTIC PROCEDURES and SELF-DIAGNOSTICS articles were performed before diagnosing a symptom. Following are some symptoms available for diagnosis.

- Erratic Timing Advance
- Timing Not Affected By Vacuum
- Engine Does Not Operate Smoothly Or Misfires At High Speed
- Engine Fails To Start
- Engine Backfires, Fails To Start
- Engine Continues To Run With Key Off
- Engine Runs Only With Key In Start Position
- Excessive Fuel Consumption
- Intermittent Spark

ERRATIC TIMING ADVANCE

Check vacuum advance mechanism and centrifugal advance weights (6.0L engine). See SYSTEM & COMPONENT TESTING article.

TIMING NOT AFFECTED BY VACUUM

Check vacuum advance mechanism and adjusting screws (6.0L engine). See SYSTEM & COMPONENT TESTING article. Check pick-up coil pivot for corrosion (6.0L engine only). See BASIC DIAGNOSTIC PROCEDURES article.

ENGINE DOES NOT OPERATE SMOOTHLY OR MISFIRES AT HIGH SPEED

Check spark plugs, spark advance, ignition system wires and connections. Check starter solenoid for shorting at terminal "S" (6.0L engine). Check for missing trigger wheel pin (6.0L engine). See BASIC DIAGNOSTIC PROCEDURES article.

ENGINE FAILS TO START

No Spark At Plugs - Check for open, loose or corroded ground wires in distributor, and check primary wiring circuits. See BASIC DIAGNOSTIC PROCEDURES article. Check for defective ignition module, cracked distributor cap and defective rotor. See BASIC DIAGNOSTIC PROCEDURES article.

ENGINE BACKFIRES, FAILS TO START

Verify ignition timing is correct, check for moisture in distributor or faulty distributor cap and verify that ignition wires are connected in proper firing order. See BASIC DIAGNOSTIC PROCEDURES article.

ENGINE CONTINUES TO RUN WITH KEY OFF

Check for defective starter motor solenoid. See SYSTEM & COMPONENT TESTING article. Check for shorted diode in alternator warning light circuit. See SYSTEM & COMPONENT TESTING article.

ENGINE RUNS ONLY WITH KEY IN START POSITION

Check resistance wire for open circuit or excessive resistance (6.0L engine). See SYSTEM & COMPONENT TESTING article.

EXCESSIVE FUEL CONSUMPTION

Check for incorrect ignition timing. Check vacuum advance mechanism and centrifugal advance weights (6.0L engine). See SYSTEM & COMPONENT TESTING article.

INTERMITTENT SPARK

Check for loose or corroded terminals. Check for loose ground connector or shorted wires in distributor (6.0L engine). Check for missing trigger wheel pin or for defective pick-up coil or ignition module (6.0L engine).

INTERMITTENTS

INTERMITTENT PROBLEM DIAGNOSIS

Intermittent fault testing requires duplicating circuit or component failure to identify the problem. These procedures may lead to the computer setting a fault code (on some systems) which may help in diagnosis.

If problem vehicle does not produce fault codes, monitor voltage or resistance values using a DVOM, while attempting to reproduce conditions causing intermittent fault. A change in status on DVOM will indicate a fault has been located.

Use a DVOM to pinpoint faults. When monitoring voltage, ensure ignition switch is in ON position or engine is running. Ensure ignition switch is in OFF position or negative battery cable is disconnected when monitoring circuit resistance. Status changes on DVOM during test procedures will indicate area of fault.

TEST PROCEDURES

Intermittent Simulation - To reproduce the conditions creating an intermittent fault, use the following methods:

- Lightly vibrate component.
- Heat component.
- Wiggle or bend wiring harness.
- Spray component with water.
- Remove/apply vacuum source.

Monitor circuit/component voltage or resistance while simulating intermittent. If engine is running, monitor for self-diagnostic codes. Use test results to identify a faulty component or circuit.

1991 ENGINE PERFORMANCE
System & Component Testing – Carbureted

Grand Wagoneer

INTRODUCTION

Before testing separate components or systems, perform procedures in BASIC DIAGNOSTIC PROCEDURES article.

MODULES, MOTORS, RELAYS & SOLENOIDS

MODULES

Ignition Module – See TIMING CONTROL SYSTEMS under IGNITION SYSTEM.

RELAYS

Starter Motor Relay – **1)** Disconnect wiring from "I" and "G" terminals. *See Fig. 1.* Measure resistance between "I" and "G" terminals with an ohmmeter. Resistance should be about 22 ohms.

2) Measure resistance between either terminal and ground post. Resistance reading should be infinite. If readings are correct, reconnect wiring. If readings are incorrect, replace relay.

3) Disconnect SOL terminal wire and connect a voltmeter between terminal and ground post. With ignition switch in START position, voltmeter should indicate battery voltage.

NOTE: Ensure transmission is in Park or Neutral with parking brake applied before connecting terminal "G" to ground.

4) If battery voltage is not present, check wiring harness, bulkhead connector, and ignition switch adjustment. If battery voltage is present and the starter relay is not working, connect wiring to "I" terminal and use a jumper wire to connect terminal "G" to ground. If relay does not "click", repair ground circuit.

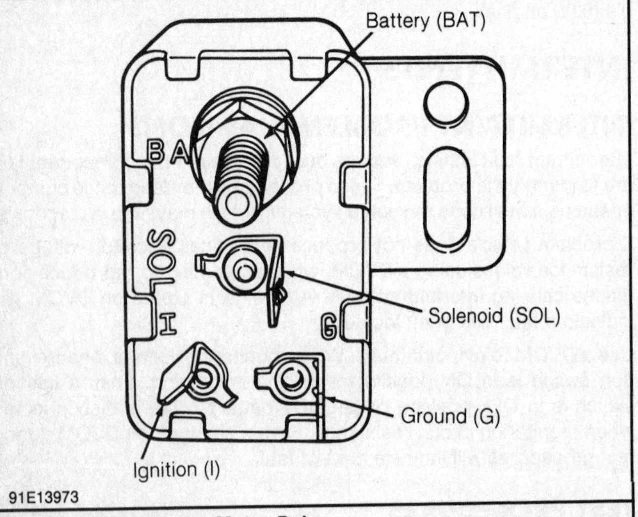
Battery (BAT)
BA
SOL
I
G
Solenoid (SOL)
Ground (G)
Ignition (I)
91E13973

Fig. 1: Testing Starter Motor Relay

FUEL SYSTEM

FUEL DELIVERY

Carburetor – See REMOVAL, OVERHAUL & INSTALLATION article for information on Motorcraft 2150 carburetor.

Fuel Pump – **1)** Before performing fuel pump test, check for kinked or bent fuel tubes or hoses that could cause restrictions. Also check for fuel leaks in supply tubes and hoses.

2) Remove air cleaner assembly. Disconnect fuel inlet fitting at carburetor. Disconnect fuel return hose at filter and plug fitting on filter. Remove any spilled fuel from engine.

3) Connect fuel pressure gauge, hose restrictor, and flexible hose between fuel filter and carburetor. Position flexible hose and hose restrictor so fuel can be discharged into a graduated container.

4) Operate engine at curb idle RPM and permit fuel to discharge into graduated container by momentarily opening hose restrictor. Close hose restrictor and allow pressure to stabilize.

5) Note fuel pump pressure reading. Fuel gauge should indicate 5.0-6.5 psi (.35-.46 kg/cm²). If fuel pump pressure is correct, go to next step. If fuel pump pressure is not within specification and fuel tubes/hoses and filter are okay, replace fuel pump.

6) Operate engine at curb idle. Open hose restrictor and allow fuel to discharge into graduated container for 30 seconds, then close restrictor. At least 16 ounces (.47 liters) of fuel should have been discharged.

7) If fuel pump volume is less than specified, repeat test using an auxiliary fuel supply and replacement fuel filter. If fuel pump volume is now correct, check for restrictions in fuel tubes/hoses and fuel tank for proper venting.

FUEL CONTROL

System and component testing information is not available from manufacturer.

IDLE CONTROL SYSTEM

The Grand Wagoneer engine uses a non-feedback carburetor system. No idle control system is used.

IGNITION SYSTEM

NOTE: For basic ignition checks, see BASIC DIAGNOSTIC PROCEDURES article.

TIMING CONTROL SYSTEMS

Ignition Coil Primary Circuit – **1)** Turn ignition on. Connect voltmeter between coil positive (+) terminal and ground. If reading is 5.5-6.5 volts, go to next step. If reading is battery voltage, go to step **4)**. If reading is lower than 5.5 volts, go to step **7)**.

2) Place ignition switch in START position. With voltmeter connected between coil positive (+) terminal and ground, observe voltmeter reading while engine is cranking. If reading is battery voltage, primary circuit is okay. If reading is less than battery voltage, go to next step.

3) Check for short or open circuit in wire attached to "I" terminal at starter motor solenoid. Also check starter solenoid for proper operation. Repair wiring or replace components as necessary.

4) With voltmeter connected between coil positive (+) terminal and ground, disconnect wire from "I" terminal at starter motor solenoid. If reading remains at battery voltage, go to next step. If reading drops to 5.5-6.5 volts, replace starter motor solenoid.

5) With voltmeter connected between coil positive (+) terminal and ground, connect a jumper wire between coil negative (–) terminal and ground. If reading drops to 5.5-6.5 volts, go to next step. If reading is still incorrect, go to step **8)**.

6) Turn ignition off. Check continuity of green wire between coil negative (–) terminal and ignition module. If continuity is okay, replace ignition module. If not, repair Green wire as necessary. Also check continuity between ignition module Black wire connector terminal and ground. Repair Black wire as necessary and go back to step **2)**.

7) With voltmeter connected between coil positive (+) terminal and ground, disconnect ignition coil capacitor. If reading is now 5.5-6.5 volts, replace ignition coil capacitor. If reading is still incorrect, go to next step.

8) Turn ignition off. Check resistance between coil positive (+) terminal and bulkhead connector (Yellow wire). If reading is 1.4 ohms or more, repair or replace primary circuit resistance wire. If reading is 1.3-1.4 ohms, go to next step.

9) With ignition off, check resistance between bulkhead connector and ignition switch terminal No. 11 (Yellow wire). If resistance is less than 0.1 ohms, replace ignition switch or repair Red ignition switch wire coming from battery. If reading is more than 0.1 ohms, repair poor connections or wiring at ignition switch or bulkhead connector.

Ignition Coil Test – 1) Check ignition coil for carbon tracking, oil leaks, or other damage. Replace coil if necessary. If coil is okay, go to next step.

2) Disconnect wiring and coil tower secondary wire from ignition coil terminals. Connect ohmmeter between coil negative (–) and positive (+) terminals. If coil resistance is 1.11-1.25 ohms at 75°F (24°C), go to next step. If coil resistance is incorrect, replace ignition coil.

3) Connect an ohmmeter between the coil tower and ignition coil negative (–) terminal. If coil resistance is 7700-9300 ohms at 75°F (24°C), ignition coil is okay. If coil resistance is incorrect, replace ignition coil.

Ignition Feed To Ignition Module – 1) Ensure ignition coil primary circuit is okay. Disconnect ignition module 2-pin and 4-pin connectors. Turn ignition on. Connect voltmeter between ground and ignition module wiring harness Yellow wire at 2-pin connector. If reading is within 0.2 volts of battery voltage, replace ignition module and go to step **3)**.

2) If reading is more than 0.2 volts of battery voltage, repair poor connections or wiring at ignition switch or bulkhead connector. After repairs check for spark at coil wire, If spark, is available end test. If spark is not available, replace ignition module.

3) Connect 2-pin connector at ignition module, leave 4-pin connector disconnected. Connect ammeter between ground and ignition module wiring harness Black wire at 4-pin connector.

4) If ammeter reading is 0.9-1.1 amps, ignition feed to ignition module is okay. If ammeter reading is higher or lower than 0.9-1.1 amps, replace ignition module.

Sensor & Ignition Module Check – 1) Turn ignition on. Disconnect secondary coil wire from distributor and hold wire with insulated pliers 1/2" from a known engine ground. Disconnect 4-pin connector from ignition module. If no spark exists, go to step **5)**. If spark exists at coil, go to next step.

2) Check resistance between terminals "C" (White wire) and "D" (Light Blue wire) at 4-pin wiring harness connector. *See Fig. 2*. If ohmmeter reading is 400-800 ohms, go to step **6)**. If ohmmeter reading is incorrect, go to next step.

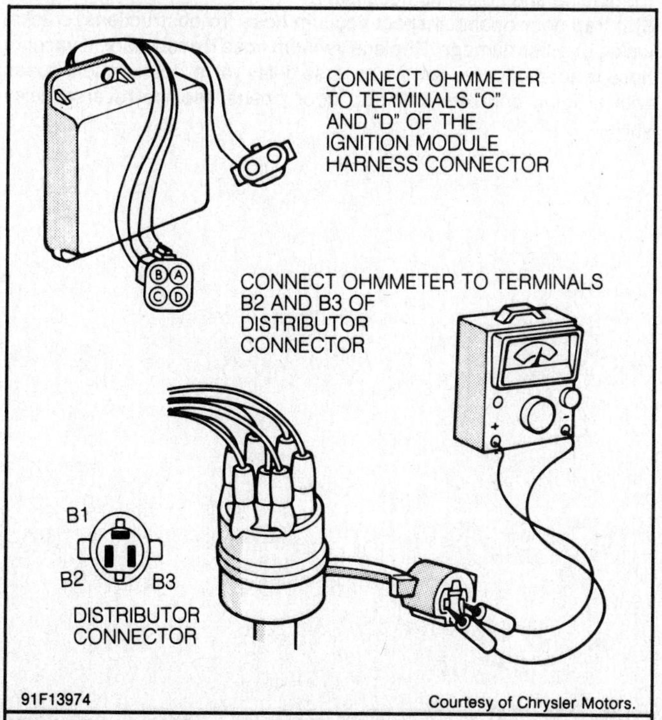
CONNECT OHMMETER TO TERMINALS "C" AND "D" OF THE IGNITION MODULE HARNESS CONNECTOR
B
A
C
D
CONNECT OHMMETER TO TERMINALS B2 AND B3 OF DISTRIBUTOR CONNECTOR
B1
B2
B3
DISTRIBUTOR CONNECTOR
91F13974
Courtesy of Chrysler Motors.

Fig. 2: Checking Sensor & Ignition Module

3) Disconnect and reconnect 3-pin connector at distributor. If ohmmeter now indicates 400-800 ohms, go to step **6)**. If ohmmeter reading is still incorrect, disconnect 3-pin connector at distributor and go to next step.

4) Connect ohmmeter between terminals B2 and B3 of distributor connector. If ohmmeter indicates 400-800 ohms, repair or replace harness between 3-pin connector and 4-pin connector. If ohmmeter reading is still incorrect, replace pick-up coil.

5) Connect ohmmeter between battery negative terminal and terminal "B" (Black wire) of ignition module 4-pin wiring harness connector. If ohmmeter reads zero (not more than .002 ohms), go back to step **2)**. If ohmmeter reading is more than zero, repair ground circuit. Check resistance at ground cable, distributor-to-engine block and ground screw in distributor

6) Connect voltmeter between terminals "C" and "D" at ignition module wiring harness connector. Crank engine and observe voltmeter. If voltmeter fluctuates, sensor and ignition module are operating properly.

7) If voltmeter does not fluctuate locate and repair fault. Check distributor trigger wheel, check for missing trigger wheel pin and for a distributor shaft that is not turning.

Centrifugal Advance Check – 1) Disconnect vacuum hose from vacuum advance mechanism and plug. Connect timing light to No. 1 spark plug and tachometer to ignition coil TACH terminal.

2) Start engine and observe timing while engine is idle. Slowly increase engine speed to 2000 RPM. timing should advance smoothly as engine speed increases.

Vacuum Advance Check – 1) Start and warm engine to normal operating temperature. Connect vacuum hose to vacuum advance mechanism. Observe timing while engine speed is at idle. Slowly increase and hold engine speed to 2000 RPM.

2) With vacuum applied, ignition timing should advance sooner than with centrifugal advance alone. At 2000 RPM, the vacuum advance should causes total advance to be more than with centrifugal advance alone.

EMISSION SYSTEMS & SUB-SYSTEMS

EXHAUST GAS RECIRCULATION (EGR)

EGR Coolant Temperature Override Valve – 1) Ensure that engine coolant temperature is 10°F (5.6°C) below the calibrated opening temperature of the valve.

2) Inspect vacuum hoses for air leaks and proper routing. Correct or replace as necessary. Disconnect hose at thermal vacuum switch and connect it to a vacuum gauge.

3) Start and run engine at 1500 RPM. No vacuum should be indicated on the gauge. If vacuum is indicated, replace EGR coolant temperature override valve. If no vacuum is indicated, continue to operate engine until coolant temperature exceeds 155°F (68.5°C).

4) Accelerate engine to 1500 RPM. Carburetor ported vacuum should be indicated on vacuum gauge. If not, replace EGR coolant temperature override valve.

EGR Thermal Vacuum Switch – 1) Locate EGR thermal vacuum switch inside air cleaner. Ensure that air cleaner intake air temperature is 40°F (4°C) below thermal vacuum switch calibrated temperature.

2) Disconnect vacuum hoses from thermal vacuum switch and connect a hand-held vacuum pump to inner port. Apply vacuum and ensure vacuum is held by thermal vacuum switch check valve. If vacuum is not held, replace switch.

3) Start engine and warm air cleaner intake air temperature to at least 55°F (13°C). Vacuum should not be maintained by thermal vacuum switch. If vacuum is maintained, replace switch.

EGR Valve – 1) Start and warm engine to normal operating temperature. With engine operating at idle, by-pass the vacuum transducer and apply manifold vacuum directly to nipple on EGR valve.

2) Notice engine idle, the engine should idle roughly or stall. If this occurs, the EGR valve is okay. Test EGR valve transducer. If idle did not change or if engine did not stall, go to next step.

3) Disconnect vacuum hose from EGR valve and connect a hand-held vacuum pump directly to EGR valve. Apply a minimum of 12 in. Hg of vacuum to EGR valve and notice engine idle.

1991 ENGINE PERFORMANCE
System & Component Testing – Carbureted (Cont.)

4) If engine now idles roughly, inspect vacuum hoses between intake manifold and EGR valve.Also check backpressure hose from EGR valve base to transducer for leaks. If no leaks are found, test EGR valve transducer.
5) If engine idle still did not change, remove EGR valve and inspect valve and exhaust passage in manifold for blockage. Clean out passage or replace EGR as necessary.
EGR Valve Transducer – 1) Disconnect transducer vacuum hoses and backpressure line. Remove EGR valve transducer and plug transducer output port. Apply 1-2 psi (.07-.14 kg/cm²) to transducer backpressure port.
2) Using a hand-held vacuum pump, apply a minimum of 12 in. Hg of vacuum to EGR valve transducer input port. If transducer will not hold vacuum, replace EGR valve transducer.

FUEL EVAPORATION

System and component testing information is not available from manufacturer.

POSITIVE CRANKCASE VENTILATION (PCV)

System and component testing information is not available from manufacturer.

THERMOSTATIC AIR CLEANER

Air Valve Motor Functional Test – 1) With engine off, detach ambient air duct at air cleaner and observe air valve position. Valve should be fully open to incoming (cool) ambient air (heat OFF position).
2) With engine cold, start engine and as engine warms, observe air valve position. Valve should be fully closed to incoming (cool) ambient air (heat ON position).
3) Depress throttle rapidly to 1/2-3/4 part throttle position and release. Air valve should briefly remain stationary and then move toward the heat OFF position and back to the ON position.
4) Loosely attach ambient air duct to air cleaner and warm engine to normal operating temperature. Remove ambient air duct and observe air valve. Valve should either fully open to ambient air, or at a mixture position that provides the correct inlet air temperature to the carburetor. Stop engine and connect ambient air duct to the air cleaner.
5) If air valve did not function as described, check snorkel for binding. Check for missing, disconnected or improperly routed vacuum hoses. Also check for air leaks at vacuum motor, thermal vacuum switch, reverse delay valve, check valve, intake manifold or vacuum hoses.
6) If air valve operates freely when moved manually and there are no vacuum hose problems or air leaks detected, connect a vacuum hose from intake manifold vacuum directly to the air valve vacuum motor and start engine.
7) If air valve does not close, replace air valve vacuum motor. If air valve closes, either the thermal vacuum switch, reverse delay valve, or check valve are defective and must be replaced.

NOTE: The reverse delay valve provides roughly 1 1/2 minutes of delay before allowing trap door to completely close.

Reverse Delay Valve Functional Test – 1) Remove vacuum hose from end of reverse delay valve that is not Black in color. Using a hand-held vacuum pump, apply 2-4 in. Hg of vacuum to valve.
2) Note time required for atmospheric pressure to pass through valve and eliminate the vacuum. Replace reverse delay valve if time required is less than 5 seconds or more than 13 seconds.
3) Replace reverse delay valve if defective. Install replacement reverse delay valve with Black colored end toward trap door vacuum motor.
Thermal Vacuum Switch – 1) Locate thermostatic air cleaner thermal vacuum switch inside air cleaner. Connect a hand-held vacuum pump to vacuum source side of switch and a vacuum gauge to air valve vacuum motor side of switch.
2) Apply 14 in. Hg of vacuum to switch. With switch temperature below 95°F (35°C), vacuum should be maintained. Heat switch above 95°F (35°C). The air vent valve should open and vacuum gauge reading should decrease to zero. Replace thermal vacuum switch if defective.
Trap Door Functional Test – 1) With engine off, remove air cleaner cover and observe trap door position. Trap door should be closed. Using a hand-held vacuum pump, apply 2-4 in. Hg to intake manifold vacuum source hose going to trap door. Trap door should open.
2) If trap door does not open, apply vacuum directly to vacuum motor on air cleaner intake duct. If door still does not open, inspect snorkel for binding and adjust as necessary.
3) If trap door opens, inspect vacuum hose fro obstructions, cracks, kinks, or other damage. Replace vacuum hose if necessary. If vacuum hose is not defective, remove reverse delay valve. Join vacuum hoses with a fitting and retest. If trap door opens, replace reverse delay valve.

1991 ENGINE PERFORMANCE
System & Component Testing – Fuel Injected

Cherokee, Comanche, Wrangler

INTRODUCTION

Before testing separate components or systems, perform procedures in BASIC DIAGNOSTIC PROCEDURES article. Since many computer-controlled and monitored components set a trouble code if they malfunction, also perform procedures in SELF-DIAGNOSTICS article.

NOTE: Testing individual components does not isolate possible short or open circuits. Perform all voltage tests with a Digital Volt-Ohmmeter (DVOM) with a minimum 10-megohm input impedance, unless stated otherwise in test procedure. Use ohmmeter to isolate wiring harness short or open circuits.

COMPUTERIZED ENGINE CONTROLS

SINGLE BOARD ENGINE CONTROLLER

Power & Ground Circuits – Check power and ground circuits using NO START TEST NS-8B: REPAIRING LOSS OF BATTERY POWER AT ENGINE CONTROLLER or DRIVEABILITY TEST DR-33A: CHECKING ENGINE CONTROLLER GROUNDS & POWER CIRCUITS test procedures in SELF-DIAGNOSTICS article.

ENGINE SENSORS & SWITCHES

Coolant Temperature Sensor – **1)** Disconnect coolant temperature sensor. Using DVOM, check sensor resistance. Resistance should be as specified in COOLANT TEMPERATURE SENSOR & MANIFOLD AIR TEMPERATURE SENSOR RESISTANCE table. Replace sensor if necessary.

2) Check continuity between engine controller wiring harness terminal No. 2 and sensor connector terminal. Also check continuity between engine controller wiring harness terminal No. 4 and sensor connector terminal. Repair wiring if an open circuit is indicated.

NOTE: Also see appropriate coolant temperature sensor tests in SELF-DIAGNOSTICS article.

COOLANT TEMPERATURE SENSOR & MANIFOLD AIR TEMPERATURE SENSOR RESISTANCE

Temperature °F (°C)	Minimum Ohms	Maximum Ohms
-40 (-40)	291,490	381,710
-4 (-20)	85,850	108,390
14 (-10)	49,250	61,430
32 (0)	29,330	35,990
50 (10)	17,990	21,810
68 (20)	11,370	13,610
77 (25)	9120	10,880
86 (30)	7370	8750
104 (40)	4900	5750
122 (50)	3330	3880
140 (60)	2310	2670
158 (70)	1630	1870
176 (80)	1170	1340
194 (90)	860	970
212 (100)	640	720
230 (110)	480	540
248 (120)	370	410

Crankshaft Position Sensor – **1)** Disconnect crankshaft position sensor. On Cherokee and Comanche, connect ohmmeter across sensor terminal "A" (Orange/Dark Blue wire) and terminal "B" (Black/Light Blue wire). On Wrangler, connect ohmmeter across sensor terminal "A" (Brown/Red wire) and terminal "B" (Red/Green wire).

2) Ohmmeter should read 125-275 ohms with engine hot. Replace sensor if reading is not as specified. Also see appropriate crankshaft position sensor tests in SELF-DIAGNOSTICS article.

Manifold Absolute Pressure Sensor – **1)** Inspect MAP sensor vacuum hose connections at throttle body and sensor. Replace or repair vacuum hose if necessary.

2) Turn ignition on, engine off. Using DVOM, check MAP sensor output voltage. On Cherokee and Comanche, connect DVOM to MAP sensor terminal "B" (Dark Green/Red wire). On Wrangler, connect DVOM to MAP sensor terminal "B" (Red/White wire).

3) Output voltage should be 4-5 volts. Voltage should drop to 1.5-2.1 volts with a hot engine operating in Neutral and at idle speed. Also check for output voltage at engine controller wiring harness terminal No. 1. If voltage is not as specified in step **2)**, repair wiring harness if necessary.

4) With ignition on, check MAP sensor supply voltage at sensor connector terminal "C" (Violet wire on Cherokee and Comanche or Brown/Yellow wire on Wrangler). Supply voltage should be 4.5-5.5 volts. Also check for supply voltage at engine controller wiring harness terminal No. 6. If supply voltage is not as specified, repair wiring harness if necessary.

5) Check continuity of MAP sensor ground circuit at sensor connector terminal "A" (Black/Light Blue wire on Cherokee and Comanche or Brown/Red wire on Wrangler) and engine controller wiring harness terminal No. 4. Repair wiring harness if necessary.

6) Check continuity of MAP sensor ground circuit at engine controller wiring harness terminal No. 4 and engine controller wiring harness terminal No. 11. If ohmmeter indicates an open circuit, go to next step.

7) Check for defective sensor ground connection. Connection is located on right side of engine block, at oil dipstick tube mounting block. If ground connection is okay, replace the engine controller.

NOTE: If terminal No. 4 has a short circuit to 12 volts, correct this condition before replacing engine controller. If necessary, perform appropriate MAP sensor tests in SELF-DIAGNOSTICS article.

Manifold Air Temperature Sensor – **1)** Disconnect coolant temperature sensor. Using DVOM, check sensor resistance. Resistance should be as specified in COOLANT TEMPERATURE SENSOR & MANIFOLD AIR TEMPERATURE SENSOR RESISTANCE table. Replace sensor if necessary.

2) Check resistance between engine controller wiring harness terminal No. 21 and sensor connector terminal. Also check resistance between engine controller wiring harness terminal No. 4 and sensor connector terminal. Repair wiring if resistance is greater than 1 ohm.

Oxygen (O_2) Sensor (Heating Element) – **1)** Disconnect oxygen sensor connector. Using an ohmmeter, check sensor heating element resistance.

2) On Comanche and Cherokee, connect ohmmeter to Black/Tan and Dark Green/Black sensor wires. On Wrangler, connect ohmmeter to Black and Dark Green/Black sensor wires.

3) Heating element resistance should be 5-7 ohms. Replace oxygen sensor if ohmmeter reads infinity.

Park/Neutral Switch (A999/727 Auto. Trans.) – **1)** Disconnect park/neutral switch. Check continuity between switch center terminal and transmission case. Continuity should exist only when transmission is in Park or Neutral.

2) Shift transmission into Reverse. Check continuity between the 2 outside terminals on switch. Continuity should exist only when transmission is in Reverse. Check continuity between each outer terminal and transmission case.

3) Continuity should not exist between either terminal and case while in Reverse. If switch continuity tests are okay, check gearshift adjustment or back-up light circuit. If switch fails continuity tests, replace park/neutral switch.

NOTE: Also see appropriate park/neutral switch input test procedures in SELF-DIAGNOSTICS article.

Park/Neutral Switch (AW-4 Auto. Trans.) – **1)** Disconnect park/neutral switch. Ensure continuity exists between terminals "B" and "C" with transmission in Park or Neutral. *See Fig. 1.*

2) Ensure continuity exists between terminals "A" and "E" with transmission in Reverse. *See Fig. 1.* Ensure continuity exists between terminals "A" and "G" with transmission in 3rd gear.

1991 ENGINE PERFORMANCE
System & Component Testing – Fuel Injected (Cont.)

3) Ensure continuity exists between terminals "A" and "H" with transmission in 1st or 2nd gear. *See Fig. 1*. If switch fails continuity tests, replace park/neutral switch.

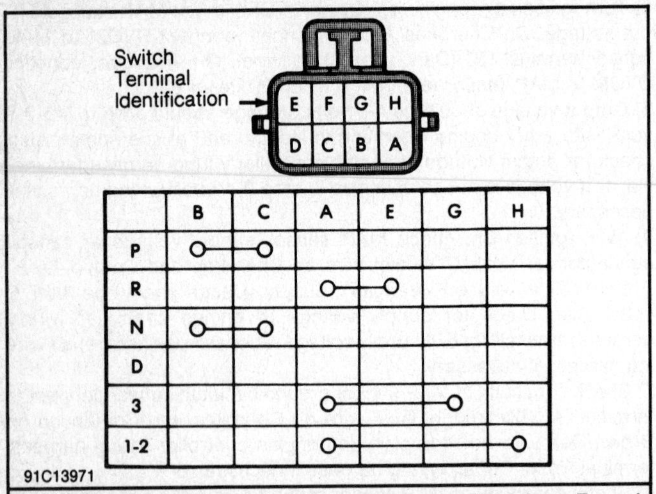
Switch
Terminal
Identification
E F G H
D C B A
B C A E G H
P
R
N
D
3
1-2
91C13971

Fig. 1: Testing Park/Neutral Switch Continuity (AW-4 Auto. Trans.)

Synchronization Signal Generator – 1) Use an analog voltmeter. DO NOT remove distributor connector from distributor. Insert voltmeter leads into backside of distributor wiring harness connector to make contact with terminals. Ensure that connector is not damaged when inserting test probes.

2) Insert positive voltmeter lead into synchronization signal output Tan/Yellow wire (Gray/Black wire on Wrangler) at the distributor wiring harness connector.

3) Insert negative voltmeter lead into ground Black/Blue wire (Brown/Red wire on Wrangler) at the distributor wiring harness connector. Set voltmeter to 15-volt DC scale.

4) With distributor cap removed, manually rotate engine until pulse ring enters sync signal generator. Turn ignition switch to ON position. With pulse positioned in the sync generator, reading should be about 5 volts.

5) If no voltage is present, check voltmeter leads for good connections If connections are okay and there is still no voltage, check for voltage at Orange supply wire (White/Black wire on Wrangler).

6) If no voltage is present at supply wire, remove engine controller and check voltage at pin No. 7. Engine controller is located on left side of engine compartment. If there is no voltage at engine controller, see appropriate synchronization sensor/circuit tests in SELF-DIAGNOSTICS article.

7) If voltage is present at engine controller pin No. 7 but not at supply wire, check continuity of supply wire between the distributor connector and the engine controller. If no continuity exists, repair wiring harness as necessary.

8) If supply wire is okay, check continuity between sync signal output wire at the distributor connector and pin No. 44 at engine controller. If no continuity exists, repair wiring harness as necessary.

9) If sync signal output wire is okay, check continuity between ground circuit wire at the distributor connector and ground. If no continuity exists, repair wiring harness as necessary. If ground wire is okay, go to next step.

10) While observing voltmeter, crank engine. Voltmeter needle should fluctuate from 0-5 volts while the engine is cranking. This verifies that stator in distributor is operating properly and that a sync (pulse) signal is being generated. If voltmeter does not fluctuate, replace synch sensor stator.

Throttle Position Sensor (TPS) – 1) Turn ignition on. Check TPS output voltage at sensor wiring harness center terminal. At idle, output voltage should be greater than 200 millivolts.

2) Gradually open throttle plate. Output voltage should gradually increase as throttle plate is opened. At wide open throttle, output voltage must be less than 4.8 volts.

NOTE: Also see appropriate throttle position sensor tests in SELF-DIAGNOSTICS article.

Vehicle Speed Sensor – See appropriate vehicle speed sensor tests in SELF-DIAGNOSTICS article.

MODULES, MOTORS, RELAYS & SOLENOIDS

MODULES

Theft Alarm Module (Cherokee) – 1) Turn ignition key to ACCY position 3 times and leave in ACCY position to activate Security Alarm Module (SAM) self-diagnostics. If parking lights and tail lights do not flash, go to step **2)**. If headlights do not flash, go to step **6)**. If horn does not sound twice, go to step **7)**. If horn sounds and headlights, parking lights and tail lights flash, go to step **8)**.

NOTE: For identifying circuits referred to in testing, see appropriate wiring diagram in WIRING DIAGRAMS article.

2) Check accessory and parking light fuses. Replace if necessary. If fuses are okay, disconnect SAM connector. Security alarm module is located on driver's side of A/C-heater housing.

NOTE: If SECURITY light comes and remains on with ignition on, the Chrysler Collision Detection (CCD) bus communication with the engine controller has been lost. After servicing vehicle ensure that system operates properly. A malfunctioning anti-theft system may keep engine from starting.

3) Check wiring side of SAM connector for battery voltage at battery, accessory, and headlight feed wires. Also check ground circuits for both ground wires.

4) If battery voltages and ground circuits are NOT okay, repair wiring harness and retest system. If battery voltages and ground circuits are okay, check for battery voltage at ignition feed wire of SAM connector.

5) If battery voltage is present, replace security alarm module and retest system. If battery voltage is not present, repair wiring harness and retest system.

6) Check headlight wiring harness and headlight relay. If wiring harness and relay are okay, replace security alarm module. If wiring harness and relay are NOT okay, repair wiring harness or replace relay and retest system.

7) Check horn, horn fuse and wiring harness. If horn, horn fuse and wiring harness are okay, replace security alarm module and retest system. If horn, horn fuse and wiring harness are not okay, repair wiring harness or replace fuse or horn and retest system.

8) Verify that SECURITY light is flashing. If SECURITY light is not flashing, check bulb and wiring harness. Repair or replace as necessary. If bulb and wiring are okay, replace security alarm module and retest system.

9) If SECURITY light is flashing, turn ignition key to OFF position. Remove illuminated entry relay from vehicle. Relay is located on a bracket behind instrument panel.

10) Check theft alarm switches by opening and closing doors and liftgate. Replace switch(es) or repair wiring harness as necessary. If switches are okay, check hood switch by opening and closing hood.

11) Replace hood switch or repair wiring harness as necessary. If hood switch is okay, unlock (with key) each front door and liftgate one at a time to test disarm switches. Replace switch(es) or repair wiring harness as necessary and retest system.

12) If disarm switches are okay, cycle power door locks to lock position and then unlock. Replace door lock switch(es), lock/unlock relay(s) or repair wiring harness as necessary and retest system.

13) If power door locks operate properly, lock and unlock vehicle with keyless entry transmitter. If power door locks do not operate properly, replace keyless entry transmitter, receiver or repair wiring harness as necessary and retest system.

14) If keyless entry system operates properly, turn ignition key to ON position and wait 30 seconds. If SECURITY light comes on and stays on, repair or replace CCD bus and wiring as necessary and retest system. If SECURITY light remains off, theft alarm system is operating properly.

NOTE: A functional SBEC-II that has been used in a vehicle equipped with theft alarm system CANNOT be used in another vehicle that is NOT equipped with theft alarm system.

MOTORS

Automatic Idle Speed (AIS) Motor – See IDLE CONTROL SYSTEM.

RELAYS

A/C Compressor Clutch Relay – See A/C COMPRESSOR CLUTCH under MISCELLANEOUS CONTROLS.

Automatic Shutdown (ASD) Relay – See appropriate ASD relay tests in SELF-DIAGNOSTICS article.

Fuel Pump Relay – See FUEL PUMP RELAY under FUEL DELIVERY.

Radiator (Cooling) Fan Relay – See RADIATOR (COOLING) FAN under MISCELLANEOUS CONTROLS.

Starter Motor Relay – Some relays have battery voltage supplied to terminal No. 30. Others have battery voltage supplied to terminals No. 87 or 87A. *See Fig. 2.* In de-energized position, relay should have continuity between terminals No. 87A and No. 30. Resistance value between terminals No. 85 and No. 86 should be 70-80 ohms for resistor type relays or 81-91 ohms for diode type relays.

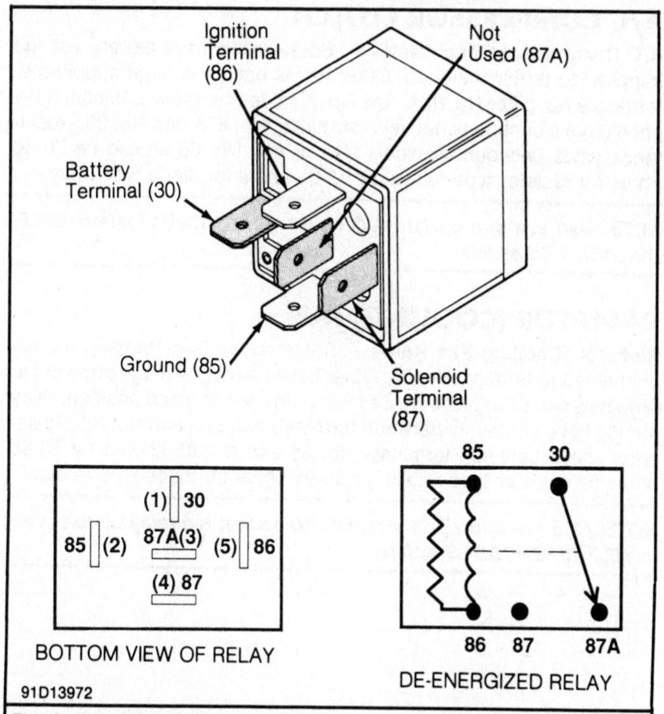
Ignition Terminal (86)
Not Used (87A)
Battery Terminal (30)
Ground (85)
Solenoid Terminal (87)
(1) 30
85 (2)
87A(3)
(5) 86
(4) 87
BOTTOM VIEW OF RELAY
85
30
86
87
87A
DE-ENERGIZED RELAY
91D13972

Fig. 2: Identifying Relay Terminals & Testing Relays

FUEL SYSTEM

FUEL DELIVERY

NOTE: Also see appropriate fuel delivery system or fuel injector control circuit tests in SELF-DIAGNOSTICS article.

Fuel System Pressure Test – **1)** Remove cap from pressure test port in fuel rail. *See Fig. 3.* Connect a 0-60 psi (0-4.22 kg/cm²) fuel pressure gauge to pressure fitting on fuel rail. Disconnect vacuum hose from fuel pressure regulator. Start engine.

2) Pressure should be approximately 39 psi (2.74 kg/cm²) with vacuum hose disconnected and 31 psi (2.18 kg/cm²) with vacuum hose connected to fuel pressure regulator.

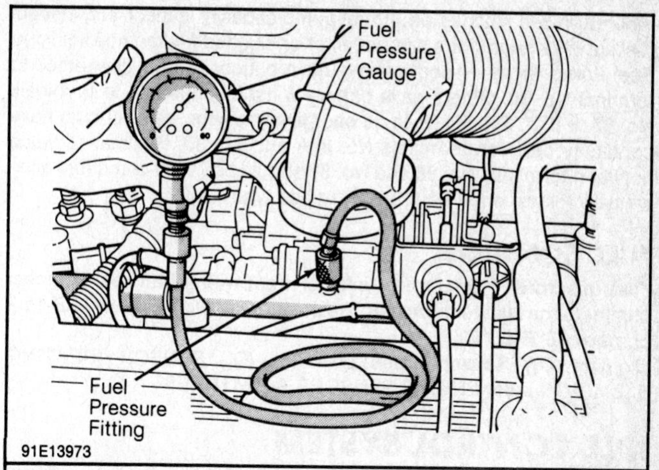
Fuel Pressure Gauge
Fuel Pressure Fitting
91E13973

Fig. 3: Testing Fuel System Pressure

3) If fuel pressure is not 8-10 psi (.56-.70 kg/cm²) higher with vacuum hose disconnected from fuel pressure regulator, inspect vacuum hose for blockage, leaks, kinks or other damage.

CAUTION: Fuel pressure will rise as high as 95 psi (6.7 kg/cm²) when fuel return line is pinched shut. Turn engine off IMMEDIATELY after pinching off fuel return line.

4) If fuel pressure is low, restart vehicle and let engine idle. Momentarily pinch hose section of fuel return line and IMMEDIATELY turn engine off. Note pressure reading on gauge.

5) If fuel pressure rises, replace fuel pressure regulator. If fuel pressure remains low, inspect fuel supply line, fuel filter, and fuel rail inlet for blockage. If fuel pressure rises above specifications, check fuel return line for kinks or blockage.

Fuel Pressure Leak Down Test – **1)** Remove cap from pressure test port in fuel rail. *See Fig. 3.* Connect a 0-60 psi (0-4.22 kg/cm²) fuel pressure gauge to pressure fitting on fuel rail. Start and run engine at idle.

2) Turn engine off and note fuel pressure reading on gauge. Leave fuel pressure gauge connected. Allow 30 minutes to elapse and then compare fuel pressure reading to reading taken when engine was off.

3) A pressure drop up to 20 psi (1.4 kg/cm²) to a range of 19-39 psi (1.3 2.7 kg/cm²) is within specification. If pressure drop is correct, the fuel pump outlet check valve and fuel pressure regulator are operating correctly.

CAUTION: Fuel pressure will rise as high as 95 psi (6.7 kg/cm²) when fuel return line is pinched shut. Turn engine off IMMEDIATELY after pinching off fuel return line.

4) If pressure drop is greater than 20 psi (1.4 kg/cm²), restart vehicle and let engine idle. Momentarily pinch shut hose section of fuel return line and IMMEDIATELY turn engine off. Note pressure reading on gauge. Allow 30 minutes to elapse and then compare fuel pressure reading to reading taken when engine was turned off.

5) If fuel pressure drops to about 20 psi (1.4 kg/cm²), replace fuel pressure regulator. If fuel pressure drops more than 20 psi (1.4 kg/cm²), fuel pressure is bleeding off past outlet check valve in fuel pump. Fuel pump must be replaced.

Fuel Pump Capacity Test – **1)** Remove cap from pressure test port in fuel rail. *See Fig. 3.* Connect a 0-60 psi (0-4.22 kg/cm²) fuel pressure gauge to pressure fitting on fuel rail. Start and run engine at idle. Note fuel pressure.

2) Pressure should be roughly 31 psi (2.18 kg/cm²) with vacuum hose connected to fuel pressure regulator and 39 psi (2.74 kg/cm²) with vacuum hose disconnected. If fuel pressure is incorrect, check fuel supply and return lines/hoses for kinks or restrictions.

3) Check fuel pump flow rate (capacity). A good fuel pump will deliver at least 2.11 pints (1 liter) of fuel per minute with the hose section of fuel return line pinched off. If fuel pump capacity is incorrect, inspect fuel supply system for a plugged filter or plugged fuel pump inlet filter.

Fuel Pump Relay – Some relays have battery voltage connected to terminal No. 30. Others have battery voltage connected to terminals No. 87 or 87A. *See Fig. 2*. In de-energized position, relay should have continuity between terminals No. 87A and No. 30. Resistance value between terminals No. 85 and No. 86 should be 70-80 ohms for resistor type relays, or 81-91 ohms for diode type relays.

FUEL CONTROL

Fuel Injectors – Disconnect injector from wiring harness. Connect ohmmeter on injector terminals. Resistance should be about 12.8-15.2 ohms at 68°F (20°C).

Oxygen (O_2) Sensor – See OXYGEN (O_2) SENSOR (HEATING ELEMENT) under ENGINE SENSORS & SWITCHES.

IDLE CONTROL SYSTEM

Automatic Idle Speed (AIS) Motor – **1)** Set parking brake and block drive wheels. Route all Exerciser Tester (7558) cables away from cooling fans, drive belt, pulleys, and exhaust components. Adjust engine idle speed to normal before disconnecting exerciser.

2) With ignition off, disconnect AIS motor connector at throttle body. Plug in exerciser tester harness connector into AIS motor. Connect Red clip of exerciser to battery positive terminal.

3) Connect Black clip to battery negative terminal. Red light on exerciser will flash if exerciser is properly connected. Start engine. Move exerciser switch to HIGH position. Engine speed should increase. Move switch to LOW position. Engine speed should decrease.

4) If engine idle speed changes while using exerciser, AIS motor is working properly. Return engine speed to normal idle and disconnect exerciser from idle speed stepper motor.

5) If engine idle did not change, turn ignition off. DO NOT disconnect exerciser from stepper motor. Remove AIS motor from throttle body. With ignition off, cycle the exerciser switch between HIGH and LOW positions. Pintle should move in and out of motor.

NOTE: When checking AIS motor operation with motor removed from throttle body, DO NOT extend pintle more than 1/4" (6.35 mm), as pintle may separate from motor. The AIS motor must be replaced if pintle separates from motor.

6) If pintle still does not move, replace AIS motor. Start engine and test replacement motor. If pintle now operates properly, check AIS motor bore in throttle body and clean if necessary. Reinstall AIS motor and retest.

7) If throttle body is clear of obstructions, use Chrysler's Diagnostic Readout Box II (DRB-II) tester and appropriate AIS (idle speed stepper) motor tests in SELF-DIAGNOSTICS article.

IGNITION SYSTEM

TIMING CONTROL SYSTEMS

Ignition timing is electronically controlled by Single Board Engine Controller II (SBEC-II). Base ignition timing is NOT adjustable with this system. The SBEC-II controlled ignition system consists of coolant temperature sensor, crankshaft position sensor, distributor (includes rotor and synchronization sensor), ignition coil, manifold absolute pressure sensor, and throttle position sensor. See ENGINE SENSORS & SWITCHES for component testing.

EMISSION SYSTEMS & SUB-SYSTEMS

CRANKCASE VENTILATION SYSTEM

System and component testing information is not available from manufacturer.

FUEL EVAPORATION

System and component testing information is not available from manufacturer.

MISCELLANEOUS CONTROLS

A/C COMPRESSOR CLUTCH

A/C Compressor Clutch Relay – Some relays have battery voltage supplied to terminal No. 30. Other haves battery voltage supplied to terminals No. 87 or No. 87A. *See Fig. 2*. In de-energized position, relay should have continuity between terminals No. 87A and No. 30. Resistance value between terminals No. 85 and No. 86 should be 70-80 ohms for resistor type relays, or 81-91 ohms for diode type relays.

NOTE: Also see appropriate A/C clutch relay circuits tests in SELF-DIAGNOSTICS article.

RADIATOR (COOLING) FAN

Radiator (Cooling) Fan Relay – Some relays have battery voltage connected to terminal No. 30. Other haves battery voltage supplied to terminals No. 87 or No. 87A. *See Fig. 2*. In de-energized position, relay should have continuity between terminals No. 87A and No. 30. Resistance value between terminals No. 85 and No. 86 should be 70-80 ohms for resistor type relays, or 81-91 ohms for diode type relays.

NOTE: Also see appropriate radiator (cooling) fan relay circuit tests in SELF-DIAGNOSTICS article.

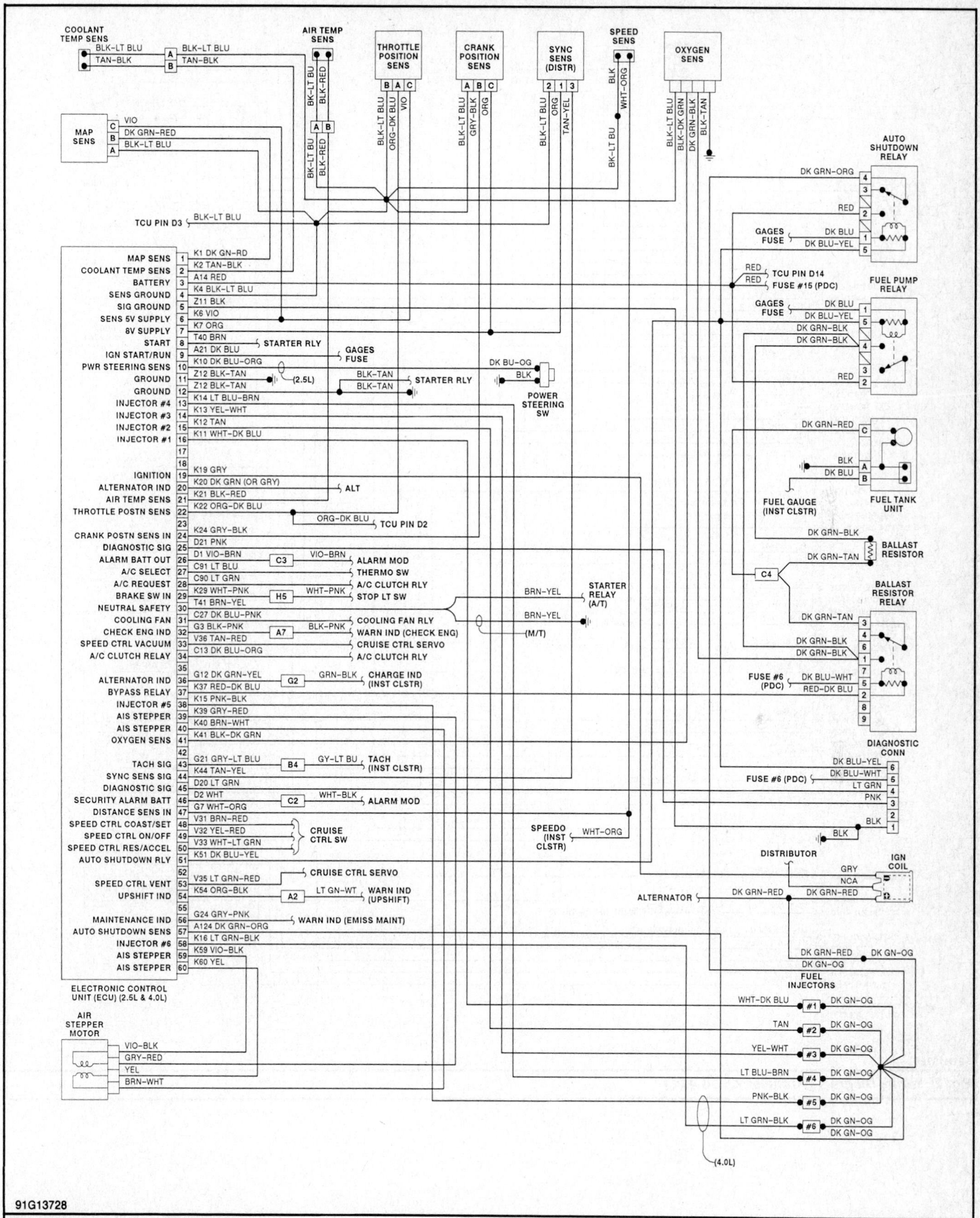

COOLANT TEMP SENS
AIR TEMP SENS
THROTTLE POSITION SENS
CRANK POSITION SENS
SYNC SENS (DISTR)
SPEED SENS
OXYGEN SENS
MAP SENS
AUTO SHUTDOWN RELAY
FUEL PUMP RELAY
FUEL TANK UNIT
BALLAST RESISTOR
BALLAST RESISTOR RELAY
DIAGNOSTIC CONN
DISTRIBUTOR
IGN COIL
FUEL INJECTORS
POWER STEERING SW
ELECTRONIC CONTROL UNIT (ECU) (2.5L & 4.0L)
AIR STEPPER MOTOR
MAP SENS
COOLANT TEMP SENS
BATTERY
SENS GROUND
SIG GROUND
SENS 5V SUPPLY
8V SUPPLY
START
IGN START/RUN
PWR STEERING SENS
GROUND
INJECTOR #4
INJECTOR #3
INJECTOR #2
INJECTOR #1
IGNITION
ALTERNATOR IND
AIR TEMP SENS
THROTTLE POSTN SENS
CRANK POSTN SENS IN
DIAGNOSTIC SIG
ALARM BATT OUT
A/C SELECT
A/C REQUEST
BRAKE SW IN
NEUTRAL SAFETY
COOLING FAN
CHECK ENG IND
SPEED CTRL VACUUM
A/C CLUTCH RELAY
BYPASS RELAY
INJECTOR #5
AIS STEPPER
OXYGEN SENS
TACH SIG
SYNC SENS SIG
SECURITY ALARM BATT
DISTANCE SENS IN
SPEED CTRL COAST/SET
SPEED CTRL ON/OFF
SPEED CTRL RES/ACCEL
AUTO SHUTDOWN RLY
SPEED CTRL VENT
UPSHIFT IND
MAINTENANCE IND
AUTO SHUTDOWN SENS
INJECTOR #6
TCU PIN D3
TCU PIN D2
TCU PIN D14
FUSE #15 (PDC)
FUSE #6 (PDC)
GAGES FUSE
STARTER RLY
STARTER RELAY (A/T)
(M/T)
(2.5L)
(4.0L)
ALT
ALARM MOD
THERMO SW
A/C CLUTCH RLY
STOP LT SW
COOLING FAN RLY
WARN IND (CHECK ENG)
CRUISE CTRL SERVO
CHARGE IND (INST CLSTR)
TACH (INST CLSTR)
CRUISE CTRL SW
WARN IND (UPSHIFT)
WARN IND (EMISS MAINT)
FUEL GAUGE (INST CLSTR)
SPEEDO (INST CLSTR)
ALTERNATOR
91G13728

Fig. 1: Wiring Diagram (Cherokee & Comanche 2.5L & 4.0L)

1991 ENGINE PERFORMANCE
Wiring Diagrams (Cont.)

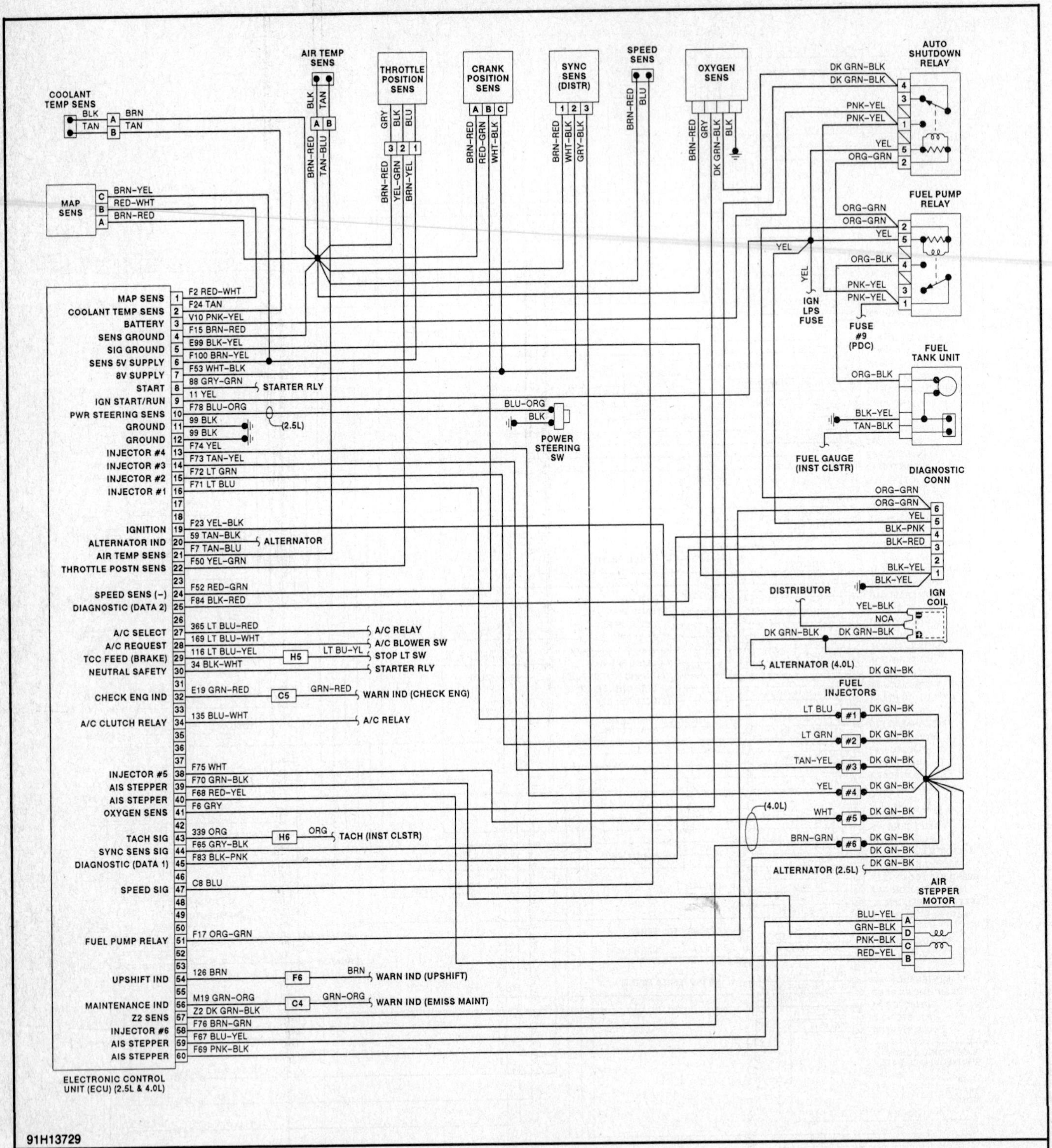
AIR TEMP SENS
THROTTLE POSITION SENS
CRANK POSITION SENS
SYNC SENS (DISTR)
SPEED SENS
OXYGEN SENS
AUTO SHUTDOWN RELAY
COOLANT TEMP SENS
MAP SENS
FUEL PUMP RELAY
IGN LPS FUSE
FUSE #9 (PDC)
FUEL TANK UNIT
POWER STEERING SW
FUEL GAUGE (INST CLSTR)
DIAGNOSTIC CONN
DISTRIBUTOR
IGN COIL
ALTERNATOR (4.0L)
FUEL INJECTORS
ALTERNATOR (2.5L)
AIR STEPPER MOTOR
MAP SENS 1 F2 RED-WHT
COOLANT TEMP SENS 2 F24 TAN
BATTERY 3 V10 PNK-YEL
SENS GROUND 4 F15 BRN-RED
SIG GROUND 5 E99 BLK-YEL
SENS 5V SUPPLY 6 F100 BRN-YEL
8V SUPPLY 7 F53 WHT-BLK
START 8 88 GRY-GRN STARTER RLY
IGN START/RUN 9 11 YEL
PWR STEERING SENS 10 F78 BLU-ORG
GROUND 11 99 BLK (2.5L)
GROUND 12 99 BLK
INJECTOR #4 13 F74 YEL
INJECTOR #3 14 F73 TAN-YEL
INJECTOR #2 15 F72 LT GRN
INJECTOR #1 16 F71 LT BLU
IGNITION 19 F23 YEL-BLK
ALTERNATOR IND 20 59 TAN-BLK ALTERNATOR
AIR TEMP SENS 21 F7 TAN-BLU
THROTTLE POSTN SENS 22 F50 YEL-GRN
SPEED SENS (-) 24 F52 RED-GRN
DIAGNOSTIC (DATA 2) 25 F84 BLK-RED
A/C SELECT 27 365 LT BLU-RED A/C RELAY
A/C REQUEST 28 169 LT BLU-WHT A/C BLOWER SW
TCC FEED (BRAKE) 29 116 LT BLU-YEL H5 LT BU-YL STOP LT SW
NEUTRAL SAFETY 30 34 BLK-WHT STARTER RLY
CHECK ENG IND 32 E19 GRN-RED C5 GRN-RED WARN IND (CHECK ENG)
A/C CLUTCH RELAY 34 135 BLU-WHT A/C RELAY
INJECTOR #5 38 F75 WHT
AIS STEPPER 39 F70 GRN-BLK
AIS STEPPER 40 F68 RED-YEL
OXYGEN SENS 41 F6 GRY
TACH SIG 43 339 ORG H6 ORG TACH (INST CLSTR)
SYNC SENS SIG 44 F65 GRY-BLK
DIAGNOSTIC (DATA 1) 45 F83 BLK-PNK
SPEED SIG 47 C8 BLU
FUEL PUMP RELAY 51 F17 ORG-GRN
UPSHIFT IND 54 126 BRN F6 BRN WARN IND (UPSHIFT)
MAINTENANCE IND 56 M19 GRN-ORG C4 GRN-ORG WARN IND (EMISS MAINT)
Z2 SENS 57 Z2 DK GRN-BLK
INJECTOR #6 58 F76 BRN-GRN
AIS STEPPER 59 F67 BLU-YEL
AIS STEPPER 60 F69 PNK-BLK
ELECTRONIC CONTROL UNIT (ECU) (2.5L & 4.0L)
91H13729

Fig. 2: Wiring Diagram (Wrangler 2.5L & 4.0L)

Cherokee, Comanche, Grand Wagoneer, Wrangler

INTRODUCTION

This article contains underhood views of vacuum hose routing. Use these vacuum diagrams during the visual inspection portion of BASIC DIAGNOSTIC PROCEDURES article. This will assist in identifying improperly routed vacuum hoses which may cause driveability and/or computer-indicated malfunctions.

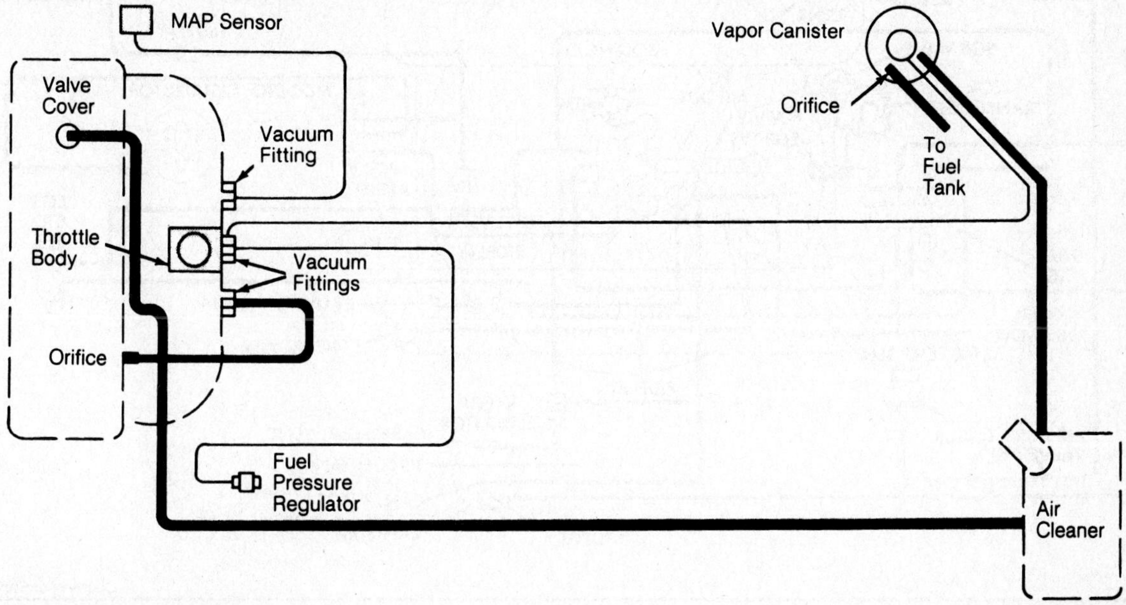
MAP Sensor
Vapor Canister
Valve Cover
Orifice
Vacuum Fitting
To Fuel Tank
Throttle Body
Vacuum Fittings
Orifice
Fuel Pressure Regulator
Air Cleaner

91H13976

Courtesy of Chrysler Motors.

Fig. 1: Engine Vacuum Diagram (2.5L)

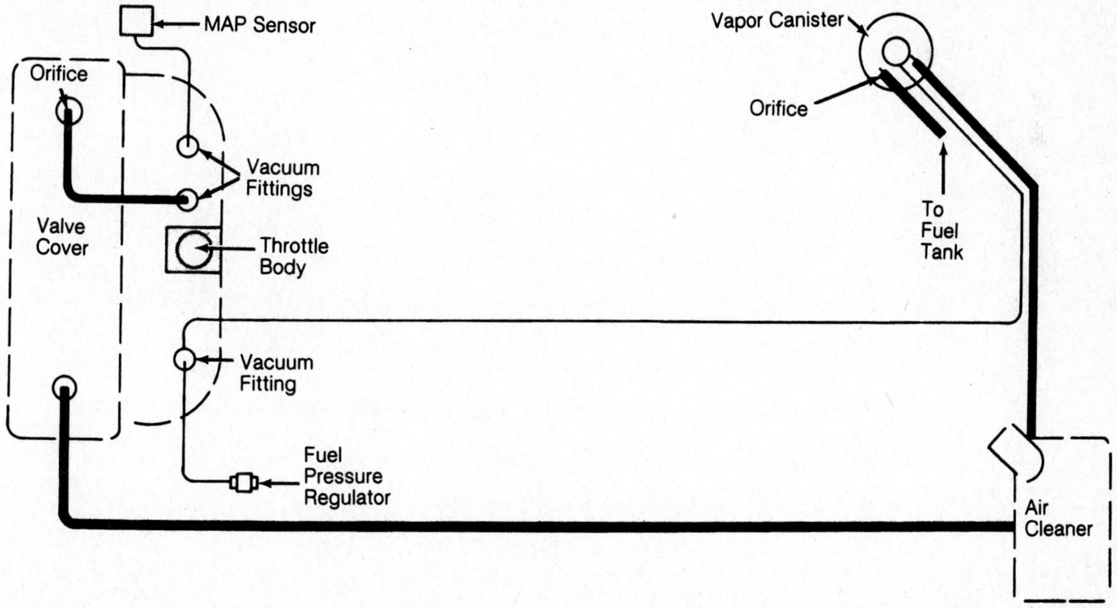
MAP Sensor
Vapor Canister
Orifice
Orifice
Vacuum Fittings
Valve Cover
Throttle Body
To Fuel Tank
Vacuum Fitting
Fuel Pressure Regulator
Air Cleaner

91I13977

Courtesy of Chrysler Motors.

Fig. 2: Engine Vacuum Diagram (4.0L)

1991 ENGINE PERFORMANCE
Vacuum Diagrams (Cont.)

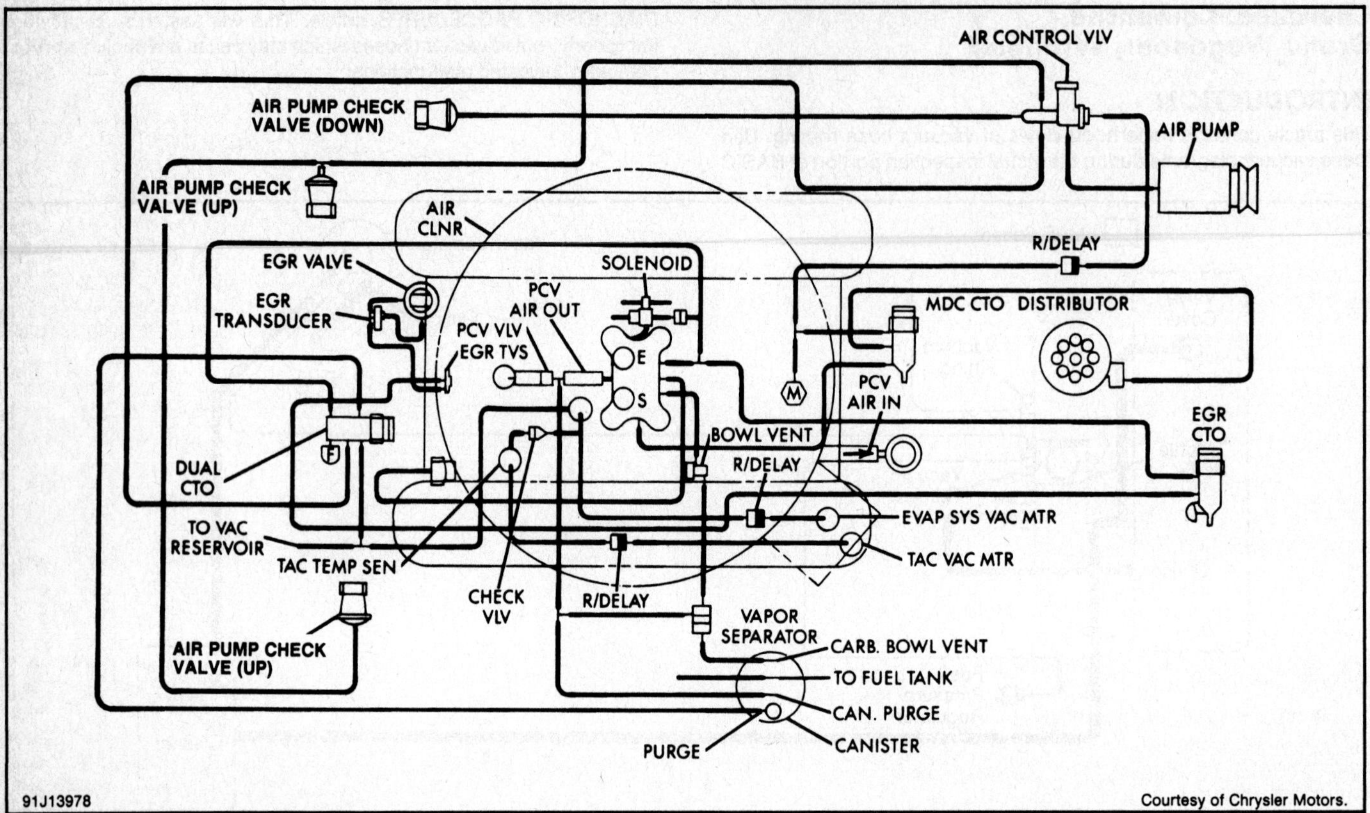
AIR CONTROL VLV
AIR PUMP CHECK
VALVE (DOWN)
AIR PUMP
AIR PUMP CHECK
VALVE (UP)
AIR
CLNR
R/DELAY
EGR VALVE
SOLENOID
EGR
TRANSDUCER
PCV
AIR OUT
MDC CTO
DISTRIBUTOR
PCV VLV
EGR TVS
E
S
M
PCV
AIR IN
F
BOWL VENT
EGR
CTO
DUAL
CTO
R/DELAY
TO VAC
RESERVOIR
EVAP SYS VAC MTR
TAC TEMP SEN
TAC VAC MTR
CHECK
VLV
R/DELAY
VAPOR
SEPARATOR
CARB. BOWL VENT
AIR PUMP CHECK
VALVE (UP)
TO FUEL TANK
CAN. PURGE
PURGE
CANISTER
91J13978
Courtesy of Chrysler Motors.

Fig. 3: Engine Vacuum Diagram (6.0L)

1991 ENGINE PERFORMANCE
Removal, Overhaul & Installation – Carbureted

Grand Wagoneer

INTRODUCTION

Removal, overhaul and installation procedures are covered in this article. If component removal and installation is primarily an unbolt and bolt-on procedure, only a torque specification may be furnished.

IGNITION SYSTEM

DISTRIBUTOR TRIGGER WHEEL & PICK-UP COIL ASSEMBLY

Removal & Installation – 1) Remove distributor cap and rotor. Using a flat washer to prevent puller from contacting other distributor components, remove trigger wheel with puller.

2) Remove pick-up coil plate screws and remove pick-up coil assembly. If vacuum advance mechanism is to be replaced, remove screws and mechanism from distributor housing.

3) To install components, reverse removal procedure. Install trigger wheel on shaft, with long portion of teeth facing up. When trigger wheel and slot in shaft are properly aligned, install pin into locating groove in shaft.

FUEL SYSTEM

CARBURETOR

Removal & Installation – 1) Remove air cleaner. Disconnect throttle cable from throttle lever. Disconnect vacuum hoses, return spring, and choke filter air tube.

2) Disconnect choke heater element wire, solenoid wire, PCV valve hose, in-line fuel filter, and choke-heated air tube at carburetor. Remove carburetor nuts, carburetor, and gasket. To install, reverse removal procedure.

Overhaul – 1) Remove air cleaner anchor screw. Note position of choke rod for assembly reference. *See Fig. 1.* Remove choke valve lever screw. Slide choke rod out of choke lever.

2) Remove 9 air horn retaining screws and carburetor identification tag. Remove air horn and gasket. Remove choke rod plastic dust seal from air horn. Remove fast idle cam retaining clip.

3) Remove choke shield. Grind off heads of choke housing cover retaining rivets. Remove retainer, cover, coil, and gasket. Remove remaining portion of rivets.

4) Remove choke housing assembly retaining screws, housing assembly, and gasket. Remove fast idle cam. Remove retaining screw, coil cover, and washer. Remove choke lever shaft and fast idle cam lever from choke housing.

5) Pry off float shaft retainer from fuel inlet seat. Remove float, float shaft retainer, and fuel inlet needle as an assembly. Remove retainer and float shaft from float lever. Remove fuel inlet needle seat and gasket.

6) Note position of main jets for reassembly reference. Remove main jets. Remove accelerator pump discharge screw, air distribution plate, booster venturi, and gasket. DO NOT remove tubes from venturi.

7) Invert main body and catch accelerator pump discharge weight and ball. Remove accelerator pump cover, pump rod, pump lever, diaphragm, and spring. Disconnect accelerator pump rod from overtravel lever. Remove rod and retainer.

8) Firmly grasp elastomer valve and pull it out of fuel bowl. *See Fig. 1.* If elastomer valve tip breaks off during removal, ensure tip is removed from fuel bowl.

9) Invert main body. Remove power valve screws, power valve cover, and gasket. Remove power valve using an 8-point socket. Remove and discard power valve gasket.

10) Remove altitude compensator mounting screws, altitude compensator assembly, and gasket from main body. Remove aneroid-to-chamber screws. Remove gasket and aneroid from chamber.

11) If removing idle mixture screws, remove idle mixture limiter cap. For reassembly reference, count and record the number of turns necessary to lightly seat mixture screws. Remove idle mixture screws.

12) Remove fast idle lever assembly from throttle shaft. Remove throttle solenoid. Remove choke diaphragm. To reassemble carburetor, reverse disassembly procedure, and perform specified adjustments.

Dry Float Level Adjustment – With float installed in fuel bowl, raise float by pressing down on float tab until fuel inlet needle is lightly seated. Using a "T" scale, measure dry float level adjustment at free end of float. Set dry float level adjustment to .328" (8.33 mm).

Accelerator Pump Rod Length Adjustment – Position accelerator pump operating rod retainer into hole No. 3 in overtravel lever. Adjust pump rod length to .185" (4.7 mm).

Accelerator Pump Stroke Adjustment – 1) Remove accelerator pump cover to remove accelerator pump rod adjuster from overtravel lever. Position adjuster in hole No. 3 in overtravel lever.

2) Energize solenoid with a 12-volt battery. Accelerator pump stroke is measured from top of accelerator pump shaft to tip of pump cover. Turn pump rod adjuster until accelerator pump shaft protrudes .165-.205" (4.2-5.2 mm) out of pump cover when solenoid is energized.

Choke Mechanism Adjustment – 1) Install choke lever and shaft bushing in choke housing (if removed). Install coil lever and lever attaching screw. Install choke rod, fast idle cam rod, and vacuum diaphragm rod to choke lever and shaft.

2) Install choke cover, coil, cover retainer, and gasket. Loosely secure cover with screws, but DO NOT completely tighten screws at this time. Align index mark on choke cover with "V" notch on housing. Tighten cover retaining screws securely.

Choke Valve & Fast Idle Cam Linkage Adjustment – 1) Open throttle to allow choke mechanism to set fast idle screw to top step of cam. Using a hand-held vacuum pump, apply vacuum to hold choke diaphragm against set screw, while using finger pressure to load choke diaphragm step in direction opposite of diaphragm.

NOTE: A vacuum leak may be noticed on choke diaphragm; this is normal. DO NOT press on linkage rods.

2) Measure clearance between air horn and top of choke valve. Initial choke valve clearance should be .078-.118" (1.98-3.00 mm). Adjust clearance by turning screw at rear of choke vacuum diaphragm.

3) Push down on fast idle cam lever. Stop when fast idle speed adjustment screw contacts second step of fast idle cam. The screw should rest against shoulder of fast idle cam high step.

4) Measure clearance between air horn wall and upper edge of choke valve. Fast idle cam adjustment should be .076" (1.93 mm). Adjust clearance by turning fast idle cam lever screw.

Choke Unloader Adjustment – 1) Hold throttle fully open, and pressure on choke valve toward closed position. Measure clearance between air horn wall and lower edge of choke valve.

2) Set choke unloader to .420" (10.67 mm). If necessary, bend unloader tang contacting fast idle cam. Bend tang toward cam to increase clearance and away from cam to decrease clearance.

3) After completing adjustment, open throttle until unloader tang is directly below fast idle cam pivot. There must be EXACTLY .070" (1.8 mm) clearance between unloader tang and edge of fast idle cam.

4) Operate throttle and inspect unloader tang to ensure it does not bind, contact or stick on any part of carburetor casting or linkage. Inspect for full throttle opening when throttle is operated from inside vehicle.

Wet Float Level Adjustment – 1) Position vehicle on a flat, level surface. Start and warm engine to normal operating temperature. Remove air cleaner anchor screw.

2) Turn engine off. Remove 9 air horn retaining screws and carburetor identification tag. Start engine, allow it to idle for one MINUTE, then turn engine off. Remove air horn and gasket.

3) Using a "T" scale, measure fuel level at a point at least 1/4" (6.35 mm) from fuel bowl wall. Set wet float level adjustment to .930" (23.62 mm). To adjust fuel level, bend float tab contacting fuel inlet valve.

4) Each time an adjustment is made, install gasket and air horn. Start engine and allow it to idle for 1 MINUTE. Turn engine off and measure

Removal, Overhaul & Installation – Carbureted (Cont.)

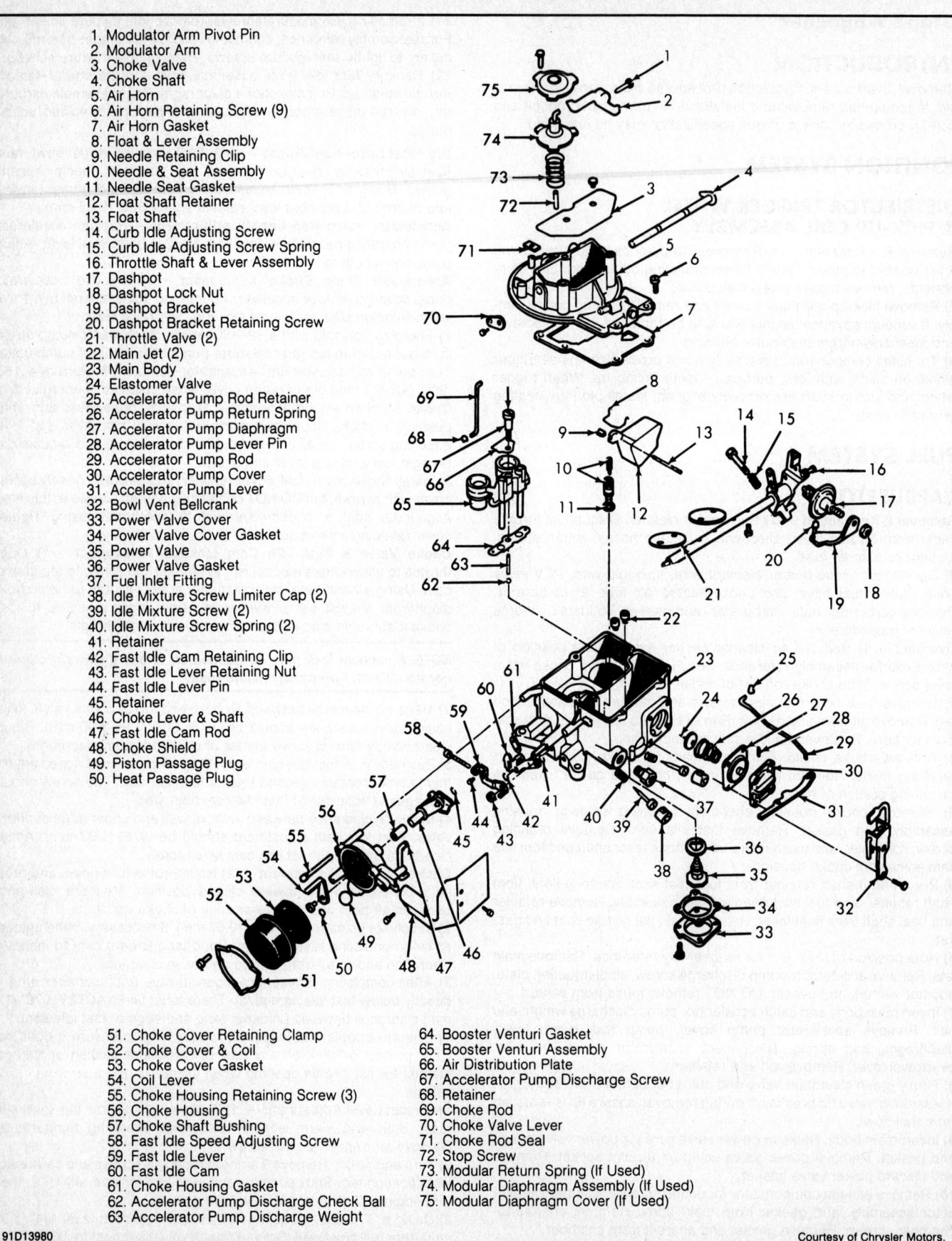

1. Modulator Arm Pivot Pin
2. Modulator Arm
3. Choke Valve
4. Choke Shaft
5. Air Horn
6. Air Horn Retaining Screw (9)
7. Air Horn Gasket
8. Float & Lever Assembly
9. Needle Retaining Clip
10. Needle & Seat Assembly
11. Needle Seat Gasket
12. Float Shaft Retainer
13. Float Shaft
14. Curb Idle Adjusting Screw
15. Curb Idle Adjusting Screw Spring
16. Throttle Shaft & Lever Assembly
17. Dashpot
18. Dashpot Lock Nut
19. Dashpot Bracket
20. Dashpot Bracket Retaining Screw
21. Throttle Valve (2)
22. Main Jet (2)
23. Main Body
24. Elastomer Valve
25. Accelerator Pump Rod Retainer
26. Accelerator Pump Return Spring
27. Accelerator Pump Diaphragm
28. Accelerator Pump Lever Pin
29. Accelerator Pump Rod
30. Accelerator Pump Cover
31. Accelerator Pump Lever
32. Bowl Vent Bellcrank
33. Power Valve Cover
34. Power Valve Cover Gasket
35. Power Valve
36. Power Valve Gasket
37. Fuel Inlet Fitting
38. Idle Mixture Screw Limiter Cap (2)
39. Idle Mixture Screw (2)
40. Idle Mixture Screw Spring (2)
41. Retainer
42. Fast Idle Cam Retaining Clip
43. Fast Idle Lever Retaining Nut
44. Fast Idle Lever Pin
45. Retainer
46. Choke Lever & Shaft
47. Fast Idle Cam Rod
48. Choke Shield
49. Piston Passage Plug
50. Heat Passage Plug

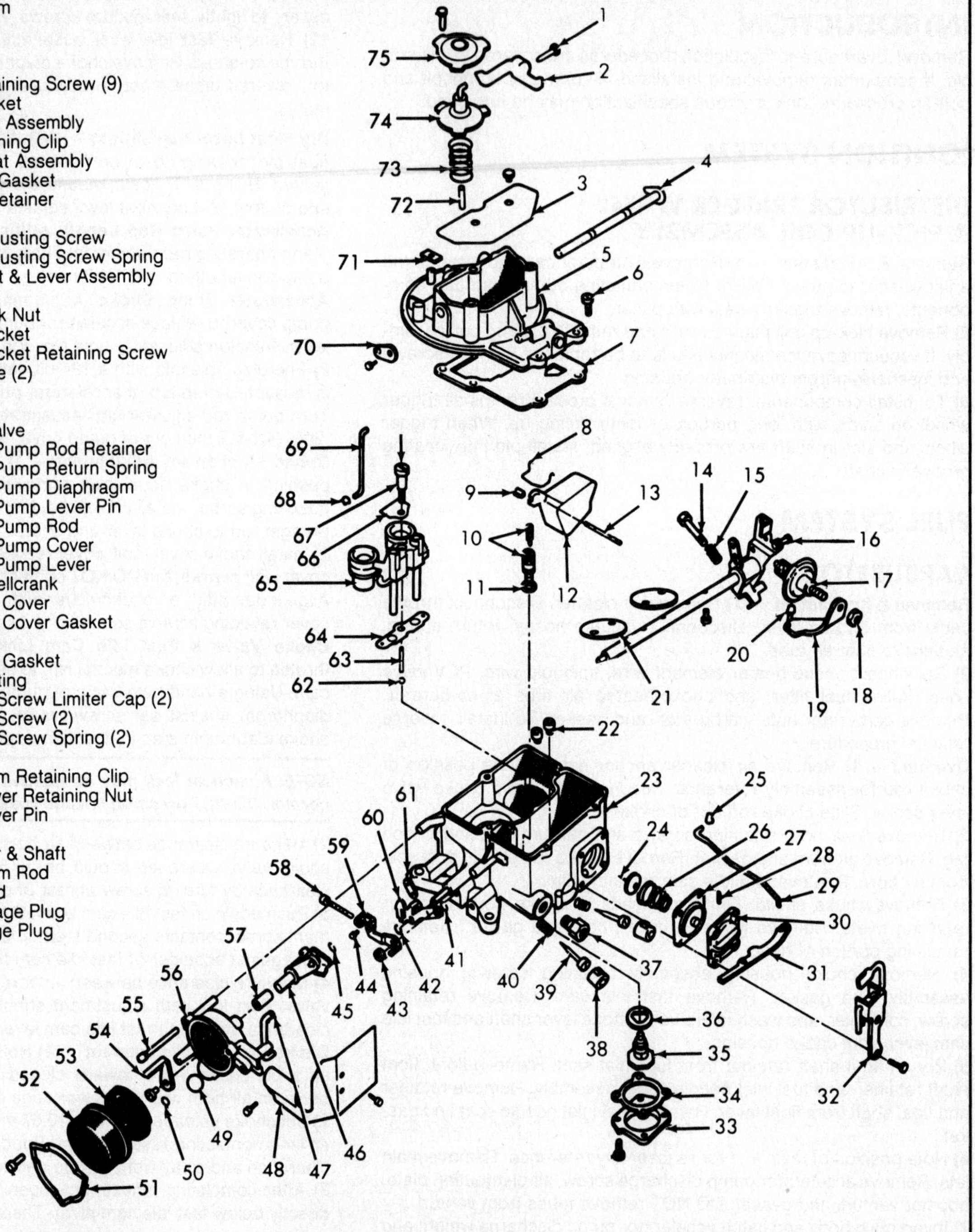

51. Choke Cover Retaining Clamp
52. Choke Cover & Coil
53. Choke Cover Gasket
54. Coil Lever
55. Choke Housing Retaining Screw (3)
56. Choke Housing
57. Choke Shaft Bushing
58. Fast Idle Speed Adjusting Screw
59. Fast Idle Lever
60. Fast Idle Cam
61. Choke Housing Gasket
62. Accelerator Pump Discharge Check Ball
63. Accelerator Pump Discharge Weight
64. Booster Venturi Gasket
65. Booster Venturi Assembly
66. Air Distribution Plate
67. Accelerator Pump Discharge Screw
68. Retainer
69. Choke Rod
70. Choke Valve Lever
71. Choke Rod Seal
72. Stop Screw
73. Modular Return Spring (If Used)
74. Modular Diaphragm Assembly (If Used)
75. Modular Diaphragm Cover (If Used)

91D13980

Courtesy of Chrysler Motors.

Fig. 1: Exploded View of 2-Barrel Carburetor (Motorcraft 2150)

fuel level once again. Once fuel level is correct, adjust idle speed and mixture.

Idle Mixture Adjustment – 1) Install idle mixture screws, then back off screws the number of turns recorded during disassembly to obtain a preliminary idle mixture adjustment. DO NOT install limiter caps at this time.

2) Install carburetor and connect tachometer to engine (TACH terminal on ignition coil). Start engine and warm to normal operating temperature. Ensure choke is OFF and engine is at curb idle speed.

3) Place transmission in Neutral. Adjust idle speed to 600 RPM. Turn idle mixture screws clockwise until a loss of RPM is noted on tachometer. Now turn idle mixture screws counterclockwise until highest RPM is obtained.

4) For final adjustment, turn both idle mixture screws clockwise in small, equal amounts until idle speed drop is 20 RPM. If final RPM differs more than 30 RPM (plus or minus) from original curb idle speed, readjust curb idle speed and repeat idle mixture adjustment procedure. Install idle mixture screw limiter caps, being careful not to disturb mixture adjustment.

Idle Speed Adjustment – 1) Connect tachometer to engine (TACH terminal on ignition coil). Start engine and warm to normal operating temperature. Ensure that choke is off and engine is at curb idle speed.

2) Place transmission in Neutral. Adjust idle speed to 600 RPM by turning hex head screw on idle solenoid carriage. Disconnect idle solenoid and adjust idle speed (anti-dieseling) screw to obtain 500 RPM. Reconnect idle solenoid.

Fast Idle Speed Adjustment – 1) Connect tachometer to engine (TACH terminal on ignition coil). Start engine and warm to normal operating temperature. Ensure choke is off and engine is at curb idle speed.

2) Place transmission in Neutral. Position fast idle cam on second step of fast idle cam. Adjust fast idle speed to 1600 RPM by turning fast idle adjustment screw.

FUEL FILTER

Removal & Installation – Disconnect negative battery cable. Disconnect fuel supply tube at carburetor. Remove and discard fuel filter. To install, reverse removal procedure.

FUEL PUMP

Removal & Installation – 1) Disconnect negative battery cable. Remove fuel tank filler cap. Disconnect fuel inlet hose and outlet tube fitting from fuel pump.

2) Remove fuel pump mounting bolts and remove fuel pump. Remove old gasket material from engine block. To install, reverse removal procedure. Start vehicle and check for leaks.

ADJUSTMENT SPECIFICATIONS

ADJUSTMENT SPECIFICATIONS

Application	Specification
Accelerator Pump Rod Length	.185" (4.7 mm)
Accelerator Pump Stroke	.165-.205" (4.2-5.2 mm)
Float Level (Dry)	.328" (8.33 mm)
Float Level (Wet)	.930" (23.62 mm)
Initial Choke Valve Clearance	.078-.118" (1.98-3.00 mm)
Fast Idle Cam Setting	.076" (1.93 mm)
Choke Cover Setting	"V" Notch
Choke Unloader	.420" (10.67 mm)
Curb Idle Speed	[1] 600 RPM
Fast Idle Speed	1600 RPM

[1] – Specification is with transmission in Drive and all brakes applied. Idle speed is 500 RPM with idle speed solenoid de-energized.

TORQUE SPECIFICATIONS

TORQUE SPECIFICATIONS

Application	Ft. Lbs. (N.m)
Carburetor Nuts	16 (22)
Fuel Pump Bolts	13 (18)
Fuel Pump Outlet Tube Fitting	18 (24)

1991 ENGINE PERFORMANCE
Removal, Overhaul & Installation – Fuel Injected

Cherokee, Comanche, Wrangler

INTRODUCTION

Removal, overhaul and installation procedures are covered in this article. If component removal and installation is primarily an unbolt and bolt-on procedure, only a torque specification may be furnished.

IGNITION SYSTEM

SYNCHRONIZATION SIGNAL GENERATOR

Removal & Installation – 1) Remove distributor cap, rotor, and distributor. Remove pulse ring mounting screws and remove pulse ring. Using pin punch and hammer, remove distributor gear roll pin.
2) Using a rubber mallet, tap distributor shaft out until distributor gear and shim are removed. Slide shaft out of distributor housing. Remove sync (synchronization) signal generator stator mounting screws and positioning arm.
3) Slide wiring harness grommet out of distributor housing. Remove synch signal generator. To install, reverse removal procedure.

FUEL SYSTEM

FUEL SYSTEM PRESSURE RELEASE

WARNING: ALWAYS relieve fuel pressure before disconnecting any fuel injection-related component. DO NOT allow fuel to contact engine or electrical components.

1) Disconnect negative battery cable. Remove fuel filler cap. Remove cap from pressure test port on fuel rail. *See Fig. 1*. Place shop towels around pressure test port to absorb spilled fuel.
2) Press the test port valve with a small screwdriver or punch wrapped in shop towels. Remove shop towels and dispose of properly. Install pressure test port cap.

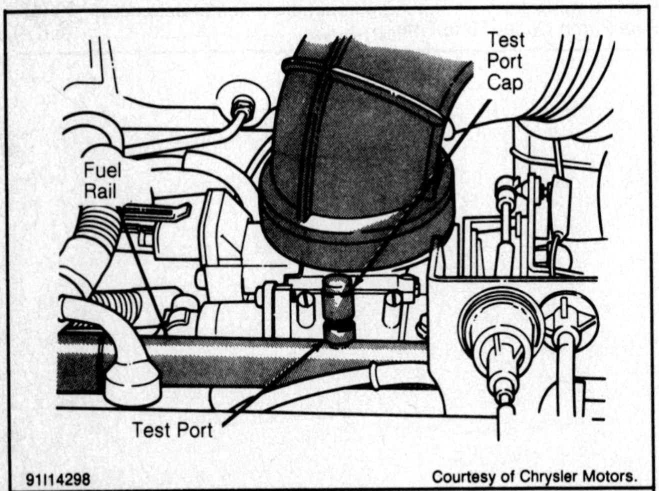
Test
Port
Cap
Fuel
Rail
Test Port
91I14298
Courtesy of Chrysler Motors.

Fig. 1: Releasing Fuel System Pressure

FUEL HOSES & CLAMPS

Removal – 1) Quick-connect fittings are used on inlet and outlet ports of fuel rail. Fitting consists of 2 "O" rings, spacer, and "O" ring retainer.
2) To disconnect quick-connect fitting, squeeze tabs against tube and pull fitting of hose/fitting assembly. Retainer should stay on fuel tube when tube is disconnected. The "O" rings and spacer should remain in connector.
Servicing Quick-Connect Fitting – A repair kit with replacement "O" ring, spacer, and retainer is available. *See Fig. 2*. To service quick-connect fitting, push disposable plug/kit assembly into quick-connect fitting until a "click" is heard. Grasp end of disposable plug and pull outward to remove it from fitting.
Installation – When installing and connecting fitting, push fuel tube into quick-connect fitting until a "click" is heard. Ensure connection is secure by firmly pulling on fuel tube. Tube should be locked in place.

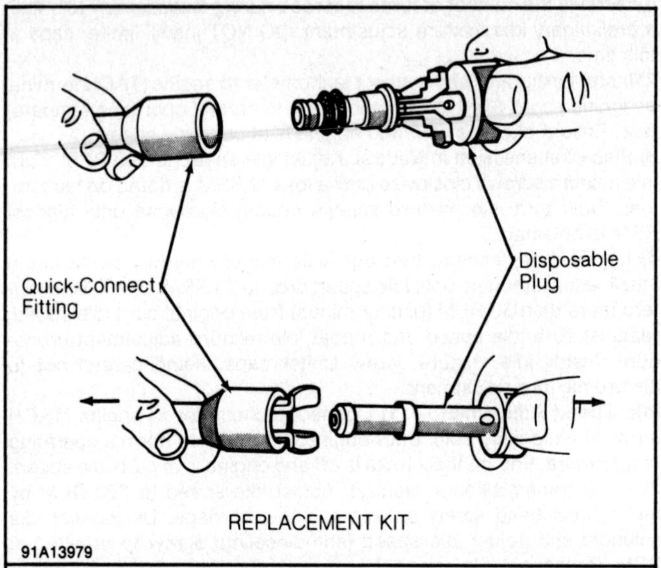
Quick-Connect
Fitting
Disposable
Plug
REPLACEMENT KIT
91A13979

Fig. 2: Quick-Connect Fitting Replacement Kit

FUEL RAILS & INJECTORS

Removal & Installation – 1) Relieve fuel system pressure. See FUEL SYSTEM PRESSURE RELEASE under FUEL SYSTEM. Remove and tag injector wiring harness connectors from each injector. Disconnect vacuum hose from fuel pressure regulator.
2) Disconnect fuel supply and fuel return lines. Remove fuel rail mounting bolts. On automatic transmission vehicles, it may be necessary to remove throttle line pressure cable and bracket.
3) Gently rock fuel rail until all injector are clear from intake manifold. Remove injector retaining clips and remove injectors. To install, reverse removal procedure. Ensure fuel injectors are properly seated in intake manifold.

FUEL FILTER

Removal & Installation – Relieve fuel pressure. See FUEL SYSTEM PRESSURE RELEASE under FUEL SYSTEM. Raise and support vehicle. Locate filter along driver-side frame rail. On Wrangler, remove fuel filter protection shield. Remove hose and clamps from both sides of filter. Remove retaining strap and remove filter. To install, reverse removal procedure.

FUEL PUMP

Removal & Installation (Cherokee & Comanche) – 1) Relieve fuel system pressure. See FUEL SYSTEM PRESSURE RELEASE under FUEL SYSTEM. Remove fuel tank filler cap, and siphon fuel out of fuel tank. Raise and support vehicle. Disconnect fuel gauge sending unit connector.
2) Disconnect fuel tank vent hose and return hoses from fuel pump/fuel gauge sending unit. Using drift punch and hammer, carefully remove fuel pump lock ring counterclockwise. Remove fuel pump/fuel gauge sending unit and "O" ring. To install, reverse removal procedure.
Removal & Installation (Wrangler) – 1) Relieve fuel system pressure. See FUEL SYSTEM PRESSURE RELEASE under FUEL SYSTEM. Remove fuel tank filler cap, and siphon fuel out of fuel tank. Raise and support vehicle. Disconnect filler vent hose and fuel filler hose from tank.

1991 ENGINE PERFORMANCE
Removal, Overhaul & Installation – Fuel Injected (Cont.)

2) Disconnect fuel gauge sending unit connector. Remove tie straps securing connector harness to fuel supply and return tubes. Disconnect fuel tank vent hose from vent tube.
3) Remove fuel tank shield or skid plate (if equipped). Support fuel tank with floor jack, and remove support strap nuts. Lower fuel tank. Remove mounting bolts, gasket, and fuel pump/fuel gauge sending unit. To install, reverse removal procedure.

THROTTLE BODY

Removal & Installation – 1) Disconnect negative battery cable. Remove air cleaner snorkel from throttle body. Disconnect automatic idle speed (stepper) motor and throttle position sensor connectors.
2) Disconnect accelerator cable, throttle cable (A/T), and speed (cruise) control cable (if equipped). Remove mounting bolts, throttle body, and gasket. To install, reverse removal procedure.

TORQUE SPECIFICATIONS

TORQUE SPECIFICATIONS

Application	ft. Lbs. (N.m)
Automatic Idle Speed Motor	[1]
Coolant Temperature Sensor	21 (28)
Crankshaft Position Sensor	[1]
Fuel Rail Bolts	20 (27)
Ignition Coil	[1]
Manifold Absolute Pressure Sensor	[1]
Manifold Air Temperature Sensor	20 (27)
Oxygen (O_2) Sensor	22 (30)
Power Steering Pressure Switch	[1]
Throttle Position Sensor	[1]
Vehicle Speed Sensor	[1]
	INCH Lbs. (N.m)
Fuel Filter Strap Bolt	108 (12)
Single-Board Engine Controller II	[2] 108 (12)
Throttle Body Bolts	108 (12)

[1] – Torque specification is not available from manufacturer.
[2] – Tighten 60-pin connector screws to 35 INCH Lbs. (4 N.m).

1991 ELECTRICAL
Alternators – Delco-Remy

Grand Wagoneer

DESCRIPTION

A rectifier bridge, connected to stator (field) windings, contains 6 diodes (3 positive and 3 negative) molded into an assembly. This rectifier bridge changes stator AC voltage into DC voltage.

Alternator field current is supplied through a diode trio connected to stator windings. A capacitor is mounted to end frame, protecting rectifier bridge and diodes from high voltage and suppressing radio interference noise.

ADJUSTMENTS

BELT TENSION

BELT ADJUSTMENT
(Tension In Lbs. (kg) Using Belt Tension Gauge)

Application	Tension
New Belts	120-160 (54.48-72.64)
Used Belts	90-115 (40.86-52.21)

TROUBLE SHOOTING

NOTE: See TROUBLE SHOOTING article in GENERAL INFORMATION.

ON-VEHICLE TESTING

NOTE: Before testing, check all terminals connections. Check alternator mounting bolts and drive belt tension. Ensure battery is fully charged.

ALTERNATOR VOLTAGE TEST

1) If battery is overcharging, attach a voltmeter across battery terminals. Run engine at a moderate speed with all accessories off. If voltmeter reads 15.5 volts or more, remove alternator for repair.
2) If battery is undercharging, turn ignition on and leave all wiring leads connected. Connect a voltmeter from alternator BAT terminal to ground. Voltmeter should read 12.5 volts. Backprobe with voltmeter between terminal No. 1 and ground. Voltmeter should read 2-4 volts. *See Fig. 1.*

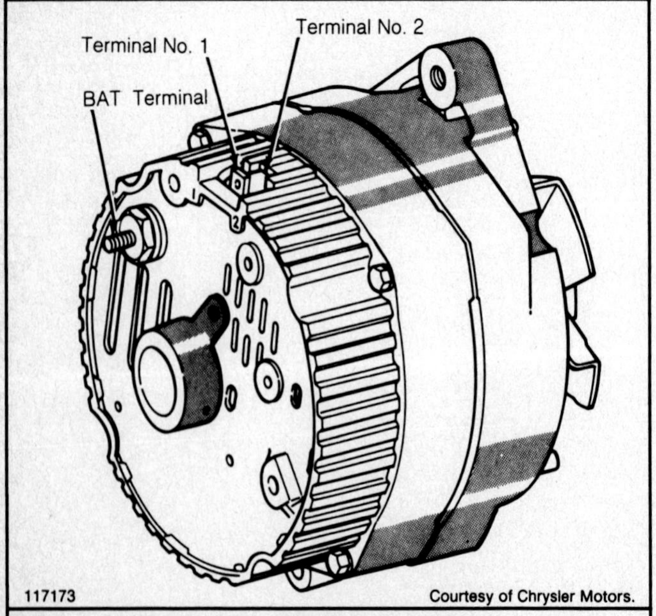
Terminal No. 2
Terminal No. 1
BAT Terminal
117173
Courtesy of Chrysler Motors.

Fig. 1: Checking Voltage at Alternator Terminal

3) Backprobe with voltmeter between terminal No. 2 and ground. Voltmeter should read 12.5 volts. A zero reading on any connection indicates an open between connection and battery. Opens in the No. 2 lead will prevent alternator from turning on.

ALTERNATOR OUTPUT TEST

1) Connect charging system tester to battery and in circuit at BAT terminal of alternator. Operate engine at 2000 RPM and adjust load (rheostat) knob on charging system tester as required to obtain maximum current output.
2) Output must be within 10 amps of rated output stamped on alternator. If not, insert a screwdriver into test hole to ground field winding. Touch tang to alternator case. *See Fig. 2.*

NOTE: DO NOT insert screwdriver more than 1" into end frame or internal damage to alternator will result.

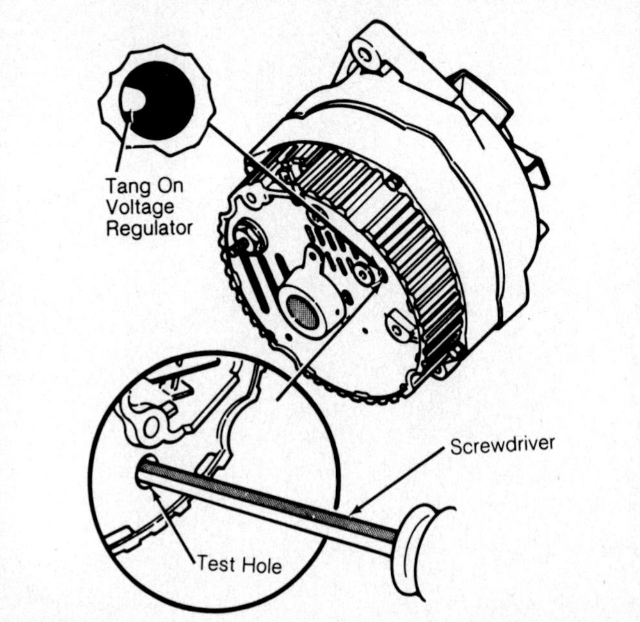
Tang On
Voltage
Regulator
Screwdriver
Test Hole
117174
Courtesy of Chrysler Motors.

Fig. 2: Locating Alternator Test Hole

3) If output increases to within 10 amps of rated output with field winding grounded, regulator is defective. If output remains below 10 amps of rated output, check field winding, diode trio, rectifier bridge, and stator.

BENCH TESTING

ROTOR FIELD WINDING TEST

Separate alternator. To check for grounded circuits, attach ohmmeter leads to rotor shaft and one slip ring (test both slip ring circuits). If any continuity is indicated, replace rotor. To test for open field, touch one ohmmeter lead to each slip ring. Resistance should measure about 2.2-3.0 ohms. If not, replace rotor.

STATOR TEST

Disconnect 3 stator winding leads from rectifier bridge and remove stator from housing. Measure resistance between stator leads. If resistances are not equal between any two leads, replace stator. Connect ohmmeter leads to any stator lead and to stator frame to check for grounded circuit. Ohmmeter reading should be infinity.

DIODE TRIO TEST

Remove diode trio from end frame. Connect an ohmmeter probe to brush terminal and other probe to one of the stator winding terminals.

Check resistance on lowest range scale. Note reading and reverse leads. If readings are the same, replace diode trio. Check other 2 stator terminals of diode trio in same manner. Connect probes between any 2 stator terminals, if resistance is zero, diode is shorted and must be replaced.

RECTIFIER BRIDGE TEST

1) Position ohmmeter with one lead touching grounded heat sink and other lead touching flat metal of diode on one of 3 terminals. Observe reading and reverse test lead connections.
2) If both readings are the same, replace rectifier bridge. A good bridge will give a high and low reading. Test all terminals (6 tests with insulated heat sink).
3) Connect ohmmeter leads to insulated heat sink and to one edge of the 3 terminals. Observe reading and reverse connections. Repeat test on all terminals (6 tests with insulated heat sink).
4) When all 12 tests have been made, testing is complete. Do not use high voltage test light to check bridge. Replace diode trio or rectifier bridge if one pair of readings is the same.

OVERHAUL

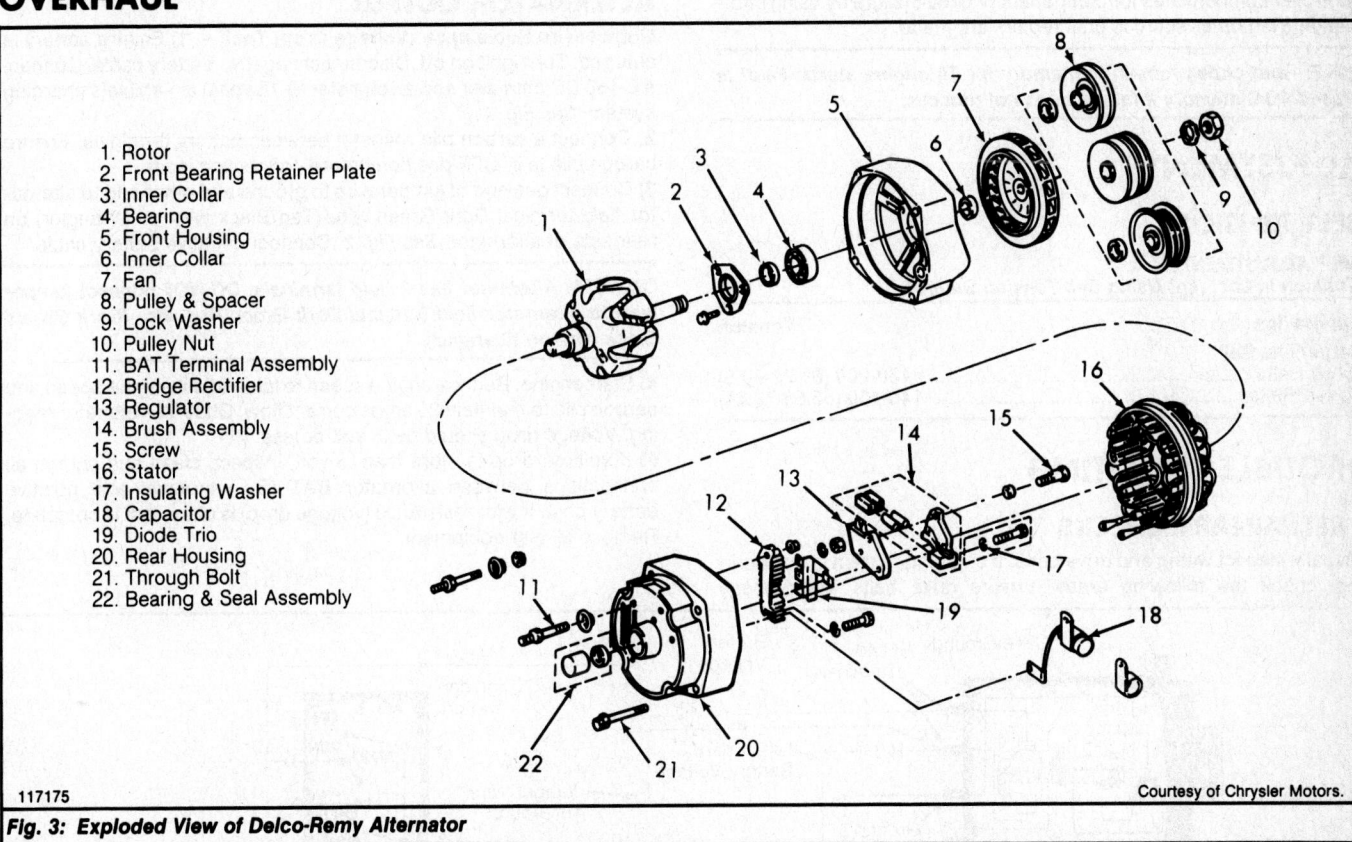

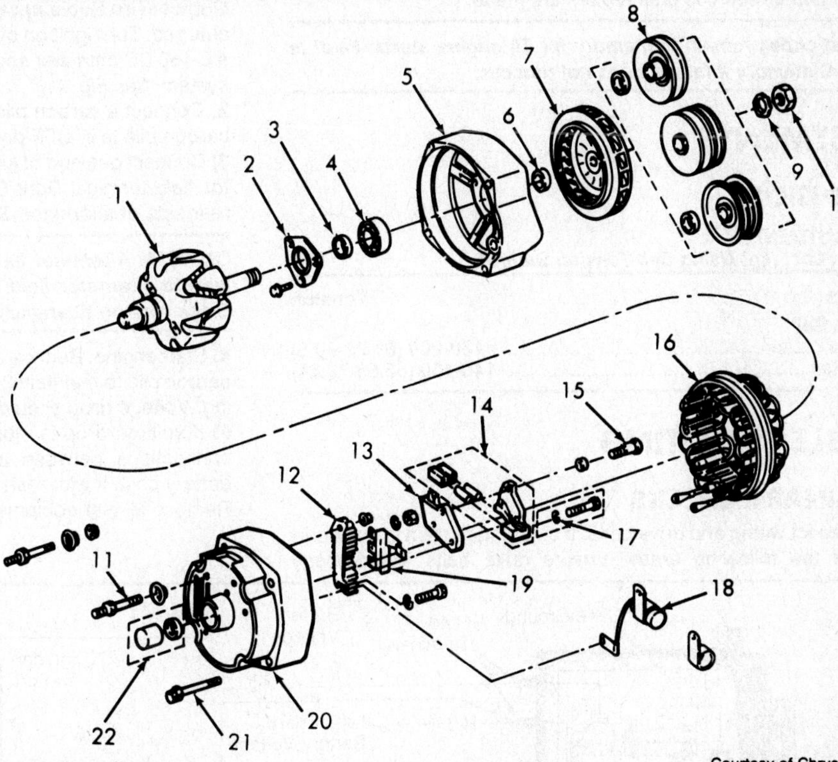
1. Rotor
2. Front Bearing Retainer Plate
3. Inner Collar
4. Bearing
5. Front Housing
6. Inner Collar
7. Fan
8. Pulley & Spacer
9. Lock Washer
10. Pulley Nut
11. BAT Terminal Assembly
12. Bridge Rectifier
13. Regulator
14. Brush Assembly
15. Screw
16. Stator
17. Insulating Washer
18. Capacitor
19. Diode Trio
20. Rear Housing
21. Through Bolt
22. Bearing & Seal Assembly

117175

Courtesy of Chrysler Motors.

Fig. 3: Exploded View of Delco-Remy Alternator

TORQUE SPECIFICATIONS

TORQUE SPECIFICATIONS

Application	Ft. Lbs. (N.m)
Adjusting Bolt	18 (24)
Pivot Bolt	33 (44)

1991 ELECTRICAL
Alternators – Nippondenso

Cherokee, Comanche, Wrangler

DESCRIPTION

Charging system consists of a Single Board Engine Controller-II (SBEC-II), alternator, CHECK ENGINE light and battery. Voltage regulation is controlled within the SBEC-II and cannot be serviced.

The SBEC-II monitors charging system input and output to ensure correct operation. The SBEC-II stores any charging system failures in memory and outputs fault code(s) when on-board diagnostics are entered.

The SBEC-II monitors several different engine control system circuits. If a problem is detected within a monitored circuit, a fault code is stored in the SBEC-II memory. The CHECK ENGINE light will illuminate and system may enter limp-in mode. In limp-in mode, engine controller compensates for component or circuit failure by using information from other sources until repairs are made.

NOTE: Fault codes remain in memory for 50 engine starts. Fault is erased from memory if failure does not reoccur.

ADJUSTMENTS

BELT TENSION

BELT ADJUSTMENT
(Tension In Lbs. (kg) Using Belt Tension Gauge)

Application	Tension
Serpentine Belt	
New Belts	180-200 (81.72-90.8)
Used Belts	140-160 (63.56-72.64)

TROUBLE SHOOTING

PRELIMINARY CHECKS

Visually inspect wiring and drive belts. If charging system is not working, check the following areas: Ensure drive belts are properly tightened. Ensure 12 volts exist at alternator field terminal with ignition on. Ensure battery cables, alternator ground cables and alternator and terminal block connections are clean and tight. Ensure alternator field circuit is not grounded (overcharging).

UNSTEADY OR LOW CHARGING

Check for loose alternator belt, defective alternator, loose alternator ground wire or corroded battery terminals.

OVERCHARGING

Check for grounded alternator field wiring or faulty alternator.

ON-VEHICLE TESTING

ALTERNATOR OUTPUT

Output Wire Resistance (Voltage Drop) Test – 1) Ensure battery is charged. Turn ignition off. Disconnect negative battery cable. Connect a 0-150 DC ammeter and a voltmeter (0-18 volts) to vehicle's charging system. *See Fig. 1.*

2) Connect a carbon pile rheostat between battery terminals. Ensure carbon pile is in OFF position before connecting leads.

3) Connect one end of jumper wire to ground and other end to alternator field terminal Dark Green wire (Tan/Black wire on Wrangler) on rear side of alternator. *See Fig. 2.* Connect negative battery cable.

CAUTION: Alternator has 2 field terminals. DO NOT connect jumper wire to alternator field terminal Dark Green/Red wire (Dark Green/Black wire on Wrangler).

4) Start engine. Reduce engine speed to idle. Adjust engine speed and carbon pile to maintain 20 amps current flow. Observe voltmeter reading. Voltage drop should be .5 volt or less.

5) If voltage drop is more than .5 volt, inspect, clean and tighten all connections between alternator BAT (B+) terminal and positive battery post. If wire resistance (voltage drop) is okay, test is complete. Remove all test equipment.

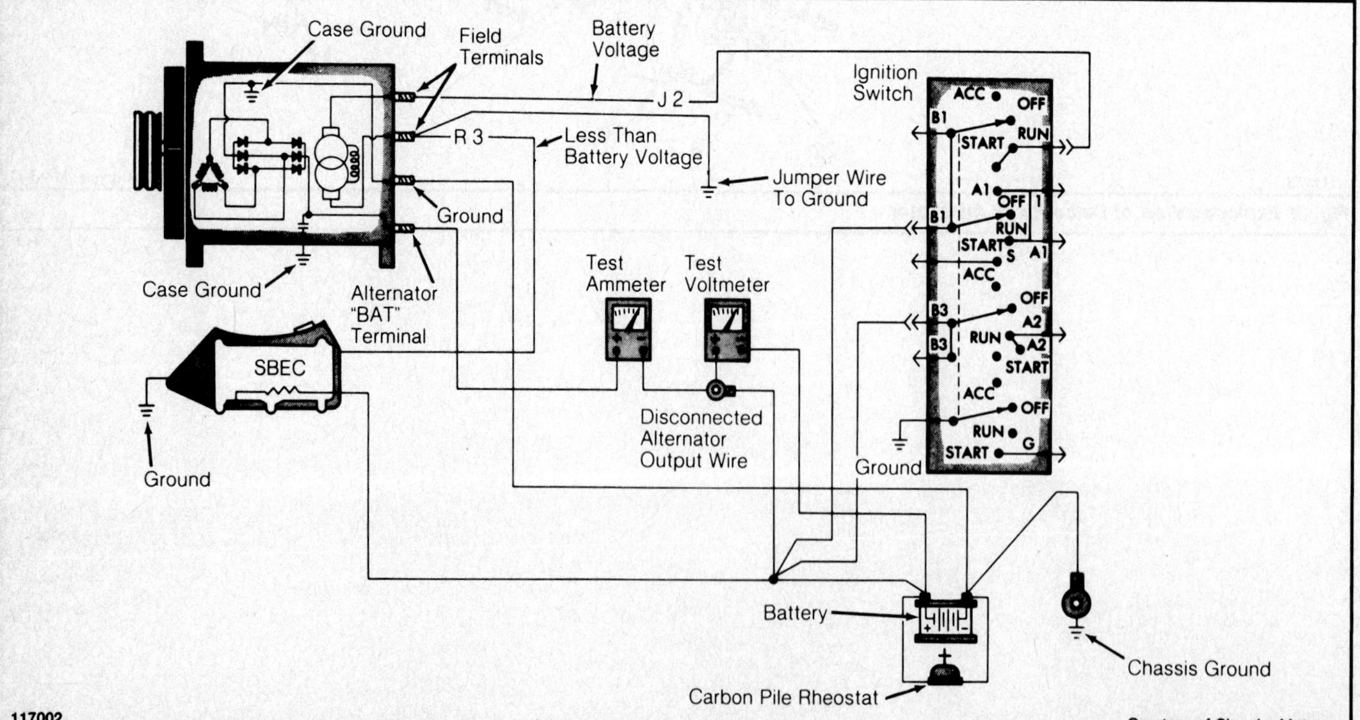
Case Ground
Field Terminals
Battery Voltage
J 2
R 3
Less Than Battery Voltage
Jumper Wire To Ground
Ignition Switch
ACC
OFF
RUN
START
B1
A1
S
B3
A2
G
Ground
Case Ground
Alternator "BAT" Terminal
Test Ammeter
Test Voltmeter
SBEC
Disconnected Alternator Output Wire
Ground
Battery
Chassis Ground
Carbon Pile Rheostat
117002
Courtesy of Chrysler Motors.

Fig. 1: Testing Alternator Output Wire Resistance

1991 ELECTRICAL
Alternators – Nippondenso (Cont.)

Current Output Test – **1)** Ensure battery is charged. Turn ignition off. Disconnect negative battery cable. Connect a 0-150 DC ammeter and a voltmeter (0-18 volts) to vehicle's charging system. *See Fig. 3.*
2) Connect a carbon pile rheostat between battery terminals. Ensure carbon pile is in OFF position before connecting leads.
3) Connect one end of jumper wire to ground and other end to alternator field terminal Dark Green wire (Tan/Black wire on Wrangler) on rear side of alternator. *See Fig. 2.* Connect negative battery cable.

CAUTION: Alternator has 2 field terminals. DO NOT connect jumper wire to alternator field terminal Dark Green/Red wire (Dark Green/Black wire on Wrangler).

4) Start engine and reduce engine speed to idle. Adjust carbon pile and engine speed until engine speed is 1250 RPM and voltmeter reads 15 volts. DO NOT allow voltage to read more than 16 volts.
5) Ammeter should read within 10 amps of rating listed on back of the alternator. If reading is not as specified, replace alternator. Remove all test equipment.

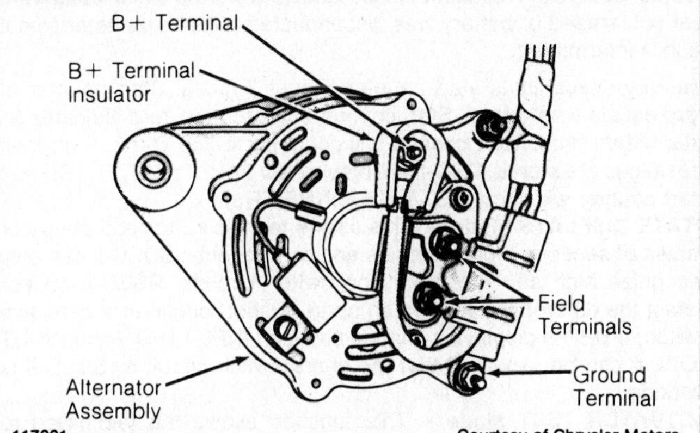
B+ Terminal
B+ Terminal Insulator
Field Terminals
Ground Terminal
Alternator Assembly

117001 Courtesy of Chrysler Motors.

Fig. 2: Identifying Alternator Terminals

ENTERING ON-BOARD DIAGNOSTICS

CAUTION: Before entering on-board diagnostics, check charging system for other problems. See PRELIMINARY CHECKS under TROUBLE SHOOTING. DO NOT connect DRB-II to vehicle with battery charger connected, as damage to DRB-II may result.

Reading Trouble Codes – Trouble codes may be read by using the CHECK ENGINE light on the instrument panel or using the DRB-II. See CHECK ENGINE LIGHT DIAGNOSTIC MODE and DIAGNOSIS USING DRB-II. A more complete diagnosis is possible using the DRB-II.

NOTE: The SBEC-II CANNOT diagnose every charging system problem. If a fault still exists after performing self-diagnostic procedures, go to ON-VEHICLE TESTING.

Trouble Code Explanation – **1)** See CHARGING SYSTEM FAULT CODES table for charging-related faults.
2) Code 12 will set if battery feed to the SBEC-II has been disconnected within last 50-100 starts. SBEC-II monitors this circuit whenever ignition is on.
3) Code 41 will set if the alternator field control fails to switch properly. SBEC-II monitors this circuit whenever ignition is on.
4) If battery temperature sense voltage goes out of range, Code 44 will set in memory. SBEC-II monitors this circuit any time ignition is on.
5) If battery voltage is more than one volt above desired control voltage for more than 20 seconds, a Code 46 will be set in memory. SBEC-II monitors this signal whenever the engine is running.
6) If battery is more than one volt below desired control voltage for more than 20 seconds, Code 47 will be set. Code 47 will also set if no significant change in voltage is detected during alternator test. The SBEC-II monitors this signal whenever engine speed is more than 1500 RPM.

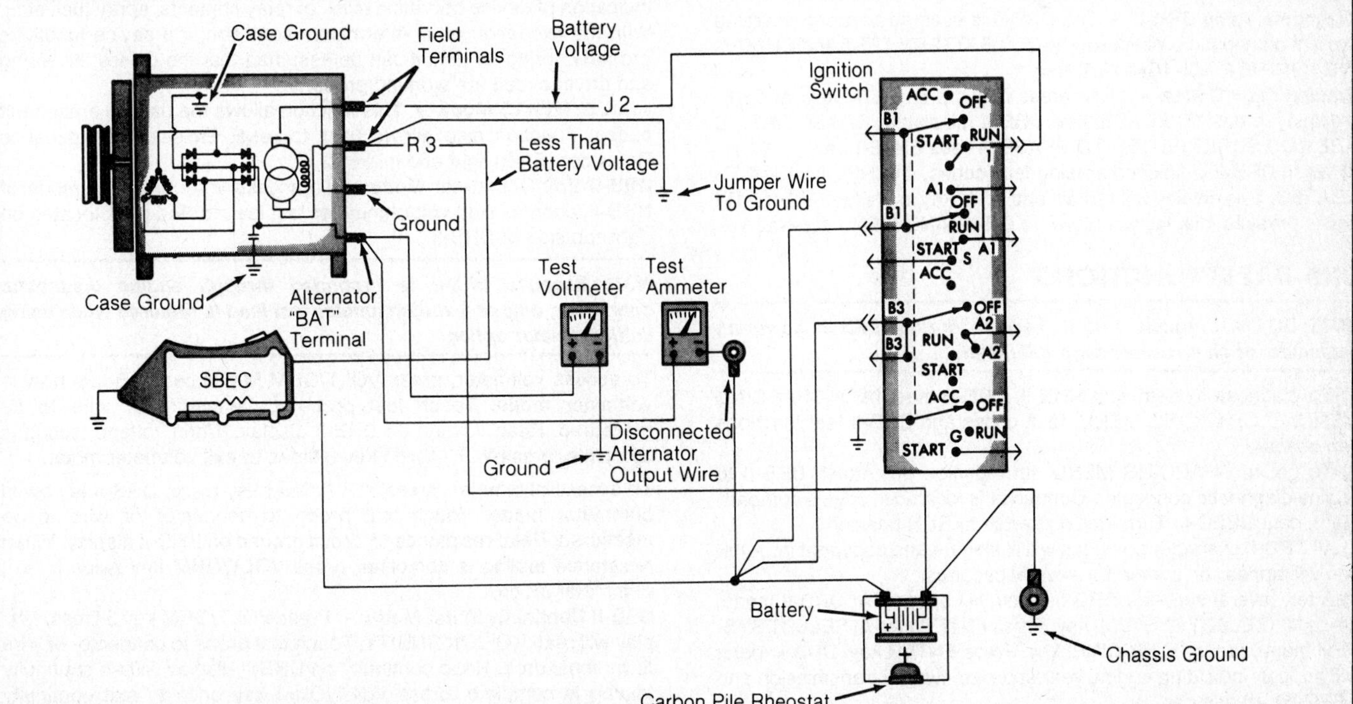
Case Ground
Field Terminals
Battery Voltage
J 2
R 3
Less Than Battery Voltage
Jumper Wire To Ground
Ground
Case Ground
Alternator "BAT" Terminal
Test Voltmeter
Test Ammeter
SBEC
Disconnected Alternator Output Wire
Ground
Ignition Switch
ACC
OFF
B1
START
RUN
1
A1
OFF
B1
RUN
START
S
A1
ACC
B3
OFF
A2
B3
RUN
A2
START
ACC
OFF
G
RUN
START
Battery
Chassis Ground
Carbon Pile Rheostat

117003 Courtesy of Chrysler Motors.

Fig. 3: Testing Alternator Current Output

1991 ELECTRICAL
Alternators – Nippondenso (Cont.)

CHARGING SYSTEM FAULT CODES

Code	Circuit	CHECK ENGINE Light Status
12	Battery Feed to SBEC-II	Off
41 [1]	Alternator Field Control	On
44 [1]	[2] Battery Temp. Sensor	On
46 [1]	High Battery Voltage	On
47 [1]	Low Battery Voltage	Off
55	End of Diagnostic Mode	Off

[1] – This code will cause limp-in mode.
[2] – Sensor inside SBEC-II. If failed, replace SBEC-II.

NOTE: Only charging system-related codes are listed here. For engine-related codes, see appropriate SELF-DIAGNOSTICS article in ENGINE PERFORMANCE.

CHECK ENGINE Light Diagnostic Mode – 1) Start engine (if possible). On models equipped with automatic transmission, place foot on brake and cycle transmission shift lever through all positions, ending in Park. On all models, turn A/C switch on and then off (if equipped).
2) Turn engine off. Without starting engine, turn ignition on, off, on, off and on. CHECK ENGINE light will come on for 2 seconds as a bulb check, followed by fault codes. Record 2-digit fault codes as displayed by flashing CHECK ENGINE light.
3) Once CHECK ENGINE light begins to flash fault codes, it cannot be stopped. Repeat step **1)** to enter diagnostic mode. Code 55 indicates end of fault code display. For more information on vehicle self-diagnostics, see appropriate SELF-DIAGNOSTICS article in ENGINE PERFORMANCE.
4) Refer to CHARGING SYSTEM FAULT CODES table to determine trouble code number to a system fault description (DRB-II display). Once trouble area is known, go to appropriate charging system test.

NOTE: CHECK ENGINE light CANNOT be used to perform actuation test mode, sensor test modes or engine running test. Fault codes can only be erased using DRB-II. Fault codes will be erased from SBEC-II memory after 50 key starts if fault does not reoccur.

Diagnosis Using DRB-II – The DRB-II is used as part of a charging system diagnostic procedure. Perform BATTERY TEST and CHARGING VERIFICATION (CH-VER) test.
Erasing Fault Codes – 1) To erase faults, press ATM key. At DRB-II display, press "2" (ERASE) key. DRB-II will display ERASE FAULTS ARE YOU SURE? (ENTER TO ERASE). Press ENTER key.
2) When DRB-II is finished erasing fault codes, it will display FAULTS ERASED. This display will remain until ATM key is pressed. After ATM key is pressed, display will return to CHARGING MENU screen.

DRB-II TEST FUNCTIONS

NOTE: DO NOT touch DRB-II keypad during DRB-II power-up sequence, or an error message will result.

1) To diagnose system with DRB-II, DRB-II must be in CHARGING MENU. At CHARGING MENU, fault codes and DRB-II test functions can be used.
2) To get to CHARGING MENU, turn ignition off. Attach DRB-II to engine diagnostic connector. Connector is located in engine compartment, near SBEC-II. Turn ignition switch to RUN position.
3) All DRB-II character positions will illuminate and copyright information will appear on screen for several seconds.
4) After several seconds DRB-II menu will appear. At DRB-II menu, press "4" (SELECT SYSTEM) key. Press ENTER key. At SELECT SYSTEM menu, press "1" (ENGINE) key. Press ENTER key. DRB-II menu will appear, indicating engine year and size, type of transmission and SBEC-II part number.
5) After several seconds AIR COND menu will appear. Press "1" (WITH A/C) or press "2" (WITHOUT A/C). DRB-II display will change to ENGINE SYSTEMS menu. At ENGINE SYSTEMS menu, press "2" (CHARGING) key. Press ENTER key.
6) Display will change to CHARGING MENU. At CHARGING menu of engine diagnostic program, specific test functions programmed into DRB-II can be performed. The following DRB-II modes can be accessed: SYSTEM TEST, READ FAULTS, STATE DISPLAYS, ACTUATOR TEST and ADJUSTMENTS.
READ FAULTS Mode – This allows technician to read and erase fault codes. A fault counter will appear along with fault displayed on DRB-II. For example, DRB-II will display 1 OF 2 FAULTS. SBEC-II will store up to 8 fault messages.

Faults are numbered in reverse order of setting. The most recent fault to occur will be number one. Vehicles without A/C will always have A/C CLUTCH RELAY CKT (circuit) stored in memory. This fault will always be number one if vehicle is not equipped with A/C. If no fault messages are stored, DRB-II will display NO FAULTS DETECTED and start counter will show 0 STARTS SINCE ERS.

A start counter will appear below DRB-II fault counter display. Start counter counts the number of times vehicle is started since faults were last set, erased or battery was disconnected. This helps determine if fault is intermittent.

Memory space limits start counter to first 3 faults. Start counter of zero equals a hard fault. Start counter of more than zero indicates an intermittent fault. Start counter will count up to 255 starts. If no fault messages are stored, DRB-II will display NO FAULTS DETECTED and start counter will show 0 STARTS SINCE ERS.
STATE DISPLAYS Mode – This allows technician to read status or values of sensors, inputs/outputs and components. SBEC-II can only recognize high and low status on switch circuits. SBEC-II cannot detect the difference between an open or short circuit or a defective switch. If DRB-II displays a change between INPUT HIGH and INPUT LOW, it can be assumed that the entire switch circuit to SBEC-II is working.
ACTUATOR TEST Mode – This function allows the technician to check operation of output circuits or devices, which SBEC-II cannot detect. DRB-II allows SBEC-II to activate these outputs or devices, so technician can check for proper operation.

Most of the tests available in this mode provide an audible or visual indication of device operation (click of relay contacts, spray fuel, etc.). With the exception of an intermittent condition, if a device functions properly during its test, it can be assumed that the device, its wiring and driver circuit are working properly.
ADJUSTMENTS Mode – This function allows the user to erase fault codes. Function also allows user to reset Emission Maintenance Reminder (EMR) light and mileage.
DRB-II Volt/Ohmmeter Mode – To access volt/ohmmeter mode of DRB-II, connect Red volt/ohmmeter test lead to Red port, located on right-top side of DRB-II.

NOTE: Because DRB-II is grounded through engine diagnostic connector, only one volt/ohmmeter test lead is required when using volt/ohmmeter option.

To access voltmeter, press VOLT/OHM key once. DRB-II is now in voltmeter mode. Touch test probe to connector or wire to be measured. Read voltage on DRB-II display. When voltage testing is complete, press VOLT/OHM key 3 times to exit voltmeter mode.

To access ohmmeter, press VOLT/OHM key twice. DRB-II is now in ohmmeter mode. Touch test probe to connector or wire to be measured. Read resistance to circuit ground on DRB-II display. When resistance testing is complete, press VOLT/OHM key twice to exit ohmmeter mode.
DRB-II Continuity Meter Mode – Press VOLT/OHM key 3 times. Display will read NO CONTINUITY. Touch test probe to connector or wire to be measured. Read continuity on DRB-II display. When continuity testing is complete, press VOLT/OHM key once to exit continuity meter mode.
VEHICLES TESTED Mode – Mode is used to show what vehicles are covered by DRB-II cartridge. To access VEHICLES TESTED mode,

turn ignition off. Attach DRB-II to engine diagnostic connector. Connector is located in engine compartment, near SBEC-II.

Turn ignition switch to RUN position. All DRB-II character positions will illuminate and copyright information will appear on screen for several seconds. After several seconds DRB-II menu will appear.

At DRB-II menu, press "1" (VEHICLES TESTED) key. Press ENTER key. DRB-II will display vehicles covered by cartridge. Screen will display for 5 seconds and return to DRB-II menu.

HOW TO USE Mode – Enter DRB-II menu display. Refer to VEHICLES TESTED MODE. At DRB-II menu, press "2" (HOW TO USE) key. Press ENTER key. A series of screens will be displayed explaining the use of DRB-II keys used to move through engine diagnostic program.

BATTERY TEST

NOTE: Perform PRELIMINARY CHECKS under TROUBLE SHOOTING before proceeding. If battery shows signs of freezing or leakage, battery posts are loose or battery has low electrolyte level, DO NOT test.

1) If battery has a built-in hydrometer, go to step **2)**. Turn ignition and all accessories off. Ensure battery voltage is 12.3 volts or more. If voltage is less than 12.3 volts, charge battery and go to step **3)**.
2) If battery hydrometer is Green, go to step **3)**. If battery hydrometer is Yellow or a bright color, replace battery and perform CHARGING VERIFICATION (CH-VER) test. If battery hydrometer is dark in color, charge battery and go to next step.
3) Ensure battery cables, terminals and posts are clean and tight. Perform a battery load test by applying a 300-amp load for 15 seconds. Wait 15 seconds to allow battery to stabilize. Apply a load equal to 50 percent of battery cold cranking rating for 15 seconds and record minimum voltage reading.
4) See MINIMUM BATTERY VOLTAGE table. If battery is below voltage, replace battery and perform CHARGING VERIFICATION (CH-VER) test. If voltage reading is okay, go to next step.

MINIMUM BATTERY VOLTAGE

Battery Temperature	Minimum Volts
70°F (21°C) Or More	9.6
60°F (16°C)	9.5
50°F (10°C)	9.4
40°F (4°C)	9.3
30°F (-1°C)	9.1
20°F (-7°C)	8.9
10°F (-12°C)	8.7
0°F (-18°C)	8.5

5) Reconnect battery cables. Inspect alternator belt tension and condition. Replace belt as necessary. Start engine. Set engine speed to 2000 RPM for 30 seconds. Turn ignition off. Connect DRB-II. Turn ignition on with engine off. Read faults.
6) If DRB-II displays BATTERY TEMP SENSOR OUT OF LIMIT, replace SBEC-II and perform CHARGING VERIFICATION (CH-VER) test. If DRB-II displays other messages, go to appropriate test. If DRB-II does not display any faults, there are either no fault messages or faults are intermittent. Go to TEST CH-5, CHECKING FOR INTERMITTENT PROBLEMS.

TEST CH-2, ALTERNATOR FIELD NOT SWITCHING PROPERLY (CODE 41)

NOTE: Perform BATTERY TEST before proceeding.

1) Put DRB-II in voltmeter mode and probe Dark Green/Red wire (Dark Green/Black wire on Wrangler) at back of alternator. If voltage is less than 10 volts, repair open circuit from ignition switch. If voltage is 10 volts or more, probe Dark Green wire (Tan/Black wire on Wrangler) at back of alternator. If voltage is less than 10 volts, go to next step. If voltage is 10 volts or more, go to step **4)**.
2) Turn ignition off. Disconnect and inspect SBEC-II connector. If connector is damaged, repair as necessary. If connector is okay, turn ignition on and probe Dark Green wire (Tan/Black wire on Wrangler) at back of alternator. If voltage is 10 volts or more, replace SBEC-II. Perform CHARGING VERIFICATION (CH-VER) test.
3) If voltage is less than 10 volts, turn ignition off and put DRB-II in ohmmeter mode. Probe Dark Green wire (Tan/Black wire on Wrangler) in alternator harness. If resistance less than 10 ohms, repair Dark Green wire (Tan/Black wire on Wrangler) for short to ground. If resistance is 10 ohms or more, replace alternator. Perform CHARGING VERIFICATION (CH-VER) test.
4) Turn ignition off. Disconnect and inspect SBEC-II connector. If connector is damaged, repair as necessary. If connector is okay, turn ignition on and put DRB-II in voltmeter mode. Probe cavity No. 20. *See Fig. 4*. If voltage is 10 volts or more, replace SBEC-II. Perform CHARGING VERIFICATION (CH-VER) test. If voltage is less than 10 volts, repair open circuit in Dark Green wire (Tan/Black wire on Wrangler). Perform CHARGING VERIFICATION (CH-VER) test.

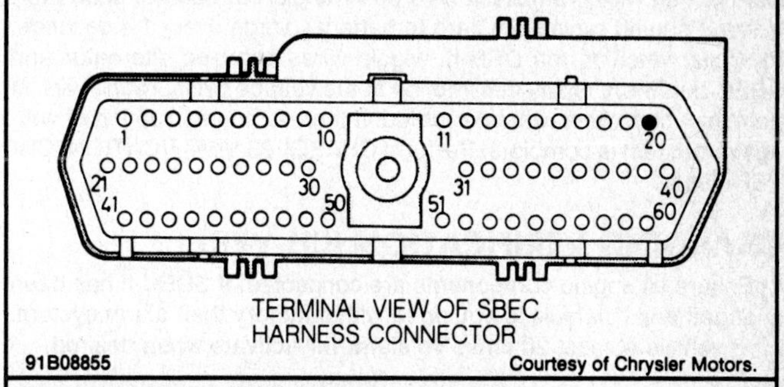
1
10
11
20
21
30
31
40
41
50
51
60
TERMINAL VIEW OF SBEC
HARNESS CONNECTOR
91B08855
Courtesy of Chrysler Motors.

Fig. 4: Identifying SBEC-II Connector Cavities

TEST CH-3, CHARGING SYSTEM VOLTAGE LOW (CODE 47)

NOTE: Perform BATTERY TEST before proceeding.

1) If alternator voltage is 15.1 volts or more, replace SBEC-II. If less than 15.1 volts, ensure no resistance is present between alternator BAT (B+) and battery positive terminal.

CAUTION: Ensure all wires are clear of moving parts.

2) Check alternator case for good connection to ground and to negative battery cable. If the ground is good, manually set engine speed to 1600 RPM. Compare voltage on DRB-II and voltage on an external meter. If difference is 1.0 volt or more, replace alternator. If difference is less than 1.0 volt, go to TEST CH-5, CHECKING FOR INTERMITTENT PROBLEMS.

TEST CH-4, CHARGING SYSTEM VOLTAGE HIGH (CODE 46)

NOTE: Perform BATTERY TEST before proceeding.

1) Turn ignition on. Put DRB-II in voltmeter mode. Probe Dark Green wire (Tan/Black wire on Wrangler) at back of alternator. If voltage is 10.0 volts or more, go to step **4)**. If voltage is less than 10.0 volts, turn ignition off. Disconnect SBEC-II connector, inspect and repair if necessary.
2) If connector is okay, turn ignition on. Probe Dark Green wire (Tan/Black wire on Wrangler) at back of alternator. If voltage is 10.0 volts or more, replace SBEC-II. Perform CHARGING VERIFICATION (CH-VER) test. If voltage is less than 10.0 volts, go to next step.
3) Turn ignition off. Disconnect alternator harness from alternator. Put DRB-II in ohmmeter mode. Probe Dark Green wire (Tan/Black wire on Wrangler) in alternator harness. If resistance is less than 10.0 ohms, repair Dark Green wire (Tan/Black wire on Wrangler) for short to ground. If resistance is 10.0 ohms or more, replace alternator. Perform CHARGING VERIFICATION (CH-VER) test.
4) With ignition on and engine off, read voltage. If voltage is less than 13.0 volts, replace SBEC-II. Perform CHARGING VERIFICATION (CH-

1991 ELECTRICAL
Alternators – Nippondenso (Cont.)

VER) test. If voltage is 13.0 volts or more, start engine and read voltage. Compare voltage readings before and after engine is running. Watch for up to 5 minutes, for a 1.0-volt difference.

5) If voltage difference is 1.0 volt or more, replace SBEC-II. Perform CHARGING VERIFICATION (CH-VER) test. If voltage difference is less than 1.0 volt, go to TEST CH-5, CHECKING FOR INTERMITTENT PROBLEMS.

TEST CH-5, CHECKING FOR INTERMITTENT PROBLEMS

NOTE: Perform TEST CH-4, CHARGING SYSTEM VOLTAGE HIGH (CODE 46) before proceeding.

1) Actuate the alternator field. Put DRB-II in voltmeter mode. Probe the Dark Green wire (Tan/Black wire on Wrangler) at back of alternator. Voltage should cycle from zero to battery voltage every 1.4 seconds.

2) While watching the DRB-II, wiggle wires between alternator and SBEC-II. If there is any interruption in the voltage cycle, repair wire at point at which cycle was interrupted. If there is no interruption of voltage cycle, test is complete. Perform CHARGING VERIFICATION (CH-VER) test.

CHARGING VERIFICATION (CH-VER)

1) Ensure all engine components are connected. If SBEC-II has been changed and if vehicle is equipped with a factory theft alarm system, start vehicle at least 20 times so alarm will activate when desired.

2) Write the Emission Maintenance Reminder (EMR) mileage into the new SBEC-II. Connect DRB-II to engine diagnostic connector and erase faults. Recheck system for fault codes.

3) If fault code(s) reset, charging system still needs repair. Check all pertinent MITCHELL TECHNICAL SERVICE BULLETINS and return to BATTERY TEST.

BENCH TESTING

NOTE: Alternators are not repairable. If necessary, replace alternator.

TORQUE SPECIFICATIONS

TORQUE SPECIFICATIONS

Application	Ft. Lbs. (N.m)
Alternator Mounting Bolts	28 (38)
Idler Pulley (Power Steering)	20 (27)

1991 ELECTRICAL
Starters – Bosch & Mitsubishi

Cherokee, Comanche
Grand Wagoneer, Wrangler

DESCRIPTION

Both Bosch and Mitsubishi starters are permanent-magnet type. A planetary gear train transmits power between starter motor and pinion shaft. Both starters are 12-volt units with solenoid mounted on starter housing.

TROUBLE SHOOTING

STARTER MOTOR NOISE

***NOTE:** To diagnose starter motor noise, see Fig. 1.*

ON-VEHICLE TESTING

COLD CRANKING TEST

***NOTE:** Ensure battery is fully charged and engine is at operating temperature. A cold engine increases starter draw amperage.*

1) Connect battery load/charging system tester to battery, and connect remote starter switch to starter relay. Set voltmeter selector to 18-volt position. Adjust ammeter reading to zero.
2) Disconnect coil wire from distributor cap. Attach coil wire to ground to prevent engine from starting. Crank engine, and note cranking voltage and amperage. Replace or repair starter if not to specification. See STARTER SPECIFICATIONS table at end of article.

STARTER RELAY TEST

2.5L & 4.0L Engines – 1) Place transmission selector in Park or Neutral (automatic only). Ensure Black/Tan wire (Black/White wire on Wrangler) has continuity to ground. Turn ignition switch to start position. Starter solenoid should work.
2) If starter solenoid does not work, check if relay clicks. If starter relay does not click, go to step **4)**. If relay clicks, ensure voltage is present at relay terminals No. 30 (battery) and 87 (starter solenoid). Also ensure voltage is present at starter solenoid.
3) If starter solenoid still does not work, check starter solenoid ground. If ground is okay, replace starter solenoid.
4) Ensure neutral safety switch wire has continuity to starter relay terminal No. 85. Ensure voltage from ignition switch is present at relay terminal No. 86.
5) If starter relay still does not work, check resistance between relay terminals No. 86 and 85. If resistance is not 70-80 ohms, replace starter relay.

6.0L Engine – 1) Disconnect connector from starter relay "I" terminal and "G" terminal. Using an ohmmeter, measure resistance between terminals. Resistance should be approximately 22 ohms. Also measure resistance between either terminal and ground. Resistance should be infinite.
2) If readings are not okay, replace relay. If readings are okay, reattach wire connectors. Remove wire connector from relay SOL terminal. Connect a voltmeter between relay SOL terminal and ground. With ignition switch in START position, voltmeter should show battery voltage.
3) If battery voltage is not present with ignition switch in START position, check for voltage at relay "I" terminal. If voltage is at "I" terminal and not SOL terminal, replace relay. If NO voltage is at "I" terminal, check wiring to ignition switch for an open circuit.
4) If starter relay still does not operate, jump "G" circuit from relay to ground. If starter relay clicks, check neutral safety switch operation. If neutral safety switch operation is okay, repair "G" wire circuit.

SOLENOID TEST

1) With a fully charged battery, connect a heavy gauge jumper wire between battery terminal and solenoid terminal wire connector at starter relay. If engine cranks, solenoid is okay.
2) If engine does not crank, check battery cable for voltage to starter solenoid BAT terminal. Jump starter relay terminals as in step **1)**, checking for voltage at solenoid terminal No. 50. Repair as necessary. If engine still does not crank, repair or replace starter.

BENCH TESTING

ARMATURE TEST

Short Circuit – Place armature in a growler. While rotating armature slowly, hold growler's blade parallel to and touching armature core. Blade vibrates if armature is shorted. Replace shorted armature.
Ground – Using growler or a self-powered test light, touch one lead to armature shaft and other lead to each commutator bar. *See Fig. 2.* If light glows at any point during procedure, armature is grounded. Replace grounded armature.

CONDITION	POSSIBLE CAUSE	CORRECTION
1. VERY HIGH FREQUENCY WHINE BEFORE ENGINE STARTS; ENGINE STARTS OK.	1. Excessive distance between pinion gear and flywheel/drive plate gear.	1. Shim starter motor toward flywheel/drive plate.
2. VERY HIGH FREQUENCY WHINE AFTER ENGINE STARTS WITH IGNITION KEY RELEASED. ENGINE STARTS OK.	2. Insufficient distance between starter motor pinion gear and flywheel/drive plate runout can cause noise to be intermittent.	2. Shim starter motor away from flywheel/drive plate. Inspect flywheel/drive plate for damage; bent, unusual wear, and excessive runout. Replace flywheel/drive plate as necessary.
3. A LOUD "WHOOP" AFTER ENGINE STARTS WHILE STARTER MOTOR IS ENGAGED.	3. Most probably cause is defective overrunning clutch. Clutch replacement normally corrects this condition	3. Replace overrunning clutch or drive assembly.
4. A "RUMBLE," "GROWL," OR "KNOCK" AS STARTER MOTOR COASTS TO STOP AFTER ENGINE STARTS.	4. Most probable cause is bent or unbalanced starter motor armature. Armature replacement normally corrects this condition.	4. Replace starter motor armature.

Courtesy of Chrysler Motors.

***Fig. 1:** Diagnosing Starter Motor Noise*

1991 ELECTRICAL
Starters – Bosch & Mitsubishi (Cont.)

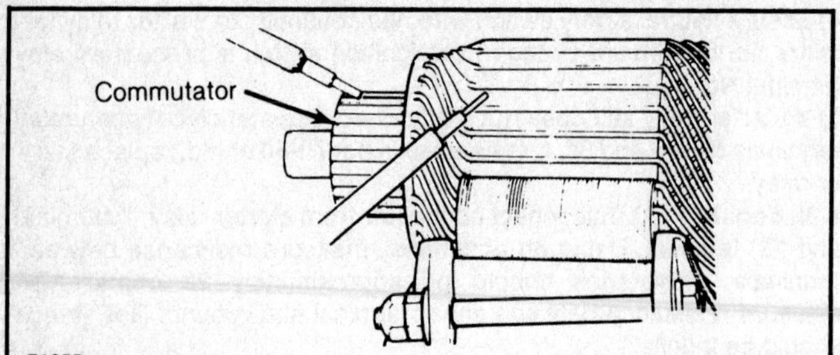
Commutator

71055 Courtesy of Chrysler Motors.

Fig. 2: Testing Starter Armature for Ground

DRIVE CLUTCH CHECK

While holding drive clutch housing, rotate pinion. Drive pinion should rotate smoothly in only one direction (pinion should engage and lock in opposite direction). If drive unit does not operate properly or if pinion is worn or burred, replace drive clutch.

REMOVAL & INSTALLATION

STARTER

Removal & Installation (2.5L) – 1) Disconnect negative battery cable. Remove exhaust pipe clamp from bracket. *See Fig. 3.* On Cherokee and Comanche models with automatic transmission, remove nut and bolt from forward end of brace rod. Remove brace rod and bracket.

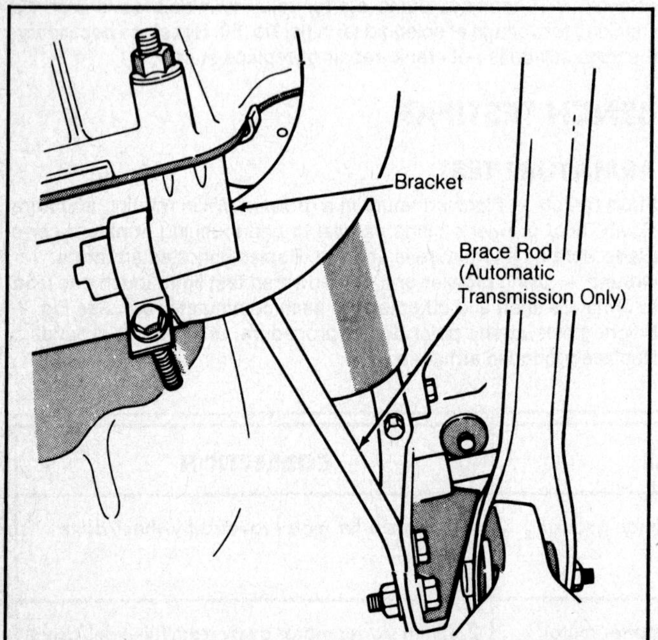
Bracket
Brace Rod
(Automatic
Transmission Only)

117176 Courtesy of Chrysler Motors.

Fig. 3: Removing 2.5L Engine Exhaust Clamp & Brace

2) On vehicles with manual transmission, remove nut, bolt and bracket from bellhousing. On all models, disconnect battery cable and solenoid wire from starter solenoid. To install, reverse removal procedure.

Removal & Installation (4.0L & 6.0L) – Disconnect negative battery cable. Raise and support vehicle. Disconnect starter battery cable and solenoid feed wire. Remove starter from flywheel housing. To install, reverse removal procedure.

STARTER SPECIFICATIONS

BOSCH STARTER SPECIFICATIONS

Application	Specification
Carbon Brush	
Minimum Length	.314" (8.0 mm)
Commutator	
Diameter	1.23-1.27" (31.2-32.3 mm)
Runout	.0004" (.01 mm)
Armature	
Core Runout	.002" (.05 mm)
End Play	.002" (.05 mm)
Cranking Test	
Test Voltage	12.5
Minimum Voltage	9.6
Amps	160
No Load Test @ 11.5 Volts	
Maximum Amps	75
Minimum RPM	2900
Solenoid Hold-In Test	
Winding Voltage	.2-2 Volts
Solenoid Pull-In Test	
Winding Voltage	6-7.3 Volts

MITSUBISHI STARTER SPECIFICATIONS

Application	Specification
Carbon Brush	
Minimum Length	.354" (9 mm)
Commutator	
Diameter	1.118-1.161" (28.4-29.5 mm)
Runout	.001" (.03 mm)
Armature	
Core Runout	.003" (.08 mm)
End Play	.023" (.58 mm)
Cranking Test	
Test Voltage	12.5
Minimum Voltage	9.6
Amps	130
No Load Test @ 11.5 Volts	
Maximum Amps	80
Minimum RPM	2500
Solenoid Hold-In Test	
Winding Voltage	3.5 Volts (Min.)
Solenoid Pull-In Test	
Winding Voltage	7.8 Volts (Max.)

TORQUE SPECIFICATIONS

TORQUE SPECIFICATIONS

Application	Ft. Lbs. (N.m)
Starter-To-Block Bolts	33 (45)

OVERHAUL

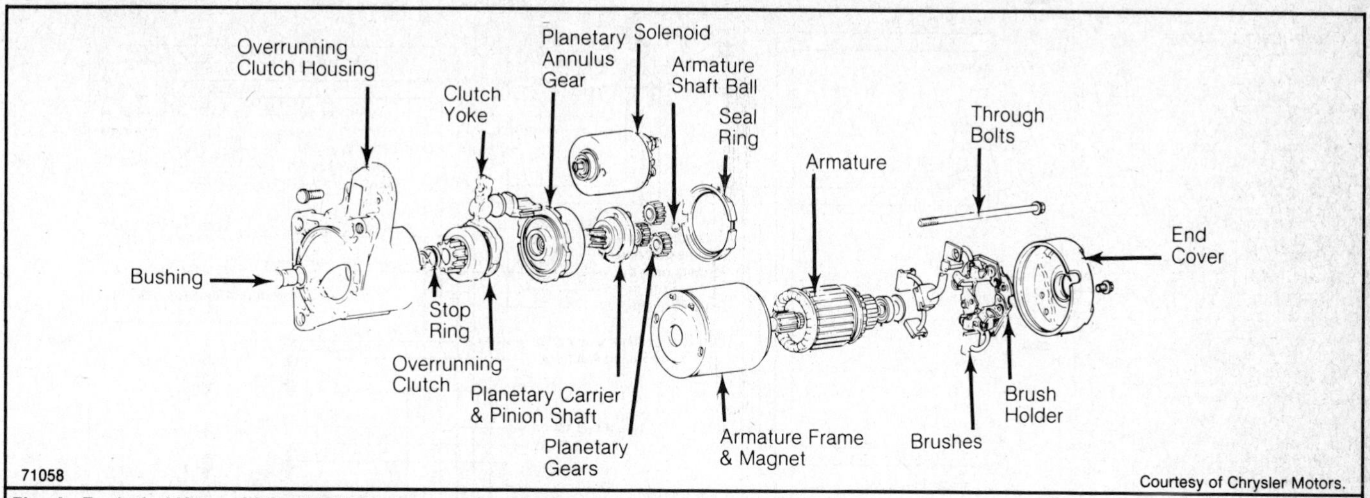
Overrunning Clutch Housing
Clutch Yoke
Planetary Annulus Gear
Solenoid
Armature Shaft Ball
Seal Ring
Armature
Through Bolts
End Cover
Bushing
Stop Ring
Overrunning Clutch
Planetary Carrier & Pinion Shaft
Planetary Gears
Armature Frame & Magnet
Brushes
Brush Holder
71058
Courtesy of Chrysler Motors.

Fig. 4: Exploded View of Mitsubishi Starter – 4.0L & 6.0L

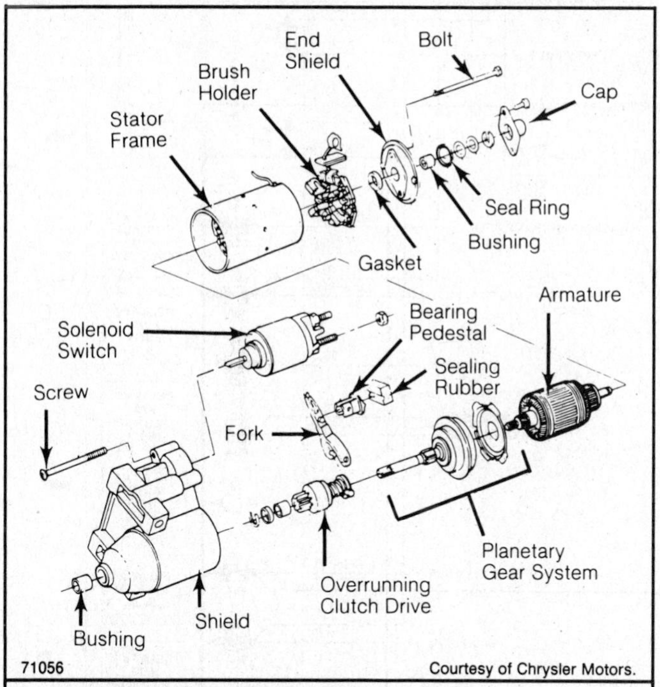
End Shield
Bolt
Brush Holder
Cap
Stator Frame
Seal Ring
Bushing
Gasket
Armature
Bearing Pedestal
Solenoid Switch
Sealing Rubber
Screw
Fork
Planetary Gear System
Overrunning Clutch Drive
Shield
Bushing
71056
Courtesy of Chrysler Motors.

Fig. 5: Exploded View of Bosch Starter – 2.5L

1991 WIRING DIAGRAMS
Cherokee & Comanche

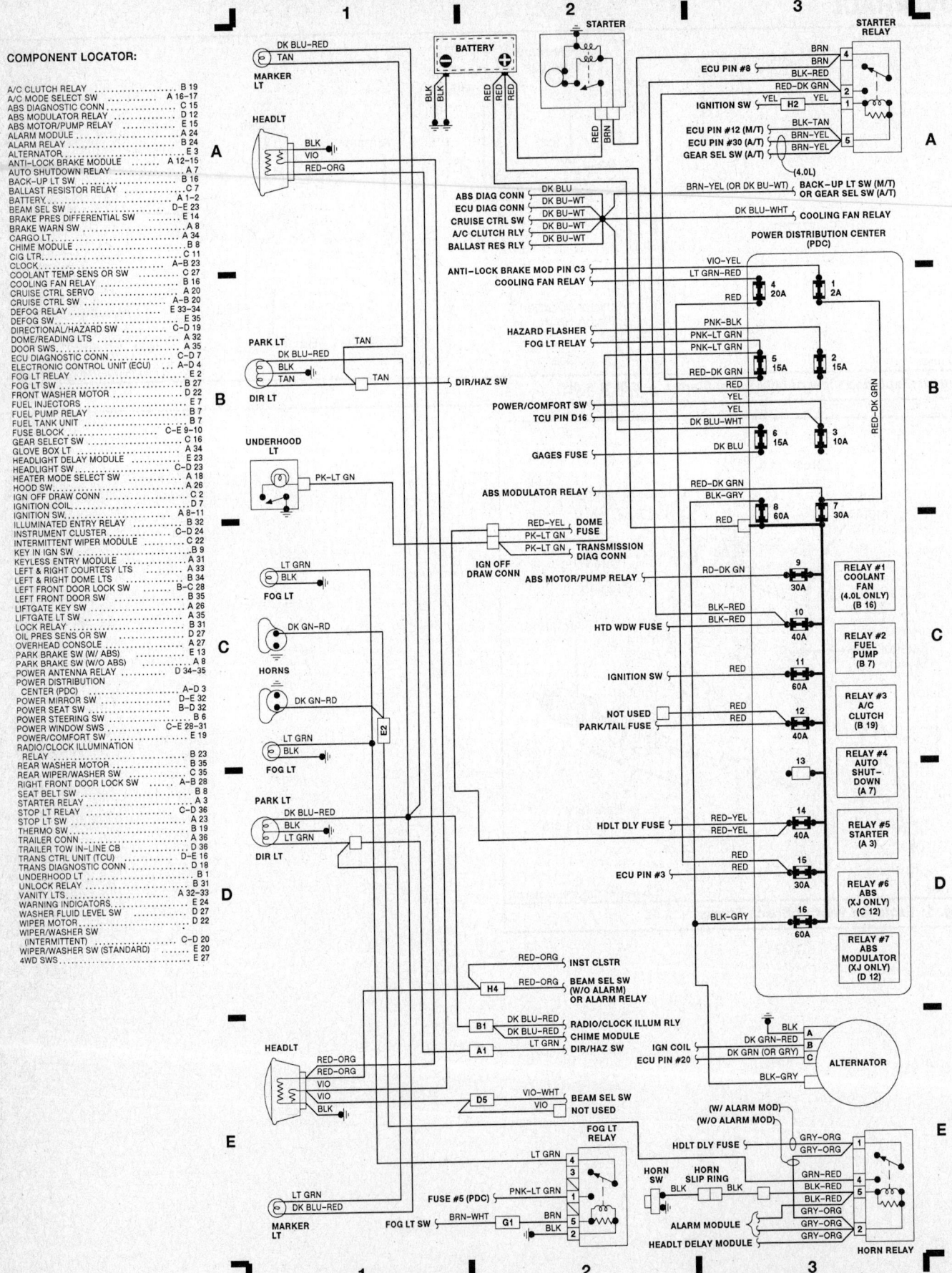

COMPONENT LOCATOR:

Component	Location
A/C CLUTCH RELAY	B 19
A/C MODE SELECT SW	A 16–17
ABS DIAGNOSTIC CONN	C 15
ABS MODULATOR RELAY	D 12
ABS MOTOR/PUMP RELAY	E 15
ALARM MODULE	A 24
ALARM RELAY	B 24
ALTERNATOR	E 3
ANTI-LOCK BRAKE MODULE	A 12–15
AUTO SHUTDOWN RELAY	A 7
BACK-UP LT SW	B 16
BALLAST RESISTOR RELAY	C 7
BATTERY	A 1–2
BEAM SEL SW	D–E 23
BRAKE PRES DIFFERENTIAL SW	E 14
BRAKE WARN SW	A 8
CARGO LT	A 34
CHIME MODULE	B 8
CIG LTR	C 11
CLOCK	A–B 23
COOLANT TEMP SENS OR SW	C 27
COOLING FAN RELAY	B 16
CRUISE CTRL SERVO	A 20
CRUISE CTRL SW	A–B 20
DEFOG RELAY	E 33–34
DEFOG SW	E 35
DIRECTIONAL/HAZARD SW	C–D 19
DOME/READING LTS	A 32
DOOR SWS	A 35
ECU DIAGNOSTIC CONN	C–D 7
ELECTRONIC CONTROL UNIT (ECU)	A–D 4
FOG LT RELAY	E 2
FOG LT SW	B 27
FRONT WASHER MOTOR	D 22
FUEL INJECTORS	E 7
FUEL PUMP RELAY	B 7
FUEL TANK UNIT	B 7
FUSE BLOCK	C–E 9–10
GEAR SELECT SW	C 16
GLOVE BOX LT	A 34
HEADLIGHT DELAY MODULE	E 23
HEADLIGHT SW	C–D 23
HEATER MODE SELECT SW	A 18
HOOD SW	A 26
IGN OFF DRAW CONN	C 2
IGNITION COIL	D 7
IGNITION SW	A 8–11
ILLUMINATED ENTRY RELAY	B 32
INSTRUMENT CLUSTER	C–D 24
INTERMITTENT WIPER MODULE	C 22
KEY IN IGN SW	B 9
KEYLESS ENTRY MODULE	A 31
LEFT & RIGHT COURTESY LTS	A 33
LEFT & RIGHT DOME LTS	B 34
LEFT FRONT DOOR LOCK SW	B–C 28
LEFT FRONT DOOR SW	B 35
LIFTGATE KEY SW	A 26
LIFTGATE LT SW	A 35
LOCK RELAY	B 31
OIL PRES SENS OR SW	D 27
OVERHEAD CONSOLE	A 27
PARK BRAKE SW (W/ ABS)	E 13
PARK BRAKE SW (W/O ABS)	A 8
POWER ANTENNA RELAY	D 34–35
POWER DISTRIBUTION CENTER (PDC)	A–D 3
POWER MIRROR SW	D–E 32
POWER SEAT SW	B–D 32
POWER STEERING SW	B 6
POWER WINDOW SWS	C–E 28–31
POWER/COMFORT SW	E 19
RADIO/CLOCK ILLUMINATION RELAY	B 23
REAR WASHER MOTOR	B 35
REAR WIPER/WASHER SW	C 35
RIGHT FRONT DOOR LOCK SW	A–B 28
SEAT BELT SW	B 8
STARTER RELAY	A 3
STOP LT RELAY	C–D 36
STOP LT SW	A 23
THERMO SW	B 19
TRAILER CONN	A 36
TRAILER TOW IN-LINE CB	D 36
TRANS CTRL UNIT (TCU)	D–E 16
TRANS DIAGNOSTIC CONN	D 18
UNDERHOOD LT	B 1
UNLOCK RELAY	B 31
VANITY LTS	A 32–33
WARNING INDICATORS	E 24
WASHER FLUID LEVEL SW	D 27
WIPER MOTOR	D 22
WIPER/WASHER SW (INTERMITTENT)	C–D 20
WIPER/WASHER SW (STANDARD)	E 20
4WD SWS	E 27

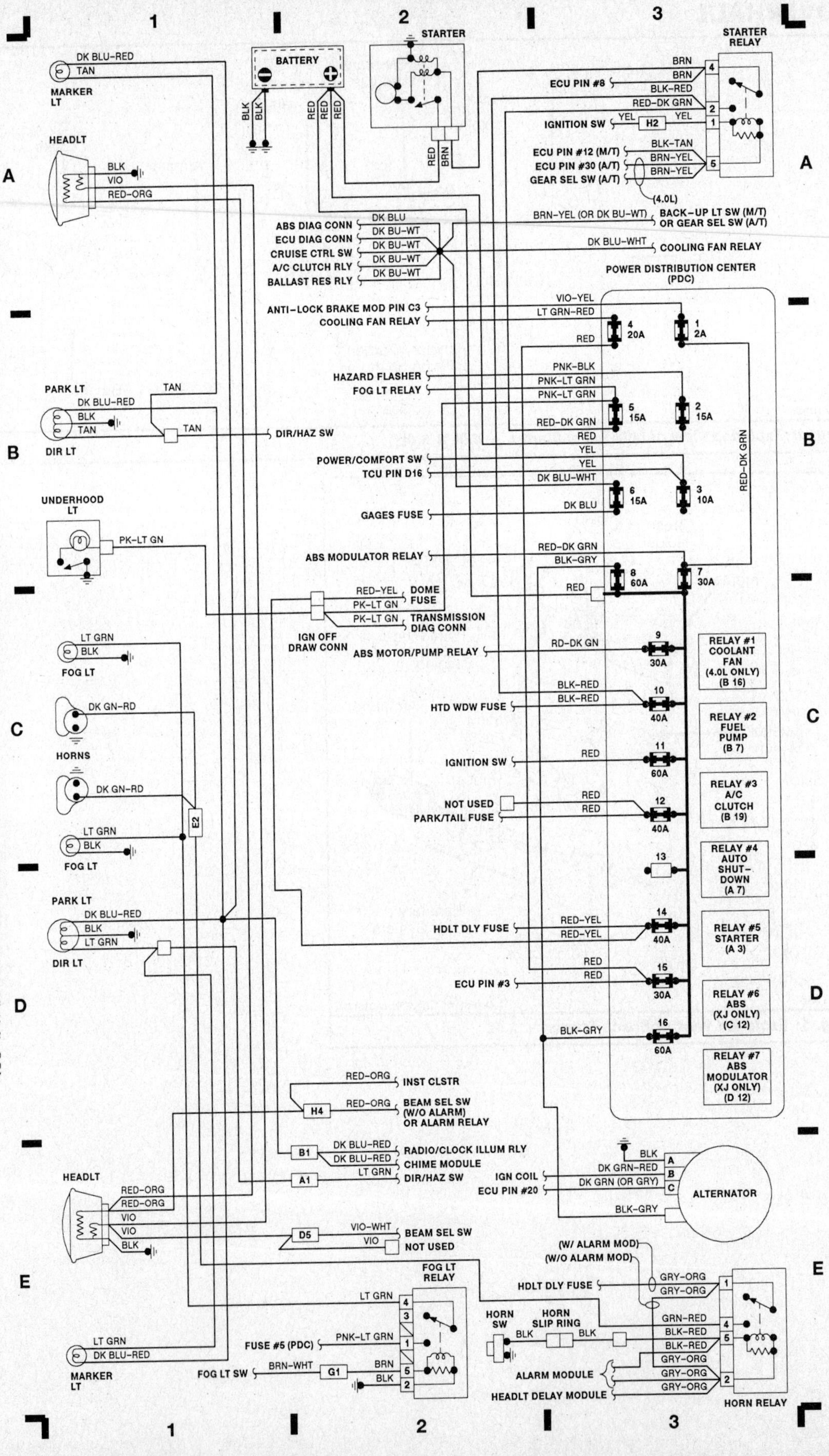
1
2
3
A
B
C
D
E
MARKER LT
DK BLU-RED
TAN
BATTERY
BLK
RED
STARTER
STARTER RELAY
BRN
BLK-RED
RED-DK GRN
ECU PIN #8
IGNITION SW
YEL
H2
ECU PIN #12 (M/T)
ECU PIN #30 (A/T)
GEAR SEL SW (A/T)
BLK-TAN
BRN-YEL
(4.0L)
HEADLT
VIO
RED-ORG
BRN-YEL (OR DK BU-WT)
BACK-UP LT SW (M/T) OR GEAR SEL SW (A/T)
ABS DIAG CONN
ECU DIAG CONN
CRUISE CTRL SW
A/C CLUTCH RLY
BALLAST RES RLY
DK BLU
DK BU-WT
DK BLU-WHT
COOLING FAN RELAY
POWER DISTRIBUTION CENTER (PDC)
VIO-YEL
LT GRN-RED
ANTI-LOCK BRAKE MOD PIN C3
20A
2A
15A
10A
60A
30A
40A
HAZARD FLASHER
FOG LT RELAY
PNK-BLK
PNK-LT GRN
PARK LT
DIR LT
DIR/HAZ SW
POWER/COMFORT SW
TCU PIN D16
GAGES FUSE
UNDERHOOD LT
PK-LT GN
ABS MODULATOR RELAY
BLK-GRY
RED-YEL
DOME FUSE
TRANSMISSION DIAG CONN
IGN OFF DRAW CONN
ABS MOTOR/PUMP RELAY
RD-DK GN
RELAY #1 COOLANT FAN (4.0L ONLY) (B 16)
FOG LT
LT GRN
HTD WDW FUSE
RELAY #2 FUEL PUMP (B 7)
DK GN-RD
HORNS
IGNITION SW
RELAY #3 A/C CLUTCH (B 19)
NOT USED
PARK/TAIL FUSE
E2
RELAY #4 AUTO SHUT-DOWN (A 7)
RELAY #5 STARTER (A 3)
HDLT DLY FUSE
ECU PIN #3
RELAY #6 ABS (XJ ONLY) (C 12)
RELAY #7 ABS MODULATOR (XJ ONLY) (D 12)
INST CLSTR
H4
BEAM SEL SW (W/O ALARM) OR ALARM RELAY
B1
RADIO/CLOCK ILLUM RLY
CHIME MODULE
A1
DIR/HAZ SW
IGN COIL
ECU PIN #20
DK GRN (OR GRY)
ALTERNATOR
D5
VIO-WHT
BEAM SEL SW
NOT USED
(W/ ALARM MOD)
(W/O ALARM MOD)
HDLT DLY FUSE
GRY-ORG
FOG LT RELAY
HORN SW
HORN SLIP RING
GRN-RED
BLK-RED
FUSE #5 (PDC)
FOG LT SW
BRN-WHT
G1
ALARM MODULE
HEADLT DELAY MODULE
HORN RELAY
1
2
3

1991 WIRING DIAGRAMS
Cherokee & Comanche (Cont.)

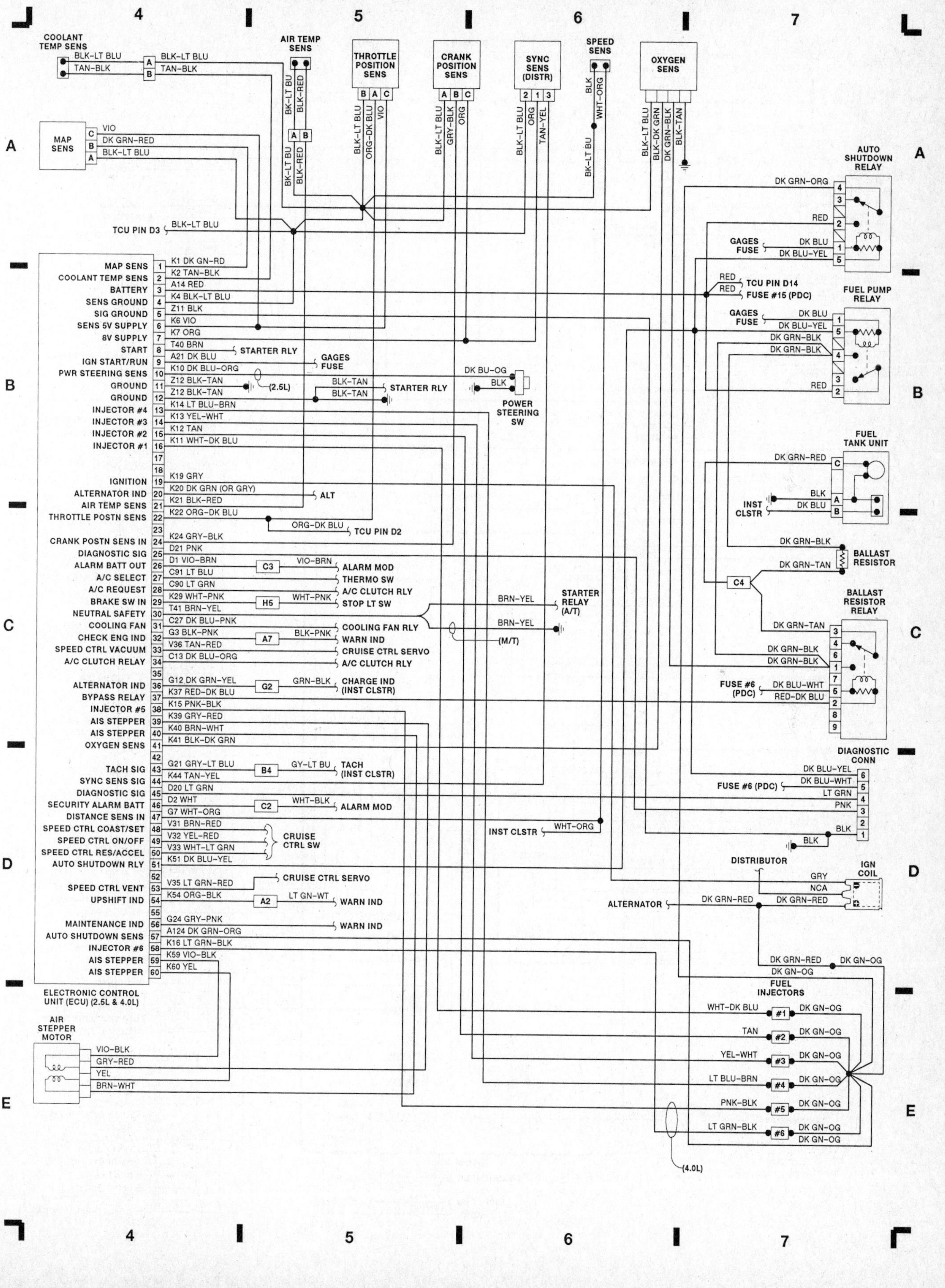
COOLANT TEMP SENS
AIR TEMP SENS
THROTTLE POSITION SENS
CRANK POSITION SENS
SYNC SENS (DISTR)
SPEED SENS
OXYGEN SENS
MAP SENS
TCU PIN D3
AUTO SHUTDOWN RELAY
GAGES FUSE
TCU PIN D14
FUSE #15 (PDC)
FUEL PUMP RELAY
STARTER RLY
POWER STEERING SW
FUEL TANK UNIT
INST CLSTR
BALLAST RESISTOR
BALLAST RESISTOR RELAY
ALT
TCU PIN D2
ALARM MOD
THERMO SW
A/C CLUTCH RLY
STOP LT SW
STARTER RELAY (A/T)
(M/T)
COOLING FAN RLY
WARN IND
CRUISE CTRL SERVO
CHARGE IND (INST CLSTR)
FUSE #6 (PDC)
DIAGNOSTIC CONN
TACH (INST CLSTR)
CRUISE CTRL SW
DISTRIBUTOR
IGN COIL
ALTERNATOR
FUEL INJECTORS
ELECTRONIC CONTROL UNIT (ECU) (2.5L & 4.0L)
AIR STEPPER MOTOR
(2.5L)
(4.0L)
1 MAP SENS K1 DK GN-RD
2 COOLANT TEMP SENS K2 TAN-BLK
3 BATTERY A14 RED
4 SENS GROUND K4 BLK-LT BLU
5 SIG GROUND Z11 BLK
6 SENS 5V SUPPLY K6 VIO
7 8V SUPPLY K7 ORG
8 START T40 BRN
9 IGN START/RUN A21 DK BLU
10 PWR STEERING SENS K10 DK BLU-ORG
11 GROUND Z12 BLK-TAN
12 GROUND Z12 BLK-TAN
13 INJECTOR #4 K14 LT BLU-BRN
14 INJECTOR #3 K13 YEL-WHT
15 INJECTOR #2 K12 TAN
16 INJECTOR #1 K11 WHT-DK BLU
19 IGNITION K19 GRY
20 ALTERNATOR IND K20 DK GRN (OR GRY)
21 AIR TEMP SENS K21 BLK-RED
22 THROTTLE POSTN SENS K22 ORG-DK BLU
24 CRANK POSTN SENS IN K24 GRY-BLK
25 DIAGNOSTIC SIG D21 PNK
26 ALARM BATT OUT D1 VIO-BRN
27 A/C SELECT C91 LT BLU
28 A/C REQUEST C90 LT GRN
29 BRAKE SW IN K29 WHT-PNK
30 NEUTRAL SAFETY T41 BRN-YEL
31 COOLING FAN C27 DK BLU-PNK
32 CHECK ENG IND G3 BLK-PNK
33 SPEED CTRL VACUUM V36 TAN-RED
34 A/C CLUTCH RELAY C13 DK BLU-ORG
36 ALTERNATOR IND G12 DK GRN-YEL
37 BYPASS RELAY K37 RED-DK BLU
38 INJECTOR #5 K15 PNK-BLK
39 AIS STEPPER K39 GRY-RED
40 AIS STEPPER K40 BRN-WHT
41 OXYGEN SENS K41 BLK-DK GRN
43 TACH SIG G21 GRY-LT BLU
44 SYNC SENS SIG K44 TAN-YEL
45 DIAGNOSTIC SIG D20 LT GRN
46 SECURITY ALARM BATT D2 WHT
47 DISTANCE SENS IN G7 WHT-ORG
48 SPEED CTRL COAST/SET V31 BRN-RED
49 SPEED CTRL ON/OFF V32 YEL-RED
50 SPEED CTRL RES/ACCEL V33 WHT-LT GRN
51 AUTO SHUTDOWN RLY K51 DK BLU-YEL
53 SPEED CTRL VENT V35 LT GRN-RED
54 UPSHIFT IND K54 ORG-BLK
56 MAINTENANCE IND G24 GRY-PNK
57 AUTO SHUTDOWN SENS A124 DK GRN-ORG
58 INJECTOR #6 K16 LT GRN-BLK
59 AIS STEPPER K59 VIO-BLK
60 AIS STEPPER K60 YEL

1991 WIRING DIAGRAMS
Cherokee & Comanche (Cont.)

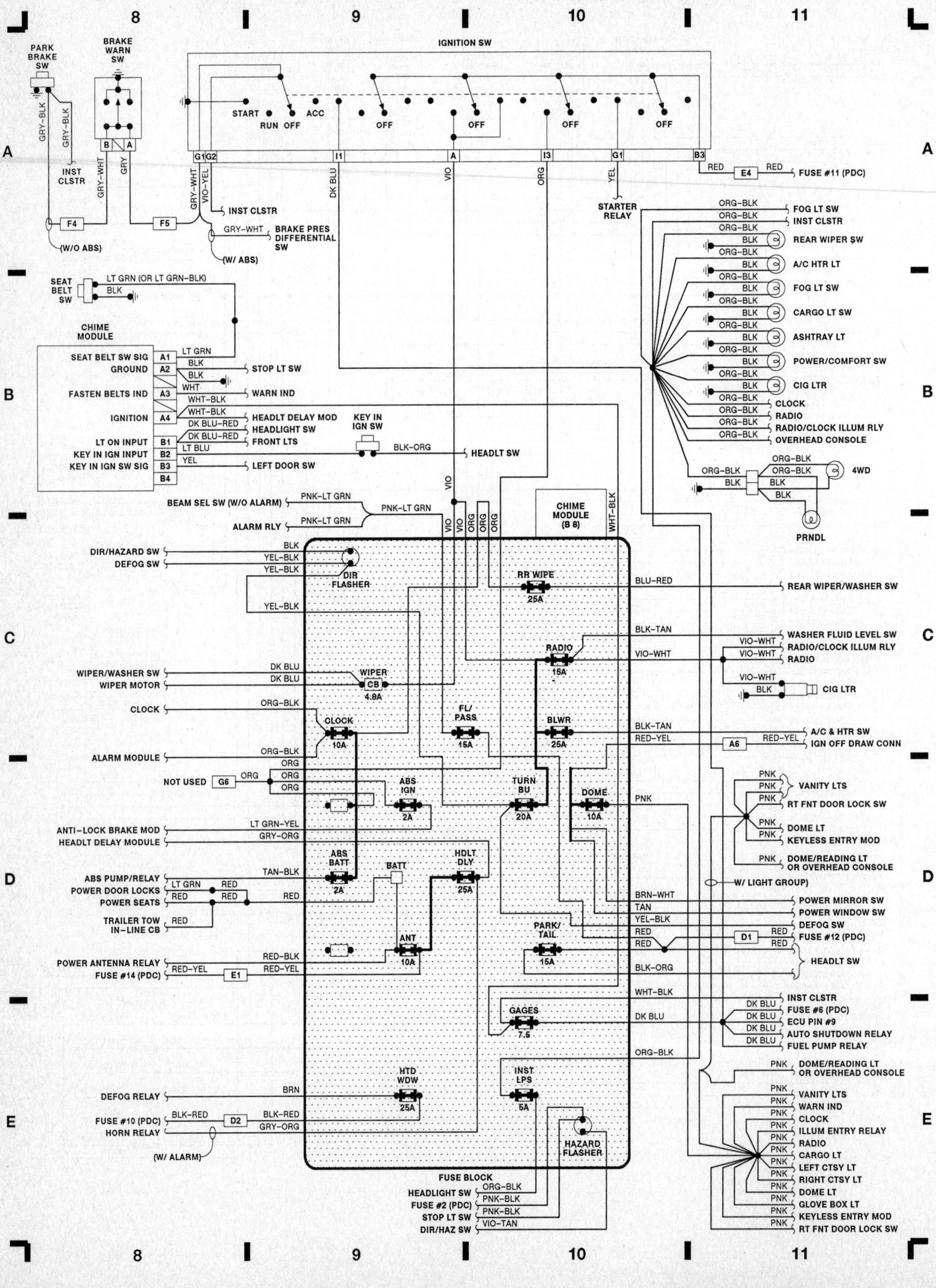

8
9
10
11
PARK BRAKE SW
BRAKE WARN SW
IGNITION SW
START
RUN
OFF
ACC
OFF
OFF
OFF
OFF
INST CLSTR
GRY-BLK
GRY-WHT
GRY
F4
F5
(W/O ABS)
(W/ ABS)
GRY-WHT
VIO-YEL
INST CLSTR
BRAKE PRES DIFFERENTIAL SW
DK BLU
VIO
ORG
YEL
STARTER RELAY
RED
E4
FUSE #11 (PDC)
ORG-BLK
BLK
FOG LT SW
INST CLSTR
REAR WIPER SW
A/C HTR LT
FOG LT SW
CARGO LT SW
ASHTRAY LT
POWER/COMFORT SW
CIG LTR
CLOCK
RADIO
RADIO/CLOCK ILLUM RLY
OVERHEAD CONSOLE
4WD
PRNDL
SEAT BELT SW
LT GRN (OR LT GRN-BLK)
CHIME MODULE
SEAT BELT SW SIG
GROUND
FASTEN BELTS IND
IGNITION
LT ON INPUT
KEY IN IGN INPUT
KEY IN IGN SW SIG
A1
A2
A3
A4
B1
B2
B3
B4
LT GRN
BLK
WHT
WHT-BLK
DK BLU-RED
LT BLU
YEL
STOP LT SW
WARN IND
HEADLT DELAY MOD
HEADLIGHT SW
FRONT LTS
LEFT DOOR SW
KEY IN IGN SW
BLK-ORG
HEADLT SW
BEAM SEL SW (W/O ALARM)
ALARM RLY
PNK-LT GRN
CHIME MODULE (B 8)
WHT-BLK
DIR/HAZARD SW
DEFOG SW
YEL-BLK
DIR FLASHER
RR WIPE
25A
BLU-RED
REAR WIPER/WASHER SW
BLK-TAN
VIO-WHT
WASHER FLUID LEVEL SW
RADIO/CLOCK ILLUM RLY
RADIO
CIG LTR
RADIO
15A
WIPER/WASHER SW
WIPER MOTOR
WIPER
CB
4.8A
CLOCK
ORG-BLK
CLOCK
10A
FL/PASS
15A
BLWR
25A
A/C & HTR SW
IGN OFF DRAW CONN
RED-YEL
A6
ALARM MODULE
NOT USED
G6
ABS IGN
2A
TURN BU
20A
DOME
10A
PNK
VANITY LTS
RT FNT DOOR LOCK SW
DOME LT
KEYLESS ENTRY MOD
DOME/READING LT OR OVERHEAD CONSOLE
W/ LIGHT GROUP
ANTI-LOCK BRAKE MOD
HEADLT DELAY MODULE
LT GRN-YEL
GRY-ORG
ABS BATT
BATT
HDLT DLY
25A
ABS PUMP/RELAY
POWER DOOR LOCKS
POWER SEATS
TRAILER TOW IN-LINE CB
TAN-BLK
LT GRN
RED
BRN-WHT
TAN
YEL-BLK
POWER MIRROR SW
POWER WINDOW SW
DEFOG SW
FUSE #12 (PDC)
D1
HEADLT SW
PARK/TAIL
15A
ANT
10A
POWER ANTENNA RELAY
FUSE #14 (PDC)
RED-BLK
E1
WHT-BLK
DK BLU
INST CLSTR
FUSE #6 (PDC)
ECU PIN #9
AUTO SHUTDOWN RELAY
FUEL PUMP RELAY
GAGES
7.5
ORG-BLK
DOME/READING LT OR OVERHEAD CONSOLE
HTD WDW
25A
INST LPS
5A
DEFOG RELAY
BRN
FUSE #10 (PDC)
HORN RELAY
BLK-RED
D2
GRY-ORG
(W/ ALARM)
HAZARD FLASHER
VANITY LTS
WARN IND
CLOCK
ILLUM ENTRY RELAY
RADIO
CARGO LT
LEFT CTSY LT
RIGHT CTSY LT
DOME LT
GLOVE BOX LT
KEYLESS ENTRY MOD
RT FNT DOOR LOCK SW
FUSE BLOCK
HEADLIGHT SW
FUSE #2 (PDC)
STOP LT SW
DIR/HAZ SW
PNK-BLK
VIO-TAN
A
B
C
D
E

1991 WIRING DIAGRAMS
Cherokee & Comanche (Cont.)

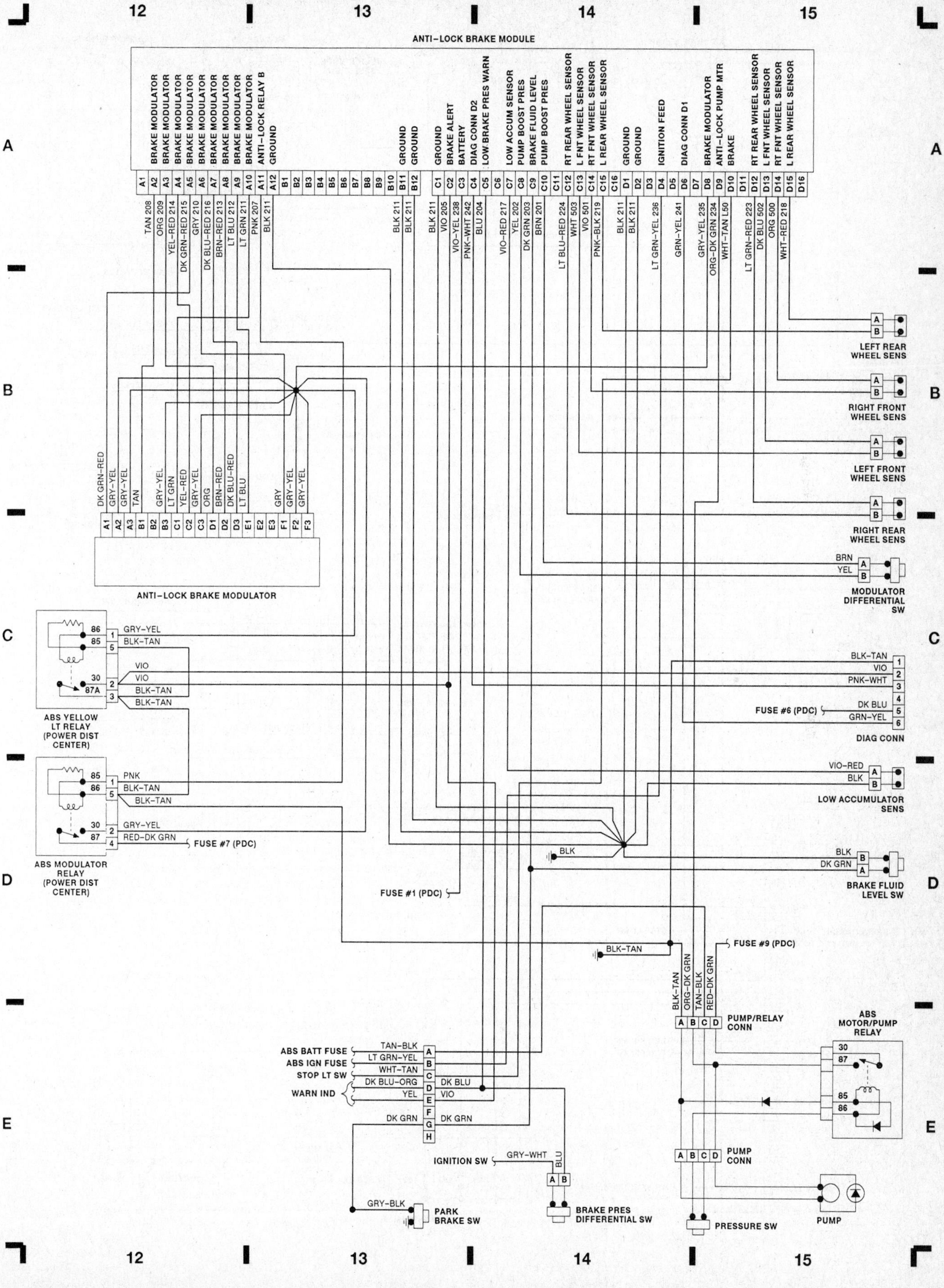
ANTI-LOCK BRAKE MODULE
ANTI-LOCK BRAKE MODULATOR
ABS YELLOW LT RELAY (POWER DIST CENTER)
ABS MODULATOR RELAY (POWER DIST CENTER)
LEFT REAR WHEEL SENS
RIGHT FRONT WHEEL SENS
LEFT FRONT WHEEL SENS
RIGHT REAR WHEEL SENS
MODULATOR DIFFERENTIAL SW
DIAG CONN
LOW ACCUMULATOR SENS
BRAKE FLUID LEVEL SW
FUSE #6 (PDC)
FUSE #7 (PDC)
FUSE #1 (PDC)
FUSE #9 (PDC)
PUMP/RELAY CONN
ABS MOTOR/PUMP RELAY
PUMP CONN
PUMP
PRESSURE SW
ABS BATT FUSE
ABS IGN FUSE
STOP LT SW
WARN IND
IGNITION SW
PARK BRAKE SW
BRAKE PRES DIFFERENTIAL SW

1991 WIRING DIAGRAMS
Cherokee & Comanche (Cont.)

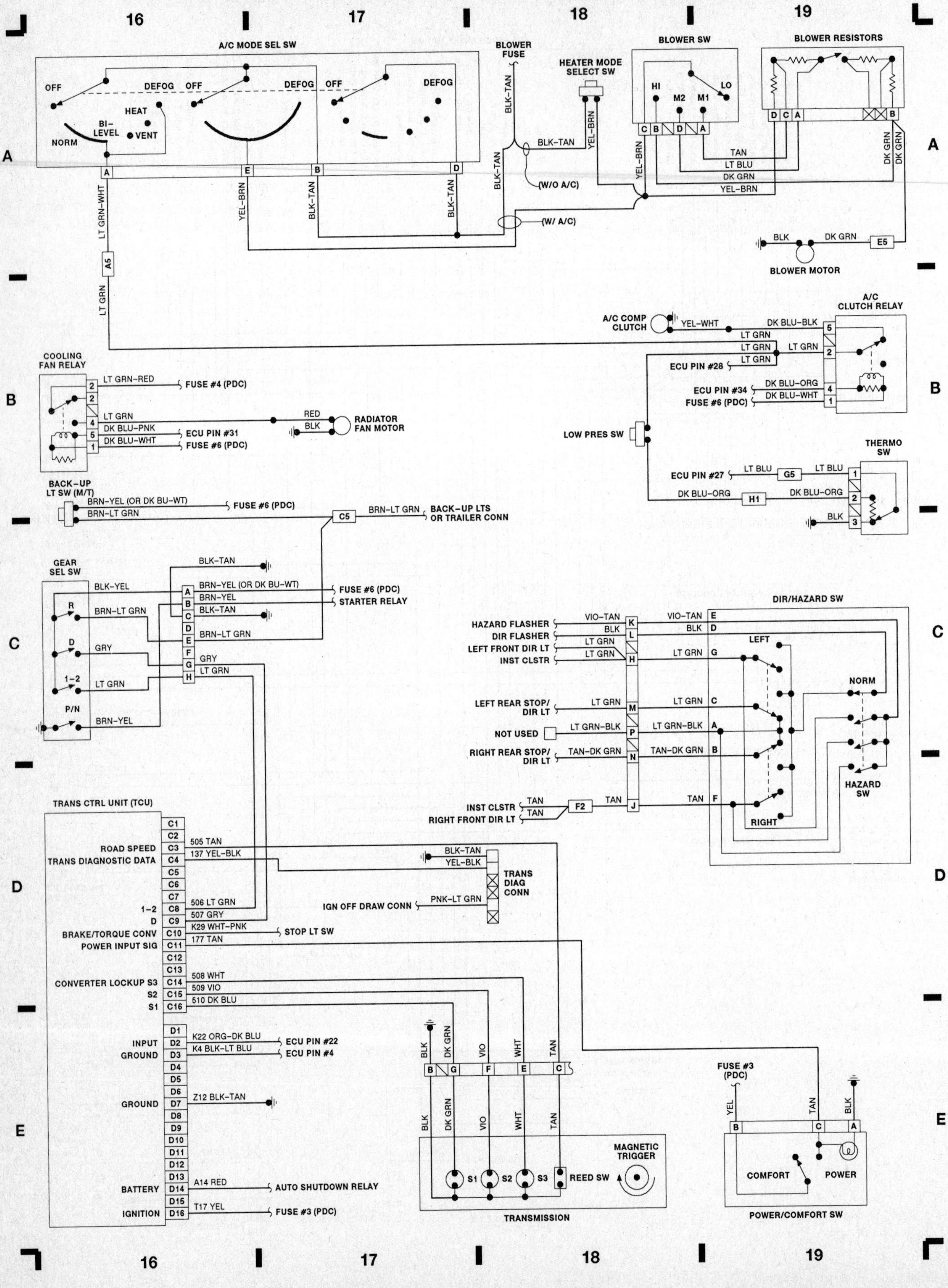
A/C MODE SEL SW
BLOWER FUSE
HEATER MODE SELECT SW
BLOWER SW
BLOWER RESISTORS
BLOWER MOTOR
A/C COMP CLUTCH
A/C CLUTCH RELAY
COOLING FAN RELAY
RADIATOR FAN MOTOR
LOW PRES SW
THERMO SW
BACK-UP LT SW (M/T)
BACK-UP LTS OR TRAILER CONN
GEAR SEL SW
FUSE #6 (PDC)
STARTER RELAY
DIR/HAZARD SW
HAZARD FLASHER
DIR FLASHER
LEFT FRONT DIR LT
INST CLSTR
LEFT REAR STOP/ DIR LT
NOT USED
RIGHT REAR STOP/ DIR LT
RIGHT FRONT DIR LT
HAZARD SW
TRANS CTRL UNIT (TCU)
ROAD SPEED
TRANS DIAGNOSTIC DATA
BRAKE/TORQUE CONV
POWER INPUT SIG
CONVERTER LOCKUP S3
INPUT
GROUND
BATTERY
IGNITION
TRANS DIAG CONN
IGN OFF DRAW CONN
STOP LT SW
ECU PIN #22
ECU PIN #4
AUTO SHUTDOWN RELAY
FUSE #3 (PDC)
MAGNETIC TRIGGER
REED SW
TRANSMISSION
COMFORT
POWER
POWER/COMFORT SW

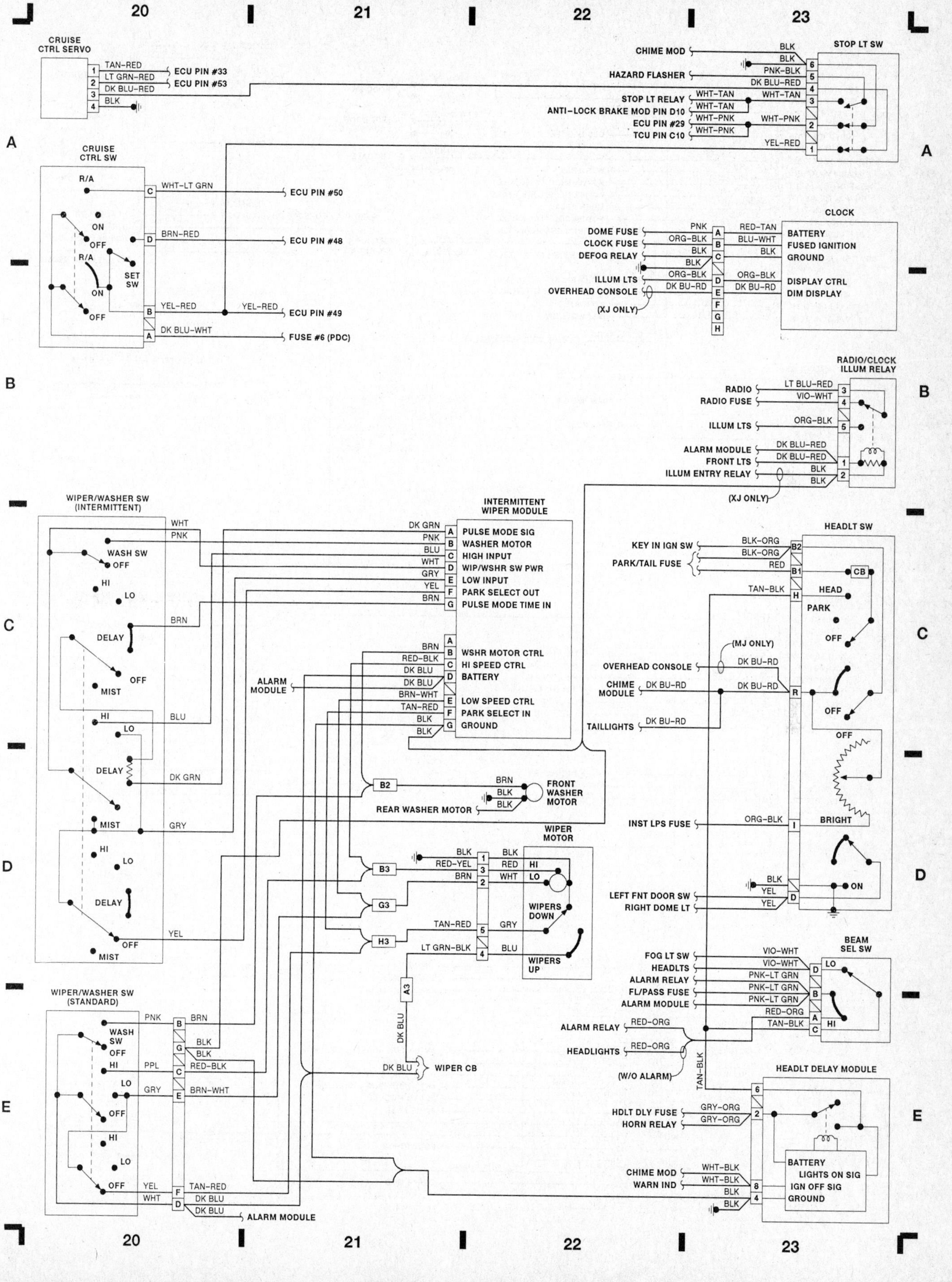

CRUISE CTRL SERVO
TAN-RED
LT GRN-RED
DK BLU-RED
BLK
ECU PIN #33
ECU PIN #53
CRUISE CTRL SW
R/A
ON
OFF
SET SW
WHT-LT GRN
BRN-RED
YEL-RED
DK BLU-WHT
ECU PIN #50
ECU PIN #48
ECU PIN #49
FUSE #6 (PDC)
CHIME MOD
HAZARD FLASHER
STOP LT RELAY
ANTI-LOCK BRAKE MOD PIN D10
ECU PIN #29
TCU PIN C10
STOP LT SW
PNK-BLK
WHT-TAN
WHT-PNK
YEL-RED
CLOCK
DOME FUSE
CLOCK FUSE
DEFOG RELAY
ILLUM LTS
OVERHEAD CONSOLE
(XJ ONLY)
BATTERY
FUSED IGNITION
GROUND
DISPLAY CTRL
DIM DISPLAY
RADIO/CLOCK ILLUM RELAY
RADIO
RADIO FUSE
ALARM MODULE
FRONT LTS
ILLUM ENTRY RELAY
WIPER/WASHER SW (INTERMITTENT)
WASH SW
HI
LO
DELAY
MIST
INTERMITTENT WIPER MODULE
PULSE MODE SIG
WASHER MOTOR
HIGH INPUT
WIP/WSHR SW PWR
LOW INPUT
PARK SELECT OUT
PULSE MODE TIME IN
WSHR MOTOR CTRL
HI SPEED CTRL
LOW SPEED CTRL
PARK SELECT IN
FRONT WASHER MOTOR
REAR WASHER MOTOR
WIPER MOTOR
WIPERS DOWN
WIPERS UP
WIPER CB
HEADLT SW
KEY IN IGN SW
PARK/TAIL FUSE
HEAD
PARK
(MJ ONLY)
CHIME MODULE
TAILLIGHTS
INST LPS FUSE
BRIGHT
LEFT FNT DOOR SW
RIGHT DOME LT
BEAM SEL SW
FOG LT SW
HEADLTS
ALARM RELAY
FL/PASS FUSE
HEADLIGHTS
(W/O ALARM)
HEADLT DELAY MODULE
HDLT DLY FUSE
HORN RELAY
WARN IND
LIGHTS ON SIG
IGN OFF SIG
WIPER/WASHER SW (STANDARD)

1991 WIRING DIAGRAMS
Cherokee & Comanche (Cont.)

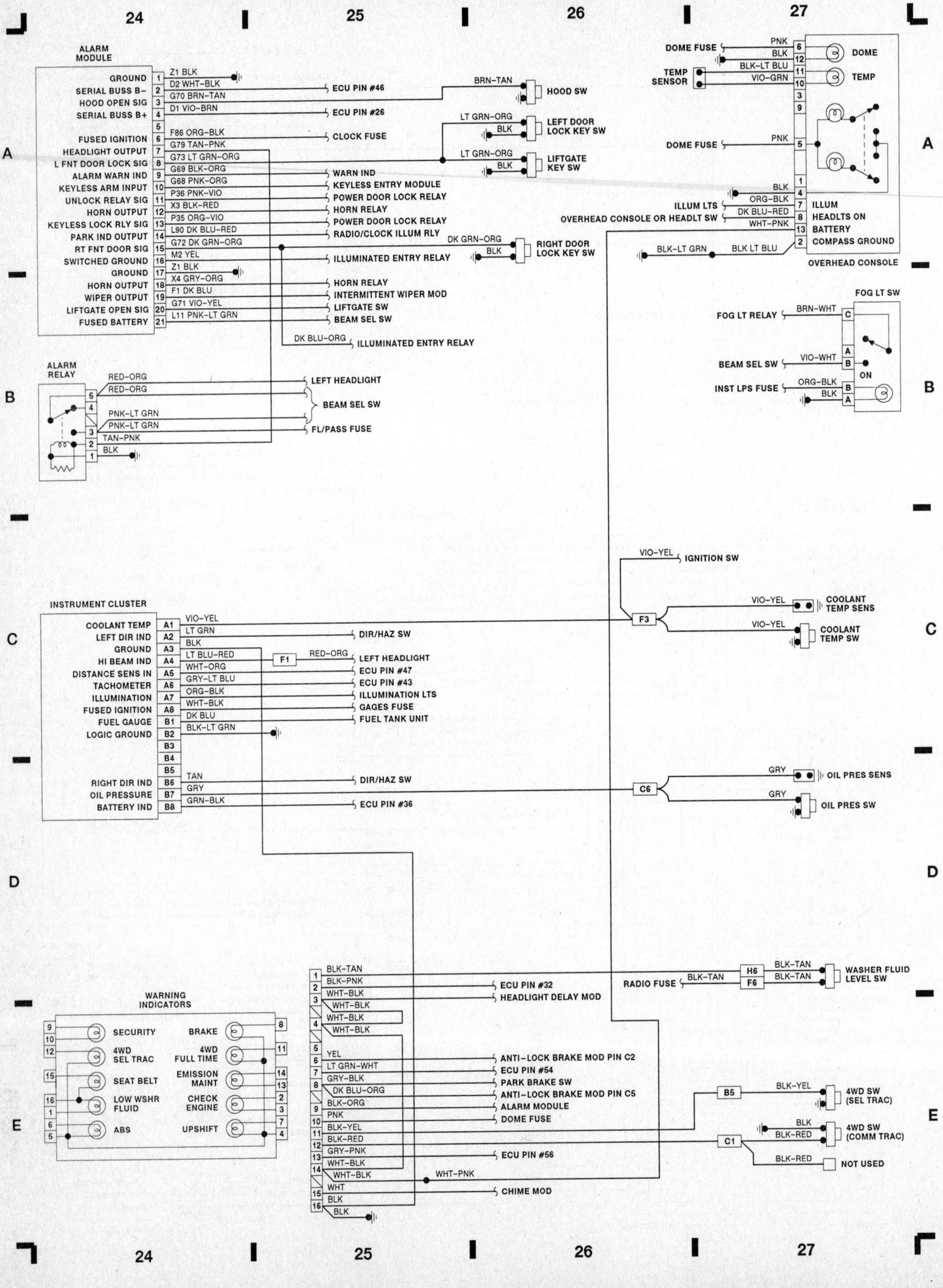
24
25
26
27
A
B
C
D
E
ALARM MODULE
GROUND 1 Z1 BLK
SERIAL BUSS B- 2 D2 WHT-BLK ECU PIN #46
HOOD OPEN SIG 3 G70 BRN-TAN
SERIAL BUSS B+ 4 D1 VIO-BRN ECU PIN #26
5
FUSED IGNITION 6 F86 ORG-BLK CLOCK FUSE
HEADLIGHT OUTPUT 7 G79 TAN-PNK
L FNT DOOR LOCK SIG 8 G73 LT GRN-ORG
ALARM WARN IND 9 G69 BLK-ORG WARN IND
KEYLESS ARM INPUT 10 G68 PNK-ORG KEYLESS ENTRY MODULE
UNLOCK RELAY SIG 11 P36 PNK-VIO POWER DOOR LOCK RELAY
HORN OUTPUT 12 X3 BLK-RED HORN RELAY
KEYLESS LOCK RLY SIG 13 P35 ORG-VIO POWER DOOR LOCK RELAY
PARK IND OUTPUT 14 L90 DK BLU-RED RADIO/CLOCK ILLUM RLY
RT FNT DOOR SIG 15 G72 DK GRN-ORG
SWITCHED GROUND 16 M2 YEL ILLUMINATED ENTRY RELAY
GROUND 17 Z1 BLK
HORN OUTPUT 18 X4 GRY-ORG HORN RELAY
WIPER OUTPUT 19 F1 DK BLU INTERMITTENT WIPER MOD
LIFTGATE OPEN SIG 20 G71 VIO-YEL LIFTGATE SW
FUSED BATTERY 21 L11 PNK-LT GRN BEAM SEL SW
DK BLU-ORG ILLUMINATED ENTRY RELAY
BRN-TAN HOOD SW
LT GRN-ORG BLK LEFT DOOR LOCK KEY SW
LT GRN-ORG BLK LIFTGATE KEY SW
DK GRN-ORG BLK RIGHT DOOR LOCK KEY SW
DOME FUSE PNK 6 DOME
BLK 12
TEMP SENSOR BLK-LT BLU 11 TEMP
VIO-GRN 10
3
9
DOME FUSE PNK 5
1
BLK 4
ILLUM LTS ORG-BLK 7 ILLUM
OVERHEAD CONSOLE OR HEADLT SW DK BLU-RED 8 HEADLTS ON
WHT-PNK 13 BATTERY
BLK-LT GRN BLK LT BLU 2 COMPASS GROUND
OVERHEAD CONSOLE
ALARM RELAY
5 RED-ORG LEFT HEADLIGHT
4 RED-ORG BEAM SEL SW
PNK-LT GRN
3 PNK-LT GRN FL/PASS FUSE
2 TAN-PNK
1 BLK
FOG LT SW
FOG LT RELAY BRN-WHT C
A
BEAM SEL SW VIO-WHT B
ON
INST LPS FUSE ORG-BLK B
BLK A
VIO-YEL IGNITION SW
F3
VIO-YEL COOLANT TEMP SENS
VIO-YEL COOLANT TEMP SW
INSTRUMENT CLUSTER
COOLANT TEMP A1 VIO-YEL
LEFT DIR IND A2 LT GRN DIR/HAZ SW
GROUND A3 BLK
HI BEAM IND A4 LT BLU-RED F1 RED-ORG LEFT HEADLIGHT
DISTANCE SENS IN A5 WHT-ORG ECU PIN #47
TACHOMETER A6 GRY-LT BLU ECU PIN #43
ILLUMINATION A7 ORG-BLK ILLUMINATION LTS
FUSED IGNITION A8 WHT-BLK GAGES FUSE
FUEL GAUGE B1 DK BLU FUEL TANK UNIT
LOGIC GROUND B2 BLK-LT GRN
B3
B4
B5
RIGHT DIR IND B6 TAN DIR/HAZ SW
OIL PRESSURE B7 GRY
BATTERY IND B8 GRN-BLK ECU PIN #36
C6
GRY OIL PRES SENS
GRY OIL PRES SW
WARNING INDICATORS
9 SECURITY
10
12 4WD SEL TRAC
15 SEAT BELT
16 LOW WSHR FLUID
1
6 ABS
5
BRAKE 8
4WD FULL TIME 11
EMISSION MAINT 14 13
CHECK ENGINE 2 3
UPSHIFT 7 4
1 BLK-TAN
2 BLK-PNK ECU PIN #32
WHT-BLK HEADLIGHT DELAY MOD
3 WHT-BLK
WHT-BLK
4 WHT-BLK
5 YEL ANTI-LOCK BRAKE MOD PIN C2
6 LT GRN-WHT ECU PIN #54
7 GRY-BLK PARK BRAKE SW
8 DK BLU-ORG ANTI-LOCK BRAKE MOD PIN C5
BLK-ORG ALARM MODULE
9 PNK DOME FUSE
10 BLK-YEL
11 BLK-RED
12 GRY-PNK ECU PIN #56
13 WHT-BLK
14 WHT-BLK WHT-PNK
WHT CHIME MOD
15 BLK
16 BLK
H6 BLK-TAN
RADIO FUSE BLK-TAN F6 BLK-TAN WASHER FLUID LEVEL SW
B5 BLK-YEL 4WD SW (SEL TRAC)
BLK
C1 BLK-RED 4WD SW (COMM TRAC)
BLK-RED NOT USED
24
25
26
27

1991 WIRING DIAGRAMS
Cherokee & Comanche (Cont.)

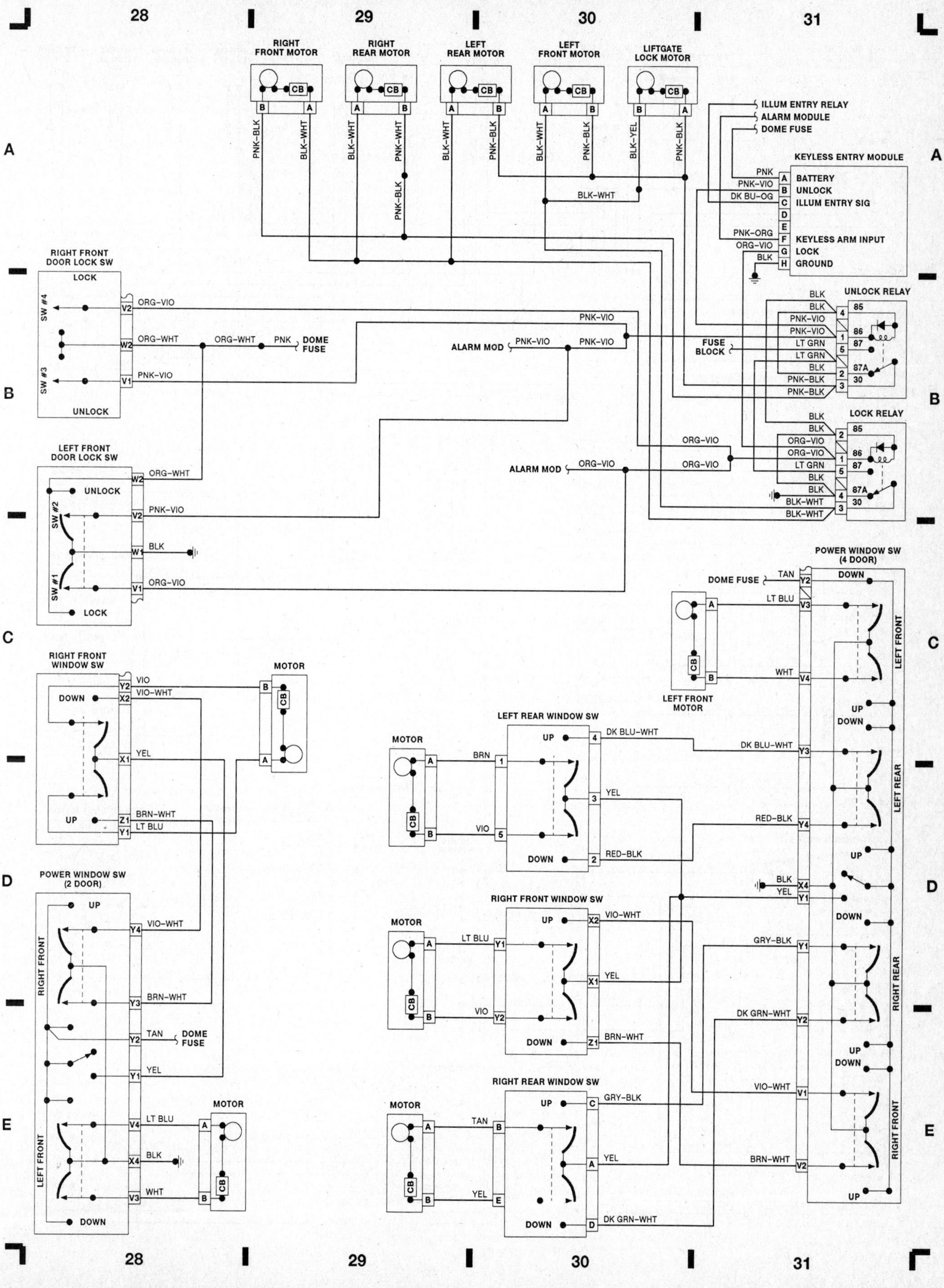
RIGHT FRONT MOTOR
RIGHT REAR MOTOR
LEFT REAR MOTOR
LEFT FRONT MOTOR
LIFTGATE LOCK MOTOR
ILLUM ENTRY RELAY
ALARM MODULE
DOME FUSE
KEYLESS ENTRY MODULE
BATTERY
UNLOCK
ILLUM ENTRY SIG
KEYLESS ARM INPUT
LOCK
GROUND
RIGHT FRONT DOOR LOCK SW
UNLOCK RELAY
FUSE BLOCK
ALARM MOD
LOCK RELAY
LEFT FRONT DOOR LOCK SW
POWER WINDOW SW (4 DOOR)
LEFT FRONT MOTOR
RIGHT FRONT WINDOW SW
MOTOR
LEFT REAR WINDOW SW
POWER WINDOW SW (2 DOOR)
RIGHT FRONT WINDOW SW
RIGHT REAR WINDOW SW
LEFT FRONT
LEFT REAR
RIGHT REAR
RIGHT FRONT

1991 WIRING DIAGRAMS
Cherokee & Comanche (Cont.)

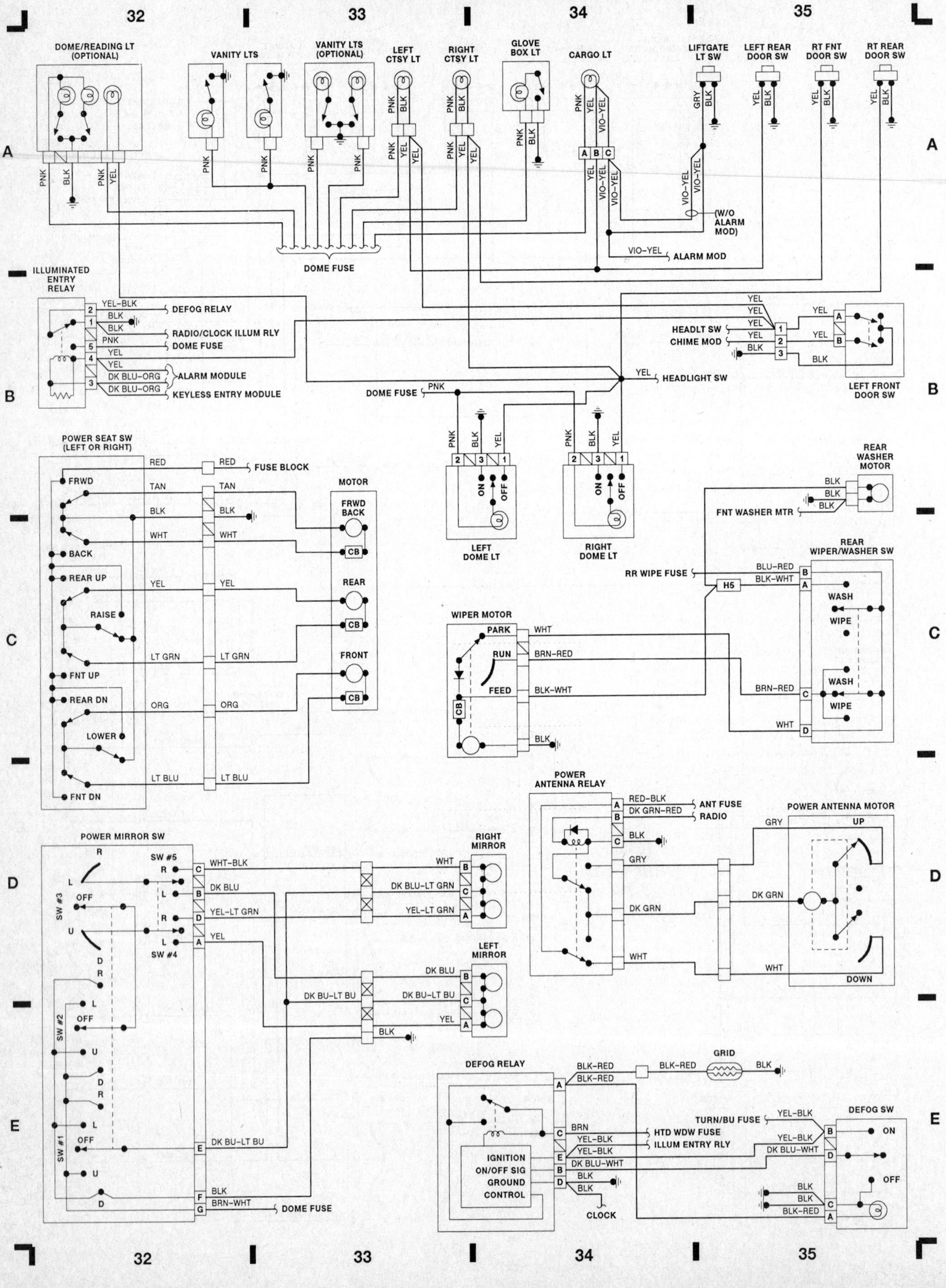
32
33
34
35
DOME/READING LT (OPTIONAL)
VANITY LTS
VANITY LTS (OPTIONAL)
LEFT CTSY LT
RIGHT CTSY LT
GLOVE BOX LT
CARGO LT
LIFTGATE LT SW
LEFT REAR DOOR SW
RT FNT DOOR SW
RT REAR DOOR SW
DOME FUSE
ALARM MOD
(W/O ALARM MOD)
ILLUMINATED ENTRY RELAY
DEFOG RELAY
RADIO/CLOCK ILLUM RLY
ALARM MODULE
KEYLESS ENTRY MODULE
HEADLT SW
CHIME MOD
HEADLIGHT SW
LEFT FRONT DOOR SW
LEFT DOME LT
RIGHT DOME LT
POWER SEAT SW (LEFT OR RIGHT)
FUSE BLOCK
MOTOR
FRWD BACK
REAR
FRONT
REAR WASHER MOTOR
FNT WASHER MTR
REAR WIPER/WASHER SW
RR WIPE FUSE
WIPER MOTOR
PARK
RUN
FEED
POWER ANTENNA RELAY
ANT FUSE
RADIO
POWER ANTENNA MOTOR
POWER MIRROR SW
RIGHT MIRROR
LEFT MIRROR
GRID
DEFOG RELAY
IGNITION ON/OFF SIG GROUND CONTROL
HTD WDW FUSE
ILLUM ENTRY RLY
TURN/BU FUSE
DEFOG SW
CLOCK
A
B
C
D
E

1991 WIRING DIAGRAMS
Cherokee & Comanche (Cont.)

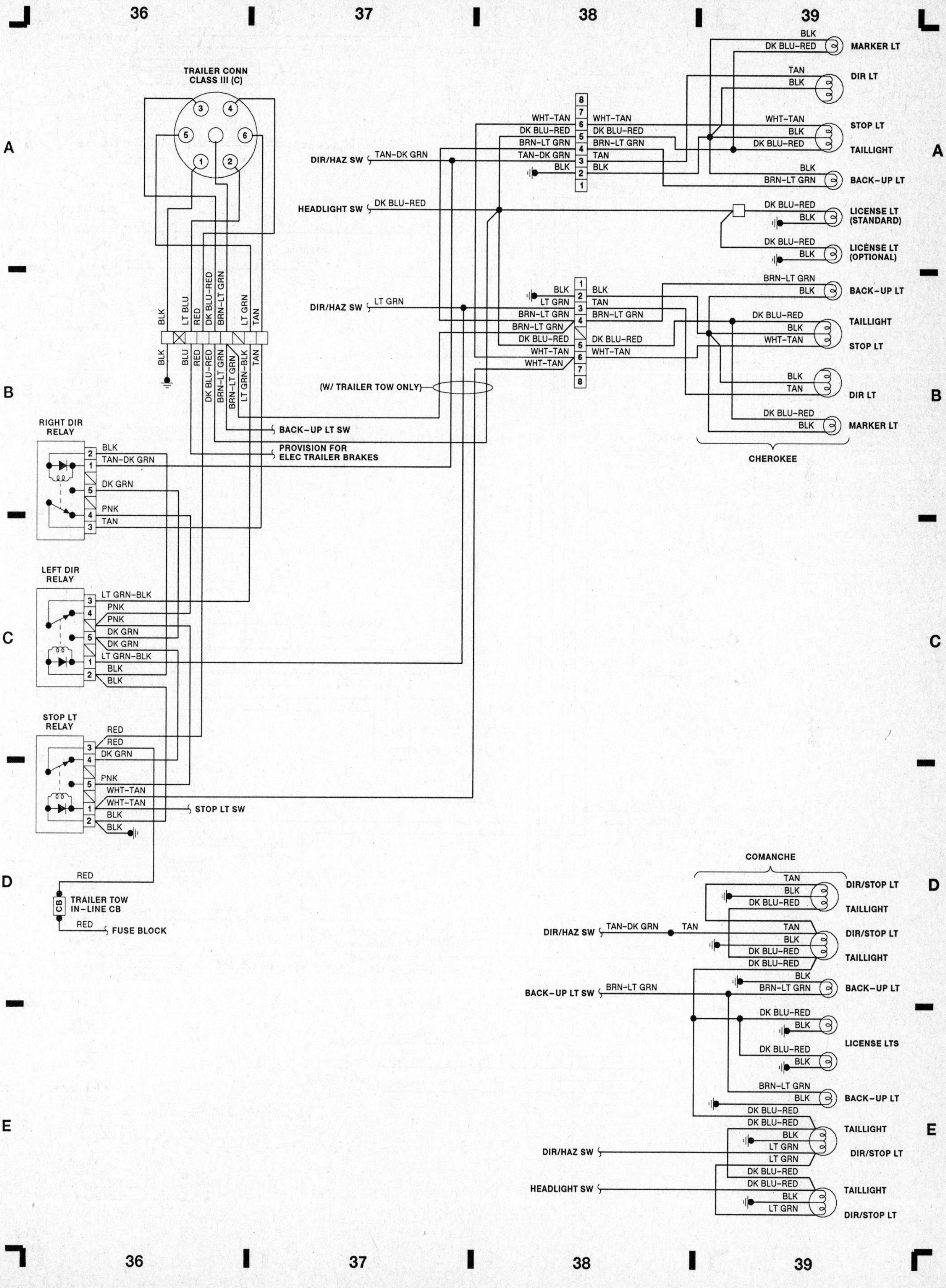
36
37
38
39
A
B
C
D
E
TRAILER CONN CLASS III (C)
DIR/HAZ SW
HEADLIGHT SW
BACK-UP LT SW
PROVISION FOR ELEC TRAILER BRAKES
(W/ TRAILER TOW ONLY)
RIGHT DIR RELAY
LEFT DIR RELAY
STOP LT RELAY
STOP LT SW
TRAILER TOW IN-LINE CB
FUSE BLOCK
MARKER LT
DIR LT
STOP LT
TAILLIGHT
BACK-UP LT
LICENSE LT (STANDARD)
LICENSE LT (OPTIONAL)
CHEROKEE
COMANCHE
DIR/STOP LT
LICENSE LTS
BLK
LT BLU
RED
DK BLU-RED
BRN-LT GRN
LT GRN
TAN
LT GRN-BLK
TAN-DK GRN
WHT-TAN
DK GRN
PNK

1991 WIRING DIAGRAMS
Grand Wagoneer

COMPONENT LOCATOR:

A/C/HEATER SW	A 8–9
ALTERNATOR	C 3
BACK–UP LT SW	B 3
BATTERY	A 1–2
BEAM SEL SW	B 5
BRAKE WARN SW	B 14
CARB BOWL VENT SOLENOID	E 3
CARB SOLENOID	E 3
CARGO LT SW	A 23
CHIME MODULE	B 8
CHOKE HEATER SW	E 3
COOLANT TEMP SENDING UNIT	A 14
COURTESY LTS	A 21
CRUISE CTRL MODULE	B–C 11
CRUISE CTRL SW	C 9–10
DEFOG SW	A 19
DEFOG TIMER	B 19
DIMMER/DOME LT SW	B 4
DIR FLASHER	C–D 6
DIR/HAZ SW	B–C 7
DISTRIBUTOR	C–D 2
DOME LT	A 22
DOOR SWS	A 20–21, A 23
FOG LT RELAY	D 3
FOG LT SW	B 19
FUEL SENDER	A 14
FUS LINKS	A 3
FUSE BLOCK	C–E 5–6
GLOVE BOX LT	A 20
HAZARD FLASHER	C–D 5
HEADLIGHT SW	B–C 4
HORN RELAY	D 3
IGNITION COIL	C 2
IGNITION KEY WARN SW	B 9
IGNITION MODULE	C 3
IGNITION SW	A 4–7
ILLUMINATION LTS	A–B 15
IN–LINE CB (TRAILER TOW)	E 21
IN–LINE FUSE (CRUISE CTRL)	C 10
INSTRUMENT CLUSTER	A–B 12
KEYLESS ENTRY MODULE	E 14
NEUTRAL SAFETY SW	B 3
OIL PRES SENS	A 14
OVERHEAD CONSOLE COMPASS	C 8
POWER DOOR LOCK SYSTEM	C–E 12–14
POWER MIRROR SYSTEM	D–E 16–17
POWER SEAT SYSTEM	C–E 14–15
POWER WINDOW SYSTEM	A–C 16–18
RADIO/ILLUM LT RELAY	C 4
REAR WIPER/WASHER SYSTEM	D–E 23
STARTER RELAY	A 3
STOP LT SW	C–D 7
TAILGATE PWR WDO SYSTEM	C–E 19
UNDERHOOD LT	A 20
VANITY LTS	A 21–22
WIPER/WASHER SYSTEMS	D–E 8–11
4WD SW	B 14

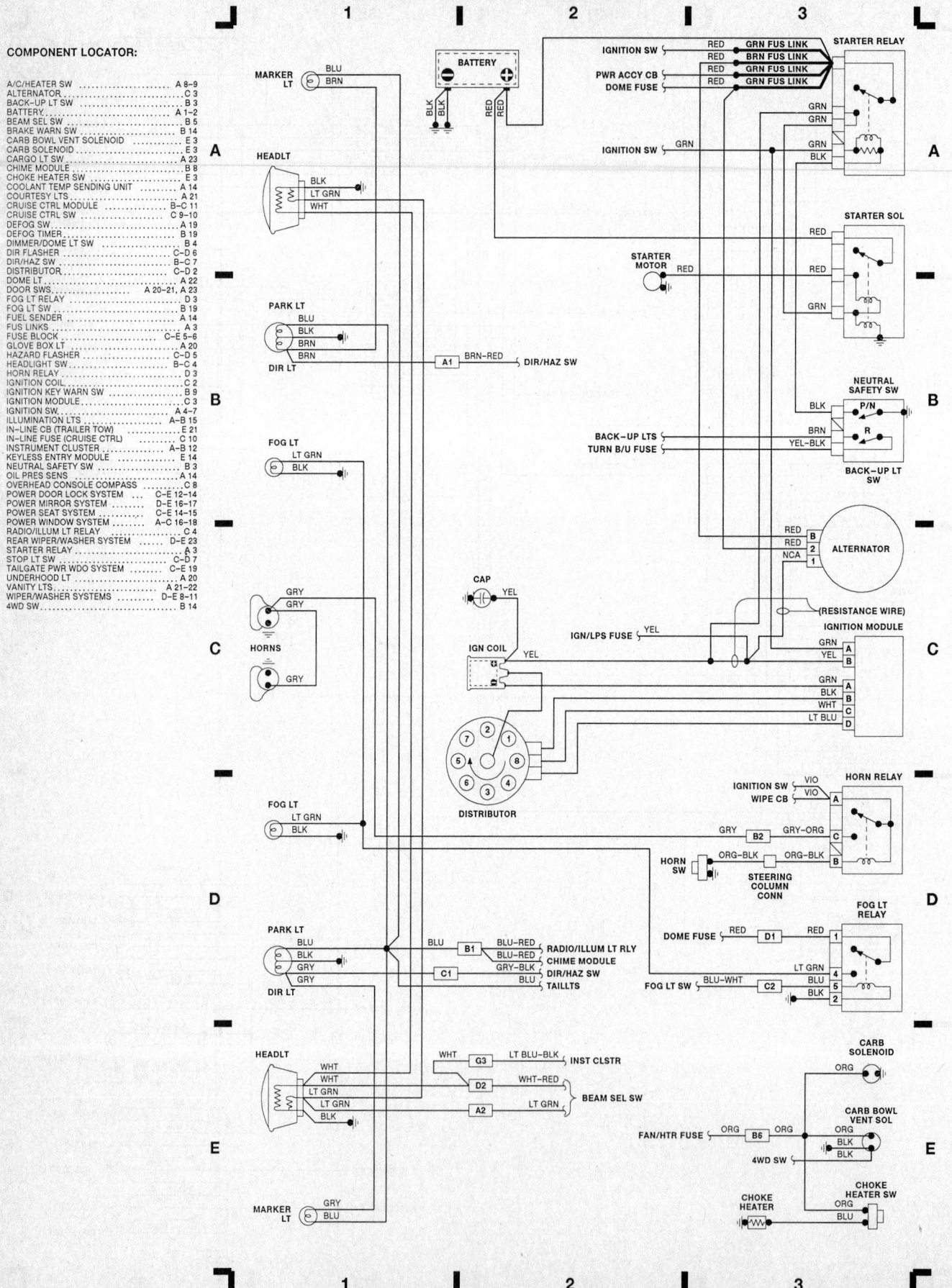

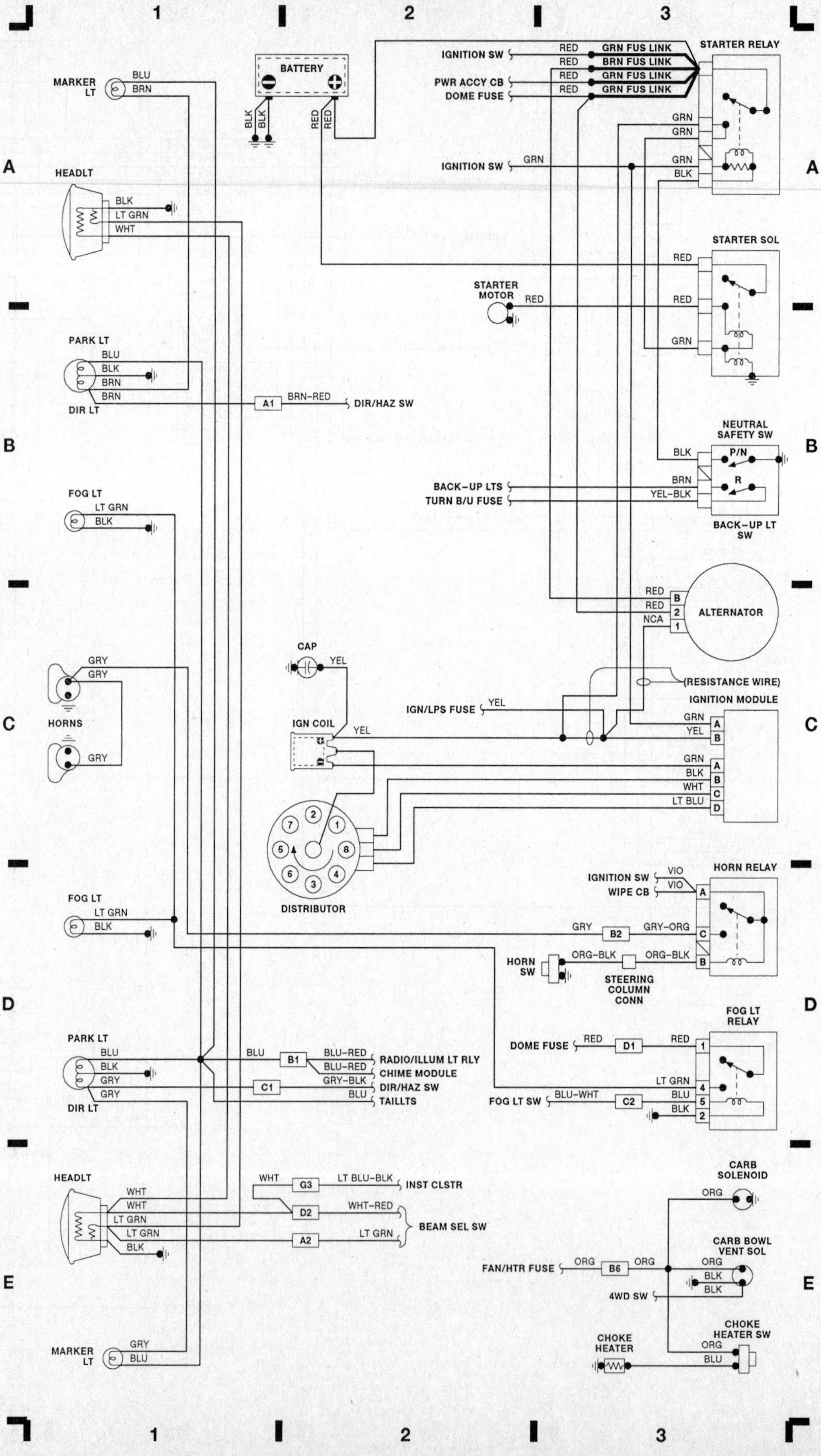
1
2
3
A
B
C
D
E
MARKER LT
BLU
BRN
BATTERY
BLK
RED
IGNITION SW
PWR ACCY CB
DOME FUSE
GRN FUS LINK
BRN FUS LINK
STARTER RELAY
GRN
HEADLT
LT GRN
WHT
STARTER SOL
STARTER MOTOR
PARK LT
DIR LT
BRN–RED
DIR/HAZ SW
A1
NEUTRAL SAFETY SW
P/N
R
BACK–UP LTS
TURN B/U FUSE
YEL–BLK
BACK–UP LT SW
FOG LT
GRY
HORNS
ALTERNATOR
NCA
CAP
YEL
(RESISTANCE WIRE)
IGN/LPS FUSE
IGNITION MODULE
IGN COIL
LT BLU
DISTRIBUTOR
HORN RELAY
VIO
WIPE CB
GRY–ORG
B2
HORN SW
ORG–BLK
STEERING COLUMN CONN
FOG LT RELAY
D1
FOG LT SW
BLU–WHT
C2
B1
C1
RADIO/ILLUM LT RLY
CHIME MODULE
GRY–BLK
TAILLTS
G3
LT BLU–BLK
INST CLSTR
D2
WHT–RED
A2
BEAM SEL SW
CARB SOLENOID
ORG
CARB BOWL VENT SOL
FAN/HTR FUSE
B6
4WD SW
CHOKE HEATER
CHOKE HEATER SW

1991 WIRING DIAGRAMS
Grand Wagoneer (Cont.)

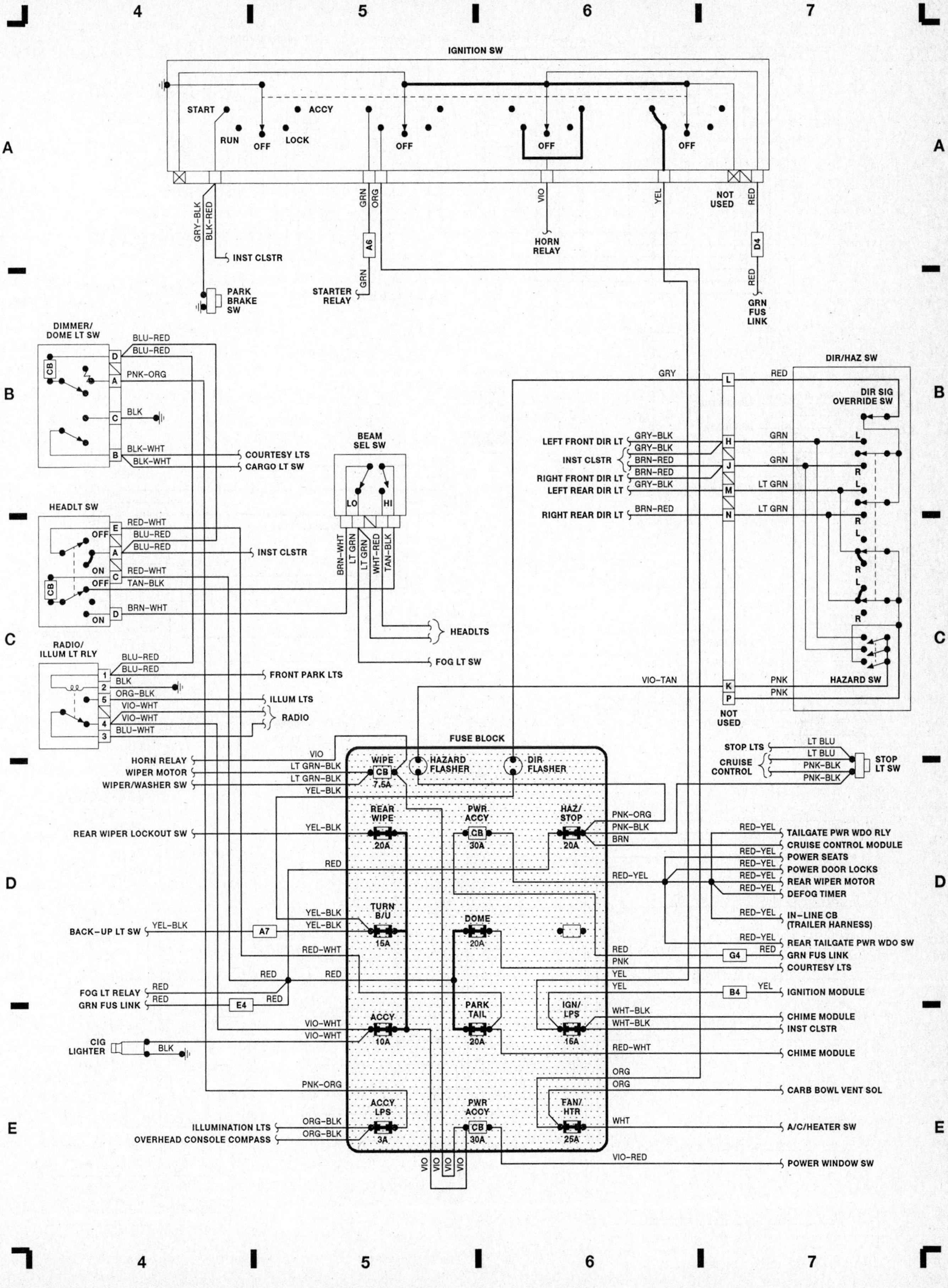
IGNITION SW
START
ACCY
RUN
OFF
LOCK
GRY-BLK
BLK-RED
INST CLSTR
PARK BRAKE SW
GRN
ORG
A6
STARTER RELAY
VIO
HORN RELAY
YEL
NOT USED
RED
D4
GRN FUS LINK
DIMMER/ DOME LT SW
BLU-RED
PNK-ORG
BLK
BLK-WHT
COURTESY LTS
CARGO LT SW
BEAM SEL SW
LO
HI
HEADLT SW
RED-WHT
TAN-BLK
BRN-WHT
LT GRN
WHT-RED
HEADLTS
FOG LT SW
RADIO/ ILLUM LT RLY
FRONT PARK LTS
ORG-BLK
VIO-WHT
ILLUM LTS
RADIO
DIR/HAZ SW
GRY
DIR SIG OVERRIDE SW
LEFT FRONT DIR LT
RIGHT FRONT DIR LT
LEFT REAR DIR LT
RIGHT REAR DIR LT
BRN-RED
LT GRN
VIO-TAN
PNK
HAZARD SW
FUSE BLOCK
WIPE CB 7.5A
HAZARD FLASHER
DIR FLASHER
HORN RELAY
WIPER MOTOR
WIPER/WASHER SW
LT GRN-BLK
YEL-BLK
STOP LTS
CRUISE CONTROL
LT BLU
PNK-BLK
STOP LT SW
REAR WIPE 20A
PWR ACCY CB 30A
HAZ/ STOP 20A
REAR WIPER LOCKOUT SW
TAILGATE PWR WDO RLY
CRUISE CONTROL MODULE
POWER SEATS
POWER DOOR LOCKS
REAR WIPER MOTOR
DEFOG TIMER
IN-LINE CB (TRAILER HARNESS)
REAR TAILGATE PWR WDO SW
GRN FUS LINK
COURTESY LTS
IGNITION MODULE
CHIME MODULE
INST CLSTR
CARB BOWL VENT SOL
A/C/HEATER SW
POWER WINDOW SW
RED-YEL
BRN
TURN B/U 15A
DOME 20A
BACK-UP LT SW
A7
G4
B4
FOG LT RELAY
E4
PARK TAIL 20A
IGN/ LPS 15A
WHT-BLK
ACCY 10A
CIG LIGHTER
ACCY LPS 3A
PWR ACCY CB 30A
FAN/ HTR 25A
WHT
VIO-RED
ILLUMINATION LTS
OVERHEAD CONSOLE COMPASS
4
5
6
7
A
B
C
D
E

1991 WIRING DIAGRAMS
Grand Wagoneer (Cont.)

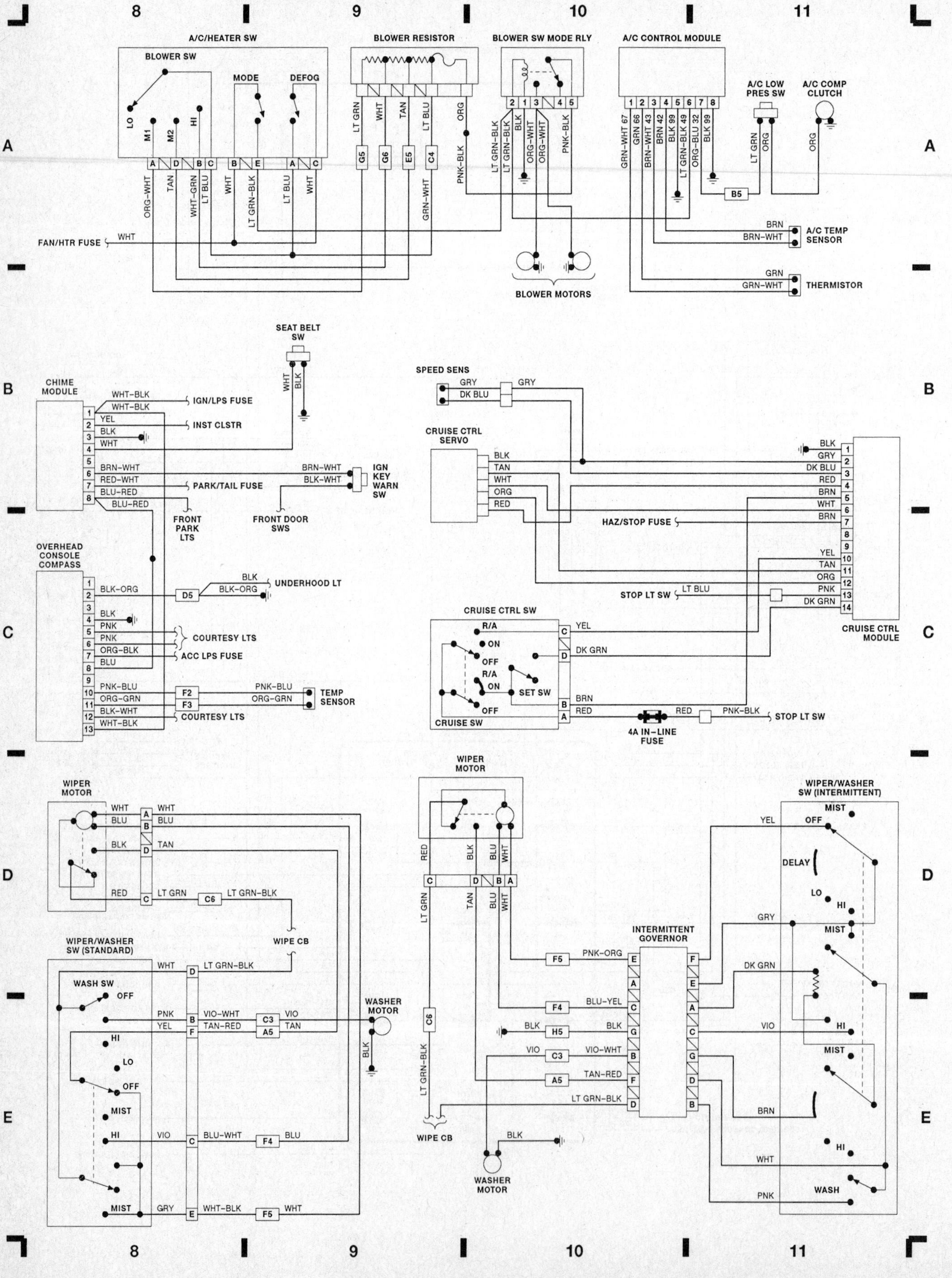
8
9
10
11
A/C/HEATER SW
BLOWER SW
MODE
DEFOG
LO
M1
M2
HI
BLOWER RESISTOR
BLOWER SW MODE RLY
A/C CONTROL MODULE
A/C LOW PRES SW
A/C COMP CLUTCH
ORG-WHT
TAN
WHT-GRN
LT BLU
WHT
LT GRN-BLK
LT GRN
TAN
GRN-WHT
ORG
PNK-BLK
ORG-WHT
PNK-BLK
GRN-WHT 67
GRN 66
BRN-WHT 43
BRN 42
BLK 99
LT GRN-BLK 49
ORG-BLU 32
B5
FAN/HTR FUSE
A/C TEMP SENSOR
THERMISTOR
BLOWER MOTORS
A
B
C
D
E
SEAT BELT SW
CHIME MODULE
WHT-BLK
IGN/LPS FUSE
INST CLSTR
YEL
BLK
BRN-WHT
RED-WHT
BLU-RED
PARK/TAIL FUSE
IGN KEY WARN SW
FRONT PARK LTS
FRONT DOOR SWS
OVERHEAD CONSOLE COMPASS
BLK-ORG
D5
UNDERHOOD LT
PNK
COURTESY LTS
ORG-BLK
BLU
ACC LPS FUSE
PNK-BLU
ORG-GRN
BLK-WHT
F2
F3
TEMP SENSOR
SPEED SENS
GRY
DK BLU
CRUISE CTRL SERVO
HAZ/STOP FUSE
STOP LT SW
CRUISE CTRL MODULE
CRUISE CTRL SW
R/A
ON
OFF
SET SW
CRUISE SW
DK GRN
4A IN-LINE FUSE
WIPER MOTOR
WIPER/WASHER SW (STANDARD)
WASH SW
MIST
C6
WIPE CB
VIO-WHT
TAN-RED
C3
A5
WASHER MOTOR
BLU-WHT
F4
F5
INTERMITTENT GOVERNOR
PNK-ORG
BLU-YEL
H5
VIO
WIPER/WASHER SW (INTERMITTENT)
DELAY
WASH

1991 WIRING DIAGRAMS
Grand Wagoneer (Cont.)

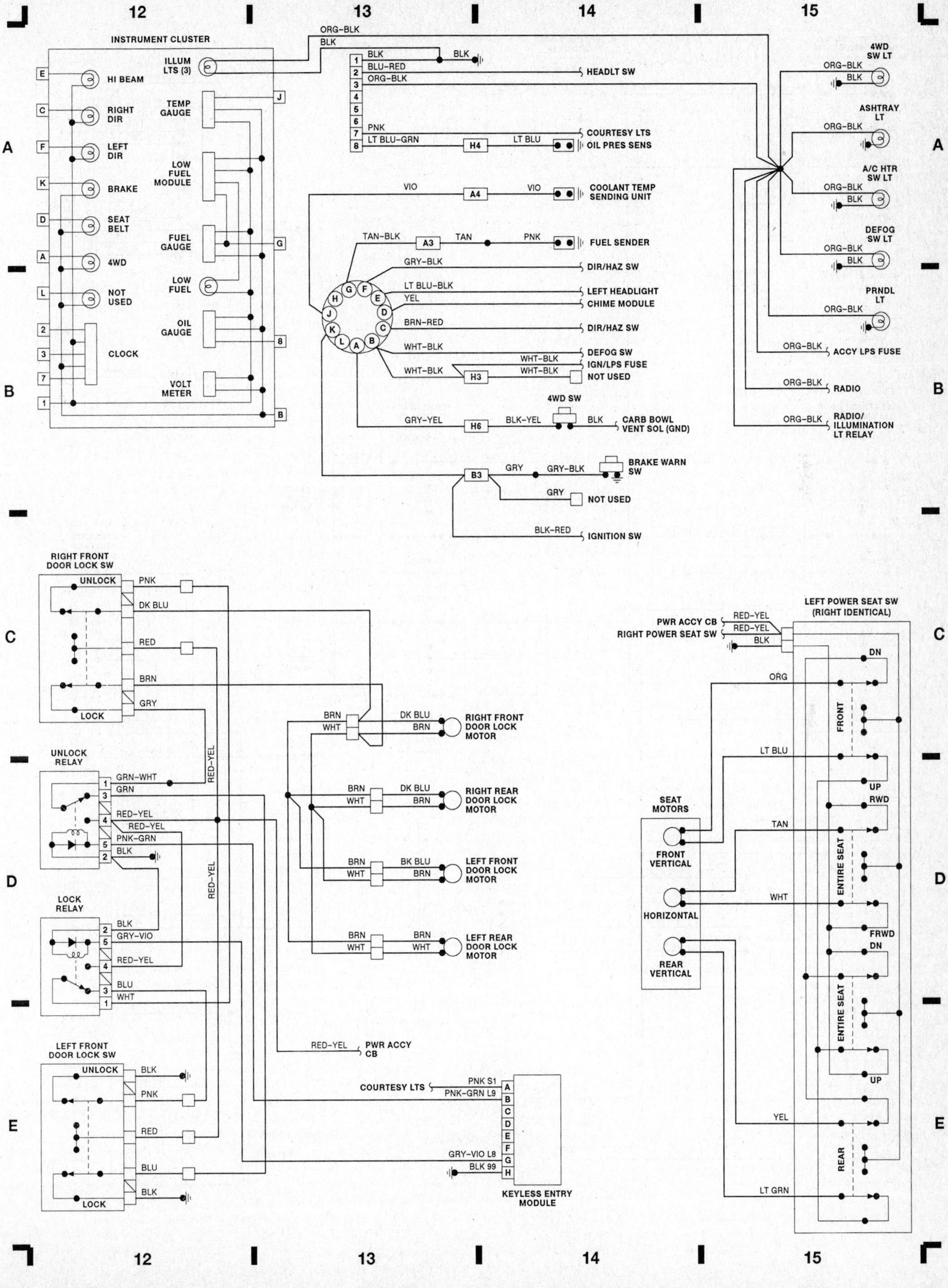
INSTRUMENT CLUSTER
HI BEAM
RIGHT DIR
LEFT DIR
BRAKE
SEAT BELT
4WD
NOT USED
CLOCK
ILLUM LTS (3)
TEMP GAUGE
LOW FUEL MODULE
FUEL GAUGE
LOW FUEL
OIL GAUGE
VOLT METER
ORG-BLK
BLK
BLU-RED
HEADLT SW
PNK
COURTESY LTS
LT BLU-GRN
LT BLU
OIL PRES SENS
VIO
COOLANT TEMP SENDING UNIT
TAN-BLK
TAN
FUEL SENDER
GRY-BLK
DIR/HAZ SW
LT BLU-BLK
LEFT HEADLIGHT
YEL
CHIME MODULE
BRN-RED
WHT-BLK
DEFOG SW
IGN/LPS FUSE
NOT USED
4WD SW
GRY-YEL
BLK-YEL
CARB BOWL VENT SOL (GND)
GRY
BRAKE WARN SW
BLK-RED
IGNITION SW
4WD SW LT
ASHTRAY LT
A/C HTR SW LT
DEFOG SW LT
PRNDL LT
ACCY LPS FUSE
RADIO
RADIO/ ILLUMINATION LT RELAY
RIGHT FRONT DOOR LOCK SW
UNLOCK
LOCK
DK BLU
RED
BRN
WHT
RIGHT FRONT DOOR LOCK MOTOR
RIGHT REAR DOOR LOCK MOTOR
BK BLU
LEFT FRONT DOOR LOCK MOTOR
LEFT REAR DOOR LOCK MOTOR
UNLOCK RELAY
GRN-WHT
GRN
RED-YEL
PNK-GRN
LOCK RELAY
GRY-VIO
BLU
PWR ACCY CB
LEFT FRONT DOOR LOCK SW
COURTESY LTS
PNK S1
PNK-GRN L9
GRY-VIO L8
BLK 99
KEYLESS ENTRY MODULE
LEFT POWER SEAT SW (RIGHT IDENTICAL)
PWR ACCY CB
RIGHT POWER SEAT SW
ORG
DN
UP
FRONT
RWD
FRWD
ENTIRE SEAT
REAR
SEAT MOTORS
FRONT VERTICAL
HORIZONTAL
REAR VERTICAL
LT GRN

1991 WIRING DIAGRAMS
Grand Wagoneer (Cont.)

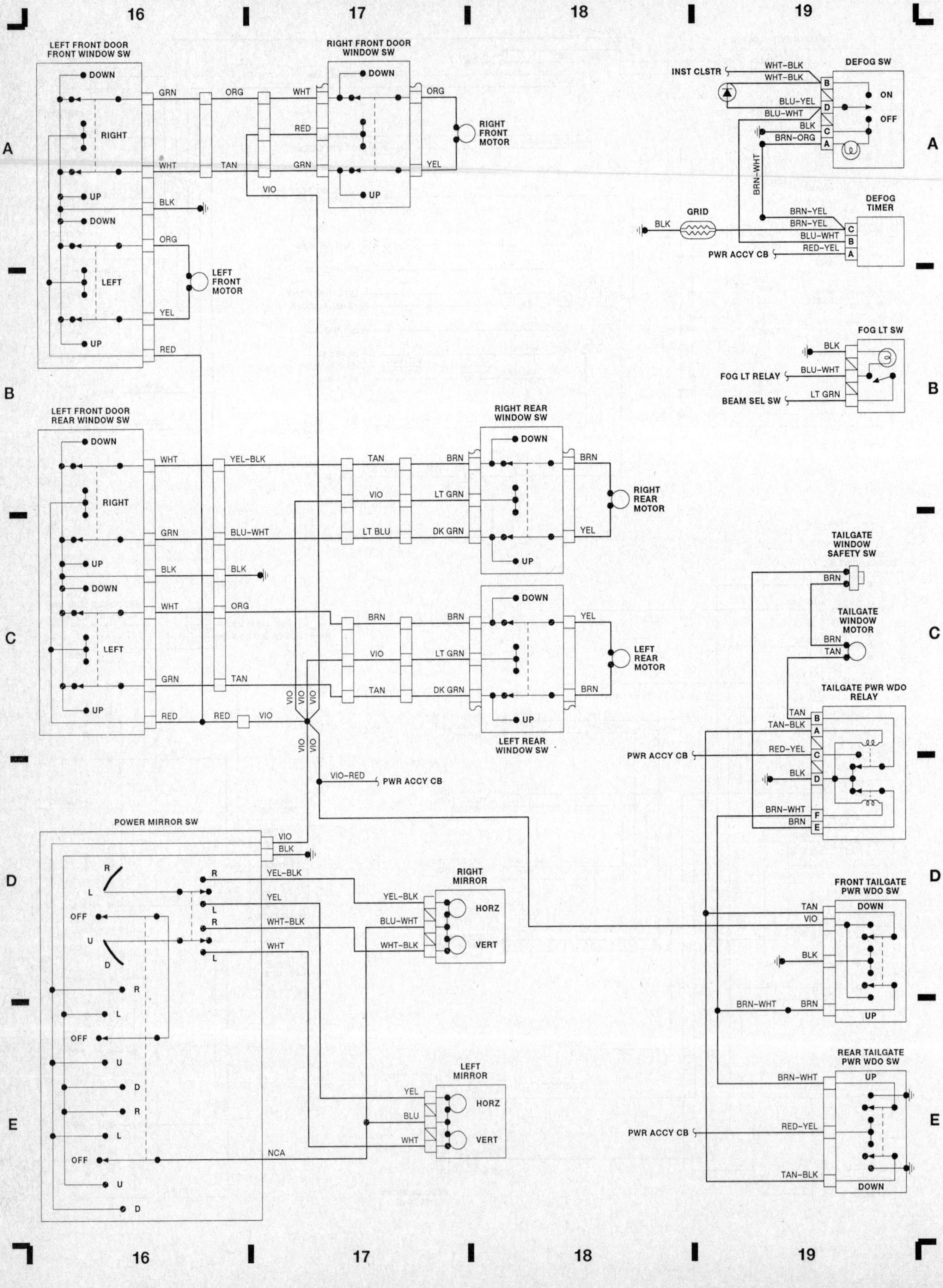
16
17
18
19
LEFT FRONT DOOR FRONT WINDOW SW
DOWN
RIGHT
UP
DOWN
LEFT
UP
GRN
ORG
WHT
TAN
GRN
BLK
ORG
YEL
RED
RIGHT FRONT DOOR WINDOW SW
DOWN
UP
ORG
RED
VIO
YEL
RIGHT FRONT MOTOR
LEFT FRONT MOTOR
INST CLSTR
WHT-BLK
WHT-BLK
BLU-YEL
BLU-WHT
BLK
BRN-ORG
DEFOG SW
ON
OFF
BRN-WHT
GRID
BLK
BRN-YEL
BRN-YEL
BLU-WHT
RED-YEL
PWR ACCY CB
DEFOG TIMER
FOG LT SW
FOG LT RELAY
BEAM SEL SW
LT GRN
LEFT FRONT DOOR REAR WINDOW SW
YEL-BLK
BLU-WHT
RIGHT REAR WINDOW SW
VIO
LT GRN
LT BLU
DK GRN
BRN
RIGHT REAR MOTOR
LEFT REAR MOTOR
LEFT REAR WINDOW SW
TAILGATE WINDOW SAFETY SW
TAILGATE WINDOW MOTOR
TAILGATE PWR WDO RELAY
TAN-BLK
VIO-RED
POWER MIRROR SW
R
L
OFF
U
D
YEL-BLK
WHT-BLK
WHT
RIGHT MIRROR
HORZ
VERT
LEFT MIRROR
BLU
NCA
FRONT TAILGATE PWR WDO SW
REAR TAILGATE PWR WDO SW
A
B
C
D
E

1991 WIRING DIAGRAMS
Grand Wagoneer (Cont.)

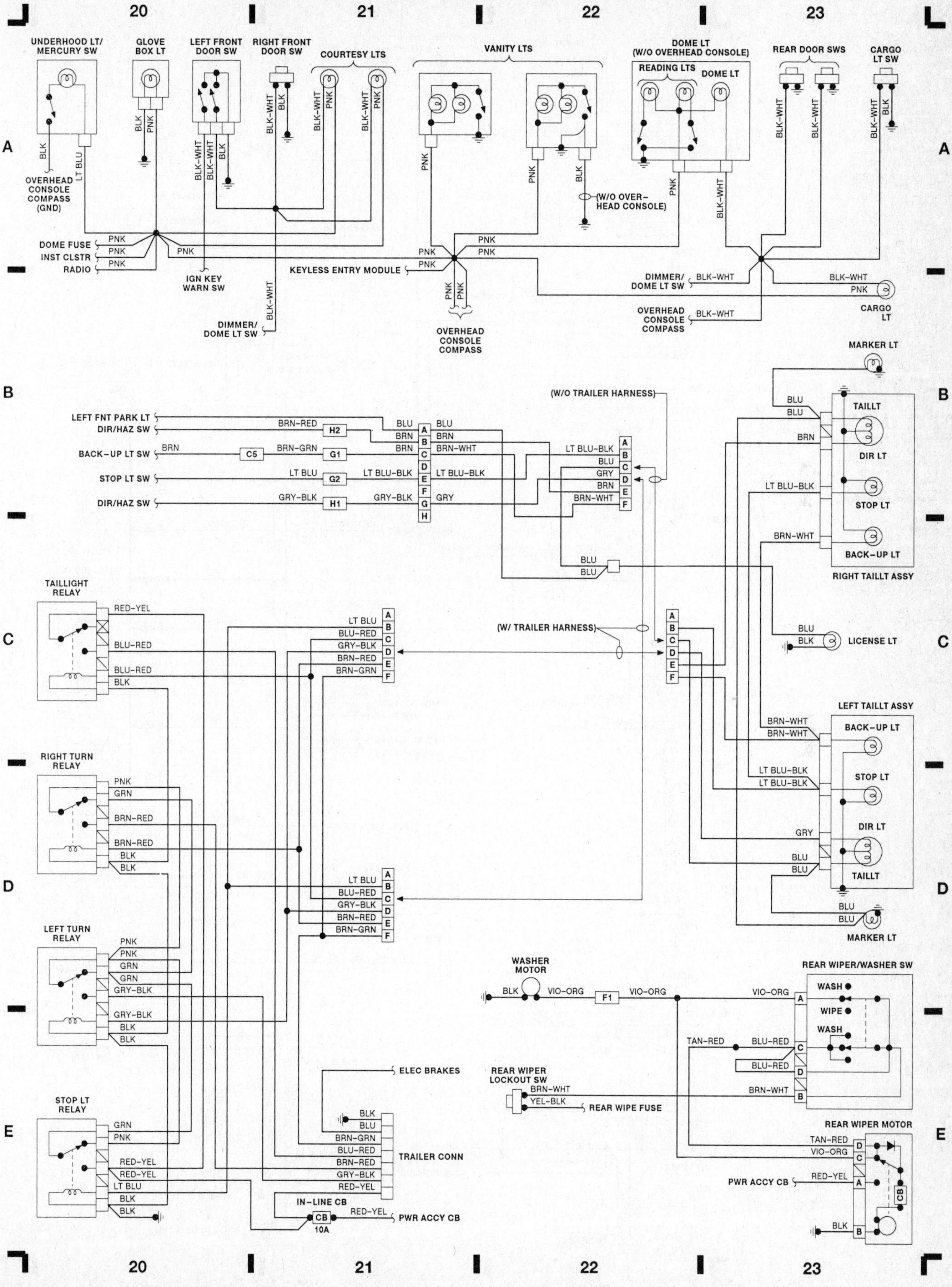
UNDERHOOD LT/ MERCURY SW
GLOVE BOX LT
LEFT FRONT DOOR SW
RIGHT FRONT DOOR SW
COURTESY LTS
VANITY LTS
DOME LT (W/O OVERHEAD CONSOLE)
READING LTS
DOME LT
REAR DOOR SWS
CARGO LT SW
OVERHEAD CONSOLE COMPASS (GND)
DOME FUSE
INST CLSTR
RADIO
IGN KEY WARN SW
DIMMER/ DOME LT SW
KEYLESS ENTRY MODULE
OVERHEAD CONSOLE COMPASS
(W/O OVER-HEAD CONSOLE)
CARGO LT
MARKER LT
(W/O TRAILER HARNESS)
LEFT FNT PARK LT
DIR/HAZ SW
BACK-UP LT SW
STOP LT SW
TAILLT
DIR LT
STOP LT
BACK-UP LT
RIGHT TAILLT ASSY
TAILLIGHT RELAY
(W/ TRAILER HARNESS)
LICENSE LT
LEFT TAILLT ASSY
RIGHT TURN RELAY
LEFT TURN RELAY
WASHER MOTOR
REAR WIPER/WASHER SW
WASH
WIPE
ELEC BRAKES
REAR WIPER LOCKOUT SW
REAR WIPE FUSE
STOP LT RELAY
TRAILER CONN
IN-LINE CB
10A
PWR ACCY CB
REAR WIPER MOTOR

1991 WIRING DIAGRAMS
Wrangler

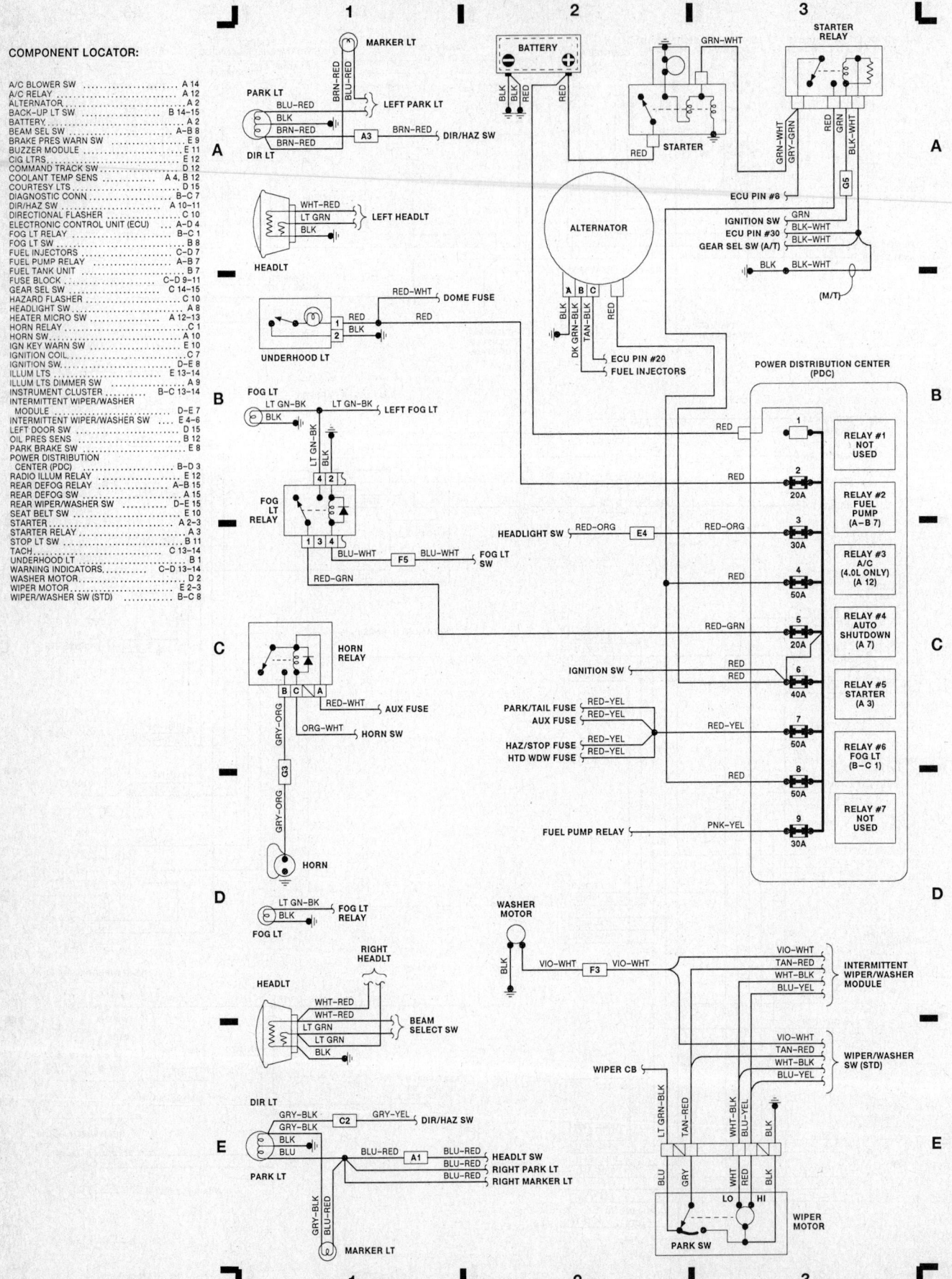

COMPONENT LOCATOR:

A/C BLOWER SW	A 14
A/C RELAY	A 12
ALTERNATOR	A 2
BACK-UP LT SW	B 14–15
BATTERY	A 2
BEAM SEL SW	A–B 8
BRAKE PRES WARN SW	E 9
BUZZER MODULE	E 11
CIG LTRS	E 12
COMMAND TRACK SW	D 12
COOLANT TEMP SENS	A 4, B 12
COURTESY LTS	D 15
DIAGNOSTIC CONN	B–C 7
DIR/HAZ SW	A 10–11
DIRECTIONAL FLASHER	C 10
ELECTRONIC CONTROL UNIT (ECU)	A–D 4
FOG LT RELAY	B–C 1
FOG LT SW	B 8
FUEL INJECTORS	C–D 7
FUEL PUMP RELAY	A–B 7
FUEL TANK UNIT	B 7
FUSE BLOCK	C–D 9–11
GEAR SEL SW	C 14–15
HAZARD FLASHER	C 10
HEADLIGHT SW	A 8
HEATER MICRO SW	A 12–13
HORN RELAY	C 1
HORN SW	A 10
IGN KEY WARN SW	E 10
IGNITION COIL	C 7
IGNITION SW	D–E 8
ILLUM LTS	E 13–14
ILLUM LTS DIMMER SW	A 9
INSTRUMENT CLUSTER	B–C 13–14
INTERMITTENT WIPER/WASHER MODULE	D–E 7
INTERMITTENT WIPER/WASHER SW	E 4–6
LEFT DOOR SW	D 15
OIL PRES SENS	B 12
PARK BRAKE SW	E 8
POWER DISTRIBUTION CENTER (PDC)	B–D 3
RADIO ILLUM RELAY	E 12
REAR DEFOG RELAY	A–B 15
REAR DEFOG SW	A 15
REAR WIPER/WASHER SW	D–E 15
SEAT BELT SW	E 10
STARTER	A 2–3
STARTER RELAY	A 3
STOP LT SW	B 11
TACH	C 13–14
UNDERHOOD LT	B 1
WARNING INDICATORS	C–D 13–14
WASHER MOTOR	D 2
WIPER MOTOR	E 2–3
WIPER/WASHER SW (STD)	B–C 8

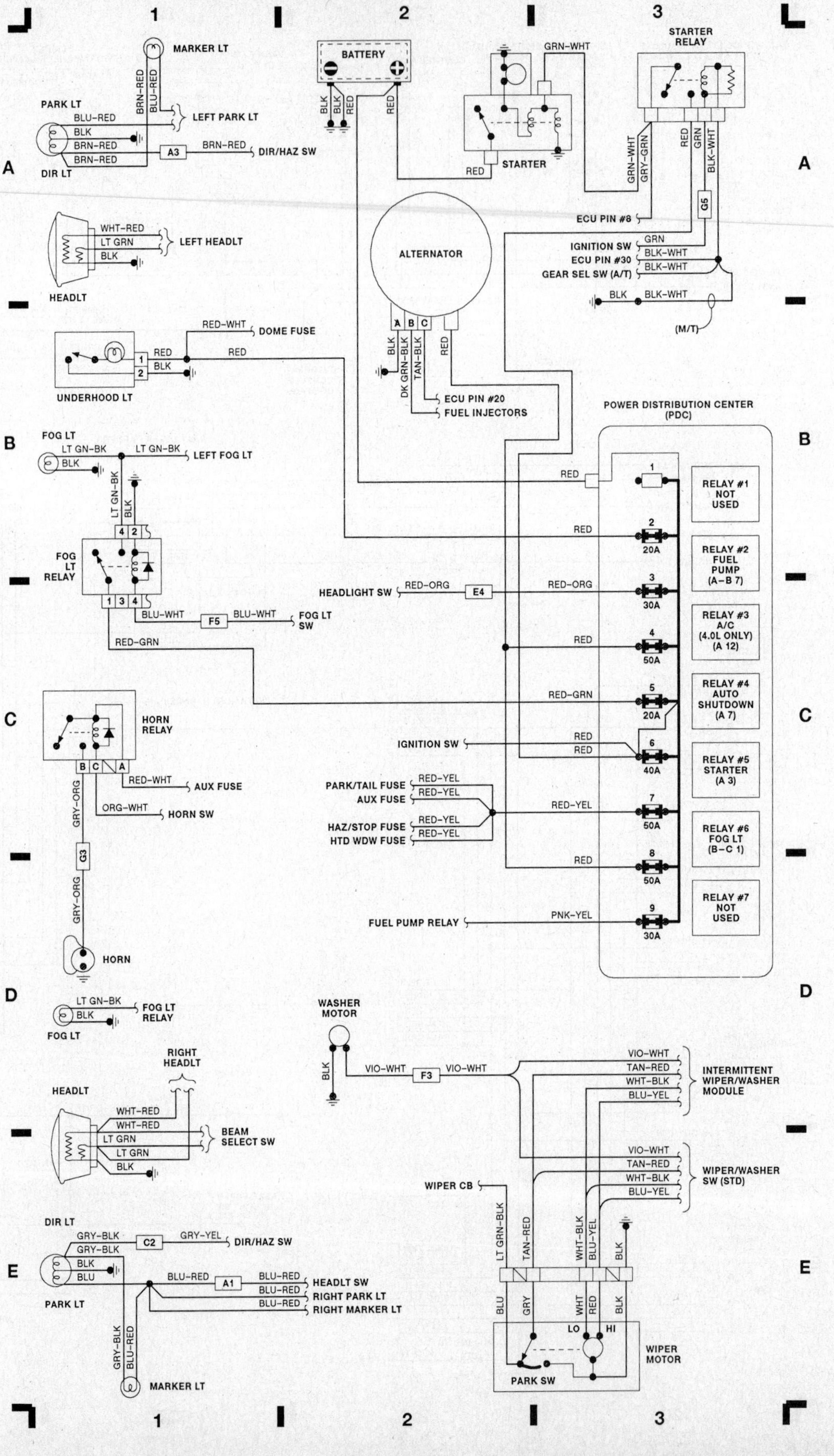
1
2
3
A
B
C
D
E
MARKER LT
PARK LT
LEFT PARK LT
DIR/HAZ SW
DIR LT
BATTERY
STARTER RELAY
STARTER
ALTERNATOR
LEFT HEADLT
HEADLT
ECU PIN #8
IGNITION SW
ECU PIN #30
GEAR SEL SW (A/T)
(M/T)
DOME FUSE
UNDERHOOD LT
ECU PIN #20
FUEL INJECTORS
POWER DISTRIBUTION CENTER (PDC)
FOG LT
LEFT FOG LT
FOG LT RELAY
FOG LT SW
HEADLIGHT SW
RELAY #1 NOT USED
RELAY #2 FUEL PUMP (A–B 7)
RELAY #3 A/C (4.0L ONLY) (A 12)
RELAY #4 AUTO SHUTDOWN (A 7)
RELAY #5 STARTER (A 3)
RELAY #6 FOG LT (B–C 1)
RELAY #7 NOT USED
HORN RELAY
AUX FUSE
HORN SW
PARK/TAIL FUSE
HAZ/STOP FUSE
HTD WDW FUSE
FUEL PUMP RELAY
HORN
WASHER MOTOR
INTERMITTENT WIPER/WASHER MODULE
RIGHT HEADLT
BEAM SELECT SW
WIPER/WASHER SW (STD)
WIPER CB
HEADLT SW
RIGHT PARK LT
RIGHT MARKER LT
WIPER MOTOR
PARK SW
LO
HI

1991 WIRING DIAGRAMS
Wrangler (Cont.)

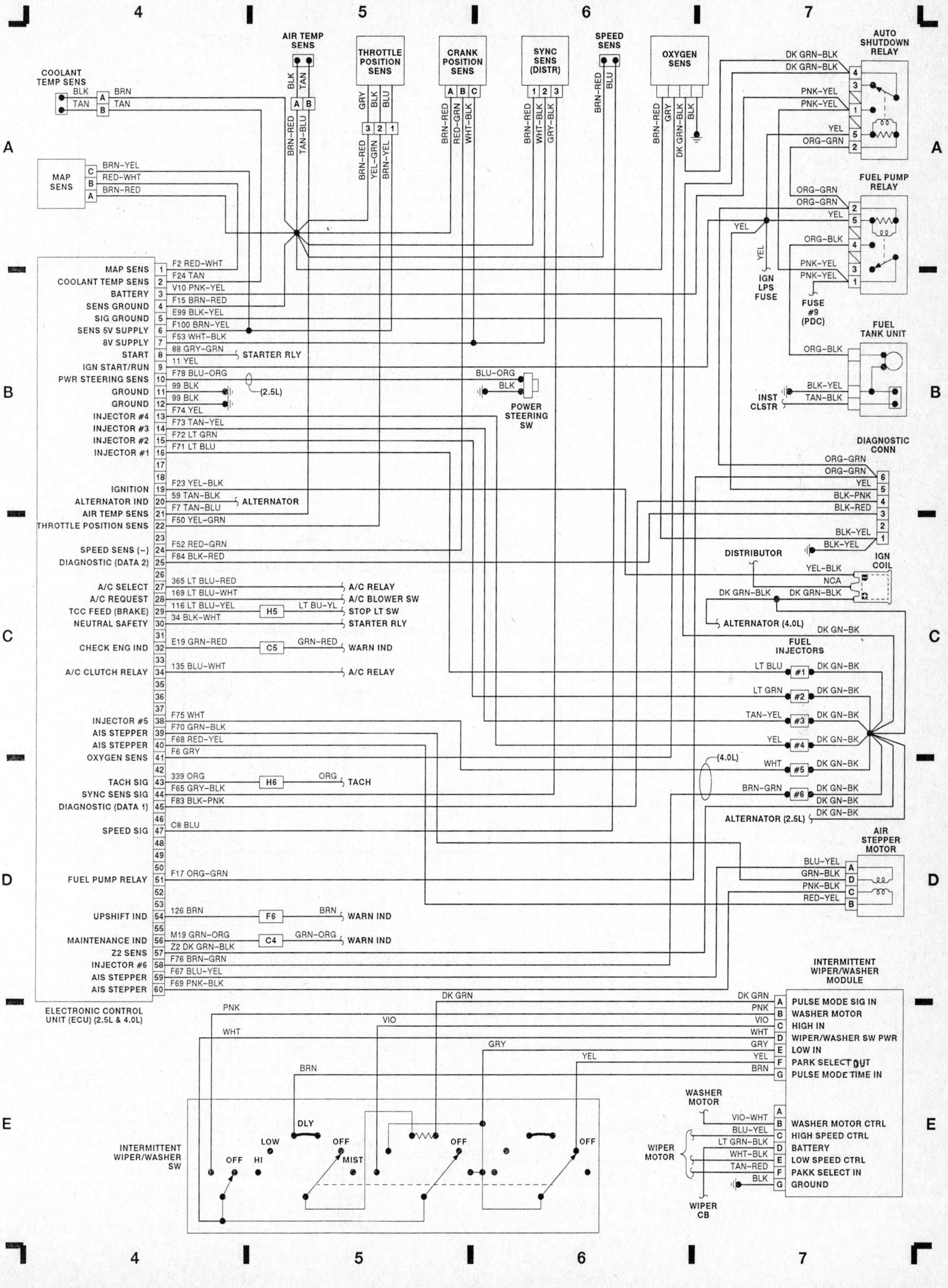
COOLANT TEMP SENS
MAP SENS
AIR TEMP SENS
THROTTLE POSITION SENS
CRANK POSITION SENS
SYNC SENS (DISTR)
SPEED SENS
OXYGEN SENS
AUTO SHUTDOWN RELAY
FUEL PUMP RELAY
FUEL TANK UNIT
IGN LPS FUSE
FUSE #9 (PDC)
INST CLSTR
POWER STEERING SW
DIAGNOSTIC CONN
DISTRIBUTOR
IGN COIL
ALTERNATOR (4.0L)
FUEL INJECTORS
ALTERNATOR (2.5L)
AIR STEPPER MOTOR
MAP SENS 1 F2 RED-WHT
COOLANT TEMP SENS 2 F24 TAN
BATTERY 3 V10 PNK-YEL
SENS GROUND 4 F15 BRN-RED
SIG GROUND 5 E99 BLK-YEL
SENS 5V SUPPLY 6 F100 BRN-YEL
8V SUPPLY 7 F53 WHT-BLK
START 8 88 GRY-GRN STARTER RLY
IGN START/RUN 9 11 YEL
PWR STEERING SENS 10 F78 BLU-ORG
GROUND 11 99 BLK
GROUND 12 99 BLK (2.5L)
INJECTOR #4 13 F74 YEL
INJECTOR #3 14 F73 TAN-YEL
INJECTOR #2 15 F72 LT GRN
INJECTOR #1 16 F71 LT BLU
IGNITION 19 F23 YEL-BLK
ALTERNATOR IND 20 59 TAN-BLK ALTERNATOR
AIR TEMP SENS 21 F7 TAN-BLU
THROTTLE POSITION SENS 22 F50 YEL-GRN
SPEED SENS (–) 24 F52 RED-GRN
DIAGNOSTIC (DATA 2) 25 F84 BLK-RED
A/C SELECT 27 365 LT BLU-RED A/C RELAY
A/C REQUEST 28 169 LT BLU-WHT A/C BLOWER SW
TCC FEED (BRAKE) 29 116 LT BLU-YEL H5 LT BU-YL STOP LT SW
NEUTRAL SAFETY 30 34 BLK-WHT STARTER RLY
CHECK ENG IND 32 E19 GRN-RED C5 GRN-RED WARN IND
A/C CLUTCH RELAY 34 135 BLU-WHT A/C RELAY
INJECTOR #5 38 F75 WHT
AIS STEPPER 39 F70 GRN-BLK
AIS STEPPER 40 F68 RED-YEL
OXYGEN SENS 41 F6 GRY
TACH SIG 43 339 ORG H6 ORG TACH
SYNC SENS SIG 44 F65 GRY-BLK
DIAGNOSTIC (DATA 1) 45 F83 BLK-PNK
SPEED SIG 47 C8 BLU
FUEL PUMP RELAY 51 F17 ORG-GRN
UPSHIFT IND 54 126 BRN F6 BRN WARN IND
MAINTENANCE IND 56 M19 GRN-ORG C4 GRN-ORG WARN IND
Z2 SENS 57 Z2 DK GRN-BLK
INJECTOR #6 58 F76 BRN-GRN
AIS STEPPER 59 F67 BLU-YEL
AIS STEPPER 60 F69 PNK-BLK
ELECTRONIC CONTROL UNIT (ECU) (2.5L & 4.0L)
INTERMITTENT WIPER/WASHER MODULE
A PULSE MODE SIG IN
B WASHER MOTOR
C HIGH IN
D WIPER/WASHER SW PWR
E LOW IN
F PARK SELECT OUT
G PULSE MODE TIME IN
WASHER MOTOR
WIPER MOTOR
WIPER CB
A
B WASHER MOTOR CTRL
C HIGH SPEED CTRL
D BATTERY
E LOW SPEED CTRL
F PAKK SELECT IN
G GROUND
INTERMITTENT WIPER/WASHER SW
OFF HI LOW DLY OFF MIST OFF OFF

1991 WIRING DIAGRAMS
Wrangler (Cont.)

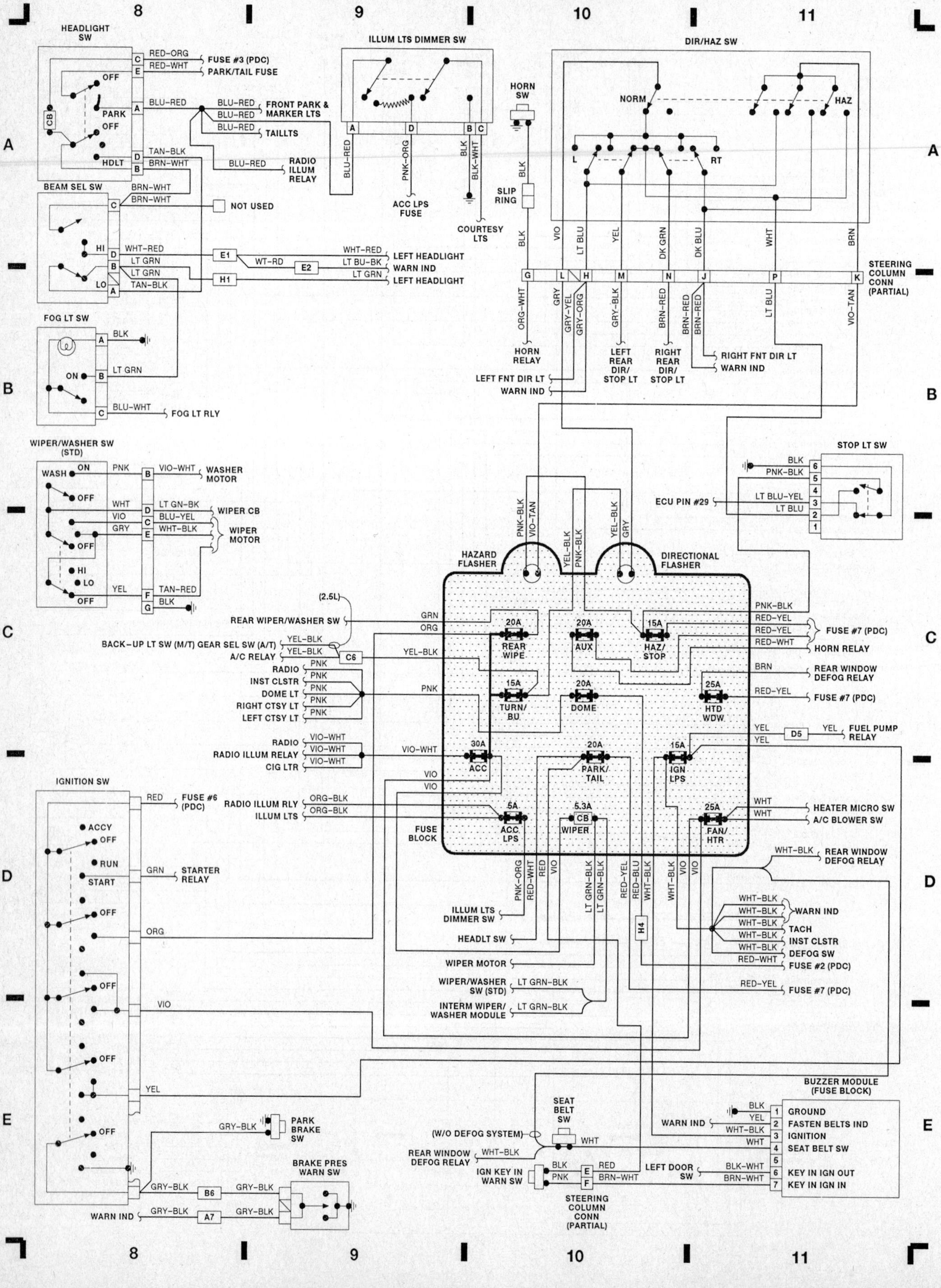
HEADLIGHT SW
ILLUM LTS DIMMER SW
HORN SW
DIR/HAZ SW
FUSE #3 (PDC)
PARK/TAIL FUSE
FRONT PARK & MARKER LTS
TAILLTS
RADIO ILLUM RELAY
BEAM SEL SW
NOT USED
ACC LPS FUSE
COURTESY LTS
SLIP RING
NORM
HAZ
LEFT HEADLIGHT
WARN IND
STEERING COLUMN CONN (PARTIAL)
FOG LT SW
FOG LT RLY
HORN RELAY
LEFT FNT DIR LT
LEFT REAR DIR/ STOP LT
RIGHT REAR DIR/ STOP LT
RIGHT FNT DIR LT
WIPER/WASHER SW (STD)
WASHER MOTOR
WIPER CB
WIPER MOTOR
STOP LT SW
ECU PIN #29
HAZARD FLASHER
DIRECTIONAL FLASHER
REAR WIPER/WASHER SW
BACK-UP LT SW (M/T) GEAR SEL SW (A/T)
A/C RELAY
RADIO
INST CLSTR
DOME LT
RIGHT CTSY LT
LEFT CTSY LT
RADIO ILLUM RELAY
CIG LTR
FUSE #7 (PDC)
REAR WINDOW DEFOG RELAY
FUEL PUMP RELAY
IGNITION SW
FUSE #6 (PDC)
RADIO ILLUM RLY
ILLUM LTS
FUSE BLOCK
HEATER MICRO SW
A/C BLOWER SW
STARTER RELAY
ILLUM LTS DIMMER SW
HEADLT SW
TACH
DEFOG SW
FUSE #2 (PDC)
INTERM WIPER/ WASHER MODULE
PARK BRAKE SW
BRAKE PRES WARN SW
SEAT BELT SW
(W/O DEFOG SYSTEM)
IGN KEY IN WARN SW
LEFT DOOR SW
BUZZER MODULE (FUSE BLOCK)
GROUND
FASTEN BELTS IND
IGNITION
KEY IN IGN OUT
KEY IN IGN IN

1991 WIRING DIAGRAMS
Wrangler (Cont.)

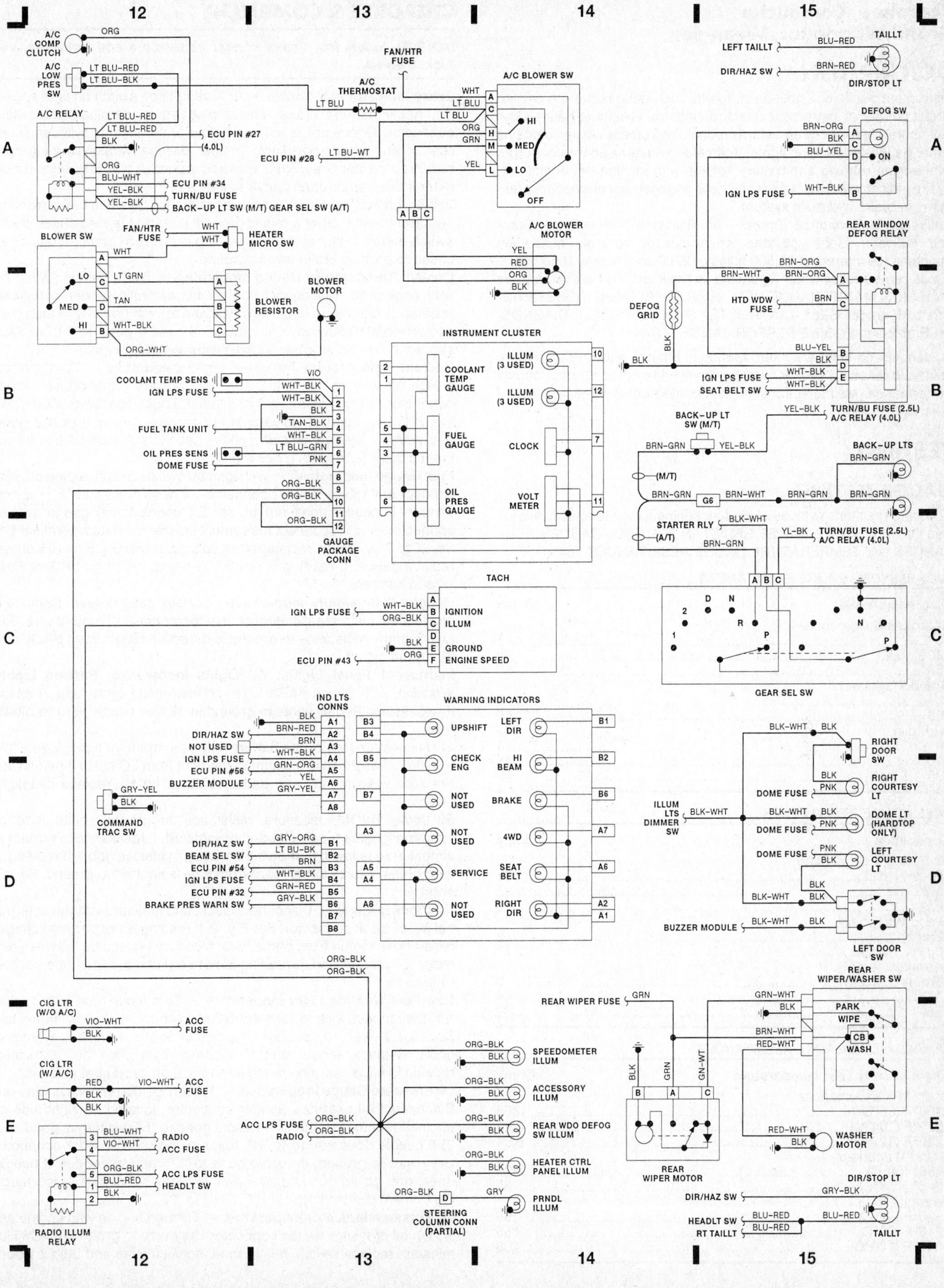
12
13
14
15
A
B
C
D
E
A/C COMP CLUTCH
ORG
A/C LOW PRES SW
LT BLU-RED
LT BLU-BLK
A/C RELAY
LT BLU-RED
LT BLU-RED
BLK
ORG
BLU-WHT
YEL-BLK
YEL-BLK
ECU PIN #27 (4.0L)
ECU PIN #34
TURN/BU FUSE
BACK-UP LT SW (M/T) GEAR SEL SW (A/T)
FAN/HTR FUSE
A/C THERMOSTAT
LT BLU
ECU PIN #28
LT BU-WT
A/C BLOWER SW
WHT
LT BLU
LT BLU
ORG
GRN
YEL
HI
MED
LO
OFF
A/C BLOWER MOTOR
YEL
RED
ORG
BLK
BLOWER SW
WHT
HEATER MICRO SW
LO
MED
HI
LT GRN
TAN
WHT-BLK
BLOWER RESISTOR
BLOWER MOTOR
ORG-WHT
LEFT TAILLT
BLU-RED
TAILLT
DIR/HAZ SW
BRN-RED
DIR/STOP LT
DEFOG SW
BRN-ORG
BLK
BLU-YEL
ON
IGN LPS FUSE
WHT-BLK
REAR WINDOW DEFOG RELAY
BRN-ORG
BRN-WHT
BRN-ORG
HTD WDW FUSE
BRN
DEFOG GRID
BLK
BLU-YEL
BLK
WHT-BLK
WHT-BLK
SEAT BELT SW
INSTRUMENT CLUSTER
ILLUM (3 USED)
COOLANT TEMP GAUGE
FUEL GAUGE
CLOCK
OIL PRES GAUGE
VOLT METER
COOLANT TEMP SENS
VIO
WHT-BLK
WHT-BLK
TAN-BLK
FUEL TANK UNIT
LT BLU-GRN
OIL PRES SENS
PNK
DOME FUSE
ORG-BLK
GAUGE PACKAGE CONN
YEL-BLK
TURN/BU FUSE (2.5L)
A/C RELAY (4.0L)
BACK-UP LT SW (M/T)
BRN-GRN
BACK-UP LTS
(M/T)
G6
STARTER RLY
BLK-WHT
(A/T)
YL-BK
GEAR SEL SW
TACH
IGNITION
ILLUM
GROUND
ENGINE SPEED
ECU PIN #43
IND LTS CONNS
WARNING INDICATORS
BRN-RED
NOT USED
GRN-ORG
ECU PIN #56
BUZZER MODULE
GRY-YEL
COMMAND TRAC SW
UPSHIFT
CHECK ENG
NOT USED
SERVICE
LEFT DIR
HI BEAM
BRAKE
4WD
SEAT BELT
RIGHT DIR
GRY-ORG
LT BU-BK
BEAM SEL SW
ECU PIN #54
GRN-RED
ECU PIN #32
GRY-BLK
BRAKE PRES WARN SW
RIGHT DOOR SW
RIGHT COURTESY LT
ILLUM LTS DIMMER SW
DOME LT (HARDTOP ONLY)
LEFT COURTESY LT
LEFT DOOR SW
REAR WIPER/WASHER SW
REAR WIPER FUSE
GRN-WHT
PARK
WIPE
CB
WASH
RED-WHT
REAR WIPER MOTOR
WASHER MOTOR
GN-WT
CIG LTR (W/O A/C)
VIO-WHT
ACC FUSE
CIG LTR (W/ A/C)
RADIO ILLUM RELAY
RADIO
ACC LPS FUSE
HEADLT SW
SPEEDOMETER ILLUM
ACCESSORY ILLUM
REAR WDO DEFOG SW ILLUM
HEATER CTRL PANEL ILLUM
PRNDL ILLUM
GRY
STEERING COLUMN CONN (PARTIAL)
RT TAILLT

1991 SAFETY EQUIPMENT
Instrument Panels

Cherokee, Comanche
Grand Wagoneer, Wrangler

DESCRIPTION

Instrument panel is supplied voltage through gauges fuse. A printed circuit on rear of instrument cluster distributes voltage to gauges and indicators. Depending on vehicle model, instrument cluster contains either gauges or warning lights. Voltmeter measures alternator output with engine running and battery voltage with ignition on, engine off. Brake indicator warns of parking brake engagement or unequal pressures in brake hydraulic system.

Emission Maintenance Timer – An Emission Maintenance Timer and Indicator Light activates when mileage reaches scheduled maintenance interval of 82,500 miles or 2700 engine operating hours. Timer can be reset when O_2 sensor is replaced. To reset timer, see EMISSION MAINTENANCE REMINDER (EMR) LIGHT RESET PROCEDURE under SELF-DIAGNOSTIC SYSTEM in SELF-DIAGNOSTICS article in ENGINE PERFORMANCE.

O_2 sensor and timer are interdependent. If timer, showing premature failure, is reset, O_2 sensor must be replaced to ensure proper engine performance. Maintenance timer is mounted on dash panel, right of steering column.

TESTING

GAUGE TESTING

Compare resistance values of malfunctioning gauge to specifications. See OIL PRESSURE GAUGE RESISTANCES, FUEL GAUGE RESISTANCES and TEMPERATURE GAUGE RESISTANCES tables.

OIL PRESSURE GAUGE RESISTANCES

Oil pressure (psi)	Ohms
Cherokee & Comanche	
0	1
40	46
80	87
Grand Wagoneer	
0	0
60	65
Wrangler	
0	1
40	46
80	90

FUEL GAUGE RESISTANCES

Application	Ohms
Cherokee & Comanche	
Empty	105
1/2 Full	33
Full	5
Grand Wagoneer	
Empty	5.5
Full	79
Wrangler	
Empty	0
1/2 Full	44
Full	89

TEMPERATURE GAUGE RESISTANCES

Application & Test Temperature	Ohms
Cherokee & Comanche	
100°F (38°C)	1365
220°F (104°C)	93.5
260°F (127°C)	55.1
Grand Wagoneer	
186° (86°C)	226
246° (118°C)	82
Wrangler	
180°F (82°C)	298
210°F (99°C)	185
240°F (116°C)	108

CHEROKEE & COMANCHE

***NOTE:** To locate instrument cluster connectors and terminals, see Figs. 1 and 3.*

Brake Indicator Inoperative – 1) Turn ignition switch on with engine off. Apply parking brake, and unplug brake warning light switch connector. Connector is located below brake master cylinder at left rear of engine compartment. Jumper between brake warning light switch connector Gray/White wire and ground. If bulb is good and indicator lights, repair open circuit to indicator.

2) With ignition switch off, measure resistance between brake warning switch connector Gray wire and ground. If reading is zero ohms, check switch and/or brake system. If reading is not zero ohms, repair open circuit to parking brake switch ground.

Coolant Temperature Gauge Inoperative – Turn ignition switch on with engine off. Disconnect coolant temperature sender connector (located at left rear of engine). If needle does not go to "C", touch connector Violet/Yellow wire to ground. If needle goes to "H", replace sender. If not, repair open Violet/Yellow wire to gauge.

Coolant Temperature Indicator Light Inoperative – Turn ignition switch on with engine off. Disconnect coolant temperature sender connector (located at left rear of engine). Touch connector Violet/Yellow wire to ground. If indicator lights, replace switch. If bulb is good and indicator light remains off, repair open Violet/Yellow wire to instrument cluster terminal A1. *See Fig. 3.*

Fuel Gauge Inoperative – With ignition switch on and engine off, disconnect fuel gauge sender connector. If needle goes to "E", replace sender. If needle does not go to "E", connect fuel gauge sender connector, and disconnect instrument cluster connector terminal B1. *See Fig. 3.* Measure resistance of sender. If reading is 5-105 ohms, replace gauge. If reading is not 5-105 ohms, repair open Dark Blue wire to sender.

Gauges & Indicators Inoperative – Check gauges fuse. Replace if blown. Test instrument cluster connector terminal A3 ground wire. *See Fig. 3.* If any resistance to ground is detected, repair open Black wire in ground circuit.

Instrument Panel Lights: All Lights Inoperative, Parking Lights Working – 1) Check PARK fuse and instrument lights fuse. Replace if necessary. Repair short to ground in 12-volt supply wire to blown fuse.

2) Using voltmeter, probe battery side of instrument lights fuse while turning headlight switch dimming rheostat from LO to HI. If results are not zero volts for LO and battery voltage for HI, replace headlight switch.

3) Using DVOM, measure resistance at ground (bulb) side of instrument lights fuse with parking lights off. If resistance to ground is almost zero (allowing for bulb filaments), system is good. If reading is zero ohms, 12 volt supply wire from fuse is shorted to ground. Repair short.

No Clock Display – Disconnect clock, and measure voltage at terminal "A" of clock connector. *See Fig. 2.* If reading is not battery voltage, repair open circuit from dome fuse. Measure resistance between terminal "C" and ground. If reading is not zero ohms, repair open circuit to ground.

Low Fuel Warning Light Inoperative – Turn ignition on with engine off. Disconnect wire to terminal B1 of instrument cluster connector. *See Fig. 3.* Wait 10 seconds. If indicator light illuminates, system is good. Replace sender unit. If indicator light does not illuminate, replace low fuel warning module (on back of instrument cluster).

Oil Pressure Gauge Inoperative – 1) Turn ignition on with engine off. Disconnect oil pressure sender connector, located on right side of engine, next to distributor. If needle goes to "H", system is good.

2) If needle does not go to "H", touch oil pressure sender connector Gray wire to ground. If needle goes to "L", replace sender. If needle does not go to "L", repair open in Gray wire circuit to gauge (instrument cluster terminal B7). *See Fig. 3.*

Oil Pressure Indicator Inoperative – Turn ignition on with engine off. Touch oil pressure switch connector Gray wire to ground. If light illuminates, replace switch. If light does not illuminate and bulb is good,

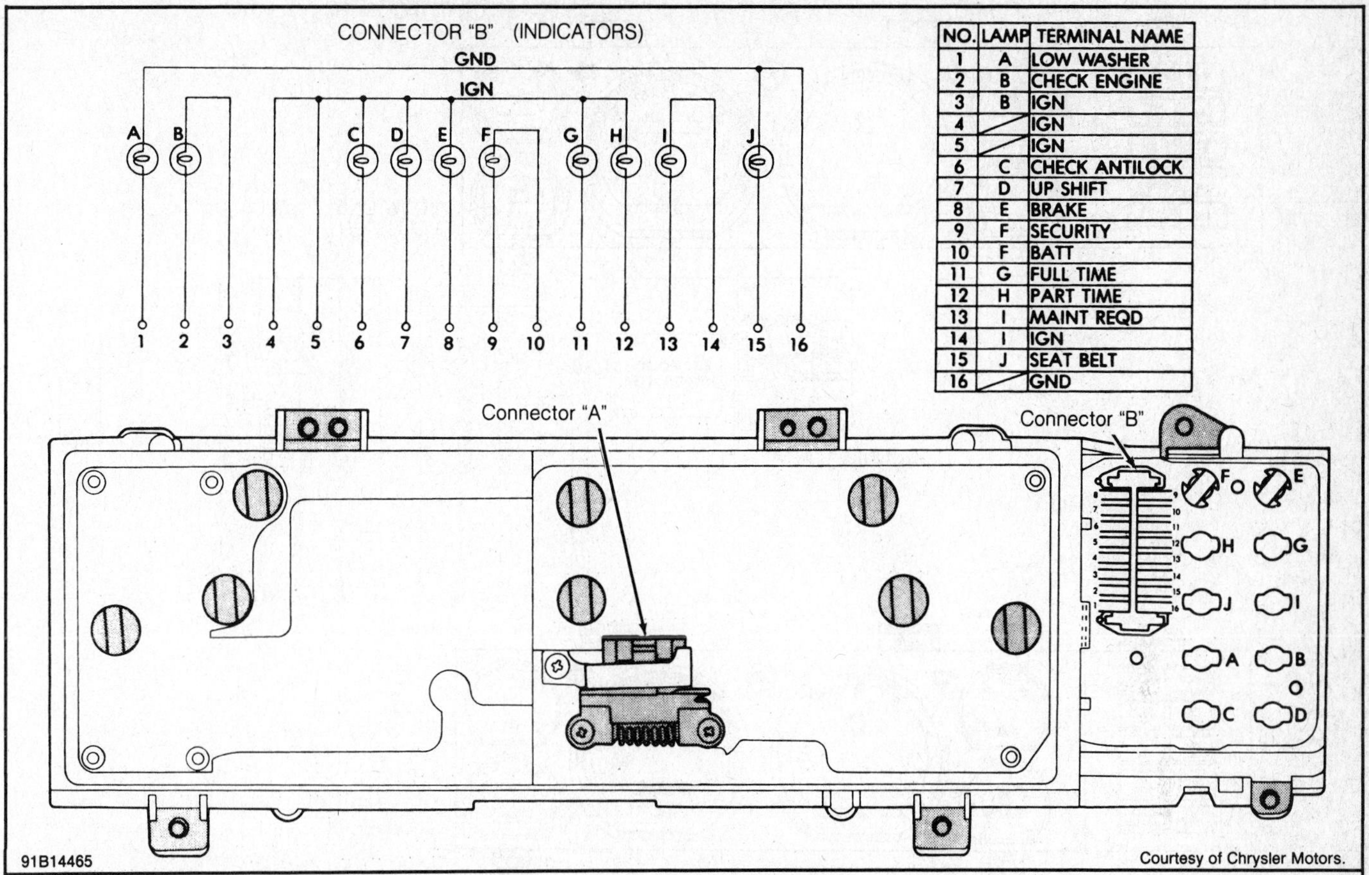
CONNECTOR "B" (INDICATORS)
GND
IGN
A B C D E F G H I J
1 2 3 4 5 6 7 8 9 10 11 12 13 14 15 16
Connector "A"
Connector "B"
91B14465
Courtesy of Chrysler Motors.

NO.	LAMP	TERMINAL NAME
1	A	LOW WASHER
2	B	CHECK ENGINE
3	B	IGN
4		IGN
5		IGN
6	C	CHECK ANTILOCK
7	D	UP SHIFT
8	E	BRAKE
9	F	SECURITY
10	F	BATT
11	G	FULL TIME
12	H	PART TIME
13	I	MAINT REQD
14	I	IGN
15	J	SEAT BELT
16		GND

Fig. 1: Identifying & Locating Instrument Cluster Connectors (Cherokee & Comanche)

repair open in Gray wire to instrument cluster connector terminal B7. *See Fig. 3.*

Part Time Or 4WD Indicator Inoperative – 1) Apply parking brake. Start engine. Place 4WD selector lever in 4WD LOCK or 4WD position. Unplug 4WD switch, and touch harness connector Black/Yellow wire to ground. If indicator light illuminates, wiring system is good. Check 4WD switch operation, and replace if defective.

2) If indicator light does not illuminate and bulb is good, repair open in Black/Yellow wire circuit to indicator light.

Tachometer Inoperative – Tachometer input is from engine ECU pin No. 43. Check Gray/Light Blue wire for short or open circuits. If wire is okay, see SELF-DIAGNOSTICS article in ENGINE PERFORMANCE.

Voltmeter (Gauge) Inoperative – Turn ignition on with engine off. If voltmeter does not indicate battery voltage, measure voltage at instrument cluster connector terminal No. A8. *See Fig. 3.* If battery voltage is present at terminal No. A8, replace voltmeter. If battery voltage is not present at terminal No. A8, repair open White/Black wire circuit to gauges fuse.

GRAND WAGONEER

Instrument Panel – Testing information is not available from manufacturer. *See Figs. 4-7.* Schematics identify individual circuits and should help with any testing.

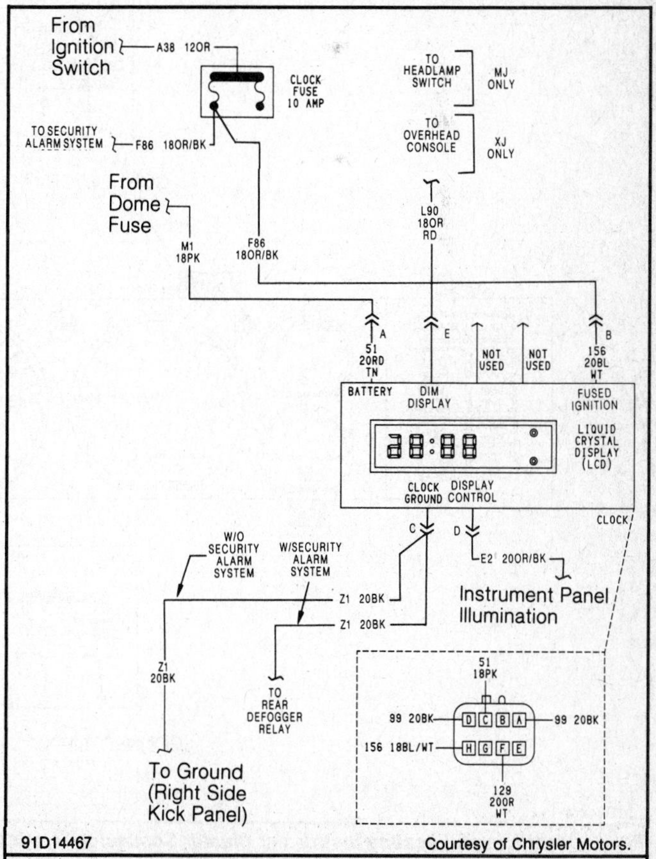
From Ignition Switch
A38 12OR
CLOCK FUSE 10 AMP
TO SECURITY ALARM SYSTEM
F86 18OR/BK
TO HEADLAMP SWITCH
MJ ONLY
TO OVERHEAD CONSOLE
XJ ONLY
From Dome Fuse
M1 18PK
F86 18OR/BK
L90 18OR RD
51 20RD TN
NOT USED
NOT USED
156 20BL WT
BATTERY
DIM DISPLAY
FUSED IGNITION
LIQUID CRYSTAL DISPLAY (LCD)
CLOCK GROUND
DISPLAY CONTROL
CLOCK
W/O SECURITY ALARM SYSTEM
W/SECURITY ALARM SYSTEM
Z1 20BK
E2 20OR/BK
Instrument Panel Illumination
Z1 20BK
TO REAR DEFOGGER RELAY
To Ground (Right Side Kick Panel)
51 18PK
99 20BK
156 18BL/WT
129 20OR WT
91D14467
Courtesy of Chrysler Motors.

Fig. 2: Clock Wiring Schematic (Cherokee & Comanche)

1991 SAFETY EQUIPMENT
Instrument Panels (Cont.)

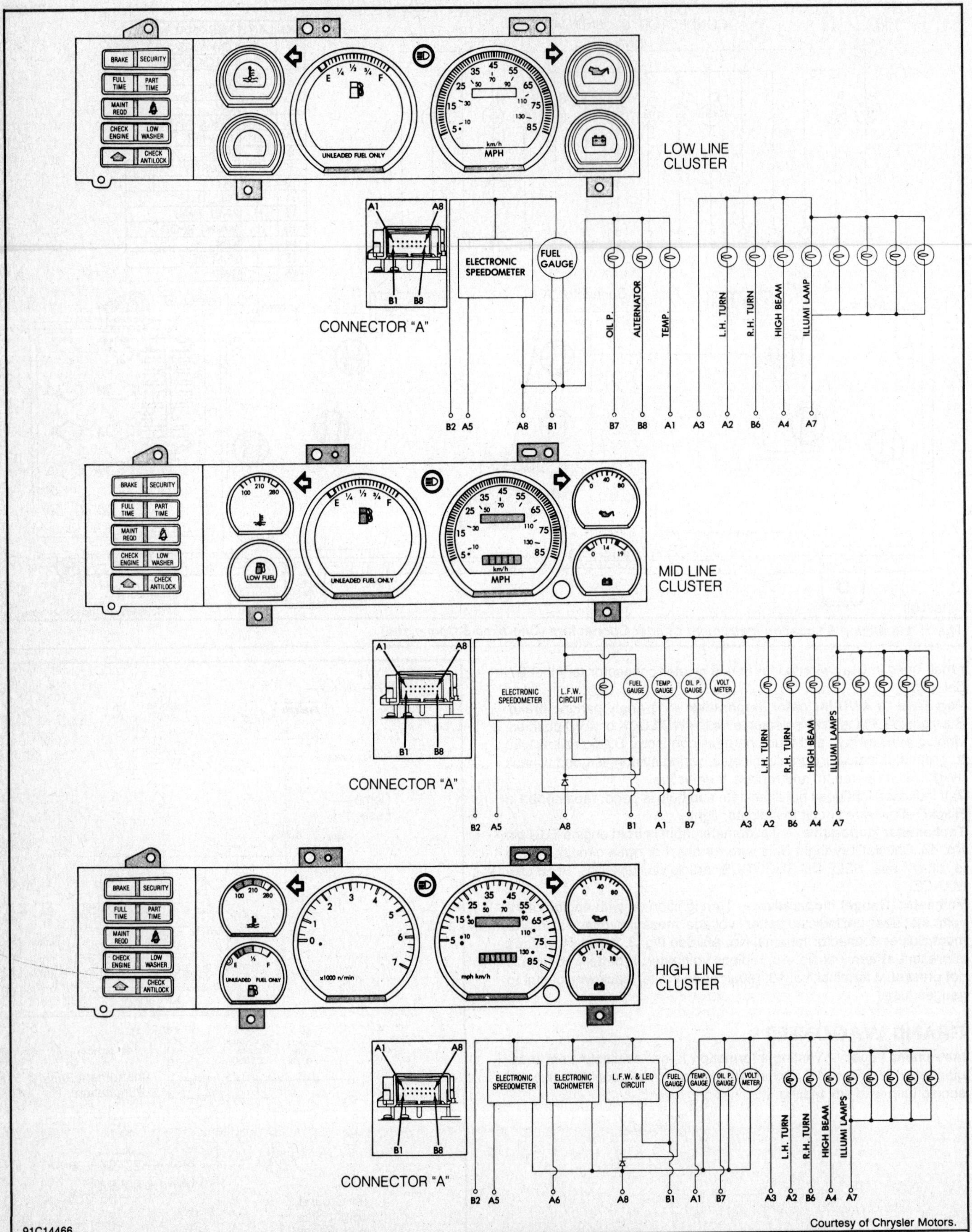
BRAKE
SECURITY
FULL TIME
PART TIME
MAINT REQD
CHECK ENGINE
LOW WASHER
CHECK ANTILOCK
UNLEADED FUEL ONLY
MPH
km/h
LOW LINE CLUSTER
A1
A8
B1
B8
CONNECTOR "A"
ELECTRONIC SPEEDOMETER
FUEL GAUGE
OIL P.
ALTERNATOR
TEMP.
L.H. TURN
R.H. TURN
HIGH BEAM
ILLUMI LAMP
B2 A5 A8 B1 B7 B8 A1 A3 A2 B6 A4 A7
LOW FUEL
MID LINE CLUSTER
L.F.W. CIRCUIT
TEMP. GAUGE
OIL P. GAUGE
VOLT METER
ILLUMI LAMPS
B2 A5 A8 B1 A1 B7 A3 A2 B6 A4 A7
x1000 r/min
mph km/h
HIGH LINE CLUSTER
ELECTRONIC TACHOMETER
L.F.W. & LED CIRCUIT
B2 A5 A6 A8 B1 A1 B7 A3 A2 B6 A4 A7

91C14466

Courtesy of Chrysler Motors.

Fig. 3: Identifying & Locating Instrument Cluster Connector Terminals (Cherokee & Comanche)

1991 SAFETY EQUIPMENT
Instrument Panels (Cont.)

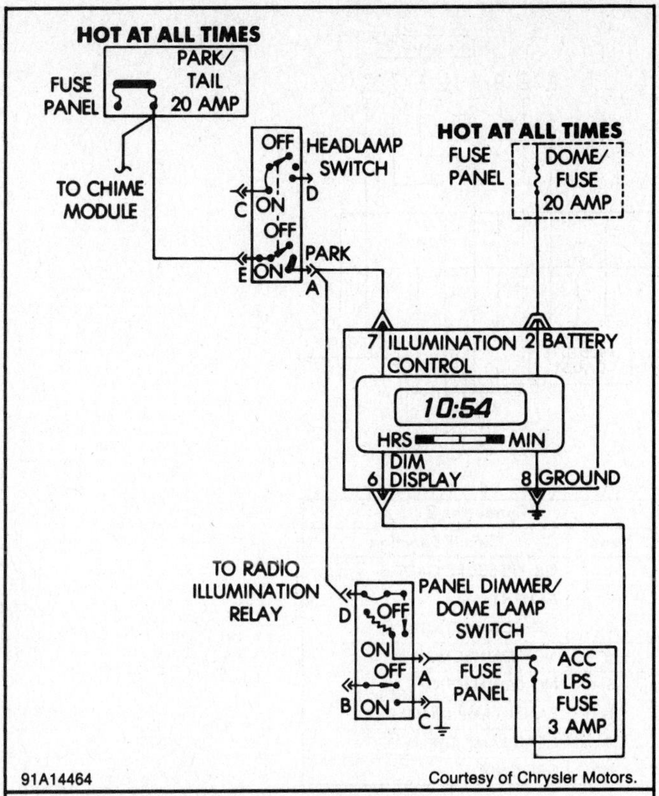
HOT AT ALL TIMES
FUSE PANEL
PARK/ TAIL 20 AMP
TO CHIME MODULE
OFF
HEADLAMP SWITCH
C
ON
D
OFF
PARK
E
ON
A
HOT AT ALL TIMES
FUSE PANEL
DOME/ FUSE 20 AMP
7 ILLUMINATION CONTROL
2 BATTERY
10:54
HRS
MIN
6 DIM DISPLAY
8 GROUND
TO RADIO ILLUMINATION RELAY
PANEL DIMMER/ DOME LAMP SWITCH
D
OFF
ON
OFF
A
B
ON
C
FUSE PANEL
ACC LPS FUSE 3 AMP
91A14464

Courtesy of Chrysler Motors.

Fig. 4: Clock Schematic (Grand Wagoneer)

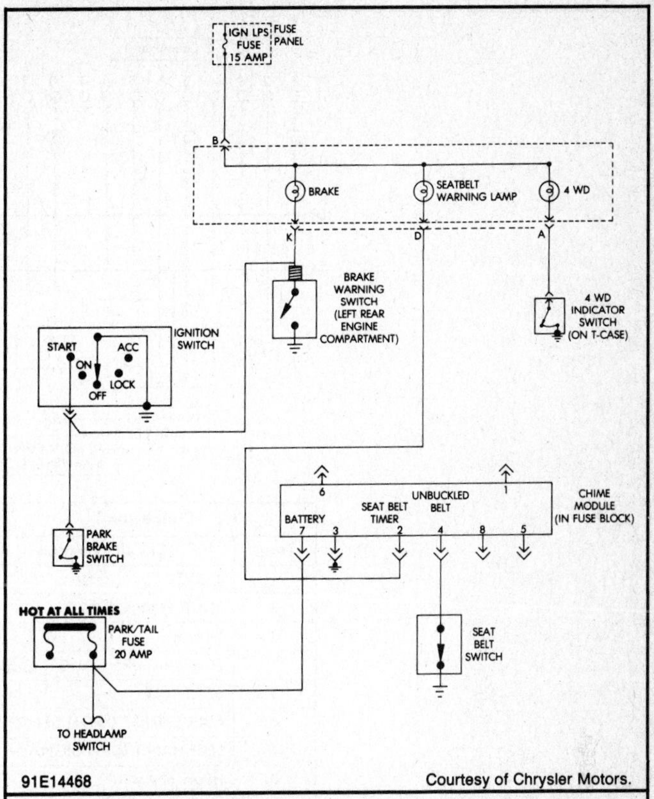
IGN LPS FUSE 15 AMP
FUSE PANEL
B
BRAKE
SEATBELT WARNING LAMP
4 WD
K
D
A
BRAKE WARNING SWITCH (LEFT REAR ENGINE COMPARTMENT)
4 WD INDICATOR SWITCH (ON T-CASE)
IGNITION SWITCH
START
ACC
ON
LOCK
OFF
PARK BRAKE SWITCH
6
1
UNBUCKLED BELT
SEAT BELT TIMER
BATTERY
7
3
2
4
8
5
CHIME MODULE (IN FUSE BLOCK)
HOT AT ALL TIMES
PARK/TAIL FUSE 20 AMP
TO HEADLAMP SWITCH
SEAT BELT SWITCH
91E14468

Courtesy of Chrysler Motors.

Fig. 6: Instrument Panel Indicator Schematic (Grand Wagoneer)

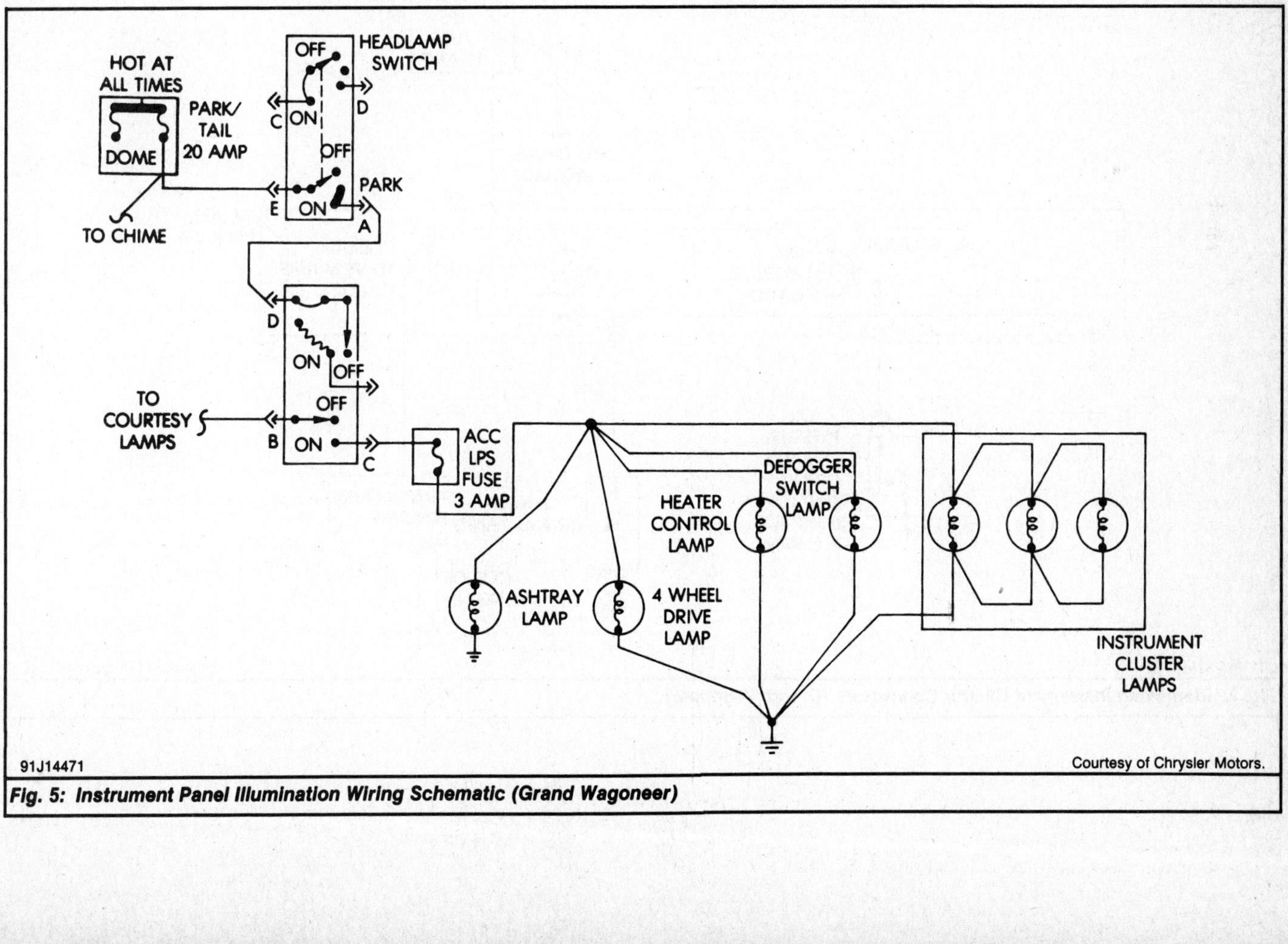
HOT AT ALL TIMES
DOME
PARK/ TAIL 20 AMP
TO CHIME
OFF
HEADLAMP SWITCH
C
ON
D
OFF
PARK
E
ON
A
D
ON
OFF
TO COURTESY LAMPS
OFF
B
ON
C
ACC LPS FUSE 3 AMP
HEATER CONTROL LAMP
DEFOGGER SWITCH LAMP
ASHTRAY LAMP
4 WHEEL DRIVE LAMP
INSTRUMENT CLUSTER LAMPS
91J14471

Courtesy of Chrysler Motors.

Fig. 5: Instrument Panel Illumination Wiring Schematic (Grand Wagoneer)

1991 SAFETY EQUIPMENT
Instrument Panels (Cont.)

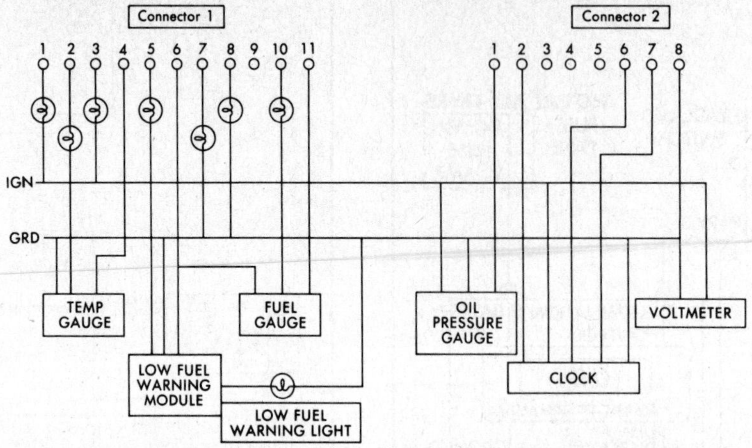
Connector 1
1 2 3 4 5 6 7 8 9 10 11
Connector 2
1 2 3 4 5 6 7 8
IGN
GRD
TEMP GAUGE
FUEL GAUGE
LOW FUEL WARNING MODULE
LOW FUEL WARNING LIGHT
OIL PRESSURE GAUGE
CLOCK
VOLTMETER

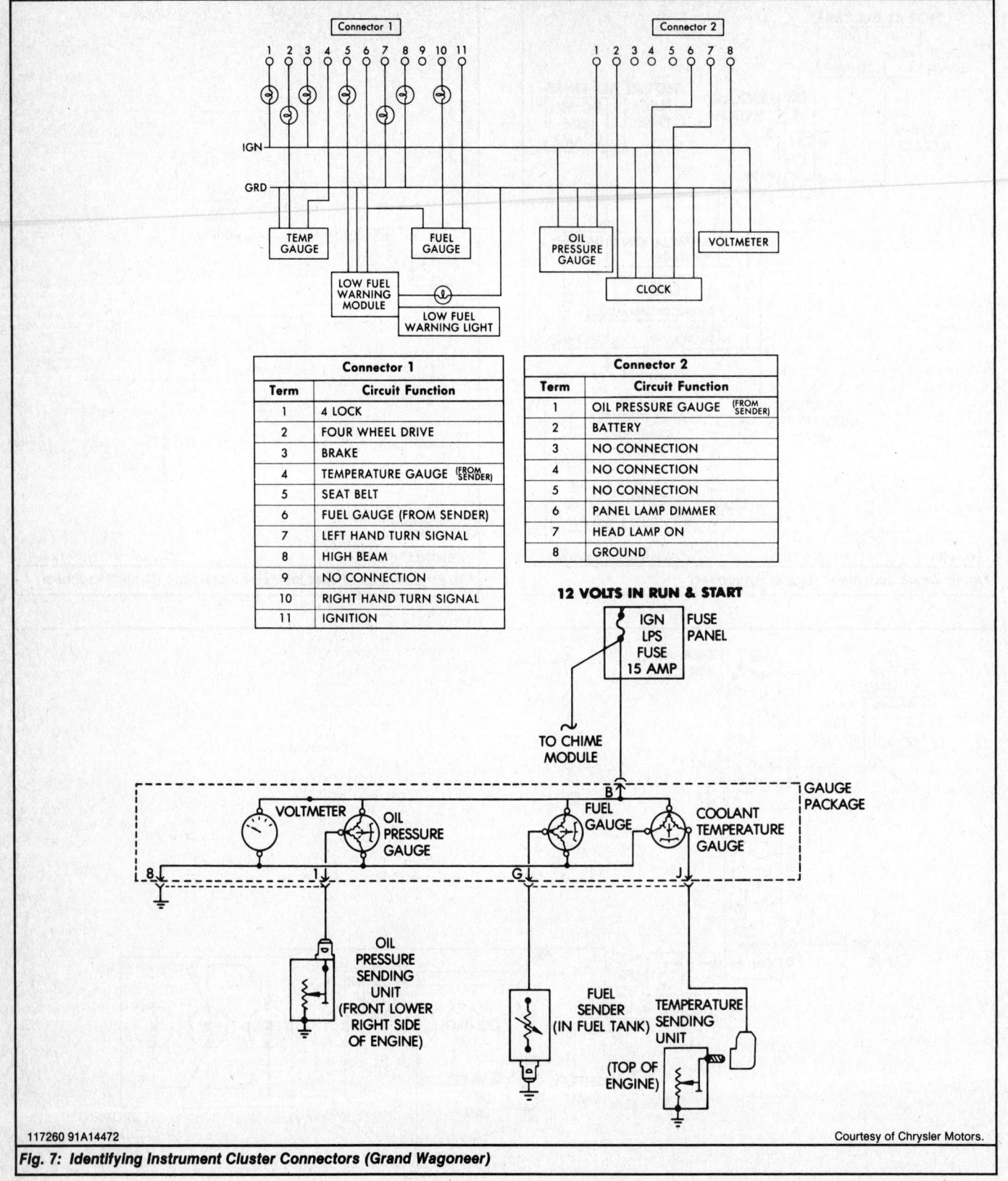

Connector 1	
Term	**Circuit Function**
1	4 LOCK
2	FOUR WHEEL DRIVE
3	BRAKE
4	TEMPERATURE GAUGE (FROM SENDER)
5	SEAT BELT
6	FUEL GAUGE (FROM SENDER)
7	LEFT HAND TURN SIGNAL
8	HIGH BEAM
9	NO CONNECTION
10	RIGHT HAND TURN SIGNAL
11	IGNITION

Connector 2	
Term	**Circuit Function**
1	OIL PRESSURE GAUGE (FROM SENDER)
2	BATTERY
3	NO CONNECTION
4	NO CONNECTION
5	NO CONNECTION
6	PANEL LAMP DIMMER
7	HEAD LAMP ON
8	GROUND

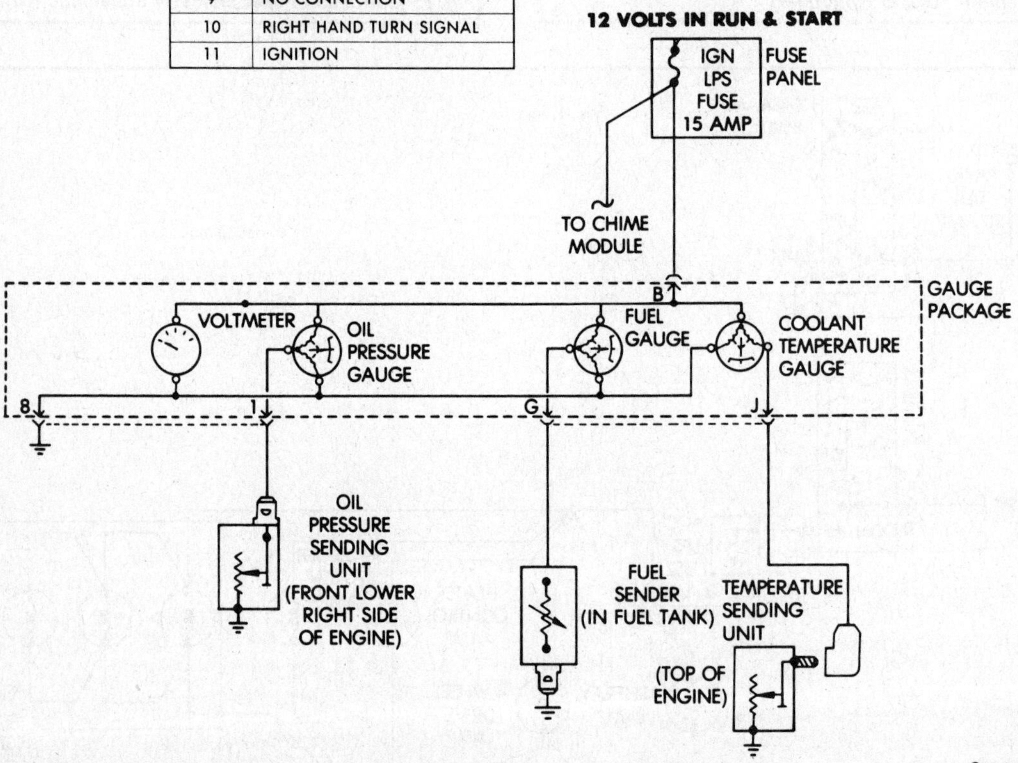
12 VOLTS IN RUN & START
IGN LPS FUSE 15 AMP
FUSE PANEL
TO CHIME MODULE
B
GAUGE PACKAGE
VOLTMETER
OIL PRESSURE GAUGE
FUEL GAUGE
COOLANT TEMPERATURE GAUGE
8
1
G
J
OIL PRESSURE SENDING UNIT (FRONT LOWER RIGHT SIDE OF ENGINE)
FUEL SENDER (IN FUEL TANK)
TEMPERATURE SENDING UNIT
(TOP OF ENGINE)

117260 91A14472

Courtesy of Chrysler Motors.

Fig. 7: Identifying Instrument Cluster Connectors (Grand Wagoneer)

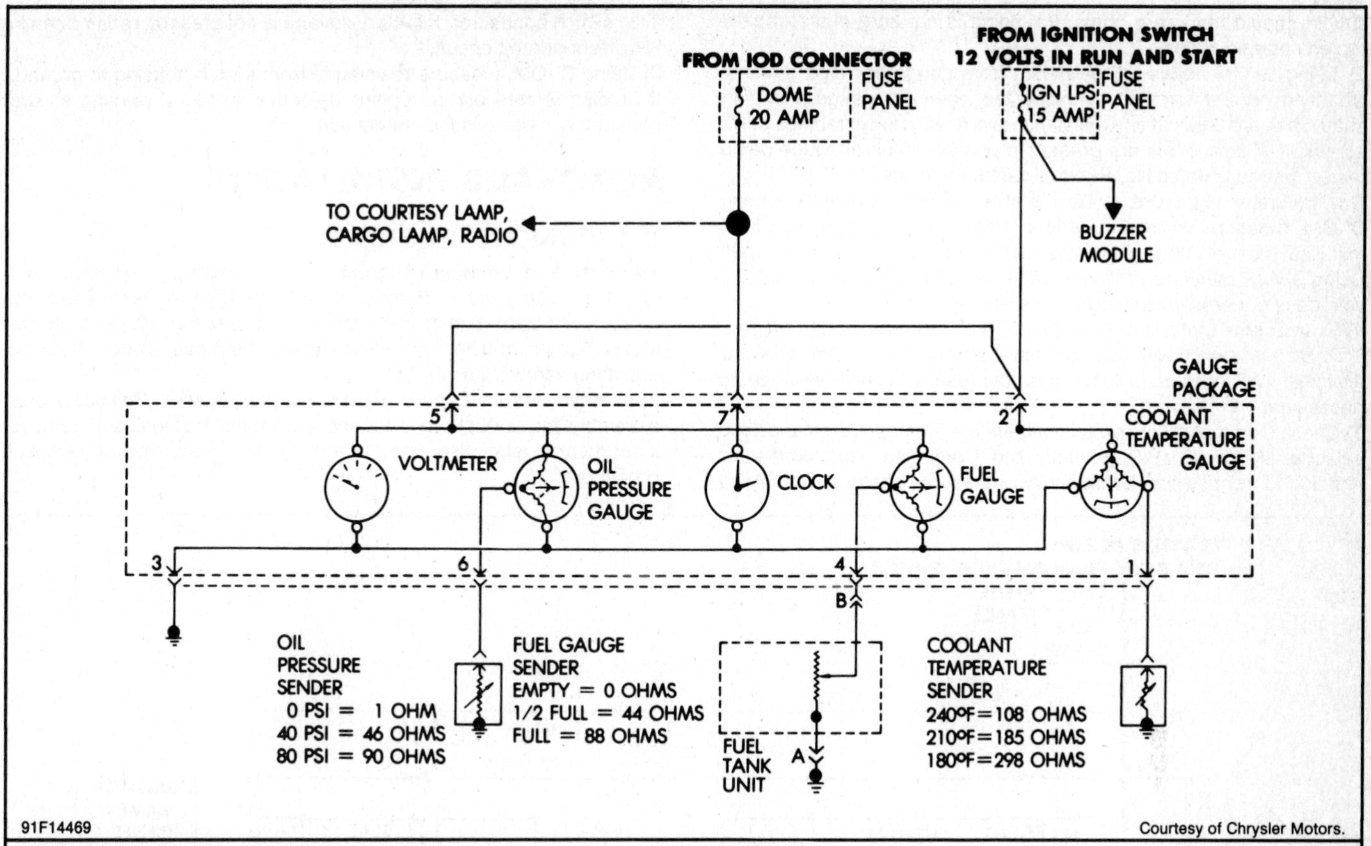

FROM IGNITION SWITCH
12 VOLTS IN RUN AND START
FROM IOD CONNECTOR
DOME
20 AMP
FUSE PANEL
IGN LPS
15 AMP
FUSE PANEL
TO COURTESY LAMP, CARGO LAMP, RADIO
BUZZER MODULE
GAUGE PACKAGE
5
7
2
COOLANT TEMPERATURE GAUGE
VOLTMETER
OIL PRESSURE GAUGE
CLOCK
FUEL GAUGE
3
6
4
1
B
OIL PRESSURE SENDER
0 PSI = 1 OHM
40 PSI = 46 OHMS
80 PSI = 90 OHMS
FUEL GAUGE SENDER
EMPTY = 0 OHMS
1/2 FULL = 44 OHMS
FULL = 88 OHMS
FUEL TANK UNIT
A
COOLANT TEMPERATURE SENDER
240°F=108 OHMS
210°F=185 OHMS
180°F=298 OHMS
91F14469
Courtesy of Chrysler Motors.

Fig. 8: Gauge Package Wiring Schematic (Wrangler)

WRANGLER

All Gauges Inoperative – 1) Check power supply to gauges with ignition on and engine off. If power is not present, check IGN/LPS (ignition/lamps) fuse. Replace if blown. Using DVOM, measure voltage at battery side of IGN/LPS fuse. If battery voltage is not present, repair open in Yellow wire circuit from ignition switch.

2) Check gauge package ground with ignition off. Separate instrument cluster connector from gauge package. Using DVOM, measure resistance from instrument cluster connector terminal No. 3 to ground. If any resistance is present, repair open in Black wire circuit to ground.

3) Check power to gauge package with ignition on and engine off. Using DVOM, measure voltage at instrument cluster connector terminals No. 2 and 5. *See Fig. 8*. If battery voltage is not present, repair open in White/Black wire circuit from fuse panel.

NOTE: If only voltmeter and oil pressure gauges are inoperative, an open exists in wire from gauge package terminal No. 2 to 5. For individual gauge testing, see GAUGE TESTING (ALL MODELS) under TESTING.

All Indicator Lights Out – Turn ignition on with engine off. Check IGN/LPS (ignition/lamps) fuse. Replace fuse if blown. Using DVOM, measure voltage at battery side of IGN/LPS fuse. If battery voltage is not present, repair open in circuit from ignition switch. Using DVOM, measure voltage at both connectors terminal No. 4 of indicator panel. *See Fig. 9*. If battery voltage is not present, repair open in White/Black wire circuit from fuse panel.

Clock Inoperative – 1) Inspect dome/courtesy light fuse. Replace if blown. Using DVOM, measure voltage at battery side of fuse. If battery voltage is not present, repair open in Red/White wire circuit from fuse No. 2 in power distribution center.

2) Separate instrument cluster connector from gauge package. Measure voltage at instrument cluster connector terminal No. 7. *See Fig. 8*. If reading is not battery voltage, repair open from fuse panel.

3) Measure resistance from gauge package terminal No. 7 to clock battery terminal. Reading should be zero ohms. If reading is not zero ohms, repair/replace printed circuit.

4) Measure resistance from clock ground terminal to gauge package terminal No. 3. If reading is not zero ohms, repair/replace printed circuit. If reading is zero ohms, replace clock.

Coolant Temperature Sender Inoperative – Turn ignition on with engine off. Disconnect coolant temperature sender connector from sender. Using DVOM, measure voltage at coolant temperature sender connector. *See Fig. 8*. If reading is not 9 volts, repair open in circuit from gauge package or from printed circuit. If reading is 9 volts and gauge does not operate, replace sender unit.

Fuel Gauge Sender Inoperative – 1) Turn ignition on with engine off. Disconnect fuel gauge sender connector from sender. Using DVOM, measure voltage at fuel gauge connector terminal "B". *See Fig. 8*. Voltage should be approximately 7.5 volts. If reading is not okay, repair open in circuit from gauge package or printed circuit.

2) Using DVOM, measure resistance from fuel gauge sender connector terminal "A" to ground. Reading on ohmmeter should be zero ohms. If reading is zero ohms and gauge does not operate, replace sender. If reading is not zero ohms, repair open in circuit from fuel gauge sender connector to ground.

Oil Pressure Sender Inoperative – Turn ignition on with engine off. Disconnect oil pressure sender connector from sender unit. Using DVOM, measure voltage at oil pressure sender connector. *See Fig. 8*. Voltage reading should be 7.5 volts. If reading is not 7.5 volts, repair open in circuit from gauge package or from printed circuit. If reading is 7.5 volts and gauge does not operate, replace sender unit.

Printed Circuit Check – 1) Turn ignition off. Disconnect gauges wiring harness connector from rear of gauge package, including voltmeter sender unit. Using DVOM, measure resistance in printed circuit from gauge package terminal No. 2 (fuel and coolant temperature gauge) or from terminal No. 5 (voltmeter and oil pressure gauge) to gauge battery terminal of suspected defective gauge. *See Fig. 8*.

1991 SAFETY EQUIPMENT
Instrument Panels (Cont.)

DVOM should read zero ohms. If reading is not zero ohms, repair/replace printed circuit.

2) Using DVOM, measure resistance from gauge package terminal No. 3 to ground terminal of suspected defective gauge. Reading should be zero ohms. If any resistance is present, repair/replace printed circuit. If zero ohms are present in printed circuit of gauge being tested, gauge is defective. Replace defective gauge.

One Indicator Light Out – Turn ignition on with engine off. Using DVOM, measure voltage at ground side of bulb socket with bulb installed. If battery voltage is not present, repair open from fuse panel. Using DVOM, measure voltage at battery side of bulb socket. If battery voltage is not present, repair/replace printed circuit.

4WD Indicator Light Out – 1) Check vacuum supply to Command Trac vacuum switch with engine running and Command Trac selector switch in 4WD position. If vacuum is not present, locate and repair as necessary.

2) Check Command Trac switch with engine running, Command Trac selector switch in 4WD position and Command Trac connector unplugged from switch. Using DVOM, measure voltage at Command Trac switch connector. If battery voltage is not present, repair open in wire from printed circuit.

3) Using DVOM, measure resistance from switch housing to ground. If reading is zero ohms, replace defective switch. If reading shows resistance, clean ground connection.

REMOVAL & INSTALLATION

INSTRUMENT CLUSTER

Removal & Installation (Cherokee & Comanche) – 1) Disconnect negative battery cable. Remove 4 instrument panel bezel attaching screws, and unsnap instrument panel bezel. *See Fig. 10.* Remove cigarette lighter housing attaching screw. Remove switch housing attaching screws. *See Fig. 11.*

2) Remove instrument panel cluster attaching screws. Pull out cluster assembly far enough to disconnect 2 multiple plugs, and remove instrument cluster. *See Figs. 12 and 13.* To install, reverse removal procedure.

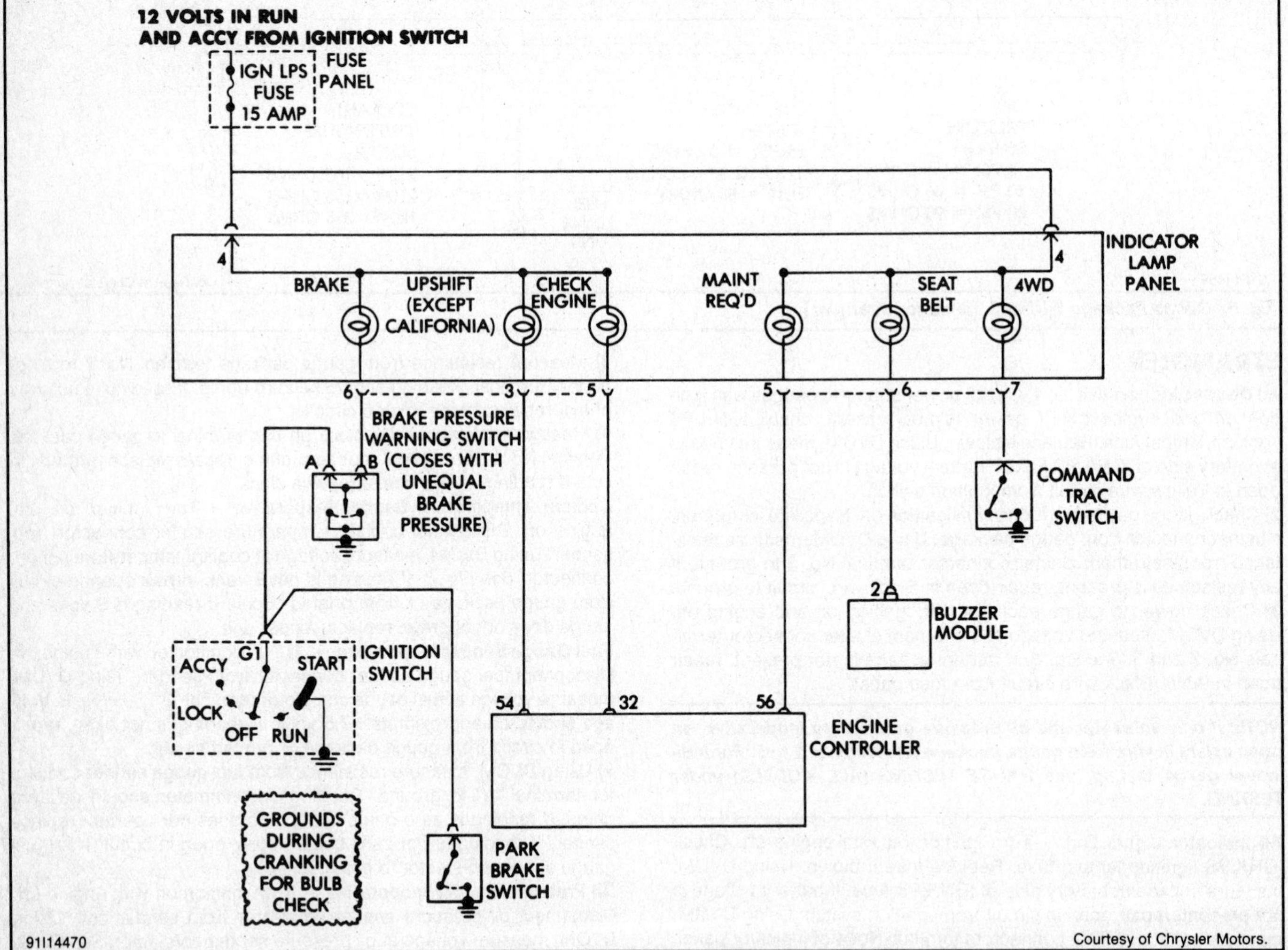
12 VOLTS IN RUN AND ACCY FROM IGNITION SWITCH
IGN LPS FUSE 15 AMP
FUSE PANEL
INDICATOR LAMP PANEL
4
4
BRAKE
UPSHIFT (EXCEPT CALIFORNIA)
CHECK ENGINE
MAINT REQ'D
SEAT BELT
4WD
6
3
5
5
6
7
BRAKE PRESSURE WARNING SWITCH
A
B (CLOSES WITH UNEQUAL BRAKE PRESSURE)
COMMAND TRAC SWITCH
2
BUZZER MODULE
G1
ACCY
START
IGNITION SWITCH
LOCK
OFF
RUN
54
32
56
ENGINE CONTROLLER
GROUNDS DURING CRANKING FOR BULB CHECK
PARK BRAKE SWITCH
91I14470
Courtesy of Chrysler Motors.

Fig. 9: Indicator Light Wiring Schematic (Wrangler)

1991 SAFETY EQUIPMENT
Instrument Panels (Cont.)

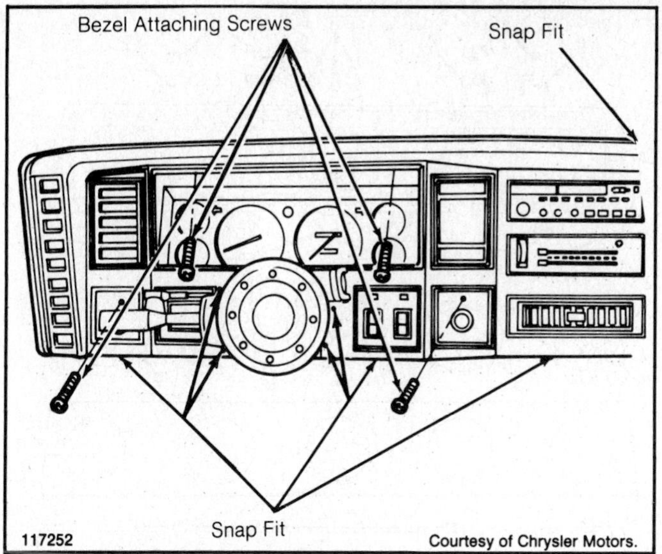
Bezel Attaching Screws
Snap Fit
Snap Fit
117252
Courtesy of Chrysler Motors.

Fig. 10: Removing Instrument Cluster Bezel (Cherokee & Comanche)

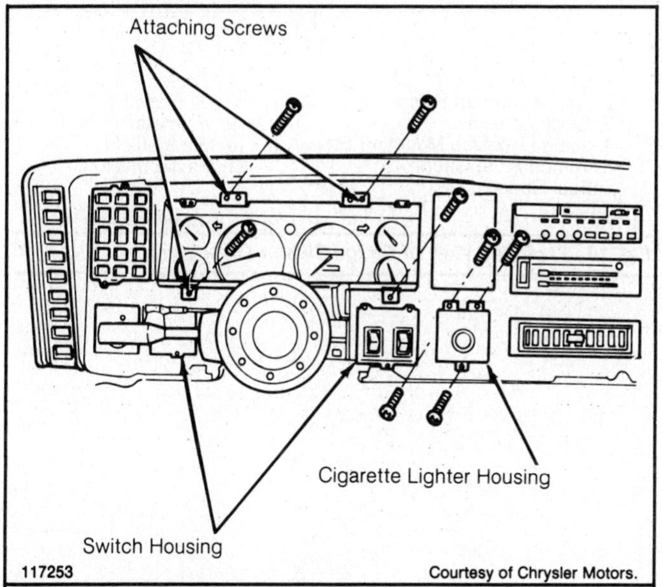
Attaching Screws
Cigarette Lighter Housing
Switch Housing
117253
Courtesy of Chrysler Motors.

Fig. 11: Removing Instrument Panel (Cherokee & Comanche)

Removal & Installation (Grand Wagoneer) – 1) Disconnect negative battery cable. Unsnap tabs holding instrument panel bezel to instrument panel, and remove bezel. Remove screws attaching instrument cluster to panel.

2) Pull instrument cluster outward. Disconnect speedometer and cluster wire harness connectors. *See Fig. 14*. Remove instrument cluster. To install, reverse removal procedure.

Removal & Installation (Wrangler) – 1) Remove 6 gauge panel mounting screws, and remove panel. Remove 6 gauge housing mounting screws, and disconnect wiring harness connector from back of gauge cluster. *See Fig. 15*.

2) Using screwdriver, remove plastic cover shield by releasing 7 tabs. Remove metal shield. Remove gauge nuts to remove individual gauges.

3) To install, reverse removal procedure. When installing gauge, place gauge contact pins over gauge screw. Gauge pins are properly driven into gauge as nut is tightened.

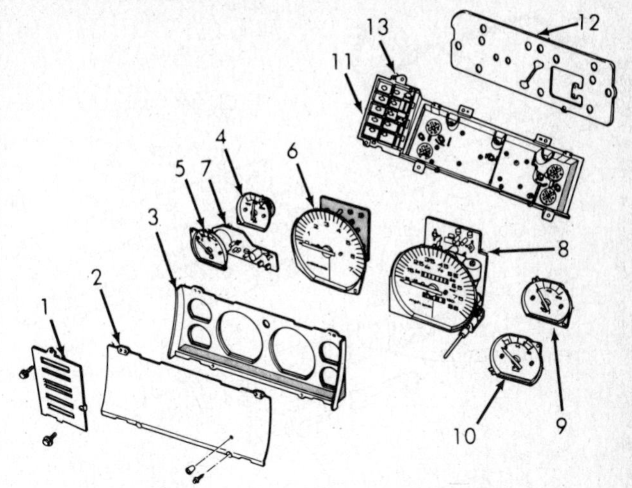
1
2
3
4
5
6
7
8
9
10
11
12
13

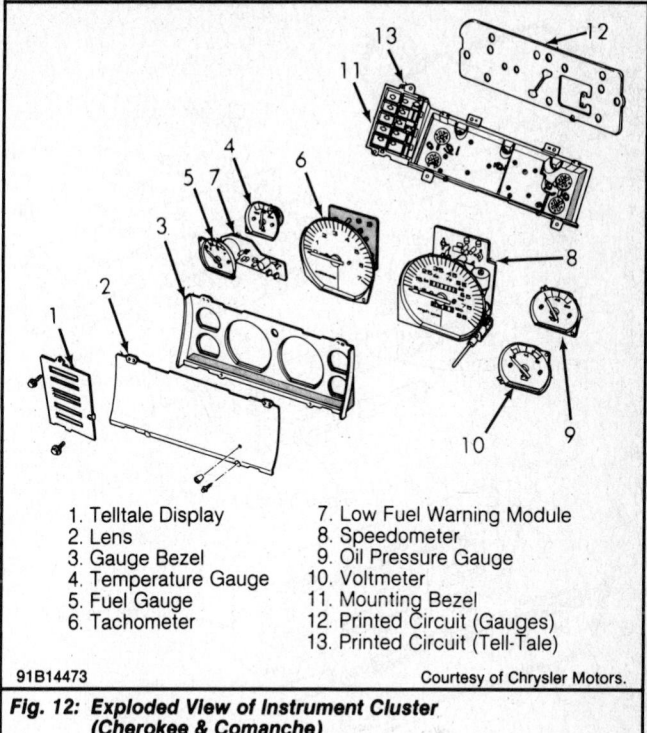

1. Telltale Display
2. Lens
3. Gauge Bezel
4. Temperature Gauge
5. Fuel Gauge
6. Tachometer
7. Low Fuel Warning Module
8. Speedometer
9. Oil Pressure Gauge
10. Voltmeter
11. Mounting Bezel
12. Printed Circuit (Gauges)
13. Printed Circuit (Tell-Tale)

91B14473 Courtesy of Chrysler Motors.

Fig. 12: Exploded View of Instrument Cluster (Cherokee & Comanche)

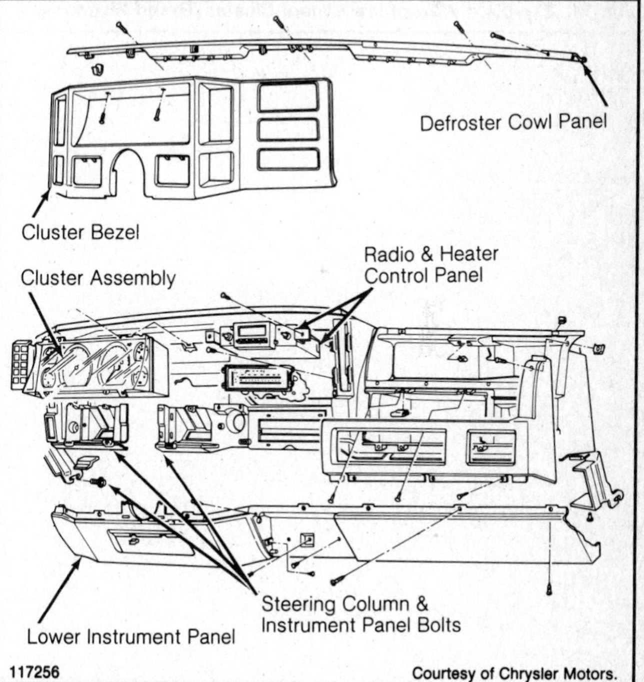
Defroster Cowl Panel
Cluster Bezel
Radio & Heater
Control Panel
Cluster Assembly
Steering Column &
Instrument Panel Bolts
Lower Instrument Panel
117256
Courtesy of Chrysler Motors.

Fig. 13: Exploded View of Instrument Panel (Cherokee & Comanche)

WIRING DIAGRAMS

See appropriate chassis wiring diagram in WIRING DIAGRAMS.

1991 SAFETY EQUIPMENT
Instrument Panels (Cont.)

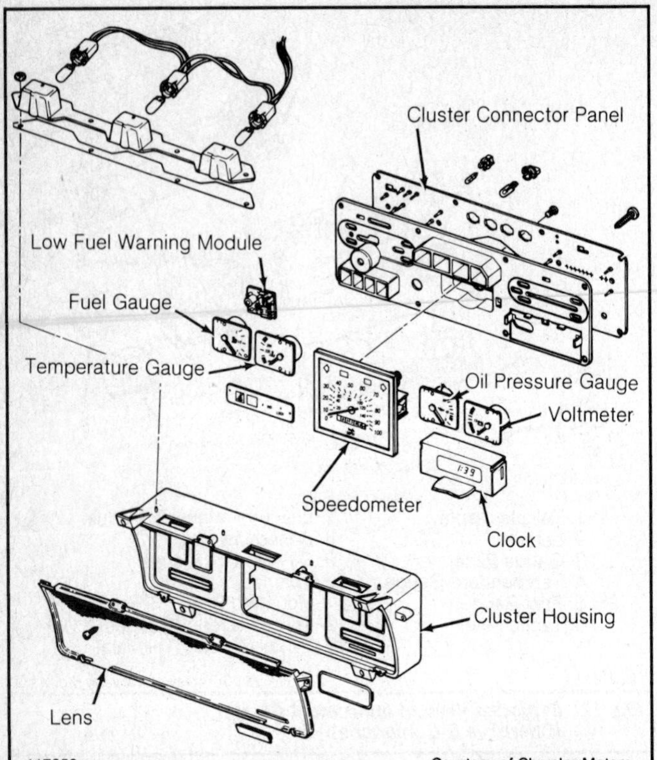
Cluster Connector Panel
Low Fuel Warning Module
Fuel Gauge
Temperature Gauge
Oil Pressure Gauge
Voltmeter
Speedometer
Clock
Cluster Housing
Lens
117258
Courtesy of Chrysler Motors.

Fig. 14: Exploded View of Instrument Cluster (Grand Wagoneer)

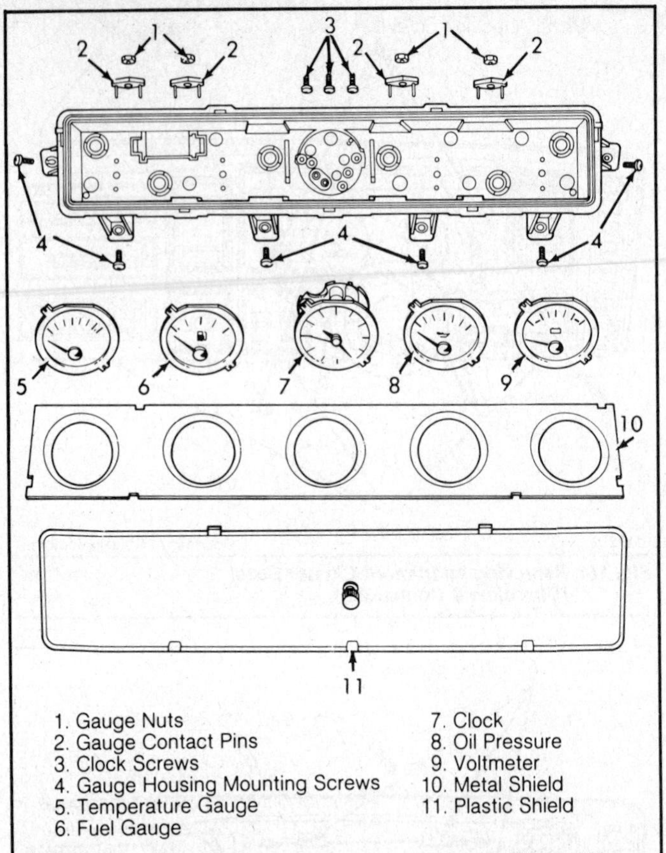
1. Gauge Nuts
2. Gauge Contact Pins
3. Clock Screws
4. Gauge Housing Mounting Screws
5. Temperature Gauge
6. Fuel Gauge
7. Clock
8. Oil Pressure
9. Voltmeter
10. Metal Shield
11. Plastic Shield
117261
Courtesy of Chrysler Motors.

Fig. 15: Exploded View of Gauge Cluster (Wrangler)

1991 SAFETY EQUIPMENT
Power Mirrors

Cherokee, Grand Wagoneer

DESCRIPTION & OPERATION

Cherokee – Mirror control switch contains 2 separate switches: operating switch and selector switch. Each mirror has 2 reversible motors. Driver operates 3 switches that control polarity of voltage to motors. Mirror select switch directs these controlled voltages.

Grand Wagoneer – Both mirrors are controlled by a dual-function switch located on left front door panel. A safety or overrun feature is designed into mirror to prevent damage to motor when mirror is moved by hand, or when mirror is operated to maximum limit.

TESTING

Cherokee – *See Figs. 1-4* for testing.

Grand Wagoneer (Motor/Switch Test) - 1) Check 30-amp circuit breaker. Check for good ground (Black) connection at base of fuse panel.

2) Using a test light, check for voltage at Violet input wire to switch. If voltage is not present, check for a broken ground wire (Black) or supply wire (Violet) between switch and fuse panel.

3) If Violet wire is okay, check for voltage at Yellow wire and White wire. If voltage is not present at both Yellow and White wires, replace power mirror.

REMOVAL & INSTALLATION

POWER MIRROR

Removal & Installation – 1) Remove interior door latch release assembly, and control panel retaining screws. Disconnect control linkage and wire harness connector. Remove latch release and control panel assembly. Remove armrest lower retaining screws.

2) Swing armrest downward to a vertical position. Disconnect armrest from upper retainer clip. Pull armrest straight out from trim panel. Remove trim panel.

3) Remove screw holding mirror trim cover. Disconnect power mirror wire harness at connector in door. Pull harness up through door. Remove 3 screws (2 screws on Grand Wagoneer) holding mirror to door. To install, reverse removal procedure.

SWITCH TEST
Slide Switch in Left (L) Position

SWITCH POSITION	TERMINALS	ZERO OHMS
Push Down (D)	A and G	Yes
	E and F	Yes
	All Others	No
Push Up (U)	A and F	Yes
	E and G	Yes
	All Others	No
Off (Normal)	All Others	No
Push Left (L)	B and G	Yes
	E and F	Yes
	All Others	No
Push Right (R)	B and F	Yes
	E and G	Yes
	All Others	No

SWITCH TEST
Slide Switch in Right (R) Position

SWITCH POSITION	TERMINALS	ZERO OHMS
Push Down (D)	D and G	Yes
	E and F	Yes
	All Others	No
Push Up (U)	D and F	Yes
	E and G	Yes
	All Others	No
Off (Normal)	All Others	No
Push Left (L)	C and G	Yes
	E and F	Yes
	All Others	No
Push Right (R)	C and F	Yes
	E and G	Yes
	All Others	No

Courtesy of Chrysler Motors

Fig. 1: Testing Power Mirror Switch (Cherokee)

1991 SAFETY EQUIPMENT
Power Mirrors (Cont.)

1. POWER INPUT—Fuse

TEST	OK	NOT OK
Open Door	Dome Lamps light	Check Dome fuse

2. POWER MIRROR SWITCH ASSEMBLY—Remove switch, unplug switch connector

TEST	OK	NOT OK
Mirror switch connector terminal F	Zero ohms	Repair open to Splice G
Mirror switch connector terminal G	Battery voltage	Repair open to Dome fuse
Jumper test leads terminal E to terminal F	—	Next step
Jumper test leads terminal G to: terminal A terminal B terminal C terminal D	Mirror moves. If OK, replace switch	Repair open to test motor and/or replace motor

Courtesy of Chrysler Motors

Fig. 2: Trouble Shooting Power Mirror (Cherokee)

WIRING DIAGRAMS

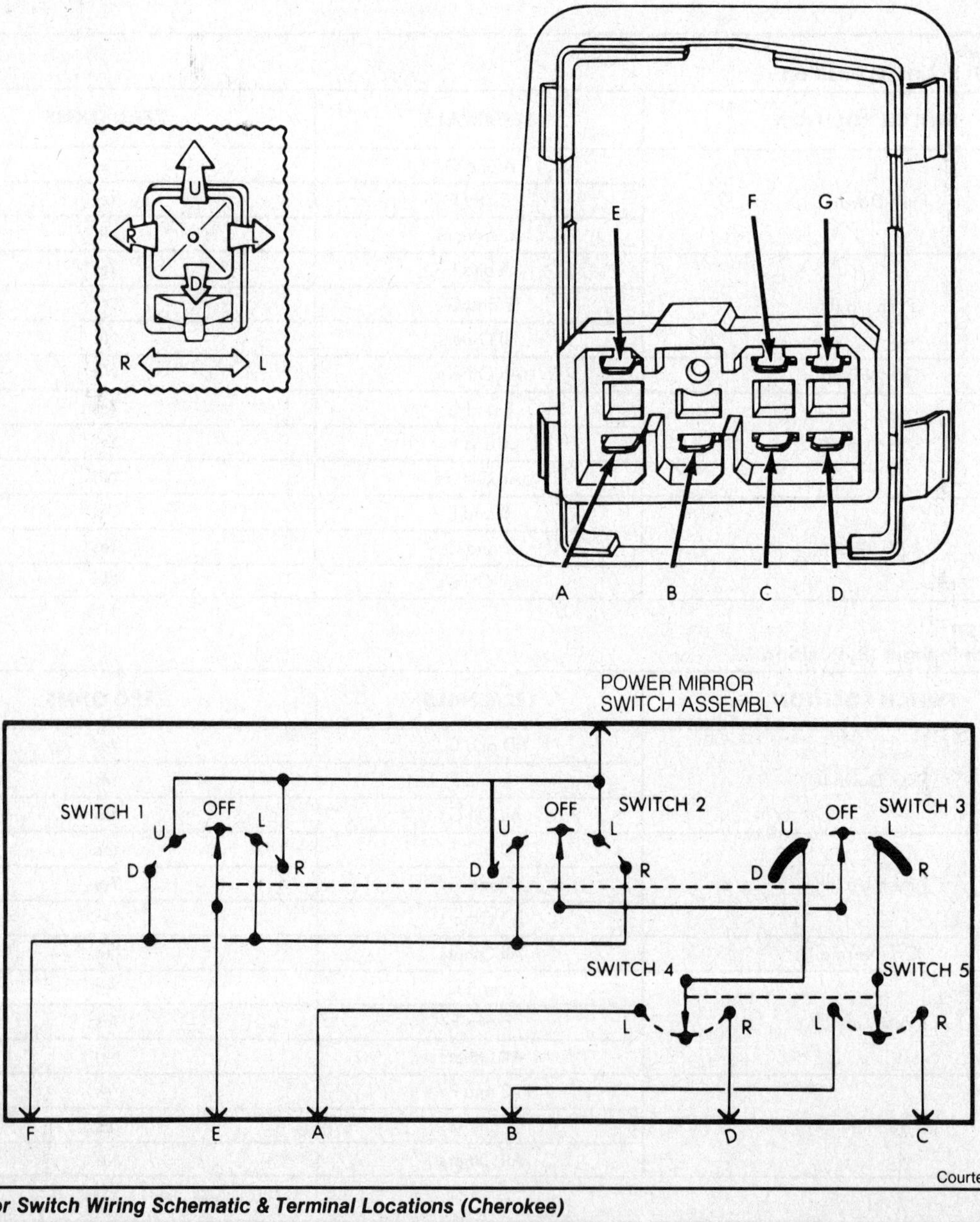
U
R
L
D
R
L
E
F
G
A
B
C
D
POWER MIRROR
SWITCH ASSEMBLY
SWITCH 1
OFF
U
L
D
R
OFF
SWITCH 2
U
L
D
R
U
OFF
SWITCH 3
L
D
R
SWITCH 4
SWITCH 5
L
R
L
R
F
E
A
B
D
C

117222 117223 117519

Courtesy of Chrysler Motors

Fig. 3: Power Mirror Switch Wiring Schematic & Terminal Locations (Cherokee)

1991 SAFETY EQUIPMENT
Power Mirrors (Cont.)

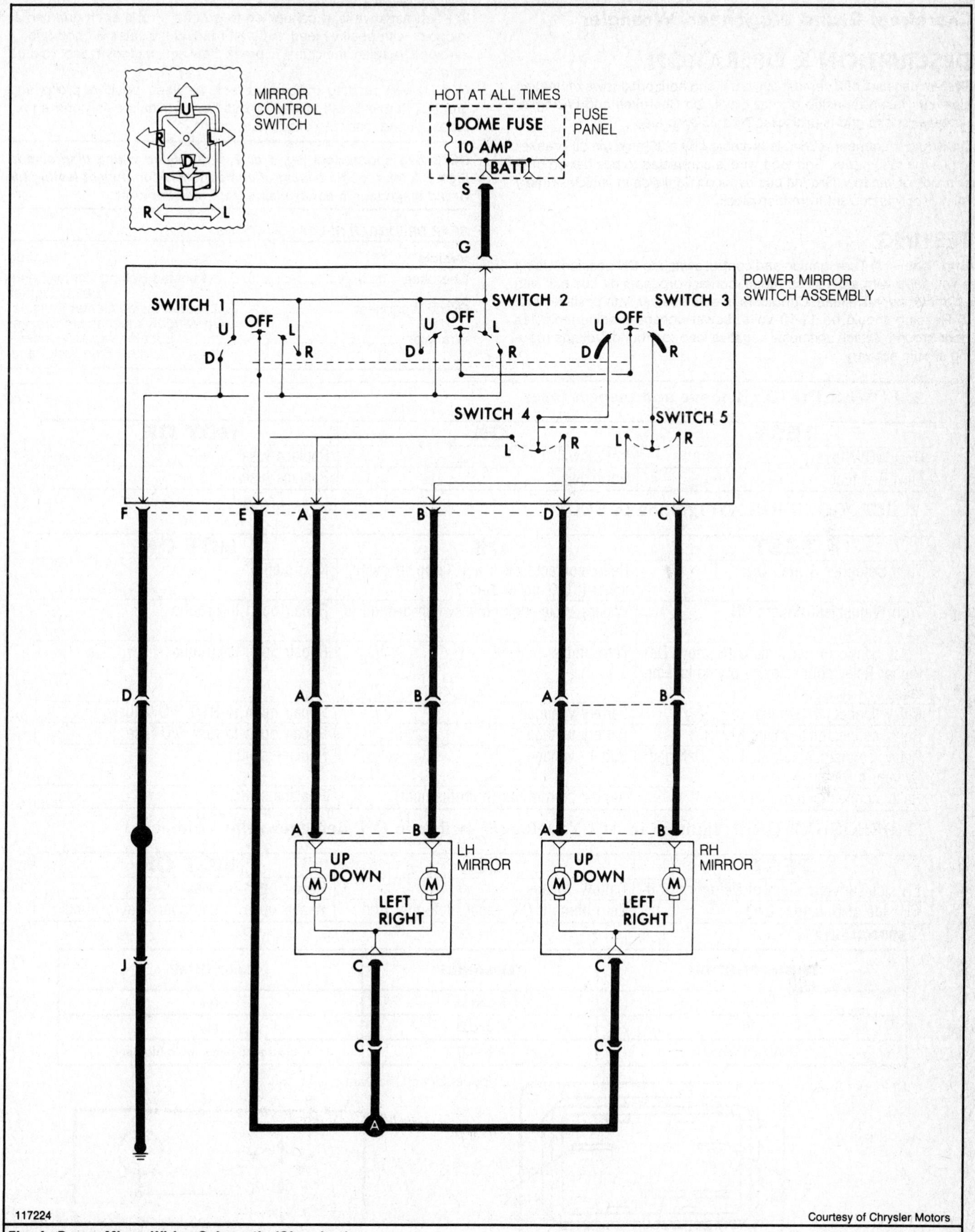
MIRROR
CONTROL
SWITCH
U
R
L
D
R
L
HOT AT ALL TIMES
DOME FUSE
10 AMP
BATT
FUSE
PANEL
S
G
POWER MIRROR
SWITCH ASSEMBLY
SWITCH 1
SWITCH 2
SWITCH 3
SWITCH 4
SWITCH 5
OFF
F
E
A
B
D
C
J
LH
MIRROR
RH
MIRROR
UP
DOWN
LEFT
RIGHT
M
117224
Courtesy of Chrysler Motors

Fig. 4: Power Mirror Wiring Schematic (Cherokee)

1991 SAFETY EQUIPMENT
Rear Window Defogger

Cherokee, Grand Wagoneer, Wrangler

DESCRIPTION & OPERATION

System consists of 2 vertical bus bars, and horizontal rows of heating elements fused to inside of rear glass. On Cherokee and Wrangler, power circuit to grid is protected by a 25-amp fuse.

On Grand Wagoneer, circuit is protected by a 30-amp circuit breaker located in fuse panel. Grid feed wire is connected to bus bar on driver's side of window. Ground bus bar is on right side of vehicle. Timer/relay receives current from fuse block.

TESTING

Grid Test – 1) Turn ignition and control switch to ON position. Using a voltmeter with a 0-15 volt range, contact ground-side bus bar with voltmeter negative lead. Contact feed-side bus bar with positive lead.
2) Reading should be 11-13 volts. Lower voltage reading indicates poor ground. Attach voltmeter negative lead to ground. Voltage reading should not vary.
3) Keep negative lead connected to ground. Probe each grid line at midpoint with positive lead. A 6-volt reading indicates a good grid. A zero-volt reading indicates a break between midpoint and voltage source.
4) A 12-volt reading indicates break between positive probe and ground. Repair break in grid or bus bar terminals using grid epoxy repair kit and following exact instructions.

NOTE: See appropriate Fig. 1 or 2, and related wiring diagrams in Figs. 3-5 for specific testing of components. Component testing for Grand Wagoneer is not available from manufacturer.

REAR DEFOGGER RELAY LOCATIONS

Vehicle	Location
Cherokee	Located Behind Center Dash, Below Lighter
Grand Wagoneer	Located Inside Center Tailgate, On Window Mechanism Bracket
Wrangler	Located Against Driver's Left Side Kick Panel

1. POWER INPUT: Remove and inspect fuses

TEST	OK	NOT OK
HTD WDW fuse	Not blown	Replace fuse
Turn B/U fuse	Not blown	Replace fuse

2. DEFOGGER RELAY: Ignition in ACCY

TEST	OK	NOT OK
Turn Defogger Switch ON	Relay contacts click and lamp in switch lights If OK, go to step 3	Next step
Turn Windshield Wipers ON	Wipers cycle, defogger switch ground is OK	Repair open to ground
Relay connector terminal D (Remove Defogger Relay connector by prying locking tabs)	Zero ohms	Repair open to ground
Relay connector terminal C	Battery voltage	Repair open to HTD WDW fuse
Relay connector terminal E	Battery voltage	Repair open to turn B/U fuse
Relay connector terminal B (Defogger Switch in ON)	Battery voltage	Replace switch
Relay connector terminal A	Almost zero ohms (bulb filament)	Replace switch

3. DEFOGGER GRID: Ignition in ACCY, defogger switch in ON, defogger relay connected

TEST	OK	NOT OK
LH side (driver's side) of Defogger Grid	Battery voltage	Repair open to relay
RH side of Defogger Grid	Zero ohms If OK, repair defogger grid	Repair open to defogger relay ground

SWITCH TEST

SWITCH POSITION	TERMINALS	ZERO OHMS
On	B and D	Yes
Off	C and D	Yes
At Rest (Normal)	A and C	Almost zero ohms (bulb filament)

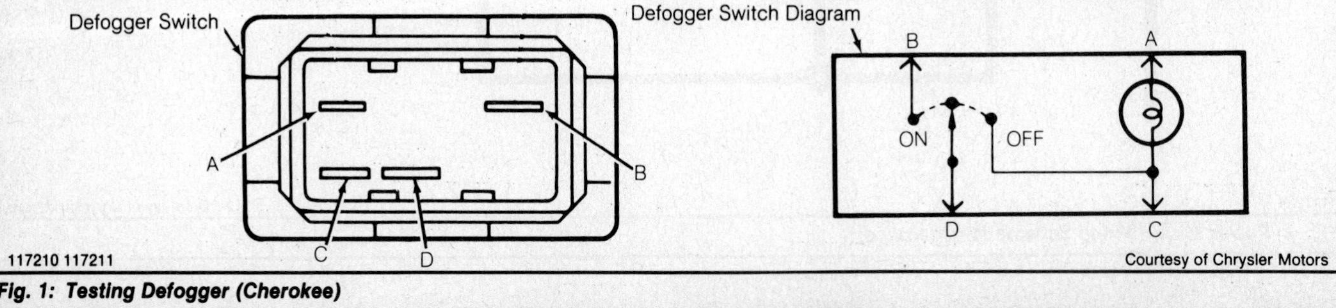
Defogger Switch
A
B
C
D
Defogger Switch Diagram
B
A
ON
OFF
D
C
117210 117211
Courtesy of Chrysler Motors

Fig. 1: Testing Defogger (Cherokee)

1991 SAFETY EQUIPMENT
Rear Window Defogger (Cont.)

1. BATTERY, IGNITION & FUSES

TEST	OK	NOT OK
HTD/WDW & IGN LPS fuses	Not blown	Replace fuses
Battery side of HTD/WDW fuse	Battery voltage	Repair open from fuse link
Ignition side of IGN LPS fuse	Battery voltage	Repair open from ignition switch NOTE: If open is before splice, seat belt buzzer will also be inoperative

2. DEFOGGER SWITCH: Defogger switch connector separated from defogger switch; turn ignition switch to RUN for voltage tests; turn ignition switch to OFF for resistance tests

TEST	OK	NOT OK
Measure voltage at defogger switch terminal B	Battery voltage	Repair open from IGN LPS fuse
Measure resistance between defogger switch connector terminal D and connector A terminal B	Zero ohms	Repair open between defogger switch connector and connector A
Turn defogger switch to ON. Measure resistance across switch terminals B and D	Zero ohms	Replace defogger switch

3. DEFOGGER RELAY: Defogger relay connector separated from defogger relay; turn defogger switch to ON; turn ignition switch to RUN for voltage tests; turn ignition switch to OFF for resistance tests

TEST	OK	NOT OK
Measure voltage at relay connector terminal C	Battery voltage	Repair open to HTD WDW fuse
Measure voltage at relay connector terminal B	Battery voltage	Repair open from defogger switch
Measure voltage at relay connector terminal E	Battery voltage	Repair open from IGN LPS fuse
Measure resistance between relay connector terminal A and LH side (driver's side) of defogger grid	Zero ohms	Repair open between relay connector and LH side of defogger grid
Measure resistance between relay connector terminal D and a clean chassis ground	Zero ohms	Repair open between relay connector and ground
Connect relay connector and measure voltage at terminal A	Battery voltage	Replace defogger relay

4. INDICATOR LAMP: Turn defogger switch to ON; turn ignition switch to RUN for voltage tests; turn ignition switch to OFF for resistance tests

TEST	OK	NOT OK
Measure resistance across bulb terminals	Zero ohms (except filament resistance)	Replace bulb
Measure voltage at defogger switch connector terminal A	Battery voltage	Repair open from defogger relay
Measure resistance from defogger switch connector terminal C to a clean chassis ground	Zero ohms	Repair open between defogger switch connector and ground

5. DEFOGGER GRID: Turn defogger switch to ON; turn ignition switch to RUN for voltage tests; turn ignition switch to OFF for resistance tests

TEST	OK	NOT OK
Measure voltage at LH side (driver's side) of Defogger Grid	Battery voltage	Repair open from defogger relay
Measure resistance for RH side of Defogger Grid to a clean chassis ground	Zero ohms	Repair open between RH side of Defogger Grid and ground

Courtesy of Chrysler Motors

Fig. 2: Testing Defogger (Wrangler)

1991 SAFETY EQUIPMENT
Rear Window Defogger (Cont.)

WIRING DIAGRAMS

For additional information, see appropriate chassis wiring diagram in WIRING DIAGRAMS

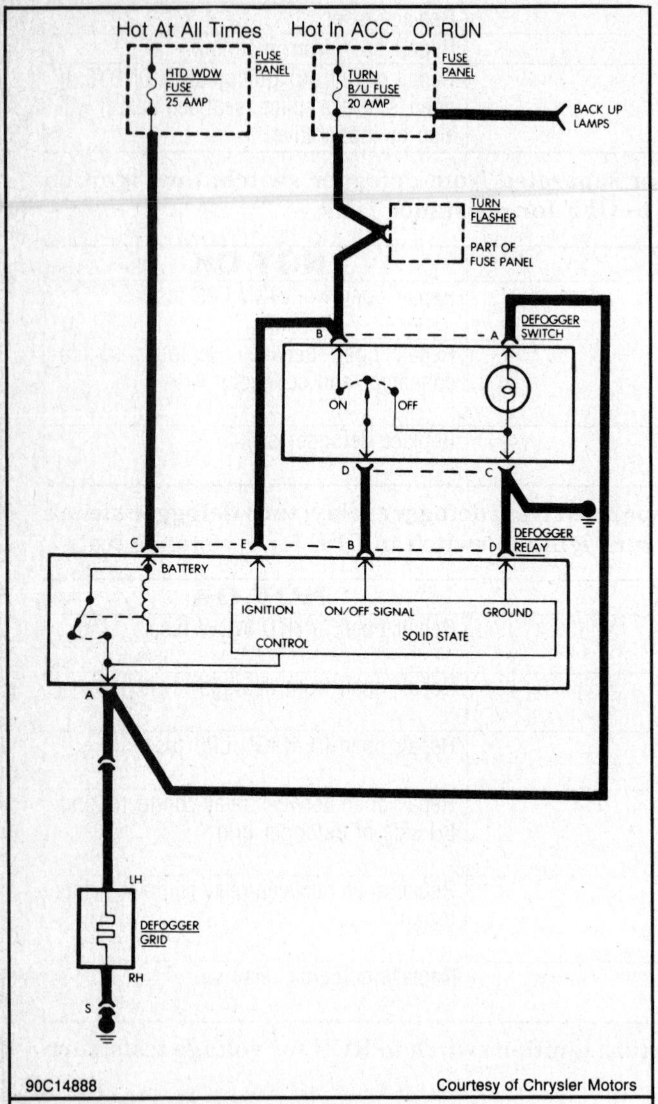
Hot At All Times
Hot In ACC Or RUN
HTD WDW FUSE 25 AMP
FUSE PANEL
TURN B/U FUSE 20 AMP
FUSE PANEL
BACK UP LAMPS
TURN FLASHER
PART OF FUSE PANEL
DEFOGGER SWITCH
ON
OFF
BATTERY
IGNITION
ON/OFF SIGNAL
GROUND
CONTROL
SOLID STATE
DEFOGGER RELAY
LH
DEFOGGER GRID
RH
90C14888
Courtesy of Chrysler Motors

Fig. 3: Defogger Wiring Schematic (Cherokee)

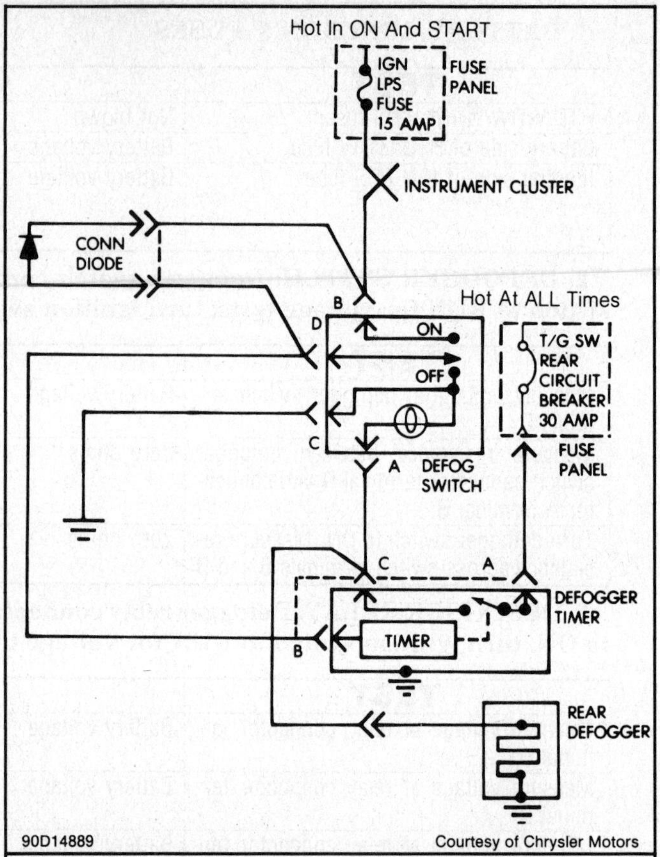
Hot In ON And START
IGN LPS FUSE 15 AMP
FUSE PANEL
INSTRUMENT CLUSTER
CONN DIODE
Hot At ALL Times
ON
OFF
DEFOG SWITCH
T/G SW REAR CIRCUIT BREAKER 30 AMP
FUSE PANEL
DEFOGGER TIMER
TIMER
REAR DEFOGGER
90D14889
Courtesy of Chrysler Motors

Fig. 4: Defogger Wiring Schematic (Grand Wagoneer)

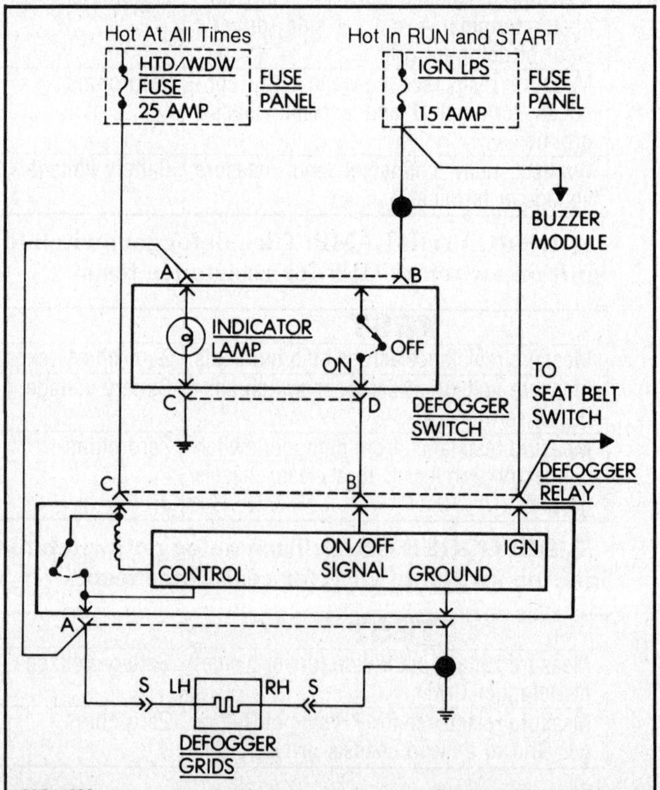
Hot At All Times
Hot In RUN and START
HTD/WDW FUSE 25 AMP
FUSE PANEL
IGN LPS 15 AMP
FUSE PANEL
BUZZER MODULE
INDICATOR LAMP
OFF
ON
DEFOGGER SWITCH
TO SEAT BELT SWITCH
DEFOGGER RELAY
ON/OFF SIGNAL
IGN
CONTROL
GROUND
LH
RH
DEFOGGER GRIDS
90G14890
Courtesy of Chrysler Motors

Fig. 5: Defogger Wiring Schematic (Wrangler)

1991 SAFETY EQUIPMENT
Steering Column Switches

Cherokee, Comanche
Grand Wagoneer, Wrangler

TESTING

HEADLIGHT DIMMER SWITCH

Cherokee & Comanche - 1) Turn headlight switch off, and disconnect dimmer switch connector. Using an ohmmeter, measure resistance at dimmer switch connector between Red wire and ground. If reading is almost zero ohms (bulb filament), go to next step. If reading is not almost zero ohms, repair open in Red wire.

2) Measure resistance at dimmer switch between Violet/White wire and ground. If reading is almost zero ohms, replace dimmer switch. If reading is not almost zero ohms, repair open in Violet/White wire.

Grand Wagoneer - 1) Ensure headlight switch fuse (No. 9 fuse in fuse panel) is okay. Disconnect dimmer switch connector. Measure voltage at dimmer switch connector between Tan/Black wire and ground. If battery voltage is present, go to next step. If battery voltage is not present, repair open in Tan/Black wire between headlight switch and dimmer switch.

2) With headlight switch on and dimmer switch in LO position, measure voltage between Light Green wire and ground. If battery voltage is present, go to next step. If battery voltage is not present, replace dimmer switch.

3) With headlight switch on and dimmer switch in HI position, measure voltage between White/Red wire and ground. Battery voltage should be present. If battery voltage is not present, replace dimmer switch.

Wrangler - 1) Ensure No. 3 fuse in power distribution center is okay. Disconnect dimmer switch connector. Measure voltage at dimmer switch connector between Brown/White wire and ground. If battery voltage is present, go to next step. If battery voltage is not present, repair open in Brown/White wire between headlight switch and dimmer switch.

2) With headlight switch on and dimmer switch in LO position, measure voltage between Light Green wire and ground. If battery voltage is present, go to next step. If battery voltage is not present, replace dimmer switch.

3) With headlight switch on and dimmer switch in HI position, measure voltage between White/Red wire and ground. Battery voltage should be present. If battery voltage is not present, replace dimmer switch.

HAZARD SWITCH

1) Ensure fuse for hazard flasher is good. Measure voltage at fuse side of flasher (side terminal). If battery voltage is present, go to next step. If battery voltage is not present, repair open circuit between fuse and hazard flasher.

2) Replace hazard flasher. Lights should flash. If lights do not flash, measure voltage at turn signal switch connector between Violet/Tan wire and ground. If battery voltage is present, replace hazard/turn signal combination switch. If battery voltage is not present, repair open in Violet/Tan wire.

HORN

Cherokee & Comanche - 1) Inspect headlight delay fuse, and replace if necessary. Relay contacts should click when horn switch is depressed. If relay clicks, go to step **4)**. If relay does not click, remove relay located on bracket (3 relays) behind instrument panel. Measure voltage at relay connector between Gray/Orange wire and ground. If battery voltage is present, go to next step. If battery voltage is not present, repair open in Gray/Orange wire.

2) Depress horn switch. Measure resistance at relay connector between Black/Red wire and ground. If reading is zero ohms, go to next step. If reading is not zero ohms, repair horn switch ground.

3) Measure resistance at relay connector between Green/Red wire and ground. Reading should be almost zero ohms (horn resistance). If resistance is okay, replace relay. If resistance is not okay, repair open in circuit between relay and horns (Green/Red wire).

4) Disconnect horn connector. Depress horn switch. Measure voltage at horn connector between Green/Red wire and ground. If battery voltage is not present, go to next step. If battery voltage is present, replace horns.

5) Measure resistance between horn bracket and chassis ground. Reading should be zero ohms. If reading is not zero ohms, check mounting screw for corrosion, and repair or replace as necessary.

Grand Wagoneer - 1) Turn ignition on. Measure voltage at relay connector between Violet wire and ground. If battery voltage is present, go to step **3)**. If battery voltage is not present, go to next step.

2) Measure voltage at ignition switch between Violet wire and ground. If battery voltage is present, replace ignition switch. If battery voltage is not present, repair open in Violet wire or replace fuse link located between starter relay and ignition switch.

3) Depress horn switch. Measure voltage at relay connector between Orange/Black wire and ground. If reading is zero volts, go to next step. If battery voltage is present, check for open in Orange/Black wire between horn switch and relay. If wire is okay, repair or replace horn switch.

4) Measure voltage at relay connector between Gray/Orange wire and ground. If battery voltage is present, go to next step. If battery voltage is not present, replace relay.

5) Connect jumper wire between horn base and chassis ground. If horn operates, clean ground connections. If horn does not operate, replace horn.

Wrangler - 1) Check 20 amp fuse (No. 2 fuse) located in fuse panel below flashers. Replace fuse as necessary. Relay contacts should click when horn switch is depressed. If relay clicks, go to step **5)**. If relay does not click, go to next step.

2) Remove relay. Relay is taped in wiring harness above fuse panel. Measure voltage at relay connector between Red/White wire and ground. If battery voltage is present, go to next step. If battery voltage is not present, repair open in Red/White wire.

3) Depress horn switch. Measure resistance at relay connector between Orange/White wire and ground. If reading is zero ohms, go to next step. If reading is not zero ohms, repair horn switch ground.

4) Measure resistance at relay connector between Gray/Orange wire and ground. Reading should be almost zero ohms (horn resistance). If resistance is okay, replace relay. If resistance is not okay, repair open in Gray/Orange wire between relay and horns.

5) Disconnect horn connector. Depress horn switch. Measure voltage at horn connector between Gray/Orange wire and ground. If battery voltage is not present, go to next step. If battery voltage is present, replace horns.

6) Measure resistance at horn connector between Black wire and chassis ground. Reading should be zero ohms. If reading is not zero ohms, repair open in Black wire to ground.

IGNITION SWITCH

1) Remove ignition switch. See IGNITION SWITCH under REMOVAL & INSTALLATION. Using an ohmmeter or self-powered test light, check ignition positions for continuity between terminals. See IGNITION SWITCH TERMINAL CONNECTIONS table. *See Fig. 1.*

2) Identify ignition switch slide bar positions by locating alignment hole in flat portion of switch, adjacent to terminals. Starting from alignment hole end of switch, positions are ACC, OFF-LOCK, OFF, ON and START. Each position has a detent stop except START position, which is spring loaded. No resistance should be between any 2 connected terminals. If switch does not function as specified, replace switch.

IGNITION SWITCH TERMINAL CONNECTIONS

Switch Position	Continuity Between	Circuit Result
ACC	A & B 2	Connected
OFF-LOCK	.....	Open
OFF	.....	Open
ON	I 1 & B 1 [1]	Connected
	A & B 2 [1]	Connected
	I 3 & B 3 [1]	Connected
START	I 1, B 1 & S	Connected
	G 1 & G 2	Grounded

[1] - Terminals B 1, B 2 and B 3 are all connected to battery circuit.

1991 SAFETY EQUIPMENT
Steering Column Switches (Cont.)

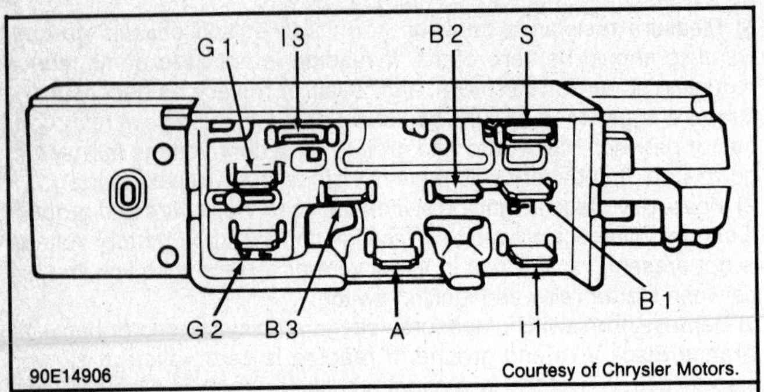
G 1
I 3
B 2
S
B 1
G 2
B 3
A
I 1
90E14906
Courtesy of Chrysler Motors.

Fig. 1: Locating Ignition Switch Terminals

TURN SIGNAL SWITCH

Cherokee & Comanche - 1) Remove and inspect 20 amp turn signal fuse (No. 4 fuse). Replace as necessary. Turn ignition switch to ACC position. Place turn signal switch in left turn signal position, and pull hazard switch out. Measure voltage at turn signal flasher between Yellow/Black wire (bottom terminal) and ground. If battery voltage is present, go to next step. If battery voltage is not present, repair open in Yellow/Black wire.

2) Replace turn signal flasher with 2-lamp, 12-volt rated flasher. Turn signals should flash. If turn signals do not flash, measure voltage at turn signal/hazard switch connector between Black wire and ground. If battery voltage is present, replace turn signal/hazard switch assembly. If battery voltage is not present, repair open circuit to hazard flasher.

Grand Wagoneer - 1) Remove and inspect HAZARD/STOP fuse (No. 5 fuse). Replace as necessary. Check operation of back-up lights. If back-up lights work, go to next step. If back-up lights do not operate, replace turn/back-up fuse (No. 1 fuse).

2) Turn ignition switch to ACC position. Place turn signal switch in left turn signal position, and pull hazard switch out. Measure voltage at turn signal flasher between Yellow/Black wire (bottom terminal) and ground. If battery voltage is present, go to next step. If battery voltage is not present, repair open circuit in Yellow/Black wire to fuse.

3) Replace turn signal flasher with 2-lamp, 12-volt rated flasher. Turn signals should flash. If turn signals do not flash, measure voltage at turn signal/hazard switch connector between Red wire and ground. If battery voltage is present, replace turn signal/hazard switch assembly. If battery voltage is not present, repair open circuit to hazard flasher.

Wrangler - Disconnect turn signal/hazard switch connector. Pull hazard switch on. Measure resistance at turn signal/hazard switch connector. Measure between specified wires with turn signal switch in correct position. See TURN SIGNAL SWITCH TEST (WRANGLER) table. If switch does not test as specified, replace switch.

TURN SIGNAL SWITCH TEST (WRANGLER)

Turn Signal Switch Position	Wire Color	Ohms
Left Turn	Violet & Yellow	Zero
	Violet & Light Blue	Zero
Right Turn	Violet & Dark Green	Zero
	Violet & Dark Blue	Zero

WIPER SWITCH

For testing information on wiper switch, see appropriate WIPER/WASHER SYSTEMS article.

REMOVAL & INSTALLATION

STEERING WHEEL

Removal & Installation - 1) Remove horn button. On sport steering wheel (round horn button), remove bushing, receiver and flex plate from steering wheel. On all models, remove steering wheel retaining nut. Mark steering wheel and shaft for reassembly reference. Using steering wheel puller, remove steering wheel.

2) To install, reverse removal procedure. Ensure marks are aligned. Tighten steering wheel nut to specification. See TORQUE SPECIFICATIONS table at end of article. Replace negative battery cable. Check horn and turn signal for correct operation. Reset clock and radio stations if necessary.

HORN BUTTON

Removal & Installation - 1) Disconnect negative battery cable. Place wheels in straight-ahead position. On standard steering wheel, remove horn button retaining screws from rear of steering wheel. Disconnect wiring from horn button, and remove horn button.

2) On sport steering wheel (round horn button), remove horn button by pulling button upward. If necessary, remove horn button internal components. Place components in order of removal. To install, reverse removal procedure.

IGNITION SWITCH

Removal - Remove lower instrument panel trim panel. Remove 2 steering column support nuts and lower steering column. Remove screws holding ignition switch to column, and lift switch off lock rod. Remove Black harness connector first, and then remove White harness connector from switch.

Installation - 1) Move position slider of switch to ACC position. Starting from alignment hole end of switch, positions are ACC, OFF-LOCK, OFF, ON and START. START position is spring loaded.

2) Position switch onto actuator rod, and loosely install switch to column bracket. Turn ignition key to ACC position and hold it there. Push switch slightly down column to remove slack in rod. Tighten switch hold-down screws.

3) Reconnect White and then Black harness connectors. Turn ignition key to test all positions, and adjust if necessary. Install 2 steering column support nuts, and install trim panel.

LOCK CYLINDER

Removal - 1) Disconnect negative battery cable. Remove horn/trim cover retaining screws from back of steering wheel. Remove steering wheel. Disconnect horn wiring. On sport steering wheel (round horn button), pull button upward, and remove horn components.

2) Remove steering wheel retaining nut and vibration dampener. Mark steering shaft and steering wheel for reassembly reference. Use proper steering wheel puller to avoid damaging shaft or threads.

3) Remove lock plate plastic cover. Compress lock plate with Lock Plate Compressor (J-23653 for standard threads or J-23653-4 for Metric threads). *See Fig. 2.* Pry retaining snap ring from steering shaft groove, and slide snap ring toward compressor.

Lock Plate
Compressor
(J-23653)
Snap Ring
90J14893
Courtesy of Chrysler Motors.

Fig. 2: Removing Lock Plate & Snap Ring

1991 SAFETY EQUIPMENT
Steering Column Switches (Cont.)

4) Unscrew and remove compressor. Remove snap ring, lock plate, canceling cam and spring from steering shaft. Remove hazard warning switch knob from side of column by pushing inward on knob and turning counterclockwise. Remove turn signal switch retaining screw. Remove turn signal/wiper switch rod.

WARNING: Lock plate is held by high pressure spring. DO NOT remove snap ring without using lock plate compressor.

5) Disconnect wire harness connector on bracket at lower end of steering column. Remove 3 turn signal switch retaining screws. Pull switch outward toward end of shaft. DO NOT dislodge dimmer switch rod.
6) Insert paper clip below retainer so retainer is flattened. *See Fig. 3.* Using needle-nose pliers, remove key warning buzzer switch and contacts as an assembly.
7) Remove lock cylinder retaining screw. Insert ignition key into lock cylinder and turn to ON position. Pull out lock cylinder.

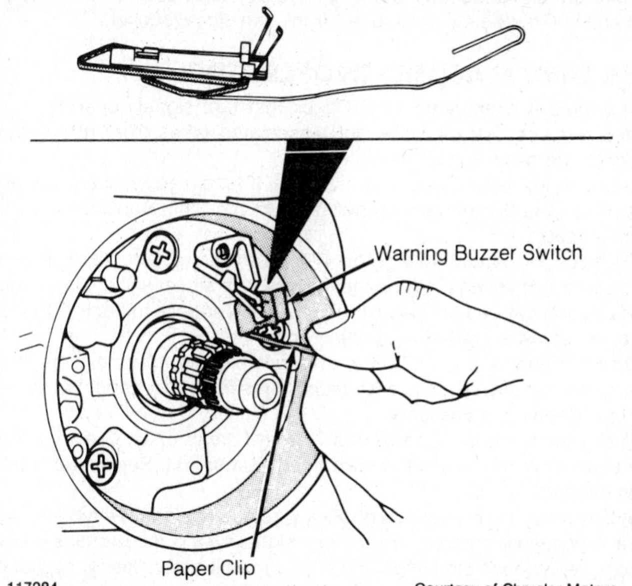
Warning Buzzer Switch
Paper Clip

117284 Courtesy of Chrysler Motors.

Fig. 3: Removing Warning Buzzer Switch

Installation – To install, reverse removal procedure. Ensure lock cylinder bottoms in bore and engages into gear for ignition switch rod by turning key. Fit warning buzzer, with contacts separated, in place. Before tightening screws, ensure dimmer switch rod is in socket in turn signal switch.

TURN SIGNAL & HAZARD FLASHER SWITCHES

Removal & Installation – **1)** Place front wheels in straight-ahead position. Disconnect negative battery cable. Remove steering wheel. See STEERING WHEEL under REMOVAL & INSTALLATION.
2) On column shift models, remove selector lever retaining pin and lever. On all models, use 2 screwdrivers to remove lock plate cover (if equipped). *See Fig. 4.*
3) Using lock plate compressor, compress lock plate. *See Fig. 2.* Remove and discard lock plate snap ring. Remove plate compressor.

WARNING: Lock plate is under strong spring tension. DO NOT attempt to remove snap ring without using lock plate compressor.

4) Remove lock plate, canceling cam, upper bearing preload spring and thrust washer. *See Fig. 4.* Depress hazard warning switch knob and rotate counterclockwise to remove.
5) On column shift models, remove gear selector cover and shift indicator light bracket screw. DO NOT remove light bracket. On tilt models, remove tilt lever.
6) On all models, disconnect switch wiring harness connector from bracket located at lower end of steering column. Wrap tape around connector for ease of switch removal.
7) Remove plastic protector from wiring harness (if equipped). Remove turn signal switch attaching screws and dimmer switch arm. Remove turn signal switch. To install, reverse removal procedure. Tighten turn signal switch screws to specification. See TORQUE SPECIFICATIONS table at end of article. Install NEW lock plate snap ring.

TORQUE SPECIFICATIONS

TORQUE SPECIFICATIONS

Application	Ft. Lbs. (N.m)
Steering Wheel Nut	25 (34)
	INCH Lbs. (N.m)
Turn Signal Mounting Screws	35 (4)

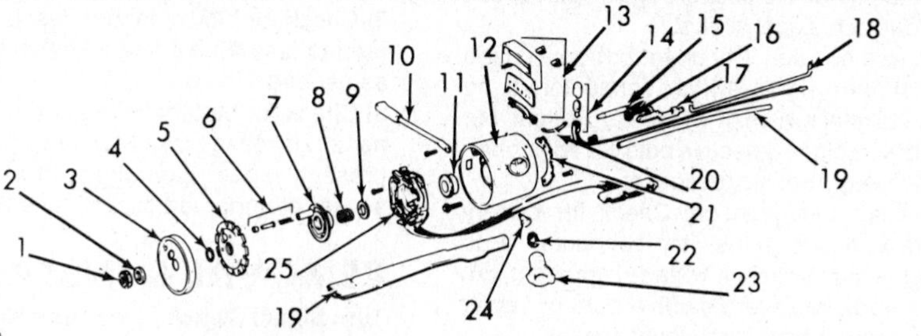
1
2
3
4
5
6
7
8
9
10
11
12
13
14
15
16
17
18
19
20
21
22
23
24
25
19

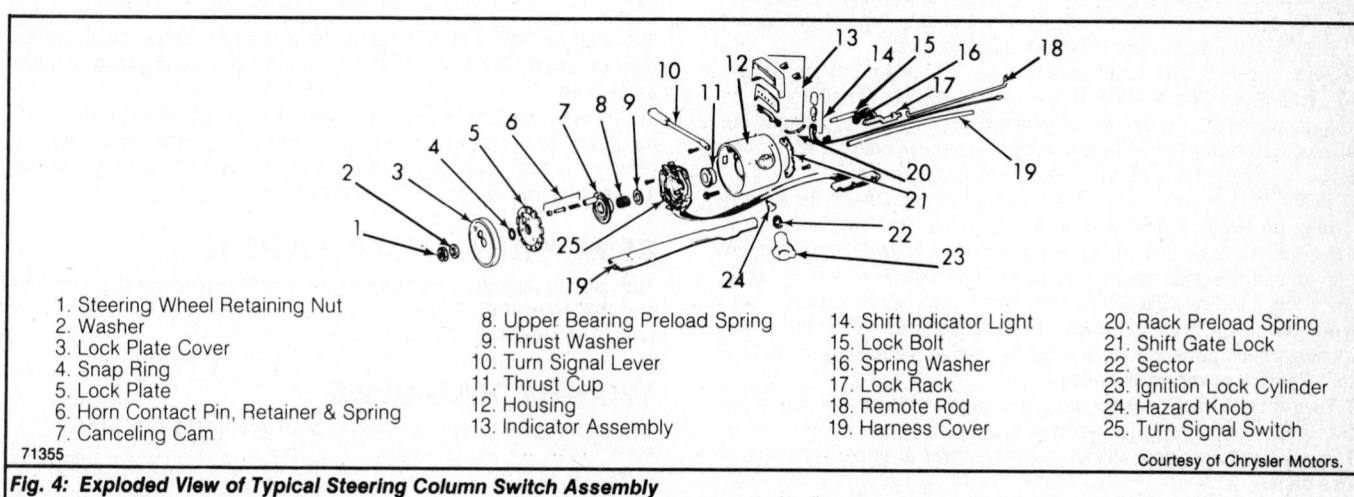

1. Steering Wheel Retaining Nut
2. Washer
3. Lock Plate Cover
4. Snap Ring
5. Lock Plate
6. Horn Contact Pin, Retainer & Spring
7. Canceling Cam
8. Upper Bearing Preload Spring
9. Thrust Washer
10. Turn Signal Lever
11. Thrust Cup
12. Housing
13. Indicator Assembly
14. Shift Indicator Light
15. Lock Bolt
16. Spring Washer
17. Lock Rack
18. Remote Rod
19. Harness Cover
20. Rack Preload Spring
21. Shift Gate Lock
22. Sector
23. Ignition Lock Cylinder
24. Hazard Knob
25. Turn Signal Switch

71355 Courtesy of Chrysler Motors.

Fig. 4: Exploded View of Typical Steering Column Switch Assembly

1991 SAFETY EQUIPMENT
Turn Signal & Hazard Flashers

Cherokee, Comanche, Grand Wagoneer, Wrangler

DESCRIPTION

The hazard flasher circuit is functional at all times. Turn signals are on a circuit separate from the hazard flashers, on a fuse controlled by the ignition switch.

TESTING

TURN SIGNALS INOPERATIVE

Cherokee & Comanche – 1) Check for blown turn signal/back-up lights fuse. If fuse is okay, check battery feed to fuse. Substitute a known good flasher unit. Replace or repair as needed.

2) Turn ignition on. Check for battery voltage on terminal "D" (Black wire) on turn signal switch connector. If no voltage is present, repair open circuit in Black wire to turn signal flasher socket at upper left of fuse panel.

3) Set turn signal lever to right turn position. Check for battery voltage on terminal "F" (Tan wire) on turn signal switch connector. If no voltage is present, replace turn signal switch. If voltage is present, but right turn signals still don't work, replace defective bulbs or repair open circuit in Tan wire to right turn signal sockets.

3) Set turn signal lever to left turn position. Check for battery voltage on terminal "G" (Light Green wire) on turn signal switch connector. If no voltage is present, replace turn signal switch. If voltage is present, but left turn signals still don't work, replace defective bulbs or repair open circuit in Light Green wire to left turn signal sockets.

Grand Wagoneer – 1) Check for blown turn signal/back-up lights fuse. If fuse is okay, check battery feed to fuse. Substitute a known good flasher unit. Replace or repair as needed.

2) Turn ignition on. Check for battery voltage on Red/Tracer wire at turn signal switch connector. If no voltage is present, repair open circuit in Gray wire to turn signal flasher socket at upper right side of fuse panel.

3) Set turn signal lever to right turn position. Check for battery voltage on Light Green wire at turn signal switch connector. If no voltage is present, replace turn signal switch. If voltage is present, but right rear turn signal doesn't work, replace defective bulb or repair open circuit in Brown/Red wire to right rear turn signal socket.

4) Leave turn signal lever in right turn position. Check for battery voltage on Green wire at turn signal switch connector. If no voltage is present, replace turn signal switch. If voltage is present, but right front turn signal doesn't work, replace defective bulb or repair open circuit in Brown/Red wire to right front turn signal socket.

5) Set turn signal lever to left turn position. Check for battery voltage on Light Green/Black wire at turn signal switch connector. If no voltage is present, replace turn signal switch. If voltage is present, but left rear turn signal doesn't work, replace defective bulb or repair open circuit in Gray/Black wire to left rear turn signal socket.

6) Leave turn signal lever in left turn position. Check for battery voltage on Green/Tracer wire at turn signal switch connector. If no voltage is present, replace turn signal switch. If voltage is present, but left front turn signal doesn't work, replace defective bulb or repair open circuit in Gray/Black wire to left front turn signal socket.

Wrangler – 1) Check for blown turn signal/back-up lights fuse. If fuse is okay, check battery feed to fuse. Substitute a known good flasher unit. Replace or repair as needed.

2) Turn ignition on. Check for battery voltage on Violet wire at turn signal switch connector. If no voltage is present, repair open circuit in Gray wire to turn signal flasher socket located at upper right side of fuse panel.

3) Set turn signal lever to right turn position. Check for battery voltage on Dark Green wire at turn signal switch connector. If no voltage is present, replace turn signal switch. If voltage is present, but right rear turn signal doesn't work, replace defective bulb or repair open circuit in Brown/Red wire to right rear turn signal socket.

4) Leave turn signal lever in right turn position. Check for battery voltage on Dark Blue wire at turn signal switch connector. If no voltage is present, replace turn signal switch. If voltage is present, but right front turn signal doesn't work, replace defective bulb or repair open circuit in Brown/Red wire to right front turn signal socket.

5) Set turn signal lever to left turn position. Check for battery voltage on Yellow wire at turn signal switch connector. If no voltage is present, replace turn signal switch. If voltage is present, but left rear turn signal doesn't work, replace defective bulb or repair open circuit in Gray/Black wire to left rear turn signal socket.

6) Leave turn signal lever in left turn position. Check for battery voltage on Light Blue wire at turn signal switch connector. If no voltage is present, replace turn signal switch. If voltage is present, but left front turn signal doesn't work, replace defective bulb or repair open circuit in Gray/Yellow wire to left front turn signal socket.

HAZARD FLASHERS INOPERATIVE

Cherokee & Comanche – 1) Check that turn signals operate. This step ensures that all bulbs and associated wires from turn signal switch are okay. Repair as necessary.

2) Check for blown hazard flasher fuse. If fuse is okay, check battery feed to fuse. Substitute a known good flasher unit. Replace or repair as needed.

3) Check for battery voltage on Violet/Tan wire at turn signal switch connector. If voltage is present, replace turn signal switch. If no voltage is present, repair open circuit in Violet/Tan wire to hazard flasher socket at lower right side of fuse panel.

Grand Wagoneer – 1) Check that turn signals operate. This step ensures that all bulbs and associated wires from turn signal switch are okay. Repair as necessary.

2) Check for blown hazard/stop fuse. If fuse is okay, check battery feed to fuse. Substitute a known good flasher unit. Replace or repair as needed.

3) Check for battery voltage on Pink wire at turn signal switch connector. If voltage is present, replace turn signal switch. If no voltage is present, repair open circuit in Violet/Tan wire to hazard flasher socket at upper left side of fuse panel.

Wrangler – 1) Check that turn signals operate to ensure that all bulbs and associated wires from turn signal switch are okay. Repair as necessary.

2) Check for blown hazard flasher fuse. If fuse is okay, check battery feed to fuse. Substitute a known good flasher unit. Replace or repair as needed.

3) Check for battery voltage on Brown wire at turn signal switch connector. If voltage is present, replace turn signal switch. If no voltage is present, repair open circuit in Violet/Tan wire to turn signal flasher socket at upper left side of fuse panel.

REMOVAL & INSTALLATION

Turn Signal Switch – For turn signal switch replacement procedure, see FRONT WIPER SWITCH under REMOVAL & INSTALLATION in WIPER/WASHER SYSTEMS article.

WIRING DIAGRAMS

See appropriate chassis wiring diagram in WIRING DIAGRAMS.

1991 SAFETY EQUIPMENT
Wiper/Washer Systems

Cherokee, Comanche, Grand Wagoneer, Wrangler

DESCRIPTION & OPERATION

All models except Grand Wagoneer use a standard wiper system with a 2-speed motor and electric washers. An optional system provides an intermittent cycle. A rear wiper/washer system is standard on Grand Wagoneer and optional on Cherokee and Wrangler.

ADJUSTMENTS

WIPER ARM ADJUSTMENT

Cherokee & Comanche – Ensure wiper shafts are in PARK position. Install driver side wiper arm onto pivot shafts so that end of wiper arm is .9-2" (23-52 mm) above lower windshield reveal molding. Install passenger side wiper arm so that its end is 1.3-2.4" (33-62 mm) above reveal molding. Blades should be parallel to lower reveal molding after installation. Install rear wiper arm (if equipped) so that midpoint of blade is .6-1.4" (15-35 mm) above lower window seal.

Grand Wagoneer – Ensure wiper shafts are in PARK position. Install driver side wiper arm onto pivot shafts so that end of wiper arm is 2-3" (51-76 mm) above lower windshield reveal molding. Install passenger side wiper arm so that its end is 1.5-3.5" (38-89 mm) above reveal molding. Blades should be parallel to wiper arms after installation. Install rear wiper arm so that it parks on rubber window molding just off glass.

Wrangler – Ensure wiper shafts are in PARK position. Install both wiper arms onto pivot shafts so that end of wiper arms are 4 1/4-5 1/8" (108-130 mm)) above lower windshield reveal molding. Blades should be parallel to each other after installation.

TESTING

FRONT WIPER MOTOR TEST

Cherokee & Comanche – **1)** Unplug wiper motor connector. Check for continuity between harness connector terminal No. 1 (Black wire) and ground. If not, repair open circuit in Black wire to ground. Reconnect wiring to motor.

2) Turn ignition switch to accessory position. With wiper switch in any position, check for battery voltage at harness connector terminal No. 4 (Light Green/Black wire). If battery voltage is not present, repair open circuit in Light Green/Black wire from fuse panel.

3) Set wiper switch to LO. Check for battery voltage at harness connector terminal No. 2 (Brown wire). If battery voltage is present, replace wiper motor. If battery voltage is not present, repair open circuit in Brown wire to wiper switch.

4) Set wiper switch to HI. Check for battery voltage at harness connector terminal No. 3 (Red/Yellow wire). If battery voltage is present, replace wiper motor. If battery voltage is not present, repair open circuit in Red/Yellow wire to wiper switch.

5) Check for battery voltage at harness connector terminal No. 5 (Tan/Red wire). Set wiper switch to OFF. Battery voltage should be present until wipers park, then drop to zero voltage. If okay, replace motor. If not, repair open circuit in Tan/Red wire to wiper switch.

Grand Wagoneer – **1)** Turn ignition switch to accessory position. With wiper switch in any position, check for battery voltage at harness connector terminal C (Light Green wire). If battery voltage is not present, repair open circuit in Light Green wire from fuse panel.

2) Set wiper switch to LO. Check for battery voltage at harness connector terminal "A" (White wire). If battery voltage is present, replace wiper motor. If battery voltage is not present, repair open circuit in White wire to wiper switch.

3) Set wiper switch to HI. Check for battery voltage at harness connector terminal "B" (Blue wire). If battery voltage is present, replace wiper motor. If battery voltage is not present, repair open circuit in Blue wire to wiper switch.

4) Check for battery voltage at harness connector terminal "D" (Tan wire). Set wiper switch to OFF. Battery voltage should be present until wipers park, then zero voltage. If okay, replace motor. If not, repair open circuit in Tan wire to wiper switch.

Wrangler – **1)** Unplug wiper motor connector. Check for continuity between harness connector terminal "E" (Black wire) and ground. If not, repair open circuit in Black wire to ground. Reconnect wiring to motor.

2) Turn ignition switch to accessory position. With wiper switch in any position, check for battery voltage at harness connector terminal "B" (Light Green/Black wire). If battery voltage is not present, repair open circuit in Light Green/Black wire from circuit breaker.

3) Set wiper switch to LO. Check for battery voltage at harness connector terminal "A" (White/Black wire). If battery voltage is present, replace wiper motor. If battery voltage is not present, repair open circuit in White/Black wire to wiper switch.

4) Set wiper switch to HI. Check for battery voltage at harness connector terminal "H" (Blue/Yellow wire). If battery voltage is present, replace wiper motor. If battery voltage is not present, repair open circuit in Blue/Yellow wire to wiper switch.

5) Check for battery voltage at harness connector terminal "D" (Tan/Red wire). Set wiper switch to OFF. Battery voltage should be present until wipers park, then zero voltage. If okay, replace motor. If not, repair open circuit in Tan/Red wire to wiper switch.

FRONT WIPER SWITCH TEST

NOTE: All terminals specified in this test are on wiper switch connector for vehicles with standard wipers. For vehicles with intermittent wipers, specified terminals are on switch side connector of intermittent module. Module is on lower instrument panel cover, near steering column.

1) Turn ignition on. Check for battery voltage on terminal "D"' White wire). If no voltage, repair open circuit in White wire from circuit breaker.

2) Set wiper switch to LO. Measure voltage at terminal "E" (Gray wire). If meter does not indicate battery voltage, replace switch.

3) Set wiper switch to HI. Measure voltage at terminal "C" (Purple wire). If meter does not indicate battery voltage, replace switch.

4) Measure voltage at terminal "F" (Yellow wire). Meter should indicate battery voltage. Set wiper switch to OFF. Meter should indicate battery voltage until wipers park, then zero. If not, replace switch.

5) For models with intermittent wipers, disconnect switch side connector from module. With an ohmmeter, measure resistance between terminals "A" (Dark Green wire) and "D" (White wire) while rotating switch from minimum to maximum delay. If resistance does not vary smoothly between 0-500,000 ohms, replace switch.

6) For models with intermittent wipers, disconnect switch side connector from module. With an ohmmeter, measure resistance between terminals "A" (Dark Green wire) and "G" (Brown wire) while rotating switch from minimum to maximum delay. If resistance does not vary smoothly between 0-500,000 ohms, replace switch.

FRONT WASHER MOTOR TEST

1) Unplug washer pump connector, under washer reservoir in engine compartment. Check for continuity between harness connector terminal "A" and ground. *See Fig. 1.* If no continuity exists, repair open circuit in Black wire to ground.

2) Connect a jumper wire between terminal "A" on washer pump and a known good ground. Supply battery voltage to washer pump terminal "B", using a jumper wire with a 15-amp in-line fuse. Replace pump if it does not operate.

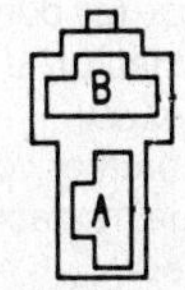
B
A

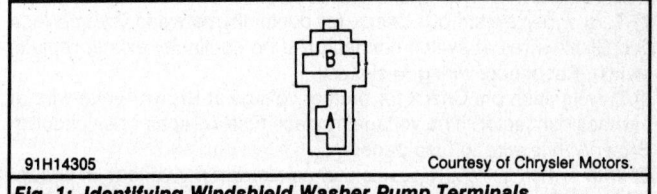

91H14305 Courtesy of Chrysler Motors.

Fig. 1: Identifying Windshield Washer Pump Terminals

1991 SAFETY EQUIPMENT
Wiper/Washer Systems (Cont.)

REAR WIPER MOTOR TEST

Cherokee - 1) Unplug harness connector at rear wiper motor. Check for continuity between Black wire on harness connector and ground. If there is no continuity, repair open circuit in Black wire to ground. Reconnect wiring to motor.

2) Turn ignition on. With rear wiper switch in any position, check for battery voltage at White wire at harness connector. If battery voltage is not present, repair open circuit in White wire from rear wiper switch.

3) Set rear wiper switch to WIPE. Check for battery voltage at Brown/Red wire at harness connector. If battery voltage is present, replace wiper motor. If battery voltage is not present, repair open circuit in Brown/Red wire to rear wiper switch.

Grand Wagoneer - 1) Unplug harness connector at rear wiper motor. Check for continuity between terminal "B" (Black wire) at harness connector and ground. If there is no continuity, repair open circuit in Black wire to ground. Reconnect wiring to motor.

2) Turn ignition on. With rear wiper switch in any position, check for battery voltage at terminal "A" (Red/Yellow wire) at harness connector. If battery voltage is not present, repair open circuit in Red/Yellow wire from rear wiper switch.

3) Set rear wiper switch to WIPER. Check for battery voltage at terminal "C" (Violet/Orange wire) at harness connector. If battery voltage is present, replace wiper motor. If battery voltage is not present, repair open circuit in Violet/Orange wire to rear wiper switch.

Wrangler - 1) Unplug harness connector at rear wiper motor. Check for continuity between terminal "B" (Black wire) at harness connector and ground. If there is no continuity, repair open circuit in Black wire to ground. Reconnect wiring to motor.

2) Turn ignition on. With rear wiper switch in any position, check for battery voltage at terminal "A" (Green wire) at harness connector. If battery voltage is not present, repair open circuit in Green wire from rear wiper switch.

3) Set rear wiper switch to WIPER. Check for battery voltage at terminal "C" (Green/White wire) at harness connector. If battery voltage is present, replace wiper motor. If battery voltage is not present, repair open circuit in Green/White wire to rear wiper switch.

REAR WIPER SWITCH TEST

Cherokee - 1) Turn ignition on. Check for battery voltage at terminal "B" (Light Blue/Red wire) at rear wiper switch harness connector. If no voltage, repair open circuit in Light Blue/Red wire to fuse panel.

2) With rear wiper switch in any position, check for battery voltage at terminal "D" (White wire). If no voltage is indicated at terminal "D" (White wire), replace switch.

3) With switch in WASH position, check for battery voltage at terminal "C" (Brown/Red wire). Repeat test with switch in WIPE position. If no voltage is indicated in each position, replace switch.

4) With switch in WASH position, check for battery voltage at terminal "A" (Black/White wire). If no voltage is indicated, replace switch.

Grand Wagoneer - 1) Turn ignition on. Check for battery voltage at terminal "B" (Brown/White wire) at rear wiper switch harness connector. If no voltage, replace fuse or repair open circuit in Brown/White wire to fuse panel.

2) With switch in WASH position, check for battery voltage at terminal "C" (Blue/Red wire). Repeat test with switch in WIPE position. If no voltage in each position, replace switch.

3) With switch in WASH position, check for battery voltage at terminal "A" (Violet/Orange wire). If no voltage, replace switch.

Wrangler - 1) Unplug harness connector at rear wiper switch. Check for continuity between Black wire at harness connector and ground. If no continuity exists, repair open circuit in Black wire to ground.

2) Turn wiper switch off. Check for continuity between Green/White and Black wires at switch connector. If no continuity exists, replace switch. Reconnect wiring to switch.

3) Turn ignition on. Check for battery voltage at Brown/White wire at harness connector. If no voltage, replace fuse or repair open circuit in Brown/White wire to fuse panel.

4) With switch in WASH position, check for battery voltage at Green/White wire at harness connector. Repeat test with switch in WIPER position. If no voltage, replace switch.

5) With switch in WASH position, check for battery voltage at Red/White wire at harness connector. If no voltage, replace switch.

REAR WASHER MOTOR TEST

1) Unplug washer pump connector, under washer reservoir in engine compartment. Check for continuity between harness connector terminal "A" (Black wire) and ground. If no continuity exists, repair open circuit in Black wire to ground.

2) Connect a jumper wire between terminal "A" on washer pump and a good ground. Supply battery voltage to washer pump terminal "B", using a jumper wire with a 15-amp in-line fuse. *See Fig. 1.* On all models except Grand Wagoneer, replace pump if it does not operate. For Grand Wagoneer, replace reservoir assembly.

REMOVAL & INSTALLATION

FRONT WIPER MOTOR

Removal & Installation (Cherokee & Comanche) - Remove wiper arms. Remove cowl trim. Disconnect washer hose. Remove cowl mounting bracket nuts and pivot pin screws. Disconnect wiring. Remove wiper motor. To install, reverse removal procedure. Adjust wiper blades. See WIPER ARM ADJUSTMENT.

Removal & Installation (Grand Wagoneer) - Remove motor adapter plate screws. Unplug wire harness connector. Remove drive link retaining clip and wiper motor. To install, reverse removal procedure. Adjust wiper blades. See WIPER ARM ADJUSTMENT under ADJUSTMENTS.

Removal & Installation (Wrangler) - 1) Remove top, if installed. Remove windshield hold-down bolts from lower corners of instrument panel. Remove wiper motor mounting screws. Disconnect wiper linkage drive arm. Remove wiper motor wire harness retaining clip. Pull motor and drive arm out through access hole.

2) Pry drive arm from motor pivot. DO NOT remove pivot attaching nut. Remove intermittent module bracket screws. Reach behind instrument panel to disconnect wiper motor harness. Remove wiper motor. To install, reverse removal procedure. Adjust wiper blades. See WIPER ARM ADJUSTMENT under ADJUSTMENTS.

FRONT WIPER SWITCH

Removal - 1) Disconnect negative battery cable. For vehicles with optional steering wheel, push and turn horn button to remove it. Remove retaining screws, bushing, receiver, flexplate and insulator. On all models, remove 3 retaining screws and steering wheel cover.

2) Disconnect horn wiring. Remove grounding pin by pulling it out gently. Remove steering wheel retaining nut and vibration damper. Mark steering shaft and steering wheel for reassembly reference. Using steering wheel puller, remove steering wheel.

CAUTION: Lock plate is retained by a high pressure spring. DO NOT remove snap ring without using a compressor tool.

3) Remove lock plate cover. Compress lock plate with Lock Plate Compressor (C4156). Remove lock plate retaining ring, lock plate, canceling cam and spring. On vehicles with optional steering wheel, remove horn button components from cancelling cam. Discard lock plate retaining ring.

4) Remove hazard warning switch knob, dimmer switch actuating arm screw and turn signal switch attaching screws. On all but Wrangler, remove lower instrument panel trim panel. On Wrangler, remove steering column shroud screws. Slide shroud toward steering wheel. On all models, apply pressure upward to shroud and downward to instrument panel to free holding tabs.

5) Remove cover under steering column. Remove PRNDL clip (if equipped). Remove 2 nuts and 4 bolts from steering column bracket. Loosen steering column brace nut at kick panel. Ease steering column downward.

6) Unplug wiper switch connector. Tape wires to wiper connector to ease harness removal. Remove wiring harness cover from column.

Pull turn signal switch out from column far enough for access to retaining screws.
7) Turn ignition switch on. Insert paper clip below key warning buzzer retainer to flatten retainer. Remove key warning buzzer and retaining clip as an assembly. DO NOT try to remove warning buzzer and retaining clip separately; clip could fall into column jacket.
8) Remove ignition lock cylinder retaining screw and lock cylinder. Remove attaching screws, housing and shroud. Ensure dimmer switch rod, lock pin and lock rack do not fall out. Remove turn signal/ wiper switch lever from housing. Remove wiper switch cover from rear of housing. Remove pivot screw and wiper switch.
Installation – 1) Install new switch. Push dimmer switch rod to ensure it is connected. Position housing to column. Ensure nylon spring retainer is forward of lock rack retaining slot. Position first tooth of gear so that it engages with first tooth of lock rack.
2) Install housing attaching screws and key lock cylinder. Carefully tighten screws while mating housing to column. Turn key to ensure lock pin extends fully when ignition switch is locked.
3) To complete installation, reverse removal procedure. Install new lock plate retaining ring. Ensure wires are flat against inside column. Ensure PRNDL cable clip is installed so that pointer aligns properly. Reinstall steering wheel and tighten nut to 25 ft. lbs. (34 N.m).

FRONT WASHER MOTOR

Removal & Installation (Except Grand Wagoneer) – Remove reservoir mounting screws and reservoir. Disconnect hose from pump. Drain reservoir. Remove filter nuts from inside reservoir. Remove washer pump motor. To install, reverse removal procedure.
Removal & Installation (Grand Wagoneer) – Remove reservoir mounting screws and reservoir. Disconnect hose from pump. Drain reservoir. Since washer pump motor is not replaceable separately, replace reservoir. To install, reverse removal procedure.

REAR WIPER MOTOR

Removal & Installation (Cherokee) – Remove wiper arm. Slide clip along hose to remove it from hose mounting. Disconnect hose. Remove pivot pin retaining nut. Remove liftgate trim panel. Disconnect wiring harness. Remove mounting screws and wiper motor. To install, reverse removal procedure.
Removal & Installation (Grand Wagoneer) – 1) Remove retaining nut and wiper arm. Remove pivot assembly retaining nut. Remove tailgate carpet and access cover. Lower tailgate.
2) While supporting glass, press safety switch on left side of tailgate and operate window switch to raise glass. Unplug motor connector. Remove reinforcement panel nut. Remove wiper motor. To install, reverse removal procedure. Tighten wiper retaining nut to 90 INCH-lbs. (10 N.m).
Removal & Installation (Wrangler) – Remove wiper arm. Remove pivot shaft retaining nut and trim cover. Unplug electrical connector. Remove mounting screws and wiper motor. To install, reverse removal procedure.

REAR WIPER SWITCH

Removal & Installation (Cherokee) – Disconnect negative battery cable. Remove 4 instrument bezel retaining screws. Pull bezel away from snap attachments. Remove switch housing panel. Unplug switch connector. Press mounting tabs and remove switch. To install, reverse removal procedure.
Removal & Installation (Grand Wagoneer) – Remove 4 screws which retain steering column to bezel. Lower bezel. Unplug connector from switch. Press retaining tangs and remove switch. To install, reverse removal procedure.
Removal & Installation (Wrangler) – Disconnect negative battery cable. Remove 6 instrument panel shroud screws. Slide shroud toward steering wheel. Pull bulb socket from bulb retainer. Press shroud upward and indicator panel downward to release holding tabs. Place shroud under steering column. Remove switch housing panel. Press switch mounting tabs and remove switch. To install, reverse removal procedure.

REAR WASHER MOTOR

Removal & Installation (Except Grand Wagoneer) – Remove reservoir mounting screws and reservoir. Disconnect hose from pump. Drain reservoir. Remove filter nuts from inside reservoir. Remove washer pump motor. To install, reverse removal procedure.
Removal & Installation (Grand Wagoneer) – Remove reservoir mounting screws and reservoir. Disconnect hose from pump. Drain reservoir. Since washer pump motor is not replaceable separately, replace reservoir. To install, reverse removal procedure.

WIRING DIAGRAMS

See appropriate chassis wiring diagram in WIRING DIAGRAMS.

1991 ENGINES
2.5L 4-Cylinder

Cherokee, Comanche, Wrangler

NOTE: For repair procedures not covered in this article, see ENGINE OVERHAUL PROCEDURES article in GENERAL INFORMATION.

ENGINE IDENTIFICATION

Engine can be identified by eighth character of Vehicle Identification Number (VIN). The VIN is stamped on a plate attached to top left corner of instrument panel.

Engine code is on a machined surface on right side of cylinder block between No. 3 and 4 cylinders. This code may be required when ordering replacement parts.

ENGINE IDENTIFICATION CODE

Engine	Code
2.5L PFI	P

Some engines are manufactured with oversize or undersize components. These engines are identified by a letter code stamped on oil filter boss near distributor. Letters are decoded as follows:

- "B" indicates all cylinder bores .010" (.25 mm) oversize.
- "C" indicates all camshaft bearing bores .010" (.25 mm) oversize.
- "M" indicates all main bearing journals .010" (.25 mm) undersize.
- "P" indicates one or more connecting rod journals .010" (.25 mm) undersize.
- "PM" indicates all crankshaft main bearing journals and one or more connecting rod journals .010" (.25 mm) undersize.

ADJUSTMENTS

VALVE CLEARANCE ADJUSTMENT

No periodic valve adjustment is required.

REMOVAL & INSTALLATION

NOTE: For reassembly reference, label all electrical connectors, vacuum hoses and fuel lines before removal. Also place mating marks on engine hood and other major assemblies before removal.

FUEL PRESSURE RELEASE

CAUTION: Fuel system is under constant pressure. This pressure must be released before disconnecting or servicing any fuel supply or return system component. Wear proper eye protection when releasing fuel system pressure.

Disconnect negative battery cable. Remove fuel filler cap. Remove cap from pressure test port on fuel rail. *See Fig. 1.* Place shop towels around pressure test port to absorb spilled fuel. Press test port valve with a small screwdriver or punch wrapped in shop towels. Remove shop towels and dispose of properly. Install pressure test port cap.

CAUTION: Always replace "O" rings, spacers and retainers whenever fuel system quick-connect fittings are disconnected. Ensure fuel connections are secure by verifying that only retainer tabs protrude from connectors, and by pulling on tubes to verify that they are secure.

COOLING SYSTEM BLEEDING

CAUTION: Engine coolant may be hot. Avoid scalding by using care. Carefully release system pressure before removing radiator cap or drain cock.

Refill cooling system. Remove coolant temperature sensor to bleed air from system while filling.

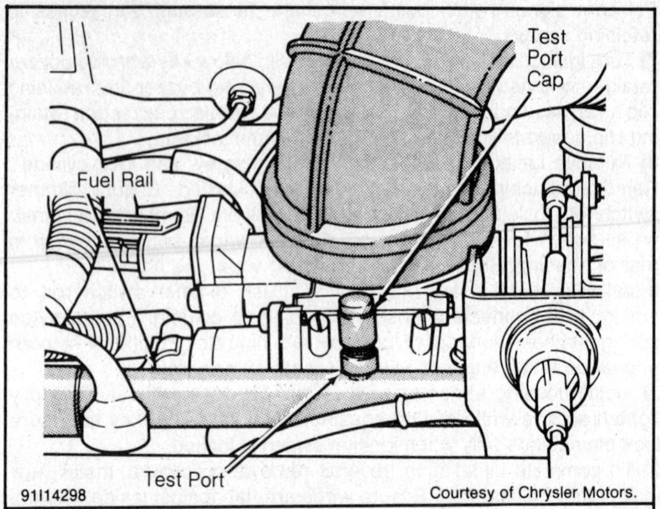
Test
Port
Cap
Fuel Rail
Test Port
91I14298
Courtesy of Chrysler Motors.

Fig. 1: Locating Fuel Pressure Bleeding Test Port

ENGINE

Removal (Cherokee & Comanche) – 1) Remove battery and air cleaner. Remove hood. Drain cooling system. Remove radiator hoses, coolant recovery hose and fan shroud. Disconnect transmission fluid cooler lines (if equipped).

2) Discharge A/C system (if equipped). Remove A/C condenser (if equipped) and radiator. Remove fan. Install a 5/16" x 1/2" bolt through fan pulley into water pump flange to maintain pulley and water pump alignment.

3) Disconnect heater hoses, throttle linkage, cruise control cable (if equipped) and throttle valve rod. Disconnect wires from starter solenoid and all fuel injection harness connections.

4) Release fuel pressure. See FUEL PRESSURE RELEASE under REMOVAL & INSTALLATION. Disconnect fuel supply and return lines at throttle body. Disconnect TDC sensor wire connector. Remove A/C service valves and cap compressor ports (if equipped).

5) Remove vacuum check valve from power brake booster (if equipped). Disconnect power steering hoses at steering gear (if equipped). Drain power steering pump reservoir. Cap power steering hoses and fittings.

6) Tag and disconnect any remaining hoses or electrical connectors. Raise and support vehicle. Disconnect exhaust pipe from exhaust manifold. Remove starter and flywheel cover.

7) On automatic transmission equipped models, mark converter and drive plate for installation reference. Remove converter-to-drive plate bolts. On all models, remove upper bellhousing bolts and loosen bottom bolts. Remove engine mount bolts.

8) Remove engine shock damper bracket. Lower vehicle. Attach lifting device to engine. Raise engine from front supports. Place support under bellhousing. Remove remaining bellhousing bolts. Remove engine.

Removal (Wrangler) – 1) Drain cooling system. Pad windshield with cloth. Raise hood and rest it against windshield frame. Remove battery. Disconnect wiring from alternator, ignition coil, distributor, oil pressure sender and fuel injection wire harness.

2) Disconnect fuel line quick-connect couplings at left inner fender panel. Remove engine ground strap. Remove air cleaner. Disconnect vacuum purge hose from vapor canister tee. Unplug idle speed actuator connector. Disconnect throttle cable and remove it from bracket.

3) Disconnect throttle rod at bellcrank. Unplug oxygen (O_2) sensor connector. Disconnect coolant hoses at radiator, intake manifold and thermostat housing. Remove fan shroud and radiator. Remove fan and spacer. Install a 5/16" x 1/2" bolt through fan pulley into water pump flange to maintain pulley and water pump alignment.

4) Remove check valve from power brake booster (if equipped). Disconnect power steering hoses at steering gear (if equipped). Drain power steering pump reservoir. Cap power steering hoses and fittings.

5) Tag and disconnect any remaining hoses or electrical connectors. Raise and support vehicle. Disconnect exhaust pipe from exhaust manifold. Remove starter. Remove flywheel housing access cover. Remove engine mount through-bolts. Remove upper bellhousing bolts. Loosen lower bellhousing bolts.

6) Lower vehicle. Attach lifting device to engine. Raise engine from front supports. Place support under bellhousing. Remove remaining bellhousing bolts. Lift engine from engine compartment.

Installation (All Models) - Remove engine mount cushions from brackets to aid alignment of engine and transmission. To complete installation, reverse removal procedure. Adjust throttle and cruise control linkage (if equipped). Tighten bolts to specification. See TORQUE SPECIFICATIONS table at end of article. Refill and check fluid levels.

INTAKE MANIFOLD

Removal - 1) Disconnect negative battery cable. Remove air inlet hose at throttle body and air cleaner. Remove power steering pump with hoses attached and wire it aside.

2) Release fuel pressure. See FUEL PRESSURE RELEASE under REMOVAL & INSTALLATION. Remove power steering pump brackets at water pump and intake manifold. Disconnect fuel supply and return lines at fuel rail.

3) Disconnect accelerator cable. Unplug cruise control connector at throttle body, using finger pressure only. Remove crankcase ventilation and manifold pressure sensor hoses. Tag and disconnect all wiring and hoses.

4) Remove bolts No. 2 through 5 securing intake manifold to cylinder head. *See Fig. 2.* Slightly loosen bolt No. 1 and nuts No. 6 and 7. Remove intake manifold. Drain coolant from manifold.

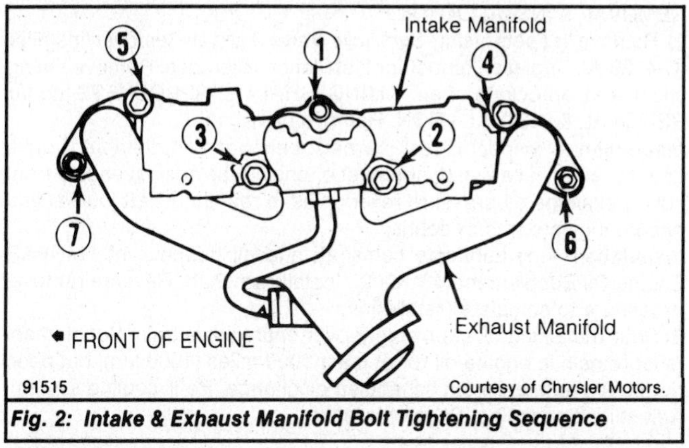
Intake Manifold
5
1
4
3
2
7
6
FRONT OF ENGINE
Exhaust Manifold
91515
Courtesy of Chrysler Motors.

Fig. 2: Intake & Exhaust Manifold Bolt Tightening Sequence

Installation - Ensure all gasket surfaces are clean. Install intake manifold. Finger-tighten all bolts. Tighten intake manifold bolts to specification in correct sequence. *See Fig. 2.* Also see TORQUE SPECIFICATIONS table at end of article. To complete installation, reverse removal procedure. Fill and bleed cooling system.

EXHAUST MANIFOLD

Removal - Disconnect negative battery cable. Remove intake manifold. See INTAKE MANIFOLD under REMOVAL & INSTALLATION. Raise and support vehicle. Disconnect exhaust pipe from exhaust manifold. Lower vehicle. Remove retaining nuts and bolts. Remove exhaust manifold.

Installation - 1) Clean all gasket surfaces. Install intake and exhaust manifolds together, using new gasket. Ensure exhaust manifold is centrally located over end studs and spacer. Tighten bolt No. 1 to specification. Tighten bolts No. 2 through 5 to specification and in sequence.

2) Install new spacers over cylinder head studs. Tighten nuts No. 6 and 7 to specification. *See Fig. 2.* Also see TORQUE SPECIFICATIONS table at end of article. To complete installation, reverse removal procedure. Start engine and check for leaks.

CYLINDER HEAD

Removal - 1) Disconnect negative battery cable. Drain cooling system. Remove accessory drive belt. Remove A/C compressor (if equipped) and wire it aside. DO NOT discharge A/C system. Remove air cleaner.

2) Remove A/C mounting bracket-to-cylinder head bolts. Loosen A/C mounting bracket-to-cylinder block bolts. Disconnect upper radiator hose and heater hoses. Remove valve cover.

3) Remove rocker arms, bridges, pivots and push rods. Tag all parts for installation reference. See ROCKER ARMS under REMOVAL & INSTALLATION. Remove manifolds. See INTAKE MANIFOLD and EXHAUST MANIFOLD under REMOVAL & INSTALLATION.

4) Tag and disconnect spark plug wires. Remove spark plugs. Remove cylinder head bolts. Remove cylinder head. Stuff clean lint free shop towels into cylinder bores.

Inspection - 1) Inspect cylinder head for cracks or damage. Using straightedge, check cylinder head for warpage in several areas. Repair or replace cylinder head if warpage exceeds specification or damage exists. See CYLINDER HEAD table under ENGINE SPECIFICATIONS at end of article.

2) Cylinder head bolts may be REUSED ONLY ONCE. If this is the first time cylinder head has been removed, put a dab of paint on the head of each bolt. If the bolts already have paint on them, or if it is unknown whether they have been used before, DISCARD THEM and replace with new ones.

Installation - 1) Clean carbon from combustion chambers and tops of pistons. Ensure all gasket surfaces are clean. Install new cylinder head gasket with numbers or word TOP upward. DO NOT apply sealant to cylinder head gasket. Ensure all holes align.

2) Install cylinder head. Apply sealing compound to threads of cylinder head bolt No. 7 before installation. Install cylinder head bolts. Tighten all bolts in 3 stages and in sequence to specification. *See Fig. 3.* See TORQUE SPECIFICATIONS table at end of article.

NOTE: During the final tightening sequence, bolt No. 7 will be tightened to a lower torque than the others.

3) To complete installation, reverse removal procedure. Install all valve train components into their original locations. Refill cooling system. Remove coolant temperature sensor to bleed air from system while filling.

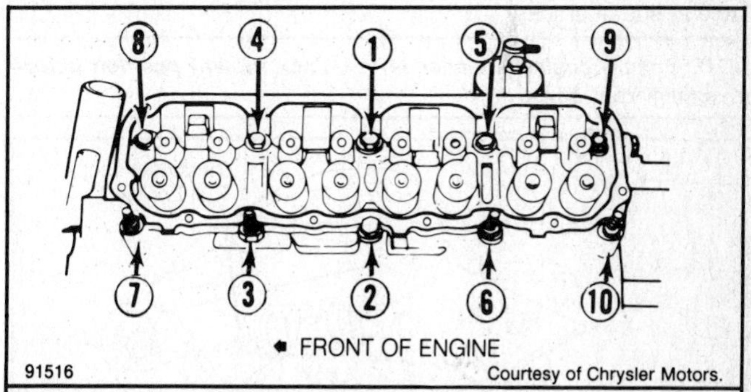
8
4
1
5
9
7
3
2
6
10
FRONT OF ENGINE
91516
Courtesy of Chrysler Motors.

Fig. 3: Cylinder Head Bolt Tightening Sequence

FRONT COVER OIL SEAL

Removal & Installation - 1) Remove drive belt. Remove vibration damper. Remove radiator shroud. Remove seal from front cover. Apply sealant to outer diameter of new seal. Coat crankshaft lightly with oil.

2) Drive seal into front cover, using Front Cover Aligner/Seal Installer (6139). Lightly coat seal contact area of vibration damper with oil. Lubricate vibration damper bolt with oil before installation. Reverse removal procedure to complete installation. See TORQUE SPECIFICATIONS table at end of article.

1991 ENGINES
2.5L 4-Cylinder (Cont.)

TIMING CHAIN & SPROCKETS

Removal - 1) Disconnect negative battery cable. Remove drive belt, fan and hub assembly. Remove fan shroud. Remove accessory drive brackets attached to timing case cover. Remove A/C compressor (if equipped) with hoses attached and wire it aside. DO NOT discharge A/C system. Remove alternator bracket assembly from cylinder head.

2) Remove vibration damper retaining bolt and washer. Remove vibration damper and key. Remove front cover retaining bolts and front cover. Cut oil pan gasket flush with face of cylinder block. Remove cut-off pieces.

3) Rotate crankshaft until timing marks on crankshaft and camshaft sprockets align. *See Fig. 4.* Remove oil slinger and camshaft sprocket retaining bolt. Remove sprockets and chain as an assembly. Remove front cover oil seal.

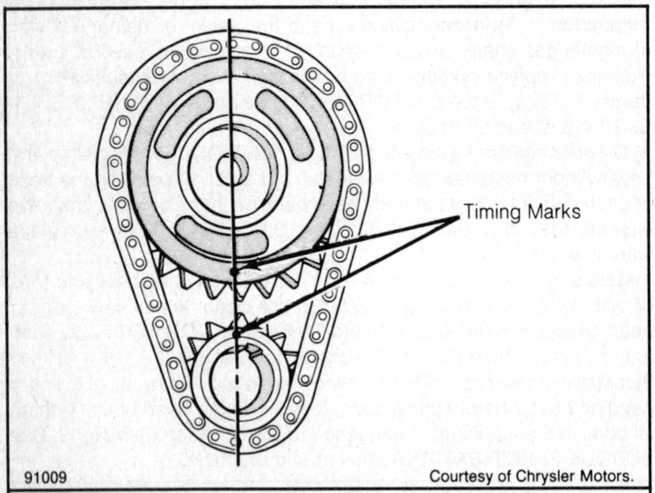
Timing Marks
91009
Courtesy of Chrysler Motors.

Fig. 4: Aligning Sprocket Timing Marks

Installation - 1) Turn tensioner lever down to unlock position. Pull tensioner block toward lever to compress spring. Turn lever up to lock position. *See Fig. 5.* Install timing chain and sprockets as an assembly. Ensure timing marks align. Install camshaft sprocket retaining bolt and washer. Tighten to specification. See TORQUE SPECIFICATIONS table at end of article.

NOTE: Ensure chain tensioner is in unlock (down) position before installing front cover.

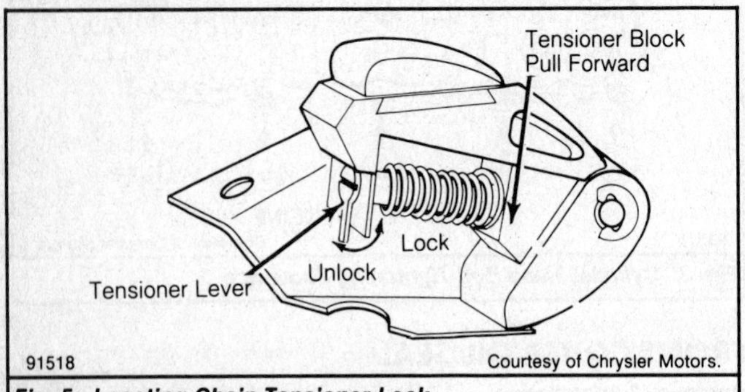
Tensioner Block
Pull Forward
Lock
Unlock
Tensioner Lever
91518
Courtesy of Chrysler Motors.

Fig. 5: Locating Chain Tensioner Lock

2) Verify proper installation by rotating crankshaft until timing mark on camshaft is at approximately one o'clock position. Timing sprockets are installed correctly if there are 20 timing chain pins between timing marks on both sprockets.

3) Clean all gasket surfaces. Install oil slinger. Apply sealing compound to both sides of front cover gasket. Install gasket onto cylinder block. Replace front section of oil pan seal with similar piece cut from new seal.

4) Coat new seal with RTV sealant and place into position. Apply sealant where oil pan and cylinder block meet. Place front cover onto cylinder block. Place Front Cover Aligner/Seal Installer (6139) in front engine cover seal area.

5) Install cover retaining bolts and tighten to specification. To complete installation, reverse removal procedure. Lubricate vibration damper retaining bolt before installation and tighten to specification. See TORQUE SPECIFICATIONS table at end of article.

ROCKER ARMS

Removal - Remove valve cover. See CYLINDER HEAD under REMOVAL & INSTALLATION. Alternately loosen cap screws one turn at a time to prevent damaging bridges. Remove bridges, pivots, rocker arms and push rods. Tag all parts for reassembly reference.

Installation - 1) Lubricate push rod ends with MOPAR Engine Oil Supplement (4318002). Install push rods into their original locations. Ensure bottom end of each push rod is centered in tappet.

2) Lubricate pivot contact area of each rocker arm with engine oil supplement. Install rocker arms, pivots and bridges into their original locations. Loosely install cap screws, then tighten alternately one turn at a time to specification. Reverse removal procedure to complete installation.

3) Pour remaining engine oil supplement over entire valve train. Supplement must remain in engine oil for at least 1000 miles (1600 km), but need not be drained until next scheduled oil change.

CAMSHAFT

Removal - 1) Disconnect negative battery cable. Drain cooling system. Discharge A/C system (if equipped). Remove A/C condenser (if equipped) and radiator. Mark distributor and engine block for installation reference. Remove distributor and ignition wiring. Remove rocker arms, bridges, pivots and push rods. See ROCKER ARMS under REMOVAL & INSTALLATION.

2) Remove tappets using Hydraulic Valve Tappet Remover/Installer (C-4129-A). Tag each tappet for installation reference. Remove timing chain and sprockets. See TIMING CHAIN & SPROCKETS under REMOVAL & INSTALLATION. Remove camshaft.

Inspection - Inspect lobes, journals, bearings and distributor drive gear for wear. If camshaft sprocket or chain rubs against engine front cover, examine oil pressure relief holes in rear camshaft journal and ensure they are free of debris.

Installation - 1) Lubricate camshaft and dip tappets into MOPAR Engine Oil Supplement (4318002). Install camshaft. Reverse removal procedure to complete installation.

2) Pour remaining oil supplement over entire valve train. Supplement must remain in engine oil for at least 1000 miles (1600 km), but need not be drained until next scheduled oil change. Refill cooling system. Adjust ignition timing. Check for leaks.

REAR CRANKSHAFT OIL SEAL

Removal - Remove transmission, clutch housing and flywheel or flexplate. Pry oil seal from housing. Avoid damage to surrounding area.

Installation - Coat outer lip of replacement seal with engine oil. Using Seal Installer (6271), install seal flush with cylinder block. Use only new bolts when installing flywheel or flexplate. Ensure felt lip is inside flywheel mounting surface to avoid tearing seal. To complete installation, reverse removal procedure. Tighten flywheel or flexplate bolts to specification, then an additional 60 degrees. See TORQUE SPECIFICATIONS table at end of article.

WATER PUMP

Removal - Disconnect negative battery cable. Drain cooling system. Remove fan shroud and drive belts. Remove fan assembly. Disconnect heater hoses and lower radiator hose at water pump. Remove water pump retaining bolts. Remove water pump.

Installation - Install water pump. Tighten bolts to specification. See TORQUE SPECIFICATIONS table at end of article. Ensure pump turns freely. Ensure belt is installed correctly to prevent engine overheating because water pump rotates in wrong direction. To complete installation, reverse removal procedure. Fill and purge air from cooling system. Remove coolant temperature sensor to bleed air from system while filling.

OIL PAN

Removal – 1) Disconnect negative battery cable. Raise and support vehicle. Drain engine oil. Disconnect exhaust pipe at exhaust manifold. Disconnect exhaust pipe hanger at catalytic converter and lower exhaust pipe. Remove starter. Remove flywheel access cover.
2) Position jack stand directly under vibration damper. Place wooden block between damper and jack stand. Remove through-bolts from engine mounts. Raise engine enough to remove oil pan. Remove oil pan retaining bolts. Remove oil pan.
Installation – Install new seals and gaskets. To complete installation, reverse removal procedure. Tighten oil pan bolts to specification. See TORQUE SPECIFICATIONS table at end of article. Fill crankcase. Start engine and check for leaks.

OVERHAUL

CYLINDER HEAD

Inspection – Inspect for cracks in combustion chambers, coolant passages, ports and exhaust valve seats. Using straightedge, check cylinder head for warpage in several areas. Repair or replace cylinder head if warpage exceeds specification or damage exists. See CYLINDER HEAD table under ENGINE SPECIFICATIONS at end of article.
Valve Springs – Use Valve Spring Tester (J-22738-02) to test each valve spring. Measure free length of each valve spring. Replace valve springs that do not meet specifications. See VALVES & VALVE SPRINGS table under ENGINE SPECIFICATIONS at end of article.
Valve Stem Oil Seals – Replace valve stem oil seals if they have deteriorated or whenever valves are serviced. Oil seals are marked INT and EXH for intake and exhaust valves, respectively. Oversize oil seals must be used with valves having .015" (.38 mm) oversize stems.
Valve Guides – Measure diameter of valve guide approximately 3/8" (10 mm) from valve spring side of head, both parallel and at right angle to long axis of head. If difference between measurements exceeds .0025" (.063 mm), or if diameter exceeds specification by .003" (.08 mm), ream valve guide for oversize valve stem. See CYLINDER HEAD table under ENGINE SPECIFICATIONS at end of article. Reface valve seats after reaming valve guides.
Valve Seats – Reface valve seats to specification. Remove only enough metal to provide smooth finish. Use tapered stones to obtain specified seat width. *See Fig. 6.* Seat width runout should not exceed .0025" (.063 mm) after refacing. See CYLINDER HEAD table under ENGINE SPECIFICATIONS at end of article.
Valves – Reface valves to specification. At least 1/32" (.79 mm) margin must remain after refacing valve. Valve stem tip can be resurfaced and chamfered when worn. DO NOT remove more than .01" (.25 mm). See VALVES & VALVE SPRINGS table under ENGINE SPECIFICATIONS at end of article.

VALVE TRAIN

Rocker Arms – Inspect pivot and valve stem contact surfaces of each rocker arm. Replace any rocker arm that is scuffed, pitted, cracked or excessively worn.
Push Rods – Inspect push rods for excessive wear. If wear is excessive because of lack of oil, replace and inspect corresponding tappet for excessive wear. Roll push rods on a flat surface to check for straightness. If wear exists along length of push rod, inspect cylinder head for obstruction.

CYLINDER BLOCK ASSEMBLY

Piston & Rod Assembly – 1) Note locations of arrow on piston crown and oil squirt hole in connecting rod. Position piston and rod assembly on support. *See Fig. 7.* Press piston pin from piston. Discard pin. Piston pin CANNOT be reused after removal. Inspect piston pin bore in connecting rod for nicks or burrs and remove as necessary.
2) Clean piston pin bore and replacement piston pin. Piston and piston pin must be at room temperature when measuring fit. Piston pin should fall through piston at room temperature. If pin jams in pin bore, replace piston.

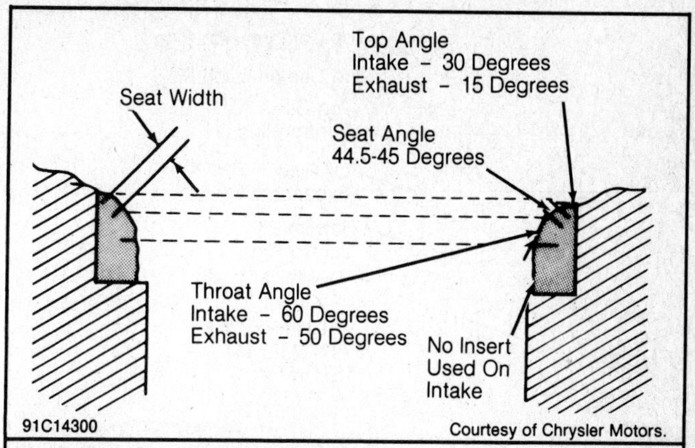
Top Angle
Intake - 30 Degrees
Exhaust - 15 Degrees
Seat Width
Seat Angle
44.5-45 Degrees
Throat Angle
Intake - 60 Degrees
Exhaust - 50 Degrees
No Insert
Used On
Intake
91C14300
Courtesy of Chrysler Motors.

Fig. 6: Checking Valve Seat Dimensions

3) Position piston on support so that arrow on piston crown will point to front of engine and connecting squirt hole will face camshaft when installed. Insert piston pin through piston pin bore and into connecting rod pin bore.
4) Press pin through rod and piston until pilot aligns with mark on support. Pin should be centered in rod. Piston pin installation requires approximately 2000 lbs. (900 kg) of force. Replace connecting rod if noticeably less force is required, or if rod moves on pin.

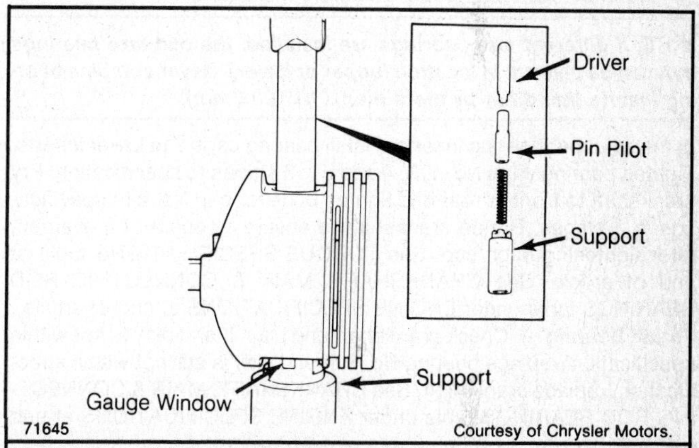
Driver
Pin Pilot
Support
Support
Gauge Window
71645
Courtesy of Chrysler Motors.

Fig. 7: Removing & Installing Piston Pin

Fitting Pistons – Measure cylinder bore 2 5/16" (59 mm) below top of bore. Measure piston diameter at right angle to piston pin at center line of pin. Piston clearance is difference between measurements. Pistons up to .004" (.10 mm) undersize may be enlarged by knurling or shot peening. Replace pistons if clearance is greater than .004" (.10 mm) or more.
Piston Rings – Install piston rings. DO NOT interchange piston rings. Top ring has a Gray scraping surface; second ring is Black. Ensure ring end gap and side clearance are within specifications. Position ring end gaps in specified area. Ring gaps may vary 20 degrees from locations illustrated. *See Fig. 8.* Also see PISTONS, PINS & RINGS table under ENGINE SPECIFICATIONS at end of article.
Rod Bearings – 1) Inspect bearings for wear or damage. Replace as necessary. Using Plastigage, check bearing clearance. See CRANKSHAFT, MAIN & CONNECTING ROD BEARINGS table under ENGINE SPECIFICATIONS at end of article. Bearings are available for standard and undersize applications.
2) If necessary, different size upper and lower bearings may be combined to obtain correct oil clearance. Tighten bolts to specification. Check rod side play. Rotate crankshaft to ensure freedom of movement. See TORQUE SPECIFICATIONS table at end of article. See CRANKSHAFT, MAIN & CONNECTING ROD BEARINGS table under ENGINE SPECIFICATIONS at end of article.

1991 ENGINES
2.5L 4-Cylinder (Cont.)

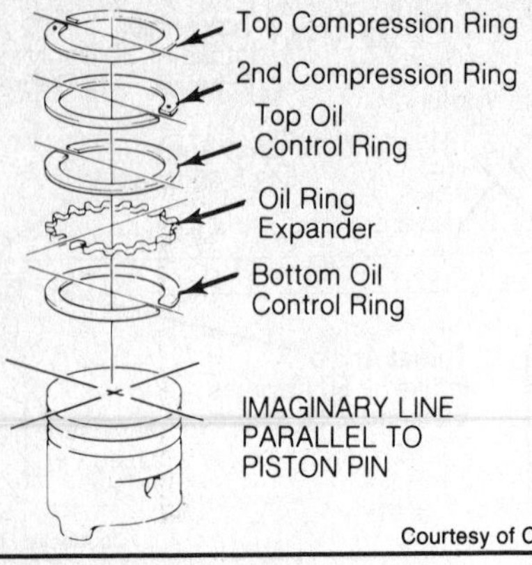
Top Compression Ring
2nd Compression Ring
Top Oil
Control Ring
Oil Ring
Expander
Bottom Oil
Control Ring
IMAGINARY LINE
PARALLEL TO
PISTON PIN
91520
Courtesy of Chrysler Motors.

Fig. 8: Positioning Piston Ring Gaps

NOTE: Never combine bearing inserts that differ by more than .001" (.03 mm) in size. Odd size inserts must be on bottom (rod cap) side.

Crankshaft & Main Bearings – 1) Inspect bearings for damage or wear. Replace as necessary. Using Plastigage, measure bearing clearance. See CRANKSHAFT, MAIN & CONNECTING ROD BEARINGS table under ENGINE SPECIFICATIONS at end of article. Bearings are available in standard and undersize. If necessary, different size upper and lower bearings may be installed to obtain correct oil clearance. Lubricate bearings before installation.

NOTE: If different size bearings are installed, the odd size bearings must all be uniform in location (upper or lower). Never combine bearing inserts that differ by more than .001" (.03 mm).

2) Install upper bearing inserts. Install bearing caps and lower inserts. Tighten bearing caps No. 1, 3, 4 and 5 in 3 stages to specification. Pry crankshaft to front or rear and tighten bolts for cap No. 2 to specification in 3 stages. Rotate crankshaft to ensure freedom of movement after tightening each cap. See TORQUE SPECIFICATIONS table at end of article. See CRANKSHAFT, MAIN & CONNECTING ROD BEARINGS table under ENGINE SPECIFICATIONS at end of article.

Thrust Bearing – Check crankshaft end play. If end play is not within specification, replace bearing No. 3. If end play is still not within specification, replace crankshaft. See CRANKSHAFT, MAIN & CONNECTING ROD BEARINGS table under ENGINE SPECIFICATIONS at end of article.

Cylinder Block – 1) Measure cylinder bore diameter crosswise to cylinder block near top of bore. Repeat measurement at bottom of bore. Subtract smaller diameter from larger diameter to determine taper. Repeat measurements for each cylinder.

2) Repeat measurements with measuring device rotated 120 degrees. Repeat this step for a total of 3 measurements. Cylinder out-of-round is the difference between measurements. Repeat for each cylinder.

3) Bore and hone cylinders for oversize pistons if taper or out-of-round exceeds specification. Move hone up and down to provide a 60-degree crosshatch pattern. DO NOT use a rigid hone or exceed 10 strokes per cylinder. See CYLINDER BLOCK table under ENGINE SPECIFICATIONS at end of article.

ENGINE OILING

ENGINE LUBRICATION SYSTEM

A distributor-driven pump supplies oil through a full-flow oil filter to an oil gallery on right side of block and intersecting lifter bores. Oil then flows to camshaft and crankshaft bearings. The rocker arms receive oil through the push rods and lifters.

Crankcase Capacity – Crankcase capacity is 4 qts. (3.8L) with oil filter change.

Oil Pressure – Normal oil pressure should be 25-35 psi (1.8-2.5 kg/cm²) at 800 RPM or 37-75 psi (2.6-5.3 kg/cm²) at 1600 RPM. Oil pressure relief occurs at 75 psi (5.3 kg/cm²).

OIL PUMP

Removal & Disassembly – Remove oil pump retaining bolts. DO NOT move oil pick-up pipe in pump body. If oil pick-up pipe is moved, pick-up pipe must be replaced to ensure an airtight seal. Remove pump cover. Disassemble pump.

Inspection – 1) Inspect for wear or damage. Place Plastigage across full width of each gear. Temporarily install cover and tighten bolts to 70 INCH lbs. (8 N.m). Remove cover. Examine Plastigage to determine end clearance.

2) Rotate gears and measure clearance between each tooth and oil pump body, directly opposite point of mesh. Replace oil pump if not within specification. See OIL PUMP SPECIFICATIONS table.

OIL PUMP SPECIFICATIONS

Application	In. (mm)
Gear End Clearance	.002-.006 (.05-.15)
Gear-to-Body Clearance	.002-.004 (.05-.10)

Reassembly & Installation – 1) Apply sealant to pick-up pipe and pump cover area prior to installation. To install pick-up tube, use Pipe Installer (7624). Ensure pick-up pipe support bracket is aligned with pump cover bolt. If relief valve is replaced, ensure replacement valve is same diameter as that removed.

2) Fill pump cavity with petroleum jelly. Install cover. Tighten cover bolts to specification. Check pump gears for freedom of rotation. Install new gasket and oil pump. Tighten retaining bolts to specification. See TORQUE SPECIFICATIONS table at end of article.

TORQUE SPECIFICATIONS

TORQUE SPECIFICATIONS

Application	Ft. Lbs. (N.m)
Camshaft Sprocket Bolt	80 (108)
Connecting Rod Cap Nuts	33 (45)
Cylinder Head Bolts [1]	
Stage 1	22 (30)
Stage 2	45 (61)
Stage 3	[2] 110 (149)
Drive Plate-To-Converter Bolts	40 (54)
Exhaust Manifold Bolts [3]	
Bolt No. 1	30 (41)
Bolt No. 2-5	23 (31)
Nut No. 6 & 7	30 (41)
Fan Bolts	18 (24)
Flexplate-To-Crankshaft Bolts	[4] 50 (68)
Flywheel-To-Crankshaft Bolts	[4] 50 (68)
Intake Manifold Bolts [3]	
Bolt No. 1	30 (41)
Bolt No. 2-5	23 (31)
Nut No. 6 & 7	30 (41)
Main Bearing Cap Bolts	
Stage 1	40 (54)
Stage 2	70 (95)
Stage 3	80 (108)
Oil Pump Retaining Bolts	
Long	17 (23)
Short	10 (14)
Oxygen (O_2) Sensor	35 (48)
Pulley-To-Vibration Damper Bolts	20 (27)
Rocker Arm Bolts	19 (26)
Throttle Body-To-Intake Bolts	16 (22)
Vibration Damper Bolt	[5] 80 (108)
Water Pump Bolts	13 (18)

[1] – Tighten in sequence. *See Fig. 3.*
[2] – All except bolt No. 7. Tighten bolt No. 7 to 100 ft. lbs (136 N.m).
[3] – Tighten bolts in sequence. *See Fig. 2.*
[4] – Tighten to specification and an additional 60 degrees.
[5] – With bolt cleaned and threads lubricated with oil.

1991 ENGINES
2.5L 4-Cylinder (Cont.)

TORQUE SPECIFICATIONS (Cont.)

Application	INCH Lbs. (N.m)
Front Cover-To-Block Bolts	62 (7)
Oil Pan Bolts	
1/4" X 20	80 (9)
5/16" X 18	132 (15)
Oil Pump Cover Bolts	70 (8)
Valve Cover Bolts	44 (5)

ENGINE SPECIFICATIONS

GENERAL SPECIFICATIONS

Application	Specification
2.5L	
Displacement	150 Cu. In. (2.5L)
Bore	3.88" (98.6 mm)
Stroke	3.19" (81.0 mm)
Compression Ratio	
Cherokee & Comanche	9.2:1
Wrangler	9.1:1
Fuel System	PFI
Horsepower @ RPM	
Cherokee	130 @ 5250
Comanche	128 @ 5250
Wrangler	123 @ 5250
Torque Ft. Lbs. @ RPM	
Cherokee	149 @ 3000
Comanche	147 @ 3000
Wrangler	139 @ 3250

CRANKSHAFT, MAIN & CONNECTING ROD BEARINGS

Application	In. (mm)
2.5L	
Crankshaft	
End Play	.0015-.0065 (.038-.165)
Runout	[1]
Main Bearings	
Journal Diameter	2.4996-2.5001 (63.490-63.503)
Journal Out-Of-Round	.0005 (.013)
Journal Taper	.0005 (.013)
Oil Clearance	.0010-.0025 (.025-.063)
Connecting Rod Bearings	
Journal Diameter	2.0934-2.0955 (53.172-53.226)
Journal Out-Of-Round	.0005 (.013)
Journal Taper	.0005 (.013)
Oil Clearance	.0015-.0025 (.038-.063)

[1] – Information not available from manufacturer.

CONNECTING RODS

Application	In. (mm)
2.5L	
Bore Diameter	
Pin Bore	.9288-.9298 (23.591-23.617)
Crankpin Bore	2.2080-2.2085 (56.083-56.096)
Center-To-Center Length	6.123-6.127 (155.52-155.62)
Maximum Bend	.003 (.08)
Maximum Twist	.006 (.15)
Side Play	.010-.019 (.25-.48)

PISTONS, PINS & RINGS

Application	In. (mm)
2.5L	
Piston	
Clearance	.0013-.0021 (.033-.053)
Diameter	[1]
Pins	
Diameter	.9304-.9309 (23.63-23.64)
Piston Fit	.0004-.0006 (.010-.015)
Rod Fit	Press Fit
Rings	
No. 1 & 2	
End Gap	.010-.020 (.25-.51)
Side Clearance	.001-.003 (.03-.08)
No. 3 (Oil)	
End Gap	.015-.055 (.38-1.40)
Side Clearance	.001-.010 (.03-.24)

[1] – Information not available from manufacturer. Replace pistons if piston clearance exceeds .004" (.10 mm).

CYLINDER BLOCK

Application	In. (mm)
2.5L	
Cylinder Bore	
Standard Diameter	3.875-3.877 (98.42-98.48)
Maximum Taper	.001 (.03)
Maximum Out-Of-Round	.001 (.03)
Minimum Deck Height	9.320 (236.73)
Maximum Deck Warpage	.008 (.20)

VALVES & VALVE SPRINGS

Application	Specification
2.5L	
Intake Valves	
Face Angle	45°
Head Diameter	1.90" (48.3 mm)
Minimum Margin	.031" (.79 mm)
Minimum Refinish Length	4.889" (124.18 mm)
Stem Diameter	.311-.312" (7.89-7.92 mm)
Valve Tip Maximum Refinish	.010" (.25 mm)
Exhaust Valves	
Face Angle	45°
Head Diameter	1.50" (38.1 mm)
Minimum Margin	.031" (.79 mm)
Minimum Refinish Length	4.917" (124.89 mm)
Stem Diameter	.311-.312" (7.90-7.92 mm)
Valve Tip Maximum Refinish	.010" (.25 mm)
Valve Springs	
Free Length	2.0" (51 mm)
Installed Height	[1]
Out-Of-Square	[1]
Pressure	Lbs. @ In. (kg @ mm)
Valve Closed	80-90 @ 1.64 (36.3-40.8 @ 41.7)
Valve Open	200 @ 1.216 (90.7 @ 30.9)

[1] – Information not available from manufacturer.

1991 ENGINES
2.5L 4-Cylinder (Cont.)

CYLINDER HEAD

Application	Specification
2.5L	
Cylinder Head Height	[1]
Maximum Warpage	.008" (.20 mm)
Valve Seats	
Intake Valve	
Seat Angle	44.5-45°
Seat Width	.040-.060" (1.02-1.52 mm)
Maximum Seat Runout	.0025" (.063 mm)
Exhaust Valve	
Seat Angle	44.5-45°
Seat Width	.040-.060" (1.02-1.52 mm)
Maximum Seat Runout	.0025" (.063 mm)
Seat Bore Diameter	[1]
Valve Guides	
Intake Valve	
Valve Guide I.D.	.313-.314" (7.95-7.98 mm)
Valve Stem-To-Guide Oil Clearance	.001-.003" (.03-.08 mm)
Exhaust Valve	
Valve Guide I.D.	.313-.314" (7.95-7.98 mm)
Valve Stem-To-Guide Oil Clearance	.001-.003" (.03-.08 mm)

[1] – Information not available from manufacturer.

CAMSHAFT

Application	In. (mm)
2.5L	
Bore Diameter	[1]
End Play	[2] 0 (0)
Journal Diameter	
No. 1.	2.029-2.030 (51.54-51.56)
No. 2.	2.019-2.020 (51.28-51.31)
No. 3.	2.009-2.010 (51.03-51.05)
No. 4.	1.999-2.000 (50.78-50.80)
Journal Runout	[3]
Lobe Height	[1]
Lobe Lift	.253 (6.43)
Oil Clearance	.001-.003 (.03-.08)

[1] – Information not available from manufacturer.
[2] – Engine running.
[3] – Information not available from manufacturer. Manufacturer specifies .001" (.03 mm) maximum base circle runout.

VALVE LIFTERS

Application	In. (mm)
2.5L	
Bore Diameter	.9055-.9065 (22.987-23.025)
Lifter Diameter	.9040-.9045 (22.962-22.974)
Oil Clearance	.001-.002 (.03-.05)

Cherokee, Comanche, Wrangler

NOTE: For repair procedures not covered in this article, see ENGINE OVERHAUL PROCEDURES article in GENERAL INFORMATION.

ENGINE IDENTIFICATION

The Vehicle Identification Number (VIN) is located on the upper left side of the dash and is visible through the windshield. The eighth character identifies engine size.

ENGINE IDENTIFICATION CODE

Engine	Code
4.0L PFI	S

Some engines are manufactured with oversize or undersize components. These engines are identified by a letter code stamped on a boss between ignition coil and distributor. Letters are decoded as follows:

- "B" indicates all cylinder bores are .010" (.25 mm) oversize.
- "C" indicates all camshaft bearing bores are .010" (.25 mm) oversize.
- "M" indicates all main bearing journals are .010" (.25 mm) undersize.
- "P" indicates one or more connecting rod journals are .010" (.25 mm) undersize.
- "PM" indicates all main journals and one or more rod journal are .010" (.25 mm) undersize.

ADJUSTMENTS

VALVE CLEARANCE ADJUSTMENT

No periodic valve adjustment is required.

REMOVAL & INSTALLATION

NOTE: For reassembly reference, label all electrical connectors, vacuum hoses and fuel lines before removal. Also place mating marks on engine hood and other major assemblies before removal.

FUEL PRESSURE RELEASE

CAUTION: Fuel system is under constant pressure. This pressure must be released before disconnecting or servicing any fuel supply or return system component. Wear proper eye protection when releasing fuel system pressure.

Disconnect negative battery cable. Remove fuel filler cap. Remove cap from pressure test port on fuel rail. *See Fig. 1.* Place shop towels around pressure test port to absorb spilled fuel. Press test port valve with a small screwdriver or punch wrapped in shop towels. Remove shop towels and dispose of properly. Install pressure test port cap.

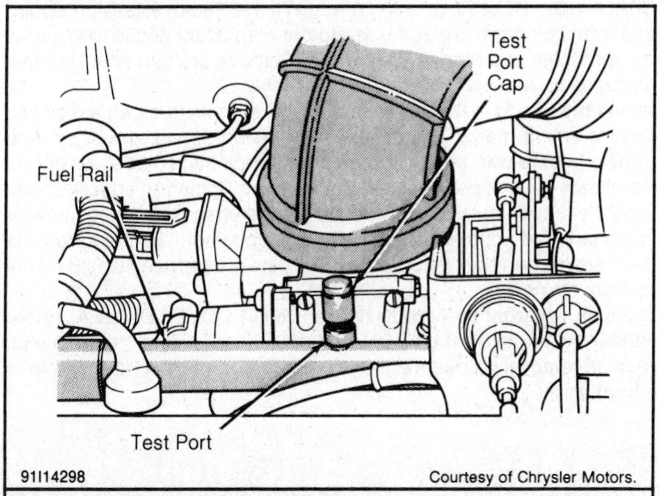
Test
Port
Cap
Fuel Rail
Test Port
91I14298
Courtesy of Chrysler Motors.

Fig. 1: Locating Fuel Pressure Bleeding Test Port

CAUTION: Always replace "O" rings, spacers and retainers whenever fuel system quick-connect fittings are disconnected. Ensure fuel connections are secure by verifying that only retaining tabs protrude from connectors, and by pulling on tubes to verify that they are locked into place.

COOLING SYSTEM BLEEDING

CAUTION: Engine coolant may be hot. Avoid scalding by using care. Carefully release system pressure before removing radiator cap or drain cock.

ENGINE

Removal – 1) Remove battery. Drain cooling system. Remove air cleaner. Unplug quick-connect vacuum hose fittings at intake manifold. Remove hood. Remove radiator hoses and radiator support. Remove fan shroud and electric fan. Unplug fan connector. Disconnect transmission cooler lines (if equipped). Remove radiator.

2) Discharge A/C system (if equipped). Remove A/C service valves. Cap compressor ports. Remove A/C condenser. Remove fan from idler pulley. Disconnect heater hoses at water pump and thermostat housing. Disconnect cruise control (if equipped) and throttle linkage. Disconnect distributor wiring, oil pressure wire and fuel injection wire harness at dash panel.

3) Disconnect line pressure cable to A/T (if equipped). Release fuel pressure. See FUEL PRESSURE RELEASE under REMOVAL & INSTALLATION. Disconnect fuel supply quick-connect fittings at fuel rail. Remove check valve from power brake booster (if equipped). Disconnect power steering hoses at steering gear (if equipped). Drain power steering pump reservoir. Cap power steering hoses and fittings.

4) Tag and disconnect any remaining vacuum hoses and electrical connectors as required. Raise and support vehicle. Disconnect exhaust pipe from exhaust manifold. Remove starter and flywheel cover. Disconnect engine speed sensor.

5) On A/T models, mark converter and drive plate for installation reference. Remove converter-to-drive plate bolts. Remove upper and loosen lower bellhousing bolts. Remove engine mount bracket bolts. Lower vehicle.

6) Attach lifting device to engine. Lift engine from front supports. Place support under bellhousing. Remove remaining bellhousing bolts. Remove engine.

Installation – 1) Remove engine mount cushions from brackets to aid alignment of engine and transmission. Replace fuel line quick-connect "O" rings, spacers and retainers.

2) Be careful not to damage trigger wheel on flywheel when installing engine into vehicle with automatic transmission. To complete installation, reverse removal procedure. Adjust throttle and cruise control linkage (if equipped). Tighten bolts to specification. See TORQUE SPECIFICATIONS table at end of article. Check and refill fluid levels.

INTAKE MANIFOLD

Removal – 1) Disconnect negative battery cable. Remove air inlet from throttle plate assembly. Remove air cleaner. Disconnect throttle and cruise control (if equipped) cables. Disconnect line pressure cable to A/T (if equipped).

2) Unplug all electrical connectors from intake manifold. Release fuel system pressure. See FUEL PRESSURE RELEASE under REMOVAL & INSTALLATION. Disconnect fuel line quick-connect fittings at fuel rail. Loosen accessory drive belt and tensioner.

3) Remove power steering pump and bracket. Wire pump aside. Remove fuel rail retaining bolts. Remove fuel rail and injector assembly. Raise and support vehicle. Disconnect exhaust pipe from manifold. Lower vehicle. Remove retaining bolts. Remove intake and exhaust manifolds as an assembly.

1991 ENGINES
4.0L 6-Cylinder (Cont.)

Installation - 1) Install new gasket. Install exhaust manifold and bolt No. 3, installed finger tight. Install intake manifold and remaining bolts loosely. Replace fuel line quick-connect "O" rings, spacers and retainers.
2) Tighten bolts to specification and in proper sequence. *See Fig. 2.* Reverse removal procedure to complete installation. See TORQUE SPECIFICATIONS table at end of article.

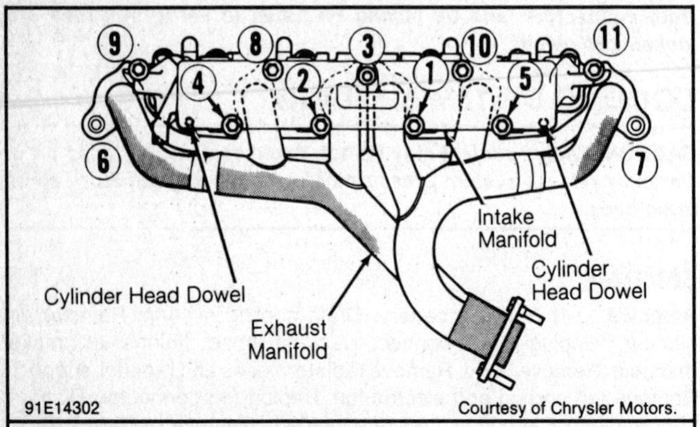
9
8
3
10
11
4
2
1
5
6
7
Intake
Manifold
Cylinder
Head Dowel
Cylinder Head Dowel
Exhaust
Manifold
91E14302
Courtesy of Chrysler Motors.

Fig. 2: Manifold Tightening Sequence

EXHAUST MANIFOLD

Removal & Installation - Remove exhaust manifold with intake manifold. See INTAKE MANIFOLD under REMOVAL & INSTALLATION.

CYLINDER HEAD

Removal - 1) Disconnect negative battery cable. Drain cooling system. Remove air cleaner, fuel pipe and vacuum advance hose. Remove molded hoses from cylinder head cover. Remove cylinder head cover.
2) Remove rocker arms, bridges, pivots and push rods. Tag all parts for reassembly reference. See ROCKER ARMS under REMOVAL & INSTALLATION. Loosen alternator drive belt. Remove alternator bracket-to-cylinder head bolt. Disconnect power steering pump bracket. DO NOT disconnect hoses. Wire power steering pump aside.
3) Remove manifolds. See INTAKE MANIFOLD and EXHAUST MANIFOLD under REMOVAL & INSTALLATION. Remove A/C compressor bolts from cylinder head (if equipped). Loosen through-bolt at bottom of A/C compressor bracket. Remove A/C compressor and wire it aside.
4) Tag and disconnect spark plug wires. Remove spark plugs. Disconnect temperature sending unit. Remove ignition coil and bracket assembly.
5) Remove cylinder head bolts. Pull bolt No. 14 out as far as it will go and hold in position with tape. Bolt No. 14 cannot be removed until head is moved forward. Remove cylinder head. Stuff clean lint free shop towels into cylinder bores.

Inspection - 1) Inspect cylinder head for cracks or damage. Using straightedge, check cylinder head for warpage in several areas. Repair or replace cylinder head if warpage exceeds specification or damage exists. See CYLINDER HEAD table under ENGINE SPECIFICATIONS at end of article.
2) Cylinder head bolts may be REUSED ONLY ONCE. If this is the first time cylinder head has been removed, put a dab of paint on the head of each bolt. If the bolts already have paint on them, of if it is unknown whether they have been used before, DISCARD THEM and replace with new ones.

Installation - 1) Clean carbon from combustion chambers and tops of pistons. Ensure all gasket surfaces are clean. Install new cylinder head gasket with numbers or word "TOP" upward. DO NOT apply gasket sealant to cylinder head gasket. Ensure all holes align. Install cylinder head.
2) Apply sealant to threads of cylinder head bolt No. 11 before installation. Install cylinder head bolts. Tighten all bolts to specification, in 3 stages and in sequence. During final tightening stage, bolt No. 11 will be tightened to a lower torque than the others. *See Fig. 3.* See TORQUE SPECIFICATIONS table at end of article.
3) To install remaining components, reverse removal procedure. Install all valve train components into original locations. Adjust A/T linkage. Refill cooling system. Start engine and check for leaks.

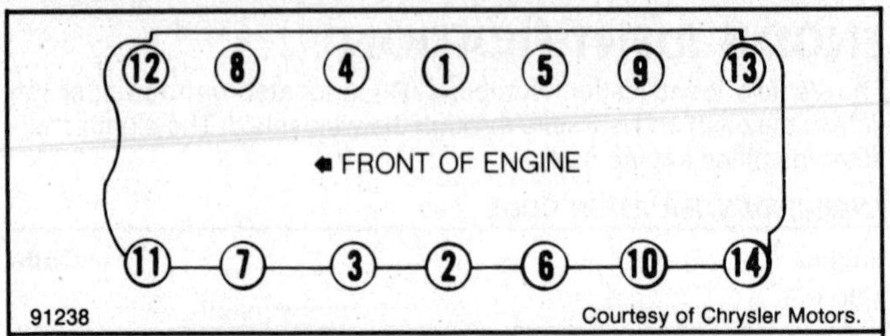
12
8
4
1
5
9
13
FRONT OF ENGINE
11
7
3
2
6
10
14
91238
Courtesy of Chrysler Motors.

Fig. 3: Cylinder Head Bolt Tightening Sequence

FRONT COVER OIL SEAL

Removal - 1) Disconnect negative battery cable. Remove drive belts, fan shroud, fan and hub assembly. Remove accessory drive pulley. Remove vibration damper retaining bolt and washer.
2) Using Puller (8068), remove vibration damper and key. Remove alternator bracket assembly and A/C compressor bracket (if equipped). Remove oil pan-to-front cover bolts. Remove cover-to-block retaining bolts. Remove front cover. Take care that tension spring and thrust pin do not fall out of camshaft preload bolt.
3) Cut oil pan gasket tabs even with face of cylinder block. Remove tabs. Remove gasket from oil pan. Remove crankshaft oil seal from front cover. Clean front cover, oil pan and cylinder block gasket surfaces.
Installation - 1) Clean all gasket surfaces. Install oil slinger. Apply sealant to both sides of front cover gasket. Install gasket onto cylinder block. Replace front section of oil pan seal with similar piece cut from new seal.
2) Coat oil pan seal with RTV sealant and place into position. Apply sealant where oil pan and cylinder block meet. Place front cover on cylinder block. Place Front Cover Aligner/Seal Installer (6139) in front engine cover seal area.
3) Ensure tension spring and thrust pin are in place in preload bolt. Install cover retaining bolts and tighten to specification. Apply sealant to seal outer diameter. Lightly coat crankshaft with oil. Drive oil seal into front cover, using Front Cover Aligner/Seal Installer (6139).
4) To complete installation, reverse removal procedure. Lubricate vibration damper retaining bolt before installation and tighten to specification. See TORQUE SPECIFICATIONS table at end of article.

TIMING CHAIN & SPROCKETS

Removal - Remove engine front cover. See FRONT COVER OIL SEAL under REMOVAL & INSTALLATION. Remove tension spring and thrust pin from preload bolt. Rotate crankshaft until timing marks on sprockets are aligned. *See Fig. 4.* Remove preload bolt. Remove timing chain and sprockets as an assembly.
Installation - 1) Install timing chain and sprockets as an assembly. Ensure timing marks align. Lubricate tension spring, thrust pin and thrust pin bore with MOPAR Engine Oil Supplement (4318002) before installation. Install preload bolt and washer. Tighten to specification.
2) Verify proper installation by rotating crankshaft until timing mark on camshaft is at approximately one o'clock position. Timing sprockets are installed correctly if 15 timing chain pins are between timing marks on both sprockets.
3) Install new front cover oil seal. See FRONT COVER OIL SEAL under REMOVAL & INSTALLATION. To install remaining components, reverse removal procedure. See TORQUE SPECIFICATIONS table at end of article.

1991 ENGINES
4.0L 6-Cylinder (Cont.)

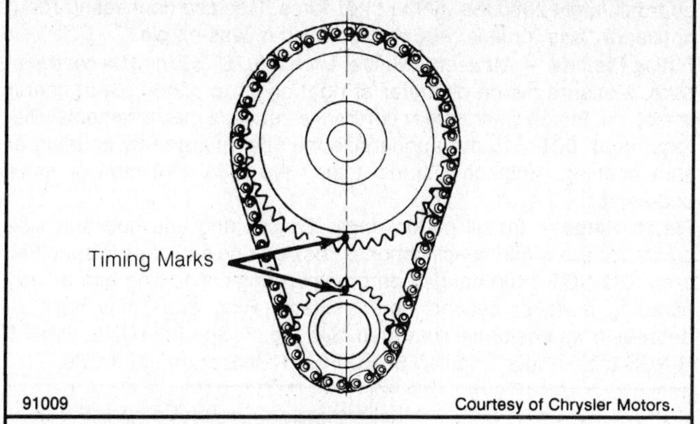
Timing Marks
91009
Courtesy of Chrysler Motors.

Fig. 4: Aligning Sprocket Timing Marks

ROCKER ARMS

Removal – Remove cylinder head cover. See CYLINDER HEAD under REMOVAL & INSTALLATION. Alternately loosen cap screws one turn at a time to prevent damaging bridges. Remove bridges, pivots, rocker arms and push rods. Tag all parts for reassembly reference.

Installation – **1)** Install all components into original locations. Ensure bottom ends of push rods are centered in tappets. Lubricate pivot contact area of rocker arms with engine oil supplement. Install cap screws loosely, and then tighten alternately one turn at a time to specification.

2) Reverse removal procedure to complete installation. See TORQUE SPECIFICATIONS table at end of article. Pour remaining oil supplement over entire valve train. Supplement must remain in engine oil for at least 1000 miles (1600 km). Refill cooling system. Adjust ignition timing. Check for leaks.

CAMSHAFT

Removal – **1)** Disconnect negative battery cable. Drain cooling system. Remove radiator and A/C condenser (if equipped), but DO NOT discharge system. Mark distributor and engine block for installation reference. Remove distributor and ignition wiring. Remove cylinder head. See CYLINDER HEAD under REMOVAL & INSTALLATION.

2) Remove tappets using Hydraulic Valve Tappet Remover/Installer (C-4129-A). Tag each tappet for installation reference. Remove timing chain and sprockets. See TIMING CHAIN & SPROCKETS under REMOVAL & INSTALLATION. Remove front bumper and/or grille as required. Remove camshaft.

Inspection – Inspect lobes, journals, bearings and distributor drive gear for wear. If camshaft sprocket or chain rubs against engine front cover, examine oil pressure relief holes in rear camshaft journal and ensure they are free of debris.

Installation – **1)** Lubricate camshaft and dip tappets into engine oil supplement. Install camshaft. Reverse removal procedure to complete installation.

2) Pour remaining oil supplement over entire valve train. Supplement must remain in engine oil for at least 1000 miles (1600 km). Refill cooling system. Adjust ignition timing. Check for leaks.

REAR CRANKSHAFT OIL SEAL

Removal – **1)** Remove transmission, clutch housing and flywheel or drive plate. Remove oil pan. See OIL PAN under REMOVAL & INSTALLATION.

2) Remove rear main bearing cap and push upper seal from groove. Ensure crankshaft is not damaged. Remove lower half of seal from bearing cap.

Installation – **1)** Clean surface of crankshaft. Apply thin coat of oil to crankshaft and seal lip. Position upper seal into groove in cylinder block. Lip of seal faces front of engine. Place lower half into bearing cap.

2) Coat both sides of lower seal end tabs with sealant. DO NOT apply sealant to lip of seal. Coat outer curved surface of lower seal with soap and lip of seal with engine oil. Position lower seal into bearing cap recess and seat firmly. Coat both chamfered edges of rear main bearing cap with sealant. DO NOT apply sealant to mating surfaces of bearing cap or cylinder block.

3) Install rear main cap in original position. Tighten bolts in 3 stages to specification. See CRANKSHAFT & MAIN BEARINGS under CYLINDER BLOCK ASSEMBLY under OVERHAUL. To install remaining components, reverse removal procedure.

WATER PUMP

Removal – Disconnect negative battery cable. Drain coolant. Remove fan shroud retaining screws and drive belts. Remove fan. Disconnect heater hoses and lower radiator hose at water pump. Remove power steering pump bracket (if equipped) at water pump boss. Remove retaining bolts and water pump.

Installation – Clean all gasket surfaces. Install water pump. Tighten bolts to specification. See TORQUE SPECIFICATIONS table at end of article. Ensure pump turns freely. Ensure belt is correctly installed or engine may overheat because pump rotates in wrong direction. To complete installation, reverse removal procedures. Fill cooling system.

OIL PAN

Removal – **1)** Disconnect negative battery cable. Raise and support vehicle at side sills. Drain engine oil. Disconnect exhaust pipe at exhaust manifold. Disconnect exhaust hanger at catalytic converter. Lower exhaust pipe. Remove starter. Remove flywheel access cover.

2) Position jack stand directly under vibration damper. Place wooden block between vibration damper and jack stand. Remove through-bolts from engine mounts. Raise engine enough to remove oil pan. Remove oil pan retaining bolts. Remove oil pan by sliding it to rear.

Installation – Install new front and rear seals and side rail gaskets. Coat inside surface of rear seal with soap. To complete installation, reverse removal procedure. Tighten oil pan bolts to specification. See TORQUE SPECIFICATIONS table at end of article. Fill crankcase. Start engine. Check for leaks.

OVERHAUL

CYLINDER HEAD

Cylinder Head Service – Inspect for cracks in combustion chambers, coolant passages, ports and exhaust valve seats. Using straightedge, check cylinder head for warpage in several areas. Repair or replace cylinder head if warpage exceeds specification or damage exists. See CYLINDER HEAD table under ENGINE SPECIFICATIONS at end of article.

Valve Springs - Use Valve Spring Tester C-647 (J-22738-02) to test each valve spring. Measure free length of each valve spring. Replace valve springs that do not meet specifications. See VALVES & VALVE SPRINGS table under ENGINE SPECIFICATIONS at end of article.

Valve Stem Oil Seals – Replace valve stem oil seals if they have deteriorated or whenever valves are serviced. Oil seals are marked "INT" and "EXH" for intake and exhaust valves, respectively.

Valve Guides – Measure diameter of valve guide approximately 3/8" (10 mm) from valve spring side of head, both parallel and at right angles to long axis of head. If difference between measurements exceeds .0025" (.063 mm), or if diameter exceeds specification by .003" (.08 mm), ream valve guide for oversize valve stem. Valve seats must be refaced after reaming valve guides. See CYLINDER HEAD table under ENGINE SPECIFICATIONS at end of article.

Valve Seats – Reface valve seats to specification. Remove only enough metal to provide smooth finish. Use tapered stones to obtain specified seat width. *See Fig. 5.* Seat width runout should not exceed .0025" (.063 mm) after refacing. See CYLINDER HEAD table under ENGINE SPECIFICATIONS at end of article.

Valves – Reface valves to specification. At least .031" (.79 mm) margin must remain after refacing valve. Valve stem tip can be resurfaced

1991 ENGINES
4.0L 6-Cylinder (Cont.)

and chamfered when worn. Do not remove more than .01" (.25 mm). See VALVES & VALVE SPRINGS table under ENGINE SPECIFICATIONS at end of article.

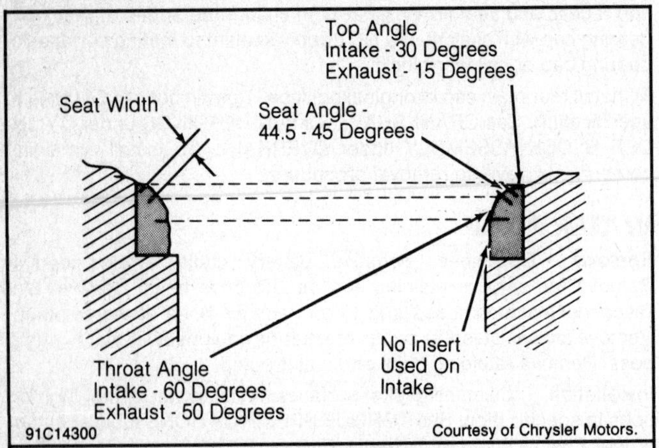
Top Angle
Intake - 30 Degrees
Exhaust - 15 Degrees
Seat Width
Seat Angle -
44.5 - 45 Degrees
No Insert
Used On
Intake
Throat Angle
Intake - 60 Degrees
Exhaust - 50 Degrees
91C14300
Courtesy of Chrysler Motors.

Fig. 5: Measuring Valve Seat Dimensions

VALVE TRAIN

Rocker Arms – Inspect pivot and valve stem contact surfaces of each rocker arm. Replace any rocker arm that is scuffed, pitted, cracked or excessively worn.

Push Rods – Inspect push rods for excessive wear. If wear is excessive because of lack of oil, replace and inspect corresponding tappet for excessive wear. Roll push rods on a flat surface to check for straightness. If wear exists along length of push rod, inspect cylinder head for obstruction.

CYLINDER BLOCK ASSEMBLY

Piston & Rod Assembly – **1)** Position piston on support. *See Fig. 6.* Press piston pin from piston. Discard pin. Piston pin CANNOT be reused after removal. Inspect piston pin bore in connecting rod for nicks and burrs and remove as necessary. Clean and dry piston pin bore and new piston pin.

2) Clean piston pin bore and replacement piston pin. Piston and piston pin must be at room temperature when measuring fit. Piston pin should fall through piston at room temperature. If pin jams in pin bore, replace piston.

3) Ensure arrow on piston crown is pointing up. Insert piston pin through piston pin bore and into connecting rod pin bore. Assemble connecting rod and piston so oil squirt hole faces camshaft and arrow on piston points to front of engine when installed.

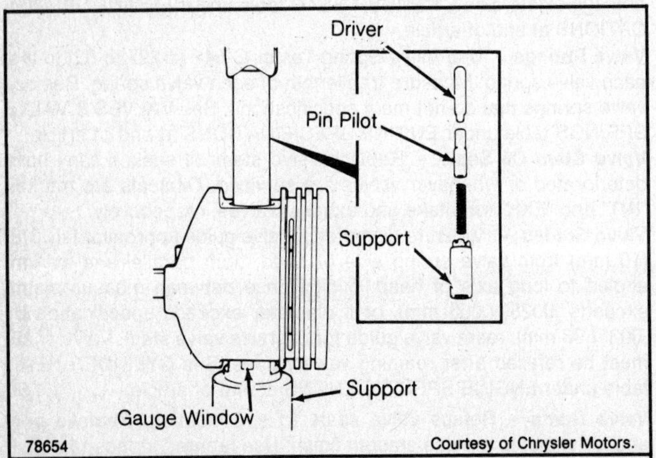
Driver
Pin Pilot
Support
Support
Gauge Window
78654
Courtesy of Chrysler Motors.

Fig. 6: Removing & Installing Piston Pin

4) Press pin through rod and piston until pilot indexes with mark on support. Pin should be centered in rod. Piston pin installation requires approximately 2000 lbs. (900 kg) of force. Replace connecting rod if noticeably less force is required, or if rod moves on pin.

Fitting Pistons – Measure cylinder bore 2 5/16" (59 mm) below top of bore. Measure piston diameter at right angle to piston pin at center line of pin. Piston clearance is difference between measurements. Pistons up to .004" (.10 mm) undersize may be enlarged by knurling or shot peening. Replace pistons if they are .004" (.10 mm) or more undersize.

Piston Rings – Install piston rings. Ensure ring end gap and side clearance are within specifications. Position ring end gaps in specified area. DO NOT interchange compression rings. Top ring has a Gray scraping surface; second ring is Black. Ring gaps may vary 20 degrees from positions illustrated. *See Fig. 7.* See PISTONS, PINS & RINGS table under ENGINE SPECIFICATIONS at end of article.

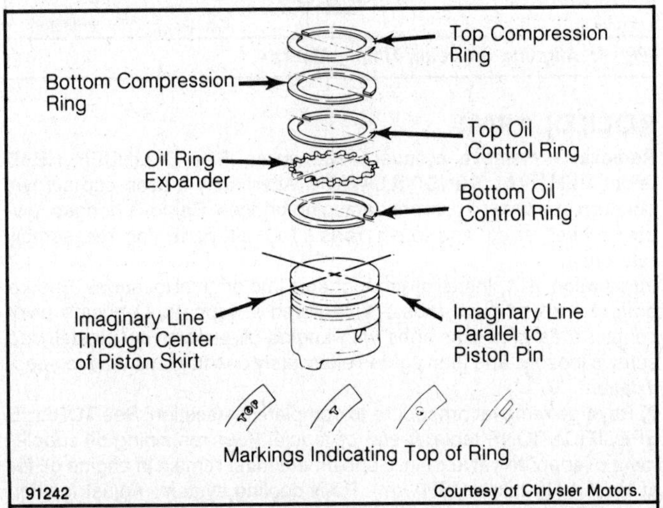
Top Compression
Ring
Bottom Compression
Ring
Top Oil
Control Ring
Oil Ring
Expander
Bottom Oil
Control Ring
Imaginary Line
Through Center
of Piston Skirt
Imaginary Line
Parallel to
Piston Pin
Markings Indicating Top of Ring
91242
Courtesy of Chrysler Motors.

Fig. 7: Positioning Piston Ring Gaps

Rod Bearings – **1)** Inspect bearings for wear or damage. Replace as necessary. Using Plastigage, check bearing clearance. See CRANKSHAFT, MAIN & CONNECTING ROD BEARINGS table under ENGINE SPECIFICATIONS at end of article. Bearings are available for standard and undersize applications.

2) If necessary, different size upper and lower bearings may be combined to obtain correct oil clearance. Lubricate bearing surfaces with oil before installation. Tighten bolts to specification. Check rod side play. Rotate crankshaft to ensure freedom of movement. See TORQUE SPECIFICATIONS table at end of article. See CRANKSHAFT, MAIN & CONNECTING ROD BEARINGS table under ENGINE SPECIFICATIONS at end of article.

NOTE: Avoid combining bearing inserts in excess of .001" (.03 mm) difference in size. Odd size inserts must be on bottom (rod cap) side.

Crankshaft & Main Bearings – **1)** Inspect bearings for wear or damage. Replace as necessary. Using Plastigage, check bearing clearance. See CRANKSHAFT, MAIN & CONNECTING ROD BEARINGS table under ENGINE SPECIFICATIONS at end of article. Bearings are available in standard and undersize. If necessary, different size upper and lower bearings may be installed to obtain correct oil clearance. Lubricate bearings before installation.

NOTE: If different size bearings are used, the odd size bearings must all be uniform in location (upper or lower). DO NOT use bearings with a thickness difference exceeding .001" (.03 mm).

2) Install upper bearing inserts. Install bearing caps and lower inserts. Tighten bearing caps in 3 stages to specification. Rotate crankshaft to ensure freedom of movement after tightening each cap. See TORQUE SPECIFICATIONS table at end of article. See CRANKSHAFT, MAIN & CONNECTING ROD BEARINGS table.

Thrust Bearing – Check crankshaft end play. If end play is not within specification, replace thrust bearing. If end play is still not within specification, replace crankshaft.

Cylinder Block – **1)** Thoroughly clean all gasket surfaces. Clean oil gallery by blowing compressed air into oil filter adapter, filter by-pass, oil gallery and crankshaft oil feed holes.

2) Measure cylinder bore diameter crosswise to cylinder block near top of bore. Repeat measurement at bottom of bore. Subtract smaller diameter from larger diameter to determine taper. Repeat measurements for each cylinder.

3) Repeat measurements with measuring device rotated 120 degrees. Repeat this step for a total of 3 measurements. Cylinder out-of-round is the difference between measurements. Repeat for each cylinder.

4) Bore and hone cylinders for oversize pistons if taper or out-of-round exceeds specification. Move hone up and down to provide a 60-degree crosshatch pattern. DO NOT use a rigid hone or exceed 10 strokes per cylinder. See CYLINDER BLOCK table under ENGINE SPECIFICATIONS at end of article.

ENGINE OILING

ENGINE LUBRICATION SYSTEM

An oil pump driven by the distributor supplies oil through a full-flow oil filter into an internal oil passage. This passage provides oil to the lifter bores and then to the camshaft and crankshaft bearings. Oil then flows to rocker arms from the hydraulic lifters and through the push rods.

Crankcase Capacity – Oil capacity is 6.0 qts. (5.7L) with filter change.

Oil Pressure – Minimum oil pressure should be 13 psi (.9 kg/cm^2) at 600 RPM. Normal oil pressure should be 37-75 psi (2.6-5.3 kg/cm^2) above 1600 RPM. Oil pressure relief is 75 psi (5.3 kg/cm^2).

OIL PUMP

Removal & Disassembly – Remove mounting bolts and oil pump. DO NOT move oil pick-up pipe in pump body. If oil pick-up pipe is moved, pick-up pipe must be replaced to ensure an airtight seal. Remove pump cover. Disassemble pump.

Inspection – Inspect for wear or damage. Place Plastigage across full width of each gear. Install cover temporarily and tighten bolts to 70 INCH lbs. (8 N.m). Remove cover. Examine Plastigage to determine end clearance. Measure clearance between each tooth and oil pump body directly opposite point of mesh. Replace oil pump if not within specifications. See OIL PUMP SPECIFICATIONS table.

OIL PUMP SPECIFICATIONS

Application	In. (mm)
Gear End Clearance	.002-.006 (.05-.15)
Gear-to-Body Clearance	.002-.004 (.05-.10)

Reassembly & Installation – **1)** Apply sealant to pick-up pipe and pump cover area prior to installation. To install pick-up pipe use Pipe Installer (7624). Ensure pick-up pipe support bracket aligns with pump cover bolt. If relief valve is replaced, ensure replacement valve is the same diameter as that removed.

2) Fill pump cavity with petroleum jelly. Install cover. Tighten cover bolts to specification. Check pump gears for freedom of rotation. Install new gasket and oil pump. Tighten retaining bolts to specification. See TORQUE SPECIFICATIONS table.

TORQUE SPECIFICATIONS

TORQUE SPECIFICATIONS

Application	Ft. Lbs. (N.m)
Camshaft Sprocket Preload Bolt	80 (108)
Connecting Rod Cap Nut	33 (45)
Cylinder Head Bolts [1]	
Stage 1	22 (30)
Stage 2	45 (61)
Stage 3	[2] 110 (149)
Intake Manifold Bolts [2]	20 (27)
Bolts No. 1-5	23 (31)
Bolts No. 6 & 7	17 (23)
Bolts No. 8-11	23 (31)
Exhaust Manifold Bolts	
Bolts No. 1-5	23 (31)
Bolts No. 6 & 7	17 (23)
Bolts No. 8-11	23 (31)
Starter Bolts	33 (45)
Fan Bolt	18 (24)
Converter-To-Flexplate Bolts	[3]
Flexplate-To-Crankshaft Bolts	55 (75)
Flywheel-To-Crankshaft Bolts	[3]
Main Bearing Cap Bolts	
Stage 1	40 (54)
Stage 2	70 (95)
Stage 3	80 (108)
Oil Pump Retaining Bolts	
Long	17 (23)
Short	10 (14)
Pulley-To-Vibration Damper Bolts	20 (27)
Rocker Arm Bolts	19 (26)
Vibration Damper Bolt [4]	80 (108)
Water Pump Bolts	13 (18)
	INCH Lbs. (N.m)
Front Cover Bolts	62 (7)
Oil Pan Bolts	
1/4" X 20	80 (9)
5/16" X 18	132 (15)
Oil Pump Cover Bolts	70 (8)
Valve Cover Bolts	55 (6)

[1] – All bolts except No. 11. Tighten bolt No. 11 to 100 ft. lbs (136 N.m) *See Fig. 3.*

[2] – Tighten in sequence. *See Fig. 2.*

[3] – Information not available from manufacturer.

[4] – With bolt cleaned and threads lubricated with oil.

ENGINE SPECIFICATIONS

GENERAL SPECIFICATIONS

Application	Specification
4.0L	
Displacement	242 Cu. In. (4.0L)
Bore	3.88" (98.6 mm)
Stroke	3.41" (81.0 mm)
Compression Ratio	8.8:1
Fuel System	PFI
Horsepower @ RPM	
Cherokee & Comanche	190 @ 4750
Wrangler	180 @ 4750
Torque Ft. Lbs. @ RPM	
Cherokee & Comanche	225 @ 4000
Wrangler	220 @ 4000

1991 ENGINES
4.0L 6-Cylinder (Cont.)

CRANKSHAFT, MAIN & CONNECTING ROD BEARINGS

Application	In. (mm)
4.0L	
Crankshaft	
End Play	.0015-.0065 (.038-.165)
Runout	[1]
Main Bearings	
Journal Diameter	2.4996-2.5001 (63.489-63.502)
Journal Out-Of-Round	.0005 (.013)
Journal Taper	.0005 (.013)
Oil Clearance	.0010-.0025 (.025-.063)
Connecting Rod Bearings	
Journal Diameter	2.0934-2.0955 (53.170-53.230)
Journal Out-Of-Round	.0005 (.013)
Journal Taper	.0005 (.013)
Oil Clearance	.0015-.0025 (.038-.064)

[1] – Information not available from manufacturer.

CONNECTING RODS

Application	In. (mm)
4.0L	
Bore Diameter	
Pin Bore	.9288-.9298 (23.591-23.617)
Crankpin Bore	2.2080-2.2085 (56.083-56.096)
Center-To-Center Length	6.123-6.127 (155.52-155.62)
Maximum Bend	.003 (.08)
Maximum Twist	.006 (.15)
Side Play	.010-.019 (.25-.48)

PISTONS, PINS & RINGS

Application	In. (mm)
4.0L	
Pistons	
Clearance	.0013-.0021 (.033-.053)
Diameter	[1]
Pins	
Diameter	.9304-.9309 (23.632-23.645)
Piston Fit	.0004-.0006 (.010-.015)
Rod Fit	Press Fit
Rings	
No. 1	
End Gap	.010-.020 (.25-.51)
Side Clearance	.0010-.0032 (.025-.081)
No. 2	
End Gap	.010-.020 (.25-.51)
Side Clearance	.0017-.0032 (.043-.081)
No. 3 (Oil)	
End Gap	.010-.025 (.25-.64)
Side Clearance	.001-.009 (.03-.23)

[1] – Information not available from manufacturer. Replace pistons if piston clearance exceeds .004" (.10 mm).

CYLINDER BLOCK

Application	In. (mm)
4.0L	
Cylinder Bore	
Standard Diameter	3.8751-3.8775 (98.42-98.48)
Maximum Taper	.001 (.03)
Maximum Out-Of-Round	.001 (.03)
Minimum Deck Height	9.429-9.435 (239.49-239.64)
Maximum Warpage	.008 (.20)

VALVES & VALVE SPRINGS

Application	Specification
4.0L	
Intake Valves	
Face Angle	45°
Head Diameter	1.91" (48.5 mm)
Minimum Margin	.031" (.79 mm)
Minimum Refinish Length	4.827" (122.61 mm)
Stem Diameter	.312" (7.93 mm)
Valve Tip Maximum Refinish	.010" (.25 mm)
Exhaust Valves	
Face Angle	45°
Head Diameter	1.5" (38 mm)
Minimum Margin	.031" (.79 mm)
Minimum Refinish Length	4.827" (122.6 mm)
Stem Diameter	.312" (7.93 mm)
Valve Tip Maximum Refinish	.010" (.25 mm)
Valve Springs	
Free Length	1.82" (46.2 mm)
Installed Height	[1]
Out-Of-Square	[1]
Pressure	Lbs. @ In. (kg @ mm)
Valve Closed	66-74 @ 1.625 (29.96-33.59 @ 41.2)
Valve Open	205-220 @ 1.2 (93.07-99.88 @ 30.48)

[1] – Information not available from manufacturer.

CYLINDER HEAD

Application	Specification
4.0L	
Cylinder Head Height	[1]
Maximum Warpage	.008" (.20 mm)
Valve Seats	
Intake Valve	
Seat Angle	44.5°
Seat Width	.040-.060" (1.02-1.52 mm)
Maximum Seat Runout	.0025" (.064 mm)
Seat Bore Diameter	[1]
Exhaust Valve	
Seat Angle	44.5°
Seat Width	.040-.060" (1.02-1.52 mm)
Maximum Seat Runout	.0025" (.064 mm)
Seat Bore Diameter	[1]
Valve Guides	
Intake Valve	
Valve Guide Cylinder Head Bore I.D.	[1]
Valve Guide I.D.	.313-.314" (7.95-7.98 mm)
Valve Guide Installed Height	[1]
Valve Stem-To-Guide Oil Clearance	.001-.003" (.03-.08 mm)
Exhaust Valve	
Valve Guide Cylinder Head Bore I.D.	[1]
Valve Guide I.D.	.312" (7.9 mm)
Valve Guide Installed Height	[1]
Valve Stem-To-Guide Oil Clearance	.001-.003" (.03-.08 mm)

[1] – Information not available from manufacturer.

1991 ENGINES
4.0L 6-Cylinder (Cont.)

CAMSHAFT

Application	In. (mm)
4.0L	
Bore Diameter	[1]
End Play [2]	0 (0)
Journal Diameter	
No. 1.	2.029-2.030 (51.54-51.56)
No. 2.	2.019-2.020 (51.28-51.31)
No. 3.	2.009-2.010 (51.03-51.05)
No. 4.	1.999-2.000 (50.78-50.80)
Journal Runout	[3]
Lobe Height	[1]
Lobe Lift	.253 (6.43)
Oil Clearance	.001-.003 (.03-.08)

[1] – Information not available from manufacturer.
[2] – Engine running.
[3] – Information not available from manufacturer. Manufacturer specifies .001" (.03 mm) maximum base circle runout.

VALVE LIFTERS

Application	In. (mm)
4.0L	
Bore Diameter	.9050-.9065 (22.987-23.025)
Lifter Diameter	.9040-.9045 (22.962-22.974)
Oil Clearance	.001-.0025 (.025-.063)

1991 ENGINES
6.0L V8

Grand Wagoneer

NOTE: For repair procedures not covered in this article, see ENGINE OVERHAUL PROCEDURES article in GENERAL INFORMATION.

ENGINE IDENTIFICATION

The Vehicle Identification Number (VIN) is located on upper left side of dash and is visible through windshield. The eighth character identifies the engine size. The tenth character identifies the model year.

ENGINE IDENTIFICATION CODE

Engine	Code
6.0L 2-Bbl.	7

Some engines are manufactured with oversize or undersize components. These engines are identified by a letter code stamped adjacent to engine code number on right valve cover. Letters are decoded as follows:

- "B" indicates all cylinder bores are .010" (.25 mm) oversize.
- "C" indicates all camshaft bearing bores are .010" (.25 mm) oversize.
- "P" indicates one or more connecting rod bearings are .010" (.25 mm) undersize.
- "M" indicates all main bearing journals are .010" (.25 mm) undersize.
- "PM" indicates all main bearings and one or more connecting rod bearings are .010" (.25 mm) undersize.

ADJUSTMENTS

VALVE CLEARANCE ADJUSTMENT

Engine uses hydraulic lifters. No adjustment is required.

REMOVAL & INSTALLATION

NOTE: For reassembly reference, label all electrical connectors, vacuum hoses and fuel lines before removal. Also place mating marks on engine hood and other major assemblies before removal.

CAUTION: Engine coolant may be hot. Avoid scalding by using care. Carefully release system pressure before removing radiator cap or drain cock.

ENGINE

Removal - 1) Remove hood and battery. Drain cooling system. Disconnect radiator and heater hoses. Disconnect transmission cooler lines. Separate fan shroud (if equipped) from radiator. Remove radiator. Remove fan. Drain fluid from power steering reservoir. Disconnect power steering hoses.

2) Discharge A/C system. Remove service valves from compressor. Remove cruise control servo and bracket as an assembly. Disconnect wire harness from engine. Disconnect fuel supply and return lines at chassis. Disconnect vacuum hose at power brake cylinder. Disconnect vacuum hose to heater damper door at intake manifold.

3) Disconnect transmission filler tube bracket at right cylinder head. DO NOT disconnect filler tube from transmission. Support engine weight with lifting device. Remove front engine mount nuts. Remove upper bellhousing bolts. Disconnect exhaust pipes at manifolds and support bracket. Remove starter. Support transmission.

4) Remove bellhousing inspection cover. Mark flexplate and converter for reassembly reference. Remove flexplate-to-converter bolts. Remove lower throttle valve and inner manual linkage support. Disconnect throttle valve rod at lower end of bellcrank. Remove remaining bellhousing bolts. Remove engine by lifting up and forward.

Installation - To install, reverse removal procedure. Adjust transmission linkage. Check and refill fluid levels. Start engine and check for leaks.

INTAKE MANIFOLD

Removal- 1) Drain coolant. Remove air cleaner. Disconnect ignition wires and remove plastic separators from brackets. Disconnect upper radiator and by-pass hoses from intake manifold. Disconnect wire from temperature sender. Remove ignition coil bracket and move it aside. Disconnect heater hose from rear of intake manifold.

2) Tag and disconnect all tubes and wires from carburetor. Disconnect throttle and throttle valve linkage from carburetor and intake manifold. Disconnect air hoses from air injection manifolds. Disconnect air pump outlet hose from diverter valve. Remove intake manifold.

Installation - Apply non-hardening sealant to both sides of gasket. Position gasket by aligning locators at rear of cylinder head. Hold rear of gasket in place and align front locators. Apply non-hardening sealant to both end seals. Reverse removal procedure to complete installation.

EXHAUST MANIFOLD

Removal - Tag and disconnect spark plug wires. Disconnect air hose at injection manifold. Raise and support vehicle. Disconnect exhaust pipes at exhaust manifolds. Remove retaining bolts and exhaust manifolds. Remove air injection manifolds.

Installation - Install manifolds. Tighten 2 center bolts to specification. Tighten outer bolts to specification. Install new exhaust pipe seals. Reverse removal procedure to complete installation.

CYLINDER HEAD

Removal - 1) Disconnect negative battery cable. Drain cooling system. Remove air cleaner. Remove intake manifold. See INTAKE MANIFOLD under REMOVAL & INSTALLATION. Disconnect and mark all hoses and electrical connections at cylinder head. Remove spark plugs. Remove cylinder head covers.

2) Remove rocker arms and push rods. See ROCKER ARMS under REMOVAL & INSTALLATION. Loosen all drive belts. Remove A/C compressor mounting bracket. Disconnect exhaust manifolds. It is not necessary to remove exhaust pipes. Disconnect negative battery cable from cylinder head.

3) Disconnect alternator support bracket from cylinder head. Remove air pump and power steering pump from mounting brackets. Remove cylinder head bolts. Remove cylinder head.

Inspection - Inspect cylinder head for cracks or damage. Using straightedge, check cylinder head for warpage in several areas. See CYLINDER HEAD table under ENGINE SPECIFICATIONS at end of article.

Installation - 1) Ensure gasket surfaces, head bolt threads and threads in cylinder block are clean. Clean carbon from combustion chambers and tops of pistons.

2) Apply non-hardening sealant to both sides of new cylinder head gasket. Install new gasket with the word TOP upward. Ensure all holes are aligned. Wire-brush cylinder head bolts. Install cylinder head.

3) Tighten cylinder head bolts in 2 stages and in proper sequence to specification. *See Fig. 1.* See TORQUE SPECIFICATIONS table at end of article. To complete installation, reverse removal procedure. Tighten bolts to specification. Refill cooling system.

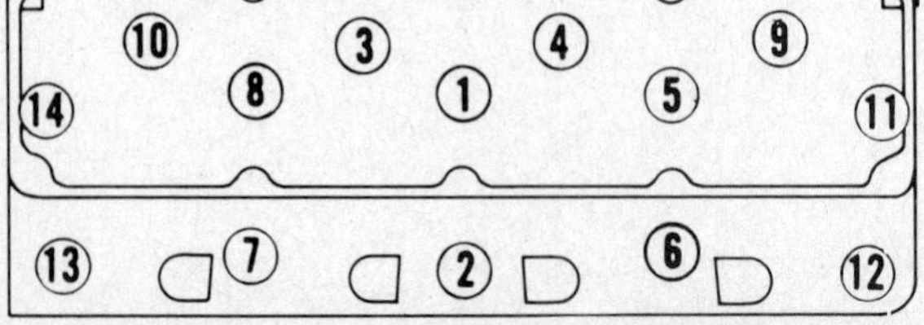
10
3
4
9
14
8
1
5
11
13
7
2
6
12

91247 Courtesy of Chrysler Motors.

Fig. 1: Cylinder Head Tightening Sequence

FRONT COVER OIL SEAL

Removal & Installation – 1) Loosen drive belts. Remove pulley and vibration damper. Remove front cover oil seal. Clean seal contact surface of vibration damper. Apply non-hardening sealer to outer diameter of new seal.

2) Using Seal Installer (7778), install seal. Lightly coat seal contact area of vibration damper with oil. Lubricate vibration damper bolt with oil before installation. Reverse removal procedure to complete installation. Tighten bolts to specification. See TORQUE SPECIFICATIONS table at end of article.

TIMING CHAIN & SPROCKETS

Removal – 1) Drain cooling system. Disconnect radiator hoses and by-pass hose. Remove drive belts, fan and hub assembly. Remove A/C compressor and bracket. Wire compressor aside. DO NOT discharge A/C system.

2) Remove alternator, bracket and idler pulley. Remove power steering pump and bracket. Remove air pump, mounting bracket and hoses as an assembly. Remove fuel pump. Disconnect heater hose at water pump. Mark distributor position and remove.

3) Remove pulley from vibration damper. Using Puller (8068), remove vibration damper. Remove front oil pan bolts. Remove front cover retaining bolts. Note length and location of bolts for reassembly reference.

4) Remove front cover and lower locating dowel pin from cylinder block. Remove crankshaft seal from cover. Cut exposed portion of oil pan gasket flush with face of cylinder block. Remove front crankshaft oil seal.

5) Remove oil slinger. Rotate crankshaft until timing marks on sprockets are aligned. *See Fig. 2.* Remove camshaft sprocket bolt, washer, distributor drive gear and fuel pump eccentric. Remove timing chain and sprockets as an assembly.

Installation – 1) Install timing chain and sprockets. Ensure timing marks are aligned. *See Fig. 2.* Install fuel pump eccentric with stamped word REAR facing camshaft.

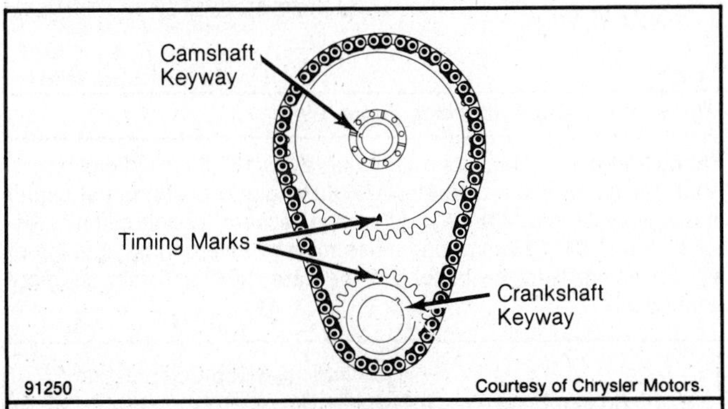

Camshaft Keyway
Timing Marks
Crankshaft Keyway
91250
Courtesy of Chrysler Motors.

Fig. 2: Aligning Sprocket Timing Marks

2) Verify proper installation by rotating crankshaft until timing mark on camshaft is at approximately 3 o'clock position. Timing sprockets are installed correctly if there are 20 timing chain pins between timing marks on both sprockets.

3) Clean gasket surfaces. Install oil slinger. Replace cut-off section of oil pan gasket with similar section cut from new gasket. Align tabs of replacement oil pan gasket and cement in place on front cover.

4) Apply non-hardening sealer to both sides of front cover gasket and install onto front cover. Apply non-hardening sealer to oil pan-to-cylinder block junctions. Install front cover onto cylinder block.

5) Install front oil pan bolts. Tighten bolts slowly and evenly until cover aligns with upper locating dowel pin. Drive lower dowel pin into cylinder block. Install and tighten remaining front cover bolts.

6) Install front cover oil seal. See FRONT COVER OIL SEAL under REMOVAL & INSTALLATION. To complete installation, reverse removal procedure. Lubricate vibration damper retaining bolt with oil prior to installation. Tighten bolts to specification. See TORQUE SPECIFICATIONS table at end of article. Refill cooling system.

ROCKER ARMS

Removal – Remove cylinder head cover. See CYLINDER HEAD under REMOVAL & INSTALLATION. Alternately loosen cap screws one turn at a time to prevent damaging bridges. Remove bridges, pivots, rocker arms and push rods. Tag all parts for reassembly reference.

Installation – Install all components into original locations. Ensure bottom ends of push rods are centered in lifters. Install cap screws loosely, then tighten alternately one turn at a time to specification. Reverse removal procedure to complete installation. See TORQUE SPECIFICATIONS table at end of article.

CAMSHAFT

Removal – 1) Drain cooling system. Remove radiator. Remove A/C condenser and receiver-drier. DO NOT discharge A/C system. Remove timing chain and sprockets. See TIMING CHAIN & SPROCKETS under REMOVAL & INSTALLATION.

2) Remove intake manifold. Remove rocker arms and push rods. See ROCKER ARMS under REMOVAL & INSTALLATION. Tag and remove hydraulic lifters. Remove hood latch support bracket. Remove bumper or grille if necessary. Remove camshaft.

Inspection – Inspect camshaft for flaking, lobe wear or worn bearing journals. Replace if not within specification. See CAMSHAFT table under ENGINE SPECIFICATIONS at end of article.

Installation – 1) Coat camshaft and lifters with an engine oil supplement prior to installation. Install fuel pump eccentric with stamped word REAR facing camshaft sprocket. Reverse removal procedure to complete installation.

2) Pour remaining oil supplement over entire valve train. Supplement must remain in engine oil for at least 1000 miles (1600 km). Tighten bolts to specification. See TORQUE SPECIFICATIONS table at end of article. Refill cooling system.

REAR CRANKSHAFT OIL SEAL

Removal – Drain engine oil. Remove starter. Remove oil pan. See OIL PAN under REMOVAL & INSTALLATION. Remove oil pan seals and gaskets. Remove rear main bearing cap. Use a brass drift to drive upper seal from groove. Remove lower half of seal from bearing cap.

Installation – 1) Clean surface of crankshaft. Apply thin coat of oil to crankshaft and seal lip. Coat block contact surface of upper seal with soap. Position upper seal into groove in cylinder block. Lip of seal should face front of engine.

2) Coat outer curved surface of lower seal with soap. Coat lip of seal with engine oil. Position lower seal into bearing cap recess. Coat both chamfered edges of rear main bearing cap with RTV silicone sealant. DO NOT apply sealant to mating surfaces of bearing cap or cylinder block.

3) Install rear main cap in original position. Tighten bolts in 4 stages to specification. See CRANKSHAFT, MAIN & CONNECTING BEARINGS table under ENGINE SPECIFICATIONS at end of article. Reverse removal procedure to complete installation.

WATER PUMP

Removal – 1) Disconnect negative battery cable. Drain radiator and remove upper radiator hose. Loosen all drive belts. Separate shroud from radiator. Install one radiator/shroud bolt to hold radiator in place.

2) Remove shroud, fan and hub. Remove A/C compressor bracket mounting stud from water pump. Remove front alternator mounting bracket. Remove 3 compressor mounting screws. Loosen nut behind and below heater hose nipple on water pump.

3) Pivot A/C compressor and bracket away from water pump. Remove front half of power steering bracket from water pump mounting stud. Disconnect all coolant hoses from water pump. Remove water pump and gasket.

Installation – Ensure gasket surfaces are clean. Check front cover cavity for corrosion. Using new gasket, install water pump. Tighten bolts to specification. See TORQUE SPECIFICATIONS table at end of article. Reverse removal procedure to complete installation. Fill cooling system.

1991 ENGINES
6.0L V8 (Cont.)

OIL PAN

Removal – Disconnect negative battery cable. Raise and support vehicle. Remove starter motor. Drain engine oil. Attach lifting device, and raise engine if necessary. Remove oil pan bolts and oil pan.

Installation – Coat inside curved surface of replacement rear seal with soap. Ensure rear seal is fully seated into recess of rear main bearing cap. To complete installation, reverse removal procedure. Tighten bolts to specification. See TORQUE SPECIFICATIONS table at end of article. Refill crankcase. Check for leaks.

OVERHAUL

CYLINDER HEAD

Cylinder Head Service – Inspect for cracks in combustion chambers, coolant passages, ports and exhaust valve seats. Using straightedge, check cylinder head for warpage in several areas. Repair or replace cylinder head if warpage exceeds specification or damage exists. See CYLINDER HEAD table under ENGINE SPECIFICATIONS at end of article.

Valve Springs - Use Valve Spring Tester (J-22738-02) to test each valve spring. Measure free length of each valve spring. Replace valve springs that do not meet specifications. See VALVES & VALVE SPRINGS table under ENGINE SPECIFICATIONS at end of article.

Valve Stem Oil Seals – Replace valve stem oil seals if they are deteriorated or whenever valves are serviced.

Valve Guides – Valve guides are an integral part of cylinder head and are not replaceable. Measure diameter of valve guide approximately 3/8" (10 mm) from valve spring side of head, both parallel and at right angle to long axis of head. If difference between measurements exceeds .0025" (.063 mm) or if diameter exceeds specification by .003" (.08 mm), ream valve guide for oversize valve stem. Reface valve seats after reaming valve guides. See CYLINDER HEAD table under ENGINE SPECIFICATIONS at end of article.

Valve Seats – Reface valve seats to specification. Remove only enough metal to provide smooth finish. Use tapered stones to obtain specified seat width. *See Fig. 3.* Seat width runout should not exceed .0025" (.063 mm) after refacing. See CYLINDER HEAD table under ENGINE SPECIFICATIONS at end of article.

Valves – Reface valves to specification. At least .031" (.79 mm) margin must remain after refacing valve .01" (.25 mm). See VALVES & VALVE SPRINGS table under ENGINE SPECIFICATIONS at end of article.

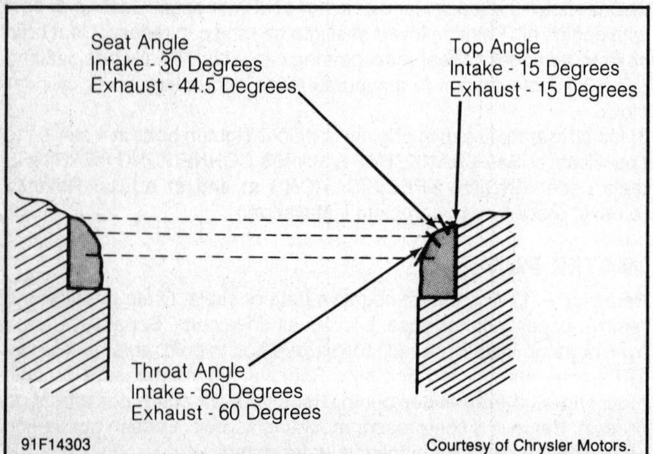
Seat Angle
Intake - 30 Degrees
Exhaust - 44.5 Degrees
Top Angle
Intake - 15 Degrees
Exhaust - 15 Degrees
Throat Angle
Intake - 60 Degrees
Exhaust - 60 Degrees
91F14303
Courtesy of Chrysler Motors.

Fig. 3: Checking Valve Seat Dimensions

VALVE TRAIN

Rocker Arms – Inspect pivot and valve stem contact surfaces of each rocker arm. Replace any rocker arm that is scuffed, pitted, cracked or excessively worn.

Push Rods – Inspect push rods for excessive wear. If wear is excessive because of lack of oil, replace and inspect corresponding tappet for excessive wear. Roll push rods on a flat surface to check for straightness. If wear exists along length of push rod, inspect cylinder head for obstruction.

CYLINDER BLOCK ASSEMBLY

Piston & Rod Assembly – **1)** Note locations of notch on piston and oil squirt hole in connecting rod. Position piston and rod assembly on support. *See Fig. 4.* Press piston pin from piston. Discard pin. Piston pin CANNOT be reused after removal. Inspect piston pin bore in connecting rod for nicks or burrs and remove as necessary.

2) Clean piston pin bore and replacement piston pin. Piston and piston pin must be at room temperature when measuring fit. Piston pin should fall through piston at room temperature. If pin jams in pin bore, replace piston.

3) Position piston on support so that notch will face front of engine and connecting squirt hole will face inward when installed. Insert piston pin through piston pin bore and into connecting rod pin bore.

4) Press pin through rod and piston until pilot indexes with mark on support. Pin should be centered in rod. Piston pin installation requires approximately 2000 lbs. (900 kg) of force. Replace connecting rod if noticeably less force is required, or if rod moves on pin.

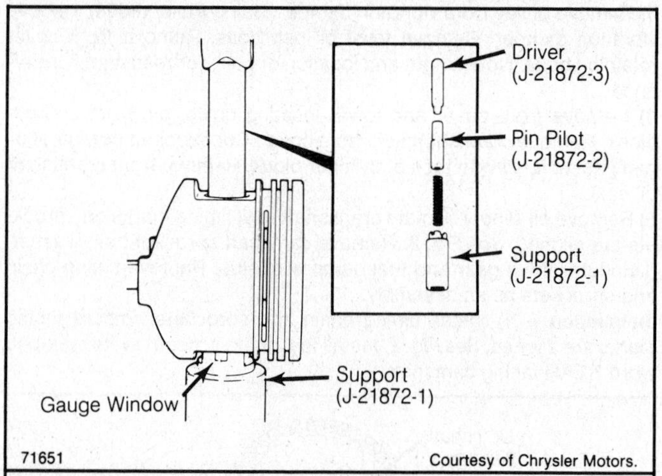
Driver
(J-21872-3)
Pin Pilot
(J-21872-2)
Support
(J-21872-1)
Support
(J-21872-1)
Gauge Window
71651
Courtesy of Chrysler Motors.

Fig. 4: Removing & Installing Piston Pin

Fitting Pistons – Measure cylinder bore 2 5/16" (59 mm) below top of bore. Measure piston diameter at right angle to piston pin at center line of pin. Piston clearance is difference between measurements. Pistons up to .004" (.10 mm) undersize may be enlarged by knurling or shot peening. Replace pistons if they are .004" (.10 mm) or more undersize.

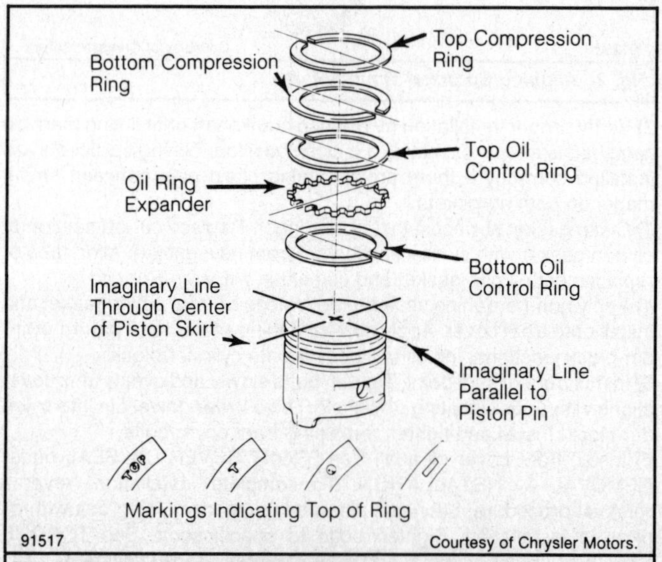
Top Compression
Ring
Bottom Compression
Ring
Top Oil
Control Ring
Oil Ring
Expander
Bottom Oil
Control Ring
Imaginary Line
Through Center
of Piston Skirt
Imaginary Line
Parallel to
Piston Pin
Markings Indicating Top of Ring
91517
Courtesy of Chrysler Motors.

Fig. 5: Positioning Piston Ring Gaps

Piston Rings – Install piston rings. Ensure ring end gap and side clearance are within specification. Position ring end gaps in specified area. *See Fig. 5*. See PISTONS, PINS & RINGS table under ENGINE SPECIFICATIONS at end of article.

Rod Bearings – **1)** Inspect bearings for wear or damage. Replace as necessary. Using Plastigage, check bearing clearance. See CRANKSHAFT, MAIN & CONNECTING ROD BEARINGS table under ENGINE SPECIFICATIONS at end of article. Bearings are available for standard and undersize applications.

2) If necessary, different size upper and lower bearings may be combined to obtain correct oil clearance. Lubricate bearing surfaces with oil before installation. Tighten bolts to specification. Check rod side play. Rotate crankshaft to ensure freedom of movement. See TORQUE SPECIFICATIONS table at end of article. See CRANKSHAFT, MAIN & CONNECTING ROD BEARINGS table at end of article.

NOTE: Never combine bearing inserts that differ by more than .001" (.03 mm).

Crankshaft & Main Bearings – **1)** Inspect bearings for wear or damage. Replace as necessary. Using Plastigage, check bearing clearance. See CRANKSHAFT, MAIN & CONNECTING ROD BEARINGS table under ENGINE SPECIFICATIONS at end of article. Bearings are available in standard and undersize. If necessary, different size upper and lower bearings may be installed to obtain correct oil clearance. Lubricate bearings before installation.

NOTE: If different size bearings are installed, the odd size bearings must all be uniform in location (upper or lower). Never combine bearing inserts that differ by more than .001" (.03 mm).

2) Install upper bearing inserts. Install bearing caps and lower inserts. Tighten bearing caps in 4 stages to specification. Rotate crankshaft to ensure freedom of movement after tightening each cap. See TORQUE SPECIFICATIONS table at end of article. See CRANKSHAFT MAIN & CONNECTING ROD BEARINGS table under ENGINE SPECIFICATIONS at end of article.

Thrust Bearing – Check crankshaft end play. If end play is not within specification, replace bearing No. 3. If end play is still not within specification, replace crankshaft.

Cylinder Block – **1)** Measure cylinder bore diameter crosswise to cylinder block near top of bore. Repeat measurement at bottom of bore. Subtract smaller diameter from larger diameter to determine taper. Repeat measurements for each cylinder.

2) Repeat measurements with measuring device rotated 120 degrees. Repeat this step for a total of 3 measurements. Cylinder out-of-round is the difference between measurements. Repeat for each cylinder.

3) Bore and hone cylinders for oversize pistons if taper or out-of-round exceeds specification. Move hone up and down to provide a 60-degree crosshatch pattern. DO NOT use a rigid hone or exceed 10 strokes per cylinder. See CYLINDER BLOCK table under ENGINE SPECIFICATIONS at end of article.

ENGINE OILING

ENGINE LUBRICATION SYSTEM

An oil pump driven by the distributor supplies oil through a full-flow oil filter into an internal oil passage. This passage provides oil to the lifter bores and then to the camshaft and crankshaft bearings. Oil then flows to rocker arms from the hydraulic lifters and through the push rods.

Crankcase Capacity – Oil capacity is 6.0 qts. (5.7L) with filter change.

Oil Pressure – Minimum oil pressure should be 13 psi (.9 kg/cm²) at 600 RPM. Normal oil pressure should be 37-75 psi (2.6-5.3 kg/cm²) above 1600 RPM. Oil pressure relief is 75 psi (5.3 kg/cm²).

OIL PUMP

Removal & Disassembly – Remove oil pan. Remove mounting bolts and oil pump. Remove pump cover. Remove drive and idler gears. Remove relief valve.

Inspection – **1)** Inspect for wear or damage. Place Plastigage across full width of each gear. Temporarily install cover without gasket. Tighten bolts to 55 INCH lbs. (6 N.m). Remove cover. Examine Plastigage to determine end clearance.

2) Measure clearance between each tooth and oil pump body directly opposite point of mesh. Replace oil pump if not within specifications. See OIL PUMP SPECIFICATIONS table.

OIL PUMP SPECIFICATIONS

Application	In. (mm)
Gear End Clearance	.002-.008 (.05-.20)
Gear-to-Body Clearance	.00052-.0025 (.013-.064 mm)

Reassembly & Installation – Fill pump cavity with petroleum jelly. Install cover. Tighten cover bolts to specification. Reverse disassembly procedure to complete assembly. Check pump gears for freedom of rotation. Install new gasket and oil pump. Tighten retaining bolts to specification. See TORQUE SPECIFICATIONS table.

TORQUE SPECIFICATIONS

TORQUE SPECIFICATIONS

Application	Ft. Lbs. (N.m)
Camshaft Sprocket Bolt	30 (41)
Connecting Rod Cap Nut	33 (45)
Cylinder Head Bolts [1]	
Stage 1	80 (108)
Stage 2	110 (149)
Drive Plate-To-Converter Bolts	22 (30)
Engine Front Cover Bolts	25 (34)
Exhaust Manifold	
2 Center Bolts	25 (34)
4 Outer Bolts	15 (20)
Exhaust Pipe-To-Manifold Nuts	20 (27)
Intake Manifold Bolts	43 (58)
Main Bearing Cap Bolts	
Stage 1	30 (41)
Stage 2	60 (81)
Stage 3	90 (122)
Stage 4	100 (136)
Rocker Arm Bolts	19 (26)
Vibration Damper Bolt	[2] 90 (122)
Starter Mounting Bolts	18 (24)
	INCH Lbs. (N.m)
Oil Pan Bolts	
1/4" X 20	84 (9)
5/16" X 18	132 (15)
Oil Pump Cover Bolts	55 (6)
Valve Cover Bolts	55 (6)
Water Pump Bolts	48 (4)

[1] – Tighten in sequence. *See Fig. 1*.
[2] – With bolt threads cleaned and lubricated.

ENGINE SPECIFICATIONS

GENERAL SPECIFICATIONS

Application	Specification
6.0L	
Displacement	360 Cu. In. (6.0L)
Bore	4.08" (103.6 mm)
Stroke	3.44" (87.4 mm)
Compression Ratio	8.25:1
Fuel System	2-Bbl.
Horsepower @ RPM	144 @ 3200
Torque Ft. Lbs. @ RPM	280 Ft. Lbs. @ 1500

1991 ENGINES
6.0L V8 (Cont.)

CRANKSHAFT, MAIN & CONNECTING ROD BEARINGS

Application	In. (mm)
6.0L	
Crankshaft	
End Play	.003-.008 (.08-.20)
Runout	[1]
Main Bearings	
Journal Diameter	[2] 2.7474-2.7489 (69.784-69.822)
Oil Clearance	[3] .001-.003 (.03-.08)
Connecting Rod Bearings	
Journal Diameter	2.0934-2.0955 (53.172-53.230)
Journal Out-Of-Round	.0005 (.013)
Journal Taper	.0005 (.013)
Oil Clearance	.001-.003 (.03-.08)

[1] – Information not available from manufacturer.
[2] – Rear main bearing 2.7464-2.7479" (69.759-69.797 mm)
[3] – Rear main bearing .002-.004" (.05-.10 mm)

CONNECTING RODS

Application	In. (mm)
6.0L	
Bore Diameter	
Pin Bore	.9288-.9298 (23.590-23.620)
Crankpin Bore	2.2080-2.2085 (56.083-56.096)
Center-To-Center Length	5.873-5.877 (149.17-149.28)
Maximum Bend	.006 (.15)
Maximum Twist	.003 (.08)
Side Play	.006-.018 (.15-.46)

PISTONS, PINS & RINGS

Application	In. (mm)
6.0L	
Pistons	
Clearance	.0012-.0020 (.030-.051)
Diameter	[1]
Pins	
Diameter	.9308-.9313 (23.649-23.655)
Piston Fit	.0003-.0005 (.008-.013)
Rod Fit	Press Fit
Rings	
No. 1	
End Gap	.010-.020 (.25-.51)
Side Clearance	.0015-.0035 (.038-.089)
No. 2	
End Gap	.010-.020 (.25-.51)
Side Clearance	.0015-.0038 (.038-.089)
No. 3 (Oil)	
End Gap	.015-.045 (.38-1.14)
Side Clearance	0-.007 (0-.18)

[1] – Information not available from manufacturer. Replace pistons if piston clearance exceeds .004" (.10 mm).

CYLINDER BLOCK

Application	In. (mm)
6.0L	
Cylinder Bore	
Standard Diameter	4.080 (103.63)
Maximum Taper	.005 (.13)
Maximum Out-Of-Round	.003 (.08)
Minimum Deck Height	9.205 (233.81)
Maximum Deck Warpage	.008 (.20)

VALVE LIFTERS

Application	In. (mm)
6.0L	
Bore Diameter	.9050-.9065 (22.987-23.025)
Lifter Diameter	.9040-.9045 (22.962-22.974)
Oil Clearance	.001-.0025 (.03-.05)

VALVES & VALVE SPRINGS

Application	Specification
6.0L	
Intake Valves	
Face Angle	29°
Head Diameter	2.020-2.030" (51.31-51.56 mm)
Minimum Margin	.031" (.79 mm)
Stem Diameter	.3715-.3725" (9.436-9.462 mm)
Exhaust Valves	
Face Angle	44°
Head Diameter	1.675-1.685" (42.55-42.80 mm)
Minimum Margin	.031" (.79 mm)
Stem Diameter	.3715-.3725" (9.436-9.462 mm)
Valve Springs	
Free Length	1.99" (50.5 mm)
Installed Height	[1]
Out-Of-Square	[1]
Pressure	Lbs. @ In. (Kg @ mm)
Valve Closed	64-72 @ 1.79 (29-33 @ 45.4)
Valve Open	202-220 @ 1.36 (92-100 @ 34.6)

[1] – Information not available from manufacturer.

CYLINDER HEAD

Application	Specification
6.0L	
Cylinder Head Height	[1]
Maximum Warpage	.008" (.20 mm)
Valve Seats	
Intake Valve	
Seat Angle	30°
Seat Width	.040-.060" (1.02-1.52 mm)
Maximum Seat Runout	.0025" (.064 mm)
Exhaust Valve	
Seat Angle	44.5°
Seat Width	.040-.060" (1.02-1.52 mm)
Maximum Seat Runout	.0025" (.064 mm)
Valve Guides	
Intake Valves	
Valve Guide I.D.	.3735-.3745" (9.487-9.512 mm)
Valve Stem-To-Guide Oil Clearance	.001-.003" (.03-.08 mm)
Exhaust Valves	
Valve Guide I.D.	.3735-.3745" (9.487-9.512 mm)
Valve Stem-To-Guide Oil Clearance	.001-.003" (.025-.076 mm)

[1] – Information not available from manufacturer.

CAMSHAFT

Application	In. (mm)
6.0L	
Bore Diameter	[1]
End Play	[2] 0 (0)
Journal Diameter	
No. 1	2.1195-2.1205 (53.835-53.861)
No. 2	2.0895-2.9050 (53.073-53.099)
No. 3	2.0595-2.0605 (52.311-52.337)
No. 4	2.0295-2.0305 (51.549-51.575)
No. 5	1.9995-2.0005 (50.787-50.813)
Journal Runout	[1]
Lobe Height	.266 (6.7564)
Lobe Lift	[1]
Oil Clearance	.001-.003 (.025-.076)

[1] – Information not available from manufacturer.
[2] – Engine running.

1991 ENGINE COOLING
Specifications & Electric Cooling Fans

Cherokee, Comanche, Grand Wagoneer, Wrangler

SPECIFICATIONS

BELT ADJUSTMENT

Cherokee, Comanche & Wrangler – Loosen rear mounting bolts of idler pulley or power steering pump (if equipped). Loosen power steering pivot bolt and lock nut (if equipped). Turn adjusting bolt to tighten belt to specification. See BELT TENSION table. Tighten bolts and lock nut to 20 ft. lbs. (27 N.m.).

Grand Wagoneer – **1)** Disconnect negative battery cable. Loosen adjustment and pivot bolts on alternator. Pry alternator away from engine to adjust belt tension to specification. See BELT TENSION table. Tighten adjustment bolt to 20 ft. lbs. (27 N.m.). Tighten pivot bolt to 28 ft. lbs (38 N.m.).

2) Loosen both power steering pump rear mounting bolts. Insert 1/2" breaker bar into square hole in bracket. Pull breaker bar to adjust tension to specification. DO NOT pry on power steering pump reservoir. See BELT TENSION table. Tighten bolts to 28 ft. lbs (38 N.m.).

3) Ensure power steering belt tension is correct. Loosen adjusting and pivot bolts on air pump. Pry air pump downward to adjust tension to specification. See BELT TENSION table. Tighten bolts to 20 ft. lbs. (27 N.m.).

BELT TENSION

BELT TENSION
Tension in Lbs. (kg) Using Strand Tension Gauge

Application	New Belt	Used Belt
Serpentine Belt	180-200 (82-91)	140-160 (64-73)
"V" Belt	120-160 (54-73)	90-115 (41-52)

COOLING SYSTEM SPECIFICATIONS

COOLING SYSTEM SPECIFICATIONS

Model	Specification
Coolant Replacement Interval	[1] 24 months
Coolant Capacity	
2.5L	[2] 10.0 qts. (9.5L)
4.0L	12.0 qts. (11.4L)
6.0L	15.5 qts. (14.7L)
Pressure Cap	12-15 psi
Thermostat Opens	
Starts	195°F (90°C)
Fully Open	218°F (103°C)

[1] – Manufacturer recommends replacing original coolant at 36 months or 52,500 miles, whichever occurs first.
[2] – On Wrangler, capacity is 9.0 qts. (8.5L).

ELECTRIC COOLING FAN

On Cherokee and Comanche 4.0L engine and heavy-duty cooling and/or air conditioning, an auxiliary electric fan operates whenever engine temperature exceeds 190°F (88°C), or whenever air conditioner is on. If Single Board Engine Controller II (SBEC-II) detects a fan control circuitry problem, a fault code will set.

NOTE: For more information on vehicle self-diagnostics, see appropriate SELF-DIAGNOSTICS article in ENGINE PERFORMANCE.

TROUBLE SHOOTING & TESTING

Electric Cooling Fan Circuit – **1)** Ensure fuses No. 4 and 6 on Power Distribution Center (PDC), near battery, are good. Ensure fan operates. See MOTOR under COMPONENT TESTING. Remove cooling fan relay from PDC. Start engine. Using a test light, check for power at terminal No. 2 (Light Green/Red wire) of PDC. If power does not appear, repair open circuit in Light Green/Red wire between terminal No. 2 and fuse No. 4.

2) Connect a jumper wire between terminal No. 2 (Light Green/Red wire) and terminal No. 4 (Light Green wire) on PDC. If fan does not operate, leave jumper wire connected. Unplug fan connector on left side of fan shroud.

3) Using a test light, check for power at Light Green wire on fan harness connector. If there is no power, repair Light Green wire between fan harness connector and terminal No. 4 on PDC. If power exists at Light Green wire, repair open circuit in Black wire on fan harness connector and ground.

4) Turn ignition off. Reconnect fan motor connector. Remove jumper wires. Reinstall relay. Connect Diagnostic Readout Box II (DRB-II) to engine diagnostic connector. Connector is located in engine compartment, next to SBEC-II.

5) Start engine. Energize fan relay circuit by warming engine until coolant temperature is higher than 190°F (88°C), or by turning air conditioning on (if equipped). If relay clicks but fan does not operate, check for poor relay connections at socket. If connections are okay, test relay. See RELAY under COMPONENT TESTING.

6) If relay does not click, put DRB-II into voltmeter mode. Measure voltage at cavity A1 (Dark Blue/White wire) in relay connector. If voltage is less than 10 volts, repair open circuit in Dark Blue/White wire between cavity A1 and fuse No. 6. If voltage is 10 volts or more, turn ignition off and reconnect relay.

7) Unplug connector from SBEC-II. Examine connector. If connector is okay, turn ignition on. With DRB-II in voltmeter mode, measure voltage at terminal No. 31 on SBEC-II harness connector. If voltage is 10 volts or more, replace SBEC-II. If voltage is less than 10 volts, repair open circuit in Dark Blue/Pink wire between SBEC-II terminal No. 31 and PDC terminal No. 5.

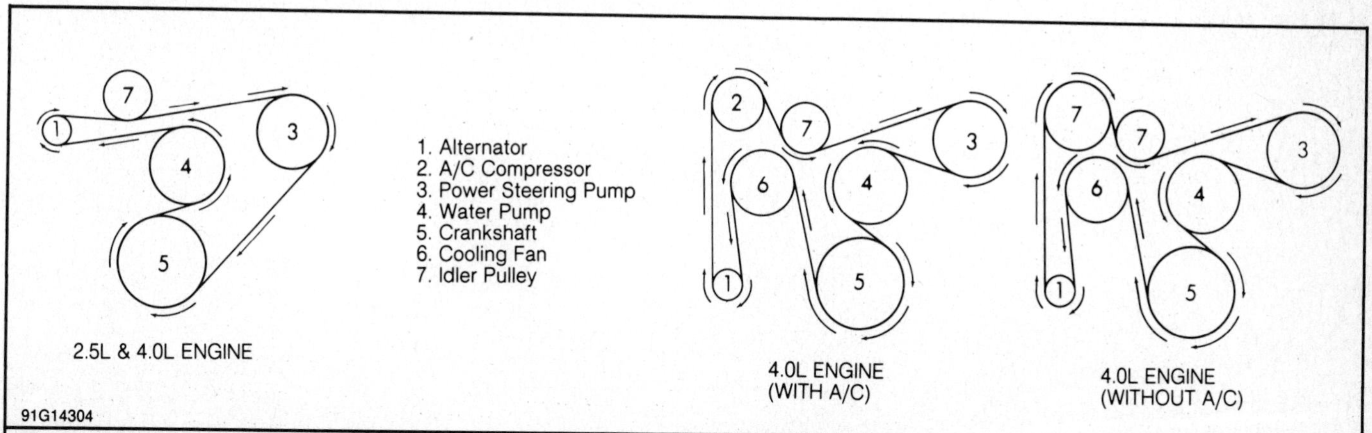
1. Alternator
2. A/C Compressor
3. Power Steering Pump
4. Water Pump
5. Crankshaft
6. Cooling Fan
7. Idler Pulley
2.5L & 4.0L ENGINE
4.0L ENGINE (WITH A/C)
4.0L ENGINE (WITHOUT A/C)
91G14304

Fig. 1: Routing Serpentine Belts (2.5L & 4.0L)

1991 ENGINE COOLING
Specifications & Electric Cooling Fans (Cont.)

COMPONENT TESTING

Motor – Unplug fan motor connector at left side of fan shroud. Connect a jumper wire from terminal "B" (Black wire) of fan motor connector to a known good engine ground. Using another jumper with a 25-amp in-line fuse, supply battery power to terminal "A" (Red wire) of fan motor connector. Service fan motor if it does not run.

Relay – **1)** Remove relay from Power Distribution Center (PDC). Connect a self-powered test light between terminals No. 2 and 4 on relay. *See Fig. 2*. Test light should indicate no continuity. Leave test light connected.

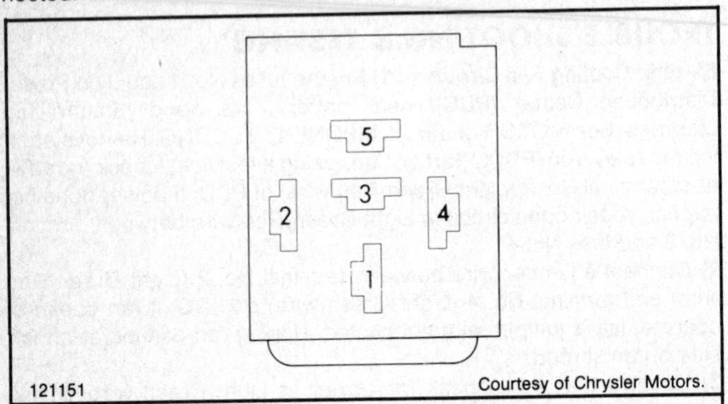
5
3
2
4
1
121151
Courtesy of Chrysler Motors.

Fig. 2: Identifying Fan Relay Connector Terminals

2) Using a jumper wire, connect relay terminal No. 5 to a good ground. Using another jumper with a 15-amp in-line fuse, supply battery power to terminal No. 1 of relay. If test light does not indicate continuity, replace relay.

WIRING DIAGRAMS

Also see appropriate chassis wiring diagram in WIRING DIAGRAMS.

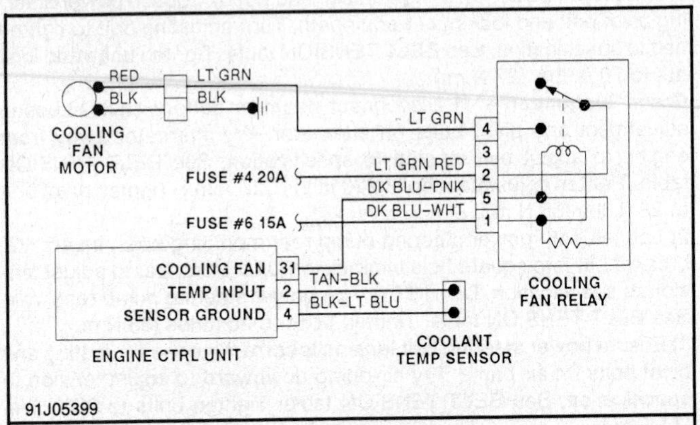
RED
BLK
LT GRN
BLK
COOLING
FAN
MOTOR
LT GRN
LT GRN RED
DK BLU-PNK
DK BLU-WHT
FUSE #4 20A
FUSE #6 15A
4
3
2
5
1
COOLING FAN
TEMP INPUT
SENSOR GROUND
31
2
4
TAN-BLK
BLK-LT BLU
ENGINE CTRL UNIT
COOLANT
TEMP SENSOR
COOLING
FAN RELAY
91J05399

Fig. 3: Electric Cooling Fan Wiring Diagram

1991 CLUTCHES RWD

Cherokee, Comanche, Wrangler

DESCRIPTION

The clutch assembly consists of a single dry-disc driven plate and a one-piece diaphragm spring-type clutch cover. The clutch is actuated through a hydraulic master cylinder and a slave cylinder, which contains a clutch release bearing. Slave cylinder and clutch release bearing must be replaced as a complete unit.

ADJUSTMENTS

HYDRAULIC SYSTEM BLEEDING

1) Fill master cylinder reservoir with DOT 3 brake fluid. Raise and support vehicle. Attach bleeder hose to bleeder screw on bleed line of slave cylinder. *See Fig. 1.* Place other end of hose in glass container 1/2 full of brake fluid. Loosen bleeder screw while holding bleeder screw fitting.

CAUTION: DO NOT allow bleed line to bend or flex when loosening bleeder screw.

2) Have an assistant depress clutch pedal to the floor. Tighten bleeder screw and release clutch pedal. Repeat bleeding procedure until fluid entering container is free of bubbles. DO NOT allow reservoir to run out of fluid during bleeding. Refill clutch master cylinder reservoir.

NOTE: No other adjustments are necessary or possible.

TROUBLE SHOOTING

NOTE: See TROUBLE SHOOTING article in GENERAL INFORMATION.

REMOVAL & INSTALLATION

TRANSMISSION

Removal - 1) Place transmission in 1st or 3rd gear. Raise and support vehicle. Drain fluid from transfer case. Support the engine with adjustable jack stand. Use wood block between pan and jack. Remove rear crossmember.

2) Disconnect transmission shift linkage, speedometer cable, transfer case vacuum lines, electrical wiring and clutch hydraulic lines. Place reference mark on drive shaft yokes and transfer case yokes for reassembly reference. Disconnect drive shafts.

3) Support transfer case with jack and lower (NOT MORE than three inches). Reaching up and around transmission case, move boot upward to access shift lever retainer.

NOTE: DO NOT remove shift lever from floor pan boot.

4) Disengage shift lever from transmission by pressing down and turning retainer counterclockwise to release it. Lift retainer out of transmission shift tower. Remove clutch housing to engine bolts. Remove transmission and transfer case.

Installation - To install, reverse removal procedure. Fill transmission with proper lubricant. Fill and bleed hydraulic clutch system. See HYDRAULIC SYSTEM BLEEDING under ADJUSTMENTS.

CLUTCH ASSEMBLY

Removal - Remove transmission. Place reference marks on clutch cover and flywheel for reassembly reference. Evenly loosen clutch cover bolts until clutch cover spring tension is released. Remove cover bolts, clutch cover, and clutch disc.

Installation - Replace all worn or damaged parts. Align clutch cover with reference marks on flywheel. Using clutch alignment shaft, align clutch disc. Tighten each cover bolt a few turns at a time to specification.

CLUTCH MASTER CYLINDER

Removal - Disconnect hydraulic line at master cylinder and plug openings. Remove cotter pin holding push rod on clutch pedal. Slide push rod off pedal pivot. Remove nuts and master cylinder.

Installation - To install, reverse removal procedure. Bleed hydraulic system. See HYDRAULIC SYSTEM BLEEDING under ADJUSTMENTS.

CLUTCH SLAVE CYLINDER

Removal - 1) Drain clutch master cylinder. Disconnect line at clutch master cylinder and clutch slave cylinder lines. Remove transmission and transfer case. Remove insulator bolts and slide insulator and insulator bracket off lines. *See Fig. 1.*

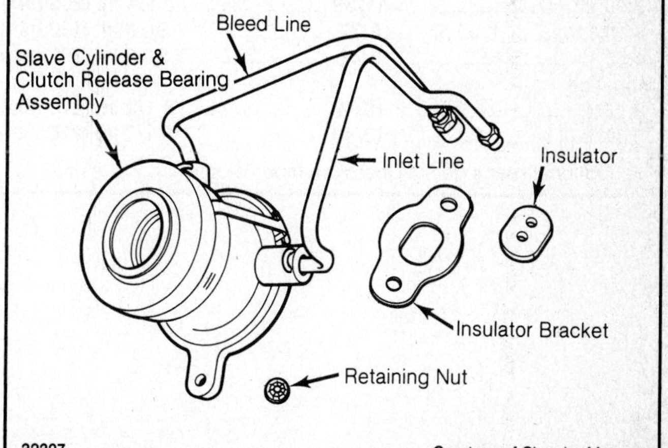
Bleed Line
Slave Cylinder &
Clutch Release Bearing
Assembly
Inlet Line
Insulator
Insulator Bracket
Retaining Nut
32327
Courtesy of Chrysler Motors.

Fig. 1: Exploded View of Clutch Release Bearing & Slave Cylinder

2) Remove retaining nut. Pry nut upward and off mounting pin on transmission front case. Remove assembly.

Installation - To install, reverse removal procedure. Bleed hydraulic system. See HYDRAULIC SYSTEM BLEEDING under ADJUSTMENTS.

PILOT BEARING

Removal & Installation - Remove clutch assembly. Using slide hammer and internal puller, remove pilot bearing. To install, lubricate pilot bearing with wheel bearing grease. Using clutch alignment shaft, install pilot bearing. Reverse removal procedure to install remaining components.

OVERHAUL

CLUTCH MASTER & SLAVE CYLINDERS

NOTE: No overhaul procedures are available. Replace defective or leaking units with new parts.

TORQUE SPECIFICATIONS

TORQUE SPECIFICATIONS

Application	Ft. Lbs. (N.m)
Clutch Cover Bolt	
4-Cylinder	23 (31)
6-Cylinder	40 (54)
Clutch Housing-To-Engine Bolt	
M12 X 1.75	55 (75)
3/8" X 16	27 (37)
7/16" X 14	43 (58)
Crossmember-To-Frame Bolt	30 (41)
Master Cylinder Mounting Nut	19 (26)
Rear Support-To-Crossmember Bolt	33 (45)

1991 DRIVE AXLES
Axle Ratio Identification

Cherokee, Comanche
Grand Wagoneer, Wrangler

The axle build date and manufacturer's number are stamped on the passenger side axle tube, near housing cover. The axle assembly part number, gear ratio and identification tag are attached to the left side of the housing cover.

AXLE RATIO & IDENTIFICATION

Axle Ratio	Pinion/Ring Gear Tooth Combinations	Ring Gear Diameter
Model 30/35		
3.07:1	14/43	7 9/16 In. (192 mm)
3.55:1	11/39	7 9/16 In. (192 mm)
3.55:1 [1]	11/39	8 1/4 In. (209 mm)
4.10:1	9/37	7 9/16 In. (192 mm)
4.56:1	9/41	7 9/16 In. (192 mm)
Model 44		
2.72:1	18/49	8 1/2 In. (216 mm)
3.31:1	13/43	8 1/2 In. (216 mm)

[1] - Optional rear axle for Cherokee models only.

1991 DRIVE AXLES
Front Axles

Cherokee, Comanche
Grand Wagoneer, Wrangler

DESCRIPTION

The Model 30 axle is used on the Command-Trac system. The Model 30 and 44 axles are used on the Selec-Trac system. All models with Command-Trac have a 2-piece axle shaft on the right side of the front differential, it is comprised of an outer axle shaft and intermediate axle shaft. All models with Selec-Trac, have a standard 1-piece axle shaft on both sides of differential.

REMOVAL & INSTALLATION

NOTE: This article covers removal and installation, and overhaul of front axle components. For information on the differential, see the 7 9/16", 8 1/4" & 8 1/2" RING GEAR article in DRIVE AXLES.

AXLE ASSEMBLY

Removal (Cherokee, Comanche & Wrangler) - 1) Raise and support vehicle. Remove wheels. Remove disc brake calipers and support them out of way. Remove rotors and brake shields.

NOTE: DO NOT allow brake hose to support the calipers.

2) Disconnect breather tube at axle. On models with Command-Trac, remove vacuum harness from shift motor and vent hose from differential housing. Remove stabilizer bar link, tie rod and drag link.
3) Remove front drive shaft. Disconnect shock absorbers and steering damper. If equipped with Anti-Lock Brake System (ABS), disconnect brake sensor.
4) Disconnect track bar. Position jack under axle. Disconnect upper and lower control arms at axle. Lower and remove axle slowly to release coil spring pressure.
Installation - Raise axle into position while guiding coil springs into position. Connect upper and lower control arms to axle. To complete installation, reverse removal procedure.
Removal (Grand Wagoneer) - 1) Raise and support vehicle. Position supports under frame rails at rear of front springs. Remove wheels. Mark front drive shaft and axle yoke for reassembly.
2) Disconnect front drive shaft at axle yoke. Secure shaft to frame with wire. Disconnect tie rods at steering knuckles. Remove shock absorbers. Remove retaining nuts and bolts from track bars at axle shaft tube brackets.
3) Disconnect breather tube at axle. Disconnect stabilizer bar link bolts at spring brackets. Remove disc brake calipers and support out of way. Remove rotors and brake shields.

NOTE: DO NOT allow brake hose to support the calipers.

4) Support axle and raise jack slightly to relieve spring tension. Remove spring "U" bolts and brackets. Loosen nuts attaching spring rear shackles to springs. Remove bolts attaching spring front shackles. Lower springs to floor. Remove axle assembly.
Installation - To install, reverse removal procedure.

AXLE SHAFT

Removal (Cherokee, Comanche & Wrangler) - 1) Raise and support vehicle. Remove wheels, caliper and rotor. Remove cotter pin, lock nut and axle hub nut.
2) Remove hub-to-steering knuckle bolts. Remove hub and rotor shield from steering knuckle. Remove left axle shaft from axle tube. On models with Command-Trac, disconnect vacuum harness. Remove vacuum motor housing.
3) Remove right axle shaft from axle tube. Ensure shift collar remains on intermediate shaft. *See Fig. 1.*
Installation - 1) Install right and left axle shafts in axle tubes. On models with Command-Trac, ensure shift collar is correctly positioned on intermediate axle shaft.

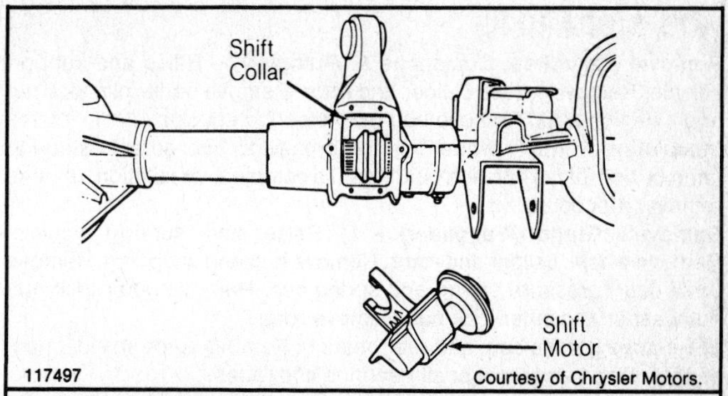
Shift
Collar
Shift
Motor
117497
Courtesy of Chrysler Motors.

***Fig. 1:** Removing Command-Trac Shift Motor*

2) Ensure outer axle shaft is completely engaged with shift collar and joined with intermediate axle shaft. *See Fig. 1.* Install shift motor. Ensure fork engages with shaft collar.
3) On all models, lubricate hub bore in steering knuckle with wheel bearing grease. Install rotor shield and hub. Tighten hub bolts. Install hub, washer and nut. Tighten hub lock nut and install cotter pin. Install rotor, caliper and wheel. Lower vehicle.
Removal (Grand Wagoneer) - 1) Raise and support vehicle. Remove wheels. Remove disc brake caliper. Remove rotor hub cover.
2) Remove axle shaft snap ring, drive gear, pressure spring and spring retainer. Using Socket (J-6893-D), remove outer lock nut, washer and inner lock nut.
3) Remove spring retainer and outer bearing. Remove rotor. Remove nuts and bolts attaching spindle and support shield. Remove spindle and support shield. Remove axle shaft.
Installation - 1) Install splined end of axle shaft in differential side gear and push shaft into place. Install spindle, support shield and rotor. Install inner wheel bearing lock nut. Install wheel, but do not tighten lug nuts.
2) Rotate wheel while tightening lock nut to 50 ft. lbs. (68 N.m). Back off inner lock nut 1/6 turn. Install washers so that inner tab is aligned with spindle keyway. Ensure peg on inner lock nut engages in nearest hole in washer.
3) Install and tighten outer lock nut. Remove wheel assembly. Install spring retainer, pressure spring and gear drive.

NOTE: Install spring retainer with cupped side of retainer facing toward center of vehicle.

4) Push drive gear inward to provide enough clearance for axle shaft snap ring. Coat rotor hub cap rim with sealant and install hub cap to rotor. Install disc brake caliper. Install wheel and lower vehicle.

INTERMEDIATE AXLE SHAFT

Removal & Installation (Cherokee, Comanche & Wrangler) - Remove outer axle. Remove differential cover and drain fluid. Remove intermediate shaft retaining clip. *See Fig. 2.* Remove intermediate shaft. To install, reverse removal procedure. Fill differential housing with 2.5 pts. (1.2L) of SAE 75W-90 gear oil.

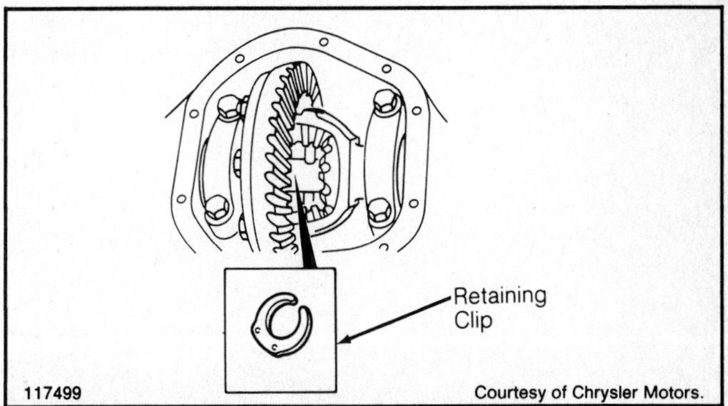
Retaining
Clip
117499
Courtesy of Chrysler Motors.

***Fig. 2:** Removing Intermediate Shaft Retaining Clip*

1991 DRIVE AXLES
Front Axles (Cont.)

HUB & BEARING

Removal (Cherokee, Comanche & Wrangler) – Raise and support vehicle. Remove wheel, caliper and rotor. Remove cotter pin, lock nut and axle hub nuts. Remove hub from steering knuckle.

Installation – Apply wheel bearing grease to hub bore in steering knuckle and install hub and bearings. To complete installation, reverse removal procedure.

Removal (Grand Wagoneer) – **1)** Raise and support vehicle. Remove wheel, caliper and rotor. Remove hub and snap ring. Remove drive gear, pressure spring and spring cup. Remove outer lock nut, nut washer and inner lock nut. Remove rotor.

2) Remove grease seal and rear bearing. Remove rotor shield if necessary. Clean and inspect all bearings and races.

Installation – **1)** Apply wheel bearing lubricant to hub bore, and repack bearings. Apply wheel bearing grease to hub cavity. Install rear bearing and grease seal in rotor. Install rotor on spindle.

NOTE: The inner lock nut has a locating peg on one side. Be sure this peg is facing outward.

2) Install inner lock nut. Install wheel, but do not tighten lug nuts. Tighten inner lock nut to 50 ft. lbs. (68 N.m), while rotating wheel. Continue rotating wheel and back off inner lock nut 1/6 turn.

3) Install nut washer and outer lock nut. Be sure the locating pin on inner washer is seated in one of the washer holes before installing outer lock nut. Tighten outer lock nut. Install spring and drive gear. Install snap ring and spring cup. Remove wheel and install caliper. Install wheel.

OVERHAUL

HUB & BEARING

NOTE: If hub is equipped with ball bearings. It CANNOT be serviced. If defective, the complete unit must be replaced.

Disassembly (Cherokee, Comanche & Wrangler) – Press hub out of carrier. Remove seals and bearings. *See Fig. 3.* Replace all worn and damaged components. If necessary, replace bearing and race as matched sets only. Remove bearing and race.

Reassembly – **1)** Install race in carrier. Apply a coating of wheel bearing grease to inside of hub bearing carrier and seals. Pack wheel bearings with wheel bearing grease. Install bearings and outer seal in the bearing carrier.

2) Press hub through the bearings into carrier. Install inner bearing seal and carrier seal. Install rotor shield on bearing carrier with retaining bolts. *See Fig. 3.*

AXLE SHAFT OUTER "U" JOINT

Remove axle shaft. Remove bearing cap and snap rings. Press out bearings caps from yoke. To install, reverse removal procedure. Pack replacement bearing caps 1/3 full of bearing grease.

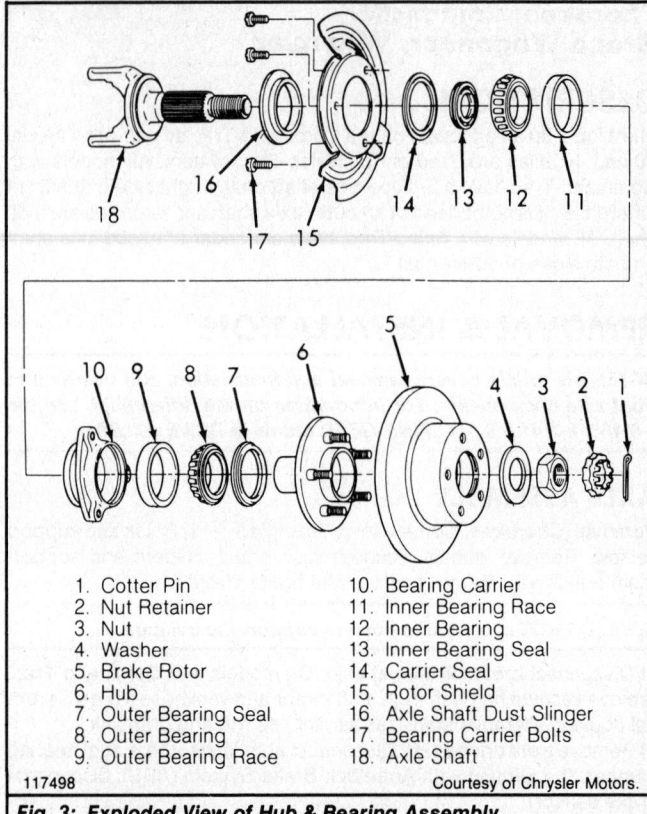

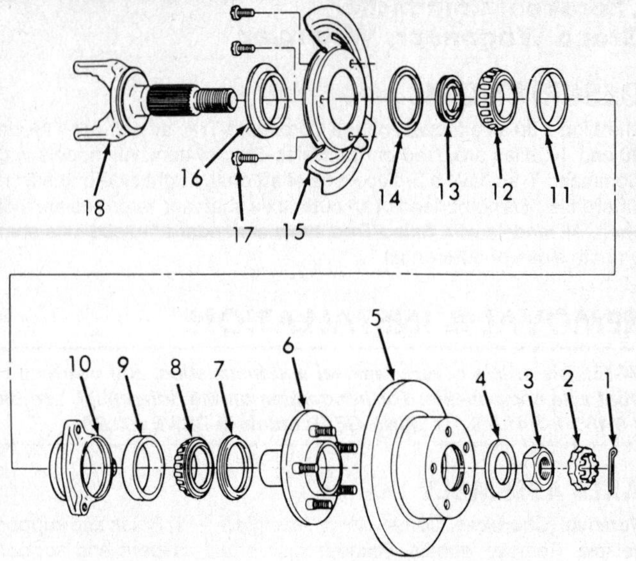
16
18
17
15
14
13
12
11
10
9
8
7
6
5
4
3
2
1

1. Cotter Pin
2. Nut Retainer
3. Nut
4. Washer
5. Brake Rotor
6. Hub
7. Outer Bearing Seal
8. Outer Bearing
9. Outer Bearing Race
10. Bearing Carrier
11. Inner Bearing Race
12. Inner Bearing
13. Inner Bearing Seal
14. Carrier Seal
15. Rotor Shield
16. Axle Shaft Dust Slinger
17. Bearing Carrier Bolts
18. Axle Shaft

117498 Courtesy of Chrysler Motors.

Fig. 3: Exploded View of Hub & Bearing Assembly (Cherokee, Comanche & Wrangler)

TORQUE SPECIFICATIONS

TORQUE SPECIFICATIONS

Applications	Ft. Lbs. (N.m)
Cherokee & Comanche	
Axle Yoke Nut	210 (285)
Hub Bolts	75 (101)
Hub Nut	175 (237)
Lower Control Arm Bolt	133 (180)
Shift Motor Bolts	8 (11)
"U" Joint Strap Bolts	14 (19)
Upper Control Arm Bolt	55 (75)
Grand Wagoneer	
Axle Shaft	
Inner Lock Nut	[1] 50 (68)
Outer Lock Nut	50 (68)
Axle Shaft-To-Yoke	16 (22)
Axle Yoke Nut	210 (285)
Shackle Bolts	100 (136)
Spring Pivot Bolts	100 (136)
Wrangler	
Axle Yoke Nut	210 (285)
Frame Bracket	105 (142)
Hub Bolts	75 (101)
Hub Nut	175 (237)
Shackle Bolts	95 (129)
Shift Motor Bolts	8 (11)
Track Bar	74 (100)
"U" Bolt At Axle Tube Retaining Nuts	90 (122)
"U" Joint Strap Bolts	14 (19)

[1] – After tightening, loosen lock nut 1/6 of a turn.

1991 DRIVE AXLES
7 9/16", 8 1/4" & 8 1/2" Ring Gear

**Cherokee, Comanche,
Grand Wagoneer, Wrangler**

DESCRIPTION

Front and rear drive axle assemblies have hypoid type gears with integral carrier housings. *See Fig. 1.* Model 30 front axle is used on Cherokee, Comanche and Wrangler. Model 35 rear axle is used on Cherokee, Comanche and Wrangler. Model 44 front and rear axles are used on Grand Wagoneer.

AXLE RATIO & IDENTIFICATION

The axle build date and manufacturer's number are stamped on the passenger side axle tube near the housing cover. The axle assembly part number, gear ratio and identification tag is attached to the left side of the housing cover. *See Fig. 2.*

AXLE RATIO & IDENTIFICATION

Axle Ratio	Pinion/Ring Gear Tooth Combinations	Ring Gear Diameter
Model 30/35		
3.07:1	14/43	7 9/16 In. (192 mm)
3.55:1	11/39	7 9/16 In. (192 mm)
3.55:1 [1]	11/39	8 1/4 In. (209 mm)
4.10:1	9/37	7 9/16 In. (192 mm)
4.56:1	9/41	7 9/16 In. (192 mm)
Model 44		
2.72:1	18/49	8 1/2 In. (216 mm)
3.31:1	13/43	8 1/2 In. (216 mm)

[1] - Optional rear axle for Cherokee only.

REMOVAL & INSTALLATION

REAR AXLE SHAFT, BEARING, SEALS & RETAINER

NOTE: To service front axle shaft, bearings, seals and retainer, see FRONT AXLES article in DRIVE AXLES.

Removal (Cherokee, Comanche & Wrangler) - 1) Raise and support vehicle. Remove rear wheel(s). Remove brake drum. Clean axle housing cover. Loosen cover bolts and drain oil. Remove cover.

2) Remove differential pinion-shaft lock screw. Remove pinion shaft from differential. Push axle in. Remove "C" clip from axle at pinion gear. Remove axle from tube. Remove axle shaft seal and bearing from axle tube.

Installation - 1) Grease bearing and install in axle tube. Apply wheel bearing grease to axle shaft seal. Install seal in axle tube. Install axle shaft.

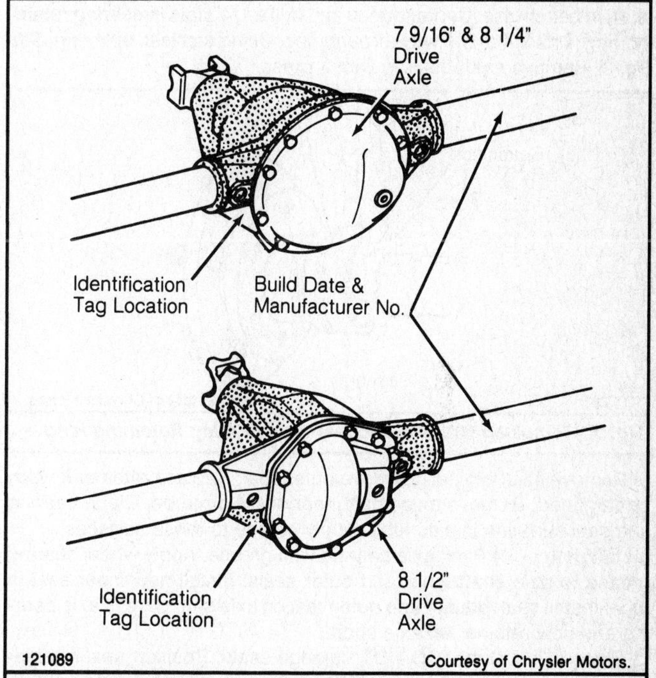
7 9/16" & 8 1/4"
Drive
Axle
Identification
Tag Location
Build Date &
Manufacturer No.
Identification
Tag Location
8 1/2"
Drive
Axle
121089
Courtesy of Chrysler Motors.

Fig. 2: Locating Drive Axle Identification Tag

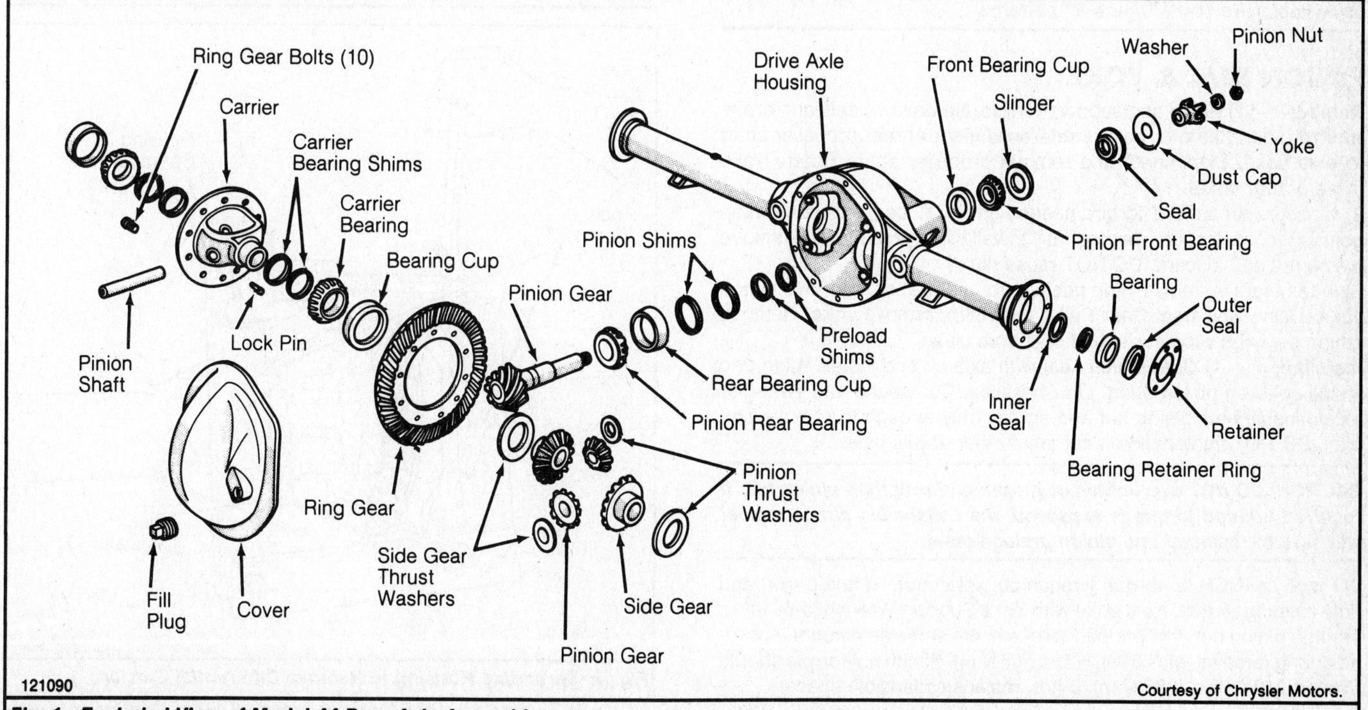
Ring Gear Bolts (10)
Carrier
Carrier
Bearing Shims
Carrier
Bearing
Bearing Cup
Pinion Shims
Pinion Gear
Drive Axle
Housing
Front Bearing Cup
Slinger
Washer
Pinion Nut
Yoke
Dust Cap
Seal
Pinion Front Bearing
Bearing
Outer
Seal
Preload
Shims
Rear Bearing Cup
Pinion Rear Bearing
Inner
Seal
Retainer
Bearing Retainer Ring
Pinion
Thrust
Washers
Pinion
Shaft
Lock Pin
Ring Gear
Side Gear
Thrust
Washers
Side Gear
Pinion Gear
Fill
Plug
Cover
121090
Courtesy of Chrysler Motors.

Fig. 1: Exploded View of Model 44 Rear Axle Assembly

1991 DRIVE AXLES
7 9/16", 8 1/4" & 8 1/2" Ring Gear (Cont.)

2) Install axle "C" clip. Pull axle out to seat "C" clip. Install pinion shaft. Install lock screw and tighten to 8.5 ft. lbs. (11 N.m). Apply RTV to axle housing cover. Tighten cover bolts to 35 ft. lbs. (47 N.m). Check oil level.

NOTE: On vehicles with Trac-Lok (limited slip) differentials, slowly drive vehicle in 10-12 "figure 8" patterns.

Removal (Grand Wagoneer) - 1) Raise and support vehicle. Remove rear wheel and brake drum. Remove outer seal retainer and brake support plate. DO NOT reuse outer seal retainer nuts.
2) Using Slide Hammer (J-2619-01), remove axle shaft. Mount axle shaft in bench vise. Center punch and drill a 1/4" hole in bearing retaining ring. Drill 3/4 of the way through ring. Using a chisel, split ring. *See Fig. 3.* Remove shaft bearing with a press.

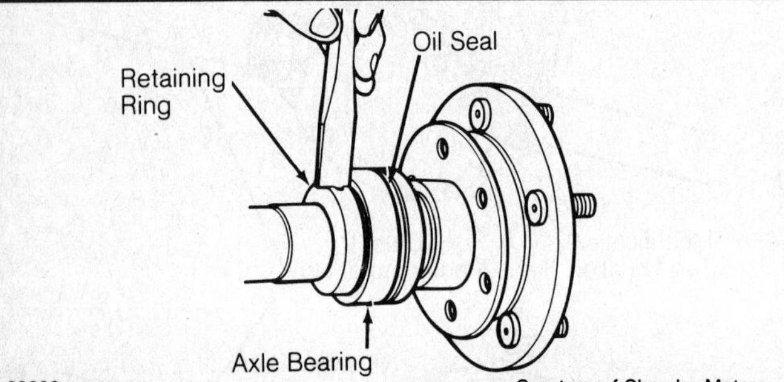
Oil Seal
Retaining Ring
Axle Bearing

29228 Courtesy of Chrysler Motors.

Fig. 3: Removing Grand Wagoneer Axle Bearing Retaining Ring

3) Remove seal retainer. Remove outer seal. Replace retainer if worn or damaged. Remove axle shaft inner seal from tube. Clean bearing and seal surfaces in axle tube. Apply grease to these surfaces.
Installation - 1) Pack axle bearing with grease. Apply wheel bearing grease to axle shaft inner and outer seals. Install new inner seal in tube. Install seal retainer and outer seal on axle shaft. Press axle bearing and new retainer on axle shaft.
2) Place axle in tube. DO NOT damage seals. Position seal retainer and brake support plate on studs. Install new nuts and tighten to 32 ft. lbs. (43 N.m). Install brake drum and wheel. Tighten lug nuts.

NOTE: On vehicles with Trac-Lok (limited slip) differentials, slowly drive vehicle in 10-12 "figure 8" patterns.

PINION SEAL & YOKE

Removal - 1) Raise and support vehicle. Remove wheels and brake rotor/drums. Stamp or paint a reference mark at rear propeller shaft to axle yoke. Disconnect and remove propeller shaft. Rotate yoke three or four times.
2) Measure amount of torque needed (in INCH lbs.) to rotate pinion gear. Record torque reading for installation procedure. Remove pinion nut and discard. DO NOT reuse nut.
3) Index mark yoke-to-pinion position for installation. Remove pinion yoke. Using Universal Gear Puller (J-22888), remove yoke. Remove pinion seal and wipe surface of seal bore clean.
Installation - 1) Coat pinion seal with axle oil and install. Align and install yoke on pinion shaft. On Cherokee, Comanche and Wrangler axles, install new pinion nut and tighten only enough to remove end play. DO NOT tighten pinion nut any further at this time.

CAUTION: DO NOT overtighten or loosen and retighten pinion nut. If required preload torque is exceeded, the collapsible pinion spacer will have to replaced and pinion preload reset.

2) Place an INCH lb. torque wrench on pinion nut. Rotate pinion and note rotating torque. Hold yoke with Yoke Support Wrench (J-8614-1). Tighten pinion nut until preload torque is the same as amount recorded during removal, plus 5 INCH lbs. (.56 N.m). Pinion nut torque should exceed 210 ft. lbs. (285 N.m). If not, replace collapsible spacer.
3) On Grand Wagoneer axles, hold yoke with Yoke Support Wrench (J-8614-1). Torque yoke nut to at least 200 ft. lbs. (271 N.m). Check pinion preload torque. Tighten pinion nut until preload torque is 10-20 INCH lbs. (1-2 N.m), or 20-40 INCH lbs. (2-5 N.m) with new bearings.
4) On all axles, align and install propeller shaft. Tighten "U" joint clamp bolts. Install brake drum/rotors and wheels. Tighten lug nuts. Check oil level.

DRIVE AXLE HOUSING

Removal - 1) Raise and support vehicle on frame rails. Remove wheels. Index mark propeller shaft and axle yoke for installation reference. Remove propeller shaft.
2) Disconnect rear track bar (if equipped) at axle bracket. Remove axle vent tube at axle. Disconnect parking brake cables at equalizer (rear axle). Remove shock absorbers. Disconnect brake hose(s).
3) On Cherokee and Comanche, support axle housing. Disconnect upper and lower control arms at axle. Lower and remove assembly to release coil spring pressure.
4) On Grand Wagoneer and Wrangler, loosen, but DO NOT remove bolts attaching spring eyes to frame brackets and shackles. Support axle housing. Remove spring "U" bolts and tie plates. Raise axle housing just enough to relieve weight from springs.
5) Remove bolts attaching springs to frame bracket and shackles. Lower springs to the floor. Lower jack slowly and remove assembly from vehicle.
Installation - Align spring mounting points and place axle in position. To install, reverse removal procedure.

DIFFERENTIAL CARRIER & PINION

Removal (Except Cherokee 8 1/4" Ring Gear) - 1) Raise and support vehicle. Remove axle housing cover and drain oil. Index mark drive axle and propeller shaft yokes for installation. Remove propeller shaft.
2) Remove wheels, brake rotor/drums and axle shafts. Mount Housing Spreader (J-24385-01) on axle housing. Mount Dial Indicator (J-8001). Spread housing enough to remove differential carrier. *See Fig. 4.*

CAUTION: Do not spread housing more than .015" (.38 mm) on Grand Wagoneer or .02" (.5 mm) on all others, or damage to housing may result.

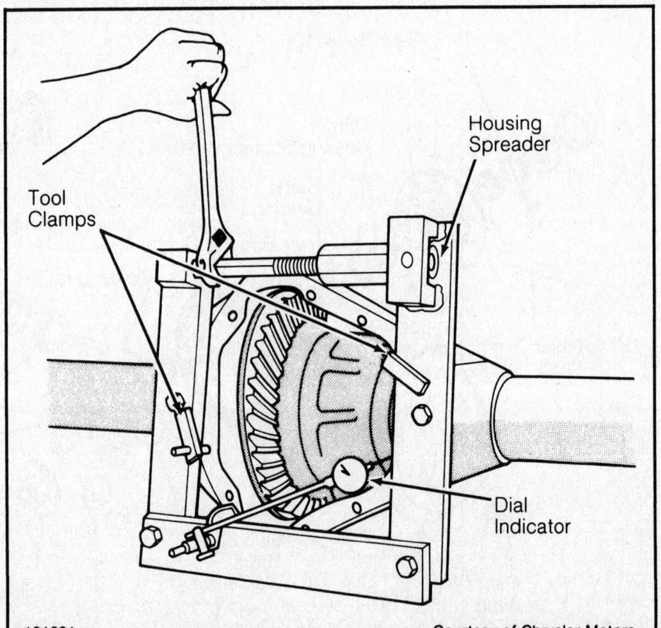
Housing Spreader
Tool Clamps
Dial Indicator

121091 Courtesy of Chrysler Motors.

Fig. 4: Spreading Housing to Remove Differential Carrier

1991 DRIVE AXLES
7 9/16", 8 1/4" & 8 1/2" Ring Gear (Cont.)

3) Index mark bearing caps for installation reference. Loosen bearing caps until almost out. Pry differential carrier loose. Remove bearing caps. Remove housing spreader. Check pinion preload and remove pinion gear assembly. See PINION SEAL & YOKE under REMOVAL & INSTALLATION.

Installation - 1) Install pinion gear, pinion bearings and seal (if removed) and adjust pinion preload. See REASSEMBLY under OVERHAUL. Spread housing as during removal.

2) Place differential carrier with bearing cups and shims in axle housing. Using a mallet, tap outer edges of drive axle bearing cups to seat differential carrier. Remove housing spreader.

3) Install bearing caps. Tighten bolts to 57 ft. lbs. (77 N.m) on Cherokee, Comanche and Wrangler or 80 ft. lbs. (108 N.m) on Grand Wagoneer. Check and adjust ring gear backlash and tooth contact. If pinion gear, bearings or seal was serviced, adjust pinion preload.

4) Apply RTV sealant to axle housing cover. Tighten cover bolts. Connect propeller shaft. Using 75W-90 gear oil, fill axle with 3.75 pts. (1.8L) for Grand Wagoneer or 2.5 pts. (1.2L) for all others.

NOTE: For differentials with Trac-Lok, add container of friction modifier (Trac-Lok additive).

Removal (Cherokee 8 1/4" Ring Gear) - 1) Remove wheels and brake drums. Mark propeller shaft for reassembly. Remove propeller shaft. Drain oil and remove housing cover. Remove pinion shaft lock screw. Remove pinion shaft.

2) Push axle shafts in and remove "C" clips. Remove axles. Measure and record differential side play, ring gear runout and pinion gear preload.

3) Mark differential gear and carrier at point of maximum runout. There should be no side play. If ring gear runout exceeds .005" (.13 mm), replace differential carrier.

4) Remove pinion yoke and seal. Mark side bearing caps and axle housing for reassembly. Remove adjuster locks. Loosen but do not remove bearing caps. Insert Hex Adjuster (C-4164) through axle tube and loosen hex adjuster on each side.

5) Remove bearing caps, adjusters and differential carrier. Keep all bearing cups, bearings and adjusters together. Using brass drift, hammer pinion shaft out of housing.

6) Drive bearing cups out of housing. Remove shim(s) from behind rear cups and record thickness. Remove bearing from pinion shaft using Bearing Puller (C-293-PA) and Bearing Remover Adapter (C-293-42).

7) Mount differential carrier in soft-jawed vise. Remove and discard ring gear bolts (LEFT-HAND thread). Using soft-faced hammer, drive ring gear off differential carrier.

Installation - 1) Install pinion gear, pinion bearings, and seal (if removed). Adjust pinion preload. See REASSEMBLY under OVERHAUL. Place differential carrier with adjusters in axle housing.

2) Install bearing caps. Check and adjust ring gear backlash and tooth contact. Preload differential carrier bearings. Tighten bolts to 100 ft. lbs. (136 N.m). Tighten adjuster lock screws to 90 INCH lbs. (10 N.m).

3) Apply RTV sealant to axle housing cover. Tighten cover bolts. Connect propeller shaft. Using 75W-90 gear oil, fill axle with 4.4 pts. (2.0L) of fluid.

NOTE: For differentials with Trac-Lok, add container of friction modifier (Trac-Lok additive).

OVERHAUL

DISASSEMBLY

NOTE: If equipped with Trac-Lok, see DIFFERENTIALS - SPICER (DANA) TRAC-LOK article in DRIVE AXLES for overhaul of limited slip unit. The following overhaul procedures apply to the drive axle gears. It is not necessary to remove complete drive axle housing to overhaul assembly.

1) Place drive axle assembly on bench. Using 2 feeler gauges, measure carrier side gear clearance. *See Fig. 5*. If side gear clearance exceeds .007" (.18 mm) on either side, replace both side gear thrust washers.

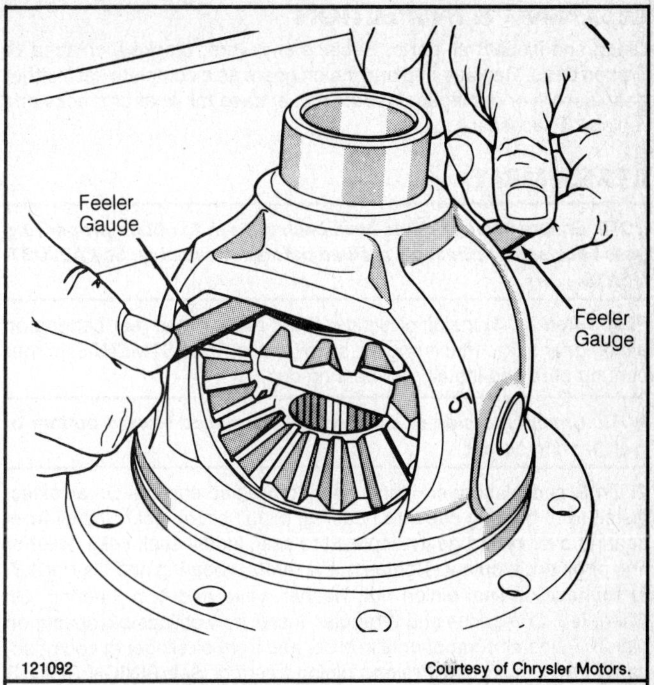
Feeler
Gauge
Feeler
Gauge
121092
Courtesy of Chrysler Motors.

Fig. 5: Checking Side Gear Clearance

2) Remove and discard ring gear bolts (LEFT-HAND thread on Cherokee 8 1/4" rear axle). Remove ring gear. On Grand Wagoneer, remove pinion shaft lock pin and remove pinion shaft. Remove pinion gears. Remove side gears and inspect.

3) On all axles, remove yoke nut, washer and pinion yoke. Keep pinion nut for pinion depth adjustment during reassembly. Remove pinion gear, pinion bearings and preload shims. On Cherokee, Comanche and Wrangler, discard collapsible spacer.

4) On all axles, remove pinion seal and rear pinion bearing cup. Remove and retain pinion depth shim located under rear bearing cup. Remove pinion front bearing race. Press off pinion gear rear bearing from pinion gear using Bearing Press Plate (J-22912-01) and hydraulic press. *See Fig. 6*. On front axles, remove inner axle housing seals.

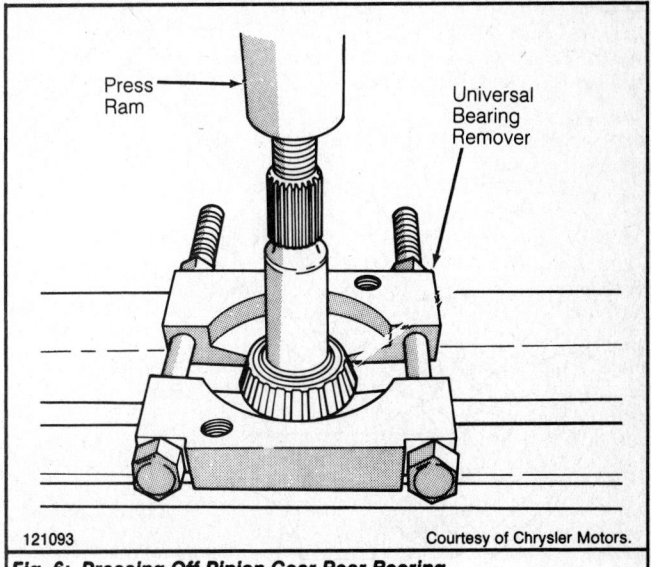

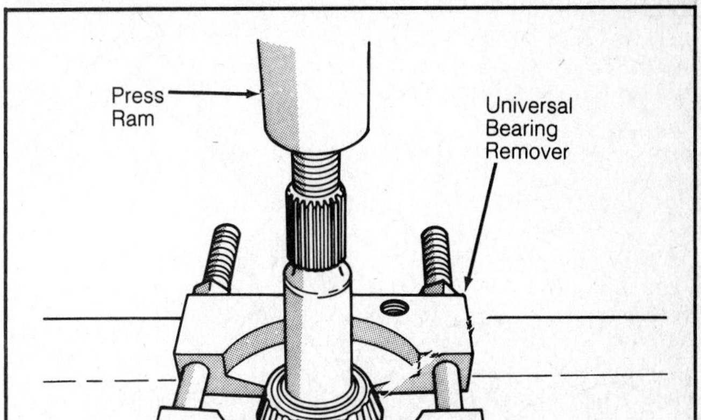
Press
Ram
Universal
Bearing
Remover
121093
Courtesy of Chrysler Motors.

Fig. 6: Pressing Off Pinion Gear Rear Bearing

1991 DRIVE AXLES
7 9/16", 8 1/4" & 8 1/2" Ring Gear (Cont.)

CLEANING & INSPECTION

Clean and inspect all parts. Replace any worn, cracked, chipped or broken parts. Replace ring and pinion gears as a complete set if either gear is worn or damaged. Inspect carrier case for wear or cracks and replace if necessary.

REASSEMBLY

NOTE: Ensure correct shims have been chosen to obtain proper ring gear backlash and bearing preload before reassembly. See ADJUSTMENTS.

Pinion Gear – 1) Install oil slinger (front axle). Press rear bearing on pinion gear shaft. Place original shim (or see ADJUSTMENTS) in rear bearing bore and install rear bearing cup.

NOTE: Chamfered side of shim must be installed toward bottom of rear bearing bore.

2) On Grand Wagoneer, install bearing preload shim(s). On all axles, install front bearing cup into housing. Install pinion gear. Install front bearing over pinion gear. Apply oil to seal. Install seal, yoke, washer and original pinion nut. Tighten nut to remove bearing end play ONLY.

3) Remove original pinion nut, washer, yoke and front bearing. On Cherokee, Comanche and Wrangler, install new collapsible spacer on pinion. Reinstall components in order and front oil slinger (if equipped) using new pinion nut. Preload pinion bearing. See PINION SEAL & YOKE under REMOVAL & INSTALLATION.

4) Make sure pinion bearing preload to 15-35 INCH lbs. (1.3-4.0 N.m). Preload is measured as the amount of torque needed to rotate the pinion gear with an INCH lb. torque wrench.

5) On Grand Wagoneer axles, hold yoke with Yoke Support Wrench (J-8614-1). Torque yoke nut to at least 200 ft. lbs. (271 N.m). Check pinion bearing preload torque. Tighten pinion nut until preload torque is 10-20 INCH lbs. (1-2 N.m), or 20-40 INCH lbs. (2-5 N.m) with new bearings.

Differential Carrier – 1) Assemble side gears with thrust washers and install into carrier. Replace side gear thrust washers if one or both side clearance is greater than .007" (.18 mm).

2) Install carrier pinion gears and thrust washers into carrier. On Grand Wagoneer, install pinion shaft and secure with lock pin. Using Bearing Puller (J-22888) and Thrust Pad (J-22888-9), remove carrier bearings. *See Fig. 7.* Note if shims are used between carrier bearing and carrier.

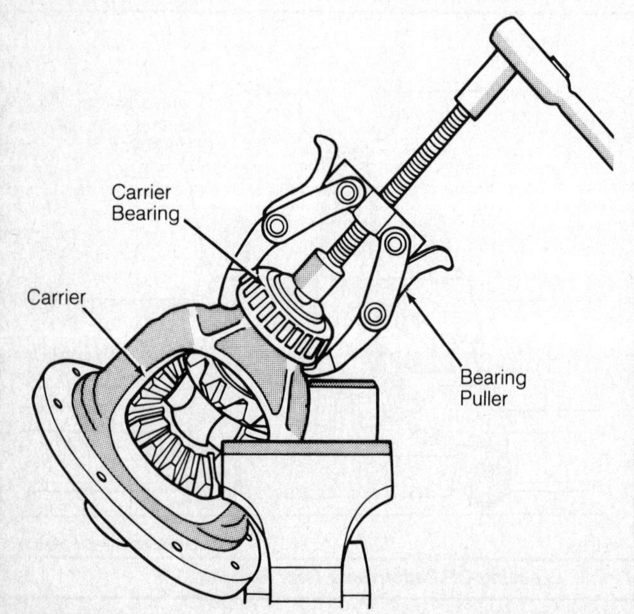
Carrier
Bearing
Carrier
Bearing
Puller

121094 Courtesy of Chrysler Motors.

Fig. 7: Removing Drive Axle Carrier Bearings

3) Install shims (if equipped) and press carrier bearings onto carrier. Using heat lamp, heat ring gear to 250°F (121°C). Install ring gear on carrier. Install new ring gear bolts (LEFT-HAND thread on Cherokee with 8 1/4" rear axle).

4) Tighten ring gear bolts to 80 ft. lbs. (108 N.m) on Cherokee, Comanche and Wrangler with 7 9/16" drive axles, 70 ft. lbs. (90 N.m) on Cherokee 8 1/4" rear axle or to 55 ft. lbs. (75 N.m) on Grand Wagoneer axles. To complete reassembly, see DIFFERENTIAL CARRIER & PINION under REMOVAL & INSTALLATION. Check ring gear backlash. See RING GEAR BACKLASH under ADJUSTMENTS.

ADJUSTMENTS

NOTE: Ring and pinion gears are serviced as matched set only. They are identified by numbers etched on gear and pinion. See Fig. 8. The first 2 numbers identify matched set. Second number on pinion gear is pinion depth variance. This number indicates amount (in thousandths of an inch) gear set varied from standard setting. Standard setting of Cherokee, Comanche and Wrangler with 7 9/16" axle is 2.095" (53.21 mm) on a rear axle, or 2.25" (57.1 mm) on a front axle. Standard setting of Grand Wagoneer is 2.625" (66.67 mm) on all axles. Variance can be a plus or minus number.

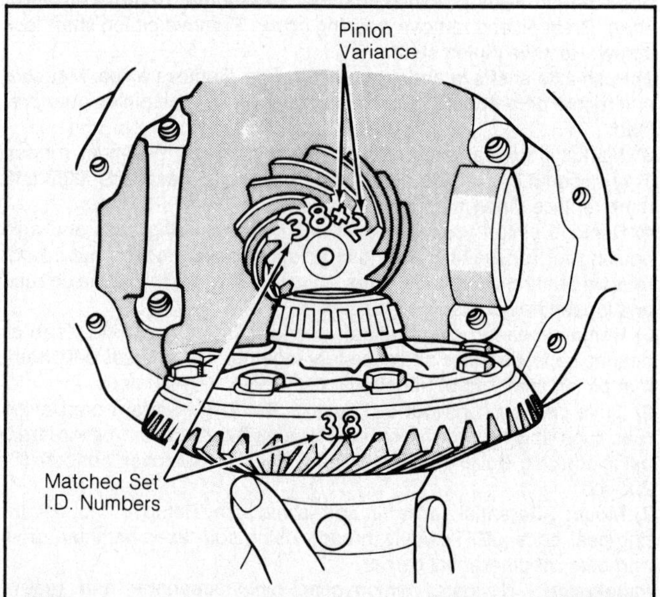
Pinion
Variance
38+2
38
Matched Set
I.D. Numbers

121095 Courtesy of Chrysler Motors.

Fig. 8: Matching Ring & Pinion Gear Set

DETERMINING CORRECT PINION STARTING SHIM

1) If original ring and pinion is being installed, use original shim. If new parts (gear set) is being installed, use following steps to determine best starting shim thickness.

2) Check numbers etched on drive pinion and ring gear. Measure thickness of original pinion shim. Note variance number on pinion gear. *See Fig. 8.* Note where the old and new pinion marking columns intersect on chart. *See Fig. 10.*

3) The intersecting figure represents the amount needed to add or subtract to the original shim. For example, if old pinion is +1 and new pinion is -3, intersecting figure is +.004" (+.10 mm). Add this amount to original shim. If old pinion is -3 and new pinion is -2, intersecting figure is -.001" (-.025 mm). *See Fig. 10.* Subtract this amount from original shim.

PINION BEARING PRELOAD

1) Apply oil to seal. Install seal, yoke, washer and original nut. Tighten pinion nut only enough to remove bearing end play. Remove original

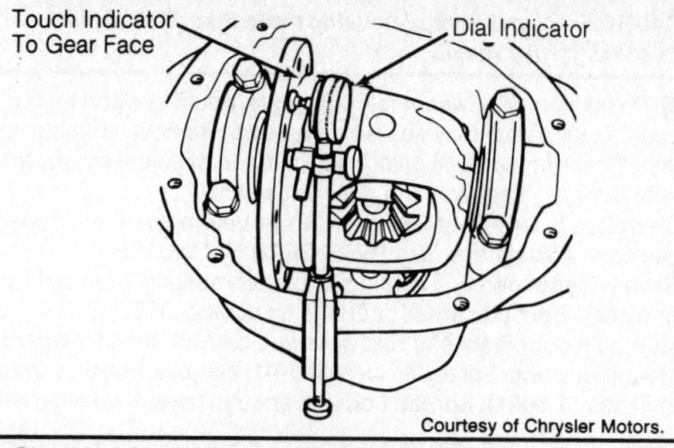

Touch Indicator
To Gear Face
Dial Indicator
71756
Courtesy of Chrysler Motors.

Fig. 9: Checking Carrier Bearing End Play & Runout

nut, washer and yoke and install new collapsible spacer. Reassemble components, including oil slinger (if equipped).

CAUTION: Never reuse collapsible spacer.

2) On Cherokee, Comanche and Wrangler, place an INCH lb. torque wrench on pinion nut. Rotate pinion and note rotating torque. Hold yoke with Yoke Support Wrench (J-8614-1). Tighten pinion nut until preload torque is 15-25 INCH lbs. (2-3 N.m). Pinion nut torque should exceed 210 ft. lbs. (285 N.m). If not, replace collapsible spacer.

CAUTION: DO NOT overtighten pinion nut. If preload torque is exceeded, collapsible spacer must be replaced and preload reset.

3) On Grand Wagoneer axles, hold yoke with Yoke Support Wrench (J-8614-1). Torque yoke nut to at least 200 ft. lbs. (271 N.m). Slowly tighten pinion nut until preload torque is 10-20 INCH lbs. (1-2 N.m), or 20-40 INCH lbs. (2-5 N.m) with new bearings.

CARRIER BEARING END PLAY

NOTE: This adjustment is not required on Cherokee 8 1/4" rear axle.

1) Place bearing cup over each carrier bearing. Install carrier assembly (without ring gear) into axle housing. Install a .142" (3.60 mm) shim on outer side of each carrier bearing cup on Cherokee, Comanche and Wrangler axles. On Grand Wagoneer axles, install a shim (which allows some side play) on each side of carrier bearing cup.

2) Install bearing caps and tighten bolts finger tight. Mount dial indicator to housing. *See Fig. 9.* Using a pry bar between shims and housing, move assembly to one side. Zero dial indicator. Pry assembly to opposite side. Record indicator reading. Do not zero or read indicator while prying.

3) Indicator reading (when divided by 2; one for each side) is the thickness of shims required. Shims are available in .002" (.050 mm) increments.

4) When all side play is eliminated, check drive gear face of carrier for runout by rotating carrier and reading dial indicator. Runout should not exceed .002" (.050 mm). Remove carrier from housing and retain shims.

RING GEAR BACKLASH

All Except Cherokee 8 1/4" Ring Gear – 1) Install carrier assembly into housing using shims selected to remove end play. Tighten bearing cap bolts evenly to 57 ft. lbs. (77 N.m) for Cherokee, Comanche and Wrangler axles, or 80 ft. lbs. (110 N.m) for Grand Wagoneer axles.

2) Attach a dial indicator to housing so button of indicator contacts drive side of ring gear tooth. Rock ring gear, and note backlash. *See Fig. 11.*

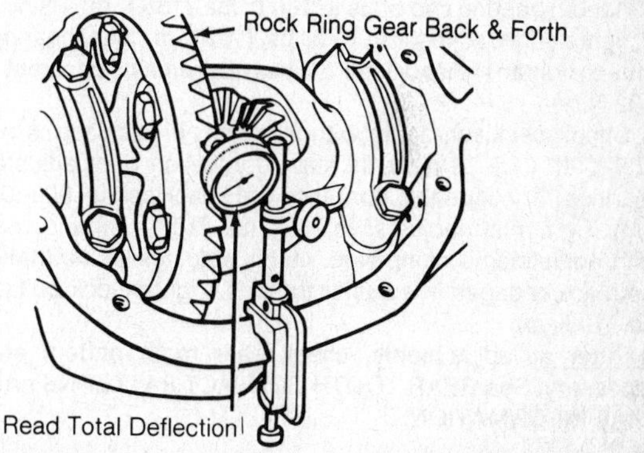

Rock Ring Gear Back & Forth
Read Total Deflection
29232
Courtesy of Chrysler Motors.

Fig. 11: Checking Ring Gear Backlash

3) Backlash should be .005-.009" (.13-.23 mm). To increase backlash, install thinner shim on ring gear side of case and a thicker shim on opposite side of case. To decrease backlash, reverse this step. DO NOT change total shim thickness.

OLD PINION MARKING	NEW PINION MARKING								
	−4	−3	−2	−1	+0	+1	+2	+3	+4
+4	+0.008	+0.007	+0.006	+0.005	+0.004	+0.003	+0.002	+0.001	0
+3	+0.007	+0.006	+0.005	+0.004	+0.003	+0.002	+0.001	0	−0.001
+2	+0.006	+0.005	+0.004	+0.003	+0.002	+0.001	0	−0.001	−0.002
+1	+0.005	+0.004	+0.003	+0.002	+0.001	0	−0.001	−0.002	−0.003
0	+0.004	+0.003	+0.002	+0.001	0	−0.001	−0.002	−0.003	−0.004
−1	+0.003	+0.002	+0.001	0	−0.001	−0.002	−0.003	−0.004	−0.005
−2	+0.002	+0.001	0	−0.001	−0.002	−0.003	−0.004	−0.005	−0.006
−3	+0.001	0	−0.001	−0.002	−0.003	−0.004	−0.005	−0.006	−0.007
−4	0	−0.001	−0.002	−0.003	−0.004	−0.005	−0.006	−0.007	−0.008

Courtesy of Chrysler Motors.

Fig. 10: Selecting Correct Pinion Starting Shim from Pinion Variance Chart

1991 DRIVE AXLES
7 9/16", 8 1/4" & 8 1/2" Ring Gear (Cont.)

4) After all adjustments, check gear tooth pattern, and adjust if necessary. See GEAR TOOTH CONTACT PATTERNS article in GENERAL INFORMATION.

Cherokee 8 1/4" Ring Gear - 1) Using hex adjuster, turn each adjuster until bearing free play is eliminated with about .010" (.25 mm) backlash. To ensure accurate adjustment, seat bearings by rotating differential carrier 1/2 turn, back and forth, 5-10 times each time adjusters are moved.

NOTE: Index gears so same teeth are meshed during all backlash measurements. It is also important to maintain specified adjuster torque to obtain accurate differential bearing preload.

2) Mount dial indicator on flange. Position indicator stem against drive side of ring gear. Check backlash every 90 degrees to find point of minimum backlash. Mark each position so backlash readings will be taken with same teeth meshed. Rotate ring gear to point of minimum backlash.

3) Tighten each adjuster to 10 ft. lbs. (14 N.m). Seat bearings as described in step **1)**. Measure backlash. If necessary, back out right or left adjuster and turn in right or left adjuster until backlash is .003-.004" (.08-.10 mm). Tighten and seat carrier bearings each time adjusters are moved.

4) Tighten bearing cap bolts to 100 ft. lbs. (136 N.m). Using hex adjuster, tighten right adjuster to 75 ft. lbs. (102 N.m). Seat bearings and continue to tighten right adjuster until torque remains constant at 75 ft. lbs. (102 N.m).

5) Check backlash again with indicator. If backlash is not between .006-.008" (.15-.20 mm), increase torque on right adjuster and seat bearings. Continue this operation until backlash is .006-.008" (.15-.20 mm). Tighten left adjuster to 75 ft. lbs. (102 N.m) and seat bearings. With adjustments completed, install adjuster locks. Make sure lock teeth are engaged in adjuster threads. Tighten lock bolts to 90 INCH lbs. (10 N.m).

6) After all adjustments, check gear tooth pattern and adjust if necessary. See GEAR TOOTH CONTACT PATTERNS article in GENERAL INFORMATION.

CARRIER BEARING PRELOAD

NOTE: Pre-loading carrier bearings may change backlash setting. Recheck backlash and adjust as necessary.

Cherokee, Comanche & Wrangler 7 9/16" Ring Gear - 1) Preload carrier bearings by adding .004" (.10 mm) to each existing shim. Mount Housing Spreader (J-24385-01) on axle housing. Mount Dial Indicator (J-8001). Spread housing enough to remove differential. *See Fig. 4.*

CAUTION: Do not spread housing more than .02" (.5 mm), or damage to housing may result.

2) Position carrier assembly into axle housing bearing bores. Tap bearing cups until fully seated in housing. Remove housing spreader. Install bearing caps, aligning marks made at disassembly. Install and tighten bolts. Recheck ring gear backlash.

Cherokee 8 1/4" Ring Gear - Carrier bearings are preloaded during backlash adjustment. See RING GEAR BACKLASH.

Grand Wagoneer - 1) Remove carrier bearing from side opposite ring gear. Preload carrier bearings by adding .015" (.38 mm) to carrier bearing mount (between ring gear and carrier). Install carrier bearing. Mount Housing Spreader (J-24385-01) on axle housing. Mount Dial Indicator (J-8001). Spread housing enough to remove differential. *See Fig. 4.*

CAUTION: Do not spread housing more than .015" (.38 mm), or damage to housing may result.

2) Position carrier assembly into axle housing bearing bores. Tap bearing cups until fully seated in housing. Remove housing spreader. Install bearing caps, aligning marks made at disassembly. Install and tighten bolts. Recheck ring gear backlash.

TORQUE SPECIFICATIONS

TORQUE SPECIFICATIONS

Application	Ft. Lbs. (N.m)
Axle Housing Cover	
Cherokee, Comanche & Wrangler	20 (27)
Grand Wagoneer	35 (47)
Differential Carrier Bearing Caps	
Cherokee, Comanche & Wrangler	
7 9/16"	57 (77)
8 1/4"	100 (136)
Grand Wagoneer	80 (108)
Leaf Spring Front Eye Bolts	105 (142)
Leaf Spring Shackle Bolts	95 (129)
Leaf Spring "U" Bolt Nuts	90 (122)
Propeller Shaft	
"U" Joint Clamp Bolts	14 (19)
Ring Gear Bolts	
Cherokee, Comanche & Wrangler	
7 9/16"	80 (108)
8 1/4"	70 (95)
Grand Wagoneer	55 (75)
Wheel Lug Nuts	75 (102)
	INCH lbs. (N.m)
Adjuster Lock Screws	
Cherokee (8 1/4" Ring Gear)	90 (10)

1991 DRIVE AXLES
Differentials – Spicer (Dana) Trac-Lok

Cherokee, Comanche
Grand Wagoneer, Wrangler

DESCRIPTION

The Trac-Lok positive traction differential is a 2-pinion, single-case type. Under normal conditions, torque to each rear wheel is divided evenly. When vehicle is driven on snow, ice or mud, torque will transfer to the wheel with the least traction.

LUBRICATION

NOTE: Use 75W-90 GL-5 plus Trac-Lok additive (friction modifier).

DIAGNOSIS & TESTING

The most common Trac-Lok condition is chatter when turning corners. Incorrect or contaminated oil is usually the cause.

Changing axle oil (with Trac-Lok additive) should correct the condition. After changing Trac-Lok differential oil, make 10 or 12 slow "figure 8" turns. If chatter persists, the clutch packs must be inspected for damage.

REMOVAL & INSTALLATION

NOTE: This article covers overhaul of Trac-Lok (positive traction) unit. For all other information, see 7 9/16", 8 1/4" & 8 1/2" RING GEAR article in DRIVE AXLES.

OVERHAUL

Disassembly – 1) Using 2 screwdrivers, remove pinion snap rings. Using a brass drift and a hammer, remove pinion shaft from case. Install Step Plate (J-23781-7) in side gear. Grease centering hole of step plate. Position Gear Rotator (J-23781-3) on step plate. Coat threads of Forcing Screw (J-8646-2) with oil.

2) Insert Forcing Screw (J-8646-2) through side gear opposite step plate. Thread screw through gear rotator until it contacts centering hole in step plate. Tighten forcing screw to relieve clutch pack tension. Remove pinion thrust washers.

3) Tighten forcing screw until all clutch pack tension is relieved. Using gear rotator, engage side gear teeth and rotate side gears until pinions can be removed.

4) Remove step plate, gear rotator, forcing screw, side gears and clutch packs. Remove clutch pack retainer clips. Mark clutch packs for reassembly reference.

Reassembly – 1) Lightly oil clutch discs. Assemble clutch pack discs. *See Fig. 2.* Assemble clutch packs on side gears.

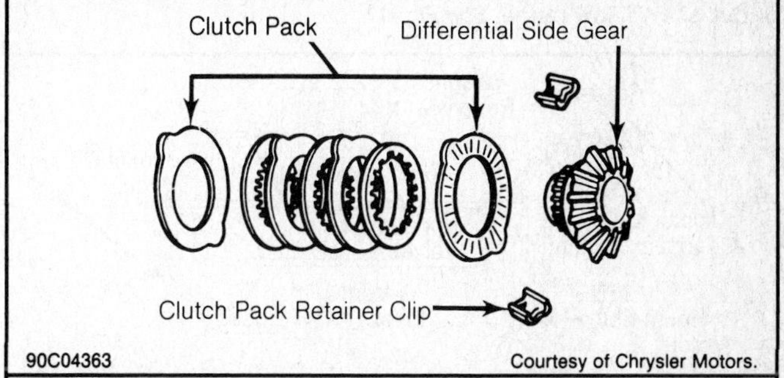
Clutch Pack
Differential Side Gear
Clutch Pack Retainer Clip
90C04363
Courtesy of Chrysler Motors.

Fig. 2: Identifying Trac-Lok Clutch Pack Assembly

2) Install clutch pack and side gear in side of case. Ensure retaining clips remain seated in case pockets. Install step plate in clutch pack just installed.

3) Install remaining side gear and clutch pack in case. Hold assembly in position and install rotating tool and forcing screw.

4) Tighten forcing screw and compress clutch packs. Install pinions. Rotate side gear with tool pawl until each pinion is aligned with pinion shaft bore.

5) Install pinion thrust washers. Remove tools. Install pinion shaft. Install snap rings on pinion shaft. Position ring gear on differential case. Install NEW ring gear bolts and tighten to 52 ft. lbs. (70 N.m).

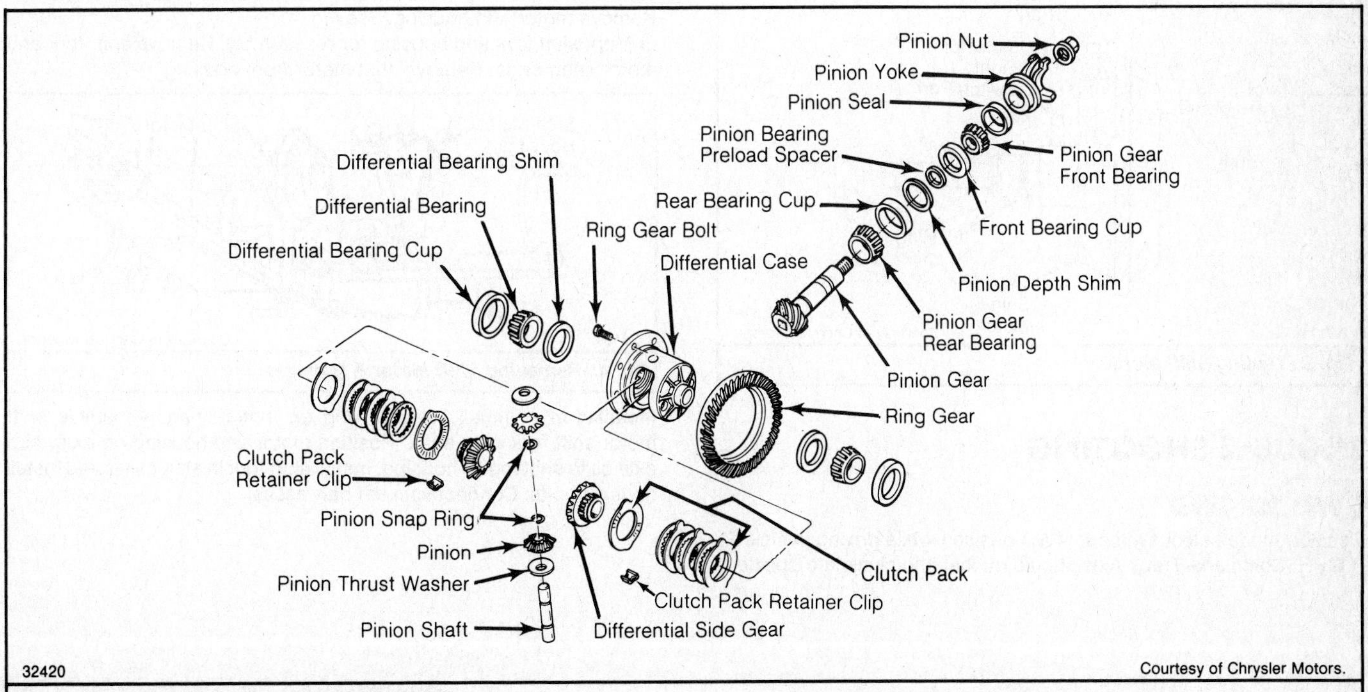
Pinion Nut
Pinion Yoke
Pinion Seal
Pinion Bearing
Preload Spacer
Pinion Gear
Front Bearing
Differential Bearing Shim
Differential Bearing
Rear Bearing Cup
Front Bearing Cup
Ring Gear Bolt
Differential Bearing Cup
Differential Case
Pinion Depth Shim
Pinion Gear
Rear Bearing
Pinion Gear
Ring Gear
Clutch Pack
Retainer Clip
Pinion Snap Ring
Pinion
Pinion Thrust Washer
Clutch Pack
Clutch Pack Retainer Clip
Pinion Shaft
Differential Side Gear
32420
Courtesy of Chrysler Motors.

Fig. 1: Exploded View of Trac-Lok Differential

1991 DRIVE AXLES
Locking Hubs – Command-Trac & Selec-Trac

Cherokee, Comanche
Grand Wagoneer, Wrangler

DESCRIPTION

The Command-Trac locking hub is used (when equipped) on all 4WD models except Grand Wagoneer. This system can be shifted between 2WD and 4WD high range, from inside the vehicle, while vehicle is moving. The vehicle speed must be reduced to 2-3 MPH, to shift into or out of 4WD low range. *See Fig. 1.*

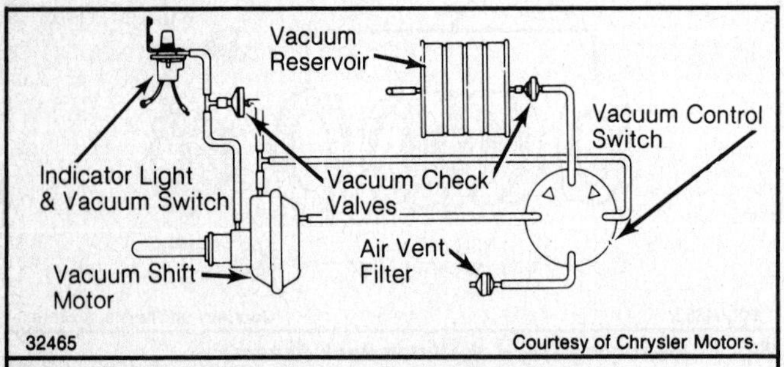
Vacuum
Reservoir
Vacuum Control
Switch
Indicator Light
& Vacuum Switch
Vacuum Check
Valves
Air Vent
Filter
Vacuum Shift
Motor
32465
Courtesy of Chrysler Motors.

Fig. 1: Command-Trac Vacuum Control System

Selec-Trac locking hub is used on all Grand Wagoneer and some 4WD Cherokee and Comanche models. Selec-Trac locking hubs allow full or part time 4WD. The system can be shifted into 2WD or 4WD modes from inside the vehicle at any speed. *See Fig. 2.*

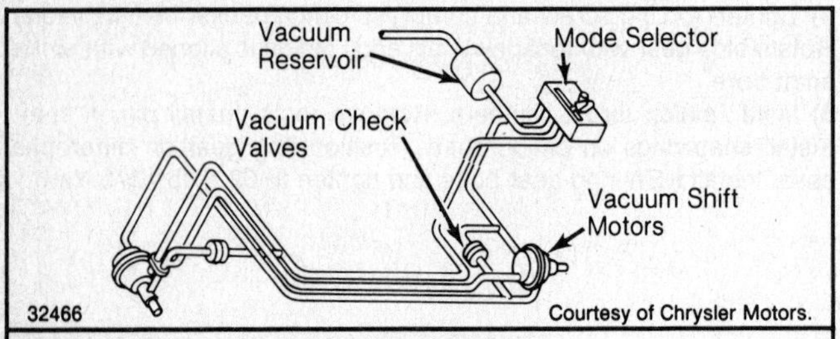
Vacuum
Reservoir
Mode Selector
Vacuum Check
Valves
Vacuum Shift
Motors
32466
Courtesy of Chrysler Motors.

Fig. 2: Selec-Trac Vacuum Control System

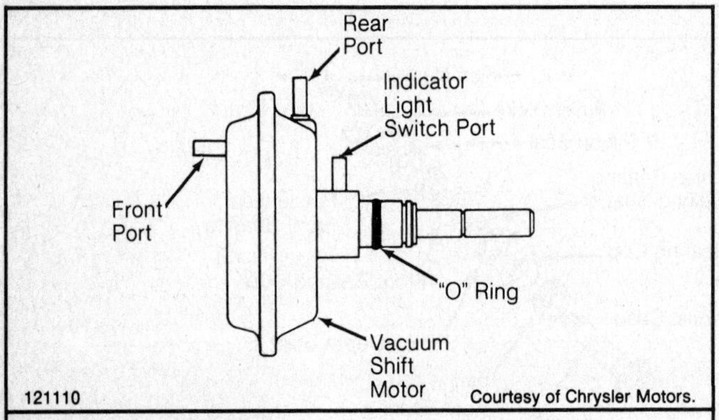
Rear
Port
Indicator
Light
Switch Port
Front
Port
"O" Ring
Vacuum
Shift
Motor
121110
Courtesy of Chrysler Motors.

Fig. 3: Testing Shift Motor

TROUBLE SHOOTING

2WD TO 4WD

Position mode select switch to 4WD position while driving vehicle 2-3 MPH (Command-Trac). Axle should ratchet and clunk into position. Transfer case should shift after axle shifts, accompanied by hissing sound from mode selector switch.

4WD TO 2WD

1) Position mode select switch to 2WD position. Transfer case should shift to 2WD and not allow shifting into 4WD or LO range. Axle should shift after transfer case shifts.
2) To determine if front axle has completed a shift out of 4WD into 2WD, position mode select switch back to 4WD position while operating vehicle at slow speed. If vehicle shifts into 2WD, axle will ratchet. If shift is not completed, transfer case will shift into 4WD and hissing sound will come from mode select switch.

ON-VEHICLE TESTING

FRONT AXLE SHIFT MOTOR

1) Raise and support vehicle. Remove vacuum harness from front axle shift motor. Apply 15 in. Hg to front port of shift motor. *See Fig. 3.* Rotate right front wheel (or rear propeller shaft on Selec-Trac) to disengage axle (2WD operation).
2) Replace shift motor if it does not hold vacuum for at least 30 seconds. If shift motor holds vacuum, remove vacuum pump. Connect vacuum pump to shift motor rear port and cap indicator light switch port. *See Fig. 3.* Apply 15 in. Hg to shift motor.
3) Replace shift motor if it does not hold vacuum for at least 30 seconds. If shift motor holds vacuum, remove cap from indicator light switch port.
4) If vacuum is present, shift motor is okay. If no vacuum is present, cap indicator light switch port and reapply 15 in. Hg to shift motor rear port. Rotate right front wheel to make sure axle shafts are engaged (4WD operation).
5) Axles must be completely engaged to open indicator light switch port. If vacuum is now present at indicator light switch port, shift motor is okay. If not, replace shift motor or repair shifter mechanism.

REMOVAL & INSTALLATION

AXLE SHIFT MOTOR & HOUSING

Removal – **1)** Raise and support vehicle. Place a drain pan under shift housing. Disconnect vacuum harness. Remove housing bolts. Remove motor and housing. *See Fig. 4.*
2) Mark shift fork and housing for reassembly. Remove shift fork and motor snap rings. Remove shift motor from housing.

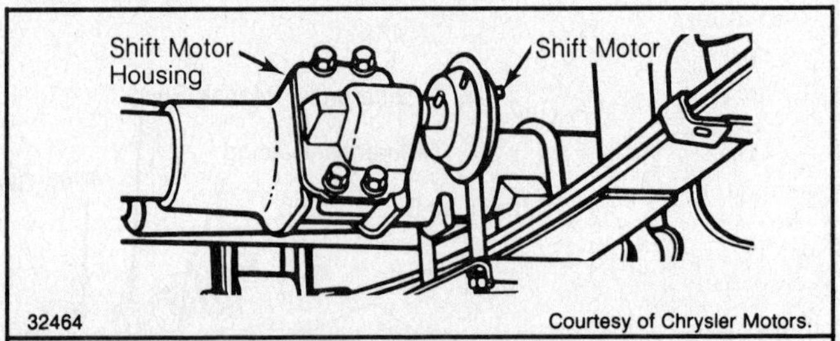
Shift Motor
Housing
Shift Motor
32464
Courtesy of Chrysler Motors.

Fig. 4: Removing Shift Motor & Housing

Installation – Install new "O" ring on motor shaft. Assemble shift motor shift fork onto shaft. Position motor and housing on axle. Add axle oil to shift motor housing. Install shift fork in shift collar and install housing bolts. Connect vacuum harnesses.

Cherokee, Comanche
Grand Wagoneer, Wrangler

DESCRIPTION

Open-end steering knuckles pivot on ball joints and allow wheels to turn.

REMOVAL & INSTALLATION

Removal - 1) Raise and support vehicle. Remove wheel, disc brake caliper, rotor, cotter pin, nut lock, and axle hub nut. Remove hub-to-steering knuckle attaching bolts. Remove hub and rotor shield from steering knuckle. Remove axle shaft from axle tube. See FRONT AXLES article.

NOTE: DO NOT disconnect caliper unless service is needed. Support caliper to prevent hose damage.

2) On models with front axle shift motor, remove outer axle shaft from right axle tube. Leave shift collar on intermediate shaft. Remove caliper anchor plate from steering knuckle. Remove steering knuckle and ball joint cotter pins. Remove ball joint nuts. Strike steering knuckle with a brass hammer and remove steering knuckle.

3) On Grand Wagoneer, remove cotter pins and retaining nut from upper ball stud yoke. Using Ball Joint Wrench (J-23447), remove split-ring seat. Remove lower cotter pin and retaining nut. Remove knuckle from axle.

Installation (Cherokee, Comanche & Wrangler) - 1) Position steering knuckle over ball joint studs and install nuts. Install new cotter pins. Install caliper anchor plate and tighten bolts. Install axle shafts into axle tubes.

2) On vehicles with front axle shift motor, ensure shift collar is correctly positioned on intermediate axle shaft, install axle into shift collar inside axle tube. Ensure axle shaft is completely engaged with shift collar.

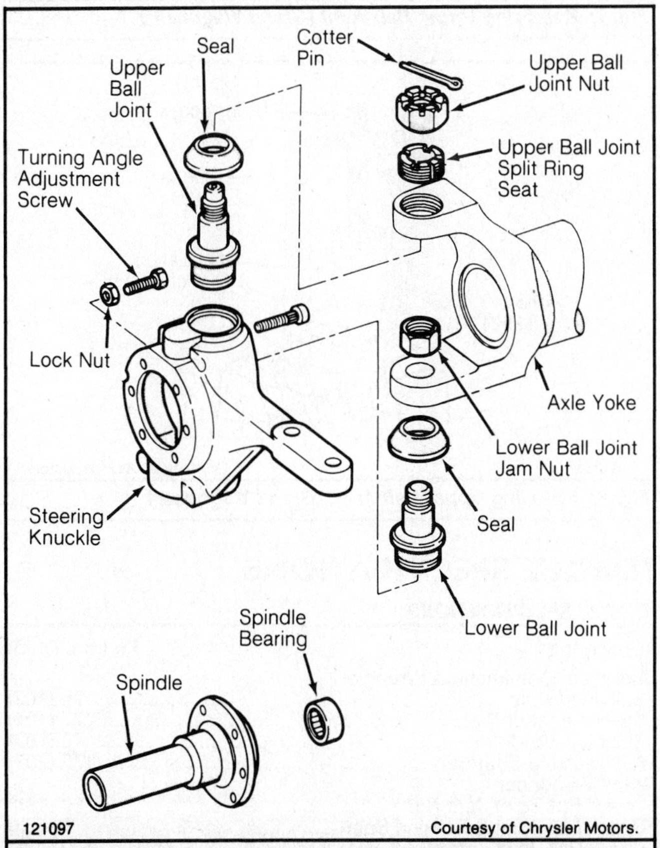
Seal
Cotter Pin
Upper Ball Joint
Upper Ball Joint Nut
Turning Angle Adjustment Screw
Upper Ball Joint Split Ring Seat
Lock Nut
Axle Yoke
Lower Ball Joint Jam Nut
Steering Knuckle
Seal
Spindle Bearing
Lower Ball Joint
Spindle
121097
Courtesy of Chrysler Motors.

Fig. 1: Exploded View of Steering Knuckle (Grand Wagoneer)

3) On all models, apply bearing grease to spindle hub bore in steering knuckle and install rotor shield and hub. Tighten spindle hub bolts. Install hub washer and nut. Tighten hub nut lock and install new cotter pin. Install rotor, caliper and wheel. Lower vehicle.

Installation (Grand Wagoneer) - 1) Place steering knuckle on lower ball joint stud. Install jam nut FINGER TIGHT only. Place upper ball joint stud through yoke. Install ball joint split-ring seat flush with yoke top surface. *See Fig. 1.*

2) Place Ball Joint Wrench (J-23447) and Adapter (J-25211-3), and gear puller over upper ball joint stud. Install Plate (J-25211-1) on steering knuckle. *See Fig. 2.* Tighten gear puller until lower ball joint is seated in lower axle yoke. Tighten lower ball joint jam nut.

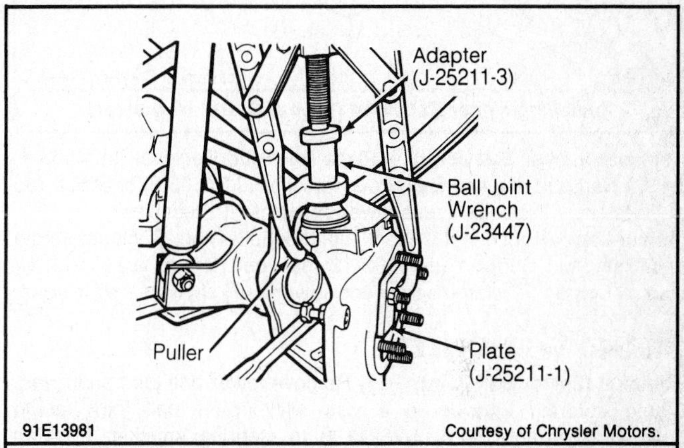
Adapter (J-25211-3)
Ball Joint Wrench (J-23447)
Puller
Plate (J-25211-1)
91E13981
Courtesy of Chrysler Motors.

Fig. 2: Installing Steering Knuckle Assembly (Grand Wagoneer)

NOTE: Never loosen nut to align cotter pin hole, TIGHTEN ONLY.

3) Remove gear puller and plate. Using Ball Joint Wrench (J-23447), tighten upper ball split-ring seat. Install and tighten upper ball joint jam nut. Install new cotter pin. Assemble remaining parts.

OVERHAUL

EXCEPT GRAND WAGONEER

Removal (Upper Ball Joint) - Place steering knuckle in soft jawed vise, place Receiver (J-34503-1) on top of upper ball joint. Place Ball Stud Remover (J-34503-3) in "C" clamp. Place "C" clamp and adapter under upper ball joint and tighten "C" clamp screw to remove ball joint. *See Fig. 3.*

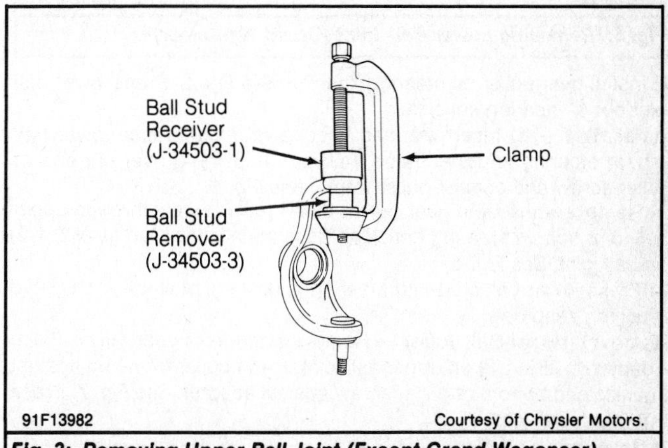
Ball Stud Receiver (J-34503-1)
Clamp
Ball Stud Remover (J-34503-3)
91F13982
Courtesy of Chrysler Motors.

Fig. 3: Removing Upper Ball Joint (Except Grand Wagoneer)

Installation - Place Ball Stud Installer (J-34503-5) on top of upper ball joint. Place Ball Stud Support (J-34503-12) between "C" clamp and yoke. Tighten "C" clamp screw and seat ball joint. *See Fig. 4*

1991 DRIVE AXLES
4WD Steering Knuckles (Cont.)

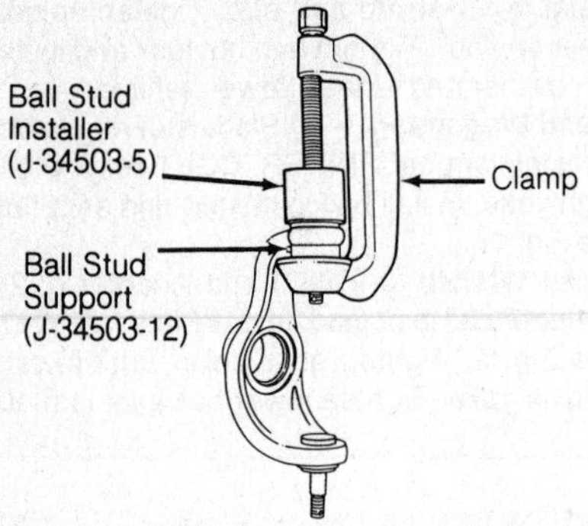
Ball Stud
Installer
(J-34503-5)
Clamp
Ball Stud
Support
(J-34503-12)

91G13983 Courtesy of Chrysler Motors.

Fig. 4: Installing Upper Ball Joint (Except Grand Wagoneer)

Removal (Lower Ball Joint) – Place Ball Stud Receiver (J-34503-1) on "C" clamp screw and Ball Stud Remover (J-34503-3) between top of yoke and "C" clamp. Press lower ball joint into receiver.

Installation – Place Installation Cup (J-34503-4) on "C" clamp screw and Ball Stud Support (J-34503-12) between top of yoke and "C" clamp. Tighten "C" clamp screw until lower ball joint is seated in yoke.

GRAND WAGONEER

Removal (Lower Ball Joint) – **1)** Remove lower ball joint snap ring. Clamp steering knuckle in a vise with upper ball joint facing downward. Attach Plate (J-25211-1) to steering knuckle. Position Adapter (J-25211-3) on lower ball joint. *See Fig. 5.*

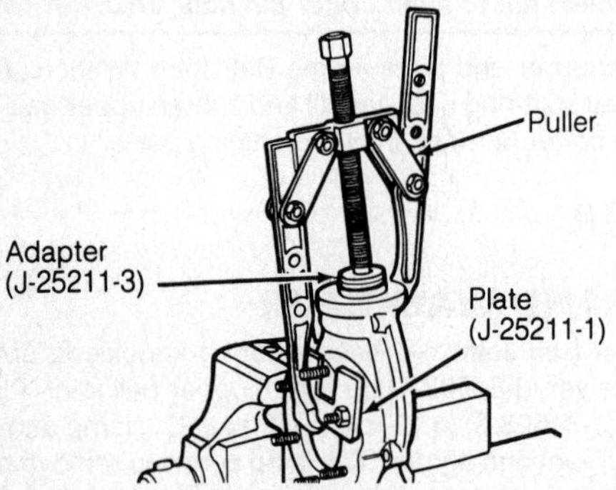
Puller
Adapter
(J-25211-3)
Plate
(J-25211-1)

91H13984 Courtesy of Chrysler Motors.

Fig. 5: Removing Lower Ball Joint (Grand Wagoneer)

2) Install gear puller on steering knuckle. *See Fig. 5*. Press lower ball joint out of steering knuckle.

Installation – **1)** Insert steering knuckle in a vise. Place lower ball joint in steering knuckle. Place Adapter (J-25211-4) over nut end of puller screw and against puller frame. *See Fig. 6*.

2) Remove arms from gear puller. Insert puller screw through upper ball joint hole in steering knuckle. Place Installation Cup (J-25211-2) on ball joint. *See Fig. 6*.

3) Press lower ball stud into steering knuckle. Install lower ball stud retaining snap ring.

Removal (Upper Ball Joint) – Remove arms from gear puller. Place Adapter (J-25211-3) on upper ball joint. Place puller frame up against knuckle and bottom of puller screw against adapter. *See Fig. 7*. Press out upper ball joint.

Installation – **1)** Place upper ball joint in steering knuckle. Install Plate (J-25211-1) on knuckle. Place Installation Cup (J-25211-2) on upper ball stud. *See Fig. 8*.

2) Install gear puller on steering knuckle. *See Fig. 8*. Press ball joint into steering knuckle.

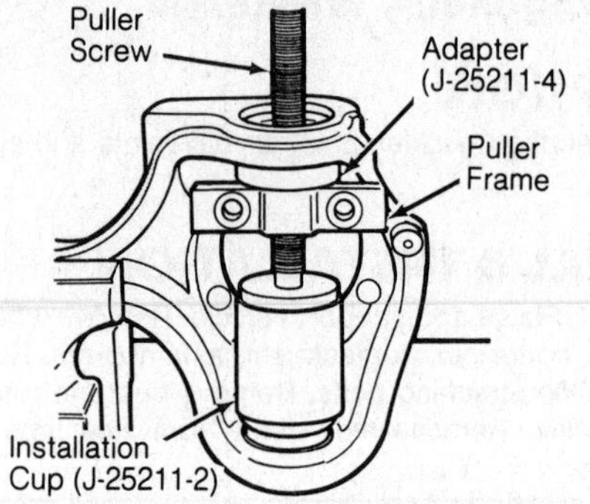
Puller
Screw
Adapter
(J-25211-4)
Puller
Frame
Installation
Cup (J-25211-2)

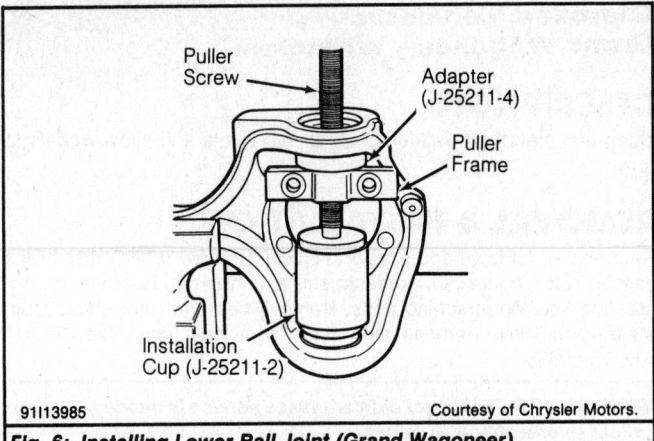

91I13985 Courtesy of Chrysler Motors.

Fig. 6: Installing Lower Ball Joint (Grand Wagoneer)

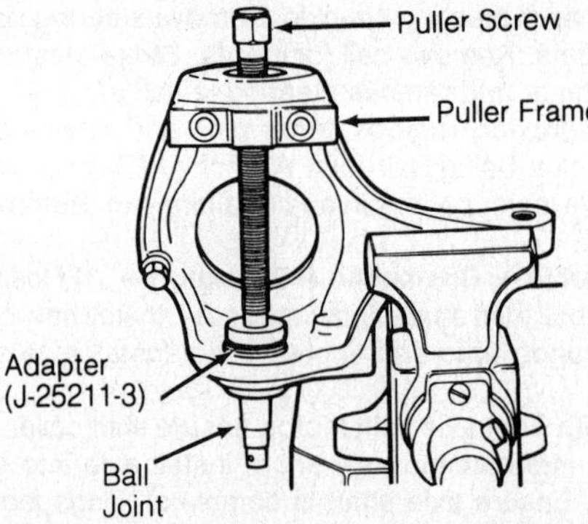
Puller Screw
Puller Frame
Adapter
(J-25211-3)
Ball
Joint

91J13986 Courtesy of Chrysler Motors.

Fig. 7: Removing Upper Ball Joint (Grand Wagoneer)

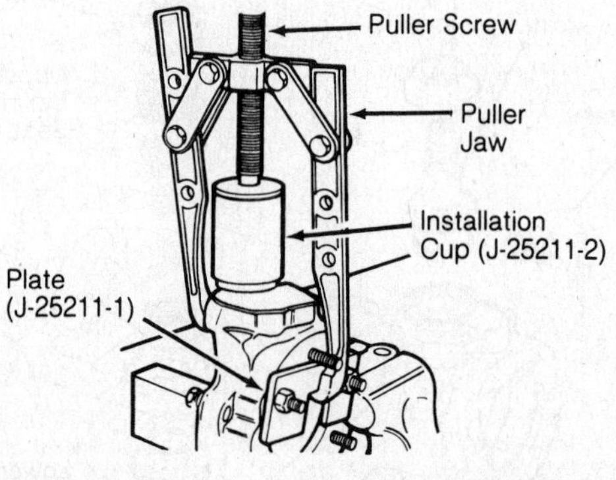
Puller Screw
Puller
Jaw
Installation
Cup (J-25211-2)
Plate
(J-25211-1)

91A13987 Courtesy of Chrysler Motors.

Fig. 8: Installing Upper Ball Joint (Grand Wagoneer)

TORQUE SPECIFICATIONS

TORQUE SPECIFICATIONS

Application	Ft. Lbs. (N.m)
Cherokee, Comanche & Wrangler	
Ball Joint Nuts	75 (102)
Caliper Anchor Plate	77 (104)
Spindle Hub Bolts	75 (102)
Axle Hub-To-Shaft nut	175 (237)
Grand Wagoneer	
Lower Ball Joint Jam Nut	80 (108)
Upper Ball Joint Split-Ring Seat	50 (68)
Upper Ball Joint Jam Nut	100 (136)

Cherokee, Comanche
Grand Wagoneer, Wrangler

DESCRIPTION

Propeller shafts are balanced, one-piece, tubular steel shafts with universal joints at each end. Single Cardan universal joints contain a spider, 4 bearing caps with needle bearings, seals and clips. The Double Cardan universal joint contains 2 spiders joined together. *See Fig. 1.*

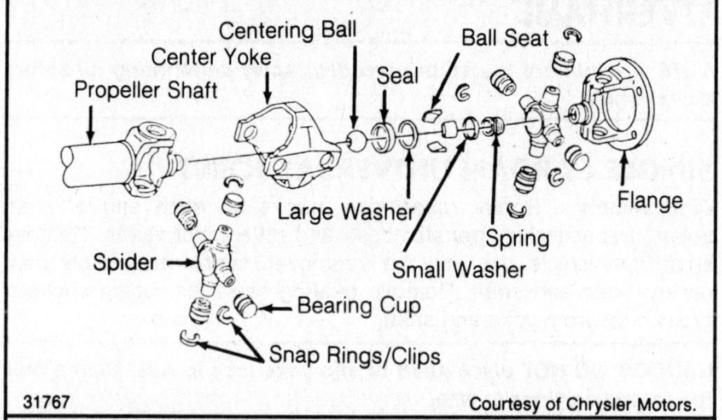

Centering Ball
Ball Seat
Center Yoke
Seal
Propeller Shaft
Large Washer
Flange
Spring
Spider
Small Washer
Bearing Cup
Snap Rings/Clips
31767
Courtesy of Chrysler Motors.

Fig. 1: Exploded View of Double Cardan Universal Joint

INSPECTION

VIBRATION

Tires & Wheels – Check tire inflation and wheel balance. Check for foreign objects in tread, damaged tread, mismatched treads or tire sizes.

Engine & Transmission Mounts – Tighten mounting bolts. If mountings are worn, replace them.

Propeller Shaft – Check shaft for damage or dents. Check for undercoating on shaft. If present, clean shaft.

Universal Joints – Check for debris or dirt. Check for loose bolts and worn bearings.

PROPELLER SHAFT RUNOUT

Remove any dirt from area around shaft where dial indicator is placed. Measure shaft runout about 3" from weld-seam on each end of shaft.

PROPELLER SHAFT RUNOUT

Application	In. (mm)
Cherokee, Comanche & Wrangler	
Front & Rear Shaft	
Front & Rear of Shaft	.010 (.25)
Center of Shaft	.015 (.38)
Grand Wagoneer	
Front Shaft	
Front & Rear of Shaft	.010 (.25)
Center of Shaft	.015 (.38)
Rear Shaft (All Areas of Shaft)	.015 (.38)

FRONT & REAR SHAFT ANGLES

NOTE: If either angle is excessive, vibration may result. On some Selec-Trac equipped vehicles, an excessive rear shaft angle may cause noise around 40-50 MPH.

NOTE: If vehicle is equipped with P205/75R15 tires, add .35" (9.0 mm) to all riding height measurements. If vehicle is equipped with P215/75R15 tires, add .79" (20.0 mm) to all riding height measurements.

Cherokee & Comanche – **1)** Measure vehicle ride height from top of axle tube to top of frame rail above axle. Front riding height should be 6.20-7.00 in. (157.5-177.8 mm). Rear riding height should be 5.70-6.50 in. (144.5-165.0 mm). Adjust ride height, if necessary.

2) Place transmission and transfer case into Neutral. Raise vehicle on hoist and allow wheels to turn freely. Turn shaft until pinion yoke is down. Attach Inclinometer Magnet (J-23498A) and Inclinometer (J-23498A) on pinion yoke bearing cap and record angle.

3) Rotate propeller shaft 90 degrees. Attach inclinometer to shaft and record angle. Inclinometer MUST face in same direction as step **2)**.

4) Difference between angles at yoke and pinion yoke is universal joint angle "B". *See Fig. 2.* Universal joint angle should be within specified range. See FRONT PROPELLER SHAFT ANGLE or REAR PROPELLER SHAFT ANGLE chart at end of article. If angle "B" is not within range, adjust axle angle.

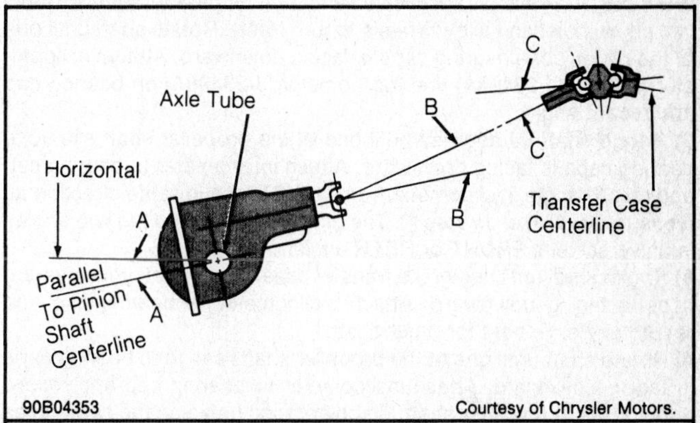

C
Axle Tube
B
C
Horizontal
B
Transfer Case Centerline
A
Parallel To Pinion Shaft Centerline
A
90B04353
Courtesy of Chrysler Motors.

Fig. 2: Front Propeller Shaft Angles (Cherokee & Comanche)

5) If angle "B" and vehicle height are correct, pinion shaft angle "A" and the rear universal joint angle "C" should also be correct. *See Fig. 2.*

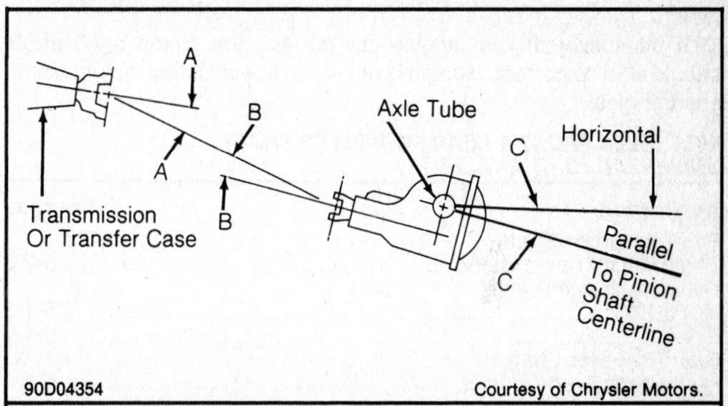

A
B
Axle Tube
Horizontal
C
A
Transmission Or Transfer Case
B
Parallel
C
To Pinion Shaft Centerline
90D04354
Courtesy of Chrysler Motors.

Fig. 3: Rear Propeller Shaft Angles (Cherokee & Comanche)

Grand Wagoneer (Front) – **1)** Place vehicle on level surface. Place Inclinometer (J-23498A) on front shaft tube. Measure and record front shaft downward incline angle. Remove inclinometer.

2) Position inclinometer on front differential housing. Measure and record drive pinion gear upward incline angle. Remove inclinometer. If pinion shaft upward angle is one degree more than shaft downward angle, the pinion shaft angle is okay.

3) If pinion shaft upward angle is LESS THAN propeller shaft downward angle by more than one degree, adjust angle. See SHAFT ANGLE under ADJUSTMENTS.

Grand Wagoneer (Rear) – **1)** Place vehicle on level surface. Place Inclinometer (J-23498A) on cylinder block, adjacent to transmission mating surface. Measure and record engine downward incline angle. Remove inclinometer.

2) Position inclinometer on rear differential housing. Measure and record drive pinion gear upward incline angle. Remove inclinometer. If pinion shaft upward angle is one degree less than the engine downward angle, the pinion shaft angle is okay.

3) If pinion shaft upward angle is GREATER THAN engine downward incline angle by more than one degree, adjust angle. See SHAFT ANGLE under ADJUSTMENTS.

1991 DRIVE AXLES
Propeller Shafts & Universal Joints (Cont.)

GRAND WAGONEER FRONT & REAR PROPELLER SHAFT ANGLES

Application	Degrees
Front Propeller Shaft	
Inspection	[1] +1 to -1
Set To	[1] +1
Rear Propeller Shaft	
Inspection	[2] -1 to +1
Set To	[2] -1

[1] - Degrees of propeller shaft angle.
[2] - Degrees of engine angle.

Wrangler - 1) Place transmission and transfer case in Neutral. Raise vehicle on hoist and allow wheels to turn freely. Rotate shaft until one of the pinion yoke bearing caps is facing downward. Attach Inclinometer Magnet (J-23498A) and Inclinometer (J-23498A) on bearing cap and record angle.
2) Rotate shaft 90 degrees until one of the propeller shaft slip yoke bearing caps is facing downward. Attach inclinometer to bearing cap and record angle. Inclinometer frame MUST face in same direction as measurement taken in step **1)**. The difference between the two angles is universal joint FRONT or REAR angle.
3) Rotate shaft until one of the transfer case output shaft yoke bearing caps is facing downward. Attach inclinometer to bearing cap and record angle. Repeat for other shaft.
4) Rotate shaft until one of the propeller shaft rear yoke bearing caps is facing downward. Attach inclinometer to bearing cap and record angle. Repeat for other shaft. The difference between the two angles is universal joint FRONT or REAR angle.
5) Compare universal joint FRONT and REAR angles. The difference between the 2 angles is the propeller shaft angle. See WRANGLER FRONT & REAR PROPELLER SHAFT UNIVERSAL JOINT ANGLES table.
6) If the universal joint angles are correct, the pinion shaft angle should also be correct. If angle is not within specification, adjust pinion shaft angles.

WRANGLER FRONT & REAR PROPELLER SHAFT UNIVERSAL JOINT ANGLES

Application	Degrees
Front Propeller Shaft	
Automatic Transmission	.5-2.5
Manual Transmission	
2.5L	.5-1.5
4.0L	0-1.0
Rear Propeller Shaft	
Automatic Transmission	.5-1.5
Manual Transmission	
2.5L	0-1.0
4.0L	.5-1.5

ADJUSTMENTS

SHAFT ANGLE

Cherokee & Comanche (Front) - 1) Adjust drive pinion gear shaft angle "A" at the lower suspension arms with shims. Adding shims will decrease pinion gear shaft angle "A" but will increase caster angle.
2) Adjustment of angle "A" is more important than caster angle. When angle "A", angle "B" and vehicle height are correct, angle "C" will also be correct.

Except Cherokee & Comanche (Front) - 1) Raise vehicle and place jack stands under frame. Place a hydraulic jack under differential housing. Raise jack to support weight of axle.
2) Loosen spring "U" bolt nuts, and install tapered shims between springs and axle spring bracket to correct angle. See FRONT PROPELLER SHAFT ANGLE or REAR PROPELLER SHAFT ANGLE chart at end of article. Torque spring "U" bolt nuts to 52 ft. lbs. (70 N.m). for Cherokee and Comanche or 100 ft. lbs. (136 N.m) for all others.

OVERHAUL

NOTE: If joints are rusted or corroded, apply penetrating oil before disassembly.

SINGLE CARDAN UNIVERSAL JOINT

Disassembly - Scribe reassembly marks on each end of shaft yokes, transmission, transfer case and differential yokes. Remove shaft from vehicle. If a slip yoke is removed, scribe reassembly mark on slip yoke and shaft. Remove bearing cap clips. Using sockets, press cups from yoke and shaft.

CAUTION: DO NOT place shaft or slip yoke tube in vise. Clamp only the forged portions in vise.

Reassembly - 1) Clean universal joint bores and yoke. Apply grease to yoke bores, bearing caps, bearings and spider contact surfaces.
2) Place spider into yoke and tap bearing cap, seal and bearings into yoke far enough to hold spider. Place a socket (smaller than cap) on side cap and place in vise.
3) Tighten vise until caps are seated in yoke. Rotate spider to make sure no binding occurs. Install cap clips and repeat procedure on remaining caps.

DOUBLE CARDAN UNIVERSAL JOINT

Disassembly - 1) Scribe reassembly marks on each end of shaft yokes, transmission, transfer case and differential yokes. Remove shaft from vehicle. If a slip yoke is removed, scribe reassembly mark on slip yoke and shaft for assembly.

CAUTION: DO NOT place shaft or slip yoke tube in vise. Clamp only the forged portions in vise.

2) Remove bearing cap clips. Using sockets, remove caps that retain "shaft end" spider in the shaft yoke. *See Fig. 1*. Repeat procedure for the remaining caps.
3) Remove the center yoke with both spiders. *See Fig. 1*. Remove caps from rear yoke along with REAR spider, bearings and seals. Remove spider from shaft if not already done.
Reassembly - Clean universal joint bores and yoke. Apply grease to the yoke bores, bearing caps, bearings and spider contact surfaces. Install rear spider to center yoke. Install ball and centering ball into center yoke after the rear spider is installed. To complete assembly, reverse disassembly.

1991 DRIVE AXLES
Propeller Shafts & Universal Joints (Cont.)

REAR PROPELLER SHAFT ANGLE

MODEL	ENGINE & TRANSMISSION	2WD OR 4WD	SHORT OR LONG BED	ANGLE A	ANGLE B	ANGLE C
Comanche						
Standard	4-CYL. A/T & M/T	2WD	SB	-1.0° to -2.0°	2.0° to 3.0°	4.5° to 5.5°
	6-CYL. A/T & M/T	2WD	SB	-1.5° to -2.5°	2.5° to 3.5°	4.5° to 5.5°
	4-CYL. A/T & M/T	4WD	SB	-2.5° to -3.5°	3.5° to 4.5°	4.5° to 5.5°
	6-CYL. A/T & M/T	4WD	SB	-3.5° to -4.5°	4.0° to 5.0°	4.5° to 5.5°
Heavy Duty	6-CYL. A/T & M/T	2WD	SB	-1.5° to -2.5°	2.5° to 3.5°	4.5° to 5.5°
	6-CYL. A/T & M/T	2WD	SB	-3.0° to -4.0°	3.5° to 4.5°	4.5° to 5.5°
Off-Road	4-CYL. A/T & M/T	4WD	SB	-2.5° to -3.5°	3.5° to 4.5°	4.5° to 5.5°
Package	6-CYL. A/T & M/T	4WD	SB	-3.5° to -4.5°	4.0° to 5.0°	4.5° to 5.5°
	6-CYL. A/T	2WD	SB	-3.0° to -4.0°	3.5° to 4.5°	4.5° to 5.5°
	6-CYL. M/T	2WD	SB	-3.5° to -4.5°	4.0° to 5.0°	4.5° to 5.5°
Standard	4-CYL. A/T & M/T	2WD	LB	0° to -1.0°	0.5° to -0.5°	6.5° to 7.5°
	6-CYL. A/T & M/T	2WD	LB	-1.0° to -2.0°	0.5° to -0.5°	6.5° to 7.5°
	4-CYL. A/T & M/T	4WD	LB	-1.5° to -2.5°	0° to 1.0°	6.5° to 7.5°
	6-CYL. A/T & M/T	4WD	LB	-2.0° to -3.0°	0.5° to 1.5°	6.5° to 7.5°
Heavy Duty	4-CYL. M/T	2WD	LB	-1.0° to -2.0°	0.5° to -0.5°	6.5° to 7.5°
	6-CYL. M/T	2WD	LB	-1.5° to -2.5°	0.5° to -0.5°	6.5° to 7.5°
	4-CYL. M/T	4WD	LB	-1.5° to -2.5°	0° to 1.0°	6.5° to 7.5°
	6-CYL. A/T & M/T	4WD	LB	-2.0° to -3.0°	0.5° to 1.5°	6.5° to 7.5°
Off-Road	4-CYL. A/T & M/T	4WD	LB	-1.5° to -2.5°	0° to 1.0	6.5° to 7.5°
Package	6-CYL. A/T & M/T	4WD	LB	-2.0° to -3.0°	0.5° to 1.5°	6.5° to 7.5°
Cherokee						
Standard	6-CYL. A/T & M/T	2WD	.....	-2.0° to -3.0°	1.5° to 2.5°	5.5° to 6.5°
	4-CYL. A/T & M/T	2WD	.....	-2.0° to -3.0°	1.5° to 2.5°	5.5° to 6.5°
	6-CYL. A/T & M/T	2WD	.....	-2.5° to -3.5°	2.0° to 3.0°	5.5° to 6.5°
	4-CYL. A/T & M/T	2WD	.....	-2.5° to -3.5°	2.0° to 3.0°	5.5° to 6.5°
Off-Road	6-CYL. A/T & M/T	4WD	.....	-4.0° to -5.0°	3.0° to 4.0°	5.5° to 6.5°
Package	4-CYL. A/T & M/T	2WD	.....	-4.0° to -5.0°	3.0° to 4.0°	5.5° to 6.5°

FRONT PROPELLER SHAFT ANGLE

MODEL	ENGINE & TRANSMISSION	2WD OR 4WD	SHORT OR LONG BED	ANGLE A	ANGLE B	ANGLE C
Comanche						
Standard	4-CYL. M/T	4WD	.....	1.5° to 2.0°	1.5° to 2.5°	-4.5° to -5.5°
	6-CYL. A/T & M/T	4WD	.....	1.5° to 2.0°	0.5° to 1.5°	-0.5° to -3.5°
Off-Road						
Package	6-CYL. A/T & M/T	4WD	.....	2.0° to 2.5°	0° to 1.0°	-3.5° to -4.5°
	4-CYL. A/T	4WD	.....	2.0° to 2.5°	0° to 1.0°	-4.0° to -5.0°
	4-CYL. M/T	4WD	.....	2.0° to 2.5°	1.5° to 2.5°	-4.5° to -5.5°
Cherokee						
Standard	4 & 6-CYL. A/T & M/T	4WD	N/A	1.0° to 2.0°	0.5° to 1.5°	-8.0° to -9.0°
Off-Road						
Package	4 & 6-CYL. M/T	4WD	N/A	1.0° to 2.0°	0.5° to 1.5°	-8.0° to -9.0°
	4 & 6-CYL. A/T	4WD	N/A	1.0° to 2.0°	0.5° to 1.5°	-3.5° to -4.5°

1991 BRAKES
Anti-Lock

Cherokee

DESCRIPTION

Bendix Anti-Lock Brake System (ABS) is used on Cherokee models equipped with Selec-Trac 4WD. This electronically operated system is designed to reduce wheel lock-up during heavy braking. System components consist of an Electronic Control Module (ECM), master cylinder/power booster unit, 4 wheel speed sensors, pump/motor assembly, 3 relays, 2 indicators lights, pressure modulator and an accumulator. *See Fig. 1*.

CAUTION: NEVER disconnect or remove any hydraulic component without depressurizing the system first. Failure to do so can lead to personal injury due to high hydraulic pressure. See DEPRESSURIZING ABS SYSTEM under REMOVAL & INSTALLATION.

OPERATION

When the ignition is turned on, the ECM is activated. Electrical circuits within the ECM activate the system and provide a self-diagnosis on the system. The indicator lights, located on the instrument panel, will illuminate until self-diagnosis is complete. If system has no faults, lights will go off.

If system has detected a fault, one or both lights will stay on to indicate a problem has been detected. With ignition on and vehicle stationary, solenoids within the pressure modulator will temporarily be activated to ensure proper operation.

Pump/motor assembly will cycle on and off to ensure pressure within accumulator is 1650-2050 psi (11,376-14,135 kPa). If pressure drops below 1050 psi (7240 kPa), a pressure switch located on accumulator block will signal ECM to deactivate ABS system. At this time, Yellow indicator light will come on. Accumulator contains enough pressure to assist stopping approximately 25-30 times.

With vehicle moving, ECM monitors wheel speed sensor by AC signals from each of the wheel speed sensors. When the ECM receives a signal from the brake switch that braking is taking place, it starts monitoring the rate of deceleration from the wheel speed sensors.

Using this information, the ECM calculates the rate of deceleration to increase, decrease or maintain hydraulic pressure to the wheels. Pressure changes are performed inside the pressure modulators by cycling (opening and closing) the solenoids (one for each front wheel or one for both rear wheels) quickly.

BLEEDING BRAKE SYSTEM

NOTE: Bleeding brake system will require 2 people. Use DOT 3 brake fluid only. Always wear safety goggles when loosening bleeder screw.

1) Ensure fluid level is at maximum level. DO NOT overfill reservoir or damage to reservoir may occur. Attach a bleeder hose to right rear wheel cylinder. Turn ignition on. Depress brake pedal and open bleeder screw. When fluid from wheel cylinder contains no air, close bleeder screw.

2) Check master cylinder reservoir fluid level and go to next wheel. When pump stops, fill reservoir to MAX mark on reservoir. DO NOT fill over this mark. DO NOT allow reservoir to go dry, or damage to pump/motor may occur. Bleeding sequence is: right rear, left rear, right front and left front.

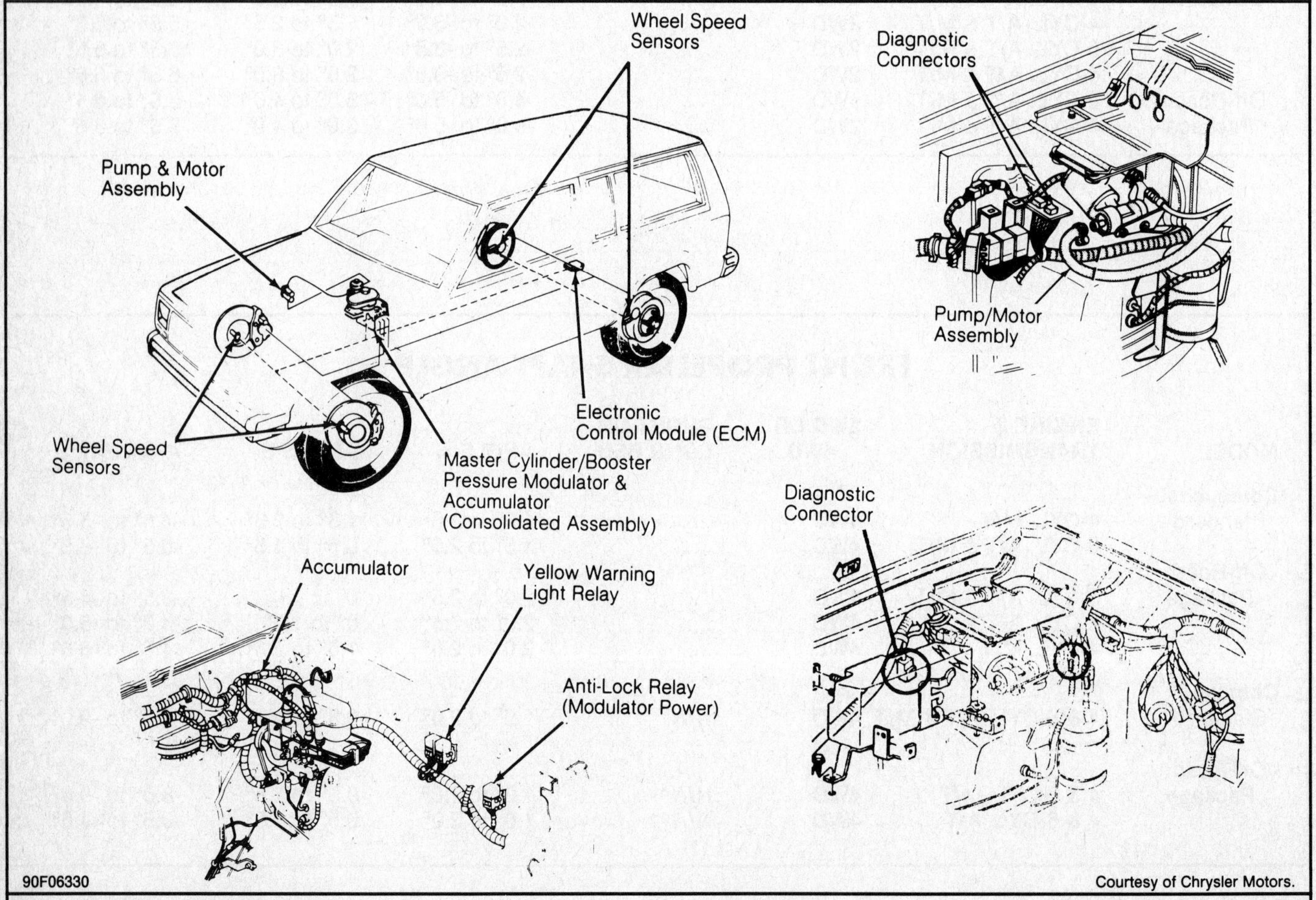
Wheel Speed
Sensors
Diagnostic
Connectors
Pump & Motor
Assembly
Pump/Motor
Assembly
Electronic
Control Module (ECM)
Wheel Speed
Sensors
Master Cylinder/Booster
Pressure Modulator &
Accumulator
(Consolidated Assembly)
Diagnostic
Connector
Accumulator
Yellow Warning
Light Relay
Anti-Lock Relay
(Modulator Power)
90F06330
Courtesy of Chrysler Motors.

Fig. 1: Locating ABS Components

REMOVAL & INSTALLATION

DEPRESSURIZING ABS SYSTEM

CAUTION: Failure to depressurize the ABS system before disconnecting or removing any hydraulic component may result in personal injury. Always wear safety goggles when loosening hydraulic line.

Turn ignition off. Depress and release brake pedal approximately 45-50 times. Brake pedal should get firmer as pressure is reduced. DO NOT turn ignition on until all components are installed and fittings are tight.

WHEEL SPEED SENSORS

Removal & Installation (Front) - 1) Raise and support front of vehicle. Note sensor wire routing for installation purposes. Clean area around sensor to prevent damage during removal. Remove wheel speed sensor. Unseat sensor wire retaining grommet.
2) Inside engine compartment, unplug sensor connector from anti-lock harness connector. Remove sensor. To install, reverse removal procedure. If polyethylene spacer strip is damaged or missing from wheel sensor, remove strip. *See Fig. 2.*
3) Using a brass feeler gauge, adjust air gap, between sensor and tone wheel to .013-.019" (.33-.48 mm). If spacer strip is attached, adjust sensor so spacer strip just touches the tone wheel.

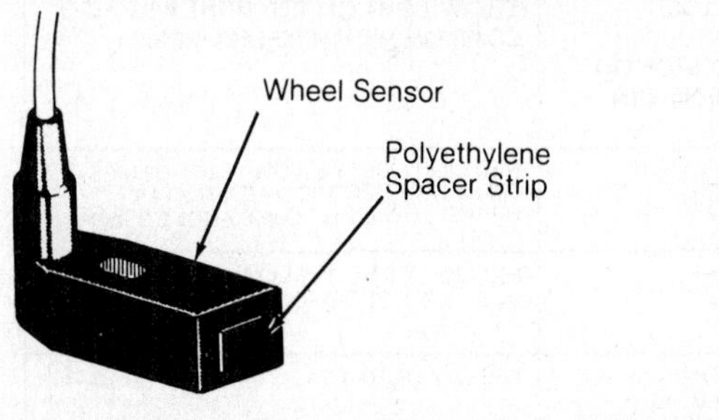
Wheel Sensor
Polyethylene
Spacer Strip

117453 Courtesy of Chrysler Motors.

Fig. 2: Identifying Polyethylene Spacer Strip

Removal & Installation (Rear) - 1) Raise and support rear of vehicle. Raise and fold rear seat forward. Pull up carpet. Unplug rear sensor connector. Push wiring through floorpan. Remove wheel and brake drum.
2) Remove rear sensor grommet from backing plate. Remove rear sensor from bracket. Remove sensor from vehicle. To install, reverse removal procedure. If polyethylene spacer strip on wheel sensor is missing or damaged, remove strip. *See Fig. 2.*
3) Using a brass feeler gauge, adjust air gap, between sensor and tone wheel to .030-.036" (.76-.91 mm). If spacer strip is attached, adjust sensor so spacer strip just touches the tone wheel.

PUMP/MOTOR ASSEMBLY

CAUTION: NEVER disconnect or remove any hydraulic component without depressurizing the system first. Failure to do so can lead to personal injury due to high hydraulic pressure. See DEPRESSURIZING ABS SYSTEM under REMOVAL & INSTALLATION.

Removal - 1) Depressurize brake system. Disconnect negative battery cable. Separate coolant pressure bottle from bracket and lay bottle out of way. Remove coolant bottle bracket retaining bolts. Rotate bracket and unplug pump/motor connector.
2) Ensure system is depressurized, and slowly loosen hydraulic lines. Remove pump/motor assembly from coolant pressure bottle bracket. Remove relay. Separate pump motor assembly from bracket.

NOTE: Excessive pump operation can lead to pump/motor assembly damage.

Installation - 1) To install, reverse removal procedure. DO NOT overfill reservoir. Ensure hydraulic lines are not contacting engine or kinked. Ensure all hydraulic lines are tight. Turn ignition on. If pump/motor assembly does not slow down, verify that the reservoir cap is removed during initial pump up.
2) Normal pump up time from zero psi is 60-80 seconds. If pump does not stop in 1 1/2 minutes, turn ignition off and check for leaks. Check for fluid in supply line to pump. Pump noise and RPM does change as pressure increases. Bleed brake system (if necessary). See BLEEDING BRAKE SYSTEM in this article.

MASTER CYLINDER/BOOSTER, MODULATOR & ACCUMULATOR ASSEMBLY

NOTE: Master cylinder/booster, modulator and accumulator are serviced as an assembly. Accumulator tank and accumulator on booster pump contain high pressure gas. DO NOT attempt to separate the components.

CAUTION: NEVER disconnect or remove any hydraulic component without depressurizing the system first. Failure to do so can lead to personal injury due to high hydraulic pressure. See DEPRESSURIZING ABS SYSTEM under REMOVAL & INSTALLATION.

Removal - 1) Depressurize brake system. Disconnect negative battery cable. Separate windshield washer reservoir from body and set aside. Remove air cleaner assembly. Unplug all electrical connectors from master cylinder/booster, modulator and accumulator assembly. Ensure system is depressurized.
2) Slowly loosen hydraulic lines from assembly. Cap lines to prevent contamination. From inside vehicle, remove lower instrument panel trim on driver's side (if needed). Unplug stoplight switch connector. Remove master cylinder push rod retaining clip. Remove assembly retaining nuts. From engine compartment, slowly remove assembly from vehicle.

NOTE: Excessive pump operation can lead to pump/motor assembly damage.

Installation - 1) To install, reverse removal procedure. Ensure bracket studs are seated in dash panel holes. Tighten mounting nuts to specification. See TORQUE SPECIFICATIONS table. Install master cylinder push rod retaining clip. DO NOT overfill master cylinder reservoir. Ensure hydraulic lines are tight. Turn ignition on to start pump. Pump RPM should slow down, indicating pump is pressurizing.
2) Normal pump up time from zero psi is 60-80 seconds. Pump will shut off when system is fully charged. If pump does not stop in 1 1/2 minutes, turn ignition off and check for leaks. Check for fluid in supply line to pump. Pump noise and RPM changes as pressure increases. Bleed brake system (if necessary). See BLEEDING BRAKE SYSTEM.

CAUTION: DO NOT let pump run dry while it is running. Pump damage will result. Check fluid level frequently and add fluid as necessary.

ELECTRONIC CONTROL MODULE (ECM)

NOTE: Proper mounting angle and position of ECM are critical. Ensure ECM is mounted onto bracket and positioned properly.

Removal & Installation - Ensure ignition is off. Fold rear seat forward and lift carpet up. Remove screws retaining ECM to floorpan and bracket. Unplug ECM connector. Remove ECM. To install, reverse removal procedure.

1991 BRAKES
Anti-Lock (Cont.)

TORQUE SPECIFICATIONS

TORQUE SPECIFICATIONS

Application	Ft. Lbs. (N.m)
Master Cylinder/Modulator & Accumulator Assembly Mounting Bracket Nut	31 (42)
Master Cylinder/Modulator & Accumulator Assembly-To-Mounting Bracket Nut	27 (37)
Wheel Lug Nuts	75 (102)
Wheel Speed Sensor Bolt	11 (15)

TESTING & TROUBLE SHOOTING

CAUTION: When testing or trouble shooting ABS system, NEVER disconnect or remove any hydraulic component without depressurizing the system first. Failure to do so can lead to personal injury due to high hydraulic pressure. See DEPRESSURIZING ABS SYSTEM under REMOVAL & INSTALLATION.

INITIAL CHECK

Before trouble shooting the ABS system, ensure tire size and type are the same. Mismatched tire size and type can lead to false wheel speed sensor readings. Pump/motor assembly may produce a clicking noise when cycling on and off. This is normal. Buzzing noise from solenoids and pump/motor may occur and is normal.

A slight pulsing sensation may be felt when brake pedal is depressed during ABS operation. This is normal. Yellow indicator light will come on if fault within ABS system is detected. Red indicator light will come on if fluid level is low, parking brake is on during operation, hydraulic pressure is low or pump/motor operates more than 4 minutes without brakes being applied.

DRIVER-INDUCED FAULT

Driver-induced fault(s) are caused by the driver improperly operating the vehicle. This causes ECM to detect a system fault. Normally this

SYSTEM FAULT	POSSIBLE CAUSE	INDICATOR LIGHT DISPLAY
LOW FLUID	SYSTEM LEAK. ACCUMULATOR CHARGE LOW OR LOST.	RED LIGHT ON. YELLOW LIGHT ON WITHIN 1/2 SECOND WHEN VEHICLE SPEED EXCEEDS 2.5 MPH.
PARKING BRAKES APPLIED	PARKING BRAKES NOT RELEASED BEFORE DRIVING VEHICLE.	RED LIGHT ON. YELLOW LIGHT ON IF VEHICLE SPEED EXCEEDS 2.5 MPH.
PRESSURE LOW AT ACCUMULATOR	ACCUMLATOR GAS CHARGE LOST. SYSTEM LEAK. PUMP/MOTOR MALFUNCTION. PROLONGED STOP ON ICY SURFACE WITH TRANSMISSION IN GEAR.	YELLOW LIGHT ON. RED LIGHT WILL ALSO COME ON WITHIN 20 SECONDS.
DIFFERENTIAL PRESSURE SWITCH (IN PROPORTIONING VALVE) ACTUATED	SYSTEM LEAK. MASTER CYLINDER MALFUNCTION. AIR IN SYSTEM.	RED LIGHT ON. YELLOW LIGHT COMES ON IN 1/2-1 SECONDS AFTER START UP. YELLOW LIGHT ON IF ABOVE 3 MPH.
PRESSURE DIFFERENTIAL AT BOOST PRESSURE DIFFERENTIAL SWITCH	BOOST MALFUNCTION. SYSTEM LEAK. NO BOOST PRESSURE.	RED LIGHT AND YELLOW LIGHT COMES ON IN 1/2-1 SECONDS.
WHEEL SENSOR FAULT (FRONT ONLY)	SENSOR-TO-TONE WHEEL SPACING INCORRECT (SPACE TOO LARGE). INTERMITTENT DAMAGE SENSOR WIRE, SENSOR OR TONE WHEEL. SENSOR AND TONE WHEEL MISALIGNED.	YELLOW LIGHT ON.
WHEEL SENSOR FAULT (FRONT OR REAR ONE OR TWO MISSING SIGNALS)	DAMAGED SENSOR, WIRE, OR CONNECTOR. SENSOR DISCONNECTED. EXCESSIVE WHEEL SPIN. MISALIGNED OR DAMAGED TONE WHEEL. OPEN SENSOR OR WIRE.	YELLOW LIGHT ON AT 15 MPH IF FAULT OCCURRED BEFORE VEHCLE DRIVE-OFF. OR, YELLOW LIGHT ON AT 8 MPH IF FAULT OCCURRED AFTER VEHICLE DRIVE-OFF.
EXCESSIVE DECAY SOLENOID OPERATION	MODULATOR/SOLENOID FAULT. WHEEL SENSOR FAULT. EXTREMELY LOW AMBIENT TEMPERATURES. VEHICLE ON ICE COVERED SURFACE. TIRES HYDROPLANING ON WATER COVERED ROAD SURFACE.	YELLOW LIGHT ON WITHIN 1-2 SECONDS.
PRESSURE MODULATOR SOLENOID FAULT	SOLENOID SHORTED OR OPEN. DECAY AND BUILD SOLENOID ON AT SAME TIME. OPEN/SHORT IN MODULATOR HARNESS.	YELLOW LIGHT ON.
PUMP/MOTOR RUN-ON	EXCESSIVE RUN TIME. RELAY SHORTED, MOTOR SWITCH SHORTED. INTERNAL LEAK. CLOG IN PUMP LINE OR RESERVOIR FILTER.	RED LIGHT ON IF PUMP RUNS MORE THAN 4 MINUTES WITH NO BRAKES APPLIED.
PUMP/MOTOR INOPERATIVE	PUMP RELAY FAULT. NO VOLTAGE TO MOTOR. DAMAGED PUMP OR MOTOR. PUMP GAS CHARGE LOST.	YELLOW LIGHT ON. RED LIGHT ON AFTER 20 SECONDS.
LOW VOLTAGE	SYSTEM VOLTAGE BELOW 9V. SHORT, OPEN IN FEED WIRES OR RELAY. FUSE BAD. POOR GROUND. LOOSE, DISCONNECTED WIRE IN SYSTEM. BATTERY LOW OR DISCHARGED	YELLOW LIGHT ON.
RELAY FAULT	RELAY SHORTED OR OPEN.	YELLOW LIGHT ON.
ECU SELF DIAGNOSTIC FEATURE INOPERATIVE (SOLENOIDS NOT TEST-EXERCISED AT START-UP)	PARKING BRAKES ON (NOT RELEASED AT DRIVE-OFF). SYSTEM COMPONENT HAS MALFUNCTIONED. LOW FLUID LEVEL/LEAK IN SYSTEM.	YELLOW LIGHT ON.

90H06331

Courtesy of Chrysler Motors.

Fig. 3: ABS Trouble Shooting Chart

is caused by driver operating vehicle with parking brake applied, spinning wheels due to high acceleration or low traction surface. Pumping or riding brake pedal may also cause a fault.

NOTE: If ABS light glows briefly, there is an excess decay of pressure. This may be caused by a long stop on ice or hydroplaning. Yellow light comes on after a 1-2 second delay. No fault code will be stored and system will return to normal after stop is complete.

VISUAL CHECK

Ensure master cylinder reservoir is full to the MAX mark on the reservoir. If reservoir is not full, check for leaks and repair if necessary. Check all mechanical components and electrical connectors. Repair or replace any defective mechanical component. Check ABS warning lights and system operation. *See Fig. 3*.

TESTING SYSTEM

If system fault is diagnosed, attach DRB-II Tester (C-4805) to diagnostic connector, located on passenger side of engine compartment. *See Fig. 1*. Retrieve fault codes using DRB-II tester. Clear codes and retest system before diagnosing.

Clear fault codes by removing 2-amp ABS-BAT fuse, located on fuse panel under dash, for 5 seconds. Install fuse. Codes can also be cleared using DRB-II. Enter ADJUSTMENTS from ABS MENU to clear codes (by pressing ATM key on DRB-II). Once codes have been cleared, road test vehicle. Check if fault codes have been reset. If codes reset, go to appropriate fault code chart. See VERIFICATION TEST VER-1A under TROUBLE SHOOTING CHARTS in this article.

DRB-II has the capability to test function of ABS system and the state of its components. Functional test monitors circuits to help isolate faults not indicated by the system's self-diagnostics, along with those which are indicated. State display of components allows ABS system to be broken down to state of each component and state of stored trouble codes.

NOTE: If ABS light glows briefly, there is an excess decay of pressure. This may be caused by a long stop on ice or hydroplaning. Yellow light comes on after a 1-2 second delay. No fault code will be stored and system will return to normal after stop is complete.

CLEARING FAULT CODES

Clear fault codes by removing 2-amp "ABS-BAT" fuse, located on fuse panel under dash, for 5 seconds. Codes can also be cleared using DRB-II. Enter ADJUSTMENTS from ABS MENU to clear codes. Erase fault codes.

FAULT MESSAGES/CODES

FAULT MESSAGES/CODES

Code	Fault Message	Fault Condition
801	SOLENOID UNDERVOLTAGE	Supply voltage to ABSM from system relay is less than 9.0 volts. Yellow ABS light is on. ABS system is inoperative.
802	PARKING BRAKE NOT SEEN	Fault is set when parking brake switch does not cycle from off to on.
805	DIFFERENTIAL PRESSURE FAULT	Differential pressure switch in proportioning valve grounds because of pressure difference between front and rear braking circuits. Red brake light is on. Yellow brake light comes on above 3-5 MPH.
806	BOOST PRESSURE FAULT	Switch grounds because of pressure difference between boost circuit and primary circuit. Red brake and Yellow ABS lights are on. ABS system is inoperative.
807	LOW ACCUMULATOR	Low accumulator switch is closed. Yellow ABS light is on. Red brake light comes on after a 20-second delay above 3 MPH. ABS system is inoperative.
808	MODULATOR FAULT	Shorted or open solenoid in modulator, or a shorted or open driver or wire. Yellow ABS light is on. ABS system is inoperative.
809	SELF-TEST FAILURE	Internal fault in ABSM. Yellow ABS light is on. ABS system is inoperative.
811	RELAY FAULT	Power is always being supplied from system power relay. Yellow ABS light is on. ABS system is inoperative.
812	PUMP/MOTOR FAULT	ABS pump runs for more than 4 minutes without input from brake switch. Red brake light is on.
813	BRAKE FAULT	Fault is set during a system test when ABSM sees brake switch always applied or never applied.
814	LOW FLUID	Brake fluid level switch is closed for more than one second or parking brake is applied for more than one second at speeds greater than 2 MPH. Red brake and Yellow ABS lights are on. ABS system is inoperative.
815	RIGHT REAR SPEED SENSOR FAULT	Missing or erratic speed sensor signal. Yellow ABS light comes on after a 2-second delay. ABS system is inoperative.
816	LEFT REAR SPEED SENSOR FAULT	Missing or erratic speed sensor signal. Yellow ABS light comes on after a 2-second delay. ABS system is inoperative.
817	RIGHT FRONT SPEED SENSOR FAULT	Missing or erratic speed sensor signal. Yellow ABS light comes on after a 2-second delay. ABS system is inoperative.
818	LEFT FRONT SPEED SENSOR FAULT	Missing or erratic speed sensor signal. Yellow ABS light comes on after a 2-second delay. ABS system is inoperative.

1991 BRAKES
Anti-Lock (Cont.)

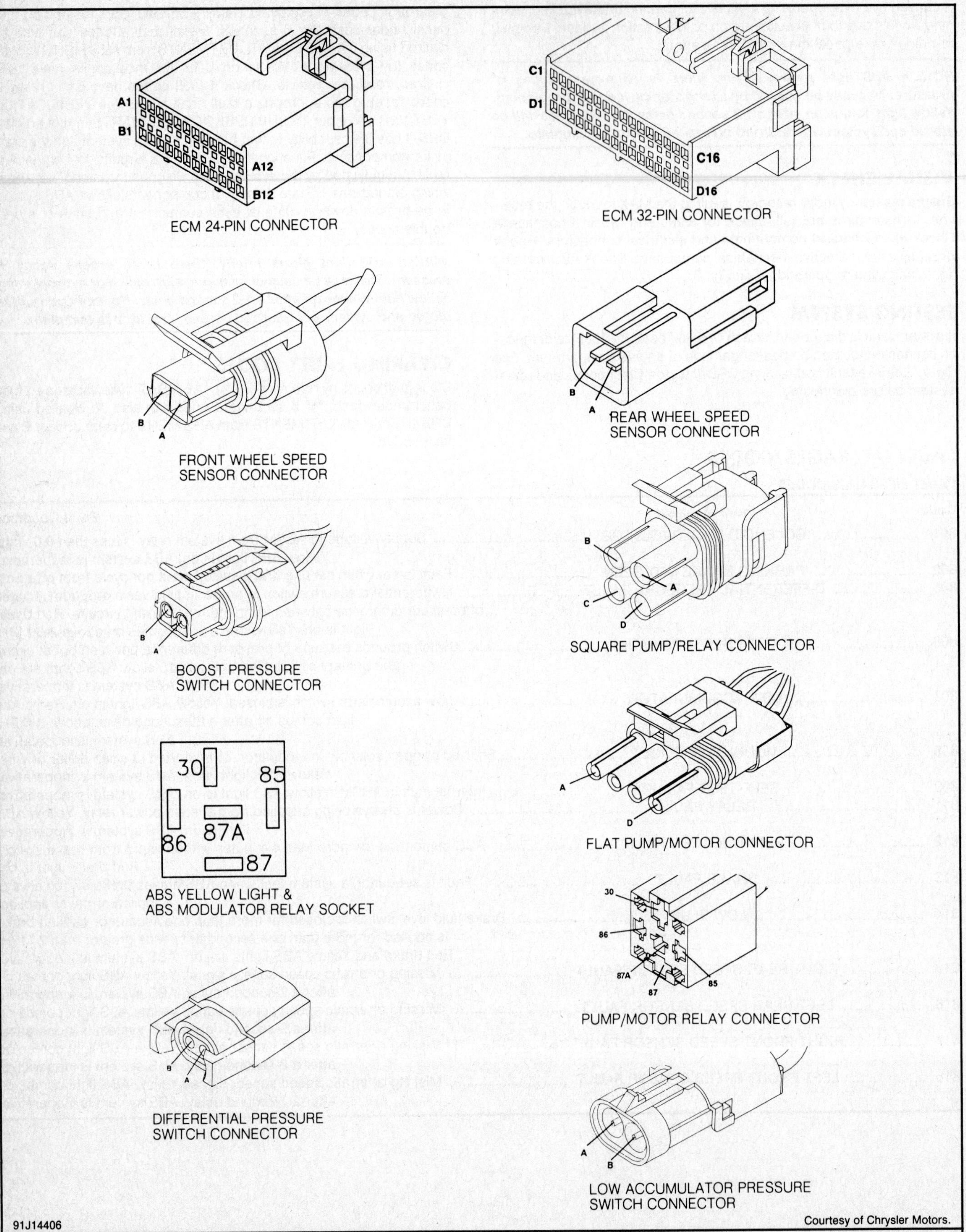
A1
B1
A12
B12
ECM 24-PIN CONNECTOR
C1
D1
C16
D16
ECM 32-PIN CONNECTOR
B
A
FRONT WHEEL SPEED
SENSOR CONNECTOR
B
A
REAR WHEEL SPEED
SENSOR CONNECTOR
B
A
BOOST PRESSURE
SWITCH CONNECTOR
B
A
C
D
SQUARE PUMP/RELAY CONNECTOR
30
85
87A
86
87
ABS YELLOW LIGHT &
ABS MODULATOR RELAY SOCKET
A
D
FLAT PUMP/MOTOR CONNECTOR
30
86
87A
87
85
PUMP/MOTOR RELAY CONNECTOR
B
A
DIFFERENTIAL PRESSURE
SWITCH CONNECTOR
A
B
LOW ACCUMULATOR PRESSURE
SWITCH CONNECTOR
91J14406
Courtesy of Chrysler Motors.

Fig. 4: Identifying Anti-Lock Brake System Connectors

WIRING DIAGRAM

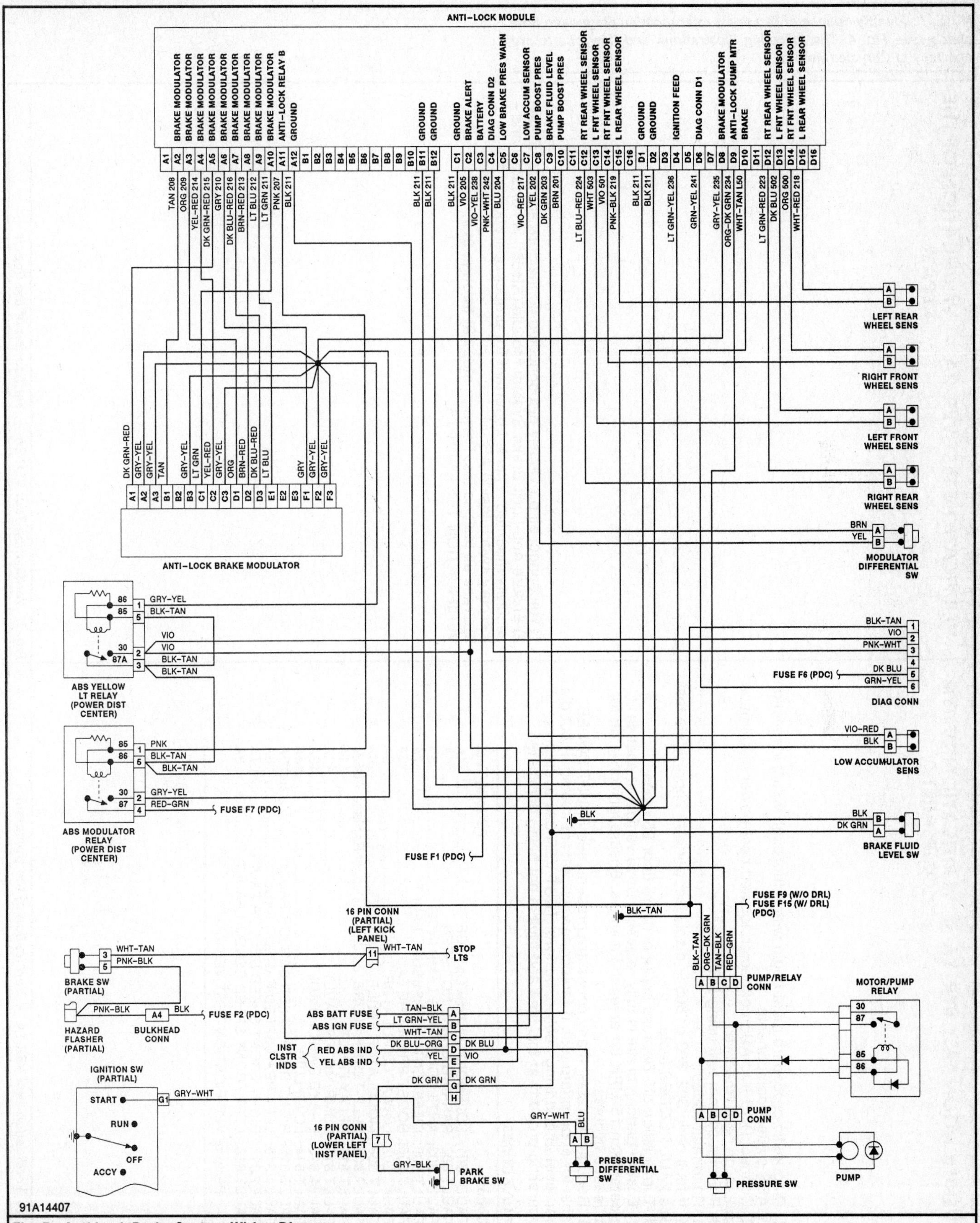
ANTI-LOCK MODULE
ANTI-LOCK BRAKE MODULATOR
LEFT REAR WHEEL SENS
RIGHT FRONT WHEEL SENS
LEFT FRONT WHEEL SENS
RIGHT REAR WHEEL SENS
MODULATOR DIFFERENTIAL SW
ABS YELLOW LT RELAY (POWER DIST CENTER)
DIAG CONN
FUSE F6 (PDC)
LOW ACCUMULATOR SENS
ABS MODULATOR RELAY (POWER DIST CENTER)
FUSE F7 (PDC)
BRAKE FLUID LEVEL SW
FUSE F1 (PDC)
16 PIN CONN (PARTIAL) (LEFT KICK PANEL)
FUSE F9 (W/O DRL) FUSE F15 (W/ DRL) (PDC)
STOP LTS
BRAKE SW (PARTIAL)
PUMP/RELAY CONN
MOTOR/PUMP RELAY
HAZARD FLASHER (PARTIAL)
BULKHEAD CONN
FUSE F2 (PDC)
ABS BATT FUSE
ABS IGN FUSE
INST CLSTR INDS
RED ABS IND
YEL ABS IND
IGNITION SW (PARTIAL)
START
RUN
OFF
ACCY
PUMP CONN
16 PIN CONN (PARTIAL) (LOWER LEFT INST PANEL)
PARK BRAKE SW
PRESSURE DIFFERENTIAL SW
PRESSURE SW
PUMP
91A14407
Fig. 5: Anti-Lock Brake System Wiring Diagram

1991 BRAKES
Anti-Lock (Cont.)

TROUBLE SHOOTING CHARTS

NOTE: *To identify connector terminals referenced in diagnostic flow charts, see Fig. 4. The following illustrations and flow charts are courtesy of Chrysler Motors.*

VERIFICATION TEST VER-1A – VERIFICATION OF THE COMPLAINT

1) Diagnostic procedure must begin with a thorough visual inspection of ABS system components.
2) Connect DRB-II to ABS connector, located near power distribution center, on right wheelwell.
3) Perform system test using DRB-II.
4) Read fault codes.
5) If fault code 802, 803 or 805 is displayed, perform appropriate test. See FAULT CODES table.
6) Turn ignition off. Depress brake pedal to floor 25 times.
7) Ensure parking brake is fully released. Drive vehicle at speeds greater than 15 MPH for at least 3 minutes. Ensure ignition is on for at least 5 minutes.
8) Read fault codes. If any codes are present, see FAULT CODES table for appropriate test. If fault code was present in step **4)** but did not reset after driving vehicle, perform TEST VER-3A. System is operating properly at this time and fault is not being duplicated.

FAULT CODES

Code	Perform Test
FAULT 801: SOLENOID UNDERVOLTAGE	4A
FAULT 802: PARKING BRAKE NOT SEEN	5A
FAULT 803: ANTILOCK/BRAKE LAMP INOP	6A
FAULT 805: DIFFERENTIAL PRESSURE FAULT	7A
FAULT 806: BOOST PRESSURE FAULT	8A
FAULT 807: LOW ACCUMULATOR	9A
FAULT 808: MODULATOR FAULT	10A
FAULT 809: SELF-TEST FAILURE	[1] Replace ABSM
FAULT 811: RELAY FAULT	11A
FAULT 812: PUMP/MOTOR FAULT	12A
FAULT 813: BRAKE SWITCH FAULT	13A
FAULT 814: LOW FLUID	14A
FAULT 815: RIGHT REAR SPEED SENSOR FAULT	15A
FAULT 816: LEFT REAR SPEED SENSOR FAULT	16A
FAULT 817: RIGHT FRONT SPEED SENSOR FAULT	17A
FAULT 818: LEFT FRONT SPEED SENSOR FAULT	18A

[1] – Perform VERIFICATION TEST VER-2A.

Fig. 6: Verification Test VER-1A – Verification of the Complaint

VERIFICATION TEST VER-2A – VERIFICATION OF THE REPAIR

1) Reconnect all previously disconnected connectors and brake lines.
2) Ensure Anti-Lock Brake System Module (ABSM) is correctly and securely mounted. This is important for proper operation of the mercury switch inside ABSM.
3) Erase all fault codes. Perform steps **3)** through **8)** in VERIFICATION TEST VER-1A.

Fig. 7: Verification Test VER-2A – Verification of the Repair

VERIFICATION TEST VER-3A – SOFT FAULT CODE TEST

At this point you have done a visual inspection, found a fault code and test driven vehicle. The fault code has not reappeared, so it is not a current or "hard" fault, but rather an intermittent or "soft" fault. Proceed as follows.

1) Refer to FAULT MESSAGES/CODES in TESTING & TROUBLE SHOOTING to determine how soft fault code was set.

2) Refer to wiring diagram to identify wiring, connectors and components that could have caused the fault.

3) Carefully inspect the entire suspect circuit. Check connectors. Check for corrosion, accident damage, and improper or missing parts.

4) Wiggle wiring harness to try to reset fault. If fault resets, perform VERIFICATION TEST VER-1A. If fault DOES NOT reset, perform VERIFICATION TEST VER-2A.

Fig. 8: Verification Test VER-3A – Soft Fault Code Test

TEST 4A – 801: SOLENOID UNDERVOLTAGE FAULT (1 OF 3)

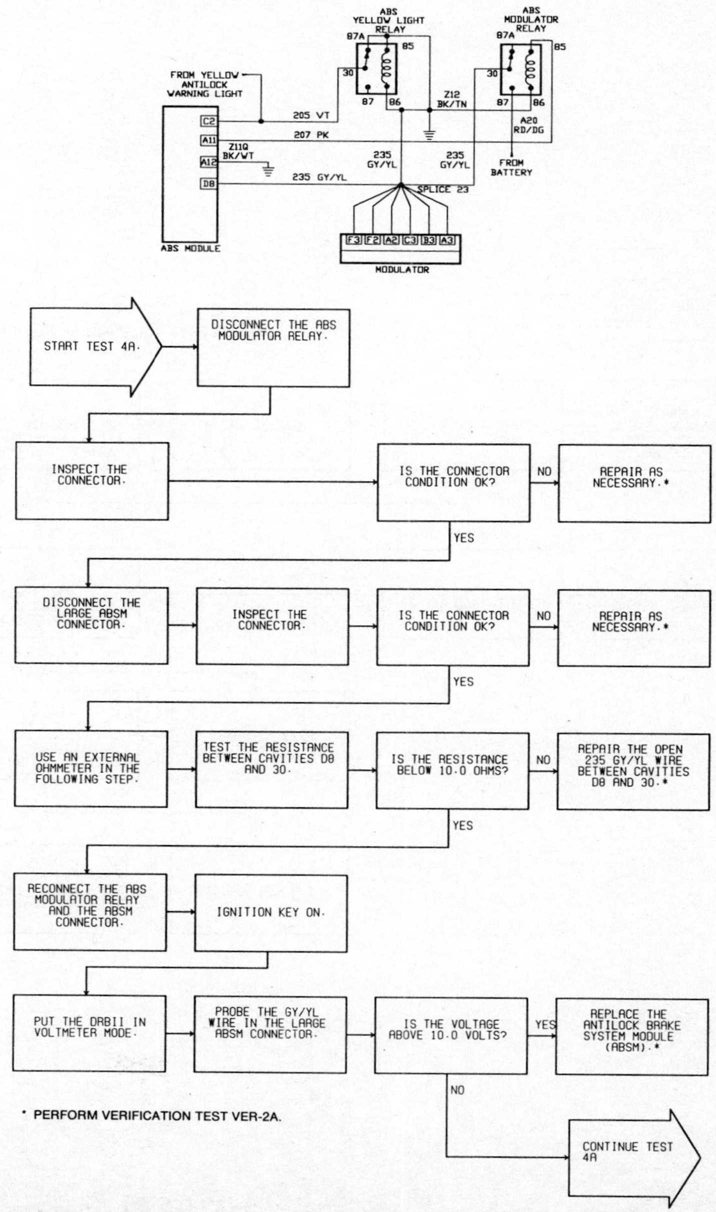
ABS YELLOW LIGHT RELAY
ABS MODULATOR RELAY
FROM YELLOW ANTILOCK WARNING LIGHT
205 VT
207 PK
Z110 BK/WT
235 GY/YL
Z12 BK/TN
A20 RD/DG
FROM BATTERY
SPLICE 23
ABS MODULE
MODULATOR
START TEST 4A.
DISCONNECT THE ABS MODULATOR RELAY.
INSPECT THE CONNECTOR.
IS THE CONNECTOR CONDITION OK?
NO
REPAIR AS NECESSARY.*
YES
DISCONNECT THE LARGE ABSM CONNECTOR.
INSPECT THE CONNECTOR.
IS THE CONNECTOR CONDITION OK?
NO
REPAIR AS NECESSARY.*
YES
USE AN EXTERNAL OHMMETER IN THE FOLLOWING STEP.
TEST THE RESISTANCE BETWEEN CAVITIES D8 AND 30.
IS THE RESISTANCE BELOW 10.0 OHMS?
NO
REPAIR THE OPEN 235 GY/YL WIRE BETWEEN CAVITIES D8 AND 30.*
YES
RECONNECT THE ABS MODULATOR RELAY AND THE ABSM CONNECTOR.
IGNITION KEY ON.
PUT THE DRBII IN VOLTMETER MODE.
PROBE THE GY/YL WIRE IN THE LARGE ABSM CONNECTOR.
IS THE VOLTAGE ABOVE 10.0 VOLTS?
YES
REPLACE THE ANTILOCK BRAKE SYSTEM MODULE (ABSM).*
NO
CONTINUE TEST 4A
* PERFORM VERIFICATION TEST VER-2A.

91C14227 91B14408

Fig. 9: Test 4A – 801: Solenoid Undervoltage Fault (1 of 3)

1991 BRAKES
Anti-Lock (Cont.)

TEST 4A – 801: SOLENOID UNDERVOLTAGE FAULT (2 OF 3)

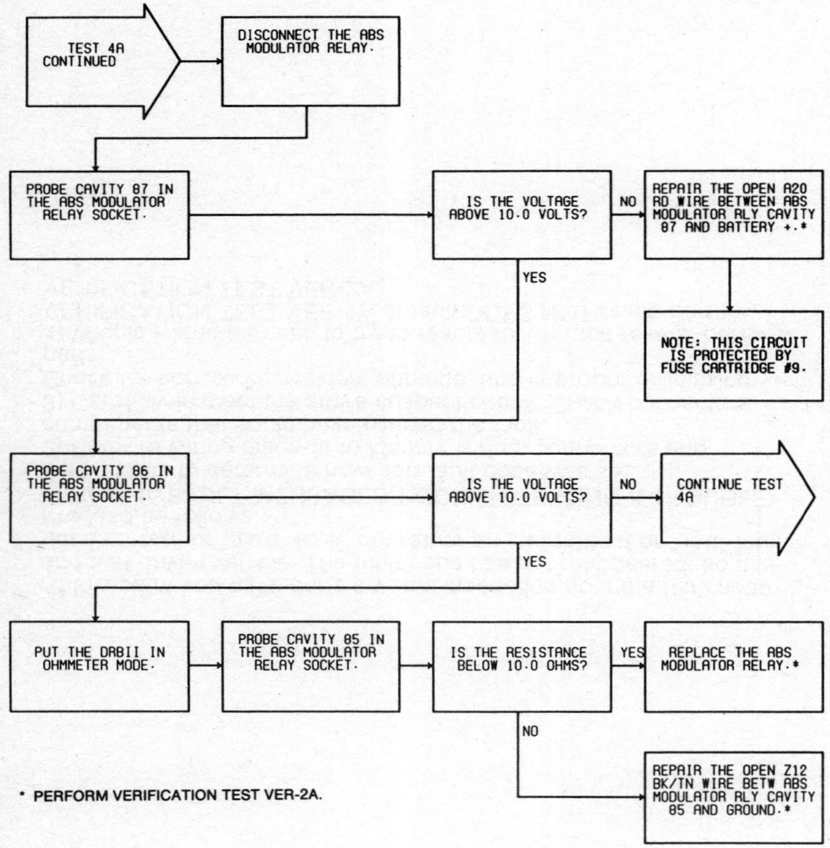
TEST 4A CONTINUED
DISCONNECT THE ABS MODULATOR RELAY.
PROBE CAVITY 87 IN THE ABS MODULATOR RELAY SOCKET.
IS THE VOLTAGE ABOVE 10.0 VOLTS?
NO
REPAIR THE OPEN A20 RD WIRE BETWEEN ABS MODULATOR RLY CAVITY 87 AND BATTERY +.*
YES
NOTE: THIS CIRCUIT IS PROTECTED BY FUSE CARTRIDGE #9.
PROBE CAVITY 86 IN THE ABS MODULATOR RELAY SOCKET.
IS THE VOLTAGE ABOVE 10.0 VOLTS?
NO
CONTINUE TEST 4A
YES
PUT THE DRBII IN OHMMETER MODE.
PROBE CAVITY 85 IN THE ABS MODULATOR RELAY SOCKET.
IS THE RESISTANCE BELOW 10.0 OHMS?
YES
REPLACE THE ABS MODULATOR RELAY.*
NO
REPAIR THE OPEN Z12 BK/TN WIRE BETW ABS MODULATOR RLY CAVITY 85 AND GROUND.*

* PERFORM VERIFICATION TEST VER-2A.

91C14409

Fig. 10: Test 4A – 801: Solenoid Undervoltage Fault (2 of 3)

TEST 4A – 801: SOLENOID UNDERVOLTAGE FAULT (3 OF 3)

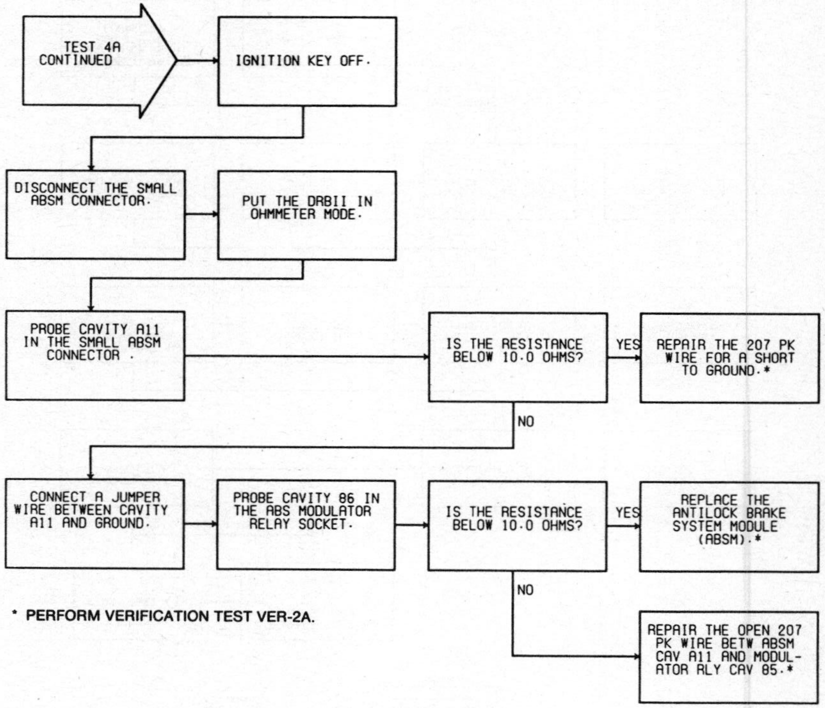
TEST 4A CONTINUED
IGNITION KEY OFF.
DISCONNECT THE SMALL ABSM CONNECTOR.
PUT THE DRBII IN OHMMETER MODE.
PROBE CAVITY A11 IN THE SMALL ABSM CONNECTOR .
IS THE RESISTANCE BELOW 10.0 OHMS?
YES
REPAIR THE 207 PK WIRE FOR A SHORT TO GROUND.*
NO
CONNECT A JUMPER WIRE BETWEEN CAVITY A11 AND GROUND.
PROBE CAVITY 86 IN THE ABS MODULATOR RELAY SOCKET.
IS THE RESISTANCE BELOW 10.0 OHMS?
YES
REPLACE THE ANTILOCK BRAKE SYSTEM MODULE (ABSM).*
NO
REPAIR THE OPEN 207 PK WIRE BETW ABSM CAV A11 AND MODULATOR RLY CAV 85.*

* PERFORM VERIFICATION TEST VER-2A.

91F14410

Fig. 11: Test 4A – 801: Solenoid Undervoltage Fault (3 of 3)

TEST 5A – 802: TESTING PARK BRAKE CIRCUIT (1 OF 2)

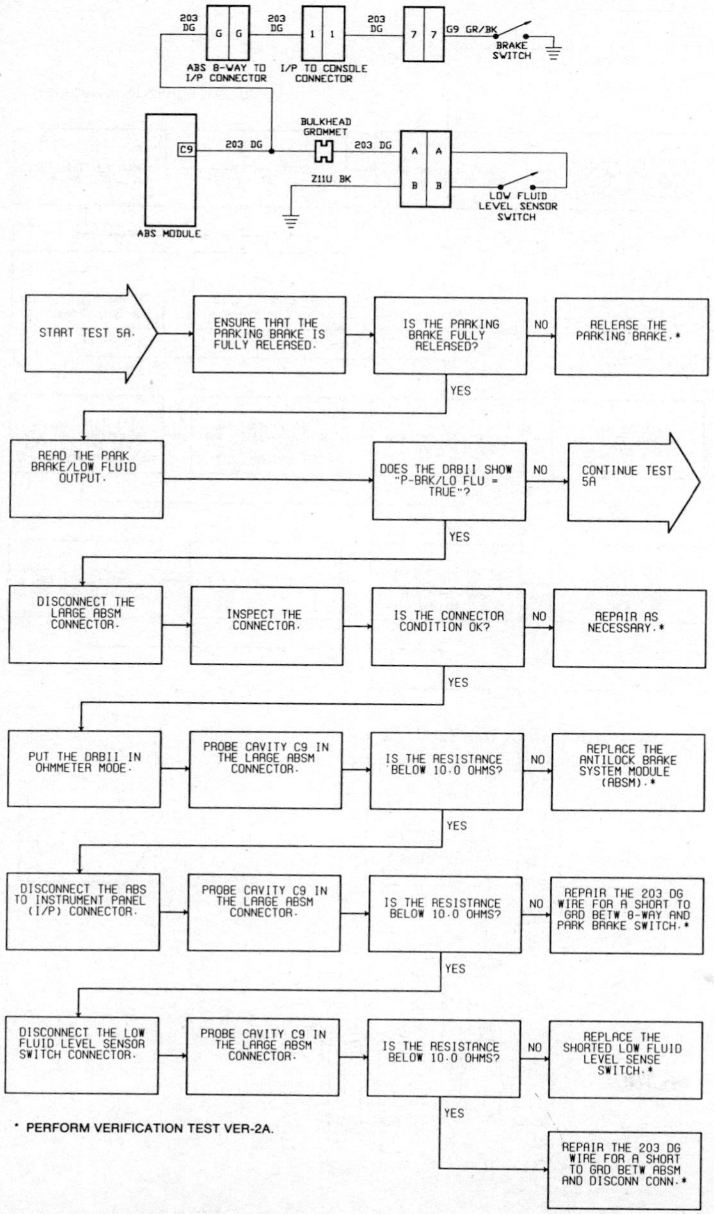
203 DG
ABS 8-WAY TO I/P CONNECTOR
I/P TO CONSOLE CONNECTOR
G9 GR/BK
BRAKE SWITCH
BULKHEAD GROMMET
203 DG
Z11U BK
LOW FLUID LEVEL SENSOR SWITCH
ABS MODULE
C9
START TEST 5A.
ENSURE THAT THE PARKING BRAKE IS FULLY RELEASED.
IS THE PARKING BRAKE FULLY RELEASED?
NO
RELEASE THE PARKING BRAKE.*
YES
READ THE PARK BRAKE/LOW FLUID OUTPUT.
DOES THE DRBII SHOW "P-BRK/LO FLU = TRUE"?
CONTINUE TEST 5A
DISCONNECT THE LARGE ABSM CONNECTOR.
INSPECT THE CONNECTOR.
IS THE CONNECTOR CONDITION OK?
REPAIR AS NECESSARY.*
PUT THE DRBII IN OHMMETER MODE.
PROBE CAVITY C9 IN THE LARGE ABSM CONNECTOR.
IS THE RESISTANCE BELOW 10.0 OHMS?
REPLACE THE ANTILOCK BRAKE SYSTEM MODULE (ABSM).*
DISCONNECT THE ABS TO INSTRUMENT PANEL (I/P) CONNECTOR.
REPAIR THE 203 DG WIRE FOR A SHORT TO GRD BETW 8-WAY AND PARK BRAKE SWITCH.*
DISCONNECT THE LOW FLUID LEVEL SENSOR SWITCH CONNECTOR.
REPLACE THE SHORTED LOW FLUID LEVEL SENSE SWITCH.*
REPAIR THE 203 DG WIRE FOR A SHORT TO GRD BETW ABSM AND DISCONN CONN.*
* PERFORM VERIFICATION TEST VER-2A.

91B14234 91G14411

Fig. 12: Test 5A – 802: Testing Park Brake Circuit (1 of 2)

TEST 5A – 802: TESTING PARK BRAKE CIRCUIT (2 OF 2)

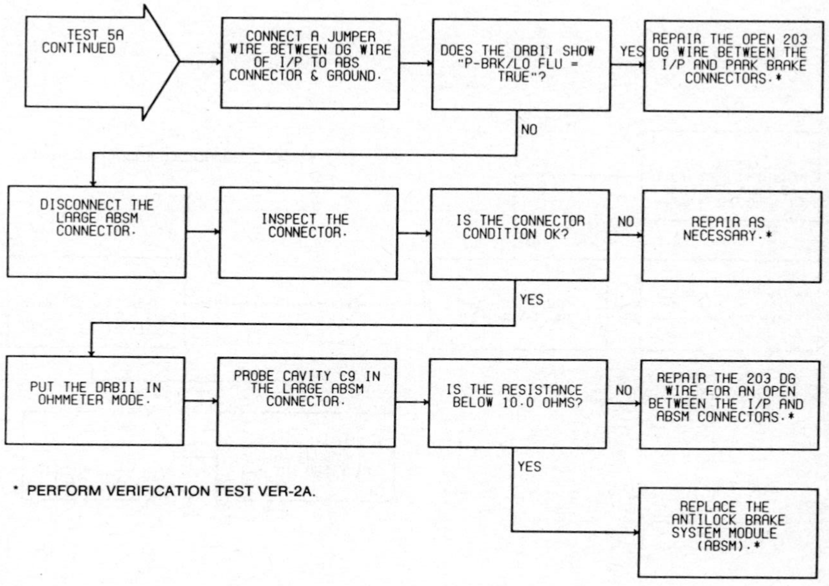
TEST 5A CONTINUED
CONNECT A JUMPER WIRE BETWEEN DG WIRE OF I/P TO ABS CONNECTOR & GROUND.
DOES THE DRBII SHOW "P-BRK/LO FLU = TRUE"?
YES
REPAIR THE OPEN 203 DG WIRE BETWEEN THE I/P AND PARK BRAKE CONNECTORS.*
NO
DISCONNECT THE LARGE ABSM CONNECTOR.
INSPECT THE CONNECTOR.
IS THE CONNECTOR CONDITION OK?
REPAIR AS NECESSARY.*
PUT THE DRBII IN OHMMETER MODE.
PROBE CAVITY C9 IN THE LARGE ABSM CONNECTOR.
IS THE RESISTANCE BELOW 10.0 OHMS?
REPAIR THE 203 DG WIRE FOR AN OPEN BETWEEN THE I/P AND ABSM CONNECTORS.*
REPLACE THE ANTILOCK BRAKE SYSTEM MODULE (ABSM).*
* PERFORM VERIFICATION TEST VER-2A.

91H14412

Fig. 13: Test 5A – 802: Testing Park Brake Circuit (2 of 2)

TEST 6A – 803: ABS WARNING LAMPS INOPERATIVE (1 OF 2)

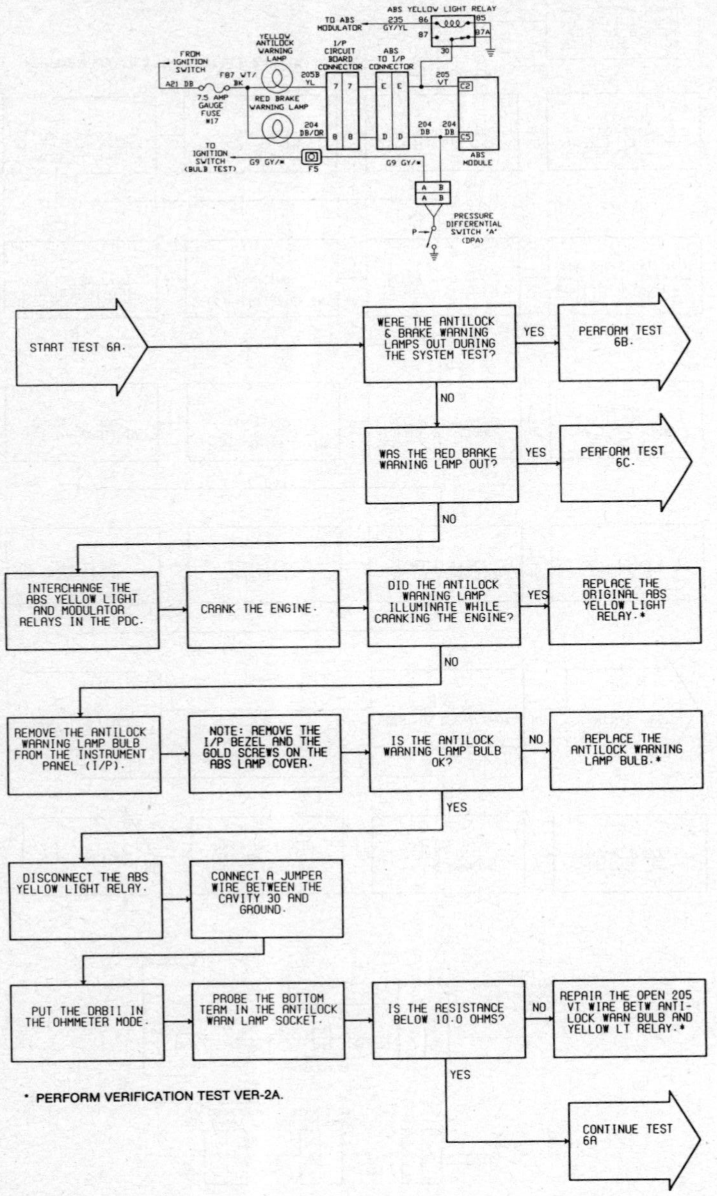
ABS YELLOW LIGHT RELAY
TO ABS MODULATOR
FROM IGNITION SWITCH
YELLOW ANTILOCK WARNING LAMP
I/P CIRCUIT BOARD CONNECTOR
ABS TO I/P CONNECTOR
7.5 AMP GAUGE FUSE #17
RED BRAKE WARNING LAMP
TO IGNITION SWITCH (BULB TEST)
ABS MODULE
PRESSURE DIFFERENTIAL SWITCH 'A' (DPA)
START TEST 6A.
WERE THE ANTILOCK & BRAKE WARNING LAMPS OUT DURING THE SYSTEM TEST?
YES
PERFORM TEST 6B.
NO
WAS THE RED BRAKE WARNING LAMP OUT?
YES
PERFORM TEST 6C.
NO
INTERCHANGE THE ABS YELLOW LIGHT AND MODULATOR RELAYS IN THE PDC.
CRANK THE ENGINE.
DID THE ANTILOCK WARNING LAMP ILLUMINATE WHILE CRANKING THE ENGINE?
YES
REPLACE THE ORIGINAL ABS YELLOW LIGHT RELAY.*
NO
REMOVE THE ANTILOCK WARNING LAMP BULB FROM THE INSTRUMENT PANEL (I/P).
NOTE: REMOVE THE I/P BEZEL AND THE GOLD SCREWS ON THE ABS LAMP COVER.
IS THE ANTILOCK WARNING LAMP BULB OK?
NO
REPLACE THE ANTILOCK WARNING LAMP BULB.*
YES
DISCONNECT THE ABS YELLOW LIGHT RELAY.
CONNECT A JUMPER WIRE BETWEEN THE CAVITY 30 AND GROUND.
PUT THE DRBII IN THE OHMMETER MODE.
PROBE THE BOTTOM TERM IN THE ANTILOCK WARN LAMP SOCKET.
IS THE RESISTANCE BELOW 10.0 OHMS?
NO
REPAIR THE OPEN 205 VT WIRE BETW ANTI-LOCK WARN BULB AND YELLOW LT RELAY.*
YES
CONTINUE TEST 6A

* PERFORM VERIFICATION TEST VER-2A.

91D14228 91I14413

Fig. 14: Test 6A – 803: ABS Warning Lamps Inoperative (1 of 2)

TEST 6A – 803: ABS WARNING LAMPS INOPERATIVE (2 OF 2)

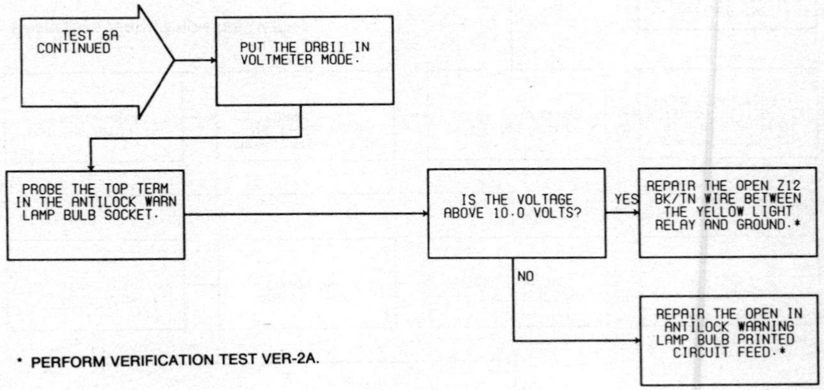
TEST 6A CONTINUED
PUT THE DRBII IN VOLTMETER MODE.
PROBE THE TOP TERM IN THE ANTILOCK WARN LAMP BULB SOCKET.
IS THE VOLTAGE ABOVE 10.0 VOLTS?
YES
REPAIR THE OPEN Z12 BK/TN WIRE BETWEEN THE YELLOW LIGHT RELAY AND GROUND.*
NO
REPAIR THE OPEN IN ANTILOCK WARNING LAMP BULB PRINTED CIRCUIT FEED.*

* PERFORM VERIFICATION TEST VER-2A.

91J14414

Fig. 15: Test 6A – 803: ABS Warning Lamps Inoperative (2 of 2)

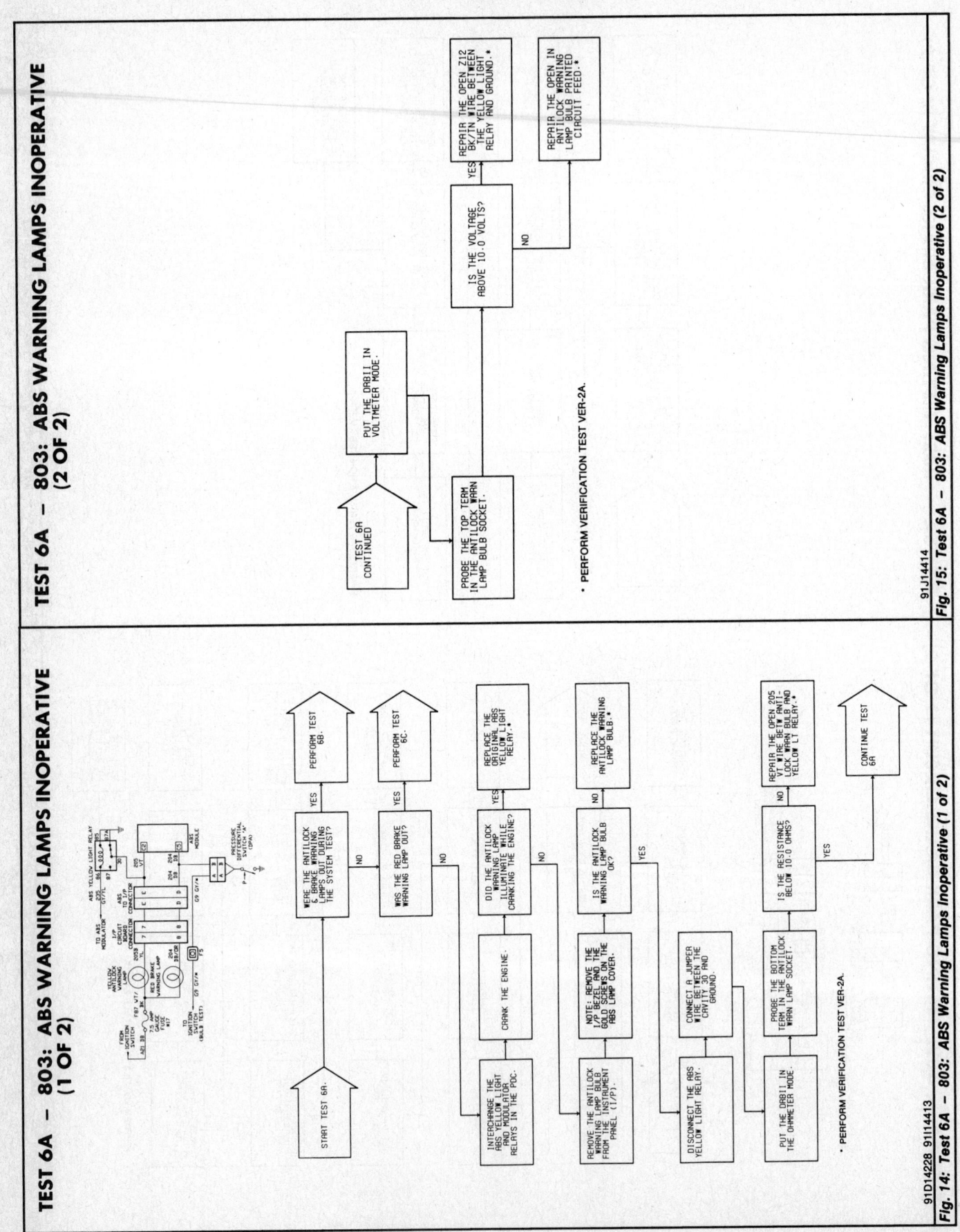

TEST 6B – 803: SOLENOID UNDERVOLTAGE FAULT

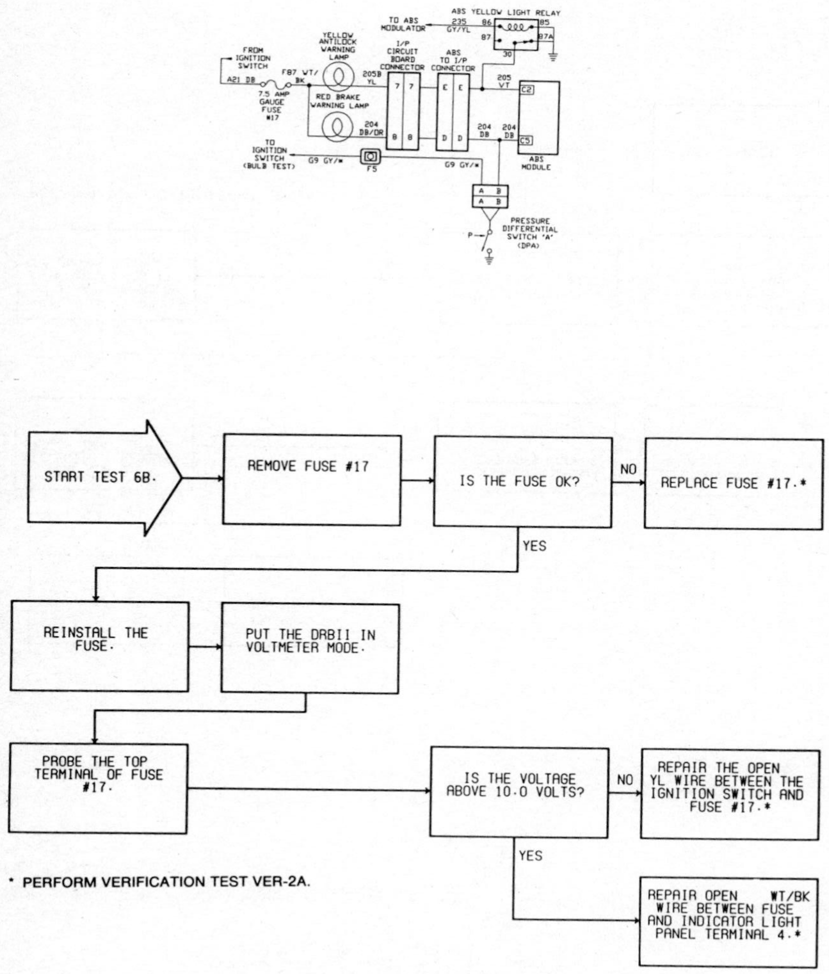
START TEST 6B.
REMOVE FUSE #17
IS THE FUSE OK?
NO
REPLACE FUSE #17.*
YES
REINSTALL THE FUSE.
PUT THE DRBII IN VOLTMETER MODE.
PROBE THE TOP TERMINAL OF FUSE #17.
IS THE VOLTAGE ABOVE 10.0 VOLTS?
NO
REPAIR THE OPEN YL WIRE BETWEEN THE IGNITION SWITCH AND FUSE #17.*
YES
REPAIR OPEN WT/BK WIRE BETWEEN FUSE AND INDICATOR LIGHT PANEL TERMINAL 4.*

* PERFORM VERIFICATION TEST VER-2A.

91D14228 91A14415

Fig. 16: Test 6B – 803: Solenoid Undervoltage Fault

TEST 6C – 803: RED BRAKE WARNING LAMP INOPERATIVE

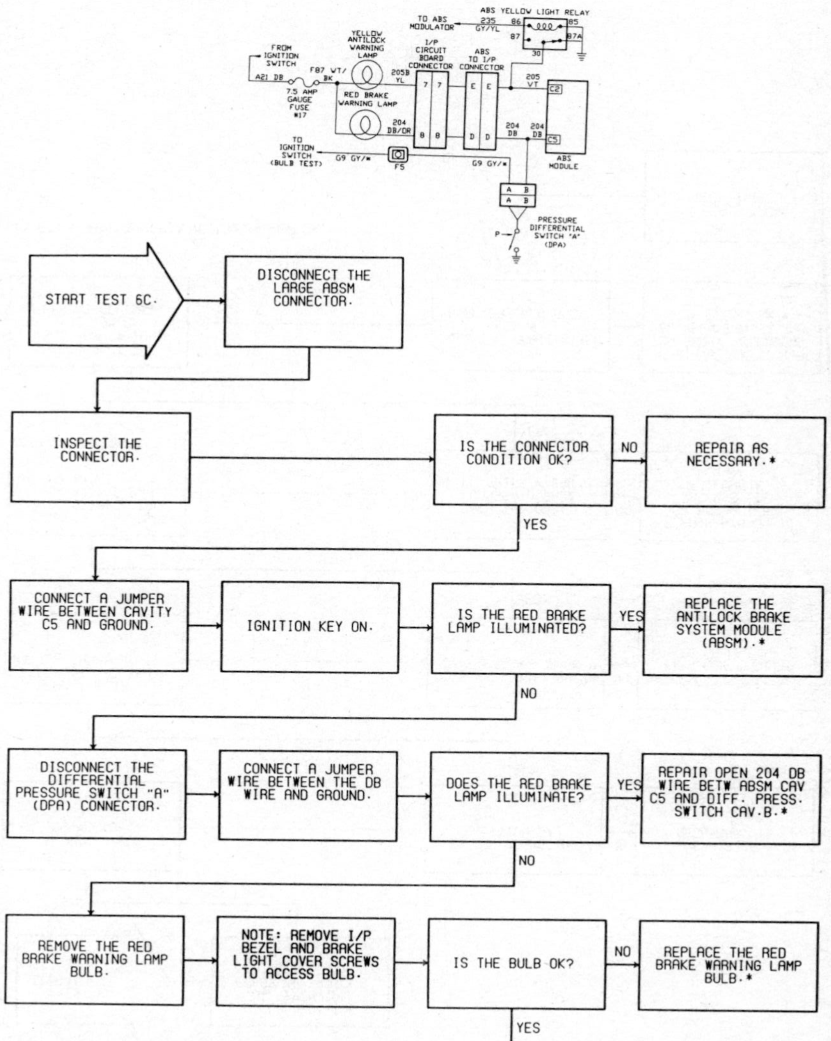
START TEST 6C.
DISCONNECT THE LARGE ABSM CONNECTOR.
INSPECT THE CONNECTOR.
IS THE CONNECTOR CONDITION OK?
NO
REPAIR AS NECESSARY.*
YES
CONNECT A JUMPER WIRE BETWEEN CAVITY C5 AND GROUND.
IGNITION KEY ON.
IS THE RED BRAKE LAMP ILLUMINATED?
YES
REPLACE THE ANTILOCK BRAKE SYSTEM MODULE (ABSM).*
NO
DISCONNECT THE DIFFERENTIAL PRESSURE SWITCH "A" (DPA) CONNECTOR.
CONNECT A JUMPER WIRE BETWEEN THE DB WIRE AND GROUND.
DOES THE RED BRAKE LAMP ILLUMINATE?
YES
REPAIR OPEN 204 DB WIRE BETW ABSM CAV C5 AND DIFF. PRESS. SWITCH CAV.B.*
NO
REMOVE THE RED BRAKE WARNING LAMP BULB.
NOTE: REMOVE I/P BEZEL AND BRAKE LIGHT COVER SCREWS TO ACCESS BULB.
IS THE BULB OK?
NO
REPLACE THE RED BRAKE WARNING LAMP BULB.*
YES
1

* PERFORM VERIFICATION TEST VER-2A.

①– Put DRB-II in voltmeter mode. Probe top terminal of Red brake warning light socket. If voltage is less than 10 volts, repair open in circuit No. 204 (Dark Blue/Orange wire) between Red brake warning lamp and Differential Pressure Switch "A" (DPA) connector. Perform VERIFICATION TEST VER-2A. If voltage is greater than 10 volts, repair printed circuit to Red brake warning lamp.

91D14228 91B14416

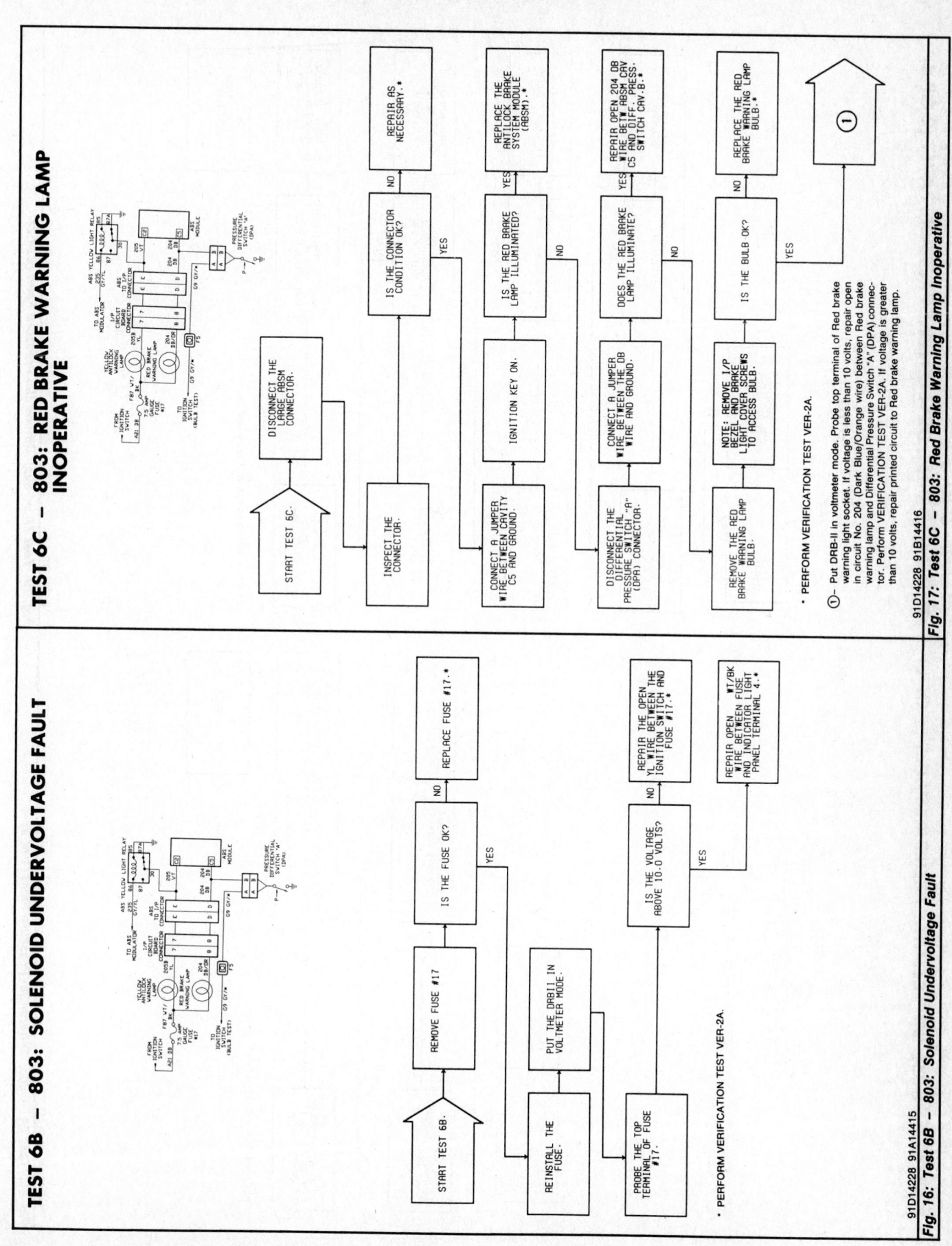

Fig. 17: Test 6C – 803: Red Brake Warning Lamp Inoperative

TEST 7A – 805: DIFFERENTIAL PRESSURE FAULT (1 OF 2)

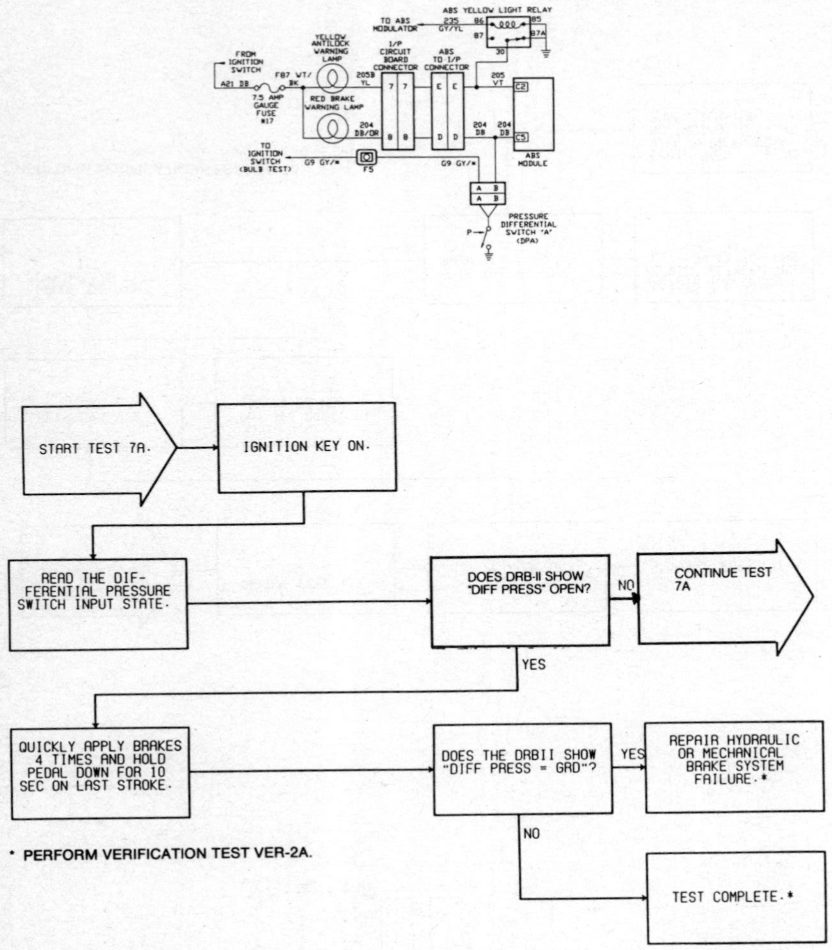
ABS YELLOW LIGHT RELAY
TO ABS MODULATOR
FROM IGNITION SWITCH
YELLOW ANTILOCK WARNING LAMP
RED BRAKE WARNING LAMP
7.5 AMP GAUGE FUSE #17
I/P CIRCUIT BOARD CONNECTOR
ABS TO I/P CONNECTOR
ABS MODULE
TO IGNITION SWITCH (BULB TEST)
PRESSURE DIFFERENTIAL SWITCH "A" (DPA)
START TEST 7A.
IGNITION KEY ON.
READ THE DIF-FERENTIAL PRESSURE SWITCH INPUT STATE.
DOES DRB-II SHOW "DIFF PRESS" OPEN?
NO
CONTINUE TEST 7A
YES
QUICKLY APPLY BRAKES 4 TIMES AND HOLD PEDAL DOWN FOR 10 SEC ON LAST STROKE.
DOES THE DRBII SHOW "DIFF PRESS = GRD"?
YES
REPAIR HYDRAULIC OR MECHANICAL BRAKE SYSTEM FAILURE.*
NO
TEST COMPLETE.*

* PERFORM VERIFICATION TEST VER-2A.

91D14228 91C14417

Fig. 18: Test 7A – 805: Differential Pressure Fault (1 of 2)

TEST 7A – 805: DIFFERENTIAL PRESSURE FAULT (2 OF 2)

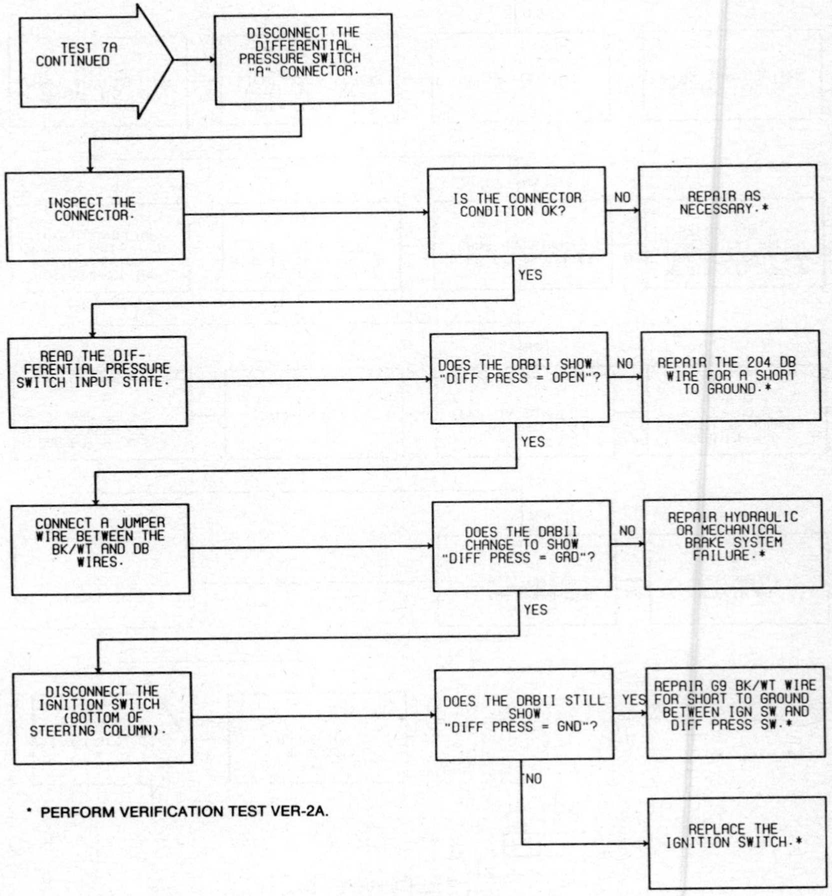
TEST 7A CONTINUED
DISCONNECT THE DIFFERENTIAL PRESSURE SWITCH "A" CONNECTOR.
INSPECT THE CONNECTOR.
IS THE CONNECTOR CONDITION OK?
NO
REPAIR AS NECESSARY.*
YES
READ THE DIF-FERENTIAL PRESSURE SWITCH INPUT STATE.
DOES THE DRBII SHOW "DIFF PRESS = OPEN"?
NO
REPAIR THE 204 DB WIRE FOR A SHORT TO GROUND.*
YES
CONNECT A JUMPER WIRE BETWEEN THE BK/WT AND DB WIRES.
DOES THE DRBII CHANGE TO SHOW "DIFF PRESS = GRD"?
NO
REPAIR HYDRAULIC OR MECHANICAL BRAKE SYSTEM FAILURE.*
YES
DISCONNECT THE IGNITION SWITCH (BOTTOM OF STEERING COLUMN).
DOES THE DRBII STILL SHOW "DIFF PRESS = GND"?
YES
REPAIR G9 BK/WT WIRE FOR SHORT TO GROUND BETWEEN IGN SW AND DIFF PRESS SW.*
NO
REPLACE THE IGNITION SWITCH.*

* PERFORM VERIFICATION TEST VER-2A.

91D14418

Fig. 19: Test 7A – 805: Differential Pressure Fault (2 of 2)

TEST 8A – 806: BOOST PRESSURE FAULT (1 OF 2)

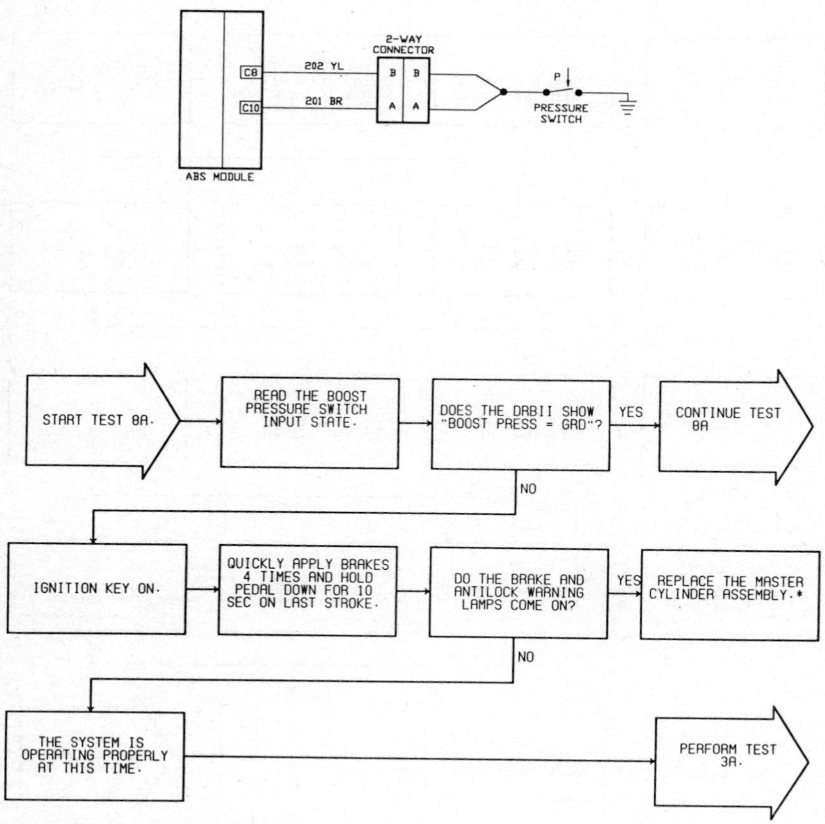
ABS MODULE
C8
C10
202 YL
201 BR
2-WAY CONNECTOR
B B
A A
P
PRESSURE SWITCH
START TEST 8A.
READ THE BOOST PRESSURE SWITCH INPUT STATE.
DOES THE DRBII SHOW "BOOST PRESS = GRD"?
YES
CONTINUE TEST 8A
NO
IGNITION KEY ON.
QUICKLY APPLY BRAKES 4 TIMES AND HOLD PEDAL DOWN FOR 10 SEC ON LAST STROKE.
DO THE BRAKE AND ANTILOCK WARNING LAMPS COME ON?
YES
REPLACE THE MASTER CYLINDER ASSEMBLY.*
NO
THE SYSTEM IS OPERATING PROPERLY AT THIS TIME.
PERFORM TEST 3A.

* PERFORM VERIFICATION TEST VER-2A.

91E14229 91E14419

Fig. 20: Test 8A – 806: Boost Pressure Fault (1 of 2)

TEST 8A – 806: BOOST PRESSURE FAULT (2 OF 2)

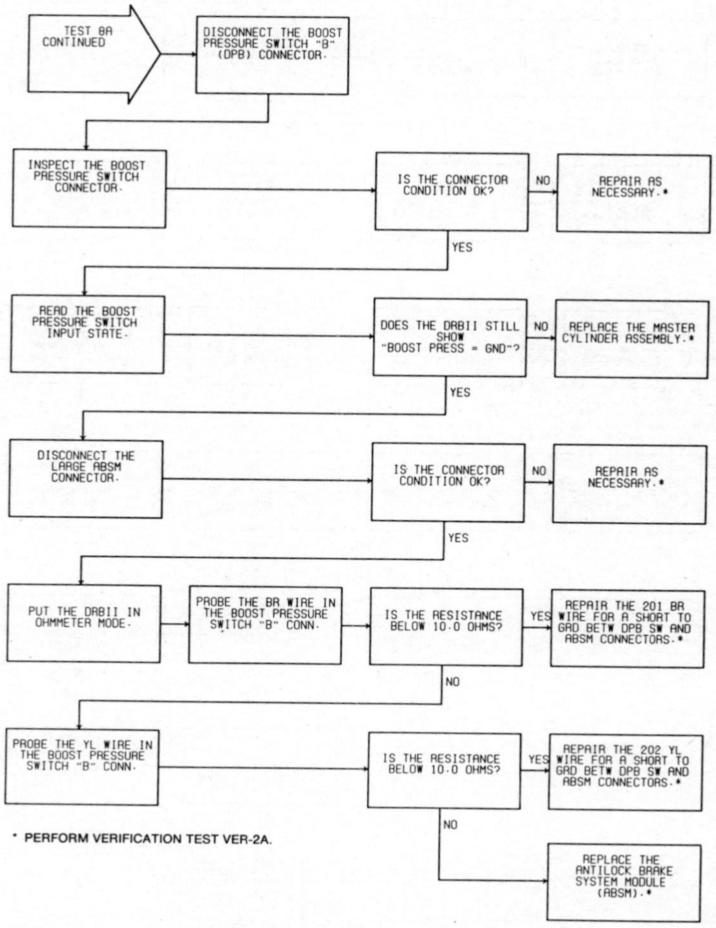
TEST 8A CONTINUED
DISCONNECT THE BOOST PRESSURE SWITCH "B" (DPB) CONNECTOR.
INSPECT THE BOOST PRESSURE SWITCH CONNECTOR.
IS THE CONNECTOR CONDITION OK?
NO
REPAIR AS NECESSARY.*
YES
READ THE BOOST PRESSURE SWITCH INPUT STATE.
DOES THE DRBII STILL SHOW "BOOST PRESS = GND"?
NO
REPLACE THE MASTER CYLINDER ASSEMBLY.*
YES
DISCONNECT THE LARGE ABSM CONNECTOR.
IS THE CONNECTOR CONDITION OK?
NO
REPAIR AS NECESSARY.*
YES
PUT THE DRBII IN OHMMETER MODE.
PROBE THE BR WIRE IN THE BOOST PRESSURE SWITCH "B" CONN.
IS THE RESISTANCE BELOW 10.0 OHMS?
YES
REPAIR THE 201 BR WIRE FOR A SHORT TO GRD BETW DPB SW AND ABSM CONNECTORS.*
NO
PROBE THE YL WIRE IN THE BOOST PRESSURE SWITCH "B" CONN.
IS THE RESISTANCE BELOW 10.0 OHMS?
YES
REPAIR THE 202 YL WIRE FOR A SHORT TO GRD BETW DPB SW AND ABSM CONNECTORS.*
NO
REPLACE THE ANTILOCK BRAKE SYSTEM MODULE (ABSM).*

* PERFORM VERIFICATION TEST VER-2A.

91H14420

Fig. 21: Test 8A – 806: Boost Pressure Fault (2 of 2)

TEST 9A – 807: LOW ACCUMULATOR FAULT

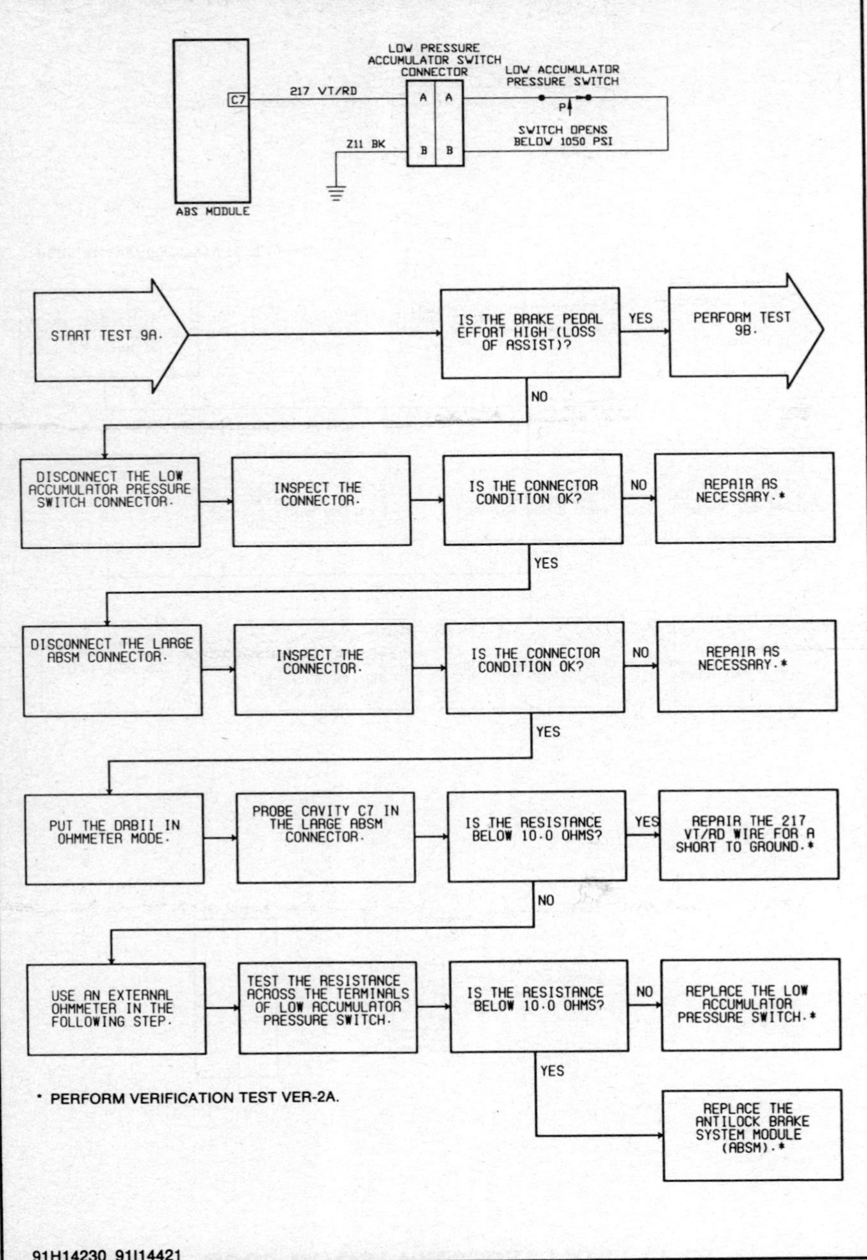
ABS MODULE
C7
217 VT/RD
Z11 BK
LOW PRESSURE ACCUMULATOR SWITCH CONNECTOR
A A
B B
LOW ACCUMULATOR PRESSURE SWITCH
P
SWITCH OPENS BELOW 1050 PSI
START TEST 9A.
IS THE BRAKE PEDAL EFFORT HIGH (LOSS OF ASSIST)?
YES
PERFORM TEST 9B.
NO
DISCONNECT THE LOW ACCUMULATOR PRESSURE SWITCH CONNECTOR.
INSPECT THE CONNECTOR.
IS THE CONNECTOR CONDITION OK?
NO
REPAIR AS NECESSARY.*
YES
DISCONNECT THE LARGE ABSM CONNECTOR.
INSPECT THE CONNECTOR.
IS THE CONNECTOR CONDITION OK?
NO
REPAIR AS NECESSARY.*
YES
PUT THE DRBII IN OHMMETER MODE.
PROBE CAVITY C7 IN THE LARGE ABSM CONNECTOR.
IS THE RESISTANCE BELOW 10.0 OHMS?
YES
REPAIR THE 217 VT/RD WIRE FOR A SHORT TO GROUND.*
NO
USE AN EXTERNAL OHMMETER IN THE FOLLOWING STEP.
TEST THE RESISTANCE ACROSS THE TERMINALS OF LOW ACCUMULATOR PRESSURE SWITCH.
IS THE RESISTANCE BELOW 10.0 OHMS?
NO
REPLACE THE LOW ACCUMULATOR PRESSURE SWITCH.*
YES
REPLACE THE ANTILOCK BRAKE SYSTEM MODULE (ABSM).*
* PERFORM VERIFICATION TEST VER-2A.
91H14230 91I14421

Fig. 22: Test 9A – 807: Low Accumulator Fault

TEST 9B – 807: LOW ACCUMULATOR FAULT

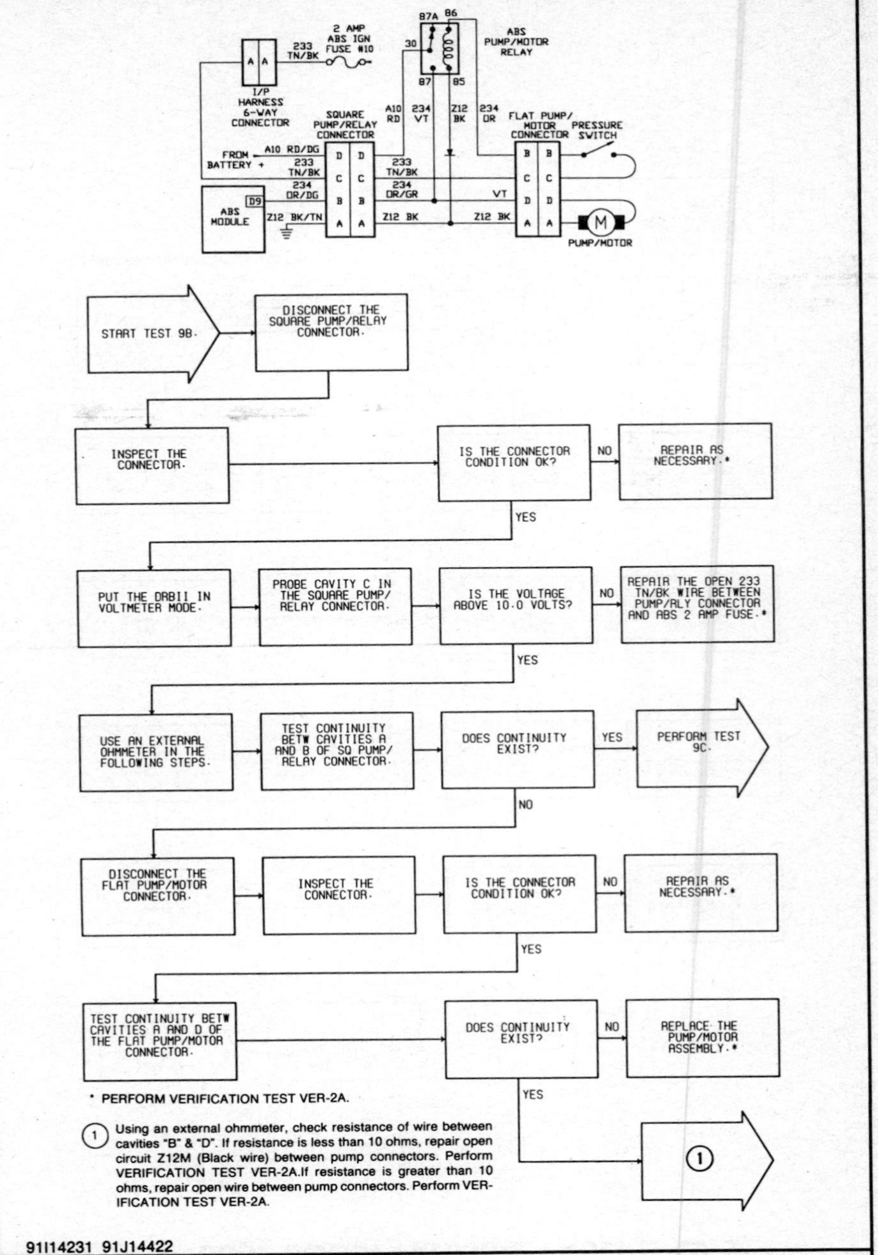
2 AMP ABS IGN FUSE #10
233 TN/BK
A A
I/P HARNESS 6-WAY CONNECTOR
FROM BATTERY +
A10 RD/DG
233 TN/BK
234 DR/DG
ABS MODULE
D9
Z12 BK/TN
SQUARE PUMP/RELAY CONNECTOR
D D
C C
B B
A A
87A 86
30
87 85
ABS PUMP/MOTOR RELAY
A10 RD
234 VT
Z12 BK
234 DR
233 TN/BK
234 DR/GR
Z12 BK
VT
Z12 BK
FLAT PUMP/ MOTOR CONNECTOR
PRESSURE SWITCH
B B
C C
D D
A A
M
PUMP/MOTOR
START TEST 9B.
DISCONNECT THE SQUARE PUMP/RELAY CONNECTOR.
INSPECT THE CONNECTOR.
IS THE CONNECTOR CONDITION OK?
NO
REPAIR AS NECESSARY.*
YES
PUT THE DRBII IN VOLTMETER MODE.
PROBE CAVITY C IN THE SQUARE PUMP/ RELAY CONNECTOR.
IS THE VOLTAGE ABOVE 10.0 VOLTS?
NO
REPAIR THE OPEN 233 TN/BK WIRE BETWEEN PUMP/RLY CONNECTOR AND ABS 2 AMP FUSE.*
YES
USE AN EXTERNAL OHMMETER IN THE FOLLOWING STEPS.
TEST CONTINUITY BETW CAVITIES A AND B OF SQ PUMP/ RELAY CONNECTOR.
DOES CONTINUITY EXIST?
YES
PERFORM TEST 9C.
NO
DISCONNECT THE FLAT PUMP/MOTOR CONNECTOR.
INSPECT THE CONNECTOR.
IS THE CONNECTOR CONDITION OK?
NO
REPAIR AS NECESSARY.*
YES
TEST CONTINUITY BETW CAVITIES A AND D OF THE FLAT PUMP/MOTOR CONNECTOR.
DOES CONTINUITY EXIST?
NO
REPLACE THE PUMP/MOTOR ASSEMBLY.*
YES
1
* PERFORM VERIFICATION TEST VER-2A.
1 Using an external ohmmeter, check resistance of wire between cavities "B" & "D". If resistance is less than 10 ohms, repair open circuit Z12M (Black wire) between pump connectors. Perform VERIFICATION TEST VER-2A. If resistance is greater than 10 ohms, repair open wire between pump connectors. Perform VERIFICATION TEST VER-2A.
91I14231 91J14422

Fig. 23: Test 9B – 807: Low Accumulator Fault

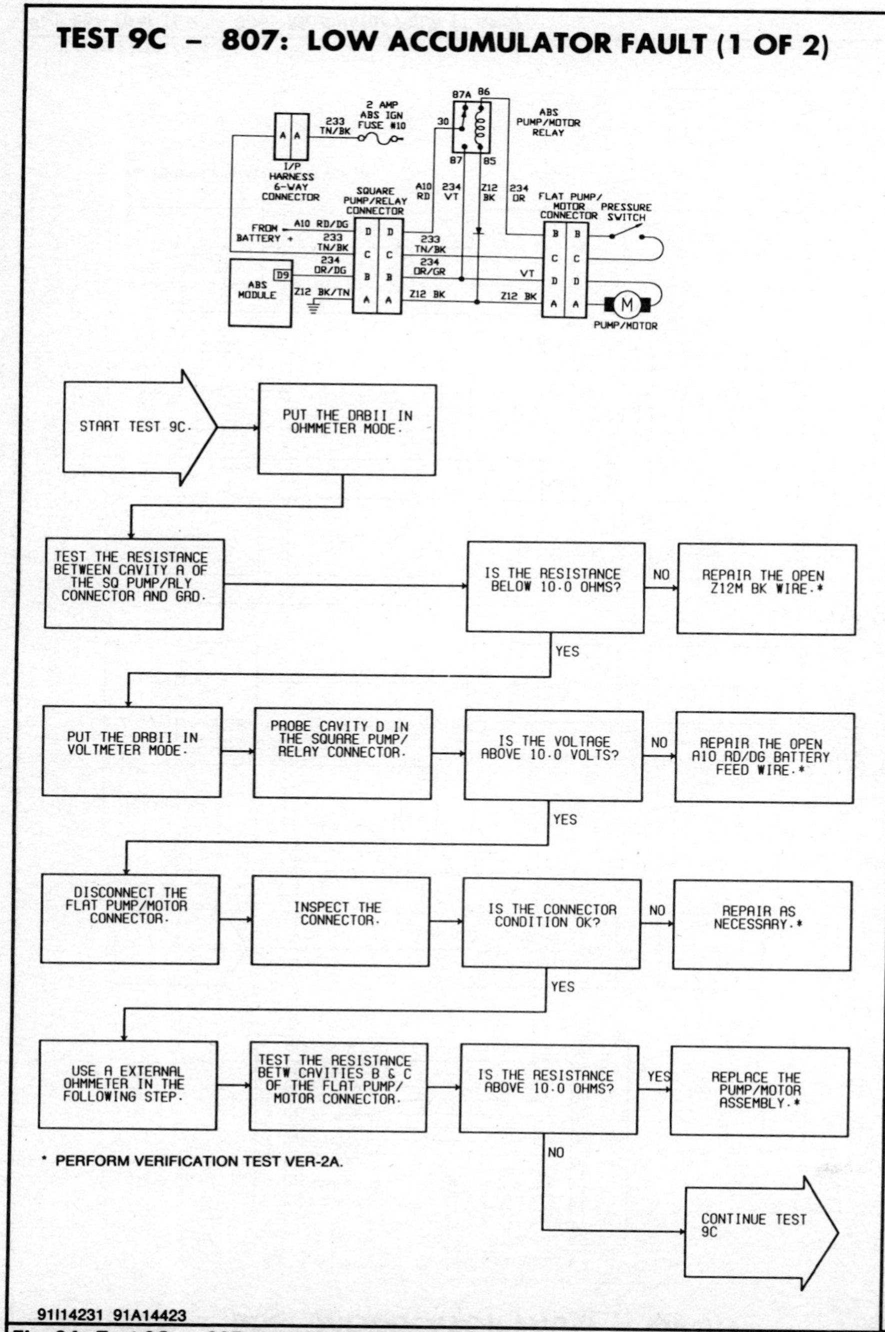
TEST 9C – 807: LOW ACCUMULATOR FAULT (1 OF 2)
2 AMP ABS IGN FUSE #10
233 TN/BK
I/P HARNESS 6-WAY CONNECTOR
FROM BATTERY +
A10 RD/DG
233 TN/BK
234 DR/DG
ABS MODULE
D9
Z12 BK/TN
SQUARE PUMP/RELAY CONNECTOR
A10 RD
234 VT
Z12 BK
234 DR
87A 86
30
87 85
ABS PUMP/MOTOR RELAY
233 TN/BK
234 DR/GR
VT
Z12 BK
Z12 BK
FLAT PUMP/MOTOR CONNECTOR
PRESSURE SWITCH
PUMP/MOTOR
START TEST 9C.
PUT THE DRBII IN OHMMETER MODE.
TEST THE RESISTANCE BETWEEN CAVITY A OF THE SQ PUMP/RLY CONNECTOR AND GRD.
IS THE RESISTANCE BELOW 10.0 OHMS?
NO
REPAIR THE OPEN Z12M BK WIRE.*
YES
PUT THE DRBII IN VOLTMETER MODE.
PROBE CAVITY D IN THE SQUARE PUMP/RELAY CONNECTOR.
IS THE VOLTAGE ABOVE 10.0 VOLTS?
NO
REPAIR THE OPEN A10 RD/DG BATTERY FEED WIRE.*
YES
DISCONNECT THE FLAT PUMP/MOTOR CONNECTOR.
INSPECT THE CONNECTOR.
IS THE CONNECTOR CONDITION OK?
NO
REPAIR AS NECESSARY.*
YES
USE A EXTERNAL OHMMETER IN THE FOLLOWING STEP.
TEST THE RESISTANCE BETW CAVITIES B & C OF THE FLAT PUMP/MOTOR CONNECTOR.
IS THE RESISTANCE ABOVE 10.0 OHMS?
YES
REPLACE THE PUMP/MOTOR ASSEMBLY.*
NO
CONTINUE TEST 9C
* PERFORM VERIFICATION TEST VER-2A.
91I14231 91A14423

Fig. 24: Test 9C – 807: Low Accumulator Fault (1 of 2)

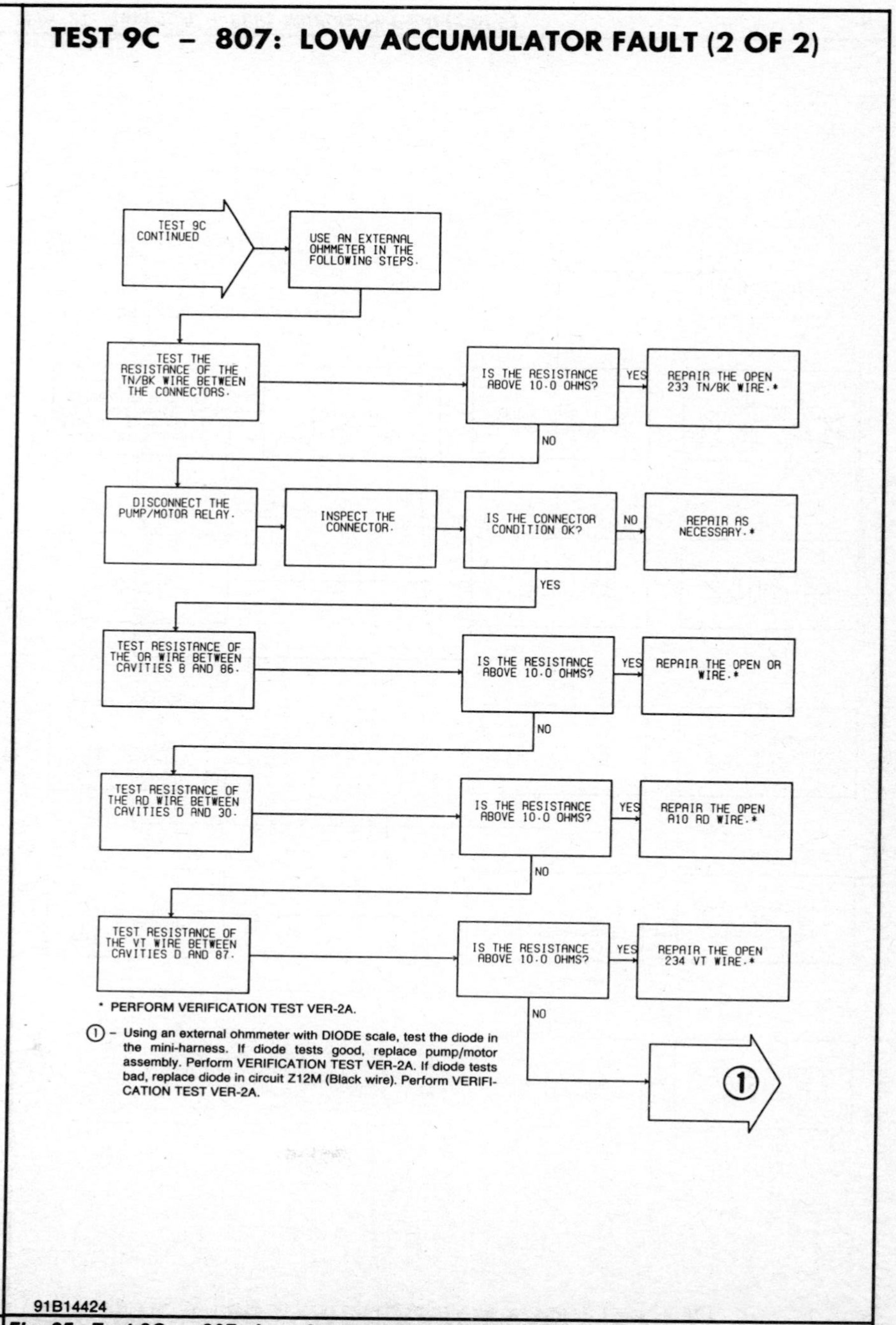
TEST 9C – 807: LOW ACCUMULATOR FAULT (2 OF 2)
TEST 9C CONTINUED
USE AN EXTERNAL OHMMETER IN THE FOLLOWING STEPS.
TEST THE RESISTANCE OF THE TN/BK WIRE BETWEEN THE CONNECTORS.
IS THE RESISTANCE ABOVE 10.0 OHMS?
YES
REPAIR THE OPEN 233 TN/BK WIRE.*
NO
DISCONNECT THE PUMP/MOTOR RELAY.
INSPECT THE CONNECTOR.
IS THE CONNECTOR CONDITION OK?
NO
REPAIR AS NECESSARY.*
YES
TEST RESISTANCE OF THE OR WIRE BETWEEN CAVITIES B AND 86.
IS THE RESISTANCE ABOVE 10.0 OHMS?
YES
REPAIR THE OPEN OR WIRE.*
NO
TEST RESISTANCE OF THE RD WIRE BETWEEN CAVITIES D AND 30.
IS THE RESISTANCE ABOVE 10.0 OHMS?
YES
REPAIR THE OPEN A10 RD WIRE.*
NO
TEST RESISTANCE OF THE VT WIRE BETWEEN CAVITIES D AND 87.
IS THE RESISTANCE ABOVE 10.0 OHMS?
YES
REPAIR THE OPEN 234 VT WIRE.*
NO
1
* PERFORM VERIFICATION TEST VER-2A.
① – Using an external ohmmeter with DIODE scale, test the diode in the mini-harness. If diode tests good, replace pump/motor assembly. Perform VERIFICATION TEST VER-2A. If diode tests bad, replace diode in circuit Z12M (Black wire). Perform VERIFICATION TEST VER-2A.
91B14424

Fig. 25: Test 9C – 807: Low Accumulator Fault (2 of 2)

1991 BRAKES
Anti-Lock (Cont.)

TEST 10A – 808: MODULATOR FAULT (1 OF 5)

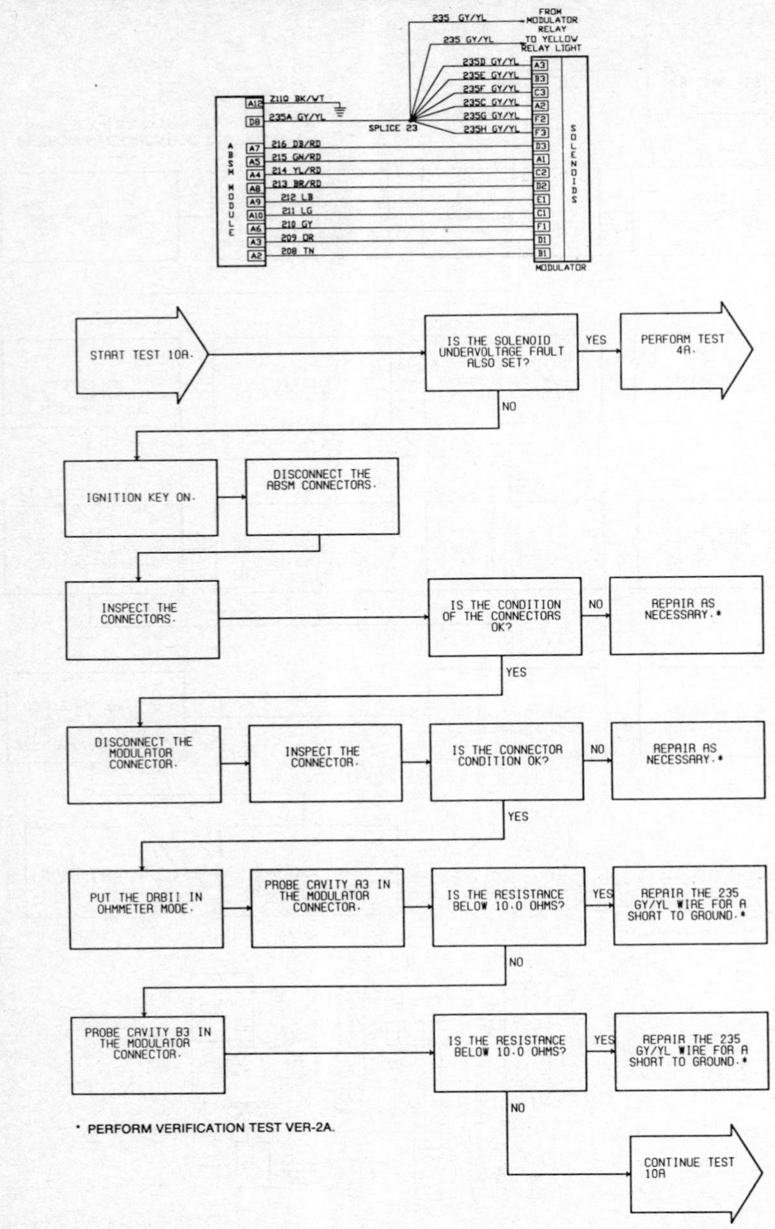
235 GY/YL
FROM MODULATOR RELAY
235 GY/YL
TO YELLOW RELAY LIGHT
Z110 BK/WT
235A GY/YL
SPLICE 23
235D GY/YL
235E GY/YL
235F GY/YL
235C GY/YL
235G GY/YL
235H GY/YL
216 DB/RD
215 GN/RD
214 YL/RD
213 BR/RD
212 LB
211 LG
210 GY
209 OR
208 TN
A12 D8 A7 A5 A4 A8 A9 A10 A6 A3 A2
ABSM MODULE
A3 B3 C3 A2 F2 F3 D3 A1 C2 D2 E1 C1 F1 D1 B1
SOLENOIDS
MODULATOR
START TEST 10A.
IS THE SOLENOID UNDERVOLTAGE FAULT ALSO SET?
YES
PERFORM TEST 4A.
NO
IGNITION KEY ON.
DISCONNECT THE ABSM CONNECTORS.
INSPECT THE CONNECTORS.
IS THE CONDITION OF THE CONNECTORS OK?
NO
REPAIR AS NECESSARY.*
YES
DISCONNECT THE MODULATOR CONNECTOR.
INSPECT THE CONNECTOR.
IS THE CONNECTOR CONDITION OK?
NO
REPAIR AS NECESSARY.*
YES
PUT THE DRBII IN OHMMETER MODE.
PROBE CAVITY A3 IN THE MODULATOR CONNECTOR.
IS THE RESISTANCE BELOW 10.0 OHMS?
YES
REPAIR THE 235 GY/YL WIRE FOR A SHORT TO GROUND.*
NO
PROBE CAVITY B3 IN THE MODULATOR CONNECTOR.
IS THE RESISTANCE BELOW 10.0 OHMS?
YES
REPAIR THE 235 GY/YL WIRE FOR A SHORT TO GROUND.*
NO
CONTINUE TEST 10A
* PERFORM VERIFICATION TEST VER-2A.

91J14232 91D14426

Fig. 26: Test 10A – 808: Modulator Fault (1 of 5)

TEST 10A – 808: MODULATOR FAULT (2 OF 5)

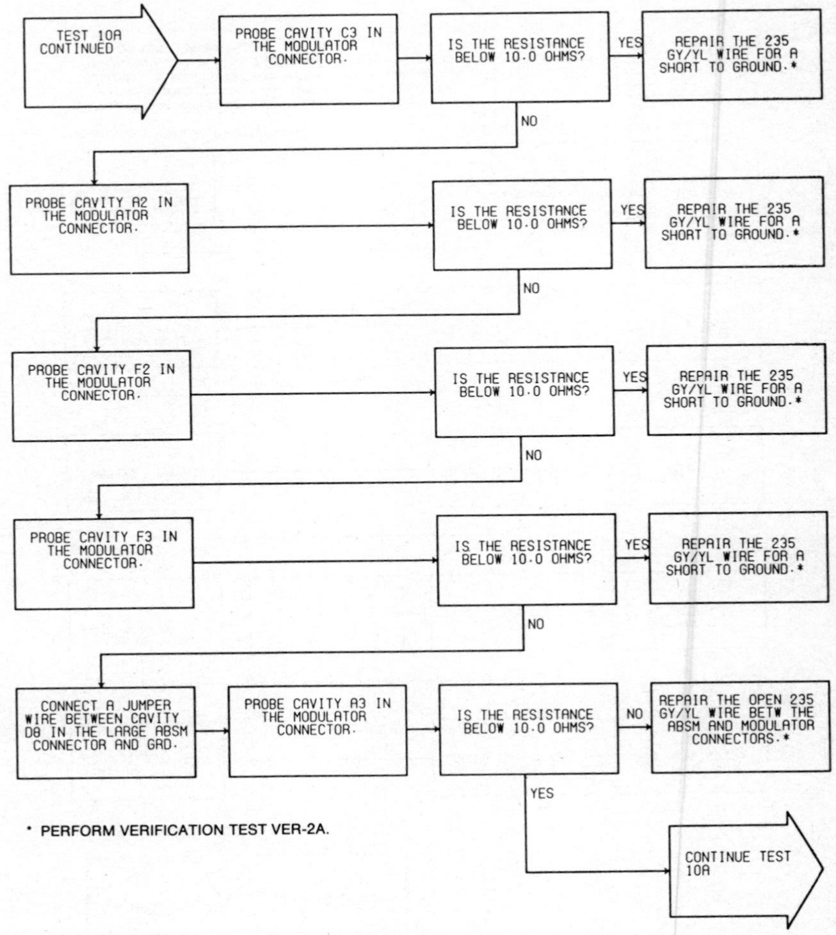
TEST 10A CONTINUED
PROBE CAVITY C3 IN THE MODULATOR CONNECTOR.
IS THE RESISTANCE BELOW 10.0 OHMS?
YES
REPAIR THE 235 GY/YL WIRE FOR A SHORT TO GROUND.*
NO
PROBE CAVITY A2 IN THE MODULATOR CONNECTOR.
IS THE RESISTANCE BELOW 10.0 OHMS?
YES
REPAIR THE 235 GY/YL WIRE FOR A SHORT TO GROUND.*
NO
PROBE CAVITY F2 IN THE MODULATOR CONNECTOR.
IS THE RESISTANCE BELOW 10.0 OHMS?
YES
REPAIR THE 235 GY/YL WIRE FOR A SHORT TO GROUND.*
NO
PROBE CAVITY F3 IN THE MODULATOR CONNECTOR.
IS THE RESISTANCE BELOW 10.0 OHMS?
YES
REPAIR THE 235 GY/YL WIRE FOR A SHORT TO GROUND.*
NO
CONNECT A JUMPER WIRE BETWEEN CAVITY D8 IN THE LARGE ABSM CONNECTOR AND GRD.
PROBE CAVITY A3 IN THE MODULATOR CONNECTOR.
IS THE RESISTANCE BELOW 10.0 OHMS?
NO
REPAIR THE OPEN 235 GY/YL WIRE BETW THE ABSM AND MODULATOR CONNECTORS.*
YES
CONTINUE TEST 10A
* PERFORM VERIFICATION TEST VER-2A.

91E14427

Fig. 27: Test 10A – 808: Modulator Fault (2 of 5)

TEST 10A – 808: MODULATOR FAULT (3 OF 5)

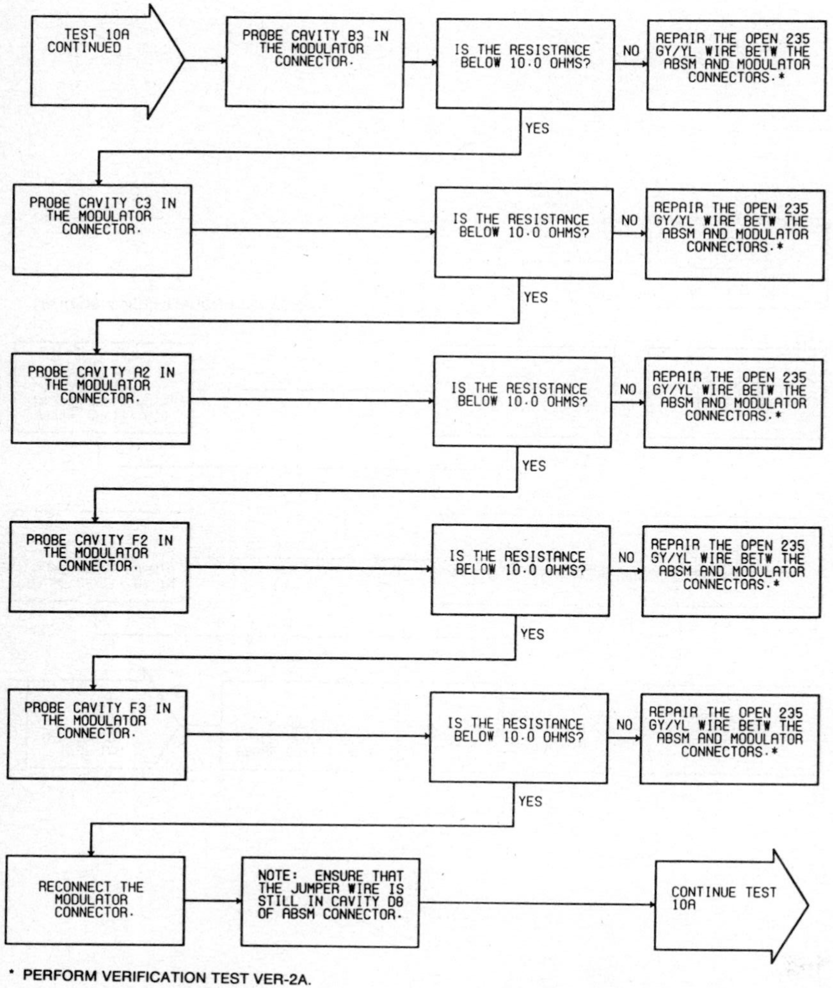
TEST 10A CONTINUED
PROBE CAVITY B3 IN THE MODULATOR CONNECTOR.
IS THE RESISTANCE BELOW 10.0 OHMS?
NO
REPAIR THE OPEN 235 GY/YL WIRE BETW THE ABSM AND MODULATOR CONNECTORS.*
YES
PROBE CAVITY C3 IN THE MODULATOR CONNECTOR.
IS THE RESISTANCE BELOW 10.0 OHMS?
NO
REPAIR THE OPEN 235 GY/YL WIRE BETW THE ABSM AND MODULATOR CONNECTORS.*
YES
PROBE CAVITY A2 IN THE MODULATOR CONNECTOR.
IS THE RESISTANCE BELOW 10.0 OHMS?
NO
REPAIR THE OPEN 235 GY/YL WIRE BETW THE ABSM AND MODULATOR CONNECTORS.*
YES
PROBE CAVITY F2 IN THE MODULATOR CONNECTOR.
IS THE RESISTANCE BELOW 10.0 OHMS?
NO
REPAIR THE OPEN 235 GY/YL WIRE BETW THE ABSM AND MODULATOR CONNECTORS.*
YES
PROBE CAVITY F3 IN THE MODULATOR CONNECTOR.
IS THE RESISTANCE BELOW 10.0 OHMS?
NO
REPAIR THE OPEN 235 GY/YL WIRE BETW THE ABSM AND MODULATOR CONNECTORS.*
YES
RECONNECT THE MODULATOR CONNECTOR.
NOTE: ENSURE THAT THE JUMPER WIRE IS STILL IN CAVITY D8 OF ABSM CONNECTOR.
CONTINUE TEST 10A

* PERFORM VERIFICATION TEST VER-2A.

91F14428

Fig. 28: Test 10A – 808: Modulator Fault (3 of 5)

TEST 10A – 808: MODULATOR FAULT (4 OF 5)

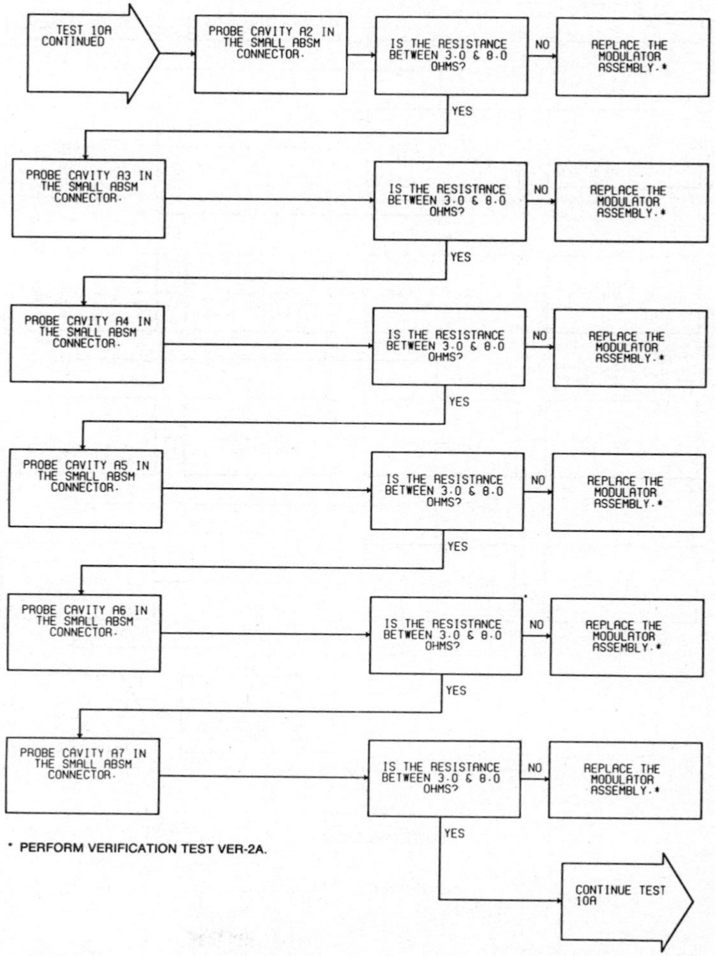
TEST 10A CONTINUED
PROBE CAVITY A2 IN THE SMALL ABSM CONNECTOR.
IS THE RESISTANCE BETWEEN 3.0 & 8.0 OHMS?
NO
REPLACE THE MODULATOR ASSEMBLY.*
YES
PROBE CAVITY A3 IN THE SMALL ABSM CONNECTOR.
IS THE RESISTANCE BETWEEN 3.0 & 8.0 OHMS?
NO
REPLACE THE MODULATOR ASSEMBLY.*
YES
PROBE CAVITY A4 IN THE SMALL ABSM CONNECTOR.
IS THE RESISTANCE BETWEEN 3.0 & 8.0 OHMS?
NO
REPLACE THE MODULATOR ASSEMBLY.*
YES
PROBE CAVITY A5 IN THE SMALL ABSM CONNECTOR.
IS THE RESISTANCE BETWEEN 3.0 & 8.0 OHMS?
NO
REPLACE THE MODULATOR ASSEMBLY.*
YES
PROBE CAVITY A6 IN THE SMALL ABSM CONNECTOR.
IS THE RESISTANCE BETWEEN 3.0 & 8.0 OHMS?
NO
REPLACE THE MODULATOR ASSEMBLY.*
YES
PROBE CAVITY A7 IN THE SMALL ABSM CONNECTOR.
IS THE RESISTANCE BETWEEN 3.0 & 8.0 OHMS?
NO
REPLACE THE MODULATOR ASSEMBLY.*
YES
CONTINUE TEST 10A

* PERFORM VERIFICATION TEST VER-2A.

91G14429

Fig. 29: Test 10A – 808: Modulator Fault (4 of 5)

TEST 10A – 808: MODULATOR FAULT (5 OF 5)

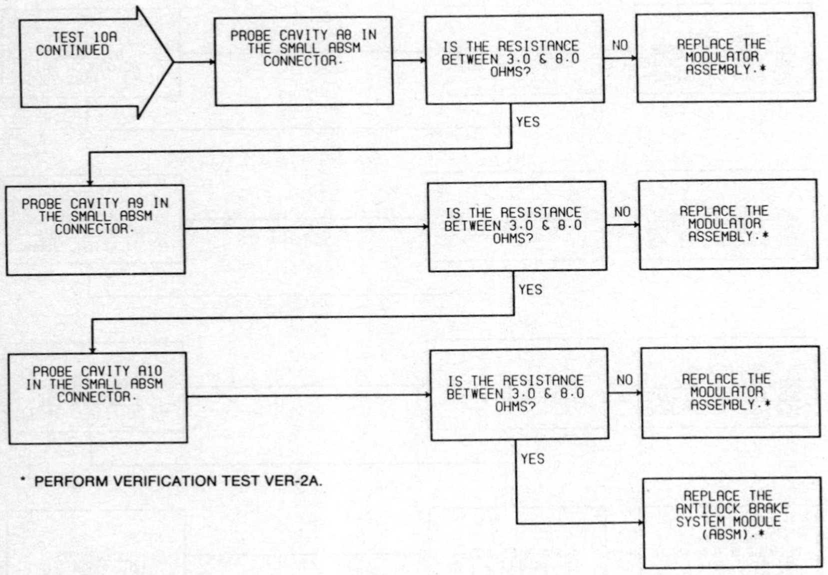
TEST 10A CONTINUED
PROBE CAVITY A8 IN THE SMALL ABSM CONNECTOR.
IS THE RESISTANCE BETWEEN 3.0 & 8.0 OHMS?
NO
REPLACE THE MODULATOR ASSEMBLY.*
YES
PROBE CAVITY A9 IN THE SMALL ABSM CONNECTOR.
IS THE RESISTANCE BETWEEN 3.0 & 8.0 OHMS?
NO
REPLACE THE MODULATOR ASSEMBLY.*
YES
PROBE CAVITY A10 IN THE SMALL ABSM CONNECTOR.
IS THE RESISTANCE BETWEEN 3.0 & 8.0 OHMS?
NO
REPLACE THE MODULATOR ASSEMBLY.*
YES
REPLACE THE ANTILOCK BRAKE SYSTEM MODULE (ABSM).*

* PERFORM VERIFICATION TEST VER-2A.

91J14430

Fig. 30: Test 10A – 808: Modulator Fault (5 of 5)

TEST 11A – 811: RELAY FAULT

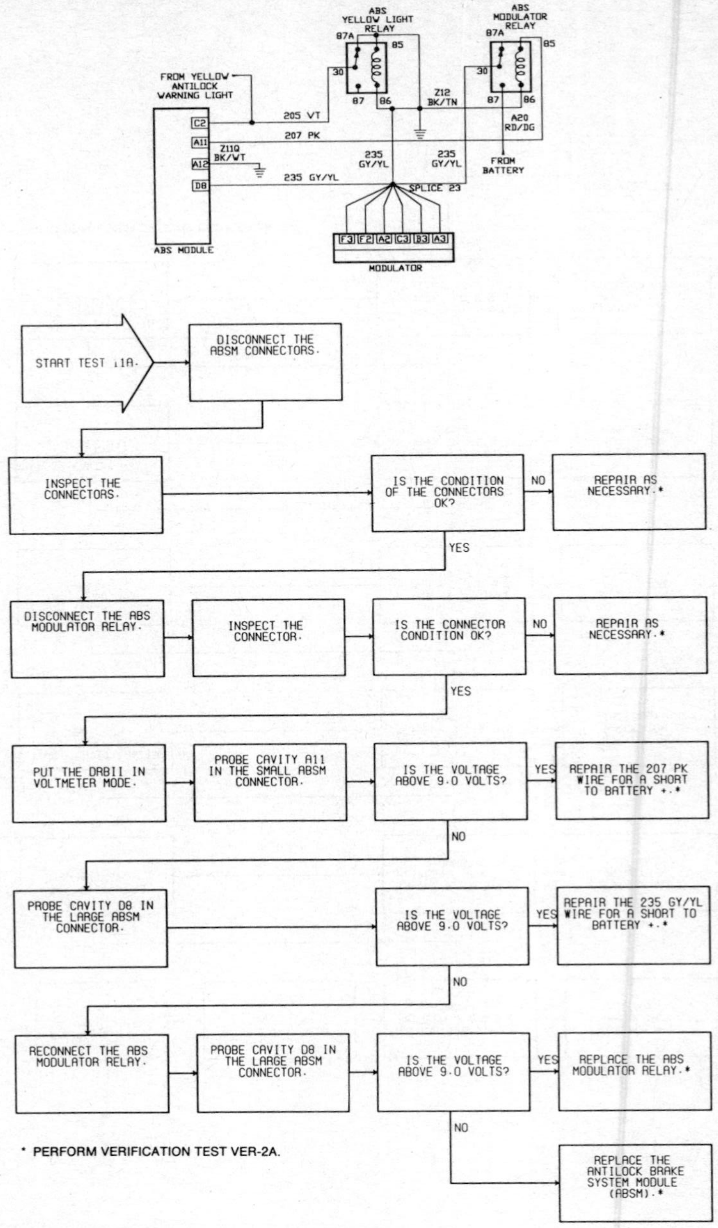
ABS YELLOW LIGHT RELAY
87A
85
30
87
86
ABS MODULATOR RELAY
87A
85
30
87
86
FROM YELLOW ANTILOCK WARNING LIGHT
C2
A11
A12
D8
ABS MODULE
205 VT
207 PK
Z11Q BK/WT
235 GY/YL
Z12 BK/TN
235 GY/YL
235 GY/YL
A20 RD/DG
FROM BATTERY
SPLICE 23
F3 F2 A2 C3 B3 A3
MODULATOR
START TEST 11A.
DISCONNECT THE ABSM CONNECTORS.
INSPECT THE CONNECTORS.
IS THE CONDITION OF THE CONNECTORS OK?
NO
REPAIR AS NECESSARY.*
YES
DISCONNECT THE ABS MODULATOR RELAY.
INSPECT THE CONNECTOR.
IS THE CONNECTOR CONDITION OK?
NO
REPAIR AS NECESSARY.*
YES
PUT THE DRBII IN VOLTMETER MODE.
PROBE CAVITY A11 IN THE SMALL ABSM CONNECTOR.
IS THE VOLTAGE ABOVE 9.0 VOLTS?
YES
REPAIR THE 207 PK WIRE FOR A SHORT TO BATTERY +.*
NO
PROBE CAVITY D8 IN THE LARGE ABSM CONNECTOR.
IS THE VOLTAGE ABOVE 9.0 VOLTS?
YES
REPAIR THE 235 GY/YL WIRE FOR A SHORT TO BATTERY +.*
NO
RECONNECT THE ABS MODULATOR RELAY.
PROBE CAVITY D8 IN THE LARGE ABSM CONNECTOR.
IS THE VOLTAGE ABOVE 9.0 VOLTS?
YES
REPLACE THE ABS MODULATOR RELAY.*
NO
REPLACE THE ANTILOCK BRAKE SYSTEM MODULE (ABSM).*

* PERFORM VERIFICATION TEST VER-2A.

91C14227 91A14431

Fig. 31: Test 11A – 811: Relay Fault

TEST 12A – 812: PUMP/MOTOR FAULT (1 OF 2)

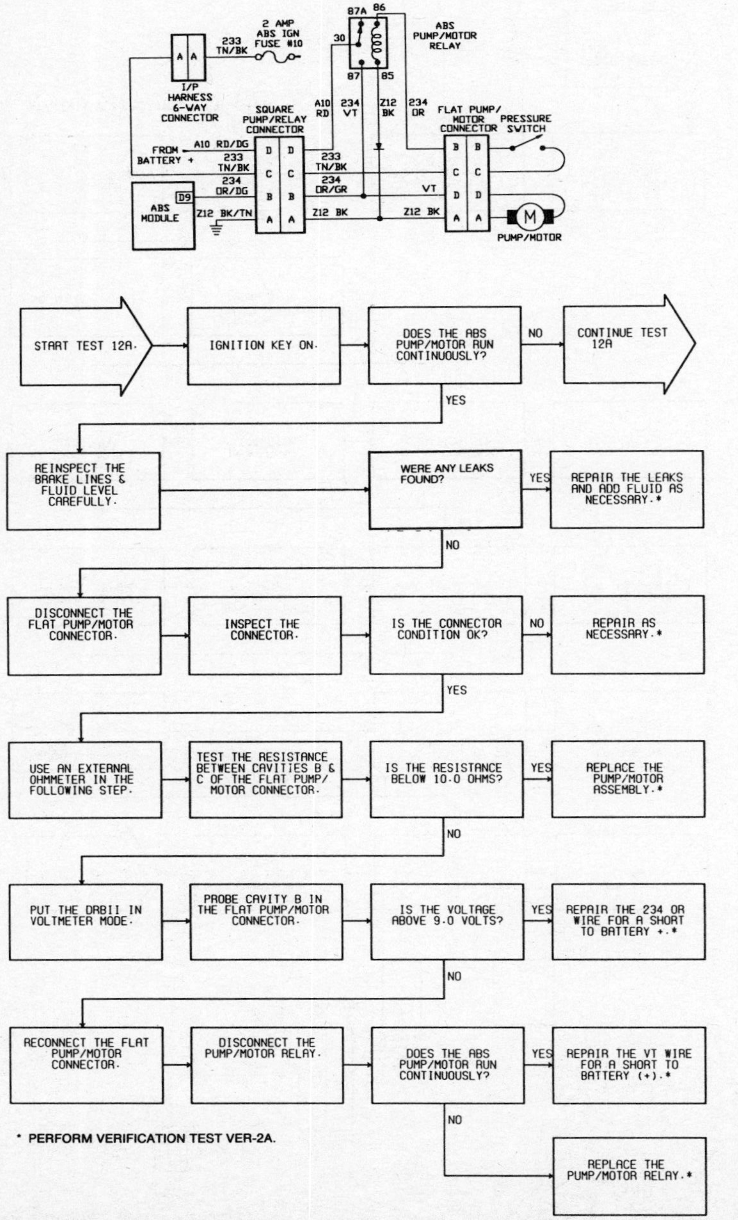
2 AMP ABS IGN FUSE #10
233 TN/BK
I/P HARNESS 6-WAY CONNECTOR
ABS PUMP/MOTOR RELAY
87A 86 30 87 85
SQUARE PUMP/RELAY CONNECTOR
FROM BATTERY +
A10 RD/DG
233 TN/BK
234 DR/DG
Z12 BK/TN
ABS MODULE
D9
A10 RD
234 VT
Z12 BK
234 DR
233 TN/BK
234 DR/GR
Z12 BK
VT
FLAT PUMP/MOTOR CONNECTOR
PRESSURE SWITCH
PUMP/MOTOR
START TEST 12A.
IGNITION KEY ON.
DOES THE ABS PUMP/MOTOR RUN CONTINUOUSLY?
NO
CONTINUE TEST 12A
YES
REINSPECT THE BRAKE LINES & FLUID LEVEL CAREFULLY.
WERE ANY LEAKS FOUND?
YES
REPAIR THE LEAKS AND ADD FLUID AS NECESSARY.*
NO
DISCONNECT THE FLAT PUMP/MOTOR CONNECTOR.
INSPECT THE CONNECTOR.
IS THE CONNECTOR CONDITION OK?
NO
REPAIR AS NECESSARY.*
YES
USE AN EXTERNAL OHMMETER IN THE FOLLOWING STEP.
TEST THE RESISTANCE BETWEEN CAVITIES B & C OF THE FLAT PUMP/MOTOR CONNECTOR.
IS THE RESISTANCE BELOW 10.0 OHMS?
YES
REPLACE THE PUMP/MOTOR ASSEMBLY.*
NO
PUT THE DRBII IN VOLTMETER MODE.
PROBE CAVITY B IN THE FLAT PUMP/MOTOR CONNECTOR.
IS THE VOLTAGE ABOVE 9.0 VOLTS?
YES
REPAIR THE 234 OR WIRE FOR A SHORT TO BATTERY +.*
NO
RECONNECT THE FLAT PUMP/MOTOR CONNECTOR.
DISCONNECT THE PUMP/MOTOR RELAY.
DOES THE ABS PUMP/MOTOR RUN CONTINUOUSLY?
YES
REPAIR THE VT WIRE FOR A SHORT TO BATTERY (+).*
NO
REPLACE THE PUMP/MOTOR RELAY.*

* PERFORM VERIFICATION TEST VER-2A.

91I14231 91B14432

Fig. 32: Test 12A – 812: Pump/Motor Fault (1 of 2)

TEST 12A – 812: PUMP/MOTOR FAULT (2 OF 2)

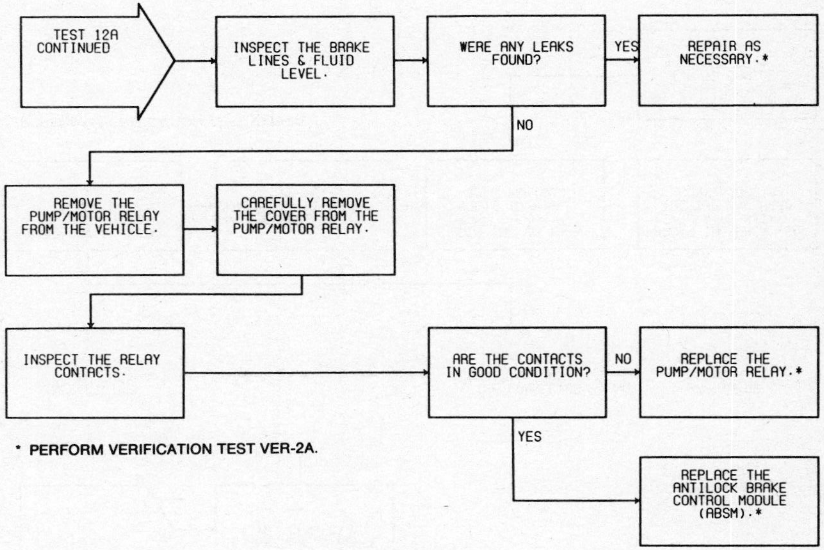
TEST 12A CONTINUED
INSPECT THE BRAKE LINES & FLUID LEVEL.
WERE ANY LEAKS FOUND?
YES
REPAIR AS NECESSARY.*
NO
REMOVE THE PUMP/MOTOR RELAY FROM THE VEHICLE.
CAREFULLY REMOVE THE COVER FROM THE PUMP/MOTOR RELAY.
INSPECT THE RELAY CONTACTS.
ARE THE CONTACTS IN GOOD CONDITION?
NO
REPLACE THE PUMP/MOTOR RELAY.*
YES
REPLACE THE ANTILOCK BRAKE CONTROL MODULE (ABSM).*

* PERFORM VERIFICATION TEST VER-2A.

91C14433

Fig. 33: Test 12A – 812: Pump/Motor Fault (2 of 2)

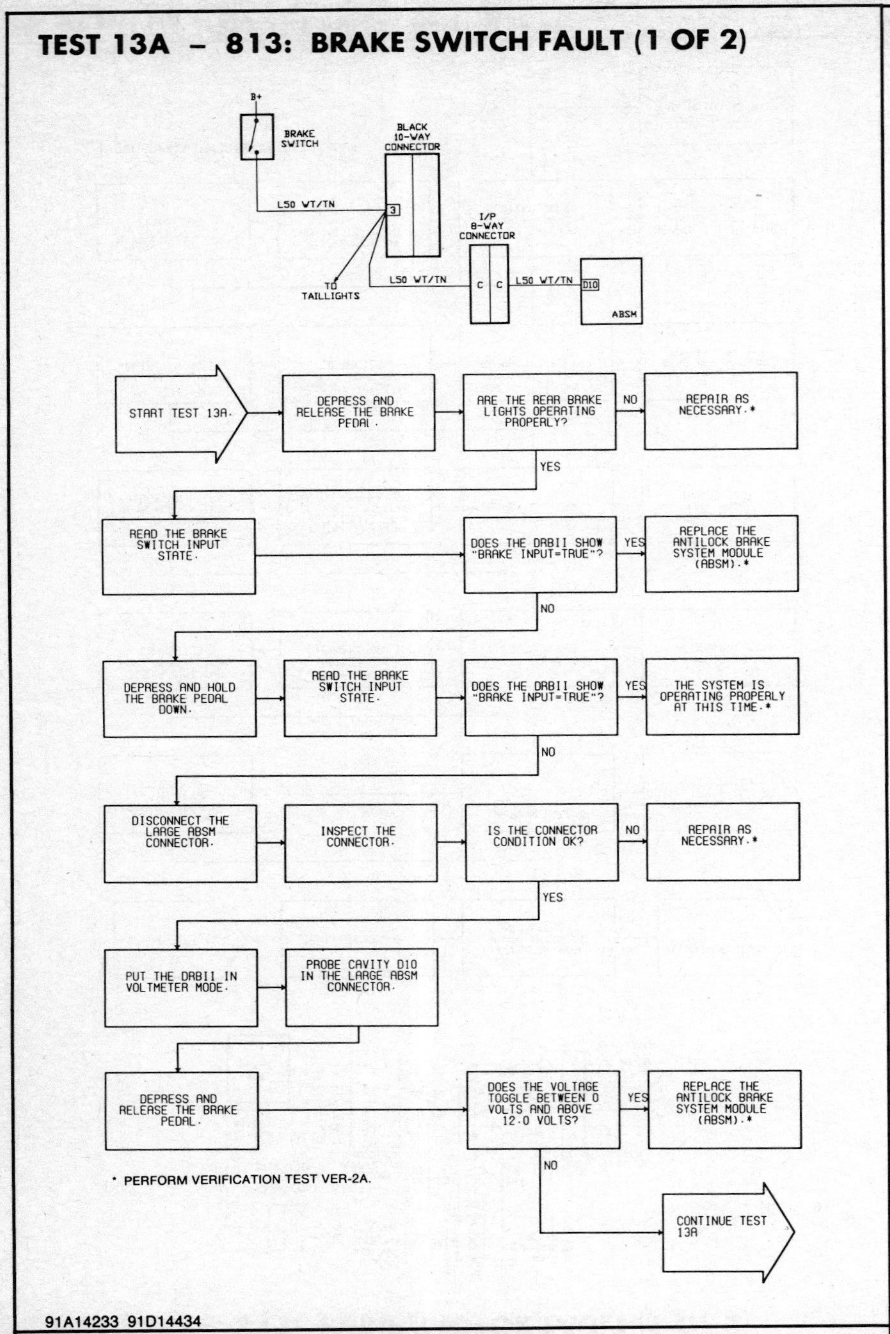
TEST 13A – 813: BRAKE SWITCH FAULT (1 OF 2)
B+
BRAKE SWITCH
BLACK 10-WAY CONNECTOR
L50 WT/TN
3
TO TAILLIGHTS
I/P 8-WAY CONNECTOR
C
C
L50 WT/TN
L50 WT/TN
D10
ABSM
START TEST 13A.
DEPRESS AND RELEASE THE BRAKE PEDAL.
ARE THE REAR BRAKE LIGHTS OPERATING PROPERLY?
NO
REPAIR AS NECESSARY.*
YES
READ THE BRAKE SWITCH INPUT STATE.
DOES THE DRBII SHOW "BRAKE INPUT=TRUE"?
YES
REPLACE THE ANTILOCK BRAKE SYSTEM MODULE (ABSM).*
NO
DEPRESS AND HOLD THE BRAKE PEDAL DOWN.
READ THE BRAKE SWITCH INPUT STATE.
DOES THE DRBII SHOW "BRAKE INPUT=TRUE"?
YES
THE SYSTEM IS OPERATING PROPERLY AT THIS TIME.*
NO
DISCONNECT THE LARGE ABSM CONNECTOR.
INSPECT THE CONNECTOR.
IS THE CONNECTOR CONDITION OK?
NO
REPAIR AS NECESSARY.*
YES
PUT THE DRBII IN VOLTMETER MODE.
PROBE CAVITY D10 IN THE LARGE ABSM CONNECTOR.
DEPRESS AND RELEASE THE BRAKE PEDAL.
DOES THE VOLTAGE TOGGLE BETWEEN 0 VOLTS AND ABOVE 12.0 VOLTS?
YES
REPLACE THE ANTILOCK BRAKE SYSTEM MODULE (ABSM).*
NO
CONTINUE TEST 13A
* PERFORM VERIFICATION TEST VER-2A.
91A14233 91D14434

Fig. 34: Test 13A – 813: Brake Switch Fault (1 of 2)

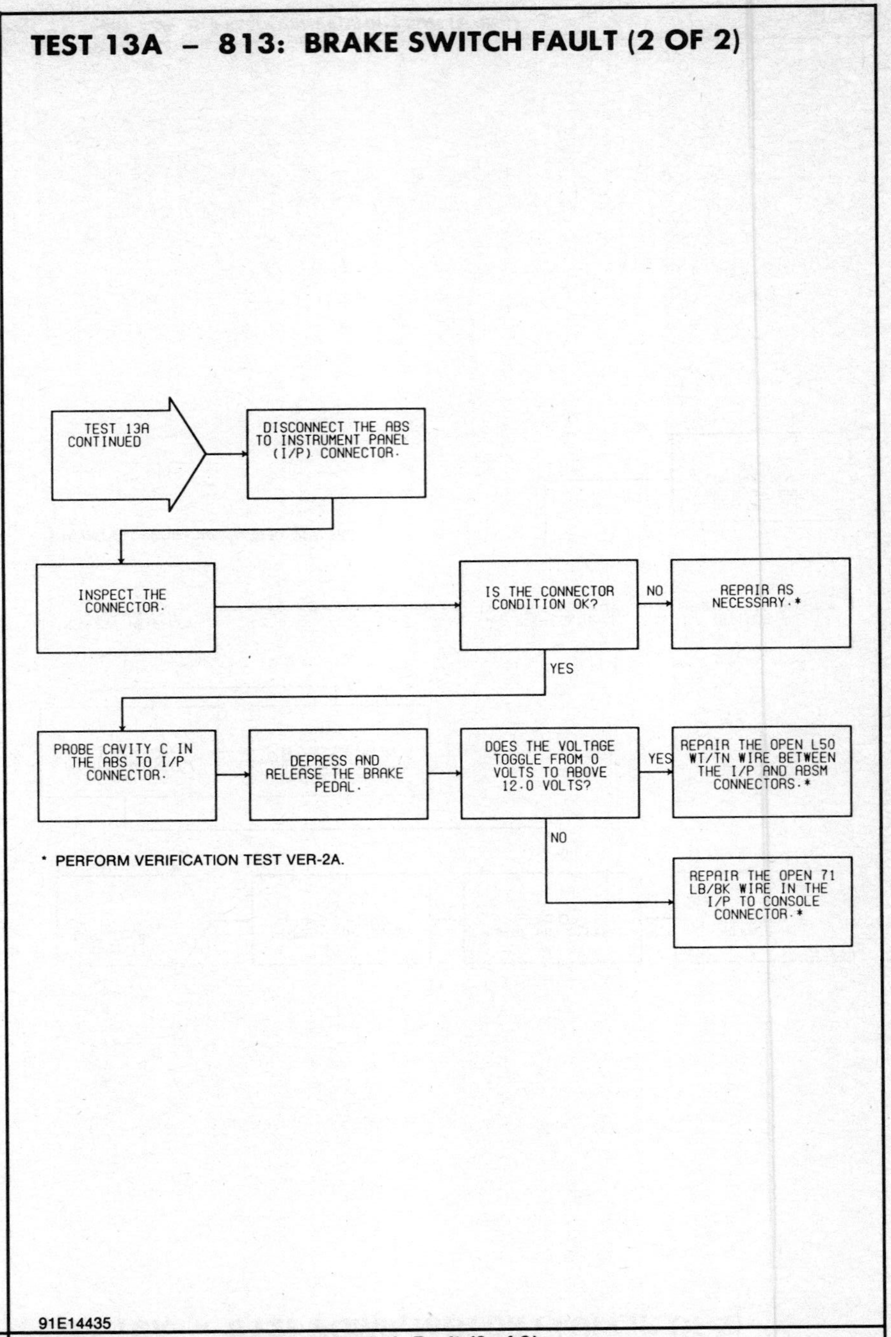
TEST 13A – 813: BRAKE SWITCH FAULT (2 OF 2)
TEST 13A CONTINUED
DISCONNECT THE ABS TO INSTRUMENT PANEL (I/P) CONNECTOR.
INSPECT THE CONNECTOR.
IS THE CONNECTOR CONDITION OK?
NO
REPAIR AS NECESSARY.*
YES
PROBE CAVITY C IN THE ABS TO I/P CONNECTOR.
DEPRESS AND RELEASE THE BRAKE PEDAL.
DOES THE VOLTAGE TOGGLE FROM 0 VOLTS TO ABOVE 12.0 VOLTS?
YES
REPAIR THE OPEN L50 WT/TN WIRE BETWEEN THE I/P AND ABSM CONNECTORS.*
NO
REPAIR THE OPEN 71 LB/BK WIRE IN THE I/P TO CONSOLE CONNECTOR.*
* PERFORM VERIFICATION TEST VER-2A.
91E14435

Fig. 35: Test 13A – 813: Brake Switch Fault (2 of 2)

TEST 14A – 814: LOW FLUID FAULT (1 OF 2)

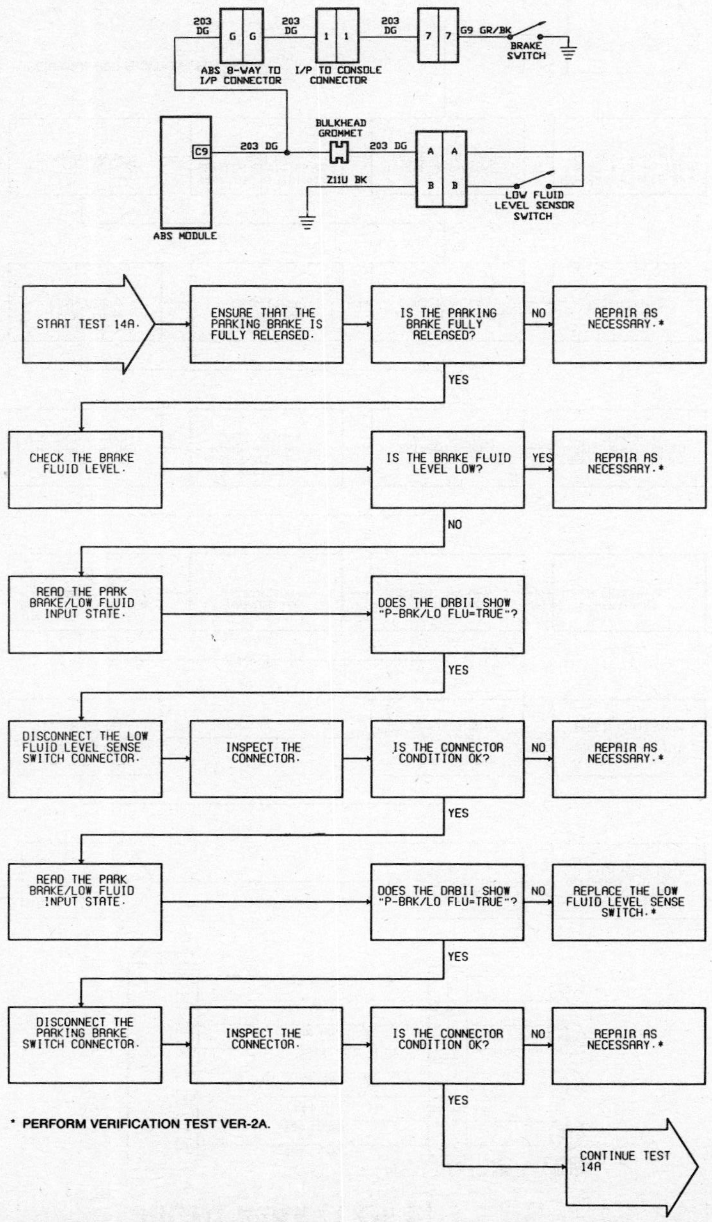
203 DG
G G
ABS 8-WAY TO I/P CONNECTOR
203 DG
1 1
I/P TO CONSOLE CONNECTOR
203 DG
7 7
G9 GR/BK
BRAKE SWITCH
C9
ABS MODULE
203 DG
BULKHEAD GROMMET
203 DG
A A
B B
Z11U BK
LOW FLUID LEVEL SENSOR SWITCH
START TEST 14A.
ENSURE THAT THE PARKING BRAKE IS FULLY RELEASED.
IS THE PARKING BRAKE FULLY RELEASED?
NO
REPAIR AS NECESSARY.*
YES
CHECK THE BRAKE FLUID LEVEL.
IS THE BRAKE FLUID LEVEL LOW?
YES
REPAIR AS NECESSARY.*
NO
READ THE PARK BRAKE/LOW FLUID INPUT STATE.
DOES THE DRBII SHOW "P-BRK/LO FLU=TRUE"?
YES
DISCONNECT THE LOW FLUID LEVEL SENSE SWITCH CONNECTOR.
INSPECT THE CONNECTOR.
IS THE CONNECTOR CONDITION OK?
NO
REPAIR AS NECESSARY.*
YES
READ THE PARK BRAKE/LOW FLUID INPUT STATE.
DOES THE DRBII SHOW "P-BRK/LO FLU=TRUE"?
NO
REPLACE THE LOW FLUID LEVEL SENSE SWITCH.*
YES
DISCONNECT THE PARKING BRAKE SWITCH CONNECTOR.
INSPECT THE CONNECTOR.
IS THE CONNECTOR CONDITION OK?
NO
REPAIR AS NECESSARY.*
YES
CONTINUE TEST 14A

* PERFORM VERIFICATION TEST VER-2A.

91B14234 91F14436

Fig. 36: Test 14A – 814: Low Fluid Fault (1 of 2)

TEST 14A – 814: LOW FLUID FAULT (2 OF 2)

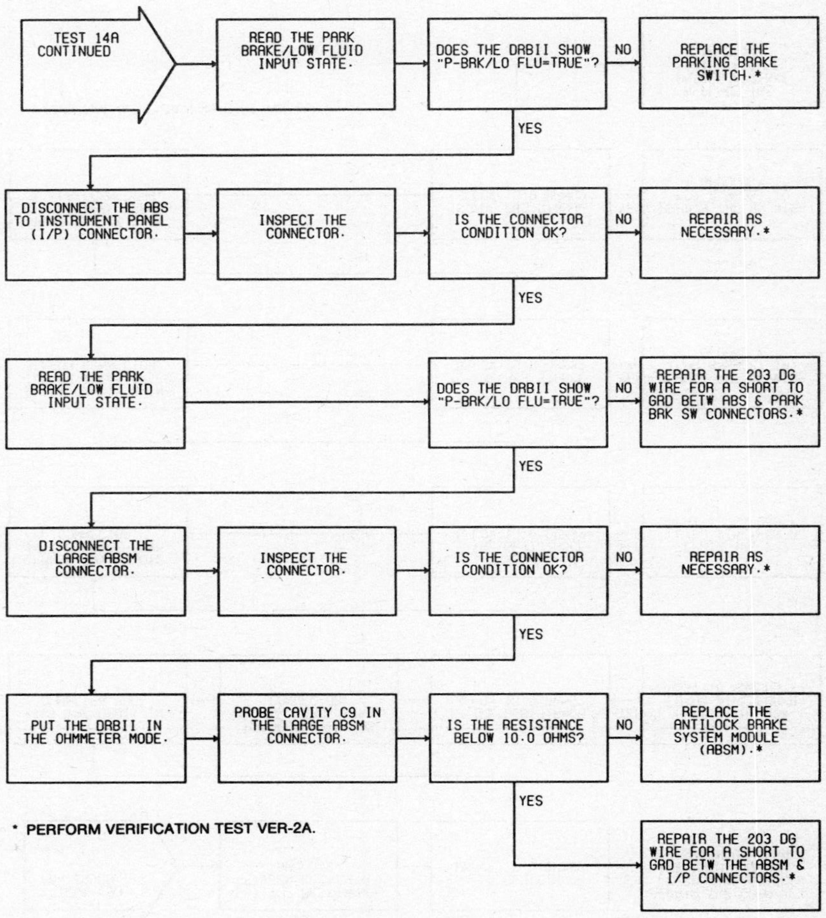
TEST 14A CONTINUED
READ THE PARK BRAKE/LOW FLUID INPUT STATE.
DOES THE DRBII SHOW "P-BRK/LO FLU=TRUE"?
NO
REPLACE THE PARKING BRAKE SWITCH.*
YES
DISCONNECT THE ABS TO INSTRUMENT PANEL (I/P) CONNECTOR.
INSPECT THE CONNECTOR.
IS THE CONNECTOR CONDITION OK?
NO
REPAIR AS NECESSARY.*
YES
READ THE PARK BRAKE/LOW FLUID INPUT STATE.
DOES THE DRBII SHOW "P-BRK/LO FLU=TRUE"?
NO
REPAIR THE 203 DG WIRE FOR A SHORT TO GRD BETW ABS & PARK BRK SW CONNECTORS.*
YES
DISCONNECT THE LARGE ABSM CONNECTOR.
INSPECT THE CONNECTOR.
IS THE CONNECTOR CONDITION OK?
NO
REPAIR AS NECESSARY.*
YES
PUT THE DRBII IN THE OHMMETER MODE.
PROBE CAVITY C9 IN THE LARGE ABSM CONNECTOR.
IS THE RESISTANCE BELOW 10.0 OHMS?
NO
REPLACE THE ANTILOCK BRAKE SYSTEM MODULE (ABSM).*
YES
REPAIR THE 203 DG WIRE FOR A SHORT TO GRD BETW THE ABSM & I/P CONNECTORS.*

* PERFORM VERIFICATION TEST VER-2A.

91G14437

Fig. 37: Test 14A – 814: Low Fluid Fault (2 of 2)

1991 BRAKES
Anti-Lock (Cont.)

TEST 15A – 815: WHEEL SPEED SENSOR FAULT – RIGHT REAR (1 OF 2)

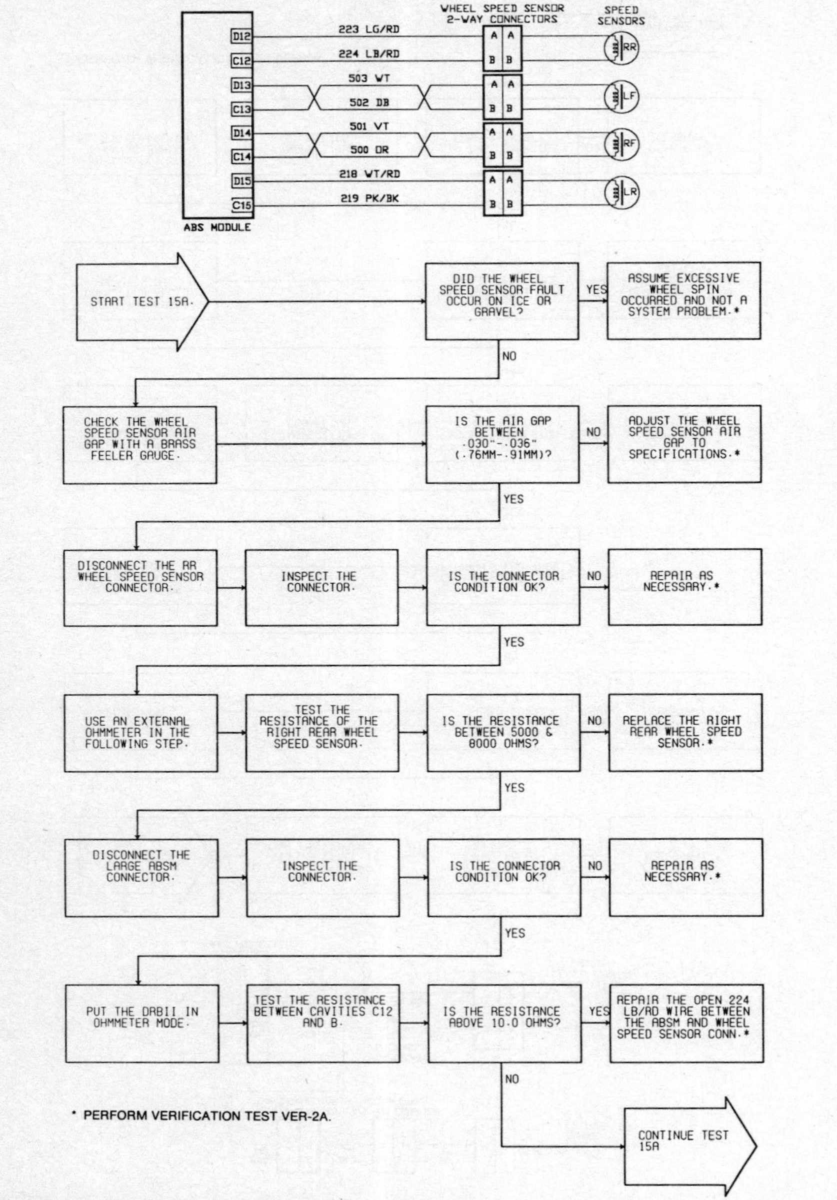
WHEEL SPEED SENSOR 2-WAY CONNECTORS
SPEED SENSORS
ABS MODULE
D12
C12
D13
C13
D14
C14
D15
C15
223 LG/RD
224 LB/RD
503 WT
502 DB
501 VT
500 DR
218 WT/RD
219 PK/BK
RR
LF
RF
LR
START TEST 15A.
DID THE WHEEL SPEED SENSOR FAULT OCCUR ON ICE OR GRAVEL?
YES
ASSUME EXCESSIVE WHEEL SPIN OCCURRED AND NOT A SYSTEM PROBLEM.*
NO
CHECK THE WHEEL SPEED SENSOR AIR GAP WITH A BRASS FEELER GAUGE.
IS THE AIR GAP BETWEEN .030"-.036" (.76MM-.91MM)?
NO
ADJUST THE WHEEL SPEED SENSOR AIR GAP TO SPECIFICATIONS.*
YES
DISCONNECT THE RR WHEEL SPEED SENSOR CONNECTOR.
INSPECT THE CONNECTOR.
IS THE CONNECTOR CONDITION OK?
NO
REPAIR AS NECESSARY.*
YES
USE AN EXTERNAL OHMMETER IN THE FOLLOWING STEP.
TEST THE RESISTANCE OF THE RIGHT REAR WHEEL SPEED SENSOR.
IS THE RESISTANCE BETWEEN 5000 & 8000 OHMS?
NO
REPLACE THE RIGHT REAR WHEEL SPEED SENSOR.*
YES
DISCONNECT THE LARGE ABSM CONNECTOR.
INSPECT THE CONNECTOR.
IS THE CONNECTOR CONDITION OK?
NO
REPAIR AS NECESSARY.*
YES
PUT THE DRBII IN OHMMETER MODE.
TEST THE RESISTANCE BETWEEN CAVITIES C12 AND B.
IS THE RESISTANCE ABOVE 10.0 OHMS?
YES
REPAIR THE OPEN 224 LB/RD WIRE BETWEEN THE ABSM AND WHEEL SPEED SENSOR CONN.*
NO
CONTINUE TEST 15A
* PERFORM VERIFICATION TEST VER-2A.

91C14235 91H14438

Fig. 38: Test 15A – 815: Wheel Speed Sensor Fault – Right Rear (1 of 2)

TEST 15A – 815: WHEEL SPEED SENSOR FAULT – RIGHT REAR (2 OF 2)

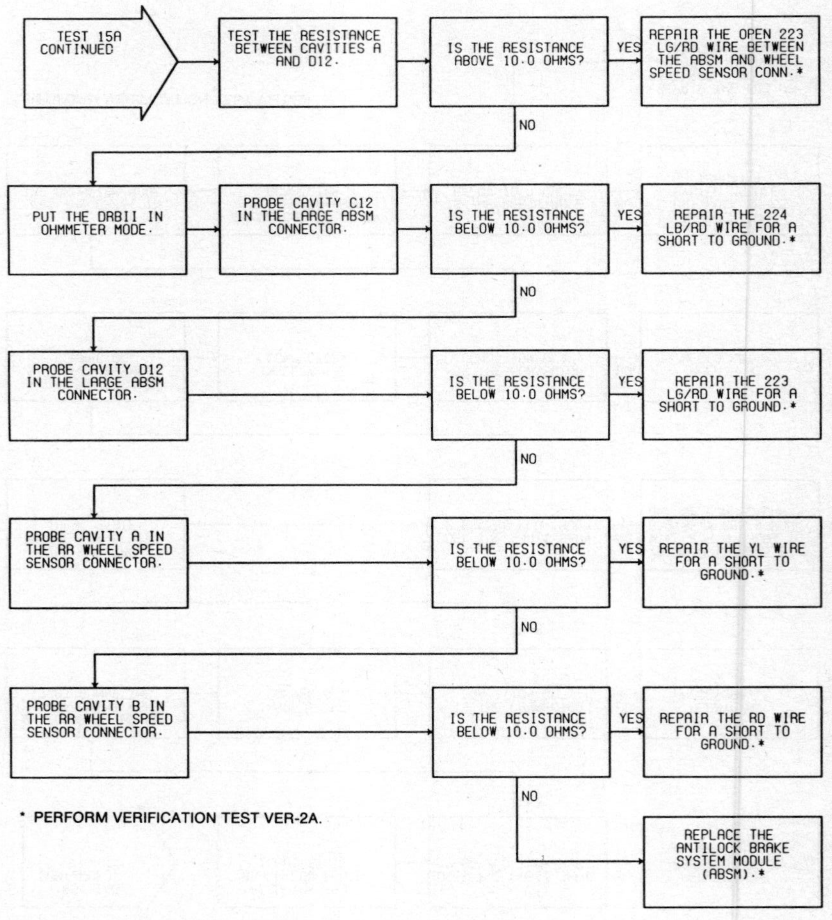
TEST 15A CONTINUED
TEST THE RESISTANCE BETWEEN CAVITIES A AND D12.
IS THE RESISTANCE ABOVE 10.0 OHMS?
YES
REPAIR THE OPEN 223 LG/RD WIRE BETWEEN THE ABSM AND WHEEL SPEED SENSOR CONN.*
NO
PUT THE DRBII IN OHMMETER MODE.
PROBE CAVITY C12 IN THE LARGE ABSM CONNECTOR.
IS THE RESISTANCE BELOW 10.0 OHMS?
YES
REPAIR THE 224 LB/RD WIRE FOR A SHORT TO GROUND.*
NO
PROBE CAVITY D12 IN THE LARGE ABSM CONNECTOR.
IS THE RESISTANCE BELOW 10.0 OHMS?
YES
REPAIR THE 223 LG/RD WIRE FOR A SHORT TO GROUND.*
NO
PROBE CAVITY A IN THE RR WHEEL SPEED SENSOR CONNECTOR.
IS THE RESISTANCE BELOW 10.0 OHMS?
YES
REPAIR THE YL WIRE FOR A SHORT TO GROUND.*
NO
PROBE CAVITY B IN THE RR WHEEL SPEED SENSOR CONNECTOR.
IS THE RESISTANCE BELOW 10.0 OHMS?
YES
REPAIR THE RD WIRE FOR A SHORT TO GROUND.*
NO
REPLACE THE ANTILOCK BRAKE SYSTEM MODULE (ABSM).*
* PERFORM VERIFICATION TEST VER-2A.

91I14439

Fig. 39: Test 15A – 815: Wheel Speed Sensor Fault – Right Rear (2 of 2)

TEST 16A – 816: WHEEL SPEED SENSOR FAULT – LEFT REAR (1 OF 2)

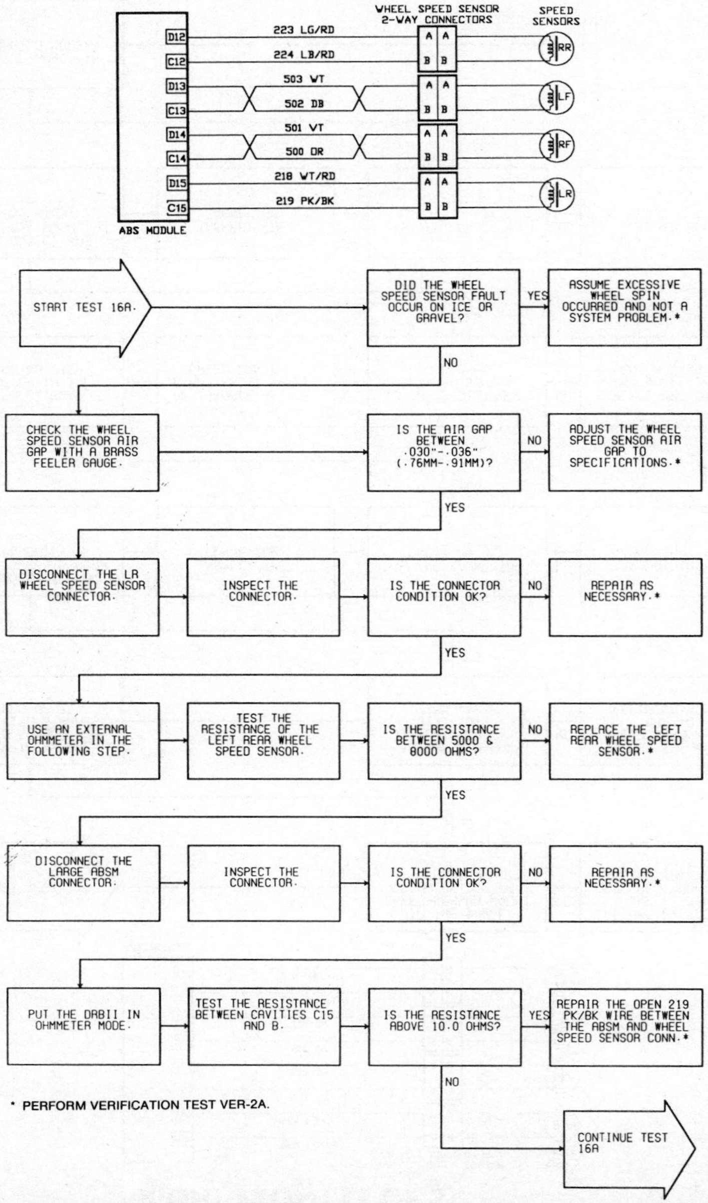
WHEEL SPEED SENSOR 2-WAY CONNECTORS
SPEED SENSORS
ABS MODULE
D12
C12
D13
C13
D14
C14
D15
C15
223 LG/RD
224 LB/RD
503 WT
502 DB
501 VT
500 DR
218 WT/RD
219 PK/BK
A
B
RR
LF
RF
LR
START TEST 16A.
DID THE WHEEL SPEED SENSOR FAULT OCCUR ON ICE OR GRAVEL?
YES
ASSUME EXCESSIVE WHEEL SPIN OCCURRED AND NOT A SYSTEM PROBLEM.*
NO
CHECK THE WHEEL SPEED SENSOR AIR GAP WITH A BRASS FEELER GAUGE.
IS THE AIR GAP BETWEEN .030"-.036" (.76MM-.91MM)?
NO
ADJUST THE WHEEL SPEED SENSOR AIR GAP TO SPECIFICATIONS.*
YES
DISCONNECT THE LR WHEEL SPEED SENSOR CONNECTOR.
INSPECT THE CONNECTOR.
IS THE CONNECTOR CONDITION OK?
NO
REPAIR AS NECESSARY.*
YES
USE AN EXTERNAL OHMMETER IN THE FOLLOWING STEP.
TEST THE RESISTANCE OF THE LEFT REAR WHEEL SPEED SENSOR.
IS THE RESISTANCE BETWEEN 5000 & 8000 OHMS?
NO
REPLACE THE LEFT REAR WHEEL SPEED SENSOR.*
YES
DISCONNECT THE LARGE ABSM CONNECTOR.
INSPECT THE CONNECTOR.
IS THE CONNECTOR CONDITION OK?
NO
REPAIR AS NECESSARY.*
YES
PUT THE DRBII IN OHMMETER MODE.
TEST THE RESISTANCE BETWEEN CAVITIES C15 AND B.
IS THE RESISTANCE ABOVE 10.0 OHMS?
YES
REPAIR THE OPEN 219 PK/BK WIRE BETWEEN THE ABSM AND WHEEL SPEED SENSOR CONN.*
NO
CONTINUE TEST 16A

* PERFORM VERIFICATION TEST VER-2A.

91C14235 91B14440

Fig. 40: Test 16A – 816: Wheel Speed Sensor Fault – Left Rear (1 of 2)

TEST 16A – 816: WHEEL SPEED SENSOR FAULT – LEFT REAR (2 OF 2)

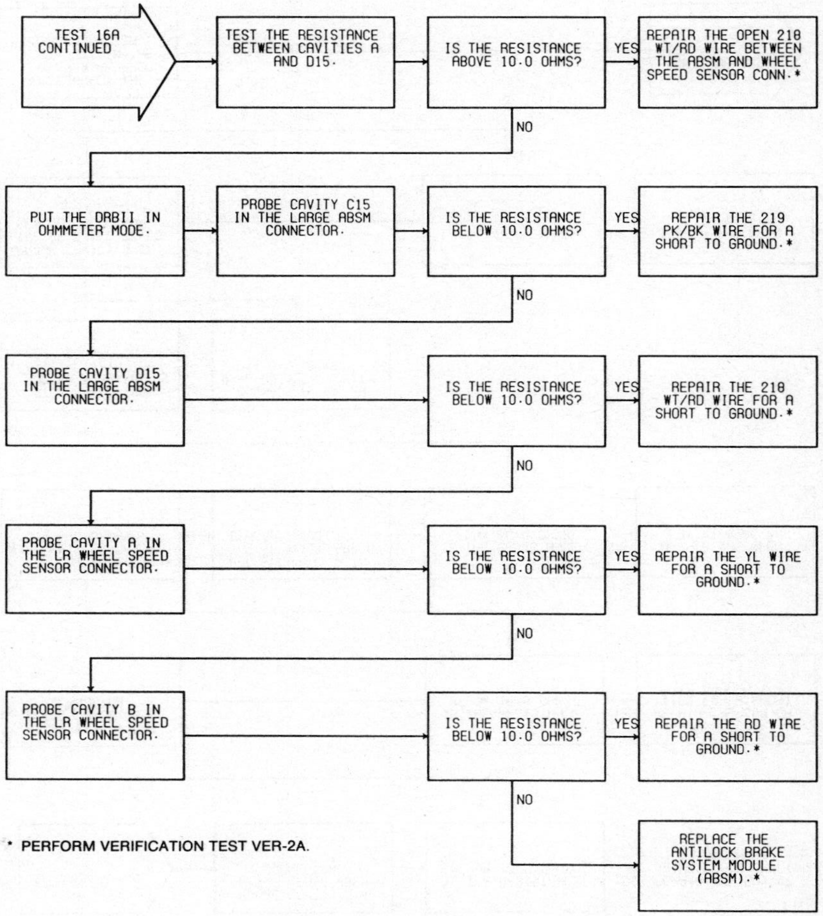
TEST 16A CONTINUED
TEST THE RESISTANCE BETWEEN CAVITIES A AND D15.
IS THE RESISTANCE ABOVE 10.0 OHMS?
YES
REPAIR THE OPEN 218 WT/RD WIRE BETWEEN THE ABSM AND WHEEL SPEED SENSOR CONN.*
NO
PUT THE DRBII IN OHMMETER MODE.
PROBE CAVITY C15 IN THE LARGE ABSM CONNECTOR.
IS THE RESISTANCE BELOW 10.0 OHMS?
YES
REPAIR THE 219 PK/BK WIRE FOR A SHORT TO GROUND.*
NO
PROBE CAVITY D15 IN THE LARGE ABSM CONNECTOR.
IS THE RESISTANCE BELOW 10.0 OHMS?
YES
REPAIR THE 218 WT/RD WIRE FOR A SHORT TO GROUND.*
NO
PROBE CAVITY A IN THE LR WHEEL SPEED SENSOR CONNECTOR.
IS THE RESISTANCE BELOW 10.0 OHMS?
YES
REPAIR THE YL WIRE FOR A SHORT TO GROUND.*
NO
PROBE CAVITY B IN THE LR WHEEL SPEED SENSOR CONNECTOR.
IS THE RESISTANCE BELOW 10.0 OHMS?
YES
REPAIR THE RD WIRE FOR A SHORT TO GROUND.*
NO
REPLACE THE ANTILOCK BRAKE SYSTEM MODULE (ABSM).*

* PERFORM VERIFICATION TEST VER-2A.

91C14441

Fig. 41: Test 16A – 816: Wheel Speed Sensor Fault – Left Rear (2 of 2)

1991 BRAKES
Anti-Lock (Cont.)

TEST 17A – 817: WHEEL SPEED SENSOR FAULT – RIGHT FRONT (1 OF 3)

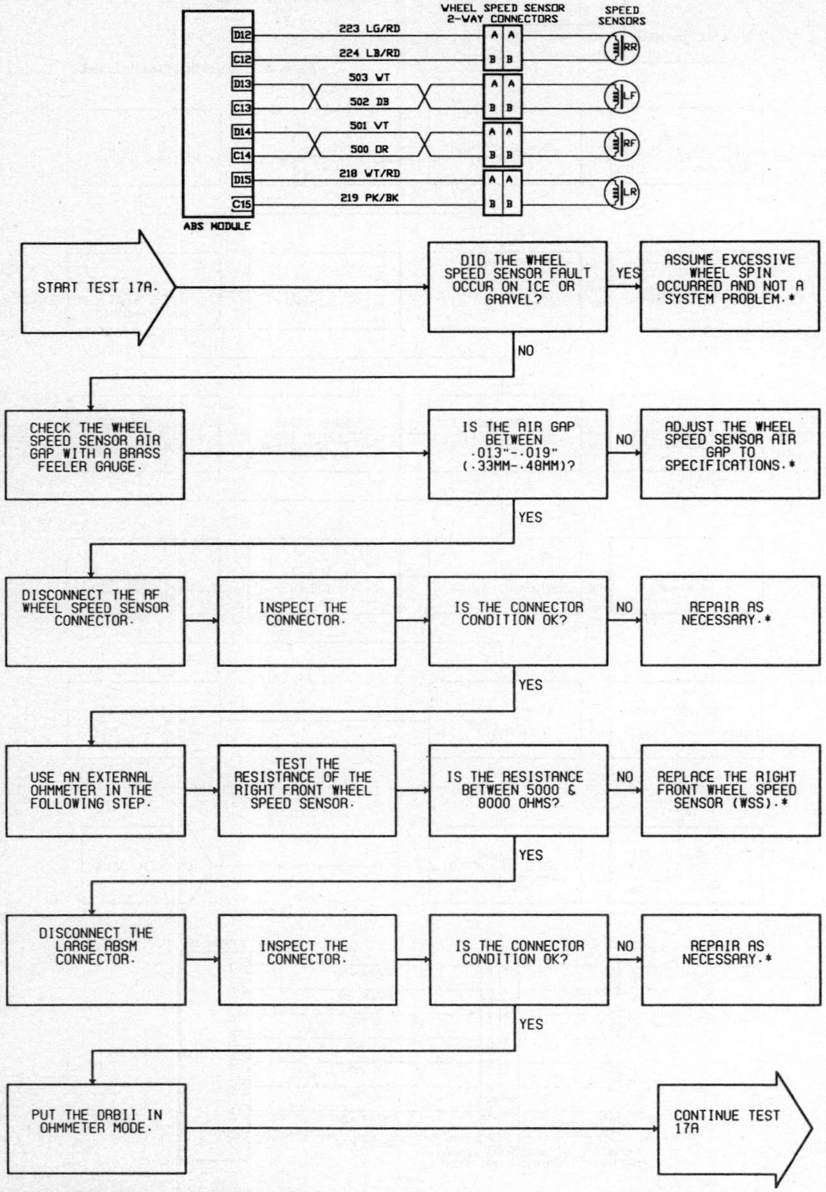
WHEEL SPEED SENSOR 2-WAY CONNECTORS
SPEED SENSORS
D12
C12
D13
C13
D14
C14
D15
C15
ABS MODULE
223 LG/RD
224 LB/RD
503 VT
502 DB
501 VT
500 DR
218 WT/RD
219 PK/BK
A
B
RR
LF
RF
LR
START TEST 17A.
DID THE WHEEL SPEED SENSOR FAULT OCCUR ON ICE OR GRAVEL?
YES
ASSUME EXCESSIVE WHEEL SPIN OCCURRED AND NOT A SYSTEM PROBLEM.*
NO
CHECK THE WHEEL SPEED SENSOR AIR GAP WITH A BRASS FEELER GAUGE.
IS THE AIR GAP BETWEEN .013"-.019" (.33MM-.48MM)?
NO
ADJUST THE WHEEL SPEED SENSOR AIR GAP TO SPECIFICATIONS.*
YES
DISCONNECT THE RF WHEEL SPEED SENSOR CONNECTOR.
INSPECT THE CONNECTOR.
IS THE CONNECTOR CONDITION OK?
NO
REPAIR AS NECESSARY.*
YES
USE AN EXTERNAL OHMMETER IN THE FOLLOWING STEP.
TEST THE RESISTANCE OF THE RIGHT FRONT WHEEL SPEED SENSOR.
IS THE RESISTANCE BETWEEN 5000 & 8000 OHMS?
NO
REPLACE THE RIGHT FRONT WHEEL SPEED SENSOR (WSS).*
YES
DISCONNECT THE LARGE ABSM CONNECTOR.
INSPECT THE CONNECTOR.
IS THE CONNECTOR CONDITION OK?
NO
REPAIR AS NECESSARY.*
YES
PUT THE DRBII IN OHMMETER MODE.
CONTINUE TEST 17A

* PERFORM VERIFICATION TEST VER-2A.

91C14235 91D14442

Fig. 42: Test 17A – 817: Wheel Speed Sensor Fault – Right Front (1 of 3)

TEST 17A – 817: WHEEL SPEED SENSOR FAULT – RIGHT FRONT (2 OF 3)

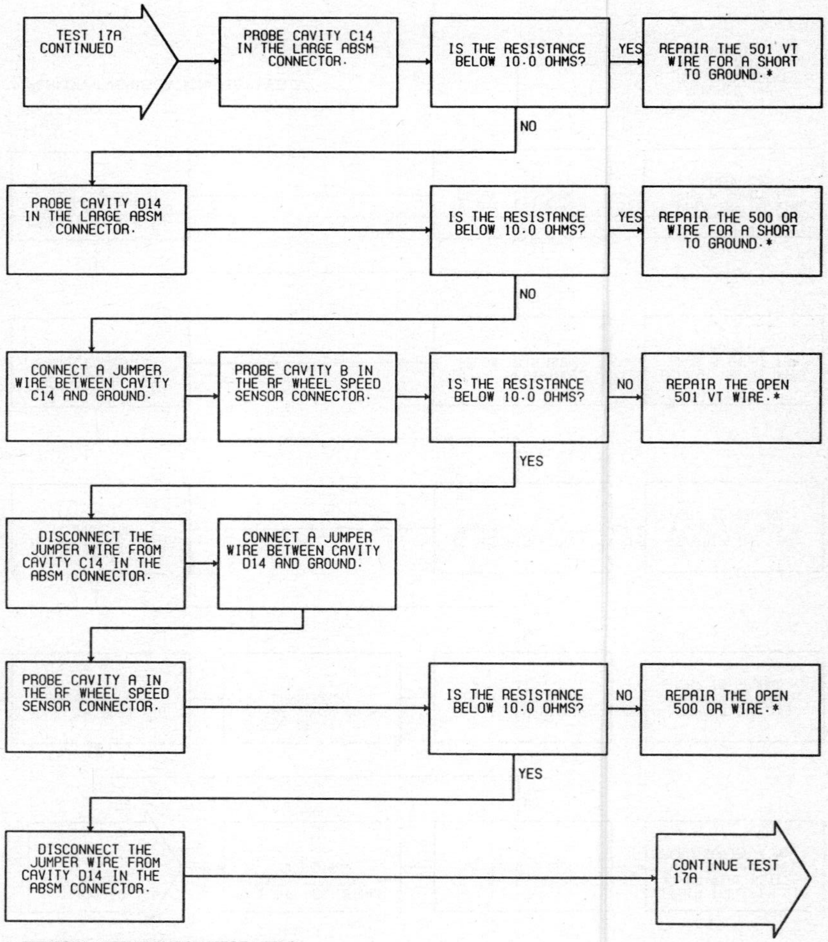
TEST 17A CONTINUED
PROBE CAVITY C14 IN THE LARGE ABSM CONNECTOR.
IS THE RESISTANCE BELOW 10.0 OHMS?
YES
REPAIR THE 501 VT WIRE FOR A SHORT TO GROUND.*
NO
PROBE CAVITY D14 IN THE LARGE ABSM CONNECTOR.
IS THE RESISTANCE BELOW 10.0 OHMS?
YES
REPAIR THE 500 OR WIRE FOR A SHORT TO GROUND.*
NO
CONNECT A JUMPER WIRE BETWEEN CAVITY C14 AND GROUND.
PROBE CAVITY B IN THE RF WHEEL SPEED SENSOR CONNECTOR.
IS THE RESISTANCE BELOW 10.0 OHMS?
NO
REPAIR THE OPEN 501 VT WIRE.*
YES
DISCONNECT THE JUMPER WIRE FROM CAVITY C14 IN THE ABSM CONNECTOR.
CONNECT A JUMPER WIRE BETWEEN CAVITY D14 AND GROUND.
PROBE CAVITY A IN THE RF WHEEL SPEED SENSOR CONNECTOR.
IS THE RESISTANCE BELOW 10.0 OHMS?
NO
REPAIR THE OPEN 500 OR WIRE.*
YES
DISCONNECT THE JUMPER WIRE FROM CAVITY D14 IN THE ABSM CONNECTOR.
CONTINUE TEST 17A

* PERFORM VERIFICATION TEST VER-2A.

91E14443

Fig. 43: Test 17A – 817: Wheel Speed Sensor Fault – Right Front (2 of 3)

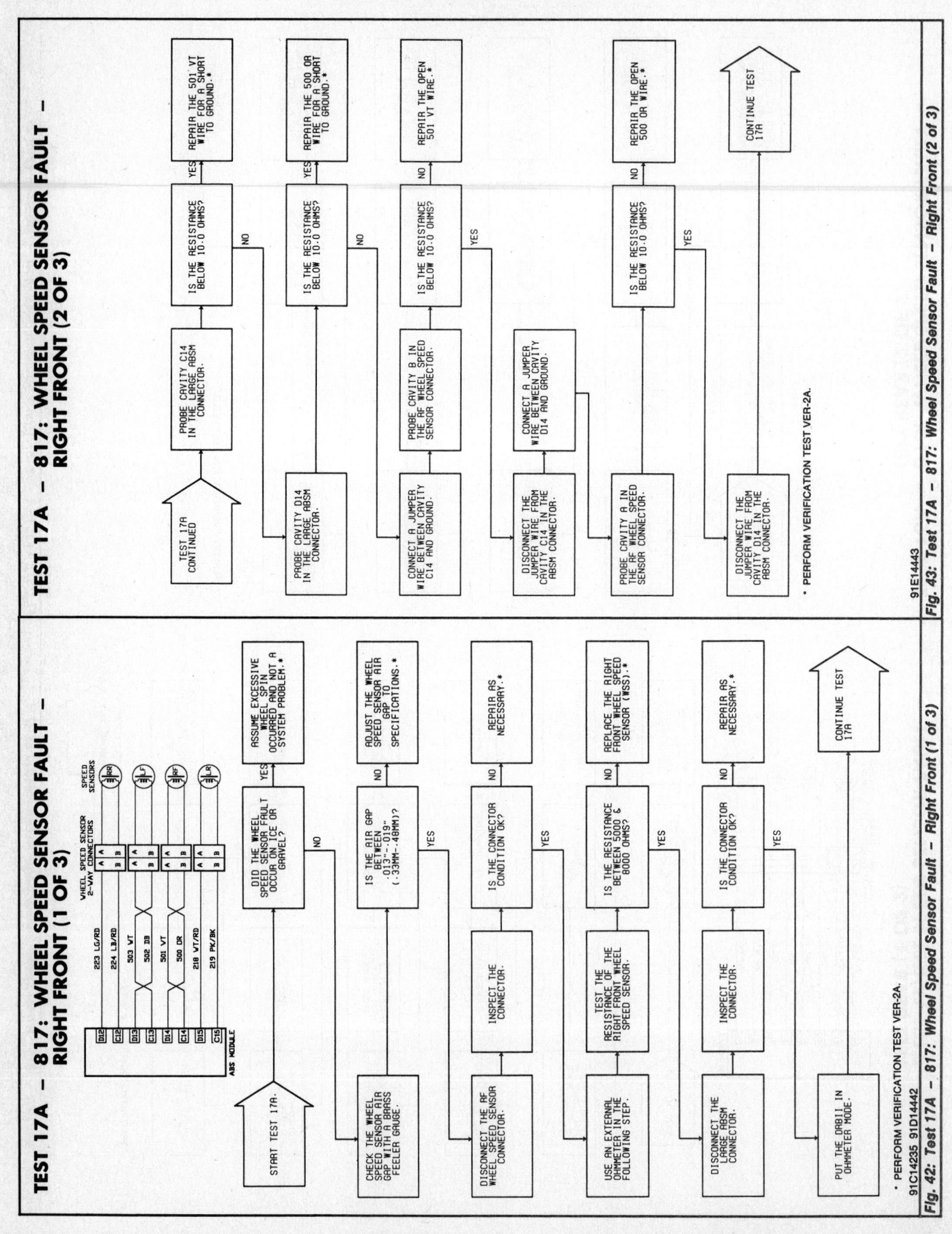

TEST 17A – 817: WHEEL SPEED SENSOR FAULT – RIGHT FRONT (3 OF 3)

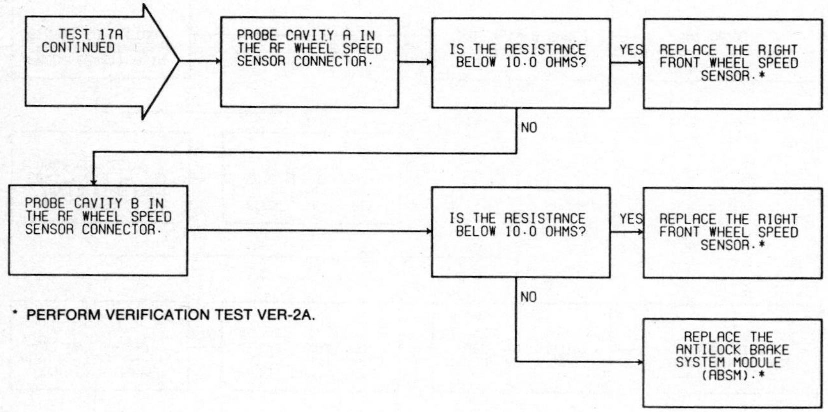
TEST 17A CONTINUED
PROBE CAVITY A IN THE RF WHEEL SPEED SENSOR CONNECTOR.
IS THE RESISTANCE BELOW 10.0 OHMS?
YES
REPLACE THE RIGHT FRONT WHEEL SPEED SENSOR.*
NO
PROBE CAVITY B IN THE RF WHEEL SPEED SENSOR CONNECTOR.
IS THE RESISTANCE BELOW 10.0 OHMS?
YES
REPLACE THE RIGHT FRONT WHEEL SPEED SENSOR.*
NO
REPLACE THE ANTILOCK BRAKE SYSTEM MODULE (ABSM).*

* PERFORM VERIFICATION TEST VER-2A.

91F14444

Fig. 44: Test 17A – 817: Wheel Speed Sensor Fault – Right Front (3 of 3)

TEST 18A – 818: WHEEL SPEED SENSOR FAULT – LEFT FRONT (1 OF 3)

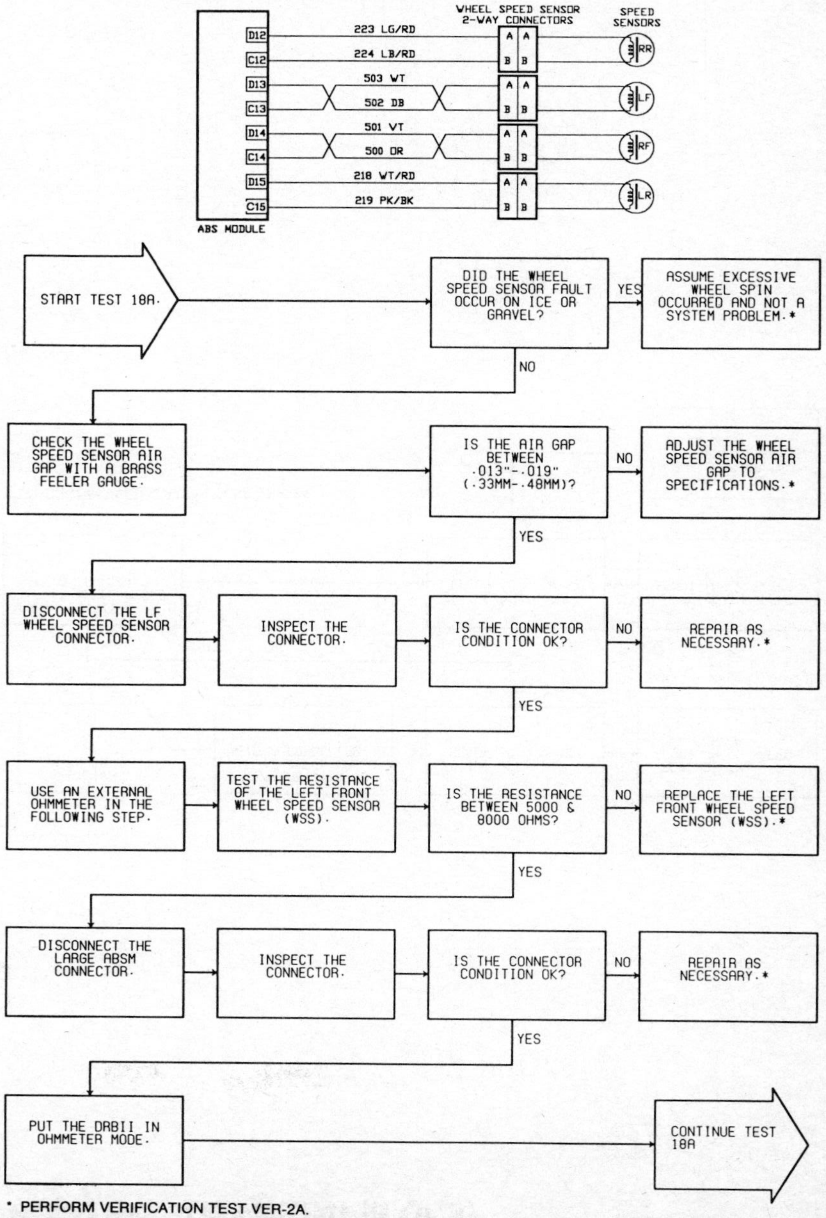
WHEEL SPEED SENSOR 2-WAY CONNECTORS
SPEED SENSORS
ABS MODULE
D12
C12
D13
C13
D14
C14
D15
C15
223 LG/RD
224 LB/RD
503 WT
502 DB
501 VT
500 OR
218 WT/RD
219 PK/BK
A A
B B
RR
LF
RF
LR
START TEST 18A.
DID THE WHEEL SPEED SENSOR FAULT OCCUR ON ICE OR GRAVEL?
YES
ASSUME EXCESSIVE WHEEL SPIN OCCURRED AND NOT A SYSTEM PROBLEM.*
NO
CHECK THE WHEEL SPEED SENSOR AIR GAP WITH A BRASS FEELER GAUGE.
IS THE AIR GAP BETWEEN .013"-.019" (.33MM-.48MM)?
NO
ADJUST THE WHEEL SPEED SENSOR AIR GAP TO SPECIFICATIONS.*
YES
DISCONNECT THE LF WHEEL SPEED SENSOR CONNECTOR.
INSPECT THE CONNECTOR.
IS THE CONNECTOR CONDITION OK?
NO
REPAIR AS NECESSARY.*
YES
USE AN EXTERNAL OHMMETER IN THE FOLLOWING STEP.
TEST THE RESISTANCE OF THE LEFT FRONT WHEEL SPEED SENSOR (WSS).
IS THE RESISTANCE BETWEEN 5000 & 8000 OHMS?
NO
REPLACE THE LEFT FRONT WHEEL SPEED SENSOR (WSS).*
YES
DISCONNECT THE LARGE ABSM CONNECTOR.
INSPECT THE CONNECTOR.
IS THE CONNECTOR CONDITION OK?
NO
REPAIR AS NECESSARY.*
YES
PUT THE DRBII IN OHMMETER MODE.
CONTINUE TEST 18A

* PERFORM VERIFICATION TEST VER-2A.

91C14235 91G14445

Fig. 45: Test 18A – 818: Wheel Speed Sensor Fault – Left Front (1 of 3)

TEST 18A – 818: WHEEL SPEED SENSOR FAULT – LEFT FRONT (2 OF 3)

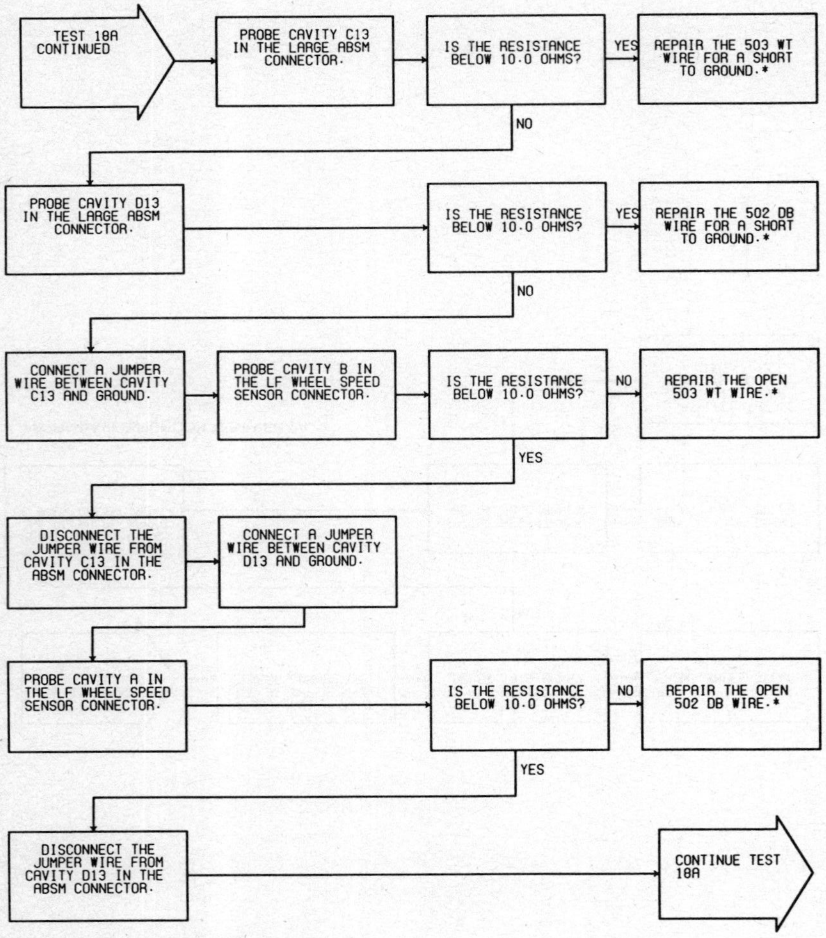
TEST 18A CONTINUED
PROBE CAVITY C13 IN THE LARGE ABSM CONNECTOR.
IS THE RESISTANCE BELOW 10.0 OHMS?
YES
REPAIR THE 503 WT WIRE FOR A SHORT TO GROUND.*
NO
PROBE CAVITY D13 IN THE LARGE ABSM CONNECTOR.
IS THE RESISTANCE BELOW 10.0 OHMS?
YES
REPAIR THE 502 DB WIRE FOR A SHORT TO GROUND.*
NO
CONNECT A JUMPER WIRE BETWEEN CAVITY C13 AND GROUND.
PROBE CAVITY B IN THE LF WHEEL SPEED SENSOR CONNECTOR.
IS THE RESISTANCE BELOW 10.0 OHMS?
NO
REPAIR THE OPEN 503 WT WIRE.*
YES
DISCONNECT THE JUMPER WIRE FROM CAVITY C13 IN THE ABSM CONNECTOR.
CONNECT A JUMPER WIRE BETWEEN CAVITY D13 AND GROUND.
PROBE CAVITY A IN THE LF WHEEL SPEED SENSOR CONNECTOR.
IS THE RESISTANCE BELOW 10.0 OHMS?
NO
REPAIR THE OPEN 502 DB WIRE.*
YES
DISCONNECT THE JUMPER WIRE FROM CAVITY D13 IN THE ABSM CONNECTOR.
CONTINUE TEST 18A

* PERFORM VERIFICATION TEST VER-2A.

91H14446

Fig. 46: Test 18A – 818: Wheel Speed Sensor Fault – Left Front (2 of 3)

TEST 18A – 818: WHEEL SPEED SENSOR FAULT – LEFT FRONT (3 OF 3)

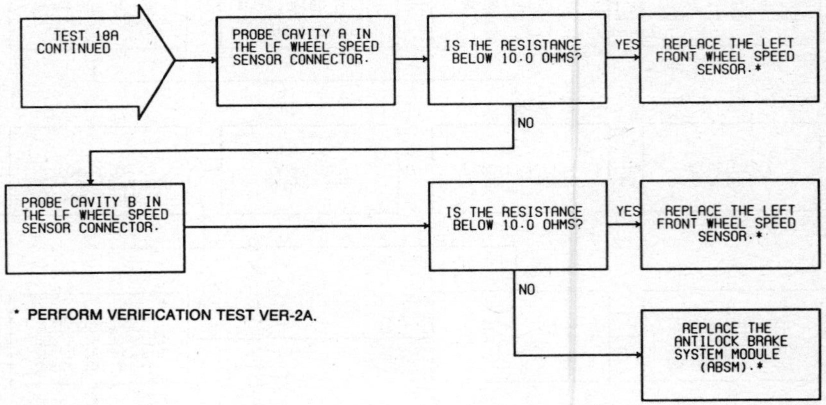
TEST 18A CONTINUED
PROBE CAVITY A IN THE LF WHEEL SPEED SENSOR CONNECTOR.
IS THE RESISTANCE BELOW 10.0 OHMS?
YES
REPLACE THE LEFT FRONT WHEEL SPEED SENSOR.*
NO
PROBE CAVITY B IN THE LF WHEEL SPEED SENSOR CONNECTOR.
IS THE RESISTANCE BELOW 10.0 OHMS?
YES
REPLACE THE LEFT FRONT WHEEL SPEED SENSOR.*
NO
REPLACE THE ANTILOCK BRAKE SYSTEM MODULE (ABSM).*

* PERFORM VERIFICATION TEST VER-2A.

91I14447

Fig. 47: Test 18A – 818: Wheel Speed Sensor Fault – Left Front (3 of 3)

1991 BRAKES
Disc & Drum

Cherokee, Comanche
Grand Wagoneer, Wrangler

DESCRIPTION

Floating caliper disc brake assembly uses a single piston caliper which floats on 2 bolts. As brake pedal is depressed, hydraulic pressure passes through a proportioning valve to brake caliper piston.

This force is transmitted to inboard brake pad, forcing it against braking surface of rotor. Pressure then moves outer caliper housing and pad inward on caliper mounting bolts, forcing outer pad against outer braking surface of rotor.

A combination proportioning valve/pressure differential switch is used on all models. Proportioning valve is not serviceable. Valve must be replaced if it malfunctions. Comanche models also use a height sensing proportioning valve. When vehicle is loaded, height sensing valve adjusts front and rear brake proportioning to maintain brake balance. As vehicle load increases (resulting in decreased vehicle height), higher brake line pressure to rear brakes is provided. Height sensing proportioning valve is not serviceable and must be replaced if it malfunctions.

WARNING: Use of aftermarket load leveling kits, air shocks or modifications changing axle-to-frame distance will provide a false reading to height sensing proportioning valve. These modifications can result in unsatisfactory brake performance, which can result in an accident.

A pressure differential brake warning light switch is used to warn vehicle operator that one side of the hydraulic system has failed. When hydraulic pressure is equal in both front and rear systems, switch piston remains centered and does not contact terminal in switch. If one side of brake system fails, hydraulic pressure moves piston toward failed side. Shoulder of piston contacts switch terminal, grounding brake warning light.

Proportioning valve operates by restricting hydraulic pressure to rear brakes at a given ratio when system hydraulic pressure reaches a certain point. This improves front-to-rear brake balance during high speed braking, when a percentage of rear weight is transferred to front wheels. Valve reduces rear brake pressure and delays rear wheel skid. On light brake application, valve allows full hydraulic pressure to rear brakes.

BLEEDING BRAKE SYSTEM

NOTE: Brake bleeding procedures for models with anti-lock brakes are not covered in this article. See ANTI-LOCK article for proper procedure.

BLEEDING SEQUENCE

Before bleeding system, exhaust all vacuum from power unit by depressing brake pedal several times. When bleeding disc brakes, air may tend to cling to caliper walls. Lightly tap caliper, while bleeding, to aid in removal of air.

Fill master cylinder with clean brake fluid. Fluid should meet DOT 3 specifications. Bleed master cylinder (if equipped) with bleeder screws. Bleed wheel cylinders and calipers in sequence. See BRAKE LINE BLEEDING SEQUENCE table.

BRAKE LINE BLEEDING SEQUENCE

Application	Sequence
All Models	RR, LR, RF, LF

MASTER CYLINDER BLEEDING

Bench Bleeding – 1) Master cylinder must be bled before installation to prevent excessive amounts of air from entering hydraulic system, creating poor brake operation.

2) Place master cylinder in soft-jawed vise. DO NOT tighten vise enough to damage master cylinder. Install bleed tubes in both outlets of master cylinder. *See Fig. 1.*

3) Fill master cylinder with clean brake fluid. Fluid should meet DOT 3 specifications. Ensure end of bleed tubes are submerged in brake fluid.

4) Using proper size rod, apply and release master cylinder until no air bubbles exist in brake fluid flow. When all air bubbles are gone from master cylinder, cap outlet ports. Install reservoir cover and seal. Install master cylinder and bleed on vehicle.

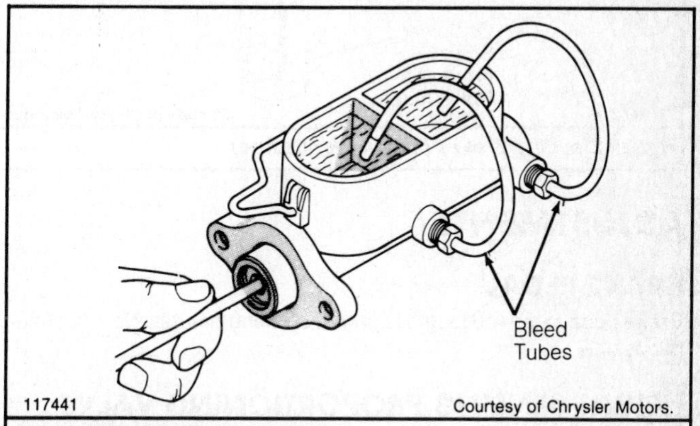
Bleed
Tubes
117441
Courtesy of Chrysler Motors.

Fig. 1: Bleeding Master Cylinder

On-Vehicle Bleeding – 1) Install master cylinder on vehicle after bench bleeding. Remove bleeder lines and install brake lines. DO NOT tighten brake lines yet.

2) Slowly force brake pedal to floor and hold in this position. Tighten brake lines, and release brake pedal. Repeat procedure until no air bubbles exist at brake lines. Tighten brake lines. Check for leaks.

PRESSURE BLEEDING

1) Clean master cylinder cap and surrounding area. Remove cap. With pressure tank at least 1/2 full, connect to master cylinder with adapters. Attach bleed hose to first bleeder valve to be serviced. See BRAKE LINE BLEEDING SEQUENCE table under BLEEDING SEQUENCE.

2) Place other end of hose in clean glass jar partially filled with clean brake fluid so end of hose is submerged in fluid.

3) Open release valve on pressure bleeder. Follow equipment manufacturer's pressure instructions or see PRESSURE BLEEDER SETTINGS table. Open bleeder screw 3/4 turn, and note fluid flow.

4) Close bleeder screw when fluid is free of bubbles. Repeat procedure on remaining wheels in proper sequence. Check brake pedal operation after bleeding has been completed.

5) Remove pressure bleeding equipment and valve retainer from hold-off valve. Ensure master cylinder is full of fluid. Check for leaks.

PRESSURE BLEEDER SETTINGS

Application	psi (kg/cm^2)
All Models	15-20 (1.1-1.4)

MANUAL BLEEDING

1) Fill master cylinder with clean brake fluid. Fluid should meet DOT 3 specifications. Install bleed hose to first bleeder valve to be serviced. See BRAKE LINE BLEEDING SEQUENCE table under BLEEDING SEQUENCE. Submerge other end of hose in clean glass jar partially filled with clean brake fluid. *See Fig. 2.*

NOTE: Ensure bleeder valve is closed when brake pedal is released. DO NOT allow master cylinder to run out of fluid.

2) Open bleeder valve 3/4 turn. Depress brake pedal slowly through full travel. Close bleeder valve, and release pedal. Repeat procedure until flow of fluid shows no signs of air bubbles.

1991 BRAKES
Disc & Drum (Cont.)

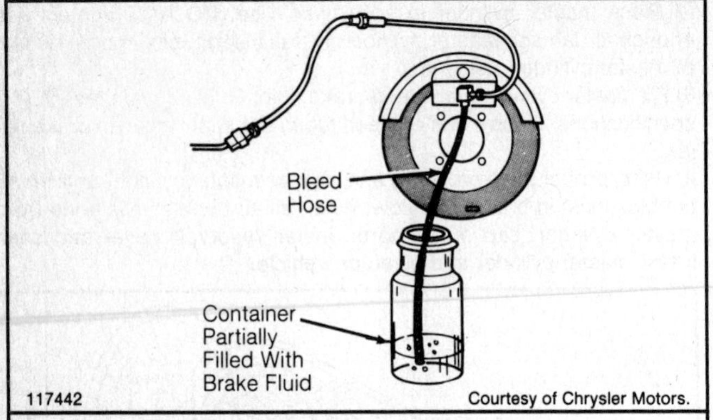
Bleed
Hose
Container
Partially
Filled With
Brake Fluid
117442
Courtesy of Chrysler Motors.

Fig. 2: Bleeding Brakes (Manual Procedure)

ADJUSTMENTS

BRAKE PEDAL

Brake pedal push rod length is preset by manufacturer. No adjustment is possible.

HEIGHT SENSING PROPORTIONING VALVE

WARNING: Vehicle must be unloaded and on level surface for accurate valve adjustment. Proportioning valve bushing must also be replaced during adjustment. Failure to observe these precautions can result in unsatisfactory brake performance, which can result in an accident.

1) Unload vehicle. Position vehicle on level surface. Raise and support vehicle. Do not allow wheels to hang free. Remove nut attaching lever to valve shaft. *See Fig. 3.*

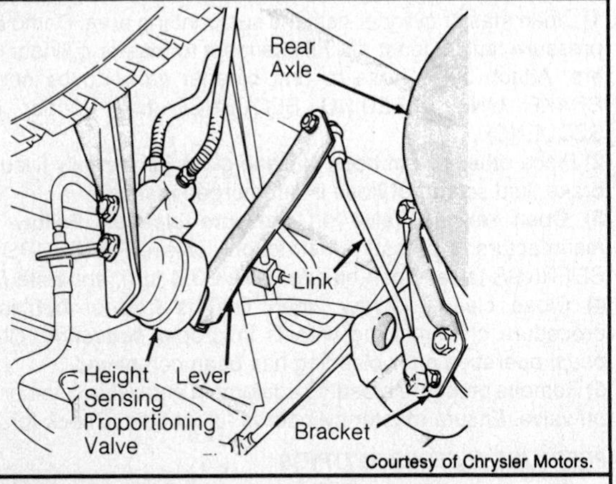
Rear
Axle
Link
Height
Sensing
Proportioning
Valve
Lever
Bracket
117444
Courtesy of Chrysler Motors.

Fig. 3: Identifying Height Sensing Proportioning Valve Assembly (Comanche)

2) Pull lever and retainer off valve shaft, and remove old bushing. Discard bushing. Clean threads and splines on valve shaft. If valve link was disconnected from axle bracket or lever, reconnect link.

NOTE: Do not attempt adjustment with link disconnected. Link must be connected to avoid false reading to valve after installation.

3) Loosen valve mounting bolts 2 turns. Turn valve shaft until shaft flat is approximately at 5:50 o'clock position. *See Fig. 4.* Install Valve Adjusting Gauge (6439). Position gauge on mounting bolt and shaft. *See Fig. 5.*

4) No clearance between gauge, shaft and bolts should exist. Gauge must be seated on shaft flat. Install retainer (if removed) in lever. Install new bushing in retainer and lever. Start bushing and lever on valve shaft.

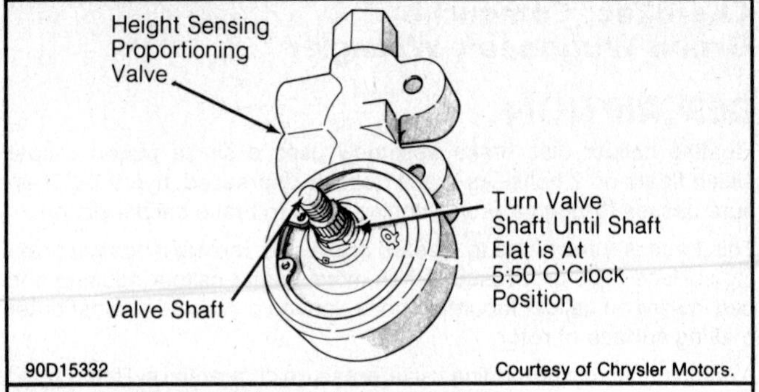
Height Sensing
Proportioning
Valve
Turn Valve
Shaft Until Shaft
Flat Is At
5:50 O'Clock
Position
Valve Shaft
90D15332
Courtesy of Chrysler Motors.

Fig. 4: Positioning Valve Shaft (Comanche)

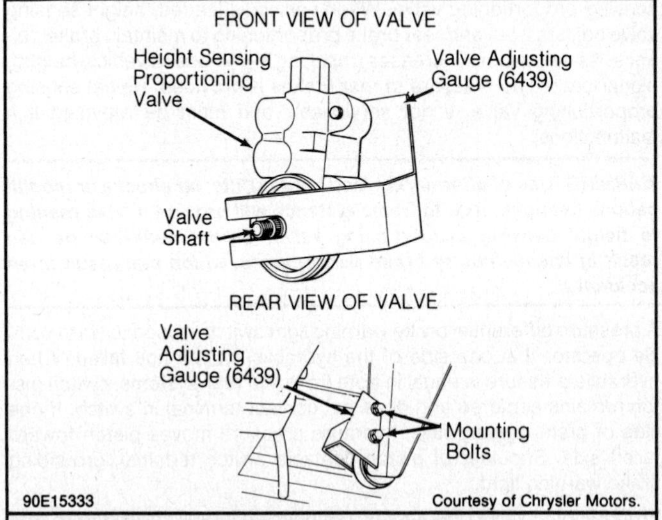
FRONT VIEW OF VALVE
Height Sensing
Proportioning
Valve
Valve Adjusting
Gauge (6439)
Valve
Shaft
REAR VIEW OF VALVE
Valve
Adjusting
Gauge (6439)
Mounting
Bolts
90E15333
Courtesy of Chrysler Motors.

Fig. 5: Installing Valve Adjusting Gauge (Comanche)

5) Press bushing and lever onto shaft with Bushing Installer (6229) or "C" clamp and a socket. *See Fig. 6.* Remove adjustment gauge and bushing installer. Tighten valve mounting bolts to 118 INCH lbs. (13 N.m). Install and tighten lever attaching nut to 100 INCH lbs. (11 N.m).

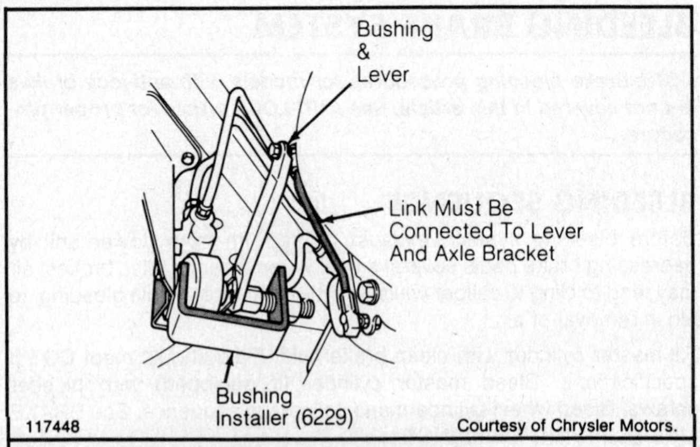
Bushing
&
Lever
Link Must Be
Connected To Lever
And Axle Bracket
Bushing
Installer (6229)
117448
Courtesy of Chrysler Motors.

Fig. 6: Installing Bushing & Lever (Comanche)

PARKING/EMERGENCY BRAKE

Cherokee, Comanche, Wagoneer & Wrangler – 1) Adjust rear brakes. See REAR BRAKE SHOES under ADJUSTMENTS. Check cable for binding, kinking or fraying. Replace cable as required. Apply and release parking brake 5 times.

2) Place parking brake lever in fifth notch. Raise and support vehicle. Position Adjustment Gauge (J-34651) on one of rear parking brake cables. *See Fig. 7*. Apply and hold a torque of 50 INCH lbs. (6 N.m) on adjustment gauge, and note position of gauge pointer.

3) If adjustment gauge pointer is not within okay band, turn parking brake cable equalizer adjustment nut in or out until pointer is within okay band. Remove tools, and lower vehicle. Ensure proper parking brake operation.

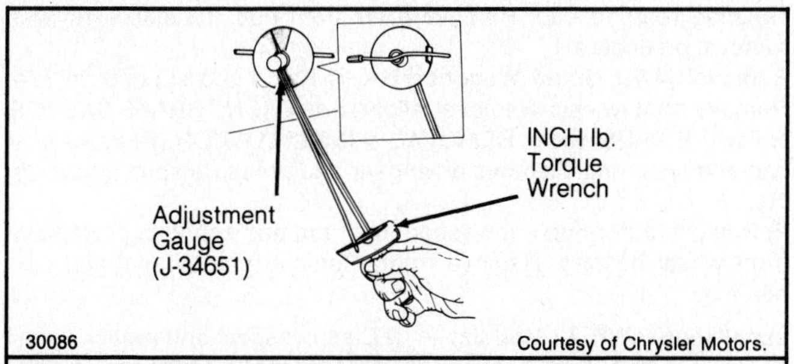

INCH lb.
Torque
Wrench
Adjustment
Gauge
(J-34651)
30086
Courtesy of Chrysler Motors.

Fig. 7: Adjusting Parking Brake (Except Grand Wagoneer)

Grand Wagoneer – 1) Adjust rear brakes. See REAR BRAKE SHOES under ADJUSTMENTS. Check cable for binding, kinking or fraying. Replace cable as required.

2) Apply and release parking brake 2-3 times. Raise and support vehicle. Loosen both lock nuts at parking brake cable equalizer. Tighten cables until wheels drag slightly when rotated by hand.

3) Loosen equalizer nut until wheels rotate freely and no drag is felt. Tighten both equalizer lock nuts. Lower vehicle, and ensure parking brake operates properly.

REAR BRAKE SHOES

NOTE: Brakes are self-adjusting. Under normal circumstances, manual adjustment is only required if shoes are removed. Replace brake shoes when lining is 1/16" on bonded linings and 1/32" from rivet on riveted linings.

1) Raise and support vehicle. Remove wheels and brake drum. Ensure right and left automatic adjuster lever and cable are properly connected.

2) Insert Brake Shoe Adjustment Gauge (J-21177-01) in drum. *See Fig. 8*. Expand gauge until inner legs contact drum braking surface. Lock gauge in position.

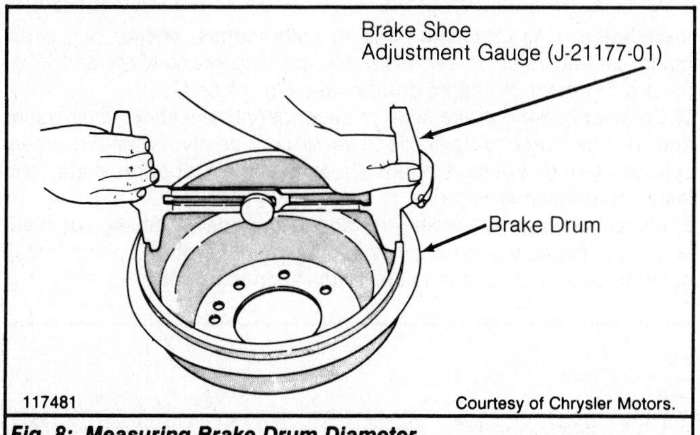

Brake Shoe
Adjustment Gauge (J-21177-01)
Brake Drum
117481
Courtesy of Chrysler Motors.

Fig. 8: Measuring Brake Drum Diameter

3) Reverse brake shoe adjustment gauge, and install it on brake shoes. *See Fig. 9*. Position gauge legs at shoe centers. If gauge does not fit (too loose or too tight), adjust brake shoes accordingly.

4) Turn star adjuster wheel (by hand) to expand or retract brake shoes. Continue adjustment until gauge outside legs have a slight drag on shoes. Repeat procedure on opposite brake shoe assembly.

5) Install brake drum and wheels. Lower vehicle. Make final adjustment by driving vehicle and making one forward stop (complete stop), followed by one reverse stop (complete stop). Repeat procedure 8-10 times to operate automatic adjusters and equalize adjustment.

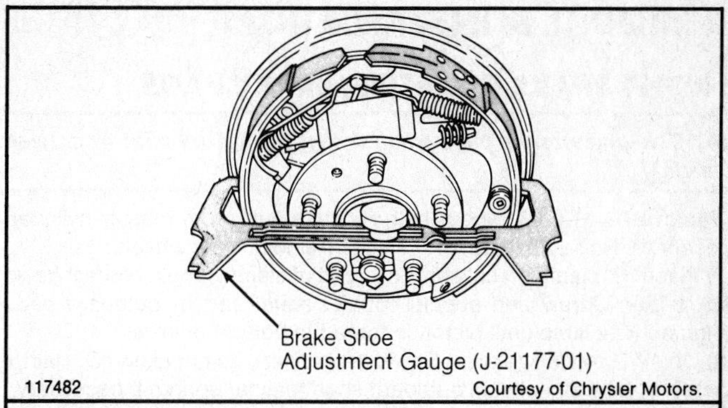

Brake Shoe
Adjustment Gauge (J-21177-01)
117482
Courtesy of Chrysler Motors.

Fig. 9: Measuring Brake Shoe Diameter

TESTING

POWER BOOSTER

Master Cylinder/Power Booster – 1) Start engine, and check power booster vacuum hose for leaks. Repair as required. Stop engine, and place gear selector in Neutral. Pump brake pedal until all vacuum reserve is depleted.

2) Press and hold brake pedal under light foot pressure. If pedal does not hold firm and falls away, master cylinder is leaking internally. Repair or replace as required. If brake pedal holds firm, proceed to next step.

3) While holding light pressure on pedal, start engine, and note pedal action. If no pedal action is noticeable, power booster or vacuum check valve is faulty. Replace check valve, and repeat test. If pedal falls away slightly then holds firm, proceed to next step.

4) Release brake pedal. Increase engine speed to 1500 RPM, close throttle and immediately stop engine. Wait at least 90 seconds and retest pedal action. Booster should provide 2 or more vacuum assisted pedal applications. If pedal action is not as specified, perform CHECK VALVE & POWER BOOSTER VACUUM test.

Check Valve & Power Booster Vacuum – 1) Disconnect vacuum hose from check valve. Remove check valve and seal from booster. Using a hand-held vacuum pump, apply 15-20 in. Hg at large end of check valve. If gauge on pump indicates any vacuum loss, valve is faulty and must be replaced. If gauge holds steady, proceed to next step.

2) Reinstall check valve and seal into power booster. Tee a vacuum gauge into vacuum hose between power booster and vacuum source. Start engine, and let idle one minute. Clamp hose shut between vacuum source and power booster.

3) Stop engine, and observe vacuum gauge. If vacuum drops more than 1 in. Hg within 15 seconds, booster diaphragm or check valve is faulty. Replace as required.

BRAKE WARNING LIGHT SYSTEM

Electrical Circuit – Disconnect wire from switch terminal, and ground wire to chassis. Turn ignition on. Warning light should come on. If light does not operate, bulb or wiring circuit is defective. Replace bulb or repair wiring as necessary. If light operates, turn off ignition, and connect wire.

Warning Light Switch – 1) Attach a bleeder hose to bleeder screw at either rear brake. Immerse other end of hose in container with brake fluid. Turn ignition on.

2) Open bleeder screw while pressure is being applied to brake pedal. Warning light should activate. Close bleeder screw before pressure is released from pedal.

3) Reapply brake pedal using moderate to heavy pressure. Light should go out. Repeat test on front brake system. System should function in same manner. Turn ignition off.

4) If light does not operate as specified for either system but comes on when electrical circuit is tested, warning light switch portion of valve is defective.

1991 BRAKES
Disc & Drum (Cont.)

REMOVAL & INSTALLATION

FRONT BRAKE CALIPER & BRAKE PADS

NOTE: Replace brake pads when lining is 1/32" (.8 mm) from rivet heads.

Removal - 1) Drain about half of brake fluid from master cylinder reservoir. Raise and support vehicle. Remove front wheels.
2) Place "C" clamp on caliper. Solid end of clamp should contact back of caliper. Screw end should contact metal part of outboard pad. Tighten "C" clamp until piston is forced to bottom of bore.
3) On 4WD models (except Grand Wagoneer), do not allow "C" clamp screw to bear directly on outboard shoe retainer spring. If necessary, use wood or metal spacer between pad and "C" clamp screw.
4) On all models, remove caliper mounting pins. Lift caliper off rotor and anchor plate.
5) On 4WD models (except Grand Wagoneer), remove outboard pad. Press one end of outboard pad inward to disengage pad lug, and rotate shoe outward until retainer spring clears caliper. Press opposite end of pad inward to disengage opposite pad lug, and rotate pad up and out of caliper. To remove inboard pad, grasp ends of pad, and tilt pad outward to release springs from caliper piston. Remove pad from piston.
6) On Grand Wagoneer, remove both brake pads and inboard pad retaining clip from caliper. On 2WD models, hold lower anti-rattle clip against anchor plate, and remove outboard brake pad. Remove inboard brake pad and both anti-rattle clips.
7) On all models, disconnect brake line at caliper, and cap hole to prevent contamination while removing caliper from vehicle.
Installation - 1) To install, reverse removal procedure. Apply a light coat of multipurpose grease to caliper sliding surfaces. Lubricate caliper mounting pins and bushings with silicone.
2) Torque caliper mounting pins to specification. See TORQUE SPECIFICATIONS table at end of article. Add brake fluid to reservoir. Apply brakes until brake pedal is firm. Check brake fluid level.

ROTOR

NOTE: DO NOT disconnect brake hose from caliper unless caliper is to be disassembled.

Removal (2WD Models) - 1) Raise and support vehicle. Remove front wheels. Remove caliper. See FRONT BRAKE CALIPER & BRAKE PADS under REMOVAL & INSTALLATION. Suspend caliper from frame or suspension.
2) Remove cap, cotter pin, nut retainer, adjusting nut and front bearing from spindle. Remove rotor from spindle. Remove grease seal and rear bearing from hub.
Installation - 1) Clean, inspect and repack wheel bearings. Replace grease seal. Coat spindle, bearing races and rotor hub cavity with grease. Clean rotor surface as required.
2) To install, reverse removal procedure. Tighten spindle nut to specification while rotating rotor to seat bearings. See TORQUE SPECIFICATIONS table at end of article. Apply brakes until brake pedal is firm. Check brake fluid level.
Removal & Installation (4WD Except Grand Wagoneer) - Raise and support vehicle. Remove front wheels. Remove caliper. See FRONT BRAKE CALIPER & BRAKE PADS under REMOVAL & INSTALLATION. Suspend caliper from frame or suspension. Remove retainers securing rotor to hub. Remove rotor from hub. To install, reverse removal procedure.
Removal (4WD Grand Wagoneer) - 1) Raise and support vehicle. Remove front wheels. Remove caliper. See FRONT BRAKE CALIPER & BRAKE PADS under REMOVAL & INSTALLATION. Remove dust cap and snap ring. Remove drive gear and pressure spring. *See Fig. 10.*
2) Remove outer nut, nut washer, inner nut and spring cup. Remove front wheel bearing. Remove rotor. Remove grease seal and rear bearing.

Installation (4WD All Models) - 1) Clean, inspect and repack wheel bearings. Apply wheel bearing grease to rotor hub cavity and spindle. Install rear bearing and new grease seal. Install rotor on spindle. Install front wheel bearing, spring cup and inner nut. Inner nut has a locating peg on one side. Ensure peg is facing outward.
2) Install wheel, but do not tighten lug nuts completely. Tighten inner nut to specification while rotating wheel. See TORQUE SPECIFICATIONS table at end of article.
3) Install nut washer and outer nut. Ensure locating peg on inner nut is seated in one of washer holes before installing outer nut. Tighten outer nut to specification.
4) Install pressure spring. Install drive gear. Push gear inward, and install snap ring. Install dust cap. Remove wheel. Install caliper. Install wheels, and lower vehicle. Apply brakes until brake pedal is firm. Check brake fluid.

REAR BRAKE SHOES

Removal (Cherokee, Comanche, Wagoneer & Wrangler) - 1) Raise and support vehicle. Remove wheels and brake drum. Remove "U" clip and washer from parking brake lever pivot pin. Place Wheel Cylinder Clamp (J-8002) over wheel cylinder.
2) Remove primary and secondary shoe return springs, hold-down spring and retainers and pins. *See Fig. 11 or 12.* Remove self-adjuster lever, adjuster and adjuster spring from brake shoes.
3) Remove brake shoes. Disconnect parking brake cable from parking brake lever, and remove lever.

Installation - 1) Lubricate backing plate ledges, anchor pin, cable guide, self-adjuster screw assembly, parking brake lever and lever pivot pin with white lithium grease. *See Fig. 11 or 12.*
2) Connect parking brake lever to secondary brake shoe with washer and "U" clip. Crimp ends of clip to secure clip on pivot. Remove wheel cylinder clamp. Position brake shoes on brake support plate, and install hold-down springs.
3) Install parking brake lever strut and spring. Install cable guide plate and adjuster cable on anchor pin. Install primary return spring. Install guide to secondary brake shoe. Install secondary return spring.

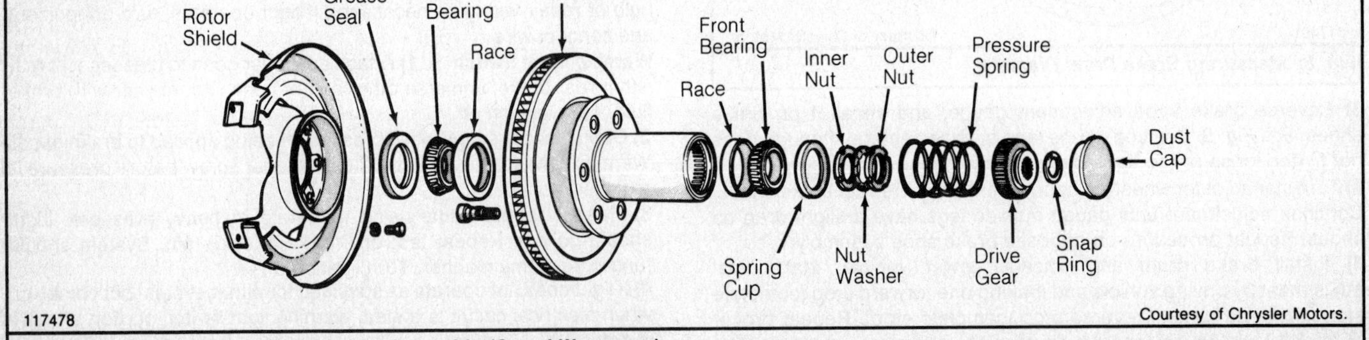
Rotor Shield
Grease Seal
Rear Bearing
Race
Rotor
Front Bearing
Race
Inner Nut
Outer Nut
Pressure Spring
Dust Cap
Spring Cup
Nut Washer
Drive Gear
Snap Ring
117478
Courtesy of Chrysler Motors.

Fig. 10: Exploded View of Rotor & Hub Assembly (Grand Wagoneer)

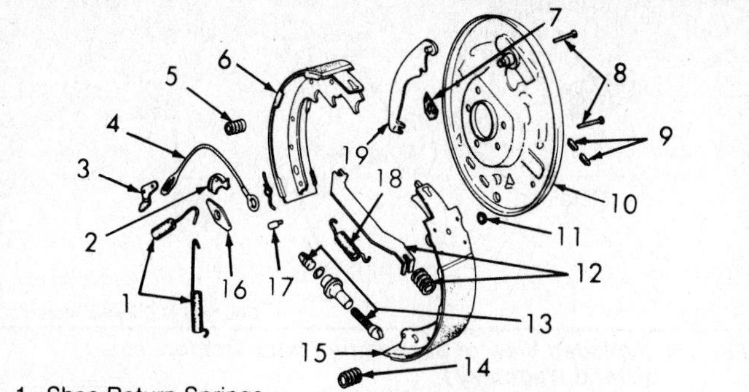

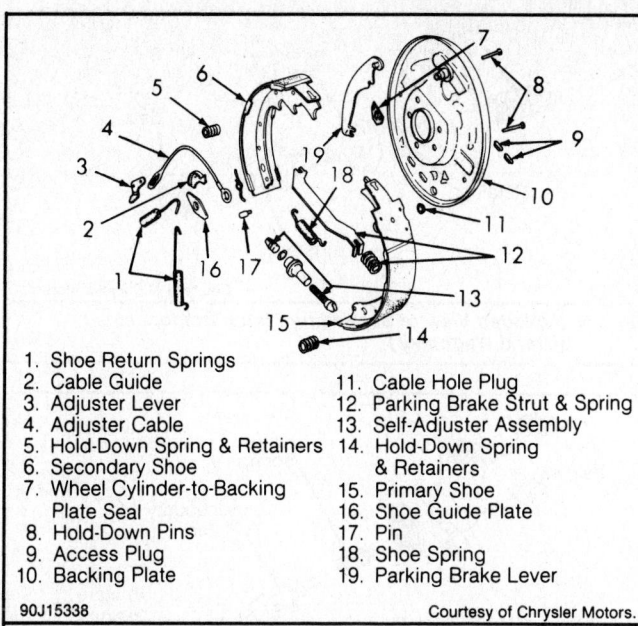

1. Shoe Return Springs
2. Cable Guide
3. Adjuster Lever
4. Adjuster Cable
5. Hold-Down Spring & Retainers
6. Secondary Shoe
7. Wheel Cylinder-to-Backing Plate Seal
8. Hold-Down Pins
9. Access Plug
10. Backing Plate
11. Cable Hole Plug
12. Parking Brake Strut & Spring
13. Self-Adjuster Assembly
14. Hold-Down Spring & Retainers
15. Primary Shoe
16. Shoe Guide Plate
17. Pin
18. Shoe Spring
19. Parking Brake Lever

90J15338 Courtesy of Chrysler Motors.

Fig. 11: Exploded View of Rear Drum Brake Assembly (Except Grand Wagoneer & Comanche W/Heavy-Duty Susp.)

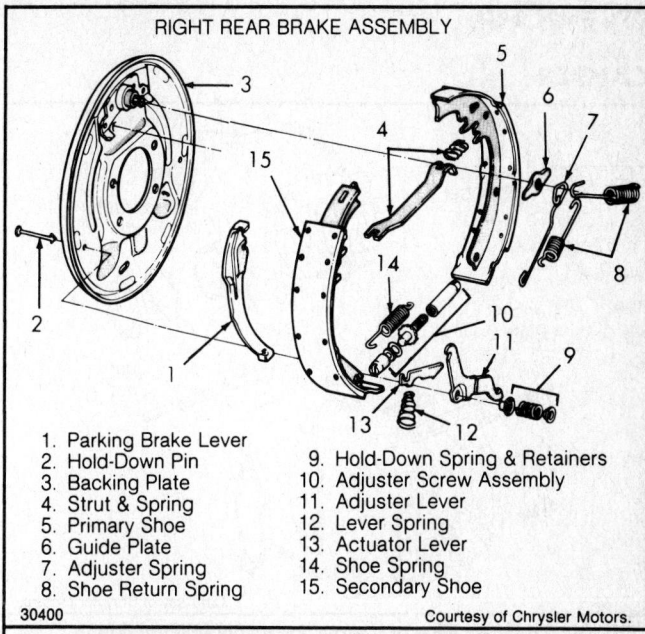

RIGHT REAR BRAKE ASSEMBLY

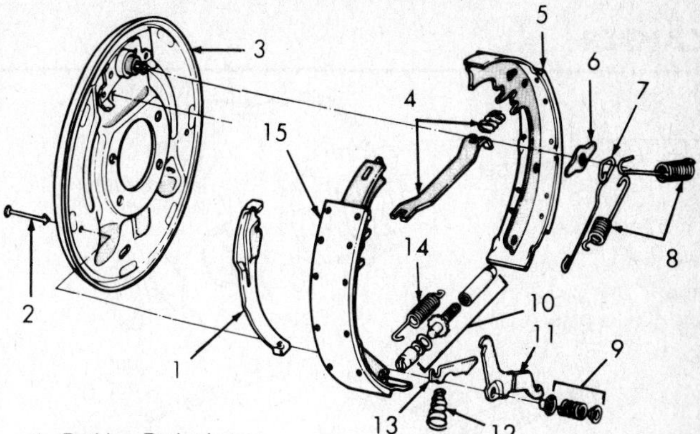

1. Parking Brake Lever
2. Hold-Down Pin
3. Backing Plate
4. Strut & Spring
5. Primary Shoe
6. Guide Plate
7. Adjuster Spring
8. Shoe Return Spring
9. Hold-Down Spring & Retainers
10. Adjuster Screw Assembly
11. Adjuster Lever
12. Lever Spring
13. Actuator Lever
14. Shoe Spring
15. Secondary Shoe

30400 Courtesy of Chrysler Motors.

Fig. 13: Exploded View of Rear Drum Brake Assembly (Grand Wagoneer)

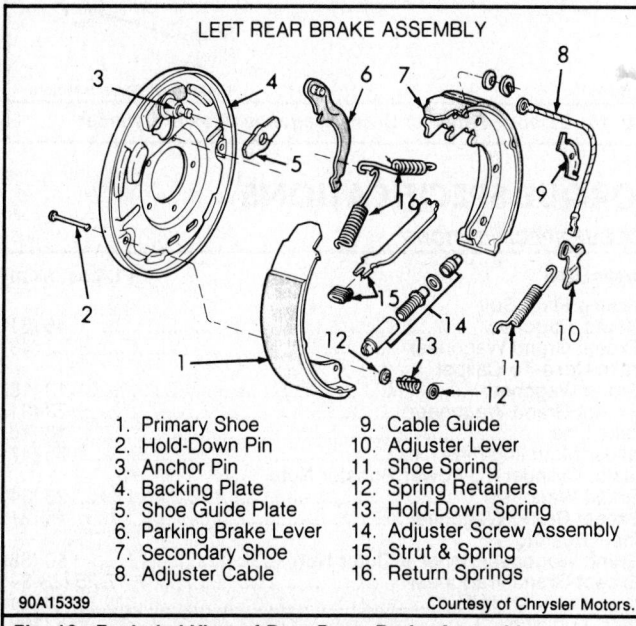

LEFT REAR BRAKE ASSEMBLY

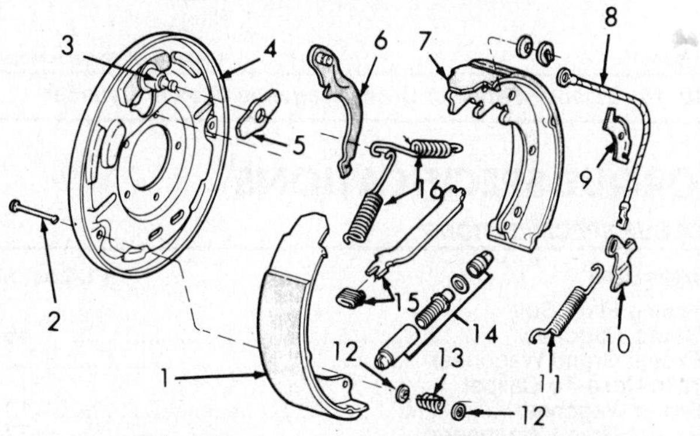

1. Primary Shoe
2. Hold-Down Pin
3. Anchor Pin
4. Backing Plate
5. Shoe Guide Plate
6. Parking Brake Lever
7. Secondary Shoe
8. Adjuster Cable
9. Cable Guide
10. Adjuster Lever
11. Shoe Spring
12. Spring Retainers
13. Hold-Down Spring
14. Adjuster Screw Assembly
15. Strut & Spring
16. Return Springs

90A15339 Courtesy of Chrysler Motors.

Fig. 12: Exploded View of Rear Drum Brake Assembly (Comanche W/Heavy-Duty Suspension)

4) Install adjuster screw, spring and lever. Connect lever to cable. Using Brake Shoe Adjustment Gauge (J-21177-01), preset brake shoe adjustment. See REAR BRAKE SHOES under ADJUSTMENTS. Install brake drums. Install wheels, and lower vehicle. Check brake fluid. Road test vehicle.

Removal (Grand Wagoneer) - 1) Raise and support vehicle. Remove wheels. Remove primary shoe return spring, automatic adjuster actuator spring and secondary shoe return spring. Remove hold-down springs and retainers. Remove brake shoes. *See Fig. 13.*

2) Disengage parking brake cable from parking brake lever. Remove parking brake strut and brake shoe assembly as a unit. Place wheel cylinder clamps over cylinders to retain pistons.

3) Inspect automatic self-adjuster lever and pivot, actuating lever, parking brake lever, self-adjuster and springs. Replace weak springs, bent levers and worn or broken parts.

Installation - 1) Clean support plate. Apply a thin film of white lithium grease to support plate ledges, anchor pin, adjuster screw threads and pivot.

2) Apply grease to adjuster lever-to-secondary brake shoe contact surface, parking brake lever pivot and portion of lever contacting secondary brake shoe.

3) Attach parking brake cable to parking brake lever on secondary shoe. Install secondary brake shoe, automatic adjuster lever and lever pivot as an assembly.

4) Install brake shoe hold-down spring. Install return spring on actuating lever tang. Large end of tapered spring should rest on brake shoe.

5) Install primary shoe and hold-down spring. Install guide plate on anchor pin. Install parking brake strut and spring on brake shoes.

6) Install adjusting screw and spring. Short end of hooked spring attaches to primary brake shoe. Long hooked end attaches to secondary brake shoe.

7) Install secondary shoe return spring, adjuster spring and primary return spring. Adjust brakes. See REAR BRAKE SHOES under ADJUSTMENTS.

8) Install drums and wheels. Lower vehicle. Check brake fluid. Road test vehicle.

1991 BRAKES
Disc & Drum (Cont.)

OVERHAUL

CALIPER

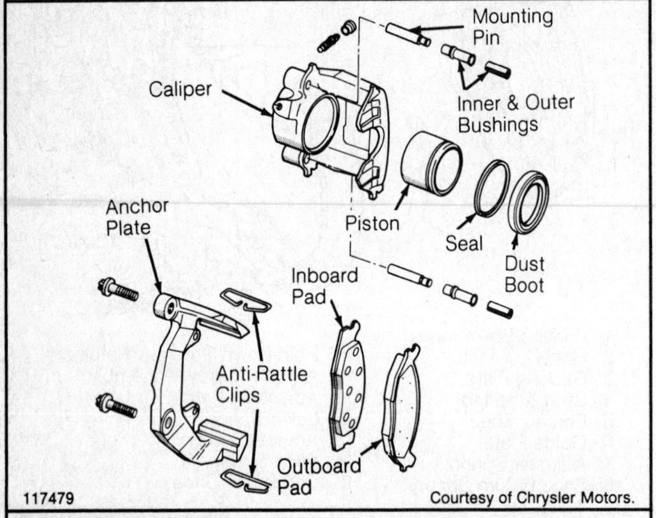
Mounting
Pin
Caliper
Inner & Outer
Bushings
Anchor
Plate
Piston
Seal
Dust
Boot
Inboard
Pad
Anti-Rattle
Clips
Outboard
Pad
117479
Courtesy of Chrysler Motors.

Fig. 14: Exploded View of Caliper Assembly (Except Grand Wagoneer)

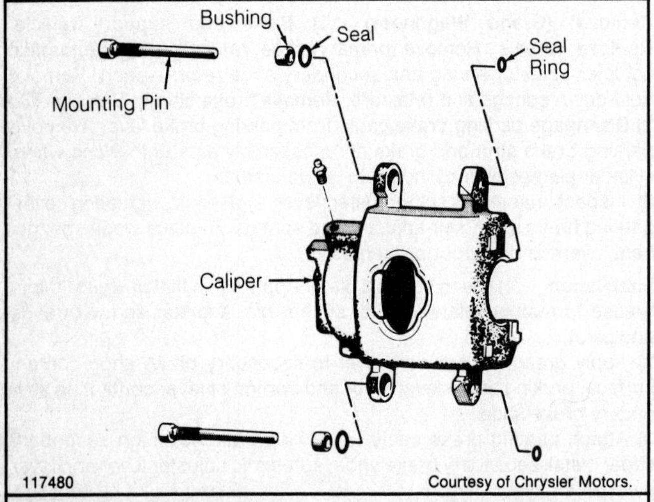
Bushing
Seal
Seal
Ring
Mounting Pin
Caliper
117480
Courtesy of Chrysler Motors.

Fig. 15: Exploded View of Caliper Assembly (Grand Wagoneer)

MASTER CYLINDER

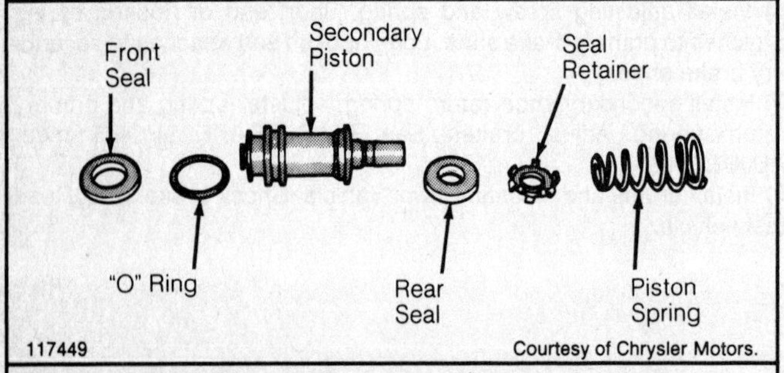
Front
Seal
Secondary
Piston
Seal
Retainer
"O" Ring
Rear
Seal
Piston
Spring
117449
Courtesy of Chrysler Motors.

Fig. 16: Exploded View of Secondary Piston Components (Except Grand Wagoneer)

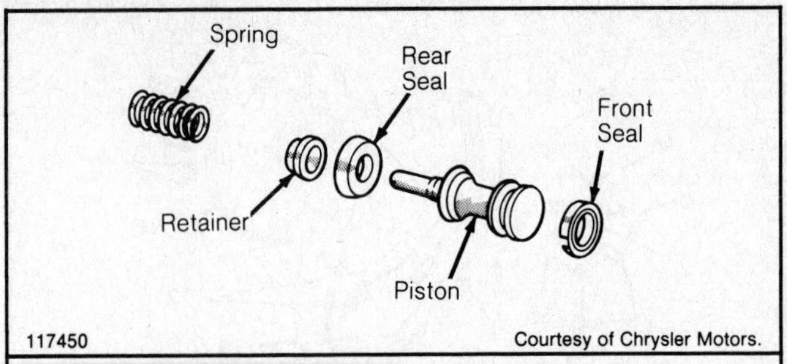
Spring
Rear
Seal
Front
Seal
Retainer
Piston
117450
Courtesy of Chrysler Motors.

Fig. 17: Exploded View of Secondary Piston Components (Grand Wagoneer)

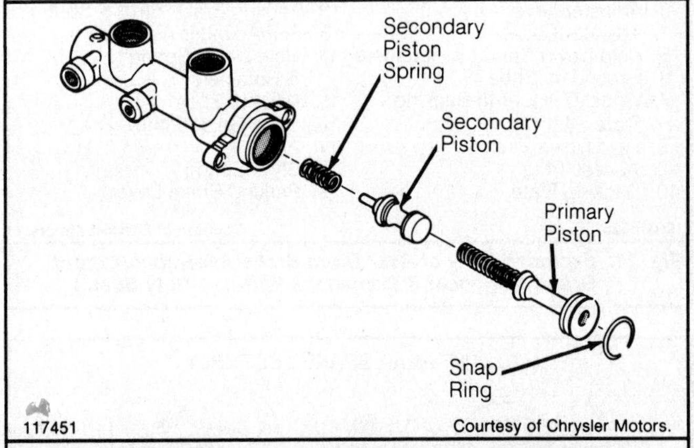
Secondary
Piston
Spring
Secondary
Piston
Primary
Piston
Snap
Ring
117451
Courtesy of Chrysler Motors.

Fig. 18: Exploded View of Grand Wagoneer Master Cylinder

TORQUE SPECIFICATIONS

TORQUE SPECIFICATIONS

Application	Ft. Lbs. (N.m)
Backing Plate Bolt	
Grand Wagoneer	45 (61)
Except Grand Wagoneer	32 (43)
Brake Hose-To-Caliper	
Grand Wagoneer	13 (18)
Except Grand Wagoneer	23 (31)
Brake Line	13 (18)
Caliper Mounting Pins	35 (47)
Master Cylinder-To-Power Booster Nuts	
Grand Wagoneer	25 (34)
Except Grand Wagoneer	15 (21)
Wheel Bearing	
Grand Wagoneer (Inner & Outer Nut)	[1] 50 (68)
Except Grand Wagoneer	[2] 17-25 (23-34)
Wheel Cylinder Bolts	18 (24)
Wheel Lug Nuts	75 (102)
	INCH Lbs. (N.m)
Brake Line-To-Master Cylinder	180 (20)

[1] – Tighten bearing nut while rotating wheel. Loosen inner nut 1/6 of a turn.
[2] – Tighten bearing nut while rotating wheel. Loosen nut 1/2 turn, and retighten to 19 INCH lbs. (2 N.m).

DISC BRAKE SPECIFICATIONS

DISC BRAKE ROTOR SPECIFICATIONS

Application	In. (mm)
Disc Diameter	
Grand Wagoneer	12.00 (304.8)
Except Grand Wagoneer	11.02 (279.9)
Lateral Runout	.005 (.13)
Parallelism	.0005 (.013)
Original Thickness	[1]
Minimum Refinish Thickness	
Cherokee & Comanche	
2WD	.86 (22)
4WD	.89 (23)
Grand Wagoneer	1.22 (31)
Wrangler	.89 (23)

[1] – Information is not available from manufacturer.

DRUM BRAKE SPECIFICATIONS

DRUM BRAKE SPECIFICATIONS

Application	In. (mm)
Drum Diameter	
Cherokee, Comanche & Wrangler	9.00 (228.6)
Cherokee W/Heavy Duty Suspension	10.00 (254.0)
Grand Wagoneer	11.00 (279.4)
Drum Width	[1]
Maximum Drum Refinish Diameter	
Cherokee, Comanche & Wrangler	9.05 (230.0)
Cherokee W/Heavy Duty Suspension	10.06 (255.5)
Grand Wagoneer	11.06 (280.9)
Wheel Cylinder Diameter	[1]
Master Cylinder Diameter	[1]

[1] – Information is not available from manufacturer.

1991 WHEEL ALIGNMENT Specifications & Procedures

Cherokee, Comanche, Grand Wagoneer, Wrangler

RIDING HEIGHT ADJUSTMENT

NOTE: On vehicles with electronic chassis controls, all systems should be functional before attempting riding height or wheel alignment adjustment.

Before adjusting alignment, check riding height. Riding height must be checked with vehicle on level floor and tires properly inflated. Bounce vehicle several times and allow suspension to settle. Visually inspect vehicle for signs of abnormal height from front to rear or side to side. Check passenger and luggage compartments for extra heavy items and remove if present. If riding height difference from side to side is more than 1" (25.4 mm), check all suspension components and repair or replace as necessary.

JACKING & HOISTING

FLOOR JACK

Vehicle may be raised by positioning jack under front or rear frame rails. *See Fig. 1.*

NOTE: Use sub-frame rail lift points to hoist vehicle. Never raise vehicle with jack under axle tubes, body side sills, steering linkage components, propeller shafts, engine/transmission oil pans, fuel tank or front suspension arms.

EMERGENCY JACKING

Cherokee & Comanche – Park vehicle on a firm, level surface. Block tire diagonally opposite tire being changed. Place automatic transmission in Park, manual transmission in Reverse. Set parking brake. Position emergency jack under front or rear axle housing. Raise vehicle.

Grand Wagoneer – Park vehicle on a firm, level surface. Block tire diagonally opposite tire being changed. Place automatic transmission in Park and set parking brake. Position emergency (bumper) jack base plate in line with bumper. Move lug wrench up and down to raise vehicle.

Wrangler – Park vehicle on a firm, level surface. Block tire diagonally opposite tire being changed. Place automatic transmission in Park, manual transmission in Reverse. Set parking brake. Position emergency jack under front or rear axle housing "U" bolts. Raise vehicle.

LIFTING VEHICLE WITH HOIST

Vehicle may be raised on single or twin-post swiveling arm, or ramp-type drive hoists. If using swiveling arm hoist, ensure lifting pads are positioned evenly at sub-frame lift points. *See Fig. 1.* All hoists should be equipped with proper adapters to support vehicle at frame rails only.

WHEEL ALIGNMENT PROCEDURES

CAMBER MEASUREMENT

Check camber to determine if any components are bent or damaged. If camber angle is not to specification, components causing the problem must be replaced. See ALIGNMENT SPECIFICATIONS at end of article. Camber is NOT adjustable.

CASTER ADJUSTMENT

Check caster angle. See ALIGNMENT SPECIFICATIONS at end of article. If caster is not to specifications, adjust by adding or removing shims at rear of lower control arms on Cherokee and Comanche, or between front axle pads and spring brackets on Grand Wagoneer and Wrangler. *See Fig. 2 or 3.*

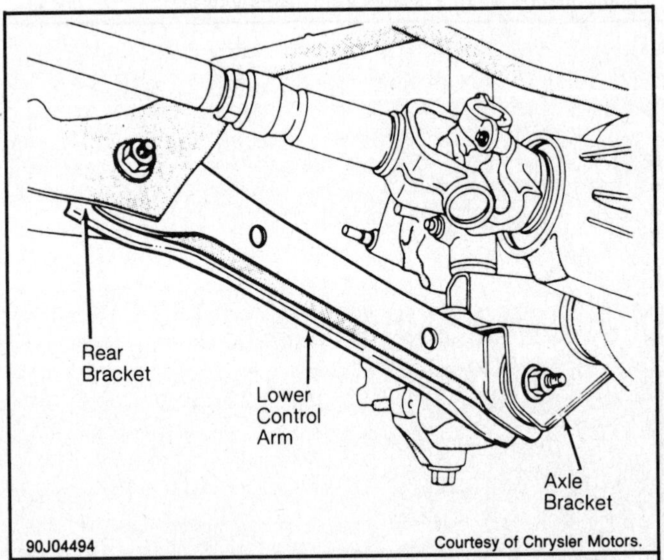
Rear
Bracket
Lower
Control
Arm
Axle
Bracket
90J04494
Courtesy of Chrysler Motors.

Fig. 2: Identifying Lower Control Arm (Cherokee & Comanche)

NOTE: On 4WD vehicles, shim adjustment will change caster angle and front drive shaft angle. If both angles cannot be adjusted to specifications, drive shaft angle has priority and should be adjusted for its specified angle. See appropriate article in DRIVE AXLES.

TOE-IN ADJUSTMENT

Cherokee & Comanche – **1)** Center front wheels straight ahead. Measure toe and compare to specifications. See ALIGNMENT SPECIFICATIONS at end of article.

2) Center steering wheel by counting the turns required to hit left and right steering stops. Center steering wheel mid-way between stops. Loosen drag link adjustment sleeve clamp bolts. *See Fig. 4.*

3) Rotate sleeve to adjust right wheel toe to specification. Position clamp bolts so threaded bolt ends face upward and to rear of vehicle.

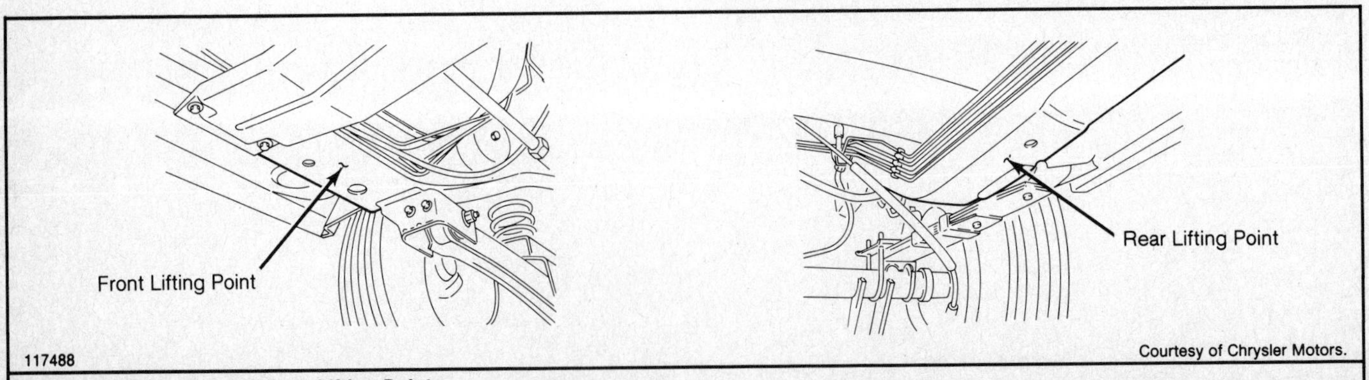
Front Lifting Point
Rear Lifting Point
117488
Courtesy of Chrysler Motors.

Fig. 1: Identifying Front & Rear Lifting Points

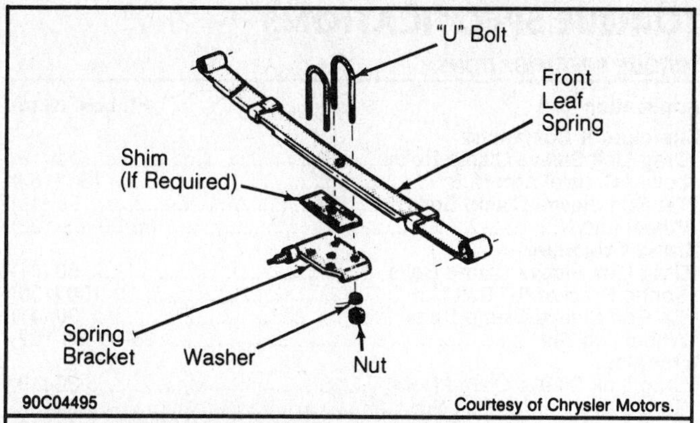
"U" Bolt
Front Leaf Spring
Shim (If Required)
Spring Bracket
Washer
Nut
90C04495
Courtesy of Chrysler Motors.

Fig. 3: Identifying Front Leaf Spring Bracket (Grand Wagoneer & Wrangler)

Tighten drag link sleeve bolts to specification. See TORQUE SPECIFICATIONS table at end of article.

4) Loosen clamp bolts at each end of tie rod. Rotate tie rod to adjust left wheel to toe specification. See ALIGNMENT SPECIFICATIONS at end of article. When adjustment is complete, position sleeve as described earlier and tighten to specifications. See TORQUE SPECIFICATIONS table at end of article.

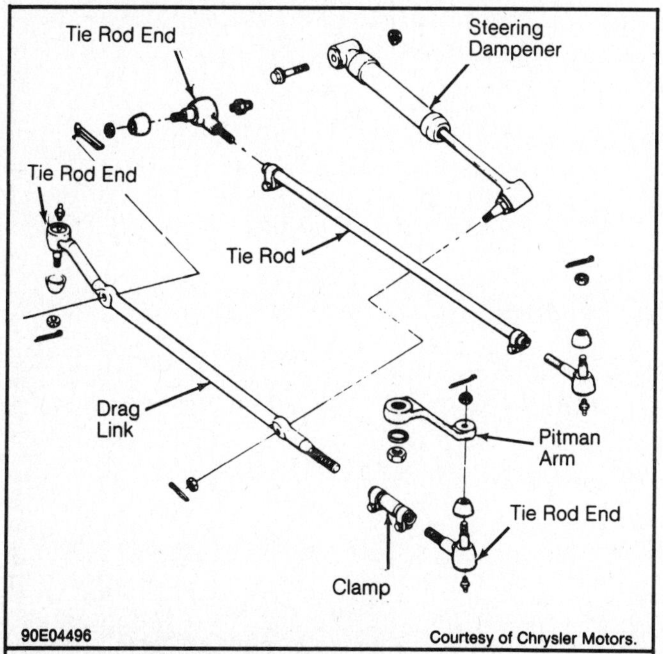
Tie Rod End
Steering Dampener
Tie Rod End
Tie Rod
Drag Link
Pitman Arm
Tie Rod End
Clamp
90E04496
Courtesy of Chrysler Motors.

Fig. 4: Exploded View of Steering Linkage (Cherokee & Comanche)

Grand Wagoneer & Wrangler – 1) Center front wheels straight ahead and lock steering wheel in centered position. Measure toe and compare to specifications. See ALIGNMENT SPECIFICATIONS at end of article.

2) Loosen tie rod adjustment sleeve clamp bolts. *See Fig. 5 or 6.* Rotate sleeve to adjust toe to specification. See ALIGNMENT SPECIFICATIONS at end of article. After adjustment, position clamp bolts so threaded ends face rearward and are angled upward. Tighten sleeve clamp to specification. See TORQUE SPECIFICATIONS table at end of article.

3) If necessary, steering wheel can be centered by adjusting the drag link adjustment sleeve. When adjustment is complete, position sleeve as described earlier and tighten to specifications. See TORQUE SPECIFICATIONS table at end of article.

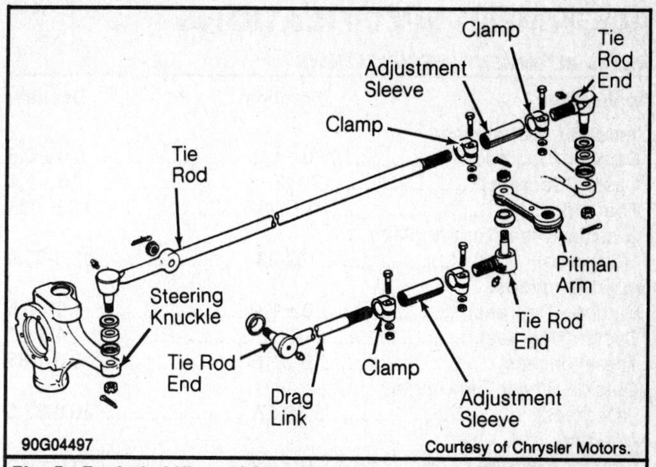
Clamp
Tie Rod End
Adjustment Sleeve
Clamp
Tie Rod
Pitman Arm
Steering Knuckle
Tie Rod End
Tie Rod End
Clamp
Drag Link
Adjustment Sleeve
90G04497
Courtesy of Chrysler Motors.

Fig. 5: Exploded View of Steering Linkage (Grand Wagoneer)

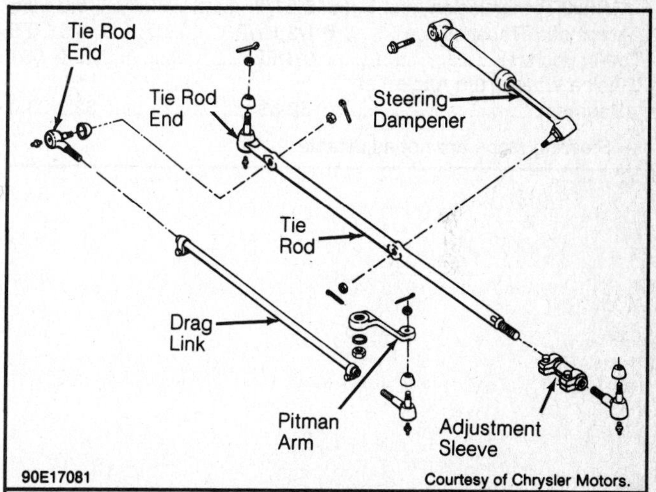
Tie Rod End
Tie Rod End
Steering Dampener
Tie Rod
Drag Link
Pitman Arm
Adjustment Sleeve
90E17081
Courtesy of Chrysler Motors.

Fig. 6: Exploded View of Steering Linkage (Wrangler)

TURNING ANGLE ADJUSTMENT

Grand Wagoneer – Check outside wheel turning angle and compare to specifications. See ALIGNMENT SPECIFICATIONS at end of article. To adjust, loosen lock nuts on turning angle adjustment screws. Turning angle adjustment screws are located at rear of each steering knuckle. Using a turntable to measure angle, adjust screws to obtain correct outside turning angle for each wheel. Tighten adjustment screw lock nuts.

1991 WHEEL ALIGNMENT Specifications & Procedures (Cont.)

ALIGNMENT SPECIFICATIONS

WHEEL ALIGNMENT SPECIFICATIONS

Application	Fraction	Decimal
Cherokee & Comanche		
Camber (Degrees)	0±1/2	0.0±0.5
Caster (Degrees)	7 1/2±1	7.5±1.0
Toe-In (Inches)	0±1/32	0.0±.031
Outside Wheel Turn Angle [1] (Degrees)	32-33	32.0-33.0
Grand Wagoneer		
Camber (Degrees)	0±1/2	0.0±0.5
Caster (Degrees)	4±1	4.0±1
Toe-In (Inches)	0-3/16	0.0-.188
Outside Wheel Turn Angle [1] (Degrees)	36-37	36.0-37.0
Wrangler		
Camber (Degrees)	0±1/2	0.0±0.5
Caster (Degrees)		
Manual Transmission	8±1/2	8.0±0.5
Automatic Transmission	6 1/2±1/2	6.5±0.5
Toe-In (Inches)	0-1/32	0.0-.031
Outside Wheel Turn Angle [1] (Degrees)	32-33	32.0-33.0

[1] – Steering stops are not adjustable.

TORQUE SPECIFICATIONS

TORQUE SPECIFICATIONS

Application	Ft. Lbs. (N.m)
Cherokee & Comanche	
Drag Link Sleeve Clamp Bolts	14 (19)
Lower Control Arm Nuts	133 (180)
Tie Rod Sleeve Clamp Bolts	36 (49)
Wheel Lug Nut	65-90 (88-122)
Grand Wagoneer	
Drag Link Sleeve Clamp Bolts	30 (41)
Spring Bracket "U" Bolt Nut	100 (136)
Tie Rod Sleeve Clamp Bolts	30 (41)
Wheel Lug Nut	65-90 (88-122)
Wrangler	
Drag Link Sleeve Clamp Bolts	36 (49)
Spring Bracket "U" Bolt Nut	90 (122)
Tie Rod Sleeve Clamp Bolts	14 (19)
Wheel Lug Nut	65-90 (88-122)

1991 SUSPENSION
Front

Cherokee, Comanche
Grand Wagoneer, Wrangler

DESCRIPTION

Cherokee and Comanche front suspensions consist of axle, 2 coil springs, track bar, stabilizer bar and upper and lower control arms. Track bar is used to minimize front axle side-to-side movement. Stabilizer bar and shock absorbers control suspension spring movement.

Grand Wagoneer and Wrangler models use leaf spring front suspension with shock absorbers, stabilizer bar and a track bar.

ADJUSTMENTS & INSPECTION

WHEEL ALIGNMENT SPECIFICATIONS & PROCEDURES

***NOTE:** See SPECIFICATIONS & PROCEDURES article in WHEEL ALIGNMENT*

WHEEL BEARING

***NOTE:** Wheel bearings on Cherokee, Comanche and Wrangler 4WD models are nonadjustable. If wheel bearings require service, see WHEEL BEARINGS under REMOVAL & INSTALLATION.*

2WD Models (Cherokee & Comanche) – 1) Raise and support vehicle. Turn wheel by hand while placing fingers of free hand on rotor shield. If any roughness is detected proceed to WHEEL BEARING under REMOVAL & INSTALLATION. Remove wheel and tire assembly.

2) Remove hub dust cap, cotter pin and nut retainer. Ensure bearings are thoroughly packed with lithium grease. Rotate hub and rotor assembly by hand, tighten retainer nut to 21 ft. lbs. (29 N.m) to seat bearings.

3) Loosen retainer nut 1/2 turn while rotating hub. Then retighten nut to 19 INCH lbs. (2 N.m). Install nut retainer and new cotter pin. Clean hub dust cap and coat inside with clean grease. Reverse removal procedure for remaining components.

4WD Models (Grand Wagoneer) – 1) Raise and support vehicle, remove wheel/tire assembly. Remove dust cover and drive gear snap ring. *See Fig. 1.* Remove drive gear, pressure spring and spring cup.

2) Remove outer lock nut using Spanner Wrench (J-6893D). Remove lock washer. Using spanner wrench, loosen inner lock nut and then tighten inner lock nut to 50 ft. lbs. (68 N.m) while rotating wheel.

3) Back off inner lock nut 55-65 degrees (1/6 of a turn) while rotating wheel. Install washer so that hole in washer is aligned with pin on inner lock nut. Install outer lock nut and tighten to 50 ft. lbs. (68 N.m). Reverse removal procedure to complete installation.

***CAUTION:** Ensure spring cup is installed with the recessed side toward the bearing and flat side facing the pressure spring.*

REMOVAL & INSTALLATION

WHEEL BEARINGS

Removal (2WD Models) – 1) Raise and support vehicle. Remove wheel assembly. Remove brake caliper and suspend caliper with wire. DO NOT allow caliper to hang on brake hose.

2) Remove hub dust cap, cotter pin, nut retainer, retainer nut, washer and outer wheel bearing. *See Fig. 1.* Remove hub and rotor assembly. Pry grease seal from hub. Remove inner wheel bearing.

Inspection – Clean bearings and hub in solvent and dry with compressed air. Inspect bearings and races for wear.

Installation – To install, reverse removal procedure. Pack bearings with wheel bearing grease. Adjust wheel bearing. See WHEEL BEARING under ADJUSTMENTS.

Removal (4WD Grand Wagoneer) – 1) Raise and support vehicle. Remove wheel assembly. Remove brake caliper and suspend caliper with wire. DO NOT allow caliper to hang on brake hose. Remove rotor from hub.

2) Remove dust cover and drive gear retaining snap ring. *See Fig. 1.* Remove drive gear, pressure spring and spring cup. Using Spanner Wrench (J-6893D), remove outer lock nut, lock washer, inner lock nut and outer wheel bearing. Remove hub. Pry grease seal from hub. Remove inner wheel bearing. Remove bearing races if necessary.

Inspection – Clean bearings and hub in solvent and dry with compressed air. Inspect bearings and races for wear.

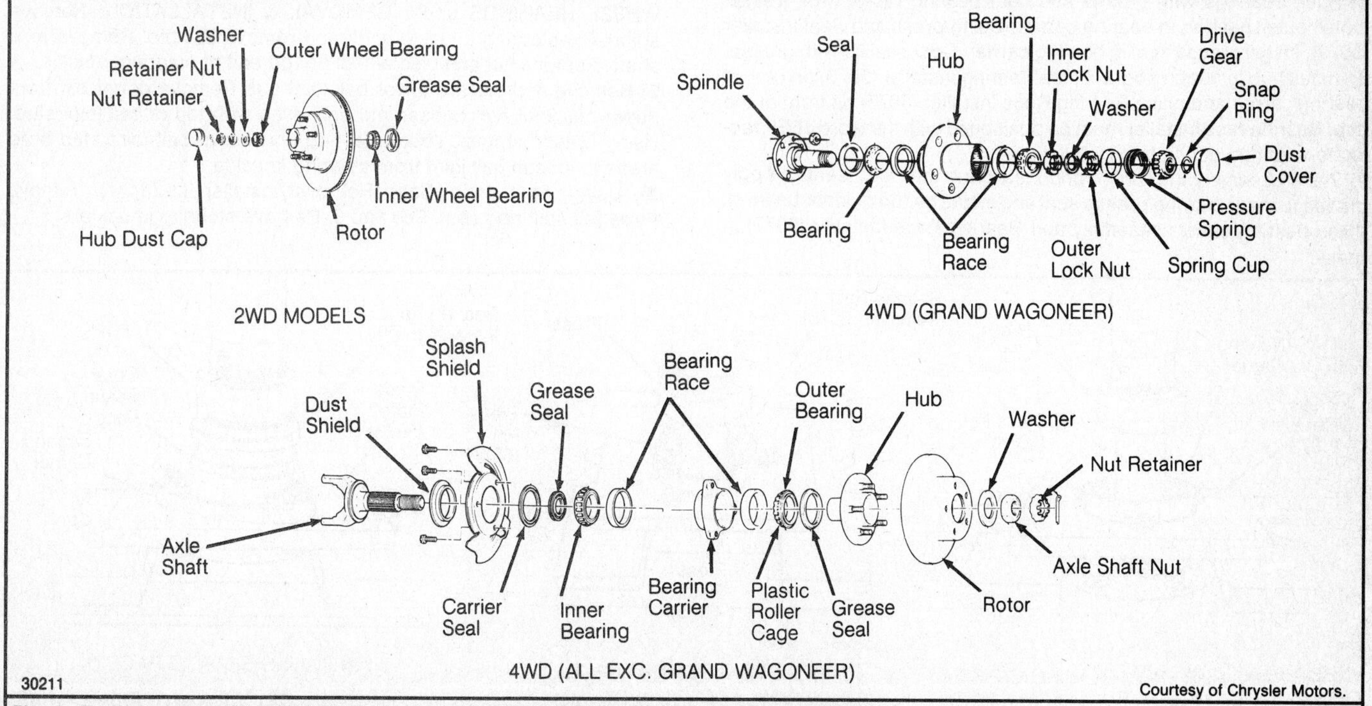
Washer
Retainer Nut
Nut Retainer
Outer Wheel Bearing
Grease Seal
Inner Wheel Bearing
Hub Dust Cap
Rotor
2WD MODELS
Spindle
Seal
Bearing
Hub
Inner
Lock Nut
Washer
Drive
Gear
Snap
Ring
Dust
Cover
Pressure
Spring
Spring Cup
Outer
Lock Nut
Bearing
Race
Bearing
4WD (GRAND WAGONEER)
Splash
Shield
Dust
Shield
Grease
Seal
Bearing
Race
Outer
Bearing
Hub
Washer
Nut Retainer
Axle
Shaft
Axle Shaft Nut
Carrier
Seal
Inner
Bearing
Bearing
Carrier
Plastic
Roller
Cage
Grease
Seal
Rotor
4WD (ALL EXC. GRAND WAGONEER)
30211
Courtesy of Chrysler Motors.

***Fig. 1:** Exploded View Of 2WD Hub/Rotor Assembly & 4WD Hub/Bearing Carrier Assembly*

1991 SUSPENSION
Front (Cont.)

Installation – To install, reverse removal procedure. Pack wheel bearings with grease. Adjust wheel bearings. See WHEEL BEARING under ADJUSTMENTS.

Removal (4WD Models Except Grand Wagoneer) – 1) Raise and support vehicle. Remove wheel assembly. Remove brake caliper and suspend caliper with wire. Remove cotter pin, nut retainer and axle shaft nut. Remove bearing carrier assembly from steering knuckle. *See Fig. 1.*

NOTE: Ball bearing-type front hub is not serviceable and must be replaced as a complete unit. Tapered roller bearing-type front hub is serviceable.

2) Inspect bearings for roughness. If bearing roughness exists, disassemble hub assembly. Install Press Plate (5073) to rear of bearing carrier. Press plate is bolted to bearing carrier. Position press plate and bearing carrier in hydraulic press.

3) Using Press Pin (5074), press hub from bearing carrier. *See Fig. 2.* If outer bearing is to be removed from hub, remove plastic roller cage from outer bearing and remove bearing rollers. *See Fig. 1.*

4) To remove bearing race from the hub, install bearing separator around bearing race. Using press and Press Pin (5074), press hub from bearing race. Remove carrier seal. *See Fig. 1.* Using Bearing Installer (5078), remove grease seal from bearing carrier.

CAUTION: Bearing installer must be positioned with the word JEEP facing toward bearing carrier during grease seal removal.

5) To remove bearing races from bearing carrier, install Press Plate (5073) to rear of bearing carrier. Press plate is bolted to bearing carrier. Position press plate and bearing carrier in hydraulic press.

6) Install Bearing Race Remover (5076) in bearing carrier between inner bearing races. Using Press Pin (5074) and press, remove inner bearing race from bearing carrier. *See Fig. 2.* Reverse components and remove outer bearing race.

Inspection – Clean bearings and hub in solvent and dry with compressed air. Inspect bearings and races for wear.

Installation – 1) Install bearing carrier on press plate. Using press and Bearing Race Installer (5077), install outer bearing race in bearing carrier. *See Fig. 2.* Bearing race should be positioned even with machined surface of bearing carrier. Repeat procedure on remaining bearing race.

2) Pack bearings with grease and coat bearing races with grease. Install outer bearing in bearing carrier. Using press and Seal Installer (5079), install grease seal in bearing carrier. Coat seal lip with grease.

3) Install hub in bearing bore. Place Bearing Installer (5078) on rear of bearing carrier and place Bearing Race Installer (5077) on front of the hub. Bearing race installer must be positioned with the word JEEP facing toward hub during hub installation.

4) Place assembly into press and install hub into the bearing. Apply grease to inner bearing grease seal and install on top of inner bearing. Place bearing carrier assembly and Bearing Race Installer (5077) in press.

5) Bearing race installer must be positioned against front of the hub. Bearing race installer must be positioned with the word JEEP toward hub during installation.

6) Place inner bearing and grease seal in bearing carrier. Using press and Seal Installer (5080), install bearing and grease seal in bearing carrier.

CAUTION: DO NOT apply excessive pressure while installing inner bearing. Final bearing preload is obtained with axle shaft nut. Ensure bearing carrier rotates smoothly and inner bearing seal seats evenly on bearing carrier.

7) Clean axle shaft and apply light coat of grease to axle shaft splines. Install dust shield and splash guard if removed. Install bearing carrier assembly.

8) Apply locking compound to bearing carrier bolts and tighten to specification. Install rotor and brake caliper. Install washer and axle nut. Tighten axle nut to specification. Install nut retainer and cotter key. Install remaining components.

NOTE: On Cherokee 4WD models with anti-lock brakes, wheel sensor clearance should be checked to provide proper brake operation. See ANTI-LOCK BRAKE WHEEL SPEED SENSOR under REMOVAL & INSTALLATION.

SHOCK ABSORBER

Removal & Installation (Grand Wagoneer) – Raise and support vehicle. Using jack, raise axle to relieve springs of axle weight. Remove upper shock absorber retaining nut and washer. Remove shock absorber-to-lower bracket bolt. Remove shock absorber and bushings. To install, reverse removal procedure.

Removal & Installation (Except Grand Wagoneer) – 1) With vehicle at normal riding height, remove nut, washer, and rubber grommet from top of shock absorber. Note component location for reassembly reference.

2) Raise and support vehicle. Remove lower shock mounting bolts from axle housing bracket. Remove shock absorber. Inspect units for damage or leakage. To install, reverse removal procedure.

STEERING KNUCKLE

Removal (Grand Wagoneer) – 1) Remove hub assembly. See WHEEL BEARINGS under REMOVAL & INSTALLATION. Remove spindle-to-steering knuckle bolts and remove spindle. Remove axle shaft. Remove nut and disconnect tie rod end at steering knuckle.

2) Remove and discard lower ball joint nut. Remove cotter pin from upper ball joint nut. Loosen nut until even with top of ball joint stud. Using brass hammer, strike steering knuckle at ball joint stud bore areas to loosen ball joint from steering knuckle.

3) Using Split Ring Seat Remover/Installer (J-23447), remove threaded split ring seat. *See Fig. 3.* Remove steering knuckle.

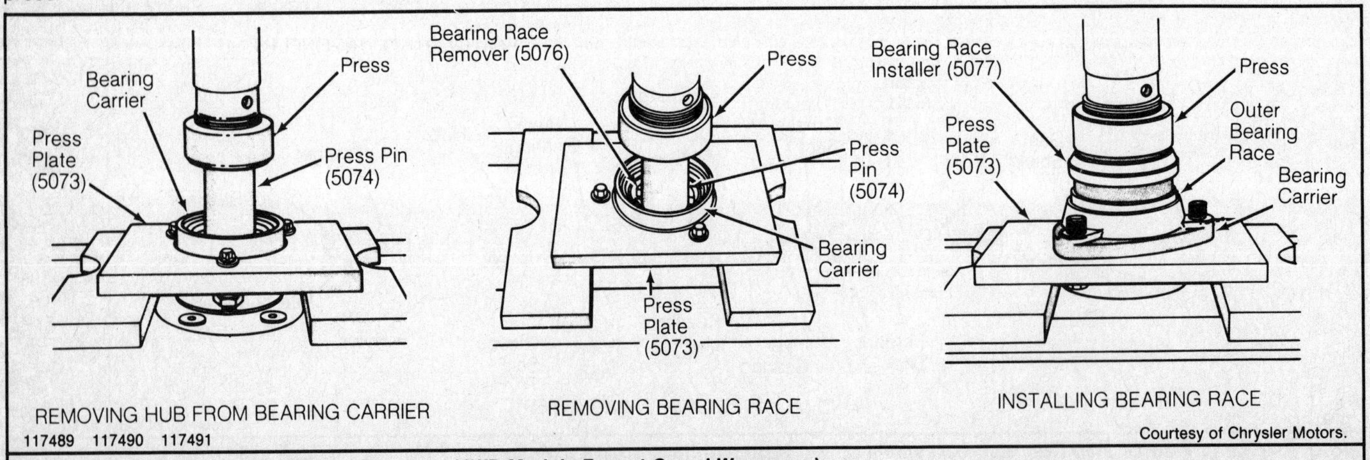
Bearing Carrier
Press
Press Plate (5073)
Press Pin (5074)
Bearing Race Remover (5076)
Press
Press Pin (5074)
Bearing Carrier
Press Plate (5073)
Bearing Race Installer (5077)
Press
Press Plate (5073)
Outer Bearing Race
Bearing Carrier
REMOVING HUB FROM BEARING CARRIER
REMOVING BEARING RACE
INSTALLING BEARING RACE
117489 117490 117491
Courtesy of Chrysler Motors.

Fig. 2: Removing & Installing Wheel Bearings (4WD Models Except Grand Wagoneer)

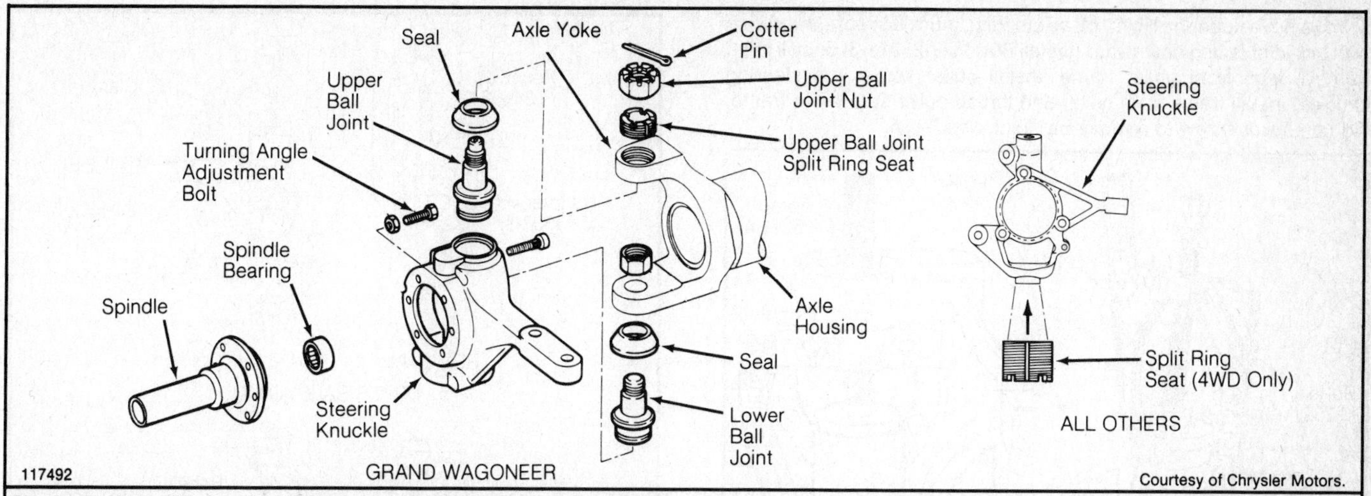
Seal
Axle Yoke
Cotter Pin
Upper Ball Joint
Upper Ball Joint Nut
Steering Knuckle
Turning Angle Adjustment Bolt
Upper Ball Joint Split Ring Seat
Spindle Bearing
Spindle
Axle Housing
Seal
Split Ring Seat (4WD Only)
Steering Knuckle
Lower Ball Joint
ALL OTHERS
117492
GRAND WAGONEER
Courtesy of Chrysler Motors.

Fig. 3: Exploded View of Steering Knuckle & Split Ring Seat (All Models)

Installation - 1) Install steering knuckle on lower ball joint stud. Install lower ball joint nut hand tight only. Tip upper steering ball joint stud into upper axle yoke. Install threaded split ring seat in axle yoke until top of split ring seat is even with axle yoke top surface.

2) Install Nut Adapter (J-23447), Button (J-25211-3) and Plate (J-25211-1) and puller on upper portion of steering knuckle. Tighten puller until lower ball joint is fully seated. *See Fig. 4.* Tighten lower ball joint nut to specification. See TORQUE SPECIFICATIONS table at end of article.

NOTE: If cotter pin holes do not align, TIGHTEN ball joint nut only. DO NOT loosen.

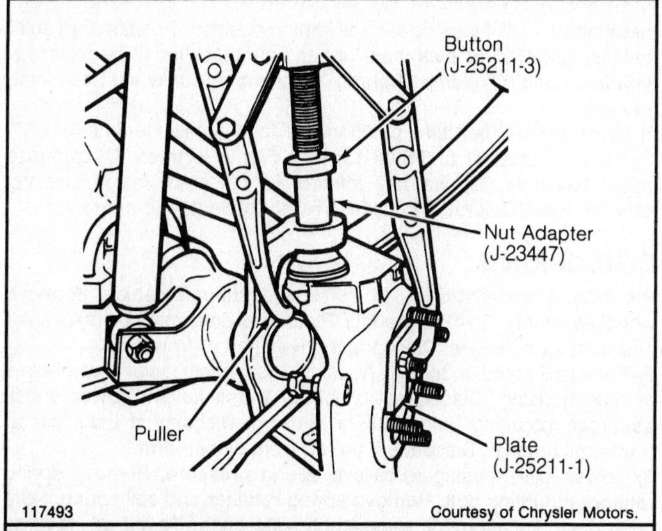
Button (J-25211-3)
Nut Adapter (J-23447)
Puller
Plate (J-25211-1)
117493
Courtesy of Chrysler Motors.

Fig. 4: Installing Steering Knuckle (Grand Wagoneer)

3) Remove puller and plate. Tighten upper ball joint split-ring seat to specification using Remover/Installer (J-23447). Tighten upper ball joint nut to specification.

4) To install remaining components, reverse removal procedure. Adjust wheel bearings. See WHEEL BEARING under ADJUSTMENTS.

Removal (Except Grand Wagoneer) - 1) Remove hub and bearing assembly and splash shield. See WHEEL BEARINGS under REMOVAL & INSTALLATION.

2) On Cherokee 4WD models, note anti-lock wheel speed sensor wire routing for installation purposes. Clean area around sensor to prevent damage during removal. Remove wheel speed sensor from knuckle.

3) On all models, remove anchor plate from steering knuckle. On each steering knuckle, remove ball joint stud cotter pin and retaining nuts. Using brass hammer, strike steering knuckle at ball joint stud bore area to loosen ball joint from steering knuckle.

Installation - To install, reverse removal procedure. On Cherokee 4WD models with anti-lock wheel speed sensor, check sensor air gap. See ANTI-LOCK BRAKE WHEEL SPEED SENSOR.

ANTI-LOCK BRAKE WHEEL SPEED SENSOR

Removal & Installation (Cherokee 4WD) - 1) Raise and support front of vehicle. Note sensor wire routing for installation purposes. Clean area around sensor to prevent damage during removal. Remove wheel speed sensor from steering knuckle. Unseat sensor wire retaining grommet.

2) Inside engine compartment, unplug sensor connector from anti-lock harness connector. Remove sensor. To install, reverse removal procedure. If polyethylene spacer strip is damaged or missing from wheel sensor, remove strip. *See Fig. 5.* Clean sensor.

3) Adjust air gap, between sensor and tone wheel to .013-.019" (.33-.48 mm) using a brass feeler gauge. If spacer strip is attached, adjust sensor so spacer strip just contacts tone wheel and tighten retaining bolt.

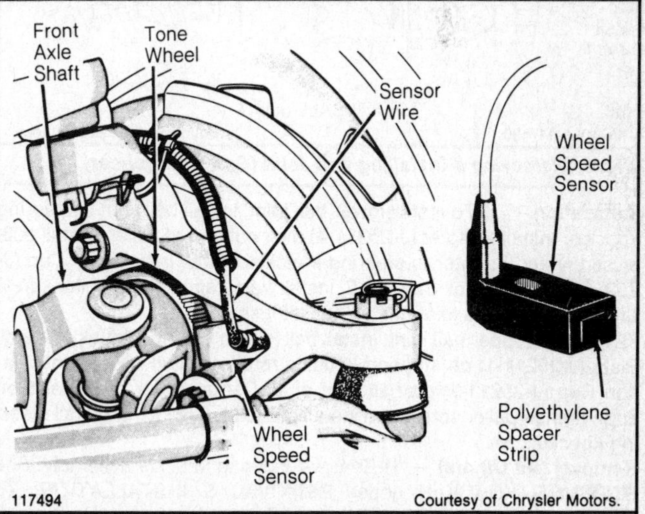
Front Axle Shaft
Tone Wheel
Sensor Wire
Wheel Speed Sensor
Wheel Speed Sensor
Polyethylene Spacer Strip
117494
Courtesy of Chrysler Motors.

Fig. 5: Locating Anti-Lock Brake Wheel Speed Sensor

UPPER & LOWER BALL JOINTS

Removal (Grand Wagoneer) - 1) Remove steering knuckle assembly. See STEERING KNUCKLE under REMOVAL & INSTALLATION.

2) To remove lower ball joint, remove snap ring from ball joint. Place steering knuckle in soft-jawed vise with ball joint facing downward. Install Plate (J-25211-1) on steering knuckle retaining studs.

1991 SUSPENSION
Front (Cont.)

3) To remove upper ball joint, place steering knuckle in soft-jawed vise with ball joint facing downward. Install Button (J-25211-3) on ball joint. Remove legs from puller frame. Install puller screw into steering knuckle. Install frame from puller and thread puller screw into frame. Tighten puller screw to remove ball joint. *See Fig. 6.*

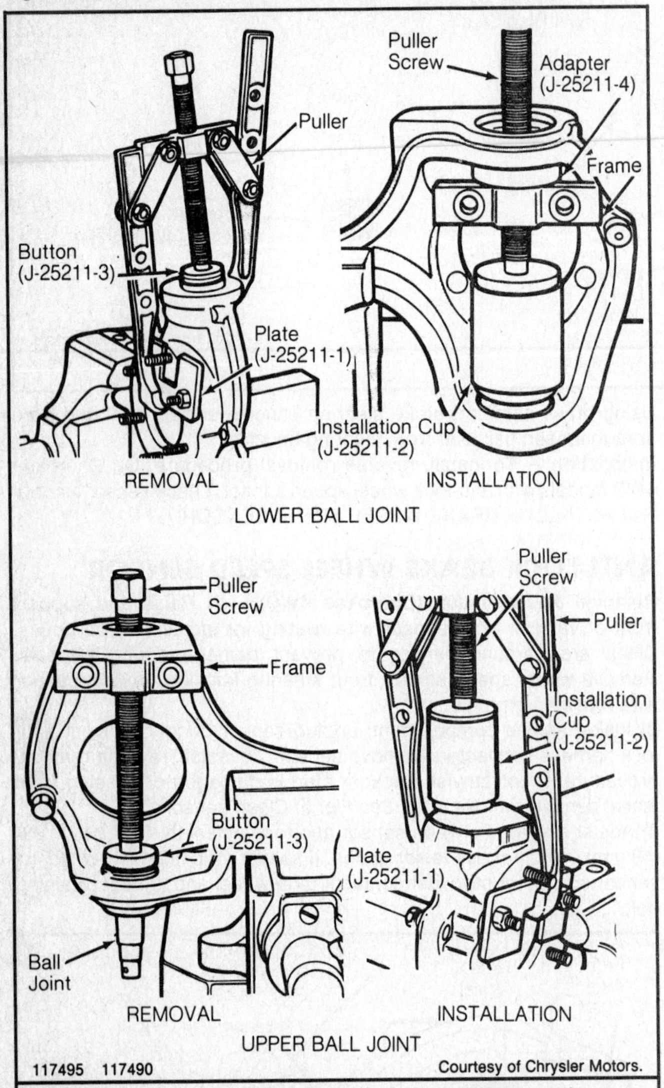
Puller
Button
(J-25211-3)
Plate
(J-25211-1)
Puller
Screw
Adapter
(J-25211-4)
Frame
Installation Cup
(J-25211-2)
REMOVAL
INSTALLATION
LOWER BALL JOINT
Puller
Screw
Frame
Button
(J-25211-3)
Ball
Joint
Puller
Screw
Puller
Installation
Cup
(J-25211-2)
Plate
(J-25211-1)
REMOVAL
INSTALLATION
UPPER BALL JOINT
117495 117490
Courtesy of Chrysler Motors.

Fig. 6: Removing & Installing Ball Joint (Grand Wagoneer)

Installation – 1) To install lower ball joint, install ball joint in steering knuckle. Install Adapter (J-25211-4) over nut end of puller. Install puller screw and adapter in steering knuckle. Install Installation Cup (J-25211-2) on ball joint. *See Fig. 6.* Install frame and tighten puller screw to install lower ball joint. Install ball joint snap ring.

2) To install upper ball joint, install ball joint in steering knuckle. Install Plate (J-25211-1) on steering knuckle retaining studs. Place Installation Cup (J-25211-2) on ball joint stud. Center puller on installation cup. Tighten puller screw and install ball joint. *See Fig. 6.* Install steering knuckle.

Removal (All Others) – 1) Remove steering knuckle assembly. See STEERING KNUCKLE under REMOVAL & INSTALLATION. To remove upper ball joint, install Receiver (J-34503-1) over top of upper ball joint. Place Adapter (J-34503-3) in "C" clamp. Install "C" clamp, adapter and receiver. Tighten "C" clamp screw to remove ball joint. *See Fig. 7.*

2) To remove lower ball joint, position Receiver (J-34503-1) onto "C" clamp and Adapter (J-34503-3) at base of clamp. *See Fig. 7.* Install "C" clamp, adapter and receiver. Tighten "C" clamp to remove ball joint. *See Fig. 7.*

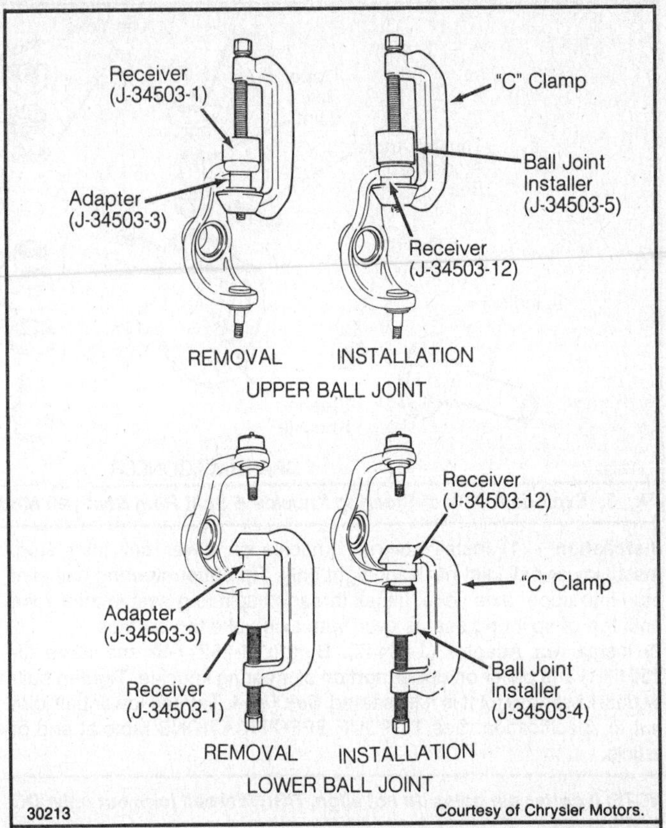
Receiver
(J-34503-1)
Adapter
(J-34503-3)
"C" Clamp
Ball Joint
Installer
(J-34503-5)
Receiver
(J-34503-12)
REMOVAL
INSTALLATION
UPPER BALL JOINT
Receiver
(J-34503-12)
"C" Clamp
Adapter
(J-34503-3)
Receiver
(J-34503-1)
Ball Joint
Installer
(J-34503-4)
REMOVAL
INSTALLATION
LOWER BALL JOINT
30213
Courtesy of Chrysler Motors.

Fig. 7: Removing & Installing Ball Joint (Except Grand Wagoneer)

Installation – 1) Place upper ball joint in position. Position Ball Joint Installer (J-34503-5) over new upper ball joint. Install Receiver (J-34503-12) and "C" clamp. Tighten "C" clamp and fully seat ball joint. *See Fig. 7.*

2) To install lower ball joint, position Ball Joint Installer (J-34503-4), "C" clamp and Receiver (J-34503-12). *See Fig. 7.* Tighten "C" clamp to install ball joint. Ensure ball joint is fully seated. Install steering knuckle. See TORQUE SPECIFICATIONS table at end of article.

COIL SPRING

Removal & Installation – 1) Raise and support vehicle. Remove wheel assembly. On 4WD models, Place reference mark on drive shaft and front axle flanges. Disconnect drive shaft at front axle.

2) Place jack stand under axle housing. Disconnect lower control arms at axle housing. Disconnect stabilizer bar links and lower shock absorber mounting bolts at axle housing. Disconnect track bar at frame rail bracket. Disconnect tie rod from pitman arm.

3) Lower axle housing to relieve spring pressure. Remove spring retainer mounting bolt. Remove spring retainer and coil spring. Note component location for reassembly reference. To install, reverse removal procedure.

LEAF SPRING

Removal & Installation – 1) Raise and support vehicle. Raise axle assembly with jack to relieve spring tension. On Wrangler, remove wheels and loosen stabilizer bar link nut. On all other models, remove stabilizer bar link from spring bracket.

2) On all models, remove spring "U" bolts and plate. Remove spring-to-front shackle bolt and spring-to-rear frame hanger bolt. Remove spring. To install, reverse removal procedure. Ensure spring center bolt is seated in axle housing. Tighten spring-to-front shackle bolt and spring-to-rear frame hanger bolt with vehicle at normal operating height. See TORQUE SPECIFICATIONS table at end of article.

UPPER CONTROL ARM & AXLE HOUSING PIVOT BUSHING

Removal & Installation - 1) Raise vehicle and remove upper control arm mounting bolt from axle housing. Disconnect control arm mounting bolt at frame rail. Remove upper control arm. Repeat procedure for opposite control arm.

2) Inspect control arm for damage or distortion and replace as needed. Check pivot bushings for excessive distortion, deterioration or wear.

3) If pivot bushing requires replacement, on 2WD models, install Spacer (J-33581-3) between ears of control arm bracket on axle housing. *See Fig. 8.*

NOTE: Spacer (J-33581-3) is not used on 4WD models as solid control arm brackets are used. DO NOT attempt to remove upper control arm pivot bushing on 2WD models without spacer. Axle bracket will be distorted if spacer is not used.

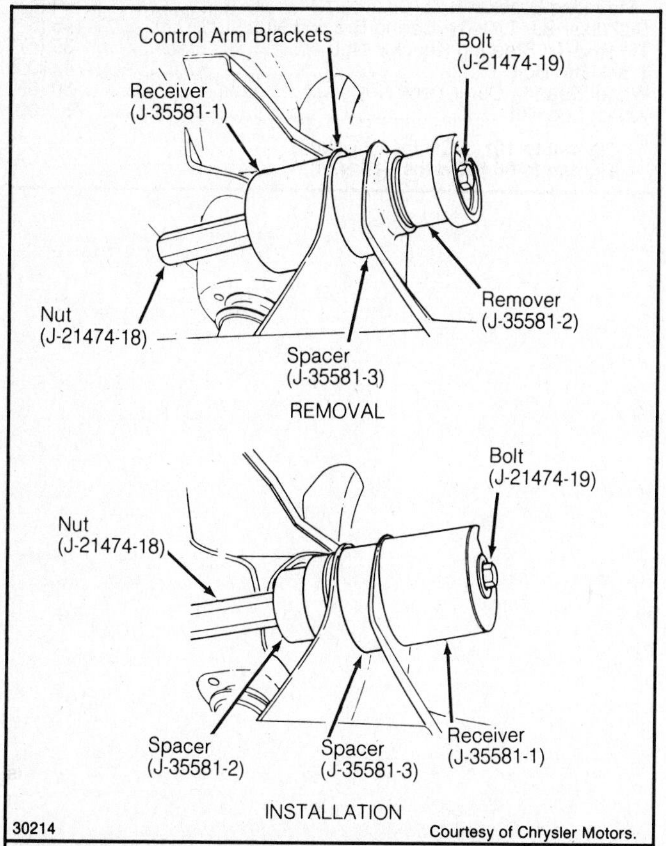
Control Arm Brackets
Bolt
(J-21474-19)
Receiver
(J-35581-1)
Remover
(J-35581-2)
Nut
(J-21474-18)
Spacer
(J-35581-3)
REMOVAL
Bolt
(J-21474-19)
Nut
(J-21474-18)
Spacer
(J-35581-2)
Spacer
(J-35581-3)
Receiver
(J-35581-1)
INSTALLATION
30214
Courtesy of Chrysler Motors.

Fig. 8: Removing & Installing Upper Control Arm Bushing

4) Install Bushing Remover/Installer Set (J-35581, which includes Spacer J-35581-3, Remover/Installer J-35581-2, Receiver J-35581-1, Bolt J-21474-19 and Nut J-21474-18) onto pivot bushing. *See Fig. 8.*

5) Rotate nut to press bushing from axle housing and into receiver. *See Fig. 8.* Once bushing is removed, remove bushing remover/installer components.

CAUTION: On 2WD models, spacer must remain installed for bushing installation.

6) Position bushing on Remover/Installer (J-35581-2) and Nut (J-21474-18). Position bushing and installer components in control arm bracket. Assemble remaining installer components. *See Fig. 8.*

7) Rotate nut to press bushing into housing until fully seated in bore. *See Fig. 8.* Remove bushing installer components. To install upper control arm, reverse removal procedure.

LOWER CONTROL ARM

Removal & Installation - Raise and support vehicle. Disconnect lower control arm mounting bolts at axle housing and frame brackets. Remove lower control arm. To install, reverse removal procedure.

TRACK BAR

Removal & Installation - 1) Raise and support vehicle. Remove cotter pin (if used) and nut at frame rail bracket. Remove track bar-to-axle housing bracket.

2) On all models except Grand Wagoneer and Wrangler, track bar is fastened to frame bracket with a tapered rod end, similar to a tie rod. Use of a puller may be necessary to free track bar from bracket. Remove track bar. To install, reverse removal procedure.

FRONT STABILIZER BAR

Removal & Installation (Grand Wagoneer) - Raise and support vehicle. Disconnect stabilizer bar from upper portion of stabilizer bar links. Remove stabilizer bar bracket-to-frame bolts. Remove brackets. Remove stabilizer bar and bushings. To install, reverse removal procedure.

Removal & Installation (Except Grand Wagoneer) - 1) Raise and support vehicle. Disconnect stabilizer bar from stabilizer bar links. Remove stabilizer bar bracket-to-frame bolts. Remove brackets. Remove stabilizer bar and bushings.

2) To install, lubricate stabilizer bar bushings and grommets with rubber lubricant. Install stabilizer bar link brackets on axle (if removed). Tighten to specification. Install stabilizer bar and brackets on the frame. DO NOT tighten bolts at this time.

3) Install stabilizer bar-to-link bolts. Tighten stabilizer bracket-to-frame bolts to specification and then tighten stabilizer bar link bolts. See TORQUE SPECIFICATIONS.

1991 SUSPENSION
Front (Cont.)

TORQUE SPECIFICATIONS

TORQUE SPECIFICATIONS

Application	Ft. Lbs. (N.m)
Cherokee & Comanche	
Axle Shaft Nut	175 (237)
Axle Shift Motor Bolt	[1]
Ball Joint Nut	75 (102)
Bearing Assembly-To-Steering Knuckle Bolt	75 (102)
Brake Caliper	
Mounting Bolt	77 (104)
Mounting Pin	30 (41)
Control Arm Bolt	
Upper	
At Axle	55 (75)
At Frame	66 (90)
Lower	133 (180)
Shock Absorber	
Lower Nut	14 (19)
Upper Nut	[2]
Stabilizer Bar	
Frame Bolt	55 (75)
Link Bolt	27 (37)
Stabilizer Bar Link-To-Bracket Bolt	70 (95)
Tie Rod-To-Steering Knuckle Nut	35 (47)
Track Bar	
Frame Rail Bracket Nut	62 (84)
Axle Mount Bolt	74 (100)
Wheel Bearing Outer Lock Nut	50 (68)
Wheel Lug Nut	75 (102)
Wheel Speed Sensor Bolt	11 (15)
Grand Wagoneer	
Ball Joint Nut	
Lower	80 (109)
Upper	100 (136)
Ball Joint Split Ring Seat	50 (68)
Shock Absorber Nut	
Lower	45 (61)
Upper	35 (47)
Spring-To-Shackle & Frame Bracket Bolt	100 (136)
Spring "U" Bolt Nut	
1/2" x 20	55 (75)
9/16" x 18	100 (136)
Stabilizer Bar	
Link Nut	55 (75)
Mounting Bracket Bolt	35 (47)
Tie Rod End Nut	60 (81)
Track Bar Nut	74 (100)
Wheel Bearing Outer Lock Nut	50 (68)
Wheel Lug Nut	75 (102)

TORQUE SPECIFICATIONS (Cont.)

Application	Ft. Lbs. (N.m)
Wrangler	
Axle Shaft Nut	175 (237)
Axle Shift Motor Bolt	[1]
Ball Joint Nut	75 (102)
Bearing Assembly-To-Steering Knuckle Bolt	75 (102)
Brake Caliper	
Mounting Bolt	77 (104)
Mounting Pin	30 (41)
Shock Absorber	
Lower Bolt	45 (61)
Upper Stud Nut	10 (14)
Spring-To-Frame Bracket Bolt	105 (142)
Spring-To-Front Shackle Bolt	95 (129)
Spring "U" Bolt Nut	90 (122)
Stabilizer Bar	
Link Bolt	45 (61)
Mounting Bracket Bolt	30 (41)
Stabilizer Bar Link-To-Spring Bracket Nut	45 (61)
Tie Rod-To-Steering Knuckle Nut	35 (47)
Track Bar Bolt	74 (100)
Wheel Bearing Outer Lock Nut	50 (68)
Wheel Lug Nut	75 (102)

[1] – Tighten to 101 INCH lbs. (11 N.m).
[2] – Tighten to 96 INCH lbs. (10 N.m).

1991 STEERING
Steering Columns

Cherokee, Comanche
Grand Wagoneer, Wrangler

DESCRIPTION & OPERATION

All models use collapsible steering columns. All columns have integral ignition switch and locking device. Optional tilt wheel is available with both automatic and manual transmissions. Transmission shift linkage is integral on all models except those with floor shift.

REMOVAL & INSTALLATION

HORN BUTTON

Removal & Installation – 1) Disconnect negative battery cable. Place wheels in straight-ahead position. On models with standard steering wheel, remove horn button retaining screws from rear of steering wheel. Disconnect wiring from horn button and remove.

2) On models with sport steering wheel (round horn button), remove horn button by pulling button upward. If necessary, remove horn internal components. Place components in order of removal. To install, reverse removal procedure.

STEERING WHEEL

Removal & Installation – 1) Remove horn button. On vehicles with sport steering wheel, remove bushing, receiver and flex plate from steering wheel. On all models, remove steering wheel retaining nut.

2) Place reference mark on steering wheel and shaft for reassembly reference. Using steering wheel puller, remove steering wheel. To install, reverse removal procedure. Align marks made during removal.

3) Tighten steering wheel nut to 25 ft. lbs. (34 N.m). Connect negative battery cable, reset clock and radio stations if applicable. Check horn, and turn signal for correct operation.

PARK-LOCK CABLE

NOTE: Park-Lock cable is used on Cherokee and Comanche model equipped with floor shift and AW4 transmission.

Removal & Installation – 1) Disconnect negative battery cable. Remove lower instrument panel trim. Remove steering column attaching nuts and lower steering column. Disconnect park-lock cable from steering column and remove cable from bracket.

2) Remove center console. Remove moldings, panels, accelerator pedal bracket and carpet screws. Pull carpet back for access to gear selector lever bell-crank, disconnect park-lock cable and remove cable. To install, reverse removal procedure.

COLUMN SHIFT TYPE STEERING COLUMN

NOTE: Steering column removal is NOT needed for, lock plate cover, lock plate, steering shaft retaining ring, canceling cam, turn signal switch, upper bearing preload spring, or ignition switch/lock cylinder removal.

Removal – 1) Disconnect negative battery cable. Remove steering wheel and horn pad. See STEERING WHEEL under REMOVAL & INSTALLATION. Remove damper assembly (if equipped). Remove turn signal lever.

2) Paint alignment marks on intermediate shaft and steering shaft for installation reference. Disconnect steering shaft from intermediate shaft. If necessary, remove lower part of instrument panel, disconnect bracket from instrument panel and lower steering column.

3) Disconnect ignition switch, dimmer switch, turn signal switch, windshield wiper switch and cruise control electrical connectors. Disconnect park-lock cable (if equipped). Disconnect steering column toe plate from instrument panel, remove steering column from vehicle.

CAUTION: When removed from vehicle, steering column must be handled very carefully. The plastic fasteners that maintain the rigidity of the energy-absorbing components could be sheared or loosened.

NOTE: On vehicles equipped with cruise control and manual transmission, take care not to damage clutch pedal cruise control switch.

Installation – 1) Align lower shaft with lower coupling and insert shaft. Raise column assembly into position onto studs. Loosely install nuts and washers in break-away capsules. Pull column rearward. Tighten nuts to specification. See TORQUE SPECIFICATIONS table at end of article.

2) Install new shift lever grommet using pliers and back-up washer to snap grommet into place. Use a multipurpose grease to aid installation. Connect gearshift cable rod to shift lever by snapping rod into grommet with pliers.

3) Adjust linkage. Place steering wheel on shaft with master splines aligned. Place damper assembly inside steering wheel (if equipped). Install steering wheel retaining nut. Tighten to 45 ft. lbs. (61 N.m).

4) Install horn pad assembly. Connect electrical connectors at steering column jacket. Connect negative battery cable. Test operation of lights and horn.

5) On models with automatic transmission, install gearshift indicator pointer. Slowly move gearshift lever from Low to Park position, pausing briefly at each position. Readjust pointer as required. Install instrument panel steering column cover.

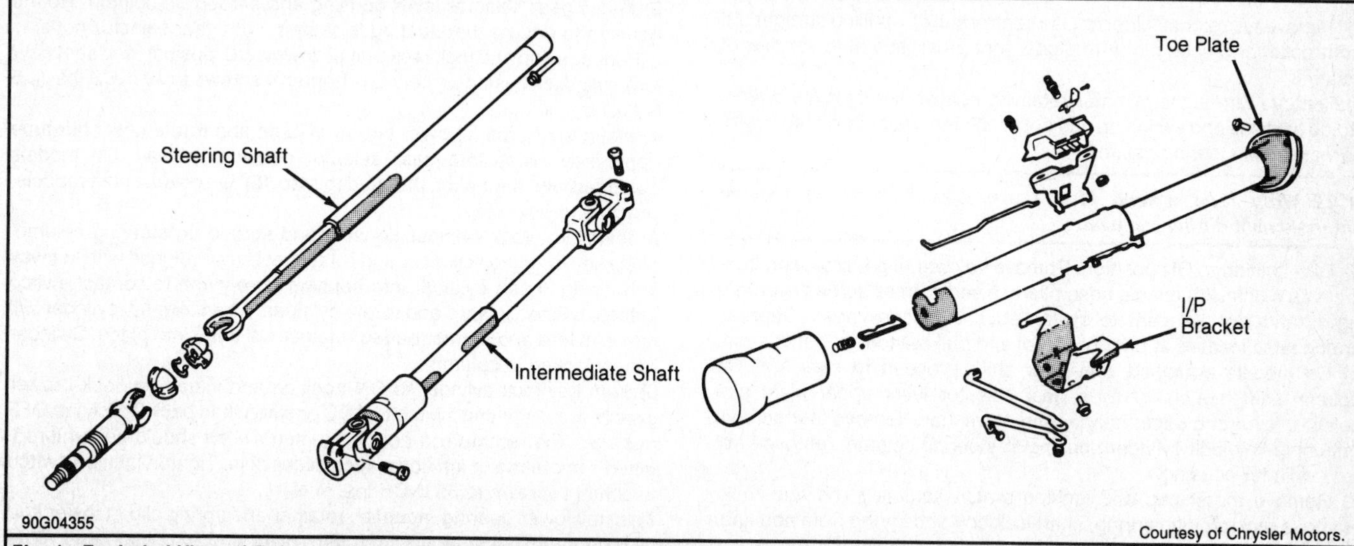
Toe Plate
Steering Shaft
I/P
Bracket
Intermediate Shaft
90G04355
Courtesy of Chrysler Motors.

Fig. 1: Exploded View of Column Steering Column & Intermediate Shaft

1991 STEERING
Steering Columns (Cont.)

FLOOR SHIFT TYPE STEERING COLUMN

Removal & Installation – Removal procedure is same as for column shift with following exceptions: In place of rotating shift bowl, a plastic shroud is fixed to lock housing. Shroud covers jacket and lock inhibitor assembly with a tab holding it in place. Replace shroud by removing key/lock housing from jacket.

OVERHAUL

NON-TILT WHEEL COLUMN

NOTE: If repairs are performed while in vehicle, DO NOT allow shaft to slip out of column.

Disassembly – **1)** If column is removed from vehicle, attach a column supporting fixture. *See Fig. 2* . If column is in vehicle, disconnect negative battery cable. Remove steering wheel. See STEERING WHEEL under REMOVAL & INSTALLATION. Remove lock plate cover.

WARNING: Lock plate is retained by a very strong spring force. Do not attempt to remove steering shaft snap ring without using appropriate lock plate depressor.

2) Depress lock plate, remove snap ring and discard. Remove lock plate, cancel cam, upper bearing preload spring and washer. Remove hazard warning switch knob, press knob inward then turn counterclockwise, remove from column.

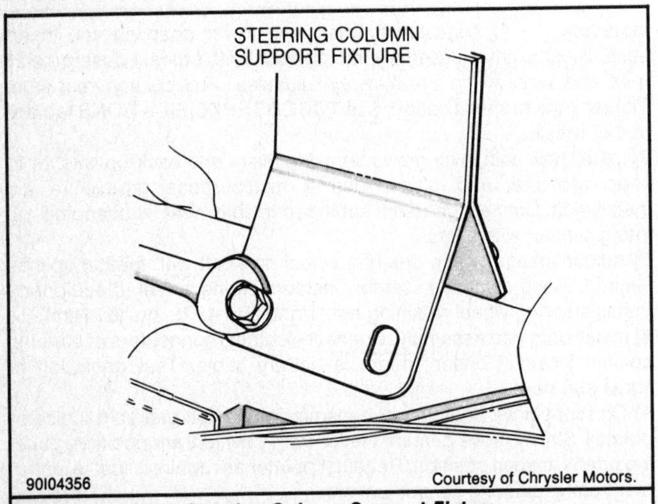
STEERING COLUMN
SUPPORT FIXTURE
90I04356
Courtesy of Chrysler Motors.

Fig. 2: Attaching Steering Column Support Fixture

3) Remove turn signal/wiper/cruise control stalk by pulling straight out from column. Disconnect turn signal wiring harness at lower end of column.

4) Remove turn signal/dimmer retaining screws and remove switch. Guide harness and switch up and out of column. Remove all other wire harnesses in steering column.

NOTE: Wrap tape around turn signal wire harness to prevent entanglement during removal.

5) Turn ignition to ON position. Remove key warning buzzer and contacts as a unit with needle nose pliers. Insert a small screwdriver into right hand slot adjacent to switch attaching screw boss. Depress spring latch located at bottom of slot and pull cylinder out of column.

6) On models equipped with floor shift, proceed to step **10)**. On column shift models, remove gear selector lever upper pivot pin, selector lever and upper bearing thrust washer. Remove four screws attaching key/lock cylinder housing to steering column, remove key/lock cylinder housing.

7) Remove thrust cap and ignition switch actuating rod and rack. Remove rack preload spring, shaft lock bolt and spring from housing. Remove shift lever detent plate from housing. *See Fig. 3.*

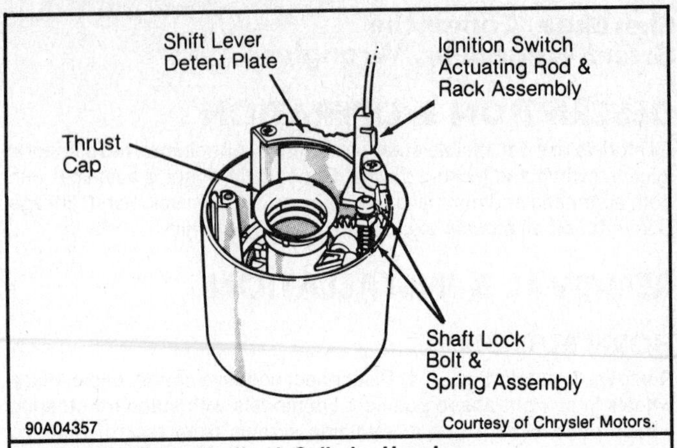
Shift Lever
Detent Plate
Ignition Switch
Actuating Rod &
Rack Assembly
Thrust
Cap
Shaft Lock
Bolt &
Spring Assembly
90A04357
Courtesy of Chrysler Motors.

Fig. 3: Identifying Key/Lock Cylinder Housing

8) Use punch to exert force on block tooth to disengage and remove lock sector. Remove gear selector lever housing and shroud from steering shaft. Remove gear selector lever spring from housing.

NOTE: Steering column must be removed from vehicle for further disassembly.

9) Remove steering shaft, if not removed earlier. Remove spring clip from lower bearing retainer, remove retainer, lower bearing, and adapter. Slide out shift tube.

10) On models equipped with floor shift, remove screws attaching key/lock cylinder and shroud to column jacket. Remove dimmer switch arm, disengage remote rod from lock rack. Remove key/lock cylinder housing to shroud screws and separate.

11) Remove and separate wave washer from key release lever pivot. Remove lock rack, lock bolt and preload spring. Use punch to exert force on block tooth to disengage and remove lock sector. Remove gear selector lever housing and shroud from steering shaft.

12) Remove steering shaft, if not removed earlier. Remove spring clip from lower bearing retainer, remove retainer, lower bearing and adapter. Slide out shift tube.

Reassembly – **1)** Coat all friction surfaces with grease. Insert key sector through key/lock cylinder hole. Install lock sector shaft. Ensure sector turns freely. Install lock rack preload spring. Assemble lock bolt and rod and install assembly in housing. Mate assembly with lock sector gear teeth. Install shift lever detent plate on housing. *See Fig. 4.*

2) Install thrust cap and ignition switch actuating rod on housing. Insert gear selector lever housing lower bearing and align indentations in shell with projections on housing. Install gear selector spring in housing.

3) Install gear selector lever housing and shroud on column. Rotate housing to ensure that bearing is seated. With gear selector housing in Park position and lock rack pulled downward, position and seat key/lock cylinder housing on column. Tighten 4 screws to 40 INCH lbs. (4.5 N.m).

4) Insert shift tube in lower end of column and rotate until shift tube upper key slides into gear selector housing keyway. On models equipped with floor shift, proceed to step **10)**. On column shift models, proceed to next step.

5) Install key/lock cylinder housing and shroud on steering column, place key in ignition cylinder and rotate until key is aligned with keyway in housing. Insert cylinder into housing far enough to contact switch actuator. Press inward and rotate cylinder. When aligned, cylinder will move inward and spring-loaded retainer will snap into place. Cylinder is now locked in column.

6) Turn key/lock cylinder to ON position and install key/lock buzzer switch. Move ignition switch to ACC position then back 2 clicks to OFF position. The remote rod hole in ignition switch should be centered. Insert remote rod in ignition switch slider hole. Tighten ignition switch to column screws to 35 INCH lbs. (4 N.m).

7) Install lower bearing, adapter, retainer and spring clip at lower end of column. Install steering shaft into lower end of column and route

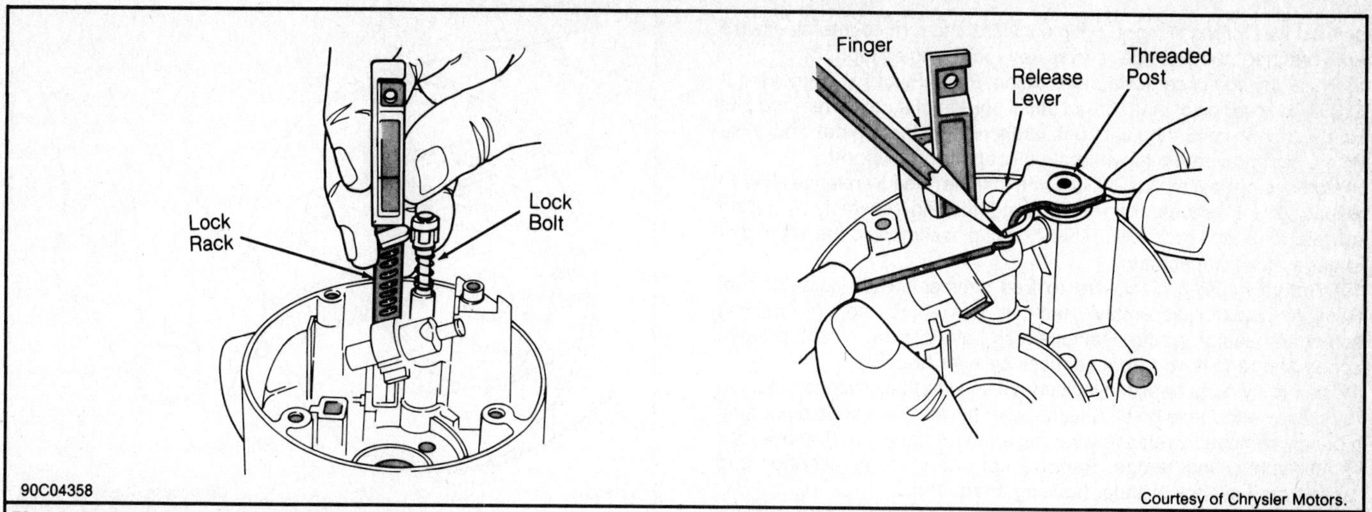
Lock
Rack
Lock
Bolt
Finger
Release
Lever
Threaded
Post
90C04358
Courtesy of Chrysler Motors.

Fig. 4: Removing Lock Rack & Bolt Release Spring

through into upper bearing. Position turn signal switch and wire harness in key/lock housing. Fold wires against connector and feed down through column. Install wiper wiring harness and route through column. Align and secure turn signal switch. Tighten screws to 35 INCH lbs. (4 N.m).

8) Install dimmer switch actuator arm and tighten screw to 35 INCH lbs. (4 N.m). Route cruise control wiring harness in column (if equipped). Install turn signal/wiper/dimmer/cruise control switch stalk on column by pressing straight in. Position thrust washer, upper bearing preload spring and cancel cam on steering column.

9) Install hazard warning switch knob. Place lock plate on shaft, depress lock plate with depressor and install new snap ring. Install steering wheel. See STEERING WHEEL under REMOVAL & INSTALLATION. Tighten steering wheel nut to 25 ft. lbs. (34 N.m).

10) On models equipped with floor shift, install key release lever return spring over threaded pivot post on housing. Insert key release finger in lock rack slot and position hole in lever over threaded pivot post. *See Fig. 4.* Ensure inner end of spring contacts release lever.

11) Raise key release lever slightly. Install lever spring between lever and boss on housing. Lubricate and place wave washer on threaded pivot post. Position shroud on key/lock housing. Tighten screws to 18 INCH lbs. (2 N.m).

12) Insert short, hooked end of remote rod in lock rack. Install assembled key/lock housing on steering column and tighten screws to 7 INCH lbs. (6 N.m). Install key/lock cylinder housing and shroud on steering column, place key in ignition cylinder and rotate until key is aligned with keyway in housing.

13) Insert cylinder into housing far enough to contact switch actuator. Press inward and rotate cylinder. When parts align, cylinder will move inward and spring-loaded retainer will snap into place. Cylinder is now locked in column.

14) Turn key/lock cylinder to ON position and install key/lock buzzer switch. Move ignition switch slider to ACC position, then back 2 clicks to OFF position. The remote rod hole in ignition switch should be centered. Insert remote rod in ignition switch slider hole and tighten ignition switch to column screws to 35 INCH lbs. (4 N.m).

15) Install lower bearing, adapter, retainer and spring clip at lower end of column. Install steering shaft into lower end of column and insert into upper bearing. Position turn signal switch and wire harness in key/lock housing. Fold wires against connector and feed down through column jacket. Install wiper wiring harness and route through column. Align and secure turn signal switch. Tighten screws to 35 INCH lbs. (4 N.m).

16) Install dimmer switch actuator arm, tighten screw to 35 INCH lbs. (4 N.m). Route cruise control wiring harness in column (if equipped). Install turn signal/wiper/dimmer/cruise control switch stalk on column by pressing straight in. Position thrust washer, upper bearing preload spring and canceling cam on steering column.

17) Install hazard warning switch knob. Place lock plate on shaft, compress plate and install new snap ring. Ensure that new snap ring is completely seated in groove before removing depressor. Install steering wheel. Tighten steering wheel nut to 25 ft. lbs. (34 N.m).

TILT WHEEL COLUMN

NOTE: Tilt steering can be disassembled in vehicle down to the column jacket. If further repairs are needed, column must be removed from vehicle.

Disassembly – 1) Remove steering wheel. See STEERING WHEEL under REMOVAL & INSTALLATION. Remove column (if required). Attach column fixture and clamp assembly in vise. *See Fig. 2.*

2) Remove tilt release lever. To remove hazard warning knob, push in knob while unscrewing. Remove ignition key light assembly. Pull knob off wiper/washer switch assembly. Remove 2 sleeve-to-wiper/washer switch retaining screws and remove sleeve.

WARNING: Lock plate is retained by a very strong spring force. Do not attempt to remove steering shaft snap ring without using appropriate lock plate depressor.

3) Rotate wiper switch shaft fully clockwise. Remove shaft by pulling straight out of wiper/washer switch. Carefully remove plastic cover from lock plate. Using Lock Plate Depressor (J-23653-A), depress lock plate. Pry retaining ring from groove, remove and discard ring.

4) Remove lock plate, canceling cam and upper bearing plate. Remove switch actuator screw and arm. Remove 3 turn signal switch attaching screws. Place shift bowl in LOW position. Wrap a piece of tape around wires to prevent snagging while removing switch and remove switch.

5) Turn key/lock cylinder to ON position. Using needle nose pliers, remove key warning buzzer switch and contacts as one unit. Remove spring and switch. DO NOT allow spring to fall into steering column. Insert a small screwdriver into the right-hand slot adjacent to switch attaching screw boss. Depress spring latch located at bottom of slot and remove key/lock cylinder.

6) Remove 3 key/lock cylinder housing cover screws and remove housing cover. Remove wiper/washer switch. Tilt lever opening shield and dimmer switch actuator rod may be removed from cap (if necessary). Remove dimmer switch mounting screws and remove switch. With ignition switch in ACC position, remove ignition switch mounting screws and remove switch.

WARNING: Tilt spring guide retainer has strong spring force.

7) Remove upper bearing race and bearing seat from steering shaft. Place column in full upward tilt position. Using a large Phillips head

1991 STEERING
Steering Columns (Cont.)

screwdriver, press tilt spring guide inward and turn counterclockwise until retainer tabs disengage from key/lock housing lug.

8) Place column in center most position. Place Pivot Pin Remover (J-21854-01) over pivot pin. Thread small portion of screw firmly into pin. Hold screw from turning with one wrench while turning nut clockwise with a second wrench to withdraw pivot pin from support.

9) Remove opposite pivot pin in same manner. Use tilt release lever to disengage lock shoes. Remove bearing housing assembly by pulling upward to extend rack fully. Move housing assembly to the left to disengage rack from actuator.

10) Rotate housing clockwise to free dimmer switch actuator rod. Remove actuator assembly. Remove lock sector spring retaining screw and sector spring. Remove lock bolt, lock rack, rack preload spring and remote rod from key/lock cylinder housing.

11) Insert a wedge between lock shoes and key/lock cylinder housing to relieve spring tension tilt release lever pin and lock shoe pin. Using a punch, remove tilt release lever pin and lock shoe pin. Remove lock shoes, spring and wedge. Remove upper and lower bearings and races from key/lock cylinder housing if required.

NOTE: Bearings and races only require removal if damaged. Remove races with hammer and punch and discard. DO NOT reuse components.

12) Remove steering shaft from upper end of steering column. Separate upper and lower steering shaft by folding shaft 90 degrees at flex joint and detaching shaft sections. Disassemble steering shaft assembly by removing centering spheres and springs. *See Fig. 5.* Remove steering column support from column. Remove shift gate from steering support (if required).

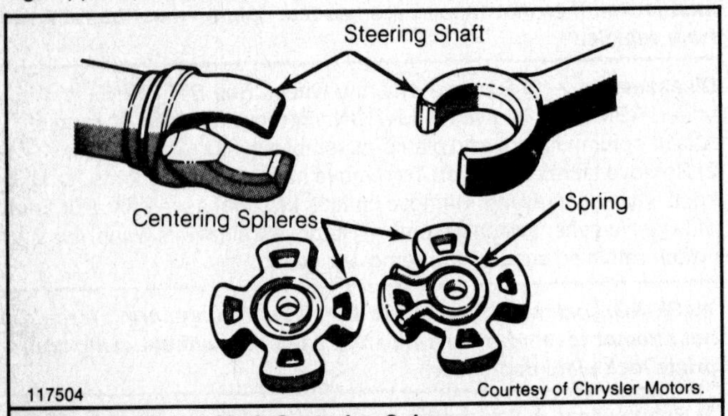
Steering Shaft
Spring
Centering Spheres
117504
Courtesy of Chrysler Motors.

Fig. 5: Identifying Shaft Centering Spheres

13) Remove retainer and bearing from lower end of steering column. Remove shift tube retaining ring and thrust washer. Using Puller (J-23073-01), remove shift tube from bowl. Insert bushing on end of puller in shift tube to force tube from bowl. DO NOT hammer shift tube as plastic joints may shear. *See Fig. 6.*

14) Tilt upper end of retainer plate toward lower end of column, turn plate counter-clockwise and remove. On column shift models, remove wave washer and shift tube spring. Remove shift bowl from steering column jacket. On floor shift models, remove column shroud from column jacket. Remove key release lever and spring from column shroud.

WARNING: Use only original or exact replacement screws, bolts and nuts to assemble steering column. Use of incorrect hardware could keep column from compressing in a collision. Column-to-instrument panel attaching nuts MUST be tightened to correct torque so that column will break away on impact

Reassembly – 1) During reassembly, coat all friction surfaces with multipurpose grease. If reassembling a floor shift type column, proceed to step **3)**. To reassemble column shift type column, install shift bowl on steering column jacket. Install shift tube spring, wave washer and retainer plate in shift bowl. Insert shift tube through lower end of column jacket and align tube key spline with shift bowl keyway.

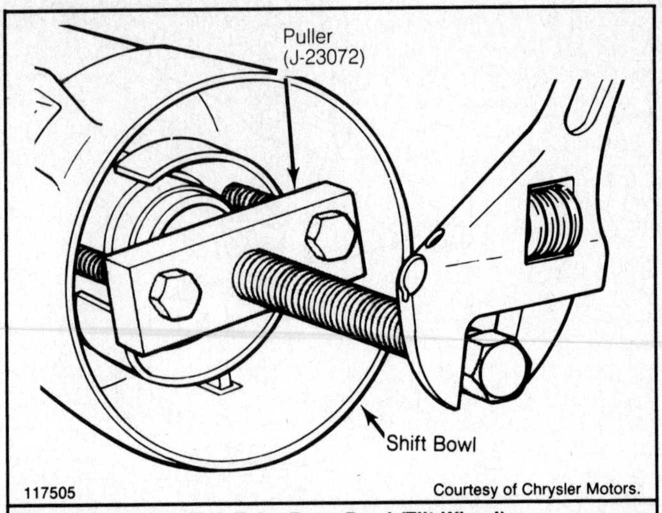
Puller
(J-23072)
Shift Bowl
117505
Courtesy of Chrysler Motors.

Fig. 6: Removing Shift Tube From Bowl (Tilt Wheel)

2) Install Puller (J-23073-01) and pull shift tube into bowl. *See Fig. 7.* Install shift tube thrust washer and retainer plate snap ring. Install column lower bearing. Attach shift gate to steering column support. Install steering column support assembly into column and tighten retaining screws alternately and evenly to 60 INCH lbs. (7 N.m).

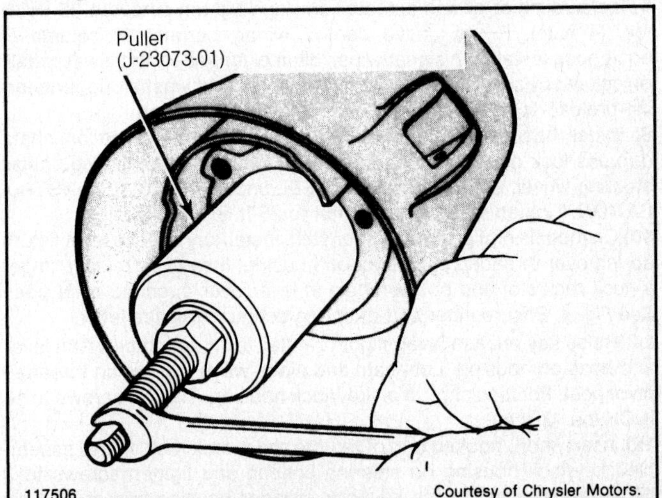
Puller
(J-23073-01)
117506
Courtesy of Chrysler Motors.

Fig. 7: Installing Shift Tube (Tilt Wheel)

3) To reassemble floor shift type column, position key release lever spring onto lever and install assembly into column shroud. Install shroud onto steering column jacket. Install retainer plate into column jacket notches.

4) Install column support into column jacket by aligning "V" on support with "V" notch in column jacket. To completely seat support, press key release lever downward while pressing support into place. Install steering column support retaining screws and tighten alternately and evenly to 60 INCH lbs. (7 N.m).

NOTE: Remaining steps apply to either column shift type or floor shift type columns

5) Install remote rod in column support rod slot. Install dimmer and ignition switches. Install new races and bearings in key/lock cylinder housing if old components were removed. Using a .18" (4.5 mm) diameter rod to aid in alignment, install lock shoes, lock shoe springs and lock shoe pin.

6) Install tilt release lever, lever spring and lever pin in key/lock cylinder housing. Insert wedge between housing and lever to relieve spring tension and ease pin installation.

7) Install lock bolt in key/lock cylinder housing and engage it in lock sector cam surface. Install lock rack, rack preload spring and replacement shim in key/lock cylinder housing. Mate square block tooth on lock rack to like tooth on lock sector. Tighten screws to 35 INCH lbs. (4 N.m).

8) Retain lock shoes in disengaged position and install key/lock housing on column support. Align pivot pin holes in key/lock cylinder housing with those in column support and install pivot pins. Seat pins fully using a hammer and punch.

CAUTION: Press housing down firmly while installing pivot pins to avoid damage to holes in column support

9) Place key/lock cylinder housing in full upward tilt position. Lubricate tilt spring guide and spring with chassis lube. Insert tilt spring guide and spring into key/lock cylinder housing. Using a large Phillips head screwdriver, install spring retainer into key/lock cylinder housing lugs.

10) Install key/lock cylinder housing cover and tighten screws to 60 INCH lbs. (7 N.m). Install gear selector indicator light assembly (if equipped). Route dimmer switch harness down through column.

11) Insert key/lock cylinder into housing far enough to contact switch actuator. Press inward and rotate cylinder. When aligned, cylinder will move inward and spring-loaded retainer will snap into place. Cylinder is now locked in column. Turn key/lock cylinder to ON position. Install key/lock buzzer switch.

12) Install turn signal switch, but DO NOT install switch retaining screws at this time. Install windshield wiper harness and switch and route harness down through column jacket. Route cruise control harness (if equipped), down through column jacket.

13) Install turn signal switch stalk by pushing straight into column. Install hazard warning knob on hazard warning switch. Install turn signal retaining screws and tighten to 33 INCH lbs. (4 N.m). Install upper bearing race in key/lock cylinder housing.

14) Install upper bearing preload spring, canceling cam and lock plate. Depress lock plate with depressor and install new snap ring. *See Fig. 8.* Install lock plate cover. Install gear selector lever and retaining pin (if equipped).

15) Install steering wheel. See STEERING WHEEL under REMOVAL & INSTALLATION. Turn key/lock cylinder to OFF position, move ignition switch downward to eliminate lash, and install switch retaining screws. Tighten screws to 35 INCH lbs. (4 N.m).

16) Depress dimmer switch slightly and insert 3/32" drill bit into adjustment hole. Loosen retaining screws, move switch upward to remove lash, and retighten screws to 35 INCH lbs. (4 N.m). Remove drill bit and test dimmer switch operation in all column tilt positions.

17) Install steering column. See appropriate type column under REMOVAL & INSTALLATION. Reconnect negative battery cable. Test ignition switch in all tilt positions. Ensure vehicle starts only in Park and Neutral.

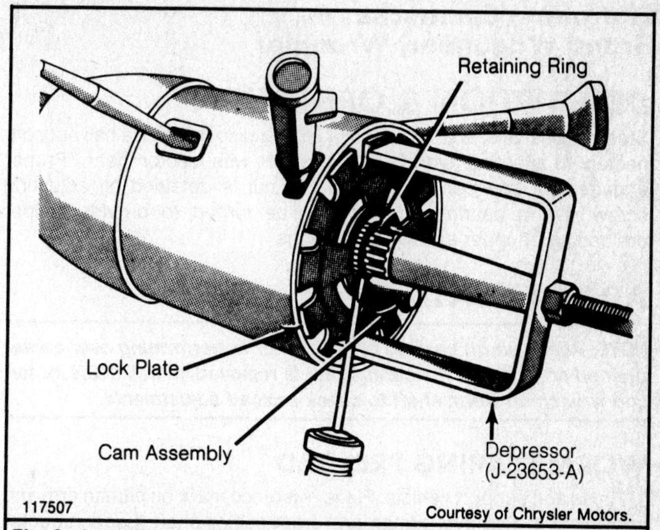

Retaining Ring
Lock Plate
Cam Assembly
Depressor
(J-23653-A)
117507
Courtesy of Chrysler Motors.

Fig. 8: Installing Lock Plate Retaining Ring

TORQUE SPECIFICATIONS

TORQUE SPECIFICATIONS

Application	Ft. Lbs. (N.m)
Flexible Coupling Bolt	17 (23)
Steering Wheel Retaining Nut	45 (61)
Support Plate Bolt	17 (23)
	INCH Lbs. (N.m)
Bearing Housing-To-Lock Housing Screw	35 (4)
Bracket-To-Column Bolt	124 (14)
Column Clamp Stud	20 (2)
Column Clamp Stud Nut	106 (12)
Hazard Switch Screw	27 (3)
Housing Cover Screw	100 (11)
Ignition Switch Screw	35 (4)
Lock Housing-To-Jacket Screw	90 (10)
Shift Tube Support Screw	60 (7)
Steering Column Lower Bracket Bolt	106 (12)
Tilt Release Spring Retaining Screw	35 (4)
Turn Signal Retaining Plate Screw	27 (3)
Upper Bracket Nut	106 (12)

1991 STEERING
Manual Recirculating Ball

Cherokee, Comanche
Grand Wagoneer, Wrangler

DESCRIPTION & OPERATION

Steering gear is a recirculating ball-type and consists of a ball nut connected to steering worm and in mesh with sector gear. Proper engagement between sector and ball nut is obtained by adjusting screw. Worm bearing adjuster can be turned to provide proper preloading of upper and lower bearings.

ADJUSTMENTS

NOTE: Adjust worm bearing preload prior to performing over-center preload adjustment. If steering gear is removed, install INCH lb. torque wrench on worm shaft to check preload adjustments.

WORM BEARING PRELOAD

1) Raise and support vehicle. Place reference mark on pitman arm and sector shaft. Remove pitman arm from sector shaft. Loosen sector shaft adjuster screw lock nut and back out adjuster screw 2-3 turns. *See Fig. 1.*

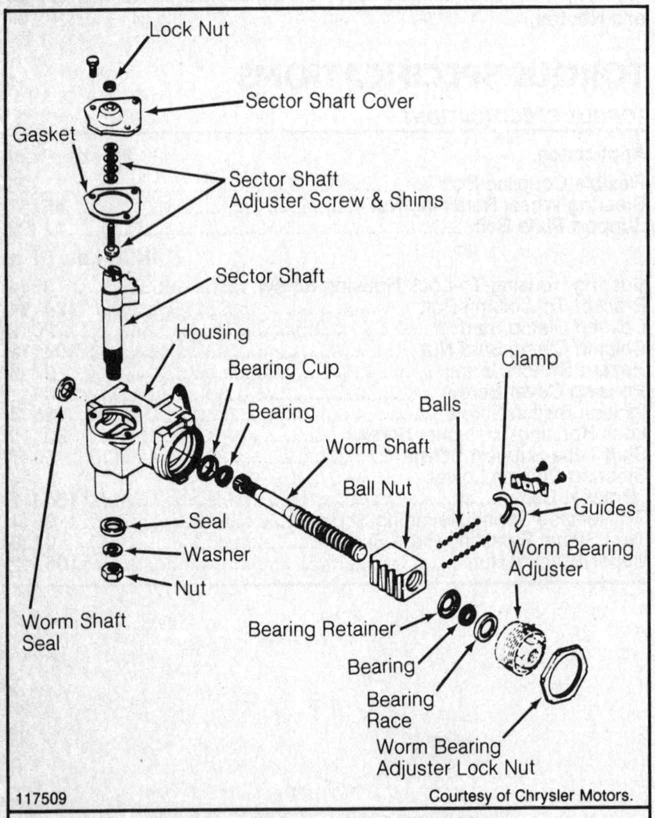
Lock Nut
Sector Shaft Cover
Gasket
Sector Shaft
Adjuster Screw & Shims
Sector Shaft
Housing
Bearing Cup
Clamp
Bearing
Balls
Worm Shaft
Ball Nut
Guides
Seal
Washer
Worm Bearing
Adjuster
Nut
Worm Shaft
Seal
Bearing Retainer
Bearing
Bearing
Race
Worm Bearing
Adjuster Lock Nut
117509
Courtesy of Chrysler Motors.

Fig. 1: Exploded View of Steering Gear Assembly

2) Remove horn button. Turn wheel to the right stop, turn wheel back 1/2 turn. Using an INCH lb. torque wrench on steering shaft nut, rotate steering shaft from right stop through a 90 degree arc and note torque wrench reading. Torque required to maintain wheel movement should be 5-8 INCH lbs. (.6-1 N.m).

NOTE: If rotating torque is exceptionally high, check steering column/shaft alignment. If alignment is okay, disassemble steering gear and repair as required.

3) If torque reading is not as specified, loosen worm bearing adjuster lock nut. *See Fig. 1.* Rotate worm bearing adjuster clockwise to increase preload or counterclockwise to decrease preload.

4) Hold worm bearing adjuster while tightening lock nut to 50 ft. lbs. (68 N.m). Recheck worm bearing preload. Adjust over-center preload.

OVER-CENTER PRELOAD

1) With worm bearing preload adjusted, turn worm shaft slowly from stop-to-stop while counting total number of turns. Turn shaft back to the exact center position.

2) Loosen lock nut and turn sector shaft adjuster screw in until all lash is taken out of sector shaft. Tighten lock nut. Rotate worm shaft slightly off center (1/2 turn). Attach an INCH lb. torque wrench to worm shaft or steering wheel nut.

3) Rotate worm shaft back through center position and note rotating torque. Rotating torque should be 4-10 INCH lbs. (.4-1.1 N.m) in excess of worm bearing preload. Maximum torque should not exceed 18 INCH lbs. (2 N.m). If rotating torque is not within specification, adjust sector shaft adjuster screw.

REMOVAL & INSTALLATION

STEERING GEAR

Removal & Installation – 1) Disconnect intermediate shaft from steering gear. Raise and support vehicle. Disconnect drag link from pitman arm. Stabilizer bar may require removal for access to drag link.

2) Mark relationship of pitman arm-to-sector shaft. Remove pitman arm retaining nut. Using puller, remove pitman arm. Remove steering gear mounting bolts and remove gear assembly.

3) To install, reverse removal procedure. Ensure all reference marks are aligned. Stake pitman arm nut against the shaft in several areas to provide safe retention.

TIE ROD END

Removal & Installation – 1) Remove cotter pins and retaining nuts at both ends of tie rod and remaining steering components. *See Figs. 2-4.* Disconnect steering damper from tie rod. Using puller, separate tie rod ends from steering knuckles and steering linkage.

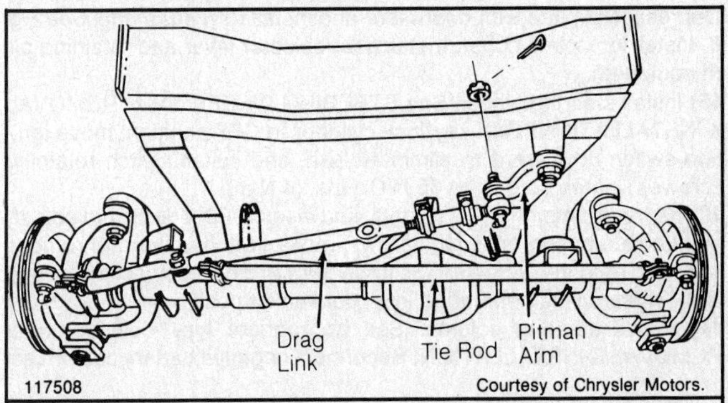
Drag
Link
Tie Rod
Pitman
Arm
117508
Courtesy of Chrysler Motors.

Fig. 2: Identifying Steering Linkage (Cherokee & Comanche)

2) Loosen clamp bolts at adjusting sleeve. Remove tie rod ends from adjusting sleeve. Note number of turns required to remove tie rod, for assembly reference.

3) To install, reverse removal procedure. Adjusting sleeve clamp bolts should be installed with threaded end of bolt toward rear of vehicle and angled slightly upward. Check and adjust toe-in. See SPECIFICATIONS & PROCEDURES article in WHEEL ALIGNMENT.

STEERING DAMPER

Removal & Installation – Place front wheels in straight-ahead position. Remove cotter pins and retaining nuts and bolts at both ends of damper and steering linkage. *See Figs. 2-4.* Remove damper assembly and rubber bushings. To install, reverse removal procedure.

DRAG LINK

Removal & Installation – Separate steering damper from drag link. Remove cotter pins and nuts from both ends of drag link. Using a puller, separate drag link from steering linkage. To install, reverse removal procedure. Ensure wheels are in straight-ahead position and pitman arm is centered prior to installation.

1991 STEERING
Manual Recirculating Ball (Cont.)

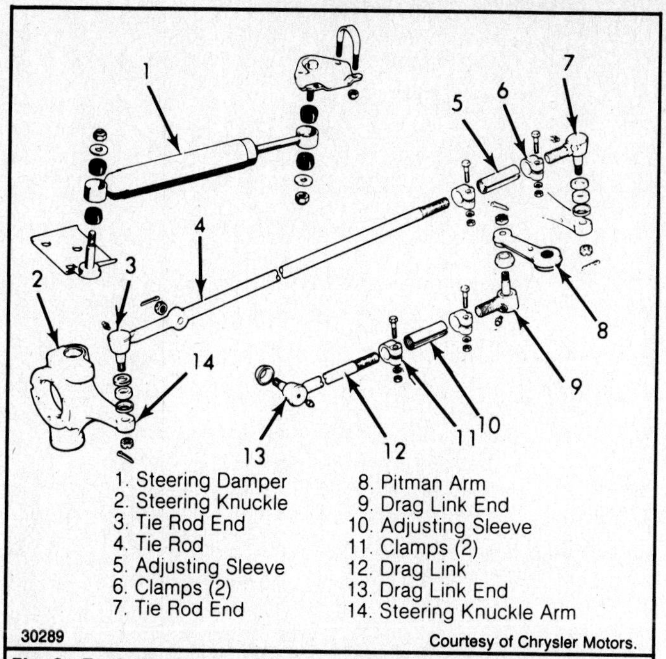
1
2
3
4
5
6
7
8
9
10
11
12
13
14
1. Steering Damper
2. Steering Knuckle
3. Tie Rod End
4. Tie Rod
5. Adjusting Sleeve
6. Clamps (2)
7. Tie Rod End
8. Pitman Arm
9. Drag Link End
10. Adjusting Sleeve
11. Clamps (2)
12. Drag Link
13. Drag Link End
14. Steering Knuckle Arm
30289
Courtesy of Chrysler Motors.

Fig. 3: Exploded View Of Steering Linkage (Grand Wagoneer)

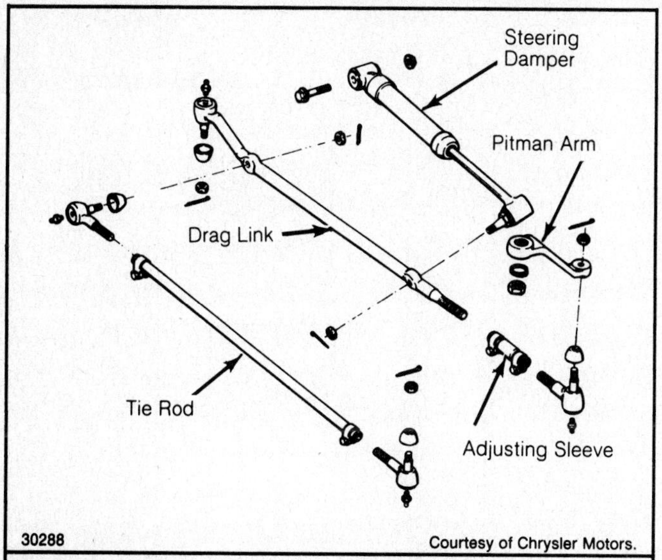
Steering Damper
Pitman Arm
Drag Link
Tie Rod
Adjusting Sleeve
30288
Courtesy of Chrysler Motors.

Fig. 4: Exploded View Of Steering Linkage (Wrangler)

OVERHAUL

DISASSEMBLY

1) Place steering gear in a vise, clamping onto one mounting tab. Worm shaft should be in a horizontal position. Rotate worm shaft from stop-to-stop while counting total number of turns. Turn shaft back to the exact center position.

2) Loosen sector shaft adjuster screw lock nut. Remove sector shaft cover bolts. Lift sector shaft cover and sector shaft from housing.

3) Loosen worm bearing adjuster lock nut. Remove worm bearing adjuster with bearing and bearing race. *See Fig. 1.* Remove ball nut and worm shaft assembly.

CAUTION: DO NOT allow ball nut to rotate down to either end of worm shaft as ball guide ends may be damaged.

4) Remove remaining bearing from the housing. Using screwdriver, pry bearing retainer from worm bearing adjuster assembly and remove bearing. Remove sector shaft adjuster screw lock nut.

5) Hold sector shaft cover and turn sector shaft adjuster screw clockwise to remove sector shaft cover. Remove sector shaft adjuster screw and shim from sector shaft. Pry out and discard both sector shaft and worm shaft seals.

CLEANING & INSPECTION

Clean components with solvent and dry with compressed air. Inspect bearings and races for signs of wear. Check ball nut and worm shaft assembly for wear and straightness.

COMPONENT SERVICE

Worm Shaft Bearing Race (In Worm Bearing Adjuster) – Using slide hammer and puller, remove bearing race from worm bearing adjuster. Using proper diameter installer, install bearing race in worm bearing adjuster.

Worm Shaft Bearing Race (In Housing) – Using a hammer and punch, remove bearing race from the housing. Using proper diameter installer, install new bearing race in the housing.

Ball Nut & Worm Shaft Assembly – Ball nut disassembly is necessary only if binding or tightness exists while rotating worm shaft. If disassembly is required, proceed as follows:

1) Remove clamp that retains ball guides. Ensure a proper area to catch the balls. Pull guides from ball nut while catching balls in clean pan. Turn ball nut over and rotate worm shaft until all balls (50) are removed.

2) Remove worm shaft from the ball nut. Wash parts and inspect worm, nut grooves, and ball bearings for indentations. Check ball guides for damage at ends where they deflect or pick up balls from helical path on worm shaft.

3) To reassemble ball nut and worm shaft, hold the ball nut with helical grooved bore in a horizontal position with ball guide holes facing upward.

4) Position ball nut so that wider/deeper side of the teeth is closer to the sector shaft cover opening after installation. Install worm shaft. Ensure worm shaft is aligned with grooves in the ball nut.

5) Rotate worm shaft until same number of shaft threads exist on both ends of ball nut. Install one ball in each guide hole on ball nut. Move worm shaft up and down and side-to-side until balls rotate into the ball nut and support the worm shaft.

6) Install guides in ball nut. Place 25 balls in a container. Install 25 balls in one guide hole while rotating the worm shaft. Repeat procedure for the remaining guide using 25 balls. Install clamps and bolts.

REASSEMBLY

1) Place gear housing in a vise with worm shaft bore horizontal and sector shaft cover opening facing upward. All bushings and worm shaft bearing races should be installed.

2) Place upper ball bearing over worm shaft. Install worm shaft and ball nut assembly into housing and up through the upper ball bearing race. Install bearing and retainer in worm bearing adjuster.

3) Install worm bearing adjuster in housing. Tighten worm bearing adjuster until a very slight amount of worm shaft end play exists. Install sector shaft adjuster screw and shim in slotted end of sector shaft.

4) Using feeler gauge, check clearance between adjuster screw and sector shaft when holding adjuster screw upward. Clearance should not exceed .002" (.05 mm). If clearance exceeds specification, a different thickness shim should be installed.

5) To lubricate gear, rotate worm shaft until ball nut is at end of travel, while forcing as much grease as possible into housing without losing it out sector shaft opening. Rotate worm shaft until ball nut is at other end, and apply more lubricant.

6) Rotate worm shaft until ball nut is at center of its travel. Install sector shaft assembly so center tooth of sector teeth enters center tooth space in ball nut.

7) Apply more lubricant in the housing. Install side cover gasket. Coat sector shaft adjuster screw with a non-hardening thread sealant. Install side cover over sector shaft by reaching through cover with a screwdriver.

1991 STEERING
Manual Recirculating Ball (Cont.)

8) Turn adjuster screw until sector shaft cover almost contacts the gasket. Install cover retaining bolts finger tight only. Turn sector shaft adjuster screw until sector shaft cover is tight against gasket and then loosen 1/2 turn. Loosely install a new lock nut onto adjuster screw.
9) Lubricate all seals with grease. Wrap sector shaft treads with single layer of tape. Install sector shaft seal in the housing. Remove tape. Install worm shaft seal. Ensure seals are fully seated.
10) Tighten sector shaft cover bolts to specification. Adjust worm bearing preload and over-center preload. See WORM BEARING PRELOAD and OVER-CENTER PRELOAD under ADJUSTMENTS.

TORQUE SPECIFICATIONS

TORQUE SPECIFICATIONS

Application	Ft. Lbs. (N.m)
Drag Link Clamp Bolt	
Cherokee & Comanche	14 (19)
Grand Wagoneer	30 (41)
Wrangler	36 (49)
Drag Link-To-Pitman Arm Nut	60 (81)
Drag Link-To-Steering Knuckle Nut	
Cherokee & Comanche	35 (47)
Drag Link-To-Tie Rod Nut	
Wrangler	35 (47)
Pitman Arm-To-Sector Shaft Nut	185 (251)
Sector Shaft Adjuster Screw Lock Nut	25 (34)
Sector Shaft Cover Bolt	45 (61)
Steering Damper Nut	
Grand Wagoneer	30 (41)
Steering Damper-To-Axle Bracket Bolt	
Cherokee, Comanche & Wrangler	55 (75)
Steering Damper-To-Drag Link Nut	
Cherokee & Comanche	35 (47)
Steering Damper-To-Tie Rod Nut	
Wrangler	53 (72)
Steering Gear-To-Frame Bolt	65 (88)
Tie Rod Clamp Bolt	
Cherokee & Comanche	36 (49)
Grand Wagoneer	30 (41)
Wrangler	14 (19)
Tie Rod End Stud Nut	
Cherokee, Comanche & Wrangler	35 (47)
Grand Wagoneer	60 (81)
Worm Bearing Adjuster Lock Nut	50 (68)

1991 STEERING
Power Recirculating Ball

Cherokee, Comanche
Grand Wagoneer, Wrangler

DESCRIPTION & OPERATION

The 2 types of Saginaw vane-type power steering pumps are vane submerged and vane non-submerged. The vanes of both pumps are driven by a rotor and move fluid from the intake to the pressure cavities of pump ring.

Centrifugal force moves vanes against inside surface of pump ring to pick up residual oil. As more oil is picked up, it is forced into cavities of thrust plate, into 2 crossover holes in pump ring and pressure plate, and into a high pressure area between pressure plate and housing end plate.

Filling the high pressure area causes oil to flow under the vanes in slots of the rotor. This forces vanes to follow inside oval surface of pump ring. As vanes rotate to small area of pump ring, oil is forced out from between vanes.

Steering gear is a variable ratio, recirculating ball type. Control valves are located inside steering gear housing.

POWER STEERING APPLICATION

Application	Type
Cherokee & Comanche	
2.5L	Non-Submerged
4.0L	Submerged
Grand Wagoneer	Submerged
Wrangler	Non-Submerged

LUBRICATION

CAPACITY

Information is not available from manufacturer.

FLUID TYPE

RECOMMENDED FLUID

Application	Type
All Models	Mopar Power Steering Fluid

FLUID LEVEL CHECK

Check fluid with engine stopped and fluid hot or cold. Fluid level must be at HOT or COLD mark on dipstick, depending on engine temperature. Use ONLY Mopar power steering fluid.

HYDRAULIC SYSTEM BLEEDING

1) Fill reservoir. Operate engine until fluid reaches operating temperature of 170°F (77°C). Turn wheels to full left position. Check fluid, and add if necessary.

2) Start and operate engine at fast idle. Recheck reservoir level. Add fluid if necessary. Turn wheels from side to side without contacting stops. Maintain fluid level just above pump body.

3) When air is removed, return wheels to straight-ahead position. Run engine 2-3 minutes. Road test vehicle. Recheck fluid level.

ADJUSTMENTS

POWER STEERING PUMP BELT

BELT TENSION SPECIFICATIONS [1]

Application	New Belt	Used Belt
Serpentine Belt	180-200	140-160
V-Belt	120-160	90-115

[1] – Tension specifications in Lbs. using Burroughs tension gauge.

WORM SHAFT THRUST BEARING PRELOAD

CAUTION: Always adjust worm shaft bearing preload before adjusting pitman shaft over-center preload torque.

1) Remove steering gear from vehicle. See STEERING GEAR under REMOVAL & INSTALLATION. Rotate gear lock-to-lock several times to drain fluid. Loosen adjuster plug lock nut. *See Fig. 1.* Using spanner wrench, turn adjuster plug clockwise until plug is seated in housing. Torque will be about 20 ft. lbs. (27 N.m).

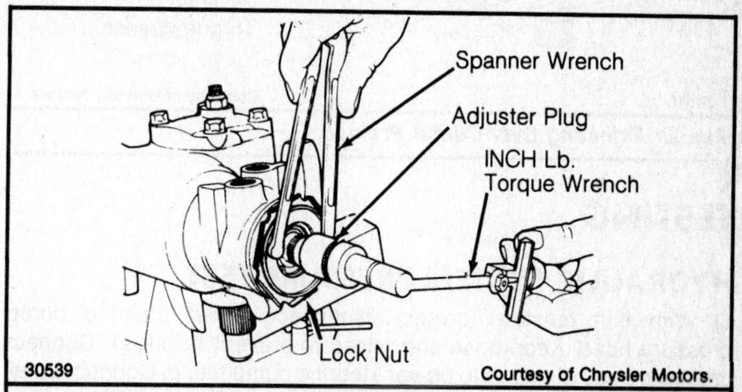
Spanner Wrench
Adjuster Plug
INCH Lb.
Torque Wrench
Lock Nut
30539
Courtesy of Chrysler Motors.

Fig. 1: Measuring Thrust Bearing Preload

2) Index mark housing opposite one hole in adjuster plug. Measure back about 1/4" (6 mm) counterclockwise from mark. Mark housing. Rotate plug counterclockwise until hole in adjuster aligns with second mark.

3) Tighten lock nut to 80 ft. lbs. (108 N.m). Ensure adjuster plug remains in position. Attach INCH Lb. torque wrench to end of stub shaft. Turn stub shaft to right stop, and then back 1/4 turn.

4) Using torque wrench, measure rotational torque required to turn shaft. Take reading with handle of torque wrench nearly vertical while turning it counterclockwise at an even rate. Reading should be 4-10 INCH lbs. (.5-1.1 N.m).

5) If torque wrench reading is not within specifications, adjustment cap may not be correctly adjusted, steering gear may be assembled incorrectly or thrust bearings and races may be defective.

PITMAN SHAFT OVER-CENTER PRELOAD

1) Rotate stub shaft from stop-to-stop and count turns. Rotate shaft in reverse direction 1/2 number turned during stop-to-stop. Ensure steering gear is centered. When steering is centered, flat area on stub shaft should face upward and be parallel with adjustment screw cover and pitman shaft master spline.

2) Over-center drag on NEW steering gear (less than 400 miles) should be equal to measured worm shaft bearing torque, plus an additional 4-8 INCH lbs. (.5-.9 N.m). Torque should NOT exceed 18 INCH lbs. (2 N.m).

3) Over-center drag on USED steering gear (more than 400 miles) should be equal to measured worm shaft bearing torque, plus an additional 4-5 INCH lbs. (.5-.6 N.m). Torque should NOT exceed 18 INCH lbs. (2 N.m).

4) Measure pitman shaft over-center preload torque by rotating torque wrench attached to stub shaft in a 45-degree arc on each side of vertical center. Record highest center-of-travel reading.

5) If necessary, adjust over-center preload torque. Loosen lock nut. *See Fig. 2.* Rotate sector shaft adjustment screw until specified reading is obtained. See LASH ADJUSTMENT PRELOAD – INCH LBS. (N.m) table. Ensure lock nut is tight when reading is obtained.

LASH ADJUSTMENT PRELOAD – INCH LBS. (N.m)

Application	Degrees	Over-Center	[1] Total
New Gears [2]	90	4-8 (.5-.9)	18 (2.0)
Used Gears [3]	90	4-5 (.5-.6)	14 (1.6)

[1] – Total preload is sum of thrust bearing and over-center preload.
[2] – In service for less than 400 miles.
[3] – In service for more than 400 miles.

1991 STEERING
Power Recirculating Ball (Cont.)

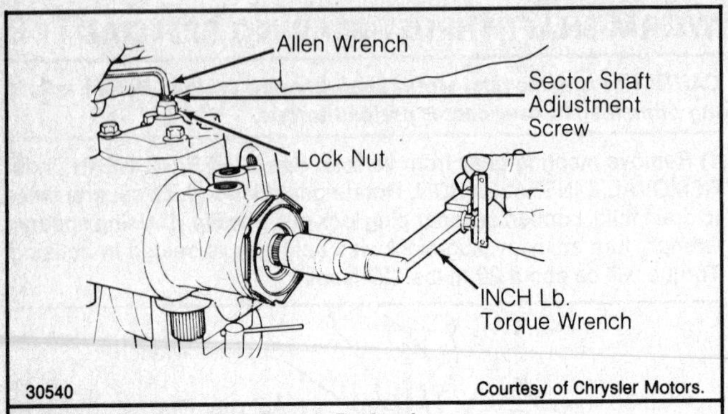
Allen Wrench
Sector Shaft
Adjustment
Screw
Lock Nut
INCH Lb.
Torque Wrench
30540
Courtesy of Chrysler Motors.

Fig. 2: Adjusting Over-Center Preload

TESTING

HYDRAULIC SYSTEM PRESSURE TEST

1) With belt tension correct, disconnect power steering pump pressure hose. Keep hose end raised to prevent fluid loss. Connect pressure hose of gauge to power steering pump fitting. Connect other hose from valve side of tester to steering gear inlet.

2) Open valve. Run engine until fluid reaches normal operating temperature of 170°F (77°C). Check fluid level. Add fluid if necessary.

3) Note pressure reading with valve open and engine idling. Pressure should be less than 150 psi (11 kg/cm²). If pressure exceeds 150 psi (11 kg/cm²), check hoses for restrictions and poppet valve for proper assembly.

4) Close and reopen gate valve completely 3 times. Record highest reading each time. DO NOT close valve longer than 5 seconds. Note if pressure is within specifications. See PRESSURE TEST SPECIFICATIONS table.

5) If all readings are within specifications and 50 psi (3.5 kg/cm²) of each other, pump is operating properly.

6) If readings exceed specifications or are not within 50 psi (3.5 kg/cm²) of each other, flow control valve in pump is sticking. Remove flow control valve. Clean or replace valve as necessary.

7) If readings are below specifications, clean or replace flow control valve. If pressures are still low, replace pump.

8) If readings are all within specifications, open valve, and turn steering wheel from right stop to left stop. Record pressure. DO NOT hold wheel against stops longer than 5 seconds.

9) Compare both readings to pump output pressure reading obtained. Readings should be same as pump output pressure. If readings are low, steering gear is leaking internally. Repair or replace as required.

PRESSURE TEST SPECIFICATIONS

Application	Idle Pressure psi (kg/cm²)	Relief Pressure psi (kg/cm²)
Wrangler	Less Than 150 (11)	1000-1100 (70-77)
All Others	Less Than 150 (11)	1350-1450 (95-102)

REMOVAL & INSTALLATION

POWER STEERING PUMP

Removal & Installation – 1) Loosen and remove pump drive belt. Disconnect pressure and return hoses from pump. Cap ends to prevent loss of fluid or contamination.

2) Remove bracket-to-engine bolts. Remove pump and mounting bracket as an assembly. To install, reverse removal procedure. Fill and bleed system. See HYDRAULIC SYSTEM BLEEDING under LUBRICATION.

STEERING GEAR

Removal – 1) Center steering gear. Disconnect intermediate shaft. Raise and support vehicle. Place drain pan under steering gear assembly. Disconnect hydraulic hoses from gear. Cap ends. Disconnect steering linkage from pitman arm.

2) Remove pitman arm from gear. Remove flexible coupling clamp bolt. Remove steering gear-to-frame bolts. Remove gear from flexible coupling and frame.

Installation – To install, reverse removal procedure. Fill pump reservoir. Bleed air from system. See HYDRAULIC SYSTEM BLEEDING under LUBRICATION.

TIE ROD END

Removal & Installation – 1) Remove cotter pins and retaining nuts at tie rod end. *See Figs. 3-5*. If necessary, disconnect steering damper from tie rod. Using puller, separate tie rod end from steering knuckle or steering linkage.

2) Loosen clamp bolts at adjusting sleeve. Remove tie rod end from adjusting sleeve. Note number of turns required to remove tie rod end for installation reference.

3) To install, reverse removal procedure. Adjusting sleeve clamp bolts should be installed with threaded end of bolt toward rear of vehicle and angled slightly upward. Check and adjust toe-in. See SPECIFICATIONS & PROCEDURES article in WHEEL ALIGNMENT.

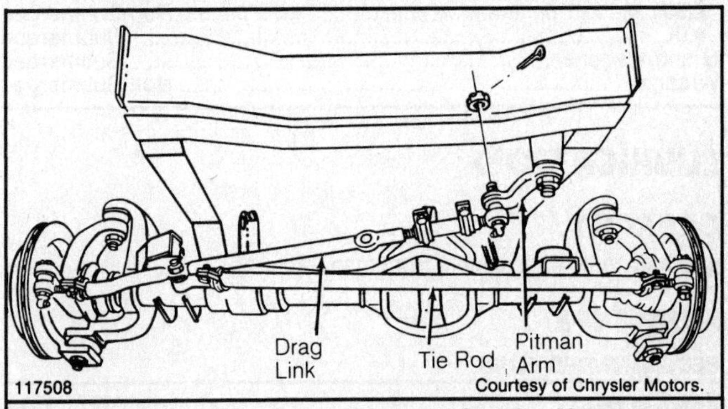
Drag
Link
Tie Rod
Pitman
Arm
117508
Courtesy of Chrysler Motors.

Fig. 3: Identifying Cherokee & Comanche Steering Linkage

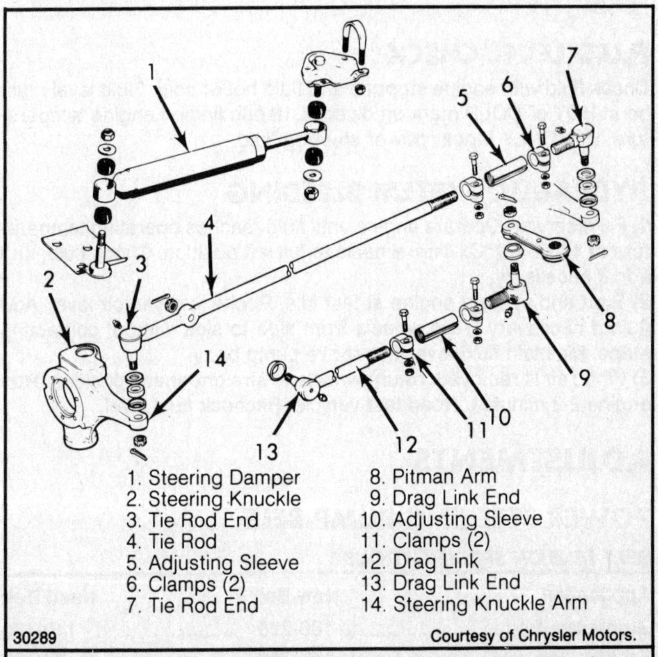
1
2
3
4
5
6
7
8
9
10
11
12
13
14
1. Steering Damper
2. Steering Knuckle
3. Tie Rod End
4. Tie Rod
5. Adjusting Sleeve
6. Clamps (2)
7. Tie Rod End
8. Pitman Arm
9. Drag Link End
10. Adjusting Sleeve
11. Clamps (2)
12. Drag Link
13. Drag Link End
14. Steering Knuckle Arm
30289
Courtesy of Chrysler Motors.

Fig. 4: Exploded View of Steering Linkage (Grand Wagoneer)

1991 STEERING
Power Recirculating Ball (Cont.)

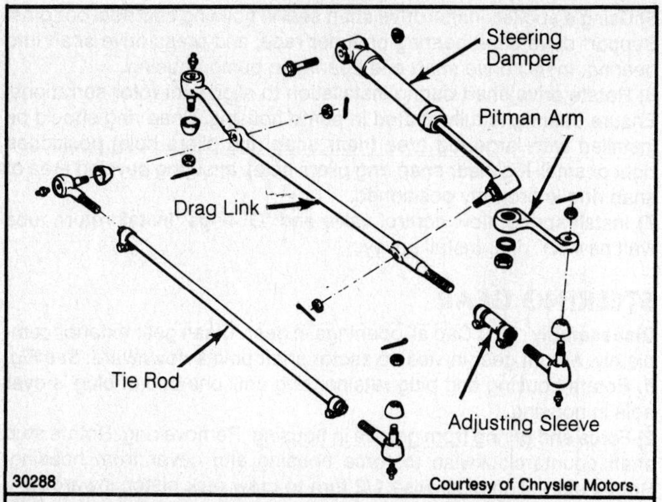
Steering
Damper
Pitman Arm
Drag Link
Tie Rod
Adjusting Sleeve
30288
Courtesy of Chrysler Motors.

Fig. 5: Exploded View of Steering Linkage (Wrangler)

STEERING DAMPER

Removal & Installation - Place front wheels in straight-ahead position. Remove cotter pins and retaining nuts and bolts at ends of damper and steering linkage. *See Figs. 3-5.* Remove damper assembly and rubber bushings. To install, reverse removal procedure.

DRAG LINK

Removal & Installation - Separate steering damper from drag link. *See Figs. 3-5.* Remove cotter pins and nuts from both ends of drag link. Using a puller, separate drag link from steering linkage. To install, reverse removal procedure. Before installation, ensure wheels are in straight-ahead position and pitman arm is centered.

OVERHAUL

SUBMERGED VANE POWER STEERING PUMP

Disassembly - **1)** Drain pump reservoir. Clean exterior of unit. Measure distance shaft protrudes from pulley, and record for assembly reference. Using pulley remover, remove pulley from shaft. Clamp pump in vise; DO NOT overtighten vise. Remove pressure line union, reservoir mounting stud and reservoir. *See Fig. 6.* Remove and discard pressure line union "O" rings.

2) Using punch and screwdriver, remove end plate retaining ring. Remove end plate and pressure plate spring. Remove "O" ring, flow control valve and spring. Note direction of pump ring installation for reassembly reference.

3) Using soft-faced hammer, tap end of drive shaft to loosen pressure plate. Remove pressure plate, pump ring, vanes, retaining ring, rotor and thrust plate assembly from body. Remove drive shaft. Using a screwdriver, pry drive shaft oil seal from housing. Remove dowel pins and seals.

Cleaning & Inspection - **1)** Clean all pump components in solvent, and blow dry. Inspect flow control valve assembly for wear, scoring, burrs and other damage. Inspect seal bore for burrs, nicks and score marks.

2) Inspect machined surfaces of body for scratches and burrs. Check "O" ring mating surfaces. Inspect drive shaft for excessive wear.

3) Inspect pump ring for roughness. Check thrust plate and pressure plate for scoring and wear. Ensure vanes slide freely but fit snugly into slots. If vanes are loose in slots, replace rotor and/or vanes.

Reassembly - **1)** Before installation, coat all "O" rings, rotor, pressure plate and end plate with petroleum jelly. Install new drive shaft seal in housing. Install "O" ring in third groove of housing. Install dowel pins in thrust plate. Install drive shaft through thrust plate and rotor. Install NEW retaining ring. Ensure rotor slides freely on drive shaft splines.

2) Install drive shaft in pump housing. Ensure thrust plate engages with dowel pins. Install pump ring on dowel pins with rotation arrow facing upward. Install vanes with rounded edges toward pump ring.

3) Lubricate outer chamfered edge of pressure plate with petroleum jelly. Install pressure plate with spring groove facing upward. To seat pressure plate, place large socket on pressure plate and press downward approximately 1/16".

4) Install end plate "O" ring in second groove of housing. Install pressure plate spring and end plate in housing. Press end plate downward, and install retaining ring. Install "O" ring, flow control valve and spring.

5) Install mounting stud and pressure line union "O" rings in rear of pump housing. Lubricate inner edge of reservoir with petroleum jelly, and install. Install mounting stud. Tighten stud to specification. Install pressure line union, and tighten to specification. See TORQUE SPECIFICATIONS table at end of article.

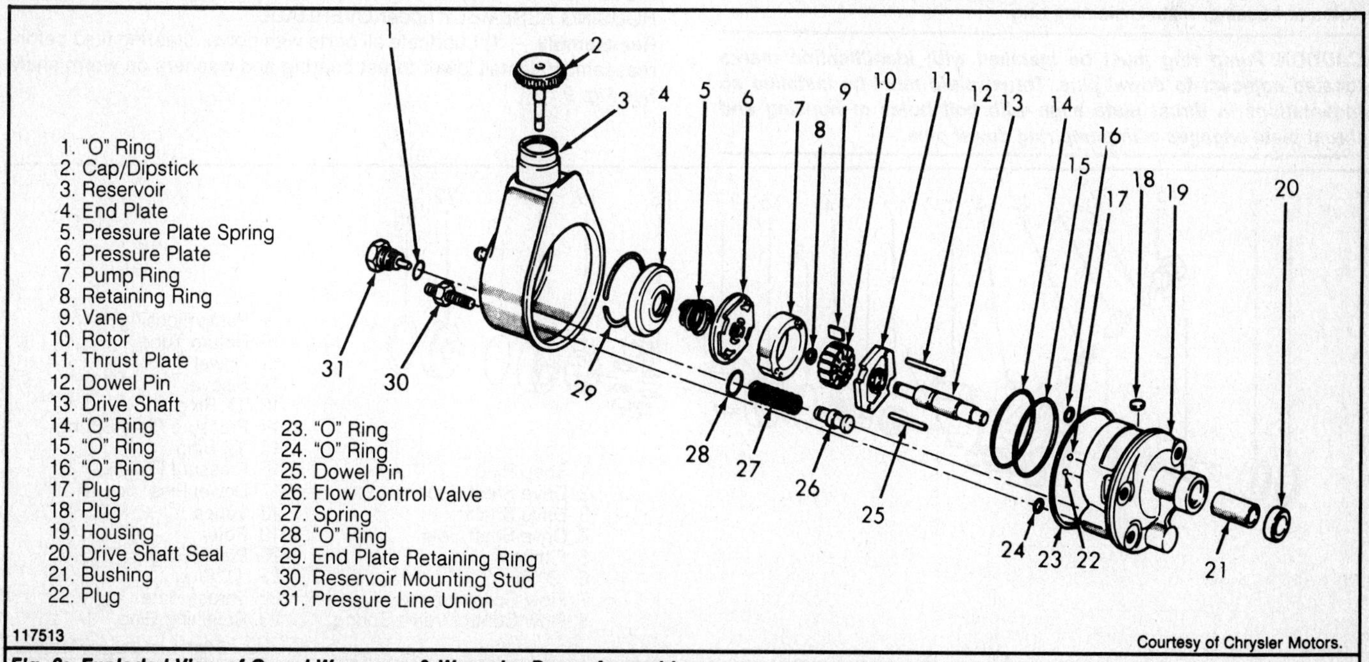
1. "O" Ring
2. Cap/Dipstick
3. Reservoir
4. End Plate
5. Pressure Plate Spring
6. Pressure Plate
7. Pump Ring
8. Retaining Ring
9. Vane
10. Rotor
11. Thrust Plate
12. Dowel Pin
13. Drive Shaft
14. "O" Ring
15. "O" Ring
16. "O" Ring
17. Plug
18. Plug
19. Housing
20. Drive Shaft Seal
21. Bushing
22. Plug
23. "O" Ring
24. "O" Ring
25. Dowel Pin
26. Flow Control Valve
27. Spring
28. "O" Ring
29. End Plate Retaining Ring
30. Reservoir Mounting Stud
31. Pressure Line Union
117513
Courtesy of Chrysler Motors.

Fig. 6: Exploded View of Grand Wagoneer & Wrangler Pump Assembly

1991 STEERING
Power Recirculating Ball (Cont.)

6) Using Pump Pulley Installer (J-25033-B), install pulley on pump shaft. Ensure shaft protrudes distance measured in disassembly procedure.
7) When replacing plastic pulley with metal pulley, install pulley flush with end of shaft. Install pump on engine, and compare alignment with adjacent pulleys. If necessary, correct alignment by using pump pulley installer to adjust shaft protrusion.

NON-SUBMERGED VANE POWER STEERING PUMP

Disassembly - 1) Remove return tube. Clean exterior of unit. Measure distance shaft protrudes through pulley, and record for reassembly reference. Using pulley remover, remove pulley from shaft. Remove fitting, "O" ring, flow control valve and spring. *See Fig. 7.*
2) Remove snap ring, drive shaft and bearing. Note direction of snap ring installation for reassembly reference. Support drive shaft bearing on inner race, and press drive shaft from bearing. Using screwdriver, remove drive shaft seal from housing.
3) Insert punch into access hole to disengage and remove retaining ring. Using a brass drift, tap on thrust plate, and remove. Remove "O" ring, pump ring, rotor and vanes. Remove dowel pins, pressure plate, "O" ring and pressure plate spring. Remove "O" ring, dowel pin and sleeve.
Cleaning & Inspection - 1) Clean all pump components in solvent, and blow dry. Inspect flow control valve assembly for wear, scoring, burrs and other damage. Inspect seal bore for burrs, nicks and score marks.
2) Inspect machined surfaces of body for scratches and burrs. Check "O" ring mating surfaces. Inspect drive shaft and sleeve for wear.
3) Inspect pump ring for roughness. Check thrust plate and pressure plate for scoring and wear. Ensure vanes slide freely but fit snugly into slots. If vanes are loose in slots, replace rotor and/or vanes.
Reassembly - 1) Lubricate all "O" rings, seals, pump ring, rotor and vanes with petroleum jelly. Install sleeve. Ensure sleeve is fully seated.
2) Install "O" ring in sleeve seat. Install small dowel pin in pump housing. Install pressure plate spring and "O" ring. Install pressure plate with dowel pin hole aligned with dowel pin holes. Install dowel pins.
3) Install pump ring with identification marks located adjacent to one dowel pin. Install rotor with counterbore toward drive shaft end of housing.
4) Install vanes with rounded edges toward pump ring. Install thrust plate "O" ring. Install thrust plate with indentations aligned with bolt holes of housing. Install retaining ring.

CAUTION: Pump ring must be installed with identification marks located adjacent to dowel pins. Thrust plate must be installed so indentations in thrust plate align with bolt holes of housing and thrust plate engages with pump ring dowel pins.

5) Using a socket, install drive shaft seal in housing until seal bottoms. Support drive shaft bearing on inner race, and press drive shaft into bearing. Install drive shaft and bearing in pump housing.
6) Rotate drive shaft during installation to align with rotor serrations. Ensure bearing is fully seated in pump housing. Snap ring should be installed with large lug area (near snap ring pliers hole) positioned right of small lug (near snap ring pliers hole), ensuring beveled area of snap ring is properly positioned.
7) Install spring, flow control valve and "O" rings. Install return tube with new "O" ring. Install pulley.

STEERING GEAR

Disassembly - 1) Cap all openings in gear. Clean gear exterior completely. Mount gear in vise so sector shaft points downward. *See Fig. 8.* Rotate housing end plug retainer ring until one end of plug is over hole in housing.
2) Force end of ring from groove in housing. Remove ring. Rotate stub shaft counterclockwise to force housing end cover from housing. Rotate stub shaft clockwise 1/2 turn to draw rack piston inward.

CAUTION: DO NOT rotate stub shaft more than necessary to remove plug as ball bearings will fall out of worm and rack piston assembly.

3) Remove end plug. Remove lock nut from sector shaft adjuster. Remove side cover. Remove and discard "O" ring or gasket from cover. Turn stub shaft until sector shaft teeth are centered in housing.
4) Using a soft-faced hammer, tap end of sector shaft to free shaft from housing. Remove sector shaft. Remove adjuster plug lock nut. Using a spanner wrench, remove adjuster plug.
5) Insert Rack Piston Arbor (C-4175) into end of rack piston assembly until arbor contacts worm shaft. Threaded arbor keeps recirculating balls from falling out of rack piston. Turn stub shaft counterclockwise to force rack piston onto arbor. Remove rack piston and arbor as an assembly.
6) Take care to keep arbor fully inserted so recirculating balls do not fall out. Remove stub shaft and valve body from housing. Remove worm shaft, worm shaft lower thrust bearing and washers from housing.
Inspection - 1) Clean all internal parts in solvent, and dry with compressed air. DO NOT steam clean hydraulic parts. Avoid wiping valve parts with cloth. Lint may cause binding of mechanism.
2) If further disassembly is required, see ADJUSTER PLUG, RACK PISTON & WORM SHAFT ASSEMBLY, VALVE BODY ASSEMBLY or HOUSING ASSEMBLY under OVERHAUL.
Reassembly - 1) Lubricate all parts with power steering fluid before reassembly. Install lower thrust bearing and washers on worm shaft. *See Fig. 9.*

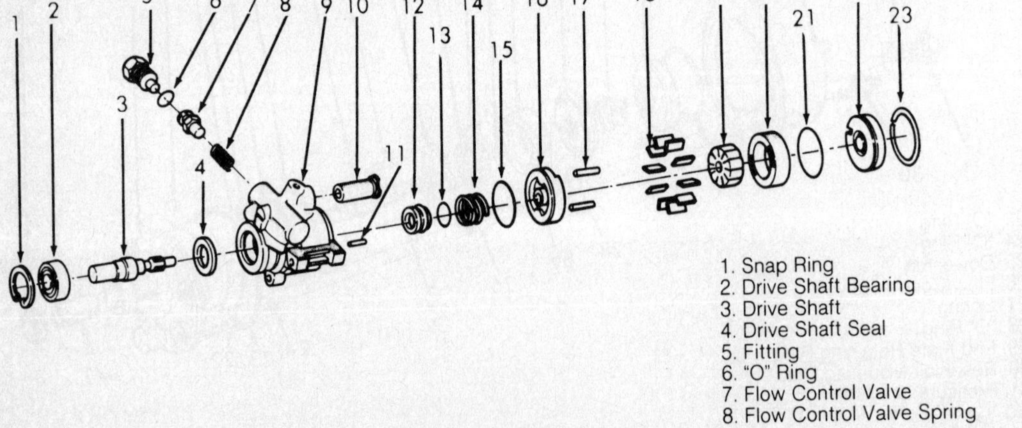
1
2
3
4
5
6
7
8
9
10
11
12
13
14
15
16
17
18
19
20
21
22
23

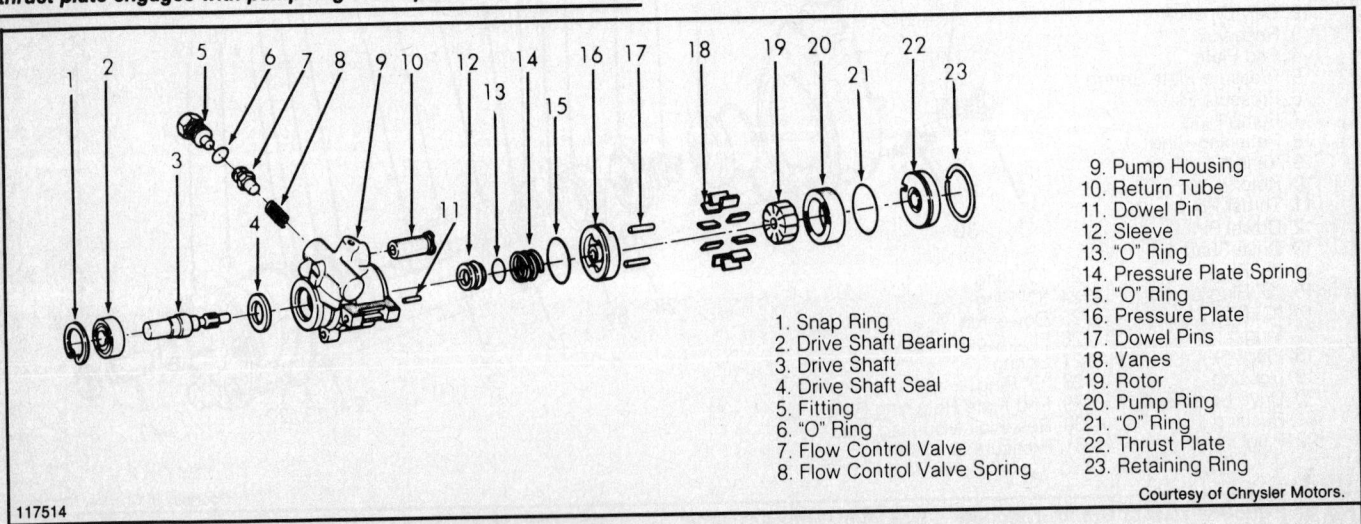

1. Snap Ring
2. Drive Shaft Bearing
3. Drive Shaft
4. Drive Shaft Seal
5. Fitting
6. "O" Ring
7. Flow Control Valve
8. Flow Control Valve Spring
9. Pump Housing
10. Return Tube
11. Dowel Pin
12. Sleeve
13. "O" Ring
14. Pressure Plate Spring
15. "O" Ring
16. Pressure Plate
17. Dowel Pins
18. Vanes
19. Rotor
20. Pump Ring
21. "O" Ring
22. Thrust Plate
23. Retaining Ring

Courtesy of Chrysler Motors.

117514

Fig. 7: Exploded View of Cherokee & Comanche Pump Assembly

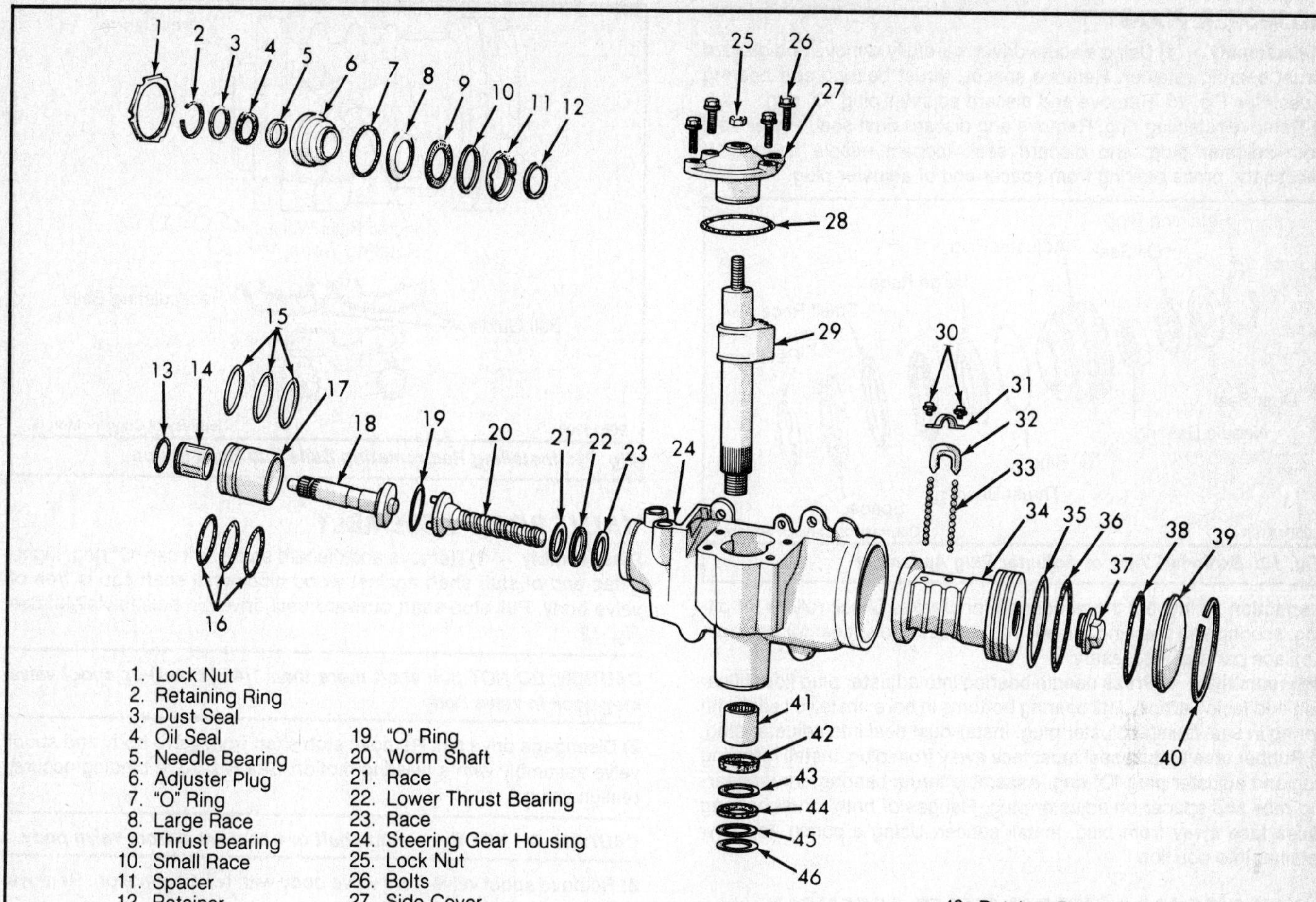

1
2
3
4
5
6
7
8
9
10
11
12
13
14
15
16
17
18
19
20
21
22
23
24
25
26
27
28
29
30
31
32
33
34
35
36
37
38
39
40
41
42
43
44
45
46

1. Lock Nut
2. Retaining Ring
3. Dust Seal
4. Oil Seal
5. Needle Bearing
6. Adjuster Plug
7. "O" Ring
8. Large Race
9. Thrust Bearing
10. Small Race
11. Spacer
12. Retainer
13. "O" Ring
14. Spool Valve
15. Teflon Rings
16. "O" Rings
17. Valve Body
18. Stub Shaft
19. "O" Ring
20. Worm Shaft
21. Race
22. Lower Thrust Bearing
23. Race
24. Steering Gear Housing
25. Lock Nut
26. Bolts
27. Side Cover
28. "O" Ring
29. Sector Shaft
30. Retainer Screws
31. Guide Clamp
32. Ball Guide
33. Recirculating Balls
34. Rack Piston
35. Oil Seal
36. "O" Ring
37. End Plug
38. "O" Ring
39. Housing End Cover
40. Retainer Ring
41. Sector Shaft Bearing
42. Upper Oil Seal
43. Steel Washer
44. Lower Oil Seal
45. Steel Washer
46. Retaining Ring

90J15197

Courtesy of Chrysler Motors.

Fig. 8: Exploded View of Saginaw Rotary Valve Power Steering Gear

NOTE: If conical thrust washers are used, ensure tapered surfaces are parallel to each other and cupped sides face toward stub shaft.

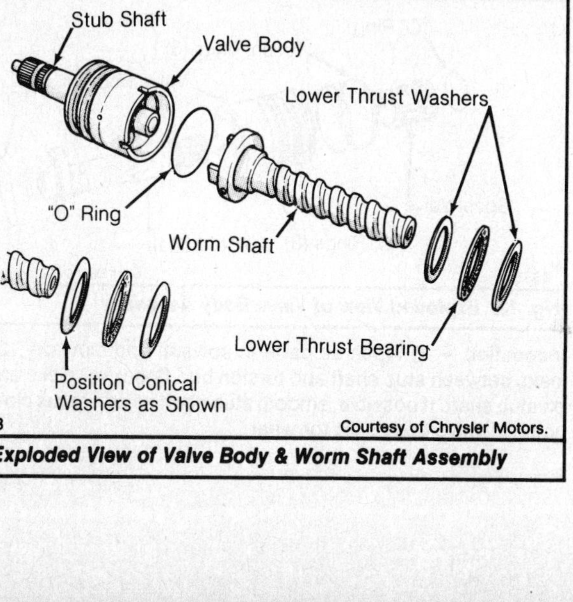

Stub Shaft
Valve Body
Lower Thrust Washers
"O" Ring
Worm Shaft
Lower Thrust Bearing
Position Conical Washers as Shown

90A15198

Courtesy of Chrysler Motors.

Fig. 9: Exploded View of Valve Body & Worm Shaft Assembly

2) Place worm shaft in valve body. Install "O" ring in valve body. Align notch in valve body with pin in worm shaft. Install valve body and worm assembly into housing. Installation is correct when fluid return port in housing is fully visible.

3) Place seal protector over stub shaft. Using new "O" ring, install adjuster plug until it seats against valve body. Remove seal protector from housing.

4) Loosely install adjuster plug lock nut. Insert rack piston (with arbor to retain recirculating balls) into housing. Align worm and rack piston. Turn stub shaft clockwise to engage worm. Maintain pressure on arbor until worm is fully engaged.

5) Rotate stub shaft clockwise to align middle rack groove in rack piston with center of sector shaft roller bearing. Remove arbor. Install a new side cover seal.

6) Thread side cover onto adjuster screw until bottomed. Back off 1/2 turn. Install sector shaft so center gear tooth meshes with center groove in rack piston. Install cover attaching bolts.

7) Install adjuster lock nut halfway onto sector shaft. Install piston and plug in rack piston. Install housing end cover "O" ring, end plug and retainer ring. Adjust worm shaft thrust bearing preload and pitman shaft over-center preload. See WORM SHAFT THRUST BEARING PRELOAD and PITMAN SHAFT OVER-CENTER PRELOAD under ADJUSTMENTS.

1991 STEERING
Power Recirculating Ball (Cont.)

ADJUSTER PLUG

Disassembly – 1) Using a screwdriver, carefully remove and discard thrust bearing retainer. Remove spacer, thrust bearing and bearing races. *See Fig. 10.* Remove and discard adjuster plug "O" ring.
2) Remove retaining ring. Remove and discard dust seal. Pry oil seal from adjuster plug, and discard seal. Inspect needle bearing. If necessary, press bearing from spacer end of adjuster plug.

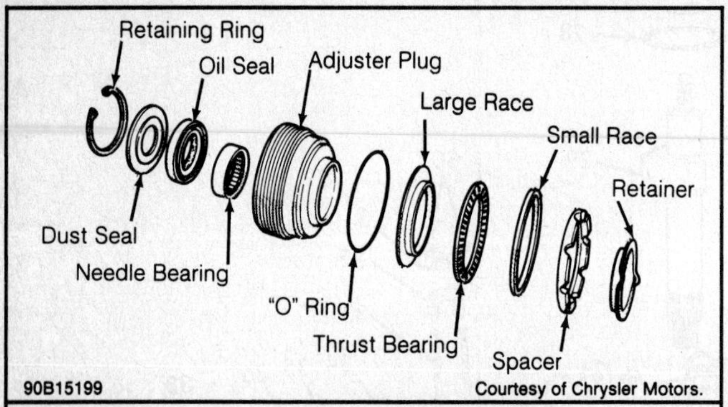
Retaining Ring
Oil Seal
Adjuster Plug
Large Race
Small Race
Retainer
Dust Seal
Needle Bearing
"O" Ring
Thrust Bearing
Spacer
90B15199
Courtesy of Chrysler Motors.

Fig. 10: Exploded View of Adjuster Plug Assembly

Inspection – Inspect thrust bearing for cracks. Check rollers for pitting, scoring and cracking. Check thrust races and spacer for damage. Replace parts as necessary.
Reassembly – 1) Press needle bearing into adjuster plug (identification end facing arbor) until bearing bottoms in bore. Install oil seal with spring in seal facing adjuster plug. Install dust seal into adjuster plug.
2) Rubber face of dust seal must face away from plug. Install retaining ring and adjuster plug "O" ring. Assemble thrust bearing, thrust bearing race and spacer on adjuster plug. Flanges of both thrust bearing races face away from plug. Install spacer. Using a punch, tap new retainer into position.

RACK PISTON & WORM SHAFT ASSEMBLY

Disassembly – Remove guide clamp, place complete unit on clean surface and remove ball guide. Remove arbor from rack piston. Remove and retain 24 recirculating balls. Remove Teflon piston rings and "O" ring seal.
Inspection – 1) Clean and dry all parts. Inspect worm shaft and rack piston grooves for scoring. Inspect recirculating balls for damage. If any ball bearings are damaged, replace entire set. Check ball guides for pinched ends.
2) Inspect lower thrust bearing races for cracking, scoring and pitting. If either race is damaged, replace worm shaft and rack piston as an assembly. Inspect rack piston teeth for chips, cracks, dents and scoring.
Reassembly – 1) Lubricate new Teflon seal and "O" ring with power steering fluid, and carefully install onto rack piston. Install worm shaft into rack piston until worm shaft touches piston shoulder.
2) Turning worm shaft counterclockwise, insert recirculating balls into rack piston hole nearest piston ring. *See Fig. 11.* Install 18 recirculating balls in ball guide, beginning with a BLACK ball, and then alternating between SILVER and BLACK. After installing each ball, press it down to provide space for next ball. Worm shaft will spiral outward as each ball is inserted.
3) Split ball guide halves, and fill one half with petroleum jelly. Install 6 remaining recirculating balls in ball guide half maintaining alternating pattern. Reassemble guide, and install in rack piston. Ensure end balls in guide are alternate of end balls in rack piston.
4) Install clamp, and tighten attaching bolts to 10 ft. lbs. (14 N.m). Insert Rack Piston Arbor (C-4175) into rack piston until it contacts worm shaft. Maintaining pressure on arbor, back worm shaft completely out of rack piston. DO NOT allow recirculating balls to drop out.

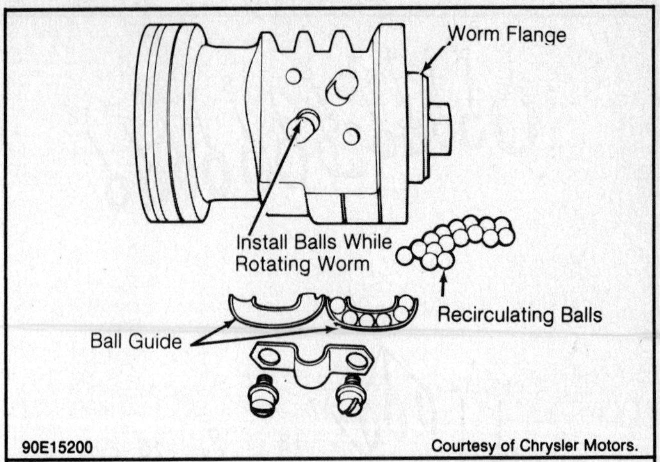
Worm Flange
Install Balls While
Rotating Worm
Recirculating Balls
Ball Guide
90E15200
Courtesy of Chrysler Motors.

Fig. 11: Installing Recirculating Balls Into Rack Piston

VALVE BODY ASSEMBLY

Disassembly – 1) Remove and discard stub shaft cap "O" ring. Lightly tap end of stub shaft against wood block until shaft cap is free of valve body. Pull stub shaft outward until drive pin hole is visible. *See Fig. 12.*

CAUTION: DO NOT pull shaft more than 1/4" (6 mm) or spool valve may cock in valve body.

2) Disengage drive pin. Remove stub shaft from valve body and spool valve assembly with a twisting motion. *See Fig. 13.* If binding occurs, realign valve.

CAUTION: DO NOT force stub shaft or spool valve from valve body.

3) Remove spool valve from valve body with twisting motion. Remove and discard all "O" and Teflon rings.

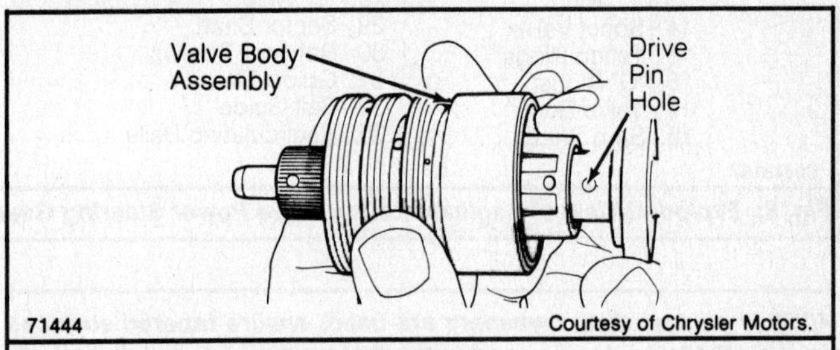
Valve Body
Assembly
Drive
Pin
Hole
71444
Courtesy of Chrysler Motors.

Fig. 12: Pulling Shaft from Valve Body

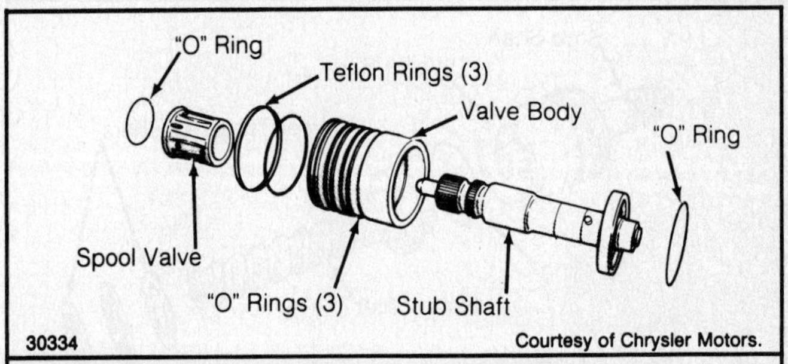
"O" Ring
Teflon Rings (3)
Valve Body
"O" Ring
Spool Valve
"O" Rings (3)
Stub Shaft
30334
Courtesy of Chrysler Motors.

Fig. 13: Exploded View of Valve Body Assembly

Inspection – 1) Wash all parts in solvent, and blow dry. Check for leaks between stub shaft and torsion bar. Check for nicks and scores on stub shaft. If possible, smooth stub shaft using crocus cloth. Check notch in valve body skirt for wear.

1991 STEERING
Power Recirculating Ball (Cont.)

NOTE: Valve body is precision built unit with selectively fitted and balanced components. If any component is faulty, entire assembly MUST be replaced.

2) Hold valve body in both hands. Tap lightly on wooden block to remove stub shaft cap, and discard "O" ring. Check spool valve fit in valve body with "O" ring removed. Lubricate spool valve with power steering fluid. Rotate spool valve in valve body. If valve does not rotate freely, replace complete valve.

Reassembly - 1) Lubricate valve body components with power steering fluid. Install new "O" rings in seal grooves. Carefully install new Teflon rings over "O" rings. DO NOT damage seal rings during installation.

NOTE: Teflon seal rings may appear distorted after installation. However, heat of operation will straighten them.

2) Lubricate spool valve "O" ring with petroleum jelly. Install on spool valve. Carefully insert spool valve into valve body.

3) Push spool valve through valve body until drive pin hole is visible at opposite end of valve body and spool valve is even with notched end of valve. Install stub shaft into spool valve and valve body.

4) Align stub shaft drive pin with spool valve locating hole. Align notch in stub shaft cap with pin in valve body. Press stub shaft and spool valve into valve body. Install stub shaft cap "O" ring into valve body. *See Fig. 9.*

CAUTION: Before installing valve body into gear housing, ensure valve body stub shaft locating pin is fully engaged in stub shaft cap notch. DO NOT allow stub shaft to disengage from valve body pin. See Fig. 14.

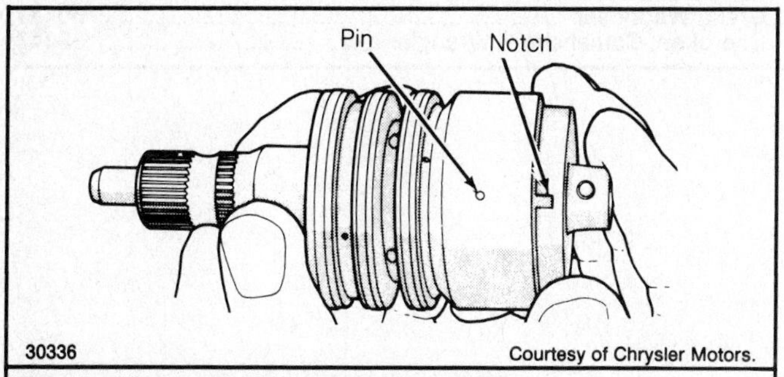
Pin
Notch
30336
Courtesy of Chrysler Motors.

Fig. 14: Aligning Pin & Notch for Stub Shaft

HOUSING ASSEMBLY

Disassembly - 1) Remove sector shaft seal retaining ring. Remove steel washer. Remove lower oil seal, steel washer and upper oil seal from housing. *See Fig. 15.* Press sector shaft bearing out of housing from lower end.

2) If hose connector seat needs replacement, use a 5/16" X 18 thread tap to tap seat. Thread connector seats ONLY 2-3 threads. Install bolt with flat washer and nut into seat. Hold bolt while tightening nut to extract seat.

Inspection - 1) If housing bore is severely worn, scored or pitted, replace housing. Minor scratches may be removed using crocus cloth. Inspect housing ball plug for fluid leakage. Seat ball plug using blunt punch.

2) Spray ball area with Loctite Solvent (7559). Dry with compressed air. Cover ball area with Loctite Sealant (290). Allow sealant to cure 2 hours.

3) Inspect all retaining ring, bearing and seal surfaces in housing. If any surface is worn or damaged, replace housing.

Reassembly - 1) Install sector shaft bearing in steering housing using Handle (C-4171) and Adapter (C-4178). *See Fig. 16.* Position bearing so identification marks face away from adapter. Press in bearing until adapter bottoms against housing. DO NOT bottom bearing in housing.

2) Install lower oil seal, steel washer and upper oil seal on handle and adapter used to install bearing. *See Fig. 17.* Lips of both seals should face toward housing bore.

3) Install steel washer and retaining ring in housing. Using handle and adapter, drive in seals until retaining ring seats in groove.

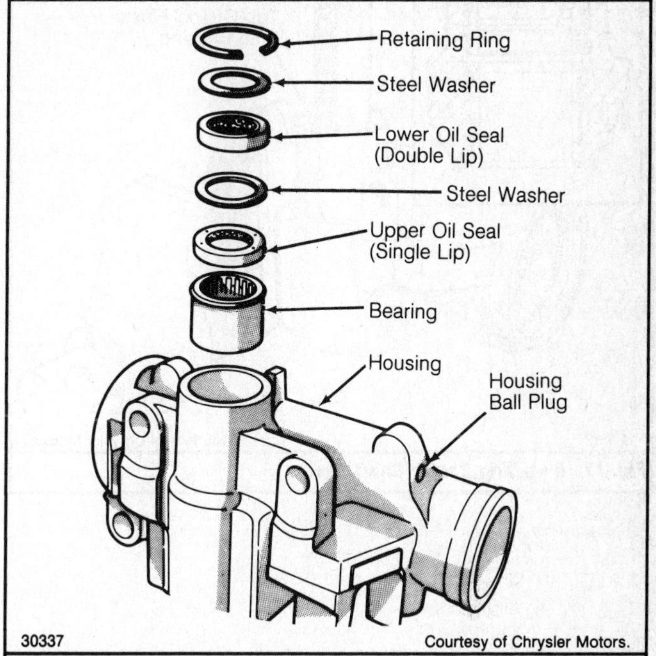
Retaining Ring
Steel Washer
Lower Oil Seal
(Double Lip)
Steel Washer
Upper Oil Seal
(Single Lip)
Bearing
Housing
Housing
Ball Plug
30337
Courtesy of Chrysler Motors.

Fig. 15: Exploded View of Gear Housing Seals & Bearing

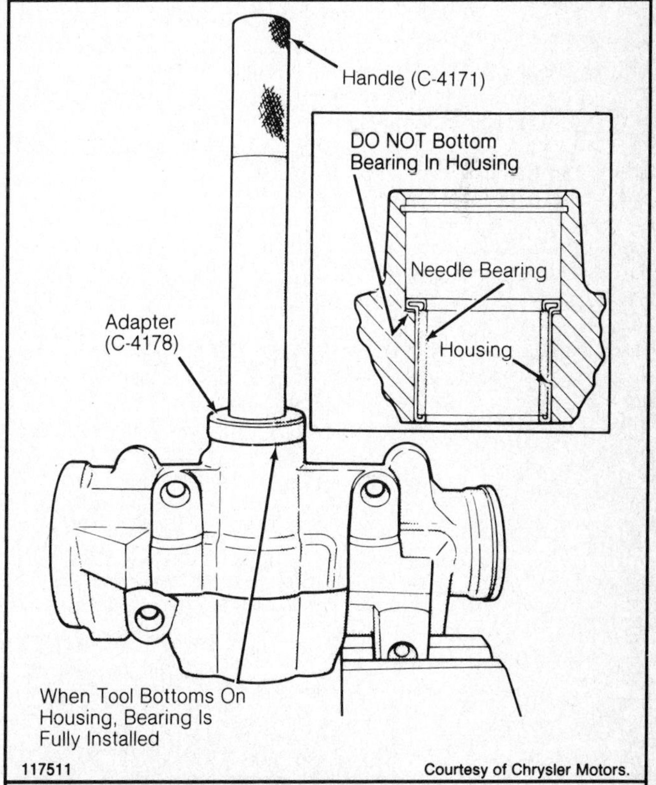
Handle (C-4171)
DO NOT Bottom
Bearing In Housing
Needle Bearing
Housing
Adapter
(C-4178)
When Tool Bottoms On
Housing, Bearing Is
Fully Installed
117511
Courtesy of Chrysler Motors.

Fig. 16: Installing Sector Shaft Bearing

1991 STEERING
Power Recirculating Ball (Cont.)

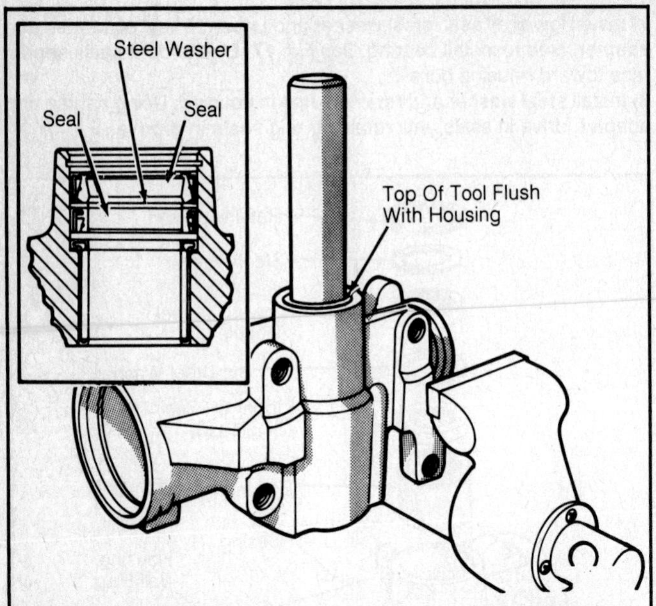
Steel Washer
Seal
Seal
Top Of Tool Flush
With Housing
117512
Courtesy of Chrysler Motors.

Fig. 17: Installing Sector Shaft Seals

TORQUE SPECIFICATIONS

TORQUE SPECIFICATIONS

Application	Ft. Lbs. (N.m)
Adjuster Plug Lock Nut	80 (108)
Drag Link Clamp Bolt	
Cherokee & Comanche	14 (19)
Grand Wagoneer	30 (41)
Wrangler	36 (49)
Drag Link-To-Pitman Arm Nut	60 (81)
Drag Link-To-Steering Knuckle Nut	
Cherokee & Comanche	35 (47)
Drag Link-To-Tie Rod Nut	
Wrangler	35 (47)
Pitman Arm Attaching Nut	185 (251)
Pressure & Return Hose Fitting	21 (29)
Pump Bracket-To-Engine Bolt	33 (45)
Pump Mounting Stud-To-Pump	35 (47)
Pump-To-Bracket Bolt	28 (38)
Pump Pressure Line Union-To-Pump	55 (75)
Rack Piston End Plug	50 (68)
Sector Shaft Adjuster Lock Nut	28 (38)
Side Cover Bolt	45 (61)
Steering Damper Nut	
Grand Wagoneer	30 (41)
Steering Damper-To-Axle Bracket Bolt	
Cherokee, Comanche & Wrangler	55 (75)
Steering Damper-To-Drag Link Nut	
Cherokee & Comanche	35 (47)
Steering Damper-To-Tie Rod Nut	
Wrangler	53 (72)
Steering Gear-To-Frame Bolt	65 (88)
Tie Rod Clamp Bolt	
Cherokee & Comanche	36 (49)
Grand Wagoneer	30 (41)
Wrangler	14 (19)
Tie Rod End Stud Nut	
Grand Wagoneer	60 (81)
Cherokee, Comanche & Wrangler	35 (47)

1991 TRANSMISSION SERVICING
Automatic Transmission

Cherokee, Comanche
Grand Wagoneer, Wrangler

IDENTIFICATION

JEEP AUTOMATIC TRANSMISSION APPLICATIONS

Model	Transmission
Cherokee & Comanche	Aisin Warner AW-4
Grand Wagoneer	Loadflite 727
Wrangler	Loadflite 929

121175

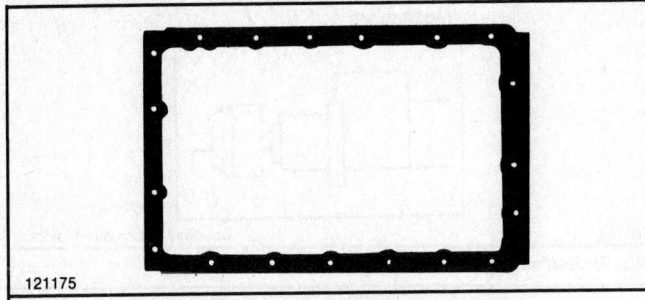

Fig. 1: AW-4 Oil Pan Gasket Identification

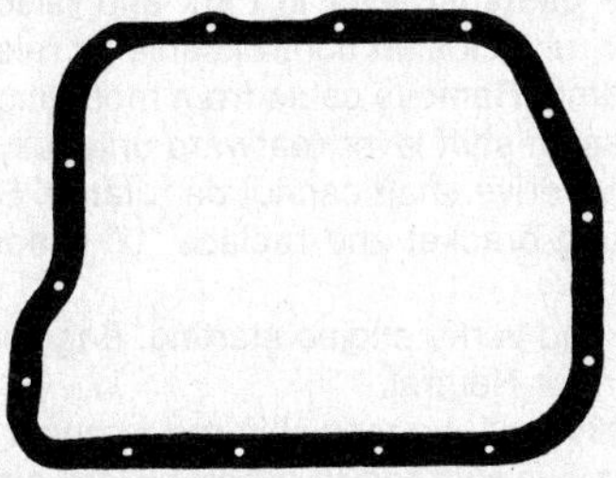

121176

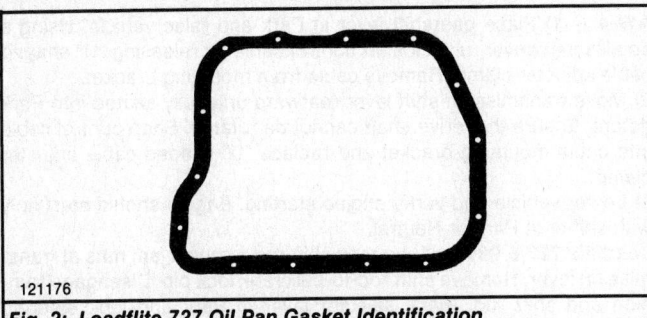

Fig. 2: Loadflite 727 Oil Pan Gasket Identification

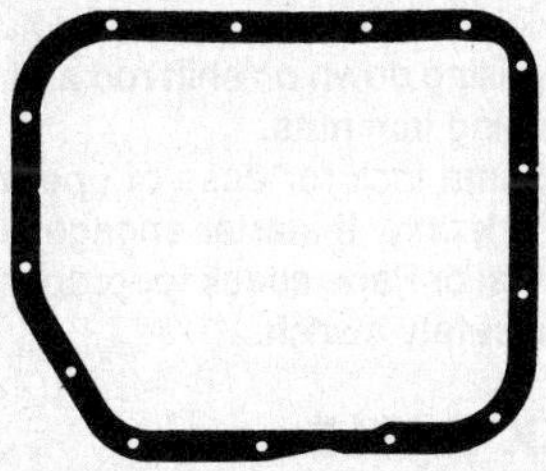

121177

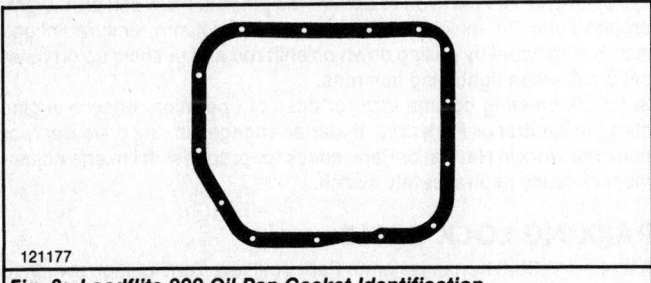

Fig. 3: Loadflite 999 Oil Pan Gasket Identification

LUBRICATION

SERVICE INTERVALS

Transmission – Check fluid level and condition of fluid at 7500 mile intervals. Change fluid, replace filter and adjust bands at 30,000 miles or 30 month intervals.

Transfer Case – Check transfer case fluid every 7500 miles and replace fluid every 30,000 miles or 30 month intervals.

CHECKING FLUID LEVEL

Transmission – Park vehicle on a level surface and apply parking brake. With engine idling at normal operating temperature, move transmission selector lever through all gears, ending in Neutral (Park for AW-4 transmission). Check fluid level. Fluid level should be between FULL and ADD mark on dipstick. Add fluid as needed. DO NOT overfill.

Transfer Case – Remove fill plug. Check oil level. If level is not up to fill plug opening, add lubricant.

RECOMMENDED FLUID

Aisin Warner AW-4 transmissions and transfer cases use Mercon type ATF. Loadflite transmissions use Dexron-II type ATF.

FLUID CAPACITY

NOTE: Transmission and converter capacities are approximate. Fluid level should always be determined by reading on dipstick, rather than amount of fluid added.

TRANSMISSION REFILL CAPACITIES

Application	Qts. (L)
All Models	8.5. (8.0)

TRANSFER CASE REFILL CAPACITIES

Application	Pts. (L)
Model 229	6.0. (2.8)
Model 231	
Wrangler	3.3 (1.5)
All Others	2.2. (1.0)
Model 242	3.0. (1.4)

DRAINING & REFILLING

Transmission – 1) Loosen oil pan bolts, tap pan to break it loose and allow fluid to drain. Remove pan and oil filter. Install new filter on bottom of valve body and tighten retaining screws to 35 INCH lbs. (4 N.m). Clean oil pan and install with new gasket. Tighten bolts to 150 INCH lbs. (17 N.m).

2) Refill transmission with approximately 5 qts. (4.7L) of ATF. Start engine and allow to run at curb idle. With vehicle on level surface, engine idling and parking brake applied, move shift selector lever through all gear ranges, ending in Neutral (Park for AW-4 transmission).

3) Recheck fluid level when transmission reaches normal operating temperature. Add fluid to FULL mark on dipstick.

Transfer Case – Remove drain plug from transfer case. Remove fill plug for easier draining. With fluid fully drained, reinstall drain plug. Fill transfer case and install fill plug. Tighten drain plug and fill plugs to 20 ft. lbs. (27 N.m).

ADJUSTMENTS

NOTE: Bands on the AW-4 transmission are not adjustable. If slippage occurs, bands must be replaced.

KICKDOWN (FRONT) BAND

Loadflite 727 & 999 – 1) Locate kickdown band adjusting screw on left side of case (near throttle lever shaft). *See Fig. 4.* Loosen adjusting

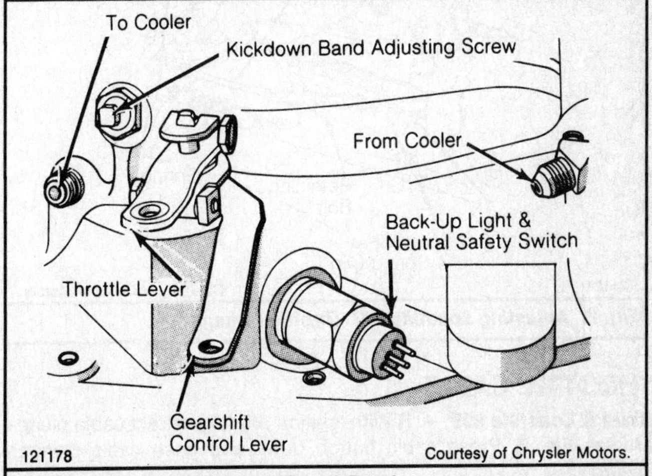
To Cooler
Kickdown Band Adjusting Screw
From Cooler
Back-Up Light &
Neutral Safety Switch
Throttle Lever
Gearshift
Control Lever

121178 Courtesy of Chrysler Motors.

Fig. 4: Adjusting Kickdown (Front) Band

1991 TRANSMISSION SERVICING
Automatic Transmission (Cont.)

screw lock nut and back off 4-5 turns. Ensure adjusting screw turns freely in case.

2) Tighten adjusting screw to 72 INCH lbs. (8 N.m). If Adapter Extension (J-24063) is used, tighten adjusting screw to 50 INCH lbs. (5 N.m). Back off adjusting screw 2 1/2 turns. Hold adjusting screw and tighten lock nut to 30 ft. lbs. (41 N.m).

LOW-REVERSE (REAR) BAND

Loadflite 727 & 999 – 1) Raise and support vehicle. Drain transmission fluid and remove oil pan. Locate low-reverse band adjusting screw on rear servo lever. *See Fig. 5.* Loosen adjusting screw lock nut. On 999 transmission, back off adjusting screw 4 turns. On 727 transmission back off adjusting screw 2 turns.

2) Tighten adjusting screw to 72 INCH lbs. (8 N.m). Hold adjusting screw and tighten lock nut to 25 ft. lbs. (34 N.m). Install oil pan and fill transmission with fluid.

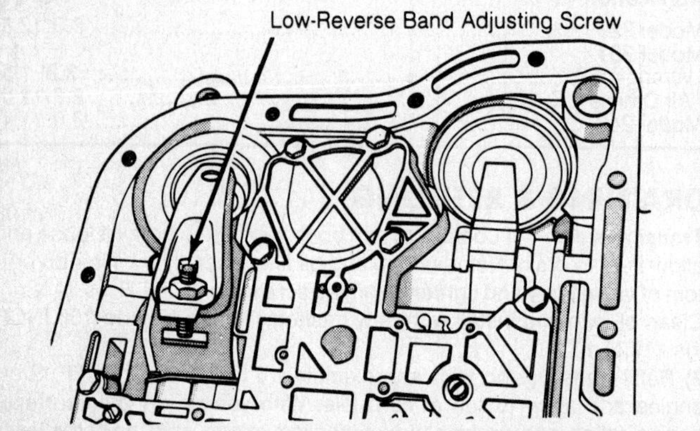
Low-Reverse Band Adjusting Screw
121197
Courtesy of Chrysler Motors.

Fig. 5: Adjusting Low-Reverse (Rear) Band

THROTTLE LINKAGE

Loadflite 727 – 1) Disconnect throttle control rod spring at carburetor. Block choke open and release fast idle cam.

2) On carburetors equipped with throttle operated solenoid valve, turn ignition on to energize solenoid. Open throttle halfway to allow solenoid to lock. Return throttle to idle position.

3) Loosen retaining bolt on throttle rod. Remove spring clip from nylon stop. Remove nylon stop and reposition at rear of link. *See Fig. 6.* Hold bellcrank in place. Push on end of link to eliminate lash. Tighten retaining bolts. Install nylon stop and spring clip. Connect throttle rod spring.

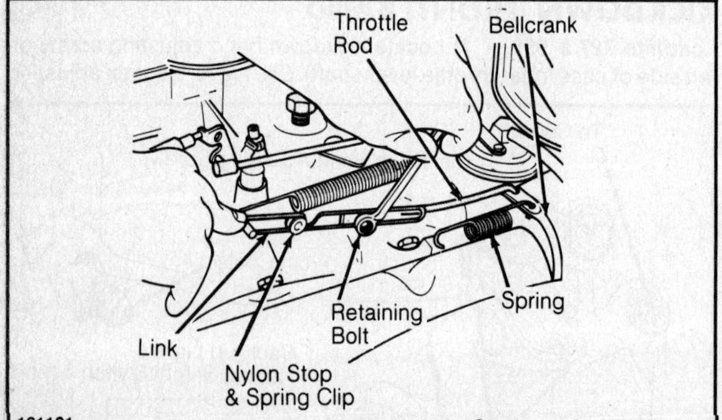
Throttle Rod
Bellcrank
Retaining Bolt
Spring
Link
Nylon Stop & Spring Clip
121181
Courtesy of Chrysler Motors.

Fig. 6: Adjusting Loadflite 727 Throttle Linkage

THROTTLE CABLE

AW-4 & Loadflite 999 – 1) With ignition off, fully retract cable plunger. *See Fig. 7.* Press cable button down and push cable plunger inward.

2) Rotate throttle lever to wide open throttle position. While holding throttle lever in position, allow cable plunger to extend. When plunger is fully extended, release throttle lever. Cable is now adjusted.

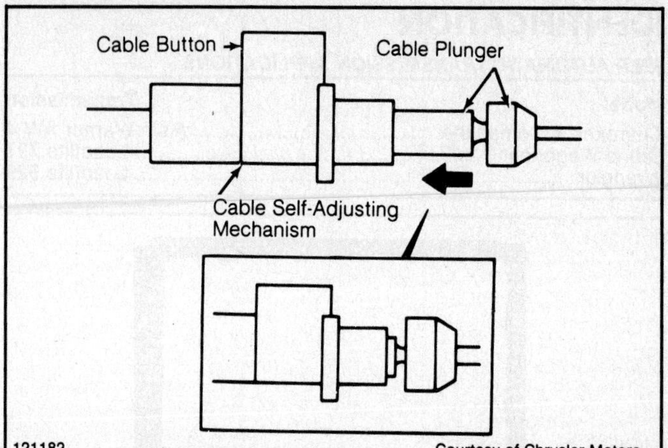
Cable Button
Cable Plunger
Cable Self-Adjusting Mechanism
121182
Courtesy of Chrysler Motors.

Fig. 7: Retracting Cable Plunger

SHIFT LINKAGE

AW-4 – 1) Place gearshift lever in Park and raise vehicle. Using a small screwdriver, unlock shift control cable by releasing "U" shaped cable adjuster clamp. Remove cable from mounting bracket.

2) Move transmission shift lever rearward until fully seated into Park detent. Ensure that drive shaft cannot be rotated. Snap control cable into cable mounting bracket and replace "U" shaped cable adjuster clamp.

3) Lower vehicle and verify engine starting. Engine should start only with shifter in Park or Neutral.

Loadflite 727 & 999 – 1) Loosen shift rod trunnion jam nuts at transmission lever. Remove shift rod-to-bellcrank lock pin. Disengage trunnion and shift rod. Place selector lever in Park and lock steering column. Move transmission shift lever to full rear Park position.

2) Adjust shift rod trunnion to obtain free pin fit in bellcrank arm. Tighten jam nuts. On vehicles with shift lever on column, ensure linkage lash is eliminated by pulling down on shift rod and pushing up on outer bellcrank when tightening jam nuts.

3) Check steering column lock for ease of operation. Ensure engine starts in Neutral or Park only. If starter engages in any drive gear, or does not work in Neutral or Park, check for proper shift linkage adjustment or faulty neutral safety switch.

PARKING LOCK CABLE

AW-4 – 1) Shift transmission to Park position. Turn ignition switch to lock position. Remove center console bezel to access cable adjustment.

2) Pull cable lock button up to release cable. *See Fig. 8.* Pull cable forward and release. Press lock button down until it snaps in place.

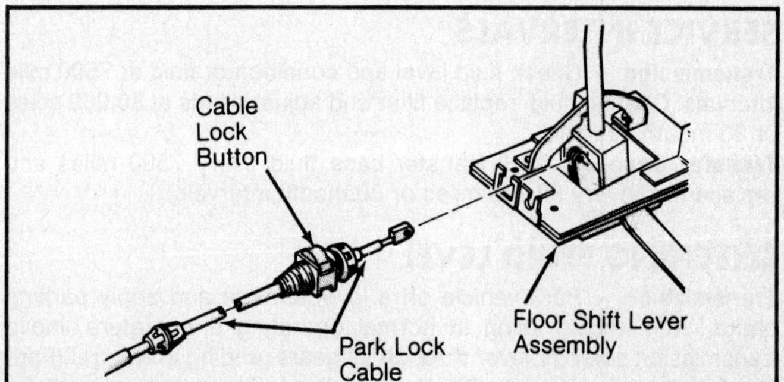
Cable Lock Button
Floor Shift Lever Assembly
Park Lock Cable
90B04353
Courtesy of Chrysler Motors.

Fig. 8: Adjusting Shift Cable

3) Verify adjustment by trying to move shifter. Shifter button and/or shifter should not move.

4) Turn ignition on. Move shifter to Neutral. If ignition switch cannot be turned to Lock position, cable is adjusted. Repeat this step with shifter in Drive.

NEUTRAL SAFETY SWITCH

AW-4 – 1) With transmission linkage properly adjusted, switch allows starter operation in Park or Neutral only.

2) To test switch, remove wire connector. Using ohmmeter, check that continuity exists between proper terminals with transmission at specified gear range. *See Fig. 9.* Replace switch if faulty.

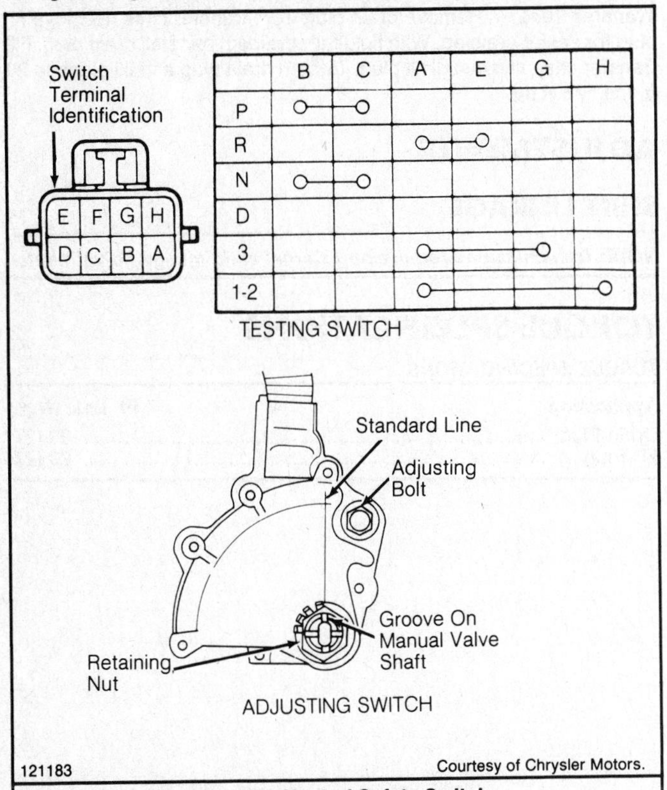

Switch
Terminal
Identification
E F G H
D C B A
B C A E G H
P
R
N
D
3
1-2
TESTING SWITCH
Standard Line
Adjusting
Bolt
Groove On
Manual Valve
Shaft
Retaining
Nut
ADJUSTING SWITCH
121183
Courtesy of Chrysler Motors.

Fig. 9: Testing & Adjusting Neutral Safety Switch

3) To replace switch, disconnect wire connector. Bend switch washer lock tabs upward and remove switch retaining nut and adjusting bolt. Remove switch assembly.

4) To install, disconnect shift linkage from transmission shift lever. Rotate shift lever all the way rearward and then forward 2 detent positions. This is the Neutral position. Install switch assembly.

5) Install adjusting bolt finger tight only. Install lock washer and retaining nut. Tighten nut to 61 INCH lbs. (7 N.m). Rotate switch to align standard line with groove of manual valve shaft. *See Fig. 9.* Tighten adjusting bolt to 108 INCH lbs. (13 N.m). Bend over lock tabs and install remaining components.

Loadflite 727 & 999 – 1) With transmission linkage properly adjusted, switch should allow starter operation in Park or Neutral only.

2) To test switch, remove wire harness and test for continuity between center pin of switch and transmission case. Continuity should only exist when transmission is in Park or Neutral.

3) Shift transmission into Reverse. Check for continuity between 2 outer switch terminals. Continuity should exist with transmission in Reverse only. With transmission in Reverse, check continuity between each outer switch terminal and transmission case. No continuity should exist between terminals and transmission case.

4) To replace switch, disconnect wire connector and unscrew from case. Move selector lever to Park and Neutral positions and check that switch operating fingers are centered in switch opening.

5) Install switch and new seal in case. Tighten switch to 24 ft. lbs. (33 N.m). Check fluid level and add as needed.

TORQUE SPECIFICATIONS

TORQUE SPECIFICATIONS

Application	Ft. Lbs. (N.m)
Kickdown (Front) Band Lock Nut	30 (41)
Low-Reverse (Rear) Band Lock Nut	25 (34)
Neutral Safety Switch (727 & 999)	24 (33)
Transfer Case Fill Plug	20 (27)
	INCH Lbs. (N.m)
Filter	35 (4)
Kickdown (Front) Band	[1] 72 (8)
Low-Reverse (Rear) Band	72 (8)
Neutral Safety Switch (AW-4)	
Retaining Nut	61 (7)
Adjusting Bolt	108 (13)
Oil Pan Bolts	150 (17)

[1] – If adapter extension is used, tighten to 50 INCH Lbs. (5 N.m). See text for complete adjusting procedure.

1991 TRANSMISSION SERVICING
Manual Transmission

Cherokee, Comanche, Wrangler

IDENTIFICATION

MANUAL TRANSMISSION APPLICATIONS

Model	Transmission
Cherokee, Comanche & Wrangler	
4-Cylinder	Aisin AX4 4-Speed
	Aisin AX5 5-Speed Overdrive
6-Cylinder	Aisin AX15 5-Speed Overdrive

LUBRICATION

SERVICE INTERVALS

Transmission – Check fluid level at 7500 mile intervals. Change fluid at 30,000 miles or 30 month intervals.

Transfer Case – Check transfer case fluid every 7500 miles and replace fluid every 30,000 miles or 30 month intervals.

CHECKING FLUID LEVEL

Transmission – Remove fill plug. Check oil level. If level is not up to fill plug opening, add lubricant.

Transfer Case – Remove fill plug. Check oil level. If level is not up to fill plug opening, add lubricant.

RECOMMENDED FLUID

Use Mercon type ATF in transfer cases. Use SAE 75W-90 gear lube with API rating of GL-5 in transmissions.

FLUID CAPACITIES

TRANSMISSION REFILL CAPACITIES

Application	Pts. (L)
AX-4 (4-Speed)	7.8 (3.7)
AX-5 (2WD 5-Speed)	7.4 (3.5)
AX-5 (4WD 5-Speed)	7.0 (3.3)
AX-15 (5-Speed)	6.7 (3.2)

TRANSFER CASE REFILL CAPACITIES

Application	Pts. (L)
Model 229	6.0. (2.8)
Model 231	
Cherokee & Comanche	2.2. (1.0)
Wrangler	3.3. (1.5)
Model 242	3.0. (1.4)

DRAINING & REFILLING

Transmission – Remove drain plug from transmission. Remove fill plug for easier draining. With fluid fully drained, reinstall drain plug. Fill transmission and install fill plug.

Transfer Case – Remove drain plug from transfer case. Remove fill plug for easier draining. With fluid fully drained, reinstall drain plug. Fill transfer case and install fill plug. Tighten drain plug and fill plugs to 20 ft. lbs. (27 N.m).

ADJUSTMENTS

SHIFT LINKAGE

NOTE: Transmissions require no external shift linkage adjustments.

TORQUE SPECIFICATIONS

TORQUE SPECIFICATIONS

Application	Ft. Lbs. (N.m)
Drain Plug	20 (27)
Fill Plug	20 (27)

1991 TRANSMISSION SERVICING
Transmission Removal & Installation

Cherokee, Comanche
Grand Wagoneer, Wrangler

MANUAL TRANSMISSION

NOTE: For manual transmission/transaxle replacement procedures, see appropriate CLUTCHES article.

TRANSFER CASE (A/T)

Removal - 1) Place transfer case in Neutral. Raise and support vehicle. Drain transfer case lubricant. Place reference mark on drive shaft yokes and transfer case yokes for reassembly reference. Disconnect drive shafts and speedometer cable.

2) Disconnect transfer case shift linkage. Disconnect vacuum hoses and electrical wiring from transfer case. Support transfer case with jack. Remove rear crossmember. Remove transfer case-to-transmission bolts. Remove transfer case.

Installation - To install, reverse removal procedure. Ensure reference marks are aligned when installing drive shafts. Fill with Mercon ATF.

AUTOMATIC TRANSMISSION

Removal - 1) Disconnect fan shroud and transmission fill tube upper bracket. Raise and support vehicle. Remove converter inspection cover and fill tube. Remove starter.

2) Mark drive shafts for installation. Disconnect drive shafts at transfer case. On V8 models, disconnect exhaust pipes from exhaust manifolds. Drain transfer case lubricant. Disconnect speedometer cable from transmission.

3) Disconnect all shift and throttle linkages from transmission and transfer case. To assist at installation, tag wiring and remove from transmission and transfer case. Mark torque converter drive plate and torque converter for reassembly reference. Remove torque converter-to-drive plate bolts.

4) Support transmission/transfer case assembly with jack and secure with chain. Remove rear transmission crossmember. On vehicles equipped with AW-4 transmission, use Oil Cooler Line Wrench (ST 7555) to disconnect oil cooler lines. Lower transmission enough to disconnect cooler lines at transmission.

5) Remove transmission-to-engine retaining bolts. Remove transmission and transfer case. Hold torque converter in position while removing transmission assembly.

Installation - To install, reverse removal procedure. Ensure all reference marks are aligned. DO NOT tighten exhaust pipe attaching bolts until crossmember has been installed and transmission jack has been removed. Fill transmission and transfer case.

TORQUE SPECIFICATIONS

TORQUE SPECIFICATIONS

Application	Ft. Lbs. (N.m)
Transfer Case-To-Crossmember Bolt	30 (41)
Transfer Case-To-Transmission Bolt	35 (47)
Transmission-To-Engine Bolt	
Upper	28 (38)
Lower	42 (57)

1991 LATEST CHANGES & CORRECTIONS CONTENTS

LATEST CHANGES & CORRECTIONS For 1991 & Earlier Models

NOTE: Latest Changes and Corrections represents a collection of last minute information and relevant technical service bulletins. Read this section and make notations in the appropriate manuals for easy reference later.

CHRYSLER MOTORS

COMPUTERIZED ENGINE CONTROLS

1) *1981-83 CHRYSLER MOTORS TIMING ADVANCE SPECIFICATIONS* – Please note that procedure for Step **3)** under POOR PERFORMANCE TEST, has been revised to read as follows:

3) Connect auxiliary gauge to vacuum supply vacuum transducer. Set vacuum and engine speed to specification. See SPARK ADVANCE SPECIFICATION table. Wait one minute for specified accumulator clock up time. Check timing. If timing is not within specification, replace computer.

SPARK ADVANCE SPECIFICATION

Computer No.	[1] RPM	Total Advance
4145472	1500	21-25°
4145478	1500	21-25°
4289024	1500	28-36°
4289043	1500	17-25°
4289067	1500	12-20°
4289069	2000	0-8°
4289075	1500	9-17°
4289077	1500	4-12°
4289081	1500	12-20°
4289083	2000	0-8°
4289086	1500	9-17°
4289089	1500	24-32°
4289091	1500	18-26°
4289094	1500	4-8°
4289097	1500	21-29°
4289099	1500	17-25°
4289103	1500	21-29°
4289145	1500	18-26°

[1] – At 16 in. Hg.

Note this change in the following DOMESTIC LIGHT TRUCKS & VANS SERVICE & REPAIR manual:
1981 SERVICE & REPAIR manual page 4-18.
1982 SERVICE & REPAIR manual page 4-19.
1983 SERVICE & REPAIR manual page 4-15.
TUNE-UP/EMISSION SERVICE & REPAIR supplement.
1981 SERVICE & REPAIR manual page 4-18.
1982 SERVICE & REPAIR manual page 4-19.
1983 SERVICE & REPAIR manual page 4-15.

ENGINES

2) *1987-90 CHRYSLER MOTORS 3.9L CAMSHAFT JOURNAL DIAMETER REVISION* – Camshaft journal specifications for 3.9L have been revised. See revised CAMSHAFT SPECIFICATIONS table.

CAMSHAFT SPECIFICATIONS

Application	In. (mm)
3.9L	
End Play	.002-.010 (.05-.25)
Journal Diameter	
3.9L	
No. 1	1.998-1.999 (50.75-50.77)
No. 2	1.982-1.983 (50.34-50.37)
No. 3	1.951-1.952 (49.56-49.58)
No. 4	1.5605-1.5615 (39.637-39.662)
Oil Clearance	
Standard	.001-.003 (.02-.08)
Wear Limit	.005 (.13)

Note these changes in the following DOMESTIC LIGHT TRUCKS & VANS publications:
1987-90 SERVICE & REPAIR manual
- 1987 – page 7-67.
- 1988 – page 7-46.
- 1989 – page CHRY 7-42.
- 1990 – page CHRY 5-32.

1987-90 ENGINE, CLUTCH & DRIVE AXLE SERVICE & REPAIR supplement
- 1987 – page 7-67.
- 1988 – page 7-46.
- 1989 – page CHRY 7-42.
- 1990 – page CHRY 5-32.

3) *1990 CHRYSLER MOTORS CAMSHAFT BEARING IDENTIFICATION REVISION* – Please note that on page CHRY 5-22 of the 1990 DOMESTIC LIGHT TRUCKS & VANS SERVICE & REPAIR manual and page CHRY 5-22 of the ENGINE, CLUTCH & DRIVE AXLE SERVICE & REPAIR supplement, camshaft bearing identification for 3.3L engines has been revised. See revised CAMSHAFT BEARING IDENTIFICATION SPECIFICATIONS table.

CAMSHAFT BEARING IDENTIFICATION SPECIFICATIONS

Application	In. (mm)
3.3L	
Camshaft Bearing I.D. [1]	
No. 1	2.000-2.001 (50.80-50.83)
No. 2	1.984-1.985 (50.39-50.42)
No. 3	1.969-1.970 (50.01-50.04)
No. 4	1.953-1.954 (49.61-49.63)

[1] – Bearings are numbered from the front of camshaft.

4) *1990 CHRYSLER MOTORS 3.9L, 5.2L & 5.9L VALVE SPRING SPECIFICATION REVISION* – Please note that on page CHRY 5-33 of the 1990 DOMESTIC LIGHT TRUCKS & VANS SERVICE & REPAIR manual and page CHRY 5-33 of the ENGINE, CLUTCH & DRIVE AXLE SERVICE & REPAIR supplement, valve spring pressure has been revised. See revised VALVE SPRING SPECIFICATIONS table.

VALVE SPRING SPECIFICATIONS

Application	Specification
3.9L, 5.2L & 5.9L	
Valve Spring Pressure	Lbs. @ In. (kg @ mm)
Valve Closed	
Intake	78-88 @ 1.687 (35-40 @ 42.85)
Exhaust	80-90 @ 1.203 (36-41 @ 30.56)

5) *1990 CHRYSLER MOTORS 3.9L, 5.2L & 5.9L CYLINDER HEAD SPECIFICATION REVISION* – Please note that on page CHRY 5-33 of the 1990 DOMESTIC LIGHT TRUCKS & VANS SERVICE & REPAIR manual and page CHRY 5-33 of the ENGINE, CLUTCH & DRIVE AXLE SERVICE & REPAIR supplement, valve guide inside diameter has been revised. See revised CYLINDER HEAD SPECIFICATIONS table.

CYLINDER HEAD SPECIFICATIONS

Application	Specification
3.9L, 5.2L & 5.9L	
Valve Guide I.D.	.374-.375" (9.50-9.53 mm)

6) *1990 CHRYSLER MOTORS CUMMINS "B" SERIES DIESEL 5.9L RING GAP SPECIFICATION REVISION* – Please note that on page CHRY 5-46 of the 1990 DOMESTIC LIGHT TRUCKS & VANS SERVICE & REPAIR manual and page CHRY 5-46 of the ENGINE, CLUTCH & DRIVE AXLE SERVICE & REPAIR supplement, ring gap specification has been revised. See revised RING GAP SPECIFICATION table.

LATEST CHANGES & CORRECTIONS For 1991 & Earlier Models (Cont.)

RING GAP SPECIFICATION

Application	In. (mm)
5.9L Diesel	
No. 3 Ring (Oil)	
End Gap	.0100-.0215 (.254-.546)

DRIVE AXLES

7 *1990 CHRYSLER MOTORS 8 1/4", 8 3/8" & 9 1/4" DRIVE AXLE ASSEMBLY SERVICE REVISION* – Removal procedures for 9 1/4" drive axle assembly have been revised to read as follows:

AXLE SHAFTS & BEARINGS

NOTE: During repairs, DO NOT heat with torch or hammer on bearing cones, cups, bores or journals.

Removal – **1)** Raise vehicle and remove wheel, tire and brake drum. Clean all dirt and foreign material from area of housing cover. Loosen housing cover attaching bolts to drain lubricant. Remove housing cover. Remove pinion gear mate shaft lock bolt and differential pinion gear mate shaft.

2) Force axle shaft toward center of vehicle. Remove "C" lock from groove in axle shaft. Pull axle shaft out of housing, using care not to damage roller bearing. Remove oil seal from housing bore.

3) To remove axle shaft bearing on 8 1/4" and 8 3/8", use Bearing Puller (C-4167). On 9 1/4", use Bearing Puller (C-4828). On 8 1/4" and 8 3/8" models, attach slide hammer to puller and remove axle shaft bearing. On 9 1/4" models, use a wrench to turn threaded shaft through puller bar and remove axle shaft bearing. On all models, if either axle or bearing shows any signs of brinnelling, spalling or pitting, replace component.

Please note this change in the following DOMESTIC LIGHT TRUCKS & VANS publications:

1986-1990 SERVICE & REPAIR manual
- 1986 – page 9-9.
- 1987 – page 9-9.
- 1988 – page 9-11.
- 1989 – page CHRY 9-11.
- 1990 – page CHRY 7-12.

1986-1990 ENGINE, CLUTCH & DRIVE AXLE SERVICE & REPAIR supplement
- 1986 – page 9-9.
- 1987 – page 9-9.
- 1988 – page 9-11.
- 1989 – page CHRY 9-11.
- 1990 – page CHRY 7-12.

STEERING

8 *1990 CHRYSLER MOTORS 5.9L DIESEL POWER STEERING SYSTEM SERVICE* – For information not covered in the 1990 DOMESTIC LIGHT TRUCKS & VANS SERVICE & REPAIR manual or ENGINE, CLUTCH & DRIVE AXLE SERVICE & REPAIR supplement, see POWER RECIRCULATING BALL article in the 1991 DOMESTIC LIGHT TRUCKS & VANS SERVICE & REPAIR publication.

TRANSMISSION SERVICING

9 *1990 CHRYSLER MOTORS CARAVAN & VOYAGER TRANSMISSION APPLICATION* – Please note that on page CHRY 12-0 of the 1990 DOMESTIC LIGHT TRUCKS & VANS SERVICE & REPAIR manual and page CHRY 12-0 of the ENGINE, CLUTCH & DRIVE AXLE SERVICE & REPAIR supplement, 3.0L vehicles are incorrectly identified as being equipped with Chrysler Torqueflite A-413 transmission. These vehicles are equipped with Chrysler Ultradrive A-604 transmission only.

10 *1990 CHRYSLER MOTORS TRANSMISSION OIL PAN GASKET APPLICATION* – Please note that on page CHRY 12-0 of the 1990 DOMESTIC LIGHT TRUCKS & VANS SERVICE & REPAIR manual and page CHRY 12-0 of the ENGINE, CLUTCH & DRIVE AXLE SERVICE & REPAIR supplement, A-518 oil pan gasket is incorrectly identified in *Fig. 2*. For correct A-518 oil pan gasket identification, refer to page CHRY 12-0, *Fig. 1*.

11 *1990 CHRYSLER MOTORS 5.9L DIESEL THROTTLE PRESSURE CABLE ADJUSTMENT* – For information not covered in the 1990 DOMESTIC LIGHT TRUCKS & VANS SERVICE & REPAIR manual or ENGINE, CLUTCH & DRIVE AXLE SERVICE & REPAIR supplement, see TRANSMISSION SERVICING article in the 1991 DOMESTIC LIGHT TRUCKS & VANS publication.

FORD MOTOR CO.

COMPUTERIZED ENGINE CONTROLS/ ENGINE PERFORMANCE

12 *1988 FORD EEC-IV CIRCUIT TEST B13 REVISION* – Step **9)** under CIRCUIT TEST B13 should be revised to read as follows.

9) Checking A/C Input Voltage – Ensure A/C is switched off. If A/C was on, rerun QUICK TEST. If code 67 or 79 is displayed, continue with this test. Install breakout box and leave ECA disconnected. With KOEO, set DVOM on 20-volt scale. Measure voltage at test pin No. 10 at the breakout box and chassis ground. If reading is greater than one volt, remove breakout box and repair short in A/C clutch power circuit. If voltage is less than one volt, replace ECA. Reconnect all components and rerun QUICK TEST.

Please note this change in the following DOMESTIC LIGHT TRUCKS & VANS publications:

1988 SERVICE & REPAIR manual page 1a-160.

1988 TUNE-UP/EMISSION SERVICE & REPAIR supplement page 1a-160.

1988 COMPUTERIZED ENGINE CONTROLS manual page 157.

13 *1990 FORD DISTRIBUTOR IDENTIFICATION* – Please note that on page FORD 1-166 of the 1990 DOMESTIC LIGHT TRUCKS & VANS SERVICE & REPAIR manual and page FORD 1-166 of the ENGINE PERFORMANCE supplement, the caption in *Fig. 2.* has been revised to identify Closed Bowl Type TFI Distributor.

ENGINES

14 *1990 FORD 2.3L, 2.9L, 3.0L, 4.9L, 5.0L, 5.8L & 7.5L UNDERSIZE CRANKSHAFT BEARING SELECTION* – Procedure for selection of undersize bearings has been revised. Please use the following revised procedure:

CONNECTING ROD & MAIN BEARINGS

1) If proper oil clearance cannot be obtained with standard bearings, try a combination of undersize bearings. DO NOT use any other bearing combination other than what is listed. See UNDERSIZE MAIN & ROD BEARING COMBINATIONS table.

2) If use of bearing combinations does not bring clearance within specification, machine of replace crankshaft as necessary. Always replace bearings in pairs.

UNDERSIZE MAIN & ROD BEARING COMBINATIONS [1]

Excess Bearing Clearance In. (mm)	Use Upper Bearing In. (mm)	Use Lower Bearing In. (mm)
.0-.0005 (.0-.013)	.001 (.025)	[2]
.0005-0010 (.013-.026)	.001 (.025)	.001 (.025)
.0010-.0015 (.026-.039)	.002 (.051)	.001 (.025)
.0015-.0020 (.039-.052)	.002 (.051)	.002 (.051)

[1] – DO NOT use any other bearing combination other than what is listed. If use of bearing combinations does not bring clearance within specification, machine of replace crankshaft as necessary.

[2] – Use standard bearing.

Please note this change in the 1990 DOMESTIC LIGHT TRUCKS & VANS SERVICE & REPAIR manual and ENGINE, CLUTCH & DRIVE

LATEST CHANGES & CORRECTIONS For 1991 & Earlier Models (Cont.)

AXLE SERVICE & REPAIR supplement on pages FORD 5-4, FORD 5-11, FORD 5-19, FORD 5-40 and FORD 5-46.

15 *1988-90 FORD 3.0L WATER PUMP & FRONT COVER SERVICE REVISION* – Please note that designation of bolts sealed with Teflon tape during installation procedures listed under ENGINE FRONT COVER has been revised. For revised Teflon seal application, *See Fig. 1.*

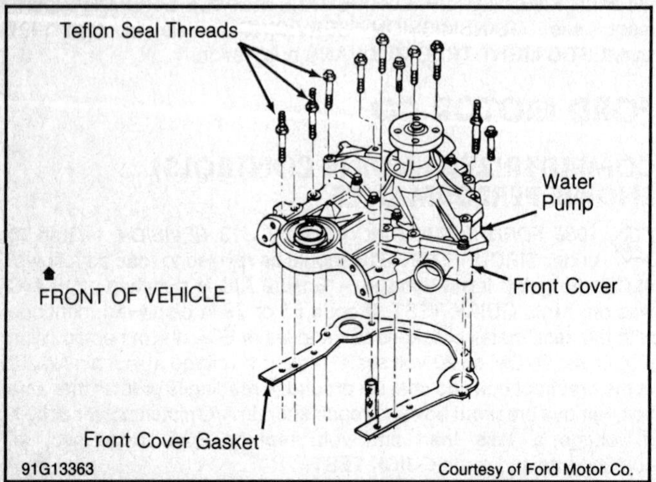
Teflon Seal Threads
Water Pump
FRONT OF VEHICLE
Front Cover
Front Cover Gasket
91G13363
Courtesy of Ford Motor Co.

Fig. 1: Installing Front Cover & Water Pump Assembly

Please note this change in the following DOMESTIC LIGHT TRUCKS & VANS publications:
1988-90 SERVICE & REPAIR manual
1988 – page 7-64.
1989 – page FORD 7-35.
1990 – page FORD 5-16.
1988-90 ENGINE, CLUTCH & DRIVE AXLE SERVICE & REPAIR supplement
1988 – page 7-64.
1989 – page FORD 7-35.
1990 – page FORD 5-16.

16 *1990 FORD 4.0L CRANKCASE CAPACITY REVISION* – Please note that on page FORD 5-26 of the 1990 DOMESTIC LIGHT TRUCKS & VANS SERVICE & REPAIR manual and page FORD 5-26 of the ENGINE, CLUTCH & DRIVE AXLE SERVICE & REPAIR supplement, oil crankcase capacity has been revised to 5.0 qts. (when oil filter is replaced).

17 *1990 FORD 4.0L CONNECTING ROD SPECIFICATION REVISION* – Please note that on page FORD 5-27 of the 1990 DOMESTIC LIGHT TRUCKS & VANS SERVICE & REPAIR manual and page FORD 5-27 of the ENGINE, CLUTCH & DRIVE AXLE SERVICE & REPAIR supplement connecting rod side play specification has been revised. See CONNECTING RODS table.

CONNECTING RODS

Application	In. (mm)
4.0L	
Side Play Service Limit	.014 (.36)

18 *1990 FORD 4.0L CYLINDER BLOCK SPECIFICATION REVISION* – Please note that on page FORD 5-28 of the 1990 DOMESTIC LIGHT TRUCKS & VANS SERVICE & REPAIR manual and page FORD 5-28 of the ENGINE, CLUTCH & DRIVE AXLE SERVICE & REPAIR supplement, cylinder block bore out-of-round specification has been revised. See CYLINDER BLOCK table.

CYLINDER BLOCK

Application	In. (mm)
4.0L	
Maximum Out-Of-Round	
Standard	.0015 (.038)
Service Limit	.005 (.13)

19 *1990 FORD 4.9L PISTON RING SPECIFICATION REVISION* – Please note that on page FORD 5-35 of the 1990 DOMESTIC LIGHT TRUCKS & VANS SERVICE & REPAIR manual and page FORD 5-35 of the ENGINE, CLUTCH & DRIVE AXLE SERVICE & REPAIR supplement, piston ring side clearance specification has been revised. See PISTON RING SPECIFICATIONS table.

PISTON RING SPECIFICATIONS

Application	In. (mm)
4.9L	
No. 1 Ring	
End Gap	.010-.020 (.25-.51)
Side Clearance	
Standard	.0019-.0036 (.048-.091)
Wear Limit	.0056 (.142)

20 *1990 FORD 5.0L & 5.8L CRANKSHAFT JOURNAL DIAMETER REVISION* – Please note that on page FORD 5-41 of the 1990 DOMESTIC LIGHT TRUCKS & VANS SERVICE & REPAIR manual and FORD 5-41 of the ENGINE, CLUTCH & DRIVE AXLE SERVICE & REPAIR supplement, crankshaft journal diameter specifications have been revised. See CRANKSHAFT JOURNAL SPECIFICATIONS table.

CRANKSHAFT JOURNAL SPECIFICATIONS

Application	In. (mm)
5.0L & 5.8L	
Main Bearings	
Journal Diameter	
5.0L	2.2482-2.2490 (57.104-57.125)
5.8L	2.9994-3.0002 (76.185-76.205)
Journal Out-Of-Round	.0006 (.015)
Journal Taper [1]	.0005 (.013)
Journal Runout	.002 (.05)

[1] – Within a 1" (25 mm) area.

21 *1990 FORD 5.0L & 5.8L PISTON PIN DIAMETER REVISION* – Please note that on page FORD 5-42 of the 1990 DOMESTIC LIGHT TRUCKS & VANS SERVICE & REPAIR manual and page FORD 5-42 of the ENGINE, CLUTCH & DRIVE AXLE SERVICE & REPAIR supplement, piston pin diameter specification has been revised. See PISTON PIN SPECIFICATIONS table.

PISTON PIN SPECIFICATIONS

Application	In. (mm)
5.0L & 5.8L	
Piston Pins	
Diameter	.9119-.9124 (23.16-23.17)
Length	3.01-3.04 (76.45-77.21)

22 *1990 FORD 5.0L & 5.8L CAMSHAFT JOURNAL DIAMETER & TIMING CHAIN DEFLECTION REVISION* – Please note that on page FORD 5-43 of the 1990 DOMESTIC LIGHT TRUCKS & VANS SERVICE & REPAIR manual and page FORD 5-43 of the ENGINE, CLUTCH & DRIVE AXLE SERVICE & REPAIR supplement, camshaft journal diameter and timing chain deflection specifications have been revised. See CAMSHAFT SPECIFICATIONS table.

CAMSHAFT SPECIFICATIONS

Application	In. (mm)
5.0L & 5.8L	
Journal Diameter	
No. 1	2.0805-2.0815 (52.845-52.870)
No. 2	2.0655-2.0665 (52.464-52.489)
No. 3	2.0505-2.0515 (52.083-52.108)
No. 4	2.0355-2.0365 (51.702-51.727)
No. 5	2.0205-2.0215 (51.321-51.346)
Timing Chain Deflection	.500 (12.70)

23 *1990 FORD 7.5L PISTON RING SPECIFICATION REVISION* – Please note that on page FORD 5-58 of the 1990 DOMESTIC LIGHT TRUCKS & VANS SERVICE & REPAIR manual and page FORD 5-58 of the ENGINE, CLUTCH & DRIVE AXLE SERVICE & REPAIR supplement, piston ring side clearance specification has been revised. See PISTON RING SPECIFICATIONS table.

PISTONS RING SPECIFICATIONS

Application	In. (mm)
7.5L	
Piston Rings	
No. 1 & 2	
End Gap	.010-.020 (.25-.51)
Side Clearance	.0025-.0045 (.064-.114)
No. 3 (Oil)	
End Gap (Steel Rail)	.010-.035 (.25-.89)
Side Clearance	Snug Fit

DRIVE AXLES

24 *1990 FORD 8 3/4" & 10 1/4" RING GEAR DIFFERENTIAL APPLICATION* – Please note that on page FORD 7-6 of the 1990 DOMESTIC LIGHT TRUCKS & VANS SERVICE & REPAIR manual and page FORD 7-6 of the ENGINE, CLUTCH & DRIVE AXLE SERVICE & REPAIR supplement, model application has been revised to include Aerostar and Ranger.

25 *1990 FORD AEROSTAR FWD & 4WD AXLE SHAFTS* – For information not covered in the 1990 DOMESTIC LIGHT TRUCKS & VANS SERVICE & REPAIR manual or 1990 ENGINE, CLUTCH & DRIVE AXLE SERVICE & REPAIR supplement, see appropriate DRIVE AXLES article in the 1991 DOMESTIC LIGHT TRUCKS & VANS publication.

BRAKES

26 *1990 FORD E150 & F150 DRUM BRAKE SPECIFICATIONS* – For information not covered in the 1990 DOMESTIC LIGHT TRUCKS & VANS SERVICE & REPAIR manual or 1990 ENGINE, CLUTCH & DRIVE AXLE SERVICE & REPAIR supplement, see appropriate DISC & DRUM article in the 1991 DOMESTIC LIGHT TRUCKS & VANS publication.

GENERAL MOTORS

ENGINE PERFORMANCE

27 *1990 GENERAL MOTORS TROUBLE SHOOTING – NO CODES* – Please note that on page GM 1-57 of the 1990 DOMESTIC LIGHT TRUCKS & VANS SERVICE & REPAIR manual and page GM 1-57 of the ENGINE PERFORMANCE supplement, HOW TO USE THIS SECTION procedures under SYMPTOMS (GASOLINE) has been revised to read as follows:

SYMPTOMS (GASOLINE)

NOTE: Also see SYMPTOMS (DIESEL) in this article.

HOW TO USE THIS SECTION

This portion of article is used only AFTER you have checked the following:

- Verify on-vehicle diagnostics work properly. Perform DIAGNOSTIC CIRCUIT CHECK as described in BASIC DIAGNOSTIC PROCEDURES article.
- Verify ECM and SERVICE ENGINE SOON light function properly.
- Verify no trouble codes are stored, or only intermittent ones.
- Verify fuel control system operates properly. Perform FIELD SERVICE MODE CHECK as described in BASIC DIAGNOSTIC PROCEDURES article.
- Perform fuel system pressure test.
- Perform visual inspection of all systems.

After performing all checks listed, verify vehicle operator complaint and locate correct symptom among those listed in this article. Not all items listed under each symptom apply to all models and systems. These procedures will normally recommend testing of a system or component on vehicle, such as EGR, EST, TCC, etc. These are covered in the SYSTEMS & COMPONENT TESTING article.

ENGINES

28 *1990 GENERAL MOTORS 2.8L VALVE SPRING SPECIFICATION REVISION* – Please note that on page GM 5-10 of the 1990 DOMESTIC LIGHT TRUCKS & VANS SERVICE & REPAIR manual and page GM 5-10 of the ENGINE, CLUTCH & DRIVE AXLE SERVICE & REPAIR supplement, valve spring pressure has been revised. See revised VALVE SPRING SPECIFICATION table.

VALVE SPRING SPECIFICATION

Application	Specification
2.8L	
Valve Spring Pressure	Lbs. @ In. (kg @ mm)
Valve Closed	81 @ 1.57 (37 @ 40.0)

29 *1990 GENERAL MOTORS 3.1L CYLINDER BLOCK SPECIFICATION REVISION* – Please note that on page GM 5-10 of the 1990 DOMESTIC LIGHT TRUCKS & VANS SERVICE & REPAIR manual and page GM 5-10 of the ENGINE, CLUTCH & DRIVE AXLE SERVICE & REPAIR supplement, cylinder bore diameter has been revised. See revised CYLINDER BLOCK SPECIFICATION table.

CYLINDER BLOCK SPECIFICATION

Application	In. (mm)
3.1L	
Cylinder Bore	
Diameter	3.5036-3.5067 (88.991-89.070)

30 *1990 GENERAL MOTORS 2.8L PISTON & RING SPECIFICATION REVISION* – Please note that on page GM 5-10 of the 1990 DOMESTIC LIGHT TRUCKS & VANS SERVICE & REPAIR manual and page GM 5-10 of the ENGINE, CLUTCH & DRIVE AXLE SERVICE & REPAIR supplement, piston ring gap and side clearance have been revised. See revised PISTON & RING SPECIFICATIONS table.

PISTON & RING SPECIFICATIONS

Application	In. (mm)
2.8L	
Pistons Rings	
No. 1	
End Gap	.010-.020 (.25-.51)
Side Clearance	.002-.004 (.05-.10)
No. 2	
End Gap	.010-.020 (.25-.51)
Side Clearance	.002-.004 (.05-.10)
No. 3 (Oil)	
End Gap	.010-.030 (.25-.75)
Side Clearance (Max.)	.0078 (.198)

31 *1990 GENERAL MOTORS 3.1L CAMSHAFT SPECIFICATION REVISION* – Please note that on page GM 5-10 of the 1990 DOMESTIC LIGHT TRUCKS & VANS SERVICE & REPAIR manual and

LATEST CHANGES & CORRECTIONS For 1991 & Earlier Models (Cont.)

page GM 5-10 of the ENGINE, CLUTCH & DRIVE AXLE SERVICE & REPAIR supplement, camshaft specifications have been revised. See revised CAMSHAFT SPECIFICATIONS table.

CAMSHAFT SPECIFICATIONS

Application	In. (mm)
3.1L	
Journal Diameter	1.8677-1.8815 (47.440-47.790)
Lobe Lift	
Intake	.2306 (5.857)
Exhaust	.2620 (6.655)
Oil Clearance	.001-.004 (.03-.10)

32 *1990 GENERAL MOTORS 3.1L CYLINDER HEAD SPECIFICATION REVISION* – Please note that on page GM 5-10 of the 1990 DOMESTIC LIGHT TRUCKS & VANS SERVICE & REPAIR manual and page GM 5-10 of the ENGINE, CLUTCH & DRIVE AXLE SERVICE & REPAIR supplement, maximum seat runout for exhaust valves has been revised. See revised CYLINDER HEAD SPECIFICATION table.

CYLINDER HEAD SPECIFICATION

Application	Specification
3.1L	
Valve Seats	
Exhaust Valve	
Seat Angle	46°
Seat Width	.067-.079" (1.70-2.01 mm)
Maximum Seat Runout	.002" (.05 mm)

33 *1990 GENERAL MOTORS 7.4L CYLINDER HEAD BOLT TIGHTENING SEQUENCE REVISION* – Please note that on page GM 5-12 of the 1990 DOMESTIC LIGHT TRUCKS & VANS SERVICE & REPAIR manual and page GM 5-12 of the ENGINE, CLUTCH & DRIVE AXLE SERVICE & REPAIR supplement, 7.4L cylinder head bolt tightening sequence illustrated in *Fig. 4.* has been revised. For revised illustration, see appropriate ENGINE article in the 1991 DOMESTIC LIGHT TRUCKS & VANS publication.

34 *1990 GENERAL MOTORS 4.3L, 5.0L & 5.7L VALVE SPRING SPECIFICATION REVISION* – Please note that on page GM 5-17 of the 1990 DOMESTIC LIGHT TRUCKS & VANS SERVICE & REPAIR manual and page GM 5-17 of the ENGINE, CLUTCH & DRIVE AXLE SERVICE & REPAIR supplement, valve spring pressure has been revised. See revised VALVE SPRING SPECIFICATIONS table.

VALVES SPRING SPECIFICATIONS

Application	Specification
4.3L, 5.0L, & 5.7L	
Valve Spring Pressure	Lbs. @ In. (kg @ mm)
Valve Open	194-206 @ 1.25 (88-93 @ 31.8)
Valve Closed	76-84 @ 1.70 (34-38 @ 43.2)

35 *1990 GENERAL MOTORS 6.2L GENERAL SPECIFICATION REVISION* – Please note that on page GM 5-25 of the 1990 DOMESTIC LIGHT TRUCKS & VANS SERVICE & REPAIR manual and page GM 5-25 of the ENGINE, CLUTCH & DRIVE AXLE SERVICE & REPAIR supplement, piston stroke specification has been revised. See revised GENERAL SPECIFICATIONS table.

GENERAL SPECIFICATIONS

Application	Specification
6.2L	
Displacement	378 Cu. In.
Bore	3.98" (101 mm)
Stroke	3.82" (97 mm)

36 *1990 GENERAL MOTORS 6.2L PISTON & RING SPECIFICATION REVISION* – Please note that on page GM 5-25 of the 1990 DOMESTIC LIGHT TRUCKS & VANS SERVICE & REPAIR manual and page GM 5-25 of the ENGINE, CLUTCH & DRIVE AXLE SERVICE & REPAIR supplement, piston and ring specifications have been revised. See revised PISTON & RING SPECIFICATIONS table.

PISTON & RING SPECIFICATIONS

Application	In. (mm)
6.2L	
Pistons	
Clearance	
Bohn Pistons	
Cylinder No. 1-6	.0035-.0045 (.089-.114)
Cylinder No. 7 & 8	.0040-.0050 (.102-.127)
Rings	
No. 1	
End Gap	.012-.022 (.30-.56)
Side Clearance	.0030-.0070 (.075-.178)
No. 2	
End Gap	.030-.040 (.75-1.01)
Side Clearance	.0015-.0031 (.038-.079)
No. 3 (Oil)	
End Gap	.010-.020 (.25-.51)
Side Clearance	.0016-.0038 (.041-.097)

37 *1990 GENERAL MOTORS 6.2L CRANKSHAFT & MAIN BEARING SPECIFICATION REVISION* – Please note that on page GM 5-25 of the 1990 DOMESTIC LIGHT TRUCKS & VANS SERVICE & REPAIR manual and page GM 5-25 of the ENGINE, CLUTCH & DRIVE AXLE SERVICE & REPAIR supplement, crankshaft and main bearing specifications have been revised. See revised CRANKSHAFT & MAIN BEARING SPECIFICATIONS table.

CRANKSHAFT & MAIN BEARING SPECIFICATIONS

Application	In. (mm)
6.2L	
Crankshaft End Play	.004-.010 (.10-.25)
Main Bearings	
Journal Diameter	
Journals No. 1-4	2.9495-2.9504 (74.917-74.940)
Journal No. 5	2.9493-2.9502 (74.912-74.935)
Journal Out-Of-Round	.0002 (.005)
Journal Taper	.0002 (.005)
Oil Clearance	
Journals No. 1-4	.0018-.0033 (.046-.084)
Journal No. 5	.0022-.0037 (.056-.094)

DRIVE AXLES

38 *1990 GENERAL MOTORS 4WD STEERING KNUCKLE SERVICE PROCEDURE REVISION* – Please note that REMOVAL & INSTALLATION procedures for all "V" Series have been revised. For revised procedure, see appropriate DRIVE AXLES article in the 1991 DOMESTIC LIGHT TRUCKS & VANS publication.

39 *1988-90 GENERAL MOTORS "K" SERIES 4WD FRONT AXLE* – For information previously not covered, see appropriate DRIVE AXLES article in the 1991 DOMESTIC LIGHT TRUCKS & VANS publication.

STEERING

40 *1990 GENERAL MOTORS LUMINA APV, SILHOUETTE & TRANSPORT POWER RACK & PINION SERVICE PROCEDURE REVISION* – Please note that rack and pinion overhaul procedures have been revised. For revised procedure, see appropriate STEERING article in the 1991 DOMESTIC LIGHT TRUCKS & VANS publication.

JEEP

ENGINE PERFORMANCE

41 *1990 JEEP A/T FLUID CAPACITY SPECIFICATION REVISION* – Please note that on page JEEP 1-3 of the 1990 DOMESTIC LIGHT TRUCKS & VANS SERVICE & REPAIR manual and page JEEP 1-3 of the ENGINE, CLUTCH & DRIVE AXLE SERVICE & REPAIR supplement, fluid capacity for AW-4 and 999 automatic transmission has been revised. See revised FLUID CAPACITIES table.

LATEST CHANGES & CORRECTIONS For 1991 & Earlier Models (Cont.)

FLUID CAPACITIES

Application	[1] Quantity
Automatic Transmission (Mercon or Dexron-II)	
AW–4	8.5 pts. (4.0L)
999	8 pts. (3.8L)

ENGINES

42 *1990 JEEP 2.5L CYLINDER HEAD INSTALLATION PROCEDURE REVISION* – Please note that on page JEEP 5-1 of the 1990 DOMESTIC LIGHT TRUCKS & VANS SERVICE & REPAIR manual and page JEEP 5-1 of the ENGINE, CLUTCH & DRIVE AXLE SERVICE & REPAIR supplement, installation procedures have been revised. For revised procedures, see appropriate ENGINE article in the 1991 DOMESTIC LIGHT TRUCKS & VANS publication.

43 *1990 JEEP 2.5L CYLINDER HEAD BOLT TORQUE REVISION* – Please note that on page JEEP 5-5 of the 1990 DOMESTIC LIGHT TRUCKS & VANS SERVICE & REPAIR manual and page JEEP 5-5 of the ENGINE, CLUTCH & DRIVE AXLE SERVICE & REPAIR supplement, torque specifications have been revised. See revised TORQUE SPECIFICATIONS table.

TORQUE SPECIFICATIONS

Application	Ft. Lbs. (N.m)
Cylinder Head Bolts	
Stage 1	22 (30)
Stage 2	45 (61)
Stage 3	[1] 110 (149)

[1] – All except bolt No. 7. Tighten bolt No. 7 to 100 ft. lbs (136 N.m).

44 *1990 JEEP 4.0 & 4.2L CYLINDER HEAD INSTALLATION PROCEDURE REVISION* – Please note that on page JEEP 5-8 of the 1990 DOMESTIC LIGHT TRUCKS & VANS SERVICE & REPAIR manual and page JEEP 5-8 of the ENGINE, CLUTCH & DRIVE AXLE SERVICE & REPAIR supplement, installation procedures have been revised. For revised procedures, see appropriate ENGINE article in the 1991 DOMESTIC LIGHT TRUCKS & VANS publication.

DRIVE AXLES

45 *1990 JEEP 7 9/16" & 8 1/2" RING GEAR SERVICE REVISION* – Please note that starting on page 7-4 of the 1990 DOMESTIC LIGHT TRUCKS & VANS SERVICE & REPAIR manual and starting on page 7-4 of the ENGINE, CLUTCH & DRIVE AXLE SERVICE & REPAIR supplement, all service procedures have been revised. For revised procedures, see appropriate DRIVE AXLES article in the 1991 DOMESTIC LIGHT TRUCKS & VANS publication.

NOTES

NOTES

NOTES

NOTES

NOTES

NOTES

NOTES